The
CROWN
Dictionary of
English Idioms

クラウン 英語イディオム 辞典

安藤貞雄［編］
edited by Ando Sadao

三省堂

編者
安藤貞雄

編集委員
永田龍男

執筆者
安藤貞雄　永田龍男

英文校閲
Paul E. Davenport

調査協力
小松泰輔　佐々木憲子　高橋美穂　永野真希子

装丁
三省堂デザイン室

『三省堂英語イディオム・句動詞大辞典』編集関係者
編　　者　安藤貞雄
編集委員　永田龍男　樋口昌幸　中川憲　田中実
英文校閲　Paul E. Davenport　Michael S. Hasegawa　Roger Northridge

まえがき

本書『クラウン英語イディオム辞典』は，姉妹編『クラウン英語句動詞辞典』とともに，『三省堂英語イディオム・句動詞大辞典』を基にしたより handy な分冊精選版で，下記の増補改訂を加えたものである．

狭義の「イディオム」は，たとえば cry wolf「虚報を伝える」のようにそれを構成する個々の語〈叫ぶ＋オオカミ〉からは推測し難い句義をもち，かつ，この2語のいずれも他の語と入れ替えられない語群をいうが，この辞典では読者の便宜を考慮し，give a sigh「ため息をつく」のような特定の名詞が特定の動詞と慣用的に結びつくコロケーション (collocation) も相当数含めてある．これは両者の境界が曖昧であるからに他ならない．

本辞典の主な増補改訂内容は次の3つにまとめられよう．

⑴ 見出しを精選し，できる限り全体をスリム化した
- 特殊なあるいは古い句見出し・句義を削除し，up-to-date なものに改めた
- 馴染みのない固有名詞や外来語表記を含む句見出しを削除した

⑵ 検索性の向上を図り user-friendly なものにした
- 相互参照 (cross-reference) を一層充実させ，引きやすいものにした
- ☞で示した参考解説を見直し，必要不可欠なものに絞った

⑶ 用例の充実・適正化を図った
- 冗長または極端に短いものや古い用例を差し替えた
- 句義のみの箇所に，得られる限り簡潔明解で馴染み深い新規用例を追加した
- 句例および「新聞見出し・リード，広告文，掲示文」を文例に差し替えた
- PC の点で配慮すべき用例および和訳を適正なものに差し替えた

この辞典の構想が検討され始めたのは，『三省堂英語イディオム・句動詞大辞典』と同時期の2007年に遡る．そして上記『大辞典』の刊行をみたのち本書執筆が開始されたのであるから，完成に足かけ7年が費やされたことになる．この間，編集委員の永田龍男氏には執筆・校正において正に寝食を顧みず全精力を傾注していただいた．また，Paul E. Davenport 氏には全用例を綿密に洗い直しかつ加筆していただいた．これらのご尽力に対してまことに感謝の念に堪えない．更に今回も三省堂辞書出版部外国語辞書第一編集室編集長の寺本衛氏，同編集室の東佐知子氏の有能かつ献身的なご援助および同編集室諸氏の綿密なご助力をいただいた．心から御礼を申し上げたい．

思えば『新クラウン英語熟語辞典』(1965) より『三省堂英語イディオム・句動詞大辞典』の集大成を経て，ここに再び書名に『クラウン』を文字通り冠する辞典への回帰をみたわけで，この間 実に半世紀近く，版を重ねること五たびとなる．蓋し感慨無量のものがある．

本辞典が姉妹編たる『クラウン英語句動詞辞典』とともに，これまで以上に数多くの読者に愛され，わが国の英語研究と学習とにいささかでも寄与することができれば，これに過ぐる喜びはない．

2014年3月　　　　安藤貞雄

凡　例

1　この辞典の内容

この辞典は，英語のイディオム，コロケーション（慣用句），諺などから成る．異形（variation）を含む総収録句見出し数は約63,800項目，用例は約50,000例である．

2　見出し

2.1　親見出し

(1) ABC順にボールド体で示した．また，同一綴りの別語は上付き番号を付した．

例：**abroad**
bank[1]　銀行
bank[2]　土手
cat

(2)《米》《英》で綴り字が異なる場合は，「米，英」の順で両形を併記した．

例：**center,**《英》**centre**
スペース節約の目的から，例文中ではどちらか一方の綴りのみを用いた．

(3)《米》《英》で発音が異なる場合は，/米｜英/の順で両音を併記した．

例：**hot** /hɑt|hɔt/　**leisure** /líːʒər|léʒə/

(4) **color, colour** /kʌ́lər/ の /-ər/ は，米音の /ɚ/（hooked schwa）と英音の /ə/（schwa）を表す．

2.2　句見出し

それぞれのイディオムは，原則として主要語のもとに集めてある．たとえば，***a dark horse*** は **horse**，***be taken aback*** は **aback** で引く．

(1) ABC順に太字イタリック体で示した．

例：***absence of mind***　うわの空
in the absence of ...がないときは

(2)（　）内の語句は句順に関与するが，[　]内の語句は句順に関与しない．

例1：***in places*** 所々に　　例2：***take place*** 起きる
in (***the***) ***place of*** ...の代わりに　　***take*** [***fill***] ***the place of*** ...に代わる

(3) *one, a person, A, B, do(ing)* などのように，語法的な関係を示すのみの語は，細字イタリック体を用いた．これらの語句は句順に関与しない．

例：***clap*** *one's* ***hands***　拍手する
may as well *A* ***as*** *B*　Bと同様Aしてもよい
give *a person* ***a call***　人に電話をかける
cannot help *doing*　...せざるをえない

(4) 見出し句の *one('s)* は（自分（の）[*i.e.* 主語と同じ人・物]）の意味，*a person('s)* は（他人（の）[*i.e.* 主語とは別の人・物]）の意味に用いた．

例：***make up*** *one's* ***mind*** 決心する
eat [***feed***] ***out of*** *a person's* ***hand***　人に従順である

(5) ２つ（以上）の同一の品詞を含む場合は，原則として最初の品詞で引く．

例：***a fly on the wall***　[２つの名詞]は **fly** で，
bright and early　[２つの形容詞]は **bright** で，

up and down ［2つの副詞］は **up** で引く.

(6) 直喩 (simile) は原則として形容詞で引く.

例：(***as***) ***cool as steel*** きわめて冷静で

(7) 同義のイディオムは, 斜線 (/) を用いて併置した.

例：***yet again / yet once more*** またもう一度

3 句義

(1) 句義内でやや異なる意味を併記する場合はセミコロン (;) で区別し, 句義が異なる場合は **1**, **2**, **3**... と太字体のアラビア数字で区別した.

(2) 語法上の注意がある場合は, 句義の前の二重角括弧内〚…〛で明示した.

例：***lay*** *a person* ***off work***〚主に受身で〛人を一時的に解雇する

4 記号・文字の特別用法

4.1 相互参照または句義中の小型大文字 (SMALL CAPITALS) は, それぞれの句見出しの主要語であり, 常に「その項を見よ」を意味する.

例：***talk through*** *one's* ***hat*** → HAT.

fall in pieces ［***powder***］ = FALL to pieces.

4.2 角括弧［ ］は, 句見出し・訳語中のある語句が直前の語句と交換可能であることを示す.

例：***it is good*** ［***bad***］ ***luck*** = ***it is good luck*** or ***it is bad luck***

吉兆［凶兆］である = 吉兆である, 凶兆である

4.3 丸括弧 ( ) には, 次の2つの特殊用法がある.

(1) 見出し句の一部が省略可能であることを示す.

例：***in*** (***rags and***) ***tatters*** = ***in rags and tatters*** or ***in tatters***

(2) 訳語のあとで細字イタリック体の語をくくっている場合は, 見出し句と慣用的に結びついて用いられる前置詞や接続詞などを示す.

例：***keep dark*** 秘密にしておく (*about*)

little dream 夢にも思わぬ (*of*, *that*)

5 略 語・記 号

5.1 一般略語・記号

Sh.	シェイクスピア	☞	解説	Gk	ギリシャ語
↔	反意句	D	オランダ語	It	イタリア語
=	同意句	F	フランス語	L	ラテン語
→	「...を見よ」	G	ドイツ語	Sp	スペイン語

5.2 主な用法指示・専門分野の略語 (五十音順)

《アイル》	アイルランド	《音》	音楽	《軍》	軍事
《アメフト》	アメリカンフットボール	《雅》	文語的な表現	《経》	経済
《医》	医学	《海》	海事	《劇》	演劇
《印》	印刷	《学俗》	学生俗語	《古》	古語
《英》	イギリス	《戯》	おどけた表現	《口》	口語
《婉曲》	婉曲表現	《ギ神》	ギリシャ神話	《豪》	オーストラリア

《古風》	古風な表現	《聖》	聖書	《文》	文語，正式表現
《詩》	詩語	《俗》	俗語	《米》	アメリカ
《狩》	狩猟	《電》	電気	《方》	方言
《宗》	宗教	《電算》	コンピューター	《法》	法律
《商》	商業	《バスケ》	バスケットボール	《論》	論理学
《スコ》	スコットランド	《卑》	卑語		

5.3　Shakespeare の作品名

Ant. & Cl. = Antony and Cleopatra
A. Y. L. = As You Like It
Coriol. = Coriolanus
Haml. = Hamlet, Prince of Denmark
1 Hen. IV = The First Part of King Henry IV
2 Hen. IV = The Second Part of King Henry IV
Hen. V = King Henry V
Hen. VIII = King Henry VIII
John = King John
Jul. Caes. = Julius Caesar
Lear = King Lear
Macb. = Macbeth
Meas. for M. = Measure for Measure
Merch. V. = The Merchant of Venice
Merry W. = The Merry Wives of Windsor
Mids. N. D. = A Midsummer-Night's Dream
Much Ado = Much Ado about Nothing
Oth. = Othello, The Moor of Venice
Rich. III = King Richard III
Rom. & Jul. = Romeo and Juliet
Sonn. = Sonnets
Tam. Shr. = The Taming of the Shrew
Temp. = The Tempest
Tr. & Cr. = Troilus and Cressida
Twel. N. = Twelfth Night
Two Gent. = The Two Gentlemen of Verona

5.4　聖書

Acts = Acts
Amos = Amos
1 Chron. = Chronicles I
2 Chron. = Chronicles II
Col. = Colossians
1 Cor. = Corinthians I
2 Cor. = Corinthians II
Dan. = Daniel
Deut. = Deuteronomy
Eccles. = Ecclesiastes
Ephes. = Ephesians
Esth. = Esther
Exod. = Exodus
Ezek. = Ezekiel
Gal. = Galatians
Gen. = Genesis
Habak. = Habakkuk
Heb. = Hebrews
Hos. = Hosea
Isa. = Isaiah
Jas. = James
Jer. = Jeremiah
Job = Job
John = John
1 John = John I
Josh. = Joshua
Jude = Jude
Judges = Judges
1 Kings = Kings I
2 Kings = Kings II
Lam. = Lamentations
Lev. = Leviticus
Luke = Luke
Mal. = Malachi
Mark = Mark
Matt. = Matthew
Mic. = Micah
Neh. = Nehemiah
Num. = Numbers
1 Pet. = Peter I
2 Pet. = Peter II
Philip. = Philippians
Prov. = Proverbs
Ps. = Psalms
Rev. = Revelation
Roms. = Romans
1 Sam. = Samuel I
2 Sam. = Samuel II
Solom. = Song of Solomon
1 Thess. = Thessalonians I
2 Thess. = Thessalonians II
1 Tim. = Timothy I
2 Tim. = Timothy II
Titus = Titus
Zech. = Zechariah
Zeph. = Zephaniah

A

A

A /eɪ/ 名 ***A1/A one*** /éɪwʌ́n/ **1** Aの第一級《英国ロイド船級協会の船名簿 (Lloyd's Register) による船級》 ▪ Miranda is a splendid *A1* clipperbuilt ship. ミランダ号はすばらしいAの第一級クリッパー型船だ.
2《英口》第一流の, 最上の ▪ This is an *A-one* steak. これは最上のステーキです ▪ I am feeling *A1*. 至極健康です.
A No. [***number***] ***1*** /éɪnʌ́mbərwʌ́n/ 《米口》第一級の, 優秀な (=《英》A one 2) ▪ It is an *A No. 1* type of project. それは第一級に属する企画である ▪ He reckoned himself as *A No. 1*. 彼は自分を最優秀と考えた.
an A.B. seaman →an ABLE-bodied seaman.
earn [***get***] ***straight A's*** 《主に米》オール優を取る ▪ Ann *got straight A's* in all her exams. アンはすべての試験でオールAを取った.
from A to Z 初めから終わりまで (=from A to IZZARD) ▪ He knows photography *from A to Z*. 彼は写真術をすっかり知りつくしている ▪ He knows Montreal *from A to Z*. 彼はモントリオールのことは何から何まで知っている.

a /ə/, **an** /ən/ 不定冠詞 ***a day*** [***week,*** etc.] ***or two*** 〚複数呼応〛1, 2日[週, など] ▪ *A day or two* are needed to complete the work. その仕事を完成するのに1, 2日必要である.

à /a/ 前 ***à la*** …のように, …をまねた ▪ Bob shot an apple off Ellen's head *à la* William Tell. ボブはウィリアム・テルをまねてエレンの頭からリンゴを射落とした. ☞F à la 'in the ... fashion'.

aback /əbǽk/ 副 ***be taken aback*** **1**《海》(帆が不意に)裏帆を打つ《逆風のため帆が帆柱に吹きつけられる状態》 ▪ The ship *was taken aback* by a squall. 船はスコールのため裏帆となった.
2 (人が)不意を打たれる, びっくりする ▪ He *was* completely *taken aback* at the question. 彼はその質問にすっかりめんくらった.
draw [***go, come***] ***aback*** 退却する ▪ All *went aback* from that time. そのときから全員退却した.
lay ... aback 《海》(後退させるため帆)を裏帆[逆帆]にする ▪ They *laid* the sails *aback* so as to make the vessel fall astern. 彼らは船を後退させるため, 帆を裏帆にした.

abandon[1] /əbǽndən/ 名 ***with*** [***in***] ***abandon*** 勝手気ままに; 思いきり, 奔放に ▪ She gave herself over to grief *with* childish *abandon*. 子供のように思いきり彼女は嘆き悲しんだ ▪ They burned private houses *with* an ardent *abandon*. 彼らは熱狂して民家を焼いた.
with gay [***reckless, wild***] ***abandon*** 羽目をはずして, 思いきり ▪ The children danced *with gay abandon*. 子供らは我を忘れてダンスした.

abandon[2] /əbǽndən/ 動 ***abandon*** *oneself* ***to*** 《文》(悲嘆・歓楽など)に身を任す ▪ When her son died, she *abandoned herself to* grief. 息子が死んだとき彼女は悲嘆にくれた ▪ Do not *abandon yourself to* despair. 自暴自棄になるな.
abandon *a person* ***to*** *his* ***fate*** 人を見捨てる, 人を成り行きに任せる ▪ We *abandoned* the girl *to her fate*. 我々はその少女を成り行きに任せた.

abase /əbéɪs/ 動 ***abase*** *oneself* 自分の品格を落とす; へりくだる ▪ *Abase yourself* before God. 神の前ではへりくだれ.

abash /əbǽʃ/ 動 ***stand*** [***be, feel***] ***abashed at*** …に狼狽する, 途方にくれる; をきまり悪がる ▪ The poor man *stood abashed at* this display of wealth. その貧しい人はこんなに富を見せつけられてあっけにとられていた.

ABC /éɪbi:sí:/ 名 (***as***) ***easy as ABC*** 実に易しい ▪ Setting up shop again is not *as easy as ABC*. 店を建て直すのはそう易しくない.
as plain as ABC 実に明白な ▪ The evidence is *as plain as ABC*. 証拠は実に明白だ.
the ABCs of (物事の)基本原則, 基礎事実[知識] ▪ I have mastered *the ABCs of* computer maintenance. コンピューターのメンテナンスのいろはに習熟した.

abdabs /ǽbdæbz/ 名 ***give*** *a person* [***get***] ***the*** (***screaming***) ***abdabs*** 《英口》人を(ひどく)いらだたせる[いらだつ] ▪ The news certainly *gave* me *the screaming abdabs*. そのニュースは確かに私をいらだたせた.

aberration /æbəréɪʃən/ 名 ***in a moment of aberration*** 気が変になって ▪ He stole a watch *in a moment of aberration*. 彼はふとした出来心で時計を盗んだ.

abeyance /əbéɪəns/ 名 ***fall*** [***go***] ***into abeyance*** (相続権などが)停止になる; (法規が一時的に)用いられなくなる ▪ This opera has *fallen into abeyance*. このオペラは一時中止になった ▪ The regulations will soon *go into abeyance*. その規則はまもなく用いられなくなるだろう.
in abeyance (一時的に)休止[停止, 中止]して ▪ The question of Mary's marriage is *in abeyance* till then. メアリーの結婚の問題はそのときまでお預けである.

abhorrence /æbhɔ́:rəns|əbhɔ́r-/ 名 ***be*** *one's* ***abhorrence*** …の大きらいなものである (↔be one's PASSION) ▪ Didactic poetry *is my abhorrence*. 教訓詩は私の大きらいなものだ.
have an abhorrence of/hold ... in abhorrence …を忌みきらう ▪ A woman *has an* in-

stinctive *abhorrence of* wrong. 女性は本能的に不正を忌みきらう ▪ In those days the Scots *were held in abhorrence* all over Europe. 当時スコットランド人はヨーロッパ中で忌みきらわれていた.

abhorrent /æbhɔ́:rənt|əbhɔ́r-/ 形 ***abhorrent from*** …に強く反対で ▪ They are *abhorrent from* blood and treason. 彼らは流血や反逆に大反対である.

abhorrent of …を忌みきらって ▪ The Greeks were *abhorrent of* excess. ギリシャ人は過度をひどくきらった.

abide /əbáɪd/ 動 ***abide by the event*** 結果に従う ▪ Do your best and *abide by the event*. 《諺》自己の最善を尽くして事の成り行きに従え,「人事を尽くして天命を待て」.

can't abide …をがまんできない ▪ I simply *can't abide* his arrogance. 彼の傲慢さは全くがまんできない.

ability /əbíləti/ 名 ***the*** [***an***] ***ability to*** *do* …をする能力 ▪ Why is *the ability to* debate even more important today? なぜ討論する能力は今日いっそう重要なのか.

to the best of *one's* ***ability*** [***abilities***] 力の及ぶかぎり ▪ I will do it *to the best of my ability*. 力の及ぶかぎりそれをやるつもりだ.

abject /ǽbdʒekt/ 形 ***in abject poverty*** ひどく貧乏で, 赤貧洗うがごとくで ▪ Lots of children are living *in abject poverty* in Uganda. ウガンダでは多くの子供がひどく貧しい生活をしている.

abjure /æbdʒʊ́ər|əb-/ 動 ***abjure the realm*** 故国放棄を誓う ▪ Such a criminal was not allowed to *abjure the realm*. そのような罪人は故国放棄を誓って国を出ることを許されなかった. ☞昔英国では反逆・神聖冒瀆以外の罪人は故国放棄を誓って国を出れば刑を免れた.

ablaze /əbléɪz/ 形 ***ablaze with*** …で燃えて; で激して ▪ The house was *ablaze with* lights. 家は灯火であかあかと輝いていた ▪ Her face was *ablaze with* anger. 彼女の顔は怒りに燃えていた.

set ... ablaze …を燃え立たせる ▪ The sight *set* his imagination *ablaze*. その光景は彼の想像を燃え立たせた ▪ The forest *was set ablaze* by lightning. 森は稲妻でパッと輝いた.

able /éɪbəl/ 形 ***an able-bodied*** [***an A.B.***] ***seaman*** 熟練した水夫, 第一級の水夫 ▪ He is *an able-bodied seaman*. 彼は熟練水夫だ.

be able to *do* 〚can に欠けた未来を表す表現・完了形を補って〛…することができる ▪ He will not *be able to* finish it by tomorrow. 彼はあすまでにそれを仕上げることはできないだろう ▪ I have not *been able to* work for three weeks. 私は3週間働けなかった.

ablution /əblú:ʃən/ 名 ***perform*** [***make***] *one's* ***ablutions*** **1**《宗》斎戒沐浴する《宗教的儀式の前または後で》 ▪ The Rajah desired leave to *perform his ablutions*. インドの王は斎戒沐浴することを許してくれと言った.

2《口・戯》体を洗う ▪ John has just *made his ablutions*. ジョンはちょうど今体を洗ったところだ.

aboard /əbɔ́:rd/ 副前 ***All aboard!*** 《米》みなさんご乗車ください!《車掌の言葉》 ▪ The conductor announced, "*All aboard!*" 車掌は「みなさんご乗車ください」と言った.

climb [***get***] ***aboard*** 《米》(電車に)乗る ▪ Her husband came running along and *climbed aboard*. 彼女の夫は走って来て電車に乗った.

come [***get***] ***aboard*** 《米口》(計画など)に参画する ▪ She asked Ted to *come aboard* the project. 彼女はテッドにその企画に参画するように依頼した.

fall [***get, run***] ***aboard*** (***of***) (船が他船の船側に)衝突する ▪ You'll *fall* [*get*] *aboard of* that coal barge. 貴船はあの石炭船に衝突することになります.

get *A* ***aboard*** (*B*) Aを(B(船・電車など)に)乗せる ▪ I'm glad I've *got* you *aboard* my boat. 君を僕のボートに乗せられてうれしいんだ ▪ They will be sure to *get* you *aboard*. 彼らはきっと君を乗船させてくれるだろうよ.

go [***come***] ***aboard*** (***of***) (船に)乗る, 乗船する ▪ He *came aboard of* my ship. 彼は私の船に乗り込んできた.

keep ... (***hard, close***) ***aboard*** (船・陸)に近く沿って航海する ▪ I was desirous of *keeping* the coast of America *close aboard*. 私はアメリカの沿岸近くに沿って航海したいと思っていた.

lay ... aboard **1**《海》(切り込み戦闘の目的で)他船に横づけする, 他船の舷側に迫る ▪ Shall we *lay* their ship *aboard*? 彼らの船に横づけにして戦おうか.

2 …を攻撃する, と競う ▪ He will *lay* them *aboard* at the inn. 彼は宿屋で彼らを襲撃するだろう.

take ... aboard …を(船に)積み込む ▪ We *took* our provisions *aboard*. 食糧を船に積み込んだ.

Welcome aboard! ご乗車[搭乗]いただきありがとうございます《特に客室乗務員の乗客に対するあいさつ》.

abode /əbóʊd/ 名 ***make*** [***take up***] *one's* ***abode*** 住居する, 住居を定める (*at, in*) ▪ The indigenous people *made their abode in* caves. 先住民は洞穴に住んだ.

abomination /əbɑ̀mənéɪʃən|əbɔ̀m-/ 名 ***have*** [***hold***] ***... in abomination*** …を忌みきらう ▪ This prince *was held in abomination* by the Persians. この君主はペルシャ人に忌みきらわれた.

abortive /əbɔ́:rtɪv/ 形 ***prove abortive*** (事が)失敗に帰する ▪ Our first design has *proved abortive*. 最初の計画は失敗に帰した.

abound /əbáʊnd/ 動 ***abound in*** *one's* ***own sense*** 自分自身の意見に従う, 自由に判断をする ▪ In this point you may *abound in your own sense*. この点については自由に判断してよい.

about /əbáʊt/ 前副 ***about and about*** 《米》似たりよったりで, ほとんど同じで ▪ This year's new fashions are all *about and about*. 今年の新しいファッションはみな似たり寄ったりだ.

about here この辺に ▪ He lives somewhere *about here*. 彼はどこかこの辺に住んでいる.

about it 《口》まあそのへんのところ ▪ I guess that's

about it. まあそんなものだなと思うよ.

at about 《米口》およそ(about) ▪ I got there *at about* three o'clock. 3時ごろそこへ着いた. ☞at を略すのはアメリカでは文語.

be about *a thing* …に従事している ▪ What *are* you *about* here? ここで何をしているのか ▪ I must *be about* my father's business. 父の仕事をしなければならない.

(***be***) ***about to*** *do* まさに…しようとして(いる) ▪ I *was* just *about to* leave when you telephoned. ちょうど帰ろうとしていたとき君から電話がかかった.

be not about to 《口》…するつもりはない《強い決意》 ▪ Sharon said: "I *am not about to* resign." 「私は辞職するつもりはない」とシャロンは言った ▪ Will she come with us?—She*'s not about to.* 彼女は我々に同行するだろうか―そのつもりはないね.

be (***out and***) ***about*** (病後などに)出歩く ▪ Beth *is* already *out and about.* ベスはもう出歩いています.

day [***week,*** etc.] ***about*** 1日[1週, など]置きに; 日[週, など]交替に ▪ We do duty *week about.* 我々は週交替に任務につく.

have ... about *one* **1** …を持ち合わせている ▪ *Have* you a pencil *about* you? 鉛筆をお持ち合わせですか.

2 …をいつも使えるようにしている ▪ He *has* his eyes *about* him. 彼はいつも目を光らせている.

have something about *one* 《口》どこか魅力がある ▪ He *has something about* him, I admit. 確かに彼にはどこか魅力がある.

that's about all [***it***] (話のしめくくりとして)まあそんなところだ ▪ So don't worry about earthquakes; *that's about it* for now. だから地震のことは心配しなくていい. まあ今のところそんなところだな.

that's about the size of it (相手の意見に答えて)そんなところさ ▪ So he's going to resign next month?—Yes, *that's about the size of it.* じゃ彼は来月辞職するのかい?―うん, そんなところさ.

that's (***just***) ***about it*** 《口》(意見を述べたあとで)まあそんなとこだ ▪ The reason we got involved in it was to help Jane. *That's just about it.* それに関わったのはジェインを助けるためだった. まあそんなとこだ.

what *one* ***is about*** 自分のやっていること, 自分の仕事 ▪ I know *what* I *am about.* 自分のやっていることは心得ている《ぬかりはないよ》 ▪ Mind *what* you *are about.* 自分の仕事に励め.

while you're about it (ことの)ついでに ▪ *While you're about it*, go buy the album. ついでにそのアルバムを買ってきてくれないか.

about-face /əbàʊtféɪs/ 名 ***be an about-face from*** 《米》…から(方針・政策など)の180度転換である ▪ His choice of that house *was an about-face from* his original intention. 彼があの家を選んだのはもとの考えとは180度の転換であった.

do an about-face 《米》回れ右する; 反転する; (…に対し政策の)180度転換をする(*on*) ▪ Soldiers *did an about-face* and marched away. 兵隊は回れ右して行進し去った ▪ We must not *do an about-face on* Iran. イランに対して変心してはならない.

above /əbʌ́v/ 前副形 ***above all*** (***things, else***) 何よりも, とりわけ, まず第一に ▪ *Above all*, don't talk to anybody about it. とりわけ, そのことは誰にも話してはなりませんよ ▪ He longed *above all else* to see his son again. 彼は何よりも息子との再会を切望した.

above and beyond …に加えて, のほかに; …より以上の, を越えた ▪ He is clever *above and beyond* his good nature. 彼は善良なのに加えて賢い ▪ He showed kindliness *above and beyond* what was expected. 彼は予期した以上の温情を見せた ▪ Many teachers are forced to go *above and beyond* the call of duty. 多くの教師はやるべき仕事以上に働くことを余儀なくされている.

all [***none***] ***of the above*** 《口》上記のすべて[どれも…ない] ▪ Courage, faithfulness and love, *all of the above* are necessary. 勇気, 誠実さ, 愛情, そのすべてが必要だ ▪ Will you have tea, coffee, or cocoa?—*None of the above*, thank you. 紅茶, コーヒー, それともココアにしますか―せっかくですが, そのどれもいりません.

be above (*doing*) (…すること)を恥じる, (高潔で)…はしない ▪ You should not *be above asking* questions. 君は質問することを恥じてはならない ▪ He *is above* such meanness. 彼はそんな卑劣なことをする人ではない.

be above *one* [*one's* ***head***] → above the HEAD(s) of.

be [***get***] ***above*** *oneself* **1** 《口》身のほどを忘れていばる ▪ In reality he *is above himself.* 実際彼は身のほどを忘れていばっている.

2 《俗》気取る, うぬぼれすぎる; 野心がありすぎる, 手に余る ▪ You *are* a little *above yourself*, my dear. You are only a little girl. お前は少しのぼせているよ, ほんの小娘にすぎないのに.

3 (馬が)肥えすぎて運動[練習]不足である ▪ Horses run best when they *are above themselves.* 馬は肥えすぎて運動不足のとき一番よく走るものだ.

feel above work 仕事を恥じる ▪ He who *feels above work* will never succeed. 仕事を恥じるような人は決して成功しない.

from above **1** 上方から; 上役から ▪ Climbing the hill, we had a fine view of the town *from above.* 丘に登ると, 上から町がきれいに眺められた.

2 天から ▪ Every good gift and every perfect gift is *from above.* あらゆるよい贈り物やあらゆる完全な贈り物は天来のものだ.

get [***rise, be***] ***above*** *oneself* 《口》うぬぼれる; 得意になる ▪ The coach never let any one player *get above himself.* コーチはどの一人の選手もうぬぼれるのを許さなかった.

go above *a person* 《米》(綴字教室で)前の者の失敗したあとをうまく綴ってその者の上席に進む ▪ If he gets it wrong, the one who is next in the class spells it if he can, and *goes above* him. 彼が綴字をまちがえば次の席の生徒ができたらその語を正しく綴り,

A

彼の上席へ進む.

one above the other (二つ)重なって, 重ねて; 上下に ▪ Put them on the table, *one above the other.* それらを重ねてテーブルの上に置きなさい.

over and above →OVER.

aboveboard /əbʌ́vbɔ̀ːrd/ 副形 ***open*** [***fair, honest***] ***and aboveboard*** 公明正大に; 公明正大な ▪ Chris's motto is to behave *open and aboveboard.* クリスのモットーは公明正大にふるまうことだ ▪ He is entirely *open and aboveboard* in his statements. 彼の申し立ては全く隠し立てがない.

abreast /əbrést/ 副 ***fall abreast of*** (遅れて)…と並ぶようになる ▪ The horse *fell abreast of* my horse. その馬は遅れて私の馬と並ぶようになった.

get abreast of (追いついて)…と並ぶようになる ▪ The lifeboat *got abreast of* the foundering ship. 救命艇は沈みかけている船の所に来て並んだ.

keep [***be, stay***] ***abreast of*** [***with***] 〚《海》では of, with はしばしば略される〛…と並行して進んで行く, に遅れないようにする ▪ You must *keep abreast with* the times. 時勢に遅れないようにしなければならない ▪ It is easy to *keep abreast of* the international situation these days. このごろは国際情勢に遅れないようにすることは易しい.

keep A abreast of [***with***] ***B*** A(人)をB(情報など)に遅れないようにする ▪ I supplement what he is learning at school in order to *keep* him *abreast with* the class. 彼がクラスの生徒たちに遅れないようにするために学校で勉強していることを補充してやっている.

abroach /əbróʊtʃ/ 副 ***set ... abroach*** **1** (たる)に飲み口をあける, をあけて流し出す ▪ Hogsheads of ale *were set abroach* in the streets. 何個ものビールの大だるが街頭で飲み口をあけられた.

2 《雅》起こす, 広げる, 公表する ▪ Have you no friend to *set* your mind *abroach*? 心の中を打ち明ける友人はいないのか ▪ Who *set* this ancient quarrel new *abroach*? この昔の口論を蒸し返したのは誰だ.

abroad /əbrɔ́ːd/ 副名 ***be all abroad*** 《口》 **1** 当惑している ▪ I'*m all abroad* with anything to do with science. 科学に関係ある事は全く何もわからない.

2 狼狽して[ぼうっとして]いる ▪ In the tenth round the champion *was all abroad.* 第10ラウンドでチャンピオンはグロッキーになった ▪ He got shellshocked, and ever since he has *been all abroad.* 彼は過度のストレスで頭が混乱し, それ以来ぼうっとしている.

3 まるで誤っている[的はずれである] ▪ You *are all abroad* in your guess. 君の推量はまるで見当違いだ.

get abroad **1** (風説が)知れ渡る ▪ The rumor soon *got abroad.* 噂はすぐに知れ渡った.

2 戸外へ出る ▪ Let us *get abroad.* 外へ出よう.

send abroad **1** 《古・詩》…を公にする, 発表する; (叫びなど)を高くあげる ▪ He has a thousand pretty phrases which he never *sends abroad.* 彼はたくさん美しい文句を知っているが, 決して発表しようとしない ▪ He *sent abroad* a shrill and terrible cry. 彼はかん高く恐ろしい叫びを高くあげた.

2 …を広く告知する ▪ Let us *send abroad* unto our brethren everywhere. いたる所のわが同胞たちに広く告知しよう.

set ... abroad (噂など)を広める ▪ They *set* the rumor *abroad.* 彼らは噂を広めた.

sound abroad (評判など)を広める ▪ The news will *be sounded abroad.* そのニュースは広まるだろう.

spread abroad (…を)広く広げる; 広がる ▪ There is a strange rumor being *spread abroad.* 妙な噂が広まっている ▪ The river *spread abroad* at the mouth. 川は河口の所で大きく広がっていた.

venture abroad 思い切って外へ出る ▪ He *ventured abroad* disguised in loud clothing and a false beard. 彼は派手な衣装と付け髭で変装し思い切って表へ出た.

absence /ǽbsəns/ 名 ***Absence makes the heart grow fonder.*** 離れていると情がいっそう深まる. ☞Thomas Haynes Bayly (1797–1839)の遺作 *Isle of Beauty* (1850)中の文.

absence of mind うわの空 (↔PRESENCE of mind) ▪ *Absence of mind* is altogether an involuntary thing. 放心は全く無意識に起こる.

after ... years' absence …年間留守の後; …年ぶりで ▪ He returned home *after 3 years' absence.* 彼は3年ぶりに家に帰った.

in a person's absence **1** 人の留守中に ▪ No one will call *in my absence.* 私の留守中には誰も来ないだろう.

2 人のいない所で ▪ Don't speak ill of a person *in their absence.* 人の陰口をきくな.

in the absence of …がない[いない]ときは; がない[いない]から ▪ *In the absence of* the principal, the vice-principal takes charge. 校長不在のときは副校長が代行する ▪ *In the absence of* evidence the prisoner was set free. 証拠がなかったので囚人は釈放された.

mark the absence 出欠を取る ▪ He *marked the absence* of the students. 彼は学生の出欠を取った.

miss the absence (***of***) **1** (…の)ない[いない]のに気がつく ▪ He *missed the absence of* his watch. 彼は時計のないのに気づいた.

2 (…が)なく[いなく]て寂しい ▪ I *miss your absence* very much. あなたがいなくてひどく寂しい.

absent[1] /ǽbsənt/ 形 ***absent without leave*** 《米》無断欠席して (→AWOL) ▪ Several men were *absent without leave.* 数人が無断欠席だった.

be absent from …を留守にする; を欠席[欠勤]する ▪ He *is* often *absent from* school [the office]. 彼はよく学校[会社]を休む ▪ He *was* unusually *absent from* home. 彼はめずらしく留守だった.

in an absent way ぼんやりして ▪ He looked at me *in an absent way* and didn't answer. 彼はぼんやりして私を見ただけで返事をしなかった.

absent[2] /æbsént/ 動 ***absent*** *oneself* ***from*** …を欠席[欠勤]する ▪ He *absented himself from* school [the office] yesterday. 彼はきのう学校[会社]を休んだ.

absolve /əbzálv|-zɔ́lv/ 動 ***absolve** oneself **from*** 自ら…を避ける ▪Many people *absolve themselves from* any action on the ground that there is too much to do. する事が多すぎるという理由で行動を避ける人が多い.

absorb /əbzɔ́:rb, -sɔ́:rb/ 動 ***be absorbed in* [*by*]** …に夢中になる ▪He *was absorbed in* a book. 彼は本を読みふけっていた ▪The boy *was absorbed by* the building of the new shed. 少年は新しい小屋を建てるのに夢中になっていた.

be absorbed into …にすっかり吸収される ▪His own followers *were* gradually *absorbed into* the English nation. 彼の家来たちすら徐々にイギリス国民にすっかり吸収された ▪Some chemicals *are* easily *absorbed into* the bloodstream. 化学薬品には血流にたやすく吸収されてしまうものがある.

abstract[1] /ǽbstrækt/ 名 ***in the abstract*** 抽象的[理論的]には (↔in the CONCRETE) ▪Cold baths are all very well *in the abstract*. 冷水浴は理屈の上では大変けっこうだ.

make an abstract of …の要約をする ▪*Make an abstract of* his book. 彼の本の要約をしなさい.

abstract[2] /æbstrǽkt/ 動 ***abstract** oneself **from*** 《文》(活躍の場など)から身を引く, 隠退する ▪Though Pascal had thus *abstracted himself from* the world, yet he could not forbear paying some attention to what was doing in it. パスカルは世間から身を引いたけれども, 世間で起こっていることに注意を払わずにはいられなかった.

abstract from** a person's **credit 人の信用をなくす ▪It *abstracts* somewhat *from his credit*. それはいくぶん彼の信用を落とす.

abstracting from …は考慮に入れないで, は別として ▪*Abstracting from* year to year changes, structural changes in Pakistan's economy have been significant. 年ごとの変動は別として, パキスタン経済の構造的変動には見るべきものがあった.

abundance /əbʌ́ndəns/ 名 ***an abundance of*** たくさんの(量・数) ▪They filled the coffin with *an abundance of* flowers. 彼らは柩(ひつぎ)にたくさんの花を入れて満たした.

in abundance たくさん, 多量に ▪Fruit grows here *in abundance*. ここは果物がたくさんなる.

live in abundance 裕福に暮らす ▪He *lives in abundance* now. 彼は今は裕福に暮らしている.

out of the abundance of the* [*one's*] *heart あふれるばかりの情けから (《聖》*Matt.* 12:34) ▪She pitied the invalid *out of the abundance of her heart*. 彼女はあふれ出る情けからその病人をあわれんだ.

there are abundance who …する人が多い ▪*There are abundance who* want a morsel of bread for themselves and their families. 自分自身や家族のために一片のパンをほしがっている人が多くいる.

abundant /əbʌ́ndənt/ 形 ***be abundant in*** …に富む ▪The land *is abundant in* minerals. その国は鉱物に富んでいる.

abuse[1] /əbjú:s/ 名 ***terms of abuse*** 悪態 ▪He addressed her in *terms of abuse*. 彼は彼女に悪態をついた.

abuse[2] /əbjú:z/ 動 ***abuse** oneself* 自慰をする ▪Many people *abuse themselves* because it gives them pleasure. 多くの人は喜びを与えてくれるので自慰をする.

abyss /əbís/ 名 ***be on the edge* [*brink*] *of an abyss*** 《文》大変な危機に瀕している ▪Our motherland *is on the edge of an abyss*. 我々の母国は大変な危機に瀕している.

look into the abyss 深淵をのぞく; 破壊[破産]寸前である ▪The "carefree" city is *looking into the abyss*. その「のんきな」都市は破産寸前だ.

accent /ǽksent|-sent/ 名 ***a cut-glass accent*** (上流社会特有の)洗練された言葉づかい ▪His secretary is very well educated, and speaks with *a cut-glass accent*. 彼の秘書は教養もあり, 話しぶりも洗練されている.

an accent you could cut with a knife 非常に目立つひどいなまり ▪My grandfather came from Poland and had *an accent you could cut with a knife*. 祖父はポーランド出身でひどいなまりがあった.

accept /əksépt/ 動 ***accept service*** 《法》(令状が非公式に送達されたものを)正式送達と認める ▪They *accepted service* of the writ. 彼らはその令状を正式送達と認めた.

accept the person* [*face*] *of …をひいきする (《聖》*Gal.*2:6) ▪God *accepteth* no *man's person*. 神は人を分け隔てなさらない.

***accept the situation* [*inevitable*]** これも運命とあきらめる ▪Will he *accept the inevitable*? 彼はこれも運命とあきらめるだろうか.

I can accept that 《口》君の言う通りだ ▪*I can accept that* and know it is true. 君の言う通りだし, それは本当だと思う.

***Please accept my apologies* [*thanks*].** 《口》お詫び[感謝]申しあげます ▪*Please accept my apologies* for the delay. 遅滞が生じたことをお詫び申しあげます.

acceptable /əkséptəbəl/ 形 ***acceptable damage* [*losses*]** 《婉曲》許容損害《戦果に比べて少ない味方の死傷者数や損害》 ▪The idea of "*acceptable losses*" has long been a part of military thinking. 許容損害という考えは, 久しく軍隊の思考法の一部であった.

the acceptable face of …の許容できる部分 ▪America is *the acceptable face of* cultural imperialism. アメリカは文化的帝国主義の許容できる部分である.

acceptance /əkséptəns/ 名 ***acceptance of persons*** えこひいき ▪The King will do justice, without *acceptance of persons*. 国王はえこひいきをせず公正な扱いをするだろう.

find* [*gain, win*] *acceptance 信用される; 賛成される (*with, in*) ▪I *found acceptance with* the

A

King. 私は国王に信任された ▪The assertion *finds acceptance in* society. その主張は社会に認められている.

with acceptance 好評で ▪He taught *with acceptance* for 20 years. 彼は20年間好評裏に教えた.

access /ǽkses/ 名 ***easy*** [***difficult***] ***of access*** 近づきやすい[にくい] ▪He is *easy of access*. 彼は近づきやすい ▪The summit is *difficult of access*. 頂上へはなかなか登れない.

gain [***obtain, get***] ***access to*** 《文》…に近づくことを許される ▪He *gained access to* the prince. 彼は王子にお目通りができた.

give access to …への立ち入り[面接, 出入り]を許す ▪This gate alone *gives access to* the house. この門以外にはその家へ入る道がない ▪The railway *gives* easy *access to* the place. 鉄道を利用すればそこへは楽に行ける.

have access to (場所・人)に近づく; に出入りする(権利がある) ▪He *has access to* my library. 彼は私の図書室へ出入りを許されている ▪Only high officials *had access to* the Emperor. 高官だけが皇帝に接することができた.

in an access of 発作的に…して ▪He struck his wife *in an access of* fury. 発作的に怒り狂って妻を打った. ☞access＝fit.

within easy access of …から楽に行ける所に ▪The library is *within easy access of* my house. その図書館へは私の家から楽に行ける.

accessible /əksésəbəl/ 形 ***accessible to*** …に動かされる; を受け入れやすい ▪He is *accessible to* reason [pity]. 彼は道理[あわれみの情]に動かされる ▪He is *accessible to* all visitors [bribery]. 彼は訪問者は誰でも[賄賂を容易に]受ける.

accessory, accessary /əksésəri/ 形 ***be*** [***be made***] ***accessory to*** …の従犯である[にさせられる] ▪The tramp *was accessory to* the murder. その浮浪者は殺人の従犯であった.

accident /ǽksədənt/ 名 ***a happy accident*** 思いがけず妊娠したこと ▪Our baby was *a happy accident*. 私たちの赤ちゃんは思いがけずにできたのよ.

Accidents will happen. 《諺》(どうしても)事故は起きるもの.

an accident waiting to happen 潜在的危険, いまにも事故[問題]が起きそうな状況[物, 人] ▪Deer on airports is *an accident waiting to happen*. 空港にシカがいるのでいつ事故が起きてもおかしくない ▪This old ladder looks like *an accident waiting to happen*. この古いはしごは今にも事故を起こしそうだ.

be in an accident 事故にあう ▪My father *was in an accident* yesterday. 父はきのう事故にあった.

by a mere accident ほんの偶然に, ふとしたことで (↔ by DESIGN, on PURPOSE) ▪It was *by a mere accident* that he was discovered. 彼が見つかったのはほんの偶然だった.

by accident 偶然, ふとしたことで ▪I met him *by accident* on Fifth Avenue. 五番街で偶然彼に出会った ▪I broke my arm *by accident*. ふとしたことで腕をくじいた.

by [***through***] ***accident of birth*** 生まれ合わせで ▪Nobody is prevented, *by accident of birth* or lack of opportunity, from achieving his potential. なんぴとも生まれ合わせや機会に恵まれないために潜在能力を延ばすのを妨げられない.

have [***meet with***] ***an accident*** 事故・奇禍・災難にあう ▪He *met with a* bad *accident* last year. 彼は昨年ひどい奇禍にあった.

more by accident than (***by***) ***design*** 故意というより幸運にも ▪*More by accident than design*, she got elected to Parliament. 故意というより幸運にも彼女は国会議員に選ばれた.

(***whether***) ***by accident or design*** 偶然か故意か ▪A woman was found dead, but *whether by accident or design* is not yet known. 女が死体で発見された. しかし, 偶然か故意かまだ不明だ.

without accident 無事に ▪Everything passed off *without accident*. 万事つつがなく済んだ.

accidentally /æksədéntəli/ 副 ***accidentally on purpose*** 《戯》わざと偶然を装って ▪He neglected the order—perhaps *accidentally on purpose*. 彼はその命令を無視したのだ—わざと偶然を装ったのかもしれないが.

acclamation /ækləméɪʃən/ 名 ***carry*** [***vote***] ***by acclamation*** 発声投票で議案を通過させる[発声投票する] ▪The proposal *was carried by acclamation*. 提案は賛成の発声で通過した.

hail ... with acclamation(***s***) …を歓呼して迎える ▪They *hailed* the king *with acclamations*. 彼らは国王を歓呼して迎えた.

acclimate /ǽkləmèɪt/ 《米》, **acclimatize** /əkláɪmətàɪz/ 動 ***acclimate*** [***acclimatize***] *oneself* ***to*** (風土・境遇)に順応する, 順化する ▪He *acclimated himself* readily *to* the harsh air. 彼はきびしい空気にすぐ順応した.

accommodate /əkɑ́mədèɪt|əkɔ́m-/ 動 ***accommodate it*** 争いを収める, 事態を収拾する ▪The king will *accommodate it* by committing my Lord Clarendon. 王はクラレンドン卿を投獄して事態を収拾するだろう.

accommodate *oneself* ***to*** …に順応する ▪You must *accommodate yourself to* new ways of living. 新しい生活様式に順応しなければならない.

get accommodated to …に順応する, 慣れる ▪It took me years to *get accommodated to* the ways of the country. その国の風習に慣れるのに私は何年もかかった.

accommodation /əkɑ̀mədéɪʃən|əkɔ̀m-/ 名 ***come to*** [***reach***] ***an accommodation*** 折り合いがつく ▪They have *come to an accommodation* at last. 彼らはついに折り合った.

for *a person's* ***accommodation*** 人の便宜のために ▪The gallery is *for the accommodation of* visitors. 階上は傍聴者のために設けてある.

accompaniment /əkʌ́mpənimənt/ 名 ***sing to the accompaniment*** (***of***) (…の)伴奏で歌う ▪ She *sang to my* piano *accompaniment*. 彼女は私のピアノに合わせて歌った.

accompany /əkʌ́mpəni/ 動 ***accompany a song*** [***the violin***] ***on the piano*** 歌[バイオリン]にピアノの伴奏をつける ▪ We *accompanied the violin on the piano*. バイオリンにピアノの伴奏をつけた.

be accompanied with …が伴う, つきものだ ▪ Poverty *is accompanied with* sickness. 貧困には病気がつきものである ▪ Lightning *is accompanied with* thunder. 稲妻には雷が伴う.

accomplished /əkámplɪʃt|əkʌ́m-/ 形 ***be accomplished in*** …にすぐれている, に堪能である ▪ He *is* thoroughly *accomplished in* Japanese painting. 彼は日本画の巨匠である.

accord /əkɔ́ːrd/ 名 ***be in*** [***out of***] ***accord with*** …と一致している[いない] ▪ Your proposal *is in accord with* my principles. 君の提案は私の主義に合っている ▪ What you are doing *is out of accord with* what you have always said. 君の今していることは, 君の常に言ってきたことと矛盾している.

be of one accord (みなが)ぴたっと一致している (= be of one MIND) ▪ They are not in one place, but they *are of one accord*. 彼らは同じ場所にはいないが, ぴたっと一致している.

of *one's* ***own accord*** 自発的に; ひとりでに (= of one's own free WILL) ▪ She had no idea of giving up Felix *of her own accord*. 彼女は自分から進んで(猫の)フィーリックスを捨てようとは全く考えていなかった ▪ The door shut *of its own accord*. 戸はひとりでに締まった.

with one accord こぞって, 一斉に; 心[声]を合わせて ▪ They rushed *with one accord* into the theater. 彼らはこぞって劇場へなだれ込んだ.

accordance /əkɔ́ːrdəns/ 名 ***in accordance with*** …に従って; と一致して ▪ *In accordance with* your wishes, I have written to him. ご希望に従い私は彼に手紙を書きました ▪ His deeds were never *in accordance with* his views. 彼の行為は彼の見解と決して一致していなかった.

accordant /əkɔ́ːrdənt/ 形 ***accordant to*** …に従って, にかなって ▪ His opinion is *accordant to* reason [the truth]. 彼の意見は道理[真実]にかなっている.

accordant with …と一致[調和]して ▪ The music was *accordant with* the words of the service. 音楽は祈りの言葉と調和していた.

according /əkɔ́ːrdɪŋ/ 副 ***according as*** 〚節を伴って〛…に従って ▪ *According as* bodies become transparent they cease to be visible. 物体は透明になるに従って見えなくなる.

according to **1** …に従って ▪ Act *according to* circumstances. 臨機応変の行動をとれ.

2 …によれば ▪ *According to* the Bible, God made the world in six days. 聖書によれば神は6日で世界を創造した.

Cut your coat according to your cloth. 《諺》布に従ってコートを裁断せよ《身分相応の暮らしをせよ》.

That's according. 《口》それは事情次第だ. ☞後に to circumstances が略されている.

account[1] /əkáʊnt/ 名 ***according to all accounts*** みなの話によれば ▪ *According to all accounts*, he spent a fortune on gambling. みなの話によれば彼はギャンブルに大金を使ったという.

balance [***settle, square***] (*one's*) ***accounts*** (***with***) (…と)差引き清算をする; に対して恨みを晴らす ▪ The EU must try harder to *balance its accounts*. EU はその勘定を清算するようもっと努力せねばならない ▪ The shot has *squared* all *accounts*. その狙撃はすべてを清算した.

be in account with *a person* 人と取引をしている ▪ I *am in account with* him. 私は彼と取引をしている.

be much account 《口》大したものである ▪ Your head *ain't much account*. 君の頭は大したものではない.

be sent [***go***] ***to*** *one's* (***long***) ***account*** 《古風・婉曲》殺される[死ぬ], あの世へ送られる[行く] ▪ He *was sent to his account* with all his imperfections on his head. 彼は罪悪のかずかずを身に負いながら殺された ▪ He has *gone to his account*. 彼はあの世へ行った. ☞最後の審判に神の前で自己の釈明をしにやられる[行く]が原義.

by [***from***] ***all accounts*** 誰に聞いても, 誰の説明でも ▪ It is a small place, *by all accounts*. 誰に聞いても, そこは狭い場所だそうです ▪ *From all accounts* he spent a fortune on gambling. 誰に聞いても彼はギャンブルで大金を費やしたという.

by [***according to***] *one's* ***own account*** 本人の言うところでは ▪ *According to her own account*, she was also a tale-teller from a very young age. 本人の話では, 彼女は非常に幼いときから告げ口屋でもあった.

call [***bring, hold***] *a person* ***to account for*** [***over***] **1** 人に(…の)釈明を求める, 責任を問う ▪ We will *call* him *to account for* his wickedness. 彼の不行跡の釈明を求めたい.

2 (…のことで)人をしかる, 非難する ▪ They decided to *bring* Dan *to account over* his rant at the referee. 彼らはダンがレフェリーに暴言を吐いたことを非難することに決めた.

charge account つけ, 掛売り ▪ May bought a new dress on her *charge account*. メイは掛売りでドレスを新調した.

charge ... to *a person's* ***account*** 人の勘定につける ▪ I have no cash; *charge* it *to my account*, will you? 手持ちの現金がないので私の勘定につけておいてくれませんか.

close an account with *a person* 人との信用取引をやめる ▪ We *closed an account with* him. 我々は彼との信用取引をやめた.

close up *one's* ***accounts*** 《米俗》死ぬ ▪ It was

A

nearly another year before he had *closed up his accounts.* ほとんど1年後に彼は死んだ.

close** one's **worldly account 俗世間との交渉を絶つ ▪ No one knows why he has *closed his worldly account.* なぜ彼が俗世間との交渉を絶ったのか誰も知らない.

doctor the accounts 説明をごまかす, 事実を曲げて説明する ▪ The embezzler tried to *doctor the accounts.* 着服者は説明をごまかそうとした.

find** one's* **[*no*]** ***account in …は割りに合う[合わない] ▪ He *found his account in* the transaction. 彼はその取引が利益になった ▪ I *find no account in* the work. その仕事は割りに合わない.

***for account of** a person* 人の金[収入]にするため ▪ A very considerable proportion are shipped *for account of* the manufacturer. 相当大きな部分が製造者の収入のため積み出される.

for the account and risk of (株式の仲買人が)…の損得をかけて(売買する)《仲買人が唯一の代理人であることを示す》 ▪ He buys and sells stocks *for the account and risk of* Mr. Smith. 彼はスミス氏の損得をかけて株を売買する.

give a bad account of …をけなす ▪ Bill was afraid she might *give a bad account of* him to her mother. ビルは彼女が母親に自分のことをけなすのではないかと心配した.

give a bad **[*poor*]** ***account of** oneself* しくじる, 失敗する ▪ He *gave a bad accout of himself* in the examination. 彼は試験でしくじった.

***give a good account of** oneself* **1** うまくやりおおす ▪ He *gave a good account of himself* as a chairman. 彼は議長として立派にやってのけた.
2 立派に申し開きをする ▪ She *gave a good account of herself* in court. 彼女は法廷で立派に申し開きをした.

give **[*render*]** **(*an*)** ***account of*** **1** …の説明をする, の始末を明らかにする ▪ I can *give* no *account of* my indigestion. 私の消化不良は何とも説明がつかない. **2** …を話す ▪ *Give* me *an account of* what you saw. 君の見たことを話してくれ.
3 …の勘定書を渡す ▪ I will *give* you *your account* tomorrow. あす(経費)勘定書を渡します.

go to** one's* **(*long*)** ***account →be sent to one's (long) ACCOUNT.

hand in** one's* ***account(s) 《米口》年貢を納める, 死ぬ ▪ He *handed in his account(s)* in 1840. 彼は1840年に死んだ. ☞account「清算書」.

have an account to settle **(*with*)** (…に)清算すべき勘定がある; (に)晴らすべき恨みがある ▪ I *have an account to settle with* him for his lies. 彼は嘘を言ったから仕返しをしてやらねばならない.

have an account with …と取引がある ▪ I *have an account with* the Midland Bank. 私はミッドランド銀行と取引がある.

hold … in much **[*little*]** ***account*** …を重んじる[軽んじる] ▪ He *held* Moses' laws *in more account.* 彼はモーセの律法をさらに重んじた.

keep account of …を記録する ▪ He *kept account of* all he did. 彼は自分の行為を全て記録した.

keep accounts 簿記をつける; 出納係を務める ▪ He *kept accounts* in Calcutta for two years. 彼はカルカッタで2年間出納係を務めた.

leave … out of account …を勘定に入れない, 無視する (↔take … into ACCOUNT) ▪ Any person who *leaves* this *out of account* is in the wrong. これを無視する人は誰でもまちがっている.

make **(*much*)** ***account of*** …を(大変)重んじる ▪ He seems to *make much account of* appearances. 彼は外見をひどく重んじているように思われる.

make no **[*light, little*]** ***account of…*** を無視する[軽んじる] ▪ At Rome this kind of bread *is made no account of.* ローマではこの種のパンは問題にされていない ▪ She is not a woman to *be made light account of.* 彼女は無視されるような女ではない.

no account 《米》 **1** 価値のない ▪ He always rode an old *no account* horse. 彼はいつも老いぼれた駄馬に乗った.
2 身分の低い人 ▪ Everybody considered him a *no account.* みなが彼を卑しい身分の者だと思った.

of much **[*some, no*]** ***account*** 重要な[いくらか重要な, つまらない] ▪ This is a matter *of some account.* これはいくらか重要な事柄だ ▪ Are all these *of no account?* これらはみなつまらないものですか.

on account 内金として ▪ He owed £50, and sent me £10 *on account.* 彼は私に50ポンド借りがあって, 10ポンド内金として送って来た.

on** a person's* ***account/on **(*the*)** ***account of*** *(a person)* **1** (ある理由)のため ▪ He stays at home now *on account of* his great age. 彼は今は高齢のため家にとじこもっている.
2 (人)の(利益の)ため (= on BEHALF of) ▪ I have come to see you *on account of* my son. 私は息子のためにあなたに会いにきました ▪ Did you go to this trouble *on my account?* 私のためにこんなに骨折ってくださったのですか.
3《口》…の勘定[負担]で ▪ They were bought and sold *on the account of* the company. それらは会社の負担[勘定]で売り買いされた.

on all accounts/on every account どう見ても; どうあっても; ぜひとも (= by all (manner of) MEANS) ▪ *On all accounts* you must do it. あなたはどうしてもそれをしなければなりません.

on no **[*not on any*]** ***account*** 《文》どうあっても…ない ▪ *On no account* are you to touch an electrical appliance with wet hands. 決して電気器具にぬれた手でさわってはなりません.

on** one's* ***own account **1** 自分の利益のために ▪ He offered the money *on his own account.* 彼は自分のためにその金を提供した.
2 自分の負担で, 独立して, 独りで ▪ He started business *on his own account.* 彼は自前で商売を始めた ▪ I did it entirely *on my own account.* 私はそれを全く自分一人の考えでやった.

on that **[*this*]** ***account*** その[この]ために, その[この]

理由で ▪ There is no reason to worry *on that account.* そのために心配するいわれはない.

open* [*start*] *an account with …と取引を始める ▪ Pen *opened an account with* a banker. ペンは銀行家と取引を始めた.

***pay* [*settle*] *one's* account** 借金を払う; 勘定をすます ▪ Please *settle your account* at your earliest convenience. 都合のつき次第お支払い願います.

place* [*pass*]… *to a person's account …を人の勘定につける ▪ It will *be placed to her account* at the last day. それは最後の(審判の)日に彼女の勘定につけられるだろう ▪ *Place* it *to my account.* 僕の勘定につけてくれ.

put…down* [*charge*] *to a person's accounts …を人の勘定につける ▪ *Put* it *down to my accounts.* それを私の勘定につけておいてください.

render* [*send in*] *an account 請求書を送付する ▪ You should *send in an account* within three months. 3か月以内に請求書を送付するべきだ.

render* (*an*) *account of → give (an) ACCOUNT of.

run up a long account against …に対し借方勘定を増やす ▪ You are *running up a long account against* us. 君は我々に対して借金を増やしている.

Short accounts make long friends. 《諺》長いつき合いに掛けは禁物.

square one's* [*an*] *account with/ square accounts with **1** 借金を返す ▪ I'm looking to *square my account with* the cable TV company. ケーブルテレビ会社に借金を返そうと思っている.

2 (人)に仕返しをする, 恨みを晴らす (*for*) ▪ I'll *square my account with* you yet. You'll never escape from our grasp. いまもなおお前に仕返しをしてやるぞ. お前は決して我々の手から逃れられはしない. ☞ →balance (one's) ACCOUNTs (with).

square* [*settle*] *accounts with → balance (one's) ACCOUNTs (with).

***state an* [*one's*] *account* [*accounts*]** (取引中の)貸借を正式に記入する ▪ By *stating his accounts* he discovered that he had been cheated. 貸借を正式に記入してみて, 彼はだまされていたと知った.

take account of **1** …を考慮する, 酌量する ▪ In making the classification we have *taken account of* that fact. 分類の際その事実を考慮した.

2 …に注意する ▪ You must *take account of* what you are doing. あなたは自分のしていることに注意しなければなりません.

take…into account …を考慮に入れる; しんしゃくする (↔leave…out of ACCOUNT) ▪ I shall *take* his youth *into account.* 彼の若いことを酌量しよう.

take no account of …を全く考慮しない, を無視する ▪ Some teachers seem to *take no account of* their students' interests. 教師の中には学生の興味など全く考慮しない者がいるようだ.

turn…to bad account 《文》…を活用しない ▪ Judges *turn* injunctions *to bad account* because they are partisans. 判事が禁止命令を活用しないのは主義の熱心な支持者だからだ.

turn* [*put*]… *to* (*one's*) (*good*) *account (うまく物)を利用する ▪ He *turned* his war experience *to good account.* 彼は自分の戦争体験を儲けの種にした ▪ He *turns* every circumstance *to account.* 彼は転んでもただでは起きない.

account[2] /əkáʊnt/ 動 ***all present and accounted for*** 《口》全員揃っている ▪ Is everyone ready to board the bus?—*All present and accounted for.* 全員バスに乗る用意が整っていますか—全員揃っています. ☞元軍隊の点呼の答え.

be accounted of 尊重される ▪ Preaching *was accounted of* in the 16th century. 16世紀には説教が尊重された.

***There is no accounting for taste*(*s*).** 《諺》人の趣味は説明できない, 「タデ食う虫も好き好き」.

accountable /əkáʊntəbəl/ 形 ***be accountable for*** …を説明せねばならない, に対して責任がある《人にのみ用いる》 ▪ He *is accountable* to me *for* the money he spends. 彼は使う金について私に使途を明らかにせねばならない ▪ You *are accountable* to him *for* the injury. 君は彼に対してその傷害の責任を負わねばならない.

be not accountable for one's actions (子供・狂人が)何をしてもしかられ[罰せられ]るべきでない ▪ He is insane. He *is not accountable for his actions.* 彼は正気ではない. 所行に責任のない身である.

accouter, 《英》**accoutre** /əkú:tər/ 動 ***be accoutered in* [*with*]** …を着ている ▪ They *were accoutered in* their best clothes. 彼らは晴着で着飾っていた.

accuracy /ǽkjərəsi/ 名 ***with accuracy*** 正確に ▪ He guessed *with accuracy.* 彼は正確に言い当てた.

accusation /ækjuzéɪʃən/ 名 ***be under an accusation*** 告訴[非難]されている ▪ He *is under a* false *accusation* of theft. 彼は窃盗という無実の罪で告訴されている.

bring* [*lay, lodge*] *an accusation against …を告訴する ▪ We *lodged an accusation against* him. 我々は彼を告訴した.

accuse /əkjú:z/ 動 ***One's looks accuse one.*** 人の顔つきで罪を犯したことがわかる ▪ *Your looks accuse* you. 君の顔つきで罪を犯したことがわかる.

accused /əkjú:zd/ 形 ***stand accused* (*of*)** (…の点で)非難されている, (…の容疑で)起訴されている ▪ She *stands accused of* dishonesty and deception. 彼女は不正直と欺きのかどで非難されている ▪ He *stands accused of* killing his mother. 彼は母を殺害した容疑で起訴されている.

accustom /əkʌ́stəm/ 動 ***accustom oneself to*** …に身を慣らす ▪ He had to *accustom himself to* long marches [sitting on the floor]. 彼は長距離行軍[床の上に座ること]に慣れねばならなかった.

***be accustomed to* [*to do*]** **1** …する習わしである ▪ The Countess *was accustomed to* keep her

A

jewels in the small casket. 伯爵夫人は宝石を小箱にしまっておく習慣だった ▪ I *am* not *accustomed to* lying. 私には嘘をつく癖はない.

2 …に慣れている ▪ We *were accustomed to* hard work [see the sun move]. つらい仕事に[太陽が動くのを見るのに]慣れていた.

become [***get***] ***accustomed to*** …に慣れる ▪ The boy soon *got accustomed to* the new method. 少年はじきに新しい方法に慣れた.

ace[1] /eɪs/ 名 ***an*** [*one's*] ***ace in the hole***/《英》***an ace up*** *one's* ***sleeve*** 《口》奥の手, 最後の切り札 ▪ I know how to keep *an ace in the hole* at work. 私は仕事においてとっておきの手を用意しておくすべをわきまえている ▪ The twenty-pound bill I keep in my shoe is *an ace up my sleeve*. 靴の中にしまっている20ポンド札が私の最後の切り札だった.

bate (*a person*) ***an ace*** (人に)ほんの少しおまけをする; (競技において, 力を平等にするため人に)ちょっぴり利を与える ▪ *Bating* him that *ace*, he was truly a great man. それだけおまけをするなんて, 彼はほんとに偉い人だった ▪ The exposer has not *bated* him *an ace*. 暴露者は彼をちっとも仮借しなかった.

have [***hold***] (***all***) ***the aces*** 《口》支配的地位にある, 支配権を握っている ▪ His employer *held all the aces*, so he was forced to quit. 彼の雇主が決定権を握っているので, 彼は退職を余儀なくされた.

have [***keep***] ***an ace up*** *one's* ***sleeve*** 《英》取って置きの切札がある ▪ Mr. White *has some aces up his sleeve* for his campaign. ホワイト氏はその運動にいくつかの切札を持っている.

play *one's* ***ace*** とっておきの手[奥の手]を使う ▪ The lawyer *played his ace* when he showed the judge the new information. 弁護士は判事に新情報を示したときとっておきの手を使った.

play *one's* ***ace well*** 駆け引きがうまい ▪ She mailed to Mark to check he could still *play his ace well*. 彼女はマークがいまも駆け引きがうまいかをチェックするためにメールした.

the ace in *one's* ***hand*** 《英》切り札, 奥の手 ▪ The difference from others is that I have *the ace in my hand*. 他の連中と違うところは, こちらには奥の手があることだ.

trump *a person's* ***ace*** 相手のエースを切り札でとる; 相手の強い手よりもさらに強い手で反撃する ▪ He did not invite me to his party but I *trumped his ace* by holding one on the same night. 彼はパーティーに招待してくれなかったが, こっちは同じ日の晩にパーティーを催して彼に反撃した.

within an ace of 《口》危うく…しようとするところ, いま少しで…するところ (= within an INCH of) ▪ I came *within an ace of* making my fortune. 私はいま少しで財産を作るところだった ▪ He was *within an ace of* being frozen to death. 彼は危うく凍死するところだった.

ace[2] /eɪs/ 動 ***ace it*** 《俗》うまくやっちまう ▪ I'm sure he'll *ace it* when he takes that bar exam. 彼はきっと司法試験でうまくやるさ. ☞「試験でAをとる」という学俗から.

ache[1] /eɪk/ 名 ***aches and pains*** 体のあちこちの軽い痛み ▪ Most of us experience *aches and pains*. 私たちの大半は体のあちこちに軽い痛みがある.

ache[2] /eɪk/ 動 ***My aching back!*** 《米》いやになっちまう ▪ I dropped and broke your favorite glass.—Oh, *my aching back!* 君の愛用のグラスを落として割った—ほんとにいやになっちまうな.

Achilles /əkíliːz/ 名 ***the*** [*one's*] ***heel of Achilles***/***the*** [*one's*] ***Achilles' heel*** (個人・国民の)弱点; (非難・攻撃を受けやすい)弱味 ▪ For him, alcohol is indeed *the heel of Achilles*. 彼にとってはアルコールはほんとうに弱点だ ▪ *His Achilles' heel* is pride. 彼の弱点は傲慢だ. ☞ Achilles はかかとだけが不死身でなかったというギリシャ伝説から.

acid /ǽsəd/ 名 ***acid rock*** 《俗》アシッドロック《大音量やビートが特徴で, 麻薬の影響を思わせる音楽》 ▪ Nick is a regular *acid rock* freak. ニックはまぎれもないアシッドロック狂だ.

acid test 厳密な吟味[証明], きびしい規準[試練] ▪ I was put to the *acid test*. 私はきびしい試験を受けた ▪ Adversity is an *acid test* of friendship. 逆境は友情の試金石である. ☞「物質が金を含むかどうかを見るための硝酸による試験」が原義.

an acid head 《俗》(幻覚症状のある) LSD 常用者 ▪ Jim is *a* regular *acid head* and sometime acts funny. ジムはまぎれもない LSD 常用者で, ときどきおかしなふるまいをする.

come the acid 《俗》無愛想にふるまう; つっけんどんに言う ▪ Why *come the acid*? なぜ無愛想なんだ.

put the acid on *a person* 《豪俗》(借金・願い事などを求めて)人に圧力をかける ▪ He *put the acid on* me for a loan of $100. 彼は私に100ドル貸せと強要した.

acknowledge /əknálɪdʒ|-nɔ́l-/ 動 ***acknowledge receipt of*** …を受け取ったことを認める ▪ I beg to *acknowledge receipt of* your letter dated Jan. 7th. 1月7日付け貴書面まさに落手いたしました ▪ Kindly *acknowledge* (*your*) *receipt*. ご入手のむねご通知ください.

be acknowledged as 〚主に受身で〛…として認識される, みなされる ▪ Wimbledon *is* widely *acknowledged as* being the premier tennis tournament. ウィンブルドンは最高のテニストーナメントであると広くみなされている.

acknowledgment /əknálɪdʒmənt|-nɔ́l-/ 名 ***bow*** *one's* ***acknowledgments of*** …に対するお礼のおじぎをする ▪ He *bowed his acknowledgments of* applause. 彼は喝采へのお礼のおじぎをした.

in acknowledgment of …のお礼に, の返事に ▪ I am sending you a small sum of money *in acknowledgment of* your help. ご援助のお礼に少額の金をお送りいたします.

acock /əkák/ 副 ***set*** *one's* ***hat acock*** 帽子の縁を上に曲げる《挑戦的な態度》 ▪ He *sets his hat acock* at matrimony. 彼は結婚を無視する態度を取っている.

acorn /éɪkɔːrn/ 名 ***Great* [*Tall*] *oaks from acorns grow.*** 《諺》大きなオークの木もドングリから育つ《大きな会社・組織も小規模から始まる》.

acquaint /əkwéɪnt/ 動 ***acquaint*** *oneself* ***with*** …に通じる; を親しく知る ▪ You must *acquaint yourself with* your new duties. 君は新しい職務に通じなくてはならない.

be acquainted of …を知らされる, 聞く ▪ I *am acquainted of* the facts. 私はそのことを聞いた.

be* [*become, get*] *acquainted with (人)と知り合いである[になる]; (物)を知っている[知る]; に精通している[する] ▪ I *am acquainted with* him. 私は彼と知り合いである ▪ He *is* well *acquainted with* the history of Japan. 彼は日本史に精通している.

make *a person* ***acquainted with*** 人に…を知らせる ▪ I will *make* him *acquainted with* my uncle's death. おじの死を彼に知らせよう.

acquaintance /əkwéɪntəns/ 名 ***a nodding* [*bowing*] *acquaintance*** **1** 会えば会釈する程度の知り合い ▪ I have *a nodding acquaintance* with the company president. 私はあの会社社長と会えば会釈する程度の知り合いだ.

2 ちょっとした知識 ▪ She has *a nodding acquaintance* with Japanese literature. 彼女は日本文学のちょっとした知識を持っている.

a passing acquaintence **1** 単なる知り合い ▪ That fellow is *a passing acquaintance* of mine. あの男は私の単なる知り合いだ.

2 =a nodding ACQUAINTANCE 2.

drop* (*an*) *acquaintance with *a person*/ ***drop*** *a person's* ***acquaintance*** 人との交際をやめる ▪ She has naturally *dropped his acquaintance*. 彼女は当然彼との交際をやめた.

make *a person's* ***acquaintance*/*make the acquaintance of*** *a person* 人と知り合いになる ▪ I am glad to *make your acquaintance*. お近づきになれてうれしゅうございます.

on* (*further*) *acquaintance (さらに)つき合ってみると ▪ *On (further) acquaintance* I found him a kind man. (さらに)つき合ってみると彼は親切な人だということがわかった.

pick acquaintance with …と偶然知り合いになる ▪ While in London I *picked acquaintance with* him. ロンドン滞在中私は偶然彼と知り合った.

renew *one's* ***acquaintance with*** …との旧交をあたためる ▪ I had a chance to *renew my acquaintance with* Smith then. 私はそのときスミスと旧交をあたためる機会を得た.

scrape* (*up*) (*an*) *acquaintance →SCRAPE[2].

acquire /əkwáɪər/ 動 ***an acquired taste*** → TASTE.

acquit /əkwít/ 動 ***acquit*** *oneself* 〚副詞(句)を伴って〛ふるまう, 演じる ▪ He *acquitted himself* well in battle. 彼は戦闘であっぱれな働きをした ▪ He *acquitted himself* to his credit. 彼は立派にふるまった.

be* [*stand*] *acquitted of …の罪なしとされる, の疑いが晴れる ▪ He *stands acquitted of* all intent to injure you. 彼は君を害する心の全然ないことが明らかになった.

acre /éɪkər/ 名 ***ancestral acres*** 《しばしば戯》先祖伝来の土地 ▪ These skills, like *ancestral acres*, were passed from father to son. これらの技術は, 先祖伝来の土地のように, 父から子へと伝えられた.

God's acre 墓地 ▪ This is their *God's acre*. ここは彼らの墓地です.

across /əkrɔ́ːs|əkrɔ́s/ 副 前 ***across a horse's back*** 馬に乗って ▪ I was *across a horse's back* then. 私はそのとき馬に乗っていた.

across each other 十文字に ▪ Lay two sticks *across each other*. 2本の棒を十文字に置きなさい.

across from 《口》…の真向かいに ▪ The store is just *across from* the post office. その店は郵便局のちょうど真向かいにある.

be across to *a person* 《俗》人の役目[責任]である ▪ It *is across to* you to help them. 彼らを援助するのは君の役目だ.

from across …の至るところから(の) ▪ This book gives golf course pictures *from across* the U.S. 本書は米国の至るところのゴルフコースの写真を示している.

right across …の至るところに ▪ There are 2 million mines scattered *right across* the region. その地域の至るところに200万の地雷が敷設してある.

act[1] /ækt/ 名 ***a balancing act*** (サーカスの)バランス芸; (対立する二者の)両立 (*between*) ▪ It's exhausting to perform *the balancing act between* work and family. 仕事と家族の両立は疲れる.

a hard* [*difficult, tough*] *act to follow 余人が真似できないようなすぐれた業績・人物 ▪ Beloved and energetic, Pope Paul VI was *a tough act to follow*. 人に愛された精力的な法王パウロ六世は, 余人が真似できないようなすぐれた人物であった.

a high-wire act 綱渡り的な行為, 危険な仕事[作業] ▪ For most of the 1850s, Douglas had performed *a* political *high-wire act*. 1850年代の大部分, ダグラスは政治的に危険な仕事を行っていた. ☞high-wire「綱渡り用の張り綱」.

act and deed 《法》(拘束力ある)証書 ▪ I deliver this as my *act and deed*. これを証書として渡します《署名のときに言う文句》.

act of God 不可抗力; 不慮の災害 ▪ He died by an *act of God* brought about by the flood. 彼は洪水による天災によって不慮の死を遂げた. ☞しばしば法律文書で使われる.

an act of faith 信念[信仰, 信頼]に基づく行為 ▪ Remembrance of the Holocaust is *an act of faith* in mankind. ホロコーストを記憶しておくことは人類への信頼を示す行為だ.

an impossible act to follow 《口》=a hard ACT to follow.

catch* [*take*]** *a person* ***in the* (*very*) *act of 人を現行中に捕える ▪ He *was caught in the (very) act of* stealing. 彼は窃盗の現行犯で捕えられ

A

た ▪ Should the throes of change *take* me *in the act of* writing it, Hyde will tear it to pieces. 万一変身の激痛がそれを書いているとき私を襲ったら，ハイドがそれをずたずたに破るであろう．

clean up** one's **act 性根を入れ替える，行いを改める ▪ If Bob doesn't *clean up his act* soon, he's going to end up in jail. もしボブがすぐに行いを改めなければ，ついには刑務所行きになるだろう．

do* [*perform, stage*] *a disappearing* [*vanishing*] *act 《口》(人が必要とされるときに)姿を消す ▪ Eric always *does a disappearing act* when he is wanted in the office. エリックは事務所で用事があるときはいつも姿を消してしまう．

do the ... act 《米口》…の[らしい]行いをする ▪ They *did the* hospitality *act* in great shape. 彼らは大いに歓待した．

get* [*put*] *one's* act [*it,* etc] *together 《口》行動に一貫性をもたせる，態勢を整える ▪ If he *got his act together* he'd be a good player. 彼が態勢を整えたならば，いい選手になるだろう ▪ The prodigal son has been trying to *get his life together*. 放蕩息子は生活を整えようと努めてきた．

get in on the act 《俗》(成功した仕事に)一枚加わる ▪ He *got in on the act* for profit. 彼は利益目あてに一枚加わった．

get into the act **1** 同様な行為をする ▪ After Iran nationalized the Anglo-Iran Oil Co., Iraq *got into the act*. イランがアングロ・イラン石油会社を国有化してから，イラクも同様なことをした．

2 《俗》＝get in on the ACT.

go into** one's **act 演技を始める; 自分らしくふるまい出す ▪ He was about to *go into his act* again. 彼は再び自分らしくふるまい出そうとしていた．

have act or part in …に加担する，の共犯者である ▪ He *had* no *act or part in* the murder of the man. 彼はその男の殺人の共犯者ではなかった．

in the act **1** 行為の最中に ▪ The cop caught the pickpocket *in the act*. 警官はすりを現行犯で捕まえた．

2 性交の現場で ▪ Her father caught them *in the act*. 彼女の父親は二人が性交している現場を見つけた．

in the* (*very*) *act of まさに…しようとして (＝on the POINT of) ▪ He was *in the very act of* starting. 彼は今まさに出発するところだった．

put on an act 《俗》芝居[狂言]をする ▪ He is just *putting on an act*. なに，ただの彼の狂言さ．

read the Riot Act →RIOT.

act[2] /ækt/ 動 ***act a good part*** 立派にふるまう ▪ He *acts a good part* whether vanquished or victorious. 彼は負けても勝っても立派にふるまう．

act** one's **age →AGE.

act in** one's **own way →in one's own WAY 1.

act on* (*the*) *behalf of** a person/**act on** a person's **behalf 人の代理を務める ▪ These agencies will *act on the behalf of* individual consumers. これらの代理店は個々の消費者の代理を務める．

action /ǽkʃən/ 名 ***a piece* [*slice*] *of the action*** **1** 《口》(活動・利益に)あずかること，(商売・取引などの)分け前，おこぼれ ▪ Everyone wants to get *a slice of the action* now that we are making a lot of money. いま我々は大いに儲けているのでみんな分け前をもらいたがっている ▪ They wanted *a piece of the action* in this land deal. 彼らはこの土地取引の利益の分け前を求めた．

2 《俗》セックス ▪ Alan also had *a piece of the action* with the slut, right? アランはそのあばずれ女とセックスもしたんだね，そうだろ?

action at a distance 隔作用; 遠隔操作 ▪ Spooky *action at a distance* is part of nature. 不気味な遠隔作用は自然の一部である．

Actions speak louder than words. 《諺》行動は言葉よりも雄弁である．

be back in action 仕事に復帰する ▪ I *was back in action* but we didn't win. 僕は仕事に復帰したが，我々は勝てなかった．

bring an action against …を相手取って訴訟を起こす ▪ They *brought an action against* the man. 彼らはその男を相手どって訴訟を起こした．

bring ... into action **1** …を活動させる; を実行する ▪ You can *bring* all your faculties *into action* in this work. あなたはこの仕事では才能を残らず働かすことができる ▪ The regulations will *be brought into action* before long. その規則はまもなく実施されるだろう．

2 戦闘を始めさせる，戦闘に参加させる ▪ The words promptly *brought* the platoon *into action*. その言葉は即座に小隊に戦闘を始めさせた．

by* [*under*] *the action of …の作用で ▪ The roof had fallen in *by the action of* the weather. 屋根は風雨の作用で落ち込んでいた．

call ... into action …を働かせる ▪ He *called into action* all of his muscles. 彼は筋肉のすべてを働かせた．

Deliberate in counsel, prompt in action. 《諺》考慮は慎重に，行動は敏速に，「初めは処女のごとく，終わりは脱兎のごとし」．

***fit the action to the word*(*s*)** →suit the ACTION to the word(s).

go into action 戦闘[行動]を開始する ▪ We immediately *went into action*. 我々はすぐに戦闘を始めた[行動に入った]．

go out of action (機械などが)動かなくなる ▪ The fighter has *gone out of action*. 戦闘機は動かなくなった．

in action 活動中，戦闘中，実行中 ▪ They are now *in action* in parliament. 彼らは今国会で活動中だ ▪ He was killed *in action*. 彼は戦死した．

industrial action ストライキ ▪ They are going to take *industrial action*. 彼らはストをかまえようとしている．

Let's see some action. 《口》実際にやってみせてくれないか ▪ Quit talking about it—*let's see some action*! 講釈はやめて—実際にやってみせてくれないか!

out of action **1** 故障して; 活動していないで ▪ How do you work this?—Sorry, it is *out of action*. どうやって動かすの?—あいにく故障中です.
2 (選手が)けがで出場できない ▪ Jim is *out of action* with a broken foot. ジムは脚を折って出場できない.
property in action 《法》(所有していないが)訴訟によって回復しうる財産 ▪ All *property in action* depends entirely upon contracts. 訴訟によって回復しうる財産はひとえに契約の如何による.
put ... in [***into***] ***action*** ...を実行に移す; を運転させる ▪ Schemes *were put in action* against his life. 彼の生命を奪う企てが実行に移された.
put ... out of action **1** (機械など)を動かなくする; (軍艦・飛行機など)の戦闘力を失わせる ▪ Antiaircraft fire *put* two of the planes immediately *out of action*. 高射砲撃により2機はすぐに戦闘不能となった.
2 (選手)をけがで出場できなくする ▪ A broken arm *put* him *out of action* for two months. 腕を折ったため彼は2か月間出場できなくなった.
see action 戦闘に参加する ▪ He *saw action* on a destroyer. 彼は駆逐艦に乗って戦闘に参加した.
spring to [***into***] ***action*** [***life***] →SPRING to life.
suit [***fit***] ***the action to the word***(***s***)/***suit*** *one's* ***actions to*** *one's* ***words*** 《文》言行を一致させる, (約束・脅迫の)言葉をすぐ実行に移す (cf. Sh., *Haml*. 3. 2. 19) ▪ *Suiting the action to the word*, he set off for the station. 言葉をすぐ実行に移して彼は駅へ向けて出発した.
swing [***go***] ***into action*** てきぱきと[威勢よく]活動し始める, 動き出す ▪ Indoor polo teams will *swing into action* here tonight. 室内ポロチームが今夜当地で威勢よく対戦を始める予定だ.
take action 作用し始める, 働き出す; 処置をとる, 行動を起こす; 訴訟を起こす ▪ He *took* prompt *action* to defend his rights. 彼は自分の権利を守るため即座に処置をとった ▪ You must *take action* in the matter. 君はその件で行動を起こさねばならない.
take action against ...を弾圧する, 弾劾する; を取り締る; を罰する ▪ They *took action against* the union. 彼らは組合を弾圧した ▪ We must *take action against* a violation. 我々は違反行為を処罰せねばならない.
take action on 《米》...の議決[決定, 実施, 解決]をする ▪ The House *took action on* the measure. 議会はその法案を議決した ▪ The Assembly had *taken* final *action on* the problem. 総会はその問題を最終的に解決した.
take an action against =bring an ACTION against.
under the action of →by the ACTION of.
where (***all***) ***the action is*** 刺激的な[重要な]活動が行われている所, 活気のある場所 ▪ *Where the action is* in New York. 活気ある場所はニューヨークだ ▪ I'd like to live *where the action is*. 活気のある場所に住みたい.

active /ǽktɪv/ 形 ***on active service*** [***duty***]
1 現役服務の; 従軍中の ▪ The War called him away from Australia *on active service*. 大戦は彼をオーストラリアから召集して従軍させた.
2 常勤[専任]で ▪ Jane still works *on active duty*. ジェインはまだ専任で働いている.

activity /æktívəti/ 名 ***be in activity*** (火山などが)活動中である ▪ The volcano *is* now *in activity*. その火山は現在活動中である.
call ... into activity ...を活動させる ▪ His interior forces *are called into activity*, and he now knows his powers. 彼の内部の力が働き始め, 彼はいまや自分の力を悟る.
show activity 活気を呈する, 色めく ▪ Business is *showing* considerable *activity*. 商売は著しい活気を呈している.
with activity 活発に ▪ He stepped back *with activity*. 彼はさっと退いた.

actor /ǽktər/ 名 ***a bad actor*** 《米口》むちゃな[手におえない]やつ[動物]; 常習犯 ▪ He is *a bad actor* when he is drunk. 彼は酔うとむちゃをする.

actual /ǽktʃuəl/ 形 *one's* ***actual*** 《英口》本物の, 純粋な ▪ I'd like to know *his actual* IQ. 彼の本当のIQが知りたい.

actuality /æktʃuǽləti/ 名 ***in actuality*** 実際に ▪ Universals are real in potentiality rather than *in actuality*. 一般概念は, 実際におけるよりも, 可能性において実在する.

Adam /ǽdəm/ 名 ***Adam's ale*** [***wine***] 《文》水 ▪ He drank *Adam's ale*. 彼は水を飲んだ[禁酒した].
(***as***) ***old as Adam*** →OLD.
not know *a person* ***from Adam*** 人(の顔)を全然知らない ▪ He did *not know* us *from Adam*. 彼は我々を全然知らなかった.
since Adam was a boy 長い間, 大昔から ▪ You're hunting up that pen you've had *since Adam was a boy*. 君はずっと前から持っていたあのペンを捜しているのだね.
the old Adam 原罪, 人性の悪; (改心・更生しない)罪深い状態 (《聖》*Roms*. 6. 6) ▪ There is a deal of *the old Adam* in me. 僕には人性の悪が多くある.

adamant /ǽdəmənt/ 名形 ***a heart of adamant*** 冷たく非情不動の心 (《聖》*Zech*. 7. 12) ▪ They had *hearts of adamant*. 彼らは石のような心を持っていた.
be adamant to ...に頑として応じない ▪ He *is adamant to* entreaties. 彼は懇願を全く聞きいれない.

adapt /ədǽpt/ 動 ***adapt*** *oneself* ***to*** ...に身を適応させる, 順応する ▪ She tried to *adapt herself to* her new surroundings. 彼女は新しい環境に順応しようと努めた.
(***be***) ***adapted for*** **1** ...に適して(いる) ▪ These clothes *are adapted for* winter wear. この服は冬着るのに適している.
2 ...用に改作される ▪ The novel *was adapted for* the stage. その小説は劇化された.
(***be***) ***adapted to*** =be ADAPTed for 1.

A

add /æd/ 動 ***add a touch of glamour*** [***class***] ***to*** …に魅惑[華(はな)]を添える ▪ Silk scarves *add a touch of glamour to* any outfit. シルクのスカーフはどのような服装にも華やぎを添えてくれる.

add weight to (議論・説)を強める ▪ This study *adds weight to* the theory that the climate is changing. この研究は気候が変わりつつあるという理論を強めるものである.

add*(*ed*) *to this [***that***] これ[それ]に加えて, その上 ▪ Sue lost her job last week and *added to that* she is pregnant again. スーは先週職を失い, その上また妊娠している.

if you add to this [***that***] = ADD(ed) to this.

I might add (前言にコメントして)ただし…だがね ▪ Your son has told me so much about you—all good, *I might add*. 息子さんは君のことをずいぶん話していたよ—ただし, 褒め言葉ばかりだがね.

to add to …に加えて ▪ *To add to* his difficulties, he lost his health. 種々の困難に加えて彼は健康を失った.

addict /ǽdɪkt/ 動 ***addict*** *oneself* ***to*** 〚名詞・動名詞を伴って〛…にふける, にやみつきになる ▪ Such persons will *addict themselves to* history. そのような人々は歴史にふけるだろう ▪ Denis *addicts himself to* lying in jest. デニスは冗談で嘘をつくことにやみつきになっている.

be addicted to 〚名詞・動名詞を伴って〛…にふけっている, の悪癖がある ▪ He *is addicted to* literature. 彼は文学に凝っている ▪ He *is addicted to* stealing. 彼は窃盗の悪癖がある.

addition /ədíʃən/ 名 ***have an addition to*** *one's* ***family*** 一人子供が増える, 子供が生まれる ▪ He *had an addition to his family*. 彼に一人子供が増えた.

in addition その上に ▪ I paid 5 dollars *in addition*. その上5ドル払った.

in addition to …に加えて, の上に ▪ *In addition to* that sum he still owes me £50. その金額の上に彼はまだ50ポンド私に借りがある.

address[1] /ǽdres|ədrés/ 名 ***a cover address*** 連絡先 ▪ I have *a cover address*, care of a bank in Chicago. 私はシカゴのある銀行気付, という連絡先を持っている.

a good address (特に都市の)高級住宅 ▪ Even now, a castle is *a good address*. 今もなお, お城は高級住宅です.

form [***mode, style***] ***of address*** (文書・口頭での)呼びかけ方, 敬称《Mr., Madam, sir など》 ▪ Your Honor is the *form of address* used when speaking to a judge. 「閣下」は裁判官に話しかけるときに用いられる敬称である.

pay *one's* ***addresses to*** (女性)に言い寄る, をくどく ▪ Many *paid their addresses to* the beautiful heiress. 美しい女相続人に言い寄った男は多かった.

to the address of 《米》(特に批評として)…に向けられた; に話しかけられた ▪ The speech was *to the address of* the farmers of the West. その演説は西部の農民に向けられたものであった.

with address 手ぎわよく ▪ He handled the problem *with address*. 問題を巧みに論じた.

address[2] /ədrés/ 動 ***address*** *oneself* ***to*** **1** …に話しかける; に手紙を出す ▪ He *addressed himself to* the reporters. 彼は報道記者たちに話しかけた.

2 (仕事など)に本気でとりかかる, 精力を傾ける ▪ You had better *address yourself to* the task. その仕事に本気でとりかかったほうがよい ▪ Let us *address ourselves to* revelry. さあ, 大いに飲めや歌えの大騒ぎをやらかそうよ.

adept /ədépt|ǽdept/ 形名 ***adept in*** [***at***] …に熟練して, がじょうずで ▪ She became *adept in* haggling over prices. 彼女は価格を値切ることがじょうずになった.

be an adept at [***in***] 《口》…の名人である ▪ He *is an adept at* lying [*in* sculpture]. 彼は嘘つきの名人[彫刻の名手]である.

adequate /ǽdɪkwət/ 形 ***be adequate to*** [***for***] **1** (任)に耐える ▪ He *is* quite *adequate to* his post. 彼はその任に十分耐える.

2 (必要)に応じうる, に十分である ▪ The supply *is* not *adequate to* the demand. 供給が需要に応じかねる.

adherence /ædhíərəns/ 名 ***give in*** *one's* ***adherence*** (***to***) (…に)加入する, 加担する ▪ Japan has *given in her adherence to* the treaty. 日本はその条約に加盟した.

adhesion /ædhíːʒən/ 名 ***give*** [***send***] ***in*** *one's* ***adhesion to*** …に加入[帰依, 同意]を申し入れる ▪ They *sent in their adhesion to* Rome. 彼らはローマへの忠誠を申し入れた ▪ He *gave in his adhesion to* the party. 彼は入党を申し入れた.

adieu /ədjúː/ 名 ***bid*** [***say***] ***adieu*** 《文・戯》いとまを告げる (*to*) ▪ The old man *bid* them *adieu*. 老人は彼らにいとまを告げた.

make [***take***] *one's* ***adieu*** いとまごいをする ▪ We *took our* last *adieu*. 我々は最後のいとまごいをした.

adit /ǽdət/ 名 ***have free adit*** 出入自由である ▪ You shall *have free adit*. あなたを出入自由にしてあげます. ☞adit = entrance.

adjacent /ədʒéɪsənt/ 形 ***be adjacent to*** …に隣接している ▪ These two men's farms *were adjacent to* each other. この二人の農場は互いに隣り合っていた.

adjourn /ədʒə́ːrn/ 動 ***adjourn without day***/***adjourn sine die*** 無期延期する ▪ The House *adjourned without day*. 議会は無期休会となった. ☞Ⓛ sine die 'without date'.

be adjourned until [***for***] (会議などが)…[の間]まで延期される ▪ The conference *was adjourned until* May 12 [*for* two weeks]. 会議は5月12日まで[2週間]延期された.

adjudge /ədʒʌ́dʒ/ 動 ***be adjudged*** (***to be***) 《文》(…だと)判定[宣告]される ▪ The company *was adjudged* (*to be*) bankrupt. その会社は破産したと宣告された ▪ Chick Evans *is adjudged* America's best golfer. チック・エバンズは米国の最優秀ゴルファーと判定されている. ☞通例 to be は省略される.

be adjudged to have *done* 《文》…したと判定される ▪ The reform *was adjudged to have* failed. 改革は失敗したと判定された.

adjust /ədʒʌ́st/ 動 ***adjust*** *oneself* 身なりを整える ▪ She quickly *adjusted herself* for the photo. 彼女は写真を撮るために素早く身なりを整えた.

adjust (*oneself*) ***to*** …に順応する ▪ The body will *adjust itself to* the climate. 体は気候に順応するものである ▪ I cannot *adjust to* my wife's mother. 私は家内の母とはうまくやってゆけない.

ad-lib, ad lib /ædlíb/ 動 アドリブ[即興]でやる ▪ Throughout the second act he had to *ad-lib* (his lines) constantly. 彼は第二幕で終始(台詞を)アドリブでやらなければならなかった.

administer /ədmínəstər/ 動 ***administer an oath to*** …に宣誓させる ▪ The *oath was administered to* him. 彼は宣誓させられた.

administer the medicine **1** 投薬する ▪ I *administered the medicine* to my boy. 私は子供にその薬を飲ませた.

2 処罰する ▪ They were forced to *administer the medicine* themselves. 彼らはやむなく自分らで処罰せねばならなかった.

admiration /ædməréɪʃən/ 名 ***a mutual admiration society*** 《戯》相互賞賛協会《互いにべた褒めしあう関係》 ▪ She characterized the Masons as *a "mutual admiration society"*. 彼女はメイスン夫妻の特徴を「相互賞賛協会」と評した. ☞Thoreau の *journal* (1851)から.

be struck with admiration (***at***) (…に)大いに感心する, 感に打たれる ▪ I *was struck with admiration at* his eloquence. 私は彼の雄弁に大いに感心した.

be the admiration of …の賞賛の的である ▪ He *is the admiration of* all the villagers. 彼はすべての村人の賞賛の的である.

in admiration 感嘆して ▪ The village people stood *in admiration*. 村人は感心して立っていた.

in admiration of [***at, for***] …に感嘆して ▪ We cried out *in admiration of* the beauty of the sight. 我々はその光景の美しさに感嘆の声をあげた.

to admiration 立派に ▪ He has succeeded *to admiration*. 彼はもののみごとに成功した.

with admiration うっとりと, 感嘆して ▪ He gazed at her *with admiration*. 彼はうっとりと彼女に見とれた.

admire /ədmáɪər/ 動 ***admire*** *a person* ***from afar*** 人をひそかに慕う ▪ That cute boy *admires* you *from afar*. あの利口な少年はあなたのことをひそかに慕っていますよ.

admission /ədmíʃən/ 名 ***Admission free.*** 入場無料 ▪ *Admission* to the lectures *free*. 聴講無料.

gain [***obtain***] ***admission*** 入場[入会, 入学]を許される ▪ He *gained admission* into the club. 彼はクラブへ入会を許された ▪ Early application is necessary to *obtain admission* to the school. その学校へ入学を許可されるには早期の出願が必要だ.

give [***grant***] ***free admission to*** …を自由に入らせる; に無料入場を許す ▪ We *give free admission to* students. 我々は学生を無料で入場させる.

make (***an***) ***admission of*** …を認める, を白状する ▪ He *made* full *admission of* his crime. 彼は罪をすっかり白状した.

on [***by***] *one's* ***own admission*** 自分も認めているように ▪ The authorities have, *on their own admission*, been lax in enforcing the law. 当局も自認しているように, その法律の執行が手ぬるかった.

admit /ədmít/ 動 ***admit*** *oneself* ***to*** …へ入る ▪ He *admitted himself to* the house. 彼はその家へ入った.

To admit one. 1枚1人限り《入場切符の文句》.

admittance /ədmítəns/ 名 ***grant*** [***refuse***] *a person* ***admittance to*** 人に(建物など)への入場を許す[断る] ▪ We *refused* him *admittance to* the house. 我々は彼がその家へ入ることを断った.

No admittance except on business. 「関係者以外立ち入り禁止」, 「無用の者入場謝絶」《掲示》.

admonish /ədmɑ́nɪʃ|-mɔ́n-/ 動 ***admonish*** *a person* ***against*** [***not to*** *do*] 人に…するなとさとす ▪ He *admonished* the boys *against* being late. 彼は生徒に遅刻するなとさとした.

ado /ədúː/ 名 ***have much ado to*** *do* …するのに苦労する ▪ I *have much ado to* keep out of debt. 借金せずにいるのがやっとこさだ.

make much ado (***in, about***) (…に)大騒ぎをする ▪ He *made much ado in* finding out his lodging. 彼は宿を見つけるのに大騒ぎした.

much ado about nothing から騒ぎ《Shakespeare の同名の劇》 ▪ As usual the media has made *much ado about nothing*. 例によってメディアはから騒ぎをした.

with much ado 大騒ぎして; やっとのことで ▪ He cleaned the house *with much ado*. 彼はやっとのことで家を掃除した.

without ado わけなく ▪ He won the race *without ado*. 彼はわけなく競走に勝った.

without more [***further***] ***ado*** あとは苦もなく; 無造作に, いきなり ▪ They were married *without more ado*. 彼らはさっさと結婚した ▪ Pay it *without further ado*. かれこれ言わずに払いたまえ.

adrenalin(e) /ədrénələn/ 名 ***get the*** [*one's*] ***adrenalin going*** [***flowing***] 興奮させる, どきどきさせる ▪ A good horror film is sure to *get your adrenalin going*. すぐれたホラー映画は必ずあなたをどきどきさせます.

adrift /ədríft/ 形 ***adrift of*** 《英口》(選手・チームが相手)にリードされて, に負けて ▪ Our team was *adrift of* the opponent. わがチームは敵に負けていた.

be all adrift **1** 《海》漂う ▪ The ship *was all adrift* for three days. その船は3日間漂っていた.

2 《口》方向がわからない, わけがわからない, 混乱している

A

▪ After what you have told me, I'*m all adrift*. 君があれだけ話してくれても，僕はさっぱりわけがわからない.

come adrift 《英》離れる，外れる (*from*) ▪ Some yachts *came adrift from* the anchors. 何艘(そう)かのヨットが錨から離れてしまった.

cut* [*cast, set*] *... adrift **1** (船)を波のまにまに漂わせる ▪ They *cut* the boat *adrift*. 彼らは船を波のまにまに漂わせた.

2 (人)を見捨てる，孤立させる ▪ The war has *cut* them *adrift* from a meaningful life. 戦争は意義ある生活から彼らを切り離してしまった.

3 関係を絶つ，縁を切る，独立させる ▪ A growing number of workers have *been cut adrift* from full-time jobs. 正社員の職を解雇される労働者が増えてきている.

get* [*come*] *adrift 流される ▪ The barrels *came adrift* in the storm. たるはそのあらしで流された.

go adrift **1** 漂流する ▪ His boat *went adrift* off Florida's coast. 彼の船はフロリダ海岸沖で漂流した.

2 脱線する ▪ You're *going adrift* from the subject. 本題から脱線しているよ.

3 なくなる，盗まれる ▪ Several books *went adrift* from the library. 数冊の書物が図書館からなくなった.

turn ... adrift …を漂流させる ▪ He fell overboard and *was turned adrift*. 彼は船から落ちて漂流した.

turn *a person* ***adrift*** 人を追い出す，お払い箱にする ▪ He *was turned adrift* by his stepmother. 彼はまま母に追い出された.

adult /ədʌ́lt|ǽdʌlt/ 名形 ***Adults only.*** (映画など)未成年者お断り.

be adult about …にまじめに取り組む ▪ Can we *be adult about* this, please? どうかこのことにはまじめに取り組もうよ.

adultery /ədʌ́ltəri/ 名 ***commit adultery*** 不貞を働く，不倫をする ▪ Is it still a sin to *commit adultery*? 不貞を働くのはいまだに罪なのだろうか.

advance[1] /ədvǽns|-vɑ́:ns/ 名 ***encourage* [*repel*]** *a person's* ***advances*** 人が接近しようとするのを歓迎する[はねつける] ▪ Far from *repelling his advances* she rather *encouraged them*. 彼女は彼の接近するのをはねつけるどころか，むしろ歓迎した.

in advance 前もって; 前金で; 立替えて ▪ Thank you *in advance*. 前もってお礼を申し上げます ▪ Send your luggage *in advance*. 手荷物は先に送っておきなさい ▪ It is necessary to pay *in advance* for the lessons. 授業料は前金で払わねばならない ▪ I am $100 *in advance* to him. 私は彼に100ドル立替えている.

in advance of …より進んで，先に立って (↔in ARREAR of) ▪ Galileo's ideas were *in advance of* the age. ガリレオの思想は時代に先んじていた ▪ *In advance of* the main army rode the drummers. 本部隊の先頭に立って鼓手隊が進んだ.

make advances **1** 金を融通する ▪ It is the business of banks to *make advances* to business firms. 企業へ金を融通するのが銀行の仕事である.

2 《口》(女性に)言い寄る ▪ Men are always looking for a chance to *make advances*. 男はいつも女に言い寄る機会をねらっている.

3 《口》親しくなろうとする，接近しようとする ▪ He *makes advances* towards [to] his superior. 彼は上役に取り入ろうとする.

4 進歩をとげる ▪ The Aztecs *made* great *advances* in the sciences, especially in astronomy. アステカ人は科学，特に天文学の面で大きな進歩をとげた.

advance[2] /ədvǽns|-vɑ́:ns/ 動 ***advance in life*** **1** 年をとる ▪ As we *advance in life* we learn the limits of our abilities. 年をとるにつれて我々は自分の能力の限界を悟るようになる.

2 立身[出世]する ▪ You should control your ego to *advance in life*. 君は立身出世したいというおのれの自我を抑制するべきだ.

advance in the world =ADVANCE in life 2.

***advance in years* [*age*]** 年をとる ▪ He has *advanced in years*. 彼は年をとった.

advance* (*money*) *on …を抵当に(金を)前貸しする; に(いくらの)手付金を打つ ▪ Please *advance* 10,000 yen *on* my salary. 1万円だけ月給の前貸ししてください ▪ He *advanced* $100 *on* the contract. その契約に100ドルの手付金を打った.

advance to the attack 進撃する ▪ We *advanced to the attack* at dawn. 夜明けに進撃した.

be advanced in years 高齢である ▪ He *is advanced in years*. 彼は高齢である.

advantage[1] /ədvǽntɪdʒ|-vɑ́:n-/ 名 ***be of great* [*no*] *advantage*** 大いに有利である[少しも有利でない] (*to*) ▪ His scholarship *was of great advantage to* him. 学識が彼には非常に有利だった.

find advantage in …は有益だと知る ▪ I *found advantage in* practising a handicraft. 私は手芸をやるのは有益だと知った.

gain* [*get, have*] *an advantage over (人)をしのぐ，(人)より有利な地歩を占める ▪ They *gained an advantage over* their opponents. 彼らは相手より有利な地歩を占めた.

get the advantage of = have the ADVANTAGE of 2.

give *A* ***an advantage* (*over*** *B*) Aを(Bよりも)優位に立たせる ▪ Stalin's position *gave* him *an advantage over* his rivals. スターリンはその地位のためにライバルたちよりも優位に立った.

have the advantage of **1** …という長所を持つ ▪ It *has the advantage of* being cheap. それは安いという長所がある.

2 …に勝る ▪ You *have the advantage of* me. 君のほうが僕よりも有利だ.

3 〚you を主語にして〛私のほうではあなたを存じあげませんが ▪ I'm afraid *you have the advantage of* me. どうもどなたか存じあげませんが.

make *one's* ***advantage of*** …を利用する ▪ The opposite party *made their advantage of* his scandal. 野党は彼のスキャンダルを利用した.

press* [*push, thrust*] *home an* [*one's*] *ad-

vantage 有利な点[好機]をうまく利用する ▪ There was no one in the room, so he *pressed home his advantage* and took the money. 部屋には誰もいなかった. そこで彼は好機を利用してその金を取った.

set ... off to advantage …を引き立たせる ▪ Japanese clothes *set* you *off to advantage*. 和服を着るとあなたは引き立って見える.

show ... to* (*good,* one's) *advantage …を実物以上によく見せる ▪ This lighting *shows* the interiors *to advantage*. この照明のためにインテリアが際立ってすばらしく見える.

***take advantage of* 1** …を利用する ▪ I *took advantage of* the fine weather to play tennis. 好天気を利用してテニスをした.

2 …につけこむ, (人)を欺く ▪ The dealer *took advantage of* the woman's ignorance and bought the picture very cheap. 商人はその女性の無知につけこんでその絵を非常に安く買った.

3 (女性)を誘惑する ▪ John *took advantage of* an innocent girl. ジョンはうぶな少女を誘惑した.

to advantage 有利に; 引き立って ▪ You look *to advantage* in Japanese clothes. あなたは和服を着ると引き立つ ▪ Armament expenditures might be used *to* better *advantage*. 軍備費はもっと有効に利用できるかもしれない.

***to* a person's *advantage*/ *to the advantage of* a person** …に有利に ▪ It turned out *to his advantage*. それは彼の利益となった.

to* (*the*) *best* [*good, better*] *advantage 最高の[よい, よりよい]状態で ▪ The party used public opinion *to* (*the*) *best advantage*. その政党は世論を最大限に利用した ▪ This dress really shows your figure *to better advantage*. このドレスを着ると, ほんとにあなたのスタイルが一層引き立ちますよ.

turn ... to* (one's) *advantage …を利用する ▪ He *turned* the situation *to his advantage*. 彼はその事態を利用した.

advantage[2] /ədvǽntɪdʒ|-vɑ́:n-/ 動 ***culturally advantaged*** 《婉曲》裕福な, 上流階級の ▪ I can't deny I had a *culturally advantaged* upbringing. 私が恵まれた家庭に育ったことは否めない.

adverse /ædvə́:rs/ 形 ***be adverse to* 1** …に反対する ▪ He *is adverse to* going to America. 彼はアメリカ行きに反対である.

2 …に不利である ▪ The judgment *was adverse to* the plaintiff. 判決は原告に不利だった.

advertisement /ædvərtáɪzmənt|ədvə́:tɪs-/ 名 ***put* [*insert*] *an advertisement in*** (新聞など)に広告を出す ▪ We *put an advertisement in* the magazine. 雑誌に広告を出した.

advice /ədváɪs/ 名 ***follow* a person's *advice*** 人の勧めに従う ▪ He *followed his friend's advice* literally. 彼は友人の勧めに忠実に従った.

give* a person *a piece* [*several bits*] *of advice 人に一つの[種々の]忠告を与える ▪ I *gave* him *a piece of advice*. 私は彼に一言忠告をした.

take* [*seek*] *advice 助言を求める ▪ He *took* medical *advice*. 医者の診察を受けた ▪ I will *seek* legal *advice* at once. すぐ弁護士に相談しよう.

take* a person's *advice 人の忠告をいれる ▪ He *took my advice* as to what he should do. 彼は身のふり方について私の意見に従った.

advise /ədváɪz/ 動 ***advise* a person *to* do** 人に…するよう勧める ▪ The doctor *advised* me *to* go to the seaside. 医者は私に海へ行くよう勧めた.

***as advised* (*in our letter of*)** 《商》(…の私どもの手紙に)述べてありますように ▪ *As advised in our letter of* March 18, we are commencing the trial production of our milk. 3月18日の手紙でお知らせいたしました通り, 私どもの牛乳の試験生産を始めます.

***be well* [*ill*] *advised to* do** …するのは賢明[愚]である ▪ He will *be well advised to* ask his father's pardon. 彼は父に謝るのが賢明であろう ▪ You would *be ill advised* only *to* wait, doing nothing. 何もしないでただ待つだけでは愚であろう.

keep* a person *advised of 《商》人に…をずっと知らせる ▪ I shall *keep* you *advised of* the state of the market. 絶えず市況をお知らせします.

advisement /ədváɪzmənt/ 名 ***take ... under advisement*** …をとくと考える, 協議する ▪ Please *take* the application *under advisement*. どうぞ申し込みをよく考え(た上で受け)てください.

advocate /ǽdvəkət/ 名 ***the devil's advocate*** (論争などのため)欠点ばかりを取りあげて反対する人 ▪ I played [acted] *the devil's advocate* to him to test the firmness of his decision. 私は彼の決心の堅さをためすためわざと彼に反対してみた ▪ Allow me to play *the devil's advocate* and express some skepticism. (議論を深めるため)故意に反対の立場をとって懐疑的な態度を表すことを許してくれ.

afar /əfɑ́:r/ 副 ***afar off*** ずっと遠くに ▪ I saw a light *afar off*. はるか彼方に明かりが見えた.

from afar 遠方から ▪ I traveled *from afar*. 私は遠方から旅して来た.

affair /əféər/ 名 ***a man of affairs*** 事務家 ▪ He is *a* well-known *man of affairs*. 彼は有名な実務家だ.

a pretty state of affairs 《口》困った事態 ▪ He hasn't got a penny and his wife's ill. It is *a pretty state of affairs*, indeed. 彼は1ペニーも持っていないし, 細君は病気だ. 本当に困った事態だ.

a state of affairs →the STATE of things.

affairs of state 国事 ▪ A prime minister is kept busy with *affairs of state*. 総理大臣は国事のため常に忙しい.

an affair of honor 《口》決闘《男子の面目に関すること》 ▪ The French called it *an affair of honor*. フランス人はそれを決闘と呼んだ.

an affair of love 不倫 ▪ Your friend intends to carry on *an affair of love*. 君の友人は不倫を続けていくつもりだ.

attend to* [*mind*] one's *own affairs いらぬ世話をしない《自分自身のことに気をつける》 ▪ I told him to *mind his own affairs*. 私は彼にいらぬ世話

A

をするなと言ってやった.

be at the head of affairs →HEAD[1].

get** one's **affairs straight 身辺の諸事(特に財政)を整理する ▪ *Getting my affairs straight*, I will make a fresh start. 私は身辺を整理して新規に出発します.

***have an affair* (*with*)** (…と)親しくする ▪ He is *having an affair with* her. 彼は彼女と親しくしている.

That's my* [*your*] *affair. それは君[僕]の知ったことではない ▪ *That's my* own *affair*. それはお前の口を出すところではない.

affected /əféktəd/ 形 ***be well* [*ill*, etc.] *affected towards*** …に対して好感[悪感情, など]を持っている ▪ He *is well affected towards* the government. 彼は政府に心服している.

affection /əfékʃən/ 名 ***gain* [*win*]** *a person's* ***affection*(*s*)** 人の愛をかち取る, 人に愛されるようになる ▪ He *gained Mary's affections* at last. 彼はついにメアリーの愛をかち取った.

have* (*an*) *affection for …を愛している ▪ He *had* a great *affection for* his daughter. 彼は娘を非常に愛していた.

set** one's **affection*(*s*) *on …を愛する, に好意を寄せる ▪ He *set his affections on* the pony. 彼はその小馬を愛した.

affectionately /əfékʃənətli/ 副 ***Yours affectionately*** さようなら, かしこ《近親間や親しい女子の間の手紙の結び》 ▪ Please be thinking of me. *Yours affectionately*. どうか私のことを想っていてください. かしこ.

affidavit /æfədéɪvət/ 名 ***make* [*take*] *an affidavit*** 《口》(証人が)供述書に偽りのないことを宣誓する ▪ I will *make affidavit* that I have returned the sum borrowed. 私は借りた金額は返したという供述書に偽りのないことを誓います ▪ I am ready to *take an affidavit* of this any day. このことについては私はいつでも進んで偽りのないことを宣誓する.

swear an affidavit 《法》(証人が)供述書に偽りのないことを宣誓する ▪ The deponent *swears an affidavit*. 供述人は供述書に偽りのないことを宣誓する.

take an affidavit **1**《法》(判事が)宣誓供述書を取る ▪ The judge *took an affidavit* from one of the employees. 判事は従業員の一人から宣誓供述書を取った.

2 →make an AFFIDAVIT.

affiliate /əfílièɪt/ 動 ***be affiliated with* [*to*]** …と近親である; と提携している; と関連がある ▪ English must *be affiliated with* Dutch. 英語はオランダ語と近親関係があるにちがいない ▪ Our society *is affiliated with* theirs. 我々の協会は彼らのと提携している ▪ This hospital *is affiliated to* our university. この病院はわが大学の付属病院である.

affinity /əfínəti/ 名 ***bear an affinity with*** …と親近性を持つ ▪ The sound of every instrument *bears a* perfect *affinity with* the rest. どの楽器の音も他のものと完全な親近性がある.

have an affinity for **1** …に魅力を感じる ▪ He *has an affinity for* politics. 彼は政治が好きだ.

2 …に親和力を持つ ▪ Basic dyes *have an affinity for* silk. 塩基性染料は絹に親和力を持っている.

affirmative /əfə́ːrmətɪv/ 名 ***in the affirmative*** 肯定的に; はいと(言う) ▪ His companion replied *in the affirmative*. 彼の友はそうだと答えた.

afflict /əflíkt/ 動 ***be afflicted by* [*at*]** …に苦しむ, 悩む ▪ She *is* greatly *afflicted at* the loss of her child. 彼女は子供の死にひどく悲しんでいる.

be afflicted with (病など)で苦しむ ▪ He *is* sorely *afflicted with* rheumatism. 彼はリューマチにかかってひどく苦しんでいる.

affluence /ǽfluəns/ 名 ***in affluence*** 富裕で ▪ He lives *in affluence*. 彼は富裕な暮らしだ.

afford /əfɔ́ːrd/ 動 ***can afford not to*** *do* 《米》…しなくとも大丈夫だ ▪ We *can afford not to* call on him. 我々は彼を訪問しなくても大丈夫だ.

can afford to *do* **1** …する余裕がある ▪ I *can afford to* keep a motorcar. 私は車を持つ余裕がある.

2《米》…しても大丈夫だ ▪ He *can afford to* sound off now. 彼は今はもう自分の意見をまくしたてても大丈夫だ.

can ill* [*not*] *afford to *do* **1** …する余裕がない; するわけにはいかない ▪ We *can ill afford to* discharge him. 彼を首にするわけにはいかない ▪ I *can't afford to* offend my employer. 雇主を怒らしてなんかいられない.

2《米》…したら大変だ ▪ The nation *can ill afford to* allow him to retire. 国民は彼を引退させたら重大なことになる.

cannot afford not to *do* 《米》…しなかったら大変なことになる ▪ The United States *cannot afford not to* stay ahead of the world. 合衆国が世界に先んじていなかったら大変である.

affront /əfrʌ́nt/ 名 ***offer an affront to*** …を侮辱する ▪ They *offered* great *affronts to* his person. 彼らは彼の体にひどい侮辱を加えた.

put an affront on …を侮辱する ▪ It was something to have *put an* open *affront on* the Eastern king. 東方の国王に公然と侮辱を加えたということはたいしたことだった.

***suffer an affront* (*at the hands of*)** (…から)侮辱を受ける ▪ He *suffered an affront at the hands of* his master. 彼は主人から侮辱を受けた.

afield /əfíːld/ 動 ***far* [*farther, further*] *afield*** ずっと遠く; 遠く離れた; はるかかなた ▪ He traveled *far afield*. 彼はずっと遠くへ旅した ▪ Reporters came from as *far afield* as Japan and China. 報道記者らははるか日本や中国からやって来た.

too far afield 遠く離れすぎて, 踏み迷って ▪ It prevents the student from straying *too far afield* in his reading. それは学生が読書においてひどく脱線するのを防ぐ.

aflame /əfléɪm/ 形 ***set … aflame*** **1** …を燃え立たせる ▪ They *set aflame* the fire already kindled. 彼らは既につけられた火をさらに燃え立たせた.

2 (血)を沸き立たせる ▪ My curiosity *was set aflame*. 私の好奇心がかき立てられた.

afloat /əflóʊt/ 形 ***keep*** [***stay***] ***afloat*** **1** (沈まないように)水に浮かんでいる ▪ He is *keeping afloat*. 彼はずっと水に浮かんでいる.

2 借金しないでいる ▪ *Keep afloat*. 借金をせずにいなさい.

3 水に浮かばせておく; 流通させておく ▪ *Keep* it *afloat*. それを水に浮かばせておけ ▪ They *kept* the bills *afloat*. 彼らは手形を流通させておいた.

set [***get***]***... afloat*** **1** …を浮かばせる ▪ They *set* the ship *afloat*. 彼らはその船を進水させた.

2 …を流布させる, 流通させる ▪ They *set* rumors *afloat* about him. 彼らは彼についての噂を流布した ▪ He *got* a newspaper *afloat*. 彼は新聞を発行した.

afoot /əfʊ́t/ 形 ***get afoot*** **1** 歩けるようになる ▪ The patient is now sufficiently strong to *get afoot*. 病人はもう歩けるほど元気になった.

2 始まる, 行われる ▪ The plan will soon *get afoot*. その計画はまもなく始まるだろう.

not know whether *one* ***is afoot or a-horseback*** 《米口》少し逆上している, 我を忘れている ▪ He did*n't know whether* he *was afoot or a-horseback*. 彼はいくぶん有頂天になっていた.

set ... afoot (計画・事業など)を起こす ▪ Inquiries *were set afoot* at once. すぐに調査が開始された.

afoul /əfáʊl/ 形 ***run*** [***fall***] ***afoul of*** 《米》…と衝突する, もつれる ▪ We *ran afoul of* the ship. 我々はその船と衝突した ▪ He went back to Italy only to *run afoul of* the police again. 彼はイタリアに戻ったが, またぞろ警察とややこしいことになった.

afraid /əfréɪd/ 形 ***be afraid for*** **1** …を心配する ▪ Parents *are afraid for* the safety of their children. 親たちは子供の安全を心配している.

2 (人)のことを気うかう ▪ She is very ill. I'*m afraid for* her. 彼女は重病だ. 彼女のことが気がかりだ.

be afraid lest ... (***should***) …しはしないかと恐れる[思う] ▪ I *am afraid lest* he (*should*) be late. 彼は遅れはしないかしら.

be afraid of …を恐れる ▪ Don't *be afraid of* making mistakes in speaking English. 英語を話すとき誤るのを恐れてはなりません.

be afraid that 《口》…ではないかと心配する ▪ Meg *was afraid that* cops would shoot her son. メグは警官が息子を撃つのではないか心配していた.

be afraid to *do* 怖がって…しない ▪ He *was afraid to* touch a rat. 彼は怖くてネズミに触れなかった.

I am [***I'm***] ***afraid*** 残念ながら…と思う ▪ *I'm afraid* it's going to rain. 雨が降るのじゃないかしら ▪ *I'm afraid* I can't help you in the matter. 残念ながらこの件についてはご助力いたしかねます ▪ Is he not coming?—*I'm afraid* not [so]. 彼は来ないのですか—どうやら来ないらしいです[そうらしいです].

aft /æft|ɑːft/ 副 ***lay aft*** 《海》船尾の方へ行く, 後退する ▪ The ship *laid aft*. 船は後退した ▪ Seaman Jones, *lay aft*! ジョーンズ船員, 船尾へ.

after /ǽftər|ɑ́ːf-/ 前 接 *A* ***after*** *A* AまたA《繰返し, 継続を表す》 ▪ Wave *after* wave came crashing on the shore. 波また波が岸辺に打ち寄せてきた ▪ I waited for her return day *after* day. 彼女の帰還を来る日も来る日も待ちわびた ▪ Hour *after* hour he toiled away at his new novel. 彼は何時間も新作小説の執筆に精を出した ▪ Car *after* car was passing. 車が次々に通っていた.

after a little しばらくの後, 少しして ▪ He opened his mouth *after a little*. 彼はしばらくして口を開いた.

after a while →WHILE.

after all **1** 最後に ▪ He came *after all* (the others). 彼は最後に来た.

2 結局, つまり ▪ He said he would not come in, but he came in *after all*. 彼は入らないと言ったが, 結局入って来た.

3 〚名詞を伴って〛…にもかかわらず ▪ *After all* my care, it was broken. 大いに注意したが, それはこわれた.

4 何と言っても ▪ I think you should invite him to your wedding; *after all*, he is your brother. 君の結婚式に彼を招待すべきだと思う. 何と言っても君のお兄さんなのだから.

after all is said and done →SAY[2].

After you. どうぞお先へ ▪ *After you*, please. どうぞお先へ.

after you with ... 《口》…についてはどうぞお先へ ▪ *After you with* the paper, please. 新聞をどうぞお先に(すんだら見せてください).

be after *A* ***for*** *B* A(人)にBをしつこく求める ▪ You *are* only *after* me *for* my money. 君は僕にお金をねだるだけだね.

be after *a person* ***to*** *do* 《米口》…するよう人に求める ▪ He *was* always *after* me *to* join the party. 彼はいつも私に入党を勧めた.

before or after 前にも後にも ▪ I was never so treated either *before or after*. 私は後にも先にもこんな扱いを受けたことがなかった.

on and after …以後 ▪ Lessons begin at 7 *on and after* May 1. 5月1日以後授業は7時に始まる.

one after another →ONE.

one after the other →ONE.

the Monday [***week, year,*** etc.] ***after next*** 次の次の月曜日[週, 年, など] ▪ Bill is not expected until *the week after next*. ビルは翌々週までは来ない.

afternoon /æ̀ftərnúːn|ɑ̀ːf-/ 名 ***an afternoon farmer*** 《口》怠け者, ぐず ▪ He is too much *an afternoon farmer* to succeed in college. 彼はぐずだから, 大学でよい成績は取れない.

again /əgén/ 副 ***again*** [***ever, time***] ***and again*** 何度も何度も ▪ *Again and again* the assailants were driven back. 攻撃軍は何度も何度も撃退された.

(***all***) ***over again*** →OVER.

as much [***many, large,*** etc.] ***again*** (***as***) (…の)2倍の量[数, 大きさ, など] ▪ Next month I am

A

to perform in a theater *as large again as* this. 来月はこの2倍の大きさの劇場で演じることになっています ▪ These shoes cost me *as much again as* the last pair I bought. この靴はこの前買った靴の2倍金がかかった.

(every) now and again →(every) NOW and then.

half again as much as 《米》…の1倍半(の量) ▪ This is almost *half again as much as* the original cost of the washer. これはその洗濯機の元の値段のほぼ1倍半だ.

half as much [many, large, etc.] ***again (as)*** (…の)1倍半の量[数, 大きさ, など] ▪ They had already increased the pile of firewood by about *half as much again*. 彼らはたき木の山を1倍半ほどすでに増やしていた ▪ The grouse is *half as large again as* a partridge. ライチョウは大きさがウズラの1倍半ある.

make again 元どおりになる ▪ The reef will *make again* a few feet ahead. 数フィート先で鉱脈は元どおりになるだろう.

on again, off again/off again, on again 変わりやすい, 定まらない, AだったりBだったり ▪ They have an *off again, on again* relationship. 彼らには定まらない関係がある ▪ As for the athletic meet, it's *on again, off again*. It depends on the weather. 運動会の件だが, あるかもしれないし, ないかもしれない. 天気次第だね.

once [over] again もう一度 ▪ They did it *once again*. 彼らはそれをもう一度した.

once and again →ONCE.

render again 《古》…を返す ▪ Please *render* me my knife *again*. 私のナイフをお返しください.

then [there] again しかしまた; また反面 ▪ It might happen. *Then again* it might not. それは起こるかもしれない. しかしまた起こらないかもしれない.

think again (再考して)考えを変える ▪ I'd advise you to *think again* before quitting your job. 仕事をやめる前に思い直してみてはどうかね.

time and again →AGAIN and again.

turn again 《古》(通例戻るために)向きを変える ▪ He *turned again* to take some minutes' exercise. 彼は数分運動するために向きを変えた.

against /əgénst/ 前 ***against payment of cost*** 代金引換えに (→CASH on delivery) ▪ Deliver this package *against payment of cost*. この荷物を代金と引換えに渡しなさい.

against the clock →against TIME.

as against →AS.

dead against …に断然反対して; に断然不利で ▪ He declared himself *dead against* the plan. 彼はその計画に断然反対だと言明した ▪ You'll find your account *dead against* you. 貸借勘定が全く自分の借りになっているのがわかりますよ.

have something [nothing] against …に嫌悪感[悪意]を抱く[抱かない] ▪ I *have something against* anyone like that. 私はあのような人には嫌悪感を抱いている ▪ I *have nothing against* Christians or Muslims. 私はキリスト教徒やイスラム教徒に悪意は抱いていない.

over against →OVER.

age /eɪdʒ/ 名 ***a golden age*** 黄金時代, 全盛期 ▪ The 70s were definitely *a golden age* for Adidas running shoes. 70年代が確実にアディダスのランニング・シューズの黄金時代だった.

a good old age かなりの年齢 (《聖》*Gen*. 15:15) ▪ Like his father, he reached *a good old age*. 父親のように彼もまたかなりの年齢に達した.

a [the] grand old age 高齢 ▪ My father died at *the grand old age* of 92. 父は92歳の高齢で亡くなった.

act [be] *one's* ***age*** 《口》年相応にふるまう ▪ Sit down and *act your age*. きちんと座ってお利口にしなさい ▪ Grandpa, it's time you stopped riding motorcycles and *acted your age*. おじいちゃん, もうバイクに乗るのをやめて, おとなしくしてもいいころだよ.

Age before beauty. 美人よりも老人が先《人(特に年長者)に道を譲るときの言葉; 階段を上がったり危険な所で先に立つ男性がするあいさつ》.

Age before honesty. 正直よりも年齢が先,「亀の甲より年の功」《特に年長者が「どうぞお先へ」とすすめられて答える言葉》.

at [to] a [the] ripe old age 《口》熟年で[に達するまで] ▪ Dad drives a car *at the ripe old age* of 75. おやじは75歳という熟年で車を運転している ▪ He began to write poems when he had lived *to a ripe old age*. 彼は熟年に達してから詩を書き始めた.

at a [the] tender age 幼い年で ▪ He maintains that money skills are best taught *at a tender age*. 金儲けの技術は幼年時に教えるのが一番よいと彼は主張する ▪ Her son died *at the tender age* of 8. 彼女の息子は8つという幼い年で死んだ.

at *one's* ***age*** (…くらい)の年で ▪ *At your age* you should be wiser. 君くらいの年ではもっと分別がほしい.

be *a person's* ***age*** ある人の年(齢)である ▪ I had a son when I *was your age*. 私は君の年のころには息子がいた.

be an age 《口》長くかかる ▪ What *an age* this girl *is* getting ready! この子は用意するのになんと長くかかるんだろう!

be [come, become] of age **1**《口》成年である[に達する]《18歳または21歳》 ▪ John will *be of age* on his next birthday. ジョンは今度の誕生日に成年になる ▪ When did he *come of age*? 彼はいつ成年に達したか.

2 (組織などが)十分発達する ▪ This company has really *come of age*. この会社も本当に発展した ▪ Travel by car *came of age* in the middle of the 20th century. 自動車旅行は20世紀の中葉に本格的になった.

be of an age (with) (…と)同じ年齢である ▪ We *are of an age*. 我々は同い年だ ▪ His wife *is of an age with* himself. 彼の妻は彼と同い年だ.

feel *one's* ***age*** 寄る年波を感じる ▪ After the

party I was *feeling my age*. パーティーのあとで私は寄る年波を感じていた.

for** one's **age 年の割りには ▪He looks old *for his age*. 彼は年の割りにはふけて見える.

***for an age* [*ages*]** 《口》長年月, ずいぶん長く ▪I haven't seen you *for ages*. ずいぶん長い間会わなかったね《久しぶりだね》.

from* [*with*] *age 老齢のため; 年を経たので; 年を経るにつれて ▪The book was yellowed *from age*. その本は古いので黄色くなっていた ▪Her eyesight got weaker *with age*. 年のせいで彼女の視力が衰えた ▪Wines get better *with age*. ワインは古くなるほどよくなる.

from age to age 代々(続いて) ▪The custom has been handed down *from age to age*. その習慣は代々伝えられてきた.

full age 成年 ▪He is of the *full age* of 18. 彼は18歳の成年である.

in all ages 今も昔も ▪It is the same *in all ages* and in all nations. それは今も昔もどこの国でも同じである.

it is an age* [*ages*] *since 《口》...して以来ほんとに久しい ▪*It is ages since* I saw you last. (この前お会いしてから)ほんとにお久しぶりですね.

look* [*show*]** *one's* ***age 年相応に見える ▪He does not *look his age*. 彼は年ほどには見えない.

of a certain age 《婉曲》(女性が)相当の年の, 若くない, 中年の ▪She is *of a certain age*, but still very beautiful. 彼女は相当の年だが, まだとても美しい.

of age ...の年齢で ▪I am 15 years *of age*. 私は15歳です ▪She is *of* tender [advanced] *age*. 彼女は若年[高齢]である ▪John is *of* driving *age*. ジョンは車の運転のできる年齢だ.

of all ages あらゆる年齢の, 老若 ▪Hairlessness affects men and women *of all ages*. 脱毛は老若男女すべてに起こる.

over age 年齢超過で ▪Next year he will be *over age* for the job. 来年で彼はこの仕事の年齢超過となる.

show** one's **age (実際よりも若く見せようとして)年が知れる ▪She *showed her age* when she dressed like a teenager. 十代の女の子の格好をしたとき彼女の年が知れた.

the age of consent →CONSENT[1].

The age of miracles is past. 《諺》奇跡の時代は終わった.

the golden age 黄金時代 (*of*) ▪Tolstoy lived in *the golden age of* Russian literature. トルストイはロシア文学の黄金時代に生きていた.

the legal* [*lawful*] *age 法定年齢, 成人年齢 ▪In most countries *the legal age* for voting is 21. たいていの国では投票できる法定年齢は21歳だ.

the third age (裕福でまだ活力のある)熟年の世代, 第三年代《約55–70歳》 ▪Some people find new partners in *the third age*. 熟年になって新しい伴侶を見つける人もいる.

through the ages 万代を通じて, 有史以来 ▪It charts celestial movements *through the ages*. それは有史以来の天体の運行を図示している.

to all ages 万世までも ▪His fame will last *to all ages*. 彼の名声は万世までも続くだろう.

under age 未成年で ▪He was rejected by the army because he was *under age*. 彼は未成年のため, 軍隊からはねられた.

What's your age? 《俗》お元気ですか ▪Hi, Rick! *What's your age?* やあ, リック! 元気かい.

with age →from AGE.

agency /éɪdʒənsi/ 名 ***by* [*through*] *the agency of*** ...の仲介[周旋, 作用]で ▪*Through the agency of* powerful friends, he finally managed to obtain the post. 有力な友だちの周旋で彼はついにその地位を得た ▪The land was fertilized *by the agency of* insects. その土地は昆虫の作用で肥沃になった.

agenda /ədʒéndə/ 名 ***a hidden agenda*** 隠れた意図, 思惑 ▪I was afraid that he had *a hidden agenda* in inviting me to his party. 彼が私をパーティーに招いてくれたのには隠れた意図があるのではと心配した.

at the top of* [*be high on*] *the agenda 主要な議題の一つで, 最優先で ▪Terrorism *is at the top of the agenda* at the European Union summit in Brussels. ブリュッセルの欧州連合のサミットではテロ行為が主要な議題の一つに上がっている ▪Sustainability is *at the top of everyone's agenda* at the moment. 現段階では万人にとって持続可能性が最優先事項だ.

move through the agenda 議事を進める ▪The Board will *move through the agenda* as quickly as possible. 委員会はできるだけ早急に議事を進めるだろう.

on* [*off*] *the [*a person's*] ***agenda*** 予定されている[いない] ▪He said the strike action is *on the agenda*. スト行動が予定されていると彼は言った ▪Foreign travel is *off the agenda* until we've got some money. 海外旅行は金がたまるまでは予定するわけにいかない.

set the agenda 予定[指針]を決める ▪Newspapers have been accused of trying to *set the agenda* for the government. 新聞は政府に代わって指針を決めようとしていると非難されてきた.

agent /éɪdʒənt/ 名 ***a free agent*** (プロスポーツの)自由契約選手, フリーエージェント ▪The Giants signed two *free agents* who had been released by the Cardinals. ジャイアンツはカーディナルズから放出された二人のフリーエージェントを雇い入れた.

Agent Orange オレンジ剤《ベトナム戦争で使用された枯れ葉剤》 ▪If things continue as they have, we'll all be eating some *Agent Orange* with our meals. こういう事態が続くなら, みんな食事とともにオレンジ剤を食べることになるだろう.

agent provocateur (挑発が目的の)おとり調査員 ▪Glen admitted he was an *agent provocateur*. 自分はおとり調査員であることをグレンは認めた. ☞F 'provocative agent'.

aggravate /ǽgrəvèɪt/ 動 ***feel aggravated*** 《口》腹立たしい ▪ He *felt aggravated* at his son's retort. 彼は息子の口答えが腹立たしかった.

aggregate /ǽgrɪgət/ 名 ***in the aggregate*** 全体として, 総計で; 概して ▪ These payments must amount, *in the aggregate*, to a vast sum. これらの支払いは総計で莫大な額に達するにちがいない.

on aggregate 《英》ゲーム数を総計すると ▪ Chelsea beat Portsmouth 4-2 *on aggregate*. チェルシーはゲーム数を総計すると4-2でポーツマスを負かした.

aggressive /əgrésɪv/ 名 ***assume* [*take*] *the aggressive*** 攻勢をとる, けんかを吹っかける ▪ He at once *assumed the aggressive*. 彼はすぐに攻勢に出た.

aggrieve /əgríːv/ 動 ***feel*** (*oneself*) ***aggrieved at* [*by*]** …を不満に思う ▪ I *felt aggrieved at* her distrust. 私は彼女の不信に対して不満を抱いた.

aghast /əgǽst|əgɑ́ːst/ 副 ***stand aghast*** (***at***) (…に)度を失っている, 肝をつぶしている ▪ He *stood aghast at* the sight. 彼はその光景にあっけにとられた.

aglow /əglóʊ/ 副形 ***be aglow with*** …で萌えて, 赤らんで ▪ The western sky *was aglow with* the setting sun. 西の空は夕日に萌えていた ▪ Her face *was aglow with* sisterly love. 彼女の顔は姉妹の愛で上気していた.

ago /əgóʊ/ 副 ***a*** (***little, short***) ***while ago*** (つい)先ほど ▪ Bill called *a short while ago*. つい先ほどビルが電話してきた.

as long ago as …の年[時代]にはすでに ▪ A steam driven vehicle was invented *as long ago as* 1784. 蒸気で走る車は1784年にはすでに発明されていた.

long ago ずっと前 ▪ He left home *long ago*. 彼はずっと前に家を出た.

no longer ago than つい[ほんの]… ▪ I met him *no longer ago than* last Sunday. 私はつい先週の日曜に彼に会った.

not long ago つい先ごろ ▪ Her mother passed away *not long ago*. つい先ごろ彼女の母が亡くなった.

some time ago しばらく前に ▪ Was your will made *some time ago*? あなたの遺言状はしばらく前に作成されたのですか.

agog /əgɑ́g|əgɔ́g/ 形 (***all***) ***agog for* [*to* do]** …したくて大変気が立って, 大騒ぎして, むずむずして ▪ They are *all agog to* know what happened. 彼らは何事が起こったか知りたくてざわめいている ▪ The boys are *all agog for* mischief. 子供らはいたずらがしたくてむずむずしている.

all agog over …のことでひどく興奮して ▪ The city was *all agog over* the opening of the football season. その町はフットボール・シーズンの幕開けでひどく興奮していた.

all agog with 《口》…で沸き立って ▪ He found the village *all agog with* expectation. 彼は村の者が期待に沸き立っているのを知った.

set ... agog …を大騒ぎさせる ▪ The news *set* the whole town *agog*. その知らせは全町を沸き立たせた.

agonize /ǽgənàɪz/ 動 ***agonize*** (*oneself*) ***over*** …で苦悩する ▪ Max *agonized himself over* the prospect of losing his wife. マックスは妻を失うかもしれないという見通しにひどく苦悩した.

agony /ǽgəni/ 名 ***an agony aunt* [*uncle*]** (新聞の)人生相談欄の(女性[男性])回答者 ▪ The *Agony Aunt* team are here to help you with your problems. 相談欄回答者チームは, 読者のさまざまの問題をお助けするために待機しています.

in agony 苦しんで; もだえて ▪ My shoes pinch; I'm *in agony*. 靴がきつくて, 痛くてたまらない.

***in an agony of joy* [*regret,* etc]** 狂喜[後悔, など]して[のあまり] ▪ He danced about the room *in an agony of joy*. 彼は狂喜して部屋を踊り回った.

pile* [*put*] *on* [*up*] *the agony 《主に英口》 **1** (同情を引くために)悲痛なことを大げさに言う; 誇張して言う ▪ As he *piled on the agony* I thought the whole house had been burnt down. 彼が大げさに話すので家は丸焼けになったものと思った.

2 いやなことをさらにひどく感じさせる ▪ The latest airfare increase just *piles on the agony* for passengers. 最近の航空運賃の値上げは搭乗客にますます負担になる.

prolong the agony (相手の知りたいことを言わないことなどにより)苦痛を長引かせる, (必要以上に)心配を長引かせる, じらす ▪ Okay, let's not *prolong the agony*. よろしい, じらさないでいこう ▪ Raising the school leaving age to 18 will also *prolong the agony* of teachers. 学校卒業年齢を18歳に上げることもまた教師の苦痛を長引かせることになるだろう.

agree /əgríː/ 動 ***agree like cats and dogs*** 犬と猫のように仲が悪い ▪ They *agree like cats and dogs*. 彼らは犬猿の間柄だ.

***agree to differ* [*disagree*]** 互いの意見の相違はしかたがないと認める ▪ We must *agree to differ* on this point. 我々はこの点については意見の相違はやむをえぬとしなければならない.

I couldn't agree (***with you***) ***more* [*less*]** 全く賛成[絶対に反対]だ ▪ *I couldn't agree more* about that. そのことでは全く賛成だ ▪ Sorry, Rob, but for once *I couldn't agree with you less*. 残念だがロブ, 今回は絶対反対だ.

agreeable /əgríːəbəl/ 形名 (***be***) ***agreeable to*** **1** …にかなった ▪ His conduct *was agreeable to* our standard. 彼の行為は我々の基準にかなっていた.

2 《口》(人が)…に乗気になって ▪ He *was agreeable to* the proposal. 彼はその提案に喜んで応じた.

3 (物が)…の気に入る ▪ It *is* quite *agreeable to* you. それは全く君の気に入るよ.

4 …に従って ▪ *Agreeable to* my promise, I have come. 私は約束どおり参りました.

5 《俗》…はけっこうで ▪ I'*m* quite *agreeable to* it. それは至極けっこうです.

do* [*make*] *the agreeable 愛想よくもてなす

▪ The Mayor *does the agreeable* to his guests. 市長は来客を愛想よくもてなします.

***make** oneself **agreeable** (**to**)* (…と)調子を合わせる; (に)愛想よくする ▪ You must *make yourself agreeable to* your master. あなたは主人のきげんを損じないようにせねばならない.

agreeably /əgríːəbli/ 副 ***agreeably to*** (命令・指図など)に従って ▪ We sent you the goods *agreeably to* your letter. お申し越しに従って品をお送りしました.

agreed /əgríːd/ 形 ***be agreed on*** …について意見が一致している ▪ All the members *are agreed on* this issue. この問題についてはメンバー全員の意見が一致している.

agreement /əgríːmənt/ 名 ***a gentleman's*** [***gentlemen's***] ***agreement*** 紳士協定《相互の信頼に基づく文章化されない約束・協定》 ▪ America will have *a "gentlemen's agreement"* with the Entente. アメリカは協商国と紳士協定を結ぶだろう.

arrive at [***come to, reach***] ***an agreement*** 協定が成立する, 話がまとまる ▪ England has *reached an agreement* with Russia on the matter. その問題についてイギリスはロシアと協定が成立した.

bring about an agreement 話をまとめる, 協定を成立させる ▪ They *brought about an agreement* regarding the matter. 彼らはその件について協定を成立させた.

by mutual agreement 双方合意の上で ▪ We separated *by mutual agreement*. 我々は双方合意で別れた.

conclude [***make, enter into***] ***an agreement*** (***with***) (…と)契約・協定を結ぶ ▪ The workers have *made an agreement with* their employers about wages. 従業員たちは雇主たちと賃金について協定を結んだ.

in agreement (***with***) (…と)一致して; (に)従って ▪ I am quite *in agreement with* what you say. 君の言われることに全く同感です ▪ We are *in agreement*. 我々は意見が一致している.

aground /əgráʊnd/ 形 ***get*** [***go, run***] ***aground*** 浅瀬に乗り上げる; 行き詰まる ▪ The steamer *ran aground* on the sands. 汽船は砂州で座礁した ▪ The scheme *got aground*. 計画は行き詰まった.

ahead /əhéd/ 副 ***ahead of*** **1** …の前方にある ▪ What does that sign just *ahead of* us say? ちょうど我々の前方にあるあの看板には何と書いてあるのか.

2 …の先の方へ ▪ Don't go too far *ahead of* me. あんまり私より先へ行かないでください ▪ I am afraid I am getting *ahead of* my story. 話が少し飛びすぎるかと思います.

3 …より先に, より早く ▪ John finished his test *ahead of* the other boys. ジョンは他の生徒より先にテストを(書き)終えた.

4 …より多く, 超過して ▪ The exports were *ahead of* the imports. 輸出額は輸入額を上回った.

be [***stay***] ***ahead*** **1** …より進んでいる (*of*) ▪ He wants to *stay ahead of* his classmates. 彼は級友たちより上位にいたいと思っている ▪ He *is ahead of* us in English. 彼は英語では我々より進んでいる.

2《米口》(物を)持合せている, 長所として持つ ▪ That was all I *was ahead*. 私の持合せはそれだけだった.

3《米》儲けて, 勝ち越して ▪ I *was ahead* $10. 10ドル勝ち越していた.

be [***stay***] ***ahead of the game***《米口》優勢である; (株式などで)儲かっている ▪ If you study hard now, you will *be ahead of the game* in college. 今一生懸命勉強すれば大学に入ってから有利だろう ▪ Newspapers diversify to *stay ahead of the game*. 新聞は優勢を保つために多角経営をしている ▪ He has invested a lot of money in the hotel to *be ahead of the game*. 彼は株で儲けるためにそのホテルに多額のお金を投資している.

come out ahead 成功する, うまくやる ▪ Grandfather said you'd *come out ahead*. おじいさんはお前は成功するだろうと言った.

dead ahead すぐ前に, 真ん前に ▪ A stock market collapse is *dead ahead*. 株式市場の崩壊は真ん前に来ている.

***get ahead and** do*《米》さっさと…する ▪ *Get ahead and* write it. さっさとそれを書きなさい.

***get ahead of** oneself* (結果が出ないうちに)先走る ▪ She *got ahead of herself* in buying a new car before she got a promotion. 彼女は昇進する前に先走って新車を買ってしまった.

get money ahead 金を(使わずに)残す ▪ He *got* a lot of *money ahead*. 彼は大金を使わずに残した.

right [***straight, dead***] ***ahead*** まん前に, ちょうど行く手に ▪ We saw a boat *right ahead*. ちょうど向こうにボートが見えた.

streets ahead ずっと前進して, ずっとまさって (*of*) ▪ He is *streets ahead of* us. 彼は我々よりはるかに進んでいる.

ahold /əhóʊld/ 名 ***get ahold of***《口》…(人)と連絡をとる; (物)を入手する ▪ Does anyone know how to *get ahold of* this company? 誰かこの会社と連絡をとる方法を知ってるかい ▪ I finally *got ahold of* that novel you mentioned. とうとう君が言ってた小説を買ったよ.

***get ahold of** oneself*《口》自分を落ち着かせる ▪ *Get ahold of yourself*, woman! 落ち着くんだ, おまえさん!

aid[1] /eɪd/ 名 ***bring … to** a person's **aid*** 人の救助に…を来させる ▪ A broadcast appeal *brought* rescue teams *to their aid*. 放送による訴えで救助隊が彼らの救助にかけつけた.

by (***the***) ***aid of*** …の助けによって ▪ We mastered English *by aid of* a grammar and a dictionary. 我々は文法書と辞書をたよりに英語を修得した.

call in** a person's **aid 人の助けを求める ▪ We *called in his aid*. 我々は彼の援助を求めた.

call [***crave***] ***… in aid*** …の助けを借りる; を援用する ▪ Imagination *craves* music *in aid*. 想像力は音楽の助けを借りる.

A

come [***go***] ***to*** *a person's* ***aid*** 人を助けに来る[行く] ▪ You never listened or *came to my aid*. 君は聞いてくれなかったし, 助けにも来てくれなかった.

give aid to …を助ける ▪ They *gave aid to* the enemy of their country. 彼らは自国の敵を援助した.

in aid of …の一助として, を扶助するために; の補いに ▪ A concert will be given *in aid of* the Nurses' Fund. 看護師基金の一助として音楽会が催されることになっている.

pray in aid of …に弁護[援助]を求める《被告が弁護に共同の利害をもっている人に求めるもの》 ▪ A corporation may *pray in aid of* him, if anything be demanded of them. 自治体は, もし何事か要求された場合は彼に援助を求めることができる.

What is [***are,*** etc.]***... in aid of?*** 《英口》〚主に現在形・過去形で〛(特に予期しないことについて)…は一体何のためなんだ, 何のつもりなんだ, …はどうしたんだ ▪ *What are* all these books *in aid of?* 一体これらの本はどうしたんだ ▪ *What's* this little handle *in aid of?* この小さいハンドルは一体何のためなのだ.

with [***without***] ***the aid of*** …の助けを借りて[借りずに] ▪ This study was carried out *with the aid of* a Government grant. この研究は政府の補助金の援助を得て遂行された ▪ Iran can survive *without the aid of* the U.S. イランは米国の援助がなくても生き延びることができる.

aid[2] /eɪd/ 動 ***aid and abet*** 《法》犯行を幇(ほう)助する ▪ The invasion *was aided and abetted* by Richard's subjects. その侵略はリチャードの臣下によって幇助せられた.

aim[1] /eɪm/ 名 ***miss*** *one's* ***aim*** ねらいがはずれる; あてがはずれる ▪ The pistol *missed its aim*. 拳銃のねらいがはずれた.

take aim **1** ねらう ▪ He *took aim* with his rifle. 彼はライフル銃でねらった.
2 《米》…を非難する; に注目する ▪ They've been *taking aim* at Ben's lack of experience. 彼らはベンの経験不足を非難してきた ▪ It seems that American car makers have decided to *take aim* at areas outside the hybrid car market. アメリカの自動車メーカーはハイブリッドカー以外の分野に注目することに決めたようだ.

the aim of the exercise →EXERCISE[1].

without aim ねらいをつけずに; 目的なしに[の] ▪ He wandered *without aim*. 彼はあてどもなくさまよった.

aim[2] /eɪm/ 動 ***aim high*** [***low***] 大望をいだく[望みが低い] ▪ You *aim* too *low*. 君は望みが低すぎる.

aim to *do* 《米》…することを目指す, するつもりである ▪ The company *aims to* set up a worsted spinning plant. 会社は毛織紡績工場を設立するつもりだ.

be aimed at …するように意図されている; することを目指す ▪ The new scheme *is aimed at* reducing unemployment. 新計画は失業を減らすことを目指すものである.

air[1] /eər/ 名 ***air miles*** 空路…マイル; 直線距離…マイル ▪ The plane blew up 400 *air miles* from its destination. 機は目的地から空路400マイルで爆発した ▪ The enemy aircraft was shot down at a point 32 *air miles* from the border. 敵機は国境から直線距離32マイルの地点で撃ち落とされた.

air rage エアレージ《搭乗客が機内で暴力行為を行うこと》 ▪ Cabin crew were often the victims of *air rage* from passengers. 客室乗務員はしばしば乗客からのエアレージの被害者となった.

airs and graces おつにすました態度; お上品ぶり ▪ Old Pitt chuckled at her *airs and graces*. ピット老人は彼女のお上品ぶりをくすくす笑った.

an air kiss キスのまね ▪ This guy blew *an air kiss* at me while I was walking. 私が歩いているとこの男が私に向かってキスのまねをした.

an air shuttle (主要都市を結ぶ)航空機の定期往復便 ▪ My uncle takes the *air shuttle* from Boston to New York once a week. おじは週1回ボストンからニューヨークまで定期往復便を利用している.

assume airs =put on AIRs (and graces).

assume an air of …を気取る ▪ He *assumes an air of* superiority when a poor man comes. 彼は貧乏人が来ると偉そうにする.

be left hanging in the air/hang in the air 《文》(問題などが)未解決のままである, 宙ぶらりんである ▪ But now only John's question *was left hanging in the air*. しかし, いまやジョンの質問だけが未解決のままになった ▪ The pupils' questions still *hang in the air*. 生徒らの質問はまだ答えられていない.

beat [***plow***] ***the air*** 空を打つ; むだ骨を折る (《聖》*1 Cor.* 9:2 6) ▪ To ask him for a subscription is like *beating the air*. 彼に寄付を請うのはまるで空を打つようなむだ骨だ.

by air 空路, 飛行機で ▪ Letters are sent from England to South Africa *by air* now. 今は手紙はイギリスから南アフリカまで空路で送られている ▪ I prefer to travel *by air*. 私は飛行機旅行のほうが好きだ.

catch some air =get some AIR 1.

change of air 転地 ▪ I merely want *change of air* and scene. 気候と場面の変化がほしいだけだ.

clear the air →CLEAR[2].

come on the air 放送される ▪ The program will *come on the air* tonight. その番組は今夜放送される.

come up for air 《米俗》一息つく, 休憩する ▪ Let's *come up for air*. 休憩しようではないか.

cut the air with a knife 重苦しい空気を感じる ▪ When the rivals were in a room together, you could have *cut the air with a knife*. ライバル同士が同室にいれば重苦しい空気が感じられるだろう.

dance on air →DANCE[2].

evaporate into thin air = vanish into thin AIR.

float on air →walk on AIR.

get air →take AIR.

get [***go***] ***off the air*** 《米》放送されなくなる, 放送をやめる ▪ *Go off the air*. 放送をやめよ ▪ His speech *got off the air* owing to the opposition of the party. 彼の演説は党の反対で放送中止となった.

get [***go***] ***on the air*** 《米》放送に出る ▪ The President will *go on the air* tonight. 大統領は今夜放送で話します.

get some air **1** 外の空気を吸う ▪ I'm going out to *get some air*. 外へ出て空気を吸うつもりだ.

2 (バスケット・スキーなどで)高くジャンプする ▪ Let's *get some air* on the skateboard. スケートボードで高くジャンプしようよ.

get the air 《米俗》解雇される; ひじ鉄をくらう ▪ He *got the air*. 彼は首になった ▪ I *got the air* from her last night. 昨夜彼女にひじ鉄をくらった.

give air to …を公表する ▪ It will do him good if you *give air to* your view. 君が見解を公表すれば彼のためになるだろう.

give *oneself* ***airs*** (***and graces***) 気取る; いばる ▪ You need not *give yourself* such *airs*. 君はそんなに気取る必要はない.

give *a person* ***the air*** 《主に米俗》解雇する, (恋人)をふる ▪ He *was given the air* before the engagement was over. 彼は契約が終らぬうちに解雇された.

go off the air (放送局が)放送をやめる ▪ The station is *going off the air*. 局は放送を終わります.

go up in the air 《口》爆発する; 腹を立てる; ひどく興奮する ▪ I asked him a simple question, and he *went* straight *up in the air*. 彼に簡単な質問をしただけなのに彼はすぐかっとなった.

grab a handful of air 《俗》(トラック・バスが)急ブレーキをかける ▪ The trucker *grabbed a handful of air* at the red traffic signal. トラック運転手は赤信号で急ブレーキをかけた. ☞手動エアブレーキから.

hit the air 《米》放送される ▪ The program *hits the air* at 7 a.m. その番組は午前7時に放送される.

hot air 《口》だぼら, 口先だけの話 ▪ His promises were all *hot air*. 彼の約束はみな口先ばかりだった.

in *one's* ***airs*** 《米俗》酒に酔って ▪ He was *in his airs*. 彼は酔っていた.

in the air **1** 空中に ▪ A plane was flying *in the air*. 飛行機が1機空を飛んでいた.

2 一般的空気となって; まもなく起こりそうで ▪ A spirit of doubt is *in the air*. 懐疑の精神が一般に流れている ▪ I get the feeling that change is *in the air*. 変化がまもなく起こりそうだという感じがする.

3 (まだ実現されないことについて)大いに噂されて ▪ There are lots of rumors *in the air* to that effect. そういう趣旨の噂が大いに立っている ▪ Federation is *in the air*. 連合が噂されている.

4 ⟦しばしば all, quite, up を伴って⟧ 漠然として, 不確かな状態で ▪ The future character of the Republic is *in the air*. 共和国の未来の性格はまだ海のものとも山のものともわからない ▪ All our holiday plans are *quite in the air*. 我々の休暇中の計画は全く未定である.

5 =up in the AIR 2.

6 《軍》支柱も適当な保護物もない ▪ The extreme left of the allied front was *in the air*. 連合軍の前線の最左翼はむき出しになっていた.

in the open air →OPEN[1].

into thin air →vanish into thin AIR.

leave ... in the air …を中ぶらりん[未定]のままにしておく ▪ We *left* the plan *in the air*. その計画を未定のままにしておいた.

live on air 《口》何も食べずにいる ▪ They expect their workmen to *live on air*. 彼らは従業員たちが食わずにいればよいと思っている.

melt into thin air →vanish into thin AIR.

off the air 放送されて[して]いない ▪ Fadiman has been *off the air* since "Information, Please" folded. ファディマンは「話の泉」が閉ざされて以来放送をやめていた.

on the air **1** 放送が始まって; 放送されて[して] ▪ We are *on the air*! さあ, 放送が始まりました《アナウンサーの言葉》 ▪ He will be *on the air* this evening. 彼は今晩放送に出るでしょう ▪ What's *on the air* this evening? 今晩の放送番組は?

2 放送中で ▪ The news is *on the air* every two hours. ニュースは2時間おきに放送される.

out of [***from***] ***thin air*** 虚空から, 何もない所から, 無から ▪ Good ideas don't come *out of thin air*. 良い考えは無からは生じない.

over the air 放送されて ▪ He made a statement *over the air* in an official capacity. 彼は公的な資格で声明をラジオ放送した.

plow the air →beat the AIR.

pluck [***pull***] ***... out of*** [***from***] ***the air*** (アイディア・答えなど)を根拠もなくでっち上げる; (名前・数字など)を思いつくまま言う, 思いつきで言う (→pluck a NUMBER out of the air) ▪ The use of the word was not accidental and he did not merely *pluck* it *out of air*. その言葉はたまたま使用されたのではないし, でっち上げただけでもなかった ▪ He had *plucked* a figure *out of the air* in respect of hidden assets. 彼は隠匿資産に関して思いつきの数字を言っていた.

punch the air ガッツポーズをとる ▪ Why do sportsmen "*punch*" *the air* when they win at tennis or score a goal? テニスで勝ったりゴールを決めたりしたとき, なぜスポーツマンはガッツポーズをとるのか.

put ... off the air …の放送をやめる ▪ They *put* commercial programs *off the air*. 彼らはコマーシャルを中止した.

put on airs (***and graces***) 気取る, 上品ぶる; いばる ▪ It's no good *putting on airs and graces* with me. I knew you when you were working in a shop! 僕にお上品ぶってもむだだ. 僕は君が店員だったころから知ってるんだ! ▪ She *puts on* high *airs* with her learning. 彼女は学問をひどく鼻にかけている.

put [***send***] ***... on the air*** …を放送する ▪ At 8.30 an amusing show *was sent on the air*. おもしろい番組が8時半に放送された.

rend the air 《文》大きな物音をたてる ▪ Thunder and lightning *rent the air*. 雷鳴と稲妻が空をつんざいた.

A

stay on the air 放送界にとどまる ▪ My job is to *stay on the air.* 私の仕事は放送業務を続けることだ.

suck air 《俗》(怖さ・酸素不足のため)ハーハーいう ▪ I bought two goldfish yesterday; they are *sucking air.* きのう金魚を2匹買ったが, 金魚は口をパクパクさせている ▪ Why are American newspapers *sucking air?* なぜアメリカの新聞は息うかいが荒くなっているのか.

take* [*get*] *air 流布する, 知れわたる ▪ The plot *took air* and was overthrown. 陰謀は知れてつぶされた.

take the air **1** (徒歩・馬・車で)戸外に出る, 新鮮な空気を吸いに外へ出る, 散歩する ▪ Mr. Smith is *taking the air* in his garden. スミス氏は庭を散歩中だ.
2 (飛行機が)離陸する ▪ The plane *took the air* vertically. 飛行機は垂直に離陸した.
3 放送を始める ▪ A lot of trouble occurred before the station *took the air* in 1973. その局が1973年に放送を始める前にいろいろと面倒が起こった.
4 《俗》(こそこそと)立ち去る ▪ The old man *took the air* into the wood. 老人は森の中に立ち去った.

take to the air **1** 飛び立つ ▪ A small flock of geese suddenly *took to the air.* ガンの小さな群れが突然飛び立った.
2 飛行家になる ▪ He has *taken to the air.* 彼は飛行家になった.

The air was blue. 《俗》ばちあたりな言葉をはく ▪ When Dad discovered the dent in his Cadillac, *the air was blue!* 親父が自分のキャデラックにへこみを発見したとき, 悪態をついた.

up in the air **1** 漠然として, 未確定で ▪ Our plans for the vacation are still *up in the air.* 休暇中の我々の計画はまだ決まらない.
2 《口》怒って, 興奮して ▪ He is *up in the air* because he was not invited. 彼は招待されなかったので怒っている.
3 《口》大喜びで ▪ She was *up in the air* because she was invited to the party. 彼女はパーティーに招待されたので大喜びだった.

vanish* [*disappear, melt, evaporate*] *into thin air 《口》すっかり消えてなくなる, 雲散霧消する (cf. Sh., *Temp.* 4. 1. 150) ▪ Since then he has *vanished into thin air.* それ以来彼は消えていなくなってしまった ▪ Something valuable and useful suddenly *evaporated into thin air.* 貴重で有用な物が突然跡形もなく消えてしまった.

walk* [*tread, float*] *on air (うれしくて)有頂天になる ▪ Since we decided to spend Christmas in Rome, they've been *treading on air.* 我々がクリスマスをローマで過ごすことに決めてからは, 彼らは有頂天で喜んでいる.

with word and air 語調を整えた(歌など) ▪ What he sang was a song *with word and air.* 彼が歌ったのは語調の整った歌だった.

air[2] /eər/ 動 ***air oneself*** **1** 戸外へ出る; 風にあたる ▪ I *aired myself* on the top. 頂上で風に吹かれた.
2 気取る ▪ A fool loves *airing himself.* ばかは気取るのが好きだ.

air one's heels 《口》ぶらつく ▪ He was *airing his heels* outside. 彼は外をぶらついていた.

air one's opinion 《口》意見を誇示する[振り回す] ▪ Have you quite finished *airing your opinion?* 君の意見の吹聴はすんだかね.

airing /éərɪŋ/ 名 ***get a full airing*** 《米》全容が明らかになる ▪ The case will *get a full airing.* その事件は全容が明らかになるだろう.

get* [*be given, have*] *an airing (意見・恨み・相違などが)公表される, 公開討論される ▪ The interesting subject of polygamy *got an airing* last week on Radio 4. 一夫多妻という興味ある題目が先週ラジオ4で公開討論された.

give ... an airing **1** (衣類)を虫干しする ▪ We must *give* our clothes *an airing.* 我々は衣類を虫干ししなければならない.
2 ...を明らかにする, 公表する ▪ He has recently *given* it *an airing* in the newspapers. 彼は最近それを新聞に公表した.

give it an airing 《口》〚命令文で〛取り去れ; 静かにせよ ▪ *Give it an airing!* 静かにせよ.

give public airing to ...を公開討論にかける ▪ They intended to *give public airing to* alternative theories. 彼らは代替の理論を公開討論にかけるつもりだった.

take an airing 戸外運動[散歩]をする ▪ I make it a rule to *take an airing* after office hours. 執務時間ののち戸外散歩をすることにしている.

aisle /aɪl/ 名 ***go* [*head, walk*] *down the aisle*** 《口》教会で結婚式をする ▪ Britain's gay couples soon can *walk down the aisle.* イギリスの同性愛のカップルはじきに教会で結婚できるようになる.

have* [*lay, send*]... (*rolling*) *in the aisles 《口》(複数の観客などを)笑いころげさせる ▪ The film [book] *sent* my friends *rolling in the aisles.* その映画を見て[本を読んで]私の友人たちは抱腹絶倒した.

rock* [*knock, lay*]... *in the aisles (人に)強い印象を与える ▪ This play has been *rocking* them *in the aisles* for days. この劇は彼らに何日も強い印象を与えている.

roll in the aisles 《口》(観客などが)笑いころげる ▪ They were *rolling in the aisles* at his jokes. 彼らは彼のジョークを聞いて笑いころげていた.

aitch /eɪtʃ/ 名 ***drop one's aitches*** → drop one's H's.

ajar /ədʒɑ́ːr/ 形副 ***ajar with the world*** 世間と調和しないで ▪ He is *ajar with the world.* 彼は世間になじまない.

set* (*nerves*) *ajar (神経)をいらだたせる ▪ The sound *set* my *nerves ajar.* その音は私の神経をいらだたせた.

akimbo /əkímboʊ/ 副 ***with* (*one's*) *arms akimbo*** 両手を腰に当て両ひじを突き出して ▪ The charwoman stood *with arms akimbo* while she gave her mistress a piece of her mind. 雑役婦は奥様に直言をしている間, 手を腰に当て両ひじを突き出し

て立っていた.

akin /əkín/ 形 ***akin to*** …と同種で, と類似で ▪ Pity is *akin to* love. 《諺》あわれみは恋愛に近い (cf. Sh., *Twel. N.* 3. 1. 119) ▪ I regard it with a feeling *akin to* contempt. 私は軽蔑に似た感情でそれをながめる.

***near akin* (*to*)** (…に)非常に似て ▪ The manufacture of paper is very *near akin to* that of linen. 紙の製造はリンネルの製造に非常によく似ている.

Pity is akin to love. →AKIN to.

alacrity /əlǽkrəti/ 名 ***show alacrity*** てきぱきする ▪ He *shows alacrity* in doing everything. 彼は何をするにもてきぱきする.

with alacrity 敏活に, てきぱきと ▪ He accepted it *with* grateful *alacrity*. 彼は感謝してさっさとそれを受け取った.

Aladdin /əlǽdən/ 名 ***Aladdin's lamp*** アラジンのランプ《こすれば何でも望むものをくれるランプ》 ▪ Goodwill is almost as expeditious and effectual as *Aladdin's lamp*. 善意はアラジンのランプとほとんど同じくらい即効がある. ☞アラビア夜話の中の「アラジンと不思議なランプ」の話から.

an* [*the*] *Aladdin's cave アラジンの洞窟, 財宝のある所 ▪ The store itself is akin to *Aladdin's cave*. その店自体がアラジンの洞窟に似ている. ☞アラジンが不思議なランプを見つけた洞窟.

alarm[1] /əlɑ́ːrm/ 名 ***a false alarm*** 《軍》危急虚報《一般的にも用いる》 ▪ We heard our house was burnt down, but it was only *a false alarm*. 我々はわが家が全焼したと聞いたが, それは虚報にすぎなかった ▪ He gave *a false alarm*. 彼は虚偽の警報を発した.

alarm and despondency (戦争などに直面しての)恐慌と意気消沈 ▪ I must get rid of what we call *alarm and despondency* in the war. いわゆる戦争の「恐慌と意気消沈」を払いのけねばならない. ☞イギリスの政治家 Winston Churchill (1874–1965) の演説から.

alarm bells start to ring 警報が鳴り始める, 心配[不安]になる ▪ *Alarm bells started to ring* when Mary said she had something to say. メアリーが言い分があると言ったとき不安になってきた.

alarms and excursions 喧騒興奮, 騒乱 ▪ There are already enough *alarms and excursions* in Southeast Asia, to say nothing of open warfare. 東南アジアでは公然の戦争はいうまでもなく, すでにたくさんの騒乱が起こっていた. ☞「軍楽のうちに軍隊舞台を横断」が原義; Elizabeth 時代の劇のト書き.

beat* [*give, ring, sound*] *the alarm 非常太鼓を打つ, 非常らっぱを吹く; 警報する, (災害で)家中・近所を騒がせる ▪ They *beat the alarm* on a gong. 彼らはどらを鳴らして急を知らせた ▪ They *sounded the alarm* of fire. 彼らは火事の警報を鳴らした ▪ The clock *rings the alarm*. その柱時計が目ざましのベルを鳴らすのだ.

in alarm 驚きあわてて, 心配して ▪ Everyone rushed out *in alarm* when the fire started. 火事が起こったときみんな驚いて飛び出した.

raise an alarm 警報する, 急を告げる ▪ He *raised an alarm* of fire. 彼は火事だと警報した.

raise* [*sound*] *the alarm 警鐘を鳴らす ▪ The government is slow to *raise the alarm* about unsafe medicines. 政府は危険な薬について警鐘を鳴らすのが遅い.

ring* [*sound*] *alarm bells/set* (*the*) *alarm bells ringing 警報を鳴らす, 心配させる, 不安にさせる ▪ Huge swarms of stinging jellyfish should *ring alarm bells*. とげのあるクラゲの大群には不安にさせられるはずだ ▪ Terrorists threats will *set alarm bells ringing* all over the world. テロリストのおどしで世界中が不安に陥るだろう.

take* (*the*) *alarm (警報に)驚く, 警戒する ▪ The town *took the alarm* before I went there. 私がそこに行く前に町の者たちは警戒した ▪ We *took alarm* at the sound. 我々はその音に驚いた.

alarm[2] /əlɑ́ːrm/ 動 ***be alarmed at* [*by*]** …に[を聞いて]驚く ▪ You *were alarmed at* the crash. 君はすさまじい音を聞いて驚いていたね.

be alarmed for …を気づかう ▪ He *is alarmed for* the safety of his brother. 彼は兄の安否を気づかっている.

albatross /ǽlbətrɑ̀s|-trɔ̀s/ 名 ***an albatross* (*a*)*round* [*about*] *one's neck*** 《口》人に旧悪を執拗に思い出させるもの, 一生ついてまわる罪の烙印 ▪ A man who killed another man has *an albatross round his neck*. 人を殺した人は旧悪の思いに苦しまねばならない. ☞S.T. Coleridge 作の *The Ancient Mariner* (1798) で老水夫の殺したアホウドリから.

alec(k) /ǽlɪk/ 名 ***a smart alec*(*k*)** 《口》(生意気な)うぬぼれ屋 ▪ He is such *a smart alec*—he thinks he can do things better than others. 彼は大のうぬぼれ屋だ—何でも人より上手にできると思っている.

alert /əlɔ́ːrt/ 名 ***on* (*full, high*) *alert*** (警察などが)厳戒態勢で ▪ Afghan troops were placed *on full alert*. アフガンの軍隊は厳戒態勢を敷いていた.

on red alert 危険[緊急非常事態]に備えて ▪ Islamabad Airport was put *on red alert* on Sunday night. 日曜日の夜, イスラマバード空港は緊急非常事態に備えていた.

on the alert (油断なく)見張って, 警戒して (*to do, for*) ▪ The men are *on the alert to* discover something wrong. その人々は何か異常を見つけようと見張っている ▪ They must be constantly *on the alert for* enemy planes. 彼らは敵機を絶えず警戒していなければならない.

algorism /ǽlgərìzəm/ 名 ***a cipher in algorism*** 零(0)の字; 有名無実の人, でくのぼう ▪ They are no more than *ciphers in algorism*. 彼らは有名無実の人々にすぎない.

alias /éɪliəs/ 名 ***go by the alias of*** …という別名を使う ▪ He *goes by the alias of* John Hall. 彼はジョン・ホールという別名を使っている.

alibi /ǽləbàɪ/ 名 ***set up* [*prove*] *an alibi*** 現場不在を証明する, アリバイを立てる ▪I *set up an alibi* for her. 私は彼女のアリバイを立てた.

Alice /ǽləs/ 名 ***like Alice in Wonderland*** 不思議の国のアリスのように《考えや計画が空想の世界にだけ存在する》 ▪Miss Denton, on going into the movies said: I feel *like Alice in wonderland*. It's like going to a fairyland. 映画界に入るときデントン嬢は言った. 不思議の国のアリスのような気分です. 妖精の国に入って行くみたいです. ☞アリスは Lewis Carroll の *Alice's Adventures in Wonderland* の主人公の少女.

alien /éɪliən/ 形 ***alien from*** …と異なる ▪This is a style *alien from* genuine English. これは真正の英文とは異なる文体である.

alien to …に反する, に合わない ▪Cruelty is quite *alien to* his nature. 残酷は彼の性質とは全く相いれない ▪Luxury is *alien to* his tastes. 贅沢は彼の趣味に合わない.

alienate /éɪliənèɪt/ 動 ***be alienated from*** …と疎遠である; と不和である ▪Young people *are* often *alienated from* the ideas of old people. 青年は老人の思想をうとんじることが多い ▪He *is alienated from* his friends. 彼は友人たちと不和である.

alight[1] /əláɪt/ 動 ***alight on** one's **feet*** 飛び降りて立つ; けがを免れる ▪He safely *alighted on his feet*. 彼は飛び降りてちゃんと立てた.

alight[2] /əláɪt/ 形 ***be alight with*** …で明々と輝く ▪Their faces *were alight with* happiness. 彼らの顔は幸福に輝いていた.

catch alight **1** 火がつく; 燃えだす ▪Some paper *caught alight* and I had to put it out. 紙に火がついたので消さなければならなかった.

2 (人が) 湧き立つ ▪At his speech, the crowd *caught alight* and cheered wildly. 彼の演説に群衆は湧き立って, 盛んに拍手した.

set* [*get*]*… alight (物)を燃やす ▪The wood was so wet that it was difficult to *set* it *alight*. その木はしめっていたので燃やすのはむずかしかった.

align /əláɪn/ 動 ***align** oneself **with*** …と同調する, 共同戦線を張る ▪We should *align ourselves with* those people. 我々はその人々と同調するべきだ.

be aligned against …に団結して反対する ▪Bush and Karzai said they *are aligned against* the Taliban. ブッシュ氏とカルザイ氏は, 我々は団結してタリバンに反対していると言った.

alignment /əláɪnmənt/ 名 ***in* [*out of*] *alignment*** 一列に並んで[並ばないで] ▪The desks are *in alignment*. 机はまっすぐに一列に並んでいる ▪Your Cadillac's wheels are *out of alignment*. あなたのキャデラックの車輪は一列に並んでいません.

in alignment with …と共同戦線を張って ▪We are *in* political *alignment with* the Popular Front. 我々は人民戦線と政治共同戦線を張っている.

alike /əláɪk/ 形 ***be alike to*** …には同じことである ▪Wealth or poverty *is alike to* him. 貧富は彼にとってはどうでもよい.

alive /əláɪv/ 形 ***alive and kicking*** 《口》元気でぴんぴんして; (組織などがいまだに)活動を続けて ▪He was very much *alive and kicking* the last time I saw him. この前会ったときは彼は非常に元気でぴんぴんしていた ▪The underground internet economy is *alive and kicking*. 地下のインターネット経済は活動を続けている. ☞魚屋が魚について言う言葉から.

alive and well 《口》 **1** 元気でぴんぴんして (= ALIVE and kicking) ▪Bin Ladin was *alive and well*. ビン・ラディンは元気でぴんぴんしていた.

2 (物が) 現存して, (いまだに)人気がある ▪It seems that the book is *alive and well*. その本はまだ人気があるらしい.

3 (遭難者などが)元気で生き続けて ▪The victim of the accident is said to be *alive and well*. その事故の遭難者は元気で生き続けていると言われている.

alive to …に敏感で ▪I have always been very *alive to* pain. 私はこれまでずっと苦痛に非常に敏感だった ▪He is *alive to* his own interests. 彼は自分の利益に抜けめがない.

alive with …が群集して; でにぎやかな ▪Our lunch was *alive with* ants. お弁当にアリがいっぱいたかっていた ▪The river is *alive with* boats. 川はボートでにぎやかだ.

all alive 《口》元気でぴんぴんして; 活気があって ▪The company were *all alive*. 一行は元気いっぱいだった ▪The city was *all alive*. 町はほんとににぎやかだった.

bring … alive **1** 興味深くする ▪The Civil War *brings* history *alive* for students. 南北戦争は学生にとって歴史を興味深いものにする.

2 = bring … (back) to LIFE.

come alive **1** (人が)生き返る; 生き生きとする ▪I've seen people really *coming alive* again. 人が生き返るのを見たことがある ▪She *came alive* as she talked about her ambition. 彼女は自分の抱負を話しているうちに生き生きとしてきた.

2 (話題・試合などが) おもしろくなる ▪The game *came alive* in the second half. 試合は後半になっておもしろくなった.

3 (場所が)活気づく, にぎやかになる ▪The city usually *came alive* after dark. その都市はたいてい日が暮れてから活気づく.

eat** a person **alive **1** (かんかんに怒って)人をさんざんにやっつける[懲らしめる] ▪Don't be scared. I'm not going to *eat* you *alive*. おびえなくてもよい. なにも取って食おうと言うんじゃない.

2 (議論・競争で)人をこてんぱんにやっつける ▪Damn, Palin *ate* him *alive*! なんてこった, ペイリン氏が彼をこてんぱんにやっつけた.

3 〚主に受身で〛(蚊・虫が)何度も刺す ▪I *was eaten alive* by bed bugs. 私はトコジラミに何度も刺された.

Heart* [*Man, Sakes*] *alive! 《口》おや!, あれっ!, おい何だと! ▪Dear *heart alive*, how his niece by marriage was startled! ほんとにまあ, 彼の義理のめいはどんなに驚いたことでしょう! ▪*Man alive!* Glad to see you! おやまあ! よくおいでくださいましたね.

keep the matter alive 一件の審議を続ける ▪ The committee *kept the matter alive.* 委員会はその件の審議を続けた.

look alive →LOOK[2].

not know** a person **is alive 《米》人が生きているのを知らない; 人の存在に気づかない ▪ Hugh has a son. But his son does *not know* he *is alive.* ヒューには息子がある. でも息子はヒューの存在を知らない.

sure as I am alive きっと, 確かに《私が生きていることほど確かに》 ▪ He is gone, *sure as I am alive.* 彼が行っちまったことはまちがいない.

all /ɔːl/ 形代名副 ***above all*** →ABOVE.

after all →AFTER.

all alone →ALONE.

all along →ALONG.

***all** A **and** B* AとBばかり ▪ He is *all* skin *and* bones. 彼は骨と皮ばかりだ.

all and sundry** [**each**]/**each and all**/**one and all 誰もかれもみな, どれもこれもみな ▪ Finally he invited *all and sundry* to partake of the cake and all. ついに彼はすべての人にケーキでも何でもお食べくださいと言った.

all a-setting 《米》よい状態で, 健康で ▪ It makes the dogs *all a-setting.* それで犬どもは強健になる.

all at once →ONCE.

all being well 万事うまくいったら, 何事もなかったら ▪ See you tomorrow, *all being well.* あすお会いしましょう, 何事もなかったら.

all but **1** ...のほかはみな ▪ *All but* one were present. 一人のほかはみな出席した ▪ He was a king in *all but* name. 彼は事実上の王様だった.

2 [[副詞的に]] ほとんど ▪ He is *all but* dead. 彼は死んだも同然だ ▪ These were *all but* unknown to the Greeks. これらはギリシャ人にはほとんど知られていなかった ▪ They were in a state of *all but* nudity. 彼らはほとんどまっ裸だった.

all** one **can **1** できるかぎり ▪ I hurried *all* I *could.* 私はできるかぎり急いだ.

2 できるかぎりのこと ▪ I will do *all* I *can* for you. 君のためにできるかぎりのことをします.

all** one **can do ...にできるのはただ...(だけ) ▪ *All* we *can do* is (to) go. 我々にできることはただ行くことだけだ ▪ It is *all* I *can do* to keep out of debt. 私は借金せずにいるのが関の山です.

all day** [**week, month, year**] **long 一日[週間, 月, 年]中 ▪ I've been working in the garden *all day long.* 一日中庭で働いていた ▪ She is growing herbs *all year long.* 彼女は一年中ハーブを栽培している.

All dressed up and nowhere to go. →DRESS[2].

all in 《口》 **1** すっかり疲れて ▪ You look *all in* today. 君はきょうは疲れきっているようだ.

2 すべてを含んで, 諸経費込みで ▪ It will cost you £100 *all in.* すべてを含めて100ポンドかかるだろう.

3 不景気で; (特にポーカーで)文無しになって ▪ I'm finished for the night; I'm *all in.* 今夜はおしまいだ. 文無しになった.

all in all **1** 何物にもまさって, 全能の, 最も重要な (《聖》 *1 Cor.* 12. 6) ▪ The glory of the Lord is *all in all.* 神の栄光は絶大である ▪ She was *all in all* to him. 彼女は彼にとってはすべてであった.

2 全体として, 概して ▪ But *all in all*, things have gone well. だが, 全体としては万事うまくいった ▪ He was a man, take him *all in all.* 彼はどの点から見てもまことの男だった.

3 すっかり ▪ Trust me not at all or *all in all.* 私を全く信用しないか, さもなくばすっかり信用してください.

***all** (**in**) **my eye** (**and Betty Martin**)* →EYE.

all in one →ONE.

all is 《米口》あらゆる面を考えてみるに ▪ *All is*, he couldn't love them. あらゆる点から考えて見て, 彼は彼らを愛することができなかったのだ.

all of 《口》[[数詞・名詞を伴って]] **1** (たっぷり)...も, ...ほども《多いことを表す句だが反語的にも用いられる (→2)》 ▪ She was *all of* six feet high. 彼女は6フィートもあった.

2 《反語》わずか..., ...だけ ▪ John was *all of* 16 when he married Jane. ジェインと結婚したときジョンはわずか16歳だった.

all** (**of**) **the ...の全部[すべて] ▪ These are *all the* books I have read so far. これは私がこれまで読んだ本の全部です.

all or nothing (中途半端でなく)全か無か ▪ I won't buy a single item of this collection; I will buy *all or nothing.* 私はこのコレクションの抜き取り買いはしない. 全部買うか全然買わないかだ.

all out →OUT[1].

all over **1** べた一面に, どこもかしこも; 《米》いたるところ (《英》 = everywhere) ▪ Things are tough *all over.* どこへ行ってもせちがらい世の中だ ▪ They came from *all over.* 彼らはあらゆるところから来た.

2 全身に; 心底から ▪ I felt a pheasant *all over.* 私はキジの頭からしっぽまでをなでた ▪ Going home that night, I was sore *all over.* その夜帰宅してから, 私は心底むくれていた.

3 《口》全体的に, すっかり; そっくり ▪ Keep your mind awake and you'll stay young *all over.* 心を常に働かせていれば, 全体的にいつまでも若々しい ▪ That's Harris *all over.* それはいかにもハリスらしい[いかにもハリスのやりそうなことだ] ▪ He is *all over* mistaken. 彼はすっかりまちがっている ▪ She is her mother *all over.* 彼女は母親そっくりだ.

4 徹底的に ▪ When he talked, he talked *all over.* 彼は話すときには徹底的に話した.

5 全く終わって; 《俗》死んで ▪ It's *all over* between us. 我々の仲はすっかり終わった ▪ The honeymoon is *all over* now. 新婚旅行は終わってしまった; 《主に米》新任早々のお手やわらかな待遇は終わった ▪ We have been *all over* that, George. ジョージ君, 我々はそのことはすっかり済んだのだ ▪ He is *all over.* 彼は死んだ.

6 ...のいたるところ, ...じゅう; いたるところに ▪ The shavings are *all over* the place. かんなくずがそこら

一面にちらかっている ▪ He is known *all over* the world. 彼は世界じゅうに知られている ▪ The news spread *all over* town. ニュースは町じゅうに広まった ▪ She was shaking *all over*. 彼女は体じゅう震えていた ▪ There were bodies *all over*. いたるところに死体があった.

7《俗》...にほれこんで ▪ You are *all over* her. 君は彼女にほれこんでいるんだ.

8 ...にへつらって ▪ That's why these people are *all over* him. それでこの人たちが彼にへつらうのだ.

9《スポーツ・口》...に完勝する ▪ The visiting team were *all over* us. 来訪チームがわがチームに完勝した.

10《口》[[形容詞的に]] 体全体のかげんが悪く, なんとなく不快で ▪ I am *all over* now. 私は今体全体のかげんが悪い.

11 (人)といちゃついて ▪ The twosome were *all over* each other on the couch. 二人組は寝椅子の上でいちゃついていた.

12 (問題・計画など)を完全にコントロールして ▪ Sarah will be *all over* the problem. セアラがその問題を完全にコントロールするだろう.

13《俗》(人)にやけに好意を示して, べたべたまとわりついて ▪ I was over his house this weekend and he was *all over* me. 今週末に彼の家へ行くと私にちやほやしてくれた.

14《俗》...して幸福で, 興奮して, 自信に満ちて ▪ I was *all over* that history test today. 今日の歴史のテストはばっちりだ.

15 (人)にのしかかって, ...と取っ組み合って ▪ All of a sudden, he was *all over* me with the broom. 突然彼は箒(ほうき)をもって私に襲いかかってきた.

***all over** oneself*《軍俗》ひどく喜んで; いばって ▪ Ronnie was *all over himself* with joy. ロニーは喜んでほくほくしていた.

all over the place [***map***]《口》いたるところに ▪ I've been *all over the place* looking for you. 君を捜していたるところを歩きまわっていたんだよ.

all over with ...はもうだめ (all up with) ▪ It's *all over with* poor John. かわいそうにジョンはもうだめだ.

all present and accounted for [《英口》***and correct***] 全員出席 ▪ The participants were *all present and accounted for* today. 参加者はきょう全員出席していた.

all right《口》**1** 申し分がない; 申し分なく ▪ That restaurant is *all right* [《俗》*all-right*]. あのレストランは申し分がない ▪ He has done it *all right*. 彼は立派にそれをやった.

2 まちがいない, 正しい ▪ We counted the invoices, and they were *all right*. 我々は仕切り状を数えたが, まちがいはなかった.

3 疑いなく, まちがいなく ▪ He will come *all right*. 彼はきっと来る.

4 よろしい (OK) ▪ *All right*. I'll come at six tomorrow. よろしい, あすの6時に来ます.

5《反語》ようし! ▪ *All right*! You'll be sorry for this. ようし, あとで悔やむな.

6 健康で, 心地よく; うれしく ▪ I'm *all right* now. Let me lie down for an hour. もうよくなりました. 1時間ほど横にならせてください ▪ Are you *all right* in that chair? そのいすで(心地)いいですか.

7 [[限定的]] 立派な, 信頼しうる ▪ He's an *all right* guy. 彼は立派な男だ.

all right, all right《口》[[all right の強調形]] 全くもって ▪ She is a smart girl *all right, all right*. 彼女はほんとに気のきいた女だ.

all round **1** 一座の者みな(に); あたり一帯に ▪ Glasses *all round*! 一座の者に杯を! ▪ Their light-hearted humor made things pleasant *all round*. 彼らの軽妙なユーモアがあたり一帯に愉快な雰囲気をかもし出した.

2 すべての点で, まんべんなく ▪ That is about square *all round*. それはすべての点で大体公平だ.

3 多方面な, 融通のきく, 平均の ▪ He is an *all round* athlete. 彼は万能選手だ.

all singing, all dancing《主に英口》非常にモダンで技術的に進歩した ▪ I have broadband now and have an *all singing, all dancing* computer. 私は今ブロードバンドに接続する非常にモダンで進歩したコンピューターを持っている. ☞ 1929年のミュージカル映画 *Broadway Melody* の宣伝文句 "All talking, All singing, All dancing" から.

all talk and no cider →TALK[1].

all the 唯一の ▪ A hut was *all the* home he ever had. 一軒の小屋が彼が持っていた唯一の家だった.

all the best →all (of) the BEST.

all the better [***worse,*** etc.] ***for*** ...のためよけいに良く[悪く, など] ▪ I feel *all the better for* a night's sleep. 一夜寝るとそれだけいっそう気分がよい ▪ He makes my pockets *all the lighter for* the extra tips. 彼のおかげで余分のチップがいるのでよけい僕の財布は軽くなる.

***all there is to** do* ...するべきことのすべて ▪ They learned *all there is to* know about it. それについて知っておくべきことはみな学んだ.

All this and heaven too.《諺》こうした良いことの上に, もっと良いことまでも. ☞「キリスト信者はこの世で幸福な生涯が得られるだけでなく, 死しては天国まで行ける」が原義.

all together →TOGETHER.

all told →TELL.

all too →TOO.

all very fine [***well***] [[通例 but 句を伴って]] まことにけっこう《不満の口調》 ▪ *All very fine*, but where's the money to come from? まことにごもっともだが, 金はどこから出るのかね.

all's for the best 何事も天の配剤だ.

All's well that ends well.《諺》終わりよければすべてよし《Shakespeare の同名の劇》.

an all time high [***low***] 空前の高さ[低さ] ▪ The price has reached *an all time high*. 値段は今までの最高に達した ▪ The party has hit *an all time low* in prestige. その党はこれまでないほど威信を失した.

and all **1** その他すべて; ...ごと, ぐるみ (including)

▪ The dog ate the bird, bones, feathers *and all.* その犬は鳥を骨・羽毛ぐるみ食べた ▪ There he sat, pipe *and all.* 彼はパイプをくわえたままそこに座っていた.
2 …などして ▪ He was exhausted *and all.* 彼は疲れはてるやら何やらだった.
3 ほんとに ▪ Her friends were a queer lot, *and all.* 彼女の友人たちはほんとに妙な人々だ.

and all that →THAT.

at all **1**〚否定文で〛少しも, 全然 ▪ I don't know him *at all.* 私は彼をちっとも知らない ▪ He was not *at all* frightened. 彼は全然おびえていなかった.
2〚疑問文で〛一体, そもそも ▪ Do you believe it *at all?* 一体君はそれを信じているのか ▪ Is she able to skate *at all?* 一体彼女はスケートができるのか.
3〚条件文で〛いやしくも, かりそめにも ▪ If you do it *at all,* do it well. どうせやるならよくやれ ▪ I don't think he works much if *at all.* かりに少しは働くとしても彼は大した働きはしないと思う.
4〚肯定文で〛ともかく ▪ The wonder is that I am here *at all.* ともかくここへ来られたのが不思議だ ▪ I am surprised that Tom succeeded *at all.* ともかくトムが成功したとは驚きだ.

(*be*) *all*…〚抽象名詞・複数名詞を伴って〛すっかり…である ▪ He *was all* astonishment. 彼はびっくり仰天した ▪ I *was all* ears. 私は耳をそばだてていた.

be all about《口》**1** …を主題としている, 意図している ▪ His book *is all about* Greece. 彼の本はギリシャを主題にしている ▪ What's this *all about?* これはいったい何事だ ▪ It's *all about* money these days. 当節はただ金を目的としている.
2 (行動・状況)に夢中になって ▪ I *am all about* pop music right now. 私は目下ポピュラー音楽に夢中だ.

be all for《口》**1** …に大賛成である (*doing*) ▪ I *am all for* your going. 君が行くことには大賛成だ ▪ I *am all for* a free Tibet. 自由なチベットに大賛成だ ▪ I *am all for banning* carrying guns. 銃の携行を禁止することに諸手を上げて賛成だ.
2 …を大いに欲しがっている ▪ He *is all for* accepting the offer. 彼はその申し出を大いに受けたがっている.

be all for nothing …に何の影響もない (*in*) ▪ *Is* his absence *all for nothing in* the prosperity of the company? 彼がいなくても会社の繁栄に何の影響もないか.

be all go →GO[1].

be all here [***there***] =be all THERE.

be all one to →be all ONE 2.

be all over the lot/《英》***be all over the shop***《米口》**1** あちこちに散らばって ▪ Why *are* your clothes *all over the lot!* なぜ君の衣服はあちこちに散らばっているのか?
2 めちゃくちゃで, 混乱して ▪ I've been so unimpressed by their campaign. They*'re all over the shop.* 彼らの選挙運動には全く感心しないね. めちゃくちゃじゃないか.

be all right with [***by***] …にちょうどよい ▪ Is tomorrow *all right with* you? あなたはあすは(都合は)いいですか.

be all that《米口》非常に魅力がある ▪ Meg thinks she'*s all that.* メグは自分はとても魅力的だと思っている.

be all the thing (一時的に)大流行している (=be (all) the RAGE) ▪ Digital *was all the thing.* デジタル方式が大流行だった.

be all there →THERE.

be all things to …に満足を与える; の望みどおり[気に入るよう]にする ▪ New York *is all things to* all people. ニューヨークは誰にも満足を与える ▪ She determined to *be all things to* her husband. 彼女は夫の気に入るようにしようと決心した.

be all up →UP[1].

each and all →ALL and sundry.

first of all →FIRST.

for all →FOR.

for all I know (***to the contrary***) →FOR all one knows.

for all of …に関するかぎり ▪ *For all of* him, they might never have met again in this world. 彼に関するかぎり, 彼らは二度と再びこの世で会えなかったかもしれない.

give … *one's* ***all*** …に全力を注ぐ[注ぐ] ▪ The singer *gave his all* in every performance. その歌手はすべての公演で全力を尽くした.

give … ***all*** *one* ***has got***《口》…を全力を尽くしてやる ▪ I'll *give* my job *all* I*'ve got.* 私は自分の仕事を全力を尽くしてやります.

give … the all clear →CLEAR[1].

in all 全部で, みなで, 総計して ▪ There are twenty teachers *in all,* including the Director. 校長を入れて, 全員で20人の先生がいる.

in all *one's* …をきわめて ▪ The sun rose *in all its* splendor. 太陽は光輝さんぜんとして上った ▪ The storm broke upon us *in all its* fury. あらしは猛威をきわめて我々を襲った.

in all *one's* ***born days*** →BORN.

It [***That***] ***is all right.*** どういたしまして; いいんだよ《感謝されたり, 詫びられたりしたときの返事》 ▪ Thank you for your gift.—*It's all right.* 結構なものをありがとう—どういたしまして ▪ I'm very sorry for being late.—*That's all right.* 遅刻してほんとうにごめんなさい—いいんだよ.

it's all right by [***with***] ***me*** いいよ, 賛成だ ▪ Shall we go to the movies tonight?—*It's all right by me.* 今夜映画を見に行こうか?—いいよ.

it's [***they're***] ***all yours*** みんなあなたの責任[もの]です ▪ These children, *they're all yours.* これらの子供たちはみんなあなたの責任です.

not all/all … not〚部分否定〛みな…とは限らない ▪ We do *not all* go. みなは行かない ▪ *All* is *not* gold that glitters.《諺》光るもの必ずしも金でない.

not … all that good [***well,*** etc.] 格別よくはない, 別にうまくはない ▪ Things are *not* going *all that well* in the camp. キャンプではあまりうまくはいっていない ▪ Capitalism may *not* be *all that good* for America. 資本主義はアメリカにとって特によいものではな

いかもしれない.

not all that** one **might** [**ought to**] **be 完全でない, 満足なものでない ▪ I may *not* be *all that* I *might be* as a husband. 私は夫として完全ではないかもしれない.

not as bad(ly) [***tall,*** etc.] ***as all that*** 言われているほど悪く[背が高く]はない ▪ Most of them are *not as rich as all that.* 彼らの大半は言われているほど金持ちじゃない ▪ He's pretty clever but *not as clever as all that.* 彼はかなり利口だが, 言われているほど利口じゃない.

not at all 少しも...でない ▪ Thank you for your trouble. —*Not at all.* お手数をおかけしました—どういたしまして (《米》You're WELCOME. に当たる) ▪ Will it bother you if I smoke?—*Not at all.* タバコを吸ったらご迷惑でしょうか—いいえ, ちっとも.

of all ⟦複数名詞を伴って⟧ 数ある...の中で ▪ Why go to Ireland, *of all* countries? 国もいろいろあろうに, どうしてアイルランドなんかへ行くのか ▪ *Of all* days on Christmas day, he was working hard. 日もあろうにクリスマスの日に彼は一生懸命働いていた.

of all the... →Of ALL the cheek!

Of all the cheek [***nerve, stupid things to do,*** etc.]***!*** よくもまあ生意気にも[厚かましくも, 愚かにも, など] ▪ *Of all the cheek*, calling me an upstart politician! よくもまあ生意気にも, 私のことを成り上がりの政治家だなんて言いおって! ▪ He said I was stupid? Well, *of all the* .... おれが間抜けだと言ったって? いやはや, 全く何という.... ☞しばしば名詞を落として of all the ...として使用される.

one and all →ALL and sundry.

take [***have*** (***got***)] ***all day*** [***morning,*** etc.] 《口》丸一日[朝中, など]かかる《わけではない》 ▪ Are you going to *take all moring* dressing? 着替えるのに朝中かかるのかい ▪ Hurry up! We *have*n't *got all day*! 急げ! 丸一日あるわけじゃないぞ!

taking all in all 全体的に見て ▪ We have had a good year's trade, *taking all in all.* 全体から見て立派な1年分の商売をした.

taking ... all in all ...を全体的に見て ▪ *Taking* him *all in all*, Balzac is the greatest French novelist. 全体的に見てバルザックはフランス最大の小説家だ.

that is all there is of ...についてはそれだけしかない ▪ *That is* just *all there is of* a personal narrative. 個々の人々を述べる場面はほんとにそれだけである.

That [***This***] ***is all there is to it.*** →THERE.

That's all. それで終わり, それだけのことだ ▪ You will be scolded. *That's all.* 君はしかられるだろう. ただそれだけのことさ ▪ *That's all* for today. きょうはこれでおしまい.

That's all I can say. 私はそう考える[思う] ▪ He is very selfish. *That's all I can say.* 彼はとても利己的だ. 僕はそう思う.

that's all she wrote 《米》それで終わりだ, それだけだ ▪ Once you harvest cilantro, *that's all she wrote.* It doesn't grow back again next year. コリアンダーの葉は, 取り入れるとそれでおしまいだ. 翌年二度と生えてくることはない.

That's all you know about it. 《口》あなたはそれについてはあまり知らない; あなたの考えはまちがっている ▪ You don't care about anybody. —*That's all you know about it.* 君は誰のこともかまわない—それは君の誤解だよ.

when all is (***said and***) ***done*** つまり, なんと言ったところで ▪ Flowers are a very small affair, *when all is done.* 花などはなんと言ってもきわめて小さな事柄だ ▪ *When all's said and done*, Peter is less to blame than John. つまるところ, ピーターはジョンほど悪くはない. ☞F quand tout est dit 'when all is said'.

with all ...をもってしても, あれほど...にもかかわらず ▪ *With all* his faults, he is a gentleman. 欠点はいろいろあっても彼は紳士だ ▪ *With all* his wealth, he is not happy. あんなに金があるのに彼は幸福でない.

all-clear /ɔ̀ːlklíər/ 名 ***give*** [***get***] ***the all-clear*** 危険は去った(着手してもよい)という合図を与える[受ける] ▪ Ben had scans today and *got the all-clear.* ベンは今日スキャナー検査を受けて危険は去ったという保証をもらった ▪ Blood tests *gave* him *the all-clear.* 血液検査で危険は去ったと診断された. ☞all-clear「空襲警報解除のサイレン[合図]」.

allege /əlédʒ/ 動 ***be alleged to*** [***be to have*** *done*] ...だ[だった]と言われている ▪ He *is alleged to* be $2,000 behind in his rent. 彼は家賃の支払いが2,000ドルも遅れていると言われている ▪ Jim *is alleged to have* threatened to shoot her to death. ジムは彼女を撃ち殺すとおどしたと言われている.

allegiance /əlíːdʒəns/ 名 ***pledge allegiance to*** ...に対して忠誠を誓う ▪ We all had to *pledge allegiance to* the flag. 我々はみなその旗に対して忠誠を誓わねばならなかった.

allergic /ələ́ːrdʒɪk/ 形 ***be allergic to*** **1** ...に対してアレルギー(体質)の ▪ He *is allergic to* avocado. 彼はアボカドに対してアレルギー体質だ.

2 《口》...が大嫌いで ▪ I'*m allergic to* math. 数学が大嫌いだ.

allergy /ǽlərdʒi/ 名 ***have an allergy for*** 《俗》...がきらい ▪ He *has an allergy for* work. 彼は仕事がきらいだ. ☞allergy「反感」.

alley /ǽli/ 名 ***an alley cat*** **1** のら猫 ▪ The beggar was (as) lean as *an alley cat.* 物乞いはのら猫のようにガリガリにやせていた.

2 《俗》誰とでも寝る女, 尻軽女 ▪ You'll have no problem dating Linda; she's *a* regular *alley cat.* リンダとデートするのはわけない. まぎれもない尻軽女だから.

(***right***) ***down*** [***up***] *one's* ***alley***/ (***right***) ***up*** *one's* ***street*** 《主に英》《米俗》趣味[能力, 利益, 願い]に全くかなって; 得意で, 専門で ▪ Skiing is *right down my alley.* スキーはほんとに好きだ ▪ Anything related to the making of handbags is *right up his alley.* 手さげかばんの製造に関する事なら何でも全く彼の得意とするところだ. ☞《野球》alley はホームランになるような球の飛ぶ想像上の線; "down the alley" とは本塁打を意味する.

strike into another alley (話が)別の方向へ入る ▪ We are now *striking into another alley*, and starting a different question. 今は話がわきへそれて, 別の問題を出してきている.

all fours /ɔ̀:lfɔ́:rz/ 名 ***on all fours*** **1**〚go, crawl などを伴って〛(動物が)四つ足で; (人が)四つんばいで ▪ He landed heavily *on all fours*. 彼はどさりと着地して両手足をついた ▪ These spies will creep, *on all fours*, like cats. スパイどもは猫のように四つんばいにはって行く.

2〚go, run などを伴って〛調子よく(歩く); (比喩などが)矛盾なくうまく相応して(いく) ▪ It is not easy to make a simile *go on all fours*. 直喩をうまく照応していかせるのは楽でない ▪ The comparison would not exactly run *on all fours* when examined. その比較は調べてみるとぴったりと照応してはいかないだろう.

3〚be, stand などを伴って〛全く同じで, 平等で; ぴたりと合って; 《英》仕返しして ▪ The quotation *is* not quite *on all fours*. その引用は(原文と)全く同じではない ▪ It must *stand on all fours* with that stipulation. それはその規定と一致しなければならない. ☞on all four extremities の意.

alliance /əláɪəns/ 名 ***an unholy alliance*** (しばしば政治で) 汚れた[いかがわしい]同盟 ▪ The parties in Tokyo have formed *an unholy alliance* to run giant political campaigns. 東京の政党は巨大な政治キャンペーンをするために汚れた協定を結んだ.

in alliance with …と連合して ▪ Japan was *in alliance with* Great Britain. 日本はイギリスと同盟していた.

make [enter into, form] an alliance with …と同盟する ▪ Russia *entered into an alliance with* France. ロシアはフランスと同盟を結んだ.

alligator /ǽləgèɪtər/ 名 ***(See you) later, alligator.*** 《戯》あとでな, じゃあね《返事は After [In a] while, crocodile!》.

all-nighter /ɔ̀:lnáɪtər/ 名 ***pull an all-nighter*** 徹夜で仕事[勉強]をする ▪ I'm sleepy, I had to *pull an all-nighter* last night. 眠い, 夕べは徹夜しなければならなかったんだ.

allocation /æ̀ləkéɪʃən/ 名 ***be under allocation*** 配給割当制になっている ▪ Sugar *is under allocation* at present. 砂糖は現在は配給制である.

put on [take off] allocation 統制する[をはずす] ▪ Textiles *were put on allocation*. 織物原料は統制になった.

allot /əlát|əlɔ́t/ 動 ***the allotted span*** 人間の寿命とされる70年(《聖》*Ps.* 90. 10) ▪ The old lady has passed *the allotted span* by nearly twenty years. その老婦人は人間の寿命をほとんど20年も越えている.

allow /əláʊ/ 動 ***allow** oneself **in*** …にふける ▪ He *allows himself in* drinking. 彼は飲酒にふけっている.

Allow me. **1**〚Allow me!〛おめでとう《Rugby 校学生語》. ☞<Allow me to congratulate you!

2《口》どうぞ; 私がいたしましょう《相手に手を貸してあげるときの丁寧な表現》 ▪ Seeing a woman trying to put her bags up on the overhead rack, he said, "*Allow me.*" 女性が網棚に荷物を上げようとしているのを見て, 彼は「私が上げましょう」と言った.

***allow me to** do* (失礼ですが)…いたします ▪ *Allow me to* introduce to you my friend Mr. Hill. 友人ヒル氏をご紹介申しあげます.

***allow ... to** do* …が…するのを許す ▪ We *allowed* the children *to* play there. 我々は子供らをそこで遊ばせておいた ▪ Fruits *are* not *allowed to* freeze. 果物類は凍らせてはいけない.

No smoking allowed. 禁煙《掲示》.

allowance /əláʊəns/ 名 ***at no allowance*** (あてがいぶちでなく)惜しみなく, 十分に, 思うままに ▪ Doctors here are prescribing it *at no allowance*. 当地の医者は思うままにそれに処方を書いている.

make allowance(s) for …を酌量する, 割引する; を見越す ▪ We must *make allowance for* his lack of experience. 我々は彼の経験不足を酌量せねばならない ▪ We must *make allowance for* the train being late. 我々は電車が遅れることを見越しておかねばならない.

make an allowance 手当を与える ▪ His father *makes* him *a* monthly *allowance*. 彼の父は彼に月々手当を与えている.

make an allowance of …の割引をする ▪ We *make an allowance of* 10% for cash payment. 現金支払ならば1割引です.

put** a person **on short allowance 人の手当を減らす ▪ They *put* the crew *on short allowance*. 彼らは船員の手当を減らした.

alloy /ǽlɔɪ/ 名 ***No joy without alloy.*** 《諺》まじり気のない喜びはない.

allure /əlʊ́ər/ 動 ***allure** a person **to** do* [***into*** *doing*] 人をそそのかして…させる ▪ I *was allured* by temptation *to* buy [*into buying*] a book. 誘惑にそそのかされてある本を買った.

allusion /əlú:ʒən/ 形 ***in allusion to*** …を暗にさして ▪ He spoke *in allusion to* the abuse. 彼はその弊風について話した.

make allusion to …を暗にほのめかす, に(直接・間接に)言及する ▪ He does not like me to *make* any *allusion to* this plan. 彼は私がこの計画のことに触れるのを好まない.

ally /əláɪ/ 動 ***ally*** (*oneself*) ***with*** …と同盟する; と提携する; と縁組する, いっしょになる ▪ America *allied herself with* Great Britain against Germany. アメリカはイギリスと同盟してドイツに対抗した ▪ The workers *allied* (*themselves*) *with* the radical party against the government. 労働者たちは急進党と提携して政府に反対した ▪ Curiosity *allied itself with* allurement. 好奇心が誘惑といっしょになった.

be allied to …と類縁である ▪ Coal *is* chemically *allied to* diamond. 石炭は化学上ダイヤと同類だ

A

▪ Love *is allied to* hatred. 愛は憎しみと似ている.

almighty /ɔːlmáɪti/ 形 ***God* [*Christ*] *Almighty!*** 《卑》(驚き・軽蔑・怒り・挫折などを表して)(こん)ちきしょう, やれやれ ▪ *Christ almighty*, get off the computer! You've been on there for ages! おいおい, コンピューターをやめなよ! ずいぶん前からかかりっきりじゃないか!

the almighty dollar 《口》万能の金, 富; 金の力 (《英》ではしばしば皮肉にアメリカ人の金儲けに汲々たるを風して用いる) ▪ In dreams they nod, and mutter "God," but mean *the almighty dollar*. 彼らは夢の中でうなずいて「神様」とつぶやくが, それは万能の金のことなのだ.

the Almighty God/God Almighty 全能の神 ▪ Jesus Christ is none other than *God Almighty* come in the flesh. イエス・キリストは, 肉体をもって現れた全能の神にほかならない.

almost /ɔ́ːlmoʊst/ 副 ***almost no* [*never, nothing*]** 《米》ほとんど…ない ▪ *Almost no* one appreciated its true significance. ほとんど誰もその真意を解する者はいなかった ▪ He is *almost never* called Pat. 彼はパットと呼ばれることはほとんどない.

aloft /əlɑ́ft|əlɔ́ft/ 副 ***go aloft*** **1**《海》檣上(しょうじょう)に登る ▪ He *went aloft* to unfurl the lighter sails. 彼は軽い帆をあげるために檣上に登った.

2《口》天国へ行く, 昇天する ▪ And now he'*s gone aloft*. そして彼はもう天国へ行ってしまった.

alone /əlóʊn/ 形副 ***all alone*** 一人ぼっちで; 独力で ▪ I was *all alone* in the house. 家に一人ぼっちだった ▪ He did it *all alone*. 彼は一人でそれをした.

go it alone →GO[2].

leave* [*let*]... *alone **1** …を(かまわずに)放っておく ▪ For heaven's sake *leave* me *alone*. どうぞお願いですから私を放っといてください ▪ He is gentle as a lamb, if only he *is let alone*. 彼は放っておきさえすれば, 非常におとなしい.

2 …に手を出さない ▪ I should *let* these shares *alone*. 私はこれらの株には手を出すべきではない.

3 …せずにおく, 言わずにおく ▪ For his other qualities I *let alone*. 彼の他の特質については, 言わずにおきます.

leave* [*let*]... *alone to do 《口》〚主に命令文で〛 **1** かまわないで…させる, 放っておいて…させる ▪ It is best to *let* [*leave*] him *alone to* do it. 彼に任せておくのが一番よい.

2 …は放っておいてもきっとする ▪ *Leave* a woman *alone to* find out that. 女性は放っておいてもきっとそれを見つけるのだ ▪ *Let* the charwoman *alone to* be the first. 掃除婦は放っておいても必ず一番やりだよ.

let alone 〚主に否定文の次に用いるが, 《英》では肯定文の次にくることもある〛 …は言うまでもなく (=to SAY nothing of) ▪ I cannot afford the time, *let alone* the expenses. 私は時間の余裕がない, 経費はもちろんのことだ ▪ He speaks Russian, *let alone* English. 彼はロシア語を話す, 英語は言うまでもない.

let* [*leave*] *well* (*enough*) *alone →WELL[2].

not alone A but* (*also*) *B 《雅》AのみならずBもまた ▪ This suggestion is *not alone* absurd *but also* malicious. この提案はばかげているばかりでなく, 悪意がある.

stand alone **1** 孤立する ▪ Can a nation *stand alone*? 国が孤立していられるか.

2 匹敵するものがない ▪ He *stands alone* in his command of English. 彼は英語が達者な点で他に匹敵するものがない.

along /əlɔ́ːŋ|əlɔ́ŋ/ 前副 ***all along*** **1** 初めから, ずっと引続き ▪ I knew that *all along*. 私はそれを初めからずっと知っていた.

2 端から端まで ▪ The wall had crumbled *all along*. 塀は端から端までくずれてしまっていた.

3 手足を伸ばして ▪ The nurse laid me *all along* again. 看護師はまた私を大の字に寝かせた.

all along the line →LINE[1].

***along about* [*toward*]** 《米口》…のころ ▪ It was *along about* 7 o'clock. 7時ごろのことだった.

along back 《米口》少し前, 最近 ▪ I've made a mistake *along back*. 最近私は誤りを犯した.

along for the ride →RIDE[1].

along here こちらの方へ ▪ He was walking *along here*. 彼はこちらの方へ歩いて来ていた.

along of **1** …といっしょに ▪ I never sailed *along of* him. 私は彼と航海したことがない. ☞《海》alongside of から来たものであろう.

2《口》…のため, のおかげで《方言ではしばしば long of》 ▪ I was quartermaster, *along of* my timber leg. おれは義足だったので操舵員だった ▪ It's all *along of* you. 全く君のおかげだ.

3《俗》(人)と ▪ I am friendly *along of* you. 私は君とは親しいよね.

along there あの方向へ ▪ The crow flew *along there*. カラスはあちらの方へ飛んで行った.

along with **1** …と共に, と協同して ▪ I would rejoice *along with* them. 彼らと共に喜び合いたい.

2 …に加えて ▪ *Along with* this, he was gentle and equitable. これに加えて彼はやさしく公正であった.

***be along* (*to*)** 《口》〚未来形で〛(…へ)やって来る, 到着する ▪ The captain *will be along* for us about sunset. 隊長は日没ごろ来てくださる ▪ *Will* he *be along to* the meeting? 彼は会に来るだろうか.

find* [*make*] *one's way along 前進する; 立身する ▪ They managed to *find their way along*. 彼らはなんとか前進して行った ▪ He worked hard to *make his way along*. 彼は立身出世するため一生懸命働いた.

right along →RIGHT[1].

alongside /əlɔ́ːŋsàɪd|əlɔ̀ŋsáɪd/ 前副 ***alongside of*** **1** …と並んで; に沿って《比喩的にも》 ▪ He walked *alongside of* his uncle. 彼はおじと並んで歩いた ▪ We walked *alongside of* the river. 我々は川に沿って歩いた.

2 …といっしょに ▪ He played *alongside of* John on the same team. 彼は同じチームでジョンといっしょにやった.

3《口》…と比較して ▪ His money doesn't look like much *alongside of* his uncle's. 彼の金はおじのと比べて多額のものとは思えない.

aloof /əlúːf/ 副 ***hold ... aloof*** …を近寄らせない ▪ Pride *holds* them *aloof*. 自尊心のため彼らは近寄れない.

stand [***remain, keep, sit, hold***] ***aloof*** (***from***) (…から)離れている; (から)超然としている; (に)よそよそしくする ▪ He *stands aloof from* the crowd. 彼は超然として俗界に交わらない ▪ Sparta *kept aloof from* this struggle. スパルタはこの争いに加わらなかった ▪ He was not the man to *stand* coldly *aloof*. 彼は冷然としてお高くとまっているような人ではなかった. ☞aloof「風上」の意; 風上にいるには船首を風上から避けておらねばならぬから「避けている」の意となった.

aloud /əláʊd/ 副 ***out aloud*** 大声で ▪ They cried *out aloud*, that he might hear them. 彼らはその男の耳に届くように大声で叫んだ.

reek [***stink***] ***aloud***《口》ぷんぷんにおう ▪ It *reeks aloud* of tobacco. それはタバコのにおいが強い ▪ The stuff *stank aloud*. その品はぷんぷんにおった.

alpha /ǽlfə/ 名 ***alpha wave*** アルファ波《リラックス時に出る1秒に8–12ヘルツの脳波》 ▪ If you stroke a cat you love for a while, you will find *alpha waves* are making you feel a lot better. 愛猫をしばらくなでてやっていると, ずっと気分が落ち着いてくるのがわかるでしょう.

from Alpha to Omega 始めから終わりまで, 徹頭徹尾 ▪ I was a gentleman *from Alpha to Omega*. 私は徹頭徹尾紳士だった.

the Alpha and Omega 初めと終わり; 全体(《聖》*Rev.* 8. 1) ▪ Sentence types are *the Alpha and Omega* of English grammar. 文型は英文法の初めであり終わりである ▪ The weather has been, since Britain was Britain, *the alpha and omega* of British conversation. イギリス始まって以来, 天気がイギリス人の会話のすべてであった.

already /ɔːlrédi/ 副 ***All right, already!***《米俗》もうわかったよ; うんざりした ▪ *All right already!* Don't rush me. もうわかったよ! そうせき立てるなよ. ☞Yiddish 語の "genuk shoyn" の訳.

also-ran /ɔ́ːlsoʊræ̀n/ 名 ***be an also-ran*** 負ける, 落伍者になる ▪ Mark *was an also-ran* in everything he tried to do. マークは手がけたあらゆることに失敗した. ☞原義は4位以下あるいは完走できなかった馬.

alt /ælt/ 名 ***in alt***《音》高音で; 大得意で, 高揚した気分で; 高ぶって; 野心的で ▪ Your ladyship's absolutely *in alt*. 奥様はすっかり夢中になっておられます ▪ I know you to be *in alt* as to your religion. あなたが宗教については高揚した気分だということを知っています ▪ Come, be a little less *in alt*, and answer a man when he speaks to you. なあ君, そんなに高ぶらないで人が話しかけたら返事ぐらいはしろよ.

altar /ɔ́ːltər/ 名 ***lead*** (*a bride*) ***to the altar*** (花嫁)と結婚式をあげる ▪ After a three-year courtship, he *led* Beth *to the altar*. 3年間の求婚ののち, 彼はベスと教会で結婚式を挙げた.

leave ... at the altar **1** 土壇場で結婚をやめる ▪ Lester *left* poor Susan *at the altar*. レスターはかわいそうに土壇場でスーザンとの結婚をやめた.

2 期待はずれに終わる ▪ Once again he didn't get his promotion and *was left at the altar*. またもや彼は昇進を逸し, 期待はずれに終わった.

sacrifice ... on the altar of **1** (他の物)を得るために…を犠牲にする ▪ Julian *sacrificed* his family life *on the altar of* his career and advancement. ジュリアンは経歴と昇進のために自分の家族の生活を犠牲にした.

2〚受身で〛(ある特定のイデオロギーや活動のために)犠牲にされる ▪ The young soldiers *were* deliberately *sacrificed on the altar of* imperialism. 若い兵士らは意図的に帝国主義の犠牲にされた.

alter /ɔ́ːltər/ 動 ***alter for the better*** [***worse***] 改善[改悪]する; 良い[悪い]方へ向かう ▪ We *altered* the system *for the better*. 我々はその制度を改善した ▪ He *altered for the worse*. 彼は人間が変わって悪くなった.

That alters the case. それでは話が変わってくる.

alternative /ɔːltə́ːrnətɪv/ 名 ***have no*** (***other***) ***alternative*** (***but to*** *do*) (…するより)ほかに道がない (→have no CHOICE 2) ▪ The judge *has no alternative but to* sentence the murderer to hanging. 裁判官は殺人者に絞首刑を宣告するほかに道がない.

have the alternative of …のどちらを選んでもよい ▪ You *have the alternative of* going or staying. 行くなりとどまるなりどちらにしてもよい.

altitude /ǽltətjùːd/ 名 ***in*** *one's* ***altitudes***《米俗》酒に酔って ▪ He was *in his altitudes*. 彼は酔っていた.

in high altitudes《米俗》大得意になって ▪ He was *in high altitudes*. 彼は大得意だった.

altogether /ɔ̀ːltəgéðər/ 副名 ***for altogether*** 永久に; 最終的に ▪ He was fled *for altogether*. 彼はとうとう逃げてしまった.

in the altogether《口》裸で (=in the BUFF, in the RAW) ▪ The child was swimming *in the altogether*. その子供は裸で泳いでいた.

taken altogether 全体的に見て, 概して ▪ *Taken altogether*, I see nothing to regret. 全体から見て, 何も遺憾な点はない ▪ *Taken altogether*, the plan has worked pretty well. 概してその計画はかなりうまくいった.

always /ɔ́ːlweɪz/ 副 ***always excepting*** ただし, …の場合を除く ▪ Everyone was tired, *always excepting* John, the eminent athlete. みんな疲れていた, ただし著名なアスリートのジョンは別だ.

always supposing (***that***) ただし…ならば ▪ I will help your project financially, *always supposing* there is no risk in it. 君の企画を財政的に援助してあげよう. ただしリスクがないとすればの話だよ.

as always いつものことだが, いつものように ▪ *As al-*

ways, Mike was late for school. 例によってマイクは遅刻した.

for always 永久に ▪ Children will bring us joy *for always*. 子供たちはいつまでも喜びをもたらすだろう.

not always 必ずしも…でない ▪ The rich are *not always* happy. 富んだ人々が必ずしも幸福ではない.

not always what** one **might** [**ought to**] **be 完全でない, 満足なものでない ▪ He is *not always what* a gentleman *ought to be*. 彼は必ずしも完璧な紳士ではない.

amaze /əméɪz/ 動 ***be amazed at*** [***by***] …に仰天する ▪ We *are amazed by* the economic development in India. 我々はインドの経済成長に仰天している.

amazement /əméɪzmənt/ 名 ***blank amazement*** 全くの仰天 ▪ A look of *blank amazement* came over his face at the sight of the ghost. その亡霊を見たときびっくり仰天した表情が彼の顔に浮かんだ.

in [***with***] ***amazement*** びっくり仰天して ▪ He stared at the girl *in amazement*. 彼は仰天して少女を見つめた.

to** person's **amazement …の大いに驚いたことには ▪ *To his amazement*, a hand appeared between the curtains. 彼がびっくり仰天したことにはカーテンの間から手が現れた.

amber /ǽmbər/ 名 ***amber gambler*** 《英口》黄信号を突破するドライバー ▪ He's short-tempered and a bit of an *amber gambler*. 彼は短気で, ちょっとした無茶なドライバーだ.

ambition /æmbíʃən/ 名 ***the height of ambition*** 最も強い望み[願い] ▪ To be an engine-driver was *the height of* his *ambition*. 機関士になることが彼の最大の願いだった.

ambitious /æmbíʃəs/ 形 ***be ambitious of*** [***for, to** do*] …を[することを]熱望する ▪ I *am ambitious to* be his pupil. 私はあの人の弟子になることを熱望している ▪ He *is ambitious of* distinction. 彼は栄達に恋々たるものがある.

ambulance /ǽmbjələns/ 名 ***ambulance chaser*** 《口》交通事故を商売の種にする弁護士, 二流弁護士 ▪ Don't hire Green. He is a notorious *ambulance chaser*. グリーンを雇っちゃだめだ. 彼は名うての交通事故専門の弁護士だ.

ambush[1] /ǽmbʊʃ/ 名 ***fall into an ambush*** 待ち伏せにあう ▪ He *fell into an ambush* on the way. 彼は途中で待ち伏せにあった.

lay [***make, construct***] ***an ambush*** 伏兵[伏勢]を置く ▪ The inhabitants of this Isle *laid an ambush* for him. この島の住民は彼に対して伏勢を置いた.

lie [***hide***] ***in ambush*** 待ち伏せする ▪ The natives *lay in ambush* in the jungle. 先住民たちはジャングルの中で待ち伏せした.

ambush[2] /ǽmbʊʃ/ 動 ***ambush** oneself* 待ち伏せする ▪ They *ambushed themselves* behind trees. 彼らは木かげに待ち伏せした.

amen /àːmén, èɪ-/ 間名 ***Amen to that!*** それに賛成(です).

say amen to …の通りだ; に全面的に賛成だ, によろしいと言う ▪ I think we had better economize from now on. —I *say amen to* that. お互いこれからは倹約したほうがよいと思う—その通りだ ▪ I'll *say amen to* everything you assert. あなたの言うことには何でも全面的に賛成する.

amenable /əmíːnəbəl/ 形 ***amenable to*** **1** (人が法律など)に従うべき, 服すべき; に従う ▪ The sovereign of this country is not *amenable to* any form of trial. この国の君主はどんな形式の裁判をも受ける義務はない ▪ She is *amenable to* reason. 彼女は道理には従う.

2 (物事が)…を受けうる; 受けやすい ▪ This case is not *amenable to* ordinary rules. この件は普通の規則で律しえない ▪ These actions are *amenable to* criticism. こうした行動は非難されやすい.

amends /əméndz/ 名 ***make amends for*** …の償いをする, 埋め合わせる ▪ He *made amends* to her *for* her loss. 彼は彼女に損害の償いをした. ☞amends は単数扱い.

amenity /əménəti/ 名 ***exchange amenities with*** …と交歓する ▪ Before he went, he *exchanged amenities with* the Mayor. 彼は立ち去る前に市長と交歓した.

American /əmérəkən/ 形 ***be American as apple-pie*** まさにアメリカ的だ ▪ For me, jazz *is American as apple-pie*. 私にとって, ジャズはまさにアメリカ的だ.

on the American plan (ホテルが)アメリカ方式で《部屋・食事込みの料金を取る方式; 実際にはこの方式のホテルはアメリカにもあまりない》(↔on the EUROPEAN plan) ▪ Is this hotel *on the American plan*? このホテルはアメリカ方式ですか.

amiss /əmís/ 副 ***be not amiss*** 悪くない, 的はずれでない, 不適当でない ▪ It may *not be amiss* to add to these remarks. これらの言葉につけ加えてもよかろう ▪ A glass of wine at supper *is not amiss*. 晩酌1杯は悪くない.

do [***deal, act***] ***amiss*** 誤った行動をする; やりそこなう; 《婉曲》悪事を働く ▪ We will punish those who *act amiss*. 悪事を働く者たちを罰するつもりだ ▪ Something has *been done amiss*. 何かしくじりがあったのだ.

go amiss **1** (事が)まずくいく, まちがう ▪ All *went amiss*. 万事不首尾だった.

2 《米俗》(物が)なくなる ▪ Something *went amiss*. 何かなくなった.

not go amiss/《英》***not come amiss*** 《口》悪くない, うまくいく ▪ A word of apology would *not go amiss*. 一言わびればうまくいく ▪ *Nothing comes amiss* to a hungry man. 《諺》すき腹にまずいものなし.

take ... amiss …を悪く取る, に腹を立てる ▪ Please don't *take* it *amiss* if I point out your errors. あなたの誤りを指摘してもどうか怒らないでくださ

い. ☞「意味を取りちがえる, 誤解する」が原義.

think amiss of …を誤解する; を悪くとる ▪ He will not *think amiss of* my conduct. 彼は私の行為を悪くはとらないだろう.

among /əmʌ́ŋ/ 前 ***among other things*** 他にもいろいろあるがその中でも; とりわけ ▪ *Among other things* hissing is considered rather rude. とりわけシューという音を出すことはだいぶ無作法と考えられている ▪ *Among other* virtues he has that of temperance. 他にも美徳はいろいろ持っているが, 彼はとりわけ節制の美徳を備えている.

among ourselves [***themselves, yourselves***] 仲間同士で, みんなで; 内密に ▪ They whispered *among themselves.* 彼らは仲間同士でささやきあった ▪ We had only 1,000 yen *among ourselves.* みんなで1,000円しか持っていなかった.

among the dead 死者の中に ▪ He is numbered *among the dead.* 彼は亡き者の数に入った.

among them, but not of them 彼らの間にまじってはいても, 彼らの一味ではない (Byron, *Childe Harold's Pilgrimage* 3. 113) ▪ I am *among them, but not of them.* 私は彼らの間にまじってはいるが, 一味ではない.

among us [***you***] みなの協力で, みんなで ▪ We had not five dollars *among us.* 我々はみなの金を合わせても5ドルなかった ▪ You have *among you* spoilt the child. 君たちはみんなして子供を甘やかしてしまった.

be among the first [***largest***] 第一[最大]のうちに入る ▪ These cities *are among the largest* in Japan. これらの都市は日本で最大の都市のうちに入る ▪ Bob *was among the first* that solved the problem. ボブはその問題を最初に解いた一人だった.

from among …の中から ▪ The chairman will be chosen *from among* the members. 議長は会員の互選による.

amorous /ǽmərəs/ 形 ***be amorous of*** …を恋している ▪ He *is amorous of* that lady. 彼はあの女性に恋している.

amount[1] /əmáʊnt/ 名 ***an amount of*** かなり(の量)の… ▪ He did *an amount of* work. 彼はかなりの仕事をした.

any amount (***of***) →ANY.

in amount 総計で; 結局 ▪ He paid more than 10 pounds *in amount.* 彼は総額10ポンド以上を払った.

no amount of... どんなに…しても効果がない ▪ *No amount of* money could persuade her to do it. どんなに金を積んでも彼女にそれをさせることはできなかった.

to the amount of …に達する, …だけの ▪ The firm has large capital *to the amount of* 500 million yen. その会社は5億円にも達する大資本を持っている.

amount[2] /əmáʊnt/ 動 ***amount to anything*** 〚否定文で〛(人が)ものになる, 成功する ▪ He'll never *amount to anything.* 彼は決してものにはなるまい.

amount to much 〚否定文・疑問文で〛たいしたものになる; たいした価値がある ▪ I don't think he can ever *amount to much.* 彼はたいしたものになんかなれないと思う ▪ Does all this *amount to much?* こんなことにたいした価値がありますか.

amount to something ひとかどの人物になる; (物が)相当の物になる ▪ All parents hope that their children will *amount to something.* すべての親は子供がひとかどの人物になるのを望んでいる ▪ Their savings will *amount to something.* 彼らの貯金は相当な額になるだろう.

amount to very little [***nothing***] ほとんど[全然]無価値である ▪ It may *amount to very little.* それはほとんど価値がないかもしれない.

amuck, amock /əmʌ́k/ 形 ***run*** [***go***] ***amuck***

1 血を求めて狂いあばれる ▪ Like a raging madman he *runs amuck* stabbing every man he meets. 彼は激怒した狂人のように狂いあばれて, 出会う人をことごとく突き刺すのだ.

2 荒れ狂う, あばれ回る ▪ The North Sea *ran amuck.* 北海は荒れ狂っていた.

3 乱暴[むちゃ]に当たり散らす (*at, against, with*) ▪ I am too discreet to *run amuck at* all I meet. 私は思慮があるから会う人ごとにむちゃに当たり散らすようなことはしない ▪ He *ran amuck with* any one who crossed him. 彼は自分に逆らう者には誰かれの別なくすぐ当たり散らした. ☞ <Malay amoq = 'furious attack'.

amuse /əmjúːz/ 動 ***amuse*** *oneself* ***by*** [***with, in***] *doing* …をしておもしろがる, おもしろく遊ぶ ▪ The children *amused themselves by making* things with paper. 子供らは紙で物を作っておもしろく遊んだ.

amuse *oneself* ***with*** (*a thing*) (ある事柄)で楽しむ, おもしろがる ▪ He *amuses himself with* a camera. 彼はカメラで楽しむ.

be amused at [***by***] …(を見て, 聞いて)おもしろがる ▪ He *was amused at* an incident. 彼はその出来事を見ておもしろがった ▪ I *am amused by* the idea. その考えを聞いておもしろかった.

be amused with …をおもしろがる ▪ He *was amused with* the idea. 彼はその着想をおもしろいと思った.

keep *a person* ***amused*** 人を退屈させない[楽しませる] (*with*) ▪ The cartoon characters of Disney have *kept* children *amused* for generations. ディズニー漫画のキャラクターは何世代にもわたって子供たちを楽しませてきた ▪ He *kept* his kids *amused with* picture books. 彼は子供を絵本で飽きさせなかった.

(***We are***) ***not amused.*** 私はおもしろくない《誰かがまじめな席でしゃれを飛ばしたとき Victoria 女王が不興げに言った言葉》 ▪ I looked upon ours as an ideal marriage. —Like Queen Victoria I *was not amused.* 私たちの結婚は理想的なものと思ってましたわ—ビクトリア女王じゃないけど, 私はおもしろくなかったよ.

You amuse me! 《反語》まあばからしい; 笑わせるね.

amusement /əmjúːzmənt/ 名 ***find amusement in*** …に興を覚える, を楽しむ ▪ Millions of people *find* their chief *amusement in* the films. 何百万という人々が主として映画を楽しむ.

for (*one's*) ***amusement*** 楽しみに ▪ I travel *for amusement.* 私は楽しみに旅行をする.

to** a person's **amusement 人がおもしろかったことに ▪ Much *to my amusement* the pair turned out to be Jewish. とてもおもしろかったことに, その二人連れはユダヤ人であることがわかった.

analogous /ənǽləgəs/ 形 ***be analogous to*** ...に類似している ▪ The gills of fishes *are analogous to* the lungs in terrestrial animals. 魚類のえらは地上動物の肺と類似している.

analogy /ənǽlədʒi/ 名 ***bear*** [***have***] ***an analogy to*** [***with***] ...と一致する, に類似する ▪ The trilobites *bear* so strong *an analogy to* those described by him. 三葉虫は彼の述べているものにきわめてよく似ている.

on the analogy of/by analogy with ...から類推して ▪ New forms are often constructed *on the analogy of* words originally unrelated. 元は無関係の語から類推して新しい語形が作られることがしばしばある.

analysis /ənǽləsəs/ 名 ***in*** [***at, on***] ***the last*** [***final***] ***analysis*** つまるところ, 結局 ▪ *At the last analysis* working for others should be the keynote of all business. 結局, 他人のために働くことがすべての事業の基調であるべきだ.

on analysis 結局 ▪ *On analysis* it gave the following results. 結局それは次のような結果となった.

anatomy /ənǽtəmi/ 名 ***like an anatomy*** 《口》骨と皮ばかりのようにやせて ▪ He is *like an anatomy.* 彼はやせて骨と皮だ.

anchor[1] /ǽŋkər/ 名 ***cast an anchor to the windward*** →WINDWARD.

come to (***an***) ***anchor*** **1** いかりを降ろす, 停泊する ▪ All the ships had *come to* (*an*) *anchor.* 船はみないかりをおろしていた.

2 落ち着く, 止まる ▪ The old lady finally *came to anchor* opposite George. 老婦人は最後にジョージの向いの席に落ち着いた ▪ He always *comes to anchor* in a pub. 彼はいつもパブへ立寄る.

weigh [***up***] ***anchor*** **1** いかりをあげる; (仕事を始めるため)腰をあげる ▪ He *weighed* his *anchor* in haste. 彼は急いで抜錨した ▪ Now, *weigh anchor* and start that packing. さあ腰をあげて, あの荷造りを始めなさい.

2 去る; 死ぬ ▪ The person responsible has *weighed anchor.* 責任者は亡くなった.

anchor[2] /ǽŋkər/ 動 ***anchor** oneself* 《口》とどまる, 座る, 休む ▪ He *anchored himself* at the hotel. 彼はホテルにとどまった.

anchor** one's **hope in [***on***] ...に望みの綱をかける ▪ He *anchored his hope in* his son's ability. 彼は息子の才能に望みを嘱していた.

be anchored in ...と強く結びついている, に根ざしている ▪ His faith *is* firmly *anchored in* the doctrines of the Church. 彼の信仰は教会の教義としっかりと結びついている.

ancient /éɪnʃənt/ 名 ***the Ancient of Days*** 「日の老いたる者」, 永遠者, 神 (《聖》*Dan.* 7.9) ▪ *The Ancient of Days* did sit. 永遠なる者が御座し給うた.

and /ənd/ 接 ***and all that*** →THAT.

And how! →HOW.

and/or および/または ▪ He will eat cake *and/or* pie. 彼はケーキおよび/またはパイを食べるだろう《ケーキとパイ, またはケーキかパイのみ食べる》.

and so forth [***on***] など, うんぬん《etc. または&c. と略す》 ▪ There came dogs, cats, horses, *and so on.* 犬, 猫, 馬などがやって来た.

and such →SUCH.

and that goes それで終わり (that is final) ▪ You can't go to the disco tonight, son, *and that goes.* 息子よ, 今夜はディスコへ行ってはならぬ. ならぬと言ったらならぬ.

and (***then***) ***some*** 《口》その上どっさり, おまけに; (しかも)それ以上で ▪ He returned from his trip to India with rare articles *and some.* 彼はインドへの旅から珍しい品をしかもどっさり持って帰って来た ▪ He was all of that *and then some.* 彼はすっかりその通りだったしそれ以上でもあった ▪ She's as attractive as Mary—*and then some.* 彼女はメアリーに劣らず魅力がある—いやメアリー以上だ.

and things →and THINGs (like that).

and to think (***that***) それなのに...とは《あきれた気持ち》 ▪ He is our representative, *and to think that* he seldom attends meetings. 彼は我々の代表だが, それなのに会合にめったに出席しないとは.

and yet それでも, それなのに ▪ It is very cold, *and yet* I must go out. 非常に寒いが, それでも私は外出しなくてはならない.

***there are** As **and** As* Aにもいろいろある ▪ *There are* books *and* books. 本にもピンからキリまである ▪ *There are* women *and* women. 女性もいろいろだ.

angel /éɪndʒəl/ 名 ***a fallen angel*** **1** 堕天使, (昔は崇拝されていたが今では)堕落した人物 ▪ I know Satan was *a fallen angel.* サタンが堕天使だったことは知っている.

2 成績不振会社[チーム], 落ち目になった会社[スポーツチーム] ▪ Derby County were this season's *fallen angels,* being sent into the Second Division after losing all their matches. ダービー・カウンティーは今シーズンの堕落天使で, 全敗したのち2部送りにされた.

an angel of a... 天使のような... ▪ Anne is very quiet and *an angel of a* girl. アンはとてももの静かな天使のような少女だ.

angel of death 死のみ使い《近うく死(の予告)の擬人化》 ▪ My father has been summoned away by the *angel of death.* 父は死のみ使いに召された.

angel of light 光の天使《明朗で優しい人》 ▪ She's an *angel of light* in the house. 彼女はその家の光の天使だ.

be an angel and お願いだから ▪ *Be an angel and* make me a cup of coffee. お願いだから私にコーヒーを1杯入れてちょうだい.

be with the angels/join the angels in heaven (人が)亡くなる ▪ Rose unexpectedly *joined the angels in heaven* Sunday May 25. ローズは突然5月25日の日曜日に亡くなった.

enough to make the angels weep 天使を泣かせるに十分な(悲しい・愚かなこと)(cf. Sh., *Meas. for M.* 2. 2. 117) ▪ The workers are not doing their jobs properly. It is *enough to make the angels weep*. 労働者たちはきちんと職務を遂行していない. これは天使を泣かせるに十分な悲しいことである.

entertain an angel unawares 偉い人とは気づかないでもてなす; 人の立派さを知らずにいる (《聖》*Heb.* 13: 2) ▪ She was *entertaining an angel unawares* in the shape of a great composer. 彼女は大作曲家をそれと知らずにもてなしていた ▪ Well, Richard, I have been *entertaining an angel unawares*. ところでリチャード君, 僕は君の立派さを知らずにいた.

Fools rush in (where angels fear to tread). 《諺》愚人は天使も踏み入ることを恐れるような所へ飛び込む,「盲ヘビにおじず」. ☞Pope, *An Essay on Criticism* 625から.

like an angel 美しく(歌うなど) ▪ She sings *like an angel*. I love her voice. 彼女は天使のように歌う. 私は彼女の声が大好きだ.

like angels' visits [angel-visits] 天使の訪れのように(まれで楽しい)(Campbell, *Pleasure of Hope* 2. 378) ▪ Letters from across the seas were *like angels' visits*. 海外からの手紙は天使の訪れのようにまれで楽しいものだった.

on the side of the angels →SIDE.

Talk of an angel and he will appear [we hear the flutter of his wings]. 噂をすれば影とやら《Talk of the DEVIL and he will appear. の上品な言い方》.

the angel in the house 家庭の天使《ひたすら夫と子供に尽くす女性》 ▪ Mrs. Ramsay clearly enacts the role of *the Angel in the House*, yet she also recognizes the limitations of this role. ラムジー夫人は明らかに家庭の天使の役割を演じている. しかし, 彼女はこの役割の限界も認めている.

anger[1] /ǽŋgər/ 名 ***in a fit of anger*** →FIT[1].

in a moment of anger 腹立ちまぎれに ▪ He beat his wife *in a moment of anger*. 彼は腹立ちまぎれに妻をなぐった.

in anger 怒って ▪ We can't govern *in anger*. 怒りにまかせて政治をすることはできない.

anger[2] /ǽŋgər/ 動 ***be angered at [by]*** …を怒る ▪ He *was angered at* the insult. 彼はその侮辱を憤った.

angle /ǽŋgəl/ 名 ***at an angle*** 曲がって, 斜めに ▪ That's why the rope hangs *at an angle*. そういうわけでロープは斜めにかかっているのだ.

at angles with …と(平行でなく)角度をなすように ▪ The portico of that detached house is *at angles with* the street. 離れ家の柱廊玄関は街路と角度をなしている.

at right angle(s) to [with] …と直角をなして ▪ These lines are *at right angles to* each other. これらの線は互いに直角をなしている ▪ The streets run *at right angle with* each other. 往来は互いに直角をなしている.

from different angles 種々異なった角度から ▪ We must view things *from different angles*. 物事は種々異なった角度から見なければならない.

know all the angles 《米》酸いも甘いもかみわけている ▪ Father *knows all the angles*. 父は酸いも甘いもかみわけている.

on the angle 斜めに ▪ The painter takes it *on the angle* rather than in front. 画家は真正面よりも斜めにそれを描く.

angry /ǽŋgri/ 形 ***be angry with*** *a person* [***at, about*** *a thing*] 人[物]に対して怒る ▪ Don't *be angry with* me, *at* what I have done. 私のしたことで私に腹を立てないでくれ.

come to angry words 激論する, けんか口論になる ▪ They *came to angry words* in the end. 彼らはしまいには激論になった.

have angry words with …と口論する ▪ I *had angry words with* her last night. 私は彼女と昨夜口論した.

anguish /ǽŋgwɪʃ/ 名 ***in [for] anguish*** 苦悶して, 苦しまぎれに ▪ The child was very badly hurt and was *in anguish* all the evening. 子供は重傷を負い一晩中苦悶した ▪ She cried out *for anguish* at parting. 彼女は別れのつらさに泣いた.

animadversion /æ̀nəmædvə́ːrʃən/ 名 ***make animadversions on*** 《文》…を批評[非難]する ▪ He *made* some *animadversions on* this ode. 彼はこの頌詩を少し酷評した.

animal /ǽnəməl/ 名 ***a different animal*** 別物, 似て非なるもの ▪ But Google is *an* entirely *different animal* from Firefox. でもグーグルはファイアフォックスとは全く別物だ.

a political animal 政治に長けた人物 ▪ The ancient Greek was *a political animal*. 古代ギリシャ人は政治の才を具えていた.

a rare animal (二つの相反する特徴・関心を具えた)まれな人物[変人] ▪ He was that *rare animal*, a scientist turned artist. 彼はあの類まれな奇人だった. もと科学者で画家に転じた.

animal passions 肉欲, 獣欲 ▪ Be very careful not to yield to *animal passions*. 肉欲に屈しないようよく気をつけなさい.

animal spirits 元気, 血気, 陽気 ▪ He has great [high] *animal spirits* and a keen sense of enjoyment. 彼は活気にあふれていて, 物事を心から楽しむことができる.

go the whole animal 徹底的にやる (=go (the) whole HOG) ▪ Let's *go the whole animal* then. では徹底的にやろうじゃないか.

A

in animal spirits 健康がすぐれて ▪ The man seemed to be *in animal spirits*. その男はきわめて健康のように見えた.

animate /ǽnəmèɪt/ 動 **(*be*) *animated by*** ... に動かされて(行動する) ▪ He worked *animated by* the determination to excel. 彼は傑出しようという決意に動かされて働いた.

(*be*) *animated with* ...で活気を与えられて(いる) ▪ They *are animated with* a spirit peculiar to the Japanese. 彼らは日本人特有の精神が旺盛である.

animation /æ̀nəméɪʃən/ 名 ***with animation*** 活気を帯びて, 活発に ▪ He spoke *with animation*. 彼は元気よく話した.

animus /ǽnəməs/ 名 ***have* [*feel, show*] (*an*) *animus against* [*towards*]** 《文》...に恨み•敵意を持っている ▪ She *has an animus against* him. 彼女は彼に恨みがある.

ankle /ǽŋkəl/ 名 ***by ankle express*** 《米口》徒歩で, 歩いて ▪ The city hall is a three-minute drive, thirty minutes *by ankle express*. 市役所は車で3分, 歩いて30分の距離だ.

on the ankle 《米俗》徒歩で, 歩いて (= on FOOT) ▪ We went there *on the ankle*. 我々はそこへ歩いて行った.

annex /ənéks/ 動 ***annexed hereto*** 《商》これに添付して ▪ We shall send you a check for five hundred dollars *annexed hereto*. ここに500ドルの小切手を添付してお送りします.

announce /ənáʊns/ 動 ***announce** oneself **as*** ...と名のる, 触れこむ ▪ He *announced himself as* sent by the king. 彼は国王からの使者だと触れこんだ.

annoy /ənɔ́ɪ/ 動 ***be* [*feel*] *annoyed with*** *a person* [***at*** *a thing*] ...に困らせられる, を不快に感じる; を怒る ▪ I *was* much *annoyed at* his intrusion. 彼の出しゃばりにはひどく弱った ▪ He *was annoyed with* his wife because the dinner was badly cooked. 彼は食事がまずかったので妻に立腹した.

annoyance /ənɔ́ɪəns/ 名 ***put*** *a person* ***to annoyance*/*be put to annoyance*** 人を当惑させる[悩まされる] ▪ We *put* him *to* much *annoyance*. 私たちは彼をひどく当惑させた.

to** one's **annoyance ...の困ったことには ▪ *To my annoyance* he refused to help me. 困ったことに彼は私を援助することを拒んだ.

anon /ənán|ənɔ́n/ 副 ***ever and anon*** → EVER and again.

another /ənʌ́ðər/ 形代 ***another matter* [*thing*] *altogether*** 全く別のこと ▪ The story is *another matter altogether*. その話は全く別のことだ.

another thing 《米》その上, もう一つ言うことがあるが ▪ *Another thing*, I wasn't eating right. その上私は十分食事をしていなかった.

Ask another! 《口》ばかなことを言うな.

Ask me another! 《口》(そんなこと)知らないよ ▪ What the deuce made her marry Bill?—*Ask me another*. いったい何だって彼女はビルとなんか結婚したのか?—そんなこと知らないよ.

from one ... to another 次々に ▪ We can convert energy *from one* form *to another*. 我々はエネルギーの形を次々に変えることができる.

just* [*like*] *another 《口》ありふれた, 月並みの ▪ That was *just another* party. あれは月並みのパーティーだった ▪ That's an idea *like another*. それはありふれた考えだ.

one after another →ONE.

one another →ONE.

one way or another →WAY.

one with another →ONE.

such another →SUCH.

take one thing with another より好みをしない[せずに取る] ▪ You must not pick and choose, but just *take one thing with another*. より好みをせずに, まんべんなくお取りください.

taking* [*taken, take*] *one* (*thing*) *with another あれこれ考え合わせてみるに; 平均してみて ▪ The qualities have turned rather to his prejudice than advantage, *take one with another*. 総合してみればそれらの特質は彼の利益になるよりもむしろ害になった ▪ *Taken one with another*, the cattle may fetch $150 a head. 平均して牛は一頭あたり150ドルになるかもしれない.

Tell me another! →TELL.

You're another. 《口》君だって同じではないか ▪ You're a humbug.—*You're another*. 君はペテン師だ—君だって同じではないか.

answer[1] /ǽnsər|ɑ́:n-/ 名 ***a dusty answer*** 《英》そっけない[役に立たない]返答 ▪ I received *a dusty answer*. 私はそっけない返事をもらった.

a straight answer to a straight question 率直な問いに対する率直な答え ▪ Can the politician give *a straight answer to a straight question*, ever? その政治家はいったい誠実な受け答えができるのか.

an answer to a maiden's prayer (相手として)特に好ましいうってつけの男; (ある目的に)特に好ましいうってつけのもの ▪ A legacy or some such *answer to a maiden's prayer* could save him from bankruptcy. 遺産とかそうしたうってつけのものがあれば彼を破産から救えるのだが.

a person's ***answer to*** ...に相当する人, 物事 ▪ She was regarded by some as *Japan's answer to* Hillary Clinton. 彼女はヒラリー•クリントン氏に相当する日本の人物であると一部の人にみなされていた.

in answer to ...に答えて; (抗議など)に応じて ▪ *In answer to* his request for help, I sent him a cheque for £100. 助けてくれという頼みに応じて, 私は彼に100ポンドの小切手を送ってやった ▪ The doctor came at once *in answer to* my telephone call. 医者は私が電話をかけたらすぐ来てくれた.

know* [*have*] *all the answers 《口》何でも知っている; 万事心得ている《自信過剰を含意》 ▪ I used to date someone who *had all the answers*, and he was such a bore. 私は万事心得ているような男とデートしていました. 彼ってとても退屈でした.

The answer is a lemon! 《口・古風》だめだよ; むだだよ ▪What! Try a thing like that on the boss? *The answer is a lemon.* なんだって! そんなことをボスに対してするって, そりゃだめだよ ▪What did the master say when you asked for a rise?—*The answer was a lemon.* 賃上げを願ったとき親方はどう言ったかね?—だめだったよ. ☞レモンは苦いことから.

the answer to** one's **prayers 待ち望んでいた人[物] ▪A new bookstore in the neigborhood is *the answer to my prayers.* 近所に本屋ができたがそれは私が待ち望んでいたものだ.

What's the answer? 我々はどうしよう ▪They may refuse to fulfil the contract. *What's the answer?* 彼らは契約履行を拒むかもしれない. 我々はどうしたらよいだろう.

won't take no for an answer/ refuse to take no for an answer 人の反対[断り]を聞き入れない ▪You're coming with me, and I *won't take no for an answer.* いっしょに来るんだ. 反対してもだめだ.

answer[2] /ǽnsər|ɑ́:n-/ 動 ***answer blows with blows*** なぐられてなぐり返す ▪I *answered blows with blows.* なぐられたからなぐり返してやった.

answer** one's **purpose → answer the PURPOSE.

answer the bell [door] 取次ぎに出る ▪The servant went to *answer the bell [door].* 使用人が取次ぎに出て行った.

answer to the name of →NAME[1].

be answered for 約束ずみである ▪*Is* your daughter *answered for*? お宅のお嬢さんは約束[婚約]ずみですか ▪These seats *are answered for.* これらの席は予約ずみです.

have a lot [much] to answer for (悪弊など)に大いに責任がある ▪People who sell drugs to young people *have a lot to answer for.* 若い人にヤクを売る人々は大いに責任がある.

*One's **prayer is answered.*** 人の願いがかなう ▪*My prayer was answered* at last. 願いがついにかなった.

answerable /ǽnsərəbəl|ɑ́:n-/ 形 ***be answerable for*** ...に対して責任がある ▪You *are answerable for* having done harm to them. 君は彼らに害を及ぼした事に対し責任がある.

ant /ænt/ 名 ***have ants in** one's **pants*** 《俗》 **1** (心配で)やきもきする; (もどかしくて)いらいらする ▪He's *got ants in his pants* about the contract. 彼はその契約が心配でやきもきしている.
2 (...と)やりたくてむずむずする (*for*) ▪Jim's *got ants in his pants for* Sally. ジムはサリーとやりたくてむずむずしている.

antagonism /æntǽgənìzəm/ 名 ***(be) in antagonism to*** ...に反対[敵対]して(いる) ▪The government placed itself *in antagonism to* them. 政府は彼らと対立した ▪It *is in* direct *antagonism to* the principles of scientific education. それは科学教育の原則にまっこうから反している.

be in [come into, be brought into] antagonism with ...と敵対している[するにいたる] ▪The Church *is in antagonism with* freedom. 教会は自由と敵対している ▪Russia *was brought into* chronic *antagonism with* Turkey. ロシアはトルコと長期にわたって反目するようになった.

antagonistic /æntæ̀gənístɪk/ 形 ***be antagonistic to*** ...に対立する ▪They *are antagonistic to* each other. 彼らは互いに相いれない.

ante /ǽnti/ 名 ***raise [up] the ante*** **1** (トランプで)賭金を引き上げる ▪Don't *up the ante* any more. You're betting far too much money already. これ以上賭金を上げるな. 君はもう賭けすぎてるよ.
2 《口》(事業などの)分担金を引き上げる ▪They *raised the ante* to compete successfully for the contract. 彼らはその請負をうまく落とすため分担金を引き上げた.
3 《口》値段を上げる ▪Sensing how keen the people looking at the house were, Bill *upped the ante* another $500. 家を見ている人々がひどく熱心なのを感じて, ビルはもう500ドル値段を上げた ▪Our aim is to *raise the ante* on teachers' salaries. 我々の目的は教員の給料の水準を引き上げることだ.

anterior /æntíəriər/ 形 ***anterior to*** (時・位置などが)...より前の ▪It was an event *anterior to* the Restoration. それは王政復古以前の出来事だった.

antic[1] /ǽntɪk/ 名 ***cut an antic*** おどける ▪He was *cutting* queer *antics.* 彼は妙におどけていた.

play [perform] (one's) antics 道化を演じる, 道化踊りをする ▪We *play our* brief *antics* in this world. 我々はこの世で短い道化踊りをする.

antic[2] /ǽntɪk/ 動 ***antic it*** 道化を演じる, 道化踊りをする ▪They might have *anticked it* with the King of Fairies. 彼らは妖精の王と道化踊りをしたかもしれない.

anticipation /æntìsəpéɪʃn/ 名 ***in anticipation (of)*** (...を)あてにして; (を)見越して ▪We are in a state of excitement *in anticipation of* political news. 我々は政治上のニュースを待ち受けてわき立っている ▪Thanking you *in anticipation.* 予めお礼を申しあげます《依頼状・問合せなどの結びの文句》.

antipathy /æntípəθi/ 名 ***have an antipathy to [against]*** ...が本能的にきらいである ▪Some people *have an antipathy to* cats. 生まれつき猫のきらいな人がいる ▪They *have a* kind of *antipathy against* the thriving of others. 彼らは他人が栄えるのを本能的にきらう.

antipodes /æntípədì:z/ 名 ***at antipodes*** 正反対で[に] ▪You are *at antipodes* with him on all points. 君は彼とすべての点で正反対である ▪We are *at* the exact *antipodes* of opinion. 我々は正反対の意見を持っている.

anvil /ǽnvəl/ 名 ***on [upon] the anvil*** 準備中で, 審議中で ▪He has now another scheme *on the anvil.* 彼は今やもう一つの計画を準備中である.

anxiety /æŋzáɪəti/ 名 ***be all anxiety*** 非常に心配している ▪ She *was all anxiety* then. そのとき彼女はひどく心配していた.

be in anxiety 心配している ▪ He *was in* great *anxiety* about the succession to the throne. 彼は王位継承について非常に心配していた.

give anxiety to …に心配をかける ▪ He *gave* terrible *anxiety to* his mother. 彼は母にひどく心配をかけた.

with anxiety 心配して ▪ He was waiting *with anxiety*. 彼は心配して待っていた.

anxious /ǽŋkʃəs/ 形 ***be anxious about*** …を心配している ▪ I *am anxious about* my health. 私は自分の健康を心配している.

be anxious for [***to** do*] …を[することを]切望する ▪ He *is anxious to* please everybody. 彼はしきりにみなを喜ばせようとしている ▪ He *is anxious for* wealth. 彼はひたすら富を得たがっている.

on the anxious seat [***bench***] 《米》大いに心配して, 気をもんで ▪ All were *on the anxious seat*, trying to learn whether their new judge was easy or tough. 今度の裁判官が打ち解けた人か手ごわい人かを知ろうとして, みんな気をもんでいた. ☞anxious seat《米》「教会・説教会などで霊的援助を願う人, 信仰を強めようとする人のため, 説教壇近くに設けた席」.

any /éni/ 形代 ***any amount*** [***number***] (***of***) 〚amount は量を表し単数扱い, number は数を表し複数扱い〛 **1** いくらでも, 際限なく ▪ He will give you *any amount of* trouble. 彼はいくらでも君に面倒をかけるだろう ▪ I will give you *any number of* pencils. 鉛筆ならいくらでもあげますよ.

2《口》たくさん ▪ Have you any sugar?—*Any amount*. 砂糖はありますか?—いくらでもあります ▪ I saw *any number of* mummies in the museum. 博物館でたくさんミイラを見た.

any and every 何もかも, すっかり ▪ I wish to read *any and every* book in this library. 私はこの図書館の本は何もかもみんな読んでみたい.

any better 少しはよい ▪ Is she *any better*? 彼女の具合は少しはいいですか.

any longer 〚主に否定文・疑問文・条件文で〛これ以上 ▪ Is it fair to leave you alone *any longer*? これ以上あなたを一人ぼっちにしていてよいか ▪ I don't smoke *any longer*. 私はもうタバコは吸いません.

any more 〚主に否定文・疑問文・条件文で〛もっと(多く) ▪ Please don't say *any more* about it. それについてはもう何も言わないでください ▪ If there is *any more* trouble, let me know. 何か困ったことがもっとありましたら, 知らせてください ▪ Are there *any more* of them? それらがもっとありますか.

any old →OLD.

any (***old***) ***how*** →HOW.

not be having any of it 全く協力する気がない ▪ We are planning a street collection but Kate *is not having any of it*. 我々は街頭募金を計画しているが, ケイトは全く協力する気がない.

not just any ただ[並]の…ではない ▪ She is *not just any* singer. She has sold more than a million copies of her first album. 彼女は並の歌手ではない. 最初のアルバムを100万枚以上も売っている.

anybody /énibàdi|-bɔ̀di/ 代 ***anybody who is anybody*** すべてのお偉方 ▪ *Anybody who is anybody* will be at the Queen's birthday celebrations. すべてのお偉方が女王の誕生日の祝賀に出席するだろう.

anybody's race [***game, contest***] 予想のつかない競走《競馬など》 ▪ It is still *anybody's race*. それはまだ予想のつかない競走だ ▪ This will be *anybody's game*. この試合は誰が勝つか予想がつくまい.

be anybody's guess →GUESS[1].

just anybody →JUST.

anyhow /énihàʊ/ 副 ***all anyhow*** **1** どんなことがあっても ▪ Although his foot pained him, he decided to work *all anyhow*. 足は痛かったが彼は万難を排して仕事をする決心をした.

2 ぞんざいで[に] ▪ She works *all anyhow*. 彼女は仕事がぞんざいだ.

feel anyhow 体の具合が悪い ▪ I *feel anyhow* today. きょうは体の調子が悪い.

anyone /éniwʌ̀n/ 代 ***anyone who is anyone*** =ANYBODY who is anybody.

be anyone's guess →be anybody's GUESS.

anyplace /énipleìs/ 副 ***get anyplace*** →GET anywhere.

anything /éniθìŋ/ 代 ***anything between** A **and** B* AとBの間で ▪ The days in summer are hot, *anything between* 30° *and* 40°. 夏日は暑くて, 30ないしは40度ある.

anything but **1** …のほかは何でも ▪ I will do *anything but* that. 私はそれ以外は何でもする.

2 少しも…でない; …とだけは決して言えない ▪ It is *anything but* pleasant. それは楽しいどころではない ▪ He is *anything but* a scholar. 彼が学者だなんてとんでもない.

anything for …のためなら何でもする ▪ *Anything for* a quiet life! 静かな生活をするためなら何でもするんだが!

Anything goes. 《口》何でもいい, 何でも許される, 何をしても[着ても]構わない ▪ What will you have tonight?—*Anything goes*. 今夜は何がいい?—何でもいいよ ▪ Must I wear a dark suit?—No, *anything goes* at that restraurant. ダークスーツを着なきゃいけないのか?—いや, あのレストランでは何を着てもいい ▪ *Anything goes* out here, dear boy. ここでは何でも許されるんだよ, 君.

anything like 〚主に否定文で〛 **1** …などではとうてい; のようなものは(何でも) ▪ *Anything like* that medicine cannot cure him. あんな薬などではとうてい彼は治らない ▪ He does not like *anything like* labor. 彼は労働といったようなものは何も好まない.

2 全然 ▪ The sum is not *anything like* adequate. その金額は決して十分でない ▪ I have not *anything like* finished it. 私はまだそれを全然終えていない.

anything of **1**〚疑問文・条件文で〛いくらか, 少しは, 少しでも ▪ Is he *anything of* a scholar? 彼は少しは学問ができるか ▪ Have you seen *anything of* my child? 私の子供をお見かけでしたか.
2〚否定文で〛少しも ▪ I have not seen *anything of* Mr. Smith lately. 近頃スミスさんに少しも会わない.
anything up to (極限数量が)多く[長く]て... ▪ It will take *anything up to* 5 months to complete the job. その仕事の完成には長くて5か月が必要だろう.
Anything you say. その通りです, そのようにします《実はそのつもりはない》 ▪ You must get out of that habit, John.—Sure, *anything you say.* その癖をやめなくちゃだめよ, ジョン—いいとも, そうしよう.
as ... as anything 何にも劣らないほど, 非常に ▪ He is *as* proud *as anything.* 彼はとても得意だ ▪ He will work *as* hard *as anything.* 彼は誰にも劣らず勉強するだろう.
can't do anything with ...に対処できない, をうまくあしらえない ▪ I *can't do anything with* my teenage daughter. 10代の娘をうまくあしらえない ▪ I *can't do anything with* my hair. 自分の髪をもてあましている.
for anything 〚I would not を伴って〛いくらくれても, 決して ▪ *I would not* do it *for anything.* 僕はどうあってもそれはしない.
for anything I know (***to the contrary***) →FOR all one knows.
if anything →IF.
If anything can go wrong, it will. 《諺》うまくいかないものは, うまくいかない.
like anything →LIKE[1].
not feel like anything 《米俗》どうも体の具合が悪い ▪ I do*n't feel like anything.* 私はどうも体の具合が悪い.
not just anything 《口》普通のこと[ただごと]ではない ▪ Gnosis is *not just anything.* 霊的直観的認識は普通のことではない.
or anything 《口》...や何か ▪ Don't worry; they don't explode *or anything.* 心配するな, 爆発なんかしないから.
So help me anything! 《口・婉曲》神も照覧あれ!, 誓って (God help me!).
too ... for anything 極度[過度]に...で ▪ You are *too* ridiculous *for anything.* 君はあまりにもばかげている.

anywhere /énihwèər/ 副 ***anywhere from*** *A* ***to*** *B* [***between*** *A* ***and*** *B*] AないしB ▪ He earns *anywhere from* 80 *to* 100 dollars a week. 彼は週に80ドルないし100ドル儲ける.
anywhere near 《口》〚否定文・疑問文で〛幾分でも, 少しでも ▪ Is this gold ring worth *anywhere near* a thousand dollars? この金の指輪は1,000ドルくらいするのですか ▪ This flower isn't *anywhere near* as beautiful as that. この花は全然あの花ほど美しくない.
if anywhere どこかにあるとすれば ▪ The best place you could live in is, *if anywhere*, either Alexandria, Arlington, or Manassas. 君が住める最良の場所は, もしどこかにあるとすれば, アレクサンドリアか, アーリントンか, マナッサスのいずれかだ.
not get [***go***] ***anywhere*** (人が)成功しない, 効果がない (→GET nowhere) ▪ He tried to solve the problem but he did*n't get anywhere.* 彼はその問題を解こうとしたが, うまくいかなかった.
not get *a person* ***anywhere*** (事が)成功しない, うまくいかない (→GET nowhere) ▪ Such methods wo*n't get* you *anywhere.* そんなやり方では何にもならないよ.

apace /əpéɪs/ 副 ***run apace*** 《雅》速く走る ▪ Ill news *runs apace.* 《諺》「悪事千里を走る」.

apart /əpɑ́:rt/ 副 ***apart from*** **1** ...は別として ▪ *Apart from* joking, what do you mean to do? 冗談はさておき, どうするつもりか.
2 ...とは別に ▪ You can hardly consider the one *apart from* the other. 甲を乙と別個に考えることはほとんどできない.
be worlds apart まるで大違いである ▪ China and the U.S.A. *are worlds apart* in their political beliefs. 中国とアメリカは政治思想が大違いである.
come apart at the seams →SEAM[1].
hold *oneself* ***apart*** 他人と交わらない ▪ Her shyness makes her *hold herself apart.* 彼女ははにかみやなので人と交わらない.
joking apart 冗談はさておき ▪ Well, *joking apart*, that's the sort of thing that could happen to kids. そう, 冗談はさておき, それは子供たちにだって起こりかねない事柄だよ.
lay [***put***] ***... apart*** =set ... APART 1, 2.
miles apart (議論が)全く食い違って[かみ合わないで] ▪ Many long-married couples are still *miles apart* in their thinking. 結婚生活の長い夫婦の中にもまだ考え方が全く食い違っている者が多い.
set ... apart **1** ...を(...のために)取りのけておく, 貯金しておく (*for*) ▪ A wise man *sets apart* some of his money *for* old age. 賢い人は老後に備えて自分の金のいくぶんかを取っておく ▪ *Set* these ropes *apart for* later use. このロープはあとで使えるように取っておきなさい ▪ This room *is set apart for* smoking. この部屋は喫煙のために特に取ってある.
2 ...を別にする, を(...から)区別する, を際立たせる (*from*) ▪ *Setting apart* the question of expense, it is too late. 経費の問題はさておいて時期が遅れた ▪ She *is set apart from* other girls by her special gifts. 彼女はその特異な才能で他の少女たちとは際立っている.
3 ...を異色あらしめる; を聖別する ▪ What *set* the company *apart* was the way it went about its work. その会社を異色あらしめたのはその事業のやり方であった.

apartment /əpɑ́:rtmənt/ 名 ***have apartments to let*** 《俗》頭がない, 愚かだ ▪ He'*s got apartments to let.* 彼は少し足りない.

apathy /ǽpəθi/ 名 ***have an apathy to*** ...に冷淡である ▪ He *has an apathy to* food. 彼は食

物をほしがらない.

ape[1] /eɪp/ 名 ***go ape*** (***crazy***)《口》 **1** 頭がおかしくなる; …に夢中になる (*over, for*) ▪ He's definitely *gone ape*, that boy. あいつは確かに頭がおかしくなってしまった, あの少年は ▪ Boys will *go ape crazy for* [*over*] the rock singer. 少年たちはそのロックシンガーに夢中になるだろう.

2《俗》かんかんに怒る ▪ She *went ape* when she saw the mess. その乱雑さを見たとき彼女はかんかんになった.

lead apes (***in hell***) 未婚のままで死ぬ; オールドミスである ▪ I must, for your love to her, *lead apes in hell*. あなたがあの人を愛していらっしゃる以上は私は未婚のまま世を終えねばなりません ▪ Poor girl, she must certainly *lead apes*. かわいそうに, 彼女は確かにオールドミスにちがいない. ☞ 地獄でサルを引き回すのが未婚女性の死後の運命と考えられたことから; ＞ape-leader (未婚女性).

play the ape へたにまねをする; ばかなまねをする; 悪ふざけをする ▪ Jones kept on *playing the ape* all the time, and spoilt everything. ジョーンズは始終悪ふざけばかりしていて, すべてを台なしにしてしまった.

play the sedulous ape (文体などを)せっせとまねる (R. L. Stevenson, *Memories and Portraits* 4-1) ▪ I have thus *played the sedulous ape* to Hazlitt, to Lamb, to Wordsworth. 私はこうしてハズリット, ラム, ワーズワスの文体をせっせとまねて書いた.

say an ape's paternoster 寒くて[怖くて]歯をガタガタ震わせる ▪ He shakes, trembles, *says an ape's paternoster*. 彼は震え, おののいて, 歯をガチガチいわせる.

ape[2] /eɪp/ 動 ***ape it*** 人まねをする, 猿真似をする ▪ The devil loves to *ape it* after God. 悪魔は神様の猿真似をすることを好む.

apeak /əpíːk/ 副 ***heave apeak***《海》 **1** (船がいかりを揚げるとき)いかりの真上に来て錨索が垂直になる ▪ The ship *hove apeak*. 船は錨索が垂直になるまでいかりの真上に寄って来た ▪ I *hove apeak* on my anchor. 船を錨索が垂直になるまでいかりに引き寄せた.

2 錨索が垂直[起きいかり]になるまで船をいかりに引き寄せる ▪ I *hove* the ship *apeak*. 船を錨索が垂直になるまでいかりに引き寄せた.

apeshit /éɪpʃɪt/ 名 ***go apeshit***《米俗》 = go APE (crazy) 2.

apex /éɪpeks/ 名 ***at the apex of*** …の絶頂に ▪ Now he was *at the apex of* his fortunes. いまや彼は運勢の絶頂にあった.

apology /əpɑ́lədʒi|əpɔ́l-/ 名 ***an apology for*** 申し訳ばかりの, 名ばかりの ▪ That single bowl of stew was *a* mere *apology for* a dinner. あのたった1杯のシチューがほんの間に合わせのごちそうだった ▪ He is *a* sorry *apology for* an actor. 彼はまことにお粗末な俳優だ.

in apology for …のおわびに; の言い訳に ▪ *In apology for* his lateness, he pleaded that his car had broken down on the way. 彼は遅刻の言い訳に途中で車が故障したのだと弁解した.

make [***offer***] ***an*** [*one's*] ***apology*** [***apologies***] 言い訳をする; わびをする ▪ I *made an apology* for my lateness. 私は遅刻をわびた ▪ I *offered my apologies* to him. 彼にわびを入れた.

make no apology [***apologies***] ***for*** …は悪いとは思っていない ▪ We *make no apology for* our way of life. 我々は自分の生活様式が悪いとは思っていない ▪ Russian parents *make no apologies for* being "hyperprotective." ロシアの親は「過保護」であることを悪いとは思っていない.

with (***many***) ***apologies to*** (他人の作品のパロディー[改作]であることをことわって)…に陳謝して ▪ To blog or not to blog: that is the question (*with apologies to* Shakespeare). ブログを公開すべきかせざるべきか, それが問題だ(シェイクスピアに陳謝して).

apoplexy /ǽpəplèksi/ 名 ***be seized with apoplexy*** 卒中にかかる ▪ He *was seized with apoplexy* at 50. 彼は50歳のとき卒中にかかった.

have a fit [***stroke***] ***of apoplexy*** 卒中を起こす ▪ He *had a fit of apoplexy*. 彼は卒中を起こした.

appall,《英》**appal** /əpɔ́ːl/ 動 ***be*** [***stand***] ***appalled at*** …にぞっとする, ぎょっとする ▪ I *was appalled at* the sight. 私はその光景を見てぎょっとした. ☞ 過去, 過去分詞は英米ともに appalled, 現在進行形も英米ともに appalling.

apparel /əpǽrəl/ 名 ***intimate apparel***《婉曲》女性の下着, 肌着 ▪ The catalog features *intimate apparel* for the grande dame. カタログは婦人用の肌着を特集している.

appeal[1] /əpíːl/ 名 ***lodge*** [***enter***] ***an appeal*** 控訴する ▪ I *lodged an appeal* against the decision. 私はその判決に対して控訴した.

make an appeal to …に訴える; に感化を及ぼす ▪ His beauty *makes a* strong *appeal to* the senses of the other sex. 彼の美しさは異性の五感に強く訴える ▪ She *made* no *appeal to* the twins. 彼女はその双生児には何の感化も及ぼさなかった ▪ We shall have to *make an appeal to* arms. 我々は武力に訴えなければならないだろう.

make an appeal to the country (国会を解散して)国民の批判に訴える ▪ Parliament would be dissolved and *an appeal made to the country*. 国会は解散されて, 国民の批判に訴えるだろう.

appeal[2] /əpíːl/ 動 ***appeal against the light*** (クリケット・テニスなどで)明るさ不十分のため試合中止を願い出る ▪ Our captain *appealed against the light*. 我々のキャプテンは明るさが不十分なため試合中止を願い出た.

appeal to Caesar →CAESAR.

appear /əpíər/ 動 ***as it appears*** 見かけの通り; 記載通りに ▪ He is quite well, *as it appears*. 彼はお見かけの通り大変丈夫です.

It appears so [***not***]. (質問に答えて)そうらしい[そうではないらしい] ▪ Is the manager going to resign? —*It appears so* [*not*]. 支配人は辞職するのかい—そうらしいね[そうではないようだ].

it appears (***to me***) ***that*** …と(私に)思われる; …

らしい ▪ *It appears to me that* something is wrong. どこか具合の悪いところがあるらしい.

So it appears. =It APPEARs so.

So it would appear. どうもそうらしいね《自信はないけれど》 ▪ She got the job, or *so it would appear.* 彼女は仕事にありついた. いや, どうもそうらしい.

strange as it may appear 不思議に思われるかもしれないが ▪ *Strange as it may appear*, it is true for all that. 奇妙に思われるかもしれないが, やはりそれは本当である.

appearance /əpíərəns/ 名 ***appearances are against*** *a person* 形勢は人に不利のようだ ▪ But all *appearances are against* him. しかし, すべての形勢は彼に不利なようだ.

appearances are (***that***) 形勢は...らしい ▪ *Appearances are that* our party will win. わが党が勝利を得るような形勢だ.

Appearances can be deceiving [***are deceitful, deceptive***]./***Appearance deceives.*** 《諺》人は見かけによらぬもの.

enter an appearance = make an APPEARANCE 1.

for appearance' sake うわべだけ, 体面上, 体裁上 ▪ Most Englishmen who go to church do so *for appearance' sake.* 教会に行く英国人のほとんどは体裁上そうしているだけだ.

give [***create***] ***the appearance of*** →put on the APPEARANCE of.

in appearance 外見[外観]は(...のようだ) ▪ *In appearance* it is a strong building. 外見は堅固な建物のようだ.

(***judging***) ***from the appearance of the sky*** 空模様から判断すれば ▪ *From the appearance of the sky*, we shall have a shower in the afternoon. この空模様では午後は夕立が来るだろう.

keep up [***save***] ***appearances*** 体裁[世間体]を繕う, 見栄を張る ▪ He was badly off, but he managed to *keep up appearances.* 彼は貧乏していたが, それでも何とかして世間体を繕った ▪ He has lost a lot of money, but still *keeps up appearances.* 彼は多額の金を失ったのにまだ見栄を張っている.

keep up the appearance of ...を取り繕う ▪ He *keeps up the appearance of* majesty. 彼は威厳を取り繕っている.

make a good [***poor***] ***appearance*** 立派に見える[みすぼらしい] ▪ He *made a good appearance.* 彼は身なりを整えていた ▪ He *made a poor appearance* at the meeting. 彼は集会で貧相だった.

make [***put in***] ***an*** [*one's*] ***appearance*** **1** 現れる, (公然と)出場する, 出頭する ▪ It was ten o'clock when he finally *made an appearance.* 彼がついに出て来たのは10時だった ▪ All men must *put in a* personal *appearance* at the Last Assize. 人はみな最後の審判には自ら出頭せねばならない ▪ The comet duly *made its appearance*, as predicted. その彗星はちょうど予測どおりに現れた.
2 (式·会などに)ちょっと顔を出す ▪ We *put in a brief appearance* at the party. 我々はその会にちょっと顔を出した.

make *one's* ***first*** [***last***] ***appearance*** 初めて現れる[なごりの出場をする] ▪ The magazine *made its first appearance* this March. その雑誌は今年の3月に初めて出た ▪ He *made his last appearance* on the stage in 2010. 2010年に彼はなごりの舞台を踏んだ.

put on [***give***] ***the appearance of*** ...らしく見せかける ▪ He *put on the appearance of* innocence. 彼は知らぬ顔をした.

save appearances →keep up APPEARANCEs.

there is every appearance of [***that***] どうも...らしい, らしく見える ▪ *There is every appearance of* (its going to) rain. どうもひと雨きそうだ ▪ *There was every appearance that* he would fail. 彼はどうも失敗しそうに見えた.

there is no appearance of ...の姿がさっぱり見えない; の模様が少しもない ▪ *There is no appearance of* the leader. 指導者の姿が全然見えない ▪ *There is no appearance of* rain. 雨の模様は少しもない.

to [***from***] ***all appearance***(***s***) 見たところでは; どう見ても ▪ *To all appearance* his statement was true. どう見てもその人の言うことは本当のようだった.

appendant /əpéndənt/ 形 ***appendant to*** [***on***] ...に付随の ▪ The land is *appendant to* a cottage. その土地はある田舎屋に付随している.

appetent /ǽpətənt/ 形 ***appetent of*** [***after***] 《文》...を熱望する, を恋しがる ▪ He is thirsty and *appetent after* glory and renown. 彼は栄光と名声を渇望している.

appetite /ǽpətàɪt/ 名 ***A good appetite is the best sauce.*** 《諺》「空腹にまずいものなし」.

get up an [*one's*] ***appetite*** 食欲を増進する ▪ She has gone for a ride to *get up her appetite.* 彼女は食欲増進のため乗馬に出た.

get up an appetite for ...する意欲を起こす ▪ I can't *get up an appetite for* teaching English. 私は英語を教える意欲が起こせない.

have a good [***poor***] ***appetite*** 食が進む[進まない] ▪ I *have a good appetite.* 私は食が進む.

have an appetite for ...欲がある, ...好きである ▪ He *has an appetite for* knowledge [music]. 彼は知識欲がある[音楽好きである].

lose [***spoil***] *one's* ***appetite*** 食欲を失う[そこなう] ▪ He has *lost his appetite.* 彼は食欲がなくなった.

to [***after***] ***the appetite of*** ...の口に合う ▪ This is *to my appetite.* これは私の口に合う.

whet *a person's* ***appetite*** (***for***) (...への)意欲[興味, 関心]をかきたてる ▪ That Schubert piece *whetted my appetite.* そのシューベルトの曲は私の関心をかき立てた ▪ His talk on English *whetted my appetite for* study. 彼の英語に関する話で勉強する意欲をかきたてられた.

whet the appetite of ...の食欲をそそる ▪ The splendid dinner *whetted the appetites of* the

A

guests. すばらしいごちそうはお客の食欲をそそった.

with a good appetite おいしそうに, 盛んに(食べる, など) ▪ He ate it *with a good appetite.* 彼はおいしそうにそれを平らげた.

work* [*stir*] *up an appetite (食べ物が)食欲をかき立てる; (人が)食欲をかき立てられる ▪ Nothing *stirs up an appetite* like the smell of a barbecue. バーベキューの匂いくらい食欲をかき立てるものはない ▪ You can definitely *work up an appetite* in this mountain air. この山の空気を吸えば断然食欲をかき立てられるよ.

applaud /əplɔ́:d/ 動 ***applaud ... to the echo*** →ECHO.

apple /ǽpəl/ 名 ***a* [*the*] *bad* [*rotten*] *apple*** →the bad APPLE.

An apple a day keeps the doctor away. 《諺》リンゴ1日1個で医者いらず.

an apple for the teacher 賄賂 ▪ Mr. Smith has sent us this box.—It's probably *an apple for the teacher.* スミスさんが我々にこの箱を送ってきた—それはたぶん賄賂だろう.

an apple of love 愛のリンゴ《トマトのこと》 ▪ Which fruit is known as *an apple of love*? どの果物が愛のリンゴとして知られているのか.

apples and oranges 《米》全く異なるもの, 水と油 ▪ Comparing Africa to America is like comparing *apples and oranges.* アフリカとアメリカを比べるのは, 水と油を比べるようなものだ.

How do you like them apples?/ How about them apples? **1**《米口》どんなもんだい《勝利・喜びの感嘆表現; 周囲の賛辞を得るために発する》 ▪ Well, I got her number. *How do you like them apples?* ところで, 彼女の電話番号がわかったよ. どんなもんだい.

2《米》こりゃびっくり[がっかり]した ▪ So Mary has married a banker? *How do you like them apples?* じゃあ, メアリーは銀行家と結婚したのか. がっかりしたな.

like a ripe apple (欲しい物が)やすやすと, いとも簡単に ▪ Independence will fall to us one day *like a ripe apple.* 独立がいつの日かやすやすと我々の手に入るだろう.

***polish apples* [*the apple*]** 《米俗》(上役などの)ごきげんをとる ▪ John *polished the apple* at work. ジョンは仕事で(上役の)ごきげんをとった. ☞学童がひいきしてもらうためによく磨いたリンゴを先生にあげる風習から.

***swallow the apple* [*olive*]** →SWALLOW[3].

The apple does not fall far from the tree. 《諺》リンゴは(リンゴの)木から遠く離れた所には落ちない, 「類は類を呼ぶ」.

the apple of *a person's* **[*the*] *eye*** ひとみ; 非常に大切なもの; 掌中の玉 (《聖》*Deut.* 32. 10, etc.) ▪ Richard was to me as an eldest son, *the apple of the eye.* リチャードは私にとっては長男のようなもので, 秘蔵っ子でした ▪ The black-currant trees were *the apple of Joseph's eye.* クロスグリの木はヨセフの掌中の玉だった.

the* [*a*] *bad* [*rotten*] *apple 他に悪影響を及ぼすもの, 不良分子 ▪ Most students are hardworking, but there are *a* few *rotten apples.* 学生たちはたいてい勤勉だが少数の不良分子がいる ▪ *The rotten apple* spoils the barrel. 《諺》一個の腐ったリンゴは樽の中のリンゴを全部だめにする,「朱に交われば赤くなる」.

the Big Apple ニューヨーク市のニックネーム ▪ The first prize is three nights in a luxurious hotel in *the Big Apple.* 一等賞はニューヨークの豪華ホテルに3泊です.

apple-cart /ǽpəlkὰ:rt/ 名 ***upset* [*overturn*] *the*** [*a person's*] ***apple-cart*** リンゴ車をひっくり返す; 転覆させる, 混乱させる, (特に)人の計画をくつがえす ▪ The moment he referred to that he *upset the apple-cart.* 彼がその事件のことに触れるやいなや大騒動になった ▪ Well, I'm afraid this letter will properly *upset your apple-cart.* この手紙は君の計画をきれいにだめにしてしまわないかね.

upset the old woman's apple-cart/ upset the apple-cart and spill the gooseberries =upset the APPLE-CART.

apple-pie /ǽpəlpàɪ/ 名 ***as American as an apple-pie*** →be AMERICAN as apple-pie.

as easy as apple-pie →(as) EASY as pie.

make an apple-pie bed シーツを折りたたんで足が十分伸ばせないようにする《悪ふざけとしてよくやる》; いろいろな物をベッドに入れて寝る者を困らせる《児童の誤用》 ▪ The girls hated the old man and plagued him by *making* him *an apple-pie bed.* 少女たちはその老人を非常にきらい, 足の伸ばせない寝床を作って老人を困らせた ▪ My sisters often *made* me *an apple-pie bed.* 姉妹たちはよくふざけて足の伸ばせない寝床を私に作ってくれた. ☞恐らく F nappe pliée 'folded sheet'から.

put ... in* (*to*) [*be in*] *apple-pie order …をきちんと整とんする[秩序整然としている] ▪ The hostess had *put* her house *in apple-pie order* before her guests arrived. 女主人はお客が来ないうちに家をきちんと整とんしていた ▪ The children's garden *was in apple-pie order.* 子供の庭はきちんと整とんされていた. ☞apple-pie をおいしくじょうずに焼くにはスライスしたリンゴをきちんとパイ皿に並べなければならないことから.

apple-tree /ǽpəltrì:/ 名 ***within two rows of apple-trees*** 《米口》ほどよい距離以内に ▪ It does not come *within two rows of apple-trees* of the point here at all. それはここの地点からほどよい距離のうちには全然入らない.

application /æ̀pləkéɪʃən/ 名 ***for external* [*internal*] *application*** 外[内服]用《薬びんの上書き文句》.

make application for …の申し込みをする ▪ He *made application for* the position. 彼はその地位を志願した ▪ Early *application for* a passage should *be made.* 乗船申し込みは早くするのがよい.

on application 申し込み次第 ▪ A complete list of new books may be had *on application* to the publisher. 新刊書総目録を当出版社への申し込みがあ

り次第進呈します.

send in a written application 願書を提出する ▪ You must *send in a written application.* あなたは願書を提出せねばならない.

show application in** one's **studies 勉学に精励する ▪ He *showed* close *application in his studies.* 彼は勉学に大いに精励した.

apply /əplái/ 動 ***apply for a church*** 教会牧師を志願する ▪ So far five preachers have *applied for* our *church.* これまでに5人の説教師がうちの教会勤務を志願している.

***apply** oneself **to** [**to** do]* …することに専念する ▪ He *applied himself* closely *to* the study of English. 彼は英語の研究に専念した ▪ He *applied himself to* comprehend two such antipodal characters. 彼はそのように正反対の二つの性格を理解しようと専念した.

apply** oneself **to** a person **for 人に…を求める[請う] ▪ We *applied ourselves to* him *for* help. 我々は彼に援助を請うた.

apply within お問い合わせは店内で《広告などの文句》 ▪ Shop assistant wanted. *Apply within.* 店員募集中. 詳しくは店内で.

appointed /əpɔ́ıntəd/ 形 ***well* [*poorly*] *appointed*** 設備の良い[悪い] ▪ This is a rare opportunity to own this *well appointed* house. いまはこの設備の良い家を所有するまれな機会です ▪ The rooms were small and *poorly-appointed.* 部屋は狭くて設備の悪いものだった.

appointment /əpɔ́ıntmənt/ 名 ***by a natural appointment*** 自然のめぐり合わせで ▪ We met *by a natural appointment.* 我々は自然のめぐり合わせで会った. ☞appointment「天命」.

by appointment **1** (…の)命により; のご用達 (*to*) ▪ *By appointment to* Her Majesty Queen Elizabeth II エリザベス2世陛下ご用達.

2 申し合わせにより, 約束により(会う, など) ▪ We met *by appointment.* 我々は約束して会った.

keep* [*break*] *an appointment 会う約束を守る[破る] ▪ I like a man who *keeps an appointment.* 私は約束を守る人が好きだ.

make an appointment **1** ある役職[地位]に任命する ▪ The president *made an appointment* of Debi Golden to Newsletter Editor. 大統領はデビ・ゴールデンをニューズレターの編集長に任命した.

2 (…と)予約[約束]する (*with*) ▪ I *made an appointment with* the doctor. 医者の予約をした.

receive a good appointment 良い職につく ▪ He *received the good appointment* of Lecturer at the University of Edinburgh. 彼はエディンバラ大学講師の良職に任ぜられた.

take up an appointment 職につく, 就任する ▪ He *took up the appointment* of professor of English literature in the University. 彼はその大学の英文学教授に就任した.

apposition /æpəzíʃən/ 名 ***in apposition to*** …と同格の[に] ▪ This noun is *in apposition to* the foregoing. この名詞は前の名詞と同格だ.

appreciate /əpríːʃièıt/ 動 ***it will be appreciated that*** 明らかに…らしい《官庁用語》 ▪ *It will be appreciated that* your motives were exemplary. 君の動機は明らかに立派であったらしい.

appreciation /əprìːʃiéıʃən/ 名 ***in appreciation of* [*for*]** …を十分認めて; の賞として ▪ We have promoted him *in appreciation of* his efforts. 我々は彼の努力を十分認めて昇進させた.

***show appreciation* (*of*)** (…に対する)感謝の意を表する ▪ He *showed appreciation of* the kindness received. 彼は受けた親切に対して謝意を表した.

with appreciation 感謝して; 同情ある理解をもって ▪ His speech was received *with appreciation.* 彼の演説は大いに受けた.

appreciative /əpríːʃətıv|-ʃiə-/ 形 ***be appreciative of*** …を認める; に感謝している ▪ He *is* always *appreciative of* kindness. 彼はいつも親切を感謝している.

apprehend /æprıhénd/ 動 ***it is apprehended that*** 《官庁用語》…と思う ▪ *It is apprehended that* the conference will prove successful. 会談は成功するものと思う.

apprehension /æprıhénʃən/ 名 ***be above** one's **apprehension*** …に理解できない ▪ This theory *is above my apprehension.* この学説は私にはわからない.

be for apprehension つかむためのものである ▪ The hand *is for apprehension.* 手は物をつかむためのものだ.

be quick* [*slow*] *of apprehension 理解が早い[遅い] ▪ He *is* very *quick of apprehension.* 彼は非常に理解が早い.

***entertain* [*have*] *apprehension*(*s*) *of* [*for*]** 〚心配の大きいとき複数〛…を気づかう ▪ We *entertain apprehensions of* failure. 我々は失敗を気づかっている ▪ He *entertains* no *apprehension for* his welfare. 彼は自分の福祉を案じていない.

in** one's **apprehension …の見るところでは ▪ *In my apprehension* he will be appointed vice-governor of this prefecture. 私の見るところでは彼は本県の副知事に任命されるだろう.

***under the apprehension that* [*lest*]** …しはしないかと気づかって ▪ I was *under the apprehension that* he might not come. 私は彼は来ないかもしれないと気づかっていた.

with apprehension 心配して[しながら] ▪ People boarded the plane *with apprehension.* 人々は不安な気持ちで飛行機に乗った.

apprehensive /æprıhénsıv/ 形 ***be apprehensive for*** (安全などを)気づかう ▪ I *am apprehensive for* his safety. 彼の安全を気づかっている.

***be apprehensive of* [*that*]** …を[しはせぬかと]恐れる, 心配する ▪ He *is apprehensive of* danger. 彼は危険を恐れている ▪ I *am apprehensive that* I may fail. 私は失敗しはしないかと心配している.

apprentice /əpréntəs/ 名 ***be an apprentice***

A

to …のへたな新米である ▪ As yet they *were apprentices to* piracy. まだ彼らは海賊には新米だった.

bind** a person **apprentice to 人を…へ徒弟にやる ▪ The boy *was bound apprentice to* a tailor. その少年は仕立屋へ徒弟にやられた.

go apprentice to …の徒弟になる ▪ I *went apprentice to* a printer. 印刷屋の徒弟になった.

apprenticeship /əpréntəsʃìp/ 名 ***serve*** [***serve out***] *one's* ***apprenticeship*** 年季を勤める[勤めあげる] ▪ Prince George was *serving his apprenticeship* in the military art. ジョージ親王は武芸に年季を入れていた ▪ He *served out his apprenticeship* with a carpenter. 彼は大工のもとで年季を勤めあげた.

apprise /əpráɪz/ 動 ***be well apprised*** よく知っている ▪ The King of England *is well apprised* in the use of them. 英国王はそれらの用法に精通している.

approach /əpróʊtʃ/ 名 ***a softly-softly approach*** 《英口》慎重なやり方[アプローチ] ▪ Others prefer *a softly-softly approach* that puts the emphasis on continuity. 他の者は持続を重視する慎重なアプローチのほうを取る.

be easy [***difficult***] ***of approach*** 近づきやすい[にくい] ▪ He *is difficult of approach*. 彼は近づきにくい人だ.

make** one's **approaches (***to***) (…に)取り入ろう[近づこう]とする ▪ He *made his approaches to* the King. 彼は国王に取り入ろうとした.

on the approach of …が近づくと ▪ *On the approach of* death he discovered the vanity of human life. 死が近づくにつれ, 彼は人生のはかなさを悟った.

appropriate[1] /əpróʊpriət/ 形 ***appropriate to*** [***for, to** do*] …に[するに]ふさわしい ▪ The speech was *appropriate to* the occasion. その演説はその場にふさわしかった ▪ Gift packages are *appropriate for* girls. 贈答用包装は女の子向きだ.

appropriate[2] /əpróʊprièɪt/ 動 ***appropriate … to** oneself* [*one's* ***own use***] 《文》…を自分用として取る; を横領する ▪ They *appropriated* the whole ship's provisions *to themselves*. 彼らは船の糧食を全部横領した ▪ The teacher always *appropriates* the best bookcase *to himself*. その先生はいつも最もよい本箱を自分用にする.

be appropriated to …に充当される ▪ The revenue *is appropriated to* the payment of University officers. 収入は大学の職員の俸給支払いに当てられる.

appropriation /əpròʊpriéɪʃən/ 名 ***make an appropriation for*** …に対して支出をする ▪ They *made an appropriation for* education. 彼らは教育に対して金をかけた.

make an appropriation of …の支出をする ▪ We *made an appropriation of* $1,000. 我々は1,000ドルの支出をした.

approval /əprú:vəl/ 名 ***for** a person's **approval*** 人の承認を求めて ▪ I submit this plan *for your approval*. この案に対してご承認を願います.

in approval 賛成[満足]して ▪ He nodded *in approval*. 彼は賛成してうなずいた.

meet with** a person's **approval 人の賛成[同意]を得る ▪ This article [step] will *meet with your approval*. この品はお気に召すでしょう[この処置は君に是認してもらえるだろう].

on approval 《商》気に入ったら買ってもらうという条件で ▪ I like the online store's policy of sale *on approval*. そのオンライン店の試用売買方式が気に入っている ▪ These goods should be sent *on approval*. これらの品は試験的に送るのがよい.

seal [***stamp***] ***of approval*** 認可[承認]のしるし ▪ Recently Ken has received a *seal of approval* from the highest places. 最近ケンは最上層部から認可のしるしをもらった ▪ Our project had the authorities' *seal of apprival*. 私たちのプロジェクトは当局の承認を得た.

with the approval …の許し[賛成]を得て ▪ It was sold *with the approval* of the authorities. それは当局の許可を得て売られた.

approve /əprú:v/ 動 ***approve** oneself* 〚補語を伴って〛…であることを立証する ▪ He *approves himself* a good teacher. 彼は立派な先生であることを示している ▪ He has *approved himself* worthy of confidence. 彼は信任されるに足るだけの働きぶりを見せた.

approve** oneself **to …に立派であることを示す ▪ The plan *approves itself to* me. その計画はよいと僕には思われる.

approved of 推賞に値する ▪ He is an *approved of* cobbler. 彼は推賞すべき靴屋だ.

April /éɪprəl/ 名 ***April showers bring*** (***forth***) ***May flowers.*** 《諺》4月の雨は5月の花を咲かせる.

***make an April fool of** a person* (4月1日の朝)エイプリルフールで人をかつぐ ▪ Mary is crazy about you? Well, they've *made an April fool of* you, John. メアリーが君に首ったけだって? そりゃ, みんながエイプリルフールで君をかついだんだよ, ジョン.

apron /éɪprən/ 名 ***a green apron*** 《皮肉》俗人説教家 ▪ It more befits *a green apron* (preacher). それは俗人説教家にもっとふさわしい.

apron-strings /éɪprənstrìŋz/ 名 ***be*** [***remain***] ***tied by apron-strings to** a person* (国・組織が自立せずに)他者に支配されている ▪ New Zealand *was tied by* colonial *apron-strings to* a "mother country". ニュージーランドは植民地として「本国」に支配されていた.

cling [***be tied, be pinned***] ***to the apron-strings*** (***of***) (…に)くっついて離れない; (の)言いなりになる, (に)屈従する ▪ He could not submit to *be tied to the apron-strings of* his wife. 彼は甘んじて妻の言いなりにはなれなかった ▪ We can't ask Sam to come. He's *tied to his mother's apron-strings*. サムを招待するわけにはいかない. 母親に頭があ

がらないんだ.

cut [***untie***] ***the apron-strings*** 依存しない, 自立する ▪ Your husband needs to *cut the apron-strings* and grow up. あなたの夫は自立して大人になる必要があります.

hold ... by the apron-strings ...を妻の権利によって所有する ▪ He *holds* the land *by the apron-strings*. 彼はその土地を妻の権利によって所有している.

apt /æpt/ 形 ***be apt at*** ...にさとい, が巧みである ▪ She *is apt at* repartee. 彼女は当意即妙の返答が非常にうまい ▪ They *are apt at* devising ways of easing toil. 彼らは巧みに労苦を減らす方法を考案する.

be apt for ...に適する ▪ The ground *is apt for* the plow. この土地は耕作に適する.

be apt to *do* **1** ...しがちである; しやすい, する傾きがある ▪ We *are apt to* think ill of others. 人はとかく他人を悪く思いがちだ ▪ He *is apt to* lose his temper. 彼は怒りやすい.

2 ...したい気持ちである《表現を和らげるのに用いる》 ▪ I *am apt to* think that he has not consulted many books. 彼はどうもあまり多くの書物を参照しなかったように思われる.

3《米》...しそうである (=be LIKELY to do) ▪ He *is apt to* succeed. 彼は成功の見込みがある ▪ It *is apt to* rain. 雨になりそうだ.

aptitude /ǽptətjù:d/ 名 ***have an aptitude for*** ...の才がある ▪ He *has an aptitude for* languages. 彼は語学の才がある.

have an aptitude to ...に染まりやすい ▪ They *have an aptitude to* vices. 彼らは悪習にすぐ染まる.

have an aptitude to *do* ...しやすい性質がある ▪ Oil *has an aptitude to* burn. 石油は燃えやすい性質がある.

Arab /ǽrəb/ 名 ***a street Arab/an Arab of the city/a city Arab/an Arab of the gutter*** 浮浪児 ▪ *City Arabs* are like tribes of free booters. 町の浮浪児どもは海賊の手合いみたいなものだ ▪ The hero began life as *a street Arab* of Glasgow. 主人公はグラスゴーの浮浪児として人生のスタートを切った.

arbitration /ɑ̀:rbətréɪʃən/ 名 ***submit*** [***refer***] ***... to arbitration*** ...を仲裁に付する ▪ The dispute *was submitted to arbitration*. その紛争は仲裁に付された.

ardent /ɑ́:rdənt/ 形 ***be ardent in*** ...に熱烈である ▪ He *was ardent in* faith. 彼は信仰が熱烈であった.

ardor /ɑ́:rdər/ 名 ***damp*** *a person's* ***ardor*** 人の熱意をさます[くじく] ▪ Hard labor is likely to *damp the ardor of* the most persistent criminal. 重労働させればいかに頑固な罪人も熱がさめるだろう.

area /éəriə/ 名 ***a disaster area*** **1** 被災地; (水害・爆発・地震などの)災害指定地域 ▪ Parts of Soweto have been declared *disaster areas* after flash floods caused havoc overnight. 鉄砲水が一夜のうちに破壊をしたあとソウェトの一部は被災地だと宣告された.

2《口》混乱した[無力な, だめな]場所[状況, 人] ▪ He was *a disaster area* as a human being. 彼は人間としてだめな人だった.

a no-go area《主に英》立ち入り禁止地帯, 無法地帯; 議論してはいけない話題 ▪ Woolwich is *a no-go area* at any time of day. ウリッジは四六時中立ち入り禁止地帯だ ▪ This topic is *a* definite *no-go area*. この話題は断然議論してはならないものだ.

a recipe for disaster →be a recipe for DISASTER.

gray [***grey***] ***area*** (知識・情報の)あいまいな部分, グレイゾーン ▪ Chris thinks he knows what is right and wrong in life—there are no *gray areas* for him. クリスは人生において何が正しく何が間違っているか承知していると思っている—彼にはグレイゾーンはないのである.

in the area of 約... ▪ I owe my parents *in the area of* 600 dollars. 両親に約600ドル借金している.

argue /ɑ́:rgju:/ 動 ***argue along lines*** 一定の理論をたどる ▪ You are *arguing along* the same old *lines*. あなたはまた昔のままの議論をやっている.

argue for [***in favor of***] ...の賛成論をする, 弁護論をする ▪ I was obliged to *argue for* his proposition. 私はやむなく彼の提案に賛成の論をした.

argue the leg off an iron pot《口》極度に議論がましい ▪ Father can, as they say, *argue the leg off an iron pot*. 父はいわゆるひどく議論がましい人だ.

argue the toss →TOSS[1].

argue *one's* ***way out of*** 議論して(ある問題)から逃れる ▪ There is no way for you to *argue your way out of* the problem. 議論してこの問題から逃げる方法はありませんよ.

argument /ɑ́:rgjəmənt|ɑ́:gju-/ 名 ***heated argument*** 怒鳴り合い, 激しい口論 ▪ Max had a *heated argument* with his father about his girlfriend. マックスはガールフレンドのことで父親と激論を交わした.

(***just***) ***for argument's sake***/(***just***) ***for the sake of argument*** 議論の糸口として ▪ Compare prices *for the sake of argument*. 議論の糸口として値段を比べてみよう.

start [***put forward, pick***] ***an argument*** 議論を始める[持ち出す] ▪ I doubt the seriousness of the people who have *put forward* those *arguments*. あんな議論を持ち出した人々の真剣さを疑う.

without argument 異議なく ▪ They passed the bill *without* further *argument*. 彼らはそれきり議論は打ち切ってその法案を通過させた.

argy-bargy /ɑ̀:rdʒibɑ́:rdʒi/ 名《英口》やかましい議論[言い争い] ▪ He got into an *argy-bargy* with the bartender. 彼はバーテンダーと言い争いを始めた.

arise /əráɪz/ 動 ***arising out of*** ...が元で ▪ *Arising out of* the Goddard case, a man was

A

summoned for threatening an ex-constable. ゴッダード事件が元となって, 一人の男が元警官をおどしたかどで召喚された.

arithmetic /əríθmətìk/ 名 ***challenge*** *a person's* ***arithmetic*** 人の計算を怪しいと言う ▪ I broadly agree—but *challenge your arithmetic.* おおむね賛成だが, 君の計算は怪しいぞ.

ark /ɑːrk/ 名 ***came*** [***have come***] ***out of the ark*** 《口》(Noah の箱船から出て来たように)非常に古い, 時代遅れだ ▪ This cheese must *have come out of the ark.* このチーズはひどく古い ▪ He must *have come out of the ark.* 彼は考えがひどく古い ▪ This clock looks as if it *came out of the ark.* この時計は古色蒼然としている.

out of the ark 《口》非常に古い, 旧式で ▪ His hat is [looks] *out of the ark.* 彼の帽子は非常に古い[古そうだ].

touch the ark/lay hands on the ark (***of*** (***the***) ***covenant***) 契約の箱に手出しをする《神聖なものを冒とくする》(《聖》*2 Sam.* 6. 6) ▪ Such a heretic will go so far as to *lay* his *hands on the ark* itself. そのような異端者は神聖なものを冒とくしさえするだろう.

went [***had gone***] ***out with the ark*** 《英》もう使用されていない, 全くの時代遅れ ▪ Such a method *went out with the ark.* そんな方法は時代遅れだ.

arm[1] /ɑːrm/ 名 ***an arm and a leg*** 《口》法外な金額 ▪ I had to pay *an arm and a leg.* 私は法外な金額を払わねばならなかった ▪ The new car cost *an arm and a leg.* その新車には途方もない金がかかった.

an arm candy 《口》(お金をもらって)パーティーなどで男性につき添う美女 ▪ The famous pop-singer entered the restaurant, accompanied by *an arm candy.* 有名なポップシンガーが美女を伴ってレストランに入ってきた.

arm in arm (***with***) (...と)腕を組み合って, 手をたずさえて ▪ The boys ran down the road *arm in arm.* 少年たちは手に手を取って道を走って行った.

as long as *one's* ***arm*** 《口》 **1** 非常に長い間 ▪ I waited *as long as my arm.* 私はずいぶん長く待った.

2 (リストが)長々しい ▪ Lucy gave him a shopping list *as long as her arm.* ルーシーは長々しい買い物メモを彼に渡した.

at arm's length **1** 腕を伸ばして届く所に, 腕を伸ばした所で (→within ARM reach) ▪ He stood *at arm's length* with the Queen. 彼は女王に少し離れて立っていた.

2 不細工に; 不利な条件で(働く) ▪ He works *at arm's length.* 彼の仕事は不細工だ.

chance *one's* ***arm*** →CHANCE[2].

cost *a person* ***an arm and a leg*** 《口》非常に高価だ ▪ This watch *cost* me *an arm and a leg.* この腕時計は目が飛び出るほど高かった.

enfold ... in *one's* ***arms*** (...を)しかと両腕にいだく ▪ She *enfolded* the child *in her arms.* 彼女はその子をしかと両腕にいだいた.

fall into *a person's* ***arms*** 人に抱かれる ▪ She *fell into his arms* and was kissed. 彼女は彼に抱かれてキスされた.

fling up *one's* ***arms in horror*** ぎょっとして両手をあげる ▪ He *flung up his arms in horror* at the news. 彼はそのニュースにぎょっとして両手をあげた.

get in *a person's* ***arms*** 《米》人と仲よくする ▪ He is *getting in her arms.* 彼は彼女と仲よくしている.

give [***offer***] *one's* ***arm*** (つかまりなさいと)...に腕を貸す (*to*) ▪ I *gave my arm to* the charming hostess of the house. 私はその家の魅力的な女主人に腕を貸した.

give *one's* ***right arm*** 右腕をやる; 大きな犠牲を払う[いとわない] (*for, to do*) ▪ During the long sermon I would have *given my right arm for* a smoke. 長い説教の間どうにも一服吸いたくてたまらなかった ▪ I'd *give my right arm to* be ambidextrous. 多芸多能な人間になれるなら右腕をやってもいい.

hold ... in *one's* ***arms*** ...を抱きかかえる ▪ My mother *held* me close *in her arms.* 母は私をしっかりと抱きかかえた.

hold (***out***)***... at arm's length*** ...を腕を伸ばしてささげる ▪ The man *held out* the dirty garment *at arm's length.* その男は汚れた衣服を腕を伸ばしてささげていた.

into *a person's* ***arms/into the arms of*** *a person* 人の所有[支配]に ▪ Ukraine headed back *into the arms of* Mother Russia. ウクライナは母国ロシアの支配下に戻った.

keep ... at arm's length 《口》...を寄せつけない, 遠ざける, よそよそしくする ▪ They were friendly, but she *kept* him *at arm's length.* 彼らは友好的ではあったが彼女は彼によそよそしくした ▪ She *kept* him *at arm's length,* thinking that he might try to kiss her. 彼女は彼がキスしようとするかもしれないと思って彼を寄せつけなかった.

make a long arm 《口》(物を取るため)腕をぐっと伸ばす ▪ Monkeys were *making long arms* for stray beans. サルたちは所々に落ちている大豆を腕を伸ばして取っていた.

offer *one's* ***arm*** →give one's ARM.

on [***upon***] *a person's* ***arm*** 人の腕によりかかって, すがって ▪ She was walking *on his arm.* 彼女は彼の腕にすがって歩いていた.

put the arm on 《口》 **1** ...に金をせびる[ねだる] (=put the BITE on, put the TOUCH on) ▪ I *put the arm on* him for $500. 彼に500ドルせびった.

2 (捕えるため)力ずくで押さえる ▪ The cop is going to *put the arm on* me. 警官は力ずくでおれを押さえるだろう.

receive [***welcome***] *a person* ***with open arms*** →with open ARMs.

one's ***right arm*** →the RIGHT arm.

take the arm (貸そうという)腕を受け入れる; 提携する ▪ She *took the* proffered *arm.* 彼女は差し出さ

れた腕を取った.

talk** a person's **arm off →TALK a person's head off.

the long arm of coincidence → COINCIDENCE.

the long* [*strong*] *arm of the law [etc.] 《雅》法(など)の長く伸びる手[力] ▪ *The long arm of the law* finally caught him. 長く伸びる法の手がついに彼を捕えた ▪ I'm afraid he can't escape *the long arm of the law*. 彼が警察の追っ手を逃れることはできまいと思う ▪ Terrorists have found it hard to escape *the long arm of* Washington. テロリストらは長く伸びる米国の勢力を逃れきれないと分かった.

the [*one's*] ***right arm*** →RIGHT[1].

throw** one's **arms around** a person's **neck 人の首に急に抱きつく ▪ Meg *threw her arms around his neck*. メグは彼の首に急に抱きついた.

twist** a person's **arm 人に圧力をかける, 強制する ▪ If you *twist my arm*, I'll stay for a second beer. そこまで勧められるなら, 帰らずにもう1杯ビールを飲もう.

under** one's **arm わきの下に, 小わきに(かかえて) ▪ He was walking with a book *under his arm*. 彼は本を1冊小わきにかかえて歩いていた.

with folded arms 腕を組んで; 手をこまねいて ▪ He looked on *with folded arms*. 彼は手をこまねいて傍観していた.

with one arm (***tied***) ***behind** one's **back*** 《口》=with one HAND (tied) behind one's back.

with open arms 諸手を上げて, 両手を広げて, 喜んで, 熱烈に, 心から歓迎して ▪ The parents received the foolish girl *with open arms*. 両親は愚かな娘を心から迎えた ▪ She instantly flew towards him *with open arms*. 彼女はすぐさま両手を広げて彼の方に走り寄った ▪ We welcomed their offer *with open arms*. 彼らの申し出に諸手を挙げて賛成した.

within arm [***arm's***] ***reach*** 手の届く所に ▪ Wood was piled *within arm reach*. たき木が手の届く所に積まれていた.

arm[2] /ɑːrm/ 動 ***armed at all points*** →at all POINTs.

(***be***) ***armed to the teeth*** 十分に武装して(いる); 武装[戦備]が十分整って(いる) ▪ We had to contend with a foe *armed to the teeth*. 我々は完全に武装した敵と戦わねばならなかった.

(***be***) ***armed with*** ...で身を固めて(いる); を用意して(いる) ▪ I *am armed with* a letter of introduction. 私は紹介状を携えています ▪ He *is armed with* full powers. 彼が全権を持っている.

armchair /ɑ́ːrmtʃèər/ 名 ***an armchair critic*** [***detective,*** etc.] (経験のない)空論的な批評家[素人探偵, など] ▪ He is what you call *an armchair critic* [*detective*]. 彼はいわゆる空論的な批評家[素人探偵]だ.

an armchair strategist 机上参謀《実戦場に出ずに指令を出す戦略家》 ▪ I'm not *an armchair strategist*. I'm speaking from direct experience. 私は机上参謀じゃない. 実体験をもとに話しているんだ.

an armchair traveler 在宅旅行家《自宅でくつろいでテレビの旅行番組を見たり旅行本を読むだけで楽しむ人》 ▪ It's much cheaper to be *an armchair traveler*. 在宅旅行家でいるほうがずっと安上がりだ.

armed /ɑːrmd/ 形 ***armed and dangerous*** 《陳腐》(銃などで)武器を持っていて危険な ▪ The murderer is at large, presumed to be *armed and dangerous*. 殺人犯はまだ捕まっておらず, 銃を所持していて危険だと考えられている.

the armed eye レンズをつけた目 (→the NAKED eye) ▪ The fixed stars appear of the same size to the naked as to *the armed eye*. 恒星は望遠鏡を使って見ても肉眼で見ても同じ大きさである.

armor, 《英》**armour** /ɑ́ːrmər/ 名 ***a chink*** [***crack***] ***in** one's **armor*** 《口》(防衛上の)弱点, 欠点, 弱み ▪ Your insecurity is *a chink in your armor*. 自信の欠如が君の弱点だ.

a knight in shining armor →KNIGHT.

armpit /ɑ́ːrmpìt/ 名 ***the armpit of the universe*** 《口》不快きわまる所 ▪ That big city is *the armpit of the universe*. その大都会は不快きわまる場所である.

up to** one's* [the***] ***armpits*** 不快な状況[仕事]に深く関わって ▪ The country was *up to its armpits* in an unwinnable war. その国は勝てない戦争に深く関わっていた ▪ The company is steeped in fraud *up to the armpits*. その会社は詐欺行為に深く関わっている.

arms /ɑːrmz/ 名 ***a call to arms*** 軍務への召集 ▪ He received *a call to arms*. 彼は軍務召集を受けた.

a deed of arms 武勲 ▪ Arthur had done no *deed of arms*. アーサーは全く武勲を立てていなかった.

At arms! →To ARMS!

be [***rise***] ***up in arms*** **1** 兵をあげて, 反旗を翻して ▪ All the tribes on the frontier *were up in arms*. 辺境の部族はこぞって兵をあげた.

2 憤激して ▪ Everyone *was up in arms* about the new parking restrictions. 新しくできた駐車制限にはみんな腹を立てていた ▪ The farmers *rose up in arms* over the reduction in the price of wheat. 農業者たちは小麦の値下げに憤激した.

bear arms **1** 武装する, 兵役に服する ▪ He is old enough to *bear arms* for his king. 彼は兵役に服して王様のために尽くすだけの年だ.

2 武器を取る, 戦う ▪ You must be *bearing arms* and resisting the wicked by fighting. 武器を取り悪者どもに抗戦していなければならぬ ▪ *Bear arms* in the cause of justice. 正義のために戦え.

3 紋章をつける ▪ He was permitted to *bear arms*. 彼は紋章をつけることを許された.

bred to arms 軍人の教育を受けて ▪ He was *bred to arms*. 彼は軍人の教育を受けた.

call ... to arms ...に武装を命じる; (軍隊)を召集[動員]する ▪ The prince *called* his men *to arms*. 親王は兵に武装を命じた ▪ England *called* her

A

troops *to arms*. イギリスは軍隊を動員した.

carry arms 武器を持つ; 銃をになう; 戦争をする ▪ No one is permitted to *carry arms*. 誰も武器を携えることは許されていない ▪ *Carry arms*! になえ銃(つつ)! ▪ Her *arms were carried* abroad. その国は外国で戦争をした.

change arms 銃をかつぎ変える ▪ *Change arms*! 肩変え!

coat of arms (盾形の)紋章; 陣羽織 ▪ His *coat of arms* was cut in a precious sardonyx stone. 彼の紋章は貴重なアカシマメノウに刻まれていた.

get under arms →under ARMS.

give up *one's* ***arms*** 降服して武器を渡す ▪ They *gave up their arms*. 彼らは降服して武器を渡した.

grant [***assign***] ***arms*** 紋章を許可する ▪ English origins must be established to *be granted* English *arms*. 英国の紋章を許可されるためには英国生まれであることが証明されなければならない.

in arms **1** 武装して ▪ Here comes Hector *in arms*. エクトルが武装してやって来る ▪ I have 100,000 men *in arms*. 私には10万の武装兵がいる. **2** 武器を取って, 剣を手にして ▪ Jonathan commanded his men to be *in arms*. ヨナタンは部下たちに武器を取るよう命じた. **3** 戦闘準備をして; 戦って ▪ They found all mankind *in* open *arms* against them. 彼らは全人類が自分らに対して公然と戦うのを知った.

in arms (***with***) 《紋章》(...と)交互に置かれ《比喩的にも》 ▪ My daughters sat *in arms with* their husbands upon my right side. 私の娘たちは夫たちと私の右側に交互に並んで座っていた.

lay down (*one's*) ***arms*** 武器を捨てる, 戦いをやめる; 降服する (*to*) ▪ After the battle, the enemy *laid down arms*. 戦争がすんで敵は武器を捨てた ▪ *Lay down your arms to* us. 我々に降参せよ.

lie upon [***on***] *one's* ***arms*** 武装したまま寝る ▪ The English army *lay on its arms* in the field. イギリス軍は戦場で武装のまま寝た.

of all arms あらゆる兵種の(うち) ▪ They numbered about 12,000 *of all arms*. 彼らは各兵種合わせて約12,000人を数えた.

rise in arms 蜂起する, 武器を持って立ち上がる《比喩的にも》 ▪ The huts and hamlets *rose in arms*. 家々村々こぞって蜂起した.

take (***up***) ***arms*** **1** 武器を取る, 武装する; 戦端を開く; 暴動を起こす (*against*) ▪ The Belgians immediately *took up arms against* them. ベルギー軍はすぐに抗戦した ▪ I was obliged to *take arms* in self-defense. 私は自衛のため戦わざるをえなかった. **2** 論戦を始める ▪ Newton *took up arms* in his own cause. ニュートンは自己の主張を弁ずるため筆を取って戦った.

To arms! 戦闘準備(せよ)! (のらっぱ) ▪ "*To arms!*" cried Mortimer.「戦闘準備!」とモーティマーは叫んだ.

turn *one's* ***arms against*** ...を攻撃する, に戦争をしかける ▪ He *turned his arms against* Naples. 彼はナポリに戦争をしかけた.

under arms 武器を取って; 武器を持って立って[進軍して]; 戦闘の陣立てをして ▪ In a moment the troops were *under arms*. ただちに軍隊は戦闘の陣立てを整えた ▪ The whole city got *under arms*. 全市をあげて武器を取った.

up in arms →be up in ARMS.

army /ɑ́ːrmi/ 名 ***an army marches on its stomach*** (軍隊も労働者も)腹が減っては戦ができぬ ▪ Napoleon famously said that *an army marches on its stomach*. ナポレオンが腹が減っては戦ができぬと言ったのは有名だ.

an army of ...の大群, 多数の ▪ *A* whole *army of* waiters was engaged for the banquet. 大勢の給仕がその宴会に雇われた.

enter [***join, go into***] ***the army*** 陸軍に入隊する ▪ Few persons desire to *enter the army*. 軍人になりたいと思う者は少ない.

in the army 陸軍軍人になって ▪ My husband and I are separated and he is *in the army*. 夫と私は別れました. 彼は陸軍に入っています.

Join the army and see the world. 軍隊に入って世の中を知ろう. ☞徴兵のスローガン《the world を the next world の意味にとって, 死ぬかもしれないとからかわれる》.

leave the army 除隊になる ▪ He *left the army*. 彼は除隊になった.

raise an army 軍を起こす; 兵を募る ▪ He *raised an army* at once. 彼はすぐに兵を起こした.

serve in the army 兵役[軍務]に服する ▪ I *served in the army* for four years. 私は4年間軍務に服した.

You and what [***whose***] ***army?*** 《口》(相手の脅しをみくびって)やれるものならやってみろ, お前一人でやれるものか ▪ One word to her and I'll nail you. —*You and whose army?* 彼女に一言でも声をかけたら, ぶん殴るぞ—やれるものならやってみろ.

around /əráund/ 前副 ***a way around*** →WAY.

all around **1** あたり一帯に, いたるところに ▪ It was foggy *all around*. あたり一帯に霧が立ちこめていた ▪ Shake hands *all around*. あたりの人々と握手しなさい. **2** すっかり; 誰に対しても ▪ The prediction seemed confirmed *all around*. その予言はすっかり確証されたようだった ▪ Be more considerate *all around*. 誰に対してももっと思いやりがあってほしい. **3** 万事に ▪ It is best *all around* for you and for me. それは君にも僕にも万事最善だ.

all the year around →all (the) YEAR round.

around and around =ROUND and round.

around here 《米》この辺り[近辺]に[で] ▪ We were under the lowest tree *around here*. 我々はこの辺で一番低い木の下にいた ▪ Everyone *around here* knows me. この辺のものはみんな俺を知っている.

be around and about 《米》...に専念する ▪ He has *been around and about* colleges all his life.

彼は大学の仕事にずっと専念してきた.

have been around 《口》 **1** 経験を積んでいる, 世故にたけている; すれている (→have been THERE) ▪ Those movie actresses *have been around.* それらの映画女優は経験を積んでいる.
2 生きてきた ▪ I*'ve been around* a lot longer than you have. 僕は君よりずっと長く生きてきたんだ.

See you around! 《米口》 また(どこかで)会いましょう, じゃあね.

arrange /əréɪndʒ/ 動 ***arrange*** *oneself* 準備する, 身を整える ▪ George hastened to *arrange himself* for the new contingencies. ジョージは急いで新しい偶発事件に備えた.

arrange for *a thing* (***to*** *do*) 物事の(…する)手はずをする ▪ The secretary must *arrange for* meeting him. 秘書が彼に会う手はずを整えねばならない ▪ Please *arrange for* the taxi *to* come there. どうぞタクシーがそこへ来るように手配してください.

it is arranged that …の手はずになっている, の都合になっている ▪ *It is arranged that* fifty persons should be present. 50人出席する手はずになっている.

arrangement /əréɪndʒmənt/ 名 ***an amicable arrangement*** 穏やかな話合い ▪ They arrived at *an amicable arrangement.* 彼らは円満に話合いがついた.

come to an arrangement 協定が成立する, 相談がまとまる ▪ We *came to an arrangement* at last. 我々はついに話し合いがついた.

make arrangements for …の手はずを整える ▪ Have you *made arrangements for* your journey yet? もう旅行の準備をしましたか.

make arrangements with *a person* ***for*** 人と…の打ち合わせをする ▪ I *made arrangements with* him *for* a meeting. 私は彼と会合の打ち合わせをした.

make the arrangements 《婉曲》 葬儀の準備をする ▪ When my father died, my mother *made the arrangements.* 父が亡くなったとき母が葬儀の手配をした.

array[1] /əréɪ/ 名 ***an array of*** ずらりと並んだ…の列 ▪ On the right we have *an array of* cliffs. 右手にはがけが連なっている.

in battle array 戦闘隊形を整えて ▪ Their infantry was drawn up *in battle array.* 彼らの歩兵は陣営を整えていた.

in beautiful [***fine***] ***array*** 《雅》 美しく身を整えて ▪ Stand up before God *in beautiful array.* 美装をして神の前に立て.

in holiday array よそ行きの服を着て ▪ The ladies were *in holiday array.* 女性たちはよそ行きの服装をしていた.

make an array 勢ぞろいする ▪ They *made an array* for a fight. 彼らは戦いに備えて勢ぞろいした.

set … in array …を配列する ▪ They *set* tables *in* orderly *array.* 彼らはテーブルをきちんと配列した.

array[2] /əréɪ/ 動 ***array*** *oneself* 着飾る ▪ Miss Smith *arrayed herself* in a silken robe. スミス嬢は絹の衣裳で着飾っていた.

array *oneself* ***against*** 〘複数主語で〙 …にこぞって反対する ▪ They *arrayed themselves against* the bill. 彼らはこぞって法案に反対した.

be arrayed (***in***) **1** (…に)身を装う; (を)着飾る ▪ Even Solomon in all his glory *was* not *arrayed* like one of these flowers. 栄華をきわめたときのソロモンでさえ, この花の一つほども着飾っていなかった.
2 (兵隊などが)整ぞろいする ▪ Soldiers *were arrayed in* order of battle. 兵隊は戦列を敷いていた.

arrear /əríər/ 名 (***be***) ***in arrears*** 滞って(いる), 遅れて(いる) ▪ Their rent *was in arrears.* 彼らの家賃は滞っていた ▪ This work *is in arrears.* この仕事は遅れている.

be paid in arrears (賃金が)後払いで支払われる ▪ Bonuses will *be paid in arrears.* ボーナスは後払いで支払われます.

fall [***go***] ***into arrears*** 滞る ▪ His studies *fell into arrears.* 彼は勉強が遅れた.

in arrear of …より遅れて (↔in ADVANCE of) ▪ In this respect we are much *in arrear of* European countries. この点では, 我々はヨーロッパ諸国よりはるかに遅れている.

in arrear(***s***) ***to*** **1** …に職務[責任]の遂行が遅れて ▪ I am two or three letters *in arrears to* different persons. 私は別々の人に対して2, 3通の手紙を出すのが遅れている.
2 …に負債[恩義]を負って ▪ I am very much *in arrear to* you for a thousand civilities. 種々ご丁重なおもてなしを受けまことにありがとうございました.

in arrear(***s***) ***with*** …が滞って ▪ You are *in arrear(s) with* your rent [your payment]. 君は家賃[支払い]が滞っている.

work off arrears 努力して徐々に遅れを取り返す; 働いて徐々に負債を返す ▪ He had to *work off arrears.* 彼は働いて徐々に負債を返さねばならなかった.

arrest[1] /ərést/ 名 ***be under*** (***an***) ***arrest*** 拘引されている ▪ Will *was under an arrest* and desired the assistance of all. ウィルは拘引されているのですべての人の援助を願った.

be under house arrest 自宅拘禁中である ▪ His brother *is under house arrest.* 彼の弟は自宅に拘禁されている.

in arrest of judgment 《法》 (陪審の答申後)誤審を理由に処置停止にして ▪ He may move the court *in arrest of judgment.* 彼は法廷を動かして処置停止にすることもできる.

place [***put***]***… under arrest*** …を拘禁する ▪ Lord Russell *was* soon after *placed under arrest.* ラッセル卿はその後まもなく拘禁された.

arrest[2] /ərést/ 動 ***arrest attention*** 注意を引く ▪ His speech failed to *arrest* public *attention.* 彼の演説は世間の人の注意を引かなかった.

arrest *a person's* ***eyes*** 人の目に留まる ▪ A black object floating *arrested his eyes.* 黒い物が浮いているのが彼の目に留まった.

arrest judgment 《法》 (陪審の答申後)誤審を理

A

由に処置停止する ▪ If the *judgment be arrested*, all the proceedings are set aside. もし誤審の理由で処置が停止されると，すべての手続きは破棄される.

arrival /əráɪvəl/ 名 ***for arrival*** 《商》着荷渡しで ▪ *For arrival* a steamer cargo was sold at 100 pounds and 5 pence. 着荷渡しで汽船の荷が100ポンド5ペンスで売られた.

on (*one's*) ***arrival*** 到着時に，着き次第 ▪ *On my arrival* at Reading, I found there Mr. Jacob. レディングに到着時に，そこにジェイコブ氏がいた.

to await arrival (受取人の)到着待ち《手紙・小包に書く文句》.

arrive /əráɪv/ 動 ***arrive on*** [***upon***] ***the scene*** [***spot***] 現場に着く ▪ A policeman *arrived on the scene*. 警官が現場にやって来た.

arrogate /ǽrəgèɪt/ 名 ***arrogate ... to*** *oneself* **1** (権力などを)私する ▪ They *arrogated to themselves* every important branch of the administration. 彼らは行政の重要部門は全部独占した.

2 うぬぼれて...があると主張する ▪ She *arrogated to herself* some importance. 彼女はいくぶん偉そうにした ▪ I don't *arrogate* so much ability *to myself*. 自分にそんな才能があるとは思っていません.

arrow[1] /ǽroʊ/ 名 ***a straight arrow*** 《米》昔気質の人，生真面目な人 ▪ Bert is remembered as *a straight arrow* by his friends. バートは友人たちから生真面目な人として記憶されている.

an arrow in the quiver 取り得るいくつかの手段[戦術]の一つ ▪ Each skill becomes *an arrow in the quiver* that we can use when needed. それぞれの技能が必要なときに使える戦術の一つになるのだ.

arrow of time/time's arrow 時間の矢《過去から現在へ時間が進む方向》 ▪ I shall use the phrase "*time's arrow*" to express this one-way property of time. 私は時間の1方向的な特質を表すために「時間の矢」という語句を使用することにする.

(***as***) ***straight as an arrow*** →STRAIGHT.

fly straight as an arrow まっすぐに飛んで行く ▪ At the sound of the thunder the child *flew straight as an arrow* to its mother. 雷の音を聞いて子供は母親の所へ矢のように飛んで行った.

shoot *one's* ***last arrow*** (競争で)もう打つ手がない ▪ We've *shot our last arrow*. There're no further steps to take against our opponent. もう打つ手はなくなった. 相手に対してこれ以上とるべき手段はない.

time's arrow =ARROW of time.

write straight arrow/ write arrow straight 正確な[良心的な]記事を書く ▪ The young journalist always aims at *writing arrow straight*. その若いジャーナリストは常に事実を正しく伝える記事を書くことを目指している.

arrow[2] /ǽroʊ/ 動 ***arrow*** *one's* ***way*** 矢のように飛んで行く ▪ Here the kingfisher *arrowed his way*. ここではカワセミが矢のように飛んで行った.

arse[1] /ɑːrs/ 名 ***a heavy arse*** 《英卑》怠け者，朝寝坊 ▪ Up, *heavy arse*! 起きろ，この朝寝坊め!

an arselicker [***kisser***] 《英卑》卑屈にペコペコするひと，おべっか遣い ▪ Niel described Mr Wood as *an "arselicker."* ウッド氏は「おべっか使い」だとニールは言った.

arse about face 《英卑》さかさまに，あべこべに ▪ The whole frame is completely *arse about face*. 骨組みはまるごと完全にあべこべになっている.

be (***right***) ***up*** *a person's* ***arse*** =(right) up a person's ARSE.

fall arse over tit 《英卑》うつぶせに倒れる ▪ I was so drunk I *fell arse over tit*. 私はひどく酔っていたのでうつぶせに倒れた.

get *one's* ***arse in gear*** 《英卑》急ぐ ▪ Now I gotta *get my arse in gear* to beautify it and make it all presentable. さて急いでそれをきれいにして体裁よくしなければならん.

get off *one's* ***arse*** 《英卑》仕事にかかる，みこしをあげる ▪ They *got off their arses* at last. 彼らはとうとうみこしをあげた.

go arse over tip/arse over tit 《英卑》逆さまになる ▪ He fell and *went arse over tip* on the ice. 彼は転んで氷の上で逆さまになった.

hang an [***the***] ***arse*** 《英卑》しりごみする，ぐずぐずする ▪ No other would *hang an arse*. 他の人なら誰もぐずぐずしないだろう.

Kiss [***Lick***] ***my arse!*** 《英卑》やだね，おとといい来い《断りの文句》 ▪ Lend me ten pounds.—*Kiss my arse*. 10ポンド貸してくれ—やだね.

lick [***kiss***] (*a person's*) ***arse*** 《英卑》(権力者などに)卑屈にペコペコする ▪ I refuse to *kiss arse* at any cost. おれはどうあっても卑屈にペコペコしないぞ ▪ He won't lend you the money until you *kiss his arse*. 彼におべっかを使うまで金は貸してくれない.

move *one's* ***arse*** 《英卑》急げ; どいてくれ ▪ *Move your arse*! We're late. 急げ! 遅れているんだ ▪ *Move your arse*. You're in the way. どいてくれ. じゃまだ.

... my arse! 《英卑》...なんかであるものか; ...なんて馬鹿な《相手の発言を強く否定する表現》 ▪ I'll be ready soon.—Ready *my arse!* You're still in bed. すぐ用意します—用意どころじゃない，まだ寝床にいるじゃないか.

not know [***can't tell***] *one's* ***arse from*** *one's* ***elbow*** 《英卑》どうしようもないばかだ ▪ If you will excuse the expression, he does *not know his arse from his elbow*. こう言っちゃ何だが，彼はどうしようもないばかだ.

(***right***) ***up*** *a person's* ***arse*** 《英卑》人の車にくっつけて走らせる ▪ The bastard's driving *right up my arse*! あの野郎，ぴたっと車をくっつけて走らせやがる!

shift *one's* ***arse*** 《英卑》 **1** 〚主に命令文で〛 = move one's ARSE.

2 怠けていないで働く ▪ John, *shift your arse* and finish the job. ジョン，怠けていないで仕事を仕上げろ.

shove [***stick, stuff***] ***... up your arse*** 《英卑》〚主に命令文で〛...を好きなようにする，勝手にする《強い拒絶》 ▪ Take your apology and *shove* it *up your arse*! 謝罪は自分でやって，勝手にするがいい.

sit on** one's **arse 《英卑》(他人が忙しくしているときに)何もしない ▪ Don't *sit* on *your arse* when other people are busy. 他の人が忙しくしてるときにぼさっとしてるんじゃない!

talk out of [***through***] *one's* ***arse*** 《英卑》ばかなことを言う, 間違ったことを言う ▪ The majority of you boys *talk through your arse*. 君たち若者大多数はばかなことを言っている.

(***with** one's*) ***arse upwards*** 《英卑》幸運で, 幸運にも ▪ This man rose *with his arse upwards*. この人はとんとん拍子に出世した.

work** one's **arse off 《英卑》しゃかりきに働く ▪ I *work my arse off* at a restaurant. レストランでしゃかりきに働いている.

(***You can***) ***shove*** [***stick***]***...up your arse!*** 《英卑》そんなものはいらん ▪ *Shove* them *up your arse*, the stupid assertions you made. そんなものはいらん, 君がしたとんまな主張なんか.

arse[2] /ɑ:rs/ 動 ***can't be arsed*** 《英卑》わざわざ...する気はない (*to do*) ▪ I *can't be arsed to* get out of bed today. きょうはわざわざ起きるつもりはない.

art /ɑ:rt/ 名 ***art for art's sake*** 芸術至上主義 ▪ Oscar Wilde believed in *art for art's sake*. オスカー・ワイルドは芸術のための芸術を信奉していた. ☞F l'art pour l'art のなぞり.

Art is long, (***and***) ***life*** (***is***) ***short.*** 《諺》芸道は長く, 人生は短い,「少年老い易く学成り難し」.

fine art 美術; 高度の技術を要する仕事; 名人芸 ▪ The contractor excels in the *fine art* of demolition. 請負人は解体という名人芸にすぐれている.

get...down [***off***] ***to a fine art*** 《口》(技術など)を完全に学び取る[自分のものにする] ▪ New Zealanders have *got* boating *down to a fine art*. ニュージーランド人たちは操船術を自家薬籠(やくろう)中のものにしている ▪ She gets money out of her father easily: she's *got* it *down to a fine art*. 彼女は父からたやすく金をもらう. 彼女はそれをうまくやる術を心得ているから.

have [***be***] ***art and*** [***or***] ***part in*** (ある事)の計画と遂行にあずかる, の共犯者である, に加担する; (漠然と)...に関係する ▪ He seems to *have art and part in* the crime. 彼はその犯罪に加担しているらしい ▪ I declare that I *had* neither *art nor part in* the affair. 断言しますが, 私はその事には全く関係はありませんでした ▪ You *are art and part* with us *in* purging heresy. あなたは異端追放については我々に加担してくださっている. ☞スコットランド法から.

the state of the art →STATE.

artful /ɑ́:rtfəl/ 形 ***come the artful over*** 《口》...をだます, だまそうとする ▪ He's always trying to *come the artful over* newcomers. 彼はいつも新来者をだまそうとしている.

article[1] /ɑ́:rtɪkəl/ 名 ***an article of faith*** (We believe で始まる宗教上の)信仰箇条, 信条 ▪ Feminists take it as *an article of faith* that only husbands abuse their wives. フェミニストたちは夫だけが妻を虐待するということを信条としている.

in the article of ...の項目の下に; に関して, 関する限り ▪ He thinks himself better, particularly *in the article of* dress. 彼は自分がよくなったと思っている, 特に服装に関して ▪ A revolution has happened *in the article of* good breeding. しつけの面において革命が行われた.

in the article of death 死のまぎわに, 臨終に ▪ Roman citizens originally made their wills only *in the article of death*. ローマ市民はもとは臨終においてのみ遺言書を書いたものだ. ☞＜L in articulo mortis のなぞり《普通このラテン語のほうを使う》.

the finished article 完成していつでも使えるもの ▪ Ron believes he is still improving and insists he is not *the finished article* yet. ロンは自分はなおも向上中で, まだ完成品ではないと主張している.

the genuine article 本物 ▪ This diamond ring is *the genuine article*. このダイヤモンドの指輪は本物だ.

article[2] /ɑ́:rtɪkəl/ 動 ***be articled to*** (年季契約で)...の徒弟になる ▪ He *was articled to* a printer. 彼は印刷屋の徒弟になった.

artifice /ɑ́:rtəfəs/ 名 ***by artifice*** 策略で ▪ They took the position *by artifice*. 彼らは策略でその陣地を取った.

artsy-fartsy /ɑ̀:rtsifɑ́:rtsi/, 《英口》 **arty-farty** /ɑ̀:rtifɑ́:rti/ 形 (人が)芸術家気取りが鼻につく; (物が)えらく芸術品めかした ▪ *Artsy-fartsy* design has been in business since 1995. 1995年以来えらく芸術品めかしたデザインが売れている.

as /əz, æz/ 副 接 前 関代 ***as a general thing*** 概して (= as a (general) RULE) ▪ I don't put much faith in your discoveries *as a general thing*. 僕はだいたい君の発見というものをたいして信用していないのだ.

as against ...に比べて, に対して ▪ The business done this year amounts to £20,000 *as against* £15,000 last year. 本年の取引は昨年の15,000ポンドに対して20,000ポンドに達する ▪ The rights of laymen *as against* priests were nothing. 司祭に比べたときの俗人の権利は取るに足らぬものであった.

as and when ...するように; ...する時《官庁用語的で, as または when だけで十分》 ▪ You may eat *as and when* you like. 君は好きな時に食べてよい ▪ The committee deals with applications for relief *as and when* they arise. その委員会は救援申請に応じて処理する.

as...as **1**〚as＋形容詞＋as＋名詞〛きわめて...で ▪ He is *as* cross *as* two sticks. 彼はひどく気むずかしい ▪ The boy is *as* good *as* gold. その少年は行いが非常に良い. ☞形容詞を強める直喩の形式; 頭韻をふむことが多く, 口語では前の as は略されることがある.

2〚as *hard* as *hard* の形で〛きわめて...で ▪ Your hand will get *as hard as hard*. 君の手はひどく固くなるだろう ▪ The house was *as* dark *as* dark. その家はまっくらだった.

3〚as＋形容詞・副詞＋as＋(簡略)節〛...と同じほど, くらい, だけ ▪ I am *as* tall *as* you (are). 私はあなたと身長は同じだ ▪ Run *as* fast *as* you can. できるだ

け速く走れ ▪ Come *as* soon *as* possible. できるだけ早く来なさい.

4〚as ... as (関係代名詞)〛 ...するだけの ▪ They planned on having *as* many children *as* came along. 彼らは生まれた子供はみな育てる計画だった ▪ I would buy *as* many books *as* I like. 好きなだけの本をみな買うのだが.

5〚命令文の形で譲歩を表す〛 ...しようとも ▪ Work *as* hard *as* you will, you will not succeed. 君はいくら働いても成功せぬだろう ▪ Be a man *as* rich *as* he is, he ought not to be idle. 人はいくら金持ちであっても怠けていてはならない.

6《米》...だけれども (although) ▪ *As* busy *as* he was, Bill had remembered the promise. 忙しかったけれど, ビルは約束を覚えていた.

as ... as any どれに[誰に]比べても少しも劣らない ▪ This pen is *as* good *as any* I have used. このペンは私の今までに使ったどのペンにも劣らず良い ▪ He is *as* honest a lad *as any*. 彼は誰にも劣らぬ正直な若者だ.

as ... as anything →ANYTHING.

as ... as before 前と同様に...で ▪ I wish you were *as* good *as before*. 君が前と同じように善良であってくれたらよいのに.

as ... as one can [possible] できるだけ... ▪ Kick the ball *as* far *as* you *can*! できるだけ遠くへボールをけってみなさい.

as ... as can be この上なく...の ▪ The weather was *as* fine *as* (it) *could be*. 天気は最高によかった.

as ... as ... can be ありうるだけ...で, この上なく...で ▪ You are *as* wrong *as* wrong *can be*. 君は大まちがいをしている ▪ I was *as* happy *as* happy *can be*. 私はこの上なく幸福だった.

as ... as ever **1** 相変わらず ▪ You study *as* hard *as ever*, don't you? 相変わらずよくご勉強ですね ▪ I feel *as* well and strong *as ever*. 相変わらず健康で元気です.

2〚動詞を伴って〛この上なく, いずれにも劣らず《あとの as は関係代名詞》 ▪ He is *as* brave a soldier *as ever* shouldered a gun. 彼は今までに銃をかついだどの兵士にも劣らず勇敢な兵士だ ▪ He is *as* great a man *as ever* lived. 彼は古来まれな偉人である.

3〚one can を伴って〛できるだけ ▪ Be *as* quick *as ever* you *can*. できるだけ早くしなさい.

as ... as heart could wish 非常に[この上なく]満足な ▪ It was *as* lovely a day *as heart could wish*. 心ゆくばかりの好天気だった.

as ... as if まるで...のように ▪ We spend *as* happy a time *as if* we had been in our own homes. 我々はまるで自分のうちにでもずっといるかのように楽しく暮らしている.

as ... as may be できるだけ...で ▪ It is well to be with such lawless people *as* little *as may be*. ああいう無法者たちとはできるだけ交わらぬようにするのがよい.

as ... as possible →POSSIBLE.

as ... as the next fellow [man] →NEXT.

(as) ... as you please とっても, この上なく (extremely) ▪ Emily sat there in her new dress, *as* pretty *as you please*. エミリーは新調のドレスをまとってそこに座っていたが, それは実にきれいだった ▪ After winning the race he was smug *as you please*. そのレースに優勝したあと, 彼はこの上もなくごきげんだった.

as between the two 両者どちらかと言えば《as for の変形》 ▪ *As between the two*, I prefer a fool to a knave. 両者のうちでは悪者より愚か者のほうがよい.

doing, as ... do この通り[実際]...しているので ▪ *Living, as* I *do*, so remote from towns, I rarely have visitors. 私はこの通り町から離れて住んでいるから, 訪問客はめったにない.

as ever is [was]《口》〚前の語を強調して〛まさしく ▪ Next week *as ever is* we'll go home. 来週こそは家へ帰ろう ▪ It was the very same Jim *as ever was*. ほかでもない, まさしくあのジムだった.

as [so] far as ... go/ as [so] far as ... is concerned →FAR.

as follows →FOLLOW.

as for ...に関しては, はどうかというに; のごときは《しばしば軽蔑的》 ▪ *As for* me, give me liberty or give me death. 私には, 自由を与えるか, それとも, 死を与えてくれ《Patrick Henry の言葉(1775)》 ▪ *As for* staying a week, it would be out of the question. 1週間滞在するといったってそれは問題になるまい.

as for my part (他人はいざ知らず)私だけは ▪ *As for my part*, I have nothing to say against it. 他人は別として私だけはそれに反対することは何もない.

as from ...から《法律・契約など正式な日付に用いる》 ▪ The agreement starts *as from* March 31st. その契約は3月31日から始まる.

as ... go →GO[2].

as one goes along やっていくうちに; 徐々に ▪ I made the story up *as* I *went along*. 私は徐々に物語を作り上げた.

as good as they make them →MAKE[2].

as how《俗》...ということを (*that*) ▪ I know *as how* you have a fancy for the boy. 私は君がその少年が好きなことを知っている.

as if あたかも...かのように, まるで...みたい **1**〚仮定法過去・仮定法過去完了で〛 ▪ He talks [talked] *as if* he knew everything. 彼は知らないことはないような話しぶりだ[だった] ▪ They look [looked] *as if* they had seen a ghost. 彼らはまるで幽霊でも見たような顔をしている[いた].

2〚主節を省略して感嘆的に〛 ▪ I'm hungry.—*As if* I hadn't fed you a couple of hours ago. 腹がすいちゃった—まるで2時間前に食事をあげなかったみたいな言いぐさね.

3〚節を簡略にして〛 ▪ They sit *as if* charmed by the music. 彼らは音楽に魅せられたようになって座っている ▪ The dog wagged his tail *as if* to tell him how glad he was. 犬はどんなに喜んでいるかを彼に知らせるかのように尾を振った.

4〚主文が現在の場合 as if の次が現在時制のことがある〛 ▪ I feel *as if* this tree knows everything. この木が何もかも知っているように思える.

as if there was no tomorrow →TOMORROW.

as in **1** …におけるように ▪ Pronounce V *as in* Victor. Victor のようにVを発音しなさい.
2《口》つまり(I mean) ▪ A: You haven't seen Bill, have you?—B: *As in*, your ex? Why would he be here?—A: I invited him. A: あなた, ビルに会ったことないでしょうね?—B: つまり, 元のご主人? どうしてここにくるの?—A: 私が招いたのよ.

as is《米》そのままで, 正札どおり ▪ Everything on sale here is sold *as is*. 当店販売の品はみな正札どおりの値段です ▪ I left it *as is*. 私はそれをそのままにしておいた ▪ All items will be sold on an "*as is*" basis. すべての品目は「正札どおり」で売ります ▪ *As is*, it is a double width comic strip. そのままでそれは大変こっけいな漫画です.

… as** one **is →Hero AS one is.

done ***as … is*** [***am,*** etc.] 実際…されているので ▪ *Written, as* it *is*, in an easy style, the book is adapted for beginners. 実際易しい文章で書いてあるから, その本は初学者に適している.

as is a《米俗》すぐれた ▪ a candy bar *as is a* candy bar 上等の棒状キャンディー.

as is often the case (***with***) →CASE.

as it is [***they are***] **1**〚文尾で〛そのあるがままに ▪ Leave it *as it is*. そのままにしておけ.
2〚文頭で, 主に仮想的な言い方が前出して〛実はそうでないので, だが実際のところは ▪ I thought things would get better, but *as it is*, they are getting worse. 事態はよくなるだろうと思っていたが, 実はそうでなくだんだん悪くなっている ▪ Had Livesey not been here, I should have seen you to the deuce. *As it is*, I have heard you. リブシーがいなかったら君なんかたたき出してやっただろうが, 実はリブシーがいたから聞いてやったんだ.
3〚文中に挿入されて〛現状では, 実際問題として ▪ The law, *as it is*, is severe on this kind of people. その法律は現在のままではこの種の人々には酷だ.

as it is called →AS we call it.

as it should be《米俗》立派で, 理想的な ▪ We are working to create a world *as it should be*. 我々は理想的な世界を作るために働いているのだ.

as it stands →as … STANDs.

as it were いわば ▪ He is, *as it were*, a grown-up baby. 彼はいわば成人した赤んぼうだ. ☞as if it were so が短縮された形.

as** one **likes [***wishes, pleases***] …が好きなように, のお好みどおりに ▪ They could worship God *as* they *liked*. 彼らは好きなように神を礼拝することができた ▪ It is just *as* you *like*. 全く君のお好みどおりだ.

as long as →LONG.

as may be そうかもしれない ▪ You have a chart, don't you?—That's *as may be*. 君は海図を持ってるだろう?—そうかもしれない.

as … never 決して…がしないほどに ▪ He suffered *as* he had *never* suffered before. 彼はそれまでになかったほど苦しんだ ▪ He delights us *as* others *never* do. 彼は他の人々には断然できないほど我々を喜ばせてくれる.

as of …の時点で, …現在で(の);《主に米》(日時)から ▪ *As of* Jan. 1951, there were 189 public schools in Hawaii. 1951年1月現在でハワイには189の公立学校があった ▪ *As of* midnight tonight we start into October 1. 今夜真夜中から10月1日が始まる.

as of now →NOW.

as of old →OLD.

as of right →RIGHT[1].

as …, so …するようにそのように…する《後続する so 節の比較の意を強調する文語体用法》 ▪ *As* two is to three, (*so*) four is to six. 2の3に対する関係と4の6に対する関係は同じである ▪ *As* rust eats iron, *so* care eats the heart. さびが鉄を腐食するように労苦は人の心を蝕む ▪ *As* is the husband, *so* is the wife. 夫が夫なら妻も妻 ▪ *As* men live, *so* they die. 生きざまは死にざま.

as … stands →STAND[2].

as things are →THING.

as things stand →as THINGs are.

as though →AS if.

as to **1**〚文頭で〛…に関しては[関して言えば](=AS for) ▪ *As to* the journey, we must decide about that later. 旅行についてはいずれ後ほど決めねばならない.
2〚しばしば間接疑問を目的語として〛…について ▪ He said nothing *as to* hours. 時間のことは彼は何も言わなかった ▪ There is no doubt *as to* who will be elected. 誰が選ばれるかについては疑いはない ▪ He said nothing *as to* whether he would come back. 彼は帰るかどうかについては何も言わなかった. ☞2 の場合 As for を使うことはできない.
3 …に応じて ▪ Will you sort the costumes *as to* color? 色に応じて衣装を分類してくれませんか.

as was《英口》〚旧名のあとにつけて〛旧… ▪ She comes from Myanmar—Burma *as was*. 彼女はミャンマー, つまり旧名ビルマの出身だ.

as we call [***put***] ***it/as … is called*** いわゆる, それが呼ばれているように ▪ We read newspapers to know "the news of the day," *as we call it*. 我々はいわゆる「その日の出来事」を知るために新聞を読む ▪ The planets, *as* these stars *are called*, move round the sun. これらの星, いわゆる惑星は太陽の回りを回転する ▪ He went to Cathay, *as* China *was* then *called*. 彼は当時の中国名であったカタイへ行った.

as … will …によくあることだが, の常として ▪ He spends all he has, *as* students *will*. 学生にありがちのことだが, 彼もあるだけ使ってしまう. ☞この will は習慣の will.

as yet (将来はともかく)今までのところまだ(=so FAR), まだ ▪ He is *as yet* a minor. 彼はまだ未成年だ ▪ *As yet*, he has not succeeded, but he will before long. 今までのところまだ彼は成功していないが, やがて成功するだろう.

as you do《英》当然のことだが, よくあることだが ▪ She said Hi to me and I said Hi too, *as you* *do*. 彼女が私にやあと言ったので，私も当然やあと返した．

as you please 好きなように ▪Do *as you please*. 好きなようにしたまえ．

As you sow, so shall you reap. 《諺》種をまいたように刈入れをする，「因果応報」．

as you were 《口》元へ!，まちがえました (Sorry, my mistake!) ▪His name is Roberts. No, *as you were*. It's Robinson. 彼の名前はロバーツだ．いや，違った，ロビンスンだ．

be as …のようである (be like)《聖書語法; 今でも雅文に用いられる》 ▪His lips *are as* lilies. 彼のくちびるはユリのようである ▪These cubs *are as* stainless snow. これらの幼獣は汚れのない雪のようだ．

being as how 《米俗》…なので (as) ▪I know you wouldn't object, *being as how* you would be one of the family. 君は家族の一人になるんだから，反対はしないだろうね．

come [***go***] ***as*** *one* ***is*** 《口》(ありのままで)着替えしないで来る[行く] ▪Just *come as* you *are*. そのまま着替えしないで来なさい．

hero [***young***, etc.] ***as*** *one* ***is*** ⟦as の前の名詞には冠詞がつかない⟧ **1** 英雄だ[若い，など]けれども ▪*Young as* he *was*, he was able. 彼は若かったが敏腕だった ▪*Woman as* she *was*, she bravely fought for the country. 彼女は女ながらも勇敢に国のために戦った．

2 英雄な[若い，など]のだから ▪*Young as* he *is*, he naturally makes such a mistake. 若いんだからそのような誤りを犯すのも無理はない．

3 ⟦通例分詞が as の前へ来て⟧ …のままで ▪He led me into the hall, *booted as* I *was*. 彼は靴をはいたままの私を広間へ案内してくれた ▪I helped her, *tottering as* she *was*, to the edge of the bank. 私は彼女がよろよろしていたのをそのまま堤防のふちまで助けて連れて行った．☞この形は元は as young as he is (彼ほど若くて)であったので，前の as が略され，前後関係で上述の三つの意味になった．

A ***is to*** *B* ***as*** *C* ***is to*** *D* AのBに対する関係はCのDに対する関係と同じである《類比 (analogy)》 ▪Day *is to* sun *as* night *is to* moon. 昼の太陽に対する関係は夜の月に対する関係と同じだ ▪Space *is to* place *as* eternity *is to* time. 空間の場所に対する関係は永遠の時間に対する関係と同じである．

it isn't as if [***as though***]/***it's not as if*** [***as though***] …というわけじゃない《あとに来る陳述を否定する》 ▪*It isn't as if* we were strangers to it. 我々はそのことを知らないわけじゃない ▪*It's not as though* anyone saw it coming. 誰かがそんなことが起こると予想していたわけじゃない．

not so [***as***]***... as*** ほど…でない ▪She is *not so* [*as*] young *as* she looks. 彼女は外見ほど若くはない ▪The result was *not so* good *as* I had expected. 結果は予期したほど良くなかった．

so as to *do* →SO.

so ... as to *do* →SO.

ascendancy, ascendency /əséndənsi/ 名 ***have*** [***get, gain, obtain***] ***ascendancy over*** …より優勢である[になる]，を支配している[する] ▪The wife gradually *gained ascendancy over* her weak-willed husband. 妻はだんだんと意志の弱い夫を支配するようになった．

ascendant, ascendent /əséndənt/ 形名 ***in the ascendant*** 支配権を握る，優勢な，日の出の勢いの; 勢力[人気]が上昇中で《誤用》 ▪The Conservative party was again *in the ascendant*. 保守党が再び支配権を握っていた．☞占星術から．

One's ***star is in the ascendant.*** 勢力[人気，運勢]が上昇中である ▪*Jim's* social *star is in the ascendant*. ジムの社交界の地位は上昇中である．

ascending /əséndɪŋ/ 形 ***in*** (***an***) ***ascending order*** (数値・重要性などが)だんだん大きくなる順序で ▪Arrange the following polynomials *in ascending order*. 次の多項式関数をだんだん大きくなる順序に配列しなさい．

ascent /əsént/ 名 ***make an ascent*** 上空へ上る; 登る ▪I have never *made an ascent* in a balloon. 私は気球で上空へ上ったことがない ▪I am going to *make an ascent* of Mt. Fuji next summer. 今度の夏は富士山に登るつもりだ．

ascribable /əskráɪbəbəl/ 形 ***be ascribable to*** …に帰せられるべきである ▪His failure *is ascribable to* incompetence. 彼の失敗は無能のためである．

ash /æʃ/ 名 (***as***) ***pale as ashes*** 《詩》極度に青白い，(顔色が)死んだように青白い ▪ghosts *as pale as ashes* きわめて青白い幽霊．

(***as***) ***white as ashes*** まっさおで ▪He went *as white as ashes*. 彼はまっさおになった．

ashes to ashes, dust to dust 灰は灰に，塵は塵に(帰す)《英国の葬式に用いる言葉》 ▪*Ashes to ashes, dust to dust*, if God won't have him the Devil must. 灰は灰に塵は塵に，もし神が受け給わねば悪魔のところへ行かねばならない．

be burnt [***reduced***] ***to ashes*** 焼けて灰になる，(家などが)灰じんに帰する ▪A great many houses *were reduced* [*burnt*] *to ashes*. 非常に多くの家が全焼した．

in sackcloth and ashes →SACKCLOTH.

lay ... in ashes …を焼いて灰にする，全滅させる ▪The whole kingdom *was laid in ashes*. 王国が全滅した．

Peace to his ashes! →PEACE to a person's ashes!

rake over old [***the***] ***ashes*** (不快な)記憶を呼びさます，古い議論をむし返す ▪I don't want to *rake over old ashes*. 私は不快な記憶を呼びさましたくない ▪John always *rakes over the ashes* of his old arguments. ジョンはいつも昔の議論をむし返す．

rise from the ashes 灰じんの中からよみがえる[復興する]; 敗北から立ち直る ▪Our party will quickly *rise from the ashes* of defeat. 我々の党は素早く敗北から立ち直るだろう．

turn to ashes in *one's* ***mouth*** まるで期待はずれの[無価値な]ものになる ▪I've been a bit stressed lately and most things *turn to ashes in my* *mouth.* 最近少々ストレス気味で，たいていのものが全然期待はずれのものになる.

turn to dust and ashes (希望が)消えうせる，だいなしになる ▪ Our hope has *turned to dust and ashes.* 我々の希望は消えうせた.

ashamed /əʃéɪmd/ 形 ***be ashamed of*** …を恥じる ▪ You ought to *be ashamed of* your ignorance. 君は自己の無知を恥ずべきだ.

be ashamed to *do* …することを恥じる，恥じてしたがらない ▪ We *are* ashamed of sin and yet not *ashamed to* sin. 我々は罪を恥じるが，それでも罪を犯すことを恥じない.

feel ashamed for …を情けなく思う，情けないやつと思う ▪ I *feel ashamed for* you. お前にはあいそが尽きた.

ashore /əʃɔ́ːr/ 副 ***be washed ashore*** 岸に打ち上げられる ▪ The wreck *was washed ashore.* 難破物は岸に打ち上げられた.

cast … ashore …を岸に打ち上げる ▪ They *were cast ashore.* 彼らは岸に打ち上げられた.

go [***get, come***] ***ashore*** **1** (船から)上陸する ▪ Soon we *went ashore.* まもなく我々は上陸した.
2 (船が)浅瀬に乗り上げる ▪ The boat may *go ashore.* 船は浅瀬に乗り上げるかもしれない.

put … ashore …を上陸させる ▪ He *put* the crew *ashore* at Sydney. 彼は乗組員をシドニーに上陸させた.

run ashore ＝go ASHORE 2.

aside /əsáɪd/ 副名 ***as*** [***in***] ***an aside*** 脇ぜりふで，こっそり ▪ Then she says to her husband, *as an aside*, "Let's get out of this place." それから彼女は「ここから出ましょうよ」とこっそり夫に言った.

aside from **1** 《米》 …の上に，に加えて (besides) ▪ *Aside from* this, the mere show is magnificent. これに加えて単に外観だけでも壮大である ▪ The city, *aside from* being a great industrial center, enjoys a high moral record. その市は大工業地である上に高い精神的歴史を持っている.
2 …のほかは，を除けば (＝EXCEPT for) ▪ *Aside from* a severe fright, Mr. Smith was uninjured. スミス氏はひどく驚いただけでけがはなかった.
3 …はさておき，を離れて ▪ *Aside from* the question of expense, the project is impracticable. 費用の問題はさておきその計画は実行不可能である ▪ That is *aside from* the subject. それは問題と関係がない.

take [***draw***] *a person* ***aside*** (内密話などのため)人をわきへ連れて行く ▪ The teacher *took* the boy *aside* and told him not to tease others. 教師は少年を脇へ呼びいじめをしないように言った.

ask[1] /æsk|ɑːsk/ 名 ***a big ask*** 《主に豪》高望み，できない相談 ▪ It is *a* pretty *big ask* to win the Cup. 優勝杯を勝ちえるというのはいささか高望みだ.

ask[2] /æsk|ɑːsk/ 動 ***a lot*** [***a great deal***] ***to ask*** 求めすぎ，頼みすぎ ▪ A chance to earn a fair living isn't *a lot to ask.* かなりの生活費をかせぐ機会を求めるのは求めすぎではない ▪ Would it be *a great deal to ask* of you? 君にお願いするのは無理だろうか.

ask an account [***a reckoning***] ***of*** …の明細[説明]を要求する ▪ We must *ask a reckoning of* the realm's revenue. 我々は国家収入の明細を要求しなければならない.

ask *a price* ***for*** …の値段を言う，いくらくれと言う ▪ What [How much] do you *ask for* it? それは値段はいくらですか.

ask for it 《口》 **1** 自業自得だ，自ら災いを招く ▪ You've been dismissed, but you did *ask for it.* 君は解雇されたが自業自得だ.
2 (女性が)求めてはずかしめを招く ▪ She was *asking for it* when she wore such a short skirt. 彼女はそんな短いスカートをはいていて自らはずかしめを招いていた.

ask for … to *do* …が…する[される]ように頼む[要求する] ▪ I *asked for* him *to* come to see me. 彼に会いに来てくれと頼んだ ▪ I *asked for* my suitcase *to* be carried to my room. 私はスーツケースを部屋まで運んでくれるように頼んだ.

ask for trouble →TROUBLE[1].

ask if [***whether***] …かと尋ねる ▪ She *asked* me *if* she might go with me. 彼女は私といっしょに行ってもいいかと尋ねた.

Ask me another! →ANOTHER.

ask … to *do* (人に)…してくれと頼む ▪ He *asked* me *to* meet him at the station. 彼は駅に出迎えてくれと私に言った.

ask too much of [***from***] 人に過大な要求をする，無理を言う ▪ I blame myself for *asking too much of* him in our first encounter. 初めて出会ったとき彼に無理を言ったことを悪かったと思っている.

ask yourself 自分に聞いてみろ，自分で決めろ ▪ Don't ask me, *ask yourself.* おれに聞くな. 自分に聞いてみろ.

be asked in church 教会で結婚の予告をしてもらう ▪ We shall *be asked in church* next Sunday. 我々は今度の日曜に結婚の予告を教会でしてもらわねばならない. ☞教会で3回まで日曜ごとに予告をして，異議があるかないかを確かめる習慣から.

couldn't ask for 《口》 …よりよいものは望めない ▪ We *couldn't* have *asked for* better weather. それ以上のいい天気は望みようもなかった.

Don't ask (***me***)***!*** 《口》(気まずくなるので)答えたくないね ▪ *Don't ask.* Silence is golden. 答えたくないね. 沈黙は金なりだ.

if you ask me 《口》言わせてもらえば，私に言わせれば ▪ Men are a bit silly, *if you ask me.* 男なんて少しばかだ，と僕は思うよ.

little [***not much***] ***to ask*** 求め[頼み]足りない ▪ It's *little to ask* of a son, certainly. それはたしかに息子に対しては求め足りないくらいだ.

(***well,***) ***I ask you*** 《口》全くひどい; 驚いたね ▪ *I ask you*, not a taxi in sight! 驚いたね，タクシーが1台も見えないなんて! ▪ Mother thinks a pink dress will suit me. *Well, I ask you*! 母はピンクの服が私に似合うと思っている. 全く驚くわ! ☞ask に強勢を置く.

you may well ask/《文・戯》 ***well may you***

A

ask (質問に対して)聞くのは当然だね[無理もないよ] ▪ What, *you may well ask*, is Neil doing here? 君が聞くのも当然だよ. なんだってニールはこんなところにいるんだろう? ▪ What is e-cash? *Well may you ask.* 電子マネーって何かって? 聞くのも無理はないね.

askance /əskǽns/ 副 ***look askance (at)/eye [view]... askance*** (人を)横目[疑い, 非難]の目で見る《嘲笑・ねたみを示すことも以前はあった》 ▪ The man *looked askance at* everything the shopman offered for sale. その人は店員が勧めたすべてのものを疑いの目で見た ▪ They *were viewed askance* by the authorities. 彼らは当局から疑いの目で見られた.

askew /əskjúː/ 副 ***hang... askew*** …をゆがめて掛ける ▪ Don't *hang* the picture *askew*. その絵をゆがめて掛けないようにしてください.

look askew at …を流し目[横目]で見る《不きげん・冷たい目で》 ▪ The boy was *looking askew at* him with his sharp gray eyes. 少年は鋭い灰色の目で彼を横目で見ていた.

asking /ǽskɪŋ|ɑ́ːsk-/ 名 ***at the asking price*** 言い値で ▪ Gone are the days of selling your home *at the asking price*. わが家を言い値で売れた時代は去ってしまった.

for the asking 《口》請求しさえすれば; (ほしいと言えば)無料で (→for an old SONG) ▪ You can have it [It is yours] *for the asking*. それはくれと言いさえすれば(ただで)あげますよ ▪ If people need food, water or diapers they are available *for the asking*. 食べ物や水, おむつが必要なら, 依頼するだけで手に入る.

aslant /əslǽnt|əslɑ́ːnt/ 前 ***run aslant*** …に抵触する ▪ It *runs aslant* all recognized conventions. それは一般に認められている一切の慣例に反する.

asleep /əslíːp/ 形副 ***be [fall] asleep at the switch [wheel]*** 《米俗》うっかりしている[する], 油断している[する], さぼっている[さぼる] ▪ If I hadn't *been asleep at the switch*, I'd have noticed the car being stolen. 私がうっかりしていなかったなら, 車が盗まれるのに気づいていただろうに.

fall asleep **1** 寝入る ▪ She *fell asleep* watching a DVD. 彼女は DVD を見ながら寝入ってしまった ▪ He *fell asleep* over the book. 彼は本を読みながら寝入った.

2 無気力な状態になる ▪ The American dream does not come to those who *fall asleep*. アメリカンドリームは無気力になってしまうような人々には実現しない《Nixon の言葉》.

fall asleep into 寝入って(ある状態)に陥る ▪ They *fall asleep into* delicious dreams. 彼らは寝入って快い夢を見る.

get [go] asleep 寝入る ▪ The baby soon *got asleep*. 赤んぼうはじきに寝入った.

lay... asleep …を寝入らせる[寝かす]《比喩的にも》 ▪ They *were* soon *laid asleep* by whispering winds. 彼らはそよ風の音でじきに寝入った ▪ The question *was laid asleep*. 問題は不問に付された.

sound asleep ぐっすり眠って, 熟睡して ▪ He's *sound asleep* snoring at this hour. 彼は今いびきをかきながらぐっすり眠っている.

aspect /ǽspekt/ 名 ***assume [take on] a new aspect*** 新局面を呈する, 面目が一変する ▪ The situation is *assuming a new aspect*. 情勢が一変しつつある.

in [under] an aspect ある面から(見るなど) ▪ View the matter *in* all its *aspects*. 事をあらゆる面からながめなさい.

aspen /ǽspən/ 名 ***tremble [shake] like an aspen (leaf)*** ぶるぶる震える ▪ She began to *shake like an aspen*. 彼女はぶるぶる震えだした.

asperity /æspérəti/ 名 ***speak with asperity*** 荒々しく[つっけんどんに]ものを言う ▪ He *spoke* to his servant *with asperity*. 彼は使用人に荒々しくものを言った.

aspersion /əspə́ːrʒən|-ʃən/ 名 ***cast aspersions on [upon]*** …を中傷する, 悪く言う ▪ They *cast aspersions upon* my character. 彼らは私の人格を中傷した.

aspire /əspáɪər/ 動 ***aspire to the hand of*** (女性)との結婚を望む ▪ He secretly *aspired to the hand of* this lady. 彼はひそかにこの女性との結婚を望んでいた.

asquint /əskwínt/ 副 ***look asquint*** **1** 斜めに見る, 斜視である ▪ He was lame in one leg and *looked asquint*. 彼は片足が不自由で斜視だった.

2 (意識的に)横目を使う ▪ He *looks asquint* at the objects of nature. 彼は自然の事物を横目で見る.

ass[1] /æs/ 名 ***a man with a paper ass*** 《米俗》口先だけのやつ, くだらねえ野郎 ▪ Neil's talking like *a man with a paper ass*. ニールは口先だけのやつみたいにしゃべっている.

a pain in the ass →a PAIN in the neck.

a piece of ass →PIECE[1].

ass backwards 《米俗》順序をまちがえて, あべこべに ▪ The whole system's been set up *ass backwards*. システム全体が順序を誤って組み立てられている.

One's ***ass is dragging.*** 《米俗》疲れきっている, しょぼくれている ▪ *My ass is dragging* a little this morning. 今朝おれはちょっぴりしょげている.

one's ***ass is grass*** 《米俗》まずいことになる, ひどい目にあう ▪ *His ass is grass* next time I see him. 今度会ったらやつはまずいことになる.

one's ***ass [butt] is in a sling*** 《米俗》ひどく困っている, まずいことになる ▪ Have that report in by five o'clock—or all *your asses are in a sling*! そのレポートを5時までにしあげなさい—さもないとおまえたち全員まずいことになるぞ.

one's ***ass is on the line*** 《米俗》(うまくいかなければ)責任を問われる ▪ *My ass is on the line* if the package arrives late. 小包の到着が遅れたら, 責任を問われる.

ass over teacups [teakettle, tincups]/ass over tip [tit] 《米俗》まっさかさまに ▪ I went tumbling *ass over teacups*. 私はまっさかさまに転がり落ちた.

be ass out 《米俗》困っている ▪ Man, I *am ass out* this month. I ain't got no kinda funds coming in. おい僕は今月困ってるんだ. 金が一円も入ってこないのでね.

be on** a person's **ass [***butt***] 《米俗》 **1** しつこくする, 悩ます ▪ He *is* always *on my ass* about something. 彼はとやかく僕のあら捜しばかりしている. **2** 車間距離を置かずに運転する ▪ He *was on my ass* all the damn time. 彼は始終人の車に追突しそうに運転した ▪ There's a Jaguar *on my ass*, making me nervous. ジャガーにおかまを掘られそうで, こっちははらはらする.

be talking out of** one's **ass 《米俗》(知らないくせに)知ったかぶりをして話している ▪ The writer of the article *is talking out of his ass*. この記事の書き手は知ったかぶりをして話している.

Bite my ass. 《米俗》＝Kiss my ASS!

bust** a person's **ass [***balls, butt, hump***] → BUST[2].

bust [***break***] *one's* ***ass*** 《米俗》猛然と努力する, うんとがんばる, しゃかりきにやる (*to do*) ▪ Bill has to *bust his ass to* win her over. ビルは彼女を味方につけるためにうんとがんばらねばならない.

bust ass out of 《米俗》大急ぎで…を飛び出す ▪ Bill *busted ass out of* the classroom and headed for home. ビルは大急ぎで飛び出して, まっすぐ家に向かった.

chew** a person's **ass (***out***) 《米俗》(へまをしたので)がみがみ言う ▪ My boss is always trying to *chew my ass* about my jeans. 社長は僕のジーンズのことでがみがみ言う.

drag [***haul, tear***] (*one's*) ***ass*** 《米俗》急ぐ, 速く動く ▪ It's time to *haul my ass* off to the airport. 空港に急いで行く時刻だ.

fall (***flat***) ***on** one's **ass*** 《米俗》ぶざまに[派手に]しくじる, 大へまをする ▪ Max totally messed up and *fell on his ass* last week. マックスは先週すっかりめちゃめちゃにして大へまをした.

get** a person's **ass 人を懲らしめる[罰する] ▪ The cops will *get his ass* for noise pollution. 警官が騒音公害のかどで彼を罰するだろう.

get** one's **ass in [***into***] ***gear*** 《米俗》急ぐ, のらくらしない, 本腰をいれる ▪ Now *get your ass in gear* and let's finish this job. さあ急いでこの仕事を済まそうぜ.

get** a person **off** his **ass 《米卑》人をしゃきっとさせる[仕事に取りかからせる] ▪ The goal here is to *get* him *off his ass*. この場合の目標は彼をしゃきっとさせることだ.

get off** one's* (dead***) ***ass*** 《米俗》のらくら[ぐずぐず]するのをやめる, けつをあげる ▪ You really should *get off your dead ass* and find a job! 君はほんとにけつをあげて勤め口を捜すべきだよ.

get [***have***] ***the*** (***red***) ***ass*** 《米俗》腹を立てる, かっとなる, 頭にくる ▪ He *had the red ass* at this guy. 彼はこの男に腹をたてた.

get your ass over here [***in here,*** etc.] 《主に米俗》(こっちなど)へ来い ▪ Jim, *get your ass over here*, please? ジム, こっちへ来てくれるか ▪ Bill, *get your ass in here*. ビル, ここへ入ってこい.

go around** one's **ass to get to** one's **elbow 《米俗》簡単なことを一番難しいやり方でする ▪ When he does projects, he always seems to *go around his ass to get to his elbow*. 彼がプロジェクトを興(おこ)すときには, いつも簡単なことを一番難しいやり方でするようだ.

haul ass 《米俗》(逃げるために)急いで動く ▪ He *hauled ass* out of the car. 彼は急いで車から降りた.

have** a person's **ass 《米俗》人をやっつける[とっちめる] ▪ They will *have his ass* soon. 彼らはじきに彼をとっちめるだろう.

have** one's **ass in a crack 《米俗》ひどく困っている ▪ I have *had my ass in a crack* two times over the last year. 私はここ1年の間で2度ひどく困ったことがあった ▪ I think he's desperate and *has his ass in a crack*. 彼はすてばちになり, ひどく困っているのだと思う.

have [***get, put***] *a person's* ***ass in a sling*** 《米俗》人を困った立場に陥れる ▪ Watch what you say, or I'll *put your ass in a sling*. 言うことに気をつけろ, さもないとやばいことになるぞ.

have [***get, put***] *one's* ***ass in a sling*** 《米俗》まずいことになる, やばいことになる ▪ Ben really *has his ass in a sling* now that he has quit his job. ベンは仕事をやめたので本当にまずいことになっている. ☞腕をつり包帯でつることから.

have ... coming out (***of***) *one's* ***ass*** 《米俗》…を腐るほどもっている, がいくらでもある ▪ If I *had* dollars *coming out my ass*, I would be involved in the bidding. ドルがいくらでもあるのだったら, その競売に参加するだろうさ.

it will be [***it's***] *a person's* ***ass*** 《米俗》人の破滅となる, ひどい目にあう ▪ When we meet, *it will be your ass*, not mine. 我々が会うとき, 君が破滅するだろうよ, 僕じゃなくて ▪ If I miss my step, *it will be my ass*. へまをやらかせば, 僕はひどい目にあうだろう. ☞ass＝end の意から.

jump through** one's **ass 《米俗》いきなりの難題にすぐに対応する, 試練を経る ▪ I had to *jump through my ass* to get stationed in San Diego. サンディエゴに配置されるためには難題に対応しなければならなかった.

kick ass and take names 《米俗》激しくやっつける[打ち負かす] ▪ The home team is *kicking ass and taking names*. ホームチームはこてんぱんにやっつけている.

kick (***some***) ***ass*** [***butt***] → KICK (a person's) ass.

kick some ass (***around***) 《米俗》(人に代わって)指図をしはじめる, (ボスとして)しごく, 締め上げる ▪ Bill is just the person to *kick some ass* over there. ビルこそあちらで指図をしはじめる適任者だろう.

A

kiss (*a person's*) ***ass*** =lick (a person's) ARSE.
Kiss my ass! 《米俗》勝手にしやがれ, くそくらえ ▪ You can *kiss my ass*. お前なんかくそくらえだ.
make an ass of *oneself* 《米俗》ばかな真似をする ▪ Tell him not to *make an ass of himself* at the party. 彼にパーティーでばかなまねをするなと言いなさい.
move your ass =get one's ASS in gear.
My ass! 《米俗》ばかな, まさか, 嘘つけ! ▪ Sold out, *my ass!* 売れてしまったって, まさか!
not give a rat's ass 全然気にしない ▪ I *don't give a rat's ass* about Valentine's day. バレンタインの日なんて, てんで気にしないね.
not know *one's* ***ass from a hole in the ground*** [***from*** *one's* ***elbow***] 《米俗》まるで無知[無能]である ▪ Critics of the war in Iraq had complained that President Bush did *not know his ass from a hole in the ground*. イラク戦争を批判する人々は, ブッシュ大統領はなんにもわかっちゃいないとこぼした.
off *a person's* ***ass*** 《米俗》人をいじめる[苦しめる]のをやめて ▪ Finally my sister is *off my ass*. ついに姉は私を苦しめるのをやめた.
on *a person's* ***ass*** 《米俗》人をいじめて[苦しめて, 追いかけて] ▪ My dad is *on my ass* about shooting in the house. おやじは家の中で発砲したことで僕をしつこくしかった.
(***out***) ***on*** *one's* ***ass*** 《米俗》(すっかり)落ちぶれて, 追い出されて, しょげて; 酔っぱらって ▪ The Senator was *out on his ass* when he lost the presidential campaign. その上院議員は大統領選に敗れたとき, すっかりしょげていた.
pull ... out of *one's* ***ass*** 《米俗》うまくごまかして切り抜ける ▪ I was unprepared for my boss's question and I had to *pull* it *out of my ass*. 社長の質問に準備していなかったので, うまくごまかして切り抜けねばならなかった.
shift *one's* ***ass*** 尻を持ち上げて働き出す ▪ I started to *shift my ass* toward the exit. 私は尻を持ち上げて出口の方へ動きはじめた.
sit on *one's* ***ass*** 《米俗》(何もせずに)じっとしたままでいる, 何もしないでいる ▪ Don't just *sit on your ass!* Get busy! ただじっと座っていてはだめだ! 仕事にかかれ!
think the sun shines out of *a person's* ***ass*** [***arse, back***] →think the SUN shines out of a person's bum.
up to *one's* ***ass in*** (厄介なこと)に深く[どっぷり]掛かり合って, のめり込んで ▪ These days I'm *up to my ass in* a damn campaign. このところいまいましいキャンペーンにのめり込んでいる.
work your ass off =work one's ARSE off.
you (***can***) ***bet your*** (***sweet***) ***ass*** 〚節を伴って〛確かだ, まちがいない ▪ *You can bet your* (*sweet*) *ass* he will win. まちがいない. 彼は勝つさ.

ass[2] /æs/ 名 ***an ass in a lion's skin*** ライオンの皮を着たロバ《おどしの鬼面をかぶった憶病者》 ▪ That candidate is *an ass in a lion's skin*. あの候補者は大きなことを言うが実は弱虫だ. ☞ライオンの皮を着たロバがいなないたため化けの皮がはげたというイソップ寓話から.
Asses have ears as well as pitchers. 《諺》ロバにも水さしにも耳がある《子供の前でもうっかりしたことは言えない》.
burial of an ass 埋葬されぬこと (《聖》*Jer*. 22. 19) ▪ He shall be buried with the *burial of an ass*. 彼は全く埋葬されないであろう.
make an ass of …をばかにする ▪ He *makes an ass of* me every time. 彼はいつも僕をばかにする.
make an ass of *oneself* 《口》ばかなことをする ▪ Don't *make* such *an ass of yourself*. そんなばかなまねはするなよ.
play the ass 《口》ばかなまねをする ▪ He *played the ass* to get some food. 彼は食物を得ようとしてばかなまねをした.

assault /əsɔ́ːlt/ 名 ***assault and battery*** 暴行殴打 ▪ You've struck me, and I shall bring an action for *assault and battery*. 君は僕をなぐったから暴行殴打で訴えてやる.
assault of [***at***] ***arms*** 剣術の試合; 銃剣術の演習[実演].
make an assault on/give an assault to …を急襲する ▪ The enemy *made an assault on* their trenches. 敵は彼らの塹壕を急襲した ▪ They *gave* several *assaults to* the outworks. 彼らは外塁を数回急襲した.
take [***gain, carry, win***]***... by assault*** 強襲して…を取る ▪ He *took* Goa *by assault*. 彼はゴアを急襲して取った.

assembly /əsémbli/ 名 ***come off the assembly line*** 仕上がる; 学校を卒業する ▪ The car had just *come off the assembly line*. その車は今仕上がったばかりだ ▪ Children *come off the assembly line* knowing little about geometry. 子供らは幾何学のことはあまり知らないで学校を卒業する.
get ... off the assembly line …の製作を完成する ▪ We *got* the tank *off the assembly line*. 我々はタンクを仕上げた.

assent /əsént/ 名 ***assent and consent*** 《英》議会の協賛 ▪ That needs the deliberate *assent and consent* of Parliament. それは国会の慎重審議の上の協賛を必要とする.
by [***with***] ***common*** [***one***] ***assent*** 一同賛成して, 満場一致で ▪ They passed the bill *with one assent*. 満場一致で議案を通した.
give *one's* ***assent to*** …に賛成[同意]する ▪ I *gave my assent to* the plan. その計画に賛成した.
nod (*one's* ***head in***) ***assent*** うなずいて賛意を示す, うんとうなずく ▪ The biologist *nodded assent*. その生物学者は賛成してうなずいた.

assert /əsə́ːrt/ 動 ***assert*** *oneself* **1** 自己(の権利・意見・存在など)を主張する ▪ He knows how to *assert himself*. 彼は自己主張の仕方を心得ている. **2** (天分などが)現れる, 頭をもたげる; 出しゃばる ▪ Justice will *assert itself*. 正義は自ら明らかになるものだ ▪ Agnostic philosophy now *asserts itself* very loudly. 今や不可知論哲学が非常にやかましく唱えられている.

assiduity /æsədjúːəti/ 名 ***with assiduity*** 精を出して, せっせと ▪ He worked *with assiduity.* 彼はせっせと働いた.

assistance /əsístəns/ 名 ***bring ... to*** *a person's* ***assistance*** =bring ... to a person's AID.

come to *a person's* ***assistance*** 人を助けに行く ▪ They were *coming to the assistance of* their friends. 彼らは友人を助けに行くところだった.

give [***render***] ***assistance to*** ...を援助する ▪ I will *give assistance to* you. 私は君を援助しよう.

associate /əsóʊʃièɪt/ 動 ***associate*** *oneself* ***in*** ...の仲間入りをする ▪ I *associated myself in* the enterprise. 私はその事業の仲間入りをした.

associate *oneself* ***with*** (提議・意見)に賛同する, を支持する; に参加する ▪ He *associated himself with* the political movement. 彼はその政治運動に参加した ▪ I *associate myself with* the proposal. その提案を支持する.

association /əsòʊsiéɪʃən/ 名 ***in association with*** ...と共同して; に関連して; と交際して ▪ The name is well known *in association with* the battle. その名はその戦いに関連して有名だ ▪ I am *in* close *association with* him. 私は彼と親密に交際している.

assume /əsjúːm/ 動 ***assume the chair*** 議長席に着く ▪ He *assumed the chair.* 彼は議長席に着いた.

assuming (***that***) 〚接続詞的に〛...と仮定して, とするならば ▪ *Assuming* the house is for sale, would you buy it? その家が売り物なら, 君は買うか.

assumption /əsʌ́mpʃən/ 名 ***go on the assumption*** (***that***) (...と)決めてかかる ▪ The teacher *went on the assumption that* the students had done their homework. 生徒は宿題をしているものと先生は決めてかかった.

on the assumption that ...という仮定のもとに ▪ The language was only pardonable *on the assumption that* it was inspired. その言葉は霊感を得たものだという仮定のもとにのみ容赦できるものだった.

assurance /əʃúrəns|əʃɔ́ːr-/ 名 ***have full assurance*** 十分な保証を得ている; 十分確信している ▪ I *have full assurance* that he will come back. 私は彼は帰って来ると確信している ▪ I *have full assurance* of its safety. 私はその安全については十分な保証を得ている.

have the assurance to *do* ずぶとくも...する ▪ He *had the assurance to* take the credit for himself. 彼は厚かましくも功を独り占めにした.

make assurance doubly [***double***] ***sure*** 念には念を入れる (cf. Sh., *Macb.* 4. 1. 83) ▪ I ran to the house in Soho, and (to *make assurance doubly sure*) destroyed my papers. 私はソーホーの家に走って行き, (念のため)書類を焼いておいた.

with assurance 確信[自信]をもって ▪ She answered the question *with assurance.* 彼女はその質問に自信をもって答えた.

assure /əʃúər|əʃɔ́ː/ 動 ***assure*** *oneself* ***of*** ...を確かめる; に確信を得る ▪ I must *assure myself of* all the circumstances. 私は事情をしっかり確かめねばならない.

assured /əʃúərd|əʃɔ́ːd/ 形 ***be*** [***rest, feel***] ***assured*** 安心する; 確信している (*that*) ▪ You may *rest assured that* they are safe. 彼らは無事だから安心しなさい ▪ I *am assured that* he is innocent. 彼が無罪だと確信している.

astern /əstə́ːrn/ 副 ***drop*** [***fall***] ***astern*** 他船に追い抜かれる, 遅れる ▪ Soon the ship *fell astern.* まもなくその船は他船に追い抜かれた.

astir /əstə́ːr/ 形 ***be astir with*** ...でざわめいている, にぎわう; で夢中になる ▪ The whole town *was astir with* the news. 町中がその知らせでざわめいていた ▪ The village *was astir with* alarm. 村の者はすわ一大事と大騒ぎだった.

astonish /əstánɪʃ|-tɔ́n-/ 動 ***astonish*** *a person's* ***weak mind*** 人を驚かす ▪ He often used to *astonish my weak mind* by his observations on this head. 彼はこの点に関する所見でよく私を驚かしたものだ. ☞19世紀ロンドンで流行した句で, weak mind にはほとんど意味はない.

astonishment /əstánɪʃmənt|-tɔ́n-/ 名 ***in*** [***with***] ***astonishment*** びっくりして ▪ He stared at me *in astonishment.* 彼はあっけにとられて私を見つめた.

to *one's* ***astonishment*** ...の驚いたことには ▪ *To his astonishment* the beggar turned out to be his own son. 彼の驚いたことにはその物乞いは自分の息子だった.

astraddle /əstrǽdəl/ 副 ***astraddle of*** [***on***] (馬など)にまたがって; (両側)にまたがって ▪ He sat *astraddle on* a big horse. 彼は大きな馬にまたがっていた ▪ The battle was fought *astraddle of* the road. 戦闘は道路の両側にまたがって行われた.

astray /əstréɪ/ 形副 ***get*** [***go***] ***astray*** 道を踏み迷う; 邪道に入る, 誤る; 堕落する ▪ Be careful not to *get astray.* 道に迷わないよう注意しなさい ▪ It is said that he has *gone astray.* 彼は堕落したそうだ.

lead ... astray 間違いを犯させる; (人を)邪道に導く, 堕落させる ▪ Don't let the experts *lead* you *astray.* 専門家に迷わされてはいけない ▪ The boy *was led astray* by bad companions. その少年は悪友によって邪道に引き入れられた.

step astray [***awry***] (正道から)踏み迷う ▪ My heedless youth has *stepped astray.* 私の無鉄砲な青春は道を踏み迷ってきた.

astride /əstráɪd/ 副 ***astride of*** ...にまたがって ▪ He was sitting *astride of* a horse. 彼は馬に乗っていた ▪ The troops are *astride of* the river. 軍隊はその川の両岸にまたがっている.

asunder /əsʌ́ndər/ 副 ***break*** [***burst***] ***asunder*** 真っ二つに[きれぎれに]割る[裂く]; 真っ二つに[きれぎれに]割れる[裂ける] ▪ He *broke* the window-

A

pane *asunder*. 彼は窓ガラスをこっぱみじんに割った ▪ The cup *broke asunder*. カップはこっぱみじんになった.

cleave ... asunder [***in two***] →CLEAVE.

come [***fall***] ***asunder*** ばらばらに崩れる ▪ The plates *fell asunder*. 皿はこっぱみじんになった.

cut [***rend, saw, tear***] ***asunder*** 真っ二つに[きれぎれに]切る[裂く, 引き切る, 引き裂く] ▪ It *rent asunder* the veil which overhung the temple. それは神殿に掛かっていた幕を二つに裂いた ▪ They put him to death by *sawing* him *asunder*. 彼らは彼をのこぎりでばらばらに切って殺害した ▪ Her heart *was torn asunder*. 彼女の胸はずたずたに裂かれた.

drive asunder ちりぢりに追い払う ▪ Parents and children *were driven asunder* by the war. 親子は戦争のためちりぢりになった.

put asunder …を引き離す; ばらばらにする ▪ I *put* the leaves of the book *asunder*. 私は本を一枚一枚ばらばらにした ▪ Let not man *put asunder* that which God has joined together. 神がいっしょにしているものを人間が引き離してはいけない.

at /ət, æt/ 前 ***At him*** [***them***]***!*** 彼[彼ら]にかかれ!, やっつけろ!

at it 《口》 **1** (せっせと)働いて, 戦って, 従事して; 忙しく; とりかかって ▪ Go *at it*! やっつけろ! ▪ Keep *at it*! 忍耐して勉強せよ ▪ He is hard *at it*. 彼はせっせとやっている ▪ After a short rest, he was *at it* again. 少し休んでから彼はまた始めた.

2 (二人が)セックスしている, やっている ▪ I found them *at it* on the sofa. 見ると二人はソファの上でやっていた.

3 (二人(以上)の人が)しゃべりまくっている ▪ It's irritating the way they are *at it*. 彼らがしゃべりまくっているさまは腹立たしい.

at that **1** その通りに (at that estimate) ▪ I will take it *at that*. その通りに受け取っておく.

2 それくらいで, それだけで《もうとやかく言わないで》 ▪ We'll let it go *at that*. それくらいでもういいとしよう.

3 しかも, おまけに ▪ I lost an arm, and the right arm *at that*. 私は腕を失なった. しかも右腕だ.

4 そのままでも ▪ *At that*, you can make a good profit. そのままでも君は大きな利益をあげることができる.

5 それにしても ▪ Tom and Helen are not strangers; but *at that*, I doubt whether he has known her long. トムとヘレンは全く知らない間柄ではない. がそれにしても彼が彼女と長い知り合いかどうか疑わしい.

6 なるほどそう言えば ▪ You are right *at that*. そう言えば君の言う通りだ.

at the East [***North, South***] 《米口》 東部[北部, 南部]地方で ▪ Slavery was defended *at the South* while it was antagonized *at the North*. 奴隷制度は北部では反対されたが, 南部では擁護された.

back at it (***again***) またやっている《通例非難して》 ▪ I thought you had stopped smoking, but I see you are *back at it again*. 君はタバコをやめたと思っていたけど, またやってるんだね.

be after *A* ***for*** *B* A(人)にBをしつこく求める[せきたてる] ▪ You *are* only *after* me *for* my money. 君は私にお金をねだるだけなんだね.

be at *A* ***about*** *B* A(人)にBのことを思い起こさせる[念を押す] ▪ He's *been at* me *about* the book he lent to me. 彼は私に貸してくれた本のことで念を押している.

where *one* ***is at*** 《米俗》 立場 ▪ He does not know *where* he *is at*. 彼は自分の立場を知らない ▪ The business world wants to know *where* it *is at*. 実業界は自己の現状を知りたく思っている. ☞《英》ではatは不要.

athirst /əθə́ːrst/ 形 (***be***) ***athirst for*** …を待ちこがれて[渇望して](いる) ▪ I *am athirst for* further news. 私は続報を待ちこがれている.

(***be***) ***athirst to*** *do* …しようと渇望して(いる) ▪ He *is athirst to* know the issue of the matter. 彼はその事件の結末を知りたがっている.

athwart /əθwɔ́ːrt/ 副 前 ***athwart*** (*a person's*) ***hawse*** 《海》(停泊している他船の)前方を横切って; 面と向かって ▪ He cocks his hat *athwart my hawse*. 彼はおれの面前で帽子を横っちょにかぶってみせる.

come [***fall***] ***athwart*** …の進路に立ちはだかるように現れる ▪ The ship *fell athwart* the Armada. その船は無敵艦隊の進路に立ちふさがった ▪ The image *comes athwart* his every thought. その姿は何を考えていてもすぐ彼の心に浮かんでくる.

go athwart **1** 思うようにいかない ▪ All *went athwart*. 万事思うようにいかなかった.

2 …をさえぎる; にさからう ▪ Things *went athwart* my purpose. 万事が私の目的をさまたげた.

lay ... athwart …を攻撃する ▪ We all *laid* them *athwart*. みんなで彼らを攻撃した.

run athwart …に斜めに[横に]ぶつかる ▪ He *ran athwart* a privateer and sank her. 彼は私掠(しりゃく)船に横にぶつかってそれを沈めた.

atmosphere /ǽtməsfìər/ 名 ***an atmosphere that one could cut with a knife*** 重苦しい緊張感や悪意に満ちた雰囲気 ▪ Meanwhile, the cockpit had *an atmosphere that one could cut with a knife*. その間操縦室は重苦しい雰囲気に包まれていた.

you can [***could***] ***cut the atmosphere with a knife*** 《口》 いかにも重苦しい雰囲気になっている ▪ Things are really hotting up, *you could cut the atmosphere with a knife*. 事態は真に危なくなって, いかにも重苦しい雰囲気になっていた.

atom /ǽtəm/ 名 ***an atom of*** 極微の ▪ There is not *an atom of* sense in what you say. 君の言うことにはもっともな点はみじんもない.

blow ... to atoms …をこっぱみじんに爆破する ▪ The building *was blown to atoms*. その建物は粉砕された.

break [***smash, shiver***]***... to*** [***into***] ***atoms*** …をこなみじんに砕く ▪ It would *shiver into atoms* some of our most potent ideas. それは我々の最も強力な思想のいくつかをこっぱみじんに打ち砕くだろう ▪ It can *break* this world *to atoms*. それはこの世

界をみじんに砕くことができる.

atonement /ətóʊnmənt/ 名 ***make atonement for*** …の償いをする ▪You must *make atonement for* the wrong you have done. 君は犯した悪行の罪滅ぼしをせねばならない.

attach /ətǽtʃ/ 動 ***attach importance*** [***weight***] ***to*** …に重きを置く ▪They *attach* too much *importance to* it. 彼らはそれを重く見すぎる.

attach itself to …にくっつく ▪Abalone *attaches itself to* rocks. アワビは岩にくっつく.

attach *oneself* ***to*** **1** (団体・党など)に所属する ▪He *attached himself to* the extreme left wing. 彼は極左翼に所属した.

2 …に愛着する ▪He *attaches himself* dearly *to* his wife. 彼は妻を深く愛している.

attached please find 同封しましたからどうぞお受け取りください《attached とはクリップで留めてあること》 ▪*Attached please find* a copy of the letter I wrote to Mr. Johnson. ジョンスン氏あての私の手紙の写しを同封しましたからお受け取りください.

(***be***) ***attached to*** **1** …に愛着[執着]して(いる) ▪A sailor *is* much *attached to* his ship. 船乗りは船に深い愛着を持っている.

2 …に属して(いる) ▪The officer *is attached to* the training squadron. その士官は練習艦隊付きだ ▪*Are* there sleeping cars *attached to* this train? この電車には寝台車がついているか.

attachment /ətǽtʃmənt/ 名 ***form an attachment for*** …が好きになる ▪He *formed an attachment for* a woman. 彼はある女を愛するようになった.

attack[1] /ətǽk/ 名 ***Attack is the best form of defense.*** 《諺》攻撃は最良の防衛.

blunt the attack (相手への)攻撃を弱める ▪The Republicans would *blunt the attack* on Obama's youth and inexperience. 共和党はオバマ氏の若さと経験不足への攻撃を弱めるだろう.

deliver [***make***] ***an attack on*** [***against***] …を攻撃する ▪They *made a* fierce *attack on* the enemy. 彼らは敵に猛攻を加えた.

have an attack of (病気)にかかる ▪The child *had an attack of* measles. 子供ははしかにかかった.

on the attack 攻撃[攻勢]に出て ▪Blackbirds are *on the attack* in Chicago. シカゴでムクドリモドキが攻撃に出ている.

attack[2] /ətǽk/ 動 ***be attacked with*** [***by***] (病気)にかかる ▪He *was attacked with* dysentery from drinking muddy water. 彼は泥水を飲んで赤痢にかかった.

attempt[1] /ətémpt/ 名 ***make an attempt at*** [***to*** *do*] …を[しようと]試みる ▪He *made an attempt at* suicide. 彼は自殺しようとした ▪He *made a* feeble *attempt to* restrain the zeal of the House of Commons. 彼は下院の熱意を押さえようと微力ながら努力した.

make an attempt on …を奪おうと企てる ▪They *made an attempt on* his life. 彼らは彼を殺害しようとした ▪The English *made an attempt on* the fortress. 英軍はその要塞の奪取を企てた.

attempt[2] /ətémpt/ 動 ***attempt the life of*** …の命を奪おうと企てる ▪The unbelieving Jews *attempted the life of* Jesus. 信仰のないユダヤ人たちはイエスの命を奪おうと企てた.

attend /əténd/ 動 ***be attended with*** (結果として)…が伴う《今は非物質的なものについてのみ言う》 ▪His plan *was attended with* great difficulties. 彼の計画には大きな困難が伴った ▪I believe that the project will *be attended with* success. そのプロジェクトはきっと成功すると思っている.

attendance /əténdəns/ 名 ***Attendance included.*** (ホテルなどで)サービス料込み.

dance attendance (***on***) →DANCE[2].

in attendance (***on***) (…に)つき添って ▪Major A was *in attendance on* the Emperor. A少佐は皇帝の侍従だった ▪The doctor is *in attendance on* him. 医者が彼についている.

include attendance サービス料を含める ▪Does the two pounds a week *include attendance*? 1週2ポンドというのはサービス料も入っているのか.

take [***check***] ***attendance*** 《米》出席を取る ▪I do not usually *take attendance*: college is not high school. 私は普通出席をとらない. 大学は高校じゃないから.

attendant /əténdənt/ 形 ***be attendant on*** **1** …につき添う, 奉仕する ▪The gentlemen *were attendant on* a great Earl. その紳士たちは偉い伯爵に奉仕していた.

2 …に伴う ▪Miseries *are attendant on* vice. 罪悪には不幸が伴う.

attention /əténʃən/ 名 ***arrest*** [***draw, attract***] ***attention*** (***to***) (…に)注意を引く ▪The *attention* of the police *was* never *attracted to* the matter. その件は全く警察の注意を引かなかった ▪Our *attention was attracted* by a singular noise. 我々は奇妙な音に気を取られた.

bring … to *a person's* ***attention*** …に人の注意を促す ▪The teacher *brought* these deficiencies *to my attention*. 先生はこれらの欠陥に私の注意を促した.

call attention (***to***) (…に)注意を引く[促す] ▪I wish to *call* your *attention to* this fact. 私はこの事実にあなたの注意を促したい.

call away [***off***] *a person's* ***attention*** 人の注意をそらす ▪*My attention was called away* to the shout. 私の注意はその叫びの方へそらされた.

catch *a person's* ***attention*** 人の注意を引く ▪An article by a friend of his *caught his attention*. 一友人の論文が彼の注意を引いた.

come to attention 気をつけ[不動]の姿勢になる ▪The soldiers *came to attention*. 兵は不動の姿勢をとった.

devote *one's* ***attention to*** …に専心する ▪He *devoted his attention to* his studies. 彼は勉学に専心した.

A

direct [***turn***] *one's* ***attention to*** …に心を向ける, を研究する, を論じる ▪ *Our attention* will *be directed* only *to* this. この事だけを論じることにする.

draw *a person's* ***attention to*** …に人の注意を引く ▪ Let me *draw your attention to* the following problem. 次の問題に君らの注意を喚起したい.

draw *oneself* ***up to attention*** 直立不動の姿勢をとる ▪ He *drew himself up to attention* and saluted. 彼は直立不動の姿勢をとって敬礼した.

for the attention of (会社などへの手紙が)…宛(あ)て, 気付 ▪ The letter is *for the attention of* Mr. Brown. この手紙はブラウン氏宛てのものです.

get [***have***] *a person's* ***undivided attention*** 人の集中した注意[世話]を受ける ▪ At the time I was the only customer, so I definately *got her undivided attention.* そのとき私は唯一の客だったので, 彼女のつきっきりの世話を受けた.

give attention to …に注意する; (勤め)を大事にやる ▪ *To* this we have already *given attention.* 我々はこのことは既に論じた ▪ You ought to *give attention to* your business. 自分の勤めを大事にやるべきである.

pay attention to **1** …に注意する, を重んじる ▪ He never *pays attention to* what she says. 彼は彼女の言うことにはいっこうかまわない.
2 …のきげんをとる ▪ Ben is *paying attention to* some young lady. ベンはある若い女性のきげんをとっている.

pay *one's* ***attentions to*** …のきげんをとる, に求愛する (= pay ATTENTION to 2) ▪ He is *paying his attentions to* an Italian countess. 彼はイタリアの伯爵夫人に求愛している.

receive [***have***] ***attention*** **1** (医師などの)手当てを受ける ▪ He *received* immediate *attention.* 彼はすぐに手当てを受けた.
2 手配を受ける ▪ Your letter shall *have* our earliest *attention.* お手紙の件はさっそく手配いたします.

spring [***jump***] (***to***) ***attention*** さっと不動の姿勢になる ▪ The soldier *sprang* (*to*) *attention.* 兵士はさっと不動の姿勢をとった.

stand (***at, to***) ***attention*** 不動の姿勢をとる[で立つ] ▪ A trooper *stood to attention.* 騎兵が不動の姿勢をとった.

turn *one's* ***attention to*** → direct one's ATTENTION to.

attentive /əténtɪv/ 形 ***be attentive to*** …に注意を払う; の世話をする, に気を配る ▪ *Be* more *attentive to* your studies. もっと勉強に精出してください ▪ She *was* very *attentive to* her little brother. 彼女は弟の世話をよくした.

attic /ǽtɪk/ 名形 ***have rats in the attic*** 《口》害をせぬ狂人である ▪ He has *had rats in the attic* since he was a boy. 彼は幼少時から気が変だ.

the attic story 《戯》頭 ▪ He is queer in *the attic story.* 彼は頭が変である.

attire /ətáɪər/ 動 ***attire*** *oneself* ***in*** 《文》…を着る, 着用する ▪ The girls *were attired in* their best clothes. 少女たちは晴れ着を着ていた.

attitude /ǽtətjù:d/ 名 ***a holier-than-thou attitude*** いかにも相手よりも徳が高いといわんばかりの態度, 独善的な態度 ▪ He was disappointed that the public has adopted *a holier-than-thou attitude* on the issue. 世間がこの問題に対して独善的な態度をとったので彼はがっかりした.

assume [***take***] ***a strong attitude toward*** [***to, on***] …に強硬な態度をとる ▪ We must *assume a strong attitude toward* the employer. 雇主に対して強硬な態度をとらねばならない.

have an attitude 《米俗》態度が悪い ▪ My dog *has an attitude.* うちの犬は強硬な態度をとる.

have an attitude problem 自己中心的[非協力的]な態度を取る, 自分勝手な人間である ▪ Ben *has an attitude problem* at school that needs to change. ベンは学校で自己中心的な態度をとっているので, それを改める必要がある ▪ Your boss *has an attitude problem.* 君の上司は自分勝手な人間だ.

strike an attitude 《古風》気取った[わざとらしい]様子をする, きざな態度をとる ▪ The actor, *striking an attitude*, quoted Shakespeare. 俳優は気取った態度でシェイクスピアを引用した.

with attitude つっぱった[自信のある, 気取った]態度で ▪ Treat everyone *with attitude* and courtesy. 万人に自信のある態度でいんぎんに接しなさい.

attorney /ətə́:rni/ 名 ***by attorney*** (委任状による)代理人で (↔in PERSON 1) ▪ I went to receive his permit *by attorney.* 私は委任状による代理人で彼の証明書を受け取りに行った ▪ No, die *by attorney.* いいえ, 死ぬのは身代わりにまかせなさい《cf. Sh., *A. Y. L.* 4.1.89》.

attribute /ətríbjət|ətríbju:t/ 動 ***be attributed to*** …のせいにされている; の作品であるとされている ▪ Their failure *is attributed to* a lack of preparation. 彼らの失敗は準備不足のせいだとされている ▪ The statement "know thyself" *is attributed to* Socrates. 「なんじ自身を知れ」という言葉はソクラテスのものであるとされている.

attune /ətjú:n/ 動 ***be attuned to*** …をよく知っている ▪ Parents should *be attuned to* their children's behavior. 親は子供のふるまいに精通すべきだ.

auction /ɔ́:kʃən/ 名 ***a Dutch auction*** 《英口》逆競り, 競り下げ競売 ▪ The U.S. Treasury uses *a Dutch auction* to sell securities. 米財務省は国債を売るために逆競りを利用する.

at auction 競売で ▪ The books were disposed of *at auction.* 書物は競売で処分された.

be [***come***] ***up for auction*** →UP[1].

on the auction block 競売にかけられて ▪ His library is going *on the auction block* in December. 彼の蔵書は12月に競売にかけられる.

put up at [***for,*** 《英》 ***to***] ***auction*** 競売に付する ▪ They *put* them *up at auction.* 彼らはそれらを競売に付した.

sell at [《英》 ***by***] ***auction*** 競売で売る ▪ These *were sold by auction.* これらは競売で売られた.

audience /ɔ́:diəns/ 名 ***a captive audience*** とらわれの聴衆《バスの乗客のようにいやでも聞かなければならない聴衆》 ▪ Can you count on having *a captive audience*? 相手がとらわれの聴衆である当てがありますか.

admit *a person* ***in audience*** →receive a person in AUDIENCE.

audience of leave いとまごいの会見 ▪ I gave him to understand that this was an *audience of leave*. 彼にこれが別れ(の会見)であることを悟らせた.

give *a person* ***an audience*** 人から聴取する, 人の言うことを聞く ▪ The committee will *give* you *an audience* to hear your plan. 委員会は君を呼んで君の計画を聴取するだろう.

grant an audience 謁見を許す (*to*) ▪ The king *granted* him *an audience* [*granted an audience to* him]. 国王は彼に拝謁を許した.

have an audience of [***with***] ...に謁見する, 拝謁する; に話しかけることを許される ▪ He *had an audience of* [*with*] the king of England. 彼は英国王に拝謁した.

receive [***admit***] *a person* ***in audience*** 人に拝謁を許す ▪ The king *admitted* him *in audience*. 国王は彼に拝謁を許した ▪ The ambassador *was received in audience* by the Emperor. 大使は皇帝に謁見を許された.

aught /ɔ:t/ 名 ***for aught I care*** 《古・詩》どうにでもなれ ▪ He may starve *for aught I care*. 彼が餓死したとてかまうものか.

for aught I know (***to the contrary***) →FOR all one knows.

augur /ɔ́:gər/ 動 ***augur well*** [***ill***] **1** 縁起がよい[悪い] (*for*) (→BODE well) ▪ This *augurs well for* our scheme. これは我々の計画の吉兆だ.

2 吉[凶]と占う (*of, for*) ▪ I *augur ill of* his success [*for* his voyage]. 彼の成功は怪しいと思う[航海はおもしろくないと思う] ▪ I *augured well for* my reception. この分なら自分は歓待されるぞと思った.

aunt /ænt|ɑ:nt/ 名 ***My giddy aunt!*** 《口》おやまあ! ▪ *My giddy aunt!* Look at that house! おやまあ! あの家をごらん!

My (***sainted***) ***aunt!*** 《軽い感嘆》おや, まあ! ▪ "*My sainted aunt!*" exclaimed Guy, with a start. 「おや!」とガイはびっくりして叫んだ.

auspice /ɔ́:spəs/ 名 ***take auspices*** 吉凶の占いをする《鳥を用いて》 ▪ *Auspices were taken* when he was appointed. 彼が任命されたとき吉凶占いがなされた.

under fair auspices さい先良く ▪ His career was begun *under fair auspices*. 彼の閲歴はさい先良く始められた.

under the auspices of ...の後援で, の賛助の下に; の主催で ▪ The meeting was held *under the auspices of* the university. その会は大学の主催で開かれた ▪ The book was published *under the auspices of* the Royal Society of Literature. その本は王立文学協会の賛助の下に出版された.

authority /əθɔ́:rəti|ɔ:θɔ́r-/ 名 ***by the authority of*** ...の権威で; の許可を得て ▪ *By whose authority* do you act? 誰の許可を得てそうするのか ▪ The locution is sanctioned *by the authority of* the best writers. その語法は一流作家たちが使っているので許されている.

carry authority 権威がある, 重きをなす ▪ Words cannot *carry authority* so weighty. 言葉にはそれほど重い権威はない.

give (***an***) ***authority for*** ...に対する典拠を示す ▪ No *authority is given for* the statement. その陳述には何ら出典が示されていない.

give *a person* (***an***) ***authority for*** [***to*** *do*] 人に...の[する]権限を与える ▪ I *gave* him *an authority to* examine it. 私は彼にそれを調べる権限を与えた.

have authority with [***over***] ...に対してにらみがきく ▪ He *has* no *authority over* his children. 彼は子供ににらみがきかない.

in authority 権勢ある ▪ The people *in authority* would try to stop him. 権勢ある人々が彼を止めようとするだろう.

on [***from***] ***good*** [***excellent***] ***authority*** 確かな筋から ▪ I have it *on good authority*. 私はそれを確かな筋から聞いている.

on *one's* (***own***) ***authority*** 自己の一存で; 自分免許の ▪ I acted *on my own authority*. 僕は僕の一存で行動した ▪ He is a doctor *on his own authority*. 彼は自分免許の博士だ.

on the authority of ...を典拠として ▪ Do not accept news *on the authority of* the papers. 新聞に出たからとて真に受けるな.

under the authority of ...の支配下で ▪ They are *under the authority of* the War Department. 彼らは陸軍省の管轄下にある.

with authority 権威をもって; 厳然と ▪ I can speak *with authority*. 私は権威をもって申しあげられます.

autumn /ɔ́:təm/ 名 ***autumn years*** 《文》(仕事しなくなった)初老期, 晩年 ▪ He spent his *autumn years* in misery. 彼は晩年をみじめに過ごした.

avail[1] /əvéɪl/ 名 ***of avail*** 役に立って; 有効で ▪ *Of* what *avail* is it? それは何の甲斐があるのか ▪ It may be *of* some *avail*. それはいくぶん役に立つかもしれない.

of little [***no***] ***avail*** あまり[少しも]役に立たない ▪ Her words were *of little avail*. 彼女の言葉はあまり役に立たなかった ▪ Every effort was *of no avail*. あらゆる努力も無駄だった.

of little or no avail あまりあるいは全く効力がない ▪ The life jacket was *of little or no avail*. 救命胴衣はほとんどあるいは全く役に立たなかった.

to little [***no***] ***avail*** あまり[少しも]成功しない ▪ I labored hard *to little avail*. 大いに骨折ったがほとんど甲斐がなかった ▪ He tried to revive the woman but *to no avail*. 彼はその女性をよみがえらせようとしたが, まるで無益だった.

without avail 無効で ▪ He tried hard to get it,

but *without avail.* 彼はそれを得ようと一生懸命やってみたが無駄だった.

avail[2] /əvéɪl/ 動 ***avail** a person **nothing*** 人になんの役にも立たない ▪Our wealth *avails* us *nothing*; all must die. 富は我々になんの役にも立たない; みんな死なねばならないのだから.

avail** oneself **of 《文》…を利用する; を無にしない ▪I *availed myself of* my position to make an excursion into North Wales. 私は自分の地位を利用して北ウェールズへ旅行した ▪Then I shall *avail myself of* your kind offer. ではお言葉に甘えさせていただきます.

available /əvéɪləbəl/ 形 ***be available for*** …に役に立つ; 《米》を望んでいる ▪A yacht *is available for* fishing. ヨットは魚釣りに役立つ ▪He *was available for* the Senate. 彼は上院議員出馬を望んでいた.

***make** a thing **available for** [**to**]* …に物を利用させる; に物を入手させる ▪He has a burning desire to *make* the best science *available to* all. 彼は最優秀の科学を万人に与えようという燃えるような願望をいだいている.

avenge /əvéndʒ/ 動 ***avenge** oneself **on*** 《文》(人)に復しゅうする ▪I will *avenge myself on* him. 彼に復しゅうしてやる.

be avenged on …に報復する (= AVENGE oneself on) ▪He swears he will *be avenged on* them sooner or later. 彼はいつかは彼らに恨みをはらしてやると断言している. ☞avenge は「公憤を感じてあだを討つ」, revenge は「私の恨みを晴らす」の意.

avenue /ǽvənjùː/ 名 ***explore every avenue/leave no avenue unexplored*** 《主に政治・商業・新聞》あらゆる手段[探究]を尽くす ▪We'll *explore every avenue* to find a way out of our difficulties. 我々は窮境から抜け出す道を見いだすためあらゆる手段を尽くすつもりだ ▪He *left no avenue unexplored.* 彼はあらゆる手段を尽くした.

the other end of the Avenue 《米》米国国会議事堂; ホワイトハウス《大統領官邸》 ▪Thus far peace prevailed between the Capitol and *the other end of the Avenue.* これまでのところ国会議事堂とホワイトハウスの間は平和であった. ☞ワシントンの Pennsylvania Avenue の一方の端に議事堂, 他方の端にホワイトハウスがあることから.

average /ǽvərɪdʒ/ 名 ***above* (*the*) *average*** 平均以上で ▪Tom's work at school is *above the average.* トムの学業は平均より上だ.

at* [*on*] (*an, the*) *average 平均して ▪Earthquake shocks occur, *on an average*, about three times a week. 地震は平均して週に3回起こる.

below* (*the*) *average 平均以下で ▪My crop is *below the average.* うちの作は平年以下だ.

on average =at (an, the) AVERAGE.

strike an average 平均を出す, 平均を取ってみる ▪It is difficult to *strike an average.* 平均を出すのはむずかしい.

strike** a person's **average →STRIKE[2].

up to the average 平均に達して ▪Jim's work at school is about *up to the average.* ジムの学業は大体平均に達している.

averse /əvɚ́ːrs/ 形 ***averse to* [*from, to do*]** (…するの)がきらいで, に反対で ▪I am not *averse to* a good dinner. ごちそうならいやではない ▪He is *averse to* coming [*to* come] here. 彼はここへ来るのをいやがっている ▪His impulses were *averse from* cruelty. 彼の情は残酷の反対であった. ☞averse from は語源的には正しいが, やや衒学的.

aversion /əvɚ́ːrʒən|-ʃən/ 名 ***have an aversion to* [*from, to do*(*ing*)]** (…すること)をきらう, に反対である ▪I *have* no *aversion to* going by different names. 私はいろいろ異なった名前で通ることがいやでない ▪Some boys *have an aversion to* hard study. 精出して勉強することが嫌いな少年もいる.

avid /ǽvɪd/ 形 ***avid of* [*for*]** …に貪慾で, をむさぼって ▪He is *avid for* food. 彼は食物に飢えている ▪A miser is *avid of* money. けちん坊は金がほしくてたまらない.

avidity /əvídəti/ 名 ***with avidity*** むさぼるように ▪I used to read magazines *with avidity.* 雑誌をむさぼるように読んだものだ.

avoid /əvɔ́ɪd/ 動 ***avoid ... like the plague*** → PLAGUE[1].

avow /əváʊ/ 動 ***avow** oneself* (***to be***) 自分が…であると公言する ▪He *avowed himself to be* a communist. 彼は共産主義者だと公言した ▪He *avowed himself* in the wrong. 彼は自分がまちがっていたと告白した.

awake[1] /əwéɪk/ 形 ***be awake to*** …に気づいている, を悟って[十分知って]いる ▪I *am* quite *awake to* all they are doing. 彼らのしていることはちゃんと知っている ▪You should *be awake to* the danger of your position. 君の立場の危険を悟るべきだ.

(***be***) ***wide awake*** **1** すっかり目がさめて ▪After drinking too much coffee, I found myself *wide awake* at 2 a.m. コーヒーを飲みすぎたあと, 2時になってもまだ目が冴(さ)えていた.

2 油断がない, よく気づいている (*to*) ▪He *is* always *wide awake to* his own interest. 彼はいつも自分の利益には抜け目がない.

awake[2] /əwéɪk/ 動 ***awake to find*** 目がさめて…と知る ▪I *awoke to find* myself famous. 私は目がさめたら有名になっていた.

awakening /əwéɪkənɪŋ/ 名 ***a rude awakening*** 《文》(不快な事実の)突然の認識, 幻滅 ▪They will get [suffer] *a rude awakening* when their family business is sold. 彼らは家業が売られたとき, 幻滅を味わうだろう.

aware /əwéər/ 形 ***be well aware*** 十分承知している (*of, that*) ▪I *am well aware of* the dangers. 危険のことは十分承知している ▪I *am well aware that* I have invited criticism. 自分が批判を招いたことは十分承知している.

awash /əwɑ́ʃ|əwɔ́ːʃ/ 形 ***set ... awash*** …を水に浸す ▪The rising water *set* everything *awash.*

差し潮がすべてのものを水に浸してしまった.

away /əwéɪ/ 副 ***Are we away?*** 《口》(もう)行こうか, さあ出発だ.

away ahead 《米》はるかに優勢で ▪He was *away ahead* on points up to the 12th round. 彼は12ラウンドまでは得点がはるかに優勢であった.

away back 《米口》ずっと昔; ...の昔に早くも; ずっと後方に ▪He insisted upon this *away back* in the Revolution. 彼は大革命の昔に早くもこのことを主張した ▪Farms and settlements were thicker *away back*. ずっと後方には農場や開拓地がもっと多かった.

away behind 《米》ずっと遅れて (=《英》far BEHIND) ▪Manufacturers of all good cars are *away behind* in their deliveries. すべての良い自動車の製造者たちからの引渡しがずっと遅れている.

away below 《米口》ずっと下方の ▪The mercury is *away below* the freezing point. 水銀柱は氷点下よりずっと下がっている.

away down 《米口》 **1** ずっと下手(しもて)の ▪*Away down* in the South is a great country called California. はるか下手の南部にカリフォルニアという大きな地域がある.

2 ずっと下位の ▪Boston is *away down* in 21st place. ボストンはずっと下って21位である.

away down east 《米口》東部沿岸のはるか北の方《Maine 州, または New England, Nova Scotia 沿岸》 ▪I am a miner, who wandered from *away down east*. おれは東部沿岸のずっと北から渡って来た鉱夫だ.

away from home →HOME.

away from it all 《口》生活の煩わしさを逃れて ▪*Away from it all*, he was able to study English peacefully. 日常生活の煩わしさを逃れて, 彼は静かに英語を研究することができた. ☞get away の get を省いたもの.

away up 《米口》 **1** ずっと上って ▪Turkeys are *away up* in price. 七面鳥はずっと値が上がっている.

2 ずっと上の ▪He lives *away up* in Canada. 彼はずっと上のカナダに住んでいる.

away with 〚動詞を省略して〛 **1** 〚命令形で〛去れ, 取り去れ; やっつけろ ▪*Away with* you this very moment! 今すぐうせろ! ▪*Away with* him! 彼を追っ払え! ▪*Away with* him, crucify him! 彼をやっつけろ, はりつけにせよ!

2 ...をがまんする; ...なしでやっていく ▪I cannot *away with* that man. あの男にはがまんできない.

(***be***) ***well away*** →WELL[2].

come away そこを離れて来る ▪*Come away*, death! 死よ, やって来い.

far and away はるかに ▪It is *far and away* the best. それは飛びぬけて一番良い.

(***for***) ***once and away*** →ONCE (and) for all.

from away 《米》遠方から ▪Capitalists *from away* are making an effort to establish an industry here. 遠方からの資本家たちが当地に事業を起こす努力をしている.

from away back 《米口》 **1** ずっと昔から; ずっと後方から ▪The Allens, *from away back*, have been founts of wisdom. アレン家の人々はずっと昔から知恵の源泉であった.

2 (人・物について)全くの, とびきりの ▪Now this Waters was a fighter *from away back*. さてこのウォーターズという男は全くの闘士だった.

have it away (***on*** *one's* ***toes***) 《英口》素早く立ち去る, 急いで逃げる ▪I *had it away on my toes* back to England, where I was arrested. 私はイングランドへ急いで逃げ戻り, そこで逮捕された.

out and away →OUT[1].

right away →RIGHT[1].

straight away →STRAIGHT.

Where away? どちらに? (In what direction?) 《船から見えた物について言う》.

Whither away? どこへ向かっているのか (Where are you going?).

awe /ɔː/ 名 ***hold*** [***keep***] *a person* ***in awe*** (***of***) 人に(...を)常に恐れさせる ▪Nations *were kept in awe of* his name. 諸国は彼の名を絶えず恐れていた.

in awe of ...を恐れかしこんで ▪American Indians often live *in awe of* nature. 北米先住民はしばしば自然を恐れかしこんで暮らす.

put *a person* ***in awe of*** 人に...を畏怖させる ▪God's majesty will *put* you *in awe of* him. 神の威厳はあなたに神を畏怖させるだろう.

stand [***be***] ***in awe of*** **1** ...を大いに恐れている, 恐れはばかっている ▪Therefore *stand in awe of* God. それゆえ神を大いに恐れよ.

2 ...に深い崇敬の念をいだく ▪My heart *stands in awe of* your words. 私の心はあなたのお言葉を深く崇敬しています.

awesome /ɔ́ːsəm/ 形 ***totally awesome*** 《俗》すごくいい, すばらしい ▪Have you seen "Last Samurai"? It is *totally awesome*. 「ラスト・サムライ」を見たかい. すっごくいいよ.

awkward /ɔ́ːkwərd/ 形 ***be awkward at*** [***with***] ...がまずい, へまだ ▪He *is awkward at* handling tools. 彼は道具の使い方がまずい.

feel awkward 間が悪い ▪I *felt awkward* as everyone except me was in evening dress. 私以外の人がみな夜会服を着ていたので間の悪い思いをした.

the awkward age 子供とも大人ともつかぬ年頃, 思春期《この時期の男女は情緒不安定で言動がぎこちないことから》 ▪She is at *the awkward age* now. 彼女は今は思春期だ.

awl /ɔːl/ 名 ***pack up*** *one's* ***awls*** 持ち物いっさいを取りまとめる ▪I'll *pack up my awls* and be gone. 家財いっさい取りまとめて出て行きます. ☞awls は alls と発音が同じであるから, 音のしゃれとする説もある.

AWOL /éɪwɑ̀l|-wɔ̀l/ 形 ***go*** [***be***] ***AWOL*** 《米》無断欠勤する ▪Bill *went AWOL* and got a good scolding by the boss. ビルは無断欠勤したのでボスにこっぴどくしかられた ▪He *went AWOL* yesterday. 彼は昨日無断欠勤した. ☞《軍》AWOL = absent

A

without leave.

awry /ərάɪ/ 副形 ***be awry from*** …に反する ▪ Nothing *is* more *awry from* the law of God. これほど神のおきてに反するものはない.

go [***run, tread***] ***awry*** (人が)誤る, まちがいをする; (物が)うまくいかない ▪ He was so just that he would not *tread awry*. 彼は非常に正しい人だったからまちがったことはしようとしなかった ▪ The marriage itself *went awry*. 結婚そのものがうまくいかなかった.

look [***glance***] ***awry*** 横目で見る; ひがんで見る ▪ Some of our party began to squint and *look awry*. 我々の仲間には横目を使い始める者もあった.

step awry →step ASTRAY.

tread the shoe awry 堕落する; 不義をする ▪ Their mother happened to *tread the shoe awry*. 彼らの母親がたまたま不義をした.

ax, 《英》 **axe** /æks/ 名 ***an*** [***the***] ***ax is hanging over…*** (人が)仕事を失いそうである, (組織が)人員を削減されそうである ▪ *The axe was hanging over* 600 jobs at the oil company last night. 昨夜, その石油会社では600以上の仕事が削減されそうになっていた.

apply the ax to …に鉈(なた)をふるう, を削減する ▪ We must *apply the ax to* our annual expenditure. 我々は歳出を削減せねばならない.

bury the ax 仲直りする, 和解する ▪ Let's *bury the ax*, shall we? 仲直りしようではないか.

face the ax 《口》首になりそうである ▪ U.S. nuclear recycling *faces the ax*. 米国核再利用が廃止されそうである ▪ Four Ministers *face the ax*. 4人の大臣が職を失いそうである.

get [***give***] ***the ax*** 《口》 **1** 首になる[する], 解雇される[する] ▪ He *got the ax* through neglect of his duties. 彼は職務怠慢で首になった ▪ His boss finally *gave* him *the ax*. 社長はついに彼を首にした.
2 退学処分を受ける[にする] ▪ Bill got caught cheating in his final exam and *got the ax*. ビルは最終試験で不正行為をして退学処分を受けた.
3 けんかをしてふられる[ふる] ▪ Jim *got the ax* from his girlfriend—they won't see each other again. ジムは彼女にふられた—二人は二度と会うことはあるまい.
4 (計画などが)中止される[する], 縮小される[する] ▪ The project *was given the ax* after succeeding at the initial stage. そのプロジェクトは初期段階で成功したあと中止された.

hang up one's ax →HANG up one's gun.

have an ax to grind 胸に一物ある; 思わくがある ▪ He evidently *has an ax to grind*. 彼はどうも胸に一物あるようだ ▪ I *have* no political *ax to grind*. 私に政治的な下心はない ▪ In suggesting the sale of the building he *had an ax to grind*. 彼がその建物を売ってはと言い出したのは, 思わくあってのことだった.

lay [***set***] ***the ax to the root of*** …を滅ぼしにかかる; の根本に斧を加える; 根本的治療をする (《聖》*Matt.* 3. 10) ▪ Two stern realists have *set the ax to the root of* the tree of hypocrisy. 二人の仮借なき現実主義者が偽善を痛撃しにかかった ▪ They *laid the ax to the root of* the evil. 彼らは悪弊の根本的治療をした.

put the ax in the helve 《古》疑い[難問, 謎]を解く.

set the axe to …を切り倒す; (計画など)を葬る ▪ Let's *set the axe to* the old tree. その老木を切り倒そう ▪ The opposition *set the axe to* the plan. 反対党はその計画を葬った.

axis /ǽksəs/ 名 ***turn on its axis*** 自転する ▪ The earth *turns on its axis* once in twenty-four hours. 地球は24時間に1回自転する.

aye /aɪ/ 副間名 ***ayes and noes*** 賛成と反対 ▪ The president counted the *ayes and noes*. 会長は賛否を数えた.

The ayes have it. 賛成者多数. ▪ *The ayes have it*, and the motion is adopted. 賛成多数, よって動議は採決されました.

B

B /biː/ 名 ***a B. and S.*** 《俗》ソーダ水で割ったブランデー(1杯) ▪ I'd like *a B. and S.* ブランデーソーダをください.

B.Y.O. 《口》(パーティーでお酒)各自持参のこと ▪ You can bring your own booze to these great *B.Y.O* restaurants. ワイン持込み可のこれらの素敵なレストランへは自分用の酒を持参してよい. ☞Bring your own.

hang a B.A. 《米俗》(ふざけて, またはあざけって)裸の尻を出す(《英》throw a MOON) ▪ Mark was angry and *hung a B.A. at* the cop. マークは怒って警官に向けて裸の尻を出した. ☞B.A. = bare-assed.

not know (a) B from a bull's foot 全く無学で字が読めない, きわめて無知で ▪ Some of those kids do*n't know B from a bull's foot*. 中には全く字の読めない子供もいる.

babe /beɪb/ 名 ***a babe in arms*** うぶな人, 世間知らず ▪ He is just *a babe in arms* in baseball terms. 彼は野球用語についてはずぶの素人だ.

a babe in Christ キリスト教への新改宗者 ▪ Even *babes in Christ* are perfect in such a sense. キリスト教へ新たに改宗した者たちですらそのような意味では完全である.

a babe in the wood(s) 単純で信じやすい子供; うぶで無経験な人 ▪ Those *babes in the woods*, uncle Sam and aunt Fanny, trusted him. その世間知らず, つまりサムおじさんとファニーおばさんはその男を信用した. ☞おじにむごく扱われた孤児が二人森へ逃げて餓死したという古い民謡から.

a babe magnet (多くの女性を惹きつける)ハンサムな青年, イケメン ▪ Max became *a babe magnet* without surgery. マックスは整形手術をせずにイケメンになった.

babes and sucklings 乳飲み子, いたいけな子供(《聖》*Ps.* 8. 2) ▪ Truth comes out of the mouths of *babes and sucklings*. 真理はいたいけな子供の口から漏れる.

Babel /béɪbəl, bǽb-/ 名 ***a babel of voices*** やかましい話し声 ▪ *A babel of voices* was heard from a schoolroom window. 教室の窓からがやがやという声が聞こえてきた. ☞Babel は《聖》*Gen.* 11にあるバベルの塔のこと; ノアの洪水のあと, 人々は天に届かせる計画で Shinar に建てようとしたが, 言語の混乱をきたしたので中止したという.

baby /béɪbi/ 名 ***a (baby) boomer*** 《主に米》ベビーブームに生まれた人 ▪ The new president is *a baby boomer*, born in 1960. 新社長は1960年生まれのベビーブーマーだ.

a baby grand 小型グランドピアノ ▪ A *baby grand* can easily fit into a smaller living room. 小型グランドピアノなら比較的狭い居間にも楽に入る.

a baby kisser 《米俗》愛嬌をふりまく選挙立候補者 ▪ He was *a baby kisser* when he ran for Presidency. 彼は大統領戦に立候補したとき盛んに愛嬌をふりまいた.

baby boom 出生率の急増; ベビーブーム ▪ China is expecting a *baby boom* this lunar year—the year of the pig. 中国はこの太陰年—亥年がベビーブームになると予期している.

be left holding the baby いやな責任を背負い込まされる; 売れない株を持たされる ▪ In a few cases they *were left holding the baby*. 2, 3回彼らはいやな責任を背負い込まされた.

empty [pour, throw] the baby out [away] with the bath(water) 《口》浴槽の水とともに赤んぼうを棄ててしまう《無用の物と一緒に大事な物を捨てる》 ▪ We shall be *emptying the baby out with the bath* by abolishing the institution. その施設を廃止すれば無用の物と共に大事な物を捨てることになる.

give** a person **the baby to hold 人に責任をなすりつけて逃げる ▪ You are not to *give* me *the baby to hold*. 僕に責任をなすりつけて逃げさせないぞ.

hand over the baby to = give a person the BABY to hold.

hold [carry] the baby いやな(またはやっかいな)役目を背負い込む ▪ We do not intend to *hold the baby*. 我々はいやな役目を背負い込むつもりはない.

It's your [his,** etc.**] baby. それは君[彼, など]のするべきことだ ▪ *It's your baby*, not mine. それは君のするべきことで, 僕の知ったことではない. ☞強勢は your [his, etc.] にある.

pass the baby 《俗》責任を押しつける(*to*) ▪ Don't *pass the baby to* me. 私に責任を押しつけないでほしい.

play the baby act 《米》幼稚な行いをする ▪ Did they *play the baby act* and go on strike? 彼らは幼稚にもストライキをやったのか.

plead the baby act 《米》言い訳[弁護]として幼年[未熟]を申し立てる ▪ He is *pleading the baby act*, and says he was a boy when he wrote it. 彼は弁解として幼少を申し立て, それを書いたときは少年だったと言っている. ☞baby act = infancy act「幼児保護法」.

smell of the baby 《軽蔑》子供じみている ▪ Do what they can, they will *smell of the baby*. 彼らが何をしても, 子供じみているだろう.

start a baby 《主に英口》妊娠する ▪ *Starting a baby* isn't always easy. 妊娠することは必ずしも容易ではない.

the baby blues 産後の鬱状態 ▪ The article says that 60% of women suffer from *the baby blues*. その論文によれば女性の6割は産後の鬱状態に悩まされるとのことだ.

wet the baby's head →HEAD[1].

bach[1] /bætʃ/ 名 ***keep bach*** 《米俗》独身生活をする ▪ Me marry? No, I'm gonna *keep bach* forever. 私が結婚するだって? いや, ずっと独身を通すつもりだ. ☞bach=bachelor.

bach[2] /bætʃ/ 動 ***bach it*** 《米俗》独身生活をする ▪ He always *bached it*. 彼は独身生活を通した.

bachelor /bǽtʃələr/ 名 ***a bachelor's wife*** 独身者が心に描く理想の妻 ▪ The *bachelor's wife* occupies a large place in our literature. 独身者が夢見る理想の妻がわが国の文学においては大きな地位を占めている.

keep bachelor('s) hall 《米》独身生活をする ▪ He *keeps bachelor hall* in a small bungalow near the village. 彼は村の近くの小さなバンガローで独身生活をしている. ☞bachelor('s) hall《米》「独身者のアパート」.

back[1] /bæk/ 名形副 ***a back number*** → NUMBER[1].

act behind** a person's **back 人の陰で暗躍する ▪ He *acted behind the manager's back*. 彼は支配人の背後で暗躍した.

as soon as** one's **back is turned →when one's BACK is turned.

at** one's [a person's] **back …の背後に[を追っかけて; を支持して] ▪ They are *at our backs*. 彼らは我々を追っかけている ▪ You knew I was *at your back*. 君は僕が後ろについていることを知っていた ▪ Caesar had the people *at his back*. カエサルは民衆の支持を得ていた.

at the back of **1** …の後ろに ▪ There is a garden *at the back of* the house. 家の後ろに庭がある. **2** …の背後に(隠れて); を支持して ▪ Some one must be *at the back of* this. この背後には誰か(黒幕が)いるにちがいない.

at the back of** one's **mind 心の奥底[片隅]に ▪ The story is permanently *at the back of my mind*. その話は永久に私の心の奥底に残っている.

back and edge 全く, あくまで; 必死に ▪ They were working *back and edge* for me. 彼らは私のために精いっぱい働いてくれていた ▪ I will have no more to do with you *back and edge*. もう君とはすっかり縁を切る.

back and forth [forward] 《米》あちこちに(行ったり来たりして)(=《英》TO and fro) ▪ The railroad made it possible for Mr. Cook to go *back and forth* to his law office. 鉄道ができてクック氏は自分の法律事務所へ行ったり来たりすることができた ▪ Barristers flitted *back and forward* through the passages. 弁護士たちは通路を足早に行ったり来たりした.

back chat [talk] 《口》(目上の人に対する)生意気[失敬]な口答え ▪ I will tolerate no *back talk* from you. 私は君に生意気な口答えは許さない ▪ Such *back talk* won't get you anywhere. そんな生意気な受け応えではらちがあかないよ.

back home 《米》うちでは, 故郷では ▪ We spend our days very quietly *back home*. うちではごく静かに日を過ごします.

one's ***back is against the wall*** 追い詰められている, 窮地に陥っている ▪ Obama is always at his best when *his back is against the wall*. オバマ氏はいつも窮地に陥っているときに一番力量を発揮する.

a person's ***back is turned*** 《口》(監督者が)背を向ける, 目を放す ▪ Jim starts to throw spitballs as soon as *the teacher's back is turned*. 先生が背を向けるや否やジムは紙つぶてを投げ始める.

one's ***back is up*** 立腹している ▪ *Dad's back is up* this morning. おやじは今朝は怒っている.

back number 時代遅れの(もの), 流行遅れの(もの) ▪ That hat is really a *back number*. あの帽子はほんとに流行遅れだ.

back of 《米口》…の後ろに[の]; の背後に[の] (=in (the) BACK of) ▪ I know the organization *back of* him. 彼の背後にある団体を知っている ▪ The house lies *back of* the Sunday school. その家は日曜学校の後ろにある.

back to back/back-to-back 《主に米口》(出来事が)連続の[して], 続けざまの[に] ▪ He saw the three movies *back to back*. 彼は立て続けに3本の映画を見た ▪ Matsui hit *back-to-back* homers at the Yankee Stadium. 松井はヤンキースタジアムで立て続けにホームランを打った.

back to back (with) (…と)背中合わせに; (と)互いに助け合って ▪ My house is *back to back with* his. 私の家は彼の家と背中合わせだ ▪ You and I must stick close, *back to back*. 君と僕とはがっちり組んで互いに助け合わなければならない.

back to front 前後を逆にして, 後ろ前に ▪ He has got his pullover on *back to front*. 彼はプルオーバーを後ろ前に着ている.

Back to the salt mines. →MINE[1].

be back of **1** …を支持する ▪ They *were* solidly *back of* Miss Jones. 彼らは結束してジョーンズ嬢を支持していた. **2** …の理由[原因]で ▪ Hard work *was back of* his success. 勤勉が彼の成功の原因だった.

be on** a person's **back →get on a person's BACK.

be [be laid, lie] on** one's **back →on one's BACK.

behind** a person's **back 〚behind を強調して〛…の陰で ▪ You're always running him down *behind his back*. 君はいつも陰で彼をけなしている ▪ The government went *behind their backs* and concluded an agreement. 政府はこっそり彼らの背後に回って協定を結んだ.

behind backs こっそりと ▪ They are always criticizing her *behind backs*. 彼らはひそかに彼女のあら捜しばかりしている.

break** one's **back 《口》懸命に働く[努力する] (=break one's NECK) ▪ I'm not going to *break my back* working for such low wages. 私はそんな低賃金で懸命に働く気はない.

break the back of **1** ...の背骨を折る, をくじく; を殺す, 不具にする ▪ The fall of the stone has *broken the back of* that horse. 石が落ちてきてその馬の背骨を折った.
2 ...には荷が重すぎる; を無力にする; を破産させる ▪ This house is enough to *break my back*. この商館はどうも私には荷が重すぎる ▪ I think we've *broken the back of* this division. 我々はこの師団を無能力にしたと思う ▪ That last loss had *broken Mr. Smith's back*. あの最近の損失のためスミス氏は破産したのだった.
3 (仕事などの)最悪[最困難]の部分を終える ▪ I have *broken the back of* the journey overland to Kyoto. 陸路の京都への旅をほとんど終えた ▪ How is your book going?—I've *broken the back of* it. 君の著書の進行状況はどうかね—とうげを越したよ. ☞動物の料理で背骨が一番むずかしい所であることから.

carry ... on *one's* ***back*** ...を背負う(て行く), おんぶする ▪ A Japanese mother used to *carry* her baby *on her back*. 以前日本の母親は赤んぼうをおんぶしたものだった.

cast *a thing* ***behind*** *one's* ***back*** 物を捨てる, 拒否する (《聖》*Neh*. 9. 26) ▪ They *cast* your law *behind their backs*. 彼らはあなたの法律を放棄した.

come [***fall***] ***off the back of a lorry***/《豪・戯》***fall off the back of a truck*** 《英口》盗まれる ▪ A boat *came off the back of a lorry*. 船が盗まれた.

cover *one's* ***back*** (非難などへの)防護策をとる ▪ Business culture today tells us to always *cover one's back*. 今日のビジネス文化は, 常に防護策をとることを教えている.

Excuse my back. 背を向けてすみません ▪ He said, "*Excuse my back*" when his back turned to the audience. 彼は聴衆に背が向くと「背中を向けてごめんなさい」と言った.

fit [***write***]***... on the back of a postage stamp*** 知っていることはほんのわずかだ ▪ What I know about Tibet could *fit on the back of a postage stamp*. チベットについて私が知っていることはほんのわずかだ.

flat on *one's* ***back*** **1** (壁・床などに)背中を付けて, あおむけで ▪ Eric fell *flat on his back*. エリックはあおむけに倒れた.
2 (病気で)臥(ふ)せって. ☞→on one's BACK.

from way back ＝from AWAY back.

get [***put, set***] *a person's* ***back up*** 《口》人を怒らせる, 頑固にする; 人に逆らう ▪ You will only *get their backs up*. 君はただ彼らを怒らすだけだろう ▪ He goes his own way if you *put his back up*. 君が彼に逆らうと彼は独自の行動をとる.

get [***put, set***] *one's* ***back up/get*** [***put, set***] ***up*** *one's* ***back*** 《口》怒る; 逆らう, 頑固になる ▪ There is no reason to *get your back up* over such a small matter. そんな小さな事に君が腹を立てることはない ▪ They *set up their backs* against the claim. 彼らはその要求に対して立腹した. ☞猫が背をそびやかして怒ることから.

get *a person* ***off*** *one's* ***back*** 《口》苦しめる[とがめる]のをやめさせる ▪ He was obliged to sell his house to *get* the creditors *off his back*. 彼は債権者が自分を苦しめるのをやめさせるために家を売ることを余儀なくされた.

get [***keep, stay***] ***off*** *a person's* ***back*** 《口》人に干渉するのをやめる; (絶えず文句を言ったり, 見張ったりして)人を苦しめるのをやめる, 悩ますのをやめる ▪ *Get off my back* and let me do my work. 私に文句を言わないで仕事をさせてください ▪ Isn't it about time you just *get off his back*? 彼をいじめるのをやめてもいいころではないか.

get [***be***] ***on*** *a person's* ***back*** 《口》人を苦しめる, 悩ます ▪ Don't *get on my back*. I've had enough. 私を苦しめないで. もうたくさんです ▪ My boss *is* always *on my back*. 親方はいつもおれに文句ばかり言っている.

get *one's* ***own back*** (***on***) 《主に英口》(...に)報復する, 仕返しをする ▪ I've *got* a little of *my own back on* him. 彼にちょっと仕返ししてやった. ☞「自分のものを取り返す」が原義.

get the back of ...の後ろへ回る ▪ John *got the back of* the enemy. ジョンは敵の後ろへ回った.

give a back (馬跳び遊戯で)飛び台になる, 背中を貸す; 背をかがめる ▪ *Give* me *a back* up this wall. この塀を登るのに君の背中を貸してくれ ▪ He was *giving a back* to Ed. 彼はエドがその上を飛べるくらいうんと背をかがめていた.

give *a person* ***the back/give the back to*** *a person* **1** 人に背を向ける, 背く; を捨て去る ▪ He has lightly *given* us *the back*. 彼は我々を軽々しく捨て去った.
2 人を無視する ▪ Emmanuel has *given* them *the back*. エマニュエルは彼らを無視した.

give [***show***] ***the back of*** *one's* ***hand to*** ...を拒絶する, 侮辱する ▪ Obama *gave the back of his hand to* Eastern Europe's pleas. オバマ氏は東欧の請願を拒絶した.

go behind *a person's* ***back*** 人の裏に回る ▪ Don't *go behind my back* complaining to the manager. 僕の裏に回って支配人に訴えたりするなよ.

have a broad back 寛大[おおらか]である ▪ It helps to *have a broad back* in show business. ショービジネスでは寛大であると役に立つ.

have *one's* ***back to*** [***against***] ***the wall***/*one's* ***back is against the wall*** 追いつめられる, (大敵に対して)苦戦する; 窮地に陥る ▪ Because of the enemy's superior numbers our troops *had their backs to the wall*. 敵が優勢であったのでわが軍は苦戦した ▪ When *his back is against the wall* he becomes very agressive. 彼は窮地に陥ると, 攻撃的になる.

have ... on *one's* ***back*** **1** (負担・夢魔など)を背負いこむ ▪ It is too much to *have* another priest *on our backs*. もう一人牧師を背負いこむのは負担過剰だ.

B

2 …に攻めかかられる ▪ We shall *have* all the powers of Europe *on our backs*. ヨーロッパのすべての強国がわが国に襲いかかってくるだろう.

have **…** ***to*** *one's* ***back*** (衣服など)を着ている ▪ She *has* no clothes *to her back*. 彼女は何も着ていない《裸である》.

in **(*****the*****)** ***back*** 後ろに; 奥に ▪ I hitchhiked to London on a lorry, my bike *in back*. 私は自転車を後ろに積んでもらってトラックでロンドンまでヒッチハイクした ▪ *In the back* two men were playing a game. 奥では二人の男がゲームをしていた.

in **(*****the*****)** ***back of*** 《米俗》…の後ろに (behind); を支持[応援]して ▪ A man appeared *in back of* them. 彼らの背後から男が現れた ▪ He has been strongly *in back of* the venture. 彼はその冒険的事業を強く支持してきた ▪ Get *in back of* your team by cheering them at the game. 試合では君のチームを声出して応援するんだ.

in **[*****at*****]** ***the back of*** *one's* ***mind*** 心の奥底に, 心のかたすみに ▪ I keep thinking *in the back of my mind* that you should first go to a college. 君はまず大学へ行くべきだという感じが私はいつもしている.

know **…** ***like the back of*** *one's* ***hand*** …に精通している ▪ He *knows* the district *like the back of his hand*. 彼はその地方を知り尽くしている.

lay *a person* ***on*** *his* ***back*** 人を(仰向けに)倒す ▪ They never look up to Heaven, till God *lay* them *on their back*. 神が彼らを仰向けに倒すまでは, 彼らは決して天を仰がない.

lie on *one's* ***back*** →on one's BACK.

like the back **(*****end*****)** ***of a bus*** 《口》[[be, look を伴って]] きわめて醜い ▪ She *looks like the back of a bus*. 彼女はとても醜い.

live off the backs of (人)を搾取する ▪ For too long big landowners have *lived off the backs of* the peasants. あまりにも長い間大地主は小作農民を搾取してきた.

make a back for =give a BACK.

Mind your back**(*****s*****)*****!*** 《口》(人などを)通らせてあげて! ▪ *Mind your backs*, please. みなさん, どうぞ通らせてあげてください.

on *a person's* ***back*** 《口》人をひどくいじめる[非難する] ▪ I have too many things to do because my supervisor is *on my back* all the time. 私の指導教官がいつもうるさく言うので, やることが多すぎる.

on **[*****upon*****]** *one's* ***back*** 《口》[[通例 be [be laid, lie] (flat) を伴って]] **1** 仰向けになって ▪ If you *lie on your back*, you can look up at the sky. 仰向けに寝ころべば空を見上げることができる.

2 病臥して ▪ They will *be laid on their backs* before a week. 彼らは1週間たたないうちに床に着くだろう ▪ He *was* flat *on his back* for 3 days. 彼は3日間病臥していた.

3 万策尽きて; 窮乏して ▪ The employers *were* flat *on their backs*. 雇い主たちはすっかりお手あげだった ▪ He *is on his back* nowadays. 彼は現在窮乏している.

on **[*****upon*****]** ***the back of*** **1** …のすぐ後ろから ▪ The child got the measles and then *on the back of* that came scarlet fever. 子供ははしかになり, それからすぐ続いて猩(しょう)紅熱にかかった ▪ *Upon the back of* these came a thousand. これらに続いて1,000名の者がやって来た.

2 …に加えて ▪ *On the back of* that her husband died. その上に彼女の夫が死んだ.

on the back of an envelope 封筒の裏の[に]; 未完成の状態で, メモ程度の段階で, (メモを封筒の裏に走り書きするように)大急ぎで ▪ He has made decisions sketched out *on the back of an envelope* again. 彼はまたしても未完成の決定を下した ▪ They cannot be done *on the back of an envelope* in a few days. それらは数日のやっつけ仕事ではできない.

out back 裏庭で (↔out FRONT 2) ▪ Last night they were *out back* having a barbecue. 昨夜彼らは裏庭でバーベキューをしていた.

pat **[*****slap*****]** *a person* ***on the back*** 《口》(賞賛の気持ちを表して)人の背中をポンとたたく, 人にお祝いを言う; (人の)したことをほめる ▪ Why don't you *pat* him *on the back*? なぜ彼をほめてあげないのか ▪ I *slapped* him *on the back* to praise him for his good shot. 私は彼がうまく当てたのをほめて背中をポンとたたいた.

put *one's* ***back into*** 《口》(ボート, 重量あげなどで)…に全力を出す, に身を入れる ▪ They *put their back into* the work. 彼らは仕事に全力を注いだ ▪ Pull, John! *Put your back into* it! ジョン, オールを引け! 全力を出してこげ!

put *a person* ***back of*** 人に…を支持させる ▪ It *put* them *back of* the United Nations. そのため彼らは国連を支持した.

put *a person's* ***back up*** →get a person's BACK up.

put *one's* ***back up/put up*** *one's* ***back*** →get one's BACK up.

put *a person* **(*****flat*****)** ***on*** *his* ***back*** 人を病臥させる; 困窮させる ▪ A bad headache *put* me *flat on my back*. ひどい頭痛で私は床についた.

put **…** ***to the back of*** *one's* ***mind*** (しばらくの間)ある考えを忘れる ▪ I try to *put* it *to the back of my mind*, but it is a recurring nightmare. 私はそれを忘れようとするのだが, 悪夢のようにまた思い出される.

ride on the back of (車など)の後ろに乗る; …の成功にあやかる, の尻馬に乗る ▪ Hugh made futile attempts to *ride on the back of* Craig's music. ヒューはクレイグの音楽の成功にあやかろうとむなしい努力をした.

Scratch my back and I will scratch yours. →(You) SCRATCH my back and I will scratch yours.

see the back of 《口》…を追い払う, 見納めする ▪ He is a terrible bore. I am always glad to *see the back of* him. 彼は恐ろしくたいくつな男だ. 私は彼がいなくなるといつも清々する ▪ I was happy to *see the back of* this snow! この雪が消えてうれしかった.

set *a person* ***back on*** *his* ***heels*** 人を驚かす, 人にショックを与える ▪ The bill for my wife's clothes *set* me *back on my heels.* 妻の衣服の請求書を見て私はびっくり仰天した.

set *a person's* ***back up*** →get a person's BACK up.

set *one's* ***back up/set up*** *one's* ***back*** →get one's BACK up.

show the back to …に後ろを見せる, から逃げる ▪ They *showed the back to* the enemy. 彼らは敵に後ろを見せた.

speak [***talk***] ***through the back of*** *one's* ***neck*** 《口》 **1** ほらを吹く, 大げさなことを言う ▪ He *talked through the back of his neck* when we missed our shots. 我々が当てそこなうと彼はとんでもないことを言った.
2 わけのわからないことを言う ▪ I wish you would not *talk through the back of your neck.* 君が愚にもつかぬことを言わないでくれたらと思うよ.

stab *a person* ***in the back*** (人の)背中を刺す; (人を)裏切る, (人の感情など)を傷つける, (人を)中傷する ▪ You were my friend until you *stabbed* me *in the back.* 僕を裏切るまで君は僕の友人だった ▪ He is the sort of man to *stab* you *in the back.* 彼は人を中傷するような人間だ.

stand back of …を支持する ▪ I *stand back of* the policy. 私はその政策を支持する.

take a back seat →BACK SEAT.

talk out of the back of *one's* ***head*** 《英口》 〚主に進行形で〛 たわごとをしゃべる ▪ He's always *talking out of the back of his head.* 彼はいつもたわごとをしゃべってばかりいる.

(***the***) ***back of beyond*** はるか遠いところ(に) ▪ It seems to be right at [in] *the back of beyond* somewhere. それはどこかほんとに遠い遠いところにあるらしい ▪ Bill lives on a small island, truly *back of beyond.* ビルはまことに遠いところの小さな島に住んでいる.

The back of my hand to…! 《口》 (軽蔑・拒絶を意味して)…などくそくらえ; はまっぴらだ ▪ *The back of my hand to* you! おまえなんかくそくらえ! ▪ *The back of my hand to* writing that! それを書くのはまっぴらだよ.

the minute *a person's* ***back is turned*** 人が背を向けたとたん ▪ The boys will start deriding him *the minute his back is turned.* 彼が背を向けたとたん少年たちは彼のことをあざけり始める.

there and back →THERE.

throw *a person* ***on his back*** 〚主に受身で〛 人を仰向けに倒す, 完全に打ちのめす ▪ I *was thrown on my back,* and I was nearly choked. 私は仰向けに投げ倒されてまるで息が詰まった.

to… and back (ある場所)までの往復 ▪ What is the fare *to* Rome *and back*? ローマまでの往復料金はいくらですか.

to the back 骨の髄まで, 全く ▪ He is Irish *to the back.* 彼は生粋のアイルランド人だ.

turn *one's* ***back*** 去る, 逃げる; 背を向ける, そっぽを向く ▪ *Sir Roger's back was* no sooner *turned* than honest Will began. サー・ロジャーが出て行くやいなや正直者のウィルは話し始めた ▪ You *turn your backs* and refuse to listen. 諸君はそっぽを向いて傾聴しようとしない.

turn *one's* [***the***] ***back on*** [***upon***] **1** (怒り・軽蔑で)…に背を向ける, を無視する ▪ He deliberately *turned his back on* me. 彼はわざと私に背を向けた.
2 …を見捨てる, と離反する ▪ His father *turned his back on* him when he was a lad. 彼の父は彼が若者だったときに彼を見捨てた.
3 …から逃げる, から去る ▪ He *turned his back upon* civilization. 彼は文明に背を向けた.

turn *one's* ***back to*** …に負ける ▪ He *turns his back to* nobody. 彼は誰にも引けを取らない.

watch *one's* [*a person's*] ***back*** 予期せぬ危険から自分の[人の]身を守る ▪ I'm tired of having to *watch my back.* 予期せぬ危険から身を守らねばならないのがいやになった ▪ He must *watch my back* and property too. 彼は私の身と財産を予期せぬ危険から守らなければならない.

when [***as soon as***] *one's* ***back is turned*** 《口》 (特に監視する人)が去ると(すぐ) ▪ *As soon as the teacher's back was turned,* the boys started fighting. 先生がいなくなるとすぐ少年たちはけんかを始めた. ☞→turn one's BACK.

with *one's* ***back to*** [***at***] ***the wall*** 追いつめられて; (大軍に対して)苦戦して ▪ He is fighting *with his back to the wall* in the election. 彼は選挙で大苦戦している.

with one arm [***hand***] ***tied behind*** *one's* ***back*** 《口》 楽々と(…が)できる ▪ I could knock you down *with one arm tied behind my back.* 君なんか片腕を背に縛りつけても簡単にたたき伏せられる.

write on the back of a postage stamp →fit… on the BACK of postage stamp.

back[2] /bæk/ 動 ***back a horse*** **1** 馬に賭ける ▪ The bookmaker asked us to *back a horse* for luck. 賭け元は我々に運だめしに馬に賭けてくれと言った.
2 運だめしに事に加わる ▪ All right, I'll *back the horse* up to £500. よし, ひとつ500ポンドだけその事業に加わろう.

back and fill 《米口》 行ったり来たりする; (考えなどが)常にぐらつく; 立ち場をあちこち変える ▪ The engine was *backing and filling* on a side-track. 機関車は待避線上で行ったり来たりしていた ▪ A decade has been consumed in *backing and filling* on the question. その問題について行きつ戻りつして10年費やしてしまった.

back *a person* ***into a corner*** →paint oneself into a CORNER.

back oars オールを逆にこぐ; 方向を逆にする ▪ We decided to *back oars* and have nothing more to do with him. 方向を逆にして彼と縁を切ることにした.

back the wrong horse →HORSE[1].

back water **1** 船を逆進させる ▪ I ordered the

men to *back water* with all their might. 私は水兵に全力をあげて逆進させるよう命じた.

2《米口》説を翻す, 前言[約束]を取り消す; 退く, 手を引く ▪ This makes business *back water.* このため商況は鈍っている ▪ Green *backed water* when John offered to fight him. ジョンがけんかを吹っかけたらグリーンは尻込みをした.

backbone /bǽkbòʊn/ 名 ***to the backbone*** 《口》骨の髄まで, 徹底して[した] ▪ They were English *to the backbone.* 彼らは生粋のイギリス人だった.

back-cap /bǽkkæ̀p/ 名 ***give*** *a person* ***a back-cap*** 《米俗》人の過去を暴露して中傷する ▪ He *gave* me *a back-cap* and ran me off the job. 彼は私の過去をあばいて中傷し私を失業させた.

backdoor /bǽkdɔ́ːr/ 名 ***by*** [***through***] ***the backdoor*** →DOOR.

background /bǽkgràʊnd/ 名 ***have a good*** [***no***] ***background*** 良家の出である[はない] ▪ I don't want her to marry Bill. He *has no background.* 彼女にビルと結婚してもらいたくない. 彼は良家の出ではないから.

keep [***remain***] ***in the background*** 黒幕になっている, 表面に出ない ▪ I'm going to *keep in the background* during the discussion. その討議中には私は表面に出ないでいるつもりです.

merge into the background (人が)背景に溶け込む, 目立たないようにふるまう ▪ She is terribly shy and usually *merges into the background.* 彼女は人見知りが激しく, たいてい目立たないようにふるまう.

back-handed /bǽkhǽndəd/ 形 ***a back-handed compliment*** 皮肉なおせじ ▪ That's rather *a back-handed compliment.* そりゃどうも皮肉なおせじですな.

backing /bǽkɪŋ/ 名 ***backing and filling*** 《米》絶えず決心を変えること ▪ After much *backing and filling* she finally agreed to sell her house. 何度も決心を変えたあとで彼女はついに自分の家を売ることに同意した.

give *one's* (***full***) ***backing to*** …を(全面的に)支援[支持]する ▪ I *give my full backing to* the government's resolutions. 政府の決議案を全面的に支持する.

backroom /bǽkrùːm/ 名 ***backroom boys***/ ***the boys in the backroom*** 《口》(戦争の背後で活動する)隠れた技術家[発明家]たち; (共同研究などの)裏方 ▪ Editors are very much the *backroom boys* of the film world. 編集者はまさに映画界の裏方だ. ☞Lord Beaverbrook が1941年3月24日に行なった兵器生産に関する演説から.

back seat /bæ̀ksíːt/ 名 ***a back seat driver*** 《口》**1** 後ろの席から運転手に一々指図をする尊大な乗客 ▪ The driver became angry with the *back seat driver.* 運転手は自分に一々指図する乗客に腹を立てた.

2《主に米》責任のない地位にいて差し出口をする人, 出しゃばり (→a MONDAY morning quarterback) ▪ You're not wanted. Stop being *a backseat driver.* 君はお呼びではない. 差し出口はよしてくれ.

take a back seat **1** 後ろの方に席を取る, 末座[陰]にいる; 下位にある; 卑下する; 一目おく (*to*) ▪ He must be content at first to *take a back seat.* 彼は初めは末座にいることに満足しなければならない ▪ His father has *taken a back seat to* his son. 父は息子に一目おいている.

2 引退する; 地位をあきらめる; 降参する; 失敗する ▪ He said that traitors should *take a back seat.* 彼は裏切者どもは引っ込むべきだと言った.

backside /bǽksàɪd/ 名 ***get off*** *one's* ***backside*** 《英口》しりを上げる ▪ *Get off your backside* and do something! しりを上げて何かしろ!

sit (***around***) ***on your backside*** 《英口》(特に他の人が忙しくしているときに)しりを据えている ▪ Are you going to *sit on your backside* and do nothing? 君はしりを据えて何もしないつもりかね?

backstairs /bǽkstèərz/ 形 ***backstairs influence*** 秘密の[陰の]勢力《特に宮廷の》 ▪ He obtained the post through [by] *backstairs influence.* 彼は陰の勢力によってその地位を得た. ☞私事について王・主人に会いたいと思う者は裏の方の階段を平素使用し守る使用人たちを取りこむことが望ましいとされたことから.

back track /bǽktræ̀k/ 名 ***make back tracks*** 《米》引き返す, 退く ▪ I'll whip you if you don't *make back tracks* at once. すぐに引きあげないとむちで打つぞ.

take the back track(***s***) 《米》引き返す, 帰る; 退く《比喩的にも》 ▪ Two days we lingered, then *took the back track.* 2日間我々はとどまって, それから帰った ▪ You are *taking the back track* on civilization. 君たちは文明から後退しつつある.

backward(**s**) /bǽkwərdz/ 副 ***backward in coming forward*** 《英口》(主張などに)遠慮がちな ▪ At first he was too *backward in coming forward.* 彼は初めは(意見を述べるのに)あまりにも遠慮がちであった ▪ Chris is not *backward in coming forward* in matters connected with music. クリスは音楽に関することでははっきり意見を言う.

backward-looking 後ろ向きの, 昔を振り返ってばかりいる ▪ Their views are traditional and *backward-looking.* 彼らの考え方は因習にとらわれていて時代遅れだ.

backward(***s***) ***and forward***(***s***) **1** 前後に, あちこち, 行ったり来たり ▪ We went *backwards and forwards* from office to bank. 我々は事務所から銀行へと行ったり来たりした.

2 しどろもどろに, ぐらついて ▪ The boy went *backward and forward* in his story. その少年の話はしどろもどろだった.

bend [***lean, fall***] ***over backward***(***s***) (***to*** *do*) 《口》**1** (行き過ぎ是正のため)反対の極端に走る; (ある傾向を直すため)行き過ぎる ▪ He is being hypercorrect, *leaning over backward to* be correct. 彼は襟を正すのに行き過ぎて, 極端に礼儀正しくなっている.

2 (人を助ける[喜ばす]ため)あらゆる努力を払う ▪ Her

parents always *bent over backward to* help her. 両親は彼女を助けるため，いつもあらゆる努力をした. ☞「体を後ろに曲げて床に手をつける動作をする」が原義.

get it backwards 誤解する，解釈を誤る ▪ You *got it backwards*. It was Ben's father and not Ben, that died. 君は誤解している. 死んだのはベンのお父さんで，ベンではない.

know ... backwards and forwards 《口》…を徹底的[完全]に知っている ▪ I *know* the book *backwards and forwards*. その本(の内容)は完全に知っている.

without a backward glance 振り返りもせずに(喜んで) ▪ He left school at 15 *without a backward glance*. 彼は15のときに喜んで学校をやめた.

backyard /bækjáːrd/ 名 ***in*** *one's* **(*own*)** ***backyard*** 《口》 **1** 家の近くに; 身近に，すぐ手近に ▪ We're living with war *in our own backyard*. 我々は身近で起こっている戦争とともに生活している ▪ He might face opposition *in his own backyard*. 彼は身内から反対されるかもしれない ▪ We have his successor *in our own backyard*. 彼の後任はすぐ手近にいる.

2 得意[専門]分野に[で] ▪ The problem is *in my own backyard*. その問題は僕の専門とするところだ.

Not in My Backyard!/NIMBY! うちの裏庭にはごめんだ《原発・ごみ処理場などが自分の家の近くに建設されることに反対する言葉》 ▪ This article takes a look at the phenomenon known as *NIMBY* or *Not in My Backyard*. この記事では例の「NIMBY—つまり，うちの裏庭にはごめんだ」現象に軽く触れている.

bacon /béɪkən/ 名 ***bring home the bacon*** 《口》 **1** 成功する，賞を持ち帰る ▪ If I fail to *bring home the bacon*, I will give you £10. もし僕が成功しなかったら，君に10ポンドやる.

2 利益を得る，働いて金を持ち帰る ▪ It was his poetry that *brought home the bacon*. 金になったのは彼の詩である ▪ After all, you *bring home the bacon*. 結局働いて金を持って帰るのは君です.

go together like bacon and eggs 完全にうまく調和する ▪ Hi Bill, that shirt and tie *go together like bacon and eggs*. やあビル，そのシャツとネクタイはぴったりと調和してるよ.

save *a person's* ***bacon*** 《主に英口》失敗[苦境]から人を救い出す ▪ This outer wear really *saved my bacon* up in Alaska! この外套は北のアラスカで本当に私を苦境から救ってくれた.

save *one's* ***bacon*** 《口》危害[難局]を(ほうほうの体で)逃れる (→save one's NECK; save one's (own) SKIN) ▪ I saw the car coming, and leapt out of the way to *save my bacon*. 私は自動車が向かって来るのを見て，通路から飛びのいてやっと助かった.

sell *one's* ***bacon*** 《口》体を売る ▪ I *sold my bacon* for 300 dollars. 300ドルで体を売った.

bad /bæd/ 形名 ***a bad egg*** **[*hat, lot*]** 《口》悪者，やくざ，ならず者，信頼できない人 ▪ Don't lend him anything; he is *a bad egg*. やつに何も貸すな，やつは信用できない ▪ In short he is *a bad hat*. 要するにあいつは悪者だ. ☞hat は head の婉曲語.

be **[*be taken*]** ***bad*** **(*with*)** (…の)病気である[になる] ▪ He *is bad with* gout. 彼は通風を病んでいる.

be in a bad mood **[*temper*]** 不きげんである，腹を立てている ▪ The manager *was in a bad mood* all day. 支配人は一日中不きげんだった.

be **[*get*]** ***in bad*** **(*with, over*)** 《主に米口》 **1** (…に)受けが悪い[悪くなる] ▪ He *is in bad with* the higher ups. 彼は上層部に受けが悪い.

2 (…と)仲が悪い[悪くなる] ▪ He *got in bad with* the other kids. 彼は他の子供たちと仲たがいした.

be **(...)** ***to the bad*** **1** …だけ借金している，赤字である ▪ I *am* £200 *to the bad*. 200ポンドの赤字だ.

2 不利である ▪ It *is* financially *to the bad*. それは財政的には不利である. ☞↔to the GOOD.

can't be bad 《口》(相手に勧めて)なかなかいいよ ▪ It *can't be bad* for free. それはただにしてはなかなかいいよ.

feel bad 気分が悪い; 後悔する，遺憾に思う (*about*) ▪ I *feel bad about* the error. その誤りを悔いている.

give up a bad job 割の悪い仕事としてやめる ▪ It is sometimes best to *give up a bad job* and start afresh. 割の悪い仕事としてやめて新規まき直しをするのも，ときにはベストだよ.

go bad **1** (食物などが)腐る ▪ Fish soon *goes bad* in hot weather. 魚は暑い時期にはすぐに腐る.

2 (演技者などが)無能になる，だめになる ▪ The player *went bad*. その選手はだめになった.

3 悪に手を染める，犯罪に走る ▪ If he keeps associating with those ruffians, he's sure to *go bad*. もし彼があんなごろつきどもといつまでもつき合っているなら，きっとワルになるに決まっている.

4 (動物が)不きげんになる，怒りっぽくなる ▪ The dog *went bad*. 犬は怒りっぽくなった.

go from bad to worse (ますます)悪化する ▪ Things *went from bad to worse*. 事態はますます悪化した.

go to the bad 堕落する; 落ちぶれる; 退化する ▪ He *went to the bad* and committed murder. 彼は落ちぶれて殺人を犯した.

have a bad hair day 《戯》 **1** 頭髪の具合が悪くて一日中不愉快である ▪ I'm *having a bad hair day*. 僕は頭髪の具合が悪くて一日中不愉快なんだ.

2 (機械が)一日中調子が悪い ▪ My PC is *having a bad hair day*. 私のパソコンは一日中調子が悪い.

have got it bad 《戯》ぞっこんに惚れ込んでいる[参っている] ▪ I realized I *have got it bad* for Jane. 僕は自分がジェインにぞっこんに惚れ込んでいるのを悟った.

(*It's*) ***too bad.*** 《口》 **1** それは残念だ，お手上げだ; …とは残念だ (*that*) ▪ *It's* (just) *too bad* she's ill. 彼女が病気だとは気の毒です ▪ *Too bad* the shoes don't fit you. 靴が合わなくて残念ですね.

2 あいにくだ，どうしようもない ▪ Well, *too bad*. We don't sell these articles. いやあいにくですが，これらの品は売りません ▪ If she doesn't like this country, that's just *too bad*. 彼女がこの国を好きでないというのであれば，それはどうしようもない.

3 (賛成できなくて)お気の毒さま ▪ If I've ruffled your feathers—well, *too bad.* 君を怒らせたとすれば—そりゃお気の毒さま.

4 ひどい[無分別な, 不正な]ことである (*that*) ▪ It was *too bad that* he did not turn up after having promised to. 彼が約束しておきながら来なかったのはひどいことだった.

my bad 《米口》 私が悪い; 私の責任だ ▪ *My bad,* man. I didn't see you. ごめんよ. 君が見えなかったんだ.

not (so, too, half) bad 《口》 なかなか良い, けっこうだ (fairly good) 《物事を控え目に言うイギリス人の癖の一つ》 ▪ Gardner is *not half* a *bad* fellow. ガードナーはなかなか良い男だ ▪ The place is *not half bad.* そこはまずまずの所だ ▪ How are you?—*Not (too) bad.* ごきげんいかが—まあまあ元気です ▪ This restaurant is *not too bad.* このレストラン, けっこういける.

not that bad/not as bad as all that 《口》 それほど悪くない 《反論》 ▪ British holidays are *not that bad.* イギリスの休暇はさほど悪くない ▪ That boy is *not as bad as all that.* あの少年はそれほどワルじゃない.

take the bad with the good 良いこともあれば悪いこともある ▪ We must *take the bad with the good.* 我々には良いことも悪いこともあるのだ. ☞the bad = bad fortune.

turn up like a bad penny →PENNY.

badger /bǽdʒər/ 名 ***badger game*** 美人局(つつもたせ); ゆすり, 恐喝 ▪ The prosecutor accused the couple of playing the *badger game.* 検事はその夫婦が美人局を働いたと告発した.

draw the badger 相手を広々した所へおびき出す ▪ Your taunts have at last *drawn the badger.* 君の痛烈な皮肉がとうとう彼をおびき出した. ☞「アナグマに犬をけしかけて巣から追い出す」が原義.

overdraw the [one's] badger 《俗》 銀行預金を出し過ぎる ▪ His checks no longer drew the cash, because he had *overdrawn his badger.* 彼の小切手はもう現金にはならなかった. 預金を引き出し過ぎていたから.

badly /bǽdli/ 副 ***be badly off*** →OFF[1].

do badly →DO[2].

bad-mouth /bǽdmáʊθ/ 名 ***put the bad-mouth on*** 《主に米口》 (人)の悪口を言う ▪ Jackie came out and *put the bad-mouth on* Hector. ジャッキーがしゃしゃり出てきてヘクターの悪口を言った.

baffle /bǽfəl/ 動 ***baffle description*** 名状しがたい ▪ The beauty of the scenery *baffles description.* その風景の美しさは名状しがたい.

be baffled in …の裏をかかれる, に失敗する ▪ He *was baffled in* his design. 彼の計画は失敗した.

bag[1] /bæg/ 名 ***a bag lady*** 《口》 女性のホームレス ▪ I saw *an* old *bag lady* feeding the pigeons in the park. ホームレスの年取った女が公園でハトにえさをやっているのを見た. ☞所持品を買い物袋に入れて歩くところから.

a bag of (skin and) bones (骨と皮ばかりのように)やせこけた人[動物] ▪ He's nothing but *a bag of skin and bones.* 彼はほんとに骨と皮ばかりだ ▪ The old woman was reduced to *a bag of bones.* 老婆はやつれて骨と皮にやせこけていた. ☞*A Bag of Bones* (1998)という Stephen King の小説の題名から.

a grab bag 雑多な寄せ集め ▪ The meeting ended in *a grab bag* of petty complaints. 会合の終わりはつまらない不満の寄せ集めになってしまった. ☞参加者がどんな景品が当たるか知らずに手を突っ込む, 催しで用意される袋.

a mixed bag 《口》 雑多な人[物] ▪ She invited *a mixed bag* of people to her party. 彼女はパーティーに様々な人々を招いた.

a stash [stuff] bag **1** マリファナを入れておく袋 ▪ Jim was caught carrying *a stash bag.* ジムはマリファナの入った袋を持っているところを見つかった.

2 (口紅・免許証などの)小物入れ ▪ I keep my keys in my *stash bag.* 鍵は小物入れに入れておく.

a (whole) bag of tricks →the whole bag of TRICKs.

an old bag 《軽蔑》 うるさい不愉快な女, おばん, 迷惑おばさん ▪ She was definitely *an old bag.* 彼女は確かにうるさいばばあだ ▪ *That old bag* is always complaining. あのおしゃべりおばさんは愚痴だらけだ.

bag and baggage 所持品[家財]いっさいを取りまとめて, いっさい合財, ひとつ残らず ▪ All the members should be expelled, *bag and baggage.* 全員一人残らず追い払わなければならない ▪ Last night our neighbors cleared out *bag and baggage.* 昨夜隣の人々は家財を取りまとめて出て行った.

bag of mystery 《俗》 ソーセージ ▪ A slice of bread was given with the "*bag of mystery*". 一切れのパンがソーセージとともに与えられた.

bags of 《口》 たくさんの (plenty of) ▪ There's *bags of* room. 余地はたくさんある ▪ He has *bags of* money. 彼は金をどっさり持っている.

bags under one's eyes 目の下の皮膚のたるみ 《睡眠不足・不健康・老齢の印》 ▪ He's only 25, but he's already got *bags under his eyes.* 彼はまだ25歳なのにもう目の下の皮膚がたるんでいる.

be a [the] bag of nerves 《口》 ひどくびくびくする; 不安である, あがる ▪ I *was a bag of nerves* when I gave a speech. 演説のときひどくあがった.

be half in the bag 酔っている ▪ He *was half in the bag* and staggering slightly. 彼はなま酔いで少しよろめいていた.

be left holding the bag 《米口》 一人で責任をとらされる, 貧乏くじを引く ▪ I *was left holding the bag* for this accident. 私はこの事故のことで全責任をとらされた.

be not one's bag **1** 《口》 興味がない, 得意ではない ▪ Boxing [Jazz] *isn't* really *my bag.* ボクシング[ジャズ]には実は興味がない.

2 自分の知ったことではない ▪ Who is Ann getting married to?—That sort of thing *is not my bag.*

アンは誰と結婚しようとしているのかな—そんなことは僕の知ったことじゃない.

bear the bag 財布を握っている, 金が自由になる ▪ My wife *bears the bag*. 財布は妻が握っている.

empty the bag 《口》袋をからにする; いっさい残らず話してしまう, 議論[討論]をし尽くす ▪ Be frank and *empty the bag*. 率直に残らず話せ. ☞Ⓕ vider le sac のなぞり.

get a poor* [*good*] *bag 猟の獲物が少ない[多い] ▪ Looks like you *got a poor bag*? 猟の獲物が少なかったようだね.

get the bag 《口》お払い箱になる (→get the SACK) ▪ It's clear he *got the bag*. 明らかに彼は首になったのだ.

give** a person **the bag **1**《口》人を解雇する, 首にする ▪ I *gave* him *the bag* two months ago. 私は2か月前に彼を首にした.
2《俗》(求婚する)人にひじ鉄をくわす ▪ She *gave* him *the bag* two weeks ago. 彼女は2週間前に彼にひじ鉄をくわした.

give** a person **the bag to hold 人を見殺しにする; 人に責任を負わせる ▪ The country will *give* Spain *the bag to hold*. その国はスペインを見殺しにするだろう.

half in the bag 酔っぱらって ▪ Jim was *half in the bag* when he came home. ジムは帰宅したとき酔っぱらっていた.

in the bag **1**《口》確実に手中にある, (成功などが)確かである; 決着がついて ▪ We thought we had the game *in the bag*. 絶対に試合に勝てると思っていた ▪ He felt the game was *in the bag*. ゲームは決着がついたように彼には思われた ▪ He felt that his election was *in the bag*. 彼は自分の当選は確実だと感じた. ☞ハンターが獲物を袋に入れるところから.
2《米口》(議案などが)成功した, 通過した ▪ The bill is *in the bag*. その議案は通過した.
3《軍》捕虜になって ▪ I went out to the Front again and got put *in the bag*. 私は再び前線に出て捕虜にされた.

in the bottom of the bag 最後の切札[手段]として ▪ I have it *in the bottom of the bag*. 私はそれを奥の手として持っている.

leave** a person **holding the bag 《口》人を空手で一人残す; 一人で責任を負わせる ▪ I don't want to *be left holding the bag*. 私は一人で責任を負わされたくない.

look like a bag-lady 汚らしく[だらしなく]見える ▪ She *looks like a bag lady* these days. 彼女は近ごろだらしなく見える.

look like an old bag だらしない格好をする ▪ Though Mom is over seventy she hates to *look like an old bag*. お袋は70歳を超えているが, だらしない格好をするのをいやがる.

make* [*secure*] *a good bag 大猟をする ▪ We *made a good bag*, instead of shooting little birds. 小さな鳥を撃つ代わりに, 我々は大猟をした.

pack** one's **bags 《口》(不和・不満などで)出て行く ▪ I'll *pack my bags* and find another job. 私はここを出て別の仕事を見つけよう.

pull out of the bag (せっぱ詰まって)名案を思いつく, 急に窮余の策を見つける ▪ He managed to *pull* something *out of the bag* to pass the exam. 試験に合格するために何とかして急に窮余の策を見つけた ▪ We've got other options we can *pull out of the bag* if it rains. もし雨なら他の案をいろいろ思いつくさ.

put* [*tie*] *on the feed bag 《俗》食事をする ▪ Come on, it's time to *put on the feed bag*. さあ, 食事をする時間だよ. ☞feed bag「飼料を入れて馬の首にかけるかいば袋」.

***set** one's **bag* (*for*)** 《米》(...に)色気[野心]を示す, (を)得ようと望む《政治的野心》 ▪ John *set his bag for* the office of mayor. ジョンは市長の職をねらった.

Somebody's cut the bag open. 《米口》(誰かが袋をあけて鳥を放したほど)猟鳥がたくさんいる ▪ *Somebody's cut the bag open* from the way they are coming. 鳥の飛んで来る様子では誰かが袋をあけて放したほど多い.

the whole bag of tricks →TRICK[1].

(Yes sir, yes sir) three bags full(, sir)! 《戯》(不満ながら)(はいはい)承知いたしました ▪ They bow to their benefactors and say loudly, "*Yes sir, yes sir, three bags full sir*." 彼らは恩人に向かってお辞儀をし, 声高に「はいはい, 承知しました」と言う. ☞伝承童謡 "Baa, baa, black sheep" の一節から.

bag[2] /bæg/ 動 ***bag it*** **1**《口》物を袋に詰める ▪ "Please *bag it*," the customer said to the clerk. 「袋に入れてください」と客は店員に言った.
2《俗》黙る; やめる, よす; うせる ▪ The story was dull, so I've decided to *bag it*. 話はつまらなかった, そこでよすことにした ▪ I've heard enough about that, so just *bag it*! そのことはうんざりするほど聞いた. だからやめてくれ.

bags I*/**《まれ》I bags*** 《学俗》(まっ先に口を出したのだから取る権利があるので)僕がもらうよ ▪ *Bags I* all the presents. 贈り物はみな僕がもらうよ ▪ *Bags I* first drink. 僕が一番に飲むんだ. ☞bag = claim.

bagger /bǽgər/ 名 ***brown bagger*** 弁当持参の人, 腰弁 ▪ *Brown baggers* eat well and save $11.7 billion each year. 腰弁らは上手に食事をして, 毎年117億ドル節約する. ☞brown bag「弁当を入れる茶色の紙袋」.

bail /beɪl/ 名 ***accept* [*allow, take*] *bail*** (治安官が保釈金を取って)保釈を許す ▪ The magistrate *accepted bail*. 治安判事は保釈を許した.

admit* [*hold*] a person *to bail 人に保釈を許す ▪ The magistrate *admitted* the prisoner *to bail*. 治安判事は囚人の保釈を許した.

***be* [*become*] *bail* (*for*)** (...の保釈)保証人となる ▪ I will *be bail for* their appearance. 私は彼らの出頭の保証人となります.

forfeit** one's **bail →save one's BAIL.

give* [*put in*] *bail 保釈金を納め(て保釈され)る

B

▪ We *gave bail* for Bill. ビルのために保釈金を納めた.

give leg bail 《戯》走って逃げる ▪ I *gave* them *leg bail* by making for a deep swamp. 私は深い沼沢の方へ向かって彼らから逃走した.

go bail for **1** …の保釈保証人となる ▪ I had to *go bail for* him. 私が彼の保釈保証人にならなければならなかった.

2《口》…を保証する ▪ I *go bail for* his honesty. 彼の正直を保証する.

go bail on …が本当であることを保証する; は確かだ ▪ He'll introduce some discipline, I'll *go bail on* that. 彼は規律を取り入れるだろう, それは確かだ.

hold *a person* ***to bail*** →admit a person to BAIL.

jump [***skip***] *one's* ***bail*** 《口》 **1**《米》保釈中に失踪する ▪ Tom *jumped his bail* and left town. トムは保釈中に失踪して町を離れてしまった ▪ The man is in jail and every one of the others *skipped his bail.* その男は入獄しているが, その他はすべて保釈中に逃亡した.

2 (出廷せずに)保釈金を放棄する ▪ I can't afford to *skip bail*—I'd lose 3,000 dollars. 出廷せずに保釈金を放棄するわけにいかない—3,000ドルをふいにしてしまう. ☞jump [skip] = evade.

make bail 保釈金を積む(*for*) ▪ He didn't think he could *make bail for* his brother. 彼は弟のために保釈金を積むことができるとは思えなかった.

(***out***) ***on bail*** (保釈金を収めて)保釈されて ▪ The suspect was *out on bail* and got arrested again. 容疑者は保釈出所中であったが, 再び逮捕された.

put up [***stand,*** 《米》 ***post***] ***bail for*** = go BAIL for.

save [***forfeit***] *one's* ***bail*** (保釈中の被告が)呼び出しに応じて出廷する[応じないため保釈金を没収される].

surrender to *one's* ***bail*** (保釈中の被告が)呼び出しに応じて出廷する ▪ The prisoner *surrendered to his bail.* 被告は呼び出しに応じて出廷した.

take bail →accept BAIL.

bait[1] /beɪt/ 名 ***bait and switch*** おとり商法《格安品をおとりに客を集め, 売り切れと言ってより高い商品を買わせる悪徳商法》 ▪ I won't buy a car from this outfit; they're notorious for their *bait and switch* tactics. この店では車を買わない, ここはおとり商法で悪名高いから. ☞《英》では switch-selling と言う.

be fishing without bait 《口》(人)が少し(頭が)おかしい ▪ Apparently the guy *is fishing without bait*: how can we believe him? どうもあいつは少しおかしいようだ. どうして彼の言うことを信じられようか.

fish or cut bait →FISH[2].

in a bait 《学俗》怒っている ▪ He is *in an* awful *bait* this morning. 彼は今朝はひどく怒っている.

jump at the bait えさに飛びつく; たやすくだまされる ▪ They offered a large reward, hoping that someone would *jump at the bait.* 彼らは誰かがまんまとだまされるようにと, 高額の報酬を出すと言った.

rise to the bait (魚が)えさを食べに浮き上がる; (人が)誘いに乗る, 挑発に乗る ▪ He *rose to the bait* and did just as he was expected to do. 彼は誘いに乗って, 期待通りにふるまった.

swallow [***take***] ***the bait*** えさを飲む; 計略に引っかかる ▪ He readily *swallowed the bait.* 彼はすぐに計略に引っかかった ▪ They tried to provoke me, but I never *took the bait.* 彼らは私を怒らせようとしたが, 私は決して挑発に乗らなかった.

bait[2] /beɪt/ 動 ***bait the hook*** (えさで)人を誘惑する ▪ She knows how to *bait the hook* to attract husbands for her daughters. 彼女は娘たちのため未来の夫たちを誘惑して引き寄せる方法を知っている.

bake /beɪk/ 動 ***As they brew, so let them bake.*** 自分がやりだした通りに続けてやらせよ ▪ I should do very imprudently to meddle, but *as they brew, so let them bake.* 私が口を出すのは不謹慎だが, 彼らが始めた通りに続けてやらせてはどうだ.

bake *a person's* ***bread*** 人をやっつける; 殺す ▪ I will *bake his bread* some day. いつかあいつをやっつけてやる.

be (***only***) ***half baked*** 《口》うすのろで(ある) ▪ He *is only half-baked*, put in with the bread and taken out with the cakes. 彼はパンとともに入れられケーキとともに出された, 半焼けだ《頭が弱い》.

baker /béɪkər/ 名 ***a baker's dozen*** →DOZEN.

balance[1] /bǽləns/ 名 ***balance in hand*** 手許金残高; 余分のもの ▪ He won with a nice *balance in hand.* 彼は余裕をもって勝った.

be [***hang, lie, tremble***] ***in the balance*** どちらになるか不安定[未決定]の状態にある, きわどい瀬戸際にある ▪ The problem *is* still *in the balance.* その問題はまだいずれとも決まらない ▪ The fate of Italy was then *trembling in the balance.* 当時イタリアの運命はきわどい瀬戸際にあった.

catch *a person* ***off*** (*his*) ***balance*** →throw a person off (his) BALANCE.

have a good balance (***at*** *one's* ***banker's***) (銀行に借金より)預金のほうが多い ▪ Father *has a good balance at his banker's.* 父は銀行に預金のほうが多い.

hold … in the balance …を不安定[未決定]にしておく ▪ We must not *hold* the issue *in the balance.* その問題を未決定の状態にしておいてはいけない.

hold the balance (二大勢力間にあって)バランスを取っている, 決定権を握っている ▪ Henry VIII *held the balance* with a stronger hand. ヘンリー八世はより強力に二国間のバランスを取った.

keep [***lose***] *one's* ***balance*** (身体・精神の)平衡を保つ[失う], 取り乱さない[取り乱す] ▪ He *lost his balance* and fell off the ladder. 彼は均衡を失いはしごから落ちた.

off (*one's*) ***balance*** **1** 平衡を失って ▪ The canoe became *off balance* and turned over. カヌーは平衡を失って転覆した.

2 気が変で, 狂って, 落ち着きがない ▪ He is quite *off his balance.* 彼は全く気が変だ.

3 度を失って，ざわついて ▪ Mr. Smith's surprise test caught the class *off balance*. スミス先生の不意打ち試験でクラスはざわついた.

on [***upon***] ***balance*** 差し引きして; すべてを考慮に入れて，結局のところ ▪ *On balance* we're £50 richer. 我々は差し引き50ポンドだけ黒字である ▪ The provisions would be, *on balance*, in our interest. 結局のところ，その条項は我々の利益になるだろう.

redress the balance →REDRESS.

strike a balance **1** 差し引き勘定する，清算する《比喩的にも》 ▪ We ought to *strike a* clear *balance* at certain set seasons. 一定の時期に清算すべきである ▪ *Striking a balance*, I should be happier here. 差し引き計算してみてここの方が幸福でしょう.

2 …の間の釣り合いを取る (*between*) ▪ I find it hard to *strike a balance between* work and play. 仕事と遊びの間の釣り合いを取るのはむずかしい.

swing [***tip, turn***] ***the balance*** = TIP the scales 1.

the balance of advantage 差し引きの勝ち味 ▪ *The balance of advantage* is with him. 差し引きの勝ち味は彼の方にある.

throw [***catch***] *a person* ***off*** (*his*) ***balance***

1 人に平衡 [バランス]を失わせる ▪ I *was thrown off balance* by the sudden gust of wind. 突然の突風でバランスを失った.

2 人に平静を失わせる; 人の意表をつく，人をあっけにとらせる，めんくらわす ▪ The minister *was thrown off balance* by the unexpected question. 大臣は予想せぬ質問に平静を失った ▪ The enemy *was thrown off balance*. 敵軍は虚をつかれた ▪ The robbers *caught* Ann *off balance* and stole her purse. 強盗はアンの意表をついて財布を奪った.

tremble in the balance →be in the BALANCE.

weighed in the balance and found wanting テストの結果不合格になる; まさかの時の試練に耐えない (《聖》*Dan*. 5. 27) ▪ You were *weighed in the balance and found wanting*. 君はテストの結果不合格になった ▪ There are many who when *weighed in the balance* are *found wanting*. まさかの時の試練に耐えない人が多い.

balance[2] /bǽləns/ 動 ***balance*** *oneself* 体の釣り合いをとる ▪ He *balanced himself* on one leg. 彼は片足で体の釣り合いをとった.

balance (*one's*) ***accounts*** (***with***) → ACCOUNT[1].

balance between (二者)の間でためらう[ちゅうちょする] ▪ I am dying, *balanced between* the darkness and the light. 私は闇と光の間でためらいながら死にかけている.

bald /bɔːld/ 形 (***as***) ***bald as a coot*** [***an egg***] →COOT.

bald-headed /bɔ̀ːldhédəd/ 形 ***go bald-headed*** 《口》(危険・障害を無視して…に)がむしゃらにぶつかっていく (*at, for*); (に)すべてをかけてやる (*into*) ▪ It is the way of a woman to *go bald-headed at* her objectives. 自分の目的に向かってがむしゃらに突進するのが女性の常である ▪ He *went bald-headed for* the enemy. 彼はがむしゃらに敵にぶつかっていった. ☞bald-headed は「かつらを着けずに」の意; 力仕事をするにはかつらは着けないことから.

snatch [***jerk***]***... bald-headed*** 《米口》…を手荒く扱う，虐待する ▪ I'll *jerk* them *bald-headed*. やつらをひどい目にあわせてやるんだ.

bale /beɪl/ 動 =BAIL.

baleful /béɪlfəl/ 形 (***as***) ***baleful as death*** 不吉な，悪意に満ちた ▪ His premonition was *baleful as death*. 彼の予感は不吉なものだった.

balk[1] /bɔːk/,《英》**baulk**[1] /bɔːlk/ 名 ***make a balk*** [***balks***] すき残しをする ▪ He that plows must *make* no *balks*. (畑を)すく人はすき残しをしてはならない.

make a balk [***balks***] ***of good ground*** 好機を捨てる，むだにする ▪ The rich Corinthian, in not inviting the poor, *made balks of good ground*. 金持ちのコリント人は貧しい人々を招かなかったので好機を捨てたわけだ.

balk[2] /bɔːk/,《英》**baulk**[2] /bɔːlk/ 動 ***be balked of*** …を得そこなう，をやりそこなう ▪ He *was balked of* his purpose. 彼は目的を遂げそこなった ▪ He *was balked of* his prey. 彼は獲物を取りそこなった.

ball[1] /bɔːl/ 名 ***a ball of fire*** 《口》精力的な腕きき ▪ As a salesman, he is *a ball of fire*. 営業マンとしては彼はばりばりの腕ききだ.

a ball of fortune 運命にほんろうされた人 ▪ He is *a ball of fortune*. 彼は世の浮き沈みを経た人である.

a different ball of wax 全く似てないもの ▪ A city-owned casino is *a different ball of wax* altogether. 都市所有のカジノは総じて全く似ていない.

a passed ball 《野球》パスボール ▪ The batter singled and went to second on *a passed ball*. バッターは単打を打ち，パスボールで二塁に進んだ.

a (***whole***) ***different*** [***new***] ***ball game*** 今までとは違う状況 ▪ If military force were to be used, then that could be *a* completely *different ball game*. もし万一軍隊を使用するのであれば，全く別な話になるだろう ▪ The Prime Minister promised that 2011 will be *whole new ball game*. 2011年は全く違った状況になると総理が約束した.

ball and chain **1** (囚人の足につけた)鎖つき鉄丸 ▪ They are forced to wear a 25 pound *ball and chain* attached to one ankle. 彼らは片方の足首に25ポンドの鎖つき鉄丸を無理にくくりつけられる.

2《俗》足手まとい《特に妻子》 ▪ Where is your *ball and chain*?—You mean my beloved daughter? In school. 君の足手まといはどこにいる—娘のことかい，学校さ.

be no ball of fire 《米口》精力家[やり手]ではない ▪ John *is* tactful and inoffensive, but decidedly *no ball of fire*. ジョンは如才なく悪意がないが，絶対にやり手ではない.

B

be on the ball 《口》理解[反応]が早い ▪Owing to lack of sleep, I'*m* not *on the ball* today. 寝不足のためにきょうは頭の働きが鈍い.

behind the eight ball 《口》窮地に陥って ▪The Dodgers got *behind the eight ball.* ドジャースは窮地に陥った. ☞Pocket Billiards で8番球に cue ball を当ててはならない; この球の後ろに来たら万事休することから.

break *a person's* ***balls*** 《卑》**1** 人を怒って非難する ▪The boss *broke my balls* for being late every day. 毎日遅刻したことで上司は私を激しくなじった.

2 →bust a person's BALLs.

break *one's* ***balls*** 《米俗》熱心に努力する (*to do*) ▪Bent is *breaking his balls to* be the big fish in the city. ベントはその町の大物になるためにしゃかりきに頑張っている.

bust *a person's* ***balls*** 《卑》人をからかう ▪Don't get offended, man, I'm just *bustin' your balls*! おい怒るなって, ただからかっているだけだから.

bust (*one's*) ***balls*** 《卑》(むだになるときがあっても)すごく頑張る ▪The cops will *bust balls* but that's it. 警官たちはしゃかりきになるだろうが, それまでさ.

carry the ball (***for***) 《米》(...のために)最も重要な[困難な]仕事をする, 推進役となる ▪He will probably *carry the ball for* the West. 彼はおそらく西欧のために難局にあたるであろう ▪Volunteers *carried the ball* in his campaign. 彼の選挙運動ではボランティアらが推進役となった. ☞ラグビーで球を持って走る者が一番重要な仕事をすることから.

catch [***take***] ***the ball before the bound*** **1** 早手回しをする, 機先を制する ▪We prevent them and *catch the ball before the bound.* 我々は彼らを阻止し機先を制する.

2 早まる ▪It is important for you not to *take the ball before the bound.* あなたは早まらないことが重要である. ☞アメフト用語から.

catch the ball on the bound 好機をつかむ ▪It was the one job in the world for him, and he *caught the ball on the bound.* それは彼には唯一の職であったので, 彼はこの好機をつかんだ.

cold enough to freeze the balls off a brass monkey 《英俗》べらぼうに寒い ▪It is *cold enough to freeze the balls off a brass monkey* here in winter. 当地は冬場はべらぼうに寒い.

crystal ball 水晶玉; 未来を占う手段 ▪So what does your *crystal ball* say about the coming election? では, 君の占いでは来たる選挙はどうなるのかね.

drop the ball 《米口》失敗をする, へまをする (*on*) ▪Every time I depend on him, he *drops the ball.* 私が彼を当てにするたびに彼はへまをやる ▪You *dropped the ball on* the project. あのプロジェクトで君は失敗をした.

eat the ball 《野球・俗》(つかんだ球をなげずに)つかんだままにする ▪The third baseman decided to *eat the ball* rather than risk a throw. 三塁手はボールを投げる危険を冒すよりも捕ったままにすることに決めた.

get *one's* ***balls chewed off*** 《卑》ぼろくそにやっつけられる ▪Why am I *getting my balls chewed off* for it? なぜおれはそのためにぼろくそにやっつけられているのか?

get on the ball 《米口》機敏[精勤, 敏腕]になる ▪He must *get on the ball* if he is to succeed. 彼は成功しようと思うなら機敏で抜け目なく行動しなければならない.

get [***set, start***] ***the ball rolling*** →start the BALL rolling.

go under the wrecking ball (鉄製ボールで)取り壊す ▪That lovely old building finally *went under the wrecking ball.* あの美しい古くからの建物がとうとう取り壊された.

have [***not have***] ***a crystal ball*** 将来を占う力がある[ない] ▪Asked about the economy, he said, "I don't *have a crystal ball.*" 経済について聞かれて, 彼は「私には未来を占う力はありません」と答えた.

have brass [***cast-iron***] ***balls*** 《俗》くそ度胸がある, むちゃをする ▪God bless him, because Carson Palmer *has brass balls.* カースン・パーマーに神の祝福あれ, だって彼はむちゃをするから.

have [***hold***] *a person* ***by the balls*** 《俗》人の急所[金玉]を握る ▪You have to pay up—they'*ve got* you *by the balls.* 君は残金を皆済しなきゃだめだ—彼らは君の急所を握っているのだ ▪The kidnappers *had* his family *by the balls* for six months. 誘拐犯は6か月にわたって彼の家族の弱みを握っていた.

have [***keep***] *one's* ***eyes on the ball*** →EYE.

have much [***it,*** etc.] ***on the ball*** 《口》大いに[など]有能である[練達している, 長所がある] ▪He will do well in that work, because he *has a lot on the ball.* 彼はその仕事を立派にやるだろう, 巧者だから ▪The manager *has nothing on the ball.* 支配人はまるで能力がない. ☞特別なスピードまたはカーブをもつ野球のピッチャーから.

have the ball at *one's* ***feet*** [***before*** *one*] 《口・古風》成功の目安が立っている; 今好機に恵まれている ▪He was chosen for the post and now *has the ball at his feet.* 彼はその地位に選ばれ今や成功の見込みが立っている. ☞フットボールでボールが足もとにころがっていることから.

have the ball in *one's* ***court*** この次は自分の責任[番]である ▪There was no way that Liz could avoid responding. She *had the ball in her court.* リズが答えずにいることはできなかった. 今度は彼女が答える番だった.

have the world by the balls 《俗》世間を牛耳っている, 圧倒的に有利な[強い]立場にいる ▪When I'm on stage I feel like I *have the world by the balls.* 舞台に立っているとき、私は世間を牛耳っているような気がする.

hit the ball 《米俗》**1** せっせとやる, 速く行く ▪These trains *hit the ball* at 150 miles an hour.

これらの列車は1時間150マイルで疾走する.

2 長くうまく働く ▪ You've got to *hit the ball*. 君は長くうまく働かなければならない. ☞おそらく野球から; あるいは鉄道のレールの先端を ball と言い「汽車が速く走る」の意から.

juggle the ball in the air 同時にいろいろなことをする ▪ He has succeeded so far by *juggling the ball in the air* at the same time. 彼は同時にいろいろなことをやって, これまでは成功してきた.

keep the ball in the air **1** (討論・その他を)うまく運ぶ ▪ The chairman *kept the ball in the air*. 議長が討論をうまく運んだ.

2 =juggle the BALL in the air.

keep the ball rolling [***up***]/ ***keep up the ball*** 《口》(会話・仕事を)だれさせないようにする, とぎれさせないようにする ▪ I put a word in now and then to *keep the ball up*. 私は会話がとぎれないようにするため時おり一言さしはさんだ ▪ The sales figures have been much better this quarter, so let's *keep the ball rolling*, guys! 今期は売り上げの数字が以前よりはずっとよくなっている. だからだれさせないようにしようぜ, みんな!

look [***peer***] ***into the crystal ball*** 未来を占う ▪ *Peer into the crystal ball* and see your future! 未来を占ってあなたの将来を見てごらん.

make a balls of 《俗》...をぶちこわす; にしくじる (make a mess of) ▪ He *made a balls of* the plan. 彼はその計画をめちゃめちゃにした.

not get *one's* ***balls in an uproar*** 《俗》大騒ぎしない, おたおたしない, 冷静でいる ▪ Now let's *not get your balls in an uproar*. さて, おたおたしないようにしようぜ.

on the ball **1**《口》油断なく見張って, 機敏にやって ▪ Get *on the ball*. ぼやぼやするな ▪ We've got to be *on the ball* to win next November. 来たる11月の選挙に勝つためには油断なく行動せねばならない ▪ If you want to finish this on time, we must keep *on the ball*. これを時間きっかりに仕上げたいなら, 絶えず機敏にやらなければならない.

2 有能である ▪ The teacher is really *on the ball*. あの教師は実に有能だ.

pick up [***take***] ***the ball and run*** (***with it***) 《主に米》(他人の)着想[計画]を引き継いで推し進める; (他の者にやらせて失敗したあとで)事の責任を取る ▪ A good proposal. We should *pick up the ball and run with it*. いい提案だ. そいつを引き継いで推し進めるべきだ ▪ You don't believe that anyone is going to *pick up the ball and run with it*. あなたは誰もが責任を取るつもりはないと思うのですね.

play ball **1** 球戯をする; 球技を始める ▪ We *played ball* for two hours. 我々は2時間球戯をした ▪ *Play ball!* プレイボール《試合開始》.

2《口》協力する, 共に働く (*with*) ▪ The Americans and British are not *playing ball*. 米英は協力していない ▪ We must *play ball with* the Americans. 我々はアメリカ国民と協力せねばならない.

put balls on 《米俗》...をもっと立派にする ▪ Rewrite it and *put balls on* it. 書き直してもっと立派にしなさい.

put much [etc.] ***on the ball*** 《野球》(投手が)投球に全力を注ぐ, 敏腕を発揮する ▪ He *put everything on the ball*. 彼は全力投球した ▪ They try to *put much on the ball*. 彼らは敏腕を発揮しようとしている.

put the ball in *a person's* ***court*** 今度は...の行動する番である ▪ The threat of further sanctions has *put the ball in North Korea's court*. 一層の制裁が加えられる兆しに, 今度は北朝鮮が打って出る番になった.

run with the ball 《口》事業を引き取って推進する ▪ If management approves the concept, we'll *run with the ball*. 経営陣がこの考えをよしとするなら, この事業を推進しよう.

start [***get, set***] ***the ball rolling*** 《口》会[運動, 本業]を開始する; の皮切りをする; 事をうまく始める ▪ He *started the* conversational *ball rolling*. 彼は話を切り出した ▪ He *set the ball rolling* by being the first to donate 1,000 dollars. 彼は最初に1,000ドル寄付して募金運動の皮切りをした ▪ The director *started the ball rolling* by a speech. 重役はあいさつをして会を始めた.

take the ball before the bound →catch the BALL before the bound.

take up the ball (話題などで)自分の番で引き取って話す, (会話・仕事で)順番を務める ▪ Rose *took up the ball*. 今度はローズが引き取って話をした.

That's the way [***That's how***] ***the ball bounces.*** 《口》これが人生というものさ (= That's the way the COOKIE crumbles).

(***the***) ***ball is in your*** [***his,*** etc.] ***court*** 今度は君[彼, など]が行動する番だ ▪ *The ball is in your court*. Look sharp. 今度は君が行動する番だ. しっかりやれよ.

The ball is with you. さあ[今度は]君の番だ.

(***the sign of***) ***the three*** (***golden***) ***balls*** 《英》質屋(の看板) ▪ My watch is at *the sign of the three golden balls*. 私の腕時計は質屋に入っている. ☞質屋は三つの金ボールを看板にしたから.

the whole ball of wax 《米口》あらゆること[もの], いっさいがっさい ▪ The union demanded higher wages, a pension plan, job security—*the whole ball of wax*. 組合は賃上げ, 年金プラン, 職の安定—つまりいっさいがっさいを要求した.

ball[2] /bɔːl/ 名 ***have*** (*oneself*) ***a ball*** 《口》楽しく過ごす ▪ He *had himself a ball* last Sunday. 彼はこの前の日曜に楽しく過ごした ▪ He is *having a ball*, criticizing the neighbors. 彼は隣人たちの悪口を言って大いに楽しんでいる.

lead (***up***) ***the ball*** 舞踏会の先導となる《出席者のうち最も著名な二人の役目》 ▪ Mr. Thornhill and my daughter *led up the ball*. ソーンヒル氏と私の娘がダンス会の先導をした.

open the ball **1** 一番に踊って舞踏会を始める ▪ The squire *opened the ball* by dancing with

John's wife. まず地方の名士がジョンの妻と踊って舞踏会が始まった.

2 (事を)始める, 口を切る ▪ Very well, I'll *open the ball* by reading out the list of members. よろしい, 私が皮切りに会員名簿を読みあげよう ▪ Bill *opened the ball* with a splendid song. ビルが一番初めにすばらしい歌を歌った.

ball[3] /bɔːl/ 動 ***ball it up*** 《米俗》楽しく過ごす ▪ Well, let's *ball it up* for a night. さあ一晩楽しく過ごそうぜ.

ball[4] /bɔːl/ 動 ***ball the jack*** 《米俗》急いで行く, 疾走する ▪ The car certainly did *ball the jack*. 車は確かに疾走した.

ballast /bǽləst/ 名 ***give ballast to*** ...を安定させる ▪ It *gave ballast to* the mind adrift on change. それは流転の波にただよう心を落ち着かせた.

have no ballast 気骨がない, すぐ影響を受ける ▪ He *has* got *no ballast* whatever. 彼は全く気骨がない.

in ballast **1** 船倉に ▪ Ninety were sick *in ballast*. 船倉で90人が船酔いしていた.

2 底荷だけ積んで ▪ They were merchantmen bound *in ballast* from Le Havre. それらはルアーブル港から底荷だけ積んで出港した商船だった.

3 底荷として ▪ Sea-coal was taken *in ballast*. 石炭が底荷として積み込まれた.

4 着実である, 安全である ▪ You can trust that firm; the partners are *in ballast*. あの会社は信用できる. 社員たちが着実だから.

ballgame /bɔ́ːlgèɪm/ 名 ***a*** (***whole***) ***new ballgame*** 完全に異なった[新しい]状況 ▪ Websites are *a whole new ballgame* for most of us. ウェブサイトなんて我々の大半のものにとって全く新しい状況だ.

ballistic /bəlístɪk/ 形 ***go ballistic*** 《俗》猛烈に怒る, 切れる ▪ Dad will *go ballistic* when he sees you dented the new car. おまえが新車にへこみをつけたことを知ったら, パパはぶち切れるだろう. ☞ 誘導ミサイルが爆発することから.

balloon /bəlúːn/ 名 ***a trial balloon*** (しばしばビジネス・政治の)測風気球, (一般大衆の反応を探るための)試案, 探り ▪ Reports of the chairman's resignation could just be *a trial balloon* to see how shareholders react. 議長辞任の報告は, 株主がどのように反応するかを探るためのものに過ぎないかもしれない ▪ The governor has put up *a trial balloon* for a tax hike. 州知事は増税の試案を発表した ▪ I decided to float *a trial balloon* to see if the idea would gain popularity. その着想が大衆受けをするかどうか探りを入れることにした ▪ John had an excellent idea, but when we sent up *a trial balloon*, the response was very negative. ジョンはすばらしい着想を得たが, 大衆の反応に探りを入れると, 返ってきたのはひどく否定的なものだった.

go over [***down***] ***like a lead balloon*** 《口》(スピーチ・提案が)失敗に終わる, (冗談が)受けない ▪ His brilliant idea *went down like a lead balloon*. 彼のすばらしい着想も失敗に終わった ▪ His joke *went over like a lead balloon*. 彼のジョークは受けなかった.

if [***when***] ***the balloon goes up*** 《口》(恐れていた)危機[大変なこと]が起こったならば[とき] ▪ They believed that *if the balloon went up*, Japan would fight. 危機が始まるならば日本は戦うだろうと彼らは信じていた ▪ *When the balloon went up*, her father was abroad. その大変なことが起こったとき彼女の父は外国にいた. ☞ 第一次世界大戦時に総攻撃を始める前に気球を上げたことから.

swell like a balloon (胃が)張る ▪ If you eat too many peas and onions, your stomach will *swell like a balloon*. 豆とタマネギを食べ過ぎると, 胃がパンパンに膨れます.

ballot /bǽlət/ 名 ***by ballot*** 投票で ▪ We elected him *by ballot*. 我々は投票で彼を選挙した.

cast a [*one's*] ***ballot*** 投票する ▪ I *cast a ballot* for him. 私は彼に1票を投じた.

cast a single ballot 《米》選挙人の総意を代表して1票を投じる《公務以外の職に選ばれたとき, 満場一致であることを示すため選挙事務官が選挙人を代表して1票を投じる》 ▪ To save time the assistant secretary *cast a single ballot* as the unanimous vote of all for Dr. Nickim. 時間節約のため書記官補がニキム博士のため選挙人の総意を代表して1票を投じた.

take a ballot 投票を行う ▪ We *took a ballot* for the office. その役を投票で決めた.

ballot box /bǽlətbɑ̀ks|-bɔ̀ks/ 名 ***stuff the ballot box*** 票の水増しをする ▪ It is a crime to *stuff the ballot box*. 票の水増しをするのは犯罪だ.

ballpark /bɔ́ːlpɑ̀ːrk/ 名 ***a ballpark estimate*** [***figure***] 《米口》およその見積もり[数字] ▪ I'd say two hundred dollars, but that's *a ballpark figure*. まあ200ドルってところだが, それは概算だよ. ☞ 野球場の入場数がいい加減であったことから.

all over the ballpark 《俗》全く焦点がぼけて, 支離滅裂で (= all over the LOT) ▪ His answers were *all over the ballpark*. 彼の答えはぐだぐだだった.

in the (***right***) ***ballpark*** 《口》(数量などが)概算で; ほぼ正しい, ほぼ当を得た ▪ Your estimate is high, but still *in the ballpark*. 君の概算は高いが, それでもほぼ正しい.

in the same ballpark as 《口》...とほぼ同等である, 比肩しうる ▪ We put gluttony *in the same ballpark as* smoking. 我々は大食いは喫煙とほぼ同等のものと考える.

out of the ballpark 《口》予想される量を超えて ▪ His estimate was completely *out of the ballpark*. 彼の見積もりは予想範囲を大きく外れていた.

balm /bɑːm/ 名 ***balm of*** [***in***] ***Gilead*** ギレアドバルサム《カンラン科の常緑樹; (それから取る)オレオ樹脂; 昔は防腐剤・外傷薬として珍重された》; 慰め, 救い, 静めるもの (《聖》*Jer*. 8. 22) ▪ The sale of the *balm of Gilead* was quite extensive. バルサムの販売は非常に手広かった.

ban /bæn/ 名 ***a blanket ban*** 全面禁止 ▪ In

certain areas *a blanket ban* was imposed on the education of Muslim girls. ある地域ではイスラム教徒の女子の教育が全面禁止になった.

***lift* [*remove*] *the ban* (*on*)** (...の)禁止を解く ▪ The Tsar *lifted the ban on* foreign travel. ロシア皇帝は海外旅行の禁を解いた.

place* [*put*]... *under the ban ...を禁止する ▪ The practice *was placed under the ban.* その慣習は禁止された ▪ He *was put under the ban* of public opinion. 彼は世論の排斥を受けた.

banana /bənǽnə|-ná:nə/ 名 ***a banana republic*** 《口》バナナ共和国《果物輸出貿易や外資への依存度が高く政治的に不安定な小国》 ▪ *A banana republic* is a derogatory term. バナナ共和国は侮蔑語である.

***a banana skin* [*peel*]** 《英》(バナナの皮から)つまずきの原因, 落とし穴 ▪ Trying to use French proved to be *a banana skin* for him. フランス語を使おうとして, 彼はかかなくてもいい恥をかいた.

banana oil 《俗》大げさな[白々しい]お世辞 ▪ Cut out the *banana oil*; flattery will get you nowhere! 白々しいお世辞はやめなさい. 追従を言っても何の役にも立たないよ.

big* [*top*] *banana 《俗》有力者, 最重要人物 (↔second BANANA) ▪ He became the *big banana* only a few years ago. 彼はほんの数年前に有力者になったばかりだ ▪ Sharapova was *top banana* at the U.S. Open. シャラポワは全米オープンでは最有力選手だった.

Cool bananas! →COOL beans!

go bananas 《口》 **1** (人が)かっとする (rave) ▪ Mom'll *go bananas* if she sees this mess. この散らかしようを見たら, おふくろは頭にくるだろうな.
2 頭がおかしくなる; (機械などが)調子が狂う ▪ We think Burt has *gone bananas*. バートは頭がおかしくなったと思う ▪ My PC is *going bananas*. 僕のパソコンは調子が狂いかけている.

second banana 《主に米俗》(寄席演芸などの)脇役; 二次的な役割の人 (↔big BANANA) ▪ Melissa used to be the *second banana* as a comedian. メリッサは以前コメディアンとしては二流だった.

slip on a banana skin 《口》失態を演じる ▪ The director has *slipped on a banana skin* in her last film. その監督は最近の映画で失態を演じた ▪ He *slipped on a banana skin* soon after getting a job. 彼は仕事に就いてすぐに失態を演じた.

band /bænd/ 名 ***be* [*feel*] *like an elastic band about to snap*** 非常にストレスが溜まっている, 限界寸前である ▪ I *felt like an elastic band about to snap*; suicide seemed to be the only way out. もう限界だと感じた. 自殺するしか解決法はないように思えた.

beat the band 《口》盛んにやる, ひどすぎるほどやる; すべてに勝る, すばらしい ▪ Doesn't that *beat the band*? それはすばらしいではないか. ☞「楽隊を負かして自分の声を聞かせる」が原義.

to beat the band/to beat all 群を抜いて, すごく ▪ She was at church praying *to beat the band.* 彼女は教会で盛んにお祈りをしていた ▪ It was raining *to beat the band.* すごい雨だった.

when the band begins to play 事態が重大化するとき ▪ It's send for the military quickly *when the band begins to play.* 情勢重大化のときは,「早く軍隊を出動させろ」だ.

bandbox /bǽndbɑ̀ks|-bɔ̀ks/ 名 **(*as*) *neat as a bandbox*** →NEAT.

***bandbox fresh* [*neat*]** きちんとした服装で ▪ Nothing looks so *bandbox fresh* on a warm summer day as a smart cotton dress. 暑い夏の日にはぱりっとした綿のドレスほどスマートに見えるものはない.

look as if* one *had just come* [*stepped*] *out of* [*from*] *a bandbox 特別身ぎれいな様子をしている ▪ He always *looks as if* he *had just come out of a bandbox.* 彼はいつもすばらしくきちんとした身なりをしている.

bandit /bǽndət/ 名 ***a one-armed bandit*** (スロットマシーンなどの)賭博機 ▪ We use the tokens, not coins, on the *one-armed bandit.* スロットマシーンには硬貨ではなくてトークンが使用される.

like a bandit 《米俗》大成功をおさめて, 意気揚々と ▪ He came out of the battle *like a bandit.* 彼は意気揚々とその闘いから出てきた.

make out like a bandit 《米俗》大成功をおさめる, ぼろもうけする; たくさんのプレゼント[お金]をもらう ▪ He invested in real estate and *made out like a bandit.* 彼は不動産に投資してぼろもうけした ▪ His kids *make out like bandits* every Christmas. 彼の子供たちは毎年クリスマスにはたくさんのプレゼントをもらう.

bandwag(g)on /bǽndwæ̀gən/ 名 ***climb* [*get, hop, jump, leap, ride*] *on* [*aboard, into*] *the bandwagon*** 《口》優勢な方を支持する; 時流に乗る; 優勢な運動に加わる ▪ He has recently *hopped on the* Wilkie *bandwagon.* 彼は最近優勢なウィルキー側についた ▪ Democratic politicians like to *get into the bandwagon.* 民主党政治家たちは優勢な方へ回るのを好む. ☞アメリカの選挙で候補者の人気をあおるため楽隊車で町をねり歩き, その候補を支持する地方の有力な指導者たちはこの車に乗って行った, という風習から.

the bandwagon effect 《心理》先陣効果《多くの人間が考え感じている方向にひきずられる傾向》 ▪ Critics allege that election polls create a "*bandwagon effect*". 選挙投票は「先陣効果」を引き起こすと批評家は断言する.

bandy /bǽndi/ 動 ***bandy words* [*blows*] *with*** ...と言い[なぐり]合いをする ▪ I *bandied blows* [*words*] *with* him. 私は彼となぐり[言い]合いをした. ☞アイルランドの bandy (ホッケーの前身)という競技から.

bane /beɪn/ 名 ***be the bane of*** ...の破滅の因である, のがんである ▪ Drink *was the bane of* his life. 酒が彼の破滅の元だった ▪ Sectarianism *is the bane of* religion. 宗閥は宗教のがんである.

bang[1] /bæŋ/ 名間副 ***bang for** one's **buck*** 《米口》(支払った)金に見合う価値，ちゃんとした見返り ▪ That boss is said to drug his workers in order to get more *bang for his buck*. あの親方はもっと多くの見返りを得るために労働者に麻薬を飲ませると言われている.

bang go →go BANG.

bang goes 《口》(希望などが)あっけなく消え去る，おじゃんだ ▪ *Bang goes* my vacation plans this summer. 今年の夏休みの計画もあっけなく消えちゃった ▪ I have to work overtime this evening. Oh well, *bang goes* my date! 今晩は残業をしないといけない. やれやれ，これでデートもおじゃんだ.

bang off 《英俗》直ちに，すぐさま ▪ I'll come *bang off*. 直ちに参ります.

bang on 《英口》(見積もり・記述などが)どんぴしゃの，ずばり的中して，当を得た (spot on) ▪ *Bang on*! よろしい (= ALL right!) ▪ As a realistic tale, it is *bang on*. 写実的な物語としてそれはすぐれている ▪ I found this estimate was *bang on*. この見積もりはどんぴしゃであることがわかった ▪ You were *bang on* when you called him a idiot. 君が彼のことをばかと呼んだのは当を得たものだった.

bang to rights →dead to RIGHTs.

come bang up against …にドスンとぶつかる ▪ The truck *came bang up against* the fence. トラックはフェンスにドスンとぶつかった.

fall bang in the middle 《口》ちょうどまん中に落ちる ▪ A bomb *fell bang in the middle* of the road. 爆弾は道路のちょうどまん中に落ちた.

get* [*give*] *a bang **1** ガンと打たれる[打つ] ▪ I *got a bang* on the head. 私は頭をガンと打たれた.
2 ぞっとするようなうれしさを感じる[与える] ▪ I *get a bang* out of this. これがぞっとするほどうれしい ▪ It *gave* me *a bang* to be with her. 彼女といっしょにいるとぞっとするほどうれしかった.

get a bang out of 《米口》大いに楽しむ[喜ぶ] ▪ Bill really *got a bang out of* the present we gave him. ビルは我々があげた贈り物を大いに喜んでくれた.

get little bang for** one's **buck 《主に米口》費やした金ほど儲かっていない ▪ The company is *getting little bang for its buck*. その会社はだんだん元手が取れなくなっている.

get more* [*better, a bigger*] *bang for the buck*/*get more bangs for** one's **bucks 《主に米口》費やした金以上のものを得る ▪ You'll definitely *get more bang for the buck* when you buy these jackets. この上着を買えば，確かに費やした金以上のものを得るでしょう. ☞bang「興奮」; buck「1ドル，金銭」.

give* [*offer, provide*] *more bang for** one's **buck 《主に米口》費やした金以上のものを与える ▪ Plasma TVs *give more "bang for your buck."* プラズマテレビは，費やした金以上のものを与える.

go bang 大音を発して爆発する[破裂する，吹っ飛ぶ，ぶつかる，閉まる] ▪ *Bang went* the gun. 鉄砲がズドンと鳴った ▪ The door *went bang*. 戸はピシャリと閉まった ▪ The airships *went bang* in the night. その飛行船は夜中に爆発した ▪ My career *went bang*, the agent said. 私の履歴は吹っ飛んでしまったと代理人が言った.

go over* [*out*] *with a bang*/*go* (*off*) *with a bang 《英》大成功を収める ▪ The play *went over with a bang*. 芝居は大成功だった ▪ The season *went with a bang*, with the Yankees taking the pennant. このシーズンは大成功を収め，ヤンキースがペナントを取った.

have* [*get*]*... bang to rights 《米俗》(ある事)に精通している，に正確である; (人)を現行犯で捕える ▪ He *has* it *bang to rights*. 彼はそれに精通している ▪ The police *got* the thief *bang to rights*. 警察は賊を現行犯逮捕した. ☞bang to rights = rightly.

not with a bang, but* (*with*) *a whimper (物事の終わりが)堂々とでなく，しょんぼりと《T. S. Eliot, *The Hollow Men* (1925)》 ▪ This is the way the world ends. *Not with a bang but a whimper*. 世界はこんなふうに終わる―堂々とでなく，しょんぼりと.

***the whole bang* (*shoot*)** 《口》全部，ありったけ，何もかも ▪ Now they have *the whole bang shoot* at their disposal. 今や彼らは全て自由に使用できる.

with a bang 《口》 **1** ズドンと，ドシンと ▪ The gun went off *with a bang*. 銃がズドンと発射された ▪ He always shuts the door *with a bang*. 彼はいつも戸をバタンと閉める.
2 威勢よく，どんどん ▪ He worked *with a bang*. 彼はどんどん働いた.
3 《米》全速力で ▪ They went off *with a bang*. 彼らは全速力で出発した.
4 うまく; 熱狂的に ▪ The new movie went over *with a bang*. 今度の映画はすごく当たった.

bang[2] /bæŋ/ 動 ***bang* (*a door*) *to*** (ドアを)バタンと閉める ▪ The *door was banged to*. ドアはバタンと閉められた. ☞to /tuː/「停止・閉鎖の状態へ」は副詞.

bang** one's **head against a brick wall → beat one's HEAD against a (stone, brick) wall.

bang ... into** a person's **head 《口》人の頭に(知識)をたたきこむ ▪ The teacher will *bang* something *into my son's head*. 先生は何か息子の頭にたたきこんでくれるだろう.

bangup /bǽŋʌ̀p/ 形 ***a bangup job*** 《米口》素晴らしい仕事 ▪ This is *a bangup job* you've done, and I thank you. 素晴らしい仕事をしてくれたね，礼を言うよ.

banish /bǽnɪʃ/ 動 ***banish ...from memory*** …をすっかり忘れてしまう ▪ The first visit to Niagara is not easily *be banished from memory*. ナイアガラを初めて訪れたときのことは容易に忘れられない.

bank[1] /bæŋk/ 名 ***a piggy bank*** (ブタの形をした)貯金箱 ▪ John's mother gave him *a piggy bank*. ジョンの母は彼に貯金箱を与えた.

break* [《米口》*burst*] *the bank **1** 《口》(賭け勝

負で)親元を倒す, 親の金を巻き上げてしまう ▪ He *broke the bank* three nights running at Paris. 彼はパリで3夜続けて親を倒した.

2〚否定文で〛高くて買えない《「胴元を破産させる」から》 ▪ Though a bit expensive, this diamond ring won't *break the bank*. 少し高価だが, このダイヤの指輪, 高くて買えないほどじゃない.

3(人を)無一文にする ▪ A few pence will not *break the bank*. 数ペンス使っても無一文にはなるまい.

can take it to the bank《米口》信頼してよい, 確かである ▪ What I am telling you is the truth. You *can take it to the bank*. 君に話しているのは本当のことだ. まちがいなく確かだよ.

cry all the way to the bank 悲しみながらも金を受け取って喜ぶ ▪ When his rich aunt died, he was *crying all the way to the bank*. 金持ちのおばが死んだとき, 彼は悲しみながらも金が入ってホクホクだった.

in the bank 銀行に預けて ▪ I have some money *in the bank*. 私は多少の金を銀行に預けてある.

laugh all the way to the bank《口》儲かって笑いが止まらない ▪ The guy who thought of this must be *laughing all the way to the bank*. これを考えついた男は儲かって笑いが止まらないにちがいない.

make bank《米俗》(短期間に)ばりばり儲ける ▪ I'll be *making bank* with my new job. 新しい仕事でばりばり儲けるぞ.

bank[2] /bæŋk/ 名 ***give*** *a person* ***down the banks***《米口》人をしかる, 責める ▪ He *gave* me *down the banks* for not telling him. 彼は私が彼に言わなかったとひどくしかった. ☞アイルランド語法.

out of bank《米口》(川が)氾濫して ▪ The river is *out of bank*. 川が氾濫している.

banker /bǽŋkər/ 名 ***banker's hour*** 銀行家の時刻《朝の10時頃》 ▪ Well, *banker's hour* today, Tom! トム君, きょうは大変出勤が遅いんですね. ☞銀行の頭取りは遅く出勤したから.

banker's hours(午前10時から午後3時までの)短い勤務時間 ▪ Hugh doesn't really work full-time. He keeps *banker's hours*. ヒューは実は8時間の基準労働をしてはいない. 10時から3時までの短時間勤務だ.

Let me be your banker. ご入り用の金をお貸ししましょう ▪ Mr. Smith, *let me be your banker*. スミスさん, ご入り用のお金をご用立てしましょう.

bankrupt /bǽŋkrʌpt/ 形 ***(be) bankrupt of***(当然あるべきもの)が全然ない, なくなった ▪ The newspapers accused the government of *being bankrupt of* ideas. 新聞は政府が無策であるといって責めた.

go bankrupt 破産する ▪ What would happen if Greece *went bankrupt*? ギリシャが破産したらどうなるだろうか.

banner /bǽnər/ 名 ***carry the banner*** **1** …の先頭に立つ; を支持[代表]する(*for*) ▪ This restaurant still *carries the banner for* English dishes. このレストランは今なおイギリス料理を代表している.

2 窮乏している ▪ I have *carried the banner* in the slum. 私は貧民街で窮乏してきた.

fight under the banner of《雅》…の旗じるしのもとに戦う ▪ We shall *fight under the banner of* freedom. 我々は自由の旗じるしのもとに戦うだろう.

follow the banner of《雅》…の旗下に加わる, の配下になる, の軍に加わる ▪ A large number *followed the banner of* a Scottish knight named Wallace. 多数がウォレスというスコットランドの騎士の旗下に参じた.

under the banner of …の旗じるしのもとに ▪ Sometimes an act of terrorism is done *under the banner of* religion. ときとしてテロ行為が宗教の旗じるしのもとになされることがある.

banns /bænz/ 名 ***ask*** [***call, publish, put up***] ***the banns***(牧師が教会で)結婚予告をして異議の有無を問う《挙式前に連続3回日曜日に行う》 ▪ *The banns* will *be asked* three Sundays successively. 結婚予告は連続3回日曜日に行われよう.

forbid the banns 結婚に異議を申し立てる《比喩的にも》 ▪ The parents of his mistress *forbad the banns*. 彼の愛人の両親が結婚に異議を申し立てた ▪ I *forbid the banns* of that marriage. 私はその結婚の異議を申し立てる.

have *one's* ***banns asked*** [***called***] 教会で結婚予告をしてもらう ▪ He *had his banns called* last Sunday. 彼は前の日曜に結婚予告をしてもらった.

baptism /bǽptɪzəm/ 名 ***a baptism of*** [***by***] ***fire***/*one's* [***the***] ***baptism of fire*** 聖霊による霊的洗礼(《聖》*Acts* 2. 3); (新兵の受ける)砲火の洗礼; 初めての厳しい試練 ▪ Audie received *his baptism of fire* as he landed in Sicily. オーディーはシチリア島に上陸したとき砲火の洗礼を浴びた ▪ The new principal got *a "baptism by fire"* from parents and teachers. 新米の校長は保護者と教師による初めての厳しい試練を受けた.

bar[1] /bɑːr/ 名 ***admission to the bar***《米》弁護士開業認可 ▪ No regular time of study was requisite for *admission to the bar*. 弁護士開業認可を得るには一定の研究期間は必要でなかった.

at (the) bar **1** 法廷で(の), 出廷中(の) ▪ These principles have been ably argued *at the bar*. これらの原則は法廷で巧みに論ぜられた.

2(法廷)弁護士(barrister)で ▪ He is *at the Bar*. 彼は法廷弁護士だ.

be called [《米》***admitted***] ***to*** [***before***] ***the bar*** [***Bar***](裁判所所属の)弁護士の免許・資格を得る ▪ He *was called to the bar* in 1885. 彼は1885年に法廷弁護士の資格を得た.

be called within the bar [***Bar***]《英》勅選弁護士(King's Counsel)に任命される ▪ He *was called within the bar* in 1885. 彼は1885年に勅選弁護士に任命された.

be tried at the bar (of)(…の)裁判を受ける ▪ He *was tried at the bar of* public opinion. 彼は世論の裁判を受けた.

behind bolt and bar →BOLT.

behind (the) bars 獄中に[で] ▪ The judge will

put [place] him *behind bars* for five years. 裁判官は彼を5年間は刑務所に入れるだろう. ☞bar「監獄の鉄格子」.

bring ... to the bar …を裁判に付す ▪ The politician *was brought to the bar.* その政治家は裁判に付された.

cross the bar この世を去る, 死ぬ ▪ I hope to see my Pilot face to face/When I have *crost the bar.* (Tennyson, *Crossing the Bar*) 私がこの世の境を越えたとき, 私の水先案内人[神]と面と向かってお会いしたいものだ. ☞bar「砂洲」(sandbar); ここではあの世とこの世の境界を指す.

eat for the bar →EAT².

go to [join] the bar 法廷弁護士 (barrister) となる ▪ He had been in India before *going to the bar.* 彼は法廷弁護士になるまではインドにいた.

in bar of …を防ぐため ▪ Danby obtained a pardon from the King *in bar of* the prosecution. ダンビーは起訴を防ぐため王からひそかに赦免を得た.

let down the bars **1** 障害を除く ▪ *Let down the bars* to success. 成功への障害を除け.
2 制約をゆるめる ▪ Governor Smith *let down the bars* on political discussions. スミス知事は政治的議論の制約をゆるめた.

practise at the bar (法廷で)弁護士をする; 弁護士を開業する ▪ I have *practised at the bar* of the House of Lords. 私は上院の懲罰制裁所で弁護士をした.

prop up the bar 《口》酒場[パブ]に入りびたる ▪ Jim is *propping up the bar* as usual. ジムは例によってパブに入りびたっている.

read [study] for the bar 法廷弁護士の修業をする ▪ His son was *reading for the bar.* 彼の息子は法廷弁護士の修業をしていた.

stand to the bar (被告が)進み出て判決を聞く ▪ Smith, *stand to the bar.* スミスさん, 進み出て判決を聞きなさい.

the bar sinister 庶出の印 ▪ That was Paston Carew, a Clinton with *the bar sinister* across the shield. あれはパストン・カルーでクリントン家の庶出の一人だった. ☞騎士道時代に庶出の騎士は自家の紋章に右上から斜めに黒い線を引いていたことから.

trial at (the) bar 全裁判官の列席する裁判; 《英》高等法院の裁判 ▪ The first instance of a *trial at bar* has just occurred at Melbourne. 全裁判官列席裁判の最初の例がちょうど今メルボルンにあった.

bar² /bɑːr/, **barring** /báːrɪŋ/ 前 ***bar [barring] none*** 例外なく, 全く ▪ This is the finest sight *bar none.* これはまたとない美しい光景だ.

bare¹ /beər/ 形 ***(as) bare as the palm of** one's **hand*** すっかりなくて ▪ So far as food is concerned, the house is *as bare as the palm of my hand.* 食物に関するかぎり, その家はすっからかんだ.

bare-faced 図々しい, 厚かましい ▪ He was *barefaced* enough to ask me for a loan. 彼は厚かましくも金を貸せと言った.

have** one's **head bare 無帽である ▪ Each *had his head bare.* 各人が無帽であった.

in** one's **bare skin 裸で ▪ The child ran about *in his bare skin.* その子は裸で走りまわった.

lay bare →LAY².

with bare hands 素手で ▪ I attacked him *with bare hands.* 私は素手で彼にかかっていった.

with bare life →LIFE.

bare² /beər/ 動 ***bare** one's **heart [soul]*** 胸の内を打ち明ける (*to*) ▪ He coudn't *bare his heart to* a girl he hardly knew. 彼はよく知りもしない娘に胸の内を打ち明けることができなかった.

bare** one's **teeth (犬などが怒って)歯をむく ▪ The dog *bared its teeth* and barked. 犬は歯をむいて吠えたてた ▪ The USA has *bared its teeth* and let its intentions be known. 米国は歯をむいておのが意図をあらわにした.

bare-bones /bèərbóʊnz/ 名 ***the bare bones*** (…の)骨子 (*of*) ▪ This book gives *the bare bones of* English grammar. 本書は英文法の骨子を与えてくれる.

barefoot /béərfʊ̀t/ 副 ***go [walk] barefoot*** はだしで行く ▪ We had better *go barefoot* along the beach. 浜辺ははだしで歩いたほうがいい.

barf /bɑːrf/ 動 ***barf** oneself **out*** うんざりさせる, むかつかせる ▪ I *barf myself out* every time I look in the mirror. 鏡を見るたびに(自分の顔に)うんざりする.

bargain¹ /báːrgən/ 名 ***a bargain hunter*** 特売品をあさる人 ▪ My wife is *a* regular *bargain hunter.* 妻はまぎれもない特売品あさり屋だ.

A bargain is a bargain. 約束は約束だ《いいかげんにはできない》.

a Dutch bargain **1** 酒の上で決める売買契約, 酒でかためる取引 ▪ I hate *a Dutch bargain* that's made in the heat of wine. 私は酒の上で取り決められる契約は大きらいだ.
2 一方的に有利な取引 ▪ In return for the occasional use of his car, you allow him the free use of your house—rather *a Dutch bargain,* isn't it? ときどき彼の車を使用する返礼に君は家を彼に自由に使わせている—これは一方にだけ有利な取引ではないか.

a wet bargain = a Dutch BARGAIN 1.

bargain and sale **1** 土地[不動産]の契約売渡し ▪ There was a *bargain and sale.* 土地の契約売渡しが行われた.
2 《米》(政治上の)不正取引 ▪ a *bargain and sale* after the Clay and Adams sort クレイおよびアダムス式の不正取引. ☞1824年の大統領選挙戦で, J. D. Adams が当選の場合は, 国務長官の椅子を与えてもらうという約束で Henry Clay が自分の持ち票を売った取引から.

be off** one's **bargain 契約を解かれる ▪ Your uncles *are off their bargain.* 君のおじたちは契約を解かれた.

beat a bargain (ひどく)値切る ▪ You must not *beat a bargain.* ひどく値切ってはならない.

buy** a thing **at a (good) bargain 物を安く買

う ▪ I *bought* it *at a bargain.* それを安く買った.

close [***conclude, settle, strike***] ***a bargain*** 取引を決める, 売買契約をする, 手を打つ ▪ The two men decided to *close a bargain*, and Jones bought the cloth. 二人は手を打つことに決め, ジョーンズはそのきれを買った ▪ *The bargain was struck* at £7,000. 7,000ポンドで手を打った.

drive a good bargain (***with***) (…を)安く買う, 得な取引をする ▪ You *drove a good bargain with* the house. 君はその家を安く買った.

drive a (***hard***) ***bargain*** (骨折って)商談を進める; (きわめて)割のよい取引をする ▪ Since the victors held all the advantages, they *drove a hard bargain* at the peace conference. 戦勝国がすべての利点を握っていたから, 彼らは平和会議で自己にきわめて有利な協定をした ▪ Tom *drove a bargain* when he sold the horse. トムはその馬を高値で売った ▪ Father *drove a hard bargain* when he bought the new house. 父はその新しい家を安く買った.

get *a thing* ***a bargain*** 《口》物を安く手に入れる ▪ I *got* this *a bargain*. これを安く買った.

hold [***keep***] *one's* ***end of the bargain up***/ ***hold*** [***keep***] ***up*** *one's* ***end of the bargain*** 約束通り自分の責任を果たす ▪ If you don't *hold your end of the bargain up*, the whole project will fail. 君が約束通り自分の責任を果たさないなら, この計画全体が失敗するだろう.

hunt for bargains 安物を探す[あさる] ▪ My wife likes to *hunt for bargains*. 妻は安物あさりが好きだ.

into [《米》***in***] ***the bargain*** おまけに, その上 ▪ Not only is he an excellent scholar, but he's a first class athlete *into the bargain*. 彼は学問がすぐれているだけでなく, その上第一級のアスリートである.

It takes two to make a bargain. 《諺》交渉が成立するには双方が合意に達しなければならない《取り決めは一人ではできない》.

keep [***live up to***] *one's* ***end of the bargain*** =hold one's end of the BARGAIN up.

make a bargain with …と売買契約をする, と取引をする ▪ I *made a bargain with* him. 私は彼と取引した.

make the best of a bad bargain 逆境に善処する; 不幸[不利]にしょげないでがまんする ▪ This isn't what I wanted at all; but I must *make the best of a bad bargain*. これは全然私のほしかったものとは違うけれども, なんとかがまんしなくてはならない.

on the bargain counter 見切品売場に《比喩的にも》 ▪ The book is dumped *on the bargain counter*. その本は見切品売場に投げ出されている ▪ The unemployed are *on the bargain counter* of the employment market. 失業者たちが職業紹介市場の投売り台に出ている.

seal a [***the***] ***bargain*** 契約の成立を祝う ▪ We signed the papers and *sealed the bargain* by drinking champagne. 我々は書類に署名し, シャンパンを飲んで契約の成立を祝った.

settle [***strike***] ***a bargain*** → close a BARGAIN.

That's [***It's***] ***a bargain!*** 承知しました ▪ You do the washing and I'll do the cooking.—Right, *it's a bargain*. あなたは洗濯をしなさい, 私は料理をしますから—はい, そうします.

throw [***include***] ***... into the bargain*** 取引におまけをつける ▪ They *threw* in a calendar *into the bargain*. 彼らはその取引にカレンダーのおまけをつけた.

bargain[2] /bɑ́ːrgən/ 動 ***bargain with*** *a person* ***over*** [***for, to*** *do*] 人と…の売買の手を打つ, 人と…する契約をする ▪ We will *bargain with* the supplier *over* prices. 我々は値段のことで納入業者と交渉するつもりだ ▪ The merchant *bargained with* him *for* it. 商人はそれを買う契約を彼と結んだ ▪ We *bargained with* the manufacturers *to* supply us with the goods. 我々はその品を供給してくれるように製造業者たちと話をつけた.

more than *one* ***bargained for*** 予期していたよりも多く ▪ Bad weather on the mountain gives climbers *more than* they *bargained for*. 山の悪天候には登山者の予想を上回る困難がある ▪ Adam got a lot *more* money *than* he *bargained for*. アダムは予期していたよりもずっと多くの報酬を得た.

bargaining /bɑ́ːrgənɪŋ/ 形 ***a bargaining chip*** [《英》***counter***] 交渉を有利にすすめる切り札 ▪ U.S. holds Iranians as *bargaining chips*. 米国はイラン人を交渉を有利にすすめる切り札としている ▪ Nora will keep it as her final *bargaining counter*. ノラは交渉を有利にすすめる最後の切り札としてそれを取っておくだろう.

barge /bɑːrdʒ/ 動 ***barge*** *one's* ***way*** 押し分けて進む ▪ He *barged his way* through the crowd. 彼は群衆を押し分けて進んだ.

barge pole /bɑ́ːrdʒpòʊl/ 名 ***not fit to be touched with*** (***the end of***) ***a barge pole*** 《口》実にいやな, 手も触れたくない ▪ He is *not fit to be touched with the end of a barge pole*. 彼は実に鼻持ちならない人物だ. ☞「はしけをあやつるさおの先で触れるにも適さない」が原義.

would not touch with (***the end of***) ***a barge pole*** → not touch ... with a ten-foot POLE.

bargee /bɑːrdʒíː/ 名 ***swear like a bargee*** 《英》(船頭みたいに)ひどく[口ぎたなく]ののしる, たんかを切る ▪ He engages in affairs with women, and *swears like a bargee*. 彼は女との情事にふけり, 口ぎたなくののしる.

bark[1] /bɑːrk/ 名 *One's* ***bark is worse than*** *one's* ***bite.*** (本心は)口ほど悪くない ▪ *My father's bark is worse than his bite*. 父は口ほど悪い人間ではありません.

bark[2] /bɑːrk/ 名 ***go*** [***come,*** etc.] ***between the bark and the tree*** 密接なもの(特に夫婦の中)へ入って仲を裂く ▪ It would be folly for me to *put* my hands *between the bark and the tree*, between you two. 私が親密なあなたがた二人の間に

手を突っ込んで仲を裂くなどは愚かなことでしょう.

have the bark on 《米口》あらけずりの, 粗野な ◦ His writing really *has the bark on* it. 彼が書いたものは実にあらけずりだ.

stick in [to] the bark 《米口》深入りしない; 立往生する ◦ A judge will not *stick to the bark* of the case. 判事はその事件には深入りしないだろう.

take the bark off 《米口》(人)をむちで打つ ◦ He is going to *take the bark off* us. 彼は我々をむちで打とうとしている.

talk the bark off a tree 《米口》激しい言葉で感情をぶちまける, 激しくののしる ◦ The miry track tempts one to *talk the bark off a tree* now and then. ぬかるみの道路を通れば, ついときおり激しくののしりたくなる.

tighter than the bark on a tree 《米口》極度にけちな ◦ You are *tighter than the bark on a tree*. 君は極度にけちだ.

bark[3] /bɑːrk/ 動 ***bark at [against] the moon*** (月に向かってほえつく, とは)いたずらに騒ぎ立てる; (上長などを)いたずらに非難する ◦ Those politicians seem to be *barking at the moon*. あの政治家たちはいたずらに騒ぎ立てているようだ.

bark up the wrong tree 《口》見当違いの追跡[攻撃]をする ◦ For the past three months the police have been *barking up the wrong tree*. この3か月の間, 警察は全く見当違いの捜査をしてきた. ☞アライグマ (raccoon) 狩りで, アライグマが逃げた木とはちがった木にむかってほえるの意.

Barking dogs seldom bite. 《諺》ほえる犬はめったに咬まない.

Go bark up another tree! 《米俗》いらぬ世話をするな (Mind your own business!).

Why keep a dog and bark yourself? → DOG[1].

barleycorn /bɑ́ːrlikɔ̀ːrn/ 名 ***every barleycorn*** すっかり, 完全に, 申し分なく (= every INCH) ◦ He is *every barleycorn* a teacher. 彼は申し分のない先生だ.

barn /bɑːrn/ 名 ***be born in a barn*** 粗野である; 武骨である ◦ I know someone who *was born in a barn*. 武骨な人を知っている ◦ *Were* you *born in a barn*? (戸を閉めずに出ていくマナーの悪さを非難して)行儀がなっていないな[出るときちゃんと閉めろよ].

between you and I and the barn 《米口》ここだけの内緒の話だが (= BETWEEN you and me and the bedpost) ◦ *Between you and I and the barn*, I am no friend of theirs. ここだけの話だが, 私は決して彼らの味方ではない.

can't hit the broadside of a barn 《野球》制球力がまるでない; まるで目標に命中しない ◦ That rookie *can't hit the broadside of a barn*, let alone strike anyone out. あのルーキーは制球力がまるでない, 三振させるなんて思いもよらない.

barn door /bɑ́ːrndɔ̀ːr/ 名 ***(as) big as a barn door*** (標的などが)とても大きい ◦ The target was *as big as a barn door*. 標的は実に大きかった.

cannot hit a barn door 射撃[弓]がへたである ◦ He loves shooting, even though he *cannot hit a barn door*. 彼は射撃はへたなくせに射撃が大好きだ.

Lock the barn door after the horse is stolen. → shut the STABLE door after the horse is stolen.

barrack-room /bǽrəkrùːm/ 名 ***a barrack-room lawyer*** 《軽蔑》(正式の訓練を受けず興味本位で入隊して)上官に迷惑をかける兵士 ◦ The young soldier is nothing more than *a barrack-room lawyer*. その若い兵士は上官に迷惑をかけてばかりいる.

barrel /bǽrəl/ 名 ***a barrel of laughs [fun]*** 《口》〚主に否定文で〛おもしろいもの, 楽しいもの ◦ It's not *a barrel of laughs* having to sit down for a chat with Gordon Brown. 座ってゴードン・ブラウンとおしゃべりしなければならないのは, 楽しいものじゃない.

be over a barrel 《口》お手あげの状態である (helpless) ◦ One day, oil producers also may *be over a barrel*. いつか産油国もお手上げの状態になるかもしれない.

give** a person **both barrels/ let** a person **have it with both barrels 《口》人を激しく非難[攻撃]する ◦ I *gave* them *both barrels* in this column. 私は彼らをこの欄で激しく攻撃した ◦ Critics *let* Doris *have it with both barrels* when they reviewed her new biography. 批評家たちはドリスの新作の伝記を書評したときに, 彼女を激しく批判した. ☞2挺の散弾銃を両手でぶっ放すことから.

have [get]** a person **over a barrel [the barrel (head)] 《口》(特に経済的に)人を意のままにする; 人を押さえる ◦ We had to admit defeat; they *had* us *over a barrel*. 我々は敗北を認めねばならなかった. 彼らは我々を押さえてしまった ◦ His wife will always *have* him *over the barrel*. 彼の妻はいつも彼を尻に敷いている. ☞溺れかけた人をたるの上に乗せて水を吐かせたことから. つまり helpless の状態を言う.

like shooting fish in a barrel →FISH[1].

more fun than a barrel of monkeys/(as) funny as a barrel of monkeys 《米》すごくおかしい[楽しい] ◦ The movie is *more fun than a barrel of monkeys*. その映画はすごくおかしい ◦ Tony was *as funny as a barrel of monkeys*. トニーはとてもおもしろい人だった.

on the barrel 《米》即座に, 遅滞なく(支払う) ◦ The cash is put *on the barrel*. 即座に現金が支払われた.

scrape (the bottom of) the barrel 《口》やむなく残った人[策]を使う ◦ We were obliged to *scrape the barrel* in our search for applicants. 我々は志願者募集にやむなく残りの策を使わなければならなかった. ☞「酒だるの底をこする」が原義.

with both barrels 猛烈に, 激しく ◦ He criticized the author *with both barrels*. 彼は著者を激しく批判した.

barrelhead /bǽrəlhèd/ 名 ***on the barrelhead*** = on the BARREL.

barren /bǽrən/ 形 ***barren of*** ...のない, を生まな

い，に乏しい ▪ The attempt was *barren of* results. その試みは効果がなかった ▪ She is *barren of* charms. 彼女は魅力に乏しい.

barricade /bæ̀rəkéɪd/ 動 ***barricade*** *oneself* [*a person*] ***in*** [***into, inside***] 自分[人]をバリケードで…の中に閉じ込める ▪ They *barricaded themselves inside* their house. 彼らは家の中にバリケードで閉じ込もった.

barrier /bǽriər/ 名 ***break the … barrier*** …の壁を破る ▪ Concorde *broke the* sound *barrier*. コンコルドは音速の壁を破った.

base[1] /beɪs/ 名 ***be*** [***go***] ***off*** (*one's*) ***base*** 《米口》気が変である[になる]; まちがっている[まちがう] ▪ She *was off her base* about it. 彼女はそのことで気がおかしくなっていた ▪ He *is* quite *off his base*. 彼は全くまちがっている. ☞野球から.

change *one's* ***base*** 《米口》退却する，出奔する ▪ His defeat caused him to *change his base* to California. 彼は敗北したためカリフォルニアに退却した. ☞McClellan 大将が1862年，Richmond を攻撃して敗北したとき，これを a change of base (基地の変更)と婉曲に言ったことから.

fill the bases →FILL[2].

get to [***reach, make***] ***first base*** **1** 1塁に出る ▪ Jeter *got to first base* and heard the cheers. ジーターは1塁に出て声援を聞いた.

2 《米口》第一歩に成功する，成功の糸口をつかむ ▪ We couldn't *get to first base* with our project. 我々の企画は成功の足がかりさえつかめなかった.

3 《主に米戯》(セックスの)第一段階まで行く《キスしたり体に触ったりする段階》 ▪ Jim hasn't even *gotten to first base* yet with his girlfriend. ジムはガールフレンドとキスする段階にさえ行っていない.

get to second base with 《主に米口》(異性)と肉体関係にまで発展する ▪ How can I *get to second base with* my new girlfriend? どうすれば僕の新しいガールフレンドと肉体関係にもちこめるだろうか.

load the bases →FILL the bases.

off (*one's*) ***base*** 《米口》 **1** 塁から離れていて; 思いがけず ▪ The pitcher caught him *off base*. 彼は離塁して投手に刺された ▪ The question caught him *off base*. 彼はその質問で不意をつかれた.

2 気が違って; まちがって，見当違いをして ▪ His answers were completely *off base*. 彼の答えは全くまちがっていた.

3 《米口》生意気な，ずうずうしい ▪ Daisy said he was *off base* when he asked for her number. 彼が電話番号を教えてくれと言ったとき，デイジーはあんたはずうずうしいと言った.

on base 塁に出て ▪ Ben promptly stole second base, but again he was left *on base*. ベンは素早く2塁に盗塁したが，またもや残塁になった.

take *one's* ***base on balls***/***take*** [***draw***] ***a base on balls*** 《野球》四球で歩く ▪ The batter *took his base on balls*. 打者は四球で出塁した.

touch all the bases/***cover*** (***all***) ***the bases*** 《米》徹底的にやる，完璧[万全]を期す ▪ This guy has *covered all the bases* he can, and he's still in trouble. この男は多芸多才であるのに，なおも面倒なことになっている. ☞「ホームランですべてのベースを確実に踏む」から.

touch base with 《口》…と連絡をとる，(連絡を取って)相談[協議]する ▪ He has also *touched base with* me repeatedly. 彼はまたたびたび私と連絡をとった ▪ I'll try to *touch base with* her when I'm in London. ロンドンに滞在中に彼女に何とか連絡を取ってみましょう.

base[2] /beɪs/ 動 ***base*** *oneself* ***on*** [***upon***] (議論の)根拠を…に置く ▪ When talking about the difference between animal behavior and human action, he explicitly *based himself upon* Aristotle. 動物のふるまいと人間の行動の違いを論じるとき，彼は議論の根拠をはっきりとアリストテレスの説に置いた.

bash[1] /bæʃ/ 名 ***have a bash at*** 《英口》(試みに)…をやってみる ▪ I'll *have a bash at* fixing my PC tonight. 今晩自分のパソコンを修理してみよう.

bash[2] /bæʃ/ 動 ***bash*** *a person's* ***head*** [***brains***] ***in*** 《英口》人を強くなぐる ▪ Shut up or I'll *bash your brains in*! 黙れ，さもないとなぐるぞ.

basics /béɪsɪks/ 名 ***back to basics*** 原点に帰って，初めからやり直して ▪ As food costs soar, it's *back to basics* for meal planners. 食費が暴騰しているので献立を考える方は原点に帰らねばならない.

go [***get***] ***back to*** (***the***) ***basics*** 基本[原点]に帰る《英国保守党の1990年代のスローガン》 ▪ Why do we need to *go back to the basics* of education? なぜ我々は教育の基本に帰る必要があるのか.

basinful /béɪsnfəl/ 名 ***have*** (***got***) ***a basinful*** これ以上は耐えられないほどの苦難にあう ▪ He's *got a basinful*. 彼はいやというほど苦難にあった.

basis /béɪsəs/ 名 ***on a first-name basis*** (ファーストネームで呼び合うほど)親しい[親密な]間柄で ▪ Practically all the guests were *on a first-name basis*. ほとんどすべての客は親しい間柄だった.

on the basis of/***on a … basis*** …を基礎として，の(基礎の)上に ▪ Among the German races society rested *on the basis of* the family. ゲルマン民族の間では社会は家族を基礎としていた ▪ He would put it *on a* new *basis*. 彼はそれを新しい基礎の上に置くだろう.

bask /bæsk|bɑːsk/ 動 ***bask in the sun*** 日なたぼっこをする ▪ She enjoyed *basking in the sun* on a springlike day in February. 彼女は2月の春のような日に日なたぼっこを楽しんだ.

basket /bǽskət|bɑ́ːskɪt/ 名 ***a basket of chips*** 愉快なこと《特に微笑》 ▪ She smiled like *a basket of chips*. 彼女は愉快そうに微笑した ▪ The seller looked as pleasant as *a basket of chips*. その売り子は実に愉快そうな顔をしていた.

be left in the basket (一番悪いリンゴのように)売れ残りになる; 無視される ▪ He has *been left in the basket*. At any rate he hasn't had an invitation yet. 彼は無視されている. とにかくまだ招待を受けていない.

basting /béɪstɪŋ/ 名 ***give** a person **a basting*** 人をなぐる ▪ If I catch you in the apple loft again, I'll *give* you *a basting*. 今度リンゴ置場にいるのを見つけたら，しこたまなぐってやる.

bat[1] /bæt/ 名 ***at a rare* [*great, fair*] *bat*** 《英》快速力で ▪ They went off *at a rare bat*. 彼らは快速力で去った. ☞bat「打撃・歩みの速度」.

at* (*the*) *bat 打者となって，打者の位置について; 出てひと働きして; やる番がきて ▪ Now you are *at bat*. Show them what you can do. さあ今度は君の番だ，彼らに君の力を見せてやれ ▪ The side first *at bat* scored another run in the ninth innings. 先攻側が9回にもう1点入れた. ☞野球から.

come to bat 打者となる; (問題・仕事・試練に)立ち向かう，矢面に立つ ▪ He *came to bat* three times. 彼は3回打者となった ▪ He *came to bat* before the Senators inquiring into his money affairs. 彼は自分の金銭問題を調査する上院の矢面に立った. ☞野球から.

cross bats with …と試合する ▪ Federer *crossed bats with* Nadal at Wimbledon. フェデラーはナダルとウィンブルドンで対戦した.

go full bat 全速力で行く ▪ Bill *went full bat* to enjoy the beauty of the those green hills. ビルはその青々とした丘の美しさを楽しむために全速力で行った.

***go* (*in*)*to bat for* [*against*]** 《米口》…を支持・弁護する[に反対する] ▪ Give me some decent evidence and I'll *go to bat for* you. ちゃんとした証拠を示してくれたら，君の弁護をしよう ▪ When the boss criticized my work, Jack really *went to bat for* me. 上司が私の仕事ぶりを非難したとき，ジャックが実によく弁護してくれた ▪ He *goes to bat against* a wrong directive. 彼はまちがった指令には反対する. ☞野球から.

go to bat for …を助ける，支持する ▪ I'd *go to bat for* him any day, because he's one of my closest friends. いつだって彼を援助するよ，一番親しい友人の一人だから.

(***hot, right***) ***from* [*off*] *the bat*** 《米口》即座に ▪ Tell me your story *hot off the bat*. すぐにお話を聞かせてください ▪ He told us, *right off the bat*, that he would not go. 彼は行かないと即座に我々に言った. ☞野球で打球がバットからすぐに離れるさまから.

off** one's **own bat **1** 自分の打撃で(点を得る) ▪ One of our adversaries scored 70 *off his own bat*. 敵の一人は自分の打撃で70点取った.
2 《口》独力で; 自己の一存で ▪ Smith has built a beautiful cottage *off his own bat*. スミスは独力で美しい田舎家を建てた ▪ He did it entirely *off his own bat*. 彼はそれを全く自己の一存でやった. ☞クリケットから.

on** one's **own bat 《俗》独立して，自力で ▪ Smith has left the company and is now *on his own bat*. スミスは会社をやめて今は独立してやっている. ☞クリケットから.

play a straight bat 《英》即答を避ける ▪ Keith *played a straight bat* to the inevitable question as to his plans. キースは彼の計画について必ず尋ねられる質問に即答を避けた.

(***right***) ***from* [*off*] *the bat*** →(hot, right) from the BAT.

Step to the bat! 《米》やれ! ☞野球から.

bat[2] /bæt/ 名 ***an old bat*** 《英口》愚かな[うるさい]女[ばばあ]，迷惑おばさん ▪ He had always referred to her as "the *old bat*". 彼はいつも彼女のことを「あのうるさいばばあ」と呼んでいた.

(***as***) ***blind as a bat*** →BLIND[1].

(***go***) ***like a bat out of hell*** 《口》まっしぐらに行く; 《空口》極度に速く飛ぶ ▪ He *went* down the street *like a bat out of hell*. 彼は猛スピードで通りを下っていった.

have bats in the* [one's] *belfry 頭が狂っている; 変人である ▪ The Sahib *had bats in the belfry* and must be humored. だんなさまは変人だったからごきげんを取らないといけなかった ▪ If I listen to her much longer, I shall *have bats in the belfry*. 彼女の言うことをこれ以上ずっと長く聞いていると私は気が変になるだろう.

take the bats 頭が変になる ▪ Have you *taken the bats*? 気でも狂ったのか.

bat[3] /bæt/ 名 ***be* [*go*] *on* [*upon*] *a bat*** 《米俗》浮かれ騒いでいる[騒ぐ]，飲み騒ぎをしている[する] ▪ He had *been on a bat* during the previous night. 彼は前夜飲み騒いでいたのだった.

bat[4] /bæt/ 名 ***sling* [*spin*] *the bat*** 《俗》外国の口語をしゃべる; 《軍俗》軍隊語をふりまわす ▪ My wife and I are going to France. She *slings the bat* like a native. 妻と私はフランスへ行きます. 妻は本国人のようにフランス語の口語をしゃべります. ☞bat (Hindi) = speech.

bat[5] /bæt/ 動 ***bat a thousand*** 《米口》〚主に進行形で〛10割を達成する; 完全に成功する ▪ No one can *bat a thousand* for the whole season. 誰にせよ全シーズン10割を達成することはできない ▪ He's *batting a thousand* so far with the new boss. 彼はこれまでのところ新しい上司に対して非常に成功している.

bat ... back and forth 《口》(思いつき・計画など)をあれこれ議論する，思い巡らす ▪ They had plenty of time to *bat* ideas *back and forth*. 彼らはいろんな考えを思い巡らす十分な時間があった.

bat five hundred 《俗》5割がたうまくやる ▪ I don't expect the government to *bat five hundred*. 政府が5割がたうまくやるとは期待していない.

bat zero 《俗》完全に失敗する，全くだめである ▪ I'm *batting zero* here. 僕はここでは全くだめだ.

***not bat an eye* [*eyelash, eyelid*]** 《口》ちっとも驚かない，びくともしない ▪ When the jury pronounced him guilty of murder, he did *not bat an eye*. 陪審員団が彼に殺人の罪ありと答申したとき，彼は平然としていた.

not* [*never*] *bat an eyelid 《口》**1** 一睡もしない ▪ I did*n't bat an eyelid*. 私はまんじりともしなかった.
2 = not BAT an eye.

without batting an eye [***eyelash, eyelid***] ちっとも驚かずに, びくともしないで ▪ John told me a lie *without batting an eyelash.* ジョンは平然として私に嘘を言った. ☞「まばたきもしない」が原義.

batch /bætʃ/ 名 ***a batch of*** 一束[一群, 一団]の, たくさんの ▪ I have *a batch of* letters to write. 私は書く手紙が一束もある ▪ There was *a* big *batch of* mail for you today. きょうはあなたにたくさん郵便が来たよ.

the best of a bad batch くずの中のえり抜き ▪ The cloth is *the best of a bad batch.* その布は粗悪品の中でも一番よいものです.

bate[1] /beɪt/ 名 ***be*** [***get***] ***in a bate*** 《英》激怒している[する] ▪ He *was in an* awful *bate.* 彼は恐ろしく怒っていた.

bate[2] /beɪt/ 動 ***bate an ace*** 少し譲歩する ▪ I can't get him to *bate an ace.* 彼に少し譲らせることもできない.

bate** one's **breath 息を殺す ▪ He *bated his breath* a little when he told the story. 彼はその話をするときはいつも息を少し殺した.

bate the wings 羽ばたきして降りる ▪ The soul *bated the wings* apace downward. 魂は羽ばたきして素早く下へ降りてきた.

not bate a jot of ...はみじんも弱めない[一文も引かぬ] ▪ Let us *not bate a jot of* zeal in our country's service. 国家への奉仕の熱情をみじんも弱めないようにしよう.

bated /béɪtəd/ 形 ***with bated breath*** 息を殺して (cf. Sh., *Merch. V.* 1. 3. 125) ▪ They listened *with bated breath* for the announcement about the winner. 彼らは優勝者の発表を息を殺して聞いていた. ☞bate＝restrain「抑える」.

bath /bæθ|bɑ:θ/ 名 ***an early bath*** 《英》終了する前に途中で帰ること ▪ Some players visited neighbouring courses while others opted for *an early bath.* 一部のプレーヤーは近所のゴルフコースへ出向いたが, 他の者は途中で切り上げることを選んだ.

have a bath (赤ちゃんが)湯浴みさせてもらう; 《英》入浴する ▪ The baby is *having a bath.* 赤ちゃんは湯浴みさせてもらっている ▪ How often do you *have a bath* in a week? 1週間に何回入浴しますか.

take a bath **1** 《主に米》入浴する ▪ He seldom *takes a bath.* 彼はめったに入浴しない.

2 《米俗》(...で)大損をする (*doing, on*) ▪ The company *took a bath investing* in that new product. 会社はその新製品に投資して大損を食らった ▪ He *took a bath* on the stock market. 彼は株式売買で大損した. ☞経済的に丸裸にされることから.

take [***have***] ***an early bath*** 《サッカー》退場を命じられる ▪ And that's his second yellow card so Taylor will *take an early bath.* それは彼の2度目のイエローカードなのでテイラーは退場を命じられるだろう.

the bath of blood 殺戮(さつりく) ▪ Once more began *the bath of blood* for the hapless race. 再び不幸な民族に対する殺戮が始まった.

bathe[1] /beɪð/ 名 ***have*** [***go for***] ***a bathe*** 《英》水泳・水浴をする[に出かける] ▪ Let us *have a bathe* in the river. 川で水浴をしよう.

bathe[2] /beɪð/ 動 ***bathe... in blood*** ...を流血に浸す ▪ His plan would have *bathed* Sparta *in blood.* 彼の計画はスパルタを流血に浸したであろう ▪ He *bathed* his hands *in blood.* 彼は手を血まみれにした《人殺しをした》.

be bathed in ...を浴びる, にひたる ▪ He *was bathed in* blood. 彼は血を浴びていた ▪ She *was bathed in* tears. 彼女は涙にくれていた.

bathroom /bǽθrù:m|bɑ́:θ-/ 名 ***go to the bathroom*** 《米》排泄する, 粗相する ▪ Dick became angry when his dog *went to the bathroom* on his carpet. ディックは飼い犬がカーペットの上に粗相したとき怒った.

baton /bætɑ́:n|bǽtən/ 名 ***hand*** [***pass***] (***on***) ***the baton*** 責任を譲渡する (*to*) ▪ I believe now is the time for him to step down gracefully and *hand on the baton to* the next generation. 今こそ彼は潔く引退して次の世代に責任を譲渡するべきときだと私は信じる.

take [***pick***] ***up the baton*** 責任を受け継ぐ ▪ The industry needs a strong leader who can *pick up the baton* that Mr. Clifford is passing. 業界はクリフォード氏が渡そうとしている責任を受け継ぐ強いリーダーが必要だ.

under the baton of (オーケストラ・合唱が)...の指揮で ▪ The orchestra came alive *under the baton of* James Ross. ジェイムズ・ロスの指揮でオーケストラが生き生きとよみがえった.

battalion /bətǽljən/ 名 ***God is for the big battalions.*** 《諺》神は大軍に味方する.

batten /bǽtən/ 動 ***batten down the hatches*** **1** 難局[トラブル]に備える ▪ Here comes the boss—*batten down the hatches.* 社長がやってきた—トラブルに備えよ.

2 黙る, 黙って控える ▪ You'll *batten down* your *hatches.* 君は黙って控えていなさい.

batter /bǽtər/ 名 ***go on the batter*** 《口》飲み騒ぐ ▪ On bank holidays we make a point of *going on the batter.* 銀行法定休日には我々は必ず飲み騒ぐことにしている.

battery /bǽtəri/ 名 ***in battery*** 砲が発砲の構えで, 砲眼から突き出されて ▪ When did you put them *in battery*? いつ砲列を発砲の構えにしたか.

lay battery to ...に砲撃を加える ▪ Mischiefs have *laid battery to* our consciences. 災いが我々の良心を襲撃した.

out of [***from***] ***battery*** (砲が)装てんのために引っこめられて ▪ The gun was *out of battery.* 大砲は装てんのため引っこめられていた.

plant battery 砲撃の準備をする ▪ They are *planting battery* to my fort. 彼らは私の要さい砲撃の準備をしている.

recharge** one's **batteries 《口》(電池に)再充電する; 英気を養う ▪ I must *recharge my batteries* before I start to write another book. 別の本を書

きはじめる前に再充電しなければならない.

***turn** a person's **battery against** [**upon**] himself* 相手の論点をとらえて逆襲する ▪ The fellow *turned my battery against myself.* その男は私の論法をとらえて逆襲した.

batting /bǽtɪŋ/ 名 ***batting average*** 打率; 成功率 ▪ Dr. Smith has a great *batting average* with her heart transplant operations. スミス博士は心臓移植手術で高い成功率を有している. ☞野球から.

battle[1] /bǽtəl/ 名 ***a battle of wills*** 意志と意志の戦い, 意地の張り合い ▪ The two countries are engaged in *a battle of wills* over energy. その二つの国はエネルギーをめぐって意志と意志の戦いをしている ▪ Refusing to eat can become the child's way of winning *a battle of wills* with her parents. 子供が食事を拒むことは両親との意地の張り合いに勝つ方法になりうる.

a battle of wits **1** 知恵比べ ▪ It was *a battle of wits* between jewelers and thieves. それは宝石商と泥棒との間の知恵比べだった.

2 勝負なしの論戦 ▪ They argued for hours but it was *a* real *battle of wits.* 彼らは何時間も議論したがほんとうの勝負なしの論戦だった.

a battle royal **1** (闘鶏2羽以上が一緒になっての)激しい乱戦 ▪ Cockerels crow till they get up *a battle royal.* 若い雄鶏は激しい乱戦になるまで鳴く.

2 激しい乱戦, 大論戦 ▪ Luther, Zwingli, and Calvin have made *a battle royal* of beliefs. ルター, ツウィングリ, カルバンは信仰の大論戦をした.

a pitched battle (計画し, 場所をしめし合わせた)正々堂々の戦い[論戦]; 激しい争い ▪ The merchants came to *a pitched battle* in the market place. 商人は市場で堂々の論戦をやりだした ▪ The "protest rally" turned into *a pitched battle* between the police and the rallyists. 「抗議集会」が警察と集会者たちとの激しい争いに変わってしまった. ☞pitch「戦陣を整える」.

a running battle 長い争い[議論] ▪ They had *a running battle* about it. 彼らはそれについて長い議論をした.

accept battle 応戦する ▪ We *accepted battle* instantly. 我々はすぐ応戦した.

an uphill battle [***struggle, task***] → UPHILL.

battle, murder, and sudden death 戦闘, 殺人, 急死 (Prayer Book, *the Litany*) ▪ From *battle, murder, and sudden death*, good God, deliver us. 神さま, 我々を戦闘, 殺人, 急死よりお救いください.

battle of nerves 神経戦 ▪ It has been a regular *battle of nerves* to get the new program accepted at the local state university. 地方の州立大学において新しいプログラムを受け入れさせるのはまさしく神経戦だった.

battle of the giants 傑出した勢力を持つ当事者同士の抗争, 両雄の激突 ▪ A *battle of giants* is about to pop in the soft-drink field. ソフトドリンクの分野でも両雄の激突が生じようとしている.

battle stations 《主に米》戦闘部署 ▪ Nor will such a network of *battle stations* immediately end the threat of nuclear attack. また, そのような戦闘部署網も直ちに核攻撃の脅威を払拭しはしないだろう.

(***be***) ***locked in battle*** 法的な争いに巻き込まれている ▪ There is still no end in sight for the two neighbors *locked in battle* over a piece of land. 狭い土地をめぐって係争中の二軒の隣同士にはまだ決着の見通しは立っていない.

do battle →join BATTLE.

fall in battle 戦死する ▪ His father *fell in battle.* 彼の父は戦死した.

fight a losing battle 負け戦をする; むだ骨を折る ▪ The doctor seems to be *fighting a losing battle* in trying to revive him. 医者は彼を生き返らせようとしているがどうもむだ骨のようだ.

fight** one's **battles over again 昔の手柄話[経歴談]などをして聞かせる ▪ The veterans *fought their battles over again* in their talks. 退役軍人たちは戦争の手柄話をした.

fight** one's **own battles 独力で戦う ▪ I appreciate the sympathy, but I can *fight my own battles.* 同情はありがたいが, 僕は独力で戦えるさ.

gain a [***the***] ***battle*** 戦いに勝つ ▪ Maria *gained the battle* with death! マライアは死との戦いに勝った!

give battle 戦う; 攻撃する ▪ The British *gave battle* to the enemy after sunset. 英軍は日没後敵を攻撃した.

give the battle 勝利を譲る, 負ける ▪ The king *gave the battle.* 国王は戦いに負けた.

half the battle 半分勝った[成功した]も同然 ▪ Youth is *half the battle.* 若さはそれだけで成功の大半である ▪ The first stroke [blow] is *half the battle.* 《諺》最初の一撃で勝負は半ば決まる.

have the battle =gain a BATTLE.

in battle array →ARRAY[1].

join [***do***] ***battle*** 争う, 戦う (*with, over*) ▪ John is preparing to *do battle with* his sister in the courts over their inheritance. ジョンは遺産のことで妹と法廷で争う準備をしている ▪ We must *do battle* for the truth. 我々は真実のために戦わなければならない.

line of battle **1** 戦列 ▪ The army was made up in the form of a *line of battle.* 軍隊は戦列の隊形に整えられた.

2 艦隊の戦列 ▪ In the *line of battle* the ships are close-hauled. 艦隊の戦列では艦は詰め開きだ.

line of battle ship 戦列艦《昔は74砲以上のもの; 本攻撃に参加できる大きさの戦艦》 ▪ It was the typical vessel—the two decker *line of battle ship* of 80 guns. それは典型的な艦—80砲の2層戦列艦であった.

lose a [***the***] ***battle*** 戦いに負ける ▪ His troops *lost the battle.* 彼の兵は敗れた.

offer battle 挑戦する ▪ He advanced with sixty thousand men to *offer battle.* 彼は挑戦するため6

万の兵を率いて前進した.

The battle is not always to the strong. 《諺》戦は強い者が勝つとは限らない (《聖》*Eccles*. 9. 11).

(***the***) ***battle lines are drawn*** 戦う準備が整った, 争点が明らかになった ▪ *The battle lines* are *being drawn* for the next election. 次の選挙を戦う準備は整っている ▪ *Battle lines were drawn* over a plan to grant legal status to gay couples in Italy. イタリアで同性愛カップルに法的資格を与える計画をめぐって争点が明らかになった.

the battle of the bulge 《戯》(中年の人, 特に女性の)やせようとする必死の戦い ▪ Jane is now fighting *the battle of the bulge* and cutting out sugar and cakes. ジェインは今やせようとする必死の戦いをしていて, 砂糖とケーキ類を断っている. ☞the Battle of the Bulge (第二次大戦末期の西部戦線でのドイツ軍の大反攻)から.

the battle of the sexes (権力をめぐる)男と女の戦い ▪ *Battle of the sexes*. Who has the bigger brain? 男と女の戦い. どちらの脳が大きいか?

trial by battle 決闘で是非を決する昔の裁判 ▪ The last *trial by battle* was waged in the court of common pleas at Westminster in 1751. 最後の決闘によって決する裁判は1751年ウェストミンスターの民事法廷で行われた.

win the battle, but lose the war 小さな勝負に勝って大事な試合に負ける ▪ The strikers may have *won the battle, but* they have *lost the war*. ストをした連中は小さな勝負では勝ったかもしれないが, 大事な試合には負けてしまった.

battle[2] /bǽtəl/ 動 ***battle it*** 戦う ▪ He was *battling it* across the table with a young Templar. 彼は食卓をはさんで若いテンプル騎士と戦っていた.

battle it out 《口》決着がつくまで戦う ▪ Try to *battle it out* on your own. 独力で決着がつくまで戦ってみろ.

battledore /bǽtəldɔ̀ːr/ 名 ***play*** (***at***) ***battledore and shuttlecock*** はねつき遊びをする ▪ I have been *playing at battledore and shuttlecock*. 私ははねつき遊びをしていました.

bauble /bɔ́ːbəl/ 名 ***hold a bauble*** 道化師の笏杖(しゃくじょう)を持つ ▪ A fool should never *hold a bauble* in his hand. 《諺》愚か者は手に笏杖を持って愚かであることを明示してはならない《自分・自覚のことを悪く言うな》.

bay[1] /beɪ/ 名 ***a little over the bay*** 《米俗》いくぶん酔って ▪ He was *a little over the bay*. 彼は少し酔っていた. ☞bay「湾」.

bay[2] /beɪ/ 名 ***at*** (***a***) ***bay/to*** (***the***) ***bay*** 触れんばかりに接近して; 進退に窮して, 困窮して, 万策尽きて ▪ Ah! that I had my lady *at* this *bay*, to kiss me. ああ! お嬢さまがこんな身近に寄り添って, 私にキスしてくださったとは ▪ The stag *at bay* is a dangerous foe. 《諺》「窮鼠(そ)猫をかむ」.

be [***stand***] ***at bay*** 追いつめられて(歯向かって)いる, 窮地に陥っている ▪ The stag *is* now *at bay*. 雄ジカは今追いつめられている ▪ He *stands at bay* against that trunk. 彼はあの幹を後ろにして追いつめられて踏みとどまってる.

bring [***drive***]***... to bay*** (猟犬が)...を追いつめる ▪ The hounds *brought* the stag *to bay*. 猟犬は雄ジカを追いつめた.

come [***turn***] ***to*** [***at***] ***bay*** 追いつめられて激しく反抗する ▪ The stag *came to bay*. 雄ジカは追いつめられて猛烈に歯向かった.

hold [***have***]***... at bay*** **1** (猟犬が)追いつめて逃がさない ▪ The hounds *held* the stag *at bay*. 猟犬が雄ジカを追いつめて逃がさなかった ▪ When *held at bay*, cowards will fight. 窮地に追いつめられると, 憶病者でも反抗する.

2 =keep ... at BAY.

keep ... at bay (猟犬・敵・危険・病気など)を寄せつけない[食い止める] ▪ The ruffian *kept* his pursurers *at bay*. 悪漢は追手を寄せつけなかった.

to (***the***) ***bay*** →at (a) BAY.

bay[3] /beɪ/ 動 ***bay*** (***at***) ***the moon*** 月にほえる, 遠ぼえする; 無益な騒ぎ[努力]をする; (上長などを)無益に非難する ▪ The member was given to *baying the moon*. その議員は無益に騒ぎたててばかりいた ▪ We are *baying at the moon*. 我々はむだな努力をしている.

bay[4] /beɪ/ 形 ***kick like a bay steer*** 《米口》激しく抗議する ▪ He came to town *kicking like a bay steer*. 彼は町に来て激しく抗議した.

bayonet[1] /béɪənət/ 名 ***at the point of the bayonet*** →POINT[1].

bayonet[2] /béɪənət, bèɪənét/ 動 ***bayonet ... into submission*** ...を武力で服従させる ▪ The King *bayonet*(*t*)*ed* the natives *into submission*. 王は原住民を武力で服従させた.

be /bi, biː/ 動 ***be a good chap*** [***a good boy, a good girl, an angel, a darling, a dear, a sport***] ***and*** *do* 《口》お願いだから...しておくれ ▪ *Be an angel*, Helen, *and* get the scissors. ヘレン, お利口だからはさみを取ってきておくれ ▪ Would you *be a good chap and* take Mary to the hospital? お願いだからメアリーを病院へ連れていってください.

be it that... 《雅》もし...であるならば (if it is that ...) ▪ *Be it that* he is honest, he will never do such a thing. 彼が正直なら, 決してそんなことはすまい.

be much [***little, nothing, something,*** etc.] ***to do with*** =HAVE much to do with.

be that as it may →MAY.

be to *do* **1** ...することになっている《予定》 ▪ We *are to* meet at 5. 5時に集まることになっている.

2 ...しなさい《命令》 ▪ You *are to* post the letter. 手紙をポストに入れなさい.

3 ...する運命である ▪ He *was* never *to* see his home again. 彼は再び郷里に帰らなかった《帰らぬ運命であった》.

4 〚if 節中で〛...するつもり, しようと思う ▪ If you *are to* become a great man, you should work hard. 偉い人になろうと思うなら, 一生懸命勉強せねばならない.

5 …すべきである《義務》 ▪ You *are to* obey your parents. 両親には従うべきである.
6〚不定詞が受身となって〛…できる《可能》 ▪ Nothing *was to* be seen but the sea and the sky. 海と空のほかは何も見えなかった.

***been there, done that*(*, seen the movie, bought the T-shirt*)** 1回で十分だ; 興味が薄れたのでもうたくさんだ (→SEEN one, seen them all) ▪ No, I don't want to climb Mount Fuji; *been there, done that.* いや, 富士山には登りたくない—1回登れば十分だ ▪ Do I like to live in the country? Not me—*been there, done that, seen the movie, bought the T-shirt.* 田舎に住みたいかって? 僕はごめんだ—いやというほど経験したので, もう興味はないね.

have been **1** 来て帰った; 行って来た ▪ *Has* the postman *been* yet? 郵便配達人はもう来たか ▪ He *has been* here. 彼はここへ来てまた帰った ▪ We *have been* there. そこへ行って来た.
2 来たことがある, 行ったことがある ▪ I *have been* there once. 一度そこへ行ったことがある.

have been and gone and done → HAVE been and done.

have been at (学校・教会など)に出席したことがある; に出席していた ▪ They *had been at* Cambridge together. 彼らは一緒にケンブリッジで学んだことがあった ▪ All his family *have been at* Eton and Oxford for two hundred years. 彼の家の者はみな200年の間イートンとオックスフォードで学んできた.

have been in **1**《主に英》…に行ったことがある ▪ I *have been in* France twice. 私はフランスに2回行ったことがある.
2 …にいたことがある ▪ He *has* never *been in* London. 彼はロンドンにいたことはない.
3 …にずっと住んでいる ▪ He *has been in* Tokyo for ten years. 彼は10年間ずっと東京に住んでいる.

have been there →THERE.

have been to **1** …に行ったことがある ▪ *Have* you ever *been to* Nikko? 君は日光に行ったことがあるか.
2〚完了を表し, just などの副詞を伴って〛…へ行って来た ▪ I *have been to* the station to see my friend off. 私は友人を見送りに駅へ行って来た.
3〚不定詞を伴って〛…しに行っていた ▪ I *have been to* see Irving today. 今日アービングに会いに行っていた.

it has to be (好ましからぬ事に対して)それも止むを得ない; それも運命である ▪ I don't like my children leaving home, but *it has to be.* 子供らが家を出て行くのはいやだが, それも仕方がない.

it was not to be そうはならなかった, そうならない運命だった ▪ We had hoped to catch him napping, but *it was not to be.* 我々は彼の虚をつきたいと思っていたが, そうはいかなかった.

Mrs. Smith [etc.] ***that is*** [***that was, that is to be***] 現在の[元の, 将来の]スミス夫人[など] ▪ We speak of her as Lady Cheyne *that is to be.* 我々は彼女を未来のレディー・チェインと言う.

to be 未来の…, …(になる)予定の ▪ She can't possibly pose as his wife-*to-be.* 彼女は彼の未来の妻に見せかけるなんてとてもできない.

Wednesday [etc.] ***was a week*** [etc.] 1週間[など]前の水曜日[など]に《今は was を省くことが多い》 ▪ He came here *Monday was a week.* 彼は1週間前の月曜にここへ来た ▪ I was in London *Monday was three weeks.* 3週間前の月曜にはロンドンにいた ▪ He went from his house *last Christmas was 4 years.* 彼はこの前のクリスマスより4年前に家を出て行った.

beach /biːtʃ/ 名 ***on the beach*** **1** (軍人・警官が)陸上勤務となって; 退職して ▪ On that page, he did post a photo of officers *on the beach.* 彼はそのページに陸上勤務の士官たちの写真を公示した.
2 (水夫などが零落して)浜辺[波止場]をうろついて ▪ There's lots of retired officers mouldering *on the beach.* 大勢の退職士官が波止場でくすぶっている.
3 失業して; 一文無しで ▪ England is always crowded with sailormen *on the beach.* イングランドはいつも失業した水夫であふれている ▪ You *on the beach,* kid? Have you got any money? 若いの, 失業してるのかい? 金はあるのかい?

bead /biːd/ 名 ***bid*** *one's* ***beads*** 祈りをささげる ▪ He was *bidding his beads* for the souls of his benefactors. 彼は恩人たちの霊に祈りをささげていた.

draw [***get, have, take***] ***a bead upon*** [***on***]《主に米》…を(小銃やピストルで)狙う, に狙いをつける ▪ Enemy snipers were *taking a bead on* the general. 敵の狙撃手は将軍に狙いをつけていた ▪ They *had a bead on* the game. 彼らは小銃で獲物をねらった. ☞bead「照星」.

pray without *one's* ***beads*** 勘定違いをする, 当てがはずれる ▪ He *prayed without his beads* in that. 彼はその点でそろばん違いをした.

say [***count, tell***] *one's* ***beads*** (じゅずをつまぐって)祈りを唱える ▪ All the people *said their beads* in a general silence. 人々はみな黙って祈りをささげた.

beak /biːk/ 名 ***birds of a beak*** 同類の鳥[人間] ▪ They were all *birds of a beak.* 彼らはみな同類だった.

be-all /bíːɔ̀ːl/ 名 ***the be-all and*** (***the***) ***end-all*** 最も大切なこと, 唯一の重要なもの (*of*) (cf. Sh., *Macb.* 1. 7. 5) ▪ Winning is not *the be-all and end-all of* life. 勝つのが人生で最も大切なことではない.

beam /biːm/ 名 ***a beam counter*** 損得勘定にしか興味がない人 ▪ The reason for America's failure is that we have *beam-counters* running our companies. 米国が失敗した理由は, 損得勘定優先の人たちが会社を経営しているからである.

a beam in [***from***] *one's* (***own***) ***eye*** 自分の目のなかの梁(はり); (自分では気づかない)自分の大欠点 (《聖》*Matt.* 7. 3) ▪ One can not see *a beam in his eye.* 人は自分の大きな欠点は見えない ▪ Let the English remove the *beam from their own eye,* before they attempt to put the mote from ours. イギリス人は我々の小さな欠点を取り除こうとする前に,

自分の大欠点を除くがよい.
broad in the beam 《口》 ヒップが大きい ▪ She is getting a bit *broad in the beam.* 彼女はヒップが少し大きくなっている. ☞beam「船の船幅」.
get off the beam **1** 方向を誤る, 正鵠(こく)を失する ▪ The general *got off the beam* in saying so. 将軍がそう言ったのは見当違いだ.
2 放送を終える ▪ He *got off the beam* at 7. 彼は7時に放送を終えた. ☞beam「ラジオ電波」.
get on the beam 放送する, 放送を始める ▪ The commercial *gets on the beam* at 3 p.m. 午後3時にコマーシャルの放送が始まる.
kick [***strike***] ***the beam*** ずっと軽い; きわめて価値が少ない, 少なくなる; 負ける ▪ Wealth opposed to love will *kick the beam.* 富は愛と比べたらずっと軽いだろう ▪ The prices of building plots *kicked the beam.* 建設地の値段がきわめて安くなった ▪ Thomson will *kick the beam.* トムスンが負けるよ. ☞秤の皿の一方がひどく軽くて, さおがはねあがることから.
off the beam **1** 方向がそれている; 《俗》 見当違いで; 《米俗》 不満足な, つまらない ▪ His plane was *off the beam.* 彼の機は航路がそれていた ▪ Any one who thinks that way is far *off the beam.* そのように考える人は誰でも大いにまちがっている.
2 放送を終えて (→get off the BEAM).
on the beam **1** 正しい方向に進んで; 《俗》 軌道に乗って, 正鵠(こく)を得て; 《米俗》 まっすぐに[で] ▪ In saying so, he was right *on the beam.* 彼がそう言ったのは正鵠を得ていた ▪ You're *on the beam.* 全くその通りだ.
2 放送して ▪ There is another program *on the beam.* もう一つ番組が放送されている.
strike the beam →kick the BEAM.

beam-ends /bìːméndz/ 名 ***on one's*** [***the***] ***beam-ends*** 〚主に be, be laid を伴って〛《口》 **1** (船が)真横に傾いて, 転覆しそうに傾いて ▪ A number of large river craft *were on their beam-ends* for want of water. 多数の大きい川船が水がないため真横に傾いていた.
2 窮境[窮乏]に陥って, 困り果てて, 病気で倒れて ▪ If I lose my job, I shall be thrown *on my beam-ends.* 失業すれば全く困り果てる ▪ He *was on his beam-ends* with rheumatism. 彼はリューマチで倒れていた.

bean /biːn/ 名 ***a hill of beans*** 《米俗》〚否定文で〛 わずかな値うちのもの ▪ He wasn't *a hill of beans* to her. 彼は彼女にとっては少しの値うちもなかった ▪ I didn't care *a hill of beans* for the girl. 私はその娘はちっとも好きでなかった.
blue beans 銃弾, たま ▪ I heard a sound like three *blue beans* in a blue bladder. がらがらの立てるような音がした.
cool beans 《俗》 (答えて)そいつはいいね ▪ Todd says he'll take us in his car.—*Cool beans.* トッドが私たちを車に乗せてくれるって—そいつはいい.
Every bean has its black. 《諺》 人にはみな欠点がある. ☞black＝a black eye.
full of beans **1** 《口》 (馬・人が)健康で, 元気で, 活気いっぱいで ▪ He does it—being *full of beans,* sir. 彼はそれをやりますよ—元気いっぱいですからね. ☞もと馬の元気なのを言ったもの; beanfed「元気に満ちた」.
2 《米口》 (人が)間違って, たわけで ▪ Don't pay any attention to Bill. He's *full of beans.* ビルの言うことには気をとめるな. やつはたわけだから.
get beans 《俗》 ひどくやられる, ひどく罰せられる, しかられる, なぐられる ▪ By gum, they don't half *get beans!* きっと, やつらをひどくやっつけてやるぞ.
give *a person* ***beans*** 《俗》 人をひどくやっつける, ひどく罰する, しかる, なぐる ▪ His elder brother *gave* him *beans* for breaking the cricket bat. 彼の兄は彼がクリケット用のバットを折ったのでひどくこらしめた ▪ His sprained ankle was *giving* him *beans.* 彼は足首をくじいてひどく苦しんでいた.
know beans (***when the bag is open***) 《米口》 もの知りである, 精通している, 聡明である ▪ One has to *know beans* to be successful in it. それに成功するためには物事に通じていなければならない.
know how many beans make five 《口》 明敏である, 抜け目がない《だまされはしない》 ▪ I didn't *know how many beans made five.* 私は世故にうとかった ▪ Old James *knows how many beans make five.* 老ジェイムズはさとくて抜け目がない. ☞昔子供に豆を使って数を教えたことから.
like beans 《口》 猛烈に (＝LIKE anything) ▪ He ran *like beans.* 彼は猛烈に走った.
mean beans/amount to a hill of beans 一文の価値もない ▪ Frankly, Nick's new invention *amounts to a hill of beans.* 率直に言えば, ニックの新発明なんて一文の価値もない.
not care a bean [***beans***] 《俗》 ちっともかまわない; 少しも好まない ▪ I do*n't care beans* for the railroad. 私は鉄道は少しも好まない ▪ I do*n't care a bean* what he says. 私は彼の言うことなんかちっとも意に介さない.
not have a bean 《英》 無一文である ▪ He is out of a job and does*n't have a bean* to spend. 彼は失業していて一文の金もない.
not know beans about 《主に米口》 …について何も知らない ▪ He does*n't know beans about* forestry. 彼は森林学のことは何も知らない.
not worth a bean 《口》 一文の値打ちもない; 一文も持っていない ▪ Has he any money?—No, he is *not worth a bean!* 彼には金があるか—いや, 一文もない.
Old bean! 《英俗》 おい大将!, やあ君! ▪ How is it going, *old bean!* 景気はどうかね, 大将!
spill the beans →SPILL².

bear¹ /beər/ 名 ***a bear garden*** 《口》 騒がしい混乱の場所 ▪ This classroom is *a bear garden* when the teacher is away. この教室は先生がいないときは騒々しい混乱の場だ.
a bear hug 強く抱きしめること《愛情の表現》 ▪ He gave Mary *an* affectionate *bear hug* the moment he met her. 彼はメアリーに会ったとたん、愛情を

込めて彼女を強く抱きしめた.

a bear in the air [***sky***] (スピード違反取締りのため上空を飛んでいる)警察のヘリコプター ▪ Slow down, buddy, there's *a bear in the air.* 相棒, スピードを落とせよ, サツのヘリが飛んでるぜ.

a bear leader 家庭教師, 貴人のお相手をする人《通常旅行している若者につき添う若者》 ▪ My son is off to France as *bear leader* to the son of a millionaire. 私の息子は百万長者の息子の家庭教師としてつき添ってフランスに行っている.

Are you there with your bears? また来ているのか; またやっているのか ▪ Marry, *are you there with your bears?* おや, またやっているんだね.

(***as***) ***busy as a hibernating bear*** →BUSY[1].

(***as***) ***cross as a bear*** (***with a sore head***) →CROSS[1].

be a bear for 《口》...が好きだ, に熱心だ ▪ He *is a bear for* work. 彼は仕事熱心だ.

be a bear for punishment 手荒な扱いや困難に耐える, 屈しない; 荒くて強じんである ▪ The boxer *is a bear for punishment.* あのボクサーはなかなかタフだ.

bear trap 《俗》(スピード違反取締りの)警察のレーダー装置 ▪ Watch out for the *bear trap* at the exit. 高速出口のレーダーに注意せよ.

Bring on *one's* ***bears!*** 《米口》なんとでもしてみろ《挑戦の文句》 ▪ He told England to *bring on her bears.* 彼はイギリスになんとでもしてくれと言った.

like [***as***] ***a bear with a sore head*** 《口》非常に不きげんな ▪ He was as sulky *as a bear with a sore head.* 彼はひどく不きげんだった.

loaded for bear **1**《口》怒って ▪ When he left here, he was really *loaded for bear.* 彼がここを去ったとき, 本当に怒っていた.

2《口》酔っぱらって ▪ By the end of the party, Bill was *loaded for bear.* パーティーが終わるまでにビルは酔っぱらっていた.

3 万全の備えをして, 手ぐすねひいて ▪ Jim is going hunting for squirrel, *loaded for bear.* ジムは周到な準備をしてリス狩りに出かけようとしている. ☞クマ撃ちには強力な弾丸を用意することから.

make a bear garden of ...を混乱の巷とする ▪ The boys *make a bear garden of* the classroom when the teacher is away. 男子生徒たちは先生がいないと教室を混乱の巷とする.

play the bear (***with***) 《口》 **1** (...に)乱暴にふるまう ▪ There is nothing but *playing the bear* among us. 我々の間では乱暴なふるまいばかりだ.

2 (...に)大損害を与える, 大破壊をする ▪ The hail has *played the bear with* the apple blossom. あられはリンゴの花を大いにいためた.

sell the skin before *one* ***has killed the bear*** 《諺》取らぬ狸の皮算用. ☞Catch the bear before you sell his skin.「皮を売る前にクマを捕えよ」.

skin the bear at once 《米口》要点に触れる, 話を要点にもっていく ▪ Now, to *skin the bear at once,* can you give me employment? ところで, 話の要点だが僕を雇ってくれますか.

take the bear by the tooth 危険なことをする ▪ You dare not *take the bear by the tooth.* 君はそんな危険なことをする勇気はあるまい.

bear[2] /beər/ 動 ***bear*** *oneself* ふるまう, 行動する; 行儀をよくする ▪ He *bore himself* like a man. 彼は男らしくふるまった.

bear and forbear /fɔ́ːrbeər/ じっとがまんする ▪ *Bear and forbear,* Epictetus used to say. じっとがまんせよ, とエピクテートスは常に言っていた. ☞Epictetus (55–135)はギリシャのストア派の哲学者.

bear ... hard [***heavy***] ...にしぶしぶ耐える, をいやに思う ▪ He *bore* it *hard* to be ignored. 彼は無視されるのにしぶしぶ耐えた.

bear inquiry [***enquiry, investigation***] 〚主に否定文で〛調査に耐える, 調査するほどの値うちがある ▪ The business won't *bear inquiry.* その事業は調査するほどの値うちはないだろう.

bear left [***right***] 《英》左側[右側]を通行する ▪ *Bear left* when you reach the school. 学校まで来たら左側を行きなさい.

bear right →BEAR left.

bear watching **1** 注目に価する; 前途有望である ▪ That young ball player will *bear watching.* あの若い野球選手は前途有望だ.

2 注視の要がある, 危ない ▪ Those tires are badly worn; they will *bear watching.* そのタイヤはひどく傷んでいるので危険だ.

bring ... to bear on [***upon***] 《文》 **1** ...に(銃砲など)を向ける; に(圧力など)を加える; に(精力など)を集中する ▪ We were unable to *bring* a gun *to bear upon* her. 我々は彼女に銃を向けることができなかった ▪ Advertisers can also *bring* pressure *to bear upon* owners and editors. 広告主はまた持ち主や編集者に圧力を加えることができる ▪ *Bring* your whole energy *to bear upon* the work. その仕事に全力を集中せよ.

2 ...に(知識など)を生かす[発揮する] ▪ This new knowledge can *be brought to bear on* the process of creating a website. この新しい知識はウェブサイトを生み出すことに生かせる.

have a (***heavy***) ***cross to bear*** →a CROSS to carry.

beard[1] /bɪərd/ 名 ***laugh at*** *a person's* ***beard*** 人を愚弄する, ばかげた嘘で人をだまそうとする ▪ By the prophet! but he *laughs at our beards.* 何ということだ, 彼は我々を愚弄しているのだ.

laugh in *one's* ***beard*** (人をからかって)ほくそえむ ▪ He *laughed in his beard* on having played a trick on the man. 彼はその男をだましてほくそえんだ.

singe the King of Spain's beard →SINGE.

speak in *one's* ***beard*** つぶやく, もぐもぐ言う ▪ He was *speaking* something *in his beard.* 彼は何かもぐもぐ言っていた.

take ... by the beard 勇敢に...を攻撃する(《聖》*1 Sam.* 17. 35) ▪ I must *take* this gigantic question *by the beard.* この巨大な問題を大胆に攻めねばならない.

***to** a person's* **beard** 人に面と向かって, 人の面前をはばからず ▪ I told him *to his beard.* 私は面と向かって彼に言った.

with the beard on the shoulder 立ち聞きする姿勢で; 不意打ち[伏兵]を警戒して見回しながら ▪ They rode *with the beard on the shoulder,* looking round. 彼らは見回して, 警戒しながら馬を進めた. ☞Spain 起源の句.

beard[2] /bɪərd/ 動 ***beard the lion*** [***a dragon,*** etc.] ***in his den*** 怖い相手と大胆に渡り合う, (敵地に乗り込んで)堂々と反対する ▪ I'm going to *beard the lion in his den,* and ask him why he hasn't increased my salary. 社長のところへ思い切って行って, なぜ給料を上げてくれなかったのか尋ねてみる.

bearer /béərər/ 名 ***the standard bearer*** 旗手, 旗頭 (*of, for*) ▪ Pastor Toby appears to be *the standard bearer of* a younger generation of clergymen. トービー牧師は若い世代の聖職者の旗手であるように思われる ▪ Doris is regarded as a *standard-bearer for* women jockeys. ドリスは女性騎手の旗頭とみなされている.

bearing[1] /béərɪŋ/ 名 ***beyond*** [***past***] (***all***) ***bearing*** とてもがまんができない ▪ This is *past bearing.* こんなことはとてもがまんができない.

bearing[2] /béərɪŋ/ 名 ***be past bearing*** (木が)もう実を結ばなくなっている; (女性が)もう子を産まなくなっている ▪ The tree [She] *is past bearing.* その木にはもう実はならない[彼女はもう子を産む年ではない].

bring** a person **to** his **bearings (分際を忘れた)人にその分を知らせる; 人を懲らしめる ▪ We must *bring* him *to his bearings.* 我々は彼の思いあがりを反省させなければならない.

find [***get***] *one's* ***bearings*** 自分の立場・位置がわかる[確定する] ▪ Look round and *get your bearings.* 見回して君の位置を知りなさい. ☞海事用語から.

get** one's **bearings back 落ち着きを取り戻す ▪ Wait until I *get my bearings back.* 私が落ち着くまで待ってください.

have no [***some***] ***bearing on*** ...に関係がない[いくらかある] ▪ It *has some bearing on* this subject. それはこの題目にいくらか関係がある.

in all its bearings あらゆる方面から ▪ I will consider the matter *in all its bearings.* その件をあらゆる方面から考えてみましょう.

in bearing 実がなる状態で ▪ The trees can be kept *in bearing* for many years. その木は長年にわたって実をならせることができる.

lose** one's **bearings 方角を失う, 道に迷う; 当惑する ▪ Somehow I *lost my bearings.* どうしたわけか道に迷った ▪ He asked me so many questions that I *lost my bearings.* 彼が非常に多くの質問をしたので当惑した.

take** one's **bearings ...の方位[位置]を確かめる; 事情[形勢]を察知する ▪ They *took the bearings of* a running horse. 彼らは走る馬の位置を確かめた ▪ *Take your bearings.* I won't hurry you. よく君の立場を考えなさい. 君をせかしはしないから.

beast /biːst/ 名 ***a beast of a*** 《口》いやな ▪ It is *a beast of a* day. ひどく天気の悪い日だ.

a beast of burden 《雅》荷物運搬用家畜, 役畜《馬・ラバ・ロバなど》 ▪ Donkeys are used as *a beast of burden* in this area. この地方ではロバは役畜として使われている.

a beast of prey →PREY[1].

make the beast with two backs 《俗》セックスをする (cf. Sh., *Oth.* 1. 1. 117) ▪ I found your daughter and Gerald *making the beast with two backs* in her room. あんたの娘とジェラルドが彼女の部屋でやってるのを見たぞ.

nail the beast 病気[不快なこと]を克服する ▪ Mr. Herbert fought hard against his cancer and eventually managed to *nail the beast.* ハーバート氏は壮絶にガンと闘い, ついにそれにうち勝った.

beat[1] /biːt/ 名 ***in*** [***out of***] ***beat*** (時計などの)打ち方が規則的で[不規則で] ▪ Set the clock *in beat.* 時計を規則的に打たせなさい ▪ The clock sounds *out of beat.* 時計の音が調子を乱している.

lie to (***a***) ***beat*** 休閑で雑草が一面にはえている ▪ The field *lies to* (*a*) *beat.* 畑は休閑で雑草が一面にはえている.

not miss a beat **1** ちゅうちょしない, ためらわない ▪ "I love you," he said, *not missing a beat.* 「君が好きだ」と彼はちゅうちょせずに言った.

2 チャンス[好機]を逃さない ▪ Ellen was playing like she *never missed a beat.* エレンは決して好機を逃さないかのようにプレーしていた.

off [***out of***] *one's* ***beat*** 持ち場違いで, 畑違いで ▪ This is *out of my beat.* これは私には畑違いだ ▪ Europe and America lay somewhere *out of their beat.* ヨーロッパとアメリカはいささか彼らの持ち場外にあった.

off (***the***) ***beat*** 調子を乱して, 不規則で ▪ A police officer is *off the beat* at last. 一人の警官がついに調子を崩した.

on the [*one's*] ***beat*** **1** 専門で, 得意で ▪ That is *on my beat.* それは私の専門だ.

2 持ち場を巡回して ▪ The policeman is *on the beat.* 警官は巡回勤務中である.

3 (時計の音が)調子が整って ▪ The clock is *on the beat.* 時計は規則正しく打っている.

out of beat →in BEAT.

pound the [***a***] ***beat*** 《口》(受持区域を)歩いてパトロールする《車などによるパトロールと対照して》 ▪ He was demoted and sent back to *pound the beat.* 彼は階級を下げられ, もとのように歩いてパトロールさせられるようになった.

beat[2] /biːt/ 動 ***be*** (***all***) ***beat up*** = be dead BEAT.

be dead beat すっかり疲れている《特に一時的に過労などで》 ▪ I *am dead beat* after a day's work. 私は一日の仕事ですっかり疲れた.

(***be***) ***hard*** [《米口》***bad***] ***to beat*** なかなか負けな

い; 及ぶものはない ▪ For loveliness it would *be hard to beat*. 美しさではそれに及ぶものはないだろう ▪ In anything over three miles he *is bad to beat*. 3マイル以上の競走なら彼は誰にも負けない.

beat a path [**track**] 度々歩いて道を踏みならす ▪ Gascoigne first *beat the path* to that perfection. ガスコインが初めてそのような完成にいたる道を作った ▪ He *beat a path* through the snow. 彼は雪の中を踏んで道を作った.

beat a track →BEAT a path.

beat a tree 木の枝をたたいて果実を落とす ▪ He *beat* his olive *trees*. 彼は彼の家のオリーブの木をたたいて果実を落とした.

beat a way through (茂み)をたたきつけて道を作る ▪ The hunters *beat a way through* the bushes. ハンターたちは茂みをたたきつけて道を開いた.

beat all 《口》全く驚く[ふしぎだ]; 天下無類だ (→beat the DUTCH) ▪ John found a box full of money. Doesn't that *beat all*? ジョンは金のいっぱい入った箱を見つけた. 全く驚くじゃないか.

beat (**all**) **creation** →CREATION.

beat ... (**all**) **hollow** →HOLLOW.

beat *a person* (**all**) **to ribands** [**sticks**] 《口》人を完全に打ち負かす ▪ I rode a race against Bob and *beat* him *all to ribands*. 私はボブと競馬をし, 完全に彼を負かした.

beat anything →BEAT everything.

beat around [《英》 **about**] **the bush** →BUSH.

beat ... at *a person's* **own game** →GAME.

beat *one's* **brains** →BRAIN.

beat *one's* **breast** [**chest**] **1** (特に申し開きのため)うぬぼれたっぷりの演説をする ▪ He *beat his breast* in an attempt to vindicate his behavior. 彼は自分の行動の申し開きをしようと, 思い入れたっぷりに演じた. **2** 《文》胸をたたいて悲しむ[怒る] ▪ At the news of his death, she *beat her breast* in grief. 彼の死の知らせに彼女は胸をたたいて悲しんだ ▪ Scholars need not *beat their breasts*. 学者たちは胸をたたいて怒らないでもよい.

beat *a person* **down** (**in price**) 人に対して値切る ▪ I managed to *beat* him *down* in price. 私はなんとか彼に値をまけさせた.

beat everything [**anything**] 《米》断然すぐれている, 何にも負けない ▪ That *beats everything* I ever heard. それは前代未聞の話だ.

beat goose (温めるため)両手をわきにはさんでたたく ▪ The laborers were *beating goose* to drive the blood into their fingers. 労働者たちは指に血をめぐらすため, 両手をわきの下にはさんでたたいていた.

beat (*one's*) **gums** [**chops**] 《米俗》(わけもなく)べらべらしゃべる ▪ Stop *beating your gums*. ばかなおしゃべりはよせ.

beat *one's* **head against a stone wall** →HEAD[1].

beat *a person's* **head in** 打撃を与えて[悩ませて]頭をかかえさす ▪ The automobile industry *beat my head in*. 私は自動車産業には頭を悩ませていた.

beat ... into fits →FIT[1].

beat it 《口》急いで行く, 去る, 逃げる; 急ぐ ▪ He will be *beating it* for Paris soon. 彼はやがて急いでパリへ出て行くだろう ▪ The murderer *beat it*, leaving him for dead. その殺人者は相手を死んだものとして捨てて逃げた.

beat it up 《俗》大いにはしゃぐ, 騒ぎ立てる ▪ His friends *beat it up* a little in the evenings. 彼の友だちは晩には少しはしゃいだ.

beat *a thing* **out of** *a person's* **head** 人に教えてある事を改めさせる ▪ I cannot *beat* the notion *out of his head*. 彼にいくら教えてもその考えを改めさせることはできない.

beat *a person* **out of sight** 人をさんざん打ち負かす ▪ He *beat* the fiddler *out of sight*. 彼はそのバイオリン弾きをさんざん負かした.

beat ... out of the field ...を競争場からたたき出す ▪ His rival *was beaten out of the field*. 彼の相手は競技場からたたき出された.

beat over the (**old**) **ground** すでに論じられた話題をまた論じる ▪ It would, in fact, be only *beating over the old ground*. それは実際すでに論じられた問題をむしかえすにすぎないだろう.

beat *one's* **swords into plowshares** →SWORD.

Beat that if you can! = Can you BEAT that?

beat the air [**wind**] 空を打つ, むだぼねを折る, 手ごたえのない戦いをする (《聖》 *1 Cor.*, 9. 26) ▪ All you are doing is to *beat the air*. 君のしていることはみなむだぼねだ.

beat the booby →BEAT goose.

beat the bounds 《英教会》教区[行政区]の境界を検分する ▪ You were provided with long willow wands with which to *beat the bounds*. あなたがたは教区の境界を検分するための柳の杖を持っていた. ☞キリスト昇天祭の日 (Ascension Day) に教区の子供たちが行列を作って柳の杖で教区の境界を打って歩いた故事から.

beat the bounds of ...を入念に調べ確かめる ▪ He has *beaten the bounds of* every aspect of man. 彼は人間のあらゆる面を入念に調べ確かめた.

beat the time of/**beat** *a person's* **time** (人)のデートを横取りする, ライバルに勝つ ▪ Johnny will get mad that you *beat his time*. 君がジョニーのデートを横取りしたので彼はかんかんに怒るだろう.

beat the wind →BEAT the air.

beat *a person* **to a frazzle** [**a jelly, a mummy, powder**] 人をくたくたに打ちのめす ▪ Two wicked men are now *beating* my poor father *to a jelly*. 二人の悪者が今私の父をめちゃくちゃに打ちのめしているところだ.

beat *a person* **to it** 《口》人の先を越す[先手を打つ] ▪ Fred applied for the job, but someone else *beat* him *to it*. フレッドはその職を志願したが, 誰か他の者が彼の先手を打った.

beat ... to the draw →DRAW[1].

beat** oneself **up 《米口》自分を責める, 罪の意識を感じる, 気がとがめる ▪ Why am I *beating myself up* over this baby? なぜ私はこの赤ちゃんのことで自分を責めているのだろうか ▪ I failed to come up to mother's expectations and I'm *beating myself up* for it. 母の期待に添えず, 気がとがめている.

beat up and down あちこち走り回る ▪ We *beat up and down* and got tired. あちこち走り回って疲れた.

beat up* (*for*) *recruits 新兵を募る ▪ He *beat up* the town *for recruits.* 彼は町を歩いて新兵を募った.

beat up the quarters of **1**《口》いきなり[不意に]…を訪問する ▪ He *beat up the quarters of* some relations. 彼は数人の親類を不意に訪問した.

2 …を騒がす; (野営中の)敵を不意打ちする ▪ He set off once more to *beat up Captain Cuttle's quarters.* 彼はカトル大尉の宿営を奇襲しようともう一度出撃した.

beat** one's **way 《米口》 **1** ただ乗りで行く; 不正入場する ▪ In America tramps often *beat their way.* アメリカでは浮浪者たちはしばしばただ乗りをする ▪ He *beat his way* to Chicago on a lake vessel. 彼は湖上船にただ乗りしてシカゴへ行った.

2 苦しい徒歩旅行をする ▪ He was *beating his way* on foot, muleback, and raft. 彼は徒歩, ラバ, いかだなどで苦しい旅をしていた.

***Can you beat that* [*it*]?** 《口》驚くじゃないか ▪ He has just come out top in the civil service exam. *Can you beat it?* 彼は公務員試験にトップ合格したところだ. 驚くだろ. ☞「これ以上のことが考えられるか」が原義.

have** a person **beat 《米俗》人にすぐれている, 人に勝つ ▪ Why, he can't *have* me *beat.* だって, 彼に私を負かすことはできないじゃないか.

***If you can't beat them*(*, join them* [*'em*]).** 《諺》みんなが悪事をやるなら(, 自分もやればいい).

(*it, that*) *beats me* [*my time*] 《口》私にはわからない, 私は閉口だ ▪ *It* clean *beats my time.* 私には全くわからない ▪ Ben shook his head, saying, "*Beats me.*" ベンは首を振って,「わからんね」と言った.

That beats everything!*/*That beats all! 《米口》それには驚いた, そんなことは信じられない ▪ Jim divorced his wife? Well, *that beats everything!* ジムが離婚したって? いや, そいつは驚きだね.

to beat the band*/*to beat all 群を抜いて, すごく ▪ She was at church praying *to beat the band.* 彼女は教会で盛んにお祈りをしていた ▪ It was raining *to beat the band.* すごい雨だった.

what beats me 私にわからないのは ▪ *What beats me* is why he commited suicide. 私にわからないのは, 彼がなぜ自殺したかだ.

you can't beat …に及ぶものはない ▪ *You can't beat* that coffeeshop for good coffee. うまいコーヒーではあの店に及ぶものはない.

beaten /bíːtən/ 形 ***off the beaten track* [*path*]** 人のあまり行かない[知らない]; 常道をはずれて ▪ We found an interesting place, *off the beaten track.* 我々は人のあまり行かないところに, 面白い場所を見つけた ▪ Everything he does is *off the beaten track.* 彼のすることはすべて常道をはずれている.

***the beaten track* [《米》 *path*]** 踏みならされた道, 常道, 通常の方法 ▪ He is a conservative person who keeps *the beaten path.* 彼は常道をたどる保守的な人間だ.

beating /bíːtɪŋ/ 名 ***give** a person **a good beating*** **1** 人をしこたまたたく ▪ He *gave* the boy *a good beating.* 彼はその少年をひどくたたいた.

2 人をひどく負かす ▪ We *gave* the enemy *a good beating.* 我々は敵をこっぴどく負かした.

take a beating **1** 退却する, なくなる ▪ They are *taking a beating.* 彼らは退却しつつある ▪ The store is *taking a* sales *beating.* その店は売上額がなくなっている.

2 (伝染病が)根絶される ▪ Malaria is *taking a beating.* マラリアが根絶されつつある.

3 打撃を受ける, ひどい目にあう ▪ He *took a* terrible *beating.* 彼はひどくやられた ▪ This team *took a* real *beating* last year, both physically and mentally. このチームは昨年肉体的にも精神的にも本当にひどい目にあった.

4 (自動車が)損傷する ▪ Your car *takes* a lot of *beating* on these rough roads. あなたの自動車はこの悪路ではひどく損傷する.

5 失敗する; 負ける, 大損する ▪ He *took a beating* in his attempt. 彼は試みに失敗した ▪ The Giants *took a beating* in last night's game. ジャイアンツは昨夜の試合で負けた ▪ The company *took a beating* last year, losing about $50,000,000. その会社は去年約5,000万ドル失って, 大損をした.

6 (心臓などが)動悸を打つ ▪ Not only the feet but the nerves *took a beating.* 足だけでなく神経もびくびくした.

take some* [*a lot of*] *beating 《口》…をしのぐことは難しい ▪ English country life *took a lot of beating.* 英国の田舎生活よりいいものはなかった.

beauty /bjúːti/ 名 ***Age before beauty.*** → AGE.

be a* (*regular*) *beauty 《口・皮肉》非常に無器用な人[信用できない人]である ▪ You*'re a beauty.* 困った人だな ▪ She *is a regular beauty.* 大変な女じゃないか.

Beauty and the Beast 美女と野獣[醜男] ▪ *Beauty and the Beast* was what they called us when we went out walking together. 我々が一緒に散歩に出たとき, 彼らは我々を「美女と野獣」と呼んだ. ☞野獣とともに暮らすことを承諾した美女の愛によって魔術が解けて野獣が美しい王子となり, 美女と結婚するというおとぎ話から.

Beauty is but* [*only*] *skin deep. 《諺》美貌はただ皮一重《外観だけで人を判断するな》.

Beauty is* [*lies*] *in the eye of the beholder. 《諺》美(貌)は見る人の目にある《美しさの基準は見る人によって異なる》 ☞あまり美しくない人などに対して

B

気休めに言うことが多い.

beauty sleep (美容に効果があるとされる)夜半前の睡眠; 決まった時間以外の睡眠 ▪ She took her *beauty sleep* before the party. パーティーの前に臨時の睡眠をとった.

Here's a beauty. 特に立派な例である.

(***that's***) ***the beauty of*** (***it***) (そこが)…のいいところ[うま味, みそ]だ ▪ *That's the beauty of it*; to offend and make up at pleasure. そこがいいところだ, 随意に怒らせたり仲直りしたりするのがさ ▪ *That's the beauty of* competition. そこが競争のうま味だよ.

beaver /bíːvər/ 名 ***an eager beaver*** 仕事の虫, はりきり屋 ▪ Meg gets to work very early. She's *a* real *eager beaver*. メグは朝早くから仕事に取りかかる. ほんとに仕事の虫だ.

(***as***) ***busy*** [***industrious***] ***as a beaver*** 《米口》全く忙しい ▪ This competitor was *as industrious as a beaver*. この競争者は全く忙しく動いた.

(***as***) ***mad as a beaver*** 《米口》ひどく怒って ▪ He is naturally *as mad as a beaver*. 彼は当然ひどく怒っている.

be (***a***) ***gone beaver*** 《米口》どうにもならない, 救いようがない, 全くだめである ▪ We *are* sure *gone beaver*. 我々はほんとに全くだめだ.

up to beaver 《米口》(最も用心深い)ビーバーでもだます知恵がある ▪ The trapper marched off, admitting that he was not yet *up to beaver*. わな猟師は自分はまだビーバーをだますだけの知恵がないことを認めて引きあげた.

work like a beaver →WORK[2].

because /bɪkʌ́z, bɪkɔ́ːz|bɪkɔ́z/ 接 (***all***) ***the better*** [***worse***, etc.] ***because*** →(all) THE better for.

because of …のため ▪ I didn't go out *because of* the rain. 私は雨のため外出しなかった.

beck /bek/ 名 ***at the beck and call of***/***at*** *a person's* ***beck and call*** (人)の言いなり[指図のまま]に ▪ A good parent isn't necessarily always *at the beck and call of* the child. よい親は必ずしも子供の言いなりにはならないものだ ▪ They move *at his beck and call*. 彼らは彼の言いなりになる.

hang upon the beck of …の命[指図]を待つ ▪ I am wholly *hanging upon your beck*. 私は全くあなたの命のままです.

have *a person* ***at*** *one's* ***beck*** 人を意のままに[あごで]使う ▪ He *has* the men *at his beck*. 彼は部下をあごで使う.

become /bɪkʌ́m/ 動 ***It ill becomes*** *a person* ***to*** *do*. …するなんて人にも似合わない ▪ *It ill becomes* you *to* complain. 不平を言うとは君にも似合わない.

becoming /bɪkʌ́mɪŋ/ 形 ***be becoming in*** *a person* (***to*** *do*) (…するのは)人にふさわしい ▪ It *is* not *becoming in* a man of his experience *to* commit such a blunder. そんな失策をするとは彼のような経験家にも似合わない.

be becoming on [***to***] (物が)…に似合う ▪ The hat *is* very *becoming on* you. その帽子はあなたによく似合ってますよ.

bed[1] /bed/ 名 ***a bed and breakfast*** **1** 朝食つきの民宿 (a B and B, B&B) ▪ Staying at [in] *a bed and breakfast* [a B and B] is a good way to meet local people. 朝食つき民宿に泊まることは地方の人々と会うよい方法である.

2 (株を買って翌朝売り戻す)株の一夜買い ▪ She bought *a bed and breakfast* and is making a go of it. 彼女は株の一夜買いをしてうまくやっている.

a bed of down [***flowers, roses***] 〚しばしば否定文で〛安楽な暮らし, 安住の地, ここちのよい所《羽・花・バラの床から》 ▪ These rocks by custom turn to *beds of down*. この岩も慣れると羽ぶとんのようになる ▪ Life as the proverb goes "is no *bed of roses*." 人生は諺にもあるように,「決してバラの床ではない」.

a bed of thorns [***nails***] 針のむしろ, つらい境遇 ▪ He lies on *a bed of thorns*. 彼はつらい立場にある.

As you make your bed, you must lie on it. 《諺》自業自得の報いを受けねばならない.

be brought to bed (***of*** *a child*) お産をする ▪ The Queen *was brought to bed of* a daughter. 王妃は女の子を出産された.

be confined to *one's* ***bed*** →keep one's BED.

be good [***bad***] ***in bed*** 《口》セックスが上手[下手]である ▪ I love John because he'*s good in bed*. 私はジョンが好きよ. だってセックスが上手なんだもの.

be put to bed with a shovel 《俗》 **1** 死んで埋葬される ▪ Poor old Jack. He *was put to bed with a shovel* last March. かわいそうなジャック老人. 彼はこの3月に死んで埋葬された.

2 ひどく酔っぱらう ▪ He wasn't just tipsy. He *was put to bed with a shovel*. 彼はほろ酔いどころじゃなかった, べろんべろんだった.

bed and board **1** 食事と宿泊 ▪ There is no city better supplied for *bed and board*. これほど食事と宿泊先の多い都市はない.

2 (妻の)夫婦生活 ▪ She separated from her *bed and board*. 彼女は夫と別居した.

climb [***get, hop***] ***into bed with*** (意外な相手)と同盟[提携]する ▪ The Liberal Democrats have *climbed into bed with* the Tories to try to win the election. 選挙に勝利しようと自由民主党は保守党と手を組んだ.

die in *one's* ***bed*** →DIE[2].

fall out of bed (気温などが)急にすごく下がる ▪ The temperature *fell out of bed* last night. 昨夜気温が急にどんと下がった.

get in [***into***] ***bed with*** …といっしょに寝る; 親密な関係になる ▪ Dell has just *got into bed with* Microsoft. デルはマイクロソフトと親密な関係になったばかりだ.

get *a person* ***into bed*** 人を説いて性交させる ▪ Finally he succeeded in *getting* Eve *into bed* with him. ついに彼は首尾よくイブを説いて性交させた.

get out of bed 起床する ▪ He *got out of bed* at

four. 彼は4時に起床した.

get out of bed on the wrong side [***the wrong way, with the left leg foremost***]/***get out on the wrong side of the bed***/***get up on*** [***out of***] ***the wrong side of the bed*** 《口》その日はきげんが悪い《ベッドの逆の側から起床する》 ▪ You must have *got out of bed on the wrong side* this morning. 君は今朝は虫のいどころが悪い. ☞通例 must have got ...の形で使う.

get (*a child*) ***to bed*** (子供を)寝かす ▪ I *got my child to bed* at nine. 9時に子供を寝かせた.

go to bed **1** 床につく, 寝る ▪ He *goes to bed* at ten. 彼は10時に就寝する.
2《俗》〚命令文で〛うるさい, 黙れ! ▪ Don't bother me! *Go to bed!* うるさい! 黙れ!
3 印刷に回される ▪ The paper *went to bed* at four. その新聞は4時に印刷に付された.
4 (いっしょに)寝る ▪ She is in the habit of *going to bed* with anybody who asks her to. 彼女は求められれば誰とでも寝るたちである.

go to bed in *one's* ***boots*** →BOOT[1].

have *one's* ***bed*** 産褥(じょく)につく ▪ Mary expects to *have her bed* in three weeks. メアリーは3週間したら産褥につく予定である.

in bed 床について, 寝て ▪ John was still *in bed*. ジョンはまだ寝ていた.

in bed with ...と提携して[ぐるになって] ▪ The company is "*in bed with*" the intelligence agency. その会社は情報部と「提携して」いる.

keep [***be confined to***] *one's* ***bed*** (病)床についている ▪ To speak plainly she *keeps her bed*. はっきり言えば彼女は床についているのです ▪ All day the sluggard *keeps his bed*. その怠け者は一日中寝床にいる.

leave *one's* ***bed*** 床を離れる; 床上げする ▪ Two days after Don Quixote *left his bed*. 2日後にドンキホーテは床を離れた.

lie [***sleep***] ***in*** [***on***] ***the bed*** *one* ***has made***/***make*** *one's* ***bed and lie in it*** 自業自得の報いを受ける ▪ It's unfortunate that it turned out badly, but Sue *made her bed and* now she must *lie in it*. 結果が悪かったのは不幸だが, スーは自業自得の報いを受けなければならない. ☞《諺》As you make your BED, you must lie on it. から.

one's ***lowly*** [***narrow***] ***bed*** 《文》墓, 奥津城(おくつき) ▪ I looked in awe upon him in *his lowly bed*. 私は奥津城に眠る彼を畏敬の念をもって眺めた.

make a [***the,*** *a person's*] ***bed*** 床を整える《床をとる, 床を片づけるの両義》 ▪ A true nurse always knows how to *make a bed*. 真の看護師は常に床のとり方を知っている ▪ He did not allow *his bed* to *be made* oftener than once a week. 彼は1週間に1度以上自分の床を片づけることを許さなかった.

make *one's* ***bed and lie in*** [***on***] ***it*** →lie in the BED one has made.

make up a bed 寝床をこしらえる, 臨時の床を用意する ▪ The *bed* could *be made up* in the usual way. 普通に床をとることができた.

no bed of roses/not a bed of roses バラの床ではない, 安楽ではない ▪ Life is*n't a bed of roses*, you know. 人生はバラの床じゃないからね.

out of bed 起きて ▪ She has not been *out of bed* since. 彼女はそれ以来起きていない.

put ... to bed **1** (子供など)を寝かす ▪ *Put* the children *to bed* now. もう子供たちを寝かしなさい.
2 (暫定的に問題・計画)にけりをつける ▪ Let's *put* this matter *to bed* quickly before we discuss more important things. もっと重要な事柄を議論する前に素早くこの問題にけりをつけよう ▪ They *put* the whole project *to bed* a month ago. 彼らはひと月前にその計画全体にけりをつけた.
3 ...が誤りであることを示す ▪ Harvey's analysis *puts* several badly thought-out economic theories *to bed*. ハービーの分析はずさんに考えられたいくつかの経済理論が誤りであることを示した.
4 組版して印刷機にかける ▪ The paper has *been put to bed* already. 新聞はすでに組版して印刷機にかけられている.

should have stood in bed 《口》(いやな日なので)家で寝ていればよかった ▪ What a horrible day! I *should have stood in bed*. なんてひどい日なんだ! 家で寝ていればよかった. ☞ボクサーの Joe Jacobs が1935年のある寒い日にはじめてワールドシリーズの野球を見たあとで言った評言. 正しくは should have stayed in bed とあるべきところ.

sick in bed 病気で床についている ▪ He's been *sick in bed* for nearly a week. 彼はここ一週間近く病気でふせっている.

take to (***a***) ***bed*** 産褥(じょく)につく ▪ Our wives *took to bed* the same day. 僕らの妻は同じ日に産褥についた.

take to *one's* ***bed*** (病気などで)床につく ▪ He *took to his bed* in March. 彼は3月に病床についた.

the bed of honor/the honor's bed 戦死者の墓 ▪ They were laid in *the bed of honor*. 彼らは戦没勇士の墓に葬られた.

You've made your bed and you must lie in [***on***] ***it.*** =As you make your BED, you must lie on it.

bed[2] /bed/ 動 ***bed*** *oneself* ***in*** ...に入り込む ▪ The bullet *bedded itself in* the wall. 弾丸は壁にめり込んだ.

Early to bed and early to rise makes a man healthy, wealthy, and wise. 《諺》早寝早起きは人を健康に裕福に賢明にする.

bed-bug /bédbʌ̀g/ 名 (***as***) ***crazy as a bed-bug*** →(as) CRAZY as a betsy bug.

bedfellow /bédfèloʊ/ 名 ***a strange bedfellow*** 気心の知れない仲間, 奇妙な仲間 (cf. Sh., *Temp.* 2. 2. 42) ▪ Misery acquaints a man with *strange bedfellows*. 不幸にあうと気心の知れぬ仲間とつき合うようになる.

make good [***bad***] ***bedfellows*** 仲のよい[悪い]相棒である ▪ Jack and Carl are so different in their views. They *make bad bedfellows.* ジャックとカールはものの見方がまるきり違う. 二人は性が合わない.

bedim /bidím/ 動 ***bedimmed with*** …に曇って ▪ Her eyes were *bedimmed with* tears. 彼女の目は涙で曇っていた.

bedpost /bédpòust/ 名 ***between you and me and the bedpost*** →BETWEEN.

bedrock /bédràk|-rɔ̀k/ 名 ***get*** [***come, be***] ***down to bedrock*** **1** 底[根本]を究める; 真相[本質]をつく ▪ *Come down to bedrock* on the problem. その問題の底を究めよ.

2《米俗》文なしになる, 資力が尽きる ▪ He must *be down to bedrock* by this time. 彼は今ごろは文なしになっているにちがいない. ☞「鉱床の底をつく」が原義.

bedroom /bédrù:m/ 名 ***have bedroom eyes*** セックスに興味があるような顔をしている ▪ Some people just *have bedroom eyes.* 人によってはセックスに興味があるような顔をしている者がいる.

bedside /bédsàid/ 名 ***be*** [***sit***] ***at*** [***by***] *a person's* ***bedside*** 人の病床にかしずく ▪ Mary's mother *sat at her bedside* while she was ill. メアリーの母は彼女の病気中看病をした.

have a good bedside manner (医者が)患者の扱い方がうまい ▪ The doctor *has a good bedside manner.* その医者は患者の扱い方がうまい.

bee /bi:/ 名 (***as***) ***brisk as bees in a tar bucket*** →TAR[1].

(***as***) ***busy as a bee*** [***a beaver*** (***building a new dam***), ***one-armed paperhanger, Grand Central Station, a cat on a hot tin roof, a fish peddler in Lent, a cranberry merchant*** (***at Thanksgiving***), ***popcorn on a skillet***] とても忙しい ▪ I don't have time to talk to you. I'm *as busy as a beaver.* お前としゃべっている暇なんかない. 目が回るほど忙しいんだ ▪ He was *as busy as a bee* trying to put the house in order. 彼は家を整頓するのに多忙を極めた.

(***as***) ***busy as a bee in a tar barrel*** → TAR[1].

be the bee's knees《英口》素晴らしく良い ▪ Really, this ice cream *is the bee's knees.* ほんとにこのアイスクリームはすごくうまい.

have a bee in *one's* ***bonnet*** [***head***] ある考えに凝っている, (大げさな, 奇異な, ばかげた)考えにつかれている; 少し気がふれている ▪ He *has a bee in his bonnet* about reforming the world single-handed. 彼は世界を一人で改革するという奇想にとりつかれている ▪ He *has a bee in his bonnet* about fresh air. 彼は新鮮な空気ということに凝っている. ☞「頭の中で一つの考えがミツバチのようにぶんぶん言っている」の意.

have bees in the head [***the brains***] =have a BEE in one's bonnet.

put a bee in *a person's* ***bonnet*** 人に着想を話して聞かす, 人に…するように促す (*about*) ▪ John *put a bee in my bonnet about* having a party for Alice. ジョンはアリスのためにパーティーを開いてやるようにと私をせきたてた.

put a bee under *one's* ***bonnet*** 奇想に凝る ▪ What new *bee* will you *put under your bonnet*? どんな新しい奇想に凝るつもりかね.

put the bee on《主に米俗》**1** …に金を貸せと言う, から金をだまし取る ▪ He *put the bee on* his daughter for $200. 彼は娘に200ドル金を貸せと言った. ☞ <sting「金をだまし取る」.

2 …を鎮圧する; を終わらせる; を打ち負かす ▪ He *put the bee on* the proceedings. 彼は訴訟手続きをやめさせた ▪ This fairy tale *puts the bee on* the lot. このおとぎ話は同類より断然すぐれている.

work like a bee (***in a hive***) せっせと[こまめに]働く ▪ Susan *works like a bee in a hive.* スーザンはミツバチのように働く.

beef /bi:f/ 名 ***beef to the heels***《口》(人が)太りすぎて ▪ She is "*beef to the heels,*" as James Joyce would put it. ジェイムズ・ジョイスなら言うだろうが, 彼女は「太りすぎ」だ. ☞「かかとまで筋肉」が原義.

have [***hold***] ***a beef against*** [***with***] …に不満を抱いている ▪ On what issue does he *have a beef against* the manager? どんな問題で彼は支配人に不満を抱いているのか?

have no beef against [***with***] …に何の不満もない ▪ I *have no beef with* Google. I like Google. グーグルに何の不満もない. グーグルは好きさ.

hound the beef《米俗》セックスの相手をあさる ▪ Me and Jed were out *hounding the beef.* おいらとジェッドは外で女をあさっていた.

put some beef into (***it***)《口》〚主に命令文で〛(それ)に一生懸命働く ▪ *Put some beef into it*—snap it up! そいつに精出して働くんだ—急いで! ▪ You *put* too much *beef into* a stroke. 君は打球に力を入れすぎる.

take on beef 体重がふえる, 重くなる ▪ I *took on beef*, but I still don't eat pork. 私は体重がふえたが, それでもポークは食べません.

What's the beef? =Where's the BEEF? 2.

Where's the beef?《米口》**1** 大切な中身はどこにある? ▪ *Where's the beef?* There's no substance in this proposal. 肝心の中身はどこだ. この提案には実質的な内容がない. ☞ 競合他社の商品をからかった, ハンバーガーチェーン Wendy's のコマーシャル.

2 何が不満なのか ▪ *Where's the beef?* No one was hurt in the accident. 何が不満なのか. その事故で誰もけがしていない.

beefed-up /bí:ftʌ̀p/ 形〚限定的〛増強した ▪ Obama got *beefed-up* protection because of the terrorist threat. オバマ氏はテロの脅威のため保安要員を増強した.

beeline /bí:làin/ 名 ***in a beeline*** 一直線に ▪ The planes flew *in a beeline.* 飛行機は一直線に飛んだ.

make [***strike, take***] ***a beeline for***《米口》…へまっすぐに行く ▪ I'm going to *strike a beeline for* home. 私は家へまっすぐに帰るつもりです. ☞ 昔ミツバチがまっすぐに飛ぶと考えられていたから; 今は誤りであることがわかっている.

beer[1] /bɪər/ 名 ***(all) beer and skittles***《口》[[主に否定文で]] 飲食遊戯の楽しみ; 遊び; 楽しくおもしろいこと ▪ Life is not *all beer and skittles.* 人生は楽しくおもしろいことばかりではない.

be in beer (ビールに)酔っている ▪ Warren *was in beer.* ウォレンはビールに酔っていた.

be small beer to [***for***] *a person* 人にとってつまらないもの ▪ Liquor licence reform *is small beer for* drinkers. 酒類販売の改正なんて酒飲みにとってはつまらない問題だ.

chronicle small beer つまらないことを記録する[話題にする, 問題にする] (cf. Sh., *Oth.* 2. 1. 161) ▪ They would *chronicle small beer* at the club. 彼らはクラブでつまらないことを語り合うのだった.

cry [***weep***] ***in*** *one's* ***beer*** 自分を哀れむ, 自分の不運を嘆く ▪ Don't *cry in your beer.* Get yourself straightened out. 自分を哀れんではだめだ. しゃきっとしろ.

make *a person* ***cry*** [***weep***] ***into*** *his* ***beer*** (なかなか取り乱さない人)を狼狽させる, うろたえさせる ▪ The defeat must have *made* American generals *weep into their beer.* その敗北は米軍の将軍らを狼狽させたにちがいない.

on the beer 飲み騒いで; 酒に酔って ▪ We had a riotous evening *on the beer.* 一晩飲み騒いだ.

think no [***not think***] ***small beer of*** *oneself*《口》うぬぼれる ▪ The pianist *doesn't think small beer of himself.* そのピアニストはなかなかうぬぼれが強い ▪ She *thinks no small beer of herself.* 彼女はうぬぼれている.

think strong beer of *oneself* →STRONG.

beer[2] /bɪər/ 動 ***be beered up***《英口》ビールを飲んで酔っ払っている ▪ He had *been beered up* before the guests came. 彼は客が来る前からビールを飲んで酔っ払っていた.

beeswax /bíːzwæks/ 名 ***Mind your own beeswax.***《米口》ほっといてくれ (＝Mind your business.). ☞beeswax (蜜蝋)は business の意図的なまちがい.

None of your beeswax.《米口》おまえの知ったことか (＝None of your business.).

beet /biːt/ 名 ***go as red as a beet***《米》(恥ずかしさ・怒りなどで)真っ赤になる ▪ When I told her the news, her face *went as red as a beet.* 彼女にそのニュースを知らせると, 彼女の顔は真っ赤になった.

beetle /bíːtəl/ 名 ***(as) blind*** [***deaf, dumb***] ***as a beetle*** ひどく目が見えなくて[耳が聞こえなくて, 口がきけなくて] ▪ They made him *as blind as a beetle.* 彼らは彼を全く盲目にした ▪ He was *as dumb as a beetle* in that matter. 彼はそのことには全く沈黙していた. ☞as deaf [dumb] as a beetle の beetle は「大うち」と考えられている.

beetle crushers《口》大きな平たい足[靴] ▪ Heavens! What *beetle crushers*! おやおや! 大そう大きな靴だなあ!

between the beetle and the block 今にも打ち砕かれそうな状態で《大うちと台盤との間にあって》 ▪ William, being thus set *between the beetle and the block*, was nothing dejected. ウィリアムはこのように今にも打ち砕かれようとしていたが, 少しも意気消沈しなかった.

beet-red /bíːtrèd/ 形 ***go*** [***turn***] ***beet-red***《口》(どぎまぎして)真っ赤になる ▪ When my mom asked me if I had kissed my boyfriend yet, I *went beet-red.* ママがもう彼とキスしたのと聞いたとき, 私は顔が真っ赤になった.

beetroot /bíːtrùːt/ 名 ***go as red as a beetroot/go beetroot (red)***《英》(恥ずかしさ・怒りなどで)真っ赤になる ▪ McCall got angry, *went as red as a beetroot.* マッコールは怒って真っ赤になった.

befall /bɪfɔ́ːl/ 動 ***it befalls that***《雅》...ということがある ▪ *It befell that* they often quarreled. 彼らはしばしばけんかをするのだった.

before /bɪfɔ́ːr/ 副前接 ***be before*** *a person* 人に記憶される ▪ Let that fact *be before* you always. その事実は常に君に記憶されるべきである.

before all (things) [***everything***] 何より先に, とりわけ ▪ In England you must *before all things* be successful. イギリスでは何よりもまず成功しなければならない ▪ He did it *before everything.* 彼はまず一番にそれをした.

before God →GOD.

before you can say Jack Robinson →JACK.

before you know it ＝before we KNOW where we are.

before you know where you are →before we KNOW where we are.

have ... before *one* 人に...が開かれている ▪ He *had* the whole world *before* him. 彼には全世界が開けていた《前途洋洋たるものがあった》.

it was [***was not***] *A* ***before*** *B* Aかかってようやく[かからぬうちに]Bした ▪ *It was not* long *before* he came. 彼はほどなく来た ▪ *It was* long *before* he came. 彼は長いことかかってようやく来た.

it will be *A* ***before*** *B* BするにはAかかるだろう ▪ *It will be* a week *before* he gets well. 彼がよくなるには1週間かかるだろう.

it will not be *A* ***before*** *B* AかからぬうちにBするだろう ▪ *It will not be* long *before* he gets well. 彼は長くかからないうちによくなるだろう.

beforehand /bɪfɔ́ːrhæ̀nd/ 副形 ***be beforehand in*** ...に早まる ▪ You *are* rather *beforehand in* your suspicions. 君は少し気を回しすぎる.

be beforehand with ...に先んじる, の機先を制する, 手回しよく...する ▪ He knew the value of *being beforehand with* an enemy. 彼は敵の機先を制することの価値を知っていた ▪ It is a good thing to *be beforehand with* packing. 手まわしよく荷作りをするのがよい.

be beforehand with the world《古》金のたくわえがある, 現金を持っている ▪ I *am* much *beforehand with the world.* 金のたくわえが多い.

get [***have***] ***... beforehand*** 金のたくわえをする[があ

る] ▪I now began to think of *getting* a little *beforehand*. 私は今や少し金をためようかと考え始めた.

befoul /bɪfáʊl/ 動 ***It is an ill bird that befouls his own nest.*** 《諺》どんな鳥も自分の巣はよごさない《内輪の恥を外へ出すな》.

beg /beg/ 動 ***beg, borrow, or steal*** 〖しばしば否定文で〗どうやっても手に入れる ▪You couldn't *beg, borrow, or steal* a job in 2011. 2011年にはどうやっても職に就けなかった ▪I haven't got a pen, sir—Well, *beg, borrow, or steal* one. ペンを持っていないのですが—それじゃあどんな手段ででも手に入れるんだな.

beg leave to *do* →I ask LEAVE to do.

beg of *a person* ***to*** *do* 人に…してくれと懇願する ▪I *beg of* you *to* change your decision. どうかご翻意くださるようお願いします.

beg pardon of *a person* 人に許しを請う ▪He *begged pardon of* me. 彼は私に許してくれと言った.

beg the question **1** 論点となっていることを真と仮定して論を進める ▪To refer to the accused as a "thief" at the outset of the trial is to *beg the question*. 裁判の初めから被告を「盗賊」と呼ぶのは, 論点となっていることを真と決めて論を進めることになる.
2 (巧みに)論点を避ける《誤用》 ▪You do not reply directly. You are just *begging the question*. 君はまともに返答をしない. 君は論点を避けているだけだ. ☞<beg は Ⓛ petitio principii の petitio の訳で take for granted の意.

beg *one's* ***way*** 道々物乞いをして行く ▪A vagabond *begged his way* across the land. 浮浪者が道々物乞いをしながら国中を歩いた.

go [***be***] (***a***) ***begging*** **1** 物もらいして歩く ▪I *went a begging* for it of those who knew me. 私は自分を知っている人々にそれをもらい歩いた.
2 買い手がつかない, もらい手がない《特にもとは重宝がられていたものについて言う》 ▪Land almost *went begging*. 土地はほとんど買い手がなかった.

I beg to differ [***disagree***] 《文》賛成しかねます ▪*I beg to differ* with you a bit there. その点は少々賛成しかねます.

I beg to inform you that .... 《商》…をお知らせ申しあげます; 拝啓《手紙の書出しで形式的文句; 今日ではあまり用いない》.

(***I***) ***beg your pardon.*** →PARDON[1].

beget /bɪgét/ 動 ***beget*** *a child* ***on*** (***the body of***) 《雅》…によって子をもうける ▪Melibeus *begot* a daughter *on* (*the body of*) his wife. メリビアスは妻によって女の子をもうけた.

beggar[1] /bégər/ 名 ***a beggar for work*** 《口》絶えず精出して働く人 ▪He is *a beggar for work*. 彼は絶えず精出して働く.

be a good beggar 寄付金[義援金]集めがうまい ▪Mr. Smith *is a good beggar*. スミス氏は寄付金集めがうまい.

Beggars must [***can***] ***not be choosers.*** 《諺》物もらいはえり好みはできない.

die a beggar のたれ死にする ▪Hands is said to have *died a beggar*. ハンズはのたれ死にしたと言われている.

Poor beggar! かわいそうに ▪*Poor beggar!* Tom is dead. かわいそうに. トムは死んだ.

Set a beggar on horseback, and he'll ride to the devil. 《諺》物乞いが馬に乗ったら馬を乗りつぶす《物乞いが急に金持ちになると, 有頂天となりやがて身を滅ぼす》.

beggar[2] /bégər/ 動 ***beggar*** (***all***) ***description*** 述べがたい, 表現[筆舌に尽く]しがたい (cf. Sh. *Ant. & Cl.* 2. 2. 203) ▪The place *beggars all description*. そこは筆舌に尽くしがたい ▪The beauty *beggared all description*. その美しさは到底筆舌の及ぶところではなかった.

beggar compare 比類がない ▪Hunger is a sauce that *beggars compare*. 空腹は無類のソースである.

beggar-my [***your***]***-neighbor*** 一人勝ちの, 人の損失で利益を得る ▪Each country was pursuing a *beggar-my-neighbor* policy. 各国が一人勝ち政策をとっていた.

I'll be beggared if ... 《俗》誓って…のようなことはない《もし…なら物乞いになる》 ▪*I'll be beggared if* I tell a lie. 私は誓って嘘は言わない.

begin /bɪgín/ 動 ***begin at the wrong end*** 初めを誤る ▪I suspected we *began at the wrong end*. 我々は初めを誤っているのだろうかと感じた.

begin close to home 手近なところから始める ▪You can *begin close to home* by visiting the American Embassy. 手近なところから始めてまずアメリカ大使館を訪問されてはどうですか. ☞home には「家」という意味はない.

begin the world →WORLD.

He who begins many things, finishes but few. 《諺》多くを始める人は, ごく少ししか完成しない.

not [***no ...***] ***begin to*** *do* 《米口》…するどころでない ▪It does *not begin to* meet the specifications. それは明細書にてんで合わない ▪I *can't begin to* describe the beauty of the scene. その景色の美しさはとても言葉で言い表せない.

to begin with 〖独立句〗 **1** まず第一に, そもそも ▪Marley was dead, *to begin with*. そもそも, マーリーは死んだ ▪*To begin with*, he's too young. まず第一に彼は若すぎる.
2 初めは ▪*To begin with*, we had very little support, but later on people began to support us. 初めは我々は支持が非常に少なかった. が, 後には人々が支持してくれ始めた.

Well begun is half done. 《諺》初めがうまくゆけば仕事は半分終わったも同然.

beginner /bɪgínər/ 名 ***beginner's luck*** 初心者の幸運[ツキ] ▪I beat you last time. My win was just *beginner's luck*. 前回は私が勝った. 私が勝ったのは初心者のツキというやつだった.

beginning /bɪgínɪŋ/ 名 ***at the beginning*** 初めから, 初めに ▪Start *at the beginning*. 初めか

らやれ ▪ He left for America *at the beginning* of June. 彼は6月の初めにアメリカへ向けて出発した.

from beginning to end 初めから終わりまで, 終始, 徹頭徹尾 ▪ The principle is pernicious *from beginning to end.* その主義は徹頭徹尾有害である ▪ He listened to my speech *from beginning to end.* 彼は私の話を初めから終わりまで傾聴した.

in the beginning (手)初めに, まず最初は ▪ *In the beginning* there were no animals. 初めには動物はいなかった ▪ You will find it rather difficult *in the beginning.* 初めはそれはややむずかしいだろう.

make a beginning 端緒を開く, 始める, 着手する ▪ School education can only *make a beginning.* 学校教育は教育の端緒を開きうるにすぎない.

make a beginning on =make a START on.

rise from humble beginnings 卑賤から身を起こす ▪ He has *risen from humble beginnings.* 彼は卑賤から身を起こした.

the beginning of the end 終わりの始まり《終末の最初のきざし》 ▪ It was *the beginning of the end* of his fame. それは彼の名声の終わりの始まりだった《それから彼の名声が下り坂となった》 ▪ Her infidelity marks *the beginning of the end* of our relationship. 彼女が不貞を働いたため私たちの関係に破綻の兆しが見えている.

begird /bɪgə́:rd/ 動 ***be begirt with*** 《文》…をめぐらす ▪ The castle *was begirt with* moats. 城には堀がめぐらしてあった.

behalf /bɪhǽf|-hɑ́:f/ 名 ***in behalf of/ in** a person's* ***behalf*** (人)のために ▪ He pleaded *in behalf of* a cause. 彼は主義のために弁じた.

in this [that] behalf 《古》これ[それ]について ▪ More could be said *in this behalf.* これについてはもっと言うこともできます.

on behalf of/on** a person's* ***behalf **1** …に代わって, を代表して ▪ *On behalf of* the company, I welcome you. 会社を代表して私があなたを歓迎します. ☞《米》ではこの意味で in behalf of を使う人もいる.

2 …のために (=in BEHALF of) ▪ I speak this *on your behalf.* 僕は君のためにこう言うのだ ▪ He works *on behalf of* the community. 彼は地域社会のために働いている.

behave /bɪhéɪv/ 動 ***behave** oneself* **1** ふるまう ▪ He *behaved himself* like a man. 彼は男らしくふるまった.

2 お行儀をよくする《今は子供に言う》 ▪ *Behave yourself,* or I will beat you. お行儀をよくしないと, たたくよ.

behave well [ill,** etc.**] to [towards] …を厚遇[冷遇, など]する ▪ They have *behaved very handsomely to* you. 彼らはあなたを非常に優遇した ▪ Did you ever *behave ill to* your father? 君は君の父を粗末にしたことがあるか.

behavior, 《英》 **behaviour** /bɪhéɪvjər/ 名 ***be [stand] on** one's* ***good [best] behavior*** **1** 謹慎中である ▪ I should be obliged to *be upon my good behavior.* やむなく謹慎せねばならないだろう.

2 最も行儀よくする, 努めて神妙にする ▪ They are visiting us this evening, so we must *be on our best behavior.* 彼らは今晩私たちを訪ねてきますから努めて行儀よくしなければなりません.

bind** a person* ***(over) to** his* ***good behavior 《法》人に謹慎を申しつける ▪ It was unjust to *bind* him *to his good behavior.* 彼に謹慎を申しつけるのは不当だった.

during good behavior 不謹慎[不都合]のないかぎりは ▪ He shall hold his office *during good behavior.* 不謹慎のない限り彼はその職についていてよい.

put** a person* ***on** his* ***good [best] behavior **1** 人に謹慎を命ずる ▪ He has *been put on his best behavior.* 彼は謹慎を命ぜられている.

2 努めて行儀よくするよう勧める ▪ That would *put* him *on his best behavior* for a couple of months. それで彼も2か月は努めて行儀よくするだろう.

behest /bɪhést/ 名 ***at** a person's* ***behest*** 《文》人の命令[強い勧め]で ▪ He runs errands *at my behest.* 彼は私の命令で使い走りをしている.

behind /bɪháɪnd/ 前副名 ***be behind** a person* ***in*** …で人より遅れをとる ▪ He *is behind* his class *in* English. 彼は英語が学級の者より遅れている.

be behind in [on, with] (仕事・支払いなど)が遅れている ▪ He *is behind in* his rent [his work]. 彼は家賃が滞って[仕事が遅れて]いる ▪ He *is behind in* fulfilling his obligation. 彼は債務の履行を怠っている ▪ The builders *are behind on* this project. 建築業者はこのプロジェクトに遅れをきたしている.

be on** one's* ***behind 《俗》座っている ▪ You've *been on your behind* all morning. 君は午前中ずっと座っていた. ☞behind「しり」.

behind** a person's* ***back →BACK[1].

far behind 《英》ずっと遅れて ▪ If Winter comes, can Spring be *far behind*? 冬来たりなば, 春遠からじ (Shelley, *Ode to the West Wind* V.14).

It is the man behind the gun that tells. 《諺》銃よりもそれを使う人がものを言う.

throw** one's* ***weight behind →WEIGHT.

behindhand /bɪháɪndhæ̀nd/ 形 ***be [get] behindhand in*** …に遅れている[遅れる] ▪ She *is behindhand in* her ideas. 彼女の思想は古い ▪ He has *got behindhand in* study. 彼は勉強が遅れた.

be behindhand in** one's* ***circumstances 暮らし向きがよくない ▪ His business faculty is small, and he *is behindhand in his circumstances.* 彼は商才に乏しく暮らし向きがよくない.

be behindhand with …が遅れている ▪ He *is behindhand with* his work [his rent]. 彼は仕事が遅れている[家賃が滞っている].

behoof /bɪhú:f/ 名 ***in [to, for, on] (the) behoof of*** …のために ▪ *For whose behoof* is this done? これは誰のためにしたのか ▪ The parlor had been turned into a bedroom *on my behoof.* 客間は私のために寝室に変えられた.

behoove /bɪhúːv/, 《英》 **behove** /bɪhə́ʊv/ 動 ***it behooves*** *a person* ***to*** *do* 《文》 …するのが人の義務である ▪ *It behooves* public officials *to* do their duty. 公務員はその職分を尽くさなければならない.

B

be-in /bíːɪ̀n/ 名 公園などでの集会《ヒッピー文化》 ▪ The youngsters really enjoyed the jazz *be-in* at the park. 若者たちは公園でのジャズ集会を心から楽しんだ.

being /bíːɪŋ/ 名形 ***bring*** [***call***] ***… into being*** …を生みだす, 生ぜしめる ▪ God *called* the heaven and earth *into being*. 神は天地を創造し給うた.

come into being 生れ出る, 生じる, 出現する; 設立される ▪ When did this world *come into being*? この世界がいつできたのか ▪ The company *came into being* in 1980. 当社は1980年に設立された.

for (***the***) ***time being*** →TIME[1].

in being 現存して, 存在して ▪ The property was given by a will in the nature of a legacy to a person *in being* at the time the will was made. その資産は遺言作成時に生存している者に対する遺産として遺言により譲与された ▪ He quoted a record not *in being*. 彼は現存しない記録を引用した.

to the very roots of *one's* ***being*** 腹の底まで, 全身が ▪ He was thrilled *to the very roots of his being*. 彼は全身がぞくぞくした.

bejabbers /bɪdʒǽbərz/, **bejabers** /bɪdʒéɪbərz/, **bejesus** /bɪdʒíːzəs/ 名 ***knock*** [***beat***] ***the bejesus out of*** 《口》 …をこっぴどく殴る (= beat the HELL out of) ▪ If I catch you doing that again, I'll *knock the bejesus out of* you. お前がまたそれをやっているのを見つけたら, ぶちのめすぞ.

scare the bejesus out of *a person* 人をびっくり仰天させる[ひどく怯えさせる] (= scare the HELL out of) ▪ This thriller will *scare the bejesus out of* you. このスリラー映画はあなたをひどく怯えさせるだろう. ☞by Jesus の婉曲語法.

beleaguer /bɪlíːgər/ 動 ***be beleaguered with*** …にとりまかれる, つきまとわれる, 悩まされる ▪ He *was beleaguered with* annoyances. 彼はいろいろいやな思いをさせられた.

belief /bɪlíːf/ 名 ***be light of belief*** 軽々しく信じがちである ▪ My brother *is light of belief*. 兄は物事を軽々しく信じる.

beggar belief (あまりに異常で)とても信じられない ▪ New regulation in Dalian *beggars belief*. 大連の新しい規制はとても信じられない.

beyond belief 信じがたい(ほど) ▪ The consequences were uproarious *beyond belief*. その結果は信じられないほど騒々しいものだった.

cherished belief [***beliefs***] 頑なにこだわる信条, まげることのない考え ▪ It is a *cherished belief* among many racists that other races are inferior to their own. 人種差別主義者は, 他の人種は自分たちの人種よりも劣っていると頑なに信じている.

easy of belief **1** 信ずるにかたくない ▪ It is *easy of belief* that he is rich. 彼が金持ちであることは容易に信じられる.
2 = be light of BELIEF.

have belief in …を信仰する, の価値を信じる ▪ I *have* strong *belief in* my religion. 自分の宗教を強く信じている ▪ I *have* no *belief in* extreme measures. 極端な手段は良いとは思わない.

to the best of *one's* ***belief*** …の信ずるかぎりでは ▪ *To the best of my belief* there is no danger. 私の信ずるかぎりでは危険はない.

believe /bɪlíːv/ 動 ***believe it or not*** 《口》 こんなことを言っては信じないだろうが ▪ *Believe it or not*, I was voted "Most Likely to Succeed." 信じられないだろうが, 僕は「最も成功しそうな人物」の投票に入選したことがある. ☞アメリカの R. Ripley が世界中の不思議な品や事実を集めて展示会を開き, これを "Believe it or not" と名づけたことから.

Believe me. ほんとに, 本当ですよ ▪ It is an old stone, *believe me*. ほんとに古い石なんですよ.

believe meanly of →think MEANLY of.

believe (***you***) ***me*** 《口》 (私が言うことは)本当ですよ ▪ And *believe you me*, I was scared! それで本当ですよ, 僕は怯えていました. ☞この表現を嫌う人もいる.

can't believe *one's* ***ears*** [***eyes***] 《口》 わが目[耳]が信じられない(くらいびっくりした) ▪ I *couldn't believe my eyes* when I got my gas bill. ガスの請求書をもらったとき, わが目が信じられなかった ▪ I *couldn't believe my ears* when Betty said I won the first prize. 私が1等賞をとったとベティーが言ったとき, わが耳が信じられなかった.

don't you believe it! 《口》 それは絶対嘘だよ ▪ Chris is dead? *Don't you believe it!* クリスが死んだって? 絶対嘘だよ.

I believe you 《口》 そうだとも ▪ He is a first class doctor?—*I believe you*, my boy. 彼は一流のお医者だね—そうだとも, 君.

I believe you, thousands wouldn't! 《英口・皮肉》 ちょっと信じられないねえ ▪ I am going to get an A plus on the final exam.—Really? *I believe you, thousands wouldn't!* ぼくは最終試験ではAプラスをとるつもりです—本当かね? ちょっと信じられないねえ.

I don't believe it! 《口》 驚いたね; やだね ▪ *I don't believe it!* Jack ran for Diet? 驚いたね. ジャックが国会議員に立候補したんだって?

If you believe that, you'll believe anything. 君がそんなことを信じるのなら, 大ばかだよ.

I'll believe it [***that***] ***when I see it.*** 《口》 実際に見るまでは信じないね ▪ Bill says he'll buy a house.—Well, *I'll believe it when I see it*. ビルは家を買うと言っている—うーん, 見るまでは信じないね.

make believe (…する)ふりをする, と想像する (*to do, that*) ▪ He *made believe* not *to* hear me. 彼は私の言うことが聞こえないふりをした ▪ Let's *make believe that* we are pirates. 我々は海賊ということにしよう《海賊ごっこをしよう》. ☞F fair croire のなぞり.

Seeing is believing. →SEEING.

would you believe (***it***) 《口》 信じられるかい; あきれるじゃないか ▪ And *would you believe*, Mary whacked her boyfriend! そしてあきれるじゃないか, メ

アリーはボーイフレンドをピシャリとぶったんだぜ.

you may not believe it こんなことを言っても信じないだろうが ▪ *You may not believe it*, but I got nominated for the Pulitzer Prize! こんなことを言っても信じないだろうが, 私はピューリツァー賞候補にノミネートされたんだよ.

you'd better believe (***it***) 《口》 確かに, 疑いなく ▪ *You'd better believe*, I'll live in clover. 私は確かに安楽に暮らすつもりですよ ▪ *You'd better believe it*. Father Christmas really does exist. 確かに, サンタクロースは本当に存在します.

believer /bɪlíːvər/ 名 ***be a*** (***great*** [***firm***]) ***believer in*** あるものが立派[重要, 貴重]だと(固く)信じる ▪ She *is a firm believer in* the power of education. 彼女は教育の力を固く信じている.

belittle /bɪlítəl/ 動 ***belittle*** *oneself* 卑下する ▪ You *betittle yourself* too much. 君は卑下しすぎる.

bell[1] /bel/ 名 ***Alarm*** [***Warning***] ***bells ring*** (***in*** *one's* ***head***). (頭の中で)警鐘が鳴る《悪いことが起こりそうだから気をつけるべきだと思いはじめる》 ▪ The *alarm bells* started *ringing* for me shortly after I opened an account with them. 彼らと取引を始めてまもなく, これは気をつけたほうがいいと思いはじめた.

answer the bell 呼び鈴に応じる, 来客の取り次ぎをする ▪ Will you *answer the bell*? お客の取次ぎをしてくれませんか.

(***as***) ***clear as a bell*** 《口》 (音などが)澄み切った, 明瞭な; 非常に聞き[理解し]やすい《水・酒などにも用いる》 ▪ His voice rings out *as clear as a bell*. 彼の声は鈴の音のように澄んでいる ▪ The whole thing was *as clear as a bell* to him. いっさいが彼には全く明白だった.

(***as***) ***sound as a bell*** →SOUND[2].

bear [***carry***] ***away the bell*** 優勝する, 賞を得る ▪ He was about to *bear away the bell*. 彼は優勝しようとしていた ▪ In that respect Julius Caesar *bore away the bell* from them. ユリウス・カエサルはその点において彼らよりまさっていた. ☞競走に勝って金の鈴を得たことから.

bear the bell 一等[最善]である; 優勝する, 成功する ▪ For pure white the lily *bears the bell*. 純白の点ではユリが一番だ ▪ Venice *bore the bell* from every city. ベネチアはすべての都市にまさっていた. ☞牛・羊の群れの中で先頭になるものに鈴をつけたことから; bear away the BELL とよく混同される.

bell, book, and candle カトリックの破門の儀式 ▪ Hold thy hand, on pain of *bell, book, and candle*. 手を控えよ, さもなくば破門にするぞ.

bells and whistles 《口》 (あると便利な)付属品 ▪ My computer has all the latest *bells and whistles*. 私のコンピューターにはいろいろと便利な付属品がついている.

by bell and book/by book and bell ミサに使用する本とベルにかけて; 確かに《中世の誓句》 ▪ He was born in Paris, *by bell and book*. 彼は確かにパリ生まれだ.

curse ... by [***with***] ***bell, book, and candle*** 鐘・書・燭破門式によって...を破門する ▪ We shall *be cursed with bell, book, and candle*. 我々は鐘・書・燭破門式によって破門されるだろう. ☞カトリックの破門式では, まず鐘を鳴らし, 破門文を読み, 最後に燭を消したから.

B

give *a person* ***a bell*** 《英》 人に電話する ▪ *Give* me *a bell* when you get home. 帰宅したらお電話ください.

hang all *one's* ***bells on one horse*** 全財産を一人の息子に残す ▪ I'll not *hang all my bells on one horse*. 私は全財産を一人息子に残すことはしない.

have had *one's* ***bell rung*** 《口》 (人が)頭を強く打たれる ▪ I know of a football player who*'s had his bell rung* once too often. 私はやりすぎてついにしたたか頭を(ボールに)打たれたフットボールのプレーヤーのことを知っている.

Hell's bells (***and buckets of blood***)***!*** ちきしょう; ぶったまげたな《怒り・驚きの叫び》 ▪ *Hell's bells*, the washing machine's overflowing again! ちきしょう, 洗濯機がまたあふれている.

ring a bell 《口》 共感を呼ぶ (*with*); 思い出させる ▪ He has a sense of the ridiculous which *rings a bell with* us. 彼はおかしみを解する心を持っていて我々の共感を呼ぶ ▪ The name *rings* no *bell* in your mind? その名前で何も思い出さないのですか? ☞頭の中にベルがあって, 何か思い当たることを聞いて鳴ると想像する.

ring [***sound***] ***alarm*** [***warning***] ***bells*** (***in*** *one's* ***head***) (事が)警鐘を鳴らす ▪ This situation is "*ringing warning bells*" in my head. この事態は私に警鐘を鳴らしている.

ring *one's* ***own bell*** 自分で自分をほめる, 自画自賛する ▪ Sidney Burton is not a person who *rings his own bell*. シドニー・バートンは自画自賛するような人ではない.

ring the bell **1** (使用人を呼ぶために)呼び鈴を鳴らす (*for*) ▪ He *rang the bell for* the servant. 彼は呼び鈴を鳴らして使用人を呼んだ.

2 《口》 うまくいく, 功を奏する ▪ This last advantage *rang the bell* with bankers. この最後の長所が銀行家の功を奏した. ☞力だめしなどでうまくいくと鐘を鳴らすことから.

3 あつらえ向きだ, ぴったりだ ▪ I'm thirsty. This cold water really *rings the bell*. のどが渇いた. この冷たい水はまさにあつらえ向きだ.

4 《口》 賞を勝ち取る, 一番である ▪ It was the shot that *rang the bell*. それは賞を勝ち取る一発であった ▪ This book *rings the bell*. この本が一番だ.

5 心に訴える, ぴんとくる ▪ His makeup just *rings the bell* for me. 彼の扮装が私にはぴんとくる.

saved by the bell 《口》 土壇場で(特に来客によって)窮地から救われる; ゴングに救われる ▪ She was *saved by the bell* when somebody came to see her. 来客があって彼女は窮地から救われた ▪ Fred was *saved by the bell* in the earlier rounds. 初めの数ラウンドではフレッドはゴングに救われた.

B

with bells on (*one's* ***toes***)《米》**1** 大喜びで, はりきって ▪ I'll be at the party *with bells on.* 大喜びでパーティーに出よう.

2 盛装して ▪ We'll be at her wedding *with bells on.* 我々は盛装して彼女の結婚式に出よう.

3 喜び勇んで, 意気揚々と ▪ She got her makeup done and arrived *with bells on.* 彼女はちゃんとお化粧をし, 意気揚々とやって来た.

4 時間通りに ▪ I'll meet you at the station *with bells on.* 時間通りに駅で君を出迎えます.

5《英戯》同類だが, 輪をかけている ▪ His latest play is melodrama *with bells on.* 彼の最新の戯曲はメロドラマに輪をかけたようなものだ.

bell[2] /bel/ 動 ***bell the cat*** 進んで難局に当たる ▪ I wonder who can *bell the cat.* 進んで難局に当たることのできるのは誰かしら. ☞イソップ寓(ぐう)話から.

belle /bel/ 名 ***the belle of the ball*** 社交界の花形の女性 ▪ Daphne will be *the belle of the ball* in that dress. そのドレスを着るとダフネは社交界の花形になるだろう.

bellows /béloʊz/ 名 ***blow the bellows/blow with bellows*** ふいごを動かす ▪ *The* four *bellows are blown* in a strange manner. 4つのふいごが奇妙な具合に動かされる.

breathe like a (***pair of***) ***bellows*** (ふいごのような)荒い息を吐いて ▪ He was sweating like a Sumo wrestler and *breathing like a bellows.* 彼は相撲取りのように汗をかき, ふいごのような荒い息をしていた.

have bellows to mend (馬が)息切れしている ▪ The horse *has bellows to mend.* 馬は息切れがする. ☞bellows＝lungs.

it's bellows to mend with ...は肺が弱い ▪ *It's bellows to mend with* his wife. 彼の妻は肺が弱い.

belly /béli/ 名 ***a belly laugh*** 腹を抱えての大笑い ▪ His jokes will give you *a belly laugh.* 彼のジョークで君たちは腹を抱えて大笑いするだろう.

go [***turn***] ***belly up***《主に米口》(魚のように腹を上に向けて)死ぬ; 失敗[破産]する ▪ My company *went belly up.* 私の会社は破産した.

have fire in the [*one's*] ***belly*** 野心を燃やす, 強い決意をもつ ▪ Max *has* a *fire in his belly* and I can bet he will do well in life. マックスは野心を燃やしているので, きっと出世すると思う.

make a god of *one's* ***belly*** 食いしんぼうだ ▪ I wish to *make a god of my belly.* 私は食いしんぼうでありたい.

The belly has no ears.《諺》ひもじい時には道理も聞こえない《衣食足りて礼節を知る》.

bellyache /bélièɪk/ 名 ***give*** *a person* ***the bellyache***《口》人をあきあきさせる, いやにさせる ▪ My next door neighbor *gives* me *the bellyache.* 僕の隣の人には全くいやになってしまう.

bellyful /bélifʊ̀l/ 名 ***get a bellyful***《口》なぐられる ▪ He *got a bellyful* from me then. そのとき彼は私にひどくたたきのめされた.

have had a bellyful of《口》...をうんざりするほど味わう ▪ I *have had a bellyful of* promises that are never kept. 私は守られもしない約束をうんざりするほどしてもらった.

belly-up /béliʌ̀p/ 副 ***go belly-up***《口》(会社・計画などが)つぶれる, だめになる, 破産する ▪ This company's about to *go belly-up.* この会社は今にも破産しそうだ ▪ Many people lost their jobs when Enron *went belly-up.* エンロンが破産したとき, 多くの人が失職した. ☞魚が死んで腹を上にして浮かぶことから.

belove /bɪlʌ́v/ 動 ***be beloved by*** [《古・詩》***of***] ...に愛される ▪ He *is beloved of* all. 彼はみなに愛されている.

below /bɪlóʊ/ 前副 ***below the belt*** (言葉・攻撃が)残酷で不公平な ▪ It is *below the belt* to mention a person's criminal record. 人の犯罪歴を口にするのは残酷で不公平だ. ☞ボクシングから.

Below there! おーい下の者!《物の落ちる場合など注意する文句》.

down below 階下で; ずっと下に ▪ The bell rang *down below.* 階下で呼び鈴が鳴った ▪ What a man in space saw *down below* was marvelous views of the earth. 宇宙飛行士がずっと下に見たものはすばらしい地球の眺めだった.

from below 下から ▪ Someone is tapping *from below.* 誰かが下からこつこつたたいている.

belt /belt/ 名 (***at***) ***full belt***《口》全速力で ▪ The steam engine is running *at full belt.* スチームエンジンは全速力で回転している.

below the belt →BELOW.

belt and braces《英口》念には念を入れる[丹念すぎる]こと《ベルトもサスペンダーも》 ▪ As always with security a *belt and braces* approach works best. 安全保障の場合いつもそうだが, 念には念を入れたアプローチが最もうまくいく.

hit [***strike***] *a person* ***below the belt***《口》人のベルトの下を打つ; 人に卑劣な仕打ちをする ▪ That's *hitting* a fellow *below the belt* with a vengeance. それこそ確かに人に卑劣な仕打ちをするというものだ. ☞ボクサーが相手のベルトの下を打つのは反則だから.

hold the belt《米》(チャンピオン)ベルトを保持する; 優勝者である ▪ He easily *held the belt* for honesty in that country. 彼はその国で正直の点では楽々と最優位を占めていた.

take a belt to《口》...をベルトでぶつ ▪ My daddy *took a belt to* my ass for being naughty. パパは言うことをきかないと言って私のおしりをベルトでぶった.

the Bible belt バイブルベルト, 聖書地帯《特に米国南部・中西部の原理主義が盛んな地域》 ▪ You wouldn't dare try to sell a sex manual in *the Bible belt.* バイブルベルトでセックス教本を売ろうとはよもや思わないでしょう.

the green belt (保護されている都市周辺の)緑地帯 ▪ The charming hotel is situated in *the green belt* of Budapest. その魅力的なホテルはブダペストの緑地帯にある.

the sun belt サンベルト《米国南部・南西部; 温かい気候のためにそう呼ばれる》 ▪ Retirees have been moving to *the sun belt* for years. 何年も前から退

職者はサンベルトへ移住している.

***tighten* [*pull in*] *one's* belt/ take [*pull*] *one's* belt in (*a notch*)** 《口》(ベルトを締めて)空腹[窮乏]をがまんする; 耐乏生活をする, 支出を切りつめる ▪ He *tightened his belt* to stave off the gnawing at his stomach. 彼は激しいおなかのひもじさを食いとめるためベルトを締めた ▪ Even the theater would have to *pull in its belt*. 劇場でさえ支出を切りつめなければならないだろう.

***under* *one's* belt** 《口》腹におさめて; 身におさめて ▪ I bore plenty of wine *under my belt*. たらふく飲んでいた ▪ He's got plenty of Latin *under his belt*. 彼はラテン語を十分身につけている.

belting /béltɪŋ/ 名 ***give** a person **a belting*** 《俗》人を(ベルトで)なぐる ▪ I saw one schoolboy *give* another *a belting*. ある学童が別の学童をなぐるのを見た.

bench /bentʃ/ 名 ***be elevated* [*raised*] *to the bench*** 判事に昇進する; 教会の監督に昇進する ▪ He *was raised to the* Episcopal *bench*. 彼は教会の監督に昇進した ▪ He *was elevated to the bench* at the young age of 40 years. 彼は40歳の若さで判事に昇進した.

be* [*sit*] *on the bench **1** 裁判官席に着いている《審理中》; 治安官である ▪ He *sits on the bench* at Poole. 彼はプールで治安官をしている.
2《野球》ゲームに参加していない, 補欠選手である ▪ How many players *sit on the bench*? 何人の選手がベンチを温めているのか?

warm* [*ride*] *the bench (選手が)ベンチを温めている ▪ Jim patiently *warmed the bench* while his teammates played. ジムはチームの仲間が試合をしている間辛抱強くベンチを温めていた.

bend[1] /bend/ 名 ***above* [*beyond*] *one's* bend** 力に及ばない;《米俗》理解できない ▪ It would be *above my bend* to tell you all I saw there. そこで見たことを全部あなたに話すことは私の力に及ばないだろう.

around the bend 通りの曲がり角に ▪ Bill's house is just *around the bend*. ビルの家はちょうど通りの曲がり角にある.

***drive* [*send*] *a person* round the bend** 《主に口》(しつこく嫌がらせをして)人を激怒させる ▪ In the end, one question *drove* him *round the bend*. 最後に, 一つの質問が彼を激怒させた.

go on the* [*a*] *bend 《俗》酒を飲んで浮かれる, 騒ぐ ▪ I *went on the bend* with an intimate friend. 私はある親友と飲み騒いだ.

go round the bend 激怒する, キレる ▪ Her safety-valve prevented her from *going round the bend*. 彼女の安全弁のおかげでキレることを免れた.

on the bend 不正手段で ▪ He will get it *on the bend*, somehow or other. 彼はなんとかして不正手段でそれを得るだろう.

round the bend **1** =around the BEND.
2《口》気が狂って, 狂気で ▪ My wife is just *round the bend*. 私の妻はまさしく気が狂っている.

bend[2] /bend/ 動 ***bend* *one's* brows** → knit one's BROWs.

***bend* *one's* eyes (*to, toward, on*)** (...の方に)目を向ける ▪ He *bent his eyes on* it. 彼はそれに目を向けた.

***bend* *one's* mind to [*on*]** ...に心を傾ける ▪ He couldn't *bend his mind to* his studies. 彼は研究に没頭することができなかった.

***bend over backward(s)* (*to* do)** → BACKWARD(S).

bend* oneself *to ...に熱中する ▪ He *bent himself to* his task. 彼は自分の仕事に熱中した.

bend* a person *to* one's *will 人を意に従わせる ▪ You will never *bend* the girl *to your will*. 君はその娘を君の意に従わせることはできないだろう.

Better bend than break. 《諺》折れるよりは曲がるほうがよい.

bended /béndəd/ 形 ***on* [*upon, with*] *bended knees*** ひざを屈して(嘆願するなど) ▪ The Chancellor spoke, dropping off the woolsack *upon* his *bended knees*. 上院議長は議長席を降りてひざまずいて言った.

bender /béndər/ 名 ***go* [*be*] *on a bender*** 《米俗》飲み(食い)騒ぎをする ▪ He *was on a bender* last night. 彼は昨夜飲み騒いでいた.

beneath /bɪníːθ/ 前 ***be beneath** a person* [*a person's* ***dignity***] 人の権威にかかわる ▪ It would *be beneath* him [*his dignity*] to accept such a menial job. そのような卑しい仕事を受け入れるのは彼の沽券(こけん)にかかわるだろう.

(*be*) *beneath contempt* 軽蔑にも値しない ▪ Such conduct *is* quite *beneath contempt*. そのような行為は全く卑しむにも足らない.

***beneath* *one's* rank** 地位を辱める ▪ He will do nothing *beneath his rank*. 彼は自分の地位を辱めるようなことはいっさいしない.

***marry beneath* one** → MARRY beneath one.

benefit /bénəfɪt/ 名 ***be of benefit to*** ...のためになる ▪ The book *wasn't of* much *benefit to* me. その本は私にはたいしてためにならなかった.

for the benefit of ...のために, に聞かせるために;《雅・反語》...の懲らしめに, あてつけに ▪ The money is to be used *for the benefit of* the poor. その金は貧者のために使うことになっている ▪ Tom thought my remark was *for his benefit*. トムは私の言葉はあてつけに言われたものと思った.

***give* A *the benefit of* B** A(人)にB(助言など)を与える ▪ You are fond of *giving* people *the benefit of* your advice. 君は人に助言を施すのが好きだ. ☞「受ける方があまり有難がらない」という含みがある.

give ... the benefit of the doubt **1** 疑わしい点は被告に有利に解釈してやる ▪ He was in the house when the money was stolen, but we *gave* him *the benefit of the doubt*. 金が盗まれたとき彼はその家にいた, が我々は善意に解釈して彼を無罪とした.
2 (疑わしい点は善意に解して)...を信じてやる ▪ I will *give* the story *the benefit of the doubt*. その話は

疑わしいが信じよう.

have no end of a benefit 《反語》ひどい目にあう ▪ I *had no end of a benefit* getting things straight. 片づけでえらい目にあった.

to the benefit of …のためになって ▪ I stopped smoking, *to the benefit of* my health. 禁煙して体のためになった.

with the benefit of hindsight 今となっては後の祭だが ▪ *With the benefit of hindsight*, that accident need never have happened. 今ではあと知恵だが, あの事故は起きなくて済んだはずだ.

without benefit of clergy 聖職裁判の特権なく; (式によって与えられる)教会の承認なく, 教会の儀式によらず; (漠然と)赦免の特権なく ▪ They were married *without benefit of clergy*. 彼らは教会の儀式によらないで結婚した ▪ She ordered him to do so, *without benefit of clergy*. 彼女は彼に赦免の特権を許さずそうせよと命じた.

bent[1] /bent/ 名 ***flee*** [***go, take***] ***to the bent*** (危険などを避けるため)荒野へ逃げる ▪ *Take to the bent*, Mr. Smith. スミスさん, 荒野へ逃げなさい.

bent[2] /bent/ 名 ***follow*** *one's* ***bent*** 気の向くことをする, 心の向くところに従う ▪ If he had *followed his bent*, he would have been a sailor. 彼が自分の好みに従ったら水夫になったであろうに.

have a bent for …が好きである ▪ Mary *has a* natural *bent for* sewing. メアリーは生まれつき裁縫が好きだ.

out of *one's* ***bent*** 専門外で; 性に合わないで; 力が及ばないで ▪ That's quite *out of my bent*. それは全く私の専門外だ.

to [***at***] ***the top of*** *one's* ***bent*** 力のかぎり, 思う存分 (cf. Sh., *Haml.* 3. 2. 401) ▪ You can amuse yourself *to the top of your bent*. 君は思う存分おもしろく遊びなさい ▪ He flattered French vanity *to the top of its bent*. 彼は思う存分フランス人のうぬぼれ心をあおった. ☞「弓を最大限度に引いて」が原義.

bent[3] /bent/ 形 ***be bent on*** [***upon***] **1** …をいつもしようと心がけている, に熱心である ▪ He *is bent on* mischief. 彼はいつもいたずらばかり考えている.

2 …しようと決心している ▪ He *is bent upon* becoming a doctor. 彼は医者になろうと決心している.

bent out of shape 《米口》 **1** かんかんに怒って; ひどくうろたえて[狼狽して] (*about, over*) ▪ He got *bent out of shape over* those cartoons. 彼はそういう漫画のことでかんかんに怒った.

2 ショックを受けた, びっくりした ▪ That conservative audience was *bent out of shape* by his speech. その保守的な聴衆は彼の演説でショックを受けた.

bereave /bɪríːv/ 動 ***be bereaved of*** (家族・親しい人)に死なれる, を失う ▪ He *was bereaved of* his mother. 彼は母を失った. ☞この意味では be bereft of よりも普通.

be bereft of …を奪われる, を失う ▪ The merchant *was bereft of* home and riches. その商人は家も富も失った.

berry /béri/ 名 (***as***) ***brown as a berry*** 《英》真っ黒に日焼けして, 小麦色で ▪ Almost all boys are *as brown as a berry* after the summer holidays. 夏休みのあとほとんどすべての少年らは真っ黒に日焼けしている.

in berry (魚が)卵をはらんで ▪ Hen lobsters were found *in berry*. 雌エビが卵をはらんでいるのがわかった. ☞berry「魚の腹子の一つ」.

berserk /bərsə́ːrk | bəzə́ːk/ 名 ***go*** [***run***] ***berserk*** 狂暴になる, 荒れ狂う ▪ The elements constantly *go berserk*. 風雨が絶えず荒れ狂う.

berth /bəːrθ/ 名 ***give a wide*** [***clear***] ***berth*** (***to***) **1** (…に)十分距離を置く ▪ The ship *gave* the other *a wide berth*. その船は(衝突しないよう)相手の船に十分な距離をおいて進んだ.

2 (…を)敬遠する, 避ける ▪ I should *give a wide berth to* the firm if I were you. もし私が君だったらその会社を避けるね. ☞berth 《海》「船が停泊中揺れ回っても他に接触しないだけの余地」.

keep a wide berth of …を敬遠する, 避ける ▪ I advise you to *keep a wide berth of* me, sir. 君は僕を避けるよう忠告する.

beseem /bɪsíːm/ 動 ***it ill*** [***well***] ***beseems*** *a person* (***to do***) 人が(…するのは)似合わない[よく似合う] ▪ *It ill beseems* you *to* leave him without help. 彼を見殺しにするとは君には似合わない.

beset /bɪsét/ 動 (***be***) ***beset with*** 《文》(困難など)につきまとわれ(る), 悩まされ(る) ▪ This is a road *beset with* robbers. ここは盗賊の出没する道路だ ▪ Human life *is beset with* sins. 人生は罪悪につきまとわれている《罪悪に陥りやすい》.

beside /bɪsáɪd/ 前 ***beside the question*** → QUESTION[1].

beside *oneself* (***with***) (…で)我を忘れて, 気が狂って, 逆上して ▪ He was *beside himself with* joy [grief]. 彼は狂喜していた[気も狂わんばかりに悲しんでいた] ▪ He is *beside himself with* anger. 彼は怒って我を忘れている.

besiege /bɪsíːdʒ/ 動 ***besieged with*** …攻めにあう ▪ The teacher was *besieged with* questions from her pupils. 先生は生徒から質問攻めにあった.

beslaver /bɪslǽvər/ 動 ***be beslavered with*** (よだれなど)をだらだら浴びせられる ▪ I *was beslavered with* compliments. 私はお世辞をたらたら浴びせられた.

besmear /bɪsmíər/ 動 ***be besmeared with*** …によごされる, …だらけになる ▪ He *is besmeared with* mud. 彼は土だらけになっている.

besom /bíːzəm/ 名 ***jump the besom*** ＝jump the BROOMSTICK. ☞besom＝broomstick.

bespangle /bɪspǽŋgəl/ 動 ***be bespangled with*** …で一面に輝く ▪ The sky *is bespangled with* stars. 空は一面星で輝いている.

bespatter /bɪspǽtər/ 動 ***be bespattered with*** …がはねかかっている ▪ The trousers *were bespattered with* mud. ズボンに泥がはね上がっている.

besprinkle /bɪspríŋkəl/ 動 ***be besprinkled***

with（水・粉などが）ふりかけられている ▪ The flowers *were besprinkled with* morning dews. 花に朝露がおりていた.

best /best/ 名形副 ***(all) for the best*** **1** 最もよいように, よかれと思って ▪ I did it (*all*) *for the best.* それが一番よいと思って私はした ▪ All (is) *for the best.* 何事も天の配剤だ《「神様のなさることに悪い事はない」というあきらめの言葉》.
2 結局一番うまくいって ▪ I lost my job, but it's *all for the best* since now I can start a new business. 職を失ったが, それがかえってよい結果になる. これで新しい仕事を始められるから.

all in one's best 晴れ着を着て ▪ He dressed himself *all in his best.* 彼は晴れ着を着た.

all (of) the best **1** 最良の質を持つもののすべて ▪ *All of the best* fruit was on display. 最上の果物がすべて展示されていた.
2《口》ごきげんよろしゅう; ご多幸を祈ります《別れ, 乾杯, 手紙の結末などで》 ▪ Goodbye then, and *all of the best* to you. ではさようなら, ごきげんよろしゅう ▪ He lifted his whisky, and said, "*All the best*, boys." 彼はウイスキーの杯を持ちあげて「諸君, ご多幸を祈る」と言った.

as best one can [《英》***may***]《米》できるかぎり, 精いっぱい ▪ He ran *as best* he *could.* 彼は精いっぱい走った ▪ I managed to keep dry *as best* I *might.* 私はなんとかしてできるだけぬれないようにした.

at best/at the best **1** いくらよく見ても, 一番よくて, せいぜい ▪ Life is, *at best*, a sea of trouble. 人生はどうせ苦難の海だ ▪ Slavery *at the best* is an undemocratic institution. 奴隷制はいくらよく見ても非民主的なものである.
2《商》最高の値段で ▪ We have orders to sell "*at best*". 最高の値段で売るように指示されている.

at one's [***its***] ***best*** 最もよい状態に; （花などが）見ごろ[満開]で; （芸術などが）盛りを極めて, 全盛で ▪ My wife died when the cherry-blossoms were *at their best.* 妻は桜花が満開のころに死んだ ▪ She was *at her best* on that day. 彼女はその日が最上のできであった ▪ Germany's art was *at its best* in this Olympic year. このオリンピックの年ドイツの芸術は全盛だった.

at the best of times **1** 最も調子[状態]のよい時でも ▪ I can't draw very well *at the best of times.* 私は最も調子のよい時でもあまりうまく描けません.
2《口》いつでも ▪ I can never resist dogs *at the best of times.* 僕はいつだって犬には目がないんだ.

at the very best 〚at best を強意して〛いくらよく見ても ▪ External evidence must, *at the very best*, be but partial. 外的証拠はいくらよく見ても部分的なものにすぎない.

Bad is the best. よいことの起こる見込みはない.

be best man 花婿付添いを務める ▪ Herbert was asked to *be best man.* ハーバートは花婿付添い役になるよう頼まれた.

be the best of friends 最高の友人[仲間]になる ▪ They were once deadly enemies and now *are the best of friends.* 彼らはかつては不倶戴天の敵同士だったが, いまや最高の仲間になっている.

best of all 何よりも ▪ He loves fishing *best of all.* 彼は何よりも魚釣りが好きだ.

best of seven《米》7つのうち4つ; 優勝 ▪ They are now believed to take the *best of seven* Series. 彼らは今やシリーズを物にすると信じられている. ☞野球の World Series では, いずれも先に4勝した方が優勝したことになる規定であることから.

do one's [***the***] ***best*** (***to do***) 全力を尽くす ▪ He *did his best to* eat. 彼は一生懸命食べた.

do [***try***] ***one's level best*** (***to do***)《口》全力を尽くす ▪ He *did his level best to* stop worrying. 心配をやめようと全力を尽くした.

(Even) the best of friends must part.《諺》とても仲の良い親友でも別れなければならない,「会うは別れの始め」.

for the best できるだけためを思って, 首尾のよいように (→(all) for the BEST) ▪ I have done everything *for the best.* 私は万事首尾のよいように取り計らった ▪ Hope *for the best.* またよい時もあろう《悲観するな》.

get [***have***] ***the best of*** **1**（議論・競技）に勝つ; をだます ▪ Alexander *had the best of* his enemies. アレクサンダーは敵に勝った.
2（取引など）で最大の利を得る, 最も得をする; 不利を最小に食いとめる, 成功する ▪ I think I *got the best of* the bargain [deal]. 私はその取引で最も得をしたと思う ▪ They *had the best of* the joke. 彼らはその冗談を最も楽しんだ.

get the best of both worlds 二物の長所[利点]を兼ね備える ▪ This house *gets the best of both worlds*—country surroundings and city convenience. この家は二物の利点を兼ね備えている—田舎の環境と都会の便利さとを.

get [***have***] ***the best of it***（競技・議論などに）勝つ ▪ In your argument the strange gentleman *had the best of it.* 君たちの議論ではよそから来た人のほうが勝ちでしたよ.

get the best out of …を最も有利[有効]に使う ▪ Tell me how to *get the best out of* the mixer. このミキサーを最も有効に使う方法を教えてください.

give a person best …に降参する, にかなわないと認める ▪ All right, I *give* you *best.* 仕方がない, 君には負けた.

give ... one's best shot →SHOT[1].

give it best《口》断念する; 敗北を認める ▪ I wanted to continue with my work, but I had to *give it best.* 仕事をまだ続けたかったが, 断念しなければならなかった.

had best do →HAD.

have the best of →get the BEST of.

how best to do どうすれば一番よいか ▪ We will teach you *how best to* prepare for an interview. 面接の最高の準備方法をお教えします.

in one's (Sunday) best →one's SUNDAY best.

in the best よくて, せいぜい ▪ This is murder

most foul, as *in the best* it is. 人殺しはどうせ卑劣なものだが, これは最も卑劣な人殺しだ.

in the best of health この上もなく健康である ▪ I hope you are *in the best of health*. この上もなくご健勝のことと存じます.

know best 一番よく知っている[心得ている] ▪ The government is sure it *knows best*. その政府は自分が一番よく心得ていると確信している.

look** one's **best 最も立派に見える ▪ He *looked his best* in uniform. 彼は制服を着ているときが最も立派だ.

make the best of …を最も利用する; の利得を収める; (不利)にできるだけ善処[がまん]する ▪ *Make the best of* your time. 君の時間を最大限に利用しなさい ▪ *Make the best of* a bad job [business]. おもしろくない事情になるべく善処せよ ▪ We'll have to *make the best of* the house. この家でがまんしなければならないだろう.

***make the best of** oneself* できるだけ魅力的に見えるようにする ▪ Margaret seeks to inspire each student to *make the best of herself*. マーガレットはそれぞれの学生ができるだけ魅力的に見えるようにするように動機づけることを目指している.

make the best of both worlds **1** 世俗的利害と精神的利害の一致を図る; 二つの相反する要求を満たす ▪ He loves his family, but he also likes golf, and tries to *make the best of both worlds*. 彼は家庭を愛しているが, 同時にゴルフも好きなので, 二つの相反する要求を満たそうと努力している.

2 異なる両陣営からよいことをせしめる ▪ There have been statesmen seeking to *make the best of both worlds*. 双方からうまい汁を吸おうとする政治家たちがこれまでにいた. ☞Charles Kingsley が *Westward Ho!* (1855)で使った.

make the best of it [***a bad bargain***] 逆境に善処する ▪ She will be sad, of course, but she must learn to *make the best of it*. 彼女はむろん悲しむだろう, しかし逆境に善処することを学ばなければならないだろう ▪ We might as well bite the bullet and *make the best of a bad bargain*. 困難に男らしく耐え, 逆境に善処したほうがいい.

make the best of the matter [***things***] 潔くあきらめる; (失望・不幸に)めげないで善処する ▪ The only thing to do is to *make the best of the matter*. 不幸を潔くあきらめるだけだ.

make the best of** one's **way 《英》できるだけ速く行く, 道を急ぐ ▪ Then we'll *make the best of our way* home, and have a glass of wine there. それからできるだけ早く家へ帰って, そこで1杯やりましょう.

May the best man win. (競技の始まる前に)一番できる人が勝ちますように ▪ The golf competition starts. *May the best man win*! ゴルフ競技が始まる. 一番できる人が勝ちますように!

of the best 最良質[最良種]の ▪ After a supper which was *of the best*, they embarked. 最高級の夕食後, 彼らは乗船した.

one of the best 良い男 ▪ The captain is *one of the best*. 船長は良い男だ.

past** one's **best 盛りを過ぎて, 最盛期を過ぎて ▪ Although Mars is dominant in the sky this month, it is well *past its best*. 火星は今月の空では群を抜いて輝いているが, もうとっくに盛りを過ぎている.

put [***set***] *one's* ***best leg*** [***foot***] ***foremost*** [***forward***] 《口》 **1** 精いっぱい急いで行く ▪ She *put her best leg foremost* to catch the bus. 彼女はバスに乗るために力いっぱい走った.

2 全力を尽くす ▪ He *set his best foot foremost* in the way of work. 彼は仕事のほうに全力を尽くした.

3 できるだけ良い印象を与える ▪ He tried hard to *put his best leg forward*. 彼はできるだけ良い印象を与えようと極力努めた.

second best 次善のもの, セカンドベスト ▪ Why may a *second best* plan not be good enough? なぜ次善の計画は十分よいものになりえないか?

the best abused 《口》最もひどくののしられた ▪ It was *the best abused* book of the year. それはその年の最もひどく悪罵された本だった.

the best is... 最もよい点は ▪ *The best is*, she has no teeth to bite. 最もよいことに彼女にはかみつく歯がない.

The best is the enemy of the good. 《諺》あまり標準が高いとかえって進歩[成功]を妨げる.

the best of a bad bunch [***lot***] 《英》悪い中でもましな人[物] ▪ Ted is *the best of a bad bunch* among defenders. テッドはディフェンダーの間では下手な中でもましなほうだ.

the best of all possible worlds 最高にすばらしい世界[状況] (Voltaire, *Candide* 1. 3) ▪ The optimist proclaims that we live in *the best of all possible worlds*. 我々は最高にすばらしい世界に住んでいると楽天論者は公言する.

the best of British (***luck***) ***to...*** うまくいきますように(祈ります) 《うまくいかないという含みがある》 ▪ I don't think you'll succeed in it, but *the best of British luck to* you, all the same. 君がこの事に成功するとは思わない, がやはりうまくいくよう祈るよ.

the best of it (出来事・しゃれなどの)最もおもしろい[驚くべき]所 ▪ *The best of it* is that all the players thought it was a complete failure. 最もおもしろかったのは出演者全員がそれを大失敗だと思ったことだ.

the best of luck 《口》せいぜいお幸せに ▪ Congratulations and *the best of luck* to you both. おめでとう, お二人ともせいぜいお幸せに.

the best part of →the better PART of.

to the best of** one's **ability [***power***] 力の及ぶかぎり, 力のかぎり ▪ I will do it *to the best of my ability*. 私は力のかぎりそれをやります.

to the best of** one's **belief [***knowledge, recollection, judgment***] 信じる[知っている, 記憶している, 判断する]かぎり ▪ *To the best of my knowledge* he is here. 私の知っているかぎり彼はここにいる ▪ *To the best of my belief* those are the actual figures. 私の信じるかぎりそれが実際の数字です.

try** one's **best →TRY[2].

***try** one's **level best** (**to** do)* →do one's level BEST (to do).

turn the best side outward できるだけ外見をよく見せる ▪Mother *turned the best side outward.* 母はできるだけ外見をよく見せた.

with the best (***of them***) 誰にも劣らず ▪He can still climb mountains *with the best.* 彼はまだ誰にも負けず山に登ることができる.

work out for the best 最後はうまくいく ▪Don't worry. Everything will *work out for the best.* 心配ご無用. 何事も結局最後はうまくいくものだ.

You know best. →KNOW[2].

bestir /bɪstə́ːr/ 動 ***bestir** oneself* 《文》奮起する, 活躍する, 努力する ▪He *bestirred himself,* but in vain. 彼は奮起しようとしたがだめだった.

bestrew /bɪstrúː/ 動 ***be bestrewn with*** 《文》…がまき散らされている ▪The street *was bestrewn with* dry leaves. 街路は枯葉で覆われていた.

bet[1] /bet/ 名 ***a good bet*** 《米》有力な見込み, 有力候補者 ▪It was *a good bet* that even meat would be off ration. 肉類でさえ統制をはずされるだろうという見込みが強かった ▪He is *a good bet* to be appointed chairman of the committee. 彼は委員長に任ぜられる有力候補だ.

a poor bet 見込みの薄い(候補者) ▪He is *a poor bet* for the job. 彼がその職につく見込みは薄い.

accept [***take up***] ***a bet*** 賭けに応じる ▪I make it a rule not to *take up a bet.* 私は賭けには応じないことにしている.

all bets are off すべてが白紙だ, 先が読めない ▪The Governor looks safe to win again, but if the press gets hold of a scandal, *all bets are off.* 州知事は再選が固いように見えるが, 新聞社がスキャンダルを手に入れたなら, すべてが白紙だ.

be a safe [***good***] ***bet*** **1** 十分見込みがある, 公算が大だ ▪It's probably *a safe bet* that the world's population will double or even triple. おそらく世界の人口は2倍あるいは3倍にさえなる公算が大きい. **2** うまく行きそうな策, 賢明な選択 ▪When you're unfamiliar with your guests' likes and dislikes, poultry *is a safe bet* for the main course. 客の好き嫌いが不明なときは, 鳥肉をメインコースにするのが無難だ.

have the bet 勝つ ▪It seemed the Frenchmen *had the bet.* フランス軍が勝ったようだった.

hedge [***cover***] *one's* ***bets*** 《口》**1** 両方に賭けて丸損を防ぐ; 防御策をとる (*against*) ▪He *hedged his bets* by buying different companies' stocks. 異なる会社の株を買って丸損を防いだ ▪I hear rumors that he has *hedged his bets against* the US dollar. 彼が米ドルに対して防御策をとったという噂を聞いた. **2** はっきりした意見を言わない, まともに答えない (*on*) ▪Bush has *hedged his bets on* Middle East peace. ブッシュ氏は中東和平についてはまともに答えなかった.

lay** a person **a bet 人と賭けをする ▪I'll *lay* you *a bet.* 君と賭けをしよう.

make a bet 賭けをする ▪He *made a bet* that he would reach the top first. 彼は自分が一番に山頂に到達すると賭けをした.

the [*one's*] ***best bet*** 《口》(ある場合の)最善のもの[策], 最も確実なこと[方法] ▪*Your best bet* is to get a bus as there're no direct trains. 直行列車がないのでバスに乗るのが一番よい.

bet[2] /bet/ 動 ***bet a nickel*** [***a cookie,** one's **last nickel,** one's **boots,** one's **neck,** one's **life***] (***that***) (…と)確信する ▪I *bet a nickel* he will win. 彼はきっと勝つ ▪You can *bet your life* the rent will go up in January. きっと1月から家賃があがるよ.

bet** a person **anything (*he* ***likes***) (***that***) …と確信する, きっと…する ▪I *bet* you *anything* you *like that* we won't be invited to the party. 我々はきっとパーティーには招待されないよ ▪He *bet* me *anything* I couldn't. 彼は絶対に私にはできないと言った.

bet** one's **bottom dollar →DOLLAR.

bet the farm [***ranch***] 《米》ほとんどすべての財産を賭ける (*on*) ▪I would *bet my farm on* becoming a Congressman. 全財産を賭けてもいい, 私は代議士になるんだ ▪Don't *bet the farm on* biofuel. バイオ燃料に全財産を賭けてはならない.

(***Do you***) ***want to bet?/How much do you want to bet?*** 《口》賭けてもそう言えるかい《怪しいね》 ▪Someday I'll be famous.—*Want to bet?* いつかおれは有名になってみせる—怪しいね.

I bet you a shilling きっと…だ ▪*I bet you a shilling* he has forgotten. 彼はきっと忘れたのだ.

I wouldn't bet on it/ (***I***) ***don't bet on it*** 《口》(相手の発言に不信を表して)そうはならないと思う ▪I hope you will be right, but *I wouldn't bet on it.* 君の言う通りだといいけど, そうはならないと思う.

I'll [***I***] ***bet*** 《口》**1** 確かに ▪*I'll bet* it will rain tomorrow. あすはきっと雨が降るよ ▪She is beautiful, *I'll bet.* 彼女は確かに美しい. **2** (相手の言う事が)信じられないよ, 疑わしいよ ▪He says he will be home early tonight.—*I'll bet!* 彼は今夜は早く帰ると言っているよ—信じられないね!

You (***can***) ***bet your*** (***sweet***) ***life*** [***bottom, ass***] 《口》きっと, 確かに, そうだとも ▪*You bet your ass* I'll be there. きっとそこへ行くぜ ▪Are you coming?—*You can bet your sweet life!* 君は来るかね—絶対行くさ.

you can bet on it きっと大丈夫だ, 当てにしていいよ ▪Will we see you at Ellen's wedding? —*You can bet on it.* エレンの結婚式では君に会えるだろうか—当てにしていいよ.

you can bet your life [***your bottom dollar***] 絶対確かだ (*on*) ▪*You can bet your bottom dollar on* the euro rising. 絶対確かだ, ユーロは上がるよ. ☞bottom dollar＝last dollar.

You want to bet on it?/Wanna bet? 《口》(相手の発言に対して)本当かい? 間違いないのか? ▪I am certain we will find some form of primitive life on Mars.—*You want to bet on it?* 火星には何らかの原始的生物が見つかると信じている―本当かい?

B **betake** /bɪtéɪk/ 動 ***betake*** *oneself* ***to***《古》…に行く, 身を投じる, とりかかる ▪ You'd better *betake yourself to* a place of safety. 安全な所へ行ったほうがよい ▪ I *betook myself to* teaching. 私は教師になった ▪ I shall *betake myself to* bed. 床につきましょう.

bethink /bɪθíŋk/ 動 ***bethink*** *oneself* ***of***《雅》…を思いつく, 思い出す ▪ I *bethought myself of* the promise I had made. 私は自分のした約束を思い出した. ☞普通は think of.

bethink *oneself* ***that***《雅》…を思いつく, 思い出す ▪ I *bethought myself that* I ought to write some letters. 私は手紙を書くべきだと思いついた.

betide /bɪtáɪd/ 動 ***Whate'er betide*** 何事が起ころうとも ▪ *Whate'er betide*, I will accomplish my purpose. 何が起ころうとも目的を達成するつもりだ.

woe betide you if →WOE.

betray /bɪtréɪ/ 動 ***betray*** *oneself* うっかり自分の本性[秘密]を表す ▪ If you say such a thing, you will *betray yourself*. そんなことを言うとお里が知れるぞ.

betsy /bétsi/ 名 (***as***) ***crazy as a betsy bug***《米口》ひどく狂って ▪ He made her *as crazy as a betsy bug*. 彼は彼女をひどく狂わせた.

better[1] /bétər/ 形副名 ***A bad excuse*** [***shift***] ***is better than none*** (***at all***).《諺》まずい言い訳でも言わぬよりはまし.

all better《米》(病気などが)すっかり良くなって《通例子供により, または子供に対して使われる》▪ "*All better* now," the doctor said to the boy. 「もうすっかり治ったよ」と医者はその少年に言った.

(***all***) ***the better for*** …のためになおさらよく, かえってよく ▪ I love him *all the better for* his faults. 欠点があるからなおさら彼が好きである ▪ He was *the better for* his failure. 彼は失敗してからよけいよくなった.

be [***get***] ***better*** **1** (病気が)快方に向かっている[だんだんよくなる] ▪ She *is better* this morning. 彼女は今朝は(病気が)よい ▪ He was blooded and *got better*. 彼は血を取ってもらって快方に向かった.

2 気分が前よりよい[よくなる] ▪ I *am better*. 前より気分がよい.

be better off →be well OFF.

be better than *one's* ***word*** →WORD.

one's ***better half***《口・戯》妻 ▪ I'll go with you if *my better half* lets me. 妻が許してくれればご一緒します.

better luck next time →better LUCK another time.

better (***off***) ***dead*** 死んだほうがまし ▪ He'd be *better off dead*. 彼は死んだほうがましだろう.

better off without …がないほうが都合がよい ▪ Jack is blind in one eye, so he's really *better off without* a car than with one. ジャックは一方の目が見えないので, ほんとうに車がないほうがよい.

better than **1** …よりすぐれた ▪ You will have to do *better than* that. 君はそれよりもうまくやらなければならないだろう.

2《口》…より多く (more than) ▪ We have received *better than* a dozen answers. 我々は1ダース以上の回答に接した. ☞この用法を嫌う人もいる.

better that way そのほうがよい ▪ He is extremely generous with his money.—*Better that way* than the other extreme. 彼は極端に金離れがよい―反対の極端よりもそのほうがよいよ.

Better (***to be***) ***safe than sorry.***《諺》はやまって後悔するより用心すぎるほうがよい.

better you than me《口》(いやなことをするはめになった相手に向かって)私でなくてよかった, 私ならいやだ ▪ I have to have an operation tomorrow.—Wow, *better you than me*! 明日手術を受けなくてはいけないんだ―わぁっ! こっちだったらごめんだな.

(***but***) ***better late than never.***《諺》(しかし)遅くともしないよりはまし.

can't do better than *do* …するのが一番よい ▪ If you want to know more about it, you *can't do better than* ask the vicar. そのことについてもっと知りたいなら司祭に尋ねるに限るよ.

do better to *do* →DO[2].

feel better =be BETTER 2.

for better or for worse/***for better, for worse*** よかれあしかれ, いかなる運命になろうとも《行く末長く》(Prayer Book, *The Form of Solemnization of Matrimony*) ▪ They have taken each other *for better or for worse*. 彼らは互いに偕老同穴のちぎりを結んだ ▪ We must take our lot *for better or for worse*. よかれあしかれ運だから仕方がない.

for the better 好転[改善, 栄転]の ▪ There is a change *for the better* in the weather today. きょうは天候が好転した ▪ His appearance is *for the better* since he gave up wearing that hat. 彼はその帽子をかぶらなくなってから風采が上がった.

get [***gain, have***] ***the better of*** …を負かす, (人)のうわ手に出る ▪ The Medes *had the better of* the Lydians. メディア軍はリディア軍に勝った ▪ He always *gets the better of* his opponent. 彼はいつも相手のうわ手に出る.

go (*a person*) ***one better***/***go*** [***do***] ***one better*** (***than***)《口》(賭けなどで)人より一つだけ上を張り込む; (人のしたことの)一つ上を行く[勝る] ▪ Whatever you possess, he can always *go one better*. あなたが何を持っていようと彼はいつもその上を行くことができる ▪ He won two prizes; I *went* him *one better* and got five. 彼は賞を二つ得た. 私はその上を行って五つ得た ▪ The urge to *go one better than* my father was strong. 父の一つ上を行こうという衝動が強かった.

had better *do* →HAD.

had better have *done* →HAD.

It is better to be born lucky than rich.《諺》金持ちに生まれるよりも幸運の星の下に生まれるほうがよい.

know any better →KNOW[2].

know better もっと思慮[分別]がある; その愚[非]なることを知っている ▪ You should *know better* at your age. 君くらいの年齢なら, もっと分別があるべきだ ▪ Our soldiers *knew better.* わが兵士たちはその手は食わなかった ▪ He is too much of a man of the world not to *know better.* 彼は世間のことをよく知っているからそんなばかなことはしない.

no better than **1** ...よりも全然よくない《not BETTER than よりも強意的》 ▪ John is *no better than* Mike at speaking French. フランス語を話すことではジョンはマイクよりもちっともうまくない.

2 ...と同様に悪い, も同然だ ▪ He is *no better than* Hitler or Stalin. 彼はヒトラーやスターリンも同然だ.

no better than *one* ***should*** [***ought to***] ***be*** 不道徳な; (特に女性が)身持ちのよくない, いかがわしい ▪ Miss Williams is rumored to be *no better than* she *should be.* ウィリアムズ嬢は身持ちがよくないと噂されている.

not better than ...よりもよくない, せいぜい...に過ぎない ▪ He's *not better than* an average pitcher. 彼は並のピッチャーよりもすぐれていない.

nothing better ...よりよいことは何もない (*than*) ▪ People think I have got *nothing better* to do *than* housework. 私には家事よりも大切なものは何もない, と世間の人は考えている.

so much the better →so MUCH 2.

Something is better than nothing. →SOMETHING.

That's better. それでよい, もう大丈夫《励まし・慰めを表す》 ▪ "*That's better*, child," he said. 「もう大丈夫だよ, 坊や」と彼は言った.

the better for →(all) the BETTER for.

the better part of →PART[1].

The better the day, the better the deed. 日がよければすることもますますよいはず《安息日を守らないことをとがめられて, 言い返す文句にもなる》.

the more [***bigger,*** etc.] ***the better*** 多い[大きい, など]ほどますますよい ▪ We are in for a lot of rain. *The more the better.* 大雨が降るだろう. 多ければ多いほどよい ▪ The general rule is *the younger the better.* 一般規則は「若いほど良い」である.

The sooner the better. →SOON.

think better of →THINK[2].

'Tis better to have loved and lost than never to have loved at all. 《諺》全く人を愛したことがないよりは, 人を愛して失った体験をするほうがよい (Tennyson, *In Memoriam A. H. H.*).

you'd better believe (***it***) →BELIEVE.

better[2] /bétər/ 動 ***better*** *oneself* 出世する, もっとよい地位[給料]を得る ▪ Young William has left the village to *better himself.* ウィリアム青年は出世するため村を出て行った.

betterment /bétərmənt/ 名 ***for*** *one's* ***betterment*** 改善[向上, 出世]のために ▪ The man worked hard *for his betterment.* 彼は出世のために一生懸命働いた.

betting /bétɪŋ/ 名 ***change the betting*** 事態[形勢, 成り行き]を変える ▪ It is not hiding the head that will *change the betting.* 頭を隠したって形勢は変わりはしない.

the betting is that 《口》おそらく...だろう ▪ *The betting is that* the governor will sign the contract. おそらく知事はその契約に署名するだろう.

What's the betting (***that***)***...?*** 《口》...の見込みはどのくらいあるだろうか ▪ *What's the betting that* Tony arrives tomorrow? トニーがあすやって来る見込みはどのくらいあるだろうか.

Betty /béti/ 名 (***all***) (***in***) ***my eye*** (***and***) ***Betty Martin*** →EYE.

between /bɪtwíːn/ 前副 ***after all there has been between*** ...が抱いてきた友情にかんがみて, してきた経験にかんがみて ▪ *After all there has been between* us, I don't want to quarrel with him. 二人はいろいろ親しくしてきたから, 彼とはけんかしたくない.

be between jobs [***projects***] 《婉曲》失業[失職]中で ▪ Jeff *is between jobs* right now. ジェフは目下失業中だ.

be caught in between 板挟みになる ▪ Mother and wife quarreled and I *was caught in between.* 母と妻が口論して, 私は板挟みになった.

between *A* ***and*** *B* AやらBやらで ▪ *Between* astonishment *and* despair, she did not know what to do. 驚きやら絶望やらで彼女はどうしてよいやらわからなかった.

between man and man →MAN[1].

between ourselves 《口》ここだけの話だが, 内緒のことで[だが] ▪ This matter is *between ourselves.* この件は内々です ▪ *Between ourselves*, he won't live long. ここだけの話だが彼は長生きはしないよ.

between the cup and the lip もう一息というところで ▪ Nothing shall come *between the cup and the lip* to defeat you. もう一息というところで君を敗北させるようなことにはしない.

between you and me/ ***between you and me and the bedpost*** [***fencepost, gatepost***] 《英戯》《口》ここだけの話だが ▪ *Between you and me and the bedpost*, he was dismissed for bribery. ここだけの話だが, 彼は収賄のかどで首になったのだ.

betwixt and between 《米俗》二流で[の] ▪ He took the lease of a house in a *betwixt and between* fashionable street. 彼はほどほどににぎやかな通りに家を借りた.

(***few and***) ***far between*** →FAR.

in between 中間に; はさまれて ▪ The trees are planted with a space of 100 yards *in between.* 木は100ヤードの間隔をおいて植えてある.

bevvy /bévi/ 動 ***be bevvied up*** 《英俗》酔っ払っている ▪ He *was* so *bevvied up* he didn't know what they were doing. 彼はひどく酔っ払っていたので, 彼らが何をやっているのかわからなかった.

bevy /bévi/ 名 ***a bevy of*** (物)の集まり, (女性)の群れ ▪ We purposely call ourselves the *Bevy of*

Beauties! 私たちは意図的に自分たちを美女の群れと自称している.

bewilderment /bɪwíldərmənt/ 名 ***in bewilderment*** 当惑して, 面くらって ▪ He gazed at it *in bewilderment.* 彼はあっけにとられてそれをじっと見た.

beyond /bɪjɑ́nd|-jɔ́nd/ 前副名 ***be*** [***get***] ***beyond*** [***past***] ***a joke*** 冗談じゃない[でなくなる]《あまり重大・迷惑でおもしろいどころじゃない》 ▪ The constant roar of trucks keeps residents awake night after night and it *is beyond a joke.* トラックが毎晩立てるひっきりなしの轟音で住民は寝られない. こいつは冗談どころじゃない ▪ Your continual lateness has *got beyond a joke.* 君のぶっ続けの遅刻はもう笑いごとではなくなった.

beyond all else 何よりも, 特に ▪ America usually has an attraction for him *beyond all else.* アメリカは通常何よりも彼をひきつける.

beyond all things 何より第一に ▪ We must do it *beyond all things.* 我々は何より第一にそれをしなければならない.

beyond money and price 金で買えないほど貴重な ▪ Health is *beyond money and price.* 健康は金で買えないほど貴重だ.

go a step beyond *a person* 人より一歩上に出る ▪ I *went a step beyond* him in displaying my principles. 自己の主義を表明することでは彼の上に出た.

go beyond *oneself* 度をはずす, 我を忘れる; 平生より上出来である ▪ He *went beyond himself* with joy. 彼は喜びのあまり我を忘れた ▪ He sometimes indeed *went beyond himself.* 彼はときとして普段よりもほんとによくやることがあった.

kick *a person* ***into the beyond*** 《米俗》人を殺す《人をあの世へ送り込む》 ▪ We *kicked* him *into the beyond.* 我々は彼をかたうけた.

(***the***) ***back of beyond*** →BACK[1].

the great beyond 《婉曲》来世, あの世 ▪ She claims that she gets messages from *the Great Beyond.* 彼女はあの世からのメッセージを受けると主張している.

bias[1] /báɪəs/ 名 ***be under*** [***have***] ***a bias*** 偏向がある, 偏している (*towards*) ▪ He *has a* strong *bias towards* that direction. 彼は非常にその方向に偏している ▪ He could not possibly *be under* any *bias.* 彼は断じてどんな偏見にもとらわれているはずはない.

on the bias 斜めに, はすかいに; バイアスに ▪ He cut the cloth *on the bias.* 彼はその布地を斜めに切った.

without bias and without favor 全く偏見なく, 公平無私に ▪ The law is applied *without bias and without favor* toward all citizens. この法律はすべての市民に公平無私に適用される.

bias[2] /báɪəs/ 動 ***be biased against*** [***in favor of***] (人)に不利な[有利な]偏見をいだいている ▪ He *is* strongly *biased against* his leader. 彼は指導者に対して強い偏見をいだいている.

bib /bɪb/ 名 《戯》*one's* [***the***] ***best bib and tucker*** (日曜などに着る)晴れ着《正しくは女子の衣服のことだが, 男子の衣服にも用いる》 ▪ Both girls and boys had on *their best bib and tucker.* 少年少女ともに晴れ着を着ていた.

Bible /báɪbəl/ 名 ***a Bible thumper*** [《英》***basher***] 《主に米口》熱狂的な聖書信奉者 ▪ I think he's just *a Bible basher.* 彼は熱狂的な聖書信奉者にすぎないと思う ▪ Hyde Park on Sunday afternoons is the paradise of crooks, cranks, and *Bible thumpers.* 日曜午後のハイドパークはごろつき, 変人, 熱狂的な宗教演説家の楽園である.

give *one's* ***bible-word*** 聖書によって誓う ▪ I *give* you *my bible-word* it was Hyde. それがハイドであったと聖書によって誓います.

on *one's* ***Bible oath*** 聖書によって誓って ▪ I say, *on my Bible oath,* that it happened exactly as I've told you. それはちょうどあなたにお話しした通りに起こったと聖書に誓って申します.

swear on a stack of Bibles 《口》誓って言う ▪ He *swore on a stack of Bibles* that he did not believe in communism. 彼は共産主義を信じていないと誓って言った.

biblical /bíblɪkəl/ 形 ***not in the biblical sense*** 《戯》(know と言っても性交したという)聖書の意味ではないが ▪ I know her but *not in the biblical sense.* 彼女は知っているが, 聖書の意味ではない.

bid[1] /bɪd/ 名 ***enter a bid*** 値をつける ▪ He *entered a bid* at an auction. 彼は競売で値をつけた.

invite bids for …の入札を求める[行う] ▪ *Bids were invited for* the construction of a new swimming pool. 新プール建設の入札が行われた.

make a bid for **1** …に入札する ▪ I *made* the largest *bid for* the article. その品に最高値をつけた. **2** (人気など)を得ようと努める ▪ He *made a bid for* the throne. 彼は王座を得ようとした ▪ He *made a bid for* election. 彼は当選しようと運動した.

bid[2] /bɪd/ 動 ***bid defiance to*** →DEFIANCE.

bid fair to *do* →FAIR.

bid *a person* ***welcome*** [***adieu, farewell, good bye, good morning***] 人にようこそ[ごきげんよう, さようなら, さよなら, おはよう]と言う ▪ I now *bid* the British public *farewell.* 私は今イギリスの公衆にお別れのあいさつをいたします ▪ He'll *bid adieu* to all the vanity of ambition. 彼はすべての空虚な野心に別れを告げるだろう.

bidding /bídɪŋ/ 名 ***at bidding*** 即座に ▪ I can write a poem *at bidding.* 即座に詩を書けます.

at *a person's* ***bidding*** 人の命に従って, 人に請われるままに ▪ He entered *at my bidding.* 彼は私の命に従って入った.

do *a person's* ***bidding*** 人の命に従う ▪ I only *did his bidding.* 私は彼の命を実行しただけである.

force the bidding (競売で)どんどん値を競り上げる ▪ The auctioneer *forced the bidding.* 競売人はどんどん値を競り上げた.

bide /baɪd/ 動 ***bide*** *one's* ***time*** (辛抱して)時[機]を待つ ▪ They held their peace and *bided* *their time*. 彼らは黙って時を待った.

let** a thing **bide 物をそのままにしておく[ほっておく] ▪ We'll *let* the crow *bide*. カラスはほっておきましょう.

big[1] /bɪɡ/ 形 ***a big cheese*** [***gun, wheel***] 《口》(組織の)重要人物, 大物 ▪ I hear he is *a big cheese* in that organization. 彼はあの組織の大物だそうだ.

a big fish in a little [***small***] ***pond*** 狭い世界の重要人物[大物] ▪ It is better to be *a big fish in a little pond* than a little fish in a big pond. 広い世界の小人物であるよりも狭い世界の大物であるほうがよい,「鶏口となるも牛後となるなかれ」.

a big girl's blouse →BLOUSE.

a big head 《英》うぬぼれ[自負心]の強い人 ▪ That's why you've got such *a big head*! それがあなたがうぬぼれの強い人である理由ですよ.

a big name [***noise***] 《口》重要人物, 大物 ▪ He is *a big name* in the world of journalism. 彼はジャーナリズムの世界では大物だ.

a big picture 全体像 ▪ This navigator gives *a big picture* of the route. このナビゲーターでこのルートの全体像がわかる.

a big shot [***wheel***] 《米口》= a BIG name.

(***as***) ***big as a barn door*** →BARN DOOR.

(***as***) ***big as a cabbage*** →as large as a CABBAGE.

(***as***) ***big as life*** →(as) large as LIFE (and twice as natural).

***be big of** a person* 〚主に反語的に〛(ふざけて, 怒って)ありがたいね, ご親切さま ▪ "That's very *big of* you," she said curtly.「そりゃどうもご親切さま」と彼女はそっけなく言った.

(***be***) ***big on*** 《俗》...に熱心[夢中]で, ...に熱中して(いる), かぶれて(いる) (= (be) HOT on 1) ▪ My dad *is big on* not spending on things we already have. おやじはすでにある物を買わないことにはまっている ▪ The small country *is* very *big on* foreign investment. その小国は海外投資に非常に力を入れている ▪ My dad *is big on* rock music and collects records. 父さんはロックが大好きでレコードを集めている.

be [***get, grow***] ***too big for** one's* ***boots*** [***shoes, breeches, britches, pants, trousers***] 非常にうぬぼれて, 気取って, いばって ▪ He is *getting too big for his britches*. 彼はひどくうぬぼれてきた ▪ Ashley doesn't *get too big for his boots*. アシュレーはいばることなんかない.

big and bold 大きくて目立つ ▪ The pattern of her dress was *big and bold*. 彼女のドレスの柄は大きくて目立っていた.

Big Brother ビッグブラザー《全体主義国家の指導者》 ▪ The physical description of *Big Brother* is reminiscent of Stalin. ビッグブラザーの身体的描写はスターリンを想起させる. ☞George Orwell の小説 *Nineteen Eighty-Four* に出てくる超大国家 Oceania の専制的統治者.

big deal **1** 一大事 ▪ This interview is a *big deal* to me. この面接は私にとって一大事なんだ ▪ What's the *big deal* about it? そんなことどうだっていいじゃないか. **2** 《口》〚Big deal! として反語的に〛大したもんだね, それがどうした《重要でも面白くもない》 ▪ John bought a new car.—*Big deal!* ジョンは新車を買ったよ—それがどうした.

big ticket 《米》〚限定的〛非常に高価な ▪ *Big ticket* item refers to retail goods that have a high selling price. 高額商品は売値が高価な小売商品を指す.

big with ...をはらんで《比喩的にも》 ▪ She was *big with* child. 彼女は妊娠していた ▪ The morning had at length arrived, *big with* the fate of Rome. ローマの命運をはらんだ朝がついにやってきた.

get big 高慢になる ▪ Never *get big* and forget the little fellow. 高慢になってかけ出し時代を忘れるな.

go over big →GO (over, down) big.

hit [***make***] (***it***) ***big*** 《口》大成功する, 非常に有名になる ▪ A Korean comics artist *made it big* in Japan. 韓国人漫画家が日本で大成功した ▪ They employed a marketing consultant to *make it big* on the internet. 彼らはインターネットで大成功するために販売促進顧問を雇った.

look big 偉そうな顔をする ▪ The Mayor liked to *look big*. 市長は偉そうな顔をするのが好きだった.

make a big deal out of [***about***] ...を大げさに考える, 騒ぎたてる ▪ Why do people *make a big deal about* nudity? 人は裸体であることになぜ大騒ぎするのか.

make a big thing (***out***) ***of*** ...を騒ぎたてる, 事だてる ▪ You don't need to *make a big thing of* me being there. 僕がそこにいたことを騒ぎたてなくてもいい.

make it big 《俗》(特に事業に)大成功する ▪ He started growing flowers two years ago, and now he has *made it big*. 彼は2年前に花作りを始めた, そして今は大成功している.

me and my big mouth 《口》まずいことを言ってしまった ▪ "*Me and my big mouth*, eh?" she said, wishing she knew when to hold her tongue.「まずいことを言っちゃった, ね?」と彼女は言って, 口をつぐむ時期を心得ていればよかったと思った.

Mr. Big →MR.

no big deal/no biggie 《口》大したことじゃない ▪ She gave a brief smile to show that it was *no big deal*. 彼女は大したことじゃないということを示すために, ちょっと微笑した.

talk big →TALK[2].

That's big of you [***him,*** etc.]. →be BIG of a person.

the big daddy 《米》(グループ中で)一番大きい[重要な]人[動物, 物] ▪ Windows is *the big daddy* of computer software. ウィンドウズはソフトウェア中の一番の大物だ ▪ The elephant is *the big daddy* of land animals. ゾウは陸上動物の中で一番の大物だ.

the big enchilada →ENCHILADA.

the Big Picture (特定の事項・問題の)大きな見通

し，展望，概観 ▪ Stand back from time to time and take a look at *the Big Picture.* ときには距離をおいて大きな見通しを見てみなさい.

the Big Three [***Four***] 《口》三つ[四つ]の大きな組織，国 ▪ General Motors, Ford and Chrysler are no longer *the "Big Three"* in the American automobile industry. GM，フォード，クライスラーはもはやアメリカの自動車産業の「ビッグスリー」ではない ▪ *The "Big Four"* in the European Union are Germany, France, Italy and the United Kingdom. ヨーロッパ連合の四大国はドイツ・フランス・イタリア・イギリスだ.

The bigger they are [***come***], ***the harder they fall.*** 《諺》権力[成功]が大きいほど，それを失うのがこたえる.

think big →THINK[2].

big[2] /bɪɡ/ 動 ***big it up*** **1**《口》(華々しく)豪遊する ▪ This time next week we'll be *bigging it up* in Nice. 来週の今はニースで豪遊しているだろうよ.

2《英俗》(拍手・声援して)応援する ▪ *Big it up* for the boys in the band! 楽団仲間に声援して応援してください.

bigot /bíɡət/ 動 ***be bigoted to*** …をかたくなに守る[墨守する] ▪ He *was bigoted to* ancient customs. 彼は古い習慣を墨守した.

big time /bíɡtàɪm/ 名 ***be in the big time*** 《口》その分野でトップクラスに入る ▪ I *was* finally *in the big time* in the last audition. 最後のオーディションで私はついにトップクラスに入った.

crack the big time 一流になる，成功する ▪ Lester managed to *crack the big time.* レスターはどうにか成功した.

have a big time 《米口》楽しく過ごす;《皮肉》ひどい目にあう ▪ I *had a big time* there. そこでは非常に愉快だった ▪ They *had a big time* when he came home drunk. 彼が酔って帰って来ると彼らはひどい目にあった.

hit [***reach, make***] ***the big time*** 有名になる ▪ Ken *hit the big time.* ケンは有名になった ▪ He has *made* [*hit*] *the big time.* 彼は大成功を収めた.

make it to the big time 一流になる，大成功する ▪ She *made it to the big time* in Alfred Hitchcock's films. 彼女はヒッチコック映画で脚光を浴びた ▪ The music CD has *made it to the big time* in New York this year. その音楽 CD は今年ニューヨークで大ヒットしている.

bike /baɪk/ 名 ***get on your*** [*one's*] ***bike*** 《英》とっとと出て行って仕事を見つける ▪ Ned was told by the boss to *get on his bike* by the end of the month. ネッドは月末までに辞めるように社長から言われた.

On yer [***your***] ***bike!*** 《英》(無礼に，おどけて)あっちへ行け，とっとと失せろ! ▪ Can I borrow ten pounds, Fred?—*On your bike!* 10ポンド貸してくれないか，フレッド—とっとと失せろ.

bile /baɪl/ 名 ***be full of bile*** 怒りと辛辣さがいっぱいで ▪ His speeches *were full of bile.* 彼のスピーチは怒りと恨みに溢れていた.

rouse [***stir***] *a person's* ***bile*** 人を怒らす ▪ The rude behavior of those officials *roused my bile.* その将校たちの無礼なふるまいに私は腹がたった.

bill[1] /bɪl/ 名 ***a clean bill of health*** 《口》**1** 完全健康証明 ▪ Even better, the doctor has given me *a clean bill of health.* さらによいことに，医者は私に完全健康証明を与えた.

2(道徳的・法的に)無実[無過失]の証明 ▪ The man was suspected of a robbery, but the police gave him *a clean bill of health.* その男は強盗の疑いをかけられたが，警察は無罪の証明をした.

a true bill 《英法》起訴陪審の公訴認定書; 真実な陳述[非難] ▪ *A true bill,* by all that is unlucky! まことに不幸なことだが真実な非難である.

answer the bill =fit the BILL.

(*as*) *phony* [***queer***] ***as a three-dollar bill*** 全くいんちきな，偽物の ▪ This guy's *as phony as a three-dollar bill.* こいつは全くのくわせ者だ.

be on the bill with …と同じ興行に出る ▪ He *was* once *on the bill with* me. 彼は昔は私と同じ興行に出ていた. ☞bill「興行」.

bring in [***lay, set***] ***a bill*** 議案を提出する ▪ He *brought in the bill* before Parliament. 彼はその法案を議会に提出した.

find a (***true***) ***bill*** (***against*** *a person*) 《法》(起訴陪審が調査の結果人を)裁判にかけるだけの証拠ありと認める;(人に対する)起訴状を受理する (↔ignore the BILL) ▪ To *find a bill,* all twelve of the jury must agree. 起訴状を受理するには陪審団の12人全員が同意しなければならない.

fit [***fill***] ***the bill*** 必要な性質[要求]にかなう，期待に添う，用が足りる ▪ The new secretary will *fill the bill* perfectly. 今度の事務員は完全に期待に添うだろう ▪ This policy will *fill the bill.* この政策は要求にかなうだろう ▪ The actor *fits the bill* nicely. その俳優はその役にピッタリだ. ☞「劇場のプログラムに大きな文字でいっぱいに書く」が原義.

foot the bill 《口》支払いをする，経費をもつ; 行為の責めを負う; 損害を償う (*for*) ▪ It was the bride's father who *footed* all *the bills.* 全経費をもったのは花嫁の父であった ▪ Why must taxpayers *foot the bill for* a public event? なぜ納税者は公共の行事の経費をもたねばならないのか. ☞「勘定書の下部 (foot) に署名して支払う」から.

head the bill →top the BILL.

ignore the bill 《法》(起訴陪審が調査の結果，人を)裁判にかけるだけの証拠なしと認める，人に対する起訴状を取り上げない (↔find a (true) BILL (against a person)).

lay a bill →bring in a BILL.

pad the bill 勘定を水増しする ▪ He *padded the bill* for his traveling expenses by exaggerating his food expenses. 彼は食事代をふくらませて旅費を水増しした.

pick up the bill 《口》他の人の分の勘定を払う ▪ Jill made a huge number of phone calls and her mother had to *pick up the bill.* ジルが電話をかけまくって, 母親がその料金の支払いをせねばならなかった.

sell** a person **a bill of goods (役に立たないもの, たやすく処分できないものを)人にだましてつかませる ▪ That salesman *sold* you *a bill of goods.* あの販売員はあなたをだましてつかませたのだ ▪ The poor sucker *was sold a bill of goods.* かわいそうにそのおめでたい人はだまされた ▪ He certainly *sold* you *a bill of goods* when he induced you to buy that old car. 彼が君にあの古自動車を勧めて買わせたのは確かにつかませたわけだよ.

set a bill →bring in a BILL.

top [head] the bill トップに大きく広告される, 主役を演じる ▪ *Topping the bill* is Colin Davis. 主役を演じるのはコリン・デイビスである.

within the bills of mortality ロンドンまたはその近くに ▪ He is living *within the bills of mortality.* 彼はロンドンのあたりに住んでいる. ☞the bills of mortality「ロンドンとその付近の週間死亡者報告書」.

bill[2] /bɪl/ 動 ***be billed to** do* …するとビラに書かれている ▪ He *is billed to* appear in the part of Hamlet. 彼はハムレット役で出演するとビラに書いてある.

bill[3] /bɪl/ 動 ***bill and coo*** 《古風》愛撫し合う; 〚しばしば進行形で〛(恋人同士が)甘い言葉を交わしながらキスする ▪ Tom and Jane *were billing and cooing* in an arbor. トムとジェインはあずまやでいちゃついていた. ☞ハトなどの恋愛行動から.

billet[1] /bílət/ 名 ***be in billets*** (兵隊が宿割りされた)宿所についている, 人家に泊まっている ▪ The soldiers *were in billets.* 兵隊たちは人家に割り当てられて泊まっていた.

Every bullet has its billet. →BULLET.

billet[2] /bílət/ 動 ***billet** (troops) **in [at, on, upon, with]*** (軍隊を)…に割り当てて宿泊させる ▪ The soldiers *were billeted on* the villagers. 兵隊たちは村人の家に割り当てて宿泊させられた.

billy-o(h) /bílioʊ/ 名 ***like billy-o*** 《口》猛烈に, ひどく, とてもうまく ▪ Sure it will rain *like billy-o.* きっと猛烈に雨が降るだろう. ☞billy-o は devil の婉曲語.

bind[1] /baɪnd/ 名 ***in a bind*** 《米口》進退に窮して, 窮地にあって (→in a (tight, bad, hot) BOX) ▪ Jack was *in a bind.* ジャックは進退に窮していた.

in a double bind 二重拘束に陥って, 板挟みになって ▪ A person who is caught *in a double-bind* cannot "win" no matter what. 板挟みになった人は何をしても「勝て」ない.

bind[2] /baɪnd/ 動 ***bind** oneself **about*** …に巻きつく; を取り巻く ▪ The hops have *bound themselves about* the poles. ホップは棒くいに巻きついた.

bind ... hand and foot →HAND and foot 1.

bind the bargain 契約を固める ▪ He *bound the bargain* with earnest money. 彼は手付金を払って契約を固めた.

***bind** oneself **to** (do)* (…すること)を誓う, 約束する ▪ He was obliged to *bind himself to* marry the girl. 彼はやむなくその娘と結婚することを誓う羽目になった.

I'll [I dare] be bound 〚主に文尾で〛確かだ, 請け合う ▪ They'll do it, *I'll be bound.* きっと彼らはそれをするだろう. ☞dare の形は1800年以後はまれ.

binge[1] /bɪndʒ/ 名 ***be [go] on the binge/ have a binge*** 《口》飲み騒ぐ, 痛飲する ▪ *Were* you *on the binge* last night? 君は昨夜飲み騒いだか ▪ We *had a* real *binge* when Jack got married. ジャックが結婚したとき, みなで飲んで実に大騒ぎをした.

binge[2] /bɪndʒ/ 動 ***binge and purge*** (拒食症で)繰り返し食べては吐く ▪ Alice had *binged and purged* for a number of years and was very thin. アリスはもう何年も前から食べては吐くを繰り返して, ひどく痩せていた.

binge-drinking 多量の酒をがぶ飲みすること ▪ *Binge-drinking* can lead to child abuse and domestic violence. 暴飲すると幼児虐待や家庭内暴力に及ぶことがある.

biological /bàɪəlάdʒɪkəl|-lɔ́dʒ-/ 形 ***biological warfare [weapons]*** 細菌戦[生物兵器] ▪ We should work for a global ban on chemical and *biological weapons.* 生化学兵器を地上から一掃するために協力すべきだ.

bird /bəːrd/ 名 ***a bird(-)brain*** 《口》ばか, とんま ▪ What *bird brain* politician comes up with these ideas? どんなとんまな政治家がこういう考えを思いつくのか.

a bird in the gilded cage 快適だが束縛の生活をする人《金ピカの籠に入れられた鳥》 ▪ He is *a* wise *bird in the gilded cage.* 彼は快適・束縛の生活をする賢人である.

a bird in the hand 確実なもの; 即座の所有物 ▪ He offered me a shilling; it was *a bird in the hand.* 彼は私に1シリングやろうと言った. それは即金であった. ☞次の諺から.

A bird in the hand is worth two in the bush. 《諺》手中の1羽はやぶの中の2羽の価値がある,「あすの百よりきょうの十」.

a bird of a different feather 独立独歩の人 ▪ She's *a bird of a different feather* who designs and makes her own clothes. 彼女は独立独歩の人で, 自分の服は自分でデザインして作る.

a bird of ill omen 不吉の鳥《カラス, フクロウ》; 凶報をもたらす人 ▪ The postman has proved *a bird of ill omen* twice this week. 郵便配達人は今週2回凶報を持って来た.

a bird of passage 渡り鳥; 流れ者《一か所に長くとどまれない人》 ▪ Sally moves nearly every year; she's *a* true *bird of passage.* サリーはほぼ毎年のように転居している. ほんものの渡り鳥だ ▪ I am only in town as *a bird of passage.* 私はただ流れ者として町にいるだけです.

a bird's eye view →BIRD'S-EYE.

(a) dicky bird 《俗》自分が何をしているかわからない人 ▪ What are you doin', are you *dicky bird?*

B

何をやってるんだい, 自分が何をしてるかわからないのかい.

A little bird told [***whispered to***] ***me.*** 《口》 風のたよりに聞いた, ある人から聞いた (《聖》 *Eccles.* 10. 20) ▪ *A little bird told me* you could be very severe. 君はときに非常にきびしいことがあるとのことだった.

An old bird is [***Old birds are***] ***not caught with chaff.*** 《諺》 古い鳥はもみがらでは捕えられない 《経験者はばかげた嘘ではだまされない》.

(***be***) ***a bird about*** 《米》 ...のたいしたファン[愛好家]で(ある) ▪ My old man *is a bird about* golf. うちのおやじはゴルフに夢中です.

be able to [***can***] ***charm the birds off a tree*** 何でもできるほどの魔力[魅力]がある ▪ Gordon *could charm a bird off a tree* if he put his mind to it. ゴードンはその気になれば何でもできるほど人を惹きつける力をもっている.

be the bird in question (人が)そのことを伝えたのだ ▪ She *is the bird in question.* 彼女がそのことを伝えた.

Birds in their little nest agree. 《諺》 巣の小鳥はけんかをしない 《けんかをしている子供に言って聞かせたりする》.

birds of a feather 同じ種類の人々, 同類 ▪ They are *birds of a feather.* 彼らは同類だ. ☞ 次の諺から.

Birds of a feather flock together. 《諺》 同じ羽の鳥は集まる, 類をもって集まる, 「類は友を呼ぶ」.

do bird 《俗》 刑に服す ▪ He's *done bird* on several occasions. 彼は数回刑に服した.

eat like a bird ごくわずかしか食べない (↔EAT like a pig) ▪ She *ate like a bird* and spoke very little. 彼女は小食で口数も少なかった.

Every bird likes its own nest the best. 《諺》 どの鳥でも自分の巣が一番好きだ.

Fine feathers make fine birds. 《諺》 美事な羽毛なら見事な鳥になる, 「馬子にも衣装」.

flip [***give, shoot***] *a person* ***the bird*** →give a person the (big) BIRD.

get the (***big***) ***bird*** 《口》 **1** (俳優などが)ブーブーやじられる; 強く[公然と]非難される ▪ The comedian was no good and soon *got the bird.* その喜劇俳優はつまらなかったのでじきにやじられた.

2 断られる; 解雇される ▪ I went up and asked for a holiday and *got the bird.* 私は行って休暇を一日くださいと言ったが断られた ▪ The boy *got the bird* for being saucy to the director. その給仕は支配人に対して生意気だったので首になった. ☞ 劇場用語から.

give *a person* ***the*** (***big***) ***bird*** **1** 《英口》 人をブーブーやじる; 強く[公然と]非難する; 《豪》 あざける ▪ Every time the speaker referred to it, they *gave* him *the bird.* 弁士がその事を言うたびに彼らは彼をやじった.

2 《米口》 (人の頼みを)断る; 人を解雇する, 追い払う ▪ He asked me to lend him five pounds, and I *gave* him *the bird.* 彼は5ポンド貸してくれと言ったが私は断った ▪ Mrs. Danby *gave* him *the bird.* ダンビー夫人は彼を首にした. ☞ 劇場用語から.

have a bird 《米口》 ショックを受ける, ひどく動揺する ▪ She *had a bird* in her bathtub; the water was cold. 彼女はバスタブに入るとショックを受けた, 冷水だったのだ.

have the bird 《口》 追っ払われる, 首になる ▪ I've *had the bird.* 私はお払い箱になった.

hear a bird sing →SING[2].

kill two birds with one stone 一石二鳥を獲る; 一挙両得をする ▪ We visited Aunt and also saw New York City on the trip, thus *killing two birds with one stone.* その旅行でおばさんを訪問し, またニューヨーク市を見た. つまり一石二鳥だった.

like a bird (鳥のように)早く軽く, 楽々と; 朗らかに ▪ My car starts *like a bird* every morning. 私の車は毎朝軽快に走りだす.

not a dicky bird 《俗》 一言も...ない, 何も...ない ▪ *Not a dicky bird* was said. 一言も言われなかった ▪ I *never* heard *a dicky bird* about him. 彼のことは一言も聞いたことがない. ☞ dicky bird (幼児語「小鳥」) は word の押韻俗語.

rise with the birds 早起きする ▪ Eve, literally, *rises with the birds.* イブは文字通り小鳥とともに起きる.

(***strictly***) ***for the birds*** 《口》 つまらない; 価値がない (bullshit) ▪ That movie is *for the birds.* その映画はつまらないよ ▪ I won't buy it. It's *strictly for the birds.* 僕はそれを買わない. つまらないから. ☞ 鳥が牛や馬の排泄物の種をついばむところから.

The bird is [***has***] ***flown.*** 相手は逃げてしまった 《捕えようとした人または捕えられていた人が逃げた》 ▪ When I got there this morning *the bird was flown.* 今朝着いたときには相手はもう逃げてしまっていた.

the birds and (***the***) ***bees*** 《婉曲》 トリとハチ 《子供に与える性の基礎知識》 ▪ His father told him about *the birds and bees* when he was a boy. 彼の父は彼が少年のとき性に関することを彼にたとえ話で説明した. ☞ 性の問題を鳥, ミツバチなどの動物の習性によって子供に説明する習慣から.

The early bird catches [***gets***] ***the worm.*** 《諺》 早起きの鳥は虫をつかまえる, 「早起きは三文の徳」.

bird's-egging /bə́ːrdzègɪŋ/ 名 ***Go on with your bird's-egging.*** 《米口》 話を続けてくれ ▪ Now *go on with your bird's-egging.* さあお話を続けてください.

That's none of *one's* ***bird's-egging.*** それは...の知ったことではない ▪ *That's none of my bird's-egging.* それは僕の知ったことではない.

bird's-eye /bə́ːrdzàɪ/ 名形 ***a bird's-eye view*** 鳥瞰(ちょうかん)図, 俯瞰図; 概要 ▪ He presented *a bird's-eye view* of the subject. 彼はその問題の概要を提出した.

get [***have, take***] ***a bird's-eye view*** (***of***) (...を)鳥瞰する; (を)概観する ▪ You can *get a bird's-eye view of* the city from the top floor of this building. このビルの最上階からこの街を鳥瞰できますよ.

birr /bəːr/ 名 ***take*** [***fetch***] *one's* ***birr*** (ジャンプするために)走ってはずみをつける ▪ He goes back to *take his birr.* 彼ははずみをつけるためあとへさがる. ☞birr「はずみ」.

birth /bəːrθ/ 名 ***a man*** [***a woman***] ***of birth*** [***of no birth***] 家柄のよい[並みの]人[女] ▪ *A woman of no birth* may marry into the purple. 女性は氏なくして玉の輿(こし)に乗ることがある.

at a birth 1度のお産で ▪ Three daughters were born *at a birth.* 女の三つ子が生まれた.

at birth 生まれた時は ▪ The baby weighed 3 kilograms *at birth.* 赤ちゃんは生まれた時は体重が3キロだった.

by birth 生まれは; 生まれながらの ▪ He is an American *by birth.* 彼は生まれはアメリカ人である ▪ He is handicapped *by birth.* 彼は生まれながら身体に障害があった.

give birth to …を生む; の原因となる ▪ She *gave birth to* a son. 彼女は息子を産んだ ▪ This spring *gives birth to* a river. この泉は流れて川となっている.

birthday /bə́ːrθdèɪ/ 名 ***in*** *one's* ***birthday suit*** [***clothes***] 《戯》生まれたままの姿で, 裸で ▪ We bathed *in our birthday suit.* 我々は裸で水浴をした. ☞in the ALTOGETHER のほうがよく用いられる.

birthright /bə́ːrθràɪt/ 名 ***sell*** *one's* ***birthright for a mess*** [***spoonful***] ***of pottage*** 一時の利益[快楽]のため永久的価値のあるものを売る (《聖》*Gen.* 25. 29-34) ▪ He *sold his birthright for a spoonful of pottage.* 彼はほんの一時の快楽のため永久的に尊いものを犠牲にした.

biscuit /bískət/ 名 ***take the biscuit*** 《口》最善[最高]である ▪ Your ability to explain clearly about everything we ask *takes the biscuit*! 何でも聞かれたことをはっきり説明できる君の能力は誰にも引けを取らない ▪ For rudeness she really *takes the biscuit.* 無作法の点では彼女が一等だ. ☞競争で一等賞をもらうことから.

bishop[1] /bíʃəp/ 名 ***The bishop has put*** [***set***] ***his foot in it.*** 料理が焦げつきました ▪ Why, madam, *the bishop has set his foot in it.* おや奥さん, お料理が焦げつきましたよ. ☞教会の主教は異端者を焼き殺したがったことから.

bishop[2] /bíʃəp/ 動 ***bishop it*** (教会の)主教の役をする ▪ They *bishop it* in England. 彼らはイギリスで教会の主教をしている.

bisque /bɪsk/ 名 ***give*** *a person* ***fifteen*** [etc.] ***and a bisque*** (比較・競技などで)人をさんざんに負かす ▪ The latest school of English poetry can *give* Byron *thirty and a bisque.* 英詩の最新派はバイロンをはるかに凌ぐものがある. ☞bisque「(テニス・ゴルフなどの)ハンディ」.

bit[1] /bɪt/ 名 ***a bit*** 《口》 **1** 少し ▪ He is *a bit* tired. 彼は少し疲れている.
2 ちょっと ▪ Just wait *a bit.* ちょっと待ってください.

a bit much 《口》不公平な, 不当な ▪ His proposal is *a bit much.* 彼の提案は不当だ ▪ It's *a bit much* of him to ask his girlfriend to wait six years. ガールフレンドに6年も待つように頼むなんて彼もあんまりだ.

a bit of a 《主に英口》 **1** ちょっとした ▪ I've got *a bit of a* problem. ちょっとした問題をかかえてましてね ▪ He is *a bit of a* poet. 彼はちょっとした詩人だ.
2 《反語》大変な ▪ You are *a bit of a* musician yourself, aren't you? 君自身たいした音楽家だね. ☞→a bit of a LAD.

a bit of all right 《俗》大変けっこうなもの《人の場合は女性に限る》 ▪ This beef is *a bit of all right.* この牛肉は大変けっこうである ▪ Jane is *a bit of all right.* ジェインはとてもいい女だ.

a bit of crackling 《英口》(セックスの対象としての)魅力的な女性, 上玉, 色女 ▪ You know her?—I do, sir. Nice *bit of crackling.* 彼女を知っているかね—知ってますよ. 上玉ですぜ.

a bit of fluff [***skirt***] 《英俗》性的に魅力的な女性, 上玉, 色女 ▪ Who is that *bit of fluff* he is dancing with? 彼と踊っているあの上玉は誰だい? ▪ He often wandered the streets in search of *a bit of skirt.* 彼はよくいい女を探して町をさまよった.

a bit of goods →a PIECE of goods.

a bit of how's your father 《英戯》性行為 ▪ He found them having *a bit of how's your father* in the kitchen. 彼は二人がキッチンで性行為をしているのを見つけた.

a bit of rough 《英俗》上流の女性と関係をもつ下層の男 ▪ She can't help falling for scruffy boys—because she likes *a bit of rough.* 彼女はだらしない若者に欺されずにはいられない—上流女好きの荒くれ男が好きだからだ.

a bit of stuff [***crumpet, tail***] 《俗・軽蔑》(セックスの対象としての)若い女, スケ ▪ She is his *bit of stuff.* 彼女はやつのスケだ.

a bit on the side **1** 《英口》浮気[不倫](の相手) ▪ Who needs *a bit on the side*? Almost all of us, it seems. 誰が浮気の相手を必要としているのかって? 我々の大半だろうね, どうやら ▪ He's married, but always looking for *a bit on the side.* 彼は結婚しているが, いつも浮気の相手を探している.
2 副収入 ▪ I earn *a bit on the side* by distributing fliers door-to-door in the evenings. 夕方戸別にちらしを配って副収入を得ている.

a bit thick [***strong***] 《英》不公平な, 受け入れがたい ▪ We thought it *a bit thick* when he called himself a genius. 彼が自分のことを天才と呼んだとき, そいつはいただけないと我々は思った.

a good bit 《諺》大いに, (かなり)長い間 ▪ Ann is *a good bit* taller than Jane. アンはジェインよりも大分背が高い ▪ How much longer will you be?—*A good bit.* どれくらい時間がかかりますか?—かなり長いことかかりますよ.

a little bit わずかに《ときとして無意味な添え言葉》 ▪ Just *a little bit*, please. ほんの少しください.

a nice bit (***of***) 《俗》たくさんの, 十分な ▪ He has *a nice bit of* money. 彼はたんまり金を持っている.

B

be* [*get*] *a bit much 公平ではない, 手に負えない ▪ It's *a bit much* for me to solve this problem. この問題を解くのは私には手に負えない.

bit by bit 一切れずつ, 少しずつ; だんだんと ▪ Pick it up *bit by bit*. 一切れずつそれを拾いあげよ ▪ They fell back *bit by bit*. じりじりと退却した.

bits and pieces [《英》***bobs***]《口》**1** 残り物, がらくた (= ODDS and ends) ▪ He is fond of collecting *bits and pieces*. 彼は何かとつまらぬものを集めるのが好きだ.
2 切れ切れのもの ▪ I overheard *bits and pieces* of their conversation. 私は偶然彼らの会話をとぎれとぎれに聞いた.
3 小物類, 身の回り品 ▪ Jane can inherit all my *bits and bobs*. ジェインは私の小物類を全部相続することができる.

bits of 貧弱で小さい (poor little) ▪ Don't get angry at their pranks—they're just *bits of* children. あの子らのいたずらに腹を立てないでちょうだい. まだほんの子供なんだから ▪ I have a few *bits of* furniture for sale. 家具をほんの2, 3点お売りします.

by bits 一時に少しずつ ▪ It is consumed *by bits*. それは一時に少しずつ消費される.

come to bits →go to BITs.

do one's bit おのれの分をつくす (= act one's PART); 応分の寄付[奉仕]をする (*for*) ▪ In wartime everyone should *do his bit*. 戦時には人はみなおのれの分をつくすべきである ▪ I'm *doing my bit for* world peace. 私は世界平和に応分の貢献をしている.

every bit **1** すべて ▪ He ate up *every bit* of it. 彼はそれをすべて食べてしまった.
2 どの点から見ても, 全く ▪ He is *every bit* a gentleman. 彼はどこから見ても紳士である.

every bit as ... as …とちょうど同じくらい ▪ He is *every bit as* strong *as* his father. 彼は全く父親と同じほど強い ▪ Her green eyes are *every bit as* beautiful *as* her red hair. 彼女の緑色の目はその赤毛とちょうど同じくらい美しい ▪ He is *every bit as* good *as* Dickens. 彼はちょうどディケンズと同じくらいすばらしい.

Every little bit helps.《諺》いかほどの寄付でも結構.

fall to bits こわれる; こなごな[きれぎれ]になる ▪ His clothes are *falling to bits*. 彼の服はぼろぼろになっている.

give a person a bit of one's mind →give a person a piece of one's MIND.

go* [*come*] *to bits こわれる ▪ In the second half our team *went* all *to bits*. 後半でわがチームはすっかりぺしゃんこになった.

in bits《口》ばらばらに, こなごなに; 疲れ切った, ばてた ▪ Your world is *in bits* already. 君の世界はすでにずたずただ ▪ Sure, I'm *in bits*. 確かに, おれはばててしまった.

It's* [*That's*] *a bit steep!《英》それって公平じゃない[ひどいよ].

juicy bits of gossip 好奇心をそそる(ときに悪意を含む)噂話 ▪ My aunt always has such *juicy bits of gossip* about her neighbors. おばはいつも隣人についておもしろいゴシップを話してくれる.

make a bit 金をためる ▪ She *makes a bit* on the side. 彼女は内職で金をためている.

not a bit/not one* (*little*) *bit 少しも…でない[でない] ▪ I'm *not a bit* tired. ちっとも疲れていない ▪ He had*n't* changed *one little bit*. 彼は少しも変わっていなかった.

not a bit of it《英口》(予想に反して)少しも(そんなことは)ない; どういたしまして ▪ By rights she should have been exhausted, but *not a bit of it*. 当然彼女は疲れきっていたはずだが, 少しもそんなことはなかった.

not a blind bit of.../not the blindest bit of《英口》(物・事などが)少しも…しない ▪ She did*n't* take *a blind bit of* notice of what he said. 彼女は彼の言葉にちっとも注意しなかった ▪ It makes *not the blindest bit of* difference to us. それは我々には全く問題ではない.

not the least* [*slightest*] *bit =not a BIT.

pick* [*pull*, etc.] *to bits …をくそみそにやっつける, ぼろくそに非難する ▪ The critic *pulled* my latest books *to bits*. その批評家は私の最新作をこっぴどくこきおろした.

***quite a bit* (*of...*)** →QUITE.

take a lot of doing →TAKE[2].

the whole bit《英口》一切合切 (= the whole ENCHILADA) ▪ It's pretty dirty. We wash *the whole bit* out, don't we? 少々汚れている. 一切合切洗い流そうか ▪ Future plans *the whole bit*. 未来はすべてを計画する.

to bits《口》こなごなに, ばらばらに, ずたずたに ▪ He broke the glass *to bits*. 彼はコップを粉砕した.

bit[2] /bɪt/ 名 ***champ* [*chomp, chafe*] *at the bit*** ⟦主に進行形で⟧ …したくていらいらする; (思い通りにならないので)いら立つ ▪ Bob *is champing at the bit* to go out. ボブは外へ出たくていらいらしている ▪ Carol *is chomping at the bit* to get out from under the control of her guardian. キャロルは後見人の支配から逃れようといら立っている. ☞馬がはやるとき, はみをかむことから.

draw bit 手綱を引いて馬を止める; 速度をゆるめる; 控え目にする ▪ Spendthrifts never *draw bit*. 道楽者は控え目にすることを知らない.

get* [*take, have*] *the bit between one's teeth*/《米》*take the bit in one's teeth 毅然として事に当たる ▪ It took ten years for young Alfred to *get the bit between his teeth*. アルフレッド青年が毅然として事に当たるのに10年かかった ▪ We need someone to *take the bit in his teeth* and go ahead. 誰か毅然として事に当たる人が必要だ.

on the bit (馬が)急いで ▪ He was going strongly and *on the bit*. 馬は激しく急いで走っていた.

take* [*get, have*] *the bit between* [*in*] *the* [*one's*] *teeth [《米》***mouth***] **1** (馬が)はみを歯でくわえて従わない, 反抗して手に負えない; 逃げだす ▪ The horse *took the bit* fairly *in his teeth*. 馬は(はみを

くわえて)すっかり言うことをきかなくなった.
2 手に負えなくなる, あくまで我意を主張する ▪ Now he has *taken the bit between his teeth* about this girl. 今や彼はこの娘について頑固に我意を主張している.
3 (ある事を)熱意と決意をもってやり出す ▪ Once he *takes the bit between his teeth*, he won't stop. いったん熱意と決意をもってやり始めたら, 彼は絶対にやめない. ☞馬がはみ (bit) をかむと手に負えなくなることから.

to bits 《口》 非常に, とても, ひどく ▪ You've beaten me *to bits*. あなたにはこてんぱんに負かされた ▪ I was thrilled *to bits* when I first met her. 私は彼女にはじめて会ったときひどくわくわくした.

up to the bit (馬が)手綱の許すかぎり全速力を出して ▪ The four went in their collars and *up to their bits*. 4頭は用意を整えて全速力を出した.

bit[3] /bɪt/ 動 ***Bit a young man and ride him on the curb.*** 《諺》 若者を御するには手綱を締めてかかれ《抑制を忘れるな》.

bitch /bɪtʃ/ 名 ***a son of a bitch*** →SON.

(as) cold [hot] as a bitch ひどく寒い[暑い] ▪ It may be *as cold as a bitch* outside. 外はやけに寒いかもしれない.

bite[1] /baɪt/ 名 ***a bite at [of] the cherry*** 《英豪》 よい物の一部, うまい口 ▪ Many people are killing themselves to get *a bite of the cherry*. 多くの人がうまい口にありつこうとやっきになっている.

a bite to eat (急いで食べる)一口の食物 ▪ I haven't had *a bite to eat* all day. 私は一日中一口も食べていない ▪ I could only snatch *a bite to eat*. 私は急いでほんの一口食べられただけだった.

another [a second] bite at [of] the cherry 《英》 (何かをする[得る])二度目の機会 ▪ Bill failed maths but he will get *another bite at the cherry*. ビルは数学を落としたが, 再試験を受ける機会を与えられるだろう.

bite and [or] sup 簡単な食事, 食べ物 ▪ He had lain concealed without either *bite or sup*. 彼は少しも食べないで隠れていた.

grab a bite to eat 急いで軽い食事をする ▪ Let's *grab a bite to eat* while waiting for the bus. バスを待っている間急いで軽い食事をしよう.

have a bite **1** 一口食べる, 軽く食べる ▪ Won't you *have a bite*, too? あなたも一口おあがり.
2 魚が食いつく ▪ I have not *had a bite* today. きょうは魚が少しもかからない.

make [take] two bites at [of] a cherry (簡単な仕事を)わざとぐずぐずする, わざと小区切りに仕事をする ▪ There's no need to *make two bites at a cherry*; we can finish it this afternoon. わざと仕事をぐずぐずする必要はない. きょうの午後終えられるから.

put the bite on =put the ARM on 1.

put the bite on *a person* 《主に米口》 人に金を貸せと言う, 金をせびる ▪ He *put the bite on* me for $100. 彼は私に100ドル貸せと言った.

take a bite out of 《米》 (金額など)の一部を取り去る[削る] ▪ We ought to have additional cuts in order to *take a bigger bite out of* the deficit. 赤字分をもっと減らすためにはさらなる経費削減をするべきだ.

bite[2] /baɪt/ 動 ***(be) bitten with [over]*** (マニア・熱狂など)にかかって(いる), ほれこんで(いる) ▪ He *is bitten with* the angling mania. 彼は魚釣り狂になっている ▪ He got *bitten over* the girl. 彼はその娘にほれこんだ.

bite *a person's* ***head off*** →HEAD[1].

bite *one's* ***lip(s)*** →LIP.

Bite me! 《米俗》 くそったれ! ▪ Have you been jilted by Ann?—Just *bite me!* 君はアンに振られたのかい?—くそったれ!

bite *one's* ***nails*** →NAIL[1].

bite *a person's* ***nose off*** →NOSE[1].

bite off more than *one* ***can chew [manage, cope with]*** 手にあまる仕事をもくろむ ▪ In trying to swim the river he *bit off more than* he *could chew*. その川を泳ぎ渡ろうとしたのは彼が手にあまる大仕事をやろうとしたことになる. ☞かみタバコから.

bite off *one's* ***own head*** →HEAD[1].

bite on granite むだ骨を折る, 骨折り損をする ▪ Your effort may end in *biting on granite*. 君の努力は徒労に終わるかもしれない.

Bite on that! 《口》 よくそれを考えてみよ! ▪ An idle man never succeeds. *Bite on that*. 怠け者は決して成功しない. よく考えてみるがいい.

bite the big one 《米俗》 **1** 腹立たしい, 困った, がっかりだ ▪ The rent is $500 a week? That *bites the big one*. 家賃は週500ドルだって? そりゃ困ったな.
2 死ぬ ▪ She was the first celebrity to *bite the big one*. 彼女は亡くなった最初のセレブだった.

bite the dust [ground, sand] 《口》 倒れる; 倒れて死ぬ; 一敗地にまみれる, 屈辱を被る ▪ May all our enemies *bite the dust*! わが敵がみな戦死しますように ▪ The road is slippery, so be careful not to *bite the ground*. 道路がすべるから, ころばぬように注意しなさい.

bite the hand that feeds *one* 恩をあだで返す ▪ It is mean of you to *bite the hand that fed* you. 君は恩をあだで返すなんて卑劣だ.

bite ... through [asunder, in two] ...をかみ割る ▪ His wife *bit* her tongue *in two*. 彼の妻は舌をかみ切った.

bite *one's* ***thumb*** →THUMB[1].

bite *one's* ***thumb at*** →THUMB[1].

bite *one's* ***tongue off*** →TONGUE.

I'll bite. 甘んじてからかわれよう ▪ What is the sun like?—All right! *I'll bite*. 太陽とはどんなものかね—よろしい, 甘んじてからかわれよう.

Once bit [bitten], twice shy. 《諺》 一度かまれると二度目には用心深くなる,「羹(あつもの)に懲りて膾(なます)を吹く」.

What's biting *a person?* 《口》 何を悩んでいるのか ▪ *What's bitting* you [him]? 君[彼]は何を悩んでいるんだ.

won't bite (you) 《戯》 怖がらなくてもよい ▪ Come a little closer, honey, I *won't bite you*.

ねえ, もう少し近くにおいでよ, 取って食いはしないよ.

biter /báɪtər/ 名 ***Great barkers are no biters.*** 《諺》ほえる犬はかみつかない.

The biter* (*is* [*gets*]) *bit. だまそうとして逆にだまされる,「ミイラ取りがミイラになる」 ▪ For Afghanistan the Ariana hijack is just a case of *the biter bit.* アフガニスタンにとってアリアナ航空ハイジャックは, まさにかもうとした者がかまれるという事例だ.

bitter /bítər/ 形名 **(*as*) *bitter as aloes*** ひどく苦い ▪ The news is *as bitter as aloes.* そのニュースはひどく苦い.

be bitter and twisted (過去の不幸な体験で)恨みつらみを抱く ▪ I *am* still *bitter and twisted* about his sarcasm during our schooldays. 私は学生時代に彼から浴びた露骨な皮肉のことでまだ恨みつらみを抱いている.

get** one's **bitters 当然の報いを受ける; 最期をとげる ▪ The wounded soldier soon *got his bitters.* 負傷兵はまもなく最期をとげた.

take the bitter with the sweet 甘いも辛いもあわせ飲む; 幸運も不運もあわせ受ける ▪ You must be prepared to *take the bitter with the sweet.* 人は甘いも辛いもあわせ飲む覚悟でなければならない.

the sweets and bitters of life →SWEET[1].

to the bitter end とことんまで ▪ We will fight it out *to the bitter end.* 我々はとことんまで戦う. ☞「錨綱の船中にある方の端まで」が原義; 綱がそこまで繰り出すと余裕がなくなることから.

black[1] /blæk/ 形名 ***a black day*** 不吉な日 (*for*) ▪ US President's visit to Israel is "*a black day*" *for* Muslims. 米国大統領のイスラエル訪問はイスラム教徒にとっては「不吉な日」である.

a black look 怒った顔 ▪ The manager gave me *a black look* when I came late this morning. 今朝遅刻すると課長が怒った顔をした.

(*as*) *black as a crow* [*death, night, ink, the grave, ebony, coal, pitch, soot, a raven, the devil, your hat, my hat, the minister's coat, the ace of spade*]/(*as*) *black as hell* [*Hades*] 真っ黒で ▪ His skin color is *as black as night.* 彼の皮膚の色は真っ黒だ ▪ Their eyes were *as black as death.* 彼らの目は真っ黒だった.

(*as*) *black as thunder* [*a thunder cloud*] 暗い; 険悪な; 不きげんな ▪ He was looking *as black as thunder.* 彼はひどく不きげんな顔をしていた ▪ He gave me a glare *as black as a thunder cloud.* 彼は険悪な目つきで私をにらんだ.

be in black 黒い服を着ている; 喪服を着ている ▪ Mrs. Smith *is in black.* スミス夫人は喪服を着ている.

(*be*) *in the black* 《口》(商売が)黒字で(ある) (↔in the RED 2) ▪ The business *is in the black.* その商売は黒字だ ▪ I *was in the black* then. 私はその時は黒字だった ▪ The company is struggling to get back *in the black.* その会社は黒字に戻そうと苦闘している.

black in the face (怒り・激情・苦闘で)顔が赤黒く(なるほど) ▪ He pulled till he was *black in the face.* 彼は顔が赤黒くなるまで激しく引っぱった ▪ He swore himself *black in the face.* 彼は顔を赤黒くしてののしった.

Black Monday **1** 暗黒の月曜日. ☞米国株式市場で株価が大暴落した日(1987年10月19日[月曜日]).

2 大混乱が起こった月曜日 ▪ Could this be another *Black Monday*? ひょっとしてきょうも暗黒の月曜日になるのだろうか.

(*down*) *in black and white* (はっきりと)文書にして, 印刷にして ▪ I had it *down in black and white.* 私はそれをはっきりと文書にしておいた ▪ The report is *in black and white.* その報告は印刷になっている.

give** a person **a black look 険悪な顔をして人を見る ▪ The boss *gave* me *a black look* this morning. 社長は今朝険悪な顔をして僕を見た.

go black (失神して)あたりがまっ暗になる ▪ I was terrified and suddenly the room *went black.* 私はぞっとした, そして急に部屋がまっ暗になった.

into the black 《口》黒字に ▪ The World Bank climbed *into the black.* 世界銀行は黒字になった.

look black **1** (事態が)険悪である ▪ Things *look black* at present. 今のところ事態は険悪である.

2 不きげんな[怒った]顔をする (*at, on, upon*) ▪ He *looked black on* me. 彼は険悪な顔をして私を見た ▪ The chief *looks black* this morning. 社長は今朝はむっとしている.

***put the black on** a person* 《米俗》人からゆすり取る ▪ He got fifteen years for *putting the black on* the gentleman. 彼はその紳士をゆすったかどで15年の懲役をくらった.

put up a black 《口》失策[へま]をやる ▪ One day she *put up a black.* ある日彼女はしくじった.

say black is** a person's **eye* [*eyebrow, nail*]/*say black is the white of** a person's **eye 人をしかりつける, 責める《腹黒いとか, 無知だとか言って》 ▪ I can *say black's your eye* though it be gray. 僕はとにかく君をしかりつけることもできる ▪ I defy anybody to *say black is my eye.* 僕を責められるなら誰でも責めてみろ.

so* [*as*] *black as** one **is painted 〚否定文・疑問文で〛評判ほど悪い ▪ He is not *so black as* he *is painted.* 彼は評判ほど悪い人ではない. ☞悪魔を真っ黒に描くことから.

swear black is white (ある目的のために)黒を白と言う ▪ He would willingly *swear black was white* if he thought it would bring any profit to himself. 彼は自分の利益になると思ったら喜んで黒を白と言うだろう.

Two blacks don't make a white. = Two WRONGs don't make a right.

black[2] /blæk/ 動 ***black** a person's **eye*** 《口》殴って目を青黒くする ▪ Smith *blacked Bill's eye* for him. スミスはビルの目を殴って青黒くしてやった.

blackboard /blǽkbɔ̀ːrd/ 名 ***the blackboard jungle*** 校内暴力 ▪ *The blackboard jungle* is teachers' ordeal. 校内暴力は教師の厳しい試練である. ☞米国の作家 Evan Hunter, *The Blackboard Jungle* (1954) より.

black dog /blǽkdɔ́ːg|-dɔ́g/ 名 ***A black dog has walked over*** *one*. 人の上を踏んで歩く ▪ *A black dog has walked over* him. 彼は意気消沈している.

get the black dog on *one's* ***back*** 《口》 不きげん[憂鬱]になる ▪ He has *got the black dog on his back* again. 彼はまた不きげんになった.

The black dog is on *one's* ***back.*** 《口》 不きげんである, ふさいでいる ▪ *The black dog was on his back*, as people say in nursery metaphor. 子供のたとえで世俗に言うように, 彼は不きげんであった.

under the black dog 《口》 不きげんで, 憂鬱で ▪ Mom was *under the black dog* again. ママはまた不きげんだった.

blacken /blǽkən/ 動 ***blacken*** *a person's* ***name*** [***image, reputation***] …に汚名を着せる [イメージを落とす, 評判を汚す] ▪ It is a plot to *blacken the name of* the Catholic Church. それはカトリック教会の名を汚そうとする陰謀だ ▪ Pervasive corruption has *blackened the image of* the nation. 汚職が広まって国家のイメージが失墜した ▪ The effort to *blacken his reputation* has begun. 彼の名声を傷つけようとする取り組みが始まった.

blacklist /blǽklìst/ 名 ***be on the blacklist***/ ***be put in the blacklist*** 要注意人物表[ブラックリスト]に載っている ▪ He found he *was on the blacklist*. 気づくと彼はブラックリストに載っていた ▪ That's where I *was put in the blacklist*. 私がブラックリストに載せられたのはそこです.

blackmail /blǽkmèɪl/ 名 ***levy blackmail*** (***on***) (…に対して)ゆすりを働く ▪ The villain *levied blackmail on* me for 10 years. その悪漢は私に対して10年間ゆすりを働いた.

blade /bleɪd/ 名 ***in the blade*** (穂になっていない)葉のうちに; 若いうちに ▪ His corn was *in the blade*. 彼の小麦は穂になっていなかった ▪ I had been betrothed while life was yet *in* bud and *blade*. 私はまだ若いつぼみのころ婚約していた.

blah /blɑː/ 名 ***blah, blah, blah*** だらだらと続くむだぐち, …とか何とか ▪ She went on complaining about her mistress—*blah, blah, blah*. 彼女は女主人のことで不満たらたらで—べちゃくちゃ, べちゃくちゃ.

blame[1] /bleɪm/ 名 ***be small blame to*** *a person* (***that***) …は人の責任ではない ▪ It *is small blame to* you *that* the meeting was not successful. 会が盛会でなかったのは君の責任ではない.

bear the blame 責めを負う, とがめを受ける ▪ He *bore the blame* of my mistake. 彼は私のあやまちの責めを負ってくれた.

get the blame 非難される (*for*) ▪ The oldest child *gets the blame for* anything and everything. 一番年上の子供は何でもかんでも非難される.

in blame of …を非難して ▪ Much is said *in blame of* him. 彼はいろいろと非難されている.

incur blame for …のために非難を招く ▪ I *incurred* great *blame for* it. 私はそのため大きな非難を招いた.

lay the blame at the door of 罪[責任]を(人)のせいにする ▪ At all times I *laid the blame at the door of* the Labour Party, the establishment. いつも責任を労働党, つまり体制側のせいにした.

lay [***fasten, put***] ***the blame on*** …に罪を着せる ▪ Don't *lay the blame* of the quarrel *on* me. けんかの罪を私に着せないでください.

shift the blame on to …に責任を転嫁する ▪ He *shifted the blame on to* the press. 彼は責任を新聞に転嫁した.

shoulder the blame for …の全責任を負う ▪ Who should *shoulder the blame for* the death of the minister? 大臣の死に対して誰が全責任を負うべきか.

take the blame (***on*** *oneself*) ***for*** …に対するとがめを受ける, 責めを負う ▪ He *took the blame for* the mistake. 彼はその誤りの責めを負った.

blame[2] /bleɪm/ 動 ***Bad workmen blame their tools.*** 《諺》へたな職人は道具に難くせをつける,「へたの道具調べ」.

be to blame for …の責めを負うべきである; は(主語)の罪である ▪ It is you that *are to blame for* it. そのことで悪いのは君だ ▪ Who *is to blame for* the accident? その事故は誰の罪か.

blame *a person* ***for*** …のため人を責める ▪ He *blamed* the teacher *for* his failure. 彼は自分が失敗したのを先生のせいにした.

Blame it! 《米俗》くそいまいましい.

blame me [***I'm blamed***] ***if I*** *do* [*don't*] …する[しないでおく]ものか ▪ *I'm blamed if I*'ll lend you more money. お前にもっと金を貸すなんてめっそうもない.

don't blame me 《口》私を責めないでほしい ▪ *Don't blame me* if we lose. もし負けても私を責めないでくれ.

I don't blame you [***her, him***] 君[彼女, 彼]が…したのも無理はない (*for doing*) ▪ He may fire you, but *I don't blame him for doing* that. 彼は君を首にするかもしれない, でもそうするのも無理もないよ.

I have only myself to blame. (誰の罪でもない)私自身が悪いのだ ▪ *I have only myself to blame* for the breakdown of my marriage. 結婚がうまく行かなかったことについては私自身が悪いのだ.

blank[1] /blæŋk/ 名形 ***a round of blank***(***s***) 空砲一発 ▪ They fired 20 *rounds of blanks*. 彼らは空砲を20発打った.

blankety blank くそいまいましい ▪ The *blankety blank* train has never been on time. くそいまいましい列車は定刻に来たためしがない.

draw a blank **1** (「空くじを引く」から)(欲しい)情報が得られない ▪ I did a search on the Web for information about an old book, but I *drew a*

B

blank. ウェブである古書の情報を捜したが，答えは得られなかった.

2《主に米》答えられない，思い出せない (*on*) ▪ He asked me her phone number and I *drew a blank*. 彼女の電話番号を聞かれたが，答えられなかった ▪ He looks familiar but I've *drawn a blank on* his name. 彼の顔は見覚えがあるが，名前が出てこない.

3（競技で）1点も取れない，1回も勝てない ▪ Arsenal *drew a blank* for the first time this season. アーセナルは今シーズン初めて1回も勝てなかった.

4《口》（求めていたものが）見つからない; 失敗する ▪ Abbas became gloomy as peace talks *drew a blank*. アッバスは和平会談が失敗したとき憂鬱になった.

fill in the blanks あとは推測する，そこから結論を出す ▪ All I need is a template so I can *fill in the blanks*. テンプレートさえあれば，あとは推測できます.

fire blanks **1**《英》空砲を撃つ;（懸命に努力したにもかかわらず）達成できない ▪ Our team did its best, but all we did was to *fire blanks*. 我がチームは最善を尽くしたが，にもかかわらず無得点に終わった.

2［主に進行形で］空砲を放つ《男が精子がないため性交しても妊娠しない》 ▪ Fertility tests showed that Tom *was firing blanks*. 生殖力検査の結果，トムは空鉄砲を放っていたことがわかった.

give** a person **a blank check 人に金額の書いていない小切手を渡す; 人に無制限の権能を与える，（金・権力などを）勝手に使わせる ▪ The architect *was given a blank check* to build and furnish the house. その建築家はその家を建ててそれに家具を備えつける無制限の権能を与えられていた.

go blank（テレビ画面・人の頭が）真っ白になる ▪ The screen suddenly *went blank*. 画面が突然に真っ白になった ▪ My brain *went blank* and I drove my car over a curb. 頭が真っ白になって歩道の縁に車を乗り上げてしまった.

in blank（証書などで）署名・記入などする個所を残した，白地式の[で] ▪ Policies were made *in blank*. 保険証券が無記名で作られた.

look blank ぽかんとしている ▪ Upon this I *looked blank*. これを聞いて私はぽかんとした.

shoot blanks **1** = fire BLANKs 2.

2《口》つまらない話をする ▪ Susan is always *shooting blanks*. スーザンはいつもつまらない話ばかりしている.

stand within the blank of ...の的になる ▪ I *stood within the blank of* his displeasure for my free speech. あまり無遠慮に言ったので彼の不きげんの的になった.

blank[2] /blæŋk/ 動 ***Blank him*** [***it***]***!*** くそいまいましい! ▪ *Blank him!* That is just like him. くそいまいましい! あいつのやりそうなことだ. ☞blank《俗》= damn.

blanket /blǽŋkət/ 名 ***on the right side of the blanket*** 嫡子で ▪ He has a child *on the right side of the blanket*. 彼には嫡子が一人いる.

on the wrong side of the blanket 庶子で，私生児で ▪ I came [was born] *on the wrong side of the blanket*. 私は庶子だ.

split the blanket《米口・戯》（夫婦が）別れる ▪ They soon *split the blanket*. 彼らはやがて夫婦別れをした.

stretch the [*one's*] ***blanket***《米口》誇張する ▪ When he gets to talking, he'll *stretch his blanket*. 彼が話をしだすと大げさになる.

wear the blanket《米口》半未開の原住民である ▪ Your father *wore the blanket*. お前のおやじは野蛮人だったのだ《人を悪罵する文句》. ☞原住民が毛布のような衣服を着ていたことから.

blast[1] /blæst|blɑːst/ 名 ***a blast from the past*** 昔のことを突然思い出させるもの ▪ The other day I met Chris after a long separation. —Oh Chris! That name is *a* real *blast from the past*! 先日久しぶりにクリスと会ったよ—ああクリス! その名前で突然昔のことを思い出した! ☞アメリカの DJ が古いレコードを掛けるときに使った表現.

at a blast 一吹きで，一気に ▪ According to the book of Joshua, *at a blast* from the ram's horns the walls of Jericho fell flat. ヨシュア記によれば，雄ヒツジの角笛を一吹きするとエリコの城壁が崩れ落ちたという ▪ The furnace melts so many tons of iron *at a blast*. その炉は一気に何トンもの鉄を溶かす.

(***at*** [***in***]) ***full blast***（衝風炉が）盛んに吹いて; 全力をあげて; 声を限りに ▪ That factory is running *full blast*. その工場は全力をあげて運転している ▪ The speeches at Hyde Park on Saturday were *in full blast*. 土曜日のハイドパークにおける演説はたけなわであった ▪ The neighbors had their televisions on *at full blast*. 隣人たちはテレビの音を最大限にしていた.

have a blast 楽しい大パーティーを催す，楽しいひとときを過ごす ▪ It was such a wonderful party and we all *had a blast*! とても素晴らしいパーティーで，みんな楽しいひとときを過ごした.

in blast（炉・人が）活動して ▪ At present four furnaces are *in blast*. 現在4つの炉が活動している.

out of blast 活動を休んで，やめて ▪ The furnaces are *out of blast*. その炉は休んでいる.

put [***lay***] ***the blast on***《米俗》...をこっぴどく批評する; をげんこつでなぐる ▪ He *put the blast on* the Democrats. 彼は民主党をひどく批評した ▪ I *put* a big *blast on* the guy. その男をげんこつでぶんなぐった.

take a blast 酔っ払う ▪ Mat *took a blast* from drinking too much wine last night. マットはゆうべワインを飲み過ぎて酔っ払った.

blast[2] /blæst|blɑːst/ 動 ***Blast it*** [***him,*** etc.]***!***《俗》こんちくしょう! ▪ Oh, *blast it!* I've forgotten my keys. ちくしょう! 鍵を忘れてきた ▪ He's always late, *blast him!* 彼はいつも遅刻する. あの野郎め!

blast my reputation if... 名誉にかけて...しない ▪ *Blast my reputation if* I had received such a letter. そんな手紙をもらったことは全然ない.

blaze[1] /bleɪz/ 名 ***burst into a blaze*** ぱっと燃え上がる ▪ The fire soon *burst into a blaze*. 火の手がまもなくぱっと燃え上がった.

go out in a blaze of glory（仕事などが）大成功に終わる，華々しく幕を閉じる ▪ The Senator *went* *out in a blaze of glory* at the age of seventy. 上院議員は70歳のときに引退の花道を飾った.

go to blazes **1**《口》〚命令文で〛こんちくしょう, くたばってしまえ《強い拒絶・放逐の言葉》 ▪ Will you lend me £20?—Certainly not. *Go to blazes*! 20ポンド貸してくれないか—貸すものか. くそくらえ!

2 急いで去る, 急に消える ▪ So much money *is gone to blazes*. 非常にたくさんの金が急に消えてしまった. ☞blazes = hell.

How* [*What, Who*] *the blazes ...? 一体どうして[何が, 誰が]...? ▪ *How the blazes* did you do it? 一体どんなにしてそれをしたのか ▪ *What the blazes* is there? 一体何があるのか.

in a blaze 烈火のようになって, ぱっと燃え上がって ▪ *In a blaze* of anger he struck me on the head. 烈火のように怒って彼は私の頭をなぐった ▪ The whole room was *in a blaze*. 部屋全体が火炎に包まれた.

like blazes 《口》猛烈に, すごく速く ▪ It was raining [snowing] *like blazes*. 猛烈に雨[雪]が降っていた ▪ Bill ran *like blazes*. ビルは風を巻いて疾走した.

like* (*blue*) *blazes 《米》猛烈に, すごく速く ▪ The rosemary was growing *like blue blazes*! ローズマリーはものすごく早く成長していた.

blaze[2] /bleɪz/ 動 ***blaze a* [*the, one's*] *way* [*path, trail*]** 《主に米》樹皮に目印をつけて森の中の道を示す; 先達となる, 新天地を開拓する ▪ The trappers *blazed their trail* through the forest. わな猟師は森の木に刻みをつけて道しるべとして行った ▪ Professor Bread has *blazed the way* for future explorers in the wilderness of philosophy. ブレッド教授は哲学の荒野での未来の探検家のために道を切り開いた. ☞blaze「切って刻み目をつける」.

***blaze about* [*abroad, forth*]** ...を触れ回る, 言い触らす ▪ He went out to *blaze* the matter *abroad*. 彼は出て行ってそのことを触れ回った.

blaze upon the world 有名になる ▪ His fame *blazed* suddenly *upon the world*. 彼の名声は急にあがった.

blazer /bléɪzər/ 名 ***run a blazer* (*on*)** 《米俗》(...を)だます ▪ They *ran a blazer on* us. 彼らは我々をだました.

bleak /bli:k/ 形 ***look bleak*** 見通しが暗い ▪ Prices dropped lower and lower, and things *looked bleak* for the company. 物価が次第に下がってきて, 会社は見通しが暗くなった.

bleed /bli:d/ 動 ***bleed to death*** 出血多量で死ぬ; (借金がかさんで)破産する ▪ If we don't get fresh orders soon, we shall *bleed to death*. 今すぐ新しい注文がこなければ, わが社は破産する.

bleed well 《方》(穀物が)収穫が多い, よくできる ▪ The corn is *bleeding well*. 小麦はよくできている.

***bleed white* [*dry*]** **1** 血の気がなくなるまで出血する; (金などを)とことんまで絞り取られる ▪ If he were cut, he would *bleed white*. もし彼が切られたなら, 血の気がなくなるまで出血するだろう.

2 (人から)とことんまで(金などを)絞り取る ▪ The money lenders absolutely *bled* him *white*. 金貸しは彼からとことんまで絞り取った.

bleeding heart 大げさに同情を示す人 ▪ A lot of *bleeding-hearts* got the idea they knew about everything. 多くの大げさに同情を示す人たちは, 自分たちは何でも知っていると思い込んだ.

make** a person's **heart bleed 《雅》いたく人のあわれみの情をそそる ▪ The sight of the children *made my heart bleed*. その子らの姿はいたく私のあわれみをそそった.

bless /bles/ 動 ***a blessed event*** おめでた《出産》 ▪ When is the *blessed event* (expected)? いつおめでたですか?

be blessed* [*blest*] *with **1** ...に恵まれている (↔ be CURSEd with) ▪ I *am blessed with* children. 私は子宝に恵まれている ▪ I hope you will always *be blessed with* good health. 私はあなたがいつも健康に恵まれますよう祈ります.

2 《反語》(厄介なもの)を持つ (= be CURSEd with) ▪ I *am blessed with* a bad memory. 私は物覚えが悪くて困る.

***bless** oneself* **1** (十字を切って)驚き・くやしさの "God bless me!" を言う ▪ How he did *bless himself*! 彼が驚いてどんなに十字を切ったことか.

2 ...を喜ぶ, 祝う (*with, in*) ▪ Old men have *blessed themselves with* this mistake. 老人たちはこのまちがいをありがたいと喜んだ ▪ The nations will *bless themselves in* him. 諸国が彼を祝うだろう.

***Bless** a person's **heart* (*alive*)!** 《口》おやまあ; 本当に《驚き・喜び・同情・感謝などを表す句》 ▪ *Bless his* old *heart*, to be sure. まあ, ほんとにね ▪ I've made you a new sweater.—*Bless your heart!* 新しいセーターを作ってあげたよ—まあ, ありがとう. ☞前に God が略されたもの.

bless** his* [*her*] ***little cotton socks 《英戯》ああ, かわいい子だ ▪ Kate, *bless her little cotton socks*, wrapped me up in a warm blanket. ケイトは, ああ, かわいい子だ, 暖かい毛布で私をくるんでくれた.

Bless me* [*you*, etc.]*!/Bless my* [*your*, etc.] *soul! (驚き・喜び・困惑などを表して)おやまあ!; ありがたや!; やあ大変! ▪ *Bless me!* I am glad to see you. おやまあ, よくおいででした ▪ "*Bless my soul!*" said John when he opened the door. 「やあ大変」とジョンは戸を開けて言った.

bless** one's **stars →thank one's (lucky) STARs.

God bless! (別れるとき)お元気で, お大事に ▪ Good night, *God bless*. おやすみ. お大事に.

(*God*) *bless you!* **1** あなたに神の加護がありますように; どうもありがとう; おやまあ!, まあかわいそうに! (など) ▪ *God bless you*, sir. I can get something to eat with this. ありがとうございます. これで何か食べるものが買えます ▪ He started sneezing violently. "*God bless you!*" she said. 彼ははげしくくしゃみをしだした. 「お大事に!」と彼女は言った.

2 (お礼・愛情を表して)どうもありがとう, かわいそうに ▪ *Bless you*, my dear. It's most kind of you to come. どうもありがとう. 来てくれてかたじけない.

B

I bless the day …したのはなんという吉日であったろう ▪ *I bless the day* I met him. 彼に会ったのはなんという吉日であったろう.

I'm [I'll be] blessed [blest] if I *do.* 私は絶対…しない ▪ *I'm blessed if I* know. 僕は絶対に知らない ▪ *I'll be blessed if* I can find it. それは絶対に見つかるまい.

to bless *oneself* ***with*** 手のひらで十字を切るための《今はたいした意味はない》 ▪ The lady hasn't got a penny *to bless herself with.* その婦人はびた一文も持っていない. ☞昔, 貨幣特に銀貨で幸運を祈って手のひらに十字を切った習慣から.

Well, I'm blessed [blest]! まあ驚いた! ▪ *Well, I'm blest!* I never expected to see you here. おや驚いた! ここで君に会おうとは思わなかった.

blessing /blésɪŋ/ 名 ***a mixed blessing*** 喜びと同時に深刻な迷惑ももたらすもの, ありがた迷惑, 痛しかゆし ▪ Moving into a new place is always *a mixed blessing.* 新しい場所へ移住するのはいつも痛しかゆしの面がある ▪ To me marriage seems to be *a mixed blessing.* 私には結婚はめでたくもあり, めでたくもなしといったもののように思われる.

ask a [the] blessing 食前(食後)の祈りをする ▪ At breakfast he never *asked a blessing* sitting. 朝食のとき彼は腰かけて食前の祈りをしたことはない.

be [turn out to be] a blessing in disguise 姿を変えた幸福である[となる], 不幸に見えても実は幸である[となる] ▪ This great calamity *was* in truth only *a blessing in disguise.* この大災害は不幸に見えたが実は幸にほかならなかった.

count *one's* ***blessings*** (不幸な時に)数々の幸せを思いだす ▪ When you feel sad, *count your blessings.* 悲しい時にはあなたの数々の幸せを思い出しなさい.

get *a person's* ***blessing*** (…に対する)人の承認[賛成, 奨励]を得る (*for*) ▪ She broke the glass. She wouldn't *get her mother's blessing for* that. 彼女はグラスを割った. そのことで母に許してもらえないだろう.

give [get] a blessing (out) 《米》しかりつける[ひどくしかられる] ▪ I'll *give* her *a* real *blessing out.* 彼女をひどくしかりつけてやる ▪ I made a mistake and I *got a blessing* from the teacher. 私は間違いをしたので, 先生にひどくしかられた.

give *one's* ***blessing*** (…を)承認[賛成, 奨励]する ▪ The government has *given its blessing* to the new plan. 政府はその新計画を正式に承認した.

invoke a blessing upon *a person* 人に恵みを授けたまえと祈る ▪ He *invoked a blessing upon* his son. 息子に恵みを授けたまえと祈った.

blight /blaɪt/ 名 ***a blight on the land*** 周囲の美観を損なうもの ▪ This crumbling building is *a blight on the land.* この崩れかけている建物は土地の美観を損なっている.

cast [put] a blight on [upon] …に暗い影を投げかける, (人の希望など)をくじく ▪ Mother's early death *cast a blight upon* my future days. 母の夭折は私の将来の日々に暗い影を投げかけた.

blind[1] /blaɪnd/ 形副名 ***a blind leader of the blind*** ＝the BLIND leading the blind.

apply [have] the blind eye 自分に都合の悪い物は見えないふりをする, わざと無視する (*to*) ▪ He thinks it wise to *apply the blind eye.* 彼は知らないふりをするのが賢明だと思っている.

(as) blind as a bat [brickbat] 盲目同然で; 先の見えない, 先を見る目がない ▪ The old scholar is *as blind as a brickbat.* その老学者は盲目同然である ▪ In judgment of character, he's *as blind as a bat.* 人物の判断では彼は全く見る目がない.

(as) blind as a beetle [a buzzard, a mole, an owl] ひどく目が見えないで ▪ Love is *blind as a beetle.* 恋は盲目である.

blind drunk ひどく酔って ▪ The man was *blind drunk.* その男はひどく酔っていた.

blind in one eye **1** →BLIND of an eye.
2《口》知恵が足りない ▪ He is *blind in one eye.* 彼は知恵が足りない.

blind of [in] an eye 一方の目が見えない ▪ He is *blind of an eye.* 彼は一方の目が見えない.

blind to …がわからない, を見る目がない ▪ He is *blind to* his own interests. 彼は自分の利害が見えない.

blind to the world 《口》ひどく酔って ▪ She was often *blind to the world.* 彼女はよく泥酔した.

come [get] on *a person's* ***blind side*** 人のほろりと参る急所を突く; 人の弱点をとらえる ▪ You *came on his blind side.* 君は彼のほろりと参る急所をうまく突いた《何かをせしめるため》 ▪ Mary can always *get on the blind side of* her grandfather. メアリーはいつもおじいさんの泣きどころをとらえることができる.

fly blind **1** 飛行機を全く計器だけに頼って飛ばす ▪ He *flew blind* in the heavy fog. 彼は濃霧の中で計器だけに頼って飛ばした.
2《口》やみくもにやる ▪ He was *flying blind* when he fixed the car. 彼は車の修繕をやみくもにやっていた.

go (at) it blind 事情を調べずにやる, 当て推量する ▪ He knew nothing about investment; he just *went at it blind.* 彼は投資については何も知らなかった. ただあてずっぽうに投資した.

go blind (ポーカーで)手の内を見ずに賭ける ▪ Mike *went* 20 pounds *blind.* マイクは手の内を見ずに20ポンド賭けた.

go blind on …をやみくもにやる ▪ Shall we be wise to *go blind on* dreadnaughts alone? 我々は弩(ど)級戦艦だけをやみくもにやっつけるのが賢明だろうか.

have the blind eye →apply the BLIND eye.

In the country of the blind, the one-eyed man is King. 《諺》盲人の国では隻眼の人が王様だ,「鳥なき里のコウモリ」.

none so blind これほど説得しがたいものはない ▪ I've told her a dozen times but there's *none so blind.* 私は彼女に何度も何度も言ったが, 全然聞こうとしない.

not make a blind bit of difference まるで関係がない ▪ The fact you are from Pakistan should *not make a blind bit of difference* when you get here. 君がここへ来れば君がパキスタン出身だという事実はまるで関係がないはずだよ.

not take a blind bit of notice 《英口》全く注目しない ▪ We did*n't take a blind bit of notice* of their objections. 我々は彼らの反対にまるで注目しなかった.

***on the blind side* (*of*)** (…の)油断しているところを, もろいところを ▪ The devil often takes saints *on their blind side.* 悪魔はしばしば聖徒たちの油断しているところをつく ▪ They approached the forts *on the blind side.* 彼らは要塞の盲点を攻めた.

***steal* [*rob*] *a person* blind** 《口》 **1** 人を無慈悲にだます, 人から大金をだまし取る ▪ I believe that children will *steal* their parents *blind.* 子供は両親を無慈悲にだますものだと私は信じている ▪ He *robbed* his aunt *blind* for years. 彼は何年もの間おばから大金をだまし取った.
2 人から身ぐるみ剥ぎ取る, すっかり巻き上げる ▪ He *was stolen blind* by a gang of thieves. 彼は窃盗団に身ぐるみ剥ぎ取られた.

the blind leading the blind 盲人を道案内する盲人《危険至極》(《聖》*Matt.* 15. 14; *Luke* 6. 39) ▪ He sets up to be a critic of the English drama: *the blind lead the blind.* 彼はイギリス劇の批評家を気取っている. 盲人を道案内する盲人とはこのことだ.

There's none so blind as those who won't see. 《諺》見ようとしない者ほど目の見えない者はいない.

***turn a blind eye* (*to*)** (見たくないものを)見ないふりする; (を)見のがしてやる ▪ She *turned a blind eye to* her son's smoking. 彼女は息子の喫煙は見ぬふりした ▪ He had stolen the money, but I *turned a blind eye.* 彼がその金を盗んだが私は見のがしてやった.

with blind staggers 《俗》(病気・酒のため)よろめき歩いて ▪ There's old Peter, going home *with blind staggers.* それ老ピーターがよろめきながら家へ帰っていくぞ.

blind[2] /blaɪnd/ 動 ***blind** oneself **to*** …を見ないふりする, に目をつぶる ▪ Wolsey could not *blind himself to* the true condition of the church. ウルジーは教会の実状に目をつぶることはできなかった.

blind a person with science 専門語を並べたてて人を煙(けむ)にまく ▪ Don't try to *blind* me *with science.* 専門語を並べたてて僕を煙にまかないでくれ.

blinder /bláɪndər/ 名 ***play a blinder*** 《英口》(特にスポーツで)素晴らしい技を見せる, ファインプレーをする ▪ Mat *plays a blinder* in every game. マットはどのゲームでもファインプレーをしてみせる.

blindfolded /bláɪndfòʊldəd/ 形 ***can do blindfolded*** (たびたびしているので)…を容易にしてのけられる (→with one HAND (tied) behind one's back 2) ▪ Max *could* sail a yacht *blindfolded.* マックスは楽々とボートの操縦ができた.

blindman /bláɪndmæn/ 名 ***a blindman's holiday*** 仕事をするには暗く灯をともすには早すぎる頃, たそがれ時 ▪ We will have *a blindman's holiday* until half past four. 4時半まではたそがれ時であろう.

blink[1] /blɪŋk/ 名 ***in the blink of an eye*** 瞬く間に, 瞬時に ▪ The thief disappeared *in the blink of an eye.* 泥棒は瞬時に姿を消した.

like* [*in*] *a blink 《口》たちまち, すぐに ▪ The wine was brought *in a blink.* 酒はすぐに出された.

on the blink 《口》(人が)調子がよくない; (店などが)左前で, つぶれそうで, (機械などが)狂って, 故障して ▪ This café looks *on the blink.* このカフェは左前のようだ ▪ This copier was totally *on the blink.* このコピー機は全く故障していた.

blink[2] /blɪŋk/ 動 ***before you can blink* (*an eyelid*)** 瞬く間に ▪ I'll be back *before you can blink.* 瞬く間に帰ってくるよ ▪ He has spent a 100 pounds *before you could blink an eyelid.* 彼は瞬く間に100ポンド使ってしまった.

blink away* [*back*] (*one's*) *tears まばたいて涙を押さえる ▪ He smiled and *blinked away his tears.* 彼はほほえみ, まばたいて涙を押さえた.

blink the fact 〖主に否定文で〗事実を見て見ぬふりする ▪ It's no use trying to *blink the fact.* その事実を見ぬふりしようとしてもだめだ.

blinker /blíŋkər/ 名 ***be in blinkers*** (馬が)目隠し皮をしている[走る]; 一方しか見ていない ▪ He *is in blinkers*, but it is about time he began to look about. 彼は一方しか見ていないが, そろそろ周囲を見始めてもいいころだ.

without blinkers 偏見なしに ▪ We are now having a fresh look, *without blinkers*, at ourselves and our country. 我々はいま偏見なしに自らと自らの国を改めて見ているのだ.

blob /blɑb|blɔb/ 名 ***make a blob*** 《口》間違いをする ▪ I was treated as if I'd *made* a string of *blobs.* 私は連続でしくじったかのように取り扱われた.

on the blob 《俗》口頭で ▪ They beg *on the blob.* 彼らは口頭でものを請う.

block[1] /blɑk|blɔk/ 名 ***a chip of* [*off*] *the old block*** →CHIP.

a chip of the same block →CHIP.

(*as*) *deaf as a block* →(as) DEAF as an adder.

be* [*come, get*] *off* [*out of*] *the* (*starting*) *blocks 《報道》スタートを切る ▪ The election campaign *is* now truly *off the starting blocks.* 選挙のキャンペーンはいまや確かにスタートを切っている ▪ The Liberal Democrats *were* first *off the blocks* with their manifesto. 自由民主党はいち早くマニフェストに取りかかった.

cut blocks with a razor (かみそりで丸太を切るように)荒仕事に利器を使う, もったいないことをする; 英才をむだに用いる ▪ That is *cutting blocks with a razor.* それは英才をむだに使うというものだ.

go on the block 《米》競売に付される ▪ The painting *went on the block* and sold for fifty thousand dollars. その絵は競売に付されて5万ドルで売られた.

***have been around the block* (*a few* [*couple of*] *times*)** 《米口》人生経験が豊かである, ある分野の知識がある ▪ Mack *has been around the* *block*, and then some. マックは人生経験が豊かだ，しかもたっぷりある．

in block 一まとめにして，全体として (en bloc) ▪ Puritans rejected *in block* the authority of creeds. 清教徒は信条の権威を全体的に拒否した．

knock** a person's **block off 《俗》(おどして)頭をぶんなぐる ▪ I'll *knock your block off* if I catch you stealing again. また盗みをしていたら頭をぶんなぐるぞ． ☞block＝head.

lay [***put***] *one's* ***head*** [***neck***] ***on the block*** (失敗すれば評判を落とすような)危険を冒す，首を賭けて誓う ▪ The day before the election I *put my head on the block* and made a few predictions. 選挙前に自分の首を賭けて，2, 3の予測をした． ☞block「断頭台」.

off** one's **block 《俗》怒って; 気が変になって (insane) (＝ off one's HEAD) ▪ The poor bloke nearly went right *off his block*. 哀れな男はほとんど正気を失いかけた．

on the block **1** 売り[競売]に出て ▪ The vacant house was *on the block*. その空き家は売りに出ていた．

2 《米》(牛が)畜殺されて，処理されて (↔ on the HOOF 1) ▪ We use the best beef *on the block*. 私どもは畜殺された最上の牛肉を使用しています．

on the [*one's*] (***starting***) ***blocks*** スタート台について，行動の用意を整えて ▪ Digital TV remains *on the starting blocks*. デジタルテレビはまだスタート台についたばかりだ．

put the blocks on …の前進を妨げる ▪ Leeds skipper vowed to *put the blocks on* super striker Henry. リーズの主将はすごいストライカーのアンリを完全に抑えると誓った．

to the block 競売に ▪ The article came *to the block*. その品は競売に出された．

block[2] /blɑk|blɔk/ 動 ***block** a person's **game*** 《米》人の計画を妨げる ▪ *Their* little *game was blocked*. 彼らのけちな計略は妨げられた．

blockade /blɑkéɪd|blɔk-/ 名 ***break*** [***lift, raise***] ***a blockade*** 封鎖を破る[解く] ▪ He *raised the blockade* of La Puebla. 彼はラ・プエブラの封鎖を解いた．

run the blockade 封鎖をくぐって出入する《特に物資を運んだり商売するため》 ▪ They afterwards became engaged in *running the blockade*. 彼らはそののち封鎖くぐりをやりだした．

blood /blʌd/ 名 ***a sporting blood*** 冒険心 ▪ When he heard about the wild boar hunt being planned, his *sporting blood* was stirred. イノシシ狩りが計画されているという話を聞いたとき，彼の冒険心が騒いだ ▪ His *sporting blood* didn't let him stay away from the races. 彼の冒険心がレースから遠ざかることを許さなかった．

after** a person's **blood/***out for*** (*a person's*) ***blood*** 《口》仕返しを狙って，危害を加えようとして ▪ The gangsters are *after your blood* now they know it was you who told the police. 警察に密告したのが君だと知って，暴力団がお礼参りをしようとしている ▪ If I found this was happening to her, I'd literally be *out for his blood*. もしもこんなことが彼女に起こっているのがわかったなら，僕は文字通り彼に危害を加えようとするだろう．

bay for (*a person's*) ***blood***/ ***bay for the blood of** a person* 《英》人の処罰を求める ▪ The tabloids have *bayed for the blood of* the killer. タブロイド紙はその殺人犯に対して厳罰を求めている ▪ There's a killer stalking the city and the local media are *baying for blood*. 殺人者がその街を歩き回っているので，土地のメディアは処罰を求めている．

blood and guts 《口》(映画・テレビなどの)暴力[流血]場面 ▪ Young people tend to enjoy movies that are full of *blood and guts*. 若い人は暴力シーンだらけの映画を楽しむ傾向がある．

blood and iron 鉄血《外交に対する武力》 ▪ During World War I Bismarck was branded as the man of "*blood and iron*". 第一次世界大戦中，ビスマルクは鉄血宰相という呼び名をつけられた ▪ It could only be settled by *blood and iron*. それは鉄血によってのみ解決されるであろう． ☞Ⓖ Blut und Eisen のなぞり．

blood and iron policy 鉄血政策，武力政策 ▪ There, nothing succeeds like a *blood-and-iron policy*. そこでは鉄血政策ほど有力なものはない．

blood and soil 血と土地《ナチスの人種主義的な農業政策・植民政策のスローガン》 ▪ *Blood and Soil* was an anti-Semitism slogan. 血と土地は反ユダヤ主義のスローガンだった． ☞Ⓖ Blut und Boden のなぞり．

one's ***blood be upon the head*** [***hands***] ***of** a person* …が死んだら人にたたるぞ; …の死は人の罪だぞ (《聖》 *Josh*. 2. 19, etc.) ▪ *My blood*, if I fall, *be on your head*! 僕が死んだら君にたたるぞ．

One's ***blood boils.*** 血が沸き立つ，憤激する ▪ *My blood boils* high. 憤激の血がひどく沸き立つ ▪ *My blood boiled* instantly at the picture. その絵を見たとたん，私のはらわたが煮えくり返った．

one's ***blood curdles*** [***runs cold***] ひどくおびえる ▪ *His blood ran cold* at the ghost. 彼はその幽霊を見てひどくおびえた．

One's ***blood freezes.*** 血も凍るほど驚く ▪ *His blood froze* when he was accused of libel. 彼は名誉毀損で訴えられたとき血も凍るほど驚いた．

A's ***blood is on*** *B's* ***hands*** [***head***] Aの死または不幸はBに責任がある ▪ *His blood is* entirely *on his father's hands*. 彼の死は全く父親の責任である．

blood is shed [***spilled***] **1** 《雅》殺人が起こる ▪ The Lord hates hands that *shed* innocent *blood*. 主は無罪の人の血を流す手を憎みたまう．

2 (変化の結果)事態が悪化する ▪ We must work something out before too much political *blood is shed*. 政策があまりにも悪化する前に何らかの道を見いださなければならない．

Blood is thicker than water. 《諺》血は水よりも濃い《ゆえに親族は優遇すべきである》．

one's ***blood is up*** 《英》頭に血がのぼる; 激昂[興奮]している ▪ He can be very violent when *his blood is up*. 頭に血がのぼったときには彼は荒れ狂うことがある ▪ It was Scott's style when *his blood was up*. それはスコットが興奮しているときの文体だった.

Blood must atone for blood. 《諺》血は血で償うべし《人を殺せば, 死んで罪ほろぼしをすべきだ》.

blood on the carpet (人間関係の)深刻なわだかまり; (組織内の争いの結果)多くのもめ事が生じること ▪ The issue is highly emotional and will cause a lot of *blood on the carpet*. 問題は非常に感情的で, 組織内に多くのもめ事を起こすだろう ▪ What if you do get *blood on the carpet*? 人間関係の深刻なわだかまりが本当に生じたら君はどうしますか?

One's ***blood runs cold*** [***freezes***]. 恐ろしくてぞっとする; ひやりとする ▪ *My blood ran cold* at the scene. 私はその光景が恐ろしくてひやっとした.

blood, sweat, and tears 血と汗と涙; 大変な苦労[困難] ▪ We've put *blood, sweat and tears* into this campaign. 我々はこのキャンペーンに血と涙と汗を注いできた ▪ This dictionary is the result of his ten years' *blood, sweat, and tears*. この辞書は彼の10年間の大変な苦労の結晶だ. ☞1940年5月13日の Winston Churchill の演説中のI have nothing to offer but blood, toil, tears, and sweat から.

blood turns to ice 血が凍る, ぞっとする ▪ As I witnessed the nationalist parades, my *blood turned to ice*. その民族主義者のパレードを見ているとき, 血が凍る思いだった.

one's ***blood will be on*** *a person* …が死んで人にたたる (《聖》*Matt.* 28. 25) ▪ *My blood will be on* you. わしはお前にたたるぞ.

Blood will have blood. 《諺》血は血を求める, 「血で血を洗う」.

Blood will tell. 血統は争われないものだ ▪ The boy comes of a courageous family and *blood will tell*. その少年は勇敢な家の生まれで血統は争われないものである.

breed [***make, stir up***] ***bad*** [***ill***] ***blood*** (***between***) (…の間に)不和をかきたてる ▪ The husband tried to *make bad blood between* his wife and her mother. 夫は妻とその母との間を不和にしようとした.

bring young blood → introduce young BLOOD.

burst a blood vessel 激怒する; ひどく興奮する ▪ When I asked my boss for more wages, he *burst a blood vessel*. 賃上げを願ったらボスは激怒した. ☞「血管を破裂させる」が原義.

corrupt in blood (反逆罪・重罪のために)血統の汚れた ▪ They became *corrupt in blood* and morals. 彼らは血統も道徳も汚れてしまった.

cry [***scream, yell***] ***blood murder*** → cry (blue) MURDER.

curdle *a person's* ***blood*** → make a person's BLOOD curdle.

draw blood **1** 採血する; 血を流させる ▪ The dog's teeth *drew blood*. 犬の歯で血が出た.
2 《口》怒らせる, 激怒させる ▪ His words *drew blood* from her. 彼の言葉が彼女を激怒させた.

draw (***the***) ***first blood*** **1** 《ボクシング》(相手に)最初に血を出させる; 《スポーツ》先制点を挙げる ▪ Gelfand *drew the first blood* in the fight. その一戦でゲルファンドは最初に血を出させた ▪ England *drew first blood* versus New Zealand. イングランドはニュージーランドに対して先制点を挙げた.
2 (相手に対して)まず優位を占める ▪ Pentax *drew the first blood* by introducing a camera called Pentax ME-F. ペンタクスはペンタクス ME-F というカメラを売り出してまず優位を占めた.

freeze [***chill, curdle***] *a person's* ***blood*** 人を(恐怖で)ぞっとさせる ▪ The scene *froze his blood*. その光景は彼をぞっとさせた.

fresh [***new, young***] ***blood*** (グループ・組織内の)若い戦力 ▪ It's time we got some *new blood* in this company. 当社は若い戦力を入れるべき時期だ.

get blood from [***out of***] ***a stone*** [《米》***turnip***] 石[カブ]から血を得る《不可能なことを企てる》 ▪ There is no money. You can't *get blood out of a turnip*. 金はない. カブから血を得ることはできない ▪ He was rude and morose and getting a smile out of him was like *getting blood out of a stone*. 彼は無礼で気難しく, 彼を微笑させるなんて, 石から血を得ようとするようなものだった.

get [***have***] *one's* [*a person's*] ***blood up*** 激昂する[させる] ▪ If you *get my blood up*, you'll be sorry for the consequences. 僕を激昂させるとあとでくやむぞ.

get ... out of *one's* ***blood*** …(の愛着)から抜け切る ▪ Tom couldn't *get* the country *out of his blood*. 彼は田舎に対する愛着から抜けられなかった ▪ She could not *get* summer laziness *out of her blood*. 彼女は夏の怠惰から抜け切れなかった.

give a blood transfusion 生き返らせる, 再び活気づける ▪ North Sea oil has *given* Britain *a blood transfusion*. 北海原油のおかげで英国は再び活気を取り戻した.

give *one's* ***blood*** 血を与える ▪ He *gave his blood* to save his mother. 彼は母を救うため血を差し出した.

give *one's* ***blood for*** …のために死ぬ ▪ The brave soldier *gave his blood for* his country. 勇敢な兵士は国のために死んだ.

have *a person's* ***blood on*** *one's* ***head*** [***hands***] 人の死に責任がある (《聖》*Josh.* 2. 19) ▪ He didn't want to *have the blood of* anyone *on his hands*. 彼は誰の死の責任も負いたくなかった.

have blue blood in *one's* ***veins*** 貴族の血が流れている ▪ He *has blue blood in his veins*. 彼には貴族の血が流れている《彼は貴族の生まれである》. ☞スペイン語 sangre azul から. 「青い血」とは白い皮膚をとおして見える静脈をさし, 純血のスペイン人であることを示した.

have *a person's* ***heart's blood*** 人の命をもらう

B

▪ I'll *have his heart's blood.* 彼の命をもらおう.

have tasted blood 最初の成功で味をしめる ▪ The masses *have tasted blood* and want more. 群衆は最初の成功で味をしめ, もっと求めている.

in blood 血で ▪ The oath was written *in blood.* その誓言は血で書かれた.

in cold [***cool***] ***blood*** 平然として, 冷静に; 冷酷に ▪ They say he murdered her *in cold blood.* 彼は彼女を平然と殺したそうである ▪ The deed was done *in cold blood.* その行為は冷酷に行われた.

in hot [***warm***] ***blood*** 激(怒)して, かっとして ▪ I struck him, I admit, but it was *in hot blood.* なるほど私は彼をなぐったが, それはかっとなってやったことだ.

in the [*one's*] ***blood*** **1** 血統を引いて ▪ I hate cats, and so did my father; it's *in the blood.* 私は猫が大きらいだが, 父もそうだった. それは親譲りだ ▪ He has courage *in his blood.* 彼の勇敢さは親譲りである.

2 性に合う, (生まれつき)好きである ▪ The sea is *in his blood.* 海は彼の性に合う ▪ Politics is *in my blood* as a hereditary trait. 私は遺伝的特性として政治が性に合っている.

into *one's* ***blood*** 性に合う ▪ Tennis runs *into my blood.* テニスは私の性に合う.

introduce [***bring***] ***young blood*** 気鋭の青年を入れる ▪ It was time to *introduce* some *young blood.* 今や気鋭の青年を入れる時であった.

let blood 手術で血を取る, 放血する《昔の療法》 ▪ In older times, in the case of fevers, the physician always *let blood* from the patient. 昔は熱病の場合は, 医者はいつも患者から血を取った.

make bad [***ill***] ***blood*** (***between***) → breed bad BLOOD (between).

make *a person's* ***blood boil*** 人を憤激させる ▪ His rude retort was enough to *make my blood boil.* 彼の無礼な返答は私を憤激させるに十分だった.

make *a person's* ***blood curdle*** [***creep, freeze, run*** [***go, turn***] ***cold***]/***curdle the*** [*a person's*] ***blood*** 人を恐ろしさでぞっとさせる, 肝を冷えさせる ▪ He used to *make our blood curdle* by reading ghost stories. 彼は怪談を読んで我々をぞっとさせるのが常だった ▪ The sight *made his blood run cold* within him. その光景は彼に血の凍る思いをさせた.

near in blood 近親で ▪ He is *near in blood* to me. 彼は私と近親である.

new blood →fresh BLOOD.

of noble blood 貴族の ▪ He is a man *of noble blood.* 彼は貴族である.

of the blood 王家の ▪ Anthony was the first prince *of the blood.* アントニーは第一王子であった.

of the blue blood 高貴な生まれの ▪ I know a gentleman *of the blue blood.* 高貴な生まれの紳士を私は知っている.

out for (*a person's*) ***blood*** = after a person's BLOOD.

restore *a person* ***to*** [***in***] ***blood*** (貴族などが本人または祖先が喪失した)称号[継承権など]を回復させる, (貴族などの)権利を回復させる ▪ Henry should *be restored to blood.* ヘンリーは権利を回復されるべきだ.

run in the blood →RUN in the family.

scent blood **1** (猟犬・野獣などが)血の味を知る ▪ Last week he was back in the lobbies, "like a shark *scenting blood.*" 先週彼は「血の味を知ったサメのように」圧力団体に戻ってきた.

2 相手の弱みにつけ込む ▪ Democrats *scenting blood* last week leapt to the attack. 民主党は相手の弱みにつけこんで, 先週攻撃に移った.

smell blood = scent BLOOD.

spill the blood of 《文》…を殺す, の血を流す ▪ Nothing justifies *spilling* innocent *blood.* 何事であれ無辜(むこ)の血を流すことは正当化されない.

spit blood [***venom, feathers***] →SPIT[2].

stir the [*a person's*] ***blood*** (人を)興奮[熱狂]させる, 血沸き肉おどる心地にする ▪ Pirate novels *stir a boy's blood.* 海賊小説は少年を興奮させる ▪ The final contest *stirred our blood.* 決勝戦は我々の血を湧かせた.

stir up bad [***ill***] ***blood*** (***between***) → breed bad BLOOD (between).

suck the blood of →SUCK[2].

sweat blood 《口》 **1** 血の汗を流す; 大変な苦労をする; 無理に苦労する (《聖》 *Luke* 22. 44) ▪ I *sweated blood* to pass the final exams. 最終試験に合格するためにしゃかりきに勉強した ▪ You have *sweat blood* for money. あなたは金を儲けるために血の汗を流した.

2 ひどく心配する, おびえる, 気をもむ, 思いわずらう ▪ I was sitting there *sweating blood* when those damned cops arrived. 私がひどく心配しながらそこに腰かけていると, その忌まわしいお巡りがやって来た ▪ Waiting for the test results, I was *sweating blood.* テストの結果待ちで気をもんでいた.

taste blood (猟犬・野獣などが)血を味わう, 初めて味を知る, 味をしめる ▪ He has *tasted blood*, so you had better give your consent at once. 彼は味をしめているのだから, あなたはすぐ承諾したほうがいい.

The blood boils. 人が怒る ▪ *The blood boils* with hate. 憎しみのため血が煮えくりかえる.

there is blood on *one's* ***hands*** …は殺人の罪がある ▪ To his horror, *there is blood on his hands.* 慄然としたことに, 彼には殺人の罪がある.

to the last drop of *one's* ***blood*** 最後の血の一滴まで, 息のあらんかぎり ▪ I will guard my property *to the last drop of my blood.* 息の通っているかぎり自分の財産を守ってみせる.

too rich for *one's* ***blood*** (物が)高価すぎる ▪ $600? Good price, but a little *too rich for my blood.* 600ドルだって? いい値段だ. でも私には高すぎる.

(***with***) ***blood in*** *one's* ***eyes*** 殺気立って ▪ I was walking down this road when a big dog *with blood in his eyes* came at me. この道を下っているとき大きな犬が殺気だって飛びかかってきた.

bloodied /blʌ́did/ 形 ***bloodied but unbowed*** →bloody but UNBOWED.

bloody /blʌ́di/ 形 ***get a bloody nose*** 鼻血が出る; ちょっぴりやっつけられる[懲らしめられる] ▪ The Tories *got a bloody nose* in the by-election. 保守党は補欠選挙でちょっぴりやられた.

give** a person **a bloody nose 人をちょっぴりやっつける[懲らしめる] ▪ They have *given* the Tories *a bloody nose*. 彼らは保守党をちょっぴりやっつけた.

not a bloody one 《卑》〚強意的に〛ただのひとつも…ない ▪ There was *not a bloody one*. ただのひとつもなかった.

wave the (bloody) shirt →SHIRT.

bloom /bluːm/ 名 ***come into bloom*** (花が)咲く, (木が)花をつける ▪ This rose *comes into bloom* later in the summer. このバラは夏の終わりに咲きます.

have a bloom on (果物)に粉がふいている ▪ The persimmons *have a bloom on* them. その柿には粉がふいている.

in bloom **1** (花が)咲いて ▪ The apple-tree is *in bloom*. リンゴの木に花が咲いている.
2 (…の)盛りで (*of*) ▪ Ann is a modern woman *in* the *bloom of* youth. アンは若い盛りの現代女性だ.

in full bloom 満開で; (火が)盛んに燃えて; 《米俗》達者[健康]で ▪ The tulips are *in full bloom* now. チューリップが今満開である.

out of bloom 花期を過ぎて ▪ Gorse is *out of bloom*. ハリエニシダは花期を過ぎた.

take the bloom off …から新鮮味[美しさ]をそぐ; を古くさくする ▪ A tall building at the back *took the bloom off* the garden. 後ろの高層ビルが庭園の美観をそいでいた.

the bloom is off the rose 《米》もはや新鮮味がなくなった, 興味が失せた ▪ *The bloom is off the rose* for many developed market economies. 多くの成熟した市場経済はもはや新鮮味がなくなった.

blossom /blɑ́səm|blɔ́s-/ 名 ***bring ... into blossom*** …に花を咲かせる ▪ Spring weather *brings* the fruit trees *into blossom*. 春の天気が果樹に花を咲かせる.

come into blossom (花が)咲き出す ▪ These old cherry trees *came into blossom* secretly in spring. これらのサクラの老木は春ひっそりと花開いた.

in blossom (花が)咲いて ▪ Plum trees are now *in blossom*. ウメは今咲いている.

in full blossom 満開で, 盛りで ▪ The flowers are *in full blossom*. 花は盛りだ ▪ The cherry tree is *in full blossom*. そのサクラは満開だ.

blot[1] /blɑt|blɔt/ 名 ***a blot in** a person's **copybook*** 履歴上の汚点 ▪ This is *a blot in his copybook*. これが彼の履歴上の汚点だ. ☞copybook「学童の習字帳」.

a blot on [in]** one's **escutcheon 家門の名折れ ▪ His brutal treatment of his daughter will always be *a blot on his escutcheon*. 彼の娘に対する残酷な扱いは常に家門の名折れであろう. ☞紋章語から.

a blot on the landscape **1** 風景[景観]を害するもの ▪ That ugly advertisement is *a blot on the landscape*. あの醜い広告は風致を害する.
2 《戯》目ざわり[じゃま]になる人[物] ▪ The only *blot on the landscape* was Lady Jane. じゃまになるのはジェイン夫人だけだった ▪ The only *blot on the landscape* is this little bit of jealousy. 唯一いやなのはこうしたちょっとばかりの嫉妬である.

hit a blot (バックギャモンで)危険にさらされているこまを取る; 欠点[弱点]をつく ▪ Here the critic has undoubtedly *hit a blot*. この点では批評家は確かに弱点をついている.

blot[2] /blɑt|blɔt/ 動 ***blot** one's **copybook*** → COPYBOOK.

blouse /blaʊs|blaʊz/ 名 ***a big girl's blouse*** 《英戯》女々しい[勇気のない, 軟弱な]男 ▪ He was screaming and acting like *a big girl's blouse*. 彼は金切り声をあげて, 勇気のない男みたいにふるまっていた ▪ He's flapping like *a big girl's blouse*. 彼はめめしい男みたいにそわそわしている.

blow[1] /bloʊ/ 名 ***a bitter blow*** 大きなショック, 精神的打撃 ▪ The defeat was *a bitter blow* to the Swedish soccer team. スウェーデンのサッカーチームにとってその敗北は大ショックだった.

a blow to** a person's **pride …にとっての屈辱 ▪ It was *a blow to Smith's pride* when his opponent took the prize. 相手が賞を取ったときはスミスには屈辱だった.

a low blow 《ボクシング》ローブロー; 反則行為, 卑劣な手段 ▪ In an argument with John, Joe bringing up his failed marriage was *a low blow*. ジョンとの論争で, ジョーが相手の結婚の失敗を持ち出したのは卑劣な手段だった.

at a [one] blow 一撃で; 一挙に, 急に, すぐに ▪ He felled the beast *at a blow*. 彼は一撃でその獣を倒した ▪ We got rid of the whole lot *at one blow*. 我々は全部を一挙に追い払った.

be at blows なぐり合い[格闘]している ▪ Jason and your brother *were at blows*. ジェイスンとあなたの弟がなぐり合いをしていた.

blow by blow (ボクシング・議論などの経過を)逐一, 詳細に(述べる) ▪ The commentator reported the match *blow by blow*. 実況放送員はその試合の経過を逐一放送した.

come [get, go] to blows なぐり合いを始める, なぐり合いになる (*over*) ▪ Robbie and Rod almost *came to blows over* Lucy. ロビーとロッドはルーシーのことで危うくなぐり合うところだった.

cushion [soften] the blow 打撃を和らげる《比喩的にも》 ▪ The way to *cushion the blow* is to raise prices slowly, not all at once. 打撃を和らげる方法は, 一挙にではなく徐々に物価を上げていくことだ.

deal a blow 一撃を加える ▪ He *dealt* me *a blow* between the eyes. 彼は私のみけんに一撃を加えた.

deal a blow to …に打撃を与える ▪ Solzhenitsyn's writings *dealt a blow to* Soviet communism. ソルジェニーツィンの著作はソビエト共産主義に打撃を与えた.

***exchange blows* (*with*)** (…と)なぐり合いをする ▪ He is too young to *exchange blows with* them. 彼はまだ若いので彼らと格闘はできない.

fall to blows 《英》 =come to BLOWs.

get a blow 新鮮な風に当たる ▪ He went by the steamer to *get a blow*. 彼はさわやかな風に当たるため汽船で行った.

get a blow in **1**《ボクシング》一撃を加える ▪ He couldn't *get a* single *blow in*. 彼はただの一撃も加え得なかった.
2《口》言葉で攻撃する; 言葉でやり返す ▪ He *got a blow in* about her flirtations. 彼は彼女の浮気のことでやり返した.

give a blow 打撃を与える (*to*) ▪ He *gave a strong blow to* his dog. 彼は自分の犬を強く叩いた.

have* [*go for*] *a blow 戸外へ出て新しい空気を吸う ▪ Let's *go for a blow* in the country. さわやかな空気を吸いに田舎へ出ましょう.

in full blow 満開で ▪ The wood-anemone was *in full blow*. アネモネが満開だった.

in one blow =at a BLOW.

strike a blow 攻撃する, 一撃を与える ▪ *A* good *blow* must *be struck* here. ここでがつんと一撃を与えなくてはならない.

***strike a blow for* [*against*]** …に加勢[反抗]する; のために[に反抗して]戦う ▪ I'm going to appoint her as manager to *strike a blow for* gender equality. 男女平等を推進させるため, 彼女を店長に任命するつもりだ.

strike the first blow 先に手を出す ▪ Neither side dared to *strike the first blow*. どちらも先に手を出す勇気はなかった.

The first blow is half the battle. 《諺》第一撃が勝負を半ば左右する.

without* (*striking*) *a blow (たいして, 全く)労せずして, 何の苦もなく; 戦わずして ▪ We were able to enter the place *without a blow*. 我々は戦わずしてそこへ入ることができた.

blow[2] /bloʊ/ 動 ***blow** oneself* 《米口》はりこむ, 奮発する ▪ The railroad *blew itself* to some fresh paint. 鉄道は奮発してペンキ塗りかえをやった.

blow a* [*one's*] *cloud タバコを吸う《エリザベス時代からの句》 ▪ *Blow thy cloud*. タバコを吸いなさい.

***blow a fuse* [*gasket*]** 《口》ヒューズを飛ばす; エンジンから蒸気が吹き出る; 怒りを爆発させる ▪ I'm just afraid that Nora's gonna *blow a gasket*. 僕はノラが激怒するんじゃないかと心配している.

blow** a person's **chances 人の機会を失わせる ▪ Getting pregnant *blew Edna's chances* of accepting a scholarship. 妊娠したためエドナは奨学金をもらう機会を逸した.

blow** a person's **cover 《口》(スパイの)正体をあばく ▪ Two years later, *his cover was blown* and he was arrested in England. 2年後彼の正体があばかれて, イングランドで逮捕された.

blow eggs 卵を産みつける ▪ The fly *blew eggs* on the body of a recently killed animal. 最近殺された動物の死体にハエが卵を産みつけた.

blow …from* (*the mouth of*) *a gun (反逆者)を銃口にくくりつけて銃殺する ▪ They will seize us and *blow* us *from guns*. 彼らは我々を捕えて銃殺にするだろう.

blow high, blow low 《米口》どんな天気にでも; どんなことがあっても ▪ *Blow high, blow low*, I need not be afraid. 何があっても, 私は恐れる必要はない.

***blow hot and cold* (*with the same breath, out of the same mouth*)** **1** ぐらぐら変わる; 定見がない ▪ These men can *blow hot and cold out of the same mouth* to serve several purposes. こういう人たちはいろいろの目的にかなうように, ころころ変わることができる ▪ They *blow hot and cold* on the question of building a subway. 彼らは地下鉄を建設する問題に関しては何ら定見がない. ☞指を温めるにもかゆを冷やすにも, 同じく息を吹きかけたという「イソップ物語」にある田舎者の話から.
2 出来不出来の波がある ▪ His team has *blown hot and cold* in their early matches. 彼のチームは最初の数試合では勝敗の波があった.

blow it **1**《口》(へまをやって)しくじる[機会をふいにする] ▪ That math test was so easy I can't understand how I could have *blown it*. その数学のテストは実に易しかったので, どうしてしくじったのか理解できない.
2《口》こんちくしょう, いまいましい《怒り, 不満を表す》 ▪ *Blow it*! You're late again! こんちくしょう, おまえ, また遅刻したな.

***Blow it out* (*your asshole* [*your ear*])!** 《米俗》くそくらえ, ばか言うな《挑戦・叱責》.

blow itself out (風などが)吹きやむ ▪ By morning the storm had *blown itself out*. 朝までにはあらしは収まっていた.

blow** one's **lines 台詞(せりふ)を忘れる ▪ Ben *blew his lines*, but Jim came to the rescue. ベンは台詞を忘れたが, ジムが助けてくれた.

Blow me! 《口》 =DAMN me!

blow me down 《英口》ああ驚いた ▪ Well, *blow me down*, if it is not Henry Brown. おや驚いた, ヘンリー・ブラウンじゃないか.

blow** a person's* [*one's*] ***mind 《口》 **1** (麻薬などで)愉快な[ぞっとするような]感じを起こさせる[起こす] ▪ This drug will *blow your mind* for an hour only. この麻薬は1時間しか快感を起こさせないだろう.
2 (麻薬のやり過ぎで)精神もうろうとなる ▪ He speaks incoherently; he seems to have *blown his mind*. 彼の言うことはしどろもどろだ. (麻薬が過ぎて)頭がもうろうとなったようだ.

blow** one's **nose →NOSE[1].

blow off* (*the*) *steam →let off (the) STEAM.

blow out** one's* [*a person's*] ***brains (ピストルなどで)頭を撃って自殺する[人を撃ち殺す] ▪ He *blew out his brains*. 彼はピストルで頭を撃って自殺した ▪ If they attempt an escape, *blow their brains* *out*. 彼らが逃げようとしたら撃ち殺せ.

blow out of the water 《口》(人・着想・企画が)全く信用できないことを暴露する, 失墜[破滅]させる ▪ Then television came along and *blew* everything *out of the water*. それからテレビがやって来て, あらゆるものを失墜させてしまった ▪ Lester's romantic plans *were blown out of the water* by Ellen. レスターのロマンチックな計画はエレンによってぶっこわされた.

blow the coals [***the fire***] 不和をあおる, 争いをあおる ▪ The Chancellor also helped to *blow the fire*. 首相もまた争いをあおるのを助けた.

blow the expense むちゃな使いかたをする; 〚命令文で〛費用なんかかまわない ▪ *Blow the expense*! 費用なんかかまうものか.

blow ... to atoms [***pieces***] **1** …をこっぱみじんに吹き飛ばす ▪ It *was blown to pieces*. それはこっぱみじんに吹き飛ばされた.

2 (鳥)を撃ってめちゃめちゃにする ▪ It *blows* pheasants *to pieces* at 20 yards. それはキジを20ヤードの所で撃ってこっぱみじんにする.

blow ... to glory [***blazes, kingdom come***] (人を)爆死させる ▪ They *were blown to blazes* by the bomb. 彼らはその爆弾で爆死した.

blow *one's* [***a***] ***top*** [***cork, fuse, gasket, lid, lump, noggin, roof,*** 《米》 ***stack, topper, wig,*** etc.] 《口》 **1** 激怒する, かっとなる ▪ My wife *blew her top* when I came home late. 私の帰りが遅かったとき妻は激怒した.

2 気が狂う, 頭がおかしくなる ▪ When she regains consciousness, she just may *blow her top*. 彼女が意識を取り返したら, 全く頭がおかしくなるかもしれない.

blow up in *a person's* ***face*** みじめに失敗する ▪ His whole scheme *blew up in his face*. 彼の計画全体がみじめにもすっかり失敗した.

blow (***wide***) ***open*** 《口》 **1** 公表する, (秘密などを)一般に暴露する; 知れる, 暴露される ▪ They have *blown* the director's plan *wide open*. 彼らは所長の計画を暴露した ▪ The true story of the stolen money *blew open*. 盗まれた金の真相がはっきりした.

2 吹き開ける[開けられる] ▪ The explosion *blew* the door *open*. 爆発で戸が吹き開けられた ▪ All of a sudden the door *blew open*. 突然扉が風で開いた.

3 (結果などを)全く未知数にする ▪ Her participation in the race *blew* it *wide open*. 彼女が競走に加わったのでその結果が全く未知数になった.

4 大きく方向転換する ▪ The city will *blow* the market *wide open*. その都市は大きく市場の方向転換を果たすだろう.

I'm [***I'll be***] ***blowed*** **1** 《俗》おやっ! 《驚きを表す》 ▪ Well, *I'll be blowed*, if she didn't cut us dead. おやっ! 彼女は我々を見て知らぬ顔をしたじゃないか.

2 決して…しない ▪ Will you subscribe?—No, *I'm blowed* if I will. 寄付してくださいませんか—いや, 絶対お断りです.

It blows a gale [***a hurricane***]. 大風が吹く ▪ *It blew a* great *gale*. 大風が吹いた.

It blows great guns (***and small arms***). 大風が吹く.

Look [***See***] ***what the wind has blown in!*** 《口・戯》まあ誰がやって来たかごらん.

puff and blow →PUFF[2].

You be blowed! 《口》くそっ! いまいましい《軽いのろい》 ▪ Do hurry up and come along.—Oh, *you be blowed!* 早く大急ぎでおいでよ—えっ, ばか言え!

blow-up /blóʊʌ̀p/ 名 ***give a blow-up*** 《口》しかる ▪ The captain *gave* him *a* grand *blow-up*. 船長は彼をはでにしかった.

blue /bluː/ 形名 ***a blue fit*** 《口》極度のいらだたしさ[不安] ▪ She would have *a blue fit* if her son were out on the sea alone. 息子が一人で海に乗り出ていたら彼女はひどく不安になるだろう.

a bolt from the blue →BOLT.

be in the blues/have a fit of the blues 気がふさいでいる ▪ He *was* much *in the blues*. 彼は非常に気がふさいでいた.

blue devils **1** ふさぎ, 憂鬱, 落胆 ▪ He has (got) the *blue devils*. 彼はふさぎの虫に取りつかれている. ☞憂鬱症になると青い魔物が見えるという.

2 《口》アルコール中毒症《アルコール中毒者の見る恐ろしい幻影》 ▪ The drunken old landlord had a fit of the *blue devils* last night. 酔いどれの老家主は昨夜アルコール中毒症に襲われた.

blue ruin 《俗》完全な破滅 ▪ The firm ended in *blue ruin*. その会社は完全に破産した.

burn blue (ロウソクが)青く燃える《死の予告か, 幽霊・悪意の存在を示すという》 ▪ When the candles *burn blue*, the devil is in the room. ロウソクが青く燃えるときは, 悪魔が部屋にいる.

by all that's blue 確かに, まちがいなく ▪ The black cat, *by all that's blue*! まちがいなく例の黒猫だ. ☞F parbleu 'by God'のなぞり.

cry [***yell***] ***blue murder*** →MURDER[1].

disappear [***go off, vanish***] ***into the blue*** 突然消える, 不意に消える ▪ He *went off into the blue* without so much as a message. 彼は伝言ひとつ残さず急に姿を消した ▪ All his worries *disappeared into the blue*. 彼の心配はすべて急に消えた.

fall in the blues 意気消沈する ▪ We should all have *fallen in the blues*. 我々はみな意気消沈したはずだ.

feel blue 気がふさぐ ▪ She has *felt blue* ever since. 彼女はそれ以来気がふさいでいる.

get [***win***] *one's* ***blue*** オックスフォード[ケンブリッジ]の代表選手となる ▪ Your son has *got his* rowing *blue*. ご令息はオックスフォード大学のボート代表選手になられました. ☞選手は blue のシャツを着ることから.

go blue (***in the face***) 《口》(寒さで)顔が青くなる ▪ His mother suddenly *went blue in the face*. 彼の母は急に(寒くて)青くなった.

have [***get***] (***a fit of***) ***the blues*** 《口》気がふさぐ, 悲しい ▪ Mike *has the blues* because his mother just passed away. マイクは母親が亡くなったので気がふさいでいる.

in the blue 《口》遠方に; 天空に ▪ He has

B

bought a house right out *in the blue*. 彼はほんとに遠い所に家を買った.

into the blue すっかり姿を消してしまう ▪ I don't know where they've gone—*into the blue*, for all I know. 彼らがどこへ行ったのか知らない—たぶん, 姿を消してしまったのだ.

into the wide [wild] blue yonder 《雅》 遠くの見知らぬところへ ▪ The pilot soared like an eagle *into the wide blue yonder*. 操縦士はワシのように遠くの見知らぬところへ舞いあがった ▪ Sailing *into the wide blue yonder*, Steve discovered his very own Treasure Island. はるか遠くまで航海に出たのち, スティーブはまさに彼だけの宝の島を発見した. ☞Robert Crawford, "Army Air Corps" (1939) という歌から.

like blue murder →MURDER[1].

look blue **1** しょげて[ふさいで]いる; 気分が悪そうである ▪ He *looks blue* at having to pay so much. 彼はそんなにたくさん支払わねばならないので浮かぬ顔をしている. **2** 非常に寒そうである ▪ They all *looked blue*, with a cold wind blowing. 冷たい風が吹いていたので, 彼らはみな寒そうであった. **3** 《米俗》 疲れきった顔をする ▪ None of them *looked blue* after the match. 試合のあと彼らは誰一人疲れきった顔をしていなかった. **4** 形勢[見込み]が悪い, 思わしくない ▪ The situation *looked blue*. 情勢は好ましくなかった.

look [see] through blue glasses 《口》 誤った, 特に悲観的な見方をする ▪ He *sees* everything *through blue glasses*. 彼は万事を悲観的に見る.

make a blue fist of 《米口》 …に悲惨な失敗をする ▪ He *made a blue fist of* taking aim. 彼はねらいを定めるのにひどく失敗した.

make the air blue =turn the air BLUE.

once in a blue moon →MOON.

out of the blue 全く予期しないところから, 思いがけなく, だしぬけに ▪ The money came right *out of the blue*. 金が全く予期しないところから出た ▪ His visit was *out of the blue*. 彼の訪問は突然だった.

sing the blues →SING[2].

take the blue ribbon 禁酒会員になる ▪ We have *taken the blue ribbon*. 我々は禁酒会員になった.

the man [gentleman, boy] in blue 警官, 水兵, アメリカ南北戦争の北軍 ▪ The crime brought upon us *the man in blue*. その犯罪のため我々の所に警官がやって来た.

till all is blue 《口》 船が港を出て青い水に消えるまで; いつまでも; 徹底的に, とことんまで ▪ Crack bottles *till all is blue*. いつまでもどんどんボトルをあけなさい ▪ We'll fight *till all is blue*. とことんまで戦おう.

till [until] one is blue in the face 〚talk, argue, scream, etc. に伴って〛 (怒り・緊張などで)疲れて顔が青くなるまで, いつまでも ▪ You may *talk till* you *are blue in the face*, but you will never make me believe what you say. 君が疲れはてるまで語っても君の言うことを僕に信じさせることはできないよ ▪ He *argued till* he *was blue in the face*. 彼は顔が青くなるまで議論した ▪ You can *talk* to him *till* you *are blue in the face*. 君は疲れるまで彼に向かってしゃべるがいい.

turn the air blue (激しく悪態をついて)空気を青くする ▪ His language positively *turned the air blue*. 彼の悪態はひどく, 本当に空気が青くなったほどだ.

vanish into the blue → disappear into the BLUE.

win one's blue →get one's BLUE.

yell blue murder cry (blue) MURDER.

Blue hen /blúːhèn/ 名 ***be a Blue hen*** デラウェア州生まれである ▪ Your mother *is a Blue hen*, no doubt. なるほど君の母は青いめんどりだ 《自分はデラウェア出身だと自慢する者に対する皮肉》. ☞Blue hen は Delaware 州の異名.

blue-peter /blùːpíːtər/ 名 ***fly [hoist] the blue-peter*** 出帆しようとしている, 出帆する, 出発する ▪ I have to *hoist the blue-peter* today. きょう出発しなければならない. ☞blue-peter は前檣に掲げる青地の小旗で, 24時間以内に出帆することを示す.

bluff[1] /blʌf/ 形名 ***a bluff game*** こけおどし ▪ It was *a bluff game* and he won. それはこけおどしの手だったが彼は勝った. ☞《米》ポーカーでこけおどしをやって相手を恐れ参らせる手.

call a person's bluff 《口》 (相手が空いばりと見て)やれるものならやってみろと挑戦する ▪ If your son threatens to run away, *call his bluff*. あなたの息子さんが家出するとおどかすなら, やれるものならやってみろと言ってやりなさい. ☞「ポーカーではったりと見て相手に手を公開させる」が原義.

make [pull, put on] a bluff (…するぞと)はったりをかける, こけおどしをする (*at doing*) ▪ He *put on a good bluff*. 彼はうまくこけおどしをやった ▪ He *made a bluff at offering* a bonus. 彼ははったりでボーナスを出すと言った.

run a bluff on 《米》 (人)にはったりをかける[かます] ▪ He's going to *run a bluff on* me, I'm afraid. 彼は私にはったりをかまそうとしているのじゃないか.

stand bluff 毅然としてひるまない ▪ He has *stood bluff* to being an old bachelor so long. 彼は非常に長い間老独身者の生活を毅然として守ってきた.

bluff[2] /blʌf/ 動 ***bluff it out*** はったりを通す, はったりで切り抜ける ▪ "I was with Bill," Eve said, deciding to *bluff it out*. イブははったりを通すことに決めて,「私はビルといっしょだったわ」と言った.

bluff one's way into はったりで(職など)に就く ▪ He *bluffed his way into* the job. 彼ははったりでその職を得た.

bluff one's way out はったりで切り抜ける ▪ He managed to *bluff his way out* the front door. 彼は何とかうまくだまして玄関から逃れ出た.

blunder[1] /blʌ́ndər/ 名 ***make a blunder*** 大失敗をする, 不注意で台なしにする ▪ Bush *made a blunder* with North Korea. ブッシュ氏は北朝鮮に対して大失敗をしでかした.

blunder[2] /blʌ́ndər/ 動 ***blunder one's way***

along (…を)まごまご歩いて行く ▪ The horse *blundered his way along* a river. 馬は川に沿ってつまずきながら進んだ.

blunt /blʌnt/ 動 ***blunt the edge of*** →dull the EDGE of.

blush[1] /blʌʃ/ 名 ***at*** (***the***) ***first blush*** ちょっと見た[聞いた, 考えた]ところでは ▪ *At the first blush* the matter seems easy. ちょっと考えたところではそれはたやすそうに思える ▪ It may sound strange *at the first blush*. ちょっと聞くとそれは奇妙に響くかもしれない. ☞blush《廃》「一見, 一瞥(べつ)」.

put *a person* ***to the blush*** 人を赤面させる, 人に面目を失わせる ▪ In conversation avoid anything that will *put* your hearer *to the blush*. 会話では聞き手を赤面させるようなことは避けなさい.

spare [***save***] *a person's* ***blushes/ spare*** [***save***] ***the blushes of*** *a person*《英》人の面目を保つ, 人に恥をかかせない ▪ The three musketeers *saved the blushes of* the Queen, when the cardinal hoped to sow mistrust between her and the King. 枢機卿が王妃と王の間に不信の種をまこうとしたとき, 三銃士は王妃の面目を保った ▪ *Spare my blushes*! あまり褒めないでくれ!《照れるから》.

blush[2] /blʌʃ/ 動 ***not blush from*** *doing* 恥じることもなく…する ▪ They have *not blushed from promoting* her as a professor. 彼らは臆面もなく彼女を教授に昇任させた.

bluster /blʌ́stər/ 動 ***bluster*** *oneself* ***into*** どなって…になる ▪ He *blustered himself into* indignation. 彼はどなって激怒した.

bluster *one's* ***way out of*** どなり立てて…から抜け出る, (難局などを)はったりで切り抜ける ▪ Can he *bluster his way out of* this mess? 彼ははったりでこの窮境を切り抜けることができるだろうか?

bluster *one's* ***way through*** どなり立てながら…を通り抜ける ▪ He *blustered his way through* the crowd. 彼はどなり立てながら人混みを通り抜けた.

bo /boʊ/ 間名 →BOO.

board /bɔːrd/ 名 ***above board*** **1**《海》生きて ▪ You're the last *above board* of that crew. 君はあの乗組員のうち最後の生き残りです.

2 公明率直で ▪ It is better to be open and *above board* over the matter. その件については率直で公明正大なほうがよい. ☞2 はトランプから.

across the board **1**《米・競馬》(賭金を)1着2着3着にわたって(賭ける) ▪ He bet $6 on the black horse *across the board*. 彼は黒馬に1, 2, 3着にわたって6ドル賭けた.

2《口》全面的な[に]; 一律の[に] ▪ The manager has promised us an *across-the-board* pay raise. 支配人は我々に一律昇給を約束した ▪ They asked for a pay increase of 5 pounds a week *across the board*. 彼らは一律に週5ポンドの賃上げを求めた.

(***as***) ***stiff as a board*** →(as) STIFF as a poker.

Back to the drawing board! はじめから[計画の]やり直しだ! ▪ Ah, well, *back to the drawing board!* よし, はじめから練り直しだ! ☞the drawing board「製図板」.

bulletin board (***system***)/***BBS***《電算》(電子)掲示板システム《ネットワーク上の情報交換板》 ▪ Many users are trying to call the *bulletin board system* (*BBS*). 多くの使用者が掲示板システムを呼び出そうとしている.

come on board (政党・会社・チームなど)のために働きはじめる ▪ Edward *came on board* as the city's new auditor. エドワードは市の監査役として働きはじめた.

fall on board =run on BOARD.

fall over board →fall OVERBOARD.

get [***go***] ***on board*** (船・飛行機・列車・バスなどに)乗る ▪ He *got on board* at once. 彼はすぐ乗った.

go [***come***] ***by the board*** **1**《海》船外に落ちる ▪ All her masts *came by the board*. その船のマストはみな折れて海中に落ちた.

2 (永久に)失われる, 見捨てられる; (計画などが)全く失敗する ▪ All I had *went by the board*. 私の財産はすっかりなくなった ▪ The plan *went by the board*. その計画はおじゃんになった.

hold the boards (芝居が)演じ続けられている, 舞台にずっとかかっている ▪ The play still *holds the boards*. その芝居はまだ演じ続けられている.

keep *one's* ***name on the board***(***s***)《大学口》ケンブリッジ大学にずっと籍をおく[のずっと一員である] ▪ He *keeps his name on the board*. 彼はケンブリッジ大学に籍をおいている.

lay (*a ship*) ***on board*** (戦うため船が)他船に横着けになる ▪ The Glorious *laid* her *on board*. グローリアス号は切り込み戦のためその船に横着けになった.

make a stern-board 船尾を先にして進む ▪ The schooner *made a stern-board* to leeward of her. スクーナー船は船尾を先にその船の風下に進んだ.

make boards 間切る《ジグザグ進路をとる》 ▪ To this and that side I *made boards*. こちら側あちら側へと私は間切った.

make short [***good***] ***boards*** 小きざみに[大きく]間切る ▪ We passed the night in *making short boards*. 我々は小きざみに間切りながら夜を過ごした.

off the (***drawing***) ***boards*** 討議されないで; 設計を終わって ▪ It took five years to get the first locomotive *off the boards*. 最初の機関車の設計を終えるのに5年かかった.

on board **1** 船上に, 船内に; 機上に; 車中に ▪ go [get, come] *on board* 船・飛行機・車に乗る ▪ The ship had 500 passengers *on board*. 船は500人の乗客を乗せていた.

2 一員に加えて, 参画して ▪ Taylor has been brought *on board* as sales manager. テイラーは販売部長として一員に加わった.

on board (***of***) **1** (船・飛行機・列車・バス・車)に乗って ▪ get *on board* a plane [car] 飛行機[車]に乗る ▪ We went *on board* just an hour before the ship sailed. 私たちは出航のほんの1時間前に乗船した ▪ He left for America *on board* (*of*) a steamer. 彼は汽船に乗ってアメリカに向かった.

B

2《米戯》馬に乗って ▪ I took a trip *on board of* a Mexican mustang. メキシコの野生馬に乗って旅をした.

on board wages 食費をもらっている《使用人について》 ▪ Servants *on board wages* provide their own victuals. 食費を支給されている使用人は自分で食べ物を用意する.

on even board with …と舷を並べて; と対等に; 仲良く ▪ He has kept himself *on even board with* all the world. 彼は世間全体と仲よくしてきた.

on the boards **1** 討議[設計]されて; 取り上げられて ▪ The 100-plus planes are still *on the boards.* 100何機が今なお設計中である ▪ It is not *on the boards* today. きょうそれは問題にされていない.

2 俳優となって ▪ He went *on the boards.* 彼は俳優になった.

on the drawing board (考え・企画・提案が)計画の途中で, 青写真の段階で ▪ The new toll road is still *on the drawing board.* 新有料道路はまだ計画中だ.

pass by the board =go by the BOARD 2.

run [***fall***] ***on board*** (他船に)衝突する; 攻撃する, 襲いかかる ▪ The San Jose *fell on board* (of) her. サンホセ号はその船に衝突した ▪ His hungry soul *falls on board* upon the Devil's cheer. 彼の飢えた魂は悪魔の食物に食いつく.

sweep the board (***clean***) (トランプに勝って)掛け金を全部勝ち取る; (競技・選挙などで)全勝する, 圧勝する ▪ He led off two captive trumps and *swept the board.* 彼はまず2枚の捕虜札を取り上げ, それから札全部を取り上げた ▪ When he got to work, he *swept the board.* 彼は仕事に取り組むと, うまくやり遂げた.

take on board **1** …を積み込む, 乗(船さ)せる ▪ He *took* the cargo *on board.* 彼は船に荷を積み込んだ ▪ We *took* the pilot *on board.* 我々は水先案内を乗せた.

2 (意見・考えなど)を理解し受け入れる ▪ Department stores need to *take on board* the views of their customers. 百貨店は顧客の意見を理解し受け入れる必要がある.

3《英》(仕事など)を引き受ける ▪ They are ready to listen and *take* your problem *on board.* 彼らは耳を傾け, あなたの問題を引き受ける用意がある.

try (*a ship*) ***by the board*** (敵船に)乗り込みを試みる ▪ The captain *tried* her *by the board.* 船長は攻撃のためその船への乗り込みを試みた.

walk [***tread***] ***the boards*** 舞台に立つ, 俳優になる (=TREAD the stage) ▪ He *trod the boards* when young. 彼は若い時分に俳優になった.

boarding /bɔ́ːrdɪŋ/ 形 ***a boarding house reach***《口》食卓上の遠くにある食べ物を素早く取る業(わざ) ▪ He developed *a boarding house reach* while he was away at camp. 彼はキャンプに行っている間に食卓上の遠くにある食べ物の早取りを覚えた.

board-nail /bɔ́ːrdnèɪl/ 名 ***bite a board-nail off*** [***in two***] くぎを板からかみ抜く[折る](ほどの勢いである) ▪ He looked as though he could *bite a board-nail off.* 彼はくぎでもかみ抜くほどのけんまくだった.

boast[1] /boʊst/ 名 ***make a boast of*** …を誇りとする ▪ She will often *make a boast of* her baby. 彼女はよく自分の赤んぼうを自慢する.

boast[2] /boʊst/ 動 ***boast** oneself* 誇る ▪ They *boasted themselves* to be Englishmen. 彼らはイギリス人たることを誇りとした.

boast it 自慢する ▪ That nation *boasts it* so. その国はひどく自慢する.

boast** oneself **of …を自慢する ▪ He *boasted himself of* his good deeds. 彼は善行を自慢した.

without boasting 自慢じゃないが ▪ *Without boasting*, my son is honest and diligent. 自慢じゃないが, 私の息子は正直で勤勉だ.

boat[1] /boʊt/ 名 ***be*** (***all***) ***in one boat***/ ***be*** (***all***) ***in the same boat***《口》**1** 立場[境遇, 運命]を共にしている ▪ My face is all muddy.—Oh, we*'re all in one boat* for that matter. 僕の顔は泥だらけだ—いや, その点ではみんな同じだ ▪ We wage earners *are all in the same boat* during these hard times. 我々賃金労働者はこの不景気の時代には誰も同じ苦境にある.

2 同じように責任がある ▪ You can't single out one for blame; they*'re all in the same boat.* 一人を選び出して責めるわけにはいかない. 彼らは同じように責任があるのだから.

burn** one's **boats →BURN[2].

by boat 船で ▪ I went *by boat.* 私は船で行った.

float** a person's **boat《口》人をわくわくさせる, 人の気を引く ▪ Find your favorite niche and do whatever *floats your boat.* お気に入りの場を見つけて, 何でも君がおもしろいと思うことをやりなさい ▪ It sounds interesting, but it doesn't *float my boat.* それはおもしろそうだが, 僕の食指は動かないね.

go [***get***] ***into a boat*** 船に乗る ▪ We *got into a boat* at once. 我々はすぐに乗船した.

miss the boat **1** ボートに乗り遅れる; 機会を取り逃がす ▪ John found that he had *missed the boat.* ジョンは機会を取り逃がしたことを知った.

2 理解し損ねる ▪ I figured I'd just *missed the boat* on those guys. 私はこの連中のことをすっかり理解し損ねたと思った.

off the boat《口・しばしば侮辱》外国からやって来たばかりで, 新参者で ▪ Joe is *off the boat* and out of a job. ジョーは外国からきたばかりで, 職にあぶれている.

push the boat out《英口》(パーティー・食事などに)お金を奮発して楽しむ[祝う] (*for*) ▪ Stan was happy to *push the boat out for* his daughter's wedding. スタンは喜んでお金を奮発して娘の結婚を祝った.

rock the boat《口》現状に(いたずらに)波風を立てる ▪ They have a tendency to *rock the boat.* 彼らは現状に波風を立てる傾向がある.

sail [***row***] ***in one*** [***the same***] ***boat*** 同じ道を行く, 行動を共にする ▪ We *sail in the same boat* as you. 我々は君たちと行動を共にする.

take a boat for ...行きの船に乗る ▪ We *took a boat for* Yokohama. 私たちは横浜行きの船に乗った.

take boat 乗船する ▪ John *took boat* at Romney. ジョンはロムニーで乗船した.

take to the boats 沈む船からボートで逃げる; あわてて事業を捨てる ▪ When the ship was wrecked offshore, we all *took to the boats*. 沖で船が難破したとき, 我々はみな沈む船からボートで逃げた.

when** one's **boat come in =when one's SHIP comes home.

boat[2] /boʊt/ 動 ***boat it*** 船で行く, ボートをこぐ ▪ They *boat it* over to Lambeth. 彼らはボートでランベスまで渡って行く.

boat the oars オールをボートに入れてこぐのをやめる ▪ *Boat the oars*!《号令》オール収め!

Bob, bob[1] /bɑb|bɔb/ 名 ***a dry*** [***wet***] ***bob*** イートン校のクリケット組[ボート組]の学生; (広く)クリケット[ボート]に熱心な人 ▪ When he was at Eton, he was famous as *a wet bob*. 彼がイートン校にいたときは, ボートの選手として有名だった.

bear a bob **1**《口》助ける; 共同して...する ▪ Every one on board had to *bear a bob*. 船上の人はみな手伝わなければならなかった.

2 折返しを歌う, コーラスに加わる ▪ I'll *bear a bob*. 私もコーラスに加わりましょう.

Bob's [***bob's***] ***your uncle***《口》万事申し分なし ▪ You have only to cook it for 30 minutes, and *Bob's your uncle*. あなたはそれを30分間焼けばよろしい. それで万事 OK です.

give the bob だます, からかう; 妨げる ▪ He really *gave* her *the bob*. 彼はうまく彼女をだました.

bob[2] /bɑb|bɔb/ 動 ***bob and weave*** (特にボクサーが)上体を上下左右に揺らす ▪ The boxer deftly *bobbed and weaved*. ボクサーは巧みに上体を上下左右に揺らした.

bob up again (***like a cork***) (失敗したり, 弱ったりした人が)元気よく立ち直る ▪ He *bobbed up again like a cork*. 彼は元気よく立ち直った.

bob up and down 絶えず上下に移動する ▪ The boat *bobbed up and down* rhythmically as the waves passed under it. ボートは波が船底を通過するとリズミカルに上下に動いた.

bobbery /bɑ́bəri/ 名 ***kick up a bobbery*** 大騒ぎを起こす ▪ He went *kicking up a bobbery*. 彼はひどく騒ぎ立てた. ☞bobbery＜Hind bāp-rē＝O father.

bode /boʊd/ 動 ***bode well*** [***ill***] (...にとって)吉[凶]兆だ, 縁起が良い[悪い] (*for, to*) ▪ His idle habits *bode ill for* his future. 彼の怠け癖で彼の将来が思いやられる ▪ The omen *boded well to* you. あなたは幸先がよかった.

bodkin /bɑ́dkən|bɔ́d-/ 副 ***ride*** [***sit, travel***] ***bodkin***《口》二人の間にはさまって乗る[座る, 旅行する] ▪ He is too big to *travel bodkin* between you and me. 彼は大きいので私とあなたの間にはさまって旅行することはできない.

body /bɑ́di|bɔ́di/ 名 ***a body man*** (政治家の)付き人 ▪ Every candidate has *a body man*. すべての候補者には付き人がいる.

a fine body of men 立派な人々 ▪ Air Force pilots are *a fine body of men*. 空軍パイロットたちは立派な人々である.

a good sort of body 好人物 ▪ The groom is *a good sort of body*. 馬丁は好人物だ.

a warm body《口》**1** これという取り柄のない人, 席を温めるだけの人 ▪ She is a lonely women who is in search of a companion or just *a warm body*. 彼女は孤独な女性で, 話し相手か, ただ席を温めるだけの人を探している.

2 (機械ではなく)血の通う人間 ▪ A warm heart makes *a warm body*. 温かい心が血の通う人を作る.

an heir of the [*one's*] ***body*** 直系の相続者 ▪ You find here a child described as *an heir of the body*. ここに直系の相続者と言われる子供がいる.

be in the body 肉体を持っている, この世にある ▪ I *am* yet *in the body*. 私はまだこの世に生きている.

body and breeches《米俗》全く, すっかり ▪ He is in love with her *body and breeches*. 彼は彼女にぞっこんにほれている ▪ He surrendered *body and breeches*. 彼はすっかり降参した.

body and soul **1** 全く, 身心を打ち込んで ▪ Devote yourself, *body and soul*, to your study. 勉強に全身全霊を打ち込みなさい.

2 身も心も, 完全に ▪ He owned the workers *body and soul*. 彼は従業員を完全に握っていた.

have body (ワインに)こくがある ▪ This wine *has body* as well as bouquet. このワインは香りがよく, こくもある.

in a body 一団となって ▪ The Cabinet resigned *in a body*. 内閣は総辞職した.

in body 親しく; 身体的には ▪ Though absent *in body*, I am with you in spirit. 肉体は離れていても, 心はあなたと共にある.

keep body and soul together《口》やっと生きていく ▪ In these days of rising prices it is difficult for us to *keep body and soul together*. どんどん物価の上がる今日では命をつないでいくことも難しい.

know where the bodies are buried 組織の秘密[スキャンダル]を握っている ▪ He *knows where the bodies are buried* at the Pentagon. 彼はペンタゴンの秘密を握っている.

over my [*a person's*] ***dead body***《口》おれの死体を越えてからにしろ《絶対にそうさせない》 ▪ I am going to buy the car, Dad. —*Over my dead body*! パパ, 僕はその車を買うよ—おれの死体を越えてからにしろ! ▪ The boss said John would come back to work *over his dead body*. 社長は「ジョンは復職したいようだがおれの死体を越えてからにしろ」と言った.

sell** one's **body 体を売る, 売春をする ▪ She *sells her body* but not her dreams. 彼女は体は売るが, 夢は売らない.

the body beautiful 理想的な肉体美 ▪ All women wish to develop *the body beautiful*. すべての女性は理想的な肉体美を作りたいと思っている.

bog[1] /bɑg|bɔg/ 名 ***bog standard*** 《英口》ありふれた, 普通の ▪ Sally drives a *bog standard* economy car. サリーはありふれた省エネ車に乗っている.

bog[2] /bɑg|bɔg/ 動 ***be* [*get*] *bogged down*** 身動きがとれない; 行きづまる (*by, with, over*) ▪ I *was bogged down by* the darkness. 私は暗闇のために身動きがとれなくなった ▪ The game *was bogged down with* fouls. ゲームは反則のために行きづまった ▪ The talks got *bogged down over* questions of sovereignty and self-rule. その会談は主権と自治の問題で行きづまった.

boggle /bɑ́gəl|bɔ́gəl/ 動 ***boggle the mind*** (複雑さ・新奇さなどで)たまげさせる, 驚愕させる ▪ The very magnitude of the Milky Way *boggles the mind.* 銀河の大きさ自体にたまげてしまう.

The mind* [*imagination*] *boggles. 《口》(そんなことは)想像もつかない ▪ He earns £2,000 a week. —*The mind boggles.* 彼は週2,000ポンドかせぐ—そんなことは想像もつかないよ.

Bohemia /boʊhíːmiə/ 名 ***a flavor of Bohemia*** 因習にとらわれない趣 ▪ There is *a flavor of Bohemia* about the place which pleases newcomers. そこには新来者を喜ばせる因習にとらわれない自由な趣がある. ☞Bohemia はジプシーの祖国と思われていたことから.

boil[1] /bɔɪl/ 名 ***at the boil*** →on the BOIL.

bring** a person **to a boil 人を激怒させる ▪ Linda *was* really *brought to a boil* by his remark. リンダは彼の言葉に本当に激怒した.

bring** a thing **to the boil 物を沸騰させる《比喩的にも》 ▪ She *brought* the kettle *to the boil.* 彼女はやかんを沸騰させた ▪ The affair *was brought to the boil* by his arrival. その事件は彼の到着によって沸騰点に達した.

come to the boil 沸騰する《比喩的にも》 ▪ Water *comes to the boil* at 100°C. 水は摂氏100度で沸騰する ▪ The row between them *came to the boil* yesterday. 彼らのけんかはきのう最も激しくなった.

give** a thing **a boil 物を煮る ▪ Mix water and whisky and *give* it *a boil.* 水とウィスキーを混ぜてそれを煮なさい.

go off the boil **1** 煮え立たなくなる ▪ The potatoes *went off the boil.* ジャガイモは煮立たなくなった.
2 《口》熱[興奮]がさめる ▪ The movement *went off the boil.* その運動は熱がさめた.

off the boil 《英》最高潮ではなくなって ▪ He was one of America's most exciting artists in the 1960s and '70s but went *off the boil* thereafter. 彼は1960年代と70年代にはアメリカの最も刺激的な芸術家の一人だったが, その後最高潮ではなくなった.

on* [*at*] *the boil 《英》 **1** (水・やかんなどが)沸騰して ▪ The kettle's just *on the boil.* やかんがちょうど沸騰してきた.
2 (状況・感情などが)最高潮で ▪ They have got an interest in keeping the scandal *on the boil.* 彼らはスキャンダルを最高に保っておくことに関心を持っている ▪ The player was obviously *on the boil* at that moment. そのプレーヤーは明らかにその時絶好調だった.

put ... on to boil ...を沸かし[煮]始める ▪ Ann *put* the kettle *on to boil.* アンはやかんを沸かし始めた.

boil[2] /bɔɪl/ 動 ***boil the pot*** →POT.

make** a person's **blood boil →BLOOD.

reach* (*the*) *boiling point (状況・感情を)制しきれなくなる; 頂点に達する ▪ Observing these events, Steinbeck's anger *reached the boiling point.* これらの事件を見て, スタインベックの怒りは頂点に達した.

boiled /bɔɪld/ 形 ***boiled as an* (*old*) *owl*** 《俗》ひどく酔って ▪ By nine o'clock he was *boiled as an owl.* 9時までに彼は酔いつぶれていた.

feel like a boiled rag 《口》すっかり気力が抜ける, ぐにゃぐにゃになる ▪ No illness makes one *feel* more *like a boiled rag* than the flu does. インフルエンザほどひどく気力の抜ける病気はない.

boiler /bɔ́ɪlər/ 名 ***burst** a person's **boiler*** 《米》人を不幸に陥れる, 破滅させる, 失敗させる ▪ Somebody will *burst their boiler.* 誰かが彼らを不幸に陥れるだろう.

burst** one's **boiler 《米》災難[不幸]にあう, 失敗する, けがをする ▪ The woodman *burst his boiler.* そのきこりはひどい目にあった.

boiling /bɔ́ɪlɪŋ/ 形副名 ***at* (*the*) *boiling point*** **1** 沸騰して, 沸騰点に達して ▪ The water is *at the boiling point.* 湯が沸騰している.
2 《口》激昂[激怒]して ▪ When Ben was asked about the story he was *at the boiling point.* ベンはその話のことを聞かれたとき激怒していた.

have a low boiling point (人が)じきに怒る ▪ He *has a low boiling point.* 彼はすぐ激怒する.

reach the boiling point 激怒する ▪ His anger *reached the boiling point.* 彼の怒りは沸点に達した.

the whole boiling 《俗》全部 ▪ I'll take *the whole boiling.* 私は全部もらいましょう.

bold /boʊld/ 形 **(*as*) *bold as brass*** 実にずうずうしい ▪ He came in *as bold as brass.* 彼は実にずうずうしく入って来た.

***I'll be bold to* (*say*)** 失礼ながらあえて(申しあげる) ▪ *I'll be bold to say* that he is not equal to the task. 失礼ながら彼はその任に耐えない者だと申しあげます.

make* [*be*] *bold to** do**/make so bold to** do 失礼ながら[あえて]...する ▪ I *make* [*am*] *bold to* say that you are drinking too much. 失礼ながらあなたは酒がすぎます《使用人が主人などに対して言う文句》 ▪ May I *make so bold* as *to* photograph you? 失礼ながら写真を撮らせていただけますか ▪ If I may *make so bold* as *to* ask, what do you mean by that? あえて質問しますけど, それはどういう意味です?

make bold with ...を失敬する, 無礼をもいとわず取る; 大胆に...に手をつける ▪ I will first *make bold with* your money. まず一番に君の金を失敬したい ▪ I *made bold with* Milton. 私は大胆にもミルトンに手をつけた.

put a bold face on →FACE[1].

boldness /bóʊldnəs/ 名 ***have the boldness to** do* 厚かましくも[大胆にも]…する ▪ He *had the boldness to* ask me for money. 彼は厚かましくも私に金をくれと言った.

bollock /bálək|bɔ́l-/ 名 ***drop a bollock*** 《英俗》大失敗をする ▪ I realized I'd *dropped a bollock* after I'd posted the letter. その手紙を投函したあとで大失敗したことに気づいた.

the dog's bollocks 《英俗》すごい, すばらしい ▪ This guitar is *the dog's bollocks*. このギターはすごい. ☞bollocks＝balls.

bolt /boʊlt/ 名 ***a bolt from [out of] the blue*** 青天のへきれき, 不意の不幸・災難 ▪ The news of the attack on the Suez Canal came like *a bolt from the blue*. スエズ運河攻撃のニュースはまるで青天のへきれきのようにやって来た ▪ There came *a bolt from the blue*—our rich bachelor uncle got married. 突然の不運がやって来た—金持ちで独身のうちのおじが結婚したのだ《遺産がもらえない》.

behind bolt and bar 厳重に監禁されて ▪ The burglar should be *behind bolt and bar*. 強盗は厳重に監禁するべきだ.

bolt upright (矢でも飲んだように)まっすぐに《立つなど》 ▪ I sat *bolt upright* in my chair. 私は体をまっすぐにしていすに座っていた.

do a bolt 《俗》逃げ出す ▪ He *did a bolt* at once. 彼はすぐ逃げ出した.

make a bolt for …の方へ逃げ出す ▪ He *made a bolt for* the car. 彼は車の方へ逃げ出した.

make a bolt for it 《口》素早く逃げ出す, 逐電する ▪ I *made a bolt for it* over the stockade. 私は矢来を越えて素早く逃げ出した.

shoot** one's **bolt 太矢を射放つ; (最後の)努力[攻撃]をする; 〚完了形・受身で〛奥の手を出し尽くす ▪ The Germans *shot their bolt* at the battle of the Bulge. ドイツ軍はバルジの戦いで最後の努力をした. ☞A fool's *bolt is* soon *shot*. 《諺》「愚者はすぐ奥の手を出しつくす」から.

bomb /bɑm|bɔm/ 名 ***a calorie bomb*** カロリー爆弾《クリスマスプディングのようにおいしいが脂肪分の高い食物》 ▪ Real Mexican food is NOT *a "calorie bomb"*. 本物のメキシコ料理はカロリー爆弾ではない.

a vitamin bomb ビタミン爆弾《ビタミンの豊富な食物》 ▪ Doctors consider kiwifruit *a* real *vitamin bomb*. キウイフルーツはビタミン豊富な食物だと医師たちは考えている.

a walking time bomb **1** 危篤状態にある人; すぐに切れる人 ▪ The doctor said he was *a walking time bomb*, and that it was a miracle he was still alive. 医師によれば彼は危険な状態で, まだ生きているのが奇跡だとのことだった ▪ He is *a walking time bomb* that could explode at any time. 彼はかんしゃく持ちでいつ怒り出すかわからない.

2 自爆をする人 ▪ With the explosives strapped to his body, the young man was *a walking time bomb*. 爆発物を体に巻きつけて, その青年は自爆した. ☞「歩く時限爆弾」.

be the bomb 《俗》すごくいい[刺激的な] ▪ Some skinny girls just think they*'re the bomb*. やせっぽちの女の子の中には自分たちがものすごくかっこいいと思っている者がいる.

cost a bomb 非常に高価だ ▪ A Persian carpet *costs a bomb*. It's out of the question. ペルシャじゅうたんはとても高価だ. 話にならんね.

drop a bomb **1** 爆弾を落とす ▪ A fighter jet had *dropped a bomb* on the bridge. ジェット戦闘機が橋に爆弾を落とした.

2 《米》爆弾宣言をする ▪ He surprised his colleagues by *dropping a bomb*. 彼は爆弾宣言をして同僚を驚かせた. ☞drop [explode] a bombshell とも言う.

3 《英俗》おならをする ▪ He *drops a bomb* wherever he is. 彼はところかまわずおならする.

go a bomb 《英》 **1** ＝go down a BOMB.

2 ＝go like a BOMB.

go down a bomb 《口》大成功である; 大人気である ▪ The party is *going down a bomb*. パーティーは大盛況だ ▪ She *went down a bomb* at the party. 彼女はパーティーで大人気だった.

go down like a bomb 《口》大きなショック[驚き, 失望; 《米》失敗]である ▪ The news of his arrival *went down like a bomb* in the village. 彼の到着のニュースは村の大きな驚きであった ▪ His jokes always *go down like a bomb*. 彼の冗談はいつもさっぱり受けない.

go like a bomb 《英口》 **1** たちまちの大成功である ▪ Suits of this sort *go like a bomb* in Paris. この種のスーツはパリでは大変な売れ行きだ.

2 (車が)とても速く走る ▪ My new car *goes like a bomb*! 僕の新車はすごく速く走る.

lay a bomb 《米俗》(演技に)失敗する ▪ I have never *laid a bomb* with this song. この歌で失敗したことはない.

like a bomb 《口》首尾よく ▪ The interview went off *like a bomb*. 面談は上首尾に終わった.

look like a bomb has hit it 《口》(部屋などが)めちゃめちゃに散らかっている ▪ My son's room *looks like a bomb has hit it*. 息子の部屋はめちゃめちゃに散らかっている.

make [earn, cost, spend] a bomb 《口》大金を儲ける[を稼ぐ, がかかる, を使う] ▪ He *made a bomb* by selling cars. 彼は車を売って大金を儲けた.

put a bomb under 《口》 **1** …の下に爆弾をしかける ▪ He tried to *put a bomb under* his uncle's car. 彼は叔父の車の下に爆弾をしかけようとした.

2 (催促状を出して人)に催促する ▪ We'd better *put a bomb under* Mr. Hall. 我々はホール氏に催促したほうがよい.

bombard /bɑmbɑ́ːrd|bɔm-/ 動 ***be bombarded with*** …で砲撃[爆撃]される; …攻めにあう ▪ Our positions *were bombarded with* shells. わが陣地は砲撃された ▪ He *was bombarded with* invitations. 彼は招待攻めにあった.

bombshell /bɑ́mʃèl|bɔ́m-/ 名 ***a bombshell***

secret (露見したら)大騒動になる機密 ▪ Mary may drop *a bombshell secret* on the family. メアリーはその家族の大変な秘密を漏らすかもしれない.

come as a bombshell 驚かす, 仰天させる ▪ The news that their son met with an accident *came as a bombshell* to the couple. 息子が事故にあったという知らせは, 二人を仰天させた.

drop a bombshell 爆弾発言をする ▪ Our daughter, a high school student, *dropped a bombshell* when she told us that she was pregnant. うちの高校生の娘が妊娠したと爆弾発言をして, 我々を驚かせた.

explode a bombshell (意見・学説などを)爆弾的に発表する ▪ He *exploded a bombshell* and stunned us. 彼は学説を爆弾的に発表して, 我々を呆然とさせた.

bonanza /bənǽnzə/ 名 ***in bonanza*** 《米》(鉱山が)富鉱で; 大当たりで ▪ The mine was *in* its greatest *bonanza*. その鉱山はまさに大当たりだった.

bond /bɑnd|bɔnd/ 名 ***be as good as*** *one's* ***bond*** (証文同様に)十分信用できる ▪ His word *is as good as his bond*. 彼の約束は十分信用できる.

enter into a bond with …と契約を結ぶ ▪ I *entered into a bond with* him. 彼と契約を結んだ.

give bond to *do* [***for***] 《米》…するべき[の]保証を与える ▪ Each must *give bond for* his appearance before the court. 各人は出廷の保証を与えなければならない.

go bond for *a person* 人の保証人となる ▪ Would he *go bond for* you? 彼は君の保証人になってくれるだろうか.

in bond 保税倉庫に入れて ▪ The whisky is bottled *in bond*. そのウイスキーはびんづめにして保税倉庫に入れられている.

in bonds 縛られて, 禁固されて ▪ The Duke was *in bonds* in London. 侯爵はロンドンで禁固中だった.

take [***release, get***]***…out of bond*** (関税を払って)…を保税倉庫から出す ▪ He *got* his next consignment of tobacco *out of bond*. 次の委託タバコを保税倉庫から出した.

bondage /bɑ́ndɪdʒ|bɔ́n-/ 名 ***in bondage*** とらわれて, 奴隷となって ▪ He was kept *in bondage*. 彼はとらわれの身になっていた.

bone /boʊn/ 名 ***a bone of contention*** [***dissention***] 争いの種 ▪ The division of the property was *a bone of contention* between the brothers. 財産分割が兄弟の間の争いの種だった. ☞犬に骨を投げ与えるとけんかになることから.

a bone to pick [***gnaw***] 論争すべきこと, 従事すべきこと, 難問題, 苦情の種 ▪ He will cast me *a bone* or two *to pick*. 彼は私に1, 2の追究すべき事柄を投げ与えるだろう ▪ I have *a bone to pick* with you. Why didn't you tell me in advance about your plan? 君に文句が1つある. なぜ君の計画を前もって言ってくれなかったのだ. ☞「骨が犬の心を捕えるように人の心を捕えるもの」が原義.

(***as***) ***dry as a bone*** →DRY[1].

(***as***) ***hard as a bone*** →HARD.

(***be***) ***all*** [***only***] ***skin and bone***(***s***) →SKIN[1].

be bone lazy [***idle***] 《英》ひどく怠惰な ▪ Jim *is bone idle*—he does nothing but watch TV all day. ジムはきわめて怠惰だ—一日中テレビを見てばかりいる. ☞lazybones (怠け者)にからませた句.

be in *a person's* ***bones*** …を予感する, 確かと感じる ▪ It *was in my bones* all summer. 夏の間じゅう私はそれを予感していた.

be on *one's* ***bones*** (ほとんど)窮乏して ▪ I'*m* right *on my bones*. 私はほんとに窮乏しているのです. ☞bones「やせて骨ばかりになっていること」.

bone of *a person's* ***bone, flesh of*** *a person's* ***flesh*** 非常に密接で, 同家族で (《聖》*Gen.* 2. 23) ▪ He is *bone of my bone, flesh of my flesh*. 彼は私の血族である.

break no bones (事故にあっても)けがはない ▪ *No bones broken*, I hope. けがはなかったろうね.

bred in the bone →BREED[2].

carry a bone in the [*one's*] ***mouth*** [***teeth***] 《海口》(船が)白泡を立てて進む ▪ Our ship *carried a bone in her mouth*. 船は白泡を立てて進んだ.

close to the bone →near the BONE.

cut [***pare***]***…*** (***down***) ***to the bone*** …をぎりぎりまで切りつめる ▪ If resources are tight, you can *cut* expenses *down to the bone*. 資金が乏しければ, 出費をぎりぎりまで切り詰めたらいい ▪ Services are already *being cut to the bone*. サービスはとっくにぎりぎりまで切りつめられている.

doesn't have [***there isn't***] ***a jealous*** [***mean, unkind,*** etc.] ***bone in*** *one's* ***body*** 少しも嫉妬(しっと)心[けちな, 不親切なところ]がない ▪ He *doesn't have a mean bone in his body*. He is accommodating, cheerful, and friendly. 彼はけちなところがない—彼は親切で陽気で愛想がいい ▪ She is an extremely caring and loving person to every one—*there isn't an unkind bone in her body*. 彼女はすべての人に対してすこぶる思いやりがあり愛情深い—彼女は不親切なところが少しもない.

(***down***) ***to the bone*** **1** (傷が)骨まで達して ▪ The laceration over the eye went *down to the bone*. 目の上の裂傷は骨まで達していた.

2 《口》骨の髄まで, 徹底的に ▪ We were chilled [frozen] *to the bone*. 我々は骨の髄まで冷えていた.

feel [***think, believe, know,*** etc.] (***it***)***…in*** *one's* ***bones*** 《口》…を直覚する, 予感がする, 直感的に確信する ▪ I *feel* (it) *in my bones* that they will never get along well together. 彼らは決して仲良くやっていかないだろうという予感がする ▪ I *thought in my bones* no good could come out of it. それからはなんの好結果も生じえないと直感的に思った.

find bones in …をなかなか信じない ▪ Some people *find bones in* the statement. その陳述をなかなか信じない人もいる.

Hard words break no bones. 《諺》きつくても言葉だけならけがはない.

have a bone in *one's* ***leg*** [***throat, arm,***

neck] 足[のど, 腕, 首]に骨を立てている ▪ I can't go, for I *have a bone in my leg*. 私は行けません. 足に骨を立てていますから ▪ He alleged that he *had a bone in his throat* and could not speak. 彼はのどに骨を立てているので話ができないと言った. ☞足[のど, 腕, 首]が使えないときの言い訳に使う文句; have a bone in my leg は特に席をあけないことを子供に言い訳するときに使う.

***have a bone to pick with** a person* 人に対して苦情がある, 人と話をつけなければならないことがある ▪ I*'ve a bone to pick with* you about your unpunctuality. 君が時間を守らないことについては君に文句がある.

in the bone 徹底的に, 骨の髄まで; 深く ▪ She was a cook *in the bone*. 彼女は徹頭徹尾料理人だった.

jump** a person's **bones 《米俗》人とセックスをする ▪ Dick doesn't love you—he just wants to *jump your bones*. ディックは君を愛していない—ただ君とセックスがしたいだけだ.

lay** one's [a person's] **bones 《米》埋葬してもらう[人を埋葬する] ▪ I am going to *lay my bones* alongside of hers. 彼女のそばに埋葬してもらうつもりだ.

***make bones of* [*about*]** …をいやがる, ためらう, に異議をもつ ▪ Elizabeth was *making* huge *bones of* sending them to Ireland. エリザベスは彼らをアイルランドへ送ることを大いにいやがった.

***make no bones of* [*about*]/*not make any bones of* [*about*]** **1** …をちゅうちょしない ▪ He *makes no bones about* admitting it. 彼はそれを認めることをためらわない ▪ She *never made any bones of* hiding in a closet. 彼女は戸だなの中へ隠れることを何とも思わなかった.
2 …を隠さない; を認める (*about, of*) ▪ Bill is poor, but he *makes no bones about* it. ビルは貧乏だが, そのことを隠さない ▪ She *makes no bones of* the fact that she is a single mother. 彼女は自分がシングルマザーだということを隠さない. ☞肉を切るとき骨を残さないことから.

make old bones **1**〚主に否定文で〛十分長生きする ▪ He'll not live to *make old bones*. 彼は長生きしないだろう.
2 ふけて見える, ふけを感じる ▪ Poor father, he's *making old bones*. お気の毒に父はふけて見えだした. ☞old bones「老体」.

near* [*close to*] *the bone **1** けちで; 困窮して ▪ He is awfully *near the bone*. 彼はひどくけちだ ▪ The family was living *near the bone*. その家は困窮した暮らしをしていた.
2 (風紀上)きわどいところまで ▪ The play was very *near the bone*. その芝居はずいぶんきわどいものだった.
3《口》痛いところを突いて, 図星をさして ▪ His comments were offensive and very *near* to *the bone*. 彼のコメントは無礼で, 痛いところを突いていた.

no bones about it ぐずぐず言わずにすぐ ▪ And *no bones about it*. そしてぐずぐず言わずすぐやれ.

No bones broken! たいしたことはないよ.

not have a ... bone in** one's **body (人)に…なところ[性格]がない ▪ He does*n't have a* deceitful [romantic, racist, etc.] *bone in his body*. 彼には人をだますような[ロマンチックな, 人種差別的な, などの]ところがない.

One end is sure to be bone. 《諺》一方の端は必ず骨だ《よいことばかりはない》.

pick a bone 骨をしゃぶる ▪ The man was starving and *picked* even the *bones*. その男は餓死しそうだったので骨さえしゃぶった.

roll the bones 《米俗》さいころ遊びをする ▪ They are *rolling the bones*. やつらはさいころ遊びをやっている. ☞bones＝dice.

skin and bone(s) →SKIN[1].

spare bones 骨惜しみする.

the bare bones of (…の)骨子, 基本, 要点 ▪ The doctor concentrated on *the bare bones of* nursing. 医師は看護の基本を中心に話した ▪ Give me *the bare bones of* the matter. 問題の要点だけ話してください.

think* (*it*)*... in** one's **bones → feel (it)... in one's BONEs.

throw a bone …にわずかな援助を与える ▪ The university *threw a bone* to the five impoverished students. その大学は5人の貧しい学生にわずかな援助を与えた ▪ *Throw* me *a bone* here!《米口》ちょっと助けてくれないか.

tickle** a person's **funny* [*crazy*] *bone 人を笑わせる, おもしろがらせる ▪ His way of telling the story *tickled my funny bone*. 彼のその話の語り口が私をおもしろがらせた.

to the bone **1** 骨の髄まで, 深く ▪ I was chilled *to the bone*. 骨の髄まで冷えきった.
2 徹底的に ▪ We cut the expenses *to the bone*. 我々は費用をぎりぎりに切りつめた.

work** one's **fingers to the bone →FINGER[1].

boner /bóʊnər/ 名 ***pull a boner*** 《米俗》大しくじりをする, とんだへまをやる《主に社交上の》 ▪ You *pulled a boner* when you spoke so disparagingly of that country. 君があの国をあんなに悪く言ったのはしくじりだった.

bonfire /bánfàɪər|bɔ́nfàɪə/ 名 ***make a bonfire of*** …を焼き捨てる ▪ *Make a bonfire of* rubbish. がらくたを焼き捨てなさい.

bonnet /bánət|bɔ́n-/ 名 ***fill** a person's **bonnet*** 人の役が勤まる; 人に匹敵する ▪ He'll never *fill John's bonnet*. 彼はとてもジョンには及ばない.

keep ... under** one's **bonnet …を秘密にしておく ▪ *Keep* what you know *under your bonnet*. 君の知っていることは秘密にしておけ.

vail* [*vale*] *the bonnet (敬意を表して)脱帽する (*to*) ▪ All nations will *vail the bonnet to* England. すべての国がイギリスに脱帽するだろう.

boo /buː/ 名 ***not say boo*** 《米口》うんともすんとも言わない ▪ I asked him a question, but he did*n't say boo*. 彼に質問をしたが, うんともすんとも言

わなかった.

wouldn't* [*cannot*] *say* [*cry*] *boo to a goose*/ *wouldn't say boo*/《豪》*wouldn't say boo to a fly 《口》(ガチョウなどにバアとも言えないほど)小心者だ, ひどく憶病である, 気が弱くて口がきけない ▪ Tim is shy and *wouldn't say boo to a goose*. ティムははにかみやで小心者だ ▪ Bob *could never say boo to a gosling* of the feminine gender. ボブは雌のガチョウの子にさえ「バア」と言えないほど憶病だった.

boodle /búːdəl/ 名 ***the whole* (*kit and*) *boodle*** 全体 ▪ There wasn't a soul of *the whole kit and boodle* that could do it. 全体の中でそれのできる者は一人もいなかった.

book[1] /bʊk/ 名 ***a talking book*** 盲人用のレコード[テープ] ▪ They received advice from *a talking book*. 彼らは盲人用のテープから助言を受けた.

at** one's **books 勉強して ▪ He is earnestly *at his books*. 彼はいま熱心に勉強している.

balance the books **1** 帳簿を精算する[締める] ▪ It's John's job to *balance the books* each quarter. 四半期ごとに帳簿を締めるのはジョンの仕事だ. **2** 勘定を精算[決済]する ▪ We can't *balance the books* till your last check clears. 君の最後の小切手が精算されるまでは勘定を決済することができない.

be borne on the books of ...によって支払われる ▪ It *was borne on the books of* his father. それは彼の父が支払った.

be in** a person's **good* [*bad, black*] *books 人の気に入りである[人にきらわれている] ▪ You will *be in father's good books* now. 君はこんどはお父さんの気に入るだろう ▪ He *is in my bad books*. 彼は私のお気に入りではない. ☞昔商店においてよい客と悪い客を別々の帳に記したことから.

(*be*) *on* [*upon*] *one's* [*the*] *books* ...の顧客である; の公式名簿に載っている《会員・患者など》 ▪ Mr. Jones has *been on our books* for many years. ジョーンズ氏は多年にわたって我々のお得意様だ ▪ She continued *on the books* as an out-patient. 彼女は外来患者として引き続き名簿に載っていた.

bring** a person **to book 《英豪》〚主に受身で〛人を罰する, 責める; 調べる ▪ He committed theft and must *be brought to book*. 彼は窃盗を犯したので罰せられなければならない ▪ Someone will *bring* you *to book* for talking like that. そのような話をしたことに対し, 誰かが君を責めるだろう. ☞book「人の悪行を記録するえんま帳」.

by my book 私の見るところでは ▪ Linda is charming *by my book*. 私の見るところではリンダは魅力的だ.

by* [*according to*] (*the*) *book 型通りに; 典拠によって; 正確に ▪ You kiss *by the book*. あなたは型通りのキスをするのね (cf. Sh., *Rom. & Jul.* 1. 5. 112) ▪ They seemed determined to go *by the book* and not rush things. 彼らは規則に則ってプレーし, あせらないと決心しているようだった.

close the book **1** (話を)終りにする, 忘れる; (...に)けりをつける (*on*) ▪ Let's *close the book on* our previous difficulties and start afresh. 以前の困難は忘れて, 新規まき直しをしよう. **2** 謎を解き明かす ▪ The detective was able to *close the book* on the murder mystery. 敏腕の探偵はその殺人事件の謎を解き明かすことができた.

close the* [*its*] *books 帳簿を締め切る; 受注を締め切る; けりをつける (*on*) ▪ The tickets were all sold, so the manager said to *close the books*. 入場券はみな売れた, そこで販売主任は受注を締め切れと言った ▪ The department store *closes its books on* the 27th of each month. そのデパートは毎月27日に帳簿を締め切る ▪ He was glad to *close the books on* the case. 彼は事件にけりがついて喜んだ.

come to the book (陪審員を務める前に)宣誓する ▪ Those appointed to be jurors *came to the book* one by one. 陪審員に任命された者が一人ずつ宣誓した.

cook the books 《俗》帳簿をごまかす ▪ He tried to hide his thefts by *cooking the books*. 彼は盗みを隠すため帳簿をごまかそうとした.

crack a book 《口》本を開いて勉強する[読む] ▪ He passed the exam without *cracking a book*. 彼は本を開いて勉強することもなく試験にパスした ▪ He hardly ever *cracked a book*. 彼は本を開いて読んだことがなかった.

earn** one's **place in the history books (偉業によって)歴史書に名を残す ▪ This discovery made him *earn his place in the history books*. この発見によって彼は歴史書に名を残すことになった.

fudge the books 事実を隠蔽する[偽って伝える] ▪ The mayor tried to *fudge the books* to make things look better. 市長は事態をよく見せようとして事実を偽って伝えようとした.

get into** a person's **good* [*bad, black*] *books 人の気に入る[人にきらわれる] ▪ He *got into the good books of* the authorities. 彼は当局に気に入られた ▪ He neglected to call on his aunt and *got into her bad books*. 彼はおばを訪問することを怠って彼女のきげんを損じた.

get* [*have, put*]... *on the books 《米》...を予定する, 計画する; の制定を準備する ▪ The Government *has* income taxes *on the books*. 政府は所得税法の制定を準備している ▪ They *put* economic controls *on the books*. 彼らは経済統制を計画した.

go off the books 《米》法律として廃止される ▪ The taxes will *go off the books*. それらの税は廃止されるだろう.

have** one's **nose* (*buried*) *in a book → NOSE[1].

hit the* [*one's*] *books 《俗》ガリ勉をする, 一心に勉強する ▪ At exam time we all *hit the books*. 試験期間には我々はみんなガリ勉をする.

in** a person's **bad* [*good*] *books 人に気に入られて[嫌われて] ▪ Mac is honest and *in his father's good books*. マックは正直者で, 父親に気に入られている.

in *a person's* ***book*** 《口》人の見るところでは ▪ *In my book* he can be entirely relied on. 私の見るところでは, 彼は全面的に信頼できる.

keep a book on =make (a) BOOK on 2.

keep books 帳簿[簿記]をつける ▪ That is when the supermarkets started *keeping books*. それがスーパーマーケットが簿記をつけ始めたころだ.

knock ... out of the books 《米》(法律など)を廃止する ▪ *Knock* the price-fixing decree *out of the books*. 公定価格を決定する法令を廃止せよ.

know *one's* ***book*** 《口》万事心得ている, 知識が正確だ ▪ Lind *knows his book* well. リンドはよくよく万事心得ている.

know ... like a book …を完全に知っている ▪ I *know* John *like a book*. I'm sure he'll come. ジョンのことはよくよく知っている. 必ず来るよ.

leave *a thing* ***on the books*** 《米》ことを採択せずにおく ▪ The U.N. voted to *leave* the resolution *on the books*. 国連はその決議を採択せずにおくことに決定した.

like a book **1** 正式の言葉で; 正確に, 注意深く ▪ He talks *like a book*. 彼は正確に話す.
2 ちゅうちょせずに ▪ Democrats would vote for the bill *like a book*. 民主党はその法案にちゅうちょなく賛成するだろう.
3 徹底的に ▪ I know him *like a book*. 彼のことはよく知っている.

(little) black book ガールフレンドの電話番号帳 ▪ Now that he's engaged to Cindy, Alan won't be needing his *little black book*. シンディーと婚約したので, アランはガールフレンドの電話番号帳は必要なくなっただろう.

make (a) book on **1** (競馬で馬)への賭け金を集める ▪ He was *making book on* Golden Star. 彼はゴールデンスター号に賭ける賭け金を集めていた.
2 《米俗》…に賭ける; を請け合う (bet) ▪ He *made a book on* the races. 彼は競馬に賭けた ▪ You can *make book on* it that he won't arrive in time. 請け合ってもいい, 彼は遅刻するさ.

off the books 除名されて ▪ His name is *off the books*. 彼の名は除かれている.

on the books **1** 記録されて, 名簿に載って.
2 《米》(法律の改正・決議案の採択などしないで)そのままにしてある ▪ These laws still remain *on the books*. これらの法律は今なお未採択のままである.
3 《米》予定されて, 計画されて ▪ There are many more programs *on the books*. もっと多くの計画が予定されている.

one for the book(s) 《口》特筆すべきもの, 注目すべきもの, 特異なもの ▪ That play is *one for the book*. その劇は特筆すべきものである.

put [get] *a person* ***into*** *a person's* ***good books*** ある人を人の気に入るようにする ▪ This gracious act on Ann's part *put* her *into Mike's good books*. このアンの丁重なふるまいで, アンはマイクのお気に入りになった.

read *a person* ***like a book*** 人(の心)を十分理解する ▪ He is not honest. I can *read* him *like a book*. 彼は正直ではない. 私には彼の心がよくわかる.

salt the books 実際より多くの収入があったように記帳する ▪ The clerk was obliged to *salt the books*. 事務員はやむなく実際より多くの収入があったように記帳した.

shut the *[one's]* ***books*** 取引を中止する, 営業を停止する ▪ The merchants are *shutting their books*. 商人たちが営業を停止しつつある.

speak by the book 〚主に否定文で〛典拠によって言う ▪ Without *speaking by the book*, I am sure there is a law against it. 典拠はないが, それを禁ずる法律が確かにあると思う.

speak [talk] like a book 《口》(あいまいでなく)正確に話す《しばしば衒学(げんがく)者について言う》; 大変ものわかったことを言う ▪ He *speaks like a book*. One gets a little weary of it at times. 彼は正確にきちんとした話をする. ときに少しあきることがあるが.

suit *a person's* ***book*** 人の希望[都合]にかなう ▪ The arrangement will *suit my book* very well indeed. その予定はほんとに私の希望通りだ ▪ I can't come because it doesn't *suit my book* just now. 今のところ都合が悪いので, 参上できません. ☞book「競馬師の賭け帳」.

swear on the book 聖書によって誓う ▪ You must *swear on the book* that it is true. 君はそれが本当であることを聖書によって誓わなければならない.

take a leaf out of *a person's* ***book*** →LEAF.

take [strike] (a name) off the books 名簿から名前を除く, 除名する; 〚主に受身で〛除名される ▪ They *took his name off the books*. 彼らは彼を除名した ▪ *His name was taken off the books*. 彼は除名された.

tear [rip] up the rule book 通常とは異なるやり方で(物事を)行う・始める ▪ What we were able to do was *tear up the rule book* and design a car that doesn't damage the environment. 我々にできることは, 通常とは異なるやり方で行って, 環境を害さない車を設計することだった.

that's [there's] a turn-up for the books 《英口》そいつは奇妙だ, 驚きだ (→a TURN-UP for the book(s)).

throw the book at 《口》…に最も重い罰を科す; 厳しく罰する ▪ The judge *threw the book at* the defendant. 判事は被告に最も重い罪を科した. ☞book「適用可能な法令がのったリスト」.

try [use, etc.***] every trick in the book*** → use every TRICK in the book.

without book 典拠なしで; そらで ▪ Every Sunday the vicar gave a sermon delivered *without book*. 毎週日曜日に教区牧師は原稿も見ずに説教を行った ▪ He is ready to assert anything *without book*. 彼はよく典拠もなしに断定する.

wrote the book on (事)をよく知っている, 第一人者である ▪ Dr. Spock *wrote the book on* babies. スポック博士は, 赤ちゃんのことをよく知っていた. ☞常に過去形で使われる.

You can't [Don't, You shouldn't] judge a book by its cover. 《諺》本を表紙で判断してはいけない《物事をうわべで判断してはいけない》.

B

book[2] /bʊk/ 動 ***be booked for [to** do]* …の[する]運命にある; の約束がある[することになっている] ▪ He *is booked for* kingdom come. 彼はもうあの世へ行く運命にある ▪ You *are booked for* the 10th of November. あなたは11月10日のお約束になっています.

be booked up 先約がある; (座席が)満席である; (先約が多くて)忙しい, ひまがない ▪ I'm sorry, sir, but the restaurant *is booked up* until the middle of next week. すみませんが, レストランは来週の中ごろまで予約でいっぱいです ▪ I should like you to go with me. *Are* you very *booked up*? あなたにいっしょに行ってもらいたいんですが, ご多忙でしょうか.

be booked (up) solid 予約満員である; (で)いっぱいである ▪ Washington hotels had *been booked solid* for months. ワシントンのホテルは数か月の間ずっと予約満員だった ▪ I'*m booked (up) solid* on worries. 心配事で頭がいっぱいです.

book it 《米》 **1**《学俗》さっさと立ち去る[帰る] ▪ Kate *booked it* to Boston. ケイトはさっさとボストンへ帰ってしまった.

2《俗》請け合う (bet) ▪ I'll be back. *Book it.* 僕は戻ってくるよ. 賭けてもいい.

book off sick 《米》(不満のため)欠勤を申し入れる ▪ Fifty men have *booked off sick* at the car factory. その自動車工場で50人の工員が不平欠勤を申し入れている.

book** one's **passage 乗船切符を買う ▪ Have you *booked your passage* from New York to London? 君はニューヨークからロンドンへの乗船切符を買ったか.

***book** a person **to** do* 人に…する約束をさせる ▪ I *booked* him *to* go there. 彼にそこへ行く約束をさせた.

boom /bu:m/ 名 ***lower the boom (on)*** 《米口》(…を)痛撃する, 非難する; (を)きびしく取り締まる ▪ The teacher *lowered the boom on* the whole class for misbehaving. 先生はクラス全員の不作法を激しく非難した.

boomerang /bú:məræŋ/ 名 ***like a boomerang*** ブーメランのように ▪ History will return *like a boomerang*. 歴史はブーメランのように戻ってくる《くりかえされる》.

boon /bu:n/ 名 ***ask a boon of** (a person)* (人)にお願いをする ▪ May I *ask a boon of* you? ひとつお願いがあります.

boost /bu:st/ 名 ***give** a person **a boost*** 人のしり押しをする《比喩的にも》 ▪ *Give* him *a boost* so that he may climb over the fence. 彼がフェンスをよじ越えられるようにしり押しをしてやれ.

boot[1] /bu:t/ 名 ***a bossy boots*** 《英》威張り散らす人 ▪ It's no fun working in an office alongside such *a bossy boots*. あんな威張り散らすやつといっしょにオフィスで働くのはうんざりだ.

a sly boots ずるいやつ ▪ That gardener is *a sly boots*. あの庭師はずるい.

(as) tough as old boots →TOUGH[1].

be in** a person's **boots 人の立場になる ▪ He has been caught at last. I shouldn't like to *be in his boots*. 彼はついに捕えられた. 彼のような状態にはなりたくないものだ.

beat** a person **out of his boots 人をすっかり負かす ▪ He can *beat* Barnes *out of his boots*. 彼はバーンズを完全に負かすことができる.

bet** one's **boots **1** 有り金を全部賭ける ▪ I will *bet my boots* that Jim will pass the examination. 有り金を全部賭けてもいい, ジムは試験に合格するさ.

2 確信している ▪ And I *bet my boots* on the day I die. 私は自分の死ぬ日を確信している.

bet your boots 《米口》大丈夫だ, 確かだ (*on*) ▪ You may *bet your boots on* that. それは確かだよ.

big in** one's **boots 《米口》威張って, 誇って ▪ They are getting *big in their boots*. 彼らはだんだんうぬぼれてきている.

boot hill 《米》(西部開拓地のガンマンなどの)墓 ▪ The cowboy is buried on the nearby boot hill. そのカウボーイは近くの墓に葬られている.

boots and saddle 馬に乗れ《騎兵に号令して》; 乗馬合図のラッパ ▪ Our trumpets blew "*Boots and saddle*" in the streets. わがラッパ隊は街頭で「乗馬ラッパ」を吹き鳴らした ▪ *Boots and saddle*! 馬に乗れ! ☞ F boute selle 'place saddle' の悪用.

die in** one's **boots/die with** one's **boots on →DIE[2].

fill** one's **boots with 《英口》(貴重な[望ましい]もの)をできるだけたくさん手に入れる ▪ The idea is to *fill their boots with* as many donations as possible. その趣向はできるだけたくさんの寄付金を集めようとするものだ.

get (the order of) the boot/be given the boot 《口》首になる; 追い出される ▪ Harris has *got the order of the boot*. ハリスは首になった ▪ The player was not sure why he *got the boot*. その選手はなぜ自分が首になったかよくわからなかった.

get too big for** one's **boots →be too BIG for one's boots.

give** a person **the boot 《口》 **1** (特に倒れている人)をける ▪ I wanted to *give* him *the boot*. 私は彼をけってやろうと思った.

2 = give a person the order of the BOOT.

give** a person **the order of the boot 《口》人を首にする; 人を追い出す; 人と縁を切る ▪ I *gave* him *the order of the boot*. 私は彼を首にした ▪ Jane has *given* her boyfriend *the order of the boot*. ジェインはボーイフレンドと縁を切った.

go down in** one's **boots 《米口》びっくりする, 恐れる ▪ You don't *go down in your boots* even a little. 君はほんの少しも怖がらないんだね.

go it boots 《米口》敏速に[活発に]行動する ▪ He yelled out, "*Go it boots.*" 彼は「敏速にやれ」とわめ

いた.

go to bed in *one's* ***boots*** 非常に酔っている ▪ If Jo drinks much more, he'll *go to bed in his boots.* もしジョーがそれ以上飲んだら酔いつぶれるだろう.

hang up *one's* ***boots*** →HANG[2].

have *one's* ***heart in*** *one's* ***boots*** →HEART.

one's ***heart goes*** [***sinks***] ***into*** *one's* ***boots*** →one's HEART is in one's boots.

in the boot 《米》開花して ▪ The wheat was *in the boot.* 小麦の花が咲いていた.

lick *a person's* ***boots/lick the boots of*** → LICK[2].

like old boots →OLD.

move [***start***] *one's* ***boots*** 《米口》出発する ▪ Now *start your boots* and go home. さあ出発して家へ帰れ.

Over shoes, over boots. →SHOE[1].

pull [***lift, raise***] *oneself* (***up***) ***by*** *one's* (***own***) ***bootstraps*** [***boottags***] →BOOTSTRAP.

put [***sink***] ***in the boot/put the boot in*** 《口》(特にすでに倒れている人を)荒々しくける《比喩的にも》 ▪ Policemen are tempted to *put the boot in* occasionally. 警官も時折けったりたたいたりしたくなる ▪ The young men who attacked the old man had *put the boot in.* 老人を襲った青年たちは(彼を)荒々しくけったのだった.

put [***stick***] ***the boot into*** 《英口》厳しく非難する ▪ An unpublished novelist *put the boot into* established reputations. 公表作品のない小説家が確立された名声(のある人)を厳しく批判した.

put [***get***] ***the boot on the wrong*** [***other***] ***leg*** 意味をはき違える, おかど違いなことをする ▪ I think he's *got the boot on the wrong leg.* 彼ははき違えたのだと思う.

seven-league boots (ヨーロッパの童話に出てくる)ひとまたぎで7リーグ(約33km) 歩ける靴 ▪ *Seven-league boots* are no longer a fairy tale by the Brothers Grimm. ひとまたぎで7リーグ歩ける靴は, もはやグリム兄弟のおとぎ話ではない.

shake [***quake, shiver, tremble***] ***in*** *one's* ***boots*** →SHAKE in one's shoes.

stand ... in *one's* ***boots*** 靴のままで(身長が)...ある ▪ I *stand* six feet *in my boots.* 私は靴のままで身長が6フィートある.

the boot is on the other leg [***foot***] 形勢が逆である; 責任はほかにある, おかど違いである《非難・責任が反対の人にある場合に言う》 ▪ You say he ought to have written to thank me, but *the boot is on the other leg.* 君は彼が私に礼状をよこすべきだったと言うが, 事情は全く逆なのだよ ▪ No, *the boot is on the other foot.* You are to remain in town and he is to go to York. いや, 話はその逆だ. 君が町に残って彼がヨークへ行くのだ. ☞靴を反対の足にはいていることにたとえて.

to boot おまけに, そのうえ ▪ She is beautiful, and a princess *to boot.* 彼女は美形で, そのうえ王女だった. ☞boot「利益」.

too big for *one's* ***boots*** 《俗》うぬぼれている ▪ Ever since Bill won the tennis tournament, he has been *too big for his boots.* ビルはテニスのトーナメントで優勝してからずっと自慢が過ぎる.

wear boots 《米》やぼったい ▪ He is a rough old fellow—*wears boots.* 彼は粗野な老人で, やぼったい.

wipe *one's* ***boots on*** →WIPE[2].

with *one's* ***heart in*** *one's* ***boots*** →HEART.

without *one's* ***boots*** 靴を脱いで ▪ I stand six feet *without my boots.* 私は靴を脱いで身長が6フィートある.

boot[2] /buːt/ 動 ***booted and spurred*** ちゃんと(乗馬の)用意して ▪ He came in *booted and spurred* at five minutes to the hour. 彼は定刻より5分前にちゃんと用意して入って来た.

bootleg /búːtlèg/ 名 ***bootleg trader*** 密輸品を安く売る業者[店] ▪ Customs are trying to stop *bootleg traders* selling their goods. 税関は密輸品業者に商品を売らせないように努力している.

bootstrap /búːtstræ̀p/ 名 ***pull*** [***lift, raise***] *oneself* (***up***) ***by*** *one's* (***own***) ***bootstraps*** 《口》(障害を乗りこえて)自力で成功[向上]する ▪ Despite many obstacles, Della has *pulled herself up by her own bootstraps.* 多くの障害を乗り越えてデラは自分の努力で成功した.

booty /búːti/ 名 ***play booty*** なれ合って悪事を働く; (競技・競馬などで)八百長をやる ▪ I bribed a jockey to *play booty.* 私は騎手に賄賂をやって八百長をやらせた.

shake *one's* ***booty*** しりをふって踊る ▪ Come on, everybody. It's time to *shake our booty* to the music. さあみんな. 音楽に合わせてしりをふって踊る時間だぜ. ☞booty「しり」.

booze /buːz/ 名 ***be on the booze*** 盛んに飲み続けて; 酔っぱらって ▪ He *was* always *on the booze.* 彼はいつも飲んでばかりいた.

bo-peep /boʊpíːp/ 名 ***have a bo-peep*** 《豪口》見る (*at*) ▪ I'm gonna *have a bo-peep at* those little beauties. そういうかわい子ちゃんたちを見るつもりだ.

play bo-peep いないいないばぁをする; (政治家などが)変幻自在の行動をする ▪ He was forced to *play bo-peep* with his creditors. 彼はやむなく債権者に対して変幻自在の行動をせざるをえなかった.

border /bɔ́ːrdər/ 名 ***on the border*** 国境近くで, 辺境地方で ▪ He joined the thieves *on the* English *border.* 彼はイギリスの国境近くで盗賊の一味に加わった.

on the borders of ...の辺境に; まさに...しようとして ▪ Buddha was born *on the borders of* Nepal. 仏陀(ぶっだ)はネパールの国境に生まれた ▪ They are *on the borders of* ruin. 彼らは破滅に瀕している.

bore[1] /bɔːr/ 名 ***a crashing bore*** 《俗》おそろしく退屈な人 ▪ Lucy's boyfriend is the most *crashing bore* I have ever met. ルーシーのボーイフレンドは今まで会ったこともないくらい退屈きわまる男だ.

bore[2] /bɔːr/ 動 ***be bored out of*** *one's* ***mind***

[**skull**]《口》うんざりして気が変になりそうだ ▪ I *was bored out of my mind* by the novel Tom lent me. トムが貸してくれた小説にうんざりして気が変になりそうだった.

be bored witless ひどく退屈する ▪ I *was bored witless* with this novel. この小説にはほとほと退屈した.

bore the ass [《英》 ***arse***] ***off*** *a person* 《卑》人をひどく退屈させる ▪ His idea of a joke *bores the arse off* me. 彼の冗談についての考えは僕をほとほと退屈させる.

bore *a person* ***to death/bore*** *a person* ***stiff*** 《口》[[主に受身で]] 人をひどくうんざりさせる, 退屈させる (→ bore a person to TEARs) ▪ The principal's talk *bored* us *to death*. 校長の話に我々はひどくうんざりした ▪ Guy says he *was bored to death* by drama classes at school. 学校の演劇のクラスはひどく退屈だとガイは言っている ▪ I *was bored stiff* with my work. 仕事にすっかり飽きてしまった.

bore[3] /bɔːr/ 動 ***bore*** *one's* ***way*** 押し分けて進む ▪ He *bored his way* through the crowd. 彼は人ごみの中を押し分けて行った.

boredom /bɔ́ːrdəm/ 名 ***die of boredom*** 死ぬほど退屈する ▪ We listened politely, even though we almost *died of boredom*. 私たちは死ぬほど退屈だったけれど, 謹聴した.

borne, born /bɔːrn/ 動 ***be born*** [***made***] ***that way*** →WAY.

be born with a silver spoon in *one's* ***mouth*** →SPOON.

be borne away (***by***) (…に)駆(か)られる ▪ He *was borne away by* anger. 彼は怒りに駆られた.

be borne in on [***upon***] *a person* 《英》人にわかってくる ▪ It *was borne in on* Jim that marriage was not a safe anchorage. 結婚は安全なよりどころではないということがジムにわかってきた.

be borne in upon 《文》(人)の肝に銘ずる, (人)が確信する《予感・警告について用いることが多い》 ▪ It *is borne in upon* me that all depends on our character. 何事も性格いかんによるということを私は強く感じている ▪ It *was borne in upon* her to beseech divine compassion in favor of the homeless. 家なき人々のため神のあわれみを乞うべきことを彼女は強く肝に銘じた.

born again 生まれ変わって, 更生して ▪ Why does a person need to be *born again*? なぜ人は生まれ変わる必要があるのか.

born and bred 生まれて育てられて; はえぬきで[の] ▪ He was *born and bred* in your house. 彼はあなたの家に生まれ育てられた ▪ He is a cockney *born and bred*. 彼ははえぬきのロンドン子だ.

born before [***ahead of***] *one's* ***time*** 月足らずで生まれて; 時世に先んじて生まれて ▪ The baby was *born before his time*. 赤んぼうは月足らずで生まれた ▪ King Alfred was *born before his time*. アルフレッド大王は時世に先んじた考えを持っていた.

born in low water 貧乏に生まれて ▪ I was *born in low water*. 私は貧乏に生まれた.

born in (***the***) ***purple*** →PURPLE.

born of …の子で, から生まれて《比喩的にも》 ▪ He was *born of* rich parents. 彼は富家に生まれた ▪ He speaks with the conviction *born of* experience. 彼は経験から得た確信をもって語る.

born rich 金持ちに生まれて ▪ He was *born rich*. 彼は金持ちの家に生まれた.

born to [***to*** *do*] …に生まれて, 生まれついて ▪ He was *born to* a large inheritance. 彼は大財産を相続する身に生まれた ▪ He was *born to* sorrows. 彼は悲運に生まれついた ▪ He was a man clearly *born to* command. 彼は(人に)命令するよう生まれついた人だった.

in all *one's* ***born days*** 《口》生まれてから今まで (since one was born) ▪ I've never *in all my born days* seen such a fool as you are. 私は生まれてこのかたお前のようなばか者を見たことがない.

not born yesterday →YESTERDAY.

There's one born every minute. 《諺》毎分ばかが一人生まれる.

borough /bɔ́ːroʊ|bʌ́rə/ 名 ***buy*** [***own***] ***a borough*** 選挙区を買収する ▪ There was a practice of *buying boroughs* and canvassing for votes. 選挙区を買収し票の獲得運動をする習慣があった.

borrow /bɑ́roʊ|bɔ́rəʊ/ 動 ***borrow trouble*** → TROUBLE[1].

borrowed plumes →PLUME[1].

live [***be***] ***on borrowed time*** →TIME[1].

borrower /bɑ́roʊər|bɔ́rəʊər/ 名 ***Neither*** (***a***) ***borrower nor a lender be.*** 借り手にも貸し手にもなるな《どちらにしても金も友も失う》(cf. Sh., *Haml.* 1. 3. 75).

bosh /bɑʃ|bɔʃ/ 名 ***talk bosh*** 《口》くだらないことを言う ▪ Everyone is *talking bosh*. みんながくだらないことを言っている.

bosom /bʊ́zəm/ 名 ***a bosom friend*** [***pal***] 親友 ▪ They were *bosom friends* then. 彼らはその時は親友であった.

come home to *a person's* ***bosom*** 深く悟る, 痛感する ▪ The fact has *come home to my bosom*. 私はその事実を痛感した.

keep ... in *one's* ***bosom*** …を胸に秘めておく ▪ I will *keep* it *in my bosom*. それを胸に秘めておこう.

of *one's* ***bosom*** 最愛の (《聖》 *Deut.* 13. 6) ▪ Then the colonel went home to the wife *of his bosom*. その後大佐は最愛の妻の所へ帰って行った.

take ... to *one's* ***bosom*** (妻)をめとる; (人)を親愛する ▪ He had *taken* the woman *to his bosom*. 彼はその女をめとっていた.

warm [***cherish, nourish***] ***a viper*** [***snake***] ***in*** *one's* ***bosom*** 恩をあだで返される ▪ Little did I know I was *cherishing a viper in my bosom*. 恩を仇で返されるとは夢にも思っていなかった. ☞「イソップ物語」から.

boss[1] /bɔːs, bɑs|bɔs/ 名 ***be*** *one's* ***own boss***

誰の支配も受けない，一匹狼である ▪ James came to York to *be his own boss*. "I wanted to live or die on my own decision," he says. ジェイムズは一匹狼になるためにヨークへやって来た.「おれは生きるも死ぬも自分で決定したかったのさ」と彼は言う.

make a boss shot 《口》撃ち損じる; 取りそこなう ▪ I am afraid I *made a boss shot* of my exam altogether. 私は試験を全くやりそこなったように思う.

show (*a person*) ***who's boss*** 《口》(人に)自分がボス[責任者]であることを見せしめる ▪ He hated the dolphin and *showed* him *who was boss*. 彼はそのイルカが嫌いで自分が親分であることをイルカに見せしめた《懲らしめたこと》.

boss[2] /bɔːs, bɑs|bɔs/ 動 ***boss it*** 《米》采配(さいはい)をふる ▪ The little fellow *bossed it* over the crowd. その小男は群衆に対して采配をふった.

boss the (***whole***) ***show*** →SHOW[1].

both /boʊθ/ 形副 ***both*** *A* ***and*** *B* AもBも ▪ *Both* brother *and* sister are dead. 兄も妹も死んだ ▪ He worked *both* by day *and* by night. 彼は昼も夜も働いた.

both ways →WAY.

have it both ways →WAY.

bother[1] /bɑ́ðər|bɔ́ðə/ 名 ***go to the bother of*** *doing* [***to*** *do*] わざわざ…する ▪ John was kind enough to *go to the bother of driving* me home. ジョンは親切にもわざわざ私を車で家まで送ってくれた ▪ I don't want to *go to the bother to* cook. 私はわざわざ料理なんかしたくない.

take [***be***] ***more bother than it's worth*** 面倒すぎてやり甲斐がない ▪ Gardening *takes more bother than it's worth*. ガーデニングは面倒すぎてやり甲斐がない.

bother[2] /bɑ́ðər|bɔ́ðə/ 動 ***bother*** *one's* ***head*** [***brains,*** *oneself*] (***about***) 〚主に否定文で〛(…に)くよくよする ▪ It is not important; don't *bother your head about* it. それは重要なことではない，そのことでくよくよするな.

bother *one's* (***pretty little***) ***head about*** … について心配する《女性に向かって》 ▪ Now, don't *bother your pretty little head about* all this. さあ，このことで心配しないでください ▪ Don't *bother your head about* me. 私のことは心配しないでくれ.

bother the life [***hell, heck***] ***out of*** (人を)やたら苛立たせる ▪ My toothache is *bothering the hell out of* me. 歯痛が私をやたら苛立たせる ▪ I stayed home, *bothering the heck out of* my aunt. 私は家にいて，おばさんをやたら苛立たせていた.

Bother you [***it***]***!*** うるさいったら!, いまいましい!

can't be bothered (***to*** *do*) 《英口》(…する)気になれない ▪ I didn't go to his party. I just *couldn't be bothered*. 私は彼のパーティーへ行かなかった. その気になれなかっただけだ ▪ The nurse *couldn't be bothered to* wash her hands. 看護師は手を洗う気になれなかった.

can't be bothered with …はごめんだ ▪ I *can't be bothered with* waiting for a bus. バスを待つのはごめんだ.

Don't bother me! 向こうへ行け; 放っといてくれ.

hot and bothered →(all) HOT and bothered, get HOT (and bothered).

I'm not bothered. 《主に英》何でもいいです ▪ What will you have to drink?—*I'm not bothered.* 飲み物は何にするかい—何でもいいよ.

(***It***) ***doesn't bother me any*** [***at all, none***]. 《俗》(私は)ちっともかまいません ▪ Do you mind if I smoke?—*It doesn't bother me any.* タバコを吸ってもいいですか?—ちっともかまいませんよ. ☞非文法的.

not bother *oneself* [*one's* ***head***] わずらわされない，気にかけない (*with, about*) ▪ I won't *bother myself with* the integrity of politicians. 私は政治家の高潔さなんか気にしない.

bottle[1] /bɑ́təl|bɔ́təl/ 名 ***a three bottle man*** 大酒にも酔わない人 ▪ He is *a three bottle man.* 彼は非常に酒に強い.

be on the bottle 《英》酒に浸って ▪ He's *been on the bottle* for days. 彼は何日も酒に浸っている.

beat the bottle アルコール依存症を克服する ▪ Recently Jeff has managed to *beat the bottle*. 最近ジェフはアルコール依存症を克服した.

bring up [《米》***raise***] ***on the bottle*** 牛乳で育てる ▪ He is a sturdy fellow though he *was brought up on the bottle*. 彼は牛乳で育てられたが頑丈な男だ.

bring your own bottle/《英》***bring a bottlle*** 《米》((くだけた)パーティーなどに)酒を持参する ▪ There is a growing trend in the country toward *bring your own bottle* restaurants. レストランに酒類持参の動向が国中で高まっている.

catch lightning in a bottle →LIGHTNING.

crack [***break***] (***open***) ***a bottle*** 《口》酒びんをあける，祝杯をあげる ▪ Let's *crack open a bottle* and celebrate. 祝杯をあげて祝おう.

fight a bottle 《俗》(大)酒をくらう ▪ He *fought a bottle* all night. 彼は夜通し大酒をくらった.

have [***show***] ***a lot of bottle*** 《英口》大変な勇気[自信]がある[を示す] ▪ Barton *showed a lot of bottle* to get results. バートンは結果を出すために大変な勇気を示した.

have the bottle to *do* 《英口》…する勇気がある (= have the NERVE (to do)) ▪ A brewer has shown it *has the bottle to* help those in need. 一人のビール醸造者が困窮している人々を援助する勇気を持っていることを示した.

hit the bottle (憂さを晴らすために)大酒を飲む ▪ Bill's been *hitting the bottle* hard since his wife left him. ビルは妻が去って以来ずっと酒浸りだ.

like *one's* ***bottle*** 酒好きである ▪ Tim still *likes his bottle*. ティムは依然として酒好きだ ▪ Mr. Blackwood was a man who *liked his bottle*. ブラックウッド氏は酒の好きな人であった.

new wine in old bottles →WINE[1].

over a [***the***] ***bottle*** 飲みながら ▪ Let us have a chat *over a bottle*. 飲みながら話しましょう.

push the bottle →PUSH².

take a bottle (赤んぼうが)哺(ほ)乳瓶で飲む ▪ What if my baby won't *take a bottle*? 赤ちゃんが哺乳瓶で飲まなかったらどうしよう.

take to the bottle 酒にふける[おぼれる], 酒をたしなむ ▪ Bob *took to the bottle* when his beloved wife died. 愛妻が亡くなったときボブは酒にふけった ▪ Ben *took to the bottle* again after Susan refused his phone calls. ベンはスーザンに電話を拒否されたあとまたぞろ酒におぼれた.

bottle² /bátəl|bɔ́təl/ 動 ***bottle it*** 《米》静かに!

bottle-washer /bátəlwàʃər|bɔ́təlwɔ̀ʃər/ 名 ***a head [chief] cook and bottle-washer*** 《俗》雑働き人《しばしば嘲笑的に》 ▪ He was *a head cook and bottle-washer*. 彼は雑役人だった.

bottom¹ /bátəm|bɔ́t-/ 名 ***at (the) bottom*** 内心は, 心底は ▪ He is a good man *at bottom*. 彼は根はよい人だ.

at the bottom of Fortune's wheel 不運のどん底に ▪ He is *at the bottom of Fortune's wheel*. 彼は不運のどん底に落ちている. ☞Fortune's wheel 運命の女神が回す運命の紡ぎ車.

at the bottom of *one's* ***heart*** 心の底では ▪ *At the bottom of my heart* I welcomed the news. 心の底では私はそのニュースを歓迎した.

at the bottom of the (career) ladder (職業の)最低の地位[どん底]から ▪ Bill started work *at the* very *bottom of the career ladder*. ビルはどん底の地位から働きはじめた ▪ Tom began *at the bottom of the ladder* as servant. トムは使用人として社会の底辺で働きはじめた.

at the bottom [top] of the pile [heap] 社会の最下層[最上層]の ▪ To people *at the bottom of the heap*, the world seems hostile. 社会の底辺にいる人々にとっては, 世間は敵のように思われる ▪ I've no idea what life *at the top of the pile* is like. 社会の上流階級の生活がどんなものか見当もつかない.

(be) at the bottom (of) (...の)どん底に(ある) ▪ Read the note *at the bottom of* the page. そのページの脚注を読みなさい.

be [lie] at the bottom of ...の根本原因[黒幕]である ▪ Jealousy *lies at the bottom of* the murder. 嫉妬(しっと)がその殺人の主因である ▪ Racist feelings *lie at the bottom of* the trouble. 人種差別の感情がこのごたごたの根本原因である.

be bumping along (at) the bottom 《英》(経済が)どん底で低迷している; 滞る ▪ The economy of the country *was* still *bumping along the bottom*. その国の経済は依然低迷している ▪ The team *is* always *bumping along at the bottom* of the league. そのチームはいつもリーグのどんじりで低迷している ▪ The housing market *was bumping along at the bottom*. 住宅供給市場はどん底で滞っている.

bet *one's* ***bottom dollar*** →DOLLAR.

one's ***bottom dollar*** →DOLLAR.

one's ***bottom drawer*** (結婚の用意に衣類・装身具などをしまっておく)たんすの一番下の引き出し ▪ Meg knitted lots of pretty things and stored them in *her bottom drawer*. メグはきれいなものをたくさん編んで, たんすの一番下の引き出しに入れておいた.

one's ***bottom line*** 最低値; 本音 ▪ *His bottom line* is still in the black. 彼の本音は未だに不明だ.

bottom up [upwards] 底を上へ向けて, 逆さまにして ▪ The boat was floating *bottom upwards*. ボートはひっくり返って浮かんでいた.

bottoms up 《口》大いに飲みたまえ《ボトルをいくつも逆さにするほど》; 乾杯! ▪ *Bottoms up*, gentlemen! みなさん, 乾杯!

examine ... to the bottom →search ... to the BOTTOM.

from the bottom of *one's* ***heart*** →HEART.

from the bottom of the barrel [heap] 《口》(残りかすのような)劣悪な人たち[もの]の中から(の) ▪ We maximize profit *from the bottom of the barrel*. 我々は劣悪なものの中から最大限の利益をあげている.

from the bottom up **1** どん底からはいあがって ▪ *From the Bottom Up* is Jean's debut album. 「どん底からはいあがって」はジーンのデビューアルバムである. **2** 初歩[基礎]から始めて, 最初から, すっかり ▪ Rodney started to study political science *from the bottom up*. ロドニーは政治学を基礎から勉強し始めた ▪ The work must be done all over again *from the bottom up*. その仕事はすっかりやり直さねばならん.

get at [to] the bottom of ...の真相を究明する[知る] ▪ The detective finally *got to the bottom of* why the man was killed. 探偵はついにその男がなぜ殺されたか真相を究明した.

get down to rock bottom ...の真相を究明する ▪ We *got down to rock bottom*. 真相を究明した.

go to the bottom (of the sea) 海底のもくずとなる, 沈む ▪ The ship *went* down *to the bottom* with all on board. その船は乗客全員と共に海底に沈んだ.

have no bottom 測り知れない, 無限の; 不安定な ▪ His energy *has no bottom*. 彼の精力は無限だ.

hit [scrape, touch] bottom 底をつく; どん底生活に陥る ▪ Steel production has *hit bottom*. 鉄鋼生産は底を突いた ▪ He's *hit bottom*. 彼はどん底生活に陥った.

knock the bottom out of →KNOCK².

Never venture all in one bottom. 《諺》一つの事業にすべてをかけるな. ☞bottom = ship.

put the bottom rail on top 《米口》境遇を逆にする《特に南北戦争後, 南部の奴隷と主人との関係が》 ▪ Some Southerners regarded public education as devices for *putting the bottom rail on top*. 南部の人々の中には公共教育を主人と奴隷との境遇を逆転させる計略とみなす者もいた.

reach [hit] the (rock) bottom 《商》(物価などが)底を突く ▪ Wheat prices have *reached the rock bottom*. 小麦相場が底をついた.

search [shift, examine, etc.***] ... to the bottom*** ...を徹底的に調べる, の真相を究明する ▪ *Examine* the matter *to the bottom*. その事件を徹底

的に調べよ.

send ... to the bottom …を沈める ▪ We *sent* several of their ships *to the bottom.* 我々は彼らの船を数隻沈めた.

stand on** one's **own bottom 独立する, 自営する ▪ It is time you learn to *stand on your own bottom.* 君はもう自立することを覚えるべき時だ. ☞《諺》Let every TUB stand on its own bottom. から.

strike bottom ＝touch BOTTOM.

the bottom drops* [*falls*] *out of** a person's **world 人の世界の基盤がくずれる《突然不幸になる[自信を失う]》 ▪ When her husband died, *the bottom dropped out of her world.* 夫が死んだとき, 彼女の世界の基盤がくずれた.

the bottom falls* [*drops*] *out of **1** …がくずれる, 崩壊する; がみじめになる ▪ *The bottom* would *fall out of* the British home front. イギリスの国内戦線がくずれるだろう ▪ *The bottom dropped out of* the day for Henry when he saw his report card. 通信簿を見たときヘンリーはみじめな気持ちになった.

2 (相場・価格などの)基盤がくずれる, 大底を突く ▪ Don't hang on to your shares till *the bottom drops* [*falls*] *out of* the market. 非常な底値になるまで, 株にしがみついていてはいけない ▪ *The bottom* has *dropped out of* the price of tin. 錫(すず)の価格が大底をついた ▪ *The bottom* has *fallen out of* the market and he lost a lot of money. 市場の基盤がくずれて, 彼は大金を失った.

***the bottom line is* (*that*)....** 《米》結局[つまるところ, 要するに]…である ▪ *The bottom line is that* we serve patients, not employees. 要は我々が奉仕するのは患者であって雇い主ではないということだ ▪ *The bottom line is* there should be a ban on smoking. 要するにタバコは禁止すべきである.

to the bottom 底まで, 根底まで ▪ Drain the cup *to the bottom.* 杯を底まで飲み干しなさい.

touch bottom (不幸・貧困などの)どん底に至る ▪ The housing market *touched bottom* months ago. 住宅供給市場は何か月も前に最悪の状態になった ▪ At last he *touched bottom* and was reduced to begging in the streets. ついに彼は貧困のどん底に落ちて, 街頭で物ごいをするようになった.

venture all in one bottom 一つの事業にすべてを賭ける ▪ He was fool enough to *venture all in one bottom.* 彼は愚かにも一つの事業にすべてを賭けた.

bottom[2] /bátəm|bɔ́t-/ 動 ***bottom** a thing **on*** 物を…の上に築く ▪ We *bottom* all our conviction *on* grounds of right reason. 我々はすべての確信を正しい道理の上に築いている.

bounce[1] /baʊns/ 名副 ***all bounce*** 大ぼら ▪ That is *all bounce.* それは大ぼらだ.

catch** a thing **on the bounce 飛びつくようにして物を(受け)取る ▪ He *caught* the ball *on the bounce.* 彼は飛びついてボールを取った.

***come bounce against* [*into*]** …にいきなりぶつかる[おどり込む] ▪ Something *came bounce against* the door. 何かがポンとドアにぶつかった.

get the* (*grand*) *bounce 《口》 **1** (きっぱりと)解雇される ▪ Did you *get the grand bounce*? 君はばっさり首にされたのかい.

2 (恋人)に捨てられる ▪ She *got the bounce* from her boyfriend. 彼女はボーイフレンドに捨てられた.

give the* (*grand*) *bounce 《口》 **1** (有無を言わさず)解雇する ▪ He has *given* her *the bounce* himself. 彼がじきじき彼女を首にした.

2 恋人を捨てる ▪ Jane *gave* Tom *the bounce.* ジェインは恋人のトムを捨てた.

have got* [*there's*] *a bounce in** one's **step 足取りがきびきびしている ▪ He's over sixty, but he *has got a bounce in his step.* 彼は60歳を超えているが, 足取りはきびきびしている.

more bounce to the ounce 使った金以上の価値, 投資額以上の見返り (more BANG for the buck) ▪ We always buy the largest packages of cat food—*more bounce to the ounce.* 私たちは一番大きいキャットフードを買っている—使った金以上の価値があるからだ. ☞炭酸清涼飲料の宣伝文句から.

on the bounce **1** 飛びはねて; 絶えずけいれん的に動いて ▪ It will not be so much *on the bounce* as formerly. それは以前ほど絶えずけいれんするようには動きはしないだろう.

2 大ぼらを吹いて ▪ He tried to achieve his object *on the bounce.* 彼は大ぼらを吹いて己の目的を達しようとした.

bounce[2] /baʊns/ 動 ***be bouncing off the walls*** 元気いっぱいで[興奮して]じっとしていられない ▪ Kids on picnics *are bouncing off the walls.* ピクニックをしている子供らは興奮してじっとしていられない.

bound[1] /baʊnd/ 名 ***at a* (*single*) *bound*** (ただ)一飛びで ▪ The horse cleared the hedge *at a bound.* 馬は一飛びで生垣を飛び越えた.

by leaps and bounds →LEAP[1].

on the bound (ボールが)はねあがって, はずんで ▪ He caught a ball *on the* first *bound.* 彼はワンバウンドでボールを捕えた.

with one bound 一飛びで; 一躍して ▪ *With one bound* the lion disappeared among the trees. 一飛びでライオンは木立の中へ消えた.

bound[2] /baʊnd/ 名 ***be within* (*the*) *bounds* (*of*)** (…の)範囲内[限界内]にある ▪ It *is within the bounds of* possibility. それはありうることだ.

beyond all bounds 限りなく ▪ He rejoiced *beyond all bounds* to see them. 彼は彼らに会って限りなく喜んだ.

***beyond the bounds* (*of*)** (…の)限界[らち]を越えて ▪ Man's imagination may extend *beyond the bounds of* space and time. 人間の想像は時空の限界を越えて広がるかもしれない ▪ It is *beyond the bounds of* human knowledge. それは人知の限界を越えている.

break bounds →BREAK[2].

go beyond* [*overstep*] *the bounds of …の限

界を越える; にもとるごとをする ▪ He *went beyond the bounds of* moderation. 彼は度を過ごした.

in bounds 《英》出入許可区域に ▪ This cafe has been placed *in bounds* for schoolboys. このカフェは生徒の出入許可区域にされている.

keep within* (*the*) *bounds **1** 度を越させない ▪ Please *keep* the noise *within bounds*. あまりやかましすぎないようにしてください ▪ She could never *keep* her temper *within bounds*. 彼女は怒りを適度に抑えることができない.

2 出入許可区域にいる; 度を越えない ▪ Please *keep within the bounds* of reason. 理性の限界を越えないでください.

know no bounds 際限がない ▪ Avarice *knows no bounds*. 強欲にはきりがない.

out of* (*all*) *bounds =out of BOUNDs 4.

out of bounds **1** 《主に英》(人が)立ち入り禁止の[に] (*to, for*) (→《米》off LIMITs) ▪ The park is *out of bounds to* students. この公園は学生立ち入り禁止です ▪ The newly restored park is still *out of bounds for* tourists. 新たに修復された公園はまだ観光客立ち入り禁止です.

2 《スポーツ》場外の[で], 定められた競技区域を越えて (↔within BOUNDs 1) ▪ His shot went *out of bounds*. 彼の一打は場外に出てしまった ▪ He had stepped *out of bounds* before he reached the goal line. 彼はゴールラインに着く前に競技区域外に出ていた.

3 (行為・使用などが)禁じられて ▪ High-fat foods are *out of bounds* on my diet. 脂肪の高い食べ物は私の食事では禁止されている.

4 礼儀にはずれて ▪ He went *out of bounds* when he called Tom a liar. 彼は礼儀にはずれてトムを嘘つきと言った.

overstep the bounds of → go beyond the BOUNDs of.

put* [*set*] *bounds to …を制限する ▪ He *sets* no *bounds to* his desires. 彼の願望にはきりがない.

within bounds **1** 《スポーツ》競技場内の[で]; 立入り自由の[で] (↔out of BOUNDs 2).

2 許される範囲内で, 抑制されて ▪ Drinking is all right as long as it's kept *within bounds*. 飲酒は抑制されている限り問題ない. ☞ →keep within (the) BOUNDs.

bound[3] /baʊnd/ 形 ***be bound and determined to*** *do* …することを固く決心している ▪ He *was bound and determined to* finish the assignment before taking on another. 彼は別の仕事に手をつける前にその仕事を済まそうと固く決心していた.

(***be***) ***bound on*** *doing* …することに決めて(いる) ▪ He *is bound on going* to Tokyo. 彼は東京に行くことに決めた.

be bound to *a person* **1** 人に恩義[義務]を負っている ▪ I *am* infinitely *bound to* my friends for their thinking of me. 私のことをいろいろ思ってくれる友人たちにはかり知れない恩義がある.

2 (…の所)に見習いに出される ▪ The son *was bound to* a master builder for several years. 息子は数年間棟梁の所に見習いに出された.

be bound to *do* **1** 必ず…するはずである, する運命にある ▪ The plan *is bound to* succeed. その計画は成功するにちがいない ▪ Man *is bound to* die. 人間は死すべき運命にある.

2 〚in honor, in duty などを伴って〛…する義務がある, 義理にも…せざるをえない (=be duty BOUND to do) ▪ I *am bound in honor to* observe it. 面目にかけてもそれを守らねばならない ▪ I *am in duty bound to* attend the meeting. その会には出席しなければならない義務がある.

3 《米》必ず…する決心である ▪ He *is bound to* come and see you. 彼は必ず君に会いに来る決心だ.

be bound up in **1** …に専心する, 夢中である ▪ He *is bound up in* his studies. 彼は勉強に夢中である.

2 …に堅く結びつけられている ▪ They *were bound up in* each other. 彼らは互いに離れられない仲だった.

(***be***) ***bound up with*** …と堅く結びつけられて(いる), 関係して(いる) ▪ The affair seemed so closely *bound up with* their interests. その事件は彼らの利害ときわめて密接な関係にあるように見えた.

be* [*feel*] *duty* [*honor*] *bound to *do* …する義務を感じる; 名誉に賭けて…しなければならないと思う ▪ I *felt duty bound to* point out the flaws in the article. 私はその製品の欠陥を指摘する義務を感じた ▪ I *was honor bound to* admit that Dean had done the work. 私は名誉に賭けて, ディーンがその仕事をやったことを認めなければならない.

I'll be bound. 《英》〚主に文尾で〛請け合うよ, きっとだ ▪ They'll regret it, *I'll be bound*. やつらは後悔するさ, 請け合ってもいい.

bound[4] /baʊnd/ 形 ***bound for*** …行きで[の] ▪ He was taken ill on a ship *bound for* Kobe. 彼は神戸行きの船上で発病した ▪ The train is *bound for* Tokyo. その電車は東京行きです.

homeward bound 帰航中で ▪ A British ship is *homeward bound*. イギリス船が帰航中である.

outward bound 外国行きで ▪ The ship was *outward bound*. その船は外国行きであった.

bound[5] /baʊnd/ 動 ***bound into favor* [*fame*]** 急に人気が出る[有名になる] ▪ Lawn tennis *bounds into favor* once again. テニスはまた急に人気が出ている ▪ He *bounded into fame*. 彼は一躍有名になった.

boundary /báʊndəri/ 名 ***beyond the boundary* (*of*)** (…の)限界を越えて ▪ It is *beyond the boundary of* human knowledge. それは人知の及ばぬところにある.

bounden /báʊndən/ 形 ***be bounden to*** *a person* ***for*** 人に…の恩を受けている ▪ I *am bounden to* him *for* my success. 私の成功は彼のおかげだ.

one's ***bounden duty*** …の本務 ▪ It was *his bounden duty* to accept the office. その役を受けるのは彼の本務であった.

bouquet /boʊkéɪ, búːkeɪ/ 名 ***hand a bou-***

quet 賞揚する，ほめる (*to*) ▪ The Secretary *handed* him *a bouquet* for his unfailing tact. 長官は彼の確実な気転を賞揚した.

throw bouquets at 《米口》…にお世辞を言う ▪ He *threw bouquets at* me regarding my ability. 彼は私の腕前について私をほめそやした.

bout /baʊt/ 名 ***have a bout with*** …と一戦を交える ▪ We *had a bout with* the enemy. 敵と一戦を交えた.

(***in***) ***this*** [***that***] ***bout*** この[その]時に ▪ The Romans did not find the enemy asleep *this bout*. ローマ軍が見るとこの時は敵は眠っていなかった.

bow[1] /boʊ/ 名 ***another string*** (***to*** *one's* ***bow***) →STRING[1].

bend a bow →draw a BOW.

bring *a person* ***to*** *one's* ***bow*** 人を臣従させる，言いなりにならせる ▪ The Dutch tried to *bring* the King *to their bow*. オランダ軍は王を自分らの言いなりにさせようとした. ☞bow (弓)と bow (敬礼)との混合.

come to *a person's* ***bow*** 人の言うままになる，臣従する ▪ They must have all men *come to their bow*. 彼らはすべての人々を臣従させねばならない. ☞句源は上に同じ.

draw [***bend***] ***a bow*** 弓を引く ▪ The Indian hunter *drew a bow*. 先住民の猟人は弓を引いた.

draw a bow at a venture あてずっぽうで弓を引く; あてずっぽうを言う (《聖》*Kings* 22. 34) (→at a VENTURE) ▪ A certain man *drew a bow at a venture*, and smote the King of Israel. ある男があてずっぽうで弓を引き，イスラエルの王を殺した ▪ I just *drew a bow at a venture*, but it evidently hit the mark. 私はあてずっぽうを言っただけなのに，どうもそれが当たったらしい.

draw [***pull***] ***the*** [***a***] ***long bow/draw with the long bow*** 《口》大ぼらを吹く，誇張して話す ▪ They *draw the long bow* better than before. 彼らは以前より大ぼらを吹くのがうまい.

have a famous bow up at the castle ほら吹きである ▪ He *has a famous bow up at the castle*. あいつはほら吹きだ.

have two [***many***] ***strings to*** *one's* ***bow*** **1** 控えの[いろいろの]手だてがある ▪ Most of them *have* so *many strings to their bow* that they are quite safe. 彼らのうちの大半はいろいろな手だてがあるので全く安全である ▪ Miss Bertram *had two strings to her bow*. バートラム嬢には控えの手だてがあった.
2 多芸多才である ▪ *Having* so *many strings to his bow*, he is bound to get on in the world. 彼は非常に多才であるから，きっと出世する.

pull the [***a***] ***long bow*** →draw the long BOW.

bow[2] /baʊ/ 名 ***make*** *one's* ***bow*** **1** おじぎをして入る，お目見えする; 正式に加入する ▪ The pianist *made his bow* to the audience. そのピアニストは聴衆にお目見えした.
2 おじぎをして退く ▪ I shall *make my bow* and go home. 私は現場を退いて家に帰ります.

take a bow (紹介・喝采に対して)おじぎをする ▪ The star of the play *took a bow* and then left the stage. その劇のスターは喝采に対しておじぎをし，そして舞台を去った.

bow[3] /baʊ/ 名 ***a shot across the bow***(***s***) → SHOT[1].

bow[4] /baʊ/ 動 ***be bowed*** (***down***) ***with*** …で曲がる，くじける ▪ Their hearts *were bowed with* grief. 彼らの心は悲嘆にくじけていた.

bow and scrape おじぎをしながら右足を後に引く; ぺこぺこする，おべっかを使う ▪ He always *bows and scrapes* to his superiors. 彼は常に上役にぺこぺこする.

bow (***down***) ***the*** [*one's*] ***ear*** [***eye***] 耳を傾ける[目を注ぐ] ▪ *Bow down your* heavenly *eye*. 天来の目を注ぎなさい ▪ *Bow down your ear*, O Lord, hear me. おお主よ，おん耳を傾けお聞きください.

bow *oneself* ***out*** (国王などの前から)おじぎをして退去する ▪ The peers *bowed themselves out*. 貴族たちは(王の前から)おじぎをして退去した.

bow *one's* ***thanks*** →THANK[1].

bow the knee →KNEE.

bow the neck to …に屈服する ▪ We can never *bow the neck to* these cruel invaders of our country. 我々はこうしたわが国への残酷な侵入者たちに決して屈服することはできない.

bow to no one 誰にも頭を下げない，誰にも負けない (*in*) ▪ I *bow to no one in* my Francophobia. 私はフランス(人)ぎらいでは誰にも負けない.

bowel /báʊəl/ 名 ***bind*** [***loosen, move***] ***the bowels*** 下痢を止める[通じをつける].

One's ***bowels are open.*** 通じがある.

One's ***bowels do not move.*** 通じがない.

bowels of mercy [***compassion***] あわれみ，同情 (《聖》*1 John* 3. 17) ▪ He was without *bowels of mercy*. 彼はあわれみがなかった ▪ We men of business must have *bowels of compassion* like any other. 我々実業家は他の人と同じようにあわれみの情を持たなければならない.

one's ***bowels yearn for*** 切に…を慕う ▪ *My bowels yearn for* my child. 私は切にわが子を慕う.

one's ***bowels yearn over*** [***upon, towards***] …にあわれみ[愛情]を強く感じている (《聖》*Gen.* 43. 30) ▪ *Joseph's bowels* did *yearn upon* his brother. ヨセフは弟に対して強い愛情をいだいていた.

have loose bowels 下痢する ▪ My cat *has loose bowels*. うちの猫は下痢している.

have no bowels (***of mercy***) 無慈悲である ▪ He is said to *have no bowels*. 彼は無慈悲だと言われている.

the bowels of the earth 地の底 ▪ Miners labor in *the bowels of the earth*. 鉱夫は地底で働く.

bow hand /bóʊhæ̀nd/ 名 ***on the bow hand*** 的をはずれて ▪ You are *on the bow hand* still. 君はまだ的をはずれている. ☞bow hand「左手」.

bowing /báʊɪŋ/ 形 ***a bowing acquaintance*** →a nodding ACQUAINTANCE.

bowl /boʊl/ 名 ***a bowl of cherries*** 《しばしば

皮肉》楽しい状況，愉快な経験 ▪ Life may be "just *a bowl of cherries*" as the old song says. 古い歌にある通り，人生はまさしく楽しいものかもしれない ▪ Living with a chronic illness isn't *a bowl of cherries*. 慢性病をかかえて生きるのは楽しいことではない. ☞Lew Brown (1893–1958)作詞，Ray Henderson (1896–1970)作曲の歌(1931)の題名.

in a goldfish bowl 金魚鉢の中で; 世間の目にさらされて ▪ A politician's life is life *in a goldfish bowl*. 政治家の生活はプライバシーを保てない生活だ.

over the bowl 宴席で; 酒を飲みながら ▪ They chatted *over the bowl*. 酒を飲みながら雑談した.

The golden bowl is broken. (《聖》 *Eccles*. 12. 6)金の鉢はこわれた《夢幻は破れた; 力尽きて死ぬ》 ▪ The mood is shattered; *the golden bowl is broken*. 気分はこわれた. 夢幻は破れた ▪ Thus they go from year to year until *the golden bowl is broken*. 彼らは死ぬまで年々このようにやっていく.

bow(-)wow /bàʊwáʊ/ 名 ***go to the bow-wows*** 堕落する，破滅する ▪ He was *going* fast *to the bow-wows*. 彼はどんどん堕落しつつあった. ☞go to the DOGs のもじり.

box[1] /bɑks|bɔks/ 名 ***a brain box*** 《英口》コンピューター; とても聡明な人，秀才 ▪ What *a brain box* you are! 君はなんと頭が切れるんだろう!

be not the sharpest tool in the box → TOOL.

hack boxes (脂・液を採るため)樹木に穴をあける ▪ It is called *hacking boxes*. それは樹木の穴あけと呼ばれる.

in a (tight, bad, hot) box 《口》窮地にあって，当惑して ▪ You are now *in a bad box*. 君は今は窮地に陥っている.

in the same box 同じ窮境[事情，立場]にある ▪ They are all *in the same box* and ought to be equally punished. 彼らはみな同じ立場にあるので同じように罰せられるべきである.

in the [a] wrong box 場所をまちがえて; 誤って ▪ You are quite *in the wrong box* there. 君はその点で全く誤っている ▪ I could see I was *in the wrong box*. 自分が場所をまちがえていることに気がついた.

knock** a pitcher **out of the box 《米》好打して投手を退かせる ▪ He *was knocked out of the box*. 彼は敵の好打のため投手を退かされた.

out of** one's **box 《口》(麻薬・酒で)狂気じみた[愚かな]ふるまいをして (= out of one's TREE) ▪ The world may think Meg *out of her box*, but she's right about her decision. メグは気が狂ったと世間は思うかもしれないが，彼女の決意は正しい.

out of the box **1**《主に米》活動を始める ▪ We want to be first *out of the box* with the latest in technology. 我々は最新の技術を最初に利用したい.
2 (コンピューター・ソフトウェアなどを)説明書を読まずにすぐ使える ▪ These laptop PCs can be used straight *out of the box*. これらのラップトップは，説明書を読まずにすぐ使えます.

right out of the box 《米》(活動を始めて)すぐに ▪ They're comfortable *right out of the box*. 彼らはすぐに快適になった.

stuff the ballot box 《米俗》不正投票をする ▪ Jeff won't win unless we *stuff the ballot box*. 我々が不正投票しない限りジェフは勝てまい.

think inside the box 型にはまった考え方をする (↔think outside the BOX) ▪ Ben is a bore; he *thinks* only *inside the box*. ベンは退屈な男だ. 型にはまった考え方しかしない.

think out of the box (職場の自己の職務範囲を超えて)全体的能率改善を考える (↔think inside the BOX) ▪ Be creative—*think out of the box*. 創造的であれ—全体的能率改善を考えよ ▪ *Thinking out of the box* would improve public education. 自由な発想をすれば公共教育の水準が上がるだろうに.

think outside the box 《米口》(難問など)を全く別な[型にはまらない，独創的な]考え方をする; 新しい観点から考える (↔think inside the BOX) ▪ The professor encourages his students to *think outside the box*. その教授は自分の学生が独創的な考え方をするように励ます ▪ Solving the difficult riddle required ideas that came from *thinking outside of the box*. 難しい謎を解くには新しい観点から考えることから生まれる着想を必要とした. ☞lateral thinking (水平思考)と呼ばれる.

box[2] /bɑks|bɔks/ 名 ***give** a person **a box on the ear(s)*** (罰として)人の横面をひっぱたく ▪ I swear I will *give* you *a box on the ears* such as you never had before in all your life. これまで一度もくらったことのないような平手打ちをきっと横面にお見舞いしてやるぞ.

box[3] /bɑks|bɔks/ 動 ***box clever [cleverly]*** 《英俗》頭を使う，抜け目なく[要領よく]ふるまう，うまく立ち回る ▪ Roy knew that he would have to *box clever* for revenge. ロイは復しゅうのためには頭を使わねばならないことを知っていた ▪ Consultants in the property sector should have *boxed clever* and invested wisely during the last decade or so. 過去10年ぐらいのあいだ不動産部門のコンサルタントは要領よくふるまって賢く投資しておくべきだった.

box** a person's **ears 人の横面を張る，懲らしめる ▪ If he does that again, I'll *box his ears*. それをまたやったら横面を張ってやる.

box it out 戦い抜く，勝負のつくまでなぐり合う，とことんまで戦う (→FIGHT it out) ▪ The Englishmen fairly *boxed it out*. イギリス人は立派に戦い抜いた.

box the compass **1** 羅針(らしん)盤の32方位を順々にまた逆に称呼する ▪ I can *box the compass*. 私は羅針盤の32方位を順次に称呼することができる.
2 (意見・方針などが)完全に一回りして元へ戻る，正反対側へ回る; あらゆる方向に変わる; すべての質問に答える; 境遇に順応する ▪ He *boxed the compass* in political views. 彼は政見を種々変えてついにもとの政見にかえった ▪ My lady reasoned in her rapid way, and *boxed the compass* all round. 奥さまは敏速に推論し，あらゆる論法を試みた ▪ She knows

how to *box her compass*. 彼女は境遇に順応する方法を知っている. ☞ 海語から.

feel boxed in 身動きできなくなった[自由を奪われた]ように感じる ▪ The girl *felt boxed in* by the crowds. 少女は人混みに自由を奪われたような気がした.

boy /bɔɪ/ 名 ***a blue-eyed boy*** 《英豪》/***a fair-haired boy*** 《米》 お気に入りの男(の子), 寵児 ▪ Ben is the *blue-eyed boy* of his father. ベンは父親のお気に入りの男の子だ ▪ Brown is *a fair-haired boy* of the administration. ブラウンは行政府のお気に入りだ.

a boy in buttons ボーイ, 給仕 ▪ The *boy in buttons* thought much of his promotion. 給仕でさえ自分の昇進を重んじた.

a boy (sent) on a man's errand 能力に余ることをさせられる人 ▪ Peter was *a boy (sent) on a man's errand* when he was knocked out by Jack. ピーターがジャックに KO されたのは力に余ったからだ.

a golden boy [girl] →GOLDEN.

a mummy's [mother's] boy 《英》/***a mamma's boy*** 《米》 お母さん子, マザコン息子 ▪ Jimmy was *a* life-long *mother's boy*. ジミーは一生涯マザコン息子だった.

a wide boy 《英口》 いかさま師, 詐欺師 ▪ Beware of Ryan; he's *a wide boy*. ライアンに注意せよ. やつはいかさま師だ.

an old boy →OLD.

boy meets girl (典型的な)男女の恋愛(話) ▪ This is the story of *Boy Meets Girl*. これは典型的な男女の恋愛話である.

boy's play →child's PLAY.

Boys will be boys. 《諺》 男の子はどこまでも男の子だ《男の子のいたずらは仕方がない》.

boys with their toys (速い車・最新の電気製品などの)おもちゃ好きな男たち ▪ Don't let the *boys with their toys* have all the fun. おもちゃ好きな男たちだけに楽しませるな.

My boy! (わが子に)ねえお前; (友だちに)やあ君 ▪ So glad to have you back, *my boy!* ねえ君, 君が戻ってきてとてもうれしいよ.

Oh, boy! 《米俗》 よう!, 本当に, むろん《愉快・驚きを表す》 ▪ I will bring a basketful of apples.—*Oh, boy!* かご一杯のリンゴを持って来ましょう—わあ, すてき!

one of the boys 《口》 **1** れっきとしたグループの一人, よいコネのある人 ▪ He listens only to *one of the boys*. 彼は良いコネのある人の言うことしか聞かない.
2 同年輩同趣味の男性社交仲間の一人 ▪ I often drink with him. He is *one of the boys*. 私はよく彼と飲む. 彼は同年輩同趣味の社交仲間の一人だ.

the boy in blue →the man in BLUE.

the boy next door 普通の人好きのする青年 ▪ He is *the* smiling *boy next door*. 彼はにこにこしている普通の人好きのする青年である.

the old boy network →NETWORK.

brace[1] /breɪs/ 名 ***in a brace of shakes*** →in a SHAKE.

splice the main brace →MAIN-BRACE.

take a brace 《米口》 (再出発をしたり, 心がけを改めたりするため)元気を出す, 奮起する ▪ I want to *take a brace* and act like a man. 私は奮起して男らしい行動をしたいと思っている.

brace[2] /breɪs/ 動 ***brace*** *oneself* [*one's* ***heart,*** *one's* ***energies***] 元気を出す, 勇気を奮い起こす ▪ *Brace yourself*, honey. The bills are on your desk. びっくりしないでね. 請求書は机の上に置いてありますから《悪いことを知らせる前に言う句》.

brace it through 《米》 押しの一手で成功する ▪ I *braced it through*. 押しの一手で成功した.

brace *oneself* ***up*** 奮起する, 気を引き締める ▪ *Brace yourself up* for a task. 奮起して仕事にかかれ.

bracket /brǽkət/ 名 ***establish a bracket*** 射距離を確定する ▪ The shell passed over the ship, to be followed by a second one which fell short, *establishing a bracket*. 砲弾は船を行き過ぎ, 次のは船に届かなかった, それで射程距離が確定した.

brag /bræg/ 名 ***play a game of brag*** ほらを吹いてだましごっこをする, ほら吹きくらべをする ▪ The two countries will *play a game of brag*. その2国はほらを吹いてだましくらべをするだろう.

brain /breɪn/ 名 ***a brain bucket*** 《俗》 オートバイ用ヘルメット ▪ You've got to wear *a brain bucket* when you drive a motorbike. オートバイに乗るときにはヘルメットを着用しなければならない.

a brain drain →DRAIN[1].

An idle [empty] brain is the devil's (work)shop. 《諺》 暇な頭は悪魔の仕事場である,「小人閑居して不善をなす」.

be the brains behind ...の原動力である, 計画[組織]した人である ▪ Sam *is the brains behind* this project. サムがこのプロジェクトの原動力だ ▪ Sebastian Faulks *is the brains behind* the new Bond novel. セバスチャン・フォークスが新しいボンド小説を書いた人だ.

beat [busy, crack, cudgel, drag, pound, puzzle, rack] *one's* ***brains*** 脳みそ・知恵をしぼる; 考えぬく (*about, for, to do, doing*) ▪ I *puzzled my brains about* choosing my line. 私は自分の専門を選ぶのに考えぬいた ▪ I *dragged my brains for* [*to* make] a song. 私は歌を一つ作ろうと脳みそをしぼった.

beat *a person's* ***brains out*** 《口》 人の頭をかち割る ▪ The criminal *beat the man's brains out*. 犯人はその人の頭をかち割った.

beat *one's* ***brains out*** **1** 《主に米口》 (長いこと)脳みそ[知恵]を絞る (*doing*) ▪ I was *beating my brains out* for about an hour *trying* to solve the problem. 1時間ばかりその問題を解こうとして脳みそをしぼった.
2 絶えず懸命に(むずかしいことを)考え出そうとする ▪ The author *beat his brains out* to find someone to publish his novel. 作者は自分の小説を出版してくれる人を見つけようと絶えず懸命に苦心した.

beat the brains out of …の頭を過度に使用させる ▪ Roosevelt *beat the brains out of* Congress. ルーズベルトは国会に仕事を過度にやらせた.

blow** a person's **brains out 銃で人の頭を撃ち抜く ▪ He *blew a neighor's brains out* with a shotgun. 彼は隣人の頭をショットガンで撃ち抜いた.

blow** one's **brains out **1** 銃で自分[人]の頭を打ち抜く ▪ He died today by *blowing his brains out.* 彼はきょう銃で自分の頭を撃ち抜いて死んだ.

2《俗》しゃかりきに働く ▪ The poor boy *blew his brains out* to better himself. 貧しい少年は出世するためにしゃかりきに働いた.

brains and** [**versus**] **brawn 頭脳と[対]体力 ▪ Rick has both *brains and brawn.* リックは頭脳も体力もある ▪ Movies and games thrive on *brains versus brawn.* 映画やゲームは頭脳対体力を素材にして栄えている.

***crack** one's **brain**(**s**)* →beat one's BRAINs.

dash** [**knock out**] a person's **brains 人の頭をぶち割る ▪ He *dashed an Athenian's brains.* 彼はアテネ人の頭をぶち割った.

dash** [**beat**] one's **brains out 《口》頭をぶっつけて死ぬ ▪ He *dashed his brains out* on the rocks. 彼は岩に頭をぶっつけて死んだ.

get** one's **brain in gear 《口》頭を働かせる ▪ I breathe deeply whenever I try to *get my brain in gear.* 私は頭を働かせるときはいつも深呼吸をする.

get** one's **brains fried 《口》 **1** 日射病にかかる ▪ They'll *get their brains fried.* 彼らは日射病にかかるだろう.

2 麻薬でふらふらする ▪ He's *got his brains fried.* 彼は麻薬でふらふらしている.

have a brain fart 《戯》すぐに物忘れする ▪ Bill is *having a brain fart* every now and again. ビルはときどきすぐに物忘れする.

have** one's **brains on ice 《口》落ち着いている ▪ If we want to be successful we must *have our brains on ice.* 成功したいと思うなら, 落ち着いていなければならない.

have** (**got**)**... on the brain あることに憑(つ)かれている, 凝っている; (ある人が)忘れられない ▪ Smith *has got* money-making *on the brain.* スミスは金儲けに凝っている ▪ Rachel will *have* the boy *on the brain.* レイチェルはその少年が忘れられないだろう.

have plenty of brains 頭が良い, たくましい知力がある ▪ He's *got plenty of brains* but no common sense. 彼は頭は良いが常識がない.

have the brain of a pigeon 愚かである ▪ If a guy is being a jerk, it's usually because he *has the brain of a pigeon.* もし男が世間知らずなふるまいをしているなら, それは通例愚か者だからだ.

make** a person's **brain**(**s**) **reel 人を仰天させる ▪ The number of stars *makes one's brain reel.* 星の数はびっくり仰天するほどだ.

out of** one's **brain 《英俗》ひどく酔って ▪ At the time, I thought he was *out of his brain.* そのときは, 彼はへべれけに酔っ払っていると思った.

pick** [**suck**] a person's **brains 人の知恵・知識を(無断で)借りる; 特殊の知識を得るため人に巧みに尋ねる ▪ Mary wants to *pick your brains* about Freud and Jung. メアリーはフロイトとユングについてあなたの知恵を借りたがっている ▪ He will *pick your brains* and try to get the better of you. 彼はあなたの知恵を借りてあなたを負かそうとするだろう.

pound** [**puzzle**] one's **brains → beat one's BRAINs.

rack** one's **brains →beat one's BRAINs.

***tax** one's [a person's] **brain**(**s**)* 頭を酷使する[人に頭を酷使させる] ▪ I have *taxed my brains* far too much for weeks. 私は何週間も頭を酷使しすぎた ▪ This problem really *taxed my brains* for two weeks. この問題には過去2週間本当に頭を酷使させられた.

turn** a person's **brain **1** めまいさせる, 頭を変にさせる ▪ His long talk is enough to *turn one's brain.* 彼の長話は人を呆然とさせるに十分である.

2 有頂天にする, 調子づかせる ▪ Success has *turned his brain.* 成功したので彼は調子づいている.

brainwash /bréɪnwɑ̀ʃ/ 動 ***brainwash** a person **into** doing* 人を洗脳して(うまく言いくるめて)…させる ▪ He systematically *brainwashed* his son *into hating* his mother. 彼は組織的に息子を洗脳して母親を憎むようにさせた.

brake /breɪk/ 名 ***jam the brake*(*s*) *on/jam on the brake*(*s*)** (自動車の)ブレーキを急に[強く]踏む; (企画など)にブレーキをかける ▪ He *jammed on the brakes*, and the car stopped. 彼が急にブレーキを踏んだので, 車が停まった ▪ The president *jammed the brake on* the project last weeek. 先週社長がその企画に待ったをかけた.

put on** [**apply**] **the brake**(**s**)/ **put the brake**(**s**) **on ブレーキをかける《比喩的にも》 ▪ The driver *put on the brakes* suddenly. 運転手は急にブレーキをかけた ▪ Mr. Smith had to *put the brake on* and take more rest. スミス氏は仕事をゆるめて, もっと休養しなければならなかった ▪ We must *put the brake on* our spending. 出費を控えないとならない.

ride the brake →RIDE².

slam the brakes on 《口》急にブレーキをかける ▪ He *slammed the brakes on.* 彼は急にブレーキをかけた.

bran /bræn/ 名 ***to the bran*** 細かく, 徹底的に(よりすぐるなど) ▪ It has been sifted *to the bran.* それは徹底的によりすぐられた.

brand /brænd/ 名 ***a brand** (**snatched, plucked**) **from the burning** [**fire**]* (《聖》 *Zech.* 3. 2)危急を救われた人物; 改宗者 ▪ He claimed the boon of *a brand snatched from the burning.* 彼は改宗者の恩恵を要求した ▪ When I realized I was through that siege, I felt like *a brand from the burning.* 私は自分がその包囲を切り抜けたことを悟ったとき, 死地から救われた人のように感じた.

the brand of Cain →CAIN.

brandy /brǽndi/ 動 ***brandy it*** ブランデーを飲みすぎる ▪ He surely had been *brandying it.* 彼は確かにブランデーを飲みすぎていた.

brass /bræs|brɑːs/ 名形 ***(as) bold as brass*** →BOLD.

brass monkey weather/ brass monkeys 《英俗》極端に寒い天候 ▪ It's *brass monkey weather* today. きょうはやけに寒い天気だね.

get [come] down to brass tacks [nails] **1** (問題の)核心に触れる ▪ She was the first to *get down to brass tacks* in the discussion. 彼女がその討論において最初に問題の核心に触れた ▪ *Come down to brass nails.* 要点を話しなさい.

2 真剣に努力を始める ▪ They were *getting down to* the *brass tacks* of mapping their fall campaigns. 彼らは秋の選挙運動の計画を立てる真剣な努力を始めていた.

have the brass (neck) to *do* 《英口》/ ***have the brass balls to*** *do* 《米俗》厚かましくも[ずうずうしくも]...する ▪ He *had the brass neck to* ask for a refund. 彼は厚かましくも払い戻し金を要求した.

part brass rags (with) 《俗》(...との)親交を解消する; (と)けんかする ▪ They'll *part brass rags* before long. 彼らはやがて親交を断つだろう. ☞「水兵がしんちゅう磨きのぼろをもう共用しない」が原義.

brass farthing /brǽsfɑ́ːrðɪŋ|brɑ́ːs-/ 名 ***be not worth a brass farthing*** 《英口》びた一文の値うちもない; (人が)びた一文も持たない ▪ It *is not worth a brass farthing.* それは一文の価値もない ▪ He *is not worth a brass farthing.* 彼はびた一文も持っていない.

not care a brass farthing 《英口》ちっともかまわない ▪ I *don't care a brass farthing* for him. 私は彼をちっとも問題にしない.

brave[1] /breɪv/ 形 ***a brave new world*** 素晴らしき新世界 (cf. Sh., *Temp.* 5. 1. 183) ▪ One day, the violence will end! *A brave new world* is coming! いつの日か暴力は終わるだろう! 素晴らしき新世界が来つつある!

put a brave face [front] on/ put on a brass face [front] (つらくても)...に平然とした顔をする ▪ He was very upset by the news but *put on a brave face.* 彼はそのニュースにショックを受けたが, 平静を装っていた.

brave[2] /breɪv/ 動 ***brave it out*** (困難などに)ひるまず立ち向かう; 勇敢に[ずうずうしく]押し通す ▪ As we felt that we had done the right thing, we could *brave it out.* 我々は正しいことをしたと思っていたので勇敢に押し通すことができた.

brawn /brɔːn/ 名 ***all brawn and no brain*** 体力はあるが, 頭はよくない ▪ This is Shorty: *all brawn and no brain,* but we love him. こちらはチビ君だ. 体力はあるが, 頭はよくない. でも彼が好きだ.

brazen /bréɪzən/ 動 ***brazen it [a thing] out*** ずうずうしく押し通す, 平気な顔をする; (悪行をして)嘘ぶく ▪ He would talk saucily, lie, and *brazen it out.* 彼はなまいきなことを言い, 嘘をつき, そして平気な顔をするのだった ▪ He *brazened out* his determination. 彼は自分の決心をずうずうしく押し通した.

brazil /brəzíl/ 名 ***(as) hard as brazil [Brazil]*** ひどく堅い ▪ My bones are *as hard as brazil.* 私の骨はひどく堅い. ☞Brazil(wood)「ブラジルウッド」の木材が非常に堅いところから.

breach /briːtʃ/ 名 ***(be) in breach of*** ...に違反して(いる) ▪ Employers can *be in breach of* an employment contract. 雇い主が雇用規約に違反することはある.

breach of duty 職務怠慢 ▪ The signalman committed a serious *breach of duty.* その信号手は重大な職務怠慢を犯した.

breach of promise 婚約破約《主として男の方から》 ▪ Margaret is going to sue Edward for *breach of promise.* マーガレットは婚約破約のかどでエドワードを訴えるつもりである.

fill the breach →step into the BREACH 2.

heal the breach (長い間の)けんかをいやす ▪ George and Jane will not speak to one another; her mother is trying to *heal the breach.* ジョージとジェインはお互いに口をきこうとしない. 彼女の母は仲直りさせようと努めている.

more honored in the breach than in the observance 守るより破った方がましな (cf. Sh., *Haml.* 1. 4. 156) ▪ The rule was at times *more honored in the breach than in the observance.* その規則は守るより破った方がましな時もあった.

mount the breach 城壁の破れ口に登る; 先頭を切る ▪ The man *mounting the breach* first, produced his plunder. その男がまず先頭を切って, 自分の分捕品を取りだした.

stand in the breach 攻撃の矢面に立つ, 難局に当たる ▪ Moses *stood in the breach.* モーセは攻撃の矢面に立った.

step into the breach **1** (人の)急場を救う ▪ Upon his release from prison, he *stepped into the breach* at once. 刑務所から釈放されるやいなや, 彼は直ちに急場を救った.

2 (劇などで)代役を務める ▪ Luckily another actor *stepped into the breach.* 幸いにも別の俳優が代役を務めた.

throw [fling] *oneself* ***into the breach*** →step into the BREACH 1.

bread /bred/ 名 ***as I live by bread*** 《口》(私がパンを食って生きているように)確かに, ほんとに ▪ I speak the truth, *as I live by bread.* 私はほんとに真実を言います.

beg *one's* ***bread*** 物乞いをする ▪ He *begged his bread* from door to door. 彼は戸ごとに物乞いをした.

Bread always falls on the buttered side. 《諺》パンはいつもバターを塗った側に落ちる《物事がうまくいかないときは, 徹底的にうまくいかない》.

bread and cheese チーズをつけたパン; 簡素な食事, 生活の資 ▪ Come and take your *bread and cheese* with me this evening. 今晩簡単な食事をし

にお越しください.

bread and circuses 《文》安価な大衆慰安物 (Juvenal, *Satires* 10. 80) ▪ They are content to live by *bread and circuses* alone. 彼らは安価な慰安物だけで暮らすのに甘んじている.

bread and water パンと水, (囚人などの)著しい粗食 ▪ They kept him on *bread and water* for a day. 彼らは彼を一日の間パンと水だけにした.

one's ***bread basket*** 《俗》胃 ▪ Tom is stuffing *his bread basket* again. トムはまたもや腹いっぱいつめ込んでいる.

bread buttered on both sides 両面にバターをぬったパン; 安楽裕福(な境遇), 大幸運, 二重の儲け ▪ Wherever he goes, he is sure to find his *bread buttered on both sides.* 彼はどこへ行っても必ず大幸運を見つける.

One's ***bread is buttered on both sides.*** = have one's BREAD buttered on both sides.

Bread is the staff of life. 《諺》パンは生命を支えるもの.

break bread **1** パンを裂く, パンをちぎって配り与える; 聖餐(さん)式に列する (《聖》 *Acts* 20. 7) ▪ They continued in *breaking* of *bread* and in prayer. 彼らはパンを裂きそして祈り続けた.
2 食事する (*with*) ▪ I have never *broken bread with* them. あの人たちと食事をしたことはない.

butter both sides of *one's* ***bread*** 《口》(同時に)二重の儲けをする ▪ He's got *both sides of his bread buttered.* 彼は二重の儲けをしている.

cast [***scatter, throw***] *one's* ***bread upon the waters*** 《文》報酬をあてにしないで善をなす, 陰徳を施す; 気前よく与える (《聖》 *Eccles.* 11. 1) ▪ The printers *cast their bread upon the waters* out of pure zeal. 印刷者たちは全くの熱意から報酬をあてにせずに善事をなした.

one's ***daily bread*** 人の日々のかて[パン] (《聖》 *Matt.* 6. 11) ▪ We must earn *our daily bread.* 我々は日々のかてを儲けなければならない.

earn [***gain***] *one's* ***bread*** (***by the sweat of*** *one's* ***brow*** [***face***]) (労働して)生計を立てる, 暮らして行く (《聖》 *Gen.* 3. 19) ▪ They *earned their bread by the sweat of their brows.* 彼らはかせいで生計を立てた.

eat the bread of affliction [***sorrow,*** etc.] 苦難[悲しみ, など]をなめる (《聖》 *Deut.* 16. 3) ▪ I do condemn thee to *eat the bread of affliction.* 私はおまえに苦難の生活をさせることにする.

eat the bread of idleness →IDLENESS.

have *one's* ***bread buttered on both sides*** 安楽裕福な身である, 両手に花の幸運にありつく ▪ Ex-attorney *has his bread buttered on both sides* in prison. 元弁護士は刑務所で両手に花の幸運にありついている.

in good bread よい生活をして, よい地位にあって ▪ Mr. Barnard is now *in good bread.* バーナード氏は今は幸福な暮らしをしている.

know on which side *one's* ***bread is buttered*** 自分の利害関係にさとい ▪ He *knows* well *on which side his bread is buttered.* 彼は自分の利害関係に全く抜け目がない.

make *one's* ***bread*** 生計を立てる ▪ He *made his bread* by writing. 彼は文筆で生計を立てた.

no bread and butter of ...の知ったことではない ▪ It is *no bread and butter of* mine. それは私の知ったことではない.

out of bread 《俗》仕事にあぶれて ▪ He is *out of bread* at present. 彼は目下失業中だ.

quarrel with *one's* ***bread and butter*** → QUARREL[2].

scatter *one's* ***bread upon the waters*** → cast one's BREAD upon the waters.

share *a person's* ***bread and salt*** 人の歓待を受ける ▪ I *shared his bread and salt.* 私は彼の歓待を受けた. ☞パンと塩は歓待の象徴.

take the bread out of *a person's* ***mouth*** **1** 人の生活の道を(競争して)奪う ▪ The invention of the spinning-jenny *took the bread out of the hand weavers' mouths.* 紡績機の発明は手織り職人たちの生活の道を奪った.
2 人の楽しもうとしているものを奪い取る ▪ He dashed forward to *take the bread out of Peel's mouth.* 彼はピールが楽しもうとしているものを奪いに飛び出してきた.

the bread-and-butter of a business 主要な収入源 ▪ With tenant farmers farm products are *the bread-and-butter of a business.* 小作農の場合, 農産物が主要な収入源だ.

the bread and wine 聖餐(さん)のパンとぶどう酒; 聖餐 ▪ He partook of *the bread and wine.* 彼は聖餐をいただいた.

the bread of life 命のかて (《聖》 *John* 6. 35) ▪ The Japanese people are at last finding *the bread of life.* 日本国民はやっと命のかてを見いだしつつある.

the greatest [***the best***] ***thing since sliced bread*** 《口・戯》賞賛される人[物], 好まれる人[物], この上もなく良い[面白い]人 ▪ My new friend is *the greatest thing since sliced bread.* 私の新しい友人はとても人に好かれている ▪ Simon seems to think his wife is *the best thing since sliced bread.* サイモンは自分の妻は最高に素敵な人だと考えているようだ.

throw *one's* ***bread upon the waters*** →cast one's BREAD upon the waters.

breadline /brédlàɪn/ 名 ***be*** [***live***] ***on the breadline*** 《英》とても貧しい生活をしている, どん底の生活をしている ▪ Half of all pensioners are *living on the breadline* in the United Kingdom. 連合王国では年金生活者たちの半分はどん底の生活をしている. ☞窮乏時に行列してパン配給を受けることから.

breadth /bredθ, bretθ/ 名 ***by a hair('s)-breadth*** →HAIR('S)-BREADTH.

break[1] /breɪk/ 名 ***a bad break*** **1** 《米口》へま, (特に社交上の)しくじり ▪ He made *a bad break* as a lawyer. 彼は弁護士としてへまをやった.

2 不運 ▪ Previously he had *a* series of *bad breaks.* その前には彼は不運続きだった.

a clean break 完全な絶縁 (*with*) ▪ He made *a clean break with* all his old associations. 彼はいっさいの古い交わりときっぱり縁を切った.

a fair break 《米》好機 ▪ When do I get *a fair break* in life? 私は人生においていつ好機に恵まれるのだろうか.

an even break 《米口》五分五分のチャンス ▪ You and I are *an even break* in this point. 君と僕とはこの点では五分五分だ.

at* (*the*) *break of day 夜明けに ▪ We started *at break of day.* 我々は夜明けに出発した.

cut *a person* ***a break*** 《米俗》人に特別な好意を示す ▪ Ohio's public colleges are *cutting* veterans *a break.* オハイオ州の公立大学は退役軍人に特別な好意を示しつつある.

***get a break* (*on*)** (...についての)好機をつかむ, 成功のチャンスにぶつかる ▪ The Herald Post *got a break on* wedding announcements. ヘラルドポスト紙は結婚発表を知る機会をつかんだ.

get a good* [*lucky*] *break 《米》運がよい ▪ He certainly *got a good break* when he began to work in that firm. 彼があの会社で働くようになったのは確かに幸運であった.

get an even break 〚主に否定文・疑問文で〛みなと同じ機会を得る ▪ When will women *get an even break* in the workplace? 女性が職場でみんなと同じチャンスを得るのはいつだろう?

get the breaks 運がよい ▪ That fellow *gets* all *the breaks.* あの男は大変運がよい.

give *a person* ***a break*** **1**《口》人を大目にみる, 人に手心を加える ▪ *Give* him *a break.* I'm sure he'll come around. 彼を大目に見てやれよ. きっと同調するさ.

2《口》人に(活躍の)好機を与える, 特別に配慮する ▪ Would you evict this tenant, or *give* him *a break?* このテナントを追い出しますか, それとも彼にチャンスを与えますか ▪ Liz begged the professor for an extension on her term paper, saying "Please *give* me *a break*". リズは期末論文の延期を願って,「特別に配慮してくださいませんか」と言った.

3 人に休憩を与える ▪ Will you *give* me *a break?* 休憩させてくれませんか.

give *a person* ***even break*** 人にみんなと同じチャンスを与える ▪ Disabled people should *be given* an *even break.* 身体の不自由な人々も平等の機会を与えられるべきである.

Give me* [*us*] *a break. 《米口》(そんなこと)信じられないね; 嘘だろ ▪ You're going to run for the Congress? *Give me a break!* 君が国会議員に立候補するって? 信じられないね!

make a break **1** すっかり変える, 中断する ▪ Army service *made a break* in his career. 軍隊勤務が彼の経歴を中断した.

2《玉突き》連続で...点をとる (*of*) ▪ He *made a break of* 80. 彼は連続で80点とった.

3 (社交上の)へまをやる (→a bad BREAK 1).

4 突進する (*for*) ▪ The deer *made a break for* the thicket. シカは茂みへ突進した.

***make a break for it* [*freedom*]** 《口》逃げようとする, 脱走する ▪ The prisoner *made a break for freedom.* 囚人は脱走した.

never give a sucker an even break 《俗》愚者には公平な機会を与えない ▪ He firmly believes in *never giving a sucker an even break.* 彼は愚者には公平な機会を与えないのはいいことだと固く信じている.

take* [*have*] *a break 《口》ちょっと(中)休みをする ▪ I *took a break* for a cigaret. 少し休んで一服した.

***tough break* [*luck,* 《俗》*beans,* 《俗》*shit*]** →a TOUGH break.

without a break 絶えず, 連綿と ▪ I have been writing since one o'clock *without a break.* 私は1時からずっと続けて書いている.

break[2] /breɪk/ 動 ***break a flag*** 旗ざおに旗を掲げる ▪ We *break* the Scottish *flag* on the flagstaff when we have visitors. 我々は訪問客があるときは旗ざおにスコットランドの旗を掲げる.

***break a horse to harness* [*saddle*]** 馬を馬車用[乗馬用]にならす ▪ The wild *horse was broken to harness.* その荒馬は馬車用にならされた.

***break a horse to the rein*(*s*)** 馬を乗りならす ▪ The *horse is* not yet *broken to the rein.* その馬はまだ乗りならされていない.

break a marriage 離婚する ▪ Henry desired to *break* his first *marriage.* ヘンリーは最初の結婚を解消したいと願った.

***break a sigh* [*smile*]** ため息をつく[急に微笑する] ▪ Jack often *broke a sigh* in the suffocating smoke. ジャックは息うまるような煙の中でしばしばため息をもらした.

break and enter (盗むため)押し入る ▪ He was had up for *breaking and entering* a shop. 彼は店に押し入ったかどでその筋へ訴えられた.

break blows with ...となぐり合いをする ▪ He *broke blows with* me. 彼は私となぐり合った.

break bounds 境界を越えて出る; らちを越える ▪ Scholars were gated for a week for *breaking bounds.* 学生たちはらちを越えたため1週間の外出禁止を命じられた.

break even 差引き損得なしである; (競技で)引き分けになる; 収支を償わせる (*on*) ▪ I'll rather *break even on* a monumental building. 私はむしろ後世に残るような建物を建てて収支を償いたい ▪ I *broke even on* the deal. 私はその取引で損得なしであった.

break *a person's* ***fall*** 人の墜落を(途中で)止める, くい止める ▪ The bush *broke his fall.* 茂みが彼の墜落をくい止めた.

break free →BREAK loose.

break gloom うさを散らす ▪ The lady tried to *break gloom* by singing songs. その女性は歌を歌って暗い気分を散らそうとした.

B

break into** a person's **mind (ある事を)悟る ▪ The truth *broke into my mind.* 私は真相を悟った.

break (it) off with 《米》…と親交を絶つ, 仲たがいする ▪ He *broke it off with* his sweetheart. 彼は恋人と仲たがいした.

Break it up! あっちへ行ってください《人だかりを解散させるときの巡査の言葉》 ▪ Come on, *break it up!* さあ, みんなどいてください.

break loose [free] **1** (つないである動物などが)離れる, 逃れる, 逃げだす (*from*) ▪ The dog *broke loose from* its chain. 犬は鎖を離れた ▪ He succeeded in *breaking free from* the jail. 彼は首尾よく脱獄した.

2 (暴力などが)わが物顔にのさばる ▪ Violence *broke loose* in the city last night. 昨夜町で暴力がわが物顔にのさばった.

break** one's **neck →NECK.

break** oneself **of (習慣など)をやめる ▪ He *broke himself of* the bad habit of smoking. 彼は喫煙の悪習をやめた.

break open …をこわして開ける[入る] ▪ The robbers *broke open* his house. 盗賊どもは彼の家をこじあけて入った.

break** one's **pick 《米》解雇される ▪ Unfortunately he *broke his pick.* 不運にも彼は首になった.

break ship (上陸した船員が)期限が切れても帰船しない ▪ In the afternoon he *broke ship*, but was undiscovered. 午後彼は上陸して期限内に帰船しなかったが, 気づかれなかった.

break soil →BREAK water.

break the ice →ICE.

break the water (魚が)水中から飛び上がる, (潜水艦が)水面に浮かび上がる ▪ The submarine *broke the water.* 潜水艦が水面に浮かびあがった.

break water [soil] (シカが)水を渡る ▪ Stags *break water* to come by fresh pasture. シカは新しい草にありつくために水を渡る.

break wind →WIND[1].

break** one's **word 約束を破る (→break one's PROMISE) ▪ He never *breaks his word.* 彼は決して約束を破らない.

break words with …と言い合いする ▪ A man may *break words with* you, sir. 人はあなたと言い合いをすることもあります.

break yard 《米》(大シカが)すみかを去る ▪ They *break yard* and start down the mountain. 彼らはすみかを去り, 山を下り始める.

without breaking stride →STRIDE.

breaker /bréɪkər/ 名 ***breakers ahead*** 《口》前途の暗礁[危険], 危険を告げる叫び ▪ Suddenly we heard a shout of "*Breakers ahead!*" 突然我々は「暗礁だ」という叫びを聞いた ▪ *Breakers ahead* in that house. あの家の前途に危険あり.

breakfast /brékfəst/ 名 ***a dog's breakfast [dinner]*** →DOG[1].

breakfast television 朝食時間帯のテレビ番組 ▪ *Breakfast television* is a good way of catching up with the latest news. 朝食時間帯のテレビ番組は, 最近のニュースに遅れなくてすむよい方法だ.

eat [have]** a person **for breakfast **1** 《口》人をしかりとばす, 非難する ▪ If I tried to pick Liz up she would *eat* me *for breakfast!* もし僕がリズを引っかけようとしたら, 彼女は僕を非難するだろう.

2 (けんか・議論・商売などで)人を簡単に打ち負かす, 難なくやり込める ▪ I could totally *eat* him *for breakfast* at golf. 彼なんかゴルフでわけなく打ち負かせるさ.

(If you) sing before breakfast, you'll cry before night [supper]. 《諺》朝食の前に歌えば, 夜[夕食]の前に泣くだろう《喜びは苦痛の始まり》.

breaking /bréɪkɪŋ/ 名 ***breaking and entering*** (窓などをこわしての)不法侵入 ▪ The man was found guilty of *breaking and entering* in the nighttime. 男は夜中に不法侵入の罪を犯していることがわかった.

break-neck /bréɪknèk/ 形 ***at (a) break-neck pace [speed]*** 危険きわまる速度で ▪ The car went *at a break-neck speed.* 自動車は無謀な速度で走った.

breast[1] /brest/ 名 ***a child at the breast*** 乳飲み子 ▪ The princess was still *a child at the breast.* 王女はまだ乳飲み子だった.

beat one's breast →BEAT[2].

give ... the breast/put ... to the breast (子供)に乳を与える ▪ She *put* the child *to the breast.* 彼女は子供に乳を飲ませた.

make a clean breast of (罪など)をすっかり打ち明ける ▪ *Make a clean breast of* it [the whole thing]. それを[それを残らず]打ち明けなさい.

past the breast 乳離れした ▪ The child is *past the breast.* その子は乳離れしている.

breast[2] /brest/ 動 ***breast it out*** あくまで抵抗する[押し通す] ▪ He *breasted it out* against difficulties. 彼は困難に対してあくまで抵抗した.

breast the tape →TAPE[1].

breast** oneself **(to) (…に)大胆に当たる ▪ The government *breasted itself to* the shock of lawless men. 政府は無法者たちの激突に大胆に当たった.

breath /breθ/ 名 ***a breath of fresh air*** 新しい息吹, 新風を吹き込むもの ▪ Okinawan writers provide *a breath of fresh air* for the Japanese literary circles. 沖縄の作家たちは日本の文壇に新風を吹き込むものである ▪ Barack Obama is welcomed as *a breath of fresh air* in the American political world. バラク・オバマ氏はアメリカの政界の新しい息吹として歓迎されている.

(a) waste of breath 言葉の空費, 話しても無駄なこと ▪ It is *waste of breath* to argue with him. 彼と議論するのは言葉の空費でなんにもならない ▪ Talking with her will be *a waste of breath.* 彼女と話しても無駄だろうよ.

above** one's **breath 声をひそめて, ささやき以上の声で ▪ He spoke *above his breath.* 彼は声をひそめて言った.

all in a breath 息をもつかず，急に；一息に ▪ *All in a breath*, back went the right hand. 急に右手が後ろへ回った ▪ She explained, *all in a breath*, that she had missed the train. 彼女は電車に乗り遅れたと一息に説明した．

at a breath 一気に，一息に《やってしまうなど》 ▪ I cannot come to the point *at a breath*. 私は一気に要点に触れることはできない．

be mentioned in the same breath 〖主に否定文で〗(...と)比べられる，匹敵できる(*with*) ▪ The true Southern watermelon is a boon apart and not to *be mentioned with* commoner things. 本物の南部のスイカは格別な恵みであり，普通のものと比べものにならない(ほど優れている) ▪ His body of work is not to *be mentioned in the same breath with* Thomas Hardy's. 彼の作品群はトマス・ハーディーのものとは比べものにならない(ほど劣っている) ▪ It's nice to *be mentioned in the same breath with* those guys. そういう男たちと同日に論じられるのはすばらしい．

below [***beneath, under***] *one's* ***breath*** (人に聞こえないくらい)声をひそめて ▪ He spoke *below his breath*. 彼はひそひそと話した ▪ He cursed his wife *under his breath*. 彼は声をひそめて妻を呪った．

catch *one's* ***breath*** **1** 固唾をのむ，(驚きなどで)息を殺す；あえぐ ▪ I *caught my breath* when I saw a green snake. アオヘビを見たとき，固唾をのんだ．
2 (走ったあとなどで)一息つく ▪ Let's sit down and *catch our breath*. 座って一息つきましょう．
3 (仕事のあとなどで)ちょっとくつろぐ ▪ We sat down over coffee to *catch our breath*. 我々は一服するために座ってコーヒーを飲んだ．

draw breath **1** 生きている ▪ He won't want for a friend as long as I *draw breath*. 私が生きているかぎり彼は友人にこと欠かないだろう．
2 ＝draw one's BREATH.

draw [***take***] *one's* [***a***] ***breath*** **1** 呼吸する；一息つく ▪ She *drew a* deep [long] *breath* before replying. 彼女は答える前に深呼吸をした ▪ A simple child lightly *draws its breath*. あどけない子供は軽やかに呼吸する ▪ *Take* a few *breaths* before jumping in. 飛び込む前に2，3回呼吸をしなさい．
2 息を吸い込む ▪ At this Mary *drew her breath*. これを見てメアリーは息を吸い込んだ．

draw *one's* ***first*** [***last***] ***breath*** 生まれる[息を引き取る] ▪ I held him in my arms as he *drew his last breath*. 彼が息を引き取ったとき彼を抱きしめた．

fetch *one's* ***breath*** 呼吸する ▪ She was *fetching her breath* in sobs. 彼女はすすり泣きながら呼吸していた．

gather breath ＝take BREATH.

get *one's* ***breath*** 息をつく ▪ At last he *got his breath* and answered. 彼はやっと息をついて答えた．

get *one's* ***breath back*** (運動のあとなどに)一息つく，呼吸が整う ▪ It took me a while to *get my breath back* after jogging half an hour. 半時間ジョギングしたあと呼吸が整うのにしばらくかかった．

get out of breath 息が切れる ▪ He *got out of breath* reading the article. 彼はその記事を読みながら息を切らした．

give up [***yield***] *one's* ***breath*** 息を引き取る ▪ The lion fell and *gave up its breath*. ライオンは倒れて死んだ．

hold *one's* ***breath*** **1** (しばらく)息を止める ▪ I *held my breath* under water. 水中で息を止めた．
2 息を殺す，固唾をのむ ▪ We *held our breath* in excitement. 私たちは興奮して固唾をのんだ．
3 〖主に否定文で〗期待する ▪ Ellen marry me? I wouldn't *hold my breath*. エレンが僕と結婚する？期待してないよ ▪ Don't *hold your breath* for his support. 彼の支持を期待してはいけない．

in a [***one, the same***] ***breath*** **1** 同時に《相反したことなど言うとき》 ▪ He says yes and no *in one breath*. 彼はうんと言ったかと思うとすぐいいやと言う．
2 口をそろえて；一息に，一気に ▪ They screamed all *in one breath*. 彼らはみないっしょに叫んだ．

in the very next breath すぐに，間をおかず ▪ First he says yes, and then *in the very next breath* he says no! 彼はうんと言ったかと思うと，その舌の根も乾かないうちにいいやと言うんだ．

keep *one's* ***breath*** ＝hold one's BREATH 1, 2.

keep [***save, spare***] *one's* ***breath to cool*** *one's* ***porridge*** →save one's BREATH (to cool one's porridge).

knock the breath out of *a person* [*a person's* ***body***] 人をあっと驚かせる ▪ The news *knocked the breath out of* him. その知らせは彼をあっと驚かせた．

lose (*one's*) ***breath*** 息切れがする ▪ If you run so fast, you may *lose your breath*. そんなに速く走ると息が切れるかもしれないよ．

mention [***speak of***] ***in the same breath*** (平凡なものと優れたものを)同日に論じる ▪ How can you *mention* Ford with Mercedes *in the same breath*? どうして君はフォードとメルセデスを同日に論じられるのかね．

not a breath of ...がちっともない ▪ There was *not a breath of* wind. 風がそよとも吹かなかった ▪ There is *not a breath of* suspicion. 一点の疑惑もない．

not to [***cannot***] ***be mentioned*** [***named***] ***in the same breath*** (***with***) (...とは)同日の論ではない；(とは)比べ物にならない(ほど劣る) ▪ This *cannot be named in the same breath with* that. これはあれとは比べ物にならない．

out of breath 息が切れて ▪ I am completely *out of breath*. すっかり息が切れた．

put *a person* ***out of breath*** 人に息切れさせる ▪ Climbing the mountain *put* him *out of breath*. その山に登ったので彼は息切れがした．

run *oneself* ***out of breath*** 走って息を切らす ▪ Jim practically *ran himself out of breath* for one hour. ジムは走ってほとんど1時間息切れがしていた．

save [***spare***] *one's* ***breath*** (***to cool*** *one's* ***porridge*** [***broth***]) 《口》〖しばしば can, may as well を伴って〗むだ口をきかない, 黙る ▪You *can save your breath*; there is no use talking to him. 黙ってらっしゃい, あの人に話したってむだです. ☞通例相手に向かって言う.

second breath **1** 息継ぎ ▪He got his head out of the water to draw a *second breath*. 彼は息継ぎをするために水から頭を出した.

2 元気の回復 ▪Their firm had sharp slumps, but seemed to have caught *second breath*. 彼らの会社はひどく落ち込んでいたが, 元気を回復したようだ.

short of breath 息切れがして ▪You won't be *short of breath* if you'll walk 3 miles daily. 毎日3マイル歩くなら, 息切れはしませんよ.

***spend* [*waste*] *one's* breath** 甲斐のないことを言う, 言ったことがむだになる (*on*) ▪I will no longer *spend my breath* in defense of it. 私はこれ以上むだ口たたいてそれを弁護しない ▪Why are you *wasting your breath on* him? 彼を説得したってむだだ.

take a* [*one's*] *breath →draw one's BREATH.

take breath 息をつく; ひと休みする ▪We stopped to *take breath*. 我々は止まって一息ついた.

take a person's breath away (驚き・喜びなどで)人をあっと言わせる, はっとさせる ▪Your offer is so generous that it *takes my breath away*. お申し込み値段は非常に気前がよいものなので驚き入りました ▪The superb scene *took my breath away*. その絶景に息をのんだ.

***the* [*a*] *breath of life to* [*for*]** …にとって必要不可欠なもの ▪He is *a breath of life to* her. 彼は彼女にとってかけがえのない大切な存在だ ▪A vanilla smell is a *breath of life for* babies. バニラのにおいは赤んぼうにとって不可欠なものだ.

the breath of one's nostrils 生命, 霊魂; 命のように大事なもの (《聖》*Gen.* 7. 22) ▪The Englishman demands freedom; it is *the breath of his nostrils*. 英国人は自由を要求する, 命ほど大事だから.

to the last breath 最後の息を引き取るまで ▪I will fight *to the last breath*. 私は死ぬまで戦う.

under one's breath →below one's BREATH.

waste one's breath →spend one's BREATH.

with bated breath →BATED.

with every* (*other*) *breath 繰り返して, 続けて ▪She screamed *with every other breath*. 彼女は何度も悲鳴をあげた.

with the* [*one's*] *last breath 死ぬまで, 最後まで《言明を強めて》 ▪I would maintain *with my last breath* that he is innocent. 彼が無罪であることを最後まで主張したい.

yield one's breath →give up one's BREATH.

breathe /briːð/ 動 ***as I live and breathe*** → LIVE[2].

breathe a word against …に対して一言不平を漏らす ▪He would never *breathe a word against* me. 彼は私に対して一言も不平を漏らすことはなかった.

***breathe again/ breathe easy* [*easier, easily*]** ほっと(一息, 安心)する ▪What you tell me makes me *breathe again*. あなたのお話を聞くとほっとしました ▪Now that exams are over with, I can *breathe easy*. 試験が終わったので, ほっとできる.

breathe down a person's neck **1** (追跡などで)人の背後に迫る ▪The police *breathed down his neck*. 警察は(追跡して)彼の背後に迫った.

2 見張る, 監視する ▪The boss is always *breathing down our necks*. ボスは常に我々を見張っている.

breathe fire and slaughter [etc.] 殺す[罰する, 報復する, など]とおどす; 《戯》立腹する (《聖》*Acts* 9. 1) ▪The policeman is *breathing fire and slaughter*. 警官は罰してやるとおどしている.

breathe freely **1** =BREATHE again.

2 気楽である, 得意の地位にある ▪The Spartans seemed to have *breathed freely* in war. スパルタ人は戦争を得意としていたようだ.

breathe fresh life into →breathe LIFE into.

breathe one's last 《文》息を引き取る ▪He *breathed his last* this morning. 彼は今朝息を引き取った.

breathe new life into →breathe LIFE into.

***not breathe a word* [*a syllable*]** 一口も漏らさない ▪You must promise *not* to *breathe a word* to anyone else. 他の誰にも一言も漏らさないとぜひ約束してください.

breather /bríːðər/ 名 ***have* [*take*] *a breather*** ひと休みする, 一息つく ▪We *took a breather* after the heavy work. 我々は激しい仕事のあとで一息ついた.

breathing /bríːðɪŋ/ 名 ***a breathing space* [*room*]** **1** (労働の間の)息つく間, 息をつく瞬間 ▪Winning this prize will give me *a* bit of *breathing space*. この賞を得たことで, ちょっと息をつく期間が得られる ▪The American loans give us *a* short *breathing room*. アメリカの資金貸付は我々に短い息抜き期間を与えてくれる.

2 憩いの場 ▪Perhaps what you need is *a* little *breathing space*. おそらくあなた方に必要なのは, 小さな憩いの場でしょう.

***a breathing spell* [*time*]** = a BREATHING space 1.

in a breathing ちょっとの間に ▪The accident happened *in a breathing*. それはちょっとの間に起こった.

breech /briːtʃ/ 名 ***be too big for one's breeches*** →be too BIG for one's boots.

wear the breeches 支配力をふるう《特に妻が夫に》 ▪It is Mrs. Smith, not Mr. Smith, who *wears the breeches* in that family. その家で支配力をふるっているのはスミス氏ではなくてスミス夫人である.

breed[1] /briːd/ 名 ***a breed apart*** 一風変わった人[物] ▪The top taxonomist is *a breed apart*. そのトップの分類学者は一風変わった人物だ.

breed[2] /briːd/ 動 ***bred for the church*** 牧師に(なるよう)育てられて ▪He was *bred for the church*. 彼は牧師に育てられた.

bred in the bone 生まれつきで[の] ▪ His idleness was *bred in the bone.* 彼の怠惰は生まれつきのものだ.

bred to a trade [***the law,*** etc.] 商売[法律, など]を仕込まれて ▪ He was *bred to the law.* 彼は弁護士の教育を受けた ▪ He is not *bred to any trade.* 彼は何業も仕込まれていない.

breed in and in 常に近親と結婚する, 同種繁殖を行う (↔BREED out and out) ▪ They *bred in and in.* それらは常に同種繁殖だった.

breed like rabbits →RABBIT[1].

breed out and out 常に近親以外と結婚する, 異種繁殖を行う (↔BREED in and in) ▪ Is it better for dogs to *breed out and out*? 犬は異種繁殖するほうがよいのだろうか.

breed true →TRUE.

Breeding will tell. 《諺》 育ち(のよし悪し)はおのずと知れる.

breeze /briːz/ 名 ***bat the breeze*** =shoot the BREEZE.

be a breeze 非常に易しい ▪ A visit to Mars will *be a breeze* in the future. 火星への旅行も将来は実に易しいものになるだろう.

create a breeze →kick up a BREEZE.

fan the breeze **1** =shoot the BREEZE.
2 《野球俗》 バットをふってボールを打ちそこなう ▪ He *fanned the breeze.* 彼はボールを打ちそこなった《ストライクになった》.

have [***get***] ***the breeze up*** [***vertical***] **1** 怒る ▪ There's no reason to *get the breeze up.* 怒る理由はない.
2 びっくりする; びくびくする ▪ We thought it was a burglar. I *had the breeze up.* 我々はそれを盗賊だと思った. 私はびくびくしていた. ☞《海》から; get the WIND up の変形.

hit [***split, take***] ***the breeze*** 《俗》 出て行く ▪ With this she *took the breeze.* こう言って彼女は出て行った.

in a breeze 《口》 楽々と ▪ The horse won *in a breeze.* その馬は楽勝した.

kick up [***create***] ***a breeze*** 《口》 一騒ぎ起こす ▪ The session *created the breeze.* その会合は一騒ぎ起こした.

shoot [***fan***] ***the breeze*** 《米口》 雑談する, だべる; だぼらを吹く ▪ Alan *fanned the breeze* with friends. アランは友人たちとだべった ▪ He *shot the breeze* for 20 minutes. 彼は20分間だぼらを吹いた.

breviary /brévièri|-viəri/ 名 ***a matter of breviary*** 疑問の余地のない事柄 (Rabelais, *Pantagruel* 4. 8) ▪ It is *a matter of breviary* with them. そのことは彼らには疑問の余地がない.

brevity /brévəti/ 名 ***Brevity is the soul of wit.*** 簡潔は機知の精髄, 「言は簡を尊ぶ」(cf. Sh., *Haml.* 2. 2. 90).

for brevity 簡潔のために, 略して ▪ He is called Sam *for brevity.* 彼は略してサムと呼ばれている.

brew /bruː/ 動 ***As you have brewed, so shall*** [***must***] ***you drink.*** 《諺》 自分のしたことの報いは自分で受けねばならない, 「自業自得」. ☞「あなたが造った酒だから, あなたが飲まねばならない」が原義.

brew mischief 悪事をもくろむ ▪ Those boys are *brewing mischief.* あの少年たちは悪事を企んでいる.

there's trouble brewing →TROUBLE[1].

bribe /braɪb/ 動 ***bribe*** *one's* ***way into*** [***out of***] 賄賂を使って...に入る[から出る] ▪ He *bribed his way into* the job. 彼は賄賂を使ってその職に就いた ▪ He allegedly *bribed his way out of* prison. 彼は賄賂を使って刑務所を出たと言われている.

brick /brɪk/ 名 ***a few bricks*** [***a brick***] ***short of a load*** 《口》 いかれた, 少し変な ▪ Some say Max is *a few bricks short of a load*! マックスはいかれていると言う人々もいる ▪ Our prime minister is *a brick short of a load.* わが国の総理は少し変だ.

(***as***) ***dry as a brick*** かさかさに乾いて ▪ The bread was *as dry as a brick.* パンはかさかさに乾いていた.

be hanging [***banging, beating***] *one's* ***head against a brick wall*** 《口》 不可能なことを試みる, むだ骨を折る ▪ I have *been banging my head against a brick wall* trying to get a refund of £150. 150ポンドの払戻金をもらおうとして長いことむだ骨を折ってきた ▪ I have *been banging my head against a brick wall* trying to convince my fellow students. 学友を納得させようと努力したが成功しなかった.

be [***come, run***] ***up against a brick wall/hit a brick wall*** 行き詰まる, (越えられない)障害[壁]にぶつかっている[ぶつかる] ▪ I can't find a job. I'*m up against a brick wall.* 職が見つからない. 壁に突き当たってしまった ▪ The police *came up against a brick wall* in their probe into the case. 警察はその事件の内偵で壁にぶち当たった.

come [***fall, be***] ***down on*** [***upon***] *a person* ***like a thousand*** [***ton, pile***] ***of bricks*** 《俗》 人をこっぴどくしかりつける ▪ The manager *came down on* me *like a ton of bricks* for coming late. 支配人は私が遅刻したのでこっぴどく私をしかりつけた.

drop a brick **1** 《英口》 へまをやる, (礼儀上の)しくじりをする ▪ Ben really *dropped a brick* when he said to Ann that he can't stand bluestockings! ベンはアンに向かって才女ががまんできないと言ったとき, まさにしくじった.
2 驚くべきニュースを伝える ▪ The doctor really *dropped a brick* when he told her the cause of her illness. 医者は彼女に病気の原因を伝えたが, それは確かにショッキングな知らせだった.

have [***wear***] ***a brick in*** *one's* ***hat*** 《米口》 酒に酔っている ▪ He *wore a brick in his hat.* 彼は酔っていた. ☞頭にれんがをのせると重いから.

hit a (***brick***) ***wall*** →hit a stone WALL.

hit *a person* ***like a thousand*** [***a ton***] ***of bricks*** =come down on a person like a thou-

B

sand of BRICKs.

hit the bricks 《俗》街を歩く; 公の場を出て行く; ストをやる; 宿がなくて夜中町を歩く ▪ The union is always *hitting the bricks*. 労働組合はストばかりやっている.

like a brick/like (***a hundred*** [***a thousand, a ton of***]) ***bricks*** 《俗》猛烈に, 活発に ▪ He works *like a brick*. 彼は猛烈に働く ▪ Just *like a thousand bricks*, I worked both late and early. 遅くても早くても私は猛烈に働いた.

like a cat on hot bricks →CAT.

make bricks without straw [***clay***] 《古風》材料なしで仕事をする; むだ骨を折る (《聖》*Exod*. 5. 7) ▪ Do you expect him to *make bricks without straw*? 彼に材料なしで仕事をさせる気か.

see through a brick wall →SEE.

shit bricks [***a brick***] 《卑》ひどく心配する ▪ He was *shitting bricks* while his wife was having her baby. 彼は妻の出産のときはひどく心配した.

wear a brick in *one's* ***hat*** →have a BRICK in one's hat.

with a brick in *one's* ***hat*** 《米口》酒に酔って ▪ He tottered along *with a brick in his hat*. 彼は酔ってよろめきながら歩いて行った.

bride /braɪd/ 名 ***Happy is the bride*** (***that***) ***the sun shines on*** (***and the corpse the rain rains on***). 《諺》太陽に照らされる花嫁(と雨が降り注ぐ死骸)は幸福である.

bridge[1] /brɪdʒ/ 名 ***a bridge of gold/ a golden bridge*** (敗軍の)容易な退却路; 困難からの容易な抜け道 ▪ Build *golden bridges* for the foe! 敵のため容易な退却路を作ってやれ.

a gold [***silver***] ***bridge*** =a BRIDGE of gold.

be a bridge between (二者)の間を繋ぐ橋 ▪ Today, Kashmir *is a bridge between* India and Pakistan. 今日カシミールはインドとパキスタンの間を繋ぐ橋である.

build bridges between ...間の橋渡しをする, を調停する ▪ The special envoy to Israel came to *build bridges between* Arabs and Jews. アラブ人とユダヤ人との間を調停するためにイスラエルへの特使が来訪した.

burn *one's* ***bridges*** [***boats***] (***behind*** *one*) →BURN[2].

burn *one's* ***bridges in front of*** *one* 自分の前の橋を燃やす《自分の将来に面倒の種をまく》 ▪ Cecil used to *burn his bridges in front of* him, making mistakes again and again. セシルは何度も誤りをくりかえして, いつも自分の将来に面倒の種をまいていた.

cross a [***that***] ***bridge when*** *one* ***comes to it*** 問題が起きたときにそれを処理する ▪ You have only to *cross a bridge when* you *come to it*. 問題が起きたときにそれを処理しさえすればよいのだ.

Don't cross the [***a***] ***bridge until*** [***till, before***] ***you come to it.*** 《諺》取越し苦労をするな.

like painting the Forth Bridge 《英》果てしなく続く仕事みたいで ▪ Obliterating chewing gum from the streets is *like painting the Forth Bridge*. チューインガムを通りから除去することは果てしなく続く仕事のようだ. ☞フォース橋はスコットランド南東部のフォース湾にかかる鉄橋. あまり大きいので, 塗り終えても最初に塗った部分を塗り直さなければならないところから.

bridge[2] /brɪdʒ/ 動 ***bridge the gap*** →GAP.

bridle /bráɪdəl/ 名 ***give*** *a horse* ***the bridle*** 馬の手綱をゆるめる, 馬を自由に活動させる ▪ I could do nothing but *give* her *the bridle* and let her run. 馬の手綱をゆるめて自由に走らせるほかなかった.

go up well to *one's* ***bridle*** (馬が命によく従って)勇んで進む ▪ Ellen was a horse *going well up to his bridle*. エレンは彼の命に従って勇んで進む馬だった.

keep *a horse* ***up into*** *his* ***bridle*** 馬に手綱の許すかぎりの全速力を保たせる ▪ *Keep* them well *up into their bridles*. 馬どもに手綱の許すかぎり全速力を出させておけ.

lay the bridle on a horse's neck =give a horse the BRIDLE.

brief /bri:f/ 名形 ***accept a brief on behalf of...*** 《法》...を弁護する ▪ He *accepted a brief on behalf of* the accused. 彼は被告を弁護した.

have plenty of briefs (弁護士が)事件の依頼が多い ▪ Mr. Todd, the lawyer, *has plenty of briefs*. 弁護士のトッド氏は事件の依頼が多い.

hold a brief for 《口》...を極力弁護する; を是認する, 支持する ▪ Dowden *holds a brief for* Shelley. ダウデンはシェリーを弁護している.

hold no brief for 《口》...を支持しない, は嫌いだ ▪ I *hold no brief for* liars. 僕は嘘つきは嫌いだ.

in brief 簡単に(言えば) ▪ Charles gave *in brief* the story of the storm. チャールズは簡単にそのあらしの話をした ▪ The weather was wet, cold and windy—*in brief*, terrlble. 天候は雨で寒くて風が強く—つまり, ひどいものだった.

take a brief (弁護士が)訴訟事件を引き受ける ▪ He was ready to *take a brief*. 彼は進んで訴訟事件を引き受けた.

brigade /brɪgéɪd/ 名 ***the black coat brigade*** 牧師たち ▪ He is one of *the black coat brigade*. 彼は牧師の一人である.

bright /braɪt/ 形 ***a bright spark*** →SPARK[1].

a bright spot (暗い状況の中で)一点明るいところ ▪ The book business may be flat, but there's at least *one bright spot*—books for teens. 出版の仕事は低調かもしれないが, 少なくとも一点明るいところがある—10代の若者向けの本だ.

(***as***) ***bright as a sixpence*** [***a button, new penny***] 《英口》ぴかぴかで; とても頭がいい; とても快活で ▪ The box is *as bright as a sixpence*. その箱はぴかぴかだ.

bright and breezy とても快活な[にこやかな] ▪ She is very *bright and breezy*. 彼女はとてもにこやかだ.

bright and clear 快晴で; 利発な ▪ The day was *bright and clear*. その日は快晴であった.

bright and early 朝早く ▪ They started out *bright and early* in an open carriage. 彼らは無蓋馬車で朝早く出かけた.

look on [see] the bright side (of) (…の)明るい面を見る, 楽観する ▪ He seems to *see* only *the bright side of* everything. 彼は万事明るい面だけを見るようだ.

bright-eyed /bráɪtàɪd/ 形 ***bright-eyed and bushy-tailed*** 《口》とてもきげんのよい ▪ He came home, *bright-eyed and bushy-tailed.* 彼はとても上きげんで帰宅した. ☞慣習的なリスの記述から.

brim /brɪm/ 名 ***to the brim*** あふれるばかりに ▪ She was filled *to the brim* with happiness. 彼女は幸福に満ちあふれていた.

brimful /brìmfól/ 形 ***brimful of*** …にあふれるばかりで ▪ He is *brimful of* new ideas. 彼は新しい思想に満ちあふれている.

brimstone /brímstòʊn/ 名 ***fire and brimstone*** →FIRE[1].

bring /brɪŋ/ 動 ***bring ... back to mind*** …を思い出す ▪ I cannot *bring* it *back to mind.* それが思い出せない.

bring down the house →HOUSE.

bring home 《競馬》(騎手が)馬に勝たせる ▪ The jockey *brought* (him) *home.* 騎手はその馬で勝った.

bring (a person) in guilty [not guilty] (陪審団が)人の有罪[無罪]を答申する ▪ The jury *brought* (him) *in guilty.* 陪審団は(彼の)有罪を答申した.

bring ... into being →BEING.

bring ... into the world [life] …を生む ▪ He *was brought into the world* on May 3, 1936. 彼は1936年5月3日に生まれた.

Bring it on! 《口》来るなら来い!

bring a person out of himself (引っ込み思案の)人を積極的になるように仕向ける ▪ There's not a single woman who can *bring* Roy *out of himself*, because he's plagued by inner turmoil. ロイを積極的にさせられる女性は一人もいない, なぜなら彼は心の不安に悩んでいるのだから.

bring a person out of his shell 人を打ち解けさせる ▪ Sports helped *bring* her *out of her shell.* スポーツのおかげで彼女は人に打ち解けてきた.

bring out the best [the worst] in a person 人に最も良い[悪い]結果をもたらす ▪ Alcohol will *bring out the worst in* people. アルコールは人々に最も悪い結果をもたらす.

bring oneself to do [doing] 〚主に否定文で〛…する気になる ▪ I cannot *bring myself to* accept your offer. 私はどうしてもあなたの申し出をお受けする気になれません ▪ He couldn't *bring himself to doing* such things. 彼はそんなことをする気になれなかった.

bring ... to bear on [upon] →BEAR[2].

bring ... to pass →PASS[1].

bring up (one's) arrears [lost ground] 遅れ[失地]を取り戻す ▪ The afternoon was spent in *bringing up my arrears* of correspondence. 午後は滞っていた書簡の返事を書いてすごした.

bring up sharp(ly) = bring a person up SHORT.

bring a person up short →SHORT.

bring up the hard way きびしく育てる ▪ Father *brought* us *up the hard way.* 父は我々をきびしく育てた.

bring ... up to date …を(現代まで)続ける ▪ The narrative has *been brought up to date.* 物語は現代のところまで続けて書かれている.

bring up wind (赤んぼうが)げっぷをする ▪ Help—my baby doesn't *bring up wind.* 助けてください—赤ちゃんがげっぷをしないんです.

brink /brɪŋk/ 名 ***from the brink of*** …の瀬戸ぎわから ▪ We saved him *from the brink of* ruin. 我々は彼を破滅の瀬戸ぎわから救った.

on the brink of …の瀬戸ぎわに ▪ The secret was *on the brink of* discovery. その秘密は危うくあばかれるところだった.

shiver on the brink 飛び込むのをためらう, いざとなって震える ▪ He stood *shivering on the brink.* 彼はいざとなってためらっていた.

to the brink of …の瀬戸ぎわへ ▪ He brought us *to the brink of* anarchy. 彼は我々を無政府の瀬戸ぎわへ追い込んだ.

briny /bráɪni/ 名 ***on the briny*** 海に ▪ I'm now *on the briny.* 私はいま海(上)にいる.

brio /brí:oʊ/ 名 ***with brio*** 生気[活気]をもって ▪ The picture is drawn *with brio.* その絵は生気はつらつと描かれている.

bristle /brísəl/ 名 ***set up one's [a person's] bristles*** 怒る[怒らせる] ▪ The Jews *set up their bristles* against God. ユダヤ人たちは神に対して憤激した ▪ His words *set their bristles up.* 彼の言葉は彼らを激怒させた.

britches /brítʃəz/ 名 ***too big for one's britches*** →be too BIG for one's boots.

Briton /brítən/ 名 ***fight like a Briton*** 不屈の勇気をもって戦う ▪ I'll never be conquered, and I'll *fight like a Briton.* 私は絶対に征服されず, 不屈の勇気をもって戦う.

work like a Briton 精出して[忍耐強く]働く ▪ Every man *works like a Briton.* すべての人が忍耐強く仕事と取り組んでいる.

broad /brɔ:d/ 形 ***(as) broad as a barn door*** ずいぶん幅がある ▪ The weight lifter's chest is *broad as a barn door.* あの重量挙げ選手は胸幅がすごく広い.

(as) broad as it is long 五十歩百歩である, 結局同じである ▪ Whether we take the bridge or the tunnel is about *as broad as it's long.* 橋を通るかトンネルを通るかどちらにしても大体同じである.

broad in the beam →BEAM.

in broad day(light) 白昼に; 公衆の前で ▪ No one can do that *in broad daylight.* 公衆の前でそれをなしうる人はいない.

B

broad-brush /brɔ́:dbrʌ̀ʃ/ 名 ***a broad-brush approach*** 大まかなアプローチ ▪ We shall take *a broad-brush approach*, and leave the detailed discussion to the following lectures. 我々は大まかなアプローチをとり，詳細な議論はのちの講義に譲ることにしよう．

broadly /brɔ́:dli/ 副 ***broadly speaking*** 概して，大ざっぱに言って ▪ *Broadly speaking*, the English are simple and friendly. 概してイギリス人は単純で友好的である．

broadside /brɔ́:dsàɪd/ 名 ***broadside on*** [***to***] …に舷側を向けて，船を横に向けて (↔END on) ▪ The most part of the time we were *broadside on*. ほとんどその間じゅう我々は船を横に向けていた ▪ We drifted down, *broadside on*. 船を横向きにして漂い下った．

broadside to [***and***] ***broadside*** (船が)並んで; 並んで，寄り添って ▪ They are *broadside and broadside*. 彼らは並んでいた．

can't hit the broadside of a barn →BARN.

fire a broadside 舷側[片舷]斉射をする ▪ Mary *fired a broadside* into his character. メアリーは彼の人格を盛んに攻撃した．

brodie /bróʊdi/ 名 ***do a brodie*** 《米俗》自殺的な跳躍をやる《がけから飛び降りるような》 ▪ He might *do a brodie* and jump off the Brooklyn Bridge. 彼は自殺的な跳躍をしてブルックリン橋から飛び降りかねない．

pull a brodie 《米俗》まちがいをやる，大へまをやる ▪ No one knows how many have *pulled a brodie* in the past century. 前の世紀に大へまをした人が何人いたか誰も知らない． ☞brodie「ブルックリン橋から飛び降りたと自称した Steve Brodie という男の名前」から．

broke /broʊk/ 形 ***be clean*** [***dead, flat, stone, stony***] ***broke*** 《口》一文なしである，破産している ▪ I'*m stony broke* myself. 僕自身，びた一文ないんだ．

broke to the (***wide, wide***) ***world*** 《口》破産して，一文なしで ▪ I found that the Treasury was *broke to the wide, wide world*. 国庫は火の車だということがわかった ▪ I've come back *broke to the world*. 私は文なしで帰って来た．

go broke 《口》文なしになる，破産する ▪ At that rate he must *go broke* soon. あの調子では彼はじきに破産するにちがいない．

go for broke (賭博で)文なしになるまでやる; 全力を出す ▪ He decided to *go for broke* in organizing textile workers. 彼は織物労働者の組合を作るのに全力を出そうと決心した．

If it ain't broke, don't fix it. [***why fix it?***] 《諺》壊れてないなら，修繕するな《いらぬおせっかいは焼くな》(→let WELL (enough) alone).

broker /bróʊkər/ 名 ***an honest broker*** (中立の立場の)調停者 ▪ He said Washington would act as *an honest broker* between the two sides. 米国政府が双方の調停者を務めるだろうと彼は言った．

broom /bru:m/ 名 ***New brooms sweep clean.***/***A new broom sweeps clean.*** 《諺》新しいほうきはきれいに掃ける《新任者は仕事ぶりがよい; 新しい間はよいものだ; 新任者は旧弊一掃に熱心である》. ☞new brooms とだけ言うことが多い．

broomstick /brú:mstɪ̀k|brʊ́m-/ 名 ***marry*** [***jump, hop***] ***over the broomstick***/***jump*** [***hop***] ***the broomstick*** 《口》同棲する，内縁関係を結ぶ ▪ Let's run away and *be married over the broomstick*. 駆け落ちして同棲しましょう．

brother[1] /brʌ́ðər/ 名 ***Am I my brother's keeper?*** 《諺》私は弟の番人でしょうか《他人のことは自分の知ったことではない》. ☞Cain が弟 Abel を殺したあと神に答えた言葉 (《聖》*Gen*. 4. 9).

be brothers under the skin → under the SKIN 2.

Big Brother →BIG[1].

brothers in arms 同一の闘争に参加する人たち，共闘の同志 ▪ The five of us were *brothers in arms* during that long strike. 我々５名はあの長期にわたるスト中には共闘の同志であった．

Oh, brother! おおすごい，わあ驚いた《Oh, sister! とは言わない》 ▪ I broke your best coffee cup.—*Oh, brother!* 君の一番よいコーヒーカップをこわしちゃった—まあ，あなたったら．

brother[2] /brʌ́ðər/ 動 ***brother it*** 兄弟として行動する ▪ You and I must *brother it*. あなたと私は兄弟として行動しなければならない．

brotherhood /brʌ́ðərhʊ̀d/ 名 ***the brotherhood of man*** 大家族としての人間社会 ▪ Peace could be achieved only by embracing the philosophy of *the brotherhood of man*. 平和の達成は，大家族としての人間社会という哲学を受け入れることによってのみ可能だろう．

brow /braʊ/ 名 ***knit*** [***bend, gather***] *one's* ***brows*** 顔をしかめる，まゆをひそめる ▪ Why do you *knit your brows*? なぜ君は顔をしかめるのか．

the sweat of (*one's*) ***brow*** →SWEAT[1].

Brown /bráʊn/ 名 ***astonish the Browns*** 偏見ある隣人たちにショックを与える ▪ If we go on to the top of the bus, our conduct will *astonish the Browns*. バスの２階へ上がれば我々の行為は偏見のある隣人たちをぎょっとさせるだろう．

Brown, Jones, and Robinson ありふれた人たち《英国中流の》 ▪ Captain *Brown, Jones, and Robinson* turned out in red cloth and gold braid. 普通の将校たちは赤服に金モールを着飾って出てきた．

brown[1] /braʊn/ 形名 (***as***) ***brown as a berry*** →BERRY.

do brown →DO[2].

do (***it***) ***up brown*** 《俗》**1** 徹底的にやっつける[だます] ▪ He is said to *be done up brown*. 彼は徹底的にやっつけられたと言われている．

2 徹底的に[見事に]やってのける ▪ Whenever they put on a party, they *do it up brown*. 彼らがパーティーを催すときはいつでも，完璧にやってのける． ☞肉をこんがり焼くところから.

do ... up brown →DO[2].

fire into the brown **1** 飛ぶ鳥の群れへ(でたらめに)撃ち込む ▪ The hunter did not *fire into the brown*, but took careful aim at some particular bird. その猟人は鳥の群れへたまをやみくもに撃ち込まず, ある特定の鳥を入念にねらった.

2 集合体へめちゃくちゃに撃ち込む ▪ We *fired into the brown* of the enemy. 敵の群れへやみくもに弾を撃ち込んだ. ☞brown「飛んでいる猟鳥の茶色の群れ」.

in a brown study (ぼんやり)物思いにふけって ▪ He is standing *in a brown study*. 彼はそこに立って黙想にふけっている. ☞brown＝gloomy.

brown[2] /braʊn/ 動 ***be browned off*** うんざり[あきあき]している; ひどくいらいらして[怒って]いる ▪ I'*m* really *browned off* that I paid £50 for a ticket. 切符に50ポンド支払ってうんざりしている ▪ I *am* really *browned off* at you. 本当に君に対して怒っている.

***brown** oneself* 日焼けする, 肌を焼く ▪ Mary *browned herself* in the sun. メアリーは太陽で肌を焼いた.

browse[1] /braʊz/ 名 (***be***) ***at browse*** (牛などが)若葉を食(は)んで(いる) ▪ The cattle are *at browse*. 牛は若葉を食んでいる.

browse[2] /braʊz/ 動 ***browse in the pages*** 本をあちこち拾い読みする ▪ *Browsing in the pages* of a book does not appeal to me. 本をあちこち拾い読みすることは僕は感心しません.

browse** one's **way 漫然と読み進む ▪ I *browsed my way* through the agony column. 尋ね人欄を漫然と読んでいった.

bruise /bru:z/ 動 ***be bruising for a bruising*** 《俗》うるさく[ばかなまねを]している(ので議論・けんかの元になる) ▪ John's *been bruising for a bruising* for a while here, looking for a fight out there. ジョンはここでしばらく前からうるさくして, 外でけんかをしかけている.

bruit /bru:t/ 動 ***bruit about*** [***abroad***] ...を広く宣伝する, 言いふらす ▪ They *bruited* the company's products *abroad*. 彼らは会社の製品を広く宣伝した.

brunt /brʌnt/ 名 ***bear*** [***take***] ***the brunt of*** ...の矢面に立つ ▪ She *bore the brunt of* the family troubles. 彼女は家庭争議の矢面に立った.

brush[1] /brʌʃ/ 名 ***a brush with death*** 一瞬死ぬ思いをすること ▪ After *a brush with death*, Cecily seemed more friendly and outgoing. 一瞬死ぬ思いをしたあと, セシリーは前よりも親しみやすく, 社交的になったようだった.

at a brush 一挙に ▪ The Chinese will carry the place *at a brush*. 中国軍は一挙にそこを占領するだろう.

at the first brush 最初の衝突[出会い]で; 一挙に ▪ So you intend to give up this poor young man *at the first brush*? それで君は一度でかわいそうにこの青年を見放すつもりなのか.

be tarred with the same brush → be TARred with the same stick.

break brush 《米》(未開地に住み)荒々しい茂みを乗り回すのに慣れる ▪ He is a *brush-breaker*. 彼は荒い茂みを乗り回すことに慣れている.

buy a brush 《俗》逃走する ▪ Let's *buy a brush*. 逃走しよう.

get a brush from ...に軽く触れる ▪ We *got a brush from* the wheel as the car passed. 車が通り過ぎるとき, 車輪が軽く我々に触れた.

give ... another brush ...に今一度ブラシをかける; をもう一度念を入れてやる ▪ *Give* the shoes *another brush*. 靴にも一度ブラシをかけなさい.

give the brush (***off***) 《米口》すげなく拒絶する ▪ She *gave* me *the brush*. 彼女は私にひじ鉄をくわした.

have a brush with ...と小ぜり合いをする, 短い鋭い競争をする ▪ We *had a brush with* the enemy. 我々は敵と小ぜり合いをした ▪ We *had a brush* down the river *with* them. 我々は彼らと川を下る競争をした.

paint with a broad brush (事を)大ざっぱに述べる ▪ The author *paints* history *with a broad brush*. 著者は歴史を大ざっぱに述べている.

brush[2] /brʌʃ/ 動 ***brush a batter back*** 《野球》(ボールを)バッターの(頭の)近くへ投げる《打たせないため》 ▪ The pitcher *brushed the batter back*. ピッチャーはバッターの頭近くへボールを投げた.

brush to one side 無視する ▪ He *brushed* my advice *to one side*. 彼は私の忠告を無視した.

brush-off /brʌ́ʃɔ̀:f|-ɔ̀f/ 名 ***get the brush-off*** 《口》(特に別れたがっている恋人に)そっけなく[すげなく]される; そっけなく拒絶される ▪ John was *getting the brush-off*. ジョンは(恋人に)すげなくされていた ▪ My application *got the brush-off*. 私の申し込みはすげなく断られた.

give the brush-off 《口》(特に恋人が別れたくて)そっけなく[すげなく]する; すげなく拒絶する ▪ Jane was *giving* her lover *the brush-off*. ジェインは恋人にそっけなくしていた ▪ He *gave* my application *the brush-off*. 彼は私の申し込みをすげなく断った.

brusque /brʌsk|brʊsk/ 動 ***brusque it*** そっけない挙動をする ▪ I'll *brusque it* a little. 少しそっけなくふるまってやろう.

bubble /bʌ́bəl/ 名 ***be on the bubble*** **1** 《米》(人が)失職しそうである, (会社が)財政援助を打ち切られそうである ▪ Max and Roy *are on the bubble* as the team plans to reduce the number of players. チームは選手の数を減らす計画なのでマックスとロイは失職しそうだ.

2 《米口》失敗しそうな ▪ This exhibition *is on the bubble*. この展覧会は潰れそうだ ▪ We'*re* always *on the bubble*, but we're optimistic as well. 我々はいつも失敗しそうだが, 同時に楽天的でもある.

blow bubbles しゃぼん玉を吹く; 空説を立てる, たわいもないことをして楽しむ ▪ Boys *blow bubbles*. 少年たちはしゃぼん玉を吹く ▪ One generation *blows bubbles* and the next breaks them. 一つの世代が

空説を立てれば次の世代はそれを破る.

bubble trouble (タイヤの)パンク ▪ I realized I had *bubble trouble*. タイヤがパンクしたなとわかった.

burst [***prick***] *a person's* ***bubble*** (人の)夢・幻想を打ち砕く ▪ (I) hate to *burst your bubble*, but I could not disagree with you more. 君の夢をぶちこわすのはいやだが, 僕は絶対不賛成だ ▪ I'm going to try and *prick the bubble of* people taking themselves too seriously. 僕は自分のことを深刻に考えすぎる人たちの幻想を打ち砕いてやろうと思っている.

prick [***burst***] ***the bubble*** **1** ばけの皮をはぐ, 偽りをあばく ▪ He was determined to *prick* this absurd *bubble*. 彼はこのばかげたばけの皮をはごうと決心していた.

2 バブルをはじけさせる; 幸せな状況に終止符を打つ ▪ The best thing to do at this point is to *burst the bubble* before it gets even larger. この時点でできる最上のことは, バブルがさらに大きくならないうちにはじけさせることだ ▪ Will rising inflation *burst the bubble*? 増大するインフレは幸せな状況に終止符を打つだろうか.

The bubble has burst. バブルがはじけた ▪ But the good times ended when *the* economic *bubble burst* in the early 1990s. しかし, 1990年代初めに経済のバブルがはじけたとき, よき時代は終わった.

bubblegum /bʌ́bəlgʌ̀m/ 名 ***bubblegum music*** 《俗》バブルガム(音楽)《ローティーンに受ける単調な歌詞のロック》 ▪ *Bubblegum music* is always neglected and denigrated. バブルガム音楽はいつも無視され軽視されている.

buck[1] /bʌk/ 名 ***a fast buck*** 《俗》あぶく銭(ぜに) ▪ Dick's all right, but his partner is just out for *a fast buck*. ディックはまともだが, 彼のパートナーはひたすらあぶく銭を儲けようとしている.

(***as***) ***hearty as a buck*** →HEARTY.

big bucks 巨額の金, 大金(おおがね) ▪ The company earns *big bucks* from China. その会社は中国でしこたま儲けている.

buck naked 《米》素っ裸で (stark naked) ▪ She stepped into the hall *buck naked*. 彼女は素っ裸で玄関に出てきた.

like a million bucks [***dollars,*** 《英》***quid***] →feel like a MILLION (dollars).

make a fast [***quick***] ***buck*** 《米》(不正をして)やすやすと大金をかせぐ ▪ You can *make a fast buck* at the casino. カジノではやすやすと大金をかせぐことができる. ☞buck「1ドル」.

Old buck! おい君!

buck[2] /bʌk/ 名 ***pass the buck*** (***to***) 《口》責任[仕事]を(人に)転嫁する ▪ A president who *passes the buck to* someone else would soon find himself in serious trouble. 誰か別な人に責任を転嫁する大統領は, じきに深刻な面倒に陥るだろう.

The buck stops here [***with me***]. 責任はここにあり, 責任はここで負う《他の人に押しつけない》 ▪ We need leaders that say *the buck stops with me*. 責任はここで負うと言うリーダーが必要だ. ☞米大統領 Harry Truman (1945–53)が机に貼りつけていた言葉.

buck[3] /bʌk/ 動 ***buck*** *one's* ***ideas up*** [***up*** *one's* ***ideas***] 《口》より抜け目なく[機敏に]なる ▪ If you want to succeed, you'll have to *buck up your ideas* a bit. 成功したいなら, もう少し抜け目のない人間にならなければだめよ.

buck the tiger →TIGER.

bucket /bʌ́kət/ 名 ***a bucket of bolts*** 《俗》ぽんこつ車 ▪ When are you going to dispose of that *bucket of bolts*? いつあのぽんこつ車を処分するのか.

a drop in the bucket →DROP[1].

by the bucket バケツで量るほど(たくさん) ▪ He has Latin *by the bucket*. 彼は多くのラテン語を知っている.

come down in buckets 《口》(雨が)土砂降りに降る ▪ The rain [It] was *coming down in buckets*. 雨が土砂降りに降っていた.

cry buckets 《口》ワーワー泣き叫ぶ ▪ The girl *cried buckets* when her cat was gone. 少女は猫がいなくなってワーワー泣き叫んだ.

give *a person* ***the bucket*** 《俗》人を首にする[解雇する] ▪ He was put about because Al had *given* him *the bucket*. アルに首にされて彼は困ってしまった.

kick the bucket 死ぬ, くたばる ▪ The old horse finally *kicked the bucket*. 年老いた馬はついに死んだ. ☞bucket は畜殺する動物を吊す木枠.

make the bucket 《米俗》まずい立場になる; 逮捕される ▪ He *made the bucket* for committing burglary. 彼は住居侵入したかどで逮捕された.

rain (***in***) ***buckets*** 《口》(雨が)土砂降りに降る ▪ Soon it began to *rain buckets*. まもなく雨が土砂降りに降りだした.

sweat buckets **1** 大汗をかく ▪ Jim *sweated buckets*. ジムは大汗をかいた.

2 非常に心配する ▪ I *sweated buckets* waiting for the result of examination. 私はおろおろしながら試験の結果を待っていた.

weep buckets 《口》さんざん涙を流させる ▪ The sad tale of unrequited love always made her *weep buckets*. 報いられない恋物語はいつも彼女にさんざん涙を流させた.

bucketsful /bʌ́kətsfʊ̀l/ 副 ***come down bucketsful*** 《口》ひどく雨が降る ▪ It was *coming down bucketsful*. 土砂降りの雨であった.

buckle[1] /bʌ́kəl/ 名 ***cover the buckle*** (特定の)ダンスをする ▪ He *covered the buckle* in gallant style. 彼は華麗にダンスをした.

cut the buckle (ダンスで)かかと[足指]でくるくる回る ▪ They *cut the buckle* as they went along. 彼らはダンスしながらかかとでくるくる回った.

make buckle and tongue meet 《米口》なんとか収支を償わせていく ▪ They *made buckle and tongue meet* by raising stock. 彼らは家畜飼育によってなんとか収支を償わせた.

buckle[2] /bʌ́kəl/ 動 ***buckle*** *oneself* ***to*** …に奮

励して当たる ▪ He *buckled himself to* the task. 彼はその仕事に奮励して当たった.

buckle-hole /bʌ́kəlhòʊl/ 名 ***reduced*** **[*starved*]** ***to the last buckle-hole*** (***of*** *one's* ***belt***) 餓えのため死に瀕している ▪ I am *reduced to the last buckle-hole of my belt.* 餓えて死にそうだ.

buckler /bʌ́klər/ 名 ***give the bucklers*** 《口》 降参する, 防衛を断念する ▪ Age *gives* youth *the bucklers.* 老年は青年にかぶとを脱ぐものだ.

take up the bucklers 戦う, 抵抗する ▪ One of them *took up the bucklers* against him. 彼らの一人が彼を相手に戦った.

buckram /bʌ́krəm/ 名 ***men*** **[*rogues*]** ***in buckram*** 架空の人物; わら人形 (cf. Sh., *1 Hen. IV.* 2. 4. 210–50) ▪ I have fought *rogues in buckram.* 私は架空の人物と戦った.

bud /bʌd/ 名 ***a bud of promise*** 《米》(社交界に出ようとする)若い娘 ▪ I know Ellen, *a bud of promise.* 私は若い娘エレンを知っている ▪ The young, unmarried girl, in sport, is called *a bud of promise.* 若い娘は戯れに前途あるつぼみと呼ばれる.

check **[*crush*]** ***in the bud*** → nip ... in the BUD.

come into bud 芽を出す; つぼみをつける ▪ The spring flowers *came into bud.* 春の花がつぼみをつけた.

give ... the bud 《米俗》 ...を打ちのめす ▪ He has *given* me *the bud.* 彼が私を打ちのめした.

in bud 芽ぐんで, 芽を出して, つぼみを持って ▪ Life was yet *in bud* and blade. 人生はまだつぼみ, 芽ばえの時であった.

in the bud 芽またはつぼみのうちに[の]; 未発に, 熟さないうちに ▪ Some flowers wither *in the bud.* つぼみのうちに枯れる花もある ▪ He is a poet *in the bud.* 彼は詩人の卵だ.

nip **[*check, crush*]** ***... in the bud*** ...をつぼみのうちに摘み取る; を未然に防ぐ, 初期のうちに防ぐ ▪ The government was able to *nip* the revolution *in the bud.* 政府は革命を未然に防ぐことができた ▪ Promising germs of freedom *were crushed in the bud.* 前途有望な自由の芽ばえが芽のうちに摘み取られた.

buddy /bʌ́di/ 名 ***good buddy*** やあ相棒《CB 無線で交信し合うトラックや車の運転手のあいさつ》 ▪ What's the Smokey situation, *good buddy*? やあ相棒, パトカーの状況はどうだい? ☞Smokey「(州警察の)パトカー」.

budget[1] /bʌ́dʒət/ 名 ***on a budget*** 予算の限られた ▪ Those *on a budget* go to Florida in the off-seasons. 予算を切りつめた人々は季節外れにフロリダへ行く.

open **[*introduce*]** ***the budget*** 政府の予算案を議会に提出する ▪ The government *opened the budget* yesterday. 政府は昨日予算案を議会に提出した.

within **[*below*]** ***budget*** 予算内で[の] ▪ We will remodel your bathroom *within* the *budget.* おたくのバスルームを予算内で模様替えいたします.

budget[2] /bʌ́dʒət/ 動 ***budget*** *one's* ***time*** 時間の使い方をよく計画する ▪ I *budget my time* carefully. 私は時間の使い方を入念に計画します.

buff[1] /bʌf/ 名 ***in buff*** **1** 裸で ▪ He slept *in buff.* 彼はすっ裸で眠った.

2 軍服を着て; 従軍して ▪ They are *in buff* for King Charles. 彼らはチャールズ王のために従軍している.

in nature's **[*the*]** ***buff*** まっ裸で ▪ The doctor examined the recruits *in nature's buff.* 医者は裸の新兵を検査した ▪ He likes to walk around the bedroom *in the buff.* 彼は裸で寝室を歩きまわるのが好きだ.

stand buff 毅然としてひるまない ▪ I must *stand buff* and out-face him. 私は毅然としてひるまず彼をおどしつけてやらなければならない.

strip ... to the buff ...をまっ裸にする; まっ裸になる《通常は腰まで裸で》 ▪ When he's *stripped to the buff*, you'll see what a wonderful build he has. 彼がまっ裸になると, 実に立派な体格であることがわかる. ☞buff「皮膚」.

wear **[*be in*]** ***buff*** 軍服を着る; 従軍する ▪ He *wore buff* in Italy. 彼はイタリアに従軍した.

buff[2] /bʌf/ 動 ***buff it*** **1** 目隠し遊びをやる ▪ I have *buffed it* fairly. 私は目隠し遊びをフェアにやった.

2 毅然と立つ, 抵抗する ▪ *Buff it* like a man. 男らしく抵抗せよ.

get buffed up (人が)体を鍛えあげる ▪ I wanted to *get buffed up* and not wear makeup. 私は体を鍛えあげ, 化粧をしないようにしたいと思った.

buffer /bʌ́fər/ 名 ***hit*** **[*run into*]** ***the buffers*** 《英口》(予定・計画が)行き詰まる, 暗礁に乗りあげる ▪ Talks on global use of energy *hit the buffers.* グローバルなエネルギー使用の話し合いは行きづまった.

buffet /bəféɪ|bʊ́feɪ/ 動 ***buffet*** *one's* ***way*** 奮闘して進む ▪ He *buffeted his way* to fortune. 彼は奮闘して金持ちになった.

buffoon /bəfúːn/ 名 ***play the buffoon*** おどける, こっけいを演ずる ▪ He laughed and *played the buffoon.* 彼は笑ったりおどけたりした.

bug[1] /bʌg/ 名 (***as***) ***cute as a bug's ear*** → CUTE as a button.

(***as***) ***snug as a bug in a rug*** →SNUG.

be a bug on **[*about, at*]** 《米》 ...に熱狂している, 巧みである ▪ She *is a bug at* languages. 彼女は語学が巧みである.

be **[*get*]** ***bitten by the bug/ catch the ... bug*** 《口》 突然強い興味[情熱]をおぼえる ▪ I *was bitten by the bug* to take pictures of the stars. 突然星の写真をとりたいという強い興味をおぼえた ▪ He *caught the* travel *bug* late in life. 彼は年輩になって旅行熱にとりつかれた.

beat the bugs 《米口》(悪魔だって)かなわない ▪ That *beats the bugs*! それには全くかなわない. ☞bugs = dickens (悪魔).

bitten by the same bug 同じ興味[趣味]をもつ

▪ Carl and I were *bitten by the same bug*. We both collect stamps. カールと僕は趣味が同じだ. 二人とも切手を収集する.

get a bug for [***about***] 《米》…の熱にとりつかれる ▪ He *got a bug for* the trailer. 彼はトレーラーハウスでの旅行に病みつきになった.

go to the bugs 《米口》滅びる ▪ Shall I let the survey *go to the bugs*? その調査はつぶさせましょうか.

have a bug for [***about***] 《米》…の熱病にとりつかれている ▪ Washington has *had a bug for* skating for the past 3 months. ワシントンはこの3か月間スケートの熱病にとりつかれていた.

have a bug on 《米口》…を怒っている ▪ Does he *have a bug on* me? 彼は私を怒っているのか.

have the ... bug 非常に…に興味を持っている ▪ He *has the* photography *bug*. 彼は写真術に非常に興味を持っている ▪ John's wife *has the* shopping *bug* and he's in a frenzy. ジョンの妻は買い物熱にうかされていて, 彼は逆上している.

put a [***the***] ***bug in*** *a person's* ***ear*** 《米口》人にヒントを与える, さりげなく知らせる[警告する] ▪ I want to *put a bug in your ear*. あなたにヒントを与えたい ▪ We *put a bug in his ear* about a new gymnasium. 新体育館のことをさりげなく彼に知らせた.

put a bug on 《米口》(人)をかつぐ ▪ They *put a bug on* me. 彼らは私をかついだ.

smell a bug 《米口》怪しいと思う (=smell a RAT) ▪ I *smell a bug*. これは怪しいぞ.

swear by no bugs 本当に誓う ▪ He *swore by no bugs* that he would make me a Consul. 彼は私を領事にすると本当に誓った. ☞bug「空想上のおばけ」.

the bug under the chip 《米口》隠れた[背後に潜んだ]動機 ▪ There are no such *bugs under the chips*. そんな底意はない.

bug[2] /bʌg/ 動 ***be bugging*** *a person* →be EATing a person.

bugged /bʌgd/ 形 ***bugged up to kill*** 《米口》悩殺するほど着飾って ▪ "*Bugged up to kill!*" exclaimed I. 「まあすごく着飾って!」と私は叫んだ.

bugger[1] /bʌ́gər/ 名 ***bugger all*** 《英卑》全く…ない (nothing) ▪ There's absolutely *bugger all* wrong with this word. この言葉は全然まずいところはない.

play silly buggers 《卑》ばかなまね[悪ふざけ]をする (*with*) ▪ Stop *playing silly buggers with* me and answer the question! おれに悪ふざけしないで, 質問に答えろ!

bugger[2] /bʌ́gər/ 動 ***bugger me/ I'm buggered*** 《英卑》こいつは驚いた! ▪ Well *I'm buggered*! I never thought he'd do that. いやこりゃ驚いた! あいつがあんなことをするなんて考えたこともない.

bugger the ... 《英卑》…なんかくそくらえ ▪ *Bugger the* dossier! We want him here! Now! 身上調査書などどうでもいい. 彼にここに来てほしいんだ. 今すぐ!

I'm buggered if ... 《英卑》…してたまるか《強い否定》(I'm damned if ...) ▪ *I'm buggered if* I know about it! そんなこと知るか.

bughouse /bʌ́ghàʊs/ 名形 ***go*** [***get***] ***bughouse*** 気が狂う ▪ We haven't *gone bughouse* yet. 我々はまだ気が狂ったわけではない ▪ The soldiers are *getting bughouse* drinking the native wine. 兵隊たちは地酒を飲んで狂気になりつつある.

build /bɪld/ 動 ***build a fire*** →make a FIRE.

build ... around the idea 《米》その考えを中心にして…を立案する ▪ I am *building* a new house *around the idea* that we should have two children. 子供が二人できるという考えを中心にして新しい家を建てている.

build on [***upon***] ***sand*** 砂の上に築く; 不安定なことをする (《聖》*Matt*. 7. 26) ▪ It is foolish to *build upon sand*. 砂上に築くのは愚かである.

built /bɪlt/ 形 ***built like a castle*** (馬が)強くがんじょうな体格で ▪ His colt is *built like a castle*. 彼の若馬はがんじょうな体格だ.

built like a tank (人が)大きくて頑強な体つきで; (建物が)頑丈な造りで; (物が)丈夫で長持ちで ▪ He is *built like a tank* and wears a tailored suit perfectly. 彼は大柄でぴったりお誂えのスーツを着用している.

built on (***the***) ***sand*** →SAND.

(***not***) ***built that way*** 《口》そのほうは得意で(ない) ▪ Don't you care for music?—Not a bit, I'm *not built that way*. 音楽は好かないのか—ちっとも好きじゃない, その方面は不得意なのだ.

bulge /bʌldʒ/ 名 ***bulge at the seams*** → burst at the SEAMs.

get [***have***] ***the bulge on*** 《口》…より勝る; に勝つ; をだます ▪ He *got the bulge on* me. 彼は僕に勝った ▪ He *has the* intellectual *bulge on* me. 彼は私より知的にまさっている. ☞bulge=advantage.

bulk[1] /bʌlk/ 名 ***break bulk*** 船倉から荷を出す, 積荷をおろし始める; 包[積荷]などの一部をくずす ▪ Then the steamer *breaks bulk*. それから船から荷がおろされる ▪ Will he *break bulk* and sell his goods by retail? 彼は積荷の一部をくずして小売りで売るのだろうか.

bulk for bulk 双方同じかさを取れば ▪ *Bulk for bulk*, gold is heavier than a fluid. 同じかさなら金は流動体より重い.

by bulk (はかりを用いないで)積荷のままで, 目分量で ▪ Do they charge carriage *by bulk*? 彼らは運賃を目分量で取るのですか.

in bulk (魚・穀類などが)ばらで, ばら荷で[の]; 大量に ▪ The ship is carrying grain *in bulk*. その船はばら積みの穀物を運んでいる ▪ The fish are *in bulk*. 魚はばらになっている.

load [***lade***] (***a ship***) ***in bulk*** (船に)荷をばらで積む ▪ *The ship is laden in bulk*: as with corn, salt, etc. その船には穀類や塩などがばらで積み込まれる.

sell ... in bulk (荷を船倉に積んだまま)まとめて売る; 大口に卸し売りする ▪ Wine *is sold* either *in bulk* or by retail. ワインは大口卸し売りか小売りにされる.

the bulk of …の大部分(数・量) ▪ *The bulk of* my debt was paid. 私の借金の大部分は支払った

▪ *The bulk of* these inventions are Edison's. これらの発明の大部分はエジソンの発明だ.

bulk[2] /bʌlk/ 動 ***bulk large*** [***small***] 大きく[小さく]見える; 重要らしい[らしくない] ▪ The weather *bulks large* in our plan. 我々の計画では天候が重大問題である.

bull /bʊl/ 名 ***a bull in a china shop*** 《口》(瀬戸物屋へ飛び込んだ雄牛のように)なんでもめちゃめちゃにしてしまう乱暴者; 熟練[用心]のいるところで手荒く無器用な人 ▪ He is very clumsy like *a bull in a china shop*. 彼はすこぶる無器用だ ▪ Don't be *a bull in a china shop*. 人に迷惑をかけるような乱暴なまねはするな.

like a bull at a (***fine-barred***) ***gate*** 猛烈に《攻撃するなど》 ▪ He attacked them *like a bull at a gate*. 彼は猛烈に彼らを攻撃した.

like a red rag to a bull/《米》 ***like waving a red flag at*** [***in front of***] ***a bull*** 《英》 雄牛に赤い旗[布]を見せるようなもので, 非常に立腹させるもので ▪ Don't mention Jim's promotion to Dick. It would be *like a red rag to a bull*! ジムが昇進したことをディックに言っちゃだめだよ. 雄牛に赤い布を見せるようなものだから ▪ Communism is *like a red rag to the bull* to him. 共産主義には彼は火のようにいきり立つ ▪ These little obstacles are just *like waving a red flag in front of a bull*. It just makes him more determined and more motivated. こんなわずかな障害は怒りを刺激するようなものだ. 彼はいっそう腹を決めていっそうやる気になるだけだ. ☞闘牛から.

make an Irish bull うっかりしてこっけいで矛盾したことを言う ▪ He often *makes an Irish bull*. 彼はよくこっけいで矛盾したことを言う. ☞たとえば「欠席のかたは手をあげてください」など.

score a bull =hit the BULL'S-EYE.

shoot [***sling, throw***] ***the bull*** 《米俗》(でたらめを)しゃべる; ほらを吹く ▪ He likes to *sling the bull*. 彼はほらを吹くのが好きだ.

take [***grab***] ***the bull by the horns*** 《口》 手ごわいものを勇敢に正面から攻撃する; 勇敢に正面から難局に当たる ▪ Let's *take the bull by the horns*, go directly to his office and state our demands. 正面から勇敢に難局に当たり, 直接彼の事務室へ行き我々の要求を述べよう. ☞下の《諺》から.

The bull must be taken by the horns. 《諺》 牛と闘うには角をつかめ《恐るべきものと闘うにはまともにぶつかるほうがかえってよい》.

tie that bull outside [***to another ashcan***] 《米俗》 信じられないね ▪ Fellers, the war's over. —*Tie that bull outside*. みなの衆, 戦争は終わったぞ—信じられないね.

bulldog /bʊ́ldɔ̀ːg|-dɔ̀g/ 名 ***of the bulldog breed*** (ブルドッグのように)決意・勇気・がんばりのある ▪ He must be *of the bulldog breed*. 彼は勇気のある人にちがいない.

bulldoze /bʊ́ldòʊz/ 動 ***bulldoze*** *one's* ***way*** 強引に進む ▪ He *bulldozed his way* through the crowd. 彼はしゃにむに人混みの中を進んでいった.

bullet /bʊ́lət/ 名 ***bite*** (***on***) ***the bullet*** 不快[困難]に男らしく耐える ▪ Be a man. *Bite the bullet*. 元気を出しなさい, 苦しみに男らしく耐えなさい.

bullet lane 《米俗》 追い越し車線 (passing lane) ▪ A white van darted out of the *bullet lane*. 白い小型トラックが追い越し車線から飛び出してきた ▪ Move over into the *bullet lane*, this car is moving too slow. 追い越し車線に移りなさい. この車はスピードが遅すぎる.

Every bullet has its billet. 《諺》 どの銃弾も宿割りが決まっている《当たるも当たらぬも天命》.

get the bullet 《口》 解雇される ▪ I am almost certain to *get the bullet*. 私が首になるのはほぼ確かだ.

give the bullet 《口》 解雇する ▪ I *gave* him *the bullet*. 私は彼を解雇した.

like a bullet from [***out of***] ***a gun*** 《口》 すぐに, 全速力で, 素早く ▪ He was off *like a bullet out of a gun*. 彼は鉄砲玉のようにとび去った.

sweat bullets 〚主に進行形で〛《米俗》 玉の汗をかく; 精神的苦痛を感じる, 非常に心配して[おびえて]いる ▪ I *was sweating bullets* when I heard your plane went down. あなたの乗った飛行機が落ちたと聞いたときにはひどく心配しました ▪ I *was sweating bullets*, sitting through the speech. そのスピーチの間, 座って玉の汗をかいていた[精神的に苦痛を感じていた].

bull-horn /bʊ́lhɔ̀ːrn/ 名 ***show the bull-horn*** 抵抗の意気を見せる ▪ He *showed the bull-horn*. 彼は抵抗の色を見せた.

bullock /bʊ́lək/ 動 ***bullock*** *one's* ***way*** 暴力をもって押し進む ▪ Sir William *bullocked his way* through Parliament. サー・ウィリアムはがむしゃらに国会議員になった.

bull's-eye /bʊ́lzàɪ/ 名 ***hit*** [***make, score***] ***the*** [***a***] ***bull's-eye*** 金的を射る, 的の中心に当てる; 大当たりを取る, 大成功を収める ▪ He has *hit the bull's-eye*. 彼はめざましい成功を収めた ▪ You *scored a bull's-eye* in selling that ground so quickly. 君はその土地を素早く売って大当たりをやった.

bully /bʊ́li/ 名間 ***A bully is always a coward.*** 《諺》 いじめっ子はきまって臆病者だ.

a bully pulpit 《米》 権力の座; 公職の権威 ▪ Becoming a senator provided him with *a bully pulpit* for his pro-gun views. 彼は上院議員になり, 銃所持支持の自説を広めるお墨付きを手にした.

Bully for you [***her, him,*** etc.]***!*** 《口》 すごいなあ《ねたみ・あざけりを含む》 ▪ I hear Bobby won the 2008 season finale.—Oh, *bully for him!* ボビーは2008年のシーズン決勝戦で優勝したんだって—わあー, そいつはすごい! ▪ You're top of your class. *Bully for you*, Alfred! 君はクラスの首席だ. すごいぞ, アルフレッド!

come the bully over 《俗》 ...をおびやかす, おどす ▪ He tried to *come the bully over* the widow. 彼は未亡人をおどそうとした.

play [***act***] ***the bully*** いばり散らす.

bulrush /búlrʌʃ/ 名 ***bow*** [***hang***] ***the head like a bulrush*** アシのように頭を下げる (《聖》*Isa.* 58. 5) ▪ Do you wish me to *hang my head like a bulrush*? 君は私にアシのように頭を下げてほしいのか.

bum /bʌm/ 名形 ***get the*** [***a***] ***bum's rush*** 《俗》おっぽり出される; 首になる ▪ You'd be lucky not to *get a bum's rush*. つまみ出されないとすれば運がいいんだろう ▪ He *got the bum's rush* from my office. 彼は私の会社からおっぽり出された.

give a bum steer 《俗》誤り導く, 誤らせる ▪ You certainly *gave* me *a bum steer* on that last investment I made. この前の僕の行った投資では確かに君の指導は誤りだったね.

give the [***a***] ***bum's rush*** 《口》(人を)おっぽり出す, 免職する ▪ The bouncer *gave* him *the bum's rush*. 用心棒はその男をおっぽり出した ▪ I *gave* him *the bum's rush*. 彼を免職にした.

on a bum 《米俗》飲み騒いで ▪ He went *on a bum* one evening and fell off the Brooklyn bridge. 彼はある晩飲み騒いでブルックリン橋から落ちた.

on the bum 《口》 **1** 浮浪して ▪ He was *on the bum*. 彼は浮浪生活をしていた.

2 飲み騒ぎして ▪ They went *on the bum*. 彼らは飲み騒いだ.

3 調子が悪く, いたんで; 不景気で ▪ My wrists are *on the bum*. 手首の調子が悪い ▪ My car went *on the bum*. 私の車が故障した ▪ Everything went *on the bum*. 万事不景気になった.

4 (金など)をせびって ▪ He always comes to me *on the bum*. 彼はいつも私の所へ金をせびりに来る.

put [***get***] ***bums on seats*** 《英口》(俳優・演劇が)多数の観客を集める ▪ Eric will *put bums on seats* when he starts playing. エリックが演技を始めたら多数の観客を呼ぶだろう. ☞bums「尻」.

bummer /bʌ́mər/ 名 ***that's*** [***it's***] ***a*** (***real***) ***bummer*** 《米俗》状況は(ほんとに)ひどい[困った, がっかりだ] ▪ *It's a bummer* to lose such a nice man. あんないいやつを失うなんてがっかりだ.

what a bummer! 《米俗》なんてこった! ▪ *What a bummer!* Today's trip was completely chaotic. なんてこった! 今日の旅行はすっかり台なしだった.

bump[1] /bʌmp/ 名 ***a bump on a log*** 退屈な[怠惰な]人 ▪ Jed is just *a bump on a log*. ジェッドはまさに怠け者だ ▪ Jack is such *a bump on a log* that most girls don't like him. ジャックはひどく退屈な男で大抵の女の子に人気がない.

go bump バタンと音がする ▪ What *went bump* in the night? 夜中にバタンと音を立てたのは何か.

have [***possess***] ***a bump of*** ...の能力[才能, 性質]がある ▪ Usually children *have* big *bumps of* curiosity. 通例子供たちは大きな好奇心をもっている ▪ He *possesses a bump of* jealousy. 彼は嫉妬するたちだ ▪ She *has* no *bump of* music. 彼女には音楽の才がない.

like a bump on a log 《米口》じっと[ぼさっと]して; 黙りこくって ▪ His wife sat there *like a bump on a log*. 彼の妻はぼさっとしてそこに座っていた ▪ Don't sit there *like a bump on a log*! Give me a hand. そこでぼさっとしているな! 手伝ってくれ.

things that go bump in the night → THING.

with a bump **1** ドスンと ▪ I landed *with a bump* and broke my left leg. 私はドスンと落っこちて, 左足を折った.

2 突如として, やぶから棒に, ハッとして ▪ The first round started *with a bump*. 第1ラウンドは突如として始まった ▪ I came back to consciousness *with a bump*. 私はハッとして意識を回復した.

bump[2] /bʌmp/ 動 ***Bump that!*** 《俗》(間違いをして)ごめん.

bumper /bʌ́mpər/ 名 ***bumper to bumper*** **1** (車が)じゅずつなぎになって, 渋滞して ▪ Being a Friday evening, it was *bumper to bumper* on the main road. 金曜日の夜とあって, 主要道路では車がじゅずつなぎになっていた ▪ Mark's expert navigation got us out of the *bumper-to-bumper* mess. マークの巧みな操縦のおかげで我々は交通渋滞から抜け出せた.

2 〚限定的に〛(保険証書が)総合の, 包括の ▪ Being a "*bumper-to-bumper*" warranty, everything excluding wear items are covered for manufacturing defects. 「総合」保障なので, 消耗品を除く製造上の欠陥を保証します.

bumpy /bʌ́mpi/ 形 ***give ... a bumpy ride*** ...を困難な目にあわせる ▪ The stock market *gave* investors *a bumpy ride* in 2001. 2001年には株式市場が投資家を苦しい目にあわせた.

have a bumpy ride 困難な目にあう, 苦労を抱えている ▪ Airlines may *have a bumpy ride* in fall and winter. 航空会社は秋と冬には困難な目にあうかもしれない.

bun /bʌn/ 名 ***get*** [***have***] ***a bun on*** 《米俗》酒に酔う[酔っている] ▪ We ought to *get a* slight *bun on*. 我々は少し酔うべきだ.

have (***got***) ***a bun in the oven*** 《英戯》妊娠して ▪ I hear Nell's *got a bun in the oven*. ネルは身重だそうだね.

take the bun 《俗》 **1** 第1位を占める, 賞を得る《よいもの, 器用なもの, おもしろいものについて言う》 ▪ The yarn fairly *takes the bun*. その話はほんとにとびきりおもしろい.

2 全く意外である ▪ Old Saunders is going to be married. That *takes the bun*! ソーンダーズ老人が結婚する. 全く意外だ.

bunch /bʌntʃ/ 名 ***a bunch of*** 《米俗》(人の)群れ ▪ *A bunch of* natives were found living in the jungle. 土着の人の群れがジャングルの中で生活しているのが見つかった.

a bunch of fives 《ボクシング・俗》握りこぶし; (一般に)手 ▪ Do you see this *bunch of fives*? このこぶしが見えるか ▪ The bouquet in *his bunch of fives* was not an agreeable perfume. 彼の手の花束はいい匂いではなかった.

give *a person* ***a bunch of fives*** 《戯》人にパンチをくらわす ▪ I *gave* him *a bunch of fives* in return and knocked him clean out. 彼にお返しのパンチをくらわせ，完全にノックアウトした.

thanks a bunch 《口・しばしば皮肉》どうもありがとう ▪ He said "*thanks a bunch*" and walked out. 彼は「どうもありがとよ」と言って，さっさと出て行った.

the best* [*pick*] *of the bunch 《口》えり抜きのもの ▪ She is *the best of the bunch*. 彼女は群中随一である ▪ Keats's "Ode to a Nightingale" is *the pick of the bunch*. キーツの「ナイチンゲールに寄す」は絶唱だ.

buncombe /bʌ́ŋkəm/ 名 ***a bid for buncombe*** 《米》選挙民の人気取りの手 ▪ The bill was another *bid for buncombe*. その議案もまた選挙民の人気取りの手だった.

make a speech for buncombe/ talk* [*speak*] *for* [*to*] *buncombe 《米》議場でおみやげ演説をする ▪ They sometimes *talked for buncombe*. 彼らはときにはおみやげ演説をした. ☞米国第16国会において Missouri Question の討議の終わりころ, Buncombe 選出の議員が,「選挙民のためにどうしても演説する」と言ったことから.

pass** a measure **for buncombe 《米》おみやげ法案を通す; 選挙民の人気取りに法案を通す ▪ The House of Representatives *passed* the bill *for buncombe*. 下院は選挙区民の人気取りのためその法案を通した.

bundle[1] /bʌ́ndəl/ 名 ***a bundle of*** 一束の，一包みの，たくさんの ▪ I have *a bundle of* letters to answer. 返事を出すべき手紙がたくさんある ▪ She has sent me *a bundle of* clothes. 彼女は私に一包みの衣類を送ってくれた.

a bundle of joy/ a bundle from heaven 《口》赤んぼう ▪ He tossed the *bundle of joy* to Rex. 彼は赤んぼうをレックスにポイと渡した.

***a bundle of laughs* [*fun*]** 《英口》〚主に否定文で〛大変おもしろい人[もの] ▪ He's a good fellow, but not exactly *a bundle of laughs*. 彼は好漢だが，あまりおもしろい男ではない ▪ Life in the Third Millennium should be just *a bundle of fun*. 21世紀の生活はまさしく楽しいものであるはずだ.

be a bundle of nerves きわめて神経過敏である ▪ I *was a bundle of nerves* then. 私はその時，極度に神経をとがらせていた.

drop** one's **bundle 《主に米》勝利[成功]をあきらめる ▪ The team was losing badly, but they did not *drop their bundle*. チームはぼろ負けしていたが，彼らは勝利をあきらめなかった.

go a* [*the*] *bundle on **1** …に大金を賭ける ▪ He *went the bundle on* a horse. 彼はある馬に大金をかけた.
2 〚しばしば否定文で〛《英口》…が好きになれない ▪ I don't *go a bundle on* her hairstyle. 彼女の髪型は好きになれない.

make a bundle 大金をかせぐ ▪ Oil companies still *make a bundle*. 石油会社は依然大金をかせいでいる ▪ Susan *made a bundle* selling real estate. スーザンは不動産を売って大金を稼いだ.

save a bundle (格安な物を買って)大金を節約する ▪ I *saved a bundle* with my bargain buys. 見切り品を買って大金を節約した.

bundle[2] /bʌ́ndəl/ 動 ***bundle** oneself **up*** 暖かそうにくるまる ▪ I *bundled myself up* in a blanket. 私は毛布にぬくぬくとくるまった.

bun-fight /bʌ́nfàɪt/ 名 ***have* (*got*) *a bun-fight on*** 《戯》お茶の会を催している ▪ My wife *has* got *a bun-fight on*. 妻はお茶の会を催している. ☞bun-fight は bun-struggle, bun-worry とも言う.

bungle /bʌ́ŋgəl/ 名 ***make a bungle of*** …をだめにする，めちゃくちゃにする ▪ He *made a* pretty *bungle of* his work. 彼は仕事をめちゃくちゃにした.

bunk[1] /bʌŋk/ 名 ***do a bunk*** 《英口》逃走する ▪ Now I'm spotted, I'll *do a bunk*. 目星をつけられたから，ずらかるよ.

bunk[2] /bʌŋk/ 動 ***bunk it*** 《主に米口》(粗末な床に)寝る ▪ We had to *bunk it* on the sand. 我々は砂上に寝なければならなかった.

bunny /bʌ́ni/ 名 ***a dumb bunny*** 愚か者 ▪ Ed is *a* regular *dumb bunny*. エドは真の愚か者だ.

fuck like bunnies 《米・禁句》矢継ぎ早にたくさん子供を産む ▪ Some of us *fuck like bunnies*. 矢継ぎ早にたくさん子供を産む者もいる.

not a happy bunny →not be a HAPPY camper.

quick like a bunny 早急に，素早く ▪ Open those bottles *quick like a bunny*. そのびんをさっさと開けろ.

bur /bəːr/ 名 ***a bur in the throat*** のどにつかえるように思われるもの; 声のしわがれ ▪ I hemmed once or twice, for it gave me *a bur in my throat*. 1, 2度えへんと言った，何かのどにつかえるようだったから.

burden /bə́ːrdən/ 名 ***be a burden to* [*on*]** …の重荷となる ▪ He *is a burden on* others. 彼は他人のやっかい者である ▪ Taxes *were a* great *burden to* the people. 課税は人民の大きな負担であった.

***bear* [*stand*] *the burden and heat* (*of the day*)** 《文》苦しい仕事に耐える，苦役に服する (《聖》*Matt*. 20. 12) ▪ He had gone to the battlefield, *stood the burden and heat of the day*. 彼は戦場に行き，苦役に耐えたのだった.

lay a burden on …に責任を負わせる ▪ The voters have *laid a burden on* him. 投票者たちは彼に責任を負わせた.

like the burden of a song (歌の折り返し句のように)何度も繰り返して ▪ Her strange smile recurred in my head *like the burden of a song*. 彼女の不思議な微笑が何度も繰り返して頭によみがえってきた.

the burden of* (*the*) *years 老いに伴う身体の衰え ▪ Old age does not mean *the burden of years*; it means the fruition of a life. 老齢は身体の衰えを意味しない. 人生の成熟を意味するのだ.

burn[1] /bəːrn/ 名 ***do a slow burn*** 徐々に怒りがこみあげてくる ▪ I *did a slow burn* when she kept me waiting for two hours. 彼女が私を2時間も待たせたとき次第に怒りが込みあげてきた.

get a good burn 《米》十分に畑の芝焼きをする ▪ If he *gets a good burn*, he will get a fair crop of corn. 十分畑焼きをしたら, トウモロコシの出来がよくなるだろう.

go for the burn 《口》(筋肉痛を起すほど)激しく運動する, 体をいじめる ▪ *Go for the burn*, not the burnout; take off at least one day a week. 燃えつきるのではなく, 体をいじめるんだ. 少なくとも週1回は休め.

burn[2] /bəːrn/ 動 ***be burned alive*** 焼け死ぬ; 火刑にされる ▪ A young woman *was burnt alive* over witchcraft. 若い女が魔術を使ったというので火刑にされた.

be burning to *do* …したくてむずむずしている ▪ He *was burning to* tell the truth. 彼は本当のことを言いたくてむずむずしていた.

burn *oneself* やけどする ▪ The child *burnt itself* while playing with matches. その子供はマッチをいじくっていてやけどした.

burn *a person* ***alive at the stake*** 人を火あぶりにする ▪ Jeanne d'Arc *was burnt alive at the stake*. ジャンヌダルクは火あぶりの刑に処せられた.

burn *one's* ***boats*** [***ship***] 背水の陣を敷く ▪ Now I have *burned my boats* with a vengeance. さあ決然として背水の陣を敷いたぞ. ☞ Julius Caesar が外征のとき敵国に上陸したら船を焼いて帰れないようにしたことから.

burn *one's* ***bridges*** (***behind*** *one*) 背水の陣を敷く ▪ It seems that you should *burn your bridges behind* you. 君は背水の陣を敷くべきだと思われる.

burn daylight 《古》日中にろうそくをともす; 時[精力]を浪費する (cf. Sh., *Merry W.* 2. 1. 54) ▪ Don't *burn daylight* about it; we have little time to spare. そのことに時間を空費してはいけない. 余分の時間はあまりないのだ.

burn ... down for a laugh 《米》…をおもしろ半分にからかう ▪ He often *burns* some one *down for a laugh*. 彼はよくおもしろ半分に人をからかう. ☞ burn「火あぶりにする」.

burn *a person's* ***eyes out*** (刑として)人の目を焼きつぶす ▪ I must *burn his eyes out*. 彼の目を焼きつぶさなければならない.

burn *a person* ***in the hand*** (刑として)人の手に焼印を押す ▪ He *was burnt in the hand* at the last assizes at Worcester. 彼はウスターのこの前の巡回裁判で手に焼印を押された.

burn like a match [***matchwood***] たやすく早く燃える ▪ The old house will *burn like a match*. その古い家はたやすく早く燃えるだろう.

burn (***metals***) ***together*** (金属を)熔接する, 焼きつぎする ▪ They *burned* the two *metals together*. 彼らはその2種の金属を熔接した.

burn *oneself* [***itself***] ***out*** **1** 《米口》精力[体力]を使い果たす ▪ Carl *burned himself out* in the first part of the race. カールはレースの序盤で力を使い果たしてしまった.
2 (物・火が)燃えつきる, 死ぬ; (怒り・熱意などが)さめる, 薄れる ▪ The building will *burn itself out* before long. 建物はやがて燃えつきるであろう ▪ His anger had been intense, but it had gradually *burnt itself out*. 彼の怒りは激しかったが, 次第に薄れていった ▪ He *burned himself out*. 彼は働きすぎて死んだ.

burn ... out of house and home → cast a person out of HOUSE and home.

burn powder → POWDER[1].

burn the [*one's*] ***candle at both ends*** **1** 二方面に精力・財力を浪費する《朝早く起きて夜遅く寝るなど》 ▪ To work all day and go to parties every night is simply *burning the candle at both ends*. 終日働き, 毎晩夜遊びに行くのは全く二方面に精力を使いはたすというものだ ▪ You must either go to bed earlier or get up later. It's folly to *burn the candle at both ends*. 君はもっと早く寝るか, もっと遅く起きるかせねばならない. 早起き遅寝は愚かだ.
2 過労で精力を使いつくす; 非常なむだ使いをする ▪ It is good to study hard, but be careful not to *burn the candle at both ends*. 一生懸命勉強するのもよいが, 過労で精力を使い果たさないよう注意しなさい.

burn the earth [***prairie, wind***] 《米口》全速力で走る ▪ I was half a mile in the lead *burning the earth*. 私は半マイル先になって全速力で走っていた.

burn the Thames → THAMES.

burn the water たいまつをともして川でサケ (salmon) を突く ▪ This amusement of *burning the water* was not without some hazard. たいまつをともしてサケを突くこの楽しみも危険がないではなかった.

burn to death 焼け死ぬ ▪ Two young boys *burnt to death* in the fire at my neighbor's house. 近所の家の火事で幼い男の子二人が焼死した.

burn *a person* ***to death*** 人を焼き殺す (→ be burnt to DEATH) ▪ Jeanne d'Arc *was burnt to death*. ジャンヌダルクは火刑に処せられた.

burn up the road 《口》車をぶっ飛ばす ▪ He *burned up the road* to see her. 彼は彼女に会うため車をぶっ飛ばした.

burn with a low blue flame **1** 《米俗》酒に酔う ▪ He is *burning with a low blue flame*. 彼は酒に酔っている.
2 心の奥で怒りをたぎらせる ▪ She was quiet, but everyone knew she would soon *burn with a low blue flame*. 彼女はもの静かにしていたが, やがてはらわたが煮えくり返ってくると誰もが承知していた.

Burn you! くたばれ! 《前に God を補う》.

One's [***The***] ***ears burn.*** 《口》(噂されて)耳がほてる《どこかで噂されているらしい》.

have ... to burn (金・時間など)がありあまるほどある ▪ I *have* money *to burn*. 金はたんまりある.

The [*One's*] ***money burns*** (***a hole***) ***in*** *one's* ***pocket.*** **1** 金が身につかない ▪ *His money burns a hole in his pocket* so fast that he has never saved a penny. 彼の金は非常に早く使われてしまうので

1ペニーも貯金していない.
2 (有り金を)非常に使いたがっている ▪ The 1,000 dollars was *burning a hole in his pocket*. 彼は1千ドルを非常に使いたがっている. ☞「金がポケットに穴をあけて出てしまう」の意.

burner /bə́ːrnər/ 名 ***a barn burner*** 白熱した試合 ▪ This year's presidential election will be *a "barn burner"*. 今年の大統領選は「白熱した試合」になるだろう.

be* [*put*] *on the back* [*front*] *burner 《口》(考え・計画など)を後回しに[最優先扱いに]する ▪ His plan *is on the back burner* for the moment. 彼の計画は当面後回しだ ▪ Sadly, the project was *put on the back burner*. 残念ながら, その計画は後回しにされた ▪ Climate change must be *put on the front burner*. 気候変動を最優先扱いにしなければならない. ☞ 料理をガスこんろの後[前]の火口にかけることから.

cook on the front burner 〚主に進行形で〛ちゃんとやっている, 順風満帆である ▪ Now you*'re cooking on the front burner*. 目下君は順調にいってるんだね.

burnt /bəːrnt/ 形 ***a burnt offering*** つましい供物, 犠牲 ▪ I made *a burnt offering* of my scruples. 私は小心翼々の心をつましくささげた.

The* [*A*] *burnt child dreads the fire. 《諺》やけどした子供は火を恐れる,「羹(あつもの)に懲りて膾(なます)を吹く」.

burr /bəːr/ 名 ***a burr under* [*in*] *one's saddle*** 《米口》目障りでしょうがないもの ▪ Someone acts thoughtlessly, and I get *a burr under my saddle*. 誰かが思慮のない行動をすると, 私は目障りでしょうがなくなる. ☞ burr「ある種の植物のいが」.

burrow /bə́ːroʊ|bʌ́rəʊ/ 動 ***burrow one's way*** 地下を掘り進む ▪ Each local body has to *burrow its own way*. 各地方団体は自分で地下を掘り進まなければならない.

burst[1] /bəːrst/, **bust** /bʌst/ 名 《俗》***at a* [*one*] *burst*** 奮励一番, 一気に ▪ With broadband you can send data *at a burst*. ブロードバンドを使えばデータを一気に発信することができる.

be* [*go*] *on the bust 《俗》飲み騒ぎする ▪ We want to *go on the bust* mildly. 我々は穏やかな酒宴をやりたい. ☞ bust のほうが普通.

in sudden bursts 時々思い出したように元気を出して ▪ He works *in sudden bursts*. 彼は時々思い出したように元気を出して働く.

burst[2] /bəːrst/ 動 ***be bursting to*** *do* 非常に…したがっている ▪ Bayne *is bursting to* play again. ベインはもう一度競技したくてうずうずしている.

be bursting with …ではち切れそうである ▪ The children *are bursting with* happiness. 子供たちは幸福ではち切れそうである.

***be full to bursting* (*with*)/ *be bursting* [*bulging*] *at the seams* (*with*)** 《口》(…で)はりさけそうである ▪ My heart *is full to bursting with* emotion. 私の胸は感動ではりさけそうだ ▪ The jail *is bursting at the seams with* more than 17,000 prisoners. その刑務所は1万7千人の囚人でパンクしそうになっている.

be ready to burst with …で破裂しそうである, でたまらない ▪ He *was ready to burst with* shame. 彼は恥ずかしくてたまらなかった.

***burst** oneself* (過労で)体をそこなう ▪ He *burst himself* while working as Congressman. 彼は下院議員として働いているときに体をそこなった.

burst a cap 《米口》雷管が破裂する《火薬に火がつかない》 ▪ I had the misfortune of having *burst a cap* at a buck. 運悪く雷管が破裂して雄ジカを打ち損ねた.

burst** one's **buttons (食べすぎ, 運動のしすぎで)胸ボタンがちぎれる ▪ Take care you don't *burst your buttons*. (あんまり食べて)ボタンがとばないよう用心しろよ.

***burst into flame*(*s*)** →FLAME.

***burst into flower* [*blossom*]** 急に花を咲かせる ▪ The orchards *burst into blossom*. 果樹園は急に花を咲かせた.

burst on the wing 《詩》急に飛び立つ ▪ The wild bird *burst on the wing*. 野鳥が急に飛び立った.

burst onto* [*upon*] *the ... scene 急に…の舞台に登場する ▪ He *burst onto the* racing *scene* in 2000. 彼は2000年に急に競馬の舞台に登場した ▪ Muhammad Ali *burst upon the scene* as a gold-medal winner at the 1960 Olympics. モハメド・アリは1960年のオリンピックの金メダル受賞者として急に舞台に登場した.

burst open **1** 破りあける ▪ The cops *burst* the door *open*. 警官らはドアを押し破ってあけた.
2 (ドアが)ぱっと開く; (つぼみが)ほころびる; (栗・さやが)はじける ▪ The door *burst open* and a stranger appeared. ドアがぱっと開いて, 見知らぬ人が現れた.

burst** one's **sides →SIDE.

burst** one's **way through …をかき分けて進む ▪ A lady will not *burst her way through* a crowd. 淑女というものは群衆の中をかき分けて進むものではない.

bury /béri/ 動 ***be buried alive*** 生き埋めにされる; 世に忘れられる, 埋もれる ▪ Our father *was buried alive* for hours. 父は何時間も生き埋めにされていた ▪ I don't have the feeling of *being buried alive* here. 私はここに埋もれているという感じは持っていません.

be buried in …にふける, に没頭する ▪ The greengrocer *was buried in* business. その八百屋は商売に没頭している ▪ I *was buried in* thought. 私は物思いにふけっていた.

be buried in oblivion 世に忘れられてしまう ▪ He *is* now *buried in oblivion*. 彼は今はすっかり世に忘れられている.

be buried under (仕事)に忙殺されている ▪ I *am buried under* a mountain of work. 私は山のような仕事に忙殺されている.

bury (*oneself*) (***away***) ***in*** …に埋もれる ▪ He *buries himself in* the country. 彼は田舎に埋もれている.

B

bury *one's* ***face*** [***head***] ***in*** (悲しみ・苦痛のため)顔を…に埋める ▪ I *buried my face in* my hands. 私は(悲しみで)両手に顔を埋めた.

bury [***hide, have***] *one's* ***head in the sand*** (***like an ostrich***) →OSTRICH.

bury *oneself* ***in*** …に没頭する, にふける ▪ Bob *buries himself in* his work to distract himself from his painful divorce. ボブはつらい離婚から心をそらすために仕事に没頭している ▪ He *buried himself in* his studies. 彼は研究に没頭した.

bury *one's* ***teeth in*** がぶりと歯をたてる ▪ Betty screamed when the dog *buried its teeth in* her leg. ベティーは犬にがぶりと足に歯をたてられ悲鳴をあげた.

have buried *a person* 親族を失った ▪ I *have buried* my wife. 私は妻を失った.

bus[1] /bʌs/ 名 ***drive the porcelain bus***/ ***drive the big white bus*** 《俗》(飲みすぎて)吐く ▪ I saw Nick *driving the porcelain bus* late Friday night. ニックが金曜の夜遅く飲み過ぎて吐いているのを見た.

like the back (***end***) ***of a bus*** →BACK[1].

miss the bus バスに乗り遅れる; 機会を取り逃す ▪ Don't *miss the bus*, I say. チャンスを逃がさないようにしなさいよ.

ride the porcelain bus 《米俗》下痢で(長いこと)便器に座る ▪ Jim was *riding the porcelain bus* all night. ジムは下痢で夜通し便器に座っていた.

bus[2] /bʌs/ 動 ***bus it*** 《俗》バスで行く, バスに乗る ▪ We may *bus it* or we may cab it. バスでもいいし, タクシーでもいい.

bush /bʊʃ/ 名 ***bang the bush***/ ***drag the bush up*** 《米口》すぐれている, 第一等である ▪ That is a cap that *bangs the bush*. それはとびきり最良の帽子だ ▪ This picture *drags the bush up* by the roots. この絵が断然すぐれている.

beat around [《英》 ***about***] ***the bush*** (用心深く)遠回しに言う, 要点を避ける; 遠回しに探る ▪ I wanted to talk about our marriage, but Joan tried to *beat around the bush*. 私は結婚のことを話したかったのだがジョーンは肝心な点を避けようとした ▪ He spent hours in *beating about the bush*. 彼は遠回しに探るのに何時間もすごした. ☞「獲物を追い出すためやぶをたたいて回る」が原義.

beat the bush [***bushes***] **1** やぶをたたいて鳥獣を追い出す; 縁の下の力持ちをする ▪ One *beat the bush* and another caught the hare. 一人が勢子(せこ)を務めもう一人がウサギを捕えた.

2 (猟人がするように)ありそうなところをくまなく探す (*for*) ▪ He was *beating the bush for* promising talent. 彼は有望なタレントをあちこち探していた.

drag the bush up →bang the BUSH.

go bush 叢林(そうりん)に入って住む[盗賊となる]; (囚人などが)奥地へ逃げる ▪ He has *gone bush*, living much like the aborigines. 彼は叢林に入って, ほとんど原住民と同じような生活をしている ▪ I decided to *go bush* down the course of the creek. 私は小川の流れを下って奥地へ逃げ込もうと決心した.

Good wine needs no (***ivy***) ***bush.*** →WINE[1].

hang out bushes 広告する ▪ They did not *hang out bushes* for their beauties. 彼女らは自分たちの美を広告しなかった. ☞「酒屋の看板の bushes (きうたの枝)を掲げる」が原義.

need no bush 宣伝はいらない ▪ Good essays *need no bush*. 良い随筆に宣伝はいらない. ☞《諺》Good WINE needs no bush. から.

take the rag off the bush ＝bang the BUSH.

bushel /bʊ́ʃəl/ 名 ***hide*** *one's* ***light*** [***candle***] ***under a bushel*** 謙遜して自己の才能・才芸を隠す (《聖》 *Matt.* 5. 10) ▪ These days it's no good *hiding your light under a bushel*. 今日では自分の才能を隠していてはだめだ.

measure *other people's* ***corn by*** *one's* ***own bushel*** 自分を標準にして人を計る ▪ We must not *measure everybody's corn by our own bushel*. 我々は自分の標準ですべての人を判断してはいけない.

under a bushel 秘密に (《聖》 *Matt.* 5. 15) ▪ You can't give a dinner *under a bushel*. 秘密に宴を催すことはできませんよ.

business /bíznəs/ 名 ***a bad business*** うまく運ばなかった成り行き, 割に合わない仕事 ▪ Extraditing our citizens to the US is *bad business*. わが国の市民をアメリカに引き渡すのは割に合わない仕事だ.

be (***back***) ***in business*** **1** 《口》(遊んでいたあとに)また仕事にありつく; 事がまたうまく行きだす ▪ We soon got the engine going. He said, "Ah, we'*re in business*." まもなくエンジンが動きだした.「またうまく動きだした」と彼は言った.

2 (再び)平常通り働いて[作動して] ▪ The plant will *be back in business* on Monday. 工場は再び月曜日には平常通り操業するだろう ▪ Our advertisers *are in business*. 我々の広告主は平常通り仕事をしている.

be not in the business of …するつもりはない (*doing*) ▪ I *am not in the business of* heavy-handed regulation. 私は高圧的な規制をするつもりはない ▪ I *am not in the business of bashing* Ben. 私はベンを激しく非難するつもりはない.

Business as usual. 営業は平常通り《事変のあった時などの掲示》. ☞Winston Churchill の The maxim of the British people is "*Business as usual*". は(1914年)以来, 第一次世界大戦時のスローガンとなり, その後広く使われるようになった.

Business before pleasure. 《諺》遊ぶよりはまず仕事.

Business is business. ビジネスはビジネス《儲けが目的で, 個人の感情など考慮すべきではない》 ▪ But *business is business* wherever you are. しかし, あなたがどこにいてもビジネスはビジネスだ.

buy [***sell***] ***out a*** [*one's*] ***business*** 店を買う[売る] ▪ He *bought out a business*. 彼は一軒の店を

買った.

come* [*get*] *to business 仕事につく; 用件に取りかかる ▪ Time to *get to business*. 用件に取りかかるべき時だ.

do a great business 大儲けする ▪ He *did a great business* with good coffee and doughnuts. 彼はうまいコーヒーとドーナツで大儲けした.

do a stroke of business 一儲けする ▪ He has *done a* good *stroke of business*. 彼は大当たりをやった.

do business 商売をする ▪ He is *doing business* for himself. 彼は独立して商売をしている.

do *one's* ***business*** 用を足す《用便をする》 ▪ See that no birds *do their business* there. 鳥たちがそこで用便をしないよう注意しなさい.

do *a person's* ***business*** (***for*** *him*) 人をやっつける, 殺す ▪ This will *do his business*. これであいつも参るだろう ▪ He *did Lord Clarendon's business*. 彼はクラレンドン卿を殺した.

do business on *one's* ***own account*** (会社員などが)各自の商売[内職]をする ▪ They are *doing business on their own account*. 彼らは個人的に内職をしている.

do business with …と取引する ▪ They *do* much *business with* South America. 彼らは南アメリカと多くの取引をしている.

do the business **1**《口》間に合う, 用が足りる ▪ That will *do the business*. (= That will DO.) それでけっこうだ ▪ It was difficult to roll the stone, but five of the boys *did the business*. その石を転がすのは難しかったが, 少年5人で見事転がせた ▪ When he cut his finger, a bandage *did the business*. 彼が指を切ったとき包帯で用が足りた.
2 期待通りのことをやる ▪ Max *does the business* on the football field. マックスはフットボールの球場では期待通りの仕事をする.
3 セックスをする ▪ He managed to *do the business* with her. 彼はなんとかしてその女とセックスした.

do the business for …をやっつける, 往生させる ▪ This will *do the business for* him. これで彼も参るだろう.

Everybody's business is nobody's business.《諺》共同責任は無責任《共同責任でやれば誰の責任でもないことになる》.

get down to business 本気で仕事にかかる; 本論に入る ▪ It's about time he *got down to business*. 彼はもう本気で仕事にかかるべき時だ ▪ Now let me *get down to business*. さあこれから本論に入らせてください.

get the business《俗》**1** ひどくしかられる ▪ Tom *got the business* for asking a dumb question to the boss. トムは社長にばかな質問をして大目玉を食った.
2 ひどい目にあう ▪ Bill *got the business* when he was caught stealing a friend's bike. ビルは友だちの自転車を盗んだのを見つかったときひどい目にあった.
3 首になる ▪ Once the new management takes over I'm sure to *get the business*. 新しい経営陣に引き継がれれば, 私はきっと首になるだろう.

get to business →come to BUSINESS.

give … the business《俗》**1** …をひどい目にあわせる; (男性)をふる, 捨てる ▪ Della *gave* John *the business* and married Bob. デラはジョンをふって, ボブと結婚した.
2 …をひどくしかる ▪ The teacher *gave* Jim *the business* when he came to school late again. ジムがまたぞろ遅刻したとき先生はジムをひどくしかった.
3 (人)を殺す ▪ The gang *gave* him *the business* when they found he had betrayed them. ギャング団は裏切られたことが分かると彼を消した.
4 …に最大限の努力をする ▪ Bill *gave* the examination *the business* but he failed it. ビルはその試験に最大限の努力を傾けたが, 受からなかった.

go about *one's* ***business*** **1** 自分の仕事をしに行く; 自分の仕事をする ▪ He left it to my management and *went about his business*. 彼はそれを私の処理にまかせて, 自分の仕事をしに行った ▪ He *went about his business* in good earnest. 彼は本気で自分の仕事をした.
2 〚命令的に〛あっちへ行け; うるさい; (人の)いらぬ世話をするな ▪ *Go about your business*; I hate the sight of you. あっちへ行け. お前を見るのもいやだ ▪ I will tell him to *go about his business*. 私は彼にいらぬ世話をするなと言ってやろう.

go into business 実業界に入る ▪ He will *go into business* when he leaves school. 彼は学校を出たら実業界に入る.

go out of business 商売をやめる; 日常の仕事をやめる ▪ My father *went out of business* after the war. 父は戦後は店をしまった.

go to business 事務につく, 出勤する ▪ What time do you *go to business* every morning? 毎朝何時にご出勤ですか.

Good business! よくやった!

have no business *doing* [***to*** *do*] **1** …する権利はない; (物が)…してはならない ▪ You *have no business to* interfere. 君には干渉する権利はない ▪ You *have no business opening* my mail! おまえなんかわしのメールを開けて見る権利もないくせに!
2 …する義務[必要]はない ▪ She *has no business to* be so just. 彼女はそんなに公正である必要はない.

have no business on《米》…に乗る権利はない ▪ He *has no business on* a horse. 彼には馬に乗る権利はない.

in business《口》仕事が整って ▪ You are *in business* to make money for yourself. 君は自分で金儲けをする仕事が整っているんだよ.

it's business as usual (不穏な情勢にもにもかかわらず)営業[事態]は平常通り ▪ *It's business as usual* for foreign students at the University. その大学の外国人学生は平常通りに勉強している.

know *one's* ***own business*** 自分のためにすべき事をちゃんと心得ている《余計な手出しをしない》 ▪ Let him alone. He *knows his own business*. 彼に構

うな. 彼は余計な手出しはしない.

like nobody's business 《口》〚強意的に〛(人間わざでないように, から)猛烈に, ひどく, すばらしく ▪ She plays the piano *like nobody's business.* 彼女はすごくピアノがうまい ▪ He snores *like nobody's business.* 彼はすごいいびきをかく.

make a great business of ...を難事と思う, 持て余す ▪ He yet *makes a great business of* the integration of those elements. 彼はまだそういう要素を統合することを持て余している.

make it *one's* ***business to*** *do* ...することにする; するのを事とする; ...するよう努力する ▪ I'll *make it my business to* go to his house and inquire. 彼の家へ行って尋ねることにします ▪ He *makes it his business to* find others' faults. 彼は他人のあら探しを事としている ▪ He *made it his business to* make charity pay off. 彼は慈善が引き合うように努力している.

mean business 《口》本気である ▪ I saw that he *meant business.* 私は彼が本気であると知った.

mind *one's* ***own business*** 《口》〚命令的に〛自分の職分を守る《人の事に干渉しない》; いらぬ世話をしない ▪ I got tired of his criticism, and told him to *mind his own business.* 私は彼の批評にあきあきしたので, 彼にいらぬ世話をするなと言った.

mix business with pleasure 〚主に否定文で〛仕事と遊びを結びつける ▪ I make it a rule never to *mix business with pleasure.* 私は決して仕事と遊びを結びつけないことにしている.

no business of mine [***yours,*** etc.]/***not my*** [***your,*** etc.] ***business*** 私の[あなたの, など]知ったことでない ▪ That's *no business of yours.* それは君の知ったことではない.

nobody's business 《米》〚強意的に〛大変なもの, たいしたもの ▪ How she knocked me for a row of pins is *nobody's business.* 彼女が私をわけなくやっつけてしまったのはすごい.

none of *one's* ***business*** ...の知ったことではない ▪ Who's that letter from?—It's *none of your business.* あの手紙は誰から来たの—お前の知ったことではないよ.

on business 用向きで, 所用で ▪ No admittance except *on business.* 無用の者入るべからず ▪ I have to go to Washington *on business.* 所用でワシントンへ行かなければならない.

out of business **1** 破産して; 失業[廃業]して ▪ The company is *out of business.* その会社は破産している.

2 作動[営業]していない ▪ The merry-go-round is *out of business* tonight. メリーゴーラウンドは今夜は動いていない.

proceed to business 議事日程に入る ▪ The Senate is ready to *proceed to business.* 上院は議事日程に入る用意が整っている.

put ... out of business (人・会社などを)破産[廃業]させる ▪ The firm *was* soon *put out of business.* その会社はまもなく破産した.

sell out a [*one's*] ***business*** →buy out a BUSINESS.

send *a person* ***about*** *his* ***business*** 人を追い返す; お払い箱にする; (余計なことをするなと)しかる ▪ Mrs. Smith *sent* him *about his business.* スミス夫人は彼をすげなく追っ払った.

set up in business **1** 開業させる, 実業で身を立てさせる ▪ My father *set* me *up in business.* 父は私に店を開かせてくれた.

2 開店[開業]する, 実業で身を立てる ▪ He *set up in business* there. 彼はそこで店を開いた.

sick of the whole business それがすっかりいやになる ▪ I am *sick of the whole business.* 私はそれがすっかりいやになった.

talk business →TALK².

What a business it is! 《俗》ほんとにやっかいなことだ! ☞business「難事」.

What business is that of mine [***yours,*** etc.]***?*** 私[あなた, など]の知ったことではない.

What is *one's* ***business?*** 職業[業務]はなんですか; 用事はなんですか ▪ *What is your business?* ご職業は? ▪ *What is your business* with him? あの人になんのご用ですか.

buskin /bʌ́skən/ 名 ***put on the buskins*** 悲劇を書く[演ずる]; 悲劇風の文体で書く ▪ Aristophanes never *put on the buskins.* アリストファネスは悲劇は決して書かなかった. ☞buskin「古代ギリシャの悲劇役者のはいた厚底の半長ぐつ」.

bust¹ /bʌst/ 形 ***go bust*** 《口》破産[破滅]する, (会社が)破産する ▪ The old man has *gone bust.* 老人は破産した ▪ Regretably our travel company *went bust.* 遺憾ながらわが旅行会社は破産した.

bust² /bʌst/ 動 ***bust a gut*** **1** 《口》大いに努力する ▪ I am going to *bust a gut* getting results. 私は結果を出そうとして精いっぱい頑張ろうと思っている.

2 《米口》ゲラゲラ笑う ▪ The show is so hilarious that I *bust a gut* every time I watch it. そのショーはとても愉快なので, 私は見るたびにゲラゲラ笑ってしまう.

bust *a person's* ***ass*** [***balls, butt, hump***] 《米俗》人をひどく非難する ▪ He's always *busting my ass* about my laziness. 彼はいつも私の怠惰をひどく非難してばかりいる.

bust *one's* ***balls*** [***butt, hump***] 《米俗》うんとがんばる, しゃかりきにやる (*to do*) ▪ I must *bust my balls to* finish my graduation thesis. 卒業論文を完成するためにはしゃかりきにやらなければならない.

bust *a person's* ***chops*** 《米俗》= BUST a person's ass.

bust *one's* ***ass*** →ASS¹.

fit to bust 《口》大いに, 大変 ▪ He stood there and laughed *fit to bust.* 彼はそこに立って笑いこけた.

or bust **1** 《米》さもなくば破滅だ ▪ In Hollywood it's either looks *or bust.* ハリウッドでは美貌でなければだめだ《美貌かまたは大きいバストかだ, の意にもなる》.

2 《口》〚前言を強調して〛絶対...だ ▪ It's boom *or bust* for the American economy. アメリカ経済の立て直しには絶対経済の好況が必要だ.

buster /bʌ́stər/ 名 ***come a buster*** 《口》ころぶ, 落ちる ▪I *came a* terrific *buster* off my motorbike. 私はオートバイから激しく転落した.

bustle /bʌ́səl/ 名 ***in a bustle*** **1** 騒いで, 雑踏して ▪The children were *in a bustle* on the playground. 子供たちが運動場で大騒ぎをしていた ▪The streets are *in a* great *bustle* all day long. 通りは一日中ひどく込み合っている.

2 せかせかして ▪She is *in a bustle* preparing for the party. 彼女はパーティーの準備でせかせかしている.

busy[1] /bízi/ 形 ***a busy bee*** 働き者でいつも陽気な人 ▪Look at her run around the kitchen! What *a busy* little *bee*! ごらん, 彼女は台所をかけずり回っている! なんという働き者でいつも陽気な人なんだ!

(as) busy as a beaver (building a new dam) →(as) busy as a BEE.

(as) busy as a hibernating bear 《皮肉》冬眠中のクマのように暇で; ひどく暇で ▪He lounged on the sofa all day, *busy as a hibernating bear.* 彼は暇をもてあまして一日中ソファでごろごろしている.

be busy about [over, with] …で忙しい ▪I *was busy over* my work. 私は仕事で忙しかった.

be [keep] busy (in) doing 忙しく…している ▪I *was busy getting* ready for the journey. 私は旅行の用意をするのに忙しかった ▪I *kept busy studying.* 私はいつも忙しく勉強した.

draw [attract] a person like bees to a honey pot 人を…に強く引きつける ▪Conflict *attracts* mercenaries *like bees to a honey pot.* 紛争が起きると傭(よう)兵がどっと集まってくる.

get busy 《口》仕事に取りかかる, 行動を始める ▪*Get busy* with your ear. 耳を働かせよ ▪We are *getting busy* right away. すぐ仕事に取りかかります.

keep (oneself) busy 忙しくしている ▪Jo *kept herself busy* with volunteer work. ジョーはボランティアの仕事で忙しくしていた.

busy[2] /bízi/ 動 ***busy oneself in doing*** …を忙しくする ▪She *busied herself in cleaning* the house. 彼女は家の掃除に忙しく立ち働いた.

busy oneself [one's hands] with [in, at, about] …を忙しくする, に忙しく働く ▪The King *busied himself in* the erection of numerous castles. 国王はたくさんの城の築造に余念がなかった ▪He *busied his hands about* many worldly things. 彼はたくさんの俗事にかまけていた.

but[1] /bʌt/ 接副前名 ***Ah, but*** →Oh, BUT.

all but →ALL.

anything but →ANYTHING.

but for …がなかったら《現在, または過去の事実の反対を仮定》 ▪*But for* his idleness, he would be a good man. 彼は怠けなければ, よい人間なんだが ▪*But for* your help, I should have failed. 君が助けてくれなかったら, 僕は失敗したところだった.

but good 《口》[[強意的に]] ひどく; とてもよく; 完全に, 徹底的に ▪John hit him *but good.* ジョンは彼をひどくぶんなぐった ▪Get rid of him *but good.* あいつをすっかりかたづけろ. ☞命令文に用いられたときは, 「失敗したら罰するぞ」というおどしを含む.

but that [[that 節中の動詞は直説法]] …しなかったら, がなかったら ▪*But that* I saw it, I could not have believed it. 見なかったら, とうてい信じられなかっただろう ▪I would go abroad *but that* I am poor. 貧乏でなければ洋行するのだが.

but that [《口》 what] **1** [[think, fear, be sure などの否定文・疑問文で]] …でないと (that ... not) ▪I'm not *sure but (that)* he may decline. 彼は断るかもしれない ▪No *fear but what* Isaac will do well in the world. アイザックはきっと出世するだろう.

2 [[doubt, deny など否定的な語を伴って]] …することを《but に意味はない; フランス語法》 ▪I do not *deny but that* he is idle. 私は彼が怠け者であることを否定しない.

cannot be but that 必ず…するにちがいない ▪It *cannot be but that* something will happen. 何かがきっと起こるにちがいない.

cannot [dare not] but do …せずにはいられない, せざるをえない ▪The superior man *dares not but* exert himself. すぐれた人はがんばらずにはいられない ▪He *cannot but* try. 彼はやってみざるをえない.

Heavens! but いやはや… 《but にほとんど意味はない》 ▪*Heavens! but* it rains! いやはや, ひどい雨だ.

I would burn the house down but たとえ家を焼こうとも ▪*I'd burn the house down but* I'll find it. どうあってもそれを必ず見つけてみせる.

it is odds [ten to one,* etc.*] but おそらく, 十中八九 ▪*It is ten to one but* Peter will come. おそらくピーターは来るだろう ▪*It is odds but* you lose. 十中八九君は負けだ.

it shall go hard but たとえどうあっても ▪*It shall go hard but* we shall demolish the theory. 我々はどうあってもきっとその理論をくつがえす.

no [not a]... but (《口》 what) [[but (= that ... not) は 関代]] …しないものはない ▪There is *no* child *but* knows him. 彼を知らない子供はいない ▪*Not a* man *but what* likes her. 彼女を好かない男はいない.

no [not, nothing]... so [such]... but (that, 《口》 what)... (逆に訳して)…しないほど…のものはない; (前から訳して)いくら…でもみな…する ▪*No* man is *so* old *but that* he may learn. 人はいくら年をとっても学問はできる ▪*Nothing* is *so* hard *but that* it becomes easy by practice. どんなにむずかしいことでも練習すれば易しくなる ▪He is *not such* a fool *but what* he can tell that. 彼はそれがわからぬほどのばかではない. ☞but だけの場合はまれ; but that は文章語.

not [never] A but B **1** BしないほどAではない; いくらAでもBする ▪He is *not* such a fool *but* he can tell that. 彼はそれを知らないほどばかではない.

2 Aすれば必ずBする ▪It *never* rains *but* it pours. 《諺》降れば必ずどしゃ降り ▪I *never* see you *but* I think of my brother. 私はあなたを見ると必ず私の弟のことを思い出す.

not but that …ないことはないが ▪He is very strong, *not but that* he will catch cold at times.

彼は非常に強い, 時々風邪を引かないわけではないが.

not that ..., but that →NOT.

nothing but →NOTHING.

nothing *A* ***but*** *B* BしなければどうしてもAしない ▪ *Nothing* would satisfy him *but* he must go there. 彼はそこへ行かなければどうしても満足しない.

Oh [***Ah, Yes***]***, but*** 〚相手の言を反ばくして〛いや ▪ *Oh, but* I did go. いやおれ実際に行ったよ.

Who knows but that [《口》 ***what***]***...?*** ...しないと誰が知ろう, ...するかもしれない ▪ *Who knows but that* he may come again? 彼はまた来るかもしれない.

Who should *A* ***but*** *B* →SHOULD.

Yes, but →Oh, BUT.

but[2] /bʌt/ 動 ***But me no buts.*** 「しかし, しかし」の連発はごめんだよ, 弁解はもうたくさんです ▪ I heartily wish I could, but—Nay, *but me no buts.* 私はほんとにそうできたらと思います. しかし—いや, しかし, しかしの連発はごめんだよ ▪ I want you to *but me no buts*; just go and do as I say. 君はあれこれ言わないでほしい. さあ僕のいう通りにするんだ. ☞最初の but は動.

butcher /bʊ́tʃər/ 名 ***have*** [***take***] ***a butcher's*** 《英俗》(一目)見る ▪ Let's *have a butcher's* at her present. 彼女のプレゼントをちょっと見てみよう. ☞脚韻俗語: butcher's hook＝look.

the butcher, the baker, the candlestick maker さまざまな商売の人 ▪ *The butcher, the baker, the candlestick maker*; And all of them gone to the fair! さまざまな商売人がみんな市場に出かけた. ☞童謡から.

butler /bʌ́tlər/ 名 ***The butler did it.*** 執事がやった; いつもの通りそうなった《キャッチフレーズ》 ▪ Of course, that's it. *The butler did it.* The butler always does it. むろんその通りだ. いつも通りそうなった. いつだってそうなるのさ. ☞優れた殺人ミステリーでは執事が殺人をやっているところから.

butt[1] /bʌt/ 名副 *one's* ***butt is on the line*** 《米》(うまくいかないと)責任を問われる ▪ If the project is late, *my butt is on the line.* このプロジェクトが遅れると, 私の責任が問われる.

Get your butt in gear. 《米俗》急げ, がんばれ《乱暴な表現》.

give (***a fish***) ***the butt*** (魚がはりにかかったとき)さおじりをてこにして魚の方へ向け魚を強く引く《比喩的にも》 ▪ *Give a fish the butt*, or she is gone forever. さおじりをてこにして魚をぐっと引きなさい, そうしないと魚は永久に逃げてしまいますよ ▪ He writes like a man who could *give the butt.* 彼は魚をぐいぐいと引きつけるように文を書く.

hustle *one's* ***butt*** 《米口》素早く動く, さっさと行動する ▪ He *hustles his butt* every day for his family. 彼は毎日家族のためにせかせかと働いている. ☞butt「尻」.

kick (*a person's*) ***ass*** [***butt***] →KICK[2].

kick (*a person's*) ***butt*** 《米》人を罰する; こてんぱんにやっつける ▪ I *kicked his butt* and then I kicked him out the door. 私は彼のけつをけり, ドアからけり出した.

save *a person's* ***butt*** 《米俗》人を救う ▪ You have the ability to *save his butt*. 君には彼を救う能力がある.

butt[2] /bʌt/ 動 ***butt*** (*oneself*) ***out*** [***into***] 先が...へ突き出る ▪ The nose of a weathercock *butts itself into* the wind. 風見の鼻の先が風の方向へ突き出ている ▪ A little square gallery *butts out* from the Tower. 四角い小バルコニーが塔から突き出ている.

butter[1] /bʌ́tər/ 名 ***be a butter-fingers/ have butterfingers*** 不器用で物をよく取り落とす ▪ What *a butter-fingers* you *are*! That's the third time you've dropped the ball. なんて不器用なんだろう, 君は! ボールを捕り損なうのはこれで3回目だぞ.

Butter to butter is no relish. 《諺》バターにバターをつけたのではなんら良い味にならない《何か実のあるものがあってこそ, 味つけの妙味がある; つき合うなら性格の違う人》.

It will cut butter when it is hot. 《口》それは溶けたバターなら切れるだろう《切れないナイフに言う》.

lay on the butter 《口》おべっかを使う ▪ *The butter was laid on* pretty thick. かなりたっぷりとおべっかが使われた.

(***look as if***) ***butter would not melt in*** *one's* ***mouth*** 《口》ひどくとり澄ましている, 虫も殺さぬ顔つきをしている《あまりにもとり澄ましている人を軽蔑して言う》 ▪ They *look as if butter would not melt in their mouths*, and yet they are among the cleverest criminals alive. 彼らは虫も殺さぬ顔つきをしているが, 世にもこうかつな犯罪人どもだ. ☞Macklin の喜劇 *The Man of the World* (1781)から.

make butter and cheese of ...を面くらわす; をだます ▪ They *made butter and cheese of* one another. 彼らは互いにだまし合った.

spread the butter too thick やたらとおべっかを使う ▪ I would not *spread the butter too thick* as it is easy to see through an act. 私はやたらとおべっかは使わない. 行いの魂胆は容易に見抜けるから.

butter[2] /bʌ́tər/ 動 ***bread buttered on both sides*** →BREAD.

Fine [***Fair, Soft***] ***words butter no parsnips.*** →PARSNIP.

have *one's* ***bread buttered for life*** 一生楽に暮らしていける ▪ He *had his bread buttered for life.* 彼は一生楽に暮らしていけた.

butter-boat /bʌ́tərbòʊt/ 名 ***empty*** [***upset***] ***the butter-boat*** 《口》盛んにおせじを浴びせる ▪ He *upset the butter-boat* into the lap of a lady. 彼は婦人に向かって盛んにおせじを浴びせた.

butterfly /bʌ́tərflàɪ/ 名 (***as***) ***gaudy as a butterfly*** 派手な ▪ Ann's scarf is *gaudy as a butterfly*. アンのスカーフはひどく派手だ.

break a butterfly on the wheel →WHEEL[1].

float [***fly***] ***like a butterfly, sting like a bee*** 見た目はひ弱そうだが, 根はすごく強い ▪ Don't be deceived by Mark's appearance—he *floats* *like a butterfly*, but *stings like a bee*. マークの外見にだまされるな—見た目はひょろひょろしてるけど, 実体はすごく強いんだ.

give** a person **butterflies in** his **stomach 人を不安にさせる ▪ His letter informing me of my mother's illness *gave* me *butterflies in my stomach*. 母の病気のことを伝える彼の手紙は私を不安にさせた.

***have butterflies* (*in the* [*one's*] *stomach* [*tummy*])** (大事を行う前に)胸がどきどきする ▪ I always *have butterflies* when I open Parliament. 私は国会を開会する時はいつも胸がどきどきします《Elizabeth 2世の言葉》.

social* [*society*] *butterfly (あちこちに出かける)社交好きの人 ▪ Linda likes dancing, singing and drinking, being the *social butterfly* that she is. リンダはダンスや歌やお酒が好きだ, なにしろあの通りの社交好きだから.

button[1] /bʌ́tən/ 名 ***a boy in buttons*** → BOY.

a hot button 《米》白熱した議論を呼ぶ問題 ▪ Rent control is the city's *hot button* for its residents. 家賃抑制が市民にとってホットな論争を呼ぶ問題である ▪ Gay marriage and abortion topped the list of *hot-button* issues. 同性同士の結婚と堕胎が熱い議論を呼ぶ問題リストのトップになった.

(as) bright as a button 《英》(特に子供や犬が)とても利口である ▪ That small dog is *as bright as a button*. あの子犬はとても利口だ ▪ The boy is *as bright as a button*. その少年はとても頭がいい.

(as) cute as a button とてもかわいい ▪ At fourteen, Jane was *as cute as a button*. 14歳のジェインはそれはそれはかわいかった.

at the touch of a button ボタンを押すだけで, いとも簡単に, 素早く ▪ The gadget provides cool filtered water *at the touch of a button*. この器具はボタンを押すだけで冷たい濾過された水が出ます.

be a button short 《英口》(知恵が)少し足りない ▪ This man *is a button short*. この男は知恵が少し足りない.

burst** one's **buttons →BURST[2].

catch** a person **by the button →hold a person by the BUTTON.

Dash my buttons. 《口》こりゃ驚いた!; くやしいっ! ▪ *Dash my buttons*, I have lost my way. ちくしょう! 道に迷ってしまった. ☞dash = damn; buttons = destiny.

have a button* [*a few buttons*] *missing*/ *have lost some of* one's *buttons 少し足りない ▪ He *has a few buttons missing*. 彼は少し足りない ▪ I think that guy *has lost some of his buttons*. あの男は少し足りないのだと思う.

have a soul above buttons 現在の職業では才能の持ちぐされだと思う ▪ My father *had a soul above buttons*. 私の父は今の職業では才能の持ちぐされだと思っていた.

***have* (*got*) *all* one's *buttons* (*on*)** 《口》頭がよい, 抜け目がない, さとい ▪ He is 83 years old, but *has all his buttons*. 彼は83歳だが頭はしっかりしている.

hold* [*catch, take*] a person *by the button 人を引き止めて放さない, 引き止めて長話をする ▪ He *held* me *by the button*. 彼は私を引き止めて長話をした.

not care a button 《主に米》少しもかまわない ▪ I do*n't care a button*. 私はちっともかまいません.

not have* (*got*) *all* one's *buttons on 《口》知恵が足りない ▪ He *has not got all his buttons on*. 彼は少し足りない. ☞buttons = wits.

not worth a button なんの価値もない ▪ These reports are *not worth a button*. これらのレポートはなんの価値もない.

on the button 《主に米口》 **1** (時刻・量に)きっちり[きっかり]と ▪ The train arrived at 7:00 *on the button*. 列車はきっかり7時に到着した.
2 全く正しい, どんぴしゃり ▪ Your suggestions are *on the button*. 君の提案は全く正しい ▪ He hit it *on the button*. 彼はそれをぴたりと言い当てた.

press* [*push*] a person's *buttons **1** 人をかっとさせる, 激怒させる ▪ Do you *press his buttons* to see how angry he can get? 彼をかっとさせて, 一体どれくらい怒るか試してみますか?
2 = press the right BUTTON.

press* [*push, touch*] *the button ボタンを押す; 《口》口火を切る ▪ He *pressed the button* for the elevator. 彼はエレベーターのボタンを押した ▪ Germany will *press the button* in the interests of peace. ドイツは平和のため口火を切るだろう.

press* [*push*] *the panic button 《英》あわてふためく; 非常手段をとる ▪ When he saw that I was angry he *pushed the panic button*. 彼は私が怒っているのを見ると, あわてふためいた.

***press* [*push*] *the right button* [*all the right buttons*]** 正しいスイッチを押す, 適切に操作・処置する ▪ You have to know how to *push all the right buttons* if you want to be a successful diplomat. 外交官として成功したければ適切に処置するすべを知っていなければならない ▪ Just show me *the right button to push*. どう処理すれば適切かぜひ示していただきたい ▪ The Foreign Minister *pressed all the right buttons* on support for Israel. 外相はイスラエルを支援するための処置をすべて適切に行った.

put** a person **into buttons 人を制服の給仕にする ▪ We don't *put* him *into buttons*. 我々は彼を給仕にはしない.

(right) on the button **1** 《主に米口》全く正しい[当を得ている] ▪ Her review of the book was *right on the button*. 彼女の書評は当を得ている.
2 = on the BUTTON 2.

take** a person **by the button →hold a person by the BUTTON.

button[2] /bʌ́tən/ 動 ***button down the back*** (衣服の)後ろにボタンがかかっている ▪ This dress *buttons down the back*. この服は後ろにボタンがある.

Button it! 《口》黙れ《無礼な言い方》 ▪ Then he said to Eve, "And you *button it.*" それから彼はイブに「君は黙れ」と言った.

button (***up***) *a person's* ***mouth*** [***lip, face***] 人を黙らせる ▪ *Button his mouth!* 彼を黙らせなさい!

button (***up***) *one's* ***mouth*** [***lip, face***] 《俗》黙っている, 口をつぐむ ▪ He *buttoned up his face.* 彼は口をつぐんだ.

buttoned-down (服装・態度などが)型にはまった, 新味のない ▪ Tom is a typical *buttoned-down* type. トムは典型的な型にはまったタイプだ.

buttoned-up 《英口》無口な, 内向的な ▪ He was too *buttoned-up* to discuss it. 彼はひどく無口でそれを議論しなかった.

buttonhole /bʌ́tənhòʊl/ 名 ***take*** *a person* ***down a buttonhole*** (***lower***) 《口》人の高慢な鼻をへし折る ▪ On my word I'll *take* you *down a buttonhole* (lower). きっとお前の高慢な鼻をへし折ってやるぞ.

buy[1] /baɪ/ 名 ***a bad*** [***good***] ***buy*** 《口》つまらぬ買物[掘り出し物] ▪ This stock is *a bad buy.* この株はつまらぬ買物だ.

buy-in (株の)買い埋め ▪ We couldn't raise the cash for a *buy-in.* 株の買い埋めをする現金を調達できなかった.

buy-out (株の)買収, 買い占め ▪ Why does a management *buyout* make sense at Honda? なぜホンダでは自社株買い占めが意味をなすのか.

on the buy 盛んに買って ▪ They are *on the buy.* 彼らは盛んに買いつけている.

buy[2] /baɪ/ 動 ***buy a packet*** →BUY it.

buy a pig in a poke →PIG[1].

buy a pup →PUP.

buy *oneself* ***in*** 株を買って(その会社に)参与する ▪ The only way is *buying yourself in.* 唯一の方法は株を買って参与することである.

buy *oneself* ***into*** 株を買って…に参与する ▪ He *bought himself into* the company. 彼は株を買ってその会社に参与した.

buy it [***a packet***] **1** 《英俗》殺される, 撃ち落とされる; 死ぬ ▪ The pilot *bought it.* パイロットは撃ち落とされた.

2 《俗》深刻に悪化する, 大変なことになる ▪ If they can't raise the money in time, they'll *buy it.* 金の工面がつかなかったら, 彼らは大変なことになるだろう.

buy it [***that***] 《主に米俗》信じる; 受け入れる; 賛成する ▪ Let's have a short break.—I'll *buy that.* 少し休みましょう—賛成.

buy *a thing* ***new*** →NEW.

buy ... over *a person's* ***head*** 人より高値をつけて…を買う ▪ Some London dealer *bought* the carpet *over my head.* あるロンドン商人が私より高値をつけてその敷き物を買った.

buy that →BUY it.

buy the farm [***ranch***] →FARM; RANCH.

buy time →TIME[1].

I'll buy it. 《俗》(難問・なぞなぞに対して)もう投げた, わからない.

buyer /báɪər/ 名 ***a buyer's market*** →MARKET.

Let the buyer beware. 《諺》買い手には用心させるがよい.

buzz[1] /bʌz/ 名 ***a buzz word*** **1** (素人にはわからないもったいぶった)専門用語 ▪ All we heard was a bunch of *buzz words* with no substance. 我々が聞いたのは内容のないたくさんの専門語だけだった.

2 今はやりの言葉, 流行語 ▪ "Green" has been the *buzz word* in all industries in recent years. 近年は「グリーン」があらゆる産業ではやり言葉になっている.

get a buzz from **1** …から電話を受ける ▪ I *got a buzz from* Bill last night. 昨夜ビルから電話を受けた.

2 …で興奮[わくわく]する ▪ Bees *get a buzz from* cocaine. ミツバチはコカインで興奮する.

get [***have***] ***a buzz on*** 《米俗》酒に酔う ▪ He *had a* good *buzz on.* 彼は相当酒に酔っていた.

get a buzz out of 《米俗》…から楽しみを得る ▪ The kids will *get a buzz out of* this toy. 子供らはこのおもちゃを楽しむだろう.

give *a person* ***a buzz*** **1** 《口》人に電話をかける ▪ I'll *give* you *a buzz* when I get to Canada. カナダに着いたら電話するよ.

2 人をわくわく[興奮]させる ▪ Coffee isn't the only drink that *gives* you *a buzz.* 人を興奮させる飲み物はコーヒーだけではない.

go with a buzz 速く進む, すらすらと進む ▪ By jove, the party simply *went with a buzz.* ほんとに, パーティーは全く順調に進行した.

buzz[2] /bʌz/ 動 ***buzz the bottle*** 《口》びんをからにする ▪ We must *buzz the bottle!* 我々はびんをあけねばならんぞ.

one's ***head*** [***mind***] ***is buzzing*** (考えが)頭の中を駆けめぐる (*with*) ▪ We have come back with *our minds buzzing with* new information. 頭の中に新しい情報を駆けめぐらせながら我々は帰ってきた.

buzzer /bʌ́zər/ 名 ***at the buzzer*** 《米》(バスケットボールなどの)試合終了のブザーが鳴ったときに ▪ Our team managed to score right *at the buzzer.* 我がチームは試合終了間際に何とか得点をあげた.

by /baɪ/ 前副 ***by and beside*** なお…の上に ▪ *By and beside* this inward comfort, I had two outward special comforts. この内的楽しみのほかに, 私は二つの特別な外的楽しみを持っていた.

by and by やがて, まもなく ▪ *By and by* some wiser man would appear. そのうち誰かもっと賢い人が現れるだろう.

by and large **1** 《海》風に向かったり離れたり ▪ They soon find one another's rate of sailing, *by and large.* それらの船は風に向かったり離れたりするときの, お互いの帆走速度がじきにわかる.

2 概して; 全般にわたって; どの点から見ても《take it が前につくのは《古》》 ▪ Take it *by and large,* we had a pleasant trip. 概して我々は愉快な旅をした ▪ Consider the matter *by and large.* その事件を

全般にわたって考察しなさい ▪ *By and large*, it is the best of its kind. どの点から見ても，それはこの種のものの中で一番良い．

by the half-hour (半時間単位で計れるほど)半時間の何倍も長く ▪ He stood watching it *by the half-hour*. 彼は半時間の何倍も長くじっとそれを立って見ていた．

without so much as (a) by-your-leave 許可も得ないで ▪ A new helper proceeded to rearrange the furniture *without so much as by-your-leave*. 今度のヘルパーは許可も得ないで家具の位置を変え始めた．

by(e) /baɪ/ 名 ***by the by(e)*** ついでながら，時に ▪ *By the bye*, he is said to go abroad next month. ところで，彼は来月洋行するそうだ．

bye /baɪ/ 名 ***draw a bye*** (テニスなどで)不戦勝を得る ▪ The latter *drew the bye* in the second round. 後者は2回戦で不戦勝を得た．

run a [one's] bye (犬の競走で犬の数がはしたなので，競走回数をそろえるためにある犬が)競走に参加していない犬と走る ▪ Sabrina *ran her bye* and she won. サブリナは非競走犬と走って勝った．

bye-bye /bàɪbáɪ/ 名 ***go bye-bye*** **1**《幼児》(特に歩きにまたは乗りに)出かける ▪ The baby wants to *go bye-bye*. 赤ちゃんが出かけたがっている．

2 =go to BYE-BYE.

go to bye-bye 《幼児》ねんねする ▪ Lie down and *go to bye-bye*. ころりんしてねんねしなさい．

bygone /báɪgɔ̀ːn|-gɔ̀n/ 名 ***Let bygones be bygones.*** 《諺》過去のことは水に流せ ▪ Can't we *let bygones be bygones* and start afresh? 過去のことは水に流して，新規蒔き直しできませんか．

bypass /báɪpæ̀s|-pɑ̀ːs/ 名 ***have had a ... bypass*** (人が…の)特質が完全に欠けている ▪ Bob *has had a* humor *bypass*. ボブはユーモアの資質に完全に欠けている．

by-word /báɪwəːrd/ 名 ***be a by-word for*** (悪いこと)の手本である ▪ He *is a by-word for* iniquity. 彼は非道の見本だ．

become a by-word 悪名が高くなる ▪ The Duke's bad manners have *become a by-word*. 公爵の不作法の悪名が高くなった．

C

C /siː/ 名 ***the big C***《口》がん ▪ *The big C* is no longer the death sentence it used to be. がんはもはやかつてそうだったような死の宣告ではない. ☞Cは cancer（がん）の頭文字.

cab /kæb/ 動 ***cab it*** タクシー[辻馬車]で行く ▪ You can *cab it*. タクシーで行きなさい.

cabbage /kǽbɪdʒ/ 名 ***as large*** [***big***] ***as a cabbage*** [***cabbages***]（草花などが）非常に大きい ▪ These roses are *as big as cabbages*. これらのバラの花は非常に大きい.

cabin /kǽbən/ 名 ***cabin fever*** 閉所性発熱《特に長い冬期の間, 荒野などで一人または数人で閉所に隔離された状態から生ずる》;《口》いらいら, 不安 ▪ We've been snowed in for a week and everyone has *cabin fever*. 1週間雪に閉じ込められてみんないらいらしている.

from log cabin to White House 丸太小屋からホワイト・ハウス（米大統領官邸）へ《微賤(せん)から権勢の地位へ昇ること; 米大統領 Abraham Lincoln の経歴から》 ▪ He started as a junior clerk and finished as managing director—a case of *from log cabin to White House*. 彼は下級事務係から身を起こして遂には専務取締役に登りつめた. 卑賤から権勢へのお手本である.

cabinet /kǽbənət/ 名 ***go into the cabinet*** 入閣する ▪ Mr. Eden *went into the cabinet*. イーデン氏は入閣した.

cable /kéɪbəl/ 名 ***bring a slip on*** *one's* ***cable***《口》いかり綱を放つ; 逃げだす ▪ He *brought a slip on his cable*. 彼は逃げだした.

by cable 海底電信[外電]で ▪ The messages have come *by cable*. その通信は外電で入った.

cut [***slip***] *one's* ***cable***(***s***)（いかりをあげる暇なく）いかり綱を切ってあわてて出港する;《俗》死ぬ ▪ The old fellow *slipped his cable* last week. 老人は先週死んだ.

cut (***the***) ***cable***(***s***) 出ていく; 中断する ▪ I want to *cut cables* and drift about. 家を出て放浪したい.

It is easier [etc.] ***for a cable to go through the needle's eye.*** 綱が針の穴を通るほうが易しい[など] ▪ *It is impossible for a cable to go through a needle's eye*. 綱が針の穴を通るのは不可能である. ☞《聖》*Matt*. 19. 24 に a camel と訳してあるのを a cable と別訳したもの.

caboodle /kəbúːdəl/ 名 ***the whole*** (***kit and***) ***caboodle***《口》何もかも, 誰もかれも, 全部 ▪ There is not a piece of china in *the whole caboodle* that I'd want. 全部のものの中にほしいと思うような陶器はひとつもない ▪ *The whole caboodle* came out and fell upon me. 全部そろって出て来て私を攻撃した ▪ Carla figures *the whole kit and caboodle* was worth about $6,000. カーラは一切合切で約6千ドルの価値があると勘定している.

cache /kæʃ/ 名 ***make a cache*** [***caches***] ***of*** ...をしまっておく, 隠したくわえる《探険家が帰りに用いるため, など》 ▪ I *made a cache of* a barrel of pork. 豚肉1たるをしまっておいた ▪ Squirrels and other rodents *make caches of* food for winter use. リスや他の齧歯(げっし)類は冬に使うために食物をたくわえておく.

cackle /kǽkəl/ 名 ***cut the cackle*** **1**《口》前置きは早く切りあげて本論[要点]に入る; 簡にして要を得る ▪ The speaker *cut the cackle* and got straight down to his talk. 講演者は前置きを早く切りあげてすぐ話に入った.
2〚命令文で〛話をやめる, 黙る ▪ *Cut the cackle*! 黙れ!

cadge /kædʒ/ 名 ***on the cadge***（知人などから）物ごいをして ▪ I bet he is *on the cadge* for something. 彼はきっと何か物ごいをしているにちがいない.

Caesar /síːzər/ 名 ***appeal to Caesar*** 最高の権威に訴える;（特に）総選挙において国民に訴える（《聖》*Acts* 25. 11） ▪ This *appeal to Caesar* worked like magic. この総選挙による国民への訴えは魔術のような働きをした.

Caesar's wife should be above suspicion. カエサルの妻は疑いをかけられるようではいけない. ☞Caesar の妻 Pompeia と Clodius との間の噂が立ったとき, Caesar が妻を離婚して言った言葉から.

like Caesar's wife カエサルの妻のように《後ろ指をさされてはならない》 ▪ A man in your position must be *like Caesar's wife*. あなたのような地位にある人は少しでも疑いをかけられるようではいけません. ☞上の句から.

Render unto Caesar the things that are Caesar's. カエサルのものはカエサルに納めよ《世俗の事と神の事とを混同してはいけない; 世俗の義務は果たせよ》（《聖》*Matt*. 22. 21）.

cage[1] /keɪdʒ/ 名 ***rattle*** *a person's* ***cage***《口》（愚弄するために）人をわざと怒らせる, 人の神経を逆なでする, に揺さぶりをかける ▪ Lamb has *rattled everyone's cage* with his intrusive personality. ラムは出しゃばりな性格のためみんなの神経を逆なでした ▪ He tried to *rattle her cage* with questions about her divorced husband. 彼は彼女を怒らせせようとして離婚した夫のことを尋ねた.

cage[2] /keɪdʒ/ 動 (***be***) ***caged in*** [***up***] おりに入れられて（いる）, 自由を束縛されて（いる） ▪ Mothers of children feel *caged up* in those high-rise flats. 子供の母親はあの高層アパートでは自由を束縛されたように感じる.

cahoot(**s**) /kəhúːts/ 名 ***be in cahoots with***

→in CAHOOTS with.

go (in) cahoots (…と)共謀する, ぐるになる; (と)山分けする (*with*) ▪ Let's *go cahoots.* 山分けしよう ▪ I will *go in cahoots with* him. 彼と共同しよう ▪ You could *go in cahoots with* a mutual friend. 君は共通の友人といっしょにやってもよい.

in cahoots with …と共謀して[ぐるになって]いる (*over*) ▪ He must be *in cahoots with* that firm. 彼はあの会社と共謀しているにちがいない ▪ They are *in cahoots with* the police *over* speed cameras. 彼らはスピードカメラのことで警察と共謀している ▪ He is working *in cahoots with* a minor official in the insurance company. 彼は保険会社の下級職員と結託して働いている.

Cain /keɪn/ 名 ***by Cain*** 《米口》ほんとに ▪ I swear *by Cain* you shall never taste wine again. 君に二度と酒を飲ませないとほんとに誓う.

raise Cain 《口》大騒ぎを起こす《騒動・異議・飲み騒ぎで》 ▪ They have been *raising Cain* and breaking things. 彼らは大騒動を起こして物をぶちこわしていた ▪ Bob *raised Cain* with me because I had kept the news from him. ボブは私がそのニュースを知らせずにおいたので, 私にやかましく言った ▪ Let's *raise* a little *Cain.* 少し飲んで騒ごうじゃないか.

the brand [mark] of Cain カインの烙印《殺人者のしるし》, 自分の名声についた犯罪や非行のしみ, 不名誉のしるし ▪ You will bear *the mark of Cain* for the rest of your life for your cruelty to her. 彼女を虐待したために, お前は死ぬまでその烙印を背負っていくことになる.

the curse of Cain 永遠流浪ののろい (《聖》*Gen.* 4) ▪ Those people had *the curse of Cain* upon their heads. その人々は永遠流浪ののろいを受けていた.

what in Cain 《米口》〚what を強調して〛一体何…? ▪ He did not know *what in Cain* to do with it. 彼は一体それをどう処理してよいかわからなかった.

cairn /keərn/ 名 ***add a stone to*** *a person's* ***cairn*** 石塚に石を加える; 故人の名を顕彰する, 霊を祭る ▪ I will *add a stone to your cairn.* 君なき後は君の名を顕彰します.

cake[1] /keɪk/ 名 ***a cake walk [cakewalk]*** 容易なこと, 朝飯前 (*for*) ▪ The race was expected to be *a cakewalk for* Al. そのレースはアルには楽勝だと思われた.

a piece of cake 《口》やさしく愉快な(仕)事 ▪ Don't worry; this job is *a piece of cake.* 心配するな, この仕事はやさしく愉快なんだから.

One's ***cake is dough.*** 《口》…の計画は失敗した; は失望した, だめだ (cf. Sh., *Tam. Shr.* 5. 1. 145) ▪ She is sorry *his cake is dough.* 女は彼が不首尾だったのを残念に思っている ▪ *My cake is* definitely *dough,* and I'm going back. 私の計画ははっきり失敗したので私は帰る.

cakes and ale [《米》***cheese***] うまい食べ物と酒, いろいろ楽しいもの; 浮かれ騒ぎ; のんきな生活 (cf. Sh., *Twel. N.* 2. 3. 123) ▪ The gardener's life, as a rule, is not all *cakes and ale.* 庭師の生活は概して楽しいことばかりではない ▪ There will be no more *cakes and ale?* もうおいしい食物や酒は出ないだろう.

can't eat *one's* ***cake and have it (too)/ can't have [keep]*** *one's* ***cake and eat it (too)*** 菓子は食べたら無くなる; 両方いいことはない ▪ They should be told that they *can't eat their cake and have it.* 両方いいことはできないということを彼らに言ってやらねばならない.

go [sell] like hot cakes 《口》どんどん売れる ▪ The boxes of fruit *sold like hot cakes.* 箱うめの果物はどんどん売れた.

hurry up the [*one's*] ***cakes*** 《米口》ことを早める[急ぐ] ▪ Go ahead and *hurry up your cakes.* どんどんやって仕事を急いでくれ.

one's ***[a] slice [cut, share] of the cake*** 《口》好ましいものの分け前 ▪ The poor are beginning to want *their share of the cake.* 貧しい人々はその良い物の分け前を欲しがり始めている.

take the cake 《口》賞を得る, 第一等である, 他にぬきんでる《今はばかげたこと, ひどいことでとびぬけている場合に皮肉に用いる》 ▪ Frank's story *took the cake.* フランクの話が第一等だった ▪ Peter's idea that we might buy a plane and fly to America *takes the cake.* 飛行機を買ってアメリカへ飛んで行けばよいというピーターの考えは最もふるっている. ☞古代ギリシャにおいて, 夜番に最も勤勉な人に勝利の賞として cake が与えられたことから; 諸説がある.

the icing on the cake/《米》***the frosting on the cake*** 《口》 **1** (好ましい)飾りもの, さらに華を添えるもの, ▪ The tie is only *icing on the cake.* ネクタイは単なる飾りものにすぎない.

2 おまけ, 付加価値, 望外の喜び ▪ The MVP winner received $5,000 as *the icing on the cake.* MVP 受賞者は副賞として5千ドル授与された ▪ Lee's transfer to a French soccer club was *the icing on the cake.* イ選手がフランスのサッカークラブに移籍されるとは喜びもひとしおだ ▪ After that refreshing shower, the rainbow was just *frosting on the cake.* すがすがしい夕立のあと虹のおまけまでついた. ☞ケーキの見栄えをよくする練り粉砂糖の上塗りから.

cake[2] /keɪk/ 動 ***(be) caked in [with]*** …がすっかり固まりついて(いる), こびりついて(いる) ▪ He *was caked in* [*with*] mud. 彼には泥がすっかりこびりついていた.

calculate /kǽlkjəlèɪt/ 動 ***be calculated for*** …に適する; を主眼としている ▪ He *is calculated for* a lawyer. 彼は弁護士にちょうどよい ▪ Cruisers *are calculated for* speed. 巡洋艦は速力を主眼にして作られている ▪ The decoration *is calculated for* effect. その装飾は効果をねらって考案されている.

be calculated to *do* **1** …しそうである, する見込みがある ▪ Such people *are calculated to* succeed. そのような人々は成功するはずだ ▪ Such a project *is calculated to* end in failure. そんな計画は失敗に終わりそうである.

2 …するようにもくろまれている ▪ This advertisement

is calculated to attract a lot of attention. この広告は多くの注意をひくようにもくろまれている.

I calculate 《米》私は思う ▪ Your aunt has two houses, *I calculate*. あなたのおばさんは2軒家を持っているんだね.

C

calendar /kǽləndər/ 名 ***on the calendar*** 日程にのぼって ▪ What's *on the calendar* for today? 今日は何が日程にのっているか.

calends /kǽləndz/ 名 ***at*** [***on, till, to***] ***the Greek calends*** 決して…しない ▪ The money shall be paid *at the Greek calends*. 金は決して払わないよ ▪ His friends looked for it only *on the Greek calends*. 彼の友だちは決してそれを捜さなかった. ☞calends (ローマ古暦のついたち) はギリシャ暦にはなかったことから.

calf /kæf|kɑːf/ 名 ***eat the calf in the cow's belly*** 《口》あまりにも早くから当てにする; 皮算用をする ▪ He would never *eat the calf in the cow's belly*. 彼は決して皮算用はしないだろう.

in calf **1** 牛が子をはらんで ▪ Their mares were in foal, their cows *in calf*. 彼らの馬も牛も子をはらんでいた.

2 (本が)子牛皮とじの[で] ▪ This book is bound *in calf*. この本は子牛皮とじだ.

kill the fatted calf 最良のもので人をもてなす, 歓迎する (《聖》*Luke* 15. 23–27) ▪ Whenever Aunt Mary comes to see us we *kill the fatted calf*. メアリーおばさんがやって来るといつでも私たちは飛び切りのもてなしをする ▪ I suppose you were expecting *the fatted calf*. 君は飛び切りの歓迎を期待していたと思う.

No one knows the luck of a lousy calf. 《諺》見込みのなさそうな少年少女でもどんなに成功するかわからない.

slip the [***her***] ***calf*** (牛が)流産する ▪ The cow *slipped her calf* again. 牛がまた流産した.

the calves of our lips 賛辞(を呈すること)(《聖》*Hos*. 14. 2) ▪ We offer unto God *the calves of our lips*. 私たちは神に賛辞を呈する.

with calf =in CALF 1.

worship the golden calf 物質的利益に傾倒する; 黄金[金持ち]を崇拝する ▪ They fell away from God to *worship the golden calf*. 彼らは神にそむいて黄金を崇拝した. ☞the golden calf は Aaron が Sinai 山に建てた黄金の偶像; 《聖》*Exod*. 32. 2–8.

call[1] /kɔːl/ 名 ***a close call/a close*** [***near, narrow***] ***shave*** **1** 危機一髪 ▪ The president survived *a close call* from a sniper's bullet. 大統領は狙撃者の弾丸から危うく難を逃れた.

2 予測[判断]困難な状況, 難題, 難問 ▪ South Africa's interest rate decision next week is *a close call*. 南アフリカの来週の利率決定は予測困難だ.

a good [***bad***] ***call*** 正しい[間違った]判定・判断; よい[つまらない]考え, 名案[愚案] ▪ The umpire made *a good call*. アンパイアは正しい判定をした ▪ Leaving kids alone is *a bad call* for parents. 子供だけを残しておくのは親としては間違った考えだ ▪ I think it is *a good call* to give him a chance. 彼にチャンスを与えるのはよい考えだと思う.

a port of call 寄港地 ▪ The chief interest of Queenstown is as *a port of call*. クイーンズタウンの主な興味は寄港地としてである.

a wake-up call **1** (ホテルで客を起こす)モーニングコール ▪ Will you give me *a wake-up call* at seven? 7時にモーニングコールをお願いします.

2 (人の目を覚まさせる)警告; 危険[難関]を人に知らせる事件 ▪ The World Trade Center bombing served as *a wake-up call* to the FBI on terrorism. 世界貿易センターへの爆撃は FBI にテロへの警告になった.

answer [***obey***] ***a*** [***the***] ***call of nature*** 《口・婉曲》便所へ行く ▪ Excuse me, I must *answer a call of nature*. ごめんください. お手洗いに行かねばなりませんから.

answer the call **1** 電話に出る ▪ My wife *answered the call* and then handed me the receiver. 妻が電話に出てそれから受話器を私に渡した.

2 点呼に答える; 要請に応える ▪ The woman *answered the call* of her name in the police court. その女は警察裁判所で自分の名前が呼ばれると返事をした ▪ Woods has *answered the call* and done an extremely good job. ウッズは要請に応えて非常に優れた仕事をした.

3 《婉曲》死ぬ, 神に召される ▪ Louis Craft *answered the call* of Almighty God on Nov. 23, 2010, at his home in Boston. ルイス・クラフトは2010年11月23日ボストンの自宅で全能の神に召された.

answer [***obey***] ***the call of duty*** 義務の要請に答える ▪ The soldiers came to *answer the call of duty*. 兵たちは義務の要請に答えてやってきた.

at call **1** 要求[請求, 申し込み]次第(に); 命令次第; すぐ手に入れうる ▪ I have $10,000 on deposit *at call*. 私は1万ドルの通知預金がある ▪ The check should be paid *at call*. 小切手は要求次第払われねばならない ▪ You can't expect to get everything you want *at call*. 欲しいものを全てすぐ手にするわけにはいかない.

2 命令[合図]に応じて; 呼べばすぐ ▪ The dog was trained to come *at call*. その犬は呼べばすぐ来るよう訓練されていた.

at *one's* ***call*** …の呼ぶ声に応じて; の自由に使える ▪ The birds came *at my call*. 鳥は私の呼び声に応じて飛んで来た ▪ He has thousands of men *at his call*. 彼は何千という部下を従えている.

feel a call to …を使命と感じる ▪ He *felt a call to* the ministry. 彼は牧師職になる使命を感じた.

feel the call of …に引きつけられる, の魅力を感じる ▪ Many Englishmen *feel the call of* the sea. イギリス人は海に引きつけられる者が多い.

give *a person* ***a call*** 人に電話をかける ▪ Just *give* him *a call*. ちょっと彼に電話しなさい.

have first call on …を最初に使う権利がある, を最初に受けることができる ▪ The owner still *has first call on* the use of the plane. 所有者にはまだ

飛行機を最初に使う権利がある.

have many calls on …を取られることが多い ▪ He *has many calls on* his money. 彼はいろいろ出費が多い ▪ I *have* too *many calls on* my time. 私は時間を取られることが多すぎる.

have* [*there is*] *no call to *do* [***for*** (*doing*)] 《口》…はお呼びでない, する必要はない; (他人の批判などに立腹して)無用[大きなお世話]だ ▪ You *have no call to* interfere. 君が干渉するなんてもってのほかだ ▪ *There is no call for* undue anxiety. 過度に心配する必要はない ▪ *There was no call for slapping* Mark. マークを平手打ちする必要はなかった.

have the call **1** 最も需要が多い ▪ Wheat *has the call.* 小麦の需要が最も多い ▪ Heifers *had the call* of the market. 若い雌牛が最も市場での需要が多かった.

2 気に入りである, 人気がある ▪ Youth *has the call.* 青年は人気がある.

make a call (***on***) (…を)訪問する ▪ She has *made a* morning *call on* Biggs. 彼女は朝ビッグズを訪問した.

make a call on *a person's* ***time*** [***money,*** etc.] 人の時間[金, など]を要する ▪ Keeping order *makes* the greatest *call on his energies.* 秩序を維持するのに彼の精力が最も多くいる.

obey a [***the***] ***call of nature*** → answer a CALL of nature.

obey the call of duty →answer the CALL of duty.

on [***upon***] ***call*** 請求次第, (医者などが)待機して ▪ *On call*, the interest on your money will be 7 percent. 当座では預金利息は7%である ▪ cotton bought *on call* 代金請求次第支払いで買った棉花 ▪ Do you know which doctor is *on call* tonight? きょうどの医者が待機してるか知ってるかい?

pay a call 訪ねる (=make a CALL (on)); 《口・婉曲》便所へ行く ▪ Clark *paid* me *a call* the other day to show me a booklet. 先日クラークが私を訪ねてきて冊子を見せてくれた ▪ He got up and *paid a call.* 彼は起きて便所に行った.

place a call to (人・所)に電話をかける ▪ Please *place a call to* Mr. Smith. どうぞスミスさんに電話をかけてください.

the call of the wild 荒野[手つかずの自然]の魅力; 野生の呼び声 ▪ We felt *the call of the wild.* 我々は荒野の魅力を感じた. ☞Jack London の同名の小説(1903)から.

within call **1** 呼べば聞こえる所に, 近くに ▪ All the beauties *within call* of the town will be present. 町の近くのすべての美人たちが出席するだろう.

2 (人の)権威に服して ▪ They are *within call* of the governor. 彼らは知事の指令下に属している.

call[2] /kɔːl/ 動 ***answer*** *one's* ***calling*** 天職を得る, 天職につく ▪ Mother Teresa *answered her calling* by laboring among the most downtrodden in Calcutta. マザー・テレサはカルカッタの最も虐げられた人々の中で働くことによって天職を実現した.

be called before …に召喚される ▪ The former White House press aide *was called before* the grand jury. ホワイトハウスの前報道補佐官は大陪審に召喚された.

(***be***) ***called on to*** *do* …せねばならない, する必要がある ▪ I felt *called on to* express my opinion on the matter. 私はその件について意見を述べねばならないと思った ▪ No one *is called on to* make such sacrifices. 誰もそんな犠牲を払う必要はない.

(***be***) ***too close to call*** (勝負の)先が読めない, 予測[判定]しがたい, 接戦である (→a close CALL 2) ▪ Tuesday's presidential election will *be too close to call.* 火曜日の大統領選は接戦になるだろう.

call for trumps 《トランプ》相手に切札を出させるよう仕向ける ▪ When you played the king, you *called for trumps.* 君がキングを出したのは, 相手に切札を出させる手だった.

call in sick 《米》(勤務先へ)病欠の電話をする ▪ She *called in sick* to the office this morning. 彼女は今朝事務所へ病欠の電話をした.

call into [***in***] ***question/call in doubt*** …に疑いをはさむ, 疑念をいだく, 異議を唱える ▪ The opposition leader *called into question* the prime minister's diplomatic skills. 野党党首は首相の外交手腕を疑問視した.

call it… 《口》値段を…とする ▪ Shall we *call it* five dollars? 値段は5ドルにしようか.

call on [***upon***] *a person* ***for*** [***to*** *do*] 人に…を頼む[することを求める] ▪ We *called upon* him *for* a speech. 彼に演説をしてくれと頼んだ ▪ The chairman *called on* Mr. Bud *to* make a few remarks. 議長はバッド氏に何かひと言言ってくれと言った.

call *a thing one's* ***own*** 物を自分のものだと言う, 所有する ▪ He doesn't have one good suit of clothes to *call his own.* 彼は自分のものといってよい服1枚すら持っていない ▪ I had hardly a moment I could *call my own.* 自分の時間としてはほとんど一刻もなかった.

call the crack 談話を切らさぬようにする ▪ He *called the crack.* 彼は談話をとだえぬようにした.

call the turn **1** (…において)支配する, 左右する, 勝つ (*in, on*) ▪ The army has always *called the turn in* politics there. そこでは陸軍が常に政治を左右してきた ▪ He *called the turn on* the last election. 彼は前の選挙で勝った.

2 (値段などが)最高になる ▪ The price of the stock actually *called the turn.* その株価は実際に最高値を呼んだ.

call things by their names (ごまかさないで)はっきり言う (→call a SPADE a spade).

call… to mind [***memory, remembrance***] …を思い出す ▪ Now you mention it, I *call* the fact *to mind* [*remembrance*]. あなたがそれを言ったので, 私はその事実を思い出した.

call *one's* ***way*** 道を進んで行く ▪ *Call your way*, the door is wide open. あなたの道を進んで行きなさい. ドアは広く開かれています.

Don't call us, we'll call you. 《口・戯》電話をくれなくてもいいよ. こちらからかけるから《相手が提供するもの[事]に興味がないときのせりふ》 ▪ *Don't call us,* John, *we will call you.* ジョン, 電話はくれなくていい. こちらからかけるから.

C

feel [***be***] ***called*** …しなければならないと思う, を天職と思う (*to do*) ▪ I *feel called to* the priesthood. 私は牧師になるのが天命だと思う.

Is that what you call it? それが…と言うのですか ▪ What do you think of his limousine?—Oh, *is that what you call it?* 彼のリムジンをどう思うかい? —えっ, あんなのがリムジンなの?

(***now***) ***that's what I call...*** これこそまさしく…だ ▪ *Now that's what I call* happiness! これこそ本物の幸せだ.

what *one* ***calls***/ ***what is called*** いわゆる ▪ She is *what* you *call* a "pinup girl." 彼女はいわゆる「美人写真むきの少女」である.

calm[1] /kɑːm/ 名 ***It falls calm*** [(***a***) ***dead calm, flat calm***]. べたなぎとなる ▪ In a few minutes *it fell dead calm.* 数分たつとべたなぎになった.

the calm before the storm あらしの前の静けさ ▪ His body stilled like *the calm before the storm.* 彼の身体はあらしの前の静けさのように小康状態になった.

calm[2] /kɑːm/ 動 ***calm*** *oneself* 心を落ち着ける ▪ Soon I *calmed myself.* やがて私は心を落ち着けた.

calumet /kǽljumèt/ 名 ***smoke the calumet of peace*** (***with***) (…と)和睦する ▪ The French desired to *smoke the calumet of peace.* フランス軍は和睦することを願った. ☞calumet (北米先住民の長い飾りぎせる)は平和の印として儀式に用いる.

camel /kǽməl/ 名 ***strain at a gnat and swallow a camel*** →STRAIN[2].

the last straw [***something***] ***that breaks the camel's back*** いよいよ耐えきれないで破滅に至らす最後の因 ▪ Now her husband's accident may prove to be *the last straw that breaks the camel's back.* 夫のこんどの事故はとうとう彼女を耐えきれず破滅させる一押しとなるかもしれない ▪ I don't know what he finally did; it was *something that broke the camel's back.* 彼が最後に何をしたのか知らないが, それが彼をいよいよ耐えきれないで破滅させた. ☞《諺》It is the last straw that breaks the camel's back.「最後に1本のワラが加わっただけでも, ラクダの首が折れてしまう」から.

cameo /kǽmiòʊ/ 名 ***a cameo role*** [***part***] 《映画》(名場面での)顔見せ役, カメオ出演《有名俳優が1場面にだけ登場して演じる脇役》 ▪ Casting a big-name actor in *a cameo role* has a hit rate of about one in a hundred. 大物俳優を名場面での顔見せ役に配してもヒットする確率は100に一つぐらいだ.

camera /kǽmərə/ 名 ***in camera*** 《法》(公開でなく)判事の私室で; 秘密に ▪ The details of the trial were heard *in camera.* その公判の詳細は非公開で尋問された.

off camera カメラに映らないところで ▪ This sort of thing is happening *off camera* all over America. この種のことは映像になっていないがアメリカ中で起きている.

on camera なまのテレビカメラの前で ▪ You must be *on camera* from seven to ten. 君は7時から10時まではなまのテレビカメラの前にいなくてはならない.

camp[1] /kæmp/ 名 ***break camp*** 野営を撤する ▪ We *broke camp* and moved on. 我々は野営を撤収して進んで行った.

make [***strike***] ***camp*** 《米》キャンプする, 野営する ▪ You've *made camp* late. 君たちは遅くキャンプしたんだね ▪ We *struck camp* in a grove. 我々は小さな森に野営した.

pitch a camp テントを張る, 野宿する ▪ There they *pitched a camp* and rested. そこで彼らはテントを張って休憩した.

strike [***break up***] (***a***) ***camp*** テントをたたむ, 撤営する ▪ We were to *strike camp* at sunrise. 日の出ころに撤営することになっていた.

take ... into camp 《米口》…をわがものにする; を負かす, だます ▪ The school *took* another contender *into camp.* その学校はもう一人の競争者を負かした ▪ The porker *was taken into camp* by Smith. その食用ブタはスミスの所有となった ▪ He *took into camp* everybody he met. 彼は出くわす人すべてをだました.

camp[2] /kæmp/ 動 ***camp it up*** 《口》(おおげさに, わざとらしく)演技する; (同性愛の男が)女っぽいしぐさをする ▪ Will Young *camped it up* for a comedy role in the West End last night. ウィル・ヤングは昨晩ウェストエンド劇場で喜劇の役を熱演した ▪ Gay men often "*camp it up*" by referring to themselves as "she", "girl", "woman", "Miss", etc. 同性愛の男性は自分のことを「彼女」,「少女」,「女」,「婦人」等々と呼んでよく女性っぽいしぐさをする.

camp on the trail [***heel***] ***of*** 《米》…にしつこくついて行く ▪ I asked him to *camp on the trails of* all kinds of beasts. 彼にあらゆる種類の家畜のあとについて行くよう頼んだ.

go camping キャンプに行く ▪ The boys have decided to *go camping* next summer. 少年たちは今度の夏キャンプに行くことに決めた.

campaign /kæmpéɪn/ 名 ***a whispering campaign*** 中傷キャンペーン ▪ John Dowd has been accused of conducting *a whispering campaign* against Ms Smith. ジョン・ダウドはスミス女史に中傷キャンペーンを行ったとして告発されている.

can[1] /kæn/ 名 ***a can of worms*** 《口》 **1** 厄介な問題[状況], 難問, 難局 (→PANDORA's box) ▪ This issue is really *a can of worms.* この件は本当に難問だ.

2 落ち着きのない人 ▪ Red Smith described Daley as restless as *a can of worms.* レッド・スミスはデイリーのことをそわそわと落ち着きがないと評した.

carry the can →take the CAN.

get a can on 《米俗》酔っ払う ▪ She used to *get a can on.* 彼女は酔っ払うのが常だった.

hand** a person **the can 《米俗》人を解雇する ▪ Yesterday the manager *handed* me *the can.* きのう支配人は私を首にした.

in the can **1** (使えるばかりに)用意ができて; (仕事などが)完了して; (契約などが)締結されて, 決定して ▪ I have a plan halfway *in the can.* 半分用意ができている案がある ▪ The new contract was *in the can.* 新契約が妥結した.

2 (フィルムが)編集[撮影]が終って ▪ The picture is *in the can.* その映画は封切りするばかりになっている ▪ The film will be *in the can* by the end of this month. その映画は月末までには撮影を終えているだろう.

not add up to a can of beans (計画などが)あまり価値がない, 目新しくない ▪ For the most part, these cars really do *not add up to a can of beans.* これらの車にはほとんど全く目新しさがない.

open* (*up*) *a can of worms 厄介な問題を表に出す, 面倒なことになる ▪ An attack on Iraq would be like *opening a can of worms.* イラク攻撃は(虫入りの缶をあけるような)厄介な問題だろう ▪ The High Court has *opened a can of worms* with this case. 最高裁は解決困難な本件を取り上げた ▪ Telling your neighbors can *open up a can of worms.* 隣人に話すと面倒なことになるかもしれないよ.

rush the can 《米俗》バー・サロンで盛んに飲む ▪ Five hundred customers a day come to *rush the can.* 1日に500人のお客がどんどん飲みに来る.

take* [*carry*] *the can 《俗》責任のないことに対して[他人の代わりに]責めを負う ▪ I am not going to *take the can* for that. 私はそのことに対して自分が責めを負うつもりはない ▪ I had to *carry the can* for my brother. 私は弟の代わりに責任を負わねばならなかった. ☞陸軍語より; 缶は中身をあけたら返す責任があることから.

can[2] /kæn/ 動 ***Can it!*** 黙れ ▪ Sit down and shut up. *Can it*, will you? 座ってだまるんだ. 口をつぐまないか.

can the racket 《米》静かにする ▪ *Can the racket*, boys! 少年たち, 静かにせよ! ☞「騒ぎを缶うめにせよ」が原義.

can[3] /kən, kæn/ 助 ***can but*** *do* ただ…するだけ ▪ We *can but* die in that case. そのときはただ死ぬだけだ.

cannot away with …をがまんできない ▪ We *cannot away with* her attitude. 我々は彼女の態度にがまんできない.

cannot but *do* →BUT[1].

cannot *do* [***be***] ***otherwise than*** …せずにはいられない ▪ We *cannot be otherwise than* touched by these expressions of thanks. 我々はこれらの感謝の言葉に感動せずにはいられない.

cannot seem to *do* →SEEM.

cannot ... too いくら…してもすぎることはない ▪ You *cannot* be *too* careful. あなたはいくら注意してもしすぎることはない ▪ We *cannot* read *too* many books. 本はいくらたくさん読んでもけっこうだ.

cannot *do A* ***without*** *doing B* **1** AすればきっとB する ▪ I *cannot* hear such a story *without weeping.* 私はそのような話を聞くと必ず泣ける.

2 BせずにはAはできない ▪ You *cannot* succeed *without persevering.* がんばらなければ成功しない.

can't be doing with …はお断りだ ▪ I *can't be doing with* that noise again. あんな騒音はもう二度とごめんだ.

can't very well *do* …するわけにはいかない ▪ I *can't very well* give you this picture. 君にこの絵をあげるわけにはいかない.

How can /kæn/ ***you?*** 君はまあひどい!

(*That*) *can't be.* まさか《驚き・不信を表す》.

canary /kənéəri/ 名 ***sing like a canary*** (…に)通報する, 仲間を売る, 内部告発する (*to, about*) ▪ Frank Blag *sang like a canary to* the authorities *about* the activities of his colleagues. フランク・ブラグは同僚の行動について当局に通報した.

cancer /kǽnsər/ 名 ***a cancer stick*** 《俗》タバコ ▪ Your *cancer sticks* will kill you and the smoke from them may kill others too. あなたのタバコはあなたを殺すだろうし, その煙は他人をも殺しかねない.

the cancer at the heart of …の病巣[がん], の奥深くにある諸悪の根源 ▪ *The cancer at the heart of* the Army goes much deeper. 軍隊の病巣はもっと深くまで進んでいる ▪ Large-scale surgery is vital to remove *the cancer at the heart of* Japan's economic system. 日本の経済制度の奥底にあるがんを取り除くには大がかりな手術が必要だ.

candidate /kǽndədèɪt/ 名 ***a candidate for a pair of wings*** 《戯・婉曲》死にかけている[死にそうな]人 ▪ My uncle looks like *a candidate for a pair of wings.* おじさんはもうすぐお迎えがくるみたいな容態だ.

a squeaky-clean candidate 清廉潔白な候補者 ▪ Americans will want *a squeaky-clean candidate* whose personal life is free from scandal. アメリカ人は, 私生活においてスキャンダルとは無縁な清廉潔白な候補者を望むだろう.

stand candidate for …に立候補する ▪ Mr. Ellison *stands candidate for* Fellow. エリスン氏は評議員に立候補している.

candle /kǽndəl/ 名 ***a lighted candle*** 宴会(の象徴) ▪ He went to every *lighted candle.* 彼はあらゆる宴会に出向いた.

be not fit to hold a candle to/ cannot hold* [*show*] *a candle to …とは比較にならない(ほど劣る); の足もとにも及ばない; に助力する力もない ▪ John isn't stupid, but he *isn't fit to hold a candle to* his brother. ジョンも愚鈍ではないが, 兄にはとてもかなわない ▪ As regards intelligence, Helen *can't hold a candle to* her sister. 聡明さにかけてはヘレンは妹の足もとにも及ばない. ☞劇場などでろうそくや明かりを持つ役の少年にちなんで.

(*be*) *not worth the candle* (仕事などが)割りに合わない; 精力[経費]を使うだけの値うちがない ▪ The game would *not be worth the candle.* その仕事は労力をかけるだけの値うちはないだろう ▪ These discoveries *are not worth the candle.* これらの発見は骨折り損のくたびれもうけだ. ☞トランプから.

burn the candle at both ends →BURN².

cannot hold* [*show*] *a candle to →be not fit to hold a CANDLE to.

hold a candle to …のために灯をかかげる; に助力する ▪ Let Plato *hold the candle to* Moses. プラトンはモーゼに助力すべきである.

hold* [*set*] *a candle to the devil 《口》(利得のため)悪事に加担する, 悪い事と知りながらする; 恐ろしくてきげんをとる ▪ As I wanted the commission, I had to *hold a candle to the devil.* 手数料がほしかったので, 悪いことと知りつつしなければならなかった ▪ I have been *holding a candle to the devil*, to show him the way to mischief. 悪いことと知りながら, 彼を災いへの道に案内した ▪ Why do you invite him to your house? It looks like *holding a candle to the devil.* なぜ彼を君の家へ招待するのか. まるで彼が恐ろしいのできげんをとるみたいだな. ☞昔老婆が St. Michael と St. Michael が踏みつけている Devil とにそれぞれ1本のろうそくを献じ, 死後天国へ行っても地獄へ行っても厚遇されようとしたという話から.

sell* [*let*] *by the candle*/*sell* [*let*] *by inch of candle ろうそく競売で売る ▪ Four acres *were let by inch of candle.* 4エーカーの土地がろうそく競売で売られた ▪ All such goods will *be sold by the candle.* そのような品はみなろうそく競売で売られるでしょう. ☞ろうそくの先から1インチの所へピンを突っ込み, ろうそくが燃えてピンが燭台へ落ちるとき最後に値をつけた人が買い手となる; フランス起源.

snuff the candle (射撃のテストとして)ろうそくの芯を弾丸で切る ▪ One of the stunts was to *snuff a candle* without putting it out. 曲芸の一つにろうそくを消さないでその芯を弾丸で切るというのがあった.

candy /kǽndi/ 名 ***(an) eye* [*(a) mind*] *candy*** 《米俗》 **1** (特に性的に)非常に魅力的な人 ▪ The girl is *an eye candy*, and she will surely attract attention. その少女はかなり魅力的だから, きっと注意を引くだろう.

2 目の保養になるもの, 見て楽しい[おもしろい]もの ▪ The computer graphics added lots of *eye candy* to that movie. CG によりその映画は見て実に楽しくなった.

like* [*as easy as*] *taking candy from a baby 《米口》造作なく[ない], 赤子の手をひねるように簡単に[な] ▪ To a thief, shoplifting may be *like taking candy from a baby.* 盗人にとって, 万引きはお茶の子さいさいかもしれない ▪ This stuff is so easy, it *is like taking candy from a baby.* この問題はいとも簡単で赤んぼうの手をひねるようなものだ.

cane¹ /keɪn/ 名 ***get the cane*** (子供が)むちで罰せられる ▪ Tom *got the cane* for telling a lie. トムは嘘をついてむちで罰せられた.

cane² /keɪn/ 動 ***cane* (*a lesson*) *into a person*** 人に(学課を)たたきこむ ▪ He *caned* mathematics *into* the boy. 彼は数学をその少年に教えこんだ.

cannon /kǽnən/ 名 ***a loose cannon* (*on the deck*)** 何をしでかすかわからない人, 要注意人物 ▪ Reid calls her *a "loose cannon"* because he never knows what she is going to do next. 彼女が次に何をしようとしているか全くわからないので, レイドは彼女のことを要注意人物と言う. ☞軍艦に取りつけられた大砲が固定されていないと, ぐるぐる回って制御が利かなくなることから.

canoe¹ /kənúː/ 名 ***paddle* one's *own canoe*** 《口》独立する; 独立に行動する; 自己の努力で成功する ▪ He had to learn to *paddle his own canoe.* 彼は独立することを覚えなければならなかった ▪ He was able to *paddle his own canoe* all by himself. 彼は全く一人の努力で成功することができた.

canoe² /kənúː/ 動 ***canoe it*** 《口》カヌーで旅する ▪ Let's take a vacation trip and *canoe it* to Lake George. 休暇旅行でジョージ湖までカヌーで行こう.

canopy /kǽnəpi/ 名 ***under the* [*God's*] *canopy*** 《米》 **1** 一体全体 (on earth) ▪ Where *under the canopy* did you come from? 君は一体どこから来たのか.

2 天の下の, 地上の ▪ No one *under God's canopy* would make any such decision. 天の下の誰一人もそんな決心をする者はない.

cant /kænt/ 名 ***be full of cant phrases*** あわれっぽい声で宗教的な句を引用する ▪ I cannot put up with him—he *is* so *full of cant phrases.* あの男にはがまんができない, あわれっぽい声で宗教的な句を引用するんだ.

canter /kǽntər/ 名 ***a preliminary canter*** 下書き, 予行 ▪ It's just the *preliminary canter*; it's an outline sketch. それは下書きにすぎません. 概略の草稿です.

win* (*a race*) *in* [*at*] *a canter (競馬の馬が)楽勝する ▪ I *won* that essay competition *in a canter.* あのエッセイ・コンテストでは楽々優勝した ▪ Hermitage *won at a canter.* エルミタージュ号は楽勝した.

cantrip /kǽntrəp/ 名 ***play* a person *a cantrip*** 人にいたずらをする ▪ Some Scottish devil put it into my head to *play* her *a cantrip.* あるスコットランドの悪魔が彼女にいたずらをしてやろうという気を私に起こさせた.

canvas /kǽnvəs/ 名 ***get the canvas on*** (船)に帆を張る ▪ We *got the canvas on* her. 我々はその船に帆を張った.

under canvas **1** テントを張って, 野営して ▪ The troops are living *under canvas* at present. 今軍隊は野営中だ.

2 帆を張って ▪ The ship was making its way *under* full *canvas.* 船は満帆をあげて航行していた ▪ The ship was *under* light *canvas.* 船は補助帆を張っていた.

win by a canvas (ボートレースで)少差で勝つ ▪ We *won by a canvas* in the race. そのボートレースで我々は少差で勝った.

cap[1] /kæp/ 名 ***a feather in*** *one's* ***cap*** → FEATHER[1].

assume [***don***] ***the black cap*** 死刑の宣告をする ▪ The judge *assumed the black cap*. 裁判官は死刑の宣告をした. ☞英国の判事は死刑の宣告をするときは, かつらに黒い四角の絹布をつける.

cap and feather days 幼年時代 ▪ I was got into the scenes of my *cap and feather days*. 私は幼年時代の舞台に入った.

cap in hand 脱帽して, かしこまって ▪ I'm not going to William, *cap in hand*, to ask for work. 私はウィリアムの所へ, かしこまって職を頼みに行くつもりはない.

fit the cap on 当てつけを自分のことと思う[思い当たる] ▪ I am glad the prisoners *fitted the cap on*. 囚人たちが思い当たるところがあってうれしい.

fling *one's* ***cap over the windmill*** →throw one's CAP over the windmill.

gain the cap 尊敬されて敬礼される ▪ Someone like that *gains his cap*. そのような人は彼に尊敬されて敬礼される.

get [***gain, win***] *one's* ***cap*** 代表選手になる ▪ He *gained his* county *cap*. 彼は州の代表選手になった.

If the cap fits, wear it. その非難[言葉]に思い当たるところがあれば自分のことと思いなさい ▪ I didn't say you were the one that started the scandal, but *if the cap fits, wear it*. 私はあなたがその醜聞を広めた元だとは言わなかったが, もしその言葉に思い当たるところがあれば自分のことと思いなさい.

kiss caps with …と同じわんで酒を飲む ▪ I wouldn't *kiss caps with* such a fellow. そんなやつとは酒を飲みたくない ☞cap＝Scotch cop (昔酒杯に用いた木製茶わん).

mount the cap and bells →wear the CAP and bells.

pop a cap 《米》射撃する ▪ Lie down. He is going to *pop a cap*. 伏せろ, 彼が発砲しようとしている.

pull caps けんかする, やかましく乱暴に争う ▪ The seven cities *pulled caps* with each other. その7都市は互いにけんかした.

put [***get***] ***on*** *one's* ***thinking*** [***considering, conjuring***] ***cap*** 《口》とくと考える, 思案する ▪ I will *put on my thinking cap* and let you know my opinion tomorrow. とくと考えてあす意見をお知らせします.

ready as a borrower's cap 即座で[に] ▪ The answer is *ready as a borrower's cap*. 返答は即座だ.

send round the cap 帽子を回して寄付金を集める ▪ We're *sending round the cap* on their behalf. 私たちは彼らのために寄付金を集めています.

throw [***fling***] *one's* ***cap over the windmill*** (特に女性が)無鉄砲なことをする, 習俗をかなぐり捨てる ▪ Since he jilted her, she has *thrown her cap over the windmill*. 彼が捨ててからは, 彼女は習俗を無視して無鉄砲になった. ☞cap は女性の礼節の象徴であることから.

throw up *one's* ***cap*** 喜んで帽子を投げあげる ▪ At the mention of a half holiday, the boys *threw up their caps* and cheered. 半休日にすると言ったら, 少年たちは大喜びで帽子を投げあげ歓声をあげた.

touch *one's* ***cap to*** …にただ軽く敬意を表する ▪ They are just *touching their caps to* tradition. 彼らはただ伝統に軽く敬意を表しているだけだ.

wear [***mount***] ***the cap and bells*** 道化師の鈴つき帽子をかぶる, 道化師である; ばかなまねをする, 笑い者になる ▪ One is bound to speak the truth, whether one *wears the cap and bells*, or a shovel hat. 人は道化師であろうが, 僧正であろうが, 真実を言わねばならない.

Where is your cap? 坊や, おじぎはどうしたの.

win *one's* ***cap*** →get one's CAP.

cap[2] /kæp/ 動 ***be capped for*** …の代表選手となる ▪ He *was capped for* England. 彼はイングランド代表選手になった. ☞England, Scotland, Ireland, Wales 代表の選手は各国の章のついた帽子をかぶったことから.

cap everything →CAP the globe.

cap the climax 上の上を行く ▪ The story was funny enough, but Bill's tale *capped the climax*. その話もけっこうおもしろかったが, ビルの話はその上を行った.

cap the globe [***the lot, everything***] 《口》すべてに勝る ▪ Well, that really *caps the globe*. しかし, ほんとに, それにはかなわない ▪ That *caps the lot*! 全くすばらしい話だな.

cap the [*one's*] ***hock*** (馬が)飛節の先を傷つけてはれあがらす ▪ The horse *capped his* own *hocks*. その馬は自分の飛節を傷つけた.

cap verses 詩句のしりとりをする, しりとりなどの詩句で答える ▪ They had amused themselves by *capping* Greek *verses*. 彼らはギリシャの詩句のしりとりをして興じた ▪ The Mayor *capped* many of the Councilor's *verses*. 市長はその市会議員の多くの詩のしりとりで答えた.

to cap it all すべてにまさって; 最後に; あげくのはてに ▪ *To cap it all*, we had a downpour. かてて加えてどしゃ降りだった.

capable /kéɪpəbəl/ 形 ***be capable of*** **1** …できる(能力・手腕・資格) ▪ He *is capable of* teaching English. 彼は英語を教える資格がある ▪ This room *is capable of* seating a hundred. この部屋は100人収容できる.

2 …を受けうる, …されうる ▪ Some animals *are capable of* instruction. 動物のなかには教育を施せるものもいる ▪ The situation *is capable of* improvement. 事態は改善することができる.

3 …しかねない ▪ He *is capable of* murder [neglecting his duty]. 彼は人を殺し[職務を怠り]かねない.

capacity /kəpǽsəti/ 名 ***at capacity*** 全生産能力で ▪ The factory is running *at* full *capacity*.

工場は全能力をあげて操業している.

beyond capacity 収容能力以上に, 超満員で ▪ The hall was crowded [filled] *beyond capacity.* 会場は超満員であった.

***in** one's **capacity** (**as**)* (...としての)資格で ▪ *In my capacity as* an officer of the law, I must do my duty and punish you. 法官としての資格で, 私は義務をつくし君を罰しなければならない ▪ I say this *in my* official *capacity.* これは役人の資格で言うのです.

in the capacity of ...の資格で ▪ He traveled *in the capacity of* tutor. 彼は家庭教師の資格で旅行した.

to capacity 満員で, 収容能力いっぱいで ▪ The hall was filled *to capacity.* 会場は満員であった.

to** one's **utmost capacity 収容能力の極限まで; 最大限の能力まで ▪ The house was crowded *to its utmost capacity.* 会場は大入り満員だった ▪ He was taxed *to his utmost capacity.* 彼は支払能力の極限まで課税された.

caper /kéɪpər/ 名 ***cut a caper*** [***capers***] ダンスで飛び上がって素早く足を交差する; 軽快におどり回る, はね回る; 浮かれ騒ぐ; ばかないたずらをする, 気まぐれな行動をする ▪ He can dance, though he does not *cut capers.* 彼は飛び上がって素早く足を交錯させるようなことはしないが, ダンスはできる ▪ He *cut a caper* for joy. 彼は小踊りして喜んだ ▪ The children are *cutting capers* in the nursery. 子供らは子供部屋でばか騒ぎしている. ☞ It caper 'shegoat'.

capital /kǽpətəl/ 名形 ***make capital out of*** ...を利用する, に乗じる ▪ If you choose to *make capital out of* this accident, there is obviously nothing I can do about it. この事件を利用しようとするなら, 私は当然どうしようもありません.

on capital 資本に対して ▪ We will pay five percent interest *on capital.* 私どもは元金に対して5パーセントの利子をお払いします.

with a capital A [***B, C,*** etc.] 《口》 **1** 大いに, 大いなる《A [B, C, etc.] は前の名詞の頭文字》 ▪ They have faith, *with a capital F.* 彼らは大いなる信仰を持っている.

2 最狭義の, 正真正銘の ▪ He only loves Art *with a capital A.* 彼は最も狭い意味で芸術が好きなだけだ.

capot /kəpɑ́t/ 動 ***Capot me!*** ちぇっ!, ちくしょう! ▪ *Capot me,* but those lads are pretty fellows. いまいましい! その若者たちは困ったものだ.

cap-out /kǽpàʊt/ 副 ***drink cap-out*** 酒杯をすっかり飲み干す ▪ *Drink* clean *cap-out.* きれいに飲み干せ.

cap-sheaf /kǽpʃìːf/ 名 ***put the cap-sheaf on*** 《米》(...を)極致[絶頂]に達せしめる ▪ That *put the cap-sheaf on* for Bill. ビルにとってはそれが最高潮となった ▪ The commissioner came this way and *put the cap-sheaf on* Michael's worldly fortune. 長官がこちらへ来て, マイケルの世俗的幸運は絶頂に達した.

captain /kǽptən|-tɪn/ 名 ***come Captain Stiff over** a person* 《俗》人に対して高慢である ▪ I shouldn't *come Captain Stiff over* him. 私は彼に対して高慢であってはいけない.

the captain of** one's **soul 自分の魂の長(おさ)(W. H. Henley, *Invictus* 4) ▪ He is *the captain of his* unconquerable *soul.* 彼は自分の不屈の魂の長である.

captive /kǽptɪv/ 形 ***lead*** [***take, hold***] *a person* ***captive*** 人を捕虜にして連れて行く[にする, にしておく] ▪ They *led* us *captive* to London. 彼らは我々をとりこにしてロンドンへ連れて行った ▪ He *was taken captive* at the first engagement. 彼は最初の交戦で捕虜になった.

captivity /kæptívəti/ 名 ***in captivity*** とりこになって ▪ Some birds do not sing *in captivity.* とりこになると歌わない鳥もいる.

lead captivity captive **1** (凱旋(がいせん)して)捕虜を連れ去る(《聖》*Judges* 5. 12) ▪ Arise, Barak, and *lead* thy *captivity captive.* 立ち上がれ, バラクよ, 敵をとりこにせよ.

2 他人を奴隷としていた者たちを捕虜にする(《聖》*Ephes.* 4. 8) ▪ When he ascended on high, he *led captivity captive* and gave gifts to men. 高い所に登るとき, 囚われ人を連れて行き, 人々に賜物を分け与えられた.

car[1] /kɑːr/ 名 ***by car/in a car*** 自動車で ▪ He went to Washington *by car.* 彼は自動車でワシントンへ行った.

hot-wire a car (キーを使わないで点火装置をショートさせて)車のエンジンをかける ▪ Thieves have outmaneuvered encryption chips by *hot-wiring cars,* or bypassing the key-ignition system. 泥棒たちは点火装置をショートさせてエンジンをかけることで, つまりキーで点火する方式をとらないで, 暗号チップの裏をかいた.

take the cars 《米》鉄道旅行に出る ▪ We then *took the cars* for Boston. それから私たちはボストンへ鉄道旅行をした.

car[2] /kɑːr/ 動 ***car it*** 《口》自動車で行く ▪ The ladies prepared to *car it* to Killarney. 婦人たちはキラーニーまで自動車で行く用意をした.

carcass /kɑ́ːrkəs/ 名 ***save** one's **carcass*** 身を全うする ▪ He lied to *save his carcass.* 彼は命惜しさに嘘をついた.

card /kɑːrd/ 名 ***a house of cards*** (カルタで組み立てた家のように)もろい仕組み; 不安定[不確実]な地位[計画] ▪ I'm afraid you've been building *a house of cards.* 君は頼りない計画を立てていたのではないかと思う ▪ It'll come down like *a house of cards.* それはカルタで作った家のようにくずれるだろう.

a knowing card すみにおけない人, 時流に明るい人 ▪ He is *a knowing card;* no one can bluff him easily. 彼はなかなかすみにおけない人物だ. 誰も彼を簡単にごまかすことはできない.

be a sure card 信頼しうる[成功する]物[人]だ; 確かな手だ ▪ That will *be a sure card* to fetch her. そうすればきっと彼女は出てくる.

be at cards トランプをしている ▪ They *are at cards* now. 彼らは今トランプをしている.

be on* [《米》 *in*] *the cards →on the CARDs, in the CARDs.

be one card* [*several cards*] *short of a full deck 《戯》少し足りない[抜けている] ▪ I think he's *one card short of a full deck.* 彼は少し抜けていると思う. ☞deck「(トランプの)一組」.

be* (*quite*) *a card (相当)変人である ▪ Crazy Charley, who *is quite a card*, entertains his shy companion by eating a spider. クレイジー・チャーリーは相当な変わり者で, クモを食べてみせて人見知りする仲間をおもしろがらせる.

be shown the red card 解雇される, 首になる ▪ Jim has *been shown the red card* and risks being banned from office. ジムは解雇され, 事務所に出入り禁止になる恐れがある.

be shown the yellow card 警告を受ける ▪ The staff will *be shown the yellow card* if they are caught making negative remarks about the corporation. 会社に対して否定的な発言をしているところを見つかれば, 職員たちは警告を受けるだろう.

A person's ***card is marked.*** 《英》(上司などに)気に入られていない, 目をつけられている ▪ *His card is marked* I fear. 彼はブラックリストに載っていると思う.

count on *one's* ***cards*** 成功を当てにする ▪ Ross *counts on his cards.* ロスは成功を当てにしている.

deal* (*out*) *the cards トランプの札を配り分ける ▪ You must *deal out the cards* this time. 今度はあなたが札を配らねばならない.

fling up *one's* ***cards*** → throw up one's CARDs.

give cards and spades 《米口》(勝負事で相手に)気前よく利点を与える, 何目か置かす; (人に)勝る ▪ He found a Chinese man who could *give* him *cards and spades.* 彼は自分に気前よく分を与えてくれることのできる中国人を見つけた. ☞cassino の得点にちなんで.

go through the* (*whole*) *card あらゆることを考慮する[試す] ▪ It's quite cumbersome to *go through the whole card.* あらゆることを試してみるのは全く煩わしい.

have a* [*another*] *card up *one's* ***sleeve*** → have a card in one's SLEEVE.

have* [*hold*] (*all*) *the cards in *one's* ***hands*** 成算がある, 奥の手がある; あらゆる有利な点を持つ ▪ Why, you're bound to win, you*'ve got all the cards in your hands.* なあに君が勝つにきまっている. 立場が有利だからね ▪ I *have all the cards in my hands.* 私には成算がある.

hold* [*keep*]** *one's* ***cards close to *one's* **[*the*] *chest*** →play one's CARDs close to one's chest.

hold the cards 相手より優勢である ▪ Cameron, relax. You *hold the cards.* キャメロン, 安心するがいい. 君は相手よりも優勢だ.

(*if you*) *play your cards right* 《口》正しくふるまう(ならば(成功する)) (→play one's CARDs well) ▪ *If you play your cards right*, you can win. 君は正しくふるまえば成功するさ.

in the cards 《米口》起こりそうである; ...する運命にある ▪ He had always felt that marriage to Helen was *in the cards.* 彼は自分がヘレンと結婚する運命にあるといつも感じていた ▪ It's *in the cards* for her to [that she will] marry John. 彼女はジョンと結婚しそうだ. ☞運勢占いに card を使うことから.

lay* (*down*)** *one's* ***cards on the table →put one's CARDs on the table.

leave *one's* ***card on*** *a person* (正式訪問の代わりに)人の元に名刺を置いて帰る ▪ As he was absent, I *left my card on* him. 彼は留守だったので, 彼に名刺を置いて帰った.

mark *a person's* ***card*** 《口》人に知らせる, 情報を与える ▪ He *marked my card* about a few things. 彼はいくつかのことを私に教えてくれた.

on the cards 《口》 **1** ありそうだ, (物事が)起こりそうだ; 噂されて ▪ It was quite *on the cards* that he would be raised to the Upper House. 彼が上院議員に昇進するということは全くありそうなことだった ▪ The success of the mine is always *on the cards.* その鉱山の成功は常に噂されている.

2 計画中で, 番付にあって ▪ The next thing *on the cards* is to elect a new chairman. 次に予定していることは新議長の選出である.

play all *one's* ***cards*** あらゆる手段を尽くす ▪ Essex had *played all his cards* now. エセックスはもうあらゆる手段を尽くしてしまっていた.

play *one's* ***best card*** 《口》奥の手を出す, 最上の策をとる ▪ Don't *play your best card* till you've heard the whole story. すっかり聞いてしまうまでは奥の手を出してはいけない.

play cards/play at* (《米》 *the*) *cards トランプをする ▪ We *played at cards.* みなでトランプをした.

play* [*keep, hold*]** *one's* ***cards close to *one's* **[*the*] *chest* [*vest*]** 《口》ひどく秘密主義である, 自分の手をなかなか知らせない ▪ He had to *play his cards close to his chest.* 彼は極力秘密主義で行かねばならなかった.

play *one's* ***cards well* [*right; badly, poorly*]** トランプがうまい[まずい]; じょうず[へた]に立ち回る; 事の処理がうまい[まずい] ▪ If you *play your cards well*, you will get a promotion. 君は物事をうまくやれば昇進するだろう ▪ If Ford *plays its cards right*, it might be a winner. フォードはきちんと対処すれば勝利者になる可能性もある ▪ If you *play your cards right*, you might get to be the boss's new secretary. 仕事をうまく処理すれば社長の新秘書になれるかもしれないよ.

play *one's* ***last card*** 最後の手を出す ▪ I have *played my last card.* 最後の手を出してしまった.

play *one's* ***winning card*** = play one's TRUMP card.

play with *one's* ***cards on the table*** 手を全部見せる, 内幕を見せる ▪ The upper classes *play with their cards on the table.* 上層階級の人たちは手の内を全部見せる.

put all the cards on the table あらゆることをさ

らけ出す《相談するときによく言う》 ▪ Let's *put all our cards on the table* and see where we are financially. 洗いざらい調べてみて，財政状態を確かめよう.

put* [*lay*] *one's* *cards on the table (持札を卓上に出して)手を見せる; 計画[考え，種]をすっかりあかす ▪ We will *put our cards on the table.* 自分の考えをすっかりあかしましょう ▪ I was rash to *lay my cards on the table.* 私が手の内をすっかり見せてしまったのは軽率であった.

show* *one's* *cards (トランプで)手の内を見せる; 計画[意図]を見せる; 考えていることを言ってしまう ▪ You had better not *show your cards.* 手のうちを見せないほうがよい.

speak by the card 慎重に正確に言う; きわめて厳密である (cf. Sh., *Haml.* 5. 1. 149) ▪ I *speak by the card* in order to avoid entanglement of words. 私は言葉がこんがらからないように正確に話します. ☞card「羅針盤の指針面」; その point (点)を言うように正確に話すこと.

stack the cards →STACK[2].

***That's the card* (*for it*).** 《口》その通りだ，そのものずばりだ，それにかぎる ▪ *That's the card!* It'll save a lot of time. それがよい. そうすれば多くの時間が省ける. ☞the card = the proper thing.

The cards are in* *one's* *hands. 切札は手の中にある; 成功の手だてを握っている; 優勢である.

the* [*a person's*] *leading* [*trump*] *card 切り札，奥の手 (→ play one's TRUMP card) ▪ In short, money's *the leading card.* 手短に言えば，金が奥の手だ.

throw* *one's* *cards on the table 知っているかぎりを率直に述べる ▪ I shall *throw* all *my cards on the table* and take his advice. すべてを率直に話して彼の助言を求めよう.

throw* [*fling*] *up* *one's* *cards 《口》持札を投げ出す; 計画を放棄する; 敗北を認める ▪ I'll *fling up my cards.* 私は計画を放棄しよう ▪ I *throw up my cards.* 僕の負けだ.

turn down one corner of the card 名刺の片すみを折る《自分自身訪問した印として》.

care[1] /keər/ 图 ***care of*** …気付[方]《通例 c/o と略して封筒の上に書く》 ▪ Mr. Andes, *c/o* Mr. B. B様方アンデス様.

give care to …に注意する ▪ *Give* more *care to* your work. 仕事にもっと注意を向けなさい.

give A into the care of B AをBに託する ▪ I have *given* the valuables *into the care of* the captain. 私は貴重品を船長に託した.

have the care of = take CARE of 1.

in care (子供が)公の保護を受けて ▪ The children are *in care.* その子供たちは公の保護を受けている.

in care of …の気付で ▪ He wants it sent to him *in care of* the American Embassy in Paris. 彼はパリの米国大使館気付でそれを送ってほしいと言っている.

in the care of …の世話になって，の保護[保管]のもとに ▪ The children were left *in the care of* their grandmother. 子供らは祖母のもとに預けられた.

just taking care of business そこそこ[まあまあ，ほどほど]のことをしている ▪ We're *just taking care of business.* We've beaten a few teams that are a little bit better than us そこそこにやってるよ. うちよりちょっと上位のチームを２つ３つ破ったんだ ▪ It's *just taking care of business.* It's not like we hate people and they hate us. まあまあです. 我々は誰もきらっていないし誰も我々をきらっていないみたいです.

leave ... in* *a person's* *care …を人の世話にゆだねる ▪ The baby *was left in Mary's care.* 赤ちゃんはメアリーの世話にゆだねられた.

leave ... to the care of* *a person …を人に託する[預ける]; を人の任務とする ▪ She *left* the child *to the care of* her sister. 彼女は子供を妹に託した ▪ I will *leave* this *to your care.* これを君にしてもらいたい.

not have* [*without*] *a care in the world 全く悩みがない[なく] ▪ He looked as if he did*n't have a care in the world.* 彼は全く悩みがないような様子だった ▪ I was in bed by 9 p.m. each night *without a care in the world.* 私は毎晩９時までには何の悩みもなく床についた.

place* [*put*]*... under* *a person's* *care …を人に預ける，託する，世話を頼む ▪ He *was placed under the care of* the nurse [the doctor]. 彼は乳母に預けられた[その医者にかけられた].

Take care. さようなら ▪ Until then, *take care,* bye for now. じゃあ，そのときまたね.

take care how …しないようにする ▪ *Take care how* you trust such people. あんな人たちを信用しないようにしなさい.

take care of **1** …の世話をする，を管理[処理]する，に気をつける; にチップをわたす ▪ Please *take care of* my house. 私の家を管理してください ▪ My secretary *takes care of* my mail. 秘書が私の郵便物を処理します ▪ Just then room service arrived and I *took care of* the waiter. ちょうどそのときルームサービスが届いたので私はウェイターにチップをわたした.

2《米》…を処分する，やっつける，取り除く;《婉曲》を殺す ▪ *Take care of* every obstacle. すべての障害を取り除きなさい ▪ I'm going to *take care of* you. 君を今にやっつけてやる ▪ This pill will *take care of* your headache. この丸薬で君の頭痛は治る ▪ Brown tried to find still another killer to *take care of* Kern. ブラウンはカーンを消すためさらに別の殺し屋を見つけようとした.

3 …を大切にする ▪ Books should *be taken* great *care of.* 書物はきわめて大切にすべきだ.

take care of* *oneself 体に気をつける ▪ *Take* good *care of yourself.* お体をたいせつに.

Take care of the pennies* [*pence*] *and the pounds will take care of themselves. 《諺》小事をゆるがせにしなければ大事はおのずからうまくゆく，「小事は大事」(= Count [Watch] the pennies, and the dollars will count themselves.).

***take care* (*that*)** 用心する，気をつける ▪ *Take*

care that you don't catch cold. 風邪をひかないよう注意しなさい.

***take care to** do* きっと…する ▪ *Take care to* do so. 必ずそうしなさい.

take ... into care (子供などを)養護ホームへ入れる ▪ We have no choice but to *take* the child *into care*. その子供は養護ホームへ入れるほかはない.

take ... under** one's* ***care …を引き受けて世話する, 預かる ▪ I *took* the child *under my care*. 私はその子供を預かった.

That takes care of that! 《米口》それで(問題は)片づいた ▪ I had no problems with either one of them, and *that takes care of that*. 彼らの誰とも問題はなかった, だからこれでもう万事解決だ.

under the care of …の世話になって; に担当されて ▪ The library is *under the care of* Mr. Green. 図書館はグリーン氏の担当である ▪ I recovered *under his care*. 私は彼の治療[看護]で治った.

without a care in the world →not have a CARE in the world.

care[2] /keər/ 動 ***any ... you care to name*** [***mention***] どんな類(たぐい)の…でも ▪ He has an encyclopedic knowledge of almost *any* topic *you care to name*. 彼はほとんどどんな主題でも該博(がいはく)な知識をもっている.

as if I cared 《口》まるで…を気にしているかのように; 全く気にならない, どうでもいい (*about, wh-*) ▪ *As If I cared about* pictures at a time like this. こんなときに写真なんかどうでもいい.

be past caring 《英口》もう興味がない (doesn't care) ▪ The room is a mess, but she *is past caring*. 部屋は散らかっているが, 彼女は気にしていない.

care nothing for …に興味を持たない; を少しもほしがらない; を問題にしない ▪ John *cares nothing for* music. ジョンは音楽に興味を持たない ▪ He *cares nothing for* the luxuries of life. 彼は生活上の贅沢品をほしがらない ▪ I *care nothing for* hardship. 私は苦難をものともしない.

couldn't care less 《口》全く無関心[平気]である ▪ He *couldn't care less* about his appearance. 彼は風采に全くむとんちゃくである.

for all [***anything***] *one* ***cares*** ちっともかまわない ▪ He may die *for anything* I *care*. 彼が死のうとおれは知らぬ ▪ I might have drowned *for all* he *cared*. 私は溺死したかもしれないが彼は平気だった.

***I don't care if I** do.* 《口》…してもよい; はい, そうします ▪ Will you have a drink?—*I don't care if I* do.「1杯いかがですか—はい, いただきます」《このように通常酒を勧められたときの答えとして》 ▪ *I don't care if I* go. 行ってもいい.

not care a bit [《主に米》***a button,*** 《主に米》***a chip, a damn,*** 《主に米》***a cent, a fig, a hang, a farthing, a pin, a rap, a straw, twopence, two coppers***] 少しもかまわない ▪ I do*n't care a bit* what he says. 彼かどう言おうと全然かまわない.

See if I care! 《口》(怒って)勝手にしろ, もう知るか.

What do I [***you, they***] ***care?*** 《口》(通例怒って)私[君, 彼ら]にはどうでもいいことだ.

Who cares?[***!***] 《口・反語》誰が気にかけるだろうか, 誰も気にしない (*about, wh-*).

Would you care for ...? …はいかがですか ▪ *Would you care for* a coffee? コーヒーを1杯いかが?

career /kəríər/ 名 *One's* ***career is run.*** 生涯は終わった.

in full career **1** 全速力で ▪ Away we went *in full career*. まっしぐらに走り去った.

2 全力を出して ▪ The science of destruction was *in full career*. 破壊の科学は全力を発揮していた.

in mid career 途中で ▪ It was stopped *in mid career*. それは途中で止められた.

make a career 出世[成功]する ▪ He *made a career* for himself. 彼は独力で出世した.

careful /kéərfəl/ 形 ***be careful about*** …にかまう; を心配する; にやかましい ▪ He *is* too *careful about* dress. 彼は服装のことにやかましすぎる.

be careful for …を心配する ▪ They *were* very *careful for* those who were to fight. 彼らは戦うことになっている人々をひどく心配した.

be careful (***in***) *doing* …するとき注意する ▪ *Be careful* (*in*) *crossing* the street. 街路を横切るときは注意しなさい.

be careful of …をたいせつにする; に注意する ▪ *Be careful of* your health. 健康に注意しなさい.

***be careful to** do* 必ず…するようにする, するよう注意する ▪ *Be careful to* use good language. 必ずよい言葉を使うようにしなさい ▪ *Be careful* not *to* catch cold. 風邪をひかないよう注意しなさい.

be careful with …に気をつける ▪ *Be careful with* the baby. 赤んぼうに気をつけてあげなさい.

careless /kéərləs/ 形 ***be careless about*** …にむとんちゃくである, をなんとも思わない ▪ He *is careless about* his personal appearance. 彼は自分の身なりにむとんちゃくである.

be careless of …に無関心である; に不注意である, を粗末にする ▪ He *was careless of* books at that time. 彼はそのころは書物には無関心であった ▪ He *is careless of* what people say. 彼は人の言うことにはむとんちゃくだ.

caricature /kǽrɪkətʃʊ̀ər/ 名 ***make a caricature of*** …を漫画風に描く ▪ He could *make a caricature of* a good face. 彼は良い顔を漫画風に描くことができた.

carl /kɑ́:rl/ 名 ***play carl again*** 《米》返報する, しっぺ返しする ▪ *Play carl* with me *again*. 私に返報してくれ.

carnal /kɑ́:rnəl/ 形 ***have carnal knowledge of*** 《法》…と性交する ▪ He *had carnal knowledge of* the widow. 彼はその未亡人と交わった.

carpet[1] /kɑ́:rpət/ 名 ***be a carpet knight*** 功績によらずに勲爵士になる ▪ Sir Bert *was* only *a carpet knight*; he got his title by bribing. サー・バートは功績なくして勲爵士になったにすぎない. 氏は賄賂

によって称号を得たのだ.

be (out) on the carpet 《米》結婚の候補となる ▪ Widow Jones *is out on the carpet.* ジョーンズ未亡人は結婚の候補となった.

beat a carpet 敷物をたたいてほこりを取る ▪ It sounds just like *beating carpets.* それはちょうど敷物をたたいているように聞こえる.

bite the carpet 激怒する, 逆上する ▪ King Henry II (1154-89) threw himself to the ground and *bit the carpet* in his rages. ヘンリー2世(1154-89)は大地に身を投げて激しく怒り狂った.

bring ... on the carpet ...を紹介する, (討議のため)...を持ち出す ▪ He *brought* another subject *on the carpet.* 彼はもう一つの題目を(討議のため)持ち出した. ☞ ＜F sur le tapis.

brush ... under [underneath, beneath] the carpet ＝SWEEP ... under the carpet.

call [put]** a person **on the carpet 人を(上役が)呼びつけてしかる ▪ The boss *called* John *on the carpet.* 社長はジョンを呼びつけてしかった. ☞ 上役の部屋にだけ carpet が敷かれていたことから.

come on the carpet 《口》現れる, 紹介される ▪ She has been more dressy since you *came on the carpet.* 君が現れてから, 彼女は前よりけばけばしい服装になった.

on the carpet **1** 審議[討議]中で, 考慮中で ▪ An important question is now *on the carpet.* 重要な問題が今審議されつつある. ☞ 会議のテーブルかけに carpet を用いたことから.

2 《口》上役に(呼びつけられて)しかられて ▪ He was *on the carpet* this morning for constantly arriving late. 彼はいつも遅刻するのでけさ上役にしかられた.

***pull the carpet (out) from under** a person* 不意に人に対する援助[支持]を打ち切る ▪ The company *pulled the carpet out from under* him by dismissing him. 会社は不意に彼を首にして援助することをやめた.

push ... under [underneath, beneath] the carpet ＝SWEEP ... under the carpet.

put** a person **on the carpet →call a person on the CARPET.

roll out the (red) carpet 儀礼をもって歓迎する ▪ They *rolled out the carpet* for the minister. 彼らは大臣を儀礼をもって歓迎した. ☞ 国王などを迎えるのに通路に red carpet を敷いたことから.

sweep [push] ... under [underneath, beneath] the carpet →SWEEP².

walk the carpet 《口》上役に(呼びつけられて)しかられる ▪ He made his servants *walk the carpet.* 彼は使用人たちを呼んでしかった. ☞ 上役の部屋にだけ carpet が敷かれていたことから.

carpet² /kɑ́rpət/ 動 ***be carpeted with*** ...で厚くおおわれる ▪ It *was carpeted with* flowers. それは花で一面におおわれていた.

carriage /kǽrɪdʒ/ 名 ***a carriage and four [pair]*** 4[2]頭立ての馬車 ▪ The party drove off in *a carriage and pair.* 一行は2頭立ての馬車で立ち去った. ☞ carriage は18世紀中葉から; 元は "coach" という語を用いた.

carriage company 《口》自家用(馬)車を持つ金持ちたち ▪ He has seen a great deal of *carriage company.* 彼は自家用(馬)車を持つ金持ちたちに大勢出会った.

carriage forward 《英》[[副詞的に]] 運賃先払いで ▪ The parcels were sent *carriage forward.* その小包は運賃先払いで送られた.

carrot /kǽrət/ 名 ***carrot-and-stick*** [[限定的]] あめとむちの (→the CARROT and the stick) ▪ a *carrot and stick* approach [method] 硬軟両用策[作戦] ▪ A *carrot and stick* approach is best with such a recalcitrant child. こんなに言うことを聞かない子にはあめとむちの両用策が最適である ▪ All organizations work on a *carrot-and-stick* policy. すべての機関はあめとむちの政策に基づいて仕事をする ▪ Governments were forced to adopt a *carrot-and-stick* approach to the trade unions. 政府は労働組合に対してあめとむちの手法をとらざるをえなかった.

***dangle a carrot in front of** a person* 人の前にニンジンをぶらさげる, 人をえさでつる (＝offer a person a CARROT) ▪ *Dangling a carrot in front of* me won't achieve anything. 私にえさをちらつかてもむだだ.

like a carrot to a donkey (ロバに対するニンジンのように)ひきつけられて, 好きで ▪ Flattery is to him *like a carrot to a donkey.* おべっかは彼には大好物だ.

offer** a person **a carrot 人をえさでつる[丸めこむ], 人にあめをちらつかせる ▪ The president *offered a carrot* of conciliation to the Iraqi president. 大統領はイラク大統領に和解というあめをちらつかせた ▪ The environmentalist *offered* the automaker *a carrot* rather than a stick. その環境保護活動家は自動車メーカーにむちよりもあめでつろうとした.

the [a] carrot and the [a] stick 「あめとむち」 ▪ The teacher made his boys work harder with *a carrot and a stick.* 先生はあめとむちで生徒をもっと勉強させた. ☞ 馬を訓練するとき好物のニンジンを与えることから.

carry¹ /kǽri/ 名 ***make a carry*** 《米》(カヌー・貨物を2水路間を結ぶ)運搬陸路を通って運ぶ ▪ They *made a carry* to the landing here. 彼らはここの陸上げ場まで運搬陸路を通って貨物を運んだ.

carry² /kǽri/ 動 ***as fast as** one's **legs can carry** one* できるだけ速く(走る, など) ▪ He went *as fast as his legs could carry* him. 彼はできるだけ速く走った.

be carried out feet first 死ぬまで(立ち退かない) ▪ We will all stay here until we *are carried out feet first.* 死ぬまでみんなここに留まろう. ☞ 足から先に出棺することから.

***carry all [everything, the world] before** one* 破竹の勢いで進む; 向かうところ敵がない; 大成功する ▪ Those teams *carried all before* them. それらのチームは向かうところ敵なしであった ▪ He has opened a restaurant and is *carrying all before* him. 彼はレストランを開いて大繁昌している ▪ When he was at Cambridge he *carried all before* him. ケンブリッジ在学中彼はすばらしい成績であった.

***carry away* [*off*] *the bell* [*palm*]** (…に)勝つ,(を)顔色なからしめる (*from*) ▪ He *carried away the palm from* us in the fencing contest. 彼はフェンシングの試合で我々に勝った ▪ The Italians have *carried away the bell from* all other nations. イタリア人はすべての他の国民にまさっていた.

carry *one's* ***candidate*** 立候補者を当選させる ▪ They *carried their candidates* in the election. 彼らは選挙で自分たちの立候補者を当選させた.

carry everything before *one* → CARRY all before one.

carry everything with it (雪崩などが)道にあるものをことごとく一掃する ▪ An avalanche *carried everything with it.* 雪崩が道にあるものを一掃した.

carry fire in one hand and water in the other 口と腹とが違う; おべっかを使う; だます ▪ *In one hand* he *carried water, in the other fire.* 彼は口と腹とが違っていた.

carry *a person* ***high*** (***and dry***) 《米》 人をやたらにいじめる, 悩ます, からかう ▪ He used to *carry* me *high and dry.* 彼はいつも私をやたらにいじめた.

carry it 勝利を得る; 勢いをたくましくする ▪ When the two come into collision, the second must *carry it* over the first. その二者が衝突すると, 第二のほうが第一に勝つにちがいない.

carry it off 《口》 平然としている; 何食わぬ顔をする ▪ He was frightened but *carrying it off* like Satan. 彼はびっくりしたが悪魔のように平気な顔をしていた ▪ He *carried it off* with a laugh. 彼は何食わぬ顔して一笑に付した.

carry it off (***well***) うまく[苦もなく]やってのける ▪ It's only a handful of authors who can *carry it off well* and Ms. Morgan is one of them. それをうまくやってのけられる作家は一握りしかいない. モーガン夫人はその一人だ.

carry off the bell [***palm***] →CARRY away the bell.

carry the world before *one* →CARRY all before one.

carry things (***off***) ***with a high hand*** → with a high HAND.

carry *A* ***through*** *B* A(人など)にB(困難など)を切り抜けさせる ▪ Our optimism *carried* us *through* the first year of defeats. 我々は楽天主義のおかげで敗北１年目を乗り切ることができた.

carry through with …をやり遂げる ▪ He *carried through with* the business. 彼はその事業をやり遂げた.

carry *a thing* ***too far*** ことを極端にやる, やりすぎる ▪ You must not *carry* a joke *too far.* 冗談は度を過ごしてはならない ▪ The mob *carried* things *too far.* 暴徒の行為はやりすぎだった.

carry true (砲の)照準が正確だ; 当たる ▪ These guns *carry true.* これらの砲は当たる.

carry *oneself* (***well,*** etc.) **1** (立派に, など)ふるまう ▪ He *carried himself* bravely in that ordeal. 彼はその試練にあたって勇敢にふるまった.

2 …の姿勢である ▪ He *carries himself* like a soldier. 彼は軍人のような姿勢である.

carry … with *one* **1** …を伴う ▪ Power *carries* responsibility *with* it. 権力は責任を伴う ▪ I never *carry* much money *with* me. 私は大金を持ち歩かない.

2 (聴衆などを)魅了して意のままにする ▪ He *carried* his audience *with* him from beginning to end. 彼は聴衆を魅了して, 初めから終わりまで(泣かせたり, 笑わせたり)意のままにした.

3 …を覚えている ▪ I *carry* the incident *with* me. 私はその事件を覚えている.

carry *oneself* ***with an air*** 気取る ▪ He *carries himself with an air.* 彼は気取るねえ.

to carry [***be carrying***] ***on with*** 今のところ[当分]持つべき ▪ Here's a few dollars *to be carrying on with.* さあ当座用の数ドルだ ▪ This broken knife will do *to carry on with.* このこわれたナイフは今のところは使える.

cart /kɑːrt/ 名 ***in the cart*** 《英口》 困ったはめになって, ひどい目にあって; 困難に陥って; 《スポーツ》 最低点を取って; 後方[不利な立場]に残されて ▪ He behaved in an irresponsible way and now he's *in the cart.* 彼は無責任なふるまいをしたので今はひどい目にあっている ▪ The fellow has run away with everything and put me right *in the cart.* その男がすべてを持ち逃げしたので, 私はほんとに困窮している ▪ We had them *in the cart* in no time. 我々はたちまち彼らを後方に残した.

keep the cart on the wheels 努力して事を運ぶ ▪ The contractor is trying to *keep the cart on the wheels.* 請負師は努力して事を運ぼうとしている.

put [***set***] ***the cart before the horse*** 《口》 本末を転倒する, 前後を誤る ▪ No, it's not bankruptcy which has caused him to drink. You've *put the cart before the horse.* いや, 破産したから彼が飲みだしたのではない. 君は前後を誤っている.

carve /kɑːrv/ 動 ***carve*** *one's* ***way to*** 自ら(運命を)開拓して…に至る ▪ He *carved his way to* renown. 彼は自ら運命を開拓して名声を得た.

case /keɪs/ 名 ***a case in point*** →POINT[1].

a clear case of …ははっきりしている ▪ It is *a clear case of* cheating. 詐欺が行われたのは明らかだ.

as is often the case (***with***) (…には)よくあることだが ▪ *As is often the case with* soldiers, I was a little too fond of liquor. 兵隊にはよくあることだが, 私は少し酒を好みすぎた ▪ He was out, *as is often the case.* よくあることだが彼は留守だった.

as the case may be 場合次第で[に応じて] ▪ We will let you know whether the experiment proves to be a success or a failure *as the case may be.* その実験が成功するか失敗するかどちらになるかお知らせします ▪ You will be paid in cash or by check *as the case may be.* その時の都合で，現金か小切手でお支払いします．

as the case stands そういう事情だから[では] ▪ *As the case stands,* you must leave tonight. そういう事情だから，君は今夜発たねばならない ▪ *As the case stands* now, it is impossible to earn much of a profit. 現状では多くの利益を得るのは不可能だ．

C

be case hardened 無神経[平気]になっている ▪ It is no use remonstrating with him, he*'s case hardened.* 彼に忠告してもむだだ．無神経になっているんだから．

be in evil case 不幸[不健康，貧困]である ▪ He *is in evil case.* 彼は健康でない．

be in good case 幸福[健全，裕福]である ▪ He *is in good case.* 彼はしあわせである．

be on [***off***] *a person's* ***case*** →get off a person's CASE, get on a person's CASE.

be on the case 《米》事件を取り調べている，事に当たっている ▪ He *is on the case.* 彼がその事件を調べている．

be the case 《英》本当である ▪ *Is* it *the case* that you've lost all your money? 君が金を全部失ったというのは本当かい ▪ Yes, that*'s the case.* はい，その通りです．

be the case with …の場合はそうである ▪ It *is* always *the case with* him. 彼はいつもそうだ．

break a case 犯人を見いだす；有罪とするに十分な証拠を集める ▪ We are about to *break the case.* 我々はその件の犯人を見つけようとしている ▪ *The case* is about to *break.* その件の犯人が見つかるところだ．

case by case 事例ごとに，一つ一つ ▪ The President has decided the issue, *case by case,* as it was raised by Congress. 大統領は問題が国会によって提出されるに応じて，一つ一つ決定を下した．☞日本語の「ケース・バイ・ケース」とは意味が違う．

come down to cases ＝get down to CASEs 1.

get down to cases 《主に米》 **1** 要点に入る ▪ Let's *get down to cases.* 本論に入りましょう．

2 真剣にことを考える ▪ The American public wants to *get down to cases.* アメリカの公衆は真剣にものを考えたいと思っている．

3 実際に仕事を始める ▪ This week the 2012 campaign *got down to cases.* 今週2012年の大統領選挙運動が実際に始まった．

4 事件を審理する ▪ Twelve Americans in a jury box would *get down to cases.* 陪審席の12人のアメリカ人が事件を審理するであろう．

get off *a person's* ***case*** 《口》余計なお世話[口出し，干渉]をやめる (↔get on a person's CASE) ▪ I really wish my dad would *get off my case* and let me be. 本当にお父さんには私に干渉するのをやめてほうっておいてほしい ▪ His critics should *get off his case* and let him do his job. 彼の批判者たちは彼のことをとやかく言うのをやめて彼に仕事をさせるべきだ．

get [***be***] ***on*** *a person's* ***case*** 《口》人のことをあれこれ言う，人に口出し[干渉]をする (↔get off a person's CASE) ▪ My wife *got on my case* and got mad at me again. 妻は私に口出ししてまたも私に腹を立てた．

have a case on 《俗》…に夢中になっている，ほれこんでいる ▪ John *had* quite *a case on* Mary. ジョンはメアリーにすっかりほれていた．

have [***put***] *a person* ***on the case*** 人に事件を取り調べさせる ▪ She won't *have* [*put*] any more men *on the case.* 彼女はこれ以上多くの人に事件を調べさせようとはするまい．

in any case どうあろうと，どのみち，ともかく ▪ *In any case* I'll come to the office tomorrow. ともかくあす事務所に参ります ▪ *In any case* you had better hear what he has to say. どっちにしろ彼の言い分を聞くべきだ．

in case **1** (…の)場合に備えて，万一に備えて；してはいけないから ▪ I must have something to fall back on, *in case* I should fail. 万一の失敗に備えて，私は何か頼るべき予備が必要だ ▪ You had better take an umbrella *in case* it (should) rain. 雨が降るといけないから，かさを持って行くべきよ ▪ Take an umbrella just *in case.* 万一に備えてかさを持って行きなさい．

2 …の場合には ▪ *In case* I forget, please remind me about it. もし忘れたらどうか思い出させてください．

in *one's* ***case*** …の場合は，については ▪ Poverty is no shame *in his case.* 彼の場合は貧困は決して恥ではない．

in case of …の場合には ▪ *In case of* fire, break the glass and push the red button. 火事の際には，ガラスをこわして，赤いボタンを押してください ▪ *In case of* my not being there, ask my brother to help you. 私がそこにいない場合は，弟に手助けを求めなさい．

in case of need →NEED[1].

in every [***this***] ***case*** すべての[この]場合に ▪ No help is needed *in this case.* この場合援助はいらない ▪ The same thing happens *in every case.* すべての場合に同じ事が起こる．

in no case 決して…ない ▪ *In no case* should it be forgotten. それは決して忘れてはならない．

in the case of **1** ＝in CASE of.

2 …の場合は，については ▪ *In the case of* Dr. X. an exception was made. X博士の場合は例外とされた．

It [***That, This***] ***is the case.*** そうである，その通りだ ▪ No, *that is* not *the case.* いや，そうではない．

It's a case. 《口》好いた同士だ ▪ He's always with that girl; *it's* really quite *a case.* 彼はいつもあの娘といっしょだ．ほんとに両想い同士だ．

keep cases 《米》 **1** (faro というかけトランプの)札箱から札の出るのを見張る，札箱を管理する ▪ He was sitting in front, *keeping cases.* 彼は前に座って札箱を管理していた．

2 厳重に見張る，見守る ▪ I'm *keeping cases* on these cattle. この牛の群を見張っている．

make out a case for [***against***] …を弁護する[責め立てる] ▪ Shakespeare *made out a* strong *case for* Shylock. シェイクスピアはシャイロックを強く弁護した ▪ The nation *made out a case against* the novelist. 国民はその小説家を非難した．

make out *one's* ***case*** 自分の正しいことを明らかにする; 自分の立場を弁明する ▪ He *made out his case.* 彼は自分の正しいことを明らかにした.

put *a person* ***on the case*** →have a person on the CASE.

put [***set***] ***the case*** **1** 事情を説明する ▪ I've *put the case* to you for consideration. 私はご考慮を願うために事情をあなたに説明しました.

2 仮定する ▪ *Put the case* that there will be no future state. 未来の国家はないと仮定せよ.

rest *one's* ***case*** 発言[陳述, 弁論, 証拠の提出]を終える ▪ Having said this, he said, "I *rest my case,*" and walked out of the chamber. こう言うと彼は「発言は以上です」と言って, 部屋から歩いて出て行った.

state a [*one's*] ***case*** (弁護士・被告が)事実をあげて訴える, 言い分を述べる; (裁判所が)上級裁判所へ陳情する ▪ He *stated his case* mildly. 彼は穏やかに言い分を述べた ▪ The judge *stated a case.* 判事が上級裁判所へ陳情した.

such being the case →SUCH.

such is the case with ... ...についてはそういう次第です ▪ *Such was the case with* Shelley. シェリーについてはそういう事情でした.

That [***This***] ***is the case.*** →It is the CASE.

cash[1] /kæʃ/ 名 ***cash and carry*** 配達なしの現金売り[の(店)] ▪ Now she shops *cash and carry* without painful backache. 今では彼女は現金払い持ち帰りの店で買物をしてもひどく背が痛むことはない ▪ This is a *cash and carry* store. ここは現金店頭渡しの店です.

cash down/cash (***down***) ***on the nail*** [***the barrel-head***] 即金で ▪ What's the price *cash down on the nail*? 値段は即金でいくらだ ▪ They bought this vessel for a song, paying part *cash down.* 彼らはこの船をただみたいな値段で買い, 一部分を即金で払った ▪ It is payable *cash on the barrelhead.* それは即金で支払うべきである ▪ It's all *cash down* at this shop, no credit given. 当店では一切現金でお支払いいただき, 掛け売りはお断りしています.

Cash is king. 《諺》資産運用は現金で保管するのが最善だ《現金を蓄えて市場の暴落を待つ方がよい》. ☞有価証券市場の価格が高すぎるときに用いる; cash と king が頭韻になっている.

Cash is trash. 《諺》資産運用を現金で保管するのは賢明でない. ☞証券取引の好機のときに用いる; cash と trash が脚韻になっている.

cash on delivery 《英》代金引換払い (→C.O.D) ▪ I received a *cash on delivery* parcel this morning. 今朝, 代金引換払いの小包を受け取った.

cash on the barrelhead 《米》即金 ▪ They won't extend credit; it's *cash on the barrelhead* or no sale. 彼らは信用貸しを延ばしてくれない. 即金か, さもなければ売ってくれないかだ.

cash up front 前払い(の[で]); 即金(払い)(の[で]) ▪ Harvey asked for *cash up front* from the buyer. ハービーは買主に前払いを要求した ▪ They require a *cash up front* payment of one hundred thousand US dollars. 彼らは10万米ドルの前払いを要求する ▪ Patients will have to pay *cash up front* before being admitted to private rooms. 患者は個室への入室許可に先立って前払いすることになっている.

cold [***hard***] ***cash*** (小切手・カードに対して)現金, 即金; (紙幣に対して)硬貨 ▪ Better still, use a debit card or *cold cash.* もっとよいのはデビットカードか現金を使うことだ ▪ The culprits are interested only in *hard cash* in every case. 犯罪者はどんな場合にも現金にしか興味がない.

in cash 現金で; 現金を所有して ▪ He bets freely when he is *in cash.* 彼は現金を持っているときは盛んにかけをする.

out [***short***] ***of cash*** 現金を切らして ▪ He was *out of cash* and could not send the five pounds. 彼は現金を切らしていて, その5ポンドを送れなかった.

strapped for cash 金欠[資金不足, 火の車]である ▪ The university is so *strapped for cash* that budget cuts are inevitable. その大学は財政難なので予算削減は避けられない.

Take the cash (***in hand***) ***and let the credit go.*** 《諺》経済的・物質的利益を先にせよ.

cash[2] /kæʃ/ 動 ***cash*** (***in***) *one's* ***chips*** [***checks***] 《口》死ぬ ▪ He has been idle since his wife *cashed in her chips.* 彼は妻が死んでからぶらぶらしている.

cast[1] /kæst|kɑːst/ 名 ***at the first cast*** 最初の試み[一撃]で ▪ He was successful *at the first cast.* 彼は一度で成功した.

give (*a person*) ***a cast*** (人を)途中で車に乗せてやる (=give a person a LIFT) ▪ The wagoner *gave* him *a cast* as far as the town. 御者は彼を町まで乗せてやった.

have a cast in one eye 片方の目が斜視である ▪ He *has a cast in* the left *eye.* 彼は左目が斜視である.

put ... in a cast (骨折した手足)にギプスをはめる ▪ The doctor *put* Richard's arm *in a cast.* 医者はリチャードの腕にギプスをはめた.

set [***stake***] ***... upon a cast*** ...をさいころの一振りにかける ▪ Their clothes *are staked upon a* single *cast.* 彼らの衣服はさいころの一振りにかけられている.

cast[2] /kæst|kɑːst/ 動 ***be cast down*** しょげる, 力を落とす ▪ For my part, I *was* horribly *cast down.* 私はとても力を落とした.

be cast for ...にうってつけである ▪ He *was cast for* the part he plays. あの人は自分の演じる役にぴたりとはまっていた.

be cast in ... mold ...の性質である ▪ He *is cast in* heroic *mold.* 彼は英雄肌だ.

cast a horoscope [***figure, nativity***] 天宮図を繰る《誕生の月日・時間から人の運命を占う》 ▪ Cardan *cast the horoscope* of our Savior. カーダンはわが救世主の運命を占った.

cast about *one's* ***eyes*** →EYE.
cast back (***to***) **1** (道を…に)引き返す; (先祖などに)立ち帰る ▪ There was some dreadful misalliance somewhere in our genealogy, and you have *cast back to* it. 我々の系図のどこかにひどく身分の低い者との結婚があり, あなたはそれに立ち帰ったのです.
2 (歴史・記憶に)さかのぼる, さかのぼって捜す ▪ He *casts back to* fiction for a helpful analogy. 彼はさかのぼって小説の中に役に立つ類似を捜し求めた.
3 遠い祖先の人に似る ▪ The boy *casts back to* his great-great grandfather. 少年はひいひいじいさん似だ.
cast in *one's* ***lot with*** →LOT.
cast ... in *a person's* ***teeth*** →TOOTH.
cast light upon →throw (a) LIGHT on.
cast *oneself* ***on*** [***upon***] …に頼る ▪ He *cast himself on* her mercy. 彼は彼女の慈悲にすがった.
cast on ... stitches …針編む ▪ I *cast on* three more *stitches*. 私はもう3針編んだ.

caste /kæst|kɑːst/ 名 ***lose caste*** 落ちぶれる, 堕落する, 社会的身分を失う; (同輩・友人に)うとまれる, 卑しめられる ▪ After being sent to prison for theft, he *lost caste* with his friends in the village. 盗みをして刑務所に入れられてのち, 彼は村の友人たちにうとまれた ▪ The aristocrat *lost caste* by becoming a tradesman. その貴族は商人に身を落とした.

castle /kǽsəl|kɑ́ːsəl/ 名 ***a castle in the air*** [***Spain***] 空中楼閣; 空想 ▪ He returned to his lodgings with his head full of *castles in the air*. 彼は頭の中に空中楼閣をいっぱいつめて下宿へ帰った. ☞F château en Espagne のなぞり; Spain はロマンチックな国と考えられていたから.
An Englishman's home [***house***] ***is his castle.*** 《諺》イギリス人の家は城である《家庭の神聖・人権の尊重を言う》.
build [***form***] ***castles in the air*** [***Spain***] 空中に楼閣を築く ▪ He is *building castles in Spain* among his books. 彼は書物に埋もれていろいろな空想にふけっている.
like a castle of cards 紙の城のように(もろく) ▪ The whole thing collapsed *like a castle of cards*. 全体がきわめてもろくつぶれた.

cat /kæt/ 名 ***a cat and bull story*** 《米》とてつもない[信じられない]話 ▪ I'll believe that *cat and bull story* when I see it. 私は見たらそのとほうもない話を信じるだろう. ☞a COCK AND BULL story を婉曲に言ったもの.
a cat and monkey trick 人を手先に使うこと ▪ So successfully was this *cat and monkey trick* performed. 人を手先に使うこの策は非常にうまくいった. ☞サルが猫を使って火中の栗を拾わせる話から.
A cat has nine lives. 《諺》猫に九生あり《たたいたくらいではなかなか死なない》.
A cat in gloves catches no mice. 《諺》慎重で丁寧にしていては, 欲しいものが 手に入らないことがある.
a cat in the meal [***tub***] 《米》隠されたもの, 陰険なもの ▪ They say there is *a cat in the meal* behind his retirement. 彼の引退には隠されたたくらみがあるということだ. ☞Webster の "bluebacked speller" にある猫とネズミの話から.
a cat in the pan →turn (the, a) CAT in the pan.
A cat may look at a king. 《諺》目上の者の前でも遠慮しなくてよいことがある; 社会的地位はどうあっても人間はみな平等である; 私はあなたに少しも劣らない《生意気な句》 ▪ What are you staring at so rudely?—You, of course! *A cat may look at a king*, mayn't he? 何をそんなに無作法に見すえているのか—もちろん, 君だよ. それくらい遠慮なくしたっていいじゃないか.
a dead cat bounce 《口》《株》(株価などの)一時的回復; 死猫の跳ね返り《政界などでの一時的な支持の回復》 ▪ The previous day's rise was just *a dead cat bounce*. 前日の上昇は一時的な回復にすぎなかった ▪ This turnaround is more than *a dead cat bounce* and we will see a gradual climb in population. この転換は一時的回復以上であり, 人口の緩やかな増加を見ることになるだろう ▪ The addition of Sarah Palin to the ticket produced at best *a dead cat bounce* in the polls for the Republicans. 公認候補者名簿にサラ・ペイリン氏を追加したのも共和党への投票にはせいぜい一時しのぎでしかなかった. ☞高所から落ちた猫が絶命していても生きて跳ねているように見えることから.
a fat cat →FAT[1].
a fraidy [***scared***] ***cat*** 《口》恐がり, 臆病者, 引っ込み思案な[人見知りする]子供 ▪ I'm such *a fraidy cat* that I haven't watched a horror movie since "Scream." 私はとっても恐がりなので「スクリーム」以来ホラー映画は見ていない.
a stroke of the cat 刑罰のむちの一打ち ▪ The judge ordered him ten *strokes of the cat*. 裁判官は彼に刑のむちを10与えるよう命じた. ☞the cat = the cat o' nine tails.
a tough cat 《俗》個性的な男; もて男 ▪ My dad's *a tough cat*. He's a Vietnam veteran and a biker. お父さんはもてるんだよ. ベトナム帰還兵でサイクリストなんだ.
agree like cats and dogs 非常に仲が悪い, 全然折り合わない ▪ They *agree like cats and dogs*. 彼らは犬猿の仲である.
All cats are gray in the dark. 《諺》暗闇ではすべての猫は灰色である,「美貌も一皮むけばみな同じ」.
(***as***) ***analogous as a cat and a cartwheel*** 猫と荷車の車輪ほど似ている; 全く似ていない (→(as) like as CHALK and cheese) ▪ They are *as analogous as a cat and a cartwheel*. それらは全く異なっている.
(***as***) ***high as a cat's back*** 《米》過度に ▪ The plan to lay off half the staff caused uproar *as high as a cat's back*. 職員の半数を解雇するという計画で大騒ぎになった.
(***as***) ***sick as a cat*** 《口》 **1** 吐き気を催して ▪ The whole family was *sick as cats*. 家族全員が吐き気を催していた.

2 ひどくいやな; きわめてうるさい ▪ I was *as sick as a cat* when I missed it. それを取り逃がしたときたまらなくいやだった. ☞ 猫が吐きやすいことから.

(as) spry as a cat きわめてすばしこい ▪ I was *spry as a cat.* 私はきわめてすばしこかった.

be like the cat that [after it] has eaten the canary/be like the cat that stole the cream →look like the CAT that has eaten the canary.

be the cat's pyjamas [whiskers] 《口》最善の人[物]である ▪ He thinks he *is the cat's pyjamas.* 彼は自分ほど立派な人物はいないと思っている. ☞ 通例些細なこと, または皮肉に用いられる.

bell the cat →BELL[2].

blow cats and dogs →rain CATs and dogs.

buy a cat in the sack 《米》=buy a PIG in a poke.

Care killed the [a] cat. 《諺》(九生あるという)猫でさえ心配のため死んだ《心配は身の毒》.

cats and dogs 《米》安くて非常に投機的な株 ▪ He bought the so-called *cats and dogs.* 彼はいわゆる安くて投機的な株を買った.

cat's meow 《米口》最高の人[もの], 素晴らしい人[もの] ▪ This watch is *the cat's meow.* この時計は最高だ.

Curiosity killed the cat. 好奇心は身を誤まる. ☞ Care killed the CAT. のもじり.

Dog my cats! 《米口》ちくしょう!, くたばりやがれ! ▪ *Dog my cats* if such an ugly set of customers can be found. そんな始末におえない連中がいてたまるか.

draw through the water with [by] a cat だまして悪ふざけをする ▪ This nation will be too wise to *be drawn* twice *through the* same *water by* the same *cat.* この国民は賢明だから, 同じ手で二度かつがれることはないだろう. ☞ 田舎者に猫にひっぱらせて池を渡らせてやれると言い, 屈強の男 4, 5 人が猫がひっぱると見せかけて, 綱を引っぱって渡らせるいたずらから.

enough to make a cat laugh 《口》きわめてこっけいな, ばかげた ▪ To see him trying to ride a bicycle is *enough to make a cat laugh.* 彼が自転車の練習をしているのを見るのは全くこっけいだ.

enough to make a cat speak (猫でもたまげて口をきくほど)実にすてきな《極めて特別なもの, 特に非常によい酒について言う》 ▪ After dinner he gave us an old liquor *enough to make a cat speak.* 夕食後, 彼はまことに素敵な古酒をふるまってくれた ▪ It is *enough to make a cat speak* French grammar to see how she tosses her head. 彼女が頭をふるさまを見るのは実にすてきだ.

grin like a Cheshire cat →CHESHIRE.

jerk [shoot, whip] the cat 《俗》酔って吐く ▪ I'm cursedly inclined to *shoot the cat.* やけに吐き気がする.

lead [live, have] a cat and dog life 《口》仲の悪い生活をする, けんかばかりして暮らす ▪ She *led a cat and dog life* with Tony. 彼女はトニーとけんかばかりして暮らした ▪ England and Ireland have *lived a cat and dog life* of it. イングランドとアイルランドはずっと仲が悪かった.

let the cat out of the bag 《口》ついうっかり秘密を漏らす ▪ Someone *let the cat out of the bag.* 誰かがつい秘密を漏らした.

like a cat in a strange garret 《米》落ち着きがない, びくびくして ▪ She acted *like a cat in a strange garret.* 彼女は不安でびくびくした行動をとった.

like a cat on hot bricks [a hot tin roof] 《口》不安で落ち着かない, びくびくして ▪ I felt *like a cat on hot bricks* all the time. 私は始終びくびくしていた ▪ You are *like a cat on hot bricks.* そわそわしていますね.

like a scalded cat 《英》脱兎のごとく, 猛烈な勢いで, 勢いよく, 激しく ▪ The car took off *like a scalded cat.* その車は急発進した.

like cats and dogs/ 《英》 ***like cat and dog*** (けんかなどに関して)激しく, すさまじく ▪ The two boys fought *like cat and dog.* 二人の少年はすさまじくなぐり合った.

Look (at) what the cat's brought [dragged] in! 《口・戯》 **1** これは珍しい人[物]が来た, 誰[何]かと思ったら ▪ "*Look what the cat dragged in,*" she laughed as she took the package. 「まあ, 何かと思ったら」と彼女は荷物を受け取って笑いながら言った.

2 (ひどい姿などで部屋に入ってきた人に対して)まあ驚いた. そんな格好で! ▪ Oh, *look what the cat's brought in!* まあ驚いた. なんて格好でしょう!

look like something the cat dragged in [brought, left] 《口》情けない様子の, 野暮な格好の, 汚らしい[みすぼらしい]姿の ▪ They're growing up healthy, even if they do *look like something the cat dragged in.* たとえ身なりはみすぼらしくても, 彼らはすくすくと育っている.

look [be] like the cat that [after it] has eaten [ate, swallowed] the canary 《米》ひどく悦に入ってすましている ▪ Each of them *looked* precisely *like the cat after it had eaten the canary.* みんなそれこそひどく悦に入ってすましていた.

look [be] like the cat that stole the cream 《口》=look like the CAT that has eaten the canary.

Muffled cats catch no mice. 《諺》手がよごれるからと言って手袋をはめては仕事ができない.

not a cat's chance 全く機会がなく ▪ There did *not* seem *a cat's chance* for Oxford. オックスフォードには勝ち目は全くないように見えた.

not have [stand] a cat in hell's chance 《口》チャンス[見込み]が全くない ▪ He did*n't have a cat in hell's chance* of winning the race. 彼はそのレースに勝つ見込みは全然なかった.

not room (enough) to swing a cat (in) →SWING[2].

play cat and mouse with 人をもてあそぶ, なぶ

る; を泳がせる ▪ If you *play cat and mouse with* your boyfriend, he'll get another girl. あなたがボーイフレンドをもてあそべば彼は別の女の子に乗りかえるよ.

poke a dead cat at *a person* 人を侮辱する, けなす ▪ He may be *poking a dead cat at* somebody who lives here. 彼はここに住んでいる誰かをけなしているのかもしれない.

pour cats and dogs →rain CATs and dogs.

put [***set***] ***the cat among the pigeons*** [***canaries***] 《口》(意外なことを言ったりしたりして)波乱[騒動]を起こす ▪ She *put the cat among the pigeons* when she said she wanted to leave school. 彼女は学校をやめると言ってみなを騒がせた.

rain [***blow***] ***cats and dogs*** 激しく雨が降る[風が吹く] ▪ It *blew* and *rained cats and dogs.* 激しく風が吹き雨が降った. ☞猫と犬は非常に仲が悪いとされていることから.

run round [***around***] ***like a scolded cat*** = run round like a blue-arsed FLY.

see [***watch***] ***which way*** [***how***] ***the cat jumps*** 《口》ひより見をする, 形勢を見る ▪ He will *see which way the cat jumps* before he declares his position. 彼は自分の立場を言明する前にまず形勢を見る ▪ I came to London merely to *see how the cat jumped.* 私はただ形勢を見るためにロンドンに来た.

shoot the cat →jerk the CAT.

That cat won't fight [***jump***]. その計画はだめだ(→That COCK won't fight).

The cat is out of the bag. 《口》秘密が漏れた; 謎は説明された ▪ I realized that *the cat was out of the bag.* 私は秘密が漏れたことを知った. ☞<let the CAT out of the bag.

The cat's got *a person's* ***tongue.*** 《口》(猫に舌を取られた, とは)黙っている, 口がきけない ▪ "*The cat's got her tongue*, I think," said her mother. 「あの子は(恥ずかしくて)口がきけないでしょう」と彼女の母は言った ▪ "Come on," said the teacher, "*Has the cat got your tongue*?" 「さあ, さあ, なぜ黙っているの」と先生は言った. ☞恐れ・憶病・はにかみなどで黙っている場合に用いる.

There is more than one way to skin a cat. →WAY.

turn (***the, a***) ***cat in*** (***the***) ***pan*** 《口》とんぼ返りをうつ; 寝返りをうつ; 私欲のために変節する ▪ The man *turned the cat in pan* once more. あいつはまた節を変えた ▪ His secretary *turned a cat in pan* and went off to a rival company. 彼の書記は寝返って敵会社の方へ行った. ☞cat = cake; pancake を焼くときにひっくり返されるから.

When [***While***] ***the cat's away, the mice will play.*** 《諺》猫がいないときにはネズミが遊ぶ,「鬼のいぬ間に洗たく」.

Who's she, the cat's mother? 《英口》 **1** 彼女って誰? 猫のお母さんのことかい? ☞子供が母親または他の女性を指すのに she を用いたときに大人が子供をたしなめて言う表現. Mother [Mom] または名前を用いるのが礼儀にかなうとされる.
2 (気取っている女性を非難して)あの人, 自分を何様だと思っているのよ.

catapult /kǽtəpʌ̀lt/ 動 ***be catapulted into*** [***to***] 急に…になる ▪ One day he *was catapulted into* fame. 彼はある日急に有名になった.

catastrophe /kətǽstrəfi/ 名 ***a walking catastrophe*** 歩く災害, 疫病神 ▪ He was *a walking catastrophe.* Far more than even Katrina, he was one of the worst disasters ever to hit America. 彼は大疫病神だった. カトリーナ台風をもはるかにしのいで, 彼は米国を襲った最悪の災害の一つだった.

catcall /kǽtkɔ̀ːl/ 名 ***utter catcalls*** 猫の鳴き声を立ててやじる ▪ The people in the gallery *uttered catcalls* and drove the actors from the stage. 天井桟敷の人々は猫の鳴き声のやじで俳優たちを退場させた.

catch[1] /kætʃ/ 名 ***a Catch-22*** [***twenty-two***] (***situation***) 身動きのとれない状況, 八方ふさがり, 行き詰まり ▪ We're in *a Catch-22 situation.* The law promotes this operation, while it places stringent requirements on it. 我々は行き詰まり状態だ. 法律ではこの操業を推進するが, 他方ではそれに厳しい要求を課している. ☞アメリカの作家 Joseph Heller の小説 (1961) から.

a shoestring catch 《野球・アメフト》地面すれすれの捕球 ▪ The leftfielder made *a shoestring catch* of a liner by Ross with two on and two outs in the fifth inning. 5回2アウトのランナー2人で, 左翼手はロスのライナーを地上すれすれで捕球した.

by catches ちょいちょい, おりおり ▪ It was written *by catches.* それはちょいちょい書かれた.

catch as catch can (レスリングの)フリースタイルの[で](どこを捕えてもよいやり方[の, で]); がむしゃらの争いの[で]; 取れるだけ取って; 行きあたりばったりの[で] ▪ Turkish wrestling is principally carried out in *catch as catch can* style. トルコのレスリングは主としてフリースタイルで行われる ▪ It was a *catch as catch can* affair. それはがむしゃらの争いであった ▪ If the firm shows signs of failing, it will be *catch as catch can* with the shareholders. もしその会社が破産のきざしを見せたら, 株主たちは取れるだけ取るだろう ▪ Leach says a lot of their trip is on a *catch as catch can* basis. リーチが言うには, 彼らの旅行の多くは行きあたりばったり式のものだ.

get a good catch of …の大漁をする ▪ We *got a good catch of* salmon. 私たちはサケの大漁をした.

have [***there is***] ***a catch*** (***in it***) 隠れた問題点[欠陥, 裏]がある ▪ *There* must *be a catch* somewhere but I can't see it. どこかに問題があるにちがいないが特定できない ▪ The plan is too good to be true and must *have a catch in it.* その案はうまくできすぎているので何か裏があるにちがいない.

no catch 《口》いやな, 無益な; むずかしい ▪ It's *no catch.* それはたいしたものではない.

What's the catch? 《口》(うますぎる話などに対して)何か問題[裏]があるのですか ▪ It left me wondering how can an airline offer fares so low—*what's the catch?* どうすれば航空会社がそんなに安く料金を設定できるのかいぶかしく思った—何か裏があるのではないか.

catch[2] /kætʃ/ 動 ***be caught between/ be*** [***get***] ***caught*** (***up***) ***in the middle*** 板ばさみになる ▪I *was caught in the middle.* 私は板ばさみになった ▪They are *getting caught up in the middle* of a broader labor fight. 彼らはより大きな労働争議に巻き込まれつつある.

be caught in (雨など)にあう ▪The party *were caught in* a shower on the way. 一行は途中でにわか雨にあった.

be [***get***] ***caught out*** **1** 妊娠する ▪I *got caught out* at last. 私はとうとう妊娠した.

2《野球》飛球を取られてアウトになる ▪Mill *was caught out* on the fly. ミルは飛球を取られてアウトになった.

be [***get***] ***caught up in*** **1** …に巻き込まれる ▪One day he will *be caught up in* the war. 彼はいつか戦争に巻き込まれるだろう.

2 …に夢中になる ▪He often *gets caught up in* comics. 彼はしばしばコミックに夢中になる.

be fairly caught まんまと見つかる ▪He *was fairly caught.* 彼はまんまと見つかった.

catch *a person doing* 人が…しているところを捕える ▪They *caught* him *stealing* it. 彼らは彼がそれを盗んでいるところを捕えた ▪You won't *catch* me *tasting* it. 僕はそれを絶対なめないよ.

catch *a person* ***a blow*** →CATCH a person one.

catch *a person* ***bending***《口・戯》人に不意打ちをくらわす, 人の虚をつく ▪I *was caught bending.* 私は不意打ちをくった. ☞かがんでいる人はけるのに都合がよいから.

catch *a person* ***cold*** →COLD.

catch *a person* ***in the*** (***very***) ***act of*** →ACT[1].

catch *a person* ***in*** *his* ***words*** 人の言葉じりをつかまえる, あげ足をとる ▪He *was caught in his words.* 彼はあげ足をとられた.

catch it (***hot***)《口》しかられる, 罰せられる ▪Anne will *catch it* (*hot*) for breaking that vase. アンはあの花びんを割ったのでしかられるだろう.

Catch me [***him***] (*doing*) (***at it***)***!***《口》それをするところを見つけられるなら見つけてみろ; 私[彼]はそんなことは絶対するものか ▪*Catch me at it* again! 二度とそんなことをするものか ▪Waste a fine day like this at the movies? *Catch me!* こんなよい天気の日をみすみす映画を見て過ごすって? 僕は絶対いやだよ.

catch *a person* ***one*** [***a blow***] 人に一撃を与える ▪I *caught* him *one* on the nose. 私は彼の鼻に一撃をくらわした.

catch that catch can →CATCH as catch can.

catch the dickens [***the devil***] ひどくしかられる, 罰せられる ▪You will *catch the devil* for it. 君はそのことでひどくしかられるぞ.

catch the post ポストを開ける時刻に間に合うようにポストに入れる ▪I wonder whether I can *catch the post.* ポストを開ける時刻に間に合うように入れられるだろうか.

catch the Speaker's eye 議長の(注意を引いて)発言の許可を得る ▪Three times he tried to *catch the Speaker's eye.* 彼は3度議長に発言許可を得ようとした.

catch the spirit of …の精神に動かされる, の精神をのみこむ ▪The men *caught the spirit of* the captain. 兵たちは隊長の意気に感じた ▪He *caught the spirit of* the age. 彼は時代の精神をのみこんだ.

catch *a person* ***upon the point of a spear*** 人をやり玉にあげる《比喩的にも》 ▪At last he *was caught upon the point of a spear.* 彼はついにやり玉にあげられた.

catch *a person* ***with*** *his* ***pants down*** 人に恥をかかせる; 人の不意をつく ▪I *caught* him *with his pants down.* 私は彼に恥をかかせた ▪It *was caught with its pants down* by the surprise attack. それは急襲によって不意をつかれた. ☞「人がズボンを脱いだところを見つける」が原義.

catch you later《口》(会話を中断するときなどに用いて)ではまたあとで ▪Teddy's last words as he left were "*Catch you later*". 別れるときのテディーの最後の言葉は「じゃ, またあとで」だった.

First catch your hare. まずことの準備手はずを整えよ ▪*First catch your hare!* You'll look a fool if you can't get anyone. まず準備をしなさい. 誰も得られなければもの笑いになるよ. ☞《諺》First catch your hare and cook it.「まず現物を手に入れよ, 処理はそれからだ」より.

No fish is caught twice with the same bait.《諺》二度と同じ手はくわない.

not catch *a person* ***dead***《口》〚主に受身で〛人が…するところは絶対見られない ▪John would*n't be caught dead* in [wearing] that tie. ジョンはそのネクタイは絶対につけないだろう.

catch-up /kǽtʃəp/ 名 ***play catch-up*** 巻き返しを図る; 追い上げる, 遅れを取り戻す[取り戻そうとする] ▪Apple Computer has *played catch-up.* アップル・コンピューターは巻き返した ▪Toronto *played catch-up* with US stock markets. トロントは合衆国の株式市場を追って上昇した.

Catherine /kǽθərən/ 名 ***turn Catherine wheels*** 側転する ▪The children *turned Catherine wheels* for our amusement. 子供らは我々の慰みに側転した.

Catholic /kǽθəlɪk/ 形 ***more Catholic than the Pope*** 教皇よりもいっそう寛容[おおらか]で ▪Teddy proved to be *more Catholic than the Pope.* テディーは教皇よりもずっと寛容だとわかった.

cat's paw /kǽtspɔ̀ː/ 名 ***make a cat's paw of*** …を手先[だし]に使う ▪She has *made a cat's paw of* you; that's plain enough. 彼女は君を手先に使ったのだ. それははっきりしている. ☞サルが猫を使って火中の栗を拾わせたという話から.

caul /kɔːl/ 名 ***be born in*** [***with***] ***a caul***《口》幸運である, 幸運に生まれついている ▪He'll never be drowned; he *was born in a caul.* 彼は決して溺死することはないだろう. 彼は幸運に生まれついているのだから. ☞caul「大網膜」は幸運を呼び水難よけと信じられていた.

C

causative /kɔ́:zətɪv/ 形 ***be causative of*** …の原因となる ▪ Intemperance *is causative of* various diseases. 不節制はいろいろの病気の原因となる.

cause /kɔ:z/ 名 ***a lost cause*** **1**(南北戦争における南軍の)失われた大義; 続ける理由[根拠]がなくなったもの《成功の見込みがない運動・企てなど》; むだ, 失敗 ▪ It is time to give up opposition as *a lost cause.* 抵抗してもむだとあきらめるときだ ▪ The war in Iraq is increasingly seen as *a lost cause.* イラクで戦争は成功の見込みがないという見方が一層増えている.

2 救いがたいもの[人], だめなもの[人] ▪ Jewish leaders have viewed Davis as *a lost cause.* ユダヤの指導者たちはデイビスをダメ男と見ていた.

for [***in***] ***a good*** [***worthy***] ***cause*** (慈善などの)良い目的のために, 大義のために ▪ The community work together *for a good cause.* その共同社会はりっぱな目的のために協力して働いている.

give (…) ***cause for*** (心配など)の種となる ▪ The state of the Empire *gave* (us) *cause for* grave concern. 帝国の状態は(我々の)深い憂慮の種となった.

have cause to *do* [***for***] …すべき理由がある, するのは当然である ▪ You *have cause to* be thankful. あなたが感謝するのは当然である ▪ We *have cause for* joy. 我々は喜ぶべき理由がある.

in the cause of …のために ▪ I will labor *in the cause of* humanity. 私は人類のために尽くします.

make common cause 協力[提携]する, 味方になる (*with*); (大義のために)共同戦線を張る (*against*) ▪ Thus the Protestants were forced to *make common cause with* the Papists. こうして新教徒はむりやりにカトリック教徒と協力させられた.

plead a [*a person's*] ***cause*** 訴訟の理由を申し立てる, 言い分を申し立てる ▪ Would to heaven that I could *plead his cause!* なんとかして彼の言い分を申し立ててやることができればなあ.

see cause to *do* …する理由を認める ▪ The Government has not *seen cause to* contribute anything towards it. 政府はそれに対して何か貢献すべき理由を認めていない.

show cause 《法》正当な理由を示す, 説明を与える; 暫定判決などに反対の理由を示す ▪ *Show cause* why they should not be held without bail. 彼らが留置されるべきでない理由を示してください.

take up a cause (社会的)運動をする ▪ They are beginning to *take up the cause* of children's rights. 彼らは子供の権利を守る運動を始めている.

the day [***hour***] ***of cause*** 裁判の日[時刻] ▪ I'll be with you in *the hour of cause.* 裁判の時刻にあなたといっしょになりましょう.

the First Cause 第一原因; 造物主, 神 ▪ God is *the First Cause.* 神は造物主である.

with [***without***] ***cause*** 理由があって[なくて] ▪ He gets angry *without cause.* 彼はわけなく腹をたてる.

caution[1] /kɔ́:ʃən/ 名 ***be a caution to*** …さえも驚く, たじろぐ ▪ The way I'll lick you will *be a caution to* the rest of your family. 私があなたを負かす負かしぶりには, あなたの家の他の人たちも驚くだろう. ☞caution「驚くべきもの」.

by way of caution 警告として ▪ I say this *by way of caution.* 念のためにこのことを申しあげる.

throw [***fing, cast***] ***caution to the wind***(***s***)/ ***throw caution out of the window*** 大胆な行動を取る, 思い切ったことをする ▪ They *threw caution to the wind* and got their reward. 彼らは思いきってやってみて褒美を手にした.

with a caution 訓戒をして ▪ The police dismissed the charge *with a caution.* 警察は将来を戒めて罪を赦した.

with caution 用心して ▪ Act *with* great *caution.* 十分注意して行動せよ.

caution[2] /kɔ́:ʃən/ 動 ***caution*** *oneself* ***against*** …を警戒する, せぬよう警戒する ▪ *Caution yourself against* errors. 誤りを犯さぬよう警戒しなさい.

caution *a person* ***not to*** *do* 人に…しないよう[するなと]警告する ▪ I *cautioned* him *not to* be late. 私は彼に遅刻するなと警告した.

cautious /kɔ́:ʃəs/ 形 ***be cautious how*** [***lest, not to*** *do*] …しないよう用心する ▪ *Be cautious how* you fall into the ditch. みぞに落ちないよう用心せよ ▪ He *is cautious lest* he should commit this offence. 彼はこの罪を犯さないように用心している ▪ *Be cautious not to* exceed it. それを越えないよう注意しなさい.

be cautious of …せぬよう用心する ▪ I will *be cautious of* giving offence. 人を怒らせないよう用心します.

cavalry /kǽvəlri/ 名 ***like the 7th Cavalry*** 第七騎兵隊のように; 衝動的に, 猛烈に, 急遽(きゅうきょ); 全滅[壊滅]状態で ▪ A consortium of community colleges charged in *like the 7th Cavalry* with an idea. 短大協会がある考えに衝動的に飛びついた ▪ A week after Election Day, the Party is looking *like the 7th Cavalry* a few hours after the Battle of the Little Bighorn. 選挙日から1週間後, その政党はリトル・ビッグホーンの戦いから数時間後の第七騎兵隊のようで見る影もない. ☞カスター将軍に率いられた第七騎兵隊(1876年 Little Bighorn でスー族により全滅)から. カスターは "impetuous George Custer" (向こう見ずなジョージ・カスター)と称される.

The cavalry are coming [***The cavalry are here***]. 助けがもうすぐ来る[助けが着いた] ▪ Don't panic—*the cavalry are coming.* うろたえるんじゃない, 助けが来るから.

cave /keɪv/ 間 ***keep cave*** 《学俗》(悪いことをしているとき)見張りをする ▪ They asked him to *keep cave* in case old Cassidy came along. みんなは老キャシディーが来ては困るので, 彼に見張りをするように頼んだ. ☞L cavē 'be thou ware' (命令法).

caveat /kɑ́:viɑ̀:t|kǽviæt/ 名 ***enter* [*file, put in*] *a caveat*** **1**《法》(...に対する)訴訟上の手続き差止めを申請する ▪ The defendant *entered a caveat.* 被告は手続き差止めを申請した.
2 警告する ▪ He *entered a caveat* against a misconception. 彼は誤解せぬよう警告した ▪ They should *put in a caveat* that he might not go to war with them. 彼らは彼が戦争をしかけないよう警告すべきである.

caviare /kæ̀viɑ́:r/ 名 ***caviare to the general* [*multitude*]** 高尚すぎて俗受けのしない逸品, 猫に小判 (cf. Sh., *Haml.* 2. 2. 457) ▪ Picasso's art is *caviare to the general.* ピカソの美術は高尚すぎて俗受けしない. ☞caviare「キャビア(チョウザメ類の腹子の塩うけ, 珍味)」.

cease[1] /si:s/ 名 ***without cease*** 果てしなく, 絶え間なく ▪ Space extends *without cease* in all directions. 空間は四方八方に果てしなく広がっている.

cease[2] /si:s/ 動 ***cease and desist***《法》(営業などを)停止する ▪ Instruct the quarreling parents to *cease and desist.* 争っている夫婦にやめるように命じなさい.

never cease to amaze ...にいつも驚き[感銘]を与える ▪ Hollywood *never ceases to amaze* the world. ハリウッドは世界に驚きを与え続けている.

without ceasing 絶えず ▪ Pray *without ceasing.* 絶えず祈りなさい.

ceiling /sí:lɪŋ/ 名 ***hit the ceiling*** →HIT[2].

set a ceiling on ...の最高限度を決める (↔put a FLOOR under) ▪ They *set a ceiling on* working hours. 彼らは労働時間の最大限を設定した.

cellar /sélər/ 名 ***down cellar***《米》地下室で[へ] ▪ He placed a young plant *down cellar.* 彼は若木を地下室に置いた.

in the cellar《競技》最下位で ▪ Our team is *in the cellar.* わがチームは最下位である.

keep a good* [*small*] *cellar ワインのたくわえが豊富[貧弱]である ▪ We *keep a good cellar* of French vintage wines. 私どもはフランスビンテージワインのたくわえが豊富です.

censor /sénsər/ 名 ***pass the censor*** 出版許可を得る ▪ Will our material *pass the censor*? 我々の資料は出版許可が得られるだろうか.

census /sénsəs/ 名 ***take a census*** (国勢)調査をする ▪ The government *took a census* of unemployment. 政府は失業調査をした.

cent /sent/ 名 ***cent percent* [《英》*per cent*]** 10割の利益[利子] ▪ He sold a score of sheep for *cent per cent.* 彼は10割の利益で羊を20頭売った.

feel like two cents《米俗》自分をつまらぬものと思う, 肩身を狭く感じる ▪ I *felt like two cents* before her. 私は彼女の前では肩身の狭い思いだった.

look like thirty cents《米》安っぽく見える ▪ He'd *look like thirty cents.* 彼は安っぽく見えるだろうよ.

not a* [*one*] *red cent《主に米》びた一文受けとらない, 払わない ▪ I would*n't* pay *a red cent* for that. 私はそんなものにはびた一文払おうとは思わない ▪ *Not* one of them gets *a red cent.* 彼らの誰も1セントたりとも受けとっていない. ☞1セント硬貨が銅製で色が赤いことから.

not care a* (*red*) *cent《米》ちっともかまわない ▪ He did*n't care a red cent* for it. 彼はそんなことはちっともかまわなかった.

not have two cents to rub together 一文無しである ▪ I've worked hard all my life and I still do*n't have two cents to rub together.* 私はずっと一生懸命働いてきたがそれでも無一文だ.

not worth a* (*red*) *cent《米》一文の値うちもない ▪ They did *not* think it *worth a cent.* 彼らはそれを一文の値うちもないと思った.

put* one's *two cents* (*worth*) *in《米》(割り込んで)自分の考えを述べる ▪ He always has to *put his two cents worth in.* 彼はいつも人の話に私見を割り込ませないと気がすまない.

one's ***two cents* (*worth*) [*two cents' worth*]** 意見, 見解 (《英》one's two penn'orth) ▪ At the meeting, Trump threw in *his two cents* on the matter. 会議でトランプはその件に関して意見を述べた ▪ You're also welcome to put in *your two cents worth.* どうかご意見もお寄せください.

center,《英》**centre** /séntər/ 名 ***catch on* (*the*) *center***《米》(蒸気機関が)止まって前方[後方]へのはずみがきかなくなる《比喩的にも》 ▪ His voice *caught on the center* occasionally. 彼の声は時々ひっかかって出なくなった.

come to the center《米俗》公然と出てくる; 顕著な地位を占める ▪ He's *come to the center.* 彼は顕著な地歩を占めた.

drive the center《米》的の中心に当てる ▪ They managed to *drive the center.* 彼らはなんとかしてうまく的の中心に当てた.

off center 真ん中より少し離れて ▪ Jane hung the picture *off center.* ジェインは絵を真ん中より少し離れたところに掛けた.

on dead center **1** 止まりセンター[死点]に[で], 静止[停滞, 膠着]状態に[で] ▪ The old problems are still stuck *on dead center.* 古い問題がいまだに真ん中で滞っている.
2 (...の)ちょうど真ん中に[で] ▪ The arrow hit the target *on dead center.* 矢は標的のど真ん中を射た.
3 的確な, 図星の ▪ Her analysis is *on dead center.* 彼女の分析は正鵠を得ている.

set ... on centers《米・建築》柱やたるきをおのおのの中心から...の間隔に置く ▪ Floor-beams three inches thick were *set* sixteen inches *on centers.* 厚さ3インチの床材がおのおのの中心から16インチの間隔に置かれた《13インチ離れて》.

the center of *a person's* ***universe*** ...にとっての最重要物[人物, 地域] ▪ A woman wishes to be *the center of her husband's universe.* 女性は夫にとって最重要人物でありたいと願う ▪ Seattle is *the center of the baseball universe* this week. 今週シアトルは野球の中心地だ.

century /séntʃəri/ 名 ***make a century*** 《クリケット》100点取る ▪ He has *made two centuries* this season. 彼は今ーズン200点取った.

make *one's* ***century*** 100まで生きる ▪ Mrs. Brown *made her century* last week. ブラウン夫人は先週100歳に達した.

C

ceremony /sérəmòʊni|sérəməni/ 名 ***stand on*** [***upon***] ***ceremony*** 儀式ばる; 堅苦しくて打ち解けない ▪ I never *stand upon ceremony* with such people. 私はそのような人々には堅苦しくしない.

without ceremony 儀式ばらないで, 打ち解けて, 無造作に ▪ *Without ceremony* the two ladies ran out of the room. いきなり女性が二人部屋から走り出た ▪ *Without* further *ceremony*, I will go on. もうあっさりと続けて話しましょう.

certain /sə́ːrtən/ 形 ***a certain age*** 相当の年齢《若くないが, はっきり言うのをはばかる場合; 主として40–60歳の婦人に言う》 ▪ He was having an affair with a lady of *a certain age*. 彼はかなりの年輩の夫人と浮気をしていた.

be certain of [***about***] ...を確信している ▪ He *is certain of* the correctness of his view. 彼は自分の見解の正しさを確信している.

be certain to *do* きっと...するだろう ▪ We *are certain to* meet him in the course of our rambles. 私たちは散歩の途中できっと彼に出会うだろう.

for certain 確かに ▪ He is *for certain* a useful member. 彼は確かに重宝な会員だ ▪ I don't know *for certain*. しかとは知りません.

in a certain condition →CONDITION[1].

make certain (***of, that***) ...を確かめる; 確実に...する ▪ I think the train leaves at 8, but you'd better *make certain*. 電車は8時発だと思うが確かめて ▪ *Make certain that* the door is locked. 確実にドアをロックしておきなさい.

morally certain まず大丈夫で, 万々まちがいなく ▪ One is not sure, only *morally certain*. 確信しているのではなく, まず大丈夫というところだ.

of a certain description いかがわしい商売の(女など) ▪ Women *of a certain description* do not do what they do openly. いかがわしい商売の女は公然とそんなことはしない.

certainly /sə́ːrtənli/ 副 ***Certainly not!*** いえいえ! ▪ Will you lend me your toothbrush?—*Certainly not!* あなたの歯ブラシを貸してくれませんか—とんでもない!

certainty /sə́ːrtənti/ 名 ***a dead certainty*** 《口》きっと勝つ馬; きっと起こること ▪ Put a fiver on the horse; he's *a dead certainty*. その馬には5ポンドかけなさい. きっと勝つから.

a moral certainty 万々まちがいないこと ▪ His bankruptcy is *a moral certainty*. 彼の破産は万々まちがいない.

for [***of, to***] (***a***) ***certainty*** 確かに, 疑いなく ▪ He will fall in love with her *to a certainty*. 彼はきっと彼女に恋するであろう ▪ I know this *for* (*a*) *certainty*. これをしかと知っている.

with certainty はっきりと ▪ I can't say *with certainty*. はっきりとは言えません.

certificate /sərtífəkət/ 名 ***try by*** (***the***) ***certificate*** (***of***) 《法》(別の法廷・権能によって書かれた)証明書によって裁判する ▪ When the issue is whether a person was absent in the army, this *is tried by the certificate of* the proper officer. 軍隊にいなかったかどうかが問題であるときは, 相当の役人の証明書によって裁判される.

cesspool /séspùːl/ 名 ***a cesspool of iniquity*** 不正のたまり ▪ Seneca speaks of Rome as *a cesspool of iniquity*. セネカはローマのことを罪悪のたまりと言っている.

chafe /tʃeɪf/ 名 ***be in a chafe*** いらいらしている ▪ There is no need for you to *be in* such *a chafe*. そんなにいらいらする必要はない.

chaff /tʃæf|tʃɑːf/ 名 ***a grain of wheat in a bushel of chaff*** →GRAIN.

be caught with chaff 〚主に否定文で〛 やすやすとだまされる, わなにかかる ▪ Frederick the Great was too old a bird to *be caught with chaff*. フリードリヒ大王は古だぬきだったからやすやすとだまされはしなかった. ☞An old BIRD is not caught with chaff. 《諺》から.

chagrin /ʃəgrín|ʃǽgrɪn/ 動 ***be chagrined at*** ...をくやしがる ▪ He *was chagrined at* his failure. 彼は失敗をくやしがった.

chain[1] /tʃeɪn/ 名 ***A chain is*** (***only***) ***as strong as its weakest link.*** 《諺》鎖の強度は一番弱い輪の強度である《事業などの各部門のどこかに弱点があると総くずれになる》.

(***a man***) ***in the chains*** (舷側の板に立ち)測船で海深を測る(人) ▪ The man *in the chains* found more water than was down in the chart. 海深を測る人がそこを測ると海図に書いてあるより深かった.

brighten the chain 旧交を温める ▪ He *brightened the chain* with Dr. Smith. 彼はスミス博士との旧交を温めた.

in chains 鎖でしばられて; 獄につながれて ▪ He is *in chains*. 彼は獄中にある.

on the chain 鎖でつながれて, 行動を制限されて ▪ We keep the dog *on the chain* all day. 犬は一日中鎖でつないでおく ▪ She keeps her servants *on the chain*. 彼女は使用人の行動を制限している.

pull [***yank***] *a person's* ***chain*** 《米口》人に余計なお節介をする; 人をからかう[ちゃかす, かつぐ, だます, いじめる, 困らす, 怒らせる] (→YANK a person's chain) ▪ My brother *pulls my chain* by doing stuff like eating my yogurt. 兄は私のヨーグルトを食べたりして私をからかう ▪ Maybe I'm just in a bad mood but your letter really *yanked my chain*. たぶん私は虫の居所が悪いだけなのだろうが, 君の手紙は本当に癇(かん)にさわった. ☞犬の鎖を引いていじめることから.

pull the chain 《英》トイレの水を流す ▪ Never forget to *pull the chain*. トイレの水を流すのを決して忘れないように.

chain[2] /tʃeɪn/ 動 ***be chained to*** ...に縛られて

▪ I am so busy that I've *been chained to* my desk all week. 私は非常に忙しくて1週間ずっと事務机に縛られていた.

chair /tʃeər/ 名 ***above* [*past*] *the Chair*** 《英》(ロンドン市参事会議員が)市長の経験があって ▪ He is *above the Chair*. あの市参事会議員はロンドン市長の経験がある.

address the chair 議長に呼びかける(Mr. Chairman! と言って)議長に謝辞など述べる ▪ It is polite to *address the chair* in a large meeting. 大きい会では議長に呼びかけるのが礼儀である.

almost* [*nearly*] *fall off* one's *chair いすから転げ落ちるほど驚く ▪ I *almost fell off my chair* when I heard of his death. 彼が死んだと聞いたとき私はびっくり仰天した ▪ She caught a glimpse of herself in the mirror and *almost fell off her chair* in shock. 彼女は鏡に映る自分の姿をちらと見てひどいショックを受けた ▪ I *nearly fell off my chair* when I heard my exam result. 試験結果を聞いていすから転げ落ちるほどびっくりした.

appeal to the chair 議長に訴え(て支援・助言を求め)る ▪ The speaker *appealing to the chair* asked for the chairman's intervention. 演説者は議長に訴えて調停を依頼した.

below the Chair 《英》(ロンドン市参事会議員が)ロンドン市長を務めたことのない ▪ The aldermen *below the Chair* were on horseback. ロンドン市長の経験のない市参事会議員たちが馬に乗っていた.

call ... to the chair ...を議長に選ぶ[指名する] ▪ Mr. Goodrich *was called to the chair*. グッドリッチ氏が議長に選ばれた.

escape the chair 《米》死刑を免れる ▪ The killer hopes to *escape the chair*. その殺人者は死刑を免れたがっている.

get* [*go*] *to the chair 《米》(電気いすで)死刑に処せられる ▪ The murderer will have to *go to the chair*. その殺人犯は死刑に処せられねばならぬだろう.

have a chair →take a CHAIR.

in the chair 議長席について, 議長を務めて ▪ Mr. Young was then *in the chair*. ヤング氏がそのとき議長をやっていた.

leave the chair 議長[司会]席を去る, 会を終える ▪ He *left the chair* in the middle of his term. 彼は在位半ばで議長職を辞した.

musical chairs **1**〚単数扱い〛いす取りゲーム ▪ *Musical chairs* has been condemned for encouraging aggression. いす取りゲームは攻撃性を助長するとして非難されている.

2 事務職員の配置転換 ▪ The candidate played *musical chairs* with his top campaign staff. その候補者はトップの選挙運動員の配置転換をした.

pass the chair →PASS[3].

past the Chair →above the CHAIR.

play first chair **1**(オーケストラ・バンドで各楽器部門の)首席[第一]奏者になる ▪ In the All-State Orchestra, Emily *plays first chair* and Sarah second. 全州オーケストラではエミリーが第一奏者, サラが第二奏者を務める.

2 指導的役割を果たす ▪ You're not the boss! You don't *play first chair*. あなたは上司ではない. あなたは第一担当者ではない.

pull up a chair 〚主に命令文で〛まあ座りなさい ▪ *Pull up a chair* and make yourself comfortable. まあ座って楽にしたまえ.

put ... in the chair **1** ...を議長[会長]に選ぶ ▪ We *put* Mr. Young *in the chair*. ヤング氏を議長に選んだ.

2《俗》...に支払わずにおく ▪ Some cab drivers have *put* him *in the chair*. 貸馬車の御者たちの中には彼に支払をしない者もいる.

send ... to the chair 《米》...を(電気いすで)死刑に処する ▪ The general *was sent to the chair* at last. 将軍はついに死刑に処せられた.

take* [*have*] *a chair いすに座る ▪ Please *take a chair*. どうぞおかけください.

take the chair 議長となる, 議事を始める ▪ Lord Crony will *take the chair* at the next meeting. クローニー卿は次の会で議長になるだろう.

chaise /ʃeɪz/ 名 ***take chaise*** (4輪の無蓋旅行用)馬車に乗る[乗って行く] ▪ From Genoa we *took chaise* for Milan. ジェノバから4輪馬車に乗ってミラノまで行った.

chalice /tʃǽləs/ 名 ***a poisoned chalice*** 《主に英》毒杯; 最初は魅力的に見えるが結局は大変なことになりそうなこと《見た目には魅力的だが失敗や不愉快な結果を招くもの》 ▪ My new task seemed interesting at first, but it turned out to be *a poisoned chalice*. 今度の仕事は当初こそおもしろそうだったが, 結局はやっかいな仕事と知れた ▪ Looking back, do you think the job was *a poisoned chalice*? 振り返ってみて, お仕事は「毒入りワイン」だとお考えですか.

chalk[1] /tʃɔːk/ 名 **(*as*) *different as chalk from cheese*** (外見だけ似て)実質は全く異なって ▪ Is badminton anything like tennis? —No, *as different as chalk from cheese*. バドミントンはテニスのようなものか—いや, 全く違う.

(*as*) *like* [*analogous*] *as chalk and cheese* (外見だけ似て)実質は全く異なって ▪ These two plants are *as like as chalk and cheese*. この二つの植物は実質は全く異なっている.

***by a long chalk* [(*long*) *chalks*]** 《英口》はるかに; 断然 ▪ His horse was the best *by long chalks*. 彼の馬が断然最良であった ▪ Ernest beat him *by a long chalk*. アーネストははるかに彼にまさっていた. ☞昔, ゲームで得点をチョークで書いたことから.

chalk and talk 《英》(教師と生徒とのくだけたやりとりによる授業に対して)伝統的な板書と説明中心の授業(の) ▪ "*Chalk and talk* as a teaching methodology is in its last days," he said. 「板書と説明の教育法は最後の日々を迎えている」と彼は言った ▪ We decided to offer online education rather than traditional *chalk and talk* classes. 伝統的な板書と説明の授業よりもオンラインの教育を提唱しようと決めた.

***come up to* (*the*) *chalk* 《米俗》再び始める; 標準に達する, 満足すべきである ▪ He soon recovered himself and *came up to the chalk* again. 彼はまもなく立ち直ってまた始めた ▪ The President does not *come up to chalk*. 大統領は標準以下である.

make chalk of one and cheese of another 両者を分けへだてする ▪ I cannot *make chalk of one and cheese of another*. 両者を分けへだてすることはできない.

no more like ... than chalk's like cheese ...とは全く異なって ▪ Tom is *no more like* you *than chalk's like cheese*. トムは君とは全く違う.

not by a long chalk 《口》全然...ない, 絶対に...ない ▪ Did he pay?—No, *not by a long chalk*. 彼は払いましたか—いいえ全然.

not know chalk from cheese チーズとチョークの区別がつかない; 全然物事がわからない ▪ They say in contempt of Tom that he does *not know chalk from cheeze*. 彼らはトムのことを軽蔑して「あいつはチーズとチョークの区別もつかない」と言う.

toe the chalk →TOE².

walk* [*stump*] *one's chalks 《俗》立ち去る, 逃げ去る, 黙って去る ▪ The prisoner has *walked his chalks*, and is off to London. 囚人は逃げ去って, ロンドンへ行っている. ☞おそらく軍隊で, 酔っていないことを証明するため兵にチョーク線上を歩かせたことから.

walk the chalk →WALK².

chalk² /tʃɔːk/ 動 ***chalk** a person's **hat*** 《米》鉄道で無賃旅行を許す ▪ I will *chalk your hat* for the journey. ご旅行での鉄道無賃乗車を許可します.

chalk on a barn door 《米口》大ざっぱな計算をする ▪ They *chalked on a barn door* and split the difference. 彼らは大ざっぱな計算をして間を取った.

***chalk one up for* [*to do*]** 《口》 **1** ...を優位とする, 支持する ▪ A 5-4 majority on the Supreme Court *chalked one up for* school principals. 連邦最高裁判は5対4の過半数で校長側を支持した. **2** 〖間投詞的に〗...の勝ちだ, よくやった; 《皮肉》結構なことだ ▪ *Chalk one up for* the kids. 子供たちの勝ち ▪ *Chalk one up to* be born with rich parents. 金持ちの両親のところに生まれて結構だったね.

challenge¹ /tʃǽləndʒ/ 名 ***rise to the challenge*** 難局[試練]に立派に対処する; 臨機の処置をとる ▪ When the lecturer didn't arrive, the chairman *rose to the challenge*. 講師が来なかったとき司会者が臨機に講演をした.

take up the challenge 挑戦を受けて立つ ▪ A number of runners *took up the challenge* set by the front-runners in the race. 数名の走者がその競走の先頭走者たちの挑戦に応じた.

challenge² /tʃǽləndʒ/ 動 ***challenge the array*** 《法》陪審団全体を忌避する ▪ We may lawfully *challenge the array*. 我々は陪審団全体を合法的に忌避することができる.

hygienically challenged 《婉曲》不衛生である, 汚れた ▪ John is gray-haired, *hygienically challenged*, drunk and low-down. ジョンは白髪で, うすよごれ, 酔っぱらっていて下劣だ.

vertically* [*socially, chronologically,* etc.] *challenged 《戯》身長的に[社会的に, 年齢的に, など]ハンディのある ▪ Nobody seriously uses *vertically challenged* for "short."「背が低い」ことを身長的にハンディがあるとまじめに言うものはいない ▪ The "*chronologically challenged*" know more than the rest of us because they've lived longer.「年齢的にハンディのある」人々は長生きしているので, 他の我々よりも多くのことを知っている.

chamber /tʃéɪmbər/ 名 ***a chamber of imagery*** いろいろな画像で飾られた部屋 (《聖》*Ezek*. 8. 12) ▪ Did some darkened *chamber of imagery* witness it? どこか暗い画像の部屋がそれの場面となったのか.

one-man Chamber of Commerce 《米》宣伝を一人で買って出ている人 ▪ From now on, I'll be a *one-man Chamber of Commerce* for Hokkaido. これからは北海道の宣伝を一人で買って出ましょう. ☞アメリカの Chamber of Commerce (商業会議所)はその町村の宣伝に関する資料を持っていることから.

champagne /ʃæmpéɪn/ 名 (***a***) ***champagne lifestyle*** 贅沢な生活ぶり(の) ▪ The woman undoubtedly led *a Champagne lifestyle*. その女性は明らかに贅沢な生活をしていた ▪ He was living *a champagne lifestyle* way beyond his means. 彼は収入以上の贅沢三昧の暮らしぶりだった.

a champagne socialist ブルジョア社会主義者, 贅沢な生活をしながら社会主義を唱える人 ▪ His opponents call him *a "champagne socialist"* because of his swanky lifestyle. 敵対者は彼のことをはでな暮らしぶりゆえに「ブルジョア社会主義者」と呼ぶ.

chance¹ /tʃæns|tʃɑːns/ 名 ***a chance in a million*** 100万分の1の[千載一遇の]チャンス, 希有の幸運 ▪ If our baby has *a chance in a million*, we want to go for it. 私たちの赤ちゃんに100万分の1でもチャンスがあるのなら, それを選びたい ▪ To be caught up in a major disaster is *a chance in a million*. 大災害に巻き込まれることはめったにない.

a chance in life 出世の機会 ▪ Some better *chance in life* will offer itself to him. 何かもっと良い出世の機会が彼に来るだろう.

a* [*the*] *chance of a snowball in hell/ a* [*the*] *chance of a fart in a windstorm 《口》〖否定文で〗実現の見込み(がない) ▪ I don't think the stock has *the chance of a snowball in hell* to recover its former glory days. 株が以前の栄光の日々を取り戻す見込みはないと思う.

a considerable chance 《米》長い間 ▪ I stood there *a considerable chance*. 長い間そこに立っていた.

a long chance 見込み[可能性]の薄いこと; あぶない賭 ▪ It would be *a long chance* for him to have missed the train. 彼が列車に乗り遅れたということはまずないだろう.

a mathematical chance きわめて少ない可能性

[低い確率] ▪ The team has only *a mathematical chance* of winning the championship. そのチームが優勝する可能性はきわめて少ない.

a smart chance of 《米口》相当の量[数]の ▪ There was *a smart chance of* Yankees in the village. 村には相当数の米国人がいた.

a sporting chance 《口》一か八かのやま; 当てにならない機会; (確実性でなく)可能性 ▪ The proposal stands *a sporting chance* of acceptance. その提案は受け入れられる可能性がある(確実とは言えないが) ▪ You have *a sporting chance*. 君には一か八かのやまがある.

against all chances 成功[勝算]の見込みがない(のに) ▪ I am sure we are to fight *against all chances*. 我々は勝算の見込みがなくても戦わねばならないのだと思う.

as chance would [will] have it 運のめぐりあわせで, 偶然にも ▪ *As chance would have it*, I met him at a dinner party. 偶然にも私は宴会で彼に会った ▪ I'm going to London tomorrow *as chance will have it*. 私はたまたまあすロンドンへ行きます.

at the first chance 機会ありしだい ▪ I intend to go there *at the first chance*. 機会がありしだいそこへ行くつもりです.

be in with a chance 勝つ見込みがある, できる見込みがある (*of doing, to do*) ▪ We *are* still *in with a chance of winning* [*to* win] the game. 我々にはまだ試合に勝つ見込みがある.

blow** one's* ***[a, the, that] chance 好機を逃す ▪ Yokohama seemed to have *blown its chance* when it lost a hard-fought match at home to Cerezo Osaka. 横浜はホームで激戦のすえセレッソ大阪に敗れたときチャンスがついえたように思われた ▪ They *blew that chance* by failing to finish first. 彼らは1位になれなくてそのチャンスを逃した.

by any chance 万一, どうかして ▪ If *by any chance* I am able to get there before you, I will wait for you. もし万一, 私があなたより先にそこへ着くことができたらお待ちしましょう.

by chance たまたま, 偶然に, 何かのはずみで ▪ I met him *by chance* in the train. 私は偶然電車の中で彼に会った.

by the merest chance ほんの偶然で, 全く偶然に ▪ He discovered it *by the merest chance*. 彼は全く偶然にそれを発見した.

chance would be a fine thing 《口》その機会があれば結構だが ▪ Why don't you apply for the job?—*Chance would be a fine thing*, but it's been promised to Johnson. 君はなぜその仕事を志願しないのか—その機会があれば結構だがそれはジョンスンに約束ずみなのだ.

drinking in the last chance saloon →the last CHANCE saloon.

fancy** one's* **[*a person's*] *chances 《口》成功の見込みありと信じる ▪ I don't *fancy your chances* at all. 君の成功の見込みは全くないと思う ▪ I *fancy my chances* with her. 彼女とうまくやれると思う.

give a chance **1** 《クリケット》打者の失策によりアウトになる機会を(野手に)与える ▪ The batsman *gave an* easy *chance* to Mr. Grace off his own bowling. 打者は自分の失策によりやすやすとアウトになる機会をグレイス氏につかませた.

2 勝負の機会を与える ▪ *Give* me *a* fair *chance*! さあ尋常に勝負せよ.

have [stand] a Chinaman's chance 《米俗》可能性が乏しい ▪ He doesn't *have a Chinaman's chance* of winning. 彼が勝つ見込みは皆無だ.

have a good chance of ...の見込みがある ▪ You *have a good chance of* success. 君には成功する見込みが十分ある.

have half a chance 五分の[わずかながら]チャンスがある ▪ I think this team *has half a chance* as well. 私はこのチームにもまだチャンスはあると思う.

have no chance of →stand no CHANCE of.

(if) given half a chance 《口》半分[少し]でも機会を与えられれば ▪ I would have voted for the man, *(if) given half a chance*. 少しでも機会が与えられていたら, あの男に投票していただろう.

jump at the chance チャンスに喜んでとびつく[応じる] (*to do, of*) ▪ Turner *jumped at the chance to* come back home. ターナーは帰郷するチャンスに喜んで応じた ▪ Many *jumped at the chance of* obtaining immigrant visas to the U.S. 多くの人が合衆国への移民ビザを得る機会にとびついた.

leave ... to chance ...を運に任せる ▪ You cannot *leave* your whole future *to chance*. あなたは未来をすべて運に任せることはできない.

mind the main chance →have an eye to the MAIN CHANCE.

no chance 《口》見込みはない; だめだ ▪ At important meetings people listen to me, but at home, *no chance*. 重要な会合では人々は私の話を聞いてくれるのだが家ではだめだ.

(not) have a chance [a dog's chance, a snowball's chance] in hell (of *doing*)/《英口》***(not) have a cat in hell's chance (of*** *doing*) 《口》全然見込みがない (→a CHANCE of a snowball in hell) ▪ I did*n't have a chance in hell of passing* the examination. 僕は試験にパスする見込みは全くなかった ▪ That last name *has not a cat in hell's chance of* success. 最後にあげた名前は成功の見込みはない ▪ We *haven't got a snowball's chance in hell of winning* the race. このレースで優勝する見込みはまるでない.

on the chance of [that] ...を予期して ▪ We will go to town *on the chance of* meeting him. 彼に会えるかもしれないから町へ行ってみよう ▪ I came *on the chance that* we could go to the cinema. 私はいっしょに映画を見に行けると思ってやってきた.

on the off chance →OFF-CHANCE.

stand a (good, fair) chance (of) 《口》(...の)見込みが(十分)ある ▪ He *stands a good chance of* winning the fight. 彼はその戦いに勝つ見込みは十

分ある.
stand *one's* ***chance*** 運[成り行き]に任せる ▪ They must *stand their chance.* 彼らは運に任せねばならない.
stand [***have***] ***no chance of*** …の見込みはない ▪ He *stands no chance of* winning. 彼には勝つ見込みはない.
take a chance of …の危険を冒す ▪ It is foolish to *take a chance of* being injured in a fight. けんかでけがをするような危険を冒すのはばかげている.
take a (***long***) ***chance/take*** (***long***) ***chances*** (…の)冒険を冒す, 危険を冒してやる, 一か八か冒険をする (*on, with*) ▪ Don't *take a chance* (*on*) going out in this weather without an umbrella. この天候にかさを持たずに出かけるような冒険はよせ ▪ Washington *took chances* rather than abandon New York without a blow. ワシントンは一撃も与えずニューヨークを放棄するより危険を冒してやるほうを選んだ ▪ I'll *take a chance on* the idea. その案をのるかそるかで実行してみます ▪ They *take long chances with* their safety. 彼らは身の安全をかけるようなことを思い切ってやる. ☞《英》take one's CHANCE 1.
take an even chance 損得五分五分の運試しをする ▪ Anyway, let's *take an even chance* and stock up with them. ともかく, 損得五分五分の運試しに, それを仕入れてみよう.
take *one's* ***chance*** **1** 運に任せてやってみる, 運試しにやる ▪ Brother, take my land, I'll *take my chance.* 兄さん, 私の土地を取りなさい. 私は運試しをやってみます.
2 機会をつかむ ▪ You must *take your chance.* 君は機会をつかまねばならない.
take no chances 《米》冒険を冒さない ▪ He is *taking no chances* of burglars getting in. 彼は強盗に入られるような危険なことはしない.
take the chance 運に任せて一か八かやってみる ▪ Let's *take the chance* and buy these goods. Prices may go up. 運試しにこの品を買ってみましょう. 値段があがるかもしれません.
the chances are against [***in favor of***] 形勢は…に不利[有利]である ▪ *The chances are* a hundred to one *against* you. 形勢はほとんど完全にあなたに不利だ ▪ *The chances were in his favor,* but he failed. 形勢は彼に有利だったが彼は失敗した.
the chances are (***that***) たぶん…らしい ▪ *The chances are that* the boss may send me to Virginia. 社長は僕をバージニアへやりそうだ.
the last chance saloon 《英》最後のチャンス, 最後の機会を与えられている ▪ The veteran lefty referred to his comeback attempt as *the Last Chance Saloon.* そのベテランの左腕投手は復帰に向けた努力を最後のチャンスだと言った ▪ Labour is drinking in *the last chance saloon* and will lose the next general election unless it changes direction. 労働党は最後のチャンスを与えられているが, 方向を変えなければ次の総選挙で敗れるだろう.

chance[2] /tʃæns|tʃɑːns/ 動 ***and chance the ducks*** [***it***] 《俗》結果はどうあろうとも; ともかくも ▪ I'll do it *and chance the ducks.* 私はそうします, 結果はどうでも ▪ He wasn't here last Sunday, *and chance it.* 彼はともかくも前の日曜には不在だった.
as it may chance 場合によっては ▪ This schedule can change *as it may chance.* この予定は場合によっては変更されることもある.
chance *one's* ***arm*** [*one's* ***mit***] 《英》運に任せてやってみる, 大冒険をする ▪ I'll *chance my arm,* and offer £10 for the horse. 思い切って運試しにその馬に10ポンド出そう.
chance it 《口》一か八かやってみる, 運を天に任せて…する ▪ I'll *chance it.* 一か八かやってみます.
chance *one's* ***luck*** 運試しをする ▪ Did you *chance your luck* at Monte Carlo? 君はモンテカルロで(カジノの)運試しをしたのか.
it chances that 偶然…する《今は通例 happen を用いる》 ▪ *It chanced that* we rode in the train. 我々はたまたまその電車に乗っていた.

chancery /tʃǽnsəri|tʃɑ́ːn-/ 名 ***get into chancery*** 《口》(ボクシングで)相手の頭をわきの下にかかえこむ[こまれる]; 動きのとれぬはめにする[なる] ▪ If you guarantee any bills for him, he'll *get* you *into chancery.* 君が彼の勘定書の保証人になったら, 彼は君を窮地に陥れるだろう.
in chancery **1**《米》衡平裁判所で審理中の ▪ The case is now *in chancery.* その案件は衡平法裁判所で目下審理中である.
2《英》大法官の支配下の ▪ a ward *in chancery* 大法官を保護者とするもの《通例親のない未成年者》 ▪ Her parents having died, she was made a ward *in chancery.* 両親が死んだので, 彼女は大法官を保護者とする身となった.
3《口》(ボクシングで)頭を相手のわきの下へかかえこまれ(ポカポカなぐられ)て; 絶対絶命になって ▪ He'll not put his head *in chancery.* 彼は頭を相手のわきの下にかかえこませないだろう ▪ What a thing it is to have your head *in chancery*! 頭を相手のわきの下にかかえこまれて絶対絶命になるのはいかにつらいことか. ☞昔の英国の最高民事裁判所の審理にかかってはなかなからちがあかなかったことから.

change[1] /tʃeɪndʒ/ 名 ***a change for the better*** [***the worse***] よくなる[悪くなる]こと ▪ It is *a change for the better.* それは改善だ.
a change of air (療養などのための)転地 ▪ He went to Bath for *a change of air.* 彼はバースへ転地した.
a change of clothes [***garments***] 衣服の着替え〚通例 change は単数形〛 ▪ Did you bring *a change of clothes* with you? 着替えを持ってきたかい ▪ She possessed as many as thirty *changes of garments.* 彼女は30着も着替えを持っていた.
a change of face [***front***] 態度[目的, 戦術]転換 ▪ The Government made *a* sudden *change of face.* 政府は急に態度を転換した.
a change of heart 心変わり, 転向, 翻意 ▪ The

move signals *a change of heart* in public policy. その動きは社会政策における転向を表している.

a change of life (女性の)更年期 ▪ Most women undergo *a change of life* in their forties. たいていの婦人は40歳台で更年期になる.

a change of pace **1** 気分転換 ▪ He read a comic book for *a change of pace.* 彼は気分転換のためコミック本を読んだ.

2《野球》チェンジアップ ▪ The batter struck out in *a change of pace.* 打者は(投手の)チェンジアップを打ってアウトになった.

a change of tide →a turn of the TIDE.

and change …と少々, プラスアルファ ▪ The mechanic said it would cost a thousand dollars *and change* to fix the crankshaft. クランク軸を修理するには千ドル少々かかるだろうと機械工は言った.

Change is as good as a rest.《諺》仕事を変えるのは休息と同じくらいによいことだ.

for **(*a*)** ***change***《口》変化のため ▪ I think I'll drink tea *for a change.* たまにはお茶を飲みたい.

get no change out of *a person*《口》**1** (人)からよい返事[結果]がもらえない; 何も聞き出せない; (けんか・議論などで)人に勝てない, 人をやっつけそこなう ▪ You won't *get* any *change out of* him. 彼からは何の返事ももらえないだろう.

2 (人から)何の援助[助言など]も得られない ▪ We *got no change out of* her. 我々は彼女から何の助言も得られなかった. ☞change「釣銭」.

get short change《口》好意的に聞いて[かまって]もらえない ▪ You'll *get short change* if you try to advise them. 彼らに助言を試みても聞いてもらえまい.

give *a person* (*his*) ***change*** 人のために尽力する; 《皮肉》人に当然の賞[罰]を与える, 返報する ▪ I could *give* you *change* for it. 私はその返礼をあなたにすることはできるのだが ▪ I *gave* him *his change.* 彼に返報してやった.

give *a person* ***no change***《口》人に何の満足も与えない, 何も知らせない ▪ He *gave* me *no change.* 彼は私に何も知らせなかった.

give short change《口》好意的に聞いて[かまって]やらない ▪ The boy *was given short change* by his relatives. 少年は親類の者にかまってもらえなかった.

go through changes 変わる, 変更を受ける ▪ Art publishing has been *going through* a lot of *changes* since I came here 20 years ago. 私が20年前にここに来て以来, 芸術出版はおおいに変化してきている.

going through changes《口》〚進行形で〛困難に直面している, 苦境に陥っている ▪ The company *is going through changes* and probably downsizing at this CES. その会社は苦境に陥っているので, おそらくこの消費者向け電気製品展示会では規模を縮小している. ☞CES＝Consumer Electronics Show.

keep the change おつりはいいよ ▪ The passengers were in a hurry so they asked the driver to *keep the change.* 乗客たちは急いでいたので運転手におつりはとっておいてくれと言った.

make a change **1** 変える, 改良する ▪ You haven't half *made a change* here. ここをずいぶんと改良したね.

2 (普段とは)ちょっと変わっている ▪ He had no money with him, which *made a change.* 彼は金の持ち合わせがなかった, それは(いつもと)ちょっと変わっていた.

make change《米》釣銭を払う ▪ The clerk *made change.* 店員は釣銭を払った.

on [***upon***] ***'change*** [***'Change***]《英》株式取引所で ▪ Scrooge's name was good *on 'change* for anything he chose to put his hand to. 王立取引所ではスクルージの名は, 彼が署名したどんな文書に対しても信用があった. ☞Exchange の略と誤解されて, 'change と書かれることが多い.

put the change on [***upon***] *a person*《口》人をだます ▪ You cannot *put the change on* me easily. 僕をやすやすとだますことはできないよ.

ring the changes **1** あることを手を変え品を変えてする; 同じことをさまざまに言い変える (*on*) ▪ You can go on working all day, provided you *ring the changes* sufficiently. 十分に手を変え品を変えれば, 一日中働き続けることができる ▪ He *rang the changes on* the subject. 彼はその問題を手を変え品を変えて説いた.

2《俗》悪い品[悪貨]を良い品[良貨]と取り代えて逃げる ▪ The man tried to *ring the changes.* その男は悪い品を良い品と取り代えて逃げようとした.

take *one's* [***the***] ***change out of***《口》(人)に仕返しをする, (こと)の仕返しをする; を罰する ▪ *Take your change out of* that! これが返答だ!《言い返し, なぐり返しなどして言う》 ▪ I shall reduce his salary and *take the change out of* him. 彼の俸給を減らして報復してやる.

work a change 変化を引き起こす, 差違を生じさせる ▪ The fact that he is now crippled has naturally *worked a change* in his living habits. 彼が今は手足が不自由であるという事実は自然彼の生活習慣に変化を生じさせた.

change[2] /tʃeɪndʒ/ 動 (***All***) ***change*** (***here***)***!*** (みなさん)お乗り換えください.

change *oneself*《米》着替える ▪ I *change myself* twice a day. 私は1日に2回着替える.

change a horse →CHANGE hand.

change for the better 良いほうに変化する ▪ Our relations with Russia will soon *change for the better.* わが国とロシアとの関係はまもなく改善されるだろう.

change for the worse 悪化する ▪ The world situation will not *change for the worse.* 世界情勢は悪化しないだろう.

change hand [***a horse***] 馬の方向を変える ▪ He suddenly *changed a horse.* 彼は急に馬の頭を向け変えた.

change *oneself* ***into*** …に化ける ▪ He *changed himself into* a peasant. 彼は農民に化けた.

change places (***with***) (…と)地位を変わる ▪ I *changed places with* him. 私は彼と地位を変わった

▪ We *changed places*. 互いに位置を入れ替わった.

channel[1] /tʃǽnəl/ 名 ***go*** [***work***] ***through*** (***the proper***) ***channels*** →through the legitimate CHANNEL.

through the legitimate [***proper***] ***channel*** 正規[正当]の経路[ルート]を経て, しかるべき手続きを踏んで ▪ He sought it *through the legitimate channel*. 彼は正規の経路を経てそれを求めた.

channel[2] /tʃǽnəl/ 動 ***half channeled over*** 生酔いで ▪ He was *half channeled over*. 彼は生酔いであった.

chant /tʃænt|tʃɑːnt/ 動 ***chant horses*** 《俗》馬をだまし売りする ▪ Jack was *chanting horses* with them. ジャックは彼らに馬をだまし売りしていた.

chant the praises [***eulogy***] ***of*** ...をのべつにほめる, 賛辞を繰り返す ▪ He *chanted the praises of* the Darwinian system. 彼はダーウィンの説を繰り返しほめた.

chapel /tʃǽpəl/ 名 ***hold chapel*** 王侯[法王, 大僧正]などが礼拝式を行う ▪ The college of cardinals *hold chapels*. 枢機卿会は礼拝式をとり行う.

keep a chapel [*one's* ***chapels***] 《口》大学で礼拝式に(1回)出席する[規定の回数だけ出席する] ▪ You must *keep your chapels*. あなたは礼拝式に規定の回数だけ出席しなくてはならない.

miss [***lose***] ***a chapel*** 礼拝式に出席しない ▪ He was blamed because he *missed a chapel*. 彼は礼拝式に出席しなかったのでしかられた.

chapter /tʃǽptər/ 名 ***a chapter of accidents*** (概して不愉快な)相つぐ不測の出来事 (→the CHAPTER of accidents) ▪ A black eye, a torn hand, blisters on your feet—my word, what *a chapter of accidents*! 目は打たれ青黒くなり, 手はひっかかれ, 足には火ぶくれができ—ほんとに, なんという不幸の連続なんだろう! ▪ The whole day was *a chapter of accidents*. 1日中不測の出来事の連続だった.

chapter and verse **1** (聖書の何章・何節という)正確な出典 ▪ The early Fathers did not care much about *chapter and verse*. 初期の教父たちは聖書の正確な出典はあまり問題にしなかった.

2 [[副詞的に]] 詳細に ▪ Give me the whole story, *chapter and verse*. その話全体を詳細に話してくれ.

give chapter and verse (***for***) ...に対する詳細な典拠を示す; を保証する, 請け合う ▪ He not only stated that this was so, but *gave chapter and verse*. 彼はそうだと言ったばかりでなく, 詳細な典拠をも示した ▪ He *gave* me *chapter and verse for* all he said. 彼は自分の言うことをすべて請け合った.

the chapter of accidents [***possibilities***] 予測しがたい事の成り行き, 偶然, 運 ▪ Away runs Jack, trusting to *the chapter of accidents*. ジャックは運にまかせて逃走する ▪ I did not suppose her refusal to be in *the chapter of possibilities*. 彼女の拒絶が万一の出来事の中に含まれていようとは思わなかった.

to [***till***] ***the end of the chapter*** 《口》最後まで; いつまでも, どこまでも ▪ Doctors will disagree on these questions *to the end of the chapter*. 博士たちはこれらの問題については, どこまでも意見を異にするであろう.

character /kǽrəktər/ 名 ***a man of character*** 人格者 ▪ He is *a man of character*. 彼は人格者だ.

(***a***) ***sterling character*** [[限定的]] 人格者(の); 第一人者(の) ▪ It's hard to pretend that the ex-president is *a sterling character*. 前大統領が人格者だとはお世辞にも言いがたい ▪ Peter Falk, the *sterling character* actor, played Columbo. 大物俳優のピーター・フォークがコロンボを演じた.

an anemic [《英》***anaemic***] ***character*** 貧血的性格, 無気力で控え目な性格, 弱々しい気質 ▪ The bigger issue is the *anemic character* of the economic recovery. より大きな問題は, 経済復興が弱々しい形質だということだ.

blacken *a person's* ***character*** 人の人格・評判などを汚す, 人に汚名を着せる, 人を悪く言う ▪ Politicians *blackened each other's character* with gusto. 政治家たちは喜んでお互いに中傷合戦をした.

by the character of ...という評判で, というので ▪ He is known in this neighborhood *by the character of* a fine gentleman. 彼はこのあたりでは立派な紳士ということで知られている.

clear *one's* [*a person's*] ***character*** 自分の[人の]身の潔白を明らかにする ▪ *Our characters* have *been cleared*. 我々の身の潔白は明らかにされた ▪ I will do my best to *clear his character*. 彼の身の潔白を明らかにするため私は最善を尽くします.

establish a character for ...という評判を打ち立てる ▪ He has *established a character for* honesty. 彼は正直という評判を打ち立てた.

get a bad [***good***] ***character*** 悪い[良い]評判を取る ▪ He has *got a bad character*. 彼は評判が悪い.

give *a person* (***a***) ***good*** [***bad***] ***character*** 人を推賞する[けなす]; (使用人などに)良い推薦状[悪い紹介]を書いてやる ▪ I *gave* him *a good character*. 彼に良い推薦状を書いてやった.

go out of character 自分の柄にないことをする ▪ He would often *go out of character*. 彼はよく柄にもないことをしたものだ.

in character はまり役で, 柄に合った; (性格上)調和して ▪ That behavior is entirely *in character* with her. それは全く彼女らしい行いです ▪ His new office would be *in character*, I think. 彼の新しい職は適職だろう.

in the character of ...の役に扮して; という資格で ▪ He made a speech *in the character of* ambassador. 彼は大使の資格で演説をした.

out of character 役に不向きで, 柄になく; (言動・言説・身分・年齢などと)調和しないで; 調子はずれで, 法外で ▪ The actor's southern accent was *out of character* with his role as Hamlet. その役者の南部なまりはハムレットの役とは調和しなかった ▪ Their prices are quite *out of character*. その店の値段は

全く法外です ▪ Self-ignorance leads a man to act *out of character*. 自己に対する無知のため人は柄にもないことをするようになる.

without a character 推薦状[人物証明]なしで ▪ I engaged him *without a character*. 私は推薦状なしで彼を雇った.

characteristic /kæ̀rəktərístɪk/ 形 ***be characteristic of*** …の特性を示している; のやりそうなことである ▪ It *is characteristic of* him to go to work before breakfast. 朝食前に仕事を始めるのはいかにも彼らしい ▪ A broad chin and large ears *are characteristic of* the Dutchman. 広いあごと大きい耳はオランダ人の特徴だ.

charge[1] /tʃɑːrdʒ/ 名 ***a charge for trouble*** 手数料 ▪ What is the *charge for trouble*? 手数料はいくらですか.

at** a person's **charge 人の費用で ▪ He went abroad *at his father's charge*. 彼は父の費用で海外へ行った.

be a charge on the public 扶助貧困者である ▪ He will *be a charge on the public*. 彼は扶助貧困者になるだろう.

bring [lay] a charge of… against (人)を…の罪で告発する ▪ They *brought a charge of* theft *against* him. 彼らは彼を窃盗罪で告発した.

free of charge 無料で ▪ You may have it *free of charge*. それは無料で得られる.

get a charge out of 《口》…にスリル[歓喜, 満足]を感じる ▪ People *get a charge out of* their children. 人々は自分の子供に大きな喜びを感じる.

give** a person **charge over [of] 人に…の管理権を与える, を受け持たせる ▪ I *gave* my brother *charge over* Jerusalem. 私は弟にエルサレムの管理権を与えた ▪ The nurse *was given charge of* the young probationers. その看護師は若い見習生たちを受け持っていた.

give** a person **in charge (to) 人を(警察に)引き渡す ▪ We *gave* the burglar *in charge to* the police. 我々は強盗を警察に引き渡した.

give** a thing **in charge (to) 物を(人に)預ける, (人の)世話に託す; 任務を(人に)命ずる ▪ Where is the gold I *gave in charge to* you? 私があなたに預けた黄金はどこにありますか ▪ He forgot nothing *given* to him *in charge*. 彼は命じられた任務は何も忘れなかった.

have [take]… in charge **1** …を引き受けている[引き受ける], 担当している[する] ▪ I *have* the education of young girls *in charge*. 私は若い娘たちの教育を引き受けている ▪ He *took* the weighty terms *in charge*. 彼はその重い条件を引き受けた.
2 《英》(警察が)引き取っている[引き取る] ▪ The police *took* the beggar *in charge*. 警察はその物乞いを引き取った.

have (the) charge of …を受け持つ, つかさどる, 預かる ▪ He *had the charge of* all the treasure. 彼が宝のすべてを保管していた ▪ Mr. Smith *has charge of* the import department. スミス氏が輸入部の主任である.

in charge of** a person/ **in** a person's **charge …に預けられて ▪ These boys are *in my charge*. この少年たちは私の担任です ▪ We left our children *in charge of* a nurse. 私たちは子供らを乳母に託した.

in (the) charge of …の担当で, の保管で, を託されて ▪ The building is *in the charge of* my uncle. その建物は私のおじが管理しています ▪ He was *in charge of* the house. 彼はその家を管理していた ▪ We placed Mr. Smith *in charge of* the class. スミス氏にそのクラスを担当させた.

lay a charge of… against → bring a CHARGE of… against.

lay… to** a person's **charge …を人の罪とする, のせいにする (《聖》*Roms*. 8. 33) ▪ You *laid* two offences *to my charge*. 君は私に二つの罪があると言った ▪ Don't *lay* her death *to my charge*. 彼女の死を私のせいにしないでください.

make a charge against …を非難する, 告訴する ▪ John Smith *made a charge against* his employer on account of his injury. ジョン・スミスはけがをしたので雇い主を告訴した.

make a charge for …の代償[代金]を請求する ▪ No *charge is made for* packing. 荷作り代はいりません.

on a [the] charge of …の罪で, の罪に問われて ▪ He was arrested *on a charge of* murder. 彼は殺人の罪で逮捕された.

on charges of …の罪で, の罪に問われて ▪ Two officers were indicted *on charges of* framing their former boss. 二人の将校が, 前の上官にぬれぎぬを着せた罪で起訴された. ☞罪が二つ以上ある場合だけでなく一つのときでも用いられる. on a [the] charge of よりも頻度が高い.

open to the charge of …のきらいがあって ▪ Office business is *open to the charge of* red-tapism. 役所仕事は形式主義のきらいがある.

prefer charges 《英・法》(…を)告訴する (*against*) ▪ She does not wish to *perfer charges against* me. 彼女は私を告訴するのを望んでいない.

put down** a sum **to** a person's **charge 金額を人の勘定につける ▪ He *put down* £500 *to my charge*. 彼は500ポンドを私の勘定につけた.

put** a thing **under** a person's **charge 物を人に預ける ▪ We *put* the house *under his charge*. 私たちは家を彼に管理してもらうことにした.

return to the charge (実戦・論戦において)攻撃を新たにする ▪ He *returns* every day *to the charge* with an increase in courage. 彼は毎日勇気を増大して攻撃を新たにする.

take charge 《口》(特に災害を与える物が)勝手に動きだす ▪ A gun *took charge* in firing. 鉄砲が自然に発砲した ▪ They were pulling the tackle, when the spar *took charge* and swung back. 彼らは複滑車を引っぱっていたが, 円材が自然に動きだして元へ戻った.

take charge of **1** …を保管する; を担当する, 引き受ける ▪ He *took charge of* the will. 彼はその遺書を保管した ▪ He will *take charge of* the office. 彼がその職分を担当するだろう ▪ His uncle determined to *take charge of* him. 彼のおじは彼を預かることに決めた.

C

2 (罪人など)を受け取る, 引き取る ▪ The police *took charge of* the robber. 警察は強盗を引き取った.

take … in charge →have … in CHARGE.

under *a person's* ***charge*** 人の監督のもとに, 保管のもとに ▪ The books are *under my charge*. その本は私が保管している.

charge[2] /tʃɑːrdʒ/ 動 ***be charged at*** 課金される, 請求される料金[利率]が…である ▪ A4 size photocopies of documents will *be charged at* ten cents per page. 文書のA4サイズのコピーは1枚につき10セント課金されます.

be charged with …で一杯である, に満ちている ▪ His poetry *is charged with* musical beauty. 彼の詩は音楽美に満ちている.

charge *a person* ***to*** *do* 人に…するよう命じる[頼む] ▪ I *charged* him *to* see that everything was all right. 彼に事故のないよう注意してくれと頼んだ ▪ They *were charged to* remain at their posts. 彼らは持ち場を守るよう命じられた.

charge … to *a person's* ***account*** → ACCOUNT[1].

charge *oneself* ***with*** (…の責任)を引き受ける ▪ He has *charged himself with* the education of some orphans. 彼は数人の孤児たちの教育を引き受けた.

chargeable /tʃáːrdʒəbəl/ 形 ***(be) chargeable on*** [***upon***] **1** …の負担すべきもので(ある); に課せらるべきもので(ある) ▪ The expense *is chargeable on* him. 経費は彼が負担すべきものだ ▪ A duty *is chargeable on* sugar. 砂糖には税が課せられるべきである.

2 (責め・罪が)…に帰せられるべきで(ある) ▪ The crime *is chargeable on* him. その罪は彼が犯したものである.

(be) chargeable to …の負担すべきもので(ある) ▪ The woman *is chargeable to* the parish. その女性は教区が扶養するべきだ.

(be) chargeable with **1** …を負担するべきで(ある); を課せられるべきで(ある) ▪ He *is chargeable with* the expense. 彼はその経費を負担するべきである ▪ Sugar *is chargeable with* duty. 砂糖には課税するべきである.

2 (責め・罪)を負わされるべきで(ある) ▪ He *is chargeable with* the crime. 彼はその犯罪に問われるべきだ.

charity /tʃǽrəti/ 名 ***(as) cold as charity*** きわめて冷淡で, 出ししぶって; きわめて冷たく (《聖》*Matt.* 24. 12) ▪ They are *as cold as charity*. 彼らはきわめて冷淡である(ひどく出ししぶる) ▪ The wind is *as cold as charity*. 風はひどく冷たい《形式的な慈善を皮肉ったもの》.

Charity begins at home. 《諺》博愛[慈善]はまず身近なところ[わが家]から (《聖》*1 Tim.* 5. 8) ▪ Well, they say *charity begins at home*. 親切は身近なところからって言うからね.

Charity covers a multitude of sins. 《諺》博愛は多くの罪業をおおう.

do [***give***] *one's* ***charity*** 施しをする ▪ He *does his charity* with privacy. 彼はひそかに施しをする.

in charity 慈善のために; (…を)哀れと思って (*with*) ▪ I gave him money *in charity*. 私は彼に金をめぐんでやった ▪ I am *in charity with* him. 私は彼を哀れと思っている.

out of charity **1** …を哀れに思って ▪ I employed him *out of charity*. 彼を哀れに思って雇ってやった.

2 (…に)悪意をもって (*with*) ▪ I am *out of charity with* Tom. 私はトムを憎んでいる.

with charity 寛大に ▪ Regard others' faults *with charity*. 他人の欠点を寛大に見なさい.

charm[1] /tʃɑːrm/ 名 ***like*** [***to***] ***a charm*** すばらしく, 完全に ▪ The medicine acted *like a charm*. その薬は不思議によくきいた.

turn on the charm (…に)魅力[愛想]を振りまく, 打算で優しくする (*to*) ▪ Chas is *turning on the charm* to secure a job at the factory. チャスは工場の仕事を確保するために愛想よくふるまう.

work like a charm 魔法のように作用する, 効験あらたかである ▪ The modem in my computer *works like a charm*. 私のパソコンのモデムは魔法のように作用している.

charm[2] /tʃɑːrm/ 動 ***be charmed to*** *do* 大喜びで…する; …すればとてもうれしい ▪ I shall *be charmed to* see you tomorrow. あす大喜びでお会いします.

be charmed with [***by***] …に魅せられる, 心酔する, が大いに気に入る ▪ I *was charmed with* your children. お子さまたちが非常に気に入りました ▪ I *was charmed by* the music. その音楽にうっとりと聞きほれた.

bear a charmed life 不死身である (cf. Sh., *Macb.* 5. 8. 12) ▪ General Gordon believed himself to *bear a charmed life*. ゴードン将軍は自分が不死身であると信じていた.

charm *one's* ***way into*** [***out of***] (魔法のように楽々と)…に入り込む[から抜け出る] ▪ He manages to *charm his way into* the hearts of her mother. 彼は首尾よく楽々と彼女の母親の心の中に忍び込む.

chary /tʃéəri/ 形 ***be chary in*** 容易に…しない ▪ The Government *were* very *chary in* putting it into force. 政府はなかなかそれを施行しなかった.

be chary of **1** …に用心する; を注意する; を大事にする ▪ I *am chary of* catching cold. 私は風邪ひきを用心している ▪ He *is chary of* his fame. 彼は自分の名声を大事にする.

2 容易に…しない, することを惜しむ ▪ He *is* very *chary of* praise. 彼はめったに人をほめない ▪ We ought to *be chary of* maligning the clergy. 我々は僧職者の悪口を言うことは控えるべきである.

chase[1] /tʃeɪs/ 名 ***cut to the chase*** 本題[核心]に入る ▪ I just *cut to the chase* and say what I've got to say. 直接本題に入って言うべきことを言おう.

give chase 追いかける, 追撃する (*to*) ▪ It *gives chase to* small birds on the wing. それは飛んでいる小鳥を追いかける ▪ Two frigates *gave* us *chase*. 2隻のフリゲート艦が我々を追いかけた.

have* [*hold*]*... in chase ...を追いかける, 追撃する; を追求する ▪ Spies *held* me *in chase*. スパイどもが私を追いかけた ▪ He then *had* subtle designs *in chase*. 彼はそのとき陰険な術策を用いていた.

in chase ...を追いかけて (*of*); 追われて ▪ We started *in chase of* the enemy. 我々は敵の追撃を始めた ▪ A hart is *in chase*. 雄ジカが追われている.

lead** a person **a (***hard, fine, merry***) ***chase*** (スピード・回り道によって)追手をひどく困らせる[苦しめる] ▪ He often *leads* them *a fine chase* over hill and dale. 彼は山越え谷越えてしばしば追手をひどく困らせる.

chase[2] /tʃeɪs/ 動 ***chase** oneself/* ***go*** (***and***) ***chase** oneself* 《口》行く, 走る; 去る, 逃げる ▪ *Chase yourself*! うせろ! ▪ You *chase yourself* below and look things over. 下へ走って行って調べてきなさい ▪ *Go and chase yourself*. (うるさい)あっち へ行け.

Go chase yourself! 《米俗》出て行け (Get out!) (→CHASE oneself).

chasm /kǽzəm/ 名 ***a yawning chasm*** 大きく口を開けた割れ目; 大きなギャップ[くいちがい] ▪ The biggest crisis in the Church and society is the *yawning chasm* between faith and life. 教会と社会との最大の危機は信仰と生活との間の大きな乖離だ.

cheap /tʃiːp/ 形名 (***as***) ***cheap as dirt*** きわめて安く ▪ I bought this hat *as cheap as dirt*. この帽子は捨て値で買った.

at a cheap rate [***fare***] 安い料金で ▪ It may serve to convey information *at a cheap rate*. それは安い料金で情報を伝えるのに役立つかもしれない.

cheap and cheerful 《英口》安いが良質の ▪ The company is advertising its cars as *cheap and cheerful*. 会社は自社の車は安いが良質だと宣伝している.

cheap and nasty 安かろう悪かろうの ▪ All these are *cheap and nasty*. これらはみな安かろう悪かろうである ▪ Most of the goods are of the *cheap and nasty* variety. 商品の大部分は, 安かろう悪かろうといった種類のものである.

cheap at the [***any***] ***price*** 《英口》価格に対して割安の, 十分値打ちがある ▪ Get your visas here! *Cheap at the price*! ここでビザをお求めください! 十分値打ちがあります.

cheap served 報いが軽くてすむ ▪ He is *cheap served*. 彼には罰が軽い.

dirt cheap 《口》安値で, 捨て値で ▪ You bought that home *dirt cheap*. あの家を安く買ったんだね.

feel cheap **1**《口》肩身が狭い感じがする, 恥ずかしく感じる ▪ When everyone except me contributed to the fund, I *felt* very *cheap*. 私以外の人がみなその基金に寄付をしたとき, 私は非常に肩身の狭い思いがした ▪ He *felt cheap* about his failure. 彼は自分の失敗を恥ずかしく思った.

2《俗》(飲み騒ぎのあとで)弱る, 気分が悪い ▪ Are you feeling any better?—*Feeling cheap* still, thanks. 少しは気分がいいか?—ありがとう, まだよくない.

get off cheap 罰が軽くてすむ; 安くてすむ ▪ If you had your car repaired for only 10 dollars, you *got off cheap*. 君が車をたった10ドルで修繕してもらったのなら, 安あがりだったね.

go cheap 《口》安売りする ▪ In the end, he *went cheap*. 最終的には彼は不利な条件で妥協した.

hold ... cheap ...を見くびる, 軽んじる ▪ Cicero *held* the Senate's intellect *cheap*. キケロは元老院の知力を見くびった ▪ I *held* his works very *cheap*. 私は彼の作品を軽蔑した.

make** oneself* (too***) ***cheap*** 自分を安っぽくする, あまりに軽々しく人に接する ▪ It is not right to let everyone come and see you. You're *making yourself cheap*. 誰もかれもみなあなたに会いに来させるのはよくない. あなたはあまり自分を安っぽくしている.

on the cheap 《英口》安く, 安あがりに; ただで(人に払わせて) ▪ We must do it *on the cheap*. それを安あがりでしなければならない ▪ He is the fellow who came on that holiday in Paris with us, *on the cheap*. 彼はただで我々とパリであの休暇を遊んだ男だ.

cheaply /tʃíːpli/ 副 ***get off cheaply*** 罰が軽くてすむ ▪ Six months' hard labor? He *got off cheaply* then. 6か月の重労働だって? それでは彼の刑は軽くてすんだんだね.

check[1] /tʃek/ 名 ***bounce a check*** 不渡り(小切手)を出す ▪ Gupta *bounced a check* and failed to make payment. グプタは不渡りを出し, 支払い不能になった.

cash (***in***) *one's* ***checks*** → CASH (in) one's chips.

checks and balances 《米》均衡抑制 ▪ Our Government's system of *checks and balances* has been subverted by party politics. 我が政府の均衡抑制方式は党略によって崩されてしまった.

draw a check (***on***) (...に対して)小切手を振り出す《比喩的にも》 ▪ He *drew a check* for £5,000 and handed it to her. 彼は5,000ポンドの小切手を書いて彼女に渡した ▪ He is *drawing a check on* our credulity, which is not likely to be honored. 彼は我々の軽信を当てこんでいるがそうは問屋がおろさない.

give a check to ...を頓座させる ▪ Tom's illness *gave a check to* our plans. トムの病気で我々の計画は頓座した.

hand [***pass***] ***in** one's* ***checks*** 《口》 **1** ばくちの数取りを座元に返す.

2 死ぬ ▪ One of the boys has *handed in his checks*. 少年たちの一人が死んだ.

3 仕事をやめる ▪ You are not going to *hand in your checks*? 君は仕事をやめるのではあるまいね.

hold* [*keep*] *... in check ...を防ぐ, くい止める, 制御する ▪ His task was to *keep* them *in check*. 彼の任務は彼らを制御することであった ▪ The king *held* the Turks *in check*. 王はトルコ軍をくい止めた.

keep a check on **1** ...を注視する, 追求する ▪ The police are *keeping a* close *check on* the movements of the suspects. 警察は容疑者の動静を厳重に注視している.

2 ...を抑制する ▪ I advise you to *keep a check on* your statements. 言説を慎まれるようお勧めする.

make out a check 小切手を書く[切る] ▪ The young man took out a checkbook, and *made out a check* for $86,000. その若い男は小切手帳を取り出して, 86,000ドルの小切手を書いた.

pass in one's checks → hand in one's CHECKs.

check[2] /tʃek/ 動 ***check and balance*** 《米》均衡抑制する ▪ Our aim is to *check and balance* the contending forces. 我々の目的は抗争している諸勢力を均衡抑制することである.

checker /tʃékər/ 名 ***That's the checker.*** 《米口》まさにそれだ ▪ *That's* just *the checker*. No wonder I like you so much. まさしくそうなのだ. 君が好きなのも当然だ.

checkmate /tʃékmèɪt/ 名 ***give checkmate*** (***to***) (相手の)王を詰める; (を)行き詰まらせる, 詰ます ▪ One of them *gave checkmate* at chess. 彼らの一人がチェスで相手の王を詰めた ▪ It *gave checkmate to* religion. それは宗教を行き詰まらせた.

play checkmate with (相手)を進退きわまらせる, (相手の)とどめを刺す ▪ He will *play checkmate with* your Majesty. 彼は陛下を窮地に陥れるでしょう.

say checkmate to (人)に「詰み」と言う, 「君の負け」と言う, 負かす ▪ Death *says checkmate to* us. 死は我々に引導を渡す ▪ Fortune often *says checkmate to* princes. 運の神はよく王侯を打ち破る.

cheek[1] /tʃiːk/ 名 ***cheek by jowl*** (ほおとあごが接しているように)ぴたりと密接して; 親密に[で] ▪ They are living *cheek by jowl*; forty in a six-roomed house. 彼らはぴたりとくっつき合って暮らしている. 40人が6部屋の家で ▪ I am living *cheek by jowl* with him in the house. 彼とその家で親密に暮らしている.

give a person cheek 人に生意気なことを言う ▪ If he *gives* me *cheek* I'll knock him down. あいつが生意気を言ったら, なぐり倒してやる.

have a cheek ずうずうしい, 無礼な ▪ Harris *has a cheek* complaining he is tired. ハリスは厚かましくも疲れたと不平を言った.

have plenty of* [*much*] *cheek つらの皮が千枚張りである, 非常に生意気である ▪ You*'ve got* too *much cheek* for a boy of ten. 君は10歳の少年にしては厚かましすぎる.

have the cheek of the devil 生意気で厚かましい ▪ That boy *has the cheek of the devil*. あの少年は生意気で厚かましい.

have the cheek to do 《口》厚かましくも[生意気にも]...する ▪ He *had the cheek to* ask me to do his work for him. 彼は厚かましくも自分の仕事を私にしてくれと言った.

None of your cheek! 生意気言うな! ▪ Now, put that book away, and *none of your cheek*. さあその本をしまえ. 生意気言うのはよせよ.

put a horse up to the cheek 手綱をくつわ鎖の第一輪にはめる(くつわをゆるめる).

to one's own cheek 《俗》自分だけのものとして, 自分だけの用に(して) ▪ Let Jim keep his earnings *to his own cheek*. ジムは自分の所得を自分だけのものにしたらよい.

turn the other cheek おとなしく侮辱を許す, 侮辱を黙って繰り返さす (《聖》*Matt.* 5. 39) ▪ When struck upon one cheek, the true Christian should *turn the other cheek*. 一方のほおをたたかれたら, 真のクリスチャンはもう一方のほおも向けるべきである.

(***with one's***) ***tongue in*** (***one's***) ***cheek*** → TONGUE.

cheek[2] /tʃiːk/ 動 ***cheek it*** 《口》ずうずうしく押し[やり]通す ▪ They persuaded me to go and beg, but I couldn't *cheek it*. 彼らは懇願しに行くよう私を説きつけたが, 私はずうずうしくそれをやり通せなかった.

cheer[1] /tʃɪər/ 名 ***be of good cheer*** 元気である, 勇敢である ▪ We *are* always *of good cheer*. 私たちはいつも元気だ ▪ Son, *be of good cheer*; thy sins are forgiven. 息子よ, しっかりなさい. あなたの罪は許されたのだ.

enjoy* [*make*] *good cheer ごちそうを食べる, 食べて愉快にする ▪ The Corinthians came to *make good cheer*. コリント人たちがごちそうを食べに来た.

give a cheer 喝采する ▪ I *gave* him *a cheer*. 私は彼に喝采した.

give three cheers (***for***) (...のために)万歳を三唱する ("Hip, hip, hurrah!" を三度繰り返す) ▪ We *gave three cheers for* the President. 大統領万歳を三唱した.

make cheer 浮かれ騒ぐ; 愉快にする ▪ We *made cheer* that day. その日は浮かれ騒いだ.

make good cheer →enjoy good CHEER.

The fewer the better cheer. 《諺》人数が少ないほど食べるものが多くてよい.

Three cheers for ...! ...万歳! ▪ *Three cheers for* the King! 国王万歳!

Two cheers! ぞっとしないな! ▪ *Two cheers* for your plan! 君の計画はぞっとしないよ.

What cheer? 《口》ごきげんいかがですか ▪ *What cheer*, Charlie? チャーリー君, ごきげんいかが.

with good cheer 喜んで; 元気よく, にこやかに ▪ He set off on his trip *with good cheer*. 彼は喜び勇んで旅に出た.

cheer[2] /tʃɪər/ 動 ***Cheer thee.*** 〚命令文で〛気を取り直せ, 元気を出せ ▪ *Cheer thee*, my boy! おい, 元気を出せ!

cheerful /tʃíərfəl/ 形 ***That's a cheerful remark.*** 《反語》そいつは聞きずてならぬ.

cheese[1] /tʃiːz/ 名 ***a big cheese*** 《口》大物, 実力者, 重要人物 ▪ The party was brimming with *big cheeses*. パーティーには大物たちがいっぱいだった.

be (***quite, just***) ***the cheese*** あつらえ向きのものである ▪ He *is quite the cheese*. 彼こそうってつけだ ▪ Nudity *is* not *the cheese* on such occasions. そのような場合には裸体は適当でない.

believe that the moon is made of green cheese →MOON.

cut the cheese 《口》(子供が)おならをする ▪ Seems Shey has *cut the cheese*, upwind, and it has wafted on the breeze. シェイがおならをしたようだ, 風上で, だから風に乗ってただよってきたのだ.

hard cheese 《口・古風》[[主に間投詞的に]] 不運 ▪ I failed the examination.—*Hard cheese*! 僕は試験に失敗した—そりゃいけなかったね! ☞話者が無関心の場合に用いる.

It is an old rat that won't eat cheese. 《諺》いくら老練な人でもおべっかには乗るものだ.

make cheeses **1** 回転してスカートをふくらませて急に座る《女子学生の遊戯》 ▪ She amused herself with *making cheeses*. 彼女はくるっと回ってスカートをふくらませ急に座って楽しんだ.

2 (女性が)腰を低くかがめておじぎする[あいさつする] ▪ She and her sister *made* these *cheeses* to pay their respects to the newcomer. 彼女と妹とは新来者に敬意を表して深くかがんでおじぎをした.

Say cheese! チーズと言ってください; はい, チーズ! 《写真をとるときに言う言葉》.

cheese[2] /tʃiːz/ 動 ***cheese it*** **1** 《俗》[[命令文で]] (話・行為を)やめろ; 逃げろ, 気をつけろ《盗賊用語》 ▪ *Cheese it*! Here's the bobby coming. 逃げろ! さつが来るぞ ▪ I say, *cheese it*, or you'll have the ceiling down. おいやめろ! でないと天じょうが落ちるぞ.

2 《米口》走り去る, 逃げる ▪ Let's *cheese it*. 逃げようじゃないか. ☞cheese は cease のなまり.

chemistry /kéməstri/ 名 ***a special*** [***strange***] ***chemistry*** (人間同士を引き寄せる)化学反応, 親和力, 相性 ▪ There has to be *a special chemistry* between me and my pupils. 私と生徒との間には特別な親和力がなければならない ▪ She is aware of the *strange chemistry* that exists between artist and model. 彼女は画家とモデルとの間に存在する不思議な相性のことをよく知っている.

cheque /tʃek/ 名 ***give a blank cheque to*** 《英》 **1** 白地小切手を与える, いくらでも支払いを引き受ける ▪ The King *gave* Holmes *a blank cheque* if he would solve the mystery. ホームズが謎の解明を引き受ければ王は報酬を惜しまなかった.

2 自由行動を許す ▪ I have not the temerity to *give a* political *blank cheque to* Lord Salisbury. 私はソールズベリー卿に政治上の自由行動を許すほどの大胆さは持ち合わせていない.

cherry /tʃéri/ 名 ***a cherry farm*** 《俗》サクランボ農園; (初犯者が収容される)矯正農場[施設] ▪ Joe got a light sentence and was sent to *a cherry farm* for six months. ジョーは軽い刑を受け, 6か月サクランボ収容所に送られた.

a second bite at the cherry (一度失敗したあとの)再挑戦, 2度目のチャンス ▪ I am lucky that I've got *a second bite at the cherry*. 再挑戦できるとはラッキーだ ▪ I had *a second bite at the cherry* but I messed up. 2度目のチャンスがあったのに, 台無しにしちゃった.

make two bites at [***of***] ***a cherry*** 分けるに値しないほど小さいものを二つに分ける; 1度でできることを2度に分けてやる; ためらう ▪ Let us toss up for the seat; there is no use *making two bites of a cherry*. コイン投げで席を決めよう. 席は小さいから二人がけにしようとしてもだめだ ▪ The cake wasn't worth *making two bites at a cherry*. そのお菓子は2度に分けて食べるほどのものではなかった.

take two bites at a cherry 仕事に不必要に長い時間をかける; 仕事を不必要に小切りにする ▪ What's the point of *taking two bites at a cherry*? 仕事をそんなに小切りにして何になるのだ.

the cherry on the cake [***the cherry on top***] 予想外の幸運, たなぼた, めっけもの ▪ To get to the final was a dream come true. Winning is *the cherry on the cake*. 決勝進出は夢の実現だった. 優勝は望外の喜びだ.

Cheshire /tʃéʃər/ 名 ***grin like a Cheshire cat*** (わけもなく)にたにた笑う ▪ Don't just stand there *grinning like a Cheshire cat*. そこに立ってわけもなくにたにた笑っているんじゃない. ☞a Cheshire cat は Lewis Carroll の童話 *Alice's Adventures in Wonderland* (1865)に出てくるにやにや笑う猫.

chest /tʃest/ 名 ***a chest of*** 箱一杯の ▪ I bought *a chest of* tools. 箱一杯の道具を買った.

chuck [***throw***] ***out a*** [*one's*] ***chest*** 《口》胸を突き出す, 度胸を示す ▪ He *threw out his chest* feeling very important. 彼は自分がとても重要人物だという気がして胸を突き出した.

get ... off *one's* ***chest*** 《口》(打ち明けて)心を軽くする; 感情や考えを述べる ▪ Come on, *get* it *off your chest*. さあ, すっかり打ち明けなさいよ.

on the [*one's*] ***chest*** 《口》(悲しみ・悩みなどが)胸につかえて ▪ She has the quarrel *on the chest*. その口論が彼女の胸につかえている ▪ His failure is *on his chest*. 彼の失敗が胸につかえている.

play ... close to *one's* ***cheat*** (物)を用心深く[秘密]にやる; を秘密にしておく ▪ You must *play* these things *close to your chest*. これらの事は秘密にやらねばだめだ.

puff out *one's* ***chest***/***puff*** *one's* ***chest out*** (誇り・見栄のため)胸をふくらませる ▪ *His chest was puffed out* with pride on the day. その日彼の胸は誇らしくふくらんでいた.

chestnut /tʃésnʌt/ 名 ***an old*** [***a hoary old***] ***chestnut*** 《主に英口》陳腐な冗談[話], 旧聞, 旧説, 繰り言 ▪ Oh, no, not *that old chestnut* again. いや, もうそのおもしろくもない冗談はごめんだ ▪ I'm tired of hearing the *old chestnut* that Hollywood doesn't finance movies about gays and AIDS. ハ

リウッドはゲイやエイズの映画に予算をつけないという旧説は聞き飽きた ▪ This show is the very model of how to give fresh life to *an old chestnut*. このショーはどのようにして古い話に新たな生命を吹き込むかのまさにモデルになるものだ.

C

pull** a person's* [the***] ***chestnuts out of the fire*** 人のために火中の栗を拾う ▪ Why should we have to *pull their chestnuts out of the fire*? いったいなぜ我々は彼らのため火中の栗を拾わねばならないのか. ☞サルのため火の中の栗を拾い出した猫の話から.

chevalier /ʃèvəlíər/ 名 ***a chevalier of industry*** [***fortune***] 山師, 詐欺師 ▪ I'm a puppet in the hands of the *chevalier of fortune*. 私は山師の手にあやつられるあやつり人形だ.

chew /tʃuː/ 動 ***be*** [***get***] ***chewed up*** 《米口》心配する ▪ Don't *get chewed up* about the new law. 新しい法律のことは心配するな.

chew the rag [***fat***] 《俗》 **1** 不平を(繰り返し)言う, 古い苦情をむし返す ▪ If anyone starts *chewing the rag*, he is immediately dismissed. もし不平を言い出す者があればすぐ首になる ▪ He was *chewing the rag* at me the whole afternoon. 彼は午後の間ずっと私に不平ばかり繰り返し言っていた.

2 不平を言う; 議論する ▪ He was *chewing the rag* at me. 彼は私に不平を言っていた ▪ We *chew the fat* over what happened weeks ago. 我々は何週も前の出来事について議論する.

3 (果てしなく)語り合う ▪ We sat there *chewing the rag* about old times. 私たちはそこに座って昔のことを語り合った.

chew** oneself **to bits inside ひどく泣いてくやしがる ▪ They lost the game and *chewed themselves to bits inside*. 彼らは試合に破れ, ひどく泣いてくやしがった.

like a piece of chewed string 《口》疲れ弱って ▪ He was *like a piece of chewed string*. 彼はぐったりしていた.

chic /ʃiːk/ 名 ***from chic*** 《口》手本によらず, 自分の頭で ▪ He drew a picture *from chic*. 彼は自分の頭で絵をかいた.

chick /tʃɪk/ 名 ***count** one's **chicks before they hatch*** [***they are hatched***] 《米》取らぬ狸の皮算用をする (→count one's CHICKENs before they are hatched) ▪ There you go again, *counting your chicks before they hatch* [*are hatched*]. また始まったな, 取らぬ狸の皮算用が.

have neither chick nor child 子供は一人もない ▪ He *has neither chick nor child* to care for. 彼には世話してやる子供が一人もない.

chicken /tʃíkɪn/ 名 ***a chicken and egg situation*** [***problem, dilemma***] ニワトリが先か卵が先かという状況[問題, ジレンマ], 二つの事柄のうちのどちらが先か原因か結論が出ない問題 ▪ Neck pain and stiffness is *a chicken-and-egg situation*. Neck stiffness can cause pain, and vice versa. 首の痛みとコリはどちらが先とは言えない. 首のコリが痛みの原因となることもあり, その逆もある ▪ Admittedly, there is *a chicken-and-egg problem* here. 実を言えば, ここに因果関係のはっきりしない問題がある. ☞"Which came first, the chicken or the egg?"「ニワトリが先か卵が先か」という古くからの謎から.

be** one's **chicken 《口》...のすることだ ▪ That's *their chicken*. それは彼らのすることだ. ☞今は That's one's PIGEON. が普通.

be no (***spring***) ***chicken*** 《口》もう若くない《女性について》 ▪ Ms. Hill *is no chicken*; she is at least fifty. ヒルさんはもう若くない, 少なくとも50歳だ.

chicken-brained [***minded***] まぬけな, 視野の狭い, 想像力のない ▪ "This is a *chicken-brained* idea," she said. 「これはばかげた考えだわ」と彼女は言った ▪ *Chicken-minded* fellows like you only see the end of the story. 君のように想像力のないものは話の結末しか見ない.

chicken-hearted/chicken-livered 臆病な, 小心な ▪ He won't be a doctor because he's too *chicken-hearted*. 彼は医者にはならないだろう, とっても気が小さいから ▪ The city councillors are too *chicken-livered* to attempt a manoeuvre like that. 市議会議員らはそんな作戦を試みるには臆病すぎる.

Chickens come home to roost. 《諺》悪行[誤り]は必ずわが身に帰ってくる《悪行などの報いが必ずある》.

Children and chicken must ever be picking. 子供とひな鳥はいつも空腹で食べたがる.

count** one's **chickens before they are hatched 取らぬ狸の皮算用をする (→count one's CHICKs before they hatch) ▪ Don't *count your chickens before they are hatched*. 取らぬ狸の皮算用はするな. ☞イソップ寓話の卵を売りに行く女の話から.

get it where the chicken got the ax 《米口》ひどくしかられる, ひどい目にあわされる ▪ I *got it* right *where the chichen got the ax*. 私はほんとにひどくしかられた. ☞get it in the NECK より少し強い表現.

get up [***rise***] ***with the chickens*** 早起きする ▪ Morning people are genetically programmed to go to bed early and *get up with the chickens*. 朝型の人は遺伝的に早寝早起きするように生体プログラムが組み込まれている.

go to bed with the chickens 《口》(夜)早く寝る ▪ Tom worked hard and *went to bed with the chickens*. トムは一生懸命働き夜は早く寝た.

like a headless chicken/《英》***like a chicken with its head cut off*** パニック[興奮, 錯乱]状態で, 取り乱して, 脇目もふらず ▪ Mr. Major is handling this election *like a headless chicken*. メイジャー氏は駆けずりまわってこの選挙を担当している.

like a trussed chicken (羽根などを胴体にくくりつけられたニワトリのように)きつく縛られて; 窮屈な衣服を着て ▪ The pirates boarded their boat and bound her naked *like a trussed chicken*. 海賊たちは彼らの船に乗り込み, 彼女を裸にしてぐるぐる巻きに縛った ▪ She wore a tanktop and tight jeans which made her look *like a trussed chicken*.

彼女はタンクトップを着てきついジーンズをはいていたが，とても窮屈そうだった．

Mother Car(e)y's chicken **1** ウミツバメ《あらしを予報すると伝えられる》 ▪ To the petrels, sailors have given the name of *Mother Carey's chickens*. 水夫たちはウミツバメをマザーケアリーのひなと呼んだ．
2 紛争をもたらす人，物議の中心人物 ▪ All this comes from your croaking; you're a *Mother Carey's chicken*. これはみな君が陰気くさい声でしゃべったから起こったのだ．君は紛争配達者だ．
3 ［複数形で］降雪 ▪ We had "*Mother Carey's Chickens*" last night. 昨夜雪が降った． ☞Mother Cary＝dear mother.

play chicken 肝[根性]だめしをする《にらみつけたりして相手を脅す; 車などで衝突寸前まで逃げない》 ▪ They *played chicken* and neither one of them blinked. 彼らはすごみあったがどちらもまばたきさえしなかった ▪ Cars narrowly missed the drunkard as he *played chicken* on the track. 車はかろうじて酔っ払いを避けたが，彼は路上で肝試しをしていたのだ ▪ The boy *played chicken* on a railroad track and was hit by a train. 少年は鉄道線路上で肝試しをしていて列車にはねられた．

run around like a headless chicken 大あわてで忙しく活動する，非常に取り乱す ▪ He's got so much work to do—he's been *running around like a headless chicken* all week. 彼は仕事が山ほどあって今週はずっとあれやこれやとばたばたしている． ☞首を切られたニワトリがしばらく走り回ることから．

chief /tʃiːf/ 名形 ***a big white chief*** 《戯》親分，重要人物 ▪ Al hopes they will soon refer to him as the *Big White Chief* in Washington. アルは間もなく彼らが自分をワシントンの重鎮と呼ぶだろうと期待している．

all chiefs and no Indians 《卑》指示を出す人ばかりで働く人がいない，「船頭多くして船山に登る」 ▪ Let's face it, people, society cannot run with *all chiefs and no Indians*. 現実を見ようではないか，君たち，社会は大将ばかりでは動かないのだ．

chief(est) of all わけても，なかんずく ▪ But *chiefest of all*, don't forget it. しかし，わけても忘れぬようにしなさい．

in chief **1** 主の，最高の ▪ The President of the USA is also the commander-*in-chief* of its armed forces. アメリカ合衆国大統領はその軍隊の最高司令官でもある ▪ She used to be the editor *in chief* of a local paper. 彼女はかつて地方紙の主筆だった．
2 主に，主として ▪ *In chief* I spend my time writing a dictionary. 私は主に辞書を執筆して過ごす．
3 王侯から直接の(借地など); 永代の(借地など)《中世法用語》 ▪ The same castle is held by you *in chief*. その城は貴家によって永代租借されている．

Too many chiefs and not enough Indians. 《諺・卑》指示を出す者が多すぎてそれを実行する人が少ない，「船頭多くして船山に登る」．

child /tʃaɪld/ 名 ***a child of nature*** 自然児; 無邪気な人，すれてない人 ▪ She is *a* pure *child of nature*, without the smallest particle of sophistication in her whole composition. 彼女は純で無邪気な子で，心身のどこにも全くすれたところがない．

a child of the forest 《米》(北米)先住民，森の民 ▪ They were fine looking *children of the forest*. 彼らは整った顔だちの先住民だった．

a child wife 幼な妻 ▪ The author opens up Poe's dark mind to show us his mad love for his *child wife*. 著者はポウの暗い精神を開いて，彼の幼な妻 (Virginia Clemm，当時13歳)への激しい愛情を示す．

a [*one's*] ***second childhood*** 第二の幼年期，もうろく ▪ I guess I'm going through *my second childhood*. 私はぼけてきているように思う．

a wild child (麻薬・酒の味を覚え悪友と交わる)非行少年[少女]，不良 ▪ Their once angelic daughter has turned into *a wild child*. かつては天使のようだった彼らの娘は非行少女になった ▪ She's held up as both a role model and *a wild child*. 彼女は模範生徒としても不良少女としても引き合いにだされる．

Children and fools speak the truth. 《諺》子供とばかは本当のことを言う[正直だ]．

children of light [***this world***] キリスト教徒[世故(せ)にたけた人たち] (《聖》*Luke* 16. 8) ▪ The *children of this world* are wiser than the *children of light*. 世故にたけた人々はキリスト教徒より賢い．

Children should be seen and [***but***] ***not heard.*** 《諺》子供は人に見てもらうだけでよいので，おしゃべりを聞いてもらうものではない《子供は上長の前では黙っているべきで，話しかけられるまではしゃべってはいけない》．

child's play →PLAY[1].

from a child [***children***] 子供のときから(ずっと) ▪ *From a child* he has been delicate. 子供のころから彼は虚弱だった ▪ It was our continual practice *from children* to keep little journals. ちょっとした日誌をつけることは我々が子供のころから続けてやってきたことであった．

get *a woman* ***with child*** 《英》女に子をはらませる ▪ He *got* Julia *with child*. 彼はジュリアに子をはらませた．

go with child 妊娠している ▪ I now *go with child*. 私は今妊娠している．

It is a wise child that knows his [***its***] ***own father.*** 《諺》自分の父親を知っているのは賢い子供である，「親の心子知らず」．

The child is father of the man. 《諺》子供はおとなの父である《三つ子の魂百まで》 ☞Wordsworth の "*My heart leaps up when I behold...*" より．

this child 《口》おれ(I, me) ▪ Not for *this child*. おれはごめんだ．

with child 妊娠して ▪ She is *with child* by the Duke. 彼女は公爵のたねを宿している．

childbed /tʃáɪldbèd/ 名 ***in childbed*** 産褥(じょく)で ▪ She died *in childbed*. 彼女は産褥で死んだ．

chill[1] /tʃɪl/ 名形 ***a chill comes over*** ...は寒

気がする ▪ Suddenly *a chill came over* me. 私は急に寒気がした.

blow chill (風が)非常に冷たい ▪ The night was dark, and the wind *blew chill.* 夜は暗く, 風は冷たかった.

cast [throw] a chill upon [over] ...に水をさす, を興ざめさせる ▪ He *cast a chill over* our joy. 彼は我々の喜びに水をあびせた ▪ The bad news *threw a chill upon* the gathering. 凶報はその集会をしゅんとさせた.

catch a chill →take a CHILL.

feel a chill →have a CHILL.

get a chill on the liver [stomach, etc.] 《口》肝臓[など]がちょっと悪くなる ▪ They'll *get a chill on their stomachs.* 彼らは胃をちょっと悪くするだろう.

give** a person **a chill 人に悪寒を覚えさす, 人を冷えこませる; 人をぞっとさせる ▪ You may *give* a baby *a chill.* 君は赤んぼうを冷えこませることもある.

have [feel] a chill 寒くてぞくぞくする ▪ I *felt a chill* in my feet. 足が寒くてぞくぞくした.

run chill 血が凍るようである ▪ My blood *ran chill* in my veins. 血管の血が凍るようだった.

send a chill [chills] up [down]** a person's **spine 恐怖で人の背すじをぞっとさせる ▪ The idea *sent a chill down my spine.* そう考えると私は恐ろしくて背すじがぞっとした.

take [catch] a chill 《主に英》冷えこむ, 寒けがする ▪ He *caught a chill* from sitting in a draft. 彼はすきま風の吹くところに座って冷えこんだ.

take the chill off (*a liquid*) 《口》(酒など)を少し温める ▪ We must *take the chill off* this wine. このワインを少し温めねばならない.

throw a chill upon [over] → cast a CHILL upon.

chill^2 /tʃɪl/ 動 ***be chilled to the bone [marrow]*** 血も凍る思いである(ぞっとする); すっかり冷えこむ ▪ We *were chilled to the bone.* 私たちはすっかり冷えこんだ.

chill** a person's **blood →CURDLE the blood.

chime /tʃaɪm/ 名 ***fall into [keep] chime with*** ...と調和する, 一致する ▪ It *falls into chime* well *with* his freedom. それは彼の自由と十分一致する ▪ Each essential *keeps chime with* the other. 各要素は互いに調和している.

chimney /tʃímni/ 名 ***in the chimney corner*** 古風な暖炉のそばの席で ▪ The old lady sat *in the chimney corner* doing crochet work. 老婦人は暖炉の火の近くの席に座ってかぎ針編みをしていた.

chin^1 /tʃɪn/ 名 ***be chin deep*** あごまでつかって ▪ He *was chin deep* in the water. 彼はあごまで水につかっていた.

chin in air あごを突き出して《怒った態度》 ▪ The squire would march up and down the deck, *chin in air.* 郷士はあごを突き出してデッキをあちこち歩くのであった.

chin in hand あごに手をあて《不きげんを示す》 ▪ He was pouting, *chin in hand.* 彼はあごに手をあて, 口をとがらせていた.

chuck** a person **under the chin (戯れに)あごの下をなでる《猫や子供への愛情表現》 ▪ The cat purrs when you *chuck* it *under the chin.* のどをなでてやるとその猫はのどをゴロゴロならす ▪ And then he had playfully *chucked* me *under the chin* and hugged me. それから彼はたわむれに私ののどをなでて抱きしめた ▪ The doctor smiled on the child, *chucking* him *under the chin.* 医者はその子にほほえみかけ, そのあごをなでた.

keep** one's **chin up 《口》元気を出す, 勇気を出してねばる ▪ *Keep your chin up.* 元気を出しなさい.

lead with** one's **chin **1**《ボクシング》あごを防御しないで戦う[打ちあう] ▪ Potts *leads with his chin,* and he doesn't flinch. ポッツはあごを防御しないで打ちあい, ひるむことはない.

2 無防備[危険]な行動をする ▪ I've been very visible; I've *led with my chin.* 私はまる見えで無防備だった.

make chin music おしゃべり[雑談]する ▪ He was *making chin music* at an old man's birthday party. 彼は老人の誕生会でおしゃべりをしていた.

stick** one's **chin out 《口》反抗する; 自ら危い目にあう ▪ The boy just *stuck his chin out* and refused to speak. 少年は反抗してものを言うことを拒んだ ▪ Don't *stick your chin out* too far. あんまり自分から危い目にあうようなことをするな. ☞反抗的にあごを突き出すことから.

take it on the chin 《米口》**1** 逆境にあって断固として耐える ▪ Millions of children must *take it on the chin.* 何百万という子供が苦しみに断固として耐えねばならない.

2 完敗する ▪ The Penguins *took it on the chin,* losing Game 3 to the Panthers, 5-2. ペンギンズ(アイスホッケーチーム)は完敗し, パンサーズに5対2で第3試合を失った. ☞ボクシングから.

take ... (right) on the chin 《口》あごに強打を受け(て堪え)る《比喩的にも》 ▪ The boxer *took* a hard one *right on the chin.* そのボクサーはあごに強打を受けた ▪ He *took* the failure *on the chin.* 彼は失敗に断固として耐えた. ☞ボクシングから.

up to the chin **1** あごのところまで深く ▪ He was buttoned *up to the chin.* 彼は服のボタンをあごのところまではめていた《詰めえりの服を着ていた》 ▪ He was *up to the chin* in the water. 彼はあごのところまで水につかっていた.

2《口》深くはまりこんで; きわめて忙しい ▪ We are *up to the chin* in the affair. 我々はその事件に深くはまりこんでいる.

wag** one's **chin →WAG^2.

with** (one's) **chin up [out] 勇気を出して, がっかりしないで ▪ He took it *with his chin out.* 彼は勇気を出して苦しみに耐えた ▪ He took the news *with chin up.* 彼はがっかりしないでそのニュースを受け取った.

chin^2 /tʃɪn/ 動 ***chin** oneself* =CHIN the bar.

chin the bar (鉄棒で)懸垂(けんすい)のひじ曲げをする

▪ He can *chin the bar* twice with one hand. 彼は片手で2回懸垂ができる.

China /tʃáɪnə/ 名 ***a china-doll complexion*** (陶磁器のように)色白の肌 ▪ The girl with *a china-doll complexion* works part time as a model. 色白の少女はパートのモデルをしている.

from China to Peru 世界の端から端まで, 世界中いたるところ (S. Johnson, *On the Vanity of Human Wishes*) ▪ These hats are being worn *from China to Peru*. これらの帽子は世界中でかぶられている.

Chinaman /tʃáɪnəmən/ 名 ***not a Chinaman's chance*** わずかな可能性[見込み]もない ▪ Gonzalez did*n't* have "*a Chinaman's chance*" of winning the election. ゴンサレスには選挙で勝つ見込みはまずなかった.

Chinese /tʃàɪníːz/ 形 ***a Chinese compliment*** 自分の心は決っているのに表面上他人の意見を尊重すること ▪ Your asking me if I take exception to your arrangements is only *a Chinese compliment*. あなたの取り決めに異議があるかとお尋ねくださるのは, 表面上私の意見を尊重してくださるにすぎません.

like Chinese water torture/like the drip-drip-drip Chinese torture (***of***) 水攻めの拷問のように(神経に障る) ▪ The incessant squawking was *like Chinese water torture*. 絶え間のない鳥の鳴き声はまるで水攻めの拷問のように神経に障った. ☞額に水をたらし続けて発狂させる昔の中国の拷問から.

chink /tʃɪŋk/ 名 ***a chink in*** *one's* ***armor*** →ARMOR.

chin-wag /tʃínwæ̀g/ 名 ***have a chin-wag*** おしゃべりをする ▪ We *had a chin-wag* with Nokia this morning. 今朝我々はノキアとおしゃべりをした.

chip /tʃɪp/ 名 ***A carpenter is known by his chips.*** 《諺》木の切片で大工ということがわかる《人の職業や趣味はその態度・話しぶりでわかる》.

a chip in porridge [***broth***] 毒にも薬にもならぬ追加物, あってもなくてもよいもの ▪ The Bill resembles the proverbial *chip in porridge*, in that it does neither good nor harm. その法案は諺に言うかゆの中のこまぎれに似て, 毒にも薬にもならない.

a chip of [***off***] ***the old block*** 父親(まれに母親)にそっくりの子《この父にしてこの子ありという場合のように, 概してよい意味》; 家族の特徴を再現している子《物にも用いる》 ▪ Young James is *a* real *chip off the old block*. ジェイムズ青年は全く父親そっくりだ ▪ The crab is its mother's child—*a chip of the old block*. そのカニは母親っ子である—母親そっくりだ.

a chip of the same block 同じ性格を受け継いだ人 (*with*) ▪ Am I not *a chip of the same block with* him? 私は彼と同じ性格を受け継いではいないか.

a chip on *one's* ***shoulder*** 《米口》けんか腰, 挑戦的態度; 不きげんな態度 ▪ He struts out with *a chip on his shoulder* and dares other youngsters to knock it off. 彼はけんか腰で闊歩し他の若者らに来るなら来いといどむ ▪ He wears *a chip on his shoulder*. 彼は不きげんな態度を取っている. ☞もと挑戦の印として肩に木片をつけて歩き, 挑戦者にたたき落とさせたことから.

(***as***) ***dry as a chip*** 乾ききって; 趣きのない, つまらない ▪ His story is *as dry as a chip*. 彼の話は無味乾燥だ.

buy chips 《俗》投資する ▪ I'll *buy chips* in a life insurance scheme. 私は生命保険業に投資します. ☞chips＝money.

call in *one's* ***chips*** コネを利用する, 影響力を行使する ▪ Lobbyists for the banks *called in their chips* and put the burden on the consumer. 銀行側の運動員たちはコネを利用して消費者に負担を押しつけた.

carry [***have***] ***a chip on*** *one's* ***shoulder*** けんか腰である ▪ They have decided to *carry a chip on their shoulders*. 彼らは挑戦的態度を取ることに決めた.

cash in *one's* ***chips*** →CASH[2].

chip and dip [***chip'n dip, chip & dip***] チップ(ア)ン(ド)ディップ《クリーム状の液体であるディップつきのポテトチップス》 ▪ Little did I know how high in fat that *chip'n dip* combination really was. チップンディップの組み合わせがどれほど高脂肪なのか知らなかった.

have had *one's* ***chips*** 《英口》負ける, 敗れる; 運がつきる; 脱落して; 死んで, 死にかけて ▪ Well, you*'ve had your chips*. You'll have to go. これでお前もおしまいだ. やめてもらわねばならん ▪ The world's oldest goldfish *has had his chips*. 世界一長生きだった金魚が死んだ ▪ The rivals *have had their chips*. ライバルたちは脱落していった.

in the chips 《口》金のある, 財産家で ▪ He is *in the chips*. 彼は財産家だ. ☞ポーカーから.

let the chips fall where they may どこに挑戦者が現れようと(かまわない); どんなことになろうとも ▪ He entered New Hampshire with a show of "*let the chips fall where they may*." 彼は「どこで挑戦者が出てもかまわない」といった調子でニューハンプシャー入りをした.

not care a chip (***for***) (…は)少しもかまわない ▪ I do*n't care a chip for* it. それは少しもかまわない.

pass in *one's* ***chips*** 《米口》死ぬ ▪ Several cowboys *passed in their chips* then. 数名のカウボーイがそのとき亡くなった.

The chip doesn't fly far from the stump. 《米口》この父[母]にしてこの子あり; 父も父なら子も子 ▪ She and her mother had the same spirit—*the chip doesn't fly far from the stump*. 彼女と母は同じ気性であった—この親にしてこの子ありである.

The chips are down./The chips get on the line. 戦争[挑戦]の幕が切って落とされる, いざという時が来る ▪ He showed his worth when *the chips were down*. いざという時には彼は真価を発揮した ▪ When *the chips get on the line* he will back down. いざという時には彼は譲るだろう.

when the chips are down →The CHIPs are down./The CHIPs get on the line.

without the chips down なんの挑戦もなく，なんの損害もなく ▪ We may be able to try it *without the chips down.* 我々はなんの挑戦も受けずにそれを試みることができるかもしれない．

chirp /tʃəːrp/ 動 ***chirp it*** 愉快にしゃべる ▪ We *chirped it* sometimes in Duke Street. 私たちはときどきデューク街で愉快にしゃべった．

chisel /tʃízəl/ 名 ***full chisel*** 《米俗》大急ぎで ▪ They went down to New Orleans *full chisel.* 彼らは全速力でニューオーリンズへ下っていった．

chock /tʃɑk|tʃɔk/ 副 ***chock full*** (***of***) (…が)ぎっしりつまって ▪ Gardens are *chock full of* flowers. 庭園には花がぎっしりいっぱい咲いている ▪ I hate people who are always *chock full of* facts. いつも事実をいっぱいつめこんでいる人は大きらいだ．

chockablock /tʃɑ́kəblɑ̀k|tʃɔ̀kəblɔ́k/ 形 ***chockablock*** (***full***) ***with*** 《口》…でいっぱいつまって《比喩的にも》 ▪ This cupboard is *chockablock with* my books. この戸棚には私の本がいっぱいつまっている．

chocolate /tʃɑ́kələt|tʃɔ́k-/ 名 ***as useless as a chocolate kettle*** 全く役に立たない，全然効果がない ▪ The investment may end up *as useless as a chocolate kettle.* その投資は最終的には全く無駄かもしれない．

choice /tʃɔɪs/ 名 ***at*** (*one's*) ***choice*** 好き勝手に，好みのままに ▪ Take them *at choice.* それを好き勝手に取りなさい ▪ You may go or stay *at your* own *choice.* あなたは行くもとどまるもご随意です．

be choice of [***over***] …をより好みする; にやかましい ▪ He *is choice of* his food [company]. 彼は食べ物にやかましい[友だちをより好みする]．

be spoilt for choice 《英》(選択肢が多くて)なかなか決められない，選ぶのに困る ▪ With so many options, she *was spoilt for choice.* 彼女は選択肢が多く選ぶのに困った ▪ Those who drive *are spoilt for choice* as to where they leave the car. 車の利用者たちはどこに車をおこうかと決めかねている．

by [***for***] ***choice*** 好んで; 選ぶとすれば，どちらかと言えば ▪ I do not live here *by choice*, but by compulsion. 私は好き好んでここに住んでいるのではない．やむをえず住んでいるのだ ▪ I should take this one *for choice.* 選ぶとすればこちらを取ります ▪ *For choice* I should infinitely prefer Chadford. どちらがよいかと言えば，チャドフォードのほうがずっと好きだ．

Every man to his choice [***taste***]. 《諺》人おのおの好みあり．

from [***out of***] ***choice*** 進んで，好んで ▪ Some people are retiring earlier *from choice.* 中には好んで早めに隠退する人もいる．

have a large [***wide***] ***choice of*** …をたくさん取りそろえている，たくさんの中より選べる ▪ We *have a large choice of* hats. 帽子は色々と取りそろえています．

have a poor choice of …が少ない，少なくて選択ができない ▪ We *have a poor choice of* hats. 帽子は少ししかおいてありません．

have *one's* ***choice*** 選ぶ権利がある，自由に選べる ▪ We *have our choice* between right and wrong. 人間は正邪のいずれを選ぶも自由である．

have no choice **1** 好みはない，より好みはしない ▪ I *have no* particular *choice.* 私には別に好みはない． **2** …するよりほかはない，より好みができない ▪ I *have no choice* in the matter. この件にはそれよりほかにしかたがない．

have no choice but to *do* …するよりほかはない ▪ We *have no choice but to* submit. 服従するよりほかはない．

make a choice 選択をする ▪ He *made the choice* after much thought. 彼はとくと考えたうえでその選択をした．

make [***take***] *one's* ***choice*** 好きなのを取る，どれかに決める ▪ *Make your choice* of whichever one you please. どれでもお好きなのをお取りください ▪ They *took their choice* from among the rings. 彼らは指輪の中からより取りした．

make choice of …を選ぶ ▪ The teacher *made choice of* a thick book. 先生は厚い本を選んだ．

of *one's* ***own choice*** 好き好んで; 自分で選んだ ▪ She married him *of her own choice.* 彼女は自分で選んで彼と結婚したのだ ▪ Mary is a girl *of his own choice.* メアリーは彼が自分で選んだ女だ．

Take your choice. どれでも好きなものを取りなさい．

there is no choice (***between***) (…の間には)甲乙がない ▪ *There is no choice between* the two. 二者の間には優劣はない．

without choice 無差別に，区別なしに ▪ His works *without choice* were condemned as heretical. 彼の作品は一律に異端的であると非難された．

choir /kwaɪər/ 名 ***join the choir invisible*** 《婉曲》昇天する ▪ My father *joined the choir invisible.* 父は昇天した． ☞the choir invisible は天国の聖歌隊. G. Eliot, *Poems* から．

choke /tʃoʊk/ 動 ***be choked with*** …でのどがつまる(思いである) ▪ Christian had *been choked with* the dust. クリスチャンはちりでのどがつまっていた ▪ He *was choked with* the thought. 彼はそう思うとのどがつまる思いだった．

choke the life out of …をしめ殺す; の活動を止める ▪ The government has nearly *choked the life out of* private schools. 政府は私立学校の息の根をほとんど止めた．

choked up 《口》怒って; 動転して ▪ He gets *choked up* about that kind of thing. 彼はそんなことに腹を立てる. ☞通例，不必要に「怒る」場合に．

Didn't that choke you? (そんなしらじらしい嘘をついて)のどがつまりはしなかったか ▪ It's a wonder *that didn't choke you!* そんなしらじらしい嘘をついてのどがつまらなかったのは不思議だ．

choker /tʃóʊkər/ 名 ***That's a choker.*** そう出られりゃ一言もない．

choose /tʃuːz/ 動 ***as you choose*** お好きなように ▪ You may do *as you choose.* 好きなようにせよ．

cannot choose but *do* …せざるをえない ▪ He

cannot choose but hear. 彼は聞かないわけにいかない.

choose** one's **own time 都合のよい時を選ぶ ▪ You may *choose your own time* in payment. 支払いはご都合のつく時でよろしい.

***choose to** do **rather than** (**to**) do* …するよりむしろ…するほうを選ぶ ▪ He *chooses to* forgo pleasure *rather than* endure pain. 彼は苦痛に耐えるよりも, むしろ快楽を捨てるほうを選ぶ.

if you choose お望みなら ▪ You may go home *if you choose.* お望みならお帰りになってもよろしい.

nothing* [*not much, not a pin*] *to choose between …の間には甲乙は全く[たいして, 少しも]ない ▪ There's *not much to choose between* those brothers. Both very worthy. その兄弟の間にはたいした違いはない. どちらもきわめて立派である ▪ There's *not a pin to choose between* me and the man. 私とその人のと間には全く優劣はない.

pick and choose →PICK[2].

chop[1] /tʃɑp|tʃɔp/ 名 ***be for the chop*** 《口》解雇され[殺され, 棄てられ]ようとしている ▪ If you don't work harder, you'll *be for the chop.* もっと精出して働かないと首になるぞ.

bust** a person's **chops 《米口》小言を言う, 批判する ▪ They *busted the lawmaker's chops* over his trip to Miami while the Congress was in session. 彼らはその議員を議会開会中のマイアミ旅行の件で批判した ▪ I don't think anybody's going to *bust my chops* for being an hour late for the appointment. 約束に1時間遅れたからと言って誰も私を非難しないと思う.

bust** one's **chops 《米口》努力する, がんばる ▪ I *busted my chops* for three years and passed all the courses. 私は3年間がんばって全課程を修了した ▪ My grandparents *busted their chops* to get into this country. 私の祖父母は苦労してこの国に入国した.

chops and changes 変転, 変移 ▪ Life is full of *chops and changes.* 人生は変転きわまりない.

first chop 《口》優秀な(もの), 第一級の(もの) ▪ The carriage was a real *first chop.* その馬車は真に最上等だった ▪ We are the *first chop* of the world. 我々は世界第一級の人物なのだ.

***get the chop* [*ax*]** 《口》 **1** 首になる ▪ He *got the ax* for negligence. 彼は怠慢のため解雇された.
2 棄てられる; 殺される ▪ He *got the chop* here. 彼はここで殺された.

give the chop 《口》 **1** 解雇する, 首にする ▪ They *gave* him *the chop.* 彼らは彼を首にした.
2 (計画などを)棄てる; (人を)殺す ▪ The committee *gave the chop* to our plan. 委員会は我々の計画を棄却した.

lick** one's **chops →LICK[2].

take a chop at …をねらい打つ, に切りかかる ▪ He *took a chop at* the dog with his stick. 彼はステッキで犬に打ちかかった.

chop[2] /tʃɑp|tʃɔp/ 動 ***chop and change*** **1** (…を)売買する《比喩的にも》 ▪ He was continually *chopping and changing* his horses. 彼は絶えず馬を売買していた ▪ They come to *chop and change* with us. 彼らは我々と取引をしに来る.
2 …を変える ▪ He *chops and changes* his mind. 彼は心をぐらぐら変える ▪ You *chop and change* all day. 君は一日中ぐらぐら気が変わるんだね.

chop logic 理屈をこねる ▪ Don't *chop logic* with me; get on with your work. 私に理屈こねてないで, どんどん仕事をやれ.

chop yarns 《俗》話をする ▪ He was very fond of *chopping yarns.* 彼は話をするのが大好きであった.

chop[3] /tʃɑp|tʃɔp/ 間形 ***chop chop*** **1** 早く早く, 急げ急げ《人を急がせるときの言葉》 ▪ Now, get to it. *Chop, chop.* さあ, さっさととりかかりなさい.
2《俗》盗難車の ▪ The arrested man said he sold the *chop-chop* vehicle parts to shops selling second-hand spare parts. 逮捕された男は盗難車の部品を中古のスペア部品を売る店に売ったと供述した ▪ Police recovered four stolen vehicles and *chop-chop* car parts in a raid. 警察はガサ入れをして盗難車4台と盗難車のパーツを押収した.
3《俗》(タバコが)密売の, 違法な ▪ Federal police searched Besnik's home and found machinery used in the manufacture of illegal "*chop chop*" tobacco. 連邦警察はベスニック宅を捜索して違法タバコ製造に用いられていた機械を見つけた.

chopper /tʃɑ́pər|tʃɔ́p-/ 名 ***get* [*give*] *the chopper*** →get the CHOP, give the CHOP.

chord /kɔːrd/ 名 ***break* [*spread*] *a chord*** 《音》和音を分散する ▪ In this case the order of *breaking the chord* is left to the taste of the performer. この場合, 和音を分散させる順序は演奏者の趣味にまかされている.

strike a chord **1** 覚えがある ▪ His voice *strikes a chord*, but I can't remember his name. 彼の声には覚えがあるが名前は思い出せない.
2 (…の)琴線に触れる, 共感を得る, 支持される (*with*) ▪ His hit record *struck a chord with* the public by appealing to their affection for automobiles. 彼のヒット曲は車への愛情に訴えて大衆の共感を得た. ☞心の琴線 (chord) を打つ (strike) が原義.

touch the right chord 巧みに感情に訴える ▪ Lyricism *touched the right chord* with those poets. 叙情調はその詩人たちの感情に強く訴えた.

chorus /kɔ́ːrəs/ 名 ***in* (*a*) *chorus*** みないっしょに, 声をそろえて ▪ Read *in chorus.* 声をそろえて読みなさい ▪ They cried out *in a chorus.* 彼らは一斉に大声で叫んだ.

join in a chorus 合唱に加わる; (賛美歌で)合唱部を歌う ▪ Mr. Smith sang the verses and everybody *joined in the chorus.* スミス氏が独唱部を歌い, みんなが合唱部を歌った.

chosen /tʃóʊzən/ 形 ***a chosen instrument*** 《英》(神意を行う)選びのうつわ (《聖》*Acts* 9. 15) ▪ This bill is the Government's *chosen instrument* for promoting industries. この法案は産業振

興のための政府の選びのうつわである.

chow /tʃaʊ/ 名 ***a chow line*** 《俗》食事[給食]を待つ人の列 ▪ Smith was in *a chow line* when the Viet Cong rocketed the camp. スミスが給食者の列にいたときベトコンがキャンプにロケット弾を打ち込んだ ▪ Look at the *chow lines* for brief reviews of area restaurants. 食事を待っている行列を見ればその地区のレストランの評判がわかる.

chowder /tʃáʊdər/ 名 ***by chowder*** 《米口》確かに ▪ I vow *by chowder* it was made of glass. それはガラス製だったとはっきり断言するよ.

run a chowder mill 《米口》チャウダー屋を営む ▪ They all *ran a chowder mill.* みんなチャウダー屋をやっていた.

Christ /kraɪst/ 名 ***before Christ*** [***B.C.***] 世紀前 ▪ He died in 250 *B.C.* 彼は紀元前250年に亡くなった. ☞しばしばスモールキャピタル B.C. で表記.

Christian /krístʃən/ 名 ***make a Christian out of*** 《俗》(人に強いて)望ましい行動[態度]をとらせる ▪ It *made Christians out of* the others. それは他の者たちに望ましい行動をとらせた.

Christmas /krísməs/ 名 (***a***) ***Christmas club*** クリスマスクラブ(の)《クリスマスの買い物用に積み立てる貯金計画》 ▪ The *Christmas club* is a savings program that was first offered by various banks during the Great Depression. クリスマスクラブとは貯金計画のことであり, 最初は大恐慌のころに種々の銀行によって提供された ▪ They put the money in the *Christmas Club* accounts. 彼らはクリスマスクラブの口座にお金を入れた.

be lit up like a Christmas tree 《口》酔っぱらって ▪ He *was lit up like a Christmas tree*, and greasy from the barbecue like everyone else. 彼は酔っぱらっており, 他のみんなと同様にバーベキューの油がついていた.

Christmas comes but once a year. 《諺》クリスマスは年に一度しか来ない《だから大いに楽しめ, 人も楽しむようにせよ, など》. ☞同名のアニメ(1936)から.

Merry Christmas! クリスマスおめでとう! ▪ *Merry Christmas*, everyone*!* みなさん, クリスマスおめでとう! ☞《英》では Happy Christmas! とも言う.

chromo /króʊmoʊ/ 名 ***take*** [***contest***] ***the chromo*** 《米口》一等である, 優勝を張り合う ▪ It *contests the chromo* with Chicago for flatness of surface. そこは地表の平たさでシカゴと優劣を争っている ▪ It *takes the chromo.* それは第一等である.

chuck[1] /tʃʌk/ 名 ***get the chuck*** 《英俗》首になる; 結婚申し込みを断られる ▪ I *got the chuck* from Barbara. バーバラに結婚の申し込みを断られた.

give *a person* ***the chuck*** 《英俗》人を首にする; 結婚申し込みを断る ▪ I *gave* him *the chuck.* 彼を首にした.

ride the chuck line 《米》冬に職がなくて野営地を次々と馬で渡って行く ▪ He was *riding the chuck line.* 彼は失業して野営地を次々に渡って行っていた.

chuck[2] /tʃʌk/ 動 ***chuck*** *oneself* ***away on*** 《口》(他人から見てつまらぬ相手)と結婚する[つき合う] ▪ He was a fool to *chuck himself away on* such a woman. 彼は愚かにもあんな女と結婚した ▪ You should not *chuck yourself away on* such a man. あんなつまらぬ男と結婚すべきでない.

chuck down *one's* ***tools*** →throw down one's TOOLs.

chuck in *one's* ***hand*** [***cards***] 《口》 **1** トランプをやめる; ...するのをやめる ▪ He *chucked his cards in* and went to bed. 彼はトランプをやめて寝た. **2** (だめだと)やめる, 敗北を認める, お手あげする ▪ As soon as the competition became more intense, he *chucked in his hand.* 競技が激しくなるや否や彼はお手あげした. ☞トランプから.

chuck it down 《英口》土砂降りである ▪ It often used to *chuck it down* all day long. 一日中土砂降りのことがよくあった.

chuck it in 《口》諦める, 断念する ▪ There were times when he almost *chucked it in.* 彼はほとんど諦めようとしたときがあった.

chuck it (***up***) 《口》やめる; よす ▪ I'll *chuck it* for tonight. 今夜はもう(仕事を)やめよう ▪ "*Chuck it,*" snapped the boy. 「よせっ!」と少年はかみつくように言った.

chuck up (***the sponge***) (競技・試みなどを)やめる; 降参する ▪ He refused to *chuck up* (*the sponge*) in the match. 彼はその試合でなかなか参ったと言わなかった. ☞ボクシングで負けたときスポンジを投げあげることから.

chuck *one's* ***weight about*** 《口》偉そうに[高慢に]ふるまう ▪ Don't start *chucking your weight about* too much. あまり偉そうなまねをするもんじゃない.

chucking-out time 《英口》(飲み屋などの)閉店時間 ▪ It is *chucking-out time* at the Circus Tavern. 居酒屋サーカスでは閉店の時間だ.

chuck-farthing /tʃʌ́kfɑ̀ːrðɪŋ/ 名 ***play*** (***at***) ***chuck-farthing*** (***with***) (...を)むちゃに投げ捨てる, (を)むちゃに賭(か)けて危険にさらす ▪ They are *playing at chuck-farthing with* their happiness. 彼らは幸福をむちゃに投げ捨てている ▪ They are *playing chuck-farthing with* the Empire. 彼らは帝国を賭けて危険にさらしている.

chuckle /tʃʌ́kəl/ 動 ***chuckle to*** *oneself* 一人でほくそえむ, 一人でくすくす笑う ▪ She *chuckled to herself* with delight. 彼女はうれしくて一人でほくそえんだ.

chum /tʃʌm/ 名 ***get*** [***make***] ***chums with*** ... と仲よしになる ▪ I *made chums with* him. 私は彼と仲よしになった.

chump /tʃʌmp/ 名 ***off*** *one's* ***chump*** 《主に英口》頭が変で; 愚かで ▪ Master has gone *off his chump.* 主人は気が狂いました ▪ He was *off his chump.* 彼は頭がおかしかった. ☞chump=head.

chunk /tʃʌŋk/ 名 ***a*** (***big, large, significant,*** etc.) ***chunk of change*** 《口》大金 ▪ I saved *a nice chunk of change.* 私はかなりの金を蓄えた ▪ The plan is expected to cost *a healthy chunk of change.* その計画は相当な大金がかかると

予想される.

a chunk of a 《米口》 **1** (人が)発育のよい; 有望な; 立派な ▪ I was *a chunk of a* boy then. 私はそのころは発育のよい少年だった ▪ You are *a chunk of a* lawyer. 君は有望な弁護士だ ▪ He spotted *a* stylish *chunk of a* woman. 彼は上品で立派な女性を見つけた.

2 (馬が)がっちりした ▪ He was riding *a* short *chunk of a* horse. 彼は背の低いがっちりした馬に乗っていた.

3 (戦いが)相当激しい ▪ He took *a chunk of a* fight now and then. 彼はときどき相当激しく戦った.

4…の類の ▪ He lives in *a* poor *chunk of a* cabin. 彼はみすぼらしい丸太小屋に住んでいる.

extinguish** a person's **chunk 《米俗》 人を殺す; 死体を消す ▪ He resolved to *extinguish her chunk*. 彼は彼女を殺そうと決心した.

church /tʃəːrtʃ/ 名 ***(as) poor as a church mouse*** →MOUSE.

at church 教会で礼拝中で ▪ She is now *at church*. 彼女は今教会で礼拝中です.

attend church 礼拝に出席する ▪ We *attend church* on Sunday. 日曜には礼拝に出席する.

between churches 礼拝と礼拝との間に, 礼拝時間の間に ▪ *Between churches* Aunt used to go down to the school and see the children. 礼拝時間の間に, おばは学校に行き子供たちに会うのが常でした.

go into [enter] the church 僧職につく, 牧師になる ▪ He decided to *go into the church*. 彼は牧師になることに決めた.

go to church **1** 教会に礼拝に行く ▪ We *go to church* on Sundays. 日曜には教会参りをする.

2 結婚する ▪ When do you intend to *go to church*? いつ結婚するつもりですか.

in church =at CHURCH.

in the church 僧職にあって, 牧師で ▪ He is *in the church*. 彼は僧職にある.

out of church 教会で礼拝していないで ▪ He is *out of church* now. 彼は今は教会で礼拝していない.

talk church 宗教じみた話をする (→talk SHOP) ▪ They were *talking church*. 彼らは宗教じみた話をしていた.

The nearer the church, the farther from God. 《諺》 教会に近いほど, 神から遠い, 「坊主の不信心」.

churchyard /tʃəːrtʃjὰːrd/ 名 ***A green [hot] Christmas [Yule] makes a full churchyard.*** →GREEN.

chute[1] /ʃuːt/ 名 ***down the chute*** 捨てられて, 浪費されて ▪ In my opinion, the government flushed millions of our tax dollars *down the chute* on these projects. 私の考えでは, 政府は我々の何百万という税金をこれらの計画に浪費した.

take the chute 《米》 道を行く ▪ They are *taking the* same *chute* every day. 彼らは毎日同じ道を行っている ▪ I *took the* wrong *chute*. 私はまちがった道を行った.

chute[2] /ʃuːt/ 動 ***chute the chute(s)*** 《口》 (車・船で)斜面をすべってプールにすべり込む; (遊園地などで)大坂すべりをする ▪ The grand finale of the show is the *chuting* of *the chute* by big elephants. そのショーの大団円は巨ゾウによる大すべり込み芸である.

cider /sáɪdər/ 名 ***all talk and no cider*** → TALK[1].

more cider and less talk →TALK[1].

cigar /sɪgάːr/ 名 ***close, but no cigar/ nice try but no cigar*** 《米口》 (答え・狙いなどが)近いがはずれ, あと一歩 ▪ *Close, but no cigar*. Actually, North Carolina won its first national championship in 1924. 近いが, はずれだ. 実際には, 1924年にノースカロライナが最初の全国優勝をはたしたのだ ▪ I've come *close, but no cigar*. 私はいい線までいったのだが, あと一歩だった[優勝[合格]できなかった] ▪ If you guessed Joe Lieberman, *nice try, but no cigar*. ジョー・リーバマンが答えだと思ったのなら, 近いが正解ではない.

cinch /sɪntʃ/ 名 ***have a cinch on*** 《米口》 …をしっかとつかまえる ▪ I *had a cinch on* what was going on. 私は情勢をしっかりとつかんでいた.

it is a cinch (that) …は確かである ▪ *It's a cinch that* the Blues will win. 青軍の勝利は確かだ.

it's a cinch 《口》 すごく簡単だ, 朝飯前だ ▪ Let's take the second question first, because *it's a cinch*. 2番目の問題を先にやろう, 簡単だから.

cinder /síndər/ 名 ***burn to cinders*** 焼いて灰にする; 焼けて灰になる ▪ They *were* just *burned to cinders* in that car accident. あの自動車事故で彼らは焼けてすっかり灰になってしまった.

to a cinder 真っ黒こげに ▪ The joint was cooked *to a cinder*. 肉片は黒こげになった.

Cinderella /sìndərélə/ 名 ***the Cinderella of*** …で継子(ままこ)扱いされるもの[こと], ないがしろにされるもの[こと] ▪ Mythography may be *the Cinderella of* cultural studies. 神話芸術は文化研究の継子であるかもしれない ▪ Skills training is *the Cinderella of* education. 技能訓練は教育でないがしろにされている.

cinema /sínəmə/ 名 ***go to a [the] cinema*** 映画(を見)に行く ▪ I *went to the cinema* yesterday. きのう映画を見に行った.

cipher /sáɪfər/ 名 ***in cipher*** 暗号で ▪ The telegram is *in cipher*. その電報は暗号によるものだ.

circle /sə́ːrkəl/ 名 ***a social circle*** 社会的集団; 社交グループ ▪ What differentiates them from housewives is that they have *a social circle* in the form of their colleagues. 彼女たちが主婦と違っているのは, 彼女たちには同僚という形の社交的サークルがあるということだ.

a vicious circle →VICIOUS.

a wide circle (of) たくさん(の) ▪ He has *a wide circle of* friends. 彼には友だちがたくさんいる. ☞has many friends より幅があり, 友情のこまやかさを表す.

argue [reason] in a circle **1** 循環論法で論じる ▪ You keep *arguing in a circle*. 君は循環論で論

じてばかりいる.

2 議論で堂々めぐりをする; 決論に達しない ▪ He would say the same thing over and over again so that we were *arguing in a circle.* 彼は同じことを何度も言うので我々は堂々めぐりをしていた.

bring ... full circle ...を元[最初]の状態に戻す ▪ It is terrific to kind of *bring* things *full circle.* いくぶん物事を元の状態に戻すのは素晴らしい.

come* [*go, turn*] *full circle (いろいろ変わったあとで)元の状態に戻る ▪ After changing my occupation many times, I have *come full circle* back to teaching. たびたび職業を変えたあと, 私はまた元の教職に戻っている.

full circle 十分な; 十分に, ぐるっと一回りして ▪ *Full circle* thinking requires considering both the positive and negative aspects of a problem. 十分な思考にはある問題の肯定・否定の両側面の考察を要する ▪ The wheel of history has come *full circle.* 歴史の車輪がぐるっと一回りして来た.

go all round the circle (話などを)遠回りする ▪ He *goes all round the circle* to come to the point. 彼は要点に触れるのに遠回りをする.

go around* [《英》*round*] *in circles **1** 堂々めぐりをする ▪ We were *going around in circles* trying to decide where to go. 我々はどこへ行くかを決めようとして堂々めぐりをしていた.

2 非常に骨を折る ▪ He *went around in circles* to correct his bad habit. 彼は悪い癖を直すのに非常に骨を折った.

3 (...するのに)うんと時間をかける ▪ Father *goes round in circles* to write an essay. 父はエッセイを書くのにうんと時間をかける.

in a circle/in circles 円形になってぐるぐると; 堂々めぐりで ▪ The girls danced *in a circle.* 少女らは円形になってダンスした ▪ I'm finding it frustrating; we're talking *in circles.* イライラしてくる, 話が堂々めぐりしているのだ.

in smart circles 流行を追う[先端的な]人々の間では ▪ Vogue's influence *in smart circles* has been legendary. トレンディーな世界におけるヴォーグ誌の影響は伝説的だ.

move in the wrong circles 悪い取り巻き連中と付き合う; 仲間を間違える ▪ He is basically good-natured but very gullible and *moving in the wrong circles.* 彼は基本的には気立てがよいのだが, とてもだまされやすいので悪い連中とつき合っている.

reason in a circle →argue in a CIRCLE.

ride circle 《米》牧場で馬を乗り回して牛を駆り集める役をする ▪ Where once you *rode circle,* a gopher couldn't graze now. 昔あなたが馬を乗り回して牛を集めていたところで, 今はジネズミ1匹も草を食うことができないだろう.

run around* [《英》*round*] *in circles いたずらにせわしく騒ぎ回る ▪ Mother is always *running around in circles.* 母はいつもいたずらにせわしく騒ぎ回っている.

***run circles round* [*around*]** = run RINGs around a person.

square the circle 与えられた円に等しい面積の正方形を求める; 不可能なことを企てる ▪ You are trying to *square the circle.* 君は不可能なことをやろうとしている.

wander in a circle ぐるっと一回りする ▪ We lost our way, and *wandered in a circle.* 私たちは道に迷ってぐるっと一回りした.

circs /sə́ːrks/ 名 ***in* [*under*] *the circs*** 《口》現在の事情では ▪ *In the circs* I would say we should not dismiss him. 今の事情では彼を解雇すべきでないと思うね.

circuit /sə́ːrkət/ 名 ***do circuits*** 《英口》サーキットトレーニングをする ▪ Lately I've been mainly *doing circuits.* 最近僕は主にサーキットトレーニングをやっている.

go on circuit 巡回裁判する ▪ Judges *go on circuit* for part of the year. 裁判官たちは1年のうちの一時期は巡回裁判に出る.

make* [*take*] *a circuit ぐるっと回る (*of*); 回り道をする ▪ Your letter *took a* considerable *circuit* to find me. あなたの手紙は私のところへ来るのに相当回り道をした ▪ The commanding officer *made a circuit of* the camp. 司令官は野営を一巡した.

make* [*go*] *the circuit of ...を歴訪する, 巡回する ▪ He *went the circuit of* the apartments. 彼は貸間を巡回した.

ride the circuit (判事・牧師が)馬で巡回する ▪ Lawyers *rode the circuits* then. その頃は弁護士は馬で巡回した.

circulation /sə̀ːrkjəléɪʃən/ 名 ***back in circulation*** **1** (人が)現役に復帰して, 返り咲いて, 以前の日常に戻って ▪ Connors is *back in circulation* after 15 years out of the tennis spotlight. コナーズは15年間テニス界のスポットライトの外にいたのち現役に復帰している ▪ Mr. Wei is *back in circulation* after 14½ years in prison. ウェイ氏は14年半の服役ののち社会復帰している.

2 (制度・流行などが)再び流通して, また出まわって ▪ A famous recording from the early years of stereo is *back in circulation,* now on CD. 以前のステレオ時代の有名なレコーディングがまた出まわっている, 今回はCDで.

be in circulation **1** 流布している; 流通[通用]している ▪ The paper money *is in circulation.* その紙幣が流通している.

2 《口》(外に出て)活動して ▪ Now he *is* back *in circulation.* 今は彼はもとのように活動している.

into circulation 流通[流布]して, 活動して, 出まわって, 発行されて ▪ The phrase went *into circulation* in the 17th century. その語句は17世紀に使われるようになった ▪ Once a false story gets *into circulation*, it's hard to kill it. 間違った話がいったん広まると, 消すのは困難だ ▪ The new 50,000 won banknote was released *into circulation* across the nation Tuesday. 火曜日5万ウォンの新札が(韓国)全国で発行された.

out of circulation (参加)活動していない ▪ Now he is *out of circulation* with his friends. 彼は今友人たちに加わって活動はしていない ▪ He is *out of circulation.* 彼は参加していません.

put ... in [into] circulation ...を流布させる; (紙幣など)を流通させる ▪ The new silver coins have *been put into circulation.* 新銀貨が発行された.

withdraw ... from circulation ...の発行[流通]を停止する ▪ This book has *been withdrawn from circulation.* この本は発行を停止されている ▪ Gold coins *were withdrawn from circulation* during the war of 1914–18. 1914–18年の大戦中, 金貨は流通を停止された.

circumstance /sə́ːrkəmstæ̀ns/ 名 ***a mere [remote, poor] circumstance*** 《米》つまらぬ人[物] ▪ King John was *a poor circumstance.* ジョン王はつまらぬ人物であった.

be not a circumstance to 《米口》...とは比較にならない, のそばへも寄れない ▪ He *is not a circumstance to* Shakespeare. 彼はシェイクスピアとは比較にならない.

Circumstances alter cases. 事情によっては一概に言えぬ[話は変わってくる] ▪ London between August and April is looked upon as a nightmare. But *circumstances alter cases.* 8月から4月までの間のロンドンはきわめて不快な地とみなされているが, 事情によっては一概には言えない.

depend on circumstances 時と場合による ▪ That *depends on circumstances.* それは時と場合による.

extenuating circumstances 《法》酌量すべき情状, 情状酌量; 特別の事情 ▪ Principals may excuse absences for *extenuating circumstances*, such as college visits. 校長は, 大学訪問など特殊事情のある場合は, 欠席を許すことがある.

fall in circumstances 落ちぶれる ▪ He has *fallen in circumstances.* 彼は落ちぶれた.

in bad [needy, reduced, straitened] circumstances 貧乏して, 困窮して ▪ I am afraid he is *in* very *bad circumstances* still. 彼はまだ非常に困窮しているのではないだろうか.

in easy [good, affluent] circumstances 安楽に[相応に, 裕福に]暮らして ▪ When men are *in easy circumstances*, they are naturally enemies to innovation. 人が安楽に暮らしているときは当然革新をきらうものである.

in [under] no circumstances / not ... in [under] any circumstances どんなことがあっても...ない ▪ *In no circumstances* must a soldier leave his post. 兵士はどんなことがあっても自己の持ち場を離れてはならない ▪ I do*n't* want you to go out *under any circumstances.* 君はなにがあっても外へ出てはいけない.

in [under] the circumstances 現状では; そういう事情で ▪ *In the circumstances* it is impossible to dismiss the secretary. 現状では, 書記を解雇することはできない ▪ *Under the circumstances*, we have decided to dismiss the secretary. そういう事情で書記を解雇することに決めた.

under ... circumstances ...の事情において(は) ▪ It will, *under* certain *circumstances*, stimulate industry. それはある場合には産業を刺激するだろう.

under no circumstances → in no CIRCUMSTANCEs.

under the circumstances → in the CIRCUMSTANCEs.

with (much) circumstance 詳細に ▪ It was told *with much circumstance.* それは詳細に述べられた.

without circumstance 儀式ばらずに, 手軽に ▪ It was done *without circumstance.* それは無造作になされた ▪ Shall we start *without circumstance*? 手軽に出発しようか.

circus /sə́ːrkəs/ 名 ***play circus*** 《米口》円を描いて回る ▪ We are *playing circus* here. 我々はここで円を描いて回っている.

see the circus 《米口》苦難に直面する; 名所見物する ▪ He took a trip into the valley to *see the circus.* 彼は名所見物のため, その盆地へ入って行った.

cit /sɪt/ 名 ***in cits*** 《米俗》平服の ▪ The thief was tackled by a soldier *in cits.* 泥棒は平服の兵士に組み付かれた.

citizen /sítəzən/ 名 ***a citizen of nature [the world]*** 世界市民 ▪ He is *a citizen of nature.* 彼は世界市民である.

a senior citizen 高齢市民, 退職者 ▪ At the age of 56, I don't think of myself as *a senior citizen.* 私は56歳で自分が高齢者だとは思っていない.

city /síti/ 名 ***a city slicker*** 《口》都会ずれした人, 世慣れた[如才ない]都会人 ▪ In the eyes of country folks, all *city slickers* are rich, arrogant and pathetically soft. 田舎の人々の目から見れば, 都会の人たちはみな金持ちで傲慢で気の毒なほどやわだ ▪ The farm shows *city slickers* how a cow is milked and how chickens lay eggs. その農場では都会の人たちに乳牛の搾乳の仕方やニワトリの産卵の様子を教える.

an automobile [a rain, river, school, spa, etc.] city 《口》自動車[雨, 川, 学校, 温泉, など](がいっぱい)の町 ▪ No one could have imagined that the land would actually turn into *an automobile city.* 誰もその土地が実際に自動車の町になるとは予想できなかっただろう ▪ Hartford is *a river city.* ハートフォードは川の町だ ▪ After the victory of the Cuban revolution, Moncada was transformed into *a school city.* キューバ革命の勝利ののちモンカダは学校の町へと変えられた ▪ The Romans founded *the spa city* of Bath. ローマ人が温泉町バースを建設した.

City of Refuge / a city of refuge 誤って人を殺した人を保護するため壁をめぐらした町, 逃れの町 ▪ If we get tired of the saints, Shakespeare is our *city of refuge.* もし我々が聖徒たちにあきたら, シェイク

スピアが我々の逃れの町になる. ☞City of Refuge は古代ユダヤの罪人保護市であった Palestine の6都市の一つ (《聖》 *Josh.* 20).

Fat City/fat city 満足な(生活)[状態], 裕福な状態 ▪ Gray lived in *Fat City*, literally and metaphorically. グレイは満ち足りて暮らした, 文字通りにも(太って)比喩的にも(満足して).

one on the city 《俗》(市が無料でくれる)コップ1杯の水 ▪ Just give me *one on the city*. ちょっとコップ1杯の水をください.

something in the City **1** ロンドンの旧市内の一かどの人物 ▪ He is *something in the City*. 彼はロンドンの旧市内の一かどの人物である.
2 《口》 いかがわしい金融業者, えたいの知れないいかさま業者, 罪人, 盗賊 ▪ She was defrauded by a *something in the City*. 彼女はいかさま業者にだまし取られた.

something in the city 町に職のある人 ▪ He always gives out he is *something in the city*. 彼は町に職をもっているといつも言っている.

the Eternal City 永遠の都 《Rome の別称》 ▪ The latest news reminds us of Rome's importance and rekindles the desire to visit *the Eternal City*. 最新のニュースで私たちはローマの重要性を思いおこし, 永遠の都を訪ねたいという希望がふたたび燃えあがった.

the inner city スラム街[地区] ▪ A lot of people look at *the inner city* and see high crime and low income. 多くの人はスラム街を見て, 犯罪の多さと収入の低さに目を向ける.

civil /sívəl/ 形 ***do the civil*** 《口》 いんぎん[丁寧]にする ▪ I have been *doing the civil*. 私は丁寧にしてきた.

civility /səvíləti/ 名 ***exchange civilities*** (***with***) (…と)時候などのあいさつをかわす ▪ I *exchanged civilities with* him. 私は彼と丁寧にあいさつをかわした.

civvy /sívi/ 形 ***in civvy street*** 《口》(軍隊にいないで)民間にいる ▪ When I was *in civvy street*, I worked in a factory. 民間にいたころ私は工場で働いていた.

clack /klæk/ 名 ***Hold your clack!*** 《俗》 黙れ! ☞clack＝tongue.

clad /klæd/ 形 (***be***) ***clad in*** …を着て(いる) ▪ The hills *are clad in* verdure. 山は緑の衣を着ている ▪ He *was clad in* rags. 彼はぼろを着ていた.

(***be***) ***clad with*** **1** (衣のように)…をまとって, におおわれて(いる) ▪ At length we entered a world of trees *clad with* chirping birds. 遂に我々はさえずる鳥の群がる森に入った ▪ Xerxes saw all the sea *clad with* his army. クセルクセスは海全体が自分の軍隊でおおわれているのを見た.
2 …を着飾って(いる) ▪ The Sphynx *is clad with* grandeur. スフィンクスは壮大さを帯びている.

claim[1] /kleɪm/ 名 ***a claim to fame*** (あまり重要でないことに関して)ちょっと誇りに思うこと, 自慢の種, 特技 ▪ Amos Glick's *claim to fame* is that he is the world's fastest banana eater. アモス・グリックの自慢はバナナの早食い世界一ということだ ▪ Buñol is a town in Spain whose *claim to fame* is the annual tomato fight it holds every August. ブニョールはスペインの街であり, その呼びものは毎年8月に行われる恒例トマト(投げ)祭りである ▪ My Uncle Hank's *claim to fame* is that he can shove his whole fist into his mouth. ハンク伯父さんの特技は握りこぶしをまるごと口の中に入れることができることだ.

have a claim on (物)を要求する権利がある, (人)に無心を言う権利がある ▪ I *have* some *claims on* his friendship. 私は彼の友情を要求する権利がある ▪ I *have a claim on* you. 僕は君には無心を言う権利がある.

have a claim to *a thing* …を要求する権利[資格]がある ▪ He *has a claim to* indemnities. 彼は賠償請求の権利がある.

have many claims on *one's* ***time*** [***purse***] いろいろなことに時間[金]をとられる ▪ I *have many claims on my purse*. いろいろなことで金がかかる.

have no claim to …を要求する権利[資格]はない ▪ He *has no claim to* scholarship. 彼は学者だなどと言えるがらではない.

jump *a person's* ***claim*** →JUMP[2].

lay claim on …を要求する ▪ He *laid* no *claim on* the intelligence of the audience. 彼は聴衆の聡明さを求めなかった.

lay claim to **1** …に対する権利[所有権]を主張する ▪ If the land belongs to you, why don't you *lay claim to* it? その土地が君のものならば, なぜその所有権を主張しないのか.
2 …をもって任ずる ▪ I do not *lay claim to* learning. 私は学者をもって任ずるものではない.

make a claim for …を請求する ▪ I *make a claim for* damages. 私は損害賠償を請求する.

make a claim on *A* ***for*** *B* AにBを請求する ▪ You can *make a claim on* the firm *for* the costs of your journey. 君は会社に君の旅行経費を請求することができる.

make a claim to …を自分のものだと言う ▪ Does anyone *make a claim to* this purse? 誰かこの財布の持ち主はいませんか.

make no claim …する能力があるとは言えない (*to, to doing, to do*) ▪ I *make no claim to* any sort of elite education. 私はどんなエリート教育も受けたとは言えない ▪ I *make no claim to having* [*to have*] an answer to the problem. その問題の解決策があるとは言えない.

put [***send***] ***in a claim for*** …に対し請求権を持ち出す ▪ He has *put in a claim for* the purse. 彼がその財布を取りに行った.

set up a claim to …に対する権利を提起する, の権利があると言う ▪ He *set up a claim to* the King. 彼は王になる権利があると言った.

stake (***out***) ***a claim*** (***to***) →STAKE[2].

claim[2] /kleɪm/ 動 ***claim*** *one's* ***pound of flesh*** →exact one's POUND of flesh.

clam /klæm/ 名 ***(as) close as a clam*** きわめてけちん坊で ▪ His father is *as close as a clam.* 彼の父はひどくけちだ.

(as) happy as a clam (at high water) 《米口》きわめて幸福に, きわめてうれしそうに ▪ A thousand African-Americans thronged the streets *happy as clams at high water.* 1,000人ものアフリカ系アメリカ人たちがきわめてうれしそうに街道に群がっていた. ☞New England の clam (ハマグリ)の産地に普通な句.

like a clam ハマグリのように(堅く口をつぐんで) ▪ You have your mouth closed *like a clam.* 君は口をハマグリのように堅く閉じている.

toot your horn if you don't sell a clam 《米口》うまくいかなくとも[成功しなくとも]続けてやる ▪ Arise and *toot your horn if you don't sell a clam.* 立ちあがって, うまくいかなくてもがんばりなさい.

clanger /klǽŋər/ 名 ***drop a clanger*** 《英口》=drop a BRICK 1.

clap[1] /klæp/ 名 ***at a [one] clap*** 《米》いっぺんに, 同時に ▪ All the candles were lighted *at one clap.* ろうそくはいっぺんに火をつけられた.

in a clap たちまち; 突然 ▪ The wind came again *in a clap.* 風がまた突然吹いて来た.

clap[2] /klæp/ 動 ***clap eyes on*** →EYE.

clap hands (暖めたり, 合図したりするため)手をたたく ▪ He *clapped his hands* for warmth. 彼は暖めるため手をたたいた ▪ He *clapped his hands*, upon which several slaves instantly appeared. 彼が手をたたくと数人の奴隷がすぐに現れた.

clap** one's **hands 拍手する ▪ Preachers hired persons to *clap their hands.* 説教家たちは拍手する人を雇った.

clap hold of …を(手荒に)つかまえる ▪ The policeman *clapped hold of* me. 警官は私を手荒につかまえた.

clap** a person **on the back (賞賛・激励のため)人の背中をたたく《比喩的にも》; 《北英》(親しみを表すため)人の背中をたたく ▪ Tom *clapped* him *on the back* to encourage him. トムは彼を激励するため背中をたたいた.

clap spurs to (馬)に急に拍車をかける ▪ He *clapped spurs to* his horse. 彼は馬に急に拍車をかけた.

clap the door to ドアをピシャリと締める ▪ He *clapped the door to.* 彼はドアをピシャリと締めた.

clapper /klǽpər/ 名 ***like the clappers (of hell)*** 《口》非常に早く; 一生懸命に ▪ He ran *like the clappers (of hell).* 彼は非常に早く走った. ☞clapper は bell を連想させ, bell は hell と韻をふむ.

claret /klǽrət/ 名 ***tap [broach]** a person's **claret*** 《俗》(げんこつでなぐって)鼻血を出させる ▪ I *tapped George's claret.* 私はジョージをげんこつでなぐって鼻血を出させた. ☞ボクシングから.

clash /klæʃ/ 名 ***a clash of Titans*** 二つの強力な敵対者の激突, 両雄対決 ▪ This contest is *a clash of titans*: between Asia and the West. この競争は東洋と西欧との両雄対決だ. ☞イギリス映画 *Clash of the Titans* (1981) から.

clasp /klæsp|klɑːsp/ 動 ***clasp** a person's **hand*** 人と握手する ▪ He *clasped her hand* with warmth. 彼は彼女と心のこもった握手をした.

clasp hands (感情をこめて)堅く握手する; 提携する ▪ My friend and I *clasped hands* on the top. 友と私は頂上で堅い握手をかわした.

clasp** one's **hands 両手の指を組み合わせる《絶望・祈り・感動のしぐさ》 ▪ You will *clasp your hands* in amazement. あなたはびっくり仰天して, 両手の指を組み合わせるでしょう.

class /klæs|klɑːs/ 名形 ***be in a class by** oneself **[of** one's **own]*** 《口》他の追随を許さない, 他のすべてのものと異なっている ▪ In English at any rate, he *is in a class by himself.* とにかく英語においては, 彼の右に出る者はない.

be in a different class from …よりずっと優れている ▪ The Phantom *is in a different class from* most wedding cars. ファントムは大半の結婚用の車よりもずっと優れている.

(be) in class 授業中で(ある) ▪ They *are in class.* 彼らは今授業中である ▪ I'll see you *in class* tomorrow. あす授業のときお会いしましょう.

be in the same class with …と同等である ▪ As an actor, Mr. A *is* not *in the same class with* Mr. B. 俳優としてはA氏はB氏に劣っている.

cut a class 授業をさぼる, ずる休みする ▪ He *cut classes* and played around on his computer instead. 彼は授業をさぼり, 代わりにコンピューターで遊んだ.

get a class →take a CLASS.

no class **1**《スポーツ》へたな, 等外で ▪ He is *no class.* 彼はだめである.

2《口》すぐれたところのない, つまらない; 野卑な ▪ Soldiers are *no class.* 兵隊たちはつまらない連中だ.

not class enough 《スポーツ》あまりうまくない ▪ He is *not class enough* to play for England. 彼はイングランドの代表選手になるほどうまくない.

obtain a class →take a CLASS.

***place ... in a class by** oneself* …を他の追随を許さぬようにする, 断然すぐれさせる ▪ The purchasing power of his income *places* him *in a class by himself.* 彼の収入での購買力で彼は断然他にすぐれている.

place ... in a class with …を…と同等の地位[同列]に置く ▪ This exploit alone *placed* Slocum *in a class with* Cook. この功績だけでスローカムをクックと同等の地位に置いた.

take a class 学級を教える ▪ He is *taking a class.* 彼はクラスを持っている.

take [obtain, get] a class 《英大学》優等で卒業する, 優等卒業学位を取る ▪ He will be lucky if he *gets a class* at all. 彼はとにかく優等で卒業したら幸運なのである ▪ He *took a* first *class* at Oxford. 彼はオックスフォードで優等で1級卒業学位を取った.

take classes in …の講習[教授]を受ける ▪ My

wife is *taking classes in* cookery. 私の妻は料理の講習を受けている.

the chattering classes 《侮蔑》おしゃべり階級《政治・社会・文化についてリベラルな意見を述べる中上流階級》(↔the silent MAJORITY 2) ▪ *The chattering classes* are deserting the party. おしゃべり階級はその政党を見捨てつつある.

(*the*) *top* [***bottom***] ***of the class*** (***of***) (...の分野)で最高[最低]で, に優れて[劣って] ▪ Her sister Karine graduated at *the top of the class of* 2010. 彼女の姉のカリンは2010年に首席で卒業した ▪ Jessie McHue graduates at *the top of the class* with a 3.973 grade point average. ジェシー・マクヒューは平均3.973という点をとり首席で卒業する.

There's a deal of class about *a person.* 《スポーツ》人が非常にすぐれている ▪ *There was a deal of class about* John. ジョンは実にすぐれていた.

travel (***by***) ***first*** [***second***] ***class*** 一[二]等で旅行する ▪ He always *travels second class*. 彼はいつも二等で旅行する.

claw[1] /klɔː/ 图 ***cut*** [***clip, pare***] ***the claws of*** ...のつめを奪う; の危害力を奪う; の活動力を奪う ▪ That will *cut his claws* pretty effectually. それで彼も悪いことがすっかりできなくなるだろう ▪ The King drew the teeth and *pared the claws of* the Peers. 国王は貴族の歯を抜き, つめをもいだ.

draw in *one's* ***claws*** 攻撃をやめる ▪ The lawyer suddenly *drew in his claws*. その弁護士は急に攻撃をやめた. ☞猫などが爪をひっこめることから.

get *one's* ***claws into*** 《口》 **1** (人を)憎んで[ねたんで]いやみを言う ▪ She's really *got her claws into* her neighbor. 彼女はほんとに隣人をねたんでいやみを言ったのだ.

2 (女性が男性を)とりこにする ▪ Once she *gets her claws into* you, you won't be able to escape. いったん彼女が君をとりこにすると君は逃げられないだろう.

in *one's* ***claws*** つかんで ▪ He has got it *in his claws*. 彼はそれをつかんでいる.

make a claw to windward 《海》船首を風上に向ける《比喩的にも》 ▪ There would be a noble opportunity to *make a claw to windward* out of the misery. その不幸からは幸福へ向かう立派な機会があるだろう.

within *one's* ***claws*** ...の手中に ▪ He has caught government *within his claws*. 彼は政治を手中に収めた ▪ That never comes *within their claws*. それは決して彼らの手中に入らない.

claw[2] /klɔː/ 動 ***Claw me and I'll claw thee.*** 僕のかゆいところをかいてくれるなら君をお返しにかいてやろう(ほめ合いでやろう) (→(You) SCRATCH my back and I will scratch yours.).

claw *one's* ***way*** **1** (しがみつきながら)進む, よじ登る ▪ We'll have to *claw our way* up the cliff. 絶壁をよじ登って進むしかないだろう.

2 (必死の努力で)成功する ▪ The Dodgers *clawed their way* to a 4-3 victory over the Oakland Athletics. ドジャースはオークランド・アスレチックスに4対3で辛勝した.

clay /kleɪ/ 图 ***as*** [***like***] ***clay in the hands of*** (***the potter***) (陶芸家の手にある土のように)...の思いのままになって (《聖》*Jer.* 18. 6) ▪ The patients were *as clay in the hands of* the doctor. 患者たちは医者の思いのままになった.

feet of clay →FOOT[1].

wet [***moisten, soak, water***] *one's* ***clay*** 《戯》1杯やる ▪ Come along. Let's *wet our clay*. さあこい, 1杯やろう. ☞clay「肉体」.

clean[1] /kliːn/ 形副 ***a clean bill of health*** 伝染病などなし[伝染の危険なし]の証明; (一般に)適当である[価値あり]という証明 ▪ The Smiths have all recovered from measles, and now have *a clean bill of health*. スミス一家はみなはしかが治ったので, 今は伝染の危険はない ▪ You must have *a clean bill of health* if you want to enter the navy. 海軍に入りたいなら, 適当であるとの証明がなければならない.

a clean sheet →SHEET[1].

(***as***) ***clean as a new pin*** ピカピカにきれいな, とても清潔な ▪ She keeps her room *as clean as a new pin*. 彼女はいつも自分の部屋をきれいにしておく.

(***as***) ***clean as a pig-sty*** 《皮肉》ひどくきたない ▪ His apartment is *as clean as a pig-sty*. 彼のアパートはひどくきたない.

by a clean sweep 完全に, 圧倒的に ▪ He won the last election *by a clean sweep*. 彼はこの前の選挙に圧倒的勝利を得た.

clean gone 《口》全く気が狂って ▪ He is *clean gone*. 彼は全く狂っている.

clean hands →HAND[1].

come clean 《俗》すっかり白状する ▪ I'll *come clean*. すっかり言ってしまいましょう.

cut clean 切れ味がよい ▪ A new knife *cuts clean*. 新しいナイフは切れ味がよい.

do the clean thing by *a person* 《米》人に対して正直にふるまう ▪ You should have *done the clean thing by* him. 君は彼に対して正直にふるまうべきだったのに.

go the clean ticket 《米》候補者名簿そのまま一人も消さずに投票する ▪ I *went the clean ticket* on the Republican nominations. 共和党の候補指名投票に候補者名簿そのまま一人も消さずに投票した.

have a clean mouth **1** 歯科医の治療がすんだ ▪ For a time at least I *have a clean mouth*. 少なくともしばらくは歯科医に用はない.

2 下品なものの言い方をしない ▪ My son *has a clean mouth*. うちの息子は下品な口はきかない.

have clean lines 形がよい ▪ That car *has clean lines*. あの自動車は形がよい.

have [***keep***] *one's* ***hands clean*** 潔白である, 身を潔白に保つ (《聖》*Ps.* 24. 4) ▪ At least I *have my hands clean* of that evil. 少なくともその悪事については私は潔白である ▪ Our countrymen *kept their hands clean*. わが国民は身を潔白に保った.

keep a clean tongue きたない口をきかない ▪ Let them *keep a clean tongue* on the subject of republicanism. 彼らは共和政体の問題についてはきたない口をきかないようにすべきである.

Keep it clean. 下品なことは言うな, 口を慎みなさい.

play with a clean deck 正直にやる, 正直である ▪ He made up to *play with a clean deck.* 彼は正直にやろうと決心した. ☞トランプからか.

squeaky clean 清廉潔白な; 輝いて清潔この上ない ▪ We expect politicians to be *squeaky clean,* but the truth is, they're human too. 我々は政治家が清廉潔白であることを期待するが, 実際には, 彼らも人間だ ▪ I like the *squeaky clean* feel of my hair. 私, 自分の髪の毛の輝いて清潔な感じがいいの.

the clean thing 《米》正直, 率直 ▪ It would have been *the clean thing* to say so openly. 率直にそう言うのが正直だったろうに.

clean[2] /kliːn/ 名 ***give ... a clean*** 《口》...に手入れする, を掃除する ▪ You must *give* it *a clean* before returning it. 君はそれを返す前にきれいに手入れせねばならない.

clean[3] /kliːn/ 動 ***clean house*** **1**《米俗》家を清掃整とんする ▪ Women helped them to *clean house.* 女たちが彼らの家の清掃整とんを手伝った.

2 刷新[浄化]する ▪ The new mayor began to *clean house.* 新らしい市長は刷新を始めた.

clean** one's **plate すっかり[きれいに]食べてしまう ▪ The hungry boy *cleaned his plate* in no time. 腹を空かせた少年は皿の料理をぺろりと平らげた.

clean the board 《口》(トランプなどに)勝って卓上のかけ金[札]を全部取ってしまう (＝sweep the BOARD (clean)); 大勝する ▪ When a man *cleaned the board,* he had something to be proud of. 勝って賭け金を全部さらってしまったときは, その人は相当の自慢の種ができたのである.

clean the slate →SLATE[1].

clean up the bases 《野球》ヒットでベース上の走者を全部生還させる ▪ He *cleaned up the bases* with a solid hit. 彼は堅実な打撃で塁上の走者を全部生還させた.

cleaner /klíːnər/ 名 ***take ... to the cleaners*** 《口》...の金をすっかり巻きあげる; をこっぴどく批判する ▪ They *took* him *to the cleaners.* 彼らは彼をこっぴどく批判した.

to the cleaners 《米俗》(ばくちなどで)すっからかんになって ▪ I went *to the cleaners.* ばくちですっからかんになった ▪ I sent him *to the cleaners.* 彼をおけらにしてやった.

cleanliness /klénlinəs/ 名 ***Cleanliness is next to godliness.*** 《諺》身体服装の清潔は敬神につぐ美徳. ☞John Wesley が *Sermon* 92, "On Dress" に引用した古言.

clear[1] /klɪər/ 形副名 ***all clear*** **1** 敵影なし,「警報解除」 ▪ The signal "*All clear*" was sounded. 警報解除の号笛が鳴った.

2 全く人なし, 障害物なし ▪ They have left in their car, so it's *all clear* now. 彼らは車で出て行ったから今は人影はない.

(*as*) *clear as crystal* (文章・談話などが)きわめて明晰(めいせき)な; 清く透明な (《聖》*Rev.* 21. 11) ▪ He manages to make his thoughts *as clear as crystal.* 彼は何とかして自分の思いをきわめて明晰なものとする ▪ He showed me a river, *clear as crystal.* 彼は清く透明な川を私に見せてくれた.

(*as*) *clear as day* [*daylight, noonday*] 火を見るよりも明らかで, きわめて明瞭で ▪ It is *as clear as day.* それはきわめて明瞭である.

(*as*) *clear as glass* ガラスのように透明な; きわめてはっきりして ▪ The beautiful river was *as clear as glass.* その美しい川はガラスのように澄みきっていた ▪ What they want is *as clear as glass.* 彼らの求めるものはきわめてはっきりしている.

(*as*) *clear as mud* →MUD.

clear cut **1** 明確[明快]な, 分かりやすい ▪ This is the first *clear-cut* evidence for cannibalism among dinosaurs. これは恐竜間で共食いがあったことを示す最初の明確な証拠だ.

2 輪郭のくっきりした, 整った ▪ His eyes were so big and *clear-cut.* 彼の眼はとても大きくてぱっちりしていた.

clear for ...にはっきり賛成で ▪ We were *clear for* the experiment [returning]. 我々はその実験[帰ること]にはっきり賛成だった.

clear from **1** ...がない ▪ I am *clear from* debts. 私には借金はない ▪ The water is *clear from* impurities. その水は不純物がない.

2 ...の罪がない ▪ I am *clear from* the blood of this woman. 私にはこの女を殺した罪はない.

clear of **1** ...がない ▪ The road was *clear of* traffic. その道路には人通りがなかった.

2 ...を逃れて, 離れて ▪ We are now *clear of* suspicion. もう私たちの容疑は晴れた ▪ The train is *clear of* the station. 電車は駅を離れた.

clear through 完全に貫いて ▪ I covered England *clear through.* イングランドをくまなく歩いた.

get clear away 逃げてしまう ▪ The burglars *got clear away* with all my wife's jewellery. 強盗どもは私の妻の宝石類を全部持って逃げてしまった.

get clear of ...を離れる, 遠ざかる; を逃れる, 避ける ▪ We *got clear of* the port. 私たちは出港した ▪ We *got clear of* the islands before sunrise. 私たちは日の出前に島々から遠ざかった ▪ I must *get clear of* these troubles. これらの困難を脱しなければならない ▪ I *got clear of* him. 私は彼を避けた.

give ... the all clear 警報解除の合図をする《比喩的にも》 ▪ The girl *gave* him *the all clear* too soon. 少女は彼に「安全」の合図を出すのが早すぎた.

***go clear* (*of*)** (...を)離れて[避けて]行く ▪ The ship did not touch, and *went clear.* 船は触れないで離れて行った.

in* (*the*) *clear (符号や暗号でなく)普通の文字で ▪ He sent a message *in the clear.* 彼は普通文字の通信を送った.

in the clear **1** 内法(うちのり)で ▪ The wooden box is three inches *in the clear.* その木箱は内法3インチである.

2 危険を脱して; 非難[巻き添え]を避けて ▪ I think

he'll be *in the clear* now. 彼はもう危険状態を脱していると思う ▪ He keeps *in the clear*. 彼は非難を避けている.

3 制限[束縛]のない; 責任[借金]なく ▪ He intends to be *in the clear* on any contracts with the firm. 彼はその会社とのどんな契約も破棄する気である.

4 潔白で; 疑い[罪, とが]がない ▪ Smith is now *in the clear*. スミスは今は容疑が晴れた.

into the clear →in the CLEAR 4.

Keep clear! 駐車禁止《掲示》 ▪ The sign read "*KEEP CLEAR*". 標識には「駐車禁止」とあった.

keep [***stay, remain***] ***clear of*** …を離れている, 避け(てい)る, さわらない ▪ I must *keep clear of* strong drink. 私は強い酒は避けねばならない ▪ *Keep clear of* the traffic. 車馬の交通から離れていなさい.

make clear 明らかにする, 説明する (→make it perfectly CLEAR) ▪ I tried to *make clear* to him that it was impossible. それが不可能なことを彼に説明しようとした.

make *oneself* ***clear*** 自分の言い分を相手にわからせる, 自分の主張を明らかにする ▪ You've *made yourself* quite *clear*. あなたの言うことはよくわかりました.

make it perfectly clear 明らかにする, 説明する (→make CLEAR) ▪ I want to *make it perfectly clear* that this policy does not permit euthanasia. この政策は安楽死を許すものではないということを明言したい.

see clear to 《主に米》…まではっきり見える ▪ They are crystal-clear and you can *see clear to* the bottom. 澄み切っていて底まではっきり見える.

sit [***stand***] ***clear of*** …から離れて座る[立つ], を避けて座る[立つ] ▪ They *sit* perfectly *clear of* each other. 彼らは互いに完全に離れて座る ▪ *Stand clear of* the doors: they'er closing. ドアが閉まります. 離れてお立ちください ▪ He *stands clear of* politics. 彼は政治には関係しない.

clear[2] /klɪər/ 動 ***be cleared out*** 金をすっかり取られてしまう, 無一文になる ▪ He *was cleared out*. 彼は一文なしになった.

clear *oneself* 身のあかしを立てる ▪ He can *clear himself*. 彼は身のあかしを立てることができる.

clear a [*one's*] ***dish*** 皿の料理を平らげてしまう ▪ Not a man among us *cleared his dish*. 我々のうち一人も料理を平らげた者はいなかった.

clear a docket 訴訟事件一覧にある事件を全部かたづける ▪ The court had *cleared* up *the docket* by sitting to midnight. 法廷は真夜中まで開いていて, 事件一覧にある事件を全部かたづけた.

clear a ship **1** 船荷をおろす ▪ Send me an exact return of what *ships are cleared*. どの船の荷がおろされたのか, 正確な報告を送ってください.

2 (軍艦上をかたづけて)戦闘の準備をする (*for action*) (→clear the DECKs for action) ▪ They *cleared the warship for action*. 彼らは戦の準備をした.

clear a [***the***] ***way*** [***street***] 道をあける, 道のじゃまものを取りのける ▪ Have you *cleared the way* to Jappa? ジャッパへ行く道のじゃまものを取りのけましたか ▪ *The streets* had to *be cleared*. 街路はじゃまものを取りのけねばならなかった.

clear an examination paper 《口》試験問題に全部答える. ☞CLEAR a dish から.

clear *one's* ***dish*** →CLEAR a dish.

clear inward →CLEAR outward.

clear of →CLEAR oneself of.

clear *oneself* ***of*** [***from***] (非難など)を払いのける ▪ I shall *clear myself of* the imputation. その汚名をすすぎましょう ▪ Why don't they *clear themselves from* the reproach? 彼らはなぜその非難を払いのけないのか ▪ The doctor *was cleared of* murdering three patients with morphine overdoses. その医者はモルヒネを過剰投与して3人の患者を殺したとの容疑が晴れた.

clear ... out of the [*one's*] ***way*** …を除去する ▪ We must *clear* the obstacle *out of our way*. 我々はその障害を除去せねばならない.

clear outward [***inward***] 出港[入港]手続きをする ▪ I have been able to *clear inward*. 私は入港手続きをすることができた.

clear *one's* [*a person's*] ***skirts*** →SKIRT.

clear the air [***atmosphere***] **1** (空気中の雲・ちりなどを)吹き払う, うっとうしさを吹き払う ▪ The storm has certainly *cleared the air*. あらしが確かにちりを吹き払った ▪ The rain *cleared the atmosphere* from dust. 雨はちりを払って空気を清めた.

2 緊張した空気を和らげる ▪ His friendly remarks seemed to *clear the air*. 彼の好意ある言葉が緊張した空気を和らげるようにみえた.

3 (暗雲・疑惑・誤解・不具などを)一掃する ▪ His declaration *cleared the air*. 彼の言明が疑惑を払った.

clear the decks for action →DECK[1].

clear the land 土地を開墾する ▪ Farmers had to *clear the land* before planting. 農夫らは種まきの前に土地を開墾しなければならなかった.

clear the room **1** 部屋の中の必要でない物や人を出す; 家具を取りのける ▪ We *cleared the room* ready for the decorators. 装飾師たちが仕事ができるように部屋の家具を取りのけた.

2 部屋を出る ▪ The doctor ordered her husband to *clear the room*. 医者は彼女の夫に退室を命じた.

clear the table →TABLE.

clear the way [***street***] →CLEAR a way.

clear the way (***for***) (…への)障害を除く ▪ The police *cleared the way for* the King. 警察は国王の通行のじゃまものを除いた ▪ The new law will *clear the way for* many educational improvements. 新法は多くの教育改善への障害を除くであろう.

clearance /klíərəns/ 名 ***make a clearance of*** …をきれいに処分する, 一掃する ▪ We *made a clearance of* stored goods. 在庫品を処分した.

cleave /kli:v/ 動 ***cleave ... asunder*** [***in two***] …を真二つに割る《比喩的にも》 ▪ It *clove* my heart *in two*. それは私の胸を真二つにした.

cleave ... to the chine …を背骨まで真二つに割る ▪ He *clove* the man *to the chine*. 彼はその男を背

骨まで真二つに割った.

cleave** one's **way through …を押し分けて進む ▪ The vessel *clove her way through* the strait. 船は狭い海峡を押し分けるようにして進んだ.

*one's **tongue cleaves to the roof of the mouth*** 舌が口蓋にへばりついて物が言えない (《聖》*Ps.* 137. 6) ▪ *His* parched *tongue clove to the roof of his mouth*, and he could not utter a word. 彼の乾ききった舌が口蓋に貼りついて, 一言も言えなかった.

cleft /kleft/ 形 ***in a cleft stick*** →STICK[1].

clerk[1] /klə:rk|klɑ:k/ 名 ***a clerk of (the) works*** 《英》(建設)現場監督 ▪ He was *a clerk of the works* for the royal residences. 彼は王室の住居の現場監督だった.

a room [desk] clerk (ホテルなど)客室[割り振り]係 ▪ He was employed as *a room clerk* in the Penn-Graft Hotel. 彼はペングラフトホテルの客室係として雇用された.

clerk[2] /klə:rk|klɑ:k/ 動 ***clerk it*** 《米口》店員を勤める ▪ He *clerked it* in a drugstore. 彼はドラッグストアの店員を勤めた.

clever /klévər/ 形副 ***(as) clever as sin*** 《口・軽蔑》とても抜け目のない[ずるい] ▪ He's *as clever as sin* and has no conscience. 彼はとてもずるくてどんな悪事もしかねない.

box clever →BOX[3].

clever at …がじょうずで ▪ He is *clever at* teaching English. 彼は英語教授がじょうずである.

clever with …を用いてじょうずで ▪ He is *clever with* the pen. 彼はペンをじょうずに使う(字がうまい).

not feeling too clever 《英口》気分があまりすぐれない ▪ I'm *not feeling too clever* today. きょうは気分があまりすぐれない.

clew /klu:/ 名 ***from clew to earing*** 横帆の下から上まで; 下から上まで, 全く, すっかり ▪ He knows it *from clew to earing*. 彼はそれをすっかり知っている.

click[1] /klɪk/ 名 ***with a click*** カチリと ▪ He shut the lid *with a click*. 彼はふたをカチリと締めた.

click[2] /klɪk/ 動 ***click** one's **heels (together)*** →HEEL[1].

climax /kláɪmæks/ 名 ***be at the climax of*** …の絶頂にある ▪ He *is at the climax of* his fame. 彼は名声の絶頂にある.

bring ... to a climax …を絶頂[最高潮]に達せしめる ▪ The meeting *was brought to an* exciting *climax*. 会は興奮の絶頂に達した.

clinch /klɪntʃ/ 名 ***get the clinch*** 《俗》牢に閉じ込められる ▪ She *got the clinch* for prostitution. 彼女は売春のかどで牢に閉じ込められた.

clincher /klíntʃər/ 名 ***That's a clincher.*** そう出られては一言もない.

clinic /klínɪk/ 名 ***a drying-out clinic*** アルコール中毒治療[矯正]クリニック ▪ Alex Rae checked into *a drying-out clinic* for his out-of-control drinking. アレックス・レイは飲酒を自制しきれないためアル中治療クリニックに入院した.

a well-women [-men] clinic/ a well-woman [-man] clinic 女性[男性]専門診療所 《婦人科の悩みを抱えた女性[性的な悩みを抱えた男性]のためのクリニック》 ▪ The first thing you should do is visit *a well-women clinic*. まずすべきことは, 女性専門クリニックに行くことです ▪ I had a screening for prostate cancer at my local *well-man clinic*. 最寄りの男性専門診療所で前立腺がんの検診を受けた.

clink /klɪŋk/ 名 ***go to clink*** 《口》入獄する ▪ He's *gone to clink*. 彼は入牢した.

in clink 《口》入牢して ▪ He's been *in clink* for pilfering. 彼はこそ泥をはたらいて入獄している.

clinker /klíŋkər/ 名 ***go down into the clinker*** だめになる, 破滅[消滅]する ▪ People would stop flying and the economy would *go* right *down into the clinker*. 人々は飛行機を利用するのをやめ, 経済はまさに破綻してしまうだろう.

clip[1] /klɪp/ 名 ***a clip joint*** 《俗》法外な代金をとる店, ぼったくりバー[店, クラブ] ▪ He was inveigled into *a clip joint*. 彼はぼったくりバーに誘い込まれた.

at a [one] clip 一息に, 一度に ▪ He did the task *at a clip*. 彼はその仕事を一息にやった ▪ It has been raining for a week *at a clip*. 1週間ぶっ続けに雨が降っている.

at a good clip 速いスピードで ▪ It went *at a good clip*. それはものすごい速さで行った.

make a clip 努力をする ▪ Come on, men, we have a job to do! *Make a clip* there! さあ, みんな, 仕事だ. しっかり働くんだぞ!

clip[2] /klɪp/ 動 ***clip the wings of*** →WING[1].

live by clipping 売春詐欺を(して生活)する《売春婦を装い事前に金を盗って姿を消す生活をする》 ▪ I've heard of some girls who run away from home and *live by clipping*. 家出をして売春詐欺をしながら暮らしている少女たちのことを聞いたことがある.

cloak /kloʊk/ 名 ***a cloak of secrecy*** 秘密のベール, 隠蔽(いんぺい) ▪ Everything has been done under *a cloak of secrecy*. すべてが秘密のベールのもとで行われた ▪ The changes leaked out last week despite *a cloak of secrecy*. その変更は隠されていたにもかかわらず先週漏えいした.

cloak and dagger **1** 陰謀, スパイ活動 ▪ They played *cloak and dagger* behind the Iron Curtain. 彼らは鉄のカーテンの背後でスパイ活動をした.

2 冒険と活劇 ▪ He wrote a historical romance of the *cloak and dagger* sort. 彼は冒険と活劇の歴史ロマンスを書いた.

3 秘密裏の, 諜報にかかわる ▪ There were no *cloak and dagger* methods used during interviews. インタビュー中隠し撮りの方法はとられなかった.

under a cloak of …におおわれて ▪ The ground was *under a cloak of* snow. 地面は雪におおわれていた.

under the cloak of …に乗じて; (の美名)に隠れて ▪ They escaped *under the cloak of* night. 彼らは夜陰に乗じて逃げた ▪ He made a good income *under the cloak of* charity. 彼は慈善の美名に隠れて相当の収入を得た.

clock[1] /klɑk|klɔk/ 名 ***against the clock*** = against TIME.

around* [*round*] *the clock*/ *the clock around 24時間ぶっ通しで ▪ He worked *round the clock.* 彼は四六時中働いた.

beat the clock 定めた時刻より早く仕事を仕上げる ▪ It is hard for me to *beat the clock.* 私には定めた時刻より早く仕事を仕上げることはむずかしい.

one's ***biological* [*body*] *clock*** **1** 体内時計 ▪ Larry relies on *his biological clock* to tell him when to get up and when to go to bed. ラリーは体内時計が起床と就寝のときを告げてくれるのに頼っている.

2 出産可能年齢 ▪ With her 40's approaching, she's aware *her biological clock* is ticking down. 40代が近づくにつれ彼女は自分の出産可能年齢が過ぎゆきつつあることに気づく.

clean *a person's* ***clock*** 《米口》人を殴る, 打ちのめす; を打ち負かす, やっつける ▪ He was 14 when he *cleaned my clock* the first time. He used to beat me unmercifully. 彼が最初に私を打ち倒したのは14歳のときだった. 彼は情け容赦なく私を殴りつづけた ▪ Lexus *cleaned Mercedes' clock* in the U.S. market. レクサスは米の市場でメルセデスに勝った.

hold the clock on (ストップウォッチで)...のタイムを計る ▪ He *held the clock on* me while I practised the 100m. 私が100m 走の練習をしている間, 彼はタイムを計った.

like a clock きわめて正確に, 規則正しく ▪ He manages my whole farm *like a clock.* 彼は私の農場全体をきちんと管理してくれる.

One* [*You*] *cannot put the clock back. 《諺》物事は元に戻すことはできない.

punch a* [*the*] (*time*) *clock 《米》(従業員が)出勤[退出]時にタイムレコーダー[タイムカード]を押す ▪ He *punches the clock* at 5 pm sharp and goes home. 彼は5時きっかりにタイムカードを押して帰宅する.

put* [*set, turn*] *back the clock **1** 時計を遅らせる ▪ In the USA we *set the clock(s) back* in November. 米国では11月に時計を遅らせる.

2 年齢を実際より若く言う ▪ He decided to *put the clock back* on his application form. 彼は願書に年齢を偽って若く書くことにした.

3 昔に立ち帰らす ▪ Reintroducing corporal punishment would be to *put back the clock* 50 years. 体罰を復活させるとすれば50年前に逆戻りすることになろう ▪ I wish I could *turn back the clock* to before the accident. できたら事故の前の状態に戻れたらなあ.

round the clock →around the CLOCK.

run out the clock 《主に米》(サッカーなどで)ボールをキープして時間切れに持って行く ▪ Our team, with a 4-0 lead, was *running out the clock.* わがチームは4対0とリードしていたので, ボールをキープして時間切れまで持って行こうとしていた.

tell the clock 時間を計る, 記録する ▪ I *told the clock.* 私は時間を計った.

watch the clock (時間を見守る, とは)終業時間を待ち遠しがる ▪ He always *watches the clock.* 彼はいつも終業時間を待ち遠しがる.

when *one's* ***clock strikes*** 臨終のときに ▪ I hope it won't be brought up against me *when my clock strikes.* 私は臨終のときにその罪に問われないように望みます.

clock[2] /klɑk|klɔk/ 動 ***clock*** (*oneself*) ***in* [*on*]** (時計装置で)出勤を記録する ▪ The workman *clocked in* at 6 a.m. その労働者は6時に出勤した ▪ His timecard had *been clocked in* by someone else. 彼のタイムカードは誰か別人に記録されていた.

clock (*oneself*) ***off* [*out*]** (時計装置で)退出を記録する ▪ He *clocked off* [*out*] at five. 彼は5時に退出した.

clockwork /klɑ́kwə̀ːrk|klɔ́k-/ 名 **(*as*) *regular*(*ly*) *as clockwork*** きわめて規則正しく ▪ The king's last years were passed *as regularly as clockwork.* 王の晩年はきわめて規則正しく過ごされた.

go clockwork*/*go* [*go off, run, work*] *like clockwork 規則正しく動く, 予定通りに進む (→like CLOCKWORK) ▪ The job *went clockwork.* 仕事は順調に進んだ ▪ The train *ran like clockwork.* 列車は予定通りに動いた.

like clockwork 自動的に; 規則正しく ▪ Everything went *like clockwork.* 万事きちんと規則正しくいった ▪ The surgeon made my toes move *like clockwork.* 外科医は私の足指が自然に動くようにしてくれた.

***with clockwork precision* [*accuracy*]** 計ったように正確に ▪ The contests were conducted *with clockwork precision.* コンテストは計ったように正確に行われた.

clog[1] /klɑg|klɔg/ 名 ***pop*** *one's* ***clogs*** 《口》死ぬ ▪ Charlie Yates *popped his clogs* 18 months ago at 92. チャーリー・イエイツは18か月前に92歳で死亡した.

clog[2] /klɑg|klɔg/ 動 ***clog the redemption*** 《英法》抵当の請戻しに制限をつける《たとえば期限をつけるなど》 ▪ The mortgagee must not *clog the redemption* after forfeiture. 抵当権者は権利剥奪後に抵当の請戻しに制限をつけてはならない.

cloister /klɔ́ɪstər/ 動 ***cloister*** *oneself* ***in*** …に閉じこもる ▪ He *cloistered himself in* the monastery. 彼はその僧院に閉じこもった.

live a cloistered life 孤独の生活をする ▪ He has always *lived a cloistered life.* 彼はいつも孤独な生活を送った.

close[1] /kloʊs/ 名 ***break*** *a person's* ***close*** 《法》人の土地に侵入する ▪ It seems I *broke his close.* 私は彼の所有地に侵入したようだ.

close[2] /kloʊz/ 名 ***bring ... to a close*** …を終わらせる ▪ We are *bringing* our entertainment *to a close.* 余興を終えようとしています.

come to a close 終わる ▪ Our pleasant trip has *come to a close*. 私たちの楽しい旅は終わった.
draw to a close 終わりに近づく ▪ Our vacation is *drawing to a close*. 休暇も終わりに近づいている.

close[3] /klous/ 形副 ***a close run*** きわどい一走 ▪ Life or death, and *a close run*. 生きるか死ぬか, きわどい一走だ. ☞run はクリケット用語. 一つの run に成功すれば1点を得る.
a close thing →THING.
(as) close as an oyster →OYSTER.
(as) close as wax →WAX[1].
at close quarters →QUARTER[1].
close by …のすぐそばに ▪ The hospital is *close by* the school. 病院は学校のすぐそばだ.
close in **1** 全く…の中に ▪ The ship was already underway, though still *close in*. その船はすでに航行していた, まだ全く入江の中にいたけれど.
2 (岸に)近く, めり込んで ▪ We were now *close in*. 我々は今や岸の近くにいた.
close on [upon] **1** ほとんど…; に近く ▪ For *close on* a generation no one had appeared to drive them away. ほとんど一世代の間, 誰も出て来て彼らを追い払う者はなかった ▪ It was getting *close upon* noon. もう正午近くになろうとしていた.
2 …に接近して ▪ They were *close upon* us. 彼らは我々に接近して来た.
close to …に密接して ▪ It is *close to* the wall. それは塀にくっついている.
come close to …に近づく, もう少しで…する ▪ They've *come close to* being perfect. 彼らはもう少しで完ぺきだった ▪ It is said that Pakistan and India *came close to* a nuclear war during the military standoff in 2002. 2002年の軍事的膠着状態のときパキスタンとインドとは核戦争寸前だったと言う.
keep [lie] close 隠れている ▪ *Lie close* during the day. 昼の間は隠れていなさい ▪ We advised him to *keep close*. 彼に隠れているよう勧めた.
keep ... close …を隠しておく ▪ She *kept* the letter *close*. 彼女はその手紙を隠しておいた.
keep oneself close 隠れている ▪ The soldier *kept himself* there *close*. その兵はそこに隠れていた.
keep close to **1** …に近接している, くっついている ▪ I *kept close to* my guide. 僕は案内人のそばにいた.
2 …に離れぬようにする ▪ *Keep close to* the point. 要点をそれぬようにしなさい.
lie close →keep CLOSE.
live close together 雑居する ▪ People *live close together* in this neighborhood. この界隈では人々は雑居している.
That's close. 《米学俗》ナンセンスだ, ばか言うなよ ▪ John's a genius.—Huh, *that's close*. ジョンは天才だ—フン, ばか言え.
too close for comfort 近すぎて怖い[心配だ] ▪ The examinations are getting *too close for comfort*. 試験がもうじきに迫って心配だ.

close[4] /klouz/ 動 ***be closed with*** …と秘密に会っている ▪ The chair *is closed with* the mayor. 議長は市長と秘密会談を行っている.
close (the) ranks [files] **1** 列[伍]間をつめる ▪ The officers will each successively *close* their rear *ranks*. 各将校は次々に自分の後列をつめるだろう.
2 陣営を固める; もっと団結を固める ▪ They suddenly *closed* their *files* and stood firm like a stone wall. 彼らは突然団結を固めて石の壁のように断固として動かなかった.
closed-door 非公開の, 秘密の ▪ The conference was *closed-door*. 会議は非公開だった.

closely /klóusli/ 副 ***keep [hold] ... closely*** …をいつもそばへ置く《ときに束縛の意がある》 ▪ Young men *are* often *kept* very *closely* by their fathers. 若者たちはよく父親のすぐそばへ置いておかれる ▪ *Hold* your horse *closely* in. 君の馬をそばに置いて押さえていなさい.

closet[1] /klάzət|klɔ́z-/ 名 ***bring ... out of the closet*** 《米俗》(ゲイなど秘密にしていたことを)公にする ▪ He has *brought* this subject *out of the closet*. 彼は秘密だったこの問題を公にした ▪ The incident has *brought out of the closet* the hidden racism that underlies British society. その出来事は英国社会に潜在する隠れた人種差別をさらけだした. ☞closet = water closet.
come out of the closet 《米俗》ゲイであることを公にする, カミングアウト[カムアウト]する; (秘密にしていたことを)公にする ▪ Many men are *coming out of the closet*. ゲイであることを公にする男性が多くなっている ▪ I'm a closet exerciser, but now I'm thinking of *coming out of the closet*. 私はかくれてトレーニングをやっているが, 今はそれを公にしようかなと思っている. ☞closet = water closet.

closet[2] /klάzət|klɔ́z-/ 動 ***be closeted together*** 密談する ▪ They *were closeted together* in the drawing room. 彼らは応接室で密談した.
be closeted with …と密談する ▪ The Austrian minister *was* recently *closeted with* the German chancellor. オーストリアの大臣は最近ドイツの首相と密談した.

cloth /klɔːθ|klɔθ/ 名 ***a cloth of state [estate]*** (王座・権威の座の)天蓋(がい) ▪ He dined in the hall under *a cloth of state*. 彼は大広間の天蓋の下で食事をした.
(be) cut [made] out of (the) whole cloth 全く事実無根である, でっち上げられたものだ ▪ I think the scandal *was cut out of whole cloth* by someone. そのスキャンダルは誰かのでっち上げだったと思う.
cut from the same [different] cloth 《主に英》同類[異種]の, 非常によく似た[全く異なる] ▪ The two men were *cut from the same cloth*. Both believed in hard work. Both had boundless faith in the American dream. 二人の男はそっくりだった. 二人とも勤勉を信じていたし, 二人ともアメリカンドリームに無限の信頼をおいていた. ☞服などが同じ[別の]生地で

作られているが原義.

cut your cloth according to → cut one's COAT according to one's cloth.

have a cloth in the wind →shake a CLOTH in the wind.

C

lay the cloth 食卓の用意をする ▪ The maid *laid the cloth* for four. お手伝いは4人分の食卓を用意した.

out of (***the***) ***whole cloth*** →make up out of WHOLE cloth.

remove the cloth (食事がすんで)テーブルクロスを取る ▪ *The cloth was removed* from the table. テーブルクロスは食卓からかたづけられた.

respect the cloth **1** 僧衣を考えて行為を慎む ▪ As he was a parson, he had to *respect the cloth*. 彼は牧師だったから, 自分の僧衣を考えて行為を慎まねばならなかった.

2 聖職者の前で言動を慎む ▪ We must *respect the cloth*. 我々は牧師さんの前では言動を慎まねばならない.

shake [***have***] ***a cloth in the wind*** **1** ぼろを着ている ▪ They all *shook a cloth in the wind*. 彼らはみなぼろを着ていた.

2 《海》 少し酔っている ▪ They *had* all *got a cloth in the wind*. 彼らはみな少し酔っていた.

wear the cloth 牧師になる ▪ He *wore the cloth* last year. 彼は昨年牧師になった.

clothe /kloʊð/ 動 ***be clothed upon*** (***with***) (…を)帯びる ▪ The name began to *be clothed upon with* detestable attributes. その名前は実にいやな特質を帯びるようになった.

be clothed with **1** …を着ている, でおおわれている ▪ The fields *were clothed with* verdure. 野原は緑でおおわれていた.

2 …におおわれる; を与えられる ▪ He *was clothed with* glory [disgrace]. 彼は栄誉をになった[恥をかいた] ▪ He *was clothed with* full powers. 彼は全権を与えられた.

clothed and in *one's* ***right mind*** 《戯》 服を着て確かな心で; (仕事などにかかれるよう)身心を整えて (《聖》 *Mark* 5. 15) ▪ I should be *clothed and in my right mind* by then. それまでには身心を整えているでしょう.

clothes /kloʊz|kloʊðz/ 名 ***Fine clothes make the man.*** 《諺》 良い服を着ると人品が良くなる, 「馬子にも衣裳」.

Good clothes open all doors. 《諺》 服装が良ければどの家でも歓迎される, 「浮世は衣装七分」.

in *one's* ***birthday clothes*** →in one's BIRTHDAY suit.

in long clothes (まだ)赤んぼうで ▪ He was *in long clothes*. 彼はまだ赤んぼうであった.

steal *a person's* ***clothes/steal the clothes of*** 《英口・報道》 (他人の考え・政策を)横取り[いいとこどり]する ▪ The BNP has successfully *stolen the clothes of* UKIP. 英国国民党は英国独立党の政策をうまく取りこんだ. ☞BNP = British National Party; UKIP = UK Independence Party.

cloud /klaʊd/ 名 ***a cloud in the sky*** [***on the horizon***] さし迫る異変の予表 ▪ There is not *a cloud in the sky*. さし当たって異変の兆しは少しもない.

a cloud of 無数の, 多数の (《聖》 *Heb*. 12. 1) ▪ He struck her before *a cloud of* witnesses. 彼は多数の目撃者の前で彼女をなぐった.

a little cloud no bigger than a man's hand 人の手ほどの小さな雲(さし迫る動乱のかすかな兆候) (《聖》 *1 Kings* 18. 44) ▪ There was a cloud, *a little cloud no bigger than a man's hand*. 人の手ほどの小さな雲があった.

blow a cloud 《口》 タバコを吸う ▪ He *blew a cloud*. 彼はタバコをふかした.

cast a cloud over …に暗い影を投げる ▪ Sorry I must *cast a cloud over* your happiness. あなたの幸福に暗い影を投げなければならないのは残念です.

drop from the clouds 意外な所から現れる ▪ There he was, —*dropped from the clouds*. 彼はそこにいた—意外な所から現れて.

Every cloud has a silver lining. 《諺》 どんな雲にもみな白い裏がある《憂いの反面に光明がある》 ▪ Don't be so depressed. *Every cloud has a silver lining* if you can only see it. そんなにしょげてはいけない. 見えさえすればどんな憂いにも光明はあるのだ.

hang over *a person* ***like a*** (***dark, poison***) ***cloud*** (不安などが)暗雲のように人を覆う, 頭から離れない, つきまとう ▪ The fear of failure *hangs over* their heads *like a* black *cloud*. 失敗の恐怖が彼らの頭にまとわりついている ▪ Those payments would *hang over* this country *like a* heavy *cloud*. それらの支払いはこの国に重くつきまとうだろう.

in the clouds **1** 天空高く ▪ I saw a kite gliding in circles *in the clouds*. 空高くトンビが1羽翼を広げて旋回していた.

2 (事物が)漠然として, 神秘的な; 空想的な; 高尚で難解な ▪ They amused themselves with phantoms *in the clouds*. 彼らは空想的な幻影をいだいて楽しんだ ▪ The House of Lords was cradled *in the clouds*. 上院は非現実的に育てられた.

3 (人が)ぼんやりして, 世事に超然として; 空想[白日夢]にふけって ▪ His head's always *in the clouds*. 彼はいつも空想にふけっている ▪ Gloria has been *in the clouds* ever since John asked her to marry him. ジョンが結婚を申し込んでからグローリアはずっと夢想にふけってきた.

lift the cloud over …の不安を消す, 疑惑を晴らす; うつ状態から抜ける ▪ *The cloud over* her *lifted* and her smile returned. 彼女は不安が解消し[疑惑が晴れ, うつが終わり]笑いが戻った ▪ We want to make sure *any cloud over* baseball *is lifted*. 野球に関するいかなる疑惑も解消されることを確認したい.

lose *oneself* ***in the clouds*** 夢想にふける ▪ He *lost himself in the clouds*. 彼は夢想にふけった.

lost in the clouds **1** (人が)夢想にふけって ▪ He is *lost in the clouds*. 彼は夢想にふけっている.

2 雲に隠れて ▪ The summit is *lost in the clouds*.

頂上は雲に隠れている.

on cloud seven [***nine***] 《口》 完全に幸福で; 完全に満足して ▪ There we were *on cloud seven*. そこでは全く幸福だった.

under a cloud **1** 容疑[疑惑]を受けて ▪ The junior clerk was *under a cloud* on that account. 年少社員がそのため容疑を受けていた.

2 おとがめを受けて, 不興を被って; 日陰の身で; 失意[苦悩]の状態にあって ▪ He will be *under a cloud* until he is judged innocent. 彼は潔白とされるまでは日陰の身だろう ▪ He was *under a cloud* at court. 彼は宮廷で不興を被っていた.

under cloud of …に乗じて ▪ I escaped *under cloud of* night. 私は夜陰に乗じて逃げた.

wait till the clouds roll by もっと良い時の来るのを待つ ▪ We must *wait till the clouds roll by*. もっと良い時が来るのを待たねばならぬ. ☞古い歌の文句.

clout /klaʊt/ 名 ***Cast not a clout till May be out.*** 《諺》 5月があけるまでは衣服を脱ぎ捨てるな 《早まってことを仕損じるな》.

give a clout on the head 頭にげんこつをくらわす ▪ He *gave* me *a clout on the head*. 彼は私の頭にげんこつをくらわした.

cloven /klóʊvən/ 形 ***show*** [***reveal***] ***the cloven hoof*** [***foot***] (悪魔が)本性[正体]を表す ▪ The Minister's speech on the new bill has *revealed the cloven hoof*. 新法案についての大臣の演説は本性を表した. ☞悪魔は割れたひづめだけは隠せないことから.

clover /klóʊvər/ 名 ***a four-leaf clover*** 四つ葉のクローバー, 幸運をもたらす(とされる)もの ▪ An office worker has had a run of good luck after finding a garden of *fourleaf clovers*. ある会社員は庭一面の四葉のクローバーを見つけてから, 幸運続きである.

be in (***the***) ***clover*** 《口》 裕福である; 安楽[贅沢]に暮らす ▪ The farmer *is in clover*. その農夫は裕福である. ☞clover は牛にとって大ごちそうであるから.

live (***like pigs***) ***in clover*** 裕福[安楽, 贅沢]に暮らす ▪ We *live like pigs in clover*. 我々は全く贅沢に暮らしている.

club[1] /klʌb/ 名 ***be on the Club*** [***club***] 《口》 共済組合から補助を受けている.

Clubs are trump. (トランプのクラブとこん棒の両意にかけて)腕力が勝つ.

in the (***pudding***) ***club*** 《俗》 妊娠して ▪ My wife was then *in the pudding club*. 私の妻はその時妊娠していました.

join the club 《俗》 妊娠している ▪ I'm pregnant and now my best friend Mary has *joined the club*. 今私はお腹に赤ちゃんがいるんだけど, 親友のメアリも妊娠したのよ.

Join [***Welcome to***] ***the club!*** (人の失敗などを慰めて)こちらもご同様さまだよ! ▪ I've failed the exam! —*Join the club!* Don't worry. 僕は試験に失敗した—こちらもご同様さまだよ. くよくよするなよ.

join the mile-high club →MILE-HIGH.

club[2] /klʌb/ 動 ***club a*** [*one's*] ***musket*** 銃をこん棒に使う ▪ The Royalist foot *clubbed their muskets*. 王党派歩兵たちは銃をこん棒に使った.

club the battalion 《主に英》 混乱させる ▪ You have completely *clubbed the battalion*. あなたがたはすっかり事態を混乱させた.

cluck /klʌk/ 名 ***cluck and grunt*** 《俗》 ハムエッグ ▪ I can only give you a quick *cluck and grunt*. 大急ぎのハムエッグしか作れませんが. ☞cluck はニワトリの, grunt はブタの鳴き声.

clue[1] /kluː/ 名 ***find*** [***get***] ***a clue to*** …への手がかりを見つける[握る] ▪ I've *found the clue to* this romance. 私はこのロマンスを解く鍵を見つけた ▪ I've *got a clue to* the accidents of life. 私は人生の偶然事を解く手がかりを握った.

clue[2] /kluː/ 動 ***be clued*** (***up***) ***in*** …に明るい[精通している], をよく知っている (*about, on*) ▪ They seemed less *clued in about* sex than us. 彼らは私たちよりセックスについて無知のようだった ▪ He's pretty *clued up on* human nature, too. 彼は人間の本質についてもかなり精通している.

clump /klʌmp/ 名 ***in clumps*** かたまって ▪ The bamboo grows *in clumps*. 竹はかたまってはえる.

cluster /klʌ́stər/ 名 ***in a cluster***/ ***in clusters*** 房になって, 群れをなして ▪ The citizens gathered together *in a cluster* at the gates. 市民たちは門のところに群がり集まった.

clutch[1] /klʌtʃ/ 名 ***disengage the clutches*** →take out the CLUTCHes.

fall [***get***] ***into the clutches of*** …の手中に落ちる; の毒手にかかる ▪ He came near *falling into the clutches of* the law. あやうく法網にかかるところだった ▪ He *fell into the clutches of* the usurer. 彼は高利貸の毒手にかかった.

get [***have***] ***a clutch on*** 《米》 …を知る, 理解する; を発見する ▪ He *has a clutch on* what is going on. 彼は情勢を知っている.

get [***be***] ***out of the clutches of*** …の手から逃れる[ている] ▪ He *got out of the clutches of* the law. 彼は法網を逃れた ▪ At last we *are out of that money-lender's clutches*. 私たちはついにその金貸しの毒手を逃れた.

in the clutch [***in a clutch situation***] 《スポーツ》 危機, ピンチ ▪ We saw how tough he was *in the clutch*. ピンチで彼がいかに強いかを見せつけられた.

in the clutches of …に堅く握られ[つかまれ]て ▪ I will not come *in his clutches*. 私は彼の手中には落ちません ▪ He is *in the clutches of* the usurer. 彼は高利貸の掌中にある.

let in the clutch (自動車の)クラッチを入れる (↔take out the CLUTCHes) ▪ Al slipped in the low gear and *let in the clutch*. アルはギアをローに入れてクラッチを入れた.

make a clutch at …をつかもう[捕えよう]とする ▪ He *made a clutch at* the military force in Scotland. 彼はスコットランドの軍隊を捕えようとした.

ride the clutch →RIDE the brake.

take out [***disengage, withdraw***] ***the***

clutches （自動車の）クラッチを切る（↔let in the CLUTCH） ▪ Always *take out the clutches* slowly while shifting gears. ギアシフトの際はいつもゆっくりとクラッチを切ること.

within (*one's*) ***clutch*** 取ろうと思えば取れるところに ▪ The golden fruit seemed *within clutch.* 黄金の果物はつかみ取れるところにあるように見えた.

clutch² /klʌtʃ/ 動 ***clutch at a straw*** → catch at a STRAW.

clutch hold of …をしっかりつかむ ▪ He *clutched hold of* my wrist. 彼は私の手首をしっかりつかまえた.

clutter /klʌ́tər/ 名 ***in a clutter*** 散乱して, ごったがえして ▪ The partridges are all *in a clutter,* one over the other. シャコは重なり合って大混乱を呈する ▪ The room is *in a clutter.* 部屋は散らかっている.

co. /koʊ, kʌ́mpəni/ 名 ***in Co.*** 《主に米口》共同して (*with*) ▪ Two foreign physicians carried out the treatment *in Co.* 二人の外国の医師が治療を共同で行った. ☞co. = company.

coach /koʊtʃ/ 名 ***a slow coach*** 活動[理解]ののろい人 ▪ Her husband was *a slow coach.* 彼女の夫はのろまだった.

drive a coach and four [***six***] [《主に英》***horses***] ***through*** (4[6]頭立の馬車を通せるほど)法律がすきだらけで堂々とくぐれる; 話が穴だらけでつじつまが合わない; 通路などが広い ▪ The corridor was so wide that you could *drive a coach and six* through it. その廊下は非常に広くて6頭立の馬車が通れるくらいだった ▪ The art of *driving a coach and six through* an Act of Parliament was then practised with far more boldness. 法令の網をくぐる術は今よりずっと大胆にその頃は行われた ▪ The adventures of Baron Munchausen are certainly interesting, but one could *drive a coach and four through* them. マンチョーゼン男爵の冒険談は確かにおもしろいが, すきだらけでつじつまが合わない ▪ The amendment would *drive a coach and horses through* the principle of schools' freedom. その修正は学校の自由の原則を骨抜きにするだろう. ☞英国国会議員 Stephen Rice の言葉から.

enough to turn a coach and six in 6頭立馬車をぐるっと回すことができるくらい(に大きい)《小さいものを大きく言おうとするときに用いる》 ▪ Is there not a hole in my belly, that you may *turn a coach and six in*? 私の腹には6頭立の馬車が回れるくらいの大穴がないか.

coal /koʊl/ 名 ***a cold coal to blow at*** やっても望みのない仕事 ▪ I won't have *a cold coal to blow at.* やっても望みのない仕事はしたくない.

(***as***) ***black as a coal*** きわめて黒く ▪ Their faces are *as black as a coal.* 彼らの顔は真っ黒だ.

bear coals →carry COALs.

blow [***stir***] ***the coals*** 怒り[争い, 悪意, 激情など]をあおり立てる ▪ He's irritated enough now; don't *blow the coals* too much. 彼は今でもいいかげん怒っているのだ. あまり怒りをあおり立ててはいけない ▪ By these means he *stirred the coals* of jealousy. こういう手段で彼は嫉妬心をあおった.

call [***haul, take, rake***] *a person* ***over the coals*** 人をしかりつける, 非難する ▪ He *was hauled over the coals* for his poor spelling. 彼は誤字当て字のため叱責された ▪ The boss *hauled* me *over the coals* for not finishing the job on time. 仕事を予定通り仕上げられなかったことで上司にこってり油を搾られた. ☞昔, 異端者の拷問として石炭の火の上を引っぱったことから.

carry [***bear***] ***coals*** (石炭運びのような)よごれ仕事をする, いやしい仕事をする; 恥辱[侮辱]をしのぶ ▪ I was engaged as a secretary, and so I'm not going to *carry coals.* 私は書記として雇われたのだからよごれ仕事はしません ▪ I will not *carry coals* any longer. もうこれ以上侮辱に甘んじられない.

carry coals to Newcastle 余計なことをする ▪ To give a tip to a millionaire is like *carrying coals to Newcastle.* 百万長者に心うけを与えるのは余計なことだ. ☞Newcastle は石炭の産地. Thomas Fuller の造句.

heap [***cast, gather***] ***coals of fire on*** *a person's* ***head*** 悪に報いるに徳をもってして相手を恥じ入らせる (《聖》 *Roms.* 12. 20) ▪ The man I had called a miser *heaped coals of fire on my head* by inviting me to dinner. 私がけちんぼうと呼んだ人が, 私を食事に招き悪に報いるに徳をもってして私を恐れ入らせた.

rake over the coals →rake over old ASHes.

stir the coals →blow the COALs.

take *a person* ***over the coals*** →call a person over the COALs.

coalface /kóʊlfèɪs/ 名 ***at the coalface*** 《主に英》現場で働いて, 実務に携わって ▪ He's written myriad books and papers based on his practical experience *at the coalface.* 彼は現場での実地経験に基づいて無数の本や論文を著した. ☞coalface「炭坑の切羽(きりは), 採炭現場」

coast /koʊst/ 名 ***clear the coast*** 沿岸から敵を一掃する, じゃまもの[危険]を取り除く ▪ We must first *clear the coast.* 我々はまず途上の危険を除かねばならない ▪ By making these distinctions, he says, he *clears the coast.* これらの区別を立てることにより, 彼は理解する上でのじゃまものはなくなると言う. ☞密貿易者の用語から.

Clear the coast! 《口》そこをのけ, じゃまだ!

from coast to coast 《米》大西洋岸から太平洋岸まで, 全国に ▪ He has made himself heard *from coast to coast.* 彼は全国に自説を聞いてもらえるようになった.

on the coast 《米》近くに, ほんの手近かに ▪ If she will only fix the day, he'll be sure to be *on the coast* with the parson. 彼女が結婚の日取りさえ決めれば彼はきっと牧師さんを連れてやってくる. ☞海語より.

skirt the coast 海岸に沿って進む ▪ Typhoon Phanfone *skirted the coast* of Japan's main island, dumping heavy rain that disrupted ferry and flight schedules. 台風ファンフォン(10号)は日本の本州の海岸沿いに進路をとって，大雨をもたらしたため船と飛行機は欠航になった ▪ As the plane *skirted the coast*, it became clear that the waters had receded. 飛行機が海岸沿いに飛んだところ，水は引いたことが明らかになった.

The coast is clear. 人目[じゃまもの]はない ▪ The thieves waited until *the coast was clear*. 盗賊どもは人目がなくなるまで待った ▪ *The coast was* now *clear* for Godwin's return. 今やゴドウィンの帰還をじゃまするものはなかった. ☞密貿易者の用語から.

coat /koʊt/ 名 ***a coat and tie*** 上着とネクタイ《最低限の正装》 ▪ I went to a school that required *a coat and tie* daily. 私は毎日上着とネクタイの着用が要求される学校に通った.

(*as*) *close as two coats of paint* 《陳腐》親密な，非常に親しい ▪ They are like peas in a pod, *as close as two coats of paint*. 彼らはそっくりでとても仲良しだ. ☞a coat of paint「ペンキの下塗り・中塗り・上塗り」.

change *one's* ***coat*** →turn one's COAT.

coat of arms →ARMS.

cut *one's* ***coat according to*** *one's* ***cloth*** 《口》 **1** 身分[資力]に応じた生活をする，収入内の生活をする ▪ We all have to *cut our coats according to our cloth*. みんな収入内の生活をしなければならない. **2** 境遇に順応する，できるだけのところでがまんする ▪ We cannot afford to advertise. We must *cut our coat according to our cloth*. 我々は広告を出す余裕はない. できるだけのところでがまんしなければならない.

dust *a person's* ***coat*** (***for*** *him*) 《口》人をどやしつける，ひどく打ちのめす ▪ If he comes here again, I'll *dust his coat for* him. 彼がまたやって来たらひどくどやしつけてやる.

hold *a person's* ***coat*** 人を支持する ▪ I'll *hold your coat*. あなたを支持します.

take off *one's* ***coat*** コートを脱いで身がまえる; 本気に取りかかる ▪ He *took off his coat* to the work. 彼はその仕事に本気で取りかかった.

trail *one's* ***coat*** 求めてごたごたを起こす，けんか腰である ▪ He is a bad-tempered fellow; he is always *trailing his coat*. 彼はたちの悪い男で，いつもけんか腰だ ▪ The Welshman *trailed his coat*. ウェールズ人はけんかを売ろうとした. ☞コートを後ろにひきずって行くことは挑戦の1方法とみなされていた. それを踏む者は挑戦に応じた.

turn [***change***] *one's* ***coat*** 変節する，改宗する ▪ They suddenly *turned their coats*. 彼らは急に変節した.

coat-tail /kóʊttèɪl/ 名 ***drag*** *one's* ***coat tails*** (***so that another may tread on them***) 人が踏むようにわざとコートのすそをひきずって行く，けんかを売ろうとする，けんか腰である ▪ He was blind drunk and *dragging his coat tails*. 彼は酔いつぶれていてけんか腰になっていた. ☞アイルランド人が Donnybrook Fair で行うこととされていた.

on *a person's* ***coat-tails*** 人に頼って ▪ He is still riding *on his* father's *coat-tails*. 彼はまだ父親のすねをかじっている.

on *one's* ***own coat-tail*** 《米》自費で ▪ My son sat *on his own coat-tail*. 私の息子は自活していた.

ride on *a person's* ***coattails*** 人につき従って利を得る，のおかげで成功[出世，当選]する，に便乗[依存]する ▪ "I *rode on my grandmother's coattails*," he said. "She loved to cook." 「(料理を学んだのは)祖母の後ろにくっついてたおかげです」と彼は言った.「彼女は料理するのが好きでした.」 ▪ Chavez-aligned candidates *rode on the president's coattails*. チャベスと共同陣営の候補者たちは大統領に便乗して当選した ▪ Hilary Clinton made it on her own merits rather than *riding on her spouse's coattails*. ヒラリー・クリントン氏は配偶者の威を借りたのではなく実力でやってのけた ▪ He's the classic case of a son who *rides on the coattails of* his parents' fame and fortune. 彼は両親の名声と財産の七光りを受けている息子の古典的な例だ.

trail *one's* ***coat-tails*** ＝trail one's COAT.

coax /koʊks/ 動 ***coax*** *a person* ***to*** *do* うまくだまして人に…させる ▪ I *coaxed* dad *to* give me leave to go out. 父をだまして外出の許可をもらった.

cob /kɑb|kɔb/ 名 ***have*** [***get***] ***a cob on*** 《英口》不きげんである[になる] ▪ Kelly was beginning to *have a cob on* about my punctuality. ケリーは私が時間通りでないことで不きげんになりかけていた ▪ That may partly explain why she's *got* such *a cob on*. それで彼女がなぜあんなに怒ったか多少は説明がつくだろう.

cobbler /kɑ́blər|kɔ́b-/ 名 ***give the cobbler's knock/knock at the cobbler's door*** 《口》すべるとき片足ですべりながら一方の足で3度ずつ氷をたたく. ☞Dickens, *Pickwick Papers* より.

Let the cobbler stick to his last. 《諺》各自おのが本業を守れ ▪ You're a lawyer, not a chef. *Let the cobbler stick to his last*. 君は弁護士でシェフではない. 口出ししないで料理のことは私にまかせろ. ☞L Ne sutor ultra crepidam 'Let the cobbler stick to his last.'「靴直し職人には自分の靴型を守らせよ」という諺から.

cobweb /kɑ́bwèb|kɔ́b-/ 名 ***blow*** (***away***) ***the cobwebs*** 《口》戸外運動[散歩]をする; 気分を一新する ▪ Let's go for a walk to *blow the cobwebs away*. 気分を一新するため散歩しよう.

brush [***clear***] ***away*** [***shake off***] ***the cobwebs*** モヤモヤを一掃する[吹き飛ばす，一掃する]，気分をすっきりさせる ▪ A nice little walk on the beach should *brush away the cobwebs*. ビーチをちょっと気持ちよく歩けば気分がすっきりする ▪ The phone rang about 3 a.m. and Jack *shook off the cobwebs* of sleep. 電話が午前3時ごろに鳴り，ジャックは眠気を振り払われた.

feel [***have***] ***a cobweb in the throat*** 《口》(特に酒を飲んだあとで)のどが乾く，飲みたい ▪ I *felt a cobweb in the throat*. のどが乾いた.

have cobwebs in the attic 《米俗》頭がからっぽである，ばかである ▪ I already know I *have cob-*

webs in the attic. 自分の頭がからっぽなのはとっくに気づいているさ.

cock[1] /kɑk|kɔk/ 名 ***a cock and bull story*** [***tale***] →COCK AND BULL.

A cock is always bold on its own dunghill. 《諺》誰でも友人や賞賛者に取り巻かれているときは勇敢なものだ.

a cock sparrow けんか好きな[生意気な]小男 ▪ When I entered I found that little *cock sparrow*, Governor Pickens, addressing the meeting. 入ったところ, あのけんかっ早い小男のピキンズ知事が会議で演説しているところだった.

As the old cock crows, the young cock learns. 《諺》親どりときを作れば若どりこれにならう,「見よう見まね」.

at (***full***) ***cock*** 銃の撃鉄をいっぱいに起こして; 十分の用意で ▪ Off he went, like a fowlingpiece *at cock*. 撃鉄をいっぱいに起こした猟銃のように[周到な準備を整えて], 彼は飛んで行った.

at half cock **1** 銃の撃鉄を半分起こして; 不十分の用意で, 早まって ▪ The gun was *at half cock*. その銃は撃鉄を十分起こしてなかった ▪ He went off *at half cock*. 彼は早まった.

2 立腹する ▪ The boss went off *at half cock* and shouted at the secretary. 社長は腹を立てて秘書をどなりつけた.

cock of the school 競技[戦闘]の大将 ▪ At cuffs I was always the *cock of the school*. なぐり合いにかけては私はいつもがき大将であった.

cock of the walk お山の大将; 羽振りの良い親分 ▪ He is *cock of the walk* in their set. 彼は彼らの仲間の大将である. ☞walk「鶏舎」.

Every cock crows on its own dunghill. 《諺》自分のふんの山の上に立てばどの雄鳥もときを作る,「陰弁慶は誰にでもできる」.

full cock いっぱいに開いて ▪ He turned on the taps *full cock*. 彼は飲み口をいっぱいにあけた.

live like a fighting cock 美食して贅沢に暮らす ▪ They *live like fighting cocks* on his labor. 彼らは彼の労働によって美食して贅沢に暮らしている.

Old cock! おい君, 大将!

on full cock =at (full) COCK.

That cock won't fight. 《俗》その手はだめだ, そうは問屋が卸さない ▪ Tell that to the marines! *That cock won't fight* with me. そんな事を誰が信ずるものか, その手はおれにはきかないよ.

the red cock will crow in ...が火事になるだろう ▪ We'll see if *the red cock* doesn't *crow in* his barnyard. 彼の納屋が火事にならないか見てみよう.

turn the cock せんをひねってあける ▪ *Turn the cock* of the conduit. 導管のせんをひねってあけよ.

cock[2] /kɑk|kɔk/ 動 ***cock the*** [***one's***] ***eye*** 目くばせする, 心得顔にちらと見る, 疑わし気にちらと見る; 片目で生意気に見る (*at*) ▪ She *cocks her eye at* any fellow that she happens to meet. 彼女はたまたま出会うどんな男にでも色目を使う ▪ He made a wry face and *cocked his eye at* me. 彼は顔をしかめて私を生意気に片目で見た.

cock the [***one's***] ***hat*** 帽子を横っちょにかぶる《生意気な態度》 ▪ *Cocking my hat* in his face, I demanded aloud. 彼に面と向かって帽子を横っちょにかぶり, 私は大声で聞きただした.

cock (***up***) ***one's ears*** (犬・馬などが)耳をぴんと立てる; 《戯》(人が)耳をそばだてる ▪ The dog barks and *cocks his ears*. 犬はほえて耳をぴんと立てる.

cock (***up***) ***the*** [***one's***] ***nose*** →NOSE[1].

cock-a-hoop /kὰkəhúːp|kɔ̀k-/ 形 ***all cock-a-hoop for*** 《口》...をやりたくて騒ぎ立てる, ほしくてわくわくしている ▪ The house-maids are *all cock-a-hoop for* it. メイドたちはそれがほしくて騒ぎ立てている.

be [***make***] ***cock-a-hoop*** 得意でいる; 勝ち誇っている ▪ You needn't *be* so *cock-a-hoop* over your victory. 君は自分の勝利をそんなに得意がる必要はない. ☞闘鶏から; 勝ったとき hoop (とさか)を立てることから.

cock and bull /kὰkənbúl|kɔ̀k-/ 名形 とてつもない(話) ▪ That is a lot of *cock and bull*. それは全くのたわごとだ.

a cock-and-bull story/***a story of a cock and bull*** とてつもない話, でたらめな話 ▪ The jury did not believe the witness' *cock-and-bull story*. 陪審団は証人のでたらめな話を信じなかった ▪ He set his audience agape with *a story of a cock and bull*. 彼はほら話をして聞く人をあ然とさせた.

cock(-)crow /kάkkròʊ|kɔ́k-/ 名 ***at cock-crow*** 鶏鳴(けいめい)どきに, 日の出どきに ▪ They wake up *at cock crow* and work until sunset. 彼らは一番鶏とともに起きて日の入りまで働く.

cocked hat /kάkthæ̀t|kɔ́kt-/ 名 ***knock*** [***beat***]... ***into a cocked hat*** 《口》 **1** ...を完全に打ちのめす[こわす]《比喩的にも》 ▪ A frigate of the modern type would *knock* a fort *into a cocked hat*. 近代式のフリゲート艦だったら要塞をかたなしに打ちこわすだろう ▪ The theory *was knocked into a cocked hat*. その理論は完全に論破された ▪ He *knocked* his opponent *into a cocked hat*. 彼は相手をぺしゃんこにやっつけた.

2 ...にはるかに勝る ▪ It will *knock* all the other achievements *into a cocked hat*. それは他のすべての業績にはるかに勝るだろう.

3〚主に受身で〛(人)をあっけにとらせる ▪ The news fairly *knocked* me *into a cocked hat*. そのニュースは全く私をあ然とさせた.

cock-fighting /kάkfàɪtɪŋ|kɔ́k-/ 名 ***beat cock-fighting*** 《俗》闘鶏に勝る, 何よりもすぐれている; 何よりもおもしろい ▪ Well, this *beats cock-fighting*. ほんとにこれは実にすてきだ ▪ I'm blest if you don't *beat cock-fighting*. ほんとに君はすばらしいじゃないか.

cock-horse /kάkhɔ̀ːrs|kɔ́k-/ 副 ***ride*** (***a***) ***cock-horse*** 人の足やひざの上に乗る, 乗って上下にゆすってもらう ▪ The child *rode a cock-horse* on a stick. 子供は棒に乗っていた.

cockle /kάkəl|kɔ́kəl/ 名 ***warm*** [***delight, rejoice, tickle***] ***the cockles of*** *a person's*

heart 人の心を喜ばせる, 人を元気づける ▪ I have just had *the cockles of my heart rejoiced* by a letter from Lyell. 私はちょうどライエルからの手紙でしみじみと喜ばされたところだ ▪ Here's a large whiskey, it will *warm the cockles of your heart* on this cold day. さあウイスキーをたっぷり1杯いかがですか, この寒い日には元気づきますよ.

cocksure /kɑ̀kʃúər|kɔ̀kʃɔ́ː/ 形 ***be cocksure of*** [***about***] **1** ...を確信する ▪ I'*m cocksure of* it. 私はそれを確信している.

2 ...に自信が強すぎる ▪ Tom *is cocksure of* everything. トムはすべてのことに自信がありすぎる.

cocoa /kóʊkoʊ/ 名 ***I should cocoa!*** 《英口》いいえとんでもない ▪ Are you going skating?—*I should cocoa!* スケートに行きますか—いいえとんでもない. ☞この cocoa は say so と rhyme するので, say so の代わりに使ったもの.

coconut /kóʊkənʌ̀t/ 名 ***have no milk in the coconut*** →MILK[1].

the milk in the coconut →MILK[1].

C.O.D., COD /siːoʊdíː/ 名 ***send ... C.O.D.*** 代金引き換え払いで送る, 配達時払い[着払い]で送る ▪ It's common for online dealers to *send* their computers *COD*. オンライン業者がコンピューターを代金引換で送るのはふつうのことだ. ☞COD = cash on delivery.

coddle /kɑ́dəl|kɔ́d-/ 動 ***coddle*** *oneself* 体を大事にしすぎる ▪ Some of them *coddle themselves*. 中には体を大事にしすぎる者もある.

code /koʊd/ 名 ***bring ... up to code*** 《米》(建物)を最新の建築基準に適合させる ▪ We've done repairs, widened the doors, redone the bathrooms, and *brought* the place *up to code*. 我々は修繕し, ドアを拡げ, 風呂を改装し, その建物が建築基準に合うようにした.

the code of honor 紳士淑女の道, 社会的道徳通念; 決闘法 ▪ The Japanese Samurai had a high *code of honor*. 日本の侍は高邁(こうまい)な武士道を具えていた.

coerce /koʊə́ːrs/ 動 ***coerce*** *a person* ***to*** *do* 人を強制[威圧]して ...させる ▪ He *coerced* those warriors *to* march. 彼はその戦士たちを強制的に前進させた.

coffee /kɔ́ːfi, kɑ́fi|kɔ́fi/ 名 ***a coffee fix*** (眠気覚ましの)コーヒー1杯 ▪ Doesn't everybody need *a coffee fix* at 8 AM? 誰もが午前8時には眠気覚ましにコーヒーが1杯要るというわけではないのか?

wake up and smell the coffee 《口》目を覚まして現実に目を向ける[行動を起こす] ▪ Anybody who hasn't started saving by their mid-40s should *wake up and smell the coffee*. 40代半ばまでに貯金を始めていない人は目を覚まして行動を起こすべきだ.

coffin /kɑ́ːfən|kɔ́fɪn/ 名 ***a coffin nail*** 《俗》タバコ ▪ Spears, who had claimed to be anti-smoking, was caught puffing *a coffin nail* in Australia. スピアーズは喫煙反対を唱えていたが, オーストラリアで喫煙中の現場を押さえられた.

drive [***add, pound, put***] ***a nail in*** *a person's* ***coffin*** →NAIL[1].

cog[1] /kɑg|kɔg/ 名 ***a cog in the machine/a*** (***mere***) ***cog in the wheel of society*** 些細だが絶対に必要な仕事をしている人,「縁の下の力持ち」 ▪ I should become *a cog in the machine*. 私は「縁の下の力持ち」になるべきだ.

miss a cog 《米》→slip a COG 2.

slip a cog **1** (仕事・計算などに)思わぬまちがいをする ▪ Patty seems dumbfounded; she must have *slipped a cog*. パティーは呆然としているようだ. きっと思わぬまちがいをしたのだろう.

2 《米》(心臓が)鼓動を乱す ▪ I felt my heart *slip a cog*. 私は心臓が鼓動を乱すのを感じた.

cog[2] /kɑg|kɔg/ 動 ***cog a die*** [***the dice***] さいころをごまかす ▪ He would *cog the dice* to a man's face. 彼は公然とさいころをごまかすのだった.

cognizance /kɑ́gnəzəns|kɔ́g-/ 名 (***be, come, fall, lie***) ***beyond*** [***out of***] ***the cognizance of*** ...の認知[審理]の範囲外にある; の管轄外にある ▪ This event *is beyond his cognizance*. この出来事は彼の知らぬところだ.

(***be, come, fall, lie***) ***under*** [***within***] ***the cognizance of*** ...の認知[審理]しうる範囲内にある; 管轄内にある ▪ That part of Christ's history *was within the cognizance of* his followers. キリストの生涯のその部分は弟子たちの認知しうる範囲内にあった ▪ Will any of their faults *come under their cognizance*? 彼らの落度のどれかに彼らは気がつくだろうか ▪ It is their duty to punish faults *under their cognizance*. 彼らの審理の範囲内の罪を罰するのは彼らの義務である.

have cognizance of **1** (観察・報知によって)...を知っている, 知る ▪ Surveyors *had* no *cognizance of* those islands. 測量師らはそれらの島を知らなかった.

2 《法》...の裁判[審理]権を持つ ▪ The spiritual courts *had cognizance of* these causes. 宗教裁判所はこれらの訴訟事件の裁判権を持っていた.

take cognizance of **1** ...を認める, に留意する, を観察の範囲に入れる ▪ The theory *takes* no *cognizance of* this. その学説はこの点を認めていない ▪ Will anyone *take cognizance of* them? 誰かそれらを見てくれるだろうか.

2 ...を受理して審理[裁判]する ▪ The court *took cognizance of* the case. 法廷はその事件を受理して審理した.

cognizant /kɑ́gnəzənt|kɔ́g-/ 形 ***cognizant of*** ...を認めて, 知って; 《法》(事件)を受理して, 審理管轄内と認めて ▪ He was *cognizant of* the fascinated gaze I bent upon him. 彼は私の注いだ魅せられたような凝視に気づいていた.

coign /kɔɪn/ 名 ***coign of vantage*** →place of VANTAGE.

coil /kɔɪl/ 名 ***in a coil*** 輪状に ▪ Wind up a rope *in a coil*. 綱を輪状に巻け ▪ The snake was lying *in a coil*. ヘビはとぐろを巻いていた.

keep a coil 大騒ぎする, 騒動を起こす ▪ They all

keep such *a coil* when they come to die. 彼らは死ぬ時になるとみな大騒ぎをする.

this mortal coil →MORTAL.

coin[1] /kɔɪn/ 名 ***pay*** *a person* (***back***) ***in*** *his* ***own coin*** 人に返報する, 仕返しをする ▪ I will *pay* him *back in his own coin.* 彼に返報してやるんだ ▪ John boxed Earnest's ears and said, "That *pays* you *in your own coin.*" ジョンはアーネストの横うらをなぐって「それでしっぺ返しだよ」と言った.

pay *a person* ***back in the same coin*** 同じ方法を使って返報する ▪ A government spokesperson said "if the option of war is exercised by India, then it will *be paid back in the same coin.*" 政府のスポークスパーソンは「もしも戦争という選択肢がインドによって行使されれば, インドは同じ方法で報復されるだろう」と言った.

the other side of the coin 事の反対の面 ▪ In a boom unemployment is reduced. *The other side of the coin* is that there are shortages of labor. ブームの時は失業は減少する. その反面労働が不足する.

toss [***flip***] ***a coin*** 硬貨を投げて(勝負を)決める ▪ Let's *toss a coin.* Heads or tails? さあ硬貨を投げて決めよう, 表か裏か. ☞日本のジャンケンに当たる. 硬貨を投げあげて左手の甲の上に受け, 右手で隠し押さえて, "Heads or tails?" (表か裏か)を尋ね, 当てたほうが勝ち; 投げる前に表裏を決めることもある.

coin[2] /kɔɪn/ 動 ***coin*** *one's* ***brains*** 頭脳で金を儲ける ▪ Can't you *coin your brains*? 頭で金を儲けられないかね.

coin it (***in***) 《口》どんどん大金を儲ける ▪ He must be *coining it* (*in*). 彼はどんどん大金を儲けているにちがいない.

coin money →MONEY.

coincidence /koʊínsədəns/ 名 ***the long arm of coincidence*** あまりにも偶然的な暗合 ▪ That is *the long arm of coincidence* indeed! それこそほんとにあまりにも偶然的な暗合だ! ☞make a long arm (腕をぐっと伸ばす)に coincidence を擬人化してつけたもの.

coincident /koʊínsədənt/ 形 ***coincident with*** …と一致して ▪ The nominal value of the coin is *coincident with* its metallic value. その貨幣の名目上の価値は金属としての価値と一致する.

coke /koʊk/ 名 ***Go and eat coke.*** 《口》ともかくどいてくれ; こんちきしょう《軽蔑・じれったさを表す》 ▪ You have made yourself a thorough nuisance this morning. *Go and eat coke.* 今朝はほんとにうるさいね. ともかくあっちへ行ってくれ.

cold /koʊld/ 名形 ***a cold in*** [***on***] ***the chest*** [***lungs***] せき風邪 ▪ I have *a cold in the chest.* せき風邪をひいているんだ.

a cold in the [*one's*] ***head*** [***nose***]/***a head cold*** 鼻風邪 ▪ She had *a cold in the head.* 彼女は鼻風邪だった.

a crying cold 涙の出る風邪 ▪ He has *a crying cold.* 彼は涙の出る風邪にかかっている.

(***as***) ***cold as a wagon-tire*** 《米口》全く冷たく; 死んで ▪ Here is the speckled snake, *as cold as a wagon-tire.* ここにそのマダラヘビが死んでいる.

(***as***) ***cold as charity*** →CHARITY.

(***as***) ***cold as fish*** [***a frog, ice, a key***] ひどく冷たく, 冷淡で ▪ He is a miser and *as cold as fish.* 彼はけちんぼうでひどく冷淡だ ▪ The room was *as cold as ice.* その部屋は氷のように冷たかった.

(***as***) ***cold as marble*** (触感・人の心が)非常に冷たい ▪ The wall felt *as cold as marble.* 壁はさわってみて非常に冷たかった ▪ His father was *as cold as marble.* 彼の父は非常に冷たい人だった.

be cold struck 体中がこわばる ▪ Horses and camels *are* often *cold struck.* 馬やラクダはよく体中がこわばる.

bring *a person* ***in from*** [***out of***] ***the cold*** 無視していたか, または関係なかった人に(事に)参加を許す ▪ We *brought* him *in from the cold.* 我々はそれまで無視していた彼を参加させた.

catch a cold **1** =catch (a) COLD.
2《口》(とくに財政的な)困難[災難]にあう ▪ I've often *caught a cold.* 私はしばしば災難にあった ▪ Japan *caught an* economic *cold* a dozen years ago. 日本は12年前に経済的困難におちいった.

catch [***get, take***] (***a***) ***cold*** 風邪をひく ▪ You'll *catch cold.* 風邪をひきますよ. ☞catch cold が最も普通. 通例無冠詞だが修飾語を伴うときは a(n) が必要 ▪ He *caught a* bad *cold.* 彼はひどい風邪をひいた.

catch *a person* ***cold*** 《口》人の虚[油断]をつく ▪ I had not studied for my class, and the teacher's question *caught* me *cold.* 私は勉強をしていなかったので, 先生の質問に虚をつかれた.

catch *one's* ***death*** (***of cold***) →DEATH.

Cold hands and a warm heart. 《諺》手は冷たくて心は温かい. ☞人の手が冷たい場合に言う.

come in from [***out of***] ***the cold*** (無視されていた人が事に)参加を許される ▪ The eight children *came in from the cold.* (それまで)除外されていた8人の子供が参加を許された.

...degrees of cold 氷点下…度 ▪ It was 5 *degrees of cold.* 氷点下5度だった.

get (***a***) ***cold*** →catch (a) COLD.

get *a person* ***cold*** →have a person COLD.

get [***go***] ***cold all over*** (恐怖・心配などで)震えあがる ▪ He *went cold all over* when he heard footsteps in the dark. 暗闇に足音を聞いて彼は震えあがった.

get [***have***] ***cold feet*** 《俗》おじけうく, いや気がさす; しょげる, 心配する ▪ Every actor *has cold feet* just before the beginning of a show. 俳優はみな芝居の始まる直前にはびくびくするものだ ▪ I *get* awfully *cold feet.* 私はひどく落胆している ▪ Don't tell me you've *got cold feet.* いや気がさしたんじゃなかろうね. ☞1890年頃できた句; 恐怖は血行を悪くし, 体の末端部を寒くするから.

give the cold shoulder →SHOULDER[1].

go cold on the deal 《口》事[契約など]を行う気が

なくなる，する熱がさめる ▪ You were eager to do the bank job. You're not going to *go cold on the deal* now? 君は銀行の仕事をしたがっていたが，今になって行く気がなくなっているんじゃないだろうね．

have a* (*bad*) *cold (ひどい)風邪にかかっている ▪ He stayed away from school because he *had a cold*. 彼は風邪をひいていたので学校を休んだ．

have* [*get*]** *a person* ***cold 《口》人にははっきりと勝る; 人を完全に握っている[思いのままにする] ▪ I know his past; so I have *got* him *cold*. 私は彼の過去を知っているから彼を完全に掌握している ▪ The Packers *had* the Eagles *cold*. パッカーズはイーグルスに完勝した．

lay* [*knock*]** *a person* ***cold 人を打って気絶させる ▪ The ball *laid* him out *cold* for a minute. ボールが当たって彼はちょっとの間失神した ▪ One of the hunters smacked into a tree, and *knocked* himself *cold*. 猟人の一人は木にぶつかって気絶した．

leave *a person* ***cold*** 《口》人になんの興味[印象]も与えない《特に脅迫・悪口などを無視するときの句》 ▪ He is saying all sorts of beastly things about me, but it *leaves* me *cold*. 彼は私のことをいろいろ悪く言っているが，私はなんともない ▪ His enthusiasm *leaves* us *cold*. 彼の熱狂は我々には少しも響かない．

leave *a person* ***out in the cold*** **1** 人を野ざらしにする ▪ The unfortunate traveler often finds himself *left out in the cold*. 不運な旅人はしばしば野ざらしにされる．
2 人を(故意に)無視する，ほっておく，のけ者にする ▪ I felt *left out in the cold* when I was not invited. 自分が招待されなかったとき，のけ者にされた気がした ▪ He *left* her *out in the cold*. 彼は彼女をほったらかしにした．

lose *one's* ***cold*** 風邪が治る ▪ I have *lost my cold*. 私は風邪が治った．

make* (*cold*) *meat of →MEAT.

open cold 《米》試演をせずにいきなりニューヨークで初日をあける ▪ The productions never *open cold* in New York. 映画製作所は試演せずにいきなりニューヨークで初日をあけることはない．

out cold 《口》意識を失って，失神して ▪ The ball knocked him *out cold* for 10 minutes. ボールが彼に当たって彼は10分失神した ▪ She fell down and was *out cold*. 彼女は倒れて失神した．

quit cold 《米》完全に捨てる，手を切る ▪ I *quit* them *cold*. 彼らと完全に手を切った ▪ I am not going to *quit cold* like you. 君のように完全に手を切るつもりはない．

stone cold 非常に冷たい《通例温かいはずのものについて言う》 ▪ He talks so much while eating that his food becomes *stone cold*. 彼は食事中話が多いので食べ物がすっかり冷たくなる．

take* (*a*) *cold →catch (a) COLD.

The proposition is cold. 《米俗》その事[問題]は終わった．

throw* [*pour*] *cold water on →WATER[1].

turn *a person* ***down cold*** 《米俗》人にきっぱりと[すげなく]断る ▪ He *turned* me *down cold*. 彼はすげなく断った．

when *A* ***sneezes,*** *B* ***catches* (*a*) *cold*** 《主に英》AがくしゃみをすればBが風邪をひく《AはBに大きな影響力をもつ》 ▪ *When* the US economy *sneezes*, Japan *catches cold* and Korea *catches* pneumonia. アメリカ経済がくしゃみをすれば，日本は風邪をひき，韓国は肺炎になる．

cole /koʊl/ 名 ***post* [*tip*] *the cole*** 《俗》現金を払う ▪ If he doesn't *tip the cole* without more ado, give him a taste of the pump. もし彼が即座に金を払わなければ，ポンプで水を浴びせてやれ．

collaboration /kəlæbəréɪʃən/ 名 ***in collaboration with*** …と共同して，と共著で ▪ He worked *in collaboration with* others. 彼は他の人々と共同して働いた．

collar /kɑ́lər|kɔ́lə/ 名 ***against* (*the*) *collar***
1 困難を冒して，疲労を押して ▪ He has been working *against the collar*. 彼は困難を冒して働いてきた ▪ The last mile up to the top was a good deal *against the collar*. 頂上までの最後の1マイルは非常に骨が折れた．
2 不本意で (= against the GRAIN) ▪ It goes *against the collar* to get up early after a late night's work. 夜遅くまで働いてから朝早く起きるのは不本意である．☞馬が坂を上るときは，collar が首をひっぱって苦しいことから．

be* [*get*] *hot under* [*around, in*] *the collar 《口》怒っている[怒る]，興奮している[する]，取り乱している[取り乱す] ▪ I *was hot under the collar* when they decided not to come last time. 前回彼らが来ないことに決めたとき私は腹が立った ▪ Dunn *got hot under the collar* as he voiced his dissent to the referee. ダンはレフリーに異議を唱えているうちに興奮してきた．

collar and tie カラーとネクタイ《きちんとした紳士の服装》 ▪ My father always put on *collar and tie* when he went out. 父は外出するときはいつもきちんと服装を整えた．

feel *a person's* ***collar*** 《俗》(警官が)犯人を逮捕する ▪ The policeman *felt the suspect's collar*. 警官は容疑者を逮捕した ▪ He has had *his collar felt* very often. 彼は何度も逮捕された．

fill *one's* ***collar*** 《米口》職務をよく果たす ▪ I am going to *fill my collar*. 職務をよく果たすつもりです．

go at the collar (馬が)首に力を入れて(車を)引き出す ▪ The horses *went at the collars* and rattled along. 馬は首に力を入れてガラガラ引いて行った．

in collar **1** 首輪をかけて; (馬が)仕事の用意をして．
2 《口》人が就職[就業]して (↔out of COLLAR 1) ▪ The workman is not *in collar* at present. その職人は今は職についていない．
3 《米俗》健康で; コンディションが良く[できて] (↔out of COLLAR 2).

in the collar (活動が)抑制されて ▪ You are *in the collar* now. Marriage has its obligations. あなたは今や行動を抑制されている．結婚にはそれ相応の義務

があるから.

out of collar **1**《口》失業して, 定職がなく (↔in COLLAR 2) ▪Her husband is *out of collar* again. 彼女の夫はまた失業している.

2《米俗》コンディションが悪く; 練習ができていないで (↔in COLLAR 3) ▪I have been *out of collar* for some time. だいぶ前から体調がよくない.

Roman collar ローマンカラー《首の後ろで留める堅くて小幅の白カラー; 聖職者がつける》 ▪The *Roman collar* symbolizes obedience. ローマンカラーは従順の象徴である.

slip **(*the*)** ***collar*** 束縛[困難, 労力]を逃れる; 仕事から手を引く ▪The Dutch will *slip the collar*. オランダ軍は(戦争から)手を引くだろう.

collateral /kəlǽtərəl/ 形 ***collateral to*** **1** …に平行の ▪The rural lanes were *collateral to* the main roads. 田舎道は本道路と平行していた.

2 …に付随的な ▪This is *collateral to* my work. これは私の仕事に付随的なものだ.

collect /kəlékt/ 動 ***collect*** *oneself* 我に返る; 気を取り直す, 落ち着く; 考えをまとめる ▪It was some time before he could *collect himself*. しばらくしてようやく彼は我に返った ▪I must *collect myself* before I deliver my thoughts. 考えを述べる前にまとめねばならない.

collect eyes (意図的に)人々の注意をひく ▪He *collected eyes* like a hostess. 彼は女主人のように人々の注意をひいた.

collection /kəlékʃən/ 名 ***make a collection*** **1** 寄付金を集める ▪The *collection* will *be made* after the sermon. 説教がすんだ後寄付金が集められる.

2 収集する ▪He is *making a collection* of stamps. 彼は切手を収集している.

take up a collection =make a COLLECTION 1.

collector /kəléktər/ 名 ***a collector's item*** [***piece***] (コレクター好みの)逸品, お宝もの ▪You should keep that commemorative stamp; it will be *a collector's item*, worth a lot of money in the future. あの記念切手はとっておくべきだ. 将来大金に値するお宝ものになるだろうから ▪The sideboard is definitely *a collector's piece* at $7,250. そのサイドボードは確かに7,250ドルの逸品だ.

college /kɑ́lɪdʒ|kɔ́l-/ 名 ***enter*** [***be in***] ***college*** 大学に入る[いる] ▪My son *is in college* now. 息子は今大学に入っています.

go to college **1** 大学に入る ▪I am *going to college* next year. 来年大学に入ります.

2 大学に在学している ▪My son is *going to* [*goes to*] *college* at the University of Chicago. 息子はシカゴ大学で勉強している.

out of college 大学を出て ▪He is *out of college* now. 彼は今は大学を出ている.

pay *one's* ***college*** 苦学して大学を出る ▪My brother has *paid his college*. 兄は苦学して大学を出た.

the old college try 目一杯[最大]の努力 ▪You have to applaud Bert for giving it *the old college try*, but was it worth the risk of further injury? バートが捨て身の努力をしたのは立派だが, さらにけがをするかもしれないという危険を冒すに値するだろうか ▪They gave it *the old college try*, but they fell way short. 彼らは精一杯やってみたが, はるかに力及ばずだった. ☞原義はパーティーなどで同じ大学の出身だと言って援助を引き出そうとすること.

collision /kəlíʒən/ 名 ***a collision course*** (列車・惑星や意見などの)衝突進路 (*with*) ▪Today no known asteroid is on *a collision course with* the Earth. 今日, 地球への衝突進路にある小惑星は知られていない ▪The new device puts Google on *a collision course with* Apple. その新しいデバイスによりグーグルとアップルは激突必至だ.

a head-on collision 正面衝突; 正面対決 ▪Clarke survived *a head-on collision* with a drunk driver. クラークは飲酒運転者と正面衝突したが命に異常はなかった ▪These plans will propel Sony toward *a head-on collision* with Microsoft. これらの計画はソニーをマイクロソフトと正面対決させることになるだろう.

come into [***be in***] ***collision*** **(*with*)** (…と)衝突する[している] ▪A freight train *came into collision with* a passenger train. 貨物列車が旅客列車と衝突した ▪Science and religion *come into collision* on the question. 科学と宗教はその問題について意見が一致しない.

collusion /kəlúːʒən/ 名 ***in collusion with*** …と結託して ▪They are acting *in collusion with* the enemy. 彼らは敵と結託して行動している.

collywobbles /kɑ́liwɑ̀bəlz|kɔ́liwɔbəlz/ 名 ***get*** [***give***] ***the collywobbles*** =get the WILLIES.

colophon /kɑ́ləfən/ 名 ***from titlepage to colophon*** (本の)全巻ことごとく ▪I read this book *from title-page to colophon*. 私はこの本を全巻通読した.

color,《英》**colour** /kʌ́lər/ 名 ***a color guard*** 軍旗衛兵, 旗手 ▪Paul Lemen was in *a color guard* when he was at high school. ポール・リーメンは高校に在学していたころ旗手グループにいた.

be given *one's* ***colors*** →get one's COLORs.

cast lively [etc.] ***colors on*** →put lively COLORs on.

change color 顔色を変える《青くなる, まれに赤くなる》; 別の色になる ▪Suddenly he *changed color*. 彼は急に顔色を変えた ▪With these words he *changed color*. こう言って彼は赤くなった ▪One star *changed color* incessantly. 一つの星が絶えず色を変えた ▪The salmon, normally silver and blue, *change color*. サケはふつう銀色や青色だが, 別の色に変わる.

collect local color (描くため)地方色を観察する ▪He is going to Jamaica to *collect local color* for his novel. 彼は小説に描く地方色の観察にジャマイカに行くつもりだ.

come off with flying colors [***colors flying***] **1** 堂々と旗を翻してがいせんする; みごとに成功する ▪ George *came off with flying colors*—more than a hundred votes over the next man. ジョージは堂々と勝利を得た—次点者より100票以上も多くの票を取って ▪ The Mayor *came off with flying colors*. 市長は大成功を収めた.
2 すばらしい成績を収める; 優等で卒業[合格, 進級]する ▪ He took part in the swimming contest, and *came off with flying colors*. 彼は水泳競技に参加して, すばらしい成績を収めた ▪ He *came off with flying colors* in his final exams. 彼は最終試験で優等で合格した.

come out in *one's* ***true colors*** (偽装などをすっかり脱いで)本性を表す ▪ Tom has been arrested as a spy. He has *come out in his true colors* at last. トムはスパイとして逮捕されてついに本性を表したのだ. ☞colors「記章」.

come through with flying colors 堂々と(難関を)切り抜ける ▪ Congratulations! You have *come through with flying colors*. おめでとう. 立派に合格しましたね.

cross the color-line 《米》皮膚の色の区別立てをしない ▪ You *cross the color-line*. あなたは皮膚の色で差別はしない.

desert the [*one's*] ***colors*** **1** 脱営する ▪ The soldier *deserted his colors*. 一兵士が脱営した.
2 支持の手を引く ▪ You'll never *desert the colors*. 君は絶対に支持の手は引かないね.

display *one's* (***true***) ***colors*** → show one's (true) COLORs.

draw the color-line 《米》皮膚の色の区別立てをする, 黒人との交際を拒む ▪ Would you Southern Democrats *draw the color-line*? あなたがた南部の民主党員は皮膚の色の区別立てをしませんか.

gain [***gather***] ***color*** (顔の)血色が出てくる, 血色が良くなる ▪ His complexion *gathered color*. 彼の顔に血色が出てきた.

get [***be given***] *one's* ***colors*** (クリケット・フットボールで英国パブリックスクールの)競技の選手になる[される] ▪ To *get his colors* is every boy's ambition. 学校で競技の選手になることはすべての少年の大望である ▪ My son at Charterhouse has *been given his* football *colors*. チャーターハウスにいる息子がフットボールの代表選手にされた. ☞学校の旗を飾った服や帽子などを着ることから.

give a false color to …の意味を変える, ゆがめる ▪ Newspapers often *give a false color to* the news. 新聞はよくニュースをゆがめる.

give [***lend***] ***color to*** (話など)をもっともらしく見せる ▪ The cut on his cheek *gave color to* his story that he had been attacked. ほおの切り傷は攻撃されたという彼の話をほんとうらしく見せた. ☞color《廃》「もっともらしさ」.

give no color for …の口実[根拠]を与えない ▪ St. Paul *gives* you *no color for* making void the law. 聖パウロは律法を無効にする口実を君に与えてはいない.

hang out false colors (船が)偽旗を掲げて国籍を偽る; 心にもないことを表明する ▪ Our female candidate will no longer *hang out false colors*. わが女性候補者はもはや偽旗を掲げることはしない.

haul down *one's* ***colors*** = strike one's COLORs.

in *one's* ***true colors*** …の真相において ▪ He showed me New York *in its true colors*. 彼はニューヨークの真相を見せてくれた ▪ Always try and see things *in their true colors*. いつも物事の真相を知るようにしなさい.

lay on the colors (***too***) ***thickly*** (絵具をこてこて塗りつけるように)仰々しく書き[ほめ]立てる ▪ Don't *lay on the colors too thickly*. そう大げさにほめ立てるな.

lend color to →give COLOR to.

lose color 血色をなくする; 健康をそこなう ▪ The child has *lost color* lately. その子はこのごろ血色がなくなった.

lower *one's* ***colors*** (旗を巻いて)下手に出る; 要求[地位, 自説]を撤回する ▪ They *lowered their colors* when they were defeated in the argument. 議論に敗れたとき彼らは自説を撤回した.

nail *one's* ***colors to*** …に旗をくぎうけにしておろさない; を固守して譲らない《決意を表明する》 ▪ He hastened to *nail his colors to* the compromise of 1870. 彼は急いで1870年の妥協より一歩も譲らぬことを表明した.

nail *one's* ***colors to the mast*** 《主に英》 **1** 不動の態度を取る決意である ▪ I'm not going to give in. I'll *nail my colors to the mast*. 私は屈服するつもりはない. とことんまで戦う決意である ▪ I've *nailed my colors to the mast*. 最後までやり通す決意だ.
2 主義主張を宣言し固守する ▪ He has *nailed his colors to the mast* and is standing as a socialist candidate. 彼は自己の主義主張を宣言し, 社会党候補として立候補している. ☞colors「軍旗」. 海戦で降伏せず戦闘続行を表明するために軍旗をマストに釘うけにしたことから.

off color →OFF[1].

paint … in bright [***high, glowing***] ***colors*** **1** …をひどく良く言う ▪ He *painted* the rector *in bright colors*. 彼は司祭をひどくほめ立てた.
2 (未来について)…を楽観的に解釈する ▪ He *painted* the country's future *in glowing colors*. 彼はその国の未来を明るく描いた.

paint … in dark colors (尾ひれをつけて)…を悪く言う ▪ He *paints* your actions *in dark colors*. 彼はあなたの行為を尾ひれをつけて悪く言う.

put false colors [***a false color***] ***on*** …を曲げる, ゆがめる ▪ You've *put a false color on* things there. 君はその点では事情をゆがめている.

put [***cast***] ***lively*** [etc.] ***colors on*** …を元気そうに[など]見せる ▪ He was desirous to *put handsome colors on* her death. 彼は彼女の死を美しく見せることを望んだ.

sail under false colors 偽りの国旗を掲げて[国籍をくらまして]走る; 偽善的行為をする, 素性をくらます ▪ They are political spies *sailing under false colors.* 彼らは素性を偽っている政治スパイである.

see the color of *a person's* ***money*** 人の金の色を拝む《約束だけでは信用できない場合に言う》 ▪ I demanded to *see the color of his money* before I started the work. 私は仕事にかかる前に彼の金の色を拝ませてほしいと言った.

show [***display***] *one's* (***true***) ***colors*** **1** 本性を表す ▪ Now you are *showing your true colors.* いよいよ君の本性を表しだしたね.
2 意見[立場]を公表する ▪ They may find some difficulty in *showing their colors.* 彼らは意見を表明するのが幾分困難かもしれない. ☞colors「記章」.

stick to *one's* ***colors*** 自分の主義[信念]を固守する ▪ He is *sticking to his colors* with obstinacy. 彼は頑固に自分の主義を固守している.

strike *one's* ***colors*** 旗をおろす; 降参する, 戦い[活動]をやめる ▪ Nothing, except my health, could have made me *strike my colors.* 健康の問題以外には, どんなことだって私に活動をやめさせられなかったろうに.

take *one's* ***color from*** …の主義主張を取り入れる; (周囲・仲間)の色に染まる ▪ He has no opinion; he just *takes his color from* the company he is in. 彼には意見はない, ただつき合い仲間の意見を取り入れるだけだ ▪ He has *taken his color from* his surroundings. 彼は周囲の色に染まっている.

true to *one's* ***colors*** (大義・目的・野望に)忠実な, 正直な ▪ He remained *true to his colors* and never once accepted a bribe. 彼は大義を守りとおし, 一度たりとも収賄のためしはなかった.

turn color 紅葉[黄葉]する, 別の色になる ▪ The leaves are *turning color* early this year. 今年は早く紅葉してきている.

under color of …を口実に, にかこつけて; の仮面のもとに ▪ A present was given *under color of* friendship. 友情にかこつけて贈物が彼に贈られた ▪ He has come here *under color of* being orthodox. 彼は正統派であるというふれこみでここへ来た.

wear *a person's* ***colors*** 人にひいきする, 人のファンである ▪ Between Tom and Dick, she clearly *wears Tom's colors.* トムとディックとでは, 彼女は明らかにトムが好みだ. ☞人の記章をつける(男が好きな女の好む色を用いたりすること)が原義.

win *one's* ***colors*** 《英》(競技の)正選手になる, 好成績をあげる ▪ At Cambridge he *won his colors* in cricket and was on the boxing team. ケンブリッジで彼はクリケットの正選手であり, ボクシング部に所属していた ▪ He has *won his colors* and is now the head boy. 彼は好成績をあげ, 現在は首席だ.

with colors flying/with flying colors りっぱに, 堂々と ▪ He passed the examination *with flying colors.* 彼はりっぱにその試験にパスした. ☞戦勝軍が軍旗をなびかせて引きあげることから.

with the colors 現役に服して; 軍隊に勤務して ▪ Five years were passed *with the colors* and four in the reserve. 5年は現役で, 4年は予備役で過ごした ▪ My brother serves *with the colors.* 兄は今軍隊にいる.

without color 偽るところなく ▪ Answer me *without color* whether it is so or not. そうであるかないか偽りなく私に答えなさい.

colt /koʊlt/ 名 ***a colt's tail*** ちぎれ雲 ▪ *Colt's tails* scudded across the sky. ちぎれ雲が飛ぶように空を渡った.

a colt's tooth **1** 馬の乳歯 ▪ Horses have the *colt's tooth* at three years old. 馬は3歳のときには, 乳歯がある.
2 若者らしい趣味[願い]; 気まぐれ[浮気]の傾向 ▪ His Majesty had *a colt's tooth* and loved another maiden. 陛下は浮気の傾向を持っておられ, また別の娘を愛された ▪ Now age has plucked out all his *colt's teeth.* 今や老齢が彼の浮気の虫をすっかり取り去った.

like a young colt 無責任で; 元気がよくて; 無器用で; 未熟で ▪ That boy frisks about the place *like a young colt.* あの少年は子馬のようにそこらをはね回る.

column /kɑ́ləm|kɔ́l-/ 名 ***dodge the column*** 《口》義務を回避する, 怠ける ▪ He is apt to *dodge the column.* 彼は義務を回避しがちである.

coma /kóʊmə/ 名 ***go*** (***off***) ***into a coma*** 意識を失う ▪ The boy *went into a coma* after the car accident. 少年は自動車事故のあと気を失った.

in a coma 昏睡に陥って ▪ The injured girl is *in a coma.* けがをした少女は昏睡に陥っている.

comb[1] /koʊm/ 名 ***cut the comb of*** …の高慢の鼻をへし折る, やりこめる ▪ Repentance has *cut our comb.* 悔恨が我々の高慢の鼻を折った ▪ I will *cut his comb* if such extravagance continues. もしそんな贅沢を続けるようなら彼をやりこめてやろう. ☞comb「とさか」; 闘鶏から.

go through [***over***]***… with a fine*** (***tooth***) ***comb*** 目のつんだくしで一面にくしけずる; …を徹底的に調査する, 細かく調べる ▪ The accountants are *going through* his books *with a toothcomb.* 会計係が彼の帳簿を徹底的に調べている ▪ We *went through* the house *with a fine comb.* その家を細かく吟味した. ☞toothcomb「目の細かいくし」.

run a comb through *one's* ***hair*** 素早く髪をすく ▪ Just let me *run a comb through my hair.* ちょっと髪を素早くすかせてください.

with a fine-tooth(***ed***) ***comb*** → FINE-TOOTH(ED).

comb[2] /koʊm/ 動 ***comb*** *a person's* ***head*** 《戯》うちのめす, なぐる ▪ He will *comb your head* with a bunch of keys. 彼は鍵たばで君をなぐるだろう.

combination /kɑ̀mbənéɪʃən|kɔ̀m-/ 名 ***in combination with*** …と結合[合同]して, 組み合って ▪ He carried on the work *in combination with* his brother. 彼は弟と共同でその仕事を経営した.

combustion /kəmbʌ́stʃən/ 名 ***throw ... into combustion*** ...を激昂[混乱, 騒乱]させる ▪ He again *threw* his country *into combustion*. 彼はまた自国に騒乱を起こした.

come[1] /kʌm/ 名 ***come and go*** 去来, 行き来 ▪ There was a constant *come and go* of visitors. 客が絶えず出入りした.

There is a come. 《米》相当植物がはえている ▪ *There is a come* in the ground. その地には相当植物がはえている.

come[2] /kʌm/ 動 ***as crazy*** [***rich, clever, stupid,*** etc.] ***as they come*** ひどく気が狂って[金持ちで, 賢くて, ばかで, など] ▪ The Boston Marathon is *as international as they come*. ボストンマラソンはずば抜けて国際的だ.

as it comes 《英》(飲み物に加えるミルク・砂糖などに関して)お任せします ▪ How do you like your tea? —*As it comes*. 紅茶はどのようなのがよろしいですか—お任せします.

come *do* →COME and do.

come alive/***come to life*** よみがえる ▪ The memorized verses *came alive* in his mind. 記憶していた詩歌が彼の心によみがえった.

come and *do*/《米口》***come*** *do* ...しに来る ▪ *Come* (*and*) see me. 遊びにおいでなさい.

Come and get it! 《米口》食事の用意ができました(さあ来て召しあがれ).

come and go **1** 行ったり来たりする《一度のとき, 繰り返すとき》 ▪ She *comes and goes* at her will. 彼女は意のままに行ったり来たりする ▪ Money *comes and goes*. 金は天下の回りもの.

2 現れたり消えたりする; (時が)来てまた去る ▪ His color *came and went*. 彼は赤くなったり青くなったりした ▪ Years *came and went*. 何年もの年月が流れた.

3 短い訪問をする; つかのまである ▪ The Smiths *came and went* in a few days. スミス夫妻は2, 3日の短い訪問をした.

come and go upon ...で自由に行動する; に頼って行く[渡る] ▪ There was considerable room to *come and go upon*. 自由に行動する余地が相当にあった ▪ You have an excellent character to *come and go upon*. 君は頼っていくべき立派な人格を持っている.

Come and have one. 《口》さあ1杯やりなさい.

come as ...に仮装する, の格好をする ▪ His wife *came as* a go-go dancer. 彼の奥さんはゴーゴーダンサーの格好をしていた.

come back to haunt ...を思い出させて苦しめる, 過去ことでさいなまれる ▪ The scene *came back to haunt* him. その光景がよみがえって彼はつらくなった ▪ Four years later, that decision has *come back to haunt* him. 4年後に彼はその決定を思い出して後悔することになった.

come close to **1** ...に接近する ▪ He had *come close to* the spirit of the new labor group. 彼は新しい労働団体の精神に接近して来ていた ▪ That chapter *comes closest to* him. その章は彼に一番ぴったりしている.

2 ほとんど...するようになる; 危うく...する (*doing*) ▪ His son *came close to fulfilling* his dream. 息子は自分の夢をほとんど実現するまでになった ▪ He *came close to being* killed in the accident. 彼はその事故で危うく死ぬところだった.

Come, come これ, これ《人に注意を与えるときの言葉》 ▪ *Come, come*, Mr. James, be careful what you are saying. これ, これ, ジェイムズ君, 言葉には注意しなさいよ.

come day, go day, God send Sunday ぶらぶらとのんきに日を送るような ▪ It's *come day, go day, God send Sunday* with him. 彼はぶらぶら日をすごしている ▪ Young Joe carried on in his *come day, go day, God send Sunday* manner. ジョー青年はぶらぶらとのんきに日を送った.

come down hard on 《口》 **1** ...をきびしくしかる[罰する] ▪ The teacher *came down hard on* the naughty boys. 先生はいたずら少年らを厳しくしかった.

2 ...に強く反対する ▪ The rector *came down hard on* drinking. 司祭は飲酒に激しく反対した.

come down in the world →go down in the WORLD.

come down on *a person* ***like a thousand of bricks*** →BRICK.

come down with the pelf [***dust, needful***] 金を出す, 支払う ▪ Rich fathers are not willing to *come down with the pelf*. 金持ちの父親は金を出したがらぬものだ.

come easy [***natural***] ***to*** ...に(学習)しやすい ▪ Learning to fly an airplane *comes easy to* Frank. 飛行機の操縦を学ぶことはフランクには易しい.

come first 一等になる; 一番大事である ▪ Tom *came first* in the race. トムはそのレースに優勝した ▪ My family *comes first*. 私の家族が一番大事だ.

Come high, come low/《米俗》***Come hell or high water*** どんなことがあっても ▪ *Come high, come low*, we are going to accomplish it. 私たちはどんなことがあってもそれを達成するつもりだ.

come in for it 《口》罰せられる, しかられる ▪ You'll *come in for it* presently. 君は今に罰せられるだろう.

come in handy [***useful, serviceable***] 役にたってくれる, 役にたつようになる ▪ There is nothing but will *come in useful* sooner or later. 遅かれ早かれ役にたたないものはない ▪ This knife may *come in handy*. このナイフは役にたつようになるかもしれない.

come in usefully [***opportunely***] (天産物が)都合よく出回る ▪ The storms *came in opportunely* to help the Welsh. あらしが都合よくあってウェールズ軍を助けた.

come in *a person's* ***way*** 人の前に現れる, 人に見つかる, 人の手に入る ▪ I am determined to do anything that *comes in my way*. 手あたり次第どんなことでもする決心だ.

come into being [***existence***] 生じる, 誕生[出現]する ▪ Northern Ireland *came into being* in 1920. 北アイルランドは1920年に誕生した ▪ The

Billy T Award *came into existence* in 1997. ビリーT大賞は1997年に設けられた. ☞Billy T Award はニュージーランドの喜劇役者に与えられる賞.

come into force [***effect, play, operation***] 有効になる, 施行される ▪ New parking regulations have *come into force* in England and Wales. 新駐車規制がイングランドとウェールズで施行された.

come into *one's* ***head*** [***mind***] (人の頭に)思い浮かぶ, する気になる ▪ The book that he had written *came into my mind.* 彼の書いた本が頭に浮かんだ ▪ It *came into my head* to jump down. 飛びおりようという考えが起きた.

come into *one's* ***own*** 本来の地位[権利]を得るようになる ▪ Agriculture has *come into its own.* 農業は本来の地位に立ち帰った ▪ Last night with the celery autumn *came into its own.* 昨夜セロリが出て秋の天下となった.

come into style →STYLE[1].

come into view [***sight***] 見えるようになる ▪ As we turned the corner, the house *came into view.* 角を曲がると, その家が見えてきた.

come it **1**《口》なしとげる, うまくやる ▪ I meant to pay him, but I couldn't *come it.* 彼に払うつもりだったができなかった.

2 偉ぶる ▪ Don't try to *come it.* 偉ぶろうとするな.

3《俗》金を貸す, 頼みを聞く; (秘密を)洩らす, 密告する; 《ボクシング》恐怖を表す, 怖がる ▪ Has he *come it?* 彼は金を貸してくれたか; 頼みを聞いてくれたか; 仲間を密告したか; (ボクシングで)怖がったか.

come it over 《俗》 **1** ...をだます; に信じさせる ▪ He tried to *come it over* me. 彼は私をだまそうとした ▪ He *came it over* them that he was a genius. 彼は天才だと彼らに信じさせた.

2 ...に勝つ, を支配する, 偉そうにする ▪ Don't try *coming it over* me. 私に対して偉そうにするな.

come it strong →STRONG.

come it with 《口》 ...に対し偉そうにする ▪ It's no use trying to *come it with* me. 私に対して偉そうにしようとしてもだめだよ.

Come light, go light. 《諺》あぶく銭は身につかぬ (→Light(ly) COME, light(ly) go).

Come now! →NOW.

come [***get***] ***off it*** [***the grass***] 《俗》(ばかな・偉そうな話などを)やめる ▪ She told me to *come off it.* 彼女は私にばか話はやめてくれと頼んだ.

come off *one's* ***perch*** 《口》鼻柱を折られる ▪ The saucy boy *came off his perch.* 生意気な少年はぎゃふんと参った.

come off second-best →SECOND-BEST.

come off well **1** うまくゆく, 成功する ▪ He *came off* very *well* in that struggle. 彼はその闘争に大勝利を収めた.

2 十分の資産を与えられる ▪ He will *come off well* when his grandmother dies. 祖母が死んだら十分な資産をもらうだろう.

come off with flying colors →COLOR.

come off with honors 優等で合格[進級, 卒業]する ▪ He *came off with honors.* 彼は優等で合格した.

Come off your perch. → come off one's PERCH.

come on down [***out, round, up***] どうぞお入りください ▪ *Come on up.* The door's open. どうぞお入りになって, ドアは開いています. ☞come in の強調, 常に命令文.

Come on in, the water's fine. 《口》お入りなさい, 水はきれいですよ《水泳・水浴している人が他の人にすすめる言葉》; おやり[加わり]なさい, それはいいですよ ▪ Are you thinking of becoming a teacher like me? *Come on in, the water's fine.* 君は僕のように先生になろうと思っているのか. ぜひなりなさい, 先生はいいよ.

come on strong →STRONG.

come on to *do* ...し始める ▪ It *came on to* rain. 雨が降り始めた.

come on top of →TOP[1].

come one, come all 《口》一人来るならみんな来い ▪ *Come one, come all,* I'm ready to take them on. 一人来るならみんな来い, 喜んでみんなと相手になる.

come out dandy →DANDY.

come out fighting [***swinging***] 攻撃的にしかける, 闘争心まるだしで戦う; (勝利のために)全力で戦い抜く ▪ Both men *came out fighting* and delivered a far more impressive debate than their first attempt. 二人とも攻撃的に論じ, 最初の試みよりもはるかに印象的な論争を展開した ▪ The chairman *came out fighting* against his critics and insisted that he had never considered resigning. 議長は, 辞職を考えたことはないと主張して批判者たちに譲らなかった.

come (***out***) ***in the open*** →OPEN[1].

come out of *oneself* (殻をやぶって)打ち解ける, 社交的になる ▪ On this last tour, he really *came out of himself.* 前の旅では彼はとてもよく打ち解けた.

Come out of that! →THAT.

come out of *one's* ***way*** (***to*** *do*) →WAY.

come out on (***the side of***) (...の側)を支持する ▪ We habitually *come out on the side of* wage-workers. 我々はいつも賃金労働者の側を支持する.

come out on the worse side of ...に負ける ▪ He will *come out on the worse side of* the fight. 彼はけんかに負けるだろう.

come out on top [***come out tops***] 1番になる, 優勝する ▪ Peterson *came out on top* by a nose while Rae and Harris tied for second place. ピータースンが鼻の差で1位になり, レイとハリスが同タイムで2位につけた.

come out strong →STRONG.

come out with it =COME it 3.

come over with the onion boat 〚主に過去形で〛(フランスのブルターニュの)玉ねぎ舟で来る《イギリス人が外国人を軽蔑して言う句》 ▪ You don't think I *came over with the onion boat,* do you? 私がブルターニュの玉ねぎ舟で来たとは思わないでしょうね.

come right →RIGHT[1].

come* (*right*) *out and say it 遠慮なく言う ▪ All right, *come out and say it.* よろしい, どんどん言ってくれ ▪ No one will *come right out and say it.* 誰もはっきりとは言わないだろう.

come right round to it 《米口》根本的事実に入る[及ぶ] ▪ It is not much better when you *come right round to it.* 根本的事実になると, そのほうはあまりすぐれていない.

come that 《英口》それに達する, それをやる ▪ I can't quite *come that.* どうもそれはやれない. ☞come＝do, attain.

come the old soldier [etc.] ***over*** …に対し老兵[など]ぶっていばる, だます ▪ He *came the royal naval officer over* us. 彼は我々に対し英国海軍将校ぶっていばった.

come to *oneself* →ONESELF.

come to bear 向けられる, 集中される, 有効に働かされる ▪ Every one fired as fast as his gun would *come to bear.* みな銃のきくかぎり早く発砲した.

come to [***on***] *one's* ***feet*** →FOOT[1].

come to little [***much***] →LITTLE; MUCH.

come to pass →PASS[1].

come to stay →STAY[2].

come to that 《口》実際; そのことになると ▪ *Come to that*, it was nothing special. 実際のところ, それはなにも特別のことではなかった.

come to think of it 〚通例 now を伴って〛考えて見れば, 思い出したが ▪ *Come to think of it*, John promised to telephone me about this time. 思い出したが, ジョンは今ごろ私に電話すると約束した ▪ *Now come to think of it*, we have here a truer explanation of Frank's failure. 考えてみれば, フランクの失敗の真の説明はここにある.

come together **1** 会合する, 集まる ▪ They *came* at last *together* and he took her in his arms. 彼らはついにいっしょになり, 彼は彼女を抱いた.
2 (夫婦として)同せいする; 同時にセックスの絶頂に達する ▪ The lovers *came together.* 恋人同士は同時に絶頂に達した.
3 和解する; うまくいく, 軌道に乗る ▪ They will *come together* again. 彼らは和解するだろう ▪ We've started to *come together* as a team. 我々はチームとしてうまくやっていけるようになった.

come unglued **1** バラバラになる ▪ The pages of the fairytale book *came unglued.* おとぎ話の本のページはバラバラになった.
2 《米口》失敗する (《英》come unstuck) ▪ With no estate tax, those plans will *come unglued.* 遺産税をとらなければ, これらの計画は失敗に終わるだろう.
3 気が動転する, 取り乱す (come unstrung) ▪ Then she tried to explain how an educated woman *came unglued* and shot a man. 次に彼女は教養のある女性がどのような次第で取り乱して男性を射殺したかを説明しようとした ▪ Hollaway stated that he *came* completely *unglued* and killed her, and that he would regret it for the rest of his life. ハラウェイは完全にわれを忘れて彼女を殺してしまった, 終生後悔するだろう, と述べた.

come unput [***unstuck***] →UNPUT; UNSTUCK.

come untied [***unwrapped***] (くくった[包んだ]ものが)解けてくる ▪ Your shoelace is *coming untied.* あなたの靴ひもは解けかけている ▪ That package is about to *come unwrapped.* その包みは解けそうになっている.

come up dry 《米》無になる, 失敗する, しくじる ▪ We just kept digging and digging and finally *came up dry.* 我々は掘削をつづけたが結局失敗だった《水は出なかった》 ▪ All attempts at getting work *came up dry.* 就職しようという試みはすべて水泡に帰した.

come up for judgment 出廷する ▪ He *came up for judgment* before a stern judge. 彼はきびしい裁判官の前に裁判を受けに出頭した.

come up in *a person's* ***opinion*** [***estimation***] 人に見直される ▪ He has *come up in my opinion.* 私は彼を見直した.

come up in the world → get up in the WORLD.

come up smiling 《口》 **1** 《ボクシング》ひどくやられてもひるまず立ち直る ▪ He *came up smiling* and ready for the next round. 彼は負けてもひるまず立ち直って次の回に備えた.
2 (失望・災難・敗北などに)めげない ▪ In spite of every misfortune, he always *comes up smiling.* あらゆる不幸にもかかわらず彼はいつもめげない ▪ His car will *come up smiling.* 彼の車は事故にも耐えるだろう.

come up (***the***) ***hard*** (***way***) 苦労してたたきあげる ▪ My father had *come up the hard way.* 父は苦労してたたきあげたのだった.

come up to sample →SAMPLE.

come (***up***) ***to*** (***the***) ***scratch*** →SCRATCH[1].

come up to time →come to TIME 2.

come what will [***may***] →WHAT.

coming and going/going and coming → COMING.

coming of age 成人になること; 成人年齢 ▪ The Jewish *coming-of-age* ceremony is supposed to take place at the more tender age of 13. ユダヤの成人式はもっと若い13歳で行われることになっている.

Coming (***right***) ***up.*** はい, ただいま; すぐに持ってまいります ▪ Two burgers, please.—*Coming right up!* ハンバーガー2個, お願いします—はい, ただいま.

Don't come the ... with *a person.* 《英口》(人)に対して…のふりをするな, …を演じるな ▪ *Don't come the* hypocrite *with* me! おれに偽善者面するのはよせ.

First come, first served. →FIRST.

get what's coming to *one* 《米口》当然の報いを受ける ▪ He certainly *got what was coming to* him. 彼は確かに当然の報いを受けけた.

have ... coming out of *one's* ***ears*** 必要以上に…がある ▪ The prosecutor declared that the defendant *had got* motives *coming out of his ears.* 被告には掃いて捨てるほど動機があると検察官は

断言した.

How come? 《口》どうしてそういうことになるのか; それはどういうわけか ▪ I understand that you skipped a class yesterday. *How come?* きのうクラスをさぼったそうだね, なぜだい ▪ *How come* you won't speak to him? 君が彼に口をきかないのはどうしてかい? ☞疑問文なのに語順がS＋Vであることに注意.

C

How comes it that ...? どうして...なのか ▪ *How comes it that* you know him? なぜ彼を知っているの.

if it comes down to it 《口》もし本当にそうせざるをえなくなれば, いざとなれば ▪ *If it comes down to it*, I'll be ready for it. もしそうなら, その準備をしよう.

if it comes to that そのことなら, それに関して言えば ▪ *If it comes to that*, I hope we'll end up as good friends. そのことなら, よき友人として終わりたい.

Let'em all come! (矢でも鉄砲でも)さあ来い!《不可避なことを喜んで受け入れる句》 ▪ "*Let'em all come!*" said George. 「さあ何でも来い」とジョージは言った.

Light(ly) come, light(ly) go./ Quickly come, quickly go. 《諺》得やすいものは失いやすい, 「あぶく銭は身につかない」(→COME light, go light).

not come to much (重要度などが)たいしたことではない ▪ One project did *not come to much*. 一つの企画はたいしたことにならなかった.

not know whether [if] one is coming or going 《口》すっかり面くらう[取り乱す]; 興奮してしまう; てんやわんやの大騒ぎでまごついている ▪ John has been so happy that he does*n't know whether* he *is coming or going*. ジョンは非常にうれしかったので, すっかりのぼせている ▪ I do*n't know if* I *am coming or going* with moving. 転居のためてんやわんやの大騒ぎでまごついている.

now I come to think of it →COME to think of it.

that comes to それ, その程度 ▪ He's not so soft as *that comes to*. 彼はそんなに優しくない. ☞comes to＝amounts to.

This is where we came in. →THIS.

to come 未来の, 将来の ▪ What does the Bible teach us about the world *to come*? 聖書は来世についてどんなことを教えてくれるか ▪ In the years *to come*, I shall think of his words very often. 将来私は彼の言葉をしばしば思い出すでしょう.

What has come over ...? はどうしたのか ▪ You look pale. *What has come over* you? 君は顔色が悪い. どうしたのか.

What's coming off? 《俗》何ごとだい, どうなってるんだ.

What's to come of ...? ...はどうなるだろう ▪ *What's to come of* him? 彼はどうなるだろう. ☞come は become のなまり.

when [if] it comes right down to it 《陳腐》ずばり[突き詰めて, 究極的に]言えば, 結局 ▪ *When it comes right down to it*, having tea is about enjoying yourself alone or in the company of others, and discovering what you like. 結局, お茶を飲むということは一人で, または他の人といっしょに楽しんで自分の好みを見いだすことだ ▪ *When it comes right down to it*, which ticket do you want? 結局どっちのチケットがほしいのかね.

when it comes to ...ということになると, の点では ▪ You can't beat Jane *when it comes to* playing the piano. ピアノの演奏では, ジェインに及ぶものはない.

when [if] it comes to the crunch [the push] 《口》せっぱつまれば, 土壇場になれば ▪ *If it comes to the crunch*, I can go back to my old job. せっぱつまれば私は昔の仕事に戻れる.

where ... comes in ...が必要とされるところ[理由] ▪ This is *where* Clinton *comes in*. ここはクリントン氏の出番だ.

where a person is coming from **1** 出身, 出自 ▪ Color, race and *where* he *is coming from*, are not important. 肌の色や人種, 出自は大事なことではない.
2 《口》人の考えの根源, (発言などの)真意, 意図 ▪ I know *where* Steve *is coming from* in the things he said. We talked about it. スティーブが言ったことの真意がわかる. それについて話したことがあるので.

comeback /kʌ́mbæ̀k/ 名 ***do [have, make, stage] a comeback*** 《口》回復する; 返り咲く; 反論する ▪ The old actor *made a* splendid *comeback* in the part of Lear. 老俳優はリア王の役で見事に返り咲いた ▪ The song has *made a comeback* thanks to a remix by the group. その歌はグループの再編成のおかげで再び流行している ▪ The Reagan campaign *made a comeback* against Ford. レーガン陣営はフォードに反論した.

comedown /kʌ́mdàʊn/ 名 ***be a comedown after*** ...より劣る ▪ Anybody but Dickens will *be a comedown after* Shakespeare. ディケンズ以外は誰でもシェイクスピアには劣るだろう.

suffer a comedown 損失を被る, 恥をかく ▪ The boy *suffered a comedown*. He was twelfth. 少年は恥をかいた. 12位だった.

comedy /kɑ́mədi|kɔ́m-/ 名 ***a comedy of errors*** 間違い続き ▪ It was *a comedy of errors*, pretty much from start to finish. ほとんど最初から最後まで間違いの連続だった. ☞Shakespeare の作品名から.

cut the comedy [crap] 《俗》〚主に命令文で〛無駄口をたたくのをやめる, ばかなことをするのをやめる ▪ Pallmeyer finally told him to *cut the comedy* and give straight answers. とうとうポールマイアーは彼に無駄口をやめて率直に答えろと言った.

comer /kʌ́mər/ 名 ***all comers*** 来る人全員(の); (競技への)参加希望者全員(の) ▪ Blaine Bussey ran 47.0 seconds in the 400 meters in an *all-comers* meet last Saturday. ブレイン・ブッシーは先週土曜日に飛び入り自由の競技会の400メートル競走を47.0秒で走った.

come-uppance /kʌ̀mʌ́pəns/ 名 ***get one's come-uppance*** 《米口》当然の報いを受ける ▪ I learned that he *got his come-uppance*. 私は彼が当然の報いを受けたことを知った.

come-upping /kʌ̀mʌ́pɪŋ/ 名 ***get*** *one's* ***come-uppings*** =get one's COME-UPPANCE.

comfort[1] /kʌ́mfərt/ 名 ***a comfort eater*** 神経性大食症患者, 摂食障害者《ストレス解消のために過食する人》 ▪ I became *a comfort eater*. Whenever I was a bit stressed, I'd turn to food. 私は摂食障害になった. ちょっとストレスがあると食べ物に依存した.

be of (***good***) ***comfort*** 元気を出す, 元気である ▪ You stand amazed, but *be of good comfort*. あなたはびっくり仰天しているが, 元気を出しなさい.

cold comfort さっぱり慰めにならぬこと, がっかりすること ▪ It is but *cold comfort* to hear that. それを聞いてがっかりだ ▪ It is *cold comfort* to know that others are ill too. 他の人々も病気だと知っても慰めにはならない.

creature [***home***] ***comforts***/***creature comforts of home*** 肉体的快楽を与えるもの, 慰楽(物); (物質的)快適さ ▪ We were steeped in the *creature comforts* of our hotel. 我々はホテルの慰楽にひたっていた ▪ Three airlines are adding some extra *creature comforts*. 三つの航空会社が乗客にくつろいでもらえるサービスを新たに提供している.

find comfort in/***take comfort from*** [***in***] ...に慰安を受ける, で自ら慰める ▪ He *finds comfort in* his children. 彼は子供たちを慰安としている.

give comfort to ...を慰める ▪ He *gave comfort to* the bereaved parent. 彼は子を失った親を慰めた.

live in comfort 安楽に暮らす ▪ We want to *live in comfort*. 我々は安楽に暮らしたい.

too ... for comfort あまりに...で危険である, 安心できない ▪ The flames got *too* close *for comfort*. 炎があまりに近くまで来て危険だった.

What comfort? ごきげんいかがですか.

comfort[2] /kʌ́mfərt/ 動 ***comfort*** *oneself* ***with*** ...で自ら慰める ▪ She *comforted herself with* the thought. 彼女はそう思って自ら慰めた.

comfortably /kʌ́mfərtəbəli/ 副 ***be comfortably off*** →be well OFF.

comic /kɑ́mɪk|kɔ́m-/ 名 ***a stand-up comic*** ピン芸人, お笑い芸人《時事ネタのジョークなどで客を笑わせるコメディアン》 ▪ You always hear truth from *a stand-up comic*. ピン芸人の言葉には常に真実がある.

coming /kʌ́mɪŋ/ 形 ***coming and going*** はさみ撃ちにして, 出口[逃げ口]をふさいで ▪ His lie put him in a position where she had him *coming and going*. 彼は嘘をついたので彼女によって窮地に追いつめられた ▪ Gee, you've got us *coming and going*. やれやれ, 困ったことをしてくれたな.

coming from you [***him, her***] 《口・皮肉》君[彼, 彼女]からそんな言葉を聞くとは ▪ Oh, this is funny *coming from you*. へえ, 君がそんなことを言うとはおもしろい.

comings and goings **1**《口》帰宅外出時間, 出入り, 行き来 ▪ Rios cautioned parents to keep track of their children's *comings and goings*. リオスは親たちに子供の外出と帰宅の時間を記録しておくように注意した.

2 消息, 動静; 活動, 行動 ▪ Neighbors could describe one another's *comings and goings* in detail. 隣人たちは互いの動静を詳細に語ることが可能だ ▪ From here you can spy on all the *comings and goings* of guests sunbathing by the pool. プール脇で日光浴をしている外来者の行動を全部ここから見ることができる.

have *a person* ***coming and going*** 人を窮地に立たせる (→COMING and going).

have [***get***] *a thing* ***coming to*** *one* 《口》(報いとして)罰[賞]を受けようとしている ▪ He's *got* a holiday *coming to* him because he's worked so hard. 彼は勤勉だったので1日休暇をもらった.

have it coming (***to*** *one*) 《口》(罰などについて)当然の報いである; 自業自得である ▪ He failed the test. He *had it coming to* him. 彼はテストに落ちた. 自業自得だ.

They must have seen you coming. だまされたんだ, 足もとを見られたんだ.

comma /kɑ́mə|kɔ́mə/ 名 ***place*** [***put, set***]***... in inverted commas*** 《英》 **1** (注意すべき語句に)引用符号をつける ▪ Borrowed words *are* often *put in inverted commas*. 借用語にはよく引用符号がつけられる.

2 ...に特別の強調を置く ▪ In speaking, he has *placed* informal expressions *in inverted commas*. 話すとき彼は口語表現に特別の強調を置いた.

command[1] /kəmǽnd|-mɑ́ːnd/ 名 ***a command performance*** 《英》御前興行《国王・大統領などの前で行う演劇・演奏》 ▪ The McGuire Sisters had *a command performance* before the queen. マクガイア・シスターズは女王の前で御前演奏を行った.

at command 自由に使いうる; 御意のままに動く ▪ He has a lot of money *at command*. 彼は自由に使える金がたくさんある ▪ I am, my dear sir, yours *at command*. あなたさまの仰せの通りにいたします.

at *a person's* ***command*** 人の御意のままに動いて, 人の自由にしうる ▪ Here I am, sir, *at your command*. 何でも御用を承ります ▪ The beer is *at your command*, Mr. Brown. ブラウンさん, ビールをご自由に召しあがってください ▪ They will go forward *at your command*. 彼らはあなたの命のままに前進するだろう.

at *one's* ***command*** 自由にしうる ▪ He offered me all the money *at his command*. 彼は自分の自由にしうる金を全部私にやろうと言った.

at the word of command 命令一下 ▪ The students rise *at the word of command*. 生徒たちは号令一下立ちあがる.

get [***obtain***] ***the command of the air*** [***sea***] 制空[制海]権を握る ▪ At last the British army *obtained the command of the air*. ついにイギリス軍が制空権を握った.

have a* (*good*) *command of …を自由自在に使いこなせる ▪ He *has a good command of* English. 彼は英語が自由自在だ.

have the command of …を見渡す, を扼(やく)す ▪ The heights *have the command of* the passes. その高地から山道が見渡せる.

***in command* (*of*)** (…を)指揮して ▪ A colonel is an officer who is *in command of* a regiment. 陸軍大佐は連隊を指揮する将校である ▪ He is *in command* in that district. 彼はその地区を統轄している.

lose command of …の支配[抑制]力を失う ▪ She *lost command of* her temper. 彼女は怒りが押さえられなくなった.

on* [*upon*] *command 命を受けて ▪ We do it *upon command.* 命を受けてそれをする.

take command of …の指揮をとる, の指揮官となる ▪ When the major was killed, the senior captain *took command of* the company. 少佐が戦死したとき, 古参大尉がその中隊の指揮をとった.

under* one's [*a person's*] *command …の指揮下に ▪ He has a hundred men *under his command.* 彼は100人を指揮下に収めている ▪ We are *under your command.* 我々はあなたの指揮下にあります.

command[2] /kəmǽnd|-mɑ́ːnd/ 動 ***command oneself*** 自制する ▪ He cannot *command himself.* 彼は自制することができない.

command a fine view (山などが)見晴らしがよい ▪ The summit *commands a fine view.* 頂上は見晴らしがよい.

command the service of …を命じて動かす ▪ A minister *commands the services of* many officials. 大臣は多くの役人を使う.

Yours to command 敬具《あなたの命のままである; 手紙の結句》.

commandment /kəmǽndmənt|-mɑ́ːnd-/ 名 ***the ten commandments*** (モーセの)十戒;《俗》10本のつめ(特に女性の) ▪ She will write *the ten commandments* on your face. 彼女はあなたの顔をつめでひっかくだろう.

commando /kəmǽndoʊ|-mɑ́ːn-/ 名 ***go commando*** 《口》下着をつけないでいる ▪ It was thought that Luke wasn't wearing underwear but it was actually Jen who admitted that she *goes commando.* ルークが下着をつけていないと思われていたが, 実際にはつけていないと認めたのはジェンだった.

on* (*the*) *commando ブール(Boer)軍の義勇民軍に勤務[従軍]して ▪ The master himself was at this time absent *on the commando.* 主人もまたその時はブール義勇民軍に従軍して留守であった.

commemoration /kəmèməréɪʃən/ 名 ***in commemoration of*** …を記念して ▪ The monument was erected *in commemoration of* the victory. その記念碑は戦勝を記念して建てられた.

commend /kəménd/ 動 ***commend me to*** 〚命令文で〛《口・反語》…がよい; (なら)…にかぎる ▪ *Commend me to* a simple life. 僕は質素な生活がよい ▪ *Commend me to* a decayed country parson for a dull dog. まぬけ者なら老いぼれの田舎牧師にかぎる.

commend* oneself *to (物が)…に良い印象を与える, の気に入る ▪ This book doesn't *commend itself to* me. この本は気に入らない.

commensurate /kəménsərət|-ʃərət/ 形 ***be commensurate with*** …とつり合う ▪ The pay *is* not *commensurate with* the work. 給料は仕事とつり合わない.

comment /kɑ́ment|kɔ́m-/ 名 ***be a comment on*** …の注釈[説明]となる ▪ Mrs. Davy's face *is a comment on* this stormy humor in her husband. デイビー夫人の顔は夫のこのかんしゃくの良い説明になる.

give comment on*/*make comments on …を論評する ▪ The paper also *gave comment on* the news. その新聞もまたそのニュースを論評した.

No comment. お答えしたくありません; 何も言うことはありません ▪ The prime minister said, "*No comment*" to the reporters. 総理大臣は「お答えできません」とレポーターに言った.

commentary /kɑ́məntèri|kɔ́məntəri/ 名 ***a running commentary* (*on*)** (本文に)対する連続した評釈; (競技・試合の)実況放送 ▪ He kept up *a running commentary on* the baseball game. 彼は野球の試合の実況放送を続けてした.

commission[1] /kəmíʃən/ 名 ***accept* [*obtain, receive*] *a commission*** 将校に任じられる ▪ He *obtained a commission* in a short time. 彼はやがて将校に任じられた.

execute a commission (頼まれた)用を達す ▪ The artist *executed a commission* for the Queen. その芸術家は女王の御用を承った.

have it in commission to do …するよう任務を受けている ▪ I *have it in commission to* support the weak. 弱い人々を援助するよう任務を受けている.

hold a commission 将校に任官している ▪ No person under 16 is eligible to *hold a commission* in the army. 16歳未満の者は陸軍将校に任官する資格はない.

in* [*into*] *commission **1** 現役の, 就役中の(軍艦など) ▪ There are always some ships *in commission* even in times of peace. 平和の時でもいつもいくらか現役艦がある.

2《口》使用されて; いつでも使用できる状態で ▪ He put the old car back *in commission* for a time. 古い自動車をまたしばらく使用するようにした.

3 →put ... into COMMISSION.

obtain a commission →accept a COMMISSION.

on commission (商品を)委託されて; 手数料で, 歩合給で ▪ He sells goods *on commission.* 彼は商品を委託販売している ▪ I have goods *on commission.* 私は商品を委託されている ▪ Earnings are strictly *on commission.* 稼ぎは厳格に歩合制だ.

on the ... commission …委員に任ぜられて ▪ He

is [serves] *on the* Historical Manuscript *commission*. 彼は史料調査委員である.

out of commission **1** 退役の, 予備の ▪ The Royal Yacht Britannia is now *out of commission*. 英国王室豪華船ブリタニア号は現在では退役している.

2《口》使えなくなって, (機械が)動かないで ▪ The wireless plant was put *out of commission* by the storm. あらしで無電局は機能を失った.

put ... into commission ...を(団体に)委任する ▪ The fund *was* for the present *put into commission*. 基金は当分管理団に委任された.

receive a commission →accept a COMMISSION.

commission[2] /kəmíʃən/ 動 ***commission*** *a person* ***to*** *do* 人に...することを委任する ▪ I have *commissioned* my bankers *to* pay my taxes while I am away. 留守中私の税金を支払うことを取引銀行に委任した.

commit /kəmít/ 動 ***commit*** *oneself* **1** 身を危うくする; のっぴきならないはめになる (*to*) ▪ The Queen would not *commit herself* by communicating secrets to a Frenchman. 女王は秘密をフランス人に伝えて身を危うくするようなことはなさらないだろう ▪ He has *committed himself to* support(ing) his brother's children. 彼は兄の子供たちを養わねばならないはめに陥った.

2 かかり合う, 累を及ぼす (*to*) ▪ The preachers had now *committed themselves* too far to recede. 説教者たちはあまり深くかかわりすぎて, 引くに引かれなかった ▪ I am not going to *commit myself to* any such policy. そんな政策にかかり合うつもりはない.

3 言質を与える; 公約する; 意見を公表する (*to, to* do [*doing*]; 約束する, の場合には *to* do が多い) ▪ Do not *commit yourself*. 言質を与えるな ▪ The President *committed himself to* solve [*solving*] the problem. 大統領はその問題の解決を公約した ▪ You have *committed yourself* on this question. この問題についてはあなたは意見を公表している.

4 身を任す, 身をゆだねる (*to*) ▪ He has *committed himself to* the cause of education. 彼は教育の業に身をゆだねた.

5 名誉を傷つける ▪ He has *committed himself* gravely. 彼は大いに名誉を傷つけた.

commit administration 遺産管理を委託する ▪ It is necessary for the magistrate to *commit administration* of the goods of the deceased. 判事は故人の遺産の管理を委託する必要がある.

commit *a person* ***for contempt*** 人を法廷[官吏]侮辱罪で投獄する ▪ Public opinion is the only thing that a judge cannot *commit for contempt*. 世論だけは裁判官が法廷侮辱罪で投獄できない.

Commit no nuisance. →NUISANCE.

commit ... to *a person's* ***hands*** ...を人に委託[委任]する ▪ You had better *commit* the matter *to his hands*. その件は彼に委任したほうがよい.

commit ... to memory →MEMORY.

commit ... to paper [***writing***] 書き留めておく, 書き留める ▪ It is well to *commit* one's thoughts *to paper*. 自分の考えを書き留めておくのは良いことである.

commit ... to prison [***an asylum,*** etc.] 刑務所[保護院, など]に入れる ▪ At last he *was committed to prison*. ついに彼は投獄された ▪ The insane man *was committed to an asylum*. 発狂した男性は保護施設に入れられた.

commit ... to the care of ...に託す[世話を頼む] ▪ I *committed* my son *to the care of* my uncle. 私は息子をおじに託した.

commit ... to the flames [***fire***] ...を火葬にする; 焼き捨てる ▪ The body *was committed to the flames*. 遺体は火葬にされた ▪ I have *committed* the letter *to the flames*. 私は手紙を焼き捨てた.

commit ... to the waves [***earth, dust, grave***] ...を水葬[埋葬]する ▪ We *committed* his body *to the grave*. 彼の遺体を埋葬した.

committee /kəmíti|kɔ̀m-/ 名 ***go into*** (***a***) ***committee*** 委員会に入る, 委員会に移る ▪ The bill *went into a committee*. 議案は委員会に移った ▪ The House *went into a committee* on the bill. 議会はその議案について委員会に入った.

in committee 委員会で審議中で ▪ The bill is now *in committee*. その議案は委員会で審議中だ.

on the committe 委員の一人で ▪ He is *on the committee*. 彼は委員の一人である.

resolve itself into a committee (議会が)委員会となる ▪ The House *resolved itself into a committee* of the whole house on the bill. 下院はその議案審議のため全院委員会となった.

common /kámən|kɔ́m-/ 形名 ***a common make of*** 粗製の ▪ This is *a common make of* goods. これは粗製品だ.

above the common 非凡な ▪ He is a man *above the common*. 彼は非凡な人である.

(***as***) ***common as an old shoe***《口》下層の, 下品な; 気さくな, 気取らない ▪ That ill-mannered girl is *as common as an old shoe*. あの不作法な少女は全く下品だ ▪ Floren was *common as an old shoe*. He'd talk to anybody, mingle with fans and sign autographs. フローレンは気さくな人だった. 誰とでも話しをしたりファンと交わったりサインをしたりした.

(***as***) ***common as dirt*** [***muck***]《英口》きわめて平凡な[ありふれた]; (女性・家族などが)俗っぽい ▪ She's *as common as muck*. 彼女はきわめて下品である ▪ White heather is *as common as dirt* round here. 白ヒースはこのあたりではとてもありふれたものだ. ☞muck は《俗》に近い.

beyond the common = out of (the) COMMON.

common ground →find common GROUND, on common GROUND.

common or garden/ common-or-garden-variety《口》ありふれた, 平凡な, 二流の ▪ It is a *common or garden* seal. それはごく平凡なアザラシ

だ. ☞園芸から.

have ... in common (***with***) **1** (...と)共通に...を持つ ▪ The two stories *have* nothing *in common.* その二つの話には共通の点は何もない ▪ They *have* many things *in common with* the species. それらはその種と共通点が多い.

2 (...と)共有している ▪ We *had* all things *in common.* すべてのものを共有していた.

in common **1** 普通に ▪ This is too good to be used *in common.* これは普通に用いられるにはあまり良すぎる.

2 共同社会の ▪ They became weary of the life *in common.* 彼らは共同社会の生活に飽きてきた.

in common parlance 平たく言えば ▪ Peter, *in common parlance*, won't work if he can possibly avoid it. 平たく言えば, ピーターはせずにすむなら仕事はしない.

in common with **1** ...と共通に ▪ I wonder what he has *in common with* them. 彼は彼らとどういう共通点があるのだろうか.

2 ...と同様に ▪ *In common with* all sensible people, I hold that it is wrong. すべての物のわかった人々と同じく私はそれはまちがいだと思う.

in the common of *a person* 《米》...に借金を負って, 恩義を受けて ▪ I am little *in your common.* 君にはあまり借金はない.

out of (***the***) ***common*** 非凡な; 異常な ▪ He has something *out of the common* about him. 彼はどこか非凡なところがある ▪ The dress is somewhat *out of the common.* その服は少し珍奇だ.

the common touch (金持ち・重要人物の) 庶民性, 親しみやすさ ▪ David Cameron has *the common touch* to unseat Prime Minister Gordon Brown. デイビッド・キャメロンにはゴードン・ブラウン首相の議席を奪う庶民性がある ▪ The minister has not lost *the common touch.* その大臣は庶民性を失っていない.

commons /kάmənz|kɔ́m-/ 名 ***be*** [***live***] ***on short commons*** 食料不足である[で暮らす], 減食している[して暮らす] ▪ Owing to the breakdown in delivery, we are (*living*) *on short commons* just now. 配給途絶のため現在減食して(暮らして)いる.

put ... on short commons ...に食料を十分与えない, 減食させる ▪ We *put* them *on short commons.* 彼らに減食させた.

commotion /kəmóʊʃən/ 名 (***be***) ***in commotion*** 動揺している; 激動している ▪ Perpetual competition for wealth keeps the world *in commotion.* 絶えざる富の取得競争が世界をいつも激動させている.

create [***cause, make***] ***a commotion*** 動揺を起こす ▪ The discovery *created a commotion* in the world. その発見は世界に動揺を起こした.

commune /kəmjú:n/ 動 ***commune with*** *oneself* [*one's* ***own heart***] 沈思内省する ▪ He would often *commune with himself.* 彼はよく沈思内省するのだった.

commune with nature 《雅》自然に親しむ, 自然と心を通い合わせる ▪ You can *commune with nature* through hiking, rock climbing, biking and fishing. あなたはハイキングやロッククライミング, サイクリング, 魚釣りによって自然に親しむことができる.

communication /kəmjù:nəkéɪʃən/ 名 ***have no communication with*** ...と文通[連絡]していない ▪ I *have no communication with* him. 彼とは文通していない.

in communication with ...と連絡して ▪ I am *in communication with* him on this subject. この問題について彼と連絡している.

place *oneself* ***in communication with*** ...へ照会する ▪ I shall *place myself in communication with* the other party. 先方へ照会しましょう.

communion /kəmjú:niən/ 名 ***deliver the communion*** 聖餐(せいさん)式を施す ▪ The priest should *deliver the communion* to him. 司祭は彼に聖餐式を施すべきである.

go to Communion 聖餐式に列する ▪ She decided not to *go to Communion.* 彼女は聖餐式に行かないことに決めた.

hold communion with ...と霊的に交わる ▪ I *hold communion with* God. 私は神と交わる《神に祈とうする》 ▪ *hold communion with* oneself (道徳的に, 霊的に)深く思索する.

in communion with **1** (教会)に属して ▪ The inhabitants of this city are *in communion with* the established church. この市の住民は国教会に属している.

2 ...と交わって ▪ An ancient author puts the reader *in communion with* the spirit of long ago. 昔の著者は読者を大昔の心と交流させる.

receive [***take***] ***the Communion*** 聖餐式を受ける ▪ They are minded to *receive the* holy *Communion.* 彼らは聖餐式を受けたい意向がある.

communist /kάmjənəst|kɔ́m-/ 形 ***go communist*** 共産化する ▪ Cuba will *go communist.* キューバは共産主義国となるだろう.

community /kəmjú:nəti/ 名 ***a close-knit community*** しっかりと結びついた地域社会(の人々) ▪ We are *a close-knit community*, and we try to take care of each other. 我々は結びつきの強い共同体であり, 互いに面倒を見あおうとしている.

compact[1] /kάmpækt|kɔ́m-/ 名 ***by*** [***from, with***] ***compact*** 契約により[から] ▪ The meaning of language is derived *from compact.* 言語の意味は契約から生ずるものである.

compact[2] /kəmpǽkt/ 形 ***compact of*** ...から作られた, から成る ▪ Milk is *compact of* three substances. ミルクは三つの物質からなっている.

companion /kəmpǽnjən/ 名 ***be*** (***not***) ***much of a companion*** 大いに気が合う(合わない) ▪ His brother *is not much of a companion* for him. 彼の兄は彼とは大して気が合わない.

company /kʌ́mpəni/ 名 ***a company man*** 会社寄り[べったり]の社員, (会社側の)イエスマン ▪ He is *a company man*; he's going to be loyal. 彼は会社側人間だ. 忠実であろうと思っている.

A man is known by the company he keeps. 《諺》友を見れば人柄がわかる.

and company **1**〚通例& Co. の形で〛…社, 商会 ▪ Dow Jones *& Co.* ダウ・ジョーンズ社 ▪ Smith *& Co.* スミス商会.
2《口・軽蔑》…たち, その他大勢 ▪ Thatcher *and company* caused great divisiveness in British society. サッチャー氏とその取り巻きは英国社会に深刻な争いの種をまいた.

bad company 悪友 ▪ You should avoid *bad company*. 悪友と交わるな.

be addicted to low company 身分の低い人々の間に入りびたる ▪ He *is addicted to low company*. 彼は卑しい人々の間に入りびたっている.

(be) good [bad, poor] company つき合っておもしろい[おもしろくない] ▪ He's very *poor company*. 彼はつき合っておもしろくない.

be in good company (ある事のできない人を慰めて)立派な人々にも…の連れは多い ▪ Don't worry if you can't play the piano. You*'re in good company*. ピアノが弾けなくてもくよくよするなよ. 立派な人々にも君の連れは大勢いるからな.

be on** one's **company manners 他人行儀でとり澄ましている ▪ He *is* always *on his company manners*. 彼はいつも他人行儀でとり澄ましている.

bear [keep]** a person **company 人の相手をする, お供をする, おつき合いする ▪ I am prepared to *keep* you *company*. お供するつもりでいます ▪ This pleasant river has *borne* us *company* for some time. この愉快な川がしばしの間私たちの相手をしてくれた.

Company in distress makes trouble less. 《諺》不幸を共にする人があれば苦しみは薄らぐ.

err [sin] in good company →transgress in good COMPANY.

favor** a person **with** one's **company 人につき合う ▪ Will you *favor* me *with* (the pleasure of) *your company* at dinner? 食事をつき合ってくださいませんか《招待の文》.

for company おつき合いに ▪ His wife wept *for company*. 妻はもらい泣きをした.

force** one's **company upon …と無理につき合う, に押しかけて行く ▪ Then I will not *force my company upon* you. それでは無理におつき合いはしません.

get [receive]** one's **company 中隊長(大尉)になる ▪ After the war, Harley *received his company*. 戦後ハーリーは大尉になった.

get into bad company 悪い人々と仲よしになる, 悪友と交わる ▪ He *got into bad company* and went to bars and dance-halls. 彼は悪友と交わり, 酒場やダンスホールへ行った.

give** a person one's **company =bear a person COMPANY.

have company 饗宴を催す ▪ We're *having company* tonight. 今夜お客があります.

have the pleasure of** a person's **company 人といっしょになる ▪ I *have the pleasure of your company* on the voyage. この航海で君といっしょだ.

in company **1** 人前で, 人中で ▪ He insulted me *in company*. 彼は人前で私を侮辱した.
2 (…と)いっしょに (*with*) ▪ We went there *in company*. 我々はいっしょにそこへ行った ▪ He came *in company with* a group of boys. 彼は少年の集団といっしょに来た.

in** a person's **company …と話していると, といっしょにいると ▪ Time passes so pleasantly *in your company*. あなたと話していると時が実に愉快に過ぎていく ▪ *In his company* I am never bored. 彼といっしょにいると決して退屈しない.

in each other's company お互いにいっしょで ▪ We are often *in each other's company*. 我々はお互いにしばしばいっしょになる.

keep** a person **company = bear a person COMPANY.

keep company with **1** …と交際する ▪ He *kept company with* the prince. 彼は王子と交際した.
2 …のお供をする ▪ I'll *keep company with* you as far as London Bridge. ロンドン橋までお供しよう.
3 (結婚の目的で)…とつき合う ▪ Our maid is *keeping company with* the milkman. うちのメイドは牛乳屋とつき合っている.

keep good [bad] company 良い友[悪い友]と交わる ▪ The teacher advised his pupils always to *keep good company*. 先生は生徒にいつも良い友だちと交わるよう忠告した.

keep to** one's **own company 独居する ▪ Uncle *keeps to his own company*. おじは独居して人と交際しない.

part company →PART[2].

present company excepted ここにいらっしゃるみなさんは別として ▪ Many people these days are selfish, *present company excepted*. 現代人には利己的な人が多い, ここにいらっしゃるみなさんは別ですが.

receive company 客を迎える, 訪問を受ける; 接待する ▪ He *receives* much *company*. 彼は来客が多い.

receive** one's **company →get one's COMPANY.

transgress [sin, err,** etc.**] in good company 立派な人々も…と同じ違反[罪, 誤り, など]を犯している ▪ In this respect he *sinned in good company*. この点においては彼ばかりでなく立派な人々も同じ罪を犯したのだ ▪ It is no disgrace to be *intoxicated in good company*. お歴々も同じように酔うのだから酔うのは少しも恥ではない.

Two's company, three's none [a crowd]. 《諺》2人は良い連れだが3人となればしっくりしない.

would rather have** a person's **room than his company →ROOM.

compare[1] /kəmpéər/ 名 ***beyond [without, past] compare*** 《雅》比類を絶して, 比類なく ▪ He was disgraced *past compare*. 彼はこの上な

C

い恥辱を受けた ▪ His piety was *beyond compare.* 彼の信心は比類がない.

compare² /kəmpéər/ 動 ***(as) compared with*** …と比べて ▪ It is a great improvement *as compared with* last year. それは昨年のと比べて格段の進歩だ.

cannot be compared to …といっしょにはならない; と似たところは全くない ▪ Your house *cannot be compared to* mine. 君の家はうちとはいっしょにならない.

cannot [do not] compare with …とは比較にならない(はるかに劣る) ▪ He *cannot compare with* Shakespeare as a writer of tragedies. 彼は悲劇作者としてシェイクスピアとは比較にならない.

compare favorably with …と比べて勝るとも劣らない ▪ It *compares favorably with* the other. それは他の方と比べて勝るとも劣らない.

compare notes →NOTE.

not to be compared with …とは比べものにならぬ ▪ This is *not to be compared with* that. これはあれとは比べものにならない.

comparison /kəmpǽrəsən/ 名 ***be without comparison*** 比肩するものがない ▪ Nikko's scenery *is without comparison.* 日光の景色は比肩するものがない.

bear [stand] comparison with …と匹敵する ▪ In point of grandeur the view *bears comparison with* any in the Alps. 壮大さの点ではそのながめはアルプス山脈中のどのながめにも匹敵する.

beyond (all) comparison → without COMPARISON.

by comparison 比べると, 割りに ▪ This one is really cheaper *by comparison.* 実際このほうが割りと安い.

Comparisons are odious. 《諺》比較はいやなもの.

draw a comparison between …を比較する ▪ The teacher *drew a comparison between* America and Russia. 先生は米国とロシアを比較した.

draw [make] comparisons 比較をする ▪ You may scold a boy, but don't *draw comparisons* with his brothers. 少年をしかってもよいが, その子の兄弟たちと比較をするな.

in comparison 割りに, 存外 ▪ This is easy *in comparison.* これは割りに易しい.

in [by] comparison with [to, of] …に比べて, 比べれば ▪ The buildings in London are small *in comparison with* the skyscrapers in New York. ロンドンの建物はニューヨークの摩天楼に比べれば小さなものだ.

institute [make] a comparison (between) (…を)比較する ▪ One might *institute a comparison between* ancient Rome and modern Britain. 古代ローマと現代ブリテンとを比較することもできよう.

pale by [in] comparison (…に)比較すると顔色がない[見劣りがする] ▪ Many problems in our area *pale in comparison* with the devastation in East Japan. わが地域での多くの問題は東日本の大災害に比べればたいしたことではないように見える.

stand comparison with → bear COMPARISON with.

there is no comparison between …は同日の論でない, (段違いで)比較にならない ▪ *There is no comparison between* the two. 二者は同日の論でない.

without [out of all, beyond (all)] comparison 比類なく ▪ His joy was *without comparison.* 彼の喜びは比類を絶していた ▪ It is, *out of all comparison,* the stronger of the two. そのほうが二つのうちで断然比較にならないほど強い.

compass /kʌ́mpəs/ 名 ***beyond*** *one's* ***compass/beyond the compass of*** *one's* ***powers*** 力に及ばぬ ▪ It is *beyond my compass.* それは私の力に及ばない.

beyond [out of, without] the compass of …の及ばぬ(ところで), の範囲外で ▪ The matter is *beyond the compass of* thought. そのことは考え及ばぬことである ▪ The sun never goes down *out of the compass of* our sight. 太陽は我々の視界の外に沈むことはない.

cast [fetch, go, take] a compass **1** ぐるっと一回りする, う回する ▪ We *went a compass* into Leicestershire. う回してレスターシャーに入った ▪ Troops of deer were *fetching a compass.* シカの群れが遠回りしていた.

2 遠回しに行動する, 遠回しにものを言う; 脱線する ▪ He always *fetches a compass.* 彼はいつも遠回しにものを言う.

Coryate's compasses 《戯》足 (legs) ▪ I resolved to try *Coryate's compasses.* 歩いてみようと決心した. ☞英国人旅行家 Thomas Coryate より.

in a small compass 小範囲内に, こじんまりと ▪ His book presents the subject *in a small compass.* 彼の本はその題目を小範囲で論じている.

take a compass →cast a COMPASS.

within compass 限度内に ▪ Keep your desires *within compass.* 欲望を控え目にしておけ ▪ I speak *within compass.* 私は控え目に言っている.

within the compass of …の範囲内に ▪ It comes *within the compass of* our beliefs. それは我々の信じうることである.

without the compass of →beyond the COMPASS of.

compassion /kəmpǽʃən/ 名 ***have [take] compassion on*** …をあわれむ, あわれみ助ける ▪ She *had compassion on* him. 彼女は彼をあわれんだ.

have compassion with (物事)に同情する ▪ We *have compassion with* the sufferings of others. 我々は他人の苦しみに同情する.

compatible /kəmpǽtəbəl/ 形 ***compatible with*** …と両立して ▪ Accuracy is not always *compatible with* haste. 正確さは必ずしも迅速さと

両立しない ▪ Leonard is not *compatible with* his father. レナードは父とは合わない.

compel /kəmpél/ 動 ***be compelled to*** *do* 仕方なく…する ▪ I *was compelled to* go there. 私は仕方なくそこへ行った.

compel *a person* ***to*** *do* 人に強いて…させる ▪ We *compelled* him *to* sign a paper. 我々は彼に強いて書類に署名させた.

compensation /kɑ̀mpənséɪʃən|kɔ̀m-/ 名 ***in compensation for*** …の償いに;《米》の報酬に ▪ I will give you this *in compensation for* your loss. あなたの損失の償いにこれをあげます.

make compensation for …の償いをする ▪ We must *make compensation for* the damage. その損害の補償をせねばならない.

competent /kɑ́mpətənt|kɔ́m-/ 形 (***be***) ***competent for*** …する資格がある ▪ Can you think of a man *competent for* the post? その地位の適任者の心あたりはありませんか ▪ He *is competent for* teaching. 彼は教える資格がある.

competition /kɑ̀mpətíʃən|kɔ̀m-/ 名 (***be***) ***in competition with*** …と競争する ▪ Our representatives *were in competition with* the best swimmers from America. わが代表たちはアメリカからの一流水泳選手たちと競争した.

put *a person* ***in*** [***into***] ***competition with*** 人を…と競争させる ▪ You should not *put* him *in competition with* me. 彼を私と競争させてはだめだ.

complain /kəmpléɪn/ 動 ***Can't complain.*** 順調[快調]だよ, 大丈夫《体調・調子などを尋ねられたときの答え》 ▪ How are you, Michael?—*Can't complain.* マイケル, どうだね?—まあまあだよ.

complaint /kəmpléɪnt/ 名 ***lodge a complaint with*** …に苦情を提起する ▪ He *lodged a complaint with* the Police Department. 彼は警察に訴え出た.

make [***lay, lodge***] ***a complaint against*** **1** …に苦情を言う ▪ We *made a complaint against* him. 我々は彼に苦情を言った.
2 …を告訴する ▪ We *lodged a complaint against* him. 我々は彼を告訴した.

complete[1] /kəmplíːt/ 形 ***complete with*** 《米》…のついた, 備えつけてある ▪ My son lives in an apartment *complete with* furniture. 息子は家具付きのアパートに住んでいる ▪ My new PC came *complete with* a keyboard and a mouse. 今度買ったパソコンはキーボードとマウス付きだった.

complete[2] /kəmplíːt/ 動 ***to complete*** (***the sum*** [***measure, catalogue***] ***of***) *one's* …のあげくに, にかてて加えて ▪ *To complete the sum of his* misery, he had his wife die. その不幸のあげくのはてに, 彼は妻に死なれた.

completion /kəmplíːʃən/ 名 ***bring*** [***carry***] ***… to completion*** …を完成する, 成就する ▪ His plan *was brought to completion.* 彼の計画は成就された.

complexion /kəmplékʃən/ 名 ***put a different*** [***another***] ***complexion on*** (事)の趣を変える ▪ Your account *puts a different complexion on* the matter. 君の話でその事件の趣が変わってくる.

compliance /kəmpláɪəns/ 名 ***in compliance with*** …に応じて ▪ *In compliance with* your order, we send this article. ご注文に従いこの品をお送りします.

complicate /kɑ́mpləkèɪt|kɔ́m-/ 動 ***be complicated with*** …と複雑に交錯する ▪ The history of England *is complicated with* the history of foreign politics. イングランドの歴史は外国との抗争の歴史と複雑に交錯している.

complicate matters 事が面倒になる ▪ That will *complicate matters.* それでは事が面倒になるだろう.

compliment /kɑ́mpləmənt|kɔ́m-/ 名 ***a backhanded*** [《米》***left-handed***] ***compliment*** 裏のある[裏でけなすような]ほめ言葉, 皮肉まじりのほめ言葉 ▪ To say, "You are not quite such a fool as you look," is *a left-handed compliment.* 「君は見かけほどのばかではないね」と言うのは裏でけなすようなおせじである ▪ The critic, in *a backhanded compliment,* once proclaimed him "the finest actor on earth from the neck up." その批評家は皮肉な賛辞で彼のことを「首から上は地上でもっとも見事な俳優」と称えた.

a two-edged compliment 二面的評言《ほめているともけなしているともとれる言葉》 ▪ We understood you were a dramatist. You seem to have missed your vocation. Rather *a two-edged compliment.* 君を劇作家だと思っていたが, どうやら天職につきそこねたようだな. ほめているともけなしているともとれるけど.

fish [***angle***] ***for compliments*** ほめてもらうように仕向ける《通例自分をけなして》 ▪ I'm not a very good cook.—Nonsense, you are merely *fishing for compliments.* 私はたいした料理人ではありません—とんでもない! 賞賛目当ての心にもないご謙遜でしょう.

give my compliments to …によろしくお伝えください ▪ Please *give my compliments to* your parents. どうぞご両親によろしく.

give the last compliment 埋葬する.

in [***out of***] ***compliment to*** …に敬意を表して ▪ Maryland was so named *in compliment to* Queen Henrietta Maria. メリーランド州はヘンリエッタ・マライア女王を称えてそう命名された.

My compliments to… …に敬意を表します; によろしく ▪ *My compliments to* your father. おとうさんによろしく ▪ *My compliments to* the chef. 《英》シェフに敬意を表します《ご馳走に対するお礼の言葉》.

pay [***pass, make***] *a person* ***a compliment*** **1** 人に賛辞を呈する, ほめる ▪ He seldom *paid* his wife *a compliment* on her cooking or apparel. 彼はめったに料理や服装で奥さんをほめたことがなかった.
2 人に敬意を表する ▪ They have *paid* him *the compliment* of electing him an honorary member. 彼に敬意を表して名誉会員に選んだ.

pay [***make, present***] (*one's*) ***compliments*** (***to***) **1** (…を)ごきげん伺いに訪問する, (に)敬意を表する

▪ The new ambassador *paid his compliments to* the King. 新大使は国王を訪問してあいさつした.
2 (...に)よろしくと言う ▪ Mr. Ruth *presents his compliments to* Sir John Sinclair. ルース氏はサー・ジョン・シンクレアによろしくと言っています ▪ *Make my compliments to* your mamma. おかあさんによろしくお伝えください.

return the compliment 返礼する, 返報する; 仕返し[報復]をする ▪ This Christmas they have *returned the compliment* and invited us. 今年のクリスマスには彼らはその返礼に私どもを招待してくれた ▪ He criticized my essay, and I *returned the compliment* when I reviewed his novel. 彼にエッセイを酷評されたので, 彼の小説を書評した際に仕返しをしてやった.

send *one's* ***compliments to*** ...によろしくと申し送る; にあいさつを送る ▪ The whole family *send their compliments to* you. 一家こぞってあなたによろしくと言ってきています.

the compliments of the season 祝賀のあいさつ《クリスマス・新年に通常用いるが, 他の場合にも用いる》 ▪ It's Chistmas Day tomorrow, so I wish you *the compliments of the season*. あすはクリスマスですから, クリスマスおめでとうを申しあげます ▪ *The compliments of the season*, my worthy masters, and a merry First of April to us all! お歴々のかたがたお祝いのごあいさつ申しあげます, そして私ども一同にも万愚節おめでとうございます.

With the compliments of... 謹呈—...より《手紙, または贈呈本の表紙裏などに記す文句》.

complimentary /kàmpləméntəri|kɔ̀m-/ 形 ***be complimentary about*** ...についておせじを言う ▪ He *was complimentary about* my work. 彼は私の作品についておせじを言った.

comport /kəmpɔ́ːrt/ 動 ***comport*** *oneself* ふるまう ▪ He *comported himself* with dignity. 彼は威厳をもってふるまった.

compose /kəmpóuz/ 動 ***be composed of*** ...から成る ▪ Water *is composed of* oxygen and hydrogen. 水は酸素と水素とから成る.

compose *oneself* **1** 態度を取る, 身[形]を構える ▪ We *composed ourselves* with modesty. 我々は謙譲に身を処した ▪ Water exactly *composes itself* to a horizontal level. 水は厳密に水平面に従う. **2** 気[心]を落ち着ける ▪ I *composed myself* to write. 私は心を落ち着けて書いた.

compose *one's* ***countenance*** [***features***] 落ち着いた顔つきをする ▪ He tried to *compose his countenance* as well as he could. 彼はできるだけ落ち着いた顔つきをしようとした.

compose *one's* ***mind*** [***thoughts***] ***for*** [***to, to*** *do*] ...するよう心を落ち着ける, する心構えをする ▪ I wanted to *compose my thoughts for* action. 私は行動をするため心を落ち着けたいと思った ▪ He *composed his mind to* do so. 彼はそうする心構えをした.

composition /kàmpəzíʃən|kɔ̀m-/ 名 ***have...in*** *one's* ***composition*** 性質に...がある ▪ He *has* a touch of madness *in his composition*. 彼は性質に少し狂気なところがある.

make a composition with ...と示談にする ▪ He *made a composition with* his creditors. 彼は債権者たちと示談にした.

composure /kəmpóuʒər/ 名 ***keep*** [***lose***] *one's* ***composure*** 落ち着きを保つ[失う] ▪ She *lost her composure* at the news. 彼女はそのニュースを聞いてどぎまぎした.

regain *one's* ***composure*** 落ち着き[平静]を取り戻す ▪ Within minutes, Sodhi *regained his composure* and continued to answer questions in a relaxed, even voice. 数分以内にソディは落ち着きを取り戻してくつろいで平静な声で質問に答えつづけた.

with great composure 落ち着きはらって, 泰然として ▪ I sat down *with great composure* and wrote to him. 落ち着きはらって座り彼に手紙を書いた.

compound /kámpaund|kɔ́m-/ 動 ***compound the felony*** →FELONY.

comprehension /kàmprɪhénʃən|kɔ̀m-/ 名 ***be slow*** [***dull***] ***of comprehension*** 理解が遅い[のみこみが悪い] ▪ He *is slow of comprehension*. 彼は理解が遅い.

beyond [***above***] *one's* ***comprehension*** 理解できない ▪ His theory is *beyond my comprehension*. 彼の理論は私には理解できない.

pass (*one's*) ***comprehension*** (...に)理解できない ▪ It *passes* human *comprehension*. それは人間の頭ではわからない.

comprise /kəmpráɪz/ 動 ***be comprised in*** ...の中にある[いる], のうちに含まれる ▪ A number of states *were comprised in* the German Empire. ドイツ帝国には多数の国が含まれていた.

compromise[1] /kámprəmàɪz|kɔ́m-/ 名 ***make*** (***a***) ***compromise with*** ...と妥協する, をまげる ▪ I have *made compromise with* him. 私は彼と妥協した ▪ He *made a compromise with* his conscience. 彼は自己の良心をまげた.

compromise[2] /kámprəmàɪz|kɔ́m-/ 動 ***compromise*** *oneself* [*one's* ***honor***] 体面を危うくする, 信用を落とす; 怪しまれる ▪ You will *compromise yourself* if you associate with these people. もしこの人たちとつき合うなら君は信用を落とすだろう ▪ You must not *compromise your honor*. 人に怪しまれるようなことをしてはならない.

compulsion /kəmpʌ́lʃən/ 名 ***by compulsion*** 強制的に ▪ We made him go there *by compulsion*. 彼を強制的にそこへ行かせた.

on [***under***] ***compulsion*** しいられて ▪ A defeated enemy usually signs a treaty *under compulsion*. 敗北した敵は通常強制されて条約に調印する.

compunction /kəmpʌ́ŋkʃən/ 名 ***without compunction*** 平気で ▪ He killed his master *without* the least *compunction*. 彼は全く平気で主人を殺した.

compute /kəmpjúːt/ 名 ***beyond compute*** 量

りえない ▪ My obligations to him are *beyond compute.* 私が彼に受けた恩は量り知れない.

computer /kəmpjúːtər/ 名 ***a computer bug*** コンピューターの不具合, バグ《プログラムに悪影響を及ぼすコンピューターシステムの欠陥》 ▪ In fact, the message was simply a display error caused by *a computer bug.* 実は, そのメッセージはバグによる表示エラーにすぎなかった.

a computer hacker 《電算》ハッカー《ネットワークに不法侵入し情報を盗む者》 ▪ *Computer hackers* pose a serious threat to national security. ハッカーたちは国家の安全に深刻な脅威を与える.

a computer nerd [***geek***] 《軽蔑》コンピューターおたく ▪ Gates, *a* high school *computer nerd* and Harvard dropout, formed Microsoft in 1975 with Paul Allen. ゲイツは, 高校時代コンピューターおたくでハーバード中退者だが, 1975年にポール・アレンとマイクロソフト社を設立した.

comrade /kɑ́mræd|kɔ́mreɪd/ 名 ***a comrade in arms*** 戦友; 苦難を共にする人 ▪ They are old *comrades in arms.* 彼らは昔から苦難を共にしてきた人たちだ.

concealment /kənsíːlmənt/ 名 ***in concealment*** 隠れて; 隠されて ▪ He has absconded and is still *in concealment.* 彼は逃亡してまだ潜伏中だ.

conceit[1] /kənsíːt/ 名 ***full of conceit*** うぬぼれが強い ▪ The man is *full of conceit.* あの男はうぬぼれが強い.

in *one's* ***own conceit*** 自分では...のつもりで ▪ He is wise *in his own conceit.* 彼は自分では賢いつもりでいる.

out of conceit with ...にいや気がさして, あいそをつかして, 不満足で ▪ He has been *out of conceit with* his own playing. 彼は自分の演技にいや気がさしている ▪ I am now *out of* all *conceit with* my former self. 私は今は以前の自分にすっかりあいそをつかしている ▪ We are *out of conceit with* our lot in life. 我々は自分の運命に不満足である.

put *a person* ***out of conceit with*** 人に...をいやにならせる ▪ Paris *put* her *out of conceit with* all the other places. パリのおかげで彼女は他の土地がすべていやになった.

conceit[2] /kənsíːt/ 動 ***be conceited about*** ...に得意になる, うぬぼれる ▪ She *is conceited about* her beauty. 彼女は自分の美しさにうぬぼれている.

conceit *oneself* ***over*** ...に得意になる ▪ He *conceits himself over* his success. 彼は自分の成功に得意になっている.

conceit *oneself* (***to be***)***...*** 自分を...と空想する ▪ He *conceited himself* (*to be*) a poet. 彼は自分を詩人だと空想した.

conceive /kənsíːv/ 動 ***cannot conceive of*** ...しようとは思いもつかない ▪ I *cannot conceive of* your beating your wife. あなたが奥さんをたたくなんて思いもつきません.

conception /kənsépʃən/ 名 ***beyond conception*** 想像も及ばぬ ▪ His wisdom is *beyond conception.* 彼の知恵は想像も及ばぬ.

have no conception of ...がわからない, を知らない ▪ I *have no conception of* what he means. 彼がどういうつもりなのかわからない ▪ I *have no conception of* what a war is like. 戦争とはどんなものか少しも知らない.

in *one's* ***conception*** ...の考えでは ▪ It has always been overrated *in my conception.* それは私の考えではいつも買いかぶられてきたと思う.

concern[1] /kənsə́ːrn/ 名 ***feel concern for*** [***about, at***] ...を案じる, 心配する ▪ I *feel concern for* his safety [*about* the matter, *at* his failure]. 彼の安全を[それについて, 彼の失敗を]案じている.

have a concern in ...に(利害)関係がある ▪ You *have a concern in* that school. 君はあの学校に関係がある《出資者の一人》.

have no concern with ...と関係がない ▪ I *have no concern with* that man. あの人とは何の関係もない.

Mind your own concerns. (余計な世話を焼かないで)自分の頭のハエを追え.

no concern of mine [***yours,*** etc.] 私[あなた, など]の知ったことではない ▪ It is *no concern of mine.* 私の知ったことではない.

of... concern 関係の; 重要な ▪ It is a matter *of* no *concern* to me. それは私には関係のない事柄です ▪ The matter is *of* great *concern.* その事は重要だ.

the whole concern すべてのもの ▪ The war smashed *the whole concern.* 戦争は何もかもめちゃめちゃにした.

with [***without***] ***concern*** 憂慮して[無関心で] ▪ He asked me *with* deep *concern.* 彼は非常に心配して私に尋ねた.

concern[2] /kənsə́ːrn/ 動 ***as concerns*** ...については ▪ *As concerns* him, I have nothing to say. 彼については何も言うことはない.

as far as... is concerned ...に関するかぎり, ...だけは ▪ *As far as* I *am concerned,* it is not true. 私に関するかぎりそれは本当でない.

(***be***) ***concerned about*** ...について心配している ▪ I *am* very (much) *concerned about* the future of this country. 私はこの国の未来について大いに心配している.

be concerned in [***with***] **1** ...に関与している, に関係している ▪ He *is concerned in* the affair. 彼はその事件に関係している ▪ His work *is concerned with* the preparation of documents. 彼の仕事は書類の作成に関係している ▪ We *are* not *concerned with* that question here. ここではその問題には触れない.

2 (酒)に酔っている, 酔う ▪ She *is* a little *concerned with* liquor. 彼女は少し酒に酔っている.

concern *oneself* ***about*** [***for, to hear, at, over***] ...について[を, を聞いて, に対して]心配する, 案じる; 〚否定文で〛とんちゃくする ▪ I *am concerned* *for* your welfare. 私はあなたの身の上を案じている ▪ I don't *concern myself about* others' opinions. 私は他人の評にはとんちゃくしない.

concern** oneself **in …に関与する, 関係する ▪ I will not *concern myself in* this affair. この事件には関係したくない.

***concern** oneself **to** do* …するよう努力する, 骨を折る ▪ Providence *concerns itself to* assert the interests of religion. 天は宗教の利益を擁護するよう骨を折る.

concern** oneself **with …に従事する, 手を出す ▪ I don't *concern myself with* politics. 私は政治には手を出さない ▪ He *concerned himself with* public work. 彼は公の仕事に従事した.

to whom it may concern 関係者各位, ご担当者殿《手紙・推薦状などで個人名が不明なときに用いる》 ▪ "*To whom it may concern*" is used, especially in American English, if you do not know the name of the person you are writing to. 「関係者各位」は宛名不明の場合に, 特にアメリカ英語で使われる.

concernment /kənsə́ːrnmənt/ 名 ***have concernment in*** [***with***] …に関係を持つ ▪ I *have* no *concernment in* that matter. 私はその件に全く関係ない.

no concernment of mine [***yours,*** etc.] 私[あなた, など]の知ったことではない ▪ That is *no concernment of yours*. それは君の知ったことではない.

of concernment 重要な ▪ This is a matter *of* vital *concernment* to me. これは私にとっては死活に関するほど重要な問題です.

concert /kɑ́nsərt|kɔ́n-/ 名 ***by concert*** 申し合わせて, しめし合わせて ▪ The thing was done *by concert*. それは申し合わせてしたことだ.

in concert 一斉に; (…と)提携して (*with*) ▪ They cried *in concert*. 彼らは一斉に叫んだ ▪ France acted *in concert with* England. フランスはイングランドと提携して行動した.

up to concert pitch **1** 合奏調にまで ▪ The piano must be tuned *up to concert pitch*. ピアノは合奏調にせねばならない.

2 平常より少し馬力をかけて ▪ I'm tuned *up to concert pitch*, so let's get the interview over. 私は平常より少し馬力をかけているから, 会談をかたづけようではないか ▪ He screwed himself *up to concert pitch*. 彼は一段と勇気を奮い起こした.

conclave /kɑ́nkleɪv|kɔ́n-/ 名 ***be*** [***sit***] ***in conclave*** (***with***) (…と)密議している[する] ▪ The headmaster *sat in conclave with* the teachers. 校長は教師たちと密議した.

conclude /kənklúːd/ 動 ***To be concluded.*** 次回完結(連載物など) (→to be CONTINUEd).

conclusion /kənklúːʒən/ 名 ***arrive at a conclusion*** 結論に達する ▪ You'll *arrive at the conclusion* that he is honest. 彼は正直であるという結論にあなたは達するだろう.

at the conclusion of …の終わりに ▪ We took a vote *at the conclusion of* the debate. 我々は討論の末採決した.

bring ... to a conclusion …を終える ▪ We *brought* it *to a* satisfactory *conclusion*. 我々はそれを満足に終えた.

come to a conclusion **1** 結論に達する ▪ We have *come to the conclusion* that you are a good boy. 君は良い少年だという結論に達した.

2 終了する ▪ The debate *came to a conclusion* at noon. 討論は正午に終了した.

draw conclusions [***the conclusion***] 推断する, 思う ▪ You will *draw the conclusion* that he has very little money. 彼は金はほとんどないと君は思うだろう.

in conclusion 終わりに臨んで, 結論として ▪ I will say, *in conclusion*, that I am delighted with this meeting. 終わりに臨み本会は非常に愉快であったと申しあげます.

jump at [***to***] ***conclusions*** →JUMP[2].

leap to a conclusion →LEAP[2].

try conclusions with …と決戦を試みる, 優劣を競う ▪ Don't *try conclusions with* such a wealthy firm. そんな富裕な会社と決戦を試みてはいけません.

concord /kɑ́nkɔːrd|kɔ́n-/ 名 ***in concord*** 仲よく ▪ The people live *in concord*. その人々は互いに仲よく暮らしている.

concrete /kɑ́nkriːt|kɔ́nf-/ 名 ***be set*** [***embedded, cast***] ***in concrete*** **1** コンクリートうめにされている ▪ The skeleton *was* wrapped in a blanket and *set in concrete* six feet beneath the earth. その白骨は地下6フィートのところで毛布に包まれコンクリートうめになっていた.

2 (政策などが)固まっている, 変更不可能である ▪ No plan *is set in concrete*, and a decision to change it could be taken virtually at the last minute. 計画は固まっていないので, 変更するという決定がほとんど土壇場で起こる可能性もある.

in the concrete 具体的に[な] (↔ in the ABSTRACT) ▪ But *in the concrete* it is far otherwise. だが具体的にはそれは大いにちがう.

condemn /kəndém/ 動 ***be condemned to*** **1** …を宣告される ▪ The criminal *was condemned to* death. 犯人は死刑を宣告された.

2 …に運命づけられる ▪ He *was condemned to* a life of suffering. 彼は病苦の生活を送るよう運命づけられていた.

One's ***looks condemn*** *one.* …がしたとその顔に書いてある ▪ *His looks condemn* him. 彼がしたと顔に書いてある.

condemnation /kɑ̀ndemnéɪʃən|kɔ̀n-/ 名 *One's* ***own conduct is*** *one's* ***condemnation.*** その人の行為がその人の罪を決める.

the final condemnation of …に対する最終的非難の根拠 ▪ The absence of pity is *the final condemnation of* the literature of our time. 哀れみの欠如が現代文学に対する最終的非難の根拠だ.

condition[1] /kəndíʃən/ 名 ***be in (a) condition to*** *do* …できる状態にある, に耐える ▪ A ghost might *be in a condition to* take a chair. 幽霊はいすに座ることができるだろう ▪ The ship *is in condition to* put to sea. その船は航海に耐える.

(be) in good [bad, poor] condition 腐っていない[いる]; 健康である[ない]; 破損しないでいる[している] ▪ The eggs arrived *in good condition.* 卵は悪くならずに到着した.

be in no condition to *do* …できない状態である, に耐えない ▪ He *is in no condition to* travel. 彼は旅行できない状態である.

in a certain [an interesting, a delicate] condition 身ごもって, 妊娠して ▪ She is *in an interesting condition.* 彼女は妊娠している.

in [out of] condition 健康[不健康で]; 良好[不良]な状態で ▪ I'm *out of condition* now. 私は今は体の調子が良くない ▪ The baseball team will be *in condition.* その野球チームは良好な状態だろう.

in the [existing] conditions →under the CONDITIONs.

on no condition どんなことがあっても…ない ▪ You must *on no condition* tell him that. どんなことがあっても彼にそれを話してはならない.

on (the) condition (that) …という条件で, もし…ならば ▪ I was allowed to go swimming *on condition that* I kept near the other boys. 他の少年らのそばを離れないという条件で水泳に行くことを許された.

On what condition …? どういう条件で ▪ *On what condition* will you agree? どういう条件で君は同意しますか.

out of condition →in CONDITION.

out of condition to *do* …できない状態で ▪ Put them *out of condition to* keep the field. 彼らが戦闘を継続できない状態にしてやれ.

under [in] the [existing] conditions 現下の事情では ▪ It cannot be done *under existing conditions.* 現下の事情ではできない.

condition[2] /kəndíʃən/ 動 ***condition each other*** 互いに依存する ▪ Health and activity *condition each other.* 健康と活動は互いに依存する.

condition … to *do* …するように(動物など)を訓練する[しつける], (動物など)に…するという条件反射を起こさせる ▪ Pavlov *conditioned* his dog *to* salivate in anticipation of food when a bell rang. パブロフは犬にベルが鳴ったとき食事を期待して唾液が出るという条件反射を起こさせた.

conditional /kəndíʃənəl/ 形 ***conditional on [upon]*** …を条件としての, 次第で ▪ His term in prison is *conditional on* his behavior. 彼の入獄刑期は彼の行状次第だ.

conducive /kəndjúːsɪv/ 形 ***be conducive to*** …に役立つ, を助成する ▪ This sport *is conducive to* our physical development. このスポーツは我々の身体の発達に役立つ.

conduct[1] /kɑ́ndʌkt|kɔ́n-/ 名 *one's* ***line of conduct*** 人のふるまい, 行動 ▪ *His line of conduct* has been honorable. 彼の行動は立派であった.

conduct[2] /kəndʌ́kt/ 動 ***conduct*** *oneself* ふるまう, 身を処する ▪ The Emperor *conducted himself* with the greatest adroitness. 皇帝はきわめて手際よくふるまわれた.

confederate /kənfédərèɪt/ 動 ***confederate*** *oneself* ***with*** …と同盟する, 共謀する ▪ The French king has *confederated himself with* the great Turk. フランス王は偉大なトルコ王と同盟した.

conference /kɑ́nfərəns|kɔ́n-/ 名 ***a round-table conference*** 円卓会議《上座・下座がない円形のテーブルでの会合》 ▪ We need to sit down at *a round table conference* to discuss the problems and find lasting solutions to them. 我々は円卓会議に出席してその問題を議論し永続的な解決策を探る必要がある.

hold a conference 会議をする ▪ They *held a conference* about it. 彼らはそれについて会議をした.

in conference 会議中で ▪ The director of this school is *in conference* now. 校長は今会議中だ.

confess /kənfés/ 動 ***be confessed of*** 司祭に告白して(罪)をゆるされる ▪ You *were* not *confessed of* one sin. 君が告白して許されていない一つの罪がある.

I confess 《口》実は…なのだ ▪ *I confess* I was surprised at it. 実はそれに驚いたのだ.

stand confessed …であることが明白である; 正体を現す ▪ Throwing off his disguise, the paladin *stood confessed.* 偽装を脱ぎ捨てて, 騎士は正体を現した ▪ She *stood confessed* as a girl. 彼女が(少年でなく)少女であることがわかった.

to confess the truth 実のところ ▪ *To confess the truth,* it had been forgotten. 本当のことを言うと, それは忘れられていた.

confession /kənféʃən/ 名 ***go to confession*** 《宗》(悔悟者が司祭に)告白に行く ▪ She is so good a Catholic and *goes to confession* regularly. 彼女はとても熱心なカトリック信者できちんと告白に行く.

hear confession(s) (司祭が)告白を聞く ▪ The priest *hears confessions* in Italian. その司祭はイタリア語でざんげを聞く.

make a confession 白状[ざんげ]する ▪ The accused man *made a* full *confession.* 被告はすっかり白状した.

(Open) confession is good for the soul. 《諺》何か過ちを犯したときには, それを正直に言えば気分が楽になる.

confidence /kɑ́nfədəns|kɔ́n-/ 名 ***a con(fidence) game [trick]*** →a con TRICK, play a CONFIDENCE trick on a person.

admit *a person* ***into*** *one's* ***confidence*** 人を腹心の友とする, 人と打ち明けてつき合う ▪ If there be such, I will *admit* him *into my confidence.* もしそのような人がいたら腹心の友としよう.

give *one's* ***confidence to*** …を信頼する ▪ I *give my confidence to* him. 彼を信頼する.

have [place, put] (*one's****) confidence in*** …を信頼する, 信じる ▪ *Have* you any *confidence* *in* these reports? 君はこれらの報道を信じるか.

***have* (*the*) *confidence to* do** …する自信がある; 大胆にも…する, 厚かましくも…する ▪ They *had* no *confidence to* meet the English in the field. 彼らは戦場で英軍にまみえる自信はなかった ▪ He *had the confidence to* say so. 彼は図々しくそう言った.

in confidence 内緒で, 秘密に ▪ She told me *in* strict *confidence* that Mr. Brown drank too much. ブラウン氏は酒を飲みすぎると彼女は絶対内緒で私に話した.

in *a person's* ***confidence*** 人の秘密にあずかって, 人に信任されて ▪ I am *in his confidence.* 私は彼の秘密にあずかっている.

make a confidence to …に打ち明ける ▪ The boy *made a confidence to* his mother. 少年は母親に打ち明けた.

place [***put***] (*one's*) ***confidence in*** → have (one's) CONFIDENCE in.

play a confidence trick on *a person* 人に信用詐欺を働く ▪ I realized later that the "salesman" had *played a confidence trick on* me. セールスマンを装った男は私に信用詐欺を働いていたことが, のちほど判明した.

take *a person* ***into*** *one's* ***confidence*** 人に秘密を打ち明ける ▪ He *took* a friend *into his confidence* concerning the matter. その件について友人にこっそり打ち明けた.

with confidence 安心して; 自信[確信]をもって; 大胆不敵にも ▪ I waited *with confidence.* 私は安心して待った.

confident /kɑ́nfədənt|kɔ́n-/ 形 ***confident in*** …に自信があって; を信頼して ▪ He was *confident in* the security of his position. 自分の地位の安全性に自信があった ▪ The commander was *confident in* his own troops. 司令官は自分の軍隊を信頼していた.

confident of …を確信して ▪ He was *confident of* victory. 彼は勝利を確信していた.

confidential /kɑ̀nfədénʃəl|kɔ̀n-/ 形 ***become confidential with*** …に打ち解ける, 打ち明け話をする ▪ Don't *become confidential with* strangers. 知らぬ人に打ち解けてはいかん.

confine[1] /kɑ́nfaɪn|kɔ́n-/ 名 ***between the confines of*** …の境に ▪ I ventured into the forest *between the confines of* night and day. 昼夜の境に危険を冒して密林に分け入った.

beyond the confines of …の限界を越えて ▪ A U.S. marshal can operate *beyond the confines of* the county. 米国の執行官は郡の外でも行動できる.

on the confines of …の境に; に瀕して ▪ He is now *on the confines of* death. 彼は今や死に瀕している ▪ He found himself *on the confines of* a mystery. 彼は自分が神秘の境にいるのを知った.

within the confines of …の限界内で[に] ▪ He worked only *within the confines of* the country. 彼は国内でだけ働いた.

confine[2] /kənfáɪn/ 動 ***be confined of*** (*a child*) お産をする ▪ She *was confined of* her first child. 彼女は初産をした.

be confined to **1** …に引き[閉じ]こもる ▪ He *was confined to* his room. 彼は部屋に閉じこもった.
2 …に限定される (→CONFINE oneself to) ▪ Road travel should *be confined to* daylight hours. 陸路の移動は昼間だけにすべきだ.

confine *oneself* ***to*** …に限定する, だけにとどめる ▪ He *confined himself to* a few remarks. 彼は少し述べただけでやめた.

confinement /kənfáɪnmənt/ 名 ***be placed under confinement*** 監禁される ▪ He *was placed under confinement.* 彼は監禁された.

in (***solitary***) ***confinement*** (一人)監禁されて ▪ The prisoner had been kept *in solitary confinement* for over a year. 囚人は1年以上も一人監禁されていたのだった.

confirmation /kɑ̀nfərméɪʃən|kɔ̀n-/ 名 ***in confirmation of*** …の確証として ▪ State something *in confirmation of* the report. その報の確証として何か述べなさい.

conflict /kɑ́nflɪkt|kɔ́n-/ 名 ***come into*** [***be in***] ***conflict with*** …と衝突する[している]; と戦う[戦っている] ▪ It *is in conflict with* the provisions of the existing treaties. それは現行条約の条項に抵触している ▪ The Japanese *were in conflict with* the Russians. 日本軍はロシア軍と戦っていた.

in conflict (…と)対立[衝突]して, 矛盾して (*with*) ▪ Brutus and Cassius are *in conflict with* each other. ブルートゥスとカシウスは互いに対立している.

conform /kənfɔ́ːrm/ 動 ***conform*** *oneself* ***to*** …に従う, 順応する ▪ We have to *conform ourselves to* the customs of society. 我々は社会の慣習に従わねばならない ▪ I will *conform myself to* the prevailing taste. 当世流行の趣味に順応します ▪ Don't *be conformed to* this world. この世の俗事に慣れてしまわないようにしなさい.

conformable /kənfɔ́ːrməbəl/ 形 ***conformable to*** **1** …に適当な, 一致して, 調和して ▪ The parts must be *conformable to* the whole. 部分は全体と調和しなければならない.
2 …に従順な ▪ You are *conformable to* the King's wishes. あなたは王の願望によく従う.

conformity /kənfɔ́ːrməti/ 名 ***in conformity with*** [***to***] …に従って, 合って ▪ It is *in conformity with* custom. それは習慣に合っている.

confound /kənfáʊnd|kɔ̀n-/ 動 ***be confounded at*** [***by***] …に狼狽する ▪ I *was confounded by* the sight. それを見て狼狽した.

confound the prophets [***critics***] 他人の予言[警告]に反してうまくいく ▪ This festival, *confounding the critics*, drew many visitors. この祭りは人々の批判に反して多くの客を集めた.

(***God***) ***confound!***/***Confound it*** [***him,*** etc.]***!*** ちぇっ!, くそいまいましい!, ちきしょう!

confront /kənfrʌ́nt/ 動 ***be confronted by***

…が目前に迫る, に直面する ▪ He *is confronted by* the event. そのことが彼の目前に迫っている.

be confronted with **1** …と対決させられる ▪ The prisoner *was confronted with* his accusers [the evidence of his guilt]. 囚人は告訴者たちと対決させられた[犯罪の証拠をつきつけられた].

2 …に直面する ▪ He *is confronted with* a difficulty. 困難に直面している.

confuse /kənfjúːz/ 動 ***be*** [***become, get***] ***confused*** (***by***) (…に心が)混乱する, (人が)あわてる ▪ He *was* utterly *confused by* his blunder. 彼は自分のしくじりにすっかりあわてた.

confusion /kənfjúːʒən/ 名 ***confusion worse confounded*** 混乱の上にもまた混乱 (Milton, *Paradise Lost* 2. 996) ▪ They made *confusion worse confounded.* 彼らは混乱の上にも混乱を重ねた ▪ The house was *confusion worse confounded.* その家はいやが上にも混乱していた.

covered with [***in***] ***confusion*** どぎまぎして, あわてふためいて (《聖》 *Jer.* 3. 25) ▪ She flushed deeply and was *covered with confusion.* 彼女はまっかになりあわてふためいた.

drink confusion to …をのろって[恨みの]杯をあげる ▪ I will *drink confusion to* him. 彼に対してのろいの杯をあげよう.

in confusion 混乱して; 狼狽して ▪ Everything was *in confusion.* 万事が混乱していた ▪ They fled *in confusion.* 彼らはうろたえて逃げた.

throw ... into confusion …を狼狽させる; 混乱させる ▪ He *was thrown into confusion.* 彼は狼狽した.

conge /koʊnʒéɪ|kɔ́nʒeɪ/ 名 ***get*** *one's* ***conge from*** …を免職になる ▪ I *got my conge from* the whipper-in. 私は猟犬係を免職になった.

give *a person his* ***conge*** 人を免職する ▪ He'll *give* me *my conge* soon. 彼はやがて私を免職するだろう.

congenial /kəndʒíːniəl/ 形 ***congenial to*** **1** …に気心の合う ▪ Few people were *congenial to* him. 彼と気心の合う人は少なかった.

2 …の性分に合う, に適した ▪ The work is *congenial to* him. その仕事は彼の性分に合う.

congratulate /kəngrǽtʃəlèɪt|-grǽtʃu-/ 動 ***congratulate*** *oneself* ***on*** …を喜ぶ ▪ I *congratulate myself on* my escape. あやういところを免れてまあよかった.

congratulation /kəngrӕtʃəl|-grӕtʃu-/ 名 ***offer*** [***accept***] *one's* ***congratulations on*** …についての祝辞を述べる[受ける] ▪ Please *accept my congratulations on* your recovery. ご全快をお祝い申しあげます ▪ I *offer my congratulations on* your success. ご成功をお祝い申しあげます.

congruous /káŋgruəs|kɔ́ŋ-/ 形 ***congruous with*** [***to***] …と合致する, に適合する, つり合う ▪ It is all *congruous with* the system. それは全くその制度と合致する.

conjecture /kəndʒéktʃər/ 名 ***hazard a conjecture*** あてずっぽうを言ってみる《大げさな言い方》 ▪ I'll *hazard a conjecture* that your daughter is at the cinema. 娘さんは映画に行っているのではないかな.

conjunction /kəndʒʌ́ŋkʃən/ 名 ***in conjunction with*** …と連合して, 共に; に加えて ▪ The President must act *in conjunction with* the court of directors. 社長は重役会と協力せねばならない ▪ Your story *in conjunction with* what I already know, fills me with fear. あなたの話は私が既に知っていることに加えて, 私をひどく心配させます.

conjuncture /kəndʒʌ́ŋktʃər/ 名 ***at*** [***in***] ***this conjuncture*** この際 ▪ It is helpful *at this* critical *conjuncture.* この危急の際にそれは役に立つ.

conjure[1] /kándʒər|kʌ́n-/ 動 ***a name to conjure with*** **1** まじないに用いる名; 有力な名 ▪ The President has permitted you to use his name! Well, that's *a name to conjure with.* 大統領が君に名前を使わせてくれるって! ほんとに, それこそ大きな力のある名前だよ.

2 変わった[奇妙な]名前 ▪ The young woman had *a name to conjure with*: Guadalcanal. その若い女性はグァダルカナルという変わった名だった.

conjure[2] /kándʒər|kʌ́n-/ 動 ***conjure*** *a person* ***by God*** [etc.] ***to*** *do* 折り入って…するよう頼む ▪ I *conjure* you *by all that is holy to* desist. 後生だからよしておくれ.

connect /kənékt/ 動 ***be connected with*** **1** …と親類関係がある, の関係者である ▪ He *is connected with* the Adams by marriage. 彼は結婚によりアダムズ家と姻戚関係がある ▪ He *is connected with* the firm. 彼はその会社の関係者だ.

2 …と関連[関係]している ▪ Many traditions *are connected with* the sea. 海に関連する伝説は多い.

be well connected 親類筋がよい ▪ They *are* of good stock and *well connected.* 彼らは家柄もよく, 親類筋もよい.

connect *oneself* ***with*** …に関係する ▪ He has *connected himself with* the firm. 彼はその会社の社員になった.

connect with the ball 《球技》ボールを打つ[蹴る] ▪ She *connected with the ball* for a base hit to drive home Northridge's first run. 彼女は安打を打ってノースリッジの最初の得点を入れた ▪ Martin *connected with the ball*, but the Bears' left fielder snagged it to end the game. マーティンは打球をとばしたがベアーズの左翼手が捕球し試合終了になった ▪ When I *connected with the ball* and heard the noise it made I knew straight away that it was a goal. 私はボールを蹴ってそれが立てる音を聞いたときゴールだとすぐにわかった.

only connect 「つながりをつける」《事実・経験・出来事などをつないである意味を見出す; 自他のつながりをつけて理解を深める, などの標語》 ▪ "*Only connect*" is the motto of Mr. Thomas's studies. 「つながりをつける」というのがトマス氏の研究のモットーである.

connection /kənékʃən/ 名 ***form a connec-***

C

tion 関係ができる, 友人ができる; 縁続きになる; (男女が)親密になる ▪ He *formed* useful *connections.* 彼は有力なコネを作った.

have* (*a*) *connection with …と関係がある ▪ What *connection* do you *have with* his being late? 君は彼の遅刻とどんな関係があるのか.

in connection with …に関連[連絡]して ▪ The trains from London to Dover run *in connection with* the steamers to Calais. ロンドンからドーバーへの列車はカレー行きの汽船と連絡して運転している ▪ I must say a few words *in connection with* this subject. この問題に関して少し言わねばならない.

in the same* [*another*] *connection 同じ[別の]ことに関して ▪ The same argument was stated *in the same connection.* 同じことに関して同様の議論がなされた.

in this connection この点について; ついでながら ▪ One fact, *in this connection*, is clear. この点については一つの事実が明らかである ▪ *In this connection* he never drinks. ちなみに, 彼は禁酒家である.

***make connection*(*s*) (*at*)** (…で)連絡[接続]する ▪ The train *makes connection* with the steamer *at* Dover. その電車はドーバーで汽船と連絡する ▪ I *made* train *connections.* 電車の乗り換えをした.

miss *one's* ***connection*** 連絡の電車などに乗りおくれる ▪ I *missed my connection.* 連絡の電車に乗りそこねた.

conniption /kənípʃən/ 名 ***have a conniption fit*** 《米》(…に)かんしゃく[ヒステリー]を起こす (*about, over*) ▪ Democrat senators *had a conniption fit over* Bush's "surge". 民主党の上院議員らはブッシュ氏の「増派」に堪忍袋の緒が切れた.

connivance /kənáɪvəns/ 名 ***by connivance of*** …の得心ずくで ▪ It was done *by connivance of* the owner. それは所有者の得心ずくでなされた.

with the connivance of …の黙許により ▪ The thing was done *with the connivance of* the principal. それは校長が黙許してさせたのだ.

conquer /káŋkər|kɔ́ŋ-/ 動 ***stoop to conquer*** →STOOP.

to conquer or to die 死ぬまで戦う ▪ We were *to conquer or to die.* 決死の戦いをする覚悟だった.

conquest /kánkwest|kɔ́ŋ-/ 名 ***make a conquest* (*of*)** (…を)征服する; (女性を)なびかせる ▪ It *made a conquest of* her heart at once. それはすぐに彼女の心を征服した ▪ We shall *be made a conquest of* by the state. 我々はその国に征服されよう.

conscience /kánʃəns | kɔ́n-/ 名 ***a bad* [*guilty*] *conscience*** やましい心 ▪ That argues *a bad conscience.* それは心のやましい証拠である ▪ *A guilty conscience* needs no accuser. 《諺》心がやましければ責める人がなくても苦しむ.

a good* [*clean, clear*] *conscience 清純な[やましくない]心; 安らかな心 ▪ *A good conscience* is a continual feast. 《諺》心にやましさがないとたえず楽しい.

by* [*in, on, o'*] *my conscience 本当に ▪ *In my conscience*, sir, I do not care for you. 本当のところ, あなたは好きでありません.

clear* [*salve, square*]** *one's* ***conscience 気がすむようにする, 気のとがめを安める ▪ I *clear my conscience*; the name of liquor for you is death. 言わねば気がすまぬから言うが, お前にとっては酒という名は死と同じなのだよ[酒は命取りになるぞ].

Conscience does make* [*makes*] *cowards of us all. 《諺》良心は我らすべてを臆病者にする.

ease *a person's* ***conscience*** 人を安心させる, 人の気を楽にさせる ▪ It *eased my conscience* to know that everyone was safe. みんな無事だと知って私は安心した.

for conscience*(') *sake 良心を安んじるため, 気休めに; 良心がとがめて; 後生だから ▪ You will suffer *for conscience sake.* 君は良心がとがめて苦しむだろう ▪ He did it *for conscience sake.* 彼は良心を安んじるためにそうした.

have a good* [*bad*] *conscience やましいところがない[うしろめたい] ▪ I *have a bad conscience.* 私はうしろめたい.

have a sin on *one's* ***conscience*** 気がすまぬことがある ▪ I *have a sin on my conscience.* 私は気がすまぬことがある.

have ... on *one's* ***conscience*** (あること)に気がとがめる ▪ The king *had* something *on his conscience.* 国王は気がとがめることがあった.

have the conscience to *do* 厚かましくも…する, …しても良心がとがめない ▪ He *had the conscience to* ask me the question. 彼は厚かましくも私にその質問をした ▪ How do you *have the conscience to* demand such a price? 君はそんな値段を要求して, よくも良心がとがめないね.

in* (*all*) *conscience 《口》**1** 道理上, 良心に顧みて ▪ The seller is bound *in conscience* to do so. 売り手は道義上そうしなくてはならない ▪ I can't, *in conscience*, do such a thing. 私は良心に顧みてそんなことはできない.

2 確かに ▪ He took long enough *in all conscience.* ほんとに彼は長くかかった.

in* [*on, o'*] *my conscience → by my CONSCIENCE.

make a conscience of *doing* ぜひ…することにする ▪ You should *make a conscience of taking* exercise. 必ず運動をすべきである.

make ... a matter of conscience …を良心的に処理する ▪ We must *make* it *a matter of conscience.* それを良心的に扱わねばならない.

my conscience! おやまあ!, とんでもない!, ちぇっ! 《驚き・反ばく・困惑を表す》 ▪ Return, sir?—*My conscience*, no. 往復(切符)ですか—いや, とんでもない ▪ *My conscience!*—It's impossible! これは驚いた—そいつは不可能だ.

prick *a person's* ***conscience*** 人に良心の呵責を感じさせる ▪ There will be attempts to *prick the enemy's conscience* by making him doubtful of the justice of his cause. 敵に彼の大義の正当性に疑

問を抱かせることによって良心の呵責を感じさせるという試みがなされるだろう.

salve [***square***] *one's* ***conscience*** → clear one's CONSCIENCE.

speak *one's* ***conscience*** 心の中を話す, 自分の考えていることを話す ▪ I can no longer be quiet but must *speak my conscience* to you. 私はもう黙っておられず, 思うところをどうしても君に話したい.

upon *one's* ***conscience*** 良心にかけて(誓う); 本当のところ ▪ Tell me, *upon your conscience*, is Tom your brother? 本当のところを教えてください, トムはあなたの弟ですか.

with an easy [***a good, a safe***] ***conscience*** やましい心なく, 安心して ▪ You may do it *with a good conscience*. 安心してそうしてよろしい.

conscious /kάnʃəs|kɔ́n-/ 形 ***be conscious*** (***to*** *oneself*) ***of*** …を(内心に)意識する, に気づく ▪ I *was conscious* (*to myself*) *of* having done everything in my power. 力の及ぶかぎりを尽くしたことを意識していた.

consecrate /kάnsəkrèɪt|kɔ́n-/ 動 ***consecrate*** *one's* ***life*** [*oneself*] ***to*** …に一生をささげる ▪ He has *consecrated his life to* the cause of education. 彼は教育のために一生をささげた.

consent[1] /kənsént/ 名 ***by common*** [***general***] ***consent*** 全員一致で, 満場一致で ▪ He was chosen leader *by general consent*. 彼は全員一致で指導者に選ばれた.

Silence gives consent. →SILENCE.

the age of consent 《法》承諾年齢《結婚などを承諾しうる年齢》 ▪ *The* present *age of consent*, which is thirteen, is altogether too low. 現在の承諾年齢は13歳だが全く低すぎる.

with [***by***] ***one consent*** 異口同音に, 満場一致で ▪ They *with one consent* began to make excuses. 彼らは異口同音に言い訳をし始めた ▪ People seem *by one consent* to open their hearts freely. 人々は申し合わせたように, 自由に心を開くように思える.

consent[2] /kənsént/ 動 ***consent to*** (*do, doing*) (…すること)に同意する, 賛成する, 承諾する ▪ I *consented to* the proposal. その提案に賛成した ▪ He *consented to* divide [*dividing*] his army. 彼は自分の軍隊を分割することに賛成した.

consentaneous /kὰnsentéɪniəs/ 形 ***consentaneous to*** [***with***] …に一致した, かなった ▪ It is *consentaneous to* reason. それは道理にかなっている ▪ It is *consentaneous with* his opinion. それは彼の意見に一致している.

consequence /kάnsəkwèns|kɔ́nsɪkwəns/ 名 ***an air of consequence*** 偉そうな態度 ▪ He gives himself *an air of consequence*. 彼は偉そうにする.

answer for the consequences 結果に責任を負う ▪ I will *answer for the consequences*. 結果に責任を負います.

in consequence したがって, その結果 ▪ I do not know what took place *in consequence*. その結果起こったことは知らない ▪ The water has *in consequence* a strong acid taste. したがってその水はひどく酸っぱい味がします.

in consequence of …の結果として, のゆえに ▪ I cannot start out *in consequence of* his sudden illness. 私は彼の急病のため出発できない.

of consequence 重大な ▪ He is a man *of consequence* in his own village. 彼は自分の村では重要な人物だ.

of little [***no***] ***consequence*** ほとんど[全く]取るに足りない, ささいな ▪ It is *of little consequence* to me. 私にとってはほとんど取るに足りない.

take the consequences 報いを受ける, 結果を甘受する ▪ If you act so foolishly, you must *take the consequences*. そんなばかな行動をすれば, その報いを受けねばならない.

consequent /kάnsəkwènt|kɔ́nsɪkwənt/ 形 ***consequent on*** [***upon, to***] …の結果起こる, に必然の ▪ This is the financial embarrassment *consequent on* the war. これは戦争の結果起こった財政難である.

consequential /kὰnsɪkwénʃəl|kɔ̀n-/ 形 ***consequential on*** [***upon***] …の推論[結論]として起こる ▪ They placed a motion *consequential upon* the resolution. 彼らはその決議の結論として起こる動議を提出した.

consider /kənsídər/ 動 ***all things considered*** すべてを考えてみると ▪ *All things considered*, I think it is most advisable for you to see him. すべてを考えてみると, あなたが彼に会うのが一番賢明であると思う.

considerable /kənsídərəbəl/ 形名 (***a***) ***considerable of*** 《米》**1** かなり多量[多数]の ▪ He lost (*a*) *considerable of* wheat and Indian corn. 彼はかなり多量の小麦とトウモロコシを失った.

2 相当大きな ▪ *Considerable of* a shock from an earthquake was felt in Boston. 相当大きな地震がボストンで感じられた.

3 (人が)相当偉い ▪ I was *considerable of* a performer at one time. 私は一時は相当な役者であった.

by considerable 《米》大いに ▪ It is inferior *by considerable*. それは大いに劣る.

considerate /kənsídərət/ 形 ***be considerate of*** [***about***] …に対して思いやりがある ▪ You should *be considerate of* other people. 他人に対して思いやりがなければならない.

consideration /kənsìdəréɪʃən/ 名 ***for a consideration*** **1** 心うけ程度の(わずかな)金で ▪ He sold it *for a consideration*. 彼はわずかな金でそれを売った.

2 報酬をもらって[もらえば] ▪ He would do anything *for a consideration*. 彼は報酬をもらえばどんなことでもするだろう.

have consideration for …を重んじる ▪ He *has* no *consideration for* others' feelings. 彼は他人の感情を重んじない.

in consideration of **1** …の報酬[返礼]として ▪ He fell to diving into the sea *in consideration of* ten shillings. 彼は10シリングの返礼として，海中にもぐり始めた ▪ We gave him 10 pounds *in consideration of* his labors. 骨折りの報酬として10ポンド彼に与えた.
2 …を考慮して，のため ▪ *In consideration of* his youth, he was acquitted. 若年のため，彼は無罪放免された.

leave … out of consideration …を考慮[計算]に入れない ▪ We *left* the distance *out of consideration*. 我々は距離は度外視した.

of consideration 重要な ▪ Nothing in this world is *of* any *consideration* in comparison with eternity. 永遠と比べればこの世に重要なものは一つもない ▪ It's *of* no *consideration* at all. それは少しも重要ではない.

on [***under***] ***no consideration*** 決して…ない，どうしても…ない ▪ *On no consideration* can I consent. どうしても承諾できない.

out of consideration for …を考慮して，に免じて ▪ *Out of consideration for* his old age, we decided to take a car instead of walking. 彼の老齢を思いやって，私たちは歩かないで車に乗ることに決めた.

take … into consideration …を考慮に入れる，酌量する ▪ The teacher *took* the fact *into consideration*. 先生はそのことを考慮に入れた ▪ We must *take* his youth *into consideration*. 我々は彼の若年であることを酌量せねばならない.

under consideration 考慮中で ▪ The proposals are still *under consideration*. その提案はまだ考究中である ▪ The Club had it *under consideration* whether they should continue their session. クラブは会議を続けるべきかどうかを考究していた.

under no consideration →on no CONSIDERATION.

consignation /kɑ̀nsaɪnéɪʃən|-sɪg-/ 名 ***to the consignation of*** (人・所)あてに[の] ▪ We have shipped the said goods *to your consignation* [*the consignation of* Nice]. 上記の貨物は貴台[ニース]あてに積み出しました.

consignment /kənsáɪnmənt/ 名 ***on consignment*** 委託販売で ▪ We shipped goods *on consignment*. 当店は商品を委託販売で積み出した.

to the consignment of = to the CONSIGNATION of.

consistent /kənsístənt/ 形 (***be***) ***consistent with*** …と両立する，と一致する ▪ Noise *is* not *consistent with* serious study. 騒音は真剣な勉強と両立しない ▪ It *is consistent with* reason. それは道理にかなっている.

console /kənsóʊl/ 動 ***console*** *oneself* ***by*** [***with***] …で自ら慰める ▪ She *consoled herself with* the thought of her noble birth. 彼女は高貴の生まれであることを考えて自ら慰めた.

consonance /kɑ́nsənəns|kɔ́n-/ 名 ***in consonance with*** …と一致して，に従って ▪ He acted *in consonance with* the requirements of the occasion. 彼は時宜(じぎ)に応じて取り計らった.

out of consonance with …と一致[調和]しないで ▪ Her angry vehemence was *out of consonance with* her ordinary serenity. 彼女の怒りの激しさは平素の落ち着きに似合わなかった.

consonant /kɑ́nsənənt|kɔ́n-/ 形 ***consonant with*** …と調和[一致]して ▪ His actions are *consonant with* his beliefs. 彼の行動は信念と一致している.

consort[1] /kɑ́nsɔːrt|kɔ́n-/ 名 ***in consort*** いっしょに ▪ They came *in consort*. 彼らは連れだって来た.

consort[2] /kənsɔ́ːrt/ 動 ***be consorted with*** …といっしょにされる ▪ Marxism *is* often *consorted with* communism in popular language. マルクス主義はよく共産主義といっしょにされる.

conspicuous /kənspíkjuəs/ 形 ***conspicuous by*** *one's* ***absence*** ないのでかえって目立つ ▪ At her funeral the images of Brutus and Cassius were *conspicuous by their absence*. 彼女の葬儀には，ブルートゥスとカシウスの姿が見えなかったのがかえって目立った. ☞この考えの起源は Tacitus, *Annals* 3 にある.

cut a conspicuous figure 異彩を放つ ▪ He *cut a conspicuous figure*. 彼は異彩を放った.

make *oneself* ***conspicuous*** 異様にふるまう; 目立つような(きざな)事をする ▪ He *made himself conspicuous* at the meeting. 彼はその会で異様なふるまいをした.

conspiracy /kənspírəsi/ 名 ***a conspiracy of silence*** 沈黙の共謀，黙殺[もみ消し]の口裏合わせ ▪ It seemed to me for a long time that there was *a conspiracy of silence* about nuclear weapons. 核兵器に関して沈黙の共謀があったと私にはずっと以前から思われていた.

in conspiracy **1** 共謀して，徒党を組んで ▪ They are *in conspiracy* against the policy of the government. 彼らは政府の政策に共謀して反対している.
2 協力[協調]して ▪ All that is great works *in* close *conspiracy*. 偉大なものはすべて緊密に協調して働く.

constable /kɑ́nstəbəl|kʌ́n-/ 名 ***outrun*** [***overrun***] ***the constable*** **1** 使いすぎて借金をする ▪ I've *outrun the constable* this quarter. 私はこの四半期は使いすぎて借金をした.
2 あまりにも早足で行く，あまりにも遠くへ行く; 度を過ごす ▪ His nag will *outrun the constable*. 彼の馬はあまりにも早足で行くだろう ▪ You have *outrun the constable* at last. 君はとうとう度を過ごした.
3 巡査[法律]から逃げる ▪ He was obliged to *outrun the constable*. 彼はやむなく巡査から逃げねばならなかった.

pay the constable 勘定を払う ▪ Who is to *pay the constable*? 誰が勘定を払うのか.

consternation /kɑ̀nstərnéɪʃən|kɔ̀n-/ 名 ***in consternation*** 胆をつぶして; 狼狽して ▪ They fled *in consternation.* 彼らはあわてて逃げた.

throw ... into consternation …を仰天させる ▪ The news *threw* me *into consternation.* そのニュースに私は胆をつぶした.

constitution /kɑ̀nstətjúːʃən|kɔ̀n-/ 名 ***by constitution*** 生まれつき ▪ He was fragile *by constitution* and died in the prime of life. 生まれつき虚弱だったので彼は人生の盛りに死んだ.

have a cold [good] constitution 冷え性である[体格が良い] ▪ He *has a good constitution.* 彼は体格が良い.

have the constitution of an ox (雄牛のように)とても丈夫である ▪ I never get sick. I *have the constitution of an ox.* 私は病気になったことがない. 雄牛並に丈夫なのだ.

constitutional /kɑ̀nstətjúːʃənəl|kɔ̀n-/ 名 ***take a [one's] constitutional*** 《口》健康のための散歩[運動]をする ▪ I saw Tom *taking a constitutional.* トムが健康のための散歩をしているのを見た. ☞《英大学》より.

constrain /kənstréɪn/ 動 ***be constrained to do*** やむなく[余儀なく]…する ▪ I *am constrained to* decline. やむなくお断りします.

feel constrained …せざるをえないと思う (*to do*); 窮屈な思いをする ▪ I *feel constrained to* ask you to forgive me. あなたに許しを請わねばならぬと思います ▪ He *felt constrained.* 彼は窮屈な思いをした.

constraint /kənstréɪnt/ 名 ***by constraint*** 無理に, 強いて ▪ This is an expression used *by constraint.* これは無理に使われた言葉だ.

feel constraint 窮屈に感じる, 窮屈な様子を見せる ▪ I *feel constraint* in his presence. 私は彼の前へ出ると窮屈に感じる.

under [in] constraint 強いられて; 束縛されて ▪ I don't like to act *under constraint.* 私は強いられて行動するのはきらいだ.

without constraint 遠慮なく ▪ He writes to me *without constraint.* 彼は遠慮なく手紙をよこす.

construction /kənstrʌ́kʃən/ 名 ***bear a construction*** (ある)解釈を許す, 意味を持つ ▪ The sentence does not *bear* such *a construction.* その文はそのようには解釈できない.

put a bad [good, false, wrong] construction on …を悪く[良く, 曲げて, 誤って]解釈する ▪ He always *puts a bad construction on* my remarks. 彼はいつも私の言うことを悪く取る ▪ He *put a false construction on* my actions. 彼は私の行動を曲解した.

put [place] a construction on …を解釈する, (ある)意味にとる ▪ You *put* such *a construction on* my words. 君は私の言葉をそんな意味に取った.

under [in course of] construction 建設中 ▪ The new railway is still *in course of construction.* 新しい鉄道はまだ建設中です ▪ We have several new warships *under construction.* 新戦艦数隻を建造中である.

consult /kənsʌ́lt/ 動 ***consult (with) one's pillow*** →PILLOW.

consultation /kɑ̀nsəltéɪʃən|kɔ̀n-/ 名 ***a hand-on-the-doorknob consultation*** ドアノブに手をかけた相談, 退室時の医療相談《診察を終えた患者が退室の間際に勃起不全など言いだしにくかった別の症状を訴えること》 ▪ One typical example, in men, is known as the "*hand on the doorknob*" *consultation.* 男性の場合, 典型的な例は退室時の相談として知られている.

consume /kənsjúːm/ 動 ***be consumed with*** すっかり…のとりこになる ▪ He *is consumed with* envy [excitement]. 彼はすっかりねたみのとりこになっている[興奮して夢中になっている].

consummate /kənsʌ́mət/ 動 ***consummate a [one's] marriage*** 結婚式をすませて床入りをする ▪ He *consummated his marriage* with the princess that day. 彼はその日王女と結婚式をすませて床入りをした.

consummation /kɑ̀nsəméɪʃən|kɔ̀n-/ 名 ***the consummation of the world [of all things]*** 世の[万物の]終極, 終えん ▪ He will be with you even to *the* very *consummation of the world.* 彼は世の終えんに至るまでもあなたと共にいるであろう.

consumption /kənsʌ́mpʃən/ 名 ***for public consumption*** (情報・娯楽などが)大衆のための ▪ That's not the sort of information that is meant *for public consumption.* それは大衆向きの類の情報ではない.

contact /kɑ́ntækt|kɔ́n-/ 名 ***be in contact with*** …と接触している; と近しくしている ▪ Our troops *are in contact with* the enemy. わが軍は敵と接触している.

break contact (電流を)断つ ▪ We make contact and then *break contact.* 我々は電流をつなぎ, それからそれを断つ.

bring A into contact with B AをBと接触させる ▪ If you *bring* fire *into contact with* gunpowder, there will be an explosion. 火を火薬に接触させれば爆発が起こる ▪ We can learn much by *being brought into contact with* other minds. 他人の心と接触することによって多くを学ぶことができる.

come in [into] contact with …と会う, 交わる ▪ He *comes in contact with* all types of men. 彼はあらゆるタイプの人たちと交わる ▪ A rope *came into contact with* some electric wires. ロープが電線と接触した.

establish one's contact with …と接触する, と連絡を取る ▪ He *established his contact with* us. 彼は我々と連絡を取った.

get in contact (with) (…と)会う; (…と)連絡する ▪ I am glad we have *got in contact.* お会いしてうれしいです.

make contact (電流を)つなぐ; 接触する (*with*) ▪ If I *make contact with* the battery, they are attracted at once. もし電流線を電池とつなげば, それらはすぐに引きつけられる ▪ I've been trying to *make* *contact with* them. 私はずっと彼らと接触しようとしてきた.

contain /kəntéɪn/ 動 ***contain*** *oneself* 自制する, がまんする ▪ He could not *contain himself* for joy. 彼はうれしくてじっとして[黙って]いられなかった ▪ Let them *contain themselves* and quit themselves like men. 彼らは自制して男らしく行動すべきだ.

contemplation /kɑ̀ntəmpléɪʃən|kɔ̀n-/ 名 ***have ... in contemplation*** ...をもくろんでいる, 計画している ▪ He *has* a new school *in contemplation.* 彼は新しい学校を計画中である.

in contemplation **1** もくろんで, 計画して ▪ A new school is *in contemplation.* 新しい学校設立が計画中である.

2 ...を予期して (*of*) ▪ They were executed *in contemplation of* careful perusal. それらは入念な精読を予期して仕上げられたものである.

3 黙想して ▪ He sat there deep *in contemplation.* 彼はそこに座って沈思黙考していた.

lost [***sunk***] ***in contemplation*** 黙想にふけって ▪ He was *lost in contemplation.* 彼は黙想にふけっていた.

under contemplation = in CONTEMPLATION 1.

contemplative /kəntémplətɪv/ 形 ***contemplative of*** **1** ...を凝視して ▪ They were *contemplative of* the mud. 彼らはその泥を見つめていた.

2 ...を熟考して ▪ They are plainly *contemplative of* a contingency. 彼らは明らかに万一の場合を考慮しているのだ.

contemporary /kəntémpərèri|-pərəri/ 形 (***be***) ***contemporary with*** ...と同時代で(ある) ▪ Scott *was contemporary with* Byron. スコットはバイロンと同時代であった.

contempt /kəntémpt/ 名 ***beneath contempt*** 軽蔑するにも足らない ▪ Such an accusation is *beneath contempt.* そんな非難は軽蔑するにも足らない.

bring ... into contempt ...を侮る, を卑しめる ▪ He would like to *bring* them *into contempt.* 彼は彼らに恥をかかせたいと思った.

fall into contempt 卑しめられる, 侮られる ▪ He *fell into contempt* as a result of his foolish behavior. 彼は愚かな行動をとったので侮られるようになった.

feel [***have a***] ***contempt for*** ...を軽蔑する ▪ I *feel contempt for* such a man. 私はそのような人を軽蔑する.

have [***hold***] ***... in contempt*** (人)を侮る, 軽蔑する; (物)を卑しむ ▪ I *hold* such people *in contempt.* 私はそんな人を軽蔑する.

in contempt of ...を軽蔑して, 無視して ▪ New evils arise every day *in contempt of* my reproofs. 私の非難などはおかまいなく, 新しい害悪が毎日現れている ▪ Some people speak *in contempt of* the government. 政府を軽蔑したことを言う人もいる.

contemptuous /kəntémptʃuəs|-tju-/ 形 ***contemptuous of*** ...を軽蔑して ▪ He is very *contemptuous of* Brown. 彼はブラウンをひどく軽蔑している.

content[1] /kəntént/ 形名 ***be content to*** *do* **1** ...することに満足している ▪ He *was content to* live a quiet life in a village. 彼は村で静かな生活をすることに満足していた.

2 進んで[喜んで]...する ▪ I should *be content to* do so. 喜んでそういたしましょう.

be content with ...に満足している ▪ He *is content with* very little. 彼は非常にわずかなもので満足している.

cry content with ...に満足する ▪ They have *cried content with* their horses. 彼らは自分らの馬に満足している.

in content 満足して ▪ Live *in* peace and *content.* 平和に満足して暮らしなさい.

to *one's* ***heart's content*** 心ゆくまで, 存分に ▪ Bob hugged his daughter *to his heart's content.* ボブは心ゆくまで娘を抱きしめた ▪ They cheered him *to his heart's content.* 彼らは彼を本人の心ゆくまで喝采した.

content[2] /kəntént/ 動 ***be contented with*** [***to*** *do*] ...に[することに]安んじる ▪ He *is contented with* his lot. 彼は運命に安んじている ▪ They *are contented to* complain. 不平を言うだけで甘んじている.

content *oneself* ***with*** [***to*** *do*] **1** ...で[することに]満足する ▪ We must *content ourselves with* dry bread. バターなしのパンで満足せねばならない.

2 ...に甘んじる, とどめる ▪ He *contents himself with* reporting the findings of other scholars. 彼は他の学者の研究結果を報告することに甘んじている ▪ I shall *content myself to* say this. こう言うだけにとどめておきます.

contention /kənténʃən/ 名 ***in contention*** 論争中で[の], 競争中で[の] (*for, in, at*) ▪ Bennet was *in contention for* the position. ベネットはポジション争いの最中だった.

contest /kəntést/ 動 ***contest the passage*** 先に通ろうと互いに争う ▪ They *contested the passage.* 彼らは道を譲れと互いに争った.

contest with [***against***] ...と競争する, 論争する ▪ He *contested with* his opponent in an argument. 彼は相手と論争した.

contestation /kɑ̀ntestéɪʃən|kɔ̀nt-/ 名 ***in contestation*** 係争中の[で] ▪ That is the point *in contestation.* それが係争中の点です.

without contestation 論争の余地なく ▪ It took its place *without contestation* among established opinions. それは論なく確立した意見の間に位置を占めた.

contested /kəntéstəd/ 形 ***hotly contested*** 激戦の, 熾烈(しれつ)な争いの ▪ Microsoft is entering a *hotly contested* area. マイクロソフトは熾烈な争いの分野に参入しつつある.

context /kɑ́ntekst|kɔ́n-/ 名 ***in the context of*** ...という文脈[状況, 背景, 枠]の中で(は) ▪ His path-breaking work is best understood *in the context of* its times. 彼の先駆的な業績はその時代背景の中でもっともよく理解できる ▪ *In the context of* a political party, political leaders do not preach. 政党の枠内では党指導者はお説教はしない.

in this context =in this CONNECTION.

contiguous /kəntígjuəs/ 形 ***contiguous to*** …に接して ▪ The country is *contiguous to* the sea. その国は海に接している.

continental /kὰntənéntəl|kɔ̀ntɪ-/ 名 ***not care*** [***give***] ***a continental*** 《米俗》少しもかまわない ▪ I do*n't care a continental* what you think. あなたがどう考えようと少しもかまわない ▪ He did*n't give a continental* for anybody. 彼は誰にもちっともかまわなかった. ☞continental は米独立戦争時に発行された紙幣で, 戦争終結前に無価値となった.

not worth a continental 一文の値うちもなく ▪ The new player is *not worth a continental.* 今度の選手は三文の値うちもない.

contingent /kəntíndʒənt/ 形 ***contingent on*** [***upon***] …を条件として生じる ▪ Our plans are *contingent upon* pleasant weather. わが計画の成否は好天候かどうかによって決まる.

contingent to …に起こりがちな ▪ Such risks are *contingent to* the trade. そのような危険はその商売に起こりがちだ.

continuance /kəntínjuəns/ 名 ***of long*** [***short, some***] ***continuance*** 久しく[少し, 相当]続いた ▪ Is the rain likely to be *of* any *continuance*? 雨は続きそうですか ▪ The strain was *of short continuance.* 緊張は少し続いただけだった.

continue /kəntínju:/ 動 ***To be continued.*** 以下次号(雑誌の記事などに用いる) (→to be CONCLUDEd).

contortion /kəntɔ́:rʃən/ 名 ***make contortions of*** …をゆがめる ▪ He *made contortions of* his face. 彼は顔をゆがめた.

contract[1] /kάntrækt|kɔ́n-/ 名 ***by*** [***according to***] ***contract*** 請負で, 契約により ▪ I think it was built *by contract.* それは請負で作られたものと思う ▪ The Austrians were *according to contract* joined with the Poles. オーストリア軍は契約によりポーランド軍と合流した.

exchange contracts 《主に英》(署名して, 家・土地などの)売買契約を結ぶ ▪ It is too late to withdraw once you have *exchanged contracts.* いったん売買契約を結んでしまうと, それを撤回するのは手遅れである.

make [***enter into***] ***a contract*** (***with***) (…と)契約を結ぶ ▪ He *made a contract with* the company for a supply of electric power. その会社と電力供給の契約を結んだ.

mess up the contract 《口》事をだめにする, やりそこなう ▪ The work has *messed up the* whole *contract.* その仕事のため万事がめちゃめちゃになった.

contract[2] /kəntrǽkt/ 動 ***contract*** *oneself* ***out*** (***of***) 契約によって(…を)脱する ▪ The landlord *contracted himself out of* the Agricultural Holdings Act. 地主は契約によって農業保有地法を離脱した.

contract with *a person* ***to*** *do* [***for***] 人と…する契約を結ぶ ▪ We *contracted with* him *to* do the woodwork. 彼に大工仕事を請け合わせた.

contradiction /kὰntrədíkʃən|kɔ̀n-/ 名 ***a contradiction in terms*** 《論》名辞矛盾 ▪ A virtuous tyrant is *a contradiction in terms.* 有徳の暴君は名辞矛盾である.

in contradiction with …と矛盾して; 反して ▪ His statements are *in contradiction with* hers. 彼の言うことは彼女の言うことと正反対である.

contradistinction /kὰntrədɪstíŋkʃən|kɔ̀n-/ 名 ***in contradistinction to*** [***from***] …と対比して ▪ We speak of sins of commission *in contradistinction to* sins of omission. 怠慢罪と対比して違法罪などと言う.

contraposition /kὰntrəpəzíʃən/ 名 ***by contraposition*** 《論》換質換位法により ▪ If all A is B, then *by contraposition* all not-B is not-A. もしすべてのAがBであるならば, 換質換位法により, すべてのBでないものはAでない.

in contraposition to [***with***] …に対置して; と反対に, 対照的に ▪ He lauds the greatness of Rome *in contraposition to* this single man. 彼はこの一人の人間と対照的にローマの偉大さをほめたたえる ▪ Place the Athenians *in contraposition with* the Spartans. アテネ人をスパルタ人に対置せよ.

contrary /kάntrèri|kɔ́ntrəri/ 名形副 ***by contraries*** 正反対に, 逆に; 予期に反して ▪ Dreams go *by contraries.* 夢はさか夢 ▪ Many things in our lives go *by contraries.* 我々の生涯には予期に反することが多い.

by rule [***reason, argument***] ***of contraries*** 反対に ▪ So *by argument of contraries* the just sovereignty approaches nearest to the divine rule. そこで正反対に正しい主権は神の統治に最も近い.

contrary to …に逆らって, に反して ▪ He left home *contrary to* his father's wishes. 彼は父の希望に逆らって家を出た ▪ Snow in summer would be *contrary to* all experience. 夏の雪はあらゆる経験に反するであろう.

contrary to (*one's*) ***expectation***(***s***) (人の)予期に反して, 意外にも ▪ *Contrary to* (*our*) *expectation*(*s*), fortunately it hardly rained in the daytime today. (我々の)予想に反して幸いなことにきょうの昼間はほとんど雨が降らなかった.

contrary to popular belief [***opinion***] 常識に反するが ▪ *Contrary to popular belief,* GM leads the field in fuel efficiency. 一般的見解に相違して, GM は燃料効率においては優位に立っている.

on the contrary ちょうど反対に, それに反して, それどころか ▪ Are you nearly done?—*On the contrary,* I have only just begun. もうほとんど終えましたか?—いやそれどころか, 今やっと始めたばかりだ.

to the contrary そうでないと(の), それと反対の ▪ I will come on Monday unless you write me *to the contrary*. 来るなとのお手紙をくださらぬかぎり月曜に来ます ▪ I have no proof *to the contrary*. そうでないとの証拠はない.

C

contrast[1] /kάntræst|kɔ́ntrɑːst/ 名 ***be a contrast to*** …の好対照となる, 反対である ▪ Tom's marks *are a* great *contrast to* John's. トムの点はジョンのと大きな対照をなしている ▪ Black *is a contrast to* white. 黒は白の反対である.

by contrast with …と対照させれば; と比べれば ▪ A child of average ability may appear dull *by contrast with* a brilliant brother. 普通の能力の子供も, すばらしい秀才の兄と比べればできない子と見えるかもしれない.

form [***present***] ***a … contrast*** (***to***) (…と)…な対照をなす ▪ It *forms a* remarkable *contrast to* the rest. それは他ときわだって違う《わけても立派だ》.

in contrast with [***to***] …と対照をなして, とは著しく違って ▪ *In contrast with* that problem, this one is easy. あの問題と全く違って, この問題は易しい.

contrast[2] /kəntræ̃st|-trάːst/ 動 ***as contrasted*** (***with***) (…と)比べて, (と)対照してみると ▪ I mean literature *as contrasted with* life. 私の言うのは人生と対比してみた文学のことなのです.

be contrasted with [***by***] …で引き立つ ▪ Her white face *was* well *contrasted with* her dark dress. 彼女の白い顔は黒い衣装で美しく引き立っていた.

contravention /kὰntrəvénʃən|kɔ̀n-/ 名 ***in contravention of*** …に違反して, を犯して ▪ He acted *in contravention of* the regulations. 彼はその規則に違反した行動をした.

contribution /kὰntrəbjúːʃən|kɔ̀n-/ 名 ***lay … under contribution*** 《軍》…に軍税を課する; に寄付[貢献]させる ▪ Did you *lay* the country *under contribution*? その国に軍税を課したか ▪ The thief *laid* the whole English border region *under contribution*. 賊はイギリスの辺境全体にわたって物品を取り立てた.

make a contribution to [***towards***] …に貢献[寄付]する ▪ He *made a* great *contribution to* science. 彼は科学に対して大きな貢献をした.

contributive /kəntríbjətɪv/ 形 ***contributive to*** …に寄与する ▪ It is *contributive to* my interests. それは私の利益を増大する.

contributory /kəntríbjətɔ̀ːri|-təri/ 形 ***contributory to*** …を得るのにあずかって力がある ▪ It is *contributory to* the result. それはその結果を得るにあずかって力がある.

control[1] /kəntróʊl/ 名 ***a control freak*** 仕切り屋, 独裁者《他人に命令し支配したいという欲望を持った人》 ▪ Some call Crean *a control freak* because he demands to oversee every aspect of the basketball program. クリーンはバスケの予定をすべて監督することを要求するので彼のことを仕切り屋と呼ぶ人もいる ▪ *Control Freaks* assert themselves constantly because they fear being out of control. 仕切り屋たちは支配できなくなるのを恐れているのでいつも出しゃばる.

be in control of …を管理している ▪ He *is in control of* the building. 彼はその建物を管理している.

beyond (*one's*) ***control*** 押さえきれない, 手に余る ▪ At the sound the horse got *beyond control*. その音を聞いて馬は制御しきれなくなった ▪ The fire was *beyond our control*. 火事は我々の手に余った.

bring [***get***] ***… under control*** …を押さえる, 静める ▪ We *brought* him *under* complete *control*. 彼を完全に押さえた ▪ The fire *was got under control*. 火は消し止められた ▪ They *got* the flood *under control*. 洪水を治めた.

Everything's under control. 《口》万事異常なし ▪ You can go to sleep now, *everything's under control*. もう寝ていいですよ, 万事異常なしですから.

get control over …を制御する ▪ The rider soon *got control over* the horse. 乗り手はすぐに馬を制御した.

get out of control 制しきれなくなる ▪ Tom *got out of control*. トムは手に負えなくなった.

have control of …を制する ▪ Those who *have control of* the skies *have control of* the world. 空を制するものは世界を制する.

have control of [***over***] *oneself* おのれを制する ▪ He *has* no *control over himself*. 彼には自制がない.

have control over …を制する, 管理する(力がある) ▪ He *has* good *control over* his class. 彼は教室の管理がよい ▪ He *has* no *control over* his passions. 自分の情欲を制しえない.

in control 支配[統御]して; 抑制して, 冷静で (*of*) ▪ North Korean leader Kim Jong Il is *in control of* the communist state. 北朝鮮の指導者金正日は共産主義国家を支配している.

keep … under control …を抑制[統御]する ▪ He *kept* his temper *under control*. 彼は怒りを押さえた.

lose control of [***over***] …を制しきれなくなる ▪ He *lost control of* his car and met with an accident. 彼は自動車の操縦ができなくなって, 事故にあった ▪ Don't *lose control of* your temper. 怒りを爆発させるな.

out of control 制御できなくなって ▪ If an airplane goes *out of control*, it will certainly crash. もし飛行機が操縦できなくなったら, きっと墜落するだろう.

under (***the***) ***control*** (***of***) (…の)管理[支配]下にあって ▪ The school is *under the* direct *control of* the Department of Education. その学校は教育省の直轄学校である.

without control 統制なく, 自由勝手に ▪ Speak *without control*. 自由に話しなさい.

control[2] /kəntróʊl/ 動 ***control*** *oneself* 自制する, 押さえる ▪ Good men can *control themselves*. 善良な人は自制することができる.

controversy /kάntrəvə̀:rsi|kɔ́n-/ 名 ***(be) in (a) controversy*** (…と)論争中で(ある) (*with*) ▪ We *are in controversy with* him. 我々は彼と論争中である ▪ The problem *was* still *in controversy*. その問題はまだ論議されていた.

beyond [out of, without] controversy 論争の余地なく, 確かに ▪ That is a fact *beyond controversy*. それは議論の余地のない事実である ▪ He was *without controversy* the ablest general. 彼はもちろん最も有能な将軍であった.

convene /kənví:n/ 動 ***convene*** *oneself* 集まる ▪ The people would frequently *convene themselves* by the sound of a bell. 人々は鐘の音を聞いてよく集まった.

convenience /kənví:niəns/ 名 ***at*** *one's* ***earliest convenience*** 都合つき次第, なるべく早く ▪ I hope you will kindly call at my office *at your earliest convenience*. ご都合つき次第事務所においでください.

at *one's* ***(own) convenience*** …の都合のよいときに ▪ You may pay the money *at your own convenience*. お金はご都合のよいときでよろしい.

await *a person's* ***convenience*** 人の都合のよい時を待つ ▪ He *awaited my convenience* in the drawing-room. 彼は応接室で私の都合のよい時を待った.

consult *a person's* ***convenience*** 人の便宜を顧慮する ▪ We must *consult his convenience*. 彼の便宜を考えねばならない.

consult *one's* ***own convenience*** 自分の都合を考える ▪ He only *consults his own convenience*. 彼は自分の都合ばかりを考える.

for convenience 便宜のため, 便利なように ▪ I keep my reference books at hand *for convenience*. 便宜のため参考図書を手もとに置いておく ▪ This house was built *for convenience*. この家は便利第一に建てられたものだ.

for convenience' sake 便宜上 ▪ *For convenience' sake* we shall divide all these items into just two categories. 便宜上, これらの項目をたった2つのカテゴリーに分けよう.

for the convenience of …の便宜のために[の] ▪ There was a shelter *for the convenience of* travelers. 旅行者の便宜のための家があった.

make a convenience of (好意をよいことに)…を道具に使う, 勝手に利用する ▪ He will *make a convenience of* me. 彼は私を道具に使うだろう.

suit *a person's* ***convenience*** 人に都合がよい; 都合のよいようにする ▪ Come at any time that *suits your convenience*. 都合のよいときにいつでも来なさい ▪ I like to *suit his convenience*. 私は彼に都合よいようにしたい.

convenient /kənví:niənt/ 形 ***convenient for*** *a person* ***to*** *do* 人が…するのは都合がよく ▪ Will it be *convenient for* you *to* see me on Friday? 金曜日に私に会うのは都合がよろしいか.

convenient to …に便利で ▪ The hotel is *convenient to* the shopping center. そのホテルはショッピングセンターに手近だ.

make it convenient to *do* 都合をつけて…する ▪ I will *make it convenient to* call on you. 都合をつけてお訪ねします.

conversant /kənvə́:rsənt/ 形 ***conversant about*** …に関連[関係]する ▪ Logic is entirely *conversant about* language. 論理学は全く言語に関係している.

conversant in **1** …を事とする, を行う ▪ Physical science is *conversant in* experiment. 自然科学は実験を(仕)事とする.

2 …に精通して ▪ Milton was *conversant in* Latin. ミルトンはラテン語に精通していた.

conversant on …に詳しい ▪ Young men are *conversant on* the subject. 青年はその件に詳しい.

conversant with **1** …を扱う ▪ Chemistry has been *conversant with* the qualities of matter. 化学は物質の諸性質を扱ってきた.

2 …と親交があって; と親しくいっしょに暮らして ▪ She has been *conversant with* many ladies of rank. 彼女は多くの貴婦人たちと親交があった.

3 …に精通して ▪ He was *conversant with* questions of finance. 彼は財政の問題に精通していた.

conversation /kὰnvərséiʃən|kɔ̀n-/ 名 ***have [hold] a conversation with*** …と語り合う ▪ I *had a* long *conversation with* him. 私は彼と長く話した.

in conversation (with) (…と)談話中で ▪ I saw him *in conversation with* a friend. 私は彼が友人と話しているのを見た.

make conversation (話題もないのに)ことさら話をする; 雑談する ▪ He could not *make conversation* with her. 彼は彼女と雑談をすることができなかった.

strike up a conversation (初対面の人と)会話を始める ▪ Rochette was too shy to *strike up a conversation*. ロシェットは内気なので自分から話しかけることができなかった.

take up the conversation (やめた[他人の])話をまた始める ▪ My uncle *took up the conversation* and told us his opinion. おじはその話をまた始めて自分の考えを言った.

conversion /kənvə́:rʒən|-ʃən/ 名 ***by conversion*** 《論》換位により ▪ If everything that is not A is B, then *by conversion*, everything that is not B is A. もしAでないものがBならば, 換位によってBでないものはAである.

convert[1] /kάnvə:rt/ 名 ***make a convert of*** …を改宗させる; をわが党に引き入れる ▪ You have *made a* perfect *convert of* me to your plan. 私を全くあなたの計画の支持者にした.

convert[2] /kənvə́:rt/ 動 ***be [get] converted*** 悔い改める, 発心(ほっしん)する; (に)改宗する, 帰依する (*from* A *to* B) ▪ He *was converted from* Protestantism *to* Catholicism. 彼は新教からカトリックに改宗した.

convert** a person **to 人を…に帰依[改宗]させる ▪I *converted* my wife *to* Christianity. 妻をキリスト教に改宗させた.

convert ... to** one's **own use …を横領する ▪He *converted* public money *to his own use*. 彼は公金を横領した.

convict /kənvíkt/ 形 ***be convict of*** (有罪)を宣せられ[証せられ, 答審され]る ▪He *was convict* by many witnesses *of* the crime of treachery. 彼は多くの証人によって裏切りの罪ありと証言された.

conviction /kənvíkʃən/ 名 ***carry conviction (to)*** (人を)信服させる(力がある) ▪This argument *carries conviction*. この議論は人を信服させる力がある ▪The story would *carry conviction to* me [my mind]. その話は私を信服させるだろう.

in the (full) conviction that …と(十分)確信して ▪I did it *in the conviction that* he would be pleased. 彼が喜ぶだろうと確信してそれをした.

open to conviction 理に服する ▪He doubts the truth of your story, but is *open to conviction*. 彼は君の話の真否を疑っているが, 話せばわかる男だ.

the conviction forces itself upon me that …と悟らざるをえない ▪*The conviction forced itself upon me that* he was a true friend. 彼は真の友だと私は悟らざるをえなかった.

under conviction(s) 罪の意識に目ざめて ▪My soul was groaning *under* deep *convictions*. 私の魂は深い罪の自覚にうめいていた.

with conviction 感服して; 確信して ▪He listened *with conviction*. 彼は感服して聞いた.

convince /kənvíns/ 動 ***convince** oneself **of*** …を確かめる ▪I must *convince myself of* the fact. その事実を確かめねばならない.

convoy /kánvɔɪ|kɔ́n-/ 名 ***under (the) convoy of*** …に護衛[護送]されて ▪The supplies were sent *under convoy of* troops. 糧食は軍隊に護衛されて送られた.

convulse /kənvʌ́ls/ 動 ***be convulsed with***
1 …で騒然となる ▪The country *was convulsed with* civil strife. その国は内乱で騒然となった.
2 …で身もだえする[けいれんする] ▪She *was convulsed with* laughter. 彼女は笑いこけた ▪He *was convulsed with* pain. 彼は苦痛で身もだえした.

convulsion /kənvʌ́lʃən/ 名 ***fall into (a fit of) convulsions*** **1** けいれんを起こす ▪The child *fell into a fit of convulsions*. その子供はけいれんを起こした.
2 どっと笑いこける ▪The audience *fell into convulsions* of laughter. 聴衆は抱腹絶倒した.

go off into convulsions = fall into (a fit of) CONVULSIONs 2.

in convulsions 大笑いして ▪Everyone was *in convulsions*. みんな腹をかかえて笑った.

throw ... into convulsions …にけいれんを起こさせる; 腹の皮をよじらせる; (国民)を動乱させる ▪The funny story *threw* us *into convulsions*. そのおかしい話は我々を笑いころげさせた ▪The nation *was thrown into convulsions*. その国は動乱状態になった.

cooee /kúːiː/ 名 ***within (a) cooee of*** 《口》…のすぐ近くに, 呼べば聞こえるところに ▪Had any of our members been *within cooee of* that, they'd have been completely buried. 仲間の誰かがあの近くにいたら完全に生き埋めになってしまっていただろう.

cook[1] /kʊk/ 名 ***the chief [head] cook and bottle-washer*** 《口・戯》(パーティーなどの)幹事役 ▪John is *the chief cook and bottle-washer* of this party. ジョンはこのパーティーの幹事役だ.

Too many cooks spoil the broth [stew]. 《諺》船頭多くして船山に登る《手伝いが多すぎるとかえってじゃまになるばかり》.

cook[2] /kʊk/ 動 ***be cooked up*** (狭い場所に)閉じこめられる ▪He *was cooked up* all day in a tiny windowless office. 彼は窓のない小さな事務室に一日中閉じこめられていた.

be cooking on gas 《英口》 = be COOKing with gas.

be cooking with gas 《米口》 **1** 快調に進む, (仕事などが)はかどる; 本調子になって (→COOK with gas) ▪Control your fear and you *are cooking with gas*, baby. 恐怖を抑えなさい, そうすれば大丈夫だよ, 君 ▪Now we *are cooking with gas*. いよいよ本調子になってきた.
2 先端的なことに通じている, 近代的になって ▪We *are cooking with gas* on this now. 我々は今ではこのことをよく知っている.

cook** a person's **goose (for** him**) →GOOSE.

cook (the,** one's**) accounts 《口》帳簿[話]を繕う ▪They *cooked the accounts* and that's how they escaped. 彼らは帳簿を繕った. それでうまく逃れた ▪*Their accounts were cooked*. 彼らの話はでっちあげたものだ.

cook with gas [electricity, radar] 《米俗》うまくやる; 正しく行動する[考える] (→be COOKing with gas) ▪Now, you are *cooking with electricity*. こんどは非常にじょうずにやっているね.

cookie, cooky /kʊ́ki/ 名 ***a [one] tough cookie*** 頑固な人, てごわい[したたかな]やつ ▪Tom is *a tough cookie*. He is not going to concede. トムは頑固なやつだ. 譲歩しようとしない ▪Lewis is *a tough cookie* and I'm the only one here who can handle him. ルイスは手ごわい男で, ここで奴を操れるのはこの俺だけだ.

bet [wager] a cooky 《米口》確かだ, まちがいない ▪I'll *bet a cooky* you can't do that. そんなことはできっこないよ.

That's the way [That's how] the cookie crumbles. 《口》物事というものはそんなものなのだ《だからあきらめなさい》. ☞不幸な事などがあったとき慰めに言う.

toss** one's **cookies 《米俗》吐く, ゲロする ▪Jordan ate some bad pizza and *tossed his cookies*. ジョーダンは悪くなったピザを食べてもどした.

cool[1] /kuːl/ 形名 ***a cool customer*** [***card, character***]《口》**1** 厚かましい人[やつ] ▪ That gardener is *a cool customer*. He's asking twenty pounds an hour. あの庭師は厚かましいやつだ. 1時間20ポンドを要求している.
2 冷静沈着な人 ▪ Mr. Black is definitely *a cool customer*. ブラック氏はたしかに冷静沈着な人だ.
(***as***) ***cool as steel*** きわめて冷静で ▪ Tom was *as cool as steel*. トムはきわめて冷静であった.
blow *one's* ***cool*** →lose one's COOL.
Cool beans [***bananas***]***!***《米俗》(驚いて)うわっ(Wow).
cool(, ***calm***) ***and collected*** 落ち着いて ▪ He became *cool and collected* at once. 彼はすぐ落ち着いた.
enjoy the cool of …の冷気を楽しむ ▪ I *enjoyed the cool of* the evening. 夕涼みをした.
get cool さめる, 涼しくなる, 涼む ▪ The dog is sweating to *get cool*. 犬は涼をとるため汗をかいている.
go cool on plans [***policies,*** etc.] …に興味を失う, 情熱がなくなってくる ▪ The strategy was abandoned after Mr Lindberg *went cool on the plan*. リンドバーグ氏が計画に熱意を失ってくるにつれて, その方策は見捨てられた.
have cool cheeks 全くずうずうしい ▪ I think he *has cool cheeks*. 彼は全くずうずうしいと思うよ.
in cool blood →in cold BLOOD.
in the cool of …の涼しいときに[所で] ▪ I go jogging in the park *in the cool of* the morning. 朝の涼しいときに公園にジョギングに行く ▪ I took a stroll *in the cool of* the forest. 森の涼しい所を散策した.
It's cool!《口》大丈夫だ, 心配ない.
keep a cool head →keep one's HEAD.
keep [***stay, remain***] ***cool*** 涼んでいる; 冷静を保つ, あわてない; 怒らない ▪ It is the role of a critic to *keep cool*. 冷静を保つのは批評家の務めだ.
keep *one's* ***cool***《俗》平静を保つ ▪ I managed to *keep my cool*. 私はなんとかして平静を保った.
leave *a person* ***cool*** →LEAVE a person cold.
lose [***blow***] *one's* ***cool*** 感情的になる, 興奮する ▪ Don't *blow your cool* like that. そんなに興奮してはいけない ▪ Pete never lost his temper, never *lost his cool*. ピートは癇癪を起こしたことがない, 冷静さを失ったためしがない.
play it cool →PLAY[2].

cool[2] /kuːl/ 動 ***cool it***《俗》落ちつく; 静まる; くつろぐ ▪ *Cool it*! Nobody's interested. 静まりなさい. 誰も興味を持ってはいませんよ ▪ I *cooled it* at a table for a while. 私はしばらくテーブルでくつろいだ.
save *one's* ***breath to cool*** *one's* ***porridge*** →BREATH.

cooler /kúːlər/ 名 ***put … in the cooler***《米口》…を棚あげする ▪ The resolution will *be put in the cooler* for a time. その決議案は当分棚あげされるだろう.

cooling-off /kùːlɪŋɔ́ːf|-ɔ́f/ 形 ***a cooling-off period*** クーリングオフ期間; 冷却期間 ▪ Luckily for me, I'm still within the *cooling-off period* when I can get my money back. ラッキーなことに, クーリングオフ期間内だったので返金してもらえた ▪ "The *cooling-off period* must begin as soon as possible," the G-8 leaders said.「冷却期間はできるだけ早急に開始されねばならない」とG8の主導者たちは述べた.

coolness /kúːlnəs/ 名 ***with coolness*** 落ち着きはらって, ずうずうしく ▪ He took possession of the territory *with coolness*. 彼はずうずうしくその地域を領有した.

coon[1] /kuːn/ 名 ***a coon's age*** 長い長い間《a long time の強意句》 ▪ He hasn't had much money in *a coon's age*. 彼は長い長い間たくさんの金は持ったことがない. ☞coon (アライグマ)は長生きだから.
a gone coon 見込みのない人 ▪ I was *a gone coon*. 僕はもうだめだった.
hunt [***skin***] ***the same old coon***《主に米口》**1** いつも同じことばかりやる ▪ I am tired of *hunting the same old coon*. 同じことばかりやるのにあきた.
2 再びアメリカホイッグ党 (Whigs) を負かす, 破る ▪ It was delightful to *skin the same old coon*. アメリカホイッグ党を再び負かすのは愉快だった.
tree the coon《米口》問題を解く, 捜していた人を追いつめる ▪ Your *coons are* fairly *treed*. 君は捜していた人をまんまと追いつめたね. ☞アライグマを木に追いつめることから.

coon[2] /kuːn/ 動 ***coon a fence*** [***log, pole***]《米口》かじりつくようにして柵[丸太, 棒]を通って行く ▪ We *cooned a log* across the stream to get to the other side. 我々はかじりつくように丸木橋を渡って川を越え, 対岸に達した.

coop /kuːp/ 名 ***fly the coop***《主に米口》急に[こっそり]去る; (刑務所などから)逃げる ▪ She apparently contacted this guy right after you *flew the coop*. 君が出たあとすぐ彼女はこの男に連絡をとったようだ ▪ It made her *fly the coop*. そのため彼女は逃げることができた. ☞coop「ニワトリやウサギなどの囲いかご」.

co-op /kóʊɑp|-ɔp/ 名 ***on the co-op*** 共同組合方式で; 共同で ▪ We did it *on the co-op*. 我々はそれを共同でやった.

cooperation /koʊɑ̀pəréɪʃən|-ɔ̀p-/ 名 ***in cooperation with*** …と共同して, 協力して ▪ We worked *in cooperation with* him. 我々は彼と協力して働いた.

coot /kuːt/ 名 (***as***) ***bald as a coot*** 額がはげあがって ▪ He was *as bald as a coot*. 彼は額がはげあがっていた.
(***as***) ***stupid as a coot*** 大まぬけで ▪ He was *as stupid as a coot*. 彼はひどいまぬけだった.

cooter /kúːtər/ 名 (***as***) ***drunk as a cooter***《口》すっかり酔っ払って ▪ I had him *as drunk as a cooter*. 彼をすっかり酔っ払わせた. ☞cooter「アメリカ南東部産のカメ」.

cop[1] /kɑp|kɔp/ 名 ***cops and robbers***《口》(子供の)警官と泥棒ごっこ; (映画・物語の)警官対犯人劇 ▪ They are playing *cops and robbers* with

C

Alexander. 彼らはアレクサンダーと警官と泥棒ごっこをしている.

no cop/not much cop 《俗》 **1** (仕事が)楽でない, 困難な ▪ It's *no cop*. 仕事は楽じゃない.

2 (物が)価値がなく ▪ This heap of bricks does*n't* look *much cop* now. このれんがの山は今ではたいした価値はなさそうだ. ☞cop＝acquisition.

on the cops 《俗》 警官になって ▪ He went *on the cops*. 彼は警官になった.

cop[2] /kɑp|kɔp/ 動 ***cop a feel*** →FEEL[1].

Cop (a load of) this! 《英俗》 〚主に命令文で〛 これをよく見ろ[聞け] ▪ Hey, *cop a load of this!* おい, これをよく見ろ.

cop anything 《口》 病気にでも何にでもかかる ▪ You might *cop anything* in that house. あの家にいたら病気でも何にでもかかるだろう.

cop hold of 《英俗》 〚主に命令文で〛 …を(しっかり)握る[つかむ] ▪ Here, girl, *cop hold of* this. さあ, 彼女, こいつをつかんでくれ.

cop it (out) 《学俗》 しかられる, 罰せられる; 死ぬ ▪ I suppose I will *cop it* for this. 私はこのためにしかられるだろうと思う.

cop** a person **one 《俗》 人に一撃をくらわす ▪ The man *copped* him *one* under the chin. その男は彼のあごの下に一撃をくらわした.

cop the bullet [sack] 《俗》 首になる ▪ I *copped the bullet*. 私は首になった.

cop the packet 《俗》 しかられる; 罰せられる; 死ぬ ▪ Sorry you *copped the packet*. あんたが罰を食ったのは気の毒だ.

get copped 警察に捕えられる ▪ Tom *got copped* for raiding an apple stall. トムはリンゴの屋台店を襲ったため警察に捕えられた.

cope /koʊp/ 名 ***under the cope of heaven*** 天下に ▪ There is no one like you *under the cope of heaven*. 天下に君のような人はいない.

copper[1] /kɑ́pər|kɔ́pə/ 名 ***cool [clear] one's coppers*** 《口》 飲みすぎののどのかわきをいやす; 二日酔いに迎え酒を飲む ▪ Bring some grog to *clear our coppers*. 飲みすぎののどのかわきをいやす水割りラム酒を持って来い ▪ He *cooled his coppers* by drinking. 彼は二日酔いの迎え酒を飲んだ. ☞coppers「口とのど」.

have hot coppers (大酒後)のどがかわく ▪ He *had hot coppers* due to excessive drinking. 彼は飲みすぎてのどがかわいた.

not care two coppers 少しもかまわない ▪ I do*n't care two coppers* who he is. 彼が誰であろうと少しもかまわない. ☞coppers「銅貨」.

copper[2] /kɑ́pər|kɔ́pə/ 動 ***copper one's pocket*** 《米俗》 着服[横領]する ▪ He *coppered his pocket* at the expense of the public. 彼は公金を横領した.

copy /kɑ́pi|kɔ́pi/ 名 ***copy of one's countenance*** 見せかけ, 偽善 ▪ I shall love a Puritan's face the worse for that *copy of your countenance*. 君のその偽善のため清教徒の顔がますますきらいになる.

keep a copy of …の写しを取っておく ▪ *Keep a copy of* your manuscript. 原稿の写しを取っておけよ.

make [take] a copy of …を複写する ▪ I *took a copy of* the letter. その手紙を複写した.

make (a) good copy 良い新聞[原稿]種になる ▪ This incident will *make (a) good copy*. この事件は良い原稿ネタになる.

make copy (out) of …を種に金儲けの原稿を書く 《通常悪い意味に用いる》 ▪ He'd *make copy out of* his father's death. 彼は自分の父の死を種にしてでも原稿を書くだろう.

copybook /kɑ́pibʊ̀k|kɔ́pi-/ 名 ***blot one's copybook*** 《口》 (特に男性が)履歴をけがす, 評判をおとす ▪ The boy *blotted his copybook* by failing all his examinations. 少年はすべての試験に落ちて(学業)成績をけがした. ☞copybook「学童の書き方練習帳」.

copyhold /kɑ́pihòʊld|kɔ́pi-/ 名 ***in copyhold*** 謄本保有権によって ▪ He holds an estate *in copyhold*. 彼は謄本保有権によって土地を持っている.

cord /kɔːrd/ 名 ***cut the cord*** ＝cut the umbilical CORD.

cut the umbilical cord **1** へその緒を切る (*with*) ▪ The paramedic grabbed a pair of scissors from his emergency kit and *cut the umbilical cord*. 救急医療隊員は応急用具からはさみをつかみ出してへその緒を切った.

2 一人立ち[独立]する, 依存をやめる (*from, with*) ▪ She does need to *cut the umbilical cord from* her parents. 彼女はどうしても両親から独立する必要がある ▪ He has finally *cut the umbilical cord with* the King. 彼はついに王との関係を絶った.

core /kɔːr/ 名 ***at the core*** 芯が ▪ The town is rotten *at the core*. その町は芯が腐っている.

be shaken to the core …の芯まで揺さぶられる, ひどいショックを受ける ▪ Americans have *been shaken to the core* by the attacks of Sept. 11. アメリカ人たちは9/11の攻撃によって衝撃を受けた ▪ Paulie *was shaken to the core* after learning the woman who raised him was his aunt, not his mother. ポーリーは自分を育ててくれたのが母ではなく叔母だとわかって非常に動揺した.

get to the core of …を徹底的に調べる ▪ It is necessary to *get to the core of* the affair. 事件を徹底的に調べる必要がある.

to the core 芯まで, 生粋の; 徹底的に ▪ He is English [loyal] *to the core*. 彼は生粋のイギリス人だ[しんそこまで忠誠である].

touch** a person **to the core 人の心底までこたえる ▪ The desertion of his dog had *touched* him *to the core*. 犬の逃げたことが彼の心のそこまでこたえた.

cork /kɔːrk/ 名 ***(as) light as a cork*** とても軽い, 軽やかに ▪ Lithium is *as light as a cork*! リチウムは非常に軽い ▪ *Light as a cork* I danced upon the waves. 実に軽やかに私は波の上で踊った.

blow *one's* ***cork*** 《俗》激怒する，キレる ▪ Jim *blew his cork* and hit him on the nose. ジムは激怒して，その男の鼻をなぐった．

pop *one's* ***cork*** 突然精神錯乱を起こす，気が変になる；興奮する，かっとなる ▪ Oh, no! She flipped her wig! She *popped her cork*! ああ! 彼女はかつらをほうり投げた．彼女はおかしくなってしまった ▪ Mr. Green *popped his cork* and accused the police officer of being a racist. グリーン氏はかっとなって警察官を人種差別者だと非難した．

corker /kɔ́ːrkər/ 名 ***That's a corker.*** 《口》それでこと[議論]は決着だ．☞corker「議論や問題を決着させるもの」．

corkscrew /kɔ́ːrkskrùː/ 動 ***corkscrew*** (***a secret***) ***out of*** 《俗》(秘密)を(人)からじりじり引き出す ▪ I *corkscrewed the secret out of* him. 私はその秘密を彼からじりじり引き出した．

corn /kɔːrn/ 名 ***acknowledge*** [***admit, confess***] ***the corn*** 罪[過失，失敗など]を認める ▪ Mr. Pater *acknowledged the corn* as regards his imprisonment. ペイター氏は自分の禁固について自分の罪を認めた ▪ He *confessed the corn*. 彼は過失を認めた．

be worth [***earn***] *one's* ***corn*** 《口》賃金だけの値うちがある ▪ All our farmhands *are worth their corn*. うちの農場の働き手はみな稼ぎ高に見合う仕事をしてくれる ▪ The laborer must *earn his corn*. 労働者は賃金に値する働きをせねばならない．

break corn 《米》トウモロコシを茎からもぎ取る ▪ Many people were employed in *breaking* down *corn*. 大勢がトウモロコシのもぎ取りに雇われた．

corn in Egypt 物の豊富なこと；(食料などの)無尽蔵 (《聖》*Gen.* 42. 2) ▪ Uncle's box has arrived; there is *corn in Egypt* today. おじさんの箱が到着した．きょうは食料がうんとあるぞ ▪ Here's an unopened tin of tobacco. *Corn in Egypt*. ここにまだ開いていないタバコのかんがある．全く無尽蔵だ．

corn in the ear [***shuck***] 《米》穂がついたままのトウモロコシ ▪ Now diseases are attacking *corn in the ear*. 目下さまざまな病菌が穂が出ているトウモロコシを侵している．

corn in the milk →in the MILK.

corn on the cob 《米》**1** 煮るのに適したまだ柔らかいトウモロコシ ▪ She got ready a pot full of *corn on the cob*. 彼女は煮物用のまだ柔らかいトウモロコシのいっぱい入った鍋を用意した．

2 穂のままのトウモロコシ ▪ She will teach you how to cook *corn on the cob*. 彼女が皮つきトウモロコシの調理法を教えてくれる．

earn *one's* ***corn*** →be worth one's CORN.

measure *other people's* ***corn by*** *one's* ***own bushel*** →BUSHEL.

tread on *a person's* ***corns*** 人(の感情)を害する；人の意見や好みを無視して怒らせる；人の痛いところにさわる ▪ We cannot avoid *treading on each other's corns*. お互いの感情を害さないわけにはいかない ▪ You deliberately try to *tread on his corns*. わざと彼の好みを無視して怒らせようとする．☞corn「足のまめ」．

Up corn, down horn. 《諺》穀物が騰貴すると牛肉の値が下がる．

corner[1] /kɔ́ːrnər/ 名 ***around*** [***round***] ***the corner*** **1** 町かどを曲がった所に；すぐ近くに ▪ I live just *round the corner*. 私はすぐ近くに住んでいる．

2 間近に(迫って)；近づいて ▪ Spring is just *around the corner*. 春はもうすぐだ ▪ There was a job just *round the corner*. 職がもうちょっとで決まりかけていた．

3 起こりそうな，実現できそうな ▪ Peace is just *around the corner*. 平和はまさに実現できそうである．

back *oneself* ***into a corner*** →paint oneself into a CORNER.

beyond the four corners of →within the four CORNERs of (a document).

carry (***up***) ***a corner*** 《米》丸太に刻み目をつける ▪ It took skill to *carry a corner*. 丸太に刻み目をつけるには熟練を要した．

come round the corner = go around the CORNER 1.

cut corners [***a corner***] **1** 《米》(かどを回らずに)近道をする；無鉄砲な追い越しをする ▪ A careless driver *cuts corners*. 不注意な運転手は無鉄砲な追い越しをする．

2 物事を最も早くする，やさしくする，安上がりにする；なくてすむものを削る ▪ We can *cut corners* on production costs. 我々は生産費を節約することができる ▪ The factory is *cutting corners* wherever possible. 会社はできるかぎりの点で最も安上がりにした．

3 便宜のため厳重な手順を省く ▪ He *cut a corner* in legal procedure. 彼は訴訟手続きに便宜上厳密な手順を省いた．

cut off a corner 近道をする ▪ If we go down this lane, we can *cut off a corner*. この小路を下って行けば近道になるでしょう．

drive [***force***] *a person* ***into a corner*** 人を窮地に追いつめる ▪ Now you've *driven* me *into a corner*. とうとう僕を窮地に追いつめたね．

establish [***make***] ***a corner*** 買い占めをやる ▪ He has *established a corner* in wheat. 彼は小麦の買い占めをした．

fight [***argue, defend, stand***] *one's* ***corner*** 《英》自分の立場を守るために戦う[論じる] ▪ She *fought her corner* with passion and was very highly regarded. 彼女は熱っぽく論陣を張り，非常に高く評価された ▪ I *argued my corner* effectively, debunked all the lies and myths, and did not yield. 私は自分の立場を効果的に論じて，ことごとく嘘や神話をあばき，一歩も引かなかった．

go around [***round***] ***the corner*** **1** かどを曲がる；とうげを越す ▪ We *went round the corner*. かどを曲った．

2 《婉曲》お手洗いに行く ▪ Excuse me, I must just *go around the corner*. ごめんなさい，ちょっとお手洗いへ．

have a corner on ...を独占する ▪ They *have a*

C

corner on modern production methods. 彼らは最新の生産方法を独占している.

have *a person* ***in*** *one's* ***corner*** 人の支持[援助]を受ける ▪ Luckily, we *have* sturdy friends *in our corner*. 幸いなことに我々には強力な味方の支持がある.

C

hole and corner こっそりなされた; 陰険な ▪ That agreement was a *hole and corner* affair. その協定は秘密のものであった.

hound *a person* ***into a corner*** 人を追いつめる ▪ I don't want to *hound* him *into a corner*. 私は彼を追い詰めたくない.

in a corner 《口》 **1** 秘密の場所で, 秘密に (《聖》 *Acts* 22. 26) ▪ It was done *in a corner*. それは秘密に行われた.

2 当惑して ▪ He is *in a* (tight) *corner*. 彼は窮地に陥っている.

in a tight corner →in a CORNER 2.

in *a person's* ***corner*** ...を支援[擁護]して, の味方で ▪ I really appreciated that he was always *in my corner*. 私は彼がずっと私を支援してくれたことを本当にありがたく思っている.

keep a corner (***for***) (...のために)少しの場所をあけておく ▪ *Keep a corner for* the pie. パイを入れる場所を少しあけておきなさい.

knock the corners off *a person* 人を丸く[円満に, 温厚に]させる, 指導育成する ▪ Good directors there *knocked the corners off* cocky young actors like me. そこの優れた監督たちは私のような生意気な若い俳優を人間的に育ててくれた.

make a corner →establish a CORNER.

on the corner 《口》 失業して, 仕事がなく ▪ The old man is *on the corner*. 老人は仕事がない.

out of the corner of *one's* ***eye*** **1** こっそりと ▪ I looked *out of the corner of my eye* to see if he was going out. 彼が出て行くかどうかこっそり見た.

2 ちらっと, 何気なく ▪ I saw *out of the corner of my eye* that a man had entered the room. 私は一人の男がその部屋へ入ったのをちらっと見た.

paint [***back, box***] *oneself* [*a person*] ***into a corner*** (自分の落ち度で)窮地に追い込まれる[人を窮地に追い込む, の首を絞める] ▪ It seems President Bush has *backed himself into a corner* with rhetorical oversimplification. ブッシュ大統領は言葉を省略しすぎたために自分の首を絞めたようだ ▪ Americans have *painted themselves into a corner* on energy. アメリカ人はエネルギー問題で自らを窮地に追い込んでしまった ▪ Liberals have *boxed* the president *into a corner* where he can't move. 自由党員たちは大統領を追い込み身動きのとれない状態にした. ☞ボクシングから.

put [***stand***] *a child* ***in the corner*** (罰として)子供を部屋の隅に立たせる ▪ The boy was whipped and made to *stand in the corner*. 少年はむち打たれ, 部屋の隅に立たされた.

the four corners of (***the world*** [***earth, globe***]) ...の津々浦々, の至るところ (《聖》 *Isa*. 11. 12) ▪ He will gather together the dispersed of Judah from *the four corners of the earth*. 彼は世界の津々浦々から分散したユダ族を集めるだろう.

trim *one's* ***corners*** 《米口》 情勢の許すかぎり冒険を冒してやる ▪ He was *trimming his corners* as closely as he dared. 彼は能(あた)うるかぎりきわどい冒険を冒してやっていた.

turn the corner **1** かどを曲がる; (競馬などが)走路の(特に最後の)かどを曲がる ▪ He has *turned the corner*. 彼はかどを曲がった; 曲がって見えなくなった《死んだ》.

2 (病気・不景気が)とうげを越す, 危機を通り抜ける ▪ He has been seriously ill, but has *turned the corner* now. 彼は重病であったが今はとうげを越した ▪ The firm *turned the corner* last year. その会社は昨年危機を通り抜けた.

within [***beyond***] ***the four corners of*** (***a document***) 〚強意的に〛 (文面)の範囲内に[外に] ▪ The spirit of the church is entombed *within the four corners of* acts of parliament. 教会の霊は法令の文面の範囲内に葬られている ▪ It is necessary to look *beyond the four corners of* the agreement. その協定文面の範囲より外を見ることが必要である.

corner[2] /kɔ́ːrnər/ 動 ***corner the market*** → MARKET.

corner-stone /kɔ́ːrnərstòʊn/ 名 ***lay the corner-stone*** 定礎式を挙げる, 起工する; 基礎を築く ▪ Jewish settlers *laid the cornerstone* of a new settlement in the West Bank. ユダヤ人入植者たちは西岸の新開地の定礎式を挙げた ▪ Machiavelli *laid the cornerstone* of modern political science. マキャベリは近代政治学の基礎を築いた.

correct[1] /kərékt/ 形 ***all present and correct*** 《口》 けっこうで, 申し分なく ▪ If it works and is *all present and correct*—lucky you. もしそれがうまく作動して申し分なければ, 君はついている. ☞《軍》准尉が閲兵の際使った句.

politically correct 政治的に正しい; 非差別的な ▪ This "*politically correct*" decision will make things difficult for the debt-ridden government. この「政治的に正しい」決定は借金まみれの政府にとっては事態を困難にするだろう ▪ The worst *politically correct* phrase is "misguided criminals". The BBC used the phrase to refer to terrorists. 最悪の非差別用語は「惑わされた犯罪者」である. BBC はこの語句をテロリストを指すのに用いたのである. ☞PC, p.c. とも表記される.

the correct thing 《俗》 当を得ていること ▪ He says *the correct thing*. 彼は当を得たことを言う.

correct[2] /kərékt/ 動 ***stand corrected*** 訂正を承認する[受けいれる] ▪ I *stand corrected* and reprove myself. 私は訂正を認めて自責する.

correction /kərékʃən/ 名 ***be subject*** [***open***] ***to correction*** 誤りがあれば訂正することにする ▪ All of the information *is subject to correction*. その情報はどれも誤っていれば訂正いたします

▪ That is my opinion, but I'*m open to correction*. それが私の意見ですが, 誤りがあれば訂正します.

beyond correction 直しようがない, 矯正できない ▪ This fellow is bad *beyond correction*. この男は不良で矯正できない.

under correction まちがったら訂正してもらうことにして ▪ I speak *under correction*, for I am not a specialist. 私はまちがっていたら訂正していただくことにして話します. 専門家ではありませんから.

correlate /kɔ́:rəlèɪt|kɔ́r-/ 動 ***be correlated with*** ...と関連する ▪ I think quick reactions *are correlated with* high intelligence. 素早く反応できることは高い知性に関連があると思う.

correspondence /kɔ̀:rəspɑ́ndəns|kɔ̀rəspɔ́n-/ 名 ***be*** [***stand***] ***in correspondence with*** ...と文通している ▪ I have *been in correspondence with* him about the matter. 私はそのことについて彼と手紙のやり取りをしてきた.

do [***attend to***] *one's* ***correspondence*** (返事を書いて)手紙の処理をする ▪ I sat down to *do my correspondence*. 手紙の処理をしようと腰を下ろした ▪ He regularly *attended to his correspondence* every morning. 彼は毎朝きちんと返信の処理をした.

drop correspondence with ...との通信を絶つ ▪ He totally *dropped correspondence with* me. 彼は全く私との通信を絶った.

have correspondence with ...と文通する ▪ I *had* a great deal of *correspondence with* him. 私は彼と盛んに文通をした.

correspondent /kɔ̀:rəspɑ́ndənt|kɔ̀rəspɔ́n-/ 名 ***a good*** [***bad, negligent***] ***correspondent*** 筆まめな[筆不精の]人 ▪ I usually try to be *a good correspondent*. 日ごろから筆まめにしようと努めている ▪ I hope you will forgive me for being *a bad correspondent*. 平素のご無沙汰をお許しください.

corridor /kɔ́:rədər|kɔ́rɪdɔ:/ 名 ***the corridors of power*** 権力の回廊, 政治権力の中心 ▪ They are also potent in *the corridors of power*. 彼らはまた権力争奪の場でも有力である. ☞C. P. Snow, *Homecomings* (1956)の造語より.

corroboration /kərɑ̀bəréɪʃən|-rɔ̀b-/ 名 ***in corroboration of*** ...を確実なものにする ▪ I shall state some facts *in corroboration of* the evidence. 証拠を確証する事実を述べます.

corruption /kərʌ́pʃən/ 名 ***proof against corruption*** 賄賂がきかない ▪ The Japanese police officers are *proof against corruption*. 日本の警察官には賄賂がきかない.

corruptive /kərʌ́ptɪv/ 形 ***corruptive of*** ...を腐敗させる, を堕落させる ▪ He acted in a manner *corruptive of* public morals. 彼は風紀を乱すような行動をした.

cost[1] /kɔ:st|kɔst/ 名 ***at a*** [***the***] ***cost of*** ...の値段で; の費用で ▪ Board and lodging will be available *at a cost of* 200 pounds a week. まかないつき下宿が1週200ポンドで得られる ▪ The monument was erected *at a cost of* $50,000. その記念碑は50,000ドルの費用で建築された.

at all costs どんな費用をかけても; ぜひとも (=at any PRICE) ▪ We must arrive there *at all costs* before midnight. 真夜中にならぬうちにぜひそこへ着かねばならない ▪ Hold the position *at all costs*. 万難を排してその陣地を守れ.

at any cost どんな犠牲を払っても, ぜひとも ▪ I will accomplish my purpose *at any cost*. ぜひとも目的を達成します.

at cost 原価で, 仕入れ値段で ▪ You may take these goods *at cost*. その品は原価でお分けしましょう.

at *a person's* ***cost*** 人の費用で; 人に損害をかけて ▪ We feasted *at the enemy's cost*. 我々は敵を破って祝宴を張った.

at the cost of **1** =at a COST of.
2 ...を犠牲にして, を捨てて ▪ It is foolish to study hard *at the cost of* your health. 健康を犠牲にして一生懸命勉強するのはばかげている ▪ He saved her life *at the cost of* his own. 自分の命を犠牲にして彼女の命を救った.

cost and freight 《商》運賃込み値段 (《略》CAF, c.a.f., C&F) ▪ The lowest offer has been $749 per ton *C&F*. 最安値の付け値は運賃込み値段で1トン749ドルだった.

cost, insurance, and freight 《商》保険料運賃込み値段 (《略》CIF, c.i.f.) ▪ The average *CIF* price was 40 US dollars per ton. 平均的な保険料運賃込み値段は1トン40米ドルだった.

count the cost 事前に危険[損失, 困難]を考慮する ▪ I had no time to *count the cost*. 私は事前に困難を考慮する時間がなかった.

to *one's* ***cost*** 迷惑[損害]を被って, 苦い経験で ▪ We soon learned *to our cost* that we were far from the island. まもなくその島からずっと離れていることを知って大いに困った ▪ Traveling is expensive, as I know *to my cost*. 苦い経験で知っているが, 旅行は金がかかるものだ.

cost[2] /kɔ:st|kɔst/ 動 ***cost*** *a person* ***a bomb*** [***an arm and a leg***] 大金がかかる ▪ I was able to find great care last year, but it *cost* me *a bomb*. 私は昨年すばらしい介護を見つけることができたが, 無茶苦茶に金がかかった ▪ Upgrading to digital television need not *cost* you *an arm and a leg*. デジタルテレビにアップするのは大金をかけないですむ.

cost *a person* ***a fortune*** [***pretty penny***] 《口》大金がかかる《特に予想外に高額のとき》 ▪ This rose wreath has *cost* me *a fortune*. 私にはこのバラの花輪は高くついた ▪ That diamond ring must have *cost* him *a pretty penny*. 彼はあのダイヤの指輪に大枚をはたいたにちがいない.

cost *a person* ***dear***(***ly***) 人に高いものにつく; (...のため)ひどい目にあう ▪ That orchard he bought *cost* him *dear*. 彼の買ったその果樹園は高いものについた ▪ This cruelty *cost* him *dearly* afterwards. この残酷な行為のため彼はのちになってひどい目にあった.

cost *a person his* ***life*** 人が...のため死ぬ[命を落とす] ▪ One false step could *cost* him *his life*. 一

歩踏みはずせば彼は死ぬだろう.

cost what it may 費用がいくらかかっても; どんなことがあっても ▪ *Cost what it may*, I will accomplish my purpose. 何があっても私は目的を達成する.

cottage /kátɪdʒ|kɔ́t-/ 名 ***love in a cottage*** →LOVE[1].

cotton /kátən|kɔ́tən/ 名 ***bless her*** [***his***] ***cotton socks*** 《英戯》 …に祝福あれ《愛情の表現》 ▪ *Bless her cotton socks* for her naivety. 彼女の純真さに神の祝福がありますように.

Cotton is king. 《米》(南部では)綿が王だ ▪ *Cotton is king*, and his enemies are vanquished. 綿が王だ, そしてその敵どもは征服されている.

sitting on high cotton 《米口》大喜びで ▪ The girls were *sitting on high cotton* because they had won the trophy. トロフィーを獲得したので少女たちは大喜びだった.

spit cotton →SPIT[2].

too high for picking cotton 《米口》少し酔って ▪ I have been *too high for picking cotton*. 私は少し酔っていた.

cottonwool /kátənwʊ̀l|kɔ́tən-/ 名 ***be*** [***live***] ***in cottonwool*** 安逸をむさぼる, 贅沢に暮らす ▪ Letty *lived in* clover and *cottonwool*. レティーは贅沢に安楽に暮らした.

keep [***wrap***]***… in cottonwool*** 《口》…を甘やかす, 大事にしすぎる ▪ His mother *keeps* him *in cottonwool*. 母親は彼を甘やかしている.

couch[1] /kaʊtʃ/ 名 ***on the couch*** 神経科の診察[治療]を受けて, 精神分析を受けて ▪ Today, on the 150th anniversary of his birth, Sigmund Freud is *on the couch* himself. 今日, 生誕150年を迎えジクムント・フロイト自身が精神分析を受ける立場にある.

couch[2] /kaʊtʃ/ 動 ***be couched in*** 《雅》…の言葉で表明されている ▪ The petition *is couched in* fitting terms. その歎願書は適切な言葉で記されている.

be couched on 《雅》…の上に伏す ▪ He *is couched on* a bed of flowers. 彼は贅沢な暮らしをしている.

be couched under …の陰に隠されている ▪ A threat *is couched under* his request. 彼の嘆願の陰に脅迫がひそんでいる.

cough[1] /kɔːf|kɔf/ 名 ***give a cough*** せき払いする《注意を引いたり, 警告のため》 ▪ I *gave a cough* as I entered the room. 入室するときせき払いをした.

cough[2] /kɔːf|kɔf/ 動 ***cough*** *one's* ***head off*** 激しくせきをする ▪ Tom has been *coughing his head off* all day. トムは一日中ひどくせきをしている.

cough it up 《俗》(隠し事などを)話してしまう ▪ You had better *cough it up* and stop trying to hide it. すっかり話してしまって隠そうとしないほうがいい.

could /kəd, kʊd/ 助 ***could be*** (そう)かもしれない ▪ Where's he staying now? A lodging house? —*Could be*. 彼は今どこにいるんだろう. 下宿屋かな—そうかもね. ☞It could be の It を略したもの.

couldn't agree more 全く同感だ[その通りだ] ▪ He's lost the fight. —I *couldn't agree more*. 彼は試合に負けたのだ—全くその通りだ.

couldn't care less →CARE[2].

I couldn't 《口》もう結構です《丁寧に断るときの言葉》 ▪ Oh, *I couldn't*, thank you. いえ, もう十分です. ありがとうございます.

council /káʊnsəl/ 名 ***at*** [***in***] ***council*** **1** 会議中で[の] ▪ The duke sat *in council* with his privy councillors. 公爵は枢密顧問官たちと会議をした ▪ He is deep *in council*. 彼は慎重審議中だ.
2 諮問機関にはかって ▪ The action taken by the Queen *in Council* is a mere formality. 枢密院に諮問して行動する主権者たる女王がとる行為はただ形式的なものにすぎない ▪ Over the years, the content and form of orders *in council* have become standardized. 国王が諮問機関にはかって発する勅令はその内容と形式が年月を経て標準的なものになってきた.

call … to council …を会議に召集する ▪ The Pope *called* the Senators *to council*. 法王は評議員を会議に召集した.

Councils of war never fight. 《諺》軍事会談は戦わない《重要事項は結論に達しない》.

counsel /káʊnsəl/ 名 ***a counsel of despair*** 窮余[苦肉]の策 ▪ Partition was, if not *a counsel of despair*, at any rate a last resort. 分割は, 苦しまぎれの策ではないとしても, とにかく最終手段だった.

a counsel of perfection (天国に入ろうとする者に対する)完全を期する戒告 (《聖》*Matt*. 19. 21); 実行できない理想案(など) ▪ I'm afraid it's rather *a counsel of perfection*. それはどうも実行不可能の理想案ではないかと思う.

hold counsel =take COUNSEL.

If the counsel be good, it matters not who gave it. 《諺》よい助言なら誰がそれを与えようと問題ではない《よい助言なら目下の者からのものでも受入れよ》,「人をもって言を廃せず」.

keep *a person's* ***counsel*** 人の考えや計画などを秘して漏らさない ▪ I'll *keep your counsel*. あなたの考えは秘密にしておきましょう.

keep *one's* (***own***) ***counsel*** (考え・意見を)黙っていてほかに漏らさない ▪ Old Sedley had *kept his own counsel*. セドリー老人は自分の考えを胸に秘めていた.

take counsel 相談する, 協議する (*with, of, together*) (《聖》*John* 11. 35) ▪ *Take counsel with* your pillow. 一晩よく考えなさい ▪ I *took counsel with* my soul. 私は心と相談した.

use counsel 注意する, 慎重にする ▪ *Use counsel* in this matter. 本件は深慮を要す.

count[1] /kaʊnt/ 名 ***at the last count*** 最新の集計では ▪ *At the last count*, Christians represented 51 percent of the population. 最新の集計では, キリスト教徒は国民の51%だった.

down for the count →out for the COUNT.

keep count of **1** …を数え続ける, の数を読んでいく ▪ I *kept count of* the meteors till midnight. 夜中まで私は流れ星を数え続けた.
2 …の数を覚えている ▪ There were so many that I

couldn't *keep count of* them. たくさんあったので数を覚えていられなかった.

lose count of …を数えきれなくなる; の数がわからなくなる ▪ I was counting the number of colleges in America, but I *lost count of* them. アメリカの大学の数を数えていたが, (あまりに多くて)数がわからなくなってしまった ▪ We *lost count of* time. 我々は時の移るのを忘れた.

on all counts 《法》訴因の全部について ▪ He was found guilty *on all counts*. 彼は訴因の全部について有罪となった.

on both [etc.] ***counts*** 《法》両方[など]の訴因について ▪ She was pronounced guilty *on two counts*. 彼女は2訴因について有罪と宣言された.

out [***down***] ***for the count*** **1** 《ボクシング》10秒以内に立ち上がれないで; ノックアウトになって, 負けて ▪ He went *down for the count*. 彼はノックアウトになった ▪ We've put them *out for the count*. 我々は彼らを負かした.

2 《口》意識を失って; ぐっすり眠って ▪ I tried to wake her, but she was *out for the count*. 私は彼女を起こそうとしたが彼女はぐっすり眠っていた.

out of count 数えきれない, 無数の ▪ They are *out of* all *count*. 彼らは全く数えきれない.

set count on …を重く見る ▪ We *set count on* the game. 我々はその試合を重く見ている.

take count of **1** 〚some, any, no などを伴って〛…を重んじる ▪ *Take no count of* what he says. 彼の言うことは問題にするな ▪ Do you *take count of* such things? そんなことを重要視するのか.

2 …を数える ▪ *Take count of* votes. 票数を数えなさい.

take the count **1** 《ボクシング》10秒を数えられるまで起き上がれない, ノックアウトになる ▪ In the eleventh round, Shakey *took the count*. 第11ラウンドでシェイキーはノックアウトになった.

2 死ぬ; 使えなくなる ▪ Resentment *takes the count* before such a speech. そのような演説を聞いては恨みは消える ▪ Our old car has *taken the count*. 我々の古車は使えなくなった. ☞ボクシングから.

count[2] /kaʊnt/ 動 ***and counting*** (数・量を表す語に続けて)そしてさらに増加[成長]しつつある ▪ 19 Kids *and Counting* is an American reality television show. 「19人と更に増え続ける子供たち」はアメリカの実生活テレビ番組である.

count *one's* ***chickens before they are hatched*** →CHICKEN.

count down the days [***hours, minutes***] (待ち望んで)指折り数える ▪ I'm *counting down the days* until the end of the exams. 試験が終わる日を指折り数えて楽しみにしている.

count for much [***a great deal***] 大いに価値がある, 大いに役に立つ ▪ Birth *counts for a great deal*. 生まれは大いに物を言う.

count for nothing [***little***] 全く[ほとんど]役に立たない, 全く[ほとんど]価値がない ▪ Knowledge without common sense *counts for little*. 常識を伴わない知識はほとんど役に立たない.

count for something 重要である, 役に立つ ▪ I hope my opinion will *count for something*. 私見がお役に立てればよいのですが.

count kin with 《米》…と近親である; と家系図を比較する ▪ William can *count kin with* him. ウィリアムは彼と家系図を比較することができる《立派な家系である》.

count noses [***heads***] 《口》人数を数える, 出席者を数える ▪ Keep still, everyone. I'm *counting heads*. みなさん, じっとしていてください. 頭数を数えているのですから.

count … on *one's* ***fingers*** [***on the fingers of one hand***] …を指折り数える, 片手の指で数えられる ▪ Such men may *be counted on your fingers*. そのような人は五指を屈するほどしかない ▪ Restaurants worthy of the name could *be counted on the fingers of one hand*. 名前に値するレストランは5つもないだろう.

count out *a measure* [*member*] 《英》(下院出席者数不足のため)議案の討議[議員の演説]を中止する ▪ Mr. Freeland *was counted out* summarily. フリーランド議員は即座に演説を中止された.

count out the House 《英》下院の出席者数不足のため(40人以下)流会[休会]を宣する ▪ *The House was counted out* at 9 o'clock. 下院は(出席者数不足のため)9時に休会を宣告された.

count … quality to ある性質が(人)にありとする ▪ We *count* this *quality to* him. 我々は彼にこの性質があると思う.

count the days [***hours***] 日[時間]を数え(て待ちこがれ)る ▪ I am *counting the days* until she comes home. 彼女が帰るまで日を数えて待っている.

count the house (劇場などの)入場者数を調べる ▪ Just try to *count the house*. ちょっと入場者数を調べてみなさい.

count to ten (心を静めるため)10まで数える ▪ Father always told me to *count to ten* when I got angry. 腹が立ったら10まで数えよと常に父は私に言った.

Who's counting? 《口》数[回数]なんか問題ではない[気にするな].

countenance /káʊntənəns/ 名 ***change*** (*one's*) ***countenance*** 顔色を変える ▪ Griffith started and *changed countenance* at once. グリフィスはぎくりとして, さっと顔色を変えた.

one's ***countenance fell*** 顔に失望の色が浮かんだ; 浮かない顔をした(《聖》*Gen.* 4. 5) ▪ *His countenance fell* and the smile of welcome disappeared. 彼の顔に失望の色が現れ歓迎の微笑は消えた.

face … out of countenance …に面と向かって度を失わせる ▪ Will he *be faced out of countenance* by a young whippersnapper? 彼は青二才ににらまれて度を失うだろうか.

give [***lend***] ***countenance to*** …の肩を持つ, を暗に奨励する, 黙許する ▪ You should not *give countenance to* wrong-doing. 君は不正な行為を暗に奨

励してはいけない.

keep** one's **countenance (驚かず)平然としている; (笑わず)澄ましている ▪ *Keeping his countenance*, he did not give them one of his looks. 平然として彼は彼らをちらっとも見なかった ▪ He looked so funny that I could not *keep my countenance*. 彼は非常におかしいふうをしていたので私は笑わずにはいられなかった.

keep* (*in*) *countenance **1** …を励ます; をまごつかせない; の顔を立てる ▪ Flora will be there to *keep* you (*in*) *countenance*. フローラがそこに来てあなたを励ますでしょう ▪ Please *keep* me *in countenance*. どうぞ私の顔を立ててください.

2 平然としている, (笑わずに)澄ましている ▪ We could not *keep in countenance*. 我々は笑わずにはいられなかった.

lose countenance **1** 落ち着きを失う, うろたえる ▪ At this question he suddenly *lost countenance*. この質問に対して彼は急にうろたえた.

2 恥をかく ▪ You made me *lose countenance* in front of everybody. 君はみなの前で僕に恥をかかせた.

out of countenance あわてて, 当惑して ▪ When we accused him of lying, he was very much *out of countenance*. 嘘をついたと言って責めたら彼は非常に狼狽した.

put ... in countenance …を励ます ▪ It *puts* the learned *in countenance*. それは博学な人々の励みになる.

put ... out of countenance …をうろたえさせる, 赤面させる, 面目を失わせる ▪ The breakfast *put* me *out of countenance*. その朝食は私をめんくらわせた ▪ You *put* her a little *out of countenance*. あなたは彼女を少し赤面させた.

counter /káʊntər/ 形副名 ***act counter to*** = run COUNTER to 1.

behind the counter 店員を勤めて ▪ She is a girl *behind the counter*. 彼女は女性店員です.

go counter to →run COUNTER to.

hunt* [*go, run*] *counter (獲物と)反対の方向に走る, 狩り進む ▪ The hound *ran counter*. 猟犬は獲物と反対の方向に走った.

nail ... to the counter →NAIL[2].

over the counter **1** (薬などの売買が)処方箋なしで, 店頭で ▪ None of the smoking deterrent products now sold *over the counter* is effective. 現在店頭で販売されている喫煙抑止製品はどれも効果がない.

2 (株取引が)店頭の; 証券業者の店先で ▪ The *over-the-counter* market had its worst setback since last November. 店頭市場は昨年11月以来最悪の下げだった.

run counter →hunt COUNTER.

run* [*go*] *counter to **1** …に逆らう; に反する ▪ Let us *go counter to* tradition rather than to Scripture. 聖書よりも伝統に逆らいましょう ▪ His plans *run counter to* mine. 彼の計画は私のに反する.

2 = hunt COUNTER.

serve* [*sit, stand*] *behind the counter 店主[店員]を勤める; 売り場に勤める ▪ He *serves behind the counter*. 彼は店員を勤めている.

under the counter = under the TABLE 2.

counterpoise /káʊntərpɔ̀ɪz/ 名 ***be in counterpoise*** 平衡を保つ, つり合いがとれている ▪ The climate *is in counterpoise* all the year around. 気候は一年中安定している.

country /kʌ́ntri/ 名 ***a country cousin*** 田舎者, お上りさん ▪ The sightseeing guide geared her tour toward *country cousins* who had never been to a big city before. 観光ガイドはツアーを大都会が初めてのお上りさんに合わせた ▪ They are afraid of being seen as *country cousins* to Harvard, Yale and Princeton. 彼らの危惧はハーバードやイェール, プリンストンに比べてノーブランド大学に見られることだ.

a country mile 《米口》 **1** 遠[長]距離にわたって ▪ There's an advantage in shopping here because you're not going to have to walk *a country mile* to get a gallon of milk. ここでは買い物が便利で, ミルクを1ガロン買うのにえんえんと歩かなくてよい ▪ That boy can hit the ball *a country mile*. あの子は打球をはるか遠くまで飛ばすことができる.

2 〚by を伴って〛 ダントツで, 楽々[ゆうゆう]と ▪ He is the best bowler in Australia *by a country mile*. 彼はオーストラリアではダントツで最優秀の(クリケット)ボーラーだ.

across* (*the*) *country **1** (道路によらず)田野を横切って; 断郊の ▪ He hastened there *across the country*. 彼は田野を横断してそこへ急いだ ▪ It's an event with many cars competing in an *across country* event. それは多くの車が田野を横断して競い合う競技である.

2 国中に ▪ They stumped *across the country*. 彼らは国中を遊説した.

an unknown country (…にとって)未知の[不得意な]分野; 苦手な話題 (*to*) ▪ Computer programming remains *a* vast *unknown country to* most outsiders. コンピュータープログラミングは門外漢には茫漠(ぼう)とした未知の世界のままだ.

in the country **1** 《クリケット》 外野に ▪ The ball landed *in the country*. ボールは飛んで外野に落ちた.

2 田舎に ▪ My family live *in the country*. 私の家族は田舎に住んでいる.

In the country of the blind, the one-eyed man is King. →BLIND[1].

It's a free country! →FREE[1].

My country, right or wrong! 祖国のためには, 正邪を問わず ▪ But *my country, right or wrong*, she is still my country. だが, 祖国のためなら正邪を問わずで, その国はまだ私の祖国だ ▪ I'm not a "*my country, right or wrong*" guy. 私は「祖国のためには正邪を問わず」といったタイプではない.

put** oneself **on* [*upon*] one's *country. 陪審の審査を要求する ▪ Such an outlaw was entitled to *put himself on his country*. そういう法益被剥奪者は陪審の審査を要求する権利があった.

So many countries, so many customs. 《諺》国の数だけ習わしの数がある,「所変われば品変わる」.

up country 《米》田舎に ▪ He lives *up country*. 彼は田舎に住んでいる.

county /káʊnti/ 名 ***another county heard from*** その場で名乗り出る[登場する]思いがけない人 ▪ Her cousin decided to contest the will—*another county heard from*. 彼女のいとこが遺書をめぐる争いに名乗りをあげることにした—思わぬ伏兵であった. ☞C. Odets の劇 *Awake and Sing* (1931)より.

coup /kuː/ 名 ***count*** (*one's*) ***coup*** **1** (北米先住民が手に持ったもので敵に)最初の一撃を与える ▪ We will run in and *count coup*. 走りこんで最初の一撃を与えよう.
2 手がらを数えたてる ▪ They danced and *counted their coups*. 彼らはダンスしたり, 手がらを数えたてたりした.

make [***pull off***] ***a great coup*** すばらしい当たりを取る, 大成功を収める ▪ She *made a great coup* in her first clothing show. 彼女は最初のドレスショーですばらしい大当たりを取った.

couple[1] /kʌ́pəl/ 名 ***a couple of*** 2個[二人]の; 数個[人]の; 2, 3の ▪ I saw *a couple of* girls walking in the park. 二人の少女が公園を散歩しているのを見た ▪ He died *a couple of* years ago. 彼は2, 3年前に死んだ.

Every couple is not a pair. 《諺》合わせものが必ずしも似合いの一対とはならない《うまくいかない夫婦もある》.

go [***hunt, run***] ***in couples*** いつも二人連れだっている ▪ They used to *hunt in couples* when they were at Oxford. オックスフォードにいたころはいつも仲良く二人連れだっていたものだ.

in a couple of turns たちまち ▪ I'll be fine *in a couple of turns*. 私はすぐに良くなるでしょう.

couple[2] /kʌ́pəl/ 動 ***be coupled to*** 〖主に受身で〗…と結合している ▪ A trailer *is coupled to* the tractor. トレーラーはトラクターに連結される.

coupled with the fact that …という事実と相まって ▪ *Coupled with the fact that* we were spearfishing, we created an interesting situation. 我々がやすを使った漁法をとっていたこともあって, 興味深い事態が生じた.

courage /kə́ːrɪdʒ|kʌ́r-/ 名 (***have***) ***the courage of*** *one's* ***convictions*** [***opinions***] 自分の正しいと信ずるところを断行する勇気[意見を堂々と主張したり実行する勇気](がある) ▪ Whatever virtues he lacks, he has at least *the courage of his opinions*. 彼がどんな美徳を欠くにせよ, 少なくとも自説を主張する勇気がある. ☞F le courage de son opinion 'the courage of his opinion'.

have the courage to *do* 勇敢[大胆]にも…する ▪ He *had the courage to* say no. 彼は勇敢にもノーと言った.

lose courage 落胆する ▪ The repeated failure has made him *lose courage*. 再三再四の失敗で彼は落胆した.

pluck [***muster, screw, summon***] ***up courage*** 勇気を奮い起こす, 勇気を出す ▪ The lady *plucked up courage*, and asked the burglar what he wanted. 婦人は勇気を振い起こし強盗に何がほしいのかと尋ねた.

take courage 勇気を出す[奮い起こす] ▪ He *took courage* and entered. 彼は元気を出して入った.

take *one's* ***courage in both hands*** 《フランス語法》勇躍して立つ, 大胆に乗り出す, 思い切ってやる ▪ He *took his courage in both hands* and said, "Anna, I love you." 彼は勇気を振り絞って「アンナ, 愛しているよ」と言った.

course /kɔːrs/ 名 ***a matter of course*** もちろんのこと, 当然のこと ▪ It was *a matter of course* that he should win the chair. 彼が勝つのは当然のことであった ▪ A black swan is *a matter of course* to it. コクチョウもそれに比べれば珍らしくない.

be blown off course 進路からはずれる; (計画などが)中止になる, 頓挫する ▪ The plane *was blown off course* by strong winds. 飛行機は強風のため進路からはずれた ▪ The UK's biggest wind power project *was blown off course* as residents fought back. 英国最大の風力発電計画は地元民たちが抵抗したため中止になった.

be on the course (船が)針路をとっている, 進航中である ▪ The ship *was on the course* he intended. 船は彼の意のままの針路をとっている.

bend *one's* ***course*** …の方に向かう[向かって行く] ▪ Homeward did they *bend their course*. 彼らは家路に向かった.

by course of (法律など)の慣例に従って, の手続きをふんで ▪ They still expect a pardon *by course of* law. 彼らはまだ法律の慣例によって赦免されることを期待している.

by the (***normal, ordinary***) ***course of nature*** → in the (normal, ordinary) COURSE of nature.

direct *one's* ***course*** (***to***) (…の方へ)進路をとる, 足を向ける ▪ He therefore *directed his course to* the convoy. だから彼は護衛艦の方へ針路をとった.

down the course 一流の競走馬でなく ▪ All our horses were *down the course*. 我々の馬はみなめぼしい競走馬ではなかった.

during the course of = in the COURSE of.

embark on a course 一連の行動を始める ▪ He *embarked on a course* of extravagant living. 彼は贅沢な生活をやり始めた.

evil courses 不品行, 放蕩 ▪ The man is given over to *evil courses*. その男は放蕩にふけっている.

follow [***take***] ***a course of action*** …という行動をとる ▪ We don't *follow a* predetermined *course of action*. 我々はあらかじめ敷かれている行動はとらない ▪ The president *took a* wrong *course of action* that sent a bad signal to the world. 大

統領は間違った行動をとって世界に悪いサインを送った.

give courses in ...の教授をする ▪ More and more colleges are *giving courses in* marriage. 結婚の講義をする大学がだんだん増加している.

go through the course 課程を終える ▪ He has *gone through the* middle school *course.* 彼は中等学校の課程を終えた.

hold (***on***) *one's* ***course*** 方向[方針]を続ける ▪ He *held on his course* up the channel. 彼は針路を続けて海峡を上って行った.

in course **1**《米》正規の課程を経た ▪ I couldn't take a degree *in course* that I wanted. 僕は正規の課程を経た学位を取れなかった.

2 順序正しく, 順当に, やがて《今は in due COURSE》 ▪ You will be promoted *in course.* あなたはそのうち昇進するだろう.

3《俗》もちろん ▪ "*In course* I did," he said. 「もちろん僕はしたよ」と彼は言った.

in course of ...中で ▪ The ship is now *in course of* construction. 船は今建造中である ▪ The goods ordered are now *in course of* shipment. ご注文の品は今荷積み中です.

in due course 当然の順序を追って; 順当に; やがて, ちょうどよいころに ▪ *In due course,* she became the mother of ten children. そのうちに彼女は10人の子供の母となった ▪ The boys got promotion *in due course.* 少年たちは順当に進級した.

in (***due***) ***course of time*** 時節が来れば; そのうち, やがて ▪ It will be known to everybody *in due course of time.* それはやがて時節が来ればすべての人に知られるであろう ▪ I will take you to Nikko *in due course of time.* そのうち日光へ連れて行ってあげる.

in full course 真っ盛りで, 最盛期で ▪ The constitutional reforms are *in full course.* 憲法改革が山場だ.

in the course of ...中に, のたつうちに; の間に ▪ *In the course of* his remarks, he made the following statement. 発言中に彼は次のような陳述をした ▪ *In the course of* a year the boy grew much stronger. 1年たつうちにその少年はずっと強くなった ▪ Difficulties arose *in the course of* our inquiry. 調査しているうちにいろいろの困難が出て来た.

in the course of things/in the ordinary course of events 自然の成り行きで, 自然に; そのうちに ▪ *In the course of things* people with other ideas came to rule. 自然の成り行きで違った思想の人々が支配し始めた.

in [***by***] ***the*** (***normal, ordinary***) ***course of nature*** 自然の成り行きとして ▪ *In the course of nature,* we must all die. 自然の成り行きとして, 我々はみな死なねばならない ▪ She cannot *by the course of nature* expect to live long. 彼女が長く生きることは当然期待できない.

keep [***hold***] (***on***) *one's* ***course*** まっすぐに行く, 方針を続ける; 自分の職分を続けていく ▪ The young man *kept his course* and paid his father's debts. 青年はまっすぐに道を進み父親の負債を払った.

☞海事用語より.

lay a [*one's*] ***course*** **1** 針路を取って進む ▪ We shall *lay our course* another way. 我々は別の針路を取って進む.

2 (何かをする)計画を立てる.

leave business [***time, life, fate,*** etc.] ***to take its own course/let business*** [***time, life, fate,*** etc.] ***take its course*** 仕事[時, 人生, 運命, など]を自然の成り行きに任せる ▪ We decided to *let business take its course.* 営業は成り行き任せにすることにした ▪ She just *left the problem to take its own course.* 彼女はその問題をただ成り行きに任せた ▪ Success is having patience enough to *let time take its course.* 成功するには時の流れにゆだねられるだけの忍耐力が必要だ ▪ You should always just *let life take its course.* 常に人生をただ成り行きに任せるほうがよいだろう ▪ Don't do anything. *Let fate take its course.* 何もするな. 運を天に任せることにしよう.

lie a [***the,*** *one's*] ***course*** (船が)針路を進む ▪ She was *lying her course* about northwest. 船はおよそ北西に針路を取っていた.

lie in *a person's* ***course*** 人の行く手にある ▪ An island *lies in our course.* 我々の行く手に島がある.

of course **1**〚文・節全体にかかり, また強意肯定に〛もちろん ▪ *Of course* I'll help you if you want me to. あなたが私にお望みなら, もちろんご援助いたします.

2 当然[自然]の成り行きとして ▪ Information is by no means always given us *of course.* 知識はいつも我々に当然与えられるものではない.

3 (いいえ)もちろん ▪ You can't give up smoking. —*Of course* I can. あなたはタバコはやめられないわね—いや, もちろんやめられるよ.

4〚形容詞的に〛当然の, あたりまえの, 月並みの ▪ I thought it a matter *of course.* それをあたりまえのことと思った ▪ Their congratulations are words *of course.* 彼らの祝辞は月並みの言葉である.

on [***off***] ***course*** (乗り物などが)予定[予想]の進路通りに[からはずれて] ▪ The hurricane veered *off course.* ハリケーンは進路からそれた.

on course for [***to*** *do*] ...の途上[過程]で, へと向かって, 成功しそうで ▪ The world is *on course for* a catastrophic six degree rise in temperature by the end of this century. 世界は今世紀末までに破滅的な6度の温度上昇へと向かっている ▪ Karzai is *on course to* win the Afghanistan election. カルザイ氏はアフガニスタン大統領選に勝利しそうである.

over the course of time そのうちに, やがて ▪ I think we have gotten better *over the course of time.* 我々は時間とともに上手になったと思う.

put *a person* ***through a course of sprouts*** 《米口》(人を訓練などで)しごく; スパルタ式の訓練をする ▪ He *put* me *through a* vigorous *course of* classical *sprouts.* 彼は古典の演習で私を猛烈にしごいた.

run [***take***] *one's* ***course*** (事態・病気・歳月など)自然に経過していく; 自然に成り行く ▪ Let things *run their course.* ことの成り行きに任せよ ▪ The year *ran its course.* その年も自然に流れていった ▪ The law must *take its course.* 法の発動をまげるわけにはいかない.

shape** one's **course →SHAPE².

stand the course 苦境[苦難]に耐える ▪ I will *stand the course* as best I can. 私は精いっぱい苦難に耐えるつもりだ. ☞杭 (stake) につないだクマに数頭の犬をけしかけるクマいじめから.

stay the course 最後まで走り[がんばり]通す ▪ He was unable to *stay the course.* 彼は最後までがんばり通せなかった. ☞競馬より.

steer [take] a middle course 中庸の道をとる, 中道をとる ▪ May shrewdly *steered a middle course* between her enemies and supporters. メイは抜け目なく敵と支持者との中道をとった.

take a course in …の教授[講義]を受ける ▪ They *took a course in* English literature. 彼らはイギリス文学の講義を受けた.

take** one's **own course 自分の思うようにやる, 独自の方針をとる ▪ My parents let me *take my own course.* 両親は自分の思うようにやらせてくれた.

The course of true love never did run smooth. 《諺》真の恋路は昔から平坦だったためしはない. ☞cf. Sh., *Merch. V.* 1. 1. 134から.

throw ... off course …を予定の方向からはずす ▪ The plane *was thrown off course.* その航空機は予定の進路方向からはずれていた.

court /kɔːrt/ 名 ***a friend at [in] court*** (宮中で)引き立ててくれる友人; 有力なつて ▪ He must have *a friend at court.* 彼は良いつてがあるはずだ.

a kangaroo court →KANGAROO.

at [to] court 宮廷で[へ] ▪ I appeared *at court* on all public days. 私は公日にはいつも宮廷に参内した ▪ I am going in state *to court* to meet the Queen. 威儀を正して女王に会見するため宮廷に行く.

be presented at court (新任の大公使・社交界の子女などが)拝謁を賜わる ▪ My grandfather *was presented at court* in London. 祖父はロンドンの宮中で拝謁を賜わった.

bring ... before the court …を表ざたにする ▪ They *brought* the matter *before the court.* 彼らはその件を表ざたにした.

bring ... into court (証拠など)を法廷に持ち出す[提出する] ▪ He *brought* new evidence *into court.* 彼は新証拠を法廷に提出した.

clear the court 傍聴人を全部退廷させる ▪ The judge ordered *the court* to *be cleared.* 判事は傍聴人全員を退廷させるよう命じた.

go to court 参内する ▪ I *went to court* to meet the Queen. 私は女王に拝謁するため参内した.

hold a court 開廷する, 裁判を行う ▪ The Supreme *Court was held* the next morning in Boston. 最高裁判所は翌朝ボストンで開廷された ▪ The Archbishop of Canterbury *held a court* at Dunstable. カンタベリーの大主教はダンスタブルで裁判を行った.

hold court **1** 謁見式を行う ▪ He *held court* at York for a week. 彼はヨークで1週間謁見を行った. **2** 開廷する ▪ Hughes sometimes *held court* by phone and failed to have a court reporter present. ヒューズはときおり電話で法廷を開き, 法廷速記者を出席させるのを怠ったことがあった. **3**《口》国王[女王]のようにふるまう; ファンに取り囲まれる, ちやほやされる ▪ Jane was *holding court* for many charmed boys. ジェインは多くの魅せられた少年たちに対して女王のようにふるまっていた ▪ After a match he generally *held court* in the locker room. 試合後彼は大抵ロッカールームでファンに囲まれる.

in court 法廷で[に] ▪ He misconducted himself *in court.* 彼は法廷でふらちを働いた ▪ The Queen appeared in person *in court.* 女王自から出廷した.

laugh ... out of court 《英口》…を一笑に付し去る, 問題にしない ▪ Public opinion is *laughing* it *out of court.* 世論はそれを一笑に付している.

make [pay] (one's) court to …のきげんをとる; (女性)に言い寄る, 求婚する ▪ I went every day to *pay my court to* the King. 私は毎日国王のごきげんをとり結びに行った ▪ I began to *pay my court to* the girl. 私はその娘に言い寄り始めた.

out of court **1** 法廷外で; 示談で ▪ The case has been settled *out of court.* その件は示談で解決した. **2** (原告の言い分が)審理の価値なしと却下された; (提案などが)一顧の価値もなく, (原告が)被審理権を失って ▪ The argument has been put *out of court.* その議論は審理の価値なしと却下された ▪ His conclusion is quite *out of court* now. 彼の結論は今は全く一顧の価値もない ▪ These gentlemen are *out of court.* これらの人々は被審理権を失っている.

present ... at court (特に社交界の子女など)の宮廷での拝謁の介添えを務める ▪ He *presented* her *at court.* 彼は彼女の宮廷拝謁の介添えをした.

put ... out of court **1** →out of COURT 2. **2** …を顧慮しない, 無視する ▪ You may *put* this *out of court.* これは無視してさしつかえない ▪ He *puts* himself *out of court.* 彼は他人に無視されるようなことをする[言う].

settle ... out of court →out of COURT 1.

take ... into court …を裁判ざたにする ▪ They *took* the matter *into court.* その件を裁判ざたにした.

take** a person **to court 人を裁判ざたにする ▪ I had to *take* him *to court.* 私は彼を裁判ざたにせねばならなかった.

(***The***) ***ball is in your [his,** etc.**] court.*** こんどは君[彼, など]が行動する番だ ▪ *Ball is in your court.* Look sharp. こんどは君が行動する番だ. しっかりやれよ. ☞テニスから.

to court →at COURT.

up (a) court 路地のつきあたりに ▪ He lives *up court.* 彼は路地のつきあたりに住んでいる.

courtesy /kə́ːrtəsi/ 名 ***by [of] courtesy*** 儀礼上; 慣例により ▪ Only *of courtesy* is the Title of Lord given to them. 「卿」という尊称はただ儀礼上

彼らに与えられているにすぎない ▪ A man calls himself *by courtesy* "Your humble servant." 人は慣例により自分を「あなたのつまらないしもべ」と呼ぶ.

by* (*the*) *courtesy of **1** …の好意[提供]により《ラジオ・テレビ番組など》 ▪ This program is presented *by courtesy of* the Arizona Humanities Council. この番組はアリゾナ人道協議会の提供によるものです.
2《米》…の許可[承諾]による《さし絵・記事などの転載許可を明記する文句》 ▪ Slides reproduced *by courtesy of* the author. スライドは著者の許可により複写.

do* [*show*]** *a person* **(*a*) *courtesy 人に親切を尽くす ▪ He has *done* me *a courtesy.* 彼は私に親切を尽くしてくれた ▪ An ointment will *do* a man *a courtesy* who has any virulent sores. 軟膏は悪性のはれものがある人にはよい.

do *a person* ***the courtesy to*** *do* [***of*** *doing*] 人に丁重にも…する ▪ He *did* me *the courtesy to* consult [*of consulting*]. 彼はわざわざ私に相談してくれた.

out of courtesy …に敬意を表して, に配慮して ▪ Most wheelchair users appreciate the favor, as long as it is done *out of courtesy* and not out of sympathy. 車いす利用者の大半は好意に感謝している, それが同情からではなく礼節からなされている限りでは.

through* (*the*) *courtesy of =by (the) COURTESY of 1.

cousin /kʌ́zən/ 名 ***a country cousin*** → COUNTRY.

a Cousin Betsy 《口》知的障害者 ▪ He never gave short measure to *a Cousin Betsy.* 彼は知能障害の人にも決して量りを少なくしたことはない.

a* (*first*) *cousin once removed いとこの子, いとこ半 ▪ She was marrying her *first cousin once removed*, or her elder cousin's son. 彼女は自分のいとこ半, つまり, 年上のいとこの息子と結婚しようとしていた.

a second cousin ふた[また]いとこ, はとこ ▪ The children of first cousins are *second cousins* to each other. いとこの子供たちは互いにふたいとこだ.

be first cousin to …に非常によく似ている ▪ That teak chest *is first cousin to* mine. あのチーク材のたんすは私のに非常によく似ている.

be second cousin to …に似ている ▪ Heroin *is second cousin to* morphine. ヘロインはモルヒネに似ている.

***call cousins* (*with*)** (…と)お互いにいとこと呼び合う; (と)いとこ[親類]だと言う ▪ He *calls cousins with* some of the "best" people in England. 彼はイギリスの最も立派な人々の幾人かと親類だと言っている ▪ My new house does not pretend to *call cousins with* a mansion house. 私の新しい家はおこがましくも大邸宅に似ているなどとは言えない.

call the king *one's* ***cousin*** 〚主に否定文で〛国王をいとこだと名乗る ▪ I wouldn't *call the king my cousin.* 私は国王のいとこだと名乗ろうとも思わない《これ以上望むところはない》.

***kissing cousin*(*s*)** 非常に似通った人[物] ▪ These two cars are *kissing cousins.* この2台の車はほんとうによく似ている.

covenant /kʌ́vənənt/ 名 ***break* [*hold, keep*] *covenant*** 契約を破る[守る] ▪ They *broke covenant* with God. 彼らは神との契約を破った ▪ If we want to be like God, then we too should *keep covenant.* 神になぞらえたくば我々も契約を守ることだ.

make* [*enter into*] *a covenant 契約を結ぶ《法律的・神学的意味にのみ》 ▪ Both of them *made a covenant.* 彼らの両方とも契約を結んだ ▪ He *entered into a covenant* for mutual support with them. 彼は彼らと相互援助の契約を結んだ.

cover[1] /kʌ́vər/ 名 ***a cover girl*** →GIRL.

a cover-up 隠蔽(工作), もみ消し ▪ The main purpose of the *cover-up* was to hide the origin of the money. 隠蔽の主な目的はお金の出所を隠すためだった.

blow *one's* ***cover*** 正体[身元]がばれる ▪ Dick changed his name so as not to *blow his cover.* ディックは身元がばれないように変名した.

blow *a person's* ***cover*** [***the cover of*** *a person*] (人)の正体[身元]を暴く ▪ A British double agent *blew the cover of* many British agents to the KGB Soviet intelligence agency. 英国の二重スパイが KGB ソ連諜報機関に多くの英国人諜報員の身元を漏洩した.

from cover to cover (本の)初めから終わりまで ▪ I have read this book *from cover to cover.* 私はこの本を初めから終わりまで読んだ.

get under cover →under COVER 1.

lay covers for …人分の膳立て[料理の用意]をする ▪ *Covers were laid for* five. 5人分の料理が用意された.

off cover (切手が)封筒からはがされて ▪ The stamp is *off cover*, in excellent condition. その切手は封筒からはがされたものでコンディションは実に良好である.

on cover (切手が)封筒にはられたままで ▪ This stamp is *on cover*, and was formerly owned by Geoffrey Mason. この切手はエンタイアでかつてジェフリー・メイスンが所有していたものだ.

put ... between covers …を本にする ▪ I've *put* these articles on science *between covers.* 私はこれらの科学に関する論文を本にした.

run to cover (経済的)危険を逃れる ▪ The sellers of stock *run to cover* by buying back the stock. 株の売り手は株を買い戻して危険を逃れる.

take cover **1** 隠れる, 避難する ▪ The rain came down so violently that we had to *take cover* in a barn. 雨が非常に激しく降ってきたので納屋に避難しなければならなかった.
2《軍》地形[地物]を利用して隠れる ▪ There was nowhere we could *take cover* from the enemy. 敵から隠れることのできる場所はなかった.

under cover **1** 援護されて, 隠れて; 内密の[に]; 変装して ▪ It is raining hard; we must get *under cover* quick. 雨が激しく降っている. 早く雨宿りせねば

ならない ▪ The enemy fought *under cover.* 敵は遮蔽物に隠れて戦った.

2 封書にして, 同封して ▪ Send the money *under cover.* その金を同封して送りなさい.

under cover to *a person*/***under*** *a person's* ***cover*** …あての手紙に同封して ▪ I send this to the postmaster *under Alice's cover* [*under cover to* Alice]. 私はアリスへの手紙に同封してこれを郵便局長に送ります.

under plain cover 差出人(内容など)が明記されていない(封書)で ▪ The company sent me a pamphlet *under plain cover* containing some erotic pictures. その会社は差出人が明記されていないパンフレットを送ってきたが, 中には何枚かの春画が入っていた.

under separate [***the same***] ***cover*** 別封で[同封で] ▪ The package will be sent to you *under separate cover.* 包みは別個にお送りします.

under (***the***) ***cover of*** **1** …に援護されて ▪ The troops advanced *under cover of* a heavy artillery bombardment. 軍隊は猛烈な大砲の砲撃に援護されて前進した ▪ They slept *under the cover of* a tree. 彼らは木の陰に眠った.

2 (やみなど)にまぎれて[乗じて] ▪ They escaped *under cover of* night. 彼らは夜陰に乗じて逃亡した.

3 …にかこつけて, 隠れて ▪ Many murders have been committed *under cover of* patriotism. 愛国心にかこつけて多くの人殺しが行われた.

within the covers of a book (現実と対比して)本の中では ▪ *Within the covers of a book* we can all be Sherlock Holmes. 本の中では我々はみんなシャーロック・ホームズになれる.

cover² /kʌ́vər/ 動 ***be*** [***remain***] ***covered*** 帽子をかぶる[かぶったままでいる] ▪ Please *be covered.* どうぞ帽子をおかぶりください.

be covered with …でおおわれ(てい)る ▪ The summit of Mt. Fuji *is covered with* snow all the year round. 富士山の頂上は一年中雪でおおわれている ▪ The goods *were covered with* tarpaulins. その貨物には防水布がかけてあった.

cover a siege 包囲軍を援護する《攻撃から守る》 ▪ The King at last consented to *cover the siege.* 国王はついに包囲軍を援護することを承諾した.

cover *one's* ***back*** [***butt, rear, tail,*** 《英》 ***ass***] 《俗》(累(るい)が及ばないように) 予防線を張る, 責任回避の言い訳[言い逃れ]をする, 取り繕う ▪ Back up your plan and *cover your back.* 君の計画を補足し, 対策を立てなさい ▪ The politician *covered his ass,* so to say, by making that pledge. 政治家はそういう誓いを立てることによって, いわば, 予防線を張った.

cover *one's* ***head***/***cover*** *oneself* 帽子をかぶる《特に脱帽後に》 ▪ *Cover your head* at once. すぐに帽子をかぶりなさい.

cover into the Treasury 《米》国庫に入れる[納める] ▪ The bribe *was covered into the Treasury.* その賄賂は国庫に入れられた.

cover shorts [***short sales***] 《株式》から売りした株の引渡し用に株を買う ▪ He was trying to *cover* his *shorts.* 彼はから売りした株の引渡し用に株を買おうとしていた.

cover *oneself* ***with*** …をになう, 招く ▪ Thus he *covered himself with* glory [shame]. かくして彼は光栄に浴した[恥をかいた].

have *a person* [*a place*] ***covered*** (人・場所)を銃の射程内に置く ▪ I also *have* you *covered.* 僕もまた君を射程内に置いている.

remain covered →be COVERed.

covert /kóʊvəːrt|kʌ́vət/ 名 ***in*** (***the***) ***covert of*** …に庇護されて ▪ He lay *in the covert of* the reeds. 彼はアシの陰に寝ていた.

under covert 庇護されて, 避難して ▪ It placed the whole palace *under covert.* それは全宮殿を保護した.

under (***the***) ***covert of*** **1** (…の陰)に援護[保護]されて ▪ The vessels had protection *under* (*the*) *covert of* walls. 船舶は墻壁の陰に庇護されていた.

2 …に隠れて, に見せかけて ▪ *Under the covert of* that name you set forth your error. その名に隠れて君は自分の誤りを開陳する.

coverture /kʌ́vərtʃʊ̀ər|-tjʊ̀ə/ 名 ***under coverture*** (夫の保護のもとにある)有夫の身分で ▪ She died *under coverture.* 彼女は有夫の身分で死んだ.

covet /kʌ́vət/ 動 ***All covet, all lose.*** 《諺》すべてを望めばすべてを失う,「大欲は無欲に似たり」.

covetous /kʌ́vətəs/ 形 ***be covetous of*** …をひどくほしがる ▪ He *is covetous of* gain. 彼は利を無性にほしがっている.

cow /kaʊ/ 名 ***a milch cow*** →MILCH.

a sacred cow (ヒンドゥー教における)聖牛; 神聖にして犯すべからざるもの[こと] ▪ He's *a sacred cow.* There's nobody who will attack Jon Stewart because he's too popular. 彼は特別扱いだ. あまりにも人気が高いのでジョン・スチュワートを攻撃しようなどと思う者はいない.

(***as***) ***awkward as a cow on a crutch*** [***on roller skates***] 非常にぎこちない[不器用な], バランスを失って ▪ The little girl was *as awkward as a cow on roller skates* when she first began riding her bicycle. その幼い女の子は初めて自転車に乗り始めたときはとてもぎこちなかった.

cow chips [***cow pies, cow patties, cow flops***] 《口》乾燥牛糞《燃料に用いた》; くだらないこと ▪ There was no firewood so we burned *cow chips* in the stove to keep warm in the winter. まきがなかったので, 冬には暖をとるためにストーブで牛糞を燃やした.

Don't have a cow. 《米口》まあまあ, そうカッカしないで; 落ち着いて ▪ Jasmine's here, man, so *don't have a cow.* ジャスミンはここにいるよ, 君, だから落ち着きなさい ▪ *Don't have a cow* about global warming. 地球温暖化に関して大騒ぎするのはやめよ.

have a cow 《米俗》憤慨する, 非常に取り乱す, いらだつ (→Don't have a COW.) ▪ She *had a cow* when she found out her son had been smoking.

息子が喫煙していたのが分かって彼女はとてもおろおろした.

like a cow's tail 牛のしっぽのように(あとについて行く, など) ▪ He is always behind, *like a cow's tail.* 彼は金魚の糞のようにいつもあとについて行く.

make cow eyes at 《口》...を非常にセンチメンタルな目で見る ▪ I can't stand anyone *making cow eyes at* me. 感傷的な目で見られるのに耐えられない.

salt the cow to catch the calf 《米口》間接の手段で目的を達する ▪ He is not forthright at all; he always *salts the cow to catch the calf.* 彼は全く正攻法でなく常に間接的手段で目的を達する.

the cow with the iron tail 《口·戯》ミルクを薄めるために使うポンプ; ミルクを混ぜた水 ▪ *The cow with the iron tail* was milked a great deal in 19th-century London. 19世紀のロンドンではミルクを薄めるポンプから大いにミルクを作り出していた.

when the cows come home 決して...しない (never) ▪ I will clean the house *when the cows come home.* 家の掃除なんかするものか.

Why buy the cow when you can get the milk for free [when milk is so cheap]? 《諺》ミルクがただで[格安で]手に入るのに牛を買うことはない《女性との関係に満足していれば結婚する必要はない》.

coward /káʊərd/ 名 ***Cowards die many times before their deaths(, The valiant never taste of death but once)./A coward dies many deaths, a brave man but one.*** 《諺》臆病者は何回も死ぬ(勇者は一度しか死なない)《臆病者は死を恐れるが, 勇者は不可避のことは受容する》(cf. Sh., *Jul. Caes.* 2. 2. 32-33).

cowboy /káʊbɔ̀ɪ/ 名 ***a cowboy driver*** 無謀運転手 ▪ *A* German *cowboy driver* is supremely dangerous to himself, to others in autos, and to people on foot. ドイツ人の無謀運転手は彼自身にも, 車に乗っている他の者にも, 歩行者にもこの上なく危険だ.

cowl /kaʊl/ 名 ***The cowl does not make the monk.*** 《諺》僧帽をかぶっただけでは修道僧にはなれない《人を外観で判断するな》.

coy /kɔɪ/ 形 ***coy of*** はにかんで...がろくにできない ▪ He is *coy of* speech. 彼ははにかんで口がきけない.

***coy to** do* 遠慮して[はにかんで]...しない ▪ Lord, make me *coy to* offend. 神様, 私を罪を犯すことのない人間にしてください.

crab[1] /kræb/ 名 ***catch a crab*** 《ボート》オールを水中深く入れすぎる《水の抵抗のためこぎ手があとへひっくり返る; したがって船がひっくり返る恐れがある》 ▪ A boat capsized because one of the rowers *caught a crab.* こぎ手の一人がオールを水中深く入れすぎたので, ボートが転覆した. ☞水をかする場合, その他にも使われるが誤用.

come off [turn out, turn up] (a case of) crabs 《俗》(物が)失敗する; 当てがはずれる ▪ If this throw *comes off crabs*, there won't be enongh to bury me. もしこのさいころの一投げが失敗すれば, 私の埋葬料もなくなるだろう. ☞crab「さいころの最低点」.

cut a crab = catch a CRAB.

turn [bend] the crab 両腕を頭上にあげてだんだん体を後へ弓なりに曲げて手のひらを地面につける ▪ In the playground we performed an exercise called "*Bend the Crab.*" 運動場で我々は「後ろそらし」という運動をした.

crab[2] /kræb/ 動 ***crab** a person's **act*** 《米口》人の計画をだめにする[くじく] ▪ He has *crabbed his* own *act.* 彼は自分の計画をだめにした.

crab** a person's **game 《米口》人の見込みをだめにしてしまう ▪ They were doing well until the police *crabbed their game.* 彼らはうまくやっていたが警察が彼らの見込みをだめにした.

crabbed /krǽbəd/ 形 ***crabbed age*** 気むずかしい年寄り (cf. Sh., *The Passionate Pilgrim*) ▪ We behold these vices in *crabbed age.* 気むずかしい年寄りにこれらの悪癖を見る.

crab(-)wise /krǽbwàɪz/ 副 ***walk crab-wise*** (カニのように)横に[斜めに]歩く ▪ He *walked crab-wise* across the room. 彼は部屋を横に歩いた.

crack[1] /kræk/ 名形 ***a crack on the head*** 頭への一撃 ▪ He received *a crack on the head.* 彼は頭を一撃された.

a dirty crack 猥談, 悪い冗談 ▪ The girls were emotionally scarred by having to endure *dirty cracks* from boys in their school hallways. 女の子たちは廊下での男子たちの猥談に耐えなければならなかったので情緒的に傷ついた.

a fair crack of the whip 《口》(何かを言ったりしたりする)平等[公正]な機会 ▪ We wanted *a fair crack of the whip.* (発言の)平等な機会がほしかった.

at crack of day/at the crack of dawn 《米》夜明けに, 朝まだき ▪ I went fishing *at the crack of dawn.* 朝早く釣りに出かけた ▪ We'll be up *at crack of day* tomorrow. 明日は夜明けには起きているだろう.

be a crack hand at 《口》...の達人である ▪ He *is a crack hand at* entertaining children. 彼は子供たちをおもしろがらせるのが実にうまい.

fall [slip] through [between] the cracks **1** (...の)対象からはずれる[もれる], をすり抜ける, から抜け落ちる (*of*) ▪ The 8-year-old's tragic death *fell through the cracks of* the city's child-welfare system. その8歳児の悲劇的な死は市の児童福祉制度の対象外だった ▪ The data *fell through the cracks of* scientific method. そのデータは科学的方法をすり抜けていた.

2 (特に組織の中で)見過ごされる, 見落とされる; あぶはち取らずに終わる ▪ Homeless war vets "*fall through the cracks*". ホームレスとなった退役軍人は社会からいわば「見捨てられ」るのだ ▪ Her boyish figure unfortunately has *slipped between the cracks* of this exhibition. 不幸なことに, 彼女のボーイッシュな姿はこのショーでは注目されなかった. ☞→fall between two STOOLs.《英》では slip through the NET.

give** a person **a crack at 《口》人に...をする機会を与える ▪ I'll *give* you *a crack at* teaching English. 君に英語を教える機会を与えよう.

have a crack 談話をする ▪ Drop in one evening and *have a crack* with us. いつか晩に話しにお立ち寄りください.

have* [*get, take*] *a crack at 《口》…を試みる ▪ If you let me *have a crack at* it, maybe I will have some success. 私にそれをやってみさせてくれたら, ひょっとしてうまくできるかもしれない ▪ My wife decided to *take a crack at* a new recipe for beef stew. 妻はビーフシチューの新しいレシピをひとつ試してみることにした.

in a crack 《口》すぐに ▪ The ghost vanished *in a crack.* 幽霊はすぐに消えた.

make* [*pull*] *a crack **1** 機知に富んだことを言う ▪ He *made a crack* about my age. 彼は私の年齢についてしゃれた冗談を言った.
2 からかう, 皮肉を言う ▪ Everybody is *making cracks* about her eyebrows. みんなが彼女の眉毛をからかっている.

on the crack 《米》ドアが少し開いて ▪ The front door was *on the crack* at that time. その時表の戸は少し開いていた ▪ The door was opened *on the crack.* ドアが少し開かれた.

paper* [*paste, smooth*] *over the cracks 一時しのぎの処置をする ▪ He *papered over the cracks* for the period of the election. 彼は選挙の期間だけ弥縫(びほう)策を講じた ▪ We'll try to camouflage the damage and *smooth over the cracks.* 何とか損害を隠し, 一時しのぎで繕うことにしよう.

***take a crack* (*at*)** (…を)試みる; (を)非難する, 攻撃する ▪ I may *take a crack at* painting some pictures. 私は絵を描いてみるかもしれない ▪ He was *taking a crack at* the British. 彼はイギリス人を非難していた.

(*the*) *crack of dawn* 夜明け, 早朝 (→at the CRACK of dawn) ▪ We played mahjong till *the crack of dawn.* 我々は明け方までマージャンをやった.

the crack of doom 最後の審判の日(の雷鳴); (一般に)終わりの合図; 世の終わり (→till the CRACK of doom) ▪ The thunderstorm was so violent that we might have thought it was *the crack of doom.* 雷雨は非常に激しく世の終わりと思われるほどだった.

till the crack of doom 世の終わりまで; 最後まで, いつまでも (cf. Sh., *Macb.* 4. 1. 117) ▪ He'll hang on *till the crack of doom* if he can. 彼はできれば世の終わりまでも続けるだろう ▪ The house is built to last *till the crack of doom.* 家はいつまでももつように建てられている.

toe a crack 《米口》 **1** つま先を床板の継ぎ目に置いて立つ ▪ He ordered them to *toe the cracks* in the kitchen floor. 彼らに台所の床板の継ぎ目につま先を置いて立つよう命じた.
2 出発線[スタートライン]につく ▪ The runners *toed the crack*, ready for the big race. ランナーたちは大レースに臨んでスタートラインについた.

walk a crack 《米口》(酔いかげんを試すために)床板の間のすき目を歩く ▪ I was able to *walk a crack* after swallowing half a gallon of whiskey. 私はウィスキーを半ガロン飲んだ後に, 床板のすき目を歩けた.

What's the crack? 《英口》どうしたの, 何が起こっているの.

crack[2] /kræk/ 動 ***a hard nut* (*to crack*)** → NUT[1].

be cracked up to be 《口》〚主に否定文・疑問文で〛…であると評判である[もてはやされる] ▪ Clearly fingerprint analysis is not the gold standard it *is cracked up to be.* 明らかに, 指紋分析は世間で言われているほどの絶対的基準ではない. ☞次項も参照.

be what* [*as, all*] *one is cracked up to be 《口》〚主に否定文で〛評判[期待]通りである ▪ He *is* not the man he *is cracked up to be.* 彼は評判ほどの人間ではない ▪ Vice in Chicago *is* not *what* it*'s cracked up to be.* シカゴの罪悪は評判ほどではない ▪ Polygamy *is* not *all* it*'s cracked up to be* after all. 結局, 一夫多妻は人が言うほどのものではない.

crack a book 《俗》〚主に否定文で〛(勉強するため)…を開ける ▪ Tom doesn't *crack a book* until the night before the exam. トムは試験の前夜にならなければ本を開けない.

crack a bottle 《口》ボトルをあける, 1杯やる ▪ He asked me to *crack a bottle* with him. 彼はいっしょに1杯飲もうと私に言った.

crack a smile →SMILE[1].

crack* (*one's*) *credit 信用を落とす, なくす ▪ Don't trust a borrower if he has *cracked his credit* once or twice. 借り主が1, 2度信用を落としたことがあるなら, 信用するな.

crack ... into repute [etc.] 《口》…をほめて有名[など]にする ▪ He *was cracked into reputation* by his patrons. 彼は後援者らにほめられて有名になった.

crack open **1** 暴露する ▪ They have enough evidence to *crack open* the corruption in the city. 彼らは市の汚職を暴露するにたる証拠を持っている.
2 たたき割る[開ける] ▪ *Crack* the shell *open.* 貝がらをたたき割りなさい.
3 論破する ▪ The lawyer will *crack* her case wide *open.* 弁護士は彼女の申し立てをすっかり論破するだろう.

crack the whip →WHIP[1].

***crack up to the nines* [*stars*]** 《口》ほめそやす ▪ His students all *crack* him *up to the nines.* 生徒たちはこぞって彼をほめそやしている.

crack wise 《俗》警句を吐く, おもしろいことを言う; 逆襲をする ▪ He *cracked wise* about the pending deal. 彼は懸案の取引について気の利いたことを言った. ☞<wisecrack.

cracked /krækt/ 形 ***Cracked pipkins are discovered by their sound.*** 《諺》割れ土びんはその音でわかる(無知はしゃべるとばれるもの). ☞pipkin「小さい土びん」.

cracker /krǽkər/ 名 ***go a cracker*** 《英》全速力を出す; ぺしゃんこになる ▪ He is *gone a cracker* over head and ears. 彼はすっかりぺしゃんこになった.

C

C

crackers /krǽkərz/ 形 ***go crackers*** 《英口》気が狂う; 熱狂する, 溺愛する ▪ She'll *go crackers*. 彼女は気が狂うだろう ▪ We *went crackers* about them. 我々はそれらに熱狂した ▪ He *went crackers* over that dog. 彼はその犬に目がなかった.

cracking /krǽkɪŋ/ 形 ***get cracking*** 《口》せっせと[急いで]やりだす; 動かしだす ▪ Let's *get cracking*! さあ(仕事を)急いでせっせとやろう. ☞cracking 「馬にむちを当てること」.

cracky /krǽki/ 間 ***by cracky*** (驚き・強調を表して)いやはや, これはこれは (→by JOVE!) ▪ It was a great day, *by cracky*. いや, 全く, すばらしい1日だったよ. ☞by Christ の婉曲表現.

cradle /kréɪdəl/ 名 ***a cradle-robber***/《英戯》***a cradle-snatcher*** 《米戯》自分よりずっと年下の異性とつき合う男性[女性] (→rob the CRADLE) ▪ His grandfather was *a cradle robber* who married a teenager. 彼の祖父はずっと年下の女性が好みで十代の少女と結婚した ▪ Trudeau, the supreme *cradle-snatcher*, was still dating girls when he was in his 30s. トルードーはひどいロリコンなので, 30歳台なのにいまだに少女とデートしていた.

from the cradle 幼時から ▪ He has been learning Greek *from the cradle*. 彼はギリシャ語を幼時から学んできた.

from the cradle to the grave 揺りかごから墓場まで, 一生を通じて ▪ This law will insure the well-being of the entire nation *from the cradle to the grave*. この法律は全国民の福利を一生保証する.

in the cradle 揺籃(ようらん)期に, 初期において ▪ Stifle the treason *in the cradle*. 反逆を初めのうちに鎮圧せよ ▪ What is learned *in the cradle* is carried to the tomb. 《諺》揺りかごの中で覚えたことは墓場まで運ばれる《幼時に習い覚えたことは死ぬまで忘れない》.

rob the cradle 《口》自分よりずっと年下の者とデート[結婚]する ▪ Everyone said she was *robbing the cradle*. みんなが「彼女はひどく若い男とデートしている」と言った.

stifle ... in the cradle →in the CRADLE.

watch over the cradle 発育[成長]を見守る ▪ He *watched over the cradle* of those seminaries. 彼はそれらの学院の成長を見守った.

craft /kræft|krɑːft/ 名 ***by craft*** たくらみ[術策]によって ▪ He got it *by craft*. 彼はたくらみによってそれを得た.

crag /kræg/ 名 ***crag and tail*** 一方が絶壁で一方がなだらかな傾斜の地形 ▪ The island presented the form of what is called "*crag and tail*." 島はいわゆる「一方絶壁で他方なだらかな傾斜」の地形を呈していた.

cram /kræm/ 動 ***cram*** *oneself* 腹いっぱい詰めこむ ▪ He *crammed himself* as he was hungry. 空腹だったので彼はたらふく食べた.

cram ... down *a person's* ***throat*** →thrust ... down a person's THROAT.

cram down *one's* ***throat*** のどに無理に押しこむ ▪ The greedy fellow actually *crammed* food *down his throat*. 食いしん坊の男は実際に食物をのどに無理に押しこんだ.

cram for the examination 試験のため詰めこみ勉強をする[させる] ▪ He *crammed* the boy *for the examination*. 彼はその少年に試験のための詰めこみ勉強をさせた ▪ He *crammed* (history) *for the exam*. 彼は試験準備に(歴史を)詰めこんだ.

cramp /kræmp/ 動 ***be cramped for room*** [***space***] 狭苦しい ▪ Our house is so full of junk that we *are cramped for space*. 我が家はがらくただらけで狭苦しい.

cramp *a person's* ***style*** 《口》人を窮屈にする, 自由な活動をはばむ ▪ His lack of a car rather *cramps his style*. 自動車を持っていないことは, 彼の自由な活動をややさまたげている ▪ The loss of his teeth *cramps his style* a good deal. 彼は歯が抜けてだいぶ不自由している.

cramp-ring /krǽmprɪ̀ŋ/ 名 ***scour the cramp-ring*** かせをはめられる, 投獄される ▪ There's little hazard of *scouring the cramp-ring*. 投獄される危険はほとんどない.

cran /kræn/ 名 ***coup the crans*** 《米》めちゃくちゃになる, 不幸な目にあう ▪ They didn't like their kirk to *coup the crans*. 彼らは自分たちの教会がめちゃくちゃになるのを好まなかった.

crane /kreɪn/ 動 ***crane*** *one's* ***neck*** [***head***] 首を長く伸ばす ▪ We *craned our necks* to see what had become of our companion. 仲間はどうなっているかを見ようと我々は首を長く伸ばした ▪ Here's the letter I have been *craning my neck* for. 首を長くして待っていた手紙が来た.

crank /kræŋk/ 名 ***a crank call*** (匿名の)迷惑[いやがらせ, 脅迫, 無言]電話 ▪ We have taken steps to keep *crank calls* to a minimum. 我々は迷惑電話を最小限にするための対策をとっている.

a crank letter (匿名の)いやがらせメール, 脅迫状 ▪ Our office is flooded with mail, including a lot of *crank letters*. うちのオフィスにはいやがらせの手紙も含めて山ほどの郵便物がくる.

cranny /krǽni/ 名 ***every nook and cranny*** →every NOOK and corner.

crap /kræp/ 名 ***Cut the crap!*** 《俗》嘘を言え, たわごとを言うな ▪ Aw, come on, Jim, *cut the crap!* やい, ジム. たわごとをぬかすな.

full of crap [***bull, shit***] 《俗》ばかなことで, 全くのたわごとで ▪ What you say is *full of crap*. ばかなことをぬかすな.

craps /kræps/ 名 ***shoot craps*** 《米》クラップばくちをする ▪ Young toughs started to *shoot craps*. 若いよた者がクラップばくちをやりだした.

crash[1] /kræʃ/ 名副 ***a crash pad*** (無料)宿泊所, 一時的住居, 仮のねぐら ▪ The company maintains several *crash pads* for unmarried employees. 会社は独身社員用の社宅を整備している.

go [***fall***] ***crash*** すさまじい音を立てて倒れる[落ちる] ▪ The stone *went crash* through the window. その石は窓からドシンと飛びこんできた.

with a crash すさまじい音を立てて ▪ The tree fell *with a crash.* その木はドシンと倒れた.

crash[2] /kræʃ/ 動 ***crash about*** [***around***] *one's* ***ears*** 急に失敗する, 崩れる ▪ Our plans *crashed about our ears.* 我々の計画は急に崩れた.

crash and burn **1** 衝突炎上する ▪ A British air-liner *crashed and burned* at Prestwick airport, killing 28 people. 英国の旅客機がプレストウィック空港で衝突炎上し, 28名が死亡した.

2 火だるまになる, 失敗する, (...に)完敗[大敗]する (*against*) ▪ First-round leader McGeorge *crashed and burned* in the second round. 第1ラウンドではリードしていたマクジョージは第2ラウンドで炎上してしまった ▪ More than a few former superstars have *crashed and burned* as coaches. 少なからざる以前の名選手がコーチとしては落第だった ▪ The Angels had *crashed and burned against* A's starter Joaquin Andujar. エンジェルスはアスレチックスの先発ホアキン・アンドゥーハルに押さえ込まれた.

3 《米口》 倒産する, つぶれる ▪ Many of the investment funds *crashed and burned* and people got very upset. 投資基金の多くが倒産してパニックになった.

4 《米口・スケートボード》 (衝突・転倒で)競技からはずされる ▪ Brian tried the first flip and *crashed and burned* hard. ブライアンは最初のとんぼ返りでひどく転倒し失格となった.

crash-dive (潜水艦などが) 急速潜航する, (飛行機などが)急降下する; 急低下[暴落]する ▪ The sub had to *crash-dive* to avoid a Japanese tanker. 潜水艦は日本のタンカーを避けるために急速潜航を余儀なくされた ▪ Some 4,000 Japanese aviators intentionally *crash-dived* their planes into U.S. ships. 約4,000人の日本軍飛行兵が意図的に米軍の艦船に急降下激突した ▪ Farther out, a pelican *crash-dived* for fish. ずっと遠くでペリカンが魚を求めて急降下した ▪ By the end of the day, the share price had *crash-dived* 61 percent. その日のうちに株価は61%暴落した.

crash the gate →break the GATE.

crash *one's* ***way*** バリバリ音を立てて無理に進む ▪ We *crashed our way* through bush. 我々はバリバリ音を立てて茂みを通った.

cravat /krəvǽt/ 名 ***wear*** [***come to***] ***a hempen cravat*** 《俗》 絞首刑にされる ▪ He will *come* some day *to a hempen cravat.* 彼はいつか絞首刑にされるだろう.

crave /kreɪv/ 動 ***crave pardon*** [***leave***] 許しを請う ▪ Let me *crave pardon* for having detained you so long. こんなに長くお引き止めしたことをおわびいたします ▪ I must *crave leave* to tell you. お許しを願って申しあげねばなりません.

craven /kréɪvən/ 形 ***cry craven*** 「参った」と叫ぶ; 降参する ▪ I will make him *cry craven.* 彼に「参った」と叫ばせてやる.

craving /kréɪvɪŋ/ 名 ***have a craving for*** ...を渇望する ▪ He *has a craving for* pleasure. 彼は快楽を渇望している.

craw /krɔː/ 名 ***stick in*** *one's* ***craw*** →STICK in one's gizzard.

crawl[1] /krɔːl/ 名 ***go at a crawl*** のろのろ歩く, 徐行する, (自動車などが)往来を流す ▪ All the cars *went at a crawl.* 車はみな徐行した.

crawl[2] /krɔːl/ 動 ***be crawling with*** ...がいっぱいある, がうようよしている ▪ The ground *was crawling with* worms. 地面には虫がうようよしていた ▪ The place *was crawling with* professors. そこには教授たちがいっぱいいた.

crawl (***home***) ***on*** *one's* ***eyebrows*** 《口》 くたくたに疲れて帰る ▪ Night after night he comes in, just *crawling home on his eyebrows.* 毎夜毎夜彼はほんとにくたくたに疲れて帰って来る. ☞《軍》より.

crawl into *a person's* ***favor*** こそこそ人に取り入る ▪ He *crawled into the master's favor.* 彼はこそこそ主人に取り入った.

crayon /kréɪɑn|-ɔn/ 名 ***in crayon***(***s***) クレヨンで描いた ▪ He showed me his picture *in crayon.* 自分の描いたクレヨン画を私に見せてくれた ▪ He is a wonderful performer *in crayons.* 彼はクレヨン画のすばらしい達人である.

craze[1] /kreɪz/ 名 ***be the craze*** 大流行である, 大もてである ▪ Mexican music *is* all *the craze* now. メキシコ音楽が今や大流行である.

have a craze for ...に夢中である ▪ Some boys *have a craze for* stamp-collecting. 少年の中には切手を集めるのに夢中の者もいる.

craze[2] /kreɪz/ 動 ***be crazed about*** ...に夢中になっている ▪ She *is crazed about* a film star. 彼女は映画スターに夢中になっている.

crazy /kréɪzi/ 形名 (***as***) ***crazy as a betsy bug*** [***a peach-orchard boar, a loon***] 《米口》 頭がおかしい, ひどく狂って ▪ He's crazy—the man's *as crazy as a Betsy bug.* 彼は狂っている. あの男は本当にいかれている. ☞Betsy bug＜bess-bug「クロツヤムシ」.

be crazy about [***over***] ...にのぼせあがっている ▪ Teen-age girls *are crazy about* that song. 10代の少女たちはその歌にのぼせあがっている ▪ I *am crazy over* a girl. ある女の子に夢中だ.

be crazy to *do* 愚かにも...する; ...したくてたまらない ▪ She *was crazy to* tell what she knew. 彼女は自分の知っていることを話したくてたまらなかった ▪ He *was crazy to* approach the lion. 彼は愚かにもライオンに近づいた.

crazy like [***as***] ***a fox*** 《口》 非常に狡猾(こうかつ)で, 抜け目のない ▪ He is *crazy like a fox*, and as hard to catch. 彼は非常に狡猾で, 捕えにくい.

give *a person* ***the crazies*** 《俗》 大騒ぎする, 大げさな[過剰な]反応を示す ▪ The jazz fans are OK, but *give* me *the crazies* at Madison Square Garden. ジャズファンはけっこうなのだが, マディソンスクエアガーデンでは過剰反応だよ.

go crazy 気が狂う ▪ He *went crazy* with drink. 彼は酒で気が狂った.

like crazy 《口》猛烈に（＝like MAD） ▪ She was beating it with her umbrella *like crazy.* 彼女はそれをかさで猛烈に打っていた.

send** a person **crazy 《口》人をひどく動転させる, 興奮[狂気に]させる ▪ Lack of sleep often *sends* people *crazy.* 睡眠不足はよく人々をひどく興奮させる.

creak[1] /kriːk/ 名 ***with a creak*** ギーッと鳴って（戸が開く） ▪ The door opened *with a creak.* 戸がギーッと鳴って開いた.

creak[2] /kriːk/ 動 ***Creaking doors hang longest.*** 《諺》きしる扉は一番長く吊り下がっている《病身者はえてして長生きする》,「柳に雪折れなし」.

cream /kriːm/ 名 ***cream of the valley*** [***wilderness***] ジン酒（gin） ▪ I will just buy some *cream of the valley* for mother. 私はちょっと母にジンを買ってあげます.

get [***skim, take***] ***the cream of*** …の粋を抜く ▪ The eldest brother *took the cream of* the properties. 長兄が資産の一番よいところを取った.

take the cream off 一番良いところを取る ▪ I'm afraid that new business is *taking the cream off* our trade. 新商売は我々の商売の一番良いところを奪っているように思う.

the cream of the crop 最も良い部分, より抜きの部分 ▪ They pride themselves on being *the cream of the crop.* 彼らは自分たちをより抜きのものであると自負している.

create /kriéɪt/ 動 ***create a part*** [***a character***] **1** 役を新しく解釈して演じる ▪ Mr. Smith *created the part* of Toby in the play. スミス氏はその劇のトービーの役を新しく解釈して演じた.
2（役者に）一定の役を与える ▪ The author *created a part* for Miss Eden. 著者はイーデン嬢に一役を与えた.

create (***bloody***) ***hell*** [***murder***] 《口》大騒ぎする; 騒動を起こす;（怒って）どなり散らす ▪ The boy's father came up to school to *create bloody murder.* 少年の父はどなり散らすつもりで学校へやってきた.

creation /kriéɪʃən/ 名 ***beat*** [《米》***lick***] (***all***) ***creation*** 《口》すべてに勝る, 天下無類である ▪ If that doesn't *beat creation!* まさに天下無類だ ▪ That *beats creation.* そいつは全く驚いた; そりゃ愉快千万だ.

in (***all***) ***creation*** 〚疑問詞を強調して〛一体全体 ▪ When *in all creation* will they be finished? 一体全体いつそれらは終わるのですか ▪ How *in creation* do you suppose I know? 一体どうして私が知っていると思うのか.

like all creation 《米口》猛烈に, ひどく ▪ He pulled *like all creation.* 彼は猛烈に引っぱった ▪ This article costs *like all creation.* この品はひどく高価である.

the lord of creation →LORD[1].

creature /kríːtʃər/ 名 ***a creature of habit*** 習慣のとりこ[奴隷] ▪ Pryce may be *a creature of habit* with lunch, but not much else. プライスは昼食に関しては習慣のとりこかもしれないが, 他のことではそうでもない.

creature comforts →COMFORT[1].

good creature(***s***) 肉体的快楽を与えるもの, 飲食物, 衣食類（＝creature COMFORTs）(《聖》*1 Tim.* 4. 4) ▪ Like many other people, he is fond of *good creatures.* 多くの他の人々のように, 彼は肉体の快楽を与えるものが好きである.

credence /kríːdəns/ 名 ***find credence with*** …に信じられる ▪ These tales *found credence with* him. これらの話は彼に信じられた.

give credence (***to***) (…を)信じる ▪ He *gave credence to* the report. 彼はその報道を信じた.

lend credence to …を信じさせる ▪ This rain *lends credence to* the weather forecast. この雨は天気予報を信じさせるものだ.

refuse credence to …を信じない ▪ I *refused credence to* the report. その報道を信じなかった.

credibility /krèdəbíləti/ 名 ***a credibility gap*** **1**（公表と実際の事実との間の）食い違い ▪ There was *a* distinct *credibility gap* between policy and achievement. 政策と成果とがはっきり食い違っていた.
2（政治家・政府などの）言行不一致;（政治家・政府などに対する）不信感 ▪ President Bush has gone beyond *a credibility gap* to a credibility chasm. ブッシュ大統領に対しては不信の溝を超えて不信の峡谷に達した.

credibly /krédəbli/ 副 ***be credibly informed*** 確かな情報を得る ▪ I *am credibly informed* that Jesuits are admitted into their clubs. イエズス会士が彼らのクラブに加入を許されたという確かな情報を得た.

credit[1] /krédət/ 名 ***add to** one's **credit*** 名声を高める ▪ This new book won't *add to your credit.* この新しい本はあなたの名声を高めはしないだろう.

at a month's [etc.] ***credit*** 1か月[など]の掛けで ▪ He buys his wool *at three months' credit.* 彼は3か月の掛けで羊毛を買う.

be a credit to …の名誉である ▪ You will *be a credit to* your school. 君は学校の名誉になるだろう.

be (***much,*** etc.) ***to the credit of*** （大いに）…の名誉である[となる];（大いに）見あげたものである ▪ It *is greatly to your credit* that you have passed such a difficult exam. そんなむずかしい試験に合格したことは大いにあなたの名誉である.

credit is due to** a person **for 人が…のために賞賛されるべきである ▪ Great *credit is due to* him *for* doing that. 彼がそれをしたのは大いにほめるべきだ.

one's credit is good for （人が）…だけの支払能力がある ▪ *His credit is good for* a million yen. 彼は百万円の融通がきく.

***do** a person **credit**/**do credit to** a person* 人の栄誉となる, 人は立派なものだ ▪ His industry *does* him *credit.* 彼の勤勉はあっぱれだ ▪ Such a book *does credit to* the writer. こういう本は著者の

名声をあげる.

extend credit to →give CREDIT.

gain (*one's*) ***credit with*** …の信用を得る ▪ You will *gain credit with* him. 君は彼の信用を得るであろう.

get credit for …の功を認められる; のために面目を施す ▪ I *got* a lot of *credit for* succeeding in the enterprise. その事業に成功して大いに面目を施した.

get the credit of …の評判をとる ▪ He's *got the credit of* being industrious. 彼は勤勉だという評判をとっている.

***give credit* 《商》掛け売りする, 信用貸しする ▪ No *credit is given* at this shop. この店では掛け売りはしません.

give *a person* ***credit for*** **1** 人が(性質など)を持っていると信じる ▪ I *gave* you *credit for* being a more sensible fellow [*for* more sense]. あなたはもっと分別のある人だと信じていた ▪ He's cleverer than I *gave* him *credit for*. 彼は思っていたよりも賢明である.

2 人に(行為など)の功ありとする, 人の手がらとする ▪ I *give* you *credit for* the scheme. その計画は君の手がらだ.

give credit to **1** …を信じる ▪ Do you *give credit to* the report? その報道を信じますか.

2 …をほめてやる, の手がらとする ▪ I must *give credit to* my daughter for decorations. 飾りつけをした娘をほめてやらねばならない.

Give credit where credit [***it***] ***is due./Credit where credit is due.*** 《諺》功績を正当に評価せよ.

give the credit of …を(人の)功績とする ▪ We *give* him *the credit of* having invented paper. 紙を発明した功績は彼のものである.

have a credit for …という評判である ▪ He *has a credit for* honesty. 彼は正直だという評判だ.

have a credit of… with …に…の預金がある ▪ I *have a credit of* a million dollars *with* the bank. その銀行に100万ドルの預金がある.

have credit **1** …に信用がある (*with*) ▪ He *has credit with* the minister. 彼はその大臣に信用がある.

2 …に預金がある (*at*) ▪ I *have credit at* the bank. その銀行に預金がある.

have [***get***] ***the credit of*** …の栄誉をになう, (名誉にも)という評判である, と認められる ▪ He *has the credit of* never breaking his word. 彼は決して約束を破らないという評判である.

in high credit (***with***) (…に)評判がよい ▪ The professor is *in high credit with* his colleagues. 教授は同僚に大いに評判がよい.

lay… to *a person's* ***credit*** …を人の手がらとする ▪ This *is laid to the credit of* the Republicans. これは共和党の手がらとされている.

lose (*one's*) ***credit with*** …の信用を失う ▪ He has *lost credit with* the minister. 彼は大臣の信用を失った.

max out *one's* ***credit card*** 《米口》カードの限度額まで使う ▪ I *maxed out my credit card* when I bought my first computer. 最初のコンピューターを買ったときクレジットカードを限度額いっぱいまで使ってしまった.

on credit 掛けで, 信用貸で ▪ Please do not ask for drinks *on credit*. 酒類の掛けはご遠慮ください《バーなどによくある掲示》 ▪ It's unwise to buy things *on credit*. 物を掛けで買うのは賢明でない.

open a credit account 掛け買いを始める, クレジットの口座を開く ▪ I *opened a credit account* at the department store. 百貨店でカード利用を始めた.

place [***put***] ***credit in*** …を信用する ▪ It's unwise to *place* too much *credit in* hearsay. 風聞を信用しすぎるのは賢明ではない.

place *a sum* ***to*** *a person's* ***credit*** 金額を人の預金とする ▪ I will *place* the sum of £900 *to your credit*. 900ポンドの金額をあなたの預金とします.

rebound to *one's* ***credit*** 賞賛すべきである, 名誉である ▪ It *rebounds to his credit* that he never accepted bribes. 彼が決して賄賂を受け取らなかったのは賞賛すべきである.

reflect credit on …の名誉[面目]となる ▪ The son's success *reflects credit on* the father. 息子の成功は父の名誉となる.

standing to *one's* ***credit*** 貸し方として, 預金として ▪ I have only £5 *standing to my credit* in the bank. 私は銀行に預金がたった5ポンドしかない.

take [***get***] ***credit for*** **1** …の手がらを横取りする ▪ You must not *take credit for* work done by him. 彼がした仕事の手がらを横取りしてはいけない.

2 …の手がらと認められる ▪ You must *take* full *credit for* the success of the meeting. 会の成功は全くあなたの手がらとしなければならない.

to *one's* ***credit*** **1** …の誉れ[名誉]となるように ▪ He has acquitted himself *to his credit*. 彼はあっぱれな働きをした ▪ The house was never known but *to its credit*. 家名が落ちたことは今だかつてない.

2 人の貸し方に ▪ I have £1,000 *to my credit*. 1,000ポンドの貸しがある.

credit[2] /krédət/ 動 ***be credited with*** 《米》…の単位をもらう ▪ I *was credited with* three hours in geography. 私は地理3時間の単位をもらった.

credit *a person's* ***account with*** 人の貸し方[預金]に…を記帳する ▪ Please *credit our account with* the returned goods. どうぞ返却品を我々の預金口座に記帳してください.

creditable /krédətəbəl/ 形 ***creditable to*** …をはずかしめない ▪ It is *creditable to* your good sense. それは君の良識をはずかしめない.

creek /kri:k/ 名 ***up a creek/up shit creek*** ひどく困って (＝up the CREEK (without a paddle)) ▪ If the check doesn't arrive tomorrow, I'll be *up a creek*. 小切手が明日届かないとお手上げになる.

up the creek (***without a paddle***) 《口》 **1** 窮地にあって ▪ I shall be *up the creek*. 僕は困るだろ

う.

2 まちがって, 不正確で ▪ The information is completely *up the creek.* その情報は全くまちがっている.

creel /kriːl/ 名 ***coup the creels*** 《米》ひっくり返る; 死ぬ, 不幸に会う ▪ If you should *coup the creels* just now! 万一君がちょうど今死んだら!

in a creel 《米》一時的な混乱状態[精神錯乱状態]で ▪ The lady('s head) is *in a creel.* 婦人(の頭)は一時的に狂錯乱状態になっている.

creep[1] /kriːp/ 名 ***give** a person **the (cold) creeps*** 《口》(いやで)人をぞっとさせる ▪ The sound of the wind at night *gives* me *the creeps.* 夜の風の音は私をぞっとさせる.

creep[2] /kriːp/ 動 ***creep and crawl*** びくびくぺこぺこする ▪ I'm not going to *creep and crawl* for a favor. 好意を受けようとしてぺこぺこする気はない.

creep into** a person's **favor 人にそっと取り入る ▪ She knows how to *creep into his favor.* 彼女はこっそり彼に取り入る方法を知っている.

creep up** a person's **sleeve = CREEP into a person's favor.

make** a person's **flesh creep (いやで)人をぞっとさせる (→make a person's SKIN crawl) ▪ The sight of a snake *makes my flesh creep.* ヘビを見ると私はぞっとする ▪ Cockroaches *make her skin crawl.* ゴキブリを見たら彼女は鳥肌が立つ.

creepy /kríːpi/ 形 ***make** a person **creepy*** 人をぞっとさせる ▪ The ghost story *made* everyone *creepy.* 幽霊話はみんなをぞっとさせた.

crest[1] /krest/ 名 ***one's **crest falls*** 意気消沈する ▪ And then *his crest fell.* それから彼は意気消沈した.

let fall** one's **crest しょげる, 意気消沈する ▪ They began to *let fall their crests.* 彼らは意気消沈し始めた.

on the crest of the wave 波がしらの上に乗って; 得意の絶頂にあって ▪ We feel as if we are *on the crest of the wave.* 我々は得意の絶頂にある.

ride the crest of a wave of 〚主に進行形で〛(人気・得意)の絶頂である ▪ The hybrid *is riding the crest of a wave of* public curiosity. ハイブリッド車は一般大衆の好奇心を集め人気の絶頂にある.

crest[2] /krest/ 動 ***crest a rise*** 丘に登る ▪ A yellow animal *crested a rise.* 黄色の動物が丘に登って来た. ☞crest=top.

crib[1] /krɪb/ 名 ***crack a crib*** 《英俗》家に押し入る ▪ He has *cracked* more *cribs* than any other living burglar. 彼ほど多くの家に押し入った強盗は現存しない. ☞盗賊語より.

use a crib 《学俗》虎の巻を使う ▪ He *used* his brother's *crib.* 彼は兄の虎の巻を使った.

crib[2] /krɪb/ 動 ***cabined, cribbed, and confined/cribbed, cabined, and confined*** 狭い所に押しこめられて, 全く束縛されて (cf. Sh., *Macb.* 3. 4. 24) ▪ One feels that sense of being "*cabined, cribb'd, confin'd.*" あの「狭い所に押しこめられた」という感じがする.

cricket /kríkət/ 名 ***(as) chirpy [lively, merry] as a cricket*** (コオロギのように)とても快活で, 陽気で ▪ Even when he was in hospital, he was *as chirpy as a cricket.* 入院している時でも彼はとても陽気だった.

Is it cricket?/Would it be cricket? それで公平かい, フェアにやれよ ▪ *Is it cricket* to criticize a dog? 犬に難癖をつけたりしてまともなやり方かね?

not (quite) cricket/(just) not cricket 《俗》公明正大[公正]でない, スポーツ精神を欠く ▪ It didn't seem *cricket* to leave the poor in that condition. 貧しい人々をその状態にほっておくことは公正とは思えなかった ▪ The treatment of Stan was *just not cricket.* スタンの処遇は公明正大ではなかった.

play cricket **1** クリケットをする ▪ The boys were *playing cricket.* 少年たちはクリケットをしていた.

2 公明正大にやる[行動する] ▪ I appeal to the Conservatives to *play cricket.* 保守党に対し公正な行動をするよう訴える.

crime /kraɪm/ 名 ***Crime doesn't pay.*** 《諺》犯罪[悪事]は割に合わない.

worse than a crime 言語道断の《誤りについて言う》 ▪ There are some mistakes *worse than a crime* in his diary. 彼の日記には言語道断の誤りもある.

criminate /krímənèɪt/ 動 ***criminate** oneself* 自ら罪のあることを明らかにする; (証人が)自分が有罪になるような[自分に不利な]証言をする ▪ He was determined not to *criminate himself.* 彼は自分を有罪にするような証言はすまいと決心していた.

crimp /krɪmp/ 名 ***put a crimp in [into]*** 《米俗》...をじゃまする, だめにする; を束縛する, 押さえる ▪ They never forgive a man who *puts a crimp into* the party. 党のじゃまをする人を彼らは決して許さない ▪ Strikes last year *put a* serious *crimp in* production. 昨年のストライキが生産をひどく押さえた.

cringe /krɪndʒ/ 名 ***by the cringe*** 《俗》(驚き・いらだたしさを表して)おやおや!, ああ! ▪ *By the cringe,* it's cold here. ああ, ここは寒い!

crisis /kráɪsəs/ 名 ***at [in] a crisis*** 危機に際して ▪ Today we stand *at a crisis* in the world's history. 今日我々は世界史の転機に際会している ▪ We are *in a* national *crisis.* 我々は国難に出くわしている.

crisp /krɪsp/ 名 ***to a crisp*** カリカリに(焼け過ぎ) ▪ The skin of the eggplant was literally roasted *to a crisp.* ナスの皮は文字通りにカリカリに焼けていた.

criss-cross /krískrɔ̀ːs|-krɔ̀s/ 形副 ***go criss-cross*** 食いちがう ▪ Everything *goes crisscross* with me. 私は万事がみな食いちがう.

critical /krítɪkəl/ 形 ***be critical of*** ...に対して批判的である ▪ He *is critical of* his wife's friends. 彼は妻の友だちをかれこれ批判する.

go critical (原子炉が)臨界に達する ▪ Monju *went critical* last year, and produced its first electricity in August this year. もんじゅは昨年臨界に達し, 今年の8月に初の電力を供給した.

in a critical condition 危篤状態で ▪ The patient is now *in a critical condition.* 患者は今危篤状態である.

criticism /krítəsìzəm/ 名 ***(be) under criticism*** 批判されて(いる) ▪ His administrative policy *is* now *under criticism.* 彼の施政方針は目下批判されている.

crock /krɑk|krɔk/ 名 ***a crock of gold*** (手の届かない)大金, 巨万の富 (→the pot of GOLD at the end of the rainbow) ▪ Roger had unfortunately dreamt of having found *a crock of gold.* 遺憾ながらロジャーは幻の大金を見つけた夢を見ていた.

crocodile /krɑ́kədàɪl|krɔ́k-/ 名 ***crocodile tears*** そら涙 ▪ She shed [wept] *crocodile tears* over his death. 彼女は彼の死にそら涙を流した. ☞ワニはえさを食べながら涙を流すとの言い伝えから.

crook[1] /krʊk/ 名形 ***a crook in** one's **lot*** 《米》不幸, 試練, 苦難 ▪ It is *a* great *crook in my* present *lot.* それは私の今の大試練だ.

by hook or by crook →HOOK[1].

go crook at [on] (人)に腹をたてる; をしかる ▪ Father *went crook at* me. 父は私に腹を立てた.

have a crook in …が曲がって[ひねくれて]いる ▪ He *has a crook in* his nose. 彼は鼻が曲がっている ▪ He *has a crook in* his character. 彼は性格がひねくれている.

on the crook 《俗》不正に, 不正手段で ▪ He bought it *on the crook.* 彼はそれを不正に入手した.

crook[2] /krʊk/ 動 ***crook** one's **[the] elbow*** 《口》酒を飲む; (特に)飲みすぎる ▪ He was fined for *crooking his elbow* too often. 彼はあまりにしばしば酒を飲みすぎたため科料に処せられた.

crook** one's **(little) finger **1** = CROOK one's elbow.

2 指をかけかぎの形に曲げる ▪ She *crooked her little finger* above the handle of the cup. 彼女は小指を曲げて茶わんの取っ手を持っていた.

3 人さし指で招く ▪ Jane *crooked her finger* at me. ジェインは人さし指で私を招いた.

4 (すぐの反応を期待して)ちょっと指し招く ▪ You just *crook your finger*, and we'll run about to do your bidding. あなたがちょっと招きの合図をしさえすれば私どもは走り回って言いつけ通りにします.

crooked /krʊ́kəd/ 形 ***a crooked sixpence*** 縁起の良いもの ▪ I've got the luck; so you must keep me by you for your *crooked sixpence.* 私には幸運がついているから私を縁起の良いものとしてあなたのそばにずっとおいてくださらねばなりません. ☞曲がった6ペンス貨を持っていると運が良いという迷信から.

(as) crooked as a dog's hind leg 《口》ひどくひねくれた ▪ He is always telling lies, and he is *crooked as a dog's hind leg.* 彼は嘘ばかりついて, ひどくひねくれている.

crop[1] /krɑp|krɔp/ 名 ***a crop of*** 多くの…; …の続出 ▪ He suffered from *a crop of* troubles. 彼は次から次へ起こる苦労に悩んだ ▪ This produced *a crop of* questions. これが元で次々と疑問が出た.

crop and root 《米》すっかり ▪ He swept away the bishops *crop and root.* 彼は監督をすっかり一掃した.

have a (close) crop 五分刈りにする ▪ You've *had a close crop.* 君は五分刈りにしたね.

in [under] crop (田畑が)作物がしつけてある ▪ About three-fourths are *under crop.* およそ4分の3に作物がしつけてある.

out of crop (田畑が)作物がしつけてない ▪ A field of 1,000 acres are *out of crop.* 1,000エーカーの畑に作物がしつけてない.

stick in** one's **crop →STICK in one's gizzard.

crop[2] /krɑp|krɔp/ 動 ***crop the causey*** 《米》街路の中心を大胆に歩く ▪ All the Covenanters now proudly *crop the causey.* 今や改革長老教会員はみな誇らしげに堂々と街路の中心を歩いている.

cropper /krɑ́pər|krɔ́p-/ 名 ***come [fall, get] a cropper*** 《口》 **1** どうと倒れる; (馬などから)落ちる ▪ He *came a cropper* yesterday while out riding. 彼は昨日馬で出ていたとき, どうと馬から落ちた.

2 大失敗をする, へまをやる ▪ He *came a cropper* in the examination. 彼は試験に落第した.

3 (誤り・しくじりの結果)災難にあう ▪ A lawyer who starts gambling is certain to *come a cropper* in the end. ばくちを始める弁護士はきっとしまいにはひどい目にあう. ☞come to GRIEF よりも口語的.

4 破産する, 破滅する; 堕落する ▪ He has *come a* terrible *cropper* over this bank smash. 彼はこの銀行破産のため恐ろしい倒産をした ▪ He *came* rather *a cropper* over a girl. 彼は女の子のことでちょっと身を持ちくずした.

cross[1] /krɔːs|krɔs/ 名形 ***a cross in life*** 人生の重荷 ▪ Doing the housework is her *cross in life.* 家事をするのは彼女には人生の重荷である.

a cross to carry [《英豪》 bear] 背負っている十字架, 耐えるべき苦難 (→bear one's CROSS) ▪ They each had *a cross to carry* that was uniquely each one's own. 彼らはみな各人各様の苦境を背負っていた ▪ Everyone in this life has *a cross to bear.* すべての生あるものには耐えねばならない十字架がある.

(as) cross as a bear (with a sore head) [as two sticks, as the Devil, as the tongs] 《口》非常に気むずかしい, きわめて不きげんで ▪ I've been *as cross as a bear* for the last week. 私はこの1週間きわめて不きげんだった.

be [go] on the cross 《俗》不正や盗みを働く[働いて暮らす] ▪ He has *been on the cross* all his life. 彼は生涯盗みを働いてきた.

(be, play,** etc.**) at cross purposes **1** (計画が)互いに食いちがって (*with*) ▪ They *are* constantly *at cross purposes with* others. 彼らはいつも他の人と計画が食いちがう.

2 (目的を誤解して)互いに反対のことをする[言う] ▪ They *were at cross purposes* with each other. 互いに誤解して反対のことをしていた ▪ We were *talking at cross purposes.* 互いに食いちがっ

たことを話していた.

bear [***carry***] *one's* ***cross*** 十字架を負う《キリスト教信仰の試練として苦難・迫害を受ける》; 苦難を忍ぶ, 犠牲を忍ぶ (《聖》*Matt.* 10. 38) ▪ You *bear your cross* patiently. あなたはしんぼう強く苦難を忍んでいる ▪ She was *carrying her cross* bravely. 彼女は勇敢に苦難を忍んでいた.

cross and [***or***] ***pile*** **1** 貨幣の表と裏 ▪ The coins thrown up will fall *cross or pile*. 投げ上げられた貨幣は表か裏を上にして落ちる.

2 (時に)貨幣, 金 ▪ He has neither *cross nor pile*. 彼はびた一文も持っていない.

Crosses are ladders that lead to heaven. 《諺》十字架は天国へのはしご《苦しみに耐えていると徳が育つ》. ☞cross を「十字架」と「苦難」に掛けてある.

die on the cross はりつけになる ▪ Christ *died on the cross*. キリストははりつけになった.

get cross with [***at***] 人[事]を怒る ▪ The teacher *got cross with* the boy for smoking. 先生はその少年が喫煙したので怒った ▪ He will *get cross at* the report. 彼はその報道を聞いたら怒るだろう.

go on the cross →be on the CROSS.

make *one's* ***cross/sign with a cross*** (非識字者が)署名代わりに × 印をかく ▪ Unable to write his name, he *made his cross* on the document. 彼は名前が書けないので書類に × 印を書いた.

No cross, no crown. 《諺》十字架を負わなければ栄冠は得られない; 「艱難汝を玉にす; 苦は楽の種」.

on the cross **1** はすかいに, 斜めに ▪ A piece of velvet was cut *on the cross* for trimming her bonnet. 彼女の帽子を飾り仕立てるため, ビロードのきれが斜めに切断された.

2 不正に, 不正手段で (↔ on the SQUARE 1) ▪ The article has been got *on the cross*. その品は不正手段で手に入れられた. ☞↔on the LEVEL.

run cross to …に反する ▪ It *runs cross to* the common belief. それは世論に反する.

shake the cross 《俗》盗みをやめる ▪ *Shake the cross* and live on the square. 盗みをやめてまっとうな暮らしをせよ.

sign with a cross →make one's CROSS.

take the cross **1** (誓いを固めるため)十字架記章を受ける ▪ Frederick II *took the cross* as a symbol of his intention to lead a crusade. フリードリヒ2世は十字軍を率いる決意のしるしに十字架記章を受けた.

2 十字軍に加わる ▪ He preached and exhorted men to *take the cross*. 彼は説教して男たちに十字軍に加わるよう熱心に勧めた.

take (***up***) *one's* ***cross*** =bear one's CROSS.

cross[2] /krɔːs|krɔs/ 動 ***be crossed in love*** 失恋する, 恋敵のため恋に破れる ▪ Poor fellow! He's *been crossed in love* three times. かわいそうなやつ! 彼は3度も失恋した.

cross *oneself* (額から胸にかけて)十字を切る《祈り・驚きのため》 ▪ She *crossed herself* to ward off evil. 彼女は災いをよけるため十字を切った.

cross a cheque **1** 小切手に(2本の)平行線を引く《普通小切手で銀行を通してのみ金が支払われる》 ▪ To *cross a cheque* you need to draw two lines in the upper left hand corner. 小切手に平行線を引くには左上の隅に2本線を引くように.

2 小切手に銀行名を記入する《特別小切手で記名の銀行を通してのみ金が支払われる》 ▪ He *crossed the cheque*, drawing two lines and writing "Barclays" in between them. 彼は小切手に2本線を引き, その間に Barclays と銀行名を記入した.

cross a fortune-teller's hand [***palm***] (***with silver***) 占い者に(金銭を)与える, 与えて占いをしてもらう ▪ Every domestic *crossed the fortune-teller's hand with silver* and looked into their future life. 使用人はみな占い者に金銀を与えて未来の生活を占った. ☞ロマ(ジプシー)の占い者に運を見てもらうとき, 銀貨の端でその手のひらに十字を描いて渡すことから.

cross and pile 貨幣を投げて決める ▪ A man may *cross and pile* for his opinions. 自分の意見を貨幣を投げて決めることもある.

cross check [***cross-check***] クロスチェック[交差検査]する ▪ You should *cross check* data across multiple sites. データは複数のサイトで交差検査すべきだ ▪ You will check, double check, triple check and *cross check* with your scouts and coaching staff throughout the week. 君は今週じゅう確認, 再確認, 再々確認をして, それからスカウトやコーチ陣と別の角度から確認することになるだろう.

cross *a person's* ***hand*** [***palm***] ***with*** 人に(銀貨)をそっとつかませる《特に賄賂として》 ▪ He *crossed their hands with* pieces of silver. 彼らに銀貨を何枚かつかませた.

cross *one's* ***heart*** (***and hope to die***) → HEART.

cross *a person's* ***luck*** 人の幸運のじゃまをする ▪ Dick has *crossed her luck*. ディックは彼女の幸運のじゃまをした.

cross *one's* ***mind*** 心に思い浮かぶ, 思いつく ▪ It never *crossed my mind* that she might be his sister. 彼女が彼の妹かもしれぬということにちっとも思いつかなかった ▪ It *crosses my mind* that I danced with her. 彼女とダンスしたことを思い出す.

Cross my heart (***and hope to die***)***!*** 《口》(感嘆して)ほんとに!, 正直なところ ▪ *Cross my heart*, I didn't hide your bicycle. ほんとに僕は君の自転車を隠したりしなかったよ ▪ I didn't tell the teacher what you said. *Cross my heart and hope to die!* 私は先生に告げ口はしなかったよ, ほんとだよ! ☞子供は十字を切りながら言う事が多い.「胸の上で十字を切る」とは本当のことを言っているという印.

cross *a person's* ***path*** →PATH.

cross swords →SWORD.

cross the [*one's*] ***t's*** →T.

get *one's* ***wires*** [《英》 ***lines***] ***crossed*** →get the LINEs crossed.

have [***keep***] *one's* ***fingers crossed*** →FINGER[1].

Wires are crossed. (合図・話が)行きちがいになっている, 逆になっている ▪ Our *wires were crossed.* 我々の話が食いちがった.

crossbones /krɔ́ːsbòʊnz|krɔ́s-/ 名 ***a skull and crossbones*** どくろ図, 大腿骨を十字に組みその上に頭がい骨を置いた図形《死の象徴; 昔は海賊の旗印, 今は毒薬びんの目印として使用》 ▪ *A skull and crossbones* was stamped on the labels of poisonous drugs. どくろ図が毒薬のラベルに押されていた.

cross-corner /krɔ́ːskɔ̀ːrnər|krɔ́s-/ 名 ***at cross-corners with*** …と真反対[正反対]で ▪ Private idiosyncracies place them *at cross-corners with* the rest of their race. 個人的特質で彼らは同種族の他の者と正反対になっている.

crosscut /krɔ́ːskʌ̀t|krɔ́s-/ 名 ***saw a crosscut*** 《米》丸太を横びきする ▪ We sometimes do what we call *sawing a crosscut.* 我々はときどき丸太の横びきと称することをする.

cross(-)fire /krɔ́ːsfàɪər|krɔ́s-/ 名 ***be [get] caught in the cross fire*** 巻き添えになる, (他人の争いに)巻き込まれる, 板挟みになる ▪ *Caught in the cross fire*, a 3-year-old girl was hit in the ribs. 巻き添えで3歳の少女が肋骨に銃弾をあびた ▪ Warner's job wasn't the only thing *caught in the cross-fire* between the House and Senate. 下院と上院の板挟みになったのはウォーナーの任務だけではなかった.

crossing /krɔ́ːsɪŋ|krɔ́s-/ 名 ***have a good [rough] crossing*** 渡航に海が静穏である[荒れる] ▪ Hope you *have a good crossing.* 航海の無事を祈ります ▪ We have as yet, touch wood, never *had a rough crossing* on this ship. これまでこの船で一祟りがありませんようにー時化(しけ)にあったことがない.

cross-purpose /krɔ̀ːspə́ːrpəs|krɔ̀s-/ 名 ***at cross-purposes*** →(be, play, etc.) at CROSS purposes.

crossroad /krɔ́ːsròʊd|krɔ́s-/ 名 ***at (a) crossroads*** 四つかどに, 交差点に ▪ He let her off *at a crossroads.* 彼は彼女を十字路で降ろした ▪ May God protect our country *at* this *crossroads* of liberty and more government control. この自由と政府による統制強化の岐路にあってわが国に神のご加護がありますように.

stand [be] at the crossroads 岐路に立つ, 危機に直面する ▪ America *stands at the crossroads.* アメリカは岐路に立っている.

crow[1] /kroʊ/ 名 ***a white crow*** きわめて珍しいこと ▪ It is a black swan and *a white crow.* それは実に珍しいことだ.

(as) black as a crow 真っ黒で ▪ The night was *as black as a crow.* 漆黒の闇夜だった.

as the [a] crow flies まっすぐに, 一直線に(行って)(→in a BEELINE) ▪ It is thirteen miles from here to London *as the crow flies.* ここからロンドンまで直線距離で13マイルだ. ☞カラスはとても賢い鳥で, 最寄りのえさ場に直行することから.

crow's feet カラスの足あと《目尻のしわ》 ▪ Strivectin reduces the appearance of fine lines, wrinkles and *crow's feet.* ストリベクチン(クリーム)は細い筋やしわ, カラスの足あとを減らす ▪ Ms Shannon doesn't just have *crow's feet*, she has crow's legs. シャノンさんにはただカラスの足あとがあるのではない, カラスの太足[目尻の太いしわ]があるのだ.

eat (boiled) crow 《主に米口》ひどくいやなことをさせられる; 屈辱を忍ぶ; 前言を取り消す, やむなく誤りを認める ▪ It was a bitter experience for him to *eat crow* after his predictions proved inaccurate. 予言が当たらなかったとき自分の誤りを認めるのは彼には苦い経験であった.

have a crow to pluck [pull, pick] (with) 《口》…に言ってやること[文句]がある; 話をつけねばならぬ問題がある ▪ I *have a crow to pluck with* the wine. 私はそのワインに文句がある ▪ I *have a crow to pull with* him. 彼に言ってやることがある.

in a crow line =as the CROW flies.

not know *a person* ***from a crow*** 人を全然知らない ▪ I *don't know* him *from a crow.* 私は彼を全然知らない.

Stone the crows! 〚間投詞的に〛《英》おやまあ!, まさか!, おったまげた ▪ *Stone the crows!*—it's freezing cold in here. いやあ驚いた! ここは凍るように寒い.

The crow thinks its own bird fairest [white]. 《諺》カラスは自分の子が一番美しいと思っている;「親の欲目」.

crow[2] /kroʊ/ 動 ***crow*** *one's* ***head off*** 《口》しきりに自慢する ▪ They *crowed their heads off* when they won the general election. 彼らは総選挙に勝った時しきりに自慢した.

crowd[1] /kraʊd/ 名 ***a crowd of*** たくさんの ▪ What *a crowd of* automobiles! なんとたくさんの自動車だこと!

far from the madding crowd →MADDING.

follow [go with] the crowd 世間の人々のすることをする, 俗衆に従う ▪ He is content to *follow the crowd.* 彼は大勢にならうことに甘んじている.

in crowds/in a crowd 大勢で ▪ They came *in crowds.* 彼らは大勢で来た.

Join the crowd! 《口》(話し手と同様な経験をした人に向かって)あなたもお仲間ですね.

may [might, will, would] pass in a crowd 《口》群の中で目だって劣りはしない; まず普通だ ▪ That *may pass in a crowd.* それはまず普通である ▪ The fellow can't keep quiet, else he *might pass in a crowd.* そいつは静かにできない. でなければ目立つような欠点はないのだが.

rise [raise *oneself****] (up) above the crowd*** 衆に抜きんでる ▪ He *rose above the crowd* in everything he did. 彼は何をしてもすべて衆に抜きんでた.

stand out from the crowd [in a crowd] 他より優れている, 卓越している ▪ The magazine *stands out from the crowd* for its food safety news. その雑誌は食の安全に関する情報で他よりも抜きんでている.

Two's company, three's a crowd. →Two's COMPANY, three's none.

crowd[2] /kraʊd/ 動 ***(be) crowded with*** …でいっぱいである(状態・結果) ▪ The train *was crowded with* passengers. 電車は乗客で満員だった. ☞be crowded by は行為受身.

crowd** a person **off a wire 《米口》人に受信できないほど速く電文を送る ▪ It takes a pretty lively man to *crowd* me *off a wire.* 私に受信できないほど速く電文を送るにはかなり活発な人でなくてはだめだ.

crowd the mourners →MOURNER.

crowd ... to the wall 《米》…をすっかり屈服させる ▪ All the Native Americans *were crowded to the wall.* 北米先住民はみんなすっかり屈服した.

crown[1] /kraʊn/ 名 ***a crown of thorns*** (キリストがかぶらされた)いばらの冠 (Matt. 27. 29); 苦難 ▪ Jesus wore *a crown of thorns* when he was nailed to the cross. イエスは十字架に釘で打ちつけられたときいばらの冠をいただいた ▪ Mr Fraser wore *a "crown of thorns"* as prime minister. フレイザー氏は首相として「いばらの冠」をいただいた.

succeed to [relinquish] the crown 王位を継ぐ[を捨てる] ▪ Henry *succeeded to the crown.* ヘンリーが王位を継いだ.

take the crown 優勝する ▪ Who will *take the crown* in wrestling? 誰がレスリングで優勝するだろうか.

the crown jewels **1** 戴冠用宝玉 ▪ The Tower of London houses *the Crown jewels* and is a big tourist attraction. ロンドン塔は戴冠用宝玉を収蔵しており多くの旅行者を引きつけている.
2 価値ある資産 ▪ The Iliad and Odyssey are *the crown jewels* of ancient literature. イーリアスとオデュッセイアは古典文学の珠玉の遺産である.

wear a crown →WEAR[2].

crown[2] /kraʊn/ 動 ***be crowned with*** **1** …を(頭に)いただいている ▪ The King *was crowned with* a golden crown. 国王は金の王冠をいただいていた ▪ Mt. Fuji *is* already *crowned with* snow. 富士山はすでに雪をいただいている.
2 (成功・勝利など)で報いられる ▪ Our labors *were crowned with* success. 我々の労苦は成功をもって報いられた.
3 (歯に)…がかぶせられる ▪ His teeth *are crowned with* special cement. 彼の歯には特殊のセメントがかぶせられている.

crown all 仕上げをする ▪ He intended to *crown all* with a finishing touch. 彼は仕上げの一筆で画龍点睛をするつもりだった.

to crown (it) all (悪い事[良い事]が続いた)あげくの果てに, その上に, 最後に ▪ *To crown all,* we missed the last train. あげくの果てに我々は最終列車に乗りおくれた ▪ *To crown it all,* a book was laid upon his coffin. 最後に1冊の本が彼の棺の上に置かれた ▪ She gave us a delicious meal and, *to crown it all,* a very rare brandy. 彼女は我々にご馳走を出し, その上に極上のブランデーをふるまった.

crucible /krúːsəbəl/ 名 ***be in the crucible of*** …のきびしい試練を受けている ▪ He *is in the crucible of* affliction. 彼は難儀の試練を受けている.

cruel /krúːəl/ 形 ***cruel to be kind*** 早く治そうとして[親切心から]ひどい目にあわす (cf. Sh., *Haml.* 3. 4. 178) ▪ A dentist has to be *cruel to be kind.* 歯科医は早く治すため(患者を)痛い目にあわさねばならない ▪ But you don't have to be *cruel to be kind.* だが親切心からでも痛いことを言ってやる必要はない.

cruise /kruːz/ 動 ***be cruising for a bruising*** 《米口》わざわざ面倒[痛い目にあうこと]を求め(ている ▪ She *was* probably *cruising for a bruising* for being such a smart-ass. 彼女はこなまいきだったのでたぶん自業自得だったのだ.

crumb /krʌm/ 名 ***a crumb of comfort*** わずかな慰め[恵み] ▪ *One crumb of comfort* is that Al Qaeda's intelligence network can't be very bright. わずかな慰めはアルカイダの諜報網があまり切れものではありえないということだ.

crumbs (that fall) from the (rich man's) table (富者の)食卓からの(こぼれる)パンくず《比喩的にも》(《聖》*Luke* 16. 21) ▪ The working man is not content with the *crumbs from the rich man's table.* 労働者は富者の食卓からこぼれるパンくずに満足しない.

to a crumb 厳密に, 完全に ▪ Please sift it *to a crumb.* それを細密に調べてください.

crumpet /krʌ́mpət/ 名 ***balmy [barmy] on [in] the crumpet/off** one's **crumpet*** 《俗》頭が変で, 気が狂って ▪ That boy is *barmy on the crumpet.* その少年は頭が変である ▪ Do they think that she is *off her crumpet*? 彼女は頭が変だと思われているのか. ☞crumpet《俗》=head.

crunch[1] /krʌntʃ/ 名 ***when it comes to the crunch*** →COME[2].

crunch[2] /krʌntʃ/ 動 ***crunch numbers*** 《口》大量の数字データを高速処理する ▪ Preparing my presentation to the client required many hours of *crunching numbers.* 顧客への提案の準備には長時間かけた大量の数字データの高速処理を要した.

crusade /kruːséɪd/ 動 ***crusade it*** 十字軍[キャンペーン]に加わる ▪ I'm not going to *crusade it.* 私はキャンペーンに参加するつもりはない.

cruse /kruːz/ 名 ***the widow's cruse*** (打ち出の小うちのような)寡婦のつぼ, 無限の供給源 (《聖》*1 Kings* 17. 10–16) ▪ It was *the widow's cruse* —carving could not lessen; nor helping diminish it. それは寡婦のつぼであった—切っても減らず, 食べ物をよそっても減らなかった.

crush[1] /krʌʃ/ 名 ***have [develop, get] a crush on*** 《口》…にほれこんでいる[ほれこむ] ▪ She *has a crush on* you. 彼女は君にほれこんでいる ▪ He *got* his first *crush on* a pretty girl. 彼は美しい少女に初恋をした ▪ Fisher *developed a crush on* him and made it clear she wanted more than friendship. フィッシャーは彼を好きになり, 友情以上を望むと明言した.

crush[2] /krʌʃ/ 動 ***crush a cup of wine*** [***a pot of ale,*** etc.] 1杯飲む ▪ Come and *crush a cup of wine*. 来て1杯やりたまえ ▪ They *crushed several bottles of wine*. 彼らはボトル数本のワインを飲んだ.

crush a fly on the wheel →break a fly on the WHEEL.

crush ... into submission →SUBMISSION.

crush *one's* ***way*** 押し進む ▪ He *crushed his way* up to her at once. 彼はすぐに彼女の所へ押し分けて進んで行った.

crust /krʌst/ 名 ***crack a crust*** 《口》かなりに暮らしていく ▪ He is *cracking a* tidy *crust*. 彼は相当に暮らしている.

earn *one's* ***crust*** 生活の資を儲ける ▪ What does he do to *earn his crust*? 彼は何をして生計を立てているか.

have the crust to *do* 《俗》厚かましくも...する ▪ He *had the crust to* ask to borrow it again. 彼は厚かましくもそれをまた借りたいと言った.

crusty /krʌ́sti/ 形 ***cut up crusty*** →CUT up rough.

crutch[1] /krʌtʃ/ 名 (***as***) ***funny as a crutch*** 《皮肉》少しもおかしくない, ひどくつまらない ▪ These kinds of jokes were "*funny as a crutch*," or "funny as a funeral." この種のジョークは全く「おかしく」も「おもしろく」もなかった.

on crutches 松葉杖で[の] ▪ A man *on crutches* died after being hit by a dump truck. 松葉杖の男性がダンプカーにはねられて死亡した ▪ He went *on crutches*. 彼は松葉杖で行った.

crutch[2] /krʌtʃ/ 動 ***crutch it*** 松葉杖で行く ▪ He's got his leg hurt and has to *crutch it*. 彼は足をけがしたので松葉杖で行かねばならない.

crux /krʌks/ 名 ***the crux of*** (***the***) ***matter*** 問題の核心 ▪ Now we come to *the crux of the matter*. さて, ここで問題は核心に触れる ▪ *The crux of matter* is an efficient speed. 問題の核心は効率のよい速度だ.

cry[1] /kraɪ/ 名 ***a far cry*** 《口》**1** 遠距離 ▪ It is *a far cry* from here to London. ここからロンドンまでは非常に遠い.

2 非常な隔たり[相違], とても及びもつかぬもの ▪ Going to school is *a far cry* from working in a shop. 通学するのと店で働くのとは大違いである ▪ I am *a far cry* from a real pro. 私は真のプロには及びもつかない.

a hue and cry →HUE.

All cry and no wool./Great cry and little wool./More cry than wool./Much cry and little wool (***as when pigs are shorn***)***.*** 《諺》鳴き声ばかりで毛は1本もなし《声ばかり大きくて実質なし》,「泰山鳴動してネズミ一匹」 ▪ It's always been the same all his life—*much cry and little wool*. 彼はこれまでいつも同じであった—声だけ大きくて何もしなかった ▪ It is "*All cry and no wool*" with them. 彼らは「口ばかりで実質がない」のである. ☞Great cry and little wool, as the Devil said when he sheared the hogs. (悪魔がブタの毛を刈ったとき言ったように, やかましくがなるばかりで毛はほとんどない)が原形.

at full cry →in full CRY.

follow in the cry やじ馬について行く, 付和雷同する ▪ In the country we are content to *follow in the cry*. 田舎ではやじ馬について行くことに満足する.

give [***raise, set up, utter***] ***a cry*** 叫ぶ, 一声立てる ▪ They *raised a cry* of "Thief! Thief!" 彼らは「泥棒! 泥棒!」と叫んだ.

give cry 追跡の声をあげる, ほえ立てる ▪ The journalists *gave cry* after the prince. 新聞記者たちは公爵追跡の声をあげた.

have a good cry 存分に泣く ▪ I sat down and *had a good cry*. 私は腰を下ろして存分に泣いた.

have *one's* ***cry out*** 泣けるだけ泣く ▪ Let her *have her cry out*. 彼女に存分に泣かせてやりなさい.

in [***at, with***] ***full cry*** まっしぐらに追いかけて; 総がかりで, 一斉に ▪ All were offering their merchandise *at full cry*. みんな一斉に商品を呼び売りしていた ▪ The whole kennel of Atheists came in *with full cry*. 無神論者連中が一斉に入って来た. ☞猟犬が獲物をかぎつけたときの叫びから.

open upon the cry ほえ立てる ▪ His admirers are sure to *open upon the cry*. 彼の賞賛者たちはきっとほえ立てるだろう.

out of cry 声[手]の届かぬところに ▪ I was *out of cry* of my companions. 私は仲間の声が聞こえない所にいた.

raise [***set up, utter***] ***a cry*** →give a CRY.

with full cry →in full CRY.

within cry of ...から呼べば聞こえる所に ▪ Each house was *within cry of* another. 家は互いに呼べば聞こえる所にあった.

cry[2] /kraɪ/ 動 ***a crying towel*** (共感の印として渡す)鼻かみ用のハンカチ ▪ What do you want me to do, get out the *crying towel*? 私にどうしてほしいのか, 同情してもらいたいとでも思っているのか.

cry *oneself* ***blind*** 目がつぶれるほど泣く ▪ I *cried myself* well-nigh *blind*. 私はほとんど目がつぶれるほど泣いた.

cry (***blue***) ***murder*** →MURDER[1].

cry *one's* ***eyes*** [***heart***] ***out*** 目もつぶれるほど[胸が裂けるほど]泣く, 激しく泣く ▪ Why are you *crying your heart out*? なぜ激しく泣いているのですか.

cry for the moon →MOON.

cry harrow [***haro***] 非難する (*on*) ▪ You *cry haro on* me for a cynic. 君は僕を皮肉屋だと言って非難する.

cry loud [***aloud***] ***for*** 大声で...を求める; を大いに必要とする ▪ These things *cry loud for* reformation. これらのことは改革を大いに必要とする ▪ Injuries and insults *cried aloud for* vengeance. 傷害と侮辱は強く報復を求めた.

cry on *a person's* ***shoulder*** (人に悩みを打ち明けて)慰め[同情]を求める ▪ She generally *cries on her brother's shoulder* when she has a problem. 彼女は悩みがあると兄に打ち明けて慰めてもらう.

cry* (*out*) *before* one *is hurt わからぬ先から不平を言う, 不平の言い方が早すぎる ▪ Don't *cry before* you*'re hurt.* 《諺》わからぬ先から不平を言うな.

***cry shame on* [*upon*]** →SHAME[1].

cry* oneself *sick 病気になるほど泣く, 泣いて病気になる ▪ She will *cry herself sick* in a closet. 彼女は私室で病気になるほど泣くだろう.

***cry to* oneself** 忍び泣きする ▪ She often *cries to herself* when she is left alone. 彼女は一人ぼっちにされるとよく忍び泣きをする.

cry* oneself *to sleep →SLEEP[1].

For crying out loud! 《口》 **1** (依頼・命令などを強めて)どうぞ, お願いだから ▪ *For crying out loud*, don't worry about money. 後生だから金の心配はしないでください.

2 (驚き・いらだち・不満を表して)おやまあ; こんちくしょう ▪ Sam has lost his bankbook.—*For crying out loud!* サムは銀行預金通帳をなくしたよ—おやまあ! ☞for Christ's sake! の婉曲表現.

give* a person *something to cry about …をさらに痛い目にあわせる ▪ Come down and I'll *give* you *something to cry about.* こちらにおいで, 泣きたいのならもっと泣かせてあげよう. ☞泣いている子供に言う言葉.

It's a crying shame. (…とは)大恥辱である (*that*) ▪ *It's a crying shame that* this has happened. こんなことが起きたとは大変な恥である.

crystal /krístəl/ 名 (***as***) ***clear as crystal*** → CLEAR[1].

crystal clear きわめて明晰[明白]で ▪ He made it *crystal clear* that he intended to do so. 彼はそうする意向であることをはっきりさせた.

crystal gazing 水晶占い ▪ *Crystal gazing* was a popular pastime in the Victorian era, together with palmistry and astrology. 水晶占いは, 手相や星占いと共に, ビクトリア時代に好まれた娯楽だった.

cub /kʌb/ 名 ***a Cub Scout*** [***cub scout***] カブスカウトのメンバー《ボーイスカウトのうち8～10歳の隊員》 ▪ The highest honor *a cub scout* can achieve is the Arrow of Light award. カブスカウト団員が得ることのできる最高の名誉は光の矢賞だ.

lick the cub into shape →LICK[2].

cubit /kjúːbət/ 名 ***add a cubit to*** one's ***stature*** 身長に1キュービットを加える; 寿命を少し延ばす (《聖》 *Matt.* 6. 27) ▪ Who, by taking thought, can *add a cubit to his stature*? 思い患ったところで, 誰が寿命をわずかでも延ばすことができようか.

cuckoo /kúːkuː|kóku:/ 名形 ***be*** [***go***] ***cuckoo*** 《米俗》気が狂う ▪ He *went cuckoo* after all his family were horribly murdered. 彼は家族全員が惨殺されたあと発狂してしまった.

the cuckoo in the nest (子供に対する愛を親から横取りする)愛の巣の侵入者; 他人の仕事や特権を横取りする者 ▪ It's not always easy spotting *the cuckoo in the nest.* 他人の仕事を乗っ取る者を見抜くのは必ずしも容易ではない. ☞カッコウは他の鳥の巣の中に卵を生む習性があることから.

cucumber /kjúːkʌmbər/ 名 (***as***) ***cool as a cucumber*** 《戯》きわめて平静で[冷静で] ▪ He was *cool as a cucumber* and made no threats at all. 彼はごく平静で少しも脅したりはしなかった.

cud /kʌd/ 名 ***chew the*** [one's] ***cud*** **1** (牛などが)反すうする ▪ The cattle stood *chewing their cuds.* 牛は立って反すうしていた.

2 《口》思いめぐらす, 思いにふける ▪ I *chewed the cud* on these tidings. この知らせについて思いめぐらした ▪ She was *chewing the cud* of some sweet thought. 彼女は何か楽しい思いにふけっていた.

cudgel[1] /kʌ́dʒəl/ 名 ***take up the cudgels against*** 《英》…に反対して攻撃する, 反論する ▪ I feel I should *take up the cudgels against* you on this. この点に関しては君に反論するべきだと感じる ▪ Women leaders should *take up the cudgels against* smoking. 女性指導者は喫煙に反対運動をするべきだ.

take up the cudgels for (***in defense of, on behalf of***) 《英》…のために勇敢に弁護する ▪ He *took up the cudgels for* his friend. 彼は友人のため勇敢に弁護した.

cudgel[2] /kʌ́dʒəl/ 動 ***cudgel*** one's ***brains*** → beat one's BRAINs.

cue /kjuː/ 名 ***give*** a person ***the*** [*his*] ***cue*** 人に暗示を与える, 人に入れ知恵する ▪ I'll *give* you *the cue* when you're to start. あなたが始めるときはきっかけを与えましょう.

in (***the right***) ***cue for*** [***to*** do] 《古》…に[することに]気分が向いて ▪ I am *in* (*the right*) *cue for* reading it. それを読むことに気が向いている ▪ Nobody was *in the cue to* dance. 誰もダンスする気分になっていなかった.

on cue ちょうどよい時に, 予定通りに ▪ Bo performed *on cue*, offering his paw when the president reached out for a shake. ボー(犬の名前)はタイミングよくふるまった. 大統領が握手に手を伸ばしたとき前足を出したのだ.

pick up a cue (役者の)渡し文句をうまく受け継ぐ ▪ The actors are not *picking up their cues* fast enough. 俳優らはキューの受け継ぎをうまくやっていない.

take one's [***the***] ***cue*** (***from***) **1** (…から)きっかけをつかむ ▪ Charles said "Bosh," and that was where Mary *took her cue* to come on the stage. チャールズが「ばかな」と言うと, それをきっかけにしてメアリーが登場した.

2 (…を)見習う ▪ *Take your cue from* her. 彼女を見習え. ☞cue「劇のせりふの渡し文句」.

cuff /kʌf/ 名 ***at cuffs*** なぐり合いをして ▪ They decided the dispute *at cuffs.* 彼らは論争をなぐり合いで決した ▪ He was *at cuffs* with a brother footman. 彼は同僚の従者となぐり合いをしていた.

give a person ***a cuff*** (通例, 人の頭を手のひらで)たたく ▪ Finally Toby lost all patience and *gave* him quite *a* hard *cuff* on the ear. とうとうトービーはがまんできなくなって彼の耳に激しくビンタをくらわせた.

go* [*fall*] *to cuffs なぐり合いを始める, けんかを始める ▪ He *fell to cuffs* with a Frenchman. 彼はフランス人となぐり合いを始めた.

off the cuff 《口》無意識の[に], 即座の[に], 即席の[に], 非公式の[に] ▪ I gave him an answer *off the cuff*. 私は彼に即座に返答した. ☞cuff「ワイシャツのカフス」, カフスにメモなどを書いたことから.

on the cuff 《口》信用借り[掛け]で; ただで ▪ Many people buy cars *on the cuff*. 車を掛けで買う人が多い.

shoot** one's **cuffs カフスを袖(そで)口から出す ▪ Don't *shoot your cuffs* like that. そんなにカフスを袖口から出してはいけません.

the cuff of the neck 首の後ろの肉の多い部分 ▪ She took hold of her son by *the cuff of the neck*. 彼女は息子の後ろ首をつかまえた.

cultivation /kʌ̀ltəvéɪʃən/ 名 ***bring ... under cultivation*** ...を開墾する ▪ They *brought* waste land *under cultivation*. 彼らは荒地を開墾した.

go out of cultivation 耕作されなくなる ▪ Much land *went out of cultivation* in Gaul. ガリアでは耕作されなくなって荒れている土地が多かった.

under cultivation 耕作されて ▪ This field has been *under cultivation* for 50 years. この畑は50年の間耕作されてきた.

culturally /kʌ́ltʃərəli/ 副 ***culturally deprived* [*disadvantaged*]** 文化的に冷遇されている;《婉曲》貧しい, 貧困層の ▪ We're educated, affluent, and sophisticated, but *culturally deprived*. 我々は教育を受けているしお金も教養もある. だが, 文化的には不平等な扱いを受けている ▪ The public school system does not provide education for the poor or *culturally deprived* until they reach first grade. 公立学校制度は, 貧窮者つまり貧困者が1年生に達するまでは彼らに教育を提供しない.

culture /kʌ́ltʃər/ 名 ***a culture vulture*** 《口・戯》文化施設巡りを(してそれを自慢)する人, 文化[教養]人気取り(の人) ▪ I have to admit I'm not really much of *a culture vulture*. 私は実はあまり文化施設巡りをしていないことを認めなければならない. ☞culture と vulture が脚韻を踏んでいる.

cumber /kʌ́mbər/ 動 ***cumber** oneself **with*** ...をもてあます ▪ I *cumbered myself with* an overcoat on a warm day. 私は暖かい日にコートを着てもてあました ▪ He *cumbered himself with* a lot of luggage. 彼はたくさんの荷物をもてあました.

cunning /kʌ́nɪŋ/ 名 ***lose** one's **cunning*** 巧みを失う (《聖》*Ps.* 137. 5) ▪ The weaver's hand *lost its cunning*. その織り手は巧みな技を失った.

cup /kʌp/ 名 ***a bitter cup*** 苦杯《人生の苦い経験》 ▪ I have tasted *a bitter cup*. 私は苦い経験をなめた.

another cup of tea 全然別のもの (= another pair of SHOEs) ▪ When it comes to classical music, that's *another cup of tea*. クラシック音楽となると, 話は全く別だ.

be a cup too low どうも元気がない, ふさいでいる《誰かが黙っているか, 物思いに沈んでいるとき》 ▪ You *are a cup too low*. What is the matter? 君はどうも元気がないな. どうしたんだ.

one's ***cup is filled* [*full*]** 幸福や不幸が極点に達する[達している](《聖》*Ps.* 23) ▪ With his family around him and no fears for the future, *his cup was filled*. 家族の者に取り巻かれ, 未来の不安もなく, 彼の幸福は絶頂に達した.

one's ***cup of tea*** 《口》〚主に否定文で〛好きなこと, 性に合うこと ▪ Mountaineering is not *my cup of tea*. 登山は私の好みではない ▪ Fishing is just *my cup of tea*. 魚釣りはまさしく僕の趣味です. ☞茶が一般の飲物となり, 多くの種類が出るようになってからできた句.

one's ***cup runs over* [*overflows*]** 《古風》幸福があふれるほどある (《聖》*Ps.* 23. 5–6); (楽・苦)があふれこぼるほどある ▪ What he finally did made *the cup run over*. 彼が最後にしたことが彼を破滅させて余りがあった.

dash the cup from** a person's **lips 《英》人が得る[楽しむ]のを妨げる; 人の目的達成をはばむ ▪ The battle *dashed the cup* of victory *from his lips*. その戦いに彼は勝利が得られなかった.

***drain the cup of sorrow* [*pleasure, life,* etc.] *to the dregs* [*the bottom*]** 悲しみの杯[歓楽の美酒, 浮世の辛酸]を飲み干す ▪ I saw him *drain the cup of suffering to the* bitter *dregs*. 私は彼が苦悩をなめ尽くすのを見た.

in** one's **cups 《文》酔って ▪ He is merry when *in his cups*. 彼は酔ったときは浮かれる.

Let this cup pass from me! この杯を私から過ぎ去らせてください《この苦難を逃れさせてください》(《聖》*Matt.* 26. 39).

My cup runneth over. 《戯》至福の境地である (《聖》Ps. 23. 5). ☞アメリカの歌手 Ed Ames のアルバムの題名で有名.

the cup that cheers but not inebriates 元気づけてくれるが酔わせない杯; 茶, 紅茶 (Cowper, *The Task* 4. 40) ▪ He had better stick to *the cup that cheers but not inebriates*. 彼は茶だけを飲むことにしたほうがよい.

***There's many a slip* (*between the cup and the lip*).** →SLIP[1].

cupboard /kʌ́bərd/ 名 ***a skeleton in the cupboard*** →a SKELETON in the closet.

cry cupboard 《口》空腹を訴える, 腹がへったと言う ▪ My belly began to *cry cupboard*. 腹の虫が鳴きだしたわい.

cupboard love 利益目あての[欲得ずくの]愛情 ▪ My cat follows me everywhere, but it's only *cupboard love*—she wants some fish. 私の猫はどこへでも私について来るが, それは欲得ずくの愛情にすぎない—つまり魚がほしいのだ. ☞「戸だなの中の食物を目あてにした愛情」が原義.

The cupboard is bare. あなたにあげるものは何もない ▪ The schools are asking for a budget increase but *the cupboard is bare.* 学校からは予算の増加請求がきているが, その財源がない. ☞Mother Goose の "*Old Mother Hubbard*" より.

C

Cupid /kjúːpəd/ 名 ***look for Cupids in the eyes of*** …の目に恋を求める ▪ He *looks for Cupids in their* crystal *eyes.* 彼らの澄みきった目に彼は恋を求める.

play Cupid 仲介役をする ▪ He has *played Cupid* for single tenants. 彼は独身の間借り人のために仲介役をした ▪ Destiny *played cupid* and brought them together again. 運命が恋のキューピッドを演じ彼らはふたたび巡り会った.

curb /kəːrb/ 名 ***keep* [*put*] *a curb on*** …を抑えておく[抑える] ▪ *Put a curb on* your anger. 怒りを抑えなさい.

on the curb 《米株式》取引所外で, 街上で ▪ They were sold *on the curb.* その株は街上で売られた ▪ More than 1,000 shares changed hands, including 300 *on the curb.* 街上での300株を含めて1,000株以上が売買された.

curdle /kə́ːrdəl/ 動 ***curdle the* [*a person's*] *blood*** (恐怖・寒さが)肝をひやす; ぞっとさせる ▪ The horror of it *curdled* all *my blood.* 恐ろしさがすっかり私の肝をひやした.

make a person's blood curdle (寒さ・恐ろしさが)人をぞっとさせる, 人の肝をひやす ▪ His account *made my blood curdle.* 彼の話に私はぞっとした.

cure[1] /kjʊər/ 名 ***An ounce of prevention* (*is worth a pound of cure*).** →OUNCE.

The cure is worse than the disease. 《諺》治療が病気そのものよりも苦しい[悪い].

cure[2] /kjʊər/ 動 ***What cannot* [*can't*] *be cured must be endured.*** 《諺》治せないものはがまんしなければならない, 「ならぬ堪忍するが堪忍」.

curiosity /kjʊ̀əriɑ́səti|-ɔ́s-/ 名 ***be dying of* [*from*] *curiosity*** 好奇心に駆られる, 知りたくてたまらない ▪ *I'm dying of curiosity*: how did it turn out, Pup? 僕は知りたくてたまらない. あれはどうなったんだい, パップ?

Curiosity killed the cat. →CAT.

out of* [*from*] *curiosity 好奇心から, 物好きに ▪ I opened the box *out of curiosity.* 私は好奇心に駆られてその箱をあけた.

curious /kjʊ́əriəs/ 形 ***curious at*** …に妙を得て ▪ The doctor is *curious at* cuts and bruises. その医者は傷にかけては妙を得ている.

curious to do しきりに…したがって ▪ I am *curious to* see the man. その人に会ってみたいものだ.

***curious to relate* [*say*]** 妙な話だが, 言うもおかしいが ▪ *Curious to relate*, he is against universal suffrage. 妙な話だが, 彼は普通選挙に反対である.

curiouser and curiouser 《俗》いよいよ出でていよいよ奇で[奇なることには] ▪ "*Curiouser and curiouser*!" cried Alice. 「いよいよますます奇妙きてれつだわ!」とアリスは叫んだ. ☞Lewis Carroll, *Alice's Adventures in Wonderland* 2の初めにある句.

curl[1] /kəːrl/ 名 ***curl of the lip*** 上くちびるを少し上げること《軽蔑・嫌悪を示す》 ▪ Disgust is shown by a *curl of the lip.* 嫌悪の情は上くちびるを少し上げることによって表される.

go out of curl **1** (頭髪の)カールがとれる ▪ Her hair *went out of curl.* 彼女の髪はカールがとれた.
2 《俗》元気を失う, がっかりする, ぺしゃんこになる ▪ If I got pneumonia, I would *go* clean *out of curl.* もし肺炎にかかったら, 私は参ってしまうでしょう.

in curl (髪が)カールになって ▪ How do you keep your hair *in curl*? どうやって髪のカールを保ちますか.

curl[2] /kəːrl/ 動 ***curl a person's hair*** → HAIR.

curl one's* [*the*] *lip (軽蔑・嫌悪を示すため)上くちびるをゆがめる, 上げる ▪ A bitter smile *curled the lip* of the President. にが笑いが大統領の上くちびるをゆがめた.

curl oneself up 丸くなって寝る, ちぢこまる ▪ We *curled ourselves up*, as it was very cold. 非常に寒かったから, 我々は丸くなって寝た.

curl up and die 身体を丸めて死ぬ, 力尽きて死ぬ[負ける], 消えてしまいたく思う ▪ The worm struggled around for a time and finally *curled up and died.* 虫はしばらくもがいていたが, ついに体を丸めて死んでしまった ▪ Colorado *curled up and died* in an 8-4 loss to the struggling Montreal Expos. コロラドは必死のモントリオール・エクスポズ相手に力尽きて8対4で敗れた ▪ When they all started laughing, he just wanted to *curl up and die*! 彼らがこぞって笑い出したとき彼は穴があったら入りたい気がした.

make a person's hair curl 《口》人をぞっとさせる, 人の肝をつぶす ▪ The play fairly *makes our hair curl.* その劇は全く身の毛をよだたせる.

curlicue /kə́ːrləkjùː/ 名 ***cut* (*up*) *a curlicue*** 《米》はね回る, ふざけ散らす ▪ I *cut up a curlicue* with my right foot. 私は右足ではね回った.

curly /kə́ːrli/ 形 ***curly dirt*** 綿ぼこり, ほこりの塊り (house moss, slut's wool) ▪ There's a mountain of *curly dirt* under here! ここの下には山のような綿ぼこりがある.

currency /kə́ːrənsi|kʌ́r-/ 名 ***acquire* [*gain, obtain*] *currency*** **1** 伝わる, 流布する ▪ A rumor that the King may abdicate has *acquired currency.* 国王は退位するかもしれないという噂が伝わった.
2 通用しだす ▪ The coin *gained currency.* その貨幣は通用しだした.

at a person's own currency 当人の言う相場通りに ▪ We accept him *at his own currency.* 彼を当人の言う相場通りに認める.

gain* [*lose*] *currency with the world (新聞などが)世間の信用を得る[失う] ▪ The paper *gained currency with the world.* その新聞は世間の信用を得た.

give currency to …を通用[流布]させる ▪ He *gave currency to* the rumor. 彼がその噂を立てた.

in common currency 一般に通用して ▪ You should learn the words *in common currency* first. まず一般に通用している語を覚えるべきである.

lose currency 流布[通用]しなくなる ▪ The rumor soon *lost currency*. 噂はすぐ消えた.

current /kə́ːrənt|kʌ́r-/ 形名 ***go [swim] against the current*** 流れに逆らう(→SWIM against the stream) ▪ "Don't be afraid to *go against the current*," he told the young people. 「時流にさからうことを恐れるな」と彼は若者たちに言った.

pass [go, run] current 一般に通用する, 世間に認められる ▪ Their language *goes current* along the sea-coast. 彼らの言語は沿岸に通用する ▪ The news *passes current*. そのニュースは一般に事実とされている.

swim with [against] the current →SWIM against the stream.

curry /kə́ːri|kʌ́ri/ 動 ***curry favor (with)*** (利益を得るため…の)きげんをとる, (に)へつらう ▪ He always seems to be *currying favor with* the boss. 彼はいつも社長のきげんをとっているように見える. ☞favor は favel (栗毛の馬)のなまったもの.

curse[1] /kəːrs/ 名 ***call down a curse [curses] on [upon]*** …にのろいをかける, 人に天罰下れと祈る ▪ I *called down curses on* his head. 彼の頭に天罰下れと祈った.

Curse upon it! ちくしょう! くそっ!

Curses(, like chickens,) come home to roost. 《諺》人をのろわば穴二つ. ☞→come home to ROOST.

lay ... under a curse = call down a CURSE on.

not care [give] a curse (for) 《口》(…など)少しもかまわない ▪ He does*n't care a curse for* his loss. 彼は自分の損失などは少しもかまわない.

not worth a curse 《口》一文の価値もない ▪ This chapter is *not worth a curse*. この章は一文の値うちもない.

put a curse on …にのろいをかける ▪ A witch *put a curse on* the prince. 魔女が王子にのろいをかけた.

under a curse のろわれて, たたりを受けて ▪ The nation is *under a curse* for disobeying God. その国は神に背いたたたりを受けている.

curse[2] /kəːrs/ 動 ***be cursed with*** (いやなもの)を持っている(↔be BLESSed with) ▪ He *is cursed with* a temper. 彼は怒りっぽい気性である ▪ He *is cursed with* an idle son. 彼は(何の因果か)怠け息子を持っている.

curse and swear 悪口雑言する ▪ He began to *curse and swear*. 彼は悪口雑言しだした.

Curse it [etc.]! ちくしょう!

curtain /kə́ːrtən/ 名 ***a curtain raiser*** 前触れ ▪ The referendum is just *a curtain-raiser* for the general election. 国民投票は総選挙の前哨戦にすぎない.

be [mean, spell] curtains (for) 《口》(…にとって)死である, を意味する ▪ If you run into a big car, it'll *mean curtains for* you. 大型車にぶつかりでもしたら君はお陀仏だろうよ ▪ It'll *be curtains for* Windows XP. ウィンドウズ XP はもう終了になるだろう ▪ The flash floods may *spell curtains for* the local drive-in movie theater. 鉄砲水は地元のドライブイン映画館の命取りになるかもしれない. ☞芝居の幕が降りることから.

behind the curtain 陰に[の], 黒幕にいて[にいる] ▪ He laid the project *behind the curtain*. 彼が陰にいて計画を立てた ▪ I will not be minister *behind the curtain*. 私は陰の大臣にはなりたくない.

bring [ring] the curtain down on …に幕引きをする, を終わらせる, 廃止する ▪ The defeat of Karl I *brought the curtain down on* the empire of the Habsburgs. カール1世の敗北によりハプスブルク家は終焉を迎えた.

call [summon] *an actor* ***before the curtain*** 幕が降りたとき観客が喝采して役者を幕前に呼び出す ▪ Macready as Richard III *was called before the curtain* at Covent Garden. リチャード3世を演じたマクレディーは, コベントガーデン座で観客の喝采で幕前に呼び出された.

draw a curtain to カーテンを引いて閉じる ▪ Please *draw the curtains to* /túː/, the light is hurting my eyes. カーテンを引いてください. 光で目が痛む[光がまぶしい]から.

draw down the curtain **1** = bring the CURTAIN down on.

2 話をやめる ▪ It's time to *draw down the curtain*. もう話をやめるべきときだ.

draw the curtain **1** 幕を引いてあける ▪ I *drew the curtain* to show my books. 幕を引きあけて蔵書を見せた ▪ I *drew my curtains* to look out. カーテンを引きあけて外を見た.

2 幕を引いて閉じる ▪ She *drew her curtains* around. 彼女は周囲に幕を引いた.

draw the [a] curtain on [over] …をカーテンを引いて隠す; (話していること)をしまいにする ▪ Better *draw the curtain on* the scene. その光景は言わないことにするほうがよい.

drop the curtain 幕を降ろす; 活動を終える ▪ Congress *dropped the curtain* Wednesday. 議会は水曜日に閉会となった.

lift [raise] the curtain **1** 幕を上げる; 活動を始める ▪ Come, let us *raise the curtain*. さあ, 活動を始めよう.

2 幕を上げて見せる; 打ち明けて知らせる ▪ The magician *lifted the curtain* to reveal the missing elephant. マジシャンは幕を上げて消えたゾウの姿をまた見せた ▪ They *lifted the curtain* on the new design yesterday. 新デザインがきのう公表された.

mean curtains (for) →be CURTAINs (for).

ring the curtain up →RING[3].

summon *an actor* ***before the curtain*** →call an actor before the CURTAIN.

take a curtain (call) (役者が)観客の喝采に応じて幕前に現れる ▪ The comedian *took a curtain* *call* last night. 昨夜その喜劇役者は観客の喝采に応じて幕前に現れた.

the curtain falls [***comes down, drops, is dropped***] (***on, upon***) (...の)演技[事, 命]が終わる, 幕が降りる ▪ *The curtain* ought to *fall* at this point. ここで話は幕となるべきである ▪ *The curtain* has *dropped upon* that scene. その出来事は終わった ▪ *The curtain* has *come down on* Blair's reign. ブレア首相の政権が終わりを告げた.

The curtain rises [***is raised***]. 幕が開く, 開演になる ▪ *The curtain rises* at 8 sharp. 幕は正8時に開く.

the final curtain (劇場の)終演; 最後, 死 ▪ I left quietly before *the final curtain.* 私は終演の前にそっと出た.

curtsy, curtsey /kə́ːrtsi/ 名 ***drop*** [***make***] ***a curtsy*** (女性が)ひざを曲げておじぎをする ▪ She *dropped* such *a* disdainful *curtsy.* 彼女はあなどりきった会釈をした ▪ In Vienna men *make curtsies.* ウィーンでは男性がひざを曲げておじぎをする.

make *one's* ***curtsy to*** (婦人が女王など)に敬礼をする ▪ She *made her curtsey* to the Queen. 彼女は女王に拝謁した.

curve /kəːrv/ 名 ***throw*** [***pitch***] *a person* ***a curve*** (***ball***)/ ***throw a curve*** (***ball***) ***at*** *a person* 《主に米口》 **1** (打者に)カーブを投げる ▪ He *threw* the Yankees *a curve*—actually, bushels of them—and guided the A's to a 2-0 win. 彼はヤンキースにカーブを投じ—実は, 多投し—2対0でアスレチックスを勝利に導いた.

2 意表をつく, 裏をかく; だます, 嘘をつく ▪ The Senate *threw* the House *a curve* in the form of an amendment. 上院は修正の形で下院の意表をついた ▪ I found she'd *thrown* me *a curve ball* when she said she'd never been married before. 彼女は結婚の経験はないと言って私をかついでいたことがわかった.

curvet /kərvét/ 名 ***cut a curvet*** (馬が)跳躍する《前足が地につかないうちに後足から躍進する》; 両足をそろえてはね回る ▪ The horses *cut a curvet.* 馬たちは跳躍した.

cushy /kʊ́ʃi/ 形 ***a cushy number*** 《口》楽な仕事[職, 地位]《しばしば金になる》 ▪ I thought it would be *a cushy number.* 私はそれは楽で金になる職だろうと思った.

all very cushy 《口》きわめて愉快で ▪ My new job is *all very cushy.* こんどの仕事はきわめて愉快だ.

cuss /kʌs/ 名 ***not care a cuss*** 《俗》少しもかまわない ▪ As for your opinion, I do*n't care a cuss* about it. 君の意見なんか, 私は少しもかまわない.

not give a tinker's cuss 《口・古風》 = not give a DAMN.

not worth a (***tinker's***) ***cuss*** 《俗》一文の価値もない ▪ His ideas are *not worth a tinker's cuss.* 彼の思想は少しの値うちもない.

take the cuss off 《俗》いくぶん事態を改善する ▪ People began to stream into the theater, enough to *take the cuss off.* 人々は劇場に入りだして, 事態がいくぶん改善された.

custody /kʌ́stədi/ 名 ***give*** *a person* ***into custody*** 人を警察官に拘引[拘禁]させる ▪ He *was given into custody.* 彼は警察官に拘引された.

give *A* ***into the custody of*** *B* AをBに託する ▪ I have *given* the valuables *into the custody of* the captain. 貴重品は船長に託した.

have (***the***) ***custody of*** (子供など)を(預かって)保護する; (物)を保管する ▪ The relatives *have custody of* the child. 親族が子供を保護している ▪ The captain *has the custody of* the valuables. 船長は貴重品を保管する.

in custody 拘引[拘留]されて ▪ He is *in custody.* 彼は拘留中である.

in the custody of ...に保管[保護]されて ▪ She was placed *in the custody of* her aunt. 彼女はおばさんの保護下におかれた ▪ The valuables are *in the custody of* the captain. 貴重品は船長に保管されている.

take *a person* ***into custody*** 人を拘引[収監]する ▪ The police have *taken* him *into custody.* 警察は彼を拘引した.

custom /kʌ́stəm/ 名 ***as is*** *one's* ***custom*** いつものように ▪ I got up at seven *as is my custom.* いつものように7時に起きた.

give *one's* ***custom to*** 《商》...に愛顧を与える, をひいきにする ▪ Please *give your custom to* us. どうぞ私どもをお引き立てください.

have *a person's* ***custom*** 《商》人にひいき[得意]にしてもらう ▪ We should very much like to *have your custom.* あなた様のお引き立てを得たいものです.

it is the custom with ... to *do* ...するのは...の習慣である ▪ *It is the custom with* us in Japan *to* do so. そうするのが日本の習慣です.

make a custom of *doing*/ ***make it a custom to*** *do* いつも...することにしている ▪ I *make a custom of getting* [*make it a custom to* get] up early. 私はいつも早く起きることにしている.

withdraw [***take away***] *one's* ***custom*** ひいきにするのをやめる ▪ I shall *withdraw my custom* from the store. その店からは買わぬようにしよう.

customer /kʌ́stəmər/ 名 ***a cool customer*** →COOL[1].

a slippery customer **1** (ぬるぬるして)つかまえどころのないもの ▪ An oyster is *a slippery customer* when it comes out of its shell. カキは殻から出たばかりでは手で捕まえうらい ▪ Flu is *a slippery customer.* The virus constantly alters its surface proteins. 感冒はとらえどころがない. ウイルスが表面のタンパク質を絶えず変えるからだ.

2 しっぽをつかませない人物, ずる賢い[信頼できない]やつ ▪ Britain's former Africa Minister sounded a note of caution, describing President Mugabe as a "*slippery customer.*" 英国の前アフリカ担当大臣は警告を発し, ムガベ大統領は信頼できない男だと述べた.

an ugly [***an awkward, a tough***] ***customer***

《口》始末に負えない人，一すじなわではいかぬやつ，やっかい者 ▪ My enemy was *an ugly customer* who looked like a boxer. 敵はボクサーのような風采の一すじなわではいかぬやつだった ▪ It was evident that he was *a* very *ugly customer*. 彼が大変なやっかい者であることは明らかだった．

Only one to a customer! 一人1個限定 ▪ "Sorry, *only one to a customer*," said the woman.「申し訳ございませんが，お一人さま1個かぎりです」とその女性は言った．

The customer is always right. 《諺》お客様はいつも正しい; お客様は神様です．

cut[1] /kʌt/ 名形 ***a cut above*** 《口》…よりも一段上; …するような人でなく ▪ She was *a cut above* the housekeeper. 彼女は家政婦より一段上だった ▪ This book is *a cut above* her previous one. この本は彼女の以前の作品よりもすぐれている ▪ He's *a cut above* that sort of work. 彼はそんな仕事をする人ではない．

a cut off the nut 《戯》菜食 ▪ I'll have *a cut off the nut*. 僕は菜食にするよ．

cut and come again 何度でも好きなだけ取って食べてよい(もの)《特に肉》(→CUT[2] and come again) ▪ A ham is a *cut and come again* dish. ハムは存分に取って食べてよい料理です ▪ We have pale sherry, old port, and *cut and come again* ドライシェリー，熟成されたポートワイン，それに好きなだけ食べてよい肉があるわ．

cut and cover 《米》すき土をすかない畝(うね)にかぶせるすき方 ▪ The *cut and cover* practice is still worse. すき土をすかない畝にかぶせる方法はさらに悪い．

cut and dried **1** (意見・計画などが)型にはまった，月並みの，融通のきかない ▪ His arguments are all *cut and dried*. 彼の議論はみな月並みである ▪ His relations with his clients were *cut and dried*. 彼と依頼人との関係は融通のきかないものだった．
2 (計画・協定などが)完全にでき上がって，ちゃんと準備された; 変更なしの ▪ The plan is now *cut and dried*. その計画は完全にでき上がっている ▪ His speech was clearly *cut and dried*. 彼の演説は明らかに前もって用意されたものであった ▪ As to your journey across Europe, you can have it all *cut and dried*. ヨーロッパ横断旅行については万事ちゃんとお膳立てしてもらえる ▪ The procedure is not quite *cut and dried*. 手順は変更できないわけではない．
3 単純明快な ▪ The matter is not as *cut and dried* as that. 事態はそんなに単純なものはない．☞もとは薬店の薬草を野生の植物と比較して言ったもの．

cut and dry ＝CUT and dried 1.

cut and paste 切り貼り(仕事)(の);《電算》カットアンドペースト(の) ▪ Moses' birth story is simply a "*cut and paste*" reworking of the life of Sargon. モーゼ生誕の物語はサルゴンの伝記を加工した「切り貼り」にすぎない ▪ For certain songs, they used a *cut-and-paste* approach. 特定の歌に関しては，彼らはカットアンドペーストの方法をとった．

cut and thrust **1** 切ったり突いたりすること，接戦，肉薄戦《比喩的にも》 ▪ You don't know the *cut and thrust* of actual life. 君は実際生活上の苦闘を知らない ▪ I leave *cut and thrust* to them. 私は肉薄戦は彼らに一任します ▪ He came through the *cut and thrust* of the film world. 彼は映画界で苦闘の末に成功した．
2 力強い，鋭い ▪ That is a *cut and thrust* style. それは力強い文体である．

cut and try 実験的 ▪ He had to work by *cut and try* methods. 彼は実験的方法でやらねばならなかった．

cut from the same cloth 非常によく似て，性格が瓜二つで ▪ My brother Ron and I are *cut from the same cloth*. 兄のロンと僕は性格がそっくりだ．

draw cuts (長短の紙片・棒切れなどの)くじを引く ▪ They *drew cuts* for who should go out of the room. 彼らは誰が部屋から出て行くかについてくじを引いた ▪ We three will *draw cuts* for the honor of going with him. 我々3人で彼のお供をする者を決めるためくじを引こう．

give** a person **the cut direct (知人を)見ても知らぬ顔して行き過ぎる ▪ He *gave* me *the cut direct* this morning. 彼は今朝私を見ながら知らぬ顔して行き過ぎた．

have* [*take*] *a cut 《米》(一片の肉で)軽い食事をする ▪ I *had a* cold *cut* at Mrs. Smith's. スミス夫人の宅で冷肉で軽い食事をした．

jump the cut 《米俗》(トランプの札を切るとき)自分に有利になるよう細工する ▪ He is a good hand at *jumping the cut*. 彼はトランプの札を自分に有利に切るのがうまい．

make a cut 削減する ▪ We must *make a cut* in this article. この記事は少し削らねばならない．

make a cut at …に打ち[切り]かかる ▪ He *made a cut at* the enemy. 彼は敵に切ってかかった．

make a double cut 《米俗・鉄道》併結列車を切り離して各々を本線と分岐線に入れる ▪ He undertook to *make a double cut*. 彼は併結列車を切り離して本線と分岐線に入れる仕事を引き受けた．

make* [*miss*] *the cut 予選を通過する[に落ちる] ▪ Sixty-eight players *made the cut* at 151. 68人の選手が151で予選を通過した ▪ Sammy Sosa *missed the cut* for the July 15 game in Chicago. サミー・ソーサはシカゴでの7月15日の(オールスター)ゲームに選出されなかった．

take a cut →have a CUT.

the cut of** one's **jib →JIB.

the* (*most*) *unkindest cut of all →UNKIND.

cut[2] /kʌt/ 動 (***be***) ***cut out for*** [***to** do*]《口》…に[することに]向くようにできて(いる)，適して(いる); 似合いで(ある) ▪ John *is cut out for* [*to* be] a doctor. ジョンは医者に向くようにできている ▪ Tom and Jane *are cut out for* each other. トムとジェインは似合い(の夫婦)だ ▪ I don't feel that he *is cut out for* the job of president. 彼は会長の職に向いていないと私は思う．

cannot* [*could not*] *cut it →CUT it 3.

C

cut a deal 取り決める, 取引する ▪ The administration is hoping to *cut a deal* with Japan. 経営陣は日本との取引を希望している.

cut a loss [*one's* ***losses***] 損害をあきらめて新しく出発する; 損な投機を良いときにやめる ▪ We'd better *cut a loss* and wait for the next opportunity. 損切りをして次のチャンスを待つほうがよかろう.

cut ... adrift →ADRIFT.

cut and carve (肉などを)切り分ける, 分割する ▪ It's an image of cow parts for learning how to *cut and carve* beef. それは牛肉の切り分け方を学ぶための牛肉の部位を示す画像である.

cut and come again 《口》(肉・料理を)好きなだけ何度でも取って食べる《比喩的にも》(→CUT[1] and come again) ▪ You can *cut and come again*. We've another joint cooked. 何度でもおあがりください. もう一つ大肉片を調理してもらいましたから ▪ There are hundreds of books to show you. You can *cut and come again*. 君に見せる本が何百冊もある. いくらでも好きなだけ見なさい.

cut and contrive (収入内でやっていけるよう)やりくり算段する ▪ She is *cutting and contriving* to make both ends meet. 彼女は収支償わせるためやりくり算段をしている.

cut and run 《口》急いで逃げる; 急いで行く ▪ Our fleet were obliged to *cut and run*. わが艦隊は大急ぎで逃げねばならなかった ▪ You'll have to *cut and run*, if you want to catch the train. 電車に間に合いたいなら急いで行かねばなりません. ☞《海》「いかりをあげる暇もなく綱を切って帆走する」が原義.

cut both [***two***] ***ways*** **1** (行為・議論が)同時に益と害をなす, よしあしである ▪ Well, frankly, that *cuts both ways*. そうだな. はっきり言って, そいつはよしわるしだ ▪ That's an argument that *cuts both ways*. それは諸刃(もろは)の刃(やいば)の議論だ.

2 相互に影響する ▪ Her refusal to meet him *cuts both ways*—he won't be responsible for supporting her. 彼女が彼に会うのを断れば相互に影響を及ぼす—彼の方では彼女を養う責任がなくなるだろうから.

cut class (授業を)無断欠席する, さぼる ▪ If you *cut* one more *class* you'll fail the course. もう1時間ずる休みをしたらこの教科を落とすことになる.

cut clean →CLEAN[1].

cut *a person* ***dead*** 《口》人にそ知らぬ顔をする, 無視する ▪ I took off my hat to her, but she *cut* me *dead*. 私は彼女に対して帽子を取ったが, 彼女はそ知らぬ顔をした.

cut *a person* ***direct*** 相手をまともに見て知らぬ顔をする ▪ She called her dog away and *cut* me *direct*. 彼女は犬を呼び, 私を見ても知らん顔をした.

cut faces いろいろの面相をする, しかめつらをする ▪ Will you *cut faces* evermore? 君はいつまでもしかめつらをしますか.

cut ... free ...を切って放つ, 自由にする ▪ He *cut* himself *free* from the ropes. 彼は綱を自分で切って自由になった ▪ *Cut* the boat *free*. ボートの綱を切り放ちなさい.

cut ... in half [***two***] ...を二つに切る ▪ I *cut* the apple *in two*. そのリンゴを二つに切った.

cut ... in [***to***] ***pieces*** **1** ...を切り刻む ▪ Don't *cut* the paper *in pieces*. 紙を切り刻んではいけない.

2 (敵)を粉砕する; を酷評する ▪ We *cut* the enemy *to pieces*. 我々は敵を粉砕した ▪ He *cut* the novel *in pieces*. 彼はその小説を酷評した.

cut ... indirect よそ見をして(人)に知らぬ顔する ▪ He *cut* me *indirect*. 彼はよそ見をして私に知らぬ顔した.

cut ... infernal かがんで靴のはき具合を直して人に知らぬ顔をする ▪ He *cut* me *infernal*. 彼はかがんで靴のはき具合を直し, 私に知らぬ顔をした.

cut ... into halves ...を二つに切る (→CUT ... in half) ▪ *Cut* the apple *into halves*. リンゴを二つに切りなさい.

cut it 《口》 **1** 逃走する, 走る ▪ Now, my lady, do *cut it*. さあ, 奥さま, どうぞお逃げください.

2 〚命令文で〛よす; 黙る ▪ *Cut it*! よせ!

3 期待に添う, うまくやり遂げる, 求められた水準に達する ▪ Robbo was a great player, but sadly he could not *cut it* as a manager. ロッボは偉大な選手だったが, 悲しいことにマネージャーとしては優れていない ▪ Seven wins don't quite *cut it*. 7勝では期待通りというわけにはいかない.

cut it fat 《口》見せびらかす, 見栄を張る ▪ Don't *cut it fat* in such a way. そんなに見せびらかすな.

cut it [*things*, etc.] ***fine*** [***close***] **1** (時間・金など)ぎりぎりいっぱいに切りつめる; きわどいことをする ▪ He never misses this train but he always *cuts it fine*. 彼はこの電車に決して乗りおくれないが, いつも時間ぎりぎりに行く ▪ This group *cut it close* to the deadline, signing a deal on Monday night to buy the former sugar refinery. このグループは締め切りぎりぎりの月曜日の夜になって以前の精糖所を購入する取引に署名した ▪ To allow only 90 seconds for this operation is *cutting it fine*. この操作にたった90秒しか与えないのはきわどい芸当である ▪ The making of clothes *was cut fine*. 服の仕立てはごく僅かな儲けにしかならなかった.

2 《米》きちんと計算する ▪ This answer is correct to the last cent; you've *cut it fine*. この答えはピタリと1セントも違わない. あなたはきちんと計算している.

cut it off 《俗》眠る ▪ You were *cutting it off*. 君は眠っていた.

cut it [***that***] ***out*** 《口》(していることを)やめる; 〚命令文で〛うるさい, やめろ ▪ Why don't you *cut it out* altogether? なぜあなたはそれをすっかりやめてしまわないのですか ▪ Aw, come on! *Cut it out*! おい, やめろ! ☞無礼な表現.

cut it short 《俗》(やって[言って]いることを)やめる; 簡単にする, 急ぐ ▪ *Cut it short*, Bill! ビル, 話をやめろ ▪ Won't you *cut it short*? 簡単に言ってくれないか.

cut loose **1** (綱・鎖)を切って放つ ▪ They *cut* a boat *loose* from the ship. 彼らは親船からボートを切り放した ▪ His horses were all *cut loose*. 彼の馬はみな放たれた.

2 (関係・束縛から)自由になる, 逃れる, 離れる ▪ He tried to *cut loose* from his domineering father. 彼は横暴な父を離れて自由になろうとした.

3《米》勝手気ままに[存分に]…する; はめをはずして祝う[楽しむ]; 遠慮なく話す ▪ You must see him when he *cuts loose*. 彼が勝手きままな行動を始めたらあなたは監督しなければならない ▪ Convention delegates *cut loose* at night. 会議の代表たちは夜ははめをはずして楽しんだ.

4《米》…し始める ▪ They *cut loose* and shouted. 彼らは叫び始めた ▪ He suddenly *cut loose* with a violent attack on the President. 彼は急に大統領を激しく攻撃しだした.

5《米》攻撃[射撃]を始める ▪ I *cut loose* at the armadillo with my trusty bow and arrow. 私は腕に覚えの矢をアルマジロに射かけた.

6 立ち去る ▪ Let's *cut loose* right away. 今すぐ出かけよう.

cut *oneself* ***loose from*** *one's* ***family*** 家族から離れて独立の身となる ▪ He determined to *cut himself loose from his family*. 彼は家族から離れて独立することに決めた.

cut *one's* ***losses*** →CUT a loss.

cut *one's* ***lucky*** [***stick***]《俗》出て行く, 行く, 逃げる ▪ It is eleven. I'd better *cut my lucky*. 11時だ, おいとまするとしよう ▪ He *cut his stick* in haste. 彼はあわてて出て行った.

cut off *one's* ***nose to spite*** *one's* ***face*** →NOSE[1].

cut *a person* ***off with a shilling*** →SHILLING.

cut *oneself* ***on*** (刃物など)で(うっかり)切る, けがをする ▪ Reportedly, the guitarist accidentally *cut himself on* a knife. 伝えられるところでは, そのギター奏者はうっかりナイフで指にけがをしたとのことだ.

cut *a person* ***out of*** *one's* ***will*** →WILL[1].

cut out (***the***) ***dead wood***《口》(絵・文の)まずいところを削る; 余剰人員を削減する ▪ We must make the questionnaires more reliable by *cutting out dead wood*. まずいところを削ってアンケートをもっと確実なものにしなくてはならない ▪ We must *cut out dead wood* for the sake of the economy. 我々は経済的理由で余剰人員を削減しなければならない.

cut out the middleman 仲介段階を省略する ▪ The Internet is going to *cut out the middleman*. インターネットのお陰で仲介業者の手を経ずにすむようになるだろう.

cut short →SHORT.

cut … sublime 高い建て物や雲を見上げて人に知らぬ顔をする ▪ He *cut* me *sublime*. 彼は上の方ばかり見て私に知らぬ顔をした.

cut *one's* ***teeth on*** →TOOTH.

cut the air [***the atmosphere***] ***with a knife*** 〚you could (have) を伴って〛(その場の特に不快な)空気を感知する ▪ When I went into the room, *you could have cut the air with a knife*. 私が部屋に入るとそこの(不快な)空気が感知できた.

Cut the crap [***shit***]***!***《口》〚命令文で〛ウソつけ, 無駄口をたたくのはやめろ ▪ It's time for us to *cut the crap* and be honest with each other and candid with our voters. だましあいはやめて, 互いに正直で投票者に率直になろう ▪ Let's *cut the crap* and get to the heart of it. 無駄口はやめて核心に入ろう.

cut … to pieces [***ribbons, shreds***] (敵)を粉砕する; めちゃめちゃに切る, 切りさいなむ; (著書など)を酷評する, めちゃくちゃにやっつける ▪ The cavalry caught the foot soldiers and *cut* them *to pieces*. 騎兵隊が歩兵隊を捕えてそれを粉砕した.

cut … to the bone **1** (商品・値段)を最低まで下げる ▪ Many products *were cut to the bone*. 多くの産物の値段がぎりぎりまで下げられた.

2 (費用など)をぎりぎりに切り詰める ▪ Our living expenses *were cut to the bone*. 我々の生活費はぎりぎりに切り詰められた.

cut to the chase 本論に移る ▪ We don't have much time left, so let's *cut to the chase*. 残り時間が少ないので本題に入ろう.

cut *a person* ***to the heart*** [***the quick***] 人の胸にこたえる, 人の心を痛ませる, 人の感情をひどく害する ▪ His ingratitude *cut* her *to the quick*. 彼の忘恩は彼女にひどくこたえた ▪ His sarcastic remark *cut* me *to the heart*. 彼の皮肉な言葉はひどく私のしゃくにさわった. ☞the quick「最も敏感な部分」.

cut to the quick →QUICK.

cut two ways →CUT both ways.

cut up rough [***crusty, nasty, rusty, savage, stiff, ugly***]《英口》(ひどく)腹を立てる, けんか腰になる, あばれる, 険悪になる ▪ Hang it! You *cut up* quite *savage*. ちくしょう! ひどく怒っていやがるな ▪ He will *cut up rough* if you don't give him what he asks for. くれと言う物をやらなければ, 彼はあばれるだろう.

cut up well [***big, fat, large, rich, warm***] **1** (肉が多くて)厚く切り取れる ▪ This turkey *cuts up well*. この七面鳥は切っても厚みがある.

2《俗》たくさん財産を残して死ぬ ▪ How did the old man *cut up*? おじいさんはどれくらい財産を残して死んだか ▪ He *cut up well*. 彼はたくさん財産を残して死んだ. ☞「人の財産が豊かで切り取れる分量が多い」が原義.

cut *one's* ***way*** 障害を切り抜けて進む ▪ The ships *cut their way* slowly. 船はゆっくりと障害を切り抜けて進んだ.

have *one's* ***work cut out*** (***for*** *one*)《英》**1** 予定された仕事がある, 手いっぱい仕事がある, 忙しい ▪ I *have my work cut out for* me. 私は仕事が手いっぱいで忙しい.

2 非常に骨が折れる, きわめてむずかしい, 苦闘せねばならない ▪ It's a big job; he'll *have his work cut out for* him. それは大きな仕事だ, 彼はその仕事に苦闘せねばならぬだろう ▪ I shall *have my work cut out* to finish that job by the end of this week. 今週の終わりまでにその仕事を終えるには大変骨が折れるだろう.

C

not cut it →CUT it 3.

cute /kjuːt/ 形 ***cute as a button*** [***a bug's ear***] ちっちゃくてかわいい ▪ Her baby is *cute as a button*. 彼女の赤ちゃんはとてもかわいい.

cylinder /sílɪndər/ 名 ***be firing*** [***operating, running***] ***on all cylinders*** エンジン全開である. フル稼働中である, 快調である ▪ The company's ad business *is running on all cylinders* across all categories. 会社の広告事業はすべての分野で順調に進んでいる.

miss on all [***four, six***] ***cylinders*** (エンジンなどが)うまく動かない; 調子が悪い ▪ The engine was *missing on all cylinders*. エンジンがうまく動いていなかった.

work [***function, fire, hit, click,*** etc.] ***on all*** [***four, six***] ***cylinders*** (内燃機関が)全力で動く; 全力で働く, 好調子で動く ▪ The machine is *working on all cylinders*. 機械は全力をあげて動いている[フル稼動している] ▪ We are not *firing on all cylinders* yet, but have still won our first four games. 我々はまだ本調子ではないが, それでも最初の4試合に勝利を収めた ▪ We just happened to *hit on* all *four cylinders* today. 我々は今日たまたま全力で働いただけだ ▪ They *clicked on* all *six cylinders* in the next game. 彼らは次の試合では好調にプレーした.

D

dab /dæb/ 名形 ***be a*** (***regular***) ***dab*** (***hand***) ***at*** [***in***] 《英口》…の名人である, がじょうずである ▪ I *am a dab in* history. 私は歴史が大得意である ▪ He *is a* (*regular*) *dab hand at* photography. 彼は写真を撮るのが非常にうまい.

dabbler /dǽbələr/ 名 (***be***) ***a dabbler in*** [***at***] …のしろうとで(ある) ▪ He *is a dabbler in* painting. 彼はしろうと絵かきである.

daddy /dǽdi/ 名 ***the daddy of them all*** (ある運動などの)元祖, 主唱者 ▪ In so many other respects, he is *the daddy of them all.* その他の多くの点において彼は元祖である.

daffy /dǽfi/ 形 ***drive*** *a person* ***daffy*** 人を悩ます, いらいらさせる ▪ He'll *drive* the pitcher *daffy.* 彼は投手を悩ますだろう.

daft /dæft|dɑːft/ 形 (***as***) ***daft as a brush*** 《口》大ばかで ▪ I remember him as a kid and he was *as daft as a brush* then. 子供のころの彼を覚えているが, そのころ彼は大ばかだった.

dagger /dǽgər/ 名 ***at*** [***with***] ***daggers drawn*** (***with***) (…と)にらみ合いの状態で, (と)角突き合いして ▪ They are *at daggers drawn with* each other. 彼らは互いに角突き合いしている ▪ Was he *at daggers drawn with* his rich uncle? 彼は金持ちのおじさんとにらみ合っていたか.

look [***glare, shoot, stare***] ***daggers at*** 《雅》(人)をすごい目でにらみつける ▪ I happened to tread on his toes, and he *looked daggers at* me. 私はつい彼の足指を踏んだ. すると彼は私をすごくにらみつけた.

speak daggers to …に(胸を刺すように)とげとげしく言う (cf. Sh., *Haml.* 3. 2. 414) ▪ I will *speak daggers to* her. 彼女に毒づいてやろう.

dainty /déɪnti/ 形 ***be born with a dainty tooth*** 生まれつき食べ物の好みが贅沢である ▪ I *was born with a dainty tooth* and a palate for wine. 生まれつき食べ物の好みが贅沢でワインの好みがうるさかった.

daisy /déɪzi/ 名 (***as***) ***fresh as a daisy*** 少しも疲れない, 元気はつらつで ▪ After that sleep you ought to be *as fresh as a daisy.* あれだけ眠ったのだから, 君は元気はつらつであるのが当然だ ▪ The whole family looked *as fresh as a daisy.* 家族全員少しも疲れた様子はなかった.

cops [***oops***]***-a-daisy/ whoops daisy*** 〚間投詞的に〛あれれ, おっとっと, ヨイショ《子供を助け起こしたり抱き上げたりするときの掛け声》 ▪ Put your socks on now—*oops-a-daisy,* don't fall off the bed. さあ靴下をはくのよ—おっとっと! ベッドから転げ落ちないでね.

out with a daisy cutter 《野球》ゴロ球でアウトになって ▪ He is *out with a daisy cutter.* 彼はゴロでアウトになった.

push (***up***) [***count***] ***daisies*** 《俗》死ぬ; 死んで埋められる ▪ I shall be *pushing daisies* long before your time comes. 私はあなたよりずっと前に死んで埋葬されているでしょう.

turn (***up***) *one's* ***toes to the daisies*** 《俗》死ぬ, 死んで葬られる ▪ Be kind to those little folks when *our toes are turned up to the daisies.* 私たちが死んだら子供たちに親切にしてやってください.

under the daisies 《俗》死んで ▪ She is drinking herself *under the daisies.* 彼女はいわば飲み死にしているようなものだ.

dak /dɑːk/**, dawk** /dɔːk/ 名 ***lay a dawk*** つぎ馬[かご]旅の用意をする ▪ *The dawk is* already *laid.* つぎ馬旅行の用意はすでにできている.

dale /deɪl/ 名 ***dale and down/ down and dale*** 《詩》谷や丘 ▪ The shining vapor sailed all night over *down and dale.* 輝く水蒸気が夜じゅう谷や丘の上を流れて行った.

hill and dale 《詩》山や谷 ▪ Its surface is fairly diversified with *hill and dale.* その表面は山や谷でかなり変化がある.

o'er [***over***] ***hill and dale/ up hill and down dale*** 《詩》山越え谷越えて (→hill and DALE) ▪ I roamed *over hill and dale.* 私は山野を跋渉(ばっしょう)した.

dalles /dælz/ 名 ***run the dalles*** 《米》急流を流れ下る ▪ Here we debarked and the men *ran the dalles.* ここで我々は下船し水兵たちは急流を流れ下った.

Dalmatian /dælméɪʃən/ 名 ***spotted like a Dalmatian*** ダルメシアンのように斑点のある; 雑多なことをやって一事に徹しない ▪ That family is *spotted like a Dalmatian.* あの家族は雑多なことをやっている.

damage /dǽmɪdʒ/ 名 ***do damage to*** …に損害を与える, を害する ▪ The storm *did* much *damage to* the crops. あらしは作物に大損害を与えた.

prove [***turn out***] ***to*** *a person's* ***damage*** 人の損害となる ▪ The enterprise *proved to my damage.* その事業は私の損害となった.

stand the damage 自腹を切る ▪ I'll *stand the damage.* 私が自腹を切ります.

sue [***prosecute***] ***for damages*** 損害賠償の訴えをする ▪ We *sued for damages* for breach of contract. 我々は契約違反の損害賠償の訴えをした.

The damage is done. もう手遅れだ[後の祭だ] ▪ Nobody's going to fix this situation. *The damage is done.* 誰もこの状況を直そうとはしない. もう手遅れだ.

to *one's* ***damage*** …の損害となって ▪ The report was spread abroad *to my* great *damage.* その報道が広がって私は大損害を受けた.

What's the damage? 《口》勘定はいくらか; 経費はいくらか ▪ *What's the damage*, old fellow? おじさん, 勘定はいくらかね.

dammit /dǽmət/ 間 〚damn it の縮約形〛 ***as ... as dammit*** 《俗》ひどく[べらぼうに]...で ▪ I was *as* poor *as dammit*. 私はひどく貧乏だった.

damn[1] /dæm/ 名 ***damn all*** 《俗》全く...ない (= no, nothing) ▪ The doctor is *damn all* use. その医者は全く役にたたない ▪ There's *damn all* you can do. あなたにできることは何もない.

do [know] damn all 《英俗》てんで何もしない[知らない] (→ DAMN all) ▪ He *knew damn all* about the Russian writer. 彼はそのロシアの作家のことは何も知らなかった.

not give [care] a damn 《俗》少しもかまわない, 少しも関心を持たない ▪ I do*n't care a damn* what you do. 君が何をしようと少しもかまわない ▪ I do*n't give a damn* about it. それには少しも関心がない.

not worth a damn なんの価値もない ▪ His work is *not worth a damn*. 彼の作品は三文の値うちもない.

damn[2] /dæm/ 動 ***be damned if one does and damned if one doesn't*** してもしなくても非難される (→a CATCH-22 (situation)) ▪ In politics, one *is* often *damned if one does and damned if one doesn't*—particularly if one is the Prime Minister. 政治では, 人は往々にしてしてもしなくても非難されるものだ—総理の場合はとりわけそうだ.

Be damned to ...! 《口》こん畜生!, ...はくそくらえ! ▪ *Be damned to* you [that]! おまえ[そんなこと]などくそくらえ!

Damn and blast! 《間》こん畜生!, え, くそっ! ▪ *Damn and blast!* The petrol's run out. こん畜生! ガソリンが切れてる.

Damn [God damn] it! 《口》ちえっ!, しまった!, じれったい! ▪ *Damn it*, I love you. こんなにかわいがっているのに(わからないのか). ☞この句は焦燥の気持ちを表すだけで呪いではない.

Damn me! 《口》きっと ▪ *Damn me* but I'll do it. きっとそれをしないではおかない.

damn right and left ...にやつ当たりに当たりちらす ▪ He *damned* his men *right and left*. 彼は部下にやたらと当たりちらした.

Damn straight! 《口》確かにそうだ ▪ Have you really never loved me?—*Damn straight!* I have never loved you! 君は本当に僕を愛してなかったの?—確かにそうよ! 一度も愛したことなんかないわ.

damn with faint praise 気のない[冷淡な]ほめ方をしてかえってけなす (Pope, *Epistle to Dr. Arbuthnot* 201) ▪ She tried to *damn* all his pictures *with faint praise*. 彼女は彼のすべての絵を気のないほめ方でかえってけなそうとした.

Damn your eyes! 《口》うるさい!, 畜生! 《強い誓言》 ▪ *Damn your eyes!* Couldn't you keep quiet? うるさい! 静かにしておれんか.

damn(ed) well 《口》きっと, 確かに ▪ They *damn well* ought to be in your hands. それらは確かに君の手中にあるべきである ▪ He *damn well* isn't going to start. 彼は確かに出発する気はない.

do [try] one's damnedest (悪い事に)全力を尽くす; 《反語》最善を尽くす ▪ Now *do your damnedest* at your peril. さあ, できるだけ悪いことをしてみろ, ただではおかぬぞ ▪ She had *done her damnedest* to please him. 彼女は彼を喜ばそうと全力を尽くした.

I'll be damned [I'm damned] if ...してたまるものか《強い否定》 ▪ *I'll be damned if* I'll give him one cent more. もうこれ以上1セントだって絶対彼にはやらぬ ▪ *I'll be damned if* it is true. それが本当でたまるものか.

May you be damned!/You damned! こん畜生!

(Well,) I'll be [I'm] damned! 《口》まあうれしい!, こん畜生!, こりゃ驚いた! ▪ "*Well, I'll be damned!*" he exclaimed when he saw the gift. 「こりゃすごい」と彼はその贈物を見て叫んだ.

damnable /dǽmnəbəl/ 形 ***damnable iteration*** (聖書からの)こじつけ引用, こじつけ (cf. Sh., *1 Hen. IV* 1. 2. 101) ▪ He uses the art of "*damnable iteration*" deliberately. 彼はことさらに「こじつけ」の術を使う.

damp /dæmp/ 名形 ***a damp squib*** しめった花火; 不発の花火 ▪ My flirting with him fell flat like *a damp squib*. 私と彼とのいちゃつきは不発の花火のように失敗した.

cast [throw] a damp over/strike a damp into ...に水をさす, を意気阻喪(そそう)させる, を頓座させる ▪ Those incidents *cast an* occasional *damp over* trade. それらの事件はときどき貿易の勢いをそいだ ▪ This news *struck a damp into* their hearts. このニュースで彼らは意気阻喪した.

go off like a damp squib しめった花火のように爆発しない (→a DAMP squib) ▪ The joke *went off like a damp squib*. その冗談は一向に効きめがなかった.

damper /dǽmpər/ 名 ***cast [put] a damper on [over]*** ...を興ざめにする, 白けさせる, に水をさす ▪ The bad news *cast a damper on* the party. その凶報でその会は興ざめとなった ▪ He wanted to go abroad, but his father *put a damper on* the idea. 彼は外遊したかったが, 父親はその考えに水をさした.

have a damper 《口》1杯やる ▪ Let's *have a damper*. さあ1杯やろうではないか.

damsel /dǽmzəl/ 名 ***a damsel in distress*** 《戯》悩める[窮地の]乙女 ▪ The subject of the *damsel in distress* is a classic theme in world literature, art, and film. 悩める乙女の主題は世界の文学・美術・映画の古典的なテーマである.

dance[1] /dæns|dɑːns/ 名 ***a dance upon nothing*** 絞首刑 ▪ It led inevitably to *a dance upon nothing*. それで必然的に絞首刑に落ち着いた.

begin [lead] the dance ダンス開始の先導をする, 先に立って踊る; (行動に)率先する ▪ You are to *lead* *the dance.* あなたが先に立って踊るべきだ ▪ He is the man who *begins the dance.* 彼こそ率先する人である.

give a dance ダンスパーティーを催す ▪ She is *giving a dance* instead of a garden party. 彼女は園遊会の代わりにダンスパーティーを催します.

lead** a person **a** (**fair, pretty, jolly, merry**) **dance《英》**1** 人に苦労させる, むだ骨を折らす, ひどい面倒をかける ▪ He has *led* me *a fair dance*, I am so tired. 彼は私にむだ骨を折らせた. だから私は非常に疲れた ▪ He ran away, leaving a mass of debts. Oh, he's *led* me *a pretty dance.* 彼はたくさんの借金を残して逃げてしまった. ほんとに彼は私にひどい面倒をかけた ▪ He's *led* us *a merry dance.* We've been looking all over for him. 彼のことは大迷惑だった. 方々を探し回ったよ.

2 人をあちこちかけずり回らせる, 人をひっぱり回す ▪ He *led* me *a dance* half way round the town before I ran him to earth at his club. 彼をクラブで見つけるまで, 私は町を半分ぐるっと回らせられた. ☞昔の複雑なダンスでみなが指導者に従ったことから; →lead a person a (hard, fine, merry) CHASE.

lead the dance →begin the DANCE.

dance[2] /dæns|dɑːns/ 動 ***dance a hornpipe*** 元気よく踊る, 小踊りする ▪ I felt like *dancing a hornpipe.* 私はうれしくて小踊りしたい気がした.

***dance after** a person's **pipe** [**piping, tune, whistle**]* →DANCE to a person's pipe.

dance and pay the piper 自分で踊って他人を楽しませたうえ笛吹き料まで払う(《聖》*Matt.* 11. 7) ▪ I will *dance and pay the piper.* 踊ったうえに笛吹きの人に料金を払います.

***dance attendance** (**on**)* **1** (...に)ひどく待たされる ▪ I'm tired of *dancing attendance on* him. 彼にひどく待たされるのにはあきた ▪ Here are a pair of your shoes, *dancing attendance* till you need them. あなたの靴がここにあります. 君が必要とするまでそれはじっと待たされているのです.

2 (付き添って人に)ちやほやする, ごきげんをとる; (人に)奴隷的に仕える, 世話をする (cf. Sh., *Hen. VIII* 5. 2. 31) ▪ He lives in town when he is not *dancing attendance on* Lady Swan. 彼はスワン夫人のごきげんをとっていないときは町に住んでいる. ☞花嫁が式に参列したすべての客と踊らなければならなかった習慣から.

dance for joy 喜びのあまり踊りだす, 狂喜する ▪ They *danced for joy* at the news. 彼らはそのニュースに狂喜した.

dance in the hot trough《米》妹や弟に先に結婚される ▪ She was to *dance in the hot trough.* 彼女は妹に先に結婚される運命だった.

dance** oneself **into ダンスして...に入る[取り入る] ▪ She *danced herself into* the King's favor. 彼女はダンスして国王の気に入りになった ▪ An obscure actor *danced himself into* the chamber of the empress. 無名の俳優がダンスして女王の間に入った.

***dance on** [**upon**] **a rope** [**nothing, the air**]* 絞首刑に処せられる ▪ If you don't take care, you will soon *dance upon nothing.* 君は気をつけないとまもなく絞首刑になるぞ.

dance on air **1**《米俗》死ぬ ▪ I will make you *dance on air.* おまえを殺してやる.

2 小躍りして喜ぶ, 非常に幸せだ, まるで宙を舞うような幸福感に浸る ▪ I'm so happy and I could *dance on air.* とても幸せで宙を舞うことだってできそうだ ▪ She was just *dancing on air*, she was so happy. 彼女は小躍りして喜んだ, それほどうれしかった.

dance** oneself **out of breath 息が切れるほど踊る ▪ He *danced himself out of breath* last night. 彼は昨夜息が切れるほど踊った.

dance to a different** [**another**] **tune 急にいつもの態度や行動を変える ▪ Now he has joined the firm, he'll have to *dance to a different tune.* この商会に入ったからには, 彼は今までの態度をがらっと変えねばならないだろう ▪ They had to *dance to another tune* later on. 彼らはあとになってがらりと態度を変えねばならなかった.

***dance to** [**after**] a person's **pipe** [**piping, tune, whistle**]* 人の笛につれて踊る; 人の望みや指揮の通りにする, 人の意のままに行動する ▪ I had the prettiest girl in the castle *dancing after my whistle.* 私は城中で一番美しい娘に私の笛につれて踊ってもらった ▪ Most of them will *dance to Rome's piping.* 彼らは大抵ローマの指揮に従うだろう.

dance** a person **up and down 人を上げたり下げたりする ▪ His mother *danced* Tom *up and down.* 母親はトムを上げたり下げたりした.

dancer /dǽnsər|dɑ́ːn-/ 名 ***track up dancers***《俗》階段を上る ▪ Come, *track up* the *dancers.* さあ, 階段を上りなさい.

dander /dǽndər/ 名 *One's **dander is up.*** 怒っている, 興奮している ▪ *His dander is up.* 彼はかんかんに怒っている ▪ You're so damned adorable when *your dander is up.* 君がかんかんに怒っているときはとても可愛いよ.

get** [**have**] one's **dander up《口》(ひどく)怒る ▪ He *had his dander up.* 彼はひどく怒った.

raise the dander 怒らせる ▪ I called Bill a skunk, that *raised* his *dander.* ビルをいやなやつだと言ったら, やつはかんかんに怒った.

dandy /dǽndi/ 名 ***come out dandy***《米》良い結果になる ▪ Everything *came out dandy.* 万事好結果になった.

for dandy《口》見栄のため, 飾りのため ▪ The gay mosquito curtain is just *for dandy.* はでな蚊帳(かや)は全く見栄のためだ.

danger /déɪndʒər/ 名 ***at danger*** (信号が)危険と出て ▪ The signal is *at danger.* 信号は危険と出ている.

(be) *on the danger list*《口》重態で(ある) ▪ The patient *is on the danger list.* その患者は重態である.

clear and present danger 明白で目前の危険 ▪ I think that publishing is protected under the First Amendment except in a case of "*clear* *and present danger*". 私見では, 出版は「明白で目前の危険」の場合のほかは米国憲法修正第1条によって保護されている.

Danger past, God forgotton. 《諺》危険が去れば神も忘れられる, 「のど元過ぎれば熱さを忘れる」.

in danger 危篤で, 危険に瀕して ▪ His life is *in danger*. 彼は危篤である ▪ The country was *in danger*. 国は危険に瀕していた.

D

in danger of …の危険[恐れ]があって ▪ He was *in danger of* losing his life. 彼は命を失う恐れがあった ▪ This bridge is *in danger of* collapsing any minute. この橋はいつくずれるかわからない危険な状態にある.

out of danger 危険を脱して ▪ Out of debt, *out of danger*. 《諺》借金がなくなれば, 危険もなくなる《danger はもと「処罰される危険」》 ▪ The doctor says he's *out of danger* now. 医者は彼はもう危険を脱したと言っている.

pull ... out of danger …を敗北[死]から救い出す ▪ We should do our best to *pull* the firm *out of danger*. 我々はその会社の倒産を救うため最善を尽くすべきである.

dangle /dǽŋgəl/ 動 ***dangle** A **before*** [***in front of***] *B* [*B's* ***eyes***] B[Bの目の前]にAを見せびらかす ▪ They *dangled* the carrot *before* the donkey. 彼らはロバにニンジンを見せびらかした ▪ A mighty temptation *was dangled before* his eyes. 大きな誘惑が彼の目の前にぶら下げられていた.

Daniel /dǽnjəl/ 名 ***a Daniel come to judgment*** ダニエル(名判官)の再来; 名判官, 深謀遠慮の人 (cf. Sh., *Merch. V.* 4. 1. 223-333) ▪ You are *a Daniel come to judgment*. 君は実に深謀遠慮だ.

Daniel in the lion's den 孤立無援, 絶体絶命の状況 (《聖》*Dan.* 6) ▪ When I first went to my class, I felt rather like *Daniel in the lion's den*. はじめて担任のクラスに行ったとき, 孤立無援の状況に置かれた感じがした.

darbies /dɑ́:rbiz/ 名 ***clap on the darbies*** 《英口》手かせをはめる ▪ The ruffian showed signs of fight, so the detective *clapped on the darbies*. 悪漢は戦意を見せたので探偵は手かせをはめた.

dare /deər/ 動 ***dare** a person's **anger and say*** 怒られる覚悟で言う ▪ I will *dare your anger and say* it. 私は君に怒られる覚悟で言いたい.

dare say 〚通例 I dare say; 間接話法として第3人称に用いられるときは, He dares to say, He dared (to) say となる. 《英》では daresay と1語で書くこともある〛 **1** あえて言う ▪ This, I *dare say*, is the best explanation. これが最善の説明であると私はあえて言いたい ▪ I *dare say* that I will do it for myself. 私はそれを自力でするとあえて言う.

2 おそらく, たぶん ▪ I *dare say* it is a lie. おそらくそれは嘘であろう ▪ He told me he had a letter, which, he *dared say*, would suit the occasion. 彼は一通の手紙を持っているが, それはおそらくその場合に適するであろうと彼は私に言った.

***dare** a person **to** do* 人にやれるならやってみろといどむ ▪ I *dare* you *to* strike me. なぐれるものならなぐってみろ ▪ He *dared* me *to* jump over the stream. 彼は私にその川を飛び越えられるなら越えてみろと言った.

How dare you ...? よくも君は…したな ▪ *How dare you* lay hands on me? よくも僕の体に手をかけたな.

I dare say →DARE say 2.

I dare swear 確信する ▪ He will succeed, *I dare swear*. 彼はきっと成功するよ.

not know what** one **dares (***to***) ***hope*** (病気が治るなどと聞いて)まさかと思う ▪ She did *not know what* she *dared hope*. 彼女はまさかと思った.

dark /dɑ:rk/ 形名 ***at*** [***before, after***] ***dark*** 夕暮時に[前に, ののちに] ▪ We don't go out much *after dark*. 日暮れてのちはあまり外出しません.

in the dark **1** 暗がりに ▪ Don't leave the child alone *in the dark*. 子供を一人暗がりに残してはいけない.

2 知らないで ▪ We were completely *in the dark* as to his future plans. 我々は彼の未来の計画については全く知らなかった.

3 隠れて; 人に知られないで; 秘密裡に ▪ I am *in the dark* to all the world. 私は世間全体に知られない人間です ▪ It was procured *in the dark*. それは秘密裡に手に入れたものだ.

keep dark 《口》 **1** 隠れている ▪ He *kept dark* for a week. 彼は1週間隠れていた.

2 秘密にしておく, 黙っている (*about*) ▪ I'll *keep dark about* it. 私はそれについては黙っております.

keep** a thing **dark 《口》物を秘密にしておく ▪ We want to *keep* it *dark* till after Easter. 私たちはそれを復活祭の後まで秘密にしておきたい.

keep [***leave***] *a person* ***in the dark*** 人に知らせずにおく ▪ She was resolved to *keep* Harriet *in the dark*. 彼女はハリエットには知らせずにおこうと決心していた ▪ You *left* us *in the dark* as to your intentions. あなたはご意向を我々に知らせてくれなかった.

keep** oneself **in the dark 隠れている, 黙っている ▪ He deliberately *kept himself in the dark* as to the event. 彼はその件については意図的に黙っていた.

the dark of the moon 月のない(暗い)時[夜] ▪ It was *the dark of the moon* when we reached camp. 我々がキャンプに着いた時は月がなくて暗かった.

the dark side of (*things*) (物事の)裏面, 悪い面 ▪ He looks upon *the dark side of things*. 彼は物事を悲観的に見る ▪ This article exposes *the dark side of* Islam. その記事はイスラムの悪い面を暴露している.

The darkest hour is that before the dawn. 《諺》一番暗いのは夜明け前だ《物事は最悪の事態になると必ず良い方へ向かう》.

The darkest place is under the candlestick. 《諺》一番暗いのは燭台の下だ, 「灯台もと暗し」.

the lights and darks 明暗, 濃淡 ▪ I tried to

portray *the lights and darks* of the desert. 私は砂漠の明暗を描写しようとした.

with dark eyes 不快[憤怒]の目で ▪ Some people look upon the project *with dark eyes*. その計画を喜ばない者もいる.

darken /dáːrkən/ 動 ***darken*** *a person's* ***door*** [***doors***] 〚主に否定に用いて〛 人の家の敷居をまたぐ《脅迫・怒りのときにのみ用いる》 ▪ You shall pack and never more *darken my doors* again. さっさと出て行きもう二度とうちの敷居をまたぐな ▪ If he dares to *darken my door* again, I'll kick him out. 彼が再びやって来でもしたらけり出してやる. ☞ 敷居に影を落とし暗くするの意.

darkness /dáːrknəs/ 名 ***cast ... into the outer darkness*** ...を放逐する; を(侮辱して)解雇する(《聖》 *Matt.* 22. 13) ▪ The car must *be cast into the outer darkness*. その車は廃棄しなければならない.

darkness visible まっ暗やみ (Milton, *Paradise Lost* 1. 63) ▪ Watch-lights shade a dismal light, "*darkness visible*." 夜番の灯火が陰鬱な光, 「まっ暗やみ」を投げかける.

darling /dáːrlɪŋ/ 名 ***My darling!*** お前!, あなた! 《愛称》.

the darling of the people 国民の寵児(ちょうじ) ▪ Henry VIII was *the darling of the people*. ヘンリー８世は国民の寵児であった.

darn[1] /dɑːrn/ 名 ***by darn*** 《俗》 ほんとに, 確かに ▪ *By darn* the captain's cleared out without speaking to me. ほんとに船長は私に何も言わずに突然立ち去った. ☞ damn の婉曲語.

not care [***give***] ***a darn*** 少しもかまわない, へっちゃらだ ▪ I *don't care a darn* about the sheep just now. 今のところ私は羊には少しも関心がない ▪ I *don't give a darn* whether she ever speaks to me again. 彼女がまた私に物を言うことがあってもなくても私は少しもかまわない.

darn[2] /dɑːrn/ 動 ***Darn it!*** 《口》 ちぇっ!, いまいましい! ▪ *Darn it!* The petrol's run out. こん畜生! ガソリンが切れた.

I'll be darned 《口》 おや, 驚いた ▪ *I'll be darned.* Tom was lost in a typhoon in the China Sea. これは驚いた. トムはシナ海の台風で死んだとさ.

I'll be [***I'm***] ***darned if*** 絶対...しない ▪ *I'll be darned if* I know. 僕は絶対知らないよ.

darned /dáːrnd/ 形 ***darned sight*** 《口》 ずっと, ひどく ▪ It is a *darned sight* more sensible to go to bed. 寝るほうがずっと気がきいている.

dart /dɑːrt/ 動 ***dart a glance*** [***look***] ***at*** ...をじろりと見る ▪ Harry *darted a glance at* the newcomer. ハリーは新来者をじろりと見た.

dart in and out すばやく出たり入ったりする ▪ The sun *darted in and out* of a morning mist. 太陽が朝霧の中にすばやく見え隠れした ▪ Thoughts *darted in and out* of his head. 彼の頭にいろいろな思いが去来した.

dart to *one's* ***feet*** はね起きる, 飛び立つ ▪ When he saw us, he *darted to his feet*. 彼は我々を見るとはね起きた.

dash[1] /dæʃ/ 名 ***a dash of*** ...をちょっぴり, の少量, の気味 ▪ Put *a dash of* salt in the soup. スープにちょっぴり塩を入れなさい ▪ His style shows *a dash of* conceit. 彼の文章は少々気どっている.

at a dash 一気に, 突進して ▪ The cavalry went off *at a dash*. 騎兵隊は突進して行った ▪ We shall lose all our lives *at a dash*. 我々はみな一気に命を失うであろう.

cut a dash 《口》 さっそうとしている; めかす; 見栄を張る ▪ In his new regimentals, he *cut a dash* in the town. 新しい軍服を着て彼はその町でさっそうとしていた ▪ What with his new car and his smart clothes, he is trying to *cut a dash*. 新しい自動車やら, しゃれた服やらで彼は見栄を張ろうとしている.

have a dash at ...を試みる ▪ You may as well *have a dash at* it. それをやってみるがよい.

make a dash at [***for***] ...に突撃する, 突進する ▪ The cavalry *made a dash at* the enemy. 騎兵は敵に突撃した ▪ They *made a dash for* the goal. 彼らはゴールに突進した.

Who the dash ...? 一体誰が...? ▪ *Who the dash* is this person? この人は一体誰ですか.

with great dash 激しい勢いで ▪ They charged *with great dash*. 彼らは激しい勢いで突撃した.

dash[2] /dæʃ/ 動 ***dash*** *a person's* ***hopes*** 人の希望を打ち砕く[くじく] ▪ Economic realities *dashed her hopes* of becoming a doctor. 経済事情が悪いため彼女は医師になる希望をくじかれた ▪ This defeat has *dashed their hopes* of success on the sea. この敗北が海上で成功するという彼らの希望を打ち砕いてしまった.

Dash it! ＝DAMN it!

Dash my buttons [***wig***]***!*** 《口》 いまいましい!, こりゃ驚いた! 《困惑と驚きを表す》 ▪ *Dash my buttons!* I have lost my way. いまいましい, 迷い子になってしまった. ☞ dash＝damn.

dash *a person's* ***spirits*** 人の意気を阻喪(そそう)させる, 悲しませる ▪ Nothing so effectively *dashes our spirits* as a few days of drizzling rain. 数日連続のぬか雨ほどひどく我々の気をめいらせるものはない.

dash ... to pieces [***fragments***] ...をこなごなに砕く ▪ The ship *was dashed to pieces*. 船はこっぱみじんになった ▪ The slate *was dashed to fragments* in the morning. スレートは翌朝粉砕されていた.

dash ... to the ground [***earth***] **1** ...をたたき落とす, 地に投げつける ▪ He *dashed* his crown *to earth*. 彼は王冠を地に投げつけた ▪ The cup *is dashed to the ground*. (口まで持っていった)杯が地にたたき落とされた.

2 ...を落胆させる, 失敗に帰させる ▪ Our hopes *are dashed to the ground*. 我々の希望はすっかり絶えてしまった ▪ Our schemes *were dashed to earth*. 我々の計画はすっかり失敗に帰した.

I must [***have to***] ***dash.*** 急いで帰らなくちゃ

D

▪ It's getting late. *I must dash.* 遅くなった. 急いで帰らなくちゃ.

date /deɪt/ 名 ***at an early date*** 近いうちに ▪ I should like to visit you *at an early date.* 近いうちにお尋ねしたいと思います.

(be) down to date ＝be up to DATE.

(be) out of date **1** 時代遅れで; 旧式で; 時期はずれで ▪ The horse and buggy *is* now *out of date.* 軽装２輪馬車はもう時代遅れである ▪ They rumored she *was out of date* for matrimony. 彼女は結婚には行き遅れだと彼らはうわさした.

2 有効期限が切れた, 賞味期限を過ぎた ▪ This fish sauce *is out of date.* この魚醤は賞味期限切れである.

be up to date 《口》 **1** 最新式である; 現代の慣習[最新の思想]に合う ▪ He *is* very *up to date* in his methods of language teaching. 彼は語学教授法においてたいへん先端をいっている ▪ That car *is* quite *up to date.* その自動車は全くモダンである.

2 抜け目がない, 十分知っている; 時勢に遅れていない ▪ We *are up to date* with our work. 我々は自分の仕事は十分知っている ▪ He *is* always *up to date* in his information about the city. 彼は街についての情報にはいつも精通している.

bring [get]... up to date **1** (簿記の記帳など)を現在までにする ▪ I have *brought* my diary *up to date.* 日記を現在まで書いた ▪ The teacher's *got* his marking *up to date* [*got up to date* with his marking]. 先生は現在までの採点をした.

2 …を現在の知識[要求, 標準]に達せしめる ▪ I tried to *bring* my volumes *up to date.* 私は自著を最新のものにしようと努めた.

get** a person **a date with 《米》 人に…との会合を取り持つ ▪ He *got* me *a date with* my husband. 彼は私と夫とのデートを取り持ってくれた.

get... up to date →bring... up to DATE.

go on a blind date 《米》 (他人の世話で)見知らぬ人とデートする (→on a blind DATE) ▪ How would you like to *go on a blind date*? 見知らぬ相手とデートをしてみないか.

go [get] out of date すたれる, 古くさくなる ▪ The idea has *gone out of date.* その思想は古くさくなった ▪ The man-of-war has *gone out of date.* その軍艦はもう旧式になった.

have (got) a date with 《米口》 …とのデートがある ▪ I *have a date with* Miss Smith. 私はスミスさんとのデートがある.

make a date for 《米口》 …の約束をする ▪ I *made a date for* dinner this evening. 私は今晩ディナーの約束をした.

on a blind date (人の取り持ちによる)見知らぬ者同士のデートで ▪ He met an actress *on a blind date.* 彼は人の取り持ちである女優とデートした.

pass [be past]** one's **sell-by date 《口》 賞味[販売有効]期限を過ぎる[が過ぎている], 盛りを過ぎる ▪ He has made a lot of errors these days. I think he *is past his sell-by date* and should retire. 彼は近ごろミスが多い. 盛りを過ぎているので引退すべきだと思う ▪ This kiwi-banana yogurt *is* a week *past its sell-by date.* このキウイバナナヨーグルトは販売期限を１週間過ぎている. ☞sell-by date は食品につける販売有効期限の年月日.

to date 今日まで(の) ▪ No progress has been made *to date.* 今日まで少しも進歩していない.

under (the) date (of) (…の)日付の ▪ We acknowledge receipt of your letter *under date* Jan. 5. １月５日付の貴信拝受しました.

write... up to date ＝bring... up to DATE 1.

daughter /dɔ́ːtər/ 名 ***be** one's **mother's [father's] daughter*** (性格が)母親[父親]そっくりである ▪ Jane *is her mother's daughter.* ジェインは母親そっくりである.

daughter(s) of the horseleech 絶えず物をねだる人, 強欲な人 (《聖》 *Prov.* 30. 15) ▪ With outstretched hands these beribboned *daughters of the horseleech* are round you. 手を差し出してこれらぼろをまとって物をねだる人々が君を取り巻く. ☞horseleech「ウマヒル」.

He that would the daughter win, must with the mother first begin. 《諺》 娘を得たいと思う者はまず母親からはじめねばならない,「将を射んと欲すれば, まず馬を射よ」.

daunt /dɔːnt/ 動 ***nothing daunted*** 少しも臆さず[恐れず] ▪ *Nothing daunted*, Anne proceeded onward to the church alone. 少しも恐れずに, アンは一人で教会への道をたどり続けた.

davy /déɪvi/ 名 ***take** one's **davy*** 《俗》 誓う ▪ I'll *take my davy* of it. 私はそれを誓ってもいい ▪ They *take their davy* that they didn't do it. 彼らはそれをしたのではないと誓言している. ☞davy＝affidavit「宣誓供述書」.

dawn[1] /dɔːn/ 名 ***at [before] dawn*** 夜明けに[夜明け前に] ▪ The attack began *at* early *dawn.* 攻撃は明けがた早く始まった.

dawn breaks 夜があける ▪ *Dawn* was *breaking* when I woke up. 私が目が覚めたときは夜があけるところだった.

dawn[2] /dɔːn/ 動 ***dawn on*** [《文》 ***upon***] *one* [*one's* ***mind,*** *one's* ***intelligence***] (考え·事実などが)わかり始める, 明らかになり始める ▪ It has *dawned upon* me that I mistook his intention. 私は彼の意図を誤解していたということがだんだんわかってきた ▪ The truth must have *dawned upon his mind* by this time. もう今ごろまでには真相が彼にわかり始めたにちがいない.

dawn on [upon]** one's **recollection 思い出されてくる ▪ It *dawned on my recollection* that he had mentioned it. 彼がそのことを言ったことがあるということが思い出されてきた.

the light dawned ついに[最後に]分かった ▪ *The light dawned* and I was really excited. ついに分かったので本当に興奮した.

day /dei/ 名 ***a [the] day after [before] the fair*** →FAIR.

a day late and a dollar short 遅すぎるし準備不足だし ▪ He showed up *a day late and a dollar short* all the time. 彼はしょっちゅう遅刻してきて準備もしていなかった.

a day of days =the DAY of days.

a day of grace 支払い猶予期間 ▪ We will allow 31 *days of grace* for the payment of premiums. 私どもは保険料の支払いに31日の支払い猶予期間を与えます.

a [*one's*] ***day off*** →OFF[1].

a day person 昼型人間 ▪ I'm *a day person*, so I go to bed early. 昼型なので早く寝ます.

a good day's work 立派な1日の仕事 ▪ I have done *a good day's work*. きょうは良い仕事をした《日当にありついた》.

against a rainy day →a RAINY day.

all day and every day 一日中毎日毎日 ▪ I worked *all day and every day* in my office. 私は事務所で一日中毎日続けて働いた.

all day long 一日中(ずっと) ▪ She shopped *all day long* looking for a new dress. 彼女は新しい服を買うため一日中店を捜し回った ▪ I spent *all day long* looking for that error in our accounts. 私は我々の帳簿の中のその誤りを捜すのに一日中かかった.

(***all***) ***in the day's work*** →WORK[1].

all (***the***) ***day/all the livelong day*** 終日, 一日中 ▪ I worked *all day* without a break. 私は一日中休まずに働いた.

another day, another dollar 今日一日のつらい仕事が終わって日当にありついた ▪ Well, I've finished for today. *Another day, another dollar*. やれやれ, 今日の仕事がやっと終わった. 今日も一日疲れたが実入りはあった.

any day (***now***) (***of the week***) **1** いつの日にでも, 今すぐにでも ▪ You may call on me *any day*. いつおいでくださってもよろしい ▪ There could be a storm *any day now*. 今にもあらしが来そうだ.
2《口》どんな場合でも; 確かに ▪ I prefer *any day* to know the worst to being buoyed up by false hopes. 私はどんな場合でも偽りの希望にささえられるよりは最悪の事態を知るほうが好きだ ▪ You are a better player than he is *any day*. 確かに君のほうが彼よりうまい.

(***as***) ***clear*** [***plain***] ***as day*** とても見えやすい, とてもわかりやすい ▪ A man stepped out from the dark. I saw his face *as clear as day*. 男が暗がりから歩み出た. その顔がはっきりと見えた.

(***as***) ***happy*** [***merry***] ***as the day is long*** → HAPPY; MERRY.

(***as***) ***honest as the day is long*** →HONEST.

at day 夜明けに ▪ This morning *at day* we fell in with a Spanish ship. 今朝夜明けに我々はスペイン船に出くわした.

at the end of the day 結局のところ, つまるところ ▪ *At the end of the day*, you must decide for yourself about it. 結局のところそれについては君自身で決めなければならない.

at the present day/at this day 現今, 今日 ▪ In Japan *at the present day* they never marry so young. 日本では今どきはそんなに早く結婚しない.

back in the day 過去に, しばらく以前に ▪ He lived around here *back in the day*. 彼は過去にこのあたりに住んでいた.

be [***take***] ***all day*** 〚主に否定文で〛(時間を)長くかける ▪ Don't *take all day* over it. そのことに時間を長くかけるな.

before day 夜明け前に ▪ They got up *before day*. 彼らは夜明け前に起きた.

between two days 《米》夜のうちに; 夜どおし (overnight) ▪ He departed *between two days*. 彼は夜のうちに出て行った ▪ We had to work *between two days*. 夜どおし働かなければならなかった.

by day 昼間は, 日中は (↔by NIGHT 1) ▪ We traveled *by day* and stayed at hotels every night. 我々は日中は旅をし毎夜ホテルに泊まった.

by day and by night 昼も夜も (→DAY and night) ▪ *By day and by night* he thought of his poor father. 彼は昼も夜も気の毒な父のことを思った.

by night and day →NIGHT.

by the day **1** 1日いくらで ▪ He is paid *by the day*. 彼は日給である ▪ The boat can be hired *by the day*. ボートは日割で借りられる.
2〚進行形に伴って〛日ごとに, 日に日に ▪ His resentment was growing *by the day*. 彼の恨みは日に日につのっていた.

call it a day **1**《口》きょうはこれでよい[終わりとする, 切りあげる] ▪ I think we have accomplished a great deal. Let's *call it a day*. 我々は大仕事をしたと思う. きょうはこれで終わりにしましょう ▪ At six you come and stay till ten and *call it a day*. あなたは6時に来て10時までとどまり, それから仕事を切りあげる.
2 引退する (= call it QUITS) ▪ He decided to *call it a day* as a teacher. 彼は教師として引退を決意した. ☞ときに call it a night とも言う. もとは, call it a half day, 一日の勤務時間が終わる前に仕事場を立ち去る, の意.

carry the day 勝利を得る; 勢いをたくましくする; (その日の仕事を)立派にやり遂げる ▪ The superior artillery of the enemy *carried the day*. 敵の優勢な大砲が勝ちを制した ▪ It was the cry of "free education" that *carried the day*. きわめて盛んになったのは「授業料無料教育」の叫びであった. ☞day「戦場での1日の戦闘」.

count the days [***hours***] (待ち望んで)指折り数える ▪ She *counted the days* till Christmas. 彼女はクリスマスまで(日がたつのを)指折り数えて待った.

day about →ABOUT.

day after day 毎日毎日, 日々 ▪ He asks me for a job *day after day*. 彼は毎日私に職をねだる.

day and night 昼夜, 不眠不休で ▪ He traveled *day and night* without stopping. 彼は昼夜を分かたず旅をした.

Day breaks [***dawns***]. 夜が明ける.

D

day by day 来る日も来る日も，毎日続けて；だんだんと，日増しに ▪ I cannot give you, *day by day*, an account of this journey. 私は毎日続けてこの旅の話をあなたにすることはできません ▪ He seems to grow a little stronger *day by day*. 彼は日増しに少しずつ強くなるようです.

day in court 《米》法廷で要求を審理してもらう権利，弁訴を聞いてもらう権利 ▪ He had his *day in court*. 彼は法廷で裁判をしてもらった.

day in, day out/day in and day out 明けても暮れても，絶えず（→WEEK in, week out; YEAR in, (and) year out） ▪ *Day in and day out* you can hear them arguing about the same thing. 君は明けても暮れても彼らが同じ事について議論しているのを聞くことができる ▪ She sat and sewed *day in, day out*. 彼女は明けても暮れても座って裁縫をした.

one's ***day off*** →a day OFF.

one's ***day out*** **1**（人の）外出日 ▪ It was *his day out*. その日は彼の外出日でした.

2《スポーツ・口》特別の好演技の日 ▪ What a marvelous game Harry played! It was certainly *his day out*. ハリーはなんとすばらしい演技をしたことか! その日は確かに彼の特別好演の日だった.

day-to-day/ day to day 毎日の，日常の ▪ What is the most common word you use on a *day to day* basis? 日常的にあなたが使用している最も普通の単語は何ですか.

One's ***days are numbered.*** →The days of... are NUMBERed.

Don't give up the day job! 《戯》（あまり上手なほうではないから）本業をやめないように.

end [***close***] *one's* ***days*** 死ぬ，一生を終える；余生を終える ▪ He will *end his days* miserably. 彼はみじめに一生を終えるだろう ▪ He decided to *end his days* in Hollywood. 彼はハリウッドで生涯を閉じようと決めた.

Every dog has his day. →DOG[1].

every other day 一日おきに ▪ Come to see me *every other day*. 一日おきにおいでなさい.

fallen on evil days 不幸[不運]に陥って（Milton, *Paradise Lost* 7. 24） ▪ Unfortunately, now we have *fallen on evil days*. 不幸にも，いま私たちは不運に陥っている.

one's ***first day out*** 出発日；初めて出勤した日；興行の初日 ▪ On *our first day out* we were followed by a tribe of very large monkeys. 猟に出かけた最初の日非常に大きなサルの一群が我々のあとをつけて来た ▪ On *his first day out* a rookie policeman was having trouble with a bum. 初めての外勤の日，新米警官は浮浪者とひともめしていた.

for days on end 幾日も続けて ▪ It has been raining *for days on end*. 雨が連日降っている.

for many a long day 長い間 ▪ We have never heard such a story *for many a long day*. そんな話は長い間聞いたことがない.

from day one 初め[初日]から，最初から ▪ He hasn't done anything right *from day one*. 彼は最初からまともに仕事ができていない ▪ It was clear to me *from day one* that we are worlds apart. 我々がまるで大違いであることは最初から明白だった.

(***from***) ***day to day*** **1** 日々，日ごとに，日増しに ▪ You have been worse *from day to day*. あなたは日ごとに悪化してきた ▪ No one knows what will happen *from day to day*. 日々何が起こるか誰もわからない. ☞DAY by day と同義だが，from day to day は漸増(ぜんぞう)の意を含むことが多い.

2 一日一日と（延ばすなど）；その日その日で（先のことを考えずに） ▪ He put it off *from day to day*. 彼はそれを一日一日と延ばした.

from one day to another 一日一日と（不安な気持ちで） ▪ I never know what is going to happen *from one day to another*. 私は一日一日とどんなことが起こるか全くわからない.

from this day forth →FROM.

get [***have***] *one's* ***day in court*** → DAY in court.

get [***gain***] ***the day*** 勝利を得る（→carry the DAY） ▪ Show us how we may *get the day* of our adversary. どうすれば敵に勝てるか教えてください.

give me (***a***)***... any day*** 《口》...のほうがずっと好きだ ▪ It's too noisy around here—*give me a* quiet place *any day*. このあたりは騒がしすぎる—静かな場所のほうがずっと好きだ.

give the (***time of***) ***day*** 「おはよう」「今晩は」などのあいさつをする ▪ He *gave* us *the time of day* in Dutch. 彼はオランダ語で「今日は」と言った.

have a good [***nice***] ***day*** [***one***] お元気で，気をつけて ▪ *Have a good day* [*one*]. じゃあね，バイバイ.

have [***get***] *one's* ***day*** 運が向く；よい日の目を見る ▪ Every dog *has his day*. 《諺》誰にでも一度は得意な時代がある.

have had *one's* ***day*** 盛んな時もあった（が今はだめ）；古くさくなった，昔の名声はない ▪ Joe *has had his day*. ジョーは盛りを過ぎてもうだめである ▪ I*'ve had my day* and I am thankful for it. 私も盛んな時があった. それに対して感謝している.

have seen better days →SEE.

Heavenly days! 《口・反語》なんてすばらしい日なんだ! ▪ *Heavenly days!* The dog has soiled the carpet again! なんてすばらしい日なんだ! 犬がまたぞろカーペットの上に粗相しちゃった!

high days and holidays 《口》祝祭日，特別な行事のある日 ▪ Yesterday was *high days and holidays* for us. 昨日は我々にとって特別な日だった.

How goes the day? 戦況はどうか ▪ *How goes the day* with us? 味方の戦況はどうか.

if a day →IF.

in a day 一日で，一朝一夕に ▪ Rome was not built *in a day*. 《諺》ローマは一日にして成らず《大事業は短い月日でできるものではない》.

in all *one's* ***born days*** →BORN.

in broad day(***light***) →BROAD.

in [***on***] *one's* ***day*** 若いときは，盛んなときは ▪ He was a great man *in his day*. 彼は若いころは利(き)け

者(もの)だった ▪ She must have been a beauty *in her day.* 彼女は若いころは美人だったにちがいない.

in days gone by 昔(は) ▪ *In days gone by*, the right to vote was not given to women. 昔は, 女性に選挙権は与えられていなかった.

in *one's* ***last days*** 滅びようとして ▪ The Kingdom was *in its last days.* その王国は滅びかけていた.

in the day of …の時節には, のときは ▪ Call upon me *in the day of* trouble. まさかのときはわが名を念じなさい ▪ Thou art my hope *in the day of* evil. なんじは災いあるときのわが希望なり.

in the days of …の時代に(は) ▪ *In the days of* the Shogunate, there was a judge named Ooka. 徳川時代に大岡という名の奉行がいた ▪ Were there giants on the earth *in the days of* old? 昔は地上に巨人がいたのか.

in (***the***) ***days to come*** 将来は ▪ *In the days to come* we shall all travel to the moon. 将来はみな月旅行するだろう.

in the good old days (幸福だった)昔は (→the good old DAYs) ▪ People always say that things were better *in the good old days.* 人々はいつも昔はよかったと言う. ☞good にはほとんど意味はない.

(***in***) ***this day and age*** (昔ならともかく)現在[現代]では, 今日では, このご時世に ▪ *In this day and age* such a thing never happens. 今日ではそんな事は絶対に起こらない.

it'll be a cold day in hell before... 《口》決してしない[起こらない]だろう ▪ He knew *it'd be a cold day in hell before* he would try cooking. 二度と料理に挑戦することはないだろうと彼にはわかっていた ▪ In fact she told me that *it'd be a cold day in hell before* she ever did that again. 事実彼女は, 自分がそんなことを再びするようなことは絶対ないだろうと私に言った.

just another day at the office 退屈な決まりきった仕事, 平凡な日課 ▪ I've passed *just another day at the office.* これまで退屈で決まりきった仕事をして過ごしてきたのだ.

(***just***) ***one*** [***some***] ***of these*** (***fine***) ***days*** そのうちに, 近日 ▪ *One of these days* you'll break your neck. そのうちに君は首を折るよ ▪ *Some of these days* I shall be obliged to give him a lesson. いつか近いうちに私は彼に説教をせねばならないだろう ▪ *One of these days* is none of these days. 《諺》「近いうちに」という言葉を使う人に限って実行しないものだ,「紺屋(こうや)のあさって」.

(***just***) ***one of those days*** 《口》運の悪い日 ▪ It rained all day last Sunday. It was *one of those days.* 前の日曜には一日中雨が降った. 運の悪い日だった.

late in the day →LATE.

live to fight another day (競技・選挙などで)次の争う機会を得る ▪ We've been defeated but we'll *live to fight another day.* 我々は負けたが次の戦いのチャンスを待とう.

lose the day 負ける ▪ They have *lost the day.* 彼らは負けた.

make a day of it 愉快に1日を送る ▪ We are going to *make a day of it.* 1日楽しく遊ぶつもりだ.

make *a person's* ***day*** 《口》人を幸せな[楽しい]気持ちにする, 人を愉しくさせる ▪ You've *made my day* by coming to see me. おいで下さってほんとにうれしゅうございます.

Make my day. やってみろ ▪ All I can say is go ahead and *make my day.* ただ言えるのは, やれるならやってみろ, ということだけだ. ☞映画『ダーティハリー』の中で使われた台詞として有名.

name the day (女性が)結婚の日を決める; 結婚を承諾する ▪ She at last *named the day.* 彼女はついに結婚の日取りを決めた.

not be *a person's* ***day*** 《口》人の不運な日 ▪ It just *wasn't my day* yesterday. 昨日はほんとに私には運の悪い日でした ▪ The car wouldn't start at all—this *is not my day.* エンジンが頑としてかからなかった—運の悪い日だ.

not be named on [***in***] ***the same day*** (***with***) (…とは)同日の談ではない ▪ My trouble *is not named on the same day with* theirs. 私の苦労は彼らの苦労とは比べものにならない《はるかに劣る》.

not have all day 《口》(…する)時間があまりない ▪ Get ready quickly. We *haven't got all day.* 早く支度しなさい. 時間があまりないから.

of a day 短命の, はかない ▪ I am a creature *of a day*, passing through life as an arrow through the air. 私は短命の生きもので矢が空中を通るようにこの世を通り過ぎます.

of other days 昔の ▪ They are men *of other days.* 彼らは昔の人々だ.

of the day **1** 当時の ▪ The scholars *of the day* didn't know it. 当時の学者たちはそれを知らなかった.
2 当代の ▪ They are eminent men *of the day.* 彼らは当代の要人である.

on *one's* ***day*** →in one's DAY.

on [***for***] ***high days and holidays*** 《英》特別な機会に[のために] (→high DAYs and holidays) ▪ The drawing room is used only *on high days and holidays.* 客間は特別の機会に限って使用される.

one day **1** (過去の)ある日 ▪ *One day* I went to see him. ある日私は彼の所へ行った.
2 いつか ▪ I'll come and see you *one day.* いつかあなたをお尋ねいたします.

open as the day →OPEN[1].

pass the time of day with →TIME[1].

put in a hard day at work/put in a hard day's work まじめによく働く, 仕事に精を出す ▪ Your son is *putting in a hard day at work* at the office. 息子さんはオフィスではまじめによく働いているよ.

save [***put aside, hold back, keep***] ***...for a rainy day*** まさかの時に備えて貯金する, 困窮に備えて蓄える (→a RAINY day) ▪ Each month the old widow *saved* a little money *for a rainy day.* 毎月年老いた寡婦はまさかの時に備えて少しずつ貯金してきた.

save the day 失敗しそうな事を成功させる; 苦境を救う ▪ There was nowhere to hold the meeting until Mr. Smith *saved the day* by offering the use of his house. その会を催す場所がなかったがスミス氏が自分の家を提供して苦境を救ってくれた.

D

see better days **1** いまより幸せな生活を満喫する ▪ I'm poor now but I'll *see better days.* いまは貧しくとも将来はいま以上の幸せな生活を送るさ.
2〚完了形で〛(古くなったり, 壊れたりして)使い物にならなくなる ▪ My PC isn't old but it *has seen better days.* 私のパソコンは古くないのに使い物にならない.

seize the day 《文》(後のことは心配せずに)やりたいことをやる, いまのチャンスをつかむ ▪ He failed to *seize the day.* 彼は目前のチャンスをつかみ損ねた.

since day one =from DAY one.

some day いつか, そのうち, 他日 ▪ You'll be a rich man *some day.* 君はいつか金持ちになるだろう.

take a day [***... days***] ***off*** 1日[...日]の休暇を取る ▪ He *took* a few *days off.* 彼は数日の休暇を取った.

take all day →be all DAY.

take each day as it comes/ take it one day at a time 毎日をあるがままに受け入れる ▪ Live life to the full and *take each day as it comes.* 人生を心ゆくままに過ごし, 毎日をあるがままに受け入れなさい.

That'll be the day! 待つだけの値打ちがある; 《反語》ありそうもないことだ, まさか ▪ He says he is thinking of inviting us to a party. *That'll be the day!* 彼は我々をパーティーに招待しようと思っていると言っている. ありそうもないことだ!

(***the***) ***day after*** [***before***] その翌日[前日]《《米》では the を略す》 ▪ He said that he had come home *the day before.* 彼はその前日帰って来たと言った.

(***the***) ***day after tomorrow*** [***before yesterday***] 明後日[一昨日]《《米》では the を略す》 ▪ If today is Wednesday, the day before yesterday was Monday and *the day after tomorrow* will be Friday. きょうが水曜日なら, おとといは月曜日であさっては金曜日だ.

the day goes against [***for***] 戦況は...に不利[有利]である ▪ *The day goes against* us. 戦況は味方に不利である.

the day of days 特にめでたい[重要な, 記念すべき]日 ▪ *The day of days*, namely, of the Coronation came at last. 特にめでたい戴冠式の日が遂に来た.

The day of ... is over [***finished***]. ...の日[時代]は終わった ▪ *The day of* military government *was over* in South America. 南米では軍政の時代は終わった.

the day of small things 小さいことの日; 小規模のもの, ささやかなもの (《聖》*Zech* 4. 10) ▪ It was *the day of small things.* The membership in 1884 was only 127. それはささやかなものであった. 1884年の会員はたった127人であった.

the good old days 古き良き時代《老人のよく使う句》 ▪ My mother often talks about *the good old days.* 母はよく「古き良き時代」のことを話します.

The longest day must have an end. 《諺》いくら長い日でも必ず終わる《不運や失敗は長く続いても必ず終わりになる》.

the other day 先日 ▪ He came to see me *the other day.* 彼は先日私を尋ねて来た.

the time of day →TIME[1].

these days この頃は ▪ *These days* such an honest man is rarely to be met with. この頃はそんな正直な人にはめったにお目にかかれない.

this day week [***year, twelvemonth,*** etc.] **1** 来週[来年]のきょう ▪ Let's go *this day week.* 来週のきょう行きましょう ▪ He will have made remarkable progress by *this day twelvemonth.* 彼は来年のきょうまでには著しい進歩を遂げているだろう.
2 先週[昨年]のきょう ▪ I was married *this day week.* 私は先週のきょう結婚した.

Those were the days. あの頃はよかった ▪ London is no longer what it used to be. *Those were the days.* ロンドンはもはや以前のロンドンではない. あの頃がなつかしい.

till [(***down, up***) ***to***] ***this day*** 今日まで ▪ *To this day* the works of Shakespeare are widely studied in British schools. 今日に至るまで英国の学校ではシェイクスピアの作品が広く学ばれている.

to a day 1日も違わず, きっかり ▪ It is three years *to a day.* ちょうど3年になる.

win the day →WIN.

without day 無期限に ▪ The meeting was postponed *without day.* 会は無期延期された.

Work while it is day. 昼のうちに働きなさい (《聖》*John* 9. 4).

daylight /déɪlàɪt/ 名 ***beat*** [***knock, thump, wallop***] ***the*** (***living***) ***daylights*** [***the tar***] ***out of*** *a person* 《口》 **1** 人をひどく懲らしめる, たたきのめす ▪ I'd *beat the daylights out of* you. 君をひどく懲らしめてやりたい ▪ They *walloped the daylights out of* him. 彼らは彼をたたきのめした. ☞しばしばおどしに用いられる; daylights《古・俗》= eyes.
2 (競技などで)対戦相手を完全に打ち負かす ▪ I want to *beat the living daylights out of* everyone else in the next golf competition. 次回のゴルフコンペではみなに圧勝したいのだ.

before [***at***] ***daylight*** 夜明け前[夜明けに] ▪ He was up *before daylight.* 彼は夜明け前に起きた ▪ *At daylight* the wind was at south west. 夜明けには風は南西であった.

begin to see daylight →see DAYLIGHT.

by daylight 明るいうちに ▪ They went home *by daylight.* 明るいうちに帰宅した.

darken *a person's* ***daylights*** 《ボクシング》目を

つぶす ▪ Damn me, I will *darken his daylights.* 畜生, やつの目をつぶしてやるぞ. ☞daylights《古・俗》=eyes.

daylight robbery ひどい強奪 ▪ Five shillings a pound for chestnuts is *daylight robbery.* 栗1ポンドが5シリングとはひどい強奪だ.

daylight saving (***time***)/***daylight time*** 夏時間, サマータイム ▪ *Daylight saving time* is common in high latitudes. サマータイムは高緯度地方で一般的である.

in broad day(***light***) →BROAD.

knock the (***living***) ***daylights out of*** *a person* →beat the (living) DAYLIGHTs out of a person.

let [***knock***] ***daylight into*** [***through***] **1** …を明るみに出す, 世間に知らせる.
2《俗》…を射ぬく, 刺す, 撃つ, (風)穴をあける ▪ I shouldn't hesitate to *let daylight into* a burglar. 私は強盗を撃ち殺すのにちゅうちょしないだろう ▪ In the language of the streets, *daylight was knocked into* the ruffian. "街" の言葉で言えば, その悪党は風穴をあけられた.

No daylight! なみなみとふちまでつぎましょう!《乾杯の前に toastmaster が言う言葉》. ☞daylight「はっきり見えるすき間(酒と杯のふちとの間など)」.

put daylight between *oneself* ***and…*** 《口》…との間に距離を置く ▪ We *put daylight between ourselves and* them. 彼らとの間には距離を置いた.

scare the (***living***) ***daylights out of*** …をびっくりさせて気絶させる ▪ It will *scare the daylights out of* you. そのためあなたはびっくりして気絶するだろう. ☞daylights=wits.

see daylight 《俗》 **1** (物事が)はっきりしてくる, わかってくる ▪ I think I begin to *see daylight.* ようやくわかりだしたと思う.
2 (困難・退屈な)終了[解決]の道が見える, 完成[解決]に近づく (*into, through*) ▪ I thought I should never finish this work, but now I am beginning to *see daylight.* この仕事はとうてい終わるまいと思っていたが, どうやら完成の道が見え始めた.

shoot full of daylight 弾丸で穴だらけにする ▪ The rear door *was shot full of daylight.* 裏口のドアが銃弾で穴だらけになっていた.

show daylight →SHOW[2].

throw daylight upon …を明らかにする, 見せる ▪ That accident *threw daylight upon* the mystery. その事件で謎が明らかになった.

wallop the (***living***) ***daylights out of*** →beat the (living) DAYLIGHTs out of a person.

daytime /déɪtàɪm/ 名 ***in the daytime*** 昼間に, 日中に ▪ They work *in the daytime.* 彼らは日中は働く.

daze /deɪz/ 名 ***in a daze*** のぼせてぼーっとして, 目がくらんで ▪ When I arrived in London, I was *in a daze* for a few days. ロンドンに着いた時私は数日間はのぼせてぼーっとしていた.

dazzle /dǽzəl/ 動 ***dazzle with science*** 《口》ボクシングで負かす; 頭で負かす ▪ Too many "consultants" try to *dazzle with science* and language. あまりにも多くの「コンサルタント」が頭と言葉で負かそうとしている.

dead /ded/ 形 ***a dead cert*** =a dead CERTAINTY.

a dead duck →DUCK[1].

a dead end 鉄道支線の終点; 行きうまり(点); (政策・行動などの)行きうまり ▪ He came to *a dead end.* 彼は行きうまりに来た ▪ His research was at *a dead end.* 彼の研究はそのとき行きうまっていた.

a dead heat (競争などで)引き分け; (値打ちなどが)互角 ▪ The Democrats have retained power only in *a dead heat.* 民主党は互角の勢力でやっと政権を維持している. ☞18世紀英国の競馬から.

a dead letter **1**《法》死文《施行されない法律・規則》 ▪ The rule about ready money was soon *a dead letter.* 即金についての規則はじきに死文となった.
2 配達不能の手紙 ▪ The mail clerk didn't know what to do with *a dead letter.* 郵便局員は一通の配達不能の手紙をどう処理してよいかわからなかった.

a dead loss →be a dead LOSS.

a dead pull [***strain***] 死力を尽くすこと ▪ He learned English by *a dead pull.* 彼は必死の努力で英語を学んだ.

a dead weight on …のやっかいな足手まとい, の重荷 ▪ Now he's *a dead weight on* the whole enterprise. 今や彼は事業全体のやっかいな邪魔者である.

(***as***) ***dead as a dodo*** 《口》(ドードー鳥のように)絶滅して, すっかり死んで; すたれて ▪ Last year's fashions are *as dead as a dodo* now. 昨年の流行は今はすっかりすたれた. ☞dodo《インド洋の諸島にいたが絶滅した鳥》.

(***as***) ***dead as a doornail*** すっかり死んで ▪ This battery is *dead as a doornail.* この電池はすっかりきれている ▪ Marley was *as dead as a doornail.* マーリーは完全に死んでしまっていた.

(***as***) ***dead as*** (***a***) ***herring*** すっかり死んで ▪ He believed her to be *dead as a herring.* 彼は彼女が完全に死んでしまったと信じていた. ☞herring「ニシン」は海水を出るとすぐ死ぬことから.

(***as***) ***dead as a salmon*** 《米口》すっかり死んで ▪ He dropped down *dead as a salmon.* 彼はばったり倒れて完全に死んだ.

(***as***) ***dead as*** (***yesterday's***) ***mutton*** [***four o'clock***] 《口》全く死んで, すたれて ▪ The man who was run over was *as dead as mutton.* 車にひかれた人は完全に死んでしまった ▪ The old colonial system is *as dead as yesterday's mutton.* 古い植民地制度はもうすっかりすたれてしまった. ☞mutton は死んだ羊の肉であることから.

at a dead set →SET[1].

at [***in the***] ***dead of*** …のさなかに ▪ I saw a sweet vision *at dead of* night. 真夜中に美しい幻を見た ▪ Why should ravens share valuable food *in the dead of* winter? なぜワタリガラスは真冬には貴重なえさを分かち合うのか.

D

be a dead loss →LOSS.
be at a dead end →a DEAD end.
better dead than red 赤になるより死んだほうがまし，共産社会よりも核戦争の脅威のほうがよい ▪ "*Better dead than red*" was a U.S. slogan from the 1950s, about fighting Communism. 「赤になるより死んだほうがまし」は戦う共産主義に対する50年代のアメリカのスローガンだった．
better red than dead 核戦争で死ぬくらいなら共産主義のほうがよい ▪ During the cold war you also had another saying: *Better red than dead.* 冷戦中に，核戦争で死ぬくらいなら共産主義のほうがましだというもうひとつの標語があった．
come back from the dead → rise from the DEAD.
dead above [between] the ears 《米俗》不注意で，うわの空で ▪ If you want your company to thrive, fire the *dead above the ears* group and hire some gifted people. あなたの会社を繁栄させたければ，不注意な連中をクビにし，才能のある人々を数人雇いなさい．
dead against →AGAINST.
dead ahead (of) すぐ目の前に，真正面に ▪ Look out! There is a cat *dead ahead of* our car. 気をつけろ! 車の真正面に猫が1匹いるぞ．
dead (and) alive 《俗》 **1** (人が)気力がなく，ふさぎこんで ▪ He is *dead and alive.* 彼は気力がない．
2 (場所が)おもしろくない，退屈な ▪ It was a *dead and alive* hole in the back of beyond. それははるか遠いところにある退屈なすみかだった．
dead and buried 死んで片づいて (《聖》*Acts* 2. 29) ▪ The blood feuds had been *dead and buried* for centuries. その宿恨(しゅくこん)は何世紀も前に消滅していた．
dead and done (with) 死んで片づいた ▪ Buddhism has been *dead and done* within India proper for centuries. 仏教はインド本土では衰滅して何世紀にもなる．
dead and gone 死んでしまって; とうの昔にすたれた[忘れられた] ▪ She was *dead and gone.* 彼女は死んでしまった ▪ Such a view is *dead and gone.* そんな見方はとっくの昔にすたれている．
dead beat →be dead BEAT.
dead from the neck up [upward] 《戯》(首から上が死んで，とは)知恵が足りない，抜けている; いつもものが言えない ▪ That anchor is *dead from the neck upward.* あのニュースキャスターは知恵が足りない．
dead from the waist down 《戯》性的興奮をおぼえない ▪ He was clearly *dead from the waist down.* 彼は明らかに性的興奮をおぼえていなかった．
dead in the water 《口》実行不可能な，成功の見込みのない ▪ With no real public support, the government's plan was *dead in the water.* 真に大衆の支持がなく政府の計画は実行不可能だった．
Dead men tell no tales. 《諺》死人に口なし(だから秘密を知っている者は殺せ)．
dead (nuts) on 《口》 **1** …が大好きで，に大熱心で ▪ He is *dead nuts on* radio. 彼はラジオが大好きだ．
2 …の名人で，のねらいを誤らない ▪ These boys were *dead on* a rat. この少年たちはネズミ捕りの名人であった ▪ He is *dead on* the bird. 彼は鳥のねらいを誤らない．
dead on one's feet →FOOT[1].
dead or alive 生きているか死んでいるか; 生きていても死んでいても ▪ I don't know if he is *dead or alive.* 彼が生きているか死んでいるか私は知らない ▪ I hope John will be found—*dead or alive*—some day. ジョンは生死にかかわらずいつか見つかってほしい．
dead (set) against …に大反対で ▪ She was *dead set against* my going abroad. 彼女は私が海外に行くことに大反対であった．
dead soldier 《口》酒，ワイン，ビールの空瓶 ▪ He drank the last of his beer and set the *dead soldier* near its mates. 彼は最後のビールを空け空瓶を他の空瓶のそばに置いた．
dead to pity [reason, shame] あわれみの心がない[道理がわからない，恥を知らない] ▪ He is *dead to shame.* 彼は恥知らずだ．
dead to rights 《米俗》確かに，ほんとに; 犯罪[過ち]を犯している最中に，現行犯で ▪ He was caught *dead to rights* and is in prison. 彼は確かに捕えられて刑務所にいる ▪ This is the thieving boy caught *dead to rights* in the act. こいつが現行犯で捕まった窃盗少年だ．☞to rights は at once の意．
dead to the wide ＝DEAD to the world 2.
dead to the world **1** 世事に無関心で ▪ Old George is *dead to the world.* ジョージ老人は世事に無関心である．
2 《俗》極度に疲れ果てて; 死んだように眠って; 意識を失って ▪ After working all day I was *dead to the world.* 一日中働いたので私はすっかり疲れ果てた ▪ He was *dead to the world.* 彼は熟睡していた．
drop dead →DROP[2].
fall dead 死んで倒れる; (風が)やむ; (ボールなどが)地に落ちて(少ししか)転ばない ▪ He *fell dead* while playing tennis. 彼はテニスをやっているとき倒れて死んだ ▪ The wind *fell dead.* 風がやんだ ▪ The ball *fell dead* in the end zone. ボールはエンドゾーンに落ちたが，少ししか転ばなかった．
flog a dead horse →HORSE[1].
for dead 死んだものとして ▪ We left him *for dead.* 彼を死んだものとして放っておいた ▪ He was given up *for dead.* 彼は死んだものとしてあきらめられた ▪ He was taken *for dead.* 彼は死んだと考えられた．
from the dead 死者の間から，死から; 無名の時期から ▪ Her voice sounded like a voice *from the dead.* 彼女の声は死者からの声のように響いた ▪ He showed great skill at cooking *from the dead.* 彼の料理の腕前は無名の時期から一流だった．
give a dead cut 《米口》捨てる，すっかり無視する (*to*) ▪ You'd *given the dead cut to* the railroad. 君は鉄道をすっかり無視していた．
go dead (on a person) 《口》(機械などが)動かなく

なる; 反応しなくなる; 発達が止まる ▪ The machine *went dead on* us. 機械は止まった ▪ My arm began to *go dead.* 私の腕はなえ始めた ▪ Your audience has *gone dead on* you. 聴衆があなたに反応しなくなった.

in* [*into*] *a dead hand (財産・土地が個人の手でなく教会などの)団体の所有で[になって] ▪ The land fell *into a dead hand.* 土地は団体の所有になった.

in the dead of →at DEAD of.

A person [*thing*] ***is dead, but*** *he* [*it*] ***won't lie down.*** 人[物]は死んだがなかなか横にならない《死んでもまだ影響を与えている》 ▪ They*'re dead, but* they *won't lie down*, both him and the business. 彼らは亡くなったがまだ影響を与えている, 彼にもその事業にも.

knock them* [*'em*] *dead 《口》大向こうをうならせる, やんやと誉めそやさせる ▪ Jackie aimed to *knock them dead.* ジャッキーは大向こうをうならせようとした. ☞'em＝hem(＝them).

Let the dead bury their dead. 死人を葬ることは死人に任せておくがよい (《聖》*Matt.* 8. 22) ▪ *Let the dead* past *bury its dead*! 死んだ過去を葬ることは過去に任せなさい《過去のことはかまわずほうっておけ》.

(*loud*) *enough to wake the dead* 死者を目覚ますほど(やかましく) ▪ The noise of the boys was *enough to wake the dead.* 少年たちの騒音は死者を目覚ますほどだった.

more dead than alive 《文》疲れ果てて, 瀕死の状態で《誇張表現》 ▪ We finally got to our destination *more dead than alive.* 我々はへとへとに疲れて目的地にたどり着いた.

Never speak ill of the dead. 《諺》死人の悪口を言ってはならない.

on the dead 《米俗》全く本気に, 正直に; 打ち明けたところ ▪ *On the dead* I'd like to learn it. ほんとのところ, それを知りたい.

over *a person's* ***dead body*** 人の最も激しい反対を押して ▪ If he tried to remove the fence it would be *over my dead body.* もし彼が柵を取りのけようとするなら, それは私の激しい反対を押すものである.

play the dead march 葬送曲を奏する ▪ They *played the dead march* as the coffin was being carried out. 彼らは出棺のとき葬送曲を奏した.

rise* [*raise*] *from the dead **1**《聖》復活する[復活させる] (→from the DEAD) ▪ Christ *rose from the dead.* キリストは復活した.
2 どん底からはい上がる ▪ The airline has *risen from the dead* under the new president. その航空会社は新社長のもとでどん底からはい上がった.

ship the dead lights (強風が来るとき)船室の窓の戸を締めて波が入らないようにする ▪ The water burst into the cabin, for *the dead lights* had not yet *been shipped.* 海水が船室にどっと流れ込んだ. 窓の戸がまだ閉められてなかったから.

shoot ... dead →SHOOT².

***stop dead* [*cold*]** →STOP².

the dead hand of the past (改革をはばむ)過去の伝統[道徳律, など]の力 ▪ You are still under the power of *the dead hand of the past.* あなたがたはまだ過去の伝統の力に押さえられている.

would* [*will*] *not be seen dead/ wouldn't be caught dead 《口》...はがまんできない ▪ I *wouldn't be seen dead* wearing a skirt so short. 私はそんなに短いスカートをはくのはがまんできない《絶対はきたくない》.

You're a long time dead. 《諺》生きているうちに楽しめ.

deaden /dédən/ 動 ***be deadened to*** ...を感じなくなる ▪ He *was deadened to* all sense of shame. 彼は全く恥知らずになっていた.

deadhead /dédhèd/ 動 ***deadhead it*** 《米口》寄生する; ただで飲食する ▪ They *deadheaded it* at all the taverns. 彼らは全ての酒場で無銭飲食した.

deadline /dédlàɪn/ 名 ***beat a deadline*** 《米》
1 非常線を突破する ▪ They were on their way to *beat a deadline.* 彼らは非常線突破の途上にあった.
2 定刻に間に合わせる ▪ Bent on *beating a deadline*, thousands jaywalk to their deaths. 定刻に間に合わせようと必死になって, 何千人もの人が交通規則を無視して街路を横切って死に至る.

make the ... deadline ...の締め切り期限に間に合わせる; の出勤時限に間に合わせる ▪ By doing an all-nighter I managed to *make the* two-day *deadline.* 徹夜で取り組んで何とか2日間の締め切り期限に間に合わせた.

meet the deadline 締め切りに間に合う ▪ I must *meet the deadline*, by hook or by crook. どうしても締め切りに間に合わなければならない.

on* (*the*) *deadline 締め切り期日に ▪ I completed a movie script *on the deadline.* 私は締め切り期日に映画台本を完成した.

put a deadline on ...に期限をつける ▪ He *put a* 35-day *deadline on* the job. その仕事に35日間の期限をつけた.

set the deadline for 締め切りを...と決める ▪ He *set the deadline for* 11 a.m. today. 彼は締め切りをきょうの午前11時と決めた.

deadlock /dédlɑ̀k/ 名 ***at a deadlock*** (折り合わぬため)行きうまりとなって ▪ The two parties are *at a deadlock.* 双方譲らず立往生している ▪ Everything is *at a deadlock* now. 今や万事が行きうまり状態である.

come to a deadlock 行きうまり状態となる ▪ There were so many carts that we almost *came to a deadlock.* ほとんど立往生するほどカートだらけだった.

end in deadlock 合意なしに[行きうまったまま]終わる ▪ The peace talks between them have *ended in deadlock* once again. 両者の和平会談は再び物別れに終わった.

deadwood /dèdwʊ́d/ 名 ***get* [*have, possess*] *the deadwood* (*on*)** 《米口》(...に)勝る, (を)押さえている, だしぬく ▪ I *have the deadwood on* him. 私は彼を押さえている ▪ He considered himself to *possess the deadwood.* 彼は自分が優位にあると考えた.

deaf /def/ 形 ***(as) deaf as an adder*** [***a beetle, a door,*** 《豪》 ***a doorknob, a doornail, a door-post, a post, a stone***] 全く耳が聞こえない ▪ He was *as deaf as an adder.* 彼は全く耳が聞こえなかった. ☞adder (マムシ)はヘビのうちで最も耳が聞こえないと考えられたから (《聖》 *Ps.* 58. 4).

(be) deaf of [***in***] ***an*** [***one***] ***ear*** 片方の耳が聞こえない ▪ He is *deaf of one ear.* 彼は片方の耳が聞こえない.

deaf and dumb 聾唖(ろうあ)の ▪ Every *deaf and dumb* child must be educated. 耳とことばの不自由な子供はみな教育されなければならない.

deaf to …を全然聞かない ▪ He is *deaf to* my advice. 彼は私の忠告を全然聞かない.

fall on deaf ears →EAR.

None so deaf as those who won't hear. 《諺》 聞こうとしない者ほど聞く耳をもたない者はいない 《聞きたくない者にいくら言ってもだめである》.

stone deaf 全く耳が聞こえない ▪ When it comes to music, I am *stone deaf.* 音楽ということになると私はまるでだめだ.

turn a deaf ear to →EAR.

deal[1] /diːl/ 名 ***a big deal*** 《口》 **1** 大きな取り引き ▪ We have made *a big deal* with the firm. その会社と大きな取り引きがまとまった.

2 《皮肉》 大したこと[もの] ▪ He made *a big deal* out of nothing. 彼は何でもないことに大騒ぎした. ☞make a big deal of「…に大騒ぎする」.

3 〚通例冠詞を省いて感嘆詞的に〛 大したものさ!, 驚くね!; それがどうした, かまうものか ▪ I earned £50 this month.—*Big deal!* 僕はこの月 50 ポンド儲けた—大したものだね! ▪ So you went to University?—Well, *big deal.* それで君は大学に入ったんだな?—それがどうした.

a deal 《口》 大いに ▪ The problem is *a deal* too difficult. この問題はひどくむずかしすぎる.

a deal of 《口》 たくさんの ▪ It saves us *a deal of* trouble. それは我々の手数を大いに省いてくれる.

a done deal 《米俗》 完了した取引, 決着のついたこと, 変更できないこと ▪ The agreement was completed, so it is *a done deal.* 同意が成立したので変更できない.

a good [***great***] ***deal*** **1** 相当の量 (*of*) ▪ *A good deal of* rain has fallen. 相当量の雨が降った ▪ He spent *a great deal of* money on doctors. 彼は医者に非常に多くの金を使った ▪ He is *a great deal of* a talker. 彼はたいした話し手である.

2 相当に, ずい分 ▪ I have traveled *a good deal* in Europe. 私はヨーロッパは相当旅行しました ▪ I bled *a great deal.* 私は多量に出血した ▪ You are *a great deal* too clever. 君はひどく賢すぎる.

a square deal →SQUARE[1].

close the deal [***sale***]/ ***close on a deal*** [***sale***] 取引[商談]をまとめる ▪ Delta and Northwest *closed the deal.* デルタ航空とノースウェスト航空の間で取引が成立した ▪ We *closed on a sale* today. 我々はきょう商談をひとつまとめた.

cut [***crack***] ***a deal*** 《米口》 (…と)契約[協定]を結ぶ, 取引する (*with*) ▪ Let's talk and *cut a deal.* 話し合って協定を結ぼう.

do a deal (***with***) 《口》 (…と)契約を結ぶ, 取引を完了する ▪ Do you think you'll *do a deal?* 君は取引が成立すると思うか.

have a deal with *a person* ***for*** 《俗》 人と…の取引をする ▪ He wanted to *have a deal with* me *for* the mare. 彼は私とその雌馬の取引をしたがった.

make a big deal about [***of, out of***] 《口》 (些細なことで)大騒ぎする[誇張する] ▪ Why does everyone *make a big deal about* inter-racial relationships? なぜみんな異人種間の関係のことで大騒ぎするのか? ▪ Why does everyone *make a big deal out of* a celebrity? なぜ誰もが有名人のことを誇張するのか ▪ The media *made a big deal of* Anna Paquin's announcement that she is bisexual. 自分は両性愛者であるというアナ・パキンの声明でメディアは大騒ぎした. ☞Anna Paquin はオスカー賞女優.

make a deal for 《俗》 …の売買取引をする ▪ He *made a deal for* some chickens in the morning. 彼は朝のうちにニワトリの売買取引をした.

make a deal with …と取引する ▪ We *made a deal with* them to supply carpets for export. 我々は輸出用じゅうたんを供給するよう彼らと取引した.

make a good deal (投機などで)当てる ▪ He *made a good deal* in that business. 彼はその仕事で一山当てた.

no big deal 《口》 大したことでない ▪ It's *no big deal* to me whether they succeed or not. 彼らが成功しようとしまいと私には大したことじゃない.

strike a deal (議論の後に)取引を決める, 手を打つ (*with*) ▪ The Pitt Department Store *struck a deal with* Adidas. ピット百貨店はアディダスと取引を決めた.

That's [***It's***] ***the*** [***a***] ***deal.*** それは取引になる, それで行こう ▪ I'll clean your room for 10 dollars a week.—O.K. *That's a deal.* 1 週間 10 ドルでお部屋の掃除をしましょう—よろしい. それで行きましょう.

wet the deal 《口》 契約[取引]を結んだ祝いに 1 杯やる ▪ We will *wet the deal.* 契約祝いに 1 杯やろう.

What is the big deal? この大騒ぎはどうしたんだ ▪ My father asked, "*What's the big deal?*"「この騒ぎは何事だ」と私の父は尋ねた.

What's the deal? 《口》 (事情・予定を尋ねて)どうなっているんだ, どうするんだ ▪ *What's the deal* with Jackie? ジャッキーはどうなってるんだ?

deal[2] /diːl/ 動 ***deal a blow*** [***blows***] 打撃を加える ▪ He *dealt* his enemy *a* hard *blow* on the chin. 彼は敵のあごにひどい一撃を加えた.

deal ... by [***towards***] *a person* 人に対して…にふるまう, 人を…に扱う ▪ The master will *deal* kindly *by* you. 主人はあなたに対して優しくふるまうでしょう ▪ I have *dealt* unjustly *towards* them. 私は彼らに不当な扱いをした.

deal *a person* ***hard measure*** 人をつらい目にあわす ▪ *Hard measure was dealt* me. 私はつらい目にあわされた.

deal them off the arm 《米俗》(食卓で)給仕をする ▪ She *dealt them off the arm* all day. 彼女は一日中給仕をした.

easy [***hard***] ***to deal with*** 与しやすい[つき合いにくい, 手に負えない] ▪ He is *easy to deal with*. 彼は与しやすい相手である.

dealer /dí:lər/ 名 ***a fair*** [***plain***] ***dealer*** 正直[率直]に行動する人 ▪ He is noted as *a plain dealer*. 彼は率直な人として有名だ.

dealing /dí:lɪŋ/ 名 ***have dealing***(***s***) ***with*** ...と取引[関係, 交渉]がある, と取引[関係, 交渉]をする ▪ I have never *had* any *dealings with* him. 私は彼と取引をしたことはない ▪ He *had dealings with* John's wife. 彼はジョンの妻と関係があった.

stop dealing at ...の店で買わないことにする ▪ I have *stopped dealing at* that shop. 私はあの店では買わないことにした.

dear /dɪər/ 形副名 ***a Dear John letter*** 《戯》縁切り状 ▪ She'd better not write him *a Dear John letter*. 彼女は彼に縁切り状を書くべきではない.

cost *a person* ***dear*** 高いものにつく; ひどい目にあう ▪ His carelessness *cost* him *dear*. 不注意のため彼はひどい目にあった.

dear knows 神のみぞ知る, 誰も知らぬ ▪ *Dear knows* when we shall see them back. いつ彼らが帰って来るか誰にもわからない ▪ He has had *dear knows* how many places. 彼はいくつかわからないほどたくさんの地位を得た.

Dear me!/Oh dear! おやまあ, あらまあ, はてね ▪ *Dear me!* What a long spell of rain! まあ, なんて長雨なんでしょう!

hold ... dear (人)をかわいいと思う, (物)を惜しく思う ▪ I will forever *hold* her *dear* to my heart. 私はいつまでも彼女を心からかわいいと思う ▪ I am a happy person and I *hold* life *dear* indeed. 私は幸福な人間でほんとに命を惜しく思う.

pay dear for →PAY dearly for.

pay (***too dear***) ***for*** *one's* ***whistle*** →WHISTLE[1].

That's [***There's***] ***a dear.*** (...してくれて)いい子だね; ね, いい子だから(しておくれ) ▪ Come with me, *there's a dear*. いい子だからいっしょにおいで.

dearly /díərli/ 副 ***pay dearly for*** →PAY[2].

dearth /də:rθ/ 名 ***a singular dearth of*** ...がひどく少ないこと《新聞》 ▪ What *a singular dearth of* information on the matter! この件についていかに知るところが少ないことか!

in time of dearth 飢饉[食物欠乏]のときに ▪ Augustus, *in time of dearth*, gave freedom to 20,000 slaves. アウグストゥスは飢饉のときに, 2万人の奴隷に自由を与えた.

deary /díəri/ 形 ***Deary me!*** まあ, ほんとに! 《Dear me! を長くしたもので, 通常, Dear me よりも悲しみの調子が強い》 ▪ Dear, *deary me!* What a disgrace upon the house! まあ, ほんとに! なんという家の恥辱でしょう!

death /deθ/ 名 (***a***) ***war to the death*** 存亡的戦争 (→to the DEATH) ▪ It was *a war to the death*. それは存亡的戦争であった.

(***as***) ***baleful as death*** →BALEFUL.

(***as***) ***pale as death*** →PALE[2].

(***as***) ***silent as death*** →(as) SILENT as the grave.

(***as***) ***sure*** [***certain***] ***as death*** (***and taxes***) 確かに, 必ず ▪ *As sure as death and taxes* I'm gonna get you back. 必ず僕は君を取り戻すつもりだ.

at death's door 死に瀕(ひん)して ▪ Mrs. Crawley has been *at death's door*. クローリー夫人は死に瀕していた.

at the point of death 死に瀕して (《聖》 *Mark* 5. 23) ▪ My little daughter is *at the point of death*. 私の幼い娘は死にかけている.

be a certain death 死は確実だ ▪ To stay here *is a certain death*. ここにとどまっているときっと死ぬ.

be burnt [***frozen,*** etc.] ***to death*** 焼け[凍え, など]死ぬ ▪ A young woman *was burnt to death* here after her car caught fire. 当地で若い女性の車が火災を起こし彼女は焼け死んだ ▪ Would you rather *be burnt to death* or *frozen to death*? あなたは焼け死にたいですか, それとも凍え死にたいですか ▪ A young woman *was burnt to death* over witchcraft. 若い女性が魔術を使ったとして火刑にされた.

be death on 《口》 **1** ...が大好きである ▪ He *is death on* brandy. 彼はブランデーが何より好きである. **2** ...が非常にうまい, の名人である ▪ He *is death on* figures. 彼は計算の名人である ▪ The dog *is death on* rats. その犬はネズミ捕りが実にうまい. **3** (薬などが)...に非常によく効く, の死因となる ▪ This medicine *is death on* colds. この薬は風邪にとてもよく効く ▪ The American people would *be death on* such a candidate. アメリカ国民はそのような候補者を葬ってしまうだろう. **4** ...をひどくきらう, 大反対である ▪ They *were death on* my viewpoint. 彼らは私のものの見方をひどくきらった.

be done to death 《口》使われすぎて面白みがない ▪ Mafia movies have *been done to death*. マフィアは映画でよく取り上げられていて面白みがなくなった.

be in at the death **1** (猟犬がキツネなどの)獲物の死を見届ける ▪ The hound *was in at the death*. 猟犬は獲物の死を見届けた. **2** (事)の結末[完成]を見届ける ▪ As he started the idea, he is determined to *be in at the death*. 彼がその案を持ち出したのだから, 彼はその完遂を見届ける決心である.

be the death of **1** ...の死因となる, を殺す ▪ That old motor-cycle will *be the death of* you one of these days. あの古いオートバイで君は近いうちに死ぬようなことになるだろう ▪ Don't make me laugh. You'll *be the death of* me. 笑わせないでください. おかしくて

死にそうだ.

2 …を死ぬほど苦しめる, うき目を見せる ▪ My son's idleness will *be the death of* me yet. 息子の怠惰のために私はまだ死ぬほど苦しむことだろう.

bring** a person **to death's door (人を)死に瀕せしめる ▪ The Prince was cured of the ailment which had *brought* him *to death's door.* 王子は自分を死に瀕せしめた疾患から快復した.

D

catch** one's **death 死病にかかる ▪ You will *catch your death* if you go out in this weather. こんな天候に外出すれば死病にかかるよ.

***catch* [*take*] *one's* death (*of cold*)** 《口》ひどい風邪をひく; 風邪をひいて死ぬ ▪ Put your overcoat on. You'll *catch your death.* コートを着なさい. 風邪をひいて死にますよ.

catch the death of it 死ぬ ▪ You will *catch the death of it.* 君は命をとられるぞ.

cheat death 命拾いする ▪ He narrowly *cheated death* in the plane crash. 飛行機事故で彼は危うく命拾いした.

dance with death 危険なことを試みる, 命がけでやってみる ▪ The crossing of the border was like *dancing with death.* その国境越えは決死行だった.

Death is the great*(*est*) [*grand*] *leveler. 《諺》死は偉大な平等主義者だ,「落ちれば同じ谷川の水」.

Death keeps no calendar. 《諺》死は暦をつけない《死は時を選ばない》.

Death will have his day. 《諺》どんな人でもいつかは死ぬ.

die a dry death →DRY[1].

die a natural death*/《英》*die a death 失敗して終わる, 廃れる ▪ I felt extremism would *die a natural death.* 過激主義は滅びるだろうと思った.

die a natural* [*violent, sudden, premature*] *death 天寿を全うして死ぬ[横死する, 頓死する, 若死にする] ▪ My grandfather *died a natural death* 5 years ago. 祖父は5年前に天寿を全うした.

die the death of …らしい死を遂げる ▪ He *died the death of* a hero. 彼は英雄らしい死を遂げた.

do** a person **to death 人を殺す, 死刑に処す ▪ Caesar *was done to death* by the conspirators. カエサルは陰謀者たちによって殺害された ▪ A boy of fifteen *was done to death* by Mr. Hawes. 15歳の少年がホーズ氏によって処刑された.

do** a thing **to death 《口》事[物]をやり[焼き]すぎる; 使い古す; いやになるほど繰り返す ▪ That song has *been done to death.* その歌は歌われすぎて古くさくなった ▪ The fish *is done to death.* 魚は焼けすぎた.

***feel* [*look*] *like death warmed over* [《英》*up*]** 《口》ひどく加減が悪いように感じる[見える]; ひどく疲れた感じである[ように見える] ▪ I still *feel like death warmed up* after my cold. 風邪を引いてから私はまだ気分がひどく悪い.

fight to the death 死ぬ気でがんばる ▪ I will *fight to the death* to not become a zombie! ふぬけにならぬように死ぬ気でがんばるぞ.

flog … to death **1** (人)を鞭打って殺す ▪ The sailor *was flogged to death.* その水夫は鞭打たれて死んだ《刑罰》.

2 (問題など)をいやになるほど討論する ▪ These plans have *been flogged to death* before they have ever been put into practice. これらの計画は実行される前にいやになるほど討論された.

go** one's **death 《米口》全力を尽くす ▪ They *went their death* to support my election. 彼らは全力を尽くして私の選挙を支援した.

hang on* [*hold on, cling*] *like* (*grim*) *death 《口》しっかりとしがみつく ▪ The rider *held on* to the reins *like grim death.* 乗馬者は手綱をしっかりとつかんでいた ▪ Come on, *hang on like death.* さあ, しっかりしがみつきなさい.

hear the death rattle 息を引き取るのを聞く ▪ *Hearing the death rattle*, they covered his face. 息を引き取るのを聞いて彼らは彼の顔をおおった.

***It is* [*We make it*] *death to** a person.* 人の刑罰は死である, 刑罰を死とする ▪ *We make it death to* him. 彼を死刑とする.

lie at death's door 死にかけている, 瀕死の状態である (→ at DEATH's door) ▪ My grandmother has *lain at death's door* for over three months. 祖母は3か月以上も生死の境をさまよっている.

meet** one's **death 死ぬ ▪ He *met his death* in a plane crash. 飛行機の墜落で死んだ.

put … to death …を殺す, 死刑に処す ▪ The prisoners *were* all *put to death.* 囚人はみな処刑された.

send** a person **to** his **death (意識的・無意識的に)人を死なせる ▪ Generals *sent* thousands *to their death.* 将官たちは何千という兵を死なせた. ☞人が複数のときは deaths とすることもある.

sign** one's **own death warrant 《口》自分で自分を滅ぼす; 自分で失敗を招く《自分の死亡証明書に署名する》 ▪ If you accept the job, you will be *signing your own death warrant.* もしその仕事を受け入れたら君は自分で破滅を招くことになるだろう.

sound* [*toll*] *the death knell (事が)…の終末を告げる (*for, of*) (→the DEATH knell) ▪ This policy will *sound the death knell of* the enforcement of the law. この政策は法律の施行の終末を告げることになろう.

***take** one's **death** (**of cold**)* → catch one's DEATH (of cold).

***take** one's **death** (**upon**)* (…に)命を賭ける, 命を賭けて誓う ▪ He *took his death upon* it that he was innocent. 彼は無罪であると命を賭けて誓った.

the death knell 終末の前兆 (*for*) ▪ The CIA chief's resignation was *the death knell for* Bush. CIA 長官の解任はブッシュ氏にとって終末の前兆だった.

the gates* [*jaws*] *of death 死の窮地[間際] ▪ Many patients might be rescued from *the jaws of death.* 多くの患者が死の瀬戸際から救われる

かもしれない.

the kiss of death 身の破滅を招くもの, 災いの種 (→KISS[1]).

thrill a person to death [***to pieces***] 人を大いに[死ぬほど]喜ばす (→to PIECEs 2).

till death us do part 死が我々二人を分かつまで (Prayer-Book, "*Solemnization of Matrimony*") ▪ *Till death us do part*, that's what the Bible says. 「死が我々二人を分かつまで」は聖書の言葉である.

to death **1** …して殺す[死ぬ] ▪ He whipped the slave *to death*. 彼はその奴隷をむちで打ち殺した ▪ The gun-man scared a woman *to death*. 殺し屋は女をおどして死なせた ▪ He drank himself *to death*. 彼は飲みすぎて死んだ ▪ He bled *to death*. 彼は出血多量で死んだ.
2 死ぬほど[ひどく]…する ▪ I am sick *to death* of your chatter. 君のおしゃべりには全くあきあきした ▪ You frightened me *to death*. 死ぬほどびっくりするじゃないか.

to the death **1** 死ぬまで ▪ The Stuarts waged war *to the death* with the Puritans. スチュアート王家は清教徒たちと死ぬまで戦った.
2 最後[とことん]まで ▪ He hunted his man *to the death*. 彼は犯人を最後まで追跡した.

We make it death to *a person*. → It is DEATH to a person.

work *oneself* ***to death*** 働きすぎて疲れ果てる, 過労のあまりへばる ▪ He has *worked himself to death* and all for a pittance! 彼は死ぬほど働いてきた. それも雀の涙ほどの収入のために!

worse than death 死よりも悪い[怖い], 全くひどい ▪ Anticipation of death is *worse than death*. 死の予想は死よりも怖い ▪ Sin is *worse than death*. 罪は死よりも悪い.

deathbed /déθbèd/ 名 ***on*** [***at***] *one's* ***deathbed*** 臨終の床に, いまわの際に ▪ *On his deathbed* he whispered a promise to his son. 彼は臨終の床で息子にささやき声で一つの約束をした.

debar /dɪbɑ́ːr/ 動 ***debar*** *a person* ***from*** *doing* 《文》〚しばしば受身で〛人が…するのを妨げる, 人の…する道を断つ ▪ Being a foreigner *debars* him *from voting*. 彼は外国人だから選挙権がない ▪ The blind *are debarred from enjoying* the light of heaven. 盲人は天の光を楽しむことができない.

debate[1] /dɪbéɪt/ 名 ***in*** [***under***] ***debate*** 討論中で ▪ The question *under debate* was a hard one. 討論中の問題は難問だった.

open the debate (討論で)まっ先に発言する ▪ Who *opened the debate*? 最初に発言したのは誰だ.

debate[2] /dɪbéɪt/ 動 ***debate in*** *one's* ***mind*** (どうしようかなどと)考える ▪ I'm still *debating in my mind* whether to go there. 私はそこへ行こうかどうしようかとまだ考えている.

debate with *oneself* (どうしようかなどと)考える ▪ He is *debating with himself* what to do. 彼はどうしたらよいか今思案中である.

debit /débət/ 動 ***debit*** *a sum* ***against*** [***to***] *a person* 金額を人の借り方に記入する ▪ We *debited* £1,000 *against* him. 我々は1,000ポンドを彼の借り方に記入した.

debit *a person* [*a person's* ***account***] ***with*** …を人の借り方に記入する ▪ We *debited* him *with* £1,000. 我々は1,000ポンドを彼の借り方に記入した.

debt /det/ 名 ***a debt of honor*** 面目上支払うべき負債《とばくの負債》 ▪ He is obliged to pay some *debts of honor*. 彼はとばくの負債を払わねばならない.

fall [***get, run***] ***into*** [***in***] ***debt*** 借金する ▪ We *ran in debt* to the shopkeeper. 店主に借金した.

get out of debt 借金を返してしまう (→out of DEBT) ▪ I *got out of debt* at last. とうとう借金を返した.

in debt 借金して ▪ I'm *in debt* to my tailor. 私は仕立屋に借金がある.

in *a person's* ***debt*** 人に借金があって, 人に恩を受けて ▪ I am *in his debt*. 私は彼に借金がある ▪ We are deeply *in your debt*. 我々はあなたに深い恩を受けています.

keep out of debt 借金せずに暮らす ▪ I manage to *keep out of debt*. なんとか借金せずにやっている.

out of debt 借金がない[なくなって] ▪ I am now *out of debt*. 私は今は借金がない.

out of *a person's* ***debt*** 人に借金がない ▪ I'll have to work a long time before I am *out of his debt*. 彼からの借金を返すまで長く働かねばなるまい.

pay the debt of [*one's* ***debt to***] ***nature*** 死ぬ ▪ He *paid his debt to nature*. 彼は死んだ ▪ One of them *paid the debt of nature*. 彼らのうちの一人が死んだ. ☞生命は天から借りたものであるとの考えから.

run into [***in***] ***debt*** →fall into DEBT.

decay /dɪkéɪ/ 名 ***fall into*** [***in, to***] ***decay*** 朽ちる, 荒廃する ▪ The estate has *fallen into* such *decay*. その地所はひどく荒廃している.

in decay 荒廃して, 朽ちて ▪ The house is *in decay*. その家は荒廃している.

deceive /dɪsíːv/ 動 ***be deceived in*** …を見そこなう, に誤りを犯す ▪ I *am* very much *deceived in* Mr. Smith, if he is not kind. スミス氏が優しくないとしたら, 私は氏を大いに見そこなっていることになる.

deceive *oneself* 思いちがいする, 誤解する ▪ You are *deceiving yourself* when you believe such a foolish thing. あなたがそんなばかなことを信じるのは誤っています ▪ She *deceived herself* with dreams of success. 彼女は成功するものと思いちがいをしていた.

decency /díːsənsi/ 名 ***Decency forbids.*** 《掲示》小便無用, など.

for decency's sake 体面[体裁]上 ▪ They are man and wife *for decency's sake*. 彼らは体裁だけの夫婦だ.

deception /dɪsépʃən/ 名 ***labor under a deception*** 誤解している ▪ You *labor under a de-*

ception. 君は誤解している.

practise deception on …をだます ▪ This is why I say that the author has *practised deception on* us. だから著者は読者をだましたと私は言うのだ.

There is no deception. 種も仕掛けもない.

decide /dɪsáɪd/ 動 ***decide for*** [***in favor of***] **1** …することに決める ▪ We *decided for* carrying out the plan. その計画を実行することに決めた

2 …に有利に判決する ▪ The tribunal *decided for* us. 裁判所は我々に有利な判決をした.

decimal /désəməl/ 形 ***on the decimal system*** 十進法で ▪ American and French money is based *on the decimal system*. アメリカとフランスの通貨は十進法に基づいている.

decision /dɪsíʒən/ 名 ***come to*** [***arrive at, reach, make, take***] ***a decision*** 決定する; 決心がつく ▪ I could not *come to* any *decision*. どんな決心もつかなかった ▪ The boy *arrived at his decision* at last. 少年はついに決心をした.

give decision against [***for, in favor of***] …に不利な[有利な]判決をする ▪ The court *gave decision against* the defendant. 法廷は被告に不利な判決をした.

give decision on (事件)の判決をする ▪ The court *gave decision on* the case. 法廷はその件の判決をした.

decisive /dɪsáɪsɪv/ 形 ***be decisive of*** (勝敗など)を決する, を終局に導く ▪ It *is decisive of* the fate of the question. それでその問題の運命が決する.

deck[1] /dek/ 名 ***All hands on deck.*** 全員仕事について, 全員甲板へ (→on DECK) ▪ "*All hands on deck*," shouted the captain. 「全員仕事につけ」と船長は叫んだ ▪ It will be *all hands on deck* to get the goods invoiced and crated. 商品の送り状を作ったり木わくに詰めるのに全員仕事にかからねばならないだろう. ☞海語から.

below decks 中甲板の下の所(へ), (通常)船倉(へ) ▪ He went *below decks* to sleep. 彼は船倉へ行って寝た.

clear the decks **1** 《口》食卓のものをすっかり平らげる; (食後)食卓のものを片づける ▪ We have been busy *clearing the decks*. 食卓のものを全部平らげるのに忙しかった.

2 場所を片づけてあける; (重要でないものを)取り除く (*of*) ▪ Hurry up and *clear the decks*. 大急ぎできれいに片づけなさい ▪ The President urged the Congress to *clear the decks of* those matters. 大統領は国会にそれらの事項を取り除くよう促した.

3 =clear the DECKs for action.

clear the decks for action 《海》甲板を片づけて戦闘準備をする; (一般に)行動[作業]の準備をする ▪ As our visitors are due in ten minutes, we must *clear the decks for action*. お客たちは10分したら到着の予定だから, その準備をしなければならない.

hit the deck 起きて仕事を始める; (身を守るために)床や地面に素早く伏せる ▪ It's time to *hit the deck*. 起きて仕事を始める時だぞ ▪ He *hit the deck* the minute he heard the shots. 銃声を聞いたとたん彼はぱっと床に身を伏せた. ☞海語から.

keep the deck (困難に屈せず)ずっとデッキにいる ▪ Only 16 boys were capable of *keeping the deck*. ずっとデッキにいられた少年はたった16人だけだった.

not play with a full deck/***play with a loaded*** [***stacked***] ***deck*** **1** 正気[まとも]でない ▪ He did*n't play with a full deck* to do that. あんなことをしたなんて彼は正気ではなかった.

2 (交渉などで)不正を行う ▪ That guy is either very clever or he's *not playing with a full deck*. あの男は非常に頭が切れるか, ズルをしているかのどちらかだ.

on deck **1** 甲板に出て ▪ Go *on deck*. 甲板に出よ《当直せよ》 ▪ All hands *on deck*! 全員甲板へ!

2 《野球・口》打順が次で, 次の打者で ▪ I went *on deck* and took up a bat. 次打者だったので, バットを取り上げた ▪ He is *on deck*. 彼は次の打者である.

3 《米口》出席して, 手近にいて; 行動[勤め]の用意ができて ▪ We hope to be *on deck* to greet you. そこにいてあなたをお迎えしたいものです ▪ The boy was *on deck* for business the next morning. その少年は翌朝の仕事の用意を整えた.

stack the deck for [***against***] 《主に米》…に有利[不利]になるように札を切る; …に(有利[不利]になるように)不正手段をとる ▪ Russian media *stacked the deck for* Yeltsin. ロシアのマスメディアはエリツィン氏に有利になるように札を切った.

sweep the decks [***deck***] →SWEEP[2].

deck[2] /dek/ 動 ***deck*** *oneself* ***out*** (***with***) (…で)身を飾りたてる ▪ They *decked themselves out with* jewels and flowers. 彼らは身を宝石や花で飾りたてた.

declaration /dèkləréɪʃən/ 名 ***take*** *one's* ***declaration*** 確言[言明]する ▪ I *take my declaration* that he said so. 彼がそう言ったと確言する.

declarative /dɪklǽrətɪv/ 形 (***be***) ***declarative of*** …を陳述して(いる) ▪ The record *is declarative of* a wish on the part of the founder. その記録は創設者の希望を陳述している.

declare /dɪkléər/ 動 ***declare*** *oneself* **1** 所信を述べる ▪ The politician could hardly *declare himself* with frankness. その政治家は率直に所信を述べることがほとんどできなかった.

2 身分を名のる, 本性[正体]を表す ▪ We will *declare ourselves* on a proper occasion. 適当なときには身分を名のります ▪ Wherever a spark fell, a little fire *declared itself*. 火の粉の落ちた所ではどこでも小火が現れた.

declare (*oneself*) ***against*** …に反対を言明する ▪ He *declares against* fish. 彼は魚はきらいだと言っている ▪ They *declared themselves against* the religion of their parents. 彼らは親たちの宗教に反対を言明した.

declare an [*one's*] ***interest*** 利害関係を明かす

▪ Here I must *declare my interest.* ここで私の利害関係を明かさねばならない.

declare (*oneself*) ***for*** [***in favor of***] …に賛成・支持を表明する ▪ Turkey *declared herself for* the Germans. トルコはドイツ軍に味方すると宣言した ▪ He *declared himself for* the plan. 彼はその計画に賛成を表明した.

declare *a person* ***to be*** 人が…であると宣言[宣告]する ▪ The judge *declared* the prisoner *to be* guilty. 判事は囚人を有罪と宣告した ▪ They *declared* him *to be* a traitor to this country. 彼らは彼を国賊だと宣言した.

declare to *one's* ***heart*** 《米口》ほんとに…だよ ▪ I *declare to my heart* if you aren't Mahaly Robinson! まあ, ほんとにマハリー・ロビンスンさんではありませんか.

declare war against [***on, upon***] →WAR.

(***Have you***) ***anything to declare?*** 課税品をお持ちですか《税関を通るときにこう質問される》.

I declare **1** まあ(あきれた)《驚きを表す》 ▪ Well, *I declare!* これは驚いた; これは弱った; まさか.

2 ほんとに…だよ ▪ Your boy is a genius, *I declare.* ほんとに君の息子さんは天才だよ.

decline[1] /dɪkláɪn/ 名 ***fall*** [***sink, go***] ***into a decline*** (特に肺病で)衰弱する ▪ He *fell into a* rapid *decline* and died. 彼は肺病で急に衰弱して死んだ.

on the decline 衰えて, 下火になって, 下り坂になって ▪ The lady had lost one eye, and the other was very much *on the decline.* 婦人は片目を失い, もう片ほうの目もひどく弱っていた.

the decline and fall 衰亡 ▪ Gibbon wrote "The History of *the Decline and Fall* of the Roman Empire." ギボンは「ローマ帝国衰亡史」を書いた.

the decline of (*one's*) ***life*** 晩年 ▪ Both were approaching *the decline of life.* 二人とも晩年に近づいていた ▪ He is in *the decline of his life.* 彼は生涯の終わりに近い.

work *oneself* ***into a decline*** 働きすぎて肺病になる ▪ He *worked himself into a decline* and died. 彼は働きすぎて肺病になって死んだ.

decline[2] /dɪkláɪn/ 動 ***decline with thanks*** 《皮肉》体よく断る; ありがたくお断りする ▪ I *declined* the offer *with thanks.* 私はその申し出をありがたくお断りした.

decorum /dɪkɔ́:rəm/ 名 ***with decorum*** 礼儀正しく ▪ The performance was conducted *with decorum.* 演奏は礼儀正しく指揮された.

decrease /dí:krì:s/ 名 ***on the decrease*** 次第に減少して ▪ The population is *on the decrease.* 人口は次第に減少している.

deduce /dɪdjú:s/ 動 ***deduce a conclusion from*** …から結論を推論する ▪ We *deduced a conclusion from* the premises. 我々はその前提から一つの結論を推論した.

deduce *one's* ***descent from*** (…から家系を引き出す, とは)…の子孫であると言う ▪ He *deduces his descent from* King Alfred. 彼はアルフレッド王の子孫であると言っている.

deduction /dɪdʌ́kʃən/ 名 ***make a deduction*** **1** 推論する ▪ From the fact it was easy to *make a deduction* about the future of the firm. その事実から会社の将来を推論することはやさしかった.

2 差し引く ▪ We can *make a deduction* of ten percent. 当店は1割の割引とさせていただきます.

deed /di:d/ 名 ***a deed of arms*** →ARMS.

all talk (***and no deed***) →TALK[1].

do the dirty deed 《戯》 **1** みだらな行いをする《セックスする》 ▪ They *did the dirty deed* on campus at night. 彼らは夜, キャンパス内でみだらな行為をした.

2 不正[不愉快]なことをする ▪ The majority of the students said that the government probably *did the dirty deed.* その学生たちの大半は, 政府はおそらく不正を行ったと言った.

one's ***good deed for the day*** (ある人の)その日の一善 ▪ I've done *my good deed for the day* already. 私はもう今日の一善は行いました. ☞ボーイスカウトなどで勧める「一日一善」から.

in (***very***) ***deed*** **1** 実際に, 本当に ▪ The chief became the chief *in deed* as well as in name. 首長は名実ともに首長となった ▪ And so *in very deed* it fell out. そして実際にそういうことになった.

2 行為において (↔in WORD) ▪ He is kind *in* word and *deed.* 彼は言行(げんこう)ともに親切である.

deem /di:m/ 動 ***deem highly*** [***meanly***] ***of*** 《文》…を尊重する[軽んじる] ▪ I *deem highly of* him. 私は彼を高く買っている.

deem (***it***) ***proper to*** *do* 《文》適宜…する ▪ I *deemed it proper to* refuse it. 適宜それを断った.

deep /di:p/ 形副名 ***ankle*** [***knee, waist***] ***deep in*** 足首[ひざ, 腰]まではまって ▪ They stood *knee deep in* mud. 彼らは泥の中にひざまで入って立っていた.

be *five* ***deep*** 5人と約束がある ▪ She *was* four *deep* already. 彼女はすでに4人と約束があった.

be deep in …に深くはまって; に夢中で; に精通して ▪ He *is deep in* debt. 彼は大きな借金がある ▪ The students *are deep in* their studies. 生徒たちは勉強に余念がない ▪ The professor *is deep in* his subject. その教授は専門のことに精通している.

be in deep (***shit***) 《俗》非常に困っている, やばいことになっている (=in deep WATER(s)) ▪ He *is* now *in deep.* 彼は今非常に困っている ▪ Our beloved country *is* now *in deep shit.* われらが愛する国は今やばいことになっている.

be in too deep 《口》抜き差しならない状態である ▪ The ambassador believes that the United States *is in too deep* in Iran. 大使は合衆国がイランに対し抜き差しならない状態にあると思っている.

deep down (***inside***) (***him*** [etc.]) 〚副詞的に〛心の奥底では ▪ *Deep down,* I also hate being in debt. 心の奥底では私もまた借金するのは嫌いだ

▪ *Deep down inside* (*him*), he knew he was wrong. 彼は心の奥では自分が誤っていると分かっていた.

deep in the water 喫水の深い ▪ The ship is *deep in the water.* その船は喫水が深い.

deep six 《俗》 **1** 水葬 ▪ Take her down to the Potomac and give her the *deep six.* 彼女をポトマック川へ連れてって水葬にしてしまえ.

2 拒絶, 破棄 ▪ They gave the new proposal the *deep six.* 彼らは新しい提案を葬り去った ▪ The budget got the *deep six* from the Governor. 予算案は知事によって拒否された. ☞墓穴の深さは普通6フィートであることから.

dig deep (***into*** *one's* ***pockets***) 《口》 (気前よく)大金を使う ▪ There is something about the rhythm of an auctioneer's call that makes one want to *dig deep into one's pockets.* 競売人の呼び声のリズムにはどこか聞いている者に大金を使いたい気にさせるところがある.

drink deep 痛飲する, 多量に飲む ▪ They *drank deep* for free. 彼らは無料で大いに酒を飲んだ.

go [***run***] ***deep*** (感情などが)根強い, 鬱積している; (問題などが)根深い, 長期化している ▪ Doubts *ran deep* on reforms crucial to the US Iraq strategy. 米国のイラク政策に不可欠な改革はなされるのかという疑念は根強くあった.

go deep into …を深く研究する[掘り下げる] ▪ He *went deep into* the subject. 彼はその問題を深く掘り下げた.

go off (***at***) ***the deep end***/ ***go*** (***in***) ***off the deep end***/ ***go*** [***jump, throw***] ***in at the deep end*** 《口》 **1** 深い所へ入る; 危険を冒す; 無鉄砲に事を始める ▪ He *went in off the deep end* of the pool. 彼はプールの深い所へ飛び込んだ.

2 自制心を失う, かっとなる ▪ He is *going off the deep end* over nothing. 彼は何でもないことにかんしゃくを起こしている.

3 困難な事態にはまり込む; 人を急に難しい事に当たらせる ▪ I *jumped in at the deep end* because my boss was absent. 社長がいなかったので私は困ったことになった ▪ Her first experience in front of the camera certainly *threw* her *in at the deep end.* カメラの前に立つのは初めての経験だったので, 彼女は確かに演技するのに難儀した. ☞「プールの深い所から入る」が原義.

in deep shit →be in DEEP (shit).

***in deep water*(*s*)** →WATER[1].

in the deep of …のさなかに ▪ *In the deep of* winter, put on lovely pastels. 真冬に愛らしいパステル調の服を着なさい.

knee [***neck***]***-deep*** **1** 深くはまって ▪ The company was *knee-deep* in debt. その会社は借金に深くはまっていた.

2 非常に忙しい ▪ I'm sitting here *neck-deep* in homework. 僕はここに座って宿題に大わらわです.

lie deep 深いところにある ▪ He lies where pearls *lie deep.* 彼は海底深く真珠のあるところに眠っている.

strike deep **1** 深い感銘を与える ▪ The speech *struck deep* into the minds of the people. その演説は人々の心に深い感銘を与えた.

2 深く根をおろす ▪ The roots of the tree *strike deep.* その木の根は深く根をおろす.

too deep for words あまりに深くて言葉に表せない ▪ His feelings were *too deep for words.* 彼の感情はあまりに深くて言葉に表せなかった.

deer /dɪər/ 名 ***and such small deer*** その他の雑魚(ざ)[つまらぬやつ]ども (cf. Sh., *Lear* 3. 4. 144) ▪ I never heed the opinions of my clerks *and such small deer.* 自分の従業員その他の雑魚たちの意見など意に介さない.

like a deer caught in the headlights (ヘッドライトに捕まったシカのように)どうしていいのか分からず混乱して ▪ As his baby began to cry, he looked *like a deer caught in the headlights.* 赤んぼうが泣き始めたとき, 彼はどうしていいか分からずおろおろしているように見えた.

default /dɪfɔ́ːlt/ 名 ***by default*** 欠席によって ▪ As the defendant failed to appear, the plaintiff requested the court clerk to enter judgement *by default.* 被告が出廷しなかったので, 原告は法廷事務官に欠席裁判の提出を求めた ▪ As the team did not appear, it lost *by default.* そのチームは出場しなかったので不戦敗となった.

go by default 欠席裁判となる ▪ The case *goes by default.* その件は欠席裁判となる.

in default (義務)不履行で ▪ The firm was *in default.* その会社は契約不履行であった.

in default of …がない場合には; がないので ▪ *In default of* tools, he used a nail. 道具がなかったのでくぎを用いた ▪ *In default of* the article, send me a substitute. その品がなければ代用品を送ってください.

make default 《法》 欠席する ▪ The defendant *made default.* 被告は欠席した.

defeat[1] /dɪfíːt/ 名 ***in defeat*** 敗北のとき ▪ You must defeat well *in defeat.* 負けるときは立派な負け方をしなければならない.

inflict a defeat on (人)を敗北させる ▪ The team *inflicted a defeat on* our team. そのチームがわがチームを負かした.

suffer [***sustain***] ***a defeat*** 敗北する ▪ Our team has never yet *suffered a defeat.* わがチームはまだ負けたことがない.

defeat[2] /dɪfíːt/ 動 ***defeat*** *one's* ***own object*** [***purpose***] 目的を果たしえない; 目的達成のじゃまになる ▪ Our system of education often *defeats its own object.* わが国の教育制度はそれ本来の目的を果たしえないことが多い.

defect /díːfekt/ 名 ***have the defects of*** *one's* ***qualities*** 長所に伴う欠点もある ▪ Anyone *has the defects of his qualities.* 誰にでも長所に伴う欠点もある.

in defect 欠乏して ▪ Rainfalls were *in defect* in July. 6月には降雨量が欠乏していた.

in defect of …がない場合には; がないので ▪ Our bodies will pine away *in defect of* daily food.

我々の体は日々の食物がなかったらやせ衰えて死ぬだろう ▪ *In defect of* mirin (sweet saké), you may use saké with sugar. みりんがない場合は砂糖を加えた酒を使ってもいい.

defective /dɪféktɪv/ 形 ***defective in*** …が欠乏して, 欠けて ▪ The dialogue is *defective in* ease and grace. その対話は気楽さと上品さに欠けている ▪ In England we are *defective in* good libraries. イギリスは良い図書館に欠けている.

defend /dɪfénd/ 動 ***defend** oneself* 自己防衛をする; 弁明する ▪ I *defended myself* with a stick. 私はステッキで自衛をした.

God defend! 神の禁じ給わんことを, そんなことがあってたまるものか (→God FORBID (that ...)!).

defense, 《英》**defence** /dɪféns/ 名 ***in defense*** **1** 禁漁になった ▪ Salmon shall be *in defense* from 8th September. サケは9月8日から禁漁になる ▪ Trout streams were put *in defense.* マスの川は禁漁になっていた.

2 防御のために ▪ He never fights except *in defense.* 彼は防御のため以外は戦わない.

in defense of …を守るために ▪ He spoke *in defense of* the woman. 彼はその女性の弁護をした ▪ He drew his sword *in defense of* the innocent. 彼は罪のない人々を守るため剣を抜いた.

make a defense **1** 防御をする ▪ They *made a* very successful *defense* against the attacks of the enemy. 彼らは敵の攻撃に対し実によく防御した.

2 弁護[弁明]をする ▪ The accused man *made* no *defense.* 被告は弁明をしなかった.

Offense is the best defense. 《諺》攻撃は最善の防御.

defensive /dɪfénsɪv/ 名 ***be [act, stand] on the defensive*** 防御態勢をとる; 守勢をとる ▪ You have to *be on the defensive* all the time. あなたはいつも防御態勢をとっていなければならない ▪ Both countries claimed that they were *acting on the defensive.* 両国が防衛行為をしているのだと主張した.

throw** a person **on the defensive 先手を打って(守備から)攻勢に転じる ▪ I *threw* her *on the defensive* by insisting that she had been away on vacation. 私は彼女が休暇で不在だったと言って攻勢に転じた.

deference /défərəns/ 名 ***in deference to*** …を尊重して, に従って ▪ The Prime Minister resigned *in deference to* the will of the House of Commons. 首相は下院の意志を尊重して辞職した.

pay [show, yield] (a) deference (to) (…に)従う; (に)敬意を表する ▪ They *paid a deference to* my skill. 彼らは私の技量に敬意を表した ▪ He often *yielded a deference to* such persons. 彼はしばしばそのような人々の言に従った.

with all (due) deference (to you) お言葉ではございますが, 失礼ながら ▪ *With all deference,* I beg to disagree. 失礼ですが, 賛成しかねます.

with deference 敬意をもって, うやうやしく ▪ Do you treat your parents *with deference*? 君は両親を敬意をもって遇しますか.

defiance /dɪfáɪəns/ 名 ***bid defiance to/set ... at defiance*** …にいどみかかる, を無視する, ものともしない ▪ The typist *set* my warning *at defiance* and went out. タイピストは私の警告を無視して出て行った ▪ The thief pulled out a knife and *bade defiance to* the policeman. 盗賊はナイフを取り出して警官にいどみかかった ▪ The Alps *bid defiance to* the elements. アルプス山脈は暴風雨をものともしない.

hurl defiance at …を無視する, 見くびる ▪ He *hurls defiance at* authority. 彼はおかみの威光を見くびっている.

in defiance of …を無視して, にかまわずに, をものともせず ▪ If a soldier acts *in defiance of* orders, he is severely punished. もし兵が命令を無視して行動すれば厳罰に処せられる ▪ He jumped into the river *in defiance of* the icy water. 彼は氷のような水をものともせず川に飛びこんだ.

set ... at defiance →bid DEFIANCE to.

stand at defiance 反抗[挑戦]する ▪ You *stand at defiance* against him. 君は彼に反抗している.

deficient /dɪfíʃənt/ 形 ***deficient in*** …に欠けて ▪ She is sadly *deficient in* knowledge about health. 彼女は健康についての知識には情けないほど欠けている ▪ The milk was *deficient in* fatty matter. そのミルクは脂肪分に欠けていた.

definition /dèfəníʃən/ 名 ***by definition*** 定義上; 当然 ▪ An adjective *by definition* modifies nouns. 形容詞は定義上名詞を修飾する ▪ You're an Oxonian, so you're an intellectual *by definition.* 君はオックスフォード大学卒業生だから, 当然知識人だ.

defy /dɪfáɪ/ 動 ***defy all comparison*** 比類がない ▪ The watch was not low-priced, but as to its action it *defied all comparison.* その時計は安くはなかったが機能に至っては比類がなかった.

defy all description →DESCRIPTION.

***I defy you to** do* 君に…ができるならやってみろ ▪ *I defy you to* strike me. おれを殴れるなら殴ってみろ.

degrade /dɪgréɪd/ 動 ***degrade** oneself* 品位を落とす ▪ He *degraded himself* by telling lies. 彼は嘘をついて品位を落とした.

degree /dɪgríː/ 名 ***a degree of*** 相当多量の ▪ *A degree of* pleasure attends eating and drinking. 飲食には相当の快楽が伴う.

by degrees だんだんと, 次第に ▪ They will raise your salary *by degrees.* 彼らはおいおい君の俸給をあげてくれるでしょう.

by one degree 1等だけ ▪ The judge reduced the penalty *by one degree* owing to extenuating circumstances. 判事は情状酌量により罪1等を減じた.

by slow degrees 徐々に(進むなど) ▪ My study has been progressing *by slow degrees.* 私の研究は徐々に進んできています.

give** a person **the third degree →THIRD.

in a [some] degree いくぶんか ▪ He is angry *in*

some degree. 彼はいくぶん怒っている.

in its degree それぞれ状況[程度]に応じて ▪ Each is good *in its degree*. おのおのそれぞれに取りえがある.

in the last degree →to the last DEGREE.

not ... in the slightest degree 少しも…でない ▪ I'm *not* interested in it *in the slightest degree*. 私は少しもそれに興味を持っていません.

of degree 程度の問題で ▪ The difference is only *of degree*. 差異はただ程度の問題にすぎない.

of high [low, every] degree 高い[低い, あらゆる]身分の ▪ People *of every degree* gathered. あらゆる身分の人々が集まった.

one degree [several degrees] under ちょっと調子が悪く ▪ I am *one degree under* today. 私は今日はちょっと調子が悪い. ☞体温が "one degree [several degrees] below normal temperature" の意味.

take a degree 学位を取る ▪ He came down without *taking a degree*. 彼は学位を取らずに退学した.

to a degree **1**《口》大いに, ひどく ▪ My father is angry *to a degree*. 父はひどく怒っている.
2《米》いくぶんは, ある程度は ▪ It is all right *to a degree*. それはある程度は良い.

to a high [very large] degree 非常に, きわめて ▪ He is vain *to a high degree*. 彼はきわめてうぬぼれが強い.

to some [a certain] degree ある程度, ちょっと, いくぶん ▪ What you say is true *to some degree*. あなたのおっしゃることはいくぶん正しい ▪ *To a certain degree*, such an appraisal is correct. ある程度そのような評価は当たっている.

to [in] the last degree 最も, 極度に ▪ His argument is far-fetched *to the last degree*. 彼の議論は極度にこじつけである.

to what degree どの程度に ▪ *To what degree* are you interested in this subject? どの程度この問題に興味を持っているのか.

dekko /dékoʊ/ 名 ***have a dekko*** 《俗》ちょっと見る ▪ Let's *have a dekko*. ちょっと見ようではないか; ちょっと見せてください. ☞dekko (Hindi) は dekhna (=look) の命令形.

delay /dɪléɪ/ 名 ***without delay*** 即刻 ▪ I must return *without delay*. 私は直ちに帰らなければならない.

deliberate /dɪlíbərət/ 形 ***Deliberate in counsel, prompt in action.*** 《諺》熟慮断行, 「始めは処女のごとく終わりは脱兎のごとし」.

deliberation /dɪlìbəréɪʃən/ 名 ***with deliberation*** ゆっくりと ▪ The iceberg rolled over *with* the utmost *deliberation*. 氷山がきわめてゆっくりとひっくり返った.

delicacy /délɪkəsi/ 名 ***feel a delicacy about*** …に気おくれを感じる, ちゅうちょする ▪ He *felt a delicacy about* doing it. 彼はそれをするにはなんとなく気おくれがした.

Hunger knows no delicacy. 《諺》ひもじいときには品(ひん)も何もあったものではない.

delicate /délɪkət/ 形 ***in a delicate condition [state of health]*** 《口》身重で, 妊娠して ▪ Mrs. Micawber was *in a delicate condition*. ミコーバー夫人は身重であった.

delict /dɪlíkt/ 名 ***in flagrant delict*** 現行犯で ▪ A person taken *in flagrant delict*, with the stolen goods on him is not bailable. 現行犯で捕えられ, 盗品を持っている者は保釈できない.

delight[1] /dɪláɪt/ 名 ***scorn delights and live laborious days*** 娯楽を捨てて刻苦の生活をする (Milton, *Lycidas* 72) ▪ For the next two months I must *scorn delights and live laborious days*. 次の2か月間は私は娯楽を捨てて刻苦の生活をせねばなりません.

take [have] (a) delight in [in** doing**, to** do**] …を[することを]喜ぶ ▪ He *takes* the greatest *delight in* philosophy. 彼は哲学を最大の楽しみにしている ▪ The naughty boy *takes a delight in pulling* the dog's tail. そのいたずらっ子は犬の尾を引っぱるのをおもしろがる.

to the delight of …の喜んだことには ▪ *To the* great *delight of* his parents he passed the examination. 彼の両親が喜んだことに, 彼は試験に合格した.

delight[2] /dɪláɪt/ 動 ***be delighted at*** …が気に入る ▪ I *am delighted at* the plan of your book. あなたの著書の趣向が気に入った.

***be delighted to** do* **1** …してうれしい ▪ I *am delighted to* meet you. お会いしてうれしく思います《初対面のあいさつ》.
2〖未来形で〗喜んで…する ▪ I shall *be delighted to* undertake the work. 私は喜んでその仕事をやろう.

be delighted with …が気に入る ▪ Charles *was delighted with* the adviser. チャールズはその顧問が気に入った.

delight to honor …を喜んで尊敬する; に栄誉を与えたもう《敬語》(《聖》*Esth.* 6. 6) ▪ Heidelberg *delighted to honor* Spinoza. ハイデルベルクはスピノザを喜んで尊敬した ▪ The king *delighted to honor* him. 王は彼に栄誉を与えられた.

delirium /dɪlíriəm/ 名 ***lapse into delirium*** 譫妄(せんもう)状態に陥る, うわごとを言いだす ▪ The patient *lapsed into delirium*. 患者はうわごとを言いだした.

deliver /dɪlívər/ 動 ***be delivered of*** 《文》 **1**(女性が子)を生む, 分娩する; (船が荷)を降ろす ▪ The queen *was* safely *delivered of* a prince. 王妃は王子を安産した ▪ The ship *was delivered of* her cargo. その船は荷を降ろした.
2(意見など)を述べる; (詩文)を生み出す ▪ I *was delivered of* a speech about virtue. 美徳についての演説をやった ▪ He *was delivered of* a few verses. 彼は詩を数首作った.

deliver a battle 戦い[攻撃]をする ▪ The Emperor *delivered a* defensive *battle*. 皇帝は防衛戦をした.

***deliver** oneself* **(*of*)** 《文》(意見・心を)述べる[吐露する] ▪ Some merchants *delivered themselves* against the Bill. その法案に反対の意見を述べた商人もあった ▪ He *delivered himself of* a long suppressed opinion. 彼は長く抑えてきた意見を発表した.

deliver the goods 《口》 **1** 自分の契約を果たす ▪ He never fails to *deliver the goods*. 彼はいつも必ず契約を果たす.

2 《米俗》 期待にこたえる[にそむかぬ] ▪ People do not mind helping someone who always *delivers the goods*. 人々はいつも期待にこたえる人を援助するに異存はない.

deliver** oneself **to (警察)に自首する ▪ He *delivered himself to* the police. 彼は警察に自首した.

deliver ... under** one's **hand and seal → HAND[1].

delivery /dɪlívəri/ 名 ***on delivery*** 現品引き替えに ▪ These goods must be paid for *on delivery*. この商品は現品引き替えに代金を払ってもらわなければならない.

take delivery of …を引き取る ▪ I *took delivery of* the goods. 私はその品を受け取った.

delude /dɪlú:d/ 動 ***delude** oneself* 思い[勘]ちがいする ▪ They *deluded themselves* with belief in their superiority. 彼らは自分らがすぐれていると思いちがいしていた.

deluge[1] /délju:dʒ/ 名 ***After us [me] the Deluge!*** (わが亡き)後は野となれ山となれ! ☞ Rossbach の戦でフランス軍がドイツ軍に破れたとき Mme. de Pompadour が Louis XV に言ったと伝えられる.

deluge[2] /délju:dʒ/ 動 ***be deluged with*** …の洪水となる, が殺到する ▪ The market *was deluged with* smuggled silks. 市場は密輸入絹製品の洪水であった ▪ He *was deluged with* offers [questions]. 彼に申し出[質問]が殺到した.

delusion /dɪlú:ʒən/ 名 ***be [labor] under a delusion (as to)*** (…について)思いちがいをしている ▪ The fellow was only *laboring under a delusion*. あいつは勘違いをしていただけなのだ ▪ You *labor under a delusion as to* that. 君はそのことで思いちがいしている.

delusions of grandeur 誇大妄想 ▪ *Delusions of grandeur* are typical in schizophrenia. 「誇大妄想」は分裂性の性格によく見られる.

demand[1] /dɪmǽnd|-mɑ́:nd/ 名 ***a demand on** one's **purse [time]*** 金のいる[時間のつぶれる]こと ▪ There are many *demands on my purse*. 金のいることが多い ▪ I have many *demands on my time*. 時間を取られることが多い.

by popular demand 多くの人々の要望にこたえて ▪ The exhibition has been extended *by popular demand* through August 15. 展示会はたくさんの人々の要求に応じて8月15日まで延長された.

in demand 需要がある ▪ Solar cells are *in* great *demand*. 太陽電池は大いに需要がある ▪ Nancy is very much *in demand* as a babysitter. ナンシーは子守りとして引っぱりだこである.

make demands on [upon] (人)に…せよと要求する ▪ Your father will *make demands on* you. お父さんは君にいろいろやれと要求するだろう.

on demand 請求[要求]あり次第 ▪ This check is payable *on demand*. この小切手は請求(一覧)払いである.

demand[2] /dɪmǽnd|-mɑ́:nd/ 動 ***demand a person's business [name]*** 人に何の用かと[氏名を]問う ▪ He *demanded my business*. 彼は私に何の用かと問うた.

demean /dɪmí:n/ 動 ***demean** oneself* **1** 品位[身分, 評判]を落とす ▪ He *demeaned himself* by a marriage with an artist's daughter. 彼は画家の娘と結婚して身分を落とした.

2 〚副詞(句)を伴って〛 ふるまう, 身を処す ▪ The prince *demeaned himself* like a kind gentleman [well]. 王子は親切な紳士のように[立派に]ふるまった.

demean** oneself **to [to** do**] …に身を落とす[身を落として…する] ▪ He *demeaned himself to* a carpenter. 彼は大工に身を落とした.

demesne /dɪméɪn/ 名 ***hold ... in demesne*** 《法》 …を直接に領有する, 自己のものとして占有する ▪ The Baron *held* the lands *in demesne*. 豪族はその土地を直領地として保有していた.

in [by] ancient demesne 昔からの領有による, 昔からの借地権による ▪ Tenants *in ancient demesne* could not be sued for their lands in the king's court. 昔からの借地権による借地人を相手取って, 高等法廷に土地返還の訴訟をすることはできなかった.

in** one's **demesne as of fee 世襲土地として所有した ▪ He died seized of the land *in his demesne as of fee*. 彼はその土地を世襲地として所有して亡くなった.

demon /dí:mən/ 名 ***a demon for work*** 《口》 激しい働き手 ▪ Robert is *a demon for work*. ロバートは仕事の鬼である.

be a demon with …に騒がれる ▪ When he was younger, he *was a demon with* the ladies. 彼は若い頃は女性に騒がれていた.

the demon drink 《戯》 悪魔の飲物《人を堕落させる酒》 ▪ *The demon drink* took hold of him. 悪魔の飲み物が彼を捕えた.

demonstration /dèmənstréɪʃən/ 名 ***give a demonstration of*** …を表示する ▪ He *gave a demonstration of* love. 彼は愛情を示した.

to demonstration 決定的に, 明確に ▪ It is clear *to demonstration* that you are mad. 君の気が狂っているということは明白だ.

demonstrative /dɪmɑ́nstrətɪv|-mɔ́n-/ 形 ***be demonstrative of*** …を実証する; の真実[存在]を証明する ▪ It *is demonstrative of* their skill. それは彼らの老練さを立証する.

demur /dɪmə́:r/ 名 ***without demur*** 異議なく ▪ He will pay *without demur*. 彼は異議なく支払うだろう.

demurrer /dɪmə́:rər/ 名 ***enter [put in] a demurrer*** 《法》 異議を申し立てる ▪ We could not *put in a demurrer.* 異議の申し立てはできなかった.

den /den/ 名 ***a den of iniquity*** 悪の巣窟(そうくつ) ▪ The gambling house is one of those *dens of iniquity* that the police warn us about. その賭博場は警察が気をつけるように言っている悪の巣窟の一つだ.

a den of thieves 盗賊の巣 (《聖》 *Matt.* 21. 13) ▪ You have made my house *a den of thieves.* あなたは私の家を盗賊の巣としてしまった.

D

denial /dɪnáɪəl/ 名 ***give a flat denial*** きっぱり断る ▪ She *gave* him *a flat denial.* 彼女は彼にきっぱり断った.

make a denial of ...を否定する ▪ He *made a* public *denial of* communism. 彼は共産主義を公然と否定した.

meet ... with flat denial ...をきっぱり否定する ▪ She *met* the charge *with flat denial.* 彼女はその罪科をきっぱり否定した.

take no denial いや応を言わせない ▪ He will *take no denial.* 彼はいや応を言わせないだろう.

Denmark /dénmɑːrk/ 名 ***Something is*** [***There is something***] ***rotten in the state of Denmark.*** →ROTTEN.

dent /dent/ 名 ***make a dent in*****/**《米》 ***put a dent in*** 《口》 ...を減らす; を損する; を弱める ▪ These expenses have *made a* big *dent in* our finances. これらの費用は我々の財政に大穴をあけた.

make a dent on ...に影響を与える ▪ The textbook *made a dent on* teachers with its novel contents. その教科書は目新しい内容で教師たちに影響を与えた.

deny /dɪnáɪ/ 動 ***deny*** *oneself a thing* 物をなしですます, 自制する ▪ He *denied himself* proper food. 彼は食うべき物も食わなかった.

deny *oneself* ***to*** ...に面会を断る ▪ She *denied herself to* all callers. 彼女はすべての来客の面会を断った.

deny *oneself* ***to be*** 自分が...であることを否定する ▪ He *denied himself to be* a communist. 彼は共産主義者ではないと言った.

not deny but that ...でないとは言わない, (that 以下)を否定しない ▪ I do *not deny but that* it may be so. そうでないだろうとは言わない.

depart /dɪpɑ́ːrt/ 動 ***depart*** (***from***) ***this life*** 世を去る ▪ He *departed* (*from*) *this life* at his house in the country. 彼は田舎の自分の家で亡くなった.

departed /dɪpɑ́ːrtəd/ 形 ***the dear departed*** 《婉曲》(葬儀で)故人 ▪ Let's meditate on the life of *the dear departed.* Pray in silence. 故人の生涯に思いをはせましょう. 黙祷.

department /dɪpɑ́ːrtmənt/ 名 (***not***) ***be*** *one's* ***department*** 《口》 自分の専門分野である[ない] ▪ Leave it to me. This *is my department.* 私に任せなさい. これは私の専門分野だ ▪ Sorry, that's *not my department.* ごめん, それって私の専門分野じゃないんだ.

departure /dɪpɑ́ːrtʃər/ 名 ***take*** *one's* ***departure*** 出発する, 発足する ▪ He *took his departure* hurriedly. 彼は急いで出発した ▪ *Taking his departure* from materialism he arrived at spiritualism. 彼は唯物主義から発して精神主義に到達した.

depend /dɪpénd/ 動 ***as if*** [***though***] *one's* ***life depends on it*** できるだけ努力して, 一生懸命に ▪ He worked *as if his life depended on it.* 彼は一生懸命に働いた.

depend on [***upon***] *a person* ***to*** *do* 人を信頼して...してもらう; 人が...することを当てにする ▪ I shall have to *depend on* you *to* do it. あなたを信頼してそうしてもらわねばならないでしょう ▪ You may *depend upon* me *to* be there early. 僕はきっとそこへ早く行くから安心しなさい.

depend upon it 《口》 確かに ▪ *Depend upon it*, the book will be a best-seller. 確かに, その本はベストセラーになるだろう.

That depends./It all depends. それは事情[場合]による《後に on circumstances が略されている》 ▪ Will you go to a movie with me tonight? —*That depends.* 今夜私と映画に行きませんか—都合によってはね.

you may depend きっと(...する) ▪ *You may depend* he will do it. きっと彼はそうするだろう.

you may depend upon it 《口》 確かに ▪ It should have been a heavier judgment, *you may depend upon it.* 確かにより重い判決のはずだったが.

dependence /dɪpéndəns/ 名 ***place*** [***put***] ***dependence on*** (人)を信頼する ▪ You can *put dependence on* him. 彼は信頼できる.

dependent /dɪpéndənt/ 形 (***be***) ***dependent on*** **1** ...に頼る ▪ Children *are* usually *dependent on* their parents. 子供たちは通常親に頼る.
2 ...による ▪ The success of the picnic *is dependent on* the weather. ピクニックの成功は天候いかんだろう.

deport /dɪpɔ́ːrt/ 動 ***deport*** *oneself* ふるまう ▪ They always *deported themselves* like gentlemen. 彼らはいつも紳士のようにふるまった.

deposit[1] /dɪpɑ́zət|-pɔ́zɪt/ 名 ***have*** *a sum* ***on*** [***upon***] ***deposit*** 銀行に金を預けている ▪ I *have* £1,000 *on deposit.* 銀行に1,000ポンド預けている.

on [***upon***] ***deposit*** (銀行に)預金して ▪ He has money *on deposit* in a savings bank. 彼は貯蓄銀行に預金している.

place *a sum* ***on*** [***upon***] ***deposit*** 銀行に金を預ける ▪ He *placed* £1,000 *on deposit* for the benefit of the infant. 彼はその幼児のために銀行に1,000ポンド預けた.

deposit[2] /dɪpɑ́zət|-pɔ́zɪt/ 動 ***deposit ... in a bank*** (金を)銀行に預ける ▪ I *deposited* £1,000 *in the bank.* 私はその銀行に1,000ポンド預けた.

depreciate /dɪpríːʃièɪt/ 動 ***depreciate*** *oneself* 卑下する ▪ You should not *depreciate yourself.* 自分を卑下してはいけない.

depression /dɪpréʃən/ 名 ***fall*** [***sink***] ***into a*** (***deep***) ***depression*** (ひどく)ふさぎ込む ▪ After the loss of her child, she *fell into a depression.* 子供を失ってから彼女はふさぎ込んでしまった.

deprive /dɪpráɪv/ 動 ***deprive*** *oneself* ***of*** …を自制する, 控える, 絶つ ▪ I *deprive myself of* the comforts of life. 私は世の楽しみを絶っている.

depth /depθ/ 名 ***a man of depth*** 学問[知恵]の深い人 ▪ He is *a man of* great *depth.* 彼は非常に学問[知恵]の深い人である.

beyond *one's* ***depth*** →out of one's DEPTH.

from the depth(***s***) 奥底[深み]からの ▪ Their prayer is a cry *from the depths* of misery. 彼らの祈りは不幸のどん底からの叫びである ▪ I think so *from the depth* of my mind. 心の底からそう思う.

go [***get***] ***out of*** [***beyond***] *one's* ***depth*** **1** 背の立たぬ深みに入る (→out of one's DEPTH) ▪ The boy *got out of his depth* and was drowned. その少年は背の立たぬ深みへ入って溺死した.

2 理解できぬことに口出しする, 力の及ばぬことをしようとする ▪ You should not *go out of your depth.* わからないことに口出しするものではない ▪ They *went beyond my depth.* 彼らは私のできないことをやり始めた.

hidden depths 隠れた才能, これまで人が気うかなかった立派な素質 ▪ He showed his *hidden depths* in the speech contest. 彼は弁論大会で隠れた才能を発揮した.

in depth 徹底的に ▪ We must discuss the matter *in depth.* その件を徹底的に討議しないといけない.

in the depth of …のさなかに ▪ The adults of the winter moth are active *in the depth of* winter. 冬蛾の成虫は真冬に活動する ▪ *In the depth of* night, something woke him. 真夜中に何かが彼を起こした.

in the depths of …の奥まった所[奥底]に ▪ *In the depths of* the forest the Aka people did not wear much clothing. 森の奥地でアカ族は衣服をあまり身につけないで暮らしていた ▪ She was down *in the depths of* despair. 彼女は絶望のどん底に沈んでいた.

out of *one's* ***depth***/ ***beyond*** *one's* ***depth*** **1** 背の立たぬ深みに ▪ When he was *out of his depth,* he was seized with cramp. 彼は足の届かぬ深みにいたとき, こむらがえりを起こした.

2 理解できないで, 力に及ばないで ▪ I went to a lecture on relativity, but I was *out of my depth.* 相対性理論についての講演を聞きに行ったが, わからなかった ▪ This mathematical problem is *beyond my depth.* この数学の問題は私にはできない.

plumb new depths 前より一層悪くなる ▪ Relations between Zimbabwe and Britain *plumbed new depths.* ジンバブエと英国の関係は前より一層悪くなった.

plumb the depths (***of***) **1** (孤独・悲しみなどの)どん底に沈む ▪ When both her children were killed, she *plumbed the depths of* sorrow. 子供が二人とも殺されたとき彼女は悲しみのどん底に沈んだ.

2 (難解なものを)深く理解する ▪ Rigo's paintings *plumb the depths of* a labyrinthian soul. リゴの絵画は入り組んだ魂を深く理解している.

3 (悪い物の)極みを示す, 行きつくところまで行く, 地に落ちる ▪ It is said that the opera *plumbed the depths of* tastelessness. そのオペラは悪趣味の極みを示していたと言われている.

sink to such depths 非常に行儀が悪くなる ▪ It is hard to believe that humans are able to *sink to such depths* of bestiality. 人間が野獣のように行儀が悪くなるとは信じがたい.

to the depth of …の深さまで ▪ The snow falls there *to the depth of* six feet. 雪はそこでは6フィートも積もる.

within *one's* ***depth*** **1** (水中の)足の届く所に ▪ He kept *within his depth.* 彼は足の届く所にずっといた.

2 力に及ぶ程度で; 理解できる程度で ▪ The tobacconist's business was *within his depth.* タバコ屋は彼にはやっていけた ▪ That problem is *within my depth.* その問題は私にわかる.

deputy /dépjəti/ 名 ***by deputy*** 代理で, 代理人によって ▪ His wars were waged *by deputy.* 彼の戦争は代理人によって行われた.

derelict /dérəlɪkt/ 形 ***be derelict of*** 《米》…を怠る ▪ He *is derelict of* his duty. 彼は自分の義務を怠っている.

derision /dɪríʒən/ 名 ***be in derision*** 嘲笑されている ▪ He *was in* daily *derision.* 彼は毎日嘲笑された.

bring ... into derision …を嘲笑の的にする, 笑い草にする ▪ British policy *was brought into derision.* イギリスの政策は笑い草にされた.

hold [***have***] ***... in derision*** …をあざける ▪ They *had* me [my statement] *in derision.* 彼らは私[私の言葉]をあざけった.

derivable /dɪráɪvəbəl/ 形 ***derivable from*** **1** …から引き出せる[得られる] ▪ A large income is *derivable from* the investment. 大きな収入がその投資から得られる.

2 …を源としている ▪ All these accidents were *derivable from* carelessness. これらの事故はみな不注意が元であった.

derive /dɪráɪv/ 動 ***be derived from*** …から来て[出て]いる ▪ The American people *are derived from* many races. アメリカ国民は多くの人種からなっている ▪ Many English words *are derived from* Latin. 英語にはラテン語から来た語が多い.

derive *oneself* ***from*** …から出る[来る] ▪ Our knowledge *derives itself from* experience. 我々の知識は経験から来るものである.

derogatory /dɪrágətɔ̀ːri|-rɔ́gətəri/ 形 ***be derogatory to*** …を減損する ▪ Your behavior *is derogatory to* your dignity. あなたのふるまいはあなたの威厳を損じる.

descend /dɪsénd/ 動 ***be descended from*** 《文》…の子孫である, 出である ▪ According to the Bible, we *are* all *descended from* Adam. 聖書に

よれば我々はみなアダムの子孫である ▪ French *is descended from* Latin. フランス語はラテン語から派生したものである.

descendant /dɪséndənt/ 形 ***in* [*on*] *the descendant*** 下り坂で, 衰えかけて ▪ Jupiter (for succeeding) was *on the Descendant.* (成功運を表す)ジュピターは下り坂であった ▪ In September, 2001, the arc of his political life was *in the descendant.* 2001年9月, 彼の政治生命の弧は衰えかけていた.

D

descent /dɪsént/ 名 ***in descent*** 《紋章》下降姿勢の ▪ This coat of arms represents a Lion *in descent.* この紋章は下降姿勢のライオンを表している. ☞Lion rampant (左の後脚で立ち上がったライオン).

***make a descent upon* [*on*]** ...を急襲する ▪ The Danes *made* numerous *descents upon* the English coast during the tenth century. デーン人は10世紀にイギリス沿岸を何度も急襲した.

of... descent ...の出で, の家柄で ▪ Stephen Baldwin reveals that he is *of* Irish *descent.* スティーブン・ボールドウィンはアイルランド出身であることを明らかにしている ▪ He is *of* good *descent.* 彼は氏も育ちもよい.

description /dɪskrípʃən/ 名 ***answer to the description*** 人相書きの(述べている)通りである ▪ I saw no one *answering to the description.* 私はその人相書きの通りの人は誰も見なかった.

beyond description 名状[記述]しがたいほど ▪ The scenery is beautiful *beyond description.* その景色は言葉に尽くせぬほど美しい ▪ The beauty is *beyond description.* その美しさは筆紙[筆舌]に尽くしがたい.

defy* [*beggar*] (*all*) *description 言葉に尽くせない ▪ The beauty *defies description.* その美しさは言葉に尽くせない.

***graphic description*(*s*)** (死人などの残酷な)詳細場面 ▪ Children shouldn't see these *graphic descriptions* of the battle. 子供は戦闘のこういう詳細場面は見ないほうがよろしい.

desert[1] /dɪzə́ːrt/ 名 ***above*** *one's* ***deserts*** 身に余る ▪ The honor is *above my deserts.* その栄誉は私の身に余るものです.

***by desert*(*s*)** 勲功によって ▪ Promotion is *by deserts.* 昇進は勲功による.

Desert and reward seldom keep company. 《諺》勲功と報償はめったに釣り合わない.

get* [*have, meet with*]** *one's* **(*just*) *deserts 当然の報い[賞罰]を受ける ▪ He has *got his deserts.* 彼は当然の報いを受けた.

give *a person his* ***deserts*** 人に相当の賞罰を与える ▪ Each should *be given his deserts.* おのおのがそれ相当の賞罰を受けるべきである.

desert[2] /dɪzə́ːrt/ 動 ***desert a sinking ship*** →leave a sinking SHIP.

deserve /dɪzə́ːrv/ 動 ***deserve better of*** ...からもっと優遇される価値がある ▪ He *deserves better of* his employer than to be pensioned off. 彼は年金で解雇されるより雇主からもっと優遇されるべきである.

deserve credit for ...を賞賛されるべきである ▪ He *deserves credit for* having done so. 彼のそうした行いは賞賛されるべきだ.

deserve ill of *a person* 人から虐待される[罰せられる]に値する; 人に対し罪がある ▪ You *deserve ill of* him. 君は彼に対して罪がある.

deserve the name of ...と呼ばれる価値がある, の名に恥じない ▪ He *deserves the name of* scholar. 彼は学者と呼ばれる価値がある.

deserve well of ...から優遇される価値がある, に功労がある ▪ The soldiers *deserve well of* their country. 兵士たちは国家に対して功労があるから賞を受けるに値する.

deserve* (*well*) *to be (*done*) 当然...されるべきである ▪ He *deserves well to be* promoted. 彼は当然昇格されるべきである.

deserving /dɪzə́ːrvɪŋ/ 形 **(*be*) *deserving of*** ...に値する ▪ He *is deserving of* credit [death]. 彼は賞賛[死]に値する.

design[1] /dɪzáɪn/ 名 ***by design*** 故意に (↔by a mere ACCIDENT) ▪ William, whether by accident or *by design*, was not admitted. ウィリアムは偶然にか故意にかわからないが, 入場を許されなかった.

***have* [*harbor*] *a design* [*designs*] *on* [*against*]** ...に対して攻撃・殺害のもくろみを持つ, をねらう; (異性)に下心がある ▪ He *has a design on* her life. 彼は彼女に対して殺意をいだいている ▪ He *has a design upon* the woman. 彼はその女を襲おうとねらっている ▪ She *has designs against* his life. 彼女は彼の命をねらっている ▪ He *had designs on* her, but she spurned him. 彼は彼女に下心を抱いていたが, ひじ鉄をくわされた.

design[2] /dɪzáɪn/ 動 ***design*** *a person* [*a thing*] ***for* [*to*** *do*] 人[物]を...に予定する, 人[物]に...させるつもりである ▪ He *designed* his son *for* [*to* be] a doctor. 彼は息子を医者にするつもりであった ▪ This message *was designed for* political effect. このメッセージは政治的効果をねらったものだ.

desire[1] /dɪzáɪər/ 名 ***at*** *a person's* ***desire*** 人の望み[依頼]により; 望み通りに ▪ I also send, *at your desire*, a general list of articles. またご希望により, 商品の総目録をお送りします ▪ *At the desire of* the Director, Mr. K. will give a special lecture tomorrow. 校長の依頼でK氏はあす特別講義をする.

***Desires are nourished by delay*(*s*).** 《諺》欲望は遅滞によって募るもの,「堰(せ)かれて募る恋の情」.

from a desire to *do* ...したさに ▪ He worked hard *from a desire to* please his parents. 彼は両親を喜ばせたいと一生懸命に働いた.

the desire of *one's* ***eyes*** 目の喜びとするもの, 掌中の玉 (《聖》*Ezek.* 24. 16) ▪ She was still *the desire of his eyes.* 彼女はまだ彼の掌中の玉であった.

the desire of the moth for the star 星を求める蛾の願い《高遠な理想》(P. B. Shelley, *To*—) ▪ Your unfulfillable ideals resemble *the desire of the moth for the star.* 君の達成不可能な理想な

ど星を求める蛾の願いの類(たぐ)いだ.

desire^2 /dɪzáɪər/ 動 ***all one can desire*** この上は望めない ▪ This book is *all one can desire*. この本はこれ以上は望めない.

leave a lot [***much, a great deal***] ***to be desired*** 遺憾な点が多々ある ▪ My daughter's taste in men *leaves a lot to be desired*. 娘の男を見る目には遺憾な点が多い.

leave something to be desired 遺憾な点が少しある ▪ The plan *leaves something to be desired*. その計画は遺憾な点が少しある.

leave nothing [***little***] ***to be desired*** 申し分がない[ほとんどない] ▪ Your composition *leaves nothing to be desired*. 君の作文は申し分がない.

desirous /dɪzáɪərəs/ 形 (***be***) ***desirous of*** …を望む ▪ He *is desirous of* going abroad. 彼は海外に行くのを望んでいる.

desist /dɪzíst/ 動 ***cease and desist*** → CEASE^2.

desk /desk/ 名 ***away from*** *one's* ***desk*** 席をはずして, 席空きで ▪ I'm sorry, but John is *away from his desk* just now. 申し訳ありませんが, ジョンはただ今, 席をはずしております.

(***be, sit***) ***at*** *one's* ***desk*** 机に向かって(いる)《勉強・書きもの・事務・読書などのため》 ▪ He passed the whole evening *at his desk*. 彼はまるひと晩を勉強して過ごした.

desolate /désələt/ 形 ***be desolate of*** …が全くない ▪ The country *was desolate of* all vegetation. その地域には草木が全くなかった.

despair /dɪspéər/ 名 ***be the despair of*** …はお手あげだ; にはかなわない ▪ The boy *is the despair of* his teachers. その子には先生がたはお手あげだ ▪ This truth *is our despair*. この真実には我々もお手上げだ.

drive *a person* ***to despair*** 人を絶望させる ▪ John's laziness *drove* his father *to despair*. ジョンの怠惰に父親は絶望した.

in (***blank***) ***despair*** (全く)絶望して ▪ He gave up the attempt *in despair*. 彼は絶望してその企てを断念した.

yield [***give way***] ***to despair*** 絶望に陥る ▪ *Yielding to despair*, she wept bitterly. 絶望に陥って, 彼女はひどく泣いた.

despatch /dɪspǽtʃ/ 名 →DISPATCH.

desperate /déspərət/ 形 ***be desperate for*** …がほしくてたまらない ▪ I *am desperate for* a cup of tea. お茶が1杯ほしくてたまらない.

Desperate diseases call for desperate remedies. 《諺》重病には荒療治が必要.

desperation /dèspəréɪʃən/ 名 ***drive*** *a person* ***to desperation*** 人を捨てばちにする; 《口》人をかんかんに怒らせる ▪ That *drove* him *to desperation*. そのため彼は捨てばちになった.

in desperation やけ[捨てばち]になって ▪ They rose *in desperation* against the King. 彼らはやけになって国王に反旗を翻した.

despite /dɪspáɪt/ 名 ***despite*** *oneself* = in SPITE of oneself.

do despite to …を侮辱する, 暴行する, 凌辱する ▪ He *did despite to* the holy relics. 彼は聖遺物を凌辱した.

(***in***) ***despite of*** …にもかかわらず, をものともせず ▪ He seized my hand *in despite of* my efforts to the contrary. そうさせまいと私が努力したにもかかわらず, 彼は私の手をとらえた. ☞despite my efforts または in spite of my efforts がふつう.

destine /déstɪn/ 動 (***be***) ***destined for*** **1** (ある目的・用途)に予定されている ▪ He *is destined for* the church. 彼は牧師になることになっている ▪ This room *is destined for* the reception of nobles. この部屋は貴族の接待にあてられる.

2 …向け[行き]である ▪ These goods *are destined for* Europe. この品はヨーロッパ向けである ▪ This ship *is destined for* Boston. この船はボストン行きだ.

(***be***) ***destined to*** [***to*** *do*] …に[するように]運命うけられて(いる) ▪ He *is destined to* the gallows. 彼は絞首刑になる運命にある ▪ English seems *destined to* be the universal language. 英語は世界語になる運命にあるように思われる.

destitute /déstətjù:t/ 形 ***be destitute of*** …を欠く, がない ▪ Some officials *are* entirely *destitute of* good feeling. 人に対する同情の全くない役人もいる ▪ Some people *are destitute of* the necessaries of life. 生活必需品を欠いている人もある.

destroy /dɪstrɔ́ɪ/ 動 ***destroy*** *oneself* 自滅[自殺]する ▪ Harry will have *destroyed himself* by then. ハリーはそのときまでに自殺しているだろう.

destruction /dɪstrʌ́kʃən/ 名 ***be*** *a person's* ***destruction*** 人を滅ぼす ▪ Gambling *was his destruction*. 賭博で彼は身を滅ぼした.

destructive /dɪstrʌ́ktɪv/ 形 ***be destructive of*** [***to***] …を破壊する(ような), を害する ▪ Drinking *is destructive of* his life. 飲酒は彼の命を滅ぼす ▪ The habit *is destructive to* health. その習慣は健康に有害だ.

desuetude /déswɪtjù:d/ 名 ***fall*** [***pass***] ***into desuetude*** 《文》(習慣・風俗が)すたれる ▪ Those customs have *fallen into desuetude*. それらの習慣はすたれてしまった.

detach /dɪtǽtʃ/ 動 ***detach*** *oneself* ***from*** …から離れる ▪ She wanted to *detach herself from* her lover. 彼女は恋人と離れたいと思った.

detail /dɪtéɪl, dí:teɪl/ 名 ***down to the last detail*** 細大もらさずに ▪ We gave him the account *down to the last detail*. 我々は彼に細大もらさず説明してあげた.

give (***a***) ***full detail of*** …を詳説する ▪ He *gave full detail of* the accident. 彼はその事故の一部始終を語った.

go [***enter***] ***into detail***(***s***) 詳細にわたって論じる; 項目を一々あげる ▪ We had to *go into detail*. 詳細に述べなければならなかった.

in detail **1**《軍》各個に, かたっぱしから ▪ He beat his enemies *in detail.* 彼は敵を各個に打ち破った. ☞detail《軍》「分隊」.
2 詳細に; 項目ごとに, 一部分ずつ ▪ He told the matter *in detail.* 彼はその事件を詳細に語った.

in every detail あらゆる細部にわたって ▪ It is complete *in every detail.* それはあらゆる細部にわたって完全である.

the gory detail《戯》あからさまな詳細 ▪ A reader asked me about *the "gory details"* of writing this book. 一人の読者が本書執筆の「あからさまな詳細」について私に尋ねた.

D

detect /dɪtékt/ 動 ***detect*** *a person* ***in*** (***the act of***) *doing* 人の現行犯を見つける ▪ He *was detected in the act of stealing.* 彼は窃盗の現行犯で見つかった.

detention /dɪténʃən/ 名 ***under detention*** 拘留されて, 拘禁中 ▪ He is *under detention.* 彼は拘留されている.

determination /dɪtə̀ːrmənéɪʃən/ 名 ***come to a determination*** 決心をする ▪ The boy *came to a determination* to run away. 少年は脱走する決心をした.

determine /dɪtə́ːrmən/ 動 ***be determined on*** …することに決心する[決める] ▪ They *were determined on* a fourth appeal to the Pope. 彼らは法王に4度目の訴えをすることに決めた.

be determined to *do* …することに決心する[決める] ▪ I'*m determined* not *to* sleep upstairs. 私は階上で寝ないことに決めた.

detestation /dìːtestéɪʃən/ 名 ***be in detestation*** 忌みきらわれている ▪ They *were in detestation.* 彼らは忌みきらわれていた.

have [***hold***]***... in detestation*** …をひどくきらう ▪ I *have* the custom *in detestation.* 私はその習慣が大きらいだ.

detour /díːtʊər/ 名 ***make a detour*** 回り道をする ▪ The main road was blocked, so we had to *make a detour.* 本街道が通行止めになっていたので回り道をしなければならなかった.

detriment /détrəmənt/ 名 ***to the detriment of*** …の不利[損害]になるような[に] ▪ The rumor is greatly *to my detriment.* その噂は私に非常に不利だ ▪ He sits up very late *to the detriment of* his health. 彼は非常に遅くまで起きて健康を害している.

without detriment to …を害することなく ▪ You should study *without detriment to* your health. 健康を害さぬように勉強すべきです.

detrimental /dètrəméntəl/ 形 ***detrimental to*** …に有害な[不利な] ▪ Lack of sleep is *detrimental to* our health. 睡眠不足は健康に害がある.

deuce /djuːs/ 名 ***a deuce of a*** →the DEUCE of a.

a deuce of a mess ひどい混乱 ▪ You must be in *a deuce of a mess* after the tornado. 大竜巻にあった後だから君はもう大変に違いない.

Deuce knows. =God KNOWs.

go to the deuce **1** 滅亡する; 落ちぶれる ▪ He has *gone to the deuce.* 彼は堕落してしまった.
2〚命令文で〛くたばってしまえ! ▪ *Go to the deuce!* くたばってしまえ!

have the deuce to pay あとでひどい目にあう ▪ You'll all *have the deuce to pay.* どいつもこいつもあとでひどい目にあうぞ.

like the deuce《口》猛烈に ▪ It is snowing *like the deuce.* 猛烈に雪が降っている.

play the deuce with《口》…をめちゃめちゃにする, ひどく害する, 苦しめる ▪ He had a strong constitution originally, but he has *played the deuce with* it. 彼は元は体が強かったのだが, すっかりこわしてしまった.

(***the***) ***deuce a*** 決して[少しも]…ない《強い否定》 ▪ *The deuce a* bit I care. ちっともかまわない ▪ *Deuce a* man was present. 一人も出席していなかった.

the deuce and all =the DEVIL and all.

The deuce is in *a person.* 人がほんとにどうかしている ▪ *The deuce is in* them. やつらはほんとにどうかしている.

the deuce is in it if I can't ... 私に…できないでどうする《きっとできる》 ▪ *The deuce is in it if I cannot* read it through. 僕にそれが通読できないでどうする.

the [***a***] ***deuce of a*** 実にひどい, いやな, どえらい; 愉快な ▪ We had *a deuce of a* time. 実に愉快なひと時だった.

(***The***) ***deuce take it!*** 畜生!, しまった!, くそっ! ▪ *The deuce take it!* There goes that bus. 畜生! あのバスが行ってしまう.

Who [***What, Where,*** etc.] ***the deuce ...?*** 一体誰[何, どこ, など]か? ▪ *Who the deuce* are you? 一体君は誰だ ▪ *Where the deuce* is he? 一体あいつはどこにいるのか?

develop /dɪvéləp/ 動 ***develop*** *oneself* 現れてくる; 発展する ▪ Irish history has *developed itself* in a manner which is unique for a country in Western Europe. アイルランドの歴史は西ヨーロッパの国としては特異な様式で現れてきた ▪ Our constitutional system *develops itself* year by year. わが国の立憲制度は年々発展する.

develop a [*one's*] ***piece***《チェス》こまを有利な位置へ持っていく《比喩的にも》 ▪ He was enabled to *develop his* superior *pieces.* 彼は自分の上級のこまを有利な位置に持っていくことができた.

develop *one's* ***game***《チェス》計画を進める, 意図する戦略を実行する ▪ He had no chance of *developing his game.* 彼は自分の戦略を実行する機会がなかった.

developer /dɪvéləpər/ 名 ***a late developer*** 遅咲きの人, 奥手な人 ▪ Thompson passed the entrance examination at the age of 28. He really is *a late developer.* トンプスンは28歳で入試に合格した. 彼は実に遅咲きの人物だ.

device /dɪváɪs/ 名 ***leave*** *a person* ***to his***

own devices →LEAVE a person to himself.

devil /dévəl/ 图 ***a bit of the devil*** 少しばかりの悪魔の性(さが) ▪ He has *a bit of the devil* in him. 彼は(女性にかけては)ちょっと油断のならない男である.

a* [*one, the*] *devil of a 《口》実にひどい, いやな, どえらい; 愉快な ▪ My new boyfriend is *a devil of a* fellow. 今度のボーイフレンドはそれは愉快な男性なのよ ▪ Being governor of New York is *one devil of a* job. ニューヨークの知事であることは実に大変な仕事である ▪ It ran downhill at *the devil of a* rate. それはひどい速度で山を走りおりた ▪ She had *a devil of a* temper. 彼女はひどく不きげんだった.

***a devil with the women* [*men*]** 女たらし[浮気女] ▪ She is *a devil with the men.* 彼女は浮気女だ.

and the devil knows what その他何やかんや ▪ He sells knives, forks, *and the devil knows what.* 彼はナイフやフォークその他何やかんやを売っている.

(*as*) *black as the devil* →(as) BLACK as a crow.

(*as*) *drunk as the devil* →(as) DRUNK as a fiddler.

as the devil hates holy water (悪魔が聖水をきらうように)ひどくきらって ▪ I hate Mr. Smith, *as the devil hates holy water.* 私は(悪魔が聖水をきらうように)スミス氏が大きらいだ.

as the devil looks over Lincoln (悪魔がリンカンを見渡しているように)きびしい顔をして ▪ She looked at me, *as the Devil looked over Lincoln.* 彼女は非常に険悪な顔をして私を見た. ☞Lincoln Cathedral の外部にある怪異な悪魔の彫刻に関連がある.

as the devil loves holy water (悪魔が聖水を好むように)ひどくきらいで ▪ We love the tax collector *as the devil loves holy water.* 我々は収税吏が大きらいだ. ☞現在は as the DEVIL hates holy water を多く用いる.

Be a devil! 《英口》(人が非とするようなことを)さあ[思い切って]やってみろ!《そそのかす言葉》 ▪ Come on, Jack, *be a devil* and have another cup. さあ, ジャック, 思い切ってもう1杯やれ.

be a devil for …狂である ▪ He *is a devil for* gambling. 彼はギャンブル狂である.

***be a devil to work* [*at fighting*]** 猛烈な働き手[闘士]である ▪ He *is a devil to work.* 彼は非常な働き手である.

be devil may care むとんちゃくである, のんきである ▪ The young man *was devil may care.* その青年はのんきであった.

***be full of the devil* [*it*]** **1** いたずらである ▪ That boy *is full of the devil.* あの少年はいたずらっ子だ. **2** 嘘八百である, 大ぼらを吹いている ▪ You could tell by her laugh she *was full of it.* 彼女の大笑いで彼女がでたらめを言っているのが分かるよ.

***be the devil* (*of it*)** 大難事だ, 厄介至極だ, たまらない ▪ That *is the devil of it.* そこが困った点だ ▪ To be cross-examined *is the* very *devil.* 根掘り葉掘り尋問されては全くたまらない.

Better the devil one knows than the devil one doesn't. 《諺》知っている悪魔のほうが知らない(もっと悪いかもしれない)悪魔よりもよい,「知らぬ仏よりなじみの鬼」.

between the devil and the deep* [《古》*dead*] (*blue*) *sea 進退両難に陥って ▪ I'm *between the devil and the deep sea*; I don't know what to say. 私は進退きわまっている. どう言ってよいかわからない. ☞《聖》*Luke* 8. 26 ff. のブタの群れと Legion と呼ばれた悪魔の群れとの話によるらしい.

devil a →(the) DEVIL a.

dine* [*sup*] *with the devil →When you dine [sup] with the DEVIL, use a long spoon.

(*Each man for himself and*) (*the*) *devil take the hindmost* [*hindermost*]. (めいめいわれがちで)おくれた者は鬼に食われろ(とばかり)《利己的な競争の標語》 ▪ It was *everybody for himself and devil take the hindmost.* それは早い者勝ちであった ▪ We can't be bothered with him at this stage—it's *devil take the hindmost.* 我々はこの段階で彼にわずらわされてはいられない—誰もが我先になのだ.

find the devil's golden tooth 《米》悪魔の犬歯を見つける《この犬歯はすべての金属を黄金に変える力がある》 ▪ One would think he'd *found the devil's golden tooth.* 人は彼が悪魔の犬歯を見つけたとでも思うだろう. ☞Massachusetts でよく用いる句; 海賊 Kidd がこのような悪魔の犬歯を得たという話による.

for the devil of it たわむれに, いたずらに ▪ The boy threw a stone at the dog just *for the devil of it.* 少年はただいたずらにその犬に石を投げただけだ.

give the devil his due 悪い人にも良いところを認めてやる[認めて公平にする]; (悪人をも)公平に評する ▪ To *give the devil his due*, Old Smith, miser as he is, has been generous to me. (悪人ながらも)公平に言えば, スミス老人はけちんぼうだが私にはいつも気前がよかった ▪ *Give the devil his due.* 《諺》盗人にも三分の理あり.

go to the devil 《口》〚命令文で〛くたばってしまえ! うるさい! 行っちまえ!《きわめて強烈な反対・拒絶・追放の文句》 ▪ *Go to the devil*! くたばっちまえ! ▪ Tom told her to *go to the devil.* トムは彼女に行っちまえと言った.

have a devil of a time 《口》ひどくつらい目にあう (→a DEVIL of a) ▪ I've just been *having a devil of a time* at the dentist's. たった今歯医者で痛い目にあって来たところだ.

have the devil's own job (…するのに)骨を折る, 一苦労する (*doing, to do*) ▪ I *had the devil's own job getting* answers to those questions. その問題に答えを得るのに一苦労した.

He that sups with the devil must have a long spoon. 《諺》悪人に接するときはよほど用心しなければならない.

hold a candle to the devil →CANDLE.

kick up the devil's delight 《口》大騒ぎを起こ

す ▪ If anybody says a word against him, I am going to *kick up the devil's delight.* もし誰かが彼を一言でも非難したら, 私は大暴れしてやる.

lack devil 闘志がない ▪ He is no coward, but *lacks devil.* 彼は決して臆病ではないが, 闘志がない.

lay the devil (呼び出した)悪魔を鎮める (↔raise the DEVIL 1) ▪ It is easier to raise *the devil* than to *lay* him. 悪魔を呼び出すほうが, 鎮めるよりも易しい.

D

like the [***a***] ***devil/like devils*** (悪魔のように)激しく, 巧みに; 極度に ▪ They will fight *like devils.* 彼らは激しく戦うであろう ▪ In the race he ran *like the* [*a*] *devil.* その競走で彼は猛烈に走った.

Needs must when the devil drives. →NEEDS.

paint the devil blacker than he is 悪者を実際より[輪をかけて]悪く言う ▪ Indeed he is bad, but there's no need to *paint the devil blacker than he is.* 確かに彼は悪い奴だが実際より悪く言う必要はない.

play devil's advocate (議論を深めるため)故意に反対の立場をとる ▪ Allow me to *play devil's advocate* and express some skepticism. 故意に反対の立場をとって懐疑的な態度を表すことを許してくれ.

play the devil with 《口》…をめちゃめちゃにする, さんざんに荒らす[こわす] ▪ The malaria has *played the devil with* his health. マラリアが彼の健康をすっかりこわしてしまった ▪ The auditor *played the devil with* the office. 会計検査官は事務所をめちゃめちゃにかきまわした.

play [***act*** (***as***)] (***the***) ***devil's advocate*** →the devil's ADVOCATE.

play the devil's tattoo →beat the devil's TATTOO.

Pull devil, pull baker! →PULL[2].

pull the devil by the tail 《口》困窮している ▪ He is always *pulling the devil by the tail.* 彼はいつも金に窮している.

raise the devil **1** 悪魔を呼び出す (↔lay the DEVIL) ▪ Do not *raise the devil* you cannot lay. 鎮めることのできない悪魔を呼び出すな.
2《口》大騒ぎを起こす; 大いに浮かれ騒ぐ (= raise CAIN) ▪ He was going to *raise the devil.* 彼は大騒ぎを起こそうとしていた.

Talk [***Speak***] ***of the devil, and he will*** [***is sure to***] ***appear.*** 《諺》噂をすれば影とやら《前半だけ言うことが多い》 ▪ Well, *talk of the devil*; here is old Jackson. ほんとに噂をすれば影とやら, ジャクソンじいさんが来た.

Talk of the devil and you'll hear the flutter of his wings. 《諺》噂をすれば影とやら.

(***the***) ***devil a*** 決して[全く, 少しも]…ない《強い否定》 ▪ *The devil a* penny they have left me. 彼らは私にただの1ペニーも残してくれなかった ▪ *Devil a* bit I care. 私は少しもかまわない ▪ *The devil a* one I found. 一つも見つからなかった.

The devil alone knows. 誰も知らない, 全くわからない ▪ *The devil alone knows* what will happen. どんなことが起こるか誰にもわからない.

the devil and all すべての(悪い)もの, いまいましいもの全部; (ときに)ひどく悪いもの ▪ He may get *the devil and all* of money. 彼は金を全部そっくり得るかもしれない ▪ Rheumatism has taken possession of your right arm, which would be *the devil and all.* 君の右腕がリューマチにかかっているが, これは全くの不幸となるであろう.

the devil (***and all***) ***to do*** 大騒ぎ ▪ Then there was *the devil and all to do*: spoons, plates, and dishes flew about the room like mad. それから大騒ぎが起こった. スプーンや小皿・大皿などが盛んに部屋中を飛んだ.

the devil (***and all***) ***to pay*** あとのたたり, あとのひどい報い ▪ If you don't pay him at once, there'll be *the devil and all to pay.* 彼にすぐ支払わなければ, あとでひどい目にあうだろう. ☞悪魔との取引では必ず悪魔に支払いをしなければならなくなるという話から.

The devil can quote [***cite***] ***Scripture for his purpose.*** →SCRIPTURE.

The devil finds work for idle hands. 《諺》悪魔は仕事のない人に仕事を見つけてくれる,「小人閑居して不善を為す」.

The devil he is [***you are,*** etc.]***!*** 彼は[あなたは, など]断じてそうでない ▪ *The devil it is.* 断じてそうではない.

the devil incarnate 悪魔の化身(のような人) ▪ Abraham Lincoln was regarded by white Southerners as *the Devil incarnate.* エイブラハム・リンカンは南部の白人から悪魔の化身とみなされていた.

the devil is in it (***if***) ***I can't…*** (私にできなければ何か故障があるのだ, から)私にできないでどうする ▪ *The devil is in it if I can't* finish it. 私にそれを仕上げることができないでどうする.

The devil is not so black as he is painted. 《諺》どんな悪い人でも評判ほど悪くはないものだ.

The devil looks after his own. 《諺》悪魔はわが子の面倒を見る,「憎まれっ子世に憚(はばか)る」.

the devil of a →a DEVIL of a.

the devil of it さらに悪いことには ▪ He lost his notebook, and *the devil of it* was that it contained his homework. 彼はノートをなくした. が, さらに困ったことにそのノートには彼の宿題が書いてあったのだ.

the devil rebuking sin 自分のことを棚に上げて人を笑う ▪ *The devil rebuking sin* with a vengeance! He is hardly sober himself. 自分のことは棚に上げて人を笑うとはこのことだ. 自分はまずしらふでないくせに.

The devil rides on a fiddlestick. から騒ぎをする ▪ Heigh, heigh! *The devil rides upon a fiddlestick*; what's the matter? ほーい, ほーい. から騒ぎをやってるな. どうしたのだ.

(***The***) ***Devil take …!*** …は悪魔にでも食われてしまえ! ▪ *Devil take* them! やつらなど悪魔に食われてしまえ!

the devil to pay (***and no pitch hot***) あとのたたり, あとの災い (= the DEVIL (and all) to pay)

▪ If you're really in trouble it's "*the devil to pay and no pitch hot.*" 本当に困ったときに,「えらいことになった」という.

The devil's children* (*have*) *the devil's luck. 《諺》悪魔の子には悪魔の運がついている,「憎まれっ子世に憚(はばか)る」.

the devil's in the details 物事の細部はその最も扱いにくい[疑わしい]面である ▪ Nick has always known that *the devil's in the details.* 物事の細部はその最も扱いにくい面であることをニックはかねてから知っていた.

the devil's own job 非常に難しいこと ▪ I had *the devil's own job* getting here. 私はここへ来るのに非常に苦労をした ▪ It is *the devil's own job* to earn enough money to live. 十分な生活費をかせぐのは非常に難しい.

the devil's* (*own*) *luck*/ *the luck of the devil →LUCK[1].

to the devil with 《口》…なんかどうでもよい ▪ I've had enough! *To the devil with* all this! もうたくさんだ! こんなことはどうでもいいんだ.

What* [*Who, When, Where,* etc.] *the devil …? 〚wh 語を強調して〛一体何[誰, いつ, どこ, どうして, なぜ]…? ▪ *What the devil* makes you cry? 一体どうしてあなたは泣いているのですか ▪ *When the devil* did he go? 一体いつ彼は行ったのですか.

when the devil is blind (悪魔が盲目になるとき, とは)決して…ない (never) ▪ They will bring it *when the devil is blind.* 彼らは永久にそれを持ってこないだろう.

When you dine* [*sup*] *with the devil, use a long spoon. 悪魔と食事をするときには長いスプーンを使え《悪人と取引するときには用心しなさい》.

whip the devil round (規則・規約の網)をくぐる ▪ They *whipped the devil round* the agreement by devious means. 彼らはずるい手を使って協定の網をくぐった. ☞次項も参照.

whip the devil round* [*around*] *the stump 《米》口実や言い逃れを作って困難やジレンマを逃れる, 克服する; まっすぐな手段でできないことをごまかしや手管(てくだ)でなし遂げる ▪ There you are now *whipping the devil round the stump.* そら, あなたは口実を作って窮地を逃れようとしてるじゃありませんか ▪ It was characteristic that he could *whip the devil round the stump.* 彼はまっすぐな手段でできないことを手管でなし遂げられるという特色があった.

wish** a person **at the devil 人がくたばればよい(と思う), 人が行ってしまえばよい(と思う) ▪ I *wish* the little animal *at the devil.* その小動物がいなくなればよいと思う.

with the devil at** one's **heels 全速力で ▪ He ran out *with the devil at his heels.* 彼は全速力で走り出た.

devoid /dɪvɔ́ɪd/ 形 ***devoid of*** …のない, 欠けた ▪ He is *devoid of* common sense. 彼は常識がない.

devoir /dəvwɑ́ːr/ 名 ***do** one's **devoir*** 本分を尽くす; 最善を尽くす ▪ Did my brother *do his devoir* as a gallant knight? 兄は勇敢な騎士としての本分を尽くしましたか.

pay* [*do, tender*] *one's devoirs to (人)に敬意を表する ▪ He *paid his devoirs to* Lady Poe. 彼はポウ夫人を訪ねて敬意を表した.

devote /dɪvóʊt/ 動 ***(be) devoted to*** **1** …に専心して[ふけって](いる) ▪ He *is devoted to* yachting. 彼はヨットに熱中している.
2《米》…だけにあてがわれて(いる), の専用[専有]で(ある) ▪ This gallery *is devoted* solely *to* ukiyoe. この画廊は浮世絵ばかりだ ▪ The magazine *is devoted to* children. その雑誌は子供向けだ.

devote oneself to …に一身をささげる, 専念する, 凝る ▪ He *devotes himself to* the study of literature. 彼は文学の研究に専念している ▪ The magazine *devotes itself to* the furtherance of theological learning. その雑誌は神学の発展に尽くしている.

devotion /dɪvóʊʃən/ 名 ***be at** one's **devotions*** お祈りをしている ▪ The priest *was at his devotions.* 司祭はお祈りをしていた.

devour /dɪváʊər/ 動 ***be devoured with*** (強い感情)で一杯である, でたまらない ▪ Mother *was devoured with* worry when I didn't come home at the usual time. 私がいつもの時間に帰らなかったとき母は心配で気が気でなかった.

***devour the way* [*course*]** 《詩》道を急ぐ; (馬が)ぐんぐん進む ▪ The horse *devoured the course* before him. 馬はぐんぐん進んだ. ☞<Ｆ dévorer l'espace.

dexterous /dékstərəs/ 形 ***be dexterous in* [*at*] *doing*** …するのがうまい ▪ He *is dexterous in handling* men. 彼は人扱いがうまい.

dial /dáɪəl/ 動 ***dial 911*** 《米》911番にかける ▪ I had to *dial 911* last night. 私は昨夜911番にかけなければならなかった. ☞米国の911番は(警察・消防署の)緊急電話番号.

dialogue, 《米》**dialog** /dáɪəlɔ̀ːg|-lɔ̀g/ 名 ***dialogue of the deaf*** 互いに相手の意見を聞こうとしない議論 ▪ The dialogue, when and if it happens, will largely remain a *dialogue of the deaf.* 対話は, もし行われたとしても, おおむねてんで勝手な対話にとどまるだろう. ☞Ｆ dialogue des sourds のなぞり.

diameter /daɪǽmətər/ 名 ***in diameter*** 直径が ▪ The stalk is an inch *in diameter.* その茎は直径1インチです.

diamond /dáɪmənd|dáɪə-/ 名 ***a diamond in the rough*/*a rough diamond*** 天然のままの磨いていないダイヤ; 磨けば光る荒削りの人, 磨かぬ玉 ▪ I should call him *a diamond in the rough.* 彼はダイヤの原石とでも言いましょうか.

a diamond of the first water (光沢・透明度が)最上等のダイヤ; 第一級の人[物] ▪ He was *a diamond of the first water.* 彼は最高級の人物であった.

diamond cut diamond (機知・悪知恵などで両者相劣らず)しのぎを削るいい勝負, 火花を散らす知恵比べ ▪ You should have heard them disputing; it was *diamond cut diamond.* 彼らが論争するのを君に聞

D

かせたかったよ. 火花を散らす知恵比べだった.

say it with diamonds 想いをダイヤモンドでお伝えください (→Say it with FLOWERs!).

diarrhea /dàɪərí:ə|-ríə/ 名 ***have verbal diarrhea/have diarrhea of the mouth*** 《口》 言葉の下痢にかかっている, しゃべりすぎる ▪ He is a nice guy but he's *got verbal diarrhea.* 彼は好漢だがしゃべりすぎだ.

D

diary /dáɪəri/ 名 ***keep a diary*** 日記をつける ▪ I'm determined to *keep a diary.* 私は日記をつけることに決めた.

diastole /daɪǽstəli/ 名 ***systole and diastole*** 心臓の収縮と膨張; (潮などの)差し引き ▪ There must be a *systole and diastole* in all inquiry. あらゆる調査には差し引きがなければならない.

dibs /dɪbz/ 名 ***have* [*put*] (*one's*) *dibs on*** 《俗》 …の分け前を要求する; を次に使用する権利を主張する ▪ I *put* (*my*) *dibs on* the magazine. 今度は僕がその雑誌を読む番だ ▪ I *have dibs on* riding the bicycle. 今度は僕がその自転車に乗る番だ.

dice[1] /daɪs/ 名 ***at dice*** ばくち[さいころ遊び]で ▪ He lost his fortune *at dice.* 彼はばくちで財産を失った.

in the dice 起こりそうで, ありそうで ▪ It is hardly *in the dice.* ほとんど起こりそうにない.

load the dice (さいころに鉛を詰めて特定の数が出るようにする, から)結果をゆがめる, (人を)有利[不利]な立場に置く, 一方的な議論をする ▪ The victim has *loaded the dice* against himself by previous actions. 被害者は以前の行動によって自分を不利な立場に置いた ▪ Everybody knows that *the dice are loaded.* みんながその結果がゆがめられている[いかさまである]ことを分かっている.

no dice 《俗》 **1** 不成功で ▪ I tried to sell him an insurance policy but it was *no dice.* 彼に保険証券を売ろうとしたが成功しなかった.
2 (要求を断るときに)もう降りる, だめだ ▪ Sorry, but I'm not interested in that, *no dice.* 申し訳ないが, それには興味がないんで, もう降りるよ.

play at dice さいころ遊びをする, ばくちをする ▪ He does not *play at dice.* 彼はさいころ遊びはしない.

dice[2] /daɪs/ 動 ***dice with death*** 死の危険を冒す ▪ He *diced with death* by driving his car so fast. 彼は命がけで車を疾走させた.

dick[1] /dɪk/ 名 ***take one's dick* (*that*)** 《俗》 …と確言する, 言明する ▪ I'll *take my dick* I heard him say so. 彼がそう言うのを聞いたと言明します. ☞dick = declaration.

up to dick 《俗》 **1** 標準的な, すぐれた, 適切な ▪ The city is *up to dick* in the matter of lunches. その町はランチの点ではすぐれている.
2 丈夫な ▪ He is not *up to dick.* 彼は病気である. ☞dick = declaration (商品の価値確言).

dick[2] /dɪk/ 名 ***a clever dick*** = a smart ALEC(K).

dickens /díkənz/ 名 ***go to the dickens*** 《俗》 滅亡する, 破産する, 落ちぶれる ▪ Business *went to the dickens.* 商売はつぶれた. ☞dickens = devil.

play the dickens with 《俗》 …をめちゃくちゃにする, ひっくり返す ▪ The child has *played the dickens with* my papers. 子供が書類をめちゃめちゃにしてしまった ▪ They *played the dickens with* Rome. 彼らはローマを破壊した.

That dickens! おやっ!, 畜生!

the dickens of a ひどい ▪ He made *the dickens of a* row about it. 彼はそのことで実に大騒ぎした.

What* [*Why,* etc.] *the dickens ...? 一体 …? ▪ *What the dickens* do you want? 一体君は何がほしいのか ▪ *Why the dickens* don't these people go to bed? この人々は一体なぜ就寝しないのか.

dicky /díki/ 形 ***all dicky with*** 《英俗》 …はすっかりだめで ▪ It is *all dicky with* Dick. ディックはもうだめだ.

dictate /díkteɪt/ 名 ***follow the dictates of*** …の命じるところに従う ▪ She *followed the dictates of* her heart and married him. 彼女は心のよしと思うところに従って彼と結婚した.

dictation /dɪktéɪʃən/ 名 ***at the dictation of*** …の指示[命令]で, の口授[口述]によって ▪ The terms were *at his own dictation.* 条件は彼自身の指示によるものであった ▪ The sketches were written *at his dictation.* その短編は彼の口述で書かれた.

***write from* [*to, under*] *a person's* dictation/take *a person's* dictation** 人の口述を書き取る ▪ I *took his dictation* all morning. 午前中ずっと彼の口述を書き取った.

dictionary /díkʃənèri|-ʃənəri/ 名 ***speak like a dictionary*** 博学な話しぶりである ▪ He *speaks like a dictionary* on the subject. その問題については彼は博学な話しぶりをする.

swallow the dictionary 普通でない(特に長い)語を使う ▪ Don't start to *swallow the dictionary* all at once. 急に長い語を使いだすのはよしてくれ.

did /dɪd/ 動 **(*Well,*) *did you* [*anybody*] *ever!*** 《口》 まあ驚いた! ▪ *Well, did you ever!* Old Miss Carter's got married. まあ驚いた! カーターさんが結婚したんだって ▪ "*Did anybody ever!*" said she. 「これは驚いた」と彼女は言った. ☞"Did you [anybody] ever hear or see the like?" の縮まったもの.

(*Well,*) *I never did.* →I NEVER did!

diddly /dídəli/ 名 ***not ...* (*jack*) *diddly/not ... diddly-squat* [*diddly-shit*]** 《米俗》 ちっとも …しない ▪ I do*n't* owe her *jack diddly squat*! 僕は彼女にびた一文も借りていない ▪ Peter did*n't* say *diddly-squat* about Jane. ピーターはジェインのことは何も言わなかった.

dido /dáɪdoʊ/ 名 ***cut* [*kick*] *up* (*one's*) *dido*(*es*)** 《俗》 ふざけ散らす, 騒ぎ回る ▪ They will be *cutting up didoes.* 彼らはふざけ散らしているだろう ▪ What a *dido* he does *kick up*! 彼はなんと騒ぎ回ることだろう!

die[1] /daɪ/ 名 **(*as*) *level as a die*** →LEVEL[1].

(as) straight [true] as a die 非常にまっすぐ[誠実]で ▪The park is full of large trees *as straight as a die.* 公園には非常にまっすぐな大木が林立している ▪He is *as true as a die.* 彼は非常に誠実だ. ☞die「(建築の)台胴(円柱下部の方形台座の腰羽目の部分)」.

(be) upon a [the] die 一か八かの状態で(ある), 危機で(ある), がかけられて(いる) ▪Here *is* more *upon the die*—a kingdom. ここではもっと大きいものが危機にある—王国だ ▪My life *is upon the die.* 私の生死がかかっている.

set ... upon the die ...を賭ける, 一か八かの状態にする ▪He *set* life and fortune *upon the die.* 彼は生命と財産を賭けた.

The die is cast [thrown]. 《諺》さいは投げられた《もうあとには引けない, ことは既に決した》 ▪*The die is cast.* I can't go back. さいは投げられた. もうあとへは引けない. ☞Caesar が Rubicon 川を渡る時に言ったとされる.

die[2] /daɪ/ 動 ***die a dog's death*** →DIE like a dog.

die by** one's **own hand 自殺する ▪The boy *died by his own hand.* その少年は自殺した.

die daily 霊的に日々に死ぬ, 毎日死ぬほどに悩む (《聖》*1 Cor.* 15. 31) ▪He *dies daily.* 彼は毎日死ぬほどに悩んでいる.

die game →GAME.

die hard なかなか滅びない; (あくまで頑強に抵抗して)なかなか死なない ▪Superstitions *die hard.* 迷信はなかなか絶えない ▪The soldiers *died hard*, each fighting to the last. 兵士たちはみな最後まで頑強に戦った.

die in a ditch →DITCH.

die in** one's **bed ベッドの上で(老齢か病気で)死ぬ (↔ die in a DITCH) ▪Very few persecutors have ever *died in their beds.* ベッドの上で死んだ迫害者は今まで非常に少なかった.

die in** one's **boots [shoes] **1** 非業の死を遂げる; (特に)絞首刑になる ▪He is said to have *died in his boots.* 彼は非業の死をとげたそうだ.
2 働きながら[執務中]死ぬ (= die in HARNESS) ▪I'd like to *die in my boots.* 私は現役のままで死にたいものだ.

die in harness →HARNESS.

die in the last ditch →DITCH.

die laughing 死ぬほど笑う ▪I nearly *died laughing.* 私はほとんど笑い死にしそうだった.

die like a dog/die a dog's death みじめな死に方をする ▪If I *die like a dog*, I'll die in my duty. 非業の死を遂げるなら, 義務を果たしながら死ぬ.

die of laughing →DIE with laughing.

die rich 金を残して死ぬ ▪Fools live poor to *die rich.* 愚者は食う物も食わずに金を残して死ぬ.

die the death of →DEATH.

***die with** one* (秘密などを)生涯[死ぬまで]漏らさない[守る] ▪His secret *died with* him. 彼は自分の秘密を死ぬまで漏らさなかった.

die with** one's **boots on =DIE in one's boots.

die with dignity 自然死する《医療機械で延命される, に対して》 ▪I prefer to *die with dignity* rather than be kept alive by breathing machines. 呼吸機械で延命されるより自然死の方がよい.

die with [of] laughing 笑い死にする, 笑いこける ▪The story made you *die with laughing.* その話はあなたを笑いこけさせた.

***die within** one* 心の中になくなる ▪His hopes *died within* him. 彼には希望がすっかりなくなった.

die worth (a million) (100万ポンド)残して死ぬ ▪He *died worth* 3 millions. 彼は300万ポンド残して死んだ.

die young 若死にする ▪Whom the gods love *die young.* 《諺》才子短命. ☞ギリシャの新喜劇の作家 Menander (メナンドロス)の言葉から.

I almost died/I just about died 《口》死ぬかと思うほどびっくりした[笑った, 狼狽した] ▪*I almost died* when he said he had married. 彼が結婚したと言ったとき死ぬかと思うほどびっくりした ▪*I just about died* laughing when I saw this picture. この絵を見たとき死ぬかと思うほど笑った.

I thought I should have died. おかしくて笑い死ぬかと思った. ☞of laughing が略されている.

(I) wish [hope] I may die./(I) hope to die. 《口》ほんとだよ ▪I didn't mean to cheat you. *Hope to die*! 君をだますつもりはなかった. ほんとだよ.

I wish I may die if 決して...ない (never)《強い否定》 ▪*I wish I may die if* I like it. 私はそれは決して好きでない.

Never say die! 弱音を吐くな, くたばるな; しっかりやれ ▪Cheer up, old man—*never say die!* おい君, 元気を出せ—くたばるな.

to die for 《口》素晴らしい, 非常に魅力的な, (物が)ほしくてたまらない ▪Kate has drop-dead looks and a voice *to die for.* ケイトは目を奪うような美貌と素晴らしい声をしている ▪The dessert is *to die for.* デザートがほしくてたまらない ▪My favorite is the sesame chicken, it's *to die for*! 私のお気に入りはセサミチキンだ, たまらなくおいしい.

would rather die (than do) 《口》(...するくらいなら)死んだほうがましだ《絶対いやだ》 ▪I'*d rather die than* say sorry. すみませんと言うくらいなら死んだほうがましだ.

diet[1] /dáɪət/ 名 ***keep diet*** →take DIET.

on a diet 規定食に制限されて ▪I'll go *on a diet.* 規定食にします ▪No cake for me, thank you! I am *on a diet.* お菓子はけっこうです. ダイエット中ですから.

put ... on a diet (患者)に規定食を取らせることにする ▪The doctor *put* the patient *on a* special *diet.* 医者は患者に特別な食事を取らせることにした.

put ... to a diet (医学上・刑罰上)...に規定食を取らせるようにする ▪He *was* put into prison and *put to his diet.* 彼は投獄され, 規定食を取らされた. ☞Ｆ mettre à la diète のなぞり.

take [keep] diet (養生のため)規定食を取る[ずっと

取る] ▪ He *keeps diet.* 彼は規定食を取っている. ☞Ⓕ observer une diète のなぞり.

diet[2] /dáɪət/ 動 ***diet** oneself **on*** …食を守る, 食事を…に規定する ▪ He *dieted himself on* vegetables. 彼は菜食を守った[食事を野菜に制限した].

differ /dífər/ 動 ***agree to differ*** →AGREE.

I beg to differ (with you). 失礼ですが私は意見がちがいます ▪ England has the worst climate.—*I beg to differ.* イングランドは気候が最も悪い—失礼ですが私はそうは思いません.

difference /dífərəns/ 名 ***bury [sink] the differences*** 不和・意見の相違などを忘れる ▪ We *buried our differences.* 私たちは不和を水に流した.

have a difference 意見の不一致がある ▪ They have not *had* even *one difference.* 彼らはただの一度も意見の不一致があったことはない.

let it make no difference それはかまわない ▪ I will *let it make no difference.* それは全くかまわない.

make a difference **1** 相違を生じる, 形勢を変える (*to*) ▪ A year or two will *make a difference.* 1, 2年で相違が生じる《違ってくる》 ▪ Does it *make* any *difference to* him whether he lives in the city or the country? 都会に住むのと田舎に住むのとで何か彼にとって違うところがあるか.

2 重要である ▪ It *makes a* great *difference* which way you go. あなたがどの道を行くかは非常に重要である.

3 差別をつける, 差別扱いする (*between*) ▪ She *makes a difference between* her own children and her stepchildren. 彼女は実の子とまま子とを差別して扱っている.

make all the difference 大変な差[雲泥の差]が生じる ▪ A little perseverance *makes all the difference* between success and failure. 少しの忍耐で成功と失敗という大変な差が生じる.

make no [little] difference **1** どうでもよい, 少しも[たいして]重要ではない, 少しも[たいして]問題ではない ▪ Success or failure *makes little difference* to me. 成否は私にはどうでもよい ▪ It *makes no difference* to me whether he comes or not. 彼が来るか来ないかは私には全く問題ではない.

2 少しも[ほとんど]差別をつけない ▪ She *makes no difference* between her son and her stepson. 彼女は実の息子と義理の息子とを差別扱いしない.

make the difference 違いが生じる, 結果[性質]が異なってくる ▪ Fifteen minutes a day will *make the difference* between starting the game or sitting on the bench. 一日15分でゲームを始めるかベンチに座るかの違いが生じる ▪ Parents *make the difference* for health. 健康については両親で結果が異なってくる.

meet [pay] the difference (株の日付間の)差額を払う ▪ You must *pay the difference* of that stock. その株のさやを払わなければならない.

settle differences 紛争を解決する ▪ Why can't you *settle* your *differences* and be friends again? なぜけんかをやめてまた親しくなれないのか.

split the difference **1** 歩み寄る, 間を取る ▪ You ask 12 shillings, I offer 8; will you *split the difference* and accept ten? 君は12シリングくれと言う, 僕は8シリング出すと言う. 間を取って10シリング取ってくれないか.

2 差額の中間を取る; 残りを等分する ▪ The two of them agreed to *split the difference* and pay $100 each. 彼ら二人は差額の中間を取って各々100ドルずつ払うことに折り合いがついた.

the same difference 《口》何の変わりもないこと (→make no DIFFERENCE) ▪ Whether you go or I go, it's *the same difference.* 君が行こうと私が行こうと, 変わりはないよ.

What's the difference? 《口》何でもないじゃないか, かまわないではないか.

with a difference ちょっと変わった, ひと味違った, 違った意味で ▪ Shaw was an artist *with a difference.* ショーは一風変わった芸術家だった ▪ It is true *with a difference.* それは別の意味で本当である.

different /dífərənt/ 形 ***(as) different as chalk from cheese [day and night, night and day]*** →CHALK[1].

(as) different as day and night [night and day] 全く異なる ▪ Although they are sisters, they are *as different as night and day.* 彼女らは姉妹だけれど, 全く似ていない.

be a different story →STORY.

be different from [《口》***to, than***]…と異なる ▪ My plan *is different from* this. 私の計画はこれとは異なる ▪ Our language *is* very *different to* theirs. 我々の言語は彼らの言語とは非常に違っている.

in a different league リーグが違う; 格が違う (→not in the same LEAGUE as) ▪ We are *in a different league* now. 我々はもう今までとは格が違うのだ.

(It's) different strokes for different folks. 《主に米・諺》人が違えば好み[生き方]も異なる. ☞stroke「ほめ言葉, おだて」.

march to (the beat of) a different drun → MARCH[2].

difficult /dífɪkəlt/ 形 ***be difficult of*** …するのがむずかしい ▪ Pork *is difficult of* digestion. 豚肉は消化しにくい.

The difficult is done at once; the impossible takes a little longer. 《諺》難しいだけのことなら即座にやってのけるが, もっと難しいことにはもう少し時間がかかる.

difficulty /dífɪkəlti/ 名 ***find [have] difficulty in*** …が困難である ▪ I *find difficulty (in)* understanding it. 私はそれを理解するのに骨が折れる ▪ Are you *having difficulty in* geometry? 君は幾何学が難しいか. ☞in は -ing の前では略してもよい.

in difficulties **1** 財政窮乏して ▪ He is *in difficulties.* 彼は金に窮している.

2 (…に)困窮して (*for*) ▪ He is *in difficulties for* men [money]. 彼は人手がなくて[金に]困窮している.

in difficulty 困って ▪ Come to me if you are *in* any *difficulty*. 何か困ったことがあったら，私の所へ来なさい.

make [***raise***] ***difficulties*** [***a difficulty***] **1** 異議を唱える，文句をつける ▪ Her father *raised difficulties* when she said so. 彼女がそう言ったとき，父は異議を唱えた ▪ They never *made* any *difficulties*. 彼らは全然文句はつけなかった.
2 困難を引き起こす.

make no difficulty of [***about***] 文句を言わずに…する ▪ He *made no difficulty of* coming to Rome. 彼は文句を言わずにローマへ来た.

under difficulties 困窮に耐えて ▪ He pursued his studies *under difficulties*. 彼は苦学力行した.

with difficulty かろうじて，やっとのことで (↔with EASE) ▪ He passed the examination *with difficulty*. 彼はやっとのことで試験にパスした.

without (***any***) ***difficulty*** 難なく，楽々と ▪ He accomplished it *without any difficulty*. 彼はそれを楽々となし遂げた.

diffident /dífɪdənt/ 形 ***be diffident of*** …に自信がない ▪ I *am diffident of* my success. 私は成功に自信がない.

dig[1] /dɪg/ 名 ***give*** *a person* ***a dig in the ribs*** 人の横腹をこづく ▪ He *gave* me *a dig in the ribs* with his stick. 彼はステッキで私の横腹をこづいた.

have a dig at **1** (人)に当てこする ▪ He is always *having* [taking] such clever *digs at* the government. 彼はいつも政府を非常に巧みに当てこすっている.
2《口》(物)を試みる ▪ I'm going to *have a dig at* German. ドイツ語をやってみようと思っています.

take a dig at =have a DIG at 1.

dig[2] /dɪg/ 動 ***dig a pit for*** →PIT[1].

dig (***deep***) ***into*** *one's* ***pocket***(***s***) [***savings***] 自分の金を出す ▪ I'll have to *dig into my savings* to buy a new car. 私は新しい車を買うのにお金を出さなければなるまい.

dig *one's* ***feet*** [***heels, toes***] ***in***《口》確固たる立場を取る; 決心・意見・態度を固守する ▪ I had *dug in my feet* over the church I went to. 私は自分の行く教会は絶対変えなかった ▪ He hinted at separation, but the wife *dug her heels in* firmly. 彼は離別をほのめかしたが，妻は頑として応じなかった.

dig for victory《英》戦勝のため食料生産をする ▪ Like our neighbours, we were *digging for victory*. 隣人たちと同じように私たちは勝つために食料生産をしていた.

dig (*oneself*) ***in*** [***into***] **1** 塹壕を掘って入る，穴を掘って隠れる ▪ The officer ordered his men to *dig themselves in*. 将校は部下の兵士に塹壕を掘って入れと命じた.
2《口》地位[地歩]をがっちり固める;《スポーツ》利点[地歩]を守るため慎重にやる ▪ He has *dug* (*himself*) *in* so cleverly there is no moving him. 彼は非常に巧みに地位を固めたからもう彼を動かすことはできない ▪ I *dug myself into* the new job. 私は新しい職にしっかり根を下ろした.

dig *a person* ***in the ribs*** →poke a person in the RIBs.

dig into *one's* ***purse*** 金を使う[与える] ▪ When you have children, you always have to *dig into your purse*. 子供があれば常に金を使わねばならない.

dig open 掘りあける; あばく ▪ They *dug* the grave *open*. 彼らはその墓をあばいた.

dig *oneself* ***out of*** (苦境)からなんとか脱出する ▪ How are you going to *dig yourself out of* this mess? この窮境からどうやって脱出するつもりかね ▪ He *dug himself out of* a mess like that. 彼はあのような困難な状況からなんとか脱出した.

dig up the hatchet →HATCHET.

dig *one's* ***way*** (***in, into, through***) 掘り進んで(入る，…へ入る，抜ける) ▪ He *dug his way through* the hill. 彼は山を掘り抜けた.

One (***really***) ***digs it!***《口》…(本当に)熱中する ▪ Planting vegetables is fun. You'll *really dig it*! 野菜を植えるのは楽しい. 本当に熱中しますよ.

digestion /daɪdʒéstʃən/ 名 ***easy*** [***slow, hard***] ***of digestion*** 消化しやすい[が遅い，しにくい] ▪ Oysters are *hard of digestion*. カキは消化しにくい ▪ Flesh roasted is *slow of digestion*. 焼き肉は消化が遅い.

have a good [***weak***] ***digestion*** 胃が強い[弱い] ▪ To *have a good digestion* is important for good health. 胃が強いことが健康にとって肝要だ.

of easy [***slow, hard***] ***digestion*** 消化しやすい[が遅い，しにくい]; 理解しやすい[が遅い，しにくい] ▪ This condition is *of easy digestion*. この条件は飲み込みやすい.

dignity /dígnəti/ 名 ***be*** [***stand***] ***on*** *one's* ***dignity*** もったいぶる，お高くとまる ▪ He *stood on his dignity* and refused to join in. 彼はお高くとまって加入することを拒絶した.

beneath [***below***] *one's* ***dignity*** 品位を落とす，威信にかかわる ▪ It is *below my dignity* to answer such a rude remark. そのような無礼な言葉に応酬するのは威信にかかわる ▪ I consider it *beneath my dignity* to ask a favor. 私は恩恵を請うことは恥と考える ▪ It fell *beneath Jane's dignity* to ask Thomas to marry her. ジェインはトマスに結婚してくれと言って自分の品位を落とした.

lose *one's* ***dignity*** 威厳を損じる; 笑われる ▪ If you're afraid of *losing your dignity*, you'll never learn to speak English well. 笑われるのを恐れていては英語をうまく話すようにはなれないでしょう.

of dignity 威厳のある，貫録のある ▪ Judge Mason was a person *of dignity*. メイスン判事は貫録のある人だった.

with dignity 厳然として; もったいぶって ▪ He answered *with dignity*. 彼はもったいぶって答えた.

dilemma /dɪlémə, daɪ-/ 名 ***on the horns of a dilemma*** →HORN.

diligence /dílədʒəns/ 名 ***Diligence is the mother of good luck*** [***fortune, hap***].《諺》

勤勉は幸運の母,「稼ぐに追いつく貧乏なし」.

do** one's **diligence/give diligence 最善の努力をする(《聖》*2 Tim.* 4. 9, 21) ▪ *Give diligence* that you may be delivered from him. 彼から救い出されるよう最善の努力をしなさい.

dim /dɪm/ 形 ***a dim religious light*** (神殿・寺院などの)幽玄なあかり, 薄暗がり (Milton, *Il Penseroso* 160) ▪ We stood in the *dim religious light* of these sanctuaries. 我々はこれらの神殿の幽玄な光の中に立った.

dim and distant おぼろげな遠い(昔, など) ▪ The origin of this practice lies in the *dim and distant* past. この慣習の起源はおぼろげな遠い過去にある.

take a dim view of 《口》 **1** …を懐疑的[悲観的]に見る; をおぼつかなく思う ▪ I myself *took a dim view of* my chances of victory. 私自身勝利の見込みはおぼつかないと思っていた.
2 …に反対の見解を持つ; を好まない; を低く評価する ▪ He *took a dim view of* his son-in-law. 彼は義理の息子を軽く見た.

dime /daɪm/ 名 ***a dime a dozen*** 《米口》きわめて多量で; 安くて ▪ Sunday night fishing stories were *a dime a dozen*. 日曜の夜には魚釣りの話が非常にたくさん出た.

drop the* [*a*] *dime on 《米口》…を警察に密告する, たれこむ ▪ He *dropped a dime on* the traces of the murderer. 彼が殺人犯の足取りを警察に密告したのだ.

get off the dime 《口》動き出す ▪ It's time this administration *got off the dime*. 現政府は動き出すべき時期だ.

not be worth a dime 《米口》ほとんど価値がない ▪ His books *are not worth a dime*. 彼の本はほとんど価値がない.

not care a dime 少しも気にしない[かまわない] ▪ I do*n't care a dime*. 僕はちっともかまわない.

not give a dime a dozen 価値なしと思う ▪ I do*n't give* it *a dime a dozen*. それは三文の値うちもないと思う.

on a dime 《米口》非常に狭い所で; すぐに ▪ Tom can turn his car *on a dime*. トムは非常に狭い所で車の向きを変えることができる ▪ His car can stop *on a dime*. 彼の車はすぐに止まることができる.

dimension /dəménʃən/ 名 ***of ... dimensions*** …の大きさの ▪ The millionaire lived in a house *of* great *dimensions*. その百万長者は大邸宅に住んでいる ▪ It is a stadium *of* vast *dimensions*. それは非常に大きなスタジアムだ.

take the dimensions of …の大きさを測る ▪ We *took the dimensions of* a field. 我々は畑の大きさを測った.

the fourth dimension 第四次元《縦横高さの三次元に加えられた時間の次元》 ▪ We exist in *the fourth dimension*, time. 私たちは第四次元, つまり時間の次元に生存している.

diminish /dɪmínɪʃ/ 動 ***hide** one's **diminished head*** 小さくなって[名声を失って]姿を隠す ▪ Crest-fallen and dejected, they *hid their diminished heads*. しょげてうちしおれ, 彼らは小さくなって姿を隠した.

din[1] /dɪn/ 名 ***make a din*** やかましく騒ぐ ▪ What *a din* those children are *making*! その子供たちはなんとやかましく騒いでいることだろう!

din[2] /dɪn/ 動 ***din in** a person's **ears*** 耳を聾せんばかりに響く ▪ The shouts of his enemies were *dinning in his ears*. 敵の叫び声が彼の耳もつぶれんばかりに響いていた.

***din into** a person/**din into** a person's **ears* [*head*]** 人にやかましくいやになるほど言いきかせる ▪ The master *dinned into* the boy that the square of six is thirty-six. 先生はその少年に, 6の2乗は36であるとくどくどと言いきかせた ▪ I need not *din into your ears* the importance of hard work. 精励の重要さを君にくどくど言いきかす必要はない.

dine /daɪn/ 動 ***dine and wine** a person* 人に酒食のもてなしをする ▪ The great man *was dined and wined* wherever he went. その偉人はいたるところで酒食のもてなしを受けた.

dine with Duke Humphrey 食事なしで済ます, 正餐(せい)[食事]を抜きにする ▪ I was obliged to *dine with Duke Humphrey* and content myself with a few buns. 私は正餐を抜きにして, 少しばかりの菓子パンで満足しなければならなかった. ☞St. Paul's の Duke Humphrey aisle をよく無一文の人々がぶらついて食事を省いたことから.

ding /dɪŋ/ 動 ***ding into the ears*** くどくど言いきかせる ▪ He *dinged into their ears* that some Americans were good. 彼は善良なアメリカ人もいるということを彼らにくどくどと言いきかせた.

huff and ding どなりちらす ▪ He *huffs and dings* at such a rate. 彼はすごい勢いでどなりちらす.

dinner /dínər/ 名 ***ask** a person **to dinner*** 人を正餐(せい)に招く ▪ I *was asked to dinner* yesterday. 私はきのう正餐に招かれた.

at dinner 食事中で ▪ They were *at dinner* when I called. 私が訪問したときは彼らは食事中だった.

Dinner is served. 《しばしば戯》(執事を気取って)食事の用意ができました ▪ "*Dinner is served*," said Sue, rather formally for a lunch.「食事の用意ができました」とスーは気取って昼食の案内をした.

dinner on the grounds 《米》(宗教集会で)各自持ち寄ったものをいっしょに食べる昼食 ▪ Well, it is time for *dinner on the grounds*. さあ, もう持ち寄り昼食の時間です.

eat** one's **dinners →EAT one's terms.

***give a dinner* (*in honor of*)** (…のために)晩餐(さん)会を催す ▪ We *gave a dinner in honor of* Mr. Smith. 我々はスミス氏のために晩餐会を催した.

hand in** one's **dinner pail 《主に米口》死ぬ ▪ The most famous organist in England *handed in his dinner-pail* yesterday. イングランドで最も有名なオルガン奏者が昨日亡くなった. ☞dinner pail

(労働者などの)桶型の弁当箱.

have dinner 食事をする ▪ We *have dinner* at 6 o'clock. 我々は6時に食事をする.

lay the dinner table [***cloth***] 食事の用意をする ▪ Before *laying the dinner cloth*, the servant should tidy the room. 食事の用意をする前に, 使用人は部屋をきれいにするべきである.

make a dog's dinner of →DOG[1].

make a good [***poor***] ***dinner*** 十分な[物足りない]食事をする ▪ I *made a good dinner* with my mother. 母と十分な食事をした.

more ... [***more often***] ***than you*** [***they,*** etc.] ***have had hot dinners*** 《口》非常に多くの..., 非常にしばしば ▪ Don't scorn his stories. He has read *more* books *than you've had hot dinners*. 彼の話を軽蔑するな. 彼は大変な読書家なんだぞ ▪ I've danced *more often than you've had hot dinners*. 私はほんとに頻繁にダンスをしました. ☞しばしば経験の乏しい者をたしなめるのに用いられる.

dint /dɪnt/ 名 ***by dint of*** ...の力で, の手段により ▪ He gained the prize *by dint of* steady application. 彼はたゆまぬ勤勉によって賞を得た.

dip[1] /dɪp/ 名 ***at the dip*** 旗[帆]を少し下げて《旗を少し下げるのは敬礼の印》 ▪ I directed him to keep the flag *at the dip*. 私は彼に旗を少し下げておくように命じた ▪ The flag was *at the dip*. 旗は敬礼のため少し下げられていた.

go for [***take***] ***a dip*** =have a DIP 1.

have a dip **1** ちょっと浴びる ▪ I think I'll go to the sea and *have a dip*. 海へ行ってちょっと泳ごうと思います.

2 ちょっとのぞく[やる] (*in, into*) ▪ I *had an* hour's *dip into* the book. その本をほんの1時間ほど読んだ.

dip[2] /dɪp/ 動 ***dip a*** [*one's*] ***toe into*** ...を慎重に試す ▪ Our company has been *dipping a toe into* the computer games market. わが社はコンピューターゲーム市場を慎重に試しているところだ.

dip deep into ...をどっさり使いこむ; を深く考究する ▪ The poor relative *dipped deep into* the family resources. 貧しい親族はその家の資産をどっさり使いこんだ ▪ The scholar *dipped deep into* Eastern lore. その学者は東洋説話を深く考究した.

dip (***deeply***) ***into*** *one's* ***purse*** [***means, pockets, savings,*** etc.] ...を盛んに使う, 資産を使いこむ ▪ In early life he had *dipped deeply into his property*. 若い時分に彼はひどく財産を使いこんだのであった.

dip into pockets すりを働く (pick) ▪ He *dips into pockets*. 彼はすりである.

dip into *a person's* ***pockets*** (物が)人の財布に相当食いこむ ▪ That has *dipped into my pockets*. そのことで私は相当の金を使った.

dip into the till (勤めている会社などから)金を盗む ▪ She *dipped into the till* and was dismissed. 彼女は会社の金を盗んで解雇された.

dip *one's* ***pen in gall*** →GALL.

dip sheep 羊を殺菌液につけて洗う ▪ He travels from farm to farm *dipping sheep*. 彼は羊を消毒液で洗いながら農場を次々と旅して行く.

dip snuff 《米》かぎタバコを吸う《かぎタバコをすくい取り歯や歯ぐきにこすりつけて》 ▪ Sam smoked his pipe, and Dick *dipped snuff*. サムはパイプを吸い, ディックはかぎタバコを吸った.

diploma /dɪplóʊmə/ 名 ***get*** *one's* ***diploma*** 免状をもらう, 大学を卒業する ▪ He *got his diploma* last year. 彼は昨年大学を卒業した.

direct /dərékt|daɪ-/ 動 ***as directed*** 指図[処方]通り(に) ▪ Correct the errors *as directed*. 指示の通りに誤りを訂正せよ.

direct *one's* ***remarks at*** ...に当てつけて言う ▪ He *directed his remarks at* me. 彼は私に当てつけて言った.

direct *a person* ***to*** *do* 人に...するよう指図する[命じる] ▪ I *directed* him *to* put the room in order. 私は彼に部屋の整とんを命じた.

direct *a thing* ***to be*** *done* 事[物]をするよう指図する[命じる] ▪ I *directed* the room *to be put* in order. 私は部屋を整とんするよう命じた.

direction /dərékʃən|daɪ-/ 名 ***follow*** *a person's* ***directions*** 人の指図に従う ▪ It is a good doctor who *follows his* own *directions*. いくら名医でも自分の指図には従わぬものだ,「医者の不養生」.

Full directions inside. 詳細な使用法在中.

give directions 指図を与える ▪ He *gave directions* to his servant. 彼は使用人に指図した.

in all directions 四方八方に ▪ They fled *in all directions*. 彼らは四方八方に逃げた.

in every direction 四方八方に ▪ People ran *in every direction* when the bomb dropped. 爆弾が落ちたとき人々は四方八方に走って逃げた.

in the direction of ...の方向へ[に] ▪ He was walking *in the direction of* the village. 彼は村の方へ歩いていた.

point *a person* ***in the right direction*** 人に正しい方向を指す, 適切なアドバイスをする ▪ The securities company *pointed* applicants *in the right direction* for funding. 証券会社は申し込み者に資産のための適切なアドバイスを行った.

under the direction of ...の指揮[指導]のもとに ▪ He did the work *under my direction*. 彼は私の指導のもとにその仕事をした ▪ He can't work well *under the direction of* another. 彼は人の監督のもとではうまく働けない.

directive /dəréktɪv|daɪ-/ 形 ***directive of*** ...を支配する, 指導する ▪ Laws are rules *directive of* our actions to the end intended by the legislator. 法律は我々の行動を立法者の意図する目的に向ける法則である.

dirge /də:rdʒ/ 名 ***like a dirge*** 悲しげに[な](葬送歌のように) ▪ Don't speak in that dismal voice; it sounds *like a dirge*. そんな陰うつな声で話さないでください. まるで葬送歌のように悲しげですから.

dirt /də:rt/ 名 (***as***) ***cheap as dirt*** →CHEAP.

(***as***) ***common as dirt*** →COMMON.

cast [***fling***] ***dirt at*** [***on***] **1** …を罵倒する, の悪口を言う ▪ They *cast dirt at* my guest. 彼らは私の客を罵倒した.
2 …に泥を投げつける ▪ The tramp *flung* the *dirt at* the door. 浮浪者は戸に泥を投げつけた.

cut dirt 《米俗》走り去る, 大急ぎで去る ▪ He *cut dirt* and ran. 彼は大急ぎで逃げ去った.

dig the dirt/dig up [***for***] ***dirt*** (人に知られたくない)秘密を暴きたてる (*on*) ▪ I was asked to *dig the dirt on* Mr. Crossley. クロスリー氏の秘密を暴きたてるように頼まれた ▪ A politician has always got to be aware that someone will *dig the dirt on* him. 政治家は自分の秘密を暴き立てる者がいるだろうと絶えず心すべきである ▪ How can I *dig up dirt on* my co-workers? どうすれば仕事仲間の秘密を暴き立てられるだろうか.

dig up some [***the***] ***dirt*** 《口》(人の)秘密を暴きたてる (*on*) ▪ The jurnalist tried to *dig up* all *the dirt on* the candidate. 新聞記者はその立候補者のすべての秘密を暴きたてようとした.

dish the dirt 《俗》ゴシップを流す, スキャンダルをふりまく ▪ Susan is notorious for *dishing the dirt*. スーザンはゴシップを流すことで名を売っている.

do *a person* ***dirt/do the dirt on*** *a person* 《口》人に卑劣な仕打ちをする, 陰険な方法で人を傷つける ▪ People had been *doing* her *dirt* for 40 years. 人々は40年の間, 彼女に卑劣な仕打ちをしてきた ▪ We found out Sean is *doing the dirt on* us. ショーンが我々に泥を塗っていることを知った.

eat dirt 《口》恥辱を忍ぶ, 恥辱を受ける ▪ Every man must *eat* a peck of *dirt* before he dies. 《諺》人はみな死ぬまでには多くの恥辱を受けねばならない ▪ He delights in making me *eat dirt*. 彼は私に恥をかかせることを非常に喜ぶ.

fling dirt about 陰口をきく, 悪口を言う ▪ He spends his time *flinging dirt about*. 彼は人の悪口を言って日を送っている.

fling dirt at [***on***] →cast DIRT at.

Fling enough dirt and some will stick. 《諺》泥をいっぱい投げつければ, いくらかはくっつく《人の悪口をたくさん言っていれば, いくらかは信じられる》.

hit pay dirt 《米》やまを当てる; 大金を儲ける, 成功する ▪ The novelist was poor, but *hit pay dirt* with his third novel. その小説家は貧しかったが, 3冊目の小説で大金を儲けた.

on top of dirt 《米口》地上の[での] ▪ I'm the ugliest man now *on top of dirt*. 私は現在この世で最も醜い人間である.

play [***go***] *a person* ***dirt*** 人に卑劣な仕打ちをする ▪ He *played* his employer *dirt*. 彼は雇い主に卑劣な仕打ちをした.

strike [***hit***] ***pay dirt*** →PAY[1].

take *a person* ***for dirt under*** *one's* ***feet*** 人をちり[あくた]のように思う ▪ You *take* us *for dirt under your feet*. 君は我々をちりのように思っている.

Throw plenty of dirt and some will be sure to stick. 《諺》たくさん人の悪口を言っていれば, そのうちいくらかは信じられるようになる.

treat *a person* ***like*** (***a piece of***) ***dirt*** 《口》人をちり[つまらないもの]のように扱う, 人をごみ扱いにする ▪ They *treated* me *like dirt* in that shop. あの店では私をちりあくた扱いにした ▪ She had *been treated like dirt*. 彼女はごみのように扱われてきた.

What's the dirt? 《俗》どんな悪口なのか; どんなニュースなのか.

dirty[1] /dəːrti/ 形副 ***a dirty old man*** → MAN[1].

dirty great [***big***] 《口》とても大きい, ばかでかい ▪ He lives in a *dirty great* house. 彼はばかでかい家に住んでいる.

dirty work いやな仕事; 不正行為 ▪ She complained that she had to do all the *dirty work* while her colleague took a two-week vacation. 彼女は同僚が2週間の休暇をとっている間に面倒な仕事を全部やらなければならないことに不平をもらした.

dirty work at the crossroads いかがわしい[不愉快な]行動 ▪ Some *dirty work at the crossroads* can be expected tonight. 今夜は何かいかがわしい事件がありそうだ.

do *a person's* [***the***] ***dirty work for him*** 人の下働きをする ▪ I am not going to *do the dirty work for him*. 私は彼の下働きをするつもりはない.

do the dirty on *a person* 《口》人に卑劣な仕打ちをする; (特に)女をかどわかして捨てる ▪ He *did the dirty on* me. 彼は私に対して卑劣な仕打ちをした ▪ He *did the dirty on* her. 彼は彼女にひどいことをして捨てた.

get *one's* ***hands dirty*** 手を汚す, 恥ずべき[違法な]ことをする ▪ She would not *get* her *hands dirty* by cheating. 彼女は人をだまして手を汚すようなことはしたくなかった.

get [***have***] ***the dirty end of the stick*** → END[1].

strike pay dirt =hit pay DIRT.

talk dirty 《口》(相手を興奮させるために)卑猥なことを言う ▪ I love it when you *talk dirty*. 君のエロ話はいいね ▪ Don't *talk dirty* in front of the class. 生徒の前で卑猥なことは言うな.

wash *one's* ***dirty linen at home*** [***in public***] →LINEN.

dirty[2] /dəːrti/ 動 ***dirty*** [***soil***] *one's* ***hands/get*** *one's* ***hands dirty*** 徳操[名声]をけがす ▪ He has never *dirtied his hands* with political intrigues. 彼は政治的陰謀で名をけがしたことがない.

dis /dɪs/ 形 ***go dis*** 《口》故障する, 狂う ▪ His brain is *going dis*. 彼の頭は狂いかけている. ☞dis =disconnected (電線が切れて).

disaccustom /dìsəkʌ́stəm/ 動 ***disaccustom*** *oneself* ***to*** …の習慣をやめる ▪ He *disaccustomed himself to* the use of a sleeping drug. 彼は睡眠薬使用の習慣をやめた.

disadvantage /dìsədvǽntɪdʒ|-vάːn-/ 名 ***at a disadvantage*** 不利な立場で; 割が悪く ▪ Our soldiers were fighting *at a disadvantage*. わが軍

は不利な条件で戦っていた ▪ Foreigners are *at a disadvantage* in this respect. この点では外国人は割が悪い.

take *a person* ***at a disadvantage*** 人に不意打ちをくわせる ▪ The suddenness of his request *took* me *at a disadvantage*. 彼の依頼が突然だったので私はめんくらった.

to disadvantage 損をして, 不利な条件で, 不利になるように ▪ We had to sell *to disadvantage*. 我々は損をして売らなければならなかった ▪ It proved *to disadvantage*. それは損になった.

to the disadvantage of ...に不利な(ように) ▪ It is a rumor *to his disadvantage*. それは彼に不利な噂だ ▪ They speak there *to the disadvantage of* our nation. 彼らはそこでわが国民を悪く言う.

under (***great***) ***disadvantages*** (多大の)不利な条件のもとに ▪ He is studying *under disadvantages*. 彼は苦学している.

disaffect /dìsəfékt/ 動 ***be disaffected towards*** ...に対して不服である ▪ He *is disaffected towards* the government. 彼は政府に対して不平をいだいている.

disagreement /dìsəgrí:mənt/ 名 ***have a disagreement with*** ...と意見が違う, けんかをする ▪ He *had a disagreement with* his partner over money. 彼は金のことで相棒とけんかをした.

in disagreement with ...と不一致で, 意見が違って ▪ I am *in disagreement with* you about the matter. 私はその件についてはあなたと意見が違う.

disappear /dìsəpíər/ 動 ***disappear into the blue*** →BLUE.

disappear into thin air →vanish into thin AIR.

do a [*one's*] ***disappearing act*** 雲がくれする ▪ The newspaper has *done a disappearing act*. 新聞がどこへ行ったのか見えない ▪ Jack is sure to *do his disappearing act*. ジャックはきっと雲がくれするよ.

disappoint /dìsəpɔ́ɪnt/ 動 ***be agreeably disappointed*** 心配が根拠のないこととわかって喜ぶ ▪ I *was agreeably disappointed*. 私は心配無用とわかってほっとした.

be disappointed at (事)に失望する ▪ I *was disappointed at* not finding her at home. 私は彼女が家にいなかったのでがっかりした.

be disappointed in ...に失望する ▪ I *was disappointed in* him [love]. 彼に失望した[失恋した].

be disappointed of ...の当てがはずれる ▪ I *was disappointed of* my purpose. 私は目的が達成できなかった.

be disappointed with (物)に失望する ▪ I *was disappointed with* the new car. 新車に失望した.

disappointment /dìsəpɔ́ɪntmənt/ 名 ***to*** *one's* ***disappointment*** ...が失望したことには ▪ *To my disappointment*, he did not come. 私の失望したことには彼は来なかった.

disapproval /dìsəprú:vəl/ 名 ***in disapproval*** 不賛成で[だと言って] ▪ He shook his head *in disapproval*. 彼は不賛成を示すため頭を横に振った.

disarm /dɪsá:rm/ 動 ***disarm*** *oneself* 武装を解く, 武器を捨てる ▪ Richard *disarmed himself*. リチャードは武器を捨てた.

disassociate /dìsəsóʊʃièɪt/ 動 ***disassociate*** *oneself* ***from*** 《文》...に賛成しない ▪ We *disassociate ourselves from* his proposal. 私たちは彼の提案には賛同しません.

disaster /dɪzǽstər|-zá:s-/ 名 ***be a recipe for disaster/be a disaster waiting to happen*** うまくいかない, 不運[大失敗, 不幸な結果]を招きそうだ ▪ Are you thinking of traveling through South America by yourself? That'*s a recipe for disaster*! 一人で南米大陸を縦断しようと考えているのか? うまくいきっこないよ ▪ Decrepit U.S. dams *are a recipe for disaster*. がたがたの米国のダムは災害を招きそうだ.

disband /dɪsbǽnd/ 動 ***disband*** *oneself* 解体する ▪ The army *disbanded itself* at once. 軍隊はすぐに解体した.

disbar /dɪsbá:r/ 動 ***disbar ... from practice*** (弁護士)を業務停止にする ▪ The lawyer *was disbarred from practice*. その弁護士は業務停止になった.

disburden /dɪsbə́:rden/ 動 ***disburden*** *oneself* [*one's* ***mind***] ***of*** ...の荷をおろしてほっとする ▪ I *disburdened myself* [*my mind*] *of* the secret. 私はその秘密を打ち明けてほっとした.

discard /dɪská:rd/ 名 ***into the discard*** 捨てられて, 廃棄されて, 忘れられて ▪ Sword and spear have gone *into the discard*. 剣とやりは廃棄された.

discharge[1] /dístʃɑ:rdʒ/ 名 ***get*** *one's* ***discharge*** 解放される; 解雇される ▪ The prisoners were glad to *get their discharges*. 囚人たちは釈放されて喜んだ.

in the discharge of ...を果たすのに ▪ He is faithful *in the discharge of* his duties. 彼は職務を果たすのに忠実である.

discharge[2] /dɪstʃá:rdʒ/ 動 ***discharge*** *oneself* 出る; 噴出する ▪ The smoke *discharged itself* through the chimney. 煙が煙突から出た ▪ We *discharged ourselves* in a symphony of laughter. 我々は一斉にどっと爆笑した.

discharge a bankrupt 破産者の破産前の債務を免除する ▪ Chapter 7 would *discharge a bankrupt* of all debts. (連邦改正破産法の)第7章は破産者のすべての債務を免除することだろう.

discharge *itself* ***into*** ...に注ぐ ▪ The Nile *discharges itself into* the Mediterranean. ナイル川は地中海に注ぐ.

discharge *oneself* ***of*** **1** (職務など)を果たす ▪ He *discharged himself of* his duties. 彼は職務を果たした.

2 (言葉など)を述べる ▪ He *discharged himself of* two pieces of news. 彼は二つのニュースを述べた.

discipline /dísəplən/ 名 ***be under disci-***

pline 風紀[紀律]が締まっている ▪ The school *is under discipline.* その学校は紀律が正しい.

keep … under discipline …を制する ▪ We must *keep* our passions *under discipline.* 我々は情欲を抑えなくてはならない.

disconnect /dìskənékt/ 動 ***be disconnected with*** …と何の関係もない ▪ The accident seems to *be disconnected with* the road condition. その事故は道路状態とは何の関係もないらしい.

D

discontent /dìskəntént/ 動 ***(be) discontented with*** …に不満で(ある) ▪ He *is discontented with* his lot. 彼は自分の境遇に不満である.

discount /dískaʊnt/ 名 ***at a discount*** **1** (額面以下に)割引して ▪ They were alike *at a discount.* それらはみな割引されていた.

2 人気が落ちて; 評判が悪く; 売れ口がなく ▪ He is now *at a discount.* 彼は今は人気が落ちている ▪ Conservative principles are *at a discount* throughout the world. 保守思想は世界中で人気がない ▪ These goods are *at a discount.* この品は売れ口がない.

at 10% discount 10パーセント[など]の割引で ▪ I bought three books *at 10% discount* on the Internet. インターネットで3冊の本を1割引で買った.

five-finger discount 《俗》万引き ▪ He used his *five-finger discount* to win his daily bread. 彼は日々の糧を万引きで調達した.

give [allow, make] a discount (on the price) (値段の)割引をする ▪ Please *allow a discount on the price* of this article. この品の値段を割引してください.

with some discount いくらか割引して ▪ Accept the story *with some discount.* その話はいくらか割引して聞きなさい.

discover /dɪskʌ́vər/ 動 ***be discovered*** 《劇》幕が開くとすでに舞台に出ている ▪ At rise of curtain wife and mother-in-law *are discovered* packing fragile articles into a barrel. 幕が開くと, 嫁と姑がすでに舞台に出てこわれやすい品をたるに詰めこんでいる.

discover *oneself* ***to*** …に名のる ▪ I *discovered myself to* them. 私は彼らに名のった.

discredit /dɪskrédət/ 名 ***be a discredit to*** …の面よごし[不面目]となる ▪ Don't *be a discredit to* the family. 一家の面よごしになるな.

bring discredit on …を汚す ▪ Such a conduct *brings discredit on* the name of Athens. そのような行為はアテネの名を汚す.

bring discredit on *oneself* 不信用[不面目]を招く ▪ You will *bring discredit on yourself.* 君は信用がなくなるよ.

fall into discredit 不評判になる ▪ The doctrine has *fallen into discredit.* その説は信じられなくなった.

throw discredit on [upon] …に対して疑惑[不審]を起こさせる ▪ These facts *throw discredit on* the document. これらの事実はその書類に対して疑惑を起こさせる.

to *one's* ***discredit*** 恥さらし[面よごし]になって ▪ A failure would have been *to my discredit.* 失敗したら恥さらしになるところだった.

discretion /dɪskréʃən/ 名 ***An ounce of discretion is worth a pound of wit.*** → OUNCE.

at discretion 自由に, 勝手に, 任意に ▪ You may believe this *at discretion.* このことは任意に信じてよい ▪ He admitted much light and air *at discretion.* 彼は思うままにたくさんの光と空気を入れた.

at the discretion of …の思うままに, 勝手に ▪ Rotterdam was *at the discretion of* those rioters. ロッテルダムはそれら暴徒の思いのままであった.

Discretion is the better part of valor. 用心は勇気の大半である, いらぬ危険を冒すのはばかげている《しばしば臆病の言い訳として用いられる》(cf. Sh., *1 Hen IV* 5. 4. 120).

it is within [in] *one's* ***discretion to*** *do* …するのはその人の任意である ▪ *It is within my discretion to* dispose of the property. その財産を処分するのは私の随意である.

leave a wide discretion (人に)広い裁量の余地を与える ▪ The instructions *leave* me *a wide discretion.* その指令は私に広い裁量の余地を与えている.

leave to the discretion of …の裁量に任す ▪ I *leave* it *to your discretion.* それは君の裁量に一任する.

on *one's* ***own discretion*** 自分の思う通りに, 適宜に ▪ You must act *on your own discretion.* 君は自由に行動してよろしい.

surrender at discretion 無条件で降服する ▪ The inhabitants *surrendered at discretion.* 住民は無条件降服した. ☞以前は "to the enemy's discretion" と言った.

throw discretion [caution] to the winds →fling … to the WINDs.

use *one's* ***discretion*** 適宜に計らう, 手加減する ▪ You may *use your discretion.* 適宜に計らってよい.

use *one's* ***own discretion*** 自分の思う通りに(適宜の)処置をとる (cf. Sh., *A.Y.L.* 1. 1. 152) ▪ You may *use your own discretion.* あなたの思う通りにしてよろしい.

with discretion 慎重に ▪ You must act *with discretion.* 慎重に行動しなければならない.

years [the age] of discretion 分別年齢《英米法では普通14歳》▪ You have reached *years [the age] of discretion.* あなたは分別年齢に達した.

discriminate /dɪskrímənèɪt/ 動 ***discriminate in favor of*** …を優遇する ▪ The law does not *discriminate in favor of* the rich. 法律は金持ちを優遇しない.

discussion /dɪskʌ́ʃən/ 名 ***beyond discussion*** 論をまたない ▪ It is *beyond discussion* that he is right. 彼が正しいことは言うまでもない.

open a discussion 討論の皮切りをやる ▪ Mr.

Smith *opened the discussion*. スミス氏がその討論の皮切りをやった.

under discussion 審議中(の) ▪ The question is *under discussion*. その問題は審議中である.

disdain[1] /dɪsdéɪn/ 名 ***with disdain*** 侮蔑の態度で ▪ No one likes to be treated *with disdain*. 侮蔑をもって扱われるのを好む者はいない.

disdain[2] /dɪsdéɪn/ 動 ***disdain to*** [***to*** *do*] ... することを潔しとしない ▪ Grey *disdained to* begging [*to* beg] his life. グレイは命ごいをするのを潔しとしなかった.

disdainful /dɪsdéɪnfəl/ 形 ***disdainful of*** ... を軽蔑して, ものともせず ▪ *Disdainful of* danger, we rushed on the foe. 危険をものともせず敵を襲った.

disease /dɪzíːz/ 名 ***catch*** [***take, suffer from***] ***a disease*** 病気にかかる ▪ He was *suffering from* no *disease*. 彼はどんな病気にもかかっていなかった.

the kissing disease 《口》キス病, 伝染性単核症 (infectious mononucleosis)《キスによって伝染すると信じられていることから》 ▪ "*Kissing disease*" is believed to spread by simply kissing. 「キス病」はただキスすることで伝染すると信じられている.

disembogue /dìsɪmbóʊg/ 動 ***disembogue*** (***itself, its waters***) ***into*** ...に注ぐ ▪ The Volga *disembogues* (*itself*) *into* the Caspian Sea. ボルガ川はカスピ海に注ぐ.

disembosom /dìsɪmbózəm/ 動 ***disembosom*** *oneself* (***of***) (...を)打ち明ける ▪ He *disembosomed himself of* the secret. 彼は秘密を打ち明けた.

disentangle /dìsɪntǽŋgəl/ 動 ***disentangle*** *oneself* ***from*** ...から縁を切る ▪ He *disentangled himself from* political affairs. 彼は政治と縁を切った.

disfavor, 《英》 **disfavour** /dɪsféɪvər/ 名 ***bring*** *a person* ***into disfavor*** (***with***)/ ***bring ... into*** *a person's* ***disfavor*** 人に(...の)不興を被らせる, 人を...に不人気にする ▪ He *brought* the officer *into* the *disfavor of* the prince. 彼はその将校に親王の不興を被らせた.

come [***fall***] ***into disfavor*** (***with***) (...の)不興を被る, (に)受けが悪くなる ▪ The government *fell into disfavor*. 政府は人気がなくなった.

in *a person's* ***disfavor***/***in disfavor with*** ...に嫌われて, 受けが悪くて ▪ He was *in his master's disfavor*. 彼は主人に受けがよくなかった ▪ The earl lived many years *in disfavor with* the King. 伯爵は何年も国王に嫌われて暮らした.

regard [***look upon***]***... with disfavor*** ...に不賛成である ▪ He *looked upon* the plan *with disfavor*. 彼はその計画に不賛成であった.

to [***in***] ***the disfavor of*** ...の不利に ▪ The action should be construed *to their disfavor*. その行動は彼らの不利になるように解釈すべきだ.

disgorge /dɪsgɔ́ːrdʒ/ 動 ***disgorge*** *oneself* 吐き出す ▪ Several vessels were *disgorging themselves*. 数隻の船が乗客を吐き出していた.

disgorge (***itself***) ***into*** (川が)...に注ぐ ▪ The Thames *disgorges itself into* the North Sea. テムズ川は北海に注ぐ.

disgrace[1] /dɪsgréɪs/ 名 ***be a disgrace to*** ... の恥である, つらよごしである ▪ You *are a disgrace to* your country. お前は国のつらよごしだ ▪ Such cruelty *is a disgrace to* civilization. そのような残虐は文明の恥辱である.

(***be***) ***in disgrace*** 不興を被って(いる), 面目を失って(いる) ▪ The boy *is in disgrace* today. その少年は今日はしかられて小さくなっている ▪ He was dismissed *in disgrace*. 彼は懲戒免職になった.

bring disgrace on ...をけがす, の面目をつぶす ▪ His conduct *brought disgrace on* his family. 彼の行為は家名をけがした.

fall into disgrace (***with***) (...の)寵を失う, 日陰の身となる ▪ He *fell into disgrace with* his master. 彼は主人の寵を失った.

disgrace[2] /dɪsgréɪs/ 動 ***disgrace*** *oneself* 恥をかく, 恥をさらす ▪ I would rather die than *disgrace myself*. 恥をかくより死んだほうがましだ.

disguise[1] /dɪsgáɪz/ 名 ***in disguise*** **1** 変装した ▪ He was really a policeman *in disguise*. 彼は実は警官が変装していたのだ ▪ Poverty is a blessing *in disguise*. 貧困は不幸と見えて実は幸福である.

2 変装して ▪ He went among the enemy *in disguise*. 彼は変装して敵中に入った.

in [***under***] ***the disguise of*** **1** ...に扮(ふん)して, 変装して ▪ He went about *in the disguise of* a sailor. 彼は水夫に変装して歩き回った.

2 ...にかこつけて, と偽って ▪ He absented himself *in the disguise of* illness. 彼は病気と偽って欠席した.

make no disguise of ...を少しも隠さない ▪ She *made no disguise of* her feelings. 彼女は感情を少しも隠そうとしなかった.

throw off *one's* ***disguise*** 仮面を脱ぎ捨てる, 正体[本心]を現す ▪ He *threw off his disguise* at last. 彼はついに正体を現した.

disguise[2] /dɪsgáɪz/ 動 ***disguise*** *oneself* ***as*** [***in, with, by*** *doing*] ...に[の服で, で, して]変装する ▪ Robin Hood *disguised himself as* a farmer. ロビンフッドは農夫に変装した ▪ He *disguised himself in* woman's clothes. 彼は女装した ▪ He *disguised himself with* a false beard. 彼はつけひげをつけて変装した ▪ He *disguised himself by wearing* glasses. 彼はめがねをかけて変装した.

disguised as ...に変装して ▪ He attempted to escape *disguised as* a farmer. 彼は農夫に変装して逃げようとした.

disgust[1] /dɪsgʌ́st/ 名 ***in disgust*** いやになって, うんざりして ▪ He resigned *in disgust*. 彼はいや気がさして辞職した.

take a disgust at [***for, toward, against***] ...に対していや気を起こす, あいそを尽かす ▪ I *took a*

D

disgust at the new servant. 私は今度の使用人にあいそを尽かした.

to** one's **disgust 実にいやなことには ▪ *To my disgust* he again asked for money. 彼はまた金をくれと言ったが私は実にいやであった.

disgust[2] /dɪsgʌ́st/ 動 ***be*** [***feel***] ***disgusted*** (***at, with, by***) (行為などに, 人に, によって)胸が悪くなる, あいそが尽きる ▪ I *am disgusted at* his behavior. 私は彼のふるまいに胸が悪くなった ▪ He *was disgusted with* his wife. 彼は妻にあいそが尽きた.

dish[1] /dɪʃ/ 名 ***a dish for the gods*** 神々に捧げたいほどうまいもの ▪ Revenge is *a dish for the gods*. 復しゅうは神々に捧げたいほどすてきなものだ.

a dish of chat [***gossip***] 雑談, 茶飲み話 ▪ Tom had *a dish of chat* with her. トムは彼女と茶飲み話をした.

dish of tea 好きな[性に合う]こと ▪ Black sorcery is my *dish of tea*. 黒魔術は私のお気に入りだ.

do [***wash***] ***the dishes*** (食べ終わった)食器を洗う ▪ I'll *do the dishes*. 私が食器を洗います.

dish[2] /dɪʃ/ 動 ***dish it out*** 《口》ぼろくそに言う; 痛めつける; しかりつける; 懲らしめる ▪ He *dished it out* in the fight. 彼はけんかでひどく(相手を)痛めつけた.

dishabille /dìsəbíːl/ 名 ***in dishabille*** 略装で, 着流しで ▪ When I entered the room, the lady was *in dishabille*. 私が部屋に入ると, 婦人はしどけない身なりをしていた.

dishearten /dɪsháːrtən/ 動 ***feel disheartened at*** …にがっかりする ▪ I *felt disheartened at* the result. 私はその結果を見てがっかりした.

dishonor, 《英》 **dishonour** /dɪsánər|-ɔ́n-/ 名 ***be a dishonor to*** …の面よごし[恥]である ▪ He *is a dishonor to* the family. 彼は一家の面よごしだ.

do (***a***) ***dishonor to*** …をはずかしめる ▪ He *did dishonor to* a woman. 彼は女性をはずかしめた.

in dishonor 不面目に[な] ▪ The criminal's family lived *in dishonor*. 罪人の家族は屈辱の生活を送った.

to the dishonor of …の恥辱となるように, に恥をかかせるように ▪ They invented lies *to the dishonor of* their enemies. 彼らは敵の恥辱となるような嘘をでっちあげた.

disinclination /dɪsìnklənéɪʃən/ 名 ***have a disinclination for*** …がきらいだ ▪ Some schoolboys *have a* strong *disinclination for* work. 勉強がひどくきらいな生徒もいる.

disincline /dìsɪnkláɪn/ 動 ***be disinclined for*** [***towards, to*** *do*] …する気がない ▪ Today I *am disinclined for* work. きょうは仕事がしたくない.

disinterest /dɪsíntərəst/ 動 ***disinterest** oneself* (***from***) (…に)関与しなくなる, (と)手を切る; 《外交》(に)干渉などの意志[権利]を捨てる ▪ The people have *disinterested themselves* entirely *from* taking part in politics. 人々は政治に参加することをすっかりやめた.

disjunctive /dɪsdʒʌ́ŋktɪv/ 名 ***in the disjunctive*** 二者択一の意味[形式]で ▪ The clause must be construed *in the disjunctive*. その条項は二者択一の意味で解釈しなければならない.

dislike /dɪsláɪk/ 名 ***have*** [***take***] ***a dislike*** (***for, to, of***) …がきらいである[をきらう] ▪ They *have a dislike of* snakes. 彼らはヘビがきらいだ.

one's ***likes and dislikes*** 人の好ききらい ▪ Everyone has *his likes and dislikes*. 人にはみな好ききらいがある.

dismal /dízməl/ 名 ***be in the dismals*** 沈んでいる, ふさいでいる ▪ He *is in the dismals*. 彼はふさいでいる.

dismay /dɪsméɪ/ 名 ***be struck with dismay*** (***at***) (…を聞いて)度を失う ▪ He *was struck with dismay at* the news. 彼はそのニュースを聞いて度を失った.

in dismay 驚き[恐れ]あわてて ▪ She lifted her hands *in dismay*. 彼女は驚きあわてて両手をあげた.

dismiss /dɪsmís/ 動 ***be dismissed*** (***from***) …を免ぜられる ▪ He *was dismissed* the army. 彼は軍職を免職になった ▪ He *was dismissed* (*from*) the service. 彼は免職になった.

disorder /dɪsɔ́ːrdər/ 名 ***fall into disorder*** 無秩序[混乱]に陥る ▪ The convoy *fell into disorder*. 護送隊は混乱に陥った.

in disorder 乱れて, 混乱して ▪ The room was *in disorder*. 部屋は乱雑になっていた ▪ The enemy retreated *in disorder*. 敵は混乱して退却した.

throw ... into disorder …を混乱に陥れる ▪ We *threw* the enemy *into disorder*. 我々は敵を混乱に陥れた.

dispatch, despatch /dɪspǽtʃ/ 名 (***a***) ***happy dispatch*** **1** 死んでかえって幸福であること ▪ Well, it is *a happy dispatch*. まあ死んでかえって幸福だったというものだ.

2 切腹 ▪ He took *a happy dispatch*. 彼は切腹した.

by dispatch 速達便で ▪ Please send the papers *by dispatch*. 書類を速達便で送ってください.

use dispatch てっとりばやくやる ▪ *Use dispatch*! てきぱきやれ!

with dispatch てきぱき ▪ He did it *with dispatch*. 彼はそれをてきぱきやった.

displacement /dɪspléɪsmənt/ 名 ***have a displacement of*** …の排水量がある ▪ The ship *has a displacement of* 1,000 tons. その船は1,000トンの排水量がある.

display[1] /dɪspléɪ/ 名 ***make a display*** (***of***) **1** (…を)見せびらかす ▪ It is bad form to *make a display of* one's learning. 学をひけらかすのはきざだ.

2 (…の)見栄を張る; (を)大げさに見せる ▪ He *made a display of* affection. 彼は愛情を大げさに表現した.

on display 陳列して ▪ Various books were *on display*. いろいろな本が陳列してあった.

display[2] /dɪspléɪ/ 動 ***display** oneself* (***in***) (…となって)現れる ▪ Her skill will *display itself* *in* a fine performance. 彼女の技量は立派な演技となって現れるでしょう.

displease /dɪsplíːz/ 動 ***be displeased with*** [***at***] …が気に入らない, に腹をたてている ▪ He *was displeased with* the knavery. 彼はその悪行に怒っていた ▪ Many *were displeased at* him. 彼を不快に思う人は多かった.

disport /dɪspɔ́ːrt/ 動 ***disport*** *oneself* 遊び興じる, 戯れる ▪ Sea-birds were *disporting themselves* in the water. 海鳥が水中で戯れていた.

disposal /dɪspóʊzəl/ 名 ***at*** [***in***] *one's* ***disposal*** 人の自由に使えて, 処理できて ▪ The money is *at your disposal.* その金はご自由に使ってください ▪ My services are *at your disposal.* 何なりとご用命ください.

have … at *one's* ***disposal*** …が自由になる ▪ I *have* much money *at my disposal.* 私には自由に使える金がたくさんある.

have disposal of …を管理する ▪ In time of war the government must *have* entire *disposal of* the people. 戦時には政府は国民を完全に掌握していなければならない.

hold … at *a person's* ***disposal*** …を預かって人の指図通りに処分する ▪ I will *hold* the money *at your disposal.* その金を預かってご指示通りに処分します.

in *one's* ***disposal*** →at one's DISPOSAL.

place … at *a person's* ***disposal*** …を人が自由に使えるようにする ▪ I will *place* any sum *at your disposal.* いくらでもご用立ていたします.

put [***leave***] ***… at*** *a person's* ***disposal*** …を人の自由使用に任せる ▪ We *left* the money *at his disposal.* 我々はその金を彼の自由使用に任せた.

dispose /dɪspóʊz/ 動 ***be disposed for*** …したい気がする, を欲している ▪ The government *is* strongly *disposed for* a Spanish war. 政府は強くスペインと戦争する気になっている.

(***be***) ***disposed to*** [***to*** *do*] **1** …したい気がする, を欲している ▪ He *is disposed to* defend the country. 彼は国を防衛したい気持ちである ▪ I *am disposed to* think so. まあそういう気がする.

2 …する傾向がある ▪ He *is disposed to* take offence at trifles. 彼は小さなことで立腹する傾向がある.

(***be***) ***ill*** [***well***] ***disposed*** **1** 気立てが悪い[良い] ▪ He *is* remarkably *ill disposed.* 彼はきわめて気立てが悪い.

2 悪意[好意]を持っている (*to, toward*) ▪ The newspapers seem *ill disposed toward* the government. 新聞は政府に悪意を持っているようだ ▪ People *are well disposed to* the king. 人々は国王に好意を持っている.

3 気分が悪い[良い] ▪ I *am well disposed* today. きょうは気分が良い.

dispose of *a daughter* (***in marriage to***) 娘を(…へ)嫁にやる ▪ They have *disposed of* her *to* a business man. 彼らは彼女を実業家に嫁がせた.

dispose … to [***to*** *do*] **1** = DISPOSE a person to.

2 …を…させる傾向がある ▪ Moisture *disposes* meat *to* rancidity. 湿気は肉を腐らせがちである.

dispose *a person* ***to*** [***to*** *do*] 心を…の[する]方に傾ける ▪ Happiness will *dispose* a man *to* benevolence. 幸福は人の心を博愛の方へ傾ける.

Man proposes, but God disposes. → MAN[1].

disposition /dìspəzíʃən/ 名 ***at*** [***in***] *one's* ***disposition*** …の自由に使いうる, 処分しうる ▪ He has considerable sums of money *at his disposition.* 彼は相当額の金を自由に使うことができる ▪ The choice is no longer *in our disposition.* その選択はもはや我々の意のままにはならない.

have the disposition of …の管理[処理]権を持つ ▪ Who *has the disposition of* this land? この土地の管理権は誰が持っているのか.

make (*one's*) ***dispositions*** 万事手配する, 用意する ▪ They *made dispositions* for defense. 彼らは防御の用意をした.

show a disposition to *do* …してみたいような意向をもらす《だいぶ色気がある》 ▪ He *shows a disposition to* undertake the work. 彼はその仕事を引き受けたがっているようだ.

dispossess /dìspəzés/ 動 ***dispossess*** *oneself* ***of*** …を捨てる ▪ We have *dispossessed ourselves of* belief in such a thing. そんなことに対する信頼を捨てた.

dispraise /dɪspréɪz/ 名 ***in dispraise of*** …をそしって, けなして ▪ He said so *in dispraise of* his friend. 彼は友人をけなしてそう言った.

dispute[1] /dɪspjúːt/ 名 ***beyond*** [***out of, past, without***] (***all***) ***dispute*** 議論の余地なく, 確かに ▪ This is *beyond all dispute* the best book on the subject. これはもちろんその問題に関する最善の書である ▪ We can, *without dispute,* sail much better. 我々は確かにずっとうまく帆走できる.

in dispute 論争中で[の]; 未解決で[の] ▪ The matter is *in dispute* now. その件は今論争中である.

dispute[2] /dɪspjúːt/ 動 ***dispute every inch of the ground*** 寸土[一歩]も譲らじと奮戦する ▪ Although the enemy outnumbered us, we *disputed every inch of the ground.* 敵は数において我々に勝っていたが, 我々は寸土も譲らじと奮戦した.

disqualify /dɪskwɑ́ləfàɪ|-kwɔ́l-/ 動 ***disqualify*** *oneself* ***for*** …の資格なしと言う ▪ The Speaker *disqualified himself for* the office. 下院議長はその職につく資格がないと言った.

disregard /dìsrɪgɑ́ːrd/ 名 ***with disregard*** おろそかに ▪ He treated me *with disregard.* 彼は私をおろそかに扱った.

disrepair /dìsrɪpéər/ 名 (***be***) ***in*** (***a state of***) ***disrepair*** 修繕を怠ってこわれて[荒れて]いる ▪ The building *was in disrepair.* その建物は修繕を怠って荒れていた.

fall into disrepair (修繕を怠って)荒廃する ▪ The tower *fell into disrepair.* 塔は荒廃した.

disrepute /dìsrɪpjú:t/ 名 ***bring*** *a person* ***into disrepute*** 人を不評判にする ▪ His misconduct *brought* him *into disrepute*. 彼は非行のため評判を落とした.

fall into disrepute 評判が落ちる[悪くなる] ▪ The hotel has *fallen into disrepute*. そのホテルは評判が悪くなった.

in disrepute 評判が悪く ▪ These remedies are now *in disrepute*. これらの治療法は今は人気がない.

D

dissatisfy /dɪssǽtəsfàɪ/ 動 ***be dissatisfied with*** [***at***] …に不満である ▪ She *is dissatisfied at* his retirement [*with* his character]. 彼女は彼の引退[性格]に不満である.

dissent /dɪsént/ 動 ***without a dissenting voice*** 一人の異議もなく(通過するなど) ▪ The bill passed *without a dissenting voice*. 法案は一人の異議もなく通過した.

disservice /dɪssə́:rvəs/ 名 ***do*** *a person* (***a***) ***disservice*** 人に損害を与える, ひどい仕打ちをする ▪ I *did* the army *a* great *disservice*. 私は軍隊に非常に迷惑をかけた.

dissident /dísədənt/ 形 ***dissident from*** …と異なる ▪ Our manners are *dissident from* theirs. 我々の風俗は彼らのとは異なる.

dissimilar /dɪssímələr/ 形 ***dissimilar to*** [《まれ》***from, with***] …と似ていない, と異なる ▪ This is quite *dissimilar to* that. これはあれとは全く違う.

distaff /dístæf|-tɑ:f/ 名 ***on the distaff side*** 母方の ▪ He is my uncle *on the distaff side*. 彼は私の母方のおじです.

distance[1] /dístəns/ 名 ***a good distance off*** かなり隔たって ▪ My friend lives *a good distance off*. 私の友はかなり隔たった所に住んでいる.

at a distance 少し離れて ▪ *At a distance* it appears like an island. 少し離れるとそれは島に見える.

at a [***the***] ***distance of*** …の距離を隔てて ▪ *At a distance of* 50 meters I couldn't tell if it was a hawk or a falcon. 50メートル離れていて, タカかハヤブサか見分けがつかなかった ▪ I'm writing a review *at the distance of* forty years. 私は40年の間をおいて書評を書いているのである.

at … distance of time …だけ時を隔てて ▪ We can see *at* our *distance of time* that it was unmistakable. それがまぎれもないものだったことは我々ほどに時を隔てていてもわかる.

be some [***no***] ***distance*** 少し遠く[すぐ近く]にある ▪ The post-office *is no* [*some*] *distance* from my house. 郵便局は家のすぐ近く[から少し遠く]にある.

from a distance 遠方から(の) ▪ The house cannot be seen *from a distance*. その家は遠方からは見えない.

go [***last***] ***the*** (***full***) ***distance*** 《野球》完投する; 《ボクシング》最終回まで戦いぬく; (一般に)最後までやりぬく ▪ He has entered the University, but he will not *go the* whole *distance*. 彼は大学に入ったが卒業まではやり通さないだろう ▪ To the surprise of the boxing world, George Foreman *went the full distance* against a much younger man. ボクシング界が驚いたことに, ジョージ・フォアマンは自分よりもずっと若い選手と最後まで戦いぬいたのだった. ☞もとボクシングの口語.

in the distance 遠くに (far away) ▪ We saw a little light *in the distance*. 遠方に小さなあかりが見えた.

keep a safe [***discreet***] ***distance*** → keep one's DISTANCE.

keep *a person* ***at a distance*** 人を遠ざける, 敬遠する; 人を近づけない ▪ *Keep* that child *at a distance*. その子供を近づけないようにしてください ▪ I *kept* him *at a* respectful *distance*. 私は彼を敬遠していた.

keep at a distance (***from***) (…に)近寄らないようにする ▪ I shall *keep at a distance from* the well. その井戸に近寄らないようにします.

keep *one's* ***distance*** 分を知ってなれなれしくしない; 遠慮[用心]して近づかない ▪ Please *keep your distance*. どうぞあまりなれなれしくしないでください ▪ We had better *keep our distance* from the Town. 町にあまり近づかないほうがよい.

know *one's* ***distance*** 身のほどを知る, 分を守る ▪ He intended to teach them to *know their distance*. 彼は彼らに分を守ることを教えるつもりだった.

last the distance →go the (full) DISTANCE.

out of distance あまりに遠く離れすぎて; 全く届かないほど ▪ We are *out of distance* from such beauties. 我々はそれほどの美点からあまりに遠く離れすぎている ▪ They beat all other people quite *out of distance*. 彼らは他の者より断然勝っていた.

out of striking distance (***from***) (…から)遠くて打てない(所に) ▪ The two camps were *out of striking distance from* each other. 両陣営は互いに砲撃が届かない位置で対峙していた.

take distance 《米口》遠くへ去る ▪ I wish those ruffians would *take distance*. あのならず者たちが遠くへ去ってくれたらなあ.

'Tis distance lends enchantment to the view. 《諺》遠くで見ると景色が魅力的に見える. (T. Campbell, *Pleasures of Hope*).

to a distance 遠方へ ▪ He has moved *to a distance*. 彼は遠方へ引っ越した.

within easy distance of …にほど遠くない所に ▪ He lives *within easy distance of* his work. 彼は仕事場にほど遠くない所に住んでいる.

within hailing [***hearing***] ***distance*** (***of***) (…から)呼べば届く[(…から)聞こえる]所に ▪ He is *within hailing distance of* us. 彼は我々から呼べば届く所にいる.

within [***in***] ***striking*** [***shouting,*** 《英》***spitting***] ***distance of*** 《口》…を打てる所に; の非常に近くに, 達成間近で ▪ Our troops are not yet *within striking distance of* the enemy. わが軍はまだ敵を攻撃できる所に来ていない ▪ His house is *within spitting distance of* the bus-stop. 彼の

家はバス停に非常に近い ▪ Vote counts show he is *in striking distance of* victory. 投票数によれば，彼は当選を間近に収めている．

within walking distance of →WALKING.

distance[2] /dístəns/ 動 ***distance*** *oneself* ***from*** …と距離を置く，…に関わらない ▪ The school was trying to *distance itself from* the PTA. 学校は PTA からは距離を置こうとしていた．

distant /dístənt/ 形 ***at no distant date*** そのうちに ▪ We shall get permission *at no distant date.* 遠からず許可を得るだろう．

be distant to [***with***] …によそよそしくする ▪ I want you to *be distant with* her. 君は彼女とは疎遠にしてもらいたい．

have a distant view of …を遠望する，を遠くから見る ▪ We *had a distant view of* Mt. Everest. 我々は遠くからエベレスト山を見た．

distaste /dıstéıst/ 名 ***have a distaste for*** …が嫌いだ ▪ He *has a distaste for* work. 彼は仕事が嫌いだ．

distasteful /dıstéıstfəl/ 形 ***distasteful to*** …が嫌いで ▪ Grammar is *distasteful to* me. 私は文法が嫌いだ．

distinct /dıstíŋkt/ 形 ***as distinct from*** …とは異なるものとして ▪ Let us consider man *as distinct from* animals. 動物とは異なるものとして人間を考察してみよう．

distinct from …とはっきり異なって ▪ Our language is quite *distinct from* theirs. 我々の言語は彼らのとは全く異なる．

distinction /dıstíŋkʃən/ 名 ***a distinction without a difference*** 無用の区別立て ▪ You seem to make *a distinction without a difference.* いらぬ区別立てをしているようです．

draw a distinction between …を区別する ▪ We must *draw a distinction between* courage and audacity. 勇気と図太さとを区別せねばならない．

gain [***win***] ***a distinction*** 殊勲章を得る ▪ He *won* many *distinctions* for bravery. 彼は勇敢な行為のためたくさんの勲章を得た．

gain [***win***] ***distinction*** 殊勲を立てる，名をあげる ▪ He *gained distinction* as a writer of fiction. 彼は小説家として名を成した．

in distinction from [***to***] …と区別して ▪ He was reasonable *in distinction to* the other men. 彼は他の人々と違ってわかりがよかった．

make distinctions (***between***) (両者を)わけへだてする，区別する ▪ It is difficult to *make* careful *distinctions between* all the meanings of a word. 単語の全ての意味を入念に区別するのは難しい．

make no distinctions (***between, of***) (…の間に)区別立てをしない，同じように扱う ▪ Law *makes no distinctions of* persons. 法は人を分け隔てしない．

of distinction 卓越した，著名な ▪ His father is a writer *of distinction.* 彼の父は文豪だ．

win (***a***) ***distinction*** →gain (a) DISTINCTION.

with distinction **1** 殊勲をもって ▪ He passed the examination *with distinction.* 彼は優等で合格した ▪ He served *with distinction.* 彼は殊勲を立てた．

2 優遇をもって ▪ He was received *with distinction.* 彼は優待された．

without distinction of rank 身分の上下の区別なく[をせずに] ▪ The prince shook hands with everyone, *without distinction of rank.* 殿下は身分の上下の区別なく，すべての人と握手した．

distinguish /dıstíŋgwıʃ/ 動 ***be distinguished for*** …で著名である，に卓越している ▪ The scientist *was distinguished for* his originality. その科学者は独創性で著名だった．

be distinguished from …と区別される，とは違いがある ▪ Silk *is distinguished from* rayon. 絹はレーヨンとは違っている．

distinguish *oneself* (***by***) (…で)著名となる，めだつ，功をたてる，傑出する ▪ He has *distinguished himself by* scholarship. 彼は学問で名をあげた ▪ At dinner his awkwardness *distingiushes itself.* 会食のときに彼の無作法は目だつ ▪ He *distinguished himself* in the battle. 彼は戦闘で手がらをたてた．

distract /dıstrǽkt/ 動 ***be distracted with*** [***by, at***] …で心を取り乱す，狂気のようになる; で激怒する ▪ Her mind *is distracted by* fear. 彼女は恐怖のため気が狂いそうである ▪ He *was distracted at* some occurrence. 彼はある出来事のため取り乱した．

drive *a person* ***distracted*** 人を悩ます，激怒させる，狂人にする ▪ Pain *drove* him *distracted.* 苦痛のため彼は気が狂いそうだった．

distraction /dıstrǽkʃən/ 名 ***drive*** *a person* ***to distraction*** 人をかっと逆上させる，人の気を狂わせる ▪ He *was driven to distraction* by pain. 彼は痛くて気が狂いそうだった．

to distraction 気も狂うほどに ▪ The princess loves you *to distraction.* 王女はあなたを気も狂うほど愛している．

distress[1] /dıstrés/ 名 ***in distress*** **1** 苦悩して ▪ He was *in* great *distress* of conscience. 彼は良心にひどく苛(さいな)まれていた．

2 (金などに)困って，困窮して ▪ The company's finances are always *in distress.* その会社の財政はいつも困窮している．

3 (船が)遭難して ▪ Any ship *in distress* may be refreshed here. 遭難船はみなここで補給が受けられる．

distress[2] /dıstrés/ 動 ***be distressed at*** …に接して非常に悲しむ[悩む] ▪ He *is distressed at* the loss of his property. 彼は財産を失って非常に悲観している．

distress *oneself* 心配する; 心痛[悲観，苦慮]する ▪ Don't *distress yourself* about the child. 子供のことを心配するには及びません．

district /dístrıkt/ 名 ***the red light district*** 赤線地帯，売春の盛んな地域 ▪ *The Red Light*

D

District is one of Amsterdam's major tourist attractions. 赤線地帯はアムステルダムの主要な観光名所の一つです.

distrust /dɪstrʌ́st/ 名 ***with distrust*** 不信[疑い]をもって ▪ The child looked at the stranger *with distrust*. 子供は見知らぬ人を疑わしげに見た.

distrustful /dɪstrʌ́stfəl/ 形 ***distrustful of*** ... を疑う; に自信がない ▪ I am *distrustful of* his motive. 私は彼の動機に疑いを持っている ▪ He is *distrustful of* himself. 彼は自分に自信が持てない.

disturb /dɪstə́ːrb/ 動 ***Please don't disturb yourself.*** どうぞお構いなく.

disturbance /dɪstə́ːrbəns/ 名 ***create [make, raise] a disturbance*** 騒動を起こす ▪ They *made a disturbance* about a trifle. 彼らはつまらないことで騒ぎ立てた.

make much [great] disturbance about ... について興奮する, 立腹する ▪ Why do you *make* so *much disturbance about* a little thing? なぜ小さなことでそんなに腹を立てるのですか.

disuse /dɪsjúːs/ 名 ***fall [come] into disuse*** すたれる ▪ The word has *fallen into disuse*. その語は使われなくなった.

from disuse 使わないため ▪ The knife has become rusty *from disuse*. そのナイフは使われずにさびた.

ditch /dɪtʃ/ 名 ***be driven to the last ditch*** 窮地に追いつめられる ▪ The government *was driven to the last ditch* by the universal call for liberty. 政府は国民全体の自由の要求にあい窮地に追いつめられた.

die in a ditch 《口》のたれ死にする (↔DIE in one's bed) ▪ I would rather *die in a ditch* than marry you. 君と結婚するよりのたれ死にしたほうがましだ.

die in the last ditch 最後の防御線で死ぬ; あくまで戦って死ぬ ▪ He'll *die in the last ditch* before he surrenders. 彼は降伏するよりは最後まで戦って死ぬだろう.

fight to the last ditch とことんまで戦う ▪ I am ready to *fight to the last ditch*. とことん戦う覚悟だ.

in the ditch 《米俗》酔いつぶれて ▪ He was really *in the ditch*. 彼はほんとに酔いつぶれていた.

lay [have, put] ... under (the) ditch 《米》(土地に)かんがい水路をつける ▪ They want to *have* a large quantity of land *under (the) ditch*. 彼らは広い土地にかんがい水路をつけたいと思っている.

like digging a ditch with a spoon [teaspoon] 全く要領悪く, 非能率的に ▪ Using a typewriter in writing a paper instead of a computer is *like digging a ditch with a spoon*. 論文を書くのにコンピューターではなくタイプライターを使うのは非能率的だ.

under ditch かんがい水路の設けてある ▪ Anyone entering land *under ditch* must pay the proprietor of the canal. かんがい水路のある土地に入る人は誰でも水路の経営者に料金を払わなければならない.

ditch-water /dɪ́tʃwɔ̀ːtər/ 名 ***(as) clear as ditch-water*** 《口》少しも明らかでない[はっきりしない] ▪ The legal implications are about *as clear as ditch water*. 法的な含みはまず明らかではない.

(as) dull as ditch-water →DULL[1].

dite /daɪt/ 名 ***not care a dite*** 少しもかまわない ▪ "I do*n't care a dite*," he said. 「少しもかまわない」と彼は言った.

dither /dɪ́ðər/ 名 ***all of a dither*** (興奮・心配で)ひどく震えて ▪ The sight of us made the poor boy *all of a dither*. 我々を見ると少年はかわいそうにぶるぶる震えた.

in a dither (不慮の出来事などで)うろたえて, おろおろして ▪ Grandpa never got *in a dither* about anything. 祖父はどんなことにもうろたえたことは一度もなかった.

ditto /dɪ́toʊ/ 名 ***in (a suit of) dittos*** 上下そろいの服を着て ▪ He was never seen *in dittos* even in September. 彼は9月でも上下そろいの服を着ていることは決してなかった.

say ditto to 《口》...に同意見だと言う, 同じことを言う; に同意する ▪ I *say ditto to* Mr. Burke. 私はバーク氏と同意見である ▪ A couple ought to *say ditto to* each other in everything. 夫婦は万事についてお互いに意見が合うべきである.

dive[1] /daɪv/ 名 ***a crash dive*** (潜水艦の)急速潜航; (望みが)急になくなること ▪ It takes about a minute for a boat to submerge with *a crash dive*. 潜水艦が急速潜航するには約1分かかる ▪ My prospect of winning the championship took *a crash dive*. 選手権を勝ち取る見込みは急にしぼんだ.

go into a nose dive 《口》 **1** (力などが)急に衰える; (人が)あきらめる, 絶望する ▪ He *went into a nose dive* on being fired. 彼は首になって絶望した.
2 (株価などが)急落[暴落]する ▪ The stock market *went into a nose dive* today. 株価が本日暴落した.

make a dive for (つかもうとして, 逃げ込もうとして)...へ突進する ▪ He *made a dive for* the ditch. 彼はみぞへ飛んで行った ▪ He *made a dive for* the gun. 彼は銃をつかもうと突進した.

take a dive **1** (...に)飛び込む, 没頭する (*into*) ▪ He *took a dive into* the subject. 彼はその問題に没頭した.
2 暴落する ▪ Morale *took a dive* as the news spread. そのニュースが広まると士気はひどく落ちた.
3 《俗》なれ合いでノックアウトになる ▪ He *took a dive* in the third round. 彼は第3ラウンド目になれ合いのノックアウトになった.

take a nose dive 《口》 **1** つぶれる, 失敗する ▪ After a really splendid first week, the Festival *took a nose(-)dive*. 実にすばらしい第一週目の後のフェスティバルは失敗だった.
2 =go into a nose DIVE 2.

dive[2] /daɪv/ 動 ***dive off the deep end*** 急にわけもなく激怒する ▪ She *dived off the deep end* again. 彼女はまた急に怒りだした.

divert /dəvə́:rt/ 動 ***divert*** *oneself* ***in*** [***with***] …で慰む, で楽しむ ▪ She *diverts herself in* singing. 彼女は気晴らしに歌を歌う ▪ He often *diverted himself with* a viol. 彼はよくビオールをひいて楽しんだ.

divest /daɪvést/ 動 ***divest*** *oneself* ***of*** 《文》 **1** …を脱ぐ ▪ The king *divested himself of* his coronation robes. 国王は戴冠式の服を脱いだ.

2 (信念・態度など)を捨てる ▪ I cannot *divest myself of* the idea. 私はその考えを捨てるわけにいかない.

divide[1] /dəváɪd/ 名 ***cross*** [***go over***] ***the*** (***great***) ***divide*** 死ぬ ▪ These hunters *went over the divide* long ago. その猟人たちはずっと前に死んだ.

divide and rule 分割統治 ▪ The King adopted the policy of *divide and rule*. 国王は分割統治の政策をとった.

divide[2] /dəváɪd/ 動 (***be***) ***divided against*** *oneself* 内輪もめしている, 分裂している (《聖》 *Mark* 3. 25) ▪ An army *divided against itself* must be an easy conquest. 内部の割れている軍隊は楽に征服されるにちがいない.

be divided between *A* ***and*** *B* AとBに分かれて(決めかねて)いる ▪ Her loyalty *is divided between* home *and* work. 彼女が忠実であるべきは家庭か仕事か二つに分かれている.

(***be***) ***divided in*** (***opinion***) (意見)が分かれている ▪ The committee *are divided in opinions*. 委員会は意見が分かれている.

divide and govern [***rule***] 分割して統治する ▪ It enabled the Prime Minister to *divide and rule*. そのため総理大臣は分割して統治することができた. ☞イタリアの政論家 Machiavelli (1469-1527)の言葉.

divide the hoof ひづめが割れている《ヘブライ語より》 ▪ The swine, though he *divides the hoof*, does not chew the cud. ブタはひづめが割れているが反芻(すう)をしない.

divide the House 《英》(議会で賛否両派に分かれて)決を採る ▪ He expressed his intention of *dividing the House* on the motion. 彼はその動議の採決を行う意図を表明した.

dividend /dívədènd/ 名 ***Honesty pays dividends.*** 《諺》 正直は利益をもたらす.

pay a dividend [***dividends***] 利益・好結果を与える ▪ My researches *paid a* good *dividend*. 私の調査は良い成果を得られた.

division /dəvíʒən/ 名 ***without a division*** 賛否の分裂なしに, 採決なしに ▪ The bill was passed *without a division*. 議案は採決なしに通過した.

divorce /dəvɔ́:rs/ 動 ***be divorced from*** **1** …と離婚する ▪ She *was divorced from* him on that day. 彼女はその日に彼と離婚した.

2 …と分離する ▪ Science cannot *be divorced from* morality. 科学は道徳と切り離すことはできない.

divorce *oneself* ***from*** …と離婚する ▪ She *divorced herself from* her husband. 彼女は夫と離婚した.

do[1] /du:/ 名 ***do's and don't's*** すべきこととしてはいけないこと《あることを行う際の心得》 ▪ Here is a list of *do's and don't's* on letter writing. ここに手紙書きの心得箇条がある.

fair do's 《口》 公平な処置 ▪ *Fair do's*! 公平にやれ ▪ That is not *fair do's*. それは公平じゃない.

There is a big do on. 《口》 大興宴が行われている ▪ *There is a big do on* at No. 2. 2号館で大宴会が行われている.

do[2] /du:/ 動 ***all*** *one* (***can***) ***do is*** *do* する(できる)ことは…だけである ▪ *All* a poet *can do* today *is* warn. 今日詩人にできることは警告することだけだ ▪ *All* I *do is* drink and fight. 俺のすることは飲んでけんかをすることだけだ.

be done with …を終える; をやめる; と手を切る ▪ I wish to *be done with* my English. 私は英語を早く片づけてしまいたい ▪ Elect whom you please to be your captain; I *am done with* it. あなたの好きな人を船長に選びなさい. 私はもうやめます ▪ I *am* quite *done with* him. 私は完全に彼と手を切った.

be up and doing →UP[1].

Can do. 《口》 できる, ぜひやる《問いに答えて》 ▪ Will you be able to get this finished by five?—*Can do*. Leave it to me. 5時までにこれを終わらせられるかね—できます. 任せてください.

can [***could***] ***do worse than*** *do* →WORSE.

could do with 《口》 …ができたらいいなと思う ▪ It's so hot I *could do with* something cold to drink. ひどく暑いので冷たい飲み物にありつけたらなあ.

do *oneself* ***a bit*** [***piece***] ***of no good*** (へまをして)損をする, 害を受ける ▪ I *did myself a bit of no good* when I married you. お前さんと結婚してわたしは損をした.

do a good thing うまいもうけをする ▪ He has *done a good thing* in shares. 彼は株でうまいもうけをした.

do a(***n***) *Obama* [etc.] オバマ[など]をまねる ▪ He contemplated *doing an* Edison. 彼はエジソンのまねをすることを考えた. ☞有名な人名であることが必要.

Do as I say, not as I do. 私の言う通りにしなさい, 私のすることはまねないで《私の行いはまずい所があるかもしれないが, 私の言うことは立派だから実行しなさい》.

do away with *oneself* 自殺する ▪ He *did away with himself* in despair. 彼は絶望して自殺した.

do badly **1** うまくいかない, 成功しない ▪ The firm has *done badly* these five years. その会社はこの5年間うまくいかなかった.

2 健康がすぐれない ▪ Father has been *doing badly* since his operation. 父は手術してからずっと体がよくない.

do badly for 《口》 …を少ししか持っていない[貰わない] (↔Do well for) ▪ The staff at that hotel *do badly for* tips. あのホテルの従業員はチップをあまり貰わない.

D

do better to *do* …するほうがよい ▪ You would *do* much *better to* wait. 君は待つほうがずっとよいだろう.
do brown **1** ほどよく焼く[煮る] ▪ The fowl *was done brown* by the cook. 鶏肉は料理人がほどよく焼いた.
2《俗》まんまとだます ▪ He was too clever for me and I *was done brown*. 彼は私には賢すぎて私はまんまとだまされた.

D

do but *do* どうぞ…だけしてください ▪ *Do but* hear me. どうぞ私の言うことだけを聞いてください.
do ... by *a person* 〚通例 do の次に well, hard などを伴って〛人に対して…にふるまう; 人を…に扱う ▪ He *did* very *well by* me. 彼は私を非常に優遇した ▪ Do to others as you would *be done by*. あなたが遇してもらいたいように他人をも遇せよ (《聖》*Luke* 6. 31) (→hard DONE by).
do *one's* **do** 《口》なすべきことを(特にじょうずに)する ▪ He has *done his do*. 彼は自分のすべきことを立派に果たした.
do *oneself* **down** 恐縮する ▪ You need not *do yourself down*; you are not to blame. 君は恐縮するには及ばない, 君が悪いんじゃない.
do drugs [**dope**] 麻薬を常用する, 麻薬中毒になる ▪ Mike doesn't *do drugs* and he doesn't smoke. マイクはヤクはやらないし, タバコも吸わない.
do for *oneself* 自分でやっていく ▪ He is old enough to *do for himself*. 彼は自分のことは一人でやれる年だ.
do *one's* **head** [**nut**] 《俗》心配する; 激怒する ▪ Don't *do your head* about such a trifle. そんなささいな事で心配するな.
do *oneself* **in** 《俗》自殺する ▪ He *did himself in* after he went bankrupt. 彼は破産のあと自殺した.
do it [**the trick**] 効を奏する ▪ It's dogged *does it*. がんばりが肝心である ▪ Gently *does it*. そっとやるのが肝心.
do much [**little,** etc.] **for** …のため大いに尽くす[あまり尽くさない, など] ▪ He has *done much for* his country. 彼は国のため大いに尽くした.
do much to *do* …することに大いに貢献する ▪ Stealthy benefactions will *do much to* make the poor happy. 陰徳は貧しい人々を幸福にすることに大いに貢献する.
do nicely →DO well.
do no more than *do* やっと…するに過ぎない ▪ The fee *did no more than* cover his expenses. その報酬はやっと彼の出費をまかなうに過ぎなかった.
do nothing but *do* →NOTHING.
Do one! 《英口》あっちへ行け!
do or die 死ぬ覚悟でやる, 倒れてのちやむ; のるかそるかだ ▪ Let us *do or die*. 死ぬ覚悟でやりましょう ▪ Well, it is *do or die* this time. ほんとに, 今度こそのるかそるかだ ▪ With a real *do-or-die* spirit the team scored two touchdowns. のるかそるかの精神でチームは2回のタッチダウンを決めた.
do *one's* **own thing** =follow one's BENT.
do *a person* **proud** 《口》**1** 人に誇りを感じさせる, 人に面目を施す ▪ His wife's cleverness *did* him *proud*. 妻の賢明さで彼は面目を施した.
2 人にへつらう ▪ They *did* him *proud*. 彼らは彼にへつらった.
3 盛んにもてなす ▪ He is a millionaire; he *does* one *proud*. 彼は百万長者で人を盛んにもてなす.
do *oneself* **proud** **1** あっぱれなふるまいをする, 面目を施す ▪ The people have *done themselves proud* in building a school house. その人々は校舎を建てるという美挙をした ▪ The sun *did himself proud*. 日が照ってすばらしかった.
2 =DO oneself well 1.
do right to *do* …するのはもっともである ▪ You *do right to* think so. 君がそう思うのはもっともだ.
do something [**things**] **for** [**to**] …をより良くする; をより楽しくする; をより魅力的にする ▪ This suit *does things to* a stout woman. このスーツは太った女性を引き立てる.
do the trick →DO it.
do *a person* [*a thing*] **to death** →DEATH.
do ... up brown 《米》(事)を申し分なくやる ▪ He *did* the historical novel *up brown*. 彼は歴史小説を立派に仕上げた.
do ... up right …をきちんと[適切に]する ▪ He determined to *do* the thing *up right*. 彼はそれをきちんとしようと決心した.
do well [**nicely**] **1** (人が)うまくやる, 成功する, 繁昌する; (物が)うまくいく ▪ He is *doing* very *well* at the Bar. 彼は法廷弁護士として立派にやっている ▪ I'm glad your affairs are *doing well*. あなたの仕事がうまくいっているのをうれしく思う.
2 (作物が)よくできる ▪ Flax *does well* after wheat. 亜麻は小麦の後ではよくできる.
3 儲ける ▪ He *did well* out of the war. 彼は戦争で大いに儲けた.
4 (健康の)経過がよい, 調子がよい ▪ Mother and child are *doing well*. 母子ともに健全だ.
5 成績がよい ▪ He *did well* in English. 彼は英語の成績がよかった ▪ He *did well* during the war. 彼は戦争中立派な働きをした.
do *a person* **well** 人をよくもてなす ▪ They *do* you very *well* here. ここの人々は非常にもてなしがよい.
do *oneself* **well** 《口》**1** (特に飲食で)贅沢する; 贅沢に暮らす ▪ He *does himself well* wherever he goes. 彼はどこへ行っても贅沢をする.
2 自分で成功する. ☞Ⓖ sich gutlich tun のなぞり.
do well by →DO ... by a person.
do well for 《口》…をたくさん持っている[貰う] (↔DO badly for) ▪ We *did well for* coal during the miners' strike. 坑夫ストの間も我々は石炭をたくさん持っていた.
do well for *oneself* 《口》(経済的に)成功する, 金回りがよい; 繁昌[栄]する ▪ John was *doing* very *well for himself*. ジョンは商売が非常に繁昌している ▪ She was *doing well for herself* as an actress.

彼女は女優として羽振りのよい暮らしをしていた.

do well out of →DO well 3.

do well to *do* [***in*** *doing*] …するのはよい ▪ You will *do well to* keep silent. あなたは黙っていたほうがよい ▪ You have *done well in keeping* the secret. 君がその秘密を守ったのはよかった.

do with *oneself* (時を)過ごす ▪ What did you *do with yourself* yesterday? 昨日はどんなふうに過ごしましたか.

Don't do anything I wouldn't do. 私のしたくないようなことをしないでね《別れのときの皮肉なあいさつ》 ▪ Be sure to enjoy yourselves, then, but *don't do anything I wouldn't do.* ではみなさん, 楽しく遊んできなさい. でも私のしたくないことをしてはいけませんよ.

don't let's →LET².

Don't "granny" [etc.] ***me!*** 《口》[[相手の言葉に抗議して]]「おばあちゃん」[など]と言わないでちょうだい! ▪ *Don't* "ever so sorry" *me.* 「相すみません」なんて言わないでください.

have [***be***] ***done*** **1** すます, 終える ▪ After we *had done* in the kitchen, we went out. 台所ですませた後, 我々は外へ出て行った.

2 やめる ▪ *Have done!* やめろ[よせ]! ▪ I wish the French would *have done.* フランス軍がやめてくれればよいのに.

have [***be***] ***done*** *doing* →be DONE doing.

have done it 《口》しくじった ▪ I *have done it* again. 私はまたしくじった[へまをやった].

have done with **1** …と縁を切る; を打ち切る; を思い切る ▪ I *have done with* you for the future. もうこれからは君とは縁を切った ▪ Be a man and *have done with* her. 君も男だ, あの女のことは思い切ってしまえ ▪ I *have done with* hard work. 骨の折れる仕事は打ち切りにした.

2 …をすます, 終える; が用ずみになる ▪ Let's start at once and *have done with* it. すぐに始めて仕上げましょう ▪ *Have* you *done with* the paper? もう新聞は用ずみですか.

3 …をやめる ▪ *Have done with* all this nonsense. こんなばかなことはやめなさい.

have enough to do to *do* …するだけで精いっぱいだ ▪ I *have enough to do to* pay my debts. 借金を払うので精いっぱいだ.

have much to do to *do* →HAVE².

have much [***little, nothing, something,*** etc.] ***to do with*** →HAVE².

have to do with →HAVE².

How is ... doing? →HOW.

I'll do you! やっつけるぞ《脅迫して》.

it does not do to *do* …するのはよくない ▪ *It does not do to* complain. 不平を言うのはよくない.

it is all [***as much as***] *one* ***can do to*** *do* …するのが関の山[精いっぱい]である ▪ *It was all* he *could do to* say a word to that girl. 彼はその娘にひとこと言うのが関の山だった.

It won't do. 《英》このままではだめだ[どうにかしなければ] ▪ I was twenty places down on the last exam. *It won't do.* 今度の試験で成績が20番下がった. どうにかしなければ.

let's don't 《米口》→LET².

make *a thing* ***do*** (ものごとで)間に合わせる ▪ It isn't large enough; but we'll *make* it *do.* 十分な大きさではないが, それで間に合わせましょう.

make do and mend 古い物を修繕して間に合わせる ▪ New cars are so expensive that most people have decided to *make do and mend.* 新車は非常に高価なので, たいていの人々は古いのを修繕して間に合わせることに決めている.

make do with …でがまんする, すます ▪ We must *make do with* cheap clothes. 我々は安い服でがまんしなければならない ▪ We *made do with* sandwiches. 私たちはサンドイッチですませた.

more than *one* ***can do to*** *do* …することなどできはしない ▪ It is *more than* I *can do to* save money. 貯金することなど思いもよらない.

No you don't. 《口》やめろ, やめて ▪ He wagged his finger in a "*no-you-don't!*" gesture. 彼は指を振って「やめろ」というジェスチャーをした.

(***not***) ***do anything for*** 《口》[[主に否定文で]] …には全然興味を起こさせない ▪ Sports cars *don't do anything for* me. スポーツカーなど僕は全然興味がない.

not know what to do with *oneself* →KNOW².

That does it. 《口》 **1** (仕事などが)これで終わり ▪ "*That does it,*" he said. 「これで終わり」と彼は言った. ☞現在形が普通.

2 それで万事おしまい[ぶちこわし]だ ▪ *That did it.* She stopped calling on me. それで万事おしまいだった. 彼女は私のうちへ来なくなった.

3 もうがまんがならない ▪ *That does it.* All you can do is criticize. もうがまんがならない. 君は非難することしかできないんだ.

That does me. それには参るよ. ☞do「負かす」.

That will do. **1** それでけっこうです (→will DO) ▪ *That will do,* thank you. それでよろしい, ありがとう.

2 もうそれでよい《もどかしさを表す》 ▪ *That will do,* Tommy! トミー, もういいよ《やめろ》.

That'll do me. それで十分だろう.

what to do どうすべきか ▪ I don't know *what to do.* 私はどうしてよいかわからない.

What's doing? **1** 何が起こって[行われて]いるか ▪ There is a crowd over there. *What's doing?* あそこに人だかりができている, どうしたんだ.

2 可能性[見通し]はどうであるか ▪ *What is doing* about going abroad? 海外行きの可能性はどうですか.

What's ... doing here [etc.]***?*** なぜ…がここ[など]にあるのか《しばしば不快を表す》 ▪ *What is* the knife *doing* on the floor? なぜナイフが床の上に転がっているのか?

What's to do? どうしたものか; どうしたのか.

will do **1** 間に合う, けっこうだ ▪ These shoes *won't do* for mountaineering. この靴は登山にはだめ

だ ▪ This sum *will do* for the present. これだけの金があれば当分間に合う.

2(これで)よい ▪ This *will do* for today. きょうはこれでよし[おしまい] ▪ It *will* never *do* to expose my ignorance. 無知をさらすのはよくない.

3《英口》よしきた，いいよ ▪ Would you fix my radio?—*Will do.* ラジオを直してくれる?—いいよ.

***will do** a person* 人にちょうどよい，人の間に合う ▪ This room *will do* me well. この部屋は私にちょうどよい.

You* [*He*, etc.] *can do the other thing. →do the other THING.

You do that.《口》できるものならやってごらん ▪ If you think you can succeed, then *you do that.* 君がうまくやれると思うのだったら，やってみれば.

dock[1] /dɑk|dɔk/ 名 ***in dock*** **1**(船が)ドックに入って ▪ The ship is *in dock* to discharge her cargo. 船は荷をおろすためドックに入っている.

2《海軍俗》入院して ▪ When *in dock*, one lay upon biscuits. 入院中は茶色の角マットレスに寝た.

in dry dock《口》失業して ▪ He is *in dry dock.* 彼は失業している.

in the dock 囚人席に立って，被告席について ▪ It was his own son *in the dock.* 彼自身の息子が囚人席に立っているのであった.

put** a person **in the dock 人を非難[告訴]する ▪ The police *put* Colin *in the dock* for the murder of a young prostitute. 警察はコリンを若い娼婦殺害のかどで告訴した.

dock[2] /dɑk|dɔk/ 動 ***dock the entail***《法》限嗣相続権を解く ▪ He could not *dock the entail.* 彼は限嗣相続権を解くことができなかった.

docket /dɑ́kət|dɔ́kɪt/ 名 ***clear the dockets*** 訴訟事件一覧にある事件を全部かたうける ▪ The court *cleared* up *the dockets* by sitting till midnight. 法廷は真夜中まで開いて事件一覧中の事件を全部かたうけた.

on the docket《米》**1**〚be placed を伴って〛処理予定事項の; 協議事項とされて ▪ The case will *be placed on the docket.* その件は審議事項とされるだろう.

2 考慮[審議，施行]中(の) ▪ One cause appeared *on the docket.* 一つの訴訟事件が審議中のようだった.

doctor[1] /dɑ́ktər|dɔ́k-/ 名 ***just what the doctor ordered***《戯》まさしく好ましい[必要な]もの ▪ After a day's work a nice meal at home is *just what the doctor ordered.* 1日働いた後の，家庭でのおいしい食事こそまさしく好ましいものだ.

see a doctor 医者に診てもらう ▪ Oughtn't you to *see a doctor*? 君は医者に診てもらうべきではないか?

send for a doctor 医者を呼びにやる ▪ *The doctor was sent for* at once. すぐ医者を呼びにやった.

under the doctor 加療中で，医者にかかって ▪ He is *under the doctor.* 彼は医者にかかっている.

***Who shall decide when doctors disagree* [*differ*]?** 学者たちの意見がまちまちでは決しようもない (A. Pope, *Moral Essays* 3. 1).

You're the doctor.《口》決定はあなたがすべきです ▪ The ayes and nays are split evenly. *You're the doctor.* 賛否相半ばしている. 決定はあなたがなすべきだ.

doctor[2] /dɑ́ktər|dɔ́k-/ 動 ***doctor** oneself* 手療治する ▪ He sent me off to *doctor myself.* 彼は私を追い払って手療治させた.

dodge /dɑdʒ|dɔdʒ/ 名 ***come a dodge over***《俗》…をだます，ごまかす ▪ Don't *come* that *dodge over* me. そんなに私をだまさないでください.

***come* [*work*] *the religious dodge over* [*on*]** *a person*《口》信心ぶって人に取り入る，人の宗教感情に訴えて援助を求める ▪ The principal *came* [*worked*] *the religious dodge over* him. 校長は信心ぶって彼に取り入った.

know* (*all*) *the dodges《口》(あらゆる)手練手管を心得ている ▪ I *know all the dodges.* 私はあらゆる手練手管を心得ている.

make a dodge 身をかわす ▪ He *made a* sudden *dodge* aside. 彼は急にわきへ身をかわした.

on the dodge《口》不正[すり，盗み]を働いて ▪ I have been *on the dodge* these 8 years. この8年不正を働いてきた.

dodo /dóʊdoʊ/ 名 ***(as) dead as a dodo*** → DEAD.

dog[1] /dɔːg/ 名 ***A black dog has walked over** one.* →BLACK DOG.

a dead dog つまらぬもの (《聖》*1 Sam.* 24. 14) ▪ You are of no more use than *a dead dog.* お前は死んだ犬のように何の役にもたたない.

a dirty dog 邪悪で狡猾な人物，卑劣なやつ ▪ You're *a dirty dog.* You've got no heart. 君は卑劣なやつだ. まるで愛情というものがない.

a dog and pony show《米口》手のこんだ客寄せショー[キャンペーン] ▪ The store's *dog and pony show* attracted a good-sized audience. その店の手のこんだ客寄せショーは多数の観衆を引きつけた.

a dog in the manger《口》いじわる者 ▪ Let me have the skates. You don't know how to skate.—Don't be *a dog in the manger.* そのスケート靴をください. あなたはスケートのしかたを知らないんだから.—いじわるしないでください. ☞かいばが食えない犬が，牛にもそれを食わせまいとして，かいばおけの中でがんばったというイソップ物語から.

a dog's body 毎日決まりきった仕事を機械的にする人 ▪ In those days I was only *a dog's body*; none of the work I did required any skill. 当時私は毎日決まりきった仕事をしていたが，技術のいる仕事は一つもなかった.

***a dog's breakfast* [*dinner*]**《英口》めちゃくちゃ，ひどい出来 ▪ The passive smoking ban is *a* complete *dog's breakfast.* 受動喫煙防止条例は全くめちゃくちゃだ.

a dog's life みじめな生活《特に過労・虐待・貧困の》 ▪ When I was working under him, he gave me *a dog's life.* 彼の下で働いていたとき，彼は私をつらい目にあわせた.

a dog's orphan 取るに足らぬもの，つまらぬもの ▪ He is nothing but *a dog's orphan*. 彼はつまらぬやつにすぎない．

A living dog is better than a dead lion. 《諺》生きている犬は死んだライオンに勝る（《聖》*Eccles.* 9. 4）．

a lucky dog 《口》幸運児 ▪ He is *a lucky dog*, because he keeps getting what he wants. 彼は果報者だ，いつも欲しいものを手に入れるのだから．

An old dog will not learn new tricks. → Old DOGs will not learn new tricks.

Any stick will do to beat a dog with. 人に難くせをつけようと思えば何とか種が見つかるものだ ▪ You complain of his untidiness; well, *any stick will do to beat a dog with*. 君は彼がだらしないとこぼすが，難くせをつけたければその種は見つかるさ．

Barking dogs seldom bite. →BARK[3].

be done [dressed] up like a dog's dinner 《英》派手に着飾っている ▪ Sally *was done up like a dog's dinner* for her date with Alfie. サリーはアルフィーとのデートのため派手に着飾っていた．

be [come out] top dog 命令する地位にある；（争いの結果）勝つ ▪ He has *been top dog* so long. 彼は久しく命令する地位にあった ▪ Taylor had *come out top dog* as the result of the struggle. テイラーは争いの結果勝ったのだった．

be under dog 下の地位にある，常に服従する地位にある ▪ He has learnt what it means to *be under dog*. 彼は人の下に立つことがいかにつらいことかを知った．

blow off *one's* ***dogs*** 《口》事業[企て]をやめる ▪ He determined to *blow off his dogs*. 彼は事業をやめる決心をした．

call off the dogs （特に法的に）攻撃[非難]をやめる ▪ The scandal has been exposed. Now, let's *call off the dogs*. その醜聞は暴かれた．もう攻撃はやめよう．

die dog for 《米口》極度に忠実である ▪ I'm the man to *die dog for* those that love me. 私は愛してくれる人々にはきわめて忠実な人間だ．

dog cheap 非常に安く ▪ You got the fowls *dog cheap* at four dollars the dozen. あなたがその鶏肉を1ダース4ドルで買ったのはばかに安い．

Dog does [will] not eat dog. 《諺》共食いはせぬもの；同族相はまず；盗人にも仁義あり．

dog eat dog 《口》食うか食われるかの戦い ▪ Premier League is a game of survival. It's *dog eat dog*. プレミアリーグは生き残りゲームだ．それは食うか食われるかの戦いだ．

Dog my cats! 《俗》これは驚いた!；畜生! ▪ Why, *dog my cats!* いやこれは驚いた!

dog on... ちぇっ，いまいましい ▪ Take that, *dog on* you! これでもくらえ，こん畜生!

Every dog has his day. 《諺》誰にでも得意の時代がある．

everybody and his dog 誰もかれも，社会全体 ▪ *Everybody and his dog* is putting out a gardening book. 誰もかれもがガーデニングの本を出している．

Fight dog, fight bear. どちらか倒れるまで戦え ▪ You must fight according to the old saying, "*Fight dog, fight bear.*"「どちらか倒れるまで戦え」という古言の通りに戦わねばならない．

Give a dog a bad name and hang him. 《諺》一度悪評が立ったら浮かばれない．

give ... to the dogs →throw ... to the DOGs.

go to see a dog (about a man) →SEE.

go to the dogs 《英口》**1** ドッグレースを見に行く ▪ We are *going to the dogs* at Wembley tomorrow. あすウェンブリーのドッグレースを見に行きます．
2 落ちぶれる，破滅する；堕落する，すさんだ生活をする ▪ Since he started drinking he has *gone* steadily *to the dogs*. 彼は酒を飲みだしてから，どんどん堕落していった ▪ This country is *going to the dogs* hand over hand. この国はどんどん破滅していっている．
3 《米》失敗する，負ける ▪ This year the polls *went to the dogs*. 今年は世論調査がうまく当たらなかった．

have not a word to throw to a dog → WORD.

He who has a mind to beat his dog will easily find a stick. 《諺》人の悪口を言おうと思えば悪口の種は楽に見つかる．

help a lame dog over a stile →HELP[2].

If you lie down with dogs, you will get up with fleas. 《諺》犬といっしょに寝たらノミといっしょに起きることになる，「朱に交われば赤くなる」．

in a dog's age 《米口》長期間，非常に長い間 ▪ That was the funniest thing I've seen *in a dog's age*! あれがこれまで長い間に見た一番奇妙なことだったんだ!

keep a dog and bark *oneself* 《口》使用人がいるのに自分で用事をせねばならぬ，怠け者の使用人をもて余す ▪ The master complained that he *kept a dog and barked himself*. 主人は怠け者の使用人をもて余しているとこぼした．

lead a dog's life みじめな生活をする ▪ He *leads a dog's life*. 彼はみじめな生活をしている．

lead *a person* ***a dog's life*** 人にみじめな生活をさせる ▪ I *led* that boy *a dog's life*. 私はあの子をつらい目にあわせた．

let loose [unlease, let slip] the dogs of war 戦いの犬を放つ，戦争を始める，戦火を引き起こす（cf. Sh., *Jul. Caes.* 3. 1. 273） ▪ It is time to *let loose* Israel's *dogs of war*, one of the world's best and most ferocious fighting forces. イスラエルの戦いの犬を放つべき時だ，世界最高の，最も獰猛な軍隊をだ．

Let sleeping dogs lie. 《諺》眠っている子を起こすな，やぶをつついてヘビを出すな（→wake a sleeping DOG） ▪ Why mention that? *Let sleeping dogs lie*. なぜその話を持ち出すんだ．そっとしておきなさい．

Let the dog see the rabbit. 《口》さあどいて私[彼，など]に...させてください ▪ Father pushed me away from the fire, and said, "*Let the dog see the rabbit.*" 父は私を暖炉から押しやって，「さあどいて

私に火に当たらせてくれ」と言った.

like a dog with two tails 大喜びで ▪ My sister was *like a dog with two tails.* 妹は大喜びだった ▪ He is *like a dog with two tails* over his son's success. 彼は息子の成功に大喜びだ.

like a dog's dinner 《英口》いきに, 派手に; けばけばしく ▪ She was dolled up *like a dog's dinner.* 彼女は派手に着飾っていた.

D

lots of dog 《口》見せびらかしたっぷり ▪ There's *lots of dog* about it. それはしゃれっ気たっぷりだ.

Love me, love my dog. 《諺》私を愛するなら私の好きな人をも愛してください(そうすればあなたの愛を受けいれます).

make a dog's dinner of 《口》...を台なしにする, めちゃくちゃにする, やりそこなう ▪ He has *made a dog's dinner of* the job. 彼はその仕事をしくじった.

***not have* [*stand*] *a dog's chance* (*of*)** (...の)機会[見込み]が少しもない ▪ He does*n't stand a dog's chance of* a new car this year. 彼は今年は新車を買う見込みは全くない. ☞a dog's chance「ごく僅かな機会[見込み]」.

Old dogs* [*An old dog*] *will not learn new tricks. 《諺》老人はなかなか新しいことには順応しないものだ.

put on* (*the*) *dog 《口》偉そうにする, いばって歩く; 上品な[金持ちの]ふりをする, 見栄を張る; 気取る ▪ I don't want to *put on dog.* 私は偉そうにしたくない ▪ They bought a house and *put on the dog.* 彼らは家を買って見栄を張った.

send... to the dogs ...を投げ捨てる ▪ Has he *sent* his wealth *to the dogs*? 彼は富を遺棄したのか.

stay until the last dog is hung 最後まで残る ▪ It was a point of honor with them to *stay until the last dog was hung.* 彼らは面目にかけても最後まで残らなければならなかった.

The black dog is on *one's* ***back.*** →BLACK DOG.

The dog it was that died. 《諺》人を傷つけようとして自分が傷つく. ☞Goldsmith の詩 *Elegy on the Death of a Mad Dog* から.

the* [*a*] *dog of Montargis モンタージーの犬《知恵があり猛烈な犬》 ▪ The dog made at him like *a dog of Montargis.* その犬はモンタージーの犬のように猛烈に彼に突っかかっていった. ☞Aubri Montidier という人の犬が主人の殺人者に対して驚くべき知恵と猛烈さを示したことから.

the dog's bollocks 《英俗》(...が)すごくいいもの, 最高のもの ▪ I still think the Beatles were *the dog's bollocks.* 私はいまもビートルズは最高だったと思っている. ☞bollocks《英卑》「睾丸」.

There are more ways of killing a dog than by hanging. 君の目的を達するにはそれより他の方法がある《普通, 人が物を傷つけるような目的》 ▪ If I dismiss him, there is almost sure to be a strike.—Then don't do it. *There are more ways of killing a dog than by hanging.* もし彼を首にすると, きっとストライキが起こるだろう—それなら, 首を切らぬことだな. 君の目的を達するには他の方法があるよ.

throw* [*give, send*]*... to the dogs 《口》...を投げ捨てる; を浪費する ▪ He *threw* diplomacy *to the dogs.* 彼は外交を投げ捨てた ▪ He just *threw* his fortune *to the dogs.* 彼は財産をすっかり浪費してしまった ▪ Some younger politicians *were thrown to the dogs.* 若手政治家が数人捨てられた.

wake a sleeping dog やぶをつついてヘビを出す, 眠っている子を起こす ▪ It is good not to *wake a sleeping dog.* 眠っている子は起こさないのがよい.

What dog is a-hanging? どうしたのか ▪ Why ring all these bells? *What dog is a-hanging?* なぜ, こんなに鐘を一斉に鳴らすのですか. どうしたのですか.

Why keep a dog and bark yourself? 《諺》犬を飼っていながらどうして自分が吠えるのか《他人がやってくれるのに自分がしても意味がない》.

***work like a dog* [*dogs*]** 身を粉にして働く, へとへとになるまで働く ▪ Life's too short to *work like a dog.* 身を粉にして働くには人生は短すぎる.

You can never scare a dog away from a greasy hide. 《諺》人の悪習はなかなか抜けぬもの.

You can't teach an old dog new tricks. 《諺》老人に新しい思想[やり方]を教えることはできない.

dog[2] /dɔːg/ 動 ***dog*** *a person's* **(*foot*)*steps*** 人のあとをつける ▪ The police *dogged his footsteps* for a month. 警察は1か月の間彼を尾行した.

dog it 《米俗》 **1** 走って逃げる ▪ Let's *dog it* out of here right now. 今すぐここからずらかろう.
2 (仕事など)手を抜く, 本気でやらない (shirk) ▪ He will *dog it* lest he hurt. 彼はけがをしないよういいかげんにやるだろう.

dog it along ゆっくりと進む ▪ We *dogged it along* from Boston to New York. 我々はボストンからニューヨークまでゆっくりと進んだ.

dogged /dɔ́ːgəd/ 形 ***It's dogged* (*that, as*) *does it.*** 《諺》がんばってこそ事は成るのだ, 「思う念力岩をも通す」. ☞dogged = dogged way of doing.

doggo /dɔ́ːgoʊ/ 副 ***lie doggo*** 《俗》静かにしている, 隠れている; 時が来るのを待つ ▪ That hunter is *lying doggo.* その猟師はじっと隠れている ▪ It is wise of him to *lie doggo* for a bit. 彼がしばらくじっとしているのは賢明だ. ☞doggo はおそらく dog から.

doggone /dɔ́ːggɔ́ːn|dɔ́ggɔ́n/ 形 ***I'll be doggone if*** 《米俗》絶対...しない ▪ *I'll be doggone if* I go. おれは絶対行かない. ☞doggone = damned.

dog-house /dɔ́ːghàʊs/ 名 ***get*** *a person* ***out of the dog-house*** 《米》人を窮境から救う ▪ We must *get* people *out of the* post-war *doghouse.* 人々を戦後の窮境から救い出さねばならない.

in *a person's* ***dog-house*** 《口》人の不興を被って ▪ He is *in his master's doghouse.* 彼は主人の不興を被っている.

in the dog-house 《口》面目を失って, 人気を落として, 不興を被って ▪ Smith has been *in the doghouse* since his wife caught him flirting with another woman. スミスは他の女性といちゃついているのを妻に見つかって以来, 妻には頭があがらない.

doing /dúːɪŋ/ (do の現在分詞・動名詞) ***nothing doing*** 《口》 **1** 取引がない; 新作がない ▪ How is business?—*Nothing doing*. 商売はどうです—今は何もありません ▪ There is *nothing doing* in this line. この方面には新作がない.
2 《口》 何事もない, 何も起こって[始まって]いない ▪ There was *nothing doing*. 何事もなかった.
3 《俗》 お断りです; いりません 《依頼・申出の拒絶》; だめだった 《計画の失敗》 ▪ "Sorry, old man; *nothing doing*." お気の毒だがお断りするよ ▪ I am all through. *Nothing doing*. 私はすみました. もういりません ▪ I looked in the dictionaries. *Nothing doing*. 私は辞書を引いたが, だめだった.
take a bit of [***a lot of, some***] ***doing*** 《口》 かなりの努力を要する, 難事である ▪ It will *take doing* to make the change occur. 変化を起こすのにはかなりの努力を要するだろう ▪ Did everything go according to plan?—*Took a bit of doing*. 万事計画通りにいきましたか—なかなかの難事でした.

doit /dɔɪt/ 名 ***not care a doit*** ちっともかまわない ▪ I do*n't care a doit* for his person. 私は彼の風采など少しもかまわない. ☞doit「昔のオランダ貨幣(8分の1 penny)」.
not worth a doit 一文の価値もない ▪ It is *not worth a doit*. それは一文の値うちもない.

doldrums /dóʊldrəmz/ 名 ***in the doldrums*** **1** 気がふさいで, 元気がなく ▪ I'm *in the doldrums* and you always cheer me up. 私はふさいでいて, あなたはいつも元気づけてくれる.
2 (船がなぎなどのため)停頓状態で, 立ち往生して ▪ I saw her *in the doldrums*. 私はその船が立ち往生しているのを見た.
3 (商売が)不景気で, 停頓して ▪ We are *in the doldrums* at present. 我々は今のところ不景気です. ☞doldrums「赤道付近の無風地帯」.
out of the doldrums **1** (経済・商売が)停滞状態から脱して ▪ The Eurozone economies will come *out of the doldrums*. ユーロ諸国の経済は停滞状態から抜け出すだろう.
2 憂鬱から抜け出して ▪ It was my wife who got me *out of the doldrums* I'd been in for two years. 2年間私が落ち込んでいた憂鬱から抜け出させてくれたのは妻だった.

dole /doʊl/ 名 (***be***) ***on the dole*** 《口》 失業手当を受けて(いる) ▪ They *are on the dole*. 彼らは失業手当を受けている.
go on [***draw***] ***the dole*** 《口》 失業手当を受ける, 政府補助を受ける ▪ A good many people *go on the dole* because they do not like work. 仕事がきらいなために政府の補助を受ける人が相当多い.

doll /dɑl/ 動 ***doll*** *oneself* [***itself,*** etc.] ***up*** 《口》 めかしこむ, いきに着飾る ▪ She *was* all *dolled up*. 彼女はすっかりめかしこんでいた ▪ He *dolled himself up* to go to the factory dance. 彼は工場のダンス会に行くため, 派手に着飾った ▪ The classrooms *were dolled up* for the parents' evening. 教室は「父母の夕べ」のため美しく飾り立てられていた.

dollar /dɑ́lər|dɔ́lə/ 名 ***bet*** *one's* ***bottom dollar*** 《米口》 **1** なけなしの金を賭ける ▪ He *bet his bottom dollar* on it. 彼は財布の底をはたいてそれにかけた.
2 絶対確かである, 確信している ▪ I'll *bet my bottom dollar* that he will come. 彼はきっと来るよ.
bet you dollars to doughnuts …はまちがいなし, と請け合う ▪ I *bet you dollars to doughnuts* that she wins. 請け合ってもいい, 彼女は勝つさ.
one's ***bottom dollar*** 《米口》 残った1ドル, なけなしの金 ▪ I parted with *my bottom dollar* to rescue her. 彼女を救うためなけなしの金を出してしまった.
dollar for dollar 〚副詞的に〛 この値段では ▪ *Dollar for dollar*, you cannot get a better coat. この値段で, これ以上のコートは手に入りませんよ.
feel [***look***] ***like a million dollars*** → MILLION.
have [***with***] ***dollar signs in*** *one's* ***eyes/see dollar signs*** 儲けを当てこんでいる ▪ Smart marketers are now seeing college students *with dollar signs in their eyes*. 抜け目のない売買人が儲けを当てこんでいる大学生といま会っている.
it is dollars to doughnuts [《口》 ***buttons***] 《米口》 ほとんど確かである ▪ *It is dollars to doughnuts* that she will succeed this time. 彼女が今度こそ成功するのはまず間違いない. ☞to doughnuts の形が普通.

domestic /dəméstɪk/ 形 ***enter domestic service*** 家事手伝いになる ▪ English girls today don't like to *enter domestic service*. 今日のイギリスの少女たちは家事手伝いになることを好まない.

domesticate /dəméstəkèɪt/ 動 ***become domesticated with*** …と家族のように親しくなる ▪ Oliver *became domesticated with* the old lady. オリバーはその老婦人と家族のように親しくなった.

domination /dɑ̀mənéɪʃən|dɔ̀m-/ 名 ***under the domination of*** = under the DOMINION of.

dominion /dəmínjən/ 名 ***exercise*** [***have***] ***dominion over*** …に支配権をふるう ▪ Man *has dominion over* the animals. 人間は動物を支配している.
under the dominion of …の支配下にあって ▪ Gaul was *under the dominion of* Rome. ガリアはローマの支配下にあった.

domino /dɑ́mənòʊ|dɔ́mɪ-/ 名 ***domino theory*** ドミノ理論, 将棋倒し理論 ▪ The *domino theory* was used by successive United States administrations to justify the need for American intervention around the world. ドミノ理論は, アメリカが世界中で干渉する必要性を正当化するために代々のアメリカ政府が利用してきたものであった.
fall [***collapse***] ***like*** (***a row of***) ***dominoes*** 次々に倒れる ▪ Under systemic risk the world's financial system may *collapse like a row of dominoes*. 制度上の危機のもとで世界の財政制度は次々に崩壊するかもしれない.

it is domino with [***for***]《俗》…はもうだめだ, 終わりだ ▪ I thought *it was domino with* me. もうだめだと思った. ☞Domino の勝負で勝った者が最後のこまを打つとき "Domino!" と言うことから.

don /dɑn|dɔn/ 名 ***a Don Juan*** ドンファン ▪ He's *a* real *Don Juan*. 彼はまさにドンファンだ. ☞Don Juan は伝説上のスペイン貴族で典型的な女たらし.

D

be a don at …の名人である ▪ He *is a don at* cricket. 彼はクリケットの名人だ.

done /dʌn/ (do の過去分詞) (***be all***) ***done and dusted***《口》(人が仕事などをすっかり)終えて ▪ Yesterday I *was all done and dusted* just after lunch. きのう私は昼食の直後にすっかり仕事を終えた.

be [《英》***have***] ***done*** *doing* **1** …をし終えた ▪ I *am done packing*. 私は荷づくりを終えた ▪ When she *had done washing*, it was a white fleece. 彼女が洗い終えるとそれは白い羊毛だった.

2〚命令文で〛よせ! ▪ *Have done crying*! 泣くのはよせ!

(***be***) ***done in*** [《英》***up***] **1**《口》疲れはてて(いる)(= DONE for 1) ▪ He looked a bit *done in*. 彼はちょっと疲れた様子だった.

2 失敗する ▪ Public schools have gradually *been done in* by a lack of quality teachers. パブリックスクールは質の良い教師の不足でだんだんだめになってきている.

(***be***) ***done to the wide*** [***world***]《口》すっかり負かされて(いる), 力尽きて(いる) ▪ He came again after appearing *done to the world* more than once. 彼は何回も力尽きたように見えた後, 立ち直った ▪ He *was done to the wide* by the end of the fifth round. 彼は第5ラウンドの終わりまでにはすっかり参った.

be done with …が終わった[完成した] ▪ You*'re* not *done with* your work until you've completed this job. 君はこの作業を終えるまでは仕事が済んだとは言えない.

be [***have***] ***done*** (***with it***) **1** やってしまう ▪ Why don't you destroy the whole house and *have done with it*? なぜ君は家を全部こわしてしまわないのか.

2 (していることを)やめる ▪ *Have done*! やめろ!

done and dusted《英口》すっかり準備ができて ▪ We're *done and dusted*. You, hurry up. こっちはすっかり準備ずみだ. そっちも急いで.

done for《口》**1** 疲れ果てて, 使い古した, ぼろぼろの ▪ This computer is just about *done for*. このコンピューターはほぼがたがただ.

2 死にかけて ▪ The patient seemed as if he was *done for*. 患者は死にかけているかのように見えた ▪ I knew I was *done for* when the boss was waiting for me. 社長が私を待っているとき, もうおしまいだと悟った.

Easier said than done. →SAY².

hard done by 〚主に be, feel, look を伴って〛不当な扱いを受けて; 冷遇されて ▪ The workers *are* certainly *hard done by*. 労働者たちは確かに冷遇されている ▪ Why do you *feel hard done by*? 君はなぜ不当な扱いを受けていると思うのか.

isn't done《口》習慣上[社交上]禁じられている, (そんなことは)しないものである, それは無作法である ▪ You must not pour your tea in the saucer to cool it—it *isn't done*. お茶をさますため受け皿に移してはいけない—そんなことはしないものだ.

No sooner said than done.《俗》言うやいなや実行される[された]; 電光石火の速さでやる[やった].

That's done it.《口》まずいことになった; うまくいったぞ ▪ "*That's done it*!" he exclaimed ruefully. 「まずいことになった!」と彼は悲しげに言った.

the done thing/《米》***the thing to do***《口》正しい[礼儀にかなった]行為 ▪ It is *the done thing* in the theater. それは劇場では礼儀にかなった行為です ▪ Wearing jeans to a funeral isn't really *the done thing*. 葬儀でのジーンズ姿は礼儀に反する ▪ You shouldn't leave the table during the meal. It's not *the thing to do*. 食事中に退席してはならない. マナーに反する.

Well begun is half done. →BEGIN.

Well done! でかした, うまいぞ ▪ "*Well done!*" exclaimed Thomas. 「でかした!」とトマスが叫んだ.

What's done is done.《諺》済んだことは済んだこと.

donkey /dɑ́ŋki|dɔ́ŋ-/ 名 (***as***) ***stubborn as a donkey*** →(as) STUBBORN as a mule.

do the donkey work 骨の折れる辛い仕事をする ▪ I could *do the donkey work* for you. 君のためなら骨の折れる辛い仕事もするよ.

donkey's years [***ears***]《英口》長い間 (→《主に米俗》a COON's age) ▪ Hello! I haven't seen you for *donkey's years*. やあ! 久しぶりだね. ☞ロバの長い耳と年とをかけたもの.

talk the hind legs off a donkey →HIND-LEG.

doodah /dúːdɑː/ 名 ***all of a doodah***《英俗》興奮して, びくびくして ▪ The evenings made her *all of a* religious *doodah*. 夕方になると彼女は宗教的に興奮してきた ▪ When the examiner sent for me, I was *all of a doodah*. 試験官に呼ばれたとき私は全くびくびくものだった. ☞doodah 米南部農村の黒人歌 *Camptown Races* の折り返し句から.

doo-doo /dúːdu/ 名 ***be in deep doo-doo***《戯》(人が)大変[厄介]なことになっている ▪ If you're breaking all the rules, you*'re in deep doo-doo*. もし君がすべての規則を破っているなら, 大変なことになるよ. ☞doo-doo《幼児》「うんち」.

doom¹ /duːm/ 名 ***doom and gloom***/***gloom and doom*** 暗い見通し, 悲観的な予測 ▪ Much of the job news these days is full of *gloom and doom*. 当節は職のニュースの多くは暗い内容ばかりだ ▪ Americans have a low tolerance for *gloom and doom*. We are the nation of optimism. アメリカ人は暗い見通しに対する許容度が低い. 我々は楽天主義の国民なのだ.

One's ***doom is sealed.*** 人の運命が決まる ▪ *His*

doom is sealed. 彼の運命は決まった.

***go to* [*know, meet*] *one's* doom** 死ぬ, 滅びる ▪ He *met his doom* at Naples. 彼はナポリで没した.

spell doom for …に悲運[破滅]をもたらす ▪ A great difficulty *spelled doom for* the country. 大きな困難がその国に破滅をもたらした.

the crack of doom →CRACK[1].

the day of doom 最後の審判[世の終わり]の日; 恐ろしい事件のある日 ▪ He thinks *the day of doom* is come, if a hail-storm passes over the village. 彼はあられがその村全体に激しく降って過ぎると, 世の終わりの日が来たのだと思う ▪ *The day of doom* approached and on Jan. 14th the King was beheaded. 運命の日が近づき, 1月14日王は斬首された.

doom[2] /du:m/ 動 ***be doomed to*** **1** …する運命にある ▪ Much poetry *is doomed to* oblivion. 多くの詩は忘れられる運命にある.

2 …の宣告を受ける ▪ He *was doomed to* death by hanging. 彼は絞首刑の宣告を受けた.

doomsday /dú:mzdèɪ/ 名 ***till Doomsday*** 《口》世の終わりまで; いつまでも ▪ He can wait *till Doomsday* before I do that. 彼がいつまで待ったって私はそんなことはしない ▪ All official men wished to postpone it *till Doomsday*. 官吏はみなそれを永久に延期したいと思った.

door /dɔ:r/ 名 ***a closed door*** 制約(するもの) ▪ I believe that there are no *closed doors* in our lives. 私たちの生活には制約などないと信じています.

A door must be either* [*either be*] *shut or open. 《諺》扉は閉まっているか開いているかのいずれかである. ☞人は二兎を追うことはできない.

answer* [*go to*] *the door 取次に出る ▪ The maid *answered the door*. お手伝いが取次に出た.

As one door closes, another one opens. 《諺》一つのドアが閉まれば, もう一つのドアが開く,「捨てる神あれば拾う神あり」.

at death's door →DEATH.

bang the door down ドアをバンとたたき割る ▪ Officers *banged the door down*. 警官たちはドアをバンとたたき割った.

bar the door …への門戸を閉ざす ▪ Canada hastily decided to *bar the door* against the inflation she felt was coming. カナダは近づいていると感じたインフレへの道を閉ざすことに急遽決めた.

be at* a person's *door 人のところに迫っている ▪ It *is at our doors*. それは我々に迫っている.

be at the door of →lie at the DOOR of.

be knocking at* a person's *door (問題・機会が)いまにも起こりそうである ▪ God told Cain to be careful, because sin *was knocking at his door*. 神はカインに, いまにもお前が罪に問われそうだから気をつけるようにと言われた.

beat a path to* a person's *door 人と話し合いたがる, いっしょに仕事をしたがる ▪ If you really become famous, people will *beat a path to your door*. あなたが本当に有名になれば, 人々があなたと話し合いたがるだろう.

behind closed doors 秘密に ▪ The Society held its meeting *behind closed doors*. その協会は内密に会を開いた.

blow the doors off 《米口》…よりもはるかによい, に勝る ▪ This boat can *blow the doors off* many so-called go-fast boats. このボートは多くのいわゆる高速ボートよりもはるかに速い ▪ Rolls-Royce's newest model will *blow the doors off* most sports cars. ロールスロイスの最新型は大半のスポーツカーなど目じゃない.

by* [*through*] *the back door 《主に英》秘密に, 不正な手段で; 裏口から ▪ He must have got the contract *through the back door*. 彼は不正な手段で契約を結んだにちがいない ▪ Are these universities selling degrees *through the back door*? これらの大学は不正に学位を金で売っているのか?

close* one's *doors **1** 入らせない, 入会させない (*to*) ▪ The club has *closed its doors to* new members. そのクラブは新会員を入会させない.

2 店を閉じる, 営業をやめる ▪ They had to *close their doors* after three months. 彼らは3か月で店を閉じなければならなかった.

***close the door on* [*upon, to*]** **1** …への道を閉ざす, を不可能にする (↔open a DOOR to 1) ▪ It *closed the door on* his success. それは彼の成功への道を閉ざした ▪ The action of the Union has *closed the door to* any settlement. 組合の行動は解決への道を閉ざしてしまった.

2 戸を締めて入れぬ[出さぬ]ようにする ▪ They *closed the door upon* him. 戸を締めて彼を入れなかった[出さぬようにした] ▪ We shall *close the door to* all beggars. 物乞いはすべて締め出します.

3 …を見せぬようにする, (臭い物)にふたをする ▪ He *closed the door on* the scene. 彼はその場面を見せぬようにした.

darken* a person's *door →DARKEN.

early doors 《英口》(特に試合・コンテストに)先だって, 前もって, あらかじめ (＝earlier on (→EARLY)) ▪ We've got to make sure we don't concede, especially *early doors*. 我々は特に先立って必ず負けを認めないようにしなければならない.

(from) door to door **1** 戸口から戸口へ ▪ The taxi took us *from door to door*. タクシーは我々を戸口から戸口へ運んでいった ▪ We went *door to door* to collect enough signatures. 十分な署名を集めるために戸口から戸口へ回った.

2 戸ごとに ▪ She went *from door to door* selling matches. 彼女は戸ごとにマッチを売って歩いた.

get the door **1** 戸をあける ▪ I'll *get the door*. 私が戸をあけます.

2 解雇される, 追い出される ▪ He *got the door* at last. 彼はとうとう首になった.

give* a person *a foot in the door 人に昇進の足がかりを与える ▪ The two novels went very well and they *gave* me *a foot in the door*. その2冊の小説がうまくいって, 私は売り出しの足がかりを得た.

go to the door →answer the DOOR.

in by the back [side] door 秘密に入る ▪ He was allowed *in by the side door.* 彼は内密に入れてもらった.

in door(s) 屋内で[に], 家の中で[に] ▪ You had better remain *in door.* 君は家の中にいたほうがよい.

it's early doors 《英口》時間はたっぷりある ▪ *It's early doors* for final countdown. 最後の秒読みには時間はたっぷりある.

D

keep open doors →OPEN[1].

lay ... at the door of *a person*/ ***lay at*** *a person's* ***door*** 《文》(責め, 落ち度など)を人のせいにする[(人)に負わせる] ▪ You have *laid* your sins *at my door.* あなたは自分の罪を私のせいにした ▪ He *lays* his love of songs *at the door of* his nurse. 彼は自分の歌好きを乳母のせいにしている.

leave a [the] door open (議論・交渉などの)余地[可能性, 機会]を残しておく (*for, to do*) ▪ Britain wants to *leave the door open to* negotiate with Iran. 英国はイランとの交渉の可能性を残しておきたいと思っている ▪ This will's terms *leave the door open for* fighting among the heirs. この遺言の約定は相続人同士で争うために交渉の余地を残している. ☞報道でよく使用される.

lie [be] at the door of (罪などが人)にある (《聖》*Gen.* 4. 7) ▪ The fault *lies* [*is*] *at your door.* その過失の罪はあなたにある.

Lock the barn [《英》stable] door after the horse is stolen [is locked]. →shut the STABLE door after the horse is stolen.

make the door (upon, against) (...に対し)戸を締めてかんぬきを掛ける ▪ *Make the door upon* a woman's wit, and it will out at the casement. 女の機知は閉じこめてかんぬきを掛けても窓から出るだろう.

next door to **1** ...の隣に ▪ He lives *next door to* us. 彼は我々の隣に住んでいる.
2 ...に近く, ほとんど ▪ What you say is *next door to* a lie. 君の言うことは嘘に近い ▪ It is *next door to* impossible. それはほとんど不可能だ.

open a [the] door to [for]/ open (new) doors to [for] **1** ...への道を開く, を可能とする (↔ close the DOOR on 1) ▪ It *opened a door to* agreements on international affairs. それは国際問題についての協定への道を開いた ▪ It *opened the door for* the most confounding atheism to break in. それは最もひどい無神論が入りこむのを可能にした ▪ Iran Pressured to *Open Doors to* U.N. Rights Investigators イラン, 国連の実情調査官への道を開くように圧力をかけられる《新聞の見出し》.
2 ...に入る機会を与える, に...する機会を与える ▪ It *opened a door to* the French to assault us. それはフランス軍にわが軍を襲撃する機会を与えた ▪ We have *opened the door to* you. あなたに入る機会を与えた.

open *one's* ***doors*** **1** 入ることを許す (*to*) ▪ Some years ago the college *opened its doors to* men. 数年前その大学は男性にも入学を許した.
2 店[商売]を始める ▪ The department store *opened its doors* 50 years ago. そのデパートは50年前に営業を始めた.

out by the back [side] door 秘密に出る ▪ He was allowed *out by the back door.* 彼はこっそり出してもらった.

out of doors [door] 戸外で[に] ▪ You should spend more time *out of doors.* 君はもっと多くの時間を戸外で過ごすべきです ▪ Turn him *out of doors.* 彼を追い出せ.

push at [against] an open door 《英》〚主に進行形で〛楽々と仕事を達成する ▪ They *are pushing at an open door* because lots of people support their campaign against the new dam. 彼らは新ダム反対のキャンペーンを多くの人が支持しているので楽々と仕事を達成しつつある.

see *a person* ***to the door*** 人を戸口まで送り出す ▪ I *saw* him *to the doors.* 彼を戸口まで送り出した.

show *a person* ***the door*** **1** 出て行けと言う ▪ When she began to storm and rage, I *showed* her *the door.* 彼女がやかましくがなり立てだしたとき, 私は出て行けと言った.
2 追い出す ▪ He was so insolent that I finally *showed* him *the door.* 非常に無礼であったので私はとうとう彼を追い出した.

shut [slam] the door in *a person's* ***face*** → FACE[1].

shut the door on [upon] = close the DOOR on.

shut the door to →close the DOOR on.

the [a] revolving door **1** 《口》人員の入れ替わりが激しい組織[会社] ▪ The university has become *a revolving door* that can't keep professors. その大学は教授を長く務めさせておくことができない人員の入れ替わりの激しい組織になってしまった.
2 《主に米》役人の「天下り」 ▪ The President promised to end *the "revolving door"* between US officials and foreign companies. 大統領はアメリカの役人と外国企業間の「天下り」を終わらせると約束した.
3 一時問題を解決したが, また同じ問題が出てくる状況, 堂々めぐり ▪ He's just one of those people caught in *the revolving door* of the justice system. 彼は司法制度のその場しのぎの対策にはまった連中の一人にすぎない.

throw open *one's* ***doors to*** →THROW[2].

two [three] doors off [away] (その家から)2軒先[3軒先]に ▪ He lives *three doors off.* 彼はそこから3軒先に住んでいる.

When one door shut [is shut], another opens [is open]. 《諺》一方の扉が閉まれ[閉まっていれ]ば, 他方の扉が開く[開いている], 「捨てる神あれば拾う[助ける]神あり」.

with [within] closed doors 門戸を閉ざして; 非公開で ▪ The inquiry was held *with closed doors.* 尋問は非公開で行われた.

with open doors →OPEN[1].

within [without] doors 屋内[外]で ▪ It happened *within doors.* それは屋内で起こった.

doornail /dɔ́ːrnèɪl/ 名 **(as) dead as a doornail** →DEAD.

doorstep /dɔ̀ːrstép/ 名 **on [at]** *a person's* **[the] doorstep** …の近くに ▪ The revolution is here *on our doorstep.* 革命は我々の近くに来ている ▪ There is a swimming pool *at his doorstep.* 彼の(家の)近くにプールがある.

dope[1] /doʊp/ 名 **give the dope** 《俗》情報を知らせる ▪ I'll *give* you *the* live *dope.* 君に最近の情報を知らせよう.

hand (out) the dope 《俗》情報を知らせる ▪ He *handed* me *the dope.* 彼は私に情報を知らせてくれた ▪ I *handed out the dope* to him. 彼に内報した.

inside dope (会社などの)内部[極秘]情報 ▪ A friend gave me the *inside dope* on that business company. ある友人があの商社の内部情報を教えてくれた.

dope[2] /doʊp/ 動 **dope** *oneself* **with** …を飲用する ▪ He *doped himself with* cocaine. 彼はコカインを飲用した.

dormant /dɔ́ːrmənt/ 形 **lie dormant** 休止[潜伏, 夏眠, 冬眠]している; (権利などが)未発効である, 使用されないでいる ▪ Many plants *lie dormant* during the winter. 冬の間は眠っている植物が多い.

dose /doʊs/ 名 **give** *a person* **a dose of** 人に…を一服盛る ▪ I *gave* him *a dose of* flattery [punishment]. 彼におべっかを言ってやった[彼を罰してやった].

give *a person* ***a dose of his own medicine*** →MEDICINE.

go through ... like a dose of salts 《米口》 **1** …を完全に打ち負かす ▪ I'll *go through* the Mexicans *like a dose of salts.* メキシコ軍を完全に打ち負かしてやる.
2 (ものを得るため)…を敏速に捜す ▪ He *went through* the pockets *like a dose of salts.* 彼はポケットを素早く捜した.

have a regular dose of …を飲みすぎる《比喩的にも》 ▪ He always *has a regular dose of* cold pills. 彼はいつも風邪薬を飲みすぎる.

(only) in small doses 《口》短い間なら ▪ Relatives are nice *in small doses,* but can be very boring if they stay a long time. 親類は短い間ならいいものだが, 長く泊まられるとつくづくうんざりする ▪ I can *only* stand horror movies *in* very *small doses.* ホラー映画はほんの少しの間しかがまんできない.

doss /dɑs|dɔs/ 名 **a doss down** 《口》寝場所 ▪ I can give you *a doss down* in the attic. あなたを屋根裏部屋に泊めてあげてもよい.

dot[1] /dɑt|dɔt/ 名形 **a mere dot of a** ほんのちっぽけな ▪ He is *a mere dot of a* child. 彼はほんのちっぽけな子供にすぎない.

dot. com. billionaires インターネットを駆使して巨万の富を築いた若い富豪 ▪ The "*dot. com. billionaires*" are amassing wealth at such a rapid pace that the old rich are struggling to keep up. ネット億万長者はすごい速度で富を蓄えていて, 古くからの金持ちは追いつくために四苦八苦している.

go [walk] dot and carry one 足をひきずって歩く《比喩的にも》(→DOT and carry one) ▪ James *walks dot and carry one.* ジェイムズは足をひきずって歩く ▪ Your words *go dot and carry one.* おまえの言葉はしどろもどろだ.

in the year dot →YEAR.

off *one's* ***dot*** 《英俗》少し足りない; 気がふれて ▪ Tom was *off his dot.* トムは気がふれていた.

on the dot 《口》時間きっかりに; 即座に ▪ He went to the station at five right *on the dot.* 彼は5時きっかりに駅へ行った ▪ Pack up *on the dot* of 4:30. 4時半きっかりに仕事をやめなさい ▪ When I buy goods I always pay *on the dot.* 品物を買うときはいつも即金です.

put dots on 《俗》…を退屈させる, あきあきさせる ▪ He *puts dots on* me. 彼は私をあきあきさせる.

to a dot 《口》完全に, 全く ▪ This is correct *to a dot.* これは全く正確だ.

to the dot of an i どこからどこまでも完全に ▪ This is correct *to the dot of an i.* これはどこまでも完全に正しい.

walk dot and carry one → go DOT and carry one.

dot[2] /dɑt|dɔt/ 動 **(be) dotted about [around]** 〚受身で〛…が点在して(いる) ▪ There were a few sheep *dotted around* in the field. 野に数頭の羊が点在していた.

be dotted (about) with …が点在している ▪ The field *was dotted (about) with* sheep. 野原には羊が点在していた.

dot and carry one **1** (加算で)点を打って位を1けた上に送る; 足をひきずって行く ▪ Long ago, children were taught to *dot and carry one* when doing arithmetic. ずっと以前, 子供たちは足し算をするとき点を打って位を1けた上に送るように教えられた ▪ His way of walking was *dot and carry one.* 彼の歩き方は足を引きずるものだった.
2 〚名詞的に〛(加算のような)算数をする人, 数える人 ▪ You old dotard *Dot-and-carry-one!* このおいぼれの算数家め!
3 〚形容詞・副詞的に〛足をひきずって; 不規則に, 発作的に ▪ My pulse went *dot and carry one.* 私の脈拍は不規則だった.

dot and go one 〚形容詞・副詞的に〛足をひきずって(いる) ▪ He left the house, limping *dot and go one.* 彼は足をひきずりながら, 家を離れていった ▪ The conversation hobbled along in the *dot-and-go-one* fashion. 談話はまるで足をひきずるように, とぎれとぎれに進んだ.

dot *a person* ***one*** 《俗》人に一発くらわす ▪ He *dotted* me *one* in the eye. やつはおれの目に一発入れた.

dot the i's 慎重にする, 几帳面にする; 詳細にわたる, はっきり言う ▪ The chairman *dotted* no *i's* but everyone knew he meant the man. 議長ははっきり

D

は言わなかったが，みなその男のことだと分かっていた.

dot the [*one's*] ***i's and cross*** [*one's*] ***the t's*** →I.

dotage /dóʊtɪdʒ/ 名 ***be in*** *one's* ***dotage*** 老いぼれている ▪The world *is in its dotage* and doomsday is certainly coming all too fast. 世界は老いぼれており，最後の審判の日は確かにじつに速やかに迫りつつある.

D

double[1] /dʌ́bəl/ 名形副 ***a double whammy*** 《口》二重苦，ダブルパンチ ▪Hong Kong tourism was hit by *a double whammy* of war and health care. 香港の観光事業は戦争と健康管理というダブルパンチに見舞われていた.

at [《米》***on***] ***the double*** **1** 駆け足で ▪They advanced *at* [*on*] *the double*. 彼らは駆け足で進んだ. **2** 急速に，速く ▪Tell that boy to come here *on the double*. その少年に急いで来いと言ってくれ.

at [《米》***on***] ***the double-quick*** 非常に速く，大急ぎで ▪They were proceeding *at the double-quick*. 彼らは非常に速く行進していた. ☞double-quick time (1分間に33インチの165歩).

be *a person's* ***double*** 人とそっくり[瓜二つ]である ▪This kid *is his double* in every way. この子はあらゆる点で彼と瓜二つだ.

carry double (馬などが)二人乗せる ▪Marriage is a beast that *carries double*. 結婚は二人を乗せる馬である.

come the double (***on…***) 《俗》(…を)裏切る; (…を)ごまかす ▪Kate *came the double on* you. ケイトは君を裏切った.

do a double take 「えっ」と見直しをする ▪He looked like my brother so much that he *did a double take*. 彼は「えっ」と見直すほど兄に似ていた.

a person's ***double/the double of*** *a person* 人によく似た人[生き写し] ▪You are *your father's double*. 君はお父さんの生き写しだね.

double or quit(***s***) [***nothing***] ばくちで負けて前の損が倍になるか勝ってそっくり取り返すかの勝負; 一か八かの勝負 ▪He offered to play *double or quits*. 彼は一か八かの勝負をやろうと言った.

double quick 駆け足で，きわめて速く ▪Bundle out *double quick*. とっとと出て行け.

double (***quick***) ***time*** 駆け足で，きわめて速く ▪The boy ran to the confectioner's in *double quick time*. その少年は大急ぎで菓子屋へ走っていった.

give the double 術策を用いて(人を)避ける[逃れる] ▪He *gave the double* to some bailiffs. 彼は謀計を用いて執行吏を逃れた.

have [***perform***] ***a double service*** 二役をする ▪This furniture *has a double service*. この家具は二役をする《seat と bed など》.

in double (同じ物を)2通 ▪I send this *in double*. 私はこれを2通送ります.

lead [***live***] ***a double life*** 二重生活をする《特に，愛人を持っている男について》 ▪He was *living a double life*—a church warden by day and a thief by night. 彼は二重生活をしていた―昼は教会委員で，夜は泥棒であった ▪He was *leading a double life*. 彼は愛人を持っていた.

make a double **1**《印》1文[1行]を繰り返す. **2** くるりと向きを変える《ウサギが追われたときなど》 ▪I *made a double* towards the stern. 私は船尾の方へくるりと向きを変えた. **3** (二連銃で)2匹[2羽]もろとも撃ち取る ▪I *made a double*, bringing down two pheasants. 二連銃でキジを2羽もろとも撃ち落とした.

on the double →at the DOUBLE.

perform a double service →have a DOUBLE service.

ride double (馬に)相乗りする ▪Please *ride double* behind the butler. 執事の後ろに相乗りしてください.

see double 物が二重に見える ▪You'd have *seen double*. (酔って)物が二重に見えたでしょう.

sleep double 二人で寝る ▪Her mistress was *sleeping double*. 彼女の女主人は(同じベッドに)二人で寝ていた.

the double lines 船報中の喪失･事故記録 ▪They were reading *the double lines*. 彼らは船報の喪失･事故欄を読んでいた.

wear a double face 表裏がある; 顔と心とが違う ▪He *wears a double face* so you never know if you can trust him. 彼は顔と心が違うから信頼できるかどうか分かりっこない.

work double tides →TIDE[1].

double[2] /dʌ́bəl/ 動 ***double in brass*** **1**《米俗》平素の楽器のほかにもう一つの楽器を奏しうる; 別の役[仕事]を兼ねる; 二つの役[仕事]を兼ねる《ジャズ用語より》 ▪The jeep *doubled in brass* as a snowplow. そのジープはまた雪かきの役をも担った ▪He *doubles in brass* as a porter and a doorman. 彼はポーターとドアマンを兼ねている. **2**《米口》本職と他の仕事を兼ねる仕事をする ▪The young man can *double in brass* by writing the magazine. 若者は本職と雑誌を書く仕事を兼ねられる.

double itself 2倍になる ▪The money *doubled itself* in time. 金はやがて2倍になった.

double (***up***) *one's* ***fists*** こぶしを握る《戦う用意》 ▪He turned swiftly, *doubling his fists*. こぶしを握りながら，素早くその方へ向いた.

double-take /dʌ́bəltèɪk/ 名 ***do a double-take*** 再考する ▪Old people *did a double-take*. 老人たちは考え直した.

double-team /dʌ́bəltìːm/ 動 ***double-team it*** 《米》いっしょに協調して行動する ▪We can *double-team it* together. 我々はいっしょに協力することができる.

doubt /daʊt/ 名〚主に否定的に〛 ***a nagging doubt*** 絶えず良心をさいなむ[つきまとって離れない]疑い ▪I had *a nagging doubt* whether these options were fully appreciated by lawyers. 私はこれらの選択肢が弁護士に十分理解されているかどうかという，つきまとって離れない疑いを抱いていた.

a shadow of doubt 〚主に否定的に〛ちょっとの疑い ▪I have no *shadow of doubt* of his guilt. 彼の有罪は少しも疑わない.

beyond a* [*the*] *shadow of doubt/beyond a* [*all*] *doubt 全く疑いなく ▪His guilt was proved *beyond a shadow of doubt.* 彼の罪は一点の疑いもなく証明された.

beyond* [*out of*] (*all*) *doubt 疑う余地なく, もちろん ▪I believe *beyond all doubt* that he is honest. 彼が正直であると私は信じて疑いません.

beyond reasonable doubt 《法》合理的疑いの余地なく ▪I do not think he was proved guilty *beyond reasonable doubt.* 彼は合理的な疑いの余地なく有罪と証明されているとは思えない.

call ... in doubt ...の疑いをもつ[さしはさむ] ▪Success of an attack on Iran *is called in doubt.* イランへの攻撃が成功するか否か, 疑われている.

cast* [*throw*] *doubt on ...に疑いを投げかける ▪The prosecutor *cast doubt on* the defendant's alibi. 検察官は被告のアリバイに疑いを投げかけた.

have* one's *doubts はたして本当[賢明]かどうか疑う ▪I *have my doubts* as to his plan. 彼の計画がよいかどうか疑問に思っている.

***have no doubt* (*that*)** ...を疑わない ▪I *have no doubt* you will win the game. 君はきっと試合に勝つよ.

in doubt 不確かで, 不安で, 迷って ▪The result is still *in doubt.* 結果はまだ確かでない ▪I am *in doubt* what to do. 私はどうしたらよいか迷っている.

make doubt 疑う, 不確かである ▪I *make* some *doubt* whether the proclamation was ever printed. その宣言は一体印刷されたかどうか私はやや疑問に思っている.

make no doubt **1** 少しも疑わない, 確信する (*of, that, but that*) ▪I *make no doubt* I can get you out of the danger. あなたをその危険から脱出させることができると確信します ▪I *make no doubt of* your passing. 君の合格は疑いなしだ.
2 確かに...する (*that*) ▪*Make no doubt that* the safe door is locked. 確実に金庫の扉に錠をおろすんだ.

no doubt **1** 確かに ▪You've *no doubt* heard the news. 君は確かにそのニュースを聞いただろう.
2 《口》十中八九, おそらく ▪*No doubt* he meant to help. おそらく彼は助けるつもりだったんだろう.

without* (*a*) *doubt 疑いなく, むろん, 確かに ▪He'll come *without doubt.* 彼はきっと来る.

doubtful /dáʊtfəl/ 形 ***(be) doubtful of* [*about*]** ...を疑わしく思う, おぼつかなく思う ▪I *am doubtful of* its truth [his passing]. 私はその真偽[彼の合格]を疑う.

in a doubtful neighborhood いかがわしい人々の所に ▪I don't like to live *in* such *a doubtful neighborhood.* そんないかがわしい人々の所に住みたくない.

doubting /dáʊtɪŋ/ 形 ***a doubting Thomas*** 証拠がないと何でも疑う人 ▪He is *a doubting Thomas* born and bred. 彼は生まれながらの何でも疑う人だ. ☞キリストの弟子 Thomas が実証を得るまではキリストの復活を信じなかったことから (《聖》*John* 20. 24-29).

dough /doʊ/ 名 ***be in the dough*** 《米俗》金を持っている ▪You *are in the dough.* あなたは金を持っている.

marry into the dough 《米俗》金持ちと結婚する ▪She *married into the dough.* 彼女は金持ちと結婚した.

dovecot /dʌ́vkɑ̀t/, **dovecote** /dʌ́vkòʊt/ 名 ***a flutter in the dovecots*** 平和な生活をかき乱すこと ▪There will be *a flutter in the dovecots* before long. 近く平和な生活に波乱が起きるだろう.

flutter the dovecots ハトの間にはばたきを起こさせる, 平和な人々を騒がせる (cf. Sh., *Coriol.* 5. 6) ▪The book *fluttered the dovecots.* その本は平和な人々を騒がせた.

down[1] /daʊn/ 形副前名 ***a down and out* [*outer*]** 《米》窮乏の人, どん底の人 ▪I am floating around with *a down and out* from Battyville. バティビルから来た窮乏の人とさすらい歩いている.

be down as 《口》...と記入されている ▪His name *is down as* Smith in the telephone book. 彼の名は電話帳にスミスと記入されている.

be down for (入学・出場などを)する人として記名されている; (予約して)...に(氏名を)書き留めている ▪You*'re down for* a speech at the meeting. 君はその会で演説する人として記名されている ▪Both the boys *were down for* the race. 少年は二人ともその競走の出場者として記名されていた ▪You *are down for* Friday. お客さまは金曜日に予約されています.

be down in the world 零落している ▪When a person *is down in the world*, an ounce of help is better than a pound of preaching. 人が零落しているときは, 1ポンドの説教よりも1オンスの援助の方がありがたい. ☞Bulwer-Lytton の言葉.

***be down on* [*upon*]** **1** 《口》...におどりかかる; を責める, どなりつける; に対して怒る, 恨みを持っている ▪The critics would have *been down on* the author. 批評家たちは著者を攻撃しただろう ▪She *was* rather *down on* me for asking him to the party. 彼女は私が彼を会に招待したと言って少し私を責めた ▪Tom *is down on* his teacher. トムは先生を恨んでいる.
2 《口》...をいじめる, につらく当たる ▪She complains that he *is* always *down on* her. 彼女は彼がいつもつらく当たるとこぼしている.
3 ...を憎む, きらう; に偏見を持つ, 反対する ▪The teacher *is down on* the pupil. 先生はその生徒に偏見を持っている.
4 《俗》...を知っている, に抜け目がない, (奸計)を見抜く ▪The Baronet *was down on* it. 准男爵はそれを見抜いていた.
5 ...に弱い ▪You don't have to *be down on* things. 君は物事を怖がることはない.
6 《口》...をすぐに見つけて指摘する ▪The teacher

was down on the boy's mistake in a flash. 先生はすぐにその生徒の誤りを見つけて指摘した.

7《口》…に(金などを)要求する (*for*) ▪ The creditors *were down on* him *for* payment of his debts. 債権者たちは彼に借金支払いを要求した.

be down to 《口》少なくなって…だけになる ▪ We *are* almost *down to* our last penny. 我々は金がすくなくなってほとんど最後の1ペニーだけになった.

D

be down to every move →MOVE[1].

be down with …で寝ている, (病)にかかっている ▪ Mary *is down with* influenza. メアリーはインフルエンザで寝ている.

be run down 体のかげんが悪い ▪ He *is* very much *run down*. 彼は非常に体のかげんが悪い.

be up and down (床から)起きて階下へ降りている ▪ He *is up and down*. 彼は起きて階下へ降りている.

down and out **1** 万策尽きて; すっかり参って, 落ちぶれはてて ▪ I'm *down and out*, but I'm no traitor to my friend. 私は万策尽きたが, 友人を決して裏切らない ▪ Everybody over 40 is *down and out*. 40歳以上の人はみなすっかり参って[疲れて]しまった.

2 無一文で, 破産して, 窮乏して ▪ Once a very rich man, he is now *down and out*. 昔は大変な金持ちであったが, 彼は今はすっかり窮乏している.

3《米》窮乏者 ▪ This is a kind of hostel for poor *down and outs*. ここは哀れな窮乏者たちの宿泊所のようなものである.

down at (the) heel(s) →HEEL[1].

down by the head →by the HEAD.

down cellar →CELLAR.

down for a count of 《ボクシング》…数える間ダウンして ▪ He was *down for a count of* five. 彼は5つ数える間倒れていた.

down for (consideration) (議案などが)再考に付せられて ▪ The bill is *down for consideration*. その法案は再考に付せられている.

down in the mouth →MOUTH[1].

down the ages [years] 各時代を通じて[後年に至るまで] ▪ They have tried, *down the ages*, to do so. 彼らは各時代を通じてそうしようとしてきた ▪ A childhood experience carried magic *down the years*. 幼年時代の経験は後年まで魔力を伴った.

down the drain [pan, plughole, toilet, tube(s)] 《口》 **1** (金が)浪費されて, どぶにすてられて; (努力が)水泡に帰して, 無価値になって (→DRAIN[1]) ▪ Don't throw money *down the drain*. 金を無駄遣いしちゃいけない ▪ Plenty of Internet dreams have gone *down the drain*. インターネットの多くの夢が水泡に帰した.

2 (取り返しがつかないほど)悪化して ▪ It is sad to see marriages going *down the tubes*. 結婚が取り返しがつかないほど悪化するのを見るのはつらい.

down there **1** (下方をさして)あれあそこに ▪ Look at the pond *down there*. あそこの池を見なさい.

2 おい, 下にいる者! ▪ Be careful. *Down there*! 気をつけろ. おい下にいる者たち!

down to …に至るまで ▪ The custom continued *down to* the present time. その習慣は現在まで続いてきた ▪ Everyone is responsible for the other, from the king *down to* the peasant. すべての人は, 国王から農夫に至るまで他の人に対して責任がある.

down town (下の)市内に, 下町に ▪ She was *down town* alone. 彼女は一人下町にいた.

down under (英国から見て)地球の反対側に, オーストラリア・ニュージーランドに ▪ The same could happen *down under*. 同じことがオーストラリア方面にも起こりうるだろう ▪ It is a gift to the Prince from *down under*. それはオーストラリア・ニュージーランドから殿下への贈り物です.

down** one's **way …の近所に ▪ *Down our way* most people have got broadband. うちの近所ではたいていの人がブロードバンドにしている.

down with [[put などの動詞を省いた命令文の形]]

1 …をやっつけろ, ぶっつぶせ, 打倒せよ ▪ *Down with* the tyrant. 暴君を打倒せよ! ▪ *Down with* the door! 戸をたたきこわせ!

2 (金など)をすぐ出せ[払え] ▪ *Down with* your money [the dust]! 金をすぐ出せ!

3 …を風下に取れ ▪ *Down with* the helm! かじを風下に取れ.

4 (ストライキを始めるとき仕事)をやめろ ▪ *Down with* the work! 仕事をやめろ.

for** so much **down 手付け金(として第1回払い込み金)いくらで ▪ He bought the house *for* $9,000 *down* and $580 a month. 彼はその家を手付け金9,000ドル, 月580ドルで買った.

go down town 下町へ行く, 買い物に行く (→DOWN town) ▪ I am *going down town* this afternoon. きょう午後から下町へ行くつもりです.

have a down on 《口》(人)を恨む, きらう; (人)に悪感情をいだく, 不当な偏見をいだく ▪ Somebody *has got a down on* him. 誰かが彼を恨んでいる ▪ The examiner *has a down on* me. 試験官は私に偏見をいだいている.

have down cold 《俗》完全に覚えている ▪ I *have* this song *down cold*. 私はこの歌を完全に覚えている. ☞cold = completely.

hit [kick]** a person **who is [when he's] down 倒れた者を打つ; 人の不幸につけこんでさらに害を与える ▪ It is just *hitting* a man *when he's down*. それはまさしく倒れた人を打つことになる.

money down →MONEY.

The cove is down. 《俗》カモは気づいた《すりの意図が感づかれたときの文句》.

up and down →UP[1].

up hill and down dale →HILL.

ups and downs →UP[1].

down[2] /daʊn/ 動 ***down tools*** →TOOL.

downer /dáʊnər/ 名 ***have a downer on*** 《英豪・口》(人)を嫌っている ▪ She knows Paul *has a downer on* her. 彼女はポールが自分を嫌っていることはわかっている.

downgrade /dáʊngrèɪd/ 名 ***on the down-***

grade 成功[勢力, 健康]を失って; 下り坂で ▪ The business seems to be *on the downgrade.* 商売は下り坂のようだ.

downhill /dáʊnhìl/ 名副 ***downhill all the way/all downhill from here*** **1** ずっと[ここからは]下り坂である; ずっと[これからは]とんとん拍子で進んで ▪ Once the police had broken his alibi, the rest was *downhill all the way.* 警察が一旦彼のアリバイをくずしてしまうとあとはもうとんとん拍子で進んだ.
2 ずっと[これからは]どんどん衰えて[堕落して]いく ▪ Once you get to my age, it's *downhill all the way.* 僕の年齢になるとどんどん衰えていくよ. ☞↔uphill all the way/all uphill from here.

go downhill 丘[坂]を下っていく; (健康・家運などが)衰えていく ▪ After he retired, he *went downhill* rapidly. 引退してのち彼は急速に衰えていった.

the downhill of life 人生の下り坂, 晩年 ▪ He foolishly took to drink to solace *the downhill of life.* 彼は愚かなことに晩年を慰めるために酒に手を出した.

Downing Street /dáʊnɪŋstrìːt/ 名 ***find favor in Downing Street*** 現英政府に受けがよい ▪ He does not *find favor in Downing Street.* 彼は現英政府の受けがよくない. ☞ダウニング街には首相官邸・外務省などがあり「現英国政府」の意に用いられる.

down(-)payment /dáʊnpéɪmənt/ 名 ***make a down-payment of... on*** ...に...の頭金を払う ▪ He *made a down-payment of* $90 *on* the machine. 彼はその機械に90ドルの頭金を払った.

require a down payment for ...に分割払いの頭金の支払いを求める ▪ How much of *a down payment* do you *require for* this new car? この新車にはいくら頭金を払えばいいのですか.

downward /dáʊnwərd/ 形 ***on the downward path*** 下落[堕落]の途上に ▪ I started *on the downward path.* 私は堕落し始めた.

downy /dáʊni/ 名 ***do the downy*** 《俗》寝床に伏す, 眠る ▪ He cut chapel to *do the downy.* 彼は礼拝出席をさぼって寝た. ☞downy = bed.

do the downy on 《口・古風》= do the DIRTY on a person.

gone to the downy 《俗》就寝して ▪ He is *gone to the downy.* 彼は就寝している.

doze /doʊz/ 名 ***fall [go off] into a doze*** (思わず)うとうとする ▪ Tired and weary, he *fell into a doze.* くたびれ果てて, 彼はついうとうとした.

dozen /dʌ́zən/ 名 ***a baker's [devil's, long, printer's] dozen*** パン屋の1ダース; 13 ▪ Instead of one kick, he got *a devil's dozen.* ひとけりでなく彼は13回けられた.

by the dozen ダースいくらで ▪ Pencils are sold *by the dozen.* 鉛筆はダース単位で売られる.

by (the) dozen(s) 何十となく ▪ They are to be had *by dozens.* それらは何十となく得られる.

daily dozen 《英口》毎日行う体操《もと12種の組み合わせから成り通例朝起きた時行う》 ▪ I would rather do a *daily dozen* than go on a diet. ダイエットするより毎日体操をするほうがいい.

give** a person **two dozen [a baker's dozen] 《俗》人を2ダース[13回]むち打つ ▪ I *gave* them *two dozen* each. 彼らをおのおの2ダースずつむち打った.

in dozens ダースずつに ▪ Pack them *in dozens.* 1ダースずつそれらを包みなさい.

nineteen to the dozen 《口》非常に早く, ひっきりなしに, 盛んに(しゃべる, など) ▪ She generally talked *nineteen to the dozen.* 彼女は概して盛んにしゃべりまくった ▪ His tongue goes *nineteen to the dozen.* 彼は早口にしゃべる. ☞12語で足りるのを19語も使うという意味から.

six (of one) and half-a-dozen (of the other) →SIX.

thirteen to the dozen (12に対し13, から)おまけで ▪ Pay it *13 to the dozen.* それをおまけをつけて払いなさい.

drachm /dræm/ 名 ***not a drachm of*** ほんのちょっぴりの...もない ▪ The rogue has *not a drachm of* love about him. その悪党にはほんのちょっぴりの愛情もない.

draft, 《主に英》**draught** /dræft|drɑːft/ 名《アメリカでは通常 draft. イギリスでは「草案・設計略図」「為替手形」の意味以外は通例 draught》.

at a [one] draft 一飲みにぐいと ▪ He drank a glass of milk *at a draft.* 彼はコップ1杯のミルクを一飲みにぐいと飲んだ.

draw [make] a draft 風を通す ▪ This smoker can *draw a draft* and keep the temperature stable. この煙突は通風がよく温度を一定に保つことができる.

draw a draft on (a bank) (銀行)宛てに手形を振り出す ▪ He *drew a draft* for $100 *on a bank.* 彼は銀行宛てに100ドルの手形を振り出した.

feel a [the] draught 《俗》 **1** (「すき間風を感じる」から)逆境に苦しむ, 困窮する ▪ When the wind changed, the Conservative party *felt the draught.* 風向きが変わって, 保守党はひどく困った.
2 歓迎されない[冷遇されている]と感じる ▪ Let's go out. I *feel a draft.* 出ていこう. (ここでは)歓迎されないようだ.

make [draw] a draft 風を通す ▪ Mother tried hard to *make a* greater *draft* up the chimney. 母は煙突の通風をもっとよくしようと一生懸命に努めた.

make a draft on [upon] **1** (銀行・資金)から金を引き出す ▪ He *made a draft on* the bank. 彼は銀行から金を引き出した.
2 (信頼・友情・忍耐など)を(強く)要求する ▪ Her Majesty *makes a* thoughtless *draft on* the loyalty of her minister. 女王陛下は無思慮にも大臣の忠誠を強要なさっている.

make out a draft of ...を起草する ▪ He *made out a draft of* the opening address. 彼は開会の辞を起草した.

on draft たるから出して ▪ Beer is sold *on draft.*

ビールはたるから出して売られる ▪ Beer *on draft* beats bottled beer any day. 生ビールはびんビールよりも文句なしにまさっている.

drag[1] /dræg/ 名 ***at drag*** 《米》動物群の後部の所[のそばに] ▪ Two or three men *at drag* urged on the sluggish animals. 群れの後部にいる2, 3人がのろい動物をせきたてた.

be a drag to [***on***] …の足手まといである ▪ You will *be a drag to* your brother. あなたは兄さんの足手まといになるだろう.

drag on the market 市場の足手まとい, 売れ残り ▪ Cameras of this kind went out of fashion and are now *drags on the market*. このタイプのカメラはすたれて, いまや売れ残りになっている.

have a drag with …の気に入っている ▪ He *had a drag with* his employer. 彼は主人に気に入られていた.

in drag 《俗》(男が)女の服を着て ▪ The boys were completely *in drag*. 少年たちはすっかり女装していた.

main drag 《米口》(都市や町の)本通り ▪ We noticed several store vacancies on the *main drag*. 本通りの店が数軒空き家になっているのに気づいた.

take a drag at [***on***] …をぐっと吸う ▪ He *took a drag at* a cigarette. 彼は巻きタバコを1服吸った.

take a drag from …からぐっと飲む ▪ He *took a drag from* the glass. 彼はコップからぐっと飲んだ.

What a drag! とても退屈だ[つまらない] ▪ Susan said *what a drag* housework was. 家事ってなんて退屈なのとスーザンが言った.

drag[2] /dræg/ 動 ***drag*** *oneself* ***along*** (疲れて)足を引きずって歩く ▪ He *dragged himself along* behind the others. 彼はみんなのあとから足を引きずって歩いた.

drag *a person* (***along***) ***kicking and screaming*** 人に嫌なことを無理やりさせる ▪ US markets are *being dragged along kicking and screaming* with much stronger overseas bourses. 米国市場は, はるかに強力な海外の金融市場のために無理やり引きずられている.

drag (*one's*) ***ass***/***drag tail*** [***it***] 《俗》立ち去る (depart) ▪ I'm *dragging my ass* out of this town. 私はこの町から立ち去るつもりだ.

drag *one's* ***brains*** [***mind***] (***for***) (…のため)知恵をしぼる ▪ She *dragged her mind for* an excuse. 彼女は言い訳を考え出すために知恵をしぼった.

drag *one's* ***feet*** [***heels***] **1** (疲れなどで)足を引きずって歩く ▪ He was *dragging his feet* with exhaustion. 彼はへとへとになって足を引きずって歩いていた.

2 さっさと行動しない; 故意にぐずぐずする; いいかげんにする ▪ They *drag their feet* in the campaign. 彼らは選挙運動を本気でやらない.

drag *one's* ***tail*** 《俗》わざとのろのろと動く[行動する] ▪ Hurry up, stop *dragging your tail*. 急げ, のろのろするんじゃない.

drag *oneself* (***up***) ***by*** *one's* (***own***) ***bootstraps*** = pull oneself (up) by one's (own) BOOTSTRAPs.

dragon /drǽgən/ 名 ***chase the dragon*** 《英俗》アヘン[ヘロイン]を吸う ▪ Jailbirds were caught *chasing the dragon* in a cell block. 囚人が独房棟でヘロインを吸っているところを見つかった.

dragon lady 《米口》猛女 ▪ Nancy is no *dragon lady*, her husband claims. ナンシーは猛女なんかじゃない, と夫は主張する.

like a dragon 猛烈に ▪ I set to the tales *like a dragon*. 私は猛然とその物語にとりかかった.

drain[1] /dreɪn/ 名 ***a brain drain*** **1** 《口》(優秀な学者・技術者の)海外への流出, 頭脳流出 ▪ There is *a brain drain* of Russian scientists to the United States. ロシアの科学者が米国に頭脳流出している.

2 大変な集中力を要する疲れる仕事 ▪ The paper I had to write was *a* regular *brain drain*. 私が書かなければならなかった論文は, まさに集中力を要するつらい仕事だった.

be a drain on …に対する消耗である ▪ It *was a drain on* his energy. それは彼の精力を消耗させた.

down the drain 《口》といを流れ下って; 浪費されて ▪ The Japanese custom of returning a gift is a lot of money *down the drain*. 贈り物の返礼をする日本の習慣は大変なお金の浪費である.

go down the drain 《口》消える; (質が)下落する; むだになる ▪ They collapsed or *went down the drain*. 彼らは倒れるかまたは姿を消した ▪ Things are *going down the drain*. 品物の質が落ちている ▪ All my savings have *gone down the drain*. 私の貯えはみなむだになってしまった.

laugh like a drain 《英》大声で笑う ▪ They were all *laughing like a drain*. 彼らはみんな高笑いしていた.

to the drains おりまで(飲み尽くして) ▪ I emptied some opiate *to the drains*. アヘン剤を飲み干した.

drain[2] /dreɪn/ 動 ***drain*** *a person* ***dry*** 人の精根を枯れさせる ▪ This work will *drain* him *dry*. この仕事は彼の精根を枯れさせるであろう.

drain ... to the dregs →drink ... to the DREGs.

dram /dræm/ 名 ***fond of a dram*** 酒が好きで ▪ He is *fond of a dram*. 彼は酒が好きだ. ☞dram「(ウィスキーなどの)一口」.

not one dram of …が少しもない ▪ He has *not one dram of* learning. 彼は学問が少しもない.

drama /drɑ́ːmə/ 名 ***make a drama out of*** 《口》…を大げさに言う ▪ US lawmakers are *making another drama out of* a crisis. 米国の議員連中はまた危機を大げさに言い立てている.

drape /dreɪp/ 動 ***drape*** *oneself* 身を包む; もたれかかる ▪ He *draped himself* in abstruse thought. 彼は深遠な思想に身を包んだ ▪ Several of the regulars *draped themselves* around the bar. 数人の常客がバーのカウンターにもたれかかっていた.

drat /dræt/ 動 ***Drat it*** [***you***, etc.]***!*** 《口》ちぇっ!, 畜生!《しばしば女性が用いる》 ▪ *Drat it!*

That's the fourth fish I've lost. 畜生! これで4匹目の魚を取り逃がした ▪ *Drat the child!* うるさいがきだ!

draw[1] /drɔː/ 名 ***a good draw*** すばらしい呼び物 ▪ Performing elephants are always *a good draw* at circuses. 芸をするゾウはサーカスではいつもすばらしい呼び物になる.

beat ... to the draw 相手より早く剣[銃]を抜く; 人より早くする, 機先を制する ▪ He *beat* his enemy *to the draw*. 彼は敵の機先を制した.

give [get, have] the draw on 《米俗》(人)より先に銃を取り出させる[出す]; 機先を制させる[する] ▪ His experience *gave* him *the draw on* his opponents. 経験のおかげで彼は相手の機先を制した.

play a draw 引き分けとなる ▪ Liverpool and Manchester United *played a draw* at 2-2. リバプールとマンチェスター・ユナイテッドは2対2で引き分けた.

quick [slow] on the draw **1** 剣[銃]を取り出すのが早い[遅い] ▪ He is *quick on the draw*. 彼は銃を取り出すのが早い.

2 反応が早い[遅い] ▪ John is *quick on the draw* and has a ready answer. ジョンは返答が早く, 即答できる.

take a draw (in a lottery) (宝くじを)引く ▪ I *took a draw* and to my delight held the winning ticket. くじを引いたら, うれしいことに当たりくじだった.

draw[2] /drɔː/ 動 ***draw a bill [check] on a bank for*** 銀行あてに...(金額)の手形[小切手]を振り出す ▪ He *drew a bill on the bank for* £1,000. 彼はその銀行あてに1,000ポンドの手形を振り出した.

draw (a) blank **1** からくじを引く ▪ He *drew a blank*. 彼はからくじを引いた.

2《口》見つからない, 何も得ない, 失敗する ▪ We looked in the desk for Father's will, but *drew a blank*. 父の遺言書を捜すため机の中を見たが見つからなかった ▪ He entered for the sweepstake, but *drew a blank*. 彼は賭け金独占の競馬に賭けたが, 何も得られなかった.

3 キツネを見つけない; ...を捜しても獲物が見つからない ▪ The meet had *drawn a blank* and returned disappointed. 狩猟団はキツネが見つからないので失望して帰った ▪ Some of these woods *were drawn blank*. これらの森をいくつか捜したが獲物は何も見つからなかった.

draw and quarter **1** 手足を馬で引っぱって四つ裂きにする; 絞首刑にしたのち, 内臓を出して体を四つ裂きにする ▪ He was hanged, *drawn and quartered*. 彼は絞首刑にされ, 内臓を出され, 四つ裂きにされた.

2 (人を)厳しく罰する ▪ If you miss another piece of homework, Bill, I'll have you *drawn and quartered*. ビル, こんど宿題をしてこなければ, 君を厳しく罰するぞ.

draw at a [one's] pipe タバコを吸う ▪ He *drew* again *at his pipe*. 彼はまたタバコを吸った.

draw bit [bridle, rein] 馬を止める; 身を引きしめる ▪ He *drew rein* in the square. 彼は四辻で馬を止めた.

draw blood **1** 血を出させる ▪ The dog's teeth *drew blood*. 犬の歯が血を出させた.

2《口》怒らせる, 激怒させる ▪ His words *drew blood* from her. 彼の言葉が彼女を激怒させた.

draw deep [light] (船の)喫水が深い[浅い] ▪ The ship *draws deep*. その船は喫水が深い.

draw ... dry ...をくみ干す, 飲み干す, 枯渇させる ▪ They *drew* the well *dry*. 彼らはその井戸をくみ干した ▪ The calf *drew* the cow *dry*. 子牛は母牛の乳を飲み干した ▪ The Persian war has *drawn dry* his coffers. ペルシャ戦争で彼の金庫は枯渇した.

draw in one's horns 金を節約する ▪ We have to *draw in our horns* a bit now that you're out of a job. 君が職を失ったので少々節約せねばならない.

draw it fine《口》**1** きわめて正確にする, 寸分たがわない; こまやかな区別立てをする ▪ You *draw it* too *fine*. あなたはあまり言葉をほじくりすぎる.

2 = CUT it fine.

draw it mild《口》**1**〚主に命令文で〛(あざけり・不信・願望の意をもって)大げさに言うなよ, まさか, 誇張しないでくれ ▪ Here, *draw it mild*! おい, 大げさに言うなよ! ▪ We told him to *draw it mild*. 彼に大げさなことを言うなと言った.

2 行動を控え目にする, 度を過ごさぬ ▪ Our ladies promised to *draw it* as *mild* as possible. 婦人たちはできるだけ控え目に行動すると約束した.

3 たるから甘口のビールを出す ▪ A pint of double X, and please *draw it mild*. ダブルXのビールを1パイント, 甘口にしてくれ. ☞↔DRAW it strong.

draw it strong 大げさに言う, 過激にやる ▪ What might the consequences be if they *drew it strong*? もし彼らが過激なことをやったらどんな結果になるだろうか. ☞「ビールの strong (辛口)の方をたるから出す」が原義.

draw light →DRAW deep.

draw near →NEAR.

draw on a cigarette タバコを吸う ▪ He stopped to *draw on a cigarette*. 彼は立ち止まって[手を休めて]タバコを吸った.

draw on one's credit 自分の信用を利用する; 借金する ▪ He *drew* largely *on his credit*. 彼は大いに借金した.

draw on a person's credulity 人の信じやすさを利用する; 人をだます ▪ He *drew on my credulity*. 彼は私をだました.

draw on a person's faith 人の信用に依存している; 信じられない ▪ The story *draws* largely *on our faith*. その話は我々には大いに疑わしい.

draw on one's imagination 想像ででっちあげる; 嘘をつく ▪ He did not know the true story, so he *drew on his imagination*. 彼は真相を知らなかったので, 作り話をした.

draw one's pen [quill] against ...をペンで攻撃する ▪ He *drew his pen against* a certain great man. 彼はある偉い人をペンで攻撃した.

draw one's pen [quill] for ...をペンで弁護する ▪ They *drew their quills for* the Whigs. 彼らはペンでホイッグ党を弁護した.

draw rein →DRAW bit.

draw short and long →SHORT.

draw the cloth 食後テーブルをかたづける，食後(特にデザートの前に)テーブル掛けを取りのける ▪ When *the cloth was drawn*, he would retire to his own apartment. 食後テーブルがかたづけられると，彼は自分の部屋へ引き取るのだった.

draw the fire of …の射撃の的となる ▪ The senator's insults *drew the fire of* his opponents. その上院議員の侮辱的言辞は反対者らの攻撃の的となった.

draw the sword against [***at***] →SWORD.

draw the winner **1** くじで勝者を決める ▪ They *drew the winner*. 彼らはくじで勝者を決めた.
2 勝馬の馬券を買い当てる; 成功する ▪ He's *drawn the winner* this time. 彼は今度こそ成功を収めた.

draw to an end [***a close, a finish***] 終わりになる ▪ The longest day must *draw to an end*. どんなに長い日でも暮れねばならない ▪ The vacation is *drawing to a close*. 休暇は終わろうとしている.

draw *oneself* ***to*** *one's* ***full height*** 居丈高になる，見識ばる ▪ He *drew himself to his full height*. 彼は居丈高になった.

draw *oneself* ***together*** 身を引き締める ▪ He *drew himself together* at the first day. 彼は初日には身を引き締めた.

draw *oneself* ***up*** (威厳・怒りを示すため)そり身になる，しゃきっと背筋を伸ばす ▪ He *drew himself up* in dignity. 彼はしゃきっと背筋を伸ばして威厳を示した ▪ He *drew himself up* proudly. 彼は誇らしげに身をそらせた.

draw up a chair 椅子を引き寄せる ▪ She *drew up a chair* beside me. 彼女は私のそばに椅子を引き寄せた.

draw *a person* ***up sharp*** [***sharply***] 人に話をピタリと止めさせる ▪ A sudden shock from an earthquake *drew* the speaker *up sharp*. 急に地震があって演説者はピタリと話をやめた.

draw *oneself* ***up to*** *one's* ***full height*** しゃきっと全身を伸ばして居丈高になる ▪ He *drew himself up to his full height* and thundered at the class. 彼はしゃきっと全身を伸ばして居丈高になり，クラス(の生徒)をどなりつけた.

hang, draw, and quarter → DRAW and quarter.

Like draws to like. 《諺》同気相求む.

drawback /drɔ́:bæ̀k/ 名 ***be a drawback to*** …の妨害になる ▪ Envy *is a drawback to* friendship. ねたみは友情の妨げになる.

drawbridge /drɔ́:brìdʒ/ 名 ***pull up the drawbridge*** (城の堀の)つり上げ橋を上げる; (家族だけで過ごすために)客を断る ▪ We shouldn't *pull up the drawbridge* and stop immigration. 我々はつり上げ橋をあげて，移民を中断するべきではない ▪ Occasionallly I want to *pull up the drawbridge*, and enjoy some time alone. ときおり客を断ってしばらく一人になることを楽しみたくなることがある.

drawer /drɔ́:ər, drɔ:r/ 名 *one's* ***bottom drawer*** 嫁入支度の衣装類 ▪ She showed me *her bottom drawer*. 彼女は嫁入支度の衣装類を私に見せた. ☞最下段の引き出しに嫁入衣裳を入れたことから. →《米》HOPE chest.

from (***out of***) ***the top drawer*** 《主に英》トップクラス(の出身)で (→ the top DRAWER) ▪ She comes *from the top drawer*. 彼女は貴族の出身である.

the top drawer 上流階級，トップクラス ▪ The Grand Hotel may be *the top drawer*, but it's not pretentious. グランドホテルはトップクラスかもしれないが，お高くはとまっていない ▪ The gentleman was certainly out of *the top drawer*. その紳士は間違いなく上流階級の出だった.

drawing /drɔ́:ɪŋ/ 名 ***a drawing card*** 大入りを取る芸能人，人気番組; 呼びもの，(野球の)好カード ▪ Cowboy music is always *a* good *drawing card*. カウボーイ音楽はいつも人気のある呼び物である.

in drawing 正確に描かれて ▪ The house is *in drawing*. その家は正確に描かれている.

out of drawing **1** (特に遠近法が)画法に反して，不正確に描かれて ▪ The building is *out of drawing*. その建物は不正確に描かれている.
2 (周囲に)調和しないで，不調和に ▪ The house is *out of drawing* with surrounding elements. その家は周囲のものと不調和である.

drawing-board /drɔ́:ɪŋbɔ̀:rd/ 名 ***Back to the drawing board!*** (計画が失敗して)振り出しに戻るんだ! ▪ We said, "Ah well, *back to the drawing board!*" 我々は「よし，振り出しに戻るんだ!」と言った. ☞the drawing board「製図板」.

drawing-room /drɔ́:ɪŋrù:m/ 名 ***hold*** [***keep***] ***a drawing-room*** 接見会を催す ▪ In the evening the queen *kept a drawing-room*. 夕方女王は接見会を催した.

drawn /drɔ:n/ 形 ***be*** [***feel*** (*oneself*)] ***drawn to*** [***toward***] …に心引かれる(思いがする) ▪ I *felt* (*myself*) *drawn to* him. 私は彼に心を引かれた.

make a drawn game of it 勝負なしになる，引き分けになる ▪ If we *make a drawn game of it*, every British heart must tremble. 我々が引き分けになったら，すべてのイギリス人の胸は震えるにちがいない.

dread /dred/ 名 ***be in dread*** (***lest***) (…しはせぬかと)恐れている ▪ I *am in dread lest* I should fail. 私は失敗しはしないかと心配している.

be [***live***] ***in dread of*** …を恐れている[暮らす] ▪ He *is in dread of* death. 彼は死を恐れている ▪ A criminal always *lives in dread of* being arrested. 罪人はいつも逮捕を恐れて暮らす.

dream[1] /dri:m/ 名 ***a dream come true*** 実現した夢，叶えられた願い ▪ Working for this company is *a dream come true* for me. この会社で働けることは私にとって夢が叶った思いです.

a dream ticket 《主に英》ドリームチケット《選挙で勝利を収めそうな一組の候補者》 ▪ Obama and Clinton are *a* real *dream ticket* for many Democrats. オバマ氏とクリントン氏は多くの民主党員にとっては真のドリームチケットだ.

***be* [*live, go about*] *in a dream* (*world*)** 夢ごこちでぼんやり暮らす; 夢[幻想]の世界にいる[住む] ▪ He must be *living in a dream world* talking about eternal world peace. 恒久的な世界平和を唱えるなんて彼は空想の世界に住んでいるにちがいない.

beyond the dreams of Croesus 想像を絶する富を所有して ▪ The banker was rich *beyond the dreams of Croesus*. その銀行家は想像を絶する富を所有していた. ☞Croesus は巨万の富の所有で知られる, Lydia 最後の王(560–546 B.C.).

beyond* one's *wildest dreams 精一杯想像[期待]した以上に ▪ Winning the lottery was *beyond her wildest dreams*. 宝くじに当たったのは彼女が夢にも思わなかった喜びだった.

go to* one's *dreams 《詩》夢路に入る, 眠る ▪ The two girls *went to their dreams*. その二人の少女は夢路に入った.

in a dream 他のことを考えていてぼんやりして ▪ The boy was *in a dream* this morning. その男の子は今朝, 心ここにあらずでぼんやりしていた.

In your dreams! 《戯》(相手の発言を受けて)夢の中の話だよ, それは無理だよ ▪ I will be a billionaire some day.—*In your dreams!* いつか億万長者になってみせる—それは夢物語だよ.

like a dream 《口》容易に, 楽々と, ものの見事に ▪ Money cannot be got *like a dream*. 金はたやすく得られるものでない.

live in a dream world →be in a DREAM (world).

look a perfect dream 非常に美しい ▪ She *looks a perfect dream*. 彼女は非常に美しい.

not* [*never*] *in* one's (*wildest*) *dreams 夢にも...しない ▪ *Never in my wildest dreams* did I think I would be awarded this prize. こんな賞を授与されるなんて夢にも思わなかった.

of* one's *dreams 夢[理想]の ▪ This is the house *of my dreams*! これこそ私の夢の家だ!

Sweet dreams! おやすみなさい!

work* [*go, run*] *like a dream 非常にうまく行く ▪ The whole plan *went like a dream*. その計画は丸ごととてもうまく行った.

dream[2] /driːm/ 動 ***dream away* [*out, through*] one's *time* [*life, hours*]** うかうか過ごす ▪ He *dreamed away his time* while young. 彼は若い時分にぼーっと時を過ごした.

***dream in color* [*Technicolor*]** 極めて非現実的である ▪ I don't just *dream in color*, I *dream in Technicolor*! 私は色つきの夢をみるだけじゃない, 極彩色の夢を見るんだ.

little dream 夢にも思わぬ (*of, that*) ▪ I *little dreamed of* seeing you here. ここであなたに会おうとは夢にも思わなかった ▪ *Little* did she *dream that* he would be a great inventor. 彼女は彼が大発明家になろうとは夢にも思わなかった.

dreg /dreg/ 名 ***drink* [*drain*]*...to the dregs*** ...を一滴も残さず飲み尽くす; (幸福・辛酸)を余すところなく味わう ▪ He *drained* the cup of bitterness *to the dregs*. 彼は世の辛酸をなめ尽くした.

not a dreg 少しもない ▪ The meteor left *not a dreg* behind. 流星は跡形を少しも残さなかった.

drench /drentʃ/ 動 **(*be*) *drenched to the skin*** ずぶぬれで(ある) ▪ He came in *drenched to the skin*. 彼はずぶぬれで入って来た.

***be drenched with* [*by, in*]** ...ですっかりぬれる ▪ I *was drenched with* the rain. 雨でびしょぬれになった.

dress[1] /dres/ 名 ***dress op*(*tional*)** 夜会服着用は随意 ▪ Admission to Dance by ticket only: *dress op*(*tional*). 舞踏会への入場は入場券所持者にかぎる. 夜会服着用は随意. 《舞踏会への招待状の文句》

in full dress 盛装して ▪ The hall was crowded with officials *in full dress*. 会場は盛装した役人でいっぱいだった.

No dress. 正装には及びません《招待状の文句》.

dress[2] /dres/ 動 ***All dressed up and* [*with*] *nowhere to go.*** 盛装はしたが行く所なし《ある行事のため盛装したが, 行事が取りやめになったような場合に言う. 比喩的にも用いられる》 ▪ Nancy found herself *all dressed up and nowhere to go*. ナンシーは気がつくと, 盛装はしたが行く所なしというありさまだった.

***dress* oneself** **1** 衣服を着る, (の)服装をする ▪ She *dressed herself* for a ride. 彼女は乗馬の服装をした.

2 晩餐(さん)のために正装する, 夜会服を着る ▪ He *dressed himself* for a ball. 彼は舞踏会のため正装した.

dress for dinner 晩餐(さん)のために服装を夜会服に改める ▪ We don't *dress for dinner*. うちでは晩餐に特別な服装はしません.

dress the house 劇場を着飾らせる《指定席券を二つおきぐらいに間隔をあけて売り, 観客を劇場全体に平均して配置して入りがよいように見せる》 ▪ Ticket sales are off so let's *dress the house*. チケットの売り上げが下がったので指定席券をとびとびに売って入りをよく見せよう.

***dress the soil* [*ground*]** (植えつけのために)土地を耕す, 土地に施肥する ▪ I have been *dressing the soil* for the spring sowing. 春の種まきに備えて土地に肥料を施しています.

***dress to death* [*to kill, to the nines, like a plush horse, like a sore finger*]** 《口》むやみに着飾る, 過度に凝った服装をする ▪ My daughter *was dressed to kill*. 私の娘はむやみに着飾っていた ▪ They *are* always *dressed* up *to the nines*. 彼女らはいつも過度に着飾っている.

***dress to* [*by*] *the right* [*the left, on the center*]** 《号令》右へ[左へ, 中へ]ならう ▪ *Dress to the right*! 右へならえ! ▪ He *dressed to the left*. 彼は左へならった.

dress up to kill →DRESS to death.

get dressed 服を着る ▪ One has to *get dressed*

to go to the restaurant or bar of the hotel. ホテルのレストランかバーに行くためには服を着なければならない.

dressing /drésɪŋ/ 名 ***give*** *a person* ***a dressing*** 人を懲らしめる, 打ちのめす; うんとしかる ▪ Our generals *gave* the enemy *a dressing*. わが将軍たちは敵をひどくやっつけた ▪ He *gave* me *a dressing* for my lecture. 彼は私の講演についてひどく非難した.

window dressing →WINDOW.

D

dressing-down /drésɪŋdáʊn/ 名 ***get a dressing-down*** 《口》ひどくやっつけられる, 打ちのめされる, うんとしかられる ▪ He *got* such *a dressing-down* that he fainted. 彼はひどく打ちのめされたので気絶した.

give *a person* ***a dressing-down*** 《口》人をひどくやっつける, 打ちのめす; うんとしかりつける ▪ They will *give* you *a* good *dressing-down*. 彼らはひどく君をしかりつけるだろう.

drib /drɪb/ 名 (***in***) ***dribs and drabs*** 《口》少量(ずつ) ▪ He borrowed money *in dribs and drabs*. 彼は金をちびちび借りた.

driblet, dribblet /dríblət/ 名 ***by*** [***in***] ***driblets*** 少しずつ ▪ He withdrew his army *in driblets*. 彼は軍隊を少しずつ撤退させた.

drift[1] /drɪft/ 名 ***catch*** [***get, take***] *a person's* ***drift*** 人の真意をつかむ ▪ If you don't *catch my drift*, let me explain. 私の真意がつかめなければ, 説明しましょう.

catch [***get, take***] ***the drift*** (***of***) (…の)大体の意味[要領]をつかむ ▪ I cannot *catch the drift of* your remarks. 君の話の主旨がつかめない.

Get my drift? 私の言いたいこと, わかった? ▪ I want you to settle down and start studying. *Get my drift?* 落ち着いて勉強を始めるんだ. わかったか.

if you catch [***get***] ***my*** [***the***] ***drift*** 《口》私の言いたいことがおわかりいただけたら ▪ I don't see people in terms of race or color, *if you catch my drift*. 私は人間を人種や肌色では見ません, 私の言いたいことがわかっていただけるなら.

on [***upon***] ***the drift*** **1** 漂って, 流されて ▪ Ships are most dreadfully put *upon the drift*. 船はとてもひどく流されている.

2 《米》放浪して ▪ The young man was *upon the drift*. その青年は放浪していた.

drift[2] /drɪft/ 動 ***let things drift*** 事態を成り行きに任せる ▪ He was content to *let things drift*. 彼は事態を成り行きに任せるに甘んじた.

drill[1] /drɪl/ 名 ***at drill*** 教練[訓練]中の ▪ The soldiers were *at drill*. 兵隊は教練中であった.

What's the drill? **1** 《米口》何事(が行われているの)か ▪ *What's the drill?* Why are all these people sitting around like this? いったい何事なの? どうしてこの人たちはこんなふうにぶらぶらしているの?

2 《口》どんなふうにやるのか ▪ *What's the drill?* Is there a lot of paperwork? どんなふうにやるの? 事務処理はどっさりありますか?

drill[2] /drɪl/ 動 ***drill*** *a thing* ***into*** 物を…に教えこむ[たたきこむ] ▪ I *drilled* it *into* him. それを彼に教えこんだ.

drink[1] /drɪŋk/ 名 (***be***) ***in drink*** 酒に酔って ▪ He is a good husband except when *in drink*. 彼は酔っている時以外は良い夫である ▪ He has a pleasant way with him *in drink*. 彼は酔うと楽しい.

be meat and drink to *one* →MEAT.

(***be***) ***the worse for drink***/(***be***) ***under the influence of drink*** =(be) in DRINK.

drive *a person* ***to drink*** 人を飲酒に追いやる ▪ Mrs. Bell's bad temper *drove* him *to drink*. ベル夫人のかんしゃくのため彼は酒飲みになった.

have [***take***] ***a drink*** 1杯やる ▪ Let's *have a drink*. 1杯やりましょう.

in the drink 水[海]に ▪ He fell *in the drink* and had to be rescued. 彼は海に落ちて, 救助してもらわなければならなかった.

nurse a drink 《口》(パーティーで)酒を手に飲むふりをする, ちびちび飲む; (酒などを)少しずつ飲んで長くもたせる ▪ Jill had been *nursing* that *drink* for hours now. ジルはもう何時間も酒を手に飲むふりをしていた ▪ Each of us *nursed* just *one drink* for the whole evening. みなたった1杯の酒で一晩中ねばった.

on the drink 酒浸りになって ▪ Her brute of a husband was always *on the drink*. 彼女のけだもののような夫はいつも酒浸りだ.

the drink talking 酒の[酔った]上での話 ▪ That's just *the drink talking*. それはただ酒の上での話にすぎない.

drink[2] /drɪŋk/ 動 ***could drink the sea dry*** ひどくのどがかわいている, 大酒飲みである ▪ He *could drink the sea dry* at a single gulp. 彼はとてものどがかわいた.

drink confusion to →CONFUSION.

drink deep **1** 大いに飲む ▪ He *drank deep* night after night. 彼は毎夜毎夜痛飲した.

2 大酒飲みである ▪ He *drinks deep*. 彼は大酒飲みである.

3 …を十分味わう (*of*) ▪ He *drank deep of* life's experience. 彼は浮世の経験を十分なめた.

drink *a person* ***down*** [***dead drunk***] 飲み相手を酔いつぶす ▪ He will *drink* the Dane *down*. 彼は飲み相手のデンマーク人を酔いつぶすだろう.

drink *oneself* ***drunk*** 飲みすぎて酔う ▪ He *drank himself drunk*. 彼は大いに飲んで酔った.

drink *one's* ***eyes out*** 酒を飲んで目をつぶす ▪ You may *drink your eyes out*. 酒を飲んで目がつぶれるかもしれません.

drink *one's* ***fill*** →FILL[1].

drink *a person's* ***health*** 人の健康[幸運]を祝って乾杯する ▪ Here is something for you to *drink my health* with. これで1杯飲め.

drink *oneself* ***ill*** 酒を飲みすぎて病気になる ▪ Father *drank himself ill*. 父は酒を飲みすぎて病気になった.

drink *oneself* ***into*** 酒を飲んで…の状態になる ▪ He *drank himself into* incoherence. 彼は酒を

飲んでくだを巻いた.

drink like a fish →FISH[1].

drink *oneself* ***out of*** 酒を飲んで…を失う ▪ He *drank himself out of* his situation. 彼は酒を飲みすぎて地位を失った.

drink *oneself* ***sleepy*** [***tame***] 酒を飲んで眠く[おとなしく]なる ▪ The vipers *drank themselves tame.* まむしは酒を飲んでおとなしくなった.

drink success to …の成功を祈って乾杯する ▪ We *drank success to* the enterprise. 我々はその事業の成功を祈って乾杯した.

drink the cup [***chalice***] ***of joy*** [***sorrow, suffering***] 喜び[悲しみ, 苦しみ]を味わい尽くす ▪ I *drank the cup of joy* watching my daughter. 私は娘を見つめながら喜びを味わい尽くした.

drink the waters →WATER[1].

drink *a person* ***to death*** [***to*** *his* ***bed***] 飲み相手を酔わせて死なせる[床につかせる] ▪ I *drank* him *to his bed* [*to death*]. 飲み比べで彼を酔わせて床につかせた[死なせた].

drink *oneself* ***to death*** 酒を飲みすぎて死ぬ, 飲み死にする ▪ He will *drink himself to death.* 彼は酒で死ぬだろう.

drink *a person* ***under the table*** →TABLE.

good to drink →GOOD to eat.

I'll drink to that! 《口》 賛成だ, それはいいね, その通りだ ▪ What do you say to going on a picnic?—*I'll drink to that!* ピクニックに行くなんて, どう?—それはいいね.

One ***must drink as*** *one* ***brews.*** 《諺》 自分でしたことの報いは自分で受けねばならぬ,「自業自得」 ▪ Antichrist shall one day *drink as* he *brewed.* 反キリスト教者はいつか己の所業への報いを受けるだろう.

not fit to be drunk 飲めない ▪ The water is *not fit to be drunk.* その水は飲めない.

drip[1] /drɪp/ 名 ***in a drip*** したたって, ぬれて ▪ He is *in* such *a drip* of perspiration. 彼は汗をポタポタたらしている.

drip[2] /drɪp/ 動 ***be dripping with*** …でびっしょりである; でいっぱいである; をちりばめている ▪ He *was dripping with* perspiration. 彼は汗びっしょりだった ▪ She *was dripping with* jewels. 彼女は宝石をいっぱい身につけていた.

drip sweat 汗をたらす ▪ He was *dripping sweat.* 彼は汗をたらしていた.

dripping wet →WET[1].

drive[1] /draɪv/ 名 ***full drive*** まっしぐらに, 全速力で, 猛烈な勢いで ▪ We rode after the Spaniards *full drive.* 馬でまっしぐらにスペイン人らのあとを追った.

go for [***take***] ***a drive*** ドライブに行く ▪ Shall we *go for a drive* around the town? 町を一回りドライブしに行きましょうか.

make a drive 《米》 特別な努力をする ▪ The school *made a* great *drive* to obtain $50,000 for its new building. 学校は新築校舎のため, 50,000 ドル集めようと大々的な運動をした.

make a drive on (品)を盛んに売る ▪ They are *making a drive on* the goods. 彼らはその品を盛んに売り込んでいる.

drive[2] /draɪv/ 動 ***Drive ahead!*** (車を)どんどん進めろ!, 前進!

drive *a person* ***ape*** 《口》 人を悩ます, 頭をおかしくさせる ▪ You are *driving* me *ape* with this crap! 君のこんなたわごとを聞いていると頭がおかしくなるよ.

drive [***send***] *a person* ***around the bend*** [***twist***] 《口》 人を逆上させる, 人を激怒させる (→send *a person* up the WALL) ▪ You will *drive* him *around the bend.* 君は彼を逆上させるだろう.

drive *a person* ***back on…*** 人をやむなくもとの…によらせる ▪ There were no cigarettes left, so I *was driven back on* my pipe. 巻きタバコが残っていなかったので, 私はやむなくもとのパイプに戻った.

drive before the wind →before the WIND.

drive *a person* ***into*** (*doing*) 人に無理に…させる ▪ Oppression *drove* them *into* rebellion. 圧制に耐えかねて彼らは政府に反抗した.

drive like Jehu 《口》 無鉄砲に車を飛ばす ▪ He *drove like Jehu* to catch the train. 彼は列車に間に合うようがむしゃらに車を飛ばした. ☞Jehu は《聖》 *2 Kings*, 9. 20 にある「車を狂って走らせる人」.

drive *a person* ***mad*** [***distracted, crazy, bananas, bonkers***] 人を狂人(のよう)にする ▪ My insults have *driven* him *mad.* 私の侮辱が彼を狂わせた ▪ His first wife, his daughters, they had *driven him bananas* with good-byes. 彼の最初の妻, 娘たち, 彼女らはさよならを言ったので彼は頭がおかしくなった.

drive on the horn 《口》 自動車の運転中不必要にクラクションを鳴らす ▪ He was scolded, *driving on the horn.* 彼は運転中に不必要にクラクションを鳴らしてしかられた.

drive *a person* ***on to*** [***to*** *do*] 人を励まして…させる ▪ His success *drove* me *on to* success. 彼の成功に励まされて私は成功した.

drive team 《米口》 連獣を御する ▪ I'll have to *drive team* with 'em. 彼らと一連の馬を御さねばならないだろう.

drive the *river* 《米口》 材木を導いて川を流下させる ▪ He *drove the* Nakamagon. 彼は材木を導いてナカマゴン川を流下させた.

drive the center [***cross, nail***] 《米口》 的に完全に当てる ▪ He was very confident of *driving the cross* with a gun. 彼は銃で完全に的に当てる自信が大いにあった.

drive *a person* ***to*** *do* 人を追いたてて…させる ▪ He *was driven to* steal by hunger. 彼は飢えに耐えかねて盗みを働いた ▪ Defeat is hard to swallow but won't *drive* me *to* drink. 敗北は忍びがたいけれど, やけ酒を飲むほどじゃない.

drive… to the last moment [***minute***] 《口》 …をぎりぎりまで延ばす ▪ He *drove* the matter *to the last moment.* 彼はその件をぎりぎりまで延ばした.

let drive at **1** (勢いよく)…をねらい打つ, に打ってかかる ▪ He *let drive at* me with a book. 彼は私をね

らって本を投げつけた ▪I *let drive at* the animal with both barrels. その動物めがけて両銃身で打った.

2 …を激しくしかる ▪She *let drive at* her husband who had lost his marriage ring. 彼女は結婚指輪をなくした夫を激しくしかった.

driven /drívən/ 形 ***be hard driven*** **1** ひどくこき使われる, ひどく忙しい目にあう ▪I shall *be hard driven* to get this finished by 5 o'clock. 5時までにこれを仕上げるにはひどく忙しい目にあうだろう.

2 窮地に追いつめられる ▪The man *was hard driven* by creditors. その人は債権者たちによって窮地に追いつめられた.

driver /dráɪvər/ 名 ***in the driver's seat*** 統御の地位にいて ▪Mr. Smith was back *in the driver's seat.* スミス氏は統御の地位に復帰した.

drop[1] /drɑp|drɔp/ 名 ***a drop in*** [***of***] ***the*** [***a***] ***bucket*** [***the ocean, the sea***] 《口》大海の一滴,「焼け石に水」,「九牛の一毛」(《聖》*Isa.* 40. 15) ▪It would be *a drop in the ocean* compared to the amount he requires. それは彼が必要とする額に比べれば, 大海の一滴にすぎないだろう.

at the drop of a hat 《口》合図と同時に, すぐに, ためらわずに, 喜んで ▪He was ready to quarrel *at the drop of a hat.* 彼はいつでもすぐにけんかをした.

drop by drop 一滴ずつ, 少しずつ ▪The water was falling *drop by drop.* 水はぽたぽたと落ちていた.

fond of a drop 酒好きで ▪He is *fond of a drop.* 彼は酒飲みである.

get [***have***] ***the drop on*** 《口》 **1** (相手)より早く銃やピストルを構えてねらう; (人)の機先を制する; 不意を打つ ▪He *got the drop on* me. 彼のほうが先に私に銃を向けた ▪They *had the drop on* the outlaw, and he surrendered quietly. 彼らはそのならず者の機先を制したので彼はおとなしく降服した.

2 (人)を支配する, 手中に収める, 人の急所を押さえる ▪I have his letter admitting his responsibility, so I've *got the drop on* him. 自分の責任を認めた彼の手紙を持っているので, 彼の急所は押さえている. ☞銃を初め上へあげて, 次に的に向けて下げることから.

have a drop 1杯やる ▪Let's *have a drop.* 1杯やろう.

have a drop in *one's* [***the***] ***eye*** 酒を1杯きこしめしているようだ, ほろ酔い気分だ ▪You *had a drop in your eye.* 君はほろ酔い気分だった.

have [***take***] ***a drop too much*** 《俗》酒に酔う ▪I went there and *had a drop too much.* 私はそこへ行って酒に酔った.

have not a drop of …を少しも持たない ▪He *has not a drop of* sympathy with me. 彼は私に少しも同情を寄せていない.

have the drop on →get the DROP on.

in drops きわめてゆっくりと, 一滴ずつ ▪He shed tears *in drops.* 彼はぽろぽろと涙をこぼした.

not touch a drop 酒を全く飲まない ▪He pledged *not* to *touch a drop* all weekend. 彼は週末はすべて禁酒することを誓った.

take a drop **1** 1杯飲む ▪I *take a drop* now and then. 私は時に1杯飲む.

2 値段が下がる ▪Stocks *took a drop.* 株が下がった.

to the last drop 一滴も残さず ▪He emptied the glass *to the last drop.* 彼はコップを一滴も残さず飲み干した.

drop[2] /drɑp|drɔp/ 動 ***be dropping like flies*** →FLY[1].

drop a bomb →BOMB.

drop a nod うなずく ▪He *dropped a nod.* 彼はうなずいた.

drop *one's* ***aitches*** →drop one's H's.

drop behind (***to the rear***) 隊列からおくれる, 落後する ▪The officers *dropped to the rear.* 将校たちは後方におくれた ▪They *dropped behind* the rest of the party. 彼らは一行の他の人々におくれた ▪He *dropped behind* in the race. 彼は競走で落後した.

drop dead **1** 倒れて死ぬ, くたばる ▪I wish she would *drop dead.* 彼女がぽっくり死ねばよいのに.

2 《卑》くたばれ! ▪*Drop dead!* くたばれ!

3 急にやめる; (急に…との)関係を断つ ▪We *dropped* the plan *dead.* 我々はその計画を急にやめた ▪He *dropped* her *dead.* 彼は彼女との関係を断った.

drop (***down***) ***on*** *one's* ***knees*** →fall (down) on one's KNEEs (to).

drop everything (別なことをするために)今していることをやめる ▪I can't just *drop everything* and jump onto the Eurostar. 今していることをやめてユーロスターに飛び乗るわけにはいかない.

drop it 《口》 **1** 〚主に命令文で〛(していることを)やめる, 黙る ▪Stop making that row. *Drop it,* I tell you! そんな大騒ぎやめなさい. やめなさいと言うのに!

2 やめる ▪Why don't you *drop it* before it's too late? あとの祭にならないうちにやめたらどうだ.

drop money 金を失う[捨てる] ▪He *dropped money* at cards. 彼はトランプで金を失った.

drop short →SHORT.

drop to the ground 倒れる ▪Some of our men *dropped to the ground,* badly wounded. わが兵の幾人かは重傷を負って倒れた.

let drop **1** 落とす ▪He *let drop* a purse. 彼は財布を落とした.

2 (故意に, またはうっかり)漏らす ▪I *let drop* a word. うっかり一言漏らした.

3 (討論・行動を)打ち切る ▪They *let drop* their debate there. 彼らはそこで討論を打ち切った.

ready [***fit***] ***to drop*** 《口》疲れて今にも倒れそうで ▪I was *ready to drop* with fatigue. 私は疲れて今にも倒れそうであった.

dropping /drápɪŋ|drɔ́p-/ 形 ***dropping wet*** びしょぬれで ▪We got into a Scotch mist and were *dropping wet.* 我々は小ぬか雨の中に出て行って, びしょぬれになった.

drove /droʊv/ 名 ***in droves*** こぞって ▪The office girls are quitting *in droves.* 女子事務員たち

がこぞってやめていく.

drown /draʊn/ 動 ***A drowning man will catch* [*clutch, grab*] *at a straw.*** 《諺》おぼれる者はわらをもつかむ.

be drowned in …に浸る, おぼれる ▪He *is drowned in* sleep [wine, tears]. 彼はぐっすり寝こんで[酒に浸って, 涙にくれて]いる ▪He *was drowned in* the river. 彼は川でおぼれた.

drown *oneself* 身投げする ▪He *drowned himself* in the river. 彼は川に身投げした.

drown *oneself* ***in*** (酒・恋などに)おぼれる, (仕事などに)熱中する ▪Be careful not to *drown yourself in* drink. 酒におぼれないよう注意しなさい ▪He tried to alleviate his condition by *drowning himself in* his work. 彼は仕事に没頭することで病状を軽減しようとした.

drown *one's* ***sorrows*** [***troubles***] 酒で悲嘆[苦労]をまぎらす; 大酒を飲む ▪He says he is *drowning his troubles.* 彼は酒で苦労をまぎらしているのだと言っている. ☞in drink を略した形.

drown *one's* ***sorrows by*** *doing* …して悲嘆をまぎらす ▪We *drowned our sorrows by reading* books. 我々は読書をして悲嘆をまぎらした.

drown *a person's* ***whisky*** 《口》人のウィスキーをたくさんの水で割る ▪Don't *drown my whisky.* 私のウィスキーにあまり水を入れないでください.

like a drowned rat →RAT.

drub /drʌb/ 動 ***drub*** *a thing* ***into*** *a person* (考えなど)を人にたたきこむ ▪I will *drub* the idea *into* him. その考えを彼にたたきこんでやります.

drubbing /drʌ́bɪŋ/ 名 ***give*** *a person* ***a drubbing*** 人をしたたかなぐる ▪He *gave* the French *a drubbing.* 彼はそのフランス人をしたたかなぐった.

drug[1] /drʌg/ 名 ***a drug in*** [***on***] ***the market*** たなざらし, あまりありふれすぎて価値のないもの ▪That type of article is now *a drug on the market.* その種の品は今ではたなざらしだ.

drug[2] /drʌg/ 動 ***be drugged out*** 《米》麻薬でトリップしている ▪He *was* always *drugged out.* 彼は常にヤクをきめていた.

be drugged up 《口》薬漬けになっている ▪I *was drugged up* after the operation. 術後は薬漬けだった.

drum[1] /drʌm/ 名 (***as***) ***tight as a drum*** →TIGHT.

beat [***bang, thump***] ***the*** (***big***) ***drum*** (***for***) 《口》(…を)大声で広告する, 宣伝する, 大声で抗議する ▪They *beat the drum for* full employment. 彼らは完全雇用を大いに宣伝した.

follow the drum 軍人になる[である] ▪I used to *follow the drum* in scarlet. 昔は緋色の服を着た兵士だった.

with drums beating and colors flying 太鼓を打ち鳴らし旗をなびかせて(堂々と) ▪They marched *with drums beating and colors flying.* 彼らは太鼓を鳴らし旗をなびかせて行進した.

drum[2] /drʌm/ 動 ***drum in*** *a person's* ***ears*** 人の耳にやかましく響く ▪The sound still *drums in my ears.* その音は今なお私の耳に強く響いている.

drum into *a person's* ***ears*** うるさく繰り返して言う ▪My father *drummed* it *into my ears.* 父はそれを私にうるさく繰り返して聞かせた.

drum into *a person's* ***head*** 何度も繰り返して人の頭にたたきこむ ▪The teacher *drummed* the lesson *into the boy's head.* 先生はやかましく繰り返してその学科を少年の頭にたたきこんだ.

drummer /drʌ́mər/ 名 ***march to*** (***the beat of***) ***a different drummer*** →MARCH to (the beat of) a different drum.

drunk /drʌŋk/ 形名 (***as***) ***drunk as a fiddler*** [***the devil, a besom, a fish, a lord, a piper, an*** [***a boiled***] ***owl, a skunk, a coot***] 《口》ひどく酔って ▪On my birthday I got *as drunk as a lord.* 私の誕生日には私はへべれけに酔った ▪He came home *as drunk as an owl.* 彼はひどく酔って帰宅した.

be drunk in charge 《法》酔って運転する ▪The police thought he *was drunk in charge.* 警察は彼が酔って運転していると思った.

be [***get***] ***drunk on*** …に酔う ▪Have you ever *got drunk on* wine? 君はワインに酔ったことがあるか.

dead drunk 酔いつぶれて ▪He was *dead drunk.* 彼は酔いつぶれていた.

drunk and disorderly [***incapable***] 《法》酔いしれて, 泥酔して ▪The constable found him *drunk and incapable* in the gutter. 警官は彼が泥酔して側溝にはまっているのを見つけた.

drunk with (喜びなど)に酔って ▪He is *drunk with* success. 彼は成功に酔っている.

falling-down [***roaring***] ***drunk*** ぐでんぐでんに酔っ払って ▪A man was *falling-down drunk* in the street. 男が通りでぐでんぐでんに酔っ払っていた.

rolling drunk 酔いのために足がふらついて ▪One young woman was *rolling drunk.* 一人の若い女性が足がふらつくほど酔っていた.

druther /drʌ́ðər/ 名 ***have*** *one's* ***druthers*** 《米口》自分の好みを言う ▪If I *had* my *druthers,* I would prefer to be a teacher. 私の好みを言うなら, 教師になりたいですね. ☞druther は would rather の縮約形.

dry[1] /draɪ/ 名形 (***as***) ***dry as a bone*** [***limekiln, chip***] 《口》ひからびて; ひどくのどが乾いて ▪The soil is *as dry as a bone.* 土地はからからに乾いている ▪I am *dry as a chip.* 私はのどがからからだ.

(***as***) ***dry as dust*** **1** (乾いて)かちかちで ▪The plaster was *dry as dust.* 壁土はかちかちだった. **2** (人・本などが)無味乾燥な, 退屈な ▪These books are all *as dry as dust.* これらの本はみな無味乾燥だ.

(***as***) ***dry as paper*** とても心地悪く, 不健康で ▪His skin looked *as dry as paper.* 彼の皮膚はとても不健康にみえた.

boil … dry …を煮つめる ▪*Boil* the fish *dry.* 魚を煮つめてください.

D

bone dry かわききって ▪ The soil is *bone dry*. 土地がすっかりかわいている.

die a dry death 血を流さずに死ぬ; 溺死以外の死に方をする (cf. Sh., *Temp*. 1. 1. 72) ▪ I would fain *die a dry death*. できることなら陸上で死にたいものだ.

dry behind the ears →EAR.

go dry 《口》禁酒する, 禁酒法をしく ▪ The United States decided to *go dry*. 合衆国は禁酒法をしくことに決定した.

in the dry (雨などに)ぬれないで; (海でなく)陸上で ▪ We managed to reach the church *in the dry*. 私たちは何とか雨に濡れずに教会にたどり着いた ▪ Most amphibious animals are less agile *in the dry*. 大抵の両生類は陸上では動きがにぶい.

in the dry tree →in the green TREE.

leave the beach dry (潮が)引く ▪ The tide *leaves the beach dry*. 潮が引く.

make dry bones live 枯木に花を咲かす ▪ He *made dry bones live*. 彼は枯木を開花させた.

pump ... dry ...をくみ干す ▪ We *pumped* the well *dry*. 我々は井戸をくみ干した.

run dry →RUN[2].

the dry bones of ... are stirred 死んだように見える...が蘇生する (《聖》*Ezek*. 37. 1–10) ▪ *The dry bones of* politics *were stirred*. 死んだように見えた政治が蘇生した.

there wasn't a dry eye in ... 涙を流さない人は...にはいなかった ▪ When he sang the mournful old folk song, *there wasn't a dry eye in* the house. 彼がうら悲しい古い民謡を歌ったとき, 涙を流さない人はその家にはいなかった.

vote dry 《米》禁酒法賛成者に投票する ▪ Every town and city will *vote dry* at the next election. 次の選挙ではどの市町も禁酒法賛成者に投票するだろう.

wring ... dry ...をきつく絞る ▪ He *wrung* the towel *dry*. 彼はタオルをきつく絞った.

dry[2] /draɪ/ 動 ***dry*** *oneself* 体をふく ▪ *Dry yourself* well after swimming. 泳いだ後で体をよくふきなさい.

dry straight 《口》結局直る ▪ I shall miss you terribly at first—but it will all *dry straight*. 初めはあなたがいなくてひどく寂しい思いをするでしょう—が, 寂しさもしまいには癒えるでしょう.

dub /dʌb/ 動 ***dub*** *a person* ***a knight*** (国王が抜いた剣で肩を軽くたたいて)人を勲爵士に叙する ▪ His Majesty *dubbed* me *a knight* in this church. 陛下はこの教会で私を勲爵士に叙してくださった.

dubious /djúːbiəs/ 形 ***be dubious of*** [***about***] ...に半信半疑である, あやふやである ▪ I *am dubious of* his honesty. 彼の正直は疑わしいと思う ▪ We *are dubious about* the weather. どうも天候があやふやである.

duck[1] /dʌk/ 名 ***a dead duck*** 《俗》もはや重要でない[興味のない, つまらない]人[思想, など] ▪ The question of women's rights is not *a dead duck*. 女性の権利の問題は重要性を失っていない ▪ He is *a dead* political *duck*. 彼は政治的にはもう無力である.

a duck of a かわいい... ▪ He is *a duck of a* fellow. 彼はかわいいやつだ ▪ She was wearing *a duck of a* bonnet. 彼女はかわいい帽子をかぶっていた.

a duck shoot 《米口》朝飯前, いともたやすいこと ▪ Learning to drive a motorcycle should be *a duck shoot* for you. バイクの運転を学ぶことは, 君にとっては朝飯前のはずだよ.

a duck's egg 《学俗》ゼロ《クリケット・試験などでの無得点》 ▪ He got *a duck's egg* at the last exam. 彼はこの前の試験で0点を取った.

a fine [***nice***] ***day for*** (***young***) ***ducks*** アヒル(の子)には好天気《雨天》 ▪ It's *a fine day for young ducks*. 雨天である.

as a duck takes to water (アヒルが水に慣れるように)容易に, 自然に ▪ The baby adapted to the bottle *as a duck takes to water*. 赤んぼうはすんなり哺乳瓶に慣れた.

Can a duck swim? →Will a DUCK swim?

duck on a [***the***] ***rock/duck on drake*** 雄ガモ落とし, 石落とし《子供の遊び; 岩に乗せた相手の石に, 石をぶつけて落とす》.

duck soup **1** =a DUCK shoot.
2 くみしやすい相手, カモ ▪ How's the new history teacher?—He's *duck soup*. 新しい歴史の教師はどうだい?—ちょろいやつだよ.

get *one's* ***ducks in a row*** 《口》すべてを用意する ▪ He *got his ducks in a row* for his trip. 彼は旅行の準備をすべて整えた.

like a (***dying***) ***duck in a thunderstorm*** 《口》目を白黒させて, びっくり仰天して; おかしいほど絶望的な顔をして ▪ No employer will ever give you a job if you go about looking *like a dying duck in a thunderstorm*. 君がひどく絶望的な顔をして歩いていては, どんな雇い主だって職を与えてはくれないだろう.

like water off a duck's back →WATER[1].

make a duck and drake [***ducks and drakes***] (***with***) = play (at) DUCK(s) and drake(s) with 1.

make ducks and drakes of [***with***] = play (at) DUCK(s) and drake(s) with 2.

play (***at***) ***duck***(***s***) ***and drake***(***s***) (***with***) 《口》 **1** (...で)水切り遊びをする ▪ They often *played at duck and drake with* smooth stones. 彼らはよくなめらかな石で水切り遊びをした.
2 (...を)やたらに投げ捨てる; (を)もてあそぶ; (を)むちゃくちゃに扱う[使う]; (金などを)湯水のように乱費する ▪ You *played at ducks and drakes with* his vows. 君は彼の誓いをもてあそんだ ▪ I will *play ducks and drakes with* this money. この金を湯水のように使ってやろう ▪ He is *playing ducks and drakes with* his chances. 彼はせっかくの機会をむだにしている.

take to ... as [***like***] ***a duck to water*** (アヒルが水に慣れるように)...に喜んで慣れる, が大好きである (→as a DUCK takes to water) ▪ He *takes to* shooting *like a duck to water*. 彼は銃猟が大好きである.

Will [***Can***] ***a duck swim?*** 《口》(当然で答える

必要のないような質問に対して)もちろんだよ, あたりまえでしょ ▪ Does a bear shit in the woods?—*Can a duck swim?* クマは森でウンチするの?—もちろんさ ▪ Does childbirth hurt?—*Will a duck swim?* お産は痛いの?—あたりまえでしょ.

duck[2] /dʌk/ 動 ***duck and dive*** 《口》(状況に対処するのに)巧妙な手を使う ▪ *Ducking and diving* is becoming a habit in the UK. 巧妙な手を使うのがイギリスでは習慣になりつつある.

ducking /dʌ́kɪŋ/ 名 ***get a ducking*** (過って)水へざぶりと落ちる, ずぶぬれになる ▪ I missed my footing and *got a ducking* in the pond. 足を踏み外して池へざぶんと落ちた ▪ I *got a* real *ducking* in that downpour. あの土砂降りですっかりずぶ濡れになった.

give** a person **a ducking 人を水中に突っこむ; 人をずぶぬれにする ▪ I'll *give* you *a* good *ducking*. たっぷり水中にぶちこんでやるぞ.

duckling /dʌ́klɪŋ/ 名 ***an ugly duckling*** →UGLY.

dude /du:d/ 動 ***dude** oneself **up*** 《米俗》飾り立てる, めかしこむ ▪ She *duded herself up* for the school dance. 彼女は学校のダンスパーティーのためにめかしこんだ.

dudgeon /dʌ́dʒən/ 名 ***in (a) high [great, deep] dudgeon*** 大いに憤慨して, たいそう立腹して ▪ He went off *in a high dudgeon*. 彼は大いに憤慨して去った.

take ... in dudgeon ...に非常に立腹する ▪ He *took* my treatment *in dudgeon*. 彼は私のあしらいに大いに立腹した.

due /dju:/ 形名 ***accrue due*** →grow DUE.

become due →fall DUE.

due at [in] ...に到着のはず ▪ The train is *due in* London at 7 a.m. 電車は午前7時にロンドンに到着するはずである ▪ He is *due at* his office next Monday. 彼は来週月曜着任のはずである.

due east [north, south, west] 真東[北, 南, 西]に ▪ Sail *due east* for twenty miles and you'll run right into Cape Good Hope. 真東に20マイル航行すれば希望峰に突き当たります.

due to **1** ...に払うべき, 当然与える[尽くす]べき ▪ A thousand yen is *due to* you. 君には1,000円の借りがある ▪ The first place is *due to* Shakespeare. 第1位は当然シェイクスピアのものである ▪ For my success my thanks are *due to* you. 私の成功についてはあなたに感謝しなければなりません.

2 ...による, のせいである ▪ The difficulty is *due to* our ignorance. その困難は我々の無知によるものである ▪ My success was *due to* your help. 私の成功はあなたの援助のおかげでした.

3 ...に帰すべきものである ▪ The discovery is *due to* Newton. その発見はニュートンの功である.

4 《口》〚副詞的に〛...の理由から, のために ▪ Some articles have risen in price, *due to* the increasing demand. 需要増加のため, 値段の上がった品もある. ☞4 の用法は不正確とされるが, 通俗に行われている.

***due to** do* **1** ...するはずになって, する約束で ▪ He is *due to* speak tonight. 彼は今夜演説するはずである.

2 《米俗》まさに...しようとして ▪ I was *due to* go out. 私はちょうど出かけようとしていた.

fall [become, come] due (手形などが)満期になる ▪ The bill *becomes due* today. その手形はきょう支払い満期となる.

give** a person **his due 人に認めるべき長所を認める, 人を公平に扱う ▪ *Give* every person *his due*. 誰でもほめるべきところはほめよ.

give the devil his due →DEVIL.

grow [accrue] due 支払い満期になろうとしている ▪ The rent was to *grow due* on the day. 家賃はその日に支払い満期になろうとしていた.

have** one's **due 当然受けるべきものを得る ▪ Everyone *has his due* in this world. 人はみなこの世では当然受けるべきものは受けられる ▪ If I *had my due*, I would not be begging. 世が世なら物乞いなどはしていない.

in due season 時が来れば; ちょうどよい時に ▪ *In due season* we shall reap. 時が来れば, 刈り入れるだろう ▪ A word spoken *in due season* is pleasant. 時宜を得た言葉は愉快である.

in due time [course] 時が熟すれば, そのうち, やがて ▪ *In due course* you will be well known. そのうちあなたは有名になるでしょう ▪ He was convinced of his mistake *in due time*. 彼はやがて自分の誤りを悟った.

pay** one's **dues **1** (成功する前に)苦労を重ねる ▪ Before she was a star, Daisy Cline *paid her dues* at many local nightclubs. スターになる前にデイジー・クラインは地元のナイトクラブで苦労を重ねた.

2 《米俗》禁固刑に服する ▪ He *paid his dues* in prison the past 2 years. 彼は過去2年間, 刑務所で禁固刑に服した.

duff /dʌf/ 名 ***be up the duff*** 《英口》妊娠している ▪ His fiancée is rumored to *be "up the duff."* 彼のフィアンセは「妊娠して」いるとの噂だ.

duke /dju:k/ 動 ***duke it out*** 《米俗》けんかをする, 競い合う (*with*) ▪ The two men were *duking it out* in the bar. 二人の男がバーでけんかをしていた.

dull[1] /dʌl/ 形 ***(as) dull as ditch-water [dish-water]*** 《口》全く沈滞して, 退屈な ▪ The lecture was *as dull as ditchwater*. 講義は全く退屈だった.

dull of ...が鈍い ▪ He is *dull of* comprehension [hearing]. 彼は理解が鈍い[耳が遠い].

dull[2] /dʌl/ 動 ***dull the edge of*** →EDGE[1].

dumb /dʌm/ 形 ***a [the] dumb blonde*** 頭の弱い金髪美人 ▪ *The dumb blonde*, beautiful and desirable, does not need brains. 美しく好ましい「愚かな金髪女性」には頭脳はいらない.

(as) dumb as a box of rocks 非常に愚かな ▪ Art is handsome, but unfortunately, he's *dumb as a box of rocks*. アートはハンサムだが, 不幸にして非常に愚か者だ.

(as) dumb as a doornail [a fish, an oys-

D

ter] 全く黙りこくって ▪ The whole family was *dumb as an oyster.* 家中の者が黙りこくっていた.

be dumb on …については無言である, 説明しない ▪ Nature *is dumb on* the point. 自然はこの点については説明しない.

dumb bunny (ナイーブな)おばかさん ▪ Nancy is a bit of a *dumb bunny* but very nice. ナンシーはかなりのおばかさんだが, とても優しい.

D

sing dumb 黙っている ▪ I'll *sing dumb.* 私は黙っていましょう.

strike** a person **dumb →STRIKE².

dummy /dʌ́mi/ 名 ***give*** [***sell***] ***the dummy*** 《ラグビー》球をパスすると見せかけて相手をあざむく ▪ He *sold the dummy* cleverly. 彼は巧みに球をパスすると見せかけて相手をあざむいた.

in dummy (***form***) 書物に似せた形で ▪ The report was presented *in dummy.* 報告書は書物に似せた形で提出された.

look like a (***stuffed***) ***dummy*** でくのぼうのように黙っている ▪ Don't stand there *looking like a stuffed dummy*! Answer my question. でくのぼうのように黙ってそこへ突っ立っていてはいけません. 私の質問に答えなさい.

spit the dummy かんしゃくを起こして幼稚にふるまう ▪ He *spat the dummy* when his wife wanted to leave him. 彼は妻が別れたいと言ったときかんしゃくを起こして幼稚なふるまいをした.

stand like a dummy でくのぼうのように立つ ▪ When he was asked a question, the idiot *stood like a dummy.* 質問されたとき, その愚か者はでくのぼうのようにぼけっと立っていた.

dump /dʌmp/ 名 (***down***) ***in the dumps*** 《口》ふさいで, 不きげんで, 意気消沈して ▪ I'm just a bit *down in the dumps.* ただちょっと元気がないだけです ▪ John is *in the dumps* and won't play with the other boys. ジョンはきげんが悪くて他の少年たちと遊ぼうとしない.

get down in the dumps →GET.

not care [***worth***] ***a dump*** 《口》ちっともかまわない[価値がない] ▪ I *don't care a dump.* 私はちっともかまわない. ☞dump《俗》「小貨幣」.

dunce /dʌns/ 名 ***wear a dunce's cap*** 愚か者の帽子をかぶる, 愚か者となる ▪ The teacher stood her in the corner of the room and made her *wear a dunce's cap* on her head. 先生は彼女を教室の片すみに立たせて, 愚か者の帽子をかぶらせた《愚か者扱いをした》.

dunghill /dʌ́ŋhìl/ 名 ***die dunghill*** 《口》めめしい死に方をする, 絞首台で悔恨の色を見せる (↔die GAME) ▪ Submit, be a wretch, and *die dunghill.* 屈服して, 卑劣漢となり, 卑怯な死にかたをせよ.

Every cock crows on its [***his***] ***own dunghill.*** →COCK¹.

(***the***) ***cock on*** [***of***] ***his own dunghill*** (家庭・教区の)お山の大将 ▪ He is *the cock of this dunghill.* 彼はここではお山の大将だ.

dunk /dʌŋk/ 名 ***a slam dunk*** 強烈な打撃 ▪ That was *a slam dunk* against governmental abuse of power. これは政府の権力乱用への強烈な打撃だった. ☞《バスケ》「強烈なダンクシュート」が原義.

duplicate /djú:plək\ət/ 名 ***in*** (***a***) ***duplicate*** 全く同様な2通にして, (正副)2通にして ▪ This was certified *in* (*a*) *duplicate.* これは書類正副2通で証明された ▪ Receipts are taken *in duplicate.* 受領証は正副2通取られる.

durance /djʊ́ərəns/ 名 ***durance vile*** 《雅》恥ずべき[忌むべき]監禁 ▪ In *durance vile* here must I wake and sleep. ここに監禁の恥辱を受けて, 寝起きしなければならない.

duration /djuréɪʃən/ 名 ***for the duration***

1《軍俗》戦争の続く間 ▪ We lived in the village *for the duration* (of the war). 戦争が終わるまでずっとその村で暮らしていた.

2 (いつまでも)長い間《退屈・もどかしさを表す》 ▪ Are we going to stop here *for the duration*? 我々はここにいつまでもずっととどまるのですか. ☞もと「第2次大戦の続く間」の意.

of long [***short***] ***duration*** 長[短]期の ▪ We hope the war will be *of short duration.* 我々は戦争が短期であることを望む.

duress /dʊrés|djuə-/ 名 ***in duress*** 厳重に束縛されて, 監禁されて ▪ Some of the missionaries had been four years *in duress.* 宣教師の中には4年間厳重に監禁されていた者もある.

under duress 《法》強要[強迫]されて ▪ He confessed, *under duress*, to several crimes. 彼は強迫されて, 数件の犯罪を自白した.

dusk /dʌsk/ 名 ***at dusk*** 日暮れに ▪ The stars begin to appear *at dusk.* 星は夕暮れに現れ始める.

dust¹ /dʌst/ 名 (***as***) ***dry as dust*** →DRY¹.

(***be***) ***out for the dust*** 《米口》金儲けに興味を持つ ▪ I'*m out for the dust.* 私は金儲けに興味がある.

bite [***eat, kiss***] ***the dust*** **1** 死ぬ, 戦死する; 死んだり負傷して地上に倒れる ▪ In the course of half an hour he had twice *bitten the dust.* 半時間の間に彼は二度も地上に倒れた.

2 打ち倒される, 一敗地にまみれる, 屈辱を忍ぶ ▪ In the annual Varsity match Oxford *bit the dust.* 例年の大学対抗試合にオックスフォードは敗戦の憂き目を見た.

buried with the dust of** one's **ancestors 祖先と同じ墓に葬られる ▪ I want to be *buried with the dust of my ancestors.* 私は先祖と同じ墓に葬られたい.

cut the dust 1杯やる ▪ I think I'll stop here and *cut the dust.* ここに寄って1杯やるとしよう.

Down with the dust! 《俗》金を出せ[払え] ▪ Come, *down with the dust!* さあ, 金を出せ! ☞dust＝money.

dust and ashes ちりあくた, つまらぬもの, 期待はずれ (《聖》*Gen.* 18. 27) ▪ Everything has been *dust and ashes* to me. このところ私にとって何もかもがつまらない ▪ All their hopes have turned to *dust and ashes.* 彼らの希望はすっかり消えてしまった.

Dust thou art, and unto dust shalt thou return. あなたはちりだからちりに帰る (《聖》 *Gen.* 3. 19).

eat dust 《米口》 非難[叱責]を甘んじて受ける ▪ You have got to *eat dust* or apologize. 君は甘んじて叱責を受けるか, 謝罪するかしなくてはならない.

eat the dust →bite the DUST.

gather dust **1** ちり[ほこり]が積もる ▪ Those books just *gather* [collect] *dust*. それらの書物はちりが積もるばかりだ.

2 〚主に進行形で〛 使われないでいる, 無視されている ▪ The old records have *been gathering dust* these ten years. 古レコードはこの10年使われずにいた.

have a little dust 《米口》 戦う, 小ぜり合いをする ▪ They wished to *have a little dust*. 彼らは戦うことを望んだ.

humble ... in* [*to*] *the dust …をはずかしめる, 一敗地にまみれさす ▪ The Navy *humbled* the pride of France *to the dust*. 海軍はフランスの誇りをくじいた ▪ My soul lies *humbled in the dust*. 私の心は恥辱を被っている.

in dust and ashes 灰をかぶって, 心から(苦行をするなど) ▪ He did penance *in dust and ashes*. 彼は灰をかぶってざんげの苦行をした. ☞ 昔ユダヤには灰をかぶって苦行をする習慣があった.

in the dust 死んで; 屈辱を受けて ▪ He is *in the dust*. 彼は死んだ.

kick up* [*raise*] *a dust 《英》 騒動を起こす, 騒ぎたてる ▪ I shouldn't *kick up a dust* about it. それについて騒ぎたてるべきではない.

kiss the dust →bite the DUST.

lay the dust ちり[ほこり]を静める; 騒動を静める ▪ It was merely to *lay the dust*. それはほこりを静めるためにすぎなかった.

leave** a person **in the dust **1** (人)を窮地に見捨てておく, 見殺しにする ▪ You will not *leave* us *in the dust*. 君は我々を見殺しにはしないだろう.

2 《口》 (レース・競争で)人をはるかに離してしまう, 圧倒する ▪ When this new product is released, it will *leave* the others *in the dust*! この新製品が発売されたら, 他のものは圧倒されてしまうぞ!

lick the dust **1** =bite the DUST.

2 はいつくばる; ひれ伏して屈服する ▪ They will *lick the dust* like a serpent. 彼らはヘビのごとくはいつくばるだろう. ☞ 《聖》 *Ps.* 72. 9; *Isa.* 49. 23.

make the dust fly 大騒ぎを起こす (→make the FEATHERs fly) ▪ As soon as he learns who dented his car, he'll *make the dust fly*. 誰が彼の車をへこませたかわかり次第, 彼は大騒ぎを起こすだろう.

not see** a person **for dust 《英口》 人がすぐいなくなる, 人が素早く去る ▪ After his treachery was discovered, we did*n't see* him *for dust*. 裏切りが発覚したあと彼は姿をくらました.

raise* [*make*] *a dust **1** 騒動を起こす; 騒ぎたてる ▪ He *raised a dust* about nothing. 彼は何でもないことで騒ぎたてた.

2 ほこりを立てる ▪ The car *made a* terrible *dust* as it passed us. 自動車は我々を通り過ぎたとき, ひどい土ぼこりを立てた.

3 《英》 真実を覆い隠す ▪ To do him justice, he was not trying to *raise a dust*. 公平に評価して, 彼は真実を覆い隠そうとはしていなかった.

shake the dust off* [*from*]** *one's* ***feet/ shake off the dust of *one's* ***feet*** 憤然として去る, 軽蔑して去る (《聖》 *Matt.* 10. 14) ▪ He was glad to *shake the dust* of the town *from his feet*. 彼は怒ってその町からさっさと出ていった ▪ He *shook off the dust* of cobbling. 彼は靴直しの仕事がいやになってやめた.

take the dust of 《米口》 **1** …の後について行く ▪ I *took his dust*. 私は彼のあとについて行った.

2 速力で…に負ける ▪ The ship does not *take the dust of* anything afloat. その船は速力ではどんな船にも負けない.

the dust of ages いく時代ものちり ▪ The books were thick with *the dust of ages*. それらの書物にはいく時代ものちりが積もっていた.

throw dust in* [*into*]** *a person's* ***eyes …の目をくらます 《真相を見させない》; をだます ▪ He had *thrown dust in* honest *Adam's eyes*. 彼は正直者のアダムをだましてきた ▪ You can easily *throw dust into his eyes*. 彼の目をくらますのはわけはない.

Watch my dust! どんなに速いか見てくれ! ▪ I can go to the store and be back in a twinkle. Just *watch my dust!* 僕は店へ行ってすぐに帰ってくることができる. ちょっとどんなに速いか見ていてください!

***when the dust has settled/ after* [*once*] *the dust settles* [*clears*]** ごたごたが収まったとき ▪ *When the dust had settled*, we found the treasure had been stolen. ごたごたが収まったとき, 我々は宝物が盗まれたことに気づいた ▪ I'll let you know *once the dust clears*. ごたごたが収まり次第君に知らせるよ.

would not see** a person **for dust 《英口》 (面倒・責任を逃れて)人は雲隠れするだろう ▪ If you asked him to lend you money, you *wouldn't see* him *for dust*. 彼に金を貸してくれと言おうものなら, 彼は雲隠れするだろう.

dust[2] /dʌst/ 動 ***dust*** *oneself* (鳥が)砂をかぶる ▪ The partridges were *dusting themselves* in the road. ヤマウズラは道路で砂をかぶっていた.

***dust** a person's **jacket* [*coat*] (*for him*)** 《口》 人をなぐる, ひっぱたく ▪ I'll *dust his jacket for him*. あいつをひっぱたいてやる.

dust** oneself **off 《英》 (困難・辛い経験のあと)立ち直る, 回復する ▪ She *dusted herself off* after failing in love. 彼女は失恋のあと, 立ち直った.

dust the eyes of …をだます, たぶらかす ▪ They *dusted our eyes* with sophistry. 彼らは詭弁(きべん)で我々をたぶらかした.

dust the floor with **1** …を思いのままに扱う ▪ I'll *dust the floor with* you, my lad. おい, きさまをおれの思いのままにしてやるぞ.

2 …を恐れ入らせる ▪ If you tell a lie, I'll *dust the*

floor with you. 嘘をついたら, 恐れ入らせるぞ.

get up and dust《米口》急ぐ, 去る, 走る ▪ The gold seekers *got up and dusted.* 金を探す人たちは急いで行った.

dusting /dʌ́stɪŋ/ 名 ***give*** [***get***] ***a dusting*** なぐる[られる] ▪ I will *give* him *a* good *dusting.* あいつをうんとなぐってやろう.

D

dustman /dʌ́stmən/ 名 ***The dustman's coming.*** 《英》眠くなってきたね《子供に言う》. ☞dustman「眠りの精」; 眠くなるとごみが目の中へ入ったように目をこすることから.

dusty /dʌ́sti/ 形 ***a dusty answer*** [***reply***] 《英》厳しくつれない返事[応答] ▪ This approach received *a dusty answer* from the judge. この申し入れは判事から厳しくつれない応答を受けた.

not [***none***] ***so dusty***《英俗》なかなか良い, まんざら捨てたものではない ▪ The pay is *not so dusty.* 給料はなかなか良い. ☞dusty = worthless.

Dutch /dʌtʃ/ 形名 ***a Dutch bargain*** →BARGAIN[1].

(***be***) ***in Dutch***《口》困ったことになる, 信用を落としている, きらわれている, 警察沙汰になる ▪ He *is in Dutch* with the police for carrying a loaded revolver. 彼は弾丸をこめた銃を持っていたので警察にあげられている ▪ I *am in Dutch* with the boss. 私は社長に受けが悪い.

beat the Dutch《口》**1** ...には全く驚く《信じがたい, 異常な場合の驚き》▪ It *beats the Dutch* how he always gets the highest marks in the class. 彼がいつもクラスで最高の成績をとるのは全く不思議だ.
2 ...には何物もかなわない, 全く降参だ ▪ You women do *beat the Dutch.* あなたがたご婦人には全くかなわない ▪ Our cargoes *beat the Dutch.* 我々の船荷は全くすばらしい ▪ It *beats the Dutch*! それには参った《さっぱりわからない》.
3 (それには)がまんがならない ▪ That *beats the Dutch*! それにはがまんがならない!

do a [***the***] ***Dutch*** (***act***)《俗》逃げる; 自殺する ▪ We *did a Dutch* with everything. 我々はすべてを持って逃げた.

double Dutch ちんぷんかんぷんなこと ▪ He talks *double Dutch* backward on a Sunday. 彼は日曜にはちんぷんかんぷんなことを逆に話す《言語上の器用さをおもしろく言った句》.

Dutch comfort《口》もっと悪くなくてよかったという慰め ▪ After all it might have been worse; that's a bit of *Dutch comfort.* 結局もっと悪かったかもしれない. それがせめてもの慰めだ.

get in Dutch《口》困ったことになる, 信用を落とす, 警察ざたになる ▪ Anyone might *get in Dutch* for a dish. 誰でもいかした女性のために面目をつぶすこともある ▪ I *got in Dutch* with the boss this morning. 今朝社長にしかられた.

go Dutch《口》自分の分は自分払い[割り勘]でいく ▪ We decided to *go Dutch* on the luncheon. 我々は昼食は割り勘でいくことに決めた.

take Dutch leave《米口》許可なく[無断で]軍を離れる ▪ You have broken the rules; you *took Dutch leave.* 君は規則を破った. 無断で軍を離れた.

talk Dutch《口》はかないこと[たわごと]を言う ▪ He may be *talking Dutch* for aught I know. 彼はあるいはたわごとを言っているかもしれない.

talk to *a person* ***like a Dutch uncle***《口》人をきびしくしかる, 人にきびしく説教する; 人をこんこんと説諭する ▪ I got mad and *talked to* him *like a Dutch uncle.* 私は激怒して, 彼を激しくしかった ▪ If you don't improve, I shall have to *talk to* you *like a Dutch uncle.* 君がよくならなければ, 私はきつく君をしからねばならんだろう.

Dutchman /dʌ́tʃmən/ 名 ***I am a Dutchman***《口》首をやる《強い否定》▪ *I am a Dutchman* if I do. 僕は絶対にしないよ ▪ It is true or *I am a Dutchman.* 絶対に本当だ, でなきゃ首をやる.

duty /djúːti/ 名 (***be***) ***in duty bound*** 義理に迫られ[つまされ]る ▪ *In duty bound*, he went to see his mother. 義理につまされて, 彼は母に会いに行った.

(***be***) ***in duty bound to*** *do* 義理上...しなければならない ▪ I *am in duty bound to* side with my benefactor. 私は義理上恩人のほうに味方しなければならない.

be [***come, go***] ***off duty*** 非番である[になる] ▪ He *comes off duty* at 5 p.m.. 彼は午後5時に勤務がとける.

be [***come, go***] ***on duty*** 当番である[上番する], 勤務中である[につく] ▪ I'*m on duty* from 8 a.m. to 4 p.m. today. きょうは午前8時から午後4時まで勤務です ▪ He *goes on duty* at 8 a.m. 彼は午前8時に出勤する.

do (***double***) ***duty as*** [***for***]《米》...の役をする ▪ This word sometimes *does duty as* a verb. この語はときには動詞の役をする ▪ He *did duty as* chair. 彼は議長の役をした.

do *one's* ***duty*** **1** 本分を尽くす ▪ England expects every man to *do his duty.* イギリスは各人がその本分を尽くすことを期待する.
2《米俗》がつがつ食う ▪ He *did his duty* after exercising. 彼は運動の後, がつがつ食った.
3《婉曲》排泄する, 大[小]便をする ▪ We're not leaving this restroom until you *do your duty.* 用がすむまでお手洗いにいてあげるからね.

do *one's* ***duty by*** ...に義理をたてる ▪ I *did my duty by* my friend Hill. 友人ヒルに義理をたてた.

do duty for ...の用を務める, の代わりになる ▪ This rock *does duty for* a table. この岩はテーブルの代わりになる.

do duty to *do* ...する役をする ▪ It *did duty to* support the roof. それは屋根を支える役をした.

Duty calls.「義務が呼ぶ」, 自分にしなければならないことがある ▪ There's nothing I would like to do better, but *duty calls.* やりたいのは山々だが, しなければならないことがあるので.

go off duty →be off DUTY.

go on duty →be on DUTY.

fail in *one's* ***duty*** 役目がたたない ▪ If I do such

a thing, I shall *fail in my duty*. そんなことをしては，私の役目がたたない．

have the duty 作業の監察をする ▪ The commander *had the duty* on Monday. 司令官は月曜に業務の監察をした．

in line of duty 職務の範囲内で，職務に従って ▪ He acted *in line of duty*. 彼は職務に従って行動した．

it is *one's* ***bounden duty to*** *do* …は義理にも…しなければならない ▪ *It is my bounden duty to* help him. 私は義理にも彼を助けなければならない．

off duty 非番で，勤務時間外で ▪ The policeman was *off duty* at the time. その時警官は勤務時間外であった．

on duty 当番で，勤務(時間)中で ▪ A watchman must not smoke while *on duty*. 夜番は勤務中はタバコをすってはならない．

present [***send***] *one's* (***humble***) ***duty to*** …に対してうやうやしく敬意を表する ▪ Please *present my humble duty to* his Grace the Archbishop. 大監督猊下に私の敬意をお伝えください．

relieve *a person* ***of*** *his* ***duties*** 《婉曲》人を解雇[くびに]する ▪ I'm afraid I must *relieve* you *of your duties*. 君を解雇しなくてはならないようだね．

shirk *one's* ***duty*** 怠ける，義務を回避する ▪ If you continue to *shirk your duty*, you can expect to be fired. 君が怠け続けるなら，君をくびにしなければならない．

take the duty 勤行[司祭]をする ▪ He *took the duty* in a church for the priest. 彼は司祭に代わって勤行をした．

dye[1] /daɪ/ 名 ***of the blackest*** [***deepest***] ***dye*** 極悪の ▪ Judas was a traitor *of the deepest dye*. ユダは極悪の裏切者であった ▪ He stood accused of crimes *of the blackest dye*. 彼は極悪罪を犯したと訴えられていた ▪ Those sinister dens seem fitted for crimes *of the blackest dye*. そういう不気味な洞窟は極悪の罪にふさわしいものに思われる．

dye[2] /daɪ/ 動 ***dye in*** (***the***) ***wool*** [《英》***grain***] **1** 生(き)染めにする《織る前に糸を染める》 ▪ I *dyed* the material *in the wool*. その材料を生染めにした． **2** (思想などを)徹底的に染みこませる ▪ He *dyed* the manners of children *in the wool*. 彼は子供の礼儀作法を徹底的に染みこませた．

dye ... of a *color* …を色に染める ▪ The rain *dyed* the river *of a* dark red. 雨は川を暗赤色に染めた．

dyed-in-the-wool (布が)生染めの; (人が)骨の髄からの ▪ Hoskins is a *dyed-in-the-wool* Labour man. ホスキンズは骨の髄からの労働党員だ．

dying /dáɪɪŋ/ 形 (***be***) ***dying for*** 《口》…がほしくてたまらない ▪ He *is dying for* a drink. 彼は1杯ほしくてたまらない．

(***be***) ***dying of*** [***with***] 《口》…で死にそうだ，でたまらない ▪ I *am dying of* curiosity. 私は知りたくてたまらない ▪ The children *were dying of* boredom. 子供たちは退屈でたまらなかった ▪ I *was dying with* tiredness. 退屈でたまらなかった．

(***be***) ***dying to*** *do* 《口》…したくてたまらない ▪ I *am dying to* see you. あなたに会いたくてたまりません《手紙の文》 ▪ I've *been dying to* see you. ほんとに会いたくてたまりませんでした《会ったときの言葉》．

till [***to***] *one's* ***dying day*** 死ぬ日まで ▪ I shall remember it *to my dying day*. それを死ぬまで覚えているでしょう．

dyke /daɪk/ 名 ***hold the dyke against*** (侵入に対して)固く防衛する ▪ We are trying to *hold the dyke against* rising prices. 我々は物価高騰を固く防ごうと努めている．

D

E

E /iː/ 名 ***give*** *a person* ***the big e*** [***E***]《英口》人にひじ鉄をくわせる, 人をそっけなく拒絶する (=give the ELBOW) ▪ She's *given* him *the big E* in front of five million viewers. 彼女は5百万人が見ているところで彼にひじ鉄をくわせた.

each /iːtʃ/ 形名 ***each and all*** それぞれみな, いずれも ▪ *Each and all* have gone to see the play. それぞれみな芝居を見に行った.

each and every (*one*) どれもみな ▪ *Each and every* boy has gone to see the game. どの少年もみな観戦に行った. ☞each または every を強調する形.

each and singular →all and SINGULAR.

(***Each man for himself and***) (***the***) ***devil take the hindmost.*** →DEVIL.

each other →OTHER.

each to each それぞれ, 互いに ▪ The sides of the two triangles are equal *each to each*. 二つの三角形の各辺はそれぞれ相等しい.

each to each his own/《米》***to each his own***《諺》誰にも自分で選ぶ権利がある,「十人十色(で)」 ▪ I wouldn't pick that color, but *to each his own*. 私ならあの色は選ばないが, 人それぞれだな.

each way →WAY.

eager /íːgər/ 形 ***an eager beaver*** →BEAVER.

eager after [***for***] …を切望して, 得たがって ▪ He seems to be *eager after* fame. 彼は名声を切望しているようだ.

eager for *a person* ***to*** *do* (人が)…するのを切望して ▪ I am *eager for* you *to* meet my sister. あなたが私の妹に会うのを切望しています.

eager in …に熱心で ▪ She is *eager in* her studies. 彼女は研究に熱心である.

eager to *do* …したがる ▪ They are *eager to* go on a trip. 彼らはしきりに旅行に行きたがっている.

eagerness /íːgərnəs/ 名 ***be all eagerness to*** *do* …したくてたまらない ▪ I *am all eagerness to* go to the cinema. 映画に行きたくてたまらない.

in *one's* ***eagerness to*** *do* …したさのあまり ▪ *In her eagerness to* help the poor, she gave them all the money. 貧しい人々を助けたいあまり, 彼女はその金をみな彼らに与えた.

eagle[1] /íːgəl/ 名 ***a flier of the eagle***《米》誇大な愛国的演説家 (→fly the EAGLE) ▪ They are *fliers of the eagle*. 彼らは大げさな愛国的演説家である. ☞eagle「米国貨幣の図案に使われているワシ」; 米国国威の象徴.

a legal eagle やり手の弁護士 ▪ I'm not *a legal eagle* yet. I'm a first-year law student. 僕はまだまだ敏腕弁護士ではない. 法律専攻の1年生だ. ☞押韻による連語.

fly the eagle《米》大げさな愛国演説をする ▪ The Fourth of July is a fair time to *fly the eagle*. 7月4日は誇大な愛国的演説をするにふさわしい時である. ☞7月4日は米国独立記念日.

make the eagle scream《米》大げさな愛国演説にふける ▪ He was *making the eagle scream*. 彼は大げさな愛国的演説をやっていた.

swoop like an eagle さっと急速におりてくる ▪ The creditors *swooped like eagles* on their victims. 債権者たちは負債者の所へわっと押しかけた.

eagle[2] /íːgəl/ 動 ***eagle it*** ワシのように飛ぶ ▪ You can't *eagle it*? 君はワシのように飛ぶわけにはいかないのか.

spread eagled 両腕を伸ばして, 大の字になって ▪ The child lay *spread eagled* on the ground where it had fallen. その子供は落ちた地面に両腕を伸ばして倒れていた.

ear /ɪər/ 名 ***a pig's ear***《口》台なし, 不手際, へま ▪ This work is *a pig's ear*. この作品はだめだ.

a roasting ear 焼きトウモロコシ《特に, 穂先》 ▪ I bought *a roasting ear* fresh off the grill. 熱々の焼きトウモロコシを買った.

about [***around***] *one's* ***ears*** (打撃・弾丸・矢の雨・大火・家などが)自分の回りに《落ちかかる, くずれかかる, など; fall (down), crumble などの動詞と共に用いる》 ▪ The roof *fell* in *about our ears*. 屋根が我々の回りに落ちてきた ▪ I had everyone *about my ears*. 私はすべての人の攻撃を受けた ▪ His dreams came *crashing around his ears*. 彼の夢はめちゃめちゃにくだけてきた.

assault the ears [***ear drums***] 耳をつんざくほどである, 耳を聾(ろう)するほどである ▪ The engine's roar *assaults the ears*. エンジンの轟音が耳をつんざく.

be all ears《口》熱心に傾聴する ▪ I'*m all ears*. 一心に耳を傾けています.

be on *one's* ***ear***《米》憤激している; 奮起する; 戦おうとしている ▪ What *are* you so *on your ear* about? 何をそんなにかっかしているのか.

be solid [***thick***] ***between the ears*** →have nothing between the EARs.

believe *one's* ***ears*** 〚主に否定的に〛自分の耳を信じる ▪ I could scarcely *believe my ears*. 私はほとんど自分の耳を信じることができなかった.

bend *a person's* ***ear*** 人に傾聴させる; (うんざりさせるほど)話す ▪ He *bent my ear* with tales of the river and the sea. 彼は川と海の話を私にしゃべりまくった.

between the ears 理解力において (→have nothing between the EARs) ▪ When you get older, you get quicker *between the ears*. 年をとれば, 理解が速くなる.

bite *a person's* ***ear***《俗》人から金を借りる ▪ I

never dreamed of *biting your ear*. 君に金を借りようなどとは夢にも思わなかった.

Blow it out your ear! 《米俗》[[不快な言葉に応えて]] そんなばかな, ふざけるな.

bore** a person's **ear 人を終生の奴隷とする ▪ *Mine ears* hast thou *bored*. あなたは私を終生の奴隷として受けいれた. ☞ユダヤの使用人が6年勤めてのち自由になることを拒むときは, 終生の奴隷の印として耳にきりで穴をあけたことから; bore「(きりなどで穴を)あける」.

bow down** one's **ear (優しく)耳を貸す (《聖》 *Ps*. 31. 2) ▪ *Bow down your ear* to me. 私の申しあげることをお聞きください.

box** a person's **ears 横つらを張る ▪ I'll *box your ears*. 横つらを張るぞ.

bring the house** [**a hornet's nest,** one's **household, a storm**] **about** one's **ears 大勢[家族全員]のごうごうたる攻撃を浴びる; 面倒を引き起こす ▪ I mildly criticized the present government and *brought the house about my ears*. 穏やかに現政府を批判したのに大勢の非難攻撃を受けた ▪ You *brought a hornet's nest about my ears*. お前はおれにとんでもないやっかいをもたらしたぞ.

by ear **1** 耳で聞いただけで, 楽譜なしで ▪ He could sing [play] *by ear* very prettily. 彼は耳で聞いただけで非常にうまく歌えた[演奏できた].
2 成り行きまかせで, ぶっつけ本番で (→play (...) by EAR) ▪ No planning, no reservations, just play it *by ear*. 計画なし, 予約なし, 成り行きまかせでやるんだ.

by the ears 《口》けんかをして, 不和で (→fall together by the EARs) ▪ Take any two men that are *by the ears*. 誰でもいいからけんかをしている二人の人を例にとってみなさい.

can** do **... on** one's **ear 《豪口》容易にやってのける ▪ Mary likes cooking. She *can* bake cake *on her ear*. メアリーは料理が好きだ. 楽々とケーキを焼ける.

***catch** [**fall on**] a person's **ear**(**s**)* 人の耳に入る, 聞こえてくる ▪ A curious sound *caught his ear*. 奇妙な音が彼の耳に入った ▪ Her words *fell* pleasantly *on my ears*. 彼女の言葉が私の耳に愉快に響いた.

clear** one's **ears (気圧の変化で聞こえにくくなった)耳をもとに戻す ▪ His descent was rapid and he could not *clear his ears*. 彼は急速に降下してきたので耳をもとに戻せなかった.

clear the ears 耳あかを取る; 《口》もっと注意して[耳を掃除して]聞く ▪ You had better *clear your ears*. よく耳を掃除して聞きなさい.

close** one's **ears to →stop one's EARs to.

come about** one's **ears 身辺に迫る, 襲う ▪ The whole ship will *come about our ears* by the run. 船の者たちがたちまち一斉に我々を襲うだろう.

come out of** one's **ears 溢(あふ)れるほどたくさんある; 多すぎて対処しきれない ▪ We miscalculated. New orders are *coming out of our ears*. 計算を間違った. 新しい注文がありすぎるんだ.

***come to** [**reach**] a person's **ear**(**s**)* 人の耳に入る ▪ If the news should *come to the old man's ears*, it would break his heart. その知らせが耳に入ったら老人は悲嘆にくれるだろう.

drag ... by the ears →pull ... by the EARs.

dry behind the ears [[主に否定文で]] 十分成熟して; 経験を積んで (↔ wet behind the EARs) ▪ They are not *dry behind the ears* yet. 彼らはまだ成熟していない.

*A person's **ears are flapping**.* 《口》誰かが聞き耳を立てている ▪ Be careful what you say—that *man's ears are flapping*. 言葉に気をつけなさい. あの男が聞き耳を立てている.

*One's **ears burn** [**are burning**].* 《口》(噂話をされるため)耳がほてる (→fell one's EARs burning) ▪ Didn't *your ears burn* yesterday? きのう君の耳はほてらなかったかい《噂をされていると思わなかったかい》 ▪ *Were your ears burning*? We were just talking about you. 耳がほてっていなかったかい? ちょうど君の噂話をしてたんだ.

*One's **ears deceive** one.* 聞き違いをする ▪ That's the train coming if *my ears* don't *deceive* me. 私の聞き違いでなければ列車が来たのだ.

eat** [**drink**] **... till ... come**(**s**) **out of** one's **ears 《口》食べ[飲み]すぎる ▪ They *ate* beef burgers *till* they *came out of their ears*. 彼らはハンバーグステーキを食べすぎた.

fall on deaf** [**indifferent**] **ears 傾聴されない, 無視される ▪ My advice *fell on deaf ears*. 私の忠告は聞いてもらえなかった.

fall together by the ears つかみ合い[けんか]を始める ▪ They *fell together by the ears*. 彼らはけんかを始めた.

feel** one's **ears burning 《口》耳がほてっている; (特に悪い)噂をされていると感じる ▪ Did you *feel your ears burning*? 耳がほてっていると感じた[誰かが自分の噂をしていると感じた]かい.

from ear to ear **1** (笑うとき両方の耳まで裂けるほど)口を大きくあけて ▪ He smiled *from ear to ear*. 彼は口を大きくあけてほほえんだ.
2 耳(下)から耳(下)まで ▪ The man had his throat cut *from ear to ear*. その男は耳下から耳下までのどを切られた.

get a thick ear 《英口》耳がはれるほどなぐられる ▪ If you tell a lie, you will *get a thick ear*. 嘘をつくとこっぴどくなぐられるよ. ☞通例おどし文句.

get** one's **ears pinned back 叱責される, しかりとばされる ▪ I'm sure I'll *get my ears pinned back* for saying that. あんなことを言ったから, きっと叱責されるだろう.

***get** one's **ears set out** [**lowered**]* 散髪して耳を出す, 髪を短くする ▪ I *got my ears set out* and my beard trimmed. 髪を刈ってひげを整えてもらった ▪ You need an appointment to *get your ears lowered* at that barber's. あの理髪店で散髪してもらうには予約が必要だ.

get up** [**go off**] **on** one's **ear 《米》奮起する; 憤慨する; 《俗》聞き耳を立てる ▪ They said I was

E

lightning when I *got up on my ear.* 私が憤慨したら，稲光のようだと彼らは言った．

get *a person* **(*up*)*on*** *his* ***ears*** 人を憤慨させる ▪ It *got* his relations *on their ears.* それは彼の親類を憤慨させた．

give *a person* ***a thick ear*** 《英口》耳がはれるほど人をなぐる ▪ He *gave* his son *a thick ear.* 彼は息子を耳がはれるほどなぐった ▪ I'll *give* you *a thick ear* if you tell a lie. 嘘をつくと耳がはれるほどぶんなぐるぞ．☞通例おどし文句．

give ear **(*to*)** (…を)傾聴する，(に)耳を傾ける ▪ *Give ear to* what I am saying. 私の言っていることをよく聞きなさい．

give *one's* ***ears for*** …のためなら何でもする，犠牲をいとわない (→give one's EYEs for) ▪ I would *give my ears for* promotion [to be promoted]. 昇進のためならなんでもやる覚悟だ．

go in **(*through*)** ***one ear and*** **(*come*)** ***out*** **(*of*)** ***the other*** 《口》右の耳から入って左の耳から抜ける; 頭に残らない ▪ The criticism *went in one ear and* came *out the other.* その批判は一方の耳に入ったが他方から抜け出てしまった ▪ Everything we try to teach the boy *goes in* at *one ear and out* at *the other.* その少年に教えようとすることはみんなすぐ忘れられてしまう．☞go in at one ear and out (at) the other の形もあるが《まれ》．

grin from ear to ear 満面の笑みを浮かべる ▪ I *grin from ear to ear* when I think about America's technological might. 米国の技術力を考えると笑みがこぼれてくる．

half an ear →listen with half an EAR (to).

have a tin ear **(*for*)** →TIN.

have an **[*a good*]** ***ear for*** (音楽など)を聞く耳がある，がわかる ▪ Some animals *have an ear for* music. 音楽のわかる動物もいる．

have an ear out **[*cocked*]** ***for*** → keep an EAR out for.

have **[*hold, keep*]** ***an*** [*one's*] ***ear to the ground*** 世論に注意する，情勢に注意する ▪ He always *has an ear to the ground.* 彼はいつも情勢に注意している ▪ The law-makers will *hold their ears* close *to the ground.* 立法者は世論によく注意するものである．☞辺境開拓者が乗馬者の近づくのを知るため耳を地面につけたことから．

have big **[*long, rabbit*]** ***ears*** 《口》ひどく物を聞きたがる，詮索好きである ▪ I've never met a fellow who *has* such *long ears* as he. 彼ほど物を聞きたがる人に会ったことがない．

have **[*take, hold*]** *a person* ***by the ears*** 人をしっかりとつかんでいる，しっかりつかまえる ▪ The Spaniard *holds* these countries *by the ear.* スペイン人はこれらの国々をしっかりとつかまえている．

have **[*gain, get, win*]** *a person's* ***ear*** 人に(好意をもって)聞いてもらえる[ようになる]，人に話してその人を動かす地位にある[になる]，人の近づきである[になる] ▪ I had the good fortune to *have his ear.* 幸いにも彼に意見を聞いてもらえた[彼の近づきになった] ▪ His eloquence has *gained* for him *the ear of* the legislature. 彼の雄弁は立法府の傾聴するところとなった ▪ He was in the perfect position to *gain the ear of* government leaders. 彼は政府の指導者に主張を聞いてもらうのに完璧な立場にいた ▪ They *got the ears of* local politicians. 彼らは地元選出の政治家たちに主張を聞いてもらった．

have *one's* ***ears glued to*** …に耳をくっつけて聞く ▪ We *had our ears glued to* the radio. 私たちはラジオにかじりついて聴いた．

have **[*get*]** *one's* ***ears on*** (CB 無線を)受信状態にしておく，(意見などを)聞く用意ができている ▪ Anybody out there *got their ears on*? 誰か聞いていますか ▪ We *have our ears on* and we are listening. 聞くつもりになって聞いている．

have half an ear on …を聞くとはなしに聞く ▪ He *had half an ear on* the radio as she was talking to him. 彼女が話しかけているとき，彼の耳はぼんやりラジオのほうにいっていた．

have itching ears (ゴシップ・新しい噂など)を聞きたがる (《聖》*2 Tim.* 4. 3) ▪ He *has itching ears.* 彼はゴシップを聞きたがる人だ．

have **[*there is*]** ***nothing between the ears*** 頭がからっぽである，脳みそがない，愚かである (→between the EARs) ▪ The biggest problem with them was *there was nothing between the ears* of either one of them. 彼らの最大の問題は二人そろって頭がからだということだった ▪ You will swear that she *has nothing between the ears.* 彼女は脳みそがないと君は断言するだろう．

have sharp ears for any gossip どんなスキャンダルも聞き漏らさない，地獄耳である ▪ Mrs. Jones is inquisitive and *has sharp ears for* any *gossip.* ジョーンズ夫人は詮索好きで地獄耳である．

have something between the ears 頭に中身がある，賢明である (→between the EARs) ▪ I'm not interested in a man unless he *has something between the ears.* 賢明な者以外興味がない．

head over ears **(*in*)** = over (head and) EARs (in).

hold an [*one's*] ***ear to the ground*** →have an EAR to the ground.

hold *a person* ***by the ears*** →have a person by the EARs.

hop off on *one's* ***ear*** 《米》しかられて去る ▪ The editor has *hopped off on his ear.* 編集者はしかられて去った．

in a pig's ear 《俗》絶対に…しない[しそうにない] ▪ You must give a donation.—*In a pig's ear* I will. 寄付をしなければなりません—絶対にしません．

in **(*the*)** ***ear*** 穂が出て ▪ Barley was *in the ear.* 大麦は穂が出ていた．

in the ears of …の聞こえる所に; に聞かれるように (《聖》*Jer.* 36. 20) ▪ They told all the words *in the ears of* the king. 彼らはその言葉をすべて王に伝えた．

incline *one's* ***ear*** **(*s*)** **(*to*)** →INCLINE.

it'd be as much as *one's* ***ears were worth*** 《口》それは…にとって非常に危険なことだ. ☞昔罰として耳を切られたことから.

keep an ear out [***cocked***] ***for*** [***toward***] … に耳を傾ける, を注意深く聞く ▪He *kept an ear out for* possible phone calls. 彼は電話があるかもしれないと思って注意して耳をそばだてていた ▪She *kept an ear cocked toward* the television. 彼女はテレビに耳を傾けていた.

keep an [*one's*] ***ear to the ground*** →have an EAR to the ground.

keep *one's* ***ears open*** = keep one's EYEs open.

lead…by the ears …を屈従させておく ▪The chiefs *led* the ignorant masses *by the ears* after them. 族長たちは無知な大衆を自分らに追従させた.

lend an ear [*one's* ***ears***] (***to***) 《文》(…に)耳を傾ける[貸す] ▪*Lend an ear to* the complaints of the poor. 貧しい人々の訴えに耳を傾けなさい ▪*Lend* me *your ears* for five minutes. 5分間私にお耳を貸してください.

listen with half an ear (***to***) (…に)耳を半分傾ける, をうわの空で聞く ▪The minister has *listened* to environmentalists but only *with half an ear*. 大臣は環境保護主義者たちの言うことを聞くには聞いたが, うわの空だった.

Little pitchers have long ears. →PITCHER.

long ears **1** ロバ; ばか ▪Hinnies and mules are categorized as *long ears*. (馬とロバの交配種である)ケッテイとラバはロバ類に分類されている ▪This *long-ears* had to be "dear-Sir'd". このばかには「だんなさま」と言わなければならなかった ▪Kings are commonly said to have long hands; I wish they had as *long ears*. 通常, 王は手が長いと言われている. 耳も長ければよかったのに. ☞Jonathan Swift の言葉; 王への皮肉.
2 詮索好きな人, 地獄耳 (→have big EARs).

make a pig's ear (***out***) ***of*** 《口》…を台なしにする; にへまをやる ▪He *made a pig's ear of* repairing his house. 彼は家の修繕をしくじった.

make *a person's* ***ears burn*** 人を当惑させる, 耳がほてる ▪Mom's stories about us as babies *made my ears burn*. 私たちが赤んぼうのころのことに関する母の話には耳がほてった.

not dry behind the ears →wet behind the EARs.

on *one's* ***ear*** 酔って ▪We shall be [get] *on our ear* soon. 我々はじきに酔うだろう.

open *a person's* ***ear***(***s***) (***to***) (…に)人の耳を傾けさせる ▪I ask that you *open his ears to* the sound of the children's laughter. 彼を子供たちの笑い声に耳を傾けさせるようお願いします.

open *one's* ***ear***(***s***) (***to***) (…に)耳を傾ける ▪I began to *open my ears* the better to understand his speech. 私は彼の演説をよりよく理解するため傾聴し始めた.

out on *one's* ***ear*** (急に)首になって; (屈辱的に)追い出されて ▪I'll be *out on my ear*. 僕は首になるだろう ▪We threw the detective *out on his ear*. 我々は探偵をたたき出した.

over (***head and***) ***ears*** (***in***) (…に)深くはまりこんで ▪He got *over head and ears in* debt. 彼は借金で首が回らないようになった ▪He is *over head and ears in* love. 彼は首ったけだ.

perk (***up***) *one's* [***it's***] ***ears*** →PRICK up one's ears.

pin back *one's* ***ears*** **1**《主に英口》注意して聞く ▪Please *pin back your ears*. よく聞いてください.
2《主に英》(勝利に貢献するために)俊足を飛ばす, 素早く走る ▪He *pinned back his ears* and darted for the corners. 彼は俊足を飛ばして, コーナーめがけて疾走した.

pin *a person's* ***ears back*** 《米口》完全に懲らしめる, しかる, 打ち負かす ▪Tomorrow we'll *pin their ears back*. あす彼らを完全に打ち負かしてやろう.

play (***…***) ***by ear*** **1** 楽譜なしで[聞いただけで](…を)演奏する ▪He could *play by ear* very prettily. 彼は楽譜なしでとてもうまく演奏することができた.
2《口》〚主に play it …の形で〛ぶっつけ本番でやる, 臨機応変にやる ▪I decided to *play it by ear*. 私は臨機応変にやろうと決めた.

prick up *one's* ***ears*** →PRICK².

pull [***drag***]***… by the ears*** …を荒々しく引っぱる[引きずる] ▪He *pulled* her *by the ears* and by the hair. 彼は彼女の耳と頭髪をつかんで荒々しく引っ張った.

pull in *one's* ***ears*** 詮索をやめる ▪Now, *pull in your ears*. This is none of your business. さあ, 詮索はやめたまえ. 君には関係ないことだ.

reach *a person's* ***ear***(***s***) →come to a person's EAR(s).

set *persons* ***by the ears*** 人々に争いを起こさせる, 人々を不和にする ▪Turkey *set* the Greeks and Bulgarians *by the ears*. トルコはギリシャ人とブルガリア人とをけんかさせた. ☞闘犬から; 双方が犬の耳をもって互いに対抗させる.

set… on *one's* ***ear*** 《米》(人・業績などが)…の注目[注意]を一身に集める ▪If true, this will *set* the Republicans *on their ear*. もし真ならば, これは共和党員の注目を一身に集めるだろう.

shake *one's* ***ears*** →SHAKE².

speak in *a person's* ***ear*** (人)にささやく, 内緒で話す ▪The messenger *spoke in her ear*. 使者は彼女にささやいた.

stop [***close, shut***] *one's* ***ears to*** …に耳をふさぐ, を聞くまいとする ▪We *stopped our ears to* his complaints. 彼の訴えを聞くまいとした ▪The shrieks of the children made us *stop our ears*. 子供たちの悲鳴のため, 我々は耳をおおった.

take *a person* ***by the ears*** →have a person by the EARs.

throw *a person* ***out on*** *his* ***ear*** 人をほうり出す ▪Ben grabbed him by the scruff of the neck

E

and *threw* him *out on his ear*! ベンは彼の首筋をつかんでほうり出した.

tickle *a person's* ***ears*** 人に気に入ることを言って喜ばす, 人におべっかを言う ▪ In order to get in his good books, you must *tickle his ears* a bit. お気に入りになろうと思えば, 少し彼におべっかを使わねばならない ▪ That will *tickle his ears* for him. そうすれば彼は大いに喜ぶでしょう.

to the ears (受容力の)極限まで ▪ My father was drunk *to the ears*. 父はへべれけに酔っていた.

turn a deaf ear to …を聞こうとしない ▪ He *turned a deaf ear to* my complaints. 彼は私の苦情を聞こうとしなかった.

up to the [*one's*] ***ears in*** **1** …にどっぷり浸かっている, 夢中である ▪ He is *up to the ears in* love. 彼は首ったけだ ▪ We are *up to the ears in* trouble. 我々は苦境に深くはまりこんでいる ▪ I am *up to my ears in* work. 私は仕事に没頭している.
2 …で多忙である ▪ She was *up to her ears in* post-graduate studies. 彼女は大学院の勉強で大忙しだった.

Walls have ears. →WALL.

wet [***not dry***] ***behind the ears*** 全くの未熟で (↔dry behind the EARs) ▪ Married! You're still *wet behind the ears*. 結婚したって! 君はまだ全くの青二才じゃないか. ☞ears「(麦などの)穂」; または, 子供が耳の後ろをふかないことからとも言われる.

win *a person's* ***ear*** →have a person's EAR.

with all *one's* ***ears*** 耳をそばだてて (→be all EARs).

with *one's* [***an, one***] ***ear to the ground*** 世論に注意して (→have an EAR to the ground) ▪ He is a politician *with one ear to the ground*. 彼は世論に注意する政治家である.

would give *one's* ***ears for*** [***to*** *do*] …が得られたら[…することができたら]耳を切られてもかまわない ▪ I *would give my ears for* a glance at the map. その地図を一目見せてもらえたら, 私は耳を切られてもかまわないんだが ▪ Many a man *would give his ears to* marry such a charming young lady. こんなに若く美しい淑女と結婚するならどんな犠牲を払っても惜しくないと思う人も多いだろう. ☞有害な意見を取り消さない人の耳を切った昔の習慣から.

You cannot make a silk purse out of a sow's ear. →PURSE.

earful /íərfʊ̀l/ 名 ***get an earful*** (***of***) 《口》 **1** …を聞く ▪ I asked him about it, and I certainly *got an earful of* it. それについて彼に尋ねた. そして確かにそれを十分聞いた.
2 大目玉を食う ▪ Have I *got an earful* for you! 君の代わりに大目玉を食ったのなんのって.

give *a person* ***an earful*** 《口》人にさんざん文句を言う ▪ He *gave* them *an earful* in his Security Council speech. 彼は安全委員会の演説で彼らに怒りをぶつけた ▪ Dad will *give* you *an earful* before you buy that CD. お父さんの文句を聞かなければ, あの CD は買えないよ.

early /ə́ːrli/ 形副 ***a small and early*** →SMALL.

An early answer will oblige. 至急ご返事願います《手紙の文句》.

an early bath →BATH.

as early as 早くも…に ▪ Printing was invented *as early as* the 15th century. 印刷術は早くも15世紀に発明された.

at an early date →DATE.

at the earliest 早くとも ▪ It will be next week *at the earliest*. 早くとも来週だろう.

at the earliest date さっそく, 至急に ▪ We will hold a meeting *at the earliest date* possible. できるだけ早い日程で会議を開こう.

bright and early →BRIGHT.

die an early death 若死にする ▪ Keats *died an early death*. キーツは若死にをした.

earlier [***early***] ***on*** 前もって, 早いころ (↔LATER on) ▪ He was ill *earlier on* in the year. その年の初めのころ病気だった ▪ It was ever so cold *early on* this week. 今週初めはとても寒かった.

early and late **1** 朝早くから夜遅くまで ▪ I was up *early and late*. 朝早くから夜遅くまで起きていた.
2 始終, 絶えず, 明けても暮れても ▪ He is studying English *early and late*. 彼は始終英語を勉強している.

early habits 早寝早起きの習慣 ▪ It is not easy to acquire *early habits*. 早寝早起きの習慣をつけるのは容易でない.

early in life 若いうちに, 若くて ▪ He died *early in life*. 彼は若くて死んだ.

early in the day 早い; (遅れずに)間に合って (↔LATE in the day) ▪ It was very *early in the day*. 非常に早い時間だった ▪ It is *early in the day* to know whether it is a success or not. それが成功かどうかを知るにはまだ早い.

early or late 遅かれ早かれ, 早晩 ▪ We shall find the truth *early or late*. 我々は遅かれ早かれ真相を知るだろう.

Early to bed and early to rise (***makes a man healthy, wealthy, and wise***). 《諺》早寝早起きは人を健康に, 金持ちに, 賢明にする ▪ With final exams coming, you'd best remember, *early to bed and early to rise*. 期末試験が近づいているので, 早寝早起きをするよう心に留めておくのがよい.

get up [***rise, wake up***] (***very***) ***early*** 俊敏である, 抜け目がない ▪ They *got up* a bit too *early* for you, my boy. 彼らは君には少しすばしこすぎたね.

it is early days yet (***to*** *do*) (…するのは)まだ早い ▪ *It is early days yet to* make up your mind. 君が決心するのはまだ早い ▪ The operation seems a success, but *it is early days yet*. 手術は成功のようだ, がそう結論するのはまだ早い. ☞days は副詞で "of day" の意.

The early bird catches the worm. →BIRD.

earn /əːrn/ 動 ***earn a base*** [***run***] 《野球》ベース[1点]をとる, 進塁[得点]する ▪ He easily *earned* *a base.* 彼はやすやすと進塁した ▪ He *earned* four *runs.* 彼は4点取った.

earn** one's **keep →KEEP[1].

***earn** one's **livelihood** [**living, daily bread**]* 生計の資をかせぐ ▪ I do not know how to *earn my daily bread.* どう暮らしを立ててよいかわからない.

***earn** one's **salt** [**salary, wages**]* 給料だけの働きがある ▪ He *earns his salt.* 彼は給料だけの値うちがある.

***have richly** [**rightly**] **earned** one's **title** [**fame**]* 称号[名声]だけの功は十分ある ▪ He *has richly earned his title.* 彼はその称号を得るだけの功は十分ある.

earner /ə́ːrnər/ 名 ***a nice little earner*** 《英口》実入りのよい商売 ▪ Surcharges become *a nice little earner.* 追加料金は実入りのよい商売になる ▪ Car insurance can be *a nice little earner.* 車の保険は実入りのよい商売になることがある.

earnest /ə́ːrnəst/ 形名 ***earnest for*** …を熱望して ▪ He seems to be very *earnest for* success. 彼は成功を非常に熱望しているようだ.

in dead** [**good, real, sad, sober**] **earnest 全く真剣に, 本気で ▪ This time he came at me *in dead earnest.* こんどは彼は全く本気で私にかかってきた ▪ Are you in jest or *in real earnest?* お前, 冗談なのか本気なのか.

in earnest 真剣に, 本式に (↔in FUN, in PLAY 1) ▪ You are reducing *in earnest* these days. 君はこのごろ真剣になって体重を減らそうとしているね ▪ It began to rain *in earnest.* 本降りになってきた.

earshot /íərʃɑ̀t|-ʃɔ̀t/ 名 ***out of earshot*** (***of***) (…の, に)聞こえない所に, 聞こえないほど遠く離れて ▪ Don't let the child get *out of earshot.* 子供を声が聞こえない所へ行かせないでください ▪ Can't hear a word! They are *out of earshot of* us. 一言も聞こえない. 我々に聞こえないほど遠く離れているのだ.

within earshot (***of***) (…から)聞こえる所に, のすぐ近くに ▪ We were *within earshot of* the hotel. 私たちはホテルから呼べば聞こえる所にいた ▪ We could not get *within earshot of* the speaker. 発言者の声が聞こえる所へ行くことができなかった.

earth /əːrθ/ 名 ***all over the earth*** 世界中に ▪ By this time the news will be *all over the earth.* もう今ごろはそのニュースは世界中に知れわたっているだろう.

an earth mother **1** 〚the Earth Mother で〛母なる大地, 大地の女神 ▪ Izanami henceforth became *the Earth Mother*, the prime goddess of Shinto. イザナミはそれ以後大地の女神になった, 神道の最高の女神である.

2 いかにも母性的な女性 ▪ Jane is *an earth-mother* barmaid. ジェインはバーテンダーでいかにも母性的な女性だった. ☞Ⓖ Erdmutter のなぞり.

bring ... down to earth …を実現する; を現実に戻す ▪ The building of a world city is about to *be brought down to earth.* 世界都市の建設が今にも実現されようとしている ▪ Let us *bring* this vision *down to earth.* この夢を現実に戻しましょう.

***bring** a person **down to earth with a bang** [**bump**]* 人に辛い現実をたたきつける, 現実に引き戻す (→come (back) down to EARTH with a bang) ▪ We thought we could win the championship, but losing in the quarter-final *brought* us *down to earth with a bump.* 我々は優勝できると思っていたが, 準々決勝戦で敗退してつらい現実に引き戻された.

bring ... to the earth …を地上に射落とす ▪ He *brought* a bird *to the earth.* 彼は鳥を地上に射落とした.

come (***back***) ***down to earth with a bang*** 突然現実に引き戻される (→bring a person down to EARTH with a bang) ▪ I *came down to earth with a bang* after the general election. 総選挙のあと私は突然現実に引き戻された.

come back** [**down**] **to earth (夢想からさめて)現実の世界に戻る, 実質的なものに触れる (→bring... down to EARTH) ▪ They *came down to earth* back home. 彼らは帰宅して現実に戻った ▪ Now you have *come down to earth.* 今や君は空論から現実に戻った.

cost** [**charge, pay**] **the earth 《英口》大金がかかる, 非常に高くつく (→pay the EARTH for) ▪ It will not *cost the earth* to save the planet but it will cost the Earth if we don't act now. この惑星を救うのに大金はかかるまいが, いま行動をおこさなければ地球が破滅するだろう.

down to earth **1** 現実的な, 実際的な ▪ His approach was *down to earth.* 彼のやり方は地に足がついたものだった.

2《口》全く, すっかり, 徹底的に (= down to the GROUND) ▪ The occupation suited my tastes *down to earth.* その職業はすっかり私の好みに合った.

drop down to earth 地上に降りる ▪ The airship *dropped* smoothly *down to earth.* 飛行船はなめらかに地上に降下した.

Earth to A! 《口》もしもしAさん《ぼうっとしている人への呼びかけ》 ▪ *Earth to* Randall. Wake up*!* これこれランドル君. 起きなさい.

fall to earth 地上に落ちる ▪ The arrow *fell to earth.* その矢は地上に落ちた.

get down to earth 現実に即して活動する ▪ Modern geographers *get down to earth.* 現代の地理学者は現実に即して活動する.

go the way of all the earth →go the WAY of all flesh.

go to** [**take**] **earth 《英》(人がいつもの所から)姿を消す; 身を隠す ▪ He could not *go to earth* like a fish in the sea. 彼は海の魚のように姿を隠すことはできなかった.

like nothing on earth →NOTHING.

***move heaven and earth to** do* →MOVE[2].

of the earth, earthy **1** 土から出て土につく (《聖》*1 Cor.* 15. 47) ▪ They are *of the earth, earthy.* 彼らは土から出て土につくものである.

2 俗臭ふんぷんとして; この俗世間の, 浮世のもので ▪ He is *of the earth, earthy.* 彼は俗物中の俗物だ ▪ Sorrow is *of the earth, earthy.* 悲哀はこの浮世のものである.

on earth **1** 地上に[で]; 〚単なる強意句として〛 この世で ▪ While one is *on earth*, one must enjoy oneself. 人は地上にいる間は, 楽しく過ごさねばならない ▪ He is the most despicable man *on earth.* 彼はこの世で最も卑しむべき男だ.
2 〚疑問・否定の強意句として〛 一体, 全然 ▪ What *on earth* is the matter? 一体どうしたんだ ▪ It is no use *on earth.* それは全く役にたたない.

on the face of the earth →FACE[1].

pay the earth for …に大金を支払う (→cost the EARTH) ▪ They're going to *pay the earth for* tickets. 彼らは入場券に大金を払おうとしている.

run to earth **1** 《英》 …をくまなく捜して見つけ出す, 捕える, 追いつめる ▪ All the men who helped to *run* the family *to earth* were rewarded. その一家を捜して見つけ出すのを助けた人々は皆褒賞をもらった.
2 (問題など)を根元まで調べあげる, 突き止める ▪ We finally *ran* the cause of the problem *to earth.* 我々は遂にその問題の原因を突き止めた. ☞キツネ狩りから.

take earth →go to EARTH.

the earth moved (for you) 《戯》 〚主に疑問文で〛 (特に性的な体験などが)すばらしかった ▪ Did *the earth move for you* last night? ゆうべはすばらしかったかい?

earthly /ɜ́ːrθli/ 形名 ***no earthly/ not an earthly*** 《口》 全く機会[見込み]がない ▪ They have now *no earthly*, as all seats have been allotted. 席はみな割り当てられたから, 彼らはもう全く見込みはない ▪ The poor goalkeeper had *not an earthly.* かわいそうに, そのゴールキーパーには全く勝てる見込みはなかった. ☞次に chance を略したもの; 次項も参照.

no earthly chance [use] 《口》 全く機会はない[役にたたない] ▪ There is *no earthly chance.* 見込みは全然ない.

of the earth, earthly →EARTH.

ease[1] /iːz/ 名 ***at (one's) ease*** **1** 《号令》 休め! ▪ *At ease*! 休め! ☞Stand at ease! の略.
2 安らかに, 気楽に, 安楽に ▪ Put your mind *at ease.* ご安心ください ▪ You may do it *at your ease.* それは気楽にやってください.
3 安心して, 楽な気持ちで, くつろいで ▪ He is quite *at ease* in fashionable society. 彼は上流社交界の中で全くくつろいでいる ▪ He felt much more *at his ease* in the saddle than afoot. 彼は歩くよりも馬に乗っているほうがずっと楽な気持ちだった.

get at one's ease 落ち着く ▪ When a man has once *got at his ease*, he grows lazy. 人は一度落ち着いてしまうと, 怠け者になる.

ill at ease 不快で; 不安で, 落ち着かなくて; 気うまりで ▪ She felt *ill at ease* after her dinner. 彼女は食後気持ちが悪かった ▪ He was *ill at ease* at the news. 彼はそのニュースを聞いて不安だった ▪ I feel *ill at ease* in the saddle. 馬上では落ち着かない ▪ I feel *ill at ease* in his company. 彼といっしょにいると気うまりだ.

march at (one's) ease 《号令》 並み足行進をする ▪ The captain commanded, "*March at ease*!" 大尉は「並み足で行進!」と命令した.

put [set] a person at his ease 安楽な気持ちにさせる, くつろがせる ▪ He *put* his visitors *at their ease.* 彼はお客たちをくつろがせた.

set one's [a person's] heart at ease 安心する[人を安心させる] ▪ You may *set your heart at ease.* ご安心ください ▪ He *set my heart at ease.* 彼は私を安心させた.

take one's ease (重荷などおろして)くつろぐ; 楽にする, 休む ▪ Now the work is finished, I can *take my ease.* 仕事が終わったから, 私はくつろげる ▪ The dog was *taking his ease* on the sofa. 犬はソファの上で休んでいた.

with ease やすやすと (↔ with DIFFICULTY) ▪ The soldiers marched 20 miles *with ease.* 兵士たちは20マイルを楽に進軍した.

ease[2] /iːz/ 動 ***ease oneself*** **1** やっかい払いをする ▪ He is trying to *ease himself* by some means or other. 彼は何とかしてやっかい払いをしようとしている.
2 安心する, うさを晴らす ▪ He *eased himself* by cursing at Ormond. 彼はオーモンドをののしってうさを晴らした.
3 排便する; 《口・婉曲》 射精する ▪ Whoever *eases himself* in Apollo's Temple shall be indicted. アポロの神殿で排便する者は誰でも起訴される ▪ He had dismounted to *ease himself.* 彼は排便するため馬から降りた.

ease all 《ボート》 **1** 漕ぐのをやめる ▪ When the boat begins to rock, it is better to *ease all.* ボートが左右に揺れ始めたら漕ぐのをやめるほうがよい.
2 《号令》 漕ぎ方やめ ▪ *Ease all*! 漕ぎ方やめ!

easier /íːziər/ 副 ***Easier said than done.*** →SAY[2].

easily /íːzəli/ 副 ***easily first*** 断然第一で ▪ He is *easily first* among the poets. 彼は詩人の中ではずばぬけて優れている.

east /iːst/ 名形副 ***about east*** 《米口》 完全に[な]; 適正に[の], 正式に[の] ▪ They must take it *about east.* 彼らはそれを完全に取らねばならない ▪ Find out what is *about east* and shape your course accordingly. 適正なものを見いだしてそれに従って自分の進路を決めなさい.

down East [east] 《米口》 (New England の)東部沿岸(に, へ), (特に) Maine 州(に, へ) ▪ They laughed at the accent of the boy from *down East.* みんなが東部沿岸から来た少年のなまりをからかって笑った ▪ I must go *down East.* 東部地方へ行かねばならない.

East is East and West is West and never the twain shall meet. →never the TWAIN shall meet.

east of …の東(方)に ▪ Japan lies *east of* China. 日本は中国の東方にある.

East, (or) West, home's best. 《諺》東でも西でも, わが家[町, 国]が一番よい.

in the east 東(部)に; 東から ▪ Japan is *in the east* of Asia. 日本はアジアの東(部)にある ▪ The sun rises *in the east.* 太陽は東から上る.

lie east and west 東西にわたって横たわる ▪ The island *lay east and west.* その島は東西に横たわっていた.

on the east (of) (…の)東に(接して), 東端に ▪ There is the Pacific *on the east.* 東に接して太平洋がある ▪ Japan is *on the east of* Asia. 日本はアジアの東端にある.

send to the East Indies for Kentish pippins 簡単なことをするのに騒ぎ回る(＝break a fly on the WHEEL) ▪ He does everything in such a round-about way—talk about *sending to the East Indies for Kentish pippins*! 彼は何事をするにも実にまだるっこい. 簡単なことをするにも大騒ぎするとは正にこのことだ.

to the east (of) (…の)東方に ▪ Japan is *to the east of* China. 日本は中国の東方にある.

easy /íːzi/ 形 ***an easy mark***/《英口》***easy meat*** →a soft MARK.

as easy as abc [ABC]/(as) easy as falling [rolling] off a log/as easy as shelling peas/as easy as easy/(as) easy as pie 《口》きわめて易しい ▪ Making money can be *as easy as ABC.* 金儲けは全く容易にできることがある ▪ Saving them will be *as easy as falling off a log.* 彼らを救うのはとても易しいだろう ▪ Why, it's *as easy as pie.* なんだ, それはひどく易しいじゃないか ▪ My job is *as easy as pie.* 私の仕事はとても易しい. ☞「pie を食べるほど簡単」の意.

breathe easy →rest EASY.

come easy (…にとって)簡単である(*for, to*) ▪ Nothing *came easy for* me. 私には簡単なことなどなかった.

Easy ahead! 《号令》静かに前進!;《海》前進微速! ▪ "*Easy ahead,*" shouts the captain. 「ゆっくりと前進」と船長は叫ぶ.

easy all ＝EASE all.

Easy come, easy go. 《諺》簡単に得たものは簡単に出ていく,「悪銭身につかず」.

Easy does it. 《口》ゆっくりやれ, 落ち着け ▪ *Easy does it,* old man. 君, 落ち着け ▪ Let's move it. *Easy does it.* さあ動かそう. 静かにね.

easy going (with) (…に対して)甘い ▪ You are too *easy going with* those people. あなたはその人たちに甘すぎる.

easy in (one's) mind 安心している ▪ I'm quite *easy in mind* about them. 彼らについては全く安心している ▪ Your mother won't be *easy in her mind* till she knows you are well. お母さんはあなたが元気だということを知るまでは安心しないでしょう.

easy in one's morals (品行が)だらしない ▪ People say she is *easy in her morals.* 彼女はだらしないそうだ.

easy keep 《米》何でも食べて太る人 ▪ She describes herself as *easy keep.* 彼女は自分を何でも食べて太る人間だと言っている.

easy money →MONEY.

easy of belief →BELIEF.

easy on the ear (音楽が)耳に優しい[快い] ▪ Bossa Nova can be *easy on the ear.* ボサノバは耳に心地よいことがある.

easy on the eye(s) 《口》**1** 見て快く, (特に女性が)美形で ▪ She is *easy on the eye(s).* 彼女は見目麗しい ▪ That kind of paper is *easy on the eyes.* その種の紙は見て快い. ☞EASY to look at から; 緩叙法的(控え目)表現.
2 (活字などが)目を疲れさせない(↔hard on the eye) ▪ This type is *easy on the eye.* この活字は目が疲れない.

easy sledding 容易な仕事, 楽々とできること(↔tough sledding) ▪ It's *easy sledding* from here on. ここから先はお茶の子さいさいだ. ☞橇(そり)で丘を下ることから.

easy to come by 容易に見つかる[手に入る, 利用できる] ▪ Good jobs aren't *easy to come by.* いい仕事にはめったにありつけない.

easy to deal with →DEAL².

easy to look at 《口》(女性が)美人で ▪ She is *easy to look at.* 彼女は美人だ.

easy with …を静かに(気をつけて)やれ ▪ *Easy with* that. それは静かにやれ.

feel easy (about) (…について)楽な気持ちである[安心する] ▪ He *feels easy about* the future. 彼は将来については安心している.

get into Easy Street 裕福になる, 繁昌する(→in EASY Street) ▪ It has taken him all his life to *get into easy street.* 彼は裕福になるのに一生かかった. ☞Easy Street は easy street と書くこともある.

get off easy 《口》最悪を免れる, 軽微ですむ, 軽い罰で逃れる ▪ Harry never *got off easy,* either. ハリーも無難にはすまなかった ▪ If you paid only a two-dollar fine, you *got off* very *easy.* たった2ドルの罰金を払っただけなら, ひどく軽い罰で逃れたわけだよ.

go easy →GO².

go easy on →GO².

go easy with **1** …を惜しむ, 控える, 節約する ▪ *Go easy with* the butter. バターを控えなさい.
2 …に慈悲深い ▪ *Go easy with* her. 彼女にやさしくしてあげなさい.

have it easy 《口》全く苦労がない ▪ I've never *had it easy.* 私は楽だったことなどない ▪ Cuba *had it easy* against South Africa. キューバは南アに楽勝だった.

Honors (are) easy. 《トランプ・口》最優位のカードは敵味方半々(である) ▪ If we have the worst of that, *honors are easy.* もし我々がそれに負けても, 最優位のカードは敵味方半々だ.

I'm easy. 《口》どちらでもよい, かまわない ▪ Do you

want coffee or tea?—Either will do. *I'm easy.* コーヒーかそれとも紅茶を飲みますか?—どちらでも結構. 私はかまいません.

in [***on***] ***Easy Street*** 繁昌して, 安楽に, 裕福に ▪ He is *in Easy Street.* 彼は裕福である ▪ Luck put him *on easy street.* 幸運にも彼は裕福になった.

in [***on***] ***easy terms*** 分割払いで ▪ The remainder is to be paid by the month *in easy terms.* 残りは月々分割払いになっています.

(***It***) ***hasn't*** [***Things haven't***] ***been easy.*** (不幸・難事などの後で)容易ではなかった, 大変だった ▪ *It* just *hasn't been easy* this year. 今年はほんとに大変だった.

It is easier to tear down than to build up. 《諺》(家を)建てるより壊す方が易しい,「千日の功名一時に滅ぶ」.

It's easy to be wise after the event./《米》 ***It's easy to be smart after the fact.*** 《諺》(愚者の)後知恵 (= Fools are wise after the EVENT.).

let *a person* ***off easy*** →LET a person off lightly.

make *a person* ***easy*** 人を安心させる ▪ I *made* her *easy* on that point. その点については彼女を安心させた.

make easy going (行くのが)楽である ▪ The road drops downhill and *makes easy going.* 道路は下りになって楽である.

make *one's* ***mind easy*** 安心する ▪ *Make your mind easy.* 安心しなさい.

of easy virtue →VIRTUE.

on easy payment plan 分割払いで ▪ The attorney got his loan *on* a three-year *easy payment plan.* 弁護士は3年間の分割払いで金を借りた.

on Easy Street →in EASY Street.

on easy terms →in EASY terms.

over easy →OVER.

rest easy 満足する, くよくよしない ▪ I cannot *rest easy* until he comes. 彼が来るまでは安心できない.

Stand easy! 《英号令》休め! ▪ The command to stand-at-ease was followed by the words *Stand easy.*「休め」の号令に続いて,「(自由に)休め」の号令が出た. ☞Stand at EASE! の後に出される号令. 位置を離れさえしなければ, もっと自由な姿勢をとって手足は動かしてもよい.

take it easy **1**《口》休む;《米》無理するなよ, じゃあね《別れるとき》 ▪ You've done enough work for today; now *take it easy.* きょうの仕事は十分に果たした. これから休みなさい.

2 (物事を)のんきに考える, あせらずに[無理をせずに, のんびり]やる; 心配しない (↔take it HARD) ▪ *Take it easy.* Make yourself at home. 気楽にして, くつろいでください.

take things easy =take it EASY 2.

want easy money ぬれ手であわ式の金儲けをしたがる ▪ He *wanted easy money.* 彼はぬれ手であわ式に金を儲けたがった.

eat[1] /iːt/ 名 ***on the eat*** 《米》食事をして ▪ The guests are *on the eat.* お客は食事をしている.

eat[2] /iːt/ 動 ***be bad eating*** まずい食べ物である ▪ This fruit *is bad eating.* この果物はまずい.

be eating *a person* 《米口》人を悩まして[怒らせて]いる (→What's EATing you?) ▪ What's *eating* Mabel? メイベルは何で怒っているのか ▪ Something *is eating* the dog. 犬は何かできげんが悪いのだ.

be good [***delicious***] ***eating*** おいしい食べ物である ▪ This fruit *is delicious eating.* この果物はおいしい.

be good to eat 食べられる, 食用になる ▪ This fish *is good to eat.* この魚は食べられる.

eat *a person* ***alive*** **1** (動物などが)...を捕食する, (虫などが)刺す, の生き血を吸う ▪ He *was* nearly *eaten alive* by a great white shark. 彼はホホジロザメにあやうく食べられるところだった ▪ I got *eaten alive* when I was camping. キャンプ中に虫に刺された.

2 ...を食いつぶす, の生き血を吸う, 脅威になる ▪ Unless they change things, they're going to *be eaten alive* by the transaction costs. 事態を変えなければ, 彼らには取引代金がのしかかるだろう.

3 (病気などが)...を苦しめる, さいなむ ▪ Her inner demons *ate* her *alive.* 内なる悪魔が彼女を苦しめた.

4 (仕事・争いで)...を打ちのめす, たたきつぶす ▪ The team *ate* them *alive* in the last Super Bowl. そのチームは前回のスーパーボウルで彼らに圧勝した.

5 ...に立腹する ▪ The critics *ate* me *alive* for it. 批評家たちはそのことで私に立腹した.

eat and run 食べてすぐ去る ▪ It's rude to *eat and run.* ご馳走になってすぐ去るのは無礼だ ▪ So we *ate and ran* fast. そういうわけで, 食事後すぐに失礼したのです, そそくさと.

eat crisp 食べるとカリカリする ▪ This cookie *eats crisp.* このクッキーは食べるとカリカリする.

eat, drink, and be merry 飲み食い浮かれ騒ぐ (《聖》*Luke* 12. 19; *Eccles.* 8. 15) ▪ It is best in the circumstances to *eat, drink, and be merry.* こんな事情のもとでは, 飲み食い浮かれ騒ぐのが一番よい.

eat earth (植民地で)土地を所有する ▪ A man can *eat* as much *earth* as he likes for 5s. a square mile. 1平方マイル5シリングで好きなだけの土地を所有することができる.

eat *one's* ***family out of doors*** 食い道楽で家族を路頭に迷わす ▪ He *ate his family out of doors.* 彼は食い道楽で家族を路頭に迷わせた.

eat *a person* ***for breakfast*** 《口》(特に女性が)男性を存分に楽しんで捨てる ▪ She would *eat* a man like him *for breakfast.* 彼女は彼のような男を存分にもてあそんで捨てるだろう.

eat for the bar 《口》弁護士になるための修業をする (→EAT one's terms) ▪ He will break loose while *eating for the bar* in London. 彼はロンドンで弁護士になる修業をしている間に脱走するだろう.

eat high on the hog =live high off the HOG.

eat it up 《米口》(観客が)見とれる; 夢中になる ▪ He started telling jokes, and the audience just *ate it up.* 彼は冗談を言い始め, 聴衆はただ引き込まれるばかりだった.

eat like …のような味がする ▪ Frog *eats like* fish. カエルは魚のような味がする.

eat like a pig [***wolf, horse***] 《口》がつがつ食べる, 大食する (↔eat like a BIRD) ▪ Though I *eat like a horse*, I am underweight. 私は大食だが体重は標準以下です ▪ Kathy is one of those lucky women who can *eat like a pig* and still stay thin. キャシーは大食いしてもすらっとしたままでいられる幸福な女性の一人だ.

eat** a person's **lunch (仕事・争いで)…を打ちのめす, たたきつぶす (= EAT a person alive 4) ▪ It was a decisive victory; he *ate the incumbent's lunch.* 決定的な勝利だった. 彼は現職に圧勝したのだ.

Eat me! 《俗》ちくしょう, クソくらえ.

eat out of** a person's **hand →HAND[1].

eat** a person **out of house and home 人を食いつぶす《しばしば戯れて大食の子供などについて》 ▪ Our sons with their good appetites will *eat* us *out of house and home* some day. 食欲旺盛な息子たちはいつか我々を食いつぶすだろう.

eat** one's **own flesh 何もせずに怠けている ▪ The fool folds his hands together and *eats his own flesh.* ばか者は手をこまねいて怠けている. ☞聖書語法.

eat** a person's **salt →SALT[1].

eat shit [***crap***] 《俗》屈辱的な扱いに甘んじる ▪ You shouldn't *eat shit* when you can eat caviar. 厚遇してもらえるときに屈辱に甘んじるべきではない.

eat** oneself **sick [***into a sickness***] 食べすぎて病気になる ▪ I may *eat myself into a sickness.* 私は食べすぎて病気になるかもしれない.

eat stick (杖で)打たれる ▪ He has *eaten* five thousand *sticks.* 彼は5,000回打たれた. ☞「棒をくらう」は中国的表現.

eat** one's **terms [***dinners***] 《英口・法》(弁護士になるため)法学院会食に出る, 弁護士になる修業をする ▪ He had *eaten his terms* [*dinners*] in Gray's Inn. 彼はグレイ法学院で弁護士になる修業を終えていた. ☞barrister になる資格の一つとして Inns of Court (法学院)の食堂で毎学期少なくとも3回は会食する必要があることから.

eat the fruit of** one's (**own**) **doings 自分の行為の報いを受ける (《聖》*Isa.* 3. 10) ▪ They will *eat the fruit of their doings.* 彼らは自分の行為の報いを受けるだろう.

Eat to live, not live to eat. 《諺》生きるために食え. 食うために生きるな,「食うだけなら犬でも食う」.

eat** a person's **way 食い込んでいく, 浸食する ▪ Evil *eats his way.* 悪が彼に食い込んでいく.

eat well **1** 美食する ▪ He *ate well* in his youth. 彼は若いころには美食した.

2 大いに食欲がある ▪ The old man *eats well* at that age. その老人はあの歳にしては食が進む.

3 食べておいしい ▪ This cake looks dull but *eats* pretty *well.* このケーキは見かけはぱっとしないが食べてみるとなかなかうまい.

eat** one's **words 《口》(恥を忍んで)前言を取り消す; 大胆な放言を取り消す ▪ After all his boasting, he had to *eat his words.* しこたま自慢したあげく, 彼は恥を忍んで前言を取り消さねばならなかった.

I could eat a horse! (馬1頭食べてしまえるくらい)私は腹ぺこだ!

I'll eat my head [***hat, hands, boots***] ***if*** もし…なら頭[帽子, 手, 靴]でも食ってみせる; そんなことは絶対しない《強い否定》 ▪ You think he will get into Parliament? *I'll eat my head if* he does. 彼が国会議員になると思うのか. 彼がなったら自分の頭でも食ってみせるよ.

not eat you 《口》取って食いはしない ▪ Come on, dear. I *won't eat you.* さあおいで, 取って食いはせんよ.

Well, don't eat me! 《戯》そう食ってかかるな.

What's eating [***bugging***] ***you*** [***him, her***]***?*** 《口》何をいらいらと怒っているのですか ▪ *What's eating you*, so early in the morning? 何が気に入らないんだね, こんなに朝早くから.

eating /íːtɪŋ/ 名 ***serial eating*** **1** 同一人物がいろんなものを連続して食べること《cereal eating にかけてある》 ▪ First she ate the peas on her plate, then the potatoes, and finally the meat—I find such *serial eating* weird. 彼女はまず自分の皿の豆を, 次にジャガイモ, 最後に肉を食べた. こんな箸を休めぬ食べ方はおかしいと思う.

2 家族が別々に食事をすること ▪ "Family time" is transformed into *serial eating.* 「家族の時間」は連続個食へと変わった.

eaves /iːvz/ 名 ***hang on the eaves of*** 軒にぶらさがっている; 危うくぶらさがっている《今にも落ちそうで》 ▪ I *hang on the eaves of* life, ready to fall. 命の軒に危うくぶらさがっていて, 今にも落ちそうだ.

ebb[1] /eb/ 名 ***at a low ebb*** 引き潮で; 下り坂で, 衰えて ▪ His fortune is said to be *at a low ebb.* 彼の身代は傾いているそうだ.

at an [***the***] ***ebb*** 引き潮で; 下り坂で, 衰えて ▪ The tide is *at an ebb.* 潮は引いている ▪ His vitality is *at the ebb.* 彼の活力は衰えている.

at ebb 《詩》(目が)乾いて ▪ My eyes have never been *at ebb* since. それ以来私の目はずっと乾くことがなかった.

at the [*one's*] ***lowest ebb*** 最低潮で, すっかり衰えて ▪ In 1929 money was *at its lowest ebb.* 1929年に金融は最低潮にあった.

Every tide has its ebb. →TIDE[1].

on the ebb **1** =at an EBB.

2 引き潮に乗じて ▪ The ship went out *on the ebb.* 船は引き潮に乗じて沖へ出た.

the ebb and flow 潮の干満; 盛衰 ▪ During the freshets *the ebb and flow* are little felt. 出水の間は潮の干満はほとんど感じられない ▪ He has gone through *the ebb and flow* of life. 彼は人生の栄枯盛衰を経験した.

ebb[2] /eb/ 動 ***ebb and flow*** 差し引きする ▪ The sea will *ebb and flow.* 潮は差し引きする

E

▪ My passions *ebb and flow* at your command. 私の感情はあなたの命令に従って差し引きします.

one's ***life is ebbing away*** 生命の潮が引きつつある, 死に瀕している ▪ He lay in the street after the accident, *his life ebbing away*. 彼は事故のあと道路に倒れたまま瀕死状態だった.

ebony /ébəni/ 名 (***as***) ***black as ebony*** → (as) BLACK as a crow.

echelon /éʃəlàn|-lɔ̀n/ 名 ***in echelon*** 梯(てい)形をなして, 梯状配列で ▪ The captain disposes the soldiers *in echelon*. 隊長は兵を梯形に配置する.

in lower echelon 下級の ▪ They are government officials *in lower echelon*. 彼らは下級公務員である.

echo /ékoʊ/ 名 ***applaud*** [***cheer***]***... to the echo*** 反響するほど喝采する, ほめそやす (cf. Sh., *Macb*. 5. 3. 53) ▪ The performance *was applauded to the echo*. 演技は反響するほど喝采された ▪ His audience *cheered* him *to the echo*. 彼の聴衆は盛んに喝采した.

eclipse /ɪklíps/ 名 ***in eclipse*** **1** (日・月が)欠けて, 食されて ▪ Often had mankind seen the sun *in eclipse*. 人類はしばしば日食を見てきた.

2 光輝を失って ▪ His eyes were *in eclipse*. 彼の目は光輝を失っていた.

in eclipse (***plumage***) (鳥が)求愛用の美しい羽毛を失って ▪ This is a bird *in eclipse* (*plumage*). これは求愛用の美毛を失った鳥だ.

suffer an eclipse 光を失う ▪ His glory *suffered a* temporary *eclipse*. 彼の名誉は一時失墜した.

under an eclipse 映えない, 影が薄い, 日陰の身で ▪ Our affairs are *under an eclipse* at present. 我々の業務は今のところ映えない.

economical /ìːkənámɪkəl|-nɔ́m-/ 形 ***be economical of*** ...を節約する ▪ *Be economical of* your time. 時間を節約せよ ▪ She *is economical of* her smiles. 彼女はなかなか微笑しない.

be economical with the truth 《戯》(人が)真実を出ししぶる, 故意に事実[情報]を隠したり嘘をついたりする; 嘘が多い ▪ Usually politicians *are economical with the truth*. ふつう政治家は本当のことをなかなか明らかにしない ▪ He was known to *be economical with the truth*. 彼は嘘が多いことで知られていた.

economy /ɪkánəmi|-kɔ́n-/ 名 ***economy of truth*** 真実に手かげんを加えること, ありのままに言わないこと ▪ I do not impute falsehood to the government, but I think there has been considerable *economy of truth*. 私は政府が嘘を言ったとは言わないが, 真実に相当手かげんを加えてきたとは思う.

it is poor economy to *do* ...するのは不経済である ▪ *It is poor economy to* use it in that way. それをそのように使うのは不経済である.

practice [***use***] ***economy*** 倹約をする ▪ Strict *economy is practised* in every department. 各省で厳重な節約がされている.

the black economy (脱税などの目的で当局の目を盗んで行われる)闇の経済 ▪ Some resort to *the black economy* to employ Ukrainians. ウクライナ人を雇うために闇の経済に頼るものもいる.

the pink economy ピンク経済《ホモセクシャルの消費者によって使われる金》 ▪ The idea that the majority of working class gays and lesbians can buy into *the pink economy* is false. 労働者階級のゲイおよびレズの大多数はピンク経済を成す購買力があるという考えは間違いだ.

ecstasy /ékstəsi/ 名 (***be***) ***in an ecstasy of*** (喜び・悲しみ)がきわまって(いる) ▪ He *was in an ecstasy of* joy [grief]. 彼は感極まって[悲嘆にくれて]いた.

(***be***) ***in ecstasies*** (***over***) (...で)有頂天になって(いる) ▪ He *was in ecstasies over* the new work. 彼は新作に有頂天になっている.

be thrown [***get, go*** (***off***)] ***into ecstasies*** 有頂天になる, (に)夢中になる (*over*) ▪ She *was thrown into ecstasies over* her new dress. 彼女は新しい服に有頂天になった.

dissolve into ecstasies 有頂天にする[なる] ▪ The sight *dissolved* me *into ecstasies*. その光景は私を有頂天にした.

Eden /íːdən/ 名 ***live in Eden*** 理想の境涯に住む ▪ They were married only last week and at present are *living in Eden*. 彼らは先週結婚したばかりで, 今は理想郷に住んでいる. ☞Eden は神が人間の始祖 Adam と Eve を初めて住まわせた所 (《聖》 *Gen*. 2. 8).

edge[1] /edʒ/ 名 ***a cutting edge*** 切り札, 問題解決になるもの[人, 考え] (→at the cutting EDGE of) ▪ We need *a cutting edge* and I'm on the lookout for a striker. 我々には切り札が必要なので, 私はストライカーを探している.

around the edges かすかに, 少しきざしが見えて (*of*) ▪ His attitude to the death penalty used to be firm, but recently I detect a slight softening *around the edges*. 彼は以前は死刑に対して断固たる態度を取っていたが, 近年ではそれにかすかな軟化がみられる.

at [***on***] ***the cutting edge of*** ...の最先端にいる (→a cutting EDGE) ▪ He was *at the cutting edge of* the Apollo moon landing programs. 彼はアポロ月着陸計画の最先端にいた ▪ This play is really *on the cutting edge of* comedy. この劇は実に喜劇の最先端をいっている.

blunt the edge of →dull the EDGE of.

by [***with***] ***the edge of the sword*** 剣を突きつけて ▪ They enforced those terms *by* [*with*] *the edge of the sword*. 彼らは剣を突きつけてその条件を強制した.

cut [***do***] ***the inside*** [***outside***] ***edge*** 《スケート》スケートの内側[外側]にかどをつけて滑る ▪ Can you *do the outside edge*? あなたはスケートの外側にかどつけして滑れますか.

dull [***blunt***] ***the edge of*** ...の鋭さや厳しさをそぐ

▪ It *dulled the edge of* pleasure [the law]. それは楽しみ[法の厳しさ]をそいだ.

edge on 〚副詞的に〛 刃[ふち]にそって ▪ The board struck him *edge on*. 板の角(かど)が彼を打った.

fray at [***around***] ***the edges*** 次第に弱くなる, 次第に不安定になる, 衰退しはじめる, 摩耗してくる ▪ The hotel has seen better days and is a bit *frayed at the edges*. そのホテルは全盛期を過ぎていて, 少しいたんできている ▪ US economic growth begins to *fray around the edges*. 合衆国の経済成長は次第に弱りかけている.

get an [***the***] ***edge of*** →have an EDGE on.

get the (***rough***) ***edge of*** *a person's* ***tongue*** (人に)ひどくしかられる ▪ I *got the rough edge of my father's tongue*. 私は父にひどくしかられた.

give an edge to (食欲など)をそそる; (議論など)の力を強める ▪ The dish *gave an edge to* my appetite. その料理は私の食欲をそそった.

give *a person* ***the edge*** 《口》 人がきわどいところで勝つと見込む ▪ They *give* the Red Sox *the edge* over the Yankees. 彼らはレッドソックスがヤンキーズに僅差で勝つと見込んでいる.

give *a person* ***the*** (***rough***) ***edge of*** *one's* ***tongue*** 《英》 人をきびしくしかる, 人に舌鋒鋭くあたる ▪ The teacher *gave* the boy *the edge of her tongue*. 先生はその少年をきびしくしかった.

go over the edge 限界を超える, 破たんする ▪ The company *went over the edge* in September 2009. その会社は2009年9月に倒産した.

have [***get***] ***an*** [***the***] ***edge on*** 《口》 **1** …に恨みをいだく ▪ You always *had an edge on* me, and for no reason. あなたはいつも私に恨みをいだいていた, しかも何の理由もないのに.

2 …に勝る, 強味をもっている, より優位にある (＝have an EDGE over) ▪ The Giants *have a* slight *edge on* the Dodgers in their pitching and batting. ジャイアンツはドジャーズより投打において少しすぐれている.

3 生意気である ▪ For a kid like you, you*'ve got a* good deal of *edge on*. 君のような子供にしては君は相当生意気だね.

have [***with***] ***an edge on*** 《口》 少し酔っている[ほろ酔いかげんで] ▪ He came to the office *with* quite *an edge on*. 彼は相当酔って事務所に来た.

have [***hold***] ***an*** [***the***] ***edge over*** 《口》 …より優位にある ▪ Germany *has a* comfortable *edge over* France on that point. その点ではドイツはフランスより十分優位にある.

have rough edges **1** (性格などが)がさつである, 無作法である ▪ He's a pretty tough person and he can *have rough edges* at times. 彼はかなり気難しい人で, ときおり無作法なことがある.

2 (仕事などが)粗削りである, 不備なところがある ▪ The ideas still *have rough edges*. その考えにはまだ問題点がある.

keep *a person* ***on the edge of*** *one's* ***chair*** [《英》 ***seat***] (本が)人を(いすから身をのりださせるほど)わくわく[興奮]させておく (→on the EDGE of one's chair) ▪ This thriller is so interesting that it will *keep* you *on the edge of your seat*. このスリラーはとてもおもしろいので, ハラハラドキドキしっぱなしになるよ.

live on the edge 無鉄砲な生き方をする ▪ Favre used to *live on the edge*, now he was the consummate family man. ファーブルは危険な生き方をしていたが, 今では完ぺきなマイホームパパだった.

lose *one's* ***edge*** 昔の切れ味を失う, 鈍る, 衰える ▪ He was *losing his edge*, despite remaining world number one between 1998 and 2003. 1998年から2003年のあいだ世界一だったにもかかわらず, 彼は衰えはじめていた.

not to put too fine an edge upon it (歯にきぬ着せないで)露骨に言えば ▪ *Not to put too fine an edge upon it*, he is mad. 露骨に言えば, 彼は狂人だ.

off the edge →over the EDGE.

on a knife [***razor's***] ***edge*** 極めて不安定な状態に ▪ The company sees its future *on a knife edge*. その会社は自らの前途を極めて不安定と見ている.

on edge **1** 興奮して, いらいらして; 心配して ▪ It set my nerves *on edge*. それは私の神経をいらだたせた ▪ They naturally felt *on edge*. 彼らは当然やきもきした.

2 しきりにしたがって, むずむずして (*to do*) ▪ We were all *on edge to* know the news. 我々はニュースが知りたくてむずむずしていた ▪ I am all *on edge* over this landscape scheme. 私はこの造園計画についてやっきになっている.

3 縦に(置く, など) ▪ He set a book *on edge*. 彼は本を縦に立てた.

on the bleeding [***leading***] ***edge*** 最先端の技術を用いた, 最先端の技術に精通している ▪ Biotechnology has long been *on the bleeding edge* of science. 生命工学はずっと前から科学の最先端にある.

on the edge (***of***) **1** (…の)縁に[へ] ▪ The house stands *on the edge of* a precipice. その家はがけの縁に立っている.

2 まさにするところで, (…に)瀕(ひん)して, (心配の余り)気が変になりそうで ▪ You are *on the edge of* a discovery. あなたは発見の一歩手前まで来ている ▪ Psychologically, I myself feel that I'm already *on the edge*. 心理的には, 私自身もう限界だと思う.

on the edge of *one's* ***chair*** [《英》 ***seat***] (話などに)非常に興奮して[興味をもって] (→keep a person on the EDGE of one's chair) ▪ The story-teller kept us *on the edge of our chairs* for hours. その語り手は何時間も私たちをひどくおもしろがらせ続けた ▪ We were all *on the edge of our seats*, glued to the box. 我々はみんなわくわくして, ボックス席に釘づけになった.

on the outside edge スケートの外側の縁で ▪ To cut figures *on the outside edge* in skating is to be an adept on the ice. スケートの外側の縁でフィギュアを描けるのは氷上の達人である.

on the thin edge of nothing 《口》 狭い所で ▪ I can't move up at all. I'm sitting *on the thin*

E

edge of nothing. 少しも寄れません. 狭い所へやっとはさまっているのです.

over [***off***] ***the edge*** **1** 行き過ぎの, 極端な, 無茶な ▪ I thought his statement was *over the edge.* 彼の発言は行き過ぎだと思った.
2 狂って ▪ He has gone *over the edge.* 彼は気が狂った ▪ If he has any more bad news, he'll be *off the edge.* 彼にこれ以上の凶報があれば, 彼は気が狂うだろう. ☞ 通例 be, go のあとにくる.

push [***drive***] *a person* ***over the edge*** 《口》(不幸が)人を狂気・絶望などに追いこむ ▪ What *drove* him *over the edge* to total despair is a mystery. 何が彼を全面的な絶望に追い込んだかは謎だ.

put [***set***] ***an edge*** (***up***)***on*** **1** ...を鋭くする, 刃をつける ▪ Let me *put an edge on* that knife. そのナイフの刃を立てさせてください ▪ He knows to *put an edge upon* his speech. 彼は自分の演説を鋭いものにするすべを知っている.
2 (食欲など)をそそる ▪ The odors from the kitchen *put an edge on* our appetites. 台所からのにおいが我々の食欲をそそった.

put to (***the edge of***) ***the sword*** →SWORD.

rough around the edges 荒削りな, やや雑な, 少しばかり欠陥がある ▪ The new teachers are a little *rough around the edges.* 新米の教師たちは少しぎこちないところがある.

set the [*a person's*] ***teeth on edge*** 歯を浮かせる; いらだたせる, 怒らせる (《聖》*Jer.* 31. 29) ▪ That apple has *set my teeth on edge.* そのリンゴで私の歯が浮いた.

take the edge off/***take off the edge*** **1** (刃物)の刃を引く ▪ That wood has *taken the edge off* this knife. その木はこのナイフの刃を引いた.
2 (力・感興など)をそぐ, 鈍らせる ▪ The delay of the expedition *took the edge off* our keenness. 探検隊の延引は我々の熱意をそいだ.

the thin edge of the wedge →WEDGE[1].

with an edge on →have an EDGE on.

with the edge of the sword →by the EDGE of the sword.

edge[2] /edʒ/ 動 ***edge*** *oneself* ***into*** **1** ...に徐々に割りこむ ▪ Bit by bit, the waiter *edged himself into* the discussion. 徐々に給仕は討論に割りこんだ.
2 ...に徐々に取り入る ▪ He *edged himself into* her affections. 彼は徐々に彼女の愛情を得た.

edge *one's* ***way*** (人ごみの中を)体を横にして進む ▪ He *edged his way* through the crowd with ease. 彼は人ごみの中を体を横にしてやすやすと進んだ.

edge(d) tool /édʒdtùːl/ 名 ***jest with edge***(***d***) ***tools*** きわどい冗談を言う《edged tools は比喩的にだけ用いる》 ▪ You had better not *jest with edge tools.* きわどい冗談は言わないほうがよい.

play with edge(***d***) ***tools*** **1** 刃物をもてあそぶ《この意味のときは edge tools のみ用いる》 ▪ Those who *play with edge tools* are apt to cut themselves. 刃物をもてあそぶ人々はけがをしがちである.
2 危険物をもてあそぶ, あぶない火遊びをする ▪ When they read these sex novels, they are *playing with edged tools.* 彼らがこれらのポルノ小説を読むのはあぶない火遊びをしていることになる.

edgeway(s) /édʒwèɪz/, **-wise** /-wàɪz/ 副 ***get*** [***slide, push***] ***in a*** [*one's*] ***word edgeway***(***s***) [***-wise***] すきを見て口をさしはさむ ▪ He *pushed in his word edgeways.* 彼はすきを見て口をはさんだ.

edification /èdəfəkéɪʃən/ 名 ***for*** *one's* ***edification*** 後学のため ▪ I will show you around the city *for your edification.* ご参考までに市内をご案内いたします.

educate /édʒəkèɪt|édju-/ 動 ***an educated guess*** →GUESS[1].

educate *oneself* 修養する, 練習する ▪ He is *educating himself* to eat tomatoes. 彼はトマトを食べる練習をしている.

educate the ear [***eye***] ***to*** ...の耳[目]を肥やす ▪ I must *educate the ear to* music. 音楽の耳を肥やさねばならない.

eel /iːl/ 名 ***a*** [*one's*] ***salt eel*** (打つのに用いる)綱のきれ ▪ With *my salt eel,* I beat my boy. 私は綱のきれで私の子供をぶった.

(***as***) ***slippery as an eel*** →SLIPPERY.

get used to ... as a skinned eel [***like an eel to skinning***] 《口・皮肉》...に初めはつらくてもじきに慣れる《繰り返される苦痛について》 ▪ It goes against the grain at first, but you will soon *get used to* it, *like an eel to skinning.* 初めは不本意であるが, じきにすっかり慣れるでしょう. ☞ ウナギは皮をむかれるときほんの少ししか痛がらないと昔考えられた.

hold the eel of ... by the tail ...を少しばかりかじっている ▪ He *holds the eel of* science *by the tail.* 彼は科学を少しばかりかじっている.

eff /ef/ 動 ***eff and blind*** 《英俗》[[主に進行形で]] 盛んに悪態をつく ▪ He started *effing and blinding.* 彼は盛んに悪態をつき始めた. ☞ eff = fuck などタブー語を使用する. blind = のろう ((God) blind me! (ちくしょう!) などに現れる).

efface /ɪféɪs/ 動 ***efface*** *oneself* 自己を葬る[没却する], 表面から退く, 権利などを放棄する ▪ As a politician he has *effaced himself* by this act of imprudence. 彼はこの軽率な行動によって政治家としての自己を葬ってしまった. ☞ <Ⓕ s'effacer.

effect /ɪfékt/ 名 ***a knock-on effect*** 連鎖反応, 波及効果, 玉突き ▪ Rising oil prices have had *a knock-on effect* on the airline. 原油の値上がりのため当該の航空会社は連鎖的影響を受けた.

bring ... to effect/***carry ... into effect*** ...を成就する, 実行する, 実施する ▪ He *brought* the work *to* good *effect.* 彼はその仕事を首尾よく成就した ▪ The law shall *be carried into effect* from May 1. その法律は5月1日から施行される.

come [***go***] ***into effect*** 実施される ▪ The regulations will *come into effect* soon. その規則はまもなく実施されるだろう.

feel the effects of →suffer from the EFFECTs

of.

for effect (聞く人・見る人への)効果をねらって; 見栄のために ▪ He did it *for effect.* 彼は見栄のためそうしたのだ ▪ They dress their shop window *for effect.* 効果をねらって店の陳列窓を飾る.

from the effects of …のせいで ▪ He lay in bed *from the effects of* the cold. 彼は寒さのため寝ていた.

(*general*) *effect and* (*minute*) *details* 大体の趣きと詳細な点, 細大 ▪ I'll observe both *effect and details.* 細大もらさず観察します.

give effect to …を実施[実行]する, 有効にする ▪ I will *give effect to* my promise. 約束を実行します ▪ They will *give effect to* the regulations. 彼らはその規則を実施するだろう.

go into effect →come into EFFECT.

have effect on …に効き目がある, こたえる ▪ Punishment *has* much *effect on* him. 処罰は彼にはたいした効き目がある ▪ Wine *has* no *effect on* him. ワインは彼には少しもこたえない.

in effect **1** 事実上, 大体, つまり, 実質的には ▪ His reply is *in effect* an apology. 彼の返事は謝罪も同然である ▪ He is *in effect* her manager. 彼は事実上彼女の支配人である.
2 (法律などが)実施されて, 効力がある ▪ The law is *in effect.* その法律は施行されている.

leave no effects 相続人に何も残さない ▪ He died *leaving no effects.* 彼は相続人に遺産を少しも残さずに死んだ.

make* [*render*]... *of no effect …を無効にする ▪ They *made* the law *of no effect.* 彼らはその法を無効にした.

no effects 預金皆無《不払い小切手に記入する文言; N/Eと略記する》 ▪ His cheque was returned to me by the bank with "*N/E*" written on it! 彼の小切手は「預金残高なし(につき無効)」と記して銀行から送り返されてきた!

of no* [*none*] *effect 無効で, 効果なく(《聖》*Matt.* 15. 6) ▪ The message was *of no effect.* その口上書は何の効き目もなかった.

put... into effect =bring... to EFFECT.

***strive* [*strain*] *after effects* [*an effect*]** 立派に見せようと骨折り過ぎる ▪ The painter has spoiled a picture by *striving after effects.* 画家は立派なものに見せようと骨折り過ぎて絵を台なしにした.

suffer from* [*feel*] *the effects of …のせいで病気になっている ▪ He *suffers from the effects of* exposure to the sun. 彼は炎天にさらされたせいで病気になっている.

take effect **1** 効力[効果]を現す, (薬などが)効く ▪ The poison will soon *take effect.* その毒は今に回るだろう ▪ The medicine *took effect.* 薬が効いた.
2 (法律などが)有効となる, 実施になる ▪ When is the new rule to *take effect*? 新規則はいつ実施になるのですか.

to no effect 何の効果もなく, …しても無効で (=in VAIN) ▪ We spoke to him *to no effect.* 我々は彼に話したがむだだった.

***to the effect* (*that*)** …という趣旨の ▪ I sent a letter *to the effect that* he was wrong. 私は彼がまちがっているという趣旨の手紙を送った ▪ He spoke *to the* same *effect.* 彼は同じ趣旨のことを話した.

to this* [*that*] *effect この[その]ような趣旨の ▪ He spoke *to that effect.* 彼はそういう趣旨のことを話した.

with effect 有効に, 効果的に; 力強く ▪ He delivered a thrust *with effect.* 彼は効果的な一突きを与えた ▪ She spoke *with effect.* 彼女は力強く弁じた.

with effect from... 《英》…から有効で, 適用されて ▪ The bus fare is going up *with effect from* May 1. バス料金は5月1日から値上げされる.

without effect 何の効果もなく ▪ I spoke to him *without effect.* 彼に話したがむだだった.

without effects 財産なく ▪ Bob was *without effects.* ボブに財産はなかった.

effective /ɪféktɪv/ 形 ***become effective*** 施行される ▪ The law *becomes effective* on Sept. 30. その法律は9月30日に施行される.

efficacious /èfəkéɪʃəs/ 形 ***efficacious against* [*in*]** …に効く, 効験がある ▪ Give me some medicine *efficacious against* [*in*] fever. 熱に効く薬をください.

efficient /ɪfíʃənt/ 形 ***be efficient in*** …に敏腕[有能]である ▪ My boyfriend *is efficient in* everything he does. 私の彼は何をしても有能である.

effigy /éfədʒi/ 名 ***execute* [*burn, hang*]... *in effigy*** (憎い人の)似姿を処刑[火あぶりに, 絞首刑に]してうっぷんを晴らす ▪ The people decided to *hang* him *in effigy.* 国民は彼の似姿を絞首刑にしてうっぷんを晴らすことにした.

effort /éfərt/ 名 ***by efforts*** 努力で ▪ It can never be gained *by efforts.* それは努力では得られない.

***make an effort* [*efforts*] (*to* do)** (…するよう)努力する, 骨を折る ▪ Please *make an effort to* come. どうぞ努めておいでください.

***make every effort to* do** 全力を尽くして…する ▪ I will *make every effort to* help you. 全力を尽くしてお助けしましょう.

put a lot of* [*some, more,* etc.] *effort into …に懸命な[多少の, もっと, など]努力をする ▪ He's *put a lot of effort into* making himself better. 彼は自分を向上させようと懸命な努力をした.

***spare no effort*(*s*)** 努力を惜しまない ▪ I shall *spare no effort* to get it. 私はそれを得るためには労力を惜しまない.

That is a pretty good effort. 《口》それはかなりの力作である, なかなかよくできている.

with* (*an*) *effort 骨折って; やっと, 無理に ▪ I made this *with effort.* 私はこれを骨折って作った.

without* (*any*) *effort (何の)労苦なく, 造作なく ▪ He lifted up the stone *without effort.* 彼はその石を造作なく持ちあげた.

effrontery /ɪfrʌ́ntəri/ 名 ***have the effron-***

***tery to** do* ずうずうしくも[厚かましくも]…する ▪ He *had the effrontery to* deny it. 彼はずうずうしくもそれを否認した.

effusive /ɪfjúːsɪv/ 形 ***be effusive in*** …をあふれるばかりに表す ▪ He *was effusive in* his gratitude. 彼はあふれるばかりの謝意を表明した.

egg[1] /eg/ 名 ***a bad egg*** 《俗》悪人; 期待はずれの人[計画] ▪ He is *a bad egg.* 彼は悪人だ ▪ The scheme was *a bad egg.* その計画は期待はずれだった.

a good egg [***scout***] 頼りになる人, 気立てのよい人 (→Good EGG!) ▪ Bob is *a good egg* and the community would be the poorer without him. ボブはいい奴で, 彼がいないと地域社会はその分味気なかろう.

a rotten egg 《口》悪いやつ; のろま ▪ Everyone knows he is *a rotten egg.* 彼が悪いやつであることを知らない者はない. ☞特に子供が「のろま」の意味に用いることが多い.

(***as***) ***full of meat as an egg*** →FULL.

(***as***) ***like as*** (***two***) ***eggs*** →(as) LIKE as two peas.

(***as***) ***safe as eggs*** きわめて確かで ▪ We've won the game *as safe as eggs.* 確実に試合に勝った.

(***as***) ***sure as eggs*** (***is*** [***are***] ***eggs***) →(as) SURE as death.

break the egg in the pocket of …の計画をだめにする ▪ This circumstance *broke the egg in the pockets of* the Whigs. この事情のためホイッグ党の計画はだめになった.

(***butter and***) ***egg money*** 農家の女性が稼ぐ金 ▪ The farmer's daughter used her *egg money* to buy a nice new dress. 農夫の娘は農場で稼いだお金を使ってすてきなドレスを新調した.

can't boil an egg 《戯》卵もゆでられない《料理ができない》 ▪ Young Brits *can't boil an egg.* 英国の若者は卵もゆでられない.

Don't put all your eggs in one basket. 《諺》全財産(全力)を一つのことに注ぎ込むな (→put all one's EGGs in one basket).

egg in your beer たなぼた, 意外な授かり物 ▪ What do you want—*egg in your beer*? 何がほしいのか—たなぼたかい?

Go fry an egg! あっちへ行け! どこかへ消えてしまえ!

Go suck an egg! 《米口》(怒って[軽蔑して])あっちへ行け! 失せろ!

Good egg! 《口》すてきだ!, でかした! (→a good EGG) ▪ *Good egg!* The bottle's coming to us. これはでかした! そのボトルは我々のところへ来るぞ.

have all** one's **eggs in one basket 一つの事業に全資産を投じている ▪ It is not wise to *have all your eggs in one basket.* 全資産を一つの事業に投じるのは賢明ではない.

have an egg from the oof bird 《口》遺産を受ける ▪ He will *have a* good-sized *egg from the oof bird* when his uncle dies. 彼はおじが死んだら大きな遺産をもらうだろう.

have egg on [***all over***] *one's* ***face*** 《口》ばかみたいだ, 面目をつぶす ▪ The robbers got away; the police *had egg on their faces.* 盗賊どもは逃げ去った. 警察はまるでばかみたいだった.

have eggs on the spit 仕事を手がけている; 非常に忙しくて手が空かない ▪ I *have* other *eggs on the spit.* 私は他の仕事を手がけている ▪ I write journals now; I *have eggs on the spit.* 私はいま日誌を書いているので忙しくて手が空かない. ☞焼きぐしで卵を焼くには素早く絶えず注意していなければならないから.

He that would have eggs must endure the cackling of hens. 《諺》卵の欲しい者はめんどりの鳴き声をがまんしなければならない《欲しいものを手に入れるためには, 不快なことも耐えなくてはならない》.

in the egg できかけの[に], 未発に[の] ▪ Crush the rebellion *in the egg.* 暴動は未然に防げ ▪ He is a thief *in the egg.* 彼はどろぼうの卵だ.

lay an egg **1** 卵を産む ▪ The hen *lays an egg* every day. そのめんどりは毎日一つ卵を産む.
2 《口》(興行・演技などに)失敗する ▪ He is *laying a* financial *egg.* 彼は財政的に失敗している.
3 《口》(航空機が)爆弾を落とす ▪ The plane really *laid an egg.* その機はほんとに爆弾を落とした.

put all** one's **eggs in one basket 全資産を一つの事業に投じる ▪ He's *put all his eggs in one basket.* 彼は全財産を一つの事業に投じた. ☞古い言い方の trust all one's goods to one ship に取って代わった.

put down eggs 卵を後の用に取っておく ▪ They *put down* several hundred *eggs.* 彼らは数百の卵を後の用に取っておいた.

take eggs for** one's **money だまされる, つかまされる ▪ Will you *take eggs for your money*? 君はだまされてもよいのか. ☞卵が豊富でつまらぬものとされた時分にできた句.

tread on [***upon***] ***eggs*** 薄氷を踏む思いをする, 薄氷を踏むようにして歩く ▪ When he went in to the master for a day off, he looked as though he were *treading upon eggs.* 彼が1日の休暇を願いに主人の部屋へ入っていったときは, まるで薄氷を踏んでいるような様子だった.

walk on eggs 慎重にふるまう ▪ I felt as if I had to *walk on eggs* in the shop. 店の中では腫れものにさわるようにふるまわなければならないような気がした.

egg[2] /eg/ 動 ***egg and crumb*** 卵黄とパン粉でおおう ▪ They *were* all *egged and crumbed.* それらはみな卵黄とパン粉でおおわれた.

egg** a person **on to [***to** do*] 人を励まして…させる; そそのかして…させる ▪ Everything conspired to *egg* them *on to* the undertaking. 万事重なって彼らはその事業をやることになった ▪ Helen *egged* him *on to* write the letter. ヘレンは彼を励ましてその手紙を書かせた. ☞egg<古ノルド語 eggja＝edge.

eggshell /égʃèl/ 名 ***walk on eggshells*** ＝tread on EGGs.

Egypt /íːdʒɪpt/ 名 ***corn in Egypt*** →CORN.

Egyptian /ɪdʒípʃən/ 形名 ***Egyptian bondage*** エジプトにおけるイスラエル人たちのような奴隷の身

▪ They conspired to call back our *Egyptian bondage*. それらが重なって奴隷時代を思い出させた.

Egyptian darkness 激しい暗やみ (《聖》*Exod.* 10. 22) ▪ It was a night of *Egyptian darkness*. それは激しい暗やみの夜だった.

spoil the Egyptians 略奪者[圧制者]から奪う; 金持ち[権力者]から奪う (《聖》*Exod.* 3. 22) ▪ Easing such priests of their jewellery is a lawful *spoiling* of *the Egyptians*. そのような司祭の宝石類を奪い取ることは, 略奪者からの合法的な奪取である.

eight /eɪt/ 形名 ***(an) eight days*** 1週間 ▪ She died about *an eight days* after this event. このことがあっておよそ1週間後に彼女は死んだ.

behind the eight ball →BALL[1].

have one over the eight →be ONE over the eight.

in eight and six/in eights and sixes 《詩学》1行8音節と6音節交互に ▪ It shall be written *in eight and six*. それは1行8音節と6音節交互に書かれます.

eighty /éɪti/ 名 ***do a one-eighty/turn one hundred and eighty degrees*** **1** 180度回転する, 回れ右をする[して反対方向へ行く] ▪ The carriage hit the curb and *did a one-eighty*. 台車は縁石にぶつかって方向を180度変えた ▪ His vehicle *turned one hundred and eighty degrees* in the air and came to rest in the ditch. 彼の車は空中で180度回転し, 溝の中でとまった.
2 (決定や意見が) 180度[根本的に]逆転する[正反対になる] ▪ My whole world *did a one-eighty*. 私の世界全体が180度回転した[根本的に変わった] ▪ The outcomes *turned one hundred and eighty degrees*. 結果は正反対になった.

either /íːðər|áɪ-/ 形接 ***either*** *A* ***or*** *B* AかBか ▪ He is *either* drunk *or* mad. 彼は酔っているか, 気が狂っているかである ▪ *Either* come in *or* go out. 入って来るか出て行くかしなさい.

Me either. 《米口》私もしません (Me neither) ▪ I don't smoke.—*Me either*. 私はタバコは吸いません—私もです.

on either side どちら側にも ▪ The cherry trees are planted *on either side* of the road. 桜が道路の両側に植えられている.

elbow[1] /élboʊ/ 名 ***at*** *one's* [*a person's*, ***the***] ***elbow*** すぐ近くに, 近くに侍って ▪ Talk of the Devil and he's *at your elbow*. 悪魔のことを話せばすぐ近くにやって来る ▪ I found *at my elbow* a pretty girl. 身近に美しい少女が侍っているのがわかった.

bend the elbow →lift the ELBOW.

bite an elbow 《米口》チャンスを逃す ▪ Ben really *bit an elbow* when he refused to go with Liz to the movie. ベンはリズといっしょに映画へ行くのを断ったときほんとにチャンスを逃した.

crook the elbow →lift the ELBOW.

elbow grease 《口》(磨いたりするような)激しい腕仕事[力仕事] ▪ The silver will look better when we've put a little *elbow grease* on it. その銀は少し骨折って磨くともっと立派に見える ▪ You must use a little *elbow grease*. 君は少し手を働かさねばならぬ.

exercise the elbow →lift the ELBOW.

from the [*one's*] ***elbow*** そばから離れて, 手近になくて ▪ You cannot spare him *from your elbow*. あなたは彼をそばから離せないのね.

give [***get***] ***the elbow*** 《口》絶縁する[される], 手を切る[切られる] (→give a person the big E) ▪ I will *give* my boyfriend *the elbow*. 私は彼氏と手を切りたい ▪ He *got the elbow*. 彼は縁を切られた.

in at elbows 《まれ》裕福で (↔out at ELBOWs) ▪ The pay hardly keeps him *in at elbows*. その給料では彼はほとんど裕福にしていることができない.

keep [***have***]***... at*** *one's* ***elbow*** ...を手近において離さない, そばにつける ▪ He *keeps* a bottle *at his elbow*. 彼はボトルをそばにおいて離さない ▪ He must *have* an advisor *at his elbow*. 彼は顧問をそばにつけねば承知しない.

lift [***bend, crook, exercise, raise, tilt, tip***] ***the*** [*one's*] ***elbow*** 《口》(過度に)酒を飲む, 左ききである《通常, 常習的な場合に言う》 ▪ He *lifted his elbow* too often himself. 彼はあまりにも頻繁に飲みすぎた.

More power to your elbow! →POWER.

not know *one's* ***arse from*** *one's* ***elbow*** → ARSE[1].

out at elbows (衣服の)ひじなどが破れてみすぼらしく; (人が)貧乏して, 尾羽打ち枯らして (↔in at ELBOWs) ▪ He was so terribly *out at elbows* that he could not command a hundred pounds. 彼は恐ろしく貧しかったので, 100ポンドの金が自由にならなかった.

rub elbows (***with***) (...と)つき合う, 接触する; (他人といっしょになって)窮屈な思いをする ▪ If you take that job you will be *rubbing elbows with* all kinds of people. 君がその仕事につけば, いろんな人々とつき合うことになる.

tilt [***tip***] ***the elbow*** →lift the ELBOW.

touch elbows (***with***) =rub ELBOWs (with).

up to the [*one's*] ***elbows*** (***in***) (仕事などに)没頭して, 忙殺されて ▪ Business is brisk now and we are *up to the elbows in* orders. 今は商売の景気がよくて, 我々は注文に忙殺されている ▪ We were *up to our elbows* making jam. 我々はせっせとジャムを作っていた. ☞「仕事がひじまで積みかさねてある」が原義.

elbow[2] /élboʊ/ 動 ***elbow*** *oneself* (***in***) 人を押し分けて入る ▪ She *elbows herself in* wherever she sees business going on. 彼女は商売が行われているのを見れば, どこへでも人を押し分けて入って行く.

elbow *oneself* ***into*** 人を押し分けて...へ入る ▪ It is rude to *elbow oneself into* a crowded room. 人を押し分けて混んだ部屋へ割りこむのは不作法である.

elbow *a person* ***out of the way*** 自分のじゃまにならぬよう人を押しのける ▪ I *elbowed* him *out of the way*. じゃまにならぬように彼を押しのけた.

elbow *one's* ***way*** (***in***) 人ごみの中を押し分けて入る; 是が非でも地位を得る ▪ He *elbowed his way* *in*. 彼は人ごみを押し分けて入りこんだ.

elbow *one's* ***way into*** [***out of, through, to, forward***] **1** 人ごみを押し分けて…へ入る[から出る, を通る, へ行く, 進む] ▪ We had to *elbow our way out of* the crowd. 私たちは人ごみの中から押し分けて出なければならなかった ▪ It is impolite to *elbow one's way through* a crowd. 人ごみの中を押し分けて通るのは無礼である ▪ By slow degrees he *elbowed his way to* the front place. 彼は徐々に人を押し分けて前面に進出した.

2 人を押し分けて…の地位に達する[から出る, を通る, へ行く, 進む] ▪ They are trying to *elbow their way into* society. 彼らは人を押し分けて社交界へ入ろうとしている.

elder /éldər/ 名 *one's* ***elders and betters*** 目上の人, 先輩 ▪ Be silent in the presence of *your elders and betters*. 目上の人たちがいるところでは静かにしておきなさい.

elect /ɪlékt/ 名 ***of the elect*** 神に選ばれた ▪ My aunt considered that she was *of the elect*. 私のおばは自分を神に選ばれた者であると考えた.

element /éləmənt/ 名 ***a strife*** [***war***] ***of the elements*** 大暴風雨, 大あらし ▪ We were watching *a war of the elements*. 我々は大暴風雨を見守っていた.

an element of 少しの ▪ There is *an element of* truth in his account. 彼の話には少しは本当のところがある.

brave the elements 悪天候に挑む, 風雨に負けずに…する ▪ They *braved the elements* to see the game. 彼らは試合を見るため風雨をものともしなかった.

from *one's* ***element*** 本来のすみかを離れて ▪ Some fishes can live a long time after removal *from their element*. 水から出された後も長く生きていられる魚類もある.

in *one's* ***element*** (魚が水中にいるように)本領内[得意の境地]にある ▪ He is *in his element* when speaking English. 彼は英語を話しているときは得意だ.

out of *one's* ***element*** (水を離れた魚のように)本領外[不得意の境地]にある ▪ England is *out of her element* on land. イギリスは陸軍は不得意である ▪ I feel *out of my element* when people begin talking economics. 私は人が経済学の話を始めると途方にくれる.

elephant /éləfənt/ 名 ***an elephant race*** **1** ゾウによるレース ▪ Charlson wanted to know whether I would be interested in riding an elephant in *an elephant race*. チャールスンは, 私がゾウレースでゾウに乗るのに興味があるかどうか知りたがっていた.

2 高速道路で2台のトラックが互いに競って併走すること ▪ The track planned to hold *an elephant race*. そのトラックは高速競争をやるつもりだった.

an elephant's memory ゾウの記憶力《抜群の記憶力, 執念深さ》 ▪ What the two have in common are *an elephant's memory*, which fuels their grudges. 両者が共通に有しているのは永続的な記憶力だ, そのため反目に油が注がれることになる.

as clumsy as an elephant 非常に不格好な, ひどくぎこちない ▪ I'm not *as clumsy as an elephant*. 私はそれほど不器用ではない.

dance like an elephant 重々しく不格好なダンスをする ▪ He *dances like an elephant*. 彼の踊り方は重々しくて不格好だ.

Elephants never forget. 《諺》ゾウは決して忘れない (→an ELEPHANT's memory).

have seen the elephant 《米俗》最近の状勢に明るい; 何でも心得ている (→see the ELEPHANT) ▪ He *has seen the elephant*. 彼は何でも知っている.

see pink elephants →PINK.

see the elephant 《米俗》世間を見る, 人生の経験を積む; (大都会などの)見物をする ▪ He makes his rounds every evening, while we *see the elephant* once a week. 我々は1週間に1度だけ見物をするのに, 彼は毎晩町を見て回っている ▪ He has *seen the elephant* in its entirety. 彼は世間の全ぼうを見ている.

show the elephant (大都会などの)名所を案内する ▪ We have not *shown* you enough of *the elephant*. 我々はあなたに町の名所を十分案内していない.

elevate /éləvèɪt/ 動 ***elevate the Host*** 《カトリック》聖体を(礼拝するため)奉挙する ▪ The Queen forbad the Archbishop to *elevate the Host* for adoration. 女王は大監督が聖体を礼拝のため奉挙するのを禁じた.

elevator /éləvèɪtər/ 名 *one's* ***elevator doesn't go all the way to the top*** (***floor***) 《口》(人が)あまり賢くない, 血の巡りが悪い ▪ I do*n't* think *his elevator goes all the way to the top floor* all the time. 彼はいつもちゃんと理解できるわけではないと思う.

eleven /ɪlévən/ 形名 ***at elevenses*** 午前11時にとる軽食のときに ▪ The hot chocolate *at elevenses* was the best I have ever had. 11時のおやつのホットココアは私がかつて味わったなかで最高だった. ☞elevenses《英口》「茶, コーヒーその他の茶菓」.

in the eleven フットボール[クリケット]の選手で ▪ Laxman should be *in the eleven*. ラクスマンはクリケットの(正)選手に入るべきだ.

play for the eleven クリケットの選手になる[される] ▪ He has been chosen to *play for* his school *eleven*. 彼は学校のクリケット選手に選ばれた.

eleventh /ɪlévənθ/ 形 ***at the eleventh hour*** きわどい時に, 最後の土壇場になって (《聖》*Matt*. 20. 1-16) ▪ I made it *at the eleventh hour*. 私はそれを土壇場になって作った ▪ God has saved you *at the eleventh hour*. 神はきわどい時にあなたをお救いになった.

eligible /élədʒəbəl/ 形 ***eligible for*** …に選ばれる資格があって, 適格で ▪ He may be *eligible for* membership of the society. 彼はその会の会員に選ばれる資格があるかもしれない ▪ He is *eligible for* a prize. 彼は賞を得る資格がある.

elite /ɪlíːt/ 名 ***of the elite*** 社会的地位の高い

▪They consider themselves to be *of the elite.* 彼らは自分たちのことを社会的地位が高いと思っている.

elixir /ɪlíksər/ 名 ***the elixir of life*** (錬金術師の)不老不死の薬; (現代の)妙薬《特にいかさまもの》 ▪He was glad to pursue *the elixir of life.* 彼は不老不死の薬を喜んで追求した. ☞Arab elixir「傷につける粉薬」.

ell /el/ 名 ***Give him an inch, and he'll take an ell.*** →Give him an INCH (and he'll take a yard).

eloquent /éləkwənt/ 形 ***eloquent of*** …をよく表して, 雄弁に物語って ▪The record is *eloquent of* national prosperity. その記録は国の繁栄を雄弁に物語っている.

else /els/ 副 ***if all else fails*** 他のすべてがだめなら ▪*If all else fails,* speak the truth. もし全部だめなら, 本当のことを話しなさい.

or else →OR.

So what else is new? 他に新しい話はないのかい, その話は聞き飽きた.

somebody [***everybody,*** etc.] ***else's*** 誰か他の人の[他のすべての人の, など] ▪This is *somebody else's* hat. これは誰か他の人の帽子です ▪If it is not my business, it is *nobody else's.* それが私のすべきことでないとしたら, 他の誰のすべきことでもない.

You and who else? 助っ人は誰だね, どうせ一人じゃできないだろ《脅しなどに対して》.

elude /ɪlú:d/ 動 ***elude enquiry*** 調査してもわからない ▪The epitaph has *eluded* a very diligent *enquiry.* その碑文は非常に克明に調べても不詳のままだ.

elude *a person's* ***grasp*** つかまえようとしてもつかまらない ▪The eel *eluded our grasp.* ウナギは我々がつかまえようとしてもつかまらなかった.

Elvis /élvɪs/ 名 ***50 million Elvis fans can't be wrong*** 《口》多くの人が信じるのだから本当に違いない. ☞もとアルバムのタイトル名; Elvis = Elvis Presley (1935–77) 米国のロックンロール歌手.

embargo /ɪmbá:rgoʊ/ 名 ***lay*** [***put, place***] ***an embargo on*** [***upon***] **1** (船舶)を抑留する, 船の出港を停止する ▪They *laid an embargo on* all ships in the Thames. 彼らはテムズ川のすべての船を停留させた.

2 …の通商を停止する ▪We *placed an embargo on* the exportation of capital. 資源の流出を停めた.

3 …を抑圧する, 阻害する ▪He *put an embargo on* free speech. 彼は言論の自由を抑圧した ▪The new taxes will *lay an embargo on* the company's future prosperity. 新課税は会社の将来の繁栄を阻害するであろう.

lay … under an embargo = lay an EMBARGO on.

lift [***raise, take off, remove***] ***an embargo on*** …の出港停止を解く; (通商)を解禁する ▪The government *lifted an embargo on* the importation of meat. 政府は肉の輸入を解禁した.

place [***put***] ***an embargo on*** →lay an EMBARGO on.

under an embargo **1** 船が抑留されて, 出港停止で ▪The ship is *under an embargo.* その船は抑留中である.

2 通商が停止されて ▪Trade was *under a* general *embargo.* 通商は全般的に停止されていた.

embark /ɪmbá:rk/ 動 ***embark*** *oneself* ***in*** …に乗り出す ▪He *embarked himself in* the enterprise. 彼はその事業に乗り出した.

embarrass /ɪmbǽrəs/ 動 (***be***) ***embarrassed by*** [***with***] …に困っている, 困る ▪They *are embarrassed by* debts. 彼らは借金で困っている ▪We *are embarrassed with* this work. 我々はこの仕事には困っている.

(***be***) ***embarrassed in*** *one's* ***affairs*** 財政困難である, 金に窮している ▪He *is embarrassed in his affairs.* 彼は財政が窮迫している.

feel embarrassed どぎまぎする, あがる ▪I *feel embarrassed* in the presence of ladies. 私は女性の前ではどぎまぎする.

financially embarrassed 《婉曲》財政困難の, 手元不如意の ▪The Browns were *financially embarrassed* most of the time. ブラウン一家はほとんどいつも金に不自由していた.

embarrassment /ɪmbǽrəsmənt/ 名 ***an embarrassment of riches*** 《文・雅》贅沢な悩み, 嬉しい悲鳴 ▪We have *an embarrasment of riches* in terms of midfielders and strikers for next year. 我々は来年のミッドフィールダーとストライカーに関しては贅沢な悩みがある.

embassy /émbəsi/ 名 ***go on an embassy*** 使命を帯びて[使節として]行く ▪He *went on an embassy* to the United States. 彼は使節としてアメリカ合衆国へ行った.

embed /ɪmbéd/ 動 ***embed*** *oneself* ***in*** …に入りこむ, 埋まる ▪A bullet *embedded itself in* the flesh. 弾丸が肉の中に入りこんだ.

ember /émbər/ 名 ***fan the embers*** 残り火をあおる《比喩的にも》 ▪When we *fanned the embers,* we found just a spark. 残り火をあおったところ一つだけ火の粉があった ▪They've forgotten their feud; don't say anything to *fan the embers.* 彼らは宿恨を忘れているのだから, 残り火をあおるようなことは言わないでください.

emblematic /èmbləmǽtɪk/ 形 ***be emblematic of*** …を象徴する ▪The crown *is emblematic of* royalty. 冠は王位を象徴する.

embolden /ɪmbóʊldən/ 動 ***embolden*** *a person* ***to*** *do* 《文》人を勇気うけて…させる ▪This popularity *emboldened* me *to* write another novel. この人気に力を得て私はもう1冊小説を書いた.

embosom /ɪmbʊ́zəm/ 動 (***be***) ***embosomed in*** [***with***] **1** …に囲まれ(る) ▪The village *is embosomed with* trees. その村は木々に囲まれている.

2 《詩》(眠り・幸福)に包まれ(る) ▪He sat *embosomed in* bliss. 彼は幸福に包まれて座っていた ▪Her image *is embosomed in* my heart with sweet memories. 彼女の姿は私の心の中で愉快な記憶に包まれている.

embroider /ɪmbrɔ́ɪdər/ 動 ***embroider a story*** 話を潤色する, 話に尾ひれをつける ▪ He is a wonderful hand at *embroidering* any *story*. 彼は話に尾ひれをつけるのがすごくうまい.

embroider *a thing* ***with*** *a pattern*/ ***embroider*** *a pattern* ***on*** *a thing* 物に模様をししゅうする ▪ She *embroidered* the handkerchief *with* flowers. ハンカチに花をししゅうした.

E

embroil /ɪmbrɔ́ɪl/ 動 ***be*** [***become***] ***embroiled in*** ...に巻きこまれる ▪ The Americans *were embroiled in* the war. アメリカ国民はその戦争に巻きこまれた.

be embroiled with ...と反目する ▪ He *is embroiled with* the chief. 彼は首長と反目している.

embryo /émbriòʊ/ 名 ***in embryo*** 未発達で; 初期で; (計画などが)熟さないで ▪ He was still a lawyer *in embryo*. 彼はまだ弁護士の卵だった ▪ The project is still *in embryo*. その計画はまだ熟さない.

emergency /ɪmə́ːrdʒənsi/ 名 ***in an*** [***case of***] ***emergency*** 非常の場合に ▪ This fire extinguisher is to be used only *in an emergency*. この消火器は非常の場合にだけ使用すべきである.

on an emergency [***emergencies***] 非常の際は ▪ *On emergencies* the law must be amended. 緊急の際にはその法律は修正されなければならない.

eminence /émənəns/ 名 ***attain eminence in*** ...で名を成す ▪ He *attained eminence in* literature. 彼は文学で名を成した.

eminent /émənənt/ 形 ***eminent for*** ...で著名で ▪ He is *eminent for* his great works. 彼は大作で著名である.

eminent in ...に卓越して ▪ They are *eminent in* science and art. 彼らは学問芸術に卓越している.

the right of eminent domain 《米》(政府などの有する)私有地強制買上権 ▪ The state must grant to the corporation *the right of eminent domain*. 国家は自治体に私有地買上権を与えなければならない.

emotion /ɪmóʊʃən/ 名 ***feel emotion at*** ...を見て感動する ▪ We *felt emotion at* the sight. 我々はその光景を見て感動した.

emperor /émpərər/ 名 ***the emperor's*** (***new***) ***clothes*** 存在しないもの, 虚妄; 知ったかぶり(の状況) ▪ The newspaper's "new facts" are similar to *the emperor's clothes*—non-existent. 新聞の言う「新事実」は王様の衣服のようだ, つまり, 実際には存在しないのだ.

emphasis /émfəsəs/ 名 ***lay*** [***place, put***] ***emphasis on*** ...を力説する, 強調する; にアクセントを置く ▪ Some schools *lay* special *emphasis on* language. 語学に特に重きを置く学校もある ▪ You *put emphasis on* the last syllable. 最後の音節にアクセントを置く.

with all the emphasis at (*one's*) ***command*** できるかぎり強調して ▪ I wish to say this *with all the emphasis at my command*. 私はできるかぎり強調してこれを言いたい.

with emphasis 力を入れて ▪ He dwelled on the subject *with emphasis*. 彼はその問題を力をこめて長々と論述した.

empire /émpaɪər/ 名 ***Empire State*** エンパイアステイト《ニューヨーク州の愛称》.

employ[1] /ɪmplɔ́ɪ/ 名 (***be***) ***in employ*** 職について(いる) ▪ We must keep ourselves *in* constant *employ*. 我々はいつも職についていなければならない.

(***be***) ***in the employ of***/(***be***) ***the employ of*** ...に雇われて[使われて](いる) ▪ He *is in Mr. Smith's employ* [*the employ of* Jones & Co.] 彼はスミス氏[ジョーンズ会社]に雇われている.

(***be***) ***out of employ*** 失職して(いる) ▪ He has *been out of employ* for a year. 彼は1年前から失業している.

have ... in *one's* ***employ*** ...を雇って[使って]いる ▪ I *have* many workers *in my employ*. 私は多くの労働者を雇っている.

take ... into *one's* ***employ*** ...を雇い入れる ▪ He *took* the young men *into his employ*. 彼はその青年たちを雇い入れた.

employ[2] /ɪmplɔ́ɪ/ 動 ***be employed about*** ...に忙しくしている ▪ She *was employed about* the house all day long. 彼女は家のことに一日中忙しくしていた.

be employed for ...に雇われている, を勤めている ▪ He *was employed for* supervising the engineering shop. 彼は機械工場の監督を勤めていた.

be employed in [***on, upon***] ...に専心する, 従事する ▪ At present I *am employed upon* totaling the accounts. 現在は私は帳簿を合計することに従事しています ▪ Mother *is employed in* preparing for the party. 母はパーティーの準備をしています.

employ *a person doing* 人を...に従事させる ▪ I *employed* him *teaching* English. 彼を英語教授に従事させた.

employ *oneself* (*doing*, ***in, on***) (...に)従事する, 専心する ▪ He was *employing himself in* the work. 彼はその仕事をしていた ▪ He *employed himself teaching* English. 彼は英語を教える仕事をしていた.

employment /ɪmplɔ́ɪmənt/ 名 ***find employment*** 就職する ▪ All this year's graduates have *found employment*. 今年の卒業生は全員就職した.

get [***obtain***] ***employment*** 就職する ▪ He *got employment* at the factory. 彼はその工場に就職した.

give employment to ...を雇う, 使う ▪ The factory *gives employment to* six hundred hands. その工場は600人の従業員を雇っている.

in employment 就職して ▪ His wife is *in employment*. 彼の妻は就職している.

in the [*one's*] ***employment of*** ...に雇われて ▪ He is *in my employment*. 彼は私に雇われている.

out of employment 失業して ▪ He threw me

out of employment. 彼は私を失業させた.

take** a person **into employment 人を雇い入れる ▪ We *took* him *into employment*. 我々は彼を雇い入れた.

emptins /émptɪnz/, **emptyings** /émptɪŋz/ 名 ***run*** (***to***) ***emptins*** [***emptyings***] 《米》もちこたえられなくなる ▪ He *runs* a great deal *to emptins* in his preaching. 彼は説教が続かなくなることがよくある ▪ Mr. Chairman, this bill is nearly played out and is *running emptyings*. 議長, 本法案はほとんどへとへとにこうきまわされ, もちこたえられなくなりつつあります.

empty[1] /émpti/ 形 ***an empty chance*** ありえぬこと ▪ The likelihood of our getting a holiday is *an empty chance*. 我々が休日を得る見込みはない.

come away empty **1** 船荷なしに出港する ▪ We had to *come away* from Sydney *empty*. 積荷なしにシドニーから出港せねばならなかった.

2 何ももらわない(で帰る) ▪ I went to see my uncle but I *came away empty*. おじの所へ遊びに行ったが何ももらわないで帰って来た.

come empty handed 贈り物を持たないで来る ▪ Aunt Jane always *comes empty handed*. ジェインおばさんはいつもおみやげを持たないで来る.

come up empty 《米》(試合に負けて)手ぶらで帰る, 結果を残せない, ぱっとしない ▪ Anderson *came up empty* in his third Olympics. アンダースンは3度目のオリンピックでは成果を出せなかった.

empty nest syndrome 巣立ち症候群《子供が成長して家を出た親に見られる憂鬱な状態》 ▪ When children leave home for school or jobs or marriage, mothers often suffer from *empty nest syndrome*. 子供が就学・就職・結婚で家を出ると, 母親はよく巣立ち症候群になる.

empty of ...がなくて, を持たなくて ▪ The room was nearly *empty of* furniture. その部屋にはほとんど家具がなかった.

Empty vessels make the most sound [***noise***]. →VESSEL.

feel empty 《口》空腹を覚える ▪ The boy *felt empty* by suppertime. 少年は夕食までには空腹を覚えた.

go away empty 何も得ないで帰る (→come away EMPTY) ▪ He *went away empty*. 彼は何ももらわないで帰った.

return empty **1** 何も得ない(で帰る) ▪ The prayers of the penitent do not *return empty*. 悔い改めた人々の祈りは決してむだになることはない.

2 (剣が)一人も殺さない ▪ The sword of Saul *returned* not *empty*. サウルの剣が一人も殺さぬことはなかった. ☞聖書語法.

empty[2] /émpti/ 名 ***be running on empty*** 燃料タンクが空になりかけている, 資源が乏しくなってきている ▪ Using up oil at the present rate, the world will soon *be running on empty*. 今の割合で石油を使い果たすと, そのうち世界は資源が枯渇してくるだろう.

run on empty **1** 空腹で活動する; (食料・ガソリンなど補給しないで)動く[動かす] ▪ I know I perform poorly when I try to *run on empty*. 空腹のまま活動すればうまくできないことはわかっている.

2 (アイデア・資源などが)枯渇する, 活気を失う, マンネリ化する ▪ Some believe the Times is *running on empty*. タイムズ紙は斬新さを失いつつあると信じている人もいる.

empty[3] /émpti/ 動 ***empty** oneself* 自己を無にする, 自己を捨てる《主としてキリストについて》 ▪ Jesus *emptied Himself* for our sake. イエスは私たちのためにおのれを捨てられた.

empty (***itself***) ***into*** (川が)...に注ぐ ▪ The river *empties itself into* the Japan Sea. その川は日本海に注ぐ.

empty** oneself **of ...を捨てる《主としてキリストについて》 ▪ He *emptied Himself of* His glory and greatness. 主は自らの栄光と偉大さを捨てたもうた.

empty-handed /èmptihǽndəd/ 形 ***come away empty-handed*** 手ぶらで[むなしく]戻る ▪ We have played well but have *come away empty-handed* from the games. うまく戦ったが, 試合で結果を残せなかった ▪ Each team had several more attacks on the goal, but both *came away empty-handed*. 両チームとももう数回ゴールをおびやかしたが, 両者とも無得点だった.

emulous /émjələs/ 形 ***be emulous of*** 《文》 **1** ...を見習って(いる); に負けまいとして(いる) ▪ Howard *is emulous of* the Grecian art. ハワードはギリシャ芸術を見習っている ▪ I *am emulous of* his feat. 私は彼の功業に負けまいとしている.

2 ...を熱望して(いる) ▪ He *is emulous of* fame. 彼は名声を熱望している.

enable /ɪnéɪbəl/ 動 ***enable** a person **to** do* 人に...することを可能にさせる[する権能を与える] ▪ God *enabled* him *to* awaken several young persons. 神は彼に数人の青年の目を覚まさせた ▪ His income *enabled* him *to* live in comfort. 収入で彼は安楽に暮らすことができた.

enamor, 《英》**enamour** /ɪnǽmər/ 動 (***be***) ***enamored of*** [***with***] 《文》 **1** (人)にほれこんで(いる) ▪ He became *enamored with* [*of*] the schoolteacher and married her. 彼は学校の先生にほれこんで, 彼女と結婚した.

2 (物)に心を奪われて(いる), 魅せられて(いる) ▪ He *is enamored with* scientific researches. 彼は科学の研究に心を奪われている ▪ He *was enamored of* your letters. 彼はあなたの手紙に魅せられていた.

enchant /ɪntʃǽnt|-tʃɑ́ːnt/ 動 ***be enchanted with*** [***by***] ...に魅せられる, うっとりとする ▪ She *was enchanted by* the flowers. 彼女はその花にうっとりとしていた ▪ I *am enchanted with* her manner. 私は彼女の態度に魅せられた.

enchantment /ɪntʃǽntmənt|-tʃɑ́ːnt-/ 名 ***lend enchantment to*** ...に魅力を添える ▪ It is distance that *lends enchantment to* the view. 眺めに魅力を添えるのは距離である《遠くから見ると眺めが魅力的になる》.

enchilada /èntʃəlɑ́:də/ 名 ***the big enchilada*** 《米口》 **1** 重要人物, 大立者, ボス ▪He was *the big enchilada* of Texas business. 彼はテキサス実業界の大立者だった.
2 重要事項, 主要項目 ▪"*The big enchilada*," she said, "is the money." 「最重要なのはお金よ」と彼女は言った.
the whole enchilada 《米口》 すべて, 一切合切 ▪It's either *the whole enchilada* or nothing. 全部か, さもなくばゼロだ ▪The rare director tries to put *the whole enchilada* on the screen. 大監督は余すところなく上映しようとしている. ☞enchilada「トルティーヤで肉やチーズ等を巻いたメキシコ料理」.

E

enclose /ɪnklóʊz/ 動 ***enclosed please find*** …を同封いたしました《手紙の文句》 ▪*Enclosed please find* a P.O. for $1,000. 1,000ドルの為替を同封いたしました.

encompass /ɪnkʌ́mpəs/ 動 ***be encompassed with*** …で取り巻かれる, 取り囲まれる ▪A castle *is encompassed with* walls. 城は塀に取り囲まれている ▪They *were encompassed with* dangers. 彼らは危険に囲まれていた.

encore /ɑ́:nkɔ:r|ɔ́ŋkɔ:/ 名 ***get*** [***receive***] ***an encore*** アンコールを受ける ▪The violinist *got an encore*. そのバイオリン奏者はアンコールを受けた. ☞[F] 'again'.
give [***sing***] ***three encores*** アンコールで3曲奏する[歌う] ▪The singer *gave three encores*. その歌手はアンコールに応えて3曲歌った.

encourage /ɪnkə́:rɪdʒ|-kʌ́r-/ 動 ***be encouraged at*** …に力を得る[元気づく] ▪He *was encouraged at* his success. 彼は成功に元気づいた.
Don't encourage *a person*. (人)を増長させてはいけない.
encourage *a person* ***to*** [***to*** *do*] 人を励まして…させる ▪He *encouraged* people *to* hostility. 彼は民衆を勇気づけて反抗させた ▪He first *encouraged* you *to* write. 彼が最初にあなたを励まして書かせたのだ.

encouragement /ɪnkə́:rɪdʒmənt|-kʌ́r-/ 名 ***give encouragement to*** …を激励[鼓舞]する ▪He *gave encouragement to* struggling students. 彼は苦学生を激励した.

encumber /ɪnkʌ́mbər/ 動 ***be encumbered with*** **1** …でふさがれている, じゃまされている ▪The river *is encumbered with* shoals. その川は砂州でふさがれている ▪The room *is encumbered with* useless furniture. 部屋は不要な家具でふさがっている.
2 《文》 …を背負わされ(てい)る, にわずらわされ(てい)る ▪He *is encumbered with* a large family. 彼は大家族という負担がある ▪I *am encumbered with* cares. 私は苦労にわずらわされている.

encumbrance /ɪnkʌ́mbrəns/ 名 ***without encumbrance*** 子供がなく ▪The widow advertised herself as "*without encumbrance*." その未亡人は「子供なし」と自称した.

end[1] /end/ 名 ***a dead end*** →DEAD.
a rear end [***rear-end***] **1** (車の)後部 ▪The brown Cadillac ended up beneath the *rear end* of the Chrysler, which hit the green Cadillac. 茶色のキャデラックはクライスラーの後部の下にめり込み, クライスラーは緑色のキャデラックにぶつかった.
2 お尻 ▪As I sat, something bumped into *my rear end*. 腰かけたところ何かがお尻にぶつかった.
a [***the***] ***tag*** [***tail***] ***end*** 《口》 端っこ, 後尾, 最下位 ▪He had only two good years at *the tag end* of the 1990s. 彼が恵まれていたのは1990年代の最後の2年間だけだった.
accomplish [***fulfil, gain***] *one's* ***end***(***s***) 目的を達する ▪They use a little violence in order to *accomplish their end*. 彼らは目的を達するためには少しの暴力は行使する.
all ends up 《口》 すっかり, 全く; やすやすと; どうにか ▪Barret beat him *all ends up* in the 1st round. バレットは第1回戦で彼をすっかり負かしてしまった.
an end in itself それ自体が目的 ▪Education should be *an end in itself*. 教育はそれ自体が目的であるべきだ ▪Terrorism is a means to an end, not *an end in itself*. テロは目的への手段であって, それ自体が目的ではない ▪To misers money is *an end in itself*. 吝嗇(りんしょく)家にとっては金自体が目的だ.
answer [***serve***] *one's* ***end***(***s***) 目的にかなう ▪This *answered my end*. これは私の目的にかなった.
at a loose [***an idle***] ***end*** [《米》 ***loose ends***] 定職がなく, ぶらぶらして; 途方にくれて, 未解決で ▪The players stood about disconsolately *at a loose end*. 選手たちは何もなすところなくやるせなさそうにあちこちに立っていた ▪Windham had been *at loose ends* after getting out of the Army. ウィンダムは除隊後, 定職に就いていなかった ▪He is living *at an idle end*. 彼は定職なく暮らしている. ☞《海》「綱のくくってない端」が何の用もなしていないことから.
at an end **1** (資源・方策が)尽きて ▪My wit is *at an end*. 私の知恵は尽きた.
2 (動作・状態が)終わって ▪The festival was *at an end*. お祭りは終わった.
3 (期間が)終わって, 尽きて ▪March is now *at an end*. 3月はもう終わった.
at an idle end →at a loose END.
at loose ends 《米》 混乱[散乱]して; ほったらかしにされて ▪My predecessor had left everything *at loose ends*. 私の前任者はすべてを混乱したままにほっておいたのだった.
at the deep end (仕事などの)一番難しいところで[に] ▪Rees was thrown in *at the deep end* for his first game. リースは初戦で剣が峰に立たされた.
at the end **1** 終わりに, ついに ▪He gave in *at the end*. 彼はついに折れた ▪I must speak out *at the end*. 最後にすっかり言ってしまわねばならない.
2 先が ▪The stick is sharp *at the end*. その棒は先がとがっている.
at the end of **1** …の突き当たりに ▪The house is *at the end of* the street. その家は通りの突き当たりにある.

2 …の終わりに ▪ Come to my house *at the end of* this month. 今月末に僕の家へ来なさい.
3 …が尽きて ▪ I am *at the end of* my patience. もはやがまんできなくなった ▪ He is *at the end of* his means. 彼は貧窮して[万策尽きて]いる.

at the end of nowhere 遠隔の地で[に], 文明の果てで[に] ▪ They've turned a harmless lake *at the end of nowhere* into a great tourist trap. 彼らは片田舎の平穏な湖を旅行者からぼったくりをする場所に変えてしまった.

at the end of the day 《口》結局のところ, とどのつまり ▪ *At the end of the day* the conference was all talk, no action. 結局, 会議なんてものは口先だけであって, 行為ではなかった.

at the end of the rope →ROPE[1].

at** one's **wits'** [**wit's**] **end →WIT[1].

be at the end of** one's **row →ROW[1].

be at the end of** one's **tether →TETHER.

(be) at [on] the receiving end 《口》 **1** (不愉快なことの)受け(取)る側で(いる), 受信側で(いる) (*of*) ▪ Those *on the receiving end of* the letters have experienced considerable fear. 手紙を受けとった人たちはかなりの恐怖を覚えた ▪ Sales assistants *are* often *at the receiving end of* verbal abuse from customers. 販売員はしばしば顧客ののののしりを聞かされる立場にある.
2 (攻撃などの)的になって(いる) (*of*) ▪ The southern suburb *was on the receiving end of* hundreds of Israeli air raids. 南の郊外は何百回ものイスラエル軍の空襲の標的だった ▪ When you *are* "*on the receiving end*" *of* something bad or unpleasant, you are the person who suffers. なにか悪いことあるいは不愉快なことの「受け取り側」であれば, 被害者だということだ.

be plunged in(to) the deep end = be thrown in(to) the deep END.

be the end 《口》どうにもがまんがならない; 最悪だ ▪ You often tell a lie. You really *are the end.* あなたはよく嘘を言う. 本当に最低だ.

be the end of …の命取りになる, を殺す ▪ Overwork will *be the end of* him. 働きすぎれば彼は死ぬだろう ▪ You'll *be the end of* me. あなたは私の命取りになるでしょう.

(be) the end of the road [line] for **1** 目的地[点](である) ▪ It *is* not *the end of the road for* me. それは私にとっては目的点ではない.
2 行きづまり(である), 終点(である) ▪ Such movements mark *the end of the road for* bourgeois literature. そのような運動はブルジョワ文学にとって行きづまりを示すものである.

be [get] thrown in(to) the deep end 奈落の底に投げ込まれる, 窮地に立たされる ▪ The new assistant *was thrown into the deep end* when Craig fell ill. クレイグが病気に倒れたとき, 新米の助手は窮地に陥った.

begin [start] at the wrong end 初めを誤る; やり方を誤る ▪ By trying persuasion on him, you have *begun at the wrong end.* 彼を説得しようとするとは君はやり方を誤ったのだ.

bring an end to …を終わらせる, やめる ▪ A chiropractor *brought an end to* the pain. 指圧師のおかげで痛みがなくなった.

bring to a dead end 行き詰まらせる, 頭打ちにする ▪ Everything has *been brought to a dead end* by the White House. すべてがホワイトハウスのために袋小路に入り込んだ.

bring ... to an end …を終わらせる ▪ The expedition *was brought to an end* by his death. その遠征は彼の死によって終わりとなった.

come to a bad [sad, sticky, happy, speedy] end 不幸に[悲しい結果に, みじめな結果に, 首尾よく, 早く]終わる ▪ He will *come to a bad end.* 彼はひどい結果に終わるだろう ▪ The event *came to a speedy end.* その事件はさっさと終わった ▪ The story *comes to a happy end.* その話はめでたしめでたしに終わる ▪ He *came to a sticky end* while hunting in Africa. 彼はアフリカで狩猟中にみじめな最期を遂げた.

come to an end 終わる; 尽きる; 死ぬ ▪ The first term *came to an end.* 一学期は終わった ▪ The fissure at length *came to an end.* 裂け目はついに終わりに達した ▪ He has *come to an* untimely *end.* 彼は非業の死を遂げた.

come to the end of …が尽きる ▪ They soon *came to the end of* their supplies. 彼らはまもなく糧食が尽きた.

end for end (こちらの端があちらになるように)逆に, くるりくるりと ▪ Please turn the table *end for end.* テーブルを反対に置き変えてください ▪ The schooner began to spin slowly, *end for end.* スクーナー船はゆっくり, くるりくるりと回り始めた.

end of the line 終点, 限界, 最期; 電話の相手 ▪ Windows 98 is the *end of the line* for the first generation of Windows products. Windows98は第一世代のウィンドウズ製品の最後のものだ.

end on 《主に海》先を向けて, 正面を向けて, まっすぐに (↔ BROADSIDE on) ▪ The boat met the next breaker *end on.* ボートは次の砕け波を正面に受けた ▪ We saw a lorry coming *end on* towards us. 荷馬車がまっすぐに我々の方へやって来るのを見た.

end to end 端と端をつないで, (縦)一列につないで ▪ The trucks stood *end to end* in the siding. 無蓋貨車は待避線に縦一列につながっていた ▪ Put the tables *end to end.* テーブルを一列に並べなさい.

ends of the earth →go to the ENDs of the earth.

for** one's **own end 自分の目的のため ▪ He has done it *for his own end.* 彼は自分の目的のためそれをした.

for [to] this [that, what, which] end この[その, 何の, どの]目的のため ▪ *For these ends* he wished to obtain arbitrary power. これらの目的のため彼は専制権力を得たいと思った ▪ *To that end* he sent his ambassador to Constantinople. その目的

E

のため彼は大使をコンスタンチノープルに派遣した.

from end to end **1** 端から端まで, 全長ずっと ▪I have trod several times *from end to end* of Italy. 私はイタリアを端から端まで数回歩いた.
2 縦に(裂く, など).

fulfil [***gain***] *one's* ***end***(***s***) →accomplish one's END(s).

gain *one's* ***end*** 目的を達する ▪Persevere and you'll *gain your end*. がんばりなさい, そうすれば目的が達せられるでしょう.

E

get (***hold of***) ***the wrong end of the stick*** →STICK[1].

get [***have***] ***the better end of*** **1**…に勝る ▪We have *got the better end of* the Devil. 我々は悪魔に勝った.
2…の有利な方を占める ▪He has *got the better end of* a bargain. 彼は取引で相手より儲かった.

get [***have***] ***the dirty*** [***thick***] ***end of the stick*** 最も困難[不愉快]な役を受け持つ; 貧乏くじを引く (→the short END (of the stick)) ▪I always *get the dirty end of the stick*. 私はいつも貧乏くじを引く.

give (***a touch of***) ***the rope's end*** むちなわで打つ; 罰する ▪I'd like to *give* him *a touch of the rope's end*. 彼をむちなわで打ってやりたい.

go off (***at***) ***the deep end*** →DEEP.

go to the ends of the earth 地の果てまでも行く; できることは何でもする ▪They will *go to the ends of the Earth* to seek out and punish terrorists. 彼らはテロリストを見つけだして罰するために地の果てまでも行くだろう ▪Is there any parent among us who wouldn't *go to the ends of the earth* to save a child? 子供を救うためなら何でもしようとしないものが私たち親の中にいるだろうか.

have the better end of →get the better END of.

have the dirty [***thick***] ***end of the stick*** →get the dirty END of the stick.

have the easy end of …を楽に終える ▪He *had the easy end of* the task. 彼はその仕事を楽に終えた.

in the end 最後に, ついに, 結局 ▪*In the end* they reached a place of safety. 結局彼らは安全な地に到達した ▪The match was won by Harrow *in the end*. 試合は結局ハロー校が勝った.

keep [***hold***] *one's* ***end up***/***keep*** [***hold***] ***up*** *one's* ***end*** 《口》 **1** (経済的に)どうにかこうにかやっていく ▪I shall *keep my end up* somehow or other. 私は経済的に何とかしてやっていきます.
2 《英口》(企て・演技などの)役割を果たす; 期待された通りに果たす; 勇敢にふるまう ▪She will be worn out trying to *hold up her end*. 彼女は自分の割り当てを果たそうとして疲れ果てるだろう.
3 (取引・対談で)うまくやってのける; (自分の腕前で)がんばり通す ▪We'll try to *keep our end up*. 僕らは対談でうまくやってのけるつもりです.
4 (議論・競争で)自己の立場を守る ▪He'll *keep his end up* somehow, but it will be a hard struggle. 彼は何かと自己の立場を守るだろうが, 苦戦するだろう. ☞クリケットから.

leave *a person* (***out***) ***on the end of the line*** 人をのけ者にする ▪He *is left out on the end of the line*. 彼はのけ者にされている.

Let that be an end to the matter./***That's the end of the matter.*** 《口》これで話はおしまいだ; もうこれ以上は言わない ▪Walsh has spoken so *let that be an end to the matter*. ウォルシュが口を割ったのでそれ以上事を荒立てないことにしよう.

make an end of [***with***] **1**…のけりをつける; をやってしまう ▪Let's *make an end of* the business. この件のけりをつけましょう ▪The government *made an end of* the insurgents. 政府は反乱者たちの片をつけた.
2…を滅ぼす, かたづける ▪They *made an end with* all the vermin. 彼らは害虫をことごとく滅ぼした ▪We must *make an end of* this pile of rubbish. この廃物の山をかたづけなければならない.

make an end run (***around***) (…を)回避する ▪Developers *made an end run around* the limit by parceling large plots into thousands of single-family lots. 開発業者たちは, 広大な土地を何千もの単身家族用の土地に分割して限度制限を回避した. ☞end run「アメリカン・フットボールでボールを持った選手が防御ラインの最も外側を回るプレー」.

make the end run 目的を遂行するよう努める ▪You were going to *make that end run*. あなたはその目的を遂行しようとしていましたね.

make the two ends of the year meet 収支を合わせる ▪He made shift to *make the two ends of the year meet*. 彼は何とか収支を合わせた. ☞次項も参照.

make (***two, both***) ***ends meet*** 収支を合わせる ▪Unless you economize, we can't *make both ends meet* any more. あなたが節約してくれないと私たちはもう収支を合わせることはできません. ☞two, both を落とすのは主に《米》.

meet a...end …な死を遂げる ▪Romeo and Juliet *met a* woeful *end*. ロミオとジュリエットは悲痛な最期を遂げた.

meet *one's* ***end*** 最期を遂げる ▪He *met his end* in the accident. 彼はその事故で最期を遂げた.

meet with an untimely end 若死にする, 早世する ▪The IT giant *met with an untimely end* last month. 情報産業の巨人は先月早世してしまった.

near *one's* ***end*** 死期に近く ▪He is *near his end*. 彼は死期が近い.

never [***not***] ***hear the end of*** 《口》自慢話をいつまでも聞かされる ▪If the Red Sox wins, we will *never hear the end of* it from their millions of fans. レッドソックスが優勝したら, 何百万人ものファンから自慢話を延々と聞かされるだろう.

no end 《口》半端じゃなく, ひどく, 大いに (much) ▪He helped me *no end*. 彼は私をすごく助けてくれた ▪You are *no end* cleverer. 君のほうがずっと賢

い.

no end of 《口》 **1** 際限なく多くの, たくさんの ▪ I have *no end of* money. 金はいくらでもある ▪ He made *no end of* excuses. 彼は際限なく言い訳をした.

2 すばらしい, すてきな ▪ Keats was *no end of* a fellow. キーツはすばらしい人であった ▪ We had *no end of* a time. 我々はすばらしく愉快に過ごした.

3 ひどい, 途方もない ▪ He is *no end of* a humbug [a fool]. 彼は途方もない詐欺師[愚か者]だ.

no end to 果てしない, たくさんの ▪ There will be *no end to* this war. この戦いには終わりがないだろう ▪ There is *no end to* such examples. そのような例は枚挙にいとまがない.

not know [***tell***] ***one end of…from the other*** …のことは全然知らない ▪ I *don't know one end of* a car *from the other.* 私は車のことは何にも知らない.

odds and ends →ODDS.

on end **1** 直立して ▪ It made my hair stand *on end.* それは私の髪をさか立たせた ▪ Columbus put the egg *on end.* コロンブスは卵をまっすぐ立てた.

2 立て続けに ▪ It rained three days *on end.* 3日続けて雨が降った.

on the end (炭層が)縦になって ▪ The coal is *on the end.* その炭層は縦になっている.

on the wrong end of 遅れをとっている, 形勢不利である, 成績不振の ▪ He came out *on the wrong end of* that game. 彼はその試合で敗れてしまった.

play both ends against the middle → PLAY[2].

put an end to …をやめる; をやめさせる, 終わらせる, 廃止する ▪ You must *put an end to* this foolish behavior. 君はこのばかげたふるまいをやめなければならない ▪ *Put a* quick *end to* this treaty. この条約をすみやかに廃止せよ.

put *a person* ***at the end of the line*** 人をのけ者にする ▪ We *were* always *put at the end of the line.* 我々はいつものけ者にされた.

reach the end of the [*one's*] ***road*** [***line***] ある状況のおしまいになる ▪ Daisy has *reached the end of the road* as a dancer. デイジーはダンサーとしてはもうおしまいだ.

right [***straight***] ***on end*** **1** 打ち続いて; 一列になって ▪ It has been raining for days *right on end.* 何日も続いて雨が降っている.

2 すぐに ▪ I am going to die *right on end.* 私はすぐにも死にそうだ.

see an end of [***to***] (通例いやなもの)の終わるのを見る ▪ We shall never *see an end of* fighting in our lifetime. 我々は生存中に戦争がなくなるのを見ることはないだろう.

see beyond [***past***] ***the end of*** *one's* ***nose*** 〚主に否定文で〛(自分のことだけを考えて)目先のことしか見えない ▪ I am not surprised that he declined to donate money to the orphanage; he can't *see beyond the end of his nose.* 彼が孤児院にお金を寄付するのを断ったことに私は驚きはしない. 彼には先のことが見えないのだ ▪ He wouldn't act the way he does if he could *see beyond the end of his nose.* 先のことが見えれば彼はあんな風にはふるまうまいに.

serve *one's* ***end(s)*** →answer one's END(s).

start at the wrong end →begin at the wrong END.

The end justifies the means. 《諺》 目的は手段を正当化する, 「嘘も方便」.

the end of civilization as we know it **1** 秩序ある社会の崩壊 ▪ Acid rain would result in *the end of civilization as we know it.* 酸性雨は現代文明の終わりをもたらすことになるだろう.

2 大袈裟な反応 ▪ Smith screams as if he's just seen *the end of civilization as we know it.* スミスは(まるで現代文明の終わりを見たかのように)大袈裟に絶叫する.

the end of the ball game 試合終了, どうにもならない状況 ▪ If this happens, then it's *the end of the ball game.* こういうことが起これば, 万事休すだ.

the [*one's*] ***end of the line*** **1** 電話の終わり ▪ There was a long silence at *my end of the line.* 電話での話が終わったとき長い沈黙があった.

2 一貫作業の終わり ▪ Articles come off *the end of the line.* 一貫作業が終わって製品が生まれる.

3 終点 ▪ I generally have an hour's wait at *the end of the line.* 通常終点で1時間待ち合わせる.

4 至る所 ▪ The buying holdback has now carried back to *the end of the line.* 買い物の手控えはどこでも一般的となった.

5 《口》 事[関係, 興味, 希望, 生命など]の終わり ▪ I am sick of baseball. It is *the end of the line.* 私は野球がいやになった. もう野球は終わりだ.

the end of the rainbow 虹の端; すべての希望のかなえられる所 ▪ To many Britons Australia is still *the end of the rainbow.* 多くのイギリス人にとってはオーストラリアは今もなお「すべての希望のかなえられる国」である.

the end of the story 《口》 (この話は)これでおしまい, 以上だ (→full STOP) ▪ That was *the end of the story*—at least the end of that story. それで話は終わりだ, 少なくとも, その話は終わりだ ▪ I don't allow you to drink around town. *The end of the story.* お前が町を飲み歩くのは許さん. 以上だ.

the end(s) of the earth 世界の果て, 地の果て ▪ She swore that she would follow him to *the ends of the earth.* 彼女は地の果てまでも彼について行くと誓った.

the end(s) of the world **1** 世界の果て (《聖》 *Ps.* 19. 4) ▪ I was coming home from some place at *the end of the world.* 私は世界の果てのある所から帰宅していた.

2 世の終わり, 離別のつらさ ▪ Hers is the head upon which all "*the ends of the world*" are come. 彼女の頭にはすべての「世の終わり」が寄せて来ているのだ ▪ She told him about *the end of the world.* 彼女は彼に離別のつらさについて話した.

3《口》大災害，重大事変 ▪ Failure wouldn't be *the end of the world*. 失敗は大した事ではないだろう.

the latter end →one's LATTER end.

the short end (***of the stick***) 損な役割，貧乏くじ ▪ We got *the short end of the stick*, but that's no excuse. 我々は貧乏くじを引いたが，それは言い訳にはならない.

the thin end of the wedge《口》くさびの刃;(将来重大な結果を招く)きっかけ，引き金，糸口 ▪ It may be *the thin end of the wedge* for more radical changes. それはより抜本的な変革の第一歩であるかもしれない.

the wrong end of the stick →get hold of the wrong end of the STICK.

There's an end of it. それだけのことです; それで終わりです.

there's no end to ...に限りがない ▪ *There is no end to* avarice. 強欲には限りがない.

to make an end 終わりに ▪ *To make an end*, here was a religious college. 終わりに，ここには宗教大学がありました.

to no end むなしくも ▪ I labored *to no end*. 私の労苦はむなしかった ▪ The priest tried to obtain it, but *to no end*. 牧師はそれを得ようとしたがむだだった.

to the bitter end →BITTER.

to the end 最後まで ▪ Stick it out *to the end*. 最後まで頑張れ.

to the end of time いつまでも ▪ That will remain a secret *to the end of time*. それはいつまでも秘密のままだろう.

to this [***that, what, which***] ***end*** →for this END.

without end 果てしのない，果てしなく，永久に ▪ Pleasant tunes are sung to thy glory *without end*. 心地よい曲があなたの栄光のためずっと歌われる.

world without end →WORLD.

end[2] /end/ 動 ***end it*** (***all***)《口》自殺する ▪ I took up the rifle to *end it all*. 私は自殺しようと小銃を取りあげた.

end or mend 廃止するか改良する; 殺したり生かしたりする ▪ My fate calls me elsewhere, to scenes where I shall *end* it *or mend* it. 私の運命は私を他の所へ，私が自分の運命を殺すか生かすかするであろう舞台へ私を呼んでいる.

end (***up***) ***in smoke*** →come to SMOKE.

end up nowhere 成功しない ▪ If you don't work hard, you'll *end up nowhere*. 一生懸命勉強しなければたいした人になれませんよ.

A ***to end all*** *A*'s [***them all***]《口・戯》最善[最悪，最もまれ]なA ▪ I have been to a party *to end all* parties. この上ないパーティーに行ってきたところだ ▪ She's had the cold *to end them all*. 彼女は最悪の風邪をひいた.

endear /ɪndíər/ 動 ***endear*** *oneself* ***to*** ...に慕われる[愛される](ようになる) ▪ He *endeared himself to* his students. 彼は生徒たちに慕われるようになった.

endeavor,《英》**endeavour** /ɪndévər/ 名 ***do*** [***make***] *one's* (***best***) ***endeavor***(***s***) 努力する; 全力を尽くす ▪ We must *do our best endeavor(s)* to give the firm satisfaction. 我々は会社に満足を与えるよう全力を尽くさなければならない.

make every endeavor あらゆる努力をする ▪ *Make every endeavor* to be here early. あらゆる努力を払ってここへ早くおいでください.

endorse /ɪndɔ́:rs/ 動 ***endorse in blank*** 裏書きだけして他の書き入れは保持者に任せる ▪ The bill *was endorsed in blank*. その手形は裏書きだけしてあった.

have *one's* ***licence endorsed***《英》(自動車運転手・居酒屋が)免許証の裏に違反を書き入れられる ▪ He *had his licence endorsed* for jumping a red light. 彼は信号無視をして運転免許証の裏に違反を記入された.

One's ***licence is endorsed.***《英》(自動車運転手・居酒屋の)免許証の裏に違反の記録がしてある.

endow /ɪndáʊ/ 動 ***be endowed with***《文》...を授けられて[付与されて]いる ▪ They *were endowed with* extraordinary gifts. 彼らは非凡な才能を付与されていた.

endue /ɪndjú:/ 動 ***be endued with***《文》...を付与されている，持っている ▪ We *are endued with* capacities of action, of happiness and misery. 我々は行動の能力，幸不幸を受けいれる能力を持っている ▪ She *is endued with* rare beauty. 彼女はまれに見る美しさを授かっている. ☞be ENDOWed with とほとんど同じだが，endued は永久不変の性質・能力について言う.

endurance /ɪndjʊ́ərəns/ 名 ***beyond*** [***past***] ***endurance*** がまんしきれないほど ▪ The pain is *beyond endurance*. その苦痛は忍びがたい ▪ Your rudeness has got *past endurance*. お前の無礼にはもうがまんがならなくなった.

Spartan endurance スパルタ式忍耐，非常な忍耐と自制 ▪ She tells him that life calls for *Spartan endurance*. 人生には並はずれた忍耐が必要だと彼女は彼に説き聞かせる.

enemy /énəmi/ 名 ***a fair-weather enemy*** 平時の敵 (↔a fair-weather FRIEND) ▪ The new party is proving to be *a fair-weather enemy* of the Government. 新政党は政府の平時の敵であることがわかってきている.

a sworn enemy 不倶戴天の敵，長年にわたる敵 ▪ He's *a sworn enemy* of democracy. 彼は民主主義にとって宿命の敵だ.

be an enemy to ...を憎む; の敵である ▪ He *is an enemy to* work. 彼は仕事が大きらいだ ▪ Idleness *is an enemy to* success. 怠惰は成功の敵である.

be no enemy to ...が大好きである ▪ He *is no enemy to* drink. 彼は酒が大好きだ.

be nobody's enemy but *one's* ***own*** 人がよくて自分が損するだけの善人である ▪ He *is nobody's enemy but his own*. 彼は自分が損するだけの善人だ.

be *one's* ***own*** (***worst***) ***enemy*** (良い人間だが)自

分にとって損な悪癖がある ▪ Unfortunately he can't stop drinking. He's *his own worst enemy*. 彼は不幸にして酒をやめられない. 自分に損な悪癖があるのだ ▪ The way he antagonizes everyone around him makes him *his own worst enemy*. 自分の周りのあらゆる人を敵にまわす様子で彼はひどく損をしている.

How goes the enemy?/ What says the enemy? 《口》何時ですか. ☞時は(遅れている)人の敵だから.

make an enemy of …を敵にまわす, の恨みを買う ▪ With his insulting manner he *makes an enemy of* all around him. 人を侮辱する態度のせいで彼は自分の周りのすべての人の恨みを買っている.

public enemy number one **1** 社会を脅かす危険人物 ▪ He is *public enemy number one* to white America. 彼は米国白人社会にとって危険人物だ.

2 悪名高い指名手配犯 ▪ He became France's *public enemy number one*. 彼はフランスでもっとも凶悪な指名手配犯になった.

the great* [*last*] *enemy 死 (《聖》*1 Cor.* 15. 26) ▪ She was on her deathbed, awaiting *the last enemy*. 彼女は死の床にあって死が訪れるのを待つばかりだった.

wish ... on** one's **worst enemy 〖否定文・疑問文で〗 憎い敵に…を願う; …になればよいと思う ▪ I wouldn't *wish* that *on my worst enemy*. 不倶戴天の敵にさえもそこまでは願わないだろう.

energy /énərdʒi/ 名 ***apply* [*bend, devote, direct*]** *one's* ***energies to*** …に精力を傾ける ▪ He *applied his energies to* the compilation of a dictionary. 彼は辞書の編集に精力を傾けた.

nurse energy 活力を蓄えておく ▪ Robinson was depressed, drinking too much, *nursing* negative *energy*. ロビンスンは気落ちして, 深酒をし, マイナスエネルギーをため込んでいた.

with energy 元気[精力的]に ▪ He worked *with energy*. 彼はせっせと働いた.

enfranchise /ɪnfrǽntʃaɪz/ 動 ***enfranchise a copyhold* [*lease-hold*] *estate*** 謄本保有の土地[貸借保有権の土地]を自由保有とする ▪ He *enfranchised a copyhold estate*. 彼は謄本保有の土地を自由保有地とした.

engage /ɪngéɪdʒ/ 動 ***be engaged in*** …に従事する, を行っている ▪ He *is engaged in* literary work. 彼は著述に従事している ▪ He *is engaged in* letter-writing. 彼は手紙を書いている.

***be engaged on* [*upon*]** 《主に英・文》…に着手している; に従事して[携わって]いる ▪ I *am engaged on* a new work. 私は新作に着手している ▪ We *are engaged on* a global war on terrorism. 我々はテロに対する世界的な戦いに加わっている.

be engaged to …と婚約する[している] ▪ The girl *was engaged to* a captain. 娘は船長と婚約していた.

be engaged with **1** …と用談している ▪ I *was engaged with* him. 私は彼と用談していた.

2 …を使っている ▪ My hands *are* now *engaged with* knife and fork. 私の両手は今ナイフとフォークでふさがっている.

engage** oneself **in …に従事する ▪ You had better *engage yourself in* studying physics. 君は物理学研究に従事すべきだ.

***engage on* [*upon*]** →be ENGAGEd on.

engage** oneself **to **1** …と婚約する ▪ He *engaged himself to* the girl. 彼はその娘と婚約した.

2 …を約束する, 言質を与える ▪ I *engage myself to* nothing. 私は何も約束しません.

3 …に雇われる ▪ He has *engaged himself to* an engineer. 彼はある技師に雇われた.

***engage** oneself **to** do* …することを約束する ▪ He has *engaged himself to* help me. 彼は私を助けることを約束した.

engagement /ɪngéɪdʒmənt/ 名 ***bring about an engagement*** 戦いを起こす, 交戦する ▪ The admiral tried to *bring about an engagement*. 海軍大将は交戦しようと努めた.

make* [*enter into*] *an engagement with …と約束をする, 契約を結ぶ ▪ He *made a* binding *engagement with* me. 彼は私と契約を結んだ.

meet** one's **engagements 負債を払う, 支払い約束を果たす ▪ I have only just enough money to *meet my engagements*. 私は負債を払うだけの金しかない.

under engagement 契約[約束]している ▪ He is *under engagement* to leave within 7 days. 彼は7日以内に立ち去る約束をしている.

English /íŋglɪʃ/ 名 ***body English*** 人の感情を表すしぐさ ▪ His *body English* is a dancer's and his metaphors are military. 彼のしぐさはダンサーのそれだが, 言葉うかいは軍隊的だ.

English as she is spoken 《戯》(外国人などに)話されている通りの英語, あるがままの口頭英語表現 ▪ A character in the film is *English as she is spoken* by students in Delhi University. その映画の一つの特徴は, デリー大学の学生がしゃべっている通りの英語表現だ.

in plain English 率直に(言えば) ▪ Tell him *in plain English* what you think. あなたの思うことを率直に彼に話しなさい ▪ *In plain English* the project is ridiculous. 率直に言えばその計画はばかげている.

not English (慣用を無視した)なっていない英語 ▪ It is *not English* to say so. そういうふうに言うのは正しい英語ではない.

the King's* [*Queen's*] *English 純正(イギリス)英語 ▪ He still thinks that to split an infinitive is to abuse *the Queen's English*. To-不定詞の間に副詞を挟むのは純正英語の誤用だと彼はまだ考えている ▪ These foreigners really murder *the Queen's English*! この外国人たちは実にひどい英語を話すものだ! ▪ You should learn to talk *the King's English*. 正しい英語を話すことを学ぶべきです.

to talk plain English わかりやすく言えば ▪ *To*

talk plain English, what you propose is dishonest. わかりやすく言えば，あなたの提案することは不正だ．

engorge /ɪngɔ́:rdʒ/ 動 ***be engorged with*** **1** …が詰め込まれている，でギューギューである ▪ The mosquito *is* already *engorged with* blood. 蚊はすでに血を腹一杯吸っている．
2《医》…で充血している ▪ His prostate *is engorged with* blood. 彼の前立腺は充血している．

engross /ɪngróʊs/ 動 ***be engrossed in***《文》…に夢中である ▪ He *is engrossed in* attending to her wants. 彼は彼女の御用を承るのに夢中である ▪ They *were engrossed in* conversation. 彼らは談話に夢中であった．

engulf /ɪngʌ́lf/ 動 ***be engulfed in*** …に飲み[巻き]こまれる ▪ Shelley *was engulfed in* the deep waters. シェリーは深い海に飲まれた ▪ She *was engulfed in* grief on the death of her mother. 彼女は母の死にあたって悲嘆にくれた．

enjoin /ɪndʒɔ́ɪn/ 動 ***enjoin** a person **to** do* 人に…するよう言いつける ▪ We *enjoined* him *to* be diligent. 我々は彼に勤勉であれと言いつけた．

enjoy /ɪndʒɔ́ɪ/ 動 ***enjoy** oneself* 楽しい思いをする，おもしろく過ごす ▪ Did you *enjoy yourself* at the party? パーティーでは楽しく過ごしましたか．

enjoy poor health [***an indifferent reputation***] 健康がすぐれない[評判がよくない] ▪ She *enjoys poor health*. 彼女は健康がすぐれない．

enjoyment /ɪndʒɔ́ɪmənt/ 名 ***be in the enjoyment of*** …を享有している ▪ I *am in the enjoyment of* good health. 私は健康を享受している．

take enjoyment in …を楽しむ，おもしろがる ▪ He *takes enjoyment in* music. 彼は音楽を楽しむ ▪ He *takes enjoyment in* teasing his sister. 彼は妹をいじめることをおもしろがっている．

enlarge /ɪnlɑ́:rdʒ/ 動 ***enlarge** oneself* **1**（範囲などが）大きくなる ▪ Glory *enlarges itself* like a circle in the water. 栄光は水中の円のように広がる．
2 思う存分談論する ▪ He *enlarged himself* on this subject. 彼はこの題目について思う存分論じた．

enlarge the heart **1**（感謝・愛情で）心を広くする（《聖》*2 Cor*. 6. 13） ▪ *My heart is enlarged* with his kindness. 彼の親切で私の心が広くなった．
2 情愛の心を広くする，愛情の範囲を広げる ▪ All *hearts were enlarged*. すべての人の情愛の心は広くなった．

enlighten /ɪnláɪtən/ 動 ***be enlightened on*** [***about***]《文》…について明るい ▪ He *is* thoroughly *enlightened on* the subject. 彼はその問題には全く明るい．

enlist /ɪnlíst/ 動 ***enlist under the banner of*** …の旗の下に参加する ▪ We *enlisted under the banner of* freedom. 我々は自由の旗の下にはせ参じた．

enmesh /ɪnméʃ/ 動 ***be*** [***get***] ***enmeshed in*** **1**（網）にかかる ▪ The 9-meter whale *got enmeshed in* a net at the Collaroy Beach near Sydney. 9メートルのクジラがシドニー近くのコラロイビーチで網にかかった．
2（困難）に陥る ▪ John *was enmeshed in* a boundary dispute with his neighbors. ジョンは隣人との境界争いに巻き込まれた．

enmity /énməti/ 名 ***at enmity with*** …に敵意をいだいて，と反目して ▪ The Jews were *at enmity with* the Samaritans. ユダヤ人はサマリア人とは犬猿の仲であった．

have (***an***) ***enmity with*** …に対して敵意を持つ ▪ He *had an enmity with* Jews. 彼はユダヤ人に対して敵意を持っていた．

enough /ɪnʌ́f/ 形副名 ***be … enough to** do* …にもする ▪ He *was* impudent *enough to* ask me for it. 彼は厚かましくも私にそれをくれと言った．

cannot … enough いくら…しても足りない ▪ I *cannot* thank you *enough*. あなたにいくら感謝しても足りません．

cry enough 敗北を認める，降参だと言う ▪ *Cry enough!* 参ったと言え．

enough about《口》…についてはもう十分だ《話題を変えよう》 ▪ Well, that's *enough about* me. Now let's talk about you. さて，私についてはそれで充分だ．これからは君のことを話し合おう．

enough already《主に米口》もう十分だ ▪ Tax *enough already*. 税金はもう十分だ．

enough and enough 十分以上に，十二分に ▪ The play has wit *enough and enough*. その芝居には十二分の機知がある．

enough and to spare →SPARE[3].

enough for anything [***all***]《口》〚形容詞のあとで〛ほんとに ▪ He is witty *enough for anything*. 彼はほんとに機知に富んでいる．

Enough is as good as a feast.《諺》物事はほどほどにせよ．

Enough is enough.《諺》もうこの程度で十分だ．

Enough of…! …をやめよ ▪ *Enough of* this folly! こんなばかなことはやめろ．

enough rope →give a person ROPE (enough).

Enough said.《口》よくわかった ▪ *Enough said*. If you want to do so, you have only to say so. よくわかった．そうしたければそう言いさえすればいい．

enough to be getting [***going***] ***on with*** 何とかやっていくに十分な ▪ The wheat flour is *enough to be getting on with*. その小麦粉は（当分）何とかやっていくには十分だ．

enough to sink a ship [***battleship***]《口》十二分に，大量に ▪ "They drank *enough to sink a ship*," he said. 「彼らの暴飲ぶりは船を沈没させるほどだった」と彼は言った．

***have enough to do to** do* …するのがやっとのことである，するのに非常に苦労する ▪ She would *have enough to do to* get home. 彼女は帰宅するのにとても苦労するだろう ▪ They *have enough to do to* live. 彼らは生きるのがやっとだ．

have had (***quite, about***) ***enough of*** …はもうたくさんである，あきた ▪ I *have had enough of* him. あいつはもうたくさんだ．

more than enough 十二分に[で] ▪ There is *more than enough* for all. みんなに十二分にあるよ.
near enough →NEAR.
not know enough to come in out of the rain =not have enough sense to come in from the RAIN.
oddly [***strangely***] ***enough*** いかにも妙なことには ▪ *Oddly enough*, he cannot read. 妙なことに, 彼は文字が読めない.
quite enough 《主に英》(うんざりするほど)十分な数量の ▪ I've had *quite enough*. もうたらふく食べた.
That's (***quite***) ***enough.*** 《口》もう十分だ, いい加減にしなさい.
well enough →WELL[2].

enrage /ɪnréɪdʒ/ 動 ***be enraged against*** [***at***] (事)に激怒する ▪ He *was enraged at* the insult. 彼はその侮辱に激怒した.
be enraged with (人)に激怒する ▪ Anna *was enraged with* you. アンナはあなたにひどく怒っていた.

enrapture /ɪnrǽptʃər/ 動 ***be enraptured at*** [***over, with***] …に狂喜する, 有頂天になる ▪ He *is enraptured with* the stroke of good fortune. 彼は思いがけない幸運に狂喜している.

enrich /ɪnrítʃ/ 動 ***enrich*** *oneself* 金持ちになる ▪ He *enriched himself* at her expense. 彼は彼女を犠牲にして金持ちになった.

enroll, 《英》 **enrol** /ɪnróʊl/ 動 ***enroll*** *oneself* 軍籍に入る; (団体に)加入する ▪ He *enrolled himself* in the guild. 彼はそのギルドに加入した.

ensconce /ɪnskɑ́ns|-skɔ́ns/ 動 ***ensconce*** *oneself* (***in***) **1** (…に)身を隠す ▪ I have *ensconced myself in* a wigwam. 小屋に身を隠した.
2 (安楽のため…に)納まる, 落ち着く ▪ He *ensconced himself in* his old study. 彼は古い書斎に落ち着いた.

enshrine /ɪnʃráɪn/ 動 ***be enshrined in*** 《文》 …の中にだいじに[尊厳なものとして]保存されている ▪ The rights of all humans *are enshrined in* the Charter of the UN. すべての人の権利は国連憲章の中に尊厳をもって記されている.

enshroud /ɪnʃráʊd/ 動 ***be enshrouded in*** …に包まれる ▪ The valley *was enshrouded in* mist. 谷は霧に包まれていた.

enslave /ɪnsléɪv/ 動 ***be enslaved to*** …の奴隷[とりこ]となる ▪ He *is enslaved to* the habit of smoking. 彼は喫煙習慣にとらわれている.

enswathe /ɪnswéɪð/ 動 ***be enswathed in*** …に包まれる ▪ The jungle *was enswathed in* mist. 密林は霧に包まれていた.

entail /ɪntéɪl/ 名 ***break*** [***cut*** (***off***)] ***the entail*** 限嗣(げんし)相続権を廃する ▪ My father might have *cut off the entail*. 私の父は限嗣相続権を捨てたかもしれない.

entangle /ɪntǽŋgəl/ 動 ***be*** [***become***] ***entangled with*** **1** …ともつれ合う, からまる ▪ The story *is entangled with* legends. その話は伝説とないまぜになっている.
2 …とかかわり合いになる ▪ He *became entangled with* a woman of easy virtue. 彼は浮気女とかかわり合いになった.
entangle *oneself* ***in*** …で身動きが取れなくなる ▪ He has *entangled himself in* debt. 彼は借金で身動きが取れなくなった.
entangle *oneself* ***with*** …とかかわり合いになる ▪ He *entangled himself with* moneylenders. 彼は金貸し屋とかかわり合いになった.

enter /éntər/ 動 ***enter*** *oneself* [*one's* ***name***] ***for*** …を志願する, に申し込む ▪ He *entered himself for* the examination. 彼はその試験に申し込んだ.
enter *a person's* ***head*** [***mind***] →HEAD[1].
enter into an agreement (***to*** *do*) (…することを)承諾する, 引き受ける ▪ The firm will *enter into an agreement to* supply 5,000 pairs of shoes. その会社は5,000足の靴を供給することを承諾するだろう.
enter into *a person's* ***labor*** 他人の努力の成果を収める[取り入れる] (《聖》 *John* 4. 38) ▪ Shakespeare *entered into their labors*. シェイクスピアは彼らの努力の成果を取り入れた.
enter into the spirit of things [***it***] (パーティーなどで談笑したり踊ったりして)楽しむ, 興じる, 盛り上がる ▪ Staff also *entered into the spirit of things* by wearing red and white clothes. 紅白の服を着て, スタッフもその場に溶けこんで楽しんだ.
enter on [***upon***] ***business*** 開業する ▪ He *entered on business* soon after. 彼はそれからまもなく開業した.
enter religion 修道院生活に入る ▪ She *entered religion*. 彼女は修道院生活に入った.

enterprise /éntərpràɪz/ 名 ***have no enterprise*** 企業心[進取の気性]がない ▪ He *has no enterprise*. 彼には進取の気性がない.

entertain /èntərtéɪn/ 動 ***entertain the inner man*** →the INNER man.

entertainment /èntərtéɪnmənt/ 名 ***find entertainment in*** …を楽しむ ▪ I *find entertainment in* reading. 私は読書を楽しんでいる.
give entertainments to …をもてなす, ごちそうする ▪ They *gave entertainments to* us. 彼らは我々をもてなした.
to the entertainment of …のおもしろかったことには ▪ He fell into the water, much *to the entertainment of* the onlookers. 彼は水中に落ちこんで, 見物人は大変おもしろがった.

enthusiasm /ɪnθjúːziæ̀zəm/ 名 ***with enthusiasm*** 熱心に, 熱意をもって ▪ He began his work *with enthusiasm*. 彼は熱心に仕事を始めた.

enthusiastic /ɪnθjùːziǽstɪk/ 形 (***be***) ***enthusiastic about*** [***for, over***] …に熱中して(いる), 熱心で(ある) ▪ He *is enthusiastic for* the scheme. 彼はその計画に熱心である ▪ We *were enthusiastic about* the plan. 私たちはその計画に熱中していた ▪ I cannot get *enthusiastic over* teaching. 私は教職に熱意が持てない.

entireness /ɪntáɪərnəs/ 名 ***in its entireness*** 全体として，全体的に ▪ We can more easily contemplate it *in its entireness*. それは全体的に観察するほうがもっとたやすい．

entirety /ɪntáɪərti/ 名 ***by entireties*** 《法》二人による全体連帯の; 不可分的に ▪ They held the land *by entireties*. 彼らはその土地全体を連帯で所有していた．

in its entirety そっくりそのまま，全部，ことごとく ▪ "Hamlet" was presented *in its entirety*. ハムレットが通し上演された ▪ He fulfilled his mission *in its entirety*. 彼は使命を完全に果たした．

entitle /ɪntáɪtəl/ 動 ***entitle*** *a person* ***to*** *do* 人に…する権利[資格]を与える ▪ You *are* not *entitled to* try any more. 君にはもう試みる権利はない．

entrance[1] /éntrəns/ 名 ***effect an*** [*one's*] ***entrance*** →make an ENTRANCE.

force an entrance into …へ無理に押し入る ▪ Our soldiers *forced an entrance into* the town. わが兵はその町に無理に押し入った．

gain [***obtain***] ***entrance*** 入り込む ▪ He easily *gained entrance*. 彼はたやすく入った．

have free entrance to …に自由に出入りが許されている ▪ I *have free entrance to* his library. 私は彼の書斎への自由な出入りが許されている．

make [***effect***] ***an*** [*one's*] ***entrance*** 入る，入りおおせる ▪ He *effected an entrance* into the hall. 彼はその広間に入りおおせた．

No entrance! 入場禁止!

obtain entrance →gain ENTRANCE.

entrance[2] /ɪntrǽns|-trɑ́:ns/ 動 ***be entranced with*** …で我を忘れる ▪ He *was entranced with* joy. 彼は喜びで有頂天になった．

entreat /ɪntrí:t/ 動 ***entreat a favor of*** *a person* 人に懇願する ▪ I *entreat* this *favor of* you. どうぞこの願いをお聞きください．

entreat (***of***) *a person* ***to*** *do* 人に…してくれと頼む ▪ I *entreat* you *to* forgive me. どうぞ私をお許しくださるようお願いします．

entrench /ɪntréntʃ/ 動 ***entrench*** *oneself*/***be entrenched*** ざんごうを掘って立てこもる; 自分の立場を固める ▪ They *entrenched themselves* opposite to the enemy. 彼らは敵と向かい合ってざんごうを掘って立てこもった ▪ He *is* safely *entrenched* behind facts. 彼は事実を盾にして自分の立場を安全に守っている．

entry /éntri/ 名 ***gain entry*** **1** = make an ENTRY 2.
2 (組織などに)加入する (*to*) ▪ The shy student *gained entry to* one of the nation's most elite institutions. そのはにかみ屋の学生は国内の最エリート校の一つに入学した．

make an entry **1** 記帳する ▪ The secretary *made an entry* of the arrangement. 書記はその取決めを記帳した．
2 (…に)入る (*into*); 登場する (*on*) ▪ They *made a* triumphal *entry into* the enemy's capital. 彼らは敵の首都に堂々と入った ▪ No actor can *make a* more regular *entry on* a stage. 彼ほどきちんと舞台に登場できる俳優はいない．

entwine /ɪntwáɪn/ 動 ***entwine*** *oneself* ***around*** [***about***] …に巻きつく ▪ A myth *entwines itself about* the personage. その人には神話がまとわりついている．

envelop /ɪnvéləp/ 動 ***be enveloped in*** …に包まれる ▪ The house *was enveloped in* flames. 家は火炎に包まれていた ▪ The event *was enveloped in* mystery. 事件は神秘[謎]に閉ざされていた．

envelop *oneself* ***in*** …にくるまる ▪ He *enveloped himself in* a blanket. 彼は毛布にくるまった．

envelope /énvəlòʊp/ 名 ***on the back of an envelope*** →BACK[1].

push (***the edge of***) ***the envelope*** 《口》可能性の限界を広げる，…の限界に挑む，許容範囲を広げる[超える] ▪ They *pushed the envelope* of flight during the 1940s and 1950s. 彼らは1940から50年代に飛行の限界を押し広げた ▪ Sony continues to *push the edge of the envelope* with new and exciting technologies. ソニーは刺激的な新技術で限界を広げ続けている ▪ Jones Soda Co. has always *pushed the envelope* on wacky flavors. ジョーンズソーダ会社は風変わりな香りを作り出すのにずっと挑戦してきた． ☞envelope「航空機の性能限界を示す範囲」.

envious /énviəs/ 形 ***be envious of*** …をうらやむ，ねたむ ▪ He *is envious of* my success [my car]. 彼は私の成功をねたんで[私の車をうらやんで]いる．

environ /ɪnváɪərən/ 動 ***be environed with*** [***by***] …に取り囲まれている ▪ The harbor *is environed with* high mountains. その港は高い山々に囲まれている ▪ We *are environed by* perils. 我々は危険に取り巻かれている．

envy[1] /énvi/ 名 ***be the envy of*** …の羨望の的である ▪ Her poodle *is the envy of* Kate. 彼女のプードル犬はケイトの羨望の的である．

feel envy at [***of***] …にねたみを感じる，をうらやましく感じる ▪ Don't *feel envy at* others for money. 金のために他人をねたんではならない ▪ I *feel* no *envy at* his success. 彼の成功は少しもうらやましくない．

green with envy →GREEN.

in envy of …をうらやんで，ねたんで ▪ The conspirators did it *in envy of* Caesar. 陰謀者たちはカエサルをねたんでそうしたのだ．

out of envy 嫉妬から，うらやましさのあまり ▪ They say such things *out of envy*. 彼らは嫉妬からそんなことを言うのだ．

envy[2] /énvi/ 動 ***envy*** *a person* ***for*** …で人をうらやましく思う ▪ He *envies* Jeter *for* his success. 彼はジーターの成功を羨んでいる．

enwrap /ɪnrǽp/ 動 ***be enwrapped in*** …に包まれる ▪ The women of the Turks *are enwrapped in* white linen. トルコの婦人は白いリンネルに包まれている．

epaulet(**te**) /èpəlét/ 名 ***win*** *one's* ***epaulets*** (下士官が)将校に昇進する ▪ He *won his epaulets* in the Revolutionary War. 彼はアメリカ独立戦争において将校に昇進した.

episcopize /ɪpískəpaɪz/ 動 ***episcopize it*** 《宗》司教として統治する ▪ He *episcopized it* over all English Catholics. 彼はイギリスのカトリック教徒全体を司教として統治した.

epitome /ɪpítəmi/ 名 ***in epitome*** **1** 梗概[摘要]の形で ▪ The description contains *in epitome* the principles of education. その記述は教育原理の概要を含んでいる.

2 縮図として ▪ The characteristics of Americans exist *in epitome* in this neighborhood. アメリカ人の特徴はこの近辺に縮図の形で存在している.

epoch /épək|í:pɔk/ 名 ***make [form, mark] an epoch*** 一時期[新時代]を画する ▪ The coming of electronic publication *marks an epoch* in human life. 電子出版の出現は人間生活に一時期を画する.

equal /í:kwəl/ 形名 ***all things [all else] being equal*** →other things being EQUAL.

(be) equal to the time of day →TIME[1].

be the equal of …に匹敵する ▪ He *is the equal of* his brother in ability. 彼は才能において兄に匹敵する.

be without (an) equal in …に並ぶ者はない ▪ He *is without an equal in* eloquence. 彼は雄弁において並ぶ者がない.

equal to **1** …に等しい, 匹敵する ▪ Three times two is *equal to* six. 3×2は6 ▪ He is *equal to* me in intelligence. 彼は知力において私に匹敵する.

2 〖名詞・動名詞を伴って〗…をする力[力量, 気力]がある, に耐えられる ▪ Her sight is *equal to* threading a needle. 彼女の視力はよくて針に糸を通すことができる ▪ He was *equal to* the task [the emergency]. 彼にはその仕事をやりとげる力量があった[彼は緊急事態に対処できた] ▪ His temper is *equal to* any trial. 彼はどんな目にあっても怒らない.

equal to *a person* 人には同じことで ▪ Success or failure is *equal to* him. 成功も失敗も彼にとってはどうでもよい.

equal to *one's* ***desire*** 人の欲望に添う ▪ No man's fortune was ever *equal to his desire*. 人の身代が欲するところにかなった例はない.

equal to the honor その栄誉にふさわしい ▪ She is *equal to the honor*. 彼女はその栄誉を受けるにふさわしい.

equal to the occasion →OCCASION.

feel equal to *doing* (体の具合で)…できる気がする ▪ I don't *feel equal to receiving* visitors. 私は客の応待ができそうにない.

first among (the) equals 同輩内の指導者, 第一人者 ▪ The patriarch is considered *first among equals* by several Orthodox churches. その司教はいくつかの正教会から同教会の第一人者だと考えられている.

have no equal in …に匹敵する[並ぶ]者がない ▪ He *has no equal in* eloquence. 彼は雄弁では並ぶ者がない.

never have *one's* ***equal*** 並ぶ者がない ▪ He *never had his equal* for integrity. 彼は誠実さの点では並ぶ者がなかった.

other [all] things being equal 《口》他の[すべての]ことが同じとして[同じならば] ▪ It is said that *other things being equal*, a tall man is more respected than a short man. 他のことが同じならば, 背の高い人のほうが低い人よりも尊敬されるといわれている.

Some are more equal than others. 一部のものは他のものよりも一層平等である. ☞George Orwell, *Animal Farm* (1945)の戒律 (Commandment) の一部. All animals are equal but some [animals] are…と続いている.

equality /ɪkwɑ́ləti|-kwɔ́l-/ 名 ***on an equality with*** (人が)…と対等で[に]; (物が)…と同格で ▪ He is *on an equality with* me. 彼は私と対等だ.

equanimity /èkwənímәti/ 名 ***with equanimity*** 平然と, 落ち着いて ▪ He bears misfortune *with equanimity*. 彼は平然と不幸に耐える.

equilibrium /ì:kwɪlíbriəm/ 名 ***find an equilibrium between*** …の間に均衡を求める ▪ We must *find an equilibrium between* work and play. 仕事と遊びとの間の均衡を求めなければならない.

keep … in an equilibrium …の勢力をつり合わせておく ▪ England *kept* both Powers *in an equilibrium*. イギリスは両強国の勢力をつり合わせておいた.

equip /ɪkwíp/ 動 ***be equipped for*** **1** …の身仕度をしている, の用意をしている (→EQUIP oneself 1) ▪ I *was equipped for* all emergencies [the journey]. すべての緊急時の用意をしていた[旅支度を整えていた].

2 …の能力[資質]がある ▪ He *is equipped for* public speaking. 彼は演説の才がある.

be equipped in …に身を固めている ▪ He *was equipped in* armor. 彼は防護服に身を固めていた.

equip *oneself* **1** (…の)身支度をする, 用意をする (*for*) ▪ He *equipped himself for* the journey. 彼は旅支度を整えた.

2 (…を)身につける (*with*) ▪ The tourist *equipped himself with* good boots. 旅行者は良い靴をはいていた.

equivalent /ɪkwívələnt/ 形名 ***be equivalent to*** …に等しい; に相当[相応]する; と同意義である ▪ Here he makes a republic *equivalent to* a democracy. ここに彼は民主主義国に等しい共和国を建設する ▪ His presence would *be equivalent to* an army of ten thousand men. 彼がいることは1万人の軍隊に相当する ▪ Silence *is equivalent to* consent. 沈黙は承諾に同じ.

be the equivalent of …と等しい ▪ That expression *is the equivalent of* the other. その表現は他の表現と等しい.

erect /ɪrékt/ 動 ***erect*** *oneself* 身を起こす, 起立する ▪ His weak form *erected itself*. 彼のぼんやりした影が立ち上がった ▪ We must *erect ourselves* to

E

intellectual dignity. 我々は奮起して知的威厳を持たなければならない.

ermine /ə́ːrmən/ 名 ***wear the ermine*** 裁判官になる[である] ▪ His ambition was to *wear the ermine* by the time he was forty. 彼の熱望は40歳になるまでに裁判官になることだった. ☞裁判官は白テンの毛皮の外衣を着るから.

err /əːr/ 動 ***err on the side of*** →SIDE.

To err is human, to forgive divine. 《文》過つは人の性(さが), 赦すは神の御心(みこころ) (Pope, *An Essay on Criticism* 525).

errand /érənd/ 名 ***an errand of mercy*** 善意の使い, (困窮者に食料・医療品を運ぶ)救出の旅 ▪ That was *an errand of mercy* to save life. それは人命救助の旅だった.

come* [*go*] *on an errand of ...の使命を帯びて来る[行く] ▪ The boy has *come on an errand of* his master. その少年は主人の使命を帯びて来た.

***do an errand* [*errands*]** →run an ERRAND.

go* [*come*] *on a fool's errand むだ骨を折る ▪ The doctor has *come on a fool's errand*. 医者は来たがむだだった.

***go* (*on*) [*run, do*] *an errand* [*errands*]** 《口》使いに行く ▪ He has *gone on an errand* for Mrs. Brown. 彼はブラウン夫人のお使いに行った ▪ Johnny earns his pocket money by *running errands* for me. ジョニーは私の走り使いをして小遣いを稼いでいる.

make an errand ちょっと行く; 行く口実を見つける ▪ He *made an errand* home to fetch it. 彼はそれを取りにちょっと家へ帰った ▪ Tom *made an errand* to leave work early. トムは仕事を早く抜けようと出かける口実を見つけた.

error /érər/ 名 ***and no* (*blooming*) *error*** 確かに, 全く《前言を強める》 ▪ She is a lady *and no blooming error*. 彼女は確かに淑女だ.

be* [*stand*] *in error 考え違いしている ▪ You *are in error* in thinking so. そう考えるのはまちがいです.

by error 誤って ▪ Your letter was delivered to my address *by error*. あなたの手紙が誤って私の所へ配達されました.

commit* [*make*] *an error まちがいをする, 失策をする ▪ He *made an error* in calculation. 彼は計算まちがいをした.

errors and omissions excepted 誤謬脱落はこの限りにあらず (E. & O.E. と略す) ▪ The above is our detailed bill for services rendered, *errors and omissions excepted*. 上記は当社が提供したサービスの詳細な請求書である. 誤謬脱落を除いては.

fall into an error 誤りをやる, 身を誤る ▪ He *fell into a* great *error*. 彼は大きな誤りに陥った.

in error 誤って, まちがって ▪ The letter was addressed *in error*. その手紙は宛名がまちがっていた.

lead** a person **into error 人を誤らせる[誤信させる] ▪ This circumstance *led* them *into error*. この事情が彼らを誤信させた.

make an error →commit an ERROR.

see the error of** one's **ways 前非を悔いる ▪ Let us hope that his prodigal son may *see the errors of his ways*. 彼の放蕩息子が前非を悔いるかもしれないと期待しよう.

stand in error →be in ERROR.

the error of** one's **ways →see the ERROR of one's ways.

eruption /ɪrʌ́ptʃən/ 名 (***be***) ***in a state of eruption*** 噴火して(いる) ▪ The volcano *is in a state of eruption*. その火山は噴火している.

burst into eruption (火山が)突然爆発する ▪ Mt. Asama *burst into eruption*. 浅間山が突然爆発した.

escape[1] /ɪskéɪp/ 名 ***effect** one's **escape*** 逃げおおせる, うまく逃げる ▪ We *effected our escape* in disguise. 我々は変装してうまく逃げおおせた.

have a narrow* [*hairbreadth*] *escape 九死に一生を得る, 危ういところを逃れる ▪ She *had a narrow escape*. 彼女はきわどいところを逃れた.

have an escape 逃げる, 逃れる ▪ He has *had an escape* from death. 彼は死を逃れた.

have** one's **escape cut off 逃げ道を断たれる ▪ He *had his escape cut off*. 彼は退路を断たれた.

***make* (*good*) one's *escape* (*from*)** (...から)逃げおおせる ▪ He successfully *made* (*good*) *his escape*. 彼はうまく逃げた.

no escape from ...から逃れる道がなく ▪ There was *no escape from* the enemies. 敵から逃れることはできなかった.

escape[2] /ɪskéɪp/ 動 ***escape* (*a person's*) *attention* [*notice*]** 〚主に否定文で〛(人の)注意を免れる, (人に)見落とされる ▪ It cannot have *escaped the professor's attention*. そのことが教授に見落とされたはずはない.

escape by a hair's breadth → by a HAIR('S)-BREADTH.

escape by the skin of** one's **teeth →by the SKIN of one's teeth.

escape** one's **lips →LIP.

escape unscathed 無傷で脱する ▪ They *escaped unscathed* from the avalanche. 彼らは雪崩から無事に逃れた.

escort /éskɔːrt/ 名 ***under escort*** 護衛[護送]されて ▪ The man has been taken to hospital *under* police *escort*. 男は警察の護衛で病院に搬送された.

escrow /éskroʊ/ 名 ***in escrow*** (契約証書・金などが条件を満たすまで, または条件を果たすため)第三者に保管されて ▪ Cash funds will be placed *in escrow* with the trustee to pay it. それを支払うため, 現金で基金が保管人によって保管される ▪ He has £1,000 *in escrow* to pay taxes. 彼は税金支払いのため, 1,000ポンドを第三者に保管してもらっている.

escutcheon /ɪskʌ́tʃən/ 名 ***a* (*dark*) *blot on** one's **escutcheon*** 家門の名折れ; (一般に)名折れ, けがれ, 面汚し ▪ That foolish deed of his will remain *a blot on his escutcheon*. 彼のあのばかげた行

為はいつまでも彼の名折れであろう.

essence /ésəns/ 名 ***in essence*** 本質において ▪ The two things are different *in essence.* その二つのものは本質において異なる.

of the essence of ...に欠くことのできない ▪ Time is *of the essence of* the contract to retrieve the situation. 時間は情勢挽回を請け負うのに欠くことのできないものである. ☞法律用語から.

essential /ɪsénʃəl/ 名 ***in essentials*** 主要な点では, 要点において ▪ Both are the same *in essentials.* 両方とも主要な点では同じである.

establish /ɪstǽblɪʃ/ 動 ***establish*** *oneself* **1** 落ち着く, おさまる ▪ He *established himself* in a new house. 彼は新しい家に落ち着いた.
2 (...としての)地位を築く (*as*); 身を立てる, 一本立ちになる ▪ He *established himself as* a prominent physician. 彼は傑出した外科医としての地位を築いた.

established /ɪstǽblɪʃt/ 形 ***get*** [***become***] ***established*** 設立される; (人が)地位を築く; (植物が)根づく ▪ Bowden *got established* as a painter. ボーデンは画家としての地位を築いた.

establishment /ɪstǽblɪʃmənt/ 名 ***be on the establishment*** 使用人である ▪ Tell this to the gardeners who *are on the establishment.* 使用人である庭師たちにこのことを伝えてくれ.

keep [***have***] ***a second*** [***separate***] ***establishment*** 《婉曲》妾宅をかまえる, めかけを囲う ▪ Everyone knows that he *has a separate establishment.* 彼が妾宅をかまえているのはみな知っている.

keep (***up***) ***an establishment*** 所帯を張る ▪ He *keeps a* large *establishment.* 彼は大所帯を張っている.

estate /ɪstéɪt/ 名 ***an estate at will*** →WILL[1].

an estate for life 終身不動産権, 終身所有地 ▪ Her *estate* in the Lighthouse was only *for life.* 灯台の彼女の不動産権は終身のものにすぎなかった《世襲でなかった》.

suffer in *one's* ***estate*** 暮らし向きが苦しい ▪ He humbly says he *suffers in his estate.* 彼は自分は暮らし向きが苦しいとへりくだって言う.

the fourth estate 第4階級, 言論出版界(の人々) ▪ The conventional mass media (or the press) is known as *the fourth estate.* 伝統的なマスメディア(もしくは出版界)は第4階級として知られている ▪ You press people have been called "*the fourth estate.*" あなたたち言論界の人々は「第4階級」と呼ばれている.

esteem[1] /ɪstíːm/ 名 ***gain*** [***get***] ***high esteem*** 非常に尊敬される ▪ He *gained high esteem* in the world. 彼は世間に非常に尊敬された.

have a great esteem for ...を非常に尊敬している ▪ I *have a great esteem for* his ability. 私は彼の手腕に大いに敬服している.

hold ... in (***high***) ***esteem*** ...を(大いに)尊重している ▪ I *hold* his learning [him] *in high esteem.* 彼の学問[彼]を大いに尊重している.

hold ... in low esteem 低く見る, 軽蔑する ▪ I *hold* liars *in low esteem.* 私は嘘つきを軽蔑する.

lower oneself in *a person's* ***esteem*** 人気を落とす, に見下げられるようになる ▪ He *lowered himself in the world's esteem* by the foolish act. 彼はその愚かな行為で, 世間に見下げられるようになった.

esteem[2] /ɪstíːm/ 動 ***esteem it an honor*** [***a privilege***] ***to*** *do* ...することを光栄[特権]と思う ▪ I *esteem it an honor to* address this audience. みなさんにお話しするのを光栄に思います.

esteem it (***as***) ***a favor*** [***an honor***] ***if*** ...ならばありがたく[光栄に]思う ▪ I should *esteem it a favor if* you would grant it. それをお許しくださればありがたく存じます ▪ I should *esteem it an honor if* you would come. おいでくだされば光栄に存じます.

estimate /éstəmət/ 名 ***at a moderate*** [***conservative***] ***estimate*** 堅く[控え目に]見積もって ▪ The property will be placed at $3,000 *at a moderate estimate.* その財産は堅く見積もって3,000ドルはあるだろう.

at a rough estimate 大ざっぱに見積もって, およそのところ ▪ *At a rough estimate,* he must have walked 20 miles. およそのところ, 彼は20マイル歩いたにちがいない.

by estimate 見積もりで, 判断で ▪ *By* general *estimate* the flour ground there had an uncommon whiteness. 大体の判断だが, そこでひかれた小麦粉はすばらしく白かった.

form an estimate of ...の見積もりを作る, 大体の判断をする ▪ You can *form an estimate of* her charm. 彼女の魅力については大体の判断がつきますよ.

estimation /èstəméɪʃən/ 名 ***be in*** (***high***) ***estimation*** (大いに)尊重されている ▪ He *is in high estimation.* 彼は大いに尊重されている.

fall [***rise***] ***in the estimation of*** ...の評価が落ちる[高まる] ▪ He has *fallen in my estimation.* 私は彼を高く買わなくなった ▪ He has *risen in the estimation of* the public. 彼の世評は高くなった.

hold [***have***] ***... in estimation*** ...を尊重する ▪ He *was held in estimation* by people. 彼は人々に尊重されていた.

in *a person's* ***estimation*** ...の見るところでは[意見では] ▪ He comes first *in my estimation.* 僕の考えでは彼が一番だ.

stand high in the estimation of ...の評判が高い ▪ He *stands high in* public *estimation.* 彼は世評が高い.

win *a person's* ***estimation*** 人の尊敬を得る ▪ She *won* public *estimation.* 彼女は世の尊敬を得た.

estrange /ɪstréɪndʒ/ 動 ***be*** [***become***] ***estranged from*** 《文》...と疎遠になる, 仲が悪くなる ▪ They *are estranged from* each other. 彼らはお互いに疎遠になった.

estrange *oneself* ***from*** ...から遠ざかる ▪ He *estranged himself from* his relatives. 彼は親族から遠ざかった.

E

et /et/ 接 ***et al.*** /etáːl|-ǽl/ …他(の著者) ▪ This issue is discussed in more detail in Quirk *et al.* この件は Quirk 他でより詳細に論じられている. ☞L 'and others'.

et cetera /etsétərə/ 副 ***without et ceteras*** かっきり ▪ The bill for our stay came to £1,000 *without et ceteras.* 私たちの滞在費は1,000ポンドかっきりになった. ☞L 'and the rest'.

etch /etʃ/ 動 ***be etched in*** [***on***] *one's* ***memory*** [***mind, heart***] 《主に雅》記憶に刻まれる, 脳裏に焼き付く ▪ It was a day that *was* permanently *etched in my memory.* それはいつまでも私の記憶に刻まれている日だ ▪ That day will *be etched on my mind* until my death. あの日のことは死ぬまで私の心に刻まれているだろう.

be etched into [***on***] 《文》印象うけられている ▪ The contrast of tender sensibility and senseless brutality *was etched into* my mind. 思いやりのある感性と無分別な残忍性との対比が私の心に印象うけられた.

be etched on [***into***] *one's* ***face*** 顔に刻まれている, 表情に出ている ▪ A look of remorse *was etched on his face.* 後悔している様子が彼の顔に出ていた.

eternity /ɪtə́ːrnəti/ 名 ***launch into eternity*** →LAUNCH².

this side of eternity この世 ▪ It would be my last experience on *this side of eternity.* それはこの世での私の最後の経験となるだろう.

etiquette /étɪkət|étɪkèt/ 名 ***it is not etiquette to*** *do* …するのは礼儀にもとる ▪ *It is not etiquette to* talk at golf. ゴルフのとき話をするのは礼儀にもとる.

eulogy /júːlədʒi/ 名 ***pronounce a eulogy on*** …に対して賛辞を呈する ▪ He *pronounced a eulogy on* the dead. 彼は故人の頌(しょう)徳演説をした.

European /jʊ̀ərəpíːən/ 形 ***on the European plan*** (ホテルが)ヨーロッパ方式の《部屋代と食事代が別》(→on the AMERICAN plan) ▪ Most American hotels are *on the European plan.* アメリカのホテルはたいていヨーロッパ方式である.

eve /iːv/ 名 (***be***) ***on the eve of*** …のまぎわに, の前夜[日]に(ある) ▪ They *were on the eve of* a general election. 彼らは総選挙の直前にあった ▪ He fell ill *on the eve of* his examination. 彼は試験の直前[前日]に病気になった.

even /íːvən/ 形副 (***back***) ***on an even keel*** →KEEL.

be even with **1** …に仕返しをする, 報復する ▪ I'll *be even with* him for cheating me. 私をだましたことに対して彼に仕返しをしてやる.

2 …と同等で, 高低が同じで, (道などが)平行して, 両端が中心と同一線上にあって, と対等で ▪ The snow *was even with* the window. 雪は窓と同じ高さであった ▪ The chimney *is* made *even with* the upright of the wall. 煙突は直立する壁と平行になっている ▪ I *was even with* my master. 私は主人と対等であった.

break even →BREAK².

even as 《雅》ちょうど…ように; ちょうど…したとき ▪ It has turned out *even as* I expected. それはちょうど私が期待した通りになった ▪ *Even as* he spoke, it began to snow. ちょうど彼が話し出したとき, 雪が降り始めた.

even if たとえ…だとして; …にもかかわらず (→EVEN though) ▪ *Even if* you do not like it, you must do it. たとえそれを好まなくとも君はそれをせねばならない.

even now 今でも ▪ *Even now* he won't believe it. 彼は今でもそれを信じない ▪ *Even now* the time has arrived. ちょうど今時が来た.

even reckoning 貸借なし ▪ *Even reckoning* makes lasting friends. 貸借なしの交際は長く続く.

even so それにしても; それはそうでも ▪ He is a poor man, but *even so* there is no reason for him to wear rags. 彼は貧乏だが, それにしてもぼろをまとう理由はない.

even Stephen/《米》***even steven***/《英》***even stevens*** 《米》全く五分五分, 損得なし, 同額[同点]で, あいこで ▪ Protection for support. *Even Stephen.* 援助に対して保護, 全く五分五分である ▪ We played hard but the game finished *even stevens.* ぼくたちは懸命にプレーしたが試合は同点引き分けに終わった. ☞押韻俗語.

even though …の事実にもかかわらず; たとえ…でも (→EVEN if) ▪ *Even though* she is over sixty, she can swim faster than us. 彼女は60歳を越えているけど, 私たちより速く泳げる.

evenly even 4で割り切れる ▪ 16 is an *evenly even* number. 16は4で割り切れる数である.

get an even break 《米》対等のチャンスを得る ▪ Do women workers *get an even break*? 女性労働者は均等な機会を得ているだろうか.

get even 《口》借金を返済する; 借りを返す ▪ Mr. MacDonald has a lot of debts, but in a few years he will *get even.* マクドナルド氏は多額の借金があるが, 数年で返済するだろう.

get even with =be EVEN with 1.

give *a person* ***an even break*** 《米》人に対等のチャンスを与える ▪ *Give* her *an even break* and she'll prove herself the greatest physician of all. 彼女に対等なチャンスを与えれば, いちばん優秀な医者だということがわかるだろう.

make all even 貸借をなくする ▪ This will *make all even.* これですべて貸借なしになる.

make even (***lines***) (字間・語間を調整して)両端揃えにする ▪ One of the compositor's jobs is to *make even lines.* 植字工の仕事の一つは両端が揃うようにすることである.

not even …でさえもしない ▪ Max never stopped working, *not even* at Christmas. マックスは仕事を決してやめなかった. クリスマスでさえも.

odd and [***or***] ***even*** →ODD.

oddly even →ODDLY.

of even date 同じ日付の《《米》で普通文, 《英》で

は主に法律文書で》 ▪ By deed *of even date* he covenanted to pay all calls. 同じ日付の証文により彼はすべての払込請求に応じると誓約した.

on even ground (***with***) (…と)対等で[に] ▪ I associate *on even ground with* him. 私は彼と対等でつきあっている.

play even →PLAY².

evening /íːvnɪŋ/ 名 ***evening by evening*** 夜な夜な, 夜ごとに ▪ The crowds thronged the Cathedral *evening by evening* to hear the Gospel. 群集は福音を聴くために夜ごと大聖堂に押しかけた.

Good evening. こんばんは.

in the evening 晩[夕方]に(は) ▪ I take a walk *in the evening*. 私は晩に散歩します.

make an evening of it 一晩愉快に過ごす, 飲みあかす ▪ Let's *make an evening of it*. 一晩愉快にやろうじゃないか.

on the evening of (*the 10th*) (10日)の晩に ▪ They met *on the evening of* the 6th. 彼らは6日の晩に会った. ☞形容詞(句)がつけば on を用いる.

the evening of life 《婉曲》人生の黄昏(たそがれ), 晩年 ▪ There are exceptions who bloom in *the evening of life*. 人生の晩年に花開く例外的な人もいる.

this [***tomorrow, yesterday***] ***evening*** 今[明, 昨]晩(に) ▪ Come to my house *this evening*. 今晩私の家へおいでなさい. ☞on を用いない.

wish *a person* ***good evening*** 人に「こんばんは」と言う ▪ He *wished* me *good evening*. 彼は私に「こんばんは」とあいさつした.

event /ɪvént/ 名 ***a*** [***the***] ***happy event*** めでたいこと, 慶事《結婚, 子供の誕生など》 ▪ This is of course *a happy event* for the couple. これはもちろん夫婦にはよろこばしいことだ.

abide by the event →ABIDE.

at all events **1** ともかくも ▪ *At all events* you had better try. ともかくも君はやってみたほうがよい.
2 どんなことがあっても ▪ He must answer for the goods *at all events*. 彼はどんなことがあってもその商品に責任を持たねばならない.

Coming events cast their shadows before. 《諺》事が起ころうとする時は前兆がある.

Fools are wise after the event. 《諺》下司(げす)のあと知恵 (= It's EASY to be wise after the event.).

in all events/in any event どうあっても ▪ You should go to school *in all events*. 君はどうあっても学校へ行くべきだ ▪ *In any event* the child is safe now. どうあってもその子はもう安全である.

in either event いずれにしても ▪ *In either event* you will lose nothing. いずれにせよ君に損はないだろう.

in (***the***) ***event*** 結果において ▪ They openly, and *in the event* successfully, resisted the installation of the new prelate. 彼らは新しい高位聖職者の就任に公然と反対し結果において成功した.

in the event of [***that***] …の場合には ▪ Close the shop *in the event of* my absence. 私が休んだら店を閉めなさい ▪ *In the event that* you cancel your booking, you will forfeit your deposit. 予約をキャンセルすれば手付金は戻らないことになる.

in the unlikely event that 万一…の場合には ▪ *In the unlikely event that* strong sanctions were imposed, Iran would find it relatively easy to survive them. 万一強い制裁が科せられたとしても, イランは比較的容易に乗り切るだろう.

quite an event 《口》重大事, なかなかの大事件 ▪ The first sight of a real mangrove swamp is *quite an event*. 本物のマングローブの沼沢地を初めて見ることはなかなかの大事である.

the course of events 事の成り行き ▪ *The course of events* made it necessary for him to go to America. 事の成り行きとして彼はアメリカへ行かねばならなかった.

ever /évər/ 副 ***all*** *a person* ***ever does is*** … はいつも…してばかりいる ▪ *All* she *ever does is* read and send email. 彼女がすることといえばEメールを読んで返信することだけだ.

as … as ever →AS.

as if … ever *do* …は絶対…しない ▪ *As if* he would *ever* do such a thing! 彼は決してそんなことはしないだろう.

Did you [***anybody***] ***ever!*** →(Well,) DID you ever!

Did you ever …? **1** …したことがあるか《反語であることが多い》 ▪ *Did you ever* meet him? あなたは彼に会ったことがありますか.
2 …とは驚いた, とはけしからん ▪ Well, *did you ever* hear such nonsense? ほんとに, そんなばかな話ってあるものか.

ever a [***an***]/***e'er a*** [***an***] 《古》ほんのひとつでも ▪ Have you *ever a* dollar? 1ドルでもお持ちですか ▪ I don't know whether you have *e'er an* one. ひとつでもお持ちかどうか知りません.

ever after …の後[から]ずっと ▪ They married and were happy *ever after*. 彼らは結婚してその後ずっと幸福であった.

ever and again 時折, 時々 ▪ *Ever and again* the husky voices of the beasts were heard. 時折そのけもののしわがれた声が聞こえた.

ever more 《文》より[なお]一層 ▪ They were becoming *ever more* anxious. 彼らはなお一層心配になってきた ▪ They waited *ever more* anxiously for his return. 彼らはなお一層心配して彼の帰りを待った.

ever now and then 時折 ▪ He did *ever now and then* raise up prophets. 彼は時折予言者たちを出現させた.

ever so **1** いかに…でも ▪ If I were *ever so* rich, I would not buy it. 私がいくら金持ちであってもそれは買わないだろう ▪ If he tries *ever so*, he will not succeed. いくらやってみても彼は成功しないだろう.
2 《口》きわめて, 非常に, ほんとに(ひどく) ▪ The lady was *ever so* angry. その女性はひどく怒っていた ▪ The boy spoke his part in the play *ever so* well. 少年は劇のせりふを非常にうまく言った ▪ There

are *ever so* many questions about it. それについてはきわめて多くの問題がある.

ever so much 大いに, 非常に ▪ I thank you *ever so much* for your advice. ご助言ほんとにありがとうございました ▪ It is *ever so much* better. そのほうがずっとよい.

ever such →SUCH.

ever the same いつも同じの.

for ever [《米》***forever***] 永久に, いつまでも ▪ He would go on talking *for ever*. 彼はいつまでも話し続けるのだった.

for ever and a day いついつまでも《昔はまじめな文に, 今は戯言に》 ▪ Farewell *for ever and a day*. 永久にさようなら.

for ever and (***for***) ***ever*** いつまでもいつまでも ▪ I shall love her *for ever and ever*. 私はいつまでも彼女を愛します.

hardly [***scarcely***] ***ever*** ほとんど…しない; きわめてまれ ▪ It *hardly ever* rains in the desert. その砂漠ではほとんど雨が降らない.

Have you ever *done?* …したことがあるか ▪ *Have you ever* seen a panda? パンダを見たことがあるか.

If ever! これはこれは, まさか《驚きを表す》 ▪ Well, *if ever!* ほんとに, 驚いた!

if ever there was one/***if ever I saw one*** そのようなものが仮にもあったとすれば, まちがいなく《前の名詞を強める》 ▪ He is a scholar, *if ever there was one*. 彼こそまさしく学者である ▪ It was a brilliant stage *if ever I saw one*. それは, まちがいなくすばらしい舞台だった.

if it were ever so →were it EVER so.

scarcely ever →hardly EVER.

seldom, if ever →SELDOM.

than ever 今までよりも ▪ He works harder *than ever*. 彼は今までよりもっと精を出して働く.

the brav*est* (***man***) ***that ever lived*** 古今無比の勇敢な人 ▪ He is *the* great*est scholar that ever lived*. 彼は古今無比の大学者である.

were it ever so/***if it were ever so*** 《俗》その必要がいかに大きくても ▪ I won't ask him for bread, not *if it were ever so*. 私はいくらほしくても, 彼にパンをくれとは言わない.

everlasting /èvərlǽstɪŋ|-lɑ́:st-/ 名 ***for everlasting*** 未来永劫(ごう)に ▪ Truth and goodness should reign *for everlasting*. 真と善は未来永劫に世を支配すべきである.

from everlasting 永遠の昔から ▪ Love and beauty have belonged to humans *from everlasting*. 愛と美は劫初から人間のものだった.

evermore /èvərmɔ́:r/ 副 ***for evermore*** 永久に ▪ Those pleasures flow from the presence of God *for evermore*. それらの楽しみは神の御前から永久に流れ出る.

every /évri/ 形 ***at every turn*** →TURN[1].

every four days [*fourth* ***day***] 4日目ごとに, 3日おきに ▪ He comes here *every* four *days*. 彼は4日目ごとにここへ来る ▪ I wrote to him *every* third *day*. 私は2日おきに彼に手紙を出した.

every few minutes [***days, hours,*** etc.] 数分[日, 時間, など]おきに ▪ He called on me *every few days*. 彼は数日おきに私を訪ねて来た.

every here and there ここかしこ ▪ A streamlet spread out *every here and there*. 細流がここかしこで広がっていた.

every last [***single***] *person* [*thing*] (人•物)が一人[一つ]残らず… ▪ *Every last* one of them came. 彼らのうち一人残らずやってきた ▪ *Every single* ticket has been sold. 入場券は一枚残らず売り切れた.

every mother's son/ every Jack/ every man Jack 一人残らず, 誰もかれも (*of*) ▪ They would hang us, *every mother's son*. 彼らは我々を一人残らず絞首にするだろう ▪ *Every mother's son of* them wishes to be considered Solomon. 彼らのうち誰もかれもソロモンと考えられることを望んでいる.

every ... not/not every ... 誰もが…するわけではない (…するのは少ない) ▪ *Every* man can*not* speak with the king. 《諺》誰でも王様と話ができるわけではない ▪ *Not every* man can be a Newton. ニュートンのような大科学者になれる人は少ない. ☞every ... not の語順は古風で, 《諺》に多い.

(***every***) ***now and then*** [***again***] →NOW.

every one **1** /évriwʌn/ 人はみな ▪ *Every one* knows it. 人はみなそれを知っている.

2 /évriwʌ́n/ どれもこれもことごとく ▪ I tried *every one* of them. 私はそれらのひとつひとつを試みた.

every other **1** ひとつおきの ▪ He comes here *every other* day. 彼は1日おきにここへ来る ▪ *Every other* boy carried a lighted torch. 少年は一人おきに火のついたたいまつを持っていた.

2 他のすべての ▪ Tom was early but *every other* boy was late. トムは早かったが, 他の少年はみな遅れた.

every second →EVERY other 1.

every single person [***thing***] →EVERY last person.

every so often →OFTEN.

every time **1** …するたびに ▪ *Every time* I meet him, he smiles at me. 会うたびに彼は私ににっこりする.

2 《口》いつでも; 例外なく; さっそく, ためらわず ▪ You can rely on him *every time*. あなたはいつでも彼に頼ることができる ▪ I desire everybody to plant it *every time*. みんなが例外なくそれを植えることを望みます.

3 《口》いかにも!, よろしいとも!

every time *one* ***turns around*** 《口》しょっちゅう, いつもいつも ▪ I can't drive you home *every time* I *turn around*. 私はそんなにいつもいつもあなたを車で家まで送るわけにいきません.

every Tom, Dick and Harry →TOM.

every way あらゆる点において ▪ This is *every way* better than that. これはあれよりあらゆる点ですぐれている.

every which way 《米》 **1** あらゆる方向に, 四方八方に ▪ She looked *every which way* for a moment. 彼女はちょっと四方八方を見た.
2 あらゆる方法を尽くして; すべての面において ▪ She has tried *every which way* to lose weight. 減量するために彼女はありとあらゆることを試みた.

nearly every ... たいていの..., 大概の... ▪ *Nearly every* Japanese speaks some English. たいていの日本人は多少英語を話す.

not every ... →EVERY ... not.

everybody /évribɑ̀di|-bɔ̀di/ 代 ***Everybody for himself*** (***and God for us all***). 《諺》(一大事のときは)みんな我先だ. ☞It's everybody for himself these days (最近ではみんな自分第一だ)のように省略されることがある.

not everybody 誰もが(できる)わけではない ▪ *Not everybody* can do this. 誰もがこれをできるわけではない.

everyone /évriwʌ̀n/ 代 ***everyone and his brother*** 《米》 大勢の人々 ▪ *Everyone and his brother* seem [seems] determined to see the movie star. 多数の人たちが映画スターをぜひ見ようとしているようだ. ☞動詞は単複呼応が見られる.

everything /évriθìŋ/ 代 ***and everything*** 《口》 等々, その他もろもろ ▪ I have my books *and everything*. ぼくは本でも何でも持っている.

before everything (***else***) 何はさておき, 何よりも ▪ Character is important *before everything* (*else*). 人格が何よりも大切だ ▪ *Before everything* you should quit smoking. 何はさておき君はタバコをやめるべきだ.

do everything but *do* いっこうに...しない ▪ The book *did everything but* sell. その本はいっこうに売れなかった.

everything and nothing 何でも屋で決まった商売のない ▪ He was a commission agent, that is, *everything and nothing*. 彼は仲買人であった, すなわち, 何でも屋で定職はなかった.

everything but the kitchen sink →SINK[1].

Everything comes to him who waits. 《諺》 待つ人にはすべての物が手に入る,「待てば海路の日和あり」.

everything happens to 悪いことは何もかも...にふりかかる ▪ Why does *everything happen to* me? なぜ悪いことはみな私にふりかかるのだろう.

everything in *one's* ***power*** → in one's POWER.

Everything in the garden is lovely [***rosy***]. 《諺》 万事うまくいっている.

Everything is going [***coming***] *one's* ***way.*** 万事望み[計画]通りにいっている.

Everything is nice in your garden! 自分のものなら何でも立派なのですね; 少し手前味噌がすぎますね.

Everything's coming up roses. 万事うまく[順調に]いっている ▪ *Everything's coming up roses* for John. ジョンにとってはすべてが順調にいっている.

have everything あらゆる魅力を持つ ▪ There was a girl who *had everything*. あらゆる魅力を持つ少女がいた.

I've seen [***heard***] ***everything.*** 《口》 (信じがたいものを見て[聞いて])驚いた.

like everything →LIKE[1].

evidence /évədəns/ 名 ***bear evidence*** (***of***) (...の)形跡を示す, (の)あとを明らかに示す ▪ The country *bore evidence of* careful cultivation. その地域は入念な耕作のあとを示していた.

believe [***credit***] ***the evidence of*** *one's* ***ears*** [***eyes***] →believe one's EARs [EYEs].

call *a person* ***in evidence*** 人を証人として呼び出す ▪ He *was called in evidence* concerning a curio. 彼はある骨董品について証人として呼び出された.

give evidence **1** 証言する ▪ Mr. Smith was called on to *give evidence*. スミス氏は証言するよう求められた.
2 (...の)形跡を示す (*of*) ▪ When the ship reached port, it *gave evidence of* the storm. 港に着いたとき, 船はあらしのあとを示していた.

in evidence **1** 人目を引いて, 目立って ▪ She likes to be much *in evidence*. 彼女は大いに人目を引くのが好きである ▪ The destroyer was first *in evidence* in the Russo-Japanese war. 駆逐艦は日露戦争において初めて目立つ働きをした.
2 はっきり見えて ▪ The child was nowhere *in evidence*. その子供はどこにも見えなかった.
3 法廷における証拠の一部となって ▪ The document is *in evidence*. その書類は法廷における証拠の一部となっている.

on evidence 証拠に基づいて ▪ You should not infer *on* slight *evidence*. わずかな証拠で推断してはならない.

on no evidence 証拠もないのに ▪ He was imprisoned *on no evidence*. 彼は証拠もないのに投獄された.

on the evidence of ...を根拠に; の証言に基づいて ▪ He was convicted mainly *on the evidence of* an FBI informant. 彼は主として FBI の通報者の証言によって有罪とされた.

produce ... in evidence ...を法廷の証拠の一部として提出する ▪ The policy must *be produced in evidence*. その保険証券は法廷の証拠の一部として提出しなければならない.

show evidence =give EVIDENCE 2.

take evidence 証人調べをする; 証拠を集める (*from*) ▪ They *took evidence from* interested bodies. 彼らは関係団体から証拠を集めた.

turn King's [***Queen's,*** 《米》 ***State's***] ***evidence*** 共犯者に対する起訴の証人となる, 共犯者に不利な証言をする ▪ He *turned State's* [*King's*] *evidence* against his pals. 彼は共犯に不利な証言をした.

evil /íːvəl/ 形 名 ***an evil eye*** 邪眼, 悪魔の目《こういう目を持っている人ににらまれると災いが来ると言う》; 邪眼の人 (《聖》 *Matt.* 20. 15) (→give a person the EVIL eye) ▪ No eye is better than *an evil eye*, dark master. 目のないほうが邪眼の人よりもよいですよ，目の見えないご主人さま ▪ What's that *evil eye* up to? あの邪眼の人は何をたくらんでいるのか.

bear* [*cast, look with*] *an evil eye 悪意の目を持つ[で見る] ▪ Patriotic citizens will *cast an evil eye* upon you as a subverter of the law. 愛国的な市民はあなたを法律の破壊者として悪意の目で見るであろう.

do evil 悪事をする ▪ He who does no good *does evil* enough. 善事をせぬ人はそれだけで悪事をすることになる.

Evil communications corrupt good manners. 朱に交われば赤くなる ▪ Remember that *evil communications corrupt good manners.* 「悪友に交われば堕落する」ということを忘れるな. ☞St. Paul の言葉(《聖》*1 Cor.* 15. 33)とされるが，ギリシャ人の王(160?–135? B.C.)Menandros の句を St. Paul が引用したものである.

Evil to him that evil thinks! 《諺》悪い考えをいだく者には災いあれ!, 「人を呪わば穴ふたつ」.

fall on evil days 《雅》不運にあう (Milton, *Paradise Lost* 7. 25) ▪ He has *fallen on evil days*, poor fellow. 気の毒に，彼は不運な目にあった.

give** a person **the evil eye 人を怒って[憎々しげに]にらみつける (→an EVIL eye) ▪ I laughed so loud, the librarians *gave* me *the evil eye*. 大笑いしたので，司書たちににらみつけられた.

Hear no evil, see no evil, speak no evil. 《諺》悪を聞くな，見るな，語るな，「見ざる，聞かざる，言わざる」.

look with an evil eye →bear an EVIL eye.

Of two evils choose the less. 《諺》二つの悪のうちなら小さい方を取れ.

***put off the evil day* [*hour*]** やりにくい事を延ばす ▪ Tell the teacher that you've broken the window. You should not *put off the evil day* any longer. 先生に君が窓をこわしたことを言いなさい. 言いにくいことをこれ以上延ばしてはいけない.

The remedy is worse than the evil. 《諺》角(つの)をためて牛を殺す.

wish** a person **evil →WISH well.

evolve /ɪválv|ɪvɔ́lv/ 動 ***evolve ...from** one's **inner consciousness*** ...を想像で作り出す《しばしば戯言的に作り話やほらについて言う》 ▪ He *evolved* a scheme *from his inner consciousness*. 彼は想像で計画をでっちあげた.

ewe /juː/ 名 ***one's ewe lamb*** 最も大切にしている所有物(《聖》*2 Sam.* 12. 3) ▪ Little Marion was *her ewe lamb*. マリオン少年は彼女の秘蔵っ子だった.

exact[1] /ɪgzǽkt/ 形 ***(be) exact to a cent*** (勘定が1セントも違わぬほどに)几帳面で ▪ He *is exact to a cent* in his dealings. 彼は取引が実に几帳面だ.

to be exact 厳密[正確]に言うと ▪ January the 5th *to be exact*. 正確に言うと1月5日.

exact[2] /ɪgzǽkt/ 動 ***exact ...from** a person* 人に...をきびしく要求する[強要する] ▪ The teacher *exacted* obedience *from* the students. 先生は生徒に服従をきつく要求した.

exactitude /ɪgzǽktətjùːd/ 名 ***with exactitude*** 正確[精密]に ▪ He measured it *with* scientific *exactitude*. 彼はそれを科学的に精密に測った.

exactly /ɪgzǽktli/ 副 ***not exactly*** 必ずしも...ではない ▪ He is *not exactly* a miser. 彼はけちんぼうというわけでもない.

exaggerate /ɪgzǽdʒərèɪt/ 動 ***have an exaggerated notion* [*sense*] *of*** ...をひどく買いかぶっている，を過大視している ▪ He *has an exaggerated notion of* my wealth. 彼は私の富をひどく買いかぶっている ▪ He *has an exaggerated sense of* his own importance. 彼は自分を過大評価している.

exaggeration /ɪgzæ̀dʒəréɪʃən/ 名 ***it is no exaggeration to say*** ...と言うのは過言ではない ▪ *It is no exaggeration to say* that he is the Newton of today. 彼は現代のニュートンであると言っても過言ではない.

exalt /ɪgzɔ́ːlt/ 動 ***exalt ...to the skies*** → praise ... to the skies (→SKY).

examination /ɪgzæ̀mənéɪʃən/ 名 ***be a good* [*bad,* etc.] *examination*** 試験がよくできた[不出来の] ▪ It *was an awful examination*. その試験はひどく不出来だった.

fail in an examination 試験に不合格になる ▪ He *failed in* the entrance *examination*. 彼は入学試験に不合格だった.

make an examination of ...を検査[審査]する ▪ The doctor *made a* careful *examination of* my eyes. 医者は私の目を綿密に検査した.

on* [*upon*] *examination **1** 調査[検査，試験]の上で ▪ Licenses are issued *on examination*. 試験の上免許証が下付される.

2 調査[検査，試験]してみると ▪ It proved *on examination* to be a candle light. それは調べてみると，ろうそくの火であるとわかった.

pass* [*succeed in*] *an examination 試験に合格する ▪ He *passed the examination*. 彼はその試験に合格した.

take* [*undergo*] *an examination 試験を受ける ▪ He *took examinations* in specified subjects. 彼は指定科目の試験を受けた.

under examination 調査[試験]中で ▪ He is a criminal *under examination*. 彼は審問中の罪人である ▪ The candidate is *under examination*. 志願者は受験中である.

examine /ɪgzǽmɪn/ 動 ***examine** oneself* 内省する ▪ Make it a duty to *examine yourself*. 反省を務めとしなさい.

example /ɪgzǽmpəl|-záːm-/ 名 ***as an example*** 一例として ▪ Take, *as an example*, Spain of today. たとえば今日のスペインを見なさい.

be without* [*beyond*] *example 前例がない，空前である ▪ It *is without example* in history. それは歴史上前例がない.

by example 手本[模範]によって ▪ You must

strive to profit yourself *by example*. 君は手本を利用するよう努力せねばならない.

by way of example 一例として，例証として ▪ Take wrestling *by way of example*. 一例としてレスリングを取ってみなさい.

Example is better than precept. 《諺》実践的模範は口だけの教訓に勝る.

follow the example of …を手本[模範]とする ▪ You should *follow Tom's example* and work harder. あなたはトムを手本として，もっと精出して勉強すべきである.

for example たとえば ▪ Many great men have risen from poverty—Lincoln and Edison, *for example*. 貧困から身を起こした偉人は多い—たとえばリンカンやエジソンである.

give an example **1** 一例をあげる ▪ Please *give* me *an example*. どうぞ一例をあげてください.
2 範を垂れる (*to*) ▪ He *gave an example to* us. 彼は我々に手本を示した.

leave an example 模範を残す ▪ He *leaves a* meritorious *example*. 彼はみごとな模範を残している.

make an example of …を見せしめに懲らしめる ▪ I shall *make an example of* the next offender. 次の反則者を見せしめに懲らしめてやる.

set an example (***to***) (…に)範を垂れる ▪ He *set an example* of diligence *to* his inferiors. 彼は部下の者たちに精励の手本を示した.

take example by **1** (他人)の例にならう，を範とする ▪ You should *take example by* me. あなたは私の例にならうべきである.
2 …を戒めとする ▪ All rebels should *take example by* his punishment. すべての反逆者は彼の処罰を戒めとすべきである.

to take [***cite***] ***an example*** 一例をあげると ▪ *To take an example*, you can travel round the world in less than two hours. 一例をあげると，2時間たらずで世界一周旅行ができる.

without example 先例のない，空前の ▪ The play was a hit *without example*. その芝居は空前の大当たりだった.

exasperate /ɪgzǽspərèɪt/ 動 ***be exasperated against*** [***at, by, with***] …に立腹する，激怒する ▪ She *was exasperated against* the informer. 彼女は密告者に激怒していた ▪ He *was exasperated at* our failure. 彼は我々の失敗に腹を立てた.

exasperation /ɪgzæ̀spəréɪʃən/ 名 ***in exasperation*** 憤激して ▪ He cried out *in exasperation*. 彼は憤激して叫んだ.

exceed /ɪksíːd/ 動 ***exceed*** (*one's*) ***belief*** とても信じられない ▪ It *exceeds my belief*. それは私にはとても信じられない.

exceed** one's **commission [***authority***] 越権行為をする ▪ He *exceeded his authority* when he did so. 彼がそうしたのは越権行為だ.

exceed** one's **instructions [***orders***] 訓令を越えたことをする ▪ The captain *exceeded his orders* when he quartered men in private houses. 大尉が兵を民家に宿泊させたのは訓令を越えた行為であった.

excellence /éksələns/ 名 ***by excellence*** 優れて，特に ▪ Cesalpin was denominated, *by excellence*, the philosopher. セサルピンは特に哲学者と呼ばれた. ☞フランス語の par excellence に相当する.

excellency /éksələnsi/ 名 ***Their*** [***Your***] ***Excellencies*** 閣下 ▪ *Their Excellencies* praise me continually. あのかたがたは絶えず私をおほめくださいます. ☞They [You] の代わりに用いる尊称; 複数形で.

Your [***His***] ***Excellency*** 閣下 ▪ *Your Excellency* has emphasized the importance of doing so. 閣下はそうすることの重要性を強調なさいました. ☞You [He] の代わりに用いる尊称，動詞は3人称単数動詞を用いる.

E

excellent /éksələnt/ 形 (***be***) ***excellent in*** …にすぐれて(いる) ▪ He *is excellent in* English. 彼は英語にすぐれている.

excelsior /eksélsiɔ̀ːr/ 名 (***as***) ***dry as excelsior*** 《米》からからに乾燥して ▪ The grass was *as dry as excelsior* in the heat. 芝生は暑さの中でかさかさに乾いていた. ☞excelsior「(詰物用の)木毛」.

except /ɪksépt/ 前 ***except for*** …があるのを除いては ▪ This is a charming book *except for* a few mistakes. これは少し誤りがあるだけで，すてきな本だ ▪ He is naked *except for* a shirt. 彼はシャツ1枚を除いて裸だ.

except that …であることを除けば[以外は] ▪ This plank will do *except that* it is too long. この厚板は長すぎる点を除けば結構である.

excepting /ɪkséptɪŋ/ 前 ***not excepting*** …も含めて，同様で ▪ All were present *not excepting* the principal. 校長も含めて全員出席した.

exception /ɪksépʃən/ 名 ***above*** [***beyond***] ***exception*** 非難[疑い]の余地のない ▪ I produce two witnesses *beyond exception*. 私は非難の余地のない二人の証人を出します.

allow [***make***] ***no exception*** 特別扱いをしない ▪ You must all take the examination; I can *make no exception*. 君たちはみな試験を受けなければならない. 特別扱いはできない.

allow [***admit***] ***of no exception*** (規則などが)例外を認めない ▪ This rule *allows of no exception*. この規則は例外を認めない.

liable [***open***] ***to exception*** 異議を唱えられる余地があって，非難を受ける余地があって ▪ The declaration is *liable to exception*. その宣言は非難される余地がある.

make an exception (***of***) (…を)例外とする，特別扱いする ▪ I will *make an exception of* your case. 君の場合は特別としよう.

subject to exception 異議を唱えられることがあって，反対[非難]されることがあって ▪ The witness is *subject to exception*. 証人は忌避されることがある.

take exception at …に腹を立てる ▪ Terry *took exception at* Martin [his remark]. テリーはマーティン[彼の意見]に腹を立てた.

take exception to [***against***] **1** …に異議を唱える, 反対する; (証人など)を忌避する ▪ We must *take exception to* the assertion. その主張に反対しなければならない ▪ He *took exception against* a witness. 彼は一人の証人を忌避した.
2 = take EXCEPTION at.

The exception proves the rule. 《諺》例外があることは規則の存在を証明する;《俗・戯》私の言い分が薄弱であればあるほど私の確信は一層強い《議論の敗北の言い訳》. ☞Every rule has an exception. の逆.

E

with (***the***) ***exception of*** …を除いて, のほかは ▪ *With the exception of* Harry, all the boys passed the examination. ハリーを除いては, すべての少年が試験にパスした.

without (***an***) ***exception*** 例外なく ▪ They are bachelors *without* (*an*) *exception*. 彼らは一人残らず独身である.

excess /ɪksés/ 名 ***an excess of** A **over** B* Bに対するAの超過(額) ▪ Vietnam has always seen *an excess of* imports *over* exports. ベトナムは常に輸出に対する輸入超過を見てきた.

carry ... to excess (抽象的なもの)をやりすぎる, の度を越す ▪ Don't *carry* your caution *to excess*. 用心の度を越えてはいけない.

commit excesses 暴飲暴食(など)をする; 乱暴狼藉(ろうぜき)を働く ▪ The troops *committed excesses* when they occupied the enemy's capital. 敵の首都を占領したときその軍隊は乱暴狼藉を働いた.

go [***run***] ***to excess*** 極端に走る, やりすぎる, 度を越す ▪ You don't *run to* the same *excess* of riot. 君はそうした度のすぎた乱行をしないよね.

have ... in excess …がありすぎる ▪ At present we *have* government *in excess*. 現在は統制がありすぎる.

in (***an***) ***excess*** 過度に, 過分に ▪ Nutritious substances, given *in excess*, kill the leaves. 栄養物質を過分に与えると葉が枯れる.

in excess of …より多く, より超過して ▪ We got £500 *in excess of* the fixed sum. 定額より500ポンド多くもらった.

to excess 過度に, すぎる ▪ He drinks *to excess*. 彼は酒を飲みすぎる ▪ He is generous *to excess*. 彼は気前がよすぎる.

exchange[1] /ɪkstʃéɪndʒ/ 名 ***Exchange is no robbery.*** 交換は強奪でない《不当な交換の弁解》.

in exchange (***for***) (…と)引き替えに ▪ I received a dictionary *in exchange*. 私は代わりに辞書をもらった ▪ I taught him English *in exchange for* Japanese. 私は彼に日本語を教えてもらう代わりに英語を教えた.

exchange[2] /ɪkstʃéɪndʒ/ 動 ***exchange words with*** …と言い合いをする, 口げんかをする ▪ It is foolish to *exchange words with* such a hypocrite. そんな偽善者と言い合いをするのはばかげている.

not exchange more than a few [***half a dozen***] ***words with*** 〚主に完了形で〛…とはあまり口をきかない ▪ I *haven't exchanged more than a few words with* my neighbor. 私は隣の人とあまり話したことはない.

excite /ɪksáɪt/ 動 ***be excited at*** [***by, over***] …に興奮する, で気が立つ(狂喜したり, 激怒したり) ▪ He *was excited* with joy *at* the victory. 彼は勝利に狂喜した ▪ He *was excited over* your conduct. 彼はあなたの行為に立腹していた.

become [***get***] ***excited*** 興奮する, 激する, 狂喜する ▪ They *got excited* at the news. 彼らはそのニュースを聞いて沸き立った.

Don't excite! 《口》落ち着きなさい.

***excite** oneself* 興奮する ▪ Don't *excite yourself*! 興奮してはいけません[落ち着きなさい].

excitement /ɪksáɪtmənt/ 名 ***cause excitement*** 騒ぎを起こす ▪ It *caused excitement* in the family. それは一家に騒ぎを起こした.

in excitement 気が立って, 興奮して, 激して ▪ He spoke *in excitement*. 彼は激して言った.

exclamation /èkskləméɪʃən/ 名 ***make exclamation against*** …を大声に非難する ▪ He *made* a horrible *exclamation against* Jack. 彼はジャックを恐ろしく大声で非難した.

exclusion /ɪksklúːʒən/ 名 ***to the exclusion of*** …を除外して ▪ Ryan is keen on football *to the exclusion of* all else. ライアンは他のものが一切眼中にないほどサッカーに夢中だ.

exclusive /ɪksklúːsɪv/ 形 ***exclusive of*** …を除いて (↔INCLUSIVE of) ▪ We need 25,000 yen *exclusive of* hotel expenses. 宿泊費を除いて25,000円必要だ.

from** A **to** B **exclusive AからBまで, ただし両端(AとB)は除く ▪ *from* 10 *to* 25 *exclusive* 10から25まで, ただし10と25は除く ▪ Write down the numbers *from* 20 *to* 30 *exclusive*. 20と30を除いて20から30までの数を書け.

exculpate /ékskʌlpèɪt/ 動 ***exculpate** oneself **from*** …は無実だと身のあかしを立てる[申し開きをする] ▪ He *exculpated himself from* the impeachment. 彼はその非難は当たらないと申し開きをした.

exculpate** a person **from a charge [***blame***] 人の無実の罪を晴らす ▪ She *exculpates* me *from blame* in this matter. この件について彼女が私の無実の罪を晴らしてくれる.

excursion /ɪkskə́ːrʒən|-ʃən/ 名 ***go on an excursion*** (***to***) (…へ)遠足[旅行]に行く ▪ We *went on a* school *excursion to* the city last year. 我々は昨年その都市へ修学旅行に行った.

make [***take***] ***an excursion*** (***to, into***) (…へ)遠足[旅行]に行く ▪ We *made an excursion into* the country. 我々は田舎へ遠足[小旅行]に行った.

excuse[1] /ɪkskjúːs/ 名 ***a poor*** [***feeble, lame, miserable, rotten, sorry***] ***excuse for*** …に関する下手な言い訳[説得力のない申し訳, 弱い口実, 貧弱な弁解, ひどい逃げ口, おそまつな理由] ▪ It's *a poor excuse for* a poor excuse. それは下手な言い訳への下手な言い訳だ ▪ That's just *a lame excuse for* bad design. それはデザインがまずいことへの説

得力のない弁明だ.

be no excuse (…は)言い訳にならない ▪ Ignorance of the law *is no excuse*. 法律を知らないことは言い訳にならない ▪ It *is no excuse* for his conduct. それは彼の行為の言い訳にはならない.

give *one's* [*a person's*] ***excuses for*** …してすまないと言う[人がすまないと思っていると言う] ▪ I *gave* him *my excuses for* being late. 私は遅くなってすみませんと彼に言った ▪ Please *give* them *my excuses for* being late. 私が遅くなってすまないと思っていると彼らに伝えてください.

have no excuse for …に対しては弁解が立たない ▪ You *have no excuse for* being late. 君が遅刻した言い訳は立たない.

in excuse of …の言い訳に ▪ You cannot plead ignorance *in excuse of* your conduct. あなたは自分の行為の言い訳として知らなかったからだと言うわけにはいかない.

make an excuse (***for***) (…の)言い訳をする ▪ I am poor at *making excuses*. 私は言い訳がへたです.

make *a person's* ***excuses*** (***to***) (…に)人の言い訳をしてやる ▪ *Make my excuses to* your mother. おかあさんに私の言い訳をしてください.

without excuse 理由なしに ▪ Those who are absent *without excuse* will be punished. 理由なしに欠席する人々は罰せられる.

excuse[2] /ɪkskjúːz/ 動 ***be excused*** 《口》席をはずす; トイレに行く ▪ May I *be excused*, sir? 先生, トイレに行かせてください.

be excused (***from***) …を免除される ▪ I want to *be excused* (*from*) my lesson. 習い事を休ませてください.

excuse *oneself* **1** あやまる, 弁解する (*for*) ▪ You must *excuse yourself for* your conduct. あなたは自分の行為に対してあやまらねばならない ▪ It is no use *excusing yourself*. 言い訳してもむだである ▪ He who *excuses himself* accuses himself. 《諺》何かの弁明をすると, それをやったと認めることになる.

2 辞退する, ごめんこうむりたいと言う (*from*) ▪ He *excused himself from* coming. 彼は来られないと言って断った.

3 中座する, 辞去する ▪ He *excused himself*. 彼は辞去した.

4 すみません[ごめんください]と言う ▪ If you pass in front of another, *excuse yourself*. 人の前を通るときはすみませんと言いなさい.

Excuse me. ごめんください, 失礼します ▪ *Excuse me*, but will you tell me the way to the station? 失礼ですが, 駅へ行く道を教えてくださいませんか.

Excuse me for *doing*. …してすみません ▪ *Excuse me for interrupting* you. お話をじゃましてすみません ▪ *Excuse me for leaving* you. ちょっと失礼いたします《中座のあいさつ》.

Excuse me for living [***breathing***]***!*** 《口》それは悪かったね, おあいにく様《非難に対する皮肉な返答》.

execute /éksəkjùːt/ 動 ***execute an estate*** (特定の法の発効により)財産権を譲る ▪ The *estate was executed* to them by authority of this act. この法令の権威によってその財産権は彼らに譲られた.

execution /èksɪkjúːʃən/ 名 (***be***) ***in execution*** 判決の執行を受けて(いる), (借金不払いのため)差し押さえをされ[身柄を拘引されて(いる) ▪ The prisoner *is in execution* at the jail. その囚人は刑務所で判決の執行を受けている.

carry … into execution …を実行[実施]する ▪ We decided to *carry* the project *into execution*. 我々はその計画を実行することに決めた.

do execution 偉力を発揮する, 偉効を奏する, (敵・食物を)大いにやっつける ▪ Her charms *do execution*. 彼女の魅力は(男を)悩殺する ▪ Our machine guns *did execution* among the enemy. わが機関銃は敵をさんざんやっつけた ▪ He *did* great *execution* among the sandwiches. 彼はサンドイッチをもりもり食った.

have execution 巧妙である, 老練である ▪ The pianist *has* marvellous *execution*. そのピアニストは驚くほど巧妙である.

have … for execution 《法》…を判決を執行するため拘置する; (借金不払いのため)差し押さえ[身柄の拘引]をする ▪ I'll *have* their bodies in prison *for execution*. 借金不払いのため彼らの身柄を拘引しよう.

put … in [***into***] ***execution*** …を実行する, 実施する ▪ We must *put* the plan *into execution*. 我々はその計画を実施せねばならない.

sue [***take***] ***forth execution against*** [***upon***] …に対して判決の執行をしてもらう; (借金不払いのため)…に対し差し押さえ[身柄の拘引]をしてもらう ▪ They *took forth execution against* the defendant. 彼らは被告に対する判決を執行してもらった ▪ He will *sue forth execution upon* the merchant. 彼はその商人を借金不払いのため差し押さえてもらうだろう.

take … in execution (借金不払いのため)…の差し押さえをする, 身柄を拘引する ▪ He *was taken in execution* on a private debt. 彼は個人的な借金のため身柄を拘引された.

exemplify /ɪgzémpləfàɪ/ 動 ***exemplify*** *A* ***by*** (***means of***) *B* BによってAを例証する, Aを示すのにBを用いる ▪ He *exemplified* his point *by* an anecdote. 彼はある逸話を引いておのれの論点を示した ▪ Elitists believed the poor *exemplified* their inferiority *by means of* their economic situation. エリート主義者たちは, 貧乏人は自らが劣っていることを彼らの経済状況によって実証していると信じていた.

exempt /ɪgzémpt/ 形 (***be***) ***exempt from*** **1** …を免れている ▪ Ecclesiastical societies *are exempt from* civil control. 教会団体は公民的統制を免れている.

2 …に免疫がある ▪ They *are* not *exempt from* earthly trouble. 彼らは浮き世の苦難に免疫がない.

3 …を免除されている ▪ Men of a certain age *are exempt from* serving in the army. ある年齢の男子は兵役を免除されている.

4 (欠点・けがれなど)がない ▪ He *is exempt from*

the common failings of humanity. 彼には人によくある欠点というものがない.

exercise[1] /éksərsàɪz/ 名 ***bring ... into exercise*** ...を働かせる, 運用する ▪ Self-dependence will *bring* his talents *into exercise*. 自己信頼は彼の才能を発揮させるであろう.

take exercise 運動をする ▪ You must *take* moderate *exercise* every day. 毎日適度な運動をせねばなりません.

the aim [***point***] ***of the exercise*** その行為の真の目的, 背後にひそむ目的 ▪ *The aim of the exercise* is to improve my mind. その行為の真の目的は精神を向上させることにある.

E

exercise[2] /éksərsàɪz/ 動 ***be exercised about*** [***over***] ...について心配する, 頭を悩ます ▪ I *was* greatly *exercised about* the result. 私はその結果について大いに心配した.

exercise *oneself* ***in*** ...の練習をする, けいこをする ▪ She was *exercising herself in* the piano. 彼女はピアノのけいこをしていた.

exercise *oneself* ***over*** [***about***] ...で頭を悩ます, 心配する ▪ Don't *exercise yourself over* the affair. このことで頭を悩まさないでください.

exert /ɪgzə́:rt/ 動 ***exert*** *oneself* 努力する ▪ Every man must *exert himself* for the general good. 人はみな世のためになるよう努力すべきである.

exertion /ɪgzə́:rʃən/ 名 ***use*** [***make, put forth***] ***exertion*** 尽力する, 骨を折る ▪ I will *use* every *exertion* to help you. 全力を尽くしてお助けしましょう.

exhale /ekshéɪl/ 動 ***exhale*** *oneself* (熱情・憤怒)をぶちまける, 吐露する ▪ I have *exhaled myself* in my journal on the sin of slavery. 私は自分の日誌に奴隷制度の罪について考えを吐露した.

exhaust /ɪgzɔ́:st/ 動 ***be exhausted with*** [***by***] ...で疲れ果てている ▪ I *was exhausted with* toil. 私は労苦で疲れ果てていた.

exhaust *oneself* ***by*** ...で力を出し尽くす ▪ He *exhausted himself by* hard work. 彼は精励して力を出し尽くした.

exhibition /èksəbíʃən/ 名 ***make an*** [***a regular***] ***exhibition of*** *oneself* 《口》(ばかなことをして)いい恥をさらす ▪ I *made an exhibition of myself*. 私はいい恥さらしをした.

on exhibition 展示[覧]されて ▪ Their pictures are *on exhibition* at the museum. 彼らの絵は美術館に展示されている.

place ... on exhibition ...を展示する ▪ He *placed* his works *on exhibition*. 彼は自分の作品を展示した.

exhort /ɪgzɔ́:rt/ 動 ***exhort*** *a person* ***to*** [***to*** *do*] ...するように人に説き勧める ▪ He *exhorted* his pupils *to* good deeds [*to* do good]. 彼は生徒に善行をするよう説き勧めた.

exhortation /ègzɔ:rtéɪʃən/ 名 ***make an exhortation*** (牧師が)戒告をする ▪ He *made an exhortation*. 彼は戒告をした.

exigency /éksədʒənsi/ 名 ***be reduced to exigency*** 危機[困難]に陥る ▪ Their country *was reduced to* great *exigency*. 彼らの国は非常な危機に陥った.

meet the exigencies of ...の急に応じる ▪ We must *meet the exigencies of* the times. 時勢の急に応じなければならない.

suit the exigency 急場の間に合う[に応じる] ▪ I am prepared to *suit the exigency*. 私は急場に応じる用意がある.

exigent /éksədʒənt/ 形 ***exigent of*** ...を要求する ▪ He is *exigent of* rest. 彼は休息を求めている.

exigible /éksədʒəbəl/ 形 ***exigible from*** [***against***] *a person* 人に要求できる ▪ This service is now *exigible from* them. 今ならこのアフターサービスを彼らに要求できる.

exile[1] /égzaɪl/ 名 ***be*** [***live***] ***in exile*** 追放[流浪]の身である[の生活をする] ▪ He *lives in exile* in England. 彼はイギリスに亡命している.

condemn *a person* ***to exile*** 人を追放[流罪]にする ▪ Dostoevsky *was condemned to exile*. ドストエフスキーは流刑に処せられた.

go into exile 追放[流浪]の身となる ▪ She was taken prisoner and *went into exile*. 彼は捕虜となり, 追放された.

send [***drive***] *a person* ***into exile*** 人を追放[流罪]にする ▪ He *was sent into exile* to a remote island. 彼は遠島に流された.

exile[2] /égzaɪl/ 動 ***exile*** *oneself* 亡命する, 流浪する ▪ Marx *exiled himself* to London. マルクスはロンドンに亡命した.

existence /ɪgzístəns/ 名 ***an empty existence*** 無意味な生活, 無為な生き方 ▪ He felt he was living a pointless and *empty existence*. 彼は, 自分は無意味で空疎な人生を送っていると思った.

bring [***call***] ***... into existence*** ...を生ぜしめる, 生み出す, 成立させる ▪ God *brought* heaven and earth *into existence*. 神は天地を生ぜしめ給うた.

come into existence 生まれる; 施行される ▪ A new spirit has *come into existence* since the War. 大戦以来新しい精神が生まれた ▪ The regulations *came into existence* on June 1st. その規則は6月1日に施行された.

in existence 現存して; この世の[にある]《しばしば最上級などを強める》 ▪ It is still *in existence*. それは今なお存在する ▪ This is the largest ship *in existence*. これは世界最大の船である.

lead a ... existence ...な生活をする ▪ He is *leading a* wretched *existence*. 彼はみじめな生活をしている.

out of existence 無くなって ▪ Many banks have gone *out of existence* in the last few years. ここ数年で多くの銀行が消滅した.

put [***snuff***] ***... out of existence*** ...を滅ぼす[殺す] ▪ He *put* the old woman *out of existence*. 彼がその老婦人を殺した.

tax ... out of existence ...を重税をかけて滅ぼす

[殺す] ▪ The government *taxed* the landed classes *out of existence.* 政府は地主階級に重税をかけて滅ぼした.

to the last hour of *one's* ***existence*** いまわの際まで ▪ I will work *to the last hour of my existence.* この世にあるかぎり働きます.

exit /égzət|éksɪt/ 名 ***make*** *one's* ***exit*** **1** 出て行く, 退場する ▪ He *made his exit* from the stage. 彼は舞台から退場した.

2 この世を去る ▪ He *made his exit* by falling under a lorry. 彼はトラックの下敷きになって死んだ.

expatriate /ekspéɪtriət|-pǽt-/ 動 ***expatriate*** *oneself* (国外へ)移住する; (特に, 帰化するため)国籍を脱する ▪ He *expatriated himself* for years in Brazil. 彼は長年ブラジルに移住していた.

expect /ɪkspékt/ 動 ***as expected*** 予想通りで ▪ This was *as expected.* これは予想通りだった.

as might be expected **(*of*)**/ ***as*** *one* ***might expect*** **(*of*)** 当然予期される通りに; さすがに ▪ *As might be expected of* a samurai, he was as good as his word. 彼はさすがに武士だけあって約束を守った.

as might have been expected 果たせるかな, 案の定 ▪ *As might have been expected*, he was an imposter. 案の定彼は詐欺師だった.

as was expected 予期した通りに ▪ He came at 7 in the morning *as was expected.* 彼は予期した通り午前7時に来た.

be expecting 《口》(近いうちに)お産がある ▪ She *is expecting.* 彼女は近いうちに出産予定だ.

be **(*only*)** ***to be expected*** 予想通りで ▪ Tom's failure *was* (*only*) *to be expected*, considering his bad grades. ひどい成績のことを考えれば, トムが落第したのは不思議ではない.

Don't expect me till you see me. 私の好きなときに(ここへ)来させてください.

I shall not expect you till I see you. あなたの好きなときにおいでください《無礼な言い方》.

What **(*else*)** ***can*** **[*do*]** ***you expect?*** 何が期待できるだろうか《何も期待できない》.

expectance, expectancy /ɪkspéktənsi/ 名 ***after long expectance*** 《古》長く待ちわびた後 ▪ *After long expectance*, they went into action. 長く待ちわびた後, 彼らは(軍事)行動に移った.

in expectancy いずれ所有するはずの ▪ The law as to "estates *in expectancy*" is the most unsatisfactory part of our jurisprudence. 「将来不動産」に関する法律はわが国の法体系で最も不満足な部分だ.

expectation /èkspektéɪʃən/ 名 ***according to*** *one's* ***expectation*(*s*)** 予期の通りに ▪ It happened *according to his expectation.* それは彼の予期した通りに起こった.

against **[*contrary to*]** (*one's*) ***expectations*** 予期に反して ▪ *Contrary to my expectations*, the enemy retreated. 予期に反して敵は退却した.

answer **[*meet, come up to, live up to*]** *a person's* ***expectation*(*s*)** …の期待に添う ▪ He did not *answer the expectations of* his friends. 彼は友人たちの期待に添わなかった.

beyond (*one's*) ***expectation*(*s*)** 予期以上で[の], 予想外の[に] ▪ The beauties of Florence in spring were *beyond his expectation.* 春のフィレンツェの美しさは彼の予想以上だった ▪ Nature perfected a cure *beyond expectation.* 自然の力で予想外に完治した.

entertain expectations of …に期待をかけている ▪ We *entertain* great *expectations of* his ability. 我々は彼の才能に大きな望みをかけている.

expectation of life **1** 平均寿命[余命] (life expectancy) ▪ What was western civilization's *expectation of life* in 1955? 1955年における西洋文明の平均余命は何年だったか.

2 ものの寿命, 耐用年数 ▪ What is the usual *expectation of life* of an LED bulb? LED電球の平均耐用年数はどれほどですか.

fall short of *one's* ***expectation*(*s*)** 期待に添わない ▪ He *falls short of our expectations.* 彼は我々が期待したほどではない.

have expectations **1** (…から)遺産相続の見込みがある (*from*) ▪ He *has expectations from* his uncle. 彼はおじから大きな遺産を受ける見込みがある.

2 …に期待する (*of*) ▪ We *have* great *expectations of* him. 我々は彼に大いに期待している.

in expectation 予期の; 予期して ▪ I have something *in expectation.* 心当たりの金が少しある ▪ We are waiting *in expectation* that there is hope for us. 我々には希望があると期待して待っている.

in expectation of …を期待して, 見越して ▪ He bought it *in expectation of* a war. 彼は戦争を見越してそれを買った.

meet *a person's* ***expectation*(*s*)** →answer a person's EXPECTATION(s).

of expectations (大きな)遺産相続の見込みのある ▪ He is a man *of expectations.* 彼は大きな遺産を受ける見込みがある.

expectorate /ɪkspéktərèɪt/ 動 ***expectorate*** *oneself* (思うことをぶちまけて)胸を晴らす ▪ He took to verses, by way of *expectorating himself.* 彼は思いをぶちまけて胸を晴らすため詩を作り始めた.

expedite /ékspədàɪt/ 動 ***expedite matters*** 事をはかどらせる ▪ That will *expedite matters.* そうすれば事がはかどる.

expedition /èkspədíʃən/ 名 ***a fishing expedition*** 《主に米》(秘密裏の)情報収集, 証拠集め ▪ He objected to any agency going on *a "fishing expedition"* merely on a suspicion. 彼は, どの機関であれ単なる疑惑に基ついて情報収集をすることに反対した.

go on an expedition 遠征[探検]の途にのぼる ▪ They *went on an expedition.* 彼らは遠征の途についた.

make an expedition 遠征する, 探検の旅をする ▪ They *made an expedition* into the interior of Australia. 彼らはオーストラリアの奥地へ探検の旅をした.

E

use expedition 素早くやる ▪ He *used* all the *expedition* possible. 彼はできるかぎり素早くやった.

with expedition 大急ぎで, さっさと ▪ I sent him to the court *with expedition*. 大急ぎで彼を宮廷へやった.

expel /ɪkspél/ 動 ***be expelled (from ...)*** (…を)放逐される ▪ He *was expelled* (*from* the school). 彼は放校[退学]になった.

expense /ɪkspéns/ 名 ***(all) expenses paid*** 〚限定的〛会社[招待者]払いの ▪ Richard won an *all-expenses-paid* trip to Milwaukee to see the game. リチャードはミルウォーキーに試合観戦に行く招待旅行にあたった.

and expenses …と雑費 ▪ He offered me $100 *and expenses*. 彼は私に100ドルと雑費を提供した.

at an expense (of) (…の)経費[損失]をかけて ▪ All operations are *at an* immense *expense of* human lives. すべての軍事行動には多大な人命の損失がある ▪ We maintained the zoo *at an* immense *expense*. 膨大な経費をかけて動物園を維持した.

at any expense どんなに費用がかかっても, どんな犠牲を払っても, どうしても ▪ I must accomplish it *at any expense*. ぜひともそれをなし遂げなければならない.

at** a person's **expense **1** 人に費用を出させて ▪ He made a trip round the world *at his father's expense*. 彼は父に費用を出させて世界一周旅行をした.

2 =at the EXPENSE of 2.

at Government [public] expense 国[公]費で ▪ He studied abroad *at Government expense*. 彼は国費で外国留学をした.

at** one's **own expense 自費で; 自分を犠牲にして ▪ He published the book *at his own expense*. 彼はその本を自費で出版した.

at the expense of **1** …の費用で ▪ He built a new house *at the expense of* £80,000. 彼は80,000ポンドの費用で新しい家を建てた.

2 …を犠牲にして, に迷惑をかけて, を傷つけて ▪ He learned French *at the expense of* his health. 彼は健康を犠牲にしてフランス語を学んだ ▪ You defend his veracity *at the expense of* understanding. 彼の言ったことが本当だというなら, 彼はばかだということになるよ ▪ We had a good laugh *at his expense*. 我々は彼をさかなに大いに笑った.

be at ... expense(s) (…の)金を使う ▪ He *was at* some *expense* on that account. 彼はそのためにいくらか金を使った.

be at the expense of …の金を使う ▪ He *was at the expense of* $100. 彼は100ドル使った.

***go to (some, great) expense to** do* …するのに(いくらか, 大きな)金を使う ▪ He *went to great expense to* employ good teachers. 彼は良い先生を雇うのに多額の金を使った.

***go to the expense of** doing* 金をかけて…までする ▪ It's foolish to *go to the expense of getting* a piano teacher. 金をかけてピアノの先生まで頼むのはばかげている.

meet** one's **expenses 費用に間に合わす[に当てる] ▪ I have no money to *meet my expenses*. 私の費用に当てる金がない.

no expense (is) spared 金に糸目をつけない, 金を惜しまない ▪ It was an all-star cast, *no expense spared* on the stage. それはスター総出演であり, 舞台費用は惜しみなく使われていた ▪ *No expense was spared* in making the party glorious. パーティーを豪華なものにするため金に糸目はつけられなかった ▪ He built himself a gorgeous house, *no expense spared*. 彼は金に糸目をつけず豪邸を建てた.

pay** a person's **expenses 人の経費を出してやる ▪ He offers to *pay my expenses* through the university. 彼は大学卒業までの私の学費を出してやろうと言っている.

put** a person **to expense 人に金を使わせる, 費用を出させる ▪ I am sorry for *putting* you *to* such *expense*. 君にこんなに散財させてすまない.

regardless of expense 費用を顧みないで, 金に飽かせて ▪ She dresses *regardless of expense*. 彼女は金に飽かせて着飾る.

spare no expense →SPARE no pains.

expensive /ɪkspénsɪv/ 形 ***come expensive*** 高くつく, 金がかかる ▪ Indeed, you *come* rather *expensive*. 実際, あなたはけっこう金がかかる.

experience[1] /ɪkspíəriəns/ 名 ***a [one's] near-death experience [NDE]*** 臨死体験 ▪ Many people were given visions of the future during *their near-death experience*. 臨死体験の間に未来図を見せられた人は多い.

an out-of-body experience [OBE] 体外[幽体]離脱体験 ▪ One in ten people has *an out-of-body experience* at some time in their lives. 10人中1人は生涯のいつか体外離脱体験をしている.

buy** one's **experience →gain one's EXPERIENCE.

by [from] experience 経験で, 経験して ▪ People learn *by experience*. 人々は経験して学ぶ ▪ I know this *from experience*. 経験でこの事を知っている.

chalk ... up to experience 《米》(失敗など)を経験として今後に生かす, 失敗を薬[教訓]にする (→put ... down to EXPERIENCE) ▪ *Chalk* this one *up to experience*. このことを経験とし(て学び)なさい.

Experience does it. 《口》経験が肝心だ.

Experience is the best teacher. 《諺》経験は最良の教師である.

Experience is the father of wisdom. 《諺》経験は知恵の父.

for the experience 経験になると思って ▪ I did it just *for the experience*. ただ経験になると思ってそれをしただけです.

gain [buy]** one's **experience 経験を積む ▪ He is *gaining his experience* by degrees. 彼はだんだんと経験を積んでいる.

gain experience in …において経験を積む ▪ I *gained experience in* commanding employees.

私は従業員を指図する経験を積んだ.
have experience of …の経験がある; を受ける ▪ He *has experience of* teaching [her kindness]. 彼は教授の経験がある[彼女の親切を受けた].
have experience with …を扱った[教えた]経験がある ▪ I *had experience with* Chinese students. 私は中国の学生を教えた経験がある.
profit by experience 経験して賢くなる[こりごりする] ▪ You may *profit by* this *experience*. この経験で賢くなるがよい[を生かすがよい].
put ... down to experience (失敗など)を経験として今後に生かす, 失敗を薬[教訓]にする (→chalk ... up to EXPERIENCE) ▪ In any sport, you *put* these things *down to experience* and make sure you learn the lesson. どんなスポーツでもこういうことを経験として生かし, 教訓を学ぶようにしなさい. ☞put down (書き記す).
relate** one's **experiences 経験談をする; 宗教的生活の体験を述べる ▪ The old man *related his experience* during the war. 老人は戦時中の経験談をした.

experience[2] /ɪkspíəriəns/ 動 ***be experienced in*** …に経験がある, 熟練している ▪ He *is experienced in* teaching. 彼は教えることに熟練している.
experience religion →get RELIGION.

experiment /ɪkspérəmənt/ 名 ***by way of experiment*** 試しに ▪ I will employ him *by way of experiment*. 試しに彼を雇ってみよう.
make [conduct, try] experiment on [in] …の実験をする ▪ He *made experiment on* electricity. 彼は電気の実験をした.

expert /ékspəːrt/ 形 ***be expert in [at, on]*** …に熟練した, の専門家で ▪ He *is expert in* carving. 彼は彫刻に熟達している ▪ They *are expert at* this work. 彼らはこの仕事の専門家である.

expiation /èkspiéɪʃən/ 名 ***in expiation of*** …の償いに, の罪滅ぼしに ▪ The Abbey was built *in expiation of* the murder of Saint Thomas. ウェストミンスター寺院は聖トマス殺害の罪滅ぼしに建てられた.
make expiation (for) (…の)償いをする ▪ He *made expiation for* our sins on the cross. 彼は十字架にかかって我々の罪の償いをした.

expiration /èkspəréɪʃən/ 名 ***at the expiration of*** …が満了のとき, が経ってから ▪ He retired *at the expiration of* his term of office. 彼は任期が満了したとき引退した ▪ The bomb was set to explode *at the expiration of* 10 minutes. 爆弾は10分経ったら爆発するようにセットされていた.

expiry /ɪkspáɪəri/ 名 ***at the expiry of*** …の満了のとき ▪ He returned to Scotland *at the expiry of* the exhibition at London. ロンドンの博覧会が終わると, 彼はスコットランドへ帰った.

explain /ɪkspléɪn/ 動 ***explain** oneself* **1** 考えをはっきり言う; 自己の立場を弁明する ▪ He succeeded in *explaining himself*. 彼は自分の立場の弁明に成功した ▪ We desired him to *explain himself*. 我々は彼に考えをはっきり言ってほしかった.
2 自分の意中を明らかにする[打ち明ける] ▪ *Explain yourself*, Adeline. アデライン, 意中を打ち明けなさい.
explain matters 事情の説明となる ▪ That *explains matters*. なるほどそれでわかった.

explanation /èksplənéɪʃən/ 名 ***come to an explanation with*** …と互いに話し合いがつく[和解する] ▪ I'll *come to an explanation with* him on the subject. その問題について彼と話し合いがつくでしょう ▪ I resolved to *come to an explanation with* her. 彼女と和解しようと心を決めた.
find an explanation of …が解ける ▪ We have *found a* complete *explanation of* the mystery. その謎がすっかり解けた.
in explanation of …の釈明[説明]に ▪ Did he say anything *in explanation of* his conduct? 彼は自分の行為の釈明に何か言ったか.

explanatory /ɪksplǽnətɔ̀ːri|-təri/ 形 ***be explanatory of*** …の説明となる ▪ These words *are explanatory of* his meaning. これらの言葉は彼が言いたいことの説明となっている.

explicit /ɪksplísət/ 形 ***be explicit in*** …が隠すところなくはっきりして ▪ He *is explicit in* his statement. 彼は腹蔵なく述べる.

explode /ɪksplóʊd/ 動 ***explode a bombshell*** →BOMBSHELL.
explode with laughter [rage,** etc.**] 爆笑する[激怒する, など] ▪ They *exploded with laughter* at the news. 彼らはそのニュースを聞いて爆笑した.

expose /ɪkspóʊz/ 動 ***be exposed to*** (方角が)…向きである ▪ The house *is exposed to* the east. その家は東向きである.
expose** oneself **to …に身をさらす, を一身に浴びる ▪ If you go there, you may *expose yourself to* danger. そこへ行けば, 君は身を危険にさらすかもしれない ▪ He *exposed himself to* severe criticism. 彼はきびしい批評を一身に浴びた.

expostulate /ɪkspɑ́stʃəlèɪt|-pɔ́stju-/ 動 ***expostulate with** a person **on [about]*** 《文》…について人に苦言[反対, 反論]を言う, 説いて聞かせる ▪ I *expostulated with* him *on* (the impropriety of) his conduct. 私は彼の行為(の不都合)について彼を諭した.

exposure /ɪkspóʊʒər/ 名 ***die of exposure*** のたれ死にする ▪ Those bandits *died of exposure*. 山賊どもはのたれ死にした.
in fear of exposure (収賄などの)発覚[露顕]を恐れて ▪ He lives *in fear of exposure*. 彼は発覚を恐れながら暮らしている.

express[1] /ɪksprés/ 形名 ***at express speed*** 特急で, 特別早く ▪ He traveled *at express speed*. 彼は特急で移動(旅行)した.
by express **1** 急行で ▪ We traveled *by express*. 急行で旅行した.
2 《米》 運送便で (↔by FREIGHT) ▪ Send it *by express*. それを運送便で発送しなさい.
3 《英》 速達便で ▪ I sent the letter *by express*.

速達便で手紙を送った.

express[2] /ɪksprés/ 動 ***express*** *oneself* **1** 話す, 意志を通じる ▪ He *expresses himself* in good English. 彼は正しい英語を話す ▪ He can't *express himself* in English. 彼は英語で意思を通じられない.
2 考えを述べる, 思想を発表する ▪ He *expressed himself* clearly. 彼は思うことをはっきり述べた.
3 顕現する, 現れる ▪ The inward beauty *expresses itself* in the outward. 内側の美は外側に現れる.

express *oneself* ***strongly*** 強い(特に否定・反対の)意見を吐く ▪ He *expresses himself strongly* in his unprinted writings. 彼は印刷されない文章では強い意見を述べる.

expression /ɪkspréʃən/ 名 ***beyond*** [***past***] ***expression*** 言葉で言い表せないような ▪ This is cruelty *beyond expression*. これは言葉では言えないほどの残酷さである.

find [***seek***] ***expression*** (***in***) (…に)表れる, 表現される ▪ Ideas *find expression in* institutions. 思想が制度となって現れる.

give expression to …を表現する ▪ Her sobs prevented her from *giving expression to* her gratitude. 彼女は泣きじゃくって感謝の言葉を言うことができなかった.

with expression 表現豊かに ▪ He plays the violin *with expression*. 彼は表現豊かにバイオリンをひく.

expressive /ɪksprésɪv/ 形 (***be***) ***expressive of*** …を表す ▪ His words *were expressive of* gratitude. 彼の言葉は感謝を表した.

extend /ɪksténd/ 動 ***extend*** *oneself* **1** (馬・走者・漕者などが)全力を出す, (一般に)全力を尽くす ▪ The horse *extended himself*. その馬は全力を出した ▪ What'll he do when he really *extends himself*? 彼が本当に全力を出すとどれほどやるだろうか.
2 (…の方へ)散開する (*to*) ▪ The battalion *extended itself to* the enemy's flank. 歩兵大隊は敵軍の側面をついて散開した.

extend a call (***to***) (…に)牧師就任を求める ▪ Plymouth Church has decided to *extend a call to* Charles Berry. プリマス教会はチャールズ・ベリーに牧師就任を求めることに決定した.

extend a warm [***cordial***] ***welcome to*** 《米》…を温かく[心から]歓迎する ▪ They *extended a cordial welcome to* me. 彼らは私を心から歓迎してくれた.

extend credit to *a person*/***extend*** *a person* ***credit*** 人に信用販売[掛け売り]をする, 人につけで売る ▪ Dressed in those rags you can't expect the store to *extend* you *credit*. そんな粗末な身なりをしていては店につけで売ってはもらえないよ. ☞extend = offer, provide.

extend help [***a helping hand***] (***to***) (…に)救いの手を差し延べる ▪ He *extended a helping hand to* the poor. 彼は貧しい人々に救いの手を差し延べた.

extension /ɪksténʃən/ 名 ***build an extension to*** …へ建て増しをする ▪ He *built an extension to* his house. 彼は家へ建て増しをした.

put an extension to …に継ぎ足し[増築, 増設]をする ▪ I am thinking of *putting an extension to* my house. 自宅を増築しようと思っている.

extent /ɪkstént/ 名 ***reach the extent*** (***of***) (…の)極点に達する ▪ We have *reached the extent of* our trip. 我々は旅の終点に達した.

to a great extent 大いに; 大部分は ▪ The adult is *to a great extent* a bundle of habits. おとなは大部分癖の固まりのようなものだ.

to an extent …の程度に[まで] ▪ I agree with you *to a* certain *extent*. ある程度まではあなたと同意見です ▪ Niel trusted her *to an* unlimited *extent*. ニールは彼女を限りなく信用した.

to some extent ある程度まで ▪ *To some extent* you are right. ある程度まで君は正しい.

to such an extent that →to the EXTENT that.

to the extent of …の程度まで, ほども ▪ I owe him *to the extent of* £100. 彼に100ポンドも借金がある ▪ I will cooperate with you *to the extent of* giving you some suggestions. 君に示唆を与える程度には協力します.

to the extent that …するほど ▪ The tides have risen *to the extent that* it's almost covered the seawall. 高潮が寄せてきて防潮堤をおおうくらいだった.

to the full [***utmost***] ***extent*** 十分[最大限]に ▪ We must utilize it *to the full extent*. 我々はそれを十分に利用しなければならない.

to the full extent of *one's* ***power*** 力の限り, 精いっぱい ▪ He works *to the full extent of his power*. 彼は力の限り働く.

To what extent ...? どの程度に ▪ *To what extent* can he be trusted? どの程度彼は信用できるか.

What is the extent of ...? …はどの程度か ▪ *What is the extent of* your debt? あなたの借金はどのくらいか.

extenuate /ɪksténjuèɪt/ 動 ***extenuating circumstances*** →CIRCUMSTANCE.

extenuation /ɪkstènjuéɪʃən/ 名 ***in extenuation of*** …の軽減のため ▪ He pleaded poverty *in extenuation of* his guilt. 彼は罪を軽くするために貧困のためだったと言い訳をした.

exterior /ekstíəriər/ 形 ***exterior to*** …の外部の; とは無関係の ▪ They are matters *exterior to* his real character. それらは彼の本性とは無関係の事柄だ.

external /ɪkstə́ːrnəl/ 形 ***for external use*** (薬が)外用で ▪ This medicine is *for external use*. この薬は外用である.

extinguish /ɪkstíŋgwɪʃ/ 動 ***take oil to extinguish a fire*** なだめようとしてかえって激させる; 火に油を注ぐ ▪ That'll be *taking oil to extinguish a fire*. それは火事を消すため油を使うようなものだ《かえって激させることになる》.

extol /ɪkstóʊl/ 動 ***extol*** *a person* ***to the skies*** [***the heavens***] 人を口をきわめてほめたたえる

▪ Some will *extol* you *to the skies*. あなたを口をきわめてほめあげる人もいるだろう.

extra /ékstrə/ 形 ***go the extra mile*** (***for***) (…のために)一層の努力をする, もうひと頑張りする ▪ Students must *go the extra mile for* college acceptance. 生徒たちは大学合格のためにはもっと努力しなければならない.

have an extra pull 有利な点[長所]を持つ ▪ *I've got an extra pull* in knowing their language. 私は彼らの国の言葉を知っているから有利である.

extract[1] /ékstrækt/ 名 ***make extracts from*** …から抜粋する ▪ I *made extracts from* the book. 私はその本から抜粋した.

extract[2] /ɪkstrǽkt/ 動 ***extract the root of*** …の根(こん)を出す ▪ *Extract the* cube *root of* 27. 27の立方根を求めよ.

extraction /ɪkstrǽkʃən/ 名 ***of*** **…** ***extraction*** …生まれの, 家柄の ▪ She comes from a family *of* ancient *extraction*. 彼女は古い家柄の出だ ▪ He is *of* Japanese *extraction*. 彼は日系である.

extraneous /ekstréɪniəs/ 形 ***extraneous to*** …に無関係の ▪ This matter is *extraneous to* the question. その事柄はその問題に無関係だ.

extravagant /ɪkstrǽvəgənt/ 形 (***be***) ***extravagant in*** [***with***] …に贅沢で(ある) ▪ She *is extravagant in* her way of living. 彼女は暮らしが贅沢である ▪ He *is extravagant with* his clothes. 彼は着道楽だ.

extreme /ɪkstríːm/ 形名 ***carry*** **…** ***to*** [***into***] ***extremes*** [***an extreme***] …を極端にやる ▪ Logic *was carried to extremes*. 理論が極端になった.

drive *a person* ***to extremes*** [***extreme measures***] 人が(無生物主語に)耐えかねて最後の手段を取る ▪ His obstinacy *drove* me *to extremes*. 彼が強情なためやむを得ず私は最後の手段を取った.

Extremes meet. 《諺》両極端は一致する.

go from one extreme to the other [***another***] 極端から極端に走る, 正反対な行動をとる ▪ There are better alternatives than *going from one extreme to another*. 極端から極端に走るよりももっとよい選択肢がある.

go to extremes **1** 極端に走る ▪ He *went to extremes* to satisfy their curiosity. 彼らの好奇心を満足させるため彼は極端なことをした.

2 最後の手段を取る ▪ I *went to extremes* without giving him fair warning. 彼には十分余裕をもって予告せずに私は最後の手段を取った.

go to the extreme of …という極端なことをやる ▪ They *went to the extreme of* a lockout. 彼らは締め出しという極端な手段に訴えた.

go to the other extreme (***of***) (…という)反対の極端なことをやる ▪ When I asked you not to talk so loud, you *went to the other extreme of* remaining silent. 私が君にそんなに大声で話さないでくれと言ったら, 君は反対に極端にもじっと黙っていた.

in extreme and mean ratio 黄金比に(A: B = B: C) ▪ Let L be the given line to be divided *in extreme and mean ratio*. Lを黄金比に分割すべき与えられた線とせよ.

in extremes **1** きわめて危険な状態に; 死に瀕して ▪ Life in a slum is fierce, and *in extremes*. スラム街の生活は激しく, きわめて危険な状態だ.

2 窮境にあって ▪ He is constantly *in extremes*. 彼は絶えず窮境にある.

in [***to***] ***the*** [***an***] ***extreme*** 極度に; 極端に ▪ They are indifferent *in the extreme*. 彼らは極度に冷淡である ▪ She was delighted *to an extreme*. 彼女は極端に喜んだ.

run to an extreme = go to EXEREMEs.

take **…** ***to extremes*** …を極端に解釈する ▪ Problems can occur when people *take* dieting *to extremes*. ダイエットを極端に考えると問題が起こる.

the extremes of fortune 運命の両極端, 激しい盛衰 ▪ He has experienced *the extremes of fortune*. 彼は運命の激しい浮沈をなめた.

to the [***an***] ***extreme*** = in the EXTREME.

extremity /ɪkstréməti/ 名 ***an extremity of*** 極度の ▪ It is *an extremity of* misery [joy]. それは極度の不幸[喜び]だ.

at the extremity of …の末端[先端に] ▪ It is situated *at the* northern *extremity of* the city. それは市の北端に位置している ▪ There is a pimple *at the extremity of* his nose. 彼の鼻の先ににきびができている.

be driven [***reduced***] ***to*** (***the last***) ***extremity*** [***extremities***] 窮地に追いつめられる; 絶体絶命になる ▪ I *was driven to extremity* for food. 私は食物に窮した.

be reduced to (***the last***) ***extremity*** → be driven to EXTREMITY.

drive *a person* ***to extremities*** = drive a person to EXTREMEs.

go to extremities = go to EXTREMEs.

in an extremity 窮地[境]にあって ▪ He is *in a* dire *extremity*. 彼はひどく窮している.

in extremities = in EXTREMEs.

in *one's* ***extremity*** 人の窮地[境]にあるとき ▪ Please help them *in their extremities*. 彼らが窮地[境]にあるときは助けてやってください.

to the last extremity 最後(の土壇場)まで; 死ぬまで ▪ He will resist *to the last extremity*. 彼は最後まで抵抗するだろう.

extricate /ékstrəkèɪt/ 動 ***extricate*** *oneself* ***from*** [***out of***] …から脱する, 抜け出す ▪ I have *extricated myself from* the group. 私はそのグループから抜け出した ▪ He managed to *extricate himself out of* the jungle. 彼はなんとか密林から脱出した.

eye /aɪ/ 名 ***a gleam*** [***glint, twinkle***] ***in*** *one's* ***eye*** **1** 《口》まだ全く漠然とした考え ▪ The proposal is only *a twinkle in my eye*. その提案はまだおぼろげな私の思いつきにすぎない ▪ Getting these

E

people pardoned was *a glint in my eye* when I wrote the book. 私がその本を書いたときには, こうした人たちを赦免されるように仕向けることは, まだ全く漠然とした考えだった.
2 まだできていない[受胎前の]子 ▪ This island was discovered when you were only *a gleam in your father's eye*. この島は君が生まれるずっと前に発見された.

a sight for sore eyes →SIGHT.

all eyes and ears 一心に見つめ耳を傾けて, 全身の注意を傾けて ▪ We are *all eyes and ears*! 私たちは一生懸命目を開き耳を傾けている.

all eyes are on …にみんな[万人]が注目している ▪ *All eyes are on* the prime minister as he prepares to give evidence. 総理大臣の証拠提示にみんなが注目している.

all eyes are turned [***focused***] ***on*** …を衆人環視である, 全員が…を注視する ▪ *All eyes are turned on* the Congressional elections. すべての目が議会選挙に注がれている.

(***all***) (***in***) ***my eye*** (***and***) (***Betty Martin***) 《俗》
1〚感嘆文で〛嘘言え!, とんでもない!, ばかばかしい! ▪ *All my eye and Betty Martin*! ばか言え!
2 全くのたわごと, ばかげたこと《特にありそうもない話について》 ▪ That is *all* (*in*) *my eye and Betty Martin*. それは全くばかげた話だ.

an eagle eye [***eagle eyes***] (どんな小さな物も見落とさない)鋭い眼力, 炯眼(けいがん)(の人) (→keep an eagle EYE on) ▪ My papers were scrutinized with *an eagle eye*. 私の書類は眼光紙背に徹するほど精査された ▪ Traffic police watch foreign cars with *eagle eyes*. 交通警察は外車をウの目タカの目で監視する ▪ Nothing escapes her *eagle eye*. 何も彼女の鋭い目から逃れない.

(***an***) ***eye for*** (***an***) ***eye*** 目には目を, (同じ方法手段による直接の)報復 (《聖》*Exod*. 21. 24) ▪ What you want is not justice, but *an eye for an eye*. 君の望むものは公正な裁きでなく, 同じ手段による直接の報復である ▪ He will retaliate on you and take *eye for eye*. 彼は君に目には目をもって報復するだろう.

apply the blind eye →BLIND[1].

be a sheet in the wind's eye →be a SHEET in the wind.

be all eyes **1** 熱心に注視する; 用心して見張る ▪ The boy *was all eyes* when he did his tricks. 彼が手品をした時その少年は一心に注視していた ▪ *Be all eyes*. 用心して見張れ.
2 穴のあくほどじろじろ見る ▪ The child *was all eyes* when the stranger came. 見知らぬ人が来たときその子供は穴のあくほどじろじろ見た.

be visible to the naked eye **1** 肉眼で見える ▪ How many stars *are visible to the naked eye* at one time? 一度に肉眼で見える星はいくつか.
2 明らかな, はっきりとした ▪ The collapse of Russian industry *was visible to the naked eye*. ロシアの産業の崩壊は目に見えていた.

before [***in front of***] *one's* ***eyes*** 自分の眼前で[に] ▪ Killing was done *before my eyes*. 殺人は私の眼前でなされた.

before the eye 目の前で, みるみる ▪ Buds unfolded *before the eye*. つぼみがみるみる開いた.

believe *one's* ***eyes***〚主に否定文で〛自分の目を信じる ▪ I could hardly *believe my eyes*. 自分の目が信じられないくらいだった ▪ I couldn't *believe my eyes* seeing what the tsunami had done to this wonderful place. このすばらしい場所が津波でどうなったかを見て, 自分の目が信じられなかった.

below *one's* ***eyes*** 眼下に ▪ We saw the whole city *below our eyes*. 眼下に全市が見えた.

by reason of the fair eyes of →for the fair EYEs of.

by the [*one's*] ***eye*** 目分量で, 目測で ▪ Estimate the distance *by the eye*. 距離を目で測りなさい ▪ He will march *by his eye*. 彼は目測で行進するだろう.

cast an eye [*one's* ***eyes***] ***over*** …の誤りを軽く調べる, にざっと目を通す ▪ The officer offered to *cast an eye over* the ledger. 役人は元帳の誤りの有無をちょっと調べようと申し出た ▪ It isn't enough just to *cast your eyes over* a second-hand car. 中古車はちょっと調べるだけでは不十分だ.

cast *one's* ***eyes about*** [***down,*** etc.]/ ***cast about*** [***down,*** etc.] *one's* ***eyes*** 見回す[見おろす, など] ▪ He *cast his eyes round* the room. 彼は部屋を見回した ▪ She *cast up her eyes to* Heaven in sorrow. 彼女は悲しんで天を見上げた.

cast *one's* ***eyes*** (***at, on, over***) (…を)見やる ▪ Jeff *cast his eyes on* her. ジェフは彼女を見やった.

cast sheep's eyes at →SHEEP.

catch *a person's* ***eye*** **1** 人の目に留まる; 人の注意を引く ▪ When I *caught Jim's eye*, he came at once to talk with me. 私が目に留まると, ジムはすぐに私に話しに来た ▪ None of the pictures *caught my eye*. どの絵も私の注意を引かなかった.
2 人と視線が合う ▪ The boy *caught his teacher's eye* and stopped talking. 少年は自分を見ている先生に気づいて話をやめた.

catch [***strike, take***] ***the eye*** (主語が)目に留まる, 目につく ▪ The building *caught the eye*. 建物が目についた.

catch the eyes of the world 世間の注目を集める, 世の耳目を引く ▪ Japan has *caught the eyes of the world* with this technology. 日本はこの技術によって世間の関心を集めた.

catch the Speaker's eye →CATCH[2].

clap [***lay, set***] ***eyes on*** 《英》〚主に否定構文で〛(偶然)…を見つける, に出会う ▪ That's the first time I've *clapped eyes on* her. 彼女にお目にかかったのはそれが初めてです ▪ I never *clapped eyes on* him again. 二度と彼に会わなかった.

close an eye〚主に否定文で〛目をつぶる ▪ I never *closed an eye*. 私は全然目をつぶらなかった.

close [***shut***] *one's* ***eyes to*** (悪い点)に目をつむる,

…をわざと見ない, 考えない ▪I *close my eyes to* petty faults. 私は小さな欠点には目をつぶる ▪The detective *shut his eyes to* their crimes. 探偵は彼らの犯罪に目をつぶった.

Close your eyes and think of England. 《主に英戯》(したくないセックスにつき合うときには)目を閉じて英国のことを考えなさい ▪"Just *close your eyes and think of England*" was Victorian mothers' advice to their daughters on the eve of their weddings. 「ただ目を閉じてお国のことを考えなさい」というのが, ビクトリア朝時代の母親が嫁ぐ前夜に娘に与える助言だった.

cock the [*one's*] ***eye*** →COCK².

cry *one's* ***eyes out*** 《口》目を泣きはらす, 長くひどく泣く ▪I *cried my eyes out* when I heard of his death. 彼が死んだと聞いて号泣した.

cut (***the***) ***eyes*** [***an eye,*** *one's* ***eye***] 《米俗》 **1** ちらりと見る, 横目で見る (*at*) ▪He *cut his eye at* the skipper as he spoke. 彼はそう言いながら船長をちらりと見た.

2 互いに見交わす ▪Strangers crossed words and *cut eyes*. 見知らぬ人々が言葉を交わし目を交わした.

do *a person* ***in the eye*** 《俗》人の目を抜く, だます ▪The jockey *did* your friend *in the eye* over that horse. 騎手はその馬のことで君の友だちをだました.

drop *one's* ***eyes*** (恥ずかしさ, 後ろめたさで)目を伏せる ▪She *dropped her eyes* when she made a mistake. 彼女は間違いをして目を伏せた.

eyes and [***or***] ***no eyes*** 観察の鋭い人と鈍い人(との差違); 見る目と見ない目《自然観察書の題名》 ▪*Eyes or no eyes*; or the art of seeing. 見る目と見ない目; 観察術《書名》.

one's ***eyes are bigger than*** *one's* ***stomach.*** 《戯》食べきれもしないのに欲ばる, 食べきれないほど注文する; (物事を)能力以上に楽しむことができると考える (→have EYEs bigger than one's stomach) ▪*Are your eyes bigger than your stomach*? Take only what you are sure you can eat. 目に入るものすべてが胃に入りますか. 確実に食べきれるだけお取りなさい.

one's ***eyes are set*** 《口》酒に酔っている, 目がすわっている ▪*His eyes were* well *set* after seven pints of beer. ビール7パイントを空けたあと彼は目がすっかりすわっていた.

eyes down 《口》(ビンゴゲームを)やり始めて; 開始《一般的にも用いる》 ▪*Eyes down* 7. 45. (ビンゴの)開始7時45分 ▪The television is switched on and then it's *eyes down*. テレビがつけられそれから「視聴始め」だ. ☞Bingo 賭博の「始め」の合図から.

one's ***eyes fall*** [***rest***] ***upon*** …が人の目にふれる ▪Then *my eyes fell upon* the box. その時その箱が私の目に留まった.

Eyes front! 《号令》(頭を右または左に向けているものに対し)頭(かしら)中!, 直れ!

one's ***eyes nearly*** [***almost, practically***] ***popped out*** (***of*** *one's* ***head***) 《口》目玉が飛び出るほど驚く, 恐れる ▪When I heard it, *my eyes nearly popped out of my head*. それを聞いて私は目玉が飛び出るほど驚いた.

one's ***eyes stood out of*** *one's* ***head*** 《口》= one's EYEs nearly popped out (of one's head).

one's ***eyes swim*** [***dance***] 人の目が舞う ▪*His eyes swam* at the sight. それを見て彼は目が舞った.

feast *one's* ***eyes on*** …を飽かず[楽しげに, 感心して]眺める ▪I *feasted my eyes on* noted pictures. 私は名画を見て楽しんだ.

Fields [***Hedges***] ***have eyes, and woods have ears.*** 《諺》野に目あり, 森に耳あり,「壁に耳あり障子に目あり」(→WALLs have ears.).

fix [***fasten***] *one's* ***eyes on*** …に注目する, をじっと見つめる ▪*The eyes* of the world *are fixed upon* the new president. 世界の注意は新大統領に向けられている.

for *a person's* ***eyes only*** マル秘[親展]で ▪The letter was marked "*for members' eyes only*." その手紙には「会員限定」と記されていた.

for [***by reason of***] ***the fair eyes of*** …のために ▪They rule not *by reason of their fair eyes*. 彼らは自分たちのために統治するのではない.

get a black eye **1** (殴打などのため)目の周りに黒あざができる ▪I *got a black eye* from running into the wall at the gym. 私は体育館で壁にぶつかって目の周りにあざをつくってしまった.

2 評判を落とす ▪The technology *got a black eye* from failed projects. その技術は計画が失敗したため味噌をつけてしまった.

get *one's* ***eye in*** 《球技》練習して目が利くようになる ▪He's *got his eye in*. 彼は練習して目が利くようになった.

get the (***big***) ***eye*** 《口》色目[感嘆の目]で見られる ▪The girl *got the eye* as she walked past the boys. その少女は少年たちの所を通り過ぎたとき感嘆の目で見られた.

give an eye to …に注目する, 留意する; に精出す ▪I will *give an eye to* the job. その仕事に精出します ▪*Give an eye to* the meat. (私のいない間)肉を見ていてください.

give *one's* ***eyes for*** …のためなら何でもする (→give one's EARs for) ▪"I'd *give my eyes for* Saddam," one old woman told me. 「サダムのためなら目玉だってくれてやるよ」と老婆が私に言った.

give *a person* ***one in the eye*** →ONE in the eye.

give the (***big***) ***eye*** 《口》 **1** 色目[感嘆の目]で見る ▪Sailors *gave the eye* to every girl in the port. 船員たちは港の娘にはみな色目を使った.

2 目くばせする ▪He clammed up when I *gave* him *the eye*. 私が目くばせしたら彼は口をつぐんだ.

give the glad eye →GLAD.

have a good eye [***an eye***] ***to*** 《口》…に抜け目がない, めざとい ▪He *has a good eye to* the main chance. 彼は金儲けの機会には抜け目がない.

have a quick eye for …を見つけるのが早い ▪He *has a quick eye for* mistakes. 彼は誤りを見

つけるのが早い.

have a roving eye (きょろきょろ)よく色目を使う; 浮気っぽい ▪ He *has a roving eye*. 彼はよく色目を使う.

have (***all***) *one's* ***eyes about*** *one* 油断なくあたりに気を配る, 抜かりがない ▪ A hunter must *have his eyes about* him. 猟師は油断なくあたりに気を配らねばならない.

have an eye for **1** …に対する鑑識眼がある ▪ He *has an eye for* the picturesque. 彼は美景を見る目がある ▪ He *has* no *eye for* proportion. 彼はつり合いがわからない.

2 …に抜け目がない ▪ He *has an eye for* a good bargain. 彼は安い買い物に抜け目がない.

have an [*one's*] ***eye on*** [***upon***] **1** …を目を離さず監視する ▪ I'll *have an eye on* you day and night. 日夜目を離さずにあなたを監視します.

2 …に目をつけている, を欲しがっている ▪ I've *had my eye on* that cottage for a quite a while. 私はその田舎家にずっと目をつけていた.

have an eye to **1** …に目をつけている, を目当てとする, に野心がある; をもくろむ ▪ He *has an eye to* the position. 彼はその地位に目をつけている ▪ He always *has an eye to* making money. 彼はいつも金儲けをもくろんでいる.

2 …に気をつける, 注目する; を慎重に考える ▪ *Have an eye to* the future. 将来に目を向けなさい ▪ He *has an eye to* the education of his boy. 彼は息子の教育を慎重に考えている.

3 …に関連する ▪ What I said about the Cretan laws *had an eye to* war only. 私がクレタ島の法律について述べたことは戦争にだけ関連があった.

have an eye to [***for, on***] ***the main chance*** →MAIN CHANCE.

have *one's* ***eye on*** →have an EYE on.

have eyes at [***in***] ***the back of*** *one's* ***head*** 《口》(一度に四方が見えるほど)きわめて目ざとい; きわめて抜け目がない ▪ He must *have eyes in the back of his head*. 彼はきわめて目ざとい.

have eyes bigger than *one's* ***stomach*** 食べきれないほど食物を注文する[皿に取る] (→one's EYEs are bigger than one's stomach) ▪ In France, we say you should not *have eyes bigger than your stomach*. フランスでは, 食べきれないほど注文するなと言われている.

have eyes in *one's* ***head*** 《口》目がよく利く; (周囲や人のしている事が)よく見える ▪ I*'ve got eyes in my head* as well as you. 僕も君に劣らず目がよく利くんだ.

have eyes like a hawk タカのような鋭い目をしている; 何ひとつ見逃さない ▪ My wife, who *has eyes like a hawk*, spotted a red-winged blackbird in the tree. 妻はタカのように視力抜群なので, 樹上にいる赤い羽根のツグミを見つけた.

have eyes like saucers (驚きなどで)目を皿のようにしている ▪ Her daughter *had eyes like saucers*. 彼女の娘は皿のように大きな目をしている.

have [***keep***] *one's* ***eyes on the ball*** **1** 《スポーツ》ボールから目を離さないでよく見る ▪ *Keep your eyes on the ball*, or you won't be able to hit it. ボールをよく見ていなさい, でなければボールは打てません.

2 《口》自分のすることに常に注意する, 油断しない ▪ If you *keep your eyes on the ball*, you will be promoted. 君が手抜かりなく働いていれば昇進するだろう.

3 (短期間)世話をする ▪ In short, we *keep our eyes on the ball* for you. つまり, 私たちが君の世話をするということだ.

have eyes only for …にだけ興味を持つ, だけを目がけている (= only have EYEs for 2) ▪ John *had eyes only for* Jane at the party. パーティーでジョンはジェインにだけ関心を持っていた.

have *a person's* [*one's*] ***eyes out on stalks*** 《英口》目玉が飛び出るほどびっくりさせる[する], ひどいショックを与える[受ける] ▪ This ghost story *had my eyes out on stalks* when I was a kid. この怪談は子供のころの私にひどいショックを与えた ▪ I *had my eyes out on stalks* on some of the pictures. 目玉が飛び出るほどびっくりしながらその絵のいくつかを見た.

have eyes to see 見る目がある; 明敏である ▪ He *has eyes to see*. 彼には観察眼がある.

have [***get***] *one's* ***eye***(***s***) (***well***) ***in*** (射撃などで)距離[方向]を正確に目測できる[できるようになる] ▪ They *had their eye well in*. 彼らは距離を正確に目測できた.

have half an eye 《口》少し目が開いている, 全くの愚鈍ではない ▪ If he *had half an eye*, he would see it. 彼が少し目が開いていたらそれはわかるだろう.

have … in *one's* ***eye***(***s***) **1** …を眼中においている, もくろんでいる; に目をつけている ▪ He *had* a position *in his eye* for Peter. 彼はピーターのために就職口を考えていた ▪ They *had* nothing *in their eyes* but their own safety. 彼らは自分自身の安全以外は眼中になかった.

2 …が目にちらつく ▪ He *had* the sun *in his eyes*. 日光が彼の目にちらついた.

have [***keep***] ***one eye on*** (ある事をしながら)一方では…に気を配る ▪ He always *has one eye on* the clock. 彼はいつも一方では時計に目を配っている ▪ As she ate, she *kept one eye on* the microwave. 彼女は食事をしながら一方では電子レンジに気を配っていた.

have [***get***] ***square eyes*** 《戯》(テレビの見過ぎで)目が四角になる, テレビ漬けである ▪ One of these days, you'll *get square eyes*! そのうち君は目が四角になるよ.

hit *a person* ***between the eyes*** 《口》人に強い印象を与える, 大いに驚かす ▪ Jane *hit* Tom right *between the eyes*. ジェインはトムに強い印象を与えた.

hit *a person* ***in the eye*** **1** 人の目をなぐる ▪ Brad could have *been hit in the eye* and blinded. ブラッドは目をなぐられて失明しかねなかった.

2 人の目を射る ▪ Robberies and murders *hit* you *in the eye* in large letters. 強盗や殺人の記事が大

きな活字で目に飛びこんできた.

hold the public eye 世間の目を引く ▪ The actress *holds the public eye* with a matchless figure and lively character. その女優は類いまれなプロポーションと陽気な性格で世間の目を引いている.

in a pig's eye →PIG[1].

in** one's* [the***] ***mind's eye*** 目がけて; 想像に浮かべて; 心眼で見れば (cf. Sh., *Haml.* 1. 2. 185) ▪ I have the little cottage *in my mind's eye.* 私は小さい田舎家を心の中で想像している ▪ He saw the completed house *in his mind's eye.* 彼は心の中で完成された家を見た ▪ Goldsmith looks beautiful *in the mind's eye.* ゴールドスミスは心眼で見れば美しく見える.

in the eye of day 《雅》白昼に, 真っ昼間に ▪ Venus shines even *in the eye of day.* 金星は白昼にも輝く.

in the eye(s) of **1** …の目で見れば ▪ He was a man of mark *in the eyes of* my family. 彼は私の家族の目には重要人物であった ▪ We are babies *in his eyes.* 我々は彼から見れば赤んぼうだ.
2 …の中心[渦中]に, の焦点で ▪ The Party leader was *in the eye of* a controversy over alleged tapping of his phones. 党首は, 電話を盗聴したとされる論争の渦中にいた.

in the eye(s) of the law [***logic***] 法律上[理論上]は, 法律[論理]の見地からは ▪ All men are equal *in the eye*(s) *of the law.* 法律上は人みな平等である.

in the eyes of the public [***world***] 大衆の見解では, 世論では, 世間の目から見れば ▪ The politician is guilty *in the eyes of the public.* その政治家は世間的には有罪だ ▪ *In the eyes of the world* he passes for a saint. 世間の目では彼は聖人で通っている.

in the public eye 人前で; 世の注目を引いて, 有名な ▪ He is unabashed *in the public eye.* 彼は人前で恥じるところがない ▪ He is now a man *in the public eye.* 彼は今問題の人となっている ▪ They are prominent *in the public eye.* 彼らは名士である. ☞in the eyes of the public と混同しないよう注意.

in the twinkling of an eye →TWINKLING.

keep an eagle eye on …を厳しく見張る, に目を光らす ▪ The executives *kept an eagle eye on* the daily fluctuations in the market. 取締役たちは市場の日々の変動に目を凝らしていた.

keep an [*one's*] ***eye on*** …を(目を離さず)監視する, (事故のないよう)…に目をつけている ▪ *Keep an eye on* the child for me for a moment. ちょっとその子供を見ていてください ▪ I *kept an eye on* every side. 私は四方八方に目を配った.

keep an eye out for 《口》…を警戒する, (望むことなど)を待ちかまえる ▪ The police *kept an eye out for* pickpockets at the fair. 警察は慈善市ですりを警戒した ▪ I *kept an eye out for* any chance passer-by. 私は偶然の通行人を待ちかまえていた.

keep** one's* ***eye in =have one's HAND in.

keep** one's* ***eye to the goal 目的から目を離さない ▪ He *keeps his eye to the goal* and pushes on. 彼は常に目的から目を離さずどんどん進んで行く.

keep** one's* ***eyes glued to 目をくぎづけにする, 目を離さないで注意深く見る ▪ As he spoke and gestured, she *kept her eyes glued to* his fists. 彼が手振りしながらしゃべっていたとき彼女は彼の拳に目をくぎづけにしていた.

keep** one's* ***eyes off **1** 恋をあきらめる ▪ You'd better *keep your eyes off.* She's spoken for. 君はもうあきらめたほうがよい. 彼女には決まった人がいる.
2 〚cannot …の形で〛 あきらめられない, ぞっこんにほれこんでいる ▪ He *could not keep his eyes off* the girl. 彼はその娘にぞっこんにほれこんでいた.
3 =take one's EYEs off. ☞人に限らず物の場合もある.

keep** one's* ***eyes open [***peeled, skinned***] 油断なく見張る, 十分気を配る ▪ *Keep* (both) *your eyes open* and grasp opportunities. 油断なく気を配って機会をつかみなさい ▪ *Keep your eyes skinned* for fear you should be robbed of your wallet. 財布を取られないようによく注意していなさい ▪ I *kept my eyes peeled* to the door. 出入り口の方を油断なく見張った ▪ Stick to him like wax, and *keep your eyes skinned.* 彼にぴったり密着して目を離さないこと.

keep half an eye on …にちらちらと目をやる《監視すること》 ▪ She *kept half an eye on* the baby while cooking. 彼女は料理しながら赤んぼうにちらちらと目をやった.

keep** one's* ***weather eye open → keep a WEATHER(-)eye open.

lay eyes on =set (one's) EYEs on.

look** a person* ***in the eye [***eyes***] (恐れずに)人(の目)をまともに見る ▪ *Look* me *in the eyes* and tell me the truth. 私の目をまともに見て本当のことを言いなさい.

look upon… with another eye …に対して異なった見解を持つ ▪ The city *looked upon* it *with another eye.* 市はそれに対し異なった見解を持っていた.

lose an eye 片目が見えなくなる ▪ He has *lost an eye.* 彼は片目を失った.

make eyes at 《口》…に色目を使う, 目くばせする ▪ He is always *making eyes at* every woman he meets. 彼は女性に会うごとにいつも色目を使う.

meet** a person's* ***eyes →MEET.

meet the eye(s) of →MEET.

one ***might put*** *a thing* ***in*** *one's* ***eye*** (***and see never the worse***) 目の中へ入れても何ともない; 取るに足らない, 存在しない ▪ All that you get you *might put in your eye and see never the worse.* 君の得るものはすべて取るに足らない.

mind** one's* ***eye →MIND[2].

My eye(s)! 《英口》こりゃ驚いた!, まあ! ▪ *My eyes,* how green! まあ, 何という緑なんだろう!

not a dry eye in the house 《戯》客のうち泣かざる者なし ▪ There was *not a dry eye in the house*. 客のうち感泣しない者はなかった.
not bat an eye →BAT[5].
one eye on →with one EYE on.
one in the eye →ONE.
only have eyes for [***on***]/ ***have eyes only for*** **1** ...しか眼中にない (*on*) ▪ She *only has eyes on* her social advancement. 彼女は社会的出世しか考えていない.
2 (特定の異性)にしか興味がない, (ただ一人の人)に惹かれている ▪ He *has eyes only for* his own wife. 彼は奥さんにしか興味がない.
open *a person's* [***the***] ***eyes*** (***to***) **1** (...に)人の目を開いてやる ▪ The Lord *opens the eyes* of the blind. 神は盲人の目を開き給う.
2 人に(...を)悟らせる ▪ It *opened the eyes* of the people to the truth. それは国民に真相を悟らせた.
open (***up***) *one's* ***eyes*** **1** 目を留める (*to*) ▪ You must *open your eyes to* their doings. 君はあの連中の所業に目を留めるべきだ.
2 (驚いて)目を見張る ▪ When I told him so, he *opened his eyes*. そう言ったら彼は目を丸くした.
3 (渦などが)その中心をあける ▪ The cloud begins to *open its eyes*. 雲が裂けて地平線の一部がはっきりする.
pipe *one's* ***eye*** →PIPE[2].
please the eye 見て美しい, 目の保養になる ▪ Flowers *please the eye*. 花は見て美しい.
put *one's* ***finger in*** *one's* ***eye*** 《軽蔑》泣く ▪ Cry, baby, cry; *put your finger in your eye*. 泣け赤んぼうよ, 泣け. 泣きべそをかけ.
roll *one's* ***eyes at*** 《口》...に色目を使う ▪ She *rolls her eyes at* every handsome young man. 彼女はすべての美青年に色目を使う.
run [***pass***] *one's* [***the***] ***eye***(***s***) ***over*** ...にざっと目を通す ▪ Would you mind *running your eye over* these accounts? この計算書にざっと目を通してくださいませんか.
see eye to eye with *a person* (***on, about***) (特に宗教界において) (...について)人と意見が合う, ひとつ心である (《聖》 *Isa*. 52. 8) ▪ I *see eye to eye with* him *on* that matter. その問題については彼と見解が一致している. ☞元は「面と向かって」の意であった.
see with *one's* ***own eyes*** 自分の目で見る ▪ I have *seen* it *with my own eyes*. 私は自分の目でそれを見た.
set an eye [*one's* ***eyes***] ***by*** 《米口》...を深く愛する; を大いに重んじる ▪ Well, they *set their eyes by* the child, of course. もちろん彼らはその子供を深く愛した.
set (*one's*) ***eyes on*** ...を見る ▪ I have never *set eyes on* him before. まだ彼を見たことはない.
shut *one's* ***eyes to*** [***on***] →SHUT.
skin the eyes off *a person* 《米俗》人をすっかり打ち負かす ▪ He could *skin the eyes off* the very devil at the game of poker. ポーカーならば彼は悪魔でもすっかり打ち負かすことができるだろう.
sleep with one eye open 片目だけ眠る, 眠りが浅い ▪ When my children started to drive, I *slept with one eye open* until they got home. 子供たちが車を運転するようになったとき, 帰宅するまでは熟睡できなかった.
strain *one's* ***eyes*** →STRAIN[2].
strike [***take***] ***the eye*** →catch the EYE.
take *one's* ***eye off the ball*** ボールから目を離す; 注意を怠る, 油断する ▪ You can't *take your eye off the ball* in a modern industry. 近代工業では手抜かりがあってはならない.
take *one's* ***eyes off*** 〚主に否定文で〛...から目を離す ▪ You must not *take your eyes off* the child for a moment. 一瞬もその子から目を離してはいけない ▪ It was so interesting that I couldn't *take my eyes off* it. 非常におもしろかったのでそれから目が離せなかった.
the eye of day [***the morning, heaven***] 太陽 ▪ *The eye of the morning* will soon peep out. 太陽はまもなく現れるだろう ▪ Sometime too hot *the eye of heaven* shines. 太陽があまりにも熱く照りつけることもある. ☞cf. Sh., *Sonn*. 18.
the eye of the storm [***hurricane***] **1** 台風の目《比喩的にも》 ▪ His new party is likely to be in *the eye of the storm* in the coming election. 今度の選挙では彼の新党が台風の目になりそうだ.
2 騒動の前のつかの間の平穏なとき ▪ This is *the eye of the storm* in the current crisis. 今は現在の危機が小休止状態だ.
the naked eye →NAKED.
there is more to ... than meets the eye はじめ見たよりも重要[注目すべきもの]である ▪ *There is more to* Mr. Middleton *than meets the eye*. ミドルトン氏は見かけよりも偉い人である.
through the eyes of ...の立場で, の目[見地]を通して ▪ Reexamine the case *through the eyes of* the two witnesses. 二人の目撃者の立場でその件を再検討せよ.
throw the eye at ...に色目を使う; をほしそうに見る ▪ You have been *throwing the eye at* my daughter. あなたは私の娘に色目を使ってきた.
to the eye 見たところでは ▪ John looks *to the eye* like a nice boy, but is really very naughty. ジョンは見たところ良い子のようだが, 実はとてもわんぱくだ.
turn a blind eye (***to***) →BLIND[1].
turn *one's* ***eyes*** (***to***) (...の方へ)目を向ける ▪ She *turned her eyes to* her son. 彼女は息子の方へ目を向けた ▪ He *turned his eyes* another way. 彼は目をわきへそらした.
under *a person's* ***eye***(***s***) 人に監視[注目]されて ▪ I had fallen *under the eye of* the government. 私は政府に監視されるようになった.
under *one's* ***eyes*** 目の前で ▪ He did not know what was passing *under his eyes*. 彼は目の前で何が起こっているかわからなかった.
up to the eyes **1** (仕事などに)没頭して ▪ George

was *up to the eyes* in work. ジョージは仕事に没頭していた ▪ They were *up to the eyes* making preparations. 彼らは準備に没頭していた.
2 全く, 深く(はまり込んで) ▪ The estate was mortgaged *up to the eyes*. その地所はすっかり抵当に入っていた ▪ He was *up to the eyes* in debt. 彼は借金で首が回らなかった.

What the eye doesn't see, the heart doesn't grieve over. 《諺》目に見えないことを心は悲しまない,「知らぬが仏」.

Where are your eyes? (それを見そこなうとは)君の目は一体どこについているのか ▪ The captain asked me *where my eyes were*. 船長は私に目はどこについているのかと尋ねた.

wipe** a person's **eye 《俗》 **1** 人の射ちそこねた獲物を射ち取る; 人を負かす, 出し抜く ▪ You shoot first; I'll stand by and *wipe your eye*. 君先に射ちたまえ, 僕はそばにいて君の射ちそこねたのを射ち取るから.
2 人のうぬぼれを打ちくだく; 人の目を打って黒くはれあがらせる ▪ Hullo, cheeky! I'll *wipe your eye* for you. おい, 生意気なやつ! 高慢な鼻をへし折ってやるぞ ▪ He *wiped the eye of* the burglar. 彼は夜盗の目をなぐって黒くはれあがらせた.

with a beady eye 注意深く, 疑いの目で ▪ When we started, bankers would look at me *with a beady eye* and say you can't run a business like that. 開業したころ, 銀行員たちは私を疑いの目で見て, そんな事業は経営不可能だとよく言った.

with a jaundiced eye (ひがみなどで)偏見の目で ▪ This is a sport most people look at *with a jaundiced eye*. これはほとんどの人が偏見をもって見るスポーツだ.

with all** one's **eyes/with all the eyes in** one's **head よく注視して ▪ I looked *with all my eyes*, but I failed to detect any difference. 私はよく注意して見たが, 何の差異も見つけられなかった.

with an eye for …に鑑識眼がある, 洞察力がある ▪ She was an artist *with an eye for* detail and a musician with an ear for subtlety. 彼女は細部への鑑識眼をそなえた画家であり, 微妙さへの耳をそなえた音楽家でもあった.

with an eye to **1** …する目的で, しようとして ▪ I bought the house *with an eye to* converting it into a school. 私は学校に改造する目的で家を買った ▪ He married his wife *with an eye to* her fortune. 彼は財産目当てに妻と結婚した.
2 …によく注意して ▪ Write a paper *with an eye to* your spelling. つづりによく注意して論文を書くこと.

with dry eyes 涙を流さないで; 平然として ▪ I could not hear it *with dry eyes*. 私はそれを涙なしには聞けなかった.

***with** one's **eyes closed** [**shut**]* 《口》 **1** きわめてたやすく[楽々と] ▪ I could do your work *with my eyes closed*. 私ならあなたの仕事を楽々とできるのだが.
2 事情を知らずに, やみくもに ▪ It won't do to go about it *with your eyes shut*. やみくもにやってはだめだよ.

with** one's **eyes** (**wide**) **open **1** 事情をよく承知の上で, 問題をよくわきまえて ▪ He was seventy, but Jane married him *with her eyes open*. 彼は70歳だったが, ジェインはそれを承知の上で結婚した.
2 目を(大きく)見開いて ▪ She stared at me *with her eyes wide open*. 彼女は目を大きく見開いて私を見つめた.

with half an eye 《口》一目で; やすやすと ▪ I saw *with half an eye* that all was over. 私は万事終わったと一目でわかった ▪ Anyone can see *with half an eye* that you're in love with her. あなたが彼女に恋していることは誰にでもやすやすとわかる.

with one eye on …に(警戒の)目をつけながら ▪ He went on working *with one eye on* her. 彼女に目をつけながら仕事を続けた.

with open eyes (欠点を)知っての上で ▪ He took her *with open eyes*. 彼はすべて承知の上で彼女を受け入れた.

with the eye(s) of …の目で(見るなど) ▪ He saw the colors *with the eye of* a painter. 彼は画家の目でその色彩を見た.

without batting an eye →not BAT an eye.

eyeball /áɪbɔ̀ːl/ 名 ***eyeball to eyeball*** (***with***) 《口》(…と)面と向かって ▪ They were sitting *eyeball to eyeball*. 彼らは顔をつき合わせて座っていた.

the hairy eyeball とがめる目つき, にらみつけ ▪ She gave me *the hairy eyeball*. 彼女は私をにらみつけた.

up to the eyeballs →up to the EARs in.

eyebrow /áɪbràʊ/ 名 ***cause eyebrows to raise*** (人を)驚かす, あきれさせる ▪ Players asked to be tested so that every long home run wouldn't *cause eyebrows to raise*. 大ホームランのたびに疑われることのないように選手たちは薬物検査を要求した.

hang** [**hold**] **on by** one's [**the**] **eyebrows 《口》 **1** (困難に際して)極度にがんばる, ねばる ▪ He *hung on by his eyebrows* until he reached his goal. 彼は目標を達成するまでねばりにねばった.
2 ようやく地位にかじりついている; 窮境にある ▪ He is only *hanging on by his eyebrows* to his present work. 彼は現在の仕事に何とかかじりついているにすぎない.

***raise an eyebrow** [**eyebrows**]* 眉を上げる《驚き・軽蔑を示す》 ▪ He hardly *raises an eyebrow* at it now. 彼は今はそれに対してほとんど驚きを示さない.

raised eyebrows しかめつら, ひんしゅく ▪ There were *raised eyebrows* when she married a noted womanizer. 彼女は有名な女たらしと結婚してひんしゅくを買った.

steeped to the eyebrows (***in***) (…を)のどまで詰めこんで, (…で)いっぱいになって ▪ They were *steeped* in goose and onions *to the eyebrows*. 彼らはガチョウの詰め物をのどまで詰めこんでいた ▪ He is *steeped to the eyebrows in* learning. 彼は学問をいっぱい詰めこんでいる.

***up to the eyebrows* (*in*)** 《俗》(...に)すっかり没して ▪ I found him *up to the eyebrows in* business. 彼は商売に没頭していた.

eyeful /áɪfʊ̀l/ 名 ***get* [*have, take*] *an eyeful* (*of*)** 《口》 **1** ...を十分見る ▪ They *got an eyeful of* life. 彼らは世の中を十分見た ▪ *Get an eyeful of* this! これをよく見なさい.

2 注目すべき[驚くべきもの]を見る[見つける] ▪ A schoolboy *got an eyeful* when he spotted a wild boar in the street. 男子生徒は珍しいものを見た. 通りで野生のイノシシを見つけたのだ.

3 目に入る ▪ The bottle broke and he *got an eyeful of* seltzer. びんが割れて炭酸水が彼の目に入った.

eyelash /áɪlæʃ/ 名 ***flutter* one's *eyelashes*** (女が)男に色目を使う ▪ She was *fluttering her eyelashes* at the man. 彼女はその男に色目を使っていた.

hang on by* one's *eyelashes = hang on by one's EYEBROWs.

eyelid /áɪlɪ̀d/ 名 ***before you can blink* (*an eyelid*)** →BLINK².

hang* (*on*) *by the eyelids **1** かろうじてかじり[すがり]ついているだけである; 危地にある ▪ The covers *hang by the eyelids*. (本の)表紙はかろうじてついている ▪ His affair *hangs by the eyelids*. 彼の一件はきわめて危うい.

2 一生懸命つかまる ▪ As they went round Cape Horn in the old days, sailors *hung by their eyelids* to the yards. 昔ホーン岬を回航するときは, 船員たちは帆げたに一生懸命かじりついた.

in the batting of an eyelid 瞬く間に ▪ *In the batting of an eyelid* the man rushed into the burning house. 瞬く間にその人は燃える家に飛びこんだ.

eyetooth, eye tooth /áɪtù:θ/ 名 ***cut* one's *eyetooth*** 世間的分別がつく, 経験を積む ▪ I *cut my eyetooth* on lawsuits. 訴訟のことは知っている. ☞「糸切り歯が生えて大人になる」が原義.

give* one's *eyeteeth for ...を手に入れるためならどんな犠牲でも払う ▪ We would *give our eyeteeth for* a place like this. 我々はこのような場所のためならどんな犠牲でも払う. ☞犬歯 (eyetooth) は, 食肉獣では獲物を引き裂くための大事な歯であることから.

F

F /ef/ 名 ***an F sharp*** 《俗》ノミ ▪ The hotel was swarming with *F sharps*. そのホテルにはノミがうようよしていた. ☞F＝flea (ノミ).

face[1] /feɪs/ 名 ***a long face*** 《口》浮かぬ顔; まじめくさった顔 ▪ You will see *long faces* enough when these taxes come to be paid. これらの税金が払われるようになると浮かぬ顔が見えるだろう. ☞しょげると口の両端と目がさがり, 顔が長くなるから. (→draw a long FACE, with a long FACE).

about face **1** くるりと, 真反対に ▪ They suddenly turned *about face*. 急にくるりと向きを変えた.
2 《米・号令》回れ右!

adopt* [*carry, put on*] *a* [*the*] *face of …の外観[姿]を呈する ▪ The problems of the world are always *putting on* new *faces*. 世界の問題はいつも新しい様相を呈しつつある ▪ It *carries* no *face of* probability. それは全然ありそうに見えない.

an alabaster face 雪のように白い顔, 透きとおった滑らかな顔 ▪ Historically, the standard of beauty was having *a* pale *alabaster face*. 歴史的には, 美の基準は透きとおった白雪のような顔をしていることだった.

at* [*in, on*] *the first face ちょっと見たところでは ▪ *At the first face*, she looks gentle and amiable. ちょっと見たところでは彼女はおとなしく優しそうだ.

be* [*go,* etc.] *blue in the face 《口》(寒さ・恐れ・驚き・疲労・激怒などで)顔が青い[青くなる], 青筋を立てる ▪ It was so cold that I *went blue in the face*. ひどく寒くて私は真っ青になった ▪ John argued hotly until he *was blue in the face*. ジョンは顔が青くなるまで激論した.

be in *a person's* ***face*** 《米口》人にあれこれ口出しをする ▪ His wife *is in his face* whatever he does. 彼が何をしようとも, 彼の奥さんは口出しをする.

be* (*more than*) *just a pretty face 《口・戯》→(not) be just a pretty FACE.

be* [*have…*] *written all over *a person's* ***face*** 顔に書いてある ▪ Disappointment *was* clearly *written all over her face*. 彼女の顔にはがっかりした様子がありありと出ていた.

before *a person's* [*one's*] ***face*** **1** …の面前に, 面前で ▪ The master scolds the servants severely *before my face*. 主人は私の面前で激しく使用人をしかる ▪ He was taken *before the face of* thirty thousand men. 彼は3万の人々の面前に連行された.
2 …の前に, より先に (《聖》*Mark* 1. 2) ▪ I send my messenger *before thy face*. 私は使いをあなたより先につかわす.

blow up* [*explode, go up*] *in *a person's* ***face*** (計画などが突然つぶれて)人の面目をつぶす ▪ The summit *blew up in China's face*. その会議で中国の面子はつぶれてしまった.

bring *a person* ***face to face with*** **1** 人を…と対決させる ▪ The judge *brought* the accused *face to face with* the accuser. 裁判官は被告を原告と対決させた.
2 人に(問題)をはじめて知らせる (→come FACE to FACE with 2) ▪ They *were brought face to face with* the horror of genocide. 彼らは大量虐殺の恐怖をはじめて知らされた.

carry a* [*the*] *face of →adopt a FACE of.

change the face of (物・事)を一変させる ▪ The great war *changed the face of* Britain. 大戦は大ブリテン島を一変させた.

come face to face with **1** …とばったり出会う ▪ We *came face to face with* a shark. 我々はサメに遭遇した.
2 (問題)に直面する, をはじめて知る[経験する] ▪ He *came face to face with* the harsh realities of rural poverty. 彼は地方の貧困の厳しい現実に直面した.

disappear* [*vanish,* 《米》*fall*] *off the face of the earth (地上から)すっかり姿を消す ▪ She has just literally *disappeared off the face of the earth*. 彼女は全く文字通り地上から消えてしまった ▪ After the fire, she *fell off the face of the earth*. 火事のあと, 彼女は姿が見えなくなった.

do* [*put on*]** *one's* **[*a*] *face 《口》(女性が)化粧する ▪ She *puts on her face* quickly. 彼女は化粧がはやい ▪ She comes to *do my face*. 彼女は私の化粧をしに来てくれる.

draw* [*pull, put on, have, make, wear*] *a long face 浮かぬ顔をする, がっかりした顔をする; まじめくさった顔をする ▪ Don't go about *drawing long faces*. 浮かぬ顔をして歩き回るな ▪ You can *pull a long face* and scold people into religion. まじめくさった顔をして人々をしかって宗教に入らせることができる ▪ He *pulled a* very *long face* when he heard the news. 彼はその知らせにひどくがっかりした顔をした.

drop from the face of the earth 消息[行方]不明になる, 失踪する ▪ Mother and child seem to have *dropped from the face of the earth*. 母子ともこつぜんと姿を消したようだ.

one's ***face doesn't fit*** 顔[性格]が(特定の仕事に)向いていない ▪ Asian models are often told they have failed to win work because *their face doesn't fit*. アジア人モデルたちは, 顔が業界向きでないので仕事をもらえないと言われることがよくある.

face down →FACE up.

face downwards うつ伏せに, 表面を下にして, 伏せて ▪ He put the open book *face downwards* on the table. 彼は開いた本を伏せてテーブルの上に置いた.

one's ***face fell*** がっかりした顔をした (《聖》*Gen*. 4. 5) ▪ *His face fell* when I told him that. 私がそれ

を話すと彼はがっかりした顔をした．

face foremost 顔から先に ▪ He fell *face foremost* to the floor. 彼はうつ伏せに床に倒れた．

one's ***face is a picture*** (驚き・怒りなどを)絵に描いたような顔をしている ▪ *His face was a picture* of total disbelief. 彼は完全な不信を絵に描いたような顔をしていた．

one's ***face is red*** 《口》(恥ずかしさ・狼狽・きまり悪さで)顔が赤くなる ▪ I made such a mess of it, and *my face is red.* すっかりへまをやって顔が真っ赤だ．

face on 顔を(その方に)向けて，うつ伏せに ▪ A boy fell *face on* into the water. 男の子がうつ伏せに水の中へ落ちた．

face to face (***with***) (…と)面と向かい合って; (と)差し向かいで; 〚形容詞的に〛(と)差し向かいの，(に)直面した ▪ We shall see God *face to face.* 神をまともに見るであろう ▪ We stood *face to face with* death. 我々は死に直面した ▪ They came *face to face* in a crowd. 彼らは人ごみの中で鉢合わせした ▪ Solemn *face to face* reality is very different from the world of her novel. 彼女が直面していた厳粛な現実は自らの小説の世界とは全く違っている．

face up [***down***] 顔を上げて[下げて]; 表を上にして[下にして] ▪ The cards were placed on the table *face down.* トランプのカードは表を下にしてテーブルの上に置かれた．

Face(***s***) ***to the right*** [***left, front***]***!*** 《号令》頭(かしら)右[左，中]!

fall (***flat***) ***on*** *one's* ***face*** 《口》 **1** 急にパッタリ倒れ伏す; ひれ伏す ▪ They *fell on their faces* to God. 彼らは神の前にひれ伏した ▪ He stumbled on a stone and *fell flat on his face.* 彼は石につまずいてパッタリ前へ倒れた．

2 顔をつぶす; こっけいなほど完全に失敗する，無残な敗北[失敗]をする ▪ He could not risk *falling on his face.* 彼は自分の顔をつぶす危険を冒すことはできなかった ▪ Efforts to increase production have *fallen on their faces.* 増産の努力は完全に失敗した ▪ He tried to tackle the problem, and *fell flat on his face.* 彼はその問題に取り組もうと努め無残にも失敗した．

3 (計画・しゃれなどが)当たらない，受けない ▪ His humor *fell flat on its face.* 彼のユーモアは全然受けなかった．

feed *one's* ***face*** 《俗》食べる ▪ They began to *feed their faces.* 彼らは食べ始めた．

fix *one's* ***face*** →FIX².

fly in the face of **1** (犬などが)…に飛びかかる; のまん前を飛ぶ ▪ The dog *flew in the face of* the stranger. その犬は見知らぬ人に飛びかかった ▪ A bat *flew in the face of* the guide. コウモリが案内人のまん前を飛んだ．

2 …に挑戦する; に(公然と)反抗する; にそむく ▪ He is *flying in the face of* danger. 彼はあえて危険を冒している ▪ He *flew in the face of* justice. 彼は裁判に反抗した．

3 …に怒る，食ってかかる ▪ When I said that her hair was dyed, she *flew in my face.* 彼女の髪は染めてあると言ったら，私に食ってかかった．

fly in the face of Providence → PROVIDENCE.

from the face of …の面前[眼前，表面]から ▪ You fled *from the face of* Esau. 君はエサウの面前から逃げた ▪ Wipe it *from the face of* the earth. 地球の表面からそれを一掃せよ．

get in *a person's* ***face*** **1** 人の顔に入る，人の顔を打つ ▪ My glove *got in his face.* 私のグラブが彼の顔にあたった．

2 《口》(態度が悪くて)人をいらいらさせる，困らせる，人の勘にさわる ▪ He *got in her face* and she slapped him. 彼は彼女の勘にさわったので，彼女は彼に平手打ちした．

get out of *a person's* ***face*** 《米口》人の面前から消える; じゃまをやめる ▪ "I'm not going to *get out of your face.* I'm going to get in your face," she said. 「あなたの前から消えるもんですか．困らせてやる」と彼女は言った．

Get out of my face! 《俗》失せろ! ▪ People heard him say, "*Get out of my face!*" 彼が「消えちまえ」と言うのが聞こえた．

give *a person* ***a red face*** 人を赤面させる，まごつかせる ▪ It still *gives* me *a red face* when I retell the story. その話を繰り返すといまでも赤面してしまう．

grind the faces of… (***in the dust***) → GRIND².

have a face as long as a fiddle ひどく陰うつな[暗い]顔をしている ▪ She *had a face as long as a fiddle* after I told her she was fired. 首だと言ってやったあと彼女はひどく浮かない顔をしていた．

have a long face →draw a long FACE.

have *one's* ***face lifted*** 美容整形を受ける ▪ Some actresses *have their face lifted* any number of times. 顔に幾度となく美容整形を受けた女優もいる．

(***have*** [***with***])***… in*** *one's* [***the***] ***face*** …をまともに(受ける[て]) ▪ The ship *had* the sun *in the face.* 船は日をまともに受けた ▪ A horse runs well *with* the wind *in his face.* 馬は風をまともに受けてよく走る．

have the face to *do* ずうずうしく[厚かましく]も…する ▪ He *had the face to* ask for it. 彼はずうずうしくもそれをくれと言った．

have two faces **1** 二心がある，表裏がある ▪ She *has two faces* so you cannot trust her. 彼女には表裏があるから信頼できない．

2 (言葉が)あいまいである ▪ His speech *had two faces.* 彼の演説は二様に取れた．

Her face is her fortune. 美貌が彼女の財産である．

in *a person's* ***face*** **1** 人の顔に，にまともに ▪ The sun was shining *in our faces.* 太陽は我々にまともに照りつけていた．

2 人の面前で，公然と (↔in one's SLEEVE) ▪ She will laugh *in your face.* 彼女はあなたの面前をはばか

らず笑うだろう.

(in) full face 正面を向いて, 顔がすっかり見えるように ▪ He was seated *full face* with a book. 彼は本を持って正面を向いて座っていた ▪ The head of Apollo on the gold coin appears *in full face*. その金貨のアポロの顔は正面を向いている.

in (the) face of **1** 《英》 …の前に ▪ He was for the first time *in face of* the sea. 彼は初めて海の前に出た.

2 …に直面して, まともに, 面と向かって ▪ *In the face of* bad example, the best of precepts are of little avail. 悪い手本を前にしては, いくら良い教えもほとんど役に立たない ▪ He remained calm *in the face of* such danger. 彼はそのような危険に直面しても相変わらず平静であった.

3 …に反対して, をはばからず, にもかかわらず ▪ He went forward *in the face of* many obstacles. 彼は多くの障害をものともせず前進した ▪ They now assert it *in the face of* facts. 彼らは今や事実を無視してそれを主張している.

4 …の面前で, の見えるところで ▪ Pray for him *in the face of* the whole congregation. 全会衆(えしゅ)の前で彼のために祈りなさい.

5 …にかんがみて; を考えると ▪ *In the face of* these facts, it is impossible to deny it. これらの事実を考えるとそれを否定することはできない.

in the face of day [the sun] (白昼)公然と, おおっぴらに ▪ They broke into private houses *in the face of day*. 彼らは公然と個人の家に押し入った.

in the first face →at the first FACE.

in your face 《口》 **1** 傍若無人な, ずうずうしい; 挑戦[反抗]的な ▪ His yakuza film is *in your face*. 彼のやくざ映画は無礼千万だ ▪ Shrek's an *in-your-face* kind of guy. シュレックは反抗的な男だ.

2 〚間投詞的に〛 くたばっちまえ, ばかめ ▪ *In your face*, you lying contractors! 嘘つきの請負人どもめ, くそくらえだ!

Is [Was] my face red! (恥ずかしさ・狼狽などで)顔が赤くなる[なった]のなんのって! ▪ Boy, *was my face red!* いやもう, 顔が赤くなったのなんのって!

keep a straight face/ keep *one's* ***face straight*** 《口》 笑わずに[真顔で]いる ▪ John looked so comical that no one could *keep a straight face*. ジョンは非常にこっけいな様子をしたので誰も笑わずにはいられなかった.

keep *(one's)* ***face*** **1** =keep a straight FACE.

2 平然[泰然]としている ▪ He was beaten, but he managed to *keep his face*. 彼は負けたが何とか平静にかまえていた.

laugh in *a person's* ***face*** →LAUGH².

laugh on the other side of *one's* ***face*** → LAUGH².

Left about face! →Right about FACE!

look ... in the face →LOOK².

lose *(one's)* ***face*** 面子(めんつ)を失う, 面目を失う 《特に2国間の関係についていうことが多い》 ▪ He refused to admit he made a mistake because he didn't want to *lose face*. 彼は面子を失いたくなかったので間違いを認めるのを拒否した ▪ He has *lost face* before all his people. 彼は全国民の前で面目を失った. ☞中国語「面子 (mianzi)」の英訳.

make a crooked [pitiful, wry, etc.] ***face*** しかめつらをする, 顔をしかめる ▪ Each guest *made a wry face*. 客はめいめい顔をしかめた.

make a long face →draw a long FACE.

make [pull] faces [a face] (at) **1** (…に)顔をしかめる, しかめつらをする ▪ He will *make faces at* those grapes. 彼はそのブドウに顔をしかめるだろう ▪ When I mentioned your name, he *pulled a face*. 君の名を言ったら彼は顔をしかめた.

2 (からかって, ふざけて, 警告的に)しかめつらをする ▪ The children sat at the table *making faces at* each other. 子供はテーブルに向かって座り, 互いにしかめつらをし合っていた ▪ What are you *making faces at* me for? しかめつらで何を私に知らせようとしているか.

3 いろいろな顔をする ▪ She was *making faces* in the glass. 彼女は鏡に向かっていろいろな顔をしていた ▪ Karl was *making faces at* me and I couldn't stop giggling. カールがおかしな顔をしていたので, 私はくすくす笑いがとまらなかった.

meet *a person* ***in the face*** 人に面と向かう ▪ I seldom *meet* him *in the face*. 私は彼に面と向かうことはめったにない.

(not) be just a pretty face 《口・戯》 (顔が良いだけの)能なし(でない) ▪ You think I'*m just a pretty face*, but you're wrong. あなたは私が能なしだと思っているが, それはまちがっている ▪ She proved that she *wasn't just a pretty face*. 彼女は能なしでない事を証明した.

off *one's* ***face*** 《口》 (酒に)ひどく酔っぱらって, (薬物で)意識がもうろうとして ▪ He was *off his face* on drugs. 彼は薬物で意識がもうろうとしていた.

off the face of the earth. → wipe ... off the FACE of the earth.

on [upon] *one's* ***face*** うつ伏せに ▪ He collapsed *upon his face*. 彼はうつ伏せに倒れた ▪ She lay *on her face*. 彼女はうつ伏せになっていた.

on [upon] the face of (書類など)の文面で, 文字の上で, 明らかな意味で ▪ An unprejudiced eye, *upon the face of* the letter, could not condemn the writer of it. 偏見のない目だったら, その手紙の文面では書いた人を非難することはできないだろう.

on [upon] the face of it 見たところ(どうも…らしい) ▪ *On the face of it* the document seemed genuine. その文書は一見したところ本物らしかった.

on the face of the earth 〚最上級・否定を伴って〛 この世の中で[に], 地球上で[に] ▪ The Ritz is the best hotel *on the face of the earth*. リッツは世界最高のホテルである.

on the first face →at the first FACE.

open *one's* ***face*** 《米俗》 口を開く, 話す (↔shut one's FACE) ▪ Don't *open your face* to this girl again. この少女に二度と話をしてはいけない.

pull a face →make FACEs (at).

F

pull a long face →draw a long FACE.
pull faces →make FACEs (at).
put a bold [***brave***] ***face on*** [***upon***] 平気な顔をして…を押し切る ▪He *put a bold face on* his inconsistency. 彼は自分の矛盾を平気で押し通した.
put a good face on [***upon***] **1** …に勇敢に耐える; をせいぜいがまんする ▪He *put on a good face* against fortune. 彼は運命に勇敢に耐えた ▪*Put a good face on* the matter. その事はせいぜいがまんしなさい.
2 …に平静を装う ▪She has run away from home, but her family are *putting a good face on* it. 彼女は家出をしたが, 家族は平静を装っている.
3 (困難・苦難など)を希望的に解釈する, 良いように繕う ▪He *put a good face on* Hugh's failure. 彼はヒューの失敗を楽観的に見た.
put a new face on/put on a new face **1** (新しい事情が)様相[局面, 形勢]を一変する ▪His announcement of his candidacy *puts an* entirely *new face on* the political campaign. 彼の立候補発表は選挙戦の形勢を全く一変した.
2 《俗》…をすっかり打ち負かす, に大勝する ▪He *put a new face on* his opponent. 彼は相手を完全に打ち負かした.
put *one's* ***best face on*** (人に)愉快な顔を装う ▪I hated him, but had to *put my best face on.* 彼が大嫌いだったが愉快そうな顔をせねばならなかった.
put [***set***] *one's* ***face against*** …に断固敵対する, 断固反対する ▪*Put your face against* the whole faction. 全徒党に断固敵対しなさい ▪I shall *set my face against* any alteration in our timetable. 時間表のどんな変更にも断固反対します.
put on a bold [***brave***] ***face*** (不運・危険に際して)平気な顔をする ▪He failed in the examination, but he *put on a bold face.* 彼は試験に失敗したが平気な顔をした.
put on a [***the***] ***face of*** →adopt a FACE of.
put on a long face →draw a long FACE.
put on *one's* [***a***] ***face*** →do one's FACE.
red in the face →go RED (in the face).
Right [***Left***] ***about face!*** 《号令》右[左]向け右[左]! ▪To the *right about face!* Forward march! 右向け右! 前へ進め!
run *one's* ***face for*** 《米》厚かましく…を掛け[顔]で得る ▪They can *run their face for* drinks. 彼らは厚かましく顔で酒を飲むことができる.
save (*one's* [*a person's*]) ***face*** 顔が立つ[顔を立てる] (↔ lose (one's) FACE) ▪He *saved* (*his*) *face* by telling a lie to his parents. 彼は両親に嘘を言って面子を保った ▪They tried to *save his face.* みなは彼の顔を立てようとした.
set a face on [***upon***] …をうまく装う, 見せかける ▪They *set a face* of civil authority *upon* tyranny. 彼らは専制政治をうまく民政に見せかけた.
set *one's* ***face*** 確固たる表情[顔つき]をする ▪The flock are proud and *set their faces* as a rock. 信徒は誇り高く, 岩のように確固たる顔つきをしていた.
set *one's* ***face against*** → put one's FACE against.
set *one's* ***face for*** …の方へ向かう, へ顔を向ける (《聖》 *Gen.* 31. 21) ▪I *set my face* resolutely *for* this man and walked towards him. 私は決然としてこの人の方に向きその方へ歩いて行った.
set *one's* ***face from*** …を去る ▪They *set their faces from* the village. 彼らは村から出て行った.
set (*one's*) ***face to*** [***towards***] **1** …の方へ向かう, に向く (《聖》 *2 Kings* 12. 17) ▪We *set our faces to* the South. 南部の方へ向かった.
2 …を志す; に着手する ▪It is high time to be *setting our faces towards* reconstructing our country. もうわが国の再建に着手すべき時だ.
set *one's* ***face to*** *do* …しようと志す ▪Attila has *set his face to* achieve the conquest of the Roman Empire. アッティラはローマ帝国の征服をなし遂げようと志した.
shield *one's* ***face*** 顔を隠す ▪Adam *shielded his face* from photographers with his right hand. アダムは右手でカメラマンたちから顔を隠した.
show a face 出しゃばる; ごう然たる[大胆な]態度を示す ▪He might have *shown a face* even to the boss. 彼は社長にさえごう然たる態度を示したかもしれぬ.
show *one's* ***face*** →SHOW one's head.
shut *one's* ***face*** 《米俗》黙る, 話をやめる (↔open one's FACE) ▪The general bade him *shut his face.* 将軍は彼に黙れと言った.
shut the door in *a person's* ***face*** **1** 人が入ることを拒む, に門前払いを食わす ▪If he comes here again, *shut the door in his face.* もし彼がまたここへ来たら, 門前払いを食わせてやれ.
2 人に取りつくすべもない態度を取る, 人のこれ以上の交渉を不可能にする; 人の計画の進展を止める ▪The action of the Union *shut the door in his face.* 組合の行動は彼のこれ以上の交渉を不可能にした ▪It is *shutting the door* of conversation *in his face.* それは彼に全然談話をさせないことになる.
stare *a person* ***in the face*** →STARE[2].
stuff [***feed***] *one's* ***face with*** 《俗》〚主に進行形で〛…をがつがつ食べる ▪She *was stuffing her face with* an apple. 彼女はリンゴをがつがつ食べていた ▪He was happily *feeding his face with* cake in a cafe. 彼はうれしそうにカフェでケーキをぱくついていた.
throw [***cast, thrust***] ***... in*** *a person's* ***face*** **1** …を人の顔に投げつける ▪He *threw* dirt *in God's face.* 彼は神の顔に泥を投げつけた ▪I *cast* his age *in his face.* この老いぼれめと彼に言ってやった.
2 人の助言[援助]を怒って断る ▪I tried to give him advice, but he *threw* it back *in my face.* 私は彼に助言しようとしたが, 彼は怒ってはねつけた.
to *a person's* ***face*** 人に面と向かって; あからさまに, ずけずけと ▪If you have anything to say, say it *to my face.* 何か言うことがあれば, 私に直接言ってください ▪He does not like to be praised *to his face.* 彼は目の前でほめられるのはきらいだ.
travel on [***upon, in***] *one's* ***face*** 《米》顔で旅を

する《金を払わずに旅をする》 ▪ I must *travel on my face* after this. 私はこれからは顔で旅をせねばならない.

turn face about くるりと振り向く, 方向転換をする［させる］ ▪ They *turned faces about* and began to make head against us. 彼らはくるりと向きを変えて, 我々の方へやって来はじめた ▪ It *turned* him *face about* from the way of destruction. それは彼を破滅の道から方向転換させた. ☞軍隊用語から.

turn** one's **face to the wall →WALL.

turn** one's **face towards ...に向かって旅をする［旅立つ］ ▪ I *turned my face towards* home. 私は故郷に向かって旅立った.

two faces of a coin コインの両面; 不即不離の両面; ものごとの2面 ▪ Kohn and Pople made contributions as closely related as the *two faces of a coin*. コーンとポープルとは硬貨の両面のように密接な関係のある貢献をした ▪ Technical education and industry are always like *two faces of a coin*. 技術教育と産業とは常にコインの両面のごときものである.

wear a long face →draw a long FACE.

what's his* [*her*] *face 《口》 何とかさん ▪ *What's her face* isn't quite the looker that Barbie is. 何とかさんはバービーのような美形じゃない ▪ Della has been going out with *what's his face*, a baseball player. デラは何とかいう野球選手とつき合っている.

wipe* [*sweep*]*... off the face of the earth 〚主に受身で〛...を地表から一掃する ▪ These evils *were wiped off the face of the earth*. これらの害悪は地表から一掃された.

wipe* [*take*] *the smile* [*grin*] *off** a person's* ***face 《口》人の得意顔を消して急にまじめにする ▪ The sad news *wiped the smile off his face*. 悲報を聞いて得意顔だった彼は急にまじめになった.

with a long face 浮かぬ［憂鬱な］顔をして (→a long FACE) ▪ She has been walking about *with a long face*. 彼女は浮かぬ顔をして歩いていた.

You should have seen his* [*her*] *face. 《口》(ひどく驚いて・怒っていて)彼［彼女］の顔は見ものだったよ.

face[2] /feɪs/ 動 ***face it*** 現実を直視する ▪ They have to *face it* and decide what to do. 彼らは現実を直視して, どうすべきか決めなければならない.

face it down 軽蔑に対して大胆に抵抗する ▪ He was years *facing it down* before he received full justice from the Government. 彼は何年も軽蔑に対し大胆に抵抗を続けてようやく政府から相応の待遇を受けた.

face* (*it*) *out **1** (弱点・誤りなどを認めず)大胆に押し通す ▪ He knew he was in the wrong, but *faced it out*. 彼は自分がまちがっていることを知っていたが, しらを切って押し通した ▪ He had the courage to *face out* the demand. 彼は勇敢にもその要求を強引に押し通した.

2 (難局などを)大胆に切り抜ける ▪ You will have to *face it out* alone. 君は一人で難局を大胆に切り抜けねばならないだろう ▪ He *faced out* the danger. 彼はその危険を大胆に切り抜けた.

face ... out of countenance ...に面と向かって度を失わせる ▪ He *was faced out of countenance* by a young whipper-snapper. 彼は青二才ににらまれて度を失った.

face* (*the*) *facts (いやな)事実を認め(て対処す)る ▪ You had better *face facts*. 君は事実を認めて対処したほうがいいよ.

face the music →MUSIC.

face to the right about 回れ右をする ▪ The rest *faced to the right about*. 他の者たちは回れ右をした.

let's face it 《口》(不都合なことでも)事実として認めよう ▪ He may be a little rude sometimes, but *let's face it*, he is very good at his job. 彼はときどき少し無作法かもしれない. がそれでもよい, 彼は仕事がとてもよくできるから.

***to face page** 20* (図版・挿絵など)20ページに向かい合わせる《21ページのこと》 ▪ I want this picture *to face page 20*. この図版を21ページに載せたい.

face value /féɪsvæ̀lju:/ 名 ***at* [*on*]** (*one's*) ***face value*** 額面通りに《比喩的にも》 ▪ Don't accept promises *at their face value*. 約束を額面通りに信用してはいけない ▪ I trusted him *on face value*. 私は彼を外見通りに信用した. ☞貨幣などの表面に書かれている金額から.

facility /fəsíləti/ 名 ***give* [*afford, accord*]** *a person* ***every facility for*** 人に...のためのあらゆる便宜を与える ▪ The library *affords* people *every facility for* study. 図書館は人々に研究のためのあらゆる便宜を与える.

have a facility for ...の才［便宜］がある ▪ He *has a facility for* remembering names. 彼は名前を覚える才がある ▪ We *have* no *facility for* taking care of such a request. 我々にはそのような依頼に応じる便宜がない.

***have facility in** doing* ...をする才能がある ▪ He *has* great *facility in learning* languages. 彼は語学を学ぶ非常な才能がある.

Practice gives facility. 《諺》練習をすれば腕前があがる.

with facility たやすく, すらすらと ▪ He wrote an essay *with* great *facility*. 彼はすらすらと随筆を書いた.

facing /féɪsɪŋ/ 名 ***go through** one's **facings*** **1**《軍》(歩兵・騎馬兵が)向きを変える ▪ In *going through one's facings*, the left heel never quits the ground. 向きを変えるとき, 左のかかとは決して地面を離れない.

2 特性［技量］の検査を受ける ▪ Grace, unwillingly, *went through her facings*. グレイスはしぶしぶ技量の検査を受けた.

3 訓練を受ける, 仕込まれる ▪ I *went through my facings* indifferently. 私は漫然と訓練を受けた. ☞facing《軍》「転回」.

put** a person **through his facings **1**《軍》(歩兵・騎馬兵に)向きを変えさせる.

2 人を試験する, の特性［技量］をためす ▪ I'll *put* him

through his facings, and tell you what I think. 彼を入念に検査してみて, 私の考えをお知らせします.

3 人を訓練する, にわざを仕込む ▪ I'll *put* you *through your facings*. 君を鍛えあげよう.

facsimile /fæksíməli/ 名 ***in facsimile*** 原物通りに; 複写で ▪ The inscription is reproduced *in facsimile*. 碑銘は原物通りに複写されている.

fact /fækt/ 名 ***a fact of life*** 人生の(避けがたい)事実, (どうにもならない)現実《the FACTs of life 1 と区別》 ▪ Domestic violence is *a* savage *fact of life* for many of the world's females. 家庭内暴力は世界中の多くの女性にとって残忍な現実だ.

F

a matter of fact 事実の問題《推測・意見の問題に対して》 ▪ He speaks of *a matter of fact*. 彼は事実を言っている.

after the fact 事後(の), 犯行後(の) (↔before the FACT) ▪ He is an accessory *after the fact*. 彼は事後従犯者だ.

(and) that's [it's] a fact 《口》[[文尾につけて]] それは事実[本当]だ ▪ Cigarette smoking is linked to cancer, *and that's a fact*. 喫煙はガンに直結する, これは事実だ.

(as a) matter of fact →MATTER[1].

before the fact 事前(の); 犯行前(の) (↔after the FACT) ▪ He is an accessory *before the fact*. 彼は事前従犯者である.

confess the fact 犯行を自白する ▪ He *confessed the fact* before Justice Russel. 彼はラッセル判事の前で犯行を自白した.

facts and figures 事実と数字; 《口》正確な情報 ▪ Here are some *facts and figures* about the drug trade. 以下, 麻薬取引に関する詳細なデータの一端を示す.

for a fact 事実として ▪ I know it *for a fact*. それを事実として知っている.

get one's facts wrong [straight, right] (…を)曲解する[正しく把握する] (*about, on*) ▪ They *got their facts wrong on* the issue. 彼らはその問題を曲解した.

hard facts 厳然たる事実, 疑問の余地もない状況 ▪ We'll start with some *hard facts* about housing. 住宅に関する厳しい実情からはじめよう.

in actual fact 実のところ, 実際に ▪ *In actual fact*, oriental politics seldom remain static. 実のところ, 東洋の政治は静的なことはめったにない.

in (point of) fact **1** 実のところ, 実際上 ▪ Great Britain is a republic *in fact*. イギリスは事実上共和国である.

2 (前言を要約して)要するに, つまり ▪ He was a thief—*in fact*, he was the greatest scoundrel I ever saw. 彼は泥棒であった—つまり私の見た最大の悪漢であった.

Is that a fact? **1** (同意・確認を表して)そうなんだ, そうだね ▪ I would talk to him about the past, and he would say, "Is that so? *Is that a fact?*" 過去のことを彼に話したら, 彼は「へえ, そうなんだ」と言っていた ▪ You mean you've flown to London three times just this month? *Is that a fact?* 今月だけで3度もロンドンに飛んだというのだね. そうだろ.

2 (不信・軽蔑などを表して)ふん, そうかい ▪ I'll be promoted over you before the year is out. —Oh yeah, *is that a fact?* 今年中に僕は君より先に昇進するだろうよ—ふーん, そうかい. ☞→(Is) THAT so?

it's a fact that 実は…だ ▪ *It's a fact that* we don't have much money. 実はあまりお金を持っていないのだ.

matter of fact [[形容詞的に]] 事務的な, 平凡な, 散文的な ▪ She is a *matter of fact* person who never gets excited over anything. 彼女は何事にも決して興奮しない平凡な人間である.

the fact (of the matter) is… 実は…である ▪ *The fact of the matter is* that I don't want to go there. 実はそこへ行きたくないのです.

the fact remains that …という事実は依然として残っている, という事実はやはり変わらない ▪ *The fact remains that* most Europeans dislike drinking, eating and working in smoky surroundings. 欧州の大半の人たちがタバコ臭い環境で飲食したり働いたりするのを好まないという事実に変わりはない. ☞that 以下は the fact と同格.

the facts of life **1** (特に子供に話す)性の事実; 生殖の基本的生理作用 ▪ It is a mistake to bring up children in ignorance of *the facts of life*. 性の知識を知らせないで子供を育てるのは誤りだ.

2 (特に不快・困難な)人生の現実 ▪ They tell us to ignore *the facts of life*. 彼らは我々に人生の苦しい現実を無視せよと言う.

the facts speak for themselves 事実がおのずからそう語っている ▪ There's no point denying your error—*the facts speak for themselves*. 自分の過失ではないと言っても無駄だ, 事実からそれは明白だから.

factor /fæktər/ 名 ***a sleaze factor*** (政界などの)醜聞[マイナス]要因, 疑惑要素 ▪ They used *the sleaze factor* to tar the Clinton administration. 例の醜聞疑惑をクリントン政権のイメージダウンに用いた.

by a factor of ten [five, etc.] 10倍[5倍, など] ▪ The amount has increased *by a factor of 10* since last year. その量は昨年から10倍増えた.

(the) feel-good factor 好況感, 満足感[要因], 好感材料 ▪ *The feel-good factor* seems to be coming back in the capital market. 好況感が資本市場に戻ってきているようだ.

factory /fæktəri/ 名 ***on the factory floor*** **1** 平工員[一般労働者]として ▪ He spent five years *on the factory floor* before being promoted to supervisor. 彼は5年間平の工員として過ごしたのち現場監督に昇進した.

2 生産現場で[に] ▪ The problem was only discovered when the system was tested *on the factory floor*. システムが生産現場でテストされてはじめて問題が発見された.

fad /fæd/ 名 ***be full of fads and fancies*** 気まぐれと幻想にあふれている ▪ History *is full of fads* *and fancies* of the day. 歴史は時代の気まぐれと幻想にあふれている ▪ The boss *is full of fads and fancies* even if he is not quite mad. 社長は気まぐれと幻想だらけだが，すっかり頭が変なわけじゃない.

fade /feɪd/ 名 ***do a fade*** 《口》姿を消す，ずらかる ▪ There are always ways to *do a fade* from your responsibilities. 責任から逃げる方法はいつでもある.

have a bit of fade 《ゴルフ》(球が)左から右に少しカーブする ▪ I struck it well and luckily it *had a bit of fade*. 私は球をしたたか打ったところ，幸運にも左から右にややカーブしてくれた.

fag[1] /fæg/ 名 ***a fag hag*** 《俗・侮蔑》ホモの男とつき合う女，「おこげ」 ▪ Have you been out clubbing with Mark and Jim again? You're turning into *a* real *fag hag*! またマークとジムといっしょにナイトクラブにいってたの? ほんとに「おこげ」になってきてるよ. ☞fag「ホモ」; hag「ばばあ」.

be too much fag 《口》あまりにも面倒[やっかい]すぎる ▪ The thing *is too much fag*. それはあまりにも面倒である.

the* [*a*] *fag end 《英口》最後の切れはし; (しまいの)はしくれ ▪ There is only *a fag end* of this cloth left. この布の最後の切れはしが残されているだけである ▪ Did you see the Davis Cup match?—Only *the fag end* of it. デビスカップの試合を見たか?—しまいのはしくれだけをね ▪ We went away at *the fag-end* of summer when all the shops were starting to close. 夏の最後に出かけたが，どこも店じまいを始めていた.

fag[2] /fæg/ 動 ***fag*** *oneself* ***to death*** 身を粉にして働く ▪ It is not necessary to *fag yourself to death*. 身を粉にして働く必要はない.

fagging /fǽgɪŋ/ 名 ***have a fagging-about*** あくせく働く ▪ I *had* such *a fagging-about* last year. 私は昨年は非常にあくせく働いた.

faggot /fǽgət/ 名 ***bear* [*carry*] *a faggot*** (異端を捨てた者がしたように)火刑のための薪を運ぶ ▪ Wolsey caused them to *carry a faggot* to the fire. ウルジーは彼らにその火の所へ火刑の薪を運ばせた.

fail[1] /feɪl/ 名 ***without fail*** **1** いつも...する ▪ Every Tuesday afternoon, *without fail*, Helga went to visit her father. 毎週火曜日の午後には，きまって，ヘルガは父親を訪ねに行った.
2 必ず...する[起こる]，きっと，ぜひ ▪ You will meet me at the airport, won't you?—Don't worry, I'll be there *without fail*. 空港で出迎えてくれるんだね?—心配無用. 必ず行くよ ▪ Come tomorrow *without fail*. あすぜひ来なさい.

fail[2] /feɪl/ 動 ***cannot fail to*** *do* きっと...する，...しないはずがない ▪ Whoever studies hard *cannot fail to* succeed. 一生懸命勉強する者は誰でも成功しないはずがない.

one's ***heart fails*** *one* →HEART.

if* [*when*] *all else fails 《文》もしも他のやり方もすべてうまくいかなかったら，万策尽きれば ▪ *If all else fails*, Musharraf will amend the constitution. 万策尽きれば，ムシャラフは憲法を改正するだろう ▪ *If all else fails* let me know. 他に方法がなければ知らせよ.

not* [*never*] *fail to *do* 必ず...する ▪ *Never* [Don't] *fail to* come. ぜひ来なさい ▪ He *never failed to* accomplish his purpose. 彼は目的を達せずにはおかなかった.

time would fail *a person* ***to*** *do* 人が...しようとすれば時間が足りないだろう ▪ *Time would fail* me *to* tell of Gideon. 私がギデオンの話をしようとすれば時間が足りないだろう.

words fail *a person* 人が(感動して)物が言えない ▪ When he said so *words failed* me. 彼がそう言ったとき私は感動して物が言えなかった.

fain /feɪn/ 形副 《古》***would fain*** *do* 喜んで...したい ▪ I *would fain* know what happiness is. 私は幸福とは何であるかを大いに知りたい.

fain(s) /feɪn(z)/ 動 ***Fain(s) I*** 《英学童》...はごめんだよ ▪ *Fains I* wicket-keeping! It's up to you. (クリケットの)三柱門守備はごめんだよ! 君がやれよ.

faint /feɪnt/ 形名 ***damn ... with faint praise*** (人・物)を一応ほめる，言葉でほめて内容でけなす ▪ She *damned* Reynolds *with faint praise*, calling him one of the best imitators in the world. 彼女はレイノルズを一応ほめて，彼のことを世界でもっとも優れた模倣者の一人だと言った.

Faint heart never won fair lady. 《諺》小心者が美人を得たためしがない.

faint in color 青ざめて，血色が悪く ▪ He was *faint in color*. 彼は血色が悪かった.

faint yet* [*but*] *pursuing 疲れながらも追求して (《聖》*Judges* 8. 4) ▪ *Faint but pursuing*, they followed the thief to London. 疲れながらも追求をゆるめず，彼らはその賊をロンドンまで追って行った.

fall* (*down*) *in a faint →FALL[2].

feel faint 気が遠くなる ▪ At the sight, I *felt faint*. それを見て私は気が遠くなった.

go off in a faint 気絶する ▪ She *went off in a faint*. 彼女は気絶した.

have not the faintest 《口》全く見当がつかない ▪ I *haven't the faintest*. 全く見当がつかぬ. ☞idea を略したもの.

in a* (*dead*) *faint (全く)失神して ▪ He fell *in a dead faint*. 彼は卒倒した.

not for the faint-hearted 臆病者には向いていない ▪ The drive along the winding coast road is *not for the faint-hearted*, particularly when it's foggy. 曲がりくねった海岸沿いの道路を運転するのは臆病者には向いていない，霧が濃いときは特にそうだ.

fair /feər/ 名形副 ***a* [*the*] *day after the fair*** あとの祭り，遅すぎて ▪ Sorry, but you've come *the day after the fair*. お気の毒ですがおいでが遅すぎましたね ▪ He [It] is *a day after the fair*. 彼は遅すぎた[それはあとの祭りだ].

a* [*the*] *day before the fair 早すぎて ▪ He came *a day before the fair*. 彼は来るのが早すぎた.

(*a*) *fair field and no favor* えこひいきなし，公平無私 ▪ All the competitions are conducted on the principle of *a fair field and no favor*. すべて

の競争はえこひいきなしの原則で行われる. ☞競馬から.

a fair-haired boy →BOY.

a fair one 女性 ▪ I heard *a fair one* cry. 私は女性が泣く声を聞いた.

a fair shake 《米俗》公正な扱い[取引, 機会] ▪ You have always given me *a fair shake*. 君はいつも僕を公正に扱ってくれた《だましたりしなかった》.

a fair treat 《口》非常によく ▪ My car is old, but it runs *a fair treat*. 私の車は古いが実によく走る.

All's fair in love and war. 《諺》恋と戦争は手段を選ばない.

F

be fair with …に公平である ▪ He *is fair with* us. 彼は我々に公平だ.

be in a fair way to [*to do*] …する見込みが十分ある ▪ He *is in a fair way to* success. 彼には成功の見込みが大いにある ▪ He *is in a fair way to* make a fool of himself. 彼はどうも笑い者になりそうだ.

be on the fair way [***road***] ***to*** [*to do*] …する見込みが大いにある ▪ The merchant *is* now *on the fair way to* make a fortune. その商人は今やひと財産作る見込みが大いにある.

bid fair to *do* 《雅》…する見込みが十分ある《悪い意味にも》 ▪ The expedition *bids fair to* be successful. その遠征は大いに成功しそうである ▪ The small farmers *bid fair to* disappear. 小農は消滅しそうだ.

by fair means or foul →MEANS.

copy [***write out***] ***fair*** 清書する ▪ I will *write* his memorials *out fair*. 彼の覚え書きを清書します.

fair and softly 丁寧に穏やかに ▪ I hope they will treat it *fair and softly*. 彼らがそれを丁寧に穏やかに扱うことを望みます.

fair and square **1** 公明正大で, 公正で ▪ He is *fair and square* in all his dealings. 彼はすることがすべて公正である.

2 正々堂々と, 公明正大に, 公正に; まっすぐに ▪ We must deal with the problem *fair and square*. その問題を公明正大に論じなければならない ▪ We struck the beach *fair and square*. 我々はまっすぐに浜に行き着いた ▪ We won the match *fair and square*. 私たちはその戦いに正々堂々と勝った.

3 (標的などについて)まともに, もろに, 真ん中に, きちんと ▪ She hit me *fair and square* on the nose. 彼女はまともに私の鼻をなぐった ▪ He got the ball *fair and square* on the nose. 彼はボールを鼻にまともに受けた ▪ He sat down *fair and square*. 彼はきちんと座った.

fair dos [***do's***] 《英口》〖間投詞的に〗(アンフェアな扱いに対して)公平[平等]にやろう ▪ *Fair do's*, Jo. You've been on the computer for hours—let your sister use it for a while! ジョー, 公平にやりなさい. 何時間もコンピューターを使ってるでしょ—ちょっと妹に使わせてあげなさい.

fair enough 《口》もっともで, なるほど ▪ He won't come because he doesn't want to. —*Fair enough*. 彼は来たくないから来ないのです—ごもっともで ▪ I don't feel like going out tonight. I've got a bit of a headache.—*Fair enough*. 今晩は外出したくない. 少し頭が痛いので—そりゃ仕方ないね.

Fair fall (***to***)***...!*** →FALL[2].

fair, fat and forty 太りかけた中年の女性 ▪ She is *fair, fat and forty*. 彼女は中年で太りかけている.

fair game →be fair GAME.

fair to middlin(***g***) 《口》(顔・質・健康などが)まあ良い方で, まず良い; 二流で ▪ The food is *fair to middling*. その食べ物はまあまあだ ▪ What's your French like?—Oh, *fair to middling*. フランス語はどの程度ですか?—ああ, まあまあです.

Fair's fair. 《口》公平[公正]にやろう; 不平等[えこひいき]なしだ《行為が公平[平等]であると主張するときの言葉》 ▪ *Fair's fair*. I'll spin a coin for it. 公平にやろう. 私が硬貨を投げ上げてきめよう ▪ *Fair's fair*. If you had done the work properly, you would not have been scolded. 公正な行為だよ. もし君が仕事をきちんとやっていたらしかられはしなかったろうに ▪ *Fair's fair*, Chris. You chose where to eat last time so it's my turn this time. クリス, 平等にやろう. 前回は君がどこで食事をするか選んだのだから, 今回は私の番だ.

fall fair ドスンと倒れる ▪ The tree *fell fair* on the ground. その木は地面にドスンと倒れた.

for fair 《米俗》全く, すっかり ▪ He must have been crazy *for fair* then. 彼はそのとき全く気が狂っていたにちがいない.

get [***have***] ***a fair crack of the whip*** →a fair CRACK of the whip.

give** a person* ***a fair crack of the whip →a fair CRACK of the whip.

have a fair field and no favor (競技が)平等公平な立場でやれる ▪ You will *have a fair field and no favor*. 平等公平な立場で(競技が)やれるさ.

have more than** one's* ***fair share of 〖主に完了形で〗(不愉快なこと)に過度に見舞われる, 弱り目にたたり目[泣きっ面にハチ]である ▪ Jane's *had more than her fair share of* bad luck recently, what with losing her job and getting divorced. 失職やら, 離婚やらで, ジェインは最近弱り目にたたり目だった.

It's a fair cop. 《英俗》捕まってしまった ▪ *It's a fair cop*. I was driving way too fast. ご用になってしまった. スピード出しすぎだったもんな. ☞悪い事をしていて捕まったときの言葉; 警官以外にも用いる.

keep fair with …と親しくする[している] ▪ I must try to *keep fair with* them. 彼らと親しくするようにせねばならない.

no fair 《米口》ルール[規則]違反で, フェアでない, 偏った ▪ In such a situation, *no fair* trial can be expected. そんな状況下では公平な裁判は期待できない.

out of fair (列などの)正しい位置を離れて ▪ The bottom member would be *out of fair*. 一番びりの人は正位置をはずれるであろう.

play fair (***with***) (…と)公正に勝負する, (に対して)公正にふるまう ▪ He doesn't know how to *play fair*. 彼は公正に勝負する方法を知らない ▪ I'd like

you to *play fair with* me. 私に対して公正にふるまってもらいたい.

see fair play/《口》***see fair*** 審判になる ▪ Mr. Weller will *see fair* (between both sides). ウェラー氏が(両方の)審判をするだろう.

speak *a person* ***fair*** 人に丁寧にものを言う ▪ The workers *spoke* him soft and *fair*. 労働者たちは彼に隠やかかつ丁寧にものを言った.

stand fair →STAND[2].

take fair aim 慎重にねらいを定める ▪ He *took fair aim* with his rifle and fired. 彼は銃を慎重にねらいを定めて発砲した.

the fair(er) sex →SEX.

The glass is at fair. 晴雨計が「晴」をさしている.

through fair and foul →FOUL[1].

to [let's] be fair 《口》〚文修飾〛公平を期するために言うならば ▪ *To be fair*, they are also mirrors of our age. 公平に言えば, 彼らも現代を映す鏡なのだ.

with *one's* ***own fair hands*** 《戯》うるわしの御手(て)にて, 御自ら, (助けを借りずに)自分自身で ▪ Did you buy this cake?—No, I made it *with my own fair hands*. このケーキは買ったの?—いいえ, 私が御自ら作ったのよ.

write out fair →copy FAIR.

fairer /feərər/ 形 ***I [You] can't say fairer than that.*** 《英口》これ以上公平な提案はありませんよ ▪ I'll wash the dishes if you cook dinner. *You can't say fairer than that*, can you? 夕食を作ってくれるなら, 皿洗いをしよう. これ以上の公平はないだろ.

fairing /féərɪŋ/ 名 ***get*** *one's* ***fairing*** 《英》相当の報いを受ける ▪ Glad he *got his fairing*. あいつが相当の報いを受けたのはうれしい.

give *a person his* ***fairing*** 《英》人に相当の報いを与える ▪ I will *give* him *his fairing*. 彼に相当の報いをするつもりである.

fairy /féəri/ 名 ***(away) with the fairies*** 夢想中で, 心ここにあらずで, 放心状態で ▪ He was *away with the fairies* because of the painkillers. 彼は鎮痛剤のためもうろうとしていた.

be [sound, read] a fairy tale (現実離れして)おとぎ話のようだ ▪ It *sounds a fairy tale*. おとぎ話のようだ.

the tooth fairy 歯の妖精《子供が抜けた乳歯を枕の下に置いておくと, それと引き換えに枕の下にお金を置いていくと信じられている妖精》 ▪ Look what *the tooth fairy* left me. Twenty-five cents! 見て, 歯の妖精が置いてってくれたのを. 25セントもだよ.

fait /feɪt/ 名 ***a fait accompli*** 既成事実 ▪ The sudden change in policy was presented to the party as *a fait accompli*, without any consultation. 突然の政策変更は, 相談なしに, 既成事実として党に提出された. ☞F 'accomplished fact'.

faith /feɪθ/ 名 ***accept ... on faith*** →take ... on FAITH.

bad faith 不信, 背信, 不誠実 ▪ It was an act of *bad faith* to betray his friend. 友を裏切るのは不信の行為であった.

break (one's) faith **1** (自分の)信念[主義]にそむく ▪ That he of all people should *break faith* with his own beliefs! まさか彼が自らの信条にもとる行為をするとは!

2 (...との)約束[誓い]を破る, (を)裏切る (*with*) ▪ They *broke faith with* their ally. 彼らは同盟国を裏切った.

by [on] *one's* ***faith*** 誓って, ほんとに ▪ I say this *on my faith*. これは断言します ▪ Strange, *by my faith*! ほんとに奇妙だ!

by the faith of ...にかけて ▪ *By the faith of* my love, I will. 私の愛にかけて, 私はします.

Carthaginian faith →Punic FAITH.

engage [pledge, plight] (one's) faith 誓いを立てる, 固く約束する ▪ He has *plighted faith* to me. 彼は私に誓いを立てた.

Faith can (re)move mountains. 信仰は山をも動かす《思う念力岩をも通す》.

give faith (to) ...を信じる ▪ I *give faith to* these wonderful stories. この不思議な話を信じます.

have faith in ...を信じている, 信仰する ▪ I *have* no *faith in* drugs. 私は薬類は信用しません.

in all good faith 正直に信じて ▪ I said *in all good faith* that my husband was dead. 私は夫が死んだと正直に信じて話しました.

in bad faith 悪意をもって, 悪意で《自分がしていることがまちがっていることを知りながら》(↔in good FAITH) ▪ They acted *in bad faith*. 彼らは不信の行為をした ▪ The court ruled that the sellers had acted *in bad faith*. 法廷は販売人たちは悪意で行動したという裁定を下した.

in good faith 誠実に, 善意で《自分がしていることは正しいと信じて》(↔in bad FAITH) ▪ I know that you have acted *in good faith*. 私はあなたが誠実に行動したことを知っている ▪ His defence was that he had acted *in good faith*. He did not know when he bought the car that it had been stolen. 彼の弁明は善意で行動したということだった. 車を買った時点では盗品だとは知らなかったのだ.

keep (one's) faith (with) **1** (...に対して)誠実である, 信義[約束]を守る ▪ England *kept faith with* her ally. イギリスは同盟国に対して信義を守った ▪ Has the company *kept faith with* its promise to invest in training? 会社は養成に投資するという約束を守ってきましたか.

2 (信念などを)忠実に守る ▪ He *keeps faith with* his religion. 彼は自分の宗教を忠実に守る.

lose faith in ...を信用しなくなる ▪ I have *lost faith in* that man. 私はあの男を信用できなくなった.

My faith! ほんとに ▪ Weapons were flourished in the wind, *my faith!* ほんとに, 武器が風上で振り回された.

of faith キリスト教の主要部分[眼目]で ▪ The uncompounded nature of God is *of faith*. 神の純一な性質がキリスト教の眼目だ.

on *one's* ***faith*** →by one's FAITH.

on the faith of (...の確実性)を信頼して; の保証で

▪The bank-note is circulated entirely *on the faith of* the issuing bank. 紙幣はもっぱら発行銀行に対する信用により流通する ▪*On the faith of* his oath they had placed themselves in his power. 彼の誓いを信用して，彼らは自己を彼の支配下においた.

pin** one's **faith to [***on***] (*a person's* ***sleeve***) …を絶対的に信頼する; を盲信する ▪I wouldn't *pin my faith to* what he says. 私だったら，彼の言うことを文句なしに信用はしないね ▪We *pinned our faith on Mary's sleeve.* 我々はメアリーをすっかり信頼した.

pledge [***plight***] (*one's*) ***faith*** → engage (one's) FAITH.

Punic faith 背信，不信 ▪*Punic faith* is faithlessness. カルタゴの誠実とは不誠実のことである. ☞昔カルタゴ人は背信的だとローマ人に考えられていたことから.

put** one's **faith in …を信じる，信じている ▪Do not *put your faith in* such a remedy. そんな療法を信じてはいけません.

shake** a person's **faith 信念をゆるがす ▪What you tell me *shakes my faith* in human nature. あなたの話は人間性に対する私の信頼をゆるがすものです.

take [***accept***]***… on faith*** (証拠を求めもせず)…を信じこむ ▪We *accepted* his story *on faith.* 我々は彼の話をそのまま信じこんだ.

faithful /féɪθfəl/ 形 ***(be) faithful to*** …に対して忠実で(ある) ▪She *is faithful to* her husband. 彼女は夫に貞節である ▪The translation *is faithful to* the original. その翻訳は原文に忠実である.

faithfully /féɪθfəli/ 副 ***deal faithfully with*** **1** …を誠実に扱う ▪He *dealt faithfully with* the servants. 彼は使用人たちを誠実に扱った.

2《皮肉》(人)を厳しくしかる; を厳しく扱う ▪*Deal faithfully with* wrongdoing. 非行を厳しく扱いなさい.

fall[1] /fɔːl/ 名 ***at a fall*** ひと追いで ▪Sometimes 10 or 12 fish are killed *at a fall.* 時にはひと追いで10から12匹の魚が殺されることもある. ☞fall＝(chase of a) whale.

(***be***) ***a fall-guy for*** …の言いなりになる人(である) ▪He *is a fall-guy for* the boss. 彼は社長の言いなりになる男だ.

be heading [***riding***] ***for a fall/be headed for a fall*** 自滅・退廃に向かっている，身をもちくずしつつある ▪Greg's *riding for a fall*—he gets to work late and spends hours talking to his friends on the phone. グレッグは自堕落な生活をしている—仕事に取り掛かるのが遅いし，友人に何時間も長電話をする.

break** a person's **fall →BREAK[2].

get a fall out of →take a FALL out of.

give [***try, wrestle***] ***a fall*** ひと勝負する ▪I must *wrestle a fall* with him. 彼とひと勝負しなければならない. ☞レスリングから.

have a loose fall クジラを取り逃がす ▪The ship *had a loose fall.* その船はクジラを取り逃がした.

head for a [*one's*] ***fall*** ＝RIDE for a fall.

Pride goes before a fall./Pride will have a fall. →PRIDE[1].

spring and fall 春と秋(に)《英国でもかなり普通に用いられる》 ▪She has been bled, *spring and fall.* 彼女は春と秋に放血してもらった.

take a fall **1** 倒れる，転倒する (＝take a SPILL) ▪Bill *took a fall* on the ice and injured his right shoulder. ビルは氷上で転倒して右肩を負傷した.

2 逮捕[起訴]される ▪Ridge *took a fall* for insider trading. リッジはインサイダー取引のため逮捕された.

take [***get***] ***a fall out of***《米口》…を一時的に打ち倒す，に勝つ ▪I will *take a fall out of* my "Universal History." 私は「世界史」を征服するつもりだ.

take the fall for《主に米口》…の身代わり[替え玉]になって責めを負う，人の罪をかぶる ▪Bob'll *take the fall for* the director—he'd do anything to save his boss. ボブは重役の身代わりになって責めを受けるだろう，彼は上司を救うためなら何でもするだろうから.

the fall of life 晩年 ▪He did not succeed till *the fall of life.* 彼は晩年になるまで成功しなかった.

the fall of the day [***year***] 日[年]の暮れ《英国でもかなり普通に用いられる》 ▪It was in *the fall of the year* that she sailed for America. その船がアメリカへ向けて出帆したのは年の暮れであった.

try [***wrestle***] ***a fall*** →give a FALL.

fall[2] /fɔːl/ 動 ***almost fall off** one's **chair*** → CHAIR.

be fallen on **1** (人が)…に遭遇する ▪We *are fallen on* evil days. 我々は不運に遭遇した.

2 …を攻撃する ▪The Dutch *were fallen on* our fleet at Chatham. オランダ軍はチャタムでわが艦隊を攻撃した.

one's ***eyes fall*** 目を伏せる ▪*His eyes fell* suddenly. 彼は急に目を伏せた.

Fair fall (***to***)***…!*** …に良いことがありますように，の幸運を祈ります (↔Foul FALL…!) ▪*Fair fall* (*to*) the Puritans! 清教徒たちの幸運を祈る.

***fall a-**doing* …しだす ▪She *fell a-crying.* 彼女は泣きだした.

fall about (***laughing, with laughter***)《口》爆笑する ▪People *fell about* when he cracked a joke. 彼が冗談を言うと人々は爆笑した.

fall abreast of →ABREAST.

***fall all over** a person* **1**《口》人に大いに注意を払う; 人を非常に丁重にもてなす ▪He *fell all over* his customers. 彼は客を非常に丁重にもてなした.

2 人にこびる ▪He *fell all over* her in the hope of getting off with her. 彼は親しくなれる期待をかけて彼女にへつらった.

***fall all over** oneself* **1** 夢中になってする (*doing*) ▪The critics *fell all over themselves raving.* 批評家たちは夢中になって激賞した.

2《口》躍起になって…しようとする ▪John *fell all over himself* to please his girlfriend. ジョンは躍起になってガールフレンドを喜ばせようとした.

fall asleep at the switch →be asleep at the SWITCH.

fall back, fall edge どんなことがあろうとも ▪*Fall*

back, fall edge, nothing shall induce me to publish it. どんなことがあろうと私は断じてそれを発表しない.

fall beneath a sword 刀にかかって死ぬ ▫ He *fell beneath* the Japanese *sword*. 彼は日本刀にかかって倒れた.

fall by the wayside **1** 中途で没落[堕落]する (《聖》*Matt.* 13. 4) ▫ Many advocates of this doctrine have *fallen by the wayside*. この説の唱道者は中途で脱落した者が多い.

2 (特に競技に)負ける ▫ Many party stalwarts *fell by the wayside* on election day. 愛党心の強い人が選挙日に多く落選した.

fall* (*down*) *at** *a person's* ***feet 人の足もとに平伏する ▫ I *fell at his feet* to worship him. 私は足もとにひれ伏して彼を拝んだ (《聖》*Rev.* 19. 10).

fall* (*down*) *in a faint 卒倒する ▫ The Premier *fell down in a faint* last night. 首相は昨夜卒倒した.

***fall down on it* [*the job*]** 《口》(仕事)に失敗する, 責任を果たしえない ▫ The government *fell down on the job* of reparation payments. 政府は賠償支払いが果たせなかった ▫ We *fell down on the job* of satisfying these people. 我々はこれらの人々を満足させることに失敗した.

fall* (*flat*) *on** *one's* ***face →FACE[1].

***fall for*...(*hook, line, and sinker*)** 《口》 **1** (話など)に釣り込まれる ▫ I *fell for* the sales talk easily. 私はその売りこみ口上にやすやすと釣り込まれた.

2 ...にだまされる ▫ Everyone *fell for* his story *hook, line, and sinker*. みんな彼の話にまんまとだまされた.

3 ...にのめりこむ, 夢中になる ▫ I *fell for* the words *hook, line, and sinker*. 私はその歌詞が心底気に入った.

***fall for* (*in a big way*)** 《口》...にぞっこんほれこむ, 参る ▫ It looks as though Bill is *falling for* your sister *in a big way*. ビルはあなたの妹さんにぞっこんほれこんでいるらしい ▫ I will not *fall for* your tears. 君が泣いたって僕は参らないよ.

fall for it 《英俗》妊娠する, できちゃう ▫ You'll *fall for it* if you don't make him use a condom. 彼にコンドームを使わせないとできちゃうよ.

fall foul of →FOUL[1].

***fall from** *one's* **lips* [*mouth, tongue*]** (言葉が)口から漏れる, 出る ▫ Not a word *fell from her lips*. 彼女は一言も言わなかった.

fall heavy on (主語のため)...は困る ▫ His death will *fall heavy on* his family. 彼の死で家族は困るだろう.

***fall in* [*into*]** *a person's* ***mind* [*heart*]** 人の心に思いつく, 思い浮かぶ ▫ It *fell into my mind* that I had neglected my promise to her. 彼女への約束を反故(ほ)にしたと思い当たった.

***fall in pieces* [*powder*]** =FALL to pieces.

fall in the rear 後方に下がる ▫ The wounded men were ordered to *fall in the rear*. 負傷兵は後方へ下がるよう命じられた. ☞軍隊用語から.

fall in** *one's* **way →in one's WAY.

***fall into error* [*sin*]** 過ちを犯す, 不品行[罪]なことをする ▫ Judge Morgan *fell into error* in accepting Mr. R's statements. モーガン判事はR氏の陳述を採用した点で過ちを犯した.

***fall into** *a person's* **hands* [*lap*]** 人の手にわたる ▫ Once the tape *fell into our hands* we had a journalistic obligation to report it. 一旦テープが手に入れば我々には新聞記者として報道する義務があった.

fall into ill health 健康を害する ▫ If you study so hard, you will *fall into ill health*. そんなにひどく勉強すると健康を害するよ.

fall into step (人と)いっしょに歩く; (...と)歩調を合わせる (*with*) ▫ She hailed me and *fell into step* as I walked. 彼女は私にあいさつし, 私が歩くのに歩調を合わせた ▫ Canada *fell into step with* the United States. カナダは合衆国と足並みをそろえてきた.

***fall into the way of** *doing* →WAY.

fall off* (*the back of*) *a lorry 《英口・婉曲》盗まれる ▫ These watches *fell off the back of a lorry*. これらの時計は盗品だ.

fall off the wagon →WAGON.

***fall on a* [*one's*] *sword* [*dagger,* etc.]** 自刃する, 自害する ▫ Saul *fell upon his sword*. サウルは自刃した.

fall on** *one's* **back あお向けに倒れる ▫ He fainted and *fell on his back*. 彼は気絶してあお向けに倒れた.

fall on deaf ears →EAR.

fall on** *one's* **face →fall (flat) on one's FACE.

fall on** *a person's* **shoulders →SHOULDER[1].

fall on stony ground 実を結ばない, 効果がない (《聖》*Matt.* 13. 5) ▫ The seed of his lesson *fell on stony ground*. 彼の教訓の種は実を結ばなかった.

fall out of the line →LINE[1].

***fall over** *oneself* **1** あわててころぶ ▫ They almost *fell over themselves* in their anxiety to get there quickly. 彼らはそこへ早く行きたいあまりにあわててころびそうだった.

2 《口》[[主に進行形で]] ...しようと切望している, やっきになっている (*to do*) ▫ They *were falling over themselves to* be helpful. 彼らは一助になることを切望している.

***fall over backward*(*s*) (*to do*)** →bend over BACKWARD(S) (to do).

***fall over one another* [*each other*]** **1** 第1位を争う ▫ Capitalists are getting ready to *fall over each other*. 資本家たちは第1位を争う準備をしている.

2 めちゃくちゃに争う ▫ They *fell over one another* when the doors were opened. 戸があいたら彼らはめちゃくちゃに押し争った.

***fall short* (*of*)** →SHORT.

fall to be 自然に...となる ▫ He *fell to be* on ill terms with his mother. 彼は母と仲が悪くなった.

fall to pieces **1** こなごなになる, めちゃめちゃにこわれる, 崩壊する ▪ The glass has *fallen to pieces.* そのコップはこっぱみじんになった ▪ After the death of Alexander his empire began to *fall to pieces.* アレクサンドロスの死後, 彼の帝国は崩壊し始めた.
2 (理論などが)くずれる, だめになる ▪ The old belief *fell to pieces.* 古い信仰がくずれ去った.
3 体をこわす ▪ He has *fallen* all *to pieces.* 彼はすっかり体をこわした.

fall to** a person's **rifle [***gun***] 人の銃によって倒れる ▪ Two lions *fell to his rifle.* 2頭のライオンが彼の銃によって倒れた.

fall under** a person's **eye [***notice, observation***] 人の目に留まる ▪ This state of affairs *fell under our observation.* この情勢が我々の目に留まった ▪ Soon it *fell under his notice.* それはまもなく彼の目に留まった.

fall under** a person's **spell [***the spell of** a person*] …に魅せられる, の虜になる ▪ They *fell under the* cultural *spell of* China in the 8th century. 連中は8世紀の中国文化の魅力にとりつかれた.

Foul fall …! …に不幸[災い]がありますように!(↔Fair FALL (to)…!) ▪ *Foul fall* the day! 当日に災いあれ!

it falls on [***upon***] *a person* ***to*** *do* 《文》…することが人の責任である, 責任となる ▪ *It fell upon* him *to* open the exhibition. 博覧会の開会をするのが彼の責任となった.

it falls out that 《文》(たまたま)…ということになる ▪ *It fell out that* the two men arrived at the same time. 二人が同時に到着するということになった.

let fall **1** (橋・ベール・いかりなどを)降ろす ▪ *Let fall* a perpendicular on the base. 基底に垂線を降ろしなさい ▪ We *let fall* the anchor. 我々はいかりを降ろした.
2 落とす ▪ He *let fall* a book. 彼は本を落とした.
3 漏らす, (わざと)口をすべらす ▪ He *let fall* something during our conversation. 彼は話の中である事を漏らした ▪ He *let fall* a hint. 彼はヒントを漏らした ▪ He *let fall* that he would be coming. 彼は自分は来ると漏らした.
4 沈澱させる ▪ On cooling, it *lets fall* a yellow matter. それはさめると黄色の物質を沈澱させる.

fallen /fɔ́ːlən/ 形 ***a fallen idol*** 墜ちた偶像 ▪ He was already *a fallen idol* in Patricia's eyes. パトリシアから見れば, 彼はすでに墜ちた偶像だった.

fallow /fǽloʊ/ 名形 ***in fallow*** 休閑の ▪ The land is *in fallow.* この土地は休閑中だ.

lay … fallow (土地)を休める ▪ We *laid* the land *fallow.* 我々はその土地を休ませた.

lie fallow **1** (土地が)休む, 休んでいる ▪ The land in China never *lies fallow.* 中国の土地は決して休まない.
2 (仕事・出産などを)休む ▪ You must *lie fallow* for a bit. あなたは少し休まねばなりません ▪ Then I *lay fallow*; but the next year I had twins. その時はお産を休んだがその翌年に双子を産んだ.

false[1] /fɔːls/ 形副 ***a false dawn*** (暁の前のはかない明かり, から)幻の暁, 幻の成功[出世, など], (…の期待をそそる)誤った兆し ▪ He was appointed Secretary of State, but it proved *a false dawn.* 彼は国務長官に任命されたが, それは幻の出世であった ▪ His victory in the French Open proved to be *a false dawn* after he failed to win another title for the next five years. その後の5年間にタイトルをとれなかったので, 全仏オープンでの彼の優勝への期待は幻となった ▪ Pioneering research a few years ago by Martin Bullman was dismissed as *a false dawn.* マーティン・ブルマンによる数年前の先駆的研究は, 偽りの夜明けとして退けられた.

a false sense of security 誤解による安心, 安全に対する誤った意識 ▪ The World Health Organisation warned that European nations must not be lulled into *a false sense of security* about bird flu. WHO(世界保健機構)は, 鳥インフルエンザに関して欧州各国は誤解して安心しないように, と警告した.

a false start **1** (陸上競技などの)フライング, 不正スタート ▪ The gun sounded, but the starter called them back because of *a false start.* 号砲が鳴ったが, スターターはフライングがあったため彼らを呼び戻した.
2 失敗スタート, 出だしのつまずき[失敗] ▪ After *a false start* when he left his first job after only a week, he was offered some modelling work. わずか1週間で最初の仕事を辞めるという出だしの失敗ののち, 彼はあるモデルの仕事を紹介された.

be false to …にそむく, に不実[不貞]である ▪ She *was false to* his trust. 彼女は彼の信頼にそむいた.

in a false position 誤解される立場に; 迷惑な立場に; 主義[意図]に反する立場に ▪ That would at once place me *in a false position.* そのため私はすぐに迷惑な立場に立たされるだろう ▪ He stands *in a false position.* 彼は自己の主義に反する立場にある.

make a false move へまをやらかす ▪ He *made a false move.* 彼はへまをやらかした.

make [***take***] ***a false step*** →STEP[1].

place [***view***] ***… in a false light*** →LIGHT[1].

play false →PLAY[2].

under false pretences 詐欺をして, だまして ▪ The police charged him with obtaining money *under false pretences.* 警察は詐欺によって金を得たとして彼を告発した.

false[2] /fɔːls/ 動 ***false a blow*** なぐるふりをする ▪ He often *falsed his blows.* 彼はよくなぐるふりをした.

fame[1] /feɪm/ 名 ***bring fame*** (***to***) (…に)名声をもたらす ▪ It *brought* him *fame* and fortune. それは彼に名声と財産をもたらした.

come to fame 有名になる ▪ He *came to* sudden *fame.* 彼は急に有名になった.

win [***achieve, earn***] ***fame*** 有名になる, 名声を博する ▪ He *won* undying *fame* for the deed. 彼はその行為で不滅の名声を博した.

fame[2] /feɪm/ 動 ***be famed for*** …で有名である

▪ He *was famed for* his learning. 彼は博学で有名であった.

familiar /fəmíljər|-iə/ 形 **(*be*) *familiar to* 1** (物が)…に親しい, よく知られて(いる) ▪ Shakespeare and Milton *are familiar to* me. シェイクスピアとミルトンのことはよく知っている ▪ The voice sounded *familiar to* me. その声は聞きなれた声だと私は思った.
2 …が日常使う, に普通で(ある) ▪ Such words *are familiar to* his tongue. そんな言葉は彼が日常使う.

(*be*) *familiar with* 1 (人が)…と親しい, 心安い ▪ I *am familiar with* him. 私は彼と親しい.
2 (人が)…になれなれしくする, に対して無遠慮にふるまう ▪ Don't *be familiar with* us. 我々になれなれしくするな.
3 (人が)…を熟知して(いる), に精通して(いる); しなれて(いる) ▪ He *is familiar with* things Japanese. 彼は日本の文物に詳しい ▪ You should *be familiar with* English. 君は英語をよく知らねばならない.

(*be*) *on familiar terms with* …と親しい仲で(ある) ▪ I *am on familiar terms with* Smith. 私はスミスと親しい仲である.

***have a familiar ring* (*to it*)** 聞き覚えがある, なじみがある ▪ I thought that name *had a familiar ring*. I went to school with that girl. その名に聞き覚えがあると思った. その娘とはいっしょに学校に行った仲だ.

***make* (*oneself*) *familiar with* 1** …と親しくなる ▪ I *made familiar with* them. 私は彼らと仲よくなった.
2 …となれなれしくする, に対し無遠慮にふるまう ▪ You should not *make* so *familiar with* the principal. 君は校長にそんなになれなれしくしてはいけない.
3 …に精通する ▪ He *made himself familiar with* the machine. 彼はその機械に精通していた.

***on familiar ground*(*s*)** 勝手のわかっている分野に ▪ Let's discuss baseball. I am *on* more *familiar ground* then. 野球の話をしよう. そのほうが僕には話がわかる.

familiarity /fəmìljǽrəti|-iǽr-/ 名 ***Familiarity breeds contempt.*** 《諺》なれすぎると侮られる[侮る]ようになる.

Familiarity breeds content. 《諺》知れば知るほど敬意を払うようになる.

with familiarity 親切に, ねんごろに ▪ Treat your friends *with familiarity*. 友人たちを親切に扱いなさい.

familiarize /fəmíljəràız|-iər-/ 動 ***familiarize oneself with*** …に精通[習熟]する ▪ *Familiarize yourself with* the spoken tongue. 口語に習熟しなさい.

family /fǽməli/ 名 ***a man of family* 1** →of FAMILY.
2 《米》家族の多い人《子供が5, 6人》 ▪ He is *a man of family*. 彼は家族が多い.

a ready-made family 既成家族《特に, 再婚相手の連れ子》 ▪ Many women don't want *a ready-made family*. 多くの女性は子連れ男との再婚を希望しない ▪ When Nanci Scharf married Nick, she also had *a ready-made family*—7-year-old Bryan and 5-year-old Jason. ナンシー・シャーフはニックと結婚したとき, 連れ子ともいっしょになった. 7歳のブライアンと5歳のジェイスンだ.

all in the family その家族の独占になっている ▪ It is *all in the family*. それはその家族の独占である ▪ Don't mention it. It's *all in the family*. お礼には及びません. それはわが家の伝統です.

be in one's family 一家に伝わる ▪ The thing *is in my family*, my sister also had twins. それは我が家の家系だ. 姉の子も双子だったから.

(*be*) *in the family* 打ち解けて(いる) ▪ Please *be in the family*. どうぞくつろいでください.

have a large family 子供が多い ▪ He *has a large famiy*. 彼は子だくさんだ.

***in a family way* 1** 家族的に, 親しく打ち解けて, 内輪同士で ▪ We should discuss our interests *in a family way*. 打ち解けて我々の利害を討議すべきである ▪ We did it *in a family way*. 我々はそれを内輪同士でやった.
2 《口》妊娠して ▪ His wife is *in a family way* again. 彼の妻はまた妊娠している.

in the family way =in a FAMILY way 2.

keep ... in the family …を内輪だけのことにする ▪ Let's *keep* it *in the family*. それは内輪だけのことにしよう.

of family 名門の, 家柄のよい ▪ He married a beautiful lady *of family*. 彼は名門の美人と結婚した.

one big happy family 《口》(仲良くやっている)和やかな一家[グループ] ▪ These singers are just *one big happy family*. There's no disagreement among them. これらの歌手たちはまさに和やかな一家みたいだ. 彼らの間には意見の不一致は存在しない.

put ... in the family way …を妊娠させる (→in a FAMILY way 2) ▪ You *put* his wife *in the family way*. 君は彼の妻を妊娠させたのだ.

run in the family →RUN[2].

sell the family silver (直ちに利益を得るために)高価なものを安く手放す, 売り食い生活をする ▪ His wife *sold the family silver* and most of her jewelry to finance her husband's election campaign. 彼の妻は, 夫の選挙キャンペーンの資金を捻出するために家宝の銀製品と宝石類のほとんどを売りはらった.

start a family (最初の)子供を持つ ▪ We *started a family*, and sent our two older children to Bishop Moore High School. 私たちは子供をもうけ, 上の二人はビショップ・ムーア高校に行かせた.

The family that prays together stays together. 《諺》ともに祈る家族はいつまでもまとまっている. ☞Al Scalpone 作品から.

famish /fǽmıʃ/ 動 ***famish ... to death*** 〚主に受身で〛…をうえ死にさせる ▪ Robert *was famished to death*. ロバートはうえ死にした.

famous /féıməs/ 形 ***be a famous hand at*** …の名手である ▪ He *is a famous hand at* shooting. 彼は猟銃の名人である.

famous as …として有名で ▪ He is *famous as* a soldier. 彼は軍人として有名である.

famous at …がじょうずな, たいしたもので ▪ He is *famous at* joking. 彼はジョークが非常にうまい.

famous for …で有名で ▪ Nikko is *famous for* its scenic beauty. 日光は風景の美で有名である.

famous for being famous (能力がないのに)名が売れている, マスコミ[メディア]有名人の ▪ Certain names are mentioned a lot and all we can gather is that they're *famous for* ... well ... *being famous*. 名前にはよく言及されるものがあり, 我々に推測できるのは彼らが有名であるのは, ええと, 有名だからだ, ということだ ▪ You can be *famous for being famous* for a while, but ultimately you have to be famous for something. しばらくはマスコミの有名人でいられるが, 究極的には何かで有名にならなければならない.

Famous last words. 《戯》よく言うよ, 眉つばものだ《他人の発言に対する不信・反対を表す》 ▪ James assured me it was always sunny in Italy in June. *Famous last words.* It rained every day of our trip. ジェイムズはイタリアでは6月にはいつも晴れていると断言した. よく言うよ. 我々の旅行中は毎日雨だった.

fan[1] /fæn/ 名 ***hit the fan*** 《口》大騒動になる (→the SHIT hits the fan) ▪ The scandal *hit the fan* when photos of an allegedly topless Jess leaked onto the Internet. ジェスのトップレス姿とされる写真がインターネットに漏れたとき, そのスキャンダルは大騒ぎになった.

fan[2] /fæn/ 動 ***fan** oneself* 扇を使う, 風を入れる ▪ He was *fanning himself* by the window. 彼は窓際で自分をあおいでいた.

fan** one's **tail →TAIL[1].

fan the air 《野球》三振する ▪ The batter *fanned the air*. バッターは三振した.

fancy[1] /fǽnsi/ 名副 ***after** one's **fancy*** 望み通りの, 気に入った ▪ I have found a house *after my fancy*. 私は気に入った家を見つけた.

at a fancy price 法外な値段で ▪ He sold it *at a fancy price*. 彼はそれを法外な値段で売った.

(be) fancy free 恋をしていない ▪ He declared himself to *be fancy free*. 彼は恋をしていないと言明した.

catch the fancy of …の気に入る; に流行する ▪ The red-haired daughter has *caught his fancy*. 赤毛の娘は彼の気に入った ▪ The song *caught the fancy of* the nation. その歌は国中に流行した.

have a fancy for [to] …が好きである ▪ The Persians *have a* great *fancy to* [*for*] black hair. ペルシャ人は黒髪が非常に好きだ.

have a fancy that ... 何となく…という気がする ▪ I *have a fancy that* he will get well. 何となく彼は全快するという気がする.

please [strike, suit, take] the fancy of** a person/**please [strike, suit, take]** a person's **fancy 《口》…の気に入る, 好みに合う ▪ This house has *taken my fancy*. この家は私の気に入った ▪ She has enough money to buy whatever *takes her fancy*. 彼女には何でも気に入ったものを買える金がある.

take a fancy to [for] …が好きになる, 気に入る ▪ I have *taken a fancy to* this house. 私はこの家が気に入った.

tickle [catch]** a person's **fancy 《口・しばしば戯》人の気に入る ▪ The handbag *tickled her fancy*. そのハンドバッグは彼女の気に入った.

to** a person's **fancy 人の気に入った ▪ It is a plan *to my fancy*. それは私の望み通りの計画だ.

fancy[2] /fǽnsi/ 動 ***Don't you fancy anything?*** (病人などに)何か食べてみたいと思わないか ▪ *Don't you fancy anything* today? きょうは何か食べてみたいものはありませんか.

Fancy** a person('s) **doing! 人がそんなことをするとは驚く, 想像もできない ▪ *Fancy* our Ann *teaching* English to the natives in Africa! うちのアンがアフリカで現地人に英語を教えるとは驚いた! ▪ *Fancy her saying* such a thing! 彼女がそんなことを言うとは!

Fancy** doing **...! …するとは驚く, 想像もつかない ▪ *Fancy meeting* you here! こんなところで君と会うなんて! ▪ *Fancy having* to wait all afternoon! 午後中ずっと待たねばならないとはね.

fancy** oneself **(as) 《口》…とうぬぼれる, を気取る ▪ He *fancies himself* a bit. 彼は少しうぬぼれている ▪ He *fancied himself as* a writer. 彼は作家だとうぬぼれていた.

Fancy that!/Just [Only] fancy! そんなことがあるなんて(実に驚く)!; 考えてもごらん(不思議だ)!

I fancy 《婉曲》…のように思う ▪ The estate is, *I fancy*, theirs yet. その地所はまだ彼らのものだと思う.

fang /fæŋ/ 名 ***take out [draw, remove] the fangs of*** …のきばを抜く, 無害にする ▪ We must *take out their fangs* somehow. どうにかして彼らが危害を加えないようにせねばならない ▪ This forthright answer *drew the fangs of* his criticism. この率直な返答で彼の批評が無力になった.

far /fɑːr/ 形副 ***a far cry*** →CRY[1].

as [so] far as **1**〚否定文では so far as も可〛…まで, だけ ▪ I went *as far as* Reading by train. レディングまで電車で行った ▪ We did not go *so far as* the bridge. 我々は橋の所までは行かなかった.

2 …するかぎりでは ▪ He will not come, *so far as* I know. 私の知るかぎりでは, 彼は来ないだろう ▪ We should teach our children, *as far as* possible, everything. 子供らにできるだけ全てのことを教えるべきだ.

as [so] far as ... be concerned …に関するかぎり ▪ *As far as* I *am concerned*, we can leave either this week or next. 私に関するかぎり我々は今週でも来週でも出発できる ▪ *So far as* length *is concerned*, time is nothing compared with eternity. 長さだけから言えば, 時間は永遠とは比べものにならない.

as [so] far as ... go …の範囲内では, かぎりにおいて

は ▪ *So far as* the style *goes*, it is all right. 文体だけならそれはけっこうです ▪ *So far as* my knowledge *goes*, there is no such word. 私の知っているかぎりではそんな語はない.

as* [*so*] *far as I can see 私の見るところでは ▪ *As far as I can see*, it's been lost in translation. 私の判断では, それは翻訳で抜け落ちたのだ.

as* [*so*] *far as in* one *lies 力の及ぶかぎり ▪ I swear to do my duty *as far as in* me *lies*. 力の及ぶかぎり義務を果たすことを誓います.

as* [*so*] *far as it goes (全面的に賛成・満足ではないが)ある程度は ▪ The Polish amnesty is fine, *as far as it goes*. ポーランドの大赦は, ある程度は, よしとされるものだ.

***as far as the eye can see* [*reach*]** 見渡すかぎり ▪ There were bluebonnets *as far as the eye could see*. 見渡すかぎり青いルピナス草が咲いていた.

(*be*) *far gone* →GONE.

(*be*) *far out* 非常に遠く離れた; 奇抜な, 前衛的な (→FAR out) ▪ David has weird ideas, but they *are*n't so *far out* that people can't identify with them. デイビッドは奇妙な考えをもっているが, 誰も共鳴できないほど突飛ではない.

by far **1** たいへん, ひどく ▪ It is too expensive *by far*. それはひどく金がかかりすぎる.
2 〚比較級, 最上級, prefer, surpass を強調して〛 はるかに ▪ This is *by far* the better of the two. このほうが二つのうちではるかに良い ▪ It attracts *by far* the largest class of readers. それは断然最も大きな読者層を引きつけている.

carry* [*take*] *... too far ...をやりすぎる ▪ You seem to have *carried* frugality *too far*. 君は倹約しすぎたようだ.

far and away はるかに (=by FAR) ▪ I was *far and away* happier when I was poor. 私は貧しかったときのほうがずっと幸福だった ▪ He's *far and away* the best boxer I've ever seen. 私がこれまで見たなかでは彼がダントツで最優秀のボクサーだ.

***far and near* [*nigh*]** 遠く近く, いたるところに ▪ They searched *far and near* for the missing airman. 彼らは行方不明の飛行士をくまなく捜した.

far and wide 遠く広く, あまねく ▪ People come from *far and wide* to hear him preach. 人々は遠近いたるところから彼の説教を聞きに来た ▪ He has traveled *far and wide*. 彼は方々を旅行している.

far away ずっと向こうに; はるかかなたに; 遠くはなれて ▪ My sister lives *far away*. 妹は遠くに住んでいる.

***far be it from me to* do** 《文》 私は決して...する気はない 《干渉・批評するときの言い訳に用いる》 ▪ *Far be it from me to* instruct the nurse in her duties, but the patient has fallen out of bed. 看護師さんの仕事を指図する気はありませんが, 患者がベッドから落ちましたよ ▪ *Far be it from me to* tell you what to do, but don't you think you should apologize? 差し出がましくどうこうすべきだと言うつもりはありませんが, 謝罪すべきだとはお考えになりませんか?

far from **1** ...から遠い ▪ We are still *far from* our subject. 我々はまだ本題から遠く離れている ▪ The station is *far from* here. 駅はここから遠い.
2 決して...なく, ...どころでなく ▪ He is *far from* honest. 彼は正直どころじゃない ▪ This work is *far from* completion. この仕事は完了どころではない ▪ It was in a *far from* unfriendly fashion. それは決して薄情でない態度であった.

***far from* [*off*] doing** ...するどころでなく, 決して...しないで ▪ The storm, so *far from abating*, increased in its fury. あらしは衰えるどころか, 猛威をますますたくましくした ▪ I am *far off being* rich. 私は金持ちどころではない.

far from it それどころではない, そんなことはとんでもない ▪ My English is not at all perfect. *Far from it*! 私の英語は決して完全ではない. それどころではない ▪ There was no objection raised—*far from it*. 反対意見は出なかった—全く気配さえなかった.

far nor near どこにも...ない ▪ There is no man *far nor near*. 誰もどこにもいない.

far or near どこにも (anywhere) ▪ I could see nothing of them *far or near*. 彼らの姿はどこにも見えなかった.

far other ずっと違った (quite unlike) ▪ What he chose was a *far other* way. 彼が選んだのはずっと違った方法であった.

far out 〚間投詞的に〛 すばらしい, やった (→(be) FAR out) ▪ The astronaut exclaimed: "*Far out*! Good work." 宇宙飛行士は「すばらしい, 上出来だ」と叫んだ.

(*few and*) *far between* ごく少なく; きわめてまれで ▪ Like angel visits, *few and far between* (T. Campbell, *Pleasures of Hope* 2. 375) 天使の訪れのように, きわめてまれで ▪ Really good cooks are *few and far between*. ほんとうに立派な料理人はごく少ない ▪ There are plenty of houses for sale, but buyers are *few and far between*. たくさんの家が売りに出ているが, 買い手はずっと少ない.

from far 遠方から ▪ I salute you *from far*. 私は遠方からあなたにあいさついたします.

from far and near 遠近から ▪ Many people gathered at the market *from far and near*. 多くの人々が遠近から市場に集まった.

go too far 《口》 (言動などが)行き過ぎる, 度が過ぎる ▪ That's *going too far*. それは言いすぎだ ▪ It is all very well to be frugal; but he *goes too far*. 倹約するのも大いにけっこうだが, 彼は極端だ.

How far ...? (距離が)どれくらい; どの程度まで ▪ *How far* is it from here? ここからどれくらいありますか ▪ *How far* can you walk? 君はどれくらい(の距離を)歩けるか ▪ I can't say *how far* his story is true. 彼の話がどこまで本当かわからない.

I'll be far* (*enough*) *if 《口》 決して...ない, ...はまっぴらごめん ▪ *I'll be far enough if* it is true. それは決して本当でない.

in so far as →SO.

***in so far* (*that*)** ...の程度に ▪ I can help you *in so far that* I can obtain you a post in a bank. 君

F

に銀行の口を見つけてあげる程度には援助ができる.

not far off [***out, wrong, short***] 《口》当たらずといえど遠からず, ほぼ正しい ▪Well, not quite, but *not far off*. うーん, その通りではないが, あまり違ってもいない.

so far **1** 現在[今]までに, 今までのところ ▪How many idioms have we studied *so far*? 今までにいくつの成句を研究したか.

2 ここまで ▪Now that we have come *so far*, let's rest a while. ここまで来たのだから少し休みましょう.

so far and no farther [***further***] そこまでだ, それ以上は無理.

F

so far as →as FAR as.

so far forth …の程度にだけ ▪They are *so far forth* orthodox that they retain it. 彼らはそれを保持しているという程度にだけ正統である.

so far(,) so good この点まで[今までのところ]は万事よろしい; それまでは良かった ▪How is the new vacuum cleaner working?—*So far so good.* 新しい電気掃除機の調子はどう?—今までのところ, とても良いよ.

thus far →THUS.

fare[1] /feər/ 名 ***(All) fares, please!*** みなさん料金をいただきます《バスなどで》. ☞fare「運賃」.

You may go farther and fare worse. 《諺》進むほど状況が悪くなることもある, やりすぎは不運のもと.

fare[2] /feər/ 動 ***fare ill*** [***badly***] **1** 運が悪い, うまくいかない ▪The enterprise *fared ill*. その事業はうまくいかなかった.

2 まずい物を食べる, 食べさせられる ▪He *fared ill* there. 彼はそこでまずい物を食べさせられた.

fare well **1** うまくいく; 運がよい ▪I *fared well*. 上首尾だった.

2 ごちそうを[十分]食べる; ごちそうのもてなしを受ける ▪You'll *fare well* in my house. 私の家で十分召しあがってください.

How do you fare? **1** いかがお暮らしですか, ごきげんいかがですか ▪*How did you fare* in London? ロンドンではいかがでしたか.

2 どんな首尾ですか ▪*How did you fare* in your exam? 試験の結果はどうでしたか.

How fares it with ...? **1** …はどんなに暮らしていますか, はごきげんいかがですか ▪*How fares it with* you? ごきげんいかがですか.

2 …はどうなっていますか, どういう首尾ですか ▪*How fared it with* you in the exam? 試験の結果はどうでしたか.

it fares ill with ... **1** …は運が悪い, うまくいかない ▪*It fared ill with* me. 私はうまくいかなかった.

2 …は(暮らしが)幸福でない ▪*It fares ill with* me. 私は不幸な暮らしをしています.

it fares well with ... **1** 運が良い, はうまくいく ▪*It fares well with* him. 彼は運が良い《うまくいっている》.

2 (暮らしが)幸福である ▪*It fares well with* me, thank you. ありがとう, 幸福にやっています.

One cannot fare well but one must cry out roast meat. 《諺》自分の幸運は触れ回らずにはいられない.

You may go farther and fare worse. 《諺》欲をかけばひどい目にあう《今持っているもので満足せよ》.

fare-you [**thee**]**-well** /féərju[ðiː]wèl/ 名 ***to (a) fare-you-well*** 《米口》極度に, 完全に; 豊かに ▪We had milk *to fare-you-well*. 私たちにはミルクが豊富にあった ▪The fellow has bluffed me *to a fare-you-well*. その男は私を極度におどしつけた ▪The man has been investigated *to a fare-thee-well*. その男は徹底的に調査された.

farewell /fèərwél/ 間名形 ***bid*** *a person* ***farewell***/ ***bid*** [***say***] ***farewell to*** *a person* 人に別れを告げる ▪I have come to *bid* you all *farewell*. みなさんに別れを告げに参りました ▪We left, *bidding* our neighbor a fond *farewell*. 我々は隣人に名残り惜しい別れを告げて立ち去りました.

Farewell to ...! …よさらば!, さようなら! ▪*Farewell to* happiness! 幸福よさようなら! ▪*Farewell to* arms! 武器よさらば!

make *one's* ***farewells*** 別れのあいさつをする ▪By the evening he had *made* all *his farewells*. 夕方までには彼は別れのあいさつを全部すませていた.

take *one's* ***farewell of*** …に別れを告げる ▪He *took his farewell of* his parents. 彼は両親に別れを告げた.

faring /féərɪŋ/ 名 ***get*** *one's* ***faring*** 当然の報いを受ける ▪The old demon *got his faring*. その年老いた鬼は当然の報いを受けた. ☞faring＝fairing (当然の報い).

farm /fɑːrm/ 名 ***a fat farm*** 肥満者農園, 減量道場《肥満者の減量のための施設・クリニックなど》 ▪Daphne gained weight and went to *a fat farm*. ダフネは太ったので減量道場に出向いた.

buy the farm 《米俗》戦死する, 死ぬ ▪That cat must have been twenty years old when he finally *bought the farm*. あの猫がついに死んだとき, 20歳になっていたに相違ない.

have [***hold, let, put, set, take,*** etc.] ***...*** ***(out) to farm*** **1** (土地など)を賃貸しする, 小作させる ▪He *let* the estate *to farm* to mean persons. 彼は地所を身分の低い人々に賃貸しした.

2 (税)の取り立ての下請けをさせる ▪Taxes may *be let out to farm* for a certain rent. 税金の取り立ては一定の上納金で下請けさせてもよい.

far-off /fɑ̀ːrɔ́ːf/ 名 ***in the far-off*** 遠方に ▪The resonance of Niagara was heard *in the far-off*. 遠方にナイアガラの響きが聞こえた.

farrow /fǽroʊ/ 形名 ***at one farrow*** 一腹で ▪A sow may bring 15 pigs *at one farrow*. 雌ブタは一腹で子を15匹生むこともある.

in [***with***] ***farrow*** (ブタが)子をはらんで ▪We have several sows *in farrow*. うちでは数匹のブタが子をはらんでいる.

fart /fɑːrt/ 名 ***let a fart*** 《卑》放屁する ▪Jack is very careful not to *let a fart*. ジャックは放屁しないよう非常に注意している.

farther /fɑ́ːrðər/ 形副 ***farther on*** もっと先に

▪ The place is 3 miles *farther on*. そこはもう3マイル先です.

go farther and fare worse →go FURTHER and fare worse.

I'll see you farther first → I'll SEE you hanged first.

nay, farther いや, それどころか ▪ *Nay, farther*, we do not scruple to assert it. いや, それどころか, 我々はためらわずそれを主張します.

No farther! もうたくさん, もうわかった.

nothing is farther from *one's* ***intention than to*** *do* …する気は全くない ▪ *Nothing is farther from my intention than to* blame you. あなたを責めようなどという気は全然ありません.

nothing is farther from *a person's* ***mind*** [***thoughts***] ***than…*** 人には…のような考えは少しもない ▪ *Nothing is farther from my mind than* boasting. 自慢話をしようなんてつもりは毛頭ない.

Thus far and no farther! ここまではよいが, これ以上はいけない (《聖》*Job* 38. 11) ▪ "*Thus far and no farther*," she said. 「ここまではいいけど, これ以上はだめです」と彼女は言った.

wish *a person* ***farther*** →WISH a person further.

farthest /fɑ́:rðɪst/ 形副 ***at*** (***the***) ***farthest*** **1** 最も遠くて ▪ It is within one, two or *at farthest* three miles of London. それはロンドンから1マイル, 2マイル, 最も遠くて3マイル以内の所にある.

2 遅くとも ▪ Supper should be ready *at the farthest* by five. 夕食は遅くとも5時までにできていなければならない.

3 せいぜい (= at (the) MOST) ▪ We found only five or six *at the farthest*. せいぜい5つ6つ見つけたばかりだ.

the farthest (*thing, person,* etc.) ***from*** …からいちばん遠い[無縁な](物, 人, など) ▪ The tournament was *the farthest* event *from* his mind. そのトーナメントは彼の考えとは無縁の試合だ.

farthing /fɑ́:rðɪŋ/ 名 ***be not worth a*** (***brass***) ***farthing*** 一文の価値もない.

not a (***brass***) ***farthing*** びた一文も[少しも]…しない ▪ They will *not* contribute *a brass farthing*. 彼らはびた一文も寄付しないだろう.

not care a (***brass***) ***farthing*** 少しもかまわぬ ▪ I do*n't care a brass farthing* where you go. あなたがどこへ行こうが私は少しもかまわない.

fasces /fǽsi:z/ 名 ***lay down*** [***resign***] ***the fasces*** 高官を辞する ▪ The proctor *laid down the fasces* of his authority. 大学学生監はその権威の職を辞した.

take the fasces 高官につく ▪ My uncle had to *take the fasces*. おじはその高位につかなければならなかった.

fashion /fǽʃən/ 名 ***after*** [***in***] ***a*** [***some***] ***fashion*** **1** 一応, どうにかこうにか, 曲がりなりに ▪ Providence has made me a lady *after a fashion*. ありがたいことに, 私もどうやら貴婦人らしくなりました ▪ She cooks *after a fashion*. 彼女はどうにか料理ができる.

2 おおよそ, 大体, ほとんど ▪ A vegetarian diet is much healthier. —That's true *after a fashion*, although I don't believe all meat is bad for you. 菜食主義の食事のほうがずっと健康的です—それは原則的に正しいが, 肉はすべて悪いとは思いません.

after [***in***] *one's* ***fashion*** 自己流で; 独特の ▪ He does everything *after his* own *fashion*. 彼は何でも自己流にやる.

after the fashion of …風[流]に ▪ These boys were dressed *after the fashion of* sailors. その少年たちは水夫のような服装をしていた ▪ The hall was warmed, *after the fashion of* a country house, by a bright open fire. その広間は田舎家風に, 盛んな直火で暖められていた.

as if it's going out of fashion → like it's going out of FASHION.

be all the fashion 大流行である ▪ New life-style *is all the fashion*. 新しいライフスタイルが大流行である.

(***be***) ***in fashion*** 流行している ▪ Solitary pilgrimages *were* much *in fashion*. 一人でする巡礼が大いにはやっていた.

(***be***) ***in*** [***out of***] ***the fashion*** 流行に従っている[いない]; 流行している[いない]; 上流の事情に通じている[いない] ▪ Her gowns *were in the fashion*. 彼女のガウンは流行に従ったものだった.

(***be***) ***out of fashion*** はやっていない, すたれている ▪ This sort of hat *is out of fashion*. この種の帽子はもうすたれた.

be the fashion to *do* …することは結構[習慣]とされている ▪ It *is the fashion to* give three cheers at the end of such a meeting. そのような会の終わりには万歳を三唱する習わしだ.

bring…into fashion …を流行させる ▪ The Hungarians *brought* them *into fashion*. ハンガリー人がそれらを流行させたのだ.

come into fashion 流行してくる ▪ Little dogs *came into fashion*. 小さい犬が流行してきた.

follow the fashion 流行に従う[を追う] ▪ He *follows the fashion* of the hour. 彼はその時の流行に従う.

get out of fashion **1** (人が)流行を捨てる ▪ They have not yet *got out of fashion*. 彼らは流行からまだ抜けていない.

2 =go out of FASHION.

go out of fashion すたれる ▪ This sort of hat has *gone out of fashion*. この種の帽子はすたれた.

grow into fashion はやってくる ▪ Sins have *grown into fashion*. 罪悪がはやってきた.

in a [***some***] ***fashion*** →after a FASHION.

in *one's* ***fashion*** →after one's FASHION.

in *one's* ***own*** [***the English, like***] ***fashion*** 自己流のやり方で[イギリス流に, 同様にして] (→after one's FASHION) ▪ He did everything *in his own fashion*. 彼は何でも自己流にやった ▪ He used his knife and fork *in the English fashion*. 彼はナイフとフォークをイギリス流に使った.

in this* [*such*] *fashion こんな[そんな]ふうに ▪ He stared at me *in this fashion*. 彼は私をこんなふうにじっと見た.

lead the fashion 流行のさきがけをする ▪ They are qualified to *lead the fashion*. 彼らは流行のさきがけをする資格がある.

like* [*as if*] *it's going out of fashion 《口》やたらに, 存分に(金を使う) ▪ Every Christmas they spend money *like it's going out of fashion*. クリスマスにはいつも彼らは思う存分に金を使う.

F

of fashion 上流[社交界]の ▪ She is a woman *of fashion*. 彼女は上流の婦人だ ▪ She longed to enter the world *of fashion*. 彼女は上流社交界入りを切望した.

set the fashion 流行を作り出す, 起こす ▪ *The fashion was set* by the upper class. その流行は上流階級によって作り出された.

fast /fæst|fɑːst/ 形 副 名 ***a fast talker*** 《米口》口のうまい人, 口達者, 能弁家 ▪ Don't trust him. He's *a fast talker* who's always out for his own good. 彼を信用しちゃだめだ. あいつは口達者で, いつも自分の利益しか求めていないんだ.

be fast with …で閉じこもっている, 寝ている ▪ He *is fast with* gout. 彼は痛風で閉じこもっている.

(*be on*) *a* [*the*] *fast track* **1** (…の)最短コース(にいる); (ビジネスマン・政治家の)出世コース(にいる), すぐに…に通じる地位(にある) (*to, for*) (→FAST-track) ▪ The youngster *is on a fast track to* success. その若者は成功への最短コースにいる ▪ Management training offers *a fast track to* the top of the company. 管理者訓練は会社トップへの出世コースを提供する ▪ Our kids *are on a fast track to* becoming unhealthy adults. うちの子は不健康な大人になる最短コースを歩んでいる ▪ The pontiff *is on the fast track to* sainthood. 司教(の地位)は聖人に直結している ▪ He seems to *be on the fast track*. 彼はすぐに出世しそうに見える.

2 素早く結果を手に入れるやり方, 緊急対処(される), 迅速な対応(をされる) ▪ The government has announced that the reforms will *be* put *on the fast track*. 政府は, 改革は緊急対処されようと発表した.

break one's fast **1** 絶食後食事をとる ▪ Students finally *broke their* long *fast* with a spaghetti supper. 学生たちはとうとう長い絶食のあとスパゲティの夕食をとった.

2 《文》朝食を食べる ▪ I must be at Hudson before I *break my fast*. 私は朝食をとる前にハドスンへ行かねばならない.

fall fast しきりに降る; (夜が)どんどん迫る ▪ Snow was *falling fast*. 雪はしきりに降っていた ▪ Night has begun to *fall fast*. 夜がどんどん迫り始めた.

fast and furious (冗談が)口をついて出て; (ゲームが)白熱化して; (歓楽が)たけなわ[狂乱的]となって ▪ The merry-making will grow *fast and furious*. 歓楽はたけなわになるであろう ▪ The first half of the game was *fast and furious* with both teams scoring three goals each. 試合の前半はスピード感にあふれており, 両チームがそれぞれ3ゴール決めた.

fast and loose →play FAST and loose.

fast and thick →THICK.

Fast bind, fast find. 《諺》締まりが固ければ失うことがない《失いたくないものには, しっかりかぎをかけておけ》. ☞fast を「しっかりと」「早く」の両義にかけた.

fast enough 《口》二つ返事で ▪ He will do it *fast enough*. 彼は二つ返事でそれをするだろう.

fast-track 〚限定的〛出世コースの; 高速の, 加速した (→(be on) a FAST track) ▪ We are introducing a *fast-track* procedure for dealing with applications. 迅速に応募を処理する方法を導入中だ.

hold fast by …に(しっかり)しがみつく ▪ He *held fast by* the parapet. 彼は欄干にしがみついた.

lead* [*live*] *a fast life 放蕩(とう)な生活をする (→live FAST 1) ▪ He *led* such *a fast life* that it has permanently affected his health. 彼は非常に放蕩な生活をしたので永久に健康に響いた.

lay ... fast …をしっかり縛りつける, 禁固する ▪ We *were laid fast* by want of horses. 馬がないのでその場にくぎうけにされた ▪ I want to *lay* that rogue *fast*. あの悪漢を禁固してやりたい.

live fast **1** 放らつな[放蕩(とう)]生活をする ▪ He has *lived* too *fast*. 彼はあまりな放蕩生活をした.

2 短時間に多くの精力を消耗する, 生き急ぐ ▪ He *lived* too *fast*. 彼はあまりにも早く多くの精力を消耗した ▪ Francis *lived* too *fast* and died too young. フランシスはあまりにも生き急いで, あまりにも若死にした.

make fast 堅く締める, 縛る, つなぐ ▪ I will *make fast* the door. 戸を堅く締めましょう ▪ He *made* a line *fast* about his neck. 彼はひもを首の回りにくくった ▪ *Make* the boat *fast*. ボートをしっかりつないでおくれ.

not so fast もっとゆっくり; もっと考えよ ▪ *Not so fast*, please. もっとゆっくり言ってください ▪ *Not so fast*, my boy; you are making a mistake. 君, もっと考えなさい. まちがっていますよ.

play fast and loose **1** 言行に定見がない; 言行が一致しない ▪ You are *playing fast and loose*. Make up your mind whether you will take it or not. 考えがぐらついている. それを取るか取らないか決めろ.

2 (…に対して)気まぐれなふるまいをする《特に男女関係について》; (を)ほんろうする; (に)無責任な行為をする, (を)おろそかに扱う, (を)不注意に[雑に]取り扱う (*with*) ▪ She *played fast and loose with* me. 彼女は私に対して気まぐれなふるまいをした ▪ He is *playing fast and loose with* his health. 彼は健康をもてあそんでいる ▪ You cannot *play fast and loose with* the agreement. 協定に対して無責任なことはできない ▪ Like many film-makers, he *plays fast and loose with* the facts to tell his own version of the story. 多くの映画製作者と同様, 物語を自己流の作品にするために彼は事実をおろそかにしている ▪ The editorial writer has *played fast and loose with* the facts. 社説の執筆者は事実をないがしろにしている.

pull a fast one →ONE.
put ... on the fast track ...を素早く結果を出すようにする ▪ Our research will *be put on the fast track*. 我々の研究は早急に結果が出されるだろう.
stand fast **1** 動かない ▪ But she *stood fast*. だが彼女は動かなかった.
2 じっと立っている ▪ He could hardly speak or *stand fast*. 彼は口もきけずじっと立ってもいられないくらいだった.
3 固持[固守]する ▪ They *stood fast*, remaining glorious martyrs to the last. 彼らは固守して最後まで栄光ある殉教者で通した.
4 (敵軍に対して)踏みとどまって固守する ▪ They had two choices, either to fly, or to *stand fast*. 彼らには二つの道があるだけだった, つまり逃げるか踏みとどまって固守するかのいずれかだった.
stick fast **1** (とがった物が)しっかりと突きささる ▪ The spear *stuck fast* in the earth. やりはしっかりと地面に突きささった.
2 (ぬかるみなどに)しっかりとはまり込む ▪ At length the ship *stuck fast* in the mud. とうとう船はどろの中へしっかりとはまり込んでしまった.
3 頑として意見を変えない ▪ We tried to change his mind but he *stuck fast*. 彼に決心を変えさせようとしたが, 彼は頑として聞かなかった.
thick and fast →THICK.

fasten /fǽsən|fɑ́:sən/ 動 ***fasten*** *oneself* ***on*** **1** ...にくっつく ▪ A stigma *fastens itself on* a man. 汚名が人につくとなかなか取れない.
2 (注意など)...に集中する ▪ My eyes *fastened themselves on* the old scarlet letter. 私の目は古い緋の文字に注がれた.
Fasten your safety belt! 《口・戯》シートベルトを締めてください《運転手がスピードを出すとき客に言う言葉》 ▪ *Fasten your safety belt!* I'm going to pass that car. シートベルトを締めろ! あの車を抜くぞ.

fat[1] /fæt/ 形名 ***a bit of fat*** 《口》 **1** 思いがけぬ幸運 ▪ Bob won some money though he had made a mistake.―What *a bit of fat*! ボブは誤りを犯したのに金をもらった―何という思いがけぬ幸運だろう!
2 (仕事・劇などの)一番良い部分[役割] ▪ What was your tutoring job like?―A real *bit of fat*. 家庭教師の仕事はどうだったかね?―全くおいしい仕事だったよ.
a fat cat 《口》金持ちの権力者 ▪ He's just another *fat cat*―a corporate tycoon from Boston. 彼も金満権力者にすぎない―ボストン出身で企業の大立者だ.
a fat chance 《口・皮肉》見込みがほとんどない, 見込みが全くない ▪ We have *a fat chance* of getting it. 我々がそれを得る見込みはほとんどない ▪ Do you think your Dad will drive us to the disco?―*Fat chance*! 君のお父さんがぼくたちをディスコに車でつれて行ってくれると思うかい―ありっこないね.
a fat lot (***of good*** [***use***]) 《俗》たんまり; 《主に反語》ほとんどない, 全くない ▪ It shows what *a fat lot* of influence Congo has got. それはコンゴがいかに勢力がないかを示している ▪ *A fat lot* you care! あなたは少しもかまってくれない ▪ She can't lift anything heavy, so she's *a fat lot of use*! 彼女は重いものはなにも持ち上げられない. よく役に立つことだ ▪ *A fat lot of good* it did me! そんなものはまるで役に立たなかった.
(***as***) ***fat as a pig*** ブタのように太って ▪ I'm getting *as fat as a pig*. 僕はブタのように太っていっている.
(***as***) ***fat as an alderman*** (特に腹部が)非常に太って ▪ You will be *as fat as an alderman*. あなたはひどく太るだろう.
(***as***) ***fat as butter*** [***a young thrush***] まるまる太った《主に, 健康的な太り方》 ▪ Your little boy will soon be *as fat as a young thrush*. お宅の坊っちゃんはじきにまるまるとお太りになりましょう.
chew the fat →CHEW the rag.
cut it too fat →CUT it fat.
cut up fat →CUT up well.
eat the fat of the land →live on the FAT of the land.
grow fat 太る; 富裕になる ▪ Laugh and *grow fat*. 《諺》笑って太れ,「心配は身の毒」.
It's not over until the fat lady sings. →it isn't over till the fat LADY sings.
live on [***off***] ***the fat of the land*** 贅沢な暮らしをする(《聖》*Gen*. 45. 18), 左うちわで暮らす ▪ For thirteen years he has *lived on the fat of the land*. 13年間彼は贅沢な暮らしをした ▪ Times have changed for the upper classes, many of whom are no longer able to *live off the fat of the land*. 上流社会にとっては時代が変わったので, 彼らの多くはもう左うちわではやっていけない. ☞「その国の最も良いものを食べる」が原義.
run to fat 太り過ぎる ▪ Mother was *running to fat*. 母は太り過ぎになっていた.
The fat [***All the fat***] ***is in the fire.*** **1** 計画はすっかり失敗した.
2 《口》へまなことをやった《きっと大目玉を食うぞ, 今に大変なことになるぞ》 ▪ I told Father that Tom and I were married, and then *the fat was in the fire*. 私はトムと結婚したと父に言いました. それで大目玉をくらいました ▪ Susie knows you've been seeing her boyfriend, so *the fat's in the fire*. スージーはあなたが彼女のボーイフレンドと会っていたことを知っているから, 今に大変なことになるわよ. ☞あぶらが火の中にこぼれると, 石炭がくすぶり, 料理がだめになることから.
wax fat and kick →WAX[3].

fat[2] /fæt/ 動 ***kill the fatted calf*** →CALF.

fatally /féɪtəli/ 副 ***end*** [***terminate***] ***fatally*** (病気が)死という結果になる ▪ Many of the cases *ended fatally*. その患者の多くが亡くなった.

fate /feɪt/ 名 ***a fate worse than death*** 《戯》 **1** 死ぬよりつらい不幸, 最悪の事態[出来事] ▪ When you're 16, an evening at home with your parents is *a fate worse than death*. 16歳にとっては自宅で両親といっしょに過ごす夕方は最悪だ.
2 (婦女の)誘惑, 暴行 ▪ The lady escaped *a fate worse than death*. その女性は暴行をまぬがれた.

as fate would have it 運悪くも ▪ *As fate would have it*, I was too late. 運悪く私は遅すぎた.

(as) sure as fate →(as) SURE as death.

buffeting of fate/the buffets of fate 不幸の襲来, 不測の災難 ▪ The brave boy accepted *the buffets of fate*. その勇敢な少年は思いがけない不幸を受け入れた.

decide [fix, seal] *a person's* ***fate*** 人の運命を決定する ▪ He waited for his mistress to *fix his fate*. 彼は愛人が彼の運命を決定してくれるのを待った.

find *one's* ***fate*** 将来の自分の妻に会う ▪ He has *found his fate*. 彼は将来自分の妻となる人に会った.

F

meet *one's* ***fate*** **1** 最期を遂げる ▪ He *met his fate* abroad. 彼は外国で最期を遂げた.
2 =find one's FATE.

seal [decide, fix] *a person's* ***fate*** 人の運命を決定する, 将来を閉ざす ▪ His father's illness *sealed his fate*. 彼の父親の病は彼の将来を閉ざした.

tempt fate/tempt the fates **1** 敢えて危険を冒す, 一か八かの賭をする, 運試しをする ▪ It's *tempting fate* to start up that mountain so late in the day. こんな遅い時刻になってあの山に登り始めるのは危険だ ▪ Driving that old car is *tempting the fates*, it's sure to break down. あのおんぼろ車で行くなんて無謀だ. きっとエン故するぞ ▪ Yankee's Jorge *tempted fate* when he stretched a single into a double against Ichiro. ヤンキーズのホルへは, イチロー相手に一か八かの走塁をして単打を2塁打にした.
2 自信たっぷりに言って不運を招く, 無謀なことをする ▪ It is *tempting fate* to say so, but we are having a pretty good season so far. こんなことを言うと後が怖いが, 今シーズンのこれまでわがチームはかなり好調だ.

the irony of fate 運命の皮肉 ▪ By *the irony of fate*, the prisoner died on the very day he was set free. 皮肉なめぐり合わせで, 囚人は釈放されたその日に死んだ.

father /fá:ðər/ 名 ***(a bit of) how's your father*** 《英口・戯》例の[あの]こと《悪事・性行為などの婉曲表現》 ▪ There was some *how's your father* going on in the outhouse. 納屋で口にするのをはばかること[セックス]が行われていた. ☞必ずしも sexual なことではなく, funny business (おかしなこと) 一般を意味することもある.

be (a) father to …に父のようにふるまう ▪ The King *is father to* his people. 王は人民に父のようにふるまう.

be *one's* ***father's son [daughter]*** 父の息子[娘]だ《父によく似ている》 ▪ You *are your father's son*, indeed. 君は全くお父さんの子だな.

founding father 創設[創始]者 ▪ We've been taught at school that Dr. Sun Wen is the *founding father* of the nation. 我々は孫文博士が国家の創設者だと学校で教わった.

from father to son 親から子へ, 先祖代々.

Like father, like son./Like mother, like daughter. 《諺》この父にしてこの子あり, 「カエルの子はカエル」.

play the heavy father to …をさとす ▪ He always *plays the heavy father to* me. 彼はいつも僕を説諭する.

sleep [lie] with *one's* ***fathers*** 故郷に葬られている (《聖》*Gen*. 47. 30); 死んでいる ▪ He *sleeps with his fathers*. 彼は地下に眠っている ▪ I'll *lie with my fathers*. 故郷に葬られたい.

talk to *a person* ***like a father*** 《口》人をさとす, 説諭する ▪ I will *talk to* her *like a father*. 彼女をさとしましょう.

the father (and mother) of a 《英口》非常に激しい ▪ I gave him *the father of a* hiding. 彼をひどく打ちのめしてやった.

The wish is father to the thought. そうあれかしと願っているとそうだと思うようになる.

fathom /fǽðəm/ 名 ***fathoms deep [down]*** ずっと深く ▪ You will sink *fathoms deep*. 君はずっと深く沈むであろう.

fatted /fǽtəd/ 形 ***kill the fatted calf*** → CALF.

fault /fɑ:lt, fɔ:lt/ 名 ***(be) at fault*** **1** (犬が)臭跡を失って(いる); 迷って(いる) ▪ The hounds *were at fault*. 猟犬どもは臭跡を失った ▪ The guide *was at fault*. 案内者は立往生した.
2 まちがって(いる) ▪ You *are at fault* in thinking so. 君がそう考えるのはまちがっている.
3 困り果てて(いる); 途方にくれて(いる) ▪ The antiquarians *were at fault* because there were so many relics. 遺物が非常に多かったので, 古物研究家たちは途方にくれた ▪ My memory *was at fault*. 私は正確には覚えていなかった.
4 《口》事態に対処できない; 失敗する ▪ He *was at fault*. 彼は失敗した.
5 《口・誤用》=(be) in FAULT.

be *one's* ***fault*** …が悪い, の罪である ▪ It *was my fault*. それは私の罪でした.

(be) in fault …に罪がある, が悪い ▪ The master *was in fault*. 雇い主に責任があった.

commit a fault あやまちを犯す ▪ He *committed a* great *fault*. 彼は大きなあやまちを犯した.

find (a) fault in …にあら[欠点]を見つける ▪ This is the only *fault* I *find in* her. 彼女に私が見いだす欠点はこれだけです.

find fault (with) **1** (…の)あら捜しをする, (を)非難する ▪ He is always ready to *find fault with* other people. 彼はいつも他人のあら捜しをしたがる.
2 (…に)文句を言う, 不平を言う ▪ He *finds fault with* everything. 彼は何事にでも不平を言う.

hit off a fault 失った臭跡を再び見つける ▪ The hounds *hit off a fault* themselves. 猟犬は失った臭跡を自分で見つけた.

lay a fault to *a person's* ***charge [at*** *a person's* ***door]*** 過失を人の罪に帰する ▪ He *laid the fault to my charge*. 彼はその過失を私の罪にした.

make a fault →commit a FAULT.

The fault is in ourselves, not in our stars. 《諺》罪は我々自身にあるのであって, 我々の星

[運命]にあるのではない.

the fault is mine [etc.]/***the fault lies with me*** [etc.] 罪は私[など]にある ▪ The governor says *the fault is his*. 罪は自分にあると知事は言っている.

to a fault 欠点と言ってよいほどに, 過度に ▪ He is generous *to a fault*. 彼は寛大にすぎる.

with all faults 《商》損傷を補償せずに, いっさい買い主の責任で《A.F. または Job A.F. と略されることがある》 ▪ It was sold *with all faults*. それは「損傷を補償せず」で売られた.

favor[1], 《英》 **favour**[1] /féɪvər/ 名 ***ask a favor*** (***of***) (…に)頼みごとをする ▪ May I *ask a favor of* you? お願いを聞いていただけませんか ▪ I don't like *asking favors*. 私は人にものを頼むのはきらいです.

awaiting the favor of your prompt attention 至急ご回答願いあげます《手紙の結び》.

be [***stand***] ***high in*** *a person's* ***favor*** 人に大いに好かれている, 気に入られている ▪ He *stands high in his teacher's favor*. 彼は先生に非常に気に入られている.

be in favor **1** はやっている ▪ What *is* now *in favor*? 今何がはやっていますか.
2 (…の)気に入って[寵愛を受けて]いる (*with*) ▪ He *is in favor with* many. 彼は多くの人に人気がある.

(***be***) ***in*** *a person's* ***favor*** **1** 人に有利で(ある) ▪ The evidence *is in his favor*. その証言は彼に有利である.
2 人に寵愛されて[気に入られて](いる) ▪ He *is in his master's favor*. 彼は主人に寵愛されている.

be out of favor (***with***) (人に)きらわれて[あいそを尽かされて]いる ▪ He *is out of favor with* his master. 彼は主人にあいそを尽かされている.

bestow *one's* ***favors on*** (男)になびく ▪ She *bestowed her favors on* the man. 彼女はその男になびいた.

bring ... into *a person's* ***favor*** …を人に気に入らせる, 寵愛させる ▪ I will *bring* you again *into his favor*. 君をまた彼の気に入りにしてやる.

buy [***sell***] ***her favors*** 女を買う[春を売る] ▪ She gets her living by *selling her favors*. 彼女は春をひさいで生計を立てている.

by favor ひいきで ▪ He won the position *by favor* rather than by merit. 彼は実力よりもひいきでその地位を得た.

by [***with***] ***favor of*** …に託して《手紙の表に書く句》 ▪ *By favor of* Mr. Smith, 12 Dec. 2013. 2013年12月12日, スミス氏に託して.

by (***the***) ***favor of*** …の援助[支持, 助成]によって ▪ *By favor of* six good rowers, we arrived at my house soon. 6人のじょうずなこぎ手のおかげで, 私たちはまもなく私の家に着いた ▪ *By the favor of* daylight we perceived a great many sails. 日光のおかげで我々は非常にたくさんの船が認められた.

by [***with***] ***your favor*** ごめんをこうむって; (こう申しては)失礼ですが ▪ *By your favor*, I shall take my leave of you now. 申し訳ありませんが, もうおいとまいたします.

call in a favor (お返しに)援助を求める ▪ She in turn *calls in a favor* to the mayor. 彼女は彼女で市長に援助を求めている.

curry favor (***with***) →CURRY.

do *a person* ***a favor*** 人にあること[親切, 頼みごとなど]をしてあげる ▪ Will you *do* me *a favor*? 私の願いを聞いてくださいませんか ▪ Will you *do* me *the favor* of calling on me? どうぞ拙宅においでください.

Do me [***us***] ***a favor!*** 《英口》 **1** (くだらない質問などに対して)よくそんなことが言えるね, バカなこと言わないでくれ ▪ Why don't you go out with Brian?—Oh, *do me a favor!* He's almost 50, and he still lives with his mother! ブライアンとデートしたらどう?—やめてよ. あの人ったら50近いのに, まだ母親と暮らしてるのよ.
2 ⟦命令文を伴って⟧ 頼むから…してくれないか《いらだちを表す》 ▪ *Do me a favor*, Melissa, and keep that mouth of yours shut. メリッサ, お願いだから, だまっていてくれ ▪ Why don't you *do us* all *a favor* and keep your opinions to yourself. もういい加減にしてくれ. 君のご高説は君だけにしまっておいてくれたまえ.

do yourself a favor ⟦しばしば and do を伴って⟧ 悪いことは言わないから, 自分の体[将来]のことを考えて《相手のためを思って提案・助言するときの言葉》 ▪ You're looking really tired. Why don't you *do yourself a favor and* take a break? ほんとに疲れてるみたいだよ. 悪いことは言わないから, 休憩したらどう ▪ *Do yourself a favor, and* wear a helmet. 悪いことは言わないから, ヘルメットをかぶりなさい.

Don't do me any favors. 《口》おせっかいはやめてくれ, 大きなお世話だ.

fall from [***out of***] ***favor*** (***with***) 《文》(…の)愛顧・支持・人気を失う ▪ Jack has *fallen out of favor with* the teacher. ジャックは先生に気に入られなくなった.

favors to come 《商》さらにこの上の愛顧[引き立て] ▪ Your order gives me reason to hope for *favors to come*. ご注文をいただきこの上ともご引き立てをお願いします.

find favor in the eyes [***sight***] ***of***/***find favor with*** …に目をかけられている, の気に入っている, に人気がある (《聖》*Deut*. 24. 1; *Luke* 1. 30) ▪ The proposal *found favor with* Beth. その提案はベスの気に入った.

gain *a person's* ***favor*** → win a person's FAVOR.

go by favor えこひいきで行われる ▪ Promotion *goes by favor*. 昇進は上官の気うけしだいである ▪ Kissing *goes by favor*. キスは好きな人にだけするものである.

go in *a person's* ***favor*** 《法》人に有利に決まる ▪ The case *went in his favor*. その訴訟は彼に有利に決まった.

heap favors upon [***on***] …に重ね重ね親切を施す ▪ My friend *heaped favors on* me. 友は私に重ね重ねの親切を尽くしてくれた.

impress *a person* ***in*** *one's* ***favor*** 人に好印象を与える[気に入られる] ▪ He has *impressed* me *in* *his favor.* 彼は私に好印象を与えた.

in** a person's **favor 人の有利になるよう, 人のために ▪ I will make an exception *in your favor.* 君だけは特別の扱いをしよう ▪ The exchange rate is not *in our favor.* 為替相場は我々に有利でない.

in favor of **1** …に有利に[で] ▪ The decision is *in favor of* the defendant. 判決は被告に有利だ.

2 …に賛成して, を支持して ▪ The bishops were *in favor of* the proposition. 監督たちはその提案に賛成だった.

3 《商》…に支払うように ▪ Please draw the check *in favor of* Brown & Co. どうぞブラウン社あての小切手を振り出してください.

4 …を弁護して; の方を好んで ▪ They wrote a letter *in favor of* us to the Queen. 彼らは我々を弁護する手紙を女王に出してくれた ▪ I abandoned poetry *in favor of* prose. 詩をやめて散文に転じた.

5 …に譲って ▪ He resigned *in favor of* his brother. 彼は弟に譲るため辞職した.

look on ... with favor …に好意を示す; に賛成する, を歓迎する ▪ They *look on* the project *with favor.* 彼らはその計画を歓迎している.

lose favor with …の愛顧を失う, にあいそを尽かされる ▪ He has *lost favor with* his master. 彼は主人の愛顧を失った.

not do** a person **any favor 〚主に進行形で再帰的〛(人)のためにならないことをする, に害を与えている (*by* (*doing*)); 不養生をする ▪ The government *isn't doing* the families of the victims *any favor by hiding* the truth about what really happened. 政府は, 実際に起こったことの真相を隠して, 犠牲者の家族に害を与えている ▪ You're not well, and you're *not doing* yourself *any favors by taking* on extra work. 君は体調がよくないのに, 余分な仕事を引き受けて不養生をしている.

out of favor **1** →be out of FAVOR (*with*).

2 好意から ▪ He gave it to you *out of favor.* 彼はそれを好意からあなたにくれたのだ.

prepossess** a person **in** one's **favor (自己に有利な先入観を人に与える, から)人に好感を与える, 人の気に入る, 〚主に受身で〛初めから人に好意をいだかせる ▪ He has *prepossessed* me *in his favor.* 彼は私の気に入った ▪ His appearance *prepossessed* me *in his favor.* 彼の容貌は初めから私に好感を持たせた.

pronounce in favor of 《法》…に賛成する, 有利な判決を下す ▪ The majority *pronounced in favor of* William's undertaking. 多数の者はウィリアムの企てに賛成した.

sell her favors →buy her FAVORs.

show undue favor to …をえこひいきする ▪ He *showed undue favor to* the student. 彼はその生徒をえこひいきした.

stand high in** a person's **favor →be high in a person's FAVOR.

turn in** a person's **favor 人に有利になってくる ▪ Luck *turned in my favor.* 運が向いてきた ▪ The tide of war *turned in favor of* the besiegers. 戦況は攻囲軍に有利になってきた.

under favor of …に乗じて, 援助されて ▪ The attack was made *under favor of* darkness. 攻撃は夜陰に乗じて行われた.

win** [**gain**] a person's **favor 人に気に入られる ▪ He *won his master's favor.* 彼は主人に気に入られた.

with favor 好意をもって, ひいきして ▪ The chairman regarded our proposal *with favor.* 議長は我々の提案に好意を寄せた.

with favor of →by (the) FAVOR of.

with your favor →by your FAVOR.

favor[2], 《英》**favour**[2] /féɪvər/ 動 ***favor** a person **in the face*** 顔がある人に似ている ▪ He *favors* you *in the face.* 彼は顔があなたに似ている.

favor** a person **with 《文・戯》人に恩恵として…を与える ▪ Will you *favor* us *with* a song? 私たちに歌を歌って聞かせてください ▪ We beg to *be favored with* your orders. なにとぞ, ご用命のほどお願いします.

favored by …に託して《手紙の添え書き》 ▪ *Favored by* Mr. Smith. スミス氏に託す.

Fortune favors the brave. 《諺》幸運は勇者に味方する.

favorable, 《英》**favourable** /féɪvərəbəl/ 形 ***favorable to*** **1** …に好都合の, に適した ▪ The soil is *favorable to* roses. 土壌はバラに適している.

2 …に好意的[賛成]で ▪ He is *favorable to* the scheme. 彼はその計画に賛成だ.

favorably, 《英》**favourably** /féɪvərəbəli/ 副 ***be favorably disposed toward(s)*** …に好意的である ▪ The King *is favorably disposed towards* him. 王は彼に好意を寄せておられる.

be favorably impressed by …から好印象を受ける ▪ I *was favorably impressed by* him. 私は彼から好印象を受けた.

favorite, 《英》**favourite** /féɪvərət/ 形名 ***a favorite son*** 《米俗》出身州の気に入りの候補, 政界の人気者, 地方の名士[政治家] ▪ Indiana is seeking the presidential nomination for its *favorite son.* インディアナ州はその州出身のお気に入りの政治家を大統領候補に指名することを求めている ▪ Let me introduce to you the *favorite son* of Russell, Kansas: Bob Dole. カンザス州, ラッセルの人気政治家, ボブ・ドール氏をご紹介いたします.

be a favorite of [***with***] …のお気に入りである, に大いにもてる ▪ He *is a favorite with* his uncle. 彼はおじさんのお気に入りである ▪ They *are favorites of* Heaven. 彼らは天の寵児だ.

play favorites →PLAY[2].

fawn /fɔːn/ 名 ***in fawn*** (雌ジカが)はらんで ▪ She is *in fawn.* そのシカははらんでいる.

fealty /fíːəlti/ 名 ***do*** [***make, swear***] (*one's*) ***fealty*** 忠誠を誓う ▪ The Bishops *swore fealty* to the King. 監督たちは国王に忠誠を誓った.

receive fealty 忠誠の誓いを受ける ▪ Solomon *received fealty* of all the people of the land. ソロモンは全国民の忠誠の誓いを受けた.

fear[1] /fɪər/ 名 ***be in fear*** (***of***) (…を)恐れている, 心配している ▪ We *were in fear of* discovery. 我々は発見されるのを恐れていた.

fear and trepidation たいへんな恐怖 ▪ I went to her with *fear and trepidation.* 私は恐る恐る彼女のところに行った.

for fear 怖がって ▪ He trembled *for fear.* 彼は怖がってふるえた ▪ He could not speak *for fear.* 彼は怖くて物が言えなかった.

for fear of **1** …を恐れて ▪ I dare not enter *for fear of* the dog. 私は犬が恐ろしくて入れない.
2 …しない[のない]ように ▪ He ran away *for fear of* being hurt. 彼はけがをしないように走って逃げた ▪ I didn't call on you *for fear of* disturbing you. 私はおじゃまになってはいけないのでお訪ねしませんでした.

for fear that *one* ***may***/***for fear lest*** *one* ***should*** …しないように; …してはいけないから, することを恐れて ▪ Walk quietly *for fear lest* the patients *should* be disturbed. 患者たちのじゃまにならぬよう, 静かに歩きなさい ▪ Take an umbrella with you *for fear that* it *may* rain. 雨が降るといけないからかさを持って行きなさい.

from [***out of***] ***fear*** 怖いから ▪ They obey *from fear.* 彼らは怖いから従っている.

go in fear of …を恐れて[心配して]いる ▪ He *went in fear of* his life. 彼は自分の命を気づかった.

have a fear of …しはしないか心配である ▪ I *have a fear of* failing. 落第しはしないかと心配です.

have [***hold***] ***no fears for*** *a person* …は人にとって少しも怖くない《易しい相手だ》 ▪ The dark *holds no fears for* a blind man. 暗がりは盲人には少しも怖くない.

in fear (***and trembling***) びくびくして ▪ We have lived *in fear* for many days. 私たちは何日もびくびくして暮らした ▪ I went to the teacher *in fear and trembling.* びくつきながら先生の所へ行った.

in fear of …を気づかって ▪ They live *in* constant *fear of* attack by the enemy. 彼らは絶えず敵の攻撃を気づかいながら暮らしている.

no fear 《口》 **1** そんなことはない ▪ Go skating on that thin ice? *No fear.* あんな薄い氷の上にスケートをしに行くかって? そんなことはないよ ▪ He will not fail, *no fear.* 彼は失敗はしない, するものか.
2 心配ない ▪ Give him but sage and butter, and there's *no fear.* 彼にセージ入りバターだけやっていれば, 心配ない.

no fear but (***that, what***) きっと…する ▪ *No fear but what* he will make a capital workman some day. 彼はいつか必ず立派な職人になるにちがいない.

out of fear →from FEAR.

play on *a person's* ***fears*** 人の恐怖心[不安]につけこむ ▪ The politician *played on people's fears* and hatred. その政治家は人々の恐怖と憎しみにつけこんだ.

put the fear of death in [***into, up***] *a person* 《口》人を縮みあがらせる; けんまくで服従させる ▪ He is trying to *put the fear of death into* us. 彼は我々を縮みあがらせようとしている.

put the fear of God into 《口》 **1** (人)をたまげるほどしかる ▪ When he comes, I'll *put the fear of God into* him. 彼が来たらたまげるほどしかってやろう.
2 (人)を怖がらす ▪ What were you doing up on the roof? You *put the fear of God into* me! 屋根の上で何をしてたんだい? 肝をつぶしたよ.

stand in fear (***of***) (…を)恐れて[心配して]いる ▪ His aunt *stood in fear of* him. 彼のおばは彼を恐れていた.

there's not much fear of …の恐れはあまりない, あまり…しそうにない ▪ *There is not much fear of* deflation. デフレの恐れはあまりない.

with fear and trembling 恐れおののいて, おずおずして, びくびくして (《聖》 *Eph.* 6. 5) ▪ I say this *with fear and trembling.* 私は恐れおののきながら, かように申しあげます.

without fear or favor えこひいきなく, 公平に ▪ Investigate the case *without fear or favor.* その件を公平に調査せよ.

fear[2] /fɪər/ 動 ***fear the worst*** 最悪の事態を予感する ▪ We *fear the worst.* 我々は最悪の事態を予感している.

He that is down need fear no fall. 《諺》落ちた者には落ちる心配はいらない. ☞need は助動詞.

need not fear but (***that***) …は心配無用である ▪ You *need not fear but* he will succeed. 彼は大丈夫, 成功する.

Never fear! 《口》心配無用, 大丈夫 ▪ I'll find the occasion, *never fear!* 私が機会を見つけます. 心配いりません.

never [***do not***] ***fear but*** (***that, what***) きっと…する ▪ *Never fear but that* you shall be paid. きっとお支払いしますよ.

fearful /fíərfəl/ 形 ***be fearful of*** …を気づかう, しはしないかと気づかう ▪ I *am fearful of* failure. 失敗を気づかっている ▪ I *am fearful of* his doing it. 彼がそれをしはしないかと恐れている.

be fearful to *do* 怖くて[心配で]…しかねる ▪ He *is fearful to* tell it to the master. 彼は怖くてそれを主人に話しかねている.

fearfully /fíərfəli/ 副 ***fearfully and wonderfully*** 恐るべく奇(くす)しく (《聖》 *Ps.* 139. 14) ▪ We are *fearfully and wonderfully* made, especially women. 私たちは恐るべく奇しく作られています, 特に女性は.

feast[1] /fiːst/ 名 ***a feast for the eyes*** [***ears***] 目[耳]のごちそう; 見て[聞いて]うれしいもの ▪ The play was *a feast for the eyes.* その芝居は目のごちそう[目の正月]だった.

a feast or a famine/***either feast or famine*** 豊富か僅少か, 大成功か大失敗か ▪ Playing the stock market is *a feast or a famine*—you'll either make a lot or lose everything. 株の投機をすると大成功か大失敗かのいずれかになる. 大もうけをする

か丸裸になるかだ.

a movable feast 移動祝祭日《日付が固定されていない祝祭日》 ▪ Easter is *a movable feast.* 復活祭は移動祝祭日だ.

give* [*make*] *a feast 宴会を催す ▪ He *makes a feast* tonight. 彼は今夜ごちそうをする.

***make a feast of* [*upon*]** …をおいしく食べる ▪ He *made a feast of* the portly grunter. 彼は肥満したブタをおいしく食べた.

***the feast of reason* (*and flow of soul*)** 高談清話(と和気あいあいの交歓) ▪ St. John mingles with my bowl, *the feast of reason and flow of soul.* 使徒ヨハネは私の大杯に高談清話と和気あいあいの交歓を混ぜ合わせる. ☞A. Pope, *Satires & Epistles of Horace Imitated*, "Satire"1. 128.

the ghost* [*spectre*] *at the feast 《英・文》過去のいやなことを思い出させて興をそぐもの[人], 興ざめの原因 ▪ John was *the spectre at the feast*, always reminding her of her broken promise. ジョンは記憶の幻影だった. 守られなかった約束のことをいつも彼女に思い出させたからだ ▪ I do think Diana will be *the ghost at the* UK royal wedding *feast.* ダイアナ元妃は英国王室にとっては結婚の祝宴に冷水をあびせるもとになると思う. ☞Macbeth が主君を殺して王位に就いた祝宴の席に自分が殺させた Banquo の亡霊が現れたことから.

feast[2] /fiːst/ 動 ***feast** one's **eyes on*** →EYE.

feat /fiːt/ 名 ***no mean feat*** 偉業, 大仕事 ▪ Arafat performed *no mean feat* for peace. アラファトは平和のために偉業を成し遂げた.

put** one's **feats in** one's **mouth 自慢話をする ▪ Every time he opens *his mouth* he *puts his feats in* it. 彼は口を開けば, 自慢話だ.

feather[1] /féðər/ 名 ***a feather in** one's **cap* [*hat*]** 誇りや光栄となるもの, 名誉; 秀作 ▪ It's *a feather in John's cap* to be chosen captain of the cricket team. クリケットチームのキャプテンに選ばれることはジョンの名誉である ▪ A new television series will be another *feather in his cap.* 新シリーズのテレビ番組もまた彼の秀作だ. ☞敵を一人殺すたびに兵士の帽子に羽をつけた習慣から.

(*as*) *light as a feather* →(as) LIGHT as air.

be in grand feather 贅沢な服装をしている ▪ She *was in grand feather* at the dance. 彼女はダンスパーティーで贅沢な服装をしていた.

be tickled with a feather じきに笑う ▪ He *is tickled with a feather.* 彼はささいなことにすぐ笑う.

could* [*might*] *have knocked** a person **down with a feather 《口・戯》(羽1本で打ち倒すことができるほど)人をびっくり仰天させた ▪ When I heard that she had run off with him, you *could have knocked* me *down with a feather.* 彼女が彼とかけ落ちしたと聞いたとき, 私はびっくり仰天した.

crop the feathers of …の高慢の鼻を折る ▪ Becky is so full of vanity that *her feathers* will *be cropped* some day. ベッキーはすごくうぬぼれてるから, いつかその高慢の鼻を折られるだろう.

cut a feather **1**《海》(船が)船首でしぶきを立てて進む ▪ If the bow be too broad, she will not *cut a feather.* 船首が広すぎると, 船はしぶきを立てないだろう.
2 敏活に動く ▪ He shambles about, for he could never *cut a feather.* 彼はよろよろ歩き回る. というのは, 決して敏活に歩けないだろうから.

cut ... out of all feather …を全く顔色なからしめる ▪ She *cut* me *out of all feather.* 彼女は私を全く顔色なからしめた.

find a white feather in** a person's **tail 人の憶病の気配を見てとる, 人の憶病を見破る (→show the white FEATHER) ▪ I've long guessed that we should *find a white feather in your tail.* 我々があなたの憶病の地金を見破るだろうと私はずっと前から察していた.

Fine feathers don't always make fine birds. 《諺》外見[言うこと]が立派でも必ずしも行為が立派とはかぎらない.

Fine feathers make fine birds. **1**《諺》衣装が立派なら引き立つ,「馬子(ま)にも衣装」 ▪ When Mary came down dressed for the dance, her father remarked, "*Fine feathers make fine birds.*" メアリーがダンスの服装をしておりて来たとき, 彼女の父は「馬子にも衣装だな」と言った.
2 外観ばかりでは真価は知れない ▪ They certainly do look very smart. But *fine feathers make fine birds.* 彼らは確かに非常にスマートに見える. が, 外観がよければよく見えるものですからね《真価はわからない》.

fur, fin,* (*and*) *feather →FUR[1].

have not* [*hardly*] *a feather to fly with 《口》破産している, 一文なしである ▪ Now he *has hardly a feather to fly with.* 今では彼はほとんど無一文である.

high feather (天気が)すばらしく良い ▪ We chose a summer day of *high feather* for the excursion. 遠足にはすばらしく天気のよい夏の日を選んだ.

in feather 羽のはえた; 羽のある; 羽で飾った ▪ All fowls *in feather* fell upon it. すっかり羽のはえた鳥がみなそれに襲いかかった.

in fine* [*good, high,* etc.] *feather 健康状態よく, 意気盛んで; きげんよく ▪ I'm *in finest feather.* 私はすばらしく健康です ▪ Never was he *in finer feather.* 彼がこれほど元気だったことはない ▪ He *in great feather* showed us round the city. 彼は大得意で, 我々にその町を案内してくれた.

in full feather 《口》 **1** (ひな鳥などが)羽がはえそろって ▪ The bird was *in full feather.* 鳥は羽がはえそろっていた.
2 盛装して ▪ He was *in full feather* last Sunday. 彼はこの前の日曜には盛装していた.
3 金をたくさん持って ▪ I am *in full feather* at present. 今は金がたんまりある.
4 =in fine FEATHER.

make the feathers fly 《口》 **1** 大騒ぎを起こす, やかましくけんかする ▪ His very presence *made the feathers fly.* 彼がいることだけで大騒ぎとなった ▪ The old woman *made the feathers fly* last night. 昨

夜その老婦人はやかましくがなり立てた.

2 (相手を)ひどく打ち懲らす, やっつける ▪ If his master had hold of him, he'd *make the feathers fly.* 主人が彼をつかまえたら, ひどくやっつけるだろう.

3 ばりばり[きびきびと]仕事をする ▪ When Mrs. Hale did her spring cleaning she *made the feathers fly.* ヘイル夫人は, 春の大掃除で, きびきびと仕事をした.

not care a feather 少しも気にしない ▪ I do*n't care a feather.* 私は少しもかまわない.

of all feather すっかり羽のはえた ▪ Birds *of all feather* flew in from the sea. すっかり羽のはえそろった鳥たちが海から飛来した.

of ... feather ...種類の ▪ I am not *of* that *feather.* 私はそのような種類の人間ではない.

ride a feather 6ストーン以下の少年である ▪ The boy *rides a feather.* その少年は6ストーン以下だ. ☞ feather = feather-weight.

rise at a feather 《米》ちょっとのことで腹を立てる ▪ He *rises at a feather* against our friends. 彼は毛ほどのことで我々の友人たちに腹を立てる.

ruffle* (*up*)** *one's* ***feathers →RUFFLE².

show* [*mount*] *the white feather 《口》憶病風を吹かす, 弱音を吐く ▪ Do you want to *show the white feather* in front of these people? この人々の前で憶病風を吹かせたいのか. ☞ 闘鶏の尾に白い羽のあるのは劣等種の印であることから.

smooth *a person's* ***ruffled feathers*** (慰めの言葉をかけて)落ち着かせる, 怒り[苛立ち]を静める ▪ I suppose Jim's explanation has *smoothed Mary's ruffled feathers* by now. 今はもうジムの説明でメアリーの怒りは静まってきたのではないか.

smooth *one's* ***rumpled* [*ruffled*] *feathers*** おもむろに落ち着きを取り戻す ▪ "It can't be helped," said Simon, as he *smoothed his rumpled feathers.* 「どうにもしかたがない」とサイモンは落ち着きを取り戻しながら言った.

(*the*) *feathers fly* 《米》ひと騒動起きる, けんか[口論]が生じる ▪ *Feathers* will *fly* if he finds out you've borrowed his car. 君が彼の車を借りたということがばれるとひと騒動起きるぞ.

feather² /féðər/ 動 ***feather an oar* [*one's oars*]** オールの水かきを水平にして水面と平行にして抜く, 斜めに空を切るようにオールを抜く ▪ He *feathered his oars* [*an oar*] with skill. 彼は巧みに, オールの水かきを水平にして抜いた.

feather *one's* ***nest*** (勤めている間に少しずつ)ふところを暖める; 私腹を肥やす; (未来の用意に)たくわえをする ▪ You must never try to *feather your nest.* あなたは決して私腹を肥やそうとしてはいけない. ☞ 鳥が羽毛で巣の裏打ちをする習慣から.

tar and feather *a person* →TAR².

featheredge /féðərèdʒ/ 名 ***not to put a featheredge on it*** 《米口》率直に言うと ▪ *Not to put a featheredge on it,* I thought I'd run away with it. 率直に言えば, 私はそれを持って逃走しようと思った.

feature /fíːtʃər/ 名 ***be feature for feature alike*** 割り符を合わせたようだ ▪ Japan and New Zealand *are feature for feature alike.* 日本とニュージーランドは符節を合するようだ.

make a feature of ...を呼び物にする, 特徴とする ▪ The paper *makes a feature of* detailed weather reports. その新聞は詳細な天気記事を呼び物にしている.

federal /fédərəl/ 形 ***make a Federal case* (*out*) *of*** 《米俗》〚主に否定文で〛...を大げさに言う, 針小棒大に騒ぎ立てる ▪ Don't *make a Federal case out of* it. それを大仰に言わないでくれ ▪ He only swore at you. There's no need to *make a federal case out of* it! 彼は君にちょっと毒ういただけだ. 針小棒大に大騒ぎする必要はないよ.

fee /fiː/ 名 ***at a pin's fee*** 〚主に否定文で〛ピン(の価値)ほどにも ▪ I do not set my life *at a pin's fee.* 私は命をピンほどにも思っていない.

fee or reward 慰労金または報償 ▪ I don't ask *fee or reward* for doing it. 私はそれをしたからって, 慰労金も報償もくれとは言いません.

***hold ... in fee* (*simple*)** 《法》(土地を)絶対相続地として所有する, 領地[封土]として所有する; 絶対正当な財産として所有する ▪ Venice *held* the gorgeous East *in fee.* ベネチアは華麗な東方(小アジアなど)を絶対正当な財産として所有した ▪ He *held* the provinces *in fee.* 彼はその国々を領地として所有していた.

feed¹ /fiːd/ 名 ***at feed*** 草を食って, 餌を食べて ▪ The cattle are out *at feed.* 牛群は外で草を食(は)んでいる.

at one feed 一食に[で] ▪ He took a pound of beef *at one feed.* 彼は一食に肉を1ポンド食べた.

(*be*) *on the feed* (魚が)餌を食べて(いる); 餌をあさって[捜して](いる) ▪ A shoal of porpoises *were on the feed.* イルカの群れが餌を食べていた ▪ Towards evening he set out *on the feed.* 夕方近くに彼は餌をあさりに出かけた.

have a feed 《米口》食べる; ごちそうを食べる ▪ Let the cow *have a feed.* 牛に飼料をやりなさい ▪ Boys *had a feed* of ice-cream. 少年たちはアイスクリームをごちそうになった.

off *one's* ***feed*** →OFF¹.

feed² /fiːd/ 動 **(*be*) *fed to the* (*back*) *teeth* [*the gills, the neck*]** 《口》あきあきして(いる) ▪ They *are fed to the gills* with doing so. 彼らはそうすることにあきあきしている. ☞ gills = mouth 《俗》.

(*be*) *fed up* (*with*) 《口》(...に)あきあきして(いる), 死ぬほど退屈して(いる) ▪ We *are fed up with* the war. 我々は戦争にはあきあきしている ▪ German prisoners looked *fed up.* ドイツの捕虜はひどく退屈のようだった.

feed *oneself* 食事をする ▪ I can't *feed myself.* 私は御飯が食べられない.

feed a cold 風邪のときたくさん食べる[食べて治す] ▪ *Feed a cold* and starve a fever. 《諺》風邪には大食, 熱には絶食がよい.

feed *a person* ***a line* [*lines*]** **1** (役者に)せりふを

教える; 言うべきことを教える ▪ Glen *fed* him *a line* at one point during the show. グレンはショーの途中の一箇所で彼にせりふを教えた.

2 人をかつぐ, 一杯食わす ▪ If someone told you different, they *fed* you *a line*. もしも誰かが別のことを言ったのなら, 君をだましたのだ.

feed at the high table →FEED well.

feed ... bare (穀物・土地の草など)を牛馬にきれいに食べさせてしまう ▪ He *fed* the land *bare*. 彼はその地の草を牛馬にきれいに食べさせてしまった.

feed ... close ...を牛馬に短く食わせる ▪ Take care to *feed* the grass *close*. 草を牛馬に短く食わせるよう注意しなさい.

F

feed *one's* ***eyes*** [***sight***] 目を楽しませる ▪ I *fed my eyes* on [with] these monuments. 私はこれらの記念物で目を楽しませた.

feed *one's* ***face*** →FACE[1].

feed fat on ...を見あきる ▪ He *fed fat on* the view. 彼はその眺めを見あきた.

feed (***full and***) ***high*** 十分に美食させる ▪ *Feed* him *full and high*. 彼に十分美食させよ.

feed high →FEED well.

feed out of *a person's* ***hand*** →eat out of a person's HAND.

feed the ear 耳を楽しませる ▪ His tongue *feeds the ear* with music. 彼は歌を歌って耳を楽しませる.

feed the fire 火をあおる《比喩的にも》 ▪ When men are disposed to quarrel, anything does to *feed the fire*. 人がけんかする気になっているときは, それをあおり立てるには何でもよい.

feed the kitty 共同積立金[準備金]に出資する ▪ Everyone *feeds the kitty* at least $3. 誰もが少なくとも3ドル出資する. ☞kitty (ギャンブル用語で「積み金」の意) を「子猫」に掛けたもの.

feed well [***high, at the high table***] 《やや戯》うまいものばかり食べる, 美食する ▪ His expansive stomach testifies to how *well* he *feeds*. 彼の便便(べんべん)たる太鼓腹は, いかに美食しているかの証しである.

Well fed, well bred. 《諺》衣食足って礼節を知る.

feeding /fíːdɪŋ/ 名 ***a feeding frenzy*** **1** (サメ・ピラニアなどによる)獲物の奪い合い; 餌取り争い(の状態) ▪ If hungry animals have *a feeding frenzy*, they fight each other to get a share of it. 飢えた動物が餌取り争いの状態になると, 分け前をとろうと互いに争う.

2《口》(特ダネを追う報道関係者の)過当競争 ▪ Her sudden tragic death sparked off *a feeding frenzy* in the media. 彼女の突然の悲劇的な死でメディアの報道合戦に火がついた.

It's feeding time at the zoo! 《戯》動物園の給食時間だ ▪ I see *it's feeding time at the zoo*. I'd better help myself to some food before it's all gone. われ先にがっついてるぞ. なくならないうちに食べておかなくっちゃ ▪ "*It's feeding time at the zoo*," she laughed, seeing her children eating hungrily. 彼女は子供たちがおなかをすかせて食べているのを見て, 「動物園のえさ時間ね」と笑いながら言った.

feel[1] /fiːl/ 名 ***by the feel*** 感じで, 気持ちで ▪ He could tell *by the feel* when the sun was rising. 彼はいつ日が昇るかを感覚で知ることができた.

cop a feel 《米俗》(相手の了解なしに)体をさわる, 痴漢行為をする (*on*) ▪ I even saw him trying to *cop a feel on* a girl's breast. 彼が少女の胸をさわろうとしているのを見たことさえある.

get a feel for ...の感触[コツ]をつかむ ▪ He's *got a feel for* the strike zone. 彼はストライクゾーンの感触をつかんだ.

get the feel of ...に探りを入れる, (意向)を打診する; を理解する ▪ We must *get the feel of* political sentiment in the state. 我々は州内の政治的感情を打診せねばならない.

have a feel さわってみる ▪ Let me *have a feel*. ちょっとさわってみさせてください.

have a ... feel 手ざわりが...である ▪ This cloth *has a* rough *feel*. この布はざらざらする.

make a feel 探りを入れる ▪ He *made an* exploratory *feel*. 彼は詮索するように探りを入れた.

to the feel 手ざわりが ▪ It is firm *to the feel*. それは手ざわりが堅い.

feel[2] /fiːl/ 動 ***feel*** *oneself* **1**〚主に否定文で〛いつものように元気である, 丈夫である ▪ I don't *feel* quite *myself* today. きょう私はどうも気分が悪い.

2 落ち着く ▪ He lost his nervousness and began to *feel himself* again. 彼は神経過敏がなくなり, また落ち着き始めた.

feel bad(***ly***) 気分が悪い; 気に病む, 後悔する; 気の毒に思う ▪ I *feel bad* today. きょうは気分が悪い ▪ He *felt bad* about the error. 彼はその誤りを後悔した ▪ I *feel bad* for you. お気の毒に思います. ☞badly の形は非標準.

feel cheap →CHEAP.

feel *one's* ***feet*** **1** 場所が(どこということが)わかる ▪ Now I begin to *feel my feet*. 今ここがどこかということがわかりかけた.

2 足が痛む ▪ In hot weather she always *felt her feet* so badly. 暑い気候になると, 彼女はいつも足がひどく痛んだ.

feel free **1** (頼みに対して)よろしい, どうぞご自由に ▪ Do you mind if I smoke?—*Feel free*. タバコを吸ってもよろしいか—どうぞご自由に ▪ If you want to read this novel, *feel free*. この小説を読みたければ, ご自由にどうぞ.

2〚しばしば命令文で〛自由に[遠慮なく]...する (*to do*) ▪ *Feel free to* ask questions if you have any. 質問があれば自由に尋ねなさい.

feel (***it***)... ***in*** *one's* ***bones*** →BONE.

feel *one's* ***legs*** [***feet, etc.***] **1** 足場がしっかりしている, しっかりと立てるようになる ▪ The trees are beginning to *feel their feet*. その木は根がつき始めた.

2 自信がつく, 腰が座る ▪ It was not until the last act that he *felt his legs*. 最後の幕になって初めて彼は自信がついた ▪ The gull flew, but was not yet well *feeling his wings*. そのカモメは飛んだがまだ自信がついていなかった.

3 落ち着く，くつろぐ ▪ Now I begin to *feel my legs*. 私はようやく楽な気持ちになり始めた．

feel like **1**《米》…したい気がする ▪ I didn't *feel like* dinner. 食事をする気にならなかった ▪ I *felt like* a ride. 馬に乗って出たい気がした．

2 …らしい，になりそうである ▪ It *feels like* rain [snow] today. きょうはどうやら雨[雪]になりそうだ．

3 …の気分である ▪ What do you *feel like*? ご気分はどうですか ▪ I *feel like* catching cold. 風邪を引いたような気がする．

4 手ざわりが…のようである ▪ It *feels like* velvet. それは手ざわりがビロードのようだ．

feel like *doing*《口》…したい気がする ▪ I *feel like going* to the zoo. 私は動物園へ行きたい気がする．

feel (***like***) *oneself* いつもの健康[力，落ち着き]である ▪ He is *feeling* (*like*) *himself* again. 彼はまたいつものように元気になっている．

feel like a new person [***man, woman***] **1** 生まれ変わったような気がする ▪ Then I *felt like a new person*. そのとき私は生まれ変わったような気がした．

2 すっかり疲れが取れて良い気持ちになる，すっかり元気になる ▪ After a vigorous massage he *felt like a new man*. 強いマッサージを受けて彼はすっかり疲れが取れて良い気持ちだった．

feel like a spot《米俗》1杯やる ▪ Do you *feel like a spot*? 1杯やらないか．

feel like death warmed up《口》非常に気分が悪い，半死の気持ちである ▪ In the airplane he *felt like death warmed up*. 飛行機の中で彼は非常に気分が悪かった．

feel like new =FEEL like a new person.

feel like nothing on earth →like NOTHING on earth.

feel *one's* ***oats*** →OAT.

feel on top of the world《口》きわめてほがらか[上きげん]である ▪ I'm *feeling on top of the world*. 私はきわめて上きげんです．

feel out of it [***things***]《口》よそ者[のけ者]のように感じる，お呼びでない者のように感じる ▪ As I have been away so long, I *feel out of things*. 長い間離れていたので私はよそ者のように感じている．

feel out of place くつろがない，場ちがいのように感じる ▪ I would *feel out of place* in his drawing-room. あの人の応接間にいるとくつろがないだろう．

feel *one's* ***own man*** =FEEL oneself 1.

feel sore (***on***) →SORE.

feel to [***to*** *do*] **1** …するような気がする ▪ I *feel to* have to take care of her. 彼女の世話をしなければならないような気がする．

2《米口》…したい気がする ▪ I *feel to* go and see it. 私は行ってそれを見たいような気がする ▪ She could not any way *feel to* it. 彼女はどうしてもそうしたい気がしなかった．☞2 はもと牧師用語．

feel *one's* ***way*** **1** 手探りで進む ▪ We must *feel our way* carefully. 我々は注意深く手探りで進まねばならない．

2 探りを入れる; 慎重に行動する ▪ I won't ask him directly to lend me his car. I'll *feel my way* first. 彼に直接自動車を貸してくれとは頼みません．まず探りを入れます ▪ Reason *feels its way* in its search for the truth. 理性は真理探究に慎重を期す．

feel *one's* ***way around*** **1** 手探りで行く ▪ The fuse had blown, so I had to *feel my way around* the room in darkness. ヒューズがとんでしまったので，真っ暗な室内を手探りで進まねばならなかった．

2 (様子を見ながら)徐々に進む ▪ How are you getting along in your new job?—I'm just *feeling my way around*. 今度の仕事はどうかね?—様子を見ながら徐々にやっているよ．

make ...felt …を思い知らせる，を発揮する ▪ Japan ought to *make* her power *felt*. 日本は国威を発揚すべきである．

make *oneself* [*one's* ***presence***] ***felt*** 実力を発揮する ▪ The new governor quickly *made his presence felt*. 新知事はただちに実力を発揮した．

feeler /fíːlər/ 名 ***put*** [***send, have, throw***] ***out a feeler*** [***feelers***] 探りを入れる，様子を調べる ▪ We should *put out a* few *feelers* to see how many people are for it. 我々は何人がそれに賛成か当たってみるべきだ ▪ Murray has *put out* a few *feelers* about employment. マリーは採用に関してちょっと探りを入れた．☞昆虫が触角 (feelers) を伸ばすことから．

feeling /fíːlɪŋ/ 名形 ***a gut feeling*** [***gut feelings***] 勘，直感 ▪ We have *a gut feeling* that Nancy is still alive and we will see her again. ナンシーはまだ生きているので，彼女とまた会うだろうという感じがする．

a [***the***] ***sinking feeling*** (***that***) (…という)いやな[悪い]予感 ▪ I had *a sinking feeling that* something was wrong with him. 彼はどこか悪いのではないかという悪い予感がした．

acquire a feeling for …の感覚を身につける，の感じをつかむ，を感覚的に理解する ▪ I *acquired a feeling for* the overall marketplace. 実業界全般の感じをつかんだ．

consult *a person's* ***feelings*** 人の感情を察する[察して決定する] ▪ Jenner *consulted his* own *feelings*. ジェナーは自分の感情を顧慮した．

get a [***the***] ***feeling*** (***that***) (なぜか分からないが)…という気がする ▪ I've just *got a feeling that* something good will happen soon. It did. なにかいいことがもうすぐ起きるという気がして，実際そうなった ▪ I *got the feeling that* he was doing something naughty. 私は，彼はなにかいたずらをしていると思った．

have a feeling …の予感がある ▪ She *had a feeling* that something unpleasant was going to happen. 彼女は何か不愉快なことが起ころうとしているという予感がした．

have (***a***) ***feeling for*** …に対する感受性がある ▪ He *has a* deep *feeling* [not much *feeling*] *for* beauty in nature and art. 彼は自然および芸術の美に対する深い感受性がある[あまりない]．

F

have mixed feelings 複雑な心境である,(気持ちや考えが)混乱している ▪I *had mixed feelings* about it and it took awhile to make up my mind. それについては気持ちが定まらず,決定にしばらくかかった.

have no [not a grain of] feeling for …に対して全然思いやりがない ▪Why do you laugh? You *have no feeling for* him? 君はなぜ笑うのか. 彼に対する思いやりは全くないのか.

in a feeling way 感動的に ▪He spoke *in a feeling way*. 彼は感動的に話をした.

vent *one's* ***feelings on*** 感情を…にぶつける,怒りのはけ口を…に向ける ▪Supporters have *vented their feelings on* internet message boards. サポーターたちは感情のはけ口をインターネットの掲示板に向けた.

with feeling 熱意をこめて; 感動して; しみじみ ▪He spoke *with feeling*. 彼は熱意をこめて話した.

feign /feɪn/ 動 ***feign*** *oneself* …のふりをする,を装う ▪He *feigns himself* mad. 彼は気がふれたふりをしている.

without feigning 偽りなく,本当に,心から ▪They please you *without feigning*. 彼らは本当にあなたを喜ばせてくれる.

feint /feɪnt/ 名 ***in feint*** 見せかけに ▪He aimed straight blows, not *in feint*, at the enemy. 彼は見せかけでなく,まっすぐに敵に打ってかかった.

make a feint 偽りの見せかけをする ▪He *made a feint* and got under my guard. 彼は偽りの見せかけをして私の監視下に入った.

make a feint of *doing* [***to*** *do*] …するふりをする ▪Jekyll was sitting down to *make a feint of breakfasting*. ジキルは座って朝食を食べるふりをしていた ▪I *made a feint to* cut them down. 私はそれらを切り倒すふりをした.

felicitate /fəlísətèɪt/ 動 ***felicitate*** *oneself* ***on*** [***that***] …を[ということを]喜ぶ ▪He *felicitated himself on* his good fortune. 彼は自分の幸運を喜んだ.

felicity /fəlísəti/ 名 ***with felicity*** 適切に,うまく ▪He expressed himself *with felicity*. 彼はうまく自分の考えを述べた.

fell[1] /fel/ 名 ***a*** [*one's*] ***fell of hair*** もつれ髪,乱れ髪 ▪Their features were half hidden under *a fell of hair*. 彼らの目鼻だちはもつれ髪の下に半ば隠れていた.

fell[2] /fel/ 形 ***at*** [***in***] ***one fell swoop*** 一挙に,一気呵成に (cf. Sh., *Macb*. 4. 3. 219, [1606]) ▪I'd prefer to do the paperwork *in one fell swoop*. At least then we know it's finished with. 事務処理は一気呵成にやるほうが好きだ. そうすれば,少なくともやり終えたということはわかる.

fellow /féloʊ/ 名 ***a fellow well-met*** 《口》仲良し ▪He is the best *fellow well-met* in the world. 彼は世界中で一番の仲良しである.

be (hail-)fellow-well-met with …と大の仲良しである ▪I *am fellow-well-met with* him. 私は彼と大の仲良しである.

be not fellows (1対のものが)ふぞろいである ▪The boots *are not fellows*. その靴はふぞろいだ.

call *a man* ***fellow*** 男を(軽蔑して)やつと呼ぶ ▪We *called* him *fellow*. 彼をやつと呼んだ.

My dear [***old***] ***fellow!*** おい君,ねえ君《親しい呼びかけ》 ▪I'll tell you how it is, *my dear fellow*. ねえ君,どういう事情かを話してあげよう.

My good fellow! ねえ君《非難・諫言の調子がある》.

not find [***meet, see***] *a person's* ***fellow*** 人に匹敵するものがない ▪I *never saw his fellow*. 彼ほどの者は見たことがない.

Poor fellow! かわいそうに,気の毒なやつ ▪He looked dreadfully weak still, *poor fellow!* まだひどく弱っている様子だった. かわいそうに.

Stone dead hath no fellow. 《諺》秘密を守ること死人に及ぶものはない,「死人に口無し」.

There's a good fellow. →THERE.

fellowship /féloʊʃìp/ 名 ***bear*** *a person* ***fellowship*** 人とつき合う ▪I *bore* him *fellowship*. 私は彼とつき合った.

the right hand of fellowship 入団[入会]許可の握手 (《聖》*Gal*. 2. 9); 交友の手 ▪The church gave him *the right hand of fellowship*. 教会は彼と握手して教団の仲間に入れた ▪I will hold forth *the right hand of fellowship* to every individual. 私はすべての人に交友の手を差し伸べようとする.

felony /féləni/ 名 ***compound the felony*** 罪の上塗りをする ▪I was already late for work; and I *compounded the felony* by losing some important papers. 私はすでに仕事に遅刻していた. その上重要な書類をなくして罪の上塗りをした.

female /fíːmeɪl/ 名 ***The female of the species is more deadly than the male.*** 《諺》雌は雄よりも強い毒を持つ.

fence /fens/ 名 ***a fence-sitter*** 日和見主義者,どっちつかずの人 ▪I'm going to be *a fence-sitter* on this. これに関しては日和見を決め込むつもりだ.

be [***belong***] ***on*** *a person's* ***side of the fence*** 《主に米口》人にくみする ▪You should *be on his side of the fence*. 君は彼にくみすべきだ.

be [***sit, stand,***] ***on the fence***/***straddle the fence*** 《主に米口》日和見をする; どっちつかずである; 中立する ▪He always *sits on the fence* till he is certain which side will win. 彼はどちらが勝つかはっきりするまではいつも日和見をする ▪McCain *straddled the fence* on the politically sensitive issue. マケイン氏は政治的に微妙な問題に関してはあいまいな態度をとった.

(***be***) ***on the other*** [etc.] ***side of the fence*** 《主に米口》反対[など]側に(ある),反対[など]党に加わって(いる) ▪Journals *on the other side of the fence* will blame him. 反対側の雑誌は彼を責めるだろう ▪You *are on the* same *side of the fence*. 君たちは同じ側に加わっている.

be under fence 《米口》柵で囲まれている ▪The premises *were under* good *fence*. その屋敷は立

派な柵に囲まれていた.

come down on one side of the fence or the other (議論などで)どちらか一方を支持する.

come down [***descend***] ***on the right side of the fence*** (形勢を見て)旗色の良いほうに味方する《政治に関して用いる》 ▪ The party has at long last *come down on the right side of the fence.* その党はやっとのことで旗色の良い方へ味方をした.

come [***climb, get***] ***off the fence*** (どちら側につくのか)態度を明らかにする, 旗幟(き)鮮明にする ▪ Wales has finally *got off the fence* and made a decision. ついにウェールズは態度を明らかにして決定を下した.

Good fences make good neighbors. 《諺》しっかりした垣根があれば隣人とうまくやっていける.

keep *a person* ***on*** [***to***] *his* ***side of the fence*** 《米口》人に分を守らせる ▪ There is nothing like *keeping* a man *to his side of the fence.* 人に分を守らせることほど良いことはない.

look after [***to***] *one's* ***fences*** **1** …との関係を修復する ▪ China is trying to *look after fences* with Russia after the recent border dispute. 最近の国境紛争の後, 中国はロシアとの関係を修復しようとしている.

2 《米》国会議員が(次の選挙に備えて)選挙区の地盤を固める[立て直す] ▪ They are at home *looking after their fences.* 彼らは郷里にあって自己の地盤の立て直しをやっている.

make fence フェンシングの身構えをする ▪ He will *make fence* at your cat. 彼はあなたの猫に対してもフェンシングの身構えをするだろう.

mend [***repair***] *one's* ***fences*** = look after one's FENCEs.

put *one's* [***the***] ***horse to*** [***at***] ***the fence*** 馬に拍車をかけて障害物を飛び越えさせる.

put ... under fence 《米口》…を柵で囲む ▪ We *put under fence* 30 acres of land. 我々は30エーカーの土地を柵で囲んだ.

ride the fence **1** 《米》柵の周囲を馬で回って牛の番をする ▪ He must hire the necessary help to *ride the fence.* 馬で柵の周囲を回って牛の番をするのに必要な人員を彼は雇わねばならない.

2 《米》(ある問題について)どっちつかずである; どちらとも決めかねる ▪ I am not going to *ride the fence* on any matter. 私はどんな問題についてもどっちつかずの態度を取るつもりはありません.

rush *one's* ***fences*** →RUSH[3].

sit [***stand***] ***on the fence*** →be on the FENCE.

stop to look at a fence 《口》(障害・いやなことをするに当たって)ちゅうちょする ▪ It is no good *stopping to look at a fence.* 障害にぶつかってちゅうちょしてもだめだ. ☞競馬の障害物競走から.

fend[1] /fend/ 名 ***make a fend*** 思い切ったことをする ▪ I *make a* good *fend* for a living. 私は暮らしのために相当思い切った冒険をやる.

fend[2] /fend/ 動 ***fend and prove*** 《英》議論する, 口論する ▪ They did not delight in *fending and proving.* 彼らは口論することを喜ばなかった.

fend for *oneself* 自活する, 一人でやっていく ▪ Now that his father is dead, he must *fend for himself.* 今や父が死んだのだから彼は自活せねばならない.

fender /féndər/ 名 ***a fender bender*** 《米口》**1** 自動車同士の(小さな)衝突事故 ▪ She was involved in *a fender bender* yesterday. 彼女はきのう自動車事故に巻き込まれた.

2 無謀な運転手 ▪ I was almost run over by *a fender bender.* 無謀運転者に危うく轢かれるところだった. ☞押韻による連語.

throw out the fender 防舷物を投げる ▪ *Throw out the fender*s; we are alongside the quay. 防舷物を投げろ. 波止場に横づけになったぞ.

feoff /fiːf/ 動 ***feoff*** *a person* ***to the use of*** (*another*) (他人)の使用を許す義務のある領地を人に与える ▪ They *were feoffed to the use of* their masters. 彼らは主人に使用を許す義務のある領土を与えられた.

ferment /fərmént/ 名 ***in a ferment*** (わき返るような)大騒ぎで ▪ The foreign embassies were all *in a ferment.* 外国大使館はみな大騒ぎしていた.

fern /fəːrn/ 名 (***as***) ***invisible as fern seed*** (シダの種子のように)見えないで ▪ Their propaganda flies about *as invisible as fern seed.* 彼らの宣伝は全く見えないで飛散する.

ferret /férət/ 動 ***go ferreting*** (シロイタチを使って)ウサギ狩りに行く; (…を)詮索する (*into*) ▪ It is foolish to *go ferreting into* people's pasts. 人の過去を詮索するのは愚かである.

fertile /fə́ːrtəl|-taɪl/ 形 (***be***) ***fertile in*** [***of***] …に富んで(いる) ▪ The plains *are fertile in* native plants. その平野には原産の植物が豊富である ▪ He *is fertile of* invention. 彼は発明の才に富んでいる.

ferule /férəl/ 名 ***under the ferule*** 処罰するとおどされながら; きびしく教育されて ▪ The boy was brought up *under the ferule.* 少年は厳格に育てられた.

fervor, 《英》**fervour** /fə́ːrvər/ 名 ***with fervor*** 熱情をこめて ▪ He preached *with fervor.* 彼は熱情こめて説教した.

festival /féstəvəl/ 名 ***hold*** [***keep, make***] ***festival*** お祭りを催す, 祝宴を行う ▪ Children are ready to *make festival.* 子供はややもすればお祭り騒ぎをする ▪ They *held* high *festival.* 彼らは盛んな祝宴を催した.

fetch[1] /fetʃ/ 名 ***cast a*** [*one's*] ***fetch*** 計略をめぐらす ▪ They *cast their fetches* how to trap me. 私をいかにしてわなにかけようかと彼らは計略をめぐらした.

take a fetch 遠大な[影響の大きい]努力をする ▪ He *took a* new *fetch* in this matter. 彼はこの件について新しい遠大な努力をした.

fetch[2] /fetʃ/ 動 ***fetch*** *a person* ***a blow*** [***box***] 《口》人に一撃をくらわす ▪ I *fetched* him *a box* on the ear. 彼の横づらを一つ張ってやった.

fetch a compass 迂回する, 遠回りする ▪ They

fetched a long *compass.* 彼らはずっと遠回りをした.

fetch and carry **1** 訓練された犬が物を持って行ったり来たりする ▪ A raven may be taught to *fetch and carry* like a spaniel. オオガラスはスパニエル犬のように物を持って行ったり来たりすることを教えこむことができる. ☞ 狩猟から.

2 (人が)忙しく使い歩きをする; 奴隷のように雑役をする (*for*) ▪ Why should I *fetch and carry for* them? どうして私が彼らのために忙しく雑役をしようか.

3 噂をあちこち持ち歩く ▪ She is very fond of *fetching and carrying.* 彼女は噂をあちこち持ち回るのが大好きです. ☞ <a fetch-and-carry telltale 「噂を持ち回るおしゃべり」.

F

fetch ... back to mind ...を思い出す ▪ Mike *fetched* it *back to mind.* マイクはそれを思い出した.

fetch much たいした値になる ▪ This won't *fetch much.* これはいくらにもなるまい.

fetch the public 世の好評を得る ▪ This play will *fetch the public.* この劇は人気を得るだろう.

fetch the water [***pump***] ポンプに迎え水をして水を吸い上げる ▪ He *fetched the pump.* 彼はポンプに迎え水をして井戸水を吸い上げた.

fetch up (***level***) ***with*** ...と(並ぶ)所まで来る, に追いつく ▪ We *fetched up level with* the campfire. 我々は野営のかがり火の所まで来た ▪ I shall soon *fetch up with* you. すぐに君に追いつく.

fetch up nowhere 《英口》成功しない ▪ If you don't work hard, you'll *fetch up nowhere.* 一生懸命働かないと成功しないよ.

Go fetch! 《口》(犬に向かって)取って来い!

fetish /fétɪʃ/ 名 ***make a fetish of*** ...を盲目的に崇拝する, に熱をあげる, ...フェチである ▪ It is silly to *make a fetish of* clothes. 衣服に熱をあげるのは愚かだ.

fetter /fétər/ 名 ***in fetters*** 足枷をかけられて, 束縛されて ▪ The king was driven *in fetters* to Babylon. 国王は足枷をはめられてバビロンに護送された.

fettle /fétəl/ 名 ***in fine*** [***good, high***] ***fettle*** 《口》 **1** すばらしい状態で, 手入れが行き届いて ▪ The old machine is still *in fine fettle.* その古い機械はまだ快調に動いている.

2 非常に元気で ▪ You appear to be *in good fettle.* あなたは非常に元気のようだ. ☞ fettle = girdle 「しっかり帯を締めている」状態から.

feud /fjuːd/ 名 ***be at feud with*** **1** ...と反目している, と憎み合っている ▪ They *were at* deadly *feud with* him. 彼らは彼とひどく反目していた.

2 ...と宿恨をいだき合っている ▪ The two families have *been at feud with* each other. その二つの家は宿恨をいだき合ってきた.

fever /fíːvər/ 名 ***at fever heat*** 猛烈に ▪ They worked *at fever heat* all night. 彼らは夜通し猛烈に働いた.

in a fever (***of***) (...の)熱に浮かされて; (で)熱狂して ▪ He was *in a fever of* impatience. 彼はひどくあせっていた.

run a fever 熱がある, 発熱する ▪ I am *running a* little *fever.* 私は少し熱がある.

few /fjuː/ 形 代 ***a few*** 《口・皮肉》ずいぶん; 確かに ▪ It will cost him *a few.* それで彼はずいぶん金がかかるだろう ▪ He was determined to astonish the natives *a few.* 彼は大いに世人にショックを与えようと決心していた.

a good few (***of***) 《口》かなりたくさん(の) ▪ There were *a good few* (*of*) apples on it. その上にはかなりたくさんのリンゴがあった.

but few 《雅》ほんの少し(の) ▪ He has *but few* chances of success. 彼には成功の見込みはまずない.

every few minutes [***days, hours,*** etc.] → EVERY.

(***few and***) ***far between*** →FAR.

have [***hoist***] ***a few*** (***in***) 《米口》ビール(などを)2, 3杯飲む ▪ He *had a* good *few in* certainly. 彼はたしかにかなり飲んだ ▪ Tom has *had a few.* トムはちょっと酔っている ▪ We stopped at Donovan's on the way home and *hoisted a few.* 帰る途中ドノバンの店に寄って, 1杯引っかけた.

have had a few (***too many***) 《口》(飲みすぎて)酔っぱらっている ▪ I *had had a few too many* beers and couldn't remember how. ビールをちょっと飲みすぎてたのでどうだったか思い出せなかった.

no fewer than ...も(の)《数の多いことを示す句》 ▪ There were *no fewer than* fifty present. 50人も出席していた.

not a few **1** 少なからず, かなり多数(の) ▪ There are *not a few* visitors. 訪問客は少なくない.

2 《口》相当に, かなり ▪ Your letter diverted him *not a few.* あなたの手紙は相当彼を楽しませた.

only a few ほんの少し(の) ▪ *Only a few* understood what he said. 彼の言うことを理解した者はほんの少ししかいなかった.

precious few ごく少数の ▪ There were *precious few* kids running about the school playground. ごく少数の児童が校庭を走り回っていた.

quite a few →QUITE.

some few **1** 少しばかり(の) ▪ *Some few* of the survivors are still living. 生き残りの人々のうち少数の人がまだ生きている.

2 《米口》かなりたくさん(の) ▪ You know *some few* useful skills. 君は役に立つ技術をかなり多く知っている.

Win a few, lose a few. 人生成功する[勝つ]ときも失敗する[負ける]ときもある.

fiber, 《英》**fibre** /fáɪbər/ 名 ***every fiber of one's being*** 全身全霊 ▪ *Every fiber of his being* revolted at the idea. 彼の全身全霊がその考えにむかついた.

of coarse [***fine***] ***fiber*** 粗野[上品]な性格の ▪ He is a man *of fine fiber.* 彼は上品な人だ.

of real fiber しっかりした気骨の ▪ You are a man *of real fiber.* 君は硬骨の士だ.

fickle /fíkəl/ 形 (***as***) ***fickle as fortune*** ひどく気まぐれで ▪ She is *as fickle as fortune.* 彼女はひどく気まぐれで当てにならない. ☞ 運命の女神 Fortuna

は気まぐれである.

fiction /fíkʃən/ 名 ***Fact* [*Truth*] *is stranger than fiction.*** 《諺》事実[真実]は小説よりも奇なり.

fiddle[1] /fídəl/ 名 **(*as*) *fit* [《米》*fine*] *as a fiddle*** 《口》非常に元気で, 丈夫で; ぴんぴんして ▪ I arrived at my destination *as fit as a fiddle*. 非常に元気で目的地に着いた.

(*be*) *on the fiddle* 《英口》(金儲けのため)不正を働いて(いる) ▪ They *were* not *on the fiddle*. 彼らは金銭上の不正は働いていなかった ▪ If he's not *on the fiddle*, how did he afford that huge car? 不正を働いていないなら, どうして彼はあんな大きな車を買えたのだ.

One's ***face is made of a fiddle.*** 《口》顔がたまらなく美しい《魅惑的である》 ▪ *His Honor's face is made of a fiddle*. 閣下のご尊顔はまことに美しい.

hang up *one's* ***fiddle*** 業務から引退する; 《米口》やめる, 中止する ▪ It was time for me to *hang up my fiddle*. 私が商売から引退するときであった ▪ *Hang up your fiddle* till next year. 来年まで中止しなさい.

hang up *one's* ***fiddle when*** *one* ***comes home*** 外ではしゃぎ内でむっつりしている ▪ He entirely *hung up his fiddle when* he *came home*. 彼は全く外よしの内わるだった.

have a face as long as a fiddle →FACE[1].

play first fiddle 《口》主役を務める; 人の上に立つ ▪ Prussia should never *play first fiddle* in the affairs of the Continent. プロイセンは欧州大陸の問題に主役を務めるべきではない.

play second fiddle 下っぱ役を務める; 人の下につく (*to*) ▪ He had to *play second fiddle to* his former subordinate. 彼は以前の部下の下役にならねばならなかった.

There's many a good tune played on an old fiddle. 《諺》老練家は経験のない活動的新人に負けはせぬ; 初老の婦人も案外良い妻になれるものだ.

fiddle[2] /fídəl/ 動 ***fiddle while Rome burns*** →ROME.

fiddler /fídələr/ 名 **(*as*) *drunk as a fiddler*** 《米》ひどく酔って ▪ He crawled out *drunk as a fiddler*. 彼はへべれけに酔ってはい出た.

fiddler's news 古臭い話 ▪ Oh, that's *fiddler's news*. おい, それは旧聞だよ.

pay the fiddler **1** (快楽などの)費用を負担する ▪ Those who dance must *pay the fiddler*. ダンスする者は楽師に支払いをしなければならない.

2 《米》自分の行為の報いを受ける ▪ He *paid the fiddler* soundly. 彼は散々に己の行為の報いを受けた.

fiddlestick /fídəlstìk/ 名 ***A fiddlestick's end!*** ばかな! ▪ Ann wounded? *A fiddlestick's end!* アンがけがしたって? ばかな!

not care a fiddlestick 少しもかまわない ▪ I don't *care a fiddlestick*. 私は少しもかまわぬ.

fidget[1] /fídʒət/ 名 **(*be*) *in a fidget*** そわそわして(いる) ▪ He *is in a fidget*. 彼はそわそわしている.

give* [*have*] *the fidgets そわそわさせる[する] ▪ A long tale *gives* a child *the fidgets*. 長い話は子供をそわそわさせる.

fidget[2] /fídʒət/ 動 ***fidget*** *a person* ***to death*** 人に死ぬほど気をもませる ▪ Her son *fidgets* her *to death*. 彼女は息子のために死ぬほど気をもむ.

fie /faɪ/ 間 ***cry fie upon*** ...に対してまあいやだと言う ▪ My relations *cried fie upon* me. 親類の人々は私に対してまあいやだと言った.

Fie for shame! →SHAME[1].

Fie upon you* [*it*]*! まあいやだね ▪ *Fie upon it*; are you afraid of the dog? いやだな, 君はその犬が怖いのかね.

fief /fiːf/ 名 ***in fief*** 封土として ▪ Faust received the seashore *in fief* for ever. ファウストは海岸を永久に封土としてもらった.

field /fiːld/ 名 ***a level playing field*** 平らな競技場; 公平な条件, 均等な機会 ▪ I don't believe that we have *a level playing field* yet in this country. 私は, この国にはまだ均等な機会は存在しないと信じている.

a single field 一騎打ち ▪ In their *single fields*, deeds of prowess never died unrecorded. 一騎打ちでは, 武勇の働きは決して記録されずとも消滅することはなかった.

be in the field **1** 《競馬》競走に出ている; 競技に参加する; 立候補している ▪ The horse *is in the field*. その馬は競走に出ている ▪ *Are* you *in the field* for the egg-and-spoon race? 君はスプーンレースに出るか ▪ Mr. Stevenson *is in the field*. スティーブンスン氏が立候補している.

2 戦闘中である, 戦場に出ている ▪ The French *were in the field* already. フランス軍はすでに戦場に出ていた.

3 《理》力の働く範囲内にある (↔out of the FIELD) ▪ A body *is in the field* of another. ある物体が他の物体の力の働く範囲内にある.

be in the possession of the field →possess the FIELD.

conquer the field 勝つ, 優勢になる ▪ The English *conquered the field*. 英軍は勝った.

cover the field **(*of*)** ...の分野を(余さず)扱う[論じる] ▪ Chapter 9 *covers the field of* pharmacogenetics. 第9章は薬理遺伝学の分野を論じる.

fight a* [*the*] *field 戦う ▪ A bloody *field was fought*. 血なまぐさい戦いが行われた.

fresh fields and pastures new 新しい活動の領域; 新天地 ▪ A criminal had better look for *fresh fields and pastures new*. 罪人は新天地を探したほうがよい. ☞Milton: *Lycidas, l.* 193から.

have a field day **1** 非常に楽しく[おもしろく]過ごす ▪ Mother *had a field day* yesterday. 母はきのう非常に楽しく過ごした ▪ They were *having a field day* with his reputation. 彼らは彼の評判をもてあそんでいた.

2 したい放題する, (特に, 批判を)したい放題する機会を得る ▪ The newspapers would *have a field day* if their affair ever became public knowledge. 彼

F

らの情事が万人の知るところとなれば，新聞各紙はすきなだけ批判する機会を得るだろう．

3 大成功を収める ▪ Our team *had a field day.* わがチームは大勝した． ☞a field day「(陸軍などの)演習日」．

have the field to *oneself* 一人舞台である，競争者がない ▪ If he gave up, I should *have the field to myself.* 彼がやめたら私の一人舞台になるのだが．

hold [***keep, maintain***] ***the field*** 陣地を維持する; 地歩を保つ; 戦闘活動を続ける ▪ The actor still *holds the field.* その俳優はまだ地歩を保っている ▪ The French forces *kept the field* no longer. フランス軍はもう戦闘を続けなかった．

F

in the field **1** 畑[野原]で ▪ No infected fruit has been found *in the field.* 畑では細菌に感染した果実は見つかっていない．

2 現場で，実地で ▪ More than 100 people were treated by rescue workers *in the field* before being brought to the hospital. 病院に搬送される前に100人以上が現場の救助隊員の治療を受けた．

3 戦場で，出征[従軍]中で ▪ Congress will not abandon our troops *in the field.* 議会は戦場の我が軍隊を見捨てることはないだろう．

4 競技に参加して，守備について ▪ Jumping second last *in the field,* he produced a winning 8.55 meters jump. 前回の競技では2位の跳躍だったが，彼は8.55メートルの優勝ジャンプを決めた．

5 専門領域で ▪ Dr. Hwang was one of the most respected scientists *in the field.* 黄博士は当該分野では最も尊敬されている科学者の一人だった． ☞be in the FIELD.

keep the field 競技に残る，戦線を維持する ▪ He *kept the field* despite his injured knee. 膝を痛めたが彼は競技に残った ▪ The battalion *kept the field* against heavy opposition. 大隊は激しい反撃に抗して戦線を維持していた．

lead the field **1**《狩》猟場でさきがけをする，猟で一等になる ▪ You were *leading the field* in hunting. あなたは狩猟で先頭を切っていた．

2《スポーツ》リードする，優勢である ▪ At the end of the second day's play, Ballesteros is *leading the field.* 2日目のプレーが終了した時点では，バレステロスがリードしている．

3 (仕事・ビジネスなどで)先陣をきっている，指導的である ▪ There are some areas of medical research where Russian scientists still *lead the field.* 医学研究ではまだロシア人科学者たちがリードしている分野がいくつかある．

leave ... in possession of the field …に負けて引きあげる ▪ We *left* the enemy *in possession of the field.* 我々は敵に負けて引きあげた．

leave *a person* ***the field*** 人との議論[競技]をやめる ▪ I will *leave* you *the field.* 君との議論はやめる．

leave the field clear for 競争をやめて…にゆずる，に[を]利する ▪ John decided not to apply for the job, which *left the field clear for* Emma. ジョンはその仕事に応募しないことに決めたので，エマに利することになった．

leave the field open 干渉しない ▪ The King has *left the field open* between Wood and the Kingdom of Ireland. 国王はウッドとアイルランド王国との間に干渉することを控えた．

lose a [***the***] ***field*** 戦いに負ける ▪ What though *the field be lost?* 戦いに負けたって何であろう．

maintain the field →hold the FIELD.

out in the field **1** (牛などが)牧場に出て ▪ The bull is *out in the field.* その雄牛は牧場に出ている．

2《クリケット・野球》守備について ▪ We've lost the toss; so we are *out in the field.* 我々はコイン投げに負けたので，守備についている．

3 (敵意をもって)うろついて ▪ Her father is *out in the field* looking for trouble. 彼女の父が余計な事をしようとしてうろついている．

out of left field 《主に米》予想外[想定外]の，思いがけない ▪ It was *out of left field* and completely unexpected. それは予想外で，全く思ってもいなかった．

out of the field 《理》(他の物体の)力の働く範囲外に (↔be in the FIELD 3) ▪ A body is *out of the field* of another. ある物体が他の物体の力の働く範囲外にある．

outside *a person's* ***field*** 人の専門外で ▪ That is *outside my field.* それは私の専門外です．

play the field 《口》(一人に限らないで)大勢と異性関係を持つ ▪ He preferred *playing the field* to going steady. 彼は一人に限るよりは大勢の女と関係するほうを好んだ ▪ She's not interested in marriage at this stage, so she's quite happy to *play the field.* 現段階では彼女は結婚には関心がないので，多くの男性とつき合って満足している．

possess [***be in the possession of***] ***the field*** 勝つ ▪ But for you, your comrades could not *possess the field.* 君がいなければ君の仲間は勝てないだろうに．

take the field (戦闘・競技・運動を)開始する; 出陣する ▪ Esmond *took the field.* エズモンドは戦闘を開始した ▪ He will *take the field* against you. 彼は君と競争するだろう．

take to the field 《球技》守備につく ▪ We *took to the field.* 我々は守備についた．

the Elysian Field(***s***) 《雅》楽土 ▪ *The Elysian field* of Roman and Greek mythology was an idyllic home for departed heroes and the blessed dead. ギリシャ・ローマ神話の楽土は，今はなき英雄や祝福された死者たちのための牧歌的故郷だった．

(***way***) ***out in left field*** →LEFT FIELD.

win the [***a***] ***field*** →WIN.

fiend /fiːnd/ 名 ***a fresh air fiend*** 換気魔，野外主義者 ▪ She is something of *a fresh air fiend,* so the bedroom window is always open, whatever the weather. 彼女はいささか換気魔なので，天候がどうであれ，寝室の窓はいつも開けてある．

fifth /fɪfθ/ 名 ***a fifth*** [***third***] ***wheel*** 蛇足，余分な物; じゃま者 (→the FIFTH wheel of a coach)

▪ If you go with those two, you'll end up feeling like *a fifth wheel.* この二人といっしょに行ったら，おじゃま虫のように感じる羽目になるよ. ☞Thomas Dekker, *Match Me London* (1631) から.

dig* [*hit, poke*] *under the fifth rib 《口》急所をひどく突く，びっくり仰天させる ▪ The totally unexpected news really *hit* me *under the fifth rib.* 全く予期せぬ知らせにびっくり仰天した. ☞下の句から.

smite *a person* ***under the fifth rib*** 人の急所（第5肋骨の下，心臓）を突いて殺す《比喩的にも》 ▪ He *smote* each bishop *under the fifth rib.* 彼はおのおのの主教の急所を突いて殺した.

***take* [*plead*] *the fifth* [*Fifth* (*Amendment*)]** 《米口・戯》米国憲法修正第5条により黙秘する，返事を回避する (*on*) ▪ He *took the fifth* when asked whether he was a Communist. 彼は共産党員かと尋ねられたとき第5条により黙秘した ▪ So who do you like best, Jenny or Kim?—Sorry, I *take the Fifth on* that. それで，誰がいちばん好きなんだ，ジェニーかキムか—申し訳ないが，その件に関しては第5条により黙秘させていただく. ☞the Fifth Amendment は「被告人は自己に不利益な証言をすることは強要されない」ことなどを決めている.

***the fifth wheel of a coach* [*a wagon*]** 予備車輪; 余計なもの，あまり使わないもの ▪ The functions of the grand juror are those of *the fifth wheel of a coach.* 大陪審官の役目は馬車の予備車輪の役目だ.

fig /fɪɡ/ 名 ***A fig* [*A fig's end*] *for ...!*** …がなんだい（つまらない） ▪ *A fig* [*A fig's end*] *for* his money! 彼の金がなんだい!

a fig leaf イチジクの葉; 隠ぺい行為，口実 ▪ Are the peace talks simply providing *a fig leaf* for the continuing aggression between the two countries? 平和会談は，2国間で継続している侵犯に口実を与えているだけなのだろうか. ☞アダムとイブがイチジクの葉で局部を隠したことから（《聖》*Gen.* 3. 7）.

full fig 《俗》麗々しく，あでやかに ▪ We all dressed ourselves up *full fig.* 我々はみなあでやかに着飾った.

in fine* [*good, great*] *fig 《口》元気で，申し分のない状態で ▪ Lord Alaric was *in great fig.* アラリック卿はきわめて元気だった ▪ The horse is *in good fig* for the race. 馬は競走に出るのに絶好調だ.

in full fig 《口》盛装して（→full FIG） ▪ We all turned out *in full fig* the other day. 先日はみな盛装して繰り出した. ☞fig＝（おそらく）figure.

***not care* [*mind*] *a fig* [*a fig's end*]** 少しもかまわない ▪ I *don't care a fig* for [about] their opinions. 彼らの意見など少しもかまわない.

not give a fig* [*a fig's end*] *for …にはびた一文も出さない ▪ I will *not give a fig's end for* it. そんな物にびた一文だって出すものか.

fight[1] /faɪt/ 名 ***a good, clean fight*** 正々堂々の闘い ▪ I want *a good clean fight,* no biting, no rabbit-punching. 噛みつきもラビットパンチもなしで，正々堂々の戦いをしたい.

a stand-up fight 正々堂々の戦い《特にボクシングでやる正々堂々のなぐり合い》 ▪ The two men settled their differences in *a stand-up fight.* その二人の男は正々堂々のなぐり合いで争いの結着をつけた.

a straight fight 《英》（特に選挙での二人の候補者による）一騎打ち，ガチンコ対決 ▪ That would be *a straight fight* between the Reagan and Roosevelt traditions. それは，レーガン流伝統とルーズベルト流伝統との一騎打ちとなるだろう.

a three-cornered fight 三つ巴(ともえ)の争い ▪ The *three-cornered fight* was part of his opponents' strategy to split the votes. その三つ巴の戦いは，票を割ろうとする敵側の戦略の一部だった.

fight or flight 対戦か退却か ▪ Some of the sculptures seem poised for *fight or flight.* 彫像の幾つかは闘争か逃走かという構えをとっているように見える.

give* [*make*] (*a*) *fight 一戦を交える ▪ They resolved to *give fight.* 彼らは一戦を交えようと決心した ▪ He *made a* good *fight* for a beginner. 彼は初心者にしては善戦した.

have a tea fight 《口》大勢の客を招いて茶話会を催す ▪ My wife is *having a tea fight* tomorrow. 妻はあす茶の会を催します.

have fight in *one* 闘志がある ▪ They still *had* plenty of *fight in* them. 彼らはまだ闘志満々だった.

pick a fight with …と論争[けんか]を始める ▪ Don't *pick a fight with* your brother. 兄さんとけんかを始めてはいけない.

put up a fight 怒る; 反対する ▪ Your father will *put up a fight* if you do such a thing 君がそんなことをすればお父さんは怒るだろう.

put up a good fight 善戦する ▪ He *put up a good fight,* but was beaten. 彼は善戦したが負けた.

show fight 戦う気勢を示す; 闘志を表す，抵抗する ▪ Wait until something happens to make her *show fight.* 彼女に抵抗させることが起こるまで待て.

spoil for a fight 〚主に進行形で〛けんかがしたくてむずむずしている，けんかの口実を得る ▪ The country has *been spoiling for a fight.* その国は戦闘をしたくてずっとうずうずしている.

take the fight out of …の[から]闘志を取り去る ▪ The news *took* all *the fight out of* the soldiers. そのニュースで兵隊は闘志をすっかりなくした.

the fight of *one's* ***life*** （強敵との）苦戦 ▪ In the last election he had *the fight of his life* against a Labor candidate. この前の選挙で彼は労働党候補に苦戦した.

fight[2] /faɪt/ 動 ***be fighting for*** *one's* ***life*** **1** (人が)生死をさまよう，に瀕している ▪ One of the passengers *was fighting for her life* last night after receiving multiple injuries in the collision. 乗客の一人は，衝突で多発性外傷を受けたため，昨晩は生死をさまよっていた.
2 (会社・組織が)生き残りのために懸命に努力している，潰れないように頑張っている ▪ With debts of over 2 million dollars, the corporation *is fighting for*

its life. 2百万ドル以上の借金をかかえて，その会社は生き残りをかけて懸命に努力している.

be fighting mad 《米口》かんかんに怒る，雷を落とす ▪ When Dad finds out you've crashed the car, he'll *be fighting mad.* お前が車をぶつけたことを知ったら，お父さんは雷を落とすぞ ▪ We should *be fighting mad* about shoddy service. なおざりなサービスに対しては怒りをぶつけるべきだ.

***can* [*can't*] *fight City Hall* [*city hall*]** お役所に勝つ[は勝てない] ▪ It was Brennan who ushered in an era where you *could fight city hall* and win. お役所相手に戦って勝利する時代をもたらしたのはブレナンだった ▪ Forget it. You *can't fight City Hall*, let alone the Federal Government. 忘れろよ. お役所には勝てないんだから. まして連邦政府には.

fight a* [*the*] *good fight (主義・道のため)善戦する，大いに活動する (《聖》*1 Tim.* 6. 12) ▪ The missionaries *fought the good fight* at the sacrifice of their health. 宣教師たちは健康を犠牲にしてその道のため善戦した.

fight a lone hand →play a LONE hand.

fight against odds 優勢な敵と戦う ▪ There is no *fighting against* such *odds.* そんな優勢な敵と戦うことはできない《衆寡敵せず》.

***fight at sharp*(*s*)** 真剣勝負をする ▪ He *fought* Captain Weazel *at sharps.* 彼はウィーゼル大尉と真剣勝負をした.

fight* *one's* *battles over again →BATTLE[1].

fight fire 《米》火を消そうと努める ▪ How many men are needed each year to *fight fires*? 消火に努めるには毎年いく人いるのか.

fight* [*meet, match*] *fire with fire 相手と同じ手口で反攻する，毒をもって毒を制す ▪ The North Koreans told the U.N. that they will *fight "Fire With Fire."* 北朝鮮は「火には火をもって」反撃すると国連に告げた.

fight* (*for*) *one's* *own hand →HAND[1].

fight* *oneself* *into 戦って…へ入る ▪ A man tried to *fight himself into* the cockpit, saying he intended to crash the plane. 一人の男が飛行機を不時着させるつもりだと言って，(乗務員と)争ってコックピットに入って行こうとした.

fight it* [etc.] *out 《口》戦って解決する; 最後まで戦う ▪ The crowd let the two men *fight it out.* 群衆はその二人をけりがつくまで戦わせた ▪ They *fought* the issue *out.* 彼らはその問題を戦って決着させた.

fight like cat and dog 《古風》(しばしば)激しくけんか[口論]する ▪ We love each other, but we *fight like cat and dog.* 我々は互いに愛しているが激しく口げんかをする.

fight on its belly 腹で戦う ▪ An army, like a snake, *fights on its belly.* 軍隊はヘビと同じく腹で戦う《腹がへっては戦えない》.

fight* *oneself* *out of 戦って…から脱する[出る] ▪ We must *fight ourselves out of* prison. 我々は戦って獄から出なければならない.

fight shy of →SHY[1].

fight* *oneself* *to 戦って…となる ▪ He *fought himself to* death. 彼は戦って死んだ.

fight to a finish 勝負がつくまで戦う，一方が倒れるまで戦う ▪ No mercy, men, we'll *fight to a finish.* 諸君，容赦はいらない. けりがつくまで戦うのだ.

***fight tooth and nail* (*against, over*)** 必死に戦う (→ TOOTH and nail) ▪ The president *fought tooth and nail against* the law in question. 大統領は当該の法案を阻止しようと必死で戦った.

fight* *one's* *way 戦いつつ進む ▪ He *fought his way* in the world. 彼は苦難と戦って進路を開拓した.

fight* *one's* *way into …へ戦って入る ▪ He *fought his way into* society. 彼は苦心して社交界に入った.

fight* *one's* *way out 戦って[もがいて]出る ▪ The theater was so crowded that I had to *fight my way out* of it. 劇場は大入りだったので私はもがくようにして出なければならなかった.

***He that fights and runs may live to fight another day* (*but he that is in battle slain can never rise to fight again*).** 《諺》戦って逃げる者は生きのびてまたいつか戦うこともある(が戦って死ぬ者はもう二度と戦うことはできない)，「命あっての物種」.

fighting /fáitɪŋ/ 形 ***a fighting chance*** 勇戦奮闘を要する機会; (…する)わずかの機会 (*of doing*) ▪ His illness is serious, but he has *a fighting chance* to recover. 彼の病気は重いが回復のわずかな見込みはある ▪ If we can raise another thousand pounds, we'll have *a fighting chance of saving* the theatre. もう千ポンド集めることができれば，劇場を救う見込みがわずかながら出てくる.

fighting fit すばらしく健康で; 苦闘に耐えうる ▪ She was *fighting fit* after 10 weeks of intense physical training. 10週間の集中的な肉体訓練をしたので彼女はきわめて健康だ ▪ This flyweight is *fighting fit.* このフライ級ボクサーは激闘に耐えうる.

go down fighting 完敗するまで戦い続ける，善戦むなしく敗れる ▪ Nicol, the top seed, *went down fighting* 6-9, 2-9, 10-9, 7-9 to Atkinson, the second seed. 第1シードのニコルは，第2シードのアトキンスンに6-9, 2-9, 10-9, 7-9で敗れた.

in fighting trim →TRIM[1].

fighting-cock /fáitɪŋkɑ̀k|-kɔ̀k/ 名 ***eat* [*feed*] *like a fighting-cock*** (闘鶏のように)うまいものばかり食う ▪ They *eat* and drink *like fighting-cocks.* 彼らはうまいものばかり飲み食いする.

feel like a fighting-cock きわめて元気である; 好調である ▪ I can eat like a horse, and *feel like a fighting-cock.* 僕はいくらでも食べられ，とても元気だ.

live like a fighting-cock 美食して贅沢に暮らす ▪ They *live like fighting-cocks* upon his labor. 彼らは彼の労働によって美食して贅沢に暮らしている.

figment /fígmənt/ 名 ***a figment of* *one's* [*the*] *imagination*** 空想の所産 ▪ Risk-free investment is *a figment of the imagination.* ノーリスクの投資なんて空想の産物だ.

figure[1] /fígjər|fígə/ 名 ***a figure of fun*** **1** 奇怪な[こっけいな]風体の人 ▪ The old woman looks *a figure of fun* in that girlish hat. その老婦人があの娘のような帽子をかぶっているとこっけいな格好だ.
2 笑いもの, 物笑いの種 ▪ She's fed up with being treated as *a figure of fun* and insists that her ideas deserve serious attention. 彼女は笑いもの扱いされるのがいやになって, 自分の考えは真剣に考慮する価値があると主張する.

at a low [***high***] ***figure*** 安[高]値で ▪ We got it *at a low figure*. 我々はそれを安値で手に入れた.

cast [***set, erect***] ***a figure*** 天象図によって占う ▪ He *set a figure* to discover if you were fled to Dover. 彼はあなたがドーバーへ逃げたかどうかを知るため, 天象図によって占った.

cut a ridiculous [***foolish, queer***] ***figure*** →make a ridiculous FIGURE.

cut an unusual figure →make a ... FIGURE.

cut no figure 《米》物の数に入らない; 名が現れない ▪ The price *cuts no figure*. その値段は物の数でない ▪ He *cuts no figure* in the world. 彼は世に名が現れていない.

figure (***of***) ***four*** 動物を捕えるわな ▪ Rabbits are entangled in *figure fours*. ウサギがわなにかかった. ☞わなの引きがねが4の形であることから.

flatter *one's* ***figure*** (服が)容姿[スタイル]を引き立たせる ▪ A woman needs a dress that *flatters her figure* and is still wearable. 女性は, 容姿を引き立たせてくれて, それでいて着やすいドレスを必要とする.

go figure →GO[2].

go [***come***] ***the big figure*** 《米口》大いに見せびらかす, 見栄を張る ▪ When a man sets about *going the big figure*, halfway measures won't answer at all. 人が見栄を張り始めると, 中途半端なことでは間に合わない.

go the whole figure 《米》極限までいく, 徹底的にやる (= go (the) whole HOG) ▪ She *goes the whole figure* for furs. 彼女は徹底的に毛皮びいきである ▪ We must *go the whole figure* with the free North. 我々は奴隷解放の北部を徹底的に支持せねばならない.

in round figures (大きな端数のない金額について)概数で ▪ I've got £300 *in round figures*. 私は概数で300ポンド持っている.

keep *one's* ***figure*** (太らないで)すらりとした格好でいる ▪ My wife still *keeps her figure*. 妻は今もなおすらりとした体型でいる.

make [《口》***cut***] ***a figure*** **1** 頭角を表す, 異彩を放つ ▪ Boys who *make a figure* at school make no figure in the world. 学校で頭角を表す少年は世に出て成功しない ▪ Benjamin *cuts* quite *a figure* with all the ladies. ベンジャミンはすべての女性たちをすっかり感嘆させている ▪ The butler had a mind to *cut a figure* in his master's absence. 執事は主人の留守中に自分の働きを見せようと思った.
2 こっけいに見える ▪ He *cut a figure* at the party. 彼はそのパーティーでこっけいな様子だった.

make [《口》***cut***] ***a ... figure*** ...の姿を呈する, 地位を占める; の印象を与える ▪ He *makes a* brilliant *figure* in the political world. 彼は政界で異彩を放っている ▪ What *a* mean, contemptible *figure* he *cut*! 彼は何というみすぼらしい, 情けない姿だったことだろう ▪ My Russian uncle *cut an* unusual *figure* among the very British audience. ロシア人のおじは, 非常に英国的な聴衆のなかで異様な様子だった.

make [《口》***cut***] ***a fine*** [***good***] ***figure*** 立派に見える; 名を成す; 体裁よくやる ▪ He *cut a good figure* in the saddle. 彼は馬に乗ると立派に見えた ▪ He will *make a fine figure* in the world. 彼は世に名を成すだろう.

make [***present,*** 《口》***cut***] ***a poor*** [***sorry***] ***figure*** みすぼらしく[かわいそうに]見える, ざまが悪い; 引き立たない ▪ She *cuts a poor figure* among them. 彼女らの中にいると彼女はみすぼらしく見える.

make [《口》 ***cut***] ***a ridiculous*** [***foolish, queer***] ***figure*** こっけいに見える; 失態を演ずる; 笑いものになる ▪ He *cut a ridiculous figure* in foreign clothes. 洋服を着ると彼はこっけいに見えた.

miss a figure 《米口》まちがい[計算ちがい]をする ▪ The salesman *missed a figure*. 店員は計算まちがいをした.

of figure 《古》地位[身分, 名声]のある ▪ Mr. Smith is a gentleman *of* some *figure*. スミス氏はかなりの名士である.

of figures 算数[計算]に長じた ▪ He is a man *of figures*. 彼は計算に長じている.

on the big figure 《米》大規模に, 大げさに ▪ He does things *on the big figure*. 彼は物事を大規模にやる.

present a figure →make a FIGURE.

put a figure on ...の正確な金額[数]を言う ▪ It is too early to *put a figure on* the extent of the storm damage. 暴風被害の程度について正確な数を言うのは尚早すぎる.

set a figure →cast a FIGURE.

What's the figure? 値段はいくらですか, 代金はいくらですか. ☞figure = price.

figure[2] /fígjər|fígə/ 動 ***figure it out*** **1** 《米口》(計算・調査によって)確かめる, 見いだす ▪ He was trying to *figure it out*. 彼はそれを調べて確かめようとしていた.
2 算出する ▪ *Figure it out* and see what it comes to. それを算出して, いくらになるか見なさい.

figure ... to *oneself* ...を心に描く ▪ He had already *figured* his bride *to himself*. 彼はすでに自分の花嫁を心に描いていた.

it [***that***] ***figures*** 《口》もっともである; ありそうなことである (likely) ▪ I like him.—*It figures*. 私は彼が好きです—ごもっともです ▪ *It figures* that a young man with a large fortune wants to marry. 財産のある青年が結婚したがるのは当然である.

file /faɪl/ 名 ***a file of men*** ある目的に選ばれた[派遣された]二人 ▪ *A file of men* on horse-back passed by. ある目的で選ばれた二人が馬で通り過ぎた.

bite [***gnaw, lick***] ***a file*** (やすりをかみくだくような)むだ骨を折る ▪ He *bit the file* of English obstinacy and broke his teeth. 彼はイギリス人の頑固さを打ちくだこうとして, 自分の歯[むだ骨]を折った. ☞やすりをかみくだこうとした毒ヘビの寓話から.

close *one's* ***files*** 縦列を詰める ▪ The Barons and Clergy suddenly *closed their files*. 貴族と聖職者たちは急に結束を固めた.

double the files 二つの伍を一つにして横列を小さくする ▪ *Double your files* to the right hand. 右手へ, 伍を重ねよ ▪ It makes her *double the files* of her diligence. そのため彼女は勤勉さを集中強化せねばならない.

F

file by file 組々に, 続々 ▪ The children were seated *file by file* according to age. 子供たちは年齢順に組々着席していた.

File left [***right***]***!*** 《号令》組々左[右](へ).

gnaw a file →bite a FILE.

in file 伍をなして; 2列縦隊で ▪ We marched *in file*. 我々は2列縦隊で行進した.

in Indian [***single***] ***file*** 1列側面縦隊で ▪ The path was so narrow that we had to walk *in Indian file*. 道は非常に狭かったので, 我々は1列側面縦隊で歩かねばならなかった. ☞北米先住民は1列縦隊になって, 前の者の歩いたあとを歩いて, 敵に人数を知らせないことから.

lick [***gnaw***] ***a file*** →bite a FILE.

on file 記録して, とじ込み整理して; (…に)提出して (*with*) ▪ This card should be kept *on file* for reference. このカードは参考用にとじ込んでおかねばならない ▪ Do you have an application *on file with* us? あなたは願書を当方に提出してありますか.

rank and file →RANK.

take the right-hand file of …の上位に立つ, 優先する ▪ There are many who may *take the right-hand file of* you. あなたの右に出る者も多い.

fill[1] /fɪl/ 名 ***drink*** [***eat,*** etc.] *one's* ***fill*** 存分に飲む[食べる, など] ▪ The dog *ate its fill*. 犬は十分食べた ▪ I *grumbled* [*wept*] *my fill*. 私は存分に不平を言った[泣いた].

get *one's* ***fill*** =drink one's FILL.

have *one's* ***fill of*** …を十分[存分に]する ▪ I *had my fill of* sorrow. 私は存分に泣いた ▪ You have *had your fill of* English grammar. 君は英文法は十分身につけた.

have had *one's* ***fill*** 満腹だ, 十二分に飲み食いした ▪ No more pudding, thanks, I*'ve had my fill*. プリンはもうけっこうです. 十分いただきました.

have had *one's* ***fill of*** (不愉快なこと)にうんざりしている, あきあきしている ▪ People *have had their fill of* empty promises and want action. 国民は空約束にはもううんざりして, 行動を望んでいる.

take *one's* ***fill*** (***of***) (…を)十分に取る ▪ We *took our fill of* the sunshine and fresh air. 我々は日光と新鮮な空気を十分に取った.

fill[2] /fɪl/ 動 ***be filled with*** …でいっぱいである ▪ I *was filled with* admiration. 私はすっかり感嘆した ▪ The bucket *was filled with* water. そのバケツは水がいっぱいになっていた.

fill an engagement 公の席へ出席の約束を果たす ▪ During the campaign he *filled* 125 *engagements*. その運動中彼は125の公の席への出席約束を果たした.

fill in the blanks 説明[解説]する ▪ Obama *filled in the blanks* on what he meant by change. オバマ氏は変革とはどういうことか説明した.

fill in (***the***) ***time*** 《口》退屈しのぎをする; (何かをする前の)暇な時間を埋める ▪ You must *fill in the time* somehow. 何とか暇な時間を埋めねばならない ▪ She is *filling in time* working in a department store till she gets married. 彼女は結婚するまでひまつぶしにデパートで働いている.

fill *one's* ***pipe*** 《俗》裕福になる, 富を得る ▪ They *filled their pipe* and left others to enjoy it. 彼らは富を得て他人がそれを享受した.

fill *a person's* ***place*** [***shoes, boots***] 人に代わる; 人の代わりをうまく果たす ▪ It is difficult to *fill his place*. 彼の代わりを果たすのはむずかしい.

fill *one's* ***place*** 勤めを果たす ▪ The servant *filled his place* well. その使用人は勤めをよく果たした.

fill the bases [***sacks***] 《野球》満塁にする ▪ He *filled the sacks* by giving Jack a base on balls. 彼はジャックを(四球で)歩かせて満塁にした.

fill the bill →fit the BILL.

fill ... to the full …をいっぱいに満たす ▪ The trunk *was filled to the full*. トランクはいっぱいに詰めこまれた.

fill *a person* ***up with a story*** 《口》話で人を感銘させ(てある事柄を信じこませ)る ▪ He has *been filled up with* so many *stories* that he believes John a perfect saint. 彼は多くの話を聞かされて感銘していて, ジョンのことを全くの聖人だと信じこんでいる.

filling at the price 《口》安くて満足な ▪ It is so *filling at the price*. それは非常に安くて満足である.

to fill up the sum of …のあげくの果てに ▪ *To fill up the sum of* my joy, I had a son. 私の喜びにかてて加えて息子ができた.

fill-in /fílɪn/ 名形 ***give*** *a person* ***a fill-in on*** 人に…について説明[報告]する ▪ He *gave* the president *a fill-in on* Europe's economic crisis. 彼は大統領にヨーロッパの経済危機について報告した.

on a fill-in basis 代理という資格で ▪ He took a job *on a fill-in basis*. 彼は代理という資格で仕事を引き受けた.

fillip[1] /fíləp/ 名 ***not worth a fillip*** 一文の価値もない ▪ Said Lord Byron: drink and love—the rest's *not worth a fillip*. バイロン卿いわく: 飲めよ, 恋せよ. その他は無意味.

fillip[2] /fíləp/ 動 ***fillip with*** (*one's*) ***fingers***/ ***fillip it*** 指先ではじく ▪ Just see me *fillip it*. 私が指先ではじくのを見ていなさい.

filly /fíli/ 名 ***slip her filly*** (女性が)流産する

▪ She is sick again—*slipping her filly.* 彼女はまた病気だ—流産して.

film /fɪlm/ 名 ***go to the films*** 映画を見に行く ▪ I'm *going to the films* this evening. 私は今晩映画を見に行きます.

filter /fíltər/ 動 ***filter through the traffic*** 《英》交通の流れの途中に自分の車を割り込ませる ▪ On a motorcycle you can *filter through the traffic.* バイクに乗っているときには車の間に割り込める.

filthy /fílθi/ 形 ***filthy lucre*** 不正利得, 不浄の金; 《戯》金 (《聖》*Titus* 1. 7) ▪ He made that judgment for the sake of *filthy lucre.* 彼は不浄の金ほしさにその判定をした.

fin[1] /fɪn/ 名 ***fur, fin, (and) feather*** →FUR[1].

give [tip] a person one's fin 《俗》(握手のため)人に手を出す ▪ Come, old fellow, *tip* us *your fin.* さあ, 君, 手を出しな《握手しよう》.

Mash me a fin. 《口》私に1ポンドくれ.

fin[2] /fɪn/ 動 ***fin it/fin one's way*** 泳ぐ ▪ In midsummer salmon *fin it* along the shore. 真夏にはサケはその海岸に沿って泳いでいく.

final /fáɪnəl/ 形名 ***have the final say*** 最後の(決定的)発言権を持つ ▪ Who *has the final say* around here? この中では誰が最後の発言権を持っているのか.

one final word [thing] 《米口》最後にひとこと ▪ *One final word* of caution. This is a very bloody and violent movie. 最後に警告をひとこと. これは血なまぐさく暴力を扱った映画である.

run [play] in the finals 決勝戦に残って競走[競技]する ▪ I *ran in the finals*, but I didn't win. 私は決勝戦に残ったが, 優勝はできなかった.

the final curtain (長く続いたものの)終幕, 終了; 死 ▪ As *the final curtain* fell on the longest match in tennis history, Agassi emerged victorious. テニス史上最長の試合に最後の幕が下りたとき, アガシが勝利者となった.

finality /faɪnǽləti/ 名 ***with finality*** 決定的に, きっぱり ▪ He spoke *with finality.* 彼はきっぱり言った.

financier /fìnənsíər|faɪnǽnsiə/ 動 ***financier a person out of*** 人から…を巻き上げる ▪ He *financiered* me *out of* my money. 彼は私から金を巻き上げた.

find[1] /faɪnd/ 名 ***make [have] a find*** 掘り出しものをする ▪ I *made a* great *find* in a second hand bookshop yesterday. きのう私は古本屋ですばらしい掘り出し物を見つけた.

find[2] /faɪnd/ 動 ***(and) all found*** (給料以外に)衣食いっさいを支給されて ▪ We are paying five pounds a week, *(and) all found.* 我々は衣食いっさい支給で週5ポンド支払っている.

and found 《米口》(その上)食住費支給 ▪ I get 12 dollars a month *and found.* 私は食住費支給で月に12ドルもらう.

be well found in (設備・供給・素養)が十分である ▪ We *are well found in* water here. ここでは水の供給は十分ある ▪ He *is well found in* classical learning. 彼は古典の素養が十分ある.

find oneself **1** 気分[心地, 体調]が…である ▪ How do you *find yourself* this morning? 今朝はご気分はいかがですか《主に病人に問う》 ▪ I *find myself* very comfortable. 非常に心地がよい.

2 (気がついてみれば)身は…である ▪ I *found myself* lying in a strange place. 気がついて見ると私は見知らぬ所に寝ころんでいた ▪ You will *find yourself* in hospital soon. 君はやがて病院に入るようになるだろう.

3 衣食を自弁する ▪ He gets 20,000 yen and *finds himself.* 彼は2万円もらい, 衣食は自弁である.

4 自己の天職[適所]を見いだす ▪ After trying various jobs, he finally *found himself* and became a newspaper reporter. いろいろの職業についてみた後, 彼はついに自分の適職を見いだし新聞記者になった.

find a way out of …から抜け出す道を発見する ▪ We could *find a way out of* the difficulty. 私は困難から抜け出す道を発見できた.

find bones in →BONE.

find Christ [Him] キリストを発見する《キリスト教の真理を霊的に体験する》 ▪ Did you *find Christ*? キリストを発見なさいましたか《教会から出るとき会衆に尋ねる文句》.

find one's feet [legs] **1** (子供・病後の人などが)立ちうる; 起き上がる ▪ The baby began to *find its feet.* 赤んぼうは立って歩けるようになった ▪ I *found my feet* again. 私はまた起き上がった ▪ We *found our legs* when the ship rolled. 船が揺れるときも立って歩けた.

2 自信がつく ▪ I have *found my feet* in the business. その商売には自信がついた.

3 自己の能力[本領]を発現する; 独立でやっていける ▪ Don't worry about me, Dad, I'm sure I'll be able to *find my feet.* パパ, 私のことは心配しないで. きっと独りでやっていけるから.

4 新しい状況に慣れる ▪ It's important to give new students a chance to *find their feet.* 新入生たちには新しい環境に慣れる機会を与えることが大事だ.

find for oneself (衣食を)自弁する ▪ You will have £30 a month, but must *find for yourself.* あなたには月に30ポンドあげるが, 衣食は自弁せねばなりません ▪ I must *find for myself* in everything. 一切自弁せねばならない.

find oneself in …を自給する ▪ You'll have to *find yourself in* milk. あなたはミルクを自給しなければならないだろう.

find it in one's heart to do →HEART.

find it in oneself to do = find it in one's HEART to do.

find it ... to do …することが…であることを知る ▪ I *found it* easy *to* read the book. 私にはその本を読むことはやさしかった.

find one's (own) level →LEVEL[1].

find true north 真北を特定する; 正しい進路を見いだす ▪ How do you *find true north* with a magnetic compass? どうやって磁気羅針盤で真北を見つけ

るのですか ▪ The team have *found true north* and will be able to produce a new model by next year. チームは進路を見出したので，来年には新機種を製造できるだろう．

find** one's **way **1** 道を求めて[捜して]行く；骨折って進む ▪ Could you *find your way* home last night? 昨夜あなたは家まで(道を捜して)帰れましたか ▪ They *found their way* up to London. 彼らは道を捜してロンドンまで行った．
2 どうにかしていく ▪ How did such a statement *find its way* into print? どうしてこんな言説が印刷されることになったのか ▪ He *found his way* out of the prison. 彼はどうにかして刑務所を脱出した．
3 結局…に到達する，にたどりつく (*to*) ▪ Rivers *find their way to* the sea. 川は結局海に出る ▪ The drunkard *finds his way* into the gutter. 大酒飲みは結局どぶみぞへ落ちる《物乞いになる》．

***find** one's **way about** [**around**]* →WAY.

find** one's **way to** a person's **heart 人の心を得る，人をくどく ▪ He knows how to *find his way to a man's heart*. 彼は人のくどき方を知っている．

***know where to find** a person* 人を理解している ▪ He did not *know where to find* his nephew. 彼はおいを理解していなかった．

*One's **sin(s) will find** one **out.*** →SIN[1].

***take** a person **as** one **find** him* →TAKE[2].

finder /fáındər/ 名 ***Finders (are) keepers./ Finders keepers (losers weepers).*** 《諺》見つけた物は自分の物 ▪ "*Finders keepers*," he said, putting the money away in his pocket. 「見つけた物は自分の物」と言って，彼はお金をポケットに入れた．☞古代ローマの法律から．

finding /fáındıŋ/ 名 ***Finding is keeping.*** 《諺》拾い物はわが物．

fine[1] /faın/ 形副名 ***all very fine*** →ALL.

all very fine and large もっともらしい；《皮肉》まことにけっこうだ ▪ The man's story was *all very fine and large*. その人の話はもっともらしかった ▪ That's *all very fine and large*. それはちとひどすぎる．☞music-hall で歌われた歌から．

be in fine fettle 元気である，順調である ▪ She *was in fine fettle* when she came back from her trip to the States. 彼女はとても元気に合衆国への旅から帰った ▪ The business *is in fine fettle* and we're even planning to expand. 仕事は順調であり，拡張さえ計画中だ．

call things by fine names 婉曲な言い方をする，婉曲な名前で呼ぶ ▪ Mary likes to *call things by fine names*. メアリーは婉曲な言い方をするのが好きだ．

do fine 元気である ▪ How are you?—I'm *doing fine*, thanks. お元気ですか?—おかげさまで．

fine and とても ▪ Mother will be *fine and* joyful. 母はとても喜ぶでしょう．

fine and dandy 《口》まことに結構(，だが…) ▪ That is all very *fine and dandy*, but I have other things to do. それはまことに結構ですが私には他に仕事があります．

(in) rain or fine →RAIN[1].

in the fine 晴れ間に ▪ I got home *in the fine*. 私は晴れ間に帰宅した．

not to put too fine a point* [*an edge*] *upon it 露骨に言えば ▪ Well, *not to put too fine a point upon it*, it's like theft. そうだな，ざっくばらんに言えばそれは窃盗のようなものだ．

***one fine day* [*morning*, etc.]** ある日[朝など] ▪ Mrs. Smith set off *one fine morning*. スミス夫人はある朝出発した．☞フランス語法．

one of these fine days いつかそのうちに ▪ You will get into trouble *one of these fine days*. いつかそのうち困ったことになるぞ．☞フランス語法．

***say fine things about* [*of*]** *a person* 人のことをほめたたえる ▪ He did nothing but *say fine things of* you. 彼はただもう君のことをほめたたえていた．

some fine day いつか ▪ *Some fine day* you will be sorry. いつか後悔しますよ．☞フランス語法．

will do me* [*us*] *fine 《口》私[私たち]は(それで)かまいません ▪ It's only for one night, so this small room *will do me fine*. たった1泊きりですから私はこの小部屋で結構です．

You're a fine one to talk! 《口》自分のことをたなに上げて，自分はどうなんだ《他人の行為を非難している本人も同様な行為をしている場合に用いる》 ▪ He's always complaining, "*You're a fine one to talk!*" 彼は「そちらこそどうなんだ」といつも不満げに言っている ▪ I'm lazy? *You're a fine one to talk!* 私が怠け者だって．君に人のことが言えるのかね．

fine[2] /faın/ 名 ***in fine*** 最後に，結局；要するに ▪ *In fine*, you will have to stay in London. 結局君はロンドンに滞在せねばなるまい ▪ We have, *in fine*, attained the power of going fast. 要するに我々は速く行く力を得たのだ．

fine[3] /faın/ 名 ***draw a fine*** 罰金をかけられる ▪ I *drew a fine* of $10. 10ドルの罰金をかけられた．

fine[4] /faın/ 動 ***fine and recover*** みつぎ金を払って借地[借家]権を回復する ▪ I have *fined and recovered* and so may be thankful. 私はみつぎ金を払って権利を回復したので感謝してよい．

fine down a lease (借地人・借家人が)みつぎ金を出して地代[家賃]の値下げを図る ▪ The tenant may, with the agreement of the landlord, *fine down his lease*. 借家人は，家主の同意のもとに，心付けを出して家賃値下げを図るだろう．

finesse /fınés/ 名 ***show finesse*** 手ぎわを見せる ▪ He *showed finesse* in dealing with people. 彼は人の扱いに手ぎわを見せた．

fine-tooth(ed) /fàıntú:θt/ 形〚限定的〛 ***with a fine-tooth(ed) comb*** 入念に，こと細かに ▪ I'd advise you to examine your insurance policy *with a fine-tooth comb* to make sure you're covered if you take your car abroad. 保険証券を綿密に調べて，車を海外にもっていっても保険が効くことを確認するよう助言します．☞fine-toothed comb「目の詰んだくし」．

finger[1] /fíŋgər/ 名 ***All** one's **fingers are thumbs.**/ One's **fingers are all thumbs.*** 無器用である; 指が器用に動かない ▪ *Her fingers are all thumbs.* 彼女は非常に無器用です ▪ *All my fingers are thumbs* today. 今朝は指が器用に動きません.

arrive at** one's **fingers' ends 困窮[窮乏]する ▪ Soon he *arrived at his fingers' ends.* まもなく彼は財政が窮乏した.

be all fingers and thumbs 《口》(一時的に)指が器用に動かない ▪ I *am all fingers and thumbs* this morning. I can't tie my shoes. 今朝は指が器用に動かない. 靴のひもが結べない.

be finger and glove with =(be) HAND and glove.

burn** one's **fingers 余計なことに手を出して[早まって]やけどをする, ひどい目にあう ▪ No more gambling for me! I *burnt my fingers* once. もうかけ事はごめんだ. 一度ひどい目にあったから.

by a finger's breadth (指の幅ほどの)ほんのわずかの差[こと]で, 危うく ▪ The bullet missed my head *by a finger's breadth.* 弾丸は紙一重の差で私の頭をそれた.

by** one's **fingers' ends 手先で, 手仕事で ▪ He is obliged to live *by his fingers' ends.* 彼はやむなく手仕事で生活している.

can* [*may*] *count ... on the fingers ...は指折って数えられる(ほど少ない) ▪ Such men *may be counted on your fingers.* そのような人は指で数えるほどしかいない.

crook** one's (**little**) **finger →CROOK[2].

cross** one's **fingers (幸運・成功を祈って片手の)人指し指の上へ中指を重ねる ▪ Jane *crossed her fingers* during the race so that John would win. ジェインは競走中ジョンが勝つようにと指を重ねて祈った.

dip** one's **finger(s) in →put one's FINGER(s) in.

*One's **fingers are all thumbs.*** → All one's FINGERs are thumbs.

*one's **fingers itch** (**for, to** do)* (...したくて)手がむずむずする (→ itchy FINGERs) ▪ *My fingers itched to* be doing it myself. 自分でそれがしたくてたまらなかった.

fingers like bananas/banana fingers 大きくて太い指 ▪ He is a clumsy man with *banana fingers.* 彼は指が太くて不器用だ.

Fingers were made before forks. 《諺》昔は指で食べていたのだ《食事は儀式ばることはない》.

***get* [*have*]... *at** one's **finger(s') ends* [*tips*]** ...をそらんじ[てい]る, に精通する[している] ▪ He's *got* the subject *at his finger tips.* 彼はその問題に精通している ▪ He *has* the poem *at his finger ends.* 彼はその詩をそらんじている.

get** one's **finger on ...を取る ▪ He *got his finger on* the armament industry. 彼は軍需産業を手に入れた.

get** one's **finger out →pull one's FINGER out.

get* [*have*] one's **fingers burnt (無分別に手を出して)手を焼く, ひどい目にあう (→burn one's FINGERs) ▪ I *got my fingers burnt* by letting him use my car. 私は彼に車を貸してひどい目にあった.

give five fingers 《米俗》鼻をつまんであざける ▪ I'll *give five fingers* to every cop. サツをみなあざけってやろう.

give** a person **the finger 《米俗》人に向けて中指を立てる; 人に怒り[軽蔑]を示す《性的侮辱を示す行為》 ▪ When the kids were told to leave the store, they *gave* the manager *the finger* and ran off. 子供たちは店から出るように言われると, 店長に中指を立てて走り去った.

have a finger in ...に関係する, 加わる ▪ He *had a finger in* all the disputes in Europe. 彼はヨーロッパのすべての論争に加わった.

have a finger in every pie すべてのことを牛耳っている ▪ She liked to *have a finger in every pie.* 彼女はすべてのことに手を出すのが好きだった ▪ You must ask for your boss's permission. He *has a finger in every pie.* 君は上司の許可を得なければならない. 彼がすべてを牛耳っているのだから.

have* [*put*] *a* [one's] *finger in the pie **1** 事に参与する, 参加する, 事に手を出す ▪ You *put your finger in* too many *pies.* 君はいろいろ手を出しすぎる.

2 手出しする, 干渉する ▪ She is always *putting her finger in my pie.* 彼女はいつも私のことに余計な手出しばかりしている.

have a* [one's] *finger on the button 核兵器のボタンを押す権限を持つ ▪ It's a question of who might *have a finger on the button.* それは, 誰が核兵器のボタンを押す権限を得るかという問題だ.

have** one's **finger on the pulse →keep one's FINGER on the pulse (of).

***have* [*get*] one's **fingers burned* [*burnt*]** → get one's FINGERs burnt.

have* [*keep*] one's **fingers crossed **1**《口》(祈願・災いよけに)人さし指と中指を重ねて十字を切る《一種のまじない》(→cross one's FINGERs) ▪ I'll *have my fingers crossed* for you. そうなるよう祈っています ▪ Washington is *keeping its fingers crossed* on the ugly situation in Berlin. ワシントンはベルリンの険悪な情勢が好転するようにと祈っている.

2 (ばれないよう祈りながら)罪のない嘘[はったり, でたらめ]を言う, ほらを吹く ▪ I made the promise, but I *had my fingers crossed,* because I knew I couldn't keep it. 約束はしたけれども, 冷や冷やしてたんだ. 守れないとわかってたので.

have** one's **fingers in the till (店員が)店の金を少しずつ盗む ▪ She *had her fingers in the till,* and lost her job. 彼女は店の金を少しずつ盗んでいたので首になった. ☞till「(店の)現金用引出し」.

have light fingers 盗みぐせがある; すりである ▪ Tom *has light fingers.* トムは盗みぐせがある.

have more ... in** one's **little finger than in** your* [etc.] ***whole body 《口》すばらしく多くの...

を持っている ▪ He *has more* wit *in his little finger than in your whole body.* 彼はすばらしい知恵者である. ☞Swift, *Polite Conversation*, "Dialogue"2; than 以下はいろいろに変化する.

have sticky fingers 《口》盗み癖がある, 人差し指が曲がっている ▪ My mother got rid of our maid because she *had sticky fingers.* 母は盗み癖があるメイドを追い出した ▪ He *has got* very *sticky fingers.* 彼にはひどい盗み癖がある.

hold up a finger 指で天をさして警告する ▪ She *held up a finger* to warn me. 彼女は指で天をさして私に警告した.

F

in** one's **fingers 握って, 支配して ▪ He has the treasures *in his fingers.* 彼がその宝を握っている.

itchy fingers 《主に英》...したくてうずうずしている (→ one's FINGERs itch (for, to do)) ▪ I had *itchy fingers* to start playing the guitar again. 私はまたギターを弾きたくてうずうずしていた.

***keep* [*have*] *one's* finger on the pulse (*of*)** ...のことは十分知っている; について最新の知識を持っている ▪ Whoever designed the new model obviously *had their finger on the pulse.* 新型モデルをデザインした人は, 明らかに最先端のことを熟知していた ▪ A statesman must *keep his finger on the pulse of* the electorate. 政治家は自分の選挙区のことは十分知っていなければならない.

keep** one's **fingers crossed **1** = have one's FINGERs crossed.
2 懐疑的に警戒している ▪ U.S. policy-makers are *keeping their fingers crossed.* アメリカの政策立案者たちは懐疑的に警戒を続けている.

lay* [*put*] *a finger on (敵意をもって)...に手を出す, 触れる ▪ You shall not *put a finger on* my daughter. 娘には指一本も触れさせはせぬぞ.

lay* [*put*] *one's* [*the*] *finger on **1** (患部・悪の原因)を的確に指摘する ▪ The osteopath *laid his finger on* the trouble at once. 整骨療法家は患部をすぐに的確に指摘した.
2 場所を突き止める ▪ I can't *put my finger on* the time-table. 時間表のありかを突き止めることができない.
3 ...に手をかける ▪ Read whatever you can *lay your finger on.* 手あたり次第に読みなさい.
4 《口》...を密告する, 訴える ▪ His enemies *put the finger on* him. 彼の敵の連中が彼を密告した.

lick** one's **fingers →LICK one's chops.

lift a finger against ...に手向かう ▪ No one *lifts a finger against* him. 誰も彼には手向かわない.

***lift* [*raise, stir*] *a finger* (*to do*)** 《口》〚否定文で〛(...するため)指一本動かす, 少しの労を取る ▪ They did not *lift a finger to* help him. 彼らは少しも彼を助ける労を取らなかった.

lift* [*throw, turn up*] *the little finger (大)酒を飲む ▪ It's a pity he *lifts the little finger* so much. 彼がそんなにひどく酒を飲むのは遺憾である. ☞酒杯を持つとき多くの人が小指を上げることから.

***look through** one's* [*the*] ***fingers at* [*upon*]** ...を見ぬふりをする; を気に留めない; をこっそり見る, おぼろげに見る ▪ I saw him snatch a bun; but I *looked through my fingers at* it. 私は彼が干しブドウ入りの甘パンを取るのを見たが, 見て見ぬふりをした.

My little finger told me. 風のたよりに聞いた (= A little BIRD told me.) ▪ *My little finger told me* that. それを風のたよりに聞いた. ☞小指がむずむずするのは何かの変化を予表すると信じられていたことから.

point a* [*the, one's*] *finger* (*of blame*) (*at*)/ *point an* [*the*] *accusing finger (...に)罪[責任あり]とする ▪ The company *pointed the finger at* him. 会社は彼にその責任があるとした.

pull* [*get, take*] *one's finger out 《俗》急ぐ; (仕事など)を始める, にとりかかる ▪ It is about time we *pulled our fingers out.* わしらはもう仕事を始める時間だ ▪ You'd better *pull your finger out,* you should have finished this job hours ago. 性根を入れてやれ, この仕事はとっくに済んでいたはずだ.

put a* [*one's*] *finger in the pie →have a FINGER in the pie.

put a finger on →lay a FINGER on.

put a* [*one's*] *finger to one's lips (人に)「黙って」の合図をする ▪ Mother *put a finger to her lips,* and we all became silent. 母が「黙って」の合図をしたので私たちはみな黙りました.

***put one's finger in the dike* [*dyke*]** 《口》迫りくる脅威をくい止める, 対策を講じる《下の例文の逸話から》 ▪ This is a famous Dutch tale about an 8-year-old boy who *put his finger in the dike* to save the city of Haarlem. これは8歳の男の子に関する有名なオランダの話であり, その子はハーレムの都市を救うために自分の指を堤防に差し込んだのだった ▪ In your opinion, is there any way to *put a finger in the dike* and stop this? 君の考えでは, なにか手を打って, これを止めることができますか?

put one's finger in the fire おせっかいして手を焼く, 失敗する ▪ You will need to *put your fingers in the fire.* あなたはどうしてもおせっかいして手を焼かねば承知しないのだね.

put one's* [*the*] *finger on →lay one's FINGER on.

put* [*dip*] *one's finger*(*s*) *in ...に干渉する ▪ They will *dip their fingers in* the suit. 彼らはその訴訟に干渉するだろう.

***raise* [*stir*] *a finger* (*to do*)** →lift a FINGER (to do).

run one's fingers through one's hair → HAIR.

slip through* [*between*] *one's fingers 指の間からすべり抜ける; 逃げる ▪ Hold it fast, it will *slip through your fingers* like an eel. それをしっかりつかんでいたまえ, ウナギみたいに指からすべり抜けてしまうから ▪ I let the chance *slip through my fingers.* 機会をのがしてしまった.

snap one's fingers at →SNAP[2].

the finger of God 神のみわざ (《聖》*Exod.* 8. 19) ▪ It was done by *the finger of God.* それは神のみ

わざであった.

throw* [*turn up*] *the little finger = lift the little FINGER.

to *one's* [***the***] ***finger ends*** [***tips***] (指の先まで)完全に ▪ Mr. Smith is a gentleman *to the finger tips*. スミス氏は全くの紳士である ▪ I reddened *to my finger tips*. 私は指の先まで真っ赤になった.

to the end of *one's* ***little finger*** (小指の先まで)完全に ▪ He is a Democrat *to the end of his little finger*. 彼は生粋の民主党員である.

twist [***turn, twirl, wind, wrap***]***... round*** [***around***] *one's* (***little***) ***finger*** 人をあごで使う, を丸め込む, 意のままに[自由に]あやつる ▪ She can *twist* her father *round her* (*little*) *finger* when she wants anything. 彼女は何かほしいときは父を丸め込むことができる ▪ There was hardly anyone that he couldn't *turn around his little finger*. 彼があごで使えない人はほとんどいなかった ▪ Women may *twist* me *round their fingers* at their pleasure. 女たちは好きなように私をあごで使うがいい ▪ You *turn, twist, and wind* me just as you like. あなたは意のままに私をあごでお使いになりますね.

with a wet finger 易々と, 苦もなく ▪ He defeated them *with a wet finger*. 彼は苦もなく彼らを負かした. ☞糸つむぎのとき絶えず人さし指につばや水をつけることから.

with *one's* ***finger in*** *one's* ***mouth* 1** (指をくわえて)何もできないで ▪ He stood *with his finger in his mouth*. 彼は何もできないで立っていた.

2 何も得[達成し]ないで ▪ He returned home *with his finger in his mouth*. 彼は何のみやげも持たずに家へ帰った.

(***with***) ***fingers crossed*** (人差し指の上に中指を)指を重ねて幸運を祈りながら (→cross one's FINGERs) ▪ He flew off to England *with fingers crossed*. 彼は幸運を祈りながら英国へ旅だった.

work *one's* ***fingers to the bone*** 骨を惜しまず[激しく]働く ▪ I *worked my fingers to the bone* to make enough money to buy a car. 私は車を買う金を儲けるため一生懸命働いた. ☞裁縫師(お針子)のことから.

wrap ... round [***around***] *one's* (***little***) ***finger*** →twist ... round one's (little) FINGER.

finger[2] /fíŋgər/ 動 ***finger in*** *a person's* ***pie*** 人にいらぬ世話をやく ▪ He sometimes *fingers in her pie*. 彼はときどき彼女にいらぬ世話をやく.

finger-nail /fíŋgərnèɪl/ 名 ***hold*** [***hang***] ***on*** (***to ...***) ***by*** *one's* ***finger-nails*** 一生懸命に(地位などに)かじりつく ▪ This country is now *holding on to* the business *by its fingernails*. この国は今その事業に懸命にかじりついている.

to the finger-nails 完全につめの先まで ▪ He is witty *to the finger-nails*. 彼は全身機知に満ちている ▪ He is a gentleman *to the finger-nails*. 彼は全くの紳士だ.

fingertip /fíŋgərtìp/ 名 ***have*** [***keep***]***... at*** *one's* ***fingertips* 1** (事情など)に精通している; (答えなど)がすぐ言える ▪ He *has* all the facts *at his fingertips*. 彼はすべての事実をよく知っている.

2 (いつでも使えるように)...を手元に持っている ▪ He *has* all the material *at his fingertips*. 彼はすべての材料を手元に持っている.

hold on (***to ...***) ***by*** *one's* ***fingertips*** = hold on (to ...) by one's FINGER-NAILs.

to the [*one's*] ***fingertips*** 全くの, 完全に ▪ He is an artist *to the fingertips*. 彼は全くの芸術家だ.

finish[1] /fínɪʃ/ 名 ***a close finish*** 接戦, 僅差の勝負 ▪ It was *a close finish* with three boats hitting the finish line within a half boat length. 大接戦で, 3艇が0.5艇差内でゴールラインを抜けた.

be in at the finish (キツネなどの)最期を見届ける, 最期の場に立ち合う ▪ The squire was determined to *be in at the finish*. 郷士はキツネの最期を見届けようと決心していた ▪ Having put all this work into the plan, I want to *be in at the finish*. この仕事をすべて計画したので, その完成が見たい. ☞狩猟から.

do the finish on ...の仕上げをする ▪ He is *doing the finish on* this splendid head. 彼はこのすばらしい頭に仕上げをしている.

give the (***last***) ***finish to*** ...の仕上げをする ▪ He *gave the last finish to* the picture. 彼はその絵の仕上げをした.

to a [***the***] ***finish*** 最後まで, とことんまで ▪ He fought *to a finish*. 彼は最後まで戦った.

finish[2] /fínɪʃ/ 動 ***be finished* 1** 仕上げの教育を受ける ▪ Where *were* you *finished*? 最終学校はどこでしたか.

2《口》仕事を終える ▪ I *am finished* for the day. きょうの仕事はすんだ.

finisher /fínɪʃər/ 名 ***the finisher of the law***《戯》死刑執行人 ▪ He was suspended by *the finisher of the law*. 彼は死刑執行人によってつるされた.

fire[1] /faɪər/ 名形 ***A burnt child dreads the fire.***《諺》やけどした子は火を恐れる《痛い思いは忘れない》.

(***a***) ***fire in*** *one's* [***the***] ***belly*** 情熱, 気概 ▪ The team needs a leader with *a fire in the belly*. そのチームには, 炎の情熱をもったリーダーが必要だ.

be a fire brand 騒動を起こす危険人物である ▪ It is a pity he *is a fire brand* in the factory. 彼がその工場で騒動を起こす危険人物であるのは残念である.

be a fire eater けんか早い人である ▪ What *a fire eater* you *are*! 君ってなんてけんか早いんだろう!

between two fires 両方[腹背]から砲[攻]撃されて; 両方から非難されて ▪ What with famine and what with war, they are, so to speak, *between two fires*. ききんやら戦争やらで, 彼らはいわば腹背から砲撃されているようなものだ.

breathe fire 怒り狂っている (*over*) ▪ France's smokers are *breathing fire over* the government's decision to raise tobacco prices by a further 20 percent in January. フランスの喫煙者たちは, 1月にタバコをさらに20パーセント値上げするという政

府の決定に烈火のごとく怒っている.

build a fire →make a FIRE.

build a fire under (いやがる人)をせき立てる ▪ Mother *built a fire under* me and got me to go on an errand. 母は僕をせき立ててお使いにやった.

by fire 火事で ▪ The forest was destroyed *by fire*. その森林は火事で焼けてしまった.

catch fire **1** 火がつく, 発火する ▪ Wooden houses *catch fire* easily. 木造家屋は火がつきやすい ▪ My tongue *catches fire* as it goes. 私の舌はしゃべっていると熱を帯びる.

2 (人が)熱する, 興奮する ▪ The audience *caught fire* at the speaker's words. 聴衆は演説者の言葉に熱狂した.

F

cease fire **1** 撃ち方やめ(のらっぱ) ▪ The bugle sounded the "*cease fire*."「撃ち方やめ」のラッパが鳴った.

2 撃ち方をやめる; 戦闘を停止する ▪ *Cease fire*! 撃ち方やめ! ▪ As soon as news of the armistice arrived, the order was given to *cease fire*. 休戦の報が着くやいなや, 戦闘停止の命令が出された.

come under fire 砲火を浴びる《比喩的にも》 ▪ His speech *came under fire* from other members of Parliament. 彼の演説は他の国会議員から攻撃を浴びた.

commence fire 撃ち方を始める ▪ *Commence fire*! 撃ち方始め!

draw fire 《主に米》標的になる, 非難される (*from*) ▪ His comments *drew fire* from African-Americans. 彼の発言はアフリカ系アメリカ人からの非難を引き起こした.

draw the fire of/draw** a person's* ***fire ...の攻撃[批判]を招く ▪ His insults *drew the fire of* his opponents. 彼の侮辱は相手の攻撃を招いた.

fight* [*meet, match*] *fire with fire → FIGHT[2].

fire and brimstone 火と硫黄, 地獄の責め苦 (《聖》 *Gen*. 19: 24, *Rev*. 19: 20); ちくしょう! ▪ It rained *fire and brimstone* from heaven. 天から火と硫黄の雨が降った ▪ *Fire and brimstone*! I shall revenge me upon thee for this! ちくしょう! この恨み, 貴様に晴らさずにおくものか!

fire and sword (戦争の)焼き払いと殺戮(さつりく); 戦禍 ▪ They put all to *fire and sword*. 彼らはすべてを焼き払い虐殺した ▪ He carried the city by *fire and sword*. 彼は焼き払いと殺害により市を占領した.

fire's gone out (恋愛などで)情熱が冷めた状態である ▪ The *fire's gone out* between them. 彼らはアツアツではなくなった.

friendly fire (味方からの)誤射, 誤爆,「友好砲撃」 ▪ Four Canadian soldiers were killed in a *friendly fire* incident by two U.S. airmen. 4人のカナダ兵が米軍の二人の航空兵による誤射のため死亡した ▪ The Bulgarian soldier was killed by a *friendly fire* from US forces. そのブルガリア兵は米軍からの誤射によって戦死した.

go* [*run*] *through fire and water 水火をもくぐる, 水火もいとわぬ (《聖》 *Ps*. 66. 12) ▪ I would *go through fire and water* to find out the truth. 真相を知るためには私は水火をもいといません.

go* [*pass*] *through* (*the*) *fire 最もきびしい試練を受ける ▪ He has *gone through the fire*. 彼はひどくきびしい試練を受けてきた.

hang fire (火器が)遅発する; (事業などが)行き悩む, ぐずぐずする ▪ The gun *hung fire*. 銃は遅発した ▪ The scheme is *hanging fire*. その計画は行き悩んでいる ▪ He is *hanging fire*. 彼は(決断がつかず)ぐずぐずしている.

have fire in** one's* ***belly 活力にあふれている, エネルギッシュである ▪ He *has fire in his belly* and a burning desire to win. 彼はとても精力的で, 勝利に対して燃えるような野心を持っている.

hold* [*keep*]** *a person's* ***feet to the fire (人)に圧力をかける, 無理じいする ▪ He *held the president's feet to the fire* and forced him to sign a welfare reform bill. 彼は大統領に圧力をかけて福祉改革法案に署名させた. ☞ 昔の度胸だめしや拷問から.

hold (*one's*) ***fire*** (いざという時まで)発砲をさし控える; (適切な時まで特に批判的)発言[行為]をさし控える ▪ He was *holding his fire* till he was certain. 彼は確かになるまで発砲を控えていた ▪ Well, *hold your fire*. He may have met with an accident. 君, 批判は慎め. 彼は事故にあったのかもしれないじゃないか.

If you play with fire, you get burned. 《諺》火遊びは火傷(やけど)の元.

keep the fire in 火を燃やしておく, 灯火をつけておく ▪ We *kept the fire in* for warmth. 暖を取るため炉火をたき続けた.

lay a fire (たきぎを積んで)火をたく用意をする ▪ Do you know how to *lay a fire*? 火をたく用意をする方法を知っていますか.

light a fire **1** (巻きタバコなどに)火をつける ▪ He *lighted a fire* and smoked. 彼はタバコに火をつけて吸った.

2 =light the FIRE.

***light a fire under** a person* 《主に米》人のしりをたたく, せかせる ▪ Michael Moore's new film may *light a fire under* Bush. マイケル・ムーアの新作映画はブッシュ氏をせきたてるかもしれない.

light** a person's* ***fire 《口》人を(性的に)興奮させる ▪ None of the girls *lighted my fire*. その娘たちの誰もぼくを興奮させなかった.

light the fire 火をたきつける ▪ *Light the fire* within. 内なる炎を燃やせ.

like fire 速く ▪ The news spread *like fire*. そのニュースは素早く広がった.

make* [*build*] *a fire 火を起こす ▪ Please *make a fire*. 火を起こしてください.

make* (*a*) *fire 砲撃をする ▪ We *made* great *fire* all night with our cannon. 我々は大砲で夜じゅう盛んに砲撃をした.

miss fire **1** (火器が)発火しない, 不発に終わる ▪ The gun *missed fire*. 銃が発火しなかった.

2 (企てに)失敗する, 効を奏さない ▪ His speech *missed fire*. 彼の演説は効を奏さなかった.

on fire **1** 燃えて, 火災を起こして ▪ The house is *on fire*. その家は燃えている.

2 怒り[熱情, 熱意]に燃えて ▪ They were *on fire* to fall on. 彼らはみなひどく食べたがっていた ▪ The orator was *on fire*. 弁士は激していた.

3《口》順調で, うまくいって ▪ He is really *on fire* and that's why the whole team is playing well. 彼は本当に好調だ. だから, チーム全体がうまくいっている.

on the fire 準備中で ▪ He has a new play *on the fire*. 彼は新しい脚本を制作中である.

open fire 砲撃を開始する; 始める ▪ The enemy *opened fire* on our lines at dawn. 敵は夜明け方わが戦線に対して砲撃を開始した ▪ She *opened fire* by saying so. 彼女はまずそう言って論争の火ぶたを切った.

pass through* (*the*) *fire →go through (the) FIRE.

play with fire 火をいじる; 危険な[あぶない]ことをする ▪ Leaving the door unlocked is *playing with fire*. 戸に錠をかけずにおくことは危険な行為だ.

pull *a person's* ***chestnuts out of the fire*** →CHESTNUT.

pull* [*snatch*]*... out of the fire …を滅亡から救い出す; (勝負など)の失敗を成功に転じる ▪ Well, I *pulled* that nation *out of the fire*. ほんとに私はその国民を滅亡から救い出したのです ▪ He *pulled* the game *out of the fire*. 彼はその試合を失敗から成功に転じた.

run through fire and water →go through FIRE and water.

save ... out of the fire 大損害[災害]から(いくらかのもの)を救い出す ▪ That would be *saving* something *out of the fire*. それは破産からかなりなものを救い出すことになるだろう.

set fire to …に火をつける; を激させる, 興奮させる ▪ He *set fire to* his house in order to collect the insurance. 彼は保険金を取るために自宅に火をつけた.

set ... on fire **1** …を燃やす ▪ He *set* his house *on fire* in order to collect the insurance. 彼は保険金を取るために自分の家を焼いた.

2 …をひどく興奮させる, の感情をあおる, 激させる ▪ The orator *set* the audience *on fire*. 弁士は聴衆の激情をあおった.

set the Thames on fire →THAMES.

set the world* [*river*] *on fire = set the THAMES on fire.

show ... the fire …を少し火にかける[熱する] ▪ Just *show* the mixture *the fire* and it will be ready to eat. そのインスタント食品はちょっと火にかけたらすぐ食べられます.

snatch ... out of the fire →pull ... out of the FIRE.

strike fire **1** (打ったり, まさつしたりして)火(花)を出す ▪ It is possible to *strike fire* from flint. 火打石から火を打ち出すことができる.

2 感激[感動]させる ▪ The orator's words *struck fire* into the hearts of his hearers. 弁士の言葉は聴衆の心を感激させた.

take fire **1** =catch FIRE.

2 興奮[熱狂, 立腹]する ▪ She *took fire* at the prospect of going to America. 彼女はアメリカ行きの見通しに興奮した.

There is no fire without smoke.《諺》煙を立てずには火は起こせない《どんなことにも少しの欠点はあるものだ》 ▪ Indeed the climate is abominable there, but *there is no fire without smoke*. なるほどそこの気候はひどいが, どんなことにも欠点はあるものだ.

There is no smoke without fire. → SMOKE[1].

under fire 砲火を浴びて; 攻撃[非難]を受けて (*from, for*) ▪ They landed *under* enemy *fire*. 敵の砲火を浴びつつ上陸した ▪ I am *under fire* whatever I do. 私は何をしても非難される ▪ The prime minister came *under fire from* hard-liners. 首相は強硬派から非難されている ▪ The senator came *under fire for* comments on homosexuality. その上院議員は同性愛に関する発言で非難されている.

Where's the fire?《口》火事はどこですか, そんなに急いでどこへ行くのですか《急いでいる人に言う言葉》.

fire[2] /faɪər/ 動 ***be fired with*** …で燃え立っている ▪ He *is fired with* enthusiasm. 彼は熱意に燃え立っている.

fire into the wrong block 目標を誤る ▪ When he began his war upon the Senate, he found he had *fired into the wrong block*. 彼が上院に戦争をしかけたとき, 自分が目標を誤ったことを知った. ☞狩猟から.

fire questions at …に質問を放つ ▪ They *fired* many *questions at* him. 彼らは彼に多くの質問を放った.

fired-up《口》[[限定的]] 興奮した, 熱狂した; 怒った ▪ A *fired-up* person has abundant energy, laughs often, and speaks enthusiastically. 熱狂した人間は, エネルギーにあふれ, よく笑い, 熱情的に話す.

firestorm /fáɪərstɔ̀ːrm/ 名 ***trigger a firestorm*** 大きな反応を引き起こす, 大反響を呼ぶ ▪ That action *triggered a firestorm* of protest from women's rights advocates. その行為がきっかけとなって女権提唱者たちから抗議が殺到した.

firing /fáɪərɪŋ/ 形 ***firing blanks***《口》(男性が)生殖能力がない ▪ He is probably sterile and *firing blanks*. 彼はたぶん男性不妊症で生殖能力がない.

in the firing line《口》解雇される危険にあって, 厳しく非難される立場にあって (→in the LINE of fire) ▪ He is *in the firing line*. 彼は首になる危険がある ▪ He found himself *in the firing line* for his sexist remarks. 彼は性差別的な発言をして厳しく非難される立場に置かれた.

on* [《英》*in*] *the firing line 非難[攻撃, 排除]されて (*for, from*) ▪ The minister found himself *on* [*in*] *the firing line from* women groups for

F

his comments about wives' status. その大臣は，妻の身分に関する発言に関して女性グループからの非難の矢面に立たされていた.

out of the firing line 非難からはずれて ▪ As a public man, the mayor cannot hope to stay *out of the firing line*. 公人として市長は非難の的にならずにはすまないだろう. ☞firing-line「攻撃の最前線」.

firm /fəːrm/ 形 ***(as) firm as a rock*** →ROCK[1].

be firm with …に対して断固たる態度をとる，厳格である ▪ The teacher *was firm with* the boys. 先生は男子生徒にきびしかった.

F

hold firm **1** なかなか負けぬ，鼻息が荒い ▪ The sellers *held firm*. 売手はなかなか負けなかった.
2 しっかとつかんでいる ▪ They *hold* truth *firm* and will not let it go. 彼らは真理をしっかりとつかまえて放そうとしない.

on firm ground 事実を確信して，確かな基礎に立脚して ▪ He is *on firm ground*. 彼は確かな基礎に立脚している.

stand firm **1** しっかりと立っている，毅然としている ▪ Eldon exhorted the king to *stand firm*. エルドンは王に毅然としているように勧めた.
2 (敵軍に対し)毅然と踏みとどまる ▪ They *stood firm* against a host of opponents. 彼らは敵の大軍に対して毅然と踏みとどまっていた.
3 (物が)しっかりと動かない ▪ Fasten the clock with a nail that it may *stand firm*. しっかりと動かないように柱時計をくぎで留めなさい.

first /fəːrst/ 形副名 ***at first*** 初めは ▪ *At first* he thought English very difficult, but later he made good progress. 彼は初めは英語を非常にむずかしいと思ったが，後には非常に上達した.

at first sight [***glance, view***] **1** 一目で，一目見て ▪ He fell in love *at first sight*. 彼は一目でほれこんだ.
2 一見したところでは ▪ *At first view* the problem seems easy. 一見したところではその問題はやさしそうだ.

at** a person's **first voice [***word***] 人の声を聞くと[人の一言で]すぐ ▪ He obeyed *at her first word*. 彼は彼女の一言ですぐ従った.

at (***the***) ***first blush*** →BLUSH[1].

be a first charge on …に対する一番の要求である ▪ The care of your wife's health must *be a first charge on* your time. あなたは奥さんの健康管理にあなたの時間を一番に使わねばなりません.

be first chop 《口》第一流[級]である ▪ This wine *is first chop*. このワインは第一級だ.

***be the first to** do* 一番に…する ▪ He *was the first to* help her. 彼が一番に彼女を助けた.

come first **1** (競争などで)1等になる (*in*) ▪ Phelps *came first in* the men's 200-meter freestyle race. フェルプスは男子競泳200メートル自由形で1位になった.
2 最も重要である (*for, with*) ▪ Family always *comes first for* me. 私にはいつでも家族が最優先だ.

feet first →FOOT[1].

first among equals (同輩内の)指導[責任]者，主導的な立場の人 ▪ When the leaders of the world met in Tokyo, the American President was still *first among equals* at the conference. 世界の指導者たちが東京で一堂に会したとき，会議では依然として米国大統領が主導役だった.

first and foremost 〚限定的〛最も顕著な; 〚副詞的に〛まず第一番に，まっ先に ▪ *First and foremost* of these sufferers were the Quakers. この受難者たちのうち最も著しいのはクェーカー教徒だった ▪ Now, *first and foremost*, understand this. そこで，まず第一に，次のことを理解しなさい.

first and last **1** 前後を通じて ▪ I have known him, *first and last*, for ten years. 前後を通じて10年の間彼を知っている.
2 総じて，大体において ▪ *First and last*, that boy's education has cost £10,000. 総じて，その少年の教育は1万ポンドかかった ▪ He is a poet *first and last*. 彼は大体において詩人だ.

First come, first served. 《諺》先着者から先に接待，「早い者勝ち」.

first, last, and all the time 《米口》終始一貫して，いつまでも(変わらず) ▪ We are against it, *first, last, and all the time*. 我々はそれに徹頭徹尾反対である ▪ They pledged *first, last, and all the time* support to him. 彼らは彼に対し終始一貫した支持を誓った. ☞もとアメリカ政党の全国大会で，州代表が大統領候補を指名する際に使ったもの.

first, midst, and last 終始一貫して，初めから終わりまで (Milton, *Paradise Lost* 5. 165) ▪ The public sympathy is with him *first, midst, and last*. 世間の同情は終始一貫して彼に向けられている.

first of all まず第一に，何よりもまず ▪ One will be judged by one's appearance *first of all*. 人は何よりもまずその風采によって判断される.

first off 《口》まず第一に; すぐに ▪ *First off*, we heard a splendid performance. まず第一に我々はすばらしい演奏を聞いた.

first or last **1** 最初にでも最後にでも ▪ You may do it *first or last*, so long as you do it. それをしさえすれば，最初にやっても最後にやってもよい.
2 《まれ》遅かれ早かれ ▪ You will have to do it *first or last*. 遅かれ早かれそれをせねばならぬでしょう.

first thing 《口》→(the) first THING.

first thing (***in the morning***) 朝早く，その日早く ▪ The boss wasn't here *first thing*. 社長はその日早くはここにいませんでした.

first thing off the bat すぐに ▪ He fired the man *first thing off the bat* when he got back. 彼は帰るとすぐその男を解雇した.

first things first 《口》 **1** 最初のことを最初に，これをまず ▪ *First things first*; have you got any money with you? まず第一に，金を持っていますか.
2 大事な事から先に; 最も大切なことを第一に ▪ "*First things first*" must be the guiding principle. 「最も大切なことを一番に」が，指導原理でなければならない.

for the first time →TIME[1].

from first to last 初めから終わりまで，終始 ▪ Long John told the story *from first to last.* ロング・ジョンはその話を初めから終わりまで話した ▪ Grey was in his place *from first to last.* グレイは終始自分の持ち場にいた．

from the first (そもそもの)初めから；まず第一に ▪ He was opposed to the plan *from the first.* 彼は初めからその計画に反対であった ▪ You are dishonest *from the first.* まず第一に君は不正直だ．

get* [*take*] *a first 《英》(大学の優等試験の)第一級に入る ▪ He *got a first* in mathematics. 彼は数学の優等試験で第一級に入った．

get to first base 《主に米・戯》〚主に否定文で〛第一歩に成功する；異性関係の第一段階になる《キス，手を握ること》(→get to first BASE) ▪ Mac hasn't even *gotten to first base* with a female. マックは女性と第一段階に至ってさえいない．

give first place to …を第一とする[主位におく] ▪ You must *give first place to* training in order to be a good runner. すぐれた走者になるためには訓練を第一とせねばならない．

give** a person* (the right of*** [***to***]) ***first refusal*** 人に第一先買権[優先的選択権]を与える ▪ Tenant farmers in Scotland are to *be given the right of first refusal* to buy their land if the landlord decides to sell. 地主が売ることに決めれば，スコットランドの小作人たちには土地を買う第一先買権が与えられることになっている．

have first call on **1** …を最初に使用する権利を持つ ▪ If the business fails, the lender generally *has first call on* the company's assets. 会社が倒産すると，一般に，債権者が会社の資産を最初に使用する権利をもっている．

2 (人)に最初に助けられる人になる ▪ My son *has first call on* my time. 私の時間は真っ先に息子にあてられる．

head* [*feet*] *first →HEAD[1]; FOOT[1].

If at first you don't succeed, (***try, try, and try again.***) 《諺》初めうまくいかなくても(何度もやってみなさい) ▪ *If at first you don't succeed,* don't give up too easily; persistence pays off in the end. 最初うまくいかなくても，簡単にあきらめてはいけない．ねばり強くやれば最後にはむくわれる．

not know the first thing about …については何も知らない ▪ He did *not know the first thing about* your departure. 彼はあなたの出発については何も知らなかった． ☞the first＝even one.

on* [*till*] *the first fine day 天気になりしだい[になるまで] ▪ It will be held *on the first fine day.* それは天気になりしだい行われる ▪ The excursion was postponed *till the first fine day.* 遠足は雨天順延となった．

put…first …を最優先にする，一番大事だと考える ▪ He always *puts* duty *first.* 彼はいつも義務を第一と考える ▪ I always *put* my children *first* and my pride second. 私はいつも子供を最優先にして，自分のプライドは二の次だ．

put first things first 最も大切なことを第一にする (→FIRST things first) ▪ She was incapable of *putting first things first.* 彼女は最も大切なことを一番にすることができなかった．

take a first →get a FIRST.

the first … but one [***two***] 最初から2[3]番目の ▪ The word occurs at the very beginning of the text, *the first* word *but one.* その語はテキストのまさに書き出し，最初から２番目，に現れる．

the first I (***have***) ***heard*** [***I knew***] ***of*** 《口》(他の人は知っているにもかかわらず)…は初耳だ ▪ This is *the first I heard of* his death. 彼の死はいま初めて聞いた．

The first stroke is half the battle. 《諺》初めがよければその事は半分でき上がったのも同じだ．

(***the***) ***first thing*** →THING.

The [***A***] ***first time for everything.*** 何事にも最初というものがある ▪ Looks like they are going to reach the moon this time.—Well, there is *a first time for everything*! こんどは月に到達しそうだね—うん，何事にも最初というものはあるからね．

the first Tuesday after the first Monday 《米》最初の月曜日のあとの最初の火曜日《(11月の)総選挙日》 ▪ *The first Tuesday after the first Monday* in November is usually when America's general elections take place. 11月の最初の月曜日のあとの火曜日は，アメリカの総選挙の行われる日です．

the firstest with the mostest 最大の数で第一番に ▪ The general's strategy was to arrive at the place of combat first and with more troops than the enemy—*the firstest with the mostest.* 将軍の戦略は敵軍を凌ぐ軍勢でもって真っ先に交戦地へ到達する，つまり最速最大作戦であった． ☞《軍》「最大の兵力で一番乗り」が原義．

till the first fine day →on the FIRST fine day.

first-name /fə́ːrstnèɪm/ 名 ***be on first-name terms*** (姓でなく)名で呼び合うほどの間柄である ▪ We *were on first-name terms.* 私たちはお互いに名で呼び合うほどの間柄であった．

first-rate /fə̀ːrstréɪt/ 形副 ***feel first-rate*** 《俗》とても気分が良い ▪ I *feel first-rate* this morning. 私は今朝はとても気分が良い．

first-rate and a half 《米》きわめて優秀で；すごく ▪ That's *first-rate and a half.* それはすごく優秀だ ▪ I do like it, *first-rate and a half.* それは大好きだ．

fish[1] /fɪʃ/ 名 ***a big fish in a little pond*** お山の大将 ▪ He is the biggest businessman in our town, but he is just *a big fish in a little pond.* 彼はわが町最大の実業家だがお山の大将にすぎない．

a big fish in a small pond ＝a big FROG in a small pond.

a cold fish (感情表出が)抑制的な人；よそよそしい[素っ気ない]人，冷血漢 ▪ It is difficult to get to know Sylvia; she's such *a cold fish.* シルビアのことはわかりにくい．ほんとに感情を表に出さないんだから．

☞Shakespeare, *The Winter's Tale* (1610) から.

a fish out of water 水から出た魚《不得意な地位にいる人》 ▪ I felt like *a fish out of water* among so many musical experts. そんなに多くの音楽専門家の間に交じっていると，私は水から出た魚のような気がした.

a little fish in a big pond ＝a little FROG in a big pond.

a nice kettle of fish →KETTLE.

a queer fish 変わり者 ▪ I always thought of him as *a queer fish.* 私はずっと彼のことを変人だと思っていた.

F

All* [*Everything*] *is fish that comes to *one's* ***net.*** 《諺》何でもござれだ，転んでもただでは起きない ▪ Being a commission agent, *all's fish that comes to my net.* 委託販売人だから私は何でもござれだ.

an easy fish to catch 取り入りやすい人 ▪ She was *an easy fish to catch.* 彼女に取り入るのはやさしかった.

(***as***) ***drunk as a fish*** →(as) DRUNK as a fiddler.

(***as***) ***mute as a fish*** →MUTE.

(***be***) ***neither fish,*** (***flesh***), ***fowl nor good red herring*** 《口》何ともつかぬあいまいなもので(ある)，どっちつかずで(ある) ▪ He is vague about his profession; he *is neither fish, fowl, nor good red herring.* 彼の職業はばく然としている. 何ともつかぬあいまいなものだ.

be neither fish nor fowl 魚でも鳥でもない，どっちつかずである ▪ He'll fit in nowhere—he'll *be neither fish nor fowl.* 彼はどこにも当てはまらないないだろう. どれとも決めがたい.

Better a big fish in a little puddle than a little fish in a big puddle. 《諺》大池の小魚よりも小池の大魚のほうがよい,「鶏口となるも牛後となるなかれ」.

cry stinking fish 《口》自分の商品[努力，一族の者]を悪く言う ▪ He is not the man to *cry stinking fish.* 彼は自分の一族の者をけなすような人ではない. ☞「自分の売る魚が腐っていると大声で言う」が原義.

drink like a fish 《口》がぶがぶ飲む，絶えず飲む ▪ He is the drinker that *drinks like a fish.* 彼は鯨飲するような酒飲みである.

Everything is fish that comes to *one's* ***net.*** →All is FISH that comes to one's net.

feed the fishes 船酔いする，船酔いして吐く ▪ He *fed the fishes* liberally. 彼は船酔いしてたくさん吐いた.

fish, flesh, and fowl →FLESH[1].

have other* [*better, bigger*] *fish to fry 《口》他にしなくてはならない[さしせまった，もっと大事な]仕事がある ▪ I can't discuss the matter any longer; I*'ve other fish to fry.* その問題をこれ以上討議することはできない，他にしなくてはならないことがあるから ▪ I didn't do the washing because I *had better fish to fry.* もっと差し迫った用事があったので洗濯をしなかった ▪ Little did I know, she *had bigger fish to fry.* 彼女にそれよりも大事な仕事があったとは少しも気うかなかった ▪ They asked me to help with the decorations, but I *had other fish to fry.* 飾りつけを手伝ってと頼まれたが他にしなければならないことがあった.

land *one's* ***fish*** 捕えた魚を引き上げる; ねらった目的物を手中に収める.

like shooting fish in a barrel 容易な[に]，造作ない[なく]，楽々と ▪ I had no trouble learning to drive. It was *like shooting fish in a barrel.* 運転できるようになるのに苦労しなかった. 実に簡単だった.

live in a fish bowl 人目にさらされる暮らしをする，プライバシーのない生活をする ▪ When you *live in a fish bowl,* everything you do will be under scrutiny. 人目にさらされて生活すれば，することのすべてが詮索されるだろう.

lots* [*plenty*] *of good fish in the sea →not be the only FISH in the sea.

make fish of one and flesh* [*fowl*] *of another いやな分けへだてをする，えこひいきする ▪ This is *making fish of one and flesh of another* with a vengeance. これこそまさしく不当な分けへだてをするというものだ.

need ... like a fish needs a bicycle ...を全く必要としない ▪ A woman *needs* a man *like a fish needs a bicycle.* 女性が男性を必要としないのは，魚が自転車を必要としないのと同様だ. ☞もとフェミニスト運動のスローガン.

not be the only fish in the sea ...だけが海の魚ではない《いくらでもいる，失望するな》 ▪ Cheer up! She *is not the only fish in the sea.* 元気を出せ. 彼女だけが女じゃない《いくらでもいる》.

play a fish 魚を遊ばせる《釣り針にかかった魚をすぐに取り込まずに泳がせる》 ▪ Don't *play the fish.* Pull it up quick. 魚を遊ばせてはだめだ. 急いで取り込め.

play *a person* ***like a fish*** 人をやすやすとあやつる ▪ He *plays* his opponent *like a fish.* 彼は相手をやすやすとあやつる.

The best fish smell when they are three days old. 《諺》いくら良い魚も3日たてば臭くなる《どんな珍客も3日たてば鼻につく》.

The best fish swim* [*are*] *near the bottom. 《諺》すべて良いものは得がたい,「虎穴に入らずんば虎児を得ず」.

There are as good fish in the sea as ever came out of it. 《諺》魚は海にいくらでもいる《落胆するな，機会はいくらでもある》.

There are plenty more fish in the sea. 《諺》海にはもっとたくさんの魚がいる《落胆するな，機会はいくらでもある》.

fish[2] /fɪʃ/ 動 ***a fishing expedition*** →EXPEDITION.

fish for *oneself* **1** 得られるだけ得る ▪ *Fish for yourself* among my stores. 私の貯えから取れるだけお取りなさい.

2 自分の利益だけを求める ▪ Such men *fish for themselves.* そんな人々は自分の利益だけを求める者

だ.

3 自分自身の努力にたよる ▪ This taught the clergy the way to *fish for themselves*. このことが聖職者に自分の努力にたよる道を教えた.

fish for compliments →COMPLIMENT.

fish in the air 空中に魚を求める ▪ It is just like *fishing in the air*. それはまるで空中に魚を求めるようなものだ.

fish in troubled* [*muddy*] *waters 火事場泥棒をする ▪ The man who interferes in Africa is *fishing in troubled waters*. アフリカに干渉する者は火事場泥棒を働いているのだ.

fish or cut bait 《米口》〚しばしば命令的に〛どちらかに決める《特に仕事・計画に加わるか否か》 ▪ Now I want you gentlemen to *fish or cut bait*. さあ諸君, どちらかに決めてもらいたい. ☞もと, 漁師が魚釣りを続けるか釣り糸を切るかの意.

fish-gut /fíʃgʌt/ 名 ***give* [*keep*]** *one's* ***own fish-guts to*** *one's* ***own sea-maws*** 《俗》余分のものや良いものは同族のものに与えよ[取っておけ] ▪ The contracts should be given to English companies; let us *keep our own fish-guts to our own sea-maws*. 請負いは英国の会社に与えるべきだ. 良いものは他人にやらずに同族のものに取っておこう.

fishy /fíʃi/ 形 ***smell fishy*** 《口》うさんくさい, まゆつばである ▪ Something *smells fishy*. なにか[どこか]あやしい.

fist /fɪst/ 名 ***clench* [*double*]** *one's* ***fist*** こぶしを握る, げんこつを固める ▪ He *clenched his fists* in a threatening manner. 彼はおどかすようにこぶしを固めた.

Give us your fist. 《口》握手しよう. ☞fist = hand.

grease *a person's* ***fist*** →GREASE a person's hand.

hand over fist →HAND over hand.

in *one's* ***fists*** 《口》…の手中にあって, しっかと握って ▪ He had the treasure *in his fists*. 彼はその宝を手中に握っていた.

***make a good* [*poor*, etc.] *fist at* [*of*]** 《口》…をうまく[へたに, など]試みる ▪ He should *make a better fist at* farming than educating. 彼は教育よりも農業のほうがうまいはずだ ▪ He *made a poor fist of* this business. 彼はこの仕事を試みたがだめだった.

put up *one's* ***fists*** (戦おうとして)こぶしを振り上げる ▪ *Put up your fists*, and fight like a man! こぶしを振り上げ男らしく戦え!

rule* [*control*]** *a person* ***with an iron fist (鉄拳でもって)人を厳しく支配する, 抑えつける ▪ Fidel Castro has *ruled* Cuba *with an iron fist* for 50 years. フィデル・カストロは50年にわたってキューバに圧政を敷いた.

shake *one's* ***fist* (*at*)** (…に向かって)こぶしを振る《激怒を表す》 ▪ I *shook my fist at* him. 私は彼に向かってこぶしを振った.

use *one's* ***fist on*** …をげんこつでなぐる ▪ He *used his fist on* me. 彼は私をげんこつでなぐった.

write a good* [*poor*, etc.] *fist 《口》文字がうまい[へた, など] ▪ Few people these days can *write a good fist*. この頃は文字のうまい人は少ない.

fisticuff /fístɪkʌ̀f/ 名 ***come* [*fall*] *to fisticuffs*** なぐり合いになる ▪ They *came to* actual *fisticuffs*. 彼らは実際になぐり合いを始めた.

fit[1] /fɪt/ 名 ***be frightened into fits*** びっくりして引きつけを起こす, びっくり仰天する ▪ He *was frightened into fits*. 彼はびっくり仰天した.

beat* [*break, knock*]... *into fits 《口》…を徹底的に負かす, さんざんにやっつける ▪ At the election he *was beaten into fits*. その選挙で彼は完敗した.

***burst into a fit of laughter* [*rage*]** わっと笑いだす[急にかっと怒る] ▪ I *burst into a fit of laughter* at his joke. 彼のジョークを聞いて吹き出したよ.

***by* [*in*] *fits and starts* [*jerks, snatches*]** 間けつ的に, とぎれとぎれに; 時々思い出したように; 発作的に ▪ He always works *by fits and starts*. 彼が時々思い出したように働くのはいつものことだ ▪ He slept only in the day *by fits and starts*. 彼は昼間にだけとぎれとぎれに眠った.

fall down in a fit 卒倒する ▪ I think he just *fell down in a fit*. 彼はまさに卒倒したのだと思う.

give *a person* ***a fit*** 《口》人を驚かす, 不意打ちをくわせる; 人を憤慨させる ▪ Your defeat is enough to *give* one *a fit*. あなたの敗北は人を驚かすに十分である ▪ His conduct *gave* her *a fit*. 彼の行為は彼女を憤慨させた.

give *a person* ***fits*** **1**《口》人をさんざんに負かす ▪ The terrorists *gave* us *fits*. テロリストたちは我々をさんざんに負かした.

2《米口》人を激しくしかる ▪ The old man *gave* us particular *fits* yesterday. 老人はきのう我々を特にひどくしかった.

3 =give a person a FIT.

go into fits 卒倒する ▪ He *went into fits* of ecstacy. 彼は恍惚状態になって気絶した.

go off into fits of 急に(笑い・怒り・涙)を発する ▪ He *went off into fits of* merriment. 彼はおもしろがって急に笑いだした.

***have a fit* [*fits*]** **1** けいれん[引きつけ]を起こす ▪ The child *had a fit* after it had been put to bed. 子供は寝かしつけられた後に引きつけを起こした.

2《口》びっくりする, ショックを受ける ▪ When I heard the noise, I *had a fit*. その音を聞いて仰天した.

3《口》激怒する ▪ I *had a fit* when he told me so. 彼がそう言ったとき私は憤慨した.

4《口》大笑いする ▪ We *had a fit* when we saw the overdressed girl. 着飾りすぎた少女を見たとき我々は大笑いした.

have a fit of …が起こってひとしきり止まらない ▪ He *had a fit of* coughing. 彼はせきをし始めてひとしきり止まらなかった.

have a thousand fits 《俗》極度に興奮する[驚く] ▪ Mother would *have a thousand fits* if she saw me here. 私がここにいるのを見たら母はびっくり仰天するでしょう.

have forty fits 《米口》ヒステリーの発作を起こす; かんしゃくを起こす ▪ I should *have forty fits* if I undertook it. それを引き受けたら私はヒステリーを起こすだろう《絶対に引き受けない》.

if the fit takes *one*/***when the fit is on*** *one* 気が向けば ▪ I go to watch a football match, *if the fit takes* me. 気が向けばサッカーの試合を見に行く.

in a fit of anger [etc.] つい腹立ちまぎれに, かっと怒って[など] ▪ He threw the book *in a fit of anger*. 彼はかっと怒って本を投げた ▪ I gave him all the money *in a fit of generosity*. つい大きな気になって金を全部彼にやった.

in a fit state [***condition***] ...(するの)にふさわしい状態で, 体調が万全で (*for, to do*) ▪ The school buildings are not *in a fit state for* pupils *to* learn in. 校舎は生徒が勉強するのに適した状態ではない ▪ Only some of them were *in a fit condition to* work. 彼らのうち働ける状態にあったのは数人だけだった.

in fits and starts [***jerks, snatches***] →by FITs and starts.

in fits (***of laughter***) 《口》笑い転げて ▪ Beecham would talk to the audience and have them *in fits of laughter*. ビーチャムはいつも観客に語りかけて笑いの渦に巻き込んだ.

scream *oneself* ***into fits*** 《口》ひどい金切声をあげる ▪ The girl *screamed herself into fits*. 少女はひどい金切声をあげた.

throw a fit 《口》大いに驚く[怒る] ▪ Mother would *throw a fit* if she saw me in these clothes. 私がこの服を着ているのを見たら母はびっくり仰天するだろう ▪ When she heard it she *threw a fit*. 彼女はそれを聞いて激怒した.

throw *a person* ***into fits*** 《口》人をひどく驚かす ▪ The proposal *threw* him *into fits*. その提案は彼をびっくり仰天させた.

when the fit is on *one* →if the FIT takes one.

fit[2] /fɪt/ 形名 ***be as fit as a fiddle***/《英》***be as fit as a flea*** 《口》元気でぴんぴんして ▪ I *am as fit as a fiddle*. 私は元気でぴんぴんしている.

(***be***) ***fit for*** **1** ...に適して(いる) ▪ He *is* just *fit for* a job as a salesperson. 彼は販売員の仕事にぴったり向いている ▪ It *is fit for* the purpose. それはその目的にかなう.

2 (能力・健康上)...に耐える ▪ He *was fit for* the post. 彼はその地位に耐えた ▪ The ship *is fit for* service. その艦は任務に耐える.

(***be***) ***fit for human consumption*** (人の)食用に適(す)《比喩的にも》 ▪ Potatoes *are*, of course, quite *fit for human consumption*. ジャガイモはもちろん食用に適している. ☞官庁語から.

(***be***) ***fit for nothing*** **1** 役に立たない ▪ This curtain *is fit for nothing*. このカーテンは役に立たない.

2 =feel FIT for nothing.

be fit to be tied 極度に怒る[いらだつ] (→FIT to be tied) ▪ He *was fit to be tied* when she came home late. 彼女が遅く帰宅すると彼はひどく怒った.

feel fit 体の具合が良い, 元気である ▪ I hope you'll be *feeling fit* again. また元気になられるよう祈ります.

feel fit for nothing 全く健康がすぐれない(で何もできない) ▪ I *feel fit for nothing* nowadays. この頃は全く健康がすぐれない.

fit and trim 健康でスリムな ▪ Her vigorous daily walks kept her *fit and trim*. 毎日きびきびとウォーキングしたので彼女は健康でスリムだった.

fit for a king [***the gods***] (王[神]に捧げるほどの)最高級の, とびきり豪華な ▪ The banquet was *fit for a king*. その宴会は実に豪華だった.

fit to be tied とても, 非常に (→be FIT to be tied) ▪ Everybody was laughing *fit to be tied*. みんな大笑いしていた.

fit to burst [***bust***] 〚副詞的に〛(はち切れそうに) 混雑した, 盛んに; 大いに ▪ A system that was set up for only six members in 1958 is *fit to bust* with 15. 1958年にわずか6人用に立ち上げられた制度は, 15人で飽和状態だ ▪ He was in the bath, singing *fit to bust*. 彼は入浴中で盛んに歌をうたっていた ▪ The man in front of me was laughing *fit to bust*. 私の前の男は大笑いしていた. ☞通例 laugh, cry, sing を修飾する.

fit to kill 《口》 **1** 〚副詞的に〛過度に, ひどく ▪ He laughed *fit to kill*. 彼はひどく笑った.

2 〚限定的〛ひどく健康[元気]で ▪ She looked *fit to kill*. 彼女はひどく元気な様子だった.

have a pink [***blue***] ***fit*** 《英口》かんかんに怒る ▪ If Dad catches you smoking, he'll *have a blue fit*. もしお前がタバコを吸っているのを見たら, おやじは青すじ立てて怒るだろう.

If the cap fits (***wear it***)./《米》***If the hat*** [***shoe***] ***fits*** (***wear it***). 《諺》身に覚えがあるなら, 非難されるべきだ ▪ I didn't actually say that you lied, but *if the cap fits, wear it*. 私は君が嘘をついたとは言わなかったが, 思い当たるところがあるなら非難を受け入れるべきだ.

keep *oneself* [*a person*] ***fit*** 体をきたえる ▪ He *keeps himself fit* with early morning runs. 彼は早朝のランニングで体をきたえている.

see fit 適当と考える ▪ We may discuss the matter this evening if you *see fit*. もし適当と考えるなら今晩その問題を討議してもよろしい.

see fit (***to*** *do*, ***that***) 《しばしば皮肉》(...することを)適当と思う; することに決める; しようとする (→THINK fit to do) ▪ If God *sees fit that* I should marry, He will provide me with a worthy husband. もし神が私が結婚するのを適当と考えられるなら立派な夫を与えてくださるでしょう ▪ Grace *saw fit to* exclude them from her invitation list. グレイスは招待者名簿から彼らを除くことに決めた.

What a fit! 《皮肉》(人の地位・服などが)何とよく似合う[合う]んだろう ▪ *What a fit!* It's roomy enough for your uncle. その服は何てよく合うんだろう! 君のおじさんが着ても大きさは十分だよ.

fit[3] /fɪt/ 動 ***fit*** *oneself* ***for*** …の準備をする ▪ You must *fit yourself for* the journey. あなたは旅行の準備をしなければなりません.

fit like a glove ぴったり合う ▪ This coat *fits* (me) *like a glove*. この上着は(僕に)ぴったりだ.

fit like fun (特に衣服などが)きちんと合う ▪ The coat *fits* you *like fun*. その上着は君にきちんと合う.

fit *oneself* ***to*** …に適応する ▪ The animal body *fits itself to* its surroundings. 動物の体はその環境に適応する.

fit together **1** 組み立てる ▪ He *fit* a rough shelter *together*. 彼はそまつな小屋を組み立てた.

2 くっついて完全になる ▪ These broken pieces of the plate don't *fit together*. 皿のこの破片はくっつかない.

fitness /fítnəs/ 名 ***the*** (***eternal***) ***fitness of things*** **1** 事物本来の合目的性《18 世紀ごろしばしば用いられた句》 ▪ *The eternal fitness of things* cannot but reflect a divine design. 物事の合理性はどうしても神の思(おぼ)し召しを映すものとなる.

2 条理に合うこと, 適切なこと ▪ My writing a postscript after so long a letter is not according to *the fitness of things*. 私がこんな長い手紙に追伸を書くのは適切でありません.

five /faɪv/ 名 ***a bunch of fives*** →BUNCH.

a five and ten 《米口》(Woolworth's のような)安売り店, 激安ショップ ▪ I bought these plates at the *five and ten*. この皿をその安売り店で買った. ☞「5 セントと 10 セント(の店)」の意.

give *a person* ***five*** 片手の掌(てのひら)同士を合わせる挨拶をする (→Give me FIVE!).

Give me a high five! 《米口》(「よくやったね」と褒めて)ハイタッチしてくれ ▪ You made it! *Give me a high five*. やったね. ハイタッチしよう!

Give [***Slip***] ***me five!*** 《主に米口》(やったぜと褒めて)手を打ち合わせてくれ ▪ You've won! *Give me five*. 優勝だ! ハイタッチをしよう.

like five hundred 《米》猛烈に ▪ I heard the boys laughing *like five hundred*. 少年たちが盛んに笑うのが聞こえた.

take five 《俗》ひと休みする ▪ It is about time for me to *take five*. もう僕がひと休みする時間だ. ☞ five＝a five-minute coffee break.

the big five 五大猟獣《アフリカに生息しかつて狩猟の対象となった5種類の大型哺乳動物》 ▪ Tourists were still pouring into Kenya to see *the* "*Big Five*" animals—lions, leopards, elephants, buffalo and rhinos. 旅行者たちは五大猟獣—ライオン, ヒョウ, ゾウ, スイギュウ, サイ—を見るためにまだケニアに殺到していた ▪ Kenya will remain a top safari destination for those who want to see *the big five*. 五大猟獣を見たい人たちにはケニアは狩猟旅行の第一の目的地でありつづけるだろう.

use [***handle***] (*one's*) ***fives*** 《俗》こぶしで戦う ▪ He *handled his fives* well. 彼はこぶしで善戦した.

fix[1] /fɪks/ 名 ***be in a fix*** **1**《口》苦しいはめに陥っている, 進退きわまっている ▪ We *are* all *in a fix*. 我々はみんな苦境に陥っている.

2《俗》妊娠している ▪ The girl was found *in a fix*. その少女は妊娠しているのがわかった.

be in a good [***bad***] ***fix*** 《米》調子がよい[悪い] ▪ They *are in a* mighty *good fix*. 彼らは絶好調だ.

be in a pretty [***nice***] ***fix*** 《口》苦境に陥っている, 進退きわまっている ▪ He wrecked his dad's car, and now he *is in a pretty fix*. 彼は父の車をこわして今困り果てている.

be out of fix 《米》(機械・体の)調子が狂っている, こわれている ▪ The axletree of the world *was out of fix*. 世界の心棒が狂っていた ▪ He *is out of fix* now. 彼は今体の調子が悪い.

get a [*one's*] ***fix*** 《俗》麻薬注射をする, きめる ▪ Heroin addicts will do anything to *get their fix*. ヘロイン中毒者はヤクを打つためには何でもする.

get [***give***] *a person* ***a fix*** 《俗》人に麻薬を注射する ▪ The local pusher *gave* Tom *a fix*. 地方の麻薬業者がトムにヤクを打った.

get a fix on **1**《口》(レーダーなどで)遠方の物を見つける ▪ I can *get a fix on* the submarine. レーダーで(遠方の)潜水艦を見つけることができる.

2 的確に理解[把握]する ▪ They never *got a fix on* what the former vice president meant by the term. 元副会長がその言葉で何を言わんとしていたのか結局わからなかった.

get into a fix 苦境に陥る ▪ I *got into a fix* with my income tax. 所得税のことで苦境に陥った.

put ... in a fix …を困らせる ▪ The demands have *put* the party *in a fix*. その要求で党は窮地に陥った.

fix[2] /fɪks/ 動 ***any way*** *one* ***can fix it*** = NOHOW you can fix it.

be fixed against …に反対と堅く決めている ▪ I *am fixed against* any periodical. 私はどんな定期刊行物にも絶対反対だ.

be fixed for **1** …を得ようと[に賛成と]堅く決めている ▪ The Government *are fixed for* us. 政府は我々の支持を堅く決めている.

2《主に米口》…を供給されている, 持っている ▪ We *are fixed for* money. 我々は金は持っている.

be fixed on [***upon***] …に堅く決めている ▪ He *was fixed upon* taking her. 彼は彼女をもらおうと堅く決めていた.

be fixed to *do* …することを堅く決めている ▪ I *am fixed* not *to* part hence without her. 私は死なば彼女もろともと堅く決心している.

be fixed up 会合約束がある ▪ I *am fixed up* today. きょうは会合の約束がある.

be fixing to *do* …しそうである ▪ It *is fixing to* rain. 雨が降りそうです.

fix a [*one's*] ***cause*** 《米》裁判の準備をする ▪ The lawyers are *fixing their causes*. 弁護士たちは裁判の準備中である.

fix a horse 《米口》競走に勝たぬよう馬をいじくる

▪ He will *fix a horse*. 彼は競走に勝たぬよう馬をいじくるつもりだ. ☞「馬に蹄(ひづめ)鉄を打つ」が原義.

fix** one's **cause →FIX a cause.

***fix** one's **eyes** [**gaze, look**] **on** [**upon**]* …を見つめる, に目を注ぐ ▪ She *fixed her eyes on* the scene. 彼女はその場面を見つめた.

fix** one's **face 顔を整える, 顔の化粧をする; メイクアップをする[し直す] ▪ I will go and *fix my face*. 顔の化粧をしに行きます.

***fix** a person's **flint for** him* →FLINT.

fix** oneself* (for***) (…の)身仕度をする ▪ She *fixed herself for* going out. 彼女は外出の身支度をした.

F

***fix** one's **hope on** [**upon**]* …に望みをかける ▪ It is of no use to *fix your hope on* such a thing. そんなことに望みをかけるのはむだである.

fix … in** one's **mind …をしっかり覚える ▪ *Fix* those facts *in your mind*. それらの事実をしっかり覚えなさい.

fix it 《口》手配する, 取り計らう ▪ You've *fixed it* among you. それはあなたがたが相談して決めたのだ.

fix it [*things*] ***up*** 《口》(…と)取り決めをする (*with*) ▪ I have *fixed it up with* the headmaster. 私は校長と取り決めをした.

***fix** one's **mind on** [**upon**]* →MIND[1].

fix** oneself **on …につきまとう, しがみつく ▪ He *fixed himself on* me as an easy victim. 彼はいいカモだとばかりに私につきまとった.

***fix on … to** do* **1** …する人に…を決める[選ぶ] ▪ We *fixed on* her *to* do it. 我々は彼女をそれをする人に決めた.

2 …するのに…を選ぶ ▪ We *fixed on* Sunday *to* start for our journey. 我々は旅行に出るのに日曜を選んだ.

fix things up →FIX it up.

fix** a person's **wagon 仕返しをする; じゃまをする, 横やりを入れる ▪ He will *fix their wagon* with a special election this fall. 彼は, 今秋の特別選挙で彼らにしっぺ返しをするだろう. ☞ fix「罰する, 立場を悪くさせる」; 後に, 軸に砂を入れることを表すために wagon が付加された.

fix** a person **with** one's **eyes 人をじっと見すえる ▪ She *fixed* him *with her* frank *eyes*. 彼女はまっすぐな目で彼をじっと見た.

nohow** one **can fix it →NOHOW you can fix it.

fixed /fɪkst/ 形 ***fixed to*** …に根がはえて, から離れられないで ▪ He is *fixed to* the place. 彼はそこに根がはえている.

have [***be of***] ***no fixed address*** [《英》 ***abode***] 《法》住所不定である.

flag /flæɡ/ 名 ***a red flag*** 《口》(警告のための)赤旗, 危険信号 ▪ Stalking is *a red flag* for potential homicide. ストーキングは殺人につながるかもしれない危険信号だ.

deny [***refuse***] ***… the honor of the flag*** 旗を降ろして相手の優越を認めることを拒む ▪ A Dutch man-of-war *refused* him *the honor of the flag*. オランダの軍艦は彼の優越を認めようとしなかった.

dip the flag 旗を少し下げてまた上げる《商船が軍艦にあったとき行う敬礼》 ▪ We *dipped the flag* with respect to a U.S. destroyer. 米軍駆逐艦に旗で敬礼した.

drop the [***a***] ***flag*** 《スポーツ》(競走の出発, または決勝の合図に)旗を振り降ろす; 出発[終了]の合図をする ▪ One of the judges there *drops a flag*. そこにいる審判の一人が決勝の合図に旗を降ろす ▪ It was difficult to *drop the flag*. 出発の合図をするのがむずかしかった.

fly the black flag →hoist the black FLAG.

fly the flag **1** 旗を掲げる ▪ The ship was *flying the* British *flag*. 船はイギリスの旗を掲げていた.

2 = show the FLAG 2.

give … the honor of the flag 旗を降ろして相手の優越を認める ▪ We *gave* Holland *the honor of the flag*. 我々は旗を降ろしてオランダの優越を認めた.

hang out the red flag 危険を知らせる; 戦闘(開始)の合図をする ▪ The Chesapeake then *hung out the red flag*. チェサピーク号はそれから戦闘の合図をした.

hang (***out***) [***hoist, raise, wave***] ***the white flag*** 白旗を掲げて降服の意を表す ▪ The government will be *hanging out the white flag*. やがて政府は白旗を掲げるであろう.

hang the flags out →put the FLAGs out.

haul down** one's **flag →lower one's FLAG.

hoist** one's **flag **1** 感情[意見]を表す ▪ The parson *hoisted his flag* by saying that he did not want to do anything. 牧師は自分は何もしたくないのだと言って自分の気持を表明した.

2 (将官が)将旗を掲げる, 艦隊司令の任に当たる ▪ I shall be ordered to *hoist my flag* here. 私はここで艦隊司令の任に当たるよう命じられるだろう.

3 居酒屋を経営する; 魚屋になる.

hoist [***fly***] ***the black flag*** 黒旗を掲げる《海賊であること, 助命なし, 処刑終了を示す》 ▪ *The black flag was hoisted* outside the prison at nine o'clock. 黒旗は9時に刑務所の外に掲げられた ▪ I would *hoist the black flag*. 海賊になりたい.

hold the flag down [***up***] タクシーのフラッグを下げておく《客なし》[上げておく《客あり》].

keep the flag flying 降参しない, 戦闘を続ける ▪ Prof. Carr *kept the flag flying* in the theological seminary. カー教授は神学校で戦い続けた.

like waving [***holding***] ***a red flag in front of a bull*** →like a red rag to a BULL.

lower [***strike***] ***one's*** [***the***] ***flag*** **1** 旗をおろす《敬意・服従・降服を示す》; (討論・競争に)敗北[誤り]を認める ▪ In the debate he had to *lower his flag*. 論戦において彼は敗北を認めねばならなかった.

2 将旗を降ろす, 艦隊司令の任を退く ▪ This morning he *struck his flag* on board the Nassan. 今朝彼はナサン号上の将旗を降ろした.

nail** one's **flag to the mast = nail one's COLORs to the mast.

put* [*hang*] *the flags out (勝利などを)祝う ▪ The whole country *put the flags out* on that day. その日，国じゅうが祝った.

raise red flags 警告を発する，警戒を促す ▪ A new Pentagon report is *raising red flags* over China's new military power. 米国国防総省の新しい報告書は中国の新軍事力に対して警戒を促している.

refuse the honor of the flag → deny ... the honor of the FLAG.

run out* [*show*] *the white flag = hang (out) the white FLAG.

show the flag **1** (英国船が)外国の港などに公式訪問する ▪ Three British vessels *showed the flag* at Aden. 3隻のイギリス船がアデン港を公式訪問した. **2** 旗幟(き)を鮮明にする ▪ The leaders must *show the flag*. 指導者たちは旗幟を鮮明にしなければならない. **3** (会合などに)出席を人に見せるためにだけ出席する ▪ We'll just *show the flag* at the party. パーティーでは出席したことを人に見せるだけにしよう.

take the checkered* [《英》 *chequered*] *flag オートレースで1着になる ▪ Jimmie Johnson *took the checkered flag* and a $1 million winner's check. ジミー・ジョンスンは1位になり，100万ドルの優勝小切手を受けとった.

the flag at half-mast (港内の)船の掲げる弔旗 (→ (at) HALF-MAST) ▪ I noticed *the flag at half-mast*. 私は船の弔旗に気がついた.

The flag falls. 出発[終了]の合図の旗が降りる ▪ He will be there when *the flag falls*. 決勝の旗が降りるときには彼はそこにいるだろう ▪ *The flag* has *fallen*. 出発の合図の旗は降りた.

The flag is down. 青ざめて悲しそうである ▪ It's Lent in your cheeks, *the flag's down*. あなたのほおには四旬節が来ていて青白い. ☞昔，Lent の期間には劇場の旗を降ろして興行をやめたことから.

under the flag of (国・組織)を代表して…の旗の下に ▪ The Korean player was forced to compete *under the flag of* Japan. その韓国の選手は日本代表として競技することを強いられた ▪ Liberals of both sexes united *under the flag of* antifascism. 男女を問わずリベラリストたちが反ファシズムの旗の下に結束した.

wave the flag 党派心(など)をあおる[発揮する] ▪ He thinks the National Theatre an expensive way of *waving the flag*. 国立劇場は愛国心高揚の金のかかる手段と彼は考えている.

wrap* [*drape*] *oneself in the flag 《主に米》錦の御旗を掲げる，私利私欲のために大義名分を振りかざす ▪ The president *wrapped himself in the flag* and achieved re-election. 大統領は錦の御旗を掲げて再選を果たした.

flagpole /flǽgpòʊl/ 名 ***run ... up the flagpole*** 《主に米》 **1** (アイディアなど)を立ち上げる，提案する ▪ Let's *run* this idea *up the flagpole*. この考えを提案しよう. **2** 〚and see who salutes [if it flutters] を伴って〛(新たな計画などの)反応をはかる ▪ "*Run it up the flagpole and see if it flutters*" is a cliche in the advertising business. 「打ち上げて反応を見よう」は広告業界では決まり文句だ.

flagrant /fléɪgrənt/ 形 ***in flagrant delict/in flagrante delicto*** 《戯》現行犯で ▪ She caught her husband *in flagrante delicto* with his secretary. 彼女は夫と秘書の情事の現場を押さえた ▪ He was taken *in flagrant delict*. 彼は現行犯で捕えられた. ☞Ⓛ flagrante delicto 'in the open act'.

flag-wagging /flǽgwæ̀gɪŋ/ 名 ***indulge in flag-wagging*** 仰々しい愛国心を愚かに振り回す ▪ They *indulge in flag-wagging* on the least excuse. 彼らはややもすれば仰々しい愛国心を振り回す.

flail /fleɪl/ 名 ***be threshed with one's own flail*** 他人を扱ったように自分が扱われる ▪ You will *be threshed with your own flail*. 他人を扱ったように自分も扱われるであろう.

flair /fleər/ 名 ***have a flair for*** …の眼識[才能]がある ▪ He *has a flair for* making money. 彼は金儲けの才能がある.

flak /flæk/ 名 ***get* [*take, catch*] (*the*) *flak*** 《口》激しく非難される (*from, for*) ▪ The prime minister still *took the flak from* his people. 首相は依然として国民から激しく非難された ▪ She *got* a lot of *flak for* neglecting her children. 彼女は，育児放棄でひどく非難された. ☞flak「対空射撃」.

run* [*come*] *into a lot of flak 激しい反対にあう (*for, from*) ▪ Mr. Hawley *ran into a lot of flak for* the suggestion. ホーリー氏はその提案で猛反対にあった ▪ The politician *ran into a lot of flak from* his rivals. その政治家は政敵からの激しい反対にあった.

flake[1] /fleɪk/ 名 ***fall in flakes*** 薄片となってはげ落ちる; (雪が)霏々(ひ)として降る ▪ The snow is *falling in flakes*. 雪がちらちら降っている.

flake[2] /fleɪk/, **flakeball** /fléɪkbɔ̀ːl/ 名 《俗》奇人，異常者，支離滅裂な人 ▪ She's just a *flake(ball)* who doesn't have a grip on the real world. 彼女は，現実世界を把握していない異常者にすぎない.

flame /fleɪm/ 名 ***a new flame*** 新しい恋人 ▪ After splitting recently with lawyer Jonathan Kron, Denise has now got *a new flame*. 弁護士のジョナサン・クロンと最近別れたのち，ドゥニーズには新しい恋人ができた.

an old flame 《口》昔の恋人，元彼氏[彼女] ▪ If a man is determined to meet *an old flame*, his wife can't stop him. 男性が昔の恋人に会おうと決意すると，妻は彼を制止できない ▪ I bumped into *an old flame* of mine on the street yesterday. きのう通りで以前の恋人にばったり出会った.

be* (*enveloped*) *in flames (家などが)火炎に包まれる ▪ The house *was in flames*. 家は火炎に包まれていた.

be in a flame 気が立っている ▪ The people *are in a flame* owing to the war news. 国民は戦争のニュースのため気が立っている.

F

burst into flame(s) パッと燃えあがる ▪ The whole house *burst into flames*. 家全体がパッと燃えあがった.

commit [condemn]... to the flames …を焼き捨てる, 火に投ずる ▪ He *committed* the letter *to the flames*. 彼は手紙を焼き捨てた.

fan the flame(s) 情熱をあおり立てる ▪ Everything she said *fanned the flames* of his anger against her. 彼女の言ったことがすべて彼女に対する彼の怒りをあおり立てた.

go down in flames **1** 炎上して墜落する ▪ The plane *went down in flames* minutes after take-off. 飛行機は離陸から数分後に炎上して墜落した.
2《口》失敗する, だめになる; 破滅する ▪ The Yankees *went down in flames* 14–5. ヤンキースは14対5で火だるまになった[大敗した].

go up in flames **1** 燃える, 焼ける ▪ The house *went up in flames*. その家は焼けた.
2 にわかに尽きる, おじゃんになる ▪ His wedding plans *went up in flames*. 彼の結婚計画はご破算になった.

in a [on] flame [flames] 燃えあがって; (傷が)はれあがって; 怒り[熱意, 熱情]に燃えて ▪ Their boat was *in a flame*. 彼らのボートは燃えあがっていた ▪ He [His heart] is *on flame*. 彼[彼の胸]は恋情に燃えている.

set [put]... on [in] flame …を燃え立たせる ▪ It *set* the nation *in flame* against the government. それは国民の政府に対する敵意をあおり立てた ▪ They *set* the ships *on flame*. 彼らは船を全部炎上させた.

shoot... down in flames 《口》(計画・考えなど)がだめだと言う; を論破する ▪ He *shot* my idea *down in flames*. 彼は私の考えはだめだと言った. ☞「飛行機を撃墜する」が原義.

flank /flæŋk/ 動 *A* ***is flanked by [with]*** *B* Aの側面にBがある ▪ The road *was flanked* on each side *by* hills. 道路の両側に小山があった.

flannel /flǽnəl/ 名 ***get [receive, win]*** *one's* ***flannels*** 選手になってチームに入る, 選手になる ▪ Jason *got his flannels* in the cricket team last term. ジェイスンは前学期にクリケット・チームの選手になった. ☞クリケット・フットボールの選手のフランネル製ユニフォームから.

flanneled /flǽnəld/ 形 ***flanneled fools and muddied oafs*** クリケット・テニス・フットボールの選手 ▪ They are *flannelled fools and muddied oafs*. 彼らはクリケット・テニス・フットボールの選手だ.

flap[1] /flæp/ 名 ***get into [be in] a flap*** 《俗》はらはらする[している], あわてる[てている] ▪ Everybody *got into a flap* at the statement. その声明を聞いてみんなあわてた.

flap[2] /flæp/ 動 ***flap*** *one's* ***mouth (about)*** (…について)ばかなこと[むだなこと]をしゃべる ▪ You go *flapping your* silly *mouth about* me. 君は僕についてばかげたことをべらべらしゃべっている.

flare[1] /fleər/ 名 ***a flare up/a flare-up*** 乱闘, 暴動 ▪ The game erupted in the 75th minute with *a flare-up* involving several players. 試合は, 開始75分後に数人のプレーヤーを含む乱闘のため騒然となった.

have a flare up **1** 急にけんかをする ▪ The two boys were *having a flare up*. その二人の少年がけんかをしていた.
2 盛んな祝会を催す ▪ Michael will *have a* real *flare up* for his birthday. マイケルは自分の誕生日のために盛んな祝会を催すでしょう.

flare[2] /fleər/ 動 ***flare a handkerchief*** 《俗》(ポケットから)ハンカチをさっと取る ▪ Just after that I *flared the handkerchief*. すぐそのあと私はそのハンカチをさっと取り出した.

flash[1] /flæʃ/ 名 ***a flash card*** フラッシュカード《数字・単語が書いてあるカード; 授業などで用いる》 ▪ Amanda used *flash cards* to teach kindergartners the alphabet. アマンダは幼稚園児にアルファベットを教えるのにフラッシュカードを用いた.

a flash of lightning **1** 電光 ▪ *A* vivid *flash of lightning* illuminated the graveyard. 強烈な稲妻が墓場を明るく照らした.
2《俗》1杯のジン ▪ *Flashes of lightning* gleamed about. ジンの酒杯が輝きわたった.

a (mere) flash in the pan 火打ち石銃の空発; 線香花火のようなはかない成功, 龍頭蛇尾; 線香花火的な努力をする人 ▪ He missed his shot by *a flash in the pan*. 火打ち石銃の火皿が空発して彼は弾丸を撃ちそこねた ▪ That brilliant poem he wrote when young was *a mere flash in the pan*. 彼が若い時に書いたあのすばらしい詩は線香花火的成功にすぎなかった ▪ The rising at Kilrush was *a mere flash in the pan*. キルラシュの反乱は単なる龍頭蛇尾に終わった. ☞軍事用語から.

(as) quick as a flash 《口》すぐさま, 即座に ▪ *As quick as a flash* he pulled out a gun and shot his attacker dead. 彼はさっとピストルを抜いて襲ってきた相手を射殺した.

hot flashes (更年期の女性の)体のほてり ▪ About 75 percent of menopausal American women experience *hot flashes*. 閉経後のアメリカ人女性の約75パーセントが体のほてりを経験している.

in [like] a flash たちまちに, 即座に ▪ Six months have gone by *like a flash*. 6か月がたちまち過ぎ去った ▪ I will be with him *in a flash*. すぐに彼の所へ参ります.

flash[2] /flæʃ/ 動 ***flash a glance [a look,*** *one's* ***eyes] at [upon]*** …をちらと見る ▪ She *flashed a* defiant *look at* him. 彼女は挑戦的な目で彼をちらと見た ▪ He *flashed his* insolent *eyes upon* her. 彼は横柄な目で彼女をちらと見た.

flash a smile at …ににこっとする ▪ The girl *flashed a smile at* me as if she recognized me. 誰か分かったみたいにその女の子は私ににっこりした ▪ My heart pounded when that beautiful girl *flashed a smile at* me. そのきれいな子が私にむかってにこっとしたので胸がどきどきした.

flash across [into, on, through] *one's* ***mind*** (考えが)急に心に浮かぶ ▪ A good idea *flashed across my mind.* いい考えが急に私の心に浮かんだ.

flash ... dead ...を光で射殺する ▪ This departing glance will *flash* you *dead.* この別れの一べつであなたはまいってしまう.

flash fire (怒り・激情で)火のように輝く ▪ His eyes *flashed fire.* 彼の目は火のように輝いた.

flash in the pan (火打ち石銃が)火皿の中で発火するだけで空発に終わる; 線香花火のように終わる, 龍頭蛇尾に終わる ▪ He attempted a joke which *flashed in the pan.* 彼はしゃれを試みたがうけなかった.

***flash into* [*on*] *one's* mind** →FLASH across one's mind.

***flash it* (*about, away*)** 《口》見栄を張る; さっそうとする ▪ They *flashed it away* in their new clothes. 彼らは新しい服を着てぱりっとしていた.

flash terror into the heart of ...の心胆を寒からしめる ▪ His name would *flash terror into the hearts of* his adversaries. 彼の名は敵の肝を冷やすであろう.

***flash through* *one's* mind** →FLASH across one's mind.

***flash upon* *a person's* sight** ちらと目に写る ▪ The scene *flashed upon my sight.* その光景はちらと私の目に写った.

flat /flæt/ 形副名 ***(as) flat as a board*** 全くぺしゃんこで ▪ Her chest was *as flat as a board.* 彼女の胸は全くのぺしゃんこ[ペチャパイ]だった. ☞「少し丸味がほしい」の意を含む.

***(as) flat as a pancake* [*a flounder*]** 《口》全く平坦で; (バストが)小さい; こてんぱんに ▪ This district is *as flat as a flounder.* この地方は全く平坦である ▪ The woman was *as flat as a pancake.* その女性の胸はぺしゃんこだった ▪ I knocked him down *flat as a pancake.* 彼をこてんぱんにたたき倒した. ☞flounder は pancake より《まれ》.

be flat broke すかんぴんの, 一文なしの ▪ Harry *was* declared *flat broke* in court today. ハリーはきょう法廷で無一文だと宣告された.

fall flat **1** ばったり倒れる[伏せる] ▪ The wounded man *fell flat* on the floor. 負傷した男は床の上にばったり倒れた.

2 (話・文などが)興を引かない; 効き目がない; 全く失敗する ▪ His speech *fell flat* on the audience. 彼の話は聴衆の興を引かなかった ▪ Your excuses *fall flat* on me. 君の言い訳は私には通らない.

3 (くわだてなどが)失敗する ▪ Their plans *fell flat* completely. 彼らの計画は完全に失敗した. ☞flat「気の抜けた」.

fall flat as a pancake 少しもおもしろくない, 興を引かない ▪ His story *fell flat as a pancake.* 彼の話は少しも人の興を引かなかった.

***fall flat on* *a person's* ears** =fall FLAT 2.

***fall* (*flat*) *on* *one's* face** →FACE[1].

***feel flat* (*as a pancake*)** 《口》元気がない, 意気消沈している ▪ I've long been *feeling flat.* 私は長い間元気がなかった.

fix a flat パンクしたタイヤを直す ▪ In garages they *fix flats.* 自動車修理場でパンクのタイヤを直してくれる.

flat down ぺったりと(座る, など) ▪ He sat *flat down* on the floor. 彼は床にぺたりと座った.

flat out 《口》 **1** 全速力で; 一生懸命に ▪ He went *flat out.* 彼は全速力で行った. ☞馬が gallop するときの姿勢から.

2 すっかり疲れて(寝ころんで) ▪ She was (lying) *flat out* in the bedroom. 彼女は疲れはてて寝室に横になっていた.

3 あからさまに, ずけずけと ▪ I haven't *flat out* asked if he's going to run for President. 彼が大統領に立候補するつもりかどうかあからさまに訊ねたことはない.

from the flat 画を手本として《彫刻などの立体模型を手本とするに対して》 ▪ He drew it *from the flat.* 彼はそれを画を手本にして描いた.

get a flat 《口》タイヤがパンクする ▪ I've *got a flat.* タイヤがパンクした.

give the flat 《米口》(求婚を)すげなく断る ▪ She *gave the flat* to her suitors. 彼女は求婚者たちをすげなく断った.

go flat (タイヤが)パンクする; (電池が)切れる; (炭酸飲料などが)気が抜ける ▪ A tire *went flat* on Interstate 95 in Springfield. スプリングフィールドの州間幹線道路95号線でタイヤがパンクした.

in no time* [*nothing*] *flat 瞬く間に ▪ She got dressed *in no time flat.* 彼女は瞬く間に服を着た.

in* [*on*] *the flat 紙に, 画布に, 絵に, 平面に (↔in RELIEF 1) ▪ He represented it *in* [*on*] *the flat.* 彼はそれを画布に描いた.

join the flats 首尾一貫させる, 統一をとる ▪ *The flats* of the new edition *are* well *joined.* 新版はうまく統一がとられている. ☞flat (舞台の背景の一部)を組み合わせて完全な背景を作ることから.

lay ... flat ...をぺしゃんこに倒す[倒壊させる] ▪ They *laid* the city *flat.* 彼らはその都市をぺしゃんこにした.

leave* *a person* *flat **1** 《口》人の所を急に去る, 急に人を見捨てる ▪ He *left* the group *flat.* 彼は急にそのグループから去った ▪ My car ran out of gas and *left* me *flat.* 車のガソリンが切れて私は途方に暮れた.

2 (話などが)おもしろくない, つまらない ▪ We listened carefully to his lecture, but it *left* us *flat.* 彼の講義を注意して聴いたが, おもしろくなかった.

3 一文無しにする ▪ The robber took all my money and *left* me *flat.* 強盗は私の全財産を奪って, 1円も残さなかった.

on the flat →in the FLAT.

on the same flat 同一水準[平面]上に.

sharps and flats **1** (ピアノ・オルガンの)黒鍵 ▪ They were thin rectangular objects like the *sharps and flats* of a piano. それらはピアノの黒鍵のように長方形の物体だった.

2 詐欺師とその被害者 ▪ There are *sharps and flats* in Paris. パリには詐欺師とその餌食になる者がいる.

3 武器に訴えること ▪ He was hasty with his *flats and sharps.* 彼は軽々しく武器に訴えた.

That's flat. 《口》断然そうだ; それが私の最終的な言葉だ ▪ I'm not coming, and *that's flat.* 私は行かないと言ったら行きません ▪ You're a liar, and *that's flat.* あなたはまさに嘘つきです.

flat-footed /flætfótəd/ 形 ***catch*** *a person* ***flat-footed*** 《口》人に不意打ちをくわせる; 人の現行犯を捕える ▪ He *was caught flat-footed.* 彼はまんまとつかまった. ☞サッカー選手が前進できないうちに相手にタックルされることから.

come out flat-footed 《口》(自分の意見などを)大胆にはっきり言う ▪ He has *come out flat-footed* for the administration. 彼は政府支持をはっきり表明した ▪ They *came out flat-footed* with the demand. 彼らはその要求を大胆に述べた. ☞flat-footed「しっかりと両足で立って」.

F

flatter /flætər/ 動 ***be flattered by*** …でひどくうれしがる ▪ He *was flattered by* her attentions. 彼女のもてなしがよいので彼はひどくうれしがった.

feel (*oneself*) ***flattered by*** …で大いにうれしがる ▪ She *felt flattered by* their approval. 彼女は彼らの賛成を得て大得意であった.

flatter but [***only***] ***to deceive*** うれしがらせを言ってあざむく ▪ A fine morning *flatters only to deceive.* 朝の好天はぬか喜びをさせるくわせものである.

flatter *oneself* (***that***) 得意になって…と思う, 虫よくも…と思う ▪ I rather *flatter myself that* I am no fool. はばかりながらばかではないつもりです ▪ I don't *flatter myself that* he will forgive me. 彼が許してくれるだろうなどと虫のよいことは考えない.

You flatter me. それはお世辞でしょう.

flatterer /flætərər/ 名 ***When flatterers meet, the devil goes to dinner.*** 《諺》おべっか者が集まれば, 悪魔は用がなくなる《おべっかは非常に有害な働きをするので悪魔は休んでいてよい》.

flattery /flætəri/ 名 ***Flattery will get you nowhere.*** 《戯》おべんちゃらを言っても何も出ないよ ▪ *Flattery will get you nowhere*; but bosses need strokes too. おべんちゃらを言っても何も出ないが, 上司も褒め言葉を必要としている.

flaunt /flɔːnt/ 動 ***flaunt it away*** [***out, forth***] 美服を見せびらかすために歩き回る; 自慢げに厚かましく人に見せつけようとする ▪ They will *flaunt it away* in a chariot and six. 彼らは6頭立ての馬車に乗って自慢げに人に見せつけるであろう.

If you've got it, flaunt it. 《口》(いいものを)もっているなら隠さず見せなさい.

flavor, 《英》**flavour** /fléɪvər/ 名 ***the flavo***(***u***)***r of the month*** [***week, year***] 《主に英》その月[週, 年]の人気者・流行の品 ▪ I don't think voters are jumping on Romney because he is *the flavor of the month.* ロムニーがその月に人気があったからといって有権者たちが彼に流れているとは思わない ▪ National bonds were *the flavor of the year.* 国債がその年の人気商品だった.

flaw /flɔː/ 名 ***pick flaws in*** =pick HOLEs in.

flay /fleɪ/ 動 ***flay*** *a person* ***alive*** =SKIN a person alive.

flea /fliː/ 名 ***a flea in*** *one's* ***ear*** 《口》苦言, いやみ, 当てこすり ▪ He went away with *a flea in his ear* like a cur. 彼はのら犬のようにしかられて逃げて行った. ☞犬が耳にノミが入るとじっとしていられず走り去ることから.

a mere flea-bite ほんのささいなこと[少量] ▪ Five pounds is *a mere flea-bite* to him. 5ポンドは彼にとってはほんの少額である.

not hurt a flea [***fly***] 虫も殺さない, 誰にもけがをさせない ▪ He was a good-hearted person who would*n't hurt a flea.* 彼は, 虫も殺さぬような思いやりのある人だった.

send *a person* ***away with a flea in*** *his* ***ear*** いやみ[苦言]を言って人を追い払う (→a FLEA in one's ear) ▪ He asked for money but I *sent* him *away with a flea in his ear.* 彼はお金を無心してきたが, 私はいやみを言って追い返した.

fleck /flek/ 動 (***be***) ***flecked with*** …ではん点をつけられる ▪ The sky *was flecked with* clouds. 空には雲が点々とあった.

flee /fliː/ 動 ***flee for it*** 逃げる ▪ Without speaking, I *fled for it.* 物を言わずに私は逃げた.

fleet /fliːt/ 形 (***be***) ***fleet of foot*** 《雅》足が速い ▪ All dance styles require *fleet of foot* movement. 全てのダンスの様式は足の速い動きを必要とする.

plow [***sow***] ***fleet*** 浅く表面に近く耕やす[種をまく] ▪ The land *is plowed fleet.* 土地は浅く耕やされている.

flesh[1] /fleʃ/ 名 ***after the flesh*** 肉によって; 世俗的に, 人間並みに (《聖》*John* 8. 15; *2 Cor.* 5. 16) ▪ Ye judge *after the flesh.* あなたがたは肉によって人をさばく ▪ He does things *after the flesh.* 彼は物事を人間並みにする.

all flesh すべての動物; すべての人間 (《聖》*Isa.* 40. 6) ▪ *All flesh* is grass. 人はみな草だ.

an arm of flesh/the arm of the flesh 肉の腕; 人の力; 物質の力; 人力による援助 (《聖》*2 Chron.* 32. 8) ▪ With him is *an arm of flesh.* 彼と共におる者は肉の腕である《肉の腕は人力で, 神と対照される》 ▪ In such peril *the arm of the flesh* could do but little. そのような危険に際しては人の力は大した働きをなしえなかった.

(***be***) ***in flesh*** 太って(いる); 肉がついて(いる) ▪ The oxen *were in flesh.* 雄牛どもはよく太っていた.

be made flesh 肉体として具現する ▪ God *was made flesh* in the form of Jesus Christ. 神はイエス・キリストの姿で肉体として具現した.

exact *one's* ***pound of flesh*** →POUND[1].

fish, flesh, and fowl 魚肉, 獣肉, 鳥肉 ▪ She never touches *fish, flesh or fowl.* 彼女は肉類には一切箸をつけない.

flesh and fell **1** 肉も皮も, 全身 ▪ He will devour them, *flesh and fell.* 彼は彼らの肉も皮も食い尽くすだろう.

2 すっかり ▪ They burned the household, *flesh and fell.* 彼らはその一家をすっかり焼いてしまった.

flesh is heir to (生身の)人間は…を受ける (cf. Sh.,

Haml. 3. 1. 62) ▪ *Flesh is heir to* many ills. 人間は多くの病苦にかかる.

flesh of *one's* ***flesh*** 密接な関係にある, 同族である (《聖》*Gen.* 2. 23) ▪ He looked on Napoleon as *flesh of his flesh.* 彼はナポレオンを自分の同族とみなしていた.

get [***gain, gather, make***] ***flesh*** 肉がつく ▪ You have *got flesh.* あなたは肉がついた.

go after [***follow***] ***strange flesh*** 背倫の肉欲にふける, 男色をあさる (《聖》*Jude* 7) ▪ Sodom and Gomorrha *followed strange flesh.* ソドムとゴモラは男色をあさった.

go the way of all flesh →WAY.

grow in flesh 肉がつく ▪ You have *grown in flesh.* あなたは肉がついた.

in flesh and blood 肉体の形で, 生き身の ▪ I saw his own person *in flesh and blood.* 私は肉体を備えた彼自身を見た.

in the flesh **1** 生きて, うつし身として (《聖》*Philip.* 1. 22) ▪ St. Paul saw Christ *in the flesh.* 聖パウロはうつし身のキリストを見た ▪ In those days Buddha himself walked *in the flesh.* その頃は仏陀ご自身が生きておられた.
2 体[肉体]の形をとって, 実物の; 自ら, 親しく ▪ No Mrs. Smith appeared *in the flesh.* スミス夫人自らは全然現れなかった ▪ It was a thrill to see a movie star *in the flesh.* 実物の映画スターを見ることはぞくぞくするような喜びであった.
3 (動物を)畜殺したままで《皮をはがないで》 ▪ We roasted the pig *in the flesh.* 皮をはがずに豚を丸焼きにした.

lose flesh 肉が落ちる, やせる (↔put on FLESH) ▪ He *loses flesh* with fretting. 彼はやきもきするからやせるのだ.

make flesh →get FLESH.

make *a person's* [***the***] ***flesh creep*** [***crawl***] 人をぞっとさせる《特に幽霊の話などで》 ▪ His ghost story *made her flesh creep.* 彼の幽霊話は彼女をぞっとさせた.

one flesh (夫婦などの)一体 (《聖》*Gen.* 2. 24) ▪ Marriage makes man and wife *one flesh.* 結婚は夫婦を一体にする ▪ She became *one flesh* with the rest of common humanity. 彼女は他の一般人と一体になった.

press (***the***) ***flesh*** 《俗》(有名人・政治家が選挙演説をして)多くの人と握手をする ▪ After announcing a $13 million clinical school for the hospital, Mr. Howard *pressed the flesh* with the locals. 1,300万ドルの看護学校について公表したのち, ハワード氏は地元民と握手をした.

put flesh on (***the bones of***) …に詳しい情報をつけ加える, に肉うけする ▪ He needs to *put flesh on* the script. 彼は台本に肉うけする必要がある ▪ We must *put flesh on the bones of* basic reform plans. 基本的な変更計画に肉うけしなければならない.

put [***take***] ***on flesh*** 肉がつく, 太る (↔lose FLESH) ▪ He was *putting on flesh.* 彼はだんだん肉がついていた.

rise [***raise***] ***in flesh and fell*** 肉体のまま生き返る[生き返らす] ▪ He *rose* up *in flesh and fell* the third day. 彼は3日目に肉体のまま生き返った.

the arm of the flesh →an arm of FLESH.

the days of his flesh 彼のこの世にいた間《the Incarnation (神の顕現)に関係した句》 ▪ Jesus himself all *the days of his flesh* endured them. イエス自身もこの世に在世中ずっとそれらを耐えしのんだ.

the flesh is weak (心ははやっていても)肉体が弱くてできない (《聖》*Matt.* 26. 41) (→The SPIRIT is willing, but (the flesh is weak).) ▪ The spirit, I trust, is willing, but *the flesh is weak.* 精神は熱していると思うのだが肉体が弱い.

the flesh-pots (***of Egypt***) (今は無き, またはうらやましい)この世の贅沢品, 良きもの (《聖》*Exod.* 16. 3) ▪ The ladies lamented *the flesh-pots of Egypt.* 女性たちは今は得られなくなったこの世の贅沢品を嘆いた.

flesh[2] /fleʃ/ 動 ***flesh*** *one's* (***maiden, virgin***) ***sword*** (初めて)剣で人を切る; 初めて戦う ▪ Antonius has *fleshed his maiden sword.* アントニウスは初めての剣を使った.

flesh *one's* ***tooth*** (犬などが)ぱくりとかみつく ▪ The dog *fleshed his tooth* in the deer's leg. 犬はシカの足にぱくりとかみついた.

flick /flɪk/ 名 ***at the flick of a switch*** **1** スイッチをパチッと入れれば ▪ The whole building can be illuminated *at the flick of a switch.* スイッチ1つをパチリと入れたら建物全体に明かりがともる.
2 《電算》すばやく簡単に ▪ Federal cops can tap e-mail *at the flick of a switch.* 連邦警察官はさっと簡単にEメールを傍受できる.

go [***take***] ***to the flicks*** 映画を見に行く[見に連れて行く] ▪ He *took* his girl *to the flicks.* 彼は恋人を映画に連れて行った.

have a flick through …をざっと見る ▪ I *had a flick through* the papers. 私は書類をざっと見た.

flier /fláɪər/ 名 ***take a flier*** 《口》ドサッと落ちる ▪ I *took a flier* straight over the handlebars. 私は自転車のハンドルを越えてドスンと落ちた.

flight /flaɪt/ 名 ***a flight of fancy*** [***imagination***] 現実とかけ離れたふるった空想[想像] ▪ In *a flight of fancy*, the poor clerk saw himself as the boss. 貧乏な事務員は空想をたくましくして自分を社長に見たてた.

a flight of stairs 一続きの階段 ▪ To get to his apartment you have to walk up four *flights of stairs.* 彼の部屋へ行くには4続きの階段を歩いて上がらねばならない.

in flight 飛行中に; 機内用の ▪ They looked like something the astronauts might have to eat *in flight.* それらは, 宇宙飛行士たちが飛行中に摂るかもしれない食べもののようだった.

in full flight 全力で疾走[逃走]中で, 一目散に逃亡して ▪ Terry was *in full flight* toward the goal. テリーはゴール目指して疾走中だった ▪ The robbers were *in full flight* before the bank manager even called the sheriff. 銀行の支店長が保安官に電話さえできないうちに強盗たちは雲を霞と逃走していた.

in the first flight 《口》先頭に立って; 重要な地位を占めて ▪ His sisters were all *in the first flight*. 彼の姉妹たちはみな先頭に立っていた.

make a* [*one's*] *flight 飛ぶ ▪ I must attempt new ways to *make my flight* to fame. 私は名声目指して飛んで行く新しい方法を試みねばならない.

on a flight 飛んでいる時 ▪ *On* long *flights* the bees remain on true bearing. 長く飛んでいる時, ミツバチはずっと正しい方向を取る.

put ... to flight ...を逃走させる ▪ The Persians *were put to flight*. ペルシャ軍は敗走した.

seek safety in flight →SAFETY.

take* (*a*) *flight **1** (空中を)飛ぶ, 飛び立つ; (天体が)走る ▪ The racket strikes and so the ball *takes flight*. ラケットで打つとボールが飛ぶ ▪ The birds *took flight*. 鳥はみな飛び立った.

2 逃げる ▪ All three men *took flight* on foot. 3人の男たちは全員歩いて逃げた.

take* [*wing*] *one's flight 飛ぶ, 飛行する ▪ They tried to *wing their flight* to fame. 彼らは名声目指して飛んで行こうと努めた.

take to flight 逃走[逃亡]する ▪ The French *took to flight*. フランス軍は敗走した.

the Flight into Egypt 《聖》エジプトへの脱出《ヘロデ王の幼児虐殺を避けてイエスとその両親がエジプトに逃れたこと》.

flinch /flɪntʃ/ 動 ***flinch one's glass*** 酒杯をあけるのを避ける ▪ Lewis, by *flinching his glass*, kept himself sober as a judge. ルイスは酒杯をあけるのを避けずっとしらふで通した.

flinch the flagon (飲まないで)酒びんを次へ回す ▪ That time you *flinched the flagon*. あのときはあなたは飲まずに酒びんを次へ回した.

flinderation /flìndəréɪʃən/ 名 ***knock* [*break*] *... to flinderation*** 《米俗》...をめちゃくちゃにこわす ▪ The vase *was knocked to flinderation*. 花びんはめちゃくちゃにこわされた.

flinders /flíndərz/ 名 ***break in flinders*** みじんに砕ける ▪ The glass *broke in flinders*. コップはみじんに砕けた.

fly in* [*be blown to*] *flinders みじんに砕け散る ▪ The glass *flew in flinders*. コップはこっぱみじんに砕け散った.

fling[1] /flɪŋ/ 名 ***a final fling*** 最後のひととき[団らん, 行動] ▪ Paris Hilton has had *a final fling* before she heads to jail. パリス・ヒルトンは収監される前に最後の団らんを楽しんだ.

at a* [*one*] *fling 一挙に, 一気に ▪ He did it *at a fling*. 彼は一気にそれをした.

have a fling at 《口》 **1** ...に石を投げつける ▪ The boys were *having a fling at* a stone lantern. 男の子らが石灯籠に石を投げていた.

2 ...をちょっと攻撃する, ののしる; をからかう; を傷つけようとする ▪ I'm going to *have a fling at* his wife. 彼の妻をからかってやろうと思っている ▪ Won't you *have a fling at* Spain? ちょっとスペインを攻撃してやらないか.

3 ...をちょっとやってみる ▪ He is going to *have a fling at* the game. 彼はそのゲームをちょっとやってみようと思っている. ☞石投げ器から石を射ることから.

have* [*embark on*] *a fling with 浮気をする ▪ About 12 years ago, when waitressing in a cafe, I *had a fling with* a customer. およそ12年前, カフェでウェイトレスをしていたころ, お客と浮気をしたことがある.

***have one's fling* (*out*)** 《口》 **1** 思う存分遊興する ▪ I should like to *have my fling out* before I marry. 結婚前に, 存分に遊んでみたいものだ.

2 (したい放題に)存分にやる ▪ Let him *have his fling*! 彼に思う存分やらせておけ!

in a fling かんしゃくを起こして ▪ He has done such a thing *in a fling*. 彼は腹だちまぎれにそんなことをしたのだ.

take one's fling =have one's FLING (out) 1.

try one's fling さいころを投げて運を試す ▪ I've *tried my fling*, and I've lost. 私はさいころを投げてみたが負けだった.

fling[2] /flɪŋ/ 動 ***fling oneself about*** おどりあがる, あばれ回る ▪ He *flung himself about* in anger. 彼は怒ってあばれ回った.

***fling oneself at a person* [*a person's head*]** (女性が)男に猛烈にもちかける, 夫にしようと追い回す ▪ In the summer of 1816, Clairmont had *flung herself at* Byron and got pregnant, only to be rejected by him. 1816年の夏, クレアモントはバイロンに捨て身で言い寄って妊娠したが, 拒絶されてしまった ▪ Susan *flung herself at the head of* my friend. スーザンは私の友人を夫にしようと猛烈にもちかけた.

fling back one's head 頭を後ろへそらす《高慢な態度》 ▪ She *flung her head back*. 彼女は頭を後ろへそらした.

fling down all one's hopes せっかくの希望をおじゃんにする, すっかり絶望にする ▪ This failure *flung down all his hopes*. この失敗で彼の望みは全く消えた.

***fling one's eyes on* [*over*]** ...をちらりとながめる[見渡す] ▪ He *flung his eyes on* the crowd. 彼は群衆をちらりとながめた.

***fling in one's cards* [*hand*]** 《口》トランプ遊びをやめる ▪ I'll *fling my cards in* and go to bed. トランプをやめて寝よう.

***fling ... in a person's teeth* [*face*]** (事実・過失)を突きつけて人を面責する; 人に(不愉快な過去のこと)をことさらに思い出させる ▪ The maxim about brevity being the soul of wit *was flung in my teeth*. 「言は簡を尊ぶ」という格言が私を非難するために突きつけられた ▪ He raked up her past history and *flung* it *in her teeth*. 彼は彼女の過去の経歴をほじくり立てて, それをことさらに彼女に思い出させた.

fling oneself into **1** ...の中へ身を投げる ▪ He *flung himself into* a chair. 彼はどしんといすに腰かけた.

2 (衣服)を大急ぎで着る ▪ I *flung myself into* my clothes. 大急ぎで服を着た.

3 (事業などに)打ち込む; 全力をあげて取りかかる ▪ She *flung herself into* the rebellion. 彼女はその反乱に身を投じた ▪ He *flung himself into* the enterprise. 彼は全力をあげてその事業に着手した.

***fling** oneself **on** [**upon**]* **1** (仕事)に猛然と取りかかる ▪ He *flung himself upon* the task. 彼はその仕事に猛然と取りかかった.

2 …に飛びかかる, 猛烈に攻撃する ▪ We *flung ourselves upon* the enemy. 敵に猛烈にかかっていった.

3 …に身をゆだねる, にすがる ▪ She *flung herself on* his compassion. 彼女は彼のあわれみにすがった.

fling ... open **1** …を急に開く, 激しく開く ▪ He *flung* the door *open*. 彼は戸を急に開いた.

2 …入場[参加]自由とする ▪ The tennis competition *was flung open* to professionals. そのテニス競技はプロにも参加自由とされた.

fling up** one's **arms** [**hands**] **in horror ぞっとして両手をあげる ▪ She *flung up her hands in horror* at the sight. 彼女はそれを見て恐ろしさに両手をあげた.

fling up** one's **hands in despair 絶望して両手をあげる ▪ I *flung up my hands in despair* when I failed another exam. ふたたび試験に失敗して私はすっかり絶望した.

fling up** one's **heels **1** 足早に行く ▪ The horse was *flinging up his heels*. 馬は足早に走っていた.

2 楽しく過ごす ▪ I *flung up my heels* last Sunday. この前の日曜は楽しく過ごした.

flint /flɪnt/ 名 ***(as) hard as (a) flint*** きわめて堅く[頑固で]; きわめて冷酷な ▪ He is *as hard as flint* where business is concerned. 彼は商売のことになると血も涙もない.

(as) true as flint 忠誠心がきわめて堅い ▪ Tom was *as true as flint*. トムはきわめて誠実だった.

***fix** a person's **flint for** him* 《俗》人を罰する, やっつける ▪ I'll *fix his flint for* him. 私が彼を懲らしめてやろう.

flay* [*skin*] *a flint 《口》(火打ち石の皮をはぐほど)けちけちする; 強欲にしぼれるだけしぼる ▪ She would *flay a flint* if she could. 彼女はできればつめにでも火をともすだろう ▪ He will *skin the flint* of a miser. 彼はけちんぼうからでもしぼれるだけしぼる.

get* [*wring*] *water from a flint 奇跡的または不可能なことをする ▪ It is hard to *get water from a flint*. 奇跡を行うことはむずかしい.

like flint きわめて堅く, 冷酷で ▪ They have hearts *like flint*. 彼らはきわめて冷酷な心をしている.

set** one's **face like a flint 堅く決心する, 確固不動の態度をとる (《聖》*Isa*. 50. 7) ▪ I have *set my face like a flint* against such an idea. そんな考えには断固反対だ.

flip /flɪp/ 動 ***flip a coin*** →toss a COIN.

***flip** one's **lid** [**wig**]* 《俗》自制を失う, かっとなる ▪ He suddenly *flipped his lid*. 彼は急に逆上した.

flipper /flípər/ 名 ***give** a person **(a tip of)** one's **[the] flipper*** 《俗》人に手を与える《握手のため》 ▪ Please *give* me *a tip of your flipper*. 握手しましょう.

flirt /fləːrt/ 動 ***flirt a* [*one's*] *fan*** 扇をあでやかに使う, ひらひら使う ▪ She *flirted her fan* with such a fury. 彼女は猛烈に扇を使った.

flirt with death 命知らずのことをやる, 大きな危険を冒す ▪ The fireman was *flirting with death*. その消防士は大きな危険を冒していた.

float[1] /floʊt/ 名 ***on the float*** 《英》浮かんで, 漂って ▪ There was a log *on the float*. 丸太が1本浮かんでいた.

float[2] /floʊt/ 動 ***float in** one's **cups*** ほろ酔いである ▪ Mr. Smith, *floating in his cups*, began a discourse. スミス氏はほろ酔いきげんで談義を始めた.

float on the wind (音楽・香りが)風に乗って漂ってくる; (風説が)流布する ▪ The sweet scent came *floating on the wind*. 芳香が風に乗って漂ってきた.

flock /flɑk|flɔk/ 名 ***a flock of*** …の群れ, たくさんの ▪ I saw *a flock of* sheep without a shepherd. 羊飼いのいない羊の群れを見た ▪ He sent me *a flock of* pamphlets. 彼は多くのパンフレットを送ってよこした.

in flocks 大勢で, 大挙して ▪ Visitors came *in flocks*. 客が大勢で来た.

like a flock of sheep 羊の群れのように《服従・集合・拡散して》 ▪ In every way they act just *like a flock of sheep*. あらゆる点で彼らは全く羊の群れのようにおとなしく行動する ▪ *Like a flock of sheep* they flock around when they sight an oncoming bus. バスが来るのを見ると, 彼らは羊の群れのように寄り集まる ▪ The rebels scattered *like a flock of sheep* on being fired upon. 反乱者たちは発砲されるとクモの子を散らすように散らばって行った.

shepherd** one's **flock (牧師が教区内の信者に)精神的指導を与える, 神の教えへと導く ▪ John Paul *shepherded his flock* by going out to them. ヨハネ・パウロは信者の群に自ら寄っていって彼らを導いた.

flog /flɑg|flɔg/ 動 ***flog a dead horse*** → HORSE[1].

flog a willing horse 《口》精いっぱい働いている人をもっと働かせようとする ▪ Why do you want to *flog a willing horse*? なぜ力いっぱい働いている人をもっと働かせようとするのか.

flog the clock 《口》時計の針を進める ▪ I got suspicious that *the clock* was *being flogged*. 私は時計の針が進められているのではないかと疑った.

flog ... to death →DEATH.

flood[1] /flʌd/ 名 ***at the flood*** 潮が満ちて, よい潮時に[で] ▪ The tide is *at the flood*. 潮が満ちている.

before the Flood (Noah の洪水以前, とは)大昔 ▪ That old car looks as if it dates from *before the Flood*. あの古自動車はまるでノアの洪水以前からあるかのようだ.

flood and field 水陸, 海陸 ▪ For a power of description of the beauties of *flood and field*, no writer can surpass Thomas Hardy. 水陸の美の描写力において, トマス・ハーディーをしのぐ者はいない.

floods of tears 涙の洪水, 滂沱(ぼうだ)の涙 ▪I found myself missing him so much I was in *floods of tears.* 自分は彼をとても愛しているのだと気づいて涙がとめどなくあふれた.

in flood はんらんして ▪The rivers were *in flood.* 川ははんらんしていた.

in full flood 盛んに, とうとうと ▪When he began to talk, all his complaints came out *in full flood.* 彼が話しだすと彼のすべての苦情がとめどなく出てきた.

reach** one's **flood 最高潮に達する ▪Wiggins *reached his flood* in his thirties and wrote little of merit thereafter. ウィギンズは30歳台で絶頂に達しその後は注目に値する作品はほとんど書けずじまいだった.

take ... at the flood …の最高潮のときを利用する, 最高潮の…に乗る ▪You must *take* a tide *at the flood.* 満ち潮に乗らねばならない.

the flood tide 盛り, 満潮時, 絶頂 ▪At *the flood tide* of his success the doctor was earning ten thousand pounds a year. 成功の絶頂時にはその医者は1年に1万ポンド儲けていた.

flood[2] /flʌd/ 動 ***be flooded with*** …がはんらんする, が殺到する ▪The office *was flooded with* applications. 願書が事務所に殺到した.

flood with tears (目が)涙にあふれる ▪His eyes *flooded with tears* of grief over his nephew's death. おいの死を悲しんで彼の目には悲しみの涙が溢れた.

floodgate /flʌ́dgèɪt/ 名 ***open* [*loose*] *floodgates of*** (愛情など)のせきを切る, 思う存分…を表す, せきを切ったように…する; の重しをとる ▪He *opened floodgates of* grief. 彼は思う存分悲嘆を表した ▪The new regime shut *the floodgates opened* by Gorbachev. 新体制は, ゴルバチョフによってはずされた重しを閉じた.

the floodgates open 重しがとれる, 事態が一変する ▪Once the six men and six women were guaranteed anonymity, *the floodgates open*ed. 6人の男性と6人の女性に匿名が保証されると, 事態が一変した.

floor[1] /flɔːr/ 名 ***bring** a person **in on the ground floor*** 人を(事業などに)発足時メンバーとして採用[配置]する, 一から始めさせる ▪He *was brought in on the ground floor* of Stratos in 1984, and remained the company's sales director until Jan. 31, 2006. 彼は, 1984年にストラトス社の発足時メンバーとして採用され, 2006年1月31日まで当社の販売担当重役だった.

clean the floor up with (人)をたたき伏せる, なぐり倒す ▪If you don't shut up, I'll *clean up the floor with* you. 黙らないと, ぶちのめすぞ.

cross the floor 《英》(議会で)反対派に加わる, 政党を変わる; (対談で)反対側につく ▪In 1904, Sir Winston Churchill *crossed the floor*, leaving the Conservative Party to join the Liberal Party. 1904年ウィンストン・チャーチルは所属政党を変更し, 保守党から自由党にくらがえした.

fall* [*drop, go, sink*] *through the floor **1** 《口》床から落ち込むほど驚く ▪I nearly *fell through the floor* when I heard a cry. 私は叫び声を聞いた時ひどく驚いた.

2 (価値が)暴落する, 底値を割る ▪By mid-December gas prices *fell through the floor.* 12月中旬までにガス料金はさらに低下した ▪There was a time in the 1980s when sterling *sank through the floor.* 1980年代ポンドが下がりつづけた時期があった. ☞→sink through the FLOOR.

four* [*three*] *on the floor 《米》(自動車の)4[3]段変速マニュアル・ギアレバー(方式の車) ▪We wanted to have *three on the floor.* (マニュアルの)3段変速式が欲しかった.

from the floor (意見・質問が)一般席[聴衆]から出されて ▪These remarks were followed by more questions *from the floor.* これらの発言につづいてさらなる質問が一般聴衆から出された.

get* [*let*] *in on the ground floor 《口》事業の元からの参加者の分け前または好条件を得る[与える] ▪He wants to *get in on the ground floor.* 彼は元からの参加者の好条件を得たいと言っている ▪He is *letting* me *in on the ground floor* of this offer. 彼は私にこの申し出について元からの参加者と同じ分け前をくれている.

get* [*obtain*] *the floor 発言権を得る ▪He first *got the floor.* 彼が一番に発言権を得た. ☞floor「議会の演壇」.

have* [*hold*] *the floor **1** 議場で発言を続ける ▪Hours later Morris still *had the floor.* 数時間後モリスはまだ発言を続けていた.

2 《口》(あまりにも多く, 他人がいやになるほど)話し続ける ▪The hostess shouldn't *hold the floor* like that at the dinner-table. 女性主催者はディナーの席であのように多弁を弄するべきでない.

keep ... off the floor …の討議を中止する ▪The delegates voted to *keep* the argument *off the floor.* 代表団はその議論を中止することを票決した.

mop the floor with →wipe the FLOOR with.

occupy the floor 議会の演壇を占めている; 発言中である ▪*The floor* at that time *was occupied.* その時は議場では発言が行われていた.

on the first floor 《米》1階に; 《英》2階に ▪The living room is *on the first floor.* 居間は1階[2階]にある.

on the floor **1** 議会にあって ▪All the members were *on the floor.* 議員らは全員議会に出席していた.

2 (映画)製作中で ▪The picture's not *on the floor* yet. その映画はまだ製作中ではない.

put* [*set*] *a floor under …の最低限を決める (↔ set a CEILING on) ▪They *put a floor under* wages. 賃金の最低限を決めた.

sink through the floor 非常に当惑する, 穴があったら入りたいと思う (→fall through the FLOOR) ▪I wanted to *sink through the floor* in shame. 恥ずかしくて穴があったら入りたかった.

take the floor **1** 発言のため起立する，起立して発言する ▪ Senator Davis *took the floor* (and spoke). デイビス上院議員は起立して発言した．
2 討論に加わる[を始める] ▪ We *took the floor* again. 我々はまた討論を始めた．
3《文》ダンスするため立ち上がる ▪ They *took the floor* for the next dance. 彼らは次のダンスをするため立ち上がった．

The floor is yours.（議長が発言を求めている者に）よろしい，どうぞ．

through the floor →fall through the FLOOR.

walk the floor 床をあちこち歩いて思案する ▪ Mr. White *walked the floor*, trying to reach a decision. ホワイト氏は結論を出そうとして床をあちこち歩いた．

wipe [***mop***] ***the floor with***《俗》 **1** …をすっかりやっつけてしまう，倒してしまう ▪ The lawyer *wiped the floor with* the prosecutor. その弁護士は検事をさんざんやっつけた．
2 …をきつくしかる ▪ The teacher *wiped the floor with* John for being late. 先生はジョンを遅刻したのできびしくしかった．

floor[2] /flɔːr/ 動 ***floor a paper*** [***an examiner***]《学俗》問題[試験官の質問]を全部答える ▪ I *floored the paper* [*the examiner*]. 私は問題全部[試験官の質問全部]に答えた．

floor it《米口》アクセルを床まで踏み込む，全速で車を走らせる ▪ Sometimes I like to *floor it* just for the joy of the loud sound my exhaust makes. ただもうエキゾーストノートを楽しむために車を全速で走らせたくなることがある．

get floored **1** 打ち倒される，やっつけられる ▪ He *got floored* with a fist. 彼はげんこで打ち倒された．
2《児童俗》すっかり参ってしまう，あわてる; 失敗する，倒れる ▪ He *got floored* by an argument. 彼は口論ですっかり参ってしまった．

flop[1] /flɑp|flɔp/ 名 ***fall flop*** パタリと落ちる ▪ It *fell flop* into the river. それは川へパタリと落ちた．

take a flop どうところぶ; 急落する ▪ I *took a* nasty *flop* on that slippery sidewalk. そのすべりやすい歩道でどうところんだ ▪ Stocks *took a flop* yesterday. きのう株は急落した．

with a flop どっかと ▪ He sat down *with a flop*. 彼はどっかと座った．

flop[2] /flɑp|flɔp/ 動 ***flop*** *oneself* ***down*** どっかとしりをおろす ▪ The old man *flopped himself down* on the grass. その老人は芝生の上にどっかとしりをおろした．

flora /flɔ́ːrə/ 名 ***flora and fauna*** 動植物 ▪ The mercury in the air is harmful to the *flora and fauna* in the biosphere. 空中の水銀は，生物圏の動植物に有害だ．

flotsam /flɑ́tsəm|flɔ́t-/ 名 ***flotsam and jetsam*** **1** 浮き荷と投げ荷《難破貨物と難船のときに船体を軽くするために海中に投げた貨物》 ▪ All the goods of the inhabitants are said to savor of *flotsam and jetsam*. その住民の所有物はみな浮き荷と投げ荷のようなところがあるそうだ．
2 がらくた，はんぱもの ▪ He has a mania for buying all sorts of *flotsam and jetsam*. 彼はあらゆる種類のがらくたの買い入れに目がない．
3 敗残者たち ▪ Starving refugees are the *flotsam and jetsam* of war. 飢えた避難民たちは戦争の敗残者である．

flounce /flaʊns/ 動 ***flounce up and down*** 上下にはねる ▪ The fish *flounced up and down* on the ground. 魚は地面を上下にはねた．

flourish[1] /flə́ːrɪʃ|flʌ́r-/ 名 ***cut a flourish*** 装飾楽句を奏する ▪ I *cut* one of my best *flourishes*. 私の最善の装飾楽句の一つを奏した．

with a flourish 麗々しく，仰々しく; 吹き[振り]立てて ▪ He introduced his guest *with a flourish*. 彼はお客を仰々しく紹介した ▪ I greeted him *with a flourish* of my cane. 杖を一振りして彼にあいさつした．

flourish[2] /flə́ːrɪʃ|flʌ́r-/ 動 ***flourish ... in*** *a person's* ***face*** …を人の鼻先に見せびらかす ▪ He *flourished* the paper *in my face*. 彼はその証書を私の鼻先に見せびらかした．

flourish like a green (***bay-***)***tree*** 大いに繁昌[繁栄]する (*Prayer Book*, Ps. 37. 36) ▪ The wicked may often seem to *flourish like a green tree*. 悪人が大いに繁栄するように見えることがよくある．

flow[1] /floʊ/ 名 ***a flow of spirits*** 大元気 ▪ He has *a flow of spirits*. 彼は大変元気がよい．

at [***on***] ***the flow***（潮が）差して ▪ The tide is *on the flow*. 潮が差している．

go [***move***] ***against the flow***《口》流れ[時流]に逆らう，他人と違うことをする (↔go with the FLOW) ▪ Rachel has *gone against the flow* of what most parents do. レイチェルはほとんどの親がすることとは異なることをした．

go with the flow 流れに身を任せる (↔go against the FLOW) ▪ I just *went with the flow* and ended up in music. なるがままにしていたら，音楽に行き着いた．

in full flow **1**（川などが）とうとうと流れて ▪ The river was *in full flow*. その川はとうとうと流れていた．
2（言葉が）よどみなく流れ出て，熱弁を振るって ▪ Tony Blair was *in full flow* on one of his favourite themes, education. トニー・ブレアは，彼の好みのテーマのうちの一つである教育について熱弁を振るった．
3（仕事などが）活発で，精力的で ▪ Elliott Carter is still *in full flow* at 92. エリオット・カーターは92歳にしてなお精力的に仕事をしている．

the flow of soul（和気あいあいの）交歓，打ち解けた温かい交わり (→the FEAST of reason (and flow of soul)) ▪ The flow of drink induces the feast of reason and *the flow of soul*. 飲み物がまわると高論清談と和気あいあいの交歓が生まれる．

flow[2] /floʊ/ 動 ***ebb and flow***（潮が）差したり引いたりする ▪ The massy waters *ebb and flow*. 広大な海水が差し引きする．

flow like water（酒などが）惜しげもなくふるまわれる

▪ Wine *flowed like water.* ワインが惜しげもなくふるまわれた.

flow with milk and honey 良い物に満ちている (《聖》 *Exod.* 3. 8) ▪ He emigrated to Canada where the land *flowed with milk and honey.* 彼は良い物が豊かなカナダへ移住した.

flower /fláʊər/ 名 ***as welcome as flowers in May*** 喜んで迎えられて, 心から歓迎されて ▪ Your phone calls are *as welcome as flowers in May.* 電話していただければ大歓迎です.

bring ... into flower …に花を咲かせる ▪ The spring rain and mild weather *brought* the daffodils *into flower.* 春の雨と温暖な天気がスイセンの花を咲かせた.

come into flower 花が咲く ▪ The tulips have *come into flower.* チューリップが咲いた.

flowers of speech 文彩, 言葉の飾り, 美辞麗句 ▪ *Flowers of speech* denote the greatness of passion or event. 文彩は感情あるいは出来事がどれほどの広がりを持っているかを示す.

in flower 開花して, 花盛りで ▪ An orchard *in flower* looks delightful. 花盛りの果樹園はよい眺めだ.

in the flower of …の盛りで[に] ▪ He was cut off *in the flower of* his youth. 彼は若い盛りに世を去った.

in the flower of *one's* ***age*** [***life***] 若い盛りで ▪ He is *in the flower of his age.* 彼は若い盛りである ▪ He is a man *in the flower of life,* about thirty. 彼は若い盛りの, 30歳ばかりの男である.

No flowers. 弔花ご辞退《死亡広告の文句》.

Say it with flowers! 思う心を花でお伝えください《花屋の標語》.

flu /fluː/ 名 ***catch the flu*** インフルエンザ(など伝染性の病気)に感染する ▪ So far, humans appear to have *caught the flu* from chickens and other poultry. これまでのところ, 人間はニワトリや他の家禽からインフルエンザに感染したようだ.

flue /fluː/ 名 ***in*** (***the***) ***flue*** 《俗》質に入って ▪ I left my stock *in flue.* 財産を質に入れたままにしておいた. ☞ flue「質物運搬用エレベーター」.

up the flue 《俗》質に入って ▪ My watch is *up the flue.* 私の時計は質に入っている.

fluff /flʌf/ 動 ***fluff*** *oneself* [*one's* ***feathers***] ***out*** [***up***] (鳥が)身ぶるいして体[羽毛]をふくらませる ▪ The bird *fluffed itself out* into a ball. 鳥は身ぶるいして体を丸くした.

fluke /fluːk/ 名 ***by a fluke*** 《口》好運にも ▪ He won *by a fluke.* 彼は運よくまぐれで勝った.

flume /fluːm/ 名 ***go*** [***be***] ***up the flume*** 《米俗》失敗する, やっつけられる, 死ぬ ▪ The great stockholder has *gone up the flume.* その大株主は失敗した.

flummery /flʌ́məri/ 名 ***all flummery*** 見せかけばかりのくだらないもの[こと], ばかなこと ▪ Take away *all* this *flummery* and get this room tidy. この見かけ倒しのがらくたを取り去ってこの部屋を整とんしなさい.

flump /flʌmp/ 名 ***with a flump*** 《口》ドサリと(置く, 落ちる) ▪ It fell *with a flump.* それはドシンと落ちた.

flurry /flə́ːri|flʌ́ri/ 名 ***in a flurry*** 狼狽して, あたふたと ▪ They are all *in a flurry.* 彼らはみなあわてふためいている.

flush[1] /flʌʃ/ 名 ***a busted flush*** 《米口》期待はずれ, 失敗 ▪ I think he is *a busted flush* and his chances of election are sub-zero. 彼は期待はずれであり, 選出される見込みはゼロ以下だと思う ▪ Stockton managed it with *a busted flush.* ストックトンのやり方は失敗だった.

in full flush 今を盛りともえ出て ▪ Young shoots are *in full flush.* 若芽が今を盛りともえ出ている.

in the first flush (***of***) (…の)初めのうちの[つかの間の]歓喜に酔って ▪ They plundered Italy *in the first flush of* victory. 彼らは最初の勝利の感激に酔って, イタリアを略奪した.

in the flush (***of***) **1** (…の)盛りで ▪ He is *in the flush of* youth. 彼は今若い盛りだ.

2 (…に)感激[歓喜]して; (感情・激情を)ほとばしらせて ▪ He was *in the flush of* triumph. 彼は勝利の感激に酔っていた ▪ He said so *in the flush of* his extravagancies for his wife. 妻に対する途方もない感情をほとばしらせて彼はそう言った.

the first flush (***of***) **1** (草・葉・花の)若ばえ ▪ A horse turned out to take *the first flush of* grass. 馬が草の若ばえを食うために出て来た.

2 →in the first FLUSH (of).

flush[2] /flʌʃ/ 形 ***be flush of*** …をたくさん持っている ▪ The West Bank *is flush of* money. ウェスト銀行には金がたくさんある.

be flush with …に気前がいい; がたんまりある ▪ The Obama campaign *is flush with* donations. オバマ氏の選挙運動は寄付金でうるおっている ▪ He *is flush with* money. 彼は金をうんと持っている《his money は不可》.

flush with …と同じ平面の, 同高の ▪ I made the shelf *flush with* the window. 私はたなを窓と同じ高さにした.

flush[3] /flʌʃ/ 動 ***be flushed*** (***with***) (…で)桜色になる; (で)得意になる ▪ His face *was flushed with* wine. 彼の顔はワインで紅潮していた ▪ He *is flushed with* victory. 彼は勝ち誇っている.

flush it 《俗》 **1** 失敗する ▪ I *flushed it* in my history course. 僕は歴史科目を落とした.

2 〚間投詞的に〛ばかな!, 嘘つけ! ▪ He has married? *Flush it!* 彼が結婚したって? そんな, ばかな!

fluster[1] /flʌ́stər/ 名 ***be*** (***all***) ***in a fluster*** (すっかり)あわてている ▪ Mother *was in a fluster.* 母はすっかりあわてていた.

fluster[2] /flʌ́stər/ 動 ***be flustered up*** あわてている, 取り乱している ▪ Jane *was* all *flustered up* before the wedding. ジェインは結婚式の前ですっかり取り乱していた.

fluster *oneself* (頭が混乱して)取り乱す, 度を失う, あわて騒ぐ ▪ I would not *fluster myself* about it.

私だったらそんなことで取り乱しはしない.

flutter[1] /flʌ́tər/ 名 ***be*** (***all***) ***in a flutter*** (興奮して)胸をどきどきさせている, あわてている ▪ When they heard it, they *were all in a flutter*. 彼らはそれを聞いてすっかりどぎまぎした ▪ No wonder her pulse *was all in a flutter*. 彼女の脈拍がどきどきと打っていたのも当然である.

be all on the flutter 《口》すっかり興奮している, 胸をどきどきさせている《女性語》 ▪ I felt sure he was going to propose to me, and I *was all on the flutter*. あの人がきっと私にプロポーズするという気がしたので, すっかり興奮してどきどきしていました.

cause a flutter →make a FLUTTER.

do [***have***] ***a flutter*** 《口》(…に)少額のかけをする, 少し張る《ばくち・トランプ・競馬・株で》(*at, in*); 飲みさわぐ ▪ I always *have a flutter at* Epsom. 私はいつもエプソム(競馬)に少し張る ▪ I *had a flutter in* mining shares. 私は鉱山株に一山張った.

fall into a flutter どぎまぎしだす ▪ The news made my heart *fall into a flutter*. そのニュースは私の胸をどきどきさせた.

Give her a flutter! 硬貨をひねり上げよ《順番などを決めるため》.

make [***cause***] ***a flutter*** 評判になる, 世間を騒がせる ▪ The rumor *made a flutter* among the ladies. その噂で女性陣は大騒ぎになった ▪ The announcement *caused a* tremendous *flutter*. その発表はすごい評判になった.

put [***throw***] *a person* ***in*** [***into***] ***a flutter*** 人をどぎまぎさせる ▪ Delight *put* her *in a flutter*. 大喜びで彼女は胸をどきどきさせた.

flutter[2] /flʌ́tər/ 動 ***flutter the dovecots*** → DOVECOT.

flutter the ribbons [***ribands***] (***of a coach***) 《俗》(馬車の)馬を追う, 走らす ▪ I used to *flutter the ribbons of the coach*. 私は以前その馬車を駆ったものだ.

flux /flʌks/ 名 ***in a state of flux*** 流動の状態にあって ▪ All things are *in a state of flux*. 万物は流転の状態にある.

fly[1] /flaɪ/ 名 ***a fly in the ointment*** 《口》全体の興をさます事情, 玉にきず (《聖》*Eccl.* 10. 1) ▪ His going with us is *a fly in the ointment*. 彼が我々といっしょに行くのは興ざめだ.

a fly on the wall 壁のハエ; (その場のことを)こっそり見聞きするもの[人] (→FLY-on-the-wall) ▪ I would love to be *a fly on the wall* at lunchtime, to hear the children ask each other what they believe. 昼食時に壁のハエになって, 子供たちが信じていることを互いに尋ねるのをそっと聞きたい.

be dropping like flies (動物・人が)ばたばた死んで[病気になって]いる ▪ The heat was deadly and cows *were dropping like flies*. 暑さは殺人的で牛がばたばた死んでいた.

break [***crush***] ***a fly on the wheel*** → WHEEL[1].

descend [***be***] ***like flies on*** [***around***] …に大量に押しかける[襲いかかる] ▪ Backpackers *descend like flies on* this historic coastal wilderness. バックパッカーが, この歴史に名高い海辺の地に押しかけてくる.

die like flies ころころ[ばたばた]死ぬ ▪ In the hold they *died like flies*. 船倉では彼らはころころ死んだ.

Don't let flies stick to your heels. 早くしないとかかとにハエがたかるぞ; ぐずぐずするな, 早くせよ ▪ *Don't let flies stick to your heels*, and don't let ten minutes get the start of you. ぐずぐずするな, 10分も遅れてはだめだよ.

drop like flies **1** =die like flies (→FLY[1]).
2 次々に倒産する[つぶれる] ▪ In the 1980s, small opera companies in this city *dropped like flies*. 1980年代この市の小歌劇団は次々に閉鎖された.

fly-on-the-wall 〚限定的〛(テレビで出演者が)撮影を意識しない; ありのままの (→a FLY on the wall) ▪ The BBC's latest *fly-on-the-wall* documentary is a surprise hit. ありのままを撮った BBC の最近のドキュメンタリーは意外なヒット作品だ.

have no flies on 《俗》活発である, 抜け目がない; 欠点がない ▪ It *has no flies on* it. それは申し分がない ▪ He *hasn't* any *flies on* him. 彼は敏活である.

rise to the fly だまされる, ペテンにかかる ▪ Say that you are ill and he *rises to the fly*. 病気だと言いなさい. そうすれば彼はそれにだまされる. ☞魚が fly (蚊ばり)を食おうと上がって来て捕えられることから.

run round [***around***] ***like a blue-arsed fly*** 《英口》忙しそうに[あわただしく, そそくさと]走り回る ▪ He is *running around like a blue-arsed fly* making preparations for his visitors. 彼はお客を迎える準備に忙しそうに走り回っている ▪ I've been *running around like a blue-arsed fly* all morning. 午前中ずっとあわただしく走り回っていた.

send *a person* ***away with a fly in*** *a person's* ***ear*** 人に耳の痛いことを言って追い払う ▪ The prince *sent* him *away with a fly in his ear*. 親王は彼に耳の痛いことを言って追い払った.

swarm like flies around (…の周りに)大挙して群がる ▪ Lobbyists *swarm like flies around* the folks on Capitol Hill. ロビイストたちは国会議員の周りに群がる.

(***there are, there's***) ***no flies on*** 《俗》 **1** …は敏活である, 抜け目がない (→have no flies on (→FLY[1])) ▪ He bought cheaply and sold at a good profit. *There are no flies on* him. 安く買って相当の利を取って売った. 彼は抜け目がない ▪ *No flies on* him. 彼は敏腕である.
2 …には欠点がない ▪ *There are no flies on* his manners. 彼の行儀には少しも欠点がない.
3 (取引)にいかがわしい点はない, うしろめたい点はない ▪ This is a bona-fide offer. *No flies on* my business. これは誠意ある売り物です. 私の商売にはいかがわしい点はありません.

You can catch more flies with honey than with vinegar. 《諺》ハエをとるには酢より蜜, 「ことを成すには威圧するより下手(したて)に出よ」.

You must lose a fly to catch a trout. 《諺》マスを捕るにはハエを失わねばならない,「肉を斬らせて骨を断つ」.

***would* [*could*] *not hurt* [*harm*] *a fly* [*flea*]** 《口》(怖いと思われている人[動物]がハエも傷つけないほど)優しい, おとなしい ▪ Tom *wouldn't hurt a fly.* トムはとてもおとなしい[優しい].

fly[2] /flaɪ/ 名 ***fly-by-night*** **1** (支払いができなくて)夜逃げする人 ▪ Hotels take credit card numbers in advance to preempt *fly-by-nights.* 夜逃げ客を防止するためホテルはクレジットカードの番号を予め控えておく. ☞もと魔女のこと.

2 〖限定的〗(人・会社などが)信頼できない, 怪しげな ▪ He's not a *fly-by-night* manager. 彼はうさんくさい支配人ではない ▪ The police raided the *fly-by-night* casino in Queens. 警察はクイーンズ地区の怪しげなカジノの強制捜索をした.

on the fly **1** 飛行中で[に], 飛んで ▪ The bird was *on the fly.* 鳥は飛んでいた.

2 《米》(打った球がフライになって)球がグランドに落ちないうちに ▪ If the ball should be caught *on the fly*, he is out. 万一ボールがグラウンドに落ちないうちに捕えられたら, 彼はアウトになる.

3 《電算》プログラムの実行中の[で] ▪ The OS can be upgraded *on the fly.* OS は実行中でもアップグレードは可能である.

4 去りぎわに, 去りながら ▪ He answered *on the fly.* 彼は出て行きながら答えた.

5 《俗》急いで ▪ We had to eat our lunch *on the fly.* 私たちは大急ぎで昼食をとらねばならなかった.

6 非常に忙しく, あちこち動いて ▪ I was *on the fly* all day long. 私は一日中非常に忙しかった.

7 《米》(じっくり考えずに)とっさに, その場で ▪ She made the decision *on the fly.* 彼女は即決した.

8 《口》こっそりと ▪ You can always get a drink *on the fly.* いつでもこっそり1杯やることができるよ.

9 《俗》飲み騒ぎをして, 遊興して ▪ I'm *on the fly* every Friday night. 毎週金曜日の夜は遊興する.

fly[3] /flaɪ/ 動 ***(be) flown down*** (ハトが)すっかり飛び疲れて(いる) ▪ One bird returned right *flown down.* 1羽のハトがすっかり飛び疲れて帰った.

be flying high **1** (人・会社が)大成功している ▪ Imitation fur *is flying high* as fabric for women's coats. 人造の毛皮が女性用コートの生地として大いに受けている.

2 《米口》(特に麻薬で)非常に興奮している ▪ The man *was* on drugs, *flying high* and crying loudly. その男は薬物を使用して, ハイになって大声で叫んでいた. ☞→FLY high/FLY a high pitch.

fly a bill 融通手形を振り出して金を集める ▪ *Fly a bill* and let him have it. 融通手形を出して彼にやれ.

fly a high pitch →FLY high.

fly a* [*the*] *kite **1** たこを揚げる ▪ One of the amusements of the prisoners was *flying kites.* 囚人たちの娯楽の一つはたこ揚げであった.

2 《口》空手形を振り出して金を集める ▪ In Ireland they often resorted to *flying the kite.* アイルランドでは空手形で金を調達するという手をよく使った.

3 《口》探りを入れる, 世論に探りを入れる ▪ I'm just *flying a kite* but do you think there would be any demand for yoga teachers? 僕は探りを入れてるだけなんだが, ヨガの教師の需要があると思うかい.

fly all to pieces at 《米口》…に対して憤激する ▪ Mr. Callaway *flew all to pieces at* me. キャラウェイ氏は私に対して憤激した.

***fly apart* [*in pieces, into fragments*]** こっぱみじんに飛び散る ▪ The glass *flew in pieces.* グラスはこっぱみじんに飛び散った.

fly at high game 大志をいだく, 望みが高い ▪ Young men should *fly at high game.* 青年は大志をいだくべきである.

fly at higher game **1** (タカが)もっと高い所の獲物に飛びかかる.

2 もっと高い望みをいだく ▪ He is *flying at higher game.* 彼はもっと高いところを望んでいる.

fly contact 有視界飛行をする ▪ Willey indicated that he planned to *fly contact.* ウィリーは有視界飛行を計画していると言った.

fly high/fly a high pitch **1** 高く飛ぶ ▪ The swallows are *flying high.* ツバメが高く飛んでいる.

2 大志をいだく; 高い地位に登ろうとする, 得意になる ▪ He is *flying high.* 彼は高い地位に登ろうとしている ▪ Tom was *flying high* when his team won. トムは自分のチームが勝って得意であった.

3 高所[高名]に達する ▪ They *fly high* in their divinity. 彼らは神学において高名である ▪ Their piety *flies the high pitch.* 彼らの信心は頂点を極めている.

4 大ばくちを打つ, 大冒険をやる. ☞↔FLY low.

fly in pieces →FLY apart.

fly in the face of →FACE[1].

fly in the teeth of …に逆らう, 挑戦する ▪ You are *flying in the teeth of* other people's rights. 君は他人の権利を無視している.

fly low **1** 低く飛ぶ ▪ The swallows are *flying low* today. きょうはツバメが低く飛んでいる.

2 高望みをしない; 控え目で引っ込みがちである ▪ You *fly* too *low.* あなたは望みが低すぎる.

3 表立つこと[悪名]を避ける, 世をはばかる ▪ He is *flying low* somewhere in the country. 彼は田舎のどこかで世を忍んでいる. ☞↔FLY high.

fly off at a tangent →TANGENT.

fly off (at) the handle →HANDLE[1].

fly off one's jib 《米口》年をとる; 健康が衰える ▪ Hanks is *flying off his jibs.* ハンクスは健康がだんだん衰えている.

fly the mags 《俗》(半ペニー貨をはじき上げて)賭けをする ▪ *Fly the mags.* If heads, we scrag him. 半ペニー貨をはじき上げろ. 表が出たら彼を絞罪にするんだ.

fly to arms 急いで武器を取る, 急いで戦闘準備をする ▪ The whole nation *flew to arms.* 全国民が急いで武器を取った.

***fly to bits* [*pieces*]** =FLY apart.

fly ... to the mark (タカが)…を隠れがまで追いつめる; とことんまで追いつめる ▪ *Fly* everything *to the* *mark*, and censure it. すべてをとことんまで追いつめて非難しなさい.

Go fly a kite! 《口》うるさいあっちへ行け[やめろ]; 去れ ▪ I told him to *go fly a kite*. うるさいあっちへ行けと私は彼に言った.

I must [***have to***] ***fly*** 《口》すぐ急いで行かねばならない ▪ Glancing at his watch, he said, "*I must fly*!" 時計をちらっと見て彼は「すぐ急いで飛んで行かねばならん」と言った.

It'll never fly. 《米》(アイディアなどが)うまくいかない[受け入れられない]だろう ▪ Critics say about his new novel that *it will never fly*. 批評家たちが彼の新作について言うには, 全然売れないだろうとのことだ.

knock ... flying ...を激しく打ち倒す ▪ They *knocked* the boy *flying* as they rushed for dinner. 食事に殺到したとき彼らはその少年を押し倒した.

let fly **1** 飛ばす, 放つ ▪ He *let fly* a torrent of abuses. 彼は罵言の雨を放った.

2 逃がしてやる ▪ They *let* the bird *fly*. 彼らはその鳥を逃がしてやった.

3 激語を放つ; どなる (*with*) ▪ A hot-tempered man *lets fly* on the least provocation. 短気な人はちょっと気にさわることがあると激語を放つ ▪ The teacher *let fly* at the disobedient boy. 先生は言うことをきかぬ少年をどなりつけた ▪ It's bad form to *let fly with* four-letter words. 4文字語を口にするのは不作法だ.

let fly at (石・弾丸・罵言・怒語で)...を攻撃する ▪ We *let fly at* the elephant. 我々はゾウを目がけてぶっ放した ▪ She *let fly at* the servant. 彼女は使用人をしかりとばした.

let fly with (石・ボールを)投げる, (弾丸・ミサイルを)発射する, (パンチを)かます ▪ She *let fly with* a pie at the statue but missed it. 彼女は銅像をめがけてパイを投げつけたが当たらなかった ▪ He *let fly with* his right foot but his shot was blocked. 彼は右足を振りぬいてシュートしたが, ブロックされた ▪ He *let fly with* a left-hook to the opponent's jaw. 彼は相手のあごへ左フックを一発見舞った.

make the dust [***feathers, fur***] ***fly*** 《口》大騒動を引き起こす, やかましくけんかをする; うまく攻撃する ▪ She'd better not interfere or he'll *make the fur fly*. 彼女は干渉しないほうがいい. さもないと彼は大騒動を引き起こすだろう.

make the money fly →MONEY.

send ... flying **1** ...を飛ばす, 飛び散らす ▪ He *sent* the ball *flying*. 彼はボールを飛ばした ▪ We *sent* the bills *flying*. 我々はビラをまき散らした.

2 ...を敗走させる ▪ We *sent* the enemy *flying* in all directions. 我々は敵を四方八方に敗走させた.

3 ...を追い払う, お払い箱にする ▪ We *sent* him *flying*. 我々は彼を追いやった.

flyer /fláɪər/ 名 ***take a flyer*** 《主に米》危険を冒す, 一か八かやってみる (*on*) ▪ Individual investors *took a flyer on* stocks. 個人投資家たちは株に一か八かを狙った.

flying /fláɪɪŋ/ 形 ***get off to a flying start*** さい先がよい ▪ The bond drive *got off to a flying start*, when he subscribed for $10,000 worth. 公債募集運動は彼が1万ドル分を申し込んでさい先が良かった.

with [***under***] ***a flying seal*** 開き封にして ▪ He handed me a letter *with a flying seal*. 彼は私に開き封の手紙を手渡した.

foal /foʊl/ 名 ***in*** [***with***] ***foal*** (馬が)子をはらんで ▪ A black mare was far gone *with foal*. 黒の雌馬は妊娠して大分経っていた.

foam[1] /foʊm/ 名 ***be in a foam*** (馬などが)全身に汗をかいている ▪ The horse *is* all *in a foam*. 馬は全身汗をかいている.

foam[2] /foʊm/ 動 ***foam at the mouth*** **1** 口から泡を吹く; 口角泡をとばす ▪ The child was in convulsions and *foamed at the mouth*. 子供はけいれんを起こし口から泡を吹いた.

2 (口から泡を吹いて)激怒する ▪ When he was insulted, he *foamed at the mouth*. 彼は侮辱されたとき激怒した.

3 非常に興奮して, 熱狂して ▪ Most of the music press *foamed at the mouth* in celebration of the latest saviour of British music. ほとんどの音楽雑誌は, 英国音楽の最新の救世主を熱狂的に祝った.

foam *oneself* ***away*** 泡となって消える ▪ Their surging charges *foamed themselves away*. 彼らの大波のような襲撃は泡となって消えた.

foam with rage 激怒する ▪ Father *foamed with rage* when I told him so. 父は私がそう言ったとき激怒した.

fob /fɑb|fɔb/ 名 ***come the fob on*** 《米俗》...をだます ▪ He *came the fob on* me. 彼は私をだました.

focus /fóʊkəs/ 名 ***bring*** [***put, throw***] ***... into*** [***in, to***] (***a***) ***focus*** ...に焦点を合わせる, を表面化する, を明らかにする ▪ *Bring* the object *into focus* if you want a good photograph. 良い写真をとりたいなら対象を焦点に合わせなさい ▪ The transactions of many individuals *are brought to a focus*. 多くの人々の所為が明らかになっている ▪ This new fact *brought into focus* three big questions. この新事実は3つの大問題を表面化した.

come into focus 表面化する, 明らかになる ▪ The pictures will *come into focus*. 実状は明らかになるだろう.

get into focus 焦点が合う; 正しく見る目ができる ▪ Finally my eyes *got into focus*. ついに私は正しく見る目ができた.

get out of focus ぼやける; ぼやけさせる ▪ The film *got out of focus*. フィルムはぼやけてきた.

have ... in focus ...を正しく捕える[認識する] ▪ They don't *have* this world conflict *in focus*. 彼らはこの世界戦争を正しく捕えていない.

in focus ピントが合って, はっきりして; 焦点となって, 表面化して ▪ This object is *in focus*. この被写体はピントが合っている ▪ The problems are *in focus*. それらの問題は表面化している.

out of focus ピントがはずれて，ぼやけて; 見当違いで ▪ The image is *out of focus*. その像はピントがはずれている ▪ His charges were wholly *out of focus*. 彼の非難は全く見当違いである.

put* [*throw*]...*into* [*in, to*] (*a*) *focus →bring ... into (a) FOCUS.

fodder /fάdər|fɔ́də/ 名 ***stand up to*** *one's* ***rack*** (***fodder or no fodder***) →RACK[1].

foeman /fóʊmən/ 名 ***a foeman worthy of*** *one's* ***steel*** 《雅》好敵手，不足のない相手 (Scott, *The Lady of the Lake* 5. 10) ▪ In Gladstone he found *a foeman worthy of his steel*. 彼はグラッドストンという好敵手を得た. ☞W.E. Gladstone (1809–98) は英国の政治家; 1868–94年に4回首相となった.

F

fog[1] /fɑg|fɔg/ 名 (***all***) ***in a*** [***the***] ***fog*** 《口》当惑して，途方にくれて ▪ I am *all in a fog* over these accounts. 私はこの勘定にすっかり当惑している.

fog[2] /fɑg|fɔg/ 動 ***be fogged in*** 《米》 **1** 霧に包まれる; 霧のため混乱する《運行中止になる》 ▪ Logan Airport *was fogged in*. ローガン空港は霧に包まれていた ▪ His plane *was fogged in* and diverted to Pittsburgh. 彼の飛行機は霧の影響を受けて，ピッツバーグに行き先変更になった ▪ The senator *was fogged in* in Washington. 上院議員は霧のためワシントンに足止めされた.

2 (意識などが)もうろうとする，ぼうっとなる ▪ My head *was fogged in* by the weather. 天候のせいで頭がぼうっとしていた.

foggy /fάgi|fɔ́gi/ 形 ***have not the foggiest*** (***notion, idea***) 《口》ちっとも知らない ▪ I *haven't the foggiest notion* where they are. 彼らがどこにいるかちっとも知らない.

foil /fɔɪl/ 名 ***act as a foil to*** [***for***] ...の引き立て役をする ▪ Dick is lazy and *acts as a foil for* his energetic brother. ディックは怠け者で，精力的な彼の兄とは対照的だ.

fold[1] /foʊld/ 名 ***bring ... back to the fold*** ...を元の信仰[団体]に復帰させる (《聖》*Jer.* 23. 3) ▪ He was celebrated for *bringing* infidels *back to the fold*. 彼は不信者を信仰に復帰させるので有名だった.

receive *a person* ***back into the fold*** 人を元の信仰[団体]に受け入れる ▪ We *received* him *back into the fold*. 彼を元の政党に受け入れた.

return [***come back***] ***to the fold*** 家に帰る; 人が元の信仰(団体)に復帰する (《聖》*John* 10) ▪ Now he has *returned to the fold*. 今は彼は元の信仰に戻っている.

fold[2] /foʊld/ 動 ***fold*** *one's* ***hands*** 手をこまぬいて何もしない ▪ An American will not *fold his hands* because he is rich. アメリカ人は金持ちだからといって何もせず怠けてはいない.

fold ... in *one's* ***arms*** [***to*** *one's* ***breast***] ...をいだく ▪ We will *fold* him *in our arms*. 彼を両腕にいだこう ▪ I *fold* all my sons *to my breast*. 私は息子をみな胸にいだきます.

fold *one's* ***tent*** 静かに[そっと]立ち去る ▪ Lieberman finished fifth and soon *folded his tent*. リーバマンは5位に終わり，ただちに撤退した. ☞Longfellow, *The Day is Done* (1844) から.

folio /fóʊliòʊ/ 名 ***in folio*** 全紙二つ折り判の ▪ The usual form of books printed in the 15th century is *in folio*. 15世紀に印刷された本の普通の型は二つ折り判である.

follow /fάloʊ|fɔ́ləʊ/ 動 ***a hard*** [***tough, difficult***] ***act to follow*** 難業，偉業; 大人物，偉人; 他の追随を許さぬ人 ▪ The new chairman knows his predecessor is *a hard act to follow*. 新議長は前任者が他の追随を許さぬ人だということを知っている ▪ Sequencing the human genome is *a hard act to follow*. ヒトゲノムを配列決定するのは世紀の難事業だ ▪ "The Godfather" I and II are *a tough act to follow*. 「ゴッドファーザー」1部および2部は傑作だ ▪ Marilyn Monroe is *a hard act to follow*. マリリン・モンローは不世出の大女優だ.

as follows 次の通りで ▪ He argued *as follows*. 彼は次のように論議した ▪ Her words were *as follows*. 彼女の言葉は次の通りであった. ☞follows は非人称動詞で常に s がつくが，まれに follow となる; しばしばコロン(:) で区切って，引用文やリスト項目が続く.

follow along the line of ...と同じ方向を行く ▪ Our business *follows along the line of* that of our predecessors. 我々の事業は先輩たちの事業と同じ方向に行っている.

follow home あくまでもやり続ける，徹底的に追求する ▪ If you *follow home* the clue, you will be able to find the culprit. 手がかりを徹底的に追って行くと，犯人が見つかるだろう.

Follow me? (私の言うことが)おわかりですか? ☞< Do you follow me?

follow my leader 《遊戯》「リーダーに従え」遊び《比喩的にも》 ▪ Englishmen are the last people to play a blind game of "*follow my leader*." イギリス人は決して盲目的に先達に従う国民ではない.

follow (***the***) ***hounds*** →HOUND[1].

follow the law [***plow, sea, stage***] 弁護士[農業，船乗り，俳優]をやる ▪ He began to *follow the sea* at 16. 彼は16歳で船乗りを始めた.

follow the string (弓が)使用の結果曲がる ▪ The bow *followed the string* slightly. 使っているうちに弓がやや反った.

Follow your copy even if it fly out of the window. どこまでも原稿通りに《植字工のモットー》.

I don't quite follow. 言われることがよくわかりません ▪ I am sorry—*I don't quite follow*. すみません—どうもおっしゃることがよくわかりません.

it does not follow that ...ということにはならない ▪ If a man writes poetry, *it does not* necessarily *follow that* he understands another's poetry. 詩を書くからといって必ずしも他人の詩がわかるとは限らない.

it follows that ...ということになる ▪ If that is true, *it follows that* he was not there. もしそれが本当なら彼はそこにはいなかったことになる.

to follow 次の料理として; 引き続いて ▪ With coffee and dessert *to follow*. コーヒーとデザートつきです.

Trade follows the flag. 貿易は国旗について行く.

folly /fáli|fɔ́li/ 名 ***commit a folly*** 失策をする, ばかなことをする ▪ A young man who is unable to *commit a folly* is already an old man. ばかなまねをすることのできない若者はすでに老人である.

have the folly to *do* 愚かにも…する ▪ I *had the folly to* trust such a man. 私は愚かにもそのような人を信頼してしまった.

to a folly ばかげた程度に ▪ They are hospitable *to a folly*. 彼らはばかげているほどもてなしがよい.

fond /fand|fɔnd/ 形 ***be fond of*** …が好きである《like より上品に聞こえることがある》 ▪ I *am* very *fond of* liqueurs. 私はリキュールが大好きだ ▪ He *is* very *fond of* classical music. 彼はクラシック音楽が大好きだ.

get fond of …が好きになる ▪ I have *got fond of* him. 私はあの人が好きになった.

fondness /fándnəs|fɔ́nd-/ 名 ***have a fondness for*** …を愛好する ▪ I *have a fondness for* him [literature]. 私は彼[文学]が好きだ.

out of fondness かわいさから ▪ She is just spoiling her children *out of fondness*. 彼女はかわいさから子供たちを甘やかしてばかりいる.

font /fant|fɔnt/ 名 ***stand at font for*** …の名うけ親となる ▪ He *stood at font for* her daughter. 彼は彼女の娘の名うけ親となった. ☞font「洗礼盤」.

food /fu:d/ 名 ***be food and drink to*** *one* = be MEAT and drink to one.

be [become] food for …のえじきとなる ▪ He has *become food for* worms. 彼はウジ虫のえじきとなった《死んだ》 ▪ The house has *become food for* the flames. その家は焼けてしまった.

food for powder 火薬のえじき; 兵士 (cf. Sh., *1 Hen. IV* 4. 2. 72) ▪ There go the poor conscripts—*food for powder*. あそこに, あわれな新兵どもが行く—弾丸のえじきさ.

food for thought 思考の材料, 考えるべき[考えさせられる]こと ▪ His plans for education are certainly *food for thought*. 彼の教育計画はたしかに考慮の材料ではある.

fool[1] /fu:l/ 名 ***A fool and his money are soon parted.*** 《諺》愚か者をだまして金を取るのは易しい.

a fool for luck 《米口》格別運のよい人 ▪ He is *a fool for luck*. 彼は格別に運がよい.

A fool's bolt is soon shot. 《諺》愚者はすぐ奥の手を出し尽くす.

A man is a fool or a physician at thirty./ Every man is a fool or his own physician at forty. 《諺》知者30[40]にして医師を要せず《30[40]歳になって自分の体の具合がわからないのはばか者だ》. ☞Plutarch が Tiberius の言として伝えている文句.

act the fool =play the FOOL.

answer a fool according to his folly 愚者には(思い上がらせないために)その愚かさに応じて答える, 愚者は愚者扱いにする(《聖》*Prov.* 25. 5).

As the fool thinks, so the bell clinks. 《諺》愚か者は自分の望むことを信じてしまう.

be a fool for *one's* ***pains*** 骨折ってばかを見る ▪ If you try to help the Smiths, you will *be a fool for your pains*. スミス家を助けようとすると骨折り損のくたびれもうけになるよ.

be a fool to …に比べると取るに足らない, の足もとにも寄りつけない ▪ This *is a fool to* that. これはあれに比べると問題にならない.

be fool enough to *do* 愚かにも…する ▪ He *is fool* [They *are fools*] *enough to* think so. 彼[彼ら]は愚かにもそう思っている.

be no [nobody's, no man's] fool なかなか抜け目がない ▪ He *is nobody's fool*. 彼はどうしてなかなか抜け目がない.

Every man has a fool in his sleeve. 《諺》誰でもどこか愚かなところがある, 弱点のない人はない.

Fool that I am! →Fool THAT one is!

fool's gold まやかしもの, 絵空事, 空理空論 ▪ She assailed his plan as "*fool's gold*." 彼女は彼の案を「まやかし」だと非難した. ☞もと黄鉄鉱(または黄銅鉱)を指す; 金色なのでしばしば金と間違えられる.

Fools rush in (where angels fear to tread). →ANGEL.

live in a fool's paradise 知らぬが仏で万事よいと思っている; たわいない夢を描いて暮らす ▪ He is *living in a fool's paradise*; in reality he hasn't a week to live. 彼は知らぬが仏だが実は彼の命は1週間もたぬ.

make a fool of …を笑いものにする ▪ She always *makes a fool of* her husband. 彼女はいつも夫を笑いものにする.

make a fool of *oneself* ばかなまねをする, 笑いものになる ▪ We all *make fools of ourselves* at times. みなときにはばかなまねをすることがある.

More fool you [him, etc.***]!***/《米》***The more fool you [him,*** etc.***]!*** あなた[彼, など]はばかげている ▪ I'll invite him to dinner.—*The more fool you.* He doesn't deserve it. 僕は彼を食事に招こうと思う—ばかだなあ君は. あいつはそれほどの人間じゃない.

not suffer fools (gladly) 愚か者を放任[黙認, 容赦]しない (→suffer FOOLs gladly) ▪ He is open and uncomplicated but he does *not suffer fools* or liars *gladly*. 彼はあけっぴろげで率直だが, 愚か者や嘘つきにはどうしてもがまんできない. ☞suffer＝allow.

play *a person* ***for a fool*** 《米口》人をこけにする ▪ Your lover's *playing* you *for a fool*. It's obvious he prefers to keep you as his mistress. あなたの恋人はあなたをばかにしてるわ. あなたを愛人としてかこっていたいのは明らかよ.

play the fool 道化の役をする; ばかなまねをする, へまをやる ▪ He is apt to *play the fool* when he drinks. 彼は飲むとばかなまねをしがちである ▪ It is about time he stopped *playing the fool*. 彼はもう金のむだ使いはやめるべきときだ.

F

play the fool of …をだます ▪ He *played the fool of* me. 彼は私をかついだ.

play the fool with …をもてあそぶ; にばかを見させる, をだます; をだめにする ▪ I was *playing the fool with* the lass. 私はその娘をもてあそんでいた ▪ Stop *playing the fool with* the PC. そのパソコンをもてあそぶのはよしなさい.

suffer fools gladly 喜んで愚か者をがまんする (《聖》 *2 Cor.* 11. 19) ▪ He doesn't *suffer fools gladly.* 彼は喜んで愚か者をがまんしはしない.

(***There is***) ***no fool like an old fool.*** 愚かな老人ほど救いがたいものはない《特に若い女に恋をする老人について》 ▪ Is he going to marry a girl of twenty at his age? Well, *there's no fool like an old fool.* 彼はあの年齢で20歳の娘と結婚するんですか. いやはや, 愚かな老人ほど救いがたいものはないね.

F

fool[2] /fuːl/ 動 ***fool around the stump*** → STUMP[1].

fool it ばかなまねをする; のらくらする ▪ I can *fool it* no longer. これ以上のらくらしてはいられない.

have (***got***) *a person* ***fooled*** 人をだます; 人を分からなくて困らせる ▪ Simon almost *had* me *fooled*! サイモンにはもう少しでだまされるところだった! ▪ Revelations of the rock star's "secret life" sure *had* me *fooled.* そのロックスターの「秘密の生活」の暴露には確かに当惑させられた.

no fooling/no foolin' 《戯》もちろん, 当然, 確かに ▪ Fans won't want to miss it, *no foolin'.* ファンはそれを見逃したくないだろうよ, 当然 ▪ *No foolin'*, folks, it's really happening. マジだぜ, 君たち, それは実際に起こっているんだ.

You could have fooled me. 《口》私はそうは思わなかっただろう(し, 今も思わない), とても信じられない; その手には乗らない ▪ Do you know it's a fake?—No! Well, *you could have fooled me.* それがにせものだということを知っているかい?—いいや! でも僕はそうとは思わなかったろうな ▪ He's bought a magnificent cruiser? *You could've fooled me.* 彼が豪華なクルーザーを買っただって? とても信じられないね.

foolish /fúːlɪʃ/ 形 ***look foolish*** 愚かに見える; きまりの悪い思いをする ▪ I was made to *look foolish* in company. 人前で恥をかかされた.

foot[1] /fʊt/ 名 ***at*** (***a***) ***foot's pace*** 歩行の速度で, 並み足で《坂を登るなど》 ▪ We proceeded *at a foot's pace.* 我々は並み足で進んだ.

at *a person's* ***feet*** **1** 人の足もとに ▪ Throwing herself *at his feet*, she cried bitterly. 彼の足もとに身を投げて彼女はさめざめと泣いた.

2 (弟子・家来・嘆願者として)ひざまずいて (《聖》 *Acts* 22. 3) ▪ Iraq was *at America's feet.* イラクはアメリカに降服した ▪ He learned the science *at Newton's feet.* 彼はその学問をニュートンのもとで習った.

3 近くにいてじゃまをする ▪ I don't want Alex *at my feet*, he's a nuisance. アレックスに近くでうろちょろしてほしくない. じゃまなんだ.

at *one's* ***feet*** 足もとの[に], 目前の[に] ▪ We don't see the miracle *at our feet.* 我々は足もとの奇跡が見えない.

at foot ページの下部に ▪ We placed the proposed correction *at foot.* 我々は提案された修正をページの下部に掲げた.

at the foot of …のふもとに; (ページ)の下部に, 脚部に; (人)のもとで ▪ Have you read the note *at the foot of* the page? あなたはページの下部にある注を読みましたか ▪ We spent a week *at the foot of* the hills. 山々のふもとで1週間過ごした《連山のときも単数が普通》.

be born with two left feet 不器用である ▪ If you *were born with two left feet*, give it time. 生まれつき不器用なら, 時間をかけてゆっくりやりなさい.

be forced on to the back foot 翻意を余儀なくされる, 前言をとりさげざるを得ない ▪ Mr. Blair has *been forced on to the back foot* over his soldiers' deployment. ブレア氏は兵士の配置に関して翻意せざるを得なかった.

be light on *one's* ***feet*** 足さばきが軽快で, すばやい ▪ He *was light on his feet* and quick to zig and zag. 彼は足さばきが軽快で, 素早くジグザグに動いた.

(***be***) ***on foot*** (計画などが)始まって(いる) (→get back on one's feet (→FOOT[1])) ▪ The plan *is on foot.* その計画は始まっている.

be quick on *one's* ***feet*** 足が速い; (行動が)機敏である ▪ Smart people *are quick on their feet.* 切れ者は行動が速い.

be run [***rushed***] ***off*** *one's* ***feet*** (足をすりへらすほど)一生懸命に働く, 大忙し[大わらわ]である ▪ There's only one secretary working for the whole accounts department and the poor woman *is run off her feet.* 会計課全体で一人しか秘書がいないので, その女性は気の毒に休む暇もなく働いていた.

begin foot 《米口》クラスのびりから始める ▪ I always *began foot.* 私はいつもクラスのびりから始めた.

beneath *a person's* ***foot*** [***feet***] → under a person's FOOT.

beside [***before***] *a person's* ***feet*** 人の足もとに, 人のそばに ▪ I saw the bloody Hector stretched *before your feet.* 血まみれのヘクターがあなたの足もとでのびているのを見た.

bound [***jump, spring, start***] ***to*** *one's* ***feet*** 飛び起きる, ぱっと立ち上がる ▪ He *sprang to his feet.* 彼はぱっと立ち上がった.

bring *a person* ***to his feet*** →raise a person to his feet (→FOOT[1]).

by foot 《米》歩いて ▪ He traveled from Boston to New York *by foot.* 彼はボストンからニューヨークへ歩いて行った.

by (***Mr.***) ***Foot's horse*** → on (Mr.) FOOT's horse.

by the [***per***] ***foot run*** (平方フィートに対し)長さ何フィートで, 長さ1フィートごとに ▪ A plasterer's work is in part measured *by the foot run.* 左官の仕事は一部長さ何フィートで計られる ▪ The wood company are selling 2 by 4 at 40 pence *per foot run.* 木材会社は縦4インチ横2インチの角材を1フィートにつ

き40ペンスで売っている.

carry [***knock, sweep***] *a person* ***off*** *his* ***feet*** 《口》 **1** (波・風が)人の足をさらう ▪ The waves *carried* him *off his feet.* 波は彼の足をさらった.

2 人を熱狂させる, 有頂天にする; 人をすっかり心服させる; 女性をぞっこんほれ込ませる ▪ The speech of the Prime Minister *carried* everyone *off his feet.* 総理大臣の演説はすべての人を熱狂させた ▪ She was hoping that some glamorous young Frenchman would come along and *sweep* her *off her feet.* 彼女は, 魅力的な若いフランス人がやってきて, 自分を愛の虜(とりこ)にしてくれることを期待していた.

catch *a person's* ***foot*** 人をつまずかせる ▪ The stone *caught his foot.* その石に彼はつまずいた.

catch *a person* ***on the wrong foot*** 人に不意打ちを食わせる ▪ You are asking me to lend you some money, but I'm afraid you've *caught* me *on the wrong foot.* 君は僕に金を貸してくれと言う. だがそう不意に言われてもね.

change *one's* ***feet*** 《口》 靴をはき替える ▪ She did not *change her feet* when she came home. 彼女は帰って来たとき靴をはき替えなかった.

change foot [***feet***] (行進中)足を踏み変える ▪ He *changed foot.* 彼は足を踏み変えた.

come [etc.] ***to*** *a person's* ***feet*** 人の足もとにひざまずく ▪ I shall never forgive you even if you *come to my feet.* お前が足もとにひざまずいたとしても決して許してやるつもりはない.

come to [***on***] *one's* ***feet*** 立ち上がる ▪ He *came on his feet* again. 彼はまた立ち上がった ▪ All the pupils *come to their feet.* 生徒はみな立ち上がる.

dead on *one's* ***feet*** 《口》 非常に疲れて, 疲れはてて ▪ She continues to work even when she's *dead on her feet.* 彼女は疲れはてていても仕事をやめない.

die on *one's* ***feet*** 崩壊する; 衰える; 動かなくなる ▪ The country may *die on its feet.* その国は崩壊するかもしれない.

drag one's feet ぐずぐずする; …をわざと遅らせる (*on*) ▪ The President has *dragged his feet on* the issue. 大統領はこの問題の解決を遅らせた.

drop [***fall***] ***on*** *one's* ***feet*** 《主に英》 (猫のように)落ちてもすっくり立つ; 首尾よく窮地を免れる; (不運続きの後)運がよくなる; 裕福である (→land on one's feet (→FOOT[1])) ▪ He seems to have *fallen on his feet* at last. 不運続きの後彼はついに運がよくなったようだ ▪ Arriving in London penniless, John *fell on his feet.* 一文なしでロンドンに着いたが, ジョンは窮地をうまく切り抜けた ▪ He *fell on his feet* in such agreeable company. 彼はそのような愉快な人々といっしょで幸運だった.

feet first **1** 足から先に ▪ He jumped into the water *feet first.* 彼は足から先に水中に飛びこんだ.

2 →be carried out feet first (→CARRY[2]).

one's ***feet haven't touched the ground*** 有頂天である, 夢見ごこちである ▪ I'm absolutely on top of the world—*my feet haven't touched the ground* since yesterday. 私は全く世界の頂点にいる. 昨日から夢見ごこちだ.

feet of clay 倒れそうな土台, もろい部分, 人格上の欠点 (《聖》 *Dan.* 2. 33) ▪ Byron, with his *feet of clay,* remained the child of his age. バイロンは人格上の欠点をもっていたが, どこまでも時代の子であった ▪ Japan may one day forge for herself *feet* of iron instead *of clay.* 日本はいつかはもろい土台でなく堅固な土台を自力で作り出すであろう ▪ Some of the greatest geniuses in history had *feet of clay.* 歴史上もっとも偉大な天才にも隠れた欠点のある人はいた.

find *one's* ***feet*** →FIND[2].

find [***get, have, know***] ***the length of*** *a person's* ***foot*** (人を操ろうとして)人の弱点を知る; 人の性格を知る ▪ You shall not *know the length of my foot.* 君に僕の弱点を知らせはしないぞ. ☞靴屋から来たたとえ.

foot to foot 足を互いにかけて, 接戦して ▪ They were fighting *foot to foot.* 彼らは接戦していた.

get back [***be***] ***on*** *one's* ***feet*** 回復する, 再起する ▪ She *got back on her feet* after about three months in a wheelchair. およそ3か月車いすで過ごしたのち, 彼女は復帰した.

get [***have***] ***cold feet*** →COLD.

get *one's* ***feet on the ground*** 《主に米》 足場を得る, 地歩を固める ▪ He did a wonderful job after he *got his feet on the ground.* 足場を得たのちは, 彼はすばらしい仕事をした.

get *one's* ***feet under the table*** [***desk***] 《英》 新しい状況[仕事]に慣れる ▪ It's better to wait until you've *got your feet* firmly *under the table* before you make any big changes. 生活を大きく変える前に, 新しい職場にしっかりと慣れるまで待つほうがよい ▪ I'm trying to *get my feet under the table* in a new business. 私は, 新しい仕事に慣れようとしているところだ.

get *one's* ***feet up*** = put one's feet out (→FOOT[1]).

get *one's* ***feet wet*** 《主に米口》 始める; 初めてする, (危険を伴うことに)手を出す[染める] ▪ It is not hard to dance once you *get your feet wet.* 一度やり始めたらダンスは難しくない ▪ Investors are encouraged to *get their feet wet* by buying just a few shares to begin with. 投資家たちは最初は数株だけから始めるよう勧められる.

get [***have***] *one's* ***foot in*** **1** 《口》 足場を得る[得て親しくなる]; (入りにくい団体などに)入る ▪ I think I can *get my foot in* with this line of goods. この種の商品で足場を得ることができると思う ▪ He has at last *got his foot in* with the people at the Manor. 彼はついに領主の邸宅の人々に近づいて親しくなった.

2 競走の足慣らしをする; (一般に)仕事に慣れる ▪ I have not yet *got my foot in.* 私はまだ仕事に慣れていない. ☞ローマの競走で走者が走る前に足慣らしをしたことから.

3 《米口》 (事を)始める, 取りかかる ▪ Let's now kick up a dust, to *get my foot in.* さあ手始めに騒ぎ立て

F

よう.

get** one's **foot on the ladder 事を始める, 着手する ▪ But for your support, I could not have *got my foot on the ladder.* ご支持がなかったら事を始めることもできなかったでしょう.

get* [*set, start, step*] *off on the right foot うまく出発させる, いかせる; うまく出発する, いく ▪ The chairman's humor *set* the meeting *off on the right foot.* 議長のユーモアで会議は滑り出しよく始まった ▪ She will *start off on the right foot* with my mother. 彼女は私の母とは初めからうまくいくだろう.

get* [*start, step*] *off on the wrong foot 出発を誤る; へまをやる ▪ He *got off on the wrong foot* when he asked the boss for a day off. 彼が社長に1日の休暇を願ったのはへまだった ▪ Once you've *stepped off on the wrong foot*, it's difficult to make a fresh start. 一度まずい踏み出しをするとスタートをし直すのは難しい.

get on** one's **feet →GET.

get* [*have*] *one* [*one's*] *foot in the door 《口》(入りにくい団体などに)入る, 足場を得る ▪ He has already *got his foot in the door* of the club. 彼はすでにそのクラブに入っている. ☞「戸に片足を突っ込んで閉じられないようにして押し入る」ことから; the door は略されることがある.

get* [*have*] *the foot of …より足が速い ▪ She *had the foot of* her pursuer. 彼女のほうが追跡者より足が速かった.

get to** one's **feet 立ち上がる ▪ The whole crowd *got to their feet* and cheered. 群衆はみな立ち上がって歓呼した.

get under** a person's **feet 人のじゃまになる ▪ Why don't you ask Kelly to sit in the other room for a while? That way she won't keep *getting under my feet.* ケリーにしばらく別の部屋で座っているよう頼んでくれ. そうすれば私のじゃまにならないから.

(go) on** one's **own feet 歩いて(行く) ▪ I *went on my own feet* to a near-by library. 近くの図書館に歩いて行った.

go (to the) foot 《米口》クラスのびりになる ▪ Tom has *gone foot* three times. トムは3回クラスのびりになった.

***have* [*keep*] *a foot in both camps* [*each camp*]** (対立する)両陣営に関係している ▪ You had best *keep a foot in both camps.* 君は両陣営に関係しているのが一番いいよ.

have a hand like a foot 無器用である ▪ There you are! You *have a hand like a foot.* そら, やった! お前は無器用だな.

have a heavy* [*lead*] *foot 《口》(車を)猛スピードで運転する ▪ I hate riding with him as he *has* such *a heavy foot.* 彼は車をすごく飛ばすので, 彼といっしょに乗るのはごめんだ.

have cold feet →get COLD feet.

have* [*keep*] one's [*both*] *feet* (*set firmly*) *on the ground (成功後も浮かれないで)地に足を(しっかりと)つけている, 実際的である, 常識に富む, 健全な考え[生き方]をする ▪ He will surely succeed, for he *has his feet set firmly on the ground.* 彼はきっと成功するだろう. 実際的な人だから ▪ She's *kept her feet firmly on the ground*—fame hasn't changed her. 彼女は健全な生き方をしていて, 名声のため変わったということはない.

have foot for 《米口》(馬が)…に適応しうる ▪ His nag *has* less *foot for* a brush than the pacer. 彼の小馬はだく足の馬ほどは叢林(そうりん)に適応しえない.

have** one's **foot in →get one's FOOT in.

have** one's **foot on** a person's [**the**] **neck 人に対する支配力を持つ, 人を押さえている (《聖》*Josh.* 10. 24) ▪ Now that we have a written confession from the rogue, we *have our foot on his neck.* その悪者から自白書を取っているのだから我々はそいつを押さえていると言える.

have leaden feet 非常に足がのろい[重い] ▪ God *has leaden feet* and comes slowly to execute wrath. 神は足がのろくて天罰の執行に来るのが遅い.

have one* [*one's*] *foot in the door →get one FOOT in the door.

have one foot in the grave 《口》墓穴に片足を突っ込んでいる, 死にかけている ▪ He *has one foot in the grave.* 彼は死にかけている.

have the foot of →get the FOOT of.

have the world at** one's **feet →WORLD.

have ... under foot …を屈服させている, 支配下においている ▪ We *have* him *under foot.* 我々は彼を服従させている.

jump in with both feet/jump in feet first (何かを)性急に突き進む, 猪突猛進する ▪ Take time to think things over before you make a decision, don't *jump* straight *in with both feet.* 決定する前にじっくり考えなさい. 性急に突き進んではいけません.

keep a foot in both camps →have a FOOT in both camps.

keep** one's **feet **1** ころばないでいる ▪ It was difficult to *keep one's feet* on the icy slopes. 氷の張った坂でころばずにいることはむずかしかった.
2 うまくいく[やる], 成功する ▪ If we carry out these orders, we shall be able to *keep our feet.* もしこれらの命令を実行すれば, 成功することができるでしょう.

keep** one's [**both**] **feet on the ground → have one's feet on the ground (→FOOT[1])

keep on** one's [**its**] **feet **1** 《口》倒れないようにする; 経済的健全を保つ ▪ The proprietor promised to *keep* the newspaper *on its feet.* 経営者はその新聞をつぶさないと約束した.
2 《ボクシング》倒れないでいる ▪ He *kept on his feet* for three rounds. 彼は第3ラウンドまでは倒れずにいた.

keep under** a person's **feet 人のじゃまをする ▪ Don't *keep under your mother's feet* while she is preparing lunch. お母さんが昼食を作っている時にじゃましてはいけません.

knock** a person **off** his **feet 人をびっくり仰天させる ▪ His death *knocked* her *off her feet.* 彼の死は彼女をびっくり仰天させた.

know the length of** a person's **foot →find the length of a person's FOOT.

land on** one's **feet**/《英》**fall on** one's **feet 無事に困難[危険]を逃れる, ツキがある, なんとかなる (→drop on one's feet (→FOOT[1])) ▪ She really *landed on her feet*—she found an apartment right in the middle of San Francisco. 彼女は本当にラッキーだった—サンフランシスコの中心部でアパートを見つけたのだ ▪ Dick takes the most awful risks, but he always seems to *fall on his feet*. ディックはいかにも危険なことをするが, いつも無難に済んでいるようだ.

lay ... at** a person's **feet ...を人に献じる ▪ He *laid* the furniture *at her feet*. 彼はその家具を彼女に献じた.

... me* [*my*] *foot! 《俗》...なんてばかな, ...などであるものか ▪ You are wrong.—Wrong *my foot!* 君はまちがっている—まちがってなどいるものか!

measure** a person's **foot by** one's **own last 自分をもって他を律する. ☞last「靴の木型」.

miss** one's **foot 足を踏みはずす, 失脚する ▪ She jumped, but *missed her foot*. 彼女は飛んだが足を踏みはずした.

not fit to wash** a person's **feet 人よりひどく劣る (《聖》*John*. 13. 5. 16) ▪ We are *not fit to wash Sidney's feet*. 我々はシドニーにはかなわない.

not put* [*set*] *a foot right まちがいをする; あやまちをする ▪ He can*not put a foot right*. 彼はどうしてもまちがいをする.

off** one's **feet 寝て, 横になって; 夢中で ▪ I was *off my feet* all day with a headache. 頭痛がして一日中寝込んでいた.

on** one's **feet **1** (特に演説のために)立ち上がって; 立って ▪ Five of them were *on their feet*. 彼らのうち5人は立っていた.

2 (病後)起きて, 元気になって; 健康で ▪ He was *on his feet* again. 彼はまた元気になった ▪ I hope you get back *on your feet* very soon. すぐに快復されるようお祈りします.

3 (経済上の失敗後)立ち直って, 自立して ▪ He stood *on his feet* at last. 彼はついに立ち直った.

on foot **1** 徒歩で; 歩兵により (↔on HORSEBACK 1) ▪ We came *on foot*. 我々は歩いて来た ▪ The English made three battles *on foot*. イギリス軍は3回歩兵戦を行った.

2 起き上がって, 動いて ▪ Everybody in Jamaica is *on foot* by six in the morning. ジャマイカの人はみな朝6時には起きている ▪ My game were *on foot* before I saw them. 獲物は私が見つけぬうちに起き上がって動いていた.

3 着手されて, 活動して ▪ An investigation is *on foot*. 調査が始まっている.

4 《米口》(牛が)生きて, 生きたまま ▪ Beef was sold in Missouri *on foot* at one dollar per hundred pounds. ミズーリでは肉牛が100ポンド1ドルで生きたままで売られた.

on* [《米》*by*] (*Mr.*) *Foot's horse 《戯》足で ▪ We took the trip *on Foot's horse*. 我々は徒歩でその旅をした.

on the wrong foot 不意に, だしぬけに ▪ We caught him *on the wrong foot*. 我々は彼に不意打ちをくらわせた.

per foot run →by the FOOT run.

pick up** one's **feet **1** 立ち上がる, みこしをあげる ▪ I think I'd better *pick up my feet* and go. みこしをあげて行くとしよう.

2 (足を引きずらずに)一歩一歩地面から離して歩く ▪ The group leader ordered the men to *pick up their feet*. グループリーダーは部下に(足を引きずらずに)きちんと歩くように命じた.

pull foot 《口》逃走する, 去る ▪ His daughter *pulled foot*, and did not return till this morning. 彼の娘が逃走して, 今朝まで帰らなかった.

put a foot upon ...をだしぬく, だます, 虐待する ▪ The man was going to *put a foot upon* the skinny dog. 男はそのやせ犬を虐待しようとしていた.

put* [*set*] *a foot wrong 《口》〚主に否定文で〛まちがいをする; あやまちをする ▪ He has never *put a foot wrong*. 彼はまちがいをしたことはない.

***put* [*set*] one's [*the*] *best foot forward* [*foremost*]** 《口》 **1** 精いっぱい急いで行く ▪ He *put his best foot forward*. 彼は大急ぎで行った.

2 全力を尽くす ▪ If you *put your best foot forward*, you should be able to finish that work by three. 全力を尽くせば3時までにはその仕事を終えることができるはずです.

3 できるだけ良い印象を与える ▪ Sitting still Tom tried to *put his best foot forward*. トムはじっと座ってできるだけ良い印象を与えようとした.

***put** one's **feet out* [*up*]** 《口》(両足を投げ出して)休む[くつろぐ] ▪ You work too hard. Just *put your feet up*. あなたは働き過ぎだ. ちょっと休みなさい.

***put** (one's) **foot at* [*into, on*]** →set (one's) FOOT at.

put** one's **foot down 《口》 **1** 足を踏みしめて立つ, 踏みとどまって進まない ▪ I *put my foot down* and refused to move until he apologized. 私は踏みとどまって, 彼があやまるまで動こうとしなかった.

2 固く主張する, 断固たる態度を取る; (防止のため)強硬策を取る ▪ When students began coming late, he *put his foot down*. 生徒が遅刻し始めたとき, 彼は強硬策を取った.

3 断固として許さない[断る] ▪ When the girl wanted to go to a party, her father *put his foot down*. 娘がパーティーに行きたいと言ったとき父は断固として許さなかった.

4 アクセルをふむ, 速度を速める ▪ I *put my foot down*, and the car gathered speed up the slope. 私はアクセルをふみ, 車はスピードをあげて坂を上がった ▪ I *put my foot down* to overtake the car in front. 前の車を追い抜くためにアクセルを踏み込んだ.

***put* [*set*] one's *foot* (*down*) *on* [*upon*]** 《口》...に断固として反対する, 強く抑える ▪ Wolsey *set his foot upon* the plan. ウルジーはその計画に強く反対した ▪ She *put her foot down upon* the least symptoms of revolt. 彼女はちょっとした反抗の徴候をも強く抑えた.

put** one's **foot in** [**into**] **it 《口》(特に社交上の)へまをやる; へまなことを言う; (うっかり踏みこんで)窮境に陥る ▪ Whenever she opens her mouth, she *puts her foot in it*. 彼女は口さえ開けばへまを言う ▪ The general *put his foot into it* again. 将軍はまたしくじった. ☞「歩いていてつい泥沼に落ちこむ」が原義.

put** one's **foot in the** [one's] **mouth 《米俗》へまなことを言う, 言いしくじる ▪ A minister *put his foot in his mouth* by saying, "The number of birth-giving machines is fixed." ある大臣が失言して「産む機械の数は決まっている」と言った.

put** one's [**the**] **foot on the neck of →set one's FOOT on the neck of.

put** one's **foot to the floor 《米》(アクセルを床まで踏み込んで)車の速度を上げる ▪ We were still going round the corner but I *put my foot to the floor*. まだコーナーを曲がりかけていたが, 速度を上げた.

put** A **on** A's **feet Aを回復[復興]させる ▪ Germany *was put on its feet*. ドイツは復興した ▪ She *was put on her feet*. 彼女は全快した.

put ... on foot →set ... on FOOT.

put one foot before** [**in front of**] **the other 《口》〚cannot, can hardly を伴って〛歩く ▪ The old man *can hardly put one foot before the other*. その老人はほとんど歩けない.

put the shoe on the right foot →SHOE[1].

raise** [**bring**] a person **to** his **feet 人を立ち[起き]上がらせる ▪ The bishops hastened to *raise* the king *to his feet*. 監督たちは急いで国王を立ち上がらせた.

recover** one's **feet →RECOVER one's legs.

reel to** one's **feet →stagger to one's feet (→FOOT[1]).

regain** one's **feet (倒れた後)起き上がる ▪ Williams went down, but *regained his feet* at the count of seven. ウィリアムズはダウンしたが, カウント7で立ち上がった.

rise to** one's **feet (主に演説・乾杯のため)立ち[起き]上がる ▪ He *rose to his feet* to greet me. 彼は立ち上がって私にあいさつした.

run a good** [etc.] **foot (馬が)相当の速さで走る ▪ He *ran a* pretty *good foot*. 馬は相当速く走った.

run** one's **feet off 活動しすぎて疲れる ▪ He *ran his feet off* doing your job as well as his. 彼は自分の仕事の上にあなたの仕事もしてすっかり疲れた.

run** [**rush**] a person **off** his **feet 《口》人をひどく活動させたり, 走り回らせたりして疲れさせる ▪ The children *ran* their mother *off her feet*. 子供らは母親をてんてこまいさせて疲れさせた.

(sell** corn) **on** [**upon**] **the foot (穀物を)茎のついたまま(売る) ▪ The tenant will not *sell* his victuals *upon the foot*. 借地人は食糧を茎のついたままは売らないだろう.

set a foot wrong →put a FOOT wrong.

***set** one's [**the**] **best foot first** [**foremost, forward**]* →put one's best FOOT forward.

***set** [**put**] (one's) **foot at** [**into, on**]* ...に行く, 着く; 入る; 上陸する, を踏む ▪ I *set foot at* Bristol from France. 私はフランスからブリストルに着いた ▪ They didn't *set foot into* the city. 彼らはその都市には足を踏み入れなかった ▪ Columbus was the first to *set foot on* the island. コロンブスが最初にその島に上陸した.

***set** one's **foot** (**down**) **on** [**upon**]* →put one's FOOT (down) on.

set foot in ...に入る ▪ He *set foot in* the hall. 彼はその会館に入った.

set foot on (国・土地など)に踏み入る ▪ You shall never *set foot on* English soil again. 君には二度とイギリスの地を踏ませない.

set** [**have, put**] one's [**the**] **foot on the neck of ...を完全に征服する; を服従させる; を服従させている ▪ He is only happy when he has *set his foot on some fellow's neck*. 彼は誰かを完全に服従させているときだけきげんが良い.

set ... off on the right foot →get off on the right FOOT.

set** [**put**] **... on** its **feet ...をちゃんと立たせる, を再起させる, 復興させる《経済上・健康上・地位上》 ▪ The money will *set* him *on his feet* again. その金は彼を再起させるであろう ▪ What you need is a good stiff drink to *put* you *on your feet*. 必要なのはあなたを回復させてくれる強い良酒です.

set** [**put**] **... on foot ...を始める, 起こす ▪ They *put on foot* the Royal Society. 彼らは王立協会を創始した ▪ He *set* the plan *on foot*. 彼はその計画を起こした.

shoot** oneself **in the foot 自滅する, 墓穴を掘る ▪ You've *shot yourself in the foot* by using that name. その名前を使ったために君は墓穴を掘ったのだ.

sit at** a person's **feet 人の教え[訓育]を受ける ▪ He *sat at the feet of* Erasmus. 彼はエラスムスの教えを受けた.

***six feet under** (**the ground**)* 《口・戯》死亡して(いる), 埋葬されて(いる) ▪ Don't say this to anybody until I'm *six feet under*. 私が死ぬまでこのことは誰にも言っちゃだめだ ▪ With the passage of time, most disputants are already *six feet under the ground*. 時が経つにつれて, ほとんどの論客たちはすでに土の下に逝ってしまった ▪ Her soul is already *six feet under*. 彼女の魂はもう土の下だ.

stagger** [**totter, reel**] **to** one's **feet よろめきながら立ち上がる ▪ She fell but *staggered to her feet*. 彼女は転んだがよろめきながら立ち上がった.

stamp** (**with**) one's **foot →STAMP[2].

stand on** one's **own** [**two**] **feet 独立する ▪ Poverty had taught him to *stand on his own feet*. 貧困が彼に独立することを教えたのであった.

step off on the right** [**wrong**] **foot →get off on the right FOOT; get off on the wrong FOOT.

sweep** a person **off his feet →carry a person

off his FEET.

***take** one's **foot** [**feet**] **in** one's **hand**(**s**)* 出る, 出て行く; 旅をする ▪ Andrew *took his foot in his hand.* アンドルーは出発した ▪ If he *takes his feet in his hands*, he will see such scenes. 彼が旅行をすれば, そのような光景を見るだろう.

take to** one's **feet 足を使う, 歩く《馬の代わりに》 ▪ I *took to my feet* and ran away. 私は足を使って走り去った.

ten feet tall →TEN.

think on** one's **feet 素早く考える, 即座に答える, 当意即妙に行動する ▪ Our teacher *thinks on his feet.* 我々の先生は即座に答えてくれる ▪ An ability to *think on your feet* is a definite advantage when you're doing live comedy shows. 当意即妙に応答する能力は, ライブでコメディショーをやっているときには明らかに強みだ.

throw** oneself **at** a person's **feet (懇願するため)人の足もとにひざまずく ▪ She *threw herself at his feet* and asked for mercy. 彼女は彼の足もとにひざまずいて慈悲を乞うた.

trample** [**tread**]... **under foot ...を踏みにじる; を踏みつけにする, 抑圧する ▪ The elephants would have *trampled* us *under foot.* そのゾウたちは我々を踏みにじっただろう ▪ He *trod* my rights *under foot.* 彼は私の権利を踏みにじった ▪ The spirit of humanity *is* too often *trod under foot* by the spirit of trade. 人間性は商売根性のためにしばしば踏みにじられる.

under foot **1** 足もとが ▪ It was wet *under foot.* 足もとは湿っていた.

2《海》船底の下に ▪ The pilot dropped anchor *under foot.* 水先案内はいかりを船底の下におろした.

3 踏みつけて, 屈服させて, 支配下に ▪ We have him *under foot.* 我々は彼を服従させている.

***under** [**beneath**] a person's **foot** [**feet**]* **1** 人の足もとに; 人に服従して, 人の意のままになって ▪ Mr. Smith is now *under my feet.* スミス氏は今は私の意のままである.

2 まつわりついて, 足手まといで ▪ The children have been *under my feet* all morning so I haven't been able to get any work done. 午前中ずっと子供たちが私にまつわりついていたので, 仕事が全くできなかった.

vote with** one's **feet (ある場所・団体から立ち去ることによって)反対[不支持]の意思表示をする ▪ Parents are *voting with their feet* and moving their children to schools where there is better discipline. 親たちは不支持を表明して, よりよい教育方針の学校に子供を転校させている ▪ The service at the market was so bad that shoppers decided to *vote with their feet.* そのマーケットのサービスは非常に悪かったので, 買い物客たちは寄りつかないことに決めた ▪ If the conference is boring, people will probably *vote with their feet.* 会議が退屈ならば, 人々はたぶん退出によって意思表示をするだろう.

walk** a person **off** his **feet →WALK a person off his legs.

with a foal at foot (雌馬が)子馬を足もとに従えて ▪ In the stable yard were two excellent mares, *with foals at foot.* うまやの囲いには子馬を足もとに従えた2頭のすばらしい雌馬がいた.

with both feet どっしりと ▪ He came down *with both feet* against the proposal. 彼はその提案に断固反対した.

*(**with** one's) **feet foremost*** **1** 足から先に ▪ We crawled *feet foremost* into our bag. 我々は足から先に寝袋に入った.

2 死んで, 死体として ▪ He was carried *feet foremost.* 彼は死んで運び出された ▪ The disease carried him out *with his feet foremost.* その病気で彼は亡くなった. ☞死体は足を先にして運び出す習慣から.

foot[2] /fʊt/ 動 ***foot** oneself* 落ち着く ▪ He *footed himself* in this land. 彼はこの国に落ち着いた.

foot it《口》**1** 歩く, 徒歩で旅をする; 走る ▪ I shall *foot it* home. 私は歩いて家へ帰ります.

2 踊る, ステップを踏む ▪ Fairies *footed it* to the cricket's song. 妖精はコオロギの歌に合わせて踊った.

foot the bill《口》支払いをする, 経費をもつ; 行為の責めを負う; 損害を償う ▪ It was the bride's father who *footed* all *the bills.* 経費のすべてをもったのは花嫁の父であった. ☞「勘定書の下部 (foot) に署名して支払う」から.

footed /fʊ́təd/ 形 ***footed as** [**with**] **the wind*** 風のように速い足をもって ▪ The horse was *footed as the wind.* 馬は風のように速かった.

footing /fʊ́tɪŋ/ 名 *(**be**) **on a ...footing*** ...の関係[立場]にある ▪ I *am on a* friendly *footing* with the President. 私は大統領と親しい間柄です ▪ Men and women should approach each other *on an* equal *footing.* 男女は対等の立場で接すべきである ▪ This country *is on a* war [peace] *footing.* この国は戦時[平時]体制にある.

*(**be**) **on a good** [**bad**] **footing with*** ...に評判が良い[悪い] ▪ He *is on a good footing with* the general manager. 彼は総支配人に受けが良い.

get** [**gain, obtain**] **a footing in ...に地歩を占める, 立脚地を得る ▪ He *got a footing in* the firm. 彼はその会社に地位を得た.

keep** one's **footing **1** ころばずにいる ▪ He *kept his footing* on the ice. 彼は氷上ですっくと立っていた.

2 足場を保つ ▪ He *keeps his footing* in society. 彼は社会に足場を保っている.

lose** [**miss**] one's **footing 足を踏みはずす, 足をすべらす ▪ He *lost his footing* and fell. 彼は足をすべらせてころんだ.

mind** one's **footing (登山のときなど)足の踏みかた[足もと]に注意する ▪ *Mind your footing*! 足もとに気をつけなさい!

pay** (**for**) one's **footing 入会金を払う, 入会のあいさつにふるまいをする ▪ He has *paid his footing*, so now he is one of us. 彼は入会金を払ったんだから

もう我々の仲間の一人だ ▪ When he joined the club, he *paid his footing*, a pint of beer for every member. 彼がクラブに入会したとき, 入会あいさつとしてすべての会員に1パイントのビールをふるまった.

place ... on a footing of equality ...を対等の立場におく ▪ It *placed* the two powers *on a footing of equality*. そのため2強国は対等の立場になった.

footlights /fʊ́tlàɪts/ 名 ***across the footlights*** 舞台越しに, 役者から観客に ▪ Otis Skinner projects himself *across the footlights*. オーティス・スキナーは観客の立場になって考える.

appear before the footlights 脚光を浴びて登場する, 舞台に立つ, 役者になる ▪ He will *appear before the footlights* only one week. 彼は1週間だけ舞台に立つことになるだろう.

behind the footlights 舞台の上で ▪ Romance can blossom *behind the footlights*. 舞台の上でロマンスが花咲くこともある.

get (it) across the footlights 《口》(俳優がしゃれなどを観客に)受けるようにする; (しゃれなどが)受ける ▪ It is doubtful whether the plan would *get across the footlights*. その企画が観客に受けるかどうか疑問だ.

get over the footlights 《口》(劇・俳優が)当たりを取る ▪ The show *got over the footlights*. そのショーは当たりを取った.

smell of the footlights 芸人くさい, 芝居じみている ▪ He *smells of the footlights*. 彼は芸人くさい.

footloose /fʊ́tlù:s/ 形 ***footloose and fancy-free*** 自由で気楽な[恋を知らない]《独身者》 ▪ He is *footloose and fancy-free*. 彼は自由で気楽(な独身者)だ ▪ I was *footloose and fancy-free* and was able to be there for him. 私は身軽で気楽だったので彼のためにそこに行くことが可能だった. ☞fancy-free (Sh., *Mids. N. D.* 2. 1. 164) から.

footprint /fʊ́tprɪnt/ 名 ***footprints on the sands of time*** →SAND.

footsie /fʊ́tsi/ 名 ***play footsie (with)*** 《口》
1 (テーブルの下で異性の足に触れ合ったりして)...といちゃつく ▪ I've never *played footsie with* her. 僕は彼女といちゃついたことはない.
2 (特に政界などで) ...と馴れ合う ▪ The mayor is *playing footsie with* the Syndicate. 市長はその企業連合と馴れ合っている.

footstep /fʊ́tstèp/ 名 ***follow [tread, walk] in** a person's **footsteps*** 人の足跡をたどる; 人の例にならう, 志を継ぐ ▪ He called upon his disciples to *follow in his footsteps*. 彼は弟子たちに自分の志を継ぐように求めた.

for /fər, fɔ:r/ 前 接 ***all out for*** 総計... ▪ *All out for* 44. 総計44です.

be for it 名前を犯罪簿に記入されている, 処罰されることになっている; のっぴきならないはめにある ▪ If anything happens to his pilot, he *is for it*. もし彼の操縦士に何か起これば, 彼は処罰を免れない ▪ The manager wants to see you.—Then I expect I'*m for it*. 支配人があなたに会いたいと言っているよ—それでは僕はしかられるにちがいない. ☞it《軍俗》= punishment.

A for A **1** Aが同じなら ▪ Bulk *for* bulk, water is heavier than oil. 量が同じなら水のほうが油より重い.
2 A対Aなら ▪ Man *for* man, the Labour leaders leave the Tories looking like political pigmies. 人間対人間なら, 労働党幹部は保守党幹部をつまらない政治家のように見させる.

for all **1**〚前置詞的に〛...にもかかわらず ▪ He is not contented *for all* his wealth. 彼は金持ちなのに満足していない.
2〚接続詞的に〛どのように...しようとも ▪ *For all* you say, I still like him. あなたが何と言おうと私はやはり彼が好きである.

for all A B 〚強い否定〛Aは(Bで)ないので[Bしないので]; AをBしないので《Bは形容詞節》 ▪ I might as well have no son, *for all* the comfort you are to me. お前はちっともわしの慰めにならないので, わしには息子はいないも同然だ ▪ *For all* the improvement I've made so far, I might as well give up singing. 今まで一向にうまくならなかったので, 歌はやめたほうがよいかもしれない.

for all [aught, what]** one **knows [can tell] 知らない[わからない]が; かもしれないが ▪ We might be in Paris *for all* he *knows*. 我々がパリにいても彼は知らないだろう ▪ He might be a Frenchman or an Italian, *for all* I *can tell*. 彼がフランス人かイタリア人か私にはわからない ▪ He might have been a crook, *for all* I *know*. 彼は詐欺師だったかもわからないが ▪ *For all* I *know to the contrary*, it may still be in existence and in use. そうでないかもしれないが, それはまだ存在していて使用されているかもしれない. ☞"to the contrary" がつくことがある.

for all me 私は構わないが; 私としては ▪ You may eat it *for all me*. それを食べても構わないよ ▪ *For all me*, I have nothing to complain of. 私としては何も不平はありません.

for all that →THAT.

for (all) the world →WORLD.

for all (the world) to see 多くの人に見られて ▪ Don't wander down the street drunk *for all (the world) to see*. 酔って往来をふらついて人目にさらすではないぞ.

for anything →ANYTHING.

for better or for worse →BETTER[1].

for it それに処すべき, それに対して ▪ There was no help *for it*. どうにもしかたがなかった. ☞it はばく然と"事態"を意味する.

for ... like まあ...として (= by WAY of) ▪ We'll put it, *for* argument *like*, that he has a cut on one cheek. 我々はまあ意見として, 彼には片ほおに切り傷があると言っておこう. ☞like = so to speak.

for the asking →ASKING.

for A to do **1** Aが...するのは ▪ It was impossible *for* them *to* send assistance to the besieged. 彼らがろう城軍に援助を送るのは不可能であった ▪ *For* her *to* submit would be impossible. 彼女が屈服す

ることはありえないだろう.

2 Aが…するのを ▪ We shall wait *for* him *to* return. 我々は彼が帰るのを待ちましょう.

3 Aが…するように ▪ He stepped aside *for* her *to* enter. 彼は彼女が入れるようにわきへよけた.

4 Aが…する《前の名詞にかかる》 ▪ Is there a house *for* foreigners *to* stop at? 外国人が泊まる家がありますか ▪ It is time *for* you *to* go to bed. もうあなたの寝る時間です.

For why? なぜかと言うに.

had it not been for = IF it had not been for.

if it were not for →IF.

***it is for** a person **to** do* 人が…すべきものである[するのが適当である, してよい] ▪ *It is for* you *to* apologize. あなたが断りを言うべきです ▪ *It is for* the guilty *to* live in fear. 罪人はびくびくして暮らして当然だ.

***it is not for** a person **to** do* 人が…する柄ではない[するのはもったいない] ▪ *It is not for* me *to* dictate to you. 私はあなたに指図する柄ではありません ▪ *It is not for* me *to* live in such a house. 私がこんな家に住むのはもったいない.

O(h) for ...! ああ…がほしい ▪ *O for* a glass of wine*!* ああ, ワインが1杯飲みたいなあ ▪ *Oh for* a fine day*!* ああ天気になってほしいなあ.

There [That] is ... for you! あれこそ[それこそ]…というものですよ ▪ *That's* gratitude *for you!* それこそ感謝の気持ちっていうものですよ ▪ *There's* a sight *for you!* あれこそ見ものですよ! ☞for you は相手の注意を引くためのもの; この表現は額面通りの意味にも皮肉にも用いられる.

there is nothing for it but →NOTHING.

too ... for **1** …にはあまり…すぎる ▪ The book is *too* difficult *for* me. その本は私にはむずかしすぎる.

2 あまり…で…できない ▪ The emotion is *too* deep *for* words. その感情はあまりに深くて言葉に表せない.

were it not for = IF it were not for.

What is** he [etc.] **for** a man [etc.]**? …はどんな…ですか ▪ *What is* she *for* a woman? 彼女はどんな女性ですか ▪ *What is* that *for* a Zenobia? それはどのゼノビアですか.

forage /fɔ́:rɪdʒ|fɔ́r-/ 名 ***(be) on the forage*** (牛馬が)食べ物をあさって(いる); (人が)食糧徴発をやって(いる) ▪ I found him *on the forage* in the kitchen. 彼は台所で食糧をあさっていた.

foray /fɔ́:reɪ|fɔ́r-/ 名 *one's **first foray into*** (不慣れな分野)への最初の進出 ▪ It will be *my first foray into* the profession. これは私の最初の専門職への進出だ ▪ Gordon is going to make *his first foray into* politics. ゴードンは初めて政界に進出しようとしている.

go on a foray 略奪に出かける; 出かける ▪ I *went on a foray* to hunt wild mushrooms at Livingston Park. リビングストン公園へキノコ狩りに出かけた.

make a foray 急襲する (*on, into*) ▪ Vikings *made a foray on* the port. バイキングはその港を急襲した.

make a foray to (ある目的で)…へ出かける ▪ He *makes* weekly *forays to* the public library. 彼は毎週公立図書館に出かける.

forbid /fərbíd/ 動 ***forbid** a person **to** do* 人が…するのを禁じる[差し止める] ▪ The rain *forbids* us *to* go out. 雨のため我々は外出できない.

God [Heaven, The Lord, The saints] forbid (that ...)! (…は)断じてない; 断じて(…で)ないように ▪ *God forbid that* he should injure you*!* 彼があなたを傷つけるということは断じてない. ☞「神が…を禁じたまわんことを」が原義; forbid は仮定法.

forbidden /fərbídən/ 形 ***forbidden fruit*** **1** 禁断の木の実 (《聖》*Gen.* 2. 17) ▪ Her cheek was still *forbidden fruit* to him. 彼女のほおは彼にはまだ禁断の木の実であった. ☞Eden の園で Adam と Eve とが食べることを禁じられていた知恵の木の実.

2 禁断の悦楽, 不倫(の相手) ▪ Cash and Carter were married to other people and their love was *forbidden fruit*. キャッシュとカーターは別の相手と結婚しており, 彼らの恋は禁断の悦楽だった.

3 盗品 ▪ Travellers would exchange their *forbidden fruit* for a fistful of kyat on the black market. 旅行者たちは, 盗品をやみ市場で多額のチャット(ミャンマーの通貨単位)とよく交換した.

taste of forbidden fruit 禁じられた欲望を満たす ▪ He decided to *taste of forbidden fruit* on his birthday. 彼は誕生日に禁じられた欲望を満たそうと決心した.

force[1] /fɔ:rs/ 名 ***a force to be reckoned with*** 軽んずべからざる勢力 ▪ Regionalism is *a force to be reckoned with* in this country. この国では地方分権主義は軽んずべからざる勢力である.

break the force of …の衝撃を緩和する ▪ The ring of coral *broke the force of* the tsunami. 環礁は津波の勢いを弱めた.

bring ... into force = put ... in FORCE.

by [with] force and arms 《法》暴力によって ▪ I broke a close *with force and arms*. 私は暴力によって所有地を侵害した. ☞<Ⓛ vi et armis.

by (main) force 力ずくで; むり押しに; 暴力で ▪ We made him do it *by force*. 我々は彼に強制的にそれをさせた.

by (the) force of …の力で, によって ▪ The hardest things become easy *by the force of* habit. いかに困難なことでも習慣の力でやさしくなる.

by the sheer force of …の力だけで ▪ He made them agree *by the sheer force of* argument. 彼は議論の力だけで, 彼らに同意させた.

come into force (法律が)実施される, 施行される ▪ The new law *comes into force* on January 1st. 新法は1月1日から施行される.

force of arms 武力(行使) ▪ They succeeded in seizing power by *force of arms*. 彼らは武力行使により権力奪取に成功した.

go out of force (法律などが)自然に効力を失う ▪ The law has *gone out of force*. その法は自然に効力を失った.

***have force to** do* …する力がある ▪ Let not her cries *have force to* move you. 彼女の泣き叫ぶ声にあなたが動かされることのないように.

have force with …に対して説得力を持つ ▪ Such arguments *have force with* the masses. そのような論法は民衆に対して有力である.

in force **1** (法律が)施行されて, 効力があって ▪ The law remains *in force*. その法はまだ効力がある ▪ The obligation stands *in force*. その債務は有効である.

2 =in great FORCE 1.

3 強力に ▪ The country was represented *in force* in the exhibition. その展覧会でその国は強力に表象していた.

4 勢いが ▪ The rain increased *in force*. 雨は勢いを増した.

(*in*) *full force* **1** 総勢で; 威力を十分発揮して ▪ The police turned out *in full force*. 警察が総勢で出動した.

2 本格的に ▪ Industrial revolution has hit the country *full force*. 産業革命がその国を本格的に襲った.

3 (法律などが)十分効力をもって ▪ This custom remains *in full force*. この習慣は十分生きている.

in great force **1** 《軍》大挙して, 多数で ▪ They entered the enemy's country *in great force*. 彼らは大挙して敵国に入った.

2 《口》大元気で, 能力を十分働かせて ▪ He was better and *in great force* again. 彼は快方に向かっていてまた大いに元気になっていた.

3 《口》(会話で)雄弁に, とうとうと ▪ Richard talked *in great force* tonight, helped by the champagne. リチャードは今夜シャンパンの勢いを借りてとうとうと弁じた.

***join forces* (*with*)** (…と)力を合わせる ▪ The two explorers *joined forces*. その二人の探検家は力を合わせた.

of force 余儀なく, 必ず ▪ I went there *of force*. 私は余儀なくそこへ行った.

of no force 無効で, 効力のない ▪ A promise made under compulsion is *of no force*. 強制されてした約束は無効である.

out in force 大挙して繰りだして, 勢ぞろいして ▪ The police were *out in force*, patrolling the streets. 警察は大量動員されて通りをパトロールしていた.

put a force upon (言葉など)に無理な解釈をする ▪ He *put a force upon* my words. 彼は私の言葉に無理な解釈をした.

put … in* [*into*] *force (法律)を実施する, 施行する ▪ He *put in force* the laws of Edward the Confessor. 彼はエドワードざんげ王の法律を施行した.

see the force of …の道理[主旨, 真意]がわかる ▪ I *see the force of* your argument. 私はあなたの議論の主旨はよくわかる ▪ I can't *see the force of* doing what one dislikes. 私はきらいなことをする道理がわからない.

stand in force →in FORCE 1.

(*the*) *driving force* (*behind*) 原動力, 推進力; 立役者 ▪ Many say Ronald Reagan was *the driving force behind* the end of the Cold War. ロナルド・レーガンが冷戦終結の立役者だったと言う人は多い.

(*the*) *force*(*s*) *of darkness* 《しばしば戯》(悪影響を与える)陰の影響力, 闇の大立者 ▪ Identifying *the forces of darkness* is not always as easy as it was in World War II. 闇の影響者をつきとめるのは, いつも第二次世界大戦中のように容易にできるわけではない ▪ The forces of light and *the forces of darkness* are constantly at odds. 光の力と闇の力とはいつも敵対している ▪ As a child, we sang songs celebrating the force of light (the good people) against *the force of darkness* (evil). 子供のころ, 私たちは闇の影響力(悪)に対する光の力(善人)をたたえる歌を歌った.

***use force* (*on*)** (人に)暴力をふるう ▪ He *used force on* me. 彼は私に暴力をふるった.

with all** one's **force 全力を出して ▪ Strike the ball *with all your force*. 力いっぱいボールを打て.

with force and arms →by FORCE and arms.

with much force 力強く; 強い説得力をもって ▪ He described the battle *with much force*. 彼はその戦闘を力強く描いた ▪ He argued *with much force*. 彼は強い説得力をもって論じた.

force[2] /fɔːrs/ 動 ***be forced to** do* やむをえず…する ▪ I shall *be forced to* proceed against you. やむをえずあなたを訴えなければならないでしょう.

be forced to be 《口》余儀なく[必然的に]…される ▪ The lead *was forced to be* cut away in many places. 導線は必然的に多くのところで切断された.

force … down** a person's **throat →thrust … down a person's THROAT.

force** a person's **hand →HAND[1].

force … into a sense (言葉)の意味をこじつける, (言葉)に無理な解釈をつける ▪ Don't *force* the words of Moses *into* such *a sense*. モーゼの言葉をそんな意味にこじつけてはいけません.

***force** oneself **on* [*upon*]** **1** …に押しかける ▪ She *forced herself upon* him. 彼女は彼の押しかけ女房になった ▪ The conviction *forced itself upon* me. 私はそう確信せざるをえなかった.

2 …に性的関係を迫る, 暴行(しようと)する ▪ Wallace *forced himself on* her in the car, the woman said. ウォーレスは車の中で私に関係を迫った, とその女性は言った ▪ He told police she had *forced herself on* him while I was asleep. 私が寝ているあいだに彼女が無理に関係をもった, と彼は警察に述べた.

force … open …をむりやりに開ける ▪ The safe *was forced open*. 金庫はこじあけられていた.

***force the pace* [*running*]** (競走で)早く相手を疲れさせるために無理してピッチをあげる; (仕事を)無理に早める ▪ Don't be *forcing the pace*. 仕事は無理に早めるばかりではいけない.

***force** a person **to** do* 人に無理に…させる ▪ He

forced me *to* go there. 彼は私を無理にそこへ行かせた.

force *one's* ***way*** 無理に進む, 押し分けて進む ▪ She determined to *force her way* into society. 彼女は無理に社交界に出て行こうと決心した ▪ You need not *force your way* out, if you are in no hurry. 急いでいないのなら, 人を押し分けて出るには及びません.

force *one's* ***way through*** …を押し分けて進む[通る] ▪ We should *force our way through* the crowd. 我々は群衆の中を押し分けて通るべきだ.

fore /fɔːr/ 形名前 ***bring … to the fore*** …を著名にする, 頭角をあらわさせる; を活躍させる ▪ The revolution *brought* many enterprising men *to the fore*. 革命で多くの進取の気性に富んだ人々が世に出た.

come to the fore 前面に現れる; 頭角を現す ▪ The question of local taxation must *come to the fore* next session. 地方税の問題が次の議会には主題となるにちがいない ▪ He has *come to the fore* recently. 彼は最近頭角を現してきた ▪ The new teaching method has *come to the fore*. 新教授法が世に出てきた.

to the fore **1** (人がその場に)いて, 近い所にいて ▪ I wish he were *to the fore* here. あの人がここにいてくれたらよいのに.

2 まだ生存して ▪ The general was still *to the fore*. 将軍はまだ生きていた.

3 (金などが)手もとにあって, すぐ役立てることができて ▪ He has two thousand pounds *to the fore*. 彼は手もとに2,000ポンド持っている.

4 よく見えて, 目立って; 顕著に ▪ Magnificent structures are there *to the fore*. 壮大な建物がそこに目立って見えていた.

5 前面に; 顕著な活躍をして ▪ We are safe while he is *to the fore*. 我々は彼が盛んに活躍している間は安全である.

foredoom /fɔːrdúːm/ 動 ***be foredoomed to*** …するものと最初から決まっている ▪ The project *was foredoomed to* failure. その企画は失敗するものと最初から決まっていた.

forefront /fɔ́ːrfrʌ̀nt/ 名 ***come to the forefront*** 世の注目を浴びる, クローズアップされる ▪ The Mayan civilization *came to the forefront* of history during the Classical (A.D 300–900) period. マヤ文明は古典時代(紀元300-900年)に歴史の最前線に踊り出た.

in the forefront (***of***) (…の)最前線に, 第一線に ▪ They were *in the forefront of* the battle. 彼らは戦闘の第一線にあった ▪ I place Pitt *in the forefront of* men of importance. 私はピットを重要人物の最前線におく.

foreground /fɔ́ːrgràʊnd/ 名 ***keep … in the foreground*** …を表面に押し出しておく ▪ We *kept* the subject *in the foreground*. 我々はその問題を前面に押し出しておいた.

forehead /fɔ́ːrhèd, fɔ́rɪd/ 名 ***have the forehead to*** *do* 厚かましくも…する ▪ He *had the forehead to* say so to my face. 彼は厚かましくも私に面と向かってそう言った.

foreign /fɔ́ːrən|fɔ́r-/ 形 ***foreign to*** …と無関係で; と性質を異にする ▪ Your argument is *foreign to* the question. あなたの議論はその問題に無関係です ▪ Lying is *foreign to* his nature. 嘘をつくことは彼の性に合わない.

forelock /fɔ́ːrlàk|-lɔ̀k/ 名 ***take*** [***seize***] ***time*** [***an occasion, an opportunity***] ***by the forelock*** 時[機会]をのがさず捕える ▪ *Time* flies with such a frightful rapidity that I am compelled to *take* it *by the forelock*. 時は非常に早く飛んで行くので私はのがさず捕えねばならない. ☞「時」は前頭部にだけ毛をはやした形で描かれることから.

touch *one's* ***forelock*** 《口》極端にうやうやしく敬礼をする ▪ The boss doesn't expect us to *touch our forelocks*. 社長は我々がひどくうやうやしい敬礼をすることを期待してはいない. ☞「前髪に触れる」は昔のうやうやしい敬礼.

foremost /fɔ́ːrmòʊst/ 副 ***first and foremost*** →FIRST.

forest /fɔ́ːrəst/ 名 ***not see the forest for the trees*** 《米》 = cannot see the WOOD for the trees.

forever /fərévər/ 副 ***forever and a day*** 《口》いつまでもいつまでも; いつも ▪ We waited for him *forever and a day*. 我々は彼をいつまでもいつまでも待った. ☞for ever and ay《廃》「永遠にいつまでも」のなまった形式.

forever and ever 永久に, いつまでも, 常に《通例精神的なものに用いる》 ▪ God will live *forever and ever*. 神は永遠に生き給う.

take (…) ***forever*** …にとって(時間が)ひどく長くかかる ▪ It *took* me *forever* to figure that out. それを理解するのに長時間かかった.

forewarn /fɔːrwɔ́ːrn/ 動 ***Forewarned is forearmed.*** 《諺》警告は警備,「備えあれば憂いなし」.

forfeit /fɔ́ːrfət/ 名 ***be the forfeit of*** …の罰として取られる ▪ His life *was the forfeit of* his crime. 彼は罪に対する罰として命を失った.

pay (***the***) ***forfeit*** (***of***) (…という)罰金を支払う ▪ He who murders *pays the forfeit of* life. 人殺しをする者は命という罰金を払う.

take (***the***) ***forfeit*** (***of***) (…という)罰金を取る, (を処罰として)没収する ▪ You have undone a faithful gentleman, by *taking forfeit of* his land. 君は土地を没収して誠実な紳士を破滅させた.

forget /fərgét/ 動 ***don't forget me to*** …によろしくお伝えください ▪ *Don't forget me to* your brother. お兄さんによろしくお伝えください.

Don't you forget it. 《口》必ず覚えていてください ▪ Even if you don't like him, he is a very important person, and *don't you forget it*. たとえ君が嫌いでも彼はとても有力な人物だ, よく覚えておきなさい.

forget *oneself* **1** おのれを顧みない, 全く没我的である.

2 身のほどを忘れる, 地位[身分]を忘れる ▪ Pooh! You *forget yourself.* ふん! 身のほどを知れ!

3 自制心を失う, かっとなる; 慎みを忘れる ▪ I must have been mad to *forget myself* like that. あんなに慎みを忘れるとは私も気が狂っていたにちがいない.

4 うっかりする, うっかりしたことをする《つい秘密をもらすなど》; 没頭する ▪ He *forgot himself* and let slip a vital secret. 彼はうっかりしてつい重大な秘密を漏らしてしまった ▪ I *forget myself* entirely when reading Shelly. シェリーの詩を読んでいてすっかりのめり込んだ.

5 意識[正気]を失う, 我を忘れる ▪ I had just *forgotten myself.* ちょっと夢うつつになっていたのだった.

6《婉曲》(子供が)大小便をもらす ▪ Little Billy *forgot himself* on our neighbor's couch. ビリー坊やは隣人宅のソファーにおもらしをした.

forget and forgive/forgive and forget (過去のことを)すっかり水に流す ▪ Come, come, Mrs. Malaprop, we must *forget and forgive.* まあまあ, マラプロップさん, 過ぎたことはすっかり水に流してしまわねばなりません.

Forget it! 《口》お構いなく!, どういたしまして! ▪ I smiled at him, and said, "*Forget it!*" 私は彼にほほえみかけて,「お構いなく!」と言った.

forget more about** a thing **than** a person **ever knew 人よりもよく知っている ▪ Tom has *forgotten more about* camping *than* most people *ever knew.* トムはキャンプについてはたいていの人々よりよく知っている.

***not forget to** do* 忘れずに…する ▪ Do*n't forget to* come. 忘れずにぜひおいでください.

not forgetting 《主に英》〚文尾につけて〛…も含めて, も忘れずに ▪ I like Bach, Mozart, and Vivaldi, *not forgetting* Telemann. 私はバッハ, モーツァルトにビバルディが好きだ, それにテレマンも.

forgetful /fərɡétfəl/ 形 ***forgetful of*** **1** …を忘れて ▪ She is dancing *forgetful of* all grief. 彼女は悲しみをすっかり忘れてダンスしている.

2 …を忘れがちである ▪ He is *forgetful of* his duties. 彼は職務を怠りがちである.

forgive /fərɡív/ 動 ***could* [*might, can, may*] *be forgiven for*** *doing* …してもやむを得ない, 無理もない ▪ You *could be forgiven for thinking* so. 君がそう考えるのも無理からぬことだ.

forgive and forget →FORGET.

forgive me, but 《丁寧な質問・反論の仕方で》失礼ですが ▪ *Forgive me, but* I am afraid you're wrong. 失礼ですが, あなたは誤っておられると思います.

fork /fɔːrk/ 名 ***a fork in the road*** 二股に分かれた道路, 分かれ道 ▪ When you come to *a fork in the road*, stay close to the river. 分かれ道に来たら, 川に近い方を行きなさい.

***in the fork*(*s*)** 《米》合流する川にはさまれて ▪ The ground *in the fork* was sown with oats. 合流する川にはさまれた土地にはオートムギがまかれていた.

play a good knife and fork →KNIFE.

forked /fɔːrkt/ 形 ***a knight of the forked order*** 妻に不義をされる夫 ▪ I should be sure to be clubbed *a knight of the forked order.* 私はきっと妻に不義をされて笑い者になるだろう. ☞forked = horned (寝取られた).

speak with* (*a*) *forked tongue →TONGUE.

forlorn /fərlɔ́ːrn/ 形 ***a forlorn hope*** **1** 急襲隊, 決死隊 ▪ The *forlorn hope* of each attack consisted of a sergeant and twelve Europeans. 各襲撃の決死隊は一人の軍曹と12人のヨーロッパ兵から成っていた.

2 絶体絶命の状態の人々 ▪ His audience was all the *forlorn hope.* 彼の聴衆はみな絶体絶命の状態の人々であった.

3 無鉄砲な暴漢 ▪ I don't want to make this realm a prey to all *forlorn hopes.* 私はこの国を無鉄砲な暴漢たちのえじきにしたくない.

4 暴挙 ▪ They never went upon *a forlorn hope.* 彼らは暴挙に出たことはない.

5 はかない望み; 成功の見込みのほとんどない事業《hope の誤解から》 ▪ She had *a forlorn hope* of a letter. 彼女は手紙が来るかとはかない望みを持っていた. ☞forlorn hope < D 'Verloren hoop' (lost troop).

form[1] /fɔːrm/ 名 ***a matter of form*** 《口》単に形式上のこと; 日常のおきまり仕事 ▪ It is only *a matter of form.* それは単なる形式上のことにすぎない.

as a matter of form 形式上, 儀礼上, 体裁上 ▪ We shall have to attend the ball just *as a matter of form.* 私たちはほんの儀礼上その舞踏会に出席せねばならないだろう ▪ You have only to sign it *as a matter of form.* 君はただほんの形式上署名しさえすればよい.

bad* [*poor*] *form 《口》無作法; きざ (↔ good FORM) ▪ It is *bad form* to write a letter in red ink. 赤インキで手紙を書くのは無作法です ▪ It is *bad form* to make a display of one's learning. 学問を見せびらかすのはきざだ.

be* [*feel*] *at the top of** one's **form 最好調である ▪ I was *feeling at the top of my form.* 私は体の調子が最も良かった.

(*be*) *in* [*on*] *form* (人や馬が競技・仕事に)好調で(ある) ▪ Willow *was* clearly *in form.* ウィロー号は明らかに調子がよかった.

(*be*) *out of form* **1** (人や馬が競技・仕事に)調子が悪い, 体の調子が悪い ▪ The player *was* certainly *out of form.* その選手は確かに調子が悪かった.

2 《野球・口》打撃の調子が悪い ▪ The batter *is out of form.* 打者は打撃の調子が悪い.

for form's sake 形式上, 形式だけ ▪ You must take the examination *for form's sake.* 君は形式上試験を受けねばならない.

good form 《口》正しい礼儀作法; 礼にかなう (↔ bad FORM) ▪ You must value *good form.* 君は正しい礼儀作法を重んじねばならない ▪ It is not *good form* to grow angry in discussion. 討論で腹を立てるのは礼を失する.

have form 《警察俗》前科がある ▪ Her husband *has form.* 彼女の夫には前科がある.

in due* [*proper*] *form 正式に, 正しい形式によって

▪ The deed was drawn up *in due form.* その証書は正式に書かれた.
in form **1** =(be) in FORM.
2 正式に, 正しい形式によって《今は in due FORM》 ▪ The publisher made an apology *in form.* 発行人は正式に謝罪した.
3 形式上, 型ばかりに ▪ The ceremony was hurried through *in form.* 式は型ばかりに大急ぎですまされた.
in full form 儀礼を整えて ▪ We went in a carriage *in full form.* 儀礼を整えて馬車で行った.
in good form 好調で; 上きげんで, 大元気で ▪ He was not *in good form* for a long walk. 彼は遠足するには調子がよくなかった ▪ My uncle was *in good form* last night. おじは昨夜は上きげんであった.
in great form **1** 儀礼を整えて ▪ These officers attended *in great form.* この役人たちは儀礼を整えて出席した.
2 =in good FORM.
in one form or another 何らかの形で ▪ An Englishman will have his gambling *in one form or another.* 英国人は何らかの形でばくちを打つものだ.
in proper form →in due FORM.
in some form or other 何らかの形で ▪ Energy remains *in some form or other.* エネルギーは何らかの形で残る.
in the form of ...という(形における), という形で ▪ We find new inventions *in the form of* toys. 新発明のおもちゃがある ▪ His new book is a story told *in the form of* letters. 彼の新著は書簡体で語られた物語である.
lose *one's* ***form*** 元気を失う, 調子が悪くなる ▪ The horse has simply *lost her form.* その馬は全く調子が悪くなってしまった.
off (*one's*) ***form*** =(be) out of FORM.
on ... form ...の成績[行動, 状勢]から判断して ▪ *On* present *form*, it looks highly unlikely. 現在の状勢からみてそれはとても無理のようだ. ☞form《競馬》「今までの馬の成績記録」.
run (***true***) ***to form*** (特によくない行動が)いつも通りである, 本来[予想]通りである (→true to FORM) ▪ If he *runs to form*, he is almost sure to win. 彼が本来通りであれば, ほぼ確実に優勝する ▪ His speech *ran true to form.* 彼の演説は例のごとくだった ▪ The story lines *ran true to form.* 話の筋は予想通りだった ▪ His actions *ran true to form.* He idled away the Sunday afternoon. 彼の行動は例によって例のごとくだった. その日曜日の午後を何もしないで過ごした.
take form and shape 形をなす ▪ That model is beginning to *take form and shape.* その模型はだんだん形をなしてきている.
take the form of ...の形を取る, となる ▪ The dialogue necessarily *takes the form of* a narrative. 対話は必然的に物語の形を取る ▪ The devil *took the form of* an angel. 悪魔は天使にばけた.
true to form 例のごとく, 例によって (→run (true) to FORM) ▪ *True to form*, he arrived at the party late. 彼は例によってパーティーに遅れて来た.
What's the form? それはどんなものですか ▪ *What's the form?*—Very quiet and enjoyable. それはどんなふうですか?—非常に静かで愉快です.

form[2] /fɔːrm/ 動 ***be formed of*** ...から成る ▪ Japan *is formed of* four large islands. 日本は4つの大きな島から成っている.
form an opinion (...について)意見を形成する, 考えをもつ (*about, on*) ▪ It doesn't take him long to *form an opinion on* a player. 選手について判断するのに彼にはあまり長くはかからない ▪ I've always wanted to *form* my own *opinion about* people. ずっと人間に関して自分の意見をもちたいと思ってきた.
form *two* [*three*, etc.] ***deep*** 2[3, など]列を作る ▪ *Form* four *deep*! 4列作れ.
Form in extended order! 散開!
form *oneself* ***into*** ...の形になる ▪ The cloud *formed itself into* a camel. 雲はラクダの形になった.
form the words ものを言う ▪ He couldn't *form the words.* 彼はものが言えなかった.
form ... to *oneself* ...を心に描く ▪ You may *form to yourself* what a calamity it was. それがどんな災難であったか想像できるでしょう.

formality /fɔːrmǽləti/ 名 ***go through due formalities*** 正式の手続きを経る[形式を踏む, 儀式を行う] ▪ He *went through* the *due formalities* of asking for a leave of absence. 彼は休暇願いの正式の手続きをした.
with formalities 慣例の儀式をもって ▪ He was installed *with* all the usual *formalities.* 彼はきちんと型通りの儀式をもって就任した.
without formality 儀式ばらないで, 非公式に (informally) ▪ He visited us *without formality.* 彼は私たちを普段着で訪問してくれた.

former /fɔ́ːrmər/ 形 ***be a shadow of*** *one's* ***former self*** →the (mere) SHADOW of one's former self.
in former times [***days***] 昔は ▪ *In former times* very few people could read the Bible. 昔は聖書の読める人は非常に少なかった.

forrader /fɑ́rədər/ 副 =FORWARDER.

forswear /fɔːrswéər/ 動 ***forswear*** *oneself* 偽誓[偽証]する ▪ I have sworn to obey the laws, and I cannot *forswear myself.* 法律に従うことを誓ったのだから, 偽誓することはできない.

fort /fɔːrt/ 名 ***hold*** (***down***) ***the fort*** **1** 砦(とりで)を守る ▪ They *held the fort* for days. 彼らは何日も砦を守った.
2《口》勢力を維持する; 作業[勤め]を続ける ▪ *Hold the fort* till I come back. 私が帰るまで作業を続けなさい. ☞アメリカの南北戦争のとき, Sherman 将軍が Corse 将軍に与えた信号.
3《米》留守を守る, 不在中の管理をする ▪ You have to *hold the fort* while your parents are out. 両親が外出中は君が留守を守らなければならない.
sell the fort 砦(とりで)を売る《敵に利点を与える》

▪ Bolt *sold the fort* to the Portuguese commander. ボールトはポルトガルの司令官に砦を売った.

forth /fɔːrθ/ 副 ***and so forth*** →AND.

back and forth あちらこちらと ▪ He was running *back and forth* in the room. 彼は部屋の中をあちらこちらと走っていた.

from this day [etc.] ***forth*** →FROM.

so far forth その程度は, そこまでは ▪ I will pay the cook *so far forth*. コックにその程度は給料を出す.

so far forth as ...の程度まで, だけは ▪ You will be paid *so far forth as* you work. あなたは働くだけは報酬を受けるだろう.

F

fortify /fɔ́ːrtəfàɪ/ 動 ***fortify** oneself* 自説を裏うける ▪ He *fortified himself* by citing many illustrations. 彼は多くの例証をあげて自説を裏うけした.

fortify** oneself **against [***with***] ...に対して[で]強化する ▪ He *fortified himself against* the cold. 彼は防寒具に身を固めた(「寒さしのぎに1杯やった」の意にもなる) ▪ I *fortified myself with* a glass of wine. 私は1杯やって元気をつけた.

fortnight /fɔ́ːrtnàɪt/ 名 ***this day*** [***Monday,*** etc.] ***fortnight*** 2週間前または後のきょう[月曜, など] ▪ It must be paid *this day fortnight*. それは2週間後のきょう支払われなければならない ▪ On *Monday fortnight* I came to London. 2週間前の月曜にロンドンへやって来ました.

would rather keep** a person **a week than a fortnight 人が大食である ▪ I *would rather keep* him *a week than a fortnight*. 彼は大食家である.

fortunate /fɔ́ːrtʃənət/ 形 ***be fortunate in*** 幸いにもよい...を持っている ▪ He *is fortunate in* his wife. 彼はよい妻を持って幸いだ.

fortune /fɔ́ːrtʃən/ 名 ***a small fortune*** 《口》大金, 一財産 ▪ A drink-drive conviction can cost you *a small fortune*. 飲酒運転で有罪と決まれば大金を払わねばならない.

a soldier of fortune (どこの国にでも雇われる)浪士; 山師; 兵卒から実力でたたきあげた軍人 ▪ He was *a soldier of fortune*. 彼は兵卒から実力でたたきあげた軍人だった.

be sitting on a fortune [***gold mine***] →be sitting on a GOLD MINE.

be worth a (***small***) ***fortune*** **1** (物が)大変価値がある, 高価である ▪ This little lot *is worth a small fortune*. この狭い土地は莫大な価値がある.
2 (人が)大金持ちである ▪ The Triston family *is worth a fortune*. トリストン家は大金持ちだ.

by good [***bad***] ***fortune*** 幸運[不運]にも ▪ *By good fortune* I was able to see him. 幸運にも私は彼に会うことができた.

Fortune favors the brave. 《諺》運命の女神は勇者に味方する.

Fortune smiles upon [***on***] ...は運がよい ▪ *Fortune smiles upon* him. 彼は運がよい.

have fortune on** one's **side 幸運である ▪ She *has fortune on her side*. 彼女は幸運である.

have good [***bad***] ***fortune*** 運がよい[運が悪い] ▪ I have *had good fortune* so far. これまでは幸運に恵まれてきた.

have the (***good***) ***fortune to** do* 幸いにも...する ▪ I *had the fortune to* succeed. 私は幸いにも成功した.

make a (***small***) ***fortune*** (***out of***) (...で)金持ちになる, 身代を作る ▪ He's *made a fortune out of* bananas. 彼はバナナで大儲けした.

make** one's **fortune 出世する, 繁昌する ▪ We might all have *made our fortunes*. 我々はみんな立身出世できたかもしれないのだが.

marry a fortune →MARRY[2].

of broken fortunes 零落(れいらく)した ▪ He is a man *of broken fortunes*. 彼は零落の人である.

of fortune 大財産のある ▪ He is an Englishman *of fortune*. 彼はイギリスの大財産家である.

seek** one's **fortune 立身出世を求める ▪ His father dying, he was driven to London to *seek his fortune*. 父が死んだので, 彼は立身出世を求めてロンドンへ行かねばならなかった.

share** a person's **fortunes 人と進退を共にする ▪ I will *share his fortunes*. 彼と運命を共にする.

spend a small fortune 相当の財産を使い果たす ▪ We've *spent a small fortune* on the garden. 私たちはその庭園にちょっとした財産を使った.

tell** a person **his fortune/ tell** a person's **fortune 人の運勢を占う ▪ I asked him to *tell* me *my fortune*. 私は彼に運勢を占ってくれと言った ▪ She *told our fortune*. 彼女は我々の運勢を見てくれた.

tell fortunes 運勢を占う ▪ She *told fortunes* for a living. 彼女は生計を得るために運勢占いをやった.

the fortune of war 武運; 一か八かの冒険 ▪ It remained only to try once more *the fortune of war*. もう一度武運を試すことのみが残っていた ▪ She was his by *the fortune of war*. 彼女は一か八かの冒険によって彼のものとなった.

try** one's **fortune 運を試す, 運試しをする ▪ We are going to *try our fortune* once more. 我々はもう一度運試しをするつもりです.

What [etc.] ***in fortune?*** 一体何? ▪ *What in fortune* were they after? 彼らは一体何を捜していたのか.

forty /fɔ́ːrti/ 名 ***as*** [***by, like***] ***forty*** 《米口》盛んに, 非常な勢いで, 強く ▪ I would have whipped him *like forty*. 私は彼を激しくむち打つところだった ▪ I stick to my principles *like forty*. 私は自分の主義を固く守ります.

forty to the dozen 非常に早く ▪ He walked off *forty to the dozen*. 彼は素早く逃亡した.

forty winks →WINK[1].

with a forty foot pole 《米》〚否定文で〛どうしても ▪ I can't touch her *with a forty foot pole*. どうしても彼女に触れることができない.

forward[1] /fɔ́ːrwərd/ 副形名 (***be***) ***forward***

in [***with***] **1** …が進んでいる ▪ He *is forward in* English, but backward in mathematics. 彼は英語は進んでいるが，数学は遅れている.
2（動物の）妊娠が進んで ▪ Eleven ewes *are forward in* lamb. 11頭の雌羊が妊娠が進んでいる ▪ The mares got *forward with* foal. 雌馬は妊娠が進んだ.

be forward to *do* 進んで…しようとする[したがる] ▪ Those who *are forward to* complain are always backward to work. 不平を言いたがる人々はきまって仕事はしたがらない.

build forward 建造し続ける ▪ God will *build forward* where his foundation is once laid. 神はその基礎が一旦すえられたところでは建造し続けるものである.

forward of《米》…の前の[に] ▪ Look at the little curls just *forward of* her cap. 彼女の帽子の前にちょっと出た小さい巻き毛をご覧よ.

from this day [etc.] ***forward*** →FROM this day forth.

no further forward（予想より）あまり進歩していない ▪ They are *no further forward* than they were 24 hours ago. 彼らは24時間前と比べあまり進んでいない.

put [***set***] *oneself* ***forward***（えらそうに）出しゃばる ▪ Who are you, that *put yourself* so *forward*? そんなに出しゃばるとは君は何者なのか.

forward[2] /fɔ́ːrwərd/ 動 ***forward*** ***…*** (***from …***) ***to***（…から）…へ転送する ▪ We *forwarded* the letter *from* Chicago *to* Springfield. 私たちは，その手紙をシカゴからスプリングフィールドへ転送した.

forwarder /fɔ́ːrwərdər/, **forrader** /fɑ́rədər/ 副 ***get any forwarder*** [***forrader***]《口・戯》〚主に否定文で〛進む，進歩する ▪ I can't tell whether they will *get any forrader*. 彼らが進歩するかどうかわからない.

get no forwarder [***forrader***]《口・戯》少しも進まない，全然進歩しない ▪ We *got no forwarder* than at first. 私たちは初めより少しも進まなかった.

foster /fɑ́stər|fɔ́s-/ 名 ***at foster*** 里子にやられて ▪ They had children out *at foster* there. 彼らは子供たちをそこへ里子に出していた.

fother /fɑ́ðər/ 名 ***fall as a fother*** (***of lead***) 壊滅的な打撃として落ちかかる ▪ Every stroke *falls as a fother*. 打撃のひとつひとつが壊滅的な打撃として落ちかかる.

foul[1] /faʊl/ 形名 ***be foul of*** …にひっかかっている ▪ The fishline *is foul of* a snag. 釣糸が流木にひっかかっている.

be she fair or foul 彼女が美しくても醜くても《この foul の意味は，この句以外は方言》 ▪ I think we shall soon see the nature of the beast, *be she fair or foul*, eh? まもなくその獣の正体がわかるような気がする，そいつが美しくしても醜くてもだ，だろ?

claim a foul 相手方に反則ありと主張する，もの言いをつける ▪ You may *claim a foul* if you see your opponent touch the ball. 相手がボールに触れるのを見たら反則だと主張してよい.

cry foul（不正・不公平に対して）異議を申し立てる ▪ Two Democrats *cried foul* over a plan to extend the duck-hunting season by nine days in Mississippi. 二人の民主党員が，カモ猟の期間をミシシッピ州では9日間延長するという案に異議を申し立てた.

fall [***go, run***] ***foul of*** [***on***] **1** …と衝突する《比喩的にも》 ▪ Henry *fell foul of* the Pope. ヘンリーは教皇と衝突した ▪ He will *run foul of* the law some day. 彼はいつか法に抵触するだろう.
2 …を攻撃する ▪ The Duke *fell foul on* [*of*] him for that. 公爵はそのため彼を攻撃した.
3 …と気まずくなる ▪ There was some foolish quarrel last year, and we *fell foul of* each other. 昨年ばかげたけんかをして，我々はお互いに気まずくなった. ☞foul「綱などがもつれること」.

for foul nor fair 決して…しない ▪ What it was, she would tell no man, *for foul nor fair*. それが何であったかは彼女は決して誰にも言おうとしなかった.

foul play 殺人，殺し ▪ It is evident that there are suspicions of *foul play*. 殺人の疑いがあることは明らかだ ▪ After examining the body the police began to suspect *foul play*. 死体を検査した後，警察は凶行の疑いを持ち始めた.

go foul of [***on***] →fall FOUL of.

go through foul or fair (***to*** *do*) 水火も辞せずに[万難を排して]（…する） ▪ He will *go through foul or fair to* achieve his ends. 彼は万難を排して自分の目的を達成するだろう.

hit foul《ボクシング》不正な打ち方をする《特にベルトの下を》; 不正な行動をする;（人に）不正な手を使う ▪ He *hit* me *foul*. 彼は私に不正な手を使った.

run foul of →fall FOUL of.

through fair and foul いかなる場合にも ▪ I will stand by you *through fair and foul*. 私はいかなる場合にもあなたに味方します.

foul[2] /faʊl/ 動 ***foul*** *one's* ***hands with*** …で手をよごす; に関係して身を汚す ▪ He *fouled his hands with* gambling. 彼はとばくで身を汚した.

foul *one's* ***own nest*** →NEST.

found /faʊnd/ 動 (***be***) ***founded on*** …に基づく ▪ The argument *is founded on* fact. その議論は事実に基づいている.

be ill [***well***] ***founded*** 根拠が薄弱[十分]である ▪ The theory *is well founded*. その学説は根拠が十分である.

foundation /faʊndéɪʃən/ 名 (***be***) ***on the foundation***《英》（財団の）給費を受けて(いる) ▪ He was placed *on the* great *foundation* of Christ's Hospital. 彼はクライスツホスピタル校の豊富な基金から給費を受けることになった.

lay [***build up***] ***the foundation of*** …の定礎式を行う，の土台をすえる ▪ He *laid the foundation of* future greatness. 彼は将来の栄達の基礎を築いた.

rock [***shake***] ***… to its foundations***/ ***rock*** [***shake***] ***the foundations of*** …を根底までゆるがす ▪ Nihilism threatened to *rock* Christinanity

F

to its foundations. 虚無主義はキリスト教を根底までゆるがす恐れがあった ▪ Two ministers' resignation might *rock the foundations of* the government. 二人の大臣の辞職は政府を根底からゆるがすかもしれない.

to the [*one's*] ***foundations*** 根底まで, 根底から ▪ The wind shook the house *to the foundations*. 風はその家の土台まで揺り動かした ▪ The empire was reeling *to its foundations*. 帝国は根底からゆらいでいた.

without foundation 根拠のない, 根も葉もない ▪ It was a rumor *without foundation*. それは根も葉もない噂だった.

F

fountain-head /fáʊntənhèd/ 名 ***at the fountain-head*** 本源から ▪ He received information *at the fountain-head*. 彼は本源から情報を受けている.

trace ... to its fountain-head ...の本源を究める ▪ He *traced* the error *to its fountain-head*. 彼はその誤りの本源を究めた.

four /fɔːr/ 名形 ***form fours*** 4列に並ぶ; 《号令》4列作れ ▪ *Form fours*! 4列作れ.

Fours left [***right***]***!*** 《号令》左[右]へ4列!

in fours 4つずつの組[群れ]になって ▪ The best things come *in fours*. 最良の物は4つずつの群れになってやってくる.

make up a four 4人一組を作る ▪ I was pleased that Emily and I could *make up a four* with her grandparents this Christmas. 今年のクリスマスには, エミリーと私と彼女の祖父母とで4人グループになれるので私はうれしかった.

on all fours →ALL FOURS.

the four corners of the earth [***world***] 世界各地 ▪ Scholars gathered wisdom and knowledge from *the four corners of the world*. 学者たちは, 世界の各地から知恵と知識を蒐集した.

within the four seas →SEA.

four-bagger /fɔːrbǽgər/ 名 ***hit a four-bagger*** 《米口》ホームランを放つ; きわめて立派にやる ▪ He *hit a four-bagger* as a prophet. 彼は予言者としてすばらしい当たりを取った.

four-square /fɔːrskwéər/ 形 ***stand four-square against*** ...に対して堂々と[恐れず]立ち向かう ▪ We *stand four-square against* our troubles. 我々は苦難には堂々と立ち向かう.

stand four-square behind 全面的に支持する, 後ろ盾になる ▪ Keyes now *stands foursquare behind* the president. キーズは今は大統領を全面的に支持している.

fowl /faʊl/ 名 ***dress a fowl*** (羽毛をむしって)家禽を下処理[下ごしらえ]する ▪ Two tons of *dressed fowls* were unloaded at Sisson for shipment to McCloud. 下処理した家禽2トンがシスンでおろされ, マクラウドに送るため船積みされた.

fox[1] /fɑks|fɔks/ 名 (***as***) ***cunning*** [***sly***] ***as a fox*** [***foxes***] (キツネのように)ひどく狡猾で, ずる賢い ▪ Those people are *as cunning as foxes*. あの連中はキツネのように狡猾だ ▪ He was *sly as a fox*. 彼はキツネのようにずる賢かった.

corner *a person* ***like a trapped fox*** = hound a person into a CORNER.

crazy like a fox 《米》(愚かに見えて)実は抜け目ない ▪ Don't underestimate him—he's *crazy like a fox*. 彼をみくびってはいけない. 実は抜け目がないんだから.

play the fox **1** ずるいことをする ▪ Tiberius *played the fox* with the Senate of Rome. ティベリウスはローマ元老院に対しずるいことをした.
2 見せかける, ずるをきめる ▪ I *played the fox* several times, pretending to be in pain. 私は数回ずるをきめて, 苦しむようなふりをした.

shoot *a person's* ***fox*** 他人の敵をやっつける ▪ Now we have no case any more. They've *shot our fox*. 今や我々にはもう問題はない. 彼らが我々の敵を撃ったからだ.

the fox and the grapes 負け惜しみ ▪ It's a case of *the fox and the grapes*. それは負け惜しみの一例である. ☞イソップ物語中の「キツネとブドウ」の話から.

fox[2] /fɑks|fɔks/ 動 ***fox ... out of*** *a person* 人から手管で...を捜し出す ▪ She will *fox* the secret *out of* them in time. 彼女はやがて手管で彼らからその秘密を探り出すであろう.

fraction /frǽkʃən/ 名 ***crumble into fractions*** くずれてばらばらになる ▪ A fine building will *crumble into fractions*. 立派な建物もくずれてばらばらになるであろう.

not a fraction of 少しの...もない ▪ The statement does *not* contain *a fraction of* truth. その陳述は少しの真実も含んでいない.

not by a fraction ちっとも...しない (not at all) ▪ He does *not* like it *by a fraction*. 彼はそれをちっとも好まない.

to a fraction 《口》完全に, きちんと ▪ They were obedient *to a fraction*. 彼らは全く従順であった ▪ This hat fits you *to a fraction*. この帽子はあなたにぴたっと合う.

fragment /frǽgmənt/ 名 ***in fragments*** 断片となって; 断片的に ▪ The glass lay *in fragments*. グラスは破片となって散乱していた.

into fragments みじんに ▪ The watch broke *into fragments*. 時計はみじんに砕けた ▪ He tore the handkerchief *into fragments*. 彼はハンカチをずたずたに裂いた.

not a fragment of ...はちっともない ▪ There is *not a fragment of* heroism about him. 彼には英雄的なところはみじんもない.

to fragments こなみじんに ▪ The glass was smashed *to fragments*. グラスはこなみじんに砕けた.

frame[1] /freɪm/ 名 ***a frame*** [***state***] ***of mind*** 気分 ▪ He is now in *a* low *frame of mind*. 彼は今気分が沈んでいる.

a frame of reference 判断[行動]基準(となる思想体系), 価値観; 《数》座標系.

frames and feelings 宗教的気分感情《特に18,

19世紀宗教文学に用いられる非難的な句》 ▪ Hence arose the substitution of *frames and feelings* for the sacraments of the church. そういうわけで, 教会の秘蹟の代わりに宗教的気分感情を代用することが始まった.

in* [*out of*] *the frame **1** 注目の的である[でない].
2 …の成功を収めそうである[でない], (仕事)に選ばれそうである[でない], (選手権などに)勝ち残っている[ていない] (*for, to do*) ▪ Who's *in the frame for* the Pakistan presidency? パキスタンの大統領に選ばれそうなのは誰か ▪ They are *out of the frame for* the championship. 彼らは決勝戦に残っていない.
3 …の容疑を受けている[ていない], 手配中である[でない] (*for*) ▪ The cops have me *in the frame for* Jason's murder. 警察にジェイスン殺害の容疑をかけられている.

frame[2] /freɪm/ 動 ***be framed for*** …に耐える[適する]ようにできている ▪ He *is framed for* severe hardships. 彼はきびしい苦難に耐えるようにできている.

be framed up for 《米口》…に適する ▪ It is a nice city, but it *is* not *framed up for* tourists. そこは立派な都市だが, 観光者には適さない.

frame ... to oneself …を想像する, 心に描く, 思い浮かべる ▪ I could *frame* the sight *to myself*. 私はその光景を思い浮かべることができた.

frame well **1** 見込みがある (*in*) ▪ He *frames well in* speaking. 彼は演説家として見込みがある.
2 うまく進んでいる ▪ The plan is *framing well*. その計画はうまく進んでいる.

frank /fræŋk/ 形 ***be frank with*** …に対して淡白だ, に打ち明けて言う ▪ He *is frank with* everybody. 彼はすべての人に対して淡白だ ▪ I will *be frank with* you. 打ち明けて言いましょう.

to be frank with you 率直に言えば ▪ *To be frank with you*, I don't like your novel. 打ち明けて言えば私はあなたの小説はきらいです.

Frankenstein /fræŋkənstàɪn/ 名 ***a Frankenstein's monster*** フランケンシュタインの怪物(のようなもの); 造り主を破滅させるもの ▪ We should prevent the perversion of science into *a Frankenstein's monster*. 科学が悪用されて破滅に至るという事態は阻止しなければならない. ☞Mary Shelley, *Frankenstein* (1818) から.

frankly /fræŋkli/ 副 ***frankly speaking*** 率直に言えば ▪ *Frankly speaking*, he is dishonest. 率直に言えば彼は不正直だ.

fraud /frɔːd/ 名 ***a pious fraud*** (宗教的教えのための)方便, 善意の偽り ▪ There were those who regarded the stories about Jesus as *a pious fraud*. イエスに関する逸話を宗教的方便だとみなす人たちもいた.

by fraud 詐欺で ▪ He gets money *by fraud*. 彼は詐欺を働いて金を得る.

in* [*to the*] *fraud of 《法》 **1** …を詐欺にかけるため ▪ He did not invest *in fraud of* his creditors. 彼は債権者たちを故意に欺こうとして投資したのではない.
2 …をそこねて, じゃまして ▪ The condition was rejected as being made *to the fraud of* marriage. その条件は結婚を妨げるように作られたとして拒否された.

fraught /frɔːt/ 形 **(*be*) *fraught with*** 《詩》 **1** …を積んで(いる) ▪ The ship *was fraught with* coal. その船には石炭が積んであった.
2 …を伴って(いる) ▪ This policy *is fraught with* danger. この政策は危険を伴う.
3 …に満ちて(いる); をはらんで(いる) ▪ His heart *was fraught with* sorrow. 彼の心は悲しみに満ちていた.

fray[1] /freɪ/ 名 ***be eager for the fray*** 事あれかしと熱心に待つ; けんか早い ▪ They *were* always *eager for the fray*. 彼らはいつも事あれかしと待ち望んでいた.

enter* [*join*] *the fray 戦い[けんか, 論争]に加わる ▪ "Now don't *join the fray*," she pleaded with her husband. 「ねえ, けんかには加わらないで」と彼女は夫に嘆願した.

the thick of the fray 戦闘の最も激しい所 ▪ The soldier dashed into *the thick of the fray*. 兵は戦闘の最も激しい所へ飛び込んでいった.

fray[2] /freɪ/ 動 ***fray one's head*** (シカが)袋角(ふくろ)を枝角にしやすくするため頭を木にこする ▪ A deer *frays her head* to renew it. シカは角を更新するため頭を木にこする.

frazzle /frǽzəl/ 名 ***burn ... to a frazzle*** (特に食物)を黒こげに焼いてしまう ▪ The meat *was burnt to a frazzle*. 肉は黒こげに焼かれた.

to a frazzle 《口》へとへとになるまで, ひどく, 徹底的に ▪ He was beaten *to a frazzle* at the last election. この前の選挙で彼はさんざんに負けた ▪ My children are wearing me *to a frazzle*. 子供らは私をへとへとに疲れさせている.

freak /friːk/ 名 ***a freak of nature*** 造化の戯れ《奇形・巨大なもの》 ▪ Many were the *freaks of nature* that I beheld there. 私がそこで見た造化の戯れは多かった.

a freak out 《俗》幻覚状態, 乱ちき騒ぎ; パニック ▪ The song exploded into *a* psychedelic *freak out*. 歌は幻覚的な大騒ぎへと変わった ▪ I had *a* minor *freak out* when I missed my flight. 飛行機に乗り遅れたとき, ちょっとパニックになった.

out of mere freak ほんの気まぐれ[物好き]から ▪ He stole her purse *out of mere freak*. 彼はほんの気まぐれで彼女の財布を盗んだ.

free[1] /friː/ 形名 ***a free and easy*** 打ち解けた会合《酒・タバコ・歌の許される》(→FREE and easy) ▪ We were invited to *a free and easy* in the Local Club. 我々は地方クラブの打ち解けた会合に招かれた.

a free ride →get a free RIDE.

a free spirit (慣習にとらわれず)自由に生きる人 ▪ From defeat rises *a free spirit*. 敗北から自由人は立ちあがる.

(*as*) *free as air* [*a bird*] 《口》常に自由で ▪ I felt *as free as a bird* when I left school. 学校を出たとき私はほんとに自由に感じた.

at one's* (*own free*) *will → at one's (own

sweet) WILL.

***feel free to** do* →FEEL[2].

for free 《口》無料で ▪ He got his book *for free.* 彼はその本をただでもらった.

free and clear 《法》(財産が)負債のない, 抵当に入っていない ▪ They owned it *free and clear.* 彼らは負債のない財産を所有していた.

free and easy **1** 打ちとけた, のんきな; ずさんな; 自由気ままな (→a FREE and easy) ▪ His style is for the most part *free and easy.* 彼の文章は大体打ちとけたものである ▪ Make yourself *free and easy.* のんびりしなさい ▪ The government minister is so *free and easy* with his own rules. その政府の大臣は自分自身の規律がゆるんでいる ▪ Dillinger led a *free and easy* life here. ディリンジャーはここで気楽な生活を送った ▪ Some of our young girls have a *free and easy* attitude to sex. 今どきの若い女の子にはセックスに奔放な態度のものもいる.

2 惜しげもなく使う (*with*) ▪ The guests were rather *free and easy with* the host's liquor. お客は主人の酒を遠慮なく飲んだ.

3 のんきに ▪ The young man lived *free and easy.* その青年はのんきに暮らした.

free and open (***with***) (…と)打ち解けて; (と)開け放しでつき合う ▪ He was *free and open with* me. 彼は私と開け放しでつき合った.

free for …する暇がある ▪ Are you *free for* lunch tomorrow? あすランチをつき合う暇があるかい?

free-for-all (飛び入り)自由の, 無料の ▪ This is a *free-for-all* race. これは飛び入り自由のレースだ.

free for [***to***] *a person* ***to*** *do* 人が自由に…してもよい ▪ It was *free for* him *to* call them to his aid. 彼は自由に彼らを呼んで助けてもらうことができた.

free from …がない, がいない; を受けない ▪ I am *free from* work today. きょうは仕事がない ▪ The village is *free from* thieves. その村には盗賊がいない ▪ The country is *free from* alien influence. その国は外国の影響を受けない.

free, gratis (***and for nothing***) 《戯》無料で ▪ Souvenirs were *free, gratis.* お土産は無料だった.

free in** one's **gait 足取りが活発で, 足早で ▪ He is *free in his gait.* 彼は足早である.

free in** one's **speech 口が軽い ▪ He is very *free in his speech.* 彼は非常に口が軽い.

free of **1** 〚be (made) を伴って〛 …に出入りを許されて; の市民権を得て ▪ He *is free of* my house [the club]. 彼は私の家[そのクラブ]に出入りを許されている ▪ He *was made free of* the city. 彼はその市の市民権を与えられた.

2 …を惜しげなく使う, 自由に使う ▪ He is *free of* his tongue. 彼は遠慮なくものを言う ▪ He is *free of* money. 彼は金を惜しげなく使う.

3 …を免除されて ▪ You may get it *free of* charge. あなたはそれを無料で手に入れることができる ▪ This house is *free of* rent. この家は家賃がいらない.

4 (負担・拘束)がない ▪ I am *free of* debt. 私は借金はない.

5 …を離れて ▪ The tugs left the steamer as soon as they were *free of* the harbor. 引き船は港を離れるやいなやその汽船から離れた.

free on board 《商》本船渡しの; 積み込み渡しの 《略語 F.O.B., f.o.b.》 (↔ FREE on rail) ▪ The goods are *free on board.* その貨物は積み込み渡しだ.

free on rail 《商》貨車渡しの[で] 《略語 F.O.R., f.o.r.》 (↔ FREE on board) ▪ We will dispatch the goods *free on rail.* 商品は貨車渡しで発送いたします.

***free to** do* 自由に…してよい ▪ You are *free to* go home. 自由に帰宅してよろしい.

free to confess ためらわず[喜んで]告白する ▪ I am *free to confess* I knew it. 私はそれを知っていたことをあっさり白状する.

***free to** a person **to** do* →FREE for a person to do.

free with **1** …を惜しげもなく使う, に大まかで, 気前がよく ▪ He is *free with* his money. 彼は金離れがよい ▪ He is *free with* his advice. 彼はどしどし忠告を与える.

2 …を勝手に使う[扱う]; になれなれしくする ▪ You are *free with* some of the rules. あなたは規則のいくつかを勝手に扱っている ▪ He is *free with* my money. 彼は私の金を勝手に使う ▪ She is *free with* us. 彼女は我々になれなれしくする.

free with** one's **hands (論争・しつけなどで)やたらに手を使う ▪ In matters of discipline he is too *free with his hands.* しつけの事になると彼はあまりにも手を使いすぎる《なぐりすぎる》.

get [***have***] ***a free hand*** 行動の自由を得る[持っている], 好きなことがやれるようになる[やれる] ▪ I haven't *got a free hand* in it yet. まだそのことで私の好きなようにはやれないのです ▪ No one ever *had a freer hand* than he. 彼ほど自由に行動できた者はいない.

get [***take***] ***a free ride*** →RIDE[1].

get…free …を解き放つ, 離れさせる ▪ He *got* one hand *free.* 彼は片手を離した ▪ The lion *got free* his hinder parts. ライオンはその後半身を束縛から自由にした.

get free (***of***) (…から)自由の身となる ▪ He *got free of* the bondage. 彼は束縛を脱した.

give a free hand 行動の自由を与える, 自由に手腕をふるわせる ▪ She *gave* me *a free hand* in arranging the concert. 彼女は私に自由に音楽会の手配をさせた.

go free **1** 解放[放免]される ▪ The prisoner *went free.* 捕虜は放免された.

2 無料である ▪ The name and address of the receiver *go free.* 受取人の住所氏名は無料だ《電報》.

have a free hand →get a FREE hand.

have** one's **hands free **1** 何も持っていない; 手がすいている ▪ I *have my hands free* now. 私は今は手がすいている.

2 何でも好きなことができる ▪ Harold *had his*

hands free. ハロルドは好きなことがやれた.

home free 《俗》成功まちがいなしで ▪ You're probably *home free* in the next election. 次の選挙ではたぶん楽勝だ.

It's a free country! ここは自由な国だ ▪ If you don't like your wages, you can go and work somewhere else. *It's a free country*. 給料が気に入らないなら, 辞めてどこかよそで働けばいい. ここは自由な国なんだから.

***keep** A **free from** B* AをBから遠ざからせる, AにBを避けさせる ▪ You had better *keep* yourself *free from* vanity. あなたは虚栄から遠ざかったほうがよい.

let ... go free …を解放する ▪ We *let* them *go free*. 我々は彼らを解放した.

make [set] ... free (人)を釈放[放免]する ▪ Lincoln *set* the slaves *free*. リンカンは奴隷を解放した.

make** a person **free of 人に自由に出入[使用]を許す; 市民権を許す ▪ I *made* him *free of* my library. 彼に私の書庫に自由に出入することを許した.

***make free to** do* 思いきって[大胆にも]…する ▪ I *made free to* ask him the question. 私は思いきって彼にその質問をした.

make free with **1** (特に他人のもの)を勝手に使う, 盗む ▪ The guests *made free with* their host's liquor. 客たちは主人の酒を遠慮なく飲んだ ▪ He *made free with* her jewels. 彼は彼女の宝石を盗んだ.

2 …を無遠慮に扱う, 勝手にいじくる ▪ I advise you not to *make* so *free with* the servants. 使用人たちを手荒に扱わないよう君に忠告する ▪ He is always *making free with* my reputation. 彼はいつも私の悪口を言っている ▪ Don't *make free with* the text. 本文にみだりに手を入れてはいけない.

3 …になれなれしくする ▪ Don't *make free with* my womenfolk. 私の家の女たちとあまりなれなれしくするな.

4 《海》…に大胆に近うく ▪ You may *make free with* the shore. あなたは海岸に大胆に近ういてもよい.

of** one's **own free will →WILL[1].

set ... free →make ... FREE.

there's no (such thing as a) free lunch →LUNCH.

with a free hand 惜しげもなく, 気前よく ▪ Drinks were poured *with a free hand*. 酒類は気前よく注がれた.

free[2] /friː/ 動 ***free** oneself **from*** …を脱する, 免れる ▪ He succeeded in *freeing himself from* financial difficulties. 彼は財政困難をうまく脱出することができた.

freedom /fríːdəm/ 名 ***give** a person **the freedom of*** 人に…へ自由に出入を許す ▪ I have *given* him *the freedom of* my library. 彼に私の書庫へ自由に出入することを許している.

have the freedom of …に自由に出入りできる, を自由に利用できる ▪ I *have the freedom of* his house. 私は彼の家へは自由に出入できる.

take [use] freedoms with …に無遠慮なふるまいをする, なれなれしくする; (女性)にいたずらする ▪ Don't *take freedoms with* me. 私にあまりなれなれしくしないで ▪ He takes advantage of opportunities to *use freedoms with* a young female. 彼は好機を利用しては若い女性に馴れ馴れしくする.

with freedom 自由に, 思いのままに ▪ He spoke *with freedom* and eloquence. 彼は思いのまま, かつ雄弁に話した.

freefall /frìːfɔ́ːl/ 名 ***go into freefall*** 暴落[急落]する, 値崩れを起こす ▪ New-technology stocks *went into freefall* last week on Wall Street. 新技術関連株が先週ウォールストリートで大暴落した.

freeze[1] /friːz/ 名 ***lift** one's **freeze on*** …の禁止を撤廃する ▪ The FCC will *lift its freeze on* station building. 連邦通信委員会が放送局建設の禁止を解くだろう.

put a freeze on …を禁止する ▪ The Reds *put a freeze on* the collective farm system. 赤軍は集団農場制度を禁止した.

put ... on [in] deep freeze …を審議未了のまま葬ってしまう, の機能を停止する ▪ The Congress *put* the matter *on deep freeze* and adjourned today. 国会はその件を審議未了のまま葬りきょう休会した.

freeze[2] /friːz/ 動 ***cold enough to freeze the balls off a brass monkey*** →BALL[1].

freeze to death **1** 凍死する ▪ The rabbit *froze to death*. そのウサギは凍死した.

2 〚主に受身で〛…を凍死させる ▪ My master *is frozen to death*. 私の主人は凍死した.

freezing /fríːzɪŋ/ 名 ***at freezing*** 氷点に ▪ The weather was *at freezing*. 天候は氷点だった.

freight[1] /freɪt/ 名 ***by freight*** 《米》普通貨物便で; 貨車で, (ときに)トラックで (↔by EXPRESS 2) ▪ Shall it be sent *by freight*? それは普通便で送りましょうか.

haul freight =pull one's FREIGHT.

pay the freight 《口》運賃を払う; 料金を払う, 大金をはたく ▪ The company *paid the freight* for the toys to be shipped. その会社が輸出するおもちゃの料金を払った ▪ For years they *paid the freight* for wildlife conservation. 何年も彼らは野生生物保護のために大金を支出した.

pull** one's **freight 《米俗》素早く[すぐに]去る ▪ He discreetly *pulled his freight*. 彼は思慮深くもすぐ去った.

freight[2] /freɪt/ 動 ***be freighted with*** …でいっぱいである, に満ちている ▪ The day *was freighted with* care. その日は心配ばかりだった.

French /frentʃ/ 形名 ***pardon [excuse]** a person's **French*** 《口・しばしば戯》人のいやな言葉を許す ▪ I broke my bloody leg, if you'll *excuse my French*. 下卑た言葉を使って失礼ですが, チキショー! 脚を折ってしまった.

take French leave **1** 無断で[黙って]去る ▪ The son *took French leave* to go back to London. 息子は無断でロンドンへ帰った.

2 無断で…する[入る] ▪ The solicitor, *taking*

French leave, led us to the library. 弁護士は無断で入って，図書室まで我々を案内してくれた. ☞18世紀フランスで招待客が主人側にあいさつせずに帰宅する習慣があったことから.

frenzy /frénzi/ 名 ***a feeding frenzy*** →FEEDING.

in a frenzy of …のあまり取り乱して ▪ She ran shrieking *in a frenzy of* grief. 彼女は悲嘆のあまり取り乱してわめきながら走った.

frequent /fríːkwənt/ 動 ***frequent the society of*** …とよく会う ▪ To be gregarious is to *frequent the society of* one's kind. 社交的であるというのは同類の人たちの社会によく出入りするということである. ☞フランス語法.

fresco /fréskoʊ/ 名 ***in fresco*** 壁画法で ▪ The sibyls were painted *in fresco* by Michelangelo. その巫女(ᵏ)たちはミケランジェロによって壁画法で描かれた.

fresh /freʃ/ 形名 ***a fresh air fiend*** →FIEND.

(as) fresh as paint [a daisy, an eel, a rose, flowers in May] 元気はつらつとして ▪ He is *as fresh as paint*. 彼はきわめて元気はつらつとしている ▪ He emerged from his car *fresh as a rose*. 彼はいかにも元気はつらつとして車から出て来た.

fresh and fair 元気で若々しい ▪ He was a *fresh and fair* old man. 彼は元気で若々しい老人であった.

fresh and sweet **1** (食べ物などが)新鮮な，活きがよい; (香りが)さわやかな ▪ The oysters were fat, *fresh and sweet*. カキは育ちがよく新鮮だった ▪ The linen on the beds smelled *fresh and sweet*. ベッドのリネンはさわやかな香りだった.

2《口》(売春婦などが)出所したばかりの ▪ Mary is *fresh and sweet* and back on the street. メアリーは出所したばかりだが，また元の売春生活に戻っている.

fresh from the irons (学校)出たての ▪ He is *fresh from the irons*. 彼は学校出たてだ.

fresh in the [one's] mind [memory] 記憶に鮮やかで ▪ The event is still *fresh in my mind*. その出来事は今なお私の記憶に鮮やかです.

fresh on the graft 《口》仕事[職業]に慣れないで，新参で ▪ He is *fresh on the graft*. 彼はその仕事には新参だ.

fresh out of [《英》***from***]《米》 **1** …を出たての，ほやほやの ▪ Those girls are *fresh from* college. その少女たちは大学出たてである ▪ The narrative was *fresh from* John's lips. その話はジョンの口から出たばかりのところだった.

2 (商品が)売り切れて; 使いきって，切らして ▪ Sorry, we're *fresh out of* sugar at present. 申し訳ございませんが，砂糖はいま切らしております.

Fresh Paint. 《英》ペンキ塗りたて (Wet Paint)《掲示》.

get fresh with 《米俗》なれなれしく[無礼を]する ▪ Don't *get fresh with* mother. 母に無礼をしないでください ▪ Don't *get fresh with* me! 私になれなれしくしないでよ.

in the fresh air 戸外で ▪ I take exercise *in the fresh air* every morning. 毎朝戸外で運動する.

in the fresh of …の初めに ▪ I am busy *in the fresh of* the year receiving reports. 年の初めは報告書の受領で忙しい ▪ I would always take a stroll *in the fresh of* the morning. いつも朝早く散歩をしたものだった.

freshen /fréʃən/ 動 ***freshen the nip*** 水で割ったブランデーを1杯飲む，水で割ったラムを1パイント飲む ▪ He went into the saloon to *freshen the nip*. 彼は水で割ったブランデーを1杯やるため居酒屋へ入った.

freshen (the) way (船の)速度を早める ▪ I *freshened way* to get home. 私は帰宅するため速力を早めた. ☞海語より.

fret[1] /fret/ 名 ***in a [the] fret*** いらいらして; ぷりぷり怒って; (子供などが)じれて，だだをこねて ▪ My master was *in* as great *a fret* as I. 主人は私と同じように非常に怒っていた.

on [upon] the fret **1** いらいらして; ぷりぷり怒って ▪ He was always *on the fret*. 彼はいつもいらいらしていた ▪ You have put him *on the fret*. あなたは彼を激怒させた.

2 酒が二次発酵をして ▪ You should not dip when any wines are *upon the fret*. どのワインも二次発酵をしているときはくみ出してはならない.

the fret and fever 焦燥興奮 ▪ You are situated amid *the fret and fever* of speculation. 君は投機の焦燥興奮の中に置かれているんだ.

the fret and fume ぷりぷり怒ること ▪ I am now delivered from *the fret and fume* of life. 今は人生の腹立たしさから救われている.

fret[2] /fret/ 動 ***Don't (you) fret!*** 《口》心配するには及ばない.

***fret** oneself* じれる，やきもきする，いらいらする，悩む (*about, over*) ▪ Don't *fret yourself about* criticism. 批判のことでやきもきするな ▪ The bishop *fretted himself* in his chair. 主教はいすに掛けていらいらした.

fret away** one's **health [life] くよくよして健康を害す[暮らす] ▪ He *fretted away his health*. 彼はくよくよして健康を害した ▪ I *fretted away my life* in banishment. 追放されてくよくよして暮らした.

fret (, fuss) and fume やきもきして怒る ▪ In secret he *fretted and fumed*. 彼はひそかにやきもきして怒っていた.

fret** one's **head off ひどく頭を悩ます (*about*) ▪ I always *fret my head off about* whether I'm being boring. 私は自分が退屈な人間ではないかといつもひどく頭を悩ますのだ.

fret** one's **heart 心を悩ます ▪ So many worries *fret my heart* to death. 心配なことがそうたくさんあっては死ぬほど悩ましくなる.

fret** oneself **ill 気をもんで病気になる ▪ She *fretted herself ill*. 彼女は気をもんで病気になった.

fret out** one's **health [life] = FRET away one's health.

I should fret! 《米俗》私の知ったことではない.

Friday /fráɪdeɪ/ 名 ***a man [girl, person]***

Friday 忠実な使用人; 雑用係 ▪ Brown worked first as *a Girl Friday*, then a Washington correspondent for the New York Post. ブラウンはまず忠実な雑用係として, 次にニューヨークポスト紙のワシントン通信員として働いた. ☞Friday は Robinson Crusoe の忠実なしもべ. 金曜日に出会ったのが名前の由来.

Black Friday **1** (株価暴落など不幸な出来事があった)暗黒の金曜日《金曜日以外にも用いる》 ▪ The percentage drop was far from the record 22.6 percent drop on Oct. 19, 1987, known as *Black Friday*. 下落の比率は, 暗黒の金曜日として知られる1987年10月19日の22.6%の下落には隔たりがあった. **2**《米》黒字の金曜日 ▪ The day after Thanksgiving is called *Black Friday*. 感謝祭の翌日は黒字の金曜日と呼ばれる. ☞感謝祭(11月の第4木曜日)の翌日の金曜日はクリスマス用の買い物をする客で混雑し, 商店が黒字になることから.

Dress Down Friday 平服の金曜日《カジュアルな服装で勤務する週末のこと (casual day)》 ▪ Leave your business suit at home and have a *Dress Down Friday* in your office. ビジネススーツは家においてきて, 会社では平服の金曜日にしなさい.

Friday the 13th 13日の金曜日《厄日とされている》 ▪ I don't fly anywhere on a *Friday the 13th*. 13日の金曜日には飛行機でどこへも行きません.

He who laughs on Friday will weep on Sunday. 喜びの後にはすぐ悲しみが来る. ☞Racine, *Les Plaideurs* (1668).

friend /frend/ 名 ***a fair-weather friend*** 羽振りがよいときの友人, 金の切れ目が縁の切れ目になる人 (↔ a fair-weather ENEMY) ▪ I had a lot of money and I knew a lot of people, but most of them turned out to be *fair-weather friends*. たくさんお金があり知り合いも多かったが, 大半は金があるときだけの友だちだった.

a flexible friend 融通の利く友人, クレジットカード ▪ "*Flexible friends*" was the nickname given long ago to our credit cards.「融通の利く友人」とは何年も前に当社のクレジットカードにつけられた愛称でした.

a friend at court →COURT.

a friend in need 困ったときの友 ▪ *A friend in need* is a friend indeed.《諺》まさかの時の友こそ真の友である.

be a friend of [to] …の味方[愛好者]である ▪ The minister *was a friend to* the young nobleman. 大臣はその若い貴族の味方だった ▪ They have *been friends of* order. 彼らは秩序を愛した.

be [make] friends with …と親しい[親しくなる]; 〚again を伴って〛と仲直りする ▪ I *am friends with* him. 私は彼と親しい ▪ Will you *make friends with* me *again*? 私と仲直りしてくれませんか.

Defend me from my friends! ひいきの引き倒しはまっぴらだ; 友だちごかしのおせっかいはごめんだ.

fast friends 親友 ▪ The two have been *fast friends* since 1981. 二人は1981年以来の親友だ.

find a friend in …が味方[友人]であることを知る ▪ You will always *find a friend in* me. 私はいつもあなたの味方になってあげます.

friend or foe 敵か味方か ▪ I can't tell whether she is *friend or foe*. 彼女は敵か味方かわからない.

have friends in high places 有力なコネがある (→know a person in high PLACEs).

keep friends with …と親しくしている ▪ You must *keep friends with* her. あなたは彼女とずっと親しくしていなければなりません.

make friends with →be FRIENDs with.

our dumb friends もの言わぬ友人, 愛玩動物[ペット] ▪ When we were chartered in 1910, dogs and cats were considered *our dumb friends*. 1910年に認可を受けたとき, 犬や猫はもの言わぬ友人と考えられていた.

Short reckonings [accounts] make long friends.《諺》短期の会計は友情を長続きさせる, 友人でいたいなら借りはすぐに返せ.

What's ... between friends? 友だちの間だもの…など何であろう ▪ *What's* a few dollars *between friends?* 友だちの間だもの, 数ドルの金なんか何でもない.

With friends like that, who needs enemies?《戯》友人がそんなひどいことをするなんて, とんだ友人もあったものだ ▪ I lent a friend a valuable book, but he never returned it. *With friends like that, who needs enemies?* 友人に貴重な本を貸したのに一向に返してくれなかった. とんだ友人もあったものだ.

friended /fréndəd/ 形 ***be well [ill] friended*** 友に恵まれている[友がいない] ▪ I have *been well friended* all my life. 私は一生涯友に恵まれていた.

friendly /fréndli/ 形 ***(be) friendly to [with]*** …に友好的である ▪ The inhabitants *were friendly to* Asians. そこの住民はアジア人に友好的だった ▪ The boy *is friendly with* dogs. その少年は犬と親しくしている.

be on friendly terms with …と親しくしている ▪ I *am on friendly terms with* the minister. 私はその大臣と懇意にしている.

friendship /fréndʃìp/ 名 ***cultivate the friendship of*** 進んで(人)との友好を求める ▪ They *cultivated the friendship of* the English. 彼らは進んで英国民との友好を求めた.

have a friendship for …を敬愛する ▪ I *had a friendship for* him. 私は彼を敬愛した.

in common friendship 友人として ▪ It ought, *in common friendship*, to be done. それは友人としてなされるべきである.

out of friendship 友情から ▪ I helped him *out of friendship*. 私は友情から彼を助けた.

fright /fraɪt/ 名 ***from [of] fright*** びっくりして ▪ He became ill *of fright*. 彼はびっくりして病気になった ▪ She fainted *from fright*. 彼女はびっくりして気絶した.

get [have] a fright 恐怖に襲われる, おびえる, 恐れ

F

る ▪ She *had* such *a fright* that she fainted. 彼女はひどくおびえて気絶した.

get the fright of *one's* ***life*** たまげる ▪ I *got the fright of my life* when the dog started growling at me. 犬が私にむかってうなり始めたときは本当にたまげた.

give *a person* ***a fright*** 人に恐怖を与える, 人の肝をつぶす ▪ It *gave* him *a fright*. それは彼の肝をつぶした.

give *a person* ***the fright of*** *one's* ***life*** 人をたまげさせる ▪ I brought them here to *give* their mother *the fright of her life*. 彼らの母親をびっくりさせるために彼らをここへ連れてきた.

in a fright ぎょっとして, 肝をつぶして ▪ He was *in* a great *fright*. 彼はひどくびっくりしていた.

look a fright 《口》(人をぎょっとさせるほど)みっともない姿である, 異様な風采をしている ▪ I'm old and weak and I know I *look a fright*. 私は年取っているし体も弱っているので, 不細工な姿であることはわかっている.

of fright →from FRIGHT.

stage fright 舞台負け, 人前であがること ▪ I always get *stage fright* in the first class of the new term. 私は新学期の最初の授業では生徒の前でいつもあがる.

take fright (***at***) (...に)ぎょっとする, びっくりする ▪ The horse *took fright at* the report of the gun. 馬は鉄砲の音に驚いた.

frighten /fráɪtən/ 動 ***be frightened at*** [***by***] ...にたまげる, を見てぎょっとする ▪ The child *was frightened at* the picture. その子は絵を見てぎょっとした.

be frightened of 《口》...を恐れている ▪ *Are* you *frightened of* earthquakes? 君は地震が怖いか. ☞習慣的恐怖を言い, be FRIGHTENed at はその時々の驚き・恐怖を言う.

be frightened out of *one's* ***wits*** [***life***] びっくり仰天する, どぎもを抜かれる ▪ We *were frightened out of our wits* by the ghost story. 我々はその怪談にすっかりどぎもを抜かれた.

be frightened to death 死ぬほどびっくりする ▪ My wife *is* sometimes *frightened to death* when she travels by air. 妻は飛行機に乗る時はときどき死ぬほど恐れることがある.

frightener /fráɪtənər/ 名 ***put the frighteners on*** 《口》おどしをかけて...させる[沈黙させる] ▪ He had seen the robbery, and the robbers had *put the frighteners on* (him). 彼はその盗みを目撃したのだった, それで盗賊どもは彼をおどして口止めした.

frill /frɪl/ 名 ***no frills*** 〚限定的〛余分な飾り[サービス]のない, 実質本意の ▪ He bought his tickets for a *no-frills* flight to London. 彼はロンドン行きの格安便のチケットを買った.

put on (*one's*) ***frills*** 《米俗》気取る ▪ He *puts on* too many *frills*. 彼は気取りすぎる.

without frills 潤色なしに, 本質のみで ▪ A wedding *without frills* is better for the bride. 花嫁にとってはごてごてしない結婚式のほうがよい.

fringe /frɪndʒ/ 名 ***the*** [***a***] ***lunatic fringe*** 狂信的異端分子, 過激派 ▪ That every reform movement has *a lunatic fringe*, is a quote of Theodore Roosevelt. あらゆる改革には狂信者がいる, というのはセオドア・ルーズベルトの言葉だ.

frisk /frɪsk/ 動 ***frisk it*** (生物が)はね回る ▪ I can *frisk it* freshly. 私は生き生きとはね回ることができる.

fritter /frítər/ 動 ***fritter away*** *one's* ***chances*** 機会をむだにする ▪ He should have won easily, but he *frittered away his chances*. 彼は当然楽勝できるはずだったが, 機会をむだにしてしまった.

fritz /frɪts/ 名 ***put the fritz on/put ... on the fritz*** 《米口》...をだめにする, やめさせる ▪ The power outage *put* the ATM *on the fritz*. 停電のためATM は取り扱い不能になった ▪ An open air performance *put* our opera house show *on the fritz*. 野外公演のため歌劇場でのショーは中止になった.

on the fritz 《米俗》故障して, うまく動かないで; 狂って ▪ The machine has gone *on the fritz*. 機械が故障した.

fro /froʊ/ 副 ***to and fro*** →TO.

frock /frɑk|frɔk/ 名 ***cast*** [***throw***] *one's* ***frock to the nettles*** →NETTLE[1].

wear the frock 僧職にある ▪ He may *wear the frock*, but his behavior is most un-Christian. なるほど彼は牧師だが, その行動はとてもキリスト教徒とはいえない.

frog /frɑg|frɔg/ 名 ***a big frog in a small pond*** 《口》小池の大ガエル; 小組織の中の大人物 ▪ As company president, he is *a big frog in a small pond*. 会社社長として彼はお山の大将だ.

a little frog in a big pond/a small frog in a large [***big, huge***] ***pond*** 大池の小ガエル; 大組織の中の小人物 ▪ In a large company he feels like *a little frog in a big pond*. 大会社の中で, 彼は大池の小ガエルのように感じている.

(***as***) ***cold as a frog*** →(as) COLD as fish.

give the frog('***s***) ***march*** [***trot***] 《口》酔いどれまたは強情な囚人をうつ伏せにして手足を持って運ぶ ▪ They *gave* the defendant *the frog's march*. 彼らは被告をうつ伏せにして手足を持って運んだ.

have a frog in the [*one's*] ***throat*** 《口》(のどを痛めたりして)しわがれ声である; 声がかれている ▪ I seem to *have a frog in the throat* this morning. 今朝は声がかれているようだ.

frolic[1] /frálɪk|frɔ́l-/ 名 ***go on a frolic*** 浮かれ騒ぐ ▪ They *went on a frolic*. 彼らは浮かれ騒いだ.

frolic[2] /frálɪk|frɔ́l-/ 動 ***frolic it*** 浮かれ騒ぐ; はね回る, ふざける ▪ She laughs and *frolics it* all the day. 彼女は一日中笑ったりふざけたりする.

from /frəm/ 前 ***from a child*** [***boy, foal***] 子供[少年, 子馬]のときから ▪ I have known him *from a child*. (彼が)子供のときから彼を知っている ▪ I have reared the horse *from a foal*. その馬を子馬のときから育てた.

from above (...の)上から ▪ He looked at me *from above* his glasses. 彼はめがね越しに私を見た.
from among ...の中から ▪ We chose him *from among* them. 我々は彼らの中から彼を選んだ.
from behind (...の)後[陰]から ▪ He appeared *from behind* the door. 彼はドアの陰から現れた.
from beneath 下の方から ▪ *From beneath* was heard a wailing sound. 下の方から泣き叫ぶ声がした.
from forth 《雅》...から出て《from と forth が互いに意味を強め補う》 ▪ He *from forth* the closet brought a heap. 彼は戸だなから一山持ち出して来た.
from here on in 《米俗》今後ずっと ▪ *From here on in*, they're all free shots. これからはずっと, 何の気がねもなく射つぞ.
from now on →NOW.
from off 《雅》...から《from と off が互いに意味を強め補う》 ▪ Knights unhorsed may rise *from off* the plain. 落馬した騎士が戦場から立ち上がることもある.
from off the streets →STREET.
from out ...から《from と out が互いに意味を強め補う》 ▪ *From out* the thick darkness below, the wind brought us a noise. 下の真っ暗やみから風が物音を我々のところへ運んで来た.
from over ...のかなたから ▪ The doll has come *from over* the sea. その人形は海の彼方からやって来た.
from rags to riches →go from RAGs to riches.
from the sublime to the ridiculous 崇高から滑稽(こっけい)へ[まで], 美から醜へ[まで] ▪ The proposals range *from the sublime to the ridiculous*. 提案は玉石混交だ. ☞Tom Paine, *The Age of Reason* (1794).
from this day [etc.] ***forth*** [***forward, onward, out***] きょう[など]から ▪ I will work hard *from this day forth*. きょうから精出して働きます ▪ *From that day forward* the Spirit of God was upon David. その日から神の霊がダビデに乗り移った.
***from** ten **to** twenty* 10から20までの ▪ I saw *from* 10 *to* 20 birds. 10羽から20羽までの鳥を見た ▪ *From* 20 *to* 30 boats were ready. 20隻から30隻までの船が用意ができていた.

front[1] /frʌnt/ 名形 ***a change of front*** 方向転換 ▪ This *change of front* is founded on the report of the Board of Education. この方向転換は教育委員会の報告に基づいている. ☞軍事用語から.
at the front **1** 前面[正面]が ▪ The tongue is loose *at the front*. 舌は前の方がぶらぶらしている.
2 戦線で, 戦場に出て ▪ He is now *at the front*. 彼は今出征中である.
3 表立って, 世評にのぼって ▪ The question is *at the front*. その問題が世評にのぼっている.
be in the front line (戦場・仕事などの)最前線にいる ▪ Sports should not *be in the front line* of politics. スポーツは政治の最前線にあるべきでない.
be in the front rank 重要[有名]である ▪ He *is in the front rank* in the political world. 彼は政界の重要人物である.
bring** a person **to the front 人を世に紹介する, を有名にする ▪ His work *brought* him *to the front*. 彼の作品が彼を有名にした.
change front (戦隊が)向きを変える ▪ The troops *changed front*. その軍隊は向きを変えた.
come to the front 前面に現れてくる, 頭角を表す, 有名になる ▪ At such a time his pride would *come to the front*. そのような時には彼の自尊心が前面に現れてくるのであった ▪ It was some years before he *came to the front* as a writer. 数年たって初めて彼は作家として有名になった.
cook on the front burner →BURNER.
display a bold front (***on***) →present a bold FRONT (on).
Files to the front! 《号令》組々前へ(進め)!
from front to back (本の)表から裏まで, 本全体に ▪ This book is scribbled in *from front to back*. この本は全体に落書きがしてある.
front and center **1**〚無冠詞で〛注目の的, 中心 ▪ Patty Davis was *front and center* in being the president's daughter and opposing his politics. パティー・デイビスは(レーガン)大統領の娘でありながら彼の政策に反対したことで注目の的だった ▪ Put things you use all the time at *front and center*. いつも使用するものを目立つところに置きなさい.
2《俗》「お呼び出しです」 ▪ *Front and center*, Reagan. The boss wants to see you. お呼び出しいたします. レーガンさん. 社長がお呼びです.
front and rear 前後を; 前後両面から ▪ We were attacked *front and rear*. 我々は前後両面から攻撃された.
front downwards うつ伏せに, 伏せて ▪ He put the open book *front downwards* on the table. 彼は本を開いたままテーブルの上に伏せて置いた.
front of 《米口》...の前に (in front of) ▪ *Front of* the fire-place was the parlor. 壁炉の前に談話室があった.
***get in front of** oneself* 《米口》急ぐ; あわてる ▪ He *got in front of himself*. 彼は大いに急いだ.
go to the front 出征する ▪ A division *went* up *to the front*. 1師団が戦線に出た.
***have the front to** do* 厚かましくも...する ▪ He *had the front to* deny the obvious fact. 彼は厚かましくもその明白な事実を否認した.
in front **1** 最前列に, まっ先に ▪ So long as the U.S. stays out *in front*, war is not likely. アメリカが一番進んでいるかぎりは戦争は起こりそうにない ▪ Please go *in front*. どうぞお先に.
2 前方[前面]に, 目の前に ▪ The upper story had the two captain's cabins *in front*. 上層には前部に船長の二つの船室があった ▪ He was determined to attack the bear *in front*. 彼はそのクマを前面から攻撃しようと決心した.
in** one's **front ...の前に[の], に向かって ▪ He forced a passage across the river *in his front*.

彼は前面の川を強行して渡った.

in (the) front of …の前面に, と向かいあって; 先頭に (↔at (the) REAR of) ▪ The proclamation was repeated *in front of* the Royal Exchange. その宣言はロンドン取引所の前で繰り返された ▪ I saw a Portuguese *in the front of* 40 men. 私は1人のポルトガル人が40人の兵の先頭にいるのを認めた.

make front to …の方に向く《比喩的にも》 ▪ The Municipals *make front to* this also. 市政府もまたこの方向に向いている.

on all fronts あらゆる分野で ▪ The program has been successful *on all fronts*. プログラムはすべてが順調にいっている.

F

on the ... front …の面[場]で ▪ They gained a great victory *on the* film *front*. 彼らは映画の面で大勝利を博した.

on the [a, one's] front burner →be on the back BURNER.

on the home front 自国では ▪ There will be heavy snow across most of France, while *on the home front* we can expect clear weather nationwide. フランスではほぼ全域で大雪となるが, わが国は全国で好天が予想される. ☞「銃後」から.

open (up) a new front 新たな地平を拓く, 新しい角度から問題に取り組む ▪ Velcade will *open up a new front* in the war against cancer. (多発性骨髄腫治療薬の)ベルケイドはがんに対する戦いに新たな地平を拓くだろう.

out front **1**《米》非常に優秀な; 大変な ▪ He is *out front* in the race. 彼はその競走で断然他を圧してすぐれている ▪ He is a crank *out front*. 彼は大変な変わり者だ.

2 (建物の)正面(入り口)で[に] (↔out BACK) ▪ I met my mom *out front* of McDonald's. マクドナルドの前でお母さんに会った.

present [display, put on, show] a bold front (on) (…に対して)ごう然とした, 大胆な態度を示す ▪ *Putting on a bold front*, I informed the robber that he could take all. 私は大胆にかまえて泥棒にみんな持って行けと言った.

present a united front against …に対して共同戦線を張る ▪ We *presented a united front against* the enemy. 我々は敵に対して共同戦線を張った.

put on [up] a (brave, good) front 見栄を張る; 世間体を繕う; 平気を装う ▪ Although they *put up a front*, they really are not well off. 彼らは見栄を張っているが, 実際は裕福ではない.

take a front seat《米口》重要な地位を占める ▪ It's time for business ethics to *take a front seat*. 今やビジネス倫理が重要な位置を占めてもよい頃だ.

to one's front 人の前方を ▪ Look *to your front*. 前方を見なさい.

to the front 前へ, 目立つ所へ ▪ He likes to be *to the front*. 彼は前の方にいるのが好きだ ▪ It was removed *to the front* of a fire. それは炉火の前へ移された.

up front《俗》**1** (車・劇場の)前の席に, 前の方に; 前面に ▪ We filed into the theater and found seats *up front*. 列になって劇場に入り, 前方に席を見つけた.

2 前払いの, 先行投資の ▪ Usually, schools get tuition money *up front* for training students. ふつう, 学校は学生指導のため前納で授業料を徴収する.

3 率直な (*about, with*) ▪ Collymore was *up front about* his mistakes. コリモアは自分の過ちを率直に認めた.

4 重要な, 中心的な ▪ *Up front* and center is the dollar, which continued its slump last week. 重要で中心的なのはドルだ. 先週ドル安がずっとつづいていたからだ.

5 (企業などの)管理部門(の) ▪ US Companies are in the *up front* of international licensing. 米国の会社は国際的使用許諾を管理している.

with a bold front 大胆に, 恐れる色なく ▪ He confronted his accuser *with a bold front*. 彼は恐れる色なく告発者と対決した.

front[2] /frʌnt/ 動 ***be fronted with*** 前面が…でできている ▪ The house *is fronted with* stone. その家は前面が石でできている.

frontier /frʌntíər|frʌ́ntɪə/ 名 ***on the frontier*** 国境に ▪ There were many forts *on the frontier*. 国境には多くの砦があった.

push back the frontiers …の最前線を推し進める, の分野を開拓する, 新発見をする (*of*) ▪ Scientists *push back the frontiers of* knowledge. 科学者たちは知識の前線を切り拓く.

roll back the frontiers …の勢いを弱める (*of*) ▪ The United States should be energetic in *rolling back the frontiers of* tyranny. 米国は専制政治の勢力を弱めるために精力的であるべきだ.

frost /frɔːst|frɔst/ 名 ***of frost***《英》氷点下の ▪ It was [We had] ten degrees *of frost*. 氷点下10度だった.

froth[1] /frɔːθ|frɔθ/ 名 ***be all froth*** 実質を欠く ▪ His talk *is all froth*. 彼の話は実質を欠く.

froth[2] /frɔːθ|frɔθ/ 動 ***froth at the mouth*** → FOAM at the mouth.

froth with rage 〚主に進行形で〛口角泡を飛ばして怒る ▪ The boss *is frothing with rage* now. 社長はいま口角泡を飛ばして怒っている.

frugal /frúːgəl/ 形 ***frugal of [with]*** …を節約する ▪ He is *frugal of* his time and money. 彼は自分の時間と金を節約する.

fruit /fruːt/ 名 ***A stolen fruit tastes sweet.***《諺》盗んだ果物は味がよい.

bear fruit 実を結ぶ; 効果を生じる ▪ Do your apple-trees *bear* much *fruit*? 君のうちのリンゴの木はたくさん実がなるかい? ▪ None of these schemes have *borne fruit*. これらの計画のうちどれ一つとして実を結ばなかった.

eat the fruit of one's (own) doings →EAT[2].

forbidden fruit →FORBIDDEN.

old (tin of) fruit《主に英俗》おい君《親しい友に対

して》 ▪ She addressed him gaily as her "dear *old tin of fruit*." 彼女は陽気に彼を「あんた」と呼びかけた.

the fruit of the body [***the loins, the womb***] 子宝, 子供 (《聖》 *Ps.* 127. 3) ▪ The Lord withheld *the fruit of the womb.* 主は子宝を与え給わなかった.

the fruits of *one's* ***labor*** 労苦の成果 ▪ He lived to see *the fruits of his labor.* 彼は長生きして自分の労苦の成果を見た.

the fruits of the earth [***the ground***] (食用の)果物野菜類 ▪ The Breton peasant can turn all *the fruits of the earth* to account. ブルターニュの小作農はすべての果物野菜類を利用する.

fruitful /frúːtfəl/ 形 (***be***) ***fruitful in*** [***of***] …に富んで(いる), を豊富に生む ▪ He *is fruitful in* good wit. 彼は良知に富んでいる ▪ The year *was fruitful in* new works. その年は新作品を豊富に生んだ.

prove fruitful 成果をあげる ▪ His studies *proved fruitful.* 彼の研究は成果をあげた.

fruition /fruíʃən/ 名 ***bring ... to fruition*** …を達成させる ▪ His hopes *were brought to fruition.* 彼の希望は達成された.

come to fruition 成就する, 実を結ぶ ▪ His hopes *came to fruition.* 彼の希望は成就した.

frustrate /frʌ́streɪt|frʌstréɪt/ 動 ***be frustrated in*** …に失敗[挫折]する ▪ He *was frustrated in* the attempt. 彼はその企てに失敗した.

fry[1] /fraɪ/ 名 ***a fry up*** 《英口》(即席の)揚げ物[炒め物]料理(を作ること) ▪ *A fry up* is still on the breakfast menu. 揚げ物料理は依然として朝食のメニューにのっている.

small [***young, lesser***] ***fry*** **1** 小魚, 若魚, 小動物 ▪ The lake swarmed with *small fry.* 湖には小魚がうようよしていた ▪ One of the *small fry* was hopping about on the grass. 小動物の1匹が草の上を飛び回っていた.

2 雑魚ども, 子供たち ▪ We spent several hours watching the *small fry* playing in the park. 我々は子供たちが公園で遊んでいるのを見て数時間過ごした ▪ Compared with Sheridan, all other playwrights were *small fry.* シェリダンと比べれば他の劇作家はみな雑魚であった.

fry[2] /fraɪ/ 動 ***fry*** *oneself* 強烈な熱情で燃える ▪ I *fried myself* in my affections. 私は強烈な愛情に燃えた.

fry out fat 《米俗》金をしぼり取る ▪ No one could *fry out* more *fat* than he. 彼ほど多くの金をしぼり取ることのできる者はいない.

fry the fat out of 《米俗》…から金をしぼり取る, (実業家など)から献金させる ▪ They *fried the fat out of* the manufacturers. 彼らは製造業者から献金をさせた.

frying-pan /fráɪɪŋpæ̀n/ 名 (***jump, leap***) ***out of the frying-pan into the fire*** 小難を逃れて大難に(陥る), 一難を逃れてもっと大きい難に(あう) ▪ They were *jumping out of the frying-pan into the fire.* 彼らは小難を逃れて大難に陥りつつあった.

fuck[1] /fʌk/ 名 ***a fuck up*** 《卑》大失敗, 混乱 ▪ This isn't a mistake, this is *a* magnitude five *fuck up.* これは過ちなんてもんじゃない, マグニチュード5の大失敗だ.

for fuck's sake **1**〘主に命令文で〙お願いだから ▪ *For fuck's sake,* get out of my way! 頼むから, そこをどいてくれ!

2 つまらない理由で ▪ He threw my proposal out *for fuck's sake.* 彼はつまらぬ理由で私の提案を却下した.

not care [***give***] ***a*** (***flying***) ***fuck*** 気にしない, へとも思わない (*about*) ▪ I really *don't give a flying fuck about* politics. おれは政治なんか全くどうでもいい.

fuck[2] /fʌk/ 動 ***fuck all*** =DAMN all.

fuck it! =DAMN it!

fuck me! =DAMN me!

fuck you/ get fucked/ go fuck yourself 《卑》くたばっちまえ, くそくらえ ▪ "*Fuck you,* you bitch!" he yelled to the male reporter. 「ふざけるな, このおかま」と彼は男性レポーターにあびせた.

fucking A 《米口》〘間投詞的に〙その通り; 驚いた ▪ *Fucking A,* man. やあ, 驚いたよ. ☞もと芝居のタイトル; A=adultery.

fucking well 絶対に, 必ず ▪ I'll *fucking well* put the play on here. 絶対ここで上演するぞ.

fuddle[1] /fʌ́dəl/ 名 ***in a fuddle*** 《俗》酒に酔って ▪ He was *in a fuddle.* 彼は酔っていた.

(***out***) ***on the fuddle*** 《主に英口》外でひとしきり飲んで ▪ He pulls out a cigar when *on the fuddle.* 彼は外で飲んでいるときは葉巻を取り出す.

fuddle[2] /fʌ́dəl/ 動 ***fuddle*** *one's* ***cap*** [***nose***] 酔う ▪ Come, let us *fuddle* all *our noses.* さあさあ, みんな酔っ払おうではないか.

fuddle it 酒を飲む ▪ The captain *fuddled it* in his cabin. 船長は船室で酒を飲んだ.

fuddle *oneself* [*one's* ***brains***] ***with*** (酒)でばかになる, 頭が悪くなる ▪ He *fuddled himself with* gin. 彼はジンでぼけた.

fudge /fʌdʒ/ 動 ***fudge a day's work*** 手早く船位[正午から次の正午までの船の位置移動]推算をやる ▪ Jack could *fudge a day's work.* ジャックは手早く船位推算をやることができた.

fuel /fjúːəl/ 名 ***add fuel to the fire*** [***the flame***] 火に油を注ぐ, 激情をあおる ▪ Difficulty *adds fuel to the flame.* 困難は情熱を更にかきたてる.

take fuel on/take on fuel (船・飛行機などに)燃料を補給する ▪ We need to land at the next major airport to *take fuel on.* 給油のために次の主要空港に着陸する必要がある ▪ We will land somewhere to *take on fuel.* 給油のためどこかに着陸しよう.

fulfil /fʊlfíl/ 動 ***fulfil*** *oneself* 自分の資質を十分

F

に発揮する, 自分の大望を完全に実現する ▪ Every man has the inalienable right to *fulfil himself.* 人はみな自己の可能性を完全に実現するという奪うべからざる権利を持つ.

full /fʊl/ 形副名 ***a full court press*** 《バスケ》フルコート•プレス《コートの全面でマンツーマンのディフェンスを行う戦法》; 《米》相手に圧力をかけること; 猛[全力]攻撃 ▪ The Obama campaign put on *a full court press* to silence critics. オバマ氏のキャンペーンは批判者を黙らせるために圧力をかけた.

allow* [*give*]...*full play →give full PLAY.

(*as*) *full of meat as an egg* 栄養物[知識]に満ちて (cf. Sh., *Rom. & Jul.* 3. 1. 24f) ▪ He is *as full of meat as an egg* where the law is concerned. 彼は法律に関するかぎり知識に満ちている.

at full stretch →STRETCH[1].

at* (*the*) *full 満ちた状態で; 十分に ▪ The moon is *at the full.* 月は満ちている ▪ He gave his reasons *at full.* 彼は理由を十分に話した.

***be full of crap* [*shit, bull*]** 《卑》くだらないことばかり言って ▪ Bill *is* always *full of crap.* ビルはいつもくだらないことばかり言っている.

be full of holes (考え•計画が)欠点[穴]だらけで ▪ This plot *is full of holes.* この陰謀は穴だらけだ.

be full of it **1** ばかげたことばかり言って ▪ The talk shows *are full of it.* トークショーは嘘ばっかりだ.
2 悪ふざけ[いたずら, いじめ]ばかりして ▪ They *become* more and more *full of it* as they get older. 彼らは大きくなるにつれてますます悪ふざけをするようになってきている. ☞be FULL of crap [shit, bull] の婉曲表現.

be full of the devil ＝be FULL of it 2.

bring ... full circle →CIRCLE.

come* [*go, turn*] *full circle →CIRCLE.

do the full Monty →MONTY.

full-bodied 熟成した, (ワインなどが)こくのある ▪ This beer is *full-bodied* and very thick. このビールはこくがあって濃厚だ.

full face (写真などで)顔が正面向きで ▪ Masks are generally made *full face.* お面はたいてい正面向きに作られている.

full frontal **1** (ヌードが)真正面向きの ▪ The showing of *full frontal* nudity in movies is common. 映画で真正面向きのヌードを見せるのは普通である.
2 正面切っての, まやかしのない ▪ They advocate *full frontal* anarchy. 彼らは正面切っての無政府主義を標榜(ひょうぼう)している.

full in the face **1** まともに ▪ He looked me *full in the face.* 彼は私の顔をまともに見た.
2 顔がふっくらして ▪ He is *full in the face.* 彼は顔がふっくらしている.

full of **1** ...でいっぱいで ▪ The bucket is *full of* water. バケツには水がいっぱい入っている ▪ He is *full of* life. 彼は元気いっぱいだ.
2 ...のことでいっぱいで, ばかり考えて ▪ He is *full of* dreams and hopes. 彼は空想と希望にふけっている ▪ He is always *full of* his own affairs. 彼はいつも自分のことでいっぱいだ.
3 (ニュースなど)で頭がいっぱいで話さずにはいられない ▪ He is *full of* the news. 彼はそのニュースで頭がいっぱいで話さずにはいられない.

full of oneself **1** 自分のことばかり考えて[言って] ▪ His son is selfish and *full of himself.* 彼の息子は利己的で自分のことばかり考えている.
2 《口》うぬぼれて, おかしいほど高慢で ▪ He is so *full of himself* that he is quite empty. 彼はひどくうぬぼれていて, 頭は全くからっぽだ. ☞18-19 世紀の諺から.

full of children 子供は十分あって (《聖》 *Ps.* 17. 14) ▪ He is *full of children.* 彼には子供は十分ある.

full of days 十分年をとって, 天寿を全うして (《聖》 *Job* 42. 17) ▪ He died *full of days.* 彼は天寿を全うした.

full of emptiness つまらぬことでいっぱいの ▪ This book is *full of emptiness.* この本はつまらぬ中身でいっぱいだ.

full of it (ニュースなどで)頭をいっぱいにして, そのことばかり考えて ▪ The boy had seen the fire there and came in *full of it.* 少年はそこの火事を見たので, そのことばかり考えて入って来た.

full of piss and vinegar →PISS[1].

***full of the Old Nick* [*the devil, it*]** 《口》絶えずいたずら[悪い事]をして ▪ The boy is *full of the devil.* その少年はいたずらばかりしている. ☞Old Nick ＝the Devil.

full of years **1** ＝FULL of days.
2 春秋に富む ▪ He is a young man *full of years.* 彼は春秋に富む青年だ.

full of years and honors 天寿を全うし功成り名遂げて ▪ He died *full of years and honors.* 彼は天寿を全うし名を遂げて死んだ.

full out 全力で (all out) ▪ She played *full out,* but when she got tired, she sat down to rest. 彼女は全力でプレーしたが疲れると座って休んだ.

Full steam ahead! →STEAM[1].

full time 全時[全日]制の, フルタイムの ▪ He worked *full time* at the company. 彼はその会社の正社員だった ▪ He went back *full time* to his professorship. 彼は専任教授に復帰した.

full up 《口》ぎっしりつまって ▪ The cemeteries are *full up.* 墓地はすっかり墓でふさがっている ▪ The car is *full up.* 電車は満員だ.

full well とてもよく ▪ They know *full well* who the real winners are. 誰が真の勝利者であるか彼らにはよくわかっている.

in full **1** 略さずに, 完全に, 全部[全額]の ▪ Write your name *in full.* あなたの名前をフルネームで書きなさい ▪ He paid the creditors *in full.* 彼は債権者たちに全額支払った.
2 詳細に, 詳しく ▪ He explained the reasons *in full.* 彼はその理由を詳細に説明した.

in full cry 《英》いっせいに吠えたてる, やかましく非難する (*over*) ▪ Demmocrats are *in full cry over* the Bush tax cut. 民主党員たちはブッシュ氏の減税を

糾弾した.

in full flow [***flood, spate***]《英》(活動が)盛んに行われて(→FLOW[1]) ▪ Their wedding preparations were *in full flow*. 彼らの結婚の準備は着々と進んでいる ▪ Exhibitions, large and small, are *in full spate* this week. 今週は大小さまざまな展示会が行われている.

(in) full force →FORCE[1].

in the full of …の盛りで ▪ He is *in the full of* his prosperity. 彼は繁昌[栄華]の絶頂にある.

of the full blood 両親が同じの ▪ They are brother and sister *of the full blood*. 彼らは両親を同じうする兄妹である.

run full《海》帆を十分にはらませて走る ▪ Our yacht *ran full* under the blue sky. 私たちのヨットは青空の下, 帆をいっぱいはらませて走った.

the full monty [***monte***]《英口》何でも全部(→go the full MONTY) ▪ Their wedding was *the full monty*. 彼らの結婚式はなんでもありだった. ☞monty の語源不明.

to the full [***fullest***] 十分に, 心ゆくまで, 最大限に ▪ We ate bread *to the full*. 私たちはパンを十分に食べた ▪ I have enjoyed myself *to the fullest*. 私は十分に楽しみました.

ful(l)ness /fólnəs/ 名 ***in its fulness*** 十分に, 全面的に ▪ He displayed his ability *in its fulness*. 彼は才能を十分に発揮した ▪ He adopts that tale *in its fulness*. 彼はその話を全面的に採用している.

in the fulness of *one's* [***the***] ***heart*** 感きわまって, 真情にあふれて ▪ *In the fulness of the heart* Americans promise more than they keep. 至情にあふれるあまりに, アメリカ人は果たせないほどの約束をする.

in the fulness of time 機が熟して, 時がたって; 予定の時に(《聖》*Gal*. 4. 4) ▪ *In the fulness of time*, the ruler of the state died. 時がたってその国の支配者は死んだ.

the fulness of …の中にあるすべてのもの(《聖》*1 Chron*. 16. 32) ▪ The earth and all *its fulness* are given into my hands. この世とその中にあるすべてのものは私の手に与えられている.

the fulness of time 適当な時, 予定の時(《聖》*Gal*. 4. 4) ▪ When *the fulness of time* was come, God sent forth his son. 機が熟したとき, 神はその御子をつかわされた.

fumble /fʌ́mbəl/ 動 ***fumble the ball***《球技》ボールを受けそこねる, お手玉をする ▪ The player often *fumbles the ball*. その選手はよくお手玉をする.

fumble *one's* ***way*** 手探りで進む ▪ He *fumbled his way* into the room. 彼は手探りで部屋へ入って来た.

fume /fjuːm/ 名 ***in a fume*** ぷりぷり怒って ▪ Father was *in a fume* this morning. 父は今朝ぷんぷん怒っていた.

the fumes of wine 頭にくる酒気 ▪ It drove away *the fumes of wine*. それは頭にくる酒気をさました.

fun /fʌn/ 名 ***all in fun*** (今思い出せば)すべて愉快で ▪ The first few years were rough, but it was *all in fun*. 最初の数年はつらかったが, 今思えばみんな楽しかった.

be full of fun **1** (人が)戯れてばかりいる ▪ The boy *was full of fun*. その少年は戯れてばかりいた.
2 (物事が)とてもおもしろい, 楽しい ▪ It *was full of fun*. それはとても楽しかった.

for fun おもしろいから, おもしろ半分に ▪ Let's play soft-ball just *for fun*. (競技のためでなく)ほんの楽しみにソフトボールをやりましょう.

for the fun of it それがおもしろいから, おもしろ半分に ▪ I go out on long trips just *for the fun of it*. ただおもしろいから長旅に出るのです.

fun and games《口》お祭り騒ぎ, 楽しい遊び《しばしば反語的》; 恋のたわむれ(→have FUN and games, not be all FUN and games) ▪ They are having *fun and games* putting up new shelves. 彼らはにぎやかに新しいたな付けをやっている ▪ Mr. Moor is having *fun and games* with Miss Smith. ムーア氏はスミス嬢と恋のたわむれをしている.

good clean fun 健全な娯楽, 無害な遊び(→It's all good clean FUN.) ▪ They're such *good clean fun* that they're much like gardening itself. それらはとても無害な遊びだから, 庭いじりそのものに大変似てるよ.

good [***great***] ***fun*** 非常におもしろいこと[人] ▪ It is *great fun* to play on the beach. 浜辺で遊ぶのは非常におもしろい ▪ He is such *good fun*. 彼はとても愉快な人です.

have fun *doing* …するのがおもしろい ▪ I *have fun getting* these answers. これらの答えを得るのがおもしろいのです.

have fun and games《戯》骨が折れる, 手こずる(*doing, with*) (→FUN and games, not be all FUN and games) ▪ We *had fun and games getting* the harvest in. 私たちは取り入れに苦労した ▪ She *had fun and games with* the kids. 彼女は子供たちに手を焼いた.

have fun with …するのがおもしろい ▪ Do I *have fun with* the dictionary? 辞書を引くのはおもしろいだろうか.

have (***great***) ***fun*** (***at***) (…がとても)おもしろい ▪ We *had great fun at* the games. ゲームがとてもおもしろかった ▪ We *had fun* on board. 船上では私たちはおもしろく過ごした.

in fun 冗談に, おもしろ半分に(↔in EARNEST) ▪ He just did it *in fun*. 彼はおもしろ半分にそうしただけだ.

it is fun *doing* …するのがおもしろい ▪ *It is* no *fun looking* at your face every day. あなたの顔を毎日見るのはおもしろくない.

It was fun while it lasted. 楽しみは終わったが心残りはない, 短かったが楽しかった ▪ The Christmas Season *was fun while it lasted*. クリスマスの季節の間, 堪能した.

It's all good clean fun.《口》単なる冗談だよ,

ちょっとふざけただけだよ ▪ "*It's all good clean fun*, and they don't take it all so seriously," said Pam.「単なる冗談だ, 彼らもたいして深刻には考えないよ」とパムは言った.

like fun 《口》 **1** 勢いよく, どしどし, おもしろいように, 大いに (→FIT like fun) ▪ They performed their task *like fun*. 彼らはどんどん仕事をした ▪ The book sold *like fun*. その本はどんどん売れた.

2 〚否定的に〛とんでもない, 実はちがう (→like HELL 3) ▪ I just walked home from down town. —*Like fun* you did. 商店街から歩いて帰宅したところだよ—よく言うよ.

F

make fun of …をからかう, 愚ろうする ▪ Then you won't *make fun of* me, will you? それでは私をからかわないでしょうね.

more fun than a barrel of monkeys 《口》 とても愉快だ, 非常に笑える ▪ Congress can be *more fun than a barrel of monkeys*. 国会ではめちゃくちゃおもしろいことがある.

not be all fun and games おもしろおかしいばかりではない (→FUN and games, have FUN and games) ▪ The major league experience *isn't all fun and games*. メジャーリーグでの経験は楽しいことばかりではない.

not see the fun **1** (…の)おもしろさがわからない, (を)おもしろいと思わない (*of*) ▪ I *don't see the fun of* being cheated. 私は人にだまされるなんておもしろいとは思わない.

2 ユーモアがわからない ▪ He *never sees the fun* in anything. 彼はものごとのユーモアが全くわからない.

out of fun =for FUN.

poke fun at 《口》 …を笑う, からかう, 嘲ろうする ▪ Everybody in the office *poked fun at* Jim. 会社の人はみなジムをからかった.

fund /fʌnd/ 名 ***be in funds*** 金を持っている ▪ When he *was in funds* he preferred a taxi. 彼は金を持っているときはタクシーにした.

be out of funds 金がない ▪ I *am* now *out of funds*. 私は今は金がない.

have a fund of **1** …を備えて[たくわえて]いる ▪ He *has an* unfailing *fund of* humor. 彼は尽きないユーモアを備えている ▪ He *has a* rare *fund of* perseverance. 彼は珍しく忍耐力がある.

2 …の基金がある ▪ The school *has a fund of* $50,000. その学校には5万ドルの基金がある.

in the funds 国[公]債で ▪ He must have a hundred thousand *in the funds*. 彼は公債で10万ポンド持っているにちがいない.

put ... in funds …に金を持たせる ▪ He tried hard to *put* the society *in funds*. 彼はその協会に金を持たせるよう非常に努力した.

raise funds 寄付を募る, 資金を調達する ▪ The church *raised* the *funds* for the pews. 教会は座席のための基金を募った.

funeral /fjúːnərəl/ 名 ***It's*** [***That's***] ***your funeral.*** それは君の問題だ《私にはかかわりのないことだ》 ▪ Your wife leaving you? Well, *it's your funeral*. 奥さんが出て行こうとしてるって? そりゃ君が対処すべきことだよ ▪ *It's* none of *your funeral*. それは君の知ったことではない. ☞《英》では主に肯定文に用いる.

one's (***own***) ***funeral*** 《俗》 人のすべきこと ▪ It's none of *my funeral*. Everyone has a right to their opinions. おれの知ったことではない. 誰だって意見を言う権利がある ▪ If they've got into debt, it's *their own funeral*. 彼らが借金したとしてもそれは自業自得だ.

would be late for *one's* ***own funeral*** いつも遅れる ▪ You*'d be late for your own funeral*. 君はいつも遅れる[遅刻する].

funk /fʌŋk/ 名 ***in a*** (***blue***) ***funk*** 《俗》 **1** おじけづいて, びっくりして ▪ Arthur was *in a blue funk* when you sent for him. アーサーはあなたが彼を呼びにやったとき, びくびくしていた ▪ He was *in a* violent *funk*. 彼はひどくおじけづいていた.

2 (気分が)落ち込んで ▪ I've been *in a blue funk* since I heard the disturbing news. 気がかりなニュースを聞いてから気分が落ち込んでいる.

put ... in a funk 《俗》 …をびくびくさせる, びっくりさせる ▪ The storm *put* him *in a funk*. 暴風は彼をおじけづかせた.

funny /fʌ́ni/ 形 ***a funny farm*** [***house***] 精神病院《差別語になることがある》 ▪ They belong on the *funny farm*. 彼らは精神病院に入っている.

feel funny 《口》 体の調子が悪い, 気持ちが変である ▪ He *felt funny* all over that morning. その日の朝彼は全く調子が悪かった.

funny bone (ひじ先の)尺骨のはし《はじくとくすぐったい感じを与える骨》 ▪ Ouch! I hit my *funny bone*. あいたっ! 尺骨のはしを打ってしまった.

funny enough/《英》***funnily*** (***enough***) おかしなことに ▪ *Funny enough*, I sense some excitement. おかしなことに, 私はいささかの興奮を感じる.

funny money にせ金, 不正な金 ▪ A man was arrested for using *funny money*. ある男がにせ金を使った罪で逮捕された.

funny strange [***weird***, 《英》 ***peculiar***] ***or funny ha-ha*** "funny" (おかしい)って「奇妙」のほう, それとも「わっはっは[おもしろい]」のほう? ☞意味の確認のために言う.

get funny with 《米口》 …に生意気な態度をとる, 変なまねをする ▪ Few whites *got funny with* Daddy. He'd punch them out. お父さんに生意気な態度を取った白人はほとんどいない. ぶちのめしてたから.

so ... it's not even funny 《口》 ただ…なんてものではない, を通りこしている ▪ I love the Red Sox *so* much *it's not even funny*. レッドソックスがただ好きだなんてものではない ▪ I am *so* burned out in politics *it is not even funny*, and want to begin to explore career switching. もう政治には燃え尽きたを通りこしているので, 転職先を探しはじめたい.

fur[1] /fəːr/ 名 ***fur, fin,*** (***and***) ***feather*** 鳥獣魚類 ▪ *Fur, fin, and feather* abound in this neighborhood. この界隈には鳥獣魚類が豊富だ.

make the fur fly 《口》 **1** 騒動を起こす, 大騒ぎす

る, 騒ぎ立てる ▪ He is going to *make the fur fly* in France. 彼はフランスで騒動を起こすつもりだ ▪ When the boss finds it out, he will *make the fur fly*. 社長がそれを知ったら騒ぎ立てるだろう.
2 大げんかをする; 紛争を起こす, 戦う ▪ Those two women are sure to *make the fur fly* whenever they meet. その二人の女は出会うといつでもきっとけんかをする. ☞動物がけんかするときは毛をとばすことから.

stroke* [*rub*] *the* [*a person's*] *fur the wrong way 人の感情を逆なでする ▪ He *stroked their fur the wrong way*. 彼は彼らの感情を逆なでした.

The fur begins to fly./The fur flies. 《口》大げんか[大騒ぎ]となる (→make the FUR fly) ▪ When George said so, *the fur began to fly*. ジョージがそう言ったとき, 大騒ぎとなった ▪ *The fur* will *fly* from the Cleveland side. クリーブランド側が大騒ぎするだろう.

fur[2] /fəːr/ 動 ***our* [*the*] *furred, four-footed and feathered friends*** 《戯》動物界 ▪ We like *our four-footed and feathered friends*. 我々は動物たちが好きだ. ☞furred または four-footed が略されることがある.

furious /fjʊ́əriəs/ 形 ***be furious at*** *a thing* [***with*** *a person*] こと[人]を猛烈に怒る ▪ He *was furious with* his mother. 彼は母に猛烈に腹を立てていた.

fast and furious →FAST.

furlough /fə́ːrloʊ/ 名 ***have* (*a*) *furlough*** 休暇を賜わる ▪ I *have a* six months' *furlough*. 私は6か月の休暇をもらっている.

on furlough 賜暇(しか)[休暇]で ▪ I will go home *on furlough*. 私は賜暇で帰国します.

furnace /fə́ːrnəs/ 名 **(*be*) *tried in the furnace*** きびしい試練を経ている[にあう] ▪ He has *been tried in the furnace* of life. 彼は人生の厳しい試練を経てきた.

furnish /fə́ːrnɪʃ/ 動 ***let ... furnished*** …を家具つきで貸す ▪ A two bedroom apartment is to *be let furnished*. 寝室が二つあるアパートを家具つきで貸します.

furniture /fə́ːrnɪtʃər/ 名 ***a piece* [*an article*] *of furniture*** 家具1点, 一つの家具 ▪ A chair is *a piece of furniture*. いすは一つの家具だ.

part of the furniture 《口》(一か所に長く勤めたり, 客であったりして)家具の一部のようになった人 ▪ The old man has been coming in this pub for many years—he's *part of the furniture*. その老人は長年このパブに来ている—いわば古参客だ.

the furniture of the mind [*one's* ***shelves,*** *one's* ***pocket***] 識見[書籍, 金銭] ▪ *The furniture of the mind* reflects our character, personality and ability. 識見は我々の品性[個性, 能力]を反映する.

furrow /fə́ːroʊ|fʌ́r-/ 名 ***plow a lonely furrow*** →PLOW[2].

sow under the furrow 休閑地に種をまいてすきで土をかぶせる ▪ Wheat *is* most commonly *sown under the furrow*. 小麦は休閑地にまいてすきで土をかけるのが最も普通である.

further /fə́ːrðər/ 形副 ***further off*** もっと向こう, もっと先 ▪ The Dutch cabin lay about a mile *further off*. オランダの小屋はおよそ1マイル更に先にあった.

further on もっと先で, もっと進んでから ▪ I will speak of it *further on*. もっと先でそのことを話します.

further to (手紙・スピーチで)…に付言して ▪ *Further to* my previous email, I'm writing to confirm that I'm unable to attend the gathering. 前回のEメールの追伸として, 集会に参加できないことを念のために書き添えます.

go further and fare worse もっと欲ばってかえってまずくなる ▪ Folks may *go further and fare worse*, as they say. 世間に言うように人はさらに欲ばって, かえって悪くなることもある.

***I'll see you further* (*first*).** →I'll SEE you hanged first.

on the further side 向こう側に ▪ The gamekeeper was *on the further side* of the river. 猟場番人は川の向こう側にいた.

till further notice →NOTICE[1].

wish *a person* ***further*** →WISH[2].

furthest /fə́ːrðəst/ 形 ***at* (*the*) *furthest*** 遅くとも ▪ He will take the town in a month *at the furthest*. 彼は遅くとも1か月でその町を占領するだろう.

fury /fjʊ́əri/ 名 ***fly into a fury*** 烈火のごとく怒る ▪ He *flew into a fury* when I said so. 私がそう言ったら彼は烈火のように怒った.

***Hell has no fury* (*like a woman scorned*).** 《諺》侮辱された女ほどの憤怒は地獄にもない ▪《しばしば like 以下を変更して用いる》*Hell has no fury like* a politician ignored. 無視された政治家ほど恐いものはない. ☞William Congreve, *The Mourning Bride* (1697).

in a fury 烈火のように怒って, 激怒して ▪ He turned upon me *in a fury*. 彼は激怒して私に食ってかかった.

in all its fury 猛威をふるって ▪ The wind blew *in all its fury*. 風は猛烈に吹きまくった ▪ The storm burst *in all its fury*. あらしがどっと起こって猛威をきわめた.

lash the sea into fury (暴風が)海に怒濤を起こさせる ▪ The storm *lashed the sea into fury*. 暴風は海に怒濤を起こさせた.

like fury 《口》猛烈に, 盛んに ▪ It rained *like fury* all the afternoon. 午後ずっと猛烈に雨が降った.

the furies of *a person's* **blood** 殺した人の怨霊 ▪ He was haunted by *the furies of her blood*. 彼は殺した彼女の怨霊につきまとわれた.

fuse /fjuːz/ 名 ***be on* [*have*] *a short fuse*** 怒りっぽい ▪ Gibson admits he *has a short fuse*. ギブスンは自分は怒りっぽいことを認めている.

***blow a fuse* 1** ヒューズを飛ばす ▪ I *blew a fuse* by switching on too many appliances at the same time. あまりに多くの電気器具にスイッチを同時に入れたものだから, ヒューズをとばしてしまった.

2《口》かっとなる ▪ Her husband "*blew a fuse*" over the news of her flirtation and hit her on the nose. 夫は彼女の浮気の噂にかっとなって彼女の鼻をなぐった.

have a long fuse がまん[辛抱]うよい, 忍耐力のある ▪ I have a temper, but I *have a long fuse*. 私は短気だが, がまんはできる.

light the fuse 導火線に火をつける, 導火線[引き金]になる ▪ Patrick Henry *lit the fuse* of the American revolution with his immortal cry for liberty or death. パトリック・ヘンリーは自由かさもなくば死をという不滅の叫びでアメリカ独立戦争の引き金となった.

F

fuss[1] /fʌs/ 名 ***fuss and bother*** (いらぬ)やきもき騒ぎ ▪ What's all this *fuss and bother*? 一体このやきもき騒ぎは何事だ?

fuss and feathers 《米口》見栄っぱりと見せびらかし ▪ She is full of *fuss and feathers*. 彼女は見栄っぱりと見せびらかしに満ちている.

get into a fuss やきもきする ▪ Don't *get into* such *a fuss* about trifles. 小さなことでそんなにやきもきするな.

kick up a fuss = make a FUSS (about, over).

make a fuss (***about, over***) (…に)大げさに騒ぎ立てる; ぶつぶつ言う ▪ She *makes a fuss* if you ask her to work. 仕事をしてくれと言えば彼女はぶつぶつ言う ▪ He *makes a* great *fuss about* nothing. 彼は何でもないことに大騒ぎする.

make a fuss of [***over***] …をちやほやする, かわいがる ▪ They always *make* such *a fuss of* me. 彼らはいつも私を大騒ぎしてもてはやす ▪ Everyone *made a fuss over* the new baby. みんなが生まれたばかりの赤ちゃんをちやほやした.

without any fuss 騒がないで, おとなしく, 静かに ▪ You had better come along *without any fuss*. 君はおとなしくついて来たまえ.

fuss[2] /fʌs/ 動 ***fuss and bother*** (必要もないのに)やきもきして騒ぎ立てる ▪ She is *fussing and bothering* about the children's health. 彼女は子供たちの健康についてやきもきして騒ぎ立てている.

not be fussed (*about*) 《英口》…のことはどうでもいい ▪ He's *not fussed about* what he wears. 彼は自分が着るものには無頓着だ.

fussy /fʌ́si/ 形 ***be fussy about*** …に小うるさい ▪ She *is fussy about* her clothes. 彼女は衣服のことに小うるさい.

fut /fʌt/ 名 ***go fut*** 《英口》失敗に帰する; くずれる; (機械などが)だめになる, 動かなくなる ▪ Did the phone really *go fut*? 電話は本当にだめになったのですか ▪ My literary ambitions have *gone fut*. 私の文学上の大望はくずれ去った.

future /fjúːtʃər/ 名形 ***at some future day*** 将来いつか ▪ It will be realized *at some future day*. それは将来いつか実現されるだろう.

for the future 将来はずっと, 今後は ▪ I'll teach him to take better care *for the future*. 彼に将来はもっと注意するように教えましょう.

have a bright [***brilliant, great***] ***future before*** *one* すばらしい将来性がある ▪ You *have a bright future before* you. あなたは前途有望である.

in (***the***) ***future*** 将来, 今後は ▪ Be more careful *in future*. 今後はもっと注意しなさい ▪ No one knows what will happen *in the future*. 将来何が起こるか誰にもわからない.

in the near [***no distant***] ***future*** 近い将来に, 遠からず ▪ The matter will be settled *in no distant future*. その問題は遠からず解決するでしょう.

once and future 永遠の, 不朽の ▪ On the all-too-rare occasion you chance to meet a *once and future* friend. ごくまれにだが, 永遠の友人に出会わないとも限らない.

(***there is***) ***no future in*** …がうまくいく見込みはない ▪ We can't hide out; *there is no future in* that. 我々は潜伏はできない. そんなことがうまくいく見込みはない.

with future 有望な ▪ He is a man *with future*. 彼は有望な人である.

G

gab /gæb/ 名 ***blow the gab*** 《俗》(秘密などを)漏らす; 密告する ▪ Never *blow the gab*. 決して秘密をしゃべってはいけない.

flash the [*one's*] ***gab*** 《俗》大言壮語する, まくしたてる ▪ He is always *flashing his gab*. 彼はいつも大ぼらを吹いている.

stow [***stop***] *one's* ***gab*** 《口》〚主に命令文で〛おしゃべりをやめる ▪ *Stow your gab*. I am tired of listening. おしゃべりはよせ. 聞きあきた.

the gift of the gab [《米》***of*** [***for***] ***gab***] 《口》達者な弁舌, 雄弁(の才), 口達者 ▪ Muhammad Ali has his legendary *gift of gab*. モハメド・アリには伝説となった雄弁の才がある ▪ With his *gift of the gab* he will make an excellent politician. 弁舌が達者だから彼は立派な政治家になるだろう.

gabble /gǽbəl/ 動 ***gabble*** *a person* ***crazy*** べちゃくちゃしゃべって人の気を変にする ▪ You *gabble* me *crazy*. 君のおしゃべりで気が変になりそうだ.

gad /gæd/ 名 ***on*** [***upon***] ***the gad*** 《口》ぶらついて, いつも出歩いて; (通例女性が)遊び歩いて ▪ The girl is always *upon the gad*. その娘はいつもぶらつき歩いている. ☞gad「出歩き」.

gaff /gæf/ 名 (***as***) ***crooked as a gaff*** ひどく曲がって ▪ The path was *as crooked as a gaff*. 小道はひどく曲がっていた. ☞gaff「かぎさお」.

blow the gaff 《口》 **1** 秘密を漏らす ▪ We were going to the theater without mother knowing, but George *blew the gaff*. 我々は母に知らせないで劇場へ行くつもりだったが, ジョージが秘密を漏らした.
2 (人を)密告する (*on*) ▪ I will take it upon myself to *blow the gaff on* the three of you. 君ら3人を密告する仕事を引き受けよう. ☞gaff「余計なおしゃべり」.

bring (***a fish***) ***to gaff*** (針にかかった魚を)引き寄せて魚かぎに掛ける ▪ When *a fish* is *being brought to gaff*, much caution is necessary. 魚を引き寄せて魚かぎに掛けているときは用心が大いに必要である. ☞gaff「魚かぎ」.

get [***give***] ***the gaff*** 《米俗》(叱責・処罰・嘲笑などの)苦難を受ける[与える] ▪ If he *gets the gaff*, he'll be flat on his back. 彼は処罰を受けたら, ぺしゃんこになるだろう ▪ *Give* us *the gaff*. We deserve it. 我々をきびしくしかってください. それが当然なのです.

stand the gaff 《米俗》(叱責・処罰・嘲笑などの)苦難に耐える, 苦難を甘んじて受ける ▪ He shut his mouth and *stood the gaff*. 彼は口を閉じてきびしい叱責を甘んじて受けた.

take the gaff ＝get the GAFF.

gaffe /gæf/ 名 ***make*** [***commit***] ***a gaffe*** へまをやる, しくじりをやる ▪ He *made a* bad *gaffe*. 彼はひどいへまをやった.

gag[1] /gæg/ 名 ***place a gag upon*** [***on***] ...を抑圧する ▪ The government *placed a gag upon* freedom of speech. 政府は言論の自由を抑圧した.

gag[2] /gæg/ 動 ***be gagging for it*** 《英口》しきりにセックスしたがっている ▪ Ben says Kate *is gagging for it*. ケイトはセックスしたがっているとベンが言っている.

be gagging to *do* 《英口》しきりに...したがる, することを切望する ▪ They *are gagging to* sign the contract. 彼らはしきりに契約に署名したがっている.

gage[1] /geɪdʒ/ 名 ***at gage*** 質[抵当]に入れて ▪ His own things were *at gage*. 彼自身の物は抵当に入っていた.

deliver [***give, leave***]***... in gage*** ...を質や抵当に入れる ▪ He *left* his shirt *in gage*. 彼はシャツを抵当に入れた.

lay [***sweep***]***... to gage*** ...を抵当や質に入れる ▪ I will *lay* my gown *to gage*. 私はガウンを抵当に入れよう ▪ She *swept* her linen *to gage*. 彼女はリンネル製品を質に入れた.

lie to gage 抵当[質]に入っている ▪ His beloved gold pocket-watch *lies to gage*. 彼が愛用する金の懐中時計は質に入っている.

throw (***down***) ***a gage*** (***of battle***) (決闘の)挑戦をする ▪ He was going to *throw down a gage of battle*. 彼は決闘の挑戦をしようとしていた.

under [***upon***] ***gage*** (***of***) (...を)質や抵当として ▪ The common people borrowed money *upon gage of* their bodies. 庶民は体を抵当にして金を借りた ▪ Thirty thousand ducats were given *under gage of* the king's jewels. 国王の宝石類を抵当として3万ダカットの金が与えられた.

gage[2] /geɪdʒ/ 名 ＝GAUGE.

gaiety /géɪəti/ 名 ***the gaiety of nations*** 大衆の愉楽; 陽気な世の風潮 (Dr. Johnson, *The Lives of the Poets*) ▪ These stories add greatly to *the gaiety of nations*. これらの話は大衆の愉楽を大いに増すものである.

gain[1] /geɪn/ 名 ***for gain*** 儲け目的で ▪ Doris denied marrying *for* financial *gain*. ドリスはお金目的で結婚したことを否定した.

ill-gotten gains 不正利得 ▪ Much of the *ill-gotten gains* was spent on equipment and real estate. 不正利得の多くは備品と不動産に使われた.

No gains without pains./***No pains, no gains.***/***No pain, no gain.*** 《諺》骨折りなければ利得なし, 「たなからぼたもちは落ちてこない」.

gain[2] /geɪn/ 動 ***gain ground*** →GROUND[1].

gain the whole world and lose *one's* (***own***) ***soul*** 全世界を得て自己の魂を失う《かえって大事な物を失う》(《聖》*Matt.* 16. 26) ▪ How does it profit a man to have *gained the whole world and lost his soul?* 全世界を得て自己の魂を失ったとすれば，どれだけ人の役に立つだろうか．

gait /geɪt/ 名 ***go*** [《米》***gang***] *one's* ***own gait*** 自分の好きなようにする ▪ He always *goes his own gait.* 彼はいつも自分の好きなようにする．

gala /géɪlə|gɑ́ː-/ 名 ***in gala*** 晴れ着を着て ▪ I love to see them *in gala.* 彼らが晴れ着を着ているのを見るのが好きだ ▪ The streets were dressed *in gala.* 町は華々しく飾られていた．

gale /geɪl/ 名 ***gales of laughter*** ドッという笑い声 ▪ Comedy Festival offers *gales of laughter.* コメディー・フェスティバルはドッという笑い声を提供します．

in the teeth of the gale 大風にもかまわず; 激しい反対を押し切って ▪ The steamer started *in the teeth of the gale.* その汽船は大風にもかまわず出帆した ▪ The committee passed the resolution *in the teeth of the gale.* 委員会は猛反対を押し切ってその決議案を通過させた．

It blows a gale. →BLOW[2].

gall /gɔːl/ 名 ***be all gall*** きわめて痛烈で，辛らつで ▪ His speech *was all gall.* 彼の演説はきわめて痛烈であった．

be (***gall and***) ***wormwood to*** → WORMWOOD.

dip *one's* ***pen in gall*** 毒筆を振るう，辛らつな[痛烈な]文を書く ▪ An anonymous writer *dips his pen in gall* in order to depict the German Emperor. 匿名の筆者がドイツ皇帝を描くため毒筆を振るっている．

have the gall to *do* 《米俗》ずうずうしくも…する ▪ He *had the gall to* ask me for money. 彼は厚かましくも私に金をくれと言った．

the gall of bitterness 最も激しい悲しみ，極度の苦しみ (《聖》*Acts* 8. 23) ▪ You are still in *the gall of bitterness.* 君はまだ極度の苦しみを受けている．

gallant /gəlǽnt/ 動 ***gallant*** (***it***) ***with*** (異性)とふざける ▪ She *gallants* (*it*) *with* every pretty fellow she comes across. 彼女は美男子に出会ったら必ずその男とふざける．

gallery /gǽləri/ 名 ***a gallery hit*** [***shot, stroke***] 大向こうを目あての演技 ▪ It was *a gallery hit* of his. それは彼の例の大向こう目あての演技だった．

a shooting gallery 射撃場; 薬物を注射する場所，シャブ打ち場 ▪ Britain's first heroin "*shooting gallery*" could be opened next year. 英国の最初の「シャブ打ち場」が来年オープンする可能性がでた．

bring down the gallery 大向こうをうならせる ▪ He *brought down the gallery.* 彼は大向こうをうならせた．

play the gallery 大向こうを演じる; わいわい連のようにさわぐ ▪ We were called in to *play the gallery* to his witty remarks. 我々は彼のしゃれに対して大向こうのようにさわぐため呼び入れられた．

play to [***for***] ***the gallery*** 大向こうを目当てに演じる; 俗衆にこびる ▪ He was *playing for the* Irish *gallery.* 彼はアイルランドの俗衆におもねっていた ▪ John is a good football player, but he is too fond of *playing to the gallery.* ジョンはフットボールがうまいが，あまりに大向こうを目当てのプレーが好きで困る．

galley /gǽli/ 名 ***condemn*** [***send***]***...to the galleys*** …をガレー船こぎの刑に処する《フランス・スペインなど地中海沿岸諸国で行われた刑の一種》 ▪ Many of them *were condemned to the galleys.* 彼らの多くはガレー船こぎの刑に処せられた．

row in the galley 奴隷の苦労をなめる ▪ He had *rowed in the galley* himself. 彼もまた奴隷の苦労をなめたことがあった．

galley-west /gǽliwést/ 副 ***knock ... galley-west*** 《米口》**1** …を混乱させる ▪ You come and *knock* my serenity *galley-west.* 君はやって来て私の平静をすっかりかき乱してしまう．

2 …をすっかり打ちのめす，こっぴどくやっつける ▪ She grabbed up the basket and *knocked* the rat *galley-west.* 彼女はかごをつかみあげて，ドブネズミをたたきのめした．

gallop /gǽləp/ 名 ***at a*** [***the***] ***gallop*** ギャロップで，全速力で ▪ He was hurrying on *at a gallop.* 彼はギャロップでどんどん急いでいた ▪ Ride *at the gallop.* 馬を全速力で走らせなさい．

at a snail's gallop →SNAIL.

(***at***) ***full gallop*** ＝at a GALLOP.

go for a gallop ギャロップ乗馬に行く ▪ Let's *go for a gallop.* ギャロップ乗馬に出かけよう．

gallows /gǽloʊz/ 名 ***cheat the gallows*** **1** (自殺などによって)うまく絞首刑を逃れる; 悪者が(つかまらないうちに)死ぬ《必ずしも罪人とは限らない》 ▪ Hitler's henchman Hermann Goering *cheated the gallows* by swallowing a cyanide capsule. ヒトラーの腹心ヘルマン・ゲーリングはシアン化物のカプセルを呑むことによって絞首刑を逃れた ▪ That ruffian is going to *cheat the gallows* at last. あの悪党もとうとうお陀仏になりそうだ．

2 (絞首刑のような)当然の厳罰を免れる ▪ He has been a rogue, but has *cheated the gallows* so far. 彼は悪漢だったが，今までは当然の厳罰を免れている．

come to the gallows 絞首刑になる ▪ When he *came to the gallows*, he said "I die a lover of my country." 彼は絞首刑になるとき「われ愛国者として死す」と言った．

gallows humo(***u***)***r*** (死など不快なことを茶化した)ブラックユーモア，気味悪い冗談 ▪ *Gallows humor* makes fun of serious or terrifying situations. ブラックユーモアは，深刻な，または恐るべき状況を笑いの種にする．

have the gallows in *one's* ***face*** 絞首刑になりそうな人相[極悪な顔] ▪ He *has the gallows in his face.* 彼のあの人相では絞首台行きだ．

if the gallows had its due 絞罪に当然なるべき者がなるとしたら ▪ *If the gallows had its due*, he would no longer be among us. 絞罪に当然なるべき

者がなるとしたら，彼はもはや我々と共にいないだろう．

send* [*condemn*]*... to the gallows …を絞首刑に処する ▪ Hanratty *was sent to the gallows* for murder and rape. ハンラッティは殺人と強姦の罪で絞首刑に処せられた．

galore /gəlɔ́ːr/ 名 ***in galore*** 《古風》たくさんに，おびただしく ▪ He found big lumps *in galore*. 彼は大きなかたまりをたくさん見つけた．

galvanize /gǽlvənàɪz/ 動 ***galvanize*** *a person* ***into action*** [***activity***] 人を急に活発に動きださせる ▪ He *was galvanized into action*. 彼は急に活発に動きだした．

galvanize ... into life [***to new life***] …を急に活気づかせる，生き返らせる ▪ Her approach always *galvanized* him *to new life*. 彼女が近づくといつも彼は急に活気づいた ▪ He *galvanized* a forgotten question *into life*. 彼は忘れられていた問題を蘇らせた．

galvanize life into …に活気を吹きこむ ▪ They tried to *galvanize life into* the market. 彼らは市場を活気づかせようとした．

gam /gæm/ 動 ***go gamming*** 《米》雑談をしに行く ▪ Probably she has *gone gamming*. たぶん彼女は世間話をしに行ったんだろう．

gambit /gǽmbət/ 名 ***an opening gambit*** (論争などの)口火，最初の一手[言葉]; 先制攻撃 ▪ He's lying and it's *an opening gambit* in his negotiations. 彼は嘘をついており，それは彼の交渉の最初の一手だ．

gamble[1] /gǽmbəl/ 名 ***on a gamble*** 《米俗》冒険的に，運任せに ▪ *On a gamble* he raised his sombrero. 彼は運任せにソンブレロを上げた．

on the gamble 《主に俗》賭博で[にふけって] ▪ He went *on the gamble*. 彼は賭博をやった．

take a gamble on …に賭けて(やって)みる (→take a (long) CHANCE) ▪ You can *take a gamble on* getting a higher rate of interest. 君は高率の利息を得ることに賭けてみてもよい．

gamble[2] /gǽmbəl/ 動 ***gamble*** *oneself* ***out of house and home*** ばくちで身代をつぶす ▪ My uncle *gambled himself out of house and home*. おじはばくちで身代をつぶした．

You may [***can***] ***gamble on that.*** 《口》確かに，請け合いだ ▪ There will be trouble for some one. *You may gamble on that*. 誰かに困ったことが起こるよ，きっと．

game /geɪm/ 名形 ***a game leg*** 《口》傷ついた足 ▪ I've got *a game leg* from last week's match. 私は先週の試合で足をけがした．

a game of chance 運任せの賭博，ギャンブル ▪ Poker involves skill and is not merely *a game of chance*. ポーカーは熟練を要し，単に運勝負ではない．

a game that [***at which***] ***two can play*** → two can play at that GAME.

a paying game 儲かる仕事[行為] ▪ Flattering him is really *a paying game*. 彼におべっかを使うことは本当に儲けになる．

a winning game 勝つ見込みのある勝負; 成功の可能性が高い投機 ▪ I know it is our job to keep fans happy by playing *a winning game*. 試合に勝ってファンを喜ばせるのが我々の仕事だとわかっている．

ahead of the game **1** 早く，早い (= early) ▪ When I got up at six, mother said, "You're *ahead of the game*." 僕が6時に起きたら，母が「(ずいぶん)早いのね」と言った．

2 《口》(試合・競争で)リードして; 優勢な，(株式などで)儲かって ▪ We know the best way to stay *ahead of the game* in the fashion business. 我々はファッション・ビジネスでリードするすべをわきまえています ▪ Woods Still *Ahead of the Game* ウッズ，依然として優勢《新聞の見出し》 ▪ After 5 kilometers I was still *ahead of the game*. 5キロを過ぎても私は依然としてリードを保っていた ▪ Sony hoped to stay *ahead of the game* with PS4. ソニーは PS4 で優位を守ろうと期した ▪ He was $60 *ahead of the game*. 彼は60ドル儲けた．

(*as*) *game as a cockerel* 勇気に富んで ▪ That boxer is *as game as a cockerel*. あのボクサーは非常に勇敢だ．

back in the game また活動的[元気]になって ▪ After about ten minutes, the player was *back in the game*. 約10分後に，選手はまた元気になった．

be a game one [***'un***] 《口》相当勇敢である ▪ He'*s a game 'un*. 彼はなかなか勇敢である．

be all part of the game …はいつものことで驚かない ▪ Making mistakes *is all part of the game*. ミスをするのはいつものことで驚かない．

be fair game **1** 正しい仕事である ▪ It *is fair game* for you to open your store in that road. あなたがその通りに店を開くのは正しい．

2 正当な獲物である; 適当なからかい(など)の的である ▪ A thief *was fair game* for any man to take a shot at. 盗人は誰でもねらい撃ってよい獲物であった ▪ The boy *is fair game* to his friends. その少年は友達のからかいの的だ．

be game for [***to*** *do*] 《口》(勇気・忍耐のいること)を進んでする元気がある，意志がある，よろこんで…する ▪ He *was* quite *game to* do that. 彼は全く進んでそれをする元気があった ▪ *Are* you *game for* a walk on the moor? 荒野を散歩する気がありますか ▪ If anyone needs a team member, I'*m game for* anywhere. チームのメンバーが必要なら，よろこんでどこにでも行きます ▪ As long as I'm home, I'*m game to* baby-sit. 家にいるときなら，喜んでベビーシッターをするよ．

be new to the game (事に)慣れていない，未経験[新参]である ▪ I see you *are new to the game*. 君が新参者であることがわかった．

be off *one's* ***game*** (馬・競技者などが)調子が悪い ▪ I'*m* quite *off my game*. 全く調子が悪い．

be on *one's* ***game*** (馬・競技者などが)調子がよい ▪ Neither man *was on his game*. 二人のどちらも調子がよくなかった．

beat ... at its own game 相手の得意分野で[相手の得意技を使って]相手を打ち破る，逆にやっつける; 相

手のお株を奪う ▪He is trying to *beat* Ferguson *at his own game*, which is a risky business for a newcomer to the league. 彼はファーガスンの土俵で勝とうとしているが，リーグへの新参者には危険な仕事だ ▪He offered a less expensive alternative with which he could *beat* the competition *at their own game*. 彼は相手の土俵で競争でもっと安く勝つ手を示した．

die game 《口》 **1** 死ぬまで勇敢に戦う ▪He did not run away, but *died game*. 彼は逃走しないで，最後まで勇敢に戦った．
2 最後まで元気と忍耐を持ち続ける ▪I shall *die game*. 私は最後まで勇気と忍耐を失いません． ☞闘鶏から; ↔die DUNGHILL.

G

fly at high game →FLY³.

game and game 一対一《テニスなどで》 ▪We were *game and game*, too. 我々も一対一だった．

game and set 《テニス》ゲームセット，勝負あり ▪*Game and set* to Djokovic. ゲームセット，ジョコビッチの勝ちだ．

game on 《口》 **1** 試合開始の[で] ▪*Game on* for the London Olympics ロンドンオリンピック開幕 ▪OK, guys, it's *game on*. Let's give it our best shot! さあ，みんな，試合開始だ．しっかりやろうぜ! ▪It's *game on* at the University's hi-tech center. 大学ハイテク・センターのこけら落としだ．
2 うまくいきそうで，有望で ▪I thought it would be *game-on* for him, really thought he would thrive. 彼はうまくいくだろうと思った，成功するだろうと本当に思った．

game over 試合終了の[で]; 万事休す，もうだめだ (→The GAME is up.) ▪It is *game over* or game on for the Prime Minister. それは首相にとって試合終了か試合開始かのいずれかだ．

game, set and match 試合終了，勝負あった; 圧勝，完全な勝利 (*to, for*) ▪It was *game, set and match to* Karlovic. カルロビッチの圧勝だった．

give the game away 《口》意図[計画など]を(うっかり，またはわざと)暴露する ▪The enemy opened fire and *gave the game away*. 敵は砲撃を始めてその意図を暴露した．

have a game with ...をばかにする; をだます; にばかを見させる ▪You are *having a game with* me. あなたは私をだまそうとしている．

have the game in *one's* ***hands*** 勝利[成功]は確実である ▪I *have the game in my hands*. 私の成功は確実である．

have the game out 最後まで試合をする ▪Tom and Jack *had the game out*. トムとジャックはその勝負をとことんまでやった．

I'm game. 《口》→be GAME for.

improve [***raise***] *one's* ***game*** (ゲームの)腕を磨く ▪Boyd vowed to *improve his game*. ボイドはゲームの腕を磨くことを誓った．

in game 冗談に ▪He spoke *in game*. 彼は冗談に話した．

like a game of dominoes (ドミノゲームのように)連鎖反応して ▪The roof first collapsed in the middle. It then spread to all sides, *like a game of dominoes*. 最初に屋根が真ん中から落ちてきた．その後，四方八方に広がった，まるで将棋倒しのようだった ▪The free-agent market is *like a game of dominoes*. When one piece falls, it leads to more movement. 自由契約市場はドミノゲームのようだ．一つが倒れると，さらなる動きにつながる．

Lookers-on see most of the game. →The outsider sees the best of the GAME.

lose a game (***to***) (...と)勝負をして負ける ▪He *lost a game to* me. 彼は私に負けた．

make game of ...をからかう，嘲弄(ちょうろう)する ▪Don't *make game of* me any longer. もうこれ以上私をからかわないでくれ．

new to the game 初心者で，未経験で ▪About one of every four participants was *new to the game* of golf. およそ4人に1人の参加者はゴルフの初心者だった．

None of your (***little***) ***games.*** その手はよせ．

off *one's* ***game*** 調子が悪くて，いつもの出来ではなくて ▪Dodge was *off his game* in the first quarter. ドッジは第1クォーターでは調子が出なかった ▪We were *off our game* today and didn't manage to score a single goal. 我々は今日いつもの調子が出ず，ほんの1ゴールも得点できなかった．

on the game **1** 《盗賊俗》押し入りをして，盗みをして ▪He pressed me to go out *on the game*. 彼は私に盗みをしに出るよう迫った．
2 《俗》(街で)売春をして ▪She goes [is] *on the game*. 彼女は街で売春をしている．

out of the game 試合に欠場して，出場機会がなくて ▪Wesley is *out of the game* because of a pulled hamstring suffered last Sunday against San Diego. ウェズリーは先の日曜日のサンディエゴ戦で足がつったため試合に欠場している．

play a good [***poor,*** etc.] ***game*** 勝負がうまい[まずい，など] ▪I *play a wretched game* at cards. 私はトランプの勝負がひどくまずい．

play a losing game 不利と知りつつがんばる ▪He seems to fight best when he is *playing a losing game*. 彼は不利と知りつつがんばっているときに最も善戦するように思われる ▪I was *playing a losing game* all the evening. 私は一晩中ずっと勝つ見込みのない勝負をしていた．

play a waiting game 時機を待つ策をとる，持久策をとる ▪He knew how to *play a waiting game*. 彼は潮待ちをする方法を心得ていた．

play a winning game 勝つ見込みのある勝負をする，勝ちいくさをする ▪John *played a winning game* all the time. ジョンはずっと勝ちいくさをした．

play *a person* ***at*** *his* ***own game*** 同じやり方[方法，手段]でやり返す ▪The men are now behind bars after the women *played* them *at their own game* and conned the cons. 女性たちが同じ手口で仕返しして犯罪者たちをだましたので，その男たちはいま刑務所にいる．

play** a person's **game **1** (無意識に)他人の利益になるようなことをする ▪ They are *playing the Papists' game*. 彼らは無意識にカトリック教徒の利益になるようなことをしている.
2 (自分の目的を達するため)ことさらに他人と同じやり方をする ▪ If *playing their* dirty *game* is the only way of winning an election, I'd rather lose. 彼らと同じ汚いやり方をするしか選挙に勝つ方法がないのなら, 私はむしろ負けたほうがよい.

play** one's **own game 自分の利を図る ▪ He is out to *play his own game*. 彼は自分の利を図りにかかっている.

play* (*silly*) *games with ...をいいかげんに扱う, もてあそぶ; をじらす, 思わせぶりをする ▪ The government is *playing games with* the taxpayers' money. 政府は納税者の金をいいかげんに扱っている ▪ Just be honest and don't *play games with* me! 正直にしゃべりなさい. 私をじらさないでくれ.

play the game 《口》正々堂々の試合をする; 公明正大な行動をする; 立派に役割を果たす ▪ You broke your promise. It's not *playing the game*. 君は約束を破った. 公明正大な行動ではない.

play the same game ＝play a person's GAME 2.

Sod* [*Blow, Bugger, Stuff*] *this* [*that*] *for a game of soldiers! 《英俗》もううんざりだ (＝blow that for a LARK) ▪ I've waited for Ann over one hour. *Sod this for a game of soldiers!* 1時間以上もアンを待った. もううんざりだ.

spoil** a person's (**little**) **game 人の意図をくじく, 人の計画を台なしにする ▪ He meant to get into favor with them, but we *spoiled his little game*. 彼は彼らに取り入る気だったが我々は彼の意図をくじいた.

spoil the game しくじる, せっかくの骨折りをむだにする ▪ I *spoiled the game*. 私はしくじった.

talk a good game 《米口》(口先では)立派なことを言う, 物知りふう[誠実そう]に話す ▪ Many can *talk a good game* about diversity, but few can resist gravitating toward their own ethnic group or social class. 多様性について立派なことを述べるものは多いが, 自分の民族的グループや社会的クラスに引かれていくのに逆らうことのできるものは少ない.

(that's a) game that* [*at which*] *two can play →two can play at that GAME.

That's** a person's **little game! それが...の手[計略, 魂胆]だな! (→your (little) GAME) ▪ So *that's your little game!* なるほど, それが君の手だな.

(the) end game 終盤, 大詰め, 最終段階 ▪ The US is now in *the end game* in Iraq. 米国はいまやイラクでの最終段階にある ▪ They are preparing for *the end game*. 彼らは終結の準備をしている. ☞チェスでほとんど勝負がついた段階のこと. 他のゲーム等への転用は20世紀半ばから.

The game is not worth the candle. →(be) not worth the CANDLE.

***The game is up* [*over*].** 《英口》もうだめだ《敗北を認める句》; 万事休す《主に悪事などの失敗について》(→GAME over) ▪ *The game is up* with us. 我々はもうだめだ.

The game is yours. 勝ちは君のものだ.

The game's afoot. 獲物はもう飛び出した; 事業は始まった.

the only game in town 《口》独占状態のもの, その種の唯一のもの, 鳥なき里のコウモリ, 頼みの綱 ▪ Once upon a time, the Rio was *the only game in town* if you wanted an MP3 player. かつてはMP3プレーヤーがほしければ, リオしかなかった ▪ In 1994, Yahoo was *the only game in town*. 1994年にはヤフーがその種の唯一のものだった.

The outsider sees the best* [*Lookers-on see most*] *of the game. 《諺》岡目八目.

throw a game わざと試合に負ける, 八百長で負ける ▪ I know Wilbur. He could never *throw a game*. ウィルバーはよく知っている. 彼には八百長なんてできまい.

throw up the game 降参する, 閉口する ▪ He has *thrown up the game*. 彼は降参した.

two can play at that game*/(*that's a*) *game that* [*at which*] *two can play 《口》その手でくればこちらにも手がある; その手はこちらも使える; そっちがその気なら, こっちもやるぞ《脅し文句》 ▪ If you tell tales, *two can play at that game*. 君が告げ口をするなら, こちらにも手があるよ ▪ Politics is *a game at which two can play*. 政治は両陣営が応酬するものだ ▪ Daisy told the teacher what I did, but *that's a game that two can play*. デイジーは僕のしたことを先生に告げ口した, でもそっちがその気なら, こっちもやるぞ.

What a game! 何ということだろう, 何とうるさいことだろう; 何とおもしろい試合だろう ▪ We've got to write all this. *What a game!* これをみな書かねばならない. 何とうるさいんだろう! ▪ *What a game!* It's going to be a matter of endurance. 何とおもしろい試合だろう! 持久力の問題になりそうだ.

What is** a person's (**little**) **game? 《口》...は何をしよう[たくらもう]としているのか, どんなペテンをしようとしているのか (→your (little) GAME) ▪ Tell me *what your little game is*. 君が何をしようとしているのか教えてくれ.

your* [a person's] (*little*) *game 《口》たくらみ, 魂胆(こんたん) (→What is a person's (little) GAME?) ▪ So [Oh] that's *your little game*, is it? ああ, そういう魂胆なのだな.

gammon /gǽmən/ 名 ***gammon and patter*** 《俗》同業者だけに通じる職業語 ▪ The *gammon and patter* of sailors can be hard for others to understand. 水夫同士が使うスラングは門外漢には分かりづらいことがある.

give** a person **gammon 《盗賊俗》相棒に盗ませている間(当人の肩を押したりそば近くにいたりして)その人の注意を引きつけておく ▪ He *gave* me *gammon*. 彼は相棒に私のポケットをすらせている間私のそばに来て私の注意を引きつけていた.

keep** a person **in gammon 《盗賊俗》相棒に盗ませている間当人に話しかけてその人の注意を引きつけてお

G

く ▪ He *kept* her *in gammon* in the backroom, while I brought off the till. 彼は裏の部屋で話をして彼女を引き止め, その間に私は現金箱を持ち去った.

gamut /gǽmət/ 名 ***run the (whole) gamut of*** ...の全域にわたる (→the whole GAMUT (of)) ▪ He *ran the whole gamut of* dissipation. 彼は放蕩の限りを尽くした ▪ He *ran the gamut of* Russian-American relations. 彼は米露関係を全体にわたって論じた.

run up and down the gamut その範囲を上下する ▪ The stocks were *running up and down the gamut* from $10 to $100 a share. その株式は1株10ドルから100ドルの間を上下していた.

the whole gamut (of) (...の)全般, 全域 ▪ He went *the whole gamut of* his tricks. 彼はありったけの妙技を演じ尽くした.

gander /gǽndər/ 名 ***take [cop, have] a gander (at)*** 《米俗》(...を)ひと目見る ▪ I wanted to *take a gander at* the offspring. 私はその結果をちょっと見ようと思った.

What is sauce for the goose is sauce for the gander. →SAUCE.

gang[1] /gæŋ/ 名 ***be of a gang*** 同類である, 同じグループに属する, 同じ利害関係を持つ ▪ They *are* all *of a gang*. 彼らはみな同じグループである.

gang[2] /gæŋ/ 動 ***gang together*** 手を組む, 団結[同盟]する ▪ Surprised MPs on both sides *ganged together* to chase the rodent away. 両陣営の議員たちは驚き一丸となってネズミを追い払った.

gangbuster /gǽŋbʌ̀stər/ 名 ***come on like gangbusters*** 《米口》精力的に取り組む (→like GANGBUSTERs) ▪ We *come on like gangbusters* for capital punishment. 我々は死刑問題に精力的に取り組んでいる.

go [do] gangbusters 《米口》大当たりする ▪ What may *go gangbusters* in one store may not *go gangbusters* in another. ある店で大ヒットするかもしれない商品が別の店ではヒットしないかもしれない.

like gangbusters 勢いよく, 爆発的に, 華々しく ▪ His new novel has been selling *like gangbusters*. 彼の新作の小説は飛ぶように売れている. ☞Gangbusters＝暴力団を取り締まる警官を描くアメリカのラジオ番組.

gang(-)way /gǽŋwèɪ/ 名 ***above [below] the gangway*** 《英下院》幹部[平]議員席に ▪ He is a member *above the gangway*. 彼は下院の幹部議員である ▪ He sits *below the gangway*. 彼は下院の平議院席についている. ☞gangway「大臣・要人席と平議員席との間の通路」.

clear the gangway 道をあける ▪ *Clear the gangway* there. そこ, 道をあけてくれ.

gantlet /gɔ́:ntlət/ 名 ＝GAUNTLET.

gaol /dʒeɪl/ 名 《英》＝JAIL.

gap /gæp/ 名 ***bridge the gap*** (...の)間隙(かんげき)をふさぐ (*between*) ▪ It's our duty to *bridge the gap between* rich and poor in an interconnected world. 互いにつながった世界における貧富の隙間をふさぐのは我々の義務である.

fill (in, up) [stop, supply] a [the] gap 欠陥を補う, 不足を満たす, 空所を満たす, 間に合わせをする ▪ I heard you were one player short, so I've come to *stop the gap*. 選手が一人不足だと聞きましたので, 私がその不足を補いに来ました ▪ The work *fills in a gap* which hitherto existed in our archaeological literature. その著作はわが国の考古学文献に今日まで存在していた欠陥を補うものである.

leave [make] a gap 間隙(すき)を生じる ▪ His going *leaves a* sad *gap* in our circle. 彼が去るので我々仲間は非常に寂しくなる ▪ His death *makes a gap* in Scottish writers. 彼の死はスコットランド文壇の大損失である.

plug the gap (必要な物を)補う, 補てんする ▪ Online learning could *plug the gap*. オンラインで学習すれば, (必要な知識が)補てんできるでしょう.

stop [supply] a gap →fill (in, up) a GAP.

the gap in the market 市場参入の好機(となる分野・製品) ▪ The company was set up to fill *the gap in the market*. この会社は市場参入を果たすために設立された.

gape /geɪp/ 名 ***give** a person **the gapes*** 人にあくびをさせる ▪ The music *gave* us *the gapes*. その音楽で我々はあくびが出た.

have [get] the gapes (ニワトリなどが)張嘴(ちょうし)病にかかる; 《戯》しきりにあくびをする ▪ As the lecture dragged on, he *got the gapes*. 講演が長びくにつれて, 彼はしきりにあくびをした.

gapeseed /géɪpsì:d/ 名 ***buy [seek, sow] gapeseed*** 《皮肉》(市場などで売買をしないで)ただぽかんとして見る ▪ Plenty of persons were *sowing gapeseed* at them. 多数の人がそれらをただぽかんとして見ていた.

garb[1] /gɑ:rb/ 名 ***in the garb (of)*** (職業・時代・国柄に特有の)服を着て ▪ He was *in the garb of* a sailor. 彼は水夫服を着ていた ▪ The book has appeared *in English garb*. その本は英訳で出た.

under the garb of ...に扮して, の衣のかげに ▪ She hid her grief *under the garb of* a nun. 彼女は尼僧の衣に悲しみを隠した.

garb[2] /gɑ:rb/ 動 ***garb** oneself **as*** ...の服を着る ▪ He *garbed himself as* a sailor. 彼は水夫の服を着た.

garb** oneself **[be garbed] in (...の服)を着る[着ている], を装う[装っている] ▪ She *is garbed in* a foreign dress. 彼女は洋装している.

garbage /gɑ́:rbɪdʒ/ 名 ***Garbage in, garbage out.*** **1** 入力がゴミなら, 出力もゴミ《省略形GIGO》 ▪ If you don't input correct data you won't get correct results: *garbage in, garbage out*. 正しいデータを入力しないと正しい結果が得られない. ゴミを入れたらゴミが出る.

2 素材がお粗末なら製品もお粗末 ▪ These meals are very poor—*garbage in, garbage out*. これらの食事はとてもまずい. 食材がお粗末なら料理もお粗末だ.

garble /gɑ́:rbəl/ 動 ***garble the coinage*** (良

貨を輸出または鋳つぶすために)貨幣をえり分ける.

garbroth /gáːrbrɔ̀ːθ|-brɔ̀θ/ 名 **(as) mean as a garbroth** 《米口》きわめて卑しい ▪ One of them was *as mean as a garbroth*. 彼らの一人はきわめて下劣な人間であった.

garden /gáːrdən/ 名 ***common or garden*** → COMMON.

cultivate *one's* ***garden*** 静かに自分の事をする (Voltaire, *Candide* 30) ▪ Still he serenely *cultivates his garden*. 依然として彼は静かに庭を耕す《自分の事をする》.

Everything in the garden's lovely [《英》***rosy***]. 《皮肉》不平を言うことは何もない ▪ *Everything in the garden's lovely*; we've plenty of debts and no assets. 愚痴をこぼすことは何もありません, 借金は多いし財産は少しもないしね.

lead *a person* ***up*** [《米》***down***] ***the garden path*** 《口》だます, 迷わす, 誘惑する ▪ Everyone has *been led up the garden path* by a misconception. すべての人が誤解のために迷わされてきた. ☞庭道はとても楽しいものなので, 知らぬ間にだまされるという考えから.

gargle /gáːrgəl/ 名 ***have a gargle*** 《口》1杯やる ▪ Let's go and *have a gargle* at the Mike's. さあマイクの店へ行って1杯やろう.

garland /gáːrlənd/ 名 ***carry*** (***away***) [***gain, get, go away with, win***] ***the garland*** (競技に)優勝する; 勝利を得る ▪ He *carried away the garland*. 彼は優勝した ▪ His left wing was *gaining garlands* at the moment. 彼の左翼はその時勝利を得つつあった.

garret /gǽrət/ 名 ***be wrong in*** *one's* ***garret*** 《俗》頭が弱い; 頭が変だ ▪ Tom *is wrong in his garret*. トムは頭が弱い. ☞garret＝head.

from cellar to garret/ from garret to kitchen 家じゅう全体に ▪ The news of his arrival circulated *from cellar to garret*. 彼が到着したというニュースは家じゅうに伝わった. ☞garret＝attic (屋根裏部屋).

One's ***garret is empty*** [***unfurnished***]. 《俗》頭がからっぽである, 頭が弱い, 愚かである.

have rats in the garret ＝have rats in the ATTIC.

garrison /gǽrəsən/ 名 ***be sent into garrison*** 守備に派遣される ▪ They *were sent into garrison* on the frontiers. 彼らは国境地方へ守備に派遣された.

go into garrison 守備につく ▪ The rest are to *go into garrison* at Mantua. 他の者はマンチュアで守備につくことになっている.

in garrison 守備について ▪ Those *in garrison* at Goletta gave up that fortress. ゴレタで守備についていた人々はその要塞を放棄した.

keep garrison 守備についている ▪ The soldiers *kept garrison*. 兵士たちは守備についていた.

garter /gáːrtər/ 名 ***cast*** *one's* ***garter*** 《米》夫を得る ▪ You might have *cast your garter*. あなたは夫が得られたかもしれないのだが.

fly the garter 石飛び遊びをする ▪ They saw his boy *flying the garter* in the horseroad. 彼らは彼の息子が馬道で石飛び遊びをやっているのを見た.

in the catching up of a garter たちまち ▪ I'll do your business *in the catching up of a garter*. あなたのご用をすぐにやります.

pricking in [***prick***] ***the garter*** (棒とひもでする)一種の詐欺的遊戯《fast and loose とも言う》 ▪ Here is *pricking in the garter*. ここに詐欺的行為が行われている. ☞見物人は棒をひもでしっかりくくったと思っているのに当人はすぐにほどいて見せる遊戯.

gas /gæs/ 名 ***All is gas and gaiters.*** 《諺》万事結構である[理想的な状態である]. ☞Dickens の *Nicholas Nickleby* 中の狂老人の言葉から.

give her the gas 《米俗》自動車の速力を出す ▪ Ralph *gave her the gas*. ラルフは自動車の速力を出した.

have gas 《米俗》腹が張る ▪ Do you *have gas*? 腹が張りますか.

lie like a gas-meter →LIE[3].

out of gas →run out of GAS.

pass gas 《婉曲》放屁する, おならをする ▪ A man *passed gas* and fanned it toward a patrolman. ある男が放屁して, パトロール警官の方へとあおいだ.

run out of gas 《主に米》ガス欠になる[である], 失速する; 意欲がなくなる《続ける精力[興味]を失う》 ▪ The American economy, which seemed to have *run out of gas* 25 years ago, is now doing so well. アメリカ経済は, 25年前に失速したようだったが, 現在はすこぶる順調だ ▪ After the game, a lot of guys mentally *ran out of gas*. 試合後, 多くの者は精神的にガス欠になった ▪ The Celtics battled hard, but in the end they simply *ran out of gas*. セルティックスが激しく戦ったが, 遂に全く精力が無くなってしまった.

step [***tramp, tread***] ***on the gas*** 《主に米口》 **1** 自動車のアクセルを踏んで速度を増す ▪ She *tramped on the gas*. 彼女はアクセルを踏んで速力を出した.

2 急ぐ, 素早くする ▪ He may *tread on the gas* with the best of them. 彼は誰にも劣らず素早くすることができる.

take the gas out of *a person* 人の高慢[うぬぼれ]をくじく, やりこめる ▪ I will *take the gas out of* him. 彼をやりこめてやろう.

talk gas 《俗》むだ話をする, だぼらを吹く ▪ He deceived me by *talking gas*. 彼はほら話で私をだました.

turn on the gas (せんをひねって)ガスを出す; 《俗》気焔をあげ始める ▪ It's cold in here; *turn on the gas* and light the fire. この中は寒いな. ガスをひねって火をつけてくれ ▪ After a few drinks he really *turns on the gas*. 2, 3杯ひっかけたら彼は怪気炎を上げ始めた.

turn out [***off***] ***the gas*** (せんをひねって)ガスを止める; 《俗》ほら吹きをやめる ▪ We didn't *turn off the gas* to Europe. 我々はヨーロッパへのガスを止めなかっ

G

た.

gash /ɡæʃ/ 名 ***cut a gash*** 《米口》偉そうにかまえる, 偉そうに見える ▪ They might be up at Headquarters *cutting a gash.* 彼らは本部にいて偉そうにかまえているかもしれない.

set up** one's **gash 《米》生意気な話し方[返答]をする ▪ The wife *set up her gash.* 妻は生意気な返事をした.

gasket /ɡǽskət/ 名 ***blow a gasket*** 《口》かんかんに怒る ▪ The father *blew a gasket* when he saw his son's poor report card. 父親は息子のお粗末な成績表を見てかんかんに怒った.

gasp[1] /ɡæsp|ɡɑːsp/ 名 ***at the*** [*one's*] ***last gasp*** 死にかかって, 死ぬ間際に; 最後の瞬間に ▪ He left her *at the last gasp.* 彼は瀕死の彼女の許を去った ▪ I'm almost *at my last gasp.* 私はほとんど死にかかっている.

breathe** one's **last gasp この世で最後の息を引き取る ▪ The authority of the Augusti *breathed its last gasp* in Rome. アウグストゥス家の権威はローマで息を引き取った.

to [***till, until***] ***the last gasp*** 最後まで, 息を引き取るまで ▪ There may be enjoyments *to the last gasp.* 息を引き取るまで楽しみはあるかもしれない ▪ The Taliban will resist *till the last gasp* of their breath. タリバンは息絶えるまで抵抗するだろう.

gasp[2] /ɡæsp|ɡɑːsp/ 動 ***gasp** one's **last*** 最後の息を引き取る ▪ They seem to be ready to *gasp their last.* 彼らは今にも息を引き取りそうに見える.

make** a person **gasp 人を息が止まるほどびっくりさせる ▪ It *made* him *gasp.* そのため彼はびっくり仰天した.

gate /ɡeɪt/ 名 ***at the gate(s)*** すぐ近くに, 間近に ▪ The criminal confessed *at the gates* of death. 犯人は死の間際にすべてを自白した.

break gates 門限に帰らない; 門限後に帰る ▪ If you *break gates* again, we shall have you rusticated. 君がまた門限に帰らないことがあれば, 一時的に放校されるだろう. ☞もと Oxford, Cambridge 大学の用語.

break [***bust, crash***] ***the gate*** 《俗》招かれないのに行く; 料金を払わずに入る; うまく入り込む ▪ Someone *broke the gate* to a community clubhouse pool. 誰かが地域クラブハウスのプールに侵入した ▪ The boys *crashed the gates.* 少年たちは料金を払わずに入った ▪ He *crashed* all *the gates* of Boston. 彼はボストン全市にうまく食い込んだ.

come [***gang, go, ride***] ***a*** [***the,*** *one's*] ***gate*** 《米》ある[その, 自分の]道を来る[行く, 乗って行く] ▪ He *went his gate.* 彼は自分の道を行った. ☞gate＝way.

from [***at***] ***the gate*** 《英》魚市場から[で] ▪ fish sold *at the gate* (ビリングズゲイトの)魚市場で売られる魚. ☞gate＝Billingsgate (地名).

get the gate →GET.

give** a person **the gate 《米俗》人を解雇する, 追い出す; 男の求婚を断る ▪ He *gave* Tom *the gate.* 彼はトムを首にした ▪ She *gave* George *the gate.* 彼女はジョージをそでにした. ☞gate＝exit (出口).

open a gate for [***to***] …に道を開く, への便宜[機会]を与える ▪ He *opened a gate for* a long war. 彼は長期戦への道を開いた.

ride a [***the,*** *one's*] ***gate*** →come a GATE.

(right) out of the (starting) gate 初め[当初, しょっぱな]から ▪ Everything went wrong *right out of the starting gate.* しょっぱなから何もかもうまくいかなかった.

some [***any***] ***gate*** 《米》どこかで, どこかに ▪ I put it *some gate.* 私はそれをどこかへ置いた.

take (the) gate 《米》道を行く; 去る ▪ He *took the gate* to London. 彼はロンドンへの道を行った ▪ It is now time for us to *take the gate.* もう我々が出て行く時です.

the gate of horn 《ギ神》正夢の出てくる門 ▪ Of all his dreams, it was the only one which came through *the gate of horn.* 彼のすべての夢のうちでそれだけが正夢の出てくる門を通って来た夢であった.

the gate(s) of death 死の入口, 死の切迫 ▪ He has been at *the gates of death.* 彼は死にかけていた.

the Pearly Gates/the pearly gates 《戯》天国への門《真珠でできた, 天国の12の門; 死んだら行くと信じられている》 ▪ When you get to *the pearly gates*, it doesn't matter how many trophies you have in your living room. 天国の門に行くときには居間にいくつトロフィーがあるかなんてどうでもいいことだ ▪ What would you like to hear St. Peter say when you arrive at *the pearly gates*? 天国の門に着いたとき聖ペテロがなんと言われるのを聞きたいですか.

this [***that***] ***gate*** 《米》こちらへ[あちらへ] ▪ Come *this gate.* こちらへおいで.

gatepost /ɡéɪtpòʊst/ 名 ***between you and me and the gatepost*** →BETWEEN you and me.

gather /ɡǽðər/ 動 ***A rolling stone gathers no moss.*** →STONE[1].

gather head →HEAD[1].

gather ... in** one's **arms …を抱きよせる ▪ He quickly *gathered* the cat *in his arms.* 彼はすばやく猫を抱きよせた.

gather strength **1** 勢いを増す, しだいに強くなる ▪ The wind was *gathering strength.* 風はだんだん強くなっていた.

2 (病人などが)元気を回復する, だんだん力がつく ▪ The sick man was slowly *gathering strength.* 病人は徐々に力がついていた.

gather to a head ＝come to a HEAD.

***gather up** oneself* ＝GATHER oneself up 1.

gather** oneself **up [***together***] **1** 勇気を奮い起こす ▪ He *gathered himself up* but in vain. 彼は勇気を奮い起こしたがだめだった.

2 (驚き・ショックの後)落ち着きを取り戻す, 気を取り直す ▪ He *gathered himself together* and said he wanted a drink. 彼は落ち着きを取り戻して, 飲み物が

1杯ほしいと言った.

gather up *one's* **(*scattered*)** ***wits*** (狼狽・驚きの後)心を落ち着ける ▪ *Gather up your wits* a little and hear me. 少し心を落ち着けて私の言うことを聞きなさい.

gather up the threads of →THREAD[1].

gather up *one's* ***thoughts*** [***strength, energies,*** etc.] 心[力, 精力, など]を奮い起こす ▪ He started up, *gathering up his thoughts*. 彼は驚いて立ち上がり, 心を奮い起こした.

gather way →WAY.

gauge, 《米》 **gage** /geɪdʒ/ 名 ***get the weather gage of*** [***on***] 《海》 …の風上に出る; より優位に立つ ▪ I *got the weather gage of* him. 私は彼より優位に立った.

have [***keep***] ***the weather gage of*** **1** 《海》 …の風上にある ▪ The ship *has the weather gage of* the boat. その船はボートの風上にある.

2 …の優位に立つ; に勝つ ▪ He *has got the weather gage of* them. 彼は彼らに勝った.

take the gauge of …を測る, 評価する ▪ I watched him and *took his gauge*. 私は彼をじっと見て人物を判断してみました ▪ The old man was *taking the gauge of* the structure. 老人はその建物を目測していた.

That is about the gauge of it. 《口》 まあそのへんのところだ.

gauntlet[1] /gɔ́ːntlət/ 名 ***cast*** **(*out*)** ***the*** [*one's*] ***gauntlet/fling out*** [***down***] ***the gauntlet/throw*** **(*down*)** ***the gauntlet*** …に(こてを投げて)挑戦する (*at, to*) ▪ I *cast* them *my gauntlet*; take it up who dares. 私は彼らに挑戦する. われと思う者は挑戦に応じよ ▪ You *fling out the gauntlet to* him who calls you coward. あなたはあなたを憶病者と呼ぶ者に挑戦する ▪ Mr. Mann *threw down the gauntlet at* the Prime Minister. マン氏は大統領に挑戦状をたたきつけた. ☞中世の騎士が挑戦するとき gauntlet (籠手(こて))を投げたことから.

pick up [***take up***] ***the gauntlet*** (投げられたこてを拾って)挑戦に応じる, けんかを買う; 弁護に立つ, 弁護を引き受ける ▪ He was not slow in *picking up the gauntlet*. 彼はすかさず挑戦に応じた ▪ Two or three of his friends *took up the gauntlet*. 彼の友人の2, 3人が彼の弁護に立った ▪ Chancellor Merkel decided to *take up the gauntlet* thrown down by the Social Democrats. メルケル首相は社会民主党がふっかけた挑戦に応じることにした.

ga(u)ntlet[2] /gɔ́ːntlət/ 名 ***run the gauntlet*** **1** むち打ちの刑を受ける《昔の水夫に対する罰, 後に学童に対する罰》 ▪ One of the boatswain's mates *ran the gauntlet* for stealing a shirt. 掌帆兵曹の一人はシャツを盗んだためむち打ちの刑を受けた.

2 多数の人の批評[非難, 攻撃]にさらされる (*of*) ▪ They are compelled to *run the gauntlet of* political persecution. 彼らは手厳しく非難されて政治的迫害を受けている ▪ The minister had to *run the gauntlet of* student protesters when he arrived at the university. 大臣は大学に到着したとき, 学生の抗議者たちから非難を浴びなければならなかった.

3 苦しい多くの試練にあう, 数々の危険を冒す ▪ To get back to our lines we had to *run the gauntlet* of all their outposts. 我々の野堡(やほう)に帰るのに我々は彼らのすべての前哨地点のかずかずの危険を冒さねばならなかった. ☞gauntlet「向かい合って2列に並ぶ兵たちの間の通路」; 罪人はこの通路を走り, 兵たちはむちまたは棍棒でこれを乱打しようとする習わしから.

gay /geɪ/ 形 ***get gay*** 《米》 過度になれなれしくする ▪ I wouldn't *get gay* round [with] her. 私は彼女に対して[彼女と]過度になれなれしくしたくない.

lead a gay life **1** 浮いた遊とう的生活をする ▪ She *led a gay life* while beauty lasted. 彼女は美しさの続く間遊とう的生活をした.

2 《俗》 売春で生活する ▪ She *led a gay life* in Paris in the 1890s. 彼女は1890年代にパリで春をひさいで生活した.

with gay abandon **1** 後先のことを考えないで, くつろいで ▪ So now I do everything *with gay abandon*. こういうわけでいま私はなんでも気楽にやっている.

2 不注意に, ずさんに ▪ Fine points such as quotation marks, apostrophes and question marks were treated *with gay abandon*. 引用符やアポストロフィ, 疑問符といったような細かいしるしの扱いはずさんだった. ☞gay「気楽な」.

gaze /geɪz/ 名 ***at gaze*** **1** (人が感嘆・期待・当惑をもって)じっと見つめて ▪ They stood *at gaze*. 彼らはじっと見つめながら立っていた.

2 (紋章中のシカが)正面向きで ▪ The hart in the coat-armor was *at gaze*. その紋章中の雄ジカは正面向きであった.

fix *one's* ***gaze on*** [***upon***] …をじっと見つめる ▪ He *fixed his gaze upon* the horizon. 彼は地平線をじっと見つめた.

set *a person* ***at gaze*** 人にじっと見つめさせる, 人の目を引く ▪ Her richly endowed bosom *set* me *at gaze*. 彼女の豊満な胸から目をそらせられなかった.

stand at gaze **1** →at GAZE 1.

2 (シカが猟犬の声を最初に聞くとき)どうしようかと迷って立つ ▪ The frightened deer *stood at gaze*. びっくりしたシカはどうしようかと当惑して立っていた.

gazette[1] /gəzét/ 名 ***be*** **(*named*)** ***in the gazette*** 破産者として官報に載っている ▪ The firm *was named in the gazette*. その企業が破産者名簿に載っていた.

go into the gazette 破産者として官報に載る ▪ The firm has *gone into the gazette*. その企業は破産者として官報に載っている.

gazette[2] /gəzét/ 動 ***be gazetted out*** **(*of*)** (…からの)辞職が官報に発表される ▪ He *was gazetted out of* the army. 彼の軍職辞任が官報に発表された.

be gazetted to …への任命が官報で発表される, に任命される ▪ He *was gazetted to* the high school. 彼はその高等学校長に任命された.

gear[1] /gɪər/ 名 ***change gears*** →shift GEARs.

get *one's* ***ass*** [***butt***] ***in gear***/《英》 ***get*** *one's*

G

arse in gear 《口》もっとしっかり[早く]やる, 気合いを入れて行う ▪ You're going to have to *get your ass in gear* and work. 君は本腰を入れて働かなければならないことになりそうだ.

get* [*have*] *one's* brain into [*in*] *gear 《口》頭を活性化させる, 明晰に思索する ▪ Merriam-Webster's Word Puzzles are a good way to *get your brain in gear* for a day's work. メリアム・ウェブスター辞典のワードパズルは1日の仕事に向けて頭を活性化させるのによいやり方だ.

get one's gears turning (機械などを)作動させる; 思いをめぐらす ▪ The stories about elk and deer hunting *got my gears turning*. エルクとシカの猟に関する話で私はいろいろ思いをめぐらした.

G

get in* [*into*] *gear/shift into gear (機械の)伝動装置がかかる, 連動しだす; 調子よく動きだす ▪ The machinery has *got into gear*. 機械の伝動装置がかかった ▪ In a week he began to *get into gear* and work better. 1週間して彼は調子がよくなりもっとよく仕事をしだした.

get* [*put, set, throw*]... *into* [*in*] *gear ...の伝動装置をかける, を連動させる ▪ They *got* the machinery *into gear*. 彼らは機械の伝動装置をかけた.

get out of gear 連動装置がはずれる; 調子が狂う ▪ Since his death everything has *got out of gear*. 彼が死んでから万事調子が狂っている.

go* [*move*] *into high gear 最大の活動を始める ▪ The political campaign *moved into high gear*. 政治運動が最高潮に達した.

go out of gear =get out of GEAR.

in gear **1** (機械が)連結して, 連動して; 円滑に運転して ▪ When wheels are *in gear*, there are three teeth of each engaged. 車輪が連動しているときは, 各車輪の3つの歯がかみ合っている.

2 調子がよく ▪ He is *in gear* now. 彼は今は調子がよい.

in high* [*full*] *gear 達者で, 丈夫で ▪ The carmaker's growth remains *in high gear* despite soaring global fuel prices. 世界的な原油高にもかかわらず, その自動車メーカーの成長は依然として着実である.

move* [*step*] *up a gear より高速のギアに入れる; より多くの精力を注ぐ, 強化する ▪ Germany *moved up a gear* to beat Portugal 3-2. ドイツはいっそう気合いを入れてポルトガルを3対2で破った.

(*on*) *top gear* 全速力で ▪ Trout retired, *top gear*, into the distance. マスは全速力で遠方へ退いた.

out of gear **1** (機械の)伝動装置がはずれて, 運転が乱れて; 調子が狂って ▪ All the machinery is *out of gear*. 機械はみな狂っている.

2 調子が狂って; 体の具合が悪く ▪ He is *out of gear* now. 彼は今体の調子が悪い.

3 設備不足で ▪ My ships are *out of gear*. 私の船は設備不足です.

set* [*put, throw*]... *into* [*in*] *gear → get... into GEAR.

shift* [*change, switch*] *gears ギアを換える《高速から低速へ, またその反対に》; 方法[速度, 態度]を変える ▪ He *shifted gears* in the middle of his speech. 彼は演説の途中で速度を変えた.

slip a gear 《俗》誤りをする ▪ He is *slipping a gear* if he's made such a promise. もし彼がそんな約束をしたのなら彼はまちがっている.

throw* [*get, put*]... *out of gear **1** ...の伝動装置をはずす; の運転を妨げる ▪ The driving-belts can be removed at pleasure when the machinery *is thrown out of gear*. 機械の伝動装置がはずれたときは, 主動ベルトは随意に取りはずすことができる.

2 ...の調子を乱す ▪ The whole system *was* completely *thrown out of gear*. そのシステム全体が完全に混乱した.

gear[2] /gɪər/ 動 ***gear level*** 平速連動をかける ▪ For average riders these tricycles should *be geared level*. 普通の乗り手の場合はこれらの三輪車は平速ギアをかけるべきである.

gearing /gíərɪŋ/ 名 ***in gearing*** =in GEAR.

out of gearing =out of GEAR.

geck /gek/ 名 ***get a geck*** 《米》だまされる ▪ You need to *get a geck* to save your village. 君の村を救うためには君はだまされなければならない.

give a person the geck 《米》人をだます; 人をまく ▪ She has *given* me *the geck* today. 彼女はきょう私をだました.

gee /dʒiː/ 間 ***Gee ho!*** 《口》(馬に)右へ回れ!(↔Haw!)

***Gee whiz*(*z*) [*whillikins*]!** 《口》おやまあ!《驚き, 感動の叫び》 ▪ They saw what we were wearing and said "*Gee whizz!*" 彼らは我々の服装を見て,「おやまあ!」と言った.

gem /dʒem/ 名 ***like a rare gem*** 宝石のように[ような]; 極めて貴重で ▪ A good teacher is *like a rare gem*. よい先生は宝石のように貴重だ.

gender /dʒéndər/ 名 ***a gender warrior*** 女性解放戦士[解放論者] ▪ She does not explicitly write or speak as *a gender warrior*. 彼女は女性解放論者の立場で明確に書いたり話したりはしない.

general /dʒénərəl/ 名形 ***as a general rule* [*thing*]** 一般に, 通例, 概して ▪ *As a general rule* prices follow demand. 一般に価格は需要に従うものである.

general post 欠員による大異動 ▪ There will be *general post* among the other members of the Cabinet. 他の閣僚の間に欠員による大異動があるだろう.

in a general way **1** 通常, 一般に, 概して, ざっと ▪ *In a general way*, he gets to the office at nine. 通例彼は9時に事務所に着く.

2 普通のやり方で ▪ He has studied *in a general way*. 彼は普通のやり方で勉強した.

in general **1** 〚副詞的に〛概して, 大体, 通常 ▪ *In general* he is a satisfactory student. 概して彼は申し分のない学生である.

2 一般の (↔in PARTICULAR) ▪ I am speaking of

students *in general*. 私は一般の学生のことを言っているのである.

in the general **1**《古》=in GENERAL 1. **2** 概説的に, 概括的に; ばく然と ▪ It is easy to speak of human nature *in the general*. ばく然と人間性を語るのは易しい.

generality /dʒènərǽləti/ 名 ***of great generality*** 普遍性の大きい ▪ "Proceeds" is a word *of great generality*. 「収益」は一般性の高い語だ ▪ To paraphrase Austen, it is a rule *of great generality* that a rich bachelor must be in want of a wife. オースティンの言葉を言い換えるなら, 金持ちの独身男性が妻を是非にと望むのはほぼ例外のない慣わしである.

the generality of …の大部分 ▪ *The generality of* his hearers were favorable to his doctrine. 聴衆は概して彼の説に賛成だった.

generally /dʒénərəli/ 副 ***generally speaking*** 概して(言えば) ▪ *Generally speaking*, girls are better linguists than boys. 概して言えば, 女子のほうが男子よりも語学はうまい.

generation /dʒènəréɪʃən/ 名 ***a lost generation*** 失われた世代《20世紀初期の米作家》; 落ちこぼれの世代《学校を退学し教養がないため職を得られない若者たち》 ▪ "We are *a lost generation*. Many of the students cannot even read," said Jimmy. 「おれたちは落ちこぼれ世代だ. 学生の多くは読むことさえできないんだ」とジミーは言った.

be wiser in** one's **generation 世故にたけている (《聖》*Luke* 16. 8) ▪ He *was wiser in his generation* than his editors. 彼は編集者たちより世故にたけていた.

from generation to generation 代々(引き続いて) ▪ The heirlooms were handed down *from generation to generation*. 家宝は代々伝わった.

generation after generation 世々, 代々 ▪ It was repeated *generation after generation* of pupils. それは代々の学童によって繰り返された.

in the 10th** [etc.] **generation 10[など]代目の ▪ His ancestors *in the 10th generation* were feudal barons. 10代前の彼の祖先は封建時代の男爵だった.

the rising [coming, young] generation (ある特定の時代の)青年(層) ▪ There is danger in *the rising generation* knowing little or nothing about the great war. 青年層が世界大戦のことをほとんど知らないという危険がある.

through successive generations 代々 ▪ It has come down *through successive generations*. それは代々伝わってきた.

generous /dʒénərəs/ 形 ***generous about [in]*** …に気前がよく ▪ Mr. Ballard is *generous about* helping students. バラード先生は気前よく生徒を助ける.

generous with** one's **money 金離れがよく ▪ He is very *generous with his money*. 彼は金離れが非常によい.

genie /dʒíːni/ 名 ***let the genie out of the bottle*** 《主に米》魔神を瓶から出してしまった《状況を決定的に変える; 通例, まずい[悪い]物を出してしまったという望ましくない変化について用いる》 ▪ By starting to release digital music, the music industry *let the genie out of the bottle*. デジタル音楽を発表することで音楽業界は状況を一変させてしまった ▪ With the Internet, we really *let the genie out of the bottle*. インターネットとともに, 魔神を瓶から出してしまった. ☞genie「魔神」; 閉じこめられていた瓶から解放してくれた人の願いごとをかなえてくれるという, アラビア夜話に出る精霊.

put the genie back in the bottle 《主に米》魔神を瓶の中に戻す《(決定的に変わってしまった)状況を元に戻す》 ▪ Taboos have been broken, and you can't *put the genie back in the bottle*. タブーは破られてしまった. 状況を元には戻せない ▪ We can't *put the* Internet *genie back in the bottle*. インターネットという魔神を瓶に戻すことはできない《インターネットで変わってしまった状況を元に戻すことはできない》.

The genie is out of the bottle. 《主に米》魔神が瓶から出てしまった《状況は決定的に変わった》; ことはばれてしまった ▪ Terrorism is rampant; *the genie is out of the bottle*. テロリズムが猛威をふるっている. 状況は激変してしまった ▪ The UK inflation *genie is out of the bottle*. 英国のインフレーションがばれてしまった.

genius /dʒíːniəs/ 名 ***a budding genius*** 未来の天才, 天才児 ▪ Tim is 8 and *a budding genius* at the piano. ティムは8才だが, ピアノの天才児だ.

be a genius in …の天才である ▪ He *is a genius in* mathematics. 彼は数学の天才である.

Genius is an infinite capacity for taking pains. 《諺》天才とは努力する無限の能力である. ☞Carlyle, *Frederick the Great* (1858).

Genius is ten percent inspiration and ninety percent perspiration. 《諺》天才とは10パーセントの霊感と90パーセントの発汗である. ☞Thomas Edison の言葉.

have a genius for …の天才がある ▪ He *has a genius for* finance [making friends]. 彼は生まれつき財政の[友を作る]才がある.

genteel /dʒentíːl/ 形 ***do the genteel*** 上品ぶる, 気取る ▪ His wife likes to *do the genteel*. 彼の細君は上品ぶるのが好きだ.

in genteel poverty 貧乏ながら上流風に ▪ He lives *in genteel poverty*. 彼は貧乏ながら上品に暮らしている.

gentle /dʒéntəl/ 形名 ***(as) gentle as a lamb*** とてもおとなしい ▪ He is a big man, but *as gentle as a lamb*. 彼は大男だがとても温和だ.

of gentle blood [birth] (貴族ではないが)生まれのよい ▪ He is *of gentle blood*. 彼は生まれがよい.

gentleman /dʒéntəlmən/ 名 ***a gentleman in brown*** 《戯》ナンキンムシ ▪ Bed bugs are known in modern polite English as "*gentlemen in brown*". ナンキンムシは現代の上品な英語では「茶

色服の紳士」として知られている.

a gentleman of the short staff 《戯》警察官, おまわりさん ▪ In the language of the *gentlemen of the short staff*, he is a "boogie", i.e. a black person. おまわりさんの言葉で言えば, 彼は「boogie」つまり黒人だ.

a gentleman's agreement →AGREEMENT.

be a gentleman 《戯》何もすることがない ▪ Now I *am* completely *a gentleman*. 今私は全く何もすることがない.

Ladies and gentlemen! →LADY[1].

my gentleman 《軽蔑・戯》例の男, ご当人.

play the gentleman 紳士ぶる ▪ Eric *played the gentleman*, helping an embarrassed Mia untie the scarf. エリックは紳士を演じて, おろおろしているミーアがスカーフをはずすのを手伝った.

quite a gentleman 全くの紳士 ▪ He is *quite a gentleman*. 彼は全くの紳士だ.

the gentleman from 《米・議会》…州選出の議員 ▪ The question was raised by *the gentleman from* Arkansas. その問題はアーカンソー州選出の議員によって提起された.

the (old) gentleman in black 《口》悪魔 ▪ *The old gentleman in black* shall take me if I do. 私がそれをしたら自分を悪魔に捕まえさせよう(私は絶対にそんなことはしない).

gently /dʒéntli/ 副 ***Gently does it.*** 静かにするのが肝心. ☞gently (＝gentle way of doing) が主語.

gentry /dʒéntri/ 名 ***the light-fingered gentry*** 《俗・戯》すりども ▪ Football crowds are a golden opportunity for *the light-fingered gentry*. フットボールの観衆はすりたちにとっては無上の好機だ.

George /dʒɔːrdʒ/ 名 ***By George!*** 本当に, 全く《穏やかな誓言または感嘆の句》 ▪ *By George*, I will make an example of him. 本当にあいつを見せしめにしてやろう.

Let George do it. 《米俗》誰か(自分より)他の者にその仕事をやらせよ ▪ Producers have a way of saying "*Let George do it*" whenever a particularly difficult villain role turns up. 映画製作者は特にむずかしい悪漢役が出てくると「誰か他の者にやらせろ」と言う癖がある. ☞F laissez faire à Georges ('let George do it') のなぞり. Georges d'Amboise はルイ12世に仕えた枢機卿(けい).

germ /dʒəːrm/ 名 ***in germ*** 芽ばえのうちで[に], まだ発達しないで[しない時期に] ▪ The idea exists *in germ* in the University. その思想は大学の中に芽生えの状態で存在する.

germane /dʒərméɪn/ 形 ***germane to*** **1** …に密接に関係して ▪ Those studies are immediately *germane to* medicine. それらの研究は直接に医術に密接な関係がある.

2 …に適合して; が適切で ▪ The illustration was hardly *germane to* the case. その例証はその場合にほとんど当てはまらなかった ▪ The document is not *germane to* be reproduced in this place. その文書はここで複写するのは適当でない.

gesture /dʒéstʃər/ 名 ***as a gesture of*** 《米》…の印に ▪ My uncle gave this to me *as a gesture of* encouragement. おじは激励の印にこれを私にくれた.

by gesture 身ぶりで ▪ I spoke to a foreigner *by gesture*. 私は外国人に身ぶりで話しかけた.

get /get/ 動 ***as ... as*** *one* ***can get (it)*** 得られるかぎりたくさんの… ▪ You really need the sun *as* much *as* you *can get it*. あなたは本当にできるだけたくさん日光を浴びる必要があります ▪ I am reading *as* many books *as* I *can get*. 私は得られるかぎりたくさんの本を読んでいます.

be as good as it gets →as GOOD as it gets.

be getting there 《口》成功への途上で, 目的成就中で; もう一息で ▪ There's still room for improvement but we*'re getting there*. まだ改善の余地はあるが, 我々は成果を上げつつある.

Can I get by, please? すみません, 通してください.

Don't get cute [smart] with me. ばか言うんじゃないよ, からかわないでくれ.

Don't get me wrong. → get a person WRONG.

get *one's* **1** 《米俗》当然の報いを受ける ▪ He will *get his* when his father finds that out. 父親がそれを知ったら, 彼は当然の罰を受けるだろう.

2 《陸軍》傷を受ける《特に致命傷》 ▪ He *got his* at the western front. 彼は西部戦線で負傷した.

get a [*one's*] ***fix*** →FIX[1].

get [have] a fix [handle] on **1** 《口》(レーダーなどで)遠方の物を見つける ▪ I can *get a fix on* the submarine. レーダーで(遠方の)潜水艦を見つけられる.

2 的確に理解[把握]する ▪ They never *got a fix on* what the former vice president meant by the term. 元副会長がその言葉で何を言わんとしていたのか結局わからなかった.

get above *oneself* (身のほどを忘れて)偉ぶる, 尊大になる, うぬぼれる ▪ He has *got above himself*. 彼はあまりにもうぬぼれている.

get *one's* ***act*** [《卑》***shit***] ***together/get it all together*** きちんと[効率的に]行動する, 本気を出す, 態勢を整える ▪ In game two the boys *got their act together* and beat Dereham 3-1. 第2試合で少年たちは態勢を整えてデレハムを3対1で破った.

get along in years →YEAR.

get anywhere [《米》***anyplace***] **1** 〚疑問文・否定文で〛(何らかの)目的を達する, 成功する, 成果をあげる; 役に立つ; 進歩する ▪ The measure won't *get anywhere* at this session. その法案はこの会期には通過しないだろう ▪ You can't *get anyplace* living like that. あなたはそんな生活をしていては成功できませんよ ▪ The best place to *get anyplace* is New York. 成功するのに最善の場所はニューヨークだ.

2 (人)に目的を達成させる, 成功させる; (人)の役に立つ; (人)を進歩させる ▪ Teaching never *gets* you *anywhere*. 教職ではあなたは決して成功できない ▪ It didn't *get* him *anywhere*. それは彼には何の役にも立たなかった.

get anywhere [《米》 ***anyplace***] ***with*** 〖主に否定文で〗 …について成功する, 役立つ ▪ He is not *getting anywhere with* his assignment. 彼は割り当てられた任務がうまくいっていない ▪ The lie-detector doesn't *get* us *anywhere with* her husband. 嘘発見器は彼女の夫については, 全然我々の役に立たない.

get away (***as***) ***clean as a whistle*** まんまと逃げ去る ▪ The bank-robber *got away as clean as a whistle*. 銀行強盗はまんまと逃げ去った.

get away from it all 《口》 日常生活のうるささを逃れる; 今までと全く違ったところへ行く ▪ He went to the country to *get away from it all*. 彼は日常生活のうるささから逃れるために田舎へ行った ▪ Do you want to *get away from it all*? 君は今までと全く違ったところへ行ってみたいですか?

get away [***by***] ***with*** (***blue***) ***murder*** 《口》 処罰や叱責を免れる; 好き勝手なことをする ▪ Some of the people in our office *get away with murder*. 我々の会社にはしかられずにすむ社員もいる.

get away with it 《主に米口》 処罰[叱責]を食わないですむ; (窮地を)うまく切り抜ける ▪ Jane is always late, but she manages to *get away with it*. ジェインはいつも遅刻するが, うまく叱責を免れている ▪ All the evidence points to his guilt, but he will *get away with it*. 証拠はみな彼の有罪を示しているが彼はうまく窮地を切り抜けるだろう.

Get away [***along, on, off***] (***with you***)***!*** 《口》 〖命令文で〗 さっさと出て行け!; 嘘つけ; ばかなことを言うな ▪ *Get away with you!* 出て行け!; ばかなことを言うな! ▪ I'm going to be prime minister. —*Get away with you!* ぼくは総理大臣になるんだ—ばかなこと言うんじゃないよ.

get back into circulation 《口》 正常の生活に戻る; 再び人とつき合うようになる ▪ It's time he *got back into circulation*. 彼はもう正常の生活に戻る時だ.

get back *one's* ***own*** →get one's own BACK (on).

get better [***worse***] 良く[悪く]なる ▪ Is your headache *getting better* or *worse*? あなたの頭痛は良くなっているのですか, 悪くなっているのですか.

get beyond caring 《口》 気にしなくなる ▪ I've *got beyond caring* how to pay the bills. 私は勘定を払うことなど気にしなくなりました.

get by *oneself* (仲間から離れて)一人になる ▪ He is eager to *get by himself*. 彼はしきりに一人になりたがっている.

get couthed up 《俗》 きちんと上品な服装をする ▪ As you're a gentleman, always *get couthed up*. 君は紳士なのだからいつもきちんと上品な服装をしなさい. ☞couth は uncouth の逆成.

get done with …を終わらせる, すませる ▪ *Get done with* it quickly. それを早くすませなさい.

get … down cold …を暗記する; を完全に覚える, 習う ▪ John *got* the text of his speech *down cold*. ジョンはスピーチの本文を暗記した ▪ I thought I had *gotten* all those formulas *down cold*. 私はそれらの公式はみな完全に覚えていると思っていた.

get down in the dumps [***mouth***] 《口》 気がふさぐ, しょげる ▪ As soon as he finds himself alone, he *gets down in the dumps*. 彼は一人になるとすぐ陰うつになる.

get down sick 《米口》 病気になる ▪ She *got down sick* with the mumps. 彼女はおたふく風邪にかかった.

get … down to a fine art 《口》 〖主に完了形で〗 …を完ぺきに行うようになる ▪ She's *got* the work *down to a fine art*. 彼女はその仕事を完ぺきに行うようになっている.

get down to bedrock →BEDROCK.

get down to it もっとも重要なこと[事実]を考える ▪ *Get down to it*, my love. 最も大切なことを考えてごらん, 恋人よ.

Get … down you. を飲み[食べ]なさい 《勧誘》 ▪ *Get* that tea *down you*. その紅茶を召しあがれ.

get *one's* ***ducks in a row*** →DUCK[1].

get forward in the world 出世する ▪ He *got forward in the world*, and gained considerable property. 彼は出世して相当な財産を得た.

get from under 《米俗》 難局を切り抜ける, 窮地を逃れる ▪ They were the first to *get from under*. 彼らは一番に窮地を逃れた.

get *a person's* ***goat*** →GOAT.

get going 《口》 **1** 動きだす, 運転しだす; (人が)活動を始める, 仕事にかかる, 急ぐ (→When the GOING gets tough, the tough get GOING.) ▪ If we expect to reach there before dark, we'd better *get going*. そこへ暮れないうちに到着しようと思えば急いだほうがよい.
2 (仕事の)調子が出る ▪ Wait till I *get going*. 私の調子が出るまで待ってください.
3 出発する, 出かける ▪ Let's *get going*. 出かけよう ▪ *Get going*! 行きなさい 《go よりも会話的》; 出て行け.

get … going …を興奮させる; を怒らせる; を勢いうかせる, おしゃべりにさせる ▪ He *got* her *going* and got her angry and she stayed on there for 10 minutes. 彼は彼女を興奮させ, 怒らせ, 彼女はそこに10分もこもりつうけた ▪ King *got* his tongue *going* on all cylinders. キングは舌をフル回転させた.

get *a thing* ***going*** (物事)を発足させる; を動きださせる ▪ Let's *get* the Badminton Club *going*. バドミントンクラブを発足させよう.

get going on 《米口》 行く ▪ You had better *get going on*! 君は行ったほうがいいぞ.

get *one's* ***head*** [***mind***] ***around*** 理解する, 受け入れる ▪ The government still has not *got its head around* the significance of its cultural policies. 政府はまだ文化政策の意義を理解していない.

get [***have***] *one's* ***head examined*** →HEAD[1].

get *a person* ***in bad*** [***wrong***] ***with*** 《口》 人を…に受けなくする; 人の不興を被らせる ▪ That will *get*

G

him *in bad with* his boss. そのため彼は主人の気受けが悪くなるだろう ▪ Be careful not to *get in wrong with* the fans. ファンの人気を失わないように注意しなさい.

get in deep (***with***) (…と)深い関わり合いをもつ ▪ It wasn't long before they had *got in deep with* each other. ほどなく彼らは深い関係になった ▪ He lost a lot of money, *got in deep with* some rather dangerous moneylenders. 彼は大金を失い, 危険な金貸しと深く関わるようになった.

get in good [***right***] (***with***) (…の)気に入りとなる ▪ The husband, jumping at a chance to *get in good*, came home from work early. 夫は気に入りとなる機会をこれ幸いと捕えて仕事から早く帰って来た.

G

get in on [***into***] ***the act*** …に加わる, 参入する ▪ Other alcohol industry players also *got in on the act* by donating water, goods, or money. 他のアルコール飲料会社も水や物資, お金を寄付することによって参加した ▪ The NBA *got into the act* as a sideshow last week. 先週, 全米バスケットボール協会も加わって協賛公演を行った.

get in the [*a person's*] ***way*** →WAY.

get in there 《口》(目的達成のため)積極的態度をとる, 一肌脱ぐ ▪ This is where the groom should *get in there* and talk to his family. ここはひとつ新郎が一肌脱いで家族と話をするべきところだ.

get into the way of *doing* →WAY.

get it 《口》 **1** しかられる, 罰せられる ▪ He'll *get it* when his mother finds it out. 母親がそれを知ったら, 彼はしかられるだろう.

2 撃たれる ▪ We *got it* in the tail section. 我々は尾翼を撃たれた.

3 電話に出る ▪ I'll *get it*. Hello! 私が電話に出ます. もしもし!

4 わかる, 理解する ▪ Put your best foot forward. *Get it*? おめかししてうまくふるまってくれよ. わかったかい.

get it across 《口》(聴衆などに)訴える, 理解される[させる] ▪ Did I *get it across*? おわかりいただけましたか ▪ They are experts at *getting it across*. 彼らは聴衆に訴えることにかけては名人である.

get (***it***) ***across the footlights*** → FOOTLIGHTS.

get it (***all***) ***together*** **1** うまく処理する; 万事満足な状態にする ▪ You've *got it all together* and begun a new life. 万事うまく処理して新生活を始めたね.

2 落ち着きを保つ ▪ He *got it all together* and called the police. 彼は始終落ち着いて警察に電話した.

3 (女性が)体格がよい ▪ She's *got it all together*. 彼女は体格がよい.

4 …とつき合う, 性的関係を持つ ▪ Rigby *got it together* with Jane, and they had a child. リグビーはジェインと関係を持ち, 彼らは一子をもうけた.

get it (***in the neck*** [***where the chicken gets the chopper***]) 《口》ひどくしかられる, ひどく罰せられる ▪ He is bound to *get it in the neck*. 彼はきっと大目玉を食うぞ.

get it on 《俗》 **1** 元気いっぱいである, 熱心にとりかかる ▪ Let's *get it on*! さあ, 始めよう.

2 (…と)性的関係をもつ (*with*) ▪ His wife Jennifer has left him and is *getting it on with* her psychiatrist. 妻のジェニファーは彼の許を去り, 精神科医と関係をもちつづけている.

get it over with (面倒なこと)をすませてしまう ▪ Invite Williams for dinner and *get it over with*. ウィリアムズを正餐(さん)に招待して返礼をすませなさい.

get it up 《俗》 **1** その気になる, やる気を出す (*for*) ▪ We had to *get it up for* the playoffs. 我々は決定戦に向けて気持ちを高めなければならなかった.

2 勃起させる ▪ I couldn't even *get it up* with her! I was so humiliated. 彼女とのときに立ちさえしなかった. 全く屈辱だった.

get lost →get LOST.

get mileage out of 《口》…を活用[利用]する, から多くのこと[もの, 恩恵, サービス]を得る ▪ Webb *got mileage out of* his trip to LA. ウェブはロスへの旅行から多くを得た ▪ Thoreau *got* a lot of *mileage out of* his brief incarceration. ソーローは短期間拘束されたことを有効に利用した.

get (***nicely***) ***left*** →LEAVE[2].

get nowhere [***no place***] **1** 成功しない, 効果がない, 何の進歩もしない ▪ Such methods will *get* you *nowhere*. そんな方法では君は成功しないだろう ▪ I spent the whole day studying this *getting nowhere*. 私はまる1日この研究に費やしたが何にもならなかった ▪ The extra session *got no place*. 臨時議会は何の成果もなかった ▪ The conference *got nowhere* fast. 会議は全く何の成果も上げなかった. ☞get nowhere fast は get nowhere の強調形.

2 (人を)成功させない; 効果を与えない; 幸福にしない; 欲しい物を得させない ▪ Flattery will *get* you *nowhere*. 君はおべっかを使っても何にもならないだろう.

get off *one's* ***butt*** 腰を上げる; 取りかかる, 始める ▪ You should *get off your butt* and work harder. そろそろもっとまじめに仕事にとりかかるべきだ.

get off *one's* ***case*** [***back, tail***] 手を引く, (干渉・いじめなどを)やめる ▪ When you tell someone to *get off your case*, you are asking the individual to leave you alone, to stop criticizing you or picking on you. 「手を引いてくれ」と誰かに言えば, 「ほうっておいてくれ」とその人に頼んでいることになる. つまり, 批判したりいじめたりするのをやめるようにと.

get off easy [***lightly***] →EASY.

get … off (*one's* ***hands***) **1** (商品)をさばく, 処分する ▪ We *get* remaindered books *off our hands* at a twentieth of the list price. 残本は表示価格の20分の1で処分する.

2 《口》(娘)を嫁にやる, かたうける ▪ He *got* his daughter *off his hands*. 彼は娘をかたうけた.

get off (***it***) 《口》〚主に命令文で〛話をやめる, ひやかし[ばかなまね, 大ぼら]をやめる ▪ Join the team or *get off it*. チームに加わるか, やめるかだ.

get off on the wrong foot →FOOT[1].

get off one しゃれを言う ▪ Henry *got off* a good *one* at the meeting today. ヘンリーはきょうの会でうまいしゃれを言った.

get ... off pat →PAT².

get off the dime 《米俗》(ちゅうちょ・遅延などのあと)動き始める, 行動を起こす, 膠着状態を打破する ▪ It's time to *get off the dime* and make a decision. ぐずぐずするのをやめて, 決断をするときだ. ☞もとダンスホールで1箇所に留まっているのをやめて移動して踊ることから; dime＝10セント硬貨のように狭い場所.

get off to a flying [***good***] ***start/get off to a flyer*** うまくすべり出す ▪ The bond drive *got off to a flying start.* 公債募集運動はすべり出しがよかった.

get off to sleep →SLEEP¹.

Get off (***with you***)***!*** 《口》嘘つけ!, ほっといてくれ! ▪ Oh, *get off!* I know better than that. ああ, ほっといてくれ! 僕はそんなばかはしないよ.

Get off with you! 去れ!, 出て行け! ▪ *Get off with you!* I am going to work. 出て行け! おれは仕事をするんだ.

get *oneself* ***on*** 自分の利益を図る ▪ He used his men as his tools to *get himself on.* 彼は部下の者を自分の利益を図るための道具に使った.

get on a fair treat →TREAT¹.

get ... on *his* [***its***] ***feet*** …を回復させる, 立ち直らせる ▪ It is difficult to *get* the car industry *on its feet.* 自動車産業を立ち直らせるのはむずかしい.

get on [***upon***] *one's* ***feet*** [***legs***] **1** (人前で演説をするため)立ち上がる ▪ The cheering became deafening when Brooke *got on his feet.* ブルックが演説のため立ち上がると耳を聾する喝采が起こった.
2 自信を得る ▪ He has *got on his feet* at last. 彼はついに自信を得た.
3 (事業など)を確立する ▪ He *got* the business *on its feet.* 彼はその事業を確立した.
4 (病後など)立ち直る, 回復する (*again*) ▪ Mother *got on her feet again.* 母は(病後)立ち直った.

get on in *one's* ***business*** 商売が繁昌する ▪ He wanted to *get on in his business* and be popular in the country. 彼は商売が繁盛し, 国じゅうで有名になることを望んだ.

get on in life [***the world***] 出世する ▪ Sam aspired to *get on in life.* サムは出世を切望していた.

get on like a house on fire すぐにうちとける, 意気投合する, とても仲がよい[親しい] ▪ We *get on like a house on fire* and it feels like we've known each other for years. 私たちはとても気が合うので, 何年も前からの知り合いのような感じがする.

get on the stick 《俗》仕事に取りかかる, 仕事を始める ▪ When I figured it out, I *got on the stick* pretty quickly. 私はそれがわかると, すぐに行動に移した. ☞stick「車のギアレバー」.

get out and around (社会活動などに)参加する, (活動のために)回る ▪ He *gets out and around* to all the schools. 彼はあらゆる学校を回っている.

get out from under 《米口》 **1** 勤め[責任]を回避する; 迫る危険を避ける ▪ You traveled like the devil to *get out from under.* 君は迫る危険を避けるため猛烈に急いで行った.
2 他人より有利な地位を占める ▪ They want to *get out from under.* 彼らは他人より優位を占めたがっている.

get out of (***a***) ***duty*** 勤めを回避する ▪ He *gets out of duty* on Saturday. 彼は土曜には勤めをさぼる.

Get out of here! 《俗》 **1** ここから出て行け.
2 そんな話はやめろ, ばか言うな ▪ *Get out of here.* You can't change the truth. ばかなこと言うんじゃない. 事実は変えられない.

Get out of it! 《俗》ばか言うな; ほら吹くな ▪ *Get out of it!* You can't do a thing like that. ばか言うな! そんなことができるもんか.

get out of *a person's* ***way*** →WAY.

get out while the getting is good よい潮時でやめる, 好機を逃さないで退く ▪ The best is *getting out while the getting is good.* 最良なのは, 頃合のよいときにやめることだ.

Get out (***with you***)***!*** あっちへ行け! 《うるさいとき》; ばかを言うな《不信の表明》 ▪ *Get out with you*; he did not say that. 嘘言え! 彼はそうは言わなかったぞ.

get over *oneself* 《口》自分がそれほどの人間ではないことを悟る ▪ He needs to *get over himself.* 彼は自分がたいした人間ではないことを悟る必要がある.

get ... over (***and done with***) 《口》(必要で不愉快な事を)片うけてしまう ▪ You might as well *get* it *over and done with.* それを片うけてしまった方がいい.

get over it 《口》乗り越える, なれっこになる; 気をもむのをやめる ▪ They've had fights before and *got over it.* 彼らは以前けんかしたことがあるが, それを乗り越えた ▪ My husband finally *got over it* because I told him that my pets and I are a package deal. 夫はやっと干渉するのをやめたが, それは私がペットと私とで一組だと言ったからだ.

get over the footlights →FOOTLIGHTS.

get *one's* ***own back*** (***on***) →BACK¹.

get past it …が老朽化する ▪ The workers *got past it.* その労働者たちは高齢になって働けなかった.

get popped 《俗》 **1** 停車させられる, 逮捕される ▪ I *got popped* by a cop doing crowd control. 群衆整理をしていたポリに停止させられた.
2 撃たれる ▪ He *got popped* and was bleeding. 彼は撃たれて出血していた.

get real →REAL.

get settled 落ち着く ▪ Drop me a line as soon as you *get settled.* 落ち着かれたらすぐ手紙をください.

get somewhere →SOMEWHERE.

get that way 《口》 **1** そのような状態になる ▪ How did you *get that way*? どうしてそのような状態になったのか.
2 そのように考える[感じる] ▪ How do you *get that way*? どうしてそのように考えるのですか.

get the gate [***air, hook***] 引導を渡される, 解雇される; 別れを告げられる (*from*) ▪ I already told you

G

you *got the gate from* here. すでに言ったように，君はもうここは首になったのだ ▪ Harry *got the gate from* Sally last night. ハリーは昨晩サリーから別れを告げられた.

get there《口》目的を達する，成功する；役に立つ ▪ He's got the guts and stamina to *get there*. 彼は目的を達するだけの勇気とねばりをもっている ▪ He thought he would *get there*. 彼は成功しようと思った.

get *a person* ***there*** その点で人を降参させる ▪ I *got* him *there*. 私がそう出たので彼は参った.

get there first（人)より先に得る，達する，為しとげる ▪ The Americans *got there first*. アメリカ人がそれを先に為しとげた.

get there with both feet《米口》完全に[すばらしく]成功する ▪ He *got there with both feet* at the start. 彼はしょっぱなからすばらしい成功を収めた.

get this《主に米口》(驚くような[興味ある]ことを言う前に)これがなんと，聞いてくれ，あのね ▪ The person I met at the party was—*get this*—Noam Chomsky! パーティーで会った人は—これがなんと—ノーム・チョムスキーだった ▪ Kev, *get this*: You're gonna be an ex-con who plays an Elvis impersonator. ケブ，よく聞きな. おまえはムショ帰りの，エルビス・プレスリーのものまね役者になるんだ.

get through the Court 破産者として放免される ▪ If you *got through the Court*, you'd be worse off. もしあなたが破産者として釈放されたなら，よけいに困窮するだろう.

get to *do* **1** …するようになる[なってくる] ▪ How did you *get to* know that? それがどうしてわかってきたのか ▪ They soon *got to* be friends. 彼らはじきに仲良くなってきた.

2《米俗》どうにか…する ▪ He *got to* go to college. 彼はどうにかして大学へ行った.

get … to *do* **1**（人)を説いて…させる；(人)に…させる[してもらう] ▪ *Get* someone *to* show you the way. 誰かに道を案内してもらいなさい ▪ It would be impossible to *get* them *to* listen to reason. 彼らに聞き分けをさせることは不可能であろう.

2（物)に…させる ▪ It is hard to *get* a tree *to* grow in a bad soil. 木を悪い土壌で生長させるのはむずかしい.

get (***to***) *doing*《口》…し始める ▪ When those two women *get* (*to*) *talking*, they go on for hours. その二人の女性が話を始めると何時間も続く.

get … to *oneself* …を独占する ▪ Lucas hoped he would *get* room 214 *to himself*. ルーカスは214号室を独占することを望んでいた.

get *oneself* ***together*** ＝GATHER oneself up.

get up and go [《米》***get, hump***]《口》**1** 素早く動き出す，活発に動き出す，極力急ぐ ▪ They will *get up and go* soon. 彼らはまもなく活発に動き出すだろう ▪ *Get up and get*, boys! みんな，できるかぎり急げ!

2 →have (a lot of [much]) GET-UP-AND-GO.

get up regardless (***of expense***)《口》むやみに着飾る；金を惜しまず贅沢な服装をさせる ▪ He'd *got* himself *up regardless*. 彼はひどく贅沢な服装だった.

get well →WELL[2].

get what's coming to *one* →COME[2].

get with it **1**《口》最新式[現代的]になる ▪ Do the latest dance, *get with it*. 最新のダンスをやれ，最新式にやれ.

2《俗》油断なく努める ▪ The students *get with it* before examinations. 生徒たちは試験の前には油断なく準備する.

get with the program《主に米》事情を理解(して行動)する ▪ Libya should *get with the program* and give up their nuclear and chemical weapons programs. リビアは状況を認識して核および科学兵器の計画を断念すべきだ.

get won (***with***)《米俗》(…と)性的関係をもつ ▪ Hey, I *got won with* a hot chick last night! あのな，ゆうべセクシーなかわい子ちゃんと寝たんだぜ.

get worse →GET better.

get *a person* ***wrong*** →WRONG.

Get you!《俗》(得意げな発言に対して軽蔑的に)よく言うよ ▪ I may be nominated for the Pulitzer Prize for Drama.—*Get you!* 僕は演劇でピューリツァー賞にノミネートされるかもしれないんだ—よく言うよ! ☞ときに Get her [him, them] も使用されることがある.

(***have***) ***got***《口》持つ (have)《俗語では have が落ちて got だけになることがある》 ▪ I*'ve got* nothing to do. 私は何もすることがない ▪ I *got* no money in my pockets. ポケットにはお金はない.

have got it badly《口》ぞっこんまいっている[ほれ込んでいる] (*over*) ▪ She'*s got it badly over* you. 彼女は君にぞっこんまいっているよ. ☞物事に熱中する場合にも用いる.

have got to *do*《口》…しなければならない (have to) ▪ I*'ve got to* write a letter. 手紙を書かなければならない ▪ Drivers *have got to* get a license to drive a car. ドライバーは車の運転免許証を所持せねばならない.

How selfish [***stupid, ungrateful,*** etc.] ***can you get?***《口》どれほど利己的[愚か，恩知らず]になれることか，よくもそんなに[愚か，恩知らず]になれるものだ《驚き・不満・非難などを表す；you は聞き手を指すとは限らない》 ▪ *How stupid can you get?* Johnson was a fine runner but he was also a fool. 何という愚か者だ. ジョンスンは足は速いが愚か者でもあった.

I get it.《口》わかりました ▪ I need butter, not margarine.—*I get it.* 私はバターがいるのです，マーガリンではありません—わかりました.

I wish you may get it./***Don't you wish you may get it?***《皮肉》そうなればけっこうだがね，うまくいけばよいけどね《他人の成功を望まないとき，またはその成功が疑わしいと思うときに言う》.

It gets me.《米俗》私にはわからない ▪ *It gets me* how he did it. 彼がそれをどのようにしたのかわからない.

it gets so (***that***)《米口》(結局)…ということになる ▪ *It gets so that* someone had to go. 結局誰かが行かなければならないということになった.

I've got it! **1** (突然に)わかったぞ! ▪ *I've got it!* How about this for a headline? わかったぞ! 見出しはこれにしてはどうだ. ☞I get it とも言う.
2 わかった, 私が引き受けた ▪ Ah, okay! *I've got it.* —Thanks! ああ, わかった. 僕がやるよ—ありがたい.
3 しめたぞ, 妙案がある ▪ In the card game I said to myself, "*I've got it.*" カードゲームで, 私は「しめたぞ. 妙案がある」と心中でつぶやいた.

Let** a person **get on with it. 《口》(やりたけりゃ)やらせておけばいい《不賛成の意を含む》 ▪ Well, then, *let* them *get on with it.* よし, それじゃあ, 彼らには勝手にそうさせておけばよい.

tell** a person **where to get** [he **gets**] **off 《口》人をずけずけとたしなめてやる; 身のほどを知らせる ▪ I *told* him *where* he *got off.* 彼をきつくたしなめてやった. ☞「(車掌が)客に降りる駅を知らせる」が原義.

There's no getting away from it. 《口》現実から逃げることはできない, 現実はその通りだ ▪ If you want decent quality you have to pay for it, *there's no getting away from that.* ほどほどの質を望むなら, その代価を払うことだ. それからは逃げられない.

What has got...? 《口》...はどうなったのか ▪ They inquired *what had got* Carr. 彼らはカーはどうなったかと尋ねた.

***What has got into** a person?* 《口》...はどうなったのか ▪ *What's got into* you today? 君は今日はどうしたのだ.

Where ... have got to? 《口》...はどうなったのか ▪ He muttered *where* his hat could *have got to.* 彼は帽子は一体どうなったのかとつぶやいた.

You get! 《口》出て行け! ▪ *You get* quick! さっさと出て行け!

you** [**we**] **get 《口》...がある[いる] ▪ *You got* plenty of time! 時間はたっぷりある.

You get what you pay for. 《諺》値段相応のものが手に入る. 掘り出し物なんてない.

You** [**They**] **should get out more. 《戯》もっと見聞を広めるべきだ ▪ They say *you should get out more*, see your friends, join a club or do something creative. 彼らは言う, もっと世界を広げなさい, 友だちと会いなさい, クラブに参加しなさい, 創造的なことをしなさい, と.

You've got me there. **1** (質問に答えて)わからないや ▪ Who was the first king of England? —*You've got me there.* イングランドの初代王は?—わかりません.
2 うまく僕のしっぽをつかまえたね; 君にうまくやられた ▪ You said you did not like coffee, didn't you? —*You've got me there.* 君はコーヒーはいらないと言ったじゃないか—これは一本取られた.

You've got something there. → SOMETHING.

getaway /gétəwèɪ/ 名形 ***a getaway car*** [***van, vehicle***] (犯行現場近くに駐車してある)逃走用の車 ▪ A hooded gunman jumped into *a getaway car* and fled with the help of an accomplice. フードをかぶってピストルをもった男が逃走用の車に飛び込み, 共犯者の協力を得て逃亡した.

make** one's [**a**] **getaway 逃走する《特に盗賊が盗品を持って》 ▪ He *made a getaway* in the car. 彼はその車で逃走した.

get-go /gétgòʊ/ 名 ***from the get-go*** 《口》最初から ▪ She was someone we were very interested in right *from the get-go.* 彼女は, 我々が最初からとても興味をもっていた人だった.

get-out /gétàʊt/ 名 ***as*** [***like***] (***all***) ***get-out*** 《米口》すっかり, 全く, ひどく ▪ She was pleased *as all get-out.* 彼女はすごく喜んだ ▪ He has a pet squirrel as black *as get-out.* 彼はほんとに真っ黒なリスをペットとして飼っている.

get-together, get together /géttəgèðər/ 名 ***have*** [***give***] ***a get together*** (小規模の)パーティー[集会]を開く ▪ Afterwards we *had a get together* at the house. そのあと家でパーティーをした.

get-up, get up /gétʌ̀p/ 名 ***One's get-up is excellent.*** 扮装が役にぴったりである ▪ *Your get-up was excellent.* あなたの扮装は役にぴったりだった.

in ... get up ...の身なりで, に扮装して ▪ Kids will absolutely love him *in* that *get up.* 彼があんな格好をしているのを子供は絶対気に入るだろう.

get-up-and-go /gètʌpəngóʊ/ 名 ***have*** (***a lot of*** [***much***]) ***get-up-and-go*** (おおいに)積極性・やる気がある ▪ It's vital for salesmen to *have get-up-and-go.* セールスマンにはやる気が肝心だ.

ghost[1] /goʊst/ 名 ***a ghost driver*** (反対車線の)逆走運転手, 幽霊ドライバー ▪ Figures show motorists face the greatest risk of encountering *a ghost driver* on the south motorway. 数値の示すところでは, 逆走ドライバーに遭遇する危険が一番高いのは南自動車道だ.

A ghost has (***just***) ***walked*** [***is walking***] ***over** a person's **grave.*** →Someone is walking on a person's GRAVE.

a ghost of (***a***) →the GHOST of (a).

a ghost patient 幽霊患者, 架空の患者 ▪ Some 30,592 so-called *ghost patients* have so far been discovered. これまでのところおよそ30,592人のいわゆる幽霊患者が見つかっている.

a ghost town ゴーストタウン ▪ The little town of Soap Lake is well on its way to becoming *a ghost town.* ソープ湖畔の, その小さい町はゴーストタウン化が進みつつある.

be only a ghost [***a mere ghost***] ***of** one's **former self*** 以前の幻影にすぎない, 以前の面影さえない ▪ Clearly the village we saw *was only a ghost of its former self.* 明らかに, 我々が見た村は以前の面影もなかった.

give [***yield***] ***up the ghost*** **1** 死ぬ; 息が絶える (《聖》*Gen.* 25. 8; *Job* 10. 18) ▪ After ten weeks in the hospital he *gave up the ghost.* 入院10週間の後彼は死んだ. ☞ghost = soul, spirit.
2 《戯》(物が)こわれる ▪ My old bicycle ran into a cart and *gave up the ghost.* 私の古い自転車は荷車にぶつかってこわれた.

3 あきらめる，断念する ▪ Vice President Gore finally *gave up the ghost* and President-elect Bush graciously donned the mantle of our new leader. ゴア副大統領はついに敗北を認め，ブッシュ次期大統領が謹んで新指導者の重責を引き受けた．

have* [*stand*] *a ghost of a chance (*of doing*) …する見込みがある ▪〚主に否定文で〛They don't *have a ghost of a chance of reaching* the playoffs. 彼らがプレーオフに進出する見込みはない．

lay a ghost 幽霊を引っこませる (↔ raise a GHOST) ▪ There the last *ghost was laid* by the parson. そこで最後の幽霊が牧師に引っこまされた．

lay the ghost… (*to rest*) …のショックを克服する，のトラウマから脱する ▪ It was important that we *laid the ghost to rest* from last week when we gave away a lot of silly goals. 不用意な得点を与えてしまった先週のショックを克服することが大事だった．

(***look***) ***as if*** *a person* ***has seen a ghost*** (幽霊でも見たように)怯えて青ざめている，真っ青な顔をしている ▪ His face was drawn and pale, *as if* he *had seen a ghost*. まるで幽霊でも見たかのように，彼の顔は引きつり青ざめていた．

look like a ghost (幽霊のように)顔が青白い ▪ When the patient arose from his bed, he *looked like a ghost*. 病人がベッドから起き上がったときは顔が青白かった．

not have the ghost of《俗》少しも知らない，わからない ▪ Who's that woman?—I do*n't have the ghost of* her. あの女は誰だ—私は少しも知りません．

raise a ghost 幽霊を出す[呼び出す] (↔ lay a GHOST) ▪ We are fighting against *ghosts raised* by ourselves. 我々は自分が呼び出した幽霊と戦っているのだ．

the ghost in the machine 機械の中の幽霊《二元論批判の言葉》 ▪ Ryle referred to Descartes' mind-body dualism as "*the Ghost in the Machine*". ライルはデカルトの心身二元論を評して「機械の中の幽霊」と呼んだ．

the [***a***] ***ghost of*** (***a***)《口》〚主に否定文で〛ほんの少しの，申し訳ばかりの (→ have a GHOST of a chance (of doing)) ▪ He had only *the ghost of* garments on. 彼はほんの少しばかりの衣服を着ていた ▪ William didn't have *the ghost of a* chance with Tom at wrestling. ウィリアムはレスリングでトムに勝つ見込みは少しもなかった ▪ There wasn't *a ghost of a* chance that Jack would win. ジャックが勝つ見込みはちっともなかった．

The ghost walks. 幽霊が出る;《劇俗》給料が出る ▪ *The ghost* doesn't *walk* this time. 今度は給料が出ない．☞cf. Sh., *Haml.* 1. 1で Horatio が幽霊にお前は「生前に地中に宝をたくわえていたため」に出るのかと尋ねるところから．

ghost[2] /goʊst/ 動 ***ghost it*** 幽霊となってさまよう ▪ After *ghosting it* for an hour, it was buried. 1時間幽霊となってさまよった後それは埋葬された．

giant /dʒáɪənt/ 名 ***a gentle giant*** 優しい[おとなしい]巨人 ▪ Ross was known by some of his colleagues as "*a gentle giant*." ロスは何人かの同僚には「優しい巨人」として知られている．

a giant refreshed 酒で元気ついた巨人 (《聖》*Ps.* 78. 65) ▪ He rose next morning, like *a giant refreshed*. 彼は翌朝酒で元気ついた巨人のように起き上がった．

There were giants in those days. 当時は巨人がいた《我々の祖先は我々よりすぐれていた》(《聖》*Gen.* 6. 4).

gib /gɪb/ 名 (***as***) ***melancholy as a gib cat***《口》ひどく憂鬱な ▪ Come, what has made you *melancholy as a gib cat*? おい，何をそんなにふさぎ込んでいるんだ．☞gib「雄猫」<Gilbert.

play fy gib おどしを言う，威嚇的に見る ▪ He *plays fy gib* with his thunderbolt of excommunication. 彼は破門という雷電をもって威嚇する．☞「猫に fie (こらっ!) と言う」が原義．

play the gib (女性が)猫のまねをする ▪ She *plays the gib* and barks and bawls at her husband. 彼女は猫のまねをして，夫に向かってがなったりわめいたりする．

gibber /dʒíbər/ 動 ***gibber like an ape*** とりとめのないことをぺちゃくちゃしゃべる ▪ Don't stand there *gibbering like an ape*. とりとめのないことをしゃべりながらそこに立っていてはいけない．

gibbet /dʒíbət/ 動 ***gibbet*** *a person* ***into*** 不面目な立場に追いこむ ▪ Thus he unwittingly *gibbeted* himself *into* infamy. このようにして彼は知らずに自分を不名誉な立場に追いこんだ．

giddy /gídi/ 形 ***Giddy up!*** (馬に)はいし，どうどう!

My giddy aunt! →AUNT.

play the giddy goat →GOAT.

giff /gɪf/ 名 ***the giffs and the gaffs***《米》与える物ともらう物; 利得と損失 ▪ I think that *the giffs and the gaffs* nearly balance one another. 利得と損失が互いにほとんど釣り合うと私は思う．

gift /gɪft/ 名 ***a gift from the gods*** 思わぬ儲けもの; 意外な幸運 (→GOD's gift (to) 1) ▪ The two days there were *a gift from the gods*. そこでの2日はもっけの幸いだった．

a Greek gift 物騒な贈り物，災いをもたらすもの (→Beware of GREEKs bearing gifts.) ▪ That house you have given him is *a Greek gift*. あなたが彼に与えたあの家は物騒な贈り物だ．

at a gift《口》ただでも(…しない) ▪ I would not have it *at a gift*. それはただでもほしくない．

be [***lie***] ***in the gift of*** …が与える権利を持つ ▪ The office *is* not *in his gift*. その職は彼が与える権利を持つものではない ▪ The position *lies in the gift of* the governor. その地位は知事が与える権利を持っている．

by [***of***] ***free gift*** ただで ▪ The property came to me *by free gift*. その財産を私はただでもらった．

Don't [***Never***] ***look a gift horse in the mouth.*** →HORSE[1].

God's gift (***to***) →GOD.

have a gift for/have the gift of …の才がある ▪ He *has a gift for* painting. 彼は絵画の才がある

▪ He *has the gift of* improvisation. 彼は歌や詩を即席に作る才を持っている.

make a gift to …に寄付する, 贈る ▪ He *made a gift* of one million dollars *to* them. 彼は100万ドルを彼らに寄贈した.

the gift of the gab →GAB.

a person ***thinks*** *he* ***is God's gift to*** 《口》自分は…の第一人者だと思っている(「うぬぼれている」の意味) ▪ He *thinks* he's *God's gift to* football. 彼はフットボールでは自分が第一人者だとうぬぼれている.

gig /gɪg/ 動 ***gig it*** 1頭立2輪馬車で行く ▪ We had to *gig it* home. 我々は1頭立2輪馬車で家に帰らなければならなかった.

giggle /gígəl/ 名 ***have a fit of*** (***the***) ***giggles*** 思わずくすくす笑いだす ▪ In the middle of a love scene, Jane *had a fit of the giggles*. ラブシーンの最中にジェインは思わずくすくす笑いだした.

(***just***) ***for a giggle*** 《口》おもしろ半分に ▪ He entered the contest *just for a giggle*. 彼はおもしろ半分にそのコンテストに参加した.

gild /gɪld/ 動 ***gild the lily*** →paint the LILY.

gild the pill →sugar the PILL.

gill /dʒɪl/ 名 ***be*** [***look***] ***rosy about the gills*** 《口》血色が良い; 健康そうである ▪ You *look* all *rosy about the gills*. 君は全く健康そうだ.

be [***look***] ***white*** [***blue, green, pale, yellow***] ***about*** [***around***] ***the gills*** 《口》 **1** 血色が悪い, 病気のようである ▪ She was *looking white about the gills*. 彼女は病気のようだった ▪ When he came back, he *was* panting a little, *pale around the gills*. 帰ってきたとき, 彼は少しあえぎ, 顔は青ざめていた. **2** 疲れて弱った顔をしている; しょげた顔をしている ▪ He *looks* a little *yellow around the gills*. 彼は少ししょげた顔をしている. ☞be, look のかわりに go を使えば「…になる」の意.

to the gills 《口》いっぱいに, 限度ぎりぎりまで, すっかり ▪ I was stuffed *to the gills* with hot dogs. 私はホットドッグですっかり満腹になった ▪ The shop is packed *to the gills* with gorgeous French antiques. その店は豪華なフランスの骨董品であふれかえっている ▪ We were bored *to the gills* waiting in a line. 列に並んで待つのに全くあきあきした.

turn red in the gills 怒る, 怒った色を見せる ▪ When he was sneered at, he *turned red in the gills*. 彼は嘲笑されたとき, 色をなして怒った.

white in the gills 《口》恐れて[病気で]血色が悪く, 元気なく, しょげて ▪ What makes you so *white in the gills*? どうしてそんなに元気がないのか.

gin[1] /dʒɪn/ 名 ***gin mill*** 《口》バー, 安酒場 ▪ His cultural milieu was Chicago's *gin mills* and back alleys. 彼の文化的環境はシカゴの安酒場と裏通りだ.

gin[2] /dʒɪn/ 動 ***gin her up*** 《米口》あおり立てる; 景気をつける, 精を出す ▪ The Apaches were *ginning her up* and making things a bit lively. アパッチ族はあおり立てて, ちょっぴり景気をつけていた.

ginger /dʒíndʒər/ 名 ***by ginger*** 《米》これはまあ! 《軽い間投句》 ▪ There, *by ginger*! I have gone splash into a moral. おやまあ! 私は説教を始めてしまった.

Ginger shall be hot in the mouth. 《諺》快楽の愛好は不滅である.

put some ginger into it 《口》速力と精力をもって働く, 少し本気に努力する ▪ We've got to finish this in two hours, so *put some ginger into it*. 2時間でこれを終えなければならないのだから, 敏活に働け.

gingerbread /dʒíndʒərbrèd/ 名 ***cake and gingerbread*** 容易でおもしろいこと ▪ Marshalling a room full of mandarins was *cake and gingerbread*. ミカンがいっぱいある部屋を整とんすることは容易でおもしろい仕事であった.

gingerly /dʒíndʒərli/ 副 ***go gingerly*** 《口》非常に用心してする ▪ *Go gingerly*—lest you do more harm than good. 大いに用心してしなさい, 益よりも害をなしてはいけないから.

gipsy, gypsy /dʒípsi/ 動 ***go gipsying*** 放浪する; キャンプに出かける ▪ I'd like to *go gypsying* around the country, from campground to campground. キャンプ場めぐりをして国じゅうを回りたい.

gird /gə:rd/ 動 ***gird*** *oneself* 帯を締める ▪ Hurry up and *gird yourself*. 急いで帯を締めなさい.

gird *oneself* (***up***) ***for*** [***to, to*** *do*] …するため緊褌一番する[身構える] ▪ He was already *girding himself for* his life's work. 彼は既に一生の仕事をしようと緊褌一番していた ▪ He *girds himself up to* any enterprise. 彼はどんな事業にも気を引き締めてかかる.

gird (***up***) *one's* ***loins*** →LOIN.

girdle /gə́:rdəl/ 名 ***A good name is better than a golden girdle.*** 《諺》良い評判は金よりよい. ☞昔, 金を帯または帯からつるされた財布の中へ入れて運ぶ習慣があったことから.

be under *a person's* ***girdle*** 人に服従している ▪ He would not *be under* any *one's girdle*. 彼は誰にも服従しようとしなかった.

have a large mouth but small girdle 出費は多いが収入は少ない ▪ He *has a large mouth but small girdle*. 彼は出費が多くて, 収入が少ない.

have [***carry, hold,*** etc.] ***… under*** *one's* ***girdle*** …を服従させる, 支配下に置く ▪ He *holds* half the Scottish church *under his girdle*. 彼はスコットランド教会の半分を支配下に置いている.

like a hen on a hot girdle →like a HEN on a hot griddle.

put [***make***] ***a girdle round*** [***around***] …を1周する; (鉄道・通信線などで)環状に巻く ▪ I'll *put a girdle around* the earth in forty minutes. 私は40分で地球を1周します.

the pin and girdle いんちき遊戯の一種 (→pricking in the GARTER) ▪ He was drawn in by those cheats of *the pin and girdle*. 彼はそのいんちき遊戯の詐欺におびき入れられた.

turn (***the buckle of***) *one's* ***girdle*** 戦う準備をする ▪ If I were angry, I might *turn the buckle* *of my girdle* behind me. 私が怒っていたら戦う準備をするかもしれないのだが. ☞昔, 戦うときは, 帯の buckle を後へ回したことから.

under the girdle (胎内にいて)まだ生まれない ▪ All children *under the girdle* at the time of marriage are held to be legitimate. 婚姻時に胎内にいる子供はすべて嫡出子とみなされる.

girl /gəːrl/ 名 ***a big girl's blouse*** →BLOUSE.

a cover girl カバーガール《雑誌などの表紙のモデル》 ▪ Marlene Dietrich is the *cover girl* of this year's Cannes poster. マレーネ・ディートリッヒが今年のカンヌ映画祭のポスターのカバーガールだ.

a good-time girl ふしだらな女, 尻軽女; 売春婦 ▪ I'm *a good-time girl* and love to go running around on the beach. 私は奔放な女で, 浜辺を駆け回るのが好きです.

a page three girl (大衆紙の)(セミ)ヌード写真モデル ▪ Lily Allen made one appearance as *a Page Three girl* in the Daily Star. リリー・アレンはヌード写真モデルとして一度デイリースター紙に載ったことがある.

a working girl **1** (独身の)働く女性, OL ▪ For the average *working girl*, a Louis Feraud suit costs the equivalent of a month's salary. 平均的な OL には, ルイ・フェローのスーツは1か月分の給料に相当する.

2 《俗》 売春婦 ▪ "I've been in the brothel business a long time, as *a working girl* myself and as a manager," she said. 「長い間, 私自身商売女としても管理人としても, 売春業界にいた」と彼女は言った.

the girl next door 隣の娘《健康で控えめな娘》 ▪ The cultural and sexual stereotype of *the girl next door* or the All-American girl indicates wholesome, unassuming femininity. 隣の娘つまり典型的アメリカ娘の文化的・性的なステレオタイプは, 健康で気取らない女性を表す. ☞その反対概念には tomboy (おてんば娘), femme fatale (妖婦型の女), girly girl ((いやに)少女っぽい娘)などがある.

girth /gəːrθ/ 名 ***in girth*** 周りが ▪ The tree is 30 feet *in girth*. その木は周りが30フィートだ.

run** a horse **head and girth (競馬で他の馬に)遅れずに走る ▪ The mare *ran* him *head and girth* the first mile. その雌馬は最初の1マイルは, 雄馬に遅れずに走った.

gist /dʒɪst/ 名 ***give* [*get, grasp*] *a gist of*** …の要点を述べる[つかむ] ▪ He *gave a gist of* the book. 彼はその本の要点を述べた.

give /gɪv/ 動 ***be given to*** →GIVEN.

Don't give me that* (*rubbish, nonsense*)*! 《口》そんな(ばかな)ことを言うな[があるものか], そんなことが信じられるか ▪ I'm leaving you.—Oh, *don't give me that!* 私はあなたと別れます—なんだと, ばかなことを言うな!

give** a person **a ring (婚約者に)指輪を贈る ▪ Anand *gave* her *a ring* as a sign of his love. アナンドは愛のしるしとして彼女に指輪を贈った.

***give and bequeath* [*devise, legate*]** 《法》遺産として与える, (遺言によって)譲り与える ▪ To Ernest Langton, Esq. I *give and bequeath* my polyglot Bible. アーネスト・ラングトン殿に, 私の数か国語で書いた聖書を譲ります.

give and take **1** 物々交換する; 公平なやり取りをする ▪ In some agrarian areas *give and take* is still practised. ある農耕地帯では物々交換がまだ行なわれている ▪ They *give and take* fair and square. 彼らは公明正大なやり取りをする.

2 互いに譲り合う, 妥協する ▪ Faculty members have to *give and take* in creating new courses. 大学職員たちは新しい講座を設けるときは互いに譲り合わなければならない ▪ Partners need to *give and take*. パートナー同士は譲り合わなければならない.

give** a person **as good as** he **brings [*one **gets***] 《口》人に当然の報い[仕返し, 言い返し]をする ▪ I have *given* him *as good as* he *brings*. 私は彼に当然の仕返しをしてやった ▪ I *gave* her *as good as* I was *getting*. 私は彼女に当然の言い返しをした.

give as good as** one **gets (言葉や打撃で)巧みに応酬する, しっぺ返しをする ▪ In cross-examination he'll *give as good as* he *gets*. 反対尋問において, 彼は巧みに応酬するだろう.

give** oneself **away **1** うっかり自分の心をさらけ出す, つい(手品などの種を)見られてしまう ▪ Mary *gives herself away* by blushing every time Peter's name is mentioned. メアリーはピーターの名前が出るごとに顔を赤くして自分の気持ちを見破られてしまう.

2 自分を悪し様に言う, 自分の弱点を不必要に言う ▪ He takes delight in *giving himself away*. 彼は自分を悪し様に言うのが楽しみなのだ.

3 他人に秘密を打ち明ける ▪ I bitterly regret *giving myself away* when I was drunk. 酔って秘密を洩らしたことをひどく後悔している.

give back* (*to* ...) *with interest (...に)利子をつけて返す《比喩的にも》 ▪ He *gave back* the money *to* me *with interest*. 彼はその金を私に利子をつけて返した ▪ She *gave back* their slanders *with interest*. 彼女は彼らの中傷を利子をつけて返した.

give** a person **bad marks 低い得点[評価]を与える, 辛口の採点をする (*for, in*) ▪ Louisiana *is* regularly *given bad marks for* education. ルイジアナ州は教育に関していつも低い評価しか得ていない.

give** a person **best →BEST.

give** one's **best (人に対して)最善を尽くす ▪ I'll *give* you *my best*. 一生懸命に働きます《社長などに対して言う》 ▪ I *gave* the enemy *the best* I had. 私は敵に対して全力を出して戦った.

***give** a person **his due* [*own*]** 人を公平に扱う, に当然の待遇をする ▪ She and I had some words; but I *gave* her *her own*. 彼女と私は少し口論したが, 私は彼女の正しいところは認めてやった ▪ To *give* mankind *their own*, they are all of them prone to folly. 人類を公平に評すれば, 彼らはみなともすればばかげた行為をしがちである.

give** a person **furiously* [*seriously*] *to think 人を深刻に考えさせる ▪ This attitude of his *gave* me *furiously to think*. 彼のこの態度は私を

深刻に考えさせた. ☞F donner furieusment à penser のなぞり.

give** a person **heart failure 人に心臓発作を起こさせる, をびっくりさせる ▪ His running style *gives* you *heart failure*. 彼の走り方には肝をつぶしてしまう.

give in** one's **notice 退職[辞職]届けを出す ▪ Richardson *gave in his notice* at work, and the company accepted his resignation with regret. リチャードスンは職場に辞職願いを提出し, 会社はやむなく彼の辞職を受け入れた.

give it a hard name and 悪く言えば ▪ *Give it a hard name and* it is fraud. 悪く言えばそれは詐欺だ.

***give it a shot** [**whirl**]* 《口》やってみる, 試みる ▪ I've never played golf but I'll *give it a shot*. ゴルフをしたことはないが, やってみよう.

***give it against** [**for**]* …に不利な[有利な]判決をする ▪ The whole company *gave it* unanimously *against* me. 全員こぞって私に不利な判決を下した.

give it** one's **best shot ベストを尽くす, できるかぎりのことをする ▪ I *gave it my best shot* and that's all I can do. 全力を出しきった, あれが私にできる限界だ.

***give** (**it**) **out** (**that**)* (…と)公表する, (と)言いふらす ▪ They *gave it out that* some were stingy. 彼らはけちな人もいると公表した ▪ She *gives it out that* he is idle. 彼女は彼は怠け者だと言いふらしている.

give it to** a person **for 《俗》人から…を盗み取る, だまし取る ▪ I *gave it to* him *for* his wallet. 私は彼の札入れを盗み取った.

***give it** (**to**) a person (**hot, right and left**)* 《口》人を(ひどく)しかる[なぐる; 罰する, やっつける] ▪ I *gave it to* the servant for his carelessness. 私は使用人が不注意なのでしかった ▪ I *gave it* him *right and left*. 私は彼をむちゃくちゃになぐった.

give it to** a person **straight 《俗》(…に関して)人に本当のことを聞かせる (*about, on*) ▪ *Give it to* me *straight*. 私に本当のことを聞かせてください ▪ President Bush *gave it to* us *straight on* the war on terror. ブッシュ大統領は対テロ戦争について率直に語った.

give it up for 《口》…に拍手してたたえる ▪ The audience *gave it up for* Donnie Simpson. 聴衆はダニー・シンプスンに大きな拍手を送った.

give me ... 《口》 **1** …がよい, のほうがよい《any day [any time] がつけられることがある》 ▪ *Give me* the man who sings over his work. 歌いながら仕事をするような人に限る ▪ *Give me* sunshine over rain *any day*. 雨降りよりも晴天のほうがよい ▪ *Give me* football *any time*—but not soccer. アメリカンフットボールは大歓迎だが, サッカーはいやだ.
2 …を呼んでください《電話で》 ▪ *Give me* the police. 警察を呼んでください.

give me** [**us**] **a break 〚間投詞的に〛《俗》冗談はやめてくれ, いい加減にしてくれ ▪ *Give me a break*, You have got me confused with somebody else. やめてくれ, 私を誰かと混同してる.

***give of** oneself [one's **time,** one's **money**]* 《英》出来る範囲内で人を助ける ▪ You must *give of yourself* to others. 君はできるだけ他人に奉仕しなければならない ▪ Hunter constantly *gives of her time* to assist others. ハンターはいつも自分の時間をさいて他人を援助している.

give of** one's **best 最善を尽くす ▪ He *gives* continually *of his best*. 彼は絶えず最善を尽くす.

give or take 《口》…は別として, (数量に関して)およそ ▪ *Give or take* a few mistakes in translation, this book is an excellent guide to English literature. 少しばかりの誤訳は別として, この本はすぐれた英文学の手引書である ▪ The average age appeared to be 30, *give or take* a few years. 平均年齢は, 数年のずれは別として, およそ30歳のようだった.

***give** oneself **out as** [**for, to be**]* …だと触れこむ ▪ He *gave himself out for* [*to be*] a doctor of philology. 彼は自分は言語学博士だと触れこんだ.

***give** a person **out to be** [**as**]* 人を…であると言う ▪ Some *gave* him *out as* a scholar. 彼を学者だと言う者もあった.

***give ... over for lost** [**dead**]* = GIVE ... up for lost.

give** oneself **over to **1** …にふける, 我を忘れる; に暮れる ▪ He has *given himself over to* drinking. 彼は酒にふけってきた ▪ She *gave herself over to* tears. 彼女は我を忘れて泣きくずれた ▪ Don't *give yourself over to* sadness. 悲嘆に暮れてはいけません.
2 …に打ち込む, 専念する ▪ You must *give yourself over to* your work. 君は仕事に打ち込まなければならない.

give something back 何か恩返しをする ▪ It's a privilege to be able to *give something back* to the city that's given so much to me. 私にかくも多くを与えてくださった市に対していくらか恩返しができるのは光栄なことです.

give** a person **something for himself 《口》人を打ちのめす, 人を責める ▪ When he told me to fuck off I *gave* him *something for himself*. 彼に失せろと言われたので打ちのめしてやった.

***give** (a child) **something to cry for** [**about**]* → give a person something to CRY about.

***give the case** [**it**] **for** [**against**]* (裁判は)…の勝ち[負け]とする ▪ He had *the case given for* him. 彼は勝訴の判決を受けた.

give** oneself **to …に身をゆだねる; をほしいままにする ▪ He *gave himself to* his work body and soul. 彼は仕事に身心を打ちこんだ ▪ They *gave themselves to* plunder. 彼らは略奪をほしいままにした.

***give ... to the world** [**the public**]* …を出版する ▪ "Pride and Prejudice" *was given to the world* in 1813. 「高慢と偏見」は1813年に出版された.

***give** a person **to understand** [**know, believe, note**]* 人に悟らせる, 知らせる[信じさせる, 認めさせる] ▪ I *gave* him *to understand* that I was satisfied. 私は満足したということを彼に知らせた ▪ He *gave* me *to believe* that his intentions were honorable. 彼は自分の意図が立派であるということを私に信じさせた.

give *oneself* ***up*** あきらめる ▪ I *gave myself up* for lost. 私はもうこれまでとあきらめた.

give up *one's* ***breath*** →BREATH.

give ... up for lost [***dead***] …を助からぬもの[死んだもの]とあきらめる ▪ The doctor *gave* him *up for dead.* 医者は彼を死ぬものとあきらめた ▪ The climbers *were given up for lost.* 登山者たちはもう助からぬものとあきらめられた.

give up the fight [(***unequal***) ***struggle***] 戦い[など]をやめる; 負ける ▪ Even the animal *gave up the unequal struggle* eventually. その動物さえ結局負けた.

G

give *oneself* ***up to*** **1** …にふける ▪ He *gave himself up to* pleasures. 彼は遊びにうつつを抜かした.

2 …に身を任せる ▪ He *gave himself up to* despair. 彼は絶望に身を任せた.

3 …に自首する ▪ He *gave himself up to* the police. 彼は警察に自首して出た.

give way **1** (懇願・主張にあって)折れる, 屈する; 譲る, 負ける ▪ Mary refused at first to marry him, but she *gave way* at last. メアリーは初めは彼と結婚するのを断ったが, ついに折れた ▪ I *gave way* to her in the matter. 私はその件では彼女に譲った.

2 (圧力・暴力にあって)くずれ(落ち)る, こわれる; (健康・精神力が)こわれる, だめになる; (足・技能などが)きかなくなる ▪ The railings *gave way* and he fell over the cliff. 手すりがくずれて, 彼はがけから落ちた ▪ The rope *gave way.* 綱が切れた ▪ All the skill of the mariners *gave way* to the violence of the tempest. 水夫たちの腕前も激しい暴風にあっては全然きかなかった ▪ His strength *gave way* under repeated wounds. たびたび負傷して彼の力も尽きた ▪ My knees *gave way.* 私は腰を抜かした.

3 (進む力に押されて)退く ▪ The crowd *gave way* before the troop of policemen. 群衆は警官隊に押されて退いた.

4 道をあける, 譲る; (…に)とって代わられる (*to*) ▪ Sophistry must *give way to* learning. 屁理屈は学問に道を譲らねばならない ▪ Sorrow *gave way to* smiles. 悲しみは変わり微笑になった.

5 自制[忍耐]を失う; 感情に負ける; (感情などに)身をゆだねてしまう (*to*) ▪ Don't *give way to* your feelings. 感情に負けてはいけません ▪ Her courage kept her from *giving way.* 彼女は勇気があったから, じっと自制することができた ▪ Don't *give way to* despair. 自暴自棄になってはいけません.

6 《海》こぎ始める; いっそう力を入れてこぐ ▪ We shoveled off and *gave way.* 我々はスタートを切ってこぎ始めた ▪ The crew began to *give way.* 乗組員はいっそう力を入れてこぎ始めた.

7 《株式》(たたかれて)値が下がる ▪ The stock afterwards *gave way.* 株はその後値が下がった.

give *a person* ***what for*** 《英口》人を激しくしかる[なじる] ▪ After about an hour, Sophie stormed up to him and *gave* him *what for.* およそ30分後にソフィーが彼のところに押しかけ, 彼をなじった.

given half a [***the***] ***chance*** 《口》機会があれば(必ずする) ▪ *Given half a chance,* a widower will remarry. 機会さえあれば, 寡婦は再婚するものだ.

He gives twice who gives quickly. 《諺》すぐに援助すれば2倍援助することになる, 「明日の百より今日の五十」.

I'll give you [***him,*** etc.] ***that.*** 《口》その点は認めよう ▪ It does look like fun, *I'll give you that.* 確かにおもしろそうだ, それは認める.

I'll give you what for! 《口》お灸をすえるぞ, おしおきをするぞ ▪ Don't make a fuss now or *I'll give you what for.* いま騒ぐな. さもないとおしおきをするぞ.

It is better [***more blessed***] ***to give than to receive.*** ものを受けるよりは与えるほうが尊いことだ(《聖》*Acts* 20. 35).

it is given to *a person* ***to*** *do* 人が…することができる, する機会を与えられている ▪ *It is* not *given to* everybody *to* study abroad. すべての人が海外で勉強する機会があるわけではない ▪ *It is given to* few (people) *to* write poetry. 詩を書ける人は少ない.

not give up the ship →SHIP[1].

What gives? 《口》どうしたんだ (What's the matter?) ▪ *What gives?*—Nothing, just a little misunderstanding. どうしたんだ?—別に, ちょっとした誤解さ. ☞Ⓖ Was gibt's? のなぞり.

What would I not give to *do*? …するためにはどんな犠牲もいとわないのだが ▪ *What would I not give to* see him again? 彼にもう一度会うためならどんな犠牲だっていとわないのだが.

would give *one's* ***eyes*** [***anything, a lot***] ***for*** [***to*** *do*] =would GIVE the world for.

would give the world [*one's* ***head,*** *one's* ***ears,*** *one's* ***right arm,*** *one's* ***right hand,*** *one's* ***back teeth,*** *one's* ***eyeteeth,*** etc.] ***for*** [***to*** *do,* ***if***] …のため[するため]ならどんな犠牲でも払うのだが ▪ Many a girl *would give the world to* have such a complexion. そのような顔の色つやを持つためならどんな犠牲をもいとわないという女の子は多い ▪ I *would give my right hand to* be able to write like Thomas Hardy. トマス・ハーディーのように書けたらどんな大犠牲でも払うんだが《R. L. Stevenson の言葉》 ▪ I *would* have *given my ears for* such a success. そんな成功のためならどんな犠牲でも払っただろうに.

given /gívən/ 形 ***be given to*** **1** …にふけっている, を事とする ▪ He *is given to* drink. 彼は酒にふけっている ▪ He *is given to* telling fantastic stories. 彼は途方もない話をするのを事とする.

2 《英》(人)に許されている, 天賦のものである ▪ It *is* not *given to* many of us to live a hundred years. 我々のうち100歳まで生きられるものは多くはない ▪ Musical ability *is given to* you. 音楽的才能は天賦のものである.

gizzard /gízərd/ 名 ***fret*** *one's* ***gizzard*** 気をもむ, 心配する ▪ He'll *fret his gizzard* green if he doesn't hear from her. 彼は彼女から手紙をもらわなければひどく気をもむだろう. ☞gizzard はもとは鳥の胃袋で「気質」の意.

grumble in the gizzard 《英口》ぶつぶつ言う, こぼす ▪He went home, *grumbling in the gizzard*. 彼はぶつぶつ言いながら帰宅した.

stick in** one's **gizzard →STICK².

glad /glæd/ 形 ***(be) glad of*** **1** …してうれしい ▪*I'm glad of* your safe arrival. あなたが無事到着してうれしい.

2 …するならうれしい ▪I shall *be glad of* your company. おつき合いくだされぱうれしく存じます.

(be) glad of heart 喜んで[いそいそして](いる) ▪I *was glad of heart* to learn of your engagement. 君が婚約したと聞いてうれしかったよ.

give** a person **a** [**the**] **glad hand →HAND¹.

give the glad eye 《口》(概して女性が)色目を使う; 歓迎のまなざしを向ける ▪The barmaid *gave* him *the glad eye*. 女性バーテンダーは彼に色目を使った ▪He was *giving the glad eye* to every voter. 彼はすべての投票者に色目を使っていた.

glad clothes [***rags***] 《口》晴れ着, 礼服《特に夜会服》 ▪We all turned out in our *glad rags* to join in the procession. 我々はみな行列に加わるため晴れ着でくり出した.

(I am) glad to meet [***see***] ***you.*** 初めまして《初対面のあいさつ》 ▪*Glad to meet you*, Mr. White. 初めまして, ホワイトさん ▪*(I am) glad to see you.* お目にかかってうれしい; よくおいでくださいました ▪*(I am) glad to* have *met you*. お目にかかれて光栄でした《別れのあいさつ》.

***I should be glad to** do* 《皮肉》ぜひ…したいものだ ▪*I should be glad to* know why. どうしてなのかぜひ知りたいものだ.

shall [***will***] ***be glad to** do* 喜んで…する ▪I *shall be glad to* come. 喜んで参ります.

glaik /gleɪk/ 名 ***get the glaik(s)*** だまされる ▪He *gets the glaik* now and then. 彼は時折だまされる. ☞glaik 語源不明.

give the glaik(s) だます ▪She *gave* me *the glaiks* when all was done. 彼女は結局のところ私をだましたわけだ.

glamor, 《英》**glamour** /glǽmər/ 名 ***cast a*** [*one's*] ***glamor over*** [***on***] **1** …に魔法をかける, の目をくらます ▪Jugglers *cast a glamor over* the eyes of the spectators. 手品師は見物人の目をくらます ▪They *cast their glamor on* him. 彼らは彼を魅了した.

2 …を魅惑的にする, 神秘的に美しくする ▪The moonlight *cast a glamor over* the garden. 月光は庭園を神秘的に美しくした.

glance¹ /glæns|glɑːns/ 名 ***at a (single) glance*** 一見して, 一目で ▪Can't you tell *at a glance* what it is? それが何であるか一目でわからないか.

at (the) first glance 最初見たときは, ちょっと見れば ▪It is less apparent *at first glance*. 最初見たときはそれははっきりわからない.

cast [***give, take***] ***a glance at*** …をちらりと見る ▪She *cast a glance at* us. 彼女は我々をちらりと見た ▪He only *gave a glance at* the papers. 彼は書類をただちらっと見ただけだった.

exchange glances (with) (…と)互いに目くばせする ▪I *exchanged glances with* her. 私は彼女と目くばせした.

give a glance to [***into, over***] …にちょっと目を通す ▪He *gave a glance into* the book. 彼はその本にざっと目を通した.

steal a glance at ちらっと盗み見る ▪He *stole a glance at* the girl standing on his side. 彼は隣に立っている娘をちらっと盗み見た.

take a glance into …を瞥(べ)見する ▪I *took a glance into* the future. 私は将来を瞥見した.

without a backward glance 振り向かず; 未練なく, 後悔せずに ▪He swept past Gebrselassie *without a backward glance* and won by 10m. 彼は振り返りもしないで一気にゲブレシラシエを抜き去り, 10メートル差で優勝した ▪My uncle Tommy went off to join the navy *without a backward glance*. トミーおじさんは未練なく海軍に入隊した.

glance² /glæns|glɑːns/ 動 ***glance** one's **eye(s)*** ちらりと[素早く]見る ▪He *glanced his* severe *eyes* around the group. 彼はその群れをきびしい目つきでちらりと見回した.

glance** one's **eye(s) down [***over, through***] …をざっと見る, にざっと目を通す ▪I *glanced my eye over* his manuscript and saw that it was rubbish. 彼の草稿にざっと目を通したら, 駄作であることがわかった.

glare¹ /gleər/ 名 ***give a stony glare*** 冷たい目で見る ▪She *gave* me *a stony glare*. 彼女は私を冷たい目で見た.

in the full glare of …のぎらぎらした光を十分浴びて; にじかにさらされて ▪He was *in the full glare of* the sun. 彼はぎらぎらする日光をじかに浴びていた ▪He was *in the full glare of* publicity. 彼はひどく世間の評判になっていた.

glare² /gleər/ 動 ***glare contempt*** [***defiance, hate***] ***at*** …を軽蔑[反抗, 憎しみ]のまなざしでにらむ ▪He *glared defiance at* the magistrate. 彼は反抗のまなざしで治安判事をにらんだ.

glass¹ /glæs|glɑːs/ 名形 ***(as) clear as glass*** →CLEAR¹.

enjoy** one's* [a***] ***glass*** 酒をたしなむ ▪He *enjoys his glass* now and then. 彼は時折酒をたしなむ.

fond of** one's* [a***] ***glass*** 酒が好きで ▪He is *fond of a glass*. 彼は酒好きである.

glasses (all) round 一座のみんなに酒杯 ▪He called for *glasses all round*. 彼は「一同に酒杯を」と求めた.

have a glass 1杯やる ▪Come up and *have a glass* with us. さあ来て我々と1杯やりなさい.

have a glass too much 少し酔う ▪I have *had a glass too much*. 私は少し酔った.

How is the glass? 晴雨計[天気]はどうか.
raise a [*one's*] ***glass to*** ...に乾杯する ▪ We *raised our glasses to* our friend. 友人に乾杯した.
see through [***as in***] ***a glass darkly*** おぼろげに見える, ぼんやりと見える (《聖》 *1 Cor*. 13. 12) ▪ I *see* the drift of it *through a glass darkly*. 私にはその大勢がおぼろげに見える.
the glass is half empty [***full***] グラスに水が半分しかない[残っている]と思う, マイナス[プラス]思考をする《と悲観的[楽天的]に考える見方》 ▪ When it comes to reading the economic tea leaves, for some *the glass is half empty*, for others it's *half full*. 経済の先行き占いということになると, 悲観的に見る人も楽天的に見る人もいる ▪ Look up at the beautiful trees and flowers and see *the glass half full*. 美しい木や花を見上げて世界は希望に溢れていると思いなさい.
through rose-colored glasses → see ... through ROSE-COLORED spectacles.
under glass フレーム[温室]内で ▪ The grapes were grown *under glass*. そのブドウは温室作りであった.

glass[2] /glæs|glɑːs/ 動 ***glass*** *oneself* 《詩》 影を映す ▪ The mountains *glass themselves* in the lake. 山々はその湖に影を映している.

glass ceiling /glæssíːlɪŋ|glɑ̀ːs-/ 名 ***break*** [***shatter, smash***] ***the glass ceiling*** ガラスの天井を打ち破る ▪ Hillary Clinton *shattered* a political *glass ceiling*. ヒラリー・クリントン氏は政界のガラスの天井を粉砕した ▪ She also *broke the* highest *glass ceiling* in the United States. 彼女は米国でいちばん高いガラスの天井をも粉砕した. ☞glass ceiling 「ガラスの天井」《女性の昇進に対する差別的障害》.

glass-house /glǽshàʊs|glɑ́ːs-/ 名 ***Those*** [***People***] ***who live*** [***One living***] ***in glass-houses should not throw stones.*** 《諺》 すねに傷もつ者は他人の批評などせぬがよい.

glazier /gléɪʒər|-ziə/ 名 ***Is your father a glazier?*** 《俗》 前に立ちふさがっちゃ見えないよ《明かり先に立ちふさがっている人に対していう》. ☞「君の父親はガラス屋か, でなければ君の体に窓をつけることもできないだろうから, そう立ちふさがっては見えないぞ」の意.

gleam /gliːm/ 名 ***a gleam*** [***glint, twinkle***] ***in*** *one's* ***eye*** →EYE.
a gleam of 〚主に否定文で〛 かすかな... ▪ There is not *a gleam of* hope. かすかな望みもない.

glee /gliː/ 名 ***full of glee*** 大喜びで, 上きげんで, 大はしゃぎで ▪ I am *full of glee* this morning. 私は今朝は非常に愉快だ.
in (***high***) ***glee*** 大喜びで, 上きげんで, 大はしゃぎで ▪ The farmer was *in high glee*. その農夫は上きげんだった.
with glee 大喜びで, 愉快に ▪ He clapped his hands *with glee*. 彼は大喜びで手をたたいた.

glim /glɪm/ 名 ***douse*** [***dowse***] ***the glim*** 《主に海俗》 〚主に命令文で〛 灯火を消す ▪ *Douse the glim* when you've finished reading. 読み終わったら明かりを消しなさい.

glimmer /glímər/ 名 ***not a glimmer*** 少しも[全く]...ない ▪ Have you any idea how to do this?—*Not a glimmer*. 君はこれの仕方を知っているか?—少しも知らない.

glimmering /glímərɪŋ/ 名 ***get*** [***have***] ***a glimmering of*** ...をうすうす知る[知っている], に感づく[感づいている] ▪ I have *got a glimmering of* the truth. 私は真相をうすうす知っている.
go glimmering 《米俗》 (名声・機会などが)消える, 消えうせる ▪ My reputation has *gone glimmering*. 私の名声は消えうせてしまった.

glimpse /glɪmps/ 名 ***by glimpses*** ちらりちらりと ▪ I saw the sight *by glimpses*. 私はその光景をちらりちらりと見た.
catch [***get***] ***a glimpse of*** ...をちらりと見る ▪ I *caught* some *glimpses of* the pirates. 私は海賊どもをちらちら見た ▪ I *got a glimpse of* the house from the window of a train. 私は列車の窓からその家をちらりと見た.
the glimpses of the moon 夜の世界; 地上の出来事, 浮世の有様 (cf. Sh., *Haml*. 1. 4. 53) ▪ To revisit *the glimpses of the moon* is not for us. (牢屋から)しゃばにまた出ることは我々にはできない.

gloaming /glóʊmɪŋ/ 名 ***in the gloaming*** たそがれに《比喩的にも》 ▪ The valley looked very attractive *in the gloaming*. 谷はたそがれに包まれて非常に美しく見えた ▪ He was happy *in the gloaming* of his life. 彼は晩年は幸福であった.

globe /gloʊb/ 名 ***the use of the globes*** (昔の) 地理天文学 ▪ He taught *the use of the globes*. 彼は地理天文学を教えた.

gloom /gluːm/ 名 ***cast a gloom over*** ...に暗影を投じる, を陰気にする ▪ The sad accident *cast a gloom over* the country. 悲しい出来事で国中が陰気になってしまった.
chase *one's* ***gloom away*** 憂鬱を払う, うさを散じる ▪ He *chased his gloom away*. 彼は自分の憂鬱を払った.
gloom and doom/ ***doom and gloom*** → DOOM[1].
pile on the gloom/ 《主に英口》 ***pile*** [***put, turn***] ***on the agony*** **1** (同情を引くため)悲痛なことを大げさに言う ▪ The prime minister *piled on the gloom* over the world economy. 総理大臣は世界経済について悲痛なことを大げさに言った.
2 さらに沈んだ気分にさせる ▪ A weak US dollar *piled on the gloom* on Wall Street. アメリカドルが弱いのでウォールストリートはいっそう重い雰囲気になった.

glory /glɔ́ːri/ 名 ***at*** *one's* ***glory*** → in one's GLORY.
bask [***bathe***] ***in reflected glory of*** *a person* 人の栄誉の余光[七光り]にあずかる ▪ He *basks in reflected glory of* the achievements of others. 彼は他の人々の業績の七光りにあずかっている.
blow [***send***] ***... to glory*** 《口》 = send ... to KINGDOM COME.

Glory be! 《俗》おやまあ!, まあうれしい!《驚き・喜びを示す》.

Glory be (***to God***) ***on high.*** いと高き所では(神に)栄光があるように (《聖》*Luke* 2. 14).

Glory to God in the highest. いと高き所にいます神に栄光があるように!

go to glory 《口》昇天する, 死ぬ; だめになる ▪ Then we should have *gone to glory*. そうなれば我々はお陀仏になっていただろう.

in all *one's* ***glory*** 栄華をきわめて; 大得意で (《聖》*Matt*. 6. 29) ▪ Even Solomon *in all his glory* was not arrayed like one of these. 栄華をきわめたソロモンでさえ, これらの一つほどにも美しく着飾ってはいなかった ▪ He was *in all his glory* as treasurer of the Society. 彼はその協会の会計として大得意だった.

in glory 栄光に包まれて, 天国に ▪ He dwells with the saints *in glory*. 彼は聖徒たちと天国に住んでいる.

in [***at***] *one's* ***glory*** **1** 全盛をきわめて ▪ He was *in his glory* surrounded by a crowd of admirers. 彼は崇拝者の群れに取り巻かれて全盛を極めていた. **2**《口》大得意で, 無上に満足し楽しんで ▪ He was *in* all *his glory* last evening. 彼は昨晩気炎万丈だった ▪ He is *in his glory* ordering small boys about. 彼は少年たちをあごで使って大得意だ.

leave *a person* ***in glory*** 人の所を去る《去って一人にする》 ▪ We *left* him *in glory*. 我々は彼の許を去って彼を一人にした.

the [*one's*] ***crowning glory*** 《口》 **1** 最後を飾る栄光, 無上の栄光 ▪ Beating Georgia that year was *the crowning glory* for me. あの年にジョージア大学を破ったのが私にとって最高の栄光だった. **2** 頭髪; かつら ▪ To save *their crowning glory* men in ancient times used to rub crocodile faeces onto their scalps. 毛髪を残すために古代の男たちはワニのふんを頭皮に塗り込んだ.

the glory days (***of***) (…の)過去の全盛期[黄金時代] ▪ The 1940s and early 1950s were *the glory days of* jazz. 1940年代および1950年代初期はジャズの黄金時代だった ▪ Long gone are *the glory days* when Genoa was a great trading sea-power. ジェノバが海上貿易の大国だった栄光の日々ははるか過去のことだ ▪ *The glory days of* NASA are over. NASAの全盛時代は終わった.

to the greater glory of god (神)の栄誉をたたえるために ▪ Two fakirs stand in uncomfortable positions *to the greater glory of their gods*. 二人の苦行僧が彼らの神々の栄誉をたたえるために窮屈な姿勢で立っている. ☞ L ad majorem Dei gloriam (イエズス会のモットー, 略 AMDG) のなぞり.

gloss /glɑs|glɔs/ 名 ***put*** [***set***] ***a gloss on*** …に光沢をつける; を取り繕う ▪ He *put a gloss on* his faults. 彼は自分の失策を取り繕った.

glout /glaʊt/ 名 ***in the glout*** 《口・古》不きげんで, 渋面作って ▪ My mamma was *in the glout* with her daughter all day. 母は一日中娘に対して不きげんだった.

glove /glʌv/ 名 ***a kid glove affair*** 盛装すべき催し[式] ▪ How do we dress?—Oh, it is *a kid glove affair*. どういう服装するのかね?—ああ, 盛装すべき催しだよ.

bite *one's* ***glove*** 必殺の復しゅうを決意する ▪ He *bit his glove* and shook his head. 彼は必殺の復しゅうを決意し頭を振った. ☞イングランドとスコットランドとの国境地方では「手袋をかむ」のは必殺の復しゅうの誓いとされた.

Excuse my gloves. (握手のとき)手袋のままで失礼します.

fight with the gloves off 真の敵意をもって戦う, 仮借せずに戦う ▪ Rival firms were *fighting with the gloves off*. 敵対会社は仮借せずに戦っていた. ☞ボクシングから.

fight with the gloves on 敵意をもたずに戦う, 手かげんしながら闘う ▪ John and James were *fighting with the gloves on*. ジョンとジェイムズは手かげんしながら闘っていた.

fit like a glove ぴったり合う ▪ The boots *fitted* me *like a glove*. そのブーツは私にぴったり合った.

go for the gloves 《俗》(競馬で)向こう見ずな賭けをする ▪ It won't be my fault tomorrow if I don't *go for the gloves*. あす向こう見ずな賭けをしなくても私の落ち度にはならないだろう.

hand in [***and***] ***glove with*** …と協力して, ぐるになって ▪ Trade union federation works *hand in glove with* German government. 労働組合連盟は, ドイツ政府と協力して働いている ▪ Some people think that bin Laden was *hand in glove with* the CIA. ビンラディンは米中央情報局と気脈を通じていたと考える者もいる.

handle with gloves off きびしく[容赦なく, 手荒に]扱う ▪ The Republican *handled* Mr. Clay *with gloves off*. その共和党員はクレー氏をきびしく扱った.

handle with (***kid, silk***) ***gloves*** やさしく[用心して]うまく扱う ▪ My aunt is so irritable that we have to *handle* her *with kid gloves*. 私のおばは非常に怒りっぽいので穏やかにうまく扱わなければならない.

handle without gloves きびしく[容赦なく, 手荒に]扱う, 遠慮なく話す ▪ The prophets *are handled without gloves*. 予見者らは容赦なく扱われる.

hang up *one's* [***the***] ***gloves*** ボクサーをやめる ▪ After losing six fights in a row he *hung up his gloves*. 6連敗したのち彼はボクサーをやめた.

have the gloves on (グローブをはめて)ボクシングをやる ▪ Shall we *have the gloves on* for half an hour? 30分間ボクシングをやろうか.

put on [***wear***] ***gloves*** 穏やかに攻撃する ▪ He *put on gloves*, when he came to the House to make a speech. 彼は議会に演説に来たときは, 穏やかに攻撃をした.

put on the gloves = have the GLOVEs on.

take off the gloves/take the gloves off 手袋を脱ぐ; (闘争・議論などに)本気でかかる, 本気になって戦う ▪ He was too polite to *take the gloves off*

G

in his assault on the poem. 彼は非常に礼儀正しいので, 本気になってその詩を攻撃はしなかった.

***take off the gloves to** a person* 人をきびしく[容赦なく, 手荒に]扱う; 人と真剣に戦う[議論する] ▪ The vicar would often *take off the gloves to* me. 教区代理牧師はよく私と真剣に議論するのだった.

take up the glove 挑戦に応じる ▪ The Czar had to *take up the glove* thus thrown in his way. ロシア皇帝はこのように自分に対してされた挑戦に応じなければならなかった. ☞挑戦には手袋を投げ, それを拾い上げて挑戦に応じたことから.

The gloves are off. 《口》事が真剣になってきた, 戦いは真剣で重大だ ▪ I warn you that *the gloves are off.* 戦いは真剣になってきたことを私は君に警告する ▪ Israel admits *the gloves are off* in dealing with Hamas. イスラエルはハマスとの交渉は真剣であると認めている.

throw (down) the glove (to) (...に)挑戦する ▪ The girl *threw down the glove to* her stepmother. 娘はまま母に挑戦した.

wear gloves →put on GLOVEs.

with kid gloves →KID[1].

with the gloves off/without the gloves 容赦せずに ▪ Our boss handles [treats] us *without the gloves.* 社長は我々を容赦せずに扱っている.

glow /gloʊ/ 名 ***(all) in [of] a glow*** 熱くほてって, 赤くほてって ▪ He was *all in a glow* with hard riding. 彼は激しく乗馬したので真っ赤にほてっていた ▪ The fire is *in a glow.* 火が赤く熾(き)っている.

glue[1] /gluː/ 名 ***stick like glue (to)*** **1** (...に)ひどくねばりつく ▪ This Sussex clay *sticks like glue to* one's clothing. このサセックスの粘土は衣服にひどくねばりつく.

2 (人に)しつこくつきまとう ▪ He *sticks like glue to* me. 彼は私にしつこくつきまとう.

The glue did not hold. 《口》あなたはしくじった, あなたは的をはずした ▪ *The glue did not hold* in at least one case. 少なくとも1件ではうまくいかなかった.

glue[2] /gluː/ 動 ***(be) glued to*** **1** ...にくっつく, しつこくつきまとう ▪ Why must you always *be glued to* me? なぜ君はいつも私につきまとわなければならないのか.

2 (目が)...に見入る; (耳が)...に聞き入る; (テレビなど)にかじりついている ▪ He had his eyes *glued to* the keyhole. 彼は鍵穴に目を見すえた ▪ His ears *were glued to* the radio. 彼の耳はラジオに聞き入った ▪ Americans grow up *glued to* the television screen. アメリカ人はテレビ画面にかじりついて成長する.

glum /glʌm/ 形 ***look glum*** 不きげんな[むっつりした, 元気のない]顔をする[して見る] (*on*) ▪ You need not *look* so *glum*, sir. そんなにむっつりした顔をなさるにはおよびません.

glut[1] /glʌt/ 名 ***a glut in [on] the market*** 供給過剰 ▪ There is *a glut* of these goods *in the market.* これらの商品は市場にだぶついている.

glut[2] /glʌt/ 動 ***glut** one's **eyes (with)*** (...を)思う存分ながめる ▪ He *glutted his eyes with* the sight. 彼はその景色を思う存分ながめた.

glut the market 市場にだぶついて売れない ▪ An excessive production of woollen goods *glutted the market.* 毛織物の過剰な生産のため市場に品がだぶついた.

glut** oneself **with **1** ...を堪能する ▪ He *glutted himself with* looking at her. 彼は心ゆくまで彼女をながめた.

2 ...を飽きるほど食べる ▪ They *glutted themselves with* rich food. 彼らはごちそうを思う存分に食べた.

glutton /glʌ́tən/ 名 ***be a glutton for punishment*** 《口》苦難[苦痛]にいくらでも堪え得る人である ▪ He must *be a glutton for punishment.* 彼は苦痛にどこまでも堪え得るにちがいない.

be a glutton for work 《口》(いやな)仕事を喜んでする人である ▪ He *is a glutton for work.* 彼はいやな仕事でもいつも喜んでする.

gluttonous /glʌ́tənəs/ 形 ***be gluttonous of*** ...をむさぼる, 欲張る, に凝る ▪ The robin *is gluttonous of* wild fruits. コマドリは野生の実をむさぼる.

gnash /næʃ/ 動 ***gnash the [**one's**] teeth*** (怒り・残念で)歯ぎしりする (《聖》*Matt.* 8. 12) ▪ He *gnashed his teeth* at them. 彼は彼らに歯ぎしりした.

gnat /næt/ 名 ***down to a gnat's eyebrow*** 細部に至るまで, 詳細に ▪ Everything was computed *down to a gnat's eyebrow.* あらゆることが細部に至るまで計算された.

strain at a gnat and swallow a camel →STRAIN[2].

gnaw /nɔː/ 動 ***gnaw ... asunder [in two]*** ...をかみ切る[二つにかみ切る] ▪ The mouse *gnawed* the cord *asunder.* ネズミは綱をかみ切った ▪ He *gnawed* the cord *in two.* 彼はその綱を二つにかみ切った.

gnome /noʊm/ 名 ***the gnomes of Zurich*** チューリッヒの子鬼ども《スイスの銀行家[金融業者]のこと》 ▪ Ziegler refers to the Swiss bankers as *the gnomes of Zurich*, Basel and Bern. ツィーグラーはスイスの銀行家たちを, チューリッヒやバーゼル, ベルンの子鬼どもと呼んでいる.

go[1] /goʊ/ 名 ***a near go*** →a NEAR escape.

a pretty go 《口》弱ったこと, えらい羽目 ▪ Here's *a pretty go*! 弱ったことになった.

a queer go 《口》妙なことだ ▪ It's *a queer go*, indeed. ほんとに妙なことだ.

a rum [jolly, nice] go 《俗》べらぼうな話, 変な話 ▪ *A* pretty *rum go.* ひどくべらぼうな話だ.

all [quite] the go 《俗・古》(一時的に)大流行で, 大はやりで ▪ The tune is *all the go* in London. その歌はロンドンで大はやりだ.

at [in] one go 《口》一度の試みで, 一気に ▪ I read the book *at one go.* その本を一気に読んだ ▪ Brown wants the job finished *in one go.* ブラウンは仕事を一気に済ませたがっている.

at the first go 《口》一気に, 一度で ▪ He got the tooth out *at the first go.* 彼は一気に歯を抜いてもらった.

be a go 《米口》計画中である, 許可[認可]されている ▪ Thanks to the unanimous vote, the new firehouse *is a go*. 満場一致で新しい消防署が認められた.

be all go 《英口》大忙しである (→It's all GO.) ▪ It *was all go* in town today. きょう町では大忙しだった.

be going spare 《英》余っている ▪ One ticket *is going spare* for Friday night. 金曜日の夜のチケットが1枚余っている.

first [***second,*** etc.] ***go*** 《英》1回目[2回目]で, 1度[2度]の試みで (on the first [second] go) ▪ I passed my driving test *first go*. 運転免許試験に一発で合格した.

from go to whoa 始めから終わりまで, 終止 ▪ It only lasted about five minutes *from go to whoa*. 開始から終了までおよそ5分しかかからなかった ▪ Norman led this tournament *from go to whoa*. ノーマンはこのトーナメントを終止リードした. ☞whoa「馬などを止めるときの掛け声」.

from the word "go" **1** 《口》最初から ▪ *From the word "go"* I have been a conservative. 初めから私は保守主義者だったのです.

2 徹頭徹尾, 全く ▪ He is French *from the word "go"*. 彼は完全にフランス人である.

full of go 元気[熱意]に満ちて ▪ He is still *full of go*. 彼はまだ元気いっぱいである

go-ahead →GO-AHEAD.

go-go 最新の, 流行の ▪ Michael Ashcroft and chums are planning to transform Carlisle into a *go-go* vehicle. マイケル・アシュクロフトと同僚たちはカーライルを最新車に変えようと計画中だ.

have a bad go of 《口》ひどい病気にかかる ▪ I *had a bad go of* cold. ひどい風邪をひいた.

have a go (***at***) 《口》 **1** …を怒って非難する ▪ Harry *had a go at* me for not telling him how it really was. 実情を告げなかったので, ハリーは私を非難した.

2 (…を)攻撃する ▪ I'll *have another go at* you. もう一度おまえを攻撃するぞ.

3 (…を)やってみる ▪ We will *have another go at* this game some day. いつかまたこの競技をやってみましょう.

have ... on the go 《英口》(計画など)をかかえて, …に携わって ▪ They *have* many projects *on the go*. 彼らは多くのプロジェクトをかかえている.

have plenty of go 《口》元気[精力]が旺盛である ▪ He is still young and *has plenty of go* in him. 彼はまだ若く元気旺盛である.

in one go =at one GO.

It is a go. 《米口》それで決まった ▪ *It's a go.* Shake. それで決まった. 握手しよう.

It's all go. 《英口》大忙しだ, てんやわんやだ. ☞→be all GO.

it's one's go (***to do***) 《俗》…の(…する)番である ▪ *It's my go to* throw the ball. 私がボールを投げる番だ.

make a go of 《口》 **1** …を成功させる, うまくやる ▪ He will *make a go of* any business he enters. 彼はどんな事業を始めても成功させる ▪ He's determined to *make a go of* the bookshop. 彼はその本屋を成功させようと決意している.

2 (恋愛・結婚生活などを)うまく[幸せに, がんばって]やっていく ▪ We decided to try and *make a go of* it for the sake of the children. 私たちは子供たちのためにがんばろうと決めた.

no go 《口》不可能で; むだで, 見込みなく ▪ I've tried to pursuade your father to come, but it's *no go*. 私はあなたのおとうさんを説得して来させようとしたが, だめだ ▪ Under the circumstances, *no go* for £100,000. こんな事情で, 10万ポンドは出せない.

on [***upon***] ***the go*** **1** 《口》忙しくして, 絶えず動き回って ▪ I've been *on the go* since daybreak. 私は夜明けからずっと動き回っている ▪ My mother is *on the go* all day long. 母は一日中絶えず活動している.

2 《古》衰えてきて, 終末に近づいて ▪ Old England is *on the go*. 老いたイギリスは衰えている.

3 《俗》ほろ酔いで ▪ He was a little bit *on the go*. 彼は少しばかりきこしめしていた.

quite the go →all the GO.

go^2 /goʊ/ 動 ***as*** [***so***] ***far as ... go*** →FAR.

as ... go …並みから言えば ▪ He is a good man, *as* the world *goes*. 彼は世間並みでいえば良い人である ▪ He is a good doctor, *as* doctors *go* nowadays. 彼は今日の医者並みで言えば良医である.

As Maine goes, so goes the nation [***union***]. 《米》メイン州で勝つ政党は全国で勝つ.

as the phrase goes →PHRASE.

as the saying goes →as the SAYING is.

be going to do →GOING.

come and go 行ったり来たりする, 出たり入ったりする ▪ Her color *came and went*. 彼女の顔は赤くなったり青くなったりした ▪ Money *comes and goes*. 金は天下の回りもの.

Don't be gone too long. 早く帰ってね, 行ってらっしゃい ▪ *Don't be gone too long.*—I'll be right back. 早く帰ってきてね—すぐ帰るよ.

Don't (***even***) ***go there.*** 《米口》(難解・不愉快だから)もうその話はやめてくれ[したくない] ▪ *Don't go there*. That topic's too hot for the holidays. もうその話はしないでくれ. その話題は休日には刺激が強すぎる.

don't go doing 《口》→GO doing 2.

enough (***...***) ***to be going*** [***to go***] ***on with*** 《英口》当面やっていけるだけ十分で[な] ▪ I have more than *enough to be going on with* now. 当面やっていけるだけ十分もっている ▪ Do you think she has *enough* money *to go on with*? 彼女は当面やっていけるだけのお金を持っていると思うかい?

get going →GET.

get going on →GET.

go doing **1** …しに行く《《米》ではこの形が標準化する傾向にある》 ▪ He *went calling* [*cycling, dancing, sightseeing*]. 彼は訪ねて[サイクリングに, ダンスに, 見物に]行った.

2 《口》…する《主に否定命令文で禁止・警告を表す》

▪ Don't *go picking* the pears. ナシをもいではいけないぞ ▪ Don't *go telling* me lies. 私に嘘を言うな.

go* (*a*) *begging →BEGGING.

go a long* [*good, great*] *way/go far **1** 遠くまで行く ▪ I am *going a long way* today. きょうは遠くまで行きます.
2 長もちする; (食料のたくわえが)もちこたえる ▪ These flowers *go a long way*. これらの花は長もちする ▪ Turnips will *go far*. カブは長くもつだろう.
3 大いに効力[威力]がある; (金など)使いでがある (*with*) ▪ A little kindness will *go a long way with* some people. 小さい親切でも大いにありがたがる人がいる ▪ Ten yen used to *go far with* us. 10円が我々には大いに使いでがあったものだ ▪ Soft and fair *goes far*. 愛想のよいのは得だ.
4 大いに役に立つ, 大いに助けとなる (*towards*) ▪ The money will *go a long way towards* my school expenses. その金は私の学資に非常に役立つだろう ▪ This *goes a good way towards* solving the problem. これはその問題の解決に大いに助けとなる.
5 (説明などが)よくわかる ▪ The explanation doesn't *go far*. その説明はよくわからない.

***go a short* [*little*] *way* (*to, towards*)** …にあまり効果がない, 大して役立たない ▪ The farm produce *goes a short way to* filling the months. 農産物はその月々を満たすのに大して役立たない.

go about to *do* …しようと努める[企てる] ▪ He has *gone about to* injure me. 彼は私を害そうと企てた ▪ We must *go about to* cure them. 我々は彼らを治そうと努めなければならない.

go abroad **1** (噂などが)広まる ▪ My fame has *gone abroad* in London. 私の名声はロンドンに広まっている.
2 外国へ行く ▪ He wants to *go abroad* again. 彼はまた外国へ行きたがっている.

go against *one's* ***heart*** 気が進まない, いやである ▪ It *went against my heart* to go there. そこへ行くのは私は気が進まなかった.

go against *one's* ***stomach*** **1** 性に合わない ▪ It *goes against my stomach* to own a fault. 過失を自認するのは私の性に合わない.
2 むかつく, 胸が悪くなる ▪ Raw fish *goes against my stomach*. 生魚を食べると私は胸がむかつく.

go all out 《口》(いましている仕事に)全力をそそぐ[傾ける], …するために全力を出す (*in, for, to do*) ▪ They *went all out to* beat the record. 彼らは記録を破るために全力をあげてやった ▪ Jordan always *goes all out* on every play. ジョーダンは常にどの試合にも全力を傾ける.

go all out on 《口》…を完全に信頼する; (人)を最もよく利用する ▪ Don't *go all out on* Max: he's not as reliable as you think. マックスを信頼しきってはだめだ. 奴はお前が思っているほど頼りにならないからな ▪ When I'm busy my youngest secretary is the one I *go all out on*. 私は忙しいときには最年少の秘書を一番よく使う. ☞ 運動競技から.

go all the way with *a person* →WAY.

go* (*all*) *to pieces →PIECE[1].

go along for the ride つき合いで[交際上, 義理で]…する (→along for the RIDE) ▪ Wheat *went along for the ride* with soybeans last week. 先週小麦(の値段)も大豆につき合って変動した.

go and *do* **1** …しに行く, 行って…する ▪ *Go and* see who it is. 誰だか見に行ってください ▪ *Go and* find your friend. 友だちを訪ねて行きなさい.
2 《口》愚かにも[不運にも]…してしまう ▪ The fool has *gone and* got married. その愚か者は無分別にも結婚した ▪ What a fool to *go and* do such a thing! 無分別にもそんなことをするとは, 何というばかだ.
3 〖命令文で〗勝手に…しろ ▪ *Go and* be miserable. 勝手にひどい目にあうがよい.
4 《口》〖単なる強調, and は省略可〗…する ▪ *Go and* try it yourself. 自分でひとつやってごらん ▪ Please *go* try it at once. ぜひすぐにやってごらんなさい.

***go* (*and*) *chew bricks* [*fly a kite, climb a tree, jump in the lake*]** 《俗》出て行け, 去れ; 静かにしろ, 黙れ ▪ *Go and chew bricks*, man. こら, 出て行け! ▪ I told the Law to *go jump in the lake*. 私は法律当局に「黙っていてくれ」と言った.

go as far as to *do* →GO so far as to do.

go as you please 《口》 **1** 〖限定的〗(競技など)規則に縛られない; (行動の)自由な ▪ It will be a *go as you please* party and there will be no need to dress up for it. それは自由な会だから, 正装する必要はないでしょう.
2 あなたの好きなようにする (do as you like) ▪ By all means, *go as you please*. ぜひあなたの思い通りになさってください.

go astray →get ASTRAY.

go at it **1** 攻撃し合う[する] ▪ Two boys *went at it*. 二人の少年が攻撃し合った.
2 懸命に取り組む ▪ He liked the work and *went at it* energetically. 彼はその仕事が気に入って, 懸命に取り組んだ.
3 セックスする ▪ I saw Mom and Dad *going at it*. パパとママがセックスしているのを見た.

go back to square one 《口》初めからやり直す ▪ Jane has long been absent from school. She has to *go back to square one*. ジェインは長く学校を休んでいる. 彼女は初めからやり直さなければならない.

go bad* [*broke, ill*] *on *a person* 《口》悪く[破産に, 病気に]なって人を困らせる ▪ My bank *went broke on* me. 銀行が倒れて私はひどい目にあった ▪ The egg *went bad on* the cook. 卵が腐っていて料理人は困った ▪ The servant *went ill on* him. 使用人が病気になって彼は困った.

go badly to market →MARKET.

***go ballistic* [*berserk*]** 《口》激怒する, キレる ▪ Amy *went ballistic* when she saw them together. 彼らがいっしょにいるのを見るとエイミーはかんかんに怒った. ☞ 弾道ミサイルが爆発することから.

go bananas →BANANA.

go belly-up 《俗》 **1** (魚が死んで)腹を上にして浮く;

死ぬ ▪ One of my daughter's goldfish *went belly-up* the other day. 先日，娘の金魚のうちの1匹が死んでしまった.

2 失敗する; 倒産する; 壊れる ▪ The production company nearly *went belly-up* twice. その制作会社は2度倒産しかけた ▪ The household air-conditioning system *went belly-up*. 家庭用空調設備が故障した.

go berserk →GO ballistic.

go (*a person*) ***better*** 《トランプ》(賭けで人より)高値を張る;《口》(人に)勝る[勝つ] ▪ I *went* him two chips *better*. (ポーカーで)私は彼より2チップだけ多く賭けた ▪ I will *go better*. 私は(相手より)高値を張ろう.

go beyond caring →get PAST caring.

go by the book [***rules***] 典拠によってやる，正確にやる ▪ If you *go by the book*, you will not be scolded. きちんと正確にやればしかられはしないだろう.

go by [***under***] ***the name*** [***title***] ***of*** …の名で通っている，通称…と言う; の作とされている ▪ He *goes by the name of* Smith. 彼はスミスの名で通っている ▪ The play *goes under the name of* Shakespeare. その劇はシェイクスピアの作とされている.

go chase *oneself* ＝GO (and) chew bricks.

go cheap 安く売られる ▪ The house *went* very *cheap*. その家は非常に安く売られた.

go down in history →HISTORY.

go down in *a person's* ***opinion*** …の評価を下げる ▪ Campbell had *gone down in people's opinion* since the affair. キャンベルはその事件以来世間の評価を落としてしまった.

go down like a lead balloon (冗談・提案などが)不人気である，受けない ▪ His policies are *going down like a lead balloon* with working people. 彼の政策は労働者の不評を買いつつある.

go down the drain [***plughole***] むだ[無価値]になる; 失墜する ▪ Everything *went down the drain* for me. 私にとってすべてが水泡に帰した ▪ The country has *gone down the drain*, politically and economically. その国は，政治的にも経済的にも，失墜してしまった.

go down well [***badly***] (***with***) (…に)好評[不評]である，(に)受けがよい[悪い] ▪ The slow-paced song *went down well with* the crowd. ゆったりとした歌は群衆に好評だった ▪ Bush's measures *went down badly with* the younger generation. ブッシュ氏の政策は若い世代には不人気だった.

go easy **1** ゆっくり行く，のんきにやる; 手かげんする，大目に見る ▪ Father is *going easy*. 父はのんきにやっている.

2 〚命令文で〛もっとゆっくり，もっと穏かに;《米》気をつけよ ▪ *Go easy*, there! I'm an invalid. あの，もっと穏かに! 私は病人ですから ▪ *Go easy*, there! That furniture is breakable. 気をつけて! その家具はこわれやすいから.

go easy on 《口》 **1** …に優しくする，をお手やわらかに処理する ▪ Don't punish the boy severely; *go easy on* him. その子を厳しく罰しないで，優しくしてね.

2 …を控え目に[注意して]扱う; を使いすぎない ▪ You will have to *go easy on* that subject. その問題は控え目に扱わねばならないでしょう ▪ You should *go easy on* politics. 政治問題は注意して論ずべきである ▪ *Go easy on* the salt. 塩は控えなさい.

go far enough 〚疑問文・否定文で〛十分満たしている(*to do*) ▪ The policy didn't *go far enough to* achieve real reform. その政策は真の改革を達成するには不十分だった.

go far to *do* …することに大いに役立つ ▪ It will *go far to* bring about the result. それはその結果をもたらすのに大いに役立つであろう.

Go fetch! →FETCH[2].

go figure 理解できない，わかんないね(I don't understand this.) (→Don't ASK (me)!) ▪ Liz wants to have a conversation, but when I try, she does all the talking. *Go figure*. リズは会話がしたいと言うが，僕が話しだすと，彼女がひとりしゃべりまくるんだ. これってどういうこと? ☞イディシュ語 gey vays 'go know' のなぞり.

go fly a kite 《口》→GO (and) chew bricks.

go for it 《口》やってみる，がんばる; がむしゃらにやる ▪ I see no reason not to *go for it*. やってみない理由はない ▪ Planning to run for mayor, Graham just *goes for it*. 市長選に立候補しているので，グレアムはまさにがむしゃらにやる.

go for the jugular [***throat***] (相手の弱点・急所に)猛攻撃をする，激しく批判する ▪ England *went for the jugular*, and there was nothing Australia could do to protect themselves. イングランドは猛攻撃し，オーストラリアは防御に何のなす術もなかった ▪ Kerry *went for the jugular* against Edwards, questioning the North Carolina senator's credentials and electability. ケリーはエドワーズを攻撃し，ノースカロライナ州上院議員の証明書と選出適格性について問いただした.

go (***for***) ***to*** *do* 《俗》〚否定文・仮定に用いて〛愚かにも[大胆にも，きびしくも]…する ▪ You wouldn't *go for to* sell Ben Gunn? 君はベン・ガンを売るようなばかなことはしないだろうね ▪ You'd never *go to* suspect her. 君なら大胆にも彼女に疑いをかけたりはしないだろう.

go from *one's* ***word*** 約束を破る ▪ They did not *go from their word*. 彼らは約束を破らなかった.

go hog wild (…に[で])夢中になる，興奮する(*over*, *for*) ▪ The media *went hog wild over* the news. メディアはそのニュースに熱狂した ▪ Downtown *went hog wild for* Chinese New Year. 中心街は中国の新年で活況を呈した.

go in and out **1** 出入りする ▪ The crowds were *going in and out* of the building. 群衆はその建物を出たり入ったりしていた.

2 行ったり来たりする ▪ The piston *went in and out*. ピストンは行ったり来たりした.

3 明滅する ▪ The shadows *went in and out*. 影は明滅した.

4 自由に出入りできる ▪ He shall *go in and out*, and find pasture. その人は門を出入りして牧草を見つ

ける (《聖》 *John* 10. 9) ▪ We will stamp your hand and you may *go in and out* as you wish. 手にスタンプを押してあげますから, それで自由に出入りしてよろしい.

Go in and win! (競技に)出て勝て! 《競技, 特になぐり合いの弱い方に対する激励語》 ▪ Sit down well in your saddle, and *go in and win.* くらにうまく乗って競馬に出て勝て.

go in* [*into*] *holes (すり切れて)穴があく ▪ These stockings are guaranteed not to *go in holes.* これらのストッキングはすり切れて穴があくことはないとの保証付きです.

go in to bat (個人・チーム全体が)打者となる ▪ Lancashire *went in to bat* at six. ランカシャー・チームは6時に打者となった.

G

***go into* one's *act* [*routine*]** 《口》お決まりのふるまいを始める ▪ Watch a salesman *going into his act*, and you can learn a lot from him. 販売員がお決まりのふるまいを始めるのをよく見なさい. そうすれば彼から多くを学ぶことができます.

go into hospital →enter (a) HOSPITAL.

go it 《口》 **1** 〚命令文で〛(戦いなどを)激しくやれ, しっかりやれ ▪ *Go it!* Hit him hard. 激しくやれ, やつをうんと打ってやれ! ▪ *Go it!* I'll help you. しっかりやりなさい. 私が手伝ってあげます.

2 激しくやる; 強く[率直に]言う ▪ They didn't half *go it.* 彼らは激しくやったよ.

3 大速力で行く, 猛烈に進む ▪ He was *going it* along the motorway. 彼は高速道路を猛烈に飛ばしていた.

4 むちゃな放蕩をする, 酒色にふける ▪ He has been *going it* for years. 彼は何年もの間むちゃな放蕩をやってきた.

5 (鳥などが)懸命に歌う ▪ The larks were *going it* this fine morning. 今朝のこと, ヒバリが懸命にさえずっていた.

6 むちゃな[とっぴな, 頑固な]ふるまいをする ▪ I heard George *going it.* 私はジョージがむちゃなふるまいをするのを聞いた.

7 惜しげもなく金を出す ▪ You are *going it*, paying £800 for a suit. スーツ1着に800ポンドも払うなんて君は金使いが荒いね.

go it alone 《口》 **1** 《トランプ》(数人を相手に)一人で勝負をする ▪ He *went it alone.* 彼は一人で数人を相手に勝負をした.

2 独力でやる[戦う]; 全責任を持つ ▪ It left Captain Davis to *go it alone.* そのためデイビス船長は孤軍奮闘させられた.

3 一人暮らしをする ▪ Wallace wants to leave home and *go it alone.* ウォーレスは家を出て一人暮らしをしたがっている. ☞euchre (ユーカートランプ)から.

***go it strong* [《まれ》*thick*]** =GO it 2, 4.

go* (*it*) *strong on →go STRONG on.

***go it with a looseness* [*rush*]** 《米》あばれる ▪ The horses are all *going it with a rush.* 馬たちはみなあばれている.

Go it you cripple! Wooden legs are cheap. あなたは不利な立場にあるのでどんなにしても競争にはならない ▪ You have no capital. Well, *go it you cripple. Wooden legs are cheap.* 君は資本が全くない. そんな不利な立場ではてんで競争にはならんよ.

go jump in the lake 《口》 = GO (and) chew bricks.

***go nowhere* (*fast*)** 進行しない, はかどらない ▪ Global economy is *going nowhere fast.* 世界経済は遅々として進んでいない.

go nuts 《口》発狂する; 熱狂する ▪ The combat veteran *went nuts* with post-traumatic stress syndrome. その戦闘経験者は外傷後ストレス症候群で気がふれた ▪ Everyone *went nuts* cheering and jumping up and down. みんな熱狂して喝采し跳びはねていた.

go off at* [*in, upon*] *a tangent →fly off at a TANGENT.

***go off at half cock* [*half-cocked*]** 準備不足のまま始める, 泥縄式にやる (→at half COCK) ▪ An over-excited colleague *went off at half cock* and ruined the scheme. 過度に興奮した仕事仲間が十分な準備なしに突き進んで, 計画をだめにしてしまった.

***go off* one's *food* [*oats*]** 《口》食欲を失う ▪ He suddenly *went off his food.* 彼は急に食欲を失った.

go off full score/ go off at score → SCORE[1].

go off like a snuff of a candle 《口》急死する ▪ It is a pity that he *went off like a snuff of a candle.* 彼が急死したのは残念だ.

go off milk (牛・羊などが)乳があがる ▪ The cows *went off milk* for a time. 牛はしばらく乳があがった.

go on* (*and on*) *about (ある事)をいつまでもしつこく話す, …についてだらだらしゃべる ▪ I was wrong. But please don't *go on about* it. 私が悪かった. でもどうかその事をいつまでも言わないでくれ ▪ He can *go on and on about* golf. 彼はゴルフのことならいくらでもだらだらしゃべれる.

go on the offensive …を攻撃[反撃]する (*against*) (→act on the OFFENSIVE) ▪ Obama *went on the offensive against* McCain on the economy. オバマ氏は経済問題に関してマケイン氏を攻撃した.

***go on to* do** 続けて…する《特に一旦やめてまた》; 次に…する ▪ I *went on to* read the book. 私は続けてその本を読んだ ▪ He *goes on to* quote two passages from Seneca. 彼は次にセネカから2箇所を引用する.

go on with the procession 《米口》続ける ▪ Don't let me interrupt you—*go on with the procession!* 君の話に僕を割りこませないで, 続けてくれ. ☞行列はアメリカの公生活での呼び物であるので go on のあとへくっつけたもの.

Go on with you. 《口》嘘つけ ▪ *Go on with you*, I know better than that! 嘘つけ, その手は食わぬぞ!

go* (*a person*) *one better →BETTER[1].

go out and about (病後)起きて出歩く ▪ I'm

glad that you can *go out and about.* あなたが(起きて)出歩けるのはうれしい.

go out like a light →LIGHT[1].

go out of *one's* ***way to*** *do* →WAY.

go (out) wilding 乱暴のかぎりをつくす; 羽目をはずす ▪It was not just poor young blacks who *went wilding.* 暴れまくったのは貧しい黒人の若者ばかりではなかった.

go (over, down) big [best, perfect] 《口》大当たりを取る; 大成功する ▪The concert *went over big.* 音楽会は非常な成功だった ▪The message *went down perfect* with the people. その教書は国民に非常に受けた.

go over the ground →GROUND[1].

go over the hill **1** (兵が)理由なく[無断]欠席する ▪Private Smith *went over the hill.* スミス上等兵は無断欠席した.

2 黙って姿を消す ▪He has *gone over the hill* with the payroll. 彼は全員の給料を奪って姿を消した.

go overboard →OVERBOARD.

go places →PLACE[1].

go postal →POSTAL.

go round [around] and round [around] **1** ぐるぐる回る ▪The wheels on the bus *go round and round.* バスの車輪はぐるぐるまわる.

2 (話が)堂々巡りする ▪Our talk *went round and round* for thirty minutes. 我々の話は30分間堂々巡りした.

go round [around] in circles 堂々巡りする ▪I have spent the whole morning *going round in circles* getting nowhere. 私は午前中堂々巡りして何の結果も得られなかった.

go round [around] the bend [twist] 《英口》気が狂う, 頭がおかしくなる; 頭にくる (→around the BEND; round the TWIST) ▪They *went around the bend* and grabbed a gun. 彼らは気がふれて銃をひっつかんだ ▪Father couldn't understand him sometimes and mother *went round the bend* with it all. 父はときどき彼の言うことがわからなくなり, 母はそれに憤慨していた.

go sixty [fifty, etc.***]*** 時速60[50, など]マイルで走る ▪We are *going sixty*, as we are. このとおり私たちは60マイル出しているんだ.

go so [as] far as to *do* …しさえもする ▪He *went so far as to* call me a fool. 彼は私をばかと呼びさえもした.

go south 《俗》悪化する, 下落する ▪As the economy *went south*, so did donations to charities. 経済が悪化するにつれて, 慈善事業への寄付も減った.

go steady →STEADY.

go this [that] far 《口》ここ[そこ]までやる, 度が過ぎる ▪I can't believe the cops *went this far.* 警官がここまでやるとは信じられない.

go through fire and water →FIRE[1].

go through *a person's* ***hands*** 人に取り扱われる ▪All these documents *go through his hands.* この書類はみな彼の取り扱いである.

go through *a person's* ***mind [head]*** …の胸に去来する ▪What was *going through my mind* is that I wanted to be there. 私が考えていたのは, そこにいたいということだった ▪Everything *went through my head.* あらゆる思いが頭を駆けめぐった.

go through *one's* ***paces*** 能力[技量, 腕前]を示す ▪The pair *went through their paces* for a television crew. そのペアはテレビの取材班に妙技を披露した.

go through the ceiling [roof] = HIT the ceiling.

go through the floor …の底が抜ける, 過去最低[最安値]になる ▪In Korea, the stock market *went through the floor*, and interest rates went through the ceiling. 韓国では株式市場は最安値を更新し, 金利は最高値を更新した.

go to (a lot of [a great deal of, much]) trouble (とても)苦労する, 骨を折る ▪Anthony *went to much trouble* to research his subject. アンソニーは彼の主題を研究するのに粉骨砕身した ▪I *went to a lot of trouble* for nothing. 骨折り損のくたびれもうけだった.

go to fetch (人)を迎えに行く; (もの)を取りに行く ▪She *went to fetch* her children at school. 彼女は学校に子供たちを迎えに行った.

go to it 《口》〚主に命令文で〛どんどんやる, 自分でやる《激励》 ▪If you have a good suggestion to give to the company, *go to it.* 会社に与える良い提案があるなら, どんどん言ってやりなさい.

go to Jericho [blazes, Hell, Hong-Kong, 《英》***Putney,*** 《英》***Bath]*** 〚主に命令文で〛うせやがれ!, どうとでもなれ! ▪She may *go to Hong-Kong* for me. 彼女がどうなったってかまやしない.

go to make …を作るのに役立つ ▪These qualities *go to make* a great man. これらの資質が偉人を作るのに役立つ.

go to *one's* ***place*** 死んで地獄へ行く (《聖》*Acts* 1. 25) ▪You'll die, and *go to your* own *place.* あなたは死ぬだろう. 死んで地獄へ行くだろう.

go to show →SHOW[2].

go to (the) bull [horse, cow, etc.***]*** (雌が)交尾する ▪What age do you think is best for the mare to *go to the horse*? 雌馬が交尾するのは何歳が一番よいと思いますか.

go under the name of →GO by the name of.

go under the plough [chain-saw, combine, mower, etc.***]*** 耕作[伐採, 農作業, 除草]される (→under the PLOW) ▪Their trees really do need to *go under the chain-saw.* その木々はどうしても伐採される必要がある ▪Jordan *went under the knife* to remedy a long-standing hip injury. ジョーダンは長患いの腰部損傷の治療のため手術を受けた.

go unheard **1** 聞きとれない ▪The cat's faint cries *went unheard.* その猫のかすかな鳴き声は聞きとれなかった.

2 無視される ▪His request *went unheard.* 彼の

依頼は無視された.

go up in smoke [***flames***] 焼ける, 炎上する; 消失する ▪ The whole building *went up in flames.* 建物が全部焼けてしまった ▪ The war caused his plans to *go up in smoke.* 戦争のため彼の計画は立ち消えとなった.

go well →WELL[2].

go west →WEST.

go where the wicked cease from troubling 悪い者がしいたげをやめる所へ行く; あの世へ行く (《聖》 *Job.* 3. 17) ▪ Hard by was the grave of our enemy, now *gone where the wicked cease from troubling.* すぐ近くには今はあの世へ行った我々の敵の墓があった.

go with a bang 《口》 = go with a SWING.

go with child [***calf, foal, young***] 人[牛, 馬, 動物]が妊娠して; が妊娠して何か月である ▪ The queen is several months *gone with child.* 女王は妊娠数か月である ▪ The mare *goes* about eleven months *with young.* その雌馬は妊娠11か月位だ.

go with the flow [***tide***] →FLOW[1], go with the TIDE.

go wrong →WRONG.

Go'er on! 《株式》 続けてやれ《同じ株を買い[売り]続けることを望む叫び声》.

Going! going! gone! 《競売》 さあ売れるぞ, 売れるぞ, そら売れた!

have been and *done*/ ***have*** (***been and***) ***gone and*** *done* →HAVE[2].

have been gone 留守をしている ▪ My son *has been gone* for a year now. せがれはもう1年も留守をしている.

have *a person* ***going there*** (***for a minute*** [***moment, while***]) (一瞬)人をだます[かつぐ] ▪ Oh man, they *had* me *going there for a minute.* やれやれ, やつらには一瞬かつがれるところだった.

have much [***a lot***] ***going for*** ...にとってたくさんの[多くの]利点[取り柄]がある ▪ The restaurant *had a lot going for* it but it didn't work. そのレストランには有利な点がたくさんあったが役に立たなかった.

have nothing going for ...にとって利点[取り柄]がない ▪ I'm afraid your proposal *has nothing going for* it. 君の提案はそれには資するところがないと思う.

Here goes! →HERE.

How goes (***it***)***?*** →HOW.

if you go to that その段となれば ▪ They look a deal prettier, *if you go to that.* きれいという段となれば, それらのほうがずっときれいだ. ☞If you come to that のほうが普通.

(***it***) ***goes without saying*** (***that***) →SAY[2].

let go **1** 放つ, 発射する ▪ He *let go* another arrow. 彼はもう1本の矢を放った.

2 打ち捨てる, 黙過する ▪ We *let* the plan *go.* 我々はその計画を捨てた ▪ It is a mistake, but *let* it *go.* それは誤りだが放っておきなさい.

3 解放する; 放出する; (つかまえている物を)放す ▪ The judge *let* the prisoner *go.* 判事は囚人を放免した ▪ *Let* me *go.* 放してください ▪ The oxygen of the acid *lets go* some heat. 酸の酸素は熱を放出する.

4 《海》 解き放つ, (いかりを)おろす ▪ They *let go* the mooring lines. 繋船の綱を解いた ▪ The ship *let go* her anchor in the Downs. 船はダウンズ停泊地にいかりをおろした.

5 解雇する ▪ I *let* my secretary *go.* 秘書を解雇した.

6 自由に進ませる ▪ We *let* the ship *go* and drove with the weather. 我々は船を自由に進ませて天候のまにまに走った.

7 やめる; 考えない ▪ *Let go* your boasting of your things. 自分のものの自慢はよしなさい.

8 自制を失う ▪ She *let go* and wailed for an hour. 彼女は自制を失って, 1時間も泣き叫んだ.

let *oneself* ***go*** →LET[2].

let go (*one's* ***hold***) ***of*** (つかまえている物)を放す ▪ *Let go of* my hand. 私の手を放してくれ.

let go with (演説など)をぶつ ▪ He *let go with* an attack upon the tactics of his opponent. 彼は相手のかけひきを攻撃した.

let it go →let GO 2.

let it go at that 《米口》 **1** それでよいことにする(説明・見積もり・結論など) ▪ Eleven will do as well as any other time; *let it go at that.* 11時ならどの時刻にも劣らずけっこうです. それでよいことにしましょう.

2 それはもう言わないことにする ▪ Very well, we will *let it go at that.* よろしい, そのことはもう言うまい.

like it's going out of fashion 《口》 →FASHION.

make things go 《口》 会や集まりを愉快にする; 事を成功させる ▪ Invite James to your party. He is sure to *make things go.* あなたの会にジェイムズを招きなさい. きっと会を愉快なものにしてくれるでしょう ▪ The new manager will certainly *make things go.* 今度の支配人はきっと事業を盛んにしてくれるさ.

must be going もう帰る[おいとまする]時です ▪ I *must be going.* 私はもうおいとまする時です.

not (***even***) ***go there*** 《口》 それには触れ(さえし)ない, これ以上話題に(さえ)しない ▪ If they'd lost this game—well, let's *not even go there.* もし彼らがこの試合に負けたら, いや, もう考えるのはよそう ▪ Does she have any children?—Please do*n't go there.* 彼女は子持ちかね?—それは聞かないでください.

Off *one* [***he, she, it***] ***goes!*** ぱっと出かける ▪ So *off* we *went* in my car. それで, 私たちは私の車でさっそうと出かけた.

so far as ... go →as FAR as ... go.

So it goes. 世の中そんなものだ.

that's how it goes = That's the way the COOKIE crumbles.

the report [***story, tale***] ***goes that*** ...という話が伝わっている, だそうだ ▪ *The story goes that* the government will resign shortly. 政府は近いうちに退くそうだ.

There you go. **1** その調子, よくやった ▪ *There*

you go. Say it twice. その調子. 2回言ってごらん.
2 ほら言っただろ, それごらん ▪ *There you go.* You lose again. ほらね. また君の負けだ.
3 はいどうぞ《相手に物を手渡すときの言葉》 ▪ Evan handed over her change. "*There you go* then." エバンはお釣りを手渡した.「はい, ではどうぞ.」
4 = There you GO again!

There you go again! またやった; また言った ▪ Don't talk too much.—*There you go* again. あまりしゃべり過ぎてはいけない—そらまた小言だ.

to go **1** 残されて ▪ His contract had six months *to go.* 彼の契約は期限がまだ6か月あった ▪ We had six miles *to go.* 我々はもう6マイル行かなければならなかった ▪ We have two months *to go* before the election. 選挙まであと2か月だ ▪ There are 175 days *to go* till the Olympic final. オリンピックの決勝まで175日だ.
2《俗》(レストランで食物が)持ち帰りの ▪ I ordered two sandwiches *to go.* 持ち帰り用のサンドイッチを二つ注文した.

to go [***be going***] ***on with*** さしあたり; まず ▪ Have you got any money with you?—Enough *to go on with.* お金の持ちあわせはありますか?—さしあたり十分あります ▪ Here's a glass of milk *to be going on with.* I'll give you something to eat later. さしあたりミルクが1杯あります. あとで何か食物をあげます.

What goes up must come down. 《諺》上がったものは落ちてくる,「山あれば谷あり」,「満つれば欠くる」.

What has gone of [***is gone with***]***...?*** ...はどうなったか; はどうしたのか ▪ *What's gone with* you? 君はどうしたの? ▪ *What has gone of* Mr. K.? K氏はどうなったのか.

What*(*ever*) *goes around comes around. 《諺》出たものは帰ってくる《「情けは人のためならず」や「因果応報」とは必ずしも一致しない》.

What's going down? 《主に米口》どうしたんだ (What's up?) ▪ *What's going down,* son?—Nothin'. I'll be okay, pop. どうしたんだね, お前?—べつに. 大丈夫だよ, パパ.

What's going on? 《口》どうしたのですか.

Where do I [***do we, does he***] ***go from here?*** 私[私たち, 彼]は次は何をしたらいいのか ▪ Tell me, *where do we go from here?* 言ってよ, 我々は次にどうしたらいいの? ▪ *Where does he go from here?* 彼は次にどうしたらいいのか?

Who goes (***there***)***?*** 誰だ!《歩哨の誰何(すいか)》 ▪ *Who goes?* Stand, or we fire. 誰だ! 止まらないと撃つぞ.

go-ahead /góʊəhèd/ 名形 ***get the go-ahead*** (***for***) (...への)前進命令[積極的支持, 許可]を得る ▪ His chances of *getting the go-ahead* are slim. 彼が許可を得る見込みは少ない.

give the go-ahead (***for***) (...への)前進命令[積極的支持, 許可]を与える ▪ *Give the go ahead for* the development of those movies. それらの映画の制作に積極的支持を与えてください.

goal /goʊl/ 名 ***a goal line stand*** ゴールライン前の強力な防御 ▪ *A goal line stand* by the home team held the visitors on the two-yard line. ホームチームによるゴールライン前の強力な防御がビジターチームを2ヤードラインに食い止めた.

an own goal 《英》**1** 自殺点, オウンゴール ▪ We have scored with three *own goals,* so luck has definitely been on our side. 我々は敵のオウンゴールで3点もらった. ツキは明らかに我々の側にあった.
2 自殺行為, 判断ミス ▪ The EU has scored some spectacular *own goals* in recent years, making life difficult for its own supporters. 欧州連合は, 近年いちじるしい判断ミスをいくつか犯して, 支持者の暮らしを困難にしてしまった.

get [***kick, score, take, win, make***] ***a goal*** ゴールを得る, ゴールにボールを入れる; 1点を得る ▪ You *scored a goal* when you said how young she looked. 彼女がほんとに若く見えると君が言ったとき, 君は1点かせいだ ▪ The ball was at Napoleon's foot; but he did not *make a goal.* ボールはナポレオンの足もとにあったが, 彼はそれをゴールに入れなかった.

move the goal 《米口》自分に好都合[相手に不利]になるように規則を不正に変える ▪ He is not honest and *moves the goal.* 彼は正直ではなく自分に有利に条件を勝手に変える ▪ Whenever we've done what our boss wants, he *moves the goal.* 上司の要求通りにしあげると, 彼は決まって更に高い要求を出す.

reach *one's* ***goal*** 目標を達成する ▪ UCLA has *reached its goal* of raising $1.2 billion in private donations more than two years ahead of schedule. UCLA は, 個人寄付を12億ドル集めるという目標を予定より2年以上早く達成した.

score an own goal 《英》**1**《サッカー》誤って味方のゴールに入れてしまう, 自殺点を入れる ▪ He *scored an own goal* when he had meant to clear the ball. 彼はボールをクリアーするつもりだったのに自殺点を入れてしまった.
2 ことが裏目に出る ▪ She *scored an own goal* when she reunited her adopted son with his real dad. 彼女は養子にした息子を実の父親に再会させたが, これが裏目に出た.

goalpost /góʊlpòʊst/ 名 ***move*** [***shift***] ***the goalposts*** (自分に都合よく)規則[条件, 政策, 目標]を変える (= move the GOAL) ▪ The Government has *moved the goalpost* again without prior notice to the Opposition. 政府はまたも野党に事前連絡なしに政策を変更した.

goat /goʊt/ 名 ***act the giddy goat*** = play the (giddy) GOAT.

be the goat 《米口》他人の罪を負う, 身代わりとなる (《聖》*Lev.* 16) ▪ I did so for no other reason than to *be the goat.* 私がそうしたのは, 他人の罪を負うためにほかならなかった.

get a person's goat 《俗》人を怒らせる, いらだたせる; 人を苦しめる ▪ The constant hammering *got his goat.* 不断のつち音が彼をいらだたせた ▪ It really *got my goat* when my family were forced to attend Fourth of July fireworks. 独立記念日の花火に家族が無理やり参加させられたときは全く頭にきた. ☞ < F prendre la chevre (乳ヤギ(貧乏人の唯一の乳の源)を奪う)から.

play the* (*giddy*) *goat 《口》 ばかなまねをする, 無責任な行動をする, むちゃをやる ▪ It is time you stopped *playing the giddy goat.* 君はもうばかなまねはやめるときだ.

ride the goat 《米口》 (秘密結社, 特に秘密共済結社に)入会を許される ▪ Harrison *rode the goat* last night at the monthly meeting of the Tammany Society. ハリスンは昨夜タマニ協会の月例会で入会した. ☞ 入会式に新会員が乗るヤギが秘密共済結社の集会所ごとに飼われていると信じられていることから.

separate the sheep and the goats → SHEEP.

G

go-between /góʊbɪtwìːn/ 名 ***act* [*serve*] *as* (*a*) *go-between*** 仲介役を務める (*in, for*) ▪ Egypt *acted as go-between in* the truce negotiations. エジプトは休戦交渉の仲介をした ▪ Leonardo will *serve as a go-between for* players and management. レオナルドが選手と経営側との仲介役として働くことになるだろう.

go-by /góʊbàɪ/ 名 ***get the* [*a*] *go-by*** 無視される, 知らぬふりをされる ▪ The measure will *get a go-by* from Congress. その法案は国会では無視されるだろう.

give the go-by 《口》 **1** 無視する, 軽蔑する; 知らぬふりをする; (困難などを)避ける ▪ I shall *give* the scheme *the go-by.* 私はその計画を無視します ▪ In two of the Latin versions the difficulty *is given the go-by.* 二つのラテン語版ではその難所は避けてある ▪ She *gave* me *the go-by* last night. 彼女は昨夜私を見て知らぬふりをした.

2 勝る, 出し抜く; 追い越す, 引き離す ▪ I *gave* him *the go-by* in a race. 私は競走で彼を追い越した.

god /gɑd|gɔd/ 名 ***a feast* [*dish*] (*fit*) *for the gods*** すばらしいごちそう《反語的にも》 ▪ Let's carve the lamb as *a feast for the gods.* すばらしいごちそうとして子羊を切り分けよう.

a God-given right 天与の権利 (*to do*) ▪ The Vatican said that bishops have *a God-given right to* ban books. バチカンは, 司教には禁書をする天与の権利があると言った.

a little tin god 地位ゆえに[おだてられて]いばっている小人 ▪ He is *a* real *little tin god.* 彼はほんとに地位ゆえにいばっている小人だ.

a sight for the gods すばらしい光景 ▪ The fierce scrimmage was *a sight for the gods.* その激しいもみ合いはすばらしい光景ではあった.

Ah* [*Oh, My, Good*] *God! なむさん!, ああ困った!, ああ悲しいかな!《強い感情・興奮を表す》 ▪ *Oh, God!* The tsunami has almost reached the shore! ああ, 大変! 津波がもうじき岸に押し寄せる!

among the gods 《口》 最上階[天井]さじき ▪ The only places I could get were *among the gods.* 私の入ることのできる場所は最上階さじきだけであった.

as God's my judge* [*witness*]/ *as God's above 神かけて, 確かに《厳粛な誓言》 ▪ *As God's my judge*, they should have killed him first. 神かけて彼らはまず彼を殺すべきだったのだ ▪ *As God's above*, I speak the truth. 神かけて私は真実を話す.

***as true as God/ as true as God is in heaven* [*above me*]** 絶対間違いない ▪ He swears that his teaching is *as true as God* Himself. 彼が誓って言うには, 彼の教えは絶対に正しいとのことだ.

be with God (死んで)神とともに[天国に]いる ▪ Susan *is with God.* スーザンは天国にいる.

before God 神かけて ▪ *Before God*, Kate, I cannot look green. ケイトさん, 私はどうしても若々しい顔になれません.

***by God* (*above*)** 神かけて, きっと ▪ *By God*, I never observed it. 神かけて, 私は断じてそれを見なかった.

***by* [*with*] *God's blessing* [*help, assistance*]** 神の恵み[神助]により ▪ Yes, verily; and *by God's help* so I will. ほんとうにそうです. そして神助により私はそうしましょう.

by God's grace →GRACE.

***by guess* (*and by God*)** →GUESS[1].

depart to God 死んで昇天する ▪ Thomas *departed to God.* トマスは昇天した.

food for the gods =a feast (fit) for the GODs.

***for God's sake* [*love*]** 後生だから, お願いだから; ほんとに, 何てことだ! ▪ *For God's sake*, will you stop rattling the spoons? お願いだから, スプーンをがちゃがちゃいわせるのはよしてよ.

God almighty =Ah GOD!

God be thanked! →THANK God!

God bless. ごきげんよう, さようなら《人と別れるときのあいさつ》 ▪ Good night, *God bless.* おやすみなさい, ごきげんよろしゅう. ☞ bless は仮定法.

(*God*) *bless his soul* [*heart*]! 《口》 →BLESS a person's heart (alive)!

(*God*) *bless* [*save*] *me* [*my life, my soul*]! おやっ!, これは大変!《驚きを表す》 ▪ *God bless my soul!* Who would have thought you would come? おやおや! きみが来るとは夢にも思わなかったよ.

God bless you! →BLESS.

God damn you* [*him, it,* etc.]*! こんちくしょう! ▪ *God damn you*, McCloy, what have you done with my papers? こんちくしょう! マクロイ, 私の書類をどうしたんだ.

God damn your* [*his, her,* etc.] *eyes! 《卑》 こんちくしょう!《怒り, 憎しみを表す》 ▪ I hate you all. *God damn your eyes!* おれはお前たちが大嫌いだ. ちくしょうめ!

God forbid* (*that ...*)*! →FORBID.

God have mercy! 《口》 おやまあ!《驚き・恐怖を表す》.

God helps those who help themselves. 《諺》 天は自ら助ける者を助ける.

God in heaven! おやまあ! これは大変!《驚き・ショックを表す》 ▪ Dear *God in heaven*, Jane, what's happened to you? おやまあ, ジェイン, どうしたの.

God knows →KNOW[2].

God love it! 《俗》ほんとに ▪ *God love it*, so it was! ほんとにそうでした.

God preserve us! →PRESERVE

God rest him [his soul] 《英》彼の霊安かれ《死者の名が出たときつけ加える句》 ▪ My father, *God rest his soul*, had never scolded me. 父は, その霊安かれ, 私をしかったことはありませんでした.

God Save the King [Queen]! →SAVE[2].

God sides with the strongest. 神は最も強い者に味方する《強者は武運が強い》.

God takes soonest those he loveth best. 《諺》神に愛されしもの若くして逝きぬ. ☞しばしば碑文に書かれる.

God tempers the wind to the shorn lamb. 《諺》弱い者には吹く風も柔らか.

God willing (and the creek don't rise) 天意にかなえば, 事情が許せば《don't は仮定法》 ▪ I'll be back on Wednesday, *God willing*. 何事もなければ私は水曜日に帰る. ☞[L] deo volente のなぞり.

God's gift (to) **1** 神からの贈り物, 天の恵み; 思いがけぬ幸運 (= godsent) ▪ Vladimir Nabokov was *God's gift to* 20th-century literature. ウラジーミル・ナボコフは20世紀の文学にとって天恵だった. **2**《皮肉》(才能・人気があると思っている)うぬぼれや (→ think one is GOD's gift to women) ▪ Manny thinks he is *God's gift to* baseball. マニーは自分は野球の申し子だと思っている ▪ This guy thinks he is *God's gift to* womankind. この男は女性にもてると思っている.

God's in his heaven; all's right with the world. 《諺》神空にしろしめす, すべて世はこともなし. ☞Robert Browning, *Pippa's Song* から.

God's own 《口》大きな ▪ The government's proposal to increase taxes caused *God's own* fuss. 増税計画を政府が出したために大騒動になった.

Good God! →Ah GOD!

If God did not exist, it would be necessary to invent Him. 《諺》神がいないのなら, 神を作ることが必要だろう《神がいてもいなくても祈ることは必要だ; 自分の運命は自分で切り開くものだ》. ☞Voltaire の言葉.

if God will =GOD willing (and the creek don't rise).

In God we trust. 《米》我々は神を信頼する《アメリカの全ての現行硬貨に刻まれている銘》 ▪ The motto "*In God we trust*" is engraved upon all American coins.「我々は神を信頼する」という銘がすべてのアメリカの硬貨に刻まれている.

in God's good time =in good TIME 1.

in God's name 〚疑問詞を強めて〛一体全体 ▪ What *in God's name* are you doing with that pizza? 一体全体君はそのピザをどうしようとしてるんだ? ▪ Just who *in God's name* is protecting our children? 一体全体誰が我々の子供を保護しているのか?

in the lap of the gods →LAP[1].

make a god of …を極端に崇拝する ▪ He *makes a god of* money. 彼は極端に金を崇拝する.

Man proposes, but God disposes. →MAN[1].

My [Oh] God →Ah GOD!

on God's earth 地球上に《on earth を強めた形》 ▪ He is found nowhere *on God's earth*. 彼は地上のどこにも見つからない.

out of God's blessing into the warm sun 良い状勢から悪い状勢へ ▪ Pray God they bring us not *out of God's blessing into the warm sun*. 彼らが我々を良い状勢から悪い状勢へ陥れぬよう神に祈ってくれ.

play God/play at pretending to be God 神のごとくふるまう, 全能であろうとする, お山の大将になろうとする ▪ "We do not have the right to *play God*," the letter to the President said.「我々には神の如くふるまう権利はない」と大統領宛の手紙にあった.

play to the Gods =play to the GALLERY.

please God **1**〚文頭で〛神様お願いです ▪ *Please God*, save us. 神よお願いです, 我々をお救いください. **2**〚文末で〛神のおぼしめしならば, うまくいけば ▪ May we meet again in Paradise, *please God*. 神のおぼしめしならば, また天国で会いましょう. ☞please は仮定法現在.

see the finger [hand] of God in 《古風》…を神のみわざと信じる ▪ Many of the soldiers *saw the hand of God in* their victory. 兵士の多くは自分たちの勝利は神のみわざだと信じた.

Thank God! →THANK[2].

The gods send nuts to those who have no teeth. 《諺》神は歯がなくなったものに堅果を贈る, 遅すぎた幸運.

There but for the Grace of God go I. →GRACE.

There is a God! 《口・戯》神様はいるんだ ▪ My worst enemy died yesterday. *There is a God!* 宿敵がきのうくたばった. 神様って本当にいるんだ!

think one is God's gift to women 《戯》自分は女性にもてるとうぬぼれる (→GOD's gift (to) 2) ▪ He *thinks* he *is God's gift to women*, and can't end a conversation with a woman without touching her somewhere. 彼は女性にもてるとうぬぼれているので, 女性と話をすれば必ず体のどこかにさわる.

to God [goodness, Heaven] 神に, 心から〚hope, wish などの動詞を伴って強調を表す〛 ▪ I *wish to God* I'd never come here. 全くこんなところには来なければよかった ▪ I *hope to God* he wins it. 彼が勝つことを心から願う.

under God 神について, 誰よりも ▪ *Under God* only Dickens could have created him. 神について, ディケンズだけが彼を創造することができただろう ▪ Yet, *under God*, I will do him some good. でも私は誰よりも, あの人のためには尽くすつもりです.

Whom the gods love die young. 《諺》神の愛する人は若死にする,「才子短命」. ☞ラテン語諺より.

with God's blessing [***help, assistance***] → by GOD's blessing.

Ye gods (***and little fishes***)***!*** これは大変《英雄詩をまねた驚き》 ▪ O *ye gods! ye gods!* Must I endure all this? おお神々よ! わたしはこんなことまで耐えなければならないのか (cf. Sh., *Jul. Caes.* 4. 3. 41).

godfather /gάdfὰːðər/ 名 ***stand godfather*** (***to***) (…の)名うけ親となる ▪ He *stood godfather to* my children. 彼は私の子供の名うけ親となってくれた.

God-speed /gάdspíːd|gɔ́d-/ 名 ***at the back of God-speed*** 世界の果てに ▪ I left him *at the back of God-speed.* 私は彼を世界の果てに残した.

bid [***wish***] *a person* ***God-speed*** 人に(旅・事業の)成功を祈る ▪ Everyone seems to *bid* us *God-speed!* 全ての人が我々に道中の安全を祈っているようだ.

going /góʊɪŋ/ 動名 ***be going*** *doing* …するつもりである ▪ I'*m going fighting* for England. イギリスのために戦うつもりだ.

(***be***) ***going*** (***in, of***) 次の誕生日で…になるところで(ある) ▪ He *is going in* eighteen. 彼は次の誕生日で18歳になるところです.

(***be***) ***going on*** (年齢・時刻が)に近い ▪ He is five, *going* (*on*) six. 彼はもうじき6歳になる.

(***be***) ***going on for*** (年齢・時刻が)…に近づいて(いる) ▪ It *is going on for* 4. もう4時に近い.

be going to *do* **1** …するだろう《未来》 ▪ I believe he *is going to* be rich one day. 彼はいつか金持ちになると思う.

2 …する《予定》 ▪ I *am going to* visit him tomorrow. あす彼を訪ねます ▪ Mother *is going to* go to the concert tonight. 母は今夜音楽会に行く.

3 …しそうである《見込み》 ▪ We *are going to* have a storm. あらしになりそうだ ▪ There *is going to* be a business depression this year. 今年は不景気になりそうだ.

4 まさに…しようとしている ▪ I *was* just *going to* get in. 私はちょうど入ろうとしているところだった.

5 …するつもりである ▪ I *am going to* take the exam. 私はその試験を受けるつもりです ▪ I *was going to* come, but I couldn't. 来るつもりだったが, 来られなかった.

6 …するのだ《命令》 ▪ You'*re going to* do as I tell you. 君は私の言う通りにするのだ.

coming and going →COMING.

enough [***something***] ***to be going on with*** 《英》当面は十分である, 当座しのぎになる ▪ What we have now is more than *enough to be going on with.* 我々は現在もっているもので当面は十分だ ▪ Not really enough, but *something to be going on with.* 本当は十分ではないが, 当座しのぎにはなる.

find… heavy going …はする[進む]のが難しい ▪ This is a good book, but I am *finding* it *heavy going.* これは良い本だが, なかなか読み進めない.

get a thing going 《口》うまくやる, よろしくやる ▪ You two have *got a thing going.* 君たち二人はよろしく[ねんごろに]したな ▪ He's *got a thing going* with his company. 彼は会社をうまく経営してきた.

good going **1** 早い[すばらしい]旅; 急速な[すばらしい]進歩 ▪ *Good going*! いいぞ, よくやった ▪ An average of 50 miles an hour is *good going.* 時速平均50マイルというのは早旅です ▪ You've made *good going* in your language study. 君は語学の研究にすばらしい進歩をとげた.

2《英口》〚主に叙述的〛いつも以上[予想以上]の出来 (= not bad going) ▪ Third place was *good going* for Walker. 3位はウォーカーとしては上出来だった.

one ***has a lot*** [***nothing***] ***going for*** 《口》…には利点がたくさんある[少しもない] ▪ I *have a lot* [*everything*] *going for* me in getting the job. その職を得るのに私には多くの利点がある[全ての点で有利だ].

have a good thing going うまくいっている, 儲かっている (*with*) ▪ I *have a good thing going with* Eddie. 私はエディーとうまくいっている ▪ Dell seems to *have a good thing going* with a more direct-sales-oriented model. デル社はより直販用のモデルで儲かっているようだ.

have a lot [***something, nothing,*** etc.] ***going for*** …にとって良いこと[有利な点]がたくさんある[いくらかある, 全くない] ▪ The lad *has a lot going for* him. その若者には優れたところがたくさんある ▪ Smoking *has nothing going for* it. 喫煙は百害あって一利なしだ.

have *a person* ***going*** 人を怒らせる ▪ I really *had* him *going.* 私はほんとに彼を怒らせた.

have something [*a thing*] ***going*** 《口》恋愛[性的]関係にある (*with*) ▪ The cop used to *have something going with* Jackie. その警官は以前ジャッキーと関係があった.

heavy going (本が)難解な ▪ I found Kant's Critique of Pure Reason (to be) very *heavy going.* 読んでみてカントの「純粋理性批判」は至極難解だとわかった.

keep going **1** (生活・活動を)続ける ▪ How does the old man *keep going*? その老人はどんな風に暮らしているの? ▪ The firm will *keep going* at least for 10 years. その会社は少なくとも10年は続くだろう.

2 (生活・活動を)続けさせる ▪ She *kept* the conversation *going.* 彼女は会話がとぎれないようにした.

there is a lot [***nothing***] ***going for*** = one has a lot GOING for.

When [***If***] ***the going gets tough, the tough get going.*** 《諺》状況が厳しくなると, 強者が活躍する,「家貧しくして孝子顕(あら)わる」. ☞tough = 'difficult'; the tough = 'the tough people'.

while the going is good 《口》足もとが明るいうちに; 状況が悪くならないうちに ▪ You may be arrested any minute. My advice is go *while the going's good.* 君はいつ逮捕されるかしれない. 私の忠告は,「形勢の良いうちに立ち去れ」である.

going(-)over /gòʊɪŋóʊvər/ 名 ***give** a person* ***a (good) going over*** **1** 人を徹底的に調べる ▪ The police *gave* the suspect *a good going over*. 警察は容疑者を徹底的に調べた.
2 人をひどく打つ; 人をひどくしかる ▪ Someone *gave* her *a* mean *going-over*. 誰かが彼女をひどくしかった.

receive [get] a (good) going-over **1** 徹底的な検討[取り調べ]を受ける ▪ The report had *received a going-over* from the American delegation. その報告はアメリカ代表団から徹底的に調べられた.
2 ひどく打たれる; ひどくしかられる ▪ I *got a good going-over* in the morning. 朝ひどくしかられた.

gold /goʊld/ 名 ***a gold digger*** 金品目あてに男をたらしこむ女性 ▪ His estranged wife was *a gold-digger*. 彼の別居した妻は金目当てに結婚していた.

a heart of gold 思いやりある広い心(の人), 高貴な広い心(の人) ▪ The King is *a heart of gold*. 国王は高貴な心の人である ▪ All my friends have *hearts of gold*. 私の友人はみな思いやりある広い心の持主である. ☞ F un cœur d'or のなぞり.

All that glitters [glistens, 《英》 ***glisters] is not gold./All is not gold that glitters [glisters, glistens].*** 光るものがすべて金とはかぎらない《外見に惑わされてはならない》.

(as) good as gold 《口》 **1** (子供が)まことにおとなしい, 行儀がよい《この意味では最初の as が落ちることが多い》 ▪ Little Jim behaved *as good as gold*. ジム少年はまことに行儀がよかった ▪ John was *good as gold* as a kid. ジョンは子供のころよい子だった.
2 全く善良で信頼できる, 申し分なく良質で ▪ She is *as good as gold*. 彼女は全く立派で信頼できる人です ▪ This is *as good as gold*. これは申し分なく優秀である ▪ Despite being 18 years old the car was *as good as gold*. 18年目だが, その車は百点満点だった.

be like gold/ 《英》 ***be like gold dust*** 《口》 稀少で貴重である ▪ Good carpenters *are like gold dust* these days. 名大工は近頃は少なくて貴重である.

be sitting on a gold mine →GOLD MINE.

be worth** one's [it's]* ***weight in gold →one's WEIGHT in gold.

black gold 石油 ▪ Endless barrels of *black gold* flowed from the wells and he became a millionaire, almost overnight. 石油が油井から際限なくあふれ出て, ほとんど一晩で, 彼は大金持ちになった.

go for gold (オリンピックなどで) 金メダルを目指す ▪ Giannini *went for gold*, got a silver—and that was a pretty good effort. ジャンニーニは金メダルを目指し, 銀を得た. なかなか立派な結果だ.

go gold 大ヒットする; (ソフトウェアが) CD の生産に入る ▪ The album *went gold* and peaked in the Top 20. そのアルバムは大ヒットし, ピーク時にはトップ20に入った ▪ The most recent version of SUSE Linux *went gold* in July. SUSE リナックスの最新版が7月に CD でリリースされた.

go off gold 金本位制を廃止する ▪ England *went off gold*. イギリスは金本位制を廃止した.

hit the gold 金的を当てる ▪ The Thai sharpshooters *hit the gold* at the world championships. 世界選手権大会でタイの射撃の名選手が金的を射止めた[金メダルを取った].

in gold 金貨で; 金で ▪ Will you have the money *in gold*? お金を金貨であげましょうか ▪ He works *in gold*. 彼は金細工師である.

like liquid gold 金銀財宝のように(貴重で, 光沢があって) ▪ Breast milk is *like liquid gold* because it has such amazing properties. 母乳はそのような驚くべき特徴を備えているので, まるで魔法の飲み物のようだ.

make a gold 標的の中心を射る ▪ The lady *made* the most *golds* at archery. その貴婦人は弓術で最も多くの金的を射た.

sell** a person* ***a gold brick 《米》 人をぺてんにかける, 人に詐欺を働く ▪ Who ever heard of their *selling* him *a gold brick*? 彼らが彼に詐欺を働いたなんて聞いた者がいるのだろうか.

shine like pure gold 金色に輝く ▪ The sun *shone like pure gold*. 太陽は金色に輝いた.

strike gold 《口》 **1** 金鉱を掘り当てる; 金持ちになる ▪ Do you love the girl? —Yes, this time I've *struck gold*. 君はその娘(こ)を愛しているのか?—うん, こんどこそ金鉱を掘り当てたんだ ▪ He *struck gold* investing in safe bonds. 彼は安全な債券に投資して金持ちになった.
2 金メダルを獲得する ▪ The United States *struck gold* today in Olympic track. きょう米国はオリンピックのトラック種目で金メダルを獲得した.

the pot [crock] of gold at the end of the rainbow 「虹の端の金の壷」, いくら探求しても得られない富[報酬]. ☞ 虹の端にあたる地面を掘れば, 金の壷が見つかるという伝説から.

there's gold in them there [thar].... 《戯》 そこの...には金が埋まっている, は儲けになる ▪ As a miner might have said, *there's gold in them there* phones. 鉱夫の言い方ならば, 電話機には金が埋まっているのだ ▪ *There's gold in them thar* databases. データベースには宝が埋まっている. ☞ thar 《北英》 = there.

think gold dust of ...を非常に重んじる ▪ He *thinks gold dust of* me. 彼は私を実に重くみている.

treat ... like gold ...を非常に丁重に扱う, 大事に世話をする ▪ They've *treated* me *like gold* and I want to thank them for their hospitality. 彼らは私をとても大事に扱ってくれたので, その歓待に感謝したい.

golden /góʊldən/ 形 ***a golden boy [girl]*** 人気者, 寵児 ▪ Jones was the former *golden boy* of track. ジョーンズはトラック競技の人気選手だった.

a golden handshake (社長・理事・重役ら幹部などへの通例高額の)退職金 ▪ The former chief executive Warner will receive *a golden handshake* worth about $3,000,000. 前最高経営責任者のウォーナーは約300万ドル相当の高額退職金を受けとるだろう ▪ The reward for dismissal was *a golden handshake* of three years' pay. 解雇の報酬は

給料３年分の退職一時金だった．

a golden oldie 昔人気のあった人[物]; 昔ヒットした歌[レコード]，懐メロ ▪ He still sings the *golden oldies*. 彼はいまでも懐メロを歌う．

***a golden parachute* [*handshake*]** (企業買収時に失職した経営者に失職する補償として支払う多額の)特別退職金(を支払う契約)，ゴールデンパラシュート ▪ Thus, directors may benefit from *a "golden parachute."* こうして，取締役たちはゴールデンパラシュートのおかげで得をするかもしれない ▪ Mr. Smith was offered *a golden parachute* for having to leave his job. スミス氏にはやむなく辞職するにあたって特別退職金が支給された．

***climb the golden stairs* [*staircase*]** 《米》なき数に入る ▪ The company has *climbed the golden stairs*. その協会はつぶれた．

golden handcuffs →HANDCUFF.

Speech is silver(n), silence is golden. 《諺》雄弁は銀であり，沈黙は金である．

the golden age →AGE.

The golden bowl is broken. →BOWL[1].

the golden rule 黄金律 (《聖》*Matt.* 7. 12の教訓「自分がしてもらいたいように他人にしてあげなさい」を指す); (ある分野における)最善の教訓 ▪ My dear boy, have you not learned *the golden rule*? おまえは黄金律を学んでいないのか ▪ Be patient. That's *the golden rule* in politics. 辛抱せよ．これが政界での黄金律である．

win golden opinions →OPINION.

goldfish /góʊldfìʃ/ 名 ***in a goldfish bowl*** →BOWL[1].

gold mine /góʊldmàɪn/ 名 ***be sitting on a gold mine* [*fortune*]** 《口》金鉱の上にいる; (自分では気うかずに)莫大な価値のあるもの[宝の山]を所有している ▪ She has a lot of his paintings, so she *is sitting on a fortune*. 彼女には彼の絵がたくさんあり，宝の山をもっているようなものだ ▪ Owning land here means he's *sitting on a gold mine*. ここに土地を持っているということは，彼は宝の山を所持しているということだ．

golf /gɑlf|gɔlf/ 名 ***a golf widow*** 《口》ゴルフウィドウ《ゴルフをするため留守がちな夫を持つ妻》 ▪ Susan said she suffered the loneliness of *a golf widow*. スーザンは自分はゴルフウィドウの寂しさに耐えていると言った．

eyes look* [*are*] *like golf balls 大きな目をしている，目を見開いている ▪ His *eyes* were so purple and swollen, they *looked like golf balls*. 彼の両目は紫色に腫れており，まるでゴルフボールのようだった．

play at golf ゴルフをやる ▪ We *played at golf*. 我々はゴルフをした．

golly /gáli|gɔ́li/ 名 ***By* [*My*] *golly!*** 《口》おやおや!，実に《驚き・強調など》 ▪ *By golly*, they will have us for breakfast. ほんとに彼らは我々を朝食用に食べるだろう． ☞golly＝God.

gone /gɔːn|gɔn/ 形 ***a gone case*** もうだめなこと ▪ He felt it was *a gone case* with him. 彼はもう万事休すと思った．

all gone (使い果たして)なくなった，払底した; 終わった ▪ The money was *all gone* in a week. お金は１週間で底をついた ▪ The tickets are *all gone* for the holidays. 休日のチケットはみな売り切れた．

(*be*) *far gone* **1** (病が)大いに進んで (*in*) ▪ He *is far gone in* consumption. 彼は肺病がひどく進んでいる．

2 深くはまり込んで，深くふけって (*in*) ▪ She *was far gone in* love. 彼女は恋に夢中であった ▪ He *is far gone in* the affair. 彼は事件に深くはまり込んでいる．

3 疲れ切って ▪ Two horses *were far gone*. ２頭の馬はへとへとに疲れていた．

4 ひどく古くなって ▪ This table *is far gone*. このテーブルは古ぼけている．

5 (気が狂うか，酔って)精神がもうろうとしている ▪ He *was far gone* when he came to the party. 彼がパーティーに来た時は前後不覚に酔っていた．

be gone **1** (素早く)去る ▪ Come, let's *be gone*. さあ，さっさと帰ろう．

2 …を越した，過ぎた ▪ He *is* just *gone* 20. 彼は20歳を越したばかりだ．

(*be*) *gone in* **1** …にはまり込んで[ふけって](いる) ▪ He *is gone in* love. 彼は恋に夢中だ ▪ She *is gone in* wickedness. 彼女は悪行にふけっている．

2 《米口》すっかり疲れて(いる) ▪ I feel all *gone in*. 私はすっかり疲れた気分だ．

be gone off 《米口》すたれる，はやらなくなる ▪ They *are* a little *gone off* these days. それらはこの頃は少しすたれた．

(*be*) *gone on* 《英口》…にほれこんで(いる) ▪ He must have *been* terribly *gone on* the woman. 彼はその女性にぞっこんほれこんでいたにちがいない ▪ They seem to *be* quite *gone on* the culture of the people. 彼らはその国民の文化にぞっこんのようだ．

(*be*) *gone up* 《米》(作物が)日照りでやけてしまう ▪ Some fields *are gone up*. 日照りでやけてしまった畑もある．

gone but not forgotten 《陳腐》過ぎ去った[死んだ]がまだ記憶に残って ▪ You are *gone but not forgotten*. We love you, Darryl. 君は逝ったが記憶の中に生きている．私たちは君を愛しているよ，ダリル．

gone dis **1** 《軍》精神薄弱になって，気がふれて ▪ I believe he has *gone dis*. 彼は気が狂ったのだと思う．

2 《口》(機械などが)故障する，狂う ▪ The machine has *gone dis*. 機械が故障した． ☞dis＝disconnected「電線などが切れて」.

(*have*) *gone on* 《婉曲》死んで ▪ We will be with Jesus, and we will be with those who *have gone on* before us. 私たちはイエスとともにあり，先に逝った人たちとともにあるだろう．

it is* [*has*] *gone midnight [etc.] 《英》真夜中[など]過ぎである ▪ *It has* just *gone ten*. ちょうど10時過ぎだ．

gong /gɔːŋ|gɔŋ/ 名 ***be all gong and no dinner*** ＝be all MOUTH and trousers.

kick the gong around アヘン[マリファナ]を吸う

▪ Everyone knows that "*kicking the gong around*" is smoking opium. 誰でも知っているように，"kicking the gong around" とはアヘンを吸うことである ▪ That's where they have their parties and *kick the gong around*. そこが彼らがパーティーを開いてマリファナを吸う場所だ.

good /gʊd/ 形 名 ***a fat lot of good*** 《皮肉》大層な役立ち ▪ *A fat lot of good* will it do me. それは私にはずいぶん役に立つことでしょう《「あまり役立たない」の意》.

a good for nothing ろくでなし，ごくつぶし ▪ He was *a* handsome *good for nothing*. 彼は美男のろくでなしだった.

a good half of …の半分より少し多く ▪ He took *a good half of* it. 彼はそれを半分より少し多く取った.

a good nature 善良な性質，よい気立て，温厚さ; 好人物 ▪ He has *a good nature* and is easy to work with. 彼は気だてがよいのでいっしょに仕事をしやすい.

a good one 《俗》〚shock, scare などを伴って〛ひどく，すごく ▪ I got *shocked a good one* and that was the last time I tried to plug anything in. ひどくビリっときて，それ以来何かをコンセントにつなごうとしたことはない ▪ I got *scared a good one* though. でもすっごく怯えちゃった.

a good time **1** 相当長い時間 ▪ It took me *a good time* to get there. そこへ着くのにかなり長くかかった.
2 愉快なとき ▪ We went to the theater and had *a good time* together. 我々は劇場に行っていっしょに楽しく過ごした.

(*a*) *good-time Charlie* [*Charley*] 陽気な楽天家，遊び好きな男，道楽者 ▪ He was *a good-time Charlie*, but he did live by a personal code. 彼は愉快な男ではあったが，個人的な規範に従って生きていた ▪ His nickname, given for hard drinking, was *Good Time Charlie*. 彼のあだ名は，大酒飲みだったので，飲んだくれ飲み助だった. ☞大文字表記で固有名詞扱い.

a good way →a long WAY (off).

all in good time. →in good TIME 1.

all to the good →to the GOOD.

as good as **1** …であるも同然で，と言わぬばかり ▪ If he gets hold of me, I am *as good as* dead. もし彼が私をつかまえたら私は死んだも同然です ▪ He *as good as* said so. 彼はそう言ったも同然だった.
2 …と同じほどよい ▪ This is *as good as* that. これはあれと同じほどよい.

as good as a play →PLAY[1].

as good as one's bond 信用できる ▪ His word is *as good as his bond*. 彼の約束は信用できる.

as good as done 終わったも同然で，ほとんど完了して ▪ The deal is *as good as done*. その取引はまとまったも同然だ.

as good as good 《口》きわめてよい ▪ I resolve to be just *as good as good*! 私はほんとにきわめてよい人間になろうと決心しているんだ!

as good as it gets **1** これ以上ないほど優れている，最高にすばらしい ▪ Canada is *as good as it gets* and every immigrant knows it. カナダは最高にすばらしい. 移住者はみんなそれがわかっている.
2 (状況が)これ以上よくなる見込みがない，これが限界だ ▪ This is *as good as it gets* and this is the end. これが限界で，これで終わりだ ▪ That was about *as good as it got* for Johnson. ジョンスンにとってほぼこれ以上よくならなかった.

as good as they make them →MAKE[2].

as good (for) 《口》(…に)よいことで ▪ By the powers, Tom Morgan, it's *as good for* you! トム・モーガン，ほんとにそれは君にはよいことだよ!

be after no good いたずらにふけっている; よからぬ事をたくらんでいる ▪ He *is after no good*. 彼はよからぬ事をたくらんでいる.

be any [some] good 《口》〚any は疑問文・否定文・条件文に用いる〛いくらか役に立つ ▪ Your feeling will *be some good*. あなたのフィーリングはいくらか役に立つだろう ▪ If it *is any good*, I will take it. もしいくらかでも役に立つならそれをもらいましょう ▪ *Is* it *any good* trying such a thing? そんなことをして何か役に立つのか.

be as good as ... as any 《口》(最善ではないが)なかなかの…である ▪ I guess now's *as good as* a time *as any*. 今が潮時だと思う ▪ This spa *is as good as* a place *as any*. この温泉はなかなかおすすめの場所である.

be as good as one's word →WORD.

Be good! 《米口・戯》気をつけてね，しっかりしてね《別れのあいさつ》(→If you can't be GOOD, be careful) ▪ Bye. *Be good*!—See you next week. じゃあ，気をつけてね—また来週.

be good at …がじょうずである ▪ He *is good at* figures [golf, telling a story]. 彼は計算[ゴルフ，話をするの]がじょうずだ.

be good enough to do …してくれる; 親切にも…する ▪ Will you *be good enough to* get me that magazine? あの雑誌を取ってくださいませんか? ▪ They *were good enough to* take me with them. 彼らは親切にも私を連れて行ってくれた.

(*be*) *good for* **1** …に効く; によい ▪ Oil *is good for* burns. 油はやけどに効く ▪ It *is good for* the health to take a walk in the morning. 朝散歩するのは健康によい.
2 (名前が)…だけの信用がある ▪ His name *is good for* £1,000. 彼の名前は1,000ポンドの信用がある《手形などで》.
3 …の額である ▪ The draft *is good for* £1,000. その手形は1,000ポンドの額である.
4 (人が)…の支払い能力がある，進んで払う ▪ He *is good for* £1,000. 彼は1,000ポンド支払える.
5 …ができる; だけ生きられる，もつ[続く] ▪ *Are* you *good for* a ten miles' walk? あなたは10マイル歩くことができるのか ▪ He *is good for* another twenty years. 彼はもう20年生きられる ▪ The horse *is good for* five years' service. その馬は5年は使える.

G

6 …の役に立つ ▪ What *is* he *good for*? 彼は何ができるのか.
7 …に有効である, 産出しうる ▪ This ticket *is good for* every amusement on the island. このチケットは島でのすべての娯楽に有効である.
(be) good for nothing 役に立たない; ろくでなしで ▪ He's *good for nothing*. 彼はろくでなしだ ▪ These *are good for nothing* clippings. これは役に立たない切れ端だ.
be good for you ためになる《you は一般的で意味がない》 ▪ *Are* the pills *good for you* if you have a headache? その丸薬は頭痛に効きますか.
be good in …がじょうずである ▪ He *is good in* English. 彼は英語がうまい.
***be good of** a person **to** do* …してくれてありがとう ▪ It *was* very *good of* you *to* help me. 助けてくださって非常にありがとうございました.
be good to go 《口》順調である, 大丈夫である ▪ Trainer Todd Hutcheson felt Bochy *was good to go*. トレーナーであるトッド・ハッチスンはボッチは大丈夫だと思った.
be good with (扱い)がじょうずである ▪ He *is good with* a rifle. 彼は射撃がうまい.
be good with** one's **hands 手仕事[手工]がうまい ▪ He *is* particularly *good with his hands*. 彼は特に手仕事がうまい.
be in good company →COMPANY.
be [get] in good with 《口》…の気に入りである[に気に入られる] ▪ The boy would *get in good with* the teacher. 少年は先生に気に入られるだろう.
be no good/not be any good 《口》役に立たない, むだである; だめである ▪ He *is no good* for anything. 彼はろくでなしだ ▪ I *am no good* about names. 私は名前を覚えることは全くだめです ▪ It *is no good* talking. 話してもむだである ▪ I'*m not any good* at parking and I've been driving a car for years. 駐車は全く下手だ, 何年も車に乗っているのに.
be on to a good thing 《口》うまくいっている, 成功している (*with*) ▪ Game makers say Nintendo *is on to a good thing*. ゲーム制作者たちの言によると任天堂は順調だ ▪ He thinks he *is on to a good thing with* that state scholarship. 彼はその州の奨学金はうまくいくと思っている.
be some good →be any GOOD.
be too good for… あまりにも良すぎて…にはもったいない ▪ I think my girlfriend *is too good for* me. 僕のガールフレンドは素晴らしすぎて僕にはもったいない.
be too good to miss [turn down] とても魅力があって断れない ▪ The money *was too good to turn down*. その金はとてもありがたくて断りきれなかった.
be up to no good **1** =be after no GOOD.
2 《米》何の役にも立たない ▪ He *is up to no good*. 彼は何の役にも立たない.
3 《口》よからぬこと[悪事, いたずら]をたくらんでいる[している] ▪ Some Iranians *are up to no good* with uranium. イラン人にはウラニウムでよからぬことをたくらんでいる者もいる ▪ She couldn't let go of her suspicion that he *was up to no good*. 彼がよからぬことをたくらんでいるのではないかという疑いを彼女は捨てることができなかった.
***bid [give]** a person **good day [morning, evening, night,** etc.]* 人にこんにちは[おはよう, 今晩は, おやすみなさい]とあいさつする ▪ They *gave* him *good day* when they met him in the street. 彼らは通りで彼に会ってこんにちはとあいさつした ▪ He *bade* a cheerful *good night* to me. 彼は快活に私に「おやすみ」と言った.
but good 《口》大いに; 徹底的に; 強力に ▪ Tom hit him *but good*. トムは彼をこっぴどくなぐった.
come good 《英口》首尾よく終わる ▪ Is this the year when Arsenal *come good*? 今年はアーセナルが首尾よく終わる年となるか.
come to good 良い結果になる, 良い実を結ぶ ▪ The scheme has *come to good*. その計画は良い実を結んだ.
come to no good 悪い結果になる, ろくなことはない ▪ Your effort will *come to no good*. あなたの努力はうまくいかないだろう ▪ That fellow will *come to no good*. あの男は不幸に終わるだろう.
do** oneself **a bit [piece] of no good →DO^2.
do (any, some) good **1** 〚any は疑問文・否定文・条件文に用いる〛好結果[効果]が(いくらか)ある ▪ The new rules may *do some good*. 新しい規則はいくらか効果があるかもしれない ▪ That won't *do any good*. それは何の効果もないだろう.
2 いくらか進歩する, 増進する, 盛んになる ▪ I'm afraid I haven't *done any good* in maths this term. 今学期は数学が全然上達しなかったと思う.
do good **1** 善を行う, 親切にする; 博愛事業を行う ▪ He *does* a lot of *good* among the poor. 彼は貧しい人々に多くの善を施す ▪ She will begin *doing good* again. 彼女はまた博愛事業を始めるだろう.
2 効果がある, ためになる, 効く (*to*) ▪ This rain will *do* much *good to* the crops. この雨は作物に大いに効くだろう.
do** a person **good 人[体]のためになる, に効く ▪ Traveling has *done* him a world of *good*. 旅行が非常に彼のためになった ▪ It *does* me *good* to see him run. 彼が走るのを見るのが私は愉快だ ▪ This medicine will *do* you *good*. この薬は君に効くだろう ▪ Much *good* may it *do* you! おためになればよいがね《反語》.
Do good by stealth and blush to find it fame [known]. 《諺》ひそかに善をなし, それが知れると照れる. ☞Pope. *Epilogue to the Satires* より.
do** a person's **heart good →HEART.
do no good **1** 善行をしない ▪ He who *does no good* does evil enough. 善行をなさない人はそれだけで悪行をなすことになる.
2 効果がない, 少しも進歩しない ▪ The animal appears to *do no good*. その動物は少しも進歩しないようだ.
3 役に立たない, むだである ▪ It will *do no good* to

send for the doctor. 医者を呼びにやるのはむだだろう.

feel good 《口》気分がよい; 元気である ▪ I began to *feel* pretty *good*. 私はかなり元気になり始めた ▪ I'm *feeling good* this morning. 今朝は気分がよい ▪ I *feel good* when I'm singing. 歌を歌っているときは気持ちがよい.

for good and all/《口》***for good*** **1** よくなるように, ためになる ▪ Money is a power *for good* in some hands. 金は持つ人次第で世を益する力となる ▪ All these things have worked together *for good*. これらの事がみないっしょになって好結果を生んだ. **2**《口》永久に; これを限りに ▪ He left Japan *for good and all*. 彼は日本を永久に去った ▪ I have given up smoking *for good and all*. 私はこれを限りにタバコをやめた.

for good measure →MEASURE[1].

for good or (for) evil [ill] よかれあしかれ ▪ We must take life *for good or for evil*. 人生はよかれあしかれ受け入れなければならない.

for** a person's **(own) good 人のためになるように《主に, 苦言など不愉快なことに関して》 ▪ You may be reprimanded or corrected but it's *for your own good*. 君はしかられたりたしなめられたりするかもしれないが, それは君自身のためなのだ ▪ *For her own good*, I started distancing myself from her. 彼女のためになるように私は彼女から距離をおくようにした.

for the good of ...のためを思って; のためになるように ▪ I'm telling you this *for your good*. 私はあなたのためを思ってこれを話しているのです ▪ He is traveling *for the good of* his health. 彼は保養のために旅行している.

give as good as you get 《口》(議論・けんかで)自信をもって人と対等につき合う ▪ A woman must *give as good as you get* to survive. 女性は, 生きぬくためには他人と対等につき合っていかなければならない.

***give** a person **good day [morning, evening, night,** etc.]* →bid a person GOOD day.

Good afternoon! →GOOD morning!

good and /gʊdn/ 《口》とても; 全く ▪ I'm *good and* hungry. 私はとても腹がへっている ▪ I have got *good and* ready. 私はすっかり用意ができている.

good and bad 善人と悪人 ▪ *Good and bad* alike respect him. 善人も悪人も等しく彼を尊敬する.

good and evil 善と悪, 正と邪 ▪ Men are not good judges of *good and evil*. 人間は正邪を正しく判断することはできない.

good and hard 《口》きわめて激しく; うんと, しっかり ▪ I hit him *good and hard*. 私は彼をきわめて激しくなぐった.

good and proper 十分な[に], 徹底的な[に] ▪ He was caught *good and proper*. 彼はまんまと捕えられた.

good comes of 善が...から生まれる ▪ *Good comes of* evil. 善が悪から生まれる《雨降って地固まる》 ▪ No *good* can *come of* idleness. 怠けていてろくなことはない.

Good day [evening]! →GOOD morning!

good enough 十分よい; (満足して)いいとも, それでいい ▪ I'm not *good enough* to even talk about her, am I? 僕は彼女のことを話す資格さえないって? ▪ *Good enough*, bye. それでいい, さよなら.

good for nothing 役に立たない; だめな (《聖》*Matt*. 5. 13) ▪ These old slippers are *good for nothing*. この古いスリッパはもう役に立たない ▪ I feel *good for nothing* today. 私はきょうは何もできない気がする.

Good for you [him, George,** etc.]**! 《口》でかした!, うまいぞ! ▪ "*Good for you!* Congratulations!" でかしたな! おめでとう! ☞for [on] のあとの(代)名詞に強勢をおく.

Good God [gracious, hallow, heavens, lack, Lord, me]! おやおや!《驚きを表す》 ▪ *Good heavens*, Slich, how can you talk such nonsense? これは驚いた. スリッチ君. どうしてそんなばかなことが言えるのかね ▪ *Good Lord!* What fools! おやおや! 何というばかどもだ.

good grief (驚き・当惑などを表して)ああ, おやおや, やれやれ ▪ Oh *good grief*, I wish you hadn't done this. あらまあ, こんなことしなきゃよかったのに. ☞"Good God" の婉曲表現.

good in parts (like the curate's egg) (牧師補の卵のように)部分的に良い《悪いものを婉曲に言う》 ▪ For most people these collections are *good in parts, like the curate's egg*. 大半の人々にとって, これらのコレクションは牧師補の卵じゃないが部分的には良い.

Good man! あっぱれだ, よくやった.

good man and true 立派な誠実な人, 温厚篤実の人 ▪ Such a thing has happened to many a *good man and true*. そのようなことは多くの立派で誠実な人にも起こっている.

Good men [folks] are scarce./ A good man is hard to find. 《諺》善人は少ない,「善人見つけがたし」.

Good morning [afternoon, evening, day]! **1**〚下降調のときに〛おはよう[こんにちは, こんばんは, こんにちは]《朝[午後, 晩, 昼間]のあいさつ》. **2**〚上昇調のときに〛さようなら!

good morning to 《口》...はお留守になる ▪ When anything is upon my heart, *good morning to* my head. 何かが心にかかっているときは, 私の頭はお留守になる.

good old 《口》なつかしの《自分の故郷などを賛美する言い回しで, good は美称》 ▪ I was born in the *good old* city of London. 私はなつかしのロンドンで生まれた ▪ In the *good old* days we used to swim in this river. なつかしい昔この川で泳いだものだった.

good old Ben [Mary,** etc.]**! 《口》(期待通りのふるまいをほめて)いいぞ, よくやった, ベン[メアリー, など] ▪ Congratulations! *Good old Ben!* おめでとう. よくやった, ベン!

good sense すぐれた分別, 良識 ▪ She had the *good sense* to say nothing. 彼女は気をきかせて黙っていた.

***good to eat* [*drink*]** 食べられる[飲める] ▪ The water of this well is *good to drink*. この井戸の水は飲める.

***had* [*were, may, might*] *as good* do (*as*)** (…するよりは)…したほうがましだ ▪ He *were as good* live at Portsmouth *as* here. 彼はここに住むくらいならポーツマスに住むほうがましだね ▪ His gold *might as good* have stayed at Peru *as* come into his custody. 彼の黄金は彼に保管されるようになるくらいならペルーにあったほうがましだ.

have a good head on* one's *shoulders →HEAD[1].

have a good innings →INNING.

***have a good mind to* do** →have a great MIND to do.

have a good one よい一日を過ごす《しばしば別れのあいさつとして》 ▪ *Have a good one*, everybody. We'll see you tomorrow. みなさん, ごきげんよう. また明日お会いしましょう.

have it good 《米口》裕福[幸福]である; 楽に暮らす ▪ Now I come to say with all my heart that I *have it good*. 楽に暮らせるようになった, と心から言えるようになった ▪ He has *had it good* these ten years. この10年彼はずっと裕福であった.

hold* [*stand*] *good **1** 有効である ▪ The ticket *holds good* for three days. そのチケットは3日間有効です.
2 当てはまる; 通用する; (議論・理由などが)成り立つ ▪ The same reason *holds good* as to the sacrament. 聖餐(さん)式についても同じ理由が成り立つ ▪ It will *stand good* in nine out of ten instances. それは10例中9例まで当てはまる.

***if* a person *knows what's good for* him** どうすれば自分のためになるか知っているなら ▪ *If* you *know what's good for* you, join us. どうすれば自分のためになるかわかっているなら, 我々の仲間になりなさい.

If you can't be good, be careful. **1** (心または行いが)正しくないなら, 秘密にしなさい.
2 《戯》[[しばしば Be good を伴って別れのあいさつとして]] じゃあ, 悪いことをするときは用心して! ☞→Be GOOD!

***it's a good thing* (*that …*)** 《口》…はいい[結構な]ことである (= a (bloody, jolly, very) good JOB) ▪ *It was a good thing that* she got herself into this other school. 幸いにも彼女はこのもう一方の学校へ入った.

It's all good. 《米俗》(慰めて)大丈夫だ, 問題ない ▪ They are constantly saying *it's all good*. 彼らは大丈夫だと始終言っている.

(*It's*) *good to be here.* (歓迎のあいさつに対して)ここに来ることができてうれしいです ▪ Thanks for the welcome! *It's good to be here*. 歓迎してくださりありがとうございます. ここに来られて光栄です.

(*It's*) *good to have you here.* 来てくださってうれしいです, ようこそいらっしゃいました《歓迎のあいさつとして》 ▪ (*It's*) *good to have you here*. I'm glad you took the time to visit my site. よく来てくださいました. わざわざ私のサイトを訪問してくださりうれしいです ▪ Welcome! *It's good to have you here*. The more the merrier. ようこそ. よく来てくださいました. 多ければ多いほど楽しいですから.

Jolly good! 《口》大いに結構! とてもすばらしい! ▪ *Jolly good!* When do we start? 大いに結構だ! いつ始めるのかね.

keep* [*remain*] *good 腐らない, もつ ▪ This fish *keeps good* for two days. この魚は2日はもつ.

like a good one 盛んに; 元気よく ▪ He worked *like a good one*. 彼は元気よく働いた.

***look* [*listen*] *good* (*to*)** 《口》(…に)有望に思われる[響く], 申し分なく良く思われる[響く] ▪ It *looks good to* me. それは私には有望に思われる ▪ That *listens good to* her. それは彼女には有望に響く.

***make a good death* [*end*]** 立派な死を遂げる ▪ They say my father *made a good end*. 私の父は立派な死を遂げたということです.

make good **1** (損害などを)償う; (不足を)補う; (経費を)支払う ▪ He *made good* the loss. 彼はその損失を償った ▪ Any deficiency in repayment shall *be made good*. 返済の不足は補います ▪ You must *make good* our pay to us. あなたは我々の給料を我々に支払わなければならない.
2 (失われた, こわれたものを)回復する, 修復する, 取り換える ▪ The place *was made good* with stonework. そこは石で修復された ▪ The company *made good* the articles damaged in transit. その会社は輸送中にこわれた商品を取り換えた.
3 (言説・非難などの)真実を証明する, 実証する ▪ I will *make good* my charge against you. 私はあなたに対する非難を実証します ▪ His argument has *been made good* on other grounds. 彼の議論は他の根拠から実証されてきた.
4 (地位などを)保持する; 確保する ▪ They can't *make good* a livelihood. 彼らは生計を維持することができない ▪ They could not *make good* their prisoner. 彼らは囚人を監禁しておくことができなかった.
5 ふさいで[埋めて]水平にする ▪ Short balks were laid upon the next step so as to *make good* up to the surface of the third step. 第3階段の表面を水平にするため, 一組の短い角材が第2階段の上に置かれた.
6 《口》(約束・義務を)果たす ▪ Will you *make good* your promise? あなたは約束を果たしますか ▪ He *made good* his escape. 彼はうまく逃げきった.
7 《口》(事を)なし遂げる; 成功する, 期待に添う ▪ I am sure he will *make good* in that job. 彼はきっとその職業で成功すると思う ▪ They can't *make good* if it is demanded of them. 彼らはそれを要求されても期待に添うことはできない.
8 (ポーカーで)他の人の賭け金と同じにするため自分の賭け金を増す ▪ If he determines to play on, he *makes good*. もし彼が続けてやることに決めたら, 彼は他の者と同額になるよう賭け金を増す.

make* one's *good nights →NIGHT.

make good time →TIME[1].

make it good upon** a person* [*a person's* ***person] 格闘したりなぐりつけたりして人に自己の主張を押しつける ▪ I will *make it good on their persons.* 彼らをなぐりつけて私の主張を押しつけてやろう ▪ I will *make it good upon* you that it is wrong. それはまちがっているということを腕力に訴えてでも君にわからせよう.

may [***might***] ***as good*** *do* (***as***) →had as GOOD do (as).

never have it so good 《口》以前よりも裕福である ▪ We have *never had it so good.* 我々は以前よりも裕福であった.

not be any good →be no GOOD.

not be much good 《口》大いに役に立つ ▪ The tool *is not much good.* その道具は大いに役に立つ.

Not so good! 《口・皮肉》何てひどいこと[失敗, まちがい]だろう!

remain good →keep GOOD.

stand good →hold GOOD.

stand** a person **in good stead →stand a person in little STEAD.

straight goods 事実, 実情 ▪ Public officials are not giving Canadians the *straight goods* about crime in this country. 役人たちはこの国の犯罪についてカナダ国民に真実を伝えていない.

that's a good boy [***girl, fellow***] 《口》よい子だから(そうしてくれ); (そうしてくれて)いい子だな《おとなにも言う》.

that's a good 'un [***one***] 《口》 **1** それはうまい《おもしろいジョークだ, うまい芸だ, 気の利いた言葉だ, など》 ▪ What! No tiara?—*That's a good one.* (ばかに着飾った女について)へえ! ティアラはかぶらないの?—こりゃあ, うまいしゃれだ!

2 《皮肉》いいことを言うよ《それは特に愚かな厚かましい行為[頼み, 提案]だ》 ▪ Dad says he's tired.—He's tired? *That's a good one.* お父さんは疲れたと言ってるよ—疲れたって? よくもそんなことが言えたものね.

That's good! 《口》それはいいですね; おいしいです《賞賛・賛同を表して》 ▪ Mmm ... *that's good!* うーん, おいしい ▪ Don't know enough about writing? Maybe *that's good!* 物を書くことについて十分知っていないって. たぶんそうでしょう.

That's no good. 《口》(適切さ・都合の点で)それはまずい[だめだ] ▪ If someone tries to touch you in a way that makes you feel uncomfortable, *that's no good.* もし誰かがあなたに不愉快を覚えさせるふうに体に触れてきたら, それは良くないことだ.

That's [***It's***] ***not good enough.*** それではいけない, かんべんしてくれ《不満足・迷惑を表して》 ▪ *That's not good enough*—it must be written down. それでは満足できない—書き留めなければだめだ ▪ My parents live in LA and even though I e-mail them a lot, *that's not good enough.* 両親はロサンゼルスに住んでいて何度も電子メールを送るが, それでは足りない.

The good die young. 《諺》善人は若死にする.

The good is the enemy of the best. 《諺》善は最善の敵なり《ほどほどで妥協しては進歩がない》.

the good old days →DAY.

think [***see***] ***good to*** *do* …するのが良いと思う, 適宜に…する ▪ Thus much I *thought good to* premise. これだけは前置きするのが良いと思った.

throw good money after bad →MONEY.

to the good 《口》 **1** 黒字で, 儲かって ▪ We were £50 *to the good.* 我々は50ポンドの黒字であった ▪ I finished the work in time, with two days *to the good.* 私はその仕事を間に合うように仕上げ, 2日儲かった.

2 一般の利益で ▪ Peace is all *to the good.* 平和は全く一般の利益である. ☞↔be (...) to the BAD.

too good to be true あまりよすぎて信じられない ▪ The result is *too good to be true.* その結果はあまりに良すぎて信じられない.

too much (***of a good thing***) →TOO.

turn [***use***] ***to good account*** …を利用[活用]する ▪ The error may yet *be turned to good account.* その間違いは今後に生かされるかもしれない.

up to no good →be after no GOOD.

were as good do (***as***) →had as GOOD do (as).

What good is ...? …は何の役に立つか ▪ *What good is* that? それが何の役に立つのか.

What is the good of ...? …が何の役に立つか ▪ *What is the good of* doing such a thing? そんなことをして何になるのか.

Would you be so good as [***good enough***] ***to*** *do?* …していただけますか《非常に丁寧な言い方》 ▪ *Would you be so good as to* listen to what I have to say? 私の言い分をお聞きいただけませんか.

You can't keep a good man [***woman***] ***down.*** 《戯》強い性格の人は必ず成功する.

your good self 《商》貴殿, お客様 ▪ Our next orders will be placed with *your good selves.* 次のご注文はみなさまの所にお届けします.

good(-)by(e) /gʊ̀dbáɪ/ 名 ***bid*** [***say, kiss, wave***] ***good-by*** さよならを言う, おいとまする; あきらめる (*to*) ▪ Then he *said good-by to* me. それから彼は私にさようならを言った ▪ We *bade* him *good-by* and went forward. 私たちは彼にいとまを告げて進んで行った ▪ You can *say goodbye to* that post. It's no longer vacant. あのポストはあきらめることだよ. もうあいてないのだから.

(***can***) ***kiss ... goodby***/ (***can***) ***kiss*** [***say***] ***goodby to*** **1** (金など)を失う ▪ If the Presidential candidate wins, we can *kiss* money *goodby*, we'll all be poor. もしその大統領候補が勝ったら, 我々はお金を失い, みんな貧乏になってしまうだろう.

2 (希望など)をあきらめる ▪ Arsenal can *kiss goodby to* any hope of winning the title if they slip up against Liverpool. リバプールとの試合でつまずけば, アーセナルはタイトルを勝ちとる希望をあきらめることになる ▪ If you become a whiner now, you *can say goodby to* all your dreams of ending up on top of the heap. いま泣き言を言う人になったら, ついには社会の勝ち組になるという夢はおさらばになってしまうよ.

G

(***It's***) ***goodbye*** (***to***) *A* ***and hello*** (***to***) *B*. AよさらばBよこんにちは; Aが廃れてBがとって代わる ▪ *It was goodbye* summer *and hello* fall as a cold front moved through the state. 寒冷前線が州を移動するにつれて, 夏よさらば, 秋よこんにちは, となった ▪ So *it was goodbye to* football *and hello to* medical school. こうして, フットボールをやめて医学校に入った.

goodness /gúdnəs/ 名 ***for goodness***(') ***sake***
1 お願いだから ▪ *For goodness sake* let me go. お願いですから私を放してください.
2 ほんとにまあ!《いらだたしさ》 ▪ *For goodness' sake*! I've already waited a half hour for you. ほんとにまあ! もう半時間もあなたを待ちましたよ. ☞goodness＝God.

Goodness gracious! おやまあ!, まあ大変!, えいくそっ!《驚き・怒りの表現》(＝GOOD God!) ▪ *Goodness gracious!* What have you done? おやまあ! なんてことをしでかしたんだ. ☞goodness＝God.

Goodness knows. →God KNOWs.

Goodness me! →Ah GOD!

have the goodness to *do* **1** 親切にも…する ▪ He *had the goodness to* show me the way. 彼は親切にも私に道を案内してくれた.
2〚命令文で〛どうぞ…してください ▪ *Have the goodness to* post this letter. どうぞこの手紙をポストへ入れてください. ☞F avoir la bonte de のなぞり.

honest to goodness →HONEST to God.

(***I wish***) ***to goodness*** ぜひ…を望む (→ to GOODNESS) ▪ *I wish to goodness* your people would give a dance. お宅でダンスパーティーを催してくださったらなあ.

in the name of goodness 神の名にかけて; 一体全体 ▪ *In the name of goodness* what is that which they speak of? 一体彼らが話しているのは何だ.

My goodness! →Ah GOD!

out of the goodness of *one's* ***heart*** 親切心[善意]から, 見返りを求めないで ▪ The reason I did it was absolutely *out of the goodness of my heart*, no other reason. 私がそれを行ったのはひとえに善意からであって, 他の理由からではない.

surely to goodness 確かに, 神かけて ▪ *Surely to goodness* she has got better now. きっと彼女はもうだいぶよくなっている.

Thank goodness! →THANK God!

to goodness 《口》〚wish, hope を強調して〛ほんとに, 心から ▪ I *wish to goodness* you'd be quiet. ほんとに静かにしてくださいよ. ☞to goodness の他に, to heaven(s), the Lord, God, Christ, hell とも言う.

goods /gʊdz/ 名 ***a piece of goods*** →PIECE[1].

by goods 《英》貨車で ▪ Please send us the articles on order *by goods*. どうか注文の品は貨車でお送りください.

catch *a person* ***with the goods*** 《口》人を現行犯で捕える ▪ Sooner or later I am going to *catch* him *with the goods*. 遅かれ早かれ, 私は彼を現行犯で捕えます.

come up with the goods/ deliver the goods 《口》(約束などを)果たす, 期待に添う, 要求にかなう ▪ They asked the Cabinet minister to *deliver the goods*. 彼らはその大臣に契約を果たしてくれと頼んだ ▪ The existing system can *deliver the goods*. 現存の制度が要求にかなう ▪ Danny is a great player. He always *comes up with the goods*. ダニーは偉大な選手だ. いつも期待を裏切らない.

damaged goods 傷物, 欠陥商品; (人が)役立たず ▪ The company is viewed as *damaged goods* and its assets must be sold off in haste. その会社は傷物と見られているので, 資産は急いで売却されなければならない ▪ After the scandal, Eric is considered *damaged goods* by the party. そのスキャンダルの後エリックは党から役立たずだとみなされている.

goods and chattels 家財道具いっさい ▪ All his *goods and chattels* were confiscated. 彼の家財道具いっさいが没収された.

have (***got***) ***the goods on*** 《米》 **1** …に不利な[犯行の決定的な]証拠をつかむ ▪ The police soon *got the goods on* the murderer. 警察はまもなくその殺人者に不利な決定的証拠をつかんだ ▪ They *had the goods on* us. 彼らは我々の犯行の決定的な証拠を握っていた.
2 …に勝る, より優越の地位に立つ ▪ Bill *had the goods on* Rayfield. ビルはレイフィールドより優越な地位に立った.

have the goods 《口》非常に有能である ▪ He *has the goods*. 彼は有能だ. ☞goods「期待したもの」.

sell *a person* ***a bill of goods*** →BILL[1].

Take the goods the gods provide. 神の与えてくれる物を享受せよ; 足るを知れ.

That fellow's the goods. あの男ならけっこうだ[その仕事にあつらえ向きだ].

goody /gúdi/ 名形 ***the goodies and*** (***the***) ***baddies*** 《口》善玉と悪玉 ▪ His novel lines up *the goodies and the baddies*. 彼の小説は善玉と悪玉を勢ぞろいさせている.

goof /gu:f/ 動 ***goof up*** 〚名詞的に〛《米口》不注意な間違い[失敗], へま, ちょんぼ; 失敗作 ▪ There was a little *goof up* in Christmas presents this year. 今年のクリスマスプレゼントにはちょっと手違いがあった ▪ The whole movie was a big *goof up*. その映画全体は駄作だった.

go-off /góʊɔ̀:f|-ɔ̀f/ 名 ***at one go-off*** いっぺんで, 一挙に, 一気に ▪ They read it *at one go-off*. 彼らはそれを一気に読んだ.

(***at the*** [*one's*]) ***first go-off*** いっぺんで; 初めに, 出ばなに; 即座に ▪ He succeeded *at his first go-off*. 彼はいっぺんで成功した ▪ He flew into the arms of his mother *first go-off*. 彼はいきなり母の両腕に身を投じた ▪ *At the first go off* I thought the work was delightful. 初めは私はその仕事は愉快だと思った.

googly /gú:gli/ 名 ***bowl*** *a person* (***with***) ***a googly*** 人を驚かす, 予想外のことをする, 不意打ちを

食らわす ▪ I *bowled* the pub *a googly* that day by arriving with a card-carrying vegan. 私はその日，筋金入りの菜食主義者といっしょに行ってそのパブを驚かせた ▪ Fred *bowled* me *a googly* when he asked me to explain those statistics in the meeting. フレッドは，会議中に統計の意味を説明するよう要求して私に不意打ちを食らわせた. ☞「人に変化球を投げる」が原義.

goose /gu:s/ 名 ***(a) gone goose*** **1**《海》窮地に見殺しにされた人，捨てられた船.
2 逃げた人，なくなった物 ▪ The burglar is *a gone goose* by now. 今はもう強盗は逃げてしまっている.
3《口》もうだめで，もう見込みなく ▪ You are *a gone goose.* あなたはもうだめです ▪ It is *gone goose* with you. 君はもう見込みがない.

a goose egg **1**《俗》ゼロ(0) ▪ His mark on his mathematics examination was *a goose egg.* 彼の数学の試験の点は0だった.
2 (たん)こぶ ▪ He's got *a* huge *goose egg* on his head. 彼は頭に大きなたんこぶをつくった.

All his geese are swans.《諺》自分の物ならガチョウもハクチョウに見える《自分の持物・親類・友人を過大評価する》.

(as) silly as a goose とても愚かで，無思慮で ▪ Some like to be sly as a fox, but never *silly as a goose.* キツネのように狡猾でありたいが，絶対ガチョウのように愚かになりたくない人もいる.

be (all) right [sound] on the goose **1** 奴隷制度問題で正統な所信をいだく《Kansas の奴隷闘争のとき奴隷制度支持者について用いられた》 ▪ They *are all sound on the goose.* 彼らは奴隷問題の正統派(奴隷制度支持者)である.
2 政治的に正統な意見を持つ，政治上穏健な思想をいだく ▪ They answered, "*All right on the goose.*" 彼らは「正統な政見を持っている」と答えた.

cannot say boo to a goose →wouldn't say BOO to a goose.

cook *one's* ***goose***《俗》見込みをだめにする ▪ He *cooked his goose* behaving like that. 彼はそんなふるまいをして見込みをなくしてしまった.

cook *a person's* ***goose (for*** *him***)***《口》人をやっつける，殺す，人の見込みをだめにする ▪ The scandal *cooked his goose.* その醜聞のため彼は破滅した ▪ A year in Formosa will *cook his goose for him.* 台湾に1年いたら，彼は往生してしまうだろう.

kill the goose that lays [laid] the golden egg(s)/ kill the goose for the golden egg(s) 金の卵を産むガチョウを殺す《現在・一時の利益のために将来の利益を犠牲にする》.(→the GOOSE that lays the golden egg(s)) ☞一度にたくさんの卵を得ようとして，毎日一つずつ金の卵を産むガチョウを殺したというイソップの話から.

pluck *a person's* ***goose (for*** *him***)*** 人の高慢の鼻をへし折る ▪ I'll take it into my hands to *pluck his goose for him.* おれがあの男の高慢の鼻をへし折ってやろう.

shoe the goose つまらぬ[むだな]ことに時を空費する ▪ I don't like to *shoe the goose.* 私はむだな仕事に時間を空費したくない.

The goose hangs high.《米口》**1** 万事[形勢]有望である，(ゲームなどが)調子がいい ▪ You bet *the goose hangs high.* 君は確かに前途有望だぞ ▪ Everything is lovely and *the goose hangs high.* 万事見通しは明るい.
2 ガチョウの値が高い ▪ *The goose* does *hang high* enough. ガチョウはほんとに値がひどく高い.

the goose that lays the golden egg(s) 人の財源，最も大事な品 ▪ *The goose that laid the golden eggs* for him was out of sight. 彼の最も大事な品が見えなくなった.

The old woman is picking her geese (and selling the feathers a penny apiece).《口》雪が降りしきっている，吹雪になっている. ☞児童に対して用いられる.

turn geese into swans/turn every goose a swan いつもほめすぎたり買いかぶったりする ▪ Local historians are apt to *turn geese into swans.* 郷土史家たちは人物や行動を買いかぶりがちである.

What is sauce for the goose is sauce for the gander. →SAUCE.

gooseberry /gú:sbèri|gózbəri/ 名 ***(as) green as gooseberry***《俗》全くの青二才で，無経験で無教育の ▪ His name was Green and he was *as green as gooseberry.* 彼の名はグリーンで全くの青二才であった.

like old gooseberry《俗》強力に，猛烈に ▪ Lay on *like old gooseberry.* 思いきりなぐってやれ.

play [do] gooseberry 若い女性のつき添い役をする，恋人の会合の立ち合い役をする ▪ The maid *played gooseberry* when Emily visited Switzerland. エミリーがスイスを訪れたとき侍女がそのつき添い役をした ▪ As she does not understand a word of English, she is the fittest person to *play gooseberry.* 彼女は英語が1語もわからないから，恋人同士の会合の立ち合い役には最も適当だ.

play (up) old gooseberry with《口》**1** …をめちゃめちゃにこわす; (人のもの)を勝手にいじって[使って]こわす ▪ A great gale *played old gooseberry with* the boats. 大風が漁船をめちゃめちゃにこわしてしまった.
2 …をひどくやっつける，へこます ▪ He began to put on airs, but I soon *played up old gooseberry with* him. 彼は偉そうにし始めたが，すぐへこませてやった.

goose-flesh, gooseflesh /gú:sflèʃ/ 名 ***be goose-flesh all over*** (ぞっとして，感動して)全身に鳥肌が立つ ▪ I *was goose-flesh all over* when you sang. 君が歌ったとき僕は全身鳥肌が立った.

get goose-flesh (恐怖・寒さで)鳥肌が立つ ▪ I *got gooseflesh* when I heard the news. 私はその知らせを聞いたとき鳥肌が立った.

go all goose-flesh (恐怖・寒さで)鳥肌になる[が立つ] ▪ They *went all goose-flesh* in terror. 彼らはぞっとして鳥肌になった.

G

Gordian /gɔ́ːrdiən/ 形 ***cut*** [***untie***] ***the Gordian knot*** 快刀乱麻を断つ, 非常手段によって難問題を解決する; 短兵急に事を処断する (→cut a KNOT; the GORDIAN knot) ▪ He *cut the Gordian knot* of hereditary right. 彼は世襲の権利という難問題を一刀両断に解決した. ☞ Phrygia の Gordius 王の結んだ結び目を解く者はアジアの王になるという神託を聞いて Alexander 大王が剣を抜いて切断した故事から.

the Gordian knot **1** 難問題 ▪ The problem was as slippery as *the Gordian knot*. その問題はいかにもつかまえにくいものだった.

2 断ちえない[堅い]きずな ▪ The strings of *the Gordian knot* have tied together commons, lords and kings. 堅いきずなのひもが平民・貴族・国王を結び合わせている.

G

gorge[1] /gɔːrdʒ/ 名 ***a full gorge*** (タカなどに与える)十分な食事 ▪ Give the capon *a full gorge* of it three times a day. その食用雄鶏に1日に3回それを十分食べさせなさい.

cast [***heave***] ***the gorge*** (***at***) (…を見て)吐き気を催す; (に対して)吐き気を催すほどきらう ▪ He *cast the gorge at* the sight. 彼はその光景を見て吐き気を催した.

one's ***gorge rises*** (***at***) (…に)胸がむかつく ▪ *My gorge rises at* his face. 彼の顔を見ると胸がむかついてくる.

make the [*a person's*] ***gorge rise*** 人に吐き気を催させる ▪ The scandal *makes my gorge rise*. その醜聞に胸がむかつく.

rouse [***stir***] ***the gorge*** ひどく怒らせる, ひどくいやがらせる ▪ The thought *stirred* all *the gorge* of this Pharisee. そう考えるとこのパリサイ人はひどく腹が立った.

gorge[2] /gɔːrdʒ/ 動 ***gorge*** *oneself* ***with***/ ***be gorged with*** …を腹いっぱい詰めこむ ▪ He has *gorged himself with* beef. 彼は牛肉を腹いっぱい詰めこんだ.

gorgeous /gɔːrdʒəs/ 形 ***drop-dead gorgeous*** あっと驚くほど美しい ▪ She's naturally *drop-dead gorgeous*. 彼女は生来あっと驚くほど美しい.

goring /gɔ́ːrɪŋ/ (gore の現在分詞) ***cut goring*** 三角形に切る ▪ The cloth is *cut goring*. その布は三角形に切られる.

gory /gɔ́ːri/ 形 ***the gory details*** 《戯》事件の恐るべき詳細 ▪ Okay, here's *the gory details* of the murder case. よろしい. 殺人事件の身の毛もよだつ詳細は次のとおりだ.

gosh /gɑʃ|gɔʃ/ 名 ***By gosh!*** えっ!, おや大変!, きっと《誓いまたは驚き》 ▪ *By gosh!* I never heard that before. おやおや! そんなことは聞いたことがない. ☞ gosh＝God; by God よりも穏やか.

by guess and by gosh 《米口》あてずっぽうで, いいかげんに ▪ He can drive *by guess and by gosh*. 彼はあてずっぽうで運転できる.

gospel /gɑ́spəl|gɔ́s-/ 名 ***accept*** [***take***] ***… as*** [***for***] ***gospel*** (***truth***) (あること)を絶対的に真であると思う (→the GOSPEL truth) ▪ Don't *accept* it *as gospel*. それを絶対に真であると思ってはならない ▪ Many people will read these articles and *take* them *for gospel truth*. 多くの人はこの記事を読んで絶対正しいと思いこむだろう.

believe in the gospel of soap and water 《戯》清潔の価値を信じる ▪ Mrs. Smith is house-proud and *believes in the gospel of soap and water*. スミス夫人は家の整頓美化に熱心で清潔の価値を信じている.

preach the gospel キリストの教えを説く ▪ Go forth and *preach the gospel*. 出かけて行って福音を説きなさい.

the gospel truth 絶対的真実 ▪ Frieda Rockett loves to sing, and that's *the gospel truth*. フリーダ・ロケットは歌うのが好きだ. それは絶対に本当だ.

goss /gɑs|gɔs/ 名 ***get goss*** 《米口》ひどくしかられる, ひどい扱いを受ける ▪ Some of them *got goss*. 彼らのうちにはひどくしかられた者もいる.

give *a person* ***goss*** 《米口》人をひどくしかる, 人にひどい扱いをする ▪ The old man will *give* you *goss*. その老人はあなたをひどくしかるでしょう.

gossip /gɑ́səp|gɔ́sɪp/ 名 ***have a gossip*** (***with***) (…と)よもやま話をする, 雑談する ▪ I *had a* good *gossip with* him. 彼と楽しく雑談した.

got /gɑt|gɔt/ (get の過去分詞) ***have got on*** 《口》…の犯行[に不利]の確証を持っている ▪ That's the gist of what we*'ve got on* the arrested man. それが逮捕された男の犯行について我々が握っている確証の大要です.

have got'em all on 《口》最新式の服装をする, きわめて粋に着飾る ▪ My word! you*'ve got'em all on*, and no mistake. おやまあ, ほんとに粋に着飾ったもんだね, 全く.

have got'em bad 《米口》すばらしく熱心である; すばらしい成功である ▪ He gets to the office the first thing in the morning; he *has got'em bad*. 彼は朝一番に会社へ行く. すばらしく熱心だ.

Where has it [***he***] ***got to?*** 《口》それ[彼]はどうなったのか.

gourd /gɔːrd|gʊəd/ 名 ***out of*** *one's* ***gourd*** 《米口》気が狂って ▪ White pumpkins? Are they *out of their gourd*? 白いカボチャだって? そいつら, 気はたしかなのか ▪ I'm drunk *out of my gourd*! 俺は酔っぱらって頭がおかしくなっている. ☞「中身がヒョウタンから出て」が原義.

govern /gʌ́vərn/ 動 ***govern*** *oneself* 自分(の感情・怒りなどを)抑制する; 自制する ▪ That made him *govern himself*. そのため彼は自制した.

The king reigns, but does not govern [***rule***]. 国王は君臨するけれども統治はしない. ☞ 英国国体を表す有名な句.

government /gʌ́vərnmənt/ 名 ***against the government*** 政府に反対して; (すべて)権威に反抗しがちで ▪ They are *against the government*. 彼らは政府に反対である.

(***be***) ***in the government service*** 官吏である

▪ I *am* now *in the government service.* 私は今は官吏です.

form a government 《英》(首相が)組閣する ▪ Wellington has finished *forming a government.* ウェリントンは組閣を完了した.

under the government of …の管理のもとで ▪ The school throve *under the* wise *government of* this headmaster. その学校はこの校長の賢明な管理のもとで栄えた.

gowk /gaʊk/ 名 ***give*** *a person* ***the gowk*** 人をばかにする ▪ You have *given* me *the gowk,* Annet. アネット, 私をばかにしましたね. ☞gowk = fool.

hunt the gowk むだな使い走りをする《特に四月ばかになって使い走りをする》 ▪ Has John sent me here to *hunt the gowk*? ジョンはむだな使い走りに私をここへ寄こしたのか.

gown /gaʊn/ 名 ***in wig and gown*** →WIG.

take the gown 聖職者[法律家]になる ▪ I have now *taken the gown* according to father's wishes. 私は今や父の希望に従って聖職についた.

town and gown →TOWN.

grab[1] /græb/ 名 ***a game of grab*** 略奪競技 ▪ They are playing *a game of grab* for the farmer's vote. 彼らはその農夫の票を奪おうと互いに競っている.

be on the grab 《口》(不正な)利得に一心になっている ▪ Bill thought I *was* still *on the grab.* ビルは私がまだ利得に汲々としていると思っていた.

By grab(s)! 《米口》ちぇっ!《穏やかなのろい》 ▪ *By grabs*; it's a human creature! ちぇっ! それは人間ではないか!

grab and keep 商業上の強奪と利己主義 ▪ The *grab and keep* of modern commercialism is horrible. 近代商業主義の強奪と利己主義は恐ろしい.

have [get] the grab on 《俗》…よりきわめて有利な地位にある[なる], 大いに勝っている[勝る] ▪ He *has the grab on* me in that respect. 彼はその点では私より大いに勝っている.

make a grab at …をひっつかむ, ひったくる ▪ We *made a grab at* the rope. 我々は綱をひっつかんだ.

up for grabs 《口》誰にでも手に入れやすい ▪ Albatrosses are *up for grabs.* アホウドリは捕えやすい.

grab[2] /græb/ 動 ***grab hold of*** …をつかむ, つかまえる ▪ The man *grabbed hold of* anything he could get. その男はつかめるものなら何でもつかんだ.

grab'er by the tail and let'er rip 《米》しようとしている仕事を立派にする ▪ We have lost the pioneer heritage of "*Grab'er by the tail and let'er rip.*" 我々は「しようとしている仕事を立派にせよ」という開拓者の伝統精神を失った.

How does ... grab you? 《口》…についてどう思いますか, ご意見はいかがですか ▪ *How does* this one *grab you?* これはいかがですか.

grabble /grǽbəl/ 動 ***grabble*** *one's* ***way*** 探りながら進む ▪ He *grabbled his way,* with one hand upon the rail. 彼は片手を手すりにかけて探りながら進んだ.

grace /greɪs/ 名 ***a saving grace*** (欠点を補う)とりえ ▪ He is a dull fellow. His only *saving grace* is that he is diligent. 彼は頭が鈍い. それを補う唯一のとりえは勤勉だということである.

be in *a person's* ***good [bad] graces/be in the good [bad] graces of*** *a person* 人の気に入っている[人にきらわれている] ▪ He *is in the good graces of* his uncle. 彼はおじさんのお気に入りだ.

by God's grace 神の恵みにより, ありがたいことに ▪ Here, *by God's grace,* is the one voice for me. ありがたいことに, ここに私に向けられた唯一の御声(みこえ)がある.

by grace of …のおかげで, のために ▪ He missed being James the Third *by grace of* his own baseness. 彼は自分の卑劣さのためにジェイムズ3世になりそこねた.

by the grace of God 神の恩寵(おんちょう)により《特に正式な文書には王号の後に》 ▪ James, *by the grace of God,* King of Great Britain. グレートブリテン王ジェイムズ.

come with ill grace 不本意[残念]ながら…となる (→ with (a) bad GRACE) ▪ It *comes with ill grace* for them to spend their time battering their former colleague. 彼らは不本意ながら元同僚を攻撃するのに時間を費やすことになる.

do grace (to) (…を)飾る, よく見せる; (の)名誉となる ▪ His conduct *does grace to* his character. 彼の行為は彼の人格に光を添える.

fall from grace 神の寵を失う, 堕落する; 罪を犯す; 流行しなくなる ▪ They are *falling from grace.* 彼らは堕落しつつある.

find grace with …に恩恵を受ける ▪ I pray that he may *find grace with* God. 願わくは彼が神の恩寵(おんちょう)に浴しますように.

get into *a person's* ***good [bad] graces/get into the good [bad] graces of*** *a person* 人に気に入られる[人にきらわれる] ▪ He is rapidly *getting into the good graces of* his aunt. 彼はどんどんおばさんのお気に入りになりつつある.

give [grant] a day's [fortnight's, etc.***] grace*** (法律上の期限以上に)1日[2週間など]の猶予を与える ▪ I will *give* you *five days' grace.* 君を5日間猶予してやろう.

grace before [after] meat 食前[後]の祈り ▪ He says *grace* both *before* and *after meat.* 彼は食事の前後に感謝の祈りをする.

have the (good) grace to *do* 潔く[体よく, 勤めと思って, ゆかしくも]…する ▪ He *had the grace to* apologize. 彼は潔く謝罪した ▪ I *had the grace to* decline it. 私は体よくそれを断った ▪ I hope you will *have the grace to* attend. 勤めと思ってご出席くださるよう望みます ▪ He *had the grace to* live a religious life. 彼はゆかしくも宗教生活を送った.

his [her, your] Grace 閣下(夫人)《公爵・公爵夫人・大主教に対して》 ▪ Is *your Grace* going to receive him? 閣下は彼にお会いになるおつもりですか.

G

in** a person's **good** [**bad**] **graces ずっと人に気に入られて[きらわれて] ▪ I must keep *in the old man's good graces.* 私はその老人のきげんをそらさないようにしなければならない.

in the year of grace →YEAR.

say grace 食前の祈りを言う《数人のときは一人が代表して》 ▪ When the company comes, *say grace,* will you? お客が来たらお前が食前のお祈りを言うんだよ.

take heart of grace (好意・寛大な扱いを受けて)勇気を出す ▪ *Take heart of grace;* I know you will master it. 勇気を出しなさい, 君はきっとそれに熟達しますよ.

the means of grace 《宗》福音を聞く機会 ▪ The shop is next door to the chapel.—Oh, handy for *the means of grace.* 店は教会堂の隣です—おや, それでは福音を聞く機会に恵まれていますね.

There but for the Grace of God go I. 神様の思し召しがなかったら, 私もまた大変なことになっていただろう《全く運がよかった》 ▪ Imagining his anguish, I say to myself, "*There but for the grace of God go I.*" 彼の苦悩に思いを馳せるにつけ, つくづく自分は運がよかったと思う ▪ When I see the miserable situation Tom is in, I say: "*There, but for the Grace of God, go I.*" トムが置かれている哀れな状況を見ると,「神のご加護がなかったら, 私もあのようになっていたかもしれない」と私は言う. ☞英国の聖職者 John Bradford (1510?-55) が刑場に引かれて行く罪人たちを見て発した言葉から.

with* (*a*) *bad* [(*an*) *ill*] *grace いやいやながら, 無愛想に; 見苦しく (→come with ill GRACE) ▪ Tom did the shopping for me, but *with a bad grace.* トムは私のために買い物をしてくれたが, いやいやながらであった ▪ He washes dishes *with bad grace.* 彼はいやいや皿洗いをする ▪ I endured my mother's kisses *with ill grace.* 私はしぶしぶ母親のキスにがまんした.

with* (*a*) *good grace 潔く, 快く ▪ He admitted defeat *with a good grace.* 彼は潔く敗北を認めた ▪ We must accept the decision *with good grace.* その決定は快く受け入れなければならない.

with an easy grace 洒々落々と ▪ He talked *with an easy grace.* 彼は洒々落々と話した.

with any grace 〚否定文・疑問文で〛ふさわしさをもって, 体面をもって ▪ We cannot *with any grace* ask him. 我々は体裁が悪くて彼には質問できない ▪ Can you, *with any grace,* ask him for money? 君は彼に金をくれと言って恥ずかしくないのか.

your Grace →his GRACE.

gracious /gréɪʃəs/ 形 ***Good*** [***Goodness***] ***gracious!*** おや!, まあ!, これは大変!, しまった!《驚きを表す》 ▪ *Good gracious!* I had no idea you were in the town. おやおや! あなたが町においでとは全く知りませんでした.

Gracious Heaven [***goodness, me***]***!/ My gracious!*** = Good GRACIOUS!

grade /greɪd/ 名 ***at grade*** 《米》(鉄道・道路の交差するとき)同一平面で ▪ A railroad crosses the highway *at grade.* 鉄道が大通りと平面交差している.

below grade 《米》標準以下の, 下等の ▪ They throw away all articles *below grade.* 彼らは劣等品を全部捨てた.

go over the grade 《米》(車が)ひっくり返る ▪ A few stages *went over the grade.* 数台の駅馬車が転覆した.

grade A 〚形容詞的に〛一級品の, 最高級の ▪ These batteries are *grade A.* この電池は一級品です ▪ They will not grant *Grade A* milk status to farms with too many flies. 当局はハエが多すぎる農場には最高級ミルクの地位は与えません.

in the 5th grade 《米》(小・中・高校の)第5学年の ▪ He is a student *in the 7th grade.* 彼は7年生(中学1年生)だ.

make a grade [***grades***] 《米》成績を取る ▪ He *made* mediocre *grades.* 彼は平凡な成績を取った ▪ He will *make a* passing *grade.* 彼は合格点は取るだろう.

make the grade 《口》 **1** 必要な成績[標準]に達する; うまくいく ▪ If you *make the grade,* you will be a college professor. もしあなたが必要な成績を収めれば大学教授になれる ▪ Many veterans can *make the grade* in business of their own. 退役軍人には各自の職業で立派にやっていける者が多い.
2 (試験・検査に)合格する ▪ These goods will *make the grade.* この商品は検査に合格するだろう.
3 (…を)努力して得る (*for*) ▪ He *made the grade for* the degree. 彼は努力してその学位を得た. ☞「線路の勾配を登りつめる, 急な坂を登りつめる」が原義.

on the down [***up***] ***grade*** → DOWNGRADE; UPGRADE.

over [***under***] ***grade*** 《米》路面より上[下]を ▪ What railroads cross your road *over* or *under grade?* 何という鉄道が道路面より上または下を交差しているのですか.

teach in the grades 《米》小学校の先生をする ▪ She *taught in the grades* for five years. 彼女は小学校の先生を5年間務めた.

up to grade 《米》標準に達する, かなり上等の ▪ The teacher said my son's work was not *up to grade.* 息子の成績は標準に達していないと先生が言われた.

with good grades 《米》好成績で ▪ He graduated from high school *with good grades.* 彼は好成績で高等学校を卒業した.

graduate /grǽdʒuèɪt/ 動 ***be graduated from*** [《英》***at***] (大学)を卒業する ▪ My son *was graduated from* King's College. 私の息子はキングズカレッジを卒業した ▪ He *was graduated at* Oxford. 彼はオックスフォードを卒業した. ☞今では "graduate from" のほうが普通.

graduate A.B. 学士の称号を得て卒業する ▪ What are the jobs after you *graduate A.B.*? 学士号を得て卒業した後はどんな仕事につきますか. ☞A.B. = Ⓛ Artium Baccalaureus 'Bachelor of Arts'.

grain /greɪn/ 名 ***a grain of*** …の一粒; ほんの少しの…《否定を強める》 ▪ He has not *a grain of* courage. 彼はちっとも勇気がない ▪ There is not *a grain of* truth in what he says. 彼の言うことには本当のところは少しもない.

a grain of wheat in a bushel of chaff 大努力[大騒ぎ]して結果はきわめて少ないこと ▪ The results were *a grain of wheat in a bushel of chaff.* (大いに努力した)結果はきわめて少なかった.

against the [*one's*] ***grain*** 木目に逆らって; 意に反して, 性に反して, 不本意で ▪ When you're having difficulty, you are probably planing "*against the grain.*" All goes smoothly when you plane "with the grain." うまくいかないときは, たぶん「木目に逆らって」鉋(かんな)をかけている.「木目に沿って」鉋をかけていれば, なめらかに行く ▪ Such provision will be *against the grain* of the people. そのような規定は国民の意に反するであろう ▪ The lectures were written *against his grain.* その講義は彼の意に反して書かれた. ☞木の木目に反してはなかなかけずれないことから.

dyed in grain 不変色に染めた, 糸のうちに染めた; 徹底的に染めた; 徹底した, 生粋の ▪ These carpets were all *dyed in grain.* このカーペットはどれも糸のうちに染められたものです ▪ She was a goddess *dyed in grain.* 彼女は生まれながらの女神であった. ☞エンジムシから取った crimson 色は, ある seed, grain から取られたものと考えられていた; これは非常に不変な徹底的に染まる色であった.

go against the grain 不本意である, 性に合わない (→against the GRAIN) ▪ It *goes against the grain* with me to dismiss him. 彼を解雇するのは私は不本意です.

in grain **1** 深紅の, さめない色に染まった ▪ These colors are *in grain.* これらの色はさめないように染まっている.

2 正真正銘の, よくよくの, 生まれながらの, 徹底した《特に軽蔑的意味の語に伴って》 ▪ He is a rogue *in grain.* 彼はよくよくの悪党だ ▪ My father was a philosopher *in grain.* 私の父は正真正銘の哲学者であった. ☞→DYE in (the) wool.

of fine [***coarse***] ***grain*** きめの細かい[粗い] ▪ He is a man *of coarse grain.* 彼は粗雑な人だ.

separate [***sift, sort*** (***out***)] ***the grain*** [***wheat***] ***from the chaff*** 良いものとつまらぬものとをより分ける ▪ They talk a lot of rubbish. You must *separate the grain from the chaff.* 彼らはたわごとをたくさんしゃべる. 良い話とたわごととをより分けなければならない.

some [***many,*** etc.] ***grains of*** いくらかの[多くの, など] ▪ We must make *some grains of* allowance. 多少のしんしゃくはしなければならない.

take … with a grain of salt →SALT[1].

grammar /grǽmər/ 名 ***be bad grammar*** 文法にかなっていない ▪ Some people still think that singular "their" *is* so-called "*bad grammar.*" 単数を受ける "their" はいわゆる「文法的間違い」だといまだに考えている人もいる.

know one's grammar ちゃんとした言葉づかいをする ▪ The boy *knows his grammar.* その少年はちゃんとした言葉うかいをする.

use good [***bad***] ***grammar*** 文法を誤らない[誤る] ▪ Tom *uses good grammar.* トムは文法を誤らない.

grampus /grǽmpəs/ 名 ***blow*** [***snore***] ***like a grampus*** 息を荒く吐く[大いびきをかく] ▪ My friend *snored like a grampus.* 友人は大いびきをかいた.

blow the grampus **1**《海》人を水浸しにする, 水をかぶせて罰する《責任を怠ったり, ずるをした場合》 ▪ The captain *blew the grampus* on him for sleeping on duty. 当直中に居眠りをしたので船長は彼に水をぶっかけて罰した.

2《口》水の中で遊び回る ▪ The children *blew the grampus* all day in the outdoor pool. 子供たちは戸外のプールで一日中バシャバシャやって遊び回った.

puff like a grampus (努力して後)ハーハーと息を切らす ▪ The stairs made him *puff like a grampus.* 階段を上るのに彼はハーハーと息を切らせた.

grand /grænd/ 形 ***a*** [***the***] ***grand old age*** 高年, ベテラン年齢《必ずしも老人ではない》 ▪ Finally, at *the grand old age* of 13, he has won his first major tournament. ついに, 彼は13才という経験をつんだ年齢になって主要なトーナメントで初優勝した.

a grand slam 大成功, 完勝;《野球》満塁ホームラン;《テニス・ゴルフ》年間主要試合完全制覇;《コントラクトブリッジ》13回のトリックのすべてに勝つこと ▪ His first hit was *a grand slam.* 彼の初安打は満塁ホームランだった ▪ Anglers on the boat recorded *a grand slam*—catching white marlin, blue marlin and sailfish on the same outing. 船の釣り人たちはグランドスラムを記録した—ニシマカジキ, ニシクロカジキ, バショウカジキを同じ巡航で釣ったのだ.

do the grand《口》着飾る, 大見栄を張る; 偉そうにする ▪ They were *doing the grand* at the theater. 彼らは劇場で偉そうにしていた.

make the grand tour 大陸旅行をする《昔, 貴族・金持ちの子弟はヨーロッパの名所・旧蹟を一巡した》 ▪ He left the University to *make the* usual *grand tour* of Europe. 彼は大学を卒業して, 通例のヨーロッパ旅行をした.

take the grand tour of …を一巡する ▪ The decanters *take the grand tour of* the table. デカンタが食卓を一通り回る.

the grand old man of《戯》…の大立者, 大御所《GOM と略される》 ▪ Professor Jakobson was *the grand old man of* linguistics. ヤーコブソン教授は言語学の大御所だった.

granddaddy /grǽndæ̀di/ 名 ***the granddaddy of them all***《口》元祖, 創始者[草分け], 同類の中で最も優れた[早い, 古い]もの (→the DADDY of them all) ▪ In the Summer Olympic Games, track and field is *the granddaddy of them all.* 夏季五輪では陸上競技が本家本元だ ▪ The Rose

Bowl is nicknamed "*The Granddaddy of Them All*" because it is the oldest bowl game. ローズボウルはいちばん古いアメリカンフットボールの大会なので「大長老」というニックネームがつけられている ▪ This old goldfish is *the granddaddy of them all*. この年寄り金魚が最古参だ.

grandeur /grǽndʒər/ 名 ***in all** one's **grandeur*** 壮麗をきわめて ▪ The mountain towered above the clouds *in all its grandeur*. その山は雲上にそびえ壮麗をきわめていた.

grandmother /grǽnmʌ̀ðər/ 名 ***teach your grandmother to suck eggs*** 《米》釈迦に説法する ▪ That's *teaching your grandmother to suck eggs*. それは釈迦に説法だ.

This beats my grandmother! これは驚いた ▪ Well, *this* does *beat my grandmother!* これはほんとに驚いた!

granite /grǽnət/ 名 ***(as) hard as granite*** きわめて堅い[がんこな] ▪ "He's nobody to me," he said in a voice *hard as granite*. 「あんなやつおれには目じゃない」と彼は断固とした声で言った.

bite on granite →BITE[2].

grant[1] /grænt|grɑːnt/ 名 ***be* [*lie*] *in grant*** 《法》(財産が)証書によってのみ譲渡できる ▪ a conveyance of a thing that *lies in grant* 証書によってのみ譲渡できるものの譲渡証書.

grant[2] /grænt|grɑːnt/ 動 ***God grant that*** 神よ願わくは…しますように ▪ *God grant that* we live long. 神よ願わくは我々が長生できますように. ☞grant は仮定法現在.

I grant you. あなたの言われる通りです.

take ... for granted …を当然のこととしておろそかにする[ありがたがらない] ▪ We *take* so many things *for granted* in this country, like having hot water whenever we need it. この国では非常に多くのことが当然視されている. たとえば, 必要なときにいつでもお湯が出ることだ ▪ I *took* the facts *for granted*. 私はその事実は当然のことと思った.

take it for granted …は当然のことと思う (*that*) ▪ I *took* (*it*) *for granted that* you would come. あなたはもちろん来ると私は思った.

this granted これはよいとして ▪ *This granted*, what's next? これはよいとして, さて次は.

grape /greɪp/ 名 ***sour grapes*** 負け惜しみ ▪ You don't want to win the prize, eh? I think it's a case of *sour grapes*. 君は賞を得たくないって? そいつは負け惜しみというやつだろう. ☞イソップ物語中の「キツネとブドウ」の話から.

grapevine /gréɪpvàɪn/ 名 ***hear ... through* [《英》*on*] *the grapevine*** …と風の噂に聞く, 口伝え[口コミ]で聞く ▪ I've *heard on the grapevine* that his marriage is unhappy. 風の便りに, 彼の結婚はうまくいっていないと聞いている ▪ I *heard through the grapevine* my new neighbor doesn't like my cat. 口伝えで聞いたんだけど, 新しくきたお隣さんはうちの猫が嫌いなんですって.

grapple /grǽpəl/ 名 ***come to grapples with*** …と組み打ちする; (難問など)と取っ組み合う ▪ He *came to grapples with* the subject. 彼はその問題と格闘した.

grasp[1] /græsp|grɑːsp/ 名 ***beyond** a person's **grasp*** 人の手の届かない所に; 人の理解の及ばない ▪ The land was *beyond his grasp*. その土地は彼には得られなかった ▪ The problem was *beyond my grasp*. その問題は私にはわからなかった.

get* [*have*] *a grasp of …がはっきりとわかる ▪ The important thing was I *got a grasp of* what I need to improve on. 大事なのは自分が何を改善しなければならないかがわかったことだ.

have a good grasp of …をよく会得している; のみこみが良く早い ▪ He *has a good grasp of* the subject. 彼はその問題をよく会得している ▪ She *has a good grasp of* things. 彼女は物わかりが良くて早い.

have a thorough grasp of …に精通している ▪ He *has a thorough grasp of* the subject. 彼はその問題に精通している.

have ... within** one's **grasp …をつかみうる所に持っている ▪ He *has* an excellent position *within his grasp*. 彼にはそう思えば得られる立派な地位がある.

in the grasp of …の手中に, 支配下に ▪ They are *in the* fatal *grasp of* despotism. 彼らはひどい圧制の支配下にある ▪ The treasure was *in the grasp of* the miser. 宝は守銭奴にしっかり握られていた.

ready to** a person's **grasp 人のすぐつかめるようになって ▪ The book lay *ready to the man's grasp*. その本はその人のすぐつかめる所にあった.

take ... out of** a person's **grasp 人の手から…を奪い取る ▪ We *took* them *out of his grasp*. 我々はそれらを彼の手から奪い取った.

within** a person's **grasp 人のつかめる所に; に理解できる ▪ It is *within everybody's grasp*. それは誰にでも理解できる ▪ He had York *within his grasp*. ヨークは彼の占領しうる所にあった.

grasp[2] /græsp|grɑːsp/ 動 ***Grasp all, lose all.*** 《諺》欲ばる人はすべてを失う.

grasp at straws わらにもすがりつく, 必死の努力をする (→catch at a STRAW; A DROWNing man will catch at a straw.) ▪ When there is no reasonable hope left, we *grasp at straws*. そこそこの希望がなければ我々はわらをもつかもうとする ▪ I don't need to *grasp at straws* to beat him. 彼を打ちのめすのにわらに頼る必要はない.

grasp the nettle →NETTLE[1].

grass /græs|grɑːs/ 名 ***(as) green as grass*** →GREEN.

as long as grass grows and water runs 《米》永久に ▪ They laid aside the promise *as long as grass grows and water runs*. 彼らは約束を永久に破棄した.

be in the grass 《米》雑草に埋もれる ▪ He is somewhat *in the grass*. 彼はいくぶん雑草に埋もれた形だ.

(be, run) at grass **1** (馬が)牧場で草を食(は)んで(いる) ▪ The horse *is at grass*. 馬が牧場で草を食んでいる.
2 (人が)職を休んで(いる), 職を離れて遊んで(いる) ▪ Let him *run at grass* for a week or so. 彼に1週間ばかり職を休ませなさい ▪ He is an author *at grass*. 彼は作家だが筆を取らないでいる.
3 自由に休暇の旅に出て(いる) ▪ I have *been at grass* in the summer. 私は夏の間自由に休暇の旅をしていた.
4 《鉱山》 坑外に出て(いる) ▪ Is Tom underground?—No, he *is at grass*. トムは地下に入っているか—いいえ, 坑外へ出ています ▪ About 70 tons of quartz *are at grass* awaiting crushing. およそ70トンの石英が坑外に出され, 破砕されるのを待っている.

between grass and hay/ between hay and grass 《米》 **1** 子供とおとなの間で ▪ He is *between grass and hay*. 彼は子供とおとなの間だ.
2 どっちつかずで ▪ The season was known as *between hay and grass*. その季節はどっちつかずの季節として知られていた.

cut** one's **own grass 《口》 自分で暮らしを立てる, 独力で生活する ▪ They make their children *cut their own grass*. 彼らは子供達に独力で生活させる.

cut the grass from under** a person's **feet 人の論拠を失わせる; (先手を打って)議論[計画, 防衛]を台なしにする, あげ足を取る ▪ I was going to offer him a job, but he *cut the grass from under my feet* by enlisting. 私は彼に職を与えようと思っていたのに, 彼は軍隊に入って, すっかり私の計画がはずれてしまった ▪ You are all this while *cutting the grass from under his feet*. 君はずっと彼のあげ足ばかり取っている.

eating its fifth grass (馬が)5歳になって ▪ The horses, *eating their fifth grass*, were sold in the year 1993. 馬どもは5歳になって1993年に売られた.

go to grass **1** (家畜が)牧場に行く ▪ The horse *went to grass*. その馬は牧場に行った.
2 《口》 仕事をやめる; 休暇を取る; 田舎に引退する ▪ In three weeks we shall *go to grass*. 3週間たったら我々は休暇を取ります.
3 《俗》 打ち倒される; 倒れる; 《米》 死ぬ, 破滅する ▪ I naturally *went to grass*. 私は当然打ちのめされた.
4 〚命令文で〛 くたばってしまえ!, うるさいっ! 《面倒な, しつこく尋ねる人に対して言う》 ▪ *Go to grass* instantly! すぐにくたばってしまえ!

go to grass (and eat mullen) 《米口》 落ちぶれる, くたばる ▪ He will have to *go to grass and eat mullen*. 彼は落ちぶれなければならないでしょう.

hear the grass grow 異常に敏感である ▪ He can *hear the grass grow*. 彼は異常に敏感だ.

hunt grass 《口》 打ち倒される ▪ When you get in with your left, I *hunt grass* every time. 君が左手で一撃をくらわすと, 僕はそのたびごとに打ち倒される.

keep off the grass **1** 芝生に入らない; 規制区域に入らない ▪ *Keep off the grass*! 芝生への立入禁止! 《掲示》 ▪ *Keep off the grass* here; this ground is used for bowls. この区域へ入らないでください. ここはローンボウリングに使われます ▪ *Keep off the grass* or pay a £70 fine. 芝生に入った場合は70ポンドの罰金が科せられます.
2 遠慮する; おせっかいしない ▪ *Keep off the grass* and don't talk about stature. 遠慮して身長のことは言わないようにしなさい ▪ *Keep off the grass*! おせっかいはよせ.

kick [push, put]... into the long grass 《英》 …をたな上げにする, うやむやにする ▪ Mr. Cameron has tried to *kick* the entire issue of tax *into the long grass*. キャメロン氏は税に関する問題すべてをたな上げしようとした.

Let not the grass grow on the path of friendship. 《諺》 友人間に無沙汰はせぬこと.

more rain more grass [rest] 《米》 雨が多けりゃ休みが多い.

neither grass nor hay = between GRASS and hay.

not let the grass grow under** one's **[the] feet 《口》 **1** ぐずぐずしない ▪ You can't (afford to) *let the grass grow under your feet*. 君はぐずぐずしてはいられない(している余裕はない).
2 怠けていない, 怠らずに仕事をしている ▪ A common phrase bosses use to inspire workers is "do*n't let the grass grow under your feet*." 上司が従業員にはっぱをかけるのによく使う言葉は「さっさとやれ」だ.

put (out) [send, turn (out)]... to grass **1** (人)に職を退かせる, 暇を出す ▪ He *was put to grass*. 彼は暇を出された.
2 (人)を休暇で遊びに出す ▪ I will *send* you *to grass* somewhere in Essex. あなたにエセックスのどこかへ休暇で遊びに行ってもらいます.
3 …を牧場へ放す; (老馬)を放つ ▪ *Turn* them *out to grass* in summer time. 夏季には彼らを牧場へ放しなさい ▪ The old horse *was turned out to grass*. その老馬は放たれた.
4 《俗》 …をなぐり倒す; を打ち倒す ▪ He *was sent to grass*, to rise no more. 彼は打ち倒されて再び起きなかった.

The grass does not grow under** one's **feet. 人がぐずぐずしない, 怠けていない.

The grass is greener on the other side (of the fence). 《諺》 (垣根の)向こう側の草のほうが緑が濃い,「隣の芝生は青い」,「隣の花は赤い」.

watch grass grow 退屈である, あきあきする ▪ "Soccer is like *watching grass grow*. Soccer is like watching paint dry," Ross says. 「サッカーは退屈だ, サッカーはあきあきする」とロスは言う.

grass-roots /græsrúːts|ɡràːs-/ 名形 ***get down to the grass-roots*** 根本まで掘り下げる; 問題の根本を究める ▪ The authorities will *get down to the grass-roots*. 当局は問題の根本を究めるだろう.

grateful /ɡréɪtfəl/ 形 ***be grateful to*** **1** …に対

してありがたく思う ▪ I *am* deeply *grateful to* you. まことにありがたく思います.

2 …にとってありがたい ▪ Your sympathy *is grateful to* me. ご同情は私にとってありがたいことです.

gratify /grǽtəfàɪ/ 動 ***be gratified at*** (物)に満足する ▪ The teacher *was gratified at* their efforts. 先生は彼らの努力に満足した.

be gratified to *do* …して満足である ▪ I *am gratified to* know that you have succeeded. ご成功を承って大満足です.

be gratified with (人)に満足する ▪ The teacher *was gratified with* the students. 先生は生徒たちに満足していた.

gratitude /grǽtətjùːd/ 名 ***express*** *one's* ***gratitude*** (***for, to***) (…に)感謝の意を表す ▪ I wish to *express my gratitude for* your assistance. ご援助に謝意を表したく存じます.

in gratitude for …を感謝して ▪ He contributed a large sum to the fund *in gratitude for* their assistance. 彼は彼らの援助に感謝してその基金に多額の寄付をした.

in token of *one's* ***gratitude*** 感謝の印に ▪ I made him a present *in token of my gratitude*. 感謝の印に彼に贈り物をした.

out of gratitude 恩返しに ▪ He acted *out of gratitude*. 彼は恩返しにそうした.

with gratitude 感謝して ▪ I look back *with gratitude* upon his kindness. 私は彼の親切を思い出して感謝します.

grave[1] /greɪv/ 名 (***as***) ***close*** [***secret***] ***as the grave*** 絶対に秘密で ▪ I kept the correspondence *as secret as the grave*. 私はその文通を絶対秘密にした.

(***as***) ***silent as the grave*** →SILENT.

be in *one's* ***grave*** 死んでいる ▪ My mother *is in her grave*. 母は死んでいます.

beyond the grave あの世で[に].

carry … to the [*one's*] ***grave*** …を死ぬまで漏らさない, 死ぬまで残す ▪ He *carried* the secret *to the grave*. 彼はその秘密を死ぬまで漏らさなかった ▪ She *carried* the mark *to her grave*. 彼女は死ぬまで傷あとが残った.

dig *one's* ***own grave*** 《口》墓穴を掘る, 自業自得である ▪ He is in prison for stealing a car.—Well, he has *dug his own grave*. 彼は車を盗んで刑務所に入っている—そりゃあ自業自得だね.

drive [***send***] *a person* ***to an early grave*** 人に絶えず健康を損なうようなことをさせる, 人を苦しめる ▪ It is enough to *drive* me *to an early grave*. 私を苦しめるのはもう十分だ[もうよしてくれ].

find *one's* ***grave*** (***in***) (…で)死ぬ ▪ He *found his grave in* France. 彼はフランスで亡くなった.

have one foot in the grave →(with) one foot in the GRAVE.

make *a person* ***turn*** (***over***) ***in*** *his* ***grave*** 《口》人を地下に泣かせる[くやしがらせる] ▪ It would *make* Jefferson *turn in his grave*. それはジェファスンを地下でくやしがらせるだろう.

(***on***) ***this side*** (***of***) ***the grave*** この世で[の] ▪ It is the greatest happiness *on this side the grave*. それはこの世での最大の幸福です.

sink into the grave (長い間苦しんで)死ぬ ▪ She gradually *sank into the grave*. 彼女は悲嘆のうちに徐々に死に至った.

Someone is walking on [***across, over***] *a person's* ***grave.*** 人の墓場になる所を誰かが歩いている《わけもなくぞっと身ぶるいするときの文句》 ▪ Lord! *Somebody is walking over my grave*. ああ, 何となくぞっと身ぶるいがする. ☞ 常に進行形で用いられる.

turn over [***roll over, spin***] ***in*** *one's* ***grave***/《英》***turn in*** *one's* ***grave*** (死者が)墓の中でのたうつ《くやしくて地下で眠れない》 ▪ He might *turn in his grave* if he knew of such an attempt. 彼がもしそのような試みを聞いたら地下でくやしがるだろう.

(***with***) ***one foot in the grave***/ ***have one foot in the grave*** 死に瀕(ひん)して ▪ I would learn something even if I *had one foot in the grave*. 私はたとえ死に瀕していても何かを学ぶつもりです ▪ I'm 77, but I don't *have one foot in the grave*. 私は77歳だが, 棺桶に片足をつっこんでなんかいない.

grave[2] /greɪv/ 形 ***fall grave*** まじめになる ▪ Suddenly she *fell grave*. 急に彼女は真剣になった.

graveyard /gréɪvjɑ̀ːrd/ 名 ***the graveyard shift*** (三交替制の)深夜勤務《通例午前0時–8時》 ▪ She's working *the graveyard shift* this week. 彼女は今週は深夜勤務だ.

gravity /grǽvəti/ 名 ***keep*** *one's* ***gravity*** 笑わないでいる, 笑いをこらえる ▪ He could hardly *keep his gravity*. 彼はほとんど笑いをこらえられなかった.

upset *a person's* ***gravity*** (おかしくてたまらず)人を吹き出させる ▪ His joke *upset my gravity*. 彼のジョークに私はつい吹き出した.

gravy /gréɪvi/ 名 ***be in the gravy*** 《俗》金がたくさんある, 何不自由ない ▪ Since he changed his job, he's *been in the gravy*. 彼は職業を変えてから, 金がたくさんできた.

board [***ride***] ***the gravy train*** [***boat***] 《俗》楽にぼろ儲けをする, 楽に経済的に成功する(→the GRAVY train) ▪ He seems to be *boarding the gravy train* by smuggling. 彼は密輸で楽にぼろ儲けをしているようだ.

By [***Good***] ***gravy!*** 《米口》おや!, 断じて! ▪ *By gravy!* I'll get up early tomorrow morning. よし! あすの朝は断然早く起きるぞ.

stew in *one's* ***own gravy*** 汗びっしょりになる ▪ We had been *stewing in our own gravy*. 我々はびっしょり汗をかいていたのだった.

the gravy train 《俗》楽にぼろ儲けする手段 ▪ He can tag along on *the gravy train*. 彼は人の後について行って楽にぼろ儲けをすることができる.

gray[1], 《主に英》**grey**[1] /greɪ/ 形名 ***a grey eminence*** (政府の)陰の助言者, 背後の実力者, 黒

幕 ▪ Both are truly *grey eminences.* 二人とも真に政界の黒幕である. ☞F éminence grise のなぞり; 元リシュリューの助言者 Joseph 神父のこと. 灰色の法衣を着ていた.

***get gray* (*hair*)** 《口》(…を)心配して白髪になる; (を)ひどく心配する[悩む] (*from, over*) ▪ They have all *got gray hair from* too much thinking. 彼らはみんな考えすぎて白髪になってしまった ▪ I won't *get gray hair over* it. 私はそのことについて心配するつもりはない.

give gray hair 《口》(人を)ひどく心配させる[悩ませる] ▪ The traffic problem *gave* the policeman *gray hair.* 交通問題はその警官をひどく悩ませた.

go gray 白髪になる ▪ Although still young, he is *going* very *gray.* まだ若いのに彼は白髪になりつつある.

gray* [*grey*] *matter (脳・脊髄の)灰白質; 《戯》頭脳, 知性 ▪ This is a list of books that stimulate the *gray matter.* これは脳を刺激する本のリストだ ▪ Like Hercule Poirot, detectives used *gray matter* to solve a million-dollar knockoff case. エルキュール・ポワロと同様, 探偵たちは百万ドルの強盗事件を解決するのに頭脳を用いた. ☞Agatha Christie の作品中の探偵 Hercule Poirot の口癖から.

grow gray in the service of …に長く仕えて白髪になる ▪ Such a man, *grown gray in the service of* a nation, should be honored. 国に長く仕えて白髪になったこのような人は栄誉を与えられるべきだ.

in the gray **1** 磨かないで, 生地のままで ▪ He left the surface *in the gray.* 彼はその表面を磨かないでおいた.
2 (シカが)灰色で, 冬衣装で ▪ The deer is now *in the gray.* シカは今は冬衣装だ.

in the gray of the morning 未明に ▪ We started *in the gray of the morning.* 我々は未明に出発した.

look gray 陰気な[絶望的な]様子をする ▪ The future *looks gray.* 将来は暗い.

the gray mare →MARE.

the men in* (*grey*) *suits →SUIT[2].

gray[2], 《主に英》**grey**[2] /greɪ/ 動 ***be grayed out*** 《電算》画面が灰色になって入力[操作]不可能になる ▪ The password entry box *is grayed out.* パスワードの入力ボックスが入力不可能になった.

graze /greɪz/ 名 ***send*** *a person* ***to graze*** 《戯》人を追い出す, に暇を出す ▪ Will you *send* the clergy all *to graze*? 聖職者をみな追い出しますか.

grease[1] /gri:s/ 名 ***chafe* [*fret, fry, melt, stew, sweat*] *in*** *one's* ***own grease*** 自分の愚行の報いを受ける ▪ There he sat *fretting in his own grease.* 彼はそこに座って自分のした愚行の報いを受けていた. ☞「火あぶりにされる」という原義から.

in the grease 脂の抜いてない ▪ He deals in furs *in the grease.* 彼は刈り取ったままの羊毛[脱脂してない毛皮]を商っている.

melt *one's* ***grease*** 激しい活動によって力を出し尽くす ▪ He *melted his grease* and so died. 彼は激しい活動で力を出し尽くして死んだ.

of grease 太った ▪ It was a hart *of grease* too. それもまた太った雄ジカだった.

The squeaky wheel gets the grease. → The squeaking WHEEL gets the oil.

grease[2] /gri:s/ 動 ***grease*** *a person's* ***hand* [*palm, fist*]/*grease*** *a person* ***in the fist*** 《口》人に賄賂を贈る, 心うけをやる (→grease the PALMs of) ▪ He will tell you the lady's name if you *grease his palm.* 彼に賄賂を使えば, その女性の名前を明かすだろう. ☞F graisser la patte à quelqu'un のなぞり.

grease the wheels →WHEEL[1].

greased /gri:st/ 形 ***like* [(*as*) *quick as*] *greased lightning*** →LIGHTNING.

greasy /grí:si, -zi/ 形 ***a greasy spoon*** 《口》(揚げ物を出す)安食堂 ▪ He usually has breakfast at *a greasy spoon* near his lodging. 彼はふつう下宿の近くの安食堂で朝食をとる ▪ I had no time to eat lunch at the restaurant and bolted down a sandwich at the *greasy spoon.* レストランで昼食をとる時間がなかったので安食堂でサンドイッチをぱくついた.

climb* (*up*) *the greasy pole 《英》(仕事で)地位を高める ▪ India is a big country and still trying to *climb* (*up*) *the greasy pole.* インドは大国だが, さらに国力を高めようとしている ▪ A bestseller teaches employees how to *climb the greasy pole* in France. ベストセラー本はサラリーマンがどうやればフランスで出世できるかを教えるものだ. ☞greasy pole「脂棒」; 脂を塗った棒で, 田舎の祭りの余興などにそれをよじ登ったりその上を歩いたりする遊具.

great /greɪt/ 形名 ***a great little man*** 小柄だが心の大きい[偉大な]人 ▪ Napoleon I was *a great little man.* ナポレオン1世は小柄だが偉人だった.

a great of 《米口》多量の, 大部分の ▪ The storm spoiled *a great of* our goods. あらしが我々の貨物の大部分を台なしにした.

a great one for …の熱心家[愛好者] ▪ He is *a great one for* reading. 彼は読書に熱心である.

be a great one for よく…する, を楽しむ (→a GREAT one for) ▪ Greene *is a great one for* practical jokes. グリーンはいたずら好きだ ▪ Waugh said the area *is a great one for* baseball. ウォーが言うには, その地区は野球が盛んなところだ.

be going great guns 大いに[ばりばり]やる; とんとん拍子にいく (→a big GUN) ▪ Mike *is going great guns* as a golfer. マイクはゴルファーとして大活躍している ▪ The aircraft industry *is going great guns.* その航空産業は順風満帆だ.

(*be*) *great at* 《口》 **1** …が非常にじょうずで(ある) ▪ He *is great at* golf. 彼はゴルフが非常にじょうずだ.
2 …に詳しい, 通じている ▪ He *is great at* history. 彼は歴史に通じている.

(*be*) *great on* 《口》 **1** =(be) GREAT at.
2 …が非常に好きで(ある), に熱心で(ある); にやかましい ▪ He *is great on* heraldry. 彼は紋章学に非常に興味を持っている ▪ He *is great on* discipline. 彼は規律がやかましい.

3 …する習慣がある, 強い傾向がある ▪ The socialists *are great on* dividing up other people's money. 社会主義者は他人の金を分割する傾向が強い.

great and good 《口・戯》偉い, 重要な(人・物など) ▪ Arthur was a *great and good* king. アーサーは偉大な王であった ▪ Our country is and always has been a *great and good* nation. わが国は偉大な国家であるし, これまでもずっとそうであった.

great and small あらゆる階級の人々; 貴賤貧富を問わず ▪ He is respected by *great and small*. 彼はあらゆる階級の人々に尊敬されている.

Great Caesar [***God, Godfrey, guns, Scott, sun***]***!*** おや!, まあ驚いた!, やれやれ!, ほんとに! ▪ *Great Caesar!* There you go again! おやまあ, またやるのだね ▪ *Great Scott!* He must be mad. まあほんとに, 彼は気が狂ったにちがいない.

G

Great minds (***think alike***)***.*** 《戯》偉い人は同じように考えるものだ ▪ I think Labour will win the election. —So do I. —Ah, *great minds think alike*. 労働党が選挙に勝つと思う—私も—ああ, 偉人は同じように考えるものだね.

great with child [***young***] 妊娠して[子をはらんで] ▪ She was then *great with child*. 彼女はその時妊娠していた ▪ A sow lay *great with young*. 雌ブタが子をはらんで寝ていた.

in the great 全体的に, ひっくるめて ▪ They built a ship *in the great*. 彼らは船をそっくり作った.

no great 《米口》あまり…ない (not much) ▪ There is *no great* to see. たいして見るものはない ▪ I care *no great* about selling it. 私はそれを売ることにあまり乗り気でない.

no great of 《米口》たいした…でない ▪ It was *no great of* a fishing ground. そこはたいした漁場ではなかった.

no great shakes 《口》月並みな, ぱっとしない, 平凡な ▪ His son was *no great shakes* as a leader. 彼の息子は指導者としては凡庸だった.

play the great I am 《口》偉いとうぬぼれて行動する ▪ The boss is *playing the great I am* again. 社長はまた偉いとうぬぼれてやっている.

run a great dog [***filly,*** etc.] 非常に速く走る, 走らせる ▪ Gallant *ran a great dog* in hare-coursing. ギャラント(犬の名)はウサギ狩りですばらしい走りを見せた ▪ He *ran a great filly*. 彼は子馬を非常に速く走らせた.

the great and the good 《戯》お偉方 ▪ So it was *the great and the good* of Europe getting together for the annual dinner. こういう次第で, 年中行事の晩餐会に集まったのは欧州のお偉方たちだった.

the great body [***majority, part***] ***of*** …の大部分 ▪ *The great body of* Cavaliers listened to it. 王党員たちの大部分がそれには耳を傾けた.

the greater [***greatest***] ***part*** (***of***) (…の)大部分, 大多数 ▪ *The greater part of* the area was covered with lofty warehouses. この地域の大部分に高い倉庫がいっぱい立てられていた ▪ *The greatest part of* our company were reprobate persons. 我々の仲間の大部分は感心できない人々であった.

the greatest happiness of the greatest number 最大多数の最大幸福 《J. Bentham (1748–1832)の唱えた功利主義の原則》.

the greatest thing since sliced bread →BREAD.

greedy /grí:di/ 形 ***be greedy for*** **1** …に強欲である ▪ The porter *is* very *greedy for* money. そのポーターは金に強欲である.

2 …を切望する, 切に求める ▪ He *is greedy for* gold [fame]. 彼は黄金[名声]を強く求めている.

be greedy of **1** …に飢えている ▪ This snake *is greedy of* milk. このヘビはミルクに飢えている.

2 = be GREEDY for.

be greedy to *do* …することを切望する ▪ He *was greedy to* know the truth. 彼はしきりに真相を知りたがっていた.

Greek /gri:k/ 形名 ***at the Greek calends*** →CALENDS.

be (***all***) ***Greek to*** 《口》(人)にさっぱりわからない, ちんぷんかんぷんである ▪ His lecture *was Greek to* me. 彼の講義は私にはさっぱりわからなかった.

Beware of Greeks bearing gifts. 《諺》人の贈り物には用心せよ. ☞ギリシャ人の贈り物とはトロイの木馬のこと (→a Greek GIFT); /b/ と /g/ が頭韻を踏んでいる ▪ *Beware of Greeks bearing gifts* or Republicans bearing tax cuts. 贈り物を贈るギリシャ人や減税をもちだす共和党員にはご用心.

The Greeks had a name [***word***] ***for it.*** それは昔からあった, 知られていた ▪ Yes, *the Greeks had a word for it*. そうね, そういうことは昔からあったのよ.

When Greek meets Greek, then comes the tug of war. 両雄相まみえれば激闘が起こる (N. Lee, *Rival Queens* 4. 2. 48).

green /gri:n/ 形名 ***A green Christmas*** [***winter***] ***makes a full*** [***fat***] ***churchyard.*** 《諺》クリスマス[冬]に暖かくて雪が降らなければ墓場がにぎわう《冬暖かいと病気がはやり死亡者が多い》.

a green old age 老いてなお元気なこと, かくしゃくたること ▪ He enjoys [is in] *a green old age*. 彼は老いてなお元気である.

(***as***) ***green as grass*** 《口》世間知らずで, 無知で; だまされやすく ▪ The young man was *as green as grass*. その青年は世間知らずだった.

be a green hand (***at***) →HAND[1].

be green about the gills →be white about the GILLs.

be green at …に未熟である ▪ He *is* still *green at* his job. 彼はまだ仕事に未熟だ.

Do you see any(***thing***) ***green in my eye?*** 《口》この目に青いところがあるかい; おれにだまされやすいところがあると思うか《あかんべえをしながら言う》 ▪ *Do you see any green in my eye* that you talk such a lot of nonsense? そんなたわごとばかりしゃべって, おれがだまされるとでも思うのか.

get the green light ゴーサインを与えられる, 許可さ

れる (*from, to do*) ▪ We *got the green light from* the Chinese government to set up a branch in Beijing. 我々は中国政府から北京に支店をつくるゴーサインを得た.

give** a person **the green light 人にゴーサインを与える, 許可する (*to do*) ▪ He's just *been given the green light to* build two large detached houses. 彼は独立した2軒の豪邸を建てるゴーサインを出してもらったばかりだ ▪ The President *gave* them *the green light*. 大統領は彼らに仕事始めの合図をした. ☞green light「進めの信号」.

go green 環境に優しい暮らしをする; 菜食主義に変える ▪ Then, almost overnight, my university *went green*. We now recycle almost everything. そして, ほとんど一晩で, 私の大学は環境にやさしくなった. いまではほとんどすべてのものをリサイクルしている ▪ Seventy-four percent of the patients have noticed a change in their health since they *went green*. 患者の74%は菜食主義に変えて以来, 健康の変化に気づいている.

green and fresh まだなまなましく, 青二才で ▪ I have *green and fresh* students for friends. 私にはまだ青二才の学生が友人としている.

green to** one's **job 仕事に慣れないで, 未熟で ▪ He is still *green to his job*. 彼はまだ自分の仕事に慣れていない.

***green with envy** [**jealousy, fear**]* (顔色が青ざめるほど)ひどくうらやんで[ねたんで, 恐れて] ▪ She is *green with envy* because you have succeeded. 彼女はあなたが成功したのでひどくねたんでいる.

greener pastures 新たな仕事[分野], より魅力的な業種 (cf. Milton, *Lycidas: pastures new* 1. 192) ▪ When the going gets rough, the investment companies turn to *greener pastures*. 値上がりがはかばかしくなくなると, 投資会社は新たな分野に転進する.

have a green thumb 《口》 **1** 草木や青い物を作るのがじょうずである ▪ Helen seems to *have a green thumb*. ヘレンは草木を作るのがじょうずなようだ. **2** (...に)生まれつき向いている, 適合性がある (*for*) ▪ He *has a green thumb for* boys. 彼は少年たちと気持ちがよく合う.

have green fingers 《英口》 = have a GREEN thumb. ☞BBC の園芸放送者であった Middleton の造語で have a GREEN thumb より多く用いられる.

in the green 少壮の[血気盛んな](時期に) ▪ Though *in the green*, he may not be equal to the task. 血気盛んだが, 彼はその任に耐えられまい.

in the green tree →TREE.

look green 病気のような[青白い]顔をしている ▪ You *look green*. 顔が青いよ.

not as green as** one **is cabbage-looking 《口》 見かけほど世間知らずでない ▪ He's *not as green as* he *is cabbage-looking*. 彼は見かけほど世間知らずではない.

see some(thing) green in** a person's **eye 《口》 人をだまし[御し]やすいと見る (→Do you see any(thing) GREEN in my eye?)

the wearing of the green アイルランド愛国精神の表明 ▪ They are hanging men and women for *the wearing of the green*. 彼らはアイルランド愛国精神を表明したかどで, 男や女を絞首刑に処している. ☞green はアイルランドの国色; the wearing of the green は1798年以来伝わるアイルランド愛国革命歌.

turn green 青白くなる ▪ My brother *turned green* at her threat. 弟は彼女のおどしで青ざめた.

green-eyed /gríːnàɪd/ 形 ***the green-eyed monster*** ねたみ (cf. Sh., *Oth*. 3. 1. 165) ▪ Many a woman is a victim of *the green-eyed monster*. ねたみに取りつかれる女性が非常に多い.

Green River /gríːnrívər/ 名 ***go up Green River*** 《米口》 死ぬ ▪ Those expressions have *gone up Green River*. それらの表現は死に絶えた.

send** a person **up Green River 《米口》 人を殺す ▪ They *sent* him *up Green River*. 彼らは彼を殺した.

green-room /gríːnrùːm/ 名 ***talk green-room*** 楽屋話をする, 劇場雑談をする ▪ We *talked green-room*. 我々は楽屋話をした. ☞green-room「出演者の控室, 楽屋」.

greenwood /gríːnwʊ̀d/ 名 ***go to the greenwood*** 追放者[悪党]となって緑林に入る ▪ I must *go to the greenwood* a banished man. 追放されて緑林に入らなければならない.

greeting /gríːtɪŋ/ 名 ***one's **best greetings to*** ...によろしく ▪ *My best greetings to* your father. お父さまによろしく ▪ He sends *his best greetings to* you. 彼はあなたによろしくと言っています.

***exchange greetings** (**with**)* (...と)あいさつを交わす ▪ We *exchanged greetings with* each other. 我々は互いにあいさつを交わした.

gridiron /grídàɪərn/ 名 ***lay** a person **on the gridiron*** 人を苦しめる, 責めさいなむ, ひどく不安にする ▪ He *laid* the prisoner *on the gridiron*. 彼は囚人を責めさいなんだ.

on the gridiron 《口》 苦しめられて, 責められて, ひどく心配させられて ▪ His name was *on the gridiron* at Westminster. 彼の名前はウェストミンスターで弾劾されていた.

grief /griːf/ 名 ***bring ... to grief*** ...をひどい目にあわす; をけがさせる; を失敗させる; を破滅させる ▪ The third Empire *brought* France *to grief*. 第3帝国はフランスに憂き目を見させた ▪ A lack of funds *brought* the undertaking *to grief*. 資金不足のためその事業は失敗した.

come to grief 《主に口》 **1** ひどい目にあう; 災難にあう ▪ If you do such a mischief, you may *come to grief*. 君がそんないたずらをすると, ひどい目にあうかもしれないぜ.
2 失敗する; 破滅する, 破産する ▪ The Panama canal scheme is likely to *come to grief*. パナマ運河計画は失敗に終わりそうだ ▪ His logic *came to grief*. 彼の論理はくずれ去った ▪ The firm *came to grief*. その会社は破産した.

3 (馬・車から)落ちる; けがをする ▪ I *came to grief* in a motor-bike race last Saturday. 私は先週の土曜にオートバイ競走で転落した ▪ He was learning to skate, but *came to grief* at the corner. 彼はスケートを習っていたが, かどの所でけがをした.

get grief 《口》(…のことで)叱責される, しかられる, がみがみ言われる (*about, for*) ▪ As a kid, Scott Tweten *got* a lot of *grief about* liking country music. 子供のころスコット・トウィーテンはカントリーミュージックが好きだったのでひどくしかられた ▪ I didn't show up once and *got* some *grief for* it. 一度出席しなかったことがあって, そのことでいささか叱責された.

give** a person **grief 《口》(…のことで)人を叱責する, しかる, 人にがみがみ言う (*about, over*) ▪ The coaching staff *gave* me *grief* for not playing offensively. コーチ陣は, 攻撃的にプレイしなかったと言って私をしかりつけた.

Good* [*Great*] *grief! 《口》おや驚いた, これは大変 ▪ May I ask you for a loan of 10 pounds?—*Good grief* no! 10ポンドお貸し願えませんか?—いやとんでもない ▪ *Great grief!* I'd forgotten that! これは大変. それを忘れていた.

Time tames the strongest grief. 《諺》時はどんな悲しみをもいやす.

grievance /gríːvəns/ 名 ***air* (*out*)** *one's* ***grievance(s)* [*a grievance*]** 苦情を持ち出す, 不満を述べる ▪ The protesters *aired their grievances* about taxes and the amount of government spending. 抗議者たちは税と政府の支出額とに不満を述べた ▪ If we *air out our grievances* we will have a better city hospital for those who need it. 苦情を表明すれば, それを必要とする人々のためにもっとよい市立病院ができるだろう.

have* [*nurse*] *a grievance against …に不平をいだいている ▪ They *have a grievance against* their chief. 彼らは長官に対して不平をいだいている.

grig /grɪg/ 名 ***(as) lively* [*merry*] *as a grig*** 《口》非常に快活で, ぴんぴんはねて, 大はしゃぎで ▪ I feel *lively as a grig* this morning. 私は今朝は非常に元気です. ☞grig「コオロギ」.

grill[1] /grɪl/ 名 ***put** a person **on the grill*** 《米》(犯人)を警察の拷問にかける ▪ He does not sound frank, so he *is put on the grill.* 彼は素直に吐かないようなので, 拷問にかけられている.

grill[2] /grɪl/ 動 ***grill in the sun* [*sunshine*]** 太陽[日光]に焼きつけられる ▪ He lay *grilling in the sunshine.* 彼は灼熱の太陽の下で寝ころんでいた.

grim /grɪm/ 形 ***hang* [*hold*] *on like grim death*** 《英口》しっかりとしがみつく ▪ Brown is *hanging on like grim death* to his role of team manager. ブラウンはチームのマネージャーとしての役割にしがみついていた.

like grim death (死神のように)頑強に; 執ように ▪ You must hang on *like grim death.* 君は頑強に頑張らなければならない.

the Grim Reaper 死, 死神 ▪ A drink a day keeps *the Grim Reaper* away. 1日にお酒を1杯飲めば死神を寄せつけない,「酒は百薬の長」. ☞死神は大鎌を持った草刈り人の姿で表される; →An APPLE a day keeps the doctor away.

grimace[1] /gríməs/ 名 ***make grimaces*** しかめつらをする ▪ Rude children *make grimaces.* 無作法な子供はしかめつらをする.

grimace[2] /grɪméɪs/ 動 ***grimace it*** しかめつらをする ▪ He *grimaced it* for a few days in a suit of sables. 彼は喪服を着て数日間顔をしかめていた.

grime /graɪm/ 動 ***grime the face of*** …の顔をよごす ▪ Soot and sweat *grime the face of* the factory worker. その工場労働者の顔はすすと汗で真っ黒に汚れている.

grin[1] /grɪn/ 名 ***on the* (*broad*) *grin*** 《口》(歯をむき出して)にやにや笑って ▪ They were all *on the broad grin.* 彼らはみなおおっぴらににやにや笑っていた.

wipe the grin off** a person's **face = wipe the smile off a person's FACE.

grin[2] /grɪn/ 動 ***grin and bear* [*abide*] *it*** 《口》笑ってこらえる ▪ If Jane won't marry me, I must just *grin and bear it.* ジェインが結婚してくれなければ, 私はただ笑ってこらえるほかはない.

grin from ear to ear (おもしろさ・満足・軽蔑を表すために)ニタッと笑う ▪ The boy *grinned from ear to ear* when I gave him the apple. リンゴをやるとその少年はニタッと笑った.

grin like a Cheshire cat →CHESHIRE.

grin on the other side of** one's **face (何でもないと思ってしたことを)後悔する ▪ You will *grin on the other side of your face* if you have to pay for it. その賠償が必要なら君はしたことを後悔するだろう.

grin through a horse-collar 馬の首輪に顔を入れて歯をむきだしてにらめっこをする《田舎の遊戯》.

grind[1] /graɪnd/ 名 ***take a grind*** 《大学俗》健康のために散歩する ▪ Let's *take a grind* for a while. しばらく散歩して運動をしようではないか.

the daily grind 毎日の決まり切った[退屈な]仕事 ▪ He just got tired of *the daily grind* and wanted to slow his life down a bit. 彼は日々の仕事にちょっと疲れて, もう少しのんびり生活したいと思った.

grind[2] /graɪnd/ 動 ***grind** one's **heel into*** …にかかとをぎりぎりひねりこむ ▪ He *ground his heel into* the ground. 彼はかかとを地面へ押しつけた.

grind … into** a person's **head 人に…をたたきこむ ▪ He *ground* Latin *into your head.* 彼はラテン語をあなたにたたきこんだ.

grind … small …をひいて粉にする ▪ He *ground* the corn *small.* 彼はその穀物をひいて粉にした.

grind** one's **teeth (嫌悪・失望・憤怒で)歯ぎしりする ▪ I *ground my teeth* at his insulting remarks. 私は彼の無礼な発言に歯ぎしりした.

***grind the faces of …* (*in the dust*)** …をしいたげる; の膏血(こうけつ)をしぼる (《聖》*Isa.* 3. 15) ▪ He *ground the faces of* the poor. 彼は貧乏人の膏血をしぼった.

***grind to a halt* [*standstill*]** じりじりと来て止まる ▪ The procession *ground to a halt.* その行列

はじりじりと来てとまった.

grind ... to pieces ...をひいてこなごなにする ▪ He *ground* chestnuts *to pieces*. 彼はクリをひいて粉にした ▪ Taxation is *grinding* us *to pieces*. 課税が我々を苦しめている.

have an ax to grind →AX.

grindstone /gráɪndstòʊn/ 名 ***at the grindstone*** 極度に, 最高度に ▪ He is a sharp hand *at the grindstone*. 彼は極度に無慈悲である ▪ He was a tight-fisted hand *at the grindstone*. 彼は極度に握り屋だった.

get back to the grindstone (いやな)仕事に戻る ▪ You'll have to *get back to the grindstone* from next Monday. 君はいやでも次の月曜から仕事に戻らなければならないだろう.

hold [***have, keep, bring, put***] *a person's* ***nose to the grindstone*** 人を間断なくこき使う, きびしく働かせる ▪ He *holds their noses to the grindstone*. 彼は彼らを絶えずこき使っている ▪ The tutor *kept the boy's nose to the grindstone* of grammar. 家庭教師は少年に文法をこつこつ勉強させた.

hold [***have, keep, bring, put***] *one's* ***nose to the grindstone*** 絶えずこつこつ働く, 勉強する ▪ Rich people need not *keep their noses to the grindstone*. 金持ちは絶えずあくせく働く必要はない ▪ *Keep your nose to the grindstone* and all will be well. 一生懸命やればすべてうまくいくだろう. ☞「研磨機に鼻が近づくほど接近して働く」より.

grip /ɡrɪp/ 名 (***be***) ***at grips*** (***with***) 《口》(...と)つかみ合って(いる), (と)取っ組み合って(いる) ▪ I found myself *at grips with* the devil. 私は悪魔とつかみ合っているのに気がついた ▪ He *is at grips with* the subject. 彼はその問題と取っ組み合っている.

be in the grip of ...につかまれている ▪ He *is in the grip of* a powerful emotion. 彼は強烈な感情にとらえられている ▪ He *is in the grip of* influenza. 彼はインフルエンザにかかっている.

bring *A* ***to grips with*** *B* AをBと取っ組ませる ▪ We *brought* him *to grips with* the devil. 我々は彼を悪魔と取っ組ませた.

come [***get***] ***to grips*** (***with***) **1** 《レスリング》(...と)取っ組み合う ▪ We have *come to grips* at last. 我々はついに取っ組み合いになった ▪ Soon you will *come to grips with* death. まもなくあなたは死と組み打ちするようになるでしょう.

2 (難問などと)取っ組み合う; (に)奮闘する ▪ The doctor *came to grips with* a case of cholera. 医者はコレラ患者と奮闘した.

feel a strong grip on *one's* ***arm*** (誰かに)ぎゅっと腕を握られる ▪ I *felt a strong grip on my arm*. 私は誰かにぎゅっと腕を握られた.

get [***take***] ***a grip of*** **1** ...を制御する ▪ Try to *get a grip of* them. They are unruly. 彼らを制御するようにしなさい. 手に負えないから.

2 ...に熟達する, を究める ▪ We must *get a grip of* the subject. 我々はその問題を究めなくてはならない.

get [***take***] ***a grip on*** ...をしっかりつかむ; を制御する ▪ You must *get a grip on* yourself. あなたは自己を抑えなければならない.

have a grip on [***of***] **1** ...を握っている, 理解している ▪ He *has a grip on* his servant. 彼は使用人をしっかりと握っている ▪ He *has a grip of* the matter. 彼はその問題をよくのみこんでいる.

2 ...の心を捕えている ▪ He *has a grip on* the audience. 彼は聴衆の心を捕えている.

have [***take***] ***a grip on*** [***upon***] *oneself* 自制している ▪ It is because he *has a grip on himself*. それは彼がおのれを制しているからである.

hold *one's* ***grip*** 《米口》自己の地位を保つ, 勇気を保つ ▪ Now *hold your grip*. さあ, くじけないで.

in grips 拘留[保護]されて ▪ We will see him *in grips*. 彼を拘留してもらうようにしよう.

in the grip of ...に支配されて ▪ The markets all across the world were *in the grip of* deep depression. 世界中の市場は深刻な不況に見舞われていた.

keep a grip on [***of***] ...をしっかりつかんでいる; を制御している ▪ I tried to *keep a grip on* my emotions. 私は感情を抑えていようと努めた.

let go *one's* ***grip on*** ...を放す ▪ He *let go his grip on* the branch. 彼はつかまえていた枝を放した.

lose grip of ...の心[興味]をつなげなくなる ▪ He has *lost grip of* his audience. 彼は聴衆の心をつなげなくなった.

lose *one's* ***grip*** (***on, of***) **1** 《口》(...の)能力[元気, 熱意]がなくなる[弱まる] ▪ I'm very tired and have *lost my grip on* the job. 私はひどく疲れて, その仕事をする力がなくなった.

2 (...を)統制[制御]できなくなる ▪ He has *lost his grip of* the business. 彼は業務の統制ができなくなった.

3 (...の)理解力がなくなる[弱まる] ▪ I've *lost my grip on* the details. 私は詳細なことは理解できなくなった ▪ His mind has *lost its grip*. 彼は理解力がなくなった.

take a (***firm***) ***grip on*** *oneself* 己を抑える《特に悲しみ, 恐れなどの感情を》 ▪ Though he failed the examination, he *took a grip on himself*. 彼は試験に失敗したが悲しみを抑えていた.

take a grip of →get a GRIP of.

take a grip on ...をしっかりつかむ ▪ He *took a grip on* the rope. 彼は綱をしっかりつかんだ.

tighten *one's* ***grip*** 統制を強化する, 支配を強める ▪ Putin *tightened his grip* on parliament and the regions by changing the rules. プーチンは, 規則を変更することによって議会と地方への統制力を強化した ▪ Avian influenza *tightened its grip* on the region in 2005. 鳥インフルエンザは2005年にその地域で大流行した.

gripe /ɡraɪp/ 名 ***be in the gripe of*** ...に苦しめられている; につかまれている ▪ He *is in the gripe of* hunger. 彼は空腹に苦しめられている.

come to gripes (***with***) (...と)取っ組み合う (=

come to GRIPs (with)) ▪ He *came to gripes with* the monster. 彼はその怪物と取っ組み合った.

griskin /grískən/ 名 ***in griskins*** ぼろぼろにちぎれて ▪ My feet were absolutely *in griskins*. 私の足は全くずたずたに裂かれていた.

grist /grɪst/ 名 ***All* [*Everything*] *is grist that comes to*** *one's* ***mill.*** 自分の所へ来るものは何でもみな利用する, 何でもござれだ ▪ The author writes on any subject; *everything is grist that comes to his mill*. その著者はどんな問題についても書く, つまり何でもござれだ.

bring grist to the [*one's*] ***mill*** 儲けの種になる, 金になる; 仕事口になる《通例本職以外の儲け》 ▪ I started photography as a hobby, but it *brings grist to the mill*. 写真を道楽として始めたのだが, それは金儲けになる.

grist for [《英》 ***to***] ***the*** [*one's*] ***mill*** **1** 儲けの種 ▪ All experience is *grist to his mill*. あらゆる経験が彼にとっては利益の種である.

2 論文の種, 証拠[傍証]資料《特定の見解を支持するために用いられる材料》 ▪ This will be a *grist for the mill* of the reader as historical detective. これは, 歴史の探偵としての読者には証拠資料になるだろう.

gristle /grísəl/ 名 ***in the gristle*** まだ骨のかたまらない, 未成熟の, 未発達の ▪ The colonists' intent was to nurture a people still *in the gristle*. 入植者たちの思惑はまだ未成熟の地元民を教化することだった ▪ This business is *in the gristle*. この事業はまだかたまっていない. ☞幼児は骨の代わりに gristle (軟骨) を持っていることから.

grit[1] /grɪt/ 名 ***be clear*** [***hard***] ***grit*** (人に)気概がある, 胆力がある ▪ Our English lads *are hard grit*. わが英国の青年は気概がある.

cut grit 《米俗》 去る, 出発する ▪ As soon as I *cut grit*, they all started too. 私が出発するとすぐ, 彼らもみな出発した.

have grit 気概がある, 胆力がある ▪ They *have grit* enough to do it. 彼らはそれをするだけの気概がある.

hit the grit 《米俗》 去る, 出発する; 道を行く, 走る ▪ We'll *hit the grit* hard now. さあ頑張って行こう.

of the true grit 《米》 真の意気のある ▪ He is *of the true grit*. 彼は真の気概がある.

put (***a little***) ***grit in the machine*** 行動を妨げる, 事務の円滑な進行を妨げる ▪ Whatever I try to do, she will spitefully *put grit in the machine*! 私が何をしようとしても, 彼女は意地悪くじゃまをするのである.

grit[2] /grɪt/ 動 ***grit*** *one's* ***teeth*** 歯ぎしりする ▪ I *gritted my teeth* as I thought of it. 私はそれを思い出して歯ぎしりした.

groan[1] /groʊn/ 名 ***give a groan*** うーんとうなる《不満のしるし》 ▪ They *gave* three *groans*. 彼らは3回うーんとうなった.

with a groan うーんとうなって ▪ He fell *with a groan*. 彼はうーんとうなって倒れた.

groan[2] /groʊn/ 動 ***groan under the weight of*** …の重みできしむ, 重みに耐えかねる; 悲鳴をあげる ▪ The bridge *groaned under the weight of* buses and cars streaming north and south. その橋は北や南へと走り抜けていくバスや車の重量を支えかねていた ▪ This kingdom is *groaning under the weight of* the influx of more than 300,000 Palestinians. この王国は30万人以上のパレスチナ人の流入で悲鳴をあげている.

groat /groʊt/ 名 ***give*** *a person* ***groats for pease*** 人にしっぺ返しをする ▪ He *gave* them *groats for pease*, and excommunicated them. 彼はしっぺ返しに彼らを破門した.

not care a groat ちっともかまわない ▪ I do*n't care a groat* what you do. 君が何をしようとちっともかまわない. ☞groat「昔の英国の4 pence 貨幣」.

not worth a groat 一文の値うちもない ▪ Your opinion is *not worth a groat*. 君の意見は一文の値うちもない.

grog /grɑg|grɔg/ 名 ***have a grog blossom*** 《口》 酔って鼻を非常に赤くしている ▪ The charwoman *had* the best *grog blossom* I've ever seen. その雑役婦は酔って真っ赤な鼻をしていた.

groove /gruːv/ 名 ***back in the groove*** もとに戻って, 復帰[復活, 復調]して ▪ I felt a little rusty at first, but then I got *back in the groove*. 最初はちょっとさびついているように感じたが, その後調子がもどってきた.

be (***stuck***) ***in a groove*** 《英》 型にはまって, 同じことの繰り返しで; 退屈で ▪ I may *be stuck in a groove* just like a needle in a scratchy vinyl gramophone record. 私は, ちょうどひっかかっているレコード盤の針のように, 溝にはまりこんで(同じことを繰り返して)いるのかもしれない ▪ He seems to *be stuck in a groove* and was too rigid, hence he was not innovative. 彼はマンネリにおちいっているようで厳密すぎた, だから斬新さに欠けたのだ.

get *one's* ***groove on*** ダンスをして楽しむ ▪ I'm going to go *get my groove on*. 私はダンスをして楽しみに行くつもりよ. ☞groove「楽しい時間」.

get [***fall***] ***into*** [***in***] ***a groove*** 狭い型にはまる; 常習になる; マンネリになる ▪ Folks are apt to *get in a groove* as they grow older. 人は年をとるにつれ狭い型にはまりがちだ.

get out of the groove マンネリの[型にはまった]生活から脱する ▪ I must *get out of the groove* here. 私はここの型にはまった生活を脱しなければならない.

in the groove 《口》 **1** 最好調で ▪ Ichiro is starting to get *in the groove* after four hits on Monday. イチローは月曜日に4安打して絶好調になりつつある.

2 流行のスタイルで ▪ The song is right *in the groove*. その歌はまさしく今流行の歌だ. ☞「蓄音機の針がみぞに入って」の意から.

run a groove 狭い型にはまる, マンネリになる ▪ His whole life *ran* in *a* narrow *groove*. 彼の生活全体は狭い型にはまっていた.

grope /groʊp/ 動 ***grope and grabble*** 手探り

で進む ▪ To wade through Hegel is to *grope and grabble.* ヘーゲルを骨折って読んでいくことは手探りで進むようなものだ.

grope** one's **way **1** 手探りで進む ▪ We *groped our way* through the dark street. 我々は暗い通りを手探りで進んだ ▪ We *groped our way* toward understanding. 我々は手探りで理解しようと努めた.

2 手探りでやってみる ▪ We are compelled to *grope our way.* 手探りでやってみるよりほかはない.

gross /groʊs/ 名 ***by the gross*** 全体で, 大量に, まとめて; 卸しで ▪ These goods are to be sold *by the gross.* これらの商品は卸しで売ることになっています.

in gross 《法》絶対独立の ▪ a common *in gross* 独立共有地《荘園に属さない》 ▪ a villein *in gross* 独立農奴《serf でない》.

ground[1] /graʊnd/ 名 ***a happy hunting ground*** 《口》望むものの(豊富に)見つかる所; (人が)成功する所 (→ go to the happy hunting GROUND(s)) ▪ The forest is *a happy hunting ground* for botanizers. その森林は植物採集家の宝庫である. ☞いくらでも狩りができるとされる, 米先住民の死後の理想郷から.

a middle ground 妥協点, 落としどころ ▪ He prides himself on having found *a middle ground* between neighbors and developers. 彼は, 近隣住民と開発業者との妥協点を見いだしたことを誇りに思っている.

be above ground **1** 生きている ▪ I will find him out if he *is above ground.* 彼が生きているなら見つけ出します.

2 埋葬されていない ▪ She died last week and *is* still *above ground.* 彼女は先週死んでまだ埋葬されていない.

be on sure ground 確かなことをつかんでいる ▪ You must *be on sure ground* before you accuse a man. 人を責める前に確証をつかむ必要がある.

be thick on the ground (数が)多い; 密集した ▪ Jobs *are* not *thick on the ground* now. 今は仕事が多くない ▪ In the city ethnic restaurants *were*n't very *thick on the ground.* 町にはエスニックレストランは大して多くなかった.

be thin on the ground (数が)少ない; まばらな ▪ Scandal *is thin on the ground* here. ここではスキャンダルは少ない ▪ The visitors were *thin on the ground.* お客は少なかった.

below ground =DEAD and buried.

break fresh [***new***] ***ground*** 未墾の地を開拓する, 新生面[新しい顧客]を開拓する ▪ We shall *break new ground* in spring by opening a shop at Liverpool. 私たちは春にはリバプールに新しい店を開いて新生面を開拓する.

break ground **1** 土を掘る; 開墾する ▪ It takes three horses to *break ground.* 開墾するのに3頭の馬がいる.

2 開拓する; 先駆者になる ▪ He *broke ground* in an all but virgin field of investigation. 彼はほとんど処女地ともいうべき研究分野を開拓した.

3 (建築・鉄道・運河などを)起工する, くわ入れする ▪ They will *break ground* on the new housing project next week. 彼らは来週新しい住宅計画のくわ入れをする.

4 事業を始める ▪ He is sending me up next week to *break ground* in Edinburgh. 彼は新事業をエジンバラで始めるため, 来週私を派遣する.

5 ざんごうを掘る ▪ We hear the French are *breaking ground.* フランス軍はざんごうを掘っているそうだ.

6 《海》いかりを巻き揚げる ▪ The men of war *broke ground.* 艦隊はいかりを揚げた.

7 《米》キャンプを捨ててよそに移る ▪ The squatter *breaks ground* many times. 無断居住者は転々とする.

bring to the ground 倒す ▪ The gales *brought* the trees *to the ground.* 強風が木々を倒した.

burn to the ground 全焼する ▪ His house (*was*) *burned to the ground.* 彼の家は全焼した.

change** one's **ground =shift one's GROUND.

come to the ground 負ける, 滅びる ▪ He *came to the ground* in the contest. 彼はその競技に負けた.

common ground → find common GROUND, on common GROUND.

cover (***the***) ***ground*** **1** (ある距離を)行く, 踏破する ▪ We've *covered* a great deal of *ground* today. 我々はきょうは長い道のりを来た.

2 (研究・報告などがある範囲に)わたる; (ある範囲を)完了する ▪ The committee's report *covers* a great deal of [a lot of, lots of] *ground.* 委員会の報告は広範囲にわたっている ▪ You cannot hope to *cover the ground* of such a vast subject in two years. そんな広範囲な内容の教科を2年で終了するなんて無理だ.

3 速く行く[走る] ▪ His new car *covers the* same *ground* in much less time than the old one. 彼の新車は旧車より同じ距離をずっと短い時間で走る.

cut more ground out from under …よりも更に有利な地位を得る ▪ Daniel tried to *cut more ground out from under* him. ダニエルは彼よりももっと優位になろうとした.

cut the ground from under** a person* [*a person's **feet] 人の論拠を失わせる; 人の(計画などの)裏をかく ▪ I *cut the ground from under* him by proving it. 私はそれを証明して彼の論拠を失わせた ▪ They intend to buy that property, but let us *cut the ground from under their feet.* 彼らはその財産を買うつもりだが, 彼らの裏をかいてやろう.

dash ... to the ground **1** …をぶちこわす ▪ In his temper the child *dashed* the cup *to the ground.* 腹を立ててその子はコップをぶつけて割った.

2 (希望など)をすっかりくじく ▪ It *dashed* our hope *to the ground.* それは我々の希望をすっかりくじいた.

down to the ground 《口》全く; すべての点で (《聖》*Judges* 20. 25) ▪ That'll suit me *down to* *the ground.* 私には全く好都合です.

drive* [*run, work*]** *oneself* ***into the ground 倒れるまで働く ▪ Chris *drove himself into the ground* of his own free will. It's tragic. クリスは自らの意志で働いて倒れてしまった. 悲惨なことだ.

fall on stony ground →FALL[2].

fall to the ground **1** 地に落ちる ▪ The apple *fell to the ground.* リンゴは地に落ちた.
2 望みが絶える, 希望が失われる ▪ Our hope *fell to the ground.* 我々の希望が失われた.
3 (計画が)やめになる, 失敗に帰する ▪ The scheme *fell to the ground.* その計画はだめになった.

find common ground 妥協点[一致点]を見いだす ▪ Since then, the two have *found common ground* and talk regularly. そのとき以来, 両者は妥協点を見いだして, 定期的に話し合っている.

from the ground up 《米口》全く, 徹底的に, 土台から最後まで ▪ We suited each other *from the ground up.* 我々はお互いに全く適合し合っていた ▪ You must work on it *from the ground up.* 一番下からこつこつやらなければならない.

gain ground **1** (兵士が)前進する; 陣地を得る, 優勢になる ▪ Rebel forces *gained ground* against the ruling Taliban. 反乱軍は支配中のタリバンに対して優位になった ▪ In all states, Obama *gained ground* among unaffiliated voters. すべての州でオバマ氏は無党派投票者の支持を固めた ▪ The cause of teetotalism is slowly *gaining ground.* 絶対禁酒運動は徐々に前進している.
2 (考え・製品などが)受け入れられる, 普及する, (説などが)受け入れられる, 広まる ▪ Linux is *gaining ground* in the server market. リナックスはサーバー市場で普及しつつある ▪ The rumor *gained ground* every day. その噂は毎日広まっていった.
3 (病人が)よくなる ▪ The patient began to *gain ground.* その病人はよくなり始めた.
4 成功する; 景気がよくなる; 威勢がよくなる ▪ Keep at it. You are *gaining ground.* それを続けなさい. 君は成功しかけている.
5 追いつく; (追われる人に)近づく, 迫る (*on*) ▪ They *gained ground on* their enemy each minute. 彼らは刻々と敵に迫った.
6 (...を)侵す, 侵略する (*on*) ▪ My melancholy *gained ground on* me. 悲しみがどんどん私に募った ▪ The Parliament was slowly *gaining ground on* the prerogative. 国会は徐々にその特権を侵していた.
7 《軍》(敵と対陣して)陣地を得る (↔lose GROUND 1) ▪ They have *gained ground* in the peninsula. 彼らはその半島に地歩を得た.

gather ground =gain GROUND.

***get ground* (*of*)** (...を)侵食する; (より)優勢になる, (に)勝つ; (追跡者を)引き離す, (追われる人に)追いつく ▪ The waves are *getting ground of* the shore inch by inch. 波は少しずつ海岸を侵食している ▪ We *got ground of* the ship apace. 我々は急速にその船に追いついた.

get off the ground (飛行機が)飛び立つ; 《口》うまくスタートする ▪ The story dramatically never *gets off the ground.* その話は劇としては決してうまくいかない ▪ The movement *got off the ground.* その運動はうまくスタートした.

get ... off the ground うまくスタート[離陸]させる ▪ Paine is hoping for $1.6 million to *get* the project *off the ground.* ペインはプロジェクトをうまくスタートさせるのに160万ドル望んでいる.

give ground **1** 退く, 衰える ▪ We must *give ground.* 我々は退却しないといけない ▪ The delirium began to *give ground.* 譫妄(せんもう)状態は去りかけた.
2 =lose GROUND 2. ☞退却して敵に領土を明け渡すことから.

go over the ground 行程を踏む; (事実を)調べる ▪ I should like to *go over the ground* again. 私はまた事実を調べたい.

go over the same ground/cover the same ground 同じことを繰り返し行う[話す, 書く, 考える] ▪ We *went over the same ground* 15 or 20 times. 我々は同じことを15〜20回繰り返した.

go to ground 隠れる ▪ The militias *went to ground* in Baghdad but violence still runs rampant. バグダッドでは市民軍は地下に潜入したが, 暴力は依然として蔓延している.

go to* (*the*) *ground =come to the GROUND.

***go to the happy hunting ground*(*s*)** 《戯》死ぬ, あの世へ行く. ☞the happy hunting ground は米先住民の「天国, 死後の理想郷」; →a happy hunting GROUND.

have ground*(*s*) *for *doing* ...する根拠がある ▪ He *has grounds for complaining.* 彼には不平を言う根拠がある.

have the ground on *one's* ***side*** (競争に)有利な地歩を占める ▪ He *got the ground on his side.* 地歩が彼に有利となった.

have the ground slide from under *one* 立脚地を失う ▪ Then I shall *have the ground slide from under* me. それでは立脚地を失うだろう.

hit the ground 《口》(危険を避けて)地に伏せる ▪ Tom was shot to death before he *hit the ground.* トムは地に伏せる前に銃撃されて死んだ.

hit the ground running **1** 精力的に1日の仕事をはじめる ▪ A decade ago I had a lot more energy. I would wake up, *hit the ground running,* and never stop until I went to bed again. 私は10年前にはずっと元気だった. 目が覚めるとすぐに仕事をはじめて, また床に就くまで休憩もとらなかった.
2 《主に米》熱心に新しいことを始める ▪ The new president tries to *hit the ground running.* 新社長は新規事業に着手しようとしている.
3 即戦力として働きうる ▪ His previous experience will allow him to *hit the ground running* when he takes over the Commerce Department. 前に経験があるから彼は商務省の引継ぎ後すぐに働けるだろう.

hold* [*keep, maintain*]** *one's* ***ground **1** 地歩

などを保つ; 一歩も引かない, 譲らない ▪ The government was strong enough to *hold its ground*. 政府は強力に地歩を保つことができた ▪ We will *hold our ground* against the enemy. 我々は敵に対して一歩も引かない ▪ He can't *keep his ground* with his students. 彼は学生の信用を保てない.

2 (病人が)力を保つ ▪ The patient is *holding his ground*. その病人は力を保っている.

hope* (*that*) *the ground would* (*open and*) *swallow *one* → wish (that) the GROUND would (open and) swallow one.

into the ground 必要以上に, がまんできないほど; 極度に, とことんまで ▪ Caution is a virtue, but don't run it *into the ground*. 用心は美徳だが, 度を過ぎてはいけない.

kiss the ground =bite the DUST.

lay a ground (表面に)下塗りをする ▪ In japanning *laying the ground*, painting and finishing are required. 漆塗りには下塗り, 絵付け, 仕上げが必要である.

lose ground **1** 地歩などを失う; 衰える (↔gain GROUND 7) ▪ They are *losing ground* in the war. 彼らは戦争で陣地を失いつつある ▪ You have *lost* some *ground* at court. あなたは宮廷における地歩を少し失った ▪ He is *losing ground* with the students. 彼は生徒の信用を失いかけている.

2 遅れる; (負けて)退く; 譲る, 負ける ▪ The leading man began to *lose ground*. 先頭の人は遅れ始めた ▪ I *lost ground* badly on today's paper. 私はきょうの答案ではひどく点が下がった.

3 (病人が)悪化する ▪ The patient began to *lose ground*. 病人は悪化し始めた.

lose ground to …に地歩を譲る ▪ Why is Nokia *losing ground to* Apple and Android? なぜノキアはアップルやアンドロイドに地歩を譲っているのか?

make up ground →make up for lost TIME.

meet *a person* ***on*** *his* ***own ground*** 相手の得意の問題で論戦する ▪ I'll *meet* him anywhere *on his own ground*. どこででも彼の得意の問題で彼と論戦しよう.

mop* [*wipe*] *the ground* (*up*) *with *a person* 《口》 **1** 人をしこたま打ちのめす《比喩的にも》 ▪ I'll *mop the ground up with* him. 彼をしこたま打ちのめしてやろう ▪ The lawyer would *wipe the ground with* him in ten minutes. その弁護士だったら10分で彼を完全にやっつけてしまうだろう.

2 人にはるかに勝ることを実証する ▪ I'll *mop the ground up with* him any day. 私はいつでも彼よりはるかに勝ることを実証します.

off the ground (飛行機が)離陸して, (計画などが)緒に就いて, 糸口がついて ▪ In maybe 4 seconds, the plane was *off the ground*. たぶん4秒くらいで飛行機は離陸した ▪ Our project is *off the ground* and running. 我々のプロジェクトは緒に就いて, 目下進行中だ.

one's **(*old*) *stamping* [*stomping*] *ground*** 《口》 人の行きつけの遊び場 ▪ The place was *his stamping ground*. そこは彼の行きつけの遊び場であった. ☞stamping ground「動物が群れ集まる所」.

on common ground (…と)同じ土台に立っている, 共通の目標[考え]をもっている (*with*) ▪ Pitcher Joey Hamilton is *on common ground with* relief pitcher White. ジョイ・ハミルトン投手は救援投手のホワイトと同じ考えをもっている.

on dangerous ground 人を怒らせそうで; やばいことを話題にして, デリケートな問題に踏み込んで ▪ You are treading *on dangerous ground* here. 君はこの件に関してデリケートな問題に踏み込んでいる ▪ Though I know I am *on dangerous ground*, why must we all suffer even if we are good? 人の怒りを買うのは承知のうえだが, 我々はみな善良なのにどうして苦しまねばならないのだろう.

on *one's* ***own ground* [*home ground, turf, patch*]** →OWN.

on safe ground 安全なことを話題にして ▪ You'll be *on safe ground* if you ask him about poetry. 彼には詩のことを聞いていれば無難だろう.

on slippery ground あやふやで ▪ The speaker was *on slippery ground* and not sure of the facts. その弁士はあやふやでその事実に確信がなかった.

on the ground **1** 場所に[で], 現場に[で] ▪ Glass was found *on the ground* where the Chevrolet had been parked. シボレーが駐車してあった場所でガラス片が発見された ▪ They're losing support *on the ground*. 彼らは現場の支持を失いつつある.

2 決闘をして ▪ He has been *on the ground* many times. 彼は何度も決闘をしたことがある.

***on the ground*(*s*) (*of, that*)** (…という)理由で ▪ He wishes to resign *on the ground of* ill health. 彼は病気のため辞職したいと思っている ▪ Something must be done *on* public *grounds*. 公共のため何かせねばならない.

open ground 土を耕す ▪ A farmer *opens ground* before sowing seeds. 農夫は種をまく前に土を耕す.

prepare the ground (…のための)下準備をする, 地盤[状況]を整える (*for, to do*) ▪ Finance ministers are meeting to *prepare the ground for* the G20 summit on 2 April. 財務大臣たちは, 4月2日のG20に向けた下準備のために会議中だ ▪ She is *preparing the ground to* run for governor. 彼女は知事選に立候補するために地盤を整えている.

rooted to the ground (驚き・恐れのため)動けないで ▪ He was so afraid that he stood *rooted to the ground*. 彼は恐ろしくてじっと動かないで(立って)いた.

run* [*drive, work*] *into the ground 《英》 **1** (計画などが)失敗する ▪ The plan quickly *ran into the ground* for a lack of funds. その計画は資金不足のためすぐに失敗に終わった.

2 徹底的に使ってだめにする; 働きすぎてへとへとにさせる (→into the GROUND) ▪ That's an oil company the politician *ran into the ground*. あれがその政治屋がしゃぶりつくした石油会社だ ▪ He *ran* himself *into the ground* in the match. 彼はその試合でがん

ばりすぎてへとへとになった.

3《米俗》…をやりすぎる, 度を過ごす ▪ The advocates of temperance have *run* it *into the ground* by their extreme measures. 禁酒唱導者たちは極端な策でことをやりすぎてしまった.

shift** one's **ground 議論[意図]を変更する, 意見を変える; 異なった計画をやってみる (cf. Sh., *Haml.* 1. 5. 156) ▪ He was willing to *shift his ground.* 彼は自らの意図を変更したいと思っていた ▪ A party cannot be permitted to *shift its ground* so often. 政党がそんなに頻繁(ひんぱん)に意見を変えることは許されない.

stand** one's **ground ＝hold one's GROUND.

strike ground 《海》測鉛線が海底に達する; (泳ぐ人が)底に届く ▪ We *struck ground* with 56 fathom of line. 56尋(ひろ)の測鉛線が海底に達した ▪ He swam and then *struck ground.* 彼は泳いだら底に足が届いた.

suit** a person **(down) to the ground → down to the GROUND; SUIT[3].

take ground ある陣地による; ある立場を取る ▪ He *took ground* before Arcot on August 21st. 彼は8月21日にアーコットの前に陣を敷いた ▪ He *took* new *ground* as to fainting. 彼は卒倒することに関して新しい見地に立った.

to the ground ＝down to the GROUND.

touch ground **1**《海》船が水底に触れる ▪ A Dutch tanker *touched ground* near Miami. マイアミの近くでオランダ籍のタンカーが浅瀬に乗り上げた.

2 (議論が)現実に触れてくる, 具体化する; (漠然とした談話の後に)本論に及ぶ ▪ Now let's *touch ground.* さあ本論に入りましょう.

***wipe the ground (up) with** a person* →mop the GROUND (up) with a person.

***wish [hope] (that) the ground would (open and) swallow** one* (きまり悪く, 恥ずかしくて)穴があったら入りたい ▪ I was so ashamed that I *hoped the ground would swallow* me. 私はとても恥ずかしくて穴があったら入りたいほどだった.

worship the ground** a person **walks [treads] on →WORSHIP[2].

ground[2] /graʊnd/ 動 ***be grounded in*** **1** …の基礎知識を与えられている ▪ The boy *was* well *grounded in* mathematics. その少年は数学の基礎知識がしっかりしていた.

2 …で座礁している ▪ The ship *is grounded in* a dangerous position. 船は危険な位置で座礁している.

be grounded on …に基礎を置いている ▪ It *is grounded on* this fact. それはこの事実に基づいている.

ground** oneself **in …の基礎を自分でつける ▪ He *grounded himself in* Latin. 彼はラテン語の基礎を独習した.

ground floor /gràʊndflɔ́ːr/ 名 ***get in [let in] on the ground floor*** 《口》**1** 発起人と同一条件で投資を許される[許す]; (事業などに)最初に加入する[させる] ▪ Evans, who *got in on the ground floor,* made a fortune in the promotion of that stock. エバンスは最初に加入したので, その株の創設で一財産作った.

2 他より先んじる[先んじさせる], 有利な地位にある[する] ▪ You, having *got in on the ground floor,* will be sure to get a useful position. 君は他に先んじたから, きっと有益な地位が得られるよ.

grounding /gráʊndɪŋ/ 名 ***have a (good) grounding in*** …の基礎が(十分)できている ▪ He *has a grounding in* English. 彼は英語の基礎が十分できている.

group /gruːp/ 名 ***a splinter group*** 分派, 分裂少数グループ ▪ Critton later joined *a splinter group* of the Black Panthers. クリットンは後にブラックパンサー党の1分派に加わった.

in a group 群がって ▪ They were standing *in a group.* 彼らは群れをなして立っていた.

in groups 三々五々群がって ▪ They walked about *in groups.* 彼らは三々五々歩き回った.

grouse /graʊs/ 名 ***grouse in the gunroom*** (人が)いつも得意になってする話 (Goldsmith, *She Stoops to Conquer* 2. 1) ▪ That people should have many a story of "*grouse in the gunroom*" is a better preparation for life. 人々が得意な話を多く持っているほうが生活する上でのよりよい備えとなる.

grouter /gráʊtər/ 名 ***on a [the] grouter*** 《俗》自分の番でないのにおせっかいに; 不正に ▪ He came in *on a grouter.* 彼は取得権のない財産利得を得た.

grove /groʊv/ 名 ***the groves of academe*** 学問の世界 ▪ Jim worked for a law firm, then returned to *the groves of academe* at Harvard. ジムは法律事務所に勤務後ハーバードで学問の世界に戻った.

grovel /grʌ́vəl|grɔ́v-/ 動 ***grovel in the dust [dirt]*** 地にはいつくばう, 頭をすりつける ▪ The Parliament *groveled in the dust* at the Cardinal's feet. 国会は枢機卿の足もとにはいつくばった.

grow /groʊ/ 動 ***be grown up with*** (土地に)…が密生している ▪ The field *was grown up with* corn. 畑には小麦が密生していた.

grow like a snow-ball 雪だるま式に大きくなる ▪ Money doesn't *grow like a snow-ball.* 金は雪だるま式には増えない.

grow on [upon]** a person's **hands (事業などが)やっかいでだんだん手に負えなくなる ▪ This business is apt to *grow upon our hands.* この事業は我々の手に負えなくなりがちだ.

grow on trees →TREE.

grow out of kind (種(しゅ)が)変質[退化]する ▪ Some plants may, when transplanted, *grow out of kind.* 植物によっては移植すると種が退化するものがある.

grow (together) into one 融合して一つになる ▪ The two races *grew together into one.* その二つの種族は融合して一つになった.

grower /gróʊər/ 名 ***a rocket-like grower*** 非常に生長が早い植物 ▪ The hedges are made of the *rocket-like grower*, the Cupresso-cyparis Leylandii. 生け垣は生長の早い植物であるレイランドヒノキで造られている.

growler /gráulər/ 名 ***rush the growler***《米俗》ビールをバケツ[びんなど]に入れて取ってくる ▪ Several boys *rushed the growler* for them. 数名の少年が彼らのためビールを取ってきた.

growth /groʊθ/ 名 ***a cancerous growth*** ガン性増殖; 異常増殖(傾向) ▪ Dr. Rajesh Kumar said there has been *a cancerous growth* of substandard colleges. ラジェシュ・クマール博士は標準以下の大学が異常増殖していると述べた.

of … growth …産の ▪ Most of the plants were *of* foreign *growth*. その植物の大部分は外来種だった.

of *one's* ***growth*** 自作の ▪ These apples are *of my* own *growth*. これらのリンゴは自作です.

grub[1] /grʌb/ 名 ***grub street/Grub Street*** 三文文士の ▪ Before "Vanity Fair" made his reputation, and indeed after, Thackeray was a *Grub Street* hack.「虚栄の市」で名声が出るまでは, 実はその後も, サッカレーは三流作家だった.

ride the grub line《米》失業カウボーイが伝統的な歓待にあずかって牧場を渡り歩く ▪ Cowboys *ride the grub line* from ranch to ranch, looking for another job. カウボーイたちは別の仕事を求めて, 牧場から牧場へと伝統的な接待にあずかって渡り歩く.

grub[2] /grʌb/ 動 ***grub it***《俗》食べる ▪ He was *grubbing it* in silence. 彼は黙って食べていた.

grudge /grʌdʒ/ 名 ***bear*** [***owe***] *a person* ***a grudge*** 人に恨みをいだく ▪ Why, I almost believed you *bore* me *a grudge*. なあんだ, 君は僕に恨みをいだいてるんだとばかり思っていたんだ.

carry grudges 不満を持つ ▪ Don't *carry grudges*. 不満を持つな.

have [***bear, hold, nurse***] ***a grudge*** (***against***) (…に対して)恨みをいだく ▪ He *had a grudge against* the Duke. 彼は公爵に恨みをいだいていた.

grudging /grʌ́dʒɪŋ/ 形 ***be grudging of*** …を惜しむ ▪ Even here he *is grudging of* praise. この場合でさえ彼は賞賛を惜しむ.

gruel /grúːəl/ 名 ***get*** [***have, take***] *one's* ***gruel***《口》罰せられる, 懲らしめられる;《ボクシング》ノックアウトされる; 殺される ▪ If he plays the fool, he'll *get his gruel*. もし彼がばかなまねをすると罰せられるだろう ▪ We may *take our gruel*. 我々は殺されるかもしれない.

give *a person his* ***gruel***《口》人を罰する, 懲らしめる;《ボクシング》人をノックアウトする; 人を殺す ▪ I *gave* the rascal *his gruel*. そのならず者を懲らしめた.

grueling,《英》**gruelling** /grúːəlɪŋ/ 名 ***get*** [***have, undergo***] ***a grueling*** ひどく罰せられる, 懲らしめられる; やっつけられる《ボクシングなどで》 ▪ The witness *underwent a grueling* at your hands. その証人はあなたの手でひどくやっつけられた.

give a grueling ひどく罰する, 懲らしめる; ひどくやっつける《ボクシングなどで》 ▪ The pugilist *gave* him *a grueling* last night. そのボクサーは昨夜彼をノックアウトした.

grumble /grʌ́mbəl/ 名 (***be***) ***all over grumble***《俗》劣っている; 不満足で(ある) ▪ It is a case of *all over grumble*. それは劣っている一例だ.

grunt /grʌnt/ 名 ***grunt work***《米口》退屈できつい仕事 ▪ Congress settled down for a month of *grunt work* on the budget. 議会は予算に関する1か月の単調な雑業に取りかかった.

guarantee[1] /gæ̀rəntíː/ 名 ***carry a guarantee*** 保証がついている ▪ This television set *carries a* three months' *guarantee* on all the parts. このテレビは全部分について3か月の保証がついている.

on a guarantee (***of***) (…の)保証つきで ▪ Our goods are sold *on a* money-back *guarantee*. 私どもの品は返金保証つきで売られています.

stand guarantee (…の)保証人になる (*for, that*) ▪ He *stood guarantee that* I should wait for the result. 彼は私にその結果を待たせる保証人となった.

under guarantee of …の保証つきで ▪ Our goods are sold *under guarantee of* money back. 私どもの商品は返金保証付きで売られています.

guarantee[2] /gæ̀rəntíː/ 動 ***be guaranteed to*** *do*《口》必ず…する結果になる ▪ What is a song that *is guaranteed to* make you cry? 必ずあなたを泣かせるに決まっている歌は何でしょうか ▪ People who are cruel to animals and children *are guaranteed to* anger me. 動物や子供をいじめる人々を見ると, 必ず私は腹が立ってくる.

guard[1] /gɑːrd/ 名 ***at open guard*** すきのある構えで ▪ This makes them lie *at open guard*. このため彼らはすきのある構えでいる.

be on [***upon***] *one's* ***guard*** →stand on one's GUARD.

catch [***take***] *a person* ***off*** *his* ***guard*** 人の油断に乗じる ▪ The police, *catching* the criminal *off his guard*, arrested him. 警察は油断に乗じて犯人を逮捕した.

come off guard 非番になる ▪ This musketeer had just *come off guard*. この銃士はちょうど非番になったところだった.

drop [***lower***] *one's* ***guard/let*** *one's* ***guard down*** 警戒をゆるめる ▪ The politician finally *dropped his guard* and showed his true emotions. その政治家はついに警戒心を解いて, 自分の真の感情を吐露した ▪ Now is not the time for anyone to *let their guard down*. 今は誰も警戒をゆるめるときではない. ☞ボクシングで「ガードを下げる」から.

a person's ***guard is up*** [***down***] 人が警戒[油断]している ▪ I hurt him last time and *his guard is up*. この前彼の感情を害したので彼警戒してるのよ ▪ He admitted his infidelity when *his guard was down*. 彼は気がゆるんでいるときの不義を認めた.

keep guard 見張りをする; 警戒をする (over) ▪ He was ordered to *keep guard* at the entrance. 彼は入口で見張り番をするよう命ぜられた ▪ The gunman *kept guard over* the victims. 銃をもった男が被害者たちを見張っていた.

keep** a person **under close guard 人を厳重に監視している ▪ You must *keep* him *under close guard*, as he is not honest. 彼は正直でないから厳重に監視していなければならない.

let** one's **guard down →drop one's GUARD.

lie on** [**upon**] one's **guard →stand on one's GUARD.

mount guard →MOUNT.

***mount guard over** [**upon**]* →MOUNT.

off guard **1** 非番で, 下番して ▪ I couldn't call her until I was *off guard*. 非番になるまで彼女に電話できなかった.

2 =off one's GUARD.

off** one's **guard 油断して, 警戒を怠って ▪ The lawyer caught the witnesses *off their guard*. 弁護士は証人たちの油断に乗じた.

on guard **1** (歩哨の任務について)上番して, 警戒[警備]して, 見張って ▪ The sentry was *on guard*. 歩哨が見張り番をしていた ▪ You must be *on guard* at 8 o'clock. 君は8時に上番しなければならない.

2 《フェンシング》受けの構えをして, 第一の姿勢をして ▪ He placed himself *on guard*. 彼は受けの構えをした.

3 =on one's GUARD.

on** one's **guard 警戒[用心]して ▪ The citizens were *on their guard* against a sudden attack. 市民たちは急襲を用心した.

put** a person **off** his **guard →throw a person off his GUARD.

put** [**set**] a person **on** his **guard 人に警戒させる, 用心させる ▪ I must *put* you *on your guard* against that man. あの人には用心してくださいよ.

put** a person **under guard →under GUARD; place ... under ARREST.

put up** one's **guard =put up one's FISTs.

relieve guard 交替して番兵に立つ ▪ At midnight another soldier came to *relieve guard* at the gate of the fort. 午前0時に別の兵士がやってきて城塞門の立哨を交替した.

row the guard (脱艦兵の見張りのため)艦の回りをボートで警戒する ▪ They *rowed the guard* around the battleship, on the lookout for deserters. 彼らは脱艦兵の見張りのために戦艦の周りをボートで巡視した.

run the guard 番兵の目をかすめて通る ▪ I doubt whether we shall *run the guard*. 我々が番兵の目をかすめて通れるかどうか疑わしい.

set a guard against ...しないよう用心する ▪ You must *set a guard against* the habit. その習慣に陥らないよう用心しなければなりません.

stand guard over ...を守る, の番兵に立つ ▪ He was *standing guard over* the treasure. 彼はその宝の番をしていた.

stand** [**be, lie**] **on** [**upon**] one's **guard 警戒する, 用心する, 注意する ▪ He *lay on his guard*. 彼は警戒していた ▪ We must *stand upon our guard*. 我々は用心しなければならない.

strike down** a person's **guard 《フェンシング》相手の受けの構えを打ち破る.

take** a person **off** his **guard →catch a person off his GUARD.

the old guard →OLD.

throw** [**put**] a person **off** his **guard 人を油断させる ▪ Temerity *puts* a man *off his guard*. 無鉄砲な人はとかく油断する.

under guard 監視されて, 見張られて ▪ Syria has put the US embassy *under guard*. シリアはアメリカ大使館を監視下に置いている.

guard[2] /gɑːrd/ 動 ***be guarded in*** ...に用心深い ▪ He *is guarded in* what he says. 彼は自分の言うことに用心深い.

guardianship /gɑ́ːrdiənʃìp/ 名 ***be under the guardianship of*** ...の保護下にある ▪ We *are under the guardianship of* the law. 我々は法律の保護下にある.

gudgeon /gʌ́dʒən/ 名 ***gape for gudgeons*** うまい嘘を信じたがる ▪ James was not so stupid as to *gape for gudgeons*. ジェイムズはうまい嘘を信じたがるほど愚かではなかった. ☞「魚のように大口を開けて釣餌を求める」が原義.

give a gudgeon (人に)うまい嘘を言う, (人を)うまい嘘でだます ▪ They *give* us *a gudgeon* and flout us. 彼らはよく我々をうまい嘘でだまし侮辱する.

swallow a gudgeon うまい嘘にだまされる ▪ Readers never *swallow* such *a gudgeon*. 読者はそんなうまい嘘にだまされない.

guernsey /gə́ːrnzi/ 名 ***get a guernsey*** 《豪口》チームの選手に選ばれる; 選ばれる, 認められる ▪ Akermanis was among the unluckiest players not to *get a guernsey*. アカマニスは不幸にも選ばれなかった選手のうちの一人だった ▪ The University of Queensland has to *get a guernsey* because it is the oldest and one of the self-proclaimed "big seven." クイーンズランド大学が選ばれるにちがいない, 一番古くて自称「ビッグセブン」の一つだから. ☞ guernsey「豪式フットボール選手が着る袖なしシャツ」.

guess[1] /ges/ 名 ***an educated guess*** 経験に基づく推測 ▪ A prognosis can necessarily be only *an educated guess*. 治療後の経過の予想はもちろん経験に基づく推測にすぎない.

at a** (**rough, wild**) **guess 大体の見当で, あてずっぽうで ▪ *At a guess* there are about 800. 大体の見当でおよそ800ある.

be anybody's** [**anyone's**] **guess 《口》(出来事・結果などが)確かでない, はっきりしない; 答えは誰にもわからない ▪ Who she'll marry *is anybody's guess*. 彼女が誰と結婚するかははっきりしない ▪ Gov. Schwarzenegger's next act *is anyone's guess*. シュワルツェネッガー知事の次の動きは誰にもわからない.

***by guess** (**and by God** [**golly, gosh**])* **1** あてずっぽうで, 大体の見当で ▪ I estimated quantity *by guess*. 私は大体の見当でその量を見積もった.

2《海軍俗》でたらめに ▪ I steered *by guess*. 私はやみくもにかじを取った.

give [***have, make***] ***a guess*** あて推量する ▪ You have *made a* lucky *guess*. あて推量がうまくあたった.

have (***got***) ***another guess coming***《口》考え直さなければならない ▪ If you think you're wiser than I, you*'ve got another guess coming*. 僕より賢いと思っているのなら君は考え直さなければならないよ.

miss *one's* ***guess***《米》推量違いをする ▪ I *missed my guess* about it. それについての私の推量はまちがっていた.

One man's guess is as good as another's. それは誰にもわからない ▪ The future is so uncertain that *one man's guess is as good as another's*. 将来は全く不明確なので誰にもわからない.

three guesses《口》…はなーん[だーれ, どーこ]だ?, 簡単な質問, 答えは簡単 ▪ You have *three guesses* as to who that person is and the first two don't count. そこで質問, その人はだーれだ. ☞"the first two don't count" は three guesses のあとの言葉遊び ▪ In 1770, Ben Franklin invented a one-handed clock that gave you *three guesses* as to the time. 1770年ベンジャミン・フランクリンは針が一つだけの時計を作った. それは簡単に時間がわかるものだった.

Your guess is as good as mine.《口》そのことは私も知らない ▪ Do you believe he will come?—*Your guess is as good as mine*. 君は彼が来ると思うか?—それは私にもわかりません ▪ *Your guess is as good as mine* on this one. この件については私も知らない.

guess^{2} /ges/ 動 ***can only guess at*** …に関しては推測できるのみである, の真相[実態]は不明である ▪ The spokesman said officials *could only guess at* the numbers of the dead in the remotest villages. 広報担当者によると, 当局は遠隔の村落の死亡者数について正確に把握できていないとのことだ.

guess right [***wrong***] うまく言い当てる[当てそこなう] ▪ You've *guessed right*. 君はうまく言い当てた.

guess what《口》驚かないで, あのね, 聞いて ▪ "Mom, Mom, *guess what, guess what*!" she screamed as she bounded into the room. 「ママ, ママ, 聞いて, 聞いて」彼女は部屋に飛びこみながら叫んだ ▪ *Guess what*? I met a very nice girl yesterday! ねえ, 聞いて. きのうとてもいい娘(こ)に出合ったんだ!

I guess《主に米口》私は思う ▪ *I guess* I'll go to bed. 私は寝ようと思う.

I guess so.《口》たぶんね, おそらくね ▪ Are you ready to move?—Yeah, *I guess so*. まもなく転居するの?—ええ, たぶんね.

keep *a person* ***guessing***《口》人をはらはらさせる, 不安な状態におく, 当惑させる ▪ He *keeps* his opponents *guessing* what he will do next. 彼は今度はどうでるだろうかと相手に気をもませておく.

You'll never guess. ＝GUESS what.

guest /gest/ 名 ***Be my guest!***《口》《人に乞われて快諾する言葉》どうぞご自由に, お安いことで ▪ May I use your phone?—*Be my guest!* お電話を貸してくださいませんか?—ええ, どうぞどうぞ ▪ Thank you very much.—*Be my guest*. ほんとにありがとうございます—どういたしまして.

guidance /gáɪdəns/ 名 ***under the guidance of*** …の指導[案内]で ▪ They marched *under the guidance of* the general. 彼らはその将官の先導で進軍した.

guide /gaɪd/ 動 ***guide the way*** 道案内をする ▪ He *guided* you *the way* to this place. 彼がここまであなたの道案内をしたのです.

guillotine /gìlətíːn/ 名 ***The guillotine falls.***《議会》討論が打ち切りとなる ▪ *The guillotine fell* at 11 p.m. 午後11時討論打ち切りとなった. ☞guillotine「議事妨害を防ぎ議案の通過を図るための討論打ち切り」.

guilt /gɪlt/ 形 [[限定的]] ***a guilt trip*** 罪の意識, 罪悪感 (*about*) ▪ I 'm on *a guilt trip about* not wishing Joe a happy birthday. ジョーに誕生日のお祝いをしなかったことを悪かったと思っている.

lay [***put***] ***a guilt trip on*** *a person*/《英口》***send*** *a person* ***on a guilt trip*** 人に罪の意識をもたせる (→a GUILT trip) ▪ Sue *sent* me *on a guilt trip* about neglecting my father. 父にかまわなかったことでスーは私に罪悪感をもたせた ▪ Mike *put a guilt trip on* all of us for not helping Amy during her time of need. エイミーが必要としているときに助けなかったことでマイクは我々全員に罪の意識をもたせた.

guiltless /gíltləs/ 形 ***be guiltless of*** **1** …の罪がない ▪ I *am guiltless of* the blood of this man. 私にはこの人を殺害した罪はない.

2 …がない; を知らない; の経験がない ▪ The windows *were guiltless of* glass. その窓にはガラスがなかった ▪ He *is guiltless of* the alphabet. 彼はアルファベットを知らない ▪ He *is guiltless of* speaking French. 彼はフランス語を話した経験がない.

guilty /gílti/ 形 (***be***) ***guilty of*** **1** …の罪がある; を犯している ▪ I *am guilty of* murder. 私は殺人を犯している ▪ You have *been guilty of* a serious blunder. 君は重大な失策をした.

2 (…の欠点)がある ▪ He *is guilty of* a weakness. 彼は一つの弱点を持っている ▪ He *is guilty of* bad taste. 彼は下品という欠点がある.

find *a person* ***guilty*** [***not guilty***]《法》人を有罪[無罪]と判決する ▪ They *found* him *guilty*. 彼らは彼を有罪と判決した.

plead guilty [***not guilty***] (***to***) →PLEAD.

guinea /gíni/ 名 ***It is a guinea to a gooseberry.*** それはほとんど確かである ▪ *It is a guinea to a gooseberry* on Sam. サムについては, それはほとんど確かである.

guise /gaɪz/ 名 ***in*** [***under***] ***the guise of*** …を装って; のふりをして ▪ He traveled *in the guise of* a monk. 彼は僧に身をやつして旅をした ▪ Predators meet children through the sites *under the guise of* friendship. 性加害者たちは友だちのふりをし

てサイトを通じて子供たちに会う.

gulf[1] /gʌlf/ 名 ***a great gulf fixed*** 大きな開き, 越えがたいみぞ (《聖》*Luke* 16. 26) ▪ Between him and Mr. Carr there was *a great gulf fixed*. 彼とカー氏との間には大きな開きがあった《彼のほうが大いにすぐれていた》.

get a gulf 《英大学俗》(優等試験に落ちて)普通及第する ▪ Well, at least I *got a gulf*—better than failing altogether! まあ, 普通及第だけはできた, 完全に落ちるよりはましとしなくちゃ!

gulf[2] /gʌlf/ 動 ***gulf it*** 《英大学俗》(優等試験に落ちて)普通及第となる[で満足する] ▪ I therefore *gulfed it*. 私はそれゆえに普通及第で満足した.

gullet /gʌ́lət/ 名 ***stick in*** *one's* ***gullet*** →STICK in one's throat.

G

gulp /gʌlp/ 名 ***at a [one, the] gulp*** 一気に, ぐいと ▪ He drained the cup *at one gulp*. 彼はコップ1杯を一気にぐいと飲み干した ▪ She took the dose *at the gulp*. 彼女は薬一服をぐいと飲んだ.

gum[1] /gʌm/ 名 ***beat*** *one's* ***gums*** 絶えずしゃべりまくる, しゃべりすぎる; むだな話をする ▪ She's always *beating her gums* and I can't get a word in edgeways! 彼女はいつもしゃべりまくって私は口を挟めない.

By [My] gum! 《口》誓って, 確かに ▪ Ay, *by gum*, I do! そうです, 私はきっといたします. ☞gum 《婉曲》= God.

come the gum game over 《米俗》…をだます ▪ Opossums and racoons *come the gum game over* the hunter, by flying for refuge to the Sweet Gum tree. フクロネズミやアライグマはモミジバフウの木に逃れて猟人をだます. ☞このことがこの句の起源.

flap *one's* ***gums*** むだ口をたたく, むだ話をする, だべる ▪ They *flapped their gums* on this one for all of 10 minutes. 彼らはこのことに関してまるまる10分もしゃべりまくった.

in the gum (絹が)製造段階にあって《まだマユのゼラチン (gum) がついたままで》.

up a gum tree →TREE.

walk and chew the gum (at the same time) (同時に)二つ以上のことをする ▪ She can't *walk and chew the gum at the same time*. 彼女は同時に二つ以上のことはできない.

gum[2] /gʌm/ 動 ***go gumming*** 《米口》ゴムを取りに行く ▪ I *went* with a lot of boys *gumming*. 私は多くの少年とともにゴムを取りに行った.

gum the game 事を狂わせる[ぶちこわす] ▪ It was not I that *gummed the game*. 事をぶちこわしたのは私ではない.

gum up the works 仕事を狂わせる[遅らせる] ▪ John *gummed up the works* by failing to arrive in time. ジョンは間に合うように来れなくて仕事を遅らせた.

gummed /gʌmd/ 形 ***fret like gummed velvet [taffeta]*** ゴム引きのビロードのようにささくれ立つ (cf. Sh., *1 Hen. IV*. 2. 2. 2) ▪ He *frets like gummed velvet*. 野郎, ゴム引きのビロードみたいにささくれ立ってやがる. ☞ゴムで堅くしたビロードやタフタは早くささくれる.

gumption /gʌ́mpʃən/ 名 ***lack gumption*** 《口》悟りが鈍い, 愚かである ▪ If you do not *lack gumption*, you'll see that you must pay the debt. もしあなたが悟りが鈍くなければ, 借金は払わなければならぬということはわかるだろう.

gum-tree /gʌ́mtrìː/ 名 ***up a (gum) tree*** →TREE.

gun /gʌn/ 名 ***a big gun/(the) big guns*** 大物, 重鎮 ▪ The Republicans are also bringing in political *big guns*. 共和党も政界の大物を動員している.

a hired gun **1** 殺し屋 ▪ Aquino was killed by *a* notorious *hired gun*. アキノ氏は名うての殺し屋に殺害された.

2 難題処理請負人 ▪ The best first step would be to find *an* aggressive *hired gun* from the outside to put in charge of the project. 最良の第一歩は外部から積極果敢な請負人を見つけて計画を任せることだろう.

a smoking gun 動かぬ[決定的]証拠 ▪ *A smoking gun* is a piece of evidence that is produced in a trial, most of the time as a surprise to the other side. 動かぬ証拠とは, 裁判で提出される証拠品であり, たいていは相手側にとって思いも寄らなかったものである ▪ The study was not *a "smoking gun"* for life on Mars. その研究は火星に生命があることの決定的証拠ではなかった.

a son of a gun →SON.

a top gun トップ(クラス), ナンバーワン, (最)重要人物 ▪ Gulf Air has again been recognized as *a top gun* in the aviation industry. ガルフエアーはまたも航空業界でナンバーワンと認められた.

(as) sure as a gun →(as) SURE as death.

beat the gun →jump the GUN.

blow great guns 《口》(風が)吹き荒れる ▪ The wind *blew great guns* and the waves ran mountain high. 風が吹き荒れ, 波が山のように高まった.

bring out [up] *one's* ***big guns*** (トランプ・議論などで)奥の手を出す ▪ He decided to *bring up his big guns*. 彼は奥の手を出すことに決めた.

carry [hold] (big) guns 強力である, 権力を握っている ▪ He *carries* too *big guns* for me. I must not engage him. 彼は私には強すぎる. 彼と戦ってはいけない.

carry the guns (for) (…の)能力[資格]がある ▪ Do you think I *carry the guns for* it? 私にその能力があるとお考えですか.

carry too many [the biggest] guns (for) (議論などで)攻撃または弁護の材料[手段]がありすぎる; (相手として…には)強すぎる ▪ He *carried too many guns for* me—he beat me. 彼は私には強すぎた—私を負かした.

come out with (all) guns blazing 目標を達成するため全力を尽くす ▪ England must *come out with all guns blazing* next season. イングランドは

来シーズンには目標達成のため全力を尽くさねばならない.

cut the gun 《俗》電気を切る[止める], モーター[エンジン]を止める ▪ *Cut the gun* and listen; I thought I heard gunshots! エンジンを切って耳を澄ませ. 何発か銃声がした気がする.

draw a gun on …を銃でおどす ▪ He *drew a gun on* me, and I obeyed him. 彼は私を銃でおどしたので彼に従いました.

give her [it] the gun 《口》極端に走る; 速力を速める ▪ When he drives his new car, he *gives it the gun*. 彼は新車を運転するときは速力を速める. ☞初期の飛行機の加速器が銃の引き金に似ていたことから.

go down with all guns firing 死力をつくして敗れる, (負けても)善戦する, 意地を見せる ▪ I don't mind losing when you're *going down with all guns firing*, but tonight we just had too many players off form. 全力を尽くして負けるのはかまわないが, 今晩は不調な選手があまりにも多すぎた ▪ Prakash *went down with all guns firing* against the fourth seed, Syed. プラカシュは第4シードのサイエド相手に善戦した.

go great guns 《口》どんどんうまくやる, 大成功を収める ▪ The book was *going great guns* in twelve countries. その本は12か国で盛んに売れた.

Great guns! これは驚いた!, しまった! ▪ But *great guns!* Is a man obliged to say everything he thinks? しかし, こりゃ驚いた. 人は思うことを洗いざらい言わなければならないのか.

guns before butter バターより大砲《国民の生活より軍備を重視する政策》 ▪ With the threat of war looming, government policy was *guns before butter*. 戦争が今にも起きそうなので, 政府の政策はバターより大砲だった.

guns or [and] butter 国民の生活重視か軍備重視か[暮らしも軍備も] ▪ Back in the Cold War, it was *guns or butter*. We got guns. 冷戦のころは暮らしか軍備かであり, 我々は軍備を選んだ ▪ Bush has spent taxpayer dollars on both *guns and butter* simultaneously. ブッシュ氏は納税者からのドルを暮らしと軍備の両方に同時に使用した.

hold [put, 《口》have] a gun to** a person's **head 人を脅して…させようとする ▪ He *held a gun to my head* to make me obey him. 彼は私を脅して彼に従わせようとした.

It is the man behind the gun that tells. 《諺》勝敗は武器よりもこれを使う人にある.

jump [beat] the gun 《スポーツ》フライングする; (…のことで)早まる, 早まったことをする (*on*) ▪ He was disqualified for *jumping the gun*. 彼はフライングをして失格した ▪ They were scheduled to be married in June, but they *beat the gun*. 彼らは6月に結婚の予定だったが, それより早く結婚した ▪ Life on Mars? Let's not *jump the gun*. 火星に生命だって? 時期尚早の議論はやめよう ▪ Don't *jump the gun on* the tax plan. 税制計画に関連して早まったことをしてはならない.

lay a gun 《砲》銃[砲]を的に向ける ▪ They *laid the guns* on [at] the enemy fort. 彼らは敵軍の要塞を標的にして砲を向けた.

reach for** one's **gun 極端に反発する ▪ When I hear anyone talk of "culture", I *reach for my gun*. 人が「教養」の話をするのを聞くと私は激しい敵意をもって反発する.

spike** a person's **guns →SPIKE.

stand by** one's **guns**/《英》**stick to** one's **guns 《口》(戦い・議論などで)一歩も譲らない, 退かない ▪ It sounds like he is going to *stand by his guns*. 彼は自説を堅持するつもりのようだ ▪ I shall *stick to my guns* though the whole world is against me. たとえ全世界が反対しようとも, 私はあくまで自説を守ります.

till [until] the last gun is fired 最後(の最後)まで ▪ He likes to stay at parties *till the last gun is fired*. 彼はパーティーで最後まで残るのが好きだ.

under the gun 《米口》 **1** 武装監視されて ▪ The hostages were *under the gun* all the time. 人質たちは四六時中武装監視されていた.
2 緊張して; (すること)を迫られて (*to do*) ▪ George Seifert was *under the gun* from the day he took the head-coaching job. ジョージ・サイファートは, ヘッドコーチに就任して以来プレッシャーを感じている ▪ We are *under the gun to* finish this project as soon as possible. 我々はできるだけ早く計画を完了することを迫られている.

with** (one's) **guns blazing/with all guns blazing 猛烈に, 全力を注いで ▪ Mike kicked down the door and went in *with guns blazing*. マイクはドアをけり倒して, 勢いよく中に入り込んだ.

gunboat /ɡʌ́nbòʊt/ 名 ***gunboat diplomacy*** 武力外交, 砲艦外交 ▪ *Gunboat diplomacy* has lost the credibility of ultimate use. 武力外交は, 最終的使用については信用を失っている.

gunflint /ɡʌ́nflìnt/ 名 ***By gunflints!*** 《米口》ほんとにまあ! ▪ Well, *by gunflints*, if you are not making a noise. まあほんとに, あなたがたは何という騒ぎ方なんだ.

gunnel /ɡʌ́nəl/ 名 ***full [packed, stuffed] to the gunnels [gunwales]*** ぎっしり詰まって, あふれるほどで (*with*) ▪ The company was *stuffed to the gunnels with* debt and obsolete stock. その会社には借金と棚卸資産が山ほどあった ▪ The ship was *full to the gunnels with* cocaine. その船にはおびただしい量のコカインが積まれていた.

gunning /ɡʌ́nɪŋ/ 名 ***be a-gunning*** 銃猟をしている ▪ He *is* now *a-gunning*. 彼は今銃猟の最中だ.

go (a-)gunning 銃猟に行く ▪ I *went gunning* the other day. 先日銃猟に行った.

gun(-)point /ɡʌ́npɔ̀ɪnt/ 名 ***at gun-point*** ピストルをつきつけて, ピストルでおどして ▪ He forced the banker *at gun-point* to open the safe. 彼は銀行員をピストルでおどしてむりやりに金庫を開けさせた.

gunshot /ɡʌ́nʃɑ̀t|-ʃɔ̀t/ 名 ***out of [beyond]***

G

gunshot (***of***) (...の)射程外に ▪ They were always *out of gunshot*. 彼らは常に射程外にあった ▪ French ships anchored *out of gunshot*. フランス艦船は射程外にいかりをおろした.

within gunshot (***of***) (...の)射程内に ▪ The ship was *within gunshot of* us at daybreak. 船は夜明け方には我々の射程内にいた.

gunwale /gʌ́nəl/ 名 ***gunwale*** (***down***) ***to*** 船べりが水面に触れるまで傾いて《比喩的にも》 ▪ The ship was rolling incessantly *gunwale to*. 船は絶えず横に揺れて船べりが水面に触れるほど傾いた ▪ He rolled himself *gunwale to* at every motion of his horse. 彼は馬が動くたびに体が水平になるほど横に揺れた.

G

gunwale under 船べりが水中に没して ▪ We continued to roll *gunwale under*. 我々は船べりを水中に没して揺れ続けた.

to the gunwales 一杯に ▪ Carnegie Hall was packed *to the gunwales* with audience last night. 昨晩カーネギーホールは聴衆で超満員だった.

gush /gʌʃ/ 名 ***a gush of*** 《米口》大量(の) ▪ We have got *a gush of* peaches in the woods. 森にはたくさんモモがある.

speak with gush 《口》ひどく感傷的に[大げさに感情をこめて]話す ▪ She *spoke with* adolescent *gush* about her latest boyfriend. 彼女は少女のように今のボーイフレンドのことを感情をこめてしゃべり立てた.

gust /gʌst/ 動 ***gust the mouth*** [***the gab***] 《米》舌を喜ばせる ▪ She had the knack to *gust the gab* of any child. 彼女はどんな子供の舌でも喜ばせるこつを知っていた.

gusto /gʌ́stoʊ/ 名 ***with*** (***a***) ***gusto*** おいしく; 楽しく ▪ He ate it *with gusto*. 彼は舌鼓を打って食べた ▪ She talked *with gusto*. 彼女は楽しげに話した.

gut[1] /gʌt/ 名形 ***a gut feeling*** 勘, 虫の知らせ ▪ My *gut feeling* is that I don't need surgery. 私の勘では手術は不要だ.

a gut reaction 直感に基づく反応 (*to*) ▪ My *gut reaction to* this case has support from the social sciences. この事件に対する私の直観的な反応は社会科学によって支持される.

a misery guts 《口》ぐちり屋, ぼやき屋, 不満たれ ▪ Come on, don't be *a misery guts*! おいおい, ぐちるのはやめろよ ▪ The image built up of Chris is that he's *a misery guts*—but he's actually a ball of energy. クリスの作られたイメージはぼやき屋だけど, 本当はエネルギーのかたまりだ.

at gut level 感覚的に, 直観的に ▪ He has a good reputation, but *at gut level* I just don't trust him. 彼は評判がよいが, 私は直感的に彼にはどうも信用がおけない.

bust a gut **1**《文・俗》ゲラゲラ(と)笑う, 爆笑する ▪ He *busted a gut* reading a comic. 彼は漫画を読みながらゲラゲラ笑った.

2《俗》大いに努力する; 心配する ▪ He is *busting a gut* over the work he has to do. 彼はしなければならない仕事に精励している.

bust [***burst***] ***a gut laughing*** **1** = bust a GUT.

2《口》抱腹絶倒する, 腹の底から笑う ▪ We *bust a gut laughing* at his joke. 私たちは彼のジョークに大笑いした.

gut talk 腹を割った話, 誠実な話 ▪ I want you to put me to the test of straight talk, of *gut talk*, of heart talk. 私の率直な話, 腹を割った話, 心からの話を試していただきたい.

hate *a person's* ***guts*** 《俗》人を憎悪する ▪ I don't dislike him. I *hate his guts*. 彼がきらいなのではない. 憎悪しているのだ.

have *a person's* ***guts for garters*** 《英口》怒って罰する, 懲らしめる ▪ I'll *have* both *their guts for garters*! 二人とも懲らしめてやる.

have guts in *one* 《口》元気がある, 活気に満ちている; 良い男である ▪ He *has guts in* him. 彼は活気に満ちている.

have no guts 《口》 **1** 中身がない; 真の価値[力]がない ▪ It's just a wordy and rambling essay that simply *has no guts*. そいつは中身もなく, くどくどとりとめのないただのエッセイだ.

2 胆力がない; 根気がない ▪ He *has no guts* for hard work. 彼は骨の折れる仕事をする気力がない.

have the guts to *do* 《口》大胆にも[勇敢にも, 肝を据えて]...する ▪ It's vital that Congress *have the guts to* make the right cuts. 議会が勇気をもって適正な削減をすることが重要だ.

not fit to carry guts to a bear 非常に劣る ▪ Well, if I'm a bear, you are*n't fit to carry guts to a bear*. そうだね, もし私がクマだとすれば, 君はクマにくず肉を持って行くだけの値うちもない. ☞「クマに guts (くず肉)を持っていくだけの資格もない」が原義.

plenty of guts 《俗》多くの胆力[勇気] ▪ He has *plenty of guts* but no bowels. 彼には勇気は大いにあるが慈悲心がない.

spill *one's* ***guts*** 《米口》秘密[私事]を漏らす, 白状[自白]する, 吐く; 事実を明らかにする ▪ I really want to *spill my guts* to her. 彼女に本当のことをどうしても打ち明けたい ▪ I hate it when you *spill your guts* to strangers. 君が私事を見知らぬ人に漏らすのはきらいだ.

sweat [***work, slog, slave***] *one's* ***guts out*** 《口》汗水流して[身を粉にして]働く, 懸命に取り組む ▪ I will not *sweat my guts out* for only £60 a week. 僕は1週間にたった60ポンドでは懸命に働く気はない ▪ I'm not going to *sweat my guts out* for such miserable pay. そんなひどい給料なんかで汗水流して働いてやるものか ▪ He *slogged his guts out* to get the report finished in time. 彼はレポートの完成を間に合わすために懸命に取り組んだ.

will have *a person's* ***guts for garters*** 《英口》人をこっぴどく罰する[懲らしめる]《脅し文句》 ▪ If I catch you stealing my apples, I'*ll have your guts for garters*. もしおれのリンゴを盗んでいるところを捕まえたら, 土手っ腹に風穴をあけてやるぞ ▪ I'*ll have his guts for garters*. あいつをこっぴどく罰してやる.

gut[2] /gʌt/ 動 ***gut it out*** 《米口》堪え忍ぶ, 頑張りぬく(＝TOUGH it out) ▪ He became dehydrated but somehow *gutted it out.* 彼は脱水症状になったが, なんとか頑張りぬいた.

gutser /gʌ́tsər/ 名 ***come a gutser*** 《口》 **1** (歩行・走行中に)転倒する ▪ Edna nearly *came a gutser* on the step. エドナは階段であわや転倒するところだった.

2 失敗する, しくじる ▪ Dick is overconfident. I hope he doesn't *come a gutser.* ディックは自信過剰だ. しくじらなければいいのだが.

gutter /gʌ́tər/ 名 ***from*** [***out of***] ***the gutter*** 卑しい素姓から ▪ You will marry your son to the girl *out of the gutter?* 息子を素姓の卑しいその娘と結婚させるのか ▪ He rose *from the gutter.* 彼は卑しい身分から出世した. ☞the gutter「貧民街」.

in the gutter 貧民街に; 極貧の環境に ▪ He will die *in the gutter.* 彼は貧困のうちに死ぬだろう.

take [***raise***]***... out of the gutter*** ...を貧しい環境から救いあげ(て育て)る ▪ He *took* the child *out of the gutter.* 彼はその子供を貧困から救いあげた.

the gutter press 《英》(煽情的で俗悪な)大衆新聞[雑誌]《性・スキャンダル・プライバシーの暴露などを扱う》 ▪ My client is sick of the lies and distortions of *the gutter press.* 私の顧客は低俗新聞のウソと歪曲に辟易している.

guy[1] /gaɪ/ 名 ***do a guy*** 《英》逃走する, 逃亡する ▪ They *did a guy* when they saw a policeman. 彼らは警官を見て逃走した.

dressed like a Guy へんてこなりをして ▪ He was *dressed like a Guy.* 彼は妙な服装をしていた.

give the guy (***to***) (...から)逃げ出す, (を)まいて逃げる ▪ Don't *give* us *the guy.* 我々をまいてはいけない.

make a guy of ...を笑いものにする ▪ They will *make a guy of* you in Latin. 彼らは君をラテン語で笑いものにするだろう.

Nice guys finish last. 《諺》品行方正な男はもてない.

No more Mr. nice guy! 《口》いいやつでいるのはもうご免だ. ☞米国の歌手 Alice Cooper (1948–)の歌の題目.

the [***a***] ***good*** [***bad***] ***guy*** 善玉[悪役], 正義の味方[憎まれ役] ▪ Whenever there's a problem at the office the boss always makes me out to be *the bad guy.* 職場で問題が起きるたびに上司はきまって私を悪玉呼ばわりするんだ.

What a guy! なんと奇異なんだろう!, なんと一風変わってるんだろう! ▪ She was in evening dress with all those imitation jewels on. *What a guy!* 彼女は模造の宝石をたくさんつけた夜会服を着ていた. なんと変わってるんだろう!

guy[2] /gaɪ/ 動 ***guy the life out of*** *a person* 《米口》人をさんざんからかう[いじめる] ▪ They *guy the life out of* us. 彼らは我々をさんざんいじめる.

gym /dʒɪm/ 名 ***a gym rat*** ジムに入りびたり[健康志向]の人, アスレチッククラブに熱心に通う人 ▪ It is a fact that Obama is something of *a gym rat.* オバマ氏がなかなかのジムマニアなのは事実だ.

gyp /dʒɪp/ 名 ***give*** *a person* ***gyp*** 《英》 **1** 人をひどくしかる, 罰する, 懲らしめる ▪ I tore my clothes and mother *gave* me *gyp.* 私が衣服を裂いたので母はひどくしかった.

2 人をひどく痛ませる ▪ This hollow tooth is *giving* me *gyp.* この穴のあいた歯がひどく痛む.

G

H

h /eɪtʃ/ 名 ***drop*** *one's* ***h's*** [***aitches***] (標準語で発音すべき語頭の) h 音を落として発音する《/hæt/ を /æt/ とする類; ロンドンなまりの特徴》 ▪ He was a very fine young man, but evidently a nobody as he *dropped his aitches* and so on. 彼は非常に立派な青年だが, h 音などを落として発音したところを見ればどうも名も無い人と思われた.

habdabs /hǽbdæ̀bz/ 名 ***get the*** (***screaming***) ***habdabs*** 《口》いらいらする; びくびくする, 心配する ▪ I *get the habdabs* every time I walk in the dark. 暗闇を歩くときはいつもびくびくする.

give *a person* ***the*** (***screaming***) ***habdabs*** 《口》人をいらいら[心配]させる ▪ It *gives* me *the habdabs* even to think about it. その事を考えるだけでも私はいらいらする.

habit /hǽbət/ 名 ***be in the habit of*** …の習慣である ▪ He *is in the habit of* rising early. 彼は早起きの習慣である.

break *a person* ***of the habit*** (***of***) 人の…する習慣[癖]を直す ▪ I will *break* my child *of the* bad *habit*. 子供の悪い癖を直してやります.

break *oneself* ***of the habit*** (***of***) (…の)習慣[癖]をやめる ▪ He has *broken himself of the habit of* drinking. 彼は酒を飲む習慣をやめた.

break off the habit (***of***) (…の)癖をやめる ▪ He *broke off the habit of* smoking. 彼はタバコを吸う習慣をやめた.

fall [***get***] ***into a bad habit*** (***of***) (…の)悪い癖がつく ▪ The world has *fallen into a bad habit of* naming everything after something else. 世間は全ての物の名を他の物に因んでつけるという悪習慣になった.

fall [***get***] ***into the habit*** (***of***) (…の)癖がつく ▪ He has *fallen into the habit of* coming to tea every Sunday. 彼は日曜毎にお茶に来る習慣になった.

form a good habit [***the habit of***] 良い習慣[…の習慣]をつける ▪ *Form the habit of* rising early. 早起きの習慣をつけなさい ▪ We must *form good habits*. 良い習慣をつけねばならない.

from (***force of***) ***habit*** 習慣(の力)で ▪ I reach into my pocket for my keys *from habit*. つい癖でポケットに手を入れて鍵を探す ▪ He got up at 6 *from force of habit*. 彼はいつもの習慣で6時に起きた.

grow into a habit 癖になる ▪ Smoking has *grown into a habit* with me. 喫煙が私の習慣になった.

grow out of a habit 癖が抜ける ▪ He has *grown out of the habit*. 彼はその癖が抜けた.

Habit is second nature. 《諺》習慣は第二の天性である. ☞ギリシャ・ローマ以来の諺.

kick the habit 《口》(麻薬などの)悪習をきっぱりすてる ▪ He *kicked the habit* when he was a G.P. 彼は開業医だった時に麻薬の悪習をきっぱりやめた.

knock the habit 麻薬(常用)をやめる ▪ He just can't *knock the habit*. 彼はどうしてもヤクをやめられない.

make a habit of …を習慣にする ▪ Don't *make a habit of* borrowing money. 借金することを習慣にしてはいけない.

of full habit 多血質の ▪ He is a man *of full habit*. 彼は多血質の人である.

Old habits die hard. 《諺》古い習慣はなかなか抜けない.

Why break the habit of a lifetime? 《英・戯》生涯の習慣をどうしてやめるのか ▪ I must stop smoking this time.—*Why break the habit of a lifetime?* 今度こそタバコをやめなくては—せっかくの習慣をどうして? ☞相手が悪い習慣をやめられるはずがないと思うときに皮肉をこめて言う.

habituate /həbítʃuèɪt/ 動 ***be habituated to*** …に慣れている ▪ Their minds *are habituated to* accurate thinking. その人たちの心は正確な思索に慣れている.

hack[1] /hæk/ 名 ***be under hack*** 《米口》(人に)支配されている ▪ He *is under hack*. 彼は人に支配されている.

bring ... to a hack 《米口》…を暴露する; に手を引かせる ▪ I've *brought* him *to a hack*. 私は彼の化けの皮をはいでやった.

take a hack at …を一番試みる ▪ Let me *take a hack at* it. 私に一番やらせてください.

under hack 当惑して ▪ He put Joe *under hack* teasing him about his girl. 彼は恋人のことでからかってジョーを困らせた.

hack[2] /hæk/ 動 *a person* ***can*** [***could***] ***hack ...*** 〚しばしば否定文で〛…をうまくやりぬくことができる, 耐える ▪ His father just *could*n't *hack* family life and suddenly left home. 彼の父はどうも家庭生活をうまくやれず突然家を出た.

hack to death めちゃめちゃに使う, 使い古す ▪ The argument is *being hacked to death* in all the radical newspapers. その議論はすべての過激な新聞にめちゃめちゃに使われている.

hackle /hǽkəl/ 名 ***a cock of a different hackle*** 異なった性質の相手[敵手] ▪ Fight it out with *a cock of a different hackle*. 異なった性質の相手と雌雄を決しなさい.

get *a person's* ***hackles up/raise*** *a person's* ***hackles*** 《口》人を怒らす ▪ I *got his hackles up* by criticizing him. 私は彼を非難して怒らせた. ☞hackles は威嚇するとき逆立つ若い雄鶏の首の羽毛.

one's ***hackles rise*** 怒る ▪ *Her hackles rose*

when she heard it. 彼女はそれを聞いて怒った.

make** a person's **hackles rise = get a person's HACKLEs up.

with the [*one's*] ***hackles up*** 《口》(雄鶏・犬が首毛を立てて)戦う身構えをして; (人が)怒って; (猟犬が)キツネに近づいて殺そうとして ▪ The cockerel stood *with his hackles up*. 若雄鶏は戦う身構えをして立った ▪ I saw Jones *with his hackles up* this morning. 私は今朝ジョーンズが怒っているのを見た ▪ There's not a single foxhound *with his hackles up*. キツネに近づいて殺そうとする猟犬は1匹もいない. ☞hackles (雄鶏の首毛)が怒ると逆立つことから.

had /həd, hæd/ (have の過去および過去分詞) ***be had*** 《俗》 **1** 裏をかかれる, だまされる, 欺かれる ▪ That lawyer is a shyster. You've *been had*. 彼はいんちき弁護士だ. まんまと一杯食わされたね.

2 買収される, 賄賂をつかまされる ▪ The lawmaker's incorruptible; he cannot *be had*. その議員は清廉潔白で, 買収されることはない.

had as lief** do* (as***) →LIEF.

***had best** do* …するのが一番よい; するにこしたことはない ▪ You *had best* go at once. 君はすぐ行くにこしたことはない.

***had better** do* **1** …した(ほう)がよい《口語では had を略すことが多い》 ▪ You *had better* go. 君は行ったほうがよい ▪ We *had better* not remain here. ここにいないほうがよい ▪ *Had*n't I *better* go? 私は行ったほうがよくはありませんか.

2 …しなさい《命令的, 目上の人には失礼な言い方》 ▪ You *had better* go home. 家に帰りなさい.

***had better have** done* …したほうがよかった ▪ You *had better have* told him so. 君は彼にそう言ったほうがよかった.

had it →HAVE had it.

had rather/had sooner **1** むしろ…する方がよい, したい ▪ I *had rather* die than endure the side effects. 薬の副作用に耐えるくらいなら死んだ方がましだ ▪ He says he *had sooner* die than deceive her. 彼は彼女を欺くよりは死を選ぶという.

2 〚that 節 (that は通例省略)を伴って〛 むしろ…してもらいたい ▪ I *had rather* you let me do the driving. 僕に運転させてくれないかな.

hades /héidiːz/ 名 ***What the hades*** [***in hades***]***...?*** 一体何…? ▪ *What the hades* are you doing there? そこで一体何をしているのか.

hail[1] /heɪl/ 名 ***hail and farewell*** 《文》出会いと別れのあいさつ ▪ I am here this evening to bid *hail and farewell* to Mr. Smith. 私は今晩はスミス氏に出会いとお別れのあいさつを申し上げにまいりました.

out of hail 声の届かない所に ▪ We warned them not to be *out of hail*. 我々は彼らに声の届かぬ所へ行かぬよう警告した.

within hail 声の届く所に ▪ The vessel came *within hail* of us. 船は我々の声の届く所へ来た ▪ When we came *within hail*, we found that they were English. 我々が声の届く所へ来ると彼らはイギリス人であることがわかった.

hail[2] /heɪl/ 動 ***within hailing distance*** (***of***) →DISTANCE[1].

hail Columbia /hèɪlkəlʌ́mbiə/ 名 ***get hail Columbia*** 《米俗》大いにしかられる ▪ I *got hail Columbia* from my father for that. そのため父から大目玉をくらった. ☞hail Columbia = hell.

give... hail Columbia 《米俗》…をひどくしかる; を撃破する ▪ We *gave* him *hail Columbia*. 彼を大いにしかった ▪ We *gave* the enemy *hail Columbia*. 敵をひどくやっつけた.

kick up [***raise***] ***hail Columbia*** 《米俗》大騒ぎを起こす ▪ People *raised hail Columbia*. 人々は大騒ぎを起こした.

play hail Columbia 《米俗》こわす, だめにする (*with*) ▪ He *played hail Columbia with* his health. 彼はからだをすっかりこわした.

hair /heər/ 名 ***a bad hair day*** 《口》物事がうまく運ばない日 ▪ This has been *a* real *bad hair day*. 今日は何もかもうまくいかない.

a hair of the (***same***) ***dog that bit** a person* 《口》二日酔いをさますための迎え酒; 毒を制する毒 ▪ I took *a hair of the dog that bit* me instead of breakfast. 私は朝食の代わりに二日酔いをさます迎え酒を飲んだ. ☞昔, 狂犬にかまれたときはその犬の毛が特効薬と考えられていたことから.

a hair shirt 故意に不自由な生活を送ること, 罪滅ぼし ▪ You don't have to wear *a hair shirt* and give up all your luxuries. 何も君が耐久生活を送り, 贅沢をやめる必要はない. ☞hair shirt はキリスト教の信者が着る固い毛織のシャツ.

a head of hair →HEAD[1].

against the hair (動物の)毛並みに逆らって; 物の自然に反して; 性分[意向]に反して ▪ To fight is to go *against the hair* of your profession. けんかをなさってはご職業柄に合いません ▪ All went utterly *against the hair* with him. 万事が全く彼の意に反した ▪ It goes *against the hair* with me. それは私の性に合わない[それはいやだ] ▪ I did it *against the hair*. 私は不本意ながらそうした.

be in** a person's **hair → get in a person's HAIR.

(***be***) ***not worth a hair*** 《口》毛ほどの価値もない ▪ This *is not worth a hair*. これは一文の値うちもない.

(***be***) ***of a hair*** 《口》(容貌・性質・職業などが)同じで(ある), よく似て(いる); 同類で(ある) ▪ They *are* notorious rascals, both *of a hair*. 彼らは名うての悪党で, 同じ穴のむじなだ.

bring down** a person's **gray hairs with sorrow to the grave 年寄りを悲しませて死なせる (《聖》*Gen*. 42. 38) ▪ The vile man deserted his parents and *brought down their gray hairs with sorrow to the grave*. その卑劣な男は両親を見捨て, 年老いた彼らを悲嘆のうちに死なせてしまった.

by a hair ほんのわずかの差で ▪ Her serve was out *by a hair*. 彼女のサーブはわずかにアウトだった.

by a single hair ごくわずかなきずなで ▪ Beauty

draws us *by a single hair.* 美はごくわずかなきずなで我々を引きつける.

by the turn of a hair →TURN[1].

comb *a person's* ***hair*** (***for him***) 《口・戯》人をひどくしかる ▪ Your wife will *comb your hair* for you. 奥さんにうんとしかられますよ.

comb [***rub, smooth***] *a person's* ***hair the wrong way*** 《口》(気にくわぬことを言って)人を怒らせる ▪ Someone seems to have *combed her hair the wrong way* this morning. 誰かが今朝彼女のごきげんを損ねたらしい.

curl *a person's* ***hair*** 《米俗》人にショックを与える; 人をたまげさせる[ぞっとさせる] ▪ The movie about monsters *curled his hair.* その怪物の映画を見て彼はぞっとした.

cut [***divide***] ***the hair*** 細かい区別立てをする ▪ He *cut the hair* between satire and flattery. 彼は風刺とへつらいの細かい区別立てをした.

do *one's* ***hair*** 髪を結う ▪ She was *doing her hair.* 彼女は髪を結っていた.

do [***put***] ***up*** *one's* ***hair*** (少女が大人風に)髪を結う; (少女が)大人になる ▪ The girl is *doing up her hair.* 少女は大人風に髪を結っている.

flyaway hair (うまくまとまらない)くせ毛の髪 ▪ All you need to do to control *flyaway hair* is follow these tips. くせ毛の調髪には次の秘訣に従えばよい.

get [***have***] ***a wild hair*** 《米俗》いても立ってもいられない ▪ She *got a wild hair* and ran into a liquor shop. がまんできなくなって彼女は酒店へ飛び込んだ.

get [***have***] *a person* ***by the short hairs*** [***by the short and curlies***] 《口》人を完全に支配する[している] ▪ She's evidently *got* her husband *by the short hairs.* 彼女は明らかに夫をしりに敷いていた. ☞「うなじの髪の毛[陰毛]をつかむ」が原義. have a person by the BALLs の婉曲な言い方.

get [***be***] ***in*** *a person's* ***hair*** 《口》人を悩ます, いらだたせる, 怒らせる ▪ Don't *get in my hair* when I'm trying to study. 一生懸命勉強中だからじゃましないでよ ▪ Grace is one person who simply *gets in my hair.* グレイスも全くしゃくにさわる人物だ ▪ The dean and the lecturer *get in each other's hair.* 学長と講師はお互いに仲が悪い.

get *A* ***out of*** *B's* ***hair*** Bのじゃまにならぬよう Aをよそへ連れていく ▪ I'll *get* the child *out of your hair.* 君のじゃまにならぬようにその子をよそへ連れていくよ.

get [***keep***] *a person* ***out of*** *one's* ***hair*** …のじゃまをしないようにする ▪ *Keep* the kids *out of my hair* for a while, will you? しばらく子供たちに私のじゃまをさせないでいてくれないか.

give *a person* ***gray hair***(***s***) 人を悩ます[心配させる] ▪ The traffic problem is enough to *give* a police officer *gray hair.* 交通問題は警官を悩ます.

hair about the heels (馬の)純血種でない(印); (人の)育ちの悪い[下品な](印) ▪ "*Hair about the heels,*" muttered the Count to himself. 「育ちが悪い」と伯爵は一人つぶやいた.

One's ***hair stands on end.*** (恐怖などで)髪の毛が立つ, 身の毛がよだつ ▪ When I saw the railway accident, *my hair stood on end.* その鉄道事故を見たとき私は身の毛がよだった.

Hairs of *one's* ***head are all numbered.*** 人の頭の毛までもみな数えられている《人の運命は神によって決まっている》(《聖》*Matt.* 10. 30) ▪ Be good to me. Maybe the *hairs of my head are all numbered.* 私に親切にしてください. 私の運命はもう決まっているかもしれないから.

hang by [***on***] ***a*** (***single***) ***hair*** →HANG[2].

harm a hair of *a person's* ***head*** 〚主に否定文・条件節で〛人を傷つける ▪ If you *harm a hair of her head,* I'll kill you. 彼女を傷つけたらおまえを殺すぞ.

have *a person* ***by the short hairs*** →get a person by the short HAIRs.

have (***got***)***… where the hair is short*** 《米口》…を支配する, ものにする ▪ You certainly *have* him *where the hair is short.* 君は確かに彼を牛耳っている ▪ I *have got* German *where the hair is short.* 私はドイツ語をものにした.

have hair 《俗》勇気[忍耐, 根性, 性的魅力]がある ▪ He's *got* a lot of *hair.* 彼はとても勇気がある.

have *one's* ***hair cut*** 散髪する ▪ I must *have my hair cut* today. きょうは散髪せねばならない.

have *a person* ***in*** *one's* ***hair*** 《米》人にうるさく悩まされる ▪ If you tell him, I will *have* him *in my hair* in no time. もし君が話したら, 私はすぐ彼にうるさく悩まされるだろう.

in *one's* ***hair*** **1** (女性が)髪をたらして ▪ I showed her to my soldiers *in her hair.* 私は兵士たちに髪をたらした姿の彼女を見せた.

2 かつら[帽子]をかぶらないで ▪ He looks better *in his* own *hair.* 彼は帽子をかぶらない方が映りがよい ▪ Benjamin Franklin once appeared at the French court *in his* own *hair.* ベンジャミン・フランクリンはかつらを着けずにフランス法廷に出廷したことがあった.

in the hair (生皮の)皮の側を外にして; (皮の)毛のついたままで ▪ The skin is dressed *in the hair.* 皮は毛のついたまま仕上げられる.

keep [***hold***] *one's* ***hair on*** (*one's* ***head***) 《英口》〚主に命令文で〛落ち着いている, 腹をたてない, 興奮しない (↔lose one's HAIR 2) ▪ *Keep your hair on,* mate. まあ君, 落ち着きたまえ ▪ They have *kept their hair on their heads.* 彼らは落ち着きはらっている. ☞「髪をかきむしるな」という忠告から; →keep one's SHIRT(s) on.

let down *one's* ***hair/let*** *one's* ***hair down*** **1** (女性が)髪を解いて肩にたらす ▪ Young women these days, with their short locks, don't have to *let their hair down* at night. 現代娘は頭髪を短くしているから夜髪を解く必要がない.

2 《俗》打ち解ける; 打ち明け話をする; くつろぐ

▪ After a few drinks we both *let down our hair.* 少し飲んでから我々は二人とも打ち解けた.
3《口》無遠慮に行動する, 自由奔放にふるまう ▪ It would be nice to *let your hair down* once in a while. 時には人目を気にせずはめをはずすのもいいだろう.
lift* [*raise*] *the hair 《米俗》頭皮をはぐ ▪ He *raised the hair* of more than one Apache. 彼はアパッチ族の頭皮を一つならずはいだ. ☞the hair「かつて北米先住民が戦利品として, 倒した敵の頭からはぎとった髪つきの皮膚」.
lose *one's* ***hair*** **1** はげになる ▪ I am *losing my hair.* 髪の毛が抜けだした.
2《口》腹をたてる, かっとなる (↔keep one's HAIR on (one's head)) ▪ Jones completely *lost his hair.* ジョーンズはすっかり腹をたてた.
make *a person's* ***hair* [*toes*] *curl*** 《米口》 **1** 人を驚嘆させる ▪ To hear him talk in so many languages is enough to *make one's hair curl.* 彼がそんなに多くの言語で話すのを聞けば全く驚くほかない.
2 人をぎょっとさせる, 身ぶるいさせる ▪ I saw a huge black cat. It *made my hair curl.* 私は大きな黒猫を見てぎょっとした ▪ The thought of talking before a large audience *makes my toes curl.* 大勢の前で話をすると考えるとぞっとする.
make *a person's* ***hair stand on end*** (恐怖などで)頭の髪を直立させる, 身の毛をよだたせる ▪ These ghost stories *make my hair stand on end.* これらの幽霊話を聞くと身の毛がよだつ.
make the hair fly 《米》大騒ぎを起こす ▪ Otherwise they would *make the hair fly.* そうしないと, 彼らは騒ぎ立てるだろう.
not a hair out of place 身だしなみを整えて ▪ He always looks perfect, *not a hair out of place.* 彼は常に身だしなみを整えて一分の隙もない.
not turn a hair **1** 馬が汗を見せない ▪ The horse had *not turned a hair* till we came to Walcot church. 馬はウォールコット教会へ来るまで汗一つ見せなかった.
2 びくともしない, 驚かない; 少しも疲れたふうを見せない ▪ When the great earthquake happened, he *never turned a hair.* 大地震のときに彼はびくともしなかった ▪ He could play the fiddle from sunset to dawn *without turning a hair.* 彼は少しの疲れも見せずに日没から夜明けまでバイオリンを演奏できた.
out of *a person's* ***hair*** 人にうるさくないよう取り除いて ▪ Keep the children occupied and *out of their mothers' hair.* 子供たちに何かさせてお母さんたちのじゃまにならぬようにしておきなさい.
pull* [*tear*]** *one's* ***hair out **1** 怒っている, 怒りで髪をかきむしる ▪ Don't *pull your hair out* over minor problems. 些細な問題でカリカリするな.
2〚主に進行形で〛非常に不安になる ▪ I *was tearing my hair out* before our final exams. 最終試験の前には心配でたまらなかった.
put hairs on *a person's* ***chest*** 《口・戯》(特に酒が)人を元気にする ▪ Have another drink. It'll *put hairs on your chest.* もう1杯やれ. 元気になるぞ.
put on a hair-shirt 犯した罪に対して自らを責める ▪ There is no need for you to *put on a hair-shirt.* 君が自分を責めるいわれはない.
put up *one's* ***hair*** →do up one's HAIR.
raise the hair →lift the HAIR.
raise the hairs on the back of *one's* ***neck*** 極めて恐ろしい ▪ The strange sound *raised the hairs on the back of my neck.* 異様な物音がして私は身の毛がよだつほど恐ろしかった.
rub *a person* ***against the hair*** 人の髪を逆なでする; 人を怒らせる, 人のきげんを損ねる ▪ You *rubbed* him *against the hair.* あなたは彼を怒らせた.
rub* [*smooth*]** *a person's* ***hair the wrong way →comb a person's HAIR the wrong way.
run *one's* ***fingers* [*hand*] *through*** *one's* ***hair*** 《口》頭をかく《緊張・不安などのしぐさ》 ▪ He was nervous and kept *running his hand through his hair.* 彼はいらついて頭をかき続けていた.
salt-and-pepper* [*pepper-and-salt*] *hair 白髪混じりの頭髪, ごま塩頭 ▪ I'm so tired of coloring my *salt-and-pepper hair.* 白髪混じりの髪を染めるのはもううんざりだ ▪ I've started to have *pepper-and-salt hair.* ごま塩頭になり始めた.
see-through hair (ホルモン障害・ストレスによる, とくに女性の)薄くなっていく髪 ▪ Fine haired people tend to have *see-through hair.* 髪が細い人はとかく髪が薄い.
split hairs →SPLIT[2].
stroke *a person* ***against the hair*** → STROKE[2].
take *one's* ***hair down*** 打ち解ける; 打ち明ける ▪ They *took their hair down* and we got the information. 彼らは打ち解けてきてその情報が得られた.
take hair off the dog 《米俗》経験を積む ▪ I've *taken* a little more *hair off the dog.* ぼくは少し経験を深めた.
tear* (*out*)** *one's* ***hair →TEAR[3].
to* (*the turn of*) *a hair 寸分たがわず, ぴったり, そっくり ▪ Her face is her mother's *to a hair.* 彼女の顔は母親の顔そっくりである ▪ I was able to guess his weight *to a hair.* 私は彼の体重をぴたりと当てることができた.
touch a hair of *a person's* ***head*** =harm a HAIR of a person's head.
turn up *one's* ***hair*** =do up one's HAIR.
with *one's* ***hair down*** 遠慮しないで ▪ It is easier to talk confidentially *with one's hair down.* 内々に遠慮なく話す方が楽だ.
within a hair of 《口》危うく...するところで ▪ He was *within a hair of* being dismissed. 彼は危うく首になるところだった.
without turning* [*never turn*] *a hair 感情[驚き]を顔に出さないで[決して出さない] ▪ When she was told her ex-husband was dying, she *never turned a hair.* 彼女は前夫の危篤を知らされても眉

H

毛ひとつ動かさなかった.

haircut /héərkʌ̀t/ 名 ***a haircut place*** 《俗》水面[地面]との間隔が狭い橋 ▪ That low bridge is such *a haircut place* I'm afraid we won't make it. あの低い橋の下を(船で)くぐるのは無理だと思うが.

hair-do /héərdù:/ 名 ***get a hair-do*** 髪をセットする ▪ She *got a* new *hair-do.* 彼女は新しく髪をセットした.

hairline /héərlàɪn/ 名 ***to a hairline*** 精密に, 寸分たがわず ▪ They are matched *to a hairline.* それらはぴたりと調和している.

hair('s)-breadth /héərzbrèdθ/ 名 ***be a hair's-breadth away from*** すんでのことで…するところだ ▪ He *was a hair's-breadth away from* getting caught. 彼は危うく捕まるところだった.

by a hair('s)-breadth きわどい[間一髪の]ところで ▪ He escaped death *by a hair's-breadth.* 彼は間一髪で死を逃れた ▪ It will help to advance the art, even if only *by a hair's-breadth.* それはほんの少しでもその技能をのばすのに役立つだろう.

not a hair's-breadth (***of***) ほんの少しも…せぬ ▪ He did *not* swerve *a hair's-breadth* from his resolution. 彼は決心をほんのちょっとも曲げなかった ▪ There is *not a hair's-breadth of* difference between them. 彼らの間には毛すじほどの違いもない.

to a hair's-breadth 寸分たがわず, ぴったりと ▪ The measurements are correct *to a hair's-breadth.* その寸法はぴたっと正確だ.

within a hair's breadth of **1** 目と鼻の先で, すぐ近くで ▪ The car slipped to *within a hair's breadth of* the precipice. 車は絶壁のすぐ近くまで横滑りした.

2 すんでのことで, 危うく(…するところ) ▪ We were *within a hair's breadth of* being killed. 我々は危うく死ぬところだった ▪ I am *within a hair's breadth of* blowing my top. 私は怒りが爆発寸前のところだ.

hairy /héəri/ 形 ***a hairy ape*** 精神的または社会的に低級な人間 ▪ They are the submerged tenth—the *hairy apes* of society. 彼らはどん底階級—つまり社会の下層の人たちだ.

a hairy wonder ひどい毛むくじゃら ▪ The old tramp was *a* sort of *hairy wonder.* その老浮浪者はひどい毛むくじゃらといった人物だった.

give *a person* ***the hair eyeball*** 《米口》人を疑わしげに見る, とがめてにらむ ▪ When I said I'd made it, she *gave* me *the hairy eyeball.* うまくいったと言ったら彼女は私に疑いの目を向けた. ☞まつ毛で目を一部覆って半眼で相手を見ることから.

hairy about [***at, in***] ***the fetlocks*** [***heel***] 《俗》育ちの悪い, 無作法な ▪ He is a bit too *hairy in the fetlocks* for my taste. 彼は少しぶしつけすぎて私の好みに合わない ▪ He was *hairy at the heel.* 彼は育ちが悪かった. ☞馬の fetlocks (球節)に毛の多いのは雑種とされたことから

halcyon /hǽlsiən/ 形 ***halcyon days*** [***time***] 《雅》冬至前後の天候の穏やかな2週間; 平穏な期間 ▪ We are having *halcyon days* at present. 我々は今は平穏な日々を送っている. ☞昔, カワセミ (halcyon) がひなをかえす冬至ころに風波の穏やかな日が続くと信じられていたことから.

hale /heɪl/ 形 ***hale and hearty*** (老人・病後の人などが)達者な ▪ His father is 65 years old, but still *hale and hearty.* 彼の父は65歳だが, まだ達者である.

half /hæf|hɑ:f/ 名形副 ***a ... and a half*** 《口》大きな…, 重要な…, 困難な… ▪ It is *a* job *and a half.* それは大仕事だ ▪ That's *a* cabbage *and a half.* でかいキャベツだね.

a half-baked boy [***girl***] 《俗》未熟[世間知らず]で愚かな少年[少女] ▪ You plan to ride a bike blindfolded, you *half-baked girl*? 目隠しして自転車に乗ってみようだって? ばかな子だよ, おまえは.

at half *seven* [etc.] 7時[など]半に ▪ We move off *at half* eight. 我々は8時半に立ち去ります.

be half-hearted about …にあまり乗り気でない ▪ I'm *half-hearted about* joining the tennis club. テニスクラブに入るのはどうも気が進まない.

be half the dancer [***singer, writer,*** etc.] *one* ***used to be*** 昔ほどダンス[歌, ものを書くの, など]がじょうずではない ▪ He's *half the tennis player* he *used to be.* 彼のテニスの腕は以前より落ちている.

(***be***) ***half way to*** …に半ば達している ▪ He who wills success *is half way to* it. 成功を決意する人は成功に半ば達している.

one's ***better*** [***other***] ***half*** 《戯》妻 ▪ She is *my better half.* 彼女は私の妻です ▪ I'm waiting for *my other half.* 連れ合いと待ち合わせをしているんだ. ☞one's more than half から; 古くは夫や親友にも用いた.

by half **1** 半分だけ ▪ We'll have to reduce emissions *by half.* 排気ガスを半分だけ減らさねばなるまい.

2 →too ... by HALF.

by halves 半分だけ; 中途半端に ▪ They should not deal with such a serious question *by halves.* 彼らはそんな重大な問題をいいかげんに扱ってはいけない.

cry halves (人の見つけたものの)山分けを要求する ▪ You cannot *cry halves* to anything that he finds. 彼の見つける物の山分けを要求することはできない.

get a half nelson on …を完全に押さえる, の急所を捕える ▪ The policeman *got a half nelson on* the robber. 警官は盗賊を完全に取り押さえた. ☞half-nelson 《レスリング》「外片羽攻め」(片腕を背後から相手のわき下に入れ, その手をえり首に押しつける).

give *a person* ***half a chance*** 《口》人にちょっとでも機会を与える ▪ *Given half a chance*, they will suck you dry. 少しでも隙を見せると彼らから金を搾り取られるぞ.

go halves (***with***)/***go half and half*** (***with***) 《口》(…と)折半する, 山分けする ▪ I will *go halves with* you in the profits. 利益は君と折半しよう ▪ We'll *go halves* on the petrol. ガソリン代は折半しよう ▪ My dad *went half and half with* me to buy my first car. 私の最初の車を買うのにパパが半分

出してくれた.

half a chance 対等のチャンス ▪ He'll talk at length if you give him *half a chance.* 彼に対等のチャンスを与えれば詳しく話すだろう.

Half a loaf is better than none [***no bread***]. 《諺》半塊のパンは全くパンがないのに勝る,「半分でもないよりはまし」.

half a minute [***tick, second,*** etc.] 《口》ほんの少しの間 ▪ I'll be with you in *half a moment.* すぐそっちへ行くよ ▪ Just give me *half a tick*, will you? ちょっと待ってくれないか.

half a mo. [***a sec.***] 《口》ちょっと待って! ▪ *Half a mo.* Stay a few minutes. ちょっと待って. 数分間いてください. ☞mo. = moment, sec. = second.

half and half **1**〚副詞的に〛半分ずつ; 半々で ▪ Let's share it *half and half.* それを半分ずつ分けましょう《動詞を修飾するときは常に動詞の後にくる》 ▪ Do you like this novel?—*Half and half* really. この小説が好きですか?—まあ半々ですね.
2〚形容詞的に〛ほろ酔いで ▪ The miller, *half and half*, came out to greet us. 粉屋はほろ酔いで我々を出迎えた.
3〚名詞的に〛ハーフアンドハーフ, (シリアル・コーヒーなどに加える)牛乳とクリームの混合物 ▪ I don't use *half-and-half* with my cereal. I'm dieting. シリアルにはハーフアンドハーフは使わない. ダイエット中だからね.

half... and half... 半分…で半分… ▪ A centaur was *half* man *and half* horse. ケンタウロスは半人半馬だった ▪ I was lying in bed *half* asleep *and half* awake. 寝ぼけてベッドに横になっていた.

half as many (...) ***again as*** …の一倍半… ▪ He has *half as many* books *again as* you. 彼はあなたの一倍半の数の書物を持っている.

half as much again (***as***) →AGAIN.

half as much [***many***] (...) ***as*** (量[数]が)…の半分… ▪ There is only *half as much* water in this bottle *as* in that one. このびんにはあのびんの水の半分しかない.

half cut 《英》ほろ酔いで; かなり酔って ▪ He can work effectively unless he is *half cut.* 彼はかなり酔いが回っていなければ手際よく働くことができる ▪ I was *half-cut* on gin and tonic. ジントニックでほろ酔いであった.

half dead 《口》疲れ果てて ▪ He looked *half dead.* 彼は疲れ果てたような顔をしていた.

half horse and half alligator 《米》粗野な田舎者(の) ▪ They are *half horse and half alligator* sort of politicians. 彼らは粗野な田舎者といった政治家だ.

half past *eight* [etc.] 8時[など]半 ▪ It was *half past* seven one evening. ある晩の7時半のことだった.

half the battle →BATTLE[1].

half the fun [***trouble,*** etc] (***of*** *doing*) 《口》(…する)楽しみ[厄介など]の大部分 ▪ *Half the pleasure of going* on a journey is in the return. 旅に出かける喜びのほとんどは帰るときの満足にある ▪ That's *half the trouble*—everybody expects too much of her. 主にそれが頭痛の種だ. みなが彼女に期待しすぎる.

have half a mind to *do* →MIND[1].

have half an eye →EYE.

in half [***halves***] 《口》半分に, 2等分に ▪ Cut the squash *in half* lengthwise. カボチャを縦に半分に切りなさい ▪ We cut a square *in halves.* 正方形を二等分した.

in half the time 予想よりずっと早く ▪ I could have done the same job *in half the time.* 私だったら同じことをもっと早くやってのけただろうに.

like a half sled on ice うまくそろわないで, 円滑にいかないで ▪ First one side getting ahead and the other *like a half sled on ice.* まず一方の側が先に出, 今度は他方が先に出てうまくそろわない.

no half measures 《英》半分どころではない程度, 望める限りの度合い《反語的に》 ▪ He entertained the visitors very well. There were *no half measures.* 彼は実に手厚く客をもてなした. これ以上望めないほどのものだった.

not [***never***] ***do anything by halves*** 徹底的にやる, 中途半端なことはしない ▪ They say Scorpios *never do anything by halves.* サソリ座の人は何事も徹底してするという.

not (***even***) ***know*** [***hear***] ***the half of it*** 《口》大事な部分は分かっていない, そんな単純は話ではない, ずっと状況は悪い ▪ They tell me things are serious but they do*n't even know the half of it.* 人は深刻な事態だというがそんな生易しいものではない ▪ I hear you're having a few problems with those guys.—A few problems? You have*n't heard the half of it!* あいつらと少々ごたごたがあるらしいが—少々だって? 分かってないなあ.

not half 《英口》 **1**《反語》半分どころではなく, 非常に, とても (very) ▪ It is*n't half* cold in this room. この部屋はとても寒い ▪ She is*n't half* attractive, your sister. とても魅力的だ, 君の姉さんは.
2 大いに, ひどく (very much) ▪ He did*n't half* swear. 彼はひどく悪態をついた ▪ It did*n't half* rain! ひどい大降りだった.
3 (問いに答えて) (はい,) ほんとに, 全く, すごく ▪ Would you like to come this evening?—*Not half.* 今晩おいでくださいませんか—はい, まいりますとも ▪ Did you like the film?—*Not half* I did. その映画が気に入ったか—すごく気に入ったよ.

not half bad 《口・古風》とても良い ▪ The weather was*n't half bad* that day. その日は天気がとても良かった.

not the half of …の半分たらず(でしかない), ほんの一部しかない, 序の口に過ぎない ▪ Oh, you have*n't* heard *the half of* it yet. いや, 大切な話はまだこれからなんだ.

on halves 《米》利益の半分を取って(貸す); 半分ずつ出し合って(借りる) ▪ Land is let *on halves.* 土地は収益折半で貸される ▪ We rented a house *on halves.* 我々は半分ずつ出し合って家を借りた.

on the half shell (カキが)上の殻を取り去って(出される) ▪ He took them *on the half shell.* 彼は上の殻を取ったカキを食べた.

one [etc.] ***and a half*** 一つ半[など] ▪ He received about *a dozen and a half* blows. 彼はおよそ1ダース半の打撃を受けた[20発近くなぐられた].

six (***of one***) ***and half-a-dozen*** (***of the other***) →SIX.

That was a game [***meal, walk,*** etc.] ***and a half!*** 《口》驚くべき試合[すばらしい食事, 長時間の道のり, など]だった ▪ *That was a walk and a half.* I'm exhausted. 長いこと歩いた. もうへとへとだ.

the better half of …の大部分, 大半 ▪ *The better half of* this job is complete. この仕事はほとんど仕上がっている.

the half of it **1** それのほんの一部分 ▪ If I told you *the half of it*, you'd be shocked. ほんの少しだけその話をしてもあなたはショックを受けるでしょう.
2《口》〚否定文で〛(あるものの)最も重要な部分[面] ▪ You haven't seen *the half of it.* 君は肝心なところがわかっていない ▪ Ill? That's not *the half of it.* 病気かだって? 病気なんて(なまぬるい)もんじゃないよ.

the other half 残りの半分; (貧乏人から見て)金持ちたち, (金持ちから見た)貧乏人たち; (特に)金持ちたち ▪ It makes a change to see how *the other half* lives. 金持ち[貧しい人]たちの暮らしを見るのは気分転換になる.

to (***the***) ***halves*** **1** 半分まで, 不十分に ▪ They do it not *to halves*, but thoroughly. 彼らはそれを中途半端ではなく徹底的にやる.
2《米》(収益を)折半するように, 山分けで ▪ The owners let their land *to the halves.* 地主は土地を収益折半で貸す.

too ... by half 《反語》ひどく…すぎる ▪ You are *too* clever *by half.* 君はひどく賢すぎる.

Well begun is half done. →BEGIN.

one's ***worse*** [***worser***] ***half*** 《戯》夫 ▪ They were as merry as *their worser halves.* 彼女らは夫たちと同じようにはしゃいだ.

halfcock /hæfkák|hà:fkɔ́k/ 名 ***go off*** (***at***) ***halfcock*** (話・行動に)早まる ▪ Now don't *go off halfcock.* もう早まったことをするなよ. ☞「銃の撃鉄を半分上げた位置で発砲する」が原義.

half-cocked /hæfkákt|hà:fkɔ́kt/ 副 ***go off half-cocked*** 《米口》(話・行動において)早まる, 不用意にしゃべる[行動する] ▪ He has *gone off half-cocked* on this one. 彼はこの件に関して早まってしまった. ☞《英》では go off at half cock.

half-mast /hæfmǽst|hà:fmá:st/ 名副 (***at***) ***half-mast***/***half-mast high*** マストの中程に, (弔意を表するために旗を)竿の中程までおろして ▪ Flags were *at half-mast* on the day of the King's funeral. 旗は国王の葬儀の日には半旗であった ▪ The flag was lowered to *half mast.* 旗は半旗の位置におろされた.

half-pay /hæfpéɪ|hà:f-/ 名 ***be placed on half-pay*** (軍人が)半給与となる《現役と退役の中間》 ▪ My cousin *was placed on half-pay.* いとこは半給与となった.

halfpenny /héɪpəni/ 名 ***a bad halfpenny*** 《口》いくら追っ払ってもしつこく帰ってくるもの, しつこく現れるもの; 何も得ないで帰って来るもの ▪ I returned, like *a bad halfpenny.* 私はしつこくまた帰って来た ▪ He turns up like *a bad halfpenny.* 彼は用もないのにうるさくやって来る. ☞ 原義は「悪い半ペニー貨」.

halfpenny under the hat 下等なばくちの一種 ▪ Tom was playing *halfpenny under the hat* with some street hoodlums. トムは町のごろつきたちと下等なばくちをやっていた.

not a halfpenny the worse 少しも悪くならない ▪ Their holiness is *not a halfpenny the worse.* 彼らの神聖さはそのためちっとも減りはしない.

not have two halfpennies to rub together 《口》金をほとんど[びた一文も]持っていない ▪ He looked as if he did*n't have two halfpennies to rub together.* 彼はまるでびた一文もないかのようだった.

turn up like a bad halfpenny → a bad HALFPENNY.

halfpennyworth /héɪpəniwə̀:rθ/ 名 ***lose the ship*** [***sheep, ewe, hog***] ***for a halfpennyworth of tar*** 些細な経費を惜しんで目的[事業]を台なしにする ▪ Don't *lose the sheep for a halfpennyworth of tar.* 些細な費用を惜しんで事業を台なしにするな. ☞もと羊などの傷口にハエがとまらぬよう tar を塗ることから, それを惜しんで羊を殺すことを意味した.

half-seas /hæfsì:z|há:f-/ 形 ***half-seas over*** **1**《海》海を半分横切って[渡って] ▪ He kept below till we were *half-seas over.* 彼は我々が海を半分渡るまで船室から出なかった.
2 ゴール[目的地]までの半ば(まで来て), 半分終えて; AとBの状態の中途(にある) ▪ I am *half-seas over* to death. 私は死への道を半分来た《人生を半分生きた》.
3《口》ほろ酔いで ▪ You had better take him home; he's *half-seas over.* あなたは彼を家へ連れて帰りなさい. かなりきこしめしているから.

half-time /hæftàim|há:f-/ 名 ***on half-time*** 半分時間[半日]勤務で ▪ The workers are *on half-time* now. 労働者は今半日勤務である.

halfway /hæfwéɪ|há:f-/ 形副 ***a halfway house*** →HOUSE.

be halfway there (仕事などを)半分終えている ▪ We*'re* not even *halfway there.* 我々の仕事はまだ半分も仕上がっていない.

go halfway 歩み寄る ▪ Let's just sort of *go halfway* and see what happens. 少し歩み寄って相手の出方を見るとしよう.

go halfway toward [***to***] *doing* …するのは半分程度である; する途上である ▪ Their proposals didn't *go halfway towards meeting* our demands. 彼らの提案は我々の要求の半分も満たしていなかった.

go halfway with [***to meet***] *a person* = meet a person HALFWAY.

meet** a person **halfway 人に歩み寄る; 人と譲り合う ▪ I'll *meet* you *halfway* with £55. 55ポンドで君と折り合おう ▪ The world *meets* nobody *halfway*. 世間は誰とも妥協しない.

meet trouble halfway =borrow TROUBLE.

hallmark /hɔ́ːlmɑ̀ːrk/ 名 ***have all the hallmarks of*** …の典型的な特徴をそなえている ▪ The theft *had all the hallmarks of* a professional job. その窃盗はどう考えてもプロの手並みだった. ☞hallmark「(金銀の純度を示す)品質検証刻印」.

halloo /həlúː/ 動 ***Don't halloo till you are out of the wood.*** →WOOD.

halt[1] /hɔːlt/ 名 ***at a halt*** 停止して, 止まって ▪ Bus services are *at a halt* because of the snow. バスは雪のために運行止めになっている.

bring ... to a halt **1** …を止める, 止まらせる ▪ He *brought* his horse *to a halt*. 彼は馬を止めた. **2** …を中止させる ▪ Economic progress *was brought to a halt*. 経済の進歩は止まった.

call a halt/call "halt" 《米》停止を命じる; やめる (*to*) ▪ The officer *called a halt*. 将校は(行進の)休止を命じた ▪ As it was getting late, we decided to *call a halt to* our game. 遅くなっていたので, 我々は試合をやめることに決めた.

come to [make] a halt 止まる ▪ The train slowly *came to a halt*. 列車はゆっくりと止まった ▪ The peace negotiations have *come to a halt*. 平和交渉は停頓した.

cry a halt (仕事などを)止める ▪ We *cried a halt* for lunch. 我々は弁当を食べるためひと休みした.

grind to a halt 《口》速度を落として止まる ▪ The work gradually got slower and *ground to a halt*. 作業はだんだん遅くなりついに止まった.

make a halt →come to a HALT.

halt[2] /hɔːlt/ 動 ***halt between two opinions*** 二つの意見のどちらとも決めかねてためらう (《聖》*1 Kings* 18. 21) ▪ I see you are *halting between two opinions*. あなたは二つの意見のどちらとも決めかねてためらっているのですね.

the halting foot of justice のろくはあるが確かな司法の足取り ▪ *Justice*, though with *halting foot*, had been on his track. 司法はのろい足取りではあるが, 彼のあとをつけていた.

halter /hɔ́ːltər/ 名 ***come to the halter*** 絞首刑になる ▪ You shall never *come to the halter*. おまえを絶対に絞首刑にさせないぞ.

halve /hæv|hɑːv/ 動 ***halve a hole*** (***with***) 《ゴルフ》(…と)同じ打数でカップに入れる ▪ *The hole was halved* in 5. どちらも5打でカップインした.

halve a round [a match] 《ゴルフ》1ラウンド[試合]に同点となる ▪ Every *round* has *been halved*, hence *the match* itself *is halved*. 毎ラウンド同点となったので, 試合そのものも引き分けとなった.

halvers /hǽvərz|hɑ́ːv-/ 名 ***go halvers*** 《米俗》等分に分ける, 山分けする ▪ They *went halvers* on the price. 彼らはその値段を半分にすることに同意した.

ham[1] /hæm/ 名 ***a ham actor*** 《俗》大根役者 ▪ He is *a ham actor* who can hardly memorize his lines. 彼はへぼ役者で台詞(せりふ)もろくに覚えられない.

ham[2] /hæm/ 動 ***ham it*** (***up***) 《口》大げさに演じる ▪ The players *hammed it up*. 役者たちは大げさに演じた.

Hamlet /hǽmlət/ 名 ***Hamlet without the Prince of Denmark*** 《文》主人公抜き[骨抜き]の芝居[行事] ▪ It's like staging *Hamlet without the Prince of Denmark*. それは骨抜きの芝居を演じるようなものだ. ☞*Hamlet* は Shakespeare の悲劇; その主人公 Hamlet はデンマークの王子.

hammer /hǽmər/ 名 (***as***) ***dead*** (***as***) ***a hammer*** 《口》すっかり死んでしまって ▪ I will soon be *dead as a hammer*. 私はまもなく死んでしまうだろう.

be [go] at it hammer and tongs **1** 激しくけんかしている[する], 激しい言い合いをしている[する] ▪ They're *going at it hammer and tongs* in the backyard. 彼らは裏庭で派手に口げんかをしている. **2** 猛烈に働いている[働く] ▪ He has to finish the work by noon and he's *going at it hammer and tongs*. 彼は正午までに仕事をすませねばならず, 今ねじり鉢巻であたっている. ☞馬蹄を作る鍛冶職人が立てる騒音から.

be down on** a person **like a hammer 人を非常に苛酷に扱う; 人を非常にきびしく罰する[しかる] ▪ The directors *were down on* him *like a hammer*. 重役たちは彼を非常に激しくしかった.

bring [put up, send] ... to the hammer …を競売に付する ▪ We decided to *bring* the property *to the hammer*. その財産を競売にかけることに決めた.

by Thor's hammer ほんとに ▪ *By Thor's hammer*, I swear I'll return some day. ほんとに私はいつかきっと帰ってくる. ☞Thor's hammer「北欧神話の Thor という神の持つ金づち」.

come [go] to the hammer 競売になる ▪ His collections *went to the hammer*. 彼の収集物が競売になった.

go [come, pass] under the hammer 競売で売られる ▪ All his precious works of art *went under the hammer*. 彼の貴重な美術品がみな競売で売られた. ☞せり売り人の槌から.

hammer and pincers 馬が後足で前足のかかとをけるときの音 ▪ The horse went *hammer and pincers*. 馬は後足で前足のかかとをけった.

hammer and tongs 激しくけんかして[攻撃して]; 猛烈な勢いで ▪ They live *hammer and tongs*. 彼らはいつもけんかしている ▪ They went at each other *hammer and tongs*. 彼らは互いに猛烈にけんかした. ☞鍛冶職人が火ばさみで鉄を火から取り出して, 押さえて盛んに打つことから.

pass under the hammer →go under the HAMMER.

put up [send] ... to the hammer →bring ... to the HAMMER.

sell ... under the hammer …を競売で売る

H

▪ He threatened to *sell* the house *under the hammer*. 彼は家を競売で売ってしまうとおどした.

up to the hammer 標準にかなう, 第一流の, すぐれた ▪ The cooking was *up to the hammer*. 料理は実に立派なものであった.

hammering /hǽmərɪŋ/ 名 ***give*** *a person* ***a*** (***good***) ***hammering*** 人を(したたか)なぐる ▪ I *gave* them *a good hammering* with my baseball bat. 野球のバットで彼らをしたたかぶった.

take a hammering 大敗を喫する, ぼろ負けする ▪ I'm relieved we did not *take a hammering*. 大負けをせずにすんでほっとした.

hammock /hǽmək/ 名 ***sling*** [***lash***] ***a hammock*** ハンモックを吊る[たたむ] ▪ We were taught how to *sling* and *lash a hammock*. ハンモックの吊り方とたたみ方を教わった.

H

hand[1] /hænd/ 名 ***a cool hand*** **1** 冷静な人, 泰然たる人 ▪ He is *a cool hand* and no mistake. 彼は確かに冷静な人だ.

2《口》ずうずうしい人 ▪ He is the *coolest hand* I've ever met. 彼ほどずうずうしい人に会ったことがない.

a firm hand 厳格な制御, 厳しい管理 ▪ What those rough kids need is *a firm hand*. あの乱暴な子供たちに必要なのは厳格なしつけだ. ☞手綱で馬を制御するイメージで, a firm hand on the reins ともいう.

a green hand 青二才, 未熟者 ▪ Being *a green hand*, I found it difficult to get a job. 未熟者だったので私は職を得るのがむずかしかった.

a hand-me-down 《口》〚主に複数形で〛兄[姉]のお下がりの物《特に服》 ▪ All my clothes are *hand-me-downs* from my three older sisters. 私の服ってみんな3人の姉ちゃんのお古ばっかりなの.

a hand's turn 《口》一働き, 一仕事 ▪ He won't do *a hand's turn*. 彼はこれっぽっちの仕事もしようとしない.

a heavy hand 厳しくかつ不公平な扱い ▪ They would use *a heavy hand* in dealing with the POW's. 彼らは捕虜に不当な扱いをしたものだった.

a man of his hands 勇敢な[熟練した, 実際的才能のある]人 ▪ I'm sure he is *a man of his hands*. 彼は間違いなく実際的才能のある人だ ▪ He loved *men of their hands*. 彼は熟練した人々を好んだ.

a safe pair of hands/safe hands 《主に英》仕事ができて大失敗はしそうにない人, 信頼できる[頼りになる]人 ▪ The lawyer has the reputation of being *a safe pair of hands*. その弁護士は腕利きとのもっぱらの評判である ▪ Leaders should have vision and yet be *safe hands*. 指導者たるものは先見の明がありしかも着実な人物でなくてはならない.

a show of hands →SHOW[1].

a steady [***firm***] ***hand on the tiller*** 正確な舵(かじ)さばき ▪ What we need is a leader with *a firm hand on the tiller*. 今必要なのは確かな舵取りができる指導者だ ▪ The question is who has *a steady hand on the tiller*. 問題は誰に正確な舵さばきができるかということだ. ☞tiller「船の舵の柄」.

accept with both hands 大喜びで受ける ▪ If I were you, I'd *accept* his offer *with both hands*. 私だったら彼の申し出は喜んで受けるだろう.

all hands **1** (船の)乗組員全員 ▪ *All hands* on board perished. 船上の乗組員全員が死んだ.

2《口》(特に共同作業をしているときの)ある団体の全員 ▪ Then *all hands* went fishing. それから全員が魚釣りに行った.

all hands down やすやすと, 余裕しゃくしゃくとして ▪ We won *all hands down*; they were six lengths behind us. 我々は楽勝した. 彼らは6艇身遅れた.

all hands to the pump 全員ポンプへ!, 全員手伝え!《緊急事態に全員を召集する言葉》 ▪ We are late with the schedule. I must call *all hands to the pump*. 予定が遅れている. 全員の手伝いを求めねばならない. ☞海語から.

An empty hand is no lure for a hawk. 《諺》ただでものをもらおうと思ってもだめだ.

an old hand **1** 老練家, 熟練家 ▪ Toots, as *an old hand*, had a desk to himself. トゥーツは熟練家としてデスクを一人で持っていた.

2 前科者 ▪ They are reformed convicts, or "*old hands*." 彼らは改心した罪人, つまり前科者だ.

(***as***) ***bare*** [***flat***] ***as*** *a person's* ***hand*** ほんとに何もなく, 平たくて ▪ The room was *as bare as your hand*. その部屋はほんとにがらんとしていた ▪ The coast is *as flat as your hand*. 沿岸はほんとに平らである.

as witness the hand of ...がここに署名して証する ▪ *As witness the hands of* the said A and B. 前記のAとBがここに署名して証明する. ☞hand＝signature.

ask [***sue***] ***for a lady's*** [***woman's***] ***hand*** 女性に結婚を申し込む ▪ He summoned up the courage to *ask for her hand*. 彼は勇気をふるって彼女に結婚を申し込んだ.

(***at***) ***close hand*** 非常に近くに ▪ As a friend he often saw the great man *at close hand*. 友人として彼はよくその偉人に近く接した.

at first hand 直接に, じかに ▪ He got the information *at first hand* from the senator himself. 彼はその情報を直接その上院議員自身から得た. ☞hand＝person.

at [《米》***on***] ***hand*** **1** 手近に, 手もとに ▪ Satan was now *at hand*. サタンは今や近くにいた ▪ I don't have my book *at hand*. 手もとに私の本がありません.

2 (時が)近づいて ▪ Christmas is (near) *at hand*. クリスマスが近づいた. ☞close, hard, near, ready を伴うことがある.

at [***on***] *a person's* ***right hand*** 人の右腕として働いて ▪ He's been *at my right hand* for 8 years. 彼は僕の右腕として8年間勤めてきた.

at the hand(***s***) ***of*** 〚receive, take, find, seek, require などの動詞を伴って〛(...の手)によって; の手から ▪ The old way of life became totally outdated *at* *the hand of* the new technology and psychology. 古い生活様式は新しい科学技術と心理学によって全く時代遅れとなってしまった ▪ I will never accept any favor *at his hands*. 彼の手からは決して恩恵を受けません ▪ He suffered a defeat *at the hands of* the enemy. 彼は敵の手によって敗北を喫した.

at third hand 間接の間接に, また聞きのまた聞きで ▪ The story was got *at third hand*. その話はまた聞きのまた聞きで得た.

be a good* [*poor, bad*] *hand at 《口》…がじょうず[へた]である ▪ He *is a good hand at* figures. 彼は計算に長じている ▪ I *am a bad hand at* criticizing people. 私は人を批評するのはへたです.

be a great hand at 《口》…が非常にじょうずである ▪ He *is a great hand at* talking. 彼は談話が非常にじょうずだ.

***be a green hand* (*at*)** (特に仕事が)未熟である ▪ She *is* still *a green hand at* music. 彼女はまだ音楽には未熟である.

be a keen hand at …に熱心である ▪ He *is a keen hand at* hunting. 彼は狩猟に熱心である.

be an old hand at 《口》…に老練である, の経験家である ▪ He *is an old hand at* fixing cars. 彼は車の修理に熟達している.

be bound hand and foot 手足を縛られ(てい)る (《聖》*John* 11. 44) ▪ He *is bound hand and foot* by that wretched document. 彼はあのいまわしい文書に縛られて動きがとれない.

be good with *one's* ***hands*** 手先が器用である ▪ Ask Tom to fix it. He's very *good with his hands*. トムにそれを直してもらって. とても器用だから.

(*be*) *hand and* [*in*] *glove* **1** (…と)きわめて親しい, 密接に協力して(いる) (*with*) ▪ The two firms *are hand in glove* over this contract. その二つの会社はこの契約については密接に協力している ▪ The doctor *is hand and glove with* the bishop. その医師は司教ときわめて親しい.
2 (…と)ぐるになって(いる) (*with*) ▪ Several police officers have been working *hand in glove with* the gamblers. 数名の警察官がその博徒とぐるになってやっていた.

be in good hands よく世話をされている ▪ Your son *is in good hands* in an American family. お宅の息子は米国のある家庭で大事にされている.

be in *a person's* ***hands*** 人に支配されている, の責任である ▪ The arrangements for the meeting *are in his hands*. 会合の手筈は彼の手に任されている.

be no hand at 《口》…は全くへたである ▪ I *am no hand at* sketching. 私はスケッチは全然だめです.

be on* [*upon, in, of*] *the mending* [*advancing, declining*] *hand だんだんよくなる方[進む方, 衰える方]である ▪ He *is on the mending hand*. 彼はだんだん快方に向かっている.

be out of *a person's* ***hands*** 人の支配[責任]を離れている ▪ The decision *is out of our hands* now. それを決める責任はもう我々の手を離れている.

be well in hand うまく制御[支配, 鎮静, 操縦, 経営]されている ▪ The situation *is well in hand*. 事態はうまくおさめられている ▪ The fire *was well in hand*. 火事はうまく消されていた.

bear* [*lend*] *a hand **1** 《古風》手を貸す, 手伝う ▪ Please *bear a hand* with this luggage. どうぞこの荷物を手伝ってください.
2 《口》急ぐ ▪ Well, *bear a hand*, or he'll be off. では急ぎなさい. そうしないと彼は行ってしまいますよ.
3 参加する (*in*) ▪ He *bore a hand in* the business. 彼はその事業に参加した.

bind* [*tie*]** *a person* ***hand and foot 人の手足を縛る ▪ The robbers left us *bound hand and foot*. 強盗の一味は我々の手足を縛ったままで立ち去った.

bite the hands that feeds *one* 飼い主の手を噛む, 恩を仇で返す ▪ I have no intention of *biting the hand that feeds* me. 私に恩を仇で返すつもりはない.

by hand **1** (機械でなく)手で ▪ This rug was made *by hand*. このじゅうたんは手製である.
2 (郵便でなく)手渡しで, 使者によって ▪ The letter was sent *by hand*, not through the post. その手紙は郵便でなく, 使者によって送られた.
3 (自然の力でなく)人工で, (母乳ではなく)ミルクで(育てるなど) ▪ The mother died, so the child was brought up *by hand*. 母親が死んだのでその子供はミルクで育てられた.
4 《米》手ずから, 手塩にかけて ▪ She brought up the child *by hand*. 彼女はその子を手ずから育てた.
5 (印刷でなく)手書きで ▪ I filled the blank *by hand*. 私はその空欄に手書きで記入した.

by* [*with*]** *one's* ***own fair hand 自分の(この)手で, 自分一人で, 独力で ▪ I made this bookshelf *with my own fair hand*. この本だなを自分一人で作ったんだよ.

by the hand 急速に, すぐに ▪ They grew rich *by the hand*. 彼らはすぐに金持ちになった.

by the hand*(*s*) *of …の手により, の手を経て ▪ Many stoics died *by their* own *hands*. 自殺したストア的禁欲主義者が多い ▪ I sent the money *by the hands of* a friend. 私は友人の手を経てその金を送った.

call *a person's* ***hand*** 《米俗》人の計画[行動]を妨害する; 人に清算を要求する ▪ Something will have to be done to *call the Russian hand*. ロシアの行動を妨害するような手を何か打たねばならない ▪ He has *called your hand*. 彼はあなたに清算を要求した. ☞トランプから.

can't keep *one's* ***hands off*** *a person* 《口》…と常にべたべたして[くっつき合って]いる ▪ They *can't keep their hands off* each other. 二人はいつもいちゃいちゃし合っている.

can't see *one's* ***hand in front of*** *one's* ***face*** (暗闇・霧のせいで)目の前も見えない, 真っ暗闇である ▪ It was so dark I *couldn't see my hand in front of my face*. 暗くて一寸先も見えないほどだった.

H

cap* [*hat*] *in hand 脱帽して, かしこまって ▪ The lad came *cap in hand* to ask for money. 若者はうやうやしくやって来て金をくださいと言った ▪ I waited *hat in hand*. かしこまって待った.

carry** one's **life in** one's **hands →LIFE.

change hands **1** 手を変える ▪ My wrist is aching. I must *change hands*. 手首が痛い. 手を変えねばならない.

2 持主を変える ▪ The servant *changed hands*. 使用人は主人が変わった ▪ The hotel has *changed hands*. そのホテルは所有者が変わった.

clean hands 清廉潔白 ▪ He died with *clean hands*. 彼は清廉潔白の身で死んだ.

Cold hands and a warm heart. →COLD.

come the heavy hand 強制的に出る; 偉そうにする ▪ He *came the heavy hand* and forbade me to go. 彼は強制的に出て私が行くのを禁じた ▪ You are as poor at tennis as I, so don't *come the heavy hand* with me. 君も僕と同じようにテニスはへただ. だから僕に対して偉そうにするな.

come to hand **1** (手紙などを)落手する; 手に入る ▪ Your letter *came to hand* yesterday morning. お手紙はきのうの朝受け取りました ▪ They eat whatever *comes to hand*. 彼らは手に入るものは何でも食べる.

2 自然に見つかる ▪ The book *came to hand* when I was turning over some papers. その本は私が書類をひっくり返しているときに見つかった.

come to** a person's **hand するのが易しい ▪ It *comes to my hand* to do it. それは私にはしやすい.

come to* (*one's*) *hands 接戦をする ▪ I want to *come to hands* with the enemy. 私は敵と接戦をしたい.

declare** one's **hand 《トランプ》手を知らせる; 自分の事情[目的]を知らせる ▪ Fanny did not *declare her hand*. ファニーは自分の目的を明かさなかった.

deliver... under** one's **hand and seal 〚主に受身で〛(契約を)署名捺印して有効とする ▪ This agreement *is delivered under my hand and seal* today. この契約は私の署名捺印により今日有効となる.

dip** one's **hand in** one's **pocket = put one's hand into one's POCKET.

***dirty** one's **hands** (**with, on**)* → soil one's HANDs (with, on).

dismiss* [*reject*]*... out of hand ...を即座に却下する ▪ We cannot *reject* his proposal *out of hand*. 彼の提案を無碍(むげ)に退けるわけにはいかない.

***do a hand's turn* (*to* do)** 〚否定文で〛ちょっと努力する[仕事をする] (→lift a FINGER (to do)) ▪ He never *did a hand's turn to* help her. 彼は彼女を助ける努力をちっともしなかった.

eat* [*feed*] *out of** a person's **hand 《口》手からえさを食う; 人に従順である, 人に扱いやすい ▪ He *eats out of my hand*. 彼は私に従順である.

everything* [*anything, whatever,* etc.] *one can lay* [*get*] *one's hands on 《口》手に入れられるものは何でも ▪ They robbed the villagers of *whatever* they *could lay their hands on*. 彼らは村人たちから何でも手当たり次第に奪った.

fall* [*get*] *into the hands of **1** ...の手中に陥る ▪ He *fell into the hands of* some bad companions. 彼は悪い仲間の手中に陥った ▪ These documents must not *get into the* wrong *hands*. これらの書類が悪人の手中に落ちることがあってはならない.

2 (急に, 意外に)...の手に入る ▪ The estate *fell into the hands of* his brother. その地所は彼の弟の所有になった.

fall on** one's **hands 両手をつく ▪ Then he *fell on his hands* and apologized. すると彼は両手をついてあやまった.

fight* (*for*) *one's own hand 自分の(利益の)ために努力する ▪ After all he is *fighting for his own hand*. 結局彼は私利のために努力しているのだ.

for** one's **own hand 自分の(利益の)ために ▪ It sure was *for my own hand*. それはやっぱり私自身の利益になった ▪ Each member of the group played *for his own hand*. その団体の人はめいめい自分のために行動した《私利を図った》.

force** a person's **hand 無理に意図を示させる[行動をとらせる, 早まらせる] ▪ If you do not give up the document, the lawyer will *force your hand*. あなたがその書類を渡さなければ, 弁護士は無理にあなたに出させるだろう ▪ He occasionally *forced his adversaries' hands*. 彼はときどき相手に早まった行動をとらせた. ☞トランプから.

from hand to hand 手から手へ, 人から人へ ▪ The word was passed *from hand to hand*. その噂は人から人へと伝わった.

from hand to mouth **1** 先の備えをしないで, 節約せずに ▪ He never saved a penny, always living *from hand to mouth*. 彼はいつも先を考えずに暮らし, 1ペニーもたくわえなかった.

2 貧乏でその日暮らしで ▪ The inhabitants live *from hand to mouth* and can hardly support themselves. 住民は貧乏でその日暮らしで, 生活ができないくらいだ.

from very good hands 確かな筋から ▪ I have the news *from very good hands*. 私は確かな筋からそのニュースを聞いた.

***gain the upper hand* (*of, over*)** →get the upper HAND (of, over).

***get a* (*good, big*) *hand* (*for*)** 《口》(...に対して) 拍手喝采を受ける ▪ Ichiro *got a hand* every time he came to the bat. イチローは打席に立つたびごとに喝采された ▪ She *got a big hand for* singing very well. 彼女はとても上手に歌って盛んに拍手された.

get** one's **hand in 《口》 **1** 練習して熟達する; 練習して技量を取り戻す (↔get one's HAND out) ▪ I'll begin milking now, to *get my hand in*. 練習して熟練するため, すぐ乳しぼりを始めます ▪ After playing no tennis for some years, it took him time to *get his hand in*. テニスを数年間やらなかったので, 練習して技量を取り戻すのに彼は時間がかかった.

2 (仕事などに)慣れる ▪ I must spend an hour at a new smartphone this evening so as to *get my hand in*. 慣れるために今晩1時間新しいスマホの練習に費やさねばならない.

3 ...に手をつける ▪ We *got our hand in* at intelligence work. 我々は情報の仕事に手をつけた.

get** one's **hand out 練習しないで腕が下がる (↔get one's HAND in) ▪ I've *got my hand out* at tennis. 私は練習しないでテニスの腕前が落ちた.

get** one's **hands dirty 率先して実務に励む, 進んで関与する, 手を汚す ▪ He always *gets his hands dirty* instead of giving orders. 彼はいつも人にさせずに自分で率先してことを成す.

***get* [*lay*] *one's* hands on** **1** ...を手に入れる ▪ He has *laid his hands on* 1,000 pounds. 彼は1,000ポンド手に入れた.

2 《口》 ...をつかまえる, 逮捕する ▪ I *got my hands on* the thief. 私は泥棒をつかまえた.

get ... in hand ...を御する; に着手する ▪ The driver has *got* the horse *in hand*. 御者は馬を御した.

get ... into** one's **hand ...を手に入れる ▪ They *got* New Haven *into their hand*. 彼らはニューヘイブンを手に入れた.

get ... off** one's **hands **1** ...をすませる; を人に譲って免れる ▪ He *got* the task *off his hands*. 彼はその仕事をすませた.

2 ...を処分する, かたづける ▪ The school *got* the troublesome boy *off their hands*. 学校はその厄介な少年を退学にした.

get out of hand 過度になる; 手に負えなくなる ▪ Government spending is *getting* a little *out of hand*. 政府の出費は少し度を過ごしつつある ▪ My son has *got* quite *out of hand*. 息子はすっかり手に負えなくなった.

get ... out of hand ...をし終える ▪ I've *got* my work *out of hand*. 私は仕事を仕上げた.

get the hands 《米口》 喝采を受ける ▪ I am the fellow who *gets the hands*. 喝采されるのはこの私だ.

get* [*gain, have, take*] *the upper hand* [*the whip(-)hand*]** (of, over***) (...より)優勢になる, (に)勝つ; (を)押さえる ▪ Curiosity began to *get the upper hand*, and I decided to have a look. 好奇心が募ってきて私はひと目見ようと決心した ▪ I've *got the upper hand over* you, Fagin. フェイギン, わしはお前に勝ったぞ ▪ Don't let them *take the upper hand*. 彼らに勝ちを譲ってはならない ▪ My wife generally *has the whip hand over* me in chess. チェスではたいてい家内の方が勝つ.

give** a person **a* [*the*] *glad hand 《口》 人を温かく歓迎する 《ただし誠意のない場合が多い》 ▪ He *gave* her *the glad hand* and invited her to dinner. 彼は彼女を温かく歓迎し夕食に招待した.

give** a person **a hand **1** 人に手を貸して助ける 《a helping hand とも言う》 ▪ A police officer *gave* him *a hand* up. 警察官が彼に手を貸して立たせた.

2 《口》 人に拍手を送る, 拍手(喝采)をする ▪ The audience *gave* the new young singer *a* big *hand*. 聴衆は若い新人歌手に大きな拍手を送った.

give** a person one's* [a***] ***hand*** **1** 人に握手の手をさし出す 《あいさつ・祝意を受けるため》 ▪ You have succeeded! *Give* me *your hand*. みごと成功しましたね. お祝い申し上げます.

2 人に(...を)堅く誓う, 請け合う (*on*) ▪ I *give* you *my hand on* that. それは堅く請け合います.

3 (女性が男性に)結婚の承認を与える ▪ She finally *gave* him *her hand* in marriage. 彼女は結局彼に結婚の承諾を与えた ▪ She *gave* him *a* cool *hand*. 彼女は彼の求婚に冷ややかに応じた.

give** one's **hand on a bargain 取り引き成立の握手をする ▪ The *bargain* was struck and he *gave his hand on* it. 取引が成立して彼は握手した.

give ... into the hands of ...をゆだねる ▪ The power *was given into the hands of* the King. その権限は王にゆだねられた.

give with one hand and take away* [*back*] *with the other 助けているようで実は足を引っ張る ▪ My parents *gave with one hand and took back with the other*. 両親は援助してくれたのだが, 反面それがうっとうしくもあった.

go down on** one's **hands and knees 非常に卑屈に嘆願する ▪ I won't *go down on my hands and knees* to such a nasty fellow. 誰があんないやなやつにひざまずいてお願いなんかするものか.

go through** a person's **hands 人に扱われる, 人の手を通る ▪ The applications all *go through his hands*. 申込書は全部彼が扱う.

grease* [*oil*] *a person's hand → GREASE[2]; OIL[2].

hand and foot **1** 手足もろとも, しっかりと ▪ Bind him *hand and foot*. 彼の手足をしっかり縛り上げよ ▪ He is bound *hand and foot* to that family. 彼はその家にしっかりと縛りつけられている.

2 忠実に, まめに ▪ They waited on him *hand and foot*. 彼らはまめまめしく彼に仕えた.

hand in hand (***with***) **1** (...と)手に手を取って, 相たずさえて; (と)歩調をそろえて ▪ They dance *hand in hand* through the streets. 彼らは街路を手を取り合って踊って通る ▪ Practice should go *hand in hand with* theory. 実際は理論と相伴うべきである ▪ Poverty tends to go *hand in hand with* disease. 貧困は病気と密接に関わり合いがちだ.

2 (...と)協同して, 協力して ▪ They worked *hand in hand with* the curate. 彼らは牧師補と協同して働いた ▪ They are *hand in hand* in their affairs. 彼らはその業務で協同している.

*one's **hand is against** another's* 人が他の人に手向かう ▪ *His hand* shall *be against every man's*. 彼にすべての人に手向かわせてやろう.

*one's **hand is in*** (良く練習して)熟練している ▪ *Is her hand* still *in*? 彼女は今も良く練習して熟練しているか.

*one's **hand is out*** (練習しないので)腕が下がっている ▪ *His hand is out* now. 彼は今は練習しないで腕が

下がっている.

hand over hand [***fist***] 《口》 **1** 《主に海》 たぐって(綱などを登る, 引き寄せる) ▪ Up went Martin *hand over hand.* マーティンは綱をたぐって登って行った ▪ He hauled in the line *hand over hand.* 彼は糸をたぐり寄せた.

2 《口》 どんどん; 大量に ▪ He made money *hand over fist.* 彼はどしどし金を儲けた. ☞hand over fist は hand over hand (水夫がロープを登るとき「手を交互に動かして」登り進むの意)という海事用語より.

hand over heart 心から, ほんとに ▪ He repeatedly declares, *hand over heart*, that adult education is important. 彼は成人教育は重要だと繰り返し心から言明している. ☞手を胸に置いて誓うことから.

hand-to-hand ［限定的］ 肉薄した, 接戦の ▪ The result of the battle was decided in *hand-to-hand* combat. 戦闘の勝負は白兵戦で決着がついた.

hand to hand [《口》 ***fist***] ［副詞的に］ **1** 相接して, 肉薄して, つかみ合って ▪ The mariners were fighting *hand to hand.* 海員たちはつかみ合いをしていた ▪ They were down on me, *hand to fist.* 彼らは私につめ寄ってなじった.

2 並んで ▪ They sat *hand to fist* and drank. 彼らは並んで腰かけて飲んだ.

hand-to-mouth 《報道》 行き当たりばったりの ▪ We are worried about the new mayor's *hand-to-mouth* responses. 今度の市長の行き当たりばったりの対応は困ったものだ.

hand under hand 手を交互に下へ動かして, 伝って (→ HAND over hand) ▪ He let himself down, *hand under hand.* 彼は綱を伝って降りた.

hands (***all***) ***round*** [***around***] 《口》 手をつないで左回り《スクエアダンスの合図の一つ》; (みんな)手をつないで ▪ "*Hands round!*" said the fiddler. 「手をつないで左回り」とバイオリン弾きが言った ▪ The press will go *hands all round* for such a thing. 新聞はそのようなことのためには手をつないでいくだろう.

One's ***hands are clean.*** 清廉潔白である (《聖》 *Ps.* 24. 4) ▪ *His hands are* comparatively *clean.* 彼は比較的清廉潔白だ.

One's ***hands are tied.*** (責任・義務上)動くことができない ▪ I'm compromised. *My hands are tied.* 私は信用を落としている. 私は動けない.

hands down 《口》 **1** 楽な, 簡単な ▪ Our team won a *hands-down* victory in the tennis tournament. テニストーナメントはわがチームの楽勝だった.

2 明らかな, 反対のない ▪ This is the *hands-down* best video of the year! これこそ衆目の一致する今年の最高傑作ビデオだ!

3 やすやすと, 楽々と ▪ We beat our opponents *hands down.* 我々は相手を楽々と打ち負かした.

4 文句なく ▪ He is, *hands down*, the best player on the team. 彼は文句なくチームのうちで一番うまい. ☞競馬で, jockey が手で鞭打ったり, はげましたりしないでも勝つ場合から.

Hands in the air./***Hands on your head.*** ＝HANDs up.

Hands off! 《口》 手を触れるな!; 手を出すな; 干渉するな!; 逃げろ! ▪ "*Hands off!*" cried Silver. 「手を触れるな」とシルバーは叫んだ ▪ *Hands off* China! 中国に干渉するな!

hands-off 《口》 不干渉の ▪ The government still maintains its *hands-off* foreign policy toward the country. 政府は依然としてその国に対する不干渉外交政策をとっている.

Hands up. **1** 手をあげなさい《賛成者など》 ▪ *Hands up*, those who have the right answer. できた人は手をあげなさい《学校で》.

2 両手をあげろ《抵抗させないため; 降伏の印》 ▪ *Hands up*—every one of you. 手をあげて神妙にしろ, お前たちみんなだ.

3 《カーリング》 雪よけやめ! 《主将の号令》 ▪ *Hands up!* Stop sweeping. やめ! スイーピングやめ!

hat in hand →cap in HAND.

have a free hand →get a FREE hand.

have a great [***good***] ***hand at*** [***for***] ...がじょうずである ▪ She *has a great hand for* the violin. 彼女はバイオリンが非常にじょうずである.

have a hand (クリケット・ビリヤードを)やる ▪ Let me *have a hand* now. こんどは僕にやらせてくれ.

have a hand for ...の才がある, が巧みである ▪ She *has a hand for* cookery. 彼女は料理の才がある.

have [***take***] ***a hand in*** **1** ...に関与する, 関係する; に一役買う ▪ I protest I *had* no *hand in* it. 私はそれには関与しなかったことを断言する ▪ We *had a hand in* the successful prosecution of the war. 我々は戦争の勝利に一役買った.

2 ...に参加する ▪ I should like to *have a hand in* this scheme. 私はこの計画に参加したいものです.

have a light hand at ...が巧みである ▪ She *has a light hand at* pastry. 彼女はケーキを作るのがじょうずです.

have a steady hand at ...するのに手が震えない, そつがない ▪ He *has a steady hand at* the helm at a time of great changes. 彼は大変革の時期にそつなく舵取りをしている.

have (***all***) ***the cards in*** *one's* ***hands*** → CARD.

have clean hands 潔白である ▪ He *has* a pure heart and *clean hands.* 彼は心が清く, 潔白である.

have [***keep***] *one's* ***hand in*** **1** ...に着手している, 従事している ▪ The government *has its hand in* the construction of roads. 政府は道路の建設に着手している.

2 (いつも練習して)熟練している ▪ Write a line or two of it every day to *keep your hand in.* 熟練しておくため, 毎日それを1行か2行書きなさい.

have *one's* ***hand in the till*** 《英口》 自分に保管の責任がある金[勤務先の金]を盗む ▪ One of the clerks *had his hand in the till.* 店員の一人がレジの金を盗んだ. ☞till 「(店の)レジ」.

have *one's* ***hands full*** 手いっぱいである, 非常に忙しい ▪ With three children to care for, Mrs.

Jones *has her hands full.* 3人の子供の世話で，ジョーンズ夫人は手いっぱいだ.

have *one's* ***hands on*** …を手に入れているようなものだ ▪ You *have your hands on* the estate. あなたはその地所を手に入れているようなものだ.

have *one's* ***hands tied*** 手がふさがっている，何でも自由にできない ▪ I can't help you. I *have my hands tied* right now. 手伝ってやれないんだ. ちょうど手がふさがっていてね.

have ... in hand →in HAND.

have ... in *one's* ***hands*** …を掌中に握っている ▪ He *has* my fate *in his hands.* 彼は私の運命を掌中に握っている.

have something in hand **1** 余分がある ▪ You'll *have something in hand.* 君には余分(な金)があるだろう.

2 楽々と勝つ ▪ The opposition was weak, and we always *had something in hand.* 反対党は弱かったので我々はいつも楽勝した.

have the upper hand (***of, over***) →get the upper HAND (of, over).

have the whip(-)hand of →WHIP[1].

have time on *one's* ***hands*** →TIME[1].

have two left hands →LEFT.

have [***hold***] ***... well in hand*** →in HAND 5.

heavy in hand →HEAVY.

hold a good hand (トランプなどで)良い手[札]を持っている ▪ He wins at cards because he always seems to *hold a good hand.* 彼はいつも良い手がくるらしく，トランプで勝つ.

hold *a person's* ***hand*** 《口》(困った時に)人を慰め助ける ▪ I don't need you to *hold my hand.* あなたに助けてもらう必要はありません.

hold [***stay***] *one's* ***hand*** (…する)手を控える; 慎む; 干渉[処罰]を控える ▪ I intended to dismiss him, but I *held my hand.* 私は彼を解雇するつもりであったが，さし控えた ▪ They *held their hands*, and the bill became law. 彼らが干渉を控えたのでその法案は法律となった.

hold hands **1** (愛情こめて)お互いの手を握り合う ▪ We sat in silence, *holding hands.* 私たちは愛情こめて手を握り合い，だまって座っていた.

2 =hold one's HAND.

hold [***keep***] ***... in hand*** **1** …を予備として持つ ▪ My father has decided to *keep* £50,000 *in hand* in case of a business emergency. 父は商売上の危急の際に備えて，5万ポンドを予備に持つことにした.

2 →in HAND 5.

hold ... in the hand …を手に持つ ▪ The book was too heavy for me to *hold in the hand.* その本は重すぎて私の手には持てなかった.

hold *a person* ***in the hollow of*** *one's* ***hand*** 人を完全に掌中に握っている ▪ He *holds* the people *in the hollow of his hand.* 彼は国民を完全に支配している.

in good [***safe***] ***hands*** 安全で，手厚く保護されて，手入れ[世話]が行き届いて ▪ Your car is *in good hands.* あなたの車は手入れが行き届いている ▪ The injured animals are *in safe hands* at the zoo. 傷ついた動物たちは動物園で無事に保護されている.

in hand **1** 手に，掌中に ▪ He went out cane *in hand.* 彼はステッキ片手に出かけた.

2 手持ちの，手元の[に] ▪ I still have some money *in hand.* 私はまだ手元に少し金がある.

3 自由になって; 余分の ▪ He had a large amount of property *in hand.* 彼は多くの財産を自由にすることができた ▪ I had plenty of time *in hand.* 時間の余裕がたっぷりあった.

4 (仕事に)取りかかって，進行中で; (問題などが)討議中で，取引中で ▪ I have a new work *in hand.* 私は新作に取りかかっている ▪ The work is well *in hand.* その仕事は着々進行中である ▪ That has no relevance to the subject *in hand.* それは討議中の問題と何の関係もない.

5 制御して，支配して; 操縦して，うまく経営して ▪ I had [held] the young man well *in hand.* 私はその青年をうまく統御していた ▪ He got the business *in hand.* 彼はその事業をうまく経営した.

in *a person's* ***hand*** 人の筆で ▪ The bond is *in his* own *hand.* その証書は彼の自筆である.

in the hands of **1** …の手に(持たせて) ▪ Don't place such books *in the hands of* young people. そんな本を若者の手に持たせてはいけない.

2 …の手中に，所有となって ▪ The castle will be *in the hands of* the enemy. その城は敵の手に落ちているだろう ▪ The property is no longer *in my hands.* その財産はもはや私の所有ではない.

3 …に握られて，の掌中にあって ▪ He is still *in the hands of* the money lenders. 彼はまだ金貸しどもの掌中にある ▪ My friend's fate is still *in the jury's hands.* 友人の運命はまだ司直の手に握られている.

4 …に処理されて; に操縦されて ▪ The students are wax *in the hands of* the teacher. 生徒は先生の扱いようでどうにでもなる.

in the turn(ing) of a hand たちまち ▪ *In the turning of a hand* they were all in flames. それらはたちまちみな燃え上がった.

into [***to***] ***the hands of*** …の手に(入る，など) ▪ A letter fell *into our hands.* 1通の手紙が私たちの手に入った.

it stands *a person* ***in hand to*** *do* 《米口》人は…する必要がある ▪ *It stands* a teacher *in hand to* remember that his is a sacred calling. 教職は神聖な職業であるということを教師は記憶する必要がある.

join hand in hand 提携する ▪ Two automobile giants *joined hand in hand.* 自動車メーカーの大手2社が提携した.

join hands **1** (親和・結婚の印に，二人が)手を握り合う，握手する ▪ The bride and bridegroom *joined hands.* 新郎と新婦は手を握り合った.

2 力を合わせる，提携する ▪ Let's *join hands* in the business. その事業に力を合わせましょう ▪ They *joined hands* with the Christians. 彼らはキリスト教徒と提携した.

join** one's [a person's] **hands **1** 両手を組む, 両手を合わせる ▪ He *joined his hands* and bent his head in prayer. 彼は合掌し頭をたれて祈った.

2 (牧師が結婚式で)二人の手を握り合わさせる ▪ The vicar *joined their* right *hands*. 牧師は二人の右手を握手させ(て結婚させ)た.

keep a tight hand on →TIGHT.

keep ... at hand ...を手元に持っている ▪ I *keep* nothing *at hand*. 何も持ち合わせていない.

keep** one's **hand in =have one's HAND in.

keep** one's **hand on ...の支配権を握っている ▪ He cannot *keep his hand on* the committee. 彼は委員会の支配権を握っていることはできない.

keep** one's **hands clean 悪に手を染めない, 正直でいる ▪ Politicians should *keep their* own *hands clean*. 政治家は常に自ら潔白であるべきだ.

keep** (one's) **hands off 干渉しない, 手を出さない ▪ The government should *keep its hands off*. 政府は手を出してはいけない ▪ *Keep your hands off* me, or I'll knock you down. 手を出すな, さもないとなぐり倒すぞ.

keep ... in hand ...を経営する, 実行する; を支配する, 制御する ▪ He *kept* the farm *in hand*. 彼はその農場を経営した ▪ I must *keep* my children well *in hand*. うちの子供らをよく見張っていなければならない.

kiss** a person's **hand(s) **1** 人に敬意を表する, あいさつする, いとまごいをする ▪ My son will *kiss your hand* in a letter of his own. 息子が直接手紙でごあいさつ申しあげます.

2 (あいさつ・いとまごい・就任式に)国王[上官]の手にキスする ▪ We had the honor of *kissing Her Majesty's hand*. 我々は畏くも女王陛下の手にキスの礼をした.

lay a cool hand on a fevered brow 《戯》病人に対して優しい看護をする ▪ She is a nurse who *lays a cool hand on a fevered brow*. 彼女は病人を優しく看護する看護師である.

lay** one's **hand to the plow → put one's HAND to the plow.

lay hands on **1** ...をつかむ, 捕える, 取る ▪ The government *laid hands on* the sum. 政府はその金額に手をつけた ▪ I would like to *lay hands on* the man. 私はその男をひっとらえたい.

2 ...に暴行する ▪ I *laid hands on* him. 私は彼に暴行した.

3 按手(あんしゅ)して祝福[堅信礼, 叙任]をする ▪ The bishop *laid hands on* me in blessing after I was ordained. 司教は叙任後私に按手して祝福した.

lay** one's **hands on **1** ...を見つける ▪ I cannot *lay my hands on* the bottle. びんが見つからない.

2 →get one's HANDs on 1, 2.

lay violent hands on →VIOLENT.

leave ... in** a person's **hands ...を人の手にゆだねる ▪ Can I *leave* the hotel bookings and so on *in your hands*? ホテルの予約をはじめ一切を君にしてもらってもいいか.

One's [***The***] ***left hand does not know what** one's* [***the***] ***right hand is doing.*** 《諺》右手のしている事を左手は知らない《ある団体のする事が不統一である》.

lend a hand →bear a HAND.

lend a (helping) hand (in, at, to** do**) (...に)手を貸す, (を)手伝う ▪ They all *lent a hand in* carrying the chairs. 彼らはみなそのいすを運ぶのを手伝った ▪ I will *lend a helping hand to* raise your position. あなたの地位をあげるのに手を貸そう.

lie (heavy) on** a person's **hands [on hand] 持て余している; 処理が人の責任になっている ▪ Time *lies heavy on my hands*. 私は時間を持て余している ▪ He made them buy the goods which *lay on hand*. 彼は売れずに持て余している品を彼らに買わせた ▪ Let's clean our boots which *lie* foul *on our hands*. 汚れて手入れが必要なブーツを磨きましょう.

lie in** a person's **hands 人にできる ▪ Correction *lies in his hands*. 矯正は彼にできる.

lift [raise] a hand 〚主に否定文で〛努力する ▪ He never *lifted a hand*. 彼は全く努力しなかった.

lift [raise] a** [one's] **hand to [against] ...に向かって手を振りあげる; を攻撃する ▪ She never *lifts a hand to* her daughter. 彼女は決して娘に手を上げない ▪ Don't *raise your hand against* your father again! 二度とお父さんに歯向かってはなりません.

light in hand 扱いやすい ▪ This horse is *light in hand*. この馬は扱いやすい.

live by** one's **hands →LIVE².

live (from) hand to mouth その日暮らしをする ▪ My family *live from hand to mouth* on what I earn. 家族は私の稼ぎで何とかつつましく暮らしている.

lose the [a] hand (トランプで)負ける ▪ Ah! I see I've *lost the hand* by that play. やれやれ, その手で負けてしまったんだな.

make (a) hand 利益を得る; 成功する ▪ We should have *made a* better *hand* of them. 我々はそれからもっと利益を得るべきであった ▪ I don't *make* much *hand* at walking. 私は徒歩ではたいした利は得られない. ☞fair, fine, good などを伴って, しばしば皮肉を表すことがある.

make a poor hand at 《口》...があまり進歩しない ▪ He *made a poor hand at* English. 彼は英語があまり進歩しなかった.

make no hand of ...のわけがわからない, がさっぱりわからない ▪ He could *make no hand of* the matter. 彼はその件はさっぱりわからなかった.

Many hands make light [quick] work. 《諺》人手が多ければ仕事は楽[早い],「仕事は多勢」.

need a firm hand 強い統制が必要である ▪ *A firm hand* will *be needed* in this emergency. この非常時には強い統制が必要であろう.

not do a hand's turn 《口》少しも動かない ▪ He does *not do a hand's turn*. 彼は縦の物を横にもしない.

not let *one's* ***left hand know what*** *one's* ***right hand does*** [***is doing***] 右手のする[してい る]ことを左手に知らせない《善行を人に知らせずにやる》(《聖》 *Matt.* 6. 3) ▪ *Don't let your left hand know what your right hand does.* 善行は黙ってやれ.

not much of a hand at …がへたで ▪ I'm *not much of a hand at* tennis. 私はテニスはへただ.

off hand 準備せずに, 即座に ▪ He made a speech *off hand.* 彼は即席演説をした.

off *a person's* ***hands*** 人の手を離れて, もう責任がなくなって ▪ The matter is *off my hands.* その件はもうかたづいた ▪ He will take this work *off my hands.* 彼はこの仕事を私の手から引き取ってくれよう.

offer *one's* ***hand*** →OFFER[2].

on all hands/on every hand あまねく, 至る所で; みんなに; 四方八方に[から] ▪ It is believed *on all hands.* それはあまねく信じられている ▪ We hear good accounts of them *on all hands.* あらゆる方面から彼らの好評判を聞く.

on either hand =on EITHER side.

on hand **1** 在庫して; 持ち合わせて ▪ We have some new goods *on hand.* 私どもでは新しい品を持ち合わせております.

2《米口》手元に ▪ How much money do you have *on hand*? 君はいくら手元に金があるか.

3《米口》出席して ▪ I'll be *on hand* when you call. お呼びになればまいります.

4 間近に(迫って) ▪ There is trouble *on hand.* 困ったことになりそうだ.

5 手がけて; 担当して ▪ We have other matters *on hand.* 我々は他のことを手がけています ▪ There's a big job *on hand* for tomorrow. あすは大仕事をしなければならない.

on *one's* [*a person's*] ***hands*** **1** 自分[人]の責任[負担]となって ▪ He had the children *on his hands* for five years. 彼はその子供たちを5年の間世話せねばならなかった ▪ This house is *on my hands* till next October. 今度の10月までこの家の世話をしなければならない.

2 自分[人]の荷厄介となって; 持て余して; (商品などが)売れ残って ▪ I have many tasks *on my hands.* 私は仕事が多くて持て余している ▪ Time hangs heavy *on my hands.* 時間がなかなか経たなくて退屈だ ▪ I have an empty house *on my hands.* 借り手がつかず空き家を1軒持て余している.

3 …の両手に(返されるなど) ▪ He had his work returned *on his hands.* 彼は作品を突き返された.

on *one's* ***hands and knees*** 四つんばいになって ▪ She crawled home *on her hands and knees.* 彼女は四つんばいになって這(は)って帰った.

on *a person's* ***right hand*** → at a person's right HAND.

on (***the***) ***one hand…, on the other*** (***hand***) 一方では…, 他方では ▪ My mother was sick *on one hand*, and myself *on the other.* 一方では母が病気であり, 他方では私自身も病気であった.

on the other hand また一方では ▪ He is clever, but *on the other hand* he makes many mistakes. 彼は賢いが, また一方では誤りをすることも多い.

One hand for *oneself* ***and one for the ship.*** 《諺》船に乗っているときは, 常に片手は体を支えるために使い, もう片手で仕事をせよ《仕事だけでなく常に我が身を守るためにも意を用いよ》.

out of hand **1** すぐに, 即座に ▪ He gave me a check *out of hand.* 彼はすぐに私に小切手をくれた.

2 手に負えないで, 手に余って ▪ The boys have got quite *out of hand.* 少年たちは全く手に負えなくなった ▪ The floods were *out of hand* in a day. 洪水は1日で手の施しようがなくなった.

3 終わって, 片づいて ▪ Do it at once and put it *out of hand.* すぐにそれをして片づけてしまいなさい ▪ The business was finally *out of hand.* その仕事はついに片づいた.

out of *one's* ***hands*** 手を離れて ▪ All the decisions will be *out of our hands.* 決定はすべて我々の手の届かないところで下されることになる.

overplay *one's* ***hand*** →OVERPLAY.

play a good hand (トランプなどを)じょうずにやる ▪ She *plays a good hand* of bridge. 彼女はブリッジがうまい.

play a lone hand →LONE.

play for *one's* ***own hand*** → for one's own HAND.

play *one's* ***hand for all it is worth*** 全力を尽くす, 精根を傾ける ▪ I'll stand my ground and *play my hand for all it is worth.* 一歩も引かずに全力を尽くすつもりだ.

play into one another's hands お互いの利益になるよう行動する ▪ The two painters lived together, *playing into one another's hands.* 二人の画家はいっしょに住んで共に感化しあった.

play (***right***) ***into the hands of*** (我知らず, はかられて)相手[敵]の利益になるよう行動する; の思うつぼにはまる ▪ They *played right into the hands of* terrorists by attacking Iraq. 彼らはイラクを攻撃してまんまとテロリストたちの思うつぼにはまってしまった ▪ Taking this bait would only *play into his hands.* うっかりこの誘いに乗ろうものなら彼の思うつぼにはまる.

put *one's* ***hand into*** [***in***] *one's* ***pocket*** → POCKET.

put *one's* ***hand on*** *one's* ***heart*** (***and***) 神かけて[心から, 誠実に](…する) (→with one's HAND on one's heart) ▪ Can you *put your hand on your heart and* say you really like your current job? 今の仕事が気に入っていると誓って言えるか.

put [***set***] *one's* ***hand*** (***to***) **1** (…するよう)努力する ▪ I will *put my hand to* redress it. 私はそれを直すよう努力します.

2 (…に)着手する, をやる ▪ Whatever he *put his hand to*, he did it with all his might. 彼はどんなことを始めても, それを全力をもってした.

3 (…に)署名する ▪ He *put his hand to* that sum. 彼はその金額に署名した.

4 (…に)手をつける《盗む》 ▪ Hardly knowing what he was doing, he *put his hand to* the money. 彼は無我夢中でその金に手をつけた.

put [***lay, set***] *one's* ***hand to the plow*** 真剣に仕事を始める(《聖》*Luke* 9. 62) ▪ Now that Japan has *put its hand to the plow*, it will not look back. 今や日本は真剣に仕事に取りかかったのだから, しりごむことはしないだろう.

put *one's* ***hand up*** (答えるため)手を上げる ▪ *Put up your hand* if you know the answer. 答えがわかっているなら手を上げなさい.

put (*one's*) ***hand***(***s***) ***on*** …を見つけ出す, 捜し出す; を思い出す ▪ I cannot *put my hand on* the book. 私はその本が見いだせない ▪ He could *put his hand on* any fact he wanted in a moment. 彼は求める事実をすぐに捜し出すことができた.

put *one's* ***hands together*** 拍手する ▪ Ladies and gentlemen, *put your hands together* for Sir Elton John! みなさま, サー・エルトン・ジョンにどうぞ拍手を!

put … in hand (仕事など)を始める, に着手する ▪ Your order has *been put in hand*. ご注文に着手させました.

put *one's* ***life in*** *a person's* ***hands***/ *one's* ***life is in*** *a person's* ***hands*** 自分の生命[人生]を他人に委ねる ▪ He decided to *put his life in God's hands*. 彼は自らの命を神に委ねることにした ▪ *My life is in your hands* now. これでもう私の命は君に預けたぞ.

put *one's* ***life in*** *one's* ***hands*** 命をかける(《聖》*Judges* 12. 3) ▪ I had to *put my life in my hands*. 私は生命をかけなければならなかった.

put the last hand to →LAST².

Put your hands up! 〚主に命令文で〛手をあげよ!《降参せよ》(→HANDs up. 2).

raise a hand →lift a HAND.

raise *one's* ***hand to*** [***against***] →lift a HAND to.

ready to *one's* ***hand*** すぐ役立つように, 手元に ▪ The book lies *ready to my hand*. その本はちゃんと手元にある.

one's ***right hand*** 人の最も頼みとする友, 右腕 ▪ His secretary was *his right hand*. 彼の秘書は彼の最も頼れる援助者だった.

One's (***right***) ***hand has lost its cunning.*** 力[技量]がなくなった(《聖》*Ps.* 137. 5) ▪ *His hand has lost* nothing of *its cunning*. 彼の技量は少しもなくなっていない.

rub *one's* ***hands*** 《主に英》→RUB².

rule with an iron hand = rule with a ROD of iron.

run *one's* ***hand through*** *one's* ***hair*** →run one's fingers through one's HAIR.

serve [***wait on***] *a person* ***hand and foot*** →HAND and foot 2.

set *one's* ***hands on*** = get one's HANDs on.

shake hands →SHAKE².

show [***reveal,*** 《米》***tip***] *one's* ***hand*** 手(のうち)を見せる, 意図を明かす ▪ You should not *show your hand* to a stranger. 見知らぬ人に意図を明かしてはいけない. ☞トランプから.

sit on *one's* ***hands*** 何もしない(でいる) ▪ They *sat on their hands* for three hours. 彼らは3時間何もしないでいた.

soil [***dirty***] *one's* ***hands*** (***with, on***) 手を汚す; いやな[恥ずべき]事をする ▪ He refused to *soil his hands with* such work. 彼はそんなつまらぬ仕事をするのをことわった.

stand *one's* ***hand*** (***to***) 《口》(…に)おごる, ふるまう ▪ I used to see her *standing her hand* liberally *to* all. 私は彼女がみんなに気前よくおごるのを見るのが常だった.

stay *a person's* ***hand*** 人の手をとめる, 人の行動を抑える ▪ We ordered them to *stay their hands* until the situation became clearer. 事情が明確になるまでは行動を抑えるようにと彼らに命じた.

stay *one's* ***hand*** 手を止める, 行動を抑える ▪ He was going to strike me, but he *stayed his hand*. 彼は私をなぐろうとしたが手を止めた.

strengthen the hand(***s***) ***of*** …を支持し助ける, 勇気うける(《聖》*1 Sam.* 23. 16); (人の)行動を強化する(↔weaken the HAND(s) of) ▪ If you are in agreement with him, it'll *strengthen his hand* enormously. もしあなたが彼と同意見であれば, 彼を大いに勇気うけるでしょう.

strike hands 契約を取り決める; 協力を約す; 人の保証人となる(《聖》*Prov.* 17. 18) ▪ He forbade us to *strike hands* with a stranger. 彼は我々が見知らぬ人と契約を取り決めるのを許さなかった.

sue for a lady's hand → ask for a lady's HAND.

sully *one's* ***hands*** 《文》手を汚す, 嫌々ながらする ▪ He had no intention of *sullying his hands* by accepting a bribe. 彼は賄賂を受け取って自分の手を汚すつもりはなかった.

take a hand (***at, in***) **1** (…に)参加する, 関与する ▪ He *took a hand at* whist [*in* a game of cards]. 彼はホイスト[トランプ]に加わった.

2 (…の)間に入る, 調停する ▪ It is time for me to *take a hand*. もう私が間に入るときだ.

take hands 手を取り合う ▪ They *took hands* together. 彼らは互いに手を取り合った.

take [***get***] *one's* ***hands off*** (***of***) (…から)手を離す ▪ *Get your hands off of* me! 私から手を離してちょうだい!

take … in hand **1** (仕事など)を担当する, 管理する; を引き受ける ▪ Smith *took* the business *in hand* and made a success of it. スミスがその業務を担当して, それをうまく成功させた ▪ You have *taken* a difficult task *in hand*. 君は困難な仕事を引き受けたね.

2 …の実行[処理]に取りかかる ▪ Tomorrow we will *take* the matter *in hand*. あすその件の処理に取りかかりましょう.

3 (人の訓育・世話)を引き受ける, (人)を預かる ▪ I

have asked him to *take* her *in hand*. 彼に彼女の世話を引き受けてくれと頼んだ.

take *one's* ***life in*** *one's* (***own***) ***hands*** → LIFE.

take matters into *one's* ***own hands*** (責任者がやらないので)事を自分でやる(ことにする) ▪ He *took matters into his own hands* and visited the principal. 彼は事を自分でやることとし, 校長を訪ねた.

take ... off *a person's* ***hands*** 人の(重荷・責任)を取り除く[引き取る]; 人から…を買い取る ▪ He offered to *take* the horse *off my hands* for $200. 彼はその馬を200ドルで私から買い取ろうと言った ▪ No one will *take* the burden *off my hands*. その重荷を私から引き取ってくれる者はいないだろう.

take ... out of *a person's* ***hands*** **1** …を人から奪い取る ▪ We'll *take* the castle *out of their hands*. 我々はその城を彼らから奪い取ってやる.
2 人から(任務・責任)を取り上げる《本人が不本意の場合が多い》 ▪ If you don't cooperate, this job will *be taken out of my hands*. 君が協力してくれなければ僕はこの仕事を取りあげられるだろう.

take the hand of (出された)…の手を握る ▪ *Take my hand*; I will lead you safely. 私の手を取りなさい. 安全に手引きしてあげます.

take the high hand (***with***) (…に)強く出る, 高飛車に出る ▪ He *took the high hand with* the woman. 彼はその女性に強く出た.

talk to [***tell it to***] ***the hand*** (***because*** [***cos***] ***the face ain't listening***) 《米口》お前の話なんか聞きたくない, 聞く耳を持たない ▪ *Talk to the hand 'cause the face don't wanna hear* it any more! もうこれ以上お前の話なぞ聞きたくもねえや ▪ Tell him to *tell it to the hand*. 聞く耳を持たんとやつに言ってやれ. ☞通例, 相手の顔の前に手をかざして言われる.

The hand that rocks the cradle rules the world. 《諺》ゆりかごを動かす手は世界を支配する《母の感化力は偉大である》.

the iron hand in the velvet glove →VELVET.

the last [***finishing***] ***hand*** 仕上げの一筆 ▪ We put *the finishing hand* to our work. 我々は作品に仕上げの筆を加えた.

through hands 終えて ▪ We'll get this work *through hands* at once. すぐこの仕事を仕上げよう.

throw in *one's* ***hand***/***throw*** *one's* ***hand in*** (競技を)投げる, 手札を捨てる; 試合[争い]から手を引く, やめる ▪ Our plucky farmers are not *throwing in their hand*. わが勇気ある農夫たちは争いから手を引くつもりはない ▪ I advised him to *throw in his hand* and return to America. 彼にやめてアメリカへ帰るよう勧めた. ☞ポーカーから.

tie *a person's* ***hands*** →TIE the hands of.

tip *one's* ***hand*** →show one's HAND.

to hand **1** 手元に, 手近に; 手の届く所に; 手中に ▪ Evidence is ready *to hand*. 証拠物件はちゃんと手元にある ▪ You'll find everything *to hand*. すべてが手の届く所にありますよ ▪ Your letter came duly *to hand*. お手紙たしかに拝受いたしました.
2 服従させて, 手なづけて ▪ He brought the hawk *to hand*. 彼はタカを手なづけた.

to *one's* ***hand*** 服従させて, 手なづけて ▪ They brought those animals *to their hand*. 彼らはそれらの動物を手なづけた.

to [***unto***] *a person's* ***hand***(***s***) …のためにちゃんとできて《当人は労せずして》 ▪ I will translate it into English *to your hand*. 私はあなたのためにそれを英語に訳してあげましょう.

try *one's* ***hand*** (***at***) (…を)やってみる, (で)腕を試す ▪ Have you ever *tried your hand at* writing a novel? 小説を書いてみたことがありますか.

turn a [*one's*] ***hand*** (***to***) →put one's HAND (to).

turn *one's* ***hand to*** 経験のないことをこなす, (本業以外の)慣れない仕事ができる ▪ She is so talented she could *turn her hand to* anything. 彼女は豊かな才能に恵まれ, 初めて手がけるどんなことでもこなせる.

under *one's* ***hand*** =ready to one's HAND.

under *a person's* ***hand***(***s***) 人の手にかかって, 世話を受けて, 治療を受けて (《聖》*Exod.* 21. 20) ▪ He died *under her hand*. 彼は彼女の手にかかって死んだ ▪ The doctor sees many patients dying *under his hands*. 医者は多くの患者が自分の治療中死んでいくのを見る.

under the hand (***and seal***) ***of*** …が署名(捺印)して ▪ The deed is executed *under the hand and seal of* the owner. 証書は所有主が署名捺印して作られる ▪ You must give a bond *under your hand and seal*. 自筆署名捺印して保証を与えねばならない.

wait on [***serve***] *a person* ***hand and foot*** → HAND and foot 2.

wash *one's* ***hands of*** …と手を切る, 関係を絶つ ▪ If you insist upon this marriage, I *wash my hands of* you. もしあなたがこの結婚を主張するなら, あなたと手を切ります ▪ I *wash my hands of* any share in this transaction. 私はこの取引とはいっさい関係を絶つ. ☞Pilate がイエスの裁判に関係しないと言って手を洗った故事から (《聖》*Matt.* 27. 24).

weaken the hand(***s***) ***of*** …の気勢をそぐ (《聖》*Jer.* 38. 4) (↔ strengthen the HAND(s) of) ▪ Thus he *weakened the hands of* the soldiers. このようにして彼は兵士たちの気勢をそいだ.

win *a woman's* ***hand*** 女性から結婚の承諾を得る ▪ He was unable to *win her hand* after all. 彼は結局彼女から結婚の承諾は得られなかった.

win hands down →WIN.

with a heavy hand **1** 強力に, 断固として; 圧制的に, 厳格に ▪ They put down the revolt *with a heavy hand*. 彼らは反乱を強力に鎮圧した ▪ Our children were brought up *with a heavy hand*. うちの子は厳しく育てられた.
2 欲張って ▪ Don't use sugar *with* such *a heavy hand*. 砂糖をそんなに欲張って使ってはいけない.

3 不器用に ▪ You can't use that precision gauge *with a heavy hand.* 不器用な者にはあの精密計器の操作は無理だ.

with a high hand 尊大に, 高飛車に (《聖》 *Exod.* 14. 8) ▪ He carries things (off) *with a high hand.* 彼はものごとに高圧的である.

with a sparing [***an unsparing***] ***hand*** 控え目に[惜しみなく] ▪ He dealt out praises *with a sparing hand.* 彼は控え目に賞賛した.

with a strong [***a firm, an iron***] ***hand*** 力ずくで; 断固として, 強力に (→with a heavy HAND 1) ▪ The owner of the factory put the strike down *with a strong hand.* 工場主はストライキを断固として鎮圧した ▪ He ruled *with a firm hand.* 彼は強力に治めた.

with an even hand 公平に ▪ He ruled *with an even hand.* 彼は公平に治めた.

H

with (***an***) ***open hand*** →OPEN[1].

with (*one's*) ***bare hands*** 武器[道具]を使わずに, 素手で ▪ He fixed a loudspeaker *with his bare hands.* 彼は道具を使わずにスピーカーを修理した ▪ The serfs rebelled *with their bare hands.* 農奴たちは素手で反乱を起こした.

with both hands **1** 両手に《相反対する双方から》 ▪ He accepted gifts *with both hands.* 彼は双方から贈物をもらった.

2 全力をあげて (《聖》 *Mic.* 7. 3) ▪ You couldn't deny that, if you tried *with both hands.* 全力をあげてやってみても, それを否定することはできないだろう.

with clean hands 清廉潔白で ▪ He retired from office *with clean hands.* 彼は清廉潔白に勤めて退職した.

with folded hands 手をこまぬいて ▪ He was watching *with folded hands.* 彼は手をこまぬいて見ていた.

with *one's* ***hand in the cookie jar***/《英》 ***with*** *one's* ***hand*** [***fingers***] ***in the till*** 《主に米口》(雇い主から)ものを盗んで ▪ Caught *with his hand in the cookie jar*, he was fired immediately. 盗みの現場を押さえられて彼は即刻首になった ▪ He finally got caught *with his hand in the till.* 遂に彼は雇い主に盗みを働く現場を押さえられた.

with *one's* ***hand on*** *one's* ***heart***/***hand on heart*** 神かけて, 誠実に (→put one's HAND on one's heart (and)) ▪ I can tell you *with my hand on my heart* that you're right. 誓って言うが君の言う通りだ ▪ Can anybody honestly say *hand on heart* that I am wrong? 誰か私が誤っていると神に誓って言えるか.

with one hand [*one's* ***hands, both hands***] (***tied***) (***behind*** *one's* ***back***) 《口》 **1** (非常に)制限されて, 不利な条件で ▪ It's got even tougher *with one hand tied behind my back.* 制限を受けて状況はずっと厳しくなった ▪ We were forced to fight *with our hands tied behind our backs.* 我々は不利な条件の下で戦わざるをえなかった.

2 何の苦労もなく, 容易に ▪ He could do my job *with one hand behind his back.* 彼なら私の仕事を楽々とすることができるだろう ▪ She could make a better dinner *with one hand.* 彼女ならもっとおいしい料理を楽々と作れるのだが. ☞誇張表現.

with *one's* ***own fair hand*** = by one's own fair HAND.

wring *one's* ***hands*** 心配だが何もしない ▪ Don't just stand by and *wring your hands.* 黙って見て手をこまねくだけではだめだ.

write a good hand 字がじょうずである ▪ She is well read and *writes a good hand.* 彼女は博識で達筆でもある.

hand[2] /hænd/ 動 ***hand in*** *one's* ***notice*** [***resignation***] 正式に辞職を表明する ▪ She's already *handed in her notice.* 彼女はもう辞表を提出した.

hand it [***the punishment***] ***out*** 《口》さんざん打ちのめす, しかる ▪ He was *handing it out* with both fists. 彼は両拳でさんざん打ちのめしていた.

hand it to *a person* 《口》 人をほめる; 人にかぶとを脱ぐ ▪ For cheek I must *hand it to* you. 厚かましさでは君にかぶとを脱がねばならない.

hand *A* ***to*** *B* ***on a silver platter***/***serve up*** *A* ***on a plate*** →have ... on a PLATE; hand ... to a person on a (silver) PLATTER.

hand(-)***weed*** 《米》 雑草を手で取る ▪ I began to *hand weed* the wheat. 小麦の中の雑草を手で取り始めた.

handbag /hǽndbæ̀g/ 名 ***handbag syndrome*** ハンドバッグ症候群《いつも同じ側の肩に重いハンドバッグを掛けていると起きる背中の痛み》.

handbagging /hǽndbæ̀gɪŋ/ 名 ***a verbal handbagging*** こっぴどくしかること ▪ The boys received *a severe verbal handbagging* from an old lady. 男の子たちは一人の老婦人からひどくしかられた. ☞Margaret Thatcher 元英国首相が気に入らない大臣をハンドバッグで打つ姿を風刺漫画家が好んで描いたことから.

handclap /hǽndklæ̀p/ 名 ***give ... a slow handclap*** (演説者・選手など)にゆっくりした拍手で不満を表明する ▪ The fans *gave* the referee *a slow handclap.* ファンはレフェリーに不満の拍手をゆっくりとした.

handcuff /hǽndkʌ̀f/ 名 ***golden handcuffs*** 《俗》現職への慰留のための特典の契約, 慰留特別優遇措置; 金の手錠《他社の引き抜きを防ぐための特別待遇》 ▪ I signed a three-year, £3 million, *golden-handcuffs* deal. 3年間300万ポンドの慰留特別加給契約にサインした.

handful /hǽndfʊ̀l/ 名 ***be a handful*** 制御しにくい, 手に負えない ▪ The boy *is a handful.* その少年は手に負えない.

by the handful ひとつかみ[ひと握り]単位で, 少量ずつ ▪ People began leaving *by the handful* during the show. 公演の途中で観客は三々五々退場し始めた.

have (***got***) ***a handful*** 手に持てるだけ持っている;

制御するに手いっぱいである ▪ I've *got a handful* of raisins. 私は干しブドウを手にいっぱい持っている ▪ I shall *have a handful* when these four boys come home for the holidays. この4人の少年が休暇で帰って来たら，その世話に手いっぱいでしょう．

handgrip /hǽndgrìp/ 名 ***be at* [*in*] *handgrips* (*with*)** (…と)つかみ合いをしている ▪ He *was at handgrips with* Destiny. 彼は運命と取っ組んでいた ▪ Two wrestlers *were at handgrips*. 二人のレスラーが取っ組み合っていた．

come to handgrips つかみ合いになる ▪ They finally *came to handgrips*. 彼らはとうとうつかみ合いになった．

handicap /hǽndikæ̀p/ 名 ***under a handicap*** 不利な条件の下で ▪ The firm is working *under a handicap*. その会社は不利な条件の下で営業している．

handkerchief /hǽŋkərtʃəf/ 名 ***drop* [*throw*] *the handkerchief* (*to*)** **1**《遊戯》人に追いかけて来いと誘いかける ▪ Boys *drop the handkerchief to* girls, and girls *to* boys in the game. そのゲームでは男の子と女の子が相互に追いかける誘いをかけあう．

2 …に求愛する，意のあることをほのめかす ▪ He must *throw his handkerchief*. 彼は気に入っていることをほのめかさねばならない．☞子供の鬼ごっこ(ハンカチを投げられた者が投げた者を追いかける)から．

with handkerchief in one hand and sword in the other 災難に同情するふりをしてしかもそれを大いに利用する．

handle[1] /hǽndəl/ 名 ***a handle to one's name*** 《口》 **1** 肩書き ▪ His Majesty has given me *a handle to my name*. 陛下は私に肩書きをくださった．

2 ニックネーム，あだ名 ▪ His height earned him *a handle to his name*, Lofty. 彼は背が高いので，Lofty「のっぽ」というニックネームがついた．

be* [*go, slip*] *off the handle 《米口》 **1** 自制心を失う，かっとなる ▪ I would *go off the handle* if something like this ever happened. こんなことが起きたら僕はキレてしまうだろう．

2 死ぬ ▪ My father means to be Mayor before he *goes off the handle*. 父は死ぬ前に市長になるつもりです．

find the handle on 《野球》(ゴロ球)をつかむ ▪ He can't *find the handle on* the ball. 彼はゴロ球はつかめない．

fly off* (*at*) *the handle 《口》 **1** かっとして我を忘れる，自制心を失う ▪ He *flies* right *off the handle* for nothing. 彼は何でもないことにすぐかっとなる ▪ His voice was apt to *fly off at the handle*. 彼の声は調子がはずれがちだった．☞ぐらぐらになった斧の刃がはずれるイメージ．

2 死ぬ ▪ Hugh *flew off the handle* at his London hotel. ヒューはロンドンのホテルで亡くなった．

get* [*have*] *a handle on 《口》分かる[分かっている]，手がかりをつかむ[つかんでいる] ▪ We need to *get a* better *handle on* consumer demand. 消費者の需要をもっと把握する必要がある ▪ All of us *have a handle on* how valuable water is. 水がどれほど貴重かは誰でも分かっている．

***give* (*a person*) *a handle* (*against one*)** (人に)かれこれ言われるような機会[口実]を与える ▪ Don't *give* him *a handle against* you. 彼にかれこれ言われるようなことをするな ▪ Your indiscreet behavior may *give a handle* to your enemies. 君の無分別な行動のため，敵にかれこれ言われることになるかもしれない．

***give* (*a person*) *a handle for* [*to*]** (人に)…する機会[口実]を与える ▪ Don't *give* your enemies *a handle for* censure. 敵に非難されるような機会を与えるな．

go off the handle →be off the HANDLE.

have two handles 二様の解釈の仕方がある，二様に取れる ▪ A dilemma is, as it were, a syllogism which *has two handles*. ジレンマ[両刀論法]とは，いわば，二様に取れる論法である．

like the handle of a jug 《米》水さしの取っ手のように(一方的で) ▪ Such judges are *like the handle of a jug*, all on one side. そのような審判官は水さしの取っ手のように全く一方的である．

slip off the handle →be off the HANDLE.

take a thing by the best handle 物事を最も良いように解釈する ▪ I like people who *take a thing by the best handle*. 物事を最もよいように解する人が好きだ．☞handle「二通り以上の解釈のうちの一つ」．

(*up*) *to the handle* 《米口》徹底的に，完全に，専心に ▪ He carried on the contest *to the handle*. 彼はその競技を徹底的にやった ▪ He was enjoying his trip *up to the handle*. 彼は旅行を心ゆくまで楽しんでいた．

handle[2] /hǽndəl/ 動 ***handle oneself*** 行儀よくする，自制する ▪ You have to learn how to *handle yourself* before you can handle others. 他人を統御できるようになるより先に自制する術を心得ておかねばならない．

handle with* (*kid, silk*) *gloves →GLOVE.

handle without gloves →GLOVE.

handshake /hǽndʃèɪk/ 名 ***a golden handshake*** →a GOLDEN parachute.

give* (*a person*) [*receive*] *a handshake (人と)握手をする[受ける] ▪ I *gave* him *a* warm *handshake*. 彼と温かい握手をした ▪ He *received a* warm *handshake* there. 彼はそこで温かい握手を受けた．

handsome /hǽnsəm/ 形副 ***do something handsome* (*toward*)** (…に)気前よくする；(に)非常に親切丁寧にする ▪ They *did something handsome toward* the city. 彼らは市に対して気前よく金を出した．

***do the handsome* (*thing*) (*by, towards*)** (…に)気前よくする；(に)非常に親切にする ▪ He *did the handsome towards* me. 彼は私に非常に気前よくしてくれた ▪ I'll *do the handsome thing by* his nephew. 彼のおいを優待しましょう．

H

Handsome is that* [*as*] *handsome does./ Pretty is as pretty does. 《諺》行いの立派な人はみめも美しい,「みめより心」《あまり美しくない女性がよく引用する》. ☞Handsome is one who does handsomely. の意.

handsomely /hǽnsəmli/ 副 ***do the thing* [*act*] *handsomely*** 気前よくする ▪We will *do the thing handsomely* and celebrate the centenary. 大いに気前よく金を出して百年祭を祝いましょう.

handspring /hǽndsprìŋ/ 名 ***turn handsprings*** とんぼ返りをする ▪The acrobats were *turning handsprings* forwards and backwards. 曲芸師たちが前後にとんぼ返りをしていた.

handwriting /hǽndràɪtɪŋ/ 名 **(*the*) *handwriting on the wall*** 壁に書かれた文字; 災いの前兆 (《聖》*Dan*. 5. 5-31) ▪Miraculous *handwriting on the wall* proclaimed to me, "This thou shalt do." 壁に書かれた不思議な文字が「なんじこれをなすべし」と私に宣言した ▪Before the stock-market crash he saw *the handwriting on the wall* and sold all his securities. 株式市場の総くずれの前に彼はその前兆を見て自分の証券を全部売ってしまった. ☞→the handwriting is on the WALL (for a person).

H

handy /hǽndi/ 形 ***come in handy*** → COME².

***handy for* [*to*]** 《口》…に便利な位置にあって ▪We are so *handy for* coming by car. 我々は自動車で来るのに便利な所に(住んで)いる.

handy-dandy /hǽndidǽndi/ 名 ***play* (*at*) *handy-dandy* (*with*)** (…と)当てっこ(遊戯)をする《両手の間に物を握り, 急に手を閉じてどっちの手に物があるかを当てさせる》 ▪He would *play handy-dandy with* us. 彼は我々と当てっこをしたものだった.

hang¹ /hæŋ/ 名 ***get out of the hang of*** (*doing*) (仕事の)仕方[こつ]を忘れる ▪You'll soon *get out of the hang of playing* the piano. じきにピアノのひき方を忘れるでしょう.

get* [*get into, acquire*] *the hang of 《口》 **1** (道具など)の操作に慣れる; (芸)に熟達する ▪The machinery is simple; you'll soon *get the hang of* it. その器械は簡単です. じきにその操作に慣れるでしょう ▪I've *acquired the hang of* English grammar. 英文法をものにした.

2 (意味・主旨・状態・計画など)を理解する ▪I don't quite *get the hang of* your argument. 私はあなたの議論がよくわからない.

3 (仕事)のこつを覚える ▪Before long I *got the hang of* it. まもなく私はその仕事のこつを覚えた. ☞hang=meaning, knack.

lose the hang of 《口》…との接触がなくなる ▪I have *lost the hang of* them. 彼らとの接触が途絶えた.

not care* [*give*] *a hang 《米》少しもかまわない, 気にしない ▪Our friends do*n't care a hang*. 我々の友は少しもかまわない ▪He *no* longer *gave a hang* what they did. 彼は彼らのすることにはもはや少しもかまわなかった.

hang² /hæŋ/ 動 ***and hang the cost* [*expense*]** 《英口》費用はいくらかかってもよい ▪We want the very best, *and hang the cost*. とびきり上等なのがほしい, 値段は問わない ▪Oh, let's get a taxi *and hang the expense*! タクシーにしよう, いくらかかってもいいから.

***Be hanged* (*to you*)!** ちくしょう!, この野郎!《怒り・くやしさ・じれったさを表す》 ▪*Be hanged to you*, can't you leave me alone? この野郎! 俺にかまうな ▪Farewell, and *be hanged!* あばよ, くたばってしまうがいい.

be* [*feel*] *hung over 《口》二日酔いである ▪He *is* terribly *hung over* after last night's party. 彼は昨夜パーティーがあってひどい二日酔いだ.

be* [*get*] *hung up 《米口》 **1** (…が)念頭から離れない, (を)必要以上に心配する; (に)夢中である[になる] (*about* [*on*]) ▪The eight-year-old boy is *getting hung up about* his hair and his clothes. その8歳の少年は自分の髪や服のことばかり考えている ▪Don't *get hung up on* the small mistakes. そんな些細なミスで気をもむな ▪*Are* you still *hung up on* that girl? 君はまだあの女の子にぞっこんなのか.

2 待たされる, 止められる ▪I'm sorry I'm late. I *got hung up* at work. 遅れてごめん. 仕事で手間取ってね ▪We *were hung up* ten miles away with a couple of punctures. 10マイル離れた所で両輪ともパンクして立往生した.

go hang **1** 絞首刑になる; くたばる ▪You'll have your mouthful of rum tomorrow and *go hang*. お前はあすラム酒を1杯飲んでくたばるだろう.

2 (どうにでもなれと)放任[無視]される ▪He let party discipline *go hang*. 彼は党紀を無視されるに任せた.

***hang** oneself* 首をつる ▪He is said to have *hanged himself*. 彼は首をつったそうである.

hang a jury 陪審員の意見を不一致にして答申ができないようにする, 陪審団が評決に達するのを妨げる ▪These jurymen *hung the jury*. この陪審員たちは評決に達するのを妨げた.

***hang a left* [*right*]** 《米口》左[右]折する ▪Hey, it's here! *Hang a right* at this corner! あっ, ここだ! この角を右に曲がって!

***hang a leg* [《俗》*the groin*]** しりごみする ▪At this answer the duke *hung the groin*. この返事に公爵はためらった.

hang between life and death 生死の境にいる ▪He *hangs between life and death*. 彼は生死の境をさまよっている.

hang by* [*on*] *a* (*single*) *hair/hang by a thread 風前のともしびである ▪His life is *hanging by a thread*. 彼の命は風前のともしびである ▪It all *hangs by a hair*. それは全く危うい状態である. ☞ギリシャの伝説 Damocles の剣の話から.

hang by the wall 壁に掛け放しになっている; 不用に属する ▪Our old cauldron *hangs by the wall*. 我が家の古い大鍋が壁に掛けっ放しになって[は使われずに放置されて]いる.

***hang* (*down*) *one's* *head* (*in shame, for shame*)** →HEAD[1].
hang fire →FIRE[1].
hang* *one's* *hat on →HAT.
***hang heavy on* *a person* [(*a person's*) *hands*]** 人が(主語)を持て余す，のために苦しむ ▪ Time *hangs heavy on my hands.* 私は時がなかなか経たないで退屈である ▪ The goods *hang heavy on our hands.* その品は売れずに当店で持て余している ▪ Life *hangs heavy on* him. 彼は命を持て余している《生きているのがつらい》.
hang ... in chains (罪人の体を)鉄わくにつるして公衆にさらす ▪ They *hanged* him *in chains* for a show. 彼を鉄わくにつるして公衆にさらした.
hang in doubt 決まらない ▪ The election *hangs in doubt.* 選挙はまだ決まらない.
hang in the balance →be in the BALANCE.
hang in the wind →WIND[1].
hang in* (*there*)/*hang* (*on*) *in there 《米口》困難に耐える ▪ *Hang in there*! It will soon be over. 困難に耐えなさい! やがて終わるでしょうから ▪ Look, just *hang on in there.* I'm sure you'll get a job soon. いいか，がんばれ. 今にきっと職があるから.
Hang it* (*all*)*! ああ腹が立つ!，ちくしょう!，ちぇっ! ▪ Well, *hang it*, there can't be much harm in it if I use common sense. こんちくしょう! おれが常識を使って悪いはずはないじゃないか.
hang it on 《俗》ことをことさらに遅らせる，長びかせる ▪ You'll have to *hang it on.* あなたはそれを長びかさなければならないだろう.
hang it up 《米》(仕事を)やめる，引退する，身を引く ▪ I've had it with this job. It's time to *hang it up.* この仕事にはもううんざりだ. そろそろやめる潮時だな.
hang* *one's* *lip →HANG the lip.
hang loose リラックスしている，のんびりしている ▪ Just *hang loose* and stop working so hard. 少しのんびりして，そんなに仕事に熱中しないこと.
hang on a* (*single*) *hair →HANG by a (single) hair.
***hang on by the skin of* *one's* *teeth* [*by* *one's* *eyebrows, eyelashes, eyelids*]** 《口》
1 (困難・障害にめげず)必死になってがんばる，かじりつく ▪ You must *hang on* to your present job *by the skin of your teeth.* 君は今の仕事に必死になってかじりついていなければならない.
2 (破滅・死・敗北に瀕して)危機一髪である ▪ The patient appeared to be *hanging on by the skin of his teeth.* 患者は死に瀕して危機一髪の状態に思えた.
hang on in there =HANG in (there).
***hang on* [*upon*] *a person's* *lips* [*words, every word*]** 人の言葉を一心に聞く ▪ They were *hanging on his lips* from beginning to end of his speech. 彼らは彼の演説の初めから終わりまで一心に聞き入っていた ▪ Everyone *hangs on his words.* みな彼の言うことをかたずをのんで聞く ▪ The girls leaned forward and *hung on her every word.* 少女たちは身を乗り出して彼女の話に熱心に聞き入った.
hang one on **1**《口》...に一撃を与える ▪ It *hangs one on* the man. それはその男には打撃だ.
2《米口》(酒を飲みに行って)ひどく酔う ▪ He went to a bar and *hung one on* last night. 彼は昨夜バーに行って酔いつぶれた.
hang out* *one's* *shingle →SHINGLE.
hang* *a person* *out to dry 《米口》責任をとらせて人を窮地に追い込む，人に非常に厳しく当たる ▪ After losing the election, the party *hung* him *out to dry.* 落選後，党は責任を取らせて彼を干した. ☞「洗濯物を外に干す」から.
hang over* *a person's* *head 人の頭上に迫る ▪ A great calamity was *hanging over her head.* 大災難が彼女の頭上に降りかかろうとしていた.
hang the* [*one's*] *lip (赤面・落胆・後悔などのため)べそをかく ▪ He began to *hang the lip.* 彼はべそをかき始めた.
hang to the ropes 《米口》あくまでがんばり続ける ▪ I advised him to *hang to the ropes.* 彼にあくまでがんばり続けるよう勧めた.
hang tough 《主に米口・報道》頑として屈しない，なかなか折れない，固く決意している ▪ You tend to give in too easy. Just *hang tough.* 君はすぐに負けを認めてしまう. ちゃんと粘り強く立ち向かえ.
***hang up* *one's* *gloves* [*boots, fiddle,* etc]** (長年続けた活動・スポーツについて)ボクシング[フットボール，音楽，など]をやめる，引退する ▪ She thinks it's time to *hang up her dancing shoes.* 彼女はちょうどダンスをやめる潮時だと考えている ▪ It is time to *hang up my boots.* 私はもう引退する時だ. ☞フットボールの試合が終わるとシューズをつるすことから.
***hang up* *one's* *gun* [*ax, hatchet, sword,* etc.]** **1** 鉄砲[おの，剣，など]をつるして使うのをやめる ▪ A little more practice, and I will *hang up my gun* over the chimney. もう少し練習したら，銃を炉だなの上にかけてもう使いません ▪ He *hung up his sword.* 彼は剣を壁にかけて使うのをやめた.
2 兵役を引退する，退役する ▪ I'm *hanging up my sword* next year and moving to Miami. 私は来年退役してマイアミに引っ越す予定だ.
hang up* *one's* *hat 《口》 **1** = hang (up) one's HAT.
2 定年退職する ▪ I'm going to *hang up my hat* next spring. 来春定年で職を退く予定だ.
Hang you! この野郎!，こんちくしょう! ▪ Stop that noise, *hang you!* この野郎! 騒ぐのをやめろ.
I'll be hanged とても驚いた ▪ Well, *I'll be hanged*, there's Betty! まあ驚いた. あそこにベティーがいるわ.
I'll be hanged if 《口》...してたまるものか; 絶対に...しない ▪ *I'll be hanged if* I'll be hazed by you. 君にこき使われてたまるか.
I'll see you hanged first. →SEE.
It's* [*That's*] *no hanging matter. 《口》これは(首をつるほどの)深刻な問題ではない ▪ I do *not* see

that *it is a hanging matter* at all. それが深刻な問題だとは到底思えない.

***leave ... hanging* (*in the air* [*in midair*]) 1** (返答など)を(人)に待たせておく ▪ I *was left hanging* for over a year with nothing sent to me. 1年以上もの間待たされたが, 何も送られてこなかった ▪ The bank *left* our loan application *hanging*. 銀行はうちの融資の申し込みを据え置きにした.

2 決定を遅らせる, 未定[未決]のままにしておく ▪ The way he did it seems to have *left* everything *hanging*. 彼の処理の仕方では, 万事の決定を遅らせてしまったように思われる ▪ The matter of the spring excursion *was left hanging in the air*. 春の遠足の件は未定のままにされた ▪ Let's *leave* this question *hanging in midair* for the time being. 当分の間この問題は未決のままにしておこう.

let it all hang out 《俗》(気持ち・考え・秘密・すべてを隠さずに)自由に話す, ぶちまける; (遠慮せず)自由にやりたいようにやる ▪ Enjoy yourself at the party. *Let it all hang out.* パーティーでは楽しく過ごしなさい. 何でも自由にしゃべりなさい.

One may as well be hanged for a sheep as* (*for*) *a lamb. →SHEEP.

thereby hangs a tale →TALE.

Well, I'm hanged! 《口》これは驚いた! ▪ *Well, I'm hanged!* Who'd have thought I'd meet you here? おやまあ! ここであなたに会うとは夢にも思わなかった.

You be hanged! 《口》くたばれ ▪ *You be hanged!* You know nothing about it. こんちくしょう! お前にはそのことは何もわかりはしないんだ.

hank /hæŋk/ 名 ***hank for hank*** 船が2隻並んで; 《俗》五分五分で, 対等で ▪ The two ships sailed *hank for hank* for some time. 両船はしばらく並んで航行した ▪ If we become partners, it must be a *hank for hank* arrangement. もし我々が組合員となるなら, それは対等の取り決めでなければならない. ☞hank 《海》「帆鐶(はんかん)」.

***have* [*keep*] *a hank on* [*upon, over*]** 《主に方》...に対して抑制力[措止力]を持つ ▪ He *had this hank over* her inclinations. 彼は彼女の好みに対してこのような抑制力を持っていた ▪ You must *keep a* good *hank upon* your horse. 馬の手綱をしっかり握っていなければならない.

hanky-panky /hæ̀ŋkipǽŋki/ 名 ***play hanky-panky with*** ...をごまかす, の目をくらます ▪ The doctor is *playing hanky-panky with* his patients. その医者は患者をごまかしている.

Hanover /hǽnoʊvər/ 名 ***Go to Hanover!*** くたばってしまえ!; うせやがれ!

send a person to Hanover 人を追っ払う ▪ The king *sent* the minister *to Hanover*. 国王はその大臣を追放した.

wish a person at Hanover 人がくたばればよい[どこへでも行ってしまえばよい]と思う ▪ I've often *wished* them *at Hanover*. やつらなんかくたばればいいとたびたび願った. ☞Hanover＝Hell.

haphazard /hæ̀phǽzərd/ 名 ***at* [*by*] *haphazard*** 偶然に; でたらめに ▪ They labor *at haphazard*. 彼らの骨折りはでたらめだ.

happen /hǽpən/ 動 ***anything can* [*might*] *happen*** 何が起きるか分からない ▪ How can you be so sure—*anything can happen*! よくもそんなに自信たっぷりでいられるものだ. 一寸先は闇なのに.

as it happens たまたま; 折よく, 折あしく ▪ *As it happens*, I've left the book at home. あいにく私はその本を家へ忘れて来た ▪ *As it happens*, they were all very clever. 何しろ, 彼らはみな聡明だった.

***happen what may* [*will*]** どんなことが起こっても ▪ *Happen what may*, I will accomplish my purpose. どんなことがあっても私は目的を達成する.

if anything should happen to me 《婉曲》もし私が死んだら ▪ *If anything should happen to me* I'd like to die at home. 万一死ぬとしたら我が家で死にたいものだ ▪ I'm afraid of what she might do *if anything should happen to me*. もし私が死んだら彼女はどうするか心配だ.

it can't happen here まさかそんなことが ▪ *It can't happen here*, I'm telling you. そんなまさか, ありえないよ, 本当に.

it has to happen to a person わざわざ...にふりかかってこなくてもよいのに ▪ The boss wants me to go to China. Why does *it have to happen to* me? 社長は私に中国へ行けと言っている. どうして私が行かなければならないのだろう.

it shouldn't happen to a dog 犬にさえあってはならないことだ《不幸・処罰・苦痛について言う》 ▪ *It shouldn't happen to a dog*, certainly not to George. 犬にさえあってはならない不幸だ, ジョージの場合なおさらだ.

***it* (*so*) *happens that*/*it* (*just*) *so happens* (*that*)** ...ということがある, たまたま...する, 偶然...ということである ▪ *It so happened that* one of them died. たまたま彼らのうちの一人が死んだ ▪ *It* often *happens that* the biter is bit. 人をだまそうとしてだまされることはよくある ▪ *It just so happened* I had a little money with me. たまたま少々持ち合わせがあった.

The unexpected always happens. 《諺》予期せぬことが起きるのは世の常《起こりうるあらゆることを予見することはできない》.

What* [*Whatever*] (*has*) *happened to ...? 《口》...は(一体)どうしたのか, どうなったか ▪ *What has happened to* George since, I wonder? ジョージはその後どうしたのかしら ▪ *What's happened to* your cousin Roy? 君のいとこのロイはその後どうしているか ▪ *Whatever happened to* your new bicycle? 君の買ったばかりの自転車は一体どうなったのか.

What's happ*(*ening*)*? 《俗》こんにちは, 元気ですか ▪ *What's happ*(*ening*)*?* How's it goin'? やあ, どうだ. うまくいっているかい.

happiness /hǽpinəs/ 名 ***have the happiness to do*** 幸いにも...する ▪ I *had the happiness to* meet a friend whom I had not seen for many years. 私は久しぶりに友人に会ってうれしかった.

happy /hǽpi/ 形 ***a happy accident*** うれしい出来事 ▪ We never dreamed of a third child—it was *a happy accident.* 3人目ができようとは夢にも思わなかった—予期せぬ喜びだった.

a [***the***] ***happy event*** 《戯》おめでたいこと, 赤ちゃんの誕生 ▪ When's *the happy event,* then?—At the end of May. ところで, 予定日はいつ?—5月の終わりよ.

(***as***) ***happy as the day is long*** [《米》***as a clam, as a king, as a lark,*** 《英》***as Larry, as a sandboy***] 《口》全く気楽な, 非常に幸福な ▪ He was *as happy as the day is long.* 彼は全く幸福であった. ☞as MERRY as the day is long (cf. Sh., *Much Ado* 2. 1. 52)のまちがった引用 ▪ He's now *as happy as a clam.* 彼はいま実に幸せだ ▪ We've been *happy as Larry* since then. あれ以来私たちはずっととても幸せに暮らしている.

be happy about 〚主に疑問文・否定文で〛…に満足している ▪ He can't *be happy about* this legislation. 彼がこの法案に満足しているはずはない.

be happy at …がうまい ▪ He *is happy at* repartee. 彼は即答がうまい.

be happy in **1** …がうまい ▪ He *is happy in* his expression. 彼は言い方がうまい.

2 幸いにも…を持っている ▪ I *was* once *happy in* a son. 私も以前には幸いにも息子がいた.

be happy to *do* **1**〚未来形で〛喜んで…する; …できればうれしい ▪ I shall *be happy to* accept your invitation. 喜んでお招きに応じます ▪ I shall *be happy to* see you. 拝顔できればしあわせです.

2〚現在形・過去形で〛…してうれしい ▪ I *am happy to* see you once more. 再び拝顔してうれしい.

couldn't be happier これほど幸せなことはほかにない, こよなく幸せである ▪ We both *couldn't be happier* since we got married. 私たち二人は結婚以来この上なく幸せに暮らしています.

Happy days! (乾杯などで)ご多幸を祈る! ▪ He raised his glass, "*Happy days!*" 彼はグラスを持ちあげて「お幸せを祈って!」と言った.

happy-go-lucky 楽天的な, のんきな ▪ He goes through life in a *happy-go-lucky* fashion. 彼はのんきな人生を送っている.

in a happy hour →in a good HOUR.

not be a happy camper [《英》***bunny***] 《米戯》いらだって, うんざりして ▪ His computer crashed a little while ago and he's *not a happy camper.* コンピューターがついさっき壊れて彼はいらだっている ▪ She has caught a cold and *is not a happy bunny.* 彼女は風邪を引いてうんざりしている.

strike the happy medium →MEDIUM.

harangue /həræ̃ŋ/ 動 ***harangue*** *a person* ***out of*** [***into***] 熱弁をふるって人から…を奪う[人に…させる] ▪ The doctor *harangues* them *out of* sense. 医師は熱弁をふるって彼らから分別を奪ってしまう ▪ The author *harangued* the nation *into* fury. 著者は熱弁で国民をあおって憤激させた.

harbinger /hɑ́ːrbɪndʒər/ 名 ***a harbinger of doom*** 災害の前触れ, 予兆 ▪ Comets have long been regarded as *harbingers of doom.* 彗星は凶事の前触れと長い間考えられてきた.

harbor, 《英》**harbour** /hɑ́ːrbər/ 名 ***give harbor to*** (罪人など)をかくまう, 庇護する ▪ They *gave harbor to* the criminal. 彼らはその犯人をかくまった.

in harbor 入港中で ▪ The ship *in harbor* is an American ship. 入港中の船はアメリカ船だ.

hard /hɑːrd/ 形副 ***a hard case*** **1** 特別苦しい事情(の人) ▪ The court can't make exceptions for *hard cases.* 法廷は特に苦しい事情を特別扱いすることはできない.

2 改心させにくい人, 常習犯, 悪人 ▪ He was a clerk and *a hard case.* 彼は事務員で悪人であった.

a hard day's night 《戯》深夜業; 夜どおしの飲み騒ぎ ▪ It's been *a hard day's night.* それは夜どおしの飲み騒ぎ[深夜業]だった.

a hard left [***right***] 急角度に曲がる左折[右折], ヘアピン型の左[右]カーブ ▪ Take *a hard right* just after the motel. モーテルを過ぎたらすぐ急角度で右折しなさい.

a hard-luck story (同情・金銭を得るための)不運な身の上話 ▪ He's always got *a hard-luck story.* 彼はいつも不運な身の上話を用意している.

a hard-sell 強引な販売[宣伝] ▪ Watch out for *a hard-sell* on souvenirs. 強引なみやげ物売りに気をつけなさい.

(***as***) ***hard as a bone*** [***steel, iron, rock***] 《口》 **1** 非常に堅く; 頑健で ▪ Owing to the intense cold, the ground was *as hard as a bone.* ひどい寒さのため, 地面はこちこちになっていた.

2 一歩も譲らない, 頑固な, 厳格な ▪ He is *as hard as a bone* in anything that concerns his own interests. 彼は自分の利害に関することならどんなことにも一歩も譲らない.

(***as***) ***hard as a brick*** 非常に堅い ▪ I wielded a pick-ax, for the ground was *as hard as a brick.* 地面がとても堅かったのでつるはしを振るった.

(***as***) ***hard as nails*** →NAIL[1].

(***as***) ***hard as the nether millstone*** →MILLSTONE.

be hard at …に熱心にあたっている ▪ He *is hard at* his study. 彼は熱心に勉強している.

be [***feel***] ***hard done by*** 《口》冷遇される ▪ That's why I *feel* so *hard done by.* そんなわけで私はひどく冷遇されている.

be hard hit →HIT[2].

be hard on [***upon***] **1** …につらくあたる ▪ Why *are* you so *hard on* Smith? あなたはどうしてスミスにそんなにつらくあたるのですか.

2 …を痛める; をこわす ▪ The dry weather has *been hard on* my garden. 干天のため私の庭園はひどい目にあった ▪ This illness *is harder on* grown-ups than *on* children. この病気は子供よりも大人に

こたえる.

be hard pressed [***pushed***] 《口》 窮している, ひどく困っている ▪ He *was* always *hard pressed* for money. 彼はいつも金に窮していた ▪ I'*m* rather *hard pushed* at present. 当面少々困っている.

be hard put (***to it***) (経済的理由などで)非常に困っている ▪ Having failed in business, he *is hard put to it*. 商売に失敗して彼は窮している ▪ He *is hard put to it* to provide for his family. 彼は家族を養うのに非常に困っている ▪ I *was hard put* to find a good excuse for leaving early. 早退するよい口実を探すのに苦労した.

be hard run 《米》 困窮している, 追いつめられている ▪ I *am hard run* at present. 私はいま困窮している.

be hard set →SET².

be hard to take 堪えがたい; 信じがたい ▪ The loss of a young child *is* very *hard to take*. 幼児の死はまことに堪えがたい.

H

be hard up against it 《米口》 多くの困苦にあう ▪ When it came to taking risks, he *was hard up against it*. 危険を冒す話になると, 彼は多くの困苦に出くわした.

be hard up (***for, to***) 《口》 (…に)ひどく困っている; 金に窮している ▪ He *is hard up for* something to say. 彼は言うことがなくて困っている ▪ I'*m hard up* a week after pay day. 私は給料日から1週間後には金がなくなる.

be too hard for …には手に負えない ▪ The boy *is too hard for* me. その少年は私の手に負えない.

be too much like hard work 困難が多すぎる, あまりに骨が折れる ▪ This job *is* a bit *too much like hard work* for me. この仕事は私にはちょっときつすぎる.

bear … hard →BEAR².

bear *a person* ***hard*** 人につらく当たる ▪ Caesar *bears* me *hard*. カエサルは私につらく当たる.

call *a person* (***hard, bad***) ***names*** →NAME¹.

come down hard on 《口》 →COME².

die hard →DIE².

give the hard word きっぱり断る ▪ I will definitely *give* them *the hard word*. 彼らにきっぱりと断るつもりだ.

go hard with [***for***] 《古風》 (事態などが人)にとって困難[危険, 苦痛]となる ▪ If you don't obey me, it will *go hard with* you. 僕に従わないと君はひどい目にあうぞ. ☞主語は通例 it.

hard and fast **1** 厳重な, 動かない ▪ Our factory has a *hard and fast* rule against smoking. 我々の工場にはタバコ厳禁の規則がある.

2 すっかり座礁して ▪ We found the ship *hard and fast*. 我々は船がすっかり座礁しているのを知った.

3 しっかりと ▪ I've got him *hard and fast*. 私は彼をしっかりとつかまえた.

4 懸命に ▪ He was running *hard and fast*. 彼は一生懸命走っていた. ☞「船がすっかり座礁して」が原義.

hard at it 《口》 物事に熱中して, 忙しく取り組んで ▪ He's been *hard at it* all day. 彼は一日中せっせと働いてきた ▪ When I entered the room, my wife and her lover were *hard at it*. 部屋に入ると妻と愛人がその真っ最中だった.

hard by 《文》 すぐ近くに[の] ▪ They lived *hard by*. 彼らは近くに住んでいた ▪ They saw many whales *hard by* their ships. 彼らは船のすぐ近くにたくさんのクジラを見た.

Hard cases make bad law (***s***). 《諺》 特別苦しい事例は悪法を作る《ある法の適用が本人をひどく苦しめるような事例では, 適用に手心を加えるから, 法そのものが悪法[無力]となる. 結局新法を作ることになる》.

hard core/hard-core 《英》 **1** (反対運動の)中核メンバー, 保守反動的少数派 ▪ The *hard core* take the trouble to go to meetings regularly. 中核メンバーはいとわずきちんと集会に出る.

2 確固たる, 妥協しない ▪ His brother is a *hard-core* political activist. 彼の兄は筋金入りの政治活動家だ.

3 性描写が露骨な, ポルノの ▪ We don't carry *hard-core* sex magazines. 当店には露骨なポルノ雑誌は置いてありません.

hard facts 厳然とした事実 ▪ These are the cold *hard facts*—not just rumors. これは冷厳なまぎれもない事実で, 単なる噂ではない.

hard-fisted **1** 体が頑強な ▪ My father is a *hard-fisted* truck driver. 父はたくましいトラック運転手だ.

2 厳しい, 辛い ▪ The *hard-fisted* teacher never allowed any nonsense. その厳格な教師はばかげた真似は決して許さなかった.

3 けちな, 握り屋で ▪ He is the most *hard-fisted* miser in this town. 彼はこの町きってのけちん坊だ.

hard going 進みにくい ▪ He found the study of law to be *hard going*. 彼は法律の研究がなかなか進まないことを知った.

hard lines 《主に英口》 虐待; 不運; つらい事 ▪ It was *hard lines* that he fell ill. 彼が病気になったのは不運であった ▪ It is *hard lines* on me that I have to go. 行かねばならないのは私にはつらい.

Hard luck./Hard lines. 《英》 運が悪かったですね, お気の毒に《人を慰めて》 ▪ Failed again.—Oh, *hard luck*. まただめだったよ—それはお気の毒に ▪ Oh, *hard lines*. That's a sad story. ついていなかったな. 残念な話だ.

hard of …しがたい ▪ The passions are *hard of* control. 激情は抑えがたい ▪ I'm a bit *hard of* hearing. 私は少し耳が遠いのです.

hard on [***upon***] **1** …に近く ▪ He is *hard on* seventy. 彼は70歳に近い ▪ My father came in *hard upon* my heels. 父は私のほとんどすぐ後について入って来た.

2 →be HARD on 1.

hard to come by …を得るのが困難で ▪ Full-time jobs are *hard to come by*. 正社員の職にはなかなか就けない.

hard to swallow 信じがたい ▪I found his story rather *hard to swallow*. 彼の話はかなり信じがたいものだった.

hard up **1**《海》うわ手かじいっぱい!《かじを風上へいっぱいに取れという号令》 ▪*Hard up* (the helm)! うわ手かじいっぱい!

2 →be HARD up (for, to).

Hard words break no bones.《諺》荒い言葉は人を傷害しない.

have a hard time *doing* [***with***] …に[で]苦労する ▪He *had a hard time making* ends meet. 彼は収支をつぐなわせるのに苦労した ▪I *had a hard time with* the police. 警察でひどい目にあった.

have a hard time (***of it***) つらい[ひどい]目にあう ▪As it rained, we *had a hard time of it*. 雨が降ったので我々はひどい目にあった.

have hard luck 不運である; ひどい扱いを受ける ▪We have *had hard luck* in the track and field events. 我々は陸上競技では運が悪かった.

have it hard《米口》多くの困苦にあう ▪She has *had it hard* and is getting discouraged. 彼女は多くの困苦にあったので気を落としている.

in hard condition 頑健な体で ▪All the lads were *in hard condition*. 若者はみな頑健だった.

in the hard 硬貨で ▪Four hundred dollars were counted out to me *in the hard*. 400ドルが硬貨で勘定されて私に渡された.

it goes hard with …がひどい目にあう ▪If this letter comes to their knowledge, *it* will *go hard with* him. もしこの手紙が彼らに知れると, 彼はひどい目にあうだろう.

it will go hard but I will *do* どうあってもきっと私は…する ▪*It will go hard but I will* find them. どうあってもそれらを見つけずにはおかない.

it will go hard if 決して…しない ▪*It will go hard if* I go. 私は決して行かない ▪*It will go hard if* he goes without her. 彼は必ず彼女といっしょに行く.

it will go hard with *A* ***before*** *B* Aはどんなに困難でも[つらくても]Bしない ▪*It will go hard with* me *before* I give up the attempt. 私はどんなにつらくても企てをやめない.

let the hardest come to the hardest 最悪の事態になっても.

make hard work of →WORK[1].

play hard to get《米》お高くとまる, なかなか近づきがたいふうをする《その実つかまえてもらいたいのだが》 ▪I loved you from the moment we met.—Then why did you *play* so *hard to get*? 出会ったときからあなたが好きだったわ—だったら, なぜあんなにお高くとまったんだ.

press [***run***] *a person* ***hard*** 人にひどく迫る, 人をひどく追いつめる ▪I *pressed* him *hard*. 私は彼に肉薄した《競技で》 ▪Who will *run* you *hard* for the Presidency? 誰が大統領のいすを目指して君に肉薄するだろうか.

run hard 懸命に走る ▪I *ran hard* to catch the 8 o'clock bus. 8時のバスに乗るために私は懸命に走った.

take it [***things***] ***hard*** 物事をひどく気にする, 痛く心に感じる (↔take it EASY 2) ▪You should not *take things* so *hard*. 君は物事をそんなにひどく気にしてはいけない.

take (***some*** [***a few***]) ***hard knocks*** ひどい目にあう ▪Democrats *took a few hard knocks*, and Republicans gained 6 seats. 民主党が苦汁をなめ, 共和党は6議席を獲得した.

the hard stuff《口》(ウィスキー・ブランデーなどの)強いアルコール飲料 ▪He likes a drop of *the hard stuff*. 彼は強い酒を1杯やるのが好きだ.

the hard way **1** 苦労して, こつこつと ▪He learns songs *the hard way*. 彼はこつこつと歌を習い覚える.

2 より難しい方法で ▪The governor won the election *the hard way* by going out to meet the people. 知事は外に出て民衆に接するという, より難しい方法で当選した.

try *one's* ***hardest*** →TRY one's best.

when hard comes to hard 最悪の事態になったら ▪They keep their mouths closed *when hard comes to hard*. 最悪の事態になるとみな口を閉じたままになる.

hardball /hɑ́ːrdbɔ̀ːl/ 名 ***play hardball*** (***with*** *a person*)《主に米》(ビジネス・政治で…に対して)強硬な態度をとる, 攻撃的な行動に出る ▪The company *played hardball with* the bank. その会社は銀行に対して強硬手段に出た. ☞hardball「(ソフトボールに対して)硬(式野)球」.

harden /hɑ́ːrdən/ 動 ***be hardened against*** …に慣れて感じない ▪He *is hardened against* pity. 彼は無情になってあわれみの情を起こさない.

harden *one's* ***heart*** (***against***) →HEART.

hardly /hɑ́ːrdli/ 副 ***can hardly*** *A* ***without*** *B* AするとたいていBする ▪I *can hardly* read the story *without* thinking of my mother. その話を読むとたいてい母を思い出す.

deal hardly with …をひどい目にあわせる ▪He has *dealt hardly with* me. 彼は私をひどい目にあわせた.

hardly [***scarcely***] ***any*** いかなる…もほとんどない ▪There is *hardly any* difference between the sexes. 性別による違いはほとんどみられない.

hardly *A* ***before*** [***when***] *B* AするかせぬうちにBする ▪She had *hardly* heard the news *before* she began to cry. 彼女はそのニュースを聞くか聞かぬうちに泣きだした. ☞Aは過去完了, Bは過去が普通.

hardly earned [***won***] 苦労して得られた ▪The victory *was hardly won*. その勝利は辛くも得られた.

speak [***think***] ***hardly of*** …を悪く言う[思う] ▪Don't *speak* so *hardly of* your friend. 自分の友人のことをそう悪く言うもんじゃない.

hare /heər/ 名 (***as***) ***mad as a March hare*** →MAD.

(***as***) ***timid as a hare*** →(as) TIMID as a rabbit.

catch [***hunt for***] ***a hare with a tabor*** 不可能なことをしようとする ▪ You shall as soon *catch a hare with a tabor.* 《諺》(そんなことができるなら)小太鼓でウサギを捕らえられる,「鳥もちで馬を刺す」.

***first catch your hare*(, *then cook him*)** まず現物を手に入れよ(, 処理はそれから) ▪ You talk as if you already had the prize; but *first catch your hare, then cook him.* 君はすでに賞を得たような話しぶりだが, まず現物を手に入れなさい. 処理はそれからでよい.

get the hare's foot to lick ほんの少ししか得ない ▪ The clergyman *got the hare's foot to lick.* 牧師はほとんど何も得なかった.

hare and hounds (紙まき)ウサギ追いごっこ《紙片をまき散らして逃げるウサギ役を猟犬役が追う遊び》 ▪ You girls shouldn't play *hare and hounds* with boys. 女の子が男の子とウサギ追いごっこなんかするものではありませんよ.

He who runs after two hares will catch neither.*/*He who hunts two hares leaves one and loses the other. 《諺》二兎を追う者は一兎をも得ず.

Here [***There***] ***the hare goes away*** [***went away***]. ここで[そこで]事は終わった. ☞イソップ物語中のウサギとカメの競走中の句から.

hold with the hare and run with the hounds = run with the HARE and hunt with the hounds.

hunt for a hare with a tabor →catch a HARE with a tabor.

run with the hare and hunt [***ride***] ***with the hounds*** 二股(ふたまた)をかける, 内股膏薬(うちまたごうやく)をする(→hunt with the HOUNDs and run with the hare) ▪ You cannot *run with the hare and ride with the hounds* in politics. 政治で内股膏薬はご法度(はっと)だ ▪ Defoe *ran with the* Tory *hare and hunted with the* Whig *hounds.* デフォーはトーリー党とホイッグ党に都合よく二股をかけた.

set the tortoise to catch the hare ほとんど不可能なことをしようとする ▪ It is no good *setting the tortoise to catch the hare.* ほとんど不可能なことをしようとしてもむだである.

start a hare (議論などが)枝葉にわたる, 話をそらすような話題を持ち出す ▪ I tried to *start a hare* three or four times. 私は3, 4回話をそらすような話題を持ち出そうとした. ☞狩猟から.

There the hare goes away [***went away***]. →Here the HARE goes away.

hark /hɑːrk/ 動 (***just***) ***hark at*** 《口》まあ…の言うことを聞きなさい《嘘・ほら話の場合に言う》 ▪ *Just hark at* him—anyone would think him a landowner to hear him talk! まあ彼の話を聞いてみなさい—彼の話を聞けば誰でも彼は地主かと思うだろうよ.

harlot /hɑ́ːrlət/ 名 ***play the harlot*** (主として女性が)淫行をする(《聖》*Hos.* 3. 3) ▪ She was blamed for *playing the harlot* with noble men. 彼女は貴族たちと淫行をしたといって非難された.

harm /hɑːrm/ 名 ***come to harm*** ひどい目にあう ▪ She is very late—I hope she hasn't *come to* any *harm.* 彼女は非常に遅い—ひどい目にあっていなければいいが.

do harm (…に)害を与える, 害になる(*to*) ▪ Too much exercise will *do* you *harm.* あまり運動しすぎるとからだに害になる ▪ Did the storm *do* any *harm to* the corn? あらしは小麦に害を与えたか.

do more harm than good 有害無益である ▪ Interfering will *do more harm than good.* 干渉は有害無益である.

do no harm*/*not do any harm 悪くない, 害にならない《むしろ有益だ》 ▪ To take a walk every morning *won't do any harm.* 毎朝散歩するのは悪くないだろう.

Harm set, harm get.*/*Harm watch, harm catch. 《諺》他人にわなをかける者は自分がそれにひっかかる,「人を呪わば穴二つ」.

in harm's way*/*into harm's way 危険なところへ, 危険に曝された場所で, 危害を加えられそうで ▪ Many brave women are willing to place themselves *in harm's way.* なかには進んで危険な場所に赴く勇敢な女性もいる.

keep ...from harm …を危害から守る ▪ The she-bear willl *keep* her young *from harm.* 雌グマは子グマらを危害から守る.

mean no harm 悪意はない ▪ I *meant no harm* when I bought a souvenir sword. 私はなんら悪意があって土産品の刀を買ったのではない.

no harm done 被害はない; 全員異常なし ▪ Sorry I stepped on your toe. —*No harm done.* 失礼, 靴のつま先を踏んでしまって—大丈夫だよ.

no harm in looking 《口》(特に夫の言い訳として)目がいくのは仕方がない ▪ Why are you staring at that salesgirl?—*No harm in looking*, dear. あの店員の女の子をじっと見て, どうなさったの?—いや, つい目がいくのだ.

out of harm's way 危害を受けない[与えない]ように[所に] ▪ They migrated in time *out of harm's way.* 彼らは折よく危害を受けない所へ移住した ▪ People send children to school to keep them *out of harm's way.* 人々は子供に悪いことをさせないように学校へやる.

there is no harm in (*doing*)/ ***it does no harm to*** *do* (…して)悪いことはない ▪ *There* can *be no harm in having* innocent recreations. 無邪気な気晴らしをして悪いはずはない ▪ He may say no, but *it does no harm to* ask. 彼は断るかもしれないが, 頼むのも悪くない.

Where is the harm in (*doing*)? (…して)どこが悪いのか ▪ *Where's the harm in trying* it? それをやってみてもかまわないじゃないか.

harmless /hɑ́ːrmləs/ 形 (***as***) ***harmless as a dove*** ハトのように柔和で(《聖》*Matt.* 10. 16) ▪ Be *as harmless as a dove.* ハトのように柔和であれ.

save *a person* ***harmless*** 人を無事に免れさせる

《損失なく, 処罰されず, 損害賠償をせずに》 ▪ He will *save* the lessee *harmless* from any claims by him. 彼は借地人に何も求めず無事に免れさせるだろう.

harmony /hɑ́ːrməni/ 名 ***in harmony*** (***with***) (…と)調和して, 仲よく ▪ They lived *in harmony with* each other for forty years. 彼らは40年間仲よく暮らした ▪ The violin and piano were *in harmony*. バイオリンとピアノは調和していた.

keep … in harmony …を調和させておく ▪ He endeavors to *keep* the body *in harmony*. 彼は体の調子を整えておくよう努める.

out of harmony (***with***) (…と)調和[一致]しないで ▪ That family is *out of harmony*. あの家は仲がむつまじくない ▪ The violin was *out of harmony with* the rest of the instruments. バイオリンは他の楽器と調和していなかった.

with [***in***] ***harmony*** 調和して ▪ They sang *with harmony*. 彼らは諧調で歌った.

harness /hɑ́ːrnəs/ 名 ***be*** [***get***] ***back in*** [***into***] ***harness*** 《主に英》休日[病気]のあと平常の仕事に戻っている[戻る] ▪ How does it feel to *be back in harness* after 6 months? 半年ぶりに仕事に戻った気分はどうだ ▪ I've got to *get back into harness* on Monday. 私は月曜には仕事に戻らねばならない. ☞ 馬が「馬具をつける」とは仕事をすること.

die in harness/die with harness on *one's* ***back*** 仕事しながら死ぬ, 死ぬまで仕事をやめない ▪ He intends to *die in harness*. 彼は死ぬまで仕事をやめないつもりである. ☞「(馬が)馬具をつけたまま死ぬ」が原義.

go into harness 日々の仕事につく ▪ If you *go into harness* at once, you will die in two years. 今すぐ日々の仕事につけば, 2年したらあなたは死ぬだろう.

in double harness 2頭立てで; 二人が協力して《夫婦のことが多い》; 結婚して ▪ Those two men work very well *in double harness*. その二人はいっしょに非常にうまく働く ▪ They ran [worked] *in double harness*. 彼らは夫婦協力して働いた ▪ It's time you went *in double harness*. 君はもう結婚すべき時だ.

in harness 日常の仕事[職務]に従事して ▪ How do you like being *in harness* again, after your year of freedom? 1年間自由の身であった後にまた日常の業務につくのはいかがですか.

in single harness 1頭立てで; 独身で ▪ I go better *in single harness*. 私は独身でいるほうがよい.

trot in double harness 《米口》夫婦として暮らす ▪ We soon began to *trot in double harness*. 我々はまもなく夫婦生活をし始めた.

work [***run***] ***in harness*** 《主に英》仲よくやっていく, いっしょに働く; 協力する, 協働する (*with*) ▪ The two friends *work in harness*. その二人の友人は仲よくやっている ▪ He had to *run in harness with* them. 彼は彼らといっしょに働かねばならなかった ▪ We will *work in harness* from now on. これからは互いに力を合わせて取り組もう.

harp /hɑːrp/ 動 ***harp on*** [***upon***] ***a*** [***one, the same,*** etc.] ***string*** ひとつのことをくどくど繰り返す ▪ They are still *harping on* that *one string*. 彼らはまだその事ばかりくどくど言っている.

harper /hɑ́ːrpər/ 名 ***Have among*** [***at***] ***you, harpers!*** そら投げるぞ, そら射つぞ《群衆の中にでたらめに投げたり, 射ったりするときに用いる》 ▪ Now *have at you, harpers!* さあ投げるぞ.

harrow[1] /hǽroʊ/ 名 ***under the harrow*** 絶えず処罰[苦難]におびやかされて ▪ He was kept *under the harrow*. 彼は絶えず苦難におびやかされていた.

harrow[2] /hǽroʊ/ 動 ***harrow Hell*** (キリストが)地獄を征服する ▪ Christ has *harrowed Hell*. キリストは地獄を征服した. ☞ harrow《古》「荒らす」.

Harry /hǽri/ 名 ***a flash Harry*** いやに派手な男 ▪ He is a bit of *a flash Harry*. 彼はいやに派手なところのある男だ.

by the lord Harry 誓って, きっと ▪ *By the lord Harry*, he is telling the truth. 確かに彼は本当のことを言っている.

play old Harry with 《口》…をこわす, 害する, 混乱させる ▪ Drink has *played old Harry with* his health. 酒が彼の健康を害してしまった. ☞ old Harry = the devil.

harvest /hɑ́ːrvəst/ 名 ***a barren harvest*** 凶作, 貧弱な収穫[成果] ▪ This field yields *a barren harvest* however hard we cultivate it. この畑はどんなに耕しても大して収穫があがらない ▪ Such a policy can only lead to *a barren harvest*. そんな政策では乏しい成果にしか繋がらない.

gather [***reap***] ***a harvest*** 収穫を取り入れる; 大儲けする ▪ We've just *gathered a* fall *harvest*. 秋の取り入れをしたところだ ▪ We *reaped a harvest* of gold medals on the first day of competition. 競技会初日に我々は金メダルをどっさり稼いだ.

make a long harvest for [***about***] ***a little corn*** 《諺》小さい事をして大きい結果を得る, 「エビでタイを釣る」 ▪ Surely you have *made a long harvest for a little corn*. 確かにエビでタイを釣ったね.

hash /hæʃ/ 名 ***fix*** *a person's* ***hash*** 《米俗》人をやっつける ▪ He'll *fix your hash*. 彼は君をやっつけるだろう.

make a hash of 《口》…をめちゃめちゃにする; をきわめてへたにやる; を(やりそこなって)だめにする ▪ The administration has *made a hash of* this country. 政府がわが国をめちゃめちゃにしてしまった ▪ Jones *made a hash of* the translation. ジョーンズはきわめてまずい翻訳をした ▪ He *made a hash of* the big match. 彼は大事な試合をぶち壊しにしてしまった.

settle *a person's* ***hash*** (***for*** *him*) 《口》 **1** 人をやっつける; 人を黙らせる; 人を殺す ▪ Another blow would have *settled his hash* (*for* him). もう一撃食らったら彼は参ってしまっていただろう.

2 人の計画[意図]をぶちこわす; 人を罰する ▪ Publish this notice in the Trade Journal; that will *settle their hash*. この告示を業界紙に出しなさい. それで彼らの意図はぶちこわしになるだろう ▪ He'll *settle your*

hash for you. 彼はあなたを罰するだろう.
sling hash →SLING².

haste /heɪst/ 名 ***Haste is*** [***makes***] ***waste.*** 《諺》せいては事をし損じる (→make WASTE).

in (*one's*) ***haste*** **1** 急いで ▪ Though I am *in haste*, I am never in a hurry. 私は急いでいるが, 決してあわててはいない.
2 大急ぎで ▪ The King levied an army *in haste*. 国王は急いで軍隊を集めた.
3 性急に, 早まって, 軽々しく ▪ I said so *in my haste*. 私は軽率にそう言った ▪ I dined today with him, but will not do so again *in haste*. 私はきょう彼と食事したが二度と軽々しくそうはしない.

in haste to *do* 早く…したがる, …することを急ぐ ▪ I am *in haste to* dine. 私は早く食事がしたい ▪ Mary was *in* no *haste to* return to Scotland. メアリーはスコットランドへ帰ることを少しも急がなかった.

in hot haste 大急ぎで; やっきになって ▪ He was *in hot haste* at the time. そのとき彼は大急ぎであった.

make haste 急ぐ, 手早くする ▪ Come on, *make haste*. さあ, 急ぎなさい ▪ It was necessary for him to *make haste* home. 彼は急いで帰宅することが必要だった.

Make haste slowly. 《諺》ゆっくり急げ,「急がば回れ」. ☞この oxymoron「矛盾語法」は L festina lente のなぞり.

make haste to *do* 急いで…する, …するのを急ぐ ▪ I *made haste to* get away. 私は急いで逃げた.

Marry in haste, (***and***) ***repent at*** [***in***] ***leisure.*** 《諺》あわてて結婚, ゆっくり後悔《あわてて結婚すると後で長々と悔やむことになる》,「縁と月日の末を待て」.

(***The***) ***more haste,*** (***the***) ***less*** [***worse***] ***speed.*** 《諺》「急がば回れ」.

hat /hæt/ 名 ***a bad hat*** →a BAD egg.

a black hat [***white hat***] 悪役[善玉] ▪ I don't think it's always bad to be *a black hat*. 悪役が必ずしも悪いとは限らないと思うが. ☞カウボーイ映画での悪役[善玉]が被るハットの色から.

a brass hat 高級将校, 高官, お偉方 ▪ All the *brass hats* were invited to the ceremony. 式典にはすべてのお偉方が招待された. ☞19世紀の英軍で上席将校が軍帽のつばに金モールをつけたことから. 集合的には big brass, top brass, the brass という.

a hard hat (労働者階級の)超保守主義者 ▪ They are counting on a large number of votes from the *hard hats*. 彼らは超保守主義労働者の多数票を当てにしている.

a ten gallon hat 《口》テンガロンハット, つばの広い大きな帽子 ▪ Those ranch hands were all wearing *ten gallon hats*. 牧場労働者はみなテンガロンハットをかぶっていた.

(***as***) ***black as a*** [*one's*] ***hat*** 真っ黒で ▪ He has a face *as black as your hat*. 彼は真っ黒な顔をしている.

at the drop of a hat →DROP¹.

be all hat and no cattle 《米口》自慢話をするばかりで行動が伴わない ▪ I feel like our new captain *is all hat and no cattle*. 新主将は口ばかりで実行力がないような気がする.

be in a [***the***] ***hat*** 窮地にある, 進退きわまっている ▪ I'*m in an* awful *hat* this time. 私は今度は恐ろしく苦境にある.

be wearing *one's* ***teacher's*** [***lawyer's,*** etc.] ***hat*** 教師[弁護士, など]の役割を臨時に果たす ▪ I *was wearing my teacher's hat* at the meeting. 会合では教師役を兼任した.

beat **...** ***into a cocked hat*** → knock ... into a COCKED HAT.

bet *one's* ***hat*** 《米口》すべてをかける, 絶対まちがいない ▪ We'll never be caught again, you can *bet your hat* on it. 我々は二度と決して捕えられないだろう. それは絶対まちがいない.

by this hat 誓って ▪ *By this hat*, he won it. 確かに彼が勝った.

fling *one's* ***hat in*** [***into***] ***the ring*** → throw one's HAT in the ring.

go [***come***] ***hat in hand to*** *do*.../*do* ... ***hat in hand*** かしこまって[謙遜して, うやうやしく]…する ▪ I have to *go hat in hand* to my brother-in-law again *to* ask for some money. 恥を忍んで義理の兄にまた金の無心に行かなくてはならない ▪ They approached the queen, *hat in hand*. 彼らはうやうやしく女王の前に進み出た.

go round with the hat/carry around the [*one's*] ***hat*** (帽子を持って)寄付金を集めて回る ▪ Please dance, and I will *carry around your hat*. どうぞ踊ってください. 私があなたのために寄付金を集めて回ります.

hang *one's* ***hat inside*** 《米口》…に落ち着く, 居を定める ▪ I'm looking for a new place to *hang my hat inside*. 新しい落ち着き先をさがしている.

hang *one's* ***hat on*** 《米口》…に頼る ▪ I always *hang my hat on* him. いつも彼に頼る.

hang [***hold***] ***on to your hat*** **1** 《口》〚主に命令文で〛気をつけて ▪ *Hold on to your hat*! I'm going to pass that car. 気をつけろ! あの車を追い越すぞ.
2 驚かないで ▪ *Hold on to your hat*! Harry asked me to marry him. 驚かないで! ハリーが私に結婚してくれと言ったの.

hang (***up***) *one's* ***hat/hang up*** *one's* ***hat in a house*** 《口》家族の一員として受け入れられる, (…に)くつろぐ《求愛すること, 妻の家に住むことを意味することが多い》; 居を定める ▪ He'll be welcome to *hang up his hat in her house*. 彼は気持ちよく彼女の家庭に受け入れてもらえるだろう ▪ He *hung up his hat in the house*. 彼はその家にくつろいだ.

(*one's*) ***hat covers*** *one's* ***family*** 《口》家族のない独り者である, 一人ぼっちで自分だけ食べていればよい ▪ *My hat covers my family*. 私は一人ぼっちだ ▪ *His hat covers his family*, doesn't it? 彼は家族のない独り者だね.

hat in hand →cap in HAND.
one's ***hat is off to***《口》…に脱帽する ▪ *My hat is off to* you students for your efforts. 君たちのがんばりには脱帽だ.
Hats off to…! …に脱帽せよ ▪ *Hats off to* France! フランスに脱帽せよ!
hats to be disposed of 失われた人命 ▪ There were many *hats to be disposed of.* 多くの人命が失われた.
have *one's* ***hat in*** [***into***] ***the ring*** →throw one's HAT in the ring.
He wears a ten-dollar hat on a five-cent head.《諺》5セントの頭に10ドルの帽子をかぶっている. ☞愚かだが金持ちの人について述べるのに用いられる.
hold your hat《口》→hang on to your HAT.
I'll [***I'd***] ***eat my*** [***old Rowley's***] ***hat***《口》(もし…なら)首でもやる《否定的強調》 ▪ If I knew as little of life as that, *I'd eat my hat.* もし私が人生をそんなに知らないなら, 首でもあげる ▪ If you don't succeed, *I'll eat my hat.* 君は断然成功疑いなしだ.
In your hat!《俗》ばか言うな!
keep under *one's* ***hat*** →under one's HAT 2.
knock…into a cocked hat →COCKED HAT.
make up the hat →pass the HAT.
My hat!《俗》おやまあ! ▪ I don't snore.—*My hat!* 僕はいびきなんかかかないよ—おやおや!
My hat to a halfpenny! きっと, 断然 ▪ *My hat to a halfpenny*, Pompey is the most worthy. 断然, ポンペイウスが最も立派である.
out of the [***a***] ***hat*** 無作為に(選んで) ▪ The winner will be chosen *out of a hat* from all the attendants. 当選者は出席者全員の中から無作為に選んで決められる.
pass [《口》***make up***] ***the hat***/《口》***pass around*** [***round***] ***the hat*** 寄付金を集める, 寄付をつのる ▪ At the club meeting they *pass the hat.* クラブの集会では彼らは寄付金集めをやる ▪ They're *passing the hat around* for Jeff's leaving present. ジェフの餞別のお金を集めているんだ ▪ We're *passing the hat round* for our fighting funds. 私たちの運動資金のカンパを集めています. ☞「帽子を回して…」という具体的な意味のときもある.
pick…out of a [***the***] ***hat***《口》(コンテストの勝者など)を無作為に選ぶ ▪ We'll *pick* one lucky winner *out of the hat.* 幸運な優勝者一人を無作為に選ぶことにしよう ▪ His parents had just *picked* such a strange name *out of a hat.* 彼の両親はこんな妙な名前をいい加減に選んでつけたのだった.
pull…out of a [*one's*] ***hat***《口》…を手品のように出す, 想像で作る ▪ I'm sure you'll *pull* an excuse *out of your hat.* 君はきっと言い訳をでっちあげるだろう.
put the tin hat on =put the LID on (it).
raise *one's* ***hat to*** 帽子をあげて…にあいさつする ▪ He *raised his hat to* me as he passed. 彼は通りすがりに帽子をあげて私にあいさつした.
send [***take***] ***round the hat*** 寄付金を集める ▪ They dispatched men to *send round the hat* in America. 彼らはアメリカで寄付金を集めるため人々を派遣した ▪ Allow me to *take round the hat* for coppers. 帽子を持って寄付金の銅貨を集めて回らせてください.
somewhere to hang *one's* ***hat*** 落ち着く[居を定める]所 ▪ I want *somewhere to hang my hat.* 私はどこか落ち着く所がほしい.
take *one's* ***hat off to***/《米》***tip*** *one's* ***hat to***《口》…に対して脱帽する《敬意・感嘆・あいさつのため》 ▪ I *take my hat off to* those who do voluntary work in their spare time. 余暇にボランティア活動をする人々に敬意を表する ▪ I *take off my hat to* him for his courage. 彼の勇気には脱帽する ▪ I *tip my hat to* you for helping me find this job. この仕事を見つけるのに手を貸してくれた君には頭が下がる.
talk through *one's* ***hat***《口》ばかげたことを言う, ありそうもない[とてつもない]話をする ▪ You don't know anything about Einstein's theory. You are just *talking through your hat.* 君はアインシュタインの理論のことは何も知らない. ただでたらめを言っているだけだ ▪ He is *talking through his hat* when he says he'll make it. 彼はうまくいくと言うが, 口から出まかせだ.
throw *one's* ***hat in the air*** →throw up one's HAT.
throw [***fling, toss, have***] *one's* ***hat in*** [***into***] ***the ring***《口》挑戦に応じる; 立候補する (*for*) ▪ He has been forced to *throw his hat into the ring for* the Presidency. 彼は大統領選挙戦にやむなく出た.
throw up *one's* ***hat*** (喜んで)帽子を投げ上げる ▪ He would *throw up his hat* if he knew about it. 彼はそれを知ったら帽子を投げ上げて喜ぶだろう.
tip *one's* ***hat*** →TIP[3].
touch *one's* ***hat*** →TOUCH[2].
under *one's* ***hat***《口》**1** 頭の中に ▪ His estate lies *under his hat.* 彼の財産は頭の中にある《知恵が彼の財産である》.
2 秘密に, 内緒に ▪ She kept it *under her hat.* 彼女はそれを秘密にしておいた ▪ This is strictly *under your hat.* このことは絶対に秘密にしてください.
wear a legal [etc.] ***hat*** 弁護士[など]の役目をする ▪ James is *wearing a Santa hat* this time. ジェイムズはこんどはサンタの役をしている.
wear a steeple-crowned hat 異端者として火刑にされる ▪ You are only fit to *wear a steeple-crowned hat.* 君なんかは異端者として火あぶりの刑にされるとちょうどいいよ. ☞inquisition (宗教裁判)ではてっぺんが(尖塔状に)とがった帽子をかぶせられた.
wear another [***a different, more than one***] ***hat***/***wear two hats*** 別の[異なった, 二つの, 二つ以上の]資格[地位]で働く; 複数の仕事を持つ ▪ I'm *wearing a different hat* today. Think of me as a coach. 今日は別の資格で来ている. 私をコーチだと思いなさい ▪ Trying to *wear more than one hat* at a time is confusing. 二足のわらじを履こうとす

るとややこしくなる ▪ She *wears two hats*; one as a housewife, and the other as a teacher. 彼女は二役をこなしている. ひとつは主婦で, もうひとつは教師だ.

wear several* [*many*] *hats いろいろなことに手を出す, 多くの職務を兼任する ▪ You are trying to *wear* too *many hats* at once. 君は一度にあまりに多くの仕事に手を出そうとしている.

***wear the black hat* [*white hat*]** 悪役をする[正しい人を装う], 悪党ぶる[善人ぶる] ▪ It is important to *wear the black hat* at times. 時に悪役を演じなければならない場合がある ▪ We will have to *wear the white hat* until the storm is over. 事態が治まるまで善人を装わねばなるまい.

with your teacher's* [*lawyer's* etc.] *hat on 教師[弁護士, など]の役割を臨時に果たして ▪ I'd like to talk to you *with your lawyer's hat on*. 君の弁護士になり代わって話したい.

H

hatband /hǽtbæ̀nd/ 名 ***(as) tight as Dick's hatband*** 非常に窮屈で, とてもきつい ▪ I'm full. My belt is *as tight as Dick's hatband*. おなか一杯だ. ベルトがきつい.

hatch[1] /hætʃ/ 名 ***batten down the hatches*** 危険[困難, 難局]に備える ▪ An economic crisis is coming, so countries are *battening down the hatches*. 経済危機が迫っているので各国はそれに備えている. ☞batten「昇降口 (hatch) 密閉用の当て木を添える」.

Down the hatch! 乾杯!, ぐっと飲みなさい! ▪ He handed her a glass of milk and said, "*Down the hatch*, Miss." 彼は彼女に1杯のミルクを渡して「お嬢さん, ぐっとお飲みなさい」と言った.

hatches, (catches,) matches, and dispatches 《戯》(新聞の)誕生[婚約, 結婚, 死亡]欄 ▪ Among the news of *hatches, matches and dispatches*, were harrowing stories of murders and rapes. 誕生・結婚・死亡欄にまじって殺人やレイプの痛ましい記事があった.

under (the) hatches **1**《海》甲板下に, 甲板下に監禁されて; 非番で ▪ He was kept *under hatches* for three days without any food. 彼は食物も与えられずに3日間甲板下に監禁された.

2 位置[境遇]が低く ▪ You have brought yourself so far *under the hatches* that there is no way you'll be able to rise again. あなたはこれまで低く身を沈めていたので再び浮かびあがる方法がない.

3 拘引[収監]されて, 束縛されて, 隷属して; 屈辱の状態で ▪ It is impossible to live in a country which is continually *under hatches*. 絶えず隷属状態にある国に住むことはできない ▪ Conscience has been kept *under hatches*. 良心はずっと束縛されてきた.

4 意気消沈して; 零落して; 難渋して ▪ If he is poor, he is *under hatches*. 貧乏なら, 彼は難渋している.

5 死んで; (この世から)葬られて; 地下[地獄]に ▪ He is dead and *under hatches*. 彼は死んで地獄にいる.

hatch[2] /hætʃ/ 動 ***hatched, matched, and dispatched*** 完成されて ▪ There's another book successfully *hatched, matched, and dispatched*. また本が首尾よくできあがった.

hatchet /hǽtʃət/ 名 ***bury the hatchet*** 武器を収める, 戦争をやめる; 仲直りする ▪ It was time to *bury the hatchet* with our enemies. 敵と講和する潮時だった. ☞アメリカ先住民が講和の儀式として tomahawk「戦闘用の斧」を埋めることから. ☞次項も参照.

dig up the hatchet 戦争[けんか]を再び始める ▪ We must hope that the U.S. and Russia will never *dig up the hatchet*. 米国とロシアが二度と戦争を再開しないことを期待せずにはいられない. ☞アメリカ先住民の習慣から.

do a hatchet job on **1** …をひどくけなす, 酷評する, に罵詈雑言(ばりぞうごん)を浴びせる ▪ He *did a hatchet job on* her latest novel in one of the papers. 彼は一つの紙上で彼女の最新作の小説を酷評した.

2 (記事など)を大幅に削除する ▪ My editor *did a hatchet job on* my article. うちの編集長は私の記事に大鉈(おおなた)を振るった. ☞20世紀初頭の米国における熾烈なギャング間の抗争から.

take up the hatchet 戦争を始める, 武器を取る ▪ They decided to *take up the hatchet* against the French. 彼らはフランス軍に対して戦争を始めることに決めた. ☞アメリカ先住民の習慣から.

throw* [*fling, sling*] *the hatchet 《俗》大ぼらを吹く ▪ They knew the captain's habit of *throwing the hatchet*. 彼らは船長の大ぼらを吹く癖を知っていた. ☞的に向かって hatchet を投げる昔のスポーツから.

throw the helve after the hatchet →send the HELVE after the hatchet.

hate[1] /heɪt/ 名 *one's* ***pet hate*** 大嫌いな人[物, こと] (= one's PET aversion) ▪ *My pet hate* is having to stand in line. 大嫌いなのは列に並んで順番を待たねばならないことだ.

hate[2] /heɪt/ 動 ***hate*** *oneself* 《口・皮肉》うぬぼれる ▪ I am such a versatile writer that I sometimes *hate myself*. 私はとても多才な作家なので, ときにうぬぼれることがある.

hate *a person's* ***guts*** →GUT[1].

hate *a person* ***like poison*** →POISON.

hatred /héɪtrəd/ 名 ***be blinded by hatred*** 判断がゆがめられるほど憎む ▪ Why *are* you so *blinded by hatred* of foreigners? 君はどうしてそんなに我を忘れるほど外国人を憎むのか?

bear *a person* ***hatred*** 人に憎悪の念をいだく ▪ He *bears* you intense *hatred*. 彼はあなたに激しい憎悪の念をいだいている.

have a hatred for …を憎悪する ▪ I *have a hatred for* such people. 私はそんな人々を憎悪する.

in hatred of/ out of hatred for …を憎んで ▪ They persecute him *out of hatred for* his father. 彼らは彼の父への恨みから彼を迫害する.

hatter /hǽtər/ 名 ***(as) mad as a hatter*** →MAD.

haul[1] /hɔːl/ 名 ***a long haul*** 時間と手間のかかる厄介な仕事 ▪ Recovering from infidelity is *a* *long haul.* 不信から撚(よ)りを戻すのは手間暇のかかる大仕事だ.

a short haul 近距離, 小旅行 ▪ It was just *a short haul* to the lake. 湖まではほんのちょっとの距離だった ▪ According to the moving company, they don't make *short hauls.* その運送業者は近場の輸送は扱わないという.

in* [*over*] *the long haul 《主に米》今後長期間にわたって, 長期的には, 結局は ▪ These toys will last *over the long haul.* このおもちゃは長い間使えるだろう ▪ *Over the long haul,* this experience will prove to be invaluable. 長い目で見ればこの経験もこの上なく貴重だとわかるだろう ▪ Calculators of this type will prove best *in the long haul.* この型の計算機が結局はベストということになろう.

make* [*get*] *a fine* [*good, big, great*] *haul 《口》大漁である; 大儲けをする; 掘り出しものをする ▪ We *made a fine haul* of prizes. 我々は賞をどっさり得た ▪ The thief *made a great haul.* 泥棒は大かせぎをした.

haul[2] /hɔːl/ 動 ***haul ass* [*butt*]** 《米俗》(車などで)急ぐ, 素早く逃亡する ▪ She *hauled ass* back to the office. 彼女は急いで会社へ取って返した ▪ It's the cops! *Haul ass!* サツだ! 逃げろ!

***haul down** one's **flag** [**colors**]* 旗を巻く; 降伏する ▪ She was beaten and *hauled down her colors.* 彼女は負けて旗を巻いた.

haul in** one's **horns →HORN.

haul** a person **over the coals →call a person over the COALs.

haunch /hɔːntʃ/ 名 ***squat* [*sit*] *on** one's **haunches*** しりをおろして座る, うずくまる ▪ A lean wolf was *squatting on its haunches.* やせたオオカミがうずくまっていた.

have[1] /hæv/ 名 ***the haves and have-nots*** 有産者と無産者; 持っている国と持っていない国; (原子力兵器を)持つ国と持たない国 ▪ It is a battle between *the haves and have-nots.* それは有産者と無産者との戦いである.

have[2] /həv, hæv/ 動 ***a has-been*** (今はもう忘れられた)過去の人 ▪ The guest was some old *has-been* whose name I didn't even know. ゲストは私がその名前さえ知らない過去の人だった.

***All** one **has to do is** (**to**) do.* 人は...しさえすればよい ▪ *All* you *have to do is* (*to*) go. あなたは行きさえすればよい.

be had of ...から得る, 買う ▪ All these books may *be had of* any bookseller. これらの本はみなどの書店でも買える.

***have** a person do* **1** 人に...してもらう[させる] ▪ I will *have* him come. 彼に来てもらいましょう.

2 人に...される ▪ He *had* his wife die. 彼は妻に死なれた.

***have** a thing done* 物を...してもらう[させる]; 物を...される ▪ I will *have* my photograph taken tomorrow. 私はあす写真をとってもらいます ▪ I *had* my purse stolen yesterday. 私はきのう財布を盗まれた.

***have** oneself* ...を楽しむ ▪ I *had myself* a good night's sleep after a day of hard work. 昼間しっかり働いたあと一晩ぐっすりと快眠をむさぼった.

have a blind trust* [*faith*] *in ...に絶対の信頼を抱く, 盲信する ▪ The elderly often *have a blind trust in* medication. お年寄りには薬を信じきっている人が多い ▪ They *have a blind faith in* the government. 政府に全幅の信頼を置いている.

have a good one ごきげんよう ▪ *Have a good one.*—You, too! ごきげんよう—あなたもね!

have a lot on 忙しい ▪ I*'ve got a lot on* at the moment. 今とても忙しくしている.

***have ... about** one* →ABOUT.

***have been and** done/ **have** (**been and**) **gone and** done* 《俗》[have done の強意形] 意外[愚か, 不運]にも...してしまった ▪ He *has been and* moved my papers. やつめ, 僕の書類を動かしやがった ▪ That you should *have* (*been and*) *gone and* done such a thing! 君がそんなことをしでかしてしまったとは.

have been had 《口》騙された, ひっかかった ▪ Shucks! I*'ve been had* again! チェッ! また一杯くわされた!

***have ... before** one* **1** ...を前途に控えている ▪ Japan *has* a bright future *before* it. 日本の前途は輝かしい ▪ He *has* all his troubles *before* him. 彼はこれからいろいろ苦労しなければならない.

2 ...を手がける ▪ We *have* a strange case *before* us. 我々は今度は妙な事件を手がける.

***have but* [*only*] *to** do* ...しさえすればよい ▪ You *have only to* go and ask him. ただ彼の所へ行って頼みさえすればよい. ☞but は文語.

have** a child **by (男性・女性)によって子供をもうける ▪ He *had* two children *by* a native woman. 彼は土地の女性によって二人子供をもうけた ▪ She *had* a bastard child *by* the defendant. 彼女は被告によって庶子を産んだ.

have everything** one's **own way →WAY.

have got 《口》持つ (have) ▪ What *have* you *got* in your bag? 君のかばんの中には何があるか.

***have* (*got*) *it made* (*in the shade*)** 《口》成功確実である ▪ He *has it made* because his father is very rich. 彼は父が大金持だから成功確実である ▪ How lucky! I*'ve got it made in the shade!* ラッキー! うまくいくぞ!

have got it up there 賢い ▪ No wonder she's succeeded. She's really *got it up there.* 彼女が成功したのは当然だ. 本当に頭がいいから.

***have got to** do* ...しなければならない ▪ I *have got to* go to a meeting. 私は会合に出なければならない.

have had it 《口》 **1** なし終えた ▪ He *hasn't had it* yet. 彼はそれをまだ終えていない《本など》.

2 殺された, (不運・過失で)やられた ▪ When they run out of ammunition, they*'ve had it.* 弾薬が尽きて彼らは殺された.

3 《皮肉》得そこねた ▪ You *have had it,* I see? どうやら君は乗りそこねたようだね.

4 もう時代遅れだ; もう生命[活動]は終わりだ ▪ The general *has had it* now. その将軍はもう盛りを過ぎた ▪ This washing machine's *had it*. この洗濯機はもう寿命がきた ▪ This old cellphone *has had it* now. この古いケータイはもう使いものにならない.

5 もうたくさんだ, うんざりする, がまんできない; 腹を立てている (*up to here with*) ▪ I've *had it up to here with* you. Get out! お前にはもううんざりだ. 出て行け! ▪ I've *had it with* your yawning. 君のあくびにはもうがまんがならない ▪ The plumber *has had it up to here with* his work. 配管工が自分の仕事に腹を立てている.

***have ... in** one* …の素質がある, …なところがある ▪ He *has* something of the hero *in* him. 彼はどこか英雄的なところがある ▪ He *has in* him the making of a great man. 彼には偉人の素質がある.

have it **1** 主張する, 言う, 表現する ▪ She will *have it* that he is wrong. 彼女は彼がまちがっていると主張してきかない ▪ Rumor *has it* that he is alive. 彼は生きているという噂だ ▪ He was drunk as a lord, as his friends *have it*. 彼は友人の言葉によればへべれけに酔っていた.

2 …する ▪ Which way do you want to *have it*? どちらにしたいのですか.

3 …ということになる (*that*) ▪ Fortune *had it that* we arrived early. 運よく我々は早く着いた.

4 解けた, わかった, 思いついた ▪ Suddenly I *had it*. 急に思いついた ▪ There you *have it*. それでおわかりでしょう.

5 叱責[処罰, 打撃, 災難]を受ける ▪ Let him *have it*. 彼をしかってやれ.

6 勝つ, 優勢である ▪ The ayes *have it*. 賛成多数である.

7 (…と)聞いている ▪ I *have it* that he will be promoted soon. 彼はまもなく昇進すると聞いている.

8 〚主に否定文で will, would を伴って〛 許す ▪ Jane wanted to go, but her mother *wouldn't have it*. ジェインは行きたかったが彼女の母が頑として許さなかった.

have it* (*all*) *over …より良い, よりもすぐれている ▪ Our team *has it over* theirs. 我々のチームは彼らのよりすぐれている ▪ A jeep *has it all over* a car on rough roads. 悪路ではジープの方が普通車よりもずっと優れている.

***have it* (*all*) *over** a person* = HAVE it on a person.

have it all** one's **own way →have everything one's own WAY.

***have it away* [*off*]** 《英口》 (…と)不義[密通]をする (*with*) ▪ The boss is *having it away with* his secretary. 社長は秘書と密通をしている ▪ John's father and Jane were *having it off*. ジョンの父とジェインは不倫していた.

have it both ways →WAY.

***have it coming* (*to** one*)** →COMING.

have it easy 楽な思いをする ▪ Women *have it easy* staying home all the time. 女性はいつも家にいて気楽だ.

have it good →GOOD.

***have it in** one* 《口》 素質[力量]がある ▪ He *had it in* him. 彼にその力量があった.

have it in for 《口》 …に悪意[恨み]をいだいている; に報復[危害]を加えようと待っている ▪ He seems to *have it in for* me. 彼は私に悪意をいだいているようだ ▪ Ever since John insulted her, she has *had it in for* him. 侮辱されて以来, 彼女はジョンを恨んでいる.

***have it in** one **to** do* …することができる ▪ He *had it in* him *to* speak so forcefully. 彼はとても力強く話すことができた.

have it off →HAVE it away.

***have it on** a person* 《米口》 人にまさっている; 人の優位に立つ ▪ They think they *have it on* us. 彼らは我々にまさっていると思っている.

have it out **1** (とことんまで論争して)決着をつける ▪ Very well, then; let's *have it out*, here and now. では, よろしい. 今ここで論じ合ってかたをつけよ.

2 事を終える, 残りを楽しむ ▪ He ran into the yard to *have it out* by himself. 残りを一人で楽しむため中庭にかけ込んだ.

***have it out of** a person* 《口》 人を罰する[やっつける]; 人に仕返しする; 人から償いを取り立てる ▪ I *had it out of* him. 彼に仕返しをした.

have it out with 《口》 **1** …と論争して[なぐり合いして]かたをつける ▪ I'm going to *have it out with* him about that five hundred pounds. 私はその500ポンドについて, 彼と論争してかたをつけるつもりです.

2 …に遠慮なく(文句を)言う; に行為の説明を求める ▪ I am going to *have it out with* her. 遠慮なく彼女に文句を言ってやるつもりだ.

***have it said* (*that*)** 〚主に否定文で〛 …と言わせる ▪ I won't *have it said that* my son is a liar. 私の息子が嘘つきだとは言わせないぞ.

have it so そうしてもらう ▪ If you will *have it so*, I have nothing to say against it. ぜひそうしろとおっしゃるなら, 異議は申しません.

***have lots* [*everything*] *going for** one* 多くの[あらゆる]利点を持っている ▪ She is sure to get a job; she *has everything going for* her. 彼女の資質は申し分ないから, きっと就職できるだろう.

***have much to do to** do* …するのに大いに骨が折れる ▪ I *have much to do to* pay my monthly bills. 月々の払いが大変です.

have much* [*little, nothing, something,* etc.] *to do with …と関係が大いにある[あまりない, 全然ない, 少しある, など] ▪ I *have a great deal to do with* the affair. 私はその事件と大いに関係がある ▪ Do you *have anything to do with* him? 君は彼と何か関係があるか.

***have not to** do* …するに及ばない ▪ You *have not to* go there. あなたはそこへ行かなくてもよい.

have nothing against …を嫌う理由がない ▪ I *have nothing against* you personally. 個人的に君が嫌いなわけではない.

have nothing on/ not have anything on

《口》 **1** …に勝るところは少しもない (↔HAVE something on 1) ▪I have *had nothing on* a lot of other pitchers. 私は多くの他の投手に勝るところは少しもなかった.
2 …を有罪にするような証拠を持たない ▪I *had nothing on* her, and did not search for her. 彼女を有罪にするような証拠がなかったので, 彼女を捜さなかった.
3 (会合・約束・用事など)がない ▪I *have nothing on* of importance at the moment. 今は大した仕事はない.
4 裸である ▪I have just taken a bath and do*n't have anything on*. 風呂に入ったところで何も着ていない.

***have ... of** a person* …を人から譲り受ける ▪He *had* the estate *of* his uncle. 彼はその地所をおじから譲り受けた.

have** a person **on toast →TOAST.

***have only to** do* →HAVE but to do.

have** a person **right** [**just**] **where** one **wants them (しばしばビジネス・政治で)…よりも有利な立場に立つ ▪It looks like we *have* them *right where* we *want them*. どうも我々が彼らをリードしているようだ.

have something against (ある理由で)反対である[している] ▪Do you *have something against* our plan? 我々の計画に反対の理由が何かあるのか.

have something on 《米口》 **1** …より勝る(ところがある) (↔HAVE nothing on 1) ▪He *has something on* me in the field of biology. 彼は生物学の分野では私にまさっている点がある.
2 …に不利な[を有罪とするような]証拠を持っている ▪I *had something on* my chief. 私は親方に不利な証拠を持っていた.

have something to do with →HAVE much to do with.

***have teething problems** [**trouble(s)**]* →TEETHING.

have the cards** [**deck**] **stacked against …に不利にカードを切られる, ついていない ▪Never give up even if you *have the deck stacked against* you. 不利な立場にいても決してあきらめないように ▪I always *have the cards stacked against* me. 私はいつもツキに見放されている.

***have to** do* …しなければならない (must) ▪I *have to* go to London tomorrow. 私はあすロンドンへ行かねばならない.

***have ... to** oneself* …を独占している ▪I *have* a room *to myself*. 私は一室を独占している.

have to do with **1** …と交渉がある ▪He *has to do with* all sorts of people. 彼はあらゆる種類の人と関係している.
2 …を相手にする, 扱う; に用がある ▪Nobody can *have to do with* him. 誰も彼を相手にできない ▪Philology *has to do with* language. 言語学は言語を取り扱う ▪We *have to do with* facts, not theories. 事実には用があるが, 空論に用はない.

have to get married 《婉曲》 女性が妊娠したため結婚する ▪They had a short engagement. They *had to get married*. 彼らの婚約期間は短かった. できちゃった婚だったので.

have what it takes to be …になるのに必要な素質を持つ ▪He *has what it takes to be* a good teacher. 彼は良い先生になる素質を持っている.

***have yet to** do* →YET.

How'll you have it? 酒は何にしますか《ウィスキーかジンか, など》.

it has to be →BE.

let** a person **have it →LET[2].

Let's have it. 話し[教え]てくれ ▪What is it? *Let's have it.* なんのことだ. 話してくれ.

not have much** [**anything**] **on あまり[少しも]忙しくない ▪I *haven't got much on* next week. 来週はあまり忙しくない.

not have two ... to rub together 《口》 金を全く[ほとんど]持っていない ▪We did*n't have two* pennies *to rub together* in those days. 当時わが家はひどく貧しかった.

to have and to hold 保有する; (妻を)いつまでも大事にする ▪I bequeath you this property *to have and to hold*. 私はあなたにこの財産を譲って保有させる ▪She is my wife *to have and to hold*. 彼女はいつまでも大事にすべき私の妻です. ☞《法》から.

***where to have** a person* どの点で負かすか ▪I didn't know *where to have* him. 私は彼をどの点で参らせたらよいかわからなかった.

will have it that …と言ってきかない (→HAVE it 1) ▪She *will have it that* alcohol is a food. 彼女はアルコールは滋養になると言ってきかない.

will not have it 受けよう[がまんしよう]としない; 認めようとしない ▪If he tries to explain, I *will not have it*. 彼が説明しようとしても, 私は聞きたくない.

You have** [**You've got**] **me there. **1** そいつは一本取られた, その点では私の負けだ ▪So *you have me there*. I was wrong and you were right. これはやられた. 僕の間違いで君の言う通りだった.
2 (質問に対して)私にはわからない ▪How many miles is five kilometers?—*You've got me there*. 5キロメートルは何マイルか—わからないや.

havoc /hǽvək/ 名 ***cry havoc*** 大破壊の号令を下す; じゅうりん[略奪]をそそのかす ▪It *cried havoc* to the superstitions of men. それは人間の迷信の打破を号令した ▪Caesar's spirit shall *cry havoc* and let slip the dogs of war. カエサルの霊は大破を号令し, 戦禍を放つであろう (cf. Sh., *Jul. Caes.* 3. 1. 273). ☞もと, 兵士に Havoc! (略奪せよ)と号令したことから.

***make havoc** (**of, among**)* (…を)破壊する, (を)荒らす ▪It *made* a most dreadful *havoc among* us. それは我々に実にひどい破壊をもたらした ▪The flood has *made* great *havoc*. 洪水は無残に壊した.

***play** [**raise**] **havoc with** [**among**]* …をこわす, めちゃめちゃにする, に大混乱を引き起こす ▪When he came on to bowl, he *played havoc with* the wickets. (クリケットの)投手になったとき, 彼は打者たち

H

をさんざんにやっつけた ▪ He's *playing havoc with* his health by sitting up all night. 彼は徹夜して体をこわしている ▪ We didn't mean to *raise havoc with* our customers. お客さまを混乱させるつもりはなかったのですけれど.

work havoc upon = make HAVOC (of, among).

***wreak havoc* (*in, with, among*)** (...を)破壊する; (を)混乱させる ▪ The fire *wreaked havoc among* some hundreds of residents. その火災は数百という住民に大損害を与えた.

haw /hɔː/ 動 ***hum and haw***/《米》***hem and haw*** →HUM.

hawk /hɔːk/ 名 **(*as*) *different as a hawk from a handspike*** 《古》非常に異なって ▪ It is *as different* from modern poetry *as a hawk from a handspike*. それは近代詩とは非常に異なっている.

(*as*) *hungry* [*keen*] *as a hawk* すっかり腹がへって; 目の鋭い, 抜け目のない ▪ My mother is *as keen as a hawk*. 母は非常に目が鋭い.

between hawk and buzzard 《古》たそがれに ▪ I entered Richmond *between hawk and buzzard*. 私はたそがれにリッチモンドに入った.

hawks and doves タカ派とハト派, 強硬論者と穏健論者 ▪ A debate is going on between the *hawks and doves* on the issue. その問題を巡ってタカ派とハト派の間で目下論争中である. ☞英国保守党右派と左派, 米国共和党と民主党両陣営にもこの2派がある.

***know* [*can tell*] *a hawk from a handsaw* (*when the wind is southerly*)** 《口》見聞が広い; 聡明な; 識別力がある ▪ He is a man who *knows a hawk from a handsaw*. 彼は識別力のある人である ▪ I *know a hawk from a handsaw when the wind is southerly*. 私は抜け目がない. ☞handsaw = おそらく heronshaw (サギ); (cf. Sh., *Haml*. 2. 2. 397).

watch like a hawk 《口》厳重に見守る ▪ The police are *watching* the criminal's house *like hawks*. 警察は犯人の家を厳重に見守っている.

hawse /hɔːz/ 名 ***athwart* (*a person's*) *hawse*** →ATHWART.

***cross* [*come across*] *the hawse*(*s*)** 《海》停泊中の船の投錨区域を横切る; じゃまする; 不和になる, けんかする ▪ We *crossed the hawses* of six of them, and were abreast of her. 我々は停泊中の6隻の船の投錨区域を横切って, その船と並んだ ▪ I'll teach them to *come across my hawse*. 彼らが私のじゃまをしたらただではおかないぞ.

hay /heɪ/ 名 ***beat the hay*** 《米口》眠る ▪ She was *beating the hay*. 彼女は眠っていた.

carry hay in one's horns きげんが悪い; (近寄ると)危険である ▪ He is sharp as thorn and *carries hay in his horns*. 彼はイバラのように鋭く近寄ると危険である. ☞角で突きがちの雄牛の角は hay で包まれていたことから; Horace の句.

***dance the hay* [*hays*]** (たくさんの物の中または周りを)ぐるぐる回る; ダンスのようにさまざまの旋回をする ▪ In our joy for him we joined hands and *danced the hay* around him. 彼を迎えたうれしさで, 私たちは手をつなぎ彼の周りをぐるぐる回った.

get on the hay wagon 《米》運動[仕事]を始める ▪ The Folk Dancing Society *got on the hay wagon*. フォークダンス協会は運動に乗り出した.

hit the hay 《米口》就寝する, 床につく ▪ We should *hit the hay* early. 我々は早く床につくべきである. ☞昔はふとんにワラ (hay) が入っていたことから.

look for a needle in a bottle of hay → NEEDLE[1].

make hay of **1** ...をめちゃめちゃにこわす ▪ He *made hay of* your arguments in two minutes. 彼は君の議論を2分間でめちゃめちゃにこわした.

2 ...を混乱させる, ひっくり返す ▪ He has *made hay of* my library. 彼は私の文庫をかき回した.

3 ...をさんざんやっつける, 楽に負かす ▪ England used to *make hay of* any opponents at football. イングランドはフットボールではどんな相手でもさんざんにやっつけたものだ. ☞干し草 (hay) を作るときは草をひっくり返したり投げ散らしたりするから.

4《米》...を利用する ▪ He *made hay of* the opportunity. 彼はその機会を利用した.

Make hay while the sun shines. 《諺》日の照るうちに草を干せ《好機を逸するな》.

make hay with ...をすっかりひっくり返す ▪ Who has been *making hay with* these papers? この書類を誰がひっくり返していたのか.

that ain't hay それは多額[重要]である ▪ He's making $5,000 a month, and *that ain't hay*. 彼は月に5,000ドル稼いでいるが, そいつは大金だ.

hayride /héɪràɪd/ 名 ***be no hayride*** (楽しいどころか)ひどいものである ▪ My life *was no hayride*. 私の人生はひどいものだった.

be on a hayride (高校生が)自動車でピクニックしている ▪ I *was on a hayride* with a girl. 私は女の子と自動車でピクニックしていた.

hayseed /héɪsìːd/ 名 ***comb* [*get*] *the hayseed out of one's hair*** 《俗》田舎臭を磨き落とす ▪ He hasn't *got the hayseed out of his hair* yet. 彼はまだ田舎から出たてのほやほやだ.

haystack /héɪstæ̀k/ 名 ***look for a needle in a haystack*** →look for a NEEDLE in a bottle of hay.

haywire /héɪwàɪər/ 名 ***go haywire*** 《口》 **1** (人が)興奮する; 気が狂う; 取り乱す; 荒れ回る ▪ They have *gone* completely *haywire* with their retail prices. 彼らは小売値段のことで全く取り乱した.

2 (機械が)狂う ▪ The machine has *gone haywire*. その機械は狂った. ☞coil of wire の扱いにくいことから.

hazard /hǽzərd/ 名 ***at all hazards* [*every hazard*]** どんな危険を冒しても, ぜひとも ▪ He determined to get rid of it *at every hazard*. 彼はどんなことがあってもそれを取り除こうと決心した.

at hazard **1** でたらめに，でまかせに，運まかせに ▪ The answers I gave *at hazard* turned out to be correct. でたらめにした答えが当たった.
2 危険に瀕して ▪ Their interests were *at hazard*. 彼らの利益は危険に瀕していた.

at [***to, with***] ***the hazard of*** …を賭して，の危険を冒して ▪ He learned Hebrew *at the hazard of* his life. 彼は身命を賭してヘブライ語を学んだ ▪ He once saved me *to the hazard of* his life. 彼はかつて自分の生命の危険を冒して私を救ってくれたことがある.

by hazard ＝at HAZARD 1.

every hazard →at all HAZARDs.

in hazard 危険に瀕して ▪ My reputation is *in hazard*. 私の名声が危険に瀕している.

make a hazard (***at***) (…を)当て推量する ▪ He *made a hazard at* the direction in which they ran. 彼は彼らの逃走した方向を推測した.

on the hazard 危険に瀕して ▪ His whole fortune was *on the hazard*. 彼の全財産が危うかった.

out of hazard 危険を脱して ▪ His life was *out of hazard*. 彼の生命は危機を脱した.

run the hazard 冒険をする，一か八かやってみる ▪ She won't *run the hazard* of losing her way. 彼女は一か八かで道に迷うような冒険はしない.

to [***with***] ***the hazard of*** →at the HAZARD of.

haze /heɪz/ 名 ***in a haze*** (頭がかすみにおおわれたように)もうろうとして[混乱して] ▪ She went around *in a haze*. 彼女はもうろうとした頭で出歩いた.

hazel /héɪzəl/ 名 ***anoint … with oil of hazel*** 《古》…をハシバミのむちでなぐる ▪ Take the *oil of hazel* and *with* it *anoint* her body. ハシバミのむちを取って彼女を打ちなさい.

he /hiː/ 代 ***a he-man*** 《口》男らしい人，たくましい男性 ▪ Our son became *a* real *he-man* after entering military service. 息子は兵役につくと見違えるほどたくましくなった.

he who [***that***] 《雅》…する人 ▪ *He that* talks much errs much. 《諺》口数の多い者はぼろを出すことも多い，「数を言えば屑を言う」.

He would! 《俗》全く彼のしそうなことだ《非難をこめて》 ▪ Oh! *He would*, eh? そうか．いかにも奴のしそうなことだな.

head[1] /hed/ 名 ***a big*** [***swelled, swollen***] ***head*** 《口》うぬぼれ，思い上がり ▪ Praising your children will only give them *a big head*. 子供をほめ過ぎると，うぬぼれさせるだけだろう.

a head cook and bottle washer 雑役使用人，臨時雑役夫; 権威を見せびらかす上役 ▪ That's our *head cook and bottle washer*, and he lets everybody know it. あれは我々の上役で，権威をみんなに見せびらかす男です.

a head-hunter 優秀な人材を探しだして引き抜く役目の人，(幹部級人材の)スカウト係 ▪ That man is *an* experienced executive *head hunter*. あの男性は経験豊かな幹部級人材スカウトである.

a head of hair (全体の)頭髪《特に豊富な》 ▪ She has *a* fine *head of hair*. 彼女は美しい頭髪をしている.

a head of steam **1** 怒り心頭 ▪ He has built up *a head of steam* at what they did. 彼らの仕打ちに彼は怒りを募らせている.
2 十分な後押し ▪ You can get *a head of steam* for an idea quickly from blogs. ブログならば意見が素早く寄せられる. ☞蒸気エンジンは蒸気の圧力が一定レベルまで到達しないと作動しないことから.

a long head →LONG.

a thick head 頭が悪い者，あまり賢くない人 ▪ You left the door unlocked, you *thick head*! ドアの鍵をかけ忘れたりなんかして，おばかさんね!

above one's head ＝over one's HEAD.

above the head(***s***) ***of*** …に(むずかしすぎて)わからない ▪ His speech was *above the heads of* the audience. 彼の演説は聴衆には難しすぎてわからなかった.

at the head of …の先頭に，の首位に，の長で ▪ At 21 he was placed *at the head of* the administration. 21歳で彼は執行部の首席にすえられた ▪ He is *at the head of* the allied Forces. 彼は連合軍総司令官である ▪ You will find it *at the head of* the page. 君はそれをそのページの一番上に見つけるだろう.

H

bang one's head against a brick wall → beat one's HEAD against a (stone, 《主に英》brick) wall.

bang their heads together ＝knock their HEADs together.

be a head case 《俗》気が狂っている ▪ The girl must *be a head case* or something. あの女の子はきっと気がおかしくなっているか何かだ.

be at the head of affairs 国政を総覧する ▪ He *is at the head of affairs* in France. 彼はフランスの国政を総覧している.

be cut shorter by the head 斬首される《頭の長さだけ切って短くする》 ▪ He *was* taken and *cut shorter by the head*. 彼は捕えられて首を切られた.

be in head 《米》(作物が)頭を出す ▪ The wheat *is in head* and the barley is beginning to turn yellow. 小麦が頭を出し大麦は色うき始めている.

be in over one's head (抜け出せない)難局に巻き込まれている，困り果てる ▪ Now she's *in over her head*, with something she said. 彼女は自分が以前言ったことで抜き差しならない状況にある ▪ I'm afraid he's *in over his head* this week. 彼は今週仕事を持て余しているように思う.

be it on a person's [***one's***] (***own***) ***head*** 人[自分](自身)の責任だ ▪ *Be it on his own head*, if people don't like him. 人が彼を好かなくてもそれは彼自身の責任だ.

be on a head trip 《俗》うぬぼれている ▪ He's *been on a head trip* since he was promoted to section chief. 彼は部長に昇進以来，天狗になっている.

bear [***keep***] ***head against*** …に屈せず抵抗する; に譲らない ▪ They were unable to *bear head against* this storm. 彼らはこのあらしに屈せず抵抗することができなかった ▪ The bream *keeps head* *against* the freshets. コイは出水に流されないでいる.

beat* [*bang, bash, butt, hit, knock, run*] *one's* *head against* [*into*] *a* (*stone,*《主に英》*brick*) *wall 《口》 **1**［［進行形で］］不可能な事［見込みのない事］をしようとする ▪ He has no intention of paying you back. You *are knocking your head against a brick wall.* 彼は君に金を返す気はない. 君は見込みのない努力をしている.

2（誰かにじゃまされて）いらいらする ▪ How come you're *beating your head against a wall?* お前たちは何をいらついているのだ.

beat *a person's* ***head off*** 《口》 頭がちぎれるまで打つ; さんざんに負かす, やっつける ▪ I'll *beat his* old *head off* at billiards. 私はあいつをビリヤードでさんざんに負かしてやる.

beat *a thing* ***into*** *a person's* ***head*** 人(の心)にあることをたたき込む, 教え込む ▪ The classics *were beaten into their heads* at school. 学校では古典が彼らの頭にたたき込まれた.

Better be the head of a dog than the tail of a lion. 《諺》 ライオンの尻尾になるよりも犬の頭になるほうがよい,「鶏口となるも牛後となるなかれ」.

bite *a person's* ***head off*** **1**（頭をもぎとるほど）猛烈に食いこむ ▪ The steel jaws had almost *bitten his head off.* 鋼鉄のあごが猛烈に彼に食いこんだ.

2 怒って返答する ▪ Just because I ask you for some money, you don't have to *bite my head off.* 私が金をくれと言うからといって, そうがみがみ言わなくてもよい.

bite off *one's* ***own head*** 他人を害そうとしてかえって自分が害を受ける ▪ I would rather *bite off my own head* than confess it. それを白状するくらいならこっちが害を受けたほうがましだ.

blow *a person's* [*one's* ***own***] ***head off*** (ピストルなどで)人を射ち殺す[自殺する] ▪ She *blew his head off* with a hunting rifle. 彼女はライフルで彼を射殺した ▪ He *blew his own head off* as a result of depression. 彼は鬱(うつ)になった末に銃で自殺を遂げた.

bother *one's* ***head*** →trouble one's HEAD.

bring* [*draw*]... *to a head …を結論に達せしめる, 要約する; (事態)を絶頂[危機]に達せしめる; (機)を熟させる, に勢力を得させる ▪ It is time to *draw* this lengthy discussion *to a head.* この長い討論に結論を下すときだ ▪ It might *bring* things *to a head* one way or the other. それはどちらにしても事態を危機に追い込むかもしれない ▪ There has been some plot, though it has not *been brought to a head.* ある陰謀が企てられていた. 熟すまでには至らなかったが.

build* [*get, work*] *up a head of steam ことを起こすに充分な活力[支持, 情熱]がだんだん高まる ▪ The movement for change has been *building up a head of steam.* 変革の機運が高まってきた.

***bury* [*have, hide*]** *one's* ***head in the sand* (*like an ostrich*)** →OSTRICH.

butt heads with *a person*/***butt heads over*** 人と角を突き合わせて議論する ▪ Rural residents grew tired of *butting heads with* developers. 村人たちは開発業者との膝詰め談判にうんざりしてきた ▪ We are still *butting heads over* the question of abortion. 我々は妊娠中絶について今なお議論中だ.

buy* [*sell*]... *over *a person's* ***head*** (家など)を住居人に相談せずに買う[売る] ▪ The house will *be sold over our head.* 家は住居人たる我々の頭越しに売られるだろう.

by a head 頭(の長さ)だけの差で; ほんのわずかの差で ▪ He is taller than I *by a head.* 彼は頭の長さだけ私より高い ▪ The horse won *by a head.* その馬は頭だけの差で勝った.

(*by*) *head and shoulders* むりやりに; 手荒く ▪ He has brought in this quotation *head and shoulders.* 彼はこの引用を無理に入れている.

by* [*down by*] *the head **1** 船首の方を後尾より深く沈めて ▪ The ship was settling *by the head.* 船は船首から沈みかけていた ▪ The vessel is too much *by the head.* その船は船首が後尾より深く沈みすぎている.

2 ほろ酔いで, きこしめして ▪ He was a little *by the head*, but not drunk. 彼は少しきこしめしていたが, 酔っぱらってはいなかった.

by the head and ears むりやりに; 手荒く ▪ He dragged in the story *by the head and ears.* 彼はその話をむりやりに引っぱり出した《得意な話など》 ▪ They dragged you out of your trenches *by the head and ears.* 彼らはあなたを塹壕(ざんごう)からむりやりに引っぱり出そうとした.

can make neither head nor tail of/《口》 ***can't make head or* [*nor*] *tail* (*out*) *of*** 全くわからない ▪ I *can make neither head nor tail of* this complicated puzzle. この込み入った謎はさっぱり分からない ▪ I *can't make head or tail of* this picture—it must be upside down. この絵はわけが分からない—きっと上下さかさまだろう.

can't get *one's* ***head round* [*around*]** 《口》 …を理解できない ▪ I *can't get my head round* why our new vacuum cleaner doesn't work. どうして買ったばかりの掃除機が動かないのかわからない.

carry *one's* ***head high*** 偉そうにする ▪ The boss *carries his head* very *high.* 社長はひどく偉そうにする.

come into* [*enter*]** *a person's* ***head 人の胸に浮かぶ ▪ It *came into my head* that he would make a good musician. 彼は立派な音楽家になるだろうと私は思った ▪ An idea *came into my head.* ある考えが私の胸に浮かんだ.

come on *one's* ***head*** さか立ちする ▪ The horse cantered down a hill and *came on his head.* 馬は小走りに小山を降りてさか立ちとなった.

come* [*draw, grow, gather*] *to a head **1**（できものに）頭ができる, 化膿する ▪ The boil *drew to a head.* はれものが化膿した.

2 結論に達する, 絶頂[危機]に達する; (機が)熟する; 勢いを増す ▪ The dispute must *come to a head* soon. その論争は早く結論に達しなくてはならない

▪ The quarrel *drew to a head* when she slapped the boy. 彼女がその少年をなぐったとき，口げんかは絶頂に達した ▪ The revolt of Sardinia was stamped out before it *grew to a head*. サルデーニャの反乱は熟さないうちに鎮定された ▪ The storm *gathered to a head* at dawn. あらしは夜明けに強まった.

come* [*fall*] *under the head of …の部[項]に入る ▪ These items *come under the head of* A. これらの項目はAの部に入る ▪ The subject *falls under the head of* rhetoric. その問題は修辞学の部に入る.

cost (*a person*) *his* ***head*** …のため生命を失う ▪ Charles's actions *cost* him *his head*. チャールズは自分の行動のため命を失った.

count heads **1** 人数を数える ▪ Just try to *count heads*. ちょっと頭数を数えてみてください.
2 大多数の見解を受け入れる ▪ What is the point of *counting heads*? You decide. 多数意見に従って何になる? 君が決めればいい.

do *one's* ***head in*** 《主に英口》いらつかせる，ひどく心配[混乱，がっかり]させる ▪ His remark really *did my head in*. 彼の言葉には全くがっかりした ▪ I've been trying to solve this mystery and it's *doing my head in*. この謎を解こうと頑張っているけど，いらいらしてきたよ.

down by the head →by the HEAD.

draw to a head →come to a HEAD.

draw ... to a head →bring ... to a HEAD.

eat *a person's* ***head off*** 人に小言を言う，人をしかる ▪ She *ate his head off* when he came home late. 彼が遅く帰って来ると，彼女は彼をしかった.

eat *one's* ***head off*** 《口》 **1** (馬などが)飼い倒れになる，飼い主を食い倒す《割りの合わないほど飼料を食う; 車などにも言う》 ▪ She does not like to have the horse *eating his head off*. 彼女は馬に食い倒されるのを好まない ▪ As there is no one to drive it, that car will *eat its head off*. 誰も運転する者がないから，その自動車は持ち腐れになるだろう.
2 (使用人·被雇人などが)仕事をせずにごくつぶしをする ▪ The driver is simply hanging round *eating his head off*. 運転手はただぶらぶらしてごくつぶしをしているだけである.
3 大食する，暴食する ▪ He *ate his head off* for the next few months and did weights. その後の数か月彼は食事を大量にとり重量挙げをした. ☞もと馬に，次に使用人に，最後に雇主について言われるようになった.

enter *a person's* ***head*** 人の頭[胸]に浮かぶ ▪ It never *entered his head* that he might be wrong. 自分がまちがっているかもしれないということに彼は思い至らなかった.

fall under the head of →come under the HEAD of.

find *one's* ***head*** 落ち着く ▪ The coracle seemed to *find her head* again. あじろ舟はまた安定に戻るように見えた.

fling *oneself* ***at the head of*** →throw oneself at the HEAD of.

from head to foot [***heel***(***s***)] **1** 頭から足まで，全身 ▪ He was dressed in black *from head to foot*. 彼は全身黒装束であった ▪ Keep your body straight *from head to heels*. 頭から足までまっすぐに伸ばしていなさい.
2 完全に，すっかり ▪ He is a gentleman *from head to foot*. 彼は全くの紳士である.

from head to toe 頭のてっぺんから足の先まで ▪ He examined me *from head to toe*. 彼は私を頭のてっぺんから足の先まで調べた.

gather to a head →come to a HEAD.

get [***have***] ***a big*** [***swelled, swollen***] ***head*** 〚しばしば否定文で〛うぬぼれる，うぬぼれている; 思い上がる，思い上がっている ▪ I'm not going to *get a big head* about my recent fame. 最近ちょっと名が売れたといっても，天狗になるつもりはない ▪ I don't want them to think I *have a swollen head*. あの人たちに思い上がっていると思われたくない.

get a head 《口》二日酔いをする ▪ If you drink too much alcohol, you *get a head*. 飲みすぎると二日酔いになる.

get (***a***) ***head*** 勢力を得る，強くなる ▪ Hydrophobia will *get head* even in the coldest weather. 恐水病は最も寒い時にも勢力を得る.

get [***have***] *one's* ***head above water*** なんとかうまく仕事をさばく ▪ I found it hard to *get my head above water*. 仕事をうまく処理するのは至難の業だった.

get *one's* ***head around*** 《英口》…を理解する ▪ I just can't *get my head around* American football. 僕にはアメフトはさっぱりわからない.

get *one's* ***head down*** 《口》 **1** 床につく，寝る ▪ I *get my head down* at 10. 私は10時に寝る.
2 (特に机に向かっての)仕事に戻る ▪ I must *get my head down* to finish this work. 私はこの仕事を仕上げるため仕事に戻らなければならない.

get [***have***] *one's* ***head examined*** 気が狂っている，すっかり誤っている ▪ You like this story? Go *get your head examined*. 君はこの物語が好きなのかい? 頭を診てもらうんだな.

get [***be***] ***in over*** *one's* ***head*** 大変難しい[複雑な]状況を扱おうとする ▪ Don't *get in over your head* when choosing a pet. ペットを選ぶ際には手に負えないものは避けること.

get ... into *a person's* ***head*** …を人の頭に入れる ▪ I can't *get* the idea *into his head*. 私はその考えを彼の頭に入れることができない.

get into *one's* ***head*** **1** (酒が)頭に回る ▪ A little wine *gets into his head*. 彼はワインをちょっと飲んでも頭にくる.
2 (考えなど)を持つようになる ▪ I can't *get* the idea *into my head*. その考えを持つようにはなれない.
3 理解する，習い覚える ▪ I just can't *get* Latin grammar *into my head*. ラテン文法はどうにも理解できない.

get it into *one's* ***head to*** *do* ... 急に何か(ばかげ

たこと)をしようと決める ▪ He *got it into his head to* have a swim at midnight. 真夜中に彼は突然ひと泳ぎしようと決めた.

get (***it***) ***into*** *one's* (***thick***) ***head that*** 《口》…と考えるようになる ▪ He has *got it into his head that* he is a genius. 彼は自分は天才だと考えるようになった ▪ She *got it into her head that* he would want to hunt. 彼女は彼が猟をしたくなるだろうと考えだした ▪ I finally *got it into my thick head that* it would never work. ついにはそれが決してうまくいくまいと思い込むようになった.

get it through *one's* (***thick***) ***head how*** …ということを理解する, ということがわかり始める ▪ I never could *get it through my thick head how* the secret had leaked out. その秘密がどのようにして漏れたのかどうしても理解できなかった.

get ... out of *a person's* ***head*** (考えなど)を人に忘れさせる[捨てさせる] ▪ I cannot *get* the wrong notion *out of his head*. 私はその誤った考えを彼に捨てさせることができない.

get ... out of *one's* (***thick***) ***head*** (考えなど)を忘れる, 捨てる ▪ You must *get out of your head* the idea that you are rich. あなたは自分は金持ちだという考えを捨てなければならない.

get ... through *a person's* ***head*** …を人に理解させる[信じさせる] ▪ We could hardly *get* our talk *through his head*. 私たちの話を彼にほとんど理解させられなかった.

get ... through *one's* ***head*** …を理解する ▪ He could not *get* it *through his head* that his wife was leaving him. 彼は妻が自分を捨てようとしているということが理解できなかった.

give a head 《口》(二日酔いの)頭痛を起こさせる ▪ The liquor *gave* me *a head*. その酒で二日酔いして頭痛がした.

give *a person* ***a head start*** 人を他より先にスタートさせる ▪ This picture book helps *give* infants *a head start* in language acquisition. この絵本は幼児に早く言語を習得させるのに役立つ.

give a horse its head 手綱を放して馬を自由に行かせる ▪ *Give the horse its head*. It will tire itself out. 手綱を放して馬を自由に行かせなさい. 馬はすっかり疲れきってしまうでしょう.

give head 《俗》オーラルセックスをする.

give *a person his* ***head*** 人に思うように[自由に]させる ▪ *Give* him *his head*; he can't work under restrictions. 彼に思うようにさせなさい. 束縛のもとでは働けないのだから.

go above [***over***] *a person's* ***head*** **1** 人にむずかしくてわからない ▪ His speech *went above the boys' heads*. 彼の話は少年たちには難しくてわからなかった ▪ What his math teacher said simply *went over his head*. 数学の先生の言っていることが彼には全く理解できなかった.

2 (人より)上位の人の助言を求める ▪ He *went above the captain's head* to ask what to do. 彼はその大尉の頭越しに上の人の所へ行ってどうすべきかを尋ねた.

go (***and***) ***put your head in a bucket*** = Go (and) jump in the LAKE.

go [***compete***] ***head to head*** (***with*** *a person*) (しばしばビジネス・スポーツで人と)直接対決する ▪ The league's top two teams *went head to head* for the championship. リーグの上位2チームが優勝をかけて直接対決した.

go off *one's* ***head*** 気が狂う ▪ He must have *gone off his head* to say such a thing. 彼がそんなことを言うとは気が狂ったにちがいない.

go out of *a person's* ***head*** (ある事を)忘れる ▪ It has quite *gone out of my head*. 私はそれをすっかり忘れていた.

go over *a person's* ***head*** = go above a person's HEAD.

go to *one's* [***the***] ***head*** **1** (酒が)酔わせる, 頭にくる ▪ The whisky *went to my head*. ウィスキーが私の頭にきた.

2 興奮させる, 逆上させる; うぬぼれさせる ▪ His successes have *gone to his head*. たびたびの成功で彼はのぼせている.

grow to a head →come to a HEAD.

hang (***down***) *one's* ***head*** (***in shame*** [***guilt***], ***for shame***) (恥ずかしさ・きまり悪さで)頭をたれる; うなだれる, 恥じる ▪ He *hung his head down* and walked away. 彼はうなだれて歩み去った ▪ He *hung down his head* and withdrew. 彼はきまり悪そうに引き下がった ▪ Tom *hung his head in shame* at failing his test for the third time. トムは3度目の不合格に恥じ入った ▪ She stammered, and *hung her head for shame*. 彼女は口ごもり顔を伏せた.

have a clear head 頭脳明晰である; (酒・疲労にやられず)頭が冴えている ▪ I want to *have a clear head* tomorrow. 私はあすは冴えた頭でいたい.

have a (***good***) [***a poor, no***] ***head for*** …の頭がある[ない] ▪ Ask her. She *has a good head for* figures. 彼女に頼めよ. 計算が得意だから ▪ He *had a poor head for* science. 彼は科学の頭がなかった.

have a (***good***) ***head for heights*** 高所でも平気でいられる ▪ It's absolutely necessary to *have a good head for heights*. 高所でも平気でいられることが絶対に必要だ ▪ I won't go up the tower. I *have* no *head for heights*. 私は塔に登るのはごめんだ. 高所恐怖症でね.

have a good [***nice, full,*** etc.] ***head of hair*** ふさふさした[濃い]髪を持っている ▪ My father *had a good head of hair* (on him). 父は濃い髪をしていた ▪ He's now 68 and still *has a full head of hair*. 彼はもう68歳だが髪はまだふさふさしている.

have a (***good***) ***head on*** *one's* ***shoulders*** **1** 良識がある, 分別がある ▪ He is the only one who *has a head on his shoulders*. 良識があるのは彼だけだ.

2 聡明である ▪ She *has a good head on her shoulders* and can be depended on. 彼女は非常

に賢く頼りがいがある.

3 抜け目がない ▪ He *had a head on his shoulders*; he was well prepared to face his future. 彼に抜かりはなく将来への備えも充分だった.

4 有能である, 実際的能力がある ▪ He *has a head on his shoulders* and can do any job well. 彼は有能だから, どんな仕事でもうまくやることができる. ☞a (good) head は one's head となることもある.

have a head (ビールなどが)泡が立つ ▪ The beer *has a* [no] *head*. そのビールは泡が立つ[気が抜けている].

have a head like a sieve 《口》ひどく忘れっぽい ▪ Really you*'ve a head like a sieve*. ほんとに君はひどく忘れっぽいね. ☞sieve「ふるい」.

***have a head* (*on one*)** 《口》二日酔いで頭が痛い ▪ I *have a* shocking *head on* me. 私は二日酔いで頭がひどく痛い.

***have* [*get*] *a head start* (*on*)** **1** …に先んずる, より出足が早い, 先に始めて優位に立つ ▪ They *had a head start on* us, but soon we caught up with them. 彼らの方が出足が早かったが, じきに我々は追いついた ▪ We want to *get a head start* in the spring election. 春の選挙で早くスタートを切って優位に立ちたいものだ.

2 早くから…する ▪ He *had a head start on* his ambition to be a doctor. 彼は早くから医者になろうという大望をいだいていた.

have* [*keep*] *a level head →LEVEL[1].

have a poor head at …がへたである ▪ He *has a poor head at* figures. 彼は計算がへただ.

have an old head on young shoulders 若くても思慮が深い[賢い] ▪ He *has an old head on young shoulders* and handles his business very well. 彼は若いが思慮深く, 事業をみごとに経営している.

(*have*) *one's head in the clouds* 夢想家で(ある), 空想にふけって(いる) ▪ He is very pleasant, but he *has his head in the clouds*. 彼は非常に快活だが, 夢想家である ▪ Don't go about all day with *your head in the clouds*. 一日中空想にふけってぶらぶらしてはいけない.

***have one's head in the sand* (*like an ostrich*)** →bury one's head in the sand like an OSTRICH.

have one's head screwed on backwards 分別がない, 非常識なふるまいをする ▪ He must have *had his head screwed on backwards* to do such a thing. そんなことをするなんて彼はきっと分別を失っていたのだろう.

have one's head screwed on the right way →have one's head SCREWed on right.

have one's head* (*stuck*) *up one's ass [《英口・卑》***arse***]《米卑》短絡的である, 自己中心的である, 周りが見えていない ▪ I would work with him if he didn't *have his head up his ass*. 彼が自分勝手でなかったらいっしょに働くのだが ▪ You're right. I did *have my head up my arse* at that time. 君の言う通りだ. あのとき僕は自分のことしか考えていなかったよ.

have no head for →have a (good) HEAD for.

head and shoulders **1** → (by) HEAD and shoulders.

2 頭と肩までの(写真など) ▪ There's a *head and shoulders* portrait of Lady Moorhead on the wall. 壁にモーヘッド夫人の肩から上の肖像画がかかっている.

3 [[しばしば above や比較級・最上級を伴って]] 頭と肩だけ(高いなど); はるかに[ずば抜けて]すぐれて ▪ He walked among them, *head and shoulders* taller than his neighbors. 彼は彼らにまじって歩いたが, 隣りの人々より頭と肩だけ高かった ▪ His was *head and shoulders* the best speech. 彼の演説が断然最もよかった ▪ He is *head and shoulders* above any other man in the office. 彼は会社の誰よりもずば抜けてすぐれている.

***head first* [*foremost*]** **1** 頭から先に, まっさかさまに ▪ He plunged *head first* into the water. 彼はまっさかさまに水の中に飛び込んだ.

2 まっしぐらに, 唐突に; 無鉄砲に ▪ Don't barge *head first* into another person's room. 人の部屋へだしぬけに飛び込んではいけない.

one's ***head is spinning like a top*** (大量の情報を詰め込むのに)頭がくらくらする, めまいがする ▪ There was so much to learn that *her head was spinning like a top*. 覚えなければならないことが山ほどあって彼女は頭がくらくらした. ☞「こまのようにくるくる回っている」が原義.

head of the river (追突レース (bumping race) の)先頭のボートの位置; 先頭の位置を占めるボート[乗組員, 大学] ▪ New College bumped Magdalen and went *head of the river*. ニューカレッジ組はモードリン組に追突し, 先頭ボートとなった.

do a person's ***head off*** 人がうんざりするほど…する ▪ He argued [cried] *her head off*. 彼は彼女がうんざりするほど議論した[泣き叫んだ].

do one's ***head off*** 《口》過度に[ひどく]…する ▪ He argued [cried, ran, studied] *his head off*. 彼は猛烈に議論した[泣き叫んだ, 走った, 勉強した].

head over ears 深くはまりこんで (→over HEAD and ears) ▪ He was *head over ears* in debt when he married her. 彼が彼女と結婚したときは借金で首が回らなかった.

head over heels*/*heels over head **1** まっさかさまに, もんどりうって ▪ He fell from the roof *head over heels*. 彼は屋根からもんどりうって落ちた.

2 《米俗》深くはまりこんで, うつつを抜かして (*in*) ▪ He fell *head over heels in* love with Helen. 彼はヘレンに首ったけほれこんだ ▪ He is *head over heels in* debt. 彼は借金で首が回らない.

3 大急ぎで, 考える暇もなく, 向こう見ずに ▪ Away he went *head over heels* like a shot rabbit. 彼は撃たれたウサギのようにめちゃくちゃに走り去った.

head scratching 困惑, とまどい ▪ His statement caused some *head scratching* among the residents. 彼の発言が住民の間にやや困惑を招いた.

head-to-head **1** 一騎打ちの ▪ The two companies are expected to go *head-to-head* in the markets. 両社は市場において一騎打ち勝負を行うと考えられている.
2 (反対案を議論するために)対峙[対決]して ▪ It is not worth arguing *head-to-head* with this person. この人物とは論議するに値しない.

head to tail (同一方向に)一列に並んで ▪ A convoy of lorries was proceeding *head to tail*. 一団のトラックが一列に並んで進んでいた.

heads and points **1** (くぎ・くさびが)交互に反対に打ちこまれて ▪ The two wedges in each groove would lie *heads and points*. おのおののみぞの二つのくさびは交互に反対に打ちこまれているだろう.
2 (人が)交互に反対に寝ころんで ▪ They lie *heads and points* one by the other against the fire. 彼らは暖炉の向かいに交互に反対に寝ころんでいる.
3 (クジラが)右往左往して ▪ Whales were blowing *heads and points*. クジラが(攻撃されて)潮を吹きながら右往左往していた.

H

Heads I win, tails I lose [***you win***]. 表なら私の勝ち, 裏なら私の負け[あなたの勝ち] ▪ Bill tossed the coin into the air and said: "*Heads I win; tails I lose.*" ビルは硬貨を空中に投げて「表なら私の勝ち, 裏なら私の負け」と言った.

Heads I win, tails you lose. 表なら私の勝ち, 裏ならあなたの負け《昔, ペテン師がぼんやり者とやった遊びの文句であり, またその遊びの名》; いずれにしても私の勝ち, 一方的な不公平な取り決め ▪ *Heads, I win. Tails, you lose.*—Wait a minute ... that doesn't sound like a fair game. 表なら僕の勝ち, 裏なら君の負け—ちょっと待て. そいつはフェアではないようだが.

head(***s***) ***or tail***(***s***) 《口》丁または半, 表または裏 ▪ One person tosses the coin up and the other calls *heads or tails* as he pleases. 一人がコインを投げ上げると, 他の人が思うままに表または裏と言う ▪ *Heads or tails?* —Heads. —Heads it is. You win. 表か裏か?—表だ—表が出た. 君の勝ちだ.

heads roll 首を据えかえる, 更迭する ▪ *Heads* should *roll* over the losses. 損失の責任をとってトップを辞任させるべきだ. ☞かつて失敗の責任をとってリーダーが打ち首になったことから.

Heads up! 《口》用心しなさい, 注意しなさい ▪ *Heads up*, boys*!* A train is coming. おい, みんな注意しなさい! 列車が来ているよ.

heads will roll 首切りがあるだろう ▪ The Company is not making a profit. *Heads will roll* for this. 会社は収益をあげていない. そのため首切りがあるだろう. ☞特におどし文句のことが多い.

Heads you win, tails I lose. どちらにしてもあなたの勝ち, 一方的な不公平な取り決め ▪ It's a case of *heads you win, tails I lose*. それは「いずれにしてもあなたの得」の一例だ.

heels over head →HEAD over heels.

hide** one's **head in the sand (***like an ostrich***) →bury one's head in the sand like an OSTRICH.

hit** one's **head against a (***stone, brick***) ***wall*** →beat one's HEAD against a wall.

hit** a person **over the head **1** 人の頭をなぐる ▪ She *hit* him *over the head* with a vase. 彼女は花瓶で彼の頭をなぐった.
2 人に(...を)くどいほど強調する, くどくど言う (*with*) ▪ We have to *hit* the employees *over the head with* this fact. 従業員たちにこの事実を繰り返し力説せねばならない.

hit the (***right***) ***nail on the head*** →NAIL[1].

hold** one's **head high 高慢にふるまう, 尊大にかまえる ▪ They *held their heads high* in the world. 彼らは世間で高慢にふるまった.

hold** one's **head up (***high***) 頭をあげている, 威厳を保つ; 意気を失わない ▪ You are out of debt; now you can *hold your head up high*. 君は借金から脱したからもう頭をあげて歩ける.

hold ... in** one's **head ...を覚えることができる ▪ He *holds* all these figures *in his head*. 彼はその数字をみな覚えることができる.

hold ... over** a person's **head →HOLD[2].

in** one's **head 顔の中で《ほとんど意味はない》 ▪ His eyes burned *in his head*. 彼の目は燃えた ▪ He had an eye *in his head* to find it. 彼はそれを見つけるだけの目を持っていた.

keep** one's **head (危機などに際して)落ち着いている ▪ I was frightened, but I still *kept my head*. 私はびっくり仰天したが, でも落ち着いていた.

keep** one's **head above (***the***) ***ground*** **1** 首を地上に出している ▪ The ferret *kept his head above the ground* for about a minute. イタチは1分間ばかり首を地上に出していた.
2 生きている, 命をつないでいる ▪ They could scarcely *keep their heads above ground*. 彼らはほとんど命をつないでいることができなかった.

keep** one's **head above water **1** 首を水上に出している ▪ Try to *keep your head above water* while learning to swim. 泳ぎを習っている間は首を水上に出しておくようにしなさい.
2 おぼれないでいる ▪ He managed to *keep his head above water*. 彼はどうにかしておぼれないでいた.
3 借金せずにいる ▪ He had difficulty *keeping his head above water*. 彼は借金せずにいるのに苦労した.
4 かろうじて生きている ▪ I think we can *keep our heads above water*. 我々は何とか命をつないでいけると私は思う.

keep head against →bear HEAD against.

keep** one's **head below the parapet 秘密を暴露しないでいる ▪ It is better to always *keep your head below the parapet*. 秘密はそっとしておくに限る. ☞parapet「(敵の攻撃を防御するための)胸壁」.

keep [***get***] ***one's head down*** **1** 身を隠している[隠す], 目につかないようにしている[する] ▪ The police officer decided to *keep his head down* until the danger was over. 警察官は危険が去るまで身を隠していようと決心した ▪ They *kept their heads down* and survived the economic recession. 彼らはひたすら自重して経済不況を乗り切った.

2 集中して取り組む, 仕事に精を出す ▪ All I had to do was *get my head down* in training. ただ練習に打ちこみさえすればよかった.

knock* [*bang*]** *one's* ***head against a brick wall → beat one's HEAD against a (stone, brick) wall.

knock ... on the head 《英口》 ...をするのをやめる ▪ Do you still go jogging?—No, I *knocked* that *on the head* a while ago. 今でもまだジョギングをやっているのか—いや, 少し前にやめたよ.

knock* [*bang*] *their heads together 《主に英口》(懲らしめて)道理を悟らせる, 分別を持たせる, (けんか・悪事を)やめさせる ▪ Those boys should have *their heads knocked together*. その少年たちは懲らしめてけんかをやめさせるべきである. ☞ 通例 have their heads knocked together の形で ▪ Someone has to *bang their heads together* somehow. 誰かが何とかして彼らをしかって仲直りさせなければならない ▪ I'd like to *bang those stupid politicians' heads together*. あの愚かな政治家を懲らしめて分別を持たせたいものだ.

laugh* [*scream, shout* etc.]** *one's* ***head off →LAUGH[2]; SCREAM[2]; SHOUT[2].

lay *one's* ***head on the block*** → put one's HEAD on the (chopping) block.

lay* [*put*]** (*one's*) ***heads together 額を集めて相談する ▪ *Lay your heads together* and think out a scheme. 額を集めて相談して案を考え出してくれ.

let *a person* ***have his head*** 《口》 人を思うようにさせる[自由にさせる] ▪ It is better to *let* a young man *have his head* for a bit. 若者にはちょっとの間気ままにさせるほうがよい.

light in the head →LIGHT[2].

lose *one's* ***head*** **1** 首を切られる ▪ He escaped *losing his head* for the murder. 彼は殺人のかどで死刑になることを免れた.

2 狼狽する, あわてる ▪ You must not *lose your head*. 君は狼狽してはいけない.

3 理性を失う; 取り乱す; かっとなる ▪ I'm sorry I *lost my head* completely. すっかり取り乱してすみません.

4 夢中になる, 気が狂う ▪ He has *lost his head* over her. 彼は彼女にすっかり夢中だ.

make head 進む, 前進する ▪ We shall *make head* with the business this year. 今年はその事業が進むだろう.

make head against **1** ...に抵抗する ▪ They *made* strong *head against* the rebels. 彼らは反乱軍に強く抵抗した.

2 ...に抗して[向かって]進む ▪ They *made head against* the enemy. 彼らは敵に向かって進んだ.

3 ...に抵抗して打ち勝つ ▪ We are always *making head against* the superstition. 我々はいつもその迷信に抗して打ち勝ちつつある.

***make head or tail of* [*out of*]** 〚主に否定文で〛 ...がわかる ▪ I cannot *make head or tail of* what you say. あなたの言われることは私にはさっぱりわからない.

make *a person's* ***head swim* [*go round, spin*]** **1** 人の目を回す ▪ I don't like these merry-go-rounds. They *make my head swim*. この回転木馬はきらいだ. 乗ると目が回るから.

2 人の頭を混乱させる ▪ If you drink too much of it, it will *make your head go round*. それをあまり飲みすぎると, 頭が混乱するよ.

3 人を驚きあきれさす ▪ When politicians talk in hundreds of millions, it *makes my head go round*. 政治家たちが何億ドルなどと話すと私は驚きあきれてしまう.

need *one's* ***head examined* [*examining*]/ *should have*** *his* ***head examined***/ 《英》 ***need*** *one's* ***head testing*** 《戯》(人の異常な意見・行動に)頭がいかれているのではないか, ばかなことを, 正気の沙汰とは思えない ▪ You spent $300 on a scarf? You *need your head examined*. スカーフ1枚に300ドルはたいたって? 気は確かか ▪ You take a boat out in this storm! You *should have your head examined*! このあらしの中でボートを出すなんて, どうかしてるのじゃないか?

nod *one's* ***head*** (承知・賛成の意味で)うなずく ▪ She *nodded her head* when I asked her to come. 私が来てくださいと言ったら彼女はうなずいた.

not be right in the head →RIGHT[1].

not know if* [*whether*]** *one* ***is on *one's* ***head or*** *one's* ***heels*** 《口》 困惑する, 狼狽する ▪ There was such a noise that I did*n't know if* I *was on my head or my heels*. 非常にやかましかったので私は困惑した.

odd in the head 気が狂って, 変で ▪ She's been *odd in the head* since her accident. 彼女はその事故以来ずっと気が狂っている.

of *one's* ***own head*** 自分で思いついて ▪ Did he do it *of his own head* or by our order? 彼はそれを自分で思いついてしたのかそれとも我々の命に従ったのか.

of the first head **1** (シカが)初めて枝角(えだづの)のはえた ▪ I saw a buck *of the first head* just now. ついさっき初めて枝角のはえたシカを見かけた.

2 新しく貴族に列せられた[位階の昇進した] ▪ He was a gentleman *of the first head*. 彼は新しく貴族になった紳士だった.

off *one's* ***head*** 《口》 **1** 激しく興奮して, 激怒して; 自制を失って ▪ When I spoke to him he went *off his head*. 私が話しかけると彼は激怒した.

2 気が狂って《一時的なもの》 ▪ He is *off his head*. 彼は気が狂っている ▪ She went *off her head*. 彼女は気が狂った ▪ Aren't you *off your head*? 気は確かか.

off the top of *one's* ***head*** →TOP[1].

on* [*upon*]** *a person's* ***head **1** (災い・恨み・恵みが)人の上にふりかかって ▪ Threats of vengeance were *on his head*. 復しゅうの恐れが彼の上にふりかかっていた.

2 (罪・責任が)人の上にかかって ▪ I don't want it

laid *on my head.* その責任を私の上にかぶせないでくれ.

3 自己の責任で, 自業自得で (*own*) ▪ If you are caught speeding, it's *on your own head.* スピード違反で捕まってもそれは自業自得だ.

on** one's **head **1** さか立ちして ▪ I can stand *on my head.* 私はさか立ちができる.

2《口・軽蔑》楽々と(できる) ▪ I can do it *on my head.* そんなことは楽にできる.

do ***... on** one's **head*** →on one's HEAD 2.

on** a person's* **(*own*)** ***head be it 《文》あとでうまくいかなくても(それは)自己の責任だ, 自業自得だ ▪ *On her own head be it* if she decides to leave college early. 彼女が大学を中退すると決めたら, あとでどうなっても自分の責任だ.

open** one's **head 《米俗》話す, 語る (↔ shut one's HEAD (up)) ▪ He never *opens his head* to anybody. 彼は決して誰にも話しかけない ▪ I'm glad you didn't *open your head* about it. あなたがそれについて話さなかったのはうれしく思います. ☞head = mouth.

out of **[*off*]** *one's* ***head*** **[*skull*]** 《口》発狂して; (深酒・薬のせいで)記憶が飛んで, 泥酔して, 頭がぼんやりして ▪ They may think Christians *out of their heads.* キリスト教徒は気が狂っていると彼らは思うかもしれない ▪ He was totally *out of his skull* on smack. 彼はヘロインのせいで完全にラリっていた.

out of** one's **own head 《口》自分で考えて[案出して] ▪ It is not easy to write *out of one's own head.* 自分で創作するのは容易でない ▪ That idea is completely *out of my own head.* その案は全く私の考え出したものです.

over head **1** 頭上高く ▪ The roof was arched *over head.* 屋根は頭上高くアーチ形をなしていた.

2 頭を沈めて ▪ He was dipped *over head* in the water. 彼は頭を沈めて水につかった.

over** a person's **head **1** (危険・悪などが)頭上に落ちかかって; 迫って ▪ Danger was hanging *over his head.* 危険が彼の頭上に落ちかかっていた.

2 (当然の資格ある)人を飛び越えて(昇進するなど); 人をさしおいて, 相談もなく, 頭越しに ▪ He was promoted *over my head.* 彼は私を飛び越えて昇進した ▪ He went *over his supervisor's head* and appealed to the president. 彼は上司の頭を飛び越して社長に直訴した.

3 人に(むずかしすぎて)わからないで, 理解できないで ▪ He talks *over my head.* 彼の話は私にはむずかしすぎてわからない ▪ This calculus homework is way *over my head.* この微積分の宿題, 僕には全くチンプンカンプンだ ▪ The lecture went completely *over his head.* その講義は彼にはさっぱりわからなかった ▪ Don't teach *over the pupils' heads.* 生徒にわからないようなことを教えてはいけない.

4 →buy ... over a person's HEAD.

over** one's **head 人の頭上に, 身を守って ▪ They must have a roof *over their heads.* 彼らは頭上に守ってくれる屋根を持たねばならない.

over head and ears **1** すっかりつかってしまって ▪ He soused her in the water *over head and ears.* 彼は彼女をすっかり水につけた.

2 深くはまりこんで ▪ He is *over head and ears* in work. 彼は仕事に夢中になっている ▪ I ran *over head and ears* into debt. 首が回らぬほど借金した.

over head and heels = over HEAD and ears 2.

per head 一人あたり ▪ In that year, Americans earned $15,000 *per head.* その年, 米国人は一人あたり1万5千ドル稼いだ.

pop into** a person's **head 急に思い出す, 思いつく ▪ It suddenly *popped into my head* that today is her birthday. 今日は彼女の誕生日だとふと気がついた.

pull **[*take*]** *one's* ***head out of the sand*** 現実を直視する ▪ You should *take your head out of the sand* on this issue. 君はこの問題に関して現実をよく見据えないといけない.

put a **(*new*)** ***head on*** 《俗》**1** (顔)にげんこを食わす, をなぐる, 攻撃する ▪ He threatened to *put a head on* the man. 彼は男をなぐってやるとおどした.

2 ...を完全に負かす, に大勝する (= put a new FACE on 2) ▪ He *put a new head on* the challenger. 彼は挑戦者に完勝した.

3 ...を黙らせる, やりこめる ▪ Kelly will *put a head on* you. ケリーはあなたをやりこめるだろう.

4《口》(ビールなどの)麦芽醸造酒をあわ立たせる ▪ Lower the glass a foot or two from the faucet to *put a head on* the beer. ビールに泡が立つようにグラスを樽の蛇口から1, 2フィート下げろ ▪ The music was loud enough to *put a new head on* the beer I was drinking. 音楽は私が飲んでいるビールに泡が立つほどの音量だった. ☞head = froth.

put **[*hold*]** ***a pistol*** **[*gun*]** ***to** a person's **head*** 人を脅す, 脅迫する ▪ They *held a gun to my head*, forcing me to sign the contract. 彼らは私を脅して無理やり契約書に署名させた ▪ Their insistence on action has *put a pistol to my head.* 実力行使をすると言って彼らに脅された.

put a pistol to** one's **head ピストル自殺をする ▪ Smith *put a pistol to his head.* スミスはピストル自殺をした.

put an idea in **[*into*]** *a person's* ***head*** 人にある考えを吹きこむ ▪ No, we're not moving—what *put that idea in your head?* いや, 引っ越さないよ—どうしてそう思うの.

put an old head on young shoulders 若い者を慎重老練にする ▪ They say you can't *put an old head on young shoulders.* 若い者を慎重老練にはできないといわれる.

put **[*raise, stick, lift*]** *one's* ***head above the parapet*** 《英》公然と意見を述べる, 秘密を暴露する, 危険を冒す ▪ Are you prepared to *raise your head above the parapet?* 敢えて意見を述べる覚悟はできているか ▪ They are reluctant to *put their head above the parapet.* 彼らは秘密を白日

の下に曝(さら)すことに気が進まない. ☞parapet「(敵の攻撃を防御するための)胸壁」.

put** one's **head down しばらく眠る ▪ I'm just going to *put my head down* for an hour. これからちょっと1時間ばかり仮眠をとる ▪ Why don't you *put your head down* for a while? しばらく横になったらどうだ.

put** one's **head into a noose →put one's neck into the NOOSE.

put** one's **head into the lion's mouth 進んで危険[冒険]に身をさらす, 虎穴に入る ▪ He had stupidly *put his head into the lion's mouth.* 愚かにも彼は進んで危険に身をさらした.

put** [**lay**] one's **head** [**neck**] **on the** (**chopping**) **block 失敗[敗北, 処罰]を覚悟の上でやる, 非難を承知で困難なことをする ▪ The government has *laid its head on the block* by drafting the new law. 政府は失敗を覚悟でその新法を作った ▪ He dutifully *laid his head on the chopping block* and died. 彼は忠義者らしく自らを危険に曝(さら)して命を落とした. ☞block「首切り台」.

put** (one's) **heads together 協議する, いっしょに解決策を見つける, 額を集めて相談する (＝lay (one's) HEADs together) ▪ We *put our heads together* to solve the problem. 我々はその問題を解決するために協議した ▪ Let's *put our heads together* and find a solution. 頭を寄せ合って解決策を探そう.

put ideas into** a person's **head 人に途方もない[実現できそうもない]考えを吹き込む ▪ I really do not want to *put ideas into her head* about God and heaven. 私は神とか天国とかの実現できそうもない考えを本当に彼女に吹き込みたくないんだ.

put ... in** [**into**] a person's **head …を人に思い出させる ▪ He *put* the fact *into my head.* 彼はその事実を私に思い出させた.

***put it into** [**in**] a person's **head to** do* 人に…する気にさせる ▪ What *put it into his head to* do such a thing? 彼はなぜそんなことをする気になったのか.

put ... out of** a person's **head …を人に忘れさせる, (考え)を人にやめさせる ▪ You said something just now that *put* everything *out of my head.* あなたが今しがた何か言ったので何もかも忘れてしまった.

put ... out of** one's **head …を忘れる, (考え)をやめにする ▪ You can *put* that idea *out of your head.* あなたはその考えはやめにしなさい ▪ Later he *put* the events *out of his head.* その後彼はその出来事のことを忘れた.

rear** [**raise**] one's (**ugly**) **head (通例悪いものが)現れる; 頭をもたげる ▪ Tuberculosis suddenly *reared its ugly head* right here. 結核が突然この地で発生した ▪ Jealousy *reared its ugly head* and destroyed their marriage. 嫉妬が醜い頭をもたげてきて彼らの結婚はおじゃんになった.

***run** one's **head against a** (**stone**) **wall** [**a post**]* = beat one's HEAD against a (stone, brick) wall.

sell ... over** a person's **head →buy ... over a person's HEAD.

shake** one's **head **1** 首を横に振る《no を意味する》 ▪ John *shook his head* when I asked him whether he was ill. 病気かと尋ねると, ジョンは首を横に振った.

2 かぶりを振る (*at*)《疑念・不賛成を示す》 ▪ All the villagers *shook their heads at* his disappearance. 村人はみな彼の失踪をいぶかって頭を振った.

show** one's **head →SHOW[2].

***shut** one's **head** (**up**)* 《米俗》〚主に命令文で〛黙る, 話をやめる (↔open one's HEAD) ▪ *Shut your head up.* 黙れ! ▪ I told them to *shut their heads up.* 私は彼らに話をやめろと言った.

snap** a person's **head off →SNAP a person's nose off.

soft** [**weak**] **in the head 愚かな; 気が変で ▪ You must be *weak in the head* if you think so. そう思うなら君は愚か者にちがいない.

stand head and shoulders above …よりはるかに力量がすぐれている ▪ She *stands head and shoulders above* the other singers. 彼女は他の歌手よりはるかにすぐれている.

stand on** one's **head **1** →on one's HEAD 1.

2《口》全力を尽くす ▪ I *stood on my head* trying to explain it. それを説明するのに全力を尽くした.

stand** [**turn**] **... on its head **1** (ことの原則・解釈)を全く逆にする, くつがえす ▪ The most effective way is to *turn* their strategy *on its head.* 最も効果的な手は彼らの戦略を逆手に利用するやり方だ.

2 …を以前と全く違う扱いをする, 完全に変える ▪ Her album *turned* the music industry *on its head.* 彼女のアルバムが音楽業界を一変させた.

standing on** one's **head →on one's HEAD.

***take it into** one's **head to** do* [**that**] **1** (急に)…しようと思いつく; する気になる ▪ He *took it into his head to* get married. 彼は結婚しようと思いついた ▪ John *took it into his head that* the room could be improved. ジョンはその部屋は改良できると思いついた.

2 (…しようと)決める, 決心する ▪ He *took it into his head to* dislike her. 彼は彼女をきらうことにした.

3 信じる[思う]ようになる ▪ He *took it into his head that* I was opposing him. 彼は私が反対していると思うようになった.

take the head (馬・人が)束縛[支配]を振り切る ▪ It's high time you *took the head* and became your own man. お前もそろそろ他人の影響を受けずに自分の主張を持ってよい頃合いだ.

talk** a person's **head off →TALK[2].

talk over** a person's **head …には分からない話をする ▪ They *talked over my head* all the time. 彼らがずっと続けていた話は僕にはさっぱり分からなかった.

***the head and front** (**of**)* (…の)頂点[絶頂]; (の)最も顕著[重要]な部分 (cf. Sh., *Oth.* 1. 3. 80); (の)本質[本体] ▪ *The head and front of* your offending is your not writing explicitly. あなたの悪い点はつまるところ, あなたがはっきりと書かないことにあるので

す ▪ This is *the head and front of* the matter. これがその問題の本質です.

the head honcho 《主に米口》トップ, 責任者 ▪ Ask Carl, he's *the head honcho* in our department. カールにお尋ねください. 彼が当部局の責任者ですから. ☞honcho は日本語の「班長」より.

throw [***fling***] *oneself* ***at the head of*** …と結婚したい意をそぶりで示す ▪ She *throws herself at the head of* every unmarried man. 彼女は未婚の男ならだれかれとなく結婚したい意をそぶりで示す.

trouble [***bother***] *one's* ***head*** 心配する ▪ Don't *trouble your head* about me. 私のことは心配しないでください.

turn *a person's* ***head*** **1** 人をうぬぼれさせる ▪ Their flattery *turned her head*. 彼らがおだてるものだから彼女はうぬぼれてしまった.
2 (成功などが)人を夢中にさせる, のぼせ上がらせる; 狂気にさせる ▪ His successes *turned his head*. たびたびの成功で彼はのぼせ上がった.

H

turn *one's* ***head*** 後ろを振り向く ▪ She *turned her head* and looked at him. 彼女は振り向いて彼を見た.

turn heads とても注目される, 非常に注目を集める, ひどく関心を惹く ▪ The beautiful girl always *turns heads* when she walks in the street. その美しい少女が通りを歩くとみなが振り向く.

Two heads are better than one. 《諺》二人いれば一人より知恵も出よう, 「三人寄れば文殊の知恵」(《聖》*Eccles*. 4. 9).

upside the head 頭[顔]の横を ▪ The police knocked suspects *upside the head* with those nightsticks. 警察は例の警棒で容疑者たちの横っ面をなぐりつけた.

use *one's* ***head*** [***bean, loaf***] 頭を使う, 常識にならう ▪ Don't be silly and *use your head*! ばかを言わずによく考えろ! ▪ If I had *used my bean*, I wouldn't be in trouble now. あのとき常識的に行動していたら, 今は困っていないだろうに.

want *a person's* ***head on a plate*** [***platter***] (怒って)人を罰してやりたい ▪ The director was furious and *wanted Jed's head on a platter*. 理事はかんかんでジェドを処罰するといきまいた.

weak in the head →soft in the HEAD.

wet the baby's head 赤んぼう誕生の祝杯をあげる ▪ We went to the pub to *wet the baby's head*. 我々は赤ちゃん誕生の祝杯をあげにパブへ行った.

with *one's* ***head in the air*** いばって ▪ He went about *with his head in the air*. 彼はいばって歩き回った.

with *one's* ***head in the clouds*** (人が)ぼんやりして, うわの空で, 空想に耽って ▪ My daughter's been walking around all day *with her head in the clouds*. 娘は朝からずっと上の空で歩き回っている.

head^{2} /hed/ 動 ***head for the devil*** 破滅への道をたどる ▪ He was *heading for the devil*. 彼は破滅への道をたどっていた.

headache /hédèɪk/ 名 ***a real headache*** 大問題, 非常に困った問題, 悩みの種 ▪ Traffic jams are *a real headache* for every driver in a big city. 交通渋滞は大都市のドライバー全員の頭痛の種だ.

have a headache 頭痛がする ▪ I *have a* slight *headache*. 私は少し頭痛がする.

header /hédər/ 名 ***take a header*** 《口》(水泳で)まっさかさまに飛び込む; まっさかさまに落ちる; (目的に)まっしぐらに突進する ▪ He *took a header* into the financial world. 彼は財界に向こう見ずに飛び込んだ ▪ I *took a header* off the ladder. 私ははしごからまっさかさまに落ちた.

headlight /hédlàɪt/ 名 ***like a rabbit*** [***deer***] ***caught in the headlights*** (水鉄砲を食らったハトのように)立ちすくんで, 非常におびえて ▪ She just stood there, *like a rabbit caught in the headlights*. 彼女はおびえきってそこにただ立ち尽くしていた.

headline /hédlàɪn/ 名 ***be in headlines*** 見出し[トップ]に書き立てられている ▪ His name *was in headlines* in the newspapers. 彼の名は新聞のトップに書き立てられていた.

crash [***grab, hit, make***] ***the headlines*** 《口》見出しに書き立てられる, 大見出しになる; 有名になる《悪名の場合も含む》 ▪ His exploits *made the headlines*. 彼の手柄は新聞に大きく書きたてられた ▪ The time will soon come when space exploration doesn't *grab the headlines*. 宇宙探検がニュースで大々的に報道されない日が今にやってくるだろう.

go into headlines 新聞に大きく取り上げられる, 有名になる ▪ The terrible event will *go into headlines*. その恐ろしい事件は新聞の大見出しにされるだろう.

headway /hédwèɪ/ 名 ***make*** [***gain***] ***headway*** (船が)進行する; 前進する, 進歩する; はかどる ▪ The labor union *made* little *headway* in its efforts to organize the entire industry. 労働組合は全産業を組織する努力があまり進まなかった ▪ We haven't *made* any *headway* with our new friends. まだ新しい友だちとの関係が全然進んでいない.

heal /hiːl/ 動 ***heal*** *a person* ***of*** 人の(病気・傷など)を治す ▪ He *was healed of* his wound. 彼は傷がいえた.

health /helθ/ 名 ***a health farm*** 健康教室, ヘルスクラブ ▪ I stayed at *a health farm* for a month to lose some weight. 体重を落とすために1か月間ヘルスクラブに滞在した.

ask after *a person's* ***health*** (人)に元気かと尋ねる ▪ He *asks after her mother's health* every time he sees her. 彼は彼女に会うたびにお母さんはお元気かと尋ねる ▪ She was very concerned, and *your health was asked after*. 彼女がとても心配して君の具合はどうかと聞いたよ.

be restored to health 全快する, 本復する ▪ The patient will *be restored to health* immediately. 患者はじきに全快するだろう.

bring back to health (…を)全快させる ▪ The doctor *brought* her *back to health*. 医者は彼女を全快させた.

fall into ill health 健康を害する ▪ If you work so hard, you will *fall into ill health.* そんなに働くと，健康を害するよ．

for** one's **health **1** 保養のため ▪ He went to Switzerland *for his health.* 彼は保養のためスイスへ行った．

2《俗》〚否定文・疑問文で〛(ただ保養のために，から)物好きで ▪ I'm not in politics *for my health.* 物好きで政治をやっているのではない．

for the good [benefit] of** one's **health 保養のため ▪ He travels *for the benefit of his health.* 彼は保養のため旅行する．

Health is better than wealth.《諺》健康は富に勝る．

in bad [ill, poor] health からだが悪く; 健康がすぐれないで ▪ My father is a veteran and he is *in bad health.* 父は退役軍人で健康を害している ▪ The child is *in poor health* because of malnutrition. その子は栄養失調でからだが悪い．

in good health 健康で ▪ I am glad to hear that your child is *in good health* now. お子さんがもう元気になられたと聞いて喜んでいます．

keep in good health 健康である; (人を)健康にしておく ▪ Exercise will *keep* you *in good health.* 運動すれば，いつも健康でいられる．

(To) your health! ご健康を祝します《乾杯するときの文句》 ▪ Here's *to your health,* and may you live long. ご健康を祝し，ご長寿を祈念いたします．

heap /hiːp/ 名 ***a heap of***《口》多数の; 多量の (→HEAPs of) ▪ She has *a heap of* male friends. 彼女には大勢の男友達がいる ▪ I have *a heap of* work to do. ぼくにはする仕事がたくさんある．

a heap sight《米口》大いに，はるかに (much) ▪ There was *a heap sight* more corn. ずっと多くのトウモロコシがあった ▪ You are *a heap sight* smarter than him. あなたは彼よりずっと賢い．

all of a heap《口》 **1** どうと，どさりと，どたりと ▪ The horse fell *all of a heap.* 馬はどうと倒れた．

2 すっかり ▪ The news struck me *all of a heap.* そのニュースはすっかり私を驚かした．

at the top [bottom] of the heap [pile] (社会・組織の)頂点で支配して[底辺で服従して]，勝ち組[負け組]で ▪ He is still enjoying his place *at the top of the heap.* 彼は今なお組織のトップで君臨する地位を享受している ▪ The homeless are *at the bottom of the pile.* ホームレスの人々は社会の底辺で耐久生活をしている ▪ Henry now finds himself *at the top of the heap.* ヘンリーは今社会の最上層にいる．

collapse [fall] in [into] a heap どさりと倒れる ▪ She *collapsed in a heap* on the floor. 彼女は急に床にばったり倒れた．

***heaps better [more, older,** etc.]*《英口》ずっとよい[多い，古い，など] ▪ Help yourself—there's *heaps more.* 自由におあがりなさい．まだたくさんありますから ▪ She looks *heaps better* than yesterday. 彼女は昨日よりずっと調子よさそうだ．

heaps of《口》多数の; 多量の (→a HEAP of)《量を表すときは単数扱い》 ▪ There are *heaps of* books on this subject. この問題についての書物はたくさんある ▪ *Heaps of* money [time] is spent on testing. たくさんの金[時間]がテストに費やされた．

in a heap 積んで，重ねて; (人が)うずくまって; ぐしゃりと;《米俗》酒に酔って ▪ We laid hay *in a heap.* 我々は干し草を積み重ねた ▪ I saw her *in a heap.* 私は彼女がうずくまっているのを見た ▪ She sank to the ground *in a heap.* 彼女はぐにゃりと地上にへたばった ▪ They were all *in a heap* after the beer blast. 彼らはみな大ビールパーティーの後で酔っていた．

in heaps 積み重なって，たくさんに ▪ The bodies lay *in heaps.* 死体が累々と積み重なっていた．

knock [strike] ... all of a heap《口》…をすっかりぺしゃんこにする; の度肝(どぎも)を抜く ▪ It *knocked* the prosecution *all of a heap.* それはその遂行を全く不能にした ▪ My new employment *struck* him *all of a heap.* 私が新たに職についたので彼は仰天した．

the bottom of the heap [pile] (社会・組織の)底辺，最下位 ▪ They are candidates from *the bottom of the heap.* 彼らは最下位層からの立候補者である．

the top of the heap [pile] →TOP[1].

hear /hɪər/ 動 ***be the first** a person **hears of*** 初耳である ▪ She's getting married next Sunday.—Well, that'*s the first* I've *heard of* it! 彼女は今度の日曜に結婚するんだ—いや，それは知らなかったな．

can't hear** oneself **think《口》騒がしくて集中できない ▪ I'm trying to study and I *can hardly hear myself think.* 勉強に集中しようとしているけど騒音に気が散って仕方がない．

(Do) you hear me?《口》よく聞くんだぞ ▪ You can't go there—*do you hear me*? そこへ行ってはいけない．わかったか．

Hear, hear! (会議で賛意を表すとき)そうだ，賛成，謹聴(きんちょう) ▪ Each time the senator spoke, he was greeted with cries of "*Hear! hear!*" 上院議員が発言するたびに「そうだ，そうだ」という叫び声がそれに和した．

hear it said (that) …だと噂に聞く ▪ We often *hear it said that* the Japanese are good workers. 日本人はよく働くと言われるのをよく耳にする．

hear say《口》(…を)話[噂]に聞く ▪ I have *heard say* that the moon influences the weather. 月が天候に影響を与えると話に聞いている．☞hear say＝hear people say.

hear tell (of, that)《口》(…を)話[噂]に聞く ▪ I never *heard tell of* a man becoming a dressmaker. 男がドレスメーカーになるという話は聞いたことがない ▪ We *heard tell that* he had sold his land. 我々は彼が土地を売ったという噂を聞いた．☞hear tell of＝hear people tell of.

hear the case (判事が)審問する ▪ The judge has *heard the case.* 判事の審問がすんだ．

hear the last [the end] of →LAST[2].

hear things 空耳がする，幻聴が起きる ▪ I think you're just *hearing things.* それはただの空耳に過ぎ

ないと思うよ.

He'll* [*They'll,* etc.] *be hearing from me. 《口》彼[彼ら, など]に小言を言って[しかって]やる ▪ He'd better apologize to you or *he'll be hearing from me.* 彼が君にあやまりもしないようなら, 私が彼にやかましく言ってやる.

I hear …だそうである ▪ *I hear* (that) he was engaged. (=He was engaged, *I hear.*) 彼は婚約したそうだ.

I hear ya/I heard that 《口》同感, その通りだ, わかった ▪ I'm tired of working here. I'd really like to quit.—Yeah, *I hear ya!* ここの仕事はもううんざりだ. やめてしまいたいよ—うん, わかる, わかる.

let's hear it for 《米口》(人に)拍手[声援]を送ろう ▪ I just want to cheer. *Let's hear it for* the girls. ぜひ喝采したい. あの少女たちに拍手を送ろうよ.

make *oneself* [*one's* ***voice***] ***heard*** **1** (叫んで先方に)聞こえるようにする ▪ I could not *make myself heard* over the noise. 騒がしくて(いくら大声を出しても)先方へ聞こえなかった.

2 (相手に)聞き入れられる ▪ Don't worry. You'll soon *make your voice heard.* 心配するな. 君の声はやがて聞き入れられるよ.

3 意見を述べる ▪ He likes to *make himself heard.* 彼は意見を述べるのが好きである.

not hear the end of …をいつまでも持ち出される(のでうるさい) ▪ We shall *never hear the end of* the affair. この件をいつまでも持ち出されるのではたまらない.

Now hear this! 《米》今から重大発表をします ▪ *Now hear this!* Everyone is ordered to abandon ship. 緊急放送! 全員船から脱出せよ.

will not hear of …を許可しない ▪ My father *will not hear of* my having a car. 父はどうしても僕に車をもたせてくれない.

you could have heard a pin drop →A PIN might have been heard to drop.

You will be hearing from me [***us***]. こちらからお知らせします ▪ *You will be hearing from us* about this in due course. この件についてはいずれこちらからお知らせします.

hearing /híərɪŋ/ 名 ***beyond*** *a person's* ***hearing*** 人に聞こえない所に, 聞こえる範囲を越えて ▪ Their conversation was *beyond my hearing.* 彼らの会話は遠くて私には聞こえなかった.

come to *a person's* ***hearing*** 人の聞くところとなる ▪ The report *came to his hearing.* その報は彼の耳に入った.

from hearing 聞き取りで ▪ Can you write down English *from hearing*? あなたは聞き取りで英語を書き留めることができますか.

gain [***get, obtain***] ***a hearing*** 発言の機会を得る; (弁明・意見など)を聞いてもらう ▪ No socialists can *get a hearing* in that conservative town. その保守的な町では社会主義者の意見は聞いてもらえない.

give [***grant***] *a person* ***a fair hearing*** 人の言うことを公平に聞いてやる ▪ Did the House *give* Adams *a fair hearing*? 議会はアダムズの言い分を公平に聞いてやったのか ▪ They refused to *grant* him *a fair hearing.* 彼の話に公平に耳を貸さなかった.

give *a person* ***a hearing*** 人の言うこと[泣き言など]を聞いてやる ▪ If only someone would *give* me *a hearing*! どなたか私の訴えを聞いてくださればと思う.

hard of hearing →HARD of.

in *a person's* ***hearing*** 人の聞いている所で, 人に聞こえよがしに ▪ Don't talk about politics *in the hearing of* strangers. 見知らぬ人の聞いている所で政治の話をするな ▪ It was said *in their hearing.* それは彼らに聞こえよがしに言われた.

obtain a hearing →gain a HEARING.

out of hearing **1** (人に)聞こえない所[距離]に ▪ As soon as they went *out of hearing,* they cursed him heartily. 彼らは誰にも聞こえない所へ行くやいなや, 思う存分彼をののしった.

2 (自分に)聞こえない所[距離]に ▪ I live *out of hearing* of the sea. 私は海の音のせぬ所に住んでいる.

within hearing **1** (他人に)聞こえる所[距離]に ▪ When we came *within hearing,* I called out to him by name. 我々が相手に聞こえる所まで来たとき, 私は大声で彼の名を呼んだ.

2 (自分に)聞こえる所[距離]に ▪ He lives *within hearing* of the sea. 彼は海の音のする所に住んでいる.

without a hearing 審問[裁判]をせずに ▪ It is cruel to condemn someone *without a hearing.* 審問をせずに罪におとすのは酷だ.

hearsay /híərsèɪ/ 名 ***from*** [***by, on***] ***hearsay*** 噂で, 噂に ▪ I have it *from hearsay.* 私はそれを噂に聞いた.

heart /hɑːrt/ 名 ***a bleeding heart*** (社会的弱者に)大げさに同情を示す人, (同情に値しない人に対して)同情しすぎる人 ▪ Stop being such *a bleeding heart.* そんなに大げさに同情するのはよせ.

a change of heart 改心; (一般的に)心変わり ▪ The workers have suffered *a change of heart.* 労働者たちは心変わりした.

a faint heart 目標達成を妨げる臆病[勇気のなさ] ▪ He had *a faint heart,* though he pretended to help so willingly. 彼はびくびくしていた. 進んで手を貸すふりをしていたけれど. ☞Faint heart never won fair lady.「気弱な男が美女を妻になし得た例(ためし)がない」という17世紀初頭の諺から.

a heart of gold →GOLD.

(*a*) *heart of oak* 樫(かし)の心材; 剛勇心; 剛勇[忠勇]の士 ▪ He was *a heart of oak* and a pillar of the land. 彼は剛勇の士であり国の柱であった ▪ *hearts of oak* 英国戦艦と海兵.

a heart of stone 冷酷無情な心[人], 無慈悲な性行(の持ち主) ▪ You'll get no sympathy from him; he has *a heart of stone.* 彼に同情してはもらえないよ. 冷酷無情だから ▪ You would need *a heart of stone* to disagree. 反対するには心を鬼にせねばなるまい.

a heavy heart 悲しい気持ち, 憂鬱 ▪ He's had *a* very *heavy heart* all week. 彼は今週ずっとひどくふさいでいる.

a man* [*woman*] *after *one's* ***own heart*** …の気に入った男性[女性] (→after a person's own HEART) ▪ He likes music—*a man after my own heart.* 彼は音楽好きで, 私の眼鏡にかなった男性です.

a stout heart 《雅》勇気, 決断力 ▪ I shall meet death with *a stout heart.* 勇敢に死に立ち向かおう.

after *a person's* ***own heart*** 人の心にかなった, 望みどおりの (《聖》 *1 Sam.* 13, 14) ▪ This is a house *after my own heart.* これは私の望みどおりの家だ ▪ Clive was a man *after our own hearts.* クライブは我々の心にかなう人物だった.

allow the heart to rule the head (理屈ではなく)感情に左右される ▪ You should not *allow the heart to rule the head* in business. ビジネスでは感情に流されてはならない.

an open heart **1** 率直さ ▪ He told his troubles with *an open heart.* 彼は抱えている悩みを率直に語った.
2 親切, 寛大さ ▪ She always helps others with *an open heart.* 彼女はいつも他人にやさしく援助の手を差し伸べる.

at heart **1** 心底は, 根は ▪ He seems surly, but he is a kind man *at heart.* 彼は無愛想に見えるけれども, 根は親切な人だ.
2 心では, 内心; ほんとうは, 真の性質は ▪ The king *at heart* preferred the Catholics to the Puritans. 国王は心では清教徒よりもカトリック教徒のほうを好んだ ▪ He was a traitor *at heart.* 彼はほんとうは反逆者であった.
3 つくづく ▪ I am sick *at heart.* 私はつくづくいやになった.
4 心にかけて ▪ I have that matter close *at heart.* 私はそのことを深く心にかけています.

at the bottom of *one's* ***heart*** = from the bottom of one's HEART.

bare *one's* ***heart*** 《文》心[感情, 心配など]をすっかり打ち明ける (*to*) ▪ One evening he *bared his heart to* me. ある晩彼は私に心をすっかり打ち明けてくれた.

be all heart とても優しい ▪ She can't bear to see anyone upset; she*'s all heart.* 彼女は人が動転するのを見るに忍びない. 実に優しい女性だ.

be of good heart 元気である, 落胆しない ▪ Let us *be of good heart* and cheer tonight. 元気を出して今夜は歓声を上げよう.

be sick at heart →SICK.

Bless *a person's* ***heart* (*alive*)!** →BLESS.

break *a person's* ***heart*** 人を悲嘆にくれさせる, 落胆させる ▪ The bad news *broke her heart.* 凶報を聞いて彼女は悲嘆にくれた.

break *one's* ***heart*** 断腸の思いをする, 悲嘆にくれる, 力を落とす ▪ He *broke his heart* from disappointed love. 彼は失恋のため傷心した.

break the heart of **1** → break a person's HEART.
2 (仕事)の最難所を越す ▪ He has *broken the heart of* the business. 彼はその仕事の峠(とうげ)を越した.

bring *a person's* ***heart into*** *his* ***mouth*** 人をびっくり[びくびく]させる ▪ The sound *brought my heart into my mouth.* その物音で私は肝を潰した ▪ Every knock *brought his heart into his mouth.* ノックの音がするたびに彼は胸がどきどきした.

by heart そらで ▪ I must get [learn] this poem *by heart.* この詩を暗記せねばならない ▪ The child has [knows] many things *by heart.* その子はたくさんのことをそらで覚えている.

cannot …for *one's* ***heart*** どうしても…できない ▪ I *cannot for my heart* leave the room. 私はどうしても部屋を去ることができない.

capture the heart of = win the HEART of.

clasp* [*hold*]*… to *one's* ***heart*** …を抱きしめる ▪ She *clasped* the child *to her heart.* 彼女は子供を抱きしめた.

close* [*near, dear*] *to *one's* ***heart*/**《米》***near and dear to*** *one's* ***heart*** 興味関心が深い, 深く愛する ▪ It was a subject *near to his heart.* それは彼には関心の深い話題であった ▪ Children are *dear to God's heart.* 神は子供をこよなく慈(いつく)しみ給う ▪ He's now at home with those *near and dear to his heart.* 彼は家に戻り深く愛する家族とともにある.

***cross* [*crisscross*]** *one's* ***heart* (*and hope to die*)** 《口》〚主に命令文・疑問文で〛胸に十字を切って誓う; 真実を請け合う, 保証する ▪ I don't know who broke the window—*cross my heart and hope to die*! 誰が窓をこわしたか知りません—十字を切って誓います!

cross *one's* ***heart and point to God*** = cross one's HEART (and hope to die).

cry from the heart 熱烈な抗議, 心からの訴え ▪ There was a *cry from the heart* of the rural people. 地方から激しい抗議の声が上がった. ☞20世紀初頭から同義のフランス語 cri de cœur も用いられるようになった.

cry* [*weep*]** *one's* ***heart out 胸がはり裂けるほど泣く ▪ Hearing the news, she *cried her heart out.* その報を聞いて彼女は胸が裂けるほど泣いた.

cut *a person* ***to the heart*** 人の胸にこたえる, 心を痛める ▪ This news *cut* him *to the heart.* このニュースは彼の胸にこたえた.

devour *one's* ***heart*** = eat one's HEART out.

do *a person's* ***heart good*** 人をうれしくさせる, 喜ばせる, 元気づける ▪ It *does my heart good* to hear something like that. そのようなことを聞けば私は元気が出る ▪ It *did* all *our hearts good* to see him get the prize. 彼が賞をもらうのを見て我々はみんな痛快だった.

eat* [*tear*]** *one's* ***heart out*/*eat* [*tear*] *out *one's* ***heart*** 《口》人知れず悲嘆[苦痛, くやしさ, あこがれ]に身をこがす (《聖》 *Eccles.* 4. 5) 《誇張表現》 ▪ He is *eating his heart out* because he could not join the expedition. 彼はその探検に加われなかっ

たので人知れずくやし涙にくれている ▪ He was *eating out his heart* with regret. 彼は悔恨のため人知れず苦悩していた.

fight** one's **heart out 死闘する ▪ She *fought her heart out* and earned her country a silver medal. 彼女は死闘を演じて母国に銀メダルをもたらした.

***find it in** one's **heart to** do* 〚通例 can, could を伴って〛 **1** ...したい気がする ▪ I *could find it in my heart to* blow the ship up. 私は船を爆破したい気がした ▪ He *found it in his heart to* pray. 彼は祈りたい気がした.

2 〚主に否定文・疑問文で〛 ...する気になる ▪ I could not *find it in my heart to* dismiss the old man. その老人を解雇する気になれなかった.

3 冷酷にも...する ▪ He could *find it in his heart to* let me stay in the coalholes. 彼は冷酷にも私を石炭入れ場にとどまらせた.

follow** one's **heart (理性に従わず)自分の望む通りにする, 感情に従って行動する ▪ Remember to never *follow your heart.* 決して感情に流されないよう肝に銘じなさい.

from** one's [**the**] **heart 心から ▪ I wish *from my heart* Mr. Smith had come home. 私は心からスミスさんが帰国したらよかったのにと思う ▪ He always speaks *from the heart.* 彼は常に誠意を持って話す ▪ This letter comes straight *from the heart.* この手紙には書き手のまごころがはっきりと現れている.

from the bottom** [**depth, ground**] **of** one's **heart 心の底から ▪ I thank you for your kindness *from the bottom of my heart.* ご親切にありがたく, 衷心よりお礼申しあげます.

gain** a person's **heart → have a person's HEART.

gather heart 勇気を奮い起こす ▪ *Gather heart,* boys! 少年たちよ, 勇気を出せ.

get** [**have**] **... by heart →by HEART.

give ... fresh heart (人)を元気づける, 励ます ▪ This perfume *gives* everyone *fresh heart.* この香水をつけると誰でも元気な気分になる.

give** a person **heart 勇気づける ▪ You have *given* me *heart.* I'll try again. 君のお陰で元気が出た. もう一度やってみるよ.

give** one's **heart to ...に思いを寄せる, を恋する ▪ She will *give her heart to* you. 彼女はあなたを恋い慕うだろう.

go to** a person's **heart 人の胸にこたえる, 人に断腸の思いをさせる, 哀れを催させる ▪ The moan *went* right *to my heart.* そのうめき声はひどく私の胸にこたえた ▪ It *went to my heart* to say no to her. 彼女に「いや」と言うのは断腸の思いだった.

go** [**get**] **to the heart of ...の核心をつかむ, の奥義を極める ▪ We must *go to the heart of* the matter. 我々は事件の核心をつかまねばならない.

***harden** [**steel**] one's **heart** (**against**)* (...に対して)心を無情にする (《聖》 *Exod.* 7. 3) ▪ For once she really *hardened her heart.* 彼女はその時に限ってほんとに心を鬼にした ▪ The doctor *hardened his heart against* the suffering he saw every day. 医師は毎日目にする患者の苦しみに無感覚になった.

have a** (**big**) **heart 《口・戯》 思いやりがある, 情け深い; 寛容である; 気前がよい ▪ *Have a heart* and give her a little more time. お情けをもって彼女にもう少し時間を与えてください ▪ *Have a heart,* Tom. Give me 2 dollars. トム, けちけちしないで2ドルくれよ ▪ He helps people in need. He *has* such *a big heart!* 彼は困っている人を救済して, 実に情け深い人だ.

have a heart of gold とても優しい ▪ She's *got a heart of gold* and does anything for anyone. 彼女は非常に優しい心の持ち主で, 誰にも何でもしてあげる.

have ... at heart **1** ...を心にかけている, 切望する, に深い関心をもつ ▪ I *have* your success most *at heart.* ご成功をもっとも切望しています ▪ I *have* your interests *at heart.* 君のことは心にかけている.

2 ...を心にいだいている, もくろんでいる ▪ The Pope *has* this design *at heart.* 教皇はこの計画をもくろんでいる.

have ... by heart →get ... by HEART.

have** [**gain, obtain, win**] a person's **heart 人の愛を得る ▪ He *gained the heart of* the Princess. 彼は王女の愛を得た.

have** [**give**] **heart failure 大ショックを受ける[与える], 自信をなくす[させる] ▪ I nearly *had heart failure* at the news of her failing the test. 彼女の不合格の報にひどくショックを受けた ▪ You *gave* me *heart failure.* Knock before you open the door. びっくりさせるじゃないか. ドアを開く前にノックしろ.

have** (one's) **heart in ...に熱意を注ぐ, 心血を注ぐ ▪ I *have* little *heart in* the affair. 私はその事にはあまり熱意を注いでいない.

***have** one's **heart in** one's **boots** [**shoes**]* 意気消沈する; 心配してびくびくする ▪ Sometimes during the war I *had my heart in my boots.* 戦争中ときどき私は意気消沈することがあった ▪ I *had my heart in my boots* lest any bad news should come. 何か悪いニュースが来はしないかと私は心配でびくびくしていた.

have** one's **heart in** one's **mouth びっくり仰天する; ぎょっとする ▪ When the directors sent for me I *had my heart in my mouth.* 重役が私を呼びに人をよこしたとき, 私はぎくっとした ▪ I *had my heart in my mouth* as I watched the fight. 私はその格闘を見ながら, 胸をどきどきさせていた.

have** one's **heart in the right place (心底は)優しく思いやりがある; (根は)正しく良い人である ▪ Though he looks surly, he *has his heart in the right place.* 無愛想に見えるけれども, 彼は心優しい人である.

have** one's **heart set on ...にすっかり決めてしまっている ▪ I *have my heart set on* this hat. 私はこの帽子にすっかり決めている.

have ... near** one's **heart ...を切望する, 欲する ▪ They *had* it *near their hearts* to up anchor and away to sea. 彼らはいかりをあげて海に乗り出すことを欲した.

have no heart **1**《口》思いやりがない, 無情である ▪The man *has no heart* nor any sense of humor. 男は無情でユーモアも解さない.

2 …する気がない (*for, to do*) ▪I *have no heart to* study English. 私は英語を研究する気がない.

have the heart to *do* **1** 勇敢にも…する, …する勇気がある ▪The Turks *had the heart to* defend themselves. トルコ国民は勇敢にも自己を防衛した ▪She didn't *have the heart to* fight him in court. 彼女は法廷で彼と争う勇気がなかった.

2〚主に疑問文・否定文で〛むざんにも…する, …する気になる ▪He *had the heart to* kill the cat. 彼はむざんにもその猫を殺した ▪I don't *have the heart to* be angry at him. 彼に対して腹をたてる気になれない.

heart and hand →(with) HEART and hand.

heart and soul **1** 熱愛, 熱情, 熱心 ▪Her *heart and soul* is in it when she plays the piano. 彼女は全霊を傾けてピアノを演奏する.

2 身も心も, 全部, 全く ▪You are mine, *heart and soul*. あなたは身も心も私のものです ▪He is *heart and soul* a Democrat. 彼は全くの民主党員である ▪He puts *heart and soul* into his work. 彼は自分の仕事に身も心も打ちこんでいる.

3 身も心も打ちこんで, 一途に ▪He has gone into the business *heart and soul*. 彼は身も心も打ちこんでその事業をやってきた ▪I believe in him, *heart and soul*. 一途に彼を信仰しています.

one's ***heart bleeds for*** …のため同情の血涙を流す ▪Oh, how *her heart bleeds for* him. 彼に同情して彼女がどれほど心を痛めていることか.

one's ***heart breaks*** 断腸の思いをする, 悲嘆にくれる ▪*His heart broke* from disappointed love. 彼は失恋のため傷心した.

one's ***heart comes*** [***is***] ***in*** [***into***] *one's* ***mouth***《口》びっくり仰天する, 胸がどきどきする ▪*My heart came into my mouth* with quite a new kind of terror. 私は今まで感じたことのない種類の恐ろしさで胸がどきどきした ▪*His heart was in his mouth* as he walked onto the stage. ステージに向かいながら彼の胸はどきどきしていた.

one's ***heart fails*** *one*/ *one's* ***heart dies within*** *one* がっかりする, 意気消沈する ▪*My heart died within* me at the news. そのニュースを聞いて私はがっかりした.

one's ***heart gives a leap*** びくり[どきっ]とする ▪*My heart gave a leap* when I first saw him. 初めて彼に会ったとき私はどきっとした.

one's ***heart goes out to***《文》…に同情する, をあわれむ ▪*My heart goes out to* all those who are hungry. 私はひもじいすべての人々に同情します.

one's ***heart is in*** [***goes into, sinks into***] *one's* ***boots*** [***shoes***]《口》落胆する, 意気消沈する; ひどく心配でまたは恐ろしくてびくびくする ▪*My heart sank into my boots* when I thought of it. 私はそれを思い出したとき, ひどく気がめいった ▪When the telephone rang, *my heart went into my boots*. 電話が鳴ったとき, 私はひどく心配でびくびくした. ☞One's heart sinks の誇張した言い方.

one's ***heart is in the right place*** = have one's HEART in the right place.

one's ***heart is not in*** 心が…にない; に熱心でない[関心がない] ▪*His heart is not in* his work at all. 彼は仕事に少しも熱心でない.

one's ***heart leaps into*** *one's* ***mouth*** [***throat***] びっくり仰天する, びっくりして胸がどきどきする ▪*My heart leapt into my mouth* at the sight. 私はその光景を見てびっくり仰天した.

one's ***heart leaps up*** 心がおどる, (うれしさで)急に心がときめく ▪*My heart leaps up* when I see a rainbow. 私は虹を見ると心がおどる ▪*Her heart leapt up* when she heard a knock, thinking it might be him. 彼女はノックの音がすると彼かもしないと思って胸が躍った.

one's ***heart misgives*** *one* →MISGIVE.

one's ***heart misses*** [***loses, skips***] ***a beat*** (恐怖などで)息を飲む, ぎくっとする ▪Someone was looking at her through the window. *Her heart missed a beat*. 誰かが窓越しに彼女を見ていた. 彼女はぎくっとした.

one's ***heart sinks*** (***low***) (***within*** *one*)《口》意気消沈する ▪*Oliver's heart sank within* him when he was left alone. 独り取り残されてオリバーは意気消沈した.

one's ***heart smites*** *one* 良心の苛責を受ける (《聖》*2 Sam*. 24. 10) ▪*Her heart smote* her for not having been kinder to him. 彼にもっと親切にしてやらなかったというので彼女は良心に責められた. ☞heart = conscience.

one's ***heart stands still*** (心臓が止まるほど)ひどくびっくりする, たまげる; ひどく心配する ▪*My heart stood still* when a bear appeared. クマが出てきた時私はたまげた.

heart to heart/heart-to-heart **1**〚限定的〛まじめで率直な, 腹を割った《通例, 忠告・叱責などする場合》▪Have you had a *heart-to-heart* talk with him? 彼と腹を割った話をしたことがあるか.

2〚副詞的に〛腹蔵なく ▪We talked face to face and *heart to heart*. 私たちは向かい合って率直に話し合った.

3〚名詞的に〛腹を割った話し合い ▪He and I had a real *heart-to-heart*. 彼と実に腹を割って話し合った.

heart whole《口》恋を知らない ▪She was *heart whole* till she met Jim. 彼女はジムに会うまで恋を知らなかった.

one's ***heart's desire*** 心から欲すること[物], 思い焦がれる人 ▪*My heart's desire* was not granted. 心からの願いは叶えられなかった.

hold ... to *one's* ***heart*** → clasp ... to one's HEART.

in (***good***) ***heart*** **1** 元気で; 健全な状態で ▪He was *in good heart* and excellent form. 彼は元気ですこぶる調子がよかった ▪He was still *in heart* to

fight. 彼はまだ戦う元気があった ▪ The lees keep the drink *in heart.* おりがその酒を腐らせないでおく.
2《主に英》(土地が)肥沃で; 生産力のある ▪ The soil was kept *in heart* by superior farming methods. 土地はすぐれた農法により肥沃にしておかれた. ☞ ↔out of HEART.

in (*one's*) ***heart*** **1** 心の底で, 心ひそかに ▪ They wish *in their heart* the temple had been built. 彼らは心の底では神殿が建てられていたらなと思っている.
2 心の中に(大事に) ▪ I shall keep his words *in my heart.* 私は彼の言葉を心に銘記しておきましょう.

in *one's* ***heart of hearts*** [***of heart***] 心の真底では, 心の底までも; 本当のところ《正しい形は of heart》 ▪ *In his heart of heart* he would have admitted that. 心の真底では彼はそれを認めたであろう ▪ Tell me, *in your heart of hearts*, what do you think of him? 教えてください. 実のところ彼をどう思いますか.

in no heart (***for***) (…する)気がしなくて ▪ I am *in no heart for* laughing. 笑う気がしない.

in the heart of …のまん中に; の奥の方に ▪ There is a park *in the heart of* the city. 市のまん中に公園がある ▪ He is *in the heart of* affairs. 彼は事の衝にあたっている.

It is a poor [***sad***] ***heart that never rejoices.***《諺》決して喜ばないような悲しい人はいない, いつも悲しそうな人でも何かに喜ぶことがあるものだ.

keep (***up***) (***a good***) ***heart*** 勇気を失わない ▪ Whatever may happen, we must *keep heart.* どんな事があっても我々は勇気を失ってはならない ▪ Now, good-by, and *keep a good heart.* ではさようなら. いつまでも元気でいてください.

know [***learn***] ***… by heart*** →by HEART.

lay … to heart **1** (忠告・注意など)を心に留める, とくと考慮する ▪ I will *lay* your advice *to heart.* ご忠告を心に留めておきます.
2 …を気にする ▪ Don't *lay* her words *to heart* too much. 彼女の言葉をあまり気にしすぎてはいけない.

learn (***off***) ***by heart*** 暗記する, 暗唱できるまで覚える ▪ We were told to *learn* the poem *by heart.* 僕らはその詩を暗誦するように言われた ▪ He finds it easy to *learn* everything *off by heart.* 彼は何でも暗記するのが得意だ.

let *one's* ***heart rule*** *one's* ***head*** 感情のままに行動する ▪ Be careful not to *let your heart rule your head.* 情に流されて行動しないようになさい.

lie at *a person's* ***heart*** **1** 人に慕われている ▪ She *lies at my heart.* 彼女を私は慕っている.
2 人の心にかかる, 念頭にある ▪ His safety *lies at my heart.* 彼の安全がいつも心にかかっている.

lie near the [*one's*] ***heart*** …に同情している ▪ Your loss *lies near my heart.* ご不幸に同情しています.

lift (***up***) *one's* [*a person's*] ***heart*** 元気を出す[出させる], 気を引き立てる ▪ They *lifted up their hearts* by singing the song. 彼らはその歌を歌って気を引き立てた.

(***Lord, God***) ***bless*** *one's* ***heart!*** おやおや! ▪ *Bless your heart*, child; you are a good girl. まあほんとに, 良い子だね.

lose heart 落胆[意気消沈]する ▪ Don't *lose heart* because you cannot solve the problem. 問題が解けないからといって力を落とすな.

lose *one's* ***heart*** (***to, over***) (…に)恋する, 心を奪われる; (に)ほれこむ ▪ She will *lose her heart to* you. 彼女はあなたに恋するだろう ▪ I *lost my heart to* the puppy. 私はその子犬にすっかりほれこんだ.

make *a person's* ***heart bleed*** →BLEED.

make *a person's* ***heart leap out of*** *his* ***mouth*** 人をびっくり仰天させる, 胸をどきどきさせる, ぎょっとさせる ▪ The sight was enough to *make my heart leap out of my mouth.* その光景は私の胸をどきどきさせるに十分であった.

move [***stir, touch***] ***the*** [*one's*] ***heart*** 心を動かす ▪ It is not the eye, but the ear that *moves the heart.* 人の心を動かすのは目ではなくて耳だ ▪ This *touched her heart* deeply. これは彼女を深く感動させた.

My heart! 君 ▪ Be of good cheer, *my heart!* 君, しっかりしたまえ!

near *a person's* ***heart*** 人に大事な, 人の愛する ▪ This is a matter *near my heart.* これは私には大事なことです.

near to *one's* ***heart*** →close to one's HEART.

nearest [***next***] ***to*** *a person's* ***heart*** 人に最も大事な, 人の最も愛する ▪ He died for the cause which was *nearest to his heart.* 彼は自分の最も愛する主義のために死んだ.

not … for *one's* ***heart*** 命にかけても…しない ▪ I would *not, for my heart*, do such a thing. 命にかけても, そんなことはしたくない.

obtain *a person's* ***heart*** → have a person's HEART.

of two hearts/of a double heart 二心をいだく ▪ They are men *of two hearts.* 彼らは二心をいだいている.

open *one's* ***heart*** **1** 心を打ち明ける ▪ She *opened her heart* to her mother. 彼女は母に心を打ちあけた.
2 愛の手を差しのべる, 同情する (*to*) ▪ People *opened their hearts to* the poor people of Africa. 人々はアフリカの貧しい人たちに愛の手を差しのべた.

out of heart **1** 元気なく, しょげて ▪ He is evidently *out of heart.* 彼はどうも元気がないようだ.
2《主に英》(土地が)やせて, 生産力がなく ▪ The land was quite *out of heart.* その土地は全くやせていた. ☞ ↔in (good) HEART.

pierce *a person's* ***heart*** 強い感情が突き抜ける, 深く感動させる ▪ The sight of a dead kitten *pierced her heart* with grief. 死んだ子猫を見て彼女は悲しみに打ち沈んだ.

pour out *one's* ***heart*** (***to***) (…に)心のうちをすっかり話す ▪ She *poured out her heart to* me. 彼女の心のうちをすっかり私に話した.

put (***fresh, new***) ***heart into*** *a person* 人に

元気をつける ▪ This speech *put fresh heart into* the troops. この演説はその軍勢に新しい士気を与えた.

put** one's **heart and soul into …に全身全霊を傾ける[ささげる] ▪ He *put* all *his heart and soul into* everything. 彼は万事に全精力を注いだ.

put** a person's **heart at rest = set…at REST.

put** one's **heart into …に熱意を注ぐ ▪ He *puts his heart into* all he does. 彼は何事をするにも熱意を注いでやる.

put** a person **in** [**into**] **heart 人を元気づける, 元気を取り戻させる ▪ I will *put* you *in heart* again. また元気を取り戻させてあげます ▪ This has *put* me *in heart.* このため私は元気づいた.

rip the heart out of = tear the HEART out of.

search the** [one's] **heart 自己の心底を探る, (行動・動機などについて)内省する ▪ He *searched his heart* for words that would make sense. 彼は心底を探って道理にかなう言葉を探した.

send** a person's **heart into** his **boots 人を意気消沈させる ▪ One glance at it *sent my heart into my boots.* それを一目見て私は意気消沈した.

set** one's **heart against …に強く反対する ▪ Her father *set his heart against* the match. 彼女の父はその結婚に強く反対した.

***set** one's **heart on** [**upon**]* **1** …を熱望する, ほしがる ▪ I have *set my heart on* going to England. 私はイギリスへ行くことを熱望している.
2 …に心を決める ▪ I have *set my heart on* that hat. 私はその帽子に決めた.

sob** one's **heart out 《口》胸がはり裂けるほど泣きじゃくる ▪ Lucy *sobbed her heart out* on his chest. ルーシーは彼の胸に抱かれて嗚咽(おえつ)した.

***steal** a person's **heart** (**away**)* 知らぬまに人の愛情をかちとる ▪ Jane *stole his heart* when he visited Britain. ジェインは彼が英国を訪れたとき彼の心を捕らえた.

steel** one's **heart → harden one's HEART (against).

stir the** [one's] **heart →move the HEART.

strike at the heart of (問題などの)核心を衝く, 最も重要な部分を攻撃して大損傷を与える ▪ This suggestion *strikes at the heart of* the problem. この提案は問題の核心を衝いている ▪ Remember the day terror *struck at the heart of* America. テロがアメリカの中枢を攻撃して大打撃を与えた日を銘記せよ.

take heart 元気を出す; 気を取り直す ▪ Come on, *take heart.* さあさあ元気を出しなさい ▪ The doctor told us to *take heart.* 医師は気を取り直せと言った.

take heart of grace 勇気を奮い起こす, 元気を出す ▪ The laborers *took heart of grace* and applied for work. 労働者たちは勇気を出して仕事を志願した.

take the heart out of …をがっかりさせる ▪ The defeat *took the heart out of* the enemy. 敵は負けてがっかりした.

take…to heart **1** …を心にかける, まじめに考える ▪ *Take* this lesson *to heart.* この教訓を心に銘記しておきなさい ▪ You must *take* the business *to heart.* その事業をまじめに考えなさい.
2 …を気[苦]にする ▪ Although our joking was all in fun, Joseph *took* it *to heart.* 我々の冗談(じょうだん)は全くおもしろ半分であったが, ジョゼフはそれを気にした ▪ He *took* his punishment *to heart.* 彼は自分の処罰を苦にした.
3 …をひどく悲しむ ▪ He has *taken* the death of his dog *to heart.* 彼は愛犬の死をひどく悲しんだ.

take…to** one's **heart 《口》…を温かく[熱烈に]歓迎する; に愛情を示す ▪ The villagers *took* the new parson *to their hearts.* 村人たちは新任の牧師を熱烈に歓迎した.

tear** a person's **heart out 人をひどく悲しませる; 人を感涙にむせばせる ▪ The sad story *tore my heart out.* その悲話を聞いて私は感涙にむせんだ.

tear** one's **heart out →eat one's HEART out.

tear** [**rip**] **the heart out of …の最も重要な部分[面]を破壊する ▪ Closing the factory will *tear the heart out of* our local economy. その工場を閉鎖すれば, この地域経済の根幹が崩れるだろう.

***the heart of the matter** [**problem**]* 問題の核心, 事件の本質 ▪ Unequal pay was *the heart of the problem.* 賃金格差が問題点の中核であった.

***to** one's **heart's content** [**desire**]* → CONTENT[1].

touch the** [one's] **heart →move the HEART.

wear** one's **heart on** one's **sleeve **1** 極端に率直である, 自分の感情や意図をあからさまに[遠慮なく, 軽々しく]見せる (cf. Sh., *Oth.* 1. 1. 64.) ▪ It does not do to *wear one's heart on one's sleeve.* 自分の感情や意図をあからさまに見せるのはよくない ▪ Do have more personal dignity. You *wear your heart on your sleeve.* もっと威厳を保ちなさい. あなたは極端に率直だ.
2 情にほだされすぎる ▪ Everyone imposes on you; you *wear your heart on your sleeve.* みんながあなたをだます. あなたはじきにほろりとするから. ☞「心臓を袖につける」が原義.

weep** one's **heart out →cry one's HEART out.

What comes from the heart goes to the heart. 《諺》一念は届くもの.

What the heart thinks, the mouth speaks. 《諺》思うことは口に出るもの.

win** a person's **heart → have a person's HEART.

win the heart of …の愛情を得る ▪ She *won* all *hearts* with her lovely smile. 彼女は美しい笑顔でみんなの愛情を得た ▪ Charming baby gifts *win the heart of* every mother. かわいいベビー用品はすべての母親のハートを射止める.

with a good heart 勇んで ▪ He went there *with a good heart.* 彼は勇んでそこへ行った.

with a heart and a half 大喜びで, 心から進んで ▪ I thank you *with a heart and a half* for your

H

kindness. ご親切に心から感謝いたします.

with a heavy heart 重い心で, しょんぼりと ▪ He just stood there *with a heavy heart*. 彼はしょんぼりとそこに立ち尽くしていた.

with a light heart →LIGHT^2.

with a sinking heart うろたえて, 不安をつのらせて ▪ *With a sinking heart* she checked the sender's name. 彼女は不安のあまり送り主の名前を調べた.

***with all** one's **heart** [**with** one's **whole heart**] (**and soul**)* **1** 《雅》 全霊で, 心をこめて ▪ I love you *with all my heart*. 心から君を愛している ▪ He goes into anything *with all his heart*. 彼は何事でも全霊で取り組む.

2 喜んで(依頼に応じるなど) ▪ I will help you *with all my heart*. 喜んでお助けいたします.

with half a heart 気乗りせず, しぶしぶと ▪ Some officials serve the government sullenly and *with half a heart*. 役人の中には不きげんにしぶしぶと宮仕えする者もある.

*(**with**) **heart and hand*** 勇んで, 喜んで, 心から進んで ▪ He will join in the project, *heart and hand*. 彼は勇んでその企画に参加するだろう.

with** one's **heart in** one's **boots 気がめいって; ひどく心配で, びくびくして ▪ "Daddy," said I *with my heart in my boots*. 「おとうちゃん」と私は落胆して言った.

with** one's **heart in** one's **mouth **1** びっくり仰天して ▪ I jumped back *with my heart in my mouth*. 私は驚いて後ずさりした.

2 ひどく恐れて, びくびくして ▪ I'm doing this *with my heart in my mouth*. おっかなびっくりでこれをしている.

work** one's **heart out 懸命に取り組む ▪ She *works her heart out* in whatever she does. 彼女は手がけるあらゆることに全力で取り組む.

young at heart →be YOUNG at heart.

you're breaking my heart 《口》 情けない人だ; それはお気の毒さま ▪ Stay away from me. *You're breaking my heart*. 私に寄りつかないでよ, 情けない人ね, あなたって.

heartbeat /hάːrtbìːt/ 名 ***a heartbeat away*** *(**from**)* (…の)すぐ近く[そば]に; (の)寸前[間際]で ▪ Our office is *a heartbeat away from* the city hall. わが社は市役所の目と鼻の先だ ▪ Success is just *a heartbeat away*. 成功は間近である ▪ The prince is only *a heartbeat away from* being king. 皇太子はもうまもなく即位する手はずである.

in a heartbeat すぐに, 直ちに ▪ A police officer arrived at the scene *in a heartbeat*. 警察官が直ちに現場に急行した.

hearth /hɑːrθ/ 名 ***hearth and home*** 《雅》 家庭 (の安らぎ) ▪ Our shop is filled with unique items to enrich your *hearth and home*. 当店ではお客様の家庭生活を豊かにする斬新な商品を多数取り揃えております.

heartstrings /hάːrtstrìŋz/ 名 ***break** [**tear at**] **the heartstrings of*** …に悲痛な思いをさせる ▪ It *tore at the heartstrings of* memory. それは記憶に悲痛な思いをさせた.

play on** a person's **heartstrings (ある目的を達するために)人の愛情[同情]に訴える ▪ Don't believe his sob stories! He's only trying to *play upon your heartstrings* to escape punishment. 彼の泣き言を信じてはいけない. 君の同情に訴えて罰を免れようとしているだけなんだ.

touch** a person's [**the**] **heartstrings**/ **tug** [**pull, pluck, tear**] **at** a person's [**the**] **heartstrings 《口》 人の感情をゆり動かす, 人を最も深く感動させる, 心の琴線に触れる; 人の心を痛める ▪ He could *touch the heartstrings of* the audience. 彼は聴衆を深く感動させることができた ▪ The songster *plucked at the heartstrings of* thousands of fans. その歌手は数千人のファンの心を揺さぶった ▪ The news of his death *tugged at everyone's heartstrings*. 彼の訃報にみなが悲嘆にくれた. ☞中世において heartstring は心臓を支える腱だと考えられていた.

hearty /hάːrti/ 形 *(**as**) **hearty as a buck** [**a young lion**]* 非常に強壮な ▪ I am well and *hearty as a buck*. 私は元気でとても丈夫です.

heat /hiːt/ 名 ***at a heat*** 一気に, 一息に ▪ He hanged twenty heretics *at a* single *heat*. 彼は20人の異端者を一気に絞首刑にした.

at heat →on HEAT.

canned heat 携帯燃料 ▪ We use *canned heat* to keep food warm. うちでは料理の保温に固形燃料を使っている.

come** [**get**] **on heat →on HEAT.

give** (a person) **the heat =turn the HEAT on (a person).

If you can't stand** [**take**] **the heat, get** [**stay**] **out of the kitchen. 《諺》 熱さをがまんできなければ台所から出よ[に近うくな] (非難に耐えられないなら関わるな), 「いやなら出て行け」. ☞米国の元大統領 Harry S Truman が1952年に行った不出馬宣言の言葉から.

in a heat =in HEAT 2.

in heat **1** さかりがついて ▪ The female is *in heat* in the winter. 雌は冬にさかりがつく.

2 (激しく)怒って ▪ He spoke *in heat*. 彼は激怒して言った.

3 温床に ▪ The tomato plants were put *in heat*. トマトの苗は温床に入れられた.

in the heat of **1** …の盛りに ▪ He went out *in the heat of* the day. 彼は日盛りに出て行った.

2 …の最中に ▪ He was killed *in the heat of* the action. 彼は戦闘の最中に戦死した.

3 …の激したはずみに, 熱して ▪ I said that *in the heat of* the moment. 私はそのときの激したはずみにそう言ったのだ.

It's not the heat, it's the humidity. 《米・諺》 湿度が高いと, いっそう暑く不快に感じられる.

keep the heat on …に圧力を加えている ▪ The government is *keeping the heat on* the opposition. 政府は野党に圧力を加えている.

on* [*at*] *heat さかりがついて ▪ The ewes came *on heat*. 雌羊はさかりがついた.

put* (*the*) *heat on*/*put on* (*the*) *heat ...に圧力を加える ▪ He wants the Administration to *put heat on* Congress. 彼は政府が国会に圧力を加えることを望んでいる.

remove the heat from →take the HEAT off.

take the heat **1** 非難される, 批判に耐える, 重圧などに打ち勝つ ▪ The workers told their boss they wouldn't *take the heat* any more. 労働者たちは社長にこれ以上の抑圧はごめんだと言った.

2 責任をとる ▪ You will have to *take the heat* for this mistake. 君はこの過失の責任を取らねばなるまい.

***take the heat off* [*out of*]** ...に圧力を加えるのをやめる ▪ He *took the heat out of* the corruption issue. 彼は汚職問題に圧力を加えるのをやめた.

the heat is off 《俗》取り締まり[調査]がゆるめられている ▪ The bookies are out of business till *the heat is off*. 取り締まりがゆるめられるまでは, 競馬の賭師どもは失業だ.

the heat is on **1** 《俗》取り締まり[調査]が強化されている ▪ *The heat is on* dope. 麻薬の取り締まりが強化されている.

2 《米俗》緊張[苦境]が続いている ▪ They will weaken when *the heat is on*. 苦境が続くと彼らは弱るだろう.

***turn* [*put*] *the heat* (*on*)** 《口》(...に)圧力をかける ▪ Taxpayers *turned the heat on* the congressmen. 納税者は国会議員に圧力をかけた.

***turn the heat on* (*a person*)** 《俗》(人に)銃を向ける ▪ He placed himself in a safe spot to *turn the heat on* John. 彼はジョンをピストルで撃つのに安全な場所に身を置いた.

***turn up the heat* (*on*)** 《口》(...への)圧力を強める ▪ The police *turned the heat up on* the gang. 警察はギャング一味に対する圧力を強化した.

with heat 激しく, 熱して ▪ He spoke *with* great *heat*. 彼はひどく激して話をした ▪ He repelled the accusation *with* some *heat*. 彼はその非難をかなり激しくはねつけた.

heath /hiːθ/ 名 ***a Heath Robinson*** 《英》(見かけは)こっけいなくらい複雑だが, 実は単純な機能しかない(器具) ▪ Dad's got this *Heath Robinson* device for slicing bread. パパはこの笑っちゃうほど複雑な器具を買ったが, ただのパン切りだ.

on one's native heath 生まれ故郷に (Scott, *Rob Roy* 34) ▪ Come and see us *on our native heath* as soon as you return home. 帰郷なさったらすぐ私たちの家へ遊びにおいでください.

heather /héðər/ 名 ***set the heather on fire*** 騒動を起こす ▪ He never really *set the heather on fire*. 彼は実際には騒動を全く起こさなかった.

heave /hiːv/ 動 ***heave* (*a ship*) *about* [*ahead, aback*]** 《海》(船)を急に回す[前進させる, 後退させる] ▪ The angry sea *heaved* the boat *about* at will. 荒波にもまれて船は波の意のままにくるくる回った.

heave* (*one's heart*) *up 《口》吐く; 吐き気がする, むかつく ▪ He was *heaving his heart up* in the kitchen. 彼は台所で吐いていた.

heave in sight **1** 《海》(船などが近づいて)見えてくる ▪ To our relief a steamer now *hove in sight*. ようやく汽船が見えて来たので我々はほっとした.

2 《口》見えてくる ▪ A most tremendous bear *hove in sight*. とても巨大なクマが姿を現した.

heave the* [*one's*] *gorge むかつく ▪ He got seasick and *heaved his gorge*. 彼は船酔いして胸がむかむかした.

***heave oneself* (*up*) *out of* [*from, off*]** よいしょと(いすなど)から立つ ▪ The old man *heaved himself up out of* his armchair. 老人はよいこらしょと肘掛けいすから立ち上がった.

heave-ho /híːvhóʊ/ 名 ***get the* (*old*) *heave-ho*** 《口》お払い箱になる; 追い出される ▪ A noisy club member *got the heave-ho*. 騒がしいクラブ員が追い出された. ☞heave-ho = よいと引け《いかりを引き揚げる際の掛け声》.

give the* (*old*) *heave-ho 《口》お払い箱にする; 追い出す ▪ The director *gave* John *the old heave-ho*. 所長はジョンを首にした.

heaven /hévən/ 名 ***a marriage* [*match*] *made in heaven*** **1** 似合いのカップル ▪ They have exactly the same likes and interests—it's *a marriage made in heaven*. 二人は好みも趣味も同じで, 似合いの夫婦だ.

2 ぴったりの相性, 調和 ▪ Strawberries and cream are *a marriage made in heaven*. イチゴとクリームは絶妙に合う.

be in heaven **1** 天国に行っている, 死んでいる ▪ Her spirit will *be in heaven*. 彼女の霊は天国へ行くだろう.

2 天にも昇る気分である, 有頂天になっている, 舞い上がっている ▪ I *was in heaven* after winning the lottery. 宝くじが当たって天にも昇る心地だった.

be in* (*the*) *seventh heaven 無上に幸福である, 高揚[至福, 恍惚(こう)]の状態である ▪ I *was* really *in seventh heaven* when I kissed her. 彼女とキスしたとき実に天にも昇る心地がした ▪ The child *was in the seventh heaven*; he had been given a bicycle for his birthday. 子供はうれしくて有頂天だった. 誕生日の祝いに自転車をもらったので. ☞the seventh heaven (第7天)は神と最も幸福な天使の住む最上層天.

before Heaven 天下晴れての ▪ They are man and wife *before Heaven*. 二人は天下晴れて夫婦だ.

***by heaven*(*s*)** 神かけて, 誓って; 必ず ▪ *By heavens*, I will have his heart's blood. 断然あいつを殺してくれる.

for heaven's sake **1** お願いだから ▪ *For heaven's sake*, save me. お願いですから私を救ってください.

2 何ていうことだ! ▪ I was almost run over by a truck.—*For heaven's sake*! 私は危うくトラックにひ

かれるところだった—まあ何ていうことです!

go to heaven 昇天する, 死ぬ ▪ Last night I dreamed I *went to heaven*. ゆうべ自分が死ぬ夢を見た.

Good [Great, Gracious] Heaven(s)! おやまあ!, おや(大変)!, まあ(とんでもない)!, 困ったなあ! ▪ *Great heaven!* What a place to stop at! おやおや! こんな所へ止まるのか! ▪ *Good heavens!* Well, he is an extraordinary man. これは驚いた! ほんとに彼は風変わりな人物です.

heaven and earth **1** 天地, 宇宙, 万物 ▪ In the beginning God created *heaven and earth*. 初めに神は天地を創造された.

2 おや! 《感嘆・驚き・恐れ》 ▪ *Heaven and earth!* what will become of me? おや! 私はどうなるんだろう.

Heaven be thanked! ありがたい ▪ *Heaven be thanked* you were not killed. あなたが殺されなかったのはありがたい.

Heaven forbid (that ...)! →God FORBID (that ...)!

Heaven [God] help you [him, etc.]***!*** →God HELP you!

Heaven knows. →God KNOWs.

heaven knows where [who, etc.] どこかわからぬ所[誰かわからぬ人, など] ▪ He has gone *heaven knows where*. 彼はどこかへ行ってしまった ▪ He is in love with *heaven knows who*. 彼は誰かに恋している.

heaven on earth この世の天国, 地上の楽園 ▪ Tahiti seemed like *heaven on earth* to her. 彼女にはタヒチはこの世の楽園に思えた.

Heaven protects children(, sailors,) and drunken men. 《諺》子供や(船乗りや)酔っぱらいは, 危険な場面でもけがを免れることが多い. ☞そのような場合の驚嘆の念を表明するのに用いられる.

Heaven speed you. 幸福[成功]を祈ります.

Heavens above! →Ah GOD!

Heavens to Betsy! = Good HEAVEN(s)!

Heaven's vengeance is slow but sure. → VENGEANCE.

in [under] heaven 〚疑問詞を伴って〛一体 ▪ *Where in heaven* were you? 君は一体どこにいたんだ.

in heaven's name →in the NAME of 1.

Inscrutable are the ways of Heaven. 天意は測りがたい,「人間万事塞翁が馬」.

move heaven and earth to *do* →MOVE[2].

praise to high heaven 熱狂的にほめる, ほめちぎる ▪ The fans *praised* him *to high heaven* and called him a football god. ファンは彼のことをほめたたえ, フットボールの神様と呼んだ.

stink [smell] to (high) heaven **1** 《口》極めて不快なにおいがする ▪ This fish *stinks to high heaven*. この魚はひどく臭い.

2 不正の臭いがする, うさんくさい ▪ The behavior of these young fellows *stinks to heaven*. この若者たちの行動はどうもうさんくさい.

thank heaven ありがたい[や]! ▪ *Thank heaven* you were not killed. 君が殺されなくてありがたい.

the heavens open 土砂降りになる ▪ It grew dark and *the heavens opened*. 暗くなって土砂降りになった.

to (high) heaven(s) ひどく, 極度に, 過度に ▪ He complained *to heaven* about the tax burden. 彼は課税が重いとひどく不満を言った.

under heaven →in HEAVEN.

heavy /hévi/ 形名 ***a heavy date*** 《米戯》逢い引き ▪ She has *a heavy date* with a man in my office. 彼女はわが社の男と深い関係になっている.

a heavy hand 手厳しい[厳格な]扱い方 ▪ The king ruled with *a heavy hand*. 国王は過酷な扱いで統治した.

a heavy hitter 《米》多くの業績を上げた実力者 ▪ His resume shows he's *a* real *heavy hitter*. 履歴書によると彼は大した実力者だ.

a heavy silence [atmosphere] 深い沈黙[気まずい雰囲気] ▪ There was *a heavy silence* for a few minutes. しばらく重苦しい沈黙が流れた.

be heavy into ...に夢中になっている, のめり込んでいる ▪ Bill *is heavy into* Bess. He's been out with her every night. ビルはベスにぞっこんで, このところ彼女と毎晩デートをしている.

come [do] the heavy 《俗》気取る; いばり散らす; 見栄を張る ▪ Smith tried to *come the heavy* with me. スミスは私に対して偉そうにしようとした.

come [do] the heavy father [uncle] 《口》父親[おじ]として(尊大に)きびしくする ▪ I never *came the heavy father* on [with] them. 父親として彼らにきびしくしたことはない.

fall heavy on ...を困らせる ▪ His death will *fall heavy on* his family. 彼が死んだら家族が困るだろう.

feel heavy 体がだるい ▪ I *feel heavy* this morning. 今朝は体がだるい.

get heavy 《口》深刻になる ▪ He shouted at me and it *got* very *heavy*. 彼は私に怒鳴りかけ, 険悪な雰囲気になった.

hang heavy on *a person* →HANG[2].

have a heavy foot 《米口》非常に速く車を運転する ▪ He *has a heavy foot*, in fact, he's a speed freak. 彼は猛烈に飛ばす. はっきり言って, スピード狂だ.

heavy going 退屈な, やっかいな, 扱いにくい ▪ I found his novel very *heavy going*. 読んでみたら彼の小説は実に退屈だった ▪ The muddy paths made our journey rather *heavy going*. 道がぬかるんでいて進むのにかなりてこずった.

heavy in [on, upon] hand **1** (馬が)気力を失い手綱にすがるようにして; 追いたてなければ進まない ▪ The horses are *heavy in hand*. 馬どもはみな気力を失っている.

2 (人が)活気がない, 不活発で; もてなしにくい, 楽しませにくい ▪ He was a kind fellow, though a trifle *heavy in hand*. 彼は親切な男だ, 少し活気はないが.

heavy with ...を積んだ, 背負った ▪ The words seem *heavy with* meaning. それらの語は多くの意味

をもっているようである ▪ The very air was *heavy with* the rich perfume of the acacias. 大気自体にもアカシアの芳香が満ち満ちていた.

heavy with child 妊娠して ▪ She is *heavy with child.* 彼女は妊娠している.

***lie* [*sit, weigh*] *heavy on* [*at*]** ...に重くのしかかる, を苦しめる ▪ These burdens *lay heavy on* the nation. これらの重荷が国民の上に重くのしかかっていた ▪ The war *weighs heavy on* the people. 戦争は国民を苦しめている.

lie* (*heavy*) *on *a person's* ***hands*** →HAND[1].

make heavy weather of →WEATHER[1].

make heavy weather with →WEATHER[1].

play the heavy line*/ *play a heavy role 《劇》悲劇的[深刻]な役割を演じる ▪ He *played the heavy line* in Hamlet. 彼はハムレットの中で悲劇的な役割を演じた.

***the heavy mob* [*brigade*]** 《英口》用心棒の連中; 殺人者の一団 ▪ He turned up at the meeting with his *heavy mob.* 彼は用心棒たちを引き連れて会合に姿を現した.

Hebrew /híːbruː/ 名 ***it's Hebrew to*** ...にはちんぷんかんぷんだ (→be (all) GREEK to) ▪ Sorry, *it's* all *Hebrew to* me. 申しわけないがそれは私にはさっぱりわからない.

heck /hek/ 名 ***a heck of a ...*** 《口》すごい..., ひどい... ▪ My brother-in-law is *a heck of a* nice guy. 義理の弟は実にいいやつだ ▪ What *a heck of a* mess! 何というひどい散らかしようだ! ☞heck は hell に対する19世紀末の婉曲語.

for the heck of it =for the DEVIL of it.

raise heck =raise the DEVIL 2.

the heck of it =the DEVIL of it.

What* [*How,* etc.] *in heck ...? 《米俗》一体何[どうして, など] ▪ *How in heck* did he do that? 一体どんなにして彼はそれをしたのか.

What the heck! かまうもんか! ▪ Oh, *what the heck!* I'll have another beer. なに, かまうもんか. ビールをもう1杯くれ.

heckle /hékəl/ 名 ***set up*** *one's* ***heckle*** 怒る ▪ Don't *set up your heckle* so soon. そうすぐに怒るな. ☞heckle＝hackle (うなじ毛); おんどりは怒ると首の羽毛を立てるから.

heckle-pin /hékəlpìn/ 名 ***be on* (*the*) *heckle-pins*** ひどく心配している, 不安がっている ▪ The lad *was on heckle-pins.* 若者はひどく心配していた.

hectic /héktɪk/ 形 ***have a hectic time*** 《口》盛んに飲み騒ぐ ▪ The lad *had a hectic time.* その若者は盛んに飲み騒いだ.

hector /héktər/ 動 ***hector*** *a person* ***into* [*out of*]** *doing* 人をおどしつけて...させる[をやめさせる] ▪ She *was hectored into marrying* Tom. 彼女はおどしつけられてトムと結婚した.

hedge /hedʒ/ 名 ***A hedge between keeps friendship green.*** 《諺》友人との間に垣根があると友情は枯れない《友人と互いのプライバシーを尊重しあえば, 友情は長続きするだろう》,「親しき仲には垣をせよ」.

be on the hedge =sit on the HEDGE.

be on the wrong* [*right, better, safer*] *side* (*of*) *the hedge まちがった[正しい, よりよい, より安全な]立場にいる ▪ We *are on the right side the hedge.* 我々は正しい立場にいる.

come down on the wrong side of the hedge 決定を誤る, 誤りを犯す ▪ The Bishop of Winchester *came down on the wrong side of the hedge.* ウィンチェスターの主教は決定を誤った.

hang* [*be hung*] *on* [*in*] *the hedge (訴訟などが)放っておかれる; たなあげにされている ▪ The business of money *hangs in the hedge.* 金の問題はたなあげにされている ▪ The distinction may *be hung on the hedge.* その区別は無視してよい.

look as if *one* ***has been dragged through a hedge backwards*** →LOOK[2].

not grow on every hedge どこにでもあるというものではない, まれである ▪ It does *not grow on every hedge.* それは珍しいものだ.

sit on the hedge 《口》日和見する ▪ He *sits on the hedge* if there's any dispute. 彼は何か論争があると日和見をする.

take a sheet off a hedge 公然と盗む ▪ He might as well *take a sheet off a hedge.* 彼はむしろ公然と盗んだほうがましだ.

take hedge 出て行く, 立ち去る ▪ They all *took hedge.* 彼らはみな出て行った.

the only stick left in *one's* ***hedge*** ただ一つ残った手段[方策, 頼み] ▪ Those two regiments were *the only stick* they had *left in their hedge.* その2個連隊だけが彼らに残された頼みであった.

hedgehog /hédʒhɔ̀ːg|-hɔ̀g/ 名 ***as prickly as a hedgehog*** すぐに腹を立てる, 激高しやすい ▪ He can be *as prickly as a hedgehog* at times. 彼はときにキレることがある.

heebie-jeebies /hìːbidʒíːbiz/ 名 ***give*** *a person* ***the heebie-jeebies*** 《口》人をびくびくさせる ▪ Walking along this street after dark *gives* me *the heebie-jeebies.* 暗くなってからこの通りを歩くとびくびくする.

heed /hiːd/ 名 ***give* [*pay*] *heed to*** ...を心に留める, 注意して聞く ▪ I'll *give heed to* what you say. あなたのおっしゃることは注意して聞きます ▪ He *paid* no *heed to* my warning. 彼は私の警告を聞かなかった.

***take heed* (*of, to*)** (...に)気をつける; (を)警戒する ▪ *Take heed,* youth flies apace. 気をつけなさい. 青春はどんどん過ぎて行きますから ▪ *Take heed of* such men. そういう人々に用心しなさい.

take no heed of ...を気に留めない; を取り合わない ▪ He *takes no heed of* danger. 彼は危険を意に介しない.

heedless /híːdləs/ 形 ***be heedless of*** ...を無視する ▪ He *is heedless of* tradition. 彼は伝統を無視する.

heel /hiːl/ 名 ***air*** *one's* ***heels*** →AIR[2].

at (*a person's*) ***heel***(***s***) **1** 人のすぐあとに，くびすを接して ▪ They arrived *at his heels.* 彼らは彼のすぐあとに到着した.
2《報道》すぐあとを追って ▪ The Chinese are *at our heels* in the race for naval power. 中国は海軍力競争で我々に肉薄している.
3《雅》すぐあとについて ▪ I kept close *at his heels.* 私は彼のすぐあとにずっとついて行った ▪ The dog followed *at heel.* 犬はすぐあとについて行った.
at the heels of →on the HEELs of.
be tied by the heels →lie by the HEELs.
bring [***call***] ***... to heel*** ...を後について来させる; を教え導く ▪ They *brought* the family *to heel.* 彼らはその家族を後について来させた ▪ Threatening them will be the easiest way of *calling* them *to heel.* 脅すのが彼らを従わせる一番手っ取り早いやり方だろう. ☞「飼い犬を足もとで従順に歩かせる」が原義.
catch ... by the heels 追っかけて...をつかまえる ▪ The thieves *were* soon *caught by the heels.* 盗賊どもはすぐに追跡されて捕えられた.
clap ... by the heels →lay ... by the HEELs.
click *one's* ***heels*** (***together***) (兵隊などが)かかとをカチリと合わせ(て敬礼す)る ▪ The police officer *clicked his heels* and bowed. 警察官はかかとをカチリと合わせて礼をした.
close [***hard***] ***on the heels*** (***of***) (...の)すぐ後について ▪ He was *close on the heels of* the gold medalist. 彼は金メダル走者にぴったりついていた ▪ The police were *hard on his heels.* 警察が彼のすぐ後を追っていた.
come [***follow***] (***hard*** [***hot, close***]) ***on the heels of*** ...のすぐ後に続く ▪ Tragedies always *come hard on the heels of* one another. 悲劇というものは次々に起きるものだ ▪ The Gulf War *followed hot on the heels of* the end of the Cold War. 冷戦の終結の直後に湾岸戦争が続いた ▪ Epidemics can *follow close on the heels of* natural disasters. 自然災害の直後に疫病が蔓延することがある.
come to heel **1** (犬が)主人のすぐあとについて行く ▪ *Come to heel!* ついて来い《犬に対して》.
2 従順である，文句なしに命令に従う; 支配[しつけ，規律など]に従う ▪ Be strong and they will soon *come to heel.* 強く出なさい．そうすれば彼らは文句なしに命令に従うでしょう ▪ Their passions are trained to *come to heel.* 彼らの激情は静まるように訓練される.
cool *one's* ***heels***《口》長く待たされる，待ちあぐむ ▪ I *cooled my heels* for a whole hour outside his office. 私は彼の事務所の外で1時間もずっと待たされた. ☞元来「歩いて熱くなった足を休めてさます」の意; 皮肉に用いられるようになったもの.
dig [***stick***] *one's* ***heels in***《口》(他人の申し入れ，命令などに)断固反対[抵抗]する; 自分の決意(など)を固く守る ▪ The son *dug his heels in* and refused to marry her. 息子は自分の決意を固く守って彼女と結婚することを断った.
down at (***the***) ***heel***(***s***) **1** 靴のかかとがすり切れて; 窮乏して，みすぼらしいふうをして ▪ Thus he ran gradually *down at the heel.* こうして彼はだんだん窮乏していった ▪ Poor chap! He looks very *down at heel.* かわいそうに，彼は非常にみすぼらしいふうをしている.
2 靴のかかとが足でつぶされて《靴をつっかける人に言う》; だらしない ▪ Her shoes were trodden *down at the heels.* 彼女の靴はかかとが足でつぶされていた.
drag *one's* ***heels*** →DRAG one's feet.
follow on [***upon***] ***the heels of*** → on the HEELs of.
get the heels of =have the HEELs of.
grind ... under *one's* ***heel*** **1** ...をくびすの下に踏みにじる ▪ He *ground* the cigarette *under his heel.* 彼はタバコをかかとで踏み消した.
2 ...を冷酷に押さえつける ▪ The King *ground* the people *under his heel.* 国王は人民を冷酷に押さえつけた.
hairy about the heel →HAIRY about the fetlocks.
have ... by the heels ...にかせをかける，禁固する，逮捕する; をはずかしめる，倒す ▪ He *has* half a dozen knights safe *by the heels.* 彼は6人の騎士を逃がさないよう監禁している.
have the heels of《口》**1** ...を追い越す，に走り勝つ ▪ He will *have the heels of* the other competitors. 彼は他の競走者に走り勝つだろう.
2 ...より速く走る ▪ His car *had the heels of* mine. 彼の自動車のほうが私のより速く走った.
3 ...に勝つ，勝る ▪ Your zeal *has got the heels of* your discretion. あなたの熱心が慎重さに勝った《熱心のあまり軽率なことをした》.
heel and toe **1** 普通の歩行(をして)《走ることに対して》 ▪ With that sort of walk, called *heel and toe,* he led her to the station.「普通の歩行」と呼ばれる歩き方で，彼は彼女を駅まで導いて行った ▪ They returned to college walking, *heel and toe.* 彼らは普通に歩いて大学に帰った.
2《ダンス》ヒールアンドトウ《つま先とかかとでするダンス》 ▪ Some one was doing a *heel and toe* step on a wooden floor. 誰かが木の床の上でつま先かかとダンスをしていた.
heels foremost [***forward***] → (with one's) HEELs foremost.
heels over head →HEAD over heels.
keep to heel =come to HEEL.
kick [***cool***] *one's* ***heels***《英口》(長く)じっと待たされる ▪ We were kept *kicking our heels* for two hours. 我々は2時間もじっと待たされた.
kick [***turn, tumble***] ***up*** *a person's* ***heels***《口》人を突き倒す; 人をつまずかせる，やっつける，殺す ▪ He *kicked up her heels.* 彼は彼女を突き倒した.
kick up *one's* ***heels***《口》**1** (馬が戯れて)後足をあげる; (人が)はね回る ▪ The horse *kicked up his heels* and made for home. 馬は後足をあげて家路をたどった.

2 はしゃぐ《特に自由を得た喜びで》 ▪ She was *kicking up her heels* with delight. 彼女は大喜びではしゃぎ回っていた.

3 束縛を振り切る ▪ Your boy will *kick up his heels* sooner or later. 息子さんは遅かれ早かれ束縛を振り切るでしょう.

4 ダンスする ▪ You spend night after night *kicking up your heels.* あなたは毎夜毎夜ダンスをして過ごしている.

kick* [*lay, tip, topple, turn*] *up* one's *heels 《俗》 死ぬ ▪ He *kicked up his heels* at last. 彼はとうとう死んだ.

knock* [*set*] a person *back on* his *heels 《口》人を(不利なことで)驚かす, 狼狽させる; 人の進歩をとめる ▪ When the coach told Tom he was a poor player, it *set* him *back on his heels.* コーチがおまえはへただと言った時トムは驚きくやしがった ▪ Jane's sickness *knocked* her *back on her heels.* ジェインは病気のため学業が進まなかった.

lay* [*clap, set*]*... by the heels **1** ...に足かせ[手かせ]をはめる ▪ He shall *be laid* fast *by the heels.* 彼にしっかりと足かせをはめてやる.

2 ...を監禁する, 投獄する ▪ We must *lay* him *by the heels.* 我々は彼を監禁しなければならない.

3 ...を逮捕する ▪ The policeman has *laid* the thief *by the heels.* 警官は盗賊を捕えた.

4 ...を打ち倒す, 動けないようにする ▪ He will *lay* the under-sheriff *by the heels.* 彼は州長官代理を打ち倒すだろう ▪ Rheumatism *laid* him *by the heels.* リューマチのため彼は引きこもった. ☞「人に足かせをはめる」が原義.

lie* [*be tied*] *by the heels 閉じ込められている ▪ Continue with it next time you *are tied by the heels.* 今度病床についたらそれを続けなさい.

lift* (*up*) [*raise*] *the* [one's] *heel against 《古》...をける; に暴行する, 恩知らずな仕打ちをする(《聖》*Ps.* 41. 9) ▪ My friend has *lifted up his heel against* me. 友人が私をけった ▪ He *raised his heel against* me. 彼は私に後足で砂をかけるようなことをした.

make a heel ける ▪ The ass replied and *made a heel.* ロバは応えてけった.

neck and heels →NECK.

on* [*upon, at*] *the heels of ...のすぐあとに; のすぐ後ろに迫って; のすぐあとをつけて ▪ One calamity follows *on the heels of* another. 泣きっ面(つら)にハチ ▪ Poverty was often *on my heels.* 私はよく貧乏に追われていた ▪ They stayed *on the heels of* the runaways. 彼らは逃亡者たちのあとをつけ続けた ▪ The police were hot [hard] *on his heels.* 警察は厳しく彼を追跡した.

***out at* (*the*) *heel*(*s*)** **1** 靴下のかかとがすり切れて[破れて] ▪ Look at that man walking with his stockings *out at heels.* かかとの破れた靴下をはいて歩くあの男を見なさい ▪ She is always *out at heel.* 彼女はいつも靴下のかかとが破れている.

2 落ちぶれて; 難渋して ▪ My present situation is a little *out at heels.* 私の現在の状態はやや左前である.

set* [*rock*] one *back on* one's *heels ...を愕然とさせる, どんでん返しに合わせる ▪ His counterpunch *rocked* his opponent *back on his heels.* 彼のカウンターパンチが形勢を逆転させた.

set ... by the heels →lay ... by the HEELs.

show a clean* [*fair*] *pair of heels **1** すたこら逃げる, どんどん逃げる ▪ The thief *showed* us *a clean pair of heels.* 盗賊は我々からすたこら逃げた.

2 《主に英》 敵に圧勝する ▪ He *showed* the world's best runners *a clean pair of heels.* 彼は世界のトップランナーたちに圧倒的な強さを見せつけた.

3 《主に英》 他に抜きん出ている, 一歩リードしている ▪ He *shows* others *a clean pair of heels* in everything he does. 彼は何事につけ他人よりも一歩リードしている.

show* one's *heels すたこら逃げる; 追い越す, あとに残す (*to*) ▪ He *showed his heels to* us. 彼は我々からすたこら逃げた ▪ My impatience has *shown its heels to* my politeness. 私のせっかちが礼儀正しさを置き去りにした《私はせっかちのあまり礼儀を忘れた》.

spin on* one's *heel =turn on one's HEEL.

stick* one's *heels in →dig one's HEELs in.

take to* one's *heels 《口》 走る, 走り去る, 逃走する ▪ I *took to my heels* and collared the gentleman. 私は走ってその紳士のえり首をつかんだ ▪ When the robber heard the dog bark, he *took to his heels.* 強盗は犬のほえるのを聞いて逃走した.

tip* [*topple, turn*] *up* one's *heels →kick up one's HEELs.

to heel **1** (犬が)すぐあとについて ▪ At a word from his owner, the dog moved *to heel.* 主人の一言で犬はすぐ後ろについて来た.

2 服従して; 追従して; 適応して ▪ The Commons, realizing that he was still master, came *to heel.* 下院は彼がまだ主君であることを悟って, 服従した ▪ It is hard to bring the eye *to heel.* 目を慣らすことがむずかしい.

tread on* [*upon*] *the heels of **1** ...のすぐあとについて行く ▪ Well, here you are at last! I've been *treading on your heels* all day. やれやれ, やっと君が見つかった. 一日中君のあとを追っていたのだぞ ▪ Repentance *treads upon his heels.* 悔恨が彼につきまとう.

2 ...のすぐあとにやって来る ▪ Success *treads upon the heels of* effort and perseverance. 成功は努力と忍耐のすぐあとにやって来る.

trip* [*strike, throw*] *up* a person's *heels 人の足をすくって倒す, 人をつまずかせる《比喩的にも》 ▪ They will *throw up his heels.* 彼らは彼の足をすくって倒すだろう ▪ Death has *tripped up his heels.* 死が彼を倒した.

tumble* [*turn*] *up* a person's *heels →kick up one's HEELs.

turn on* [*upon*] one's *heel 急にくるりと向きを変える, くびすをめぐらす; 怒って立ち去る ▪ Taking offence at what I said, he *turned on his heel* and

H

left the room. 彼は私の言ったことを怒って急にくびすをめぐらして部屋を出た.

under the heel of《文》...に踏みつけられて; にしいたげられて, に支配されて ▪ They were *under the heel of* a cruel invader. 彼らは残酷な侵入者に踏みにじられていた ▪ She has long kept her husband *under her heel*. 彼女は長いこと夫をしりに敷いてきた.

(***with*** *one's*) ***heels foremost*** [***forward***]《口》死体になって ▪ He left the house *heels foremost*. 彼は死んで家から運び出された ▪ He came out of prison *with his heels forward*. 彼は刑務所から死んで運び出された.

height /haɪt/ 名 ***at a height of*** ...の高度で, 身長が...で ▪ A hawk, flying *at a height of* 50 feet, spotted a rat on the ground. 1羽のタカが50フィートの高さを飛んでいて地上に1匹のネズミを見つけた ▪ She stands *at a height of* 5 feet 2 inches. 彼女は身長が5フィート2インチある.

at the height of ...の絶頂で; が最高潮に, たけなわで ▪ The sport was *at its height*. 競技はたけなわであった ▪ He was *at the height of* his powers. 彼はもっとも脂の乗った時であった.

in height 高さが, 身長が ▪ I am 2 meters *in height*. 私は身長が2メートルです.

in the height of ...のまっ盛りに, の絶頂に ▪ I don't like to travel *in the height of* summer. 私は夏の盛りに旅行するのは好まない ▪ He was *in the height of* his vigor. 彼は元気の絶頂にあった.

in the heights 天に ▪ Praise Him *in the heights*. 天のエホバをほめたたえなさい.

the dizzy [***dizzying***] ***heights of***《主に米》目がくらむような高所, 頂点; 高い地位 ▪ He ascended to *the dizzy heights of* worldwide fame. 彼は世界的な名声の頂点に上り詰めた ▪ He has reached *the dizzying heights of* wealth. 彼は大富豪にのし上がった. ☞逆に全く取るに足らない低い地位を指して《戯》に用いることもある ▪ I was promoted to *the dizzying heights of* chief guard. 小生は守衛長に昇進した.

the height of folly 愚の骨頂 ▪ Trying to drive through a blizzard is *the height of folly*. 吹雪の中を車で通り抜けようとするのは愚の骨頂だ.

heir /eər/ 名 ***be heir to*** ...を継承する(身である), を譲り受ける (cf. Sh., *Haml.* 3. 1. 63) ▪ He *is heir to* a large fortune. 彼は莫大な財産を譲り受ける身である ▪ Cancer used to be the most incurable of all the ills that flesh *is heir to*. がんは人間のかかる病気のうちでもっとも治しにくいものだった.

fall heir to ...を相続する, 受けつぐ ▪ He has *fallen heir to* his father's bad temper. 彼は父の短気を受けついだ ▪ He *fell heir to* a certain estate. 彼はある地所を相続した.

hell /hel/ 名 ***a*** [***the***] ***hell of a***《口》大変な ▪ They kicked up *a hell of a* row. 彼らはどえらい騒ぎを起こした ▪ I have got *a hell of a* lot of money. 私にはどっさり金がある.

a hell on earth **1** この世の地獄《悲惨な所》 ▪ The place became *a hell on earth*. そこはこの世の地獄になった.

2 悪のはびこる所 ▪ These restaurants are little *hells on earth*. これらのレストランは悪のはびこる小地獄だ.

a hellraiser 大騒ぎする人, 酒乱の人 ▪ He used to be *a hellraiser*, but he's stopped drinking. 彼は酒乱だったが今は酒をやめている.

a living hell 極端に不快な状況, 生き地獄 ▪ The workplace is *a living hell* for some. 職場を生き地獄と感じる人もいる.

all (***gone***) ***to hell***《口》全く滅びて ▪ My plan is *all gone to hell*. 私の計画はすっかりおじゃんになった.

All hell breaks [***bursts, is let***] ***loose.***《口》大騒動となる; 阿修羅(あしゅら)の巷(ちまた)となる, 阿修羅のごとくあばれる ▪ When a cornered submarine surfaces, *all hell bursts loose*. 追いつめられた潜水艦が水面に浮かび上がると, ひどいありさまになる ▪ I will then sit back while *all hell breaks loose*. 大騒動になっている間私は座っていよう ▪ *All hell was let loose* when the bombs started falling. 爆弾が落ち始めると大騒動になった.

(***as***) ***... as hell***《口》ひどく, 非常に ▪ She was *as* mad *as hell*. 彼女はひどく怒っていた.

as much chance [***hope***] ***as a snowball*** [***snowflake***] ***in hell***《口》機会[見込み]は全くない ▪ Has he any chance of recovery?—*As much chance as a snowflake in hell*. 彼が全快する見込みがあるか?—全然ないね.

be hell for ...を熱愛する, 強く求める ▪ He *is hell for* efficiency. 彼は効率を強く求める.

be hell on《米俗》**1** ...にきわめて厳重である, きびしい ▪ Mammy has always *been hell on* dignity. 母はいつも品位についてはきびしかった.

2 ...にひどく有害[破壊的]である ▪ The sun *is hell on* my skin. 陽射しは私の肌には大敵だ ▪ The acidity *was hell on* my throat. 酸味のためにのどがやられた.

beat [***blast, kick, knock, lick***] (***the***) ***hell out of*** **1**《口》...をこっぴどく打ちのめす; (物)を手荒に扱う; を撃ち従える ▪ Two boys *beat the hell out of* each other. 二人の男の子が互いをたたきのめしあった ▪ He will *knock the hell out of* you. 彼は君に打ち勝つでしょう ▪ They *kicked the hell out of* the robber. 彼らは賊をたたきのめした.

2 ...にはさっぱりわからない ▪ Why did this happen? It *beats the hell out of* me. なぜこんなことが起きたのだろう. 私にはさっぱりわからない.

3《俗》...をうまくやる ▪ I just happened to *knock the hell out of* it. 私はそれをうまくやってのけたばかりだ.

catch [***get***] ***hell***《米口》お目玉を食う, 罰を受ける ▪ You are going to *catch hell* if Mom finds out you used her car. ママの車を使ったことが知れたらしかられるぞ.

come [***in spite of***] ***hell or high water***《口》どんな事があっても (→HELL and high water) ▪ I'm determined to finish the job *come hell or high water*. どんな事があってもその仕事をしてしまう決心である ▪ We will have the cattle *in spite of hell or high water*. ぜひ牛を手に入れよう.

for the hell of it 《口》戯れに, いたずらに, ほんの冗談で; くやしまぎれに ▪ He decided to dye his hair bright blue, just *for the hell of it*. 彼はただ面白半分に髪を真っ青に染めることにした ▪ He broke all the windows just *for the hell of it*. 彼はやけくそになって窓をみなこわした.

from hell to breakfast 《米俗》徹底的に ▪ This will zap your wrinkles *from hell to breakfast*. これを使えばしわが強力にやっつけられます.

get hell しかりつけられる; 懲らしめられる, 罰せられる ▪ I *got hell* for breaking the window. 私は窓をこわしてひどくしかられた.

get the hell out **1** うまく死を逃れる ▪ The others *got the hell out*. 他の者たちはうまく死を免れた.
2 急いで立ち去る (*of*) ▪ *Get the hell out of* here. ここから急いで立ち去れ.

give *a person* ***hell*** 《口》 **1** 人を不愉快でいたたまれないようにする ▪ I don't object to *being given hell* for it. それで不愉快な目にあわされても異議はない.
2 ひどい目にあわせる, 罰する, 打ちこらす, ひどくしかりつける ▪ I will *give* him *hell* next time I see him. 今度会ったらひどく彼をしかりつけてやろう.
3 (体の一部が)死にそうに痛い ▪ These new shoes are *giving* me *hell*. この新しい靴を履いていると足がひどく痛い.

go through hell/be put through hell 修羅場をくぐる, 地獄を見る ▪ I have been *going through hell* ever since I was fired. 私は首になってからずっと修羅場をくぐってきた.

go through [to] hell and back 《口》極めて不快な[辛い]経験に耐える, 修羅場を通り抜ける (→have been to HELL and back) ▪ Phew! I feel like I have *gone through hell and back*. やれやれ! やっと何とか切り抜けられたようだ.

go through hell and high water to *do* 《口》万難を排して…する (→HELL and high water) ▪ He *went through hell and high water to* rescue his sister from drowning. 彼は万難を排して溺れかかった妹を救った.

Go to hell! 《口》 **1** 行っちまえ!, うせやがれ! ▪ What are you doing here? *Go to hell!* ここで何をしてるんだ, うせやがれ!
2 くたばってしまえ!; ばか言え! 《拒絶・不同意》 ▪ Oh, *go to hell!* Don't talk such nonsense! ああ, くだらない! そんなばかな話はよせ.

go [shot] to hell/go to hell in a handbasket [bucket, basket, handcart] 《米口》急速に悪化する, あっという間に悪化の一途をたどる ▪ Your health will *go to hell in a handbasket* if you start drinking again. また飲み始めたら君の健康状態はあっという間に悪化するぞ.

have a [the] hell of a time 《口》 **1** 非常につらい, または不愉快な目にあう ▪ I've just *had a hell of a time* with the dentist. 私はちょうど今歯医者さんの所で痛い目にあったところです.
2 非常に愉快に過ごす ▪ We *had the hell of a time*—lots of pretty girls and lots of drinks. 我々は非常に愉快だった—美しい女の子が大勢いたし飲み物もうんとあったので.

have been to hell and back とてもつらい経験をした ▪ What a terrible day! I feel like I *have been to hell and back*. 何ともひどい1日だった. 地獄を見てきたような心地がする.

hell and [or] high water あらゆる障害[困難] ▪ We'll be there in time, come *hell or high water*. 我々はどんな障害があろうとも, 必ずそこへ間に合うように行く ▪ He has been through *hell and high water*. 彼は非常な難儀をした.

hell broke(n) loose 《口》混乱[無秩序, 反乱]の恐ろしい状態, 阿修羅(あしゅら)の巷(ちまた) ▪ For a time it was *hell broken loose*. 一時はそれはまるで阿修羅の巷であった.

hell for breakfast 《俗》猛烈な勢いで ▪ The cans went snorting out, *hell for breakfast* after the sub. 爆雷はうなりを立てて, 猛烈な勢いで潜水艦めがけて行った.

hell for leather 《英口》猛烈なスピード[勢い]で ▪ The horse went *hell for leather*. 馬は全速力で走った.

Hell hath no fury like a woman scorned. 《諺》軽蔑された女性の怒りほど恐ろしいものはない《男性に拒絶された女性がひどく怒って復しゅうに燃えることがある》. ☞William Congreve, *The Mourning Bride* (1697)の中の台詞から.

Hell is paved with good intentions. 《諺》 →INTENTION.

Hell mend *a person*! 《口》ちくしょう! ▪ *Hell mend* him, you might think. こんちくしょう! あいつめ, とお考えでしょう.

hell on wheels/hell-on-wheels **1** 交通地獄 ▪ We had *hell on wheels* all day here. 終日この場所は交通地獄だった.
2 (町が)無法で, ぶっそうな ▪ Detroit is still *hell on wheels*. デトロイトはまだぶっそうな町だ.
3 (馬などが)癖の悪い, 手に負えない; きびしい, おかんむりの ▪ That horse is sure *hell on wheels*. あれは確かに癖の悪い馬だ ▪ The boy is *hell on wheels* to deal with. 彼は実に扱いにくい少年だ ▪ Watch out—the boss's *hell on wheels* this week. 気をつけろ, ボスは今週荒れているからな.

hell or high water →HELL and high water.

hell to pay 前途の大難事 ▪ If he's late there'll be *hell to pay*. もし彼が遅刻すれば, 大変ひどい目にあうだろう.

hell to split 《米俗》大急ぎで, 猛烈な勢いで ▪ Jim was cutting across country from the head-gates *hell to split*. ジムは水門から全速力で田野を突っ切って進んでいた.

hell west and crooked 《米俗》ぺしゃんこに, 徹底的に ▪ Now all this knocked me *hell west* *and crooked*. さて, これらのことで私はぺしゃんこに参ってしまった.

Hell's bells! 《英口》(困って[驚いて])これは困った, なんということだ ▪ Oh, *hell's bells!* Now I'm getting a headache. ああ, なんてこった! こいつは頭が痛い ▪ Oh, *hell's bells!* Didn't you do anything while I was away? まあどうしましょう! 私の留守中何もしていないの?

hell's delight 大混乱, 阿修羅(あしゅら)の巷(ちまた), 大騒動 ▪ Just listen to the *hell's delight* that is going on over there. あそこで起こっている大騒動の音をちょっと聞きなさい.

hell's teeth 〚間投詞的に〛《英口》くそっ, なんてことだ《怒り•驚きを表す》 ▪ *Hell's teeth*, look at the time! I'm going to be late for school! 大変, もうこんな時間だ. 学校におくれちゃう.

hope* [*wish*] *to hell 《口》強く望む[願う] ▪ I *wish to hell* you would speak to the director for me. お願いですから私に免じて重役に話してください.

I'll see you in hell first. → I'll SEE you hanged first.

in spite of hell or high water = come HELL or high water.

kick up hell →raise HELL.

kick up hell's delight →raise HELL's delight.

like hell 《口》 **1** 猛烈に, 必死に, やけに ▪ We all worked *like hell* to get the job done. 仕事を片付けようとみんな猛烈にがんばった ▪ I ran *like hell* to catch the train. 列車に間に合うように必死に走った.
2 ひどく《意味を持たない単なる強勢》 ▪ I shall miss you *like hell*. あなたがいないとひどく寂しいでしょう.
3 全然[絶対に]…ない, …なんてとんでもない ▪ Did you go?—*Like hell* (I did). 君は行ったか?—行くものか ▪ You want me to say sorry? *Like hell* I will! 僕に謝れだって? 誰が謝るものか!

move hell to *do* 《口》(悪事を)するために全力を尽くす ▪ I'd *move hell to* ruin him if I could. できれば全力を尽くして彼を破滅させてやるんだが.

not ... in hell 全く…ない ▪ There's *not* a hope *in hell*. 見込みは全くない ▪ She does*n't* have a hope *in hell* of passing the exams. 彼女が試験に合格する見込みは全然ない.

Oh hell! ちくしょう!

one hell of a 《口》すごい ▪ He had *one hell of a* row with his neighbor. 彼は近所の人と派手なけんかをおっぱじめた ▪ He's *one hell of a* nice guy. 彼はすごくいい奴だ.

play* ((《英》) *merry*) *hell with 《俗》 **1** …をめちゃめちゃにする; 大損害を与える, 損傷する; 怒って強く抗議する ▪ The new manager is *playing hell with* everything. 新任の支配人は万事をひっくり返している ▪ He is *playing hell with* his health. 彼は健康をひどく害している ▪ The power failure *played merry hell with* our computer systems. 停電のおかげでわが社のコンピューター•システムに大きな支障が生じた ▪ The drunkard *played merry hell with* the sheriff in the jug. 酔っ払いはブタ箱の中で保安官に毒づいた.
2 …を打ち負かす, 虐待する ▪ He *played hell with* them. 彼は彼らを打ち負かした.

put* a person *through hell 人を苦しめる[悩ます] ▪ He *put* me *through hell* with his foul odor. 彼はひどい匂いをぷんぷんさせて悩ませた.

quicker than hell could scorch a feather 《米俗》電光石火のように, 素早く ▪ I'll be in his hair *quicker than hell could scorch a feather*. たちまちのうちに彼を怒らせてやるぞ.

raise* [*kick up*] *hell **1**《主に米口》騒いで迷惑をかける; 大騒動を起こす ▪ Several boys were *kicking up hell* in the street. 通りで数人の男の子たちが大騒ぎをしていた ▪ They *raised hell* about the tax increase. 増税に関して彼らは大騒動を起こした.
2 (撤回を求めて)怒って抗議する, 声を上げて不満を言う ▪ He *raised hell* when he found out he would have his pay cut. 減給と知って彼は猛烈に抗議した.

raise hell with 《俗》…を非難する, しかる, に不平を言う ▪ They *raised hell with* their leadership. 彼らは指導者を非難した.

raise* [*kick up*] *hell's delight 《口》大騒動を起こす, 大騒ぎをする ▪ Tomorrow when I meet them, I'm going to *raise hell's delight*. あす彼らに会ったとき, 大騒動を起こしてやるつもりだ.

scare* [*annoy*, etc.] *the hell out of 《口》ひどくおびえ[いらいら, など]させる ▪ The sight of a man with a gun *scared the hell out of* me. 銃をもった男の姿にぎょっとした.

see* a person *in hell first 《口》(相手の提案に対して)その人は断じていやだ ▪ You want me to invite that guy? I'll *see* him *in hell first*. あいつを招けだって? 絶対にいやだ.

shot* [*blown*] *to hell →go to HELL.

the child* [*house, mother*, etc.] *from hell 《戯》ひどい, 最悪の, 最も不快な子供[家, 母親, など] ▪ His mother really is *the mother-in-law from hell*. 彼の母親は実に最低の姑(しゅうとめ)だ.

the hell of a →a HELL of a.

do ***the hell out of*** *a person* 《米俗》人を徹底的に…する ▪ The noise scared *the hell out of* him. その音は彼をすっかりおびえさせた.

(The) hell with ...! …は全くいまいましい ▪ *The hell with* you, my friend. 君は全くいまいましいね ▪ *Hell with* that noise. あの音がやかましくてたまらん.

there'll be (merry) hell to pay*/(*there'll be (all)*) *hell to pay 《口》(その行動の結果)ひどく面倒なことが起きる, 地獄を見る ▪ You'd better do it right away, or *there'll be all hell to pay*. 君は今すぐした方が身のためだ, さもないととんでもないことになる.

till* [*until*] *hell freezes (over) 《口》いつまでも, 永久に ▪ I'll wait *till hell freezes over* for your answer. ずっとあなたのご返事を待っています.

(to) hell and gone **1** きわめて遠方[行けないほどの遠方](へ); いつまでも ▪ A flood occurs and carries them *to hell and gone*. 洪水があってそれらを遠い遠い所へ運んで行く.

2〚強調形〛ずっと, ひどく(遠く) ▪ He would be *to hell and gone* away from here by now. 彼は今頃までにはここからひどく遠くへ行っているだろう.

To [***The***] ***hell with ...!*** 《口》…を葬れ ▪ *To hell with* the capitalists! 資本家どもをやっつけろ.

What the hell! ええままよ, どうにでもなれ! ▪ *What the hell*, I may as well go. ままよ, 行ってもよかろう.

What [***When, Where, Who, Why, How***] ***the*** [***in***] ***hell ...?*** 一体何[いつ, どこ, 誰, なぜ, どうして]…? ▪ *What the hell* do you want? 一体あなたは何がほしいのか.

when hell freezes (***over***) 絶対に…しない (never) ▪ I'll do it *when hell freezes over*. 私はそれを絶対にしません. ☞「地獄が凍結したら…する」とは「決して…しない」こと.

wish to hell →hope to HELL.

hell-bent /hélbènt/ 形 (***be***) ***hell-bent on*** [***for***] 《口》…を堅く[必死に]決意して(いる) ▪ All the Jews *are hell-bent for* Israel. ユダヤ人はこぞってイスラエル支持を堅く決意している ▪ He *is hell-bent on* winning her love. 彼は彼女の愛を得ようと必死の決意をしている.

be hell-bent to *do* 《米俗》…しようとがむしゃらに決意している ▪ I *am hell-bent to* get back again. 私はどうしてもまた帰るつもりです.

go hell-bent for 《米俗》…を強く支持する; に全力を尽す ▪ The Democrats were *going hell-bent for* Roosevelt. 民主党はルーズベルトを強力に支持していた.

hell-bent for breakfast 《米俗》猛烈な勢いで ▪ I was going *hell-bent for breakfast*. 私は猛烈な速力で走っていた.

hello /həlóʊ|heləʊ/ 間 名 ***a golden hello*** (有望な新入社員として確保するために支払われる)多額の手当[支度金] ▪ We pay *a golden hello* to attract promising recruits to our firm. 当社への有望な新入社員の確保に高額の手当を出している.

Hello, there! やあ! 《目下の者・同年輩の友だち同士の親しみあるあいさつ》 ▪ *Hello, there!* How are you? やあ, ごきげんいかが.

say hello to …によろしく伝える ▪ *Say hello to* your father. おとうさんによろしく.

helm /helm/ 名 ***assume the helm*** →take the HELM.

(***be***) ***at the helm*** かじを取って(いる); 指導にあたる, 主宰して(いる) ▪ He *is at the helm* of state. 彼は国政を主宰している ▪ Now we have got a strong man *at the helm*. 我々は今度強い人を指導者に得た.

leave the helm かじを捨てる; 仕事を投げ出す ▪ I *left the helm* and rushed to the stern. かじを捨てて船尾へ急行した ▪ He finally *left the helm*. 彼はとうとう仕事を投げ出した.

Mind your helm! 気をつけよ!, 用心せよ! ▪ Now you'd better *mind your helm!* さあ気をつけたほうが身のためだぞ.

No talking to the man at the helm! かじを取っている人に話しかけるな! 《大事な仕事をしている人をじゃまするな》.

take [***assume***] ***the helm*** 指導にあたる, 責任の地位につく ▪ He *took the helm* of state. 彼は国政を主宰した《政権を握った》.

help[1] /help/ 名 ***be beyond help*** (患者が)助かる見込みがない, 救いようがない ▪ The poor patient *is beyond help*. 気の毒に, その患者の容態は手の施しようがない.

be of help 役に立つ ▪ Can I *be of* any *help* to you? 何か手伝いましょうか.

by help of (…の助け)により ▪ *By help of* favorable circumstances, he has succeeded. 順境のおかげで彼は成功した.

there is no help for …は何とも仕方がない ▪ *There is no help for* the situation he is in. 彼がおかれている情勢は何とも仕方がない.

there is no help for it but to *do* …するよりほかはない ▪ *There was no help for it but to* wait till he returned. 彼が戻るまで待つよりほかはなかった. ☞help「治療法」.

There's no help for it. 《主に英》もう施す手がない ▪ *There's no help for it.* We'll have to call the plumber. もうお手上げだ. 水道屋に電話しなくては.

help[2] /help/ 動 ***cannot help*** …はどうにも仕方がない ▪ One *cannot help* the shape of one's nose. 自分の鼻の形はどうにも仕方がない ▪ It's too bad, but it *can't be helped*. 気の毒だがどうにも仕方がない.

cannot help *a person* [*a person's*] *doing* 人が…するのはどうしようもない ▪ I *cannot help* him [*his*] *being* foolish. 彼が愚かなのはどうしようもない.

cannot help *doing* …せざるをえない《cannot but do よりは口語的》 ▪ I *could not help laughing* at the idea. その考えを笑わざるをえなかった.

cannot help but *do* …せざるをえない ▪ I *could not help but* laugh. 私は笑わずにはいられなかった.

God help you [***him,*** etc.]***!*** かわいそうに ▪ She says (*God help her*) she was wedded to a fool. 彼女は(かわいそうに)愚か者と結婚させられたと言っている.

Heaven [***God***] ***help*** *a person* ***if*** [***when***] …ならば[のときには]人は大変な目にあうぞ, もうだめだ ▪ *Heaven help* us *if* there is another war! もう一度戦争が起こった, 我々は大変な目にあうぞ ▪ *God help* us *when* faith silences reason. 信仰によって理性が沈黙するようになったら, もうおしまいだ. ☞help は願望を表す仮定法現在.

Heaven [***God***] ***helps those who help themselves.*** 《諺》天は自ら助くる者を助く.

help *oneself* **1** 必要なことを自分でする ▪ She is old and cannot *help herself*. 彼女は年取っているので必要なことが自分でできない.

2 困難から脱する ▪ I shall be unable to *help myself*. 私は困難を切り抜けることができないだろう.

3〚命令文で〛お好きなように; (飲食物を) 自由に取っておあがりなさい ▪ *Help yourself!* お好きなように(しなさ

H

い)!

4〖cannot を伴って〗自分をどうにかする ▪ They merely read books, because they *couldn't help themselves.* 彼らはどうにもしようがなかったのでただ本を読んだだけだった.

help a lame dog [***lamb***] (***over a stile***) (金に)困っている人を助ける ▪ He is always *helping lame dogs* (*over stiles*). 彼はいつも困った人々を助けている ▪ I can *help a lame lamb over a stile.* 私は金に困った人を助けることができる.

help matters 役に立つ, 効果がある ▪ Words will not *help matters.* 言葉だけでは何の役にも立たない.

help** oneself* (to***) **1** (…を)自分で取って食べる ▪ Please *help yourself to* the cake. どうぞご自由にお菓子をお取りください ▪ I will *help myself to* the wine. 手じゃくで1杯やろう.

2 (…を)勝手に取る; (を)勝手に使う; (を)横領する ▪ One must *help oneself,* as there is no salesman. 販売員がいないから, 客は勝手に取らなければならない ▪ He *helped himself* freely *to* the furniture. 彼はその家具を遠慮なく使った.

(***not***) ***if*** *one* ***can help it*** せずにすむものならなるべく(しない) ▪ Don't use slang *if* you *can help it.* なるべく俗語は使わないようにしなさい ▪ He does *not* talk *if* he *can help it.* 彼はなるべく話はしない.

not more than [***as little as***] *one* ***can help*** なるべく…しない ▪ Don't be *longer than* you *can help.* なるべく手間を取らぬように ▪ Your name will appear *as little as* I *can help.* お名前はなるべく出さないようにします.

So help me (***God***)***!*** 神も照覧あれ!, 神に誓って(申します)!《断言・誓約に添える》 ▪ I do swear that I will be faithful to Her Majesty. *So help me God!* 女王陛下に忠実たることを堅く誓います. 神も照覧あれ! ▪ It was, *so help me,* the most difficult problem. それは神に誓って[断然]もっとも困難な問題であった. ☞as I speak the truth を補って解す.

helping /hélpɪŋ/ 形 ***give a helping hand*** →give a person a HAND.

helve /helv/ 名 ***fly off the helve*** 《米口》(特に立腹して)自制を失う, かっとなる (＝fly off (at) the HANDLE) ▪ He would *fly off the helve* during his paroxysms of declamation. 彼は弁舌が熱してくると逆上するのであった.

send [***throw***] ***the helve after the hatchet/ send the ax*** [***hatchet***] ***after the helve*** 賭けで損をした上に残りの金を全部賭ける, 泥棒に追銭(おいせん)をする ▪ He foolishly *threw the helve after the hatchet.* 愚かにも彼は損した上に残りの金を全部賭けた.

hem[1] /hem/ 名 ***kiss the hem of*** *a person's* ***garment*** 人におもねる ▪ I don't expect staff to *kiss the hem of my garment.* 職員におもねってもらおうとは思わない.

hem[2] /hem/ 動 ***hem and haw*** [***hawk, ha***] 《米》 **1** えへんえへんと言う《注意を引くため, 単なる咳払いで》 ▪ I *hemmed and hawed*—but the Queen never stopped reading. 私はえへんえへんと咳払いした—が女王は読書をやめなかった.

2 口ごもる, 言葉を濁す; ためらう ▪ Asked why he was late, John only *hemmed and hawed.* 遅刻の理由を尋ねられたがジョンはただ口ごもってごまかした.

hemming and hawing 《米》むにゃむにゃ[もごもご]言うこと, 口ごもり, ちゅうちょ ▪ Stop *hemming and hawing,* and just tell her. もごもご言うのはやめて, 彼女に打ち明けなさい ▪ No *hemming and hawing,* please. どうかはっきり言ってください ▪ This is no time for *hemming and hawing.* 今はためらっている場合ではない.

hen /hen/ 名 ***a hen is on*** 《米口》重大なことが起きようとしている ▪ Keep cool, boys, there's *a hen on.* みんな, 落ち着け, 重大な事が起きようとしている.

a hen party [***night***] 《英口》女性だけの社交パーティー (→a STAG party) ▪ I attended *a hen party* to celebrate the forthcoming marriage of a friend. 友人の近うく結婚を祝う女性だけのパーティーに出席した ▪ I'm currently trying to hold *a hen night* for my friend. お友だちのために女の子だけのパーティーを目下計画中なの.

(***as***) ***mad as a wet hen*** →(as) MAD as hops.

(***as***) ***scarce*** [***rare***] ***as hen's teeth/scarcer than hen's teeth*** 《米俗》きわめて乏しい ▪ Horses are *scarcer than hen's teeth* round here. この辺では馬はきわめて乏しい ▪ Payphones are becoming *as rare as hen's teeth* around here. この辺りでは公衆電話が珍しくなっている. ☞ニワトリに歯がないことから.

like a hen on a hot griddle [***girdle***] そわそわして, ひどく落ち着きがなく ▪ She shifted from one foot to another *like a hen on a hot girdle.* 彼女はそわそわして足を左右に踏み変えた. ☞girdle「一種のパン焼き用なべ」.

like [***as***] ***a hen with one chick***(***en***) こまかいことにばかり気を使う, 騒ぎたてる ▪ She hovers over that child *like a hen with one chicken.* 彼女はその子につきまとって, うるさく世話をやく ▪ Karl is busy *as a hen with one chick.* カールは小さいことに大騒ぎする.

sell *one's* ***hen on*** [***of***] ***a rainy day*** 損な商売をする, 損をして売る ▪ He will never *sell his hen of a rainy day.* 彼は決して損な商売はしないだろう. ☞雨が降る日はニワトリが悪く見えるということから.

hence /hens/ 副名 ***…days*** [***weeks,*** etc.] ***hence*** 《文》今から…日[週間, など]あとに ▪ The truth will only be known several *years hence.* 真相は数年後になるまで分からないだろう.

from hence 《雅》ここ[今]から; それで ▪ He went *from hence* into the other world. 彼はこの世からあの世へ行った.

go [***depart, pass***] ***hence*** 《雅》みまかる, 死ぬ ▪ The old man *passed hence.* 老人は他界した.

Hence with…! …を持ち去れ; とともに去れ ▪ *Hence with* her, out of doors. 彼女とともに戸外へ去れ ▪ *Hence with* him! 彼を連れ去れ.

hep /hep/ 形 ***be hep to*** 《米俗》…を知っている, に通じている ▪ He *is* not *hep to* what is going on. 彼は現況を知らない.

get hep to 《米俗》…を理解する, 知る ▪ I'm *getting hep to* the fact. 私はその事実がわかりかけている.

put *a person* ***hep to*** 《米俗》人に…を教える[知らせる] ▪ Let me *put* you *hep to* this. 君に次のことを教えてやろう.

her /həːr/ 代 ***her indoors*** →INDOORS.

herd /həːrd/ 名 ***break herd*** 群れを離れる; 独立の道を行く ▪ They dare not *break herd*, afraid of the ridicule. 彼らは嘲笑を恐れて群を離れられない.

herds and flocks 牛と羊の群れ ▪ Our *herds and flocks* have become multitudinous. 我々の牛羊の群は多数になった.

ride herd on 《米》牛群の外がわを馬で回って…の番をする; を見張る, 観察する ▪ I thought you were *riding herd on* the hotel desk in town. あなたは町でホテルの受付番をしているのだと思っていた ▪ He is *riding herd on* the play. 彼はその演技をじっと見ている.

the common [***vulgar***] ***herd*** 大衆, 俗衆 (→the VULGAR herd) ▪ Don't imitate *the common herd*. 俗衆のまねをするな.

here /hɪər/ 副名 ***be here to stay*** →STAY².

be up to here 《口》 **1** とてもできないほど多くの仕事を持つ ▪ We *are up to here* in the shop. 店では私たちの手にあまるほど多くの仕事がある.

2 がまんできないほど多くの事を持つ ▪ She'*s up to here* with the children. 彼女は子供たちをもてあましている.

3 (食物・感情で)いっぱいである ▪ I can't eat any more. I'*m up to here*. もう食べられません. 腹いっぱいです.

here a little and there a little 折にふれては少しずつ(教える, など) ▪ I have learned *here a little and there a little*. これまで折にふれて少しずつ身につけてきた.

here and now 今この場で ▪ Please do this *here and now*. 今この場でこれをしてください.

here and there **1** あちこち ▪ He stays *here and there*, never in one place. 彼はあちこちに転々とし, 決して1箇所にとどまらない.

2 ときどき ▪ Fine paintings can be found *here and there* in our churches. わが国の教会では立派な絵がときどき見つかる.

here below この世 ▪ Man wants but little *here below*. 人間はこの世ではわずかあれば足りる.

Here goes! 《口》さあやるぞ!, それっ! ▪ Since it must be done, *here goes!* しなければならないんだから, さあやるぞ ▪ You deal.—O.K. *Here goes*. 君トランプを配ってくれ—よし, さあやるぞ.

Here goes nothing! 《口》ええい, やっちまえ!《見込みのないことなどをする時の発声》 ▪ "*Here goes nothing!*" said Bill at the beginning of the race. 「ええい, やっちまえ!」とビルは競走の初めに言った.

Here I am. ただいま, さあ着いた ▪ Well, *here I am*, home again after three weeks away in the North. ああ. ただいま. 3週間北へ行っていて戻ってきたところだ.

Here I go! →HERE goes!

here is [***here's***] ***where…*** 《米》ここが…するところだ ▪ *Here's where* I feel pain. ここが痛む箇所だ.

Here it is! さあここにある; さあこれをあげる ▪ May I have another?—Yes, *here it is!* もう一つもらえないか—いいよ, はいどうぞ.

here, there, and everywhere 至る所に; 絶えず動き回って ▪ The enemy was *here, there, and everywhere*. 敵は至る所にいた ▪ We were soon scattered *here, there, and everywhere*. 我々はじきに至る所に散らばった.

here today and gone tomorrow 絶えず動いて ▪ My little cousin was *here today and gone tomorrow*. いとこは絶えず動き回っていた.

Here we are! 《口》(我々の求めていたものは)さあここにあります ▪ Have you seen my glasses anywhere?—Oh yes, *here we are!* 私の眼鏡をどこかで見たかね?—ああ, ここにありますよ.

Here we are again! また出てまいりました《道化役が舞台に現れたときに言うきまり文句》.

here we are (***at***) 《口》さあ(…へ)来ました ▪ *Here we are at* the station. さあ駅へ着いたぞ.

Here we [***you***] ***go*** (***again***). 《口》また始まった《いやなこと, 退屈なことなどが再度ある時に言う》 ▪ I was engaged once, but it didn't work out.—*Here we go* again. 僕は一度婚約したんだが, うまくいかなかった—また(泣き事が)始まった.

Here you are! 《口》(探し物など出しながら)はいここにあります ▪ If you are looking for bargains, *here you are!* 掘り出し物をお探しなら, ここにあります.

Here you go. 《口》(相手に物を差し出して)はい, これをどうぞ ▪ *Here you go*. Here's your hamburger and beer. では, どうぞ. ご注文のハンバーガーとビールです.

here's a health to 《口》…の健康を祝します《乾杯の文句》 ▪ *Here's a health to* our friends. 我々の友人の健康を祝します.

Here's at you! **1** ご健康[幸福]を祝します《乾杯の文句》 ▪ Well, *here's at you*, may you live long and die happy! ではご健康を祝して, どうぞ長生きし, 幸福に一生を終えられますように.

2 《米口》よしっ!, 賛成! ▪ Then the response came—"*Here's at you!*" それから「賛成」という返答があった.

Here's cheers [***fortune, fun, God bless us, good luck, hearts and flowers, how, into your face, jolly good luck, looking at you, looking to you, luck to you, the best, the best of luck, the very best, towards you***]***!*** ＝HERE's at you! 1.

Here's something for you. これをあげよう ▪ *Here's* a little *something for you* from Kyoto.—Oh, how nice! ささやかな京都のお土産です—まあ, すてき.

H

here's to …の健康を祝します《乾杯の文句》 ▪ *Here's to* all the wanderers! すべて放浪する人たちに乾杯!

Here's where you want it. (頭を指したり, 手を頭に当てて)ここが必要なのだ《頭を使わねばいけない》 ▪ Come on, *here's where you want it*, son.—I know, Dad. さあ, お前, 頭を使うんだ—わかっているよ, 父さん.

I'm out of here. 《俗》(ほっとして)さあこれで, もう帰る[行く]よ ▪ It's five o'clock. *I'm out of here*! 5時になった. さあ帰れるぞ!

in here ここでは, この中に, ここに ▪ It is very warm *in here*. この中は非常に暖かい.

Look* [*See*] *here. おい!, ねえ!; おいこら《命令・諫言・叱責のぶっきらぼうな呼びかけ》 ▪ Now, *look here*! I'll have no feelings. おいこら! わしは情け容赦はないぞ.

near here →NEAR.

neither here nor there **1** (どっちみち)取るに足らぬ, つまらない ▪ But even if he does, that is *neither here nor there*. しかしたとえ彼がしても, それは取るに足らぬことだ.
2 要点をはずれて; 無関係で; 問題外で ▪ What you have said is *neither here nor there*. 君の言ったことは本論をはずれている ▪ I know you like him, but that is *neither here nor there*. 君は彼が好きなのは分かっている, がそれは何の関係もないことだ.
3 どうでもよい《少し捨てばち的》 ▪ It's all right. It's *neither here nor there*. けっこうです. それはどうでもよいんです. ☞cf. Sh., *Oth.* 4. 3. 59.

See here. →Look HERE.

this here 《口》この, ここにある ▪ *This here* picture was painted by Monet. こちらの絵はモネの作だ.

hero /híːroʊ|híər-/ 名 ***an* [*the*] *unsung hero*** 陰の英雄 ▪ Among all those who have done distinguished service, he is *a* true *unsung hero*. 彼こそ我らの影の功労者中の功労者だ.

make a hero of (人)を英雄扱いする, もてはやす ▪ They *made a hero of* the new champion. みんなで新チャンピオンを祭り上げた.

No man is a hero to his valet. 《諺》英雄もその使用人にはただの人, 英雄も常に接すればただの人.

heronshaw /hérənʃɔː/ 名 ***know a hawk from a heronshaw*** →know a HAWK from a handsaw (when the wind is southerly).

herring /hérɪŋ/ 名 ***a red herring*** **1** くん製ニシン.
2 (故意に)注意をそらすもの ▪ After that *red herring* let's get back to our subject. その故意の脱線から本題に帰ろう ▪ Please don't throw in *a red herring*. 本題から注意をそらす話を投げ込まないでください. ☞キツネの道へ「くん製ニシン」を投げると, 臭跡が消えて犬が迷うとされることから.

***as close as herrings* (*in a barrel*)** →like HERRINGs (in a barrel).

(*as*) *dead as a herring* よくよく死んで ▪ All hope of anything of that sort is *dead as a herring*. そのようなどんな望みも全くない.

(*as*) *thick as herrings* ひどく密集して ▪ Salmon are in shoals *as thick as herrings*. サケがぎっしり群れをなしている.

(*as*) *thin as a herring* ひどく薄い ▪ He was a very small man, *as thin as a herring*. 彼はとても小柄な男でひどく痩せていた.

(*be*) *neither fish,* (*flesh,*) *fowl, nor good red herring* →FISH[1].

***draw a red herring across* (*the path* [*track*])** 本題から注意をそらそうとする ▪ He was purposely *drawing a red herring across* the trail of the discussion. 彼はわざと本題から注意をそらそうとしていた.

Every herring should hang by its own head. 《諺》人はみな自分自身の力量によるべきだ.

I like not barrel or herring それが大きらいだ.

***like* [*as close as*] *herrings* (*in a barrel*)** すし詰めにして ▪ People were jammed inside *like herrings in a barrel*. 人々はその中へすし詰めにされていた.

the herring pond 《戯》大西洋 ▪ He crossed *the herring pond* for the fifth time. 彼は5度目の大西洋横断をした.

throw* (*out*) *a sprat to catch a herring →SPRAT.

hesitate /hézətèɪt/ 動 ***He who hesitates is lost.*** 《諺》ちゅうちょすると好機を逸してしまう《断固として事をなすべきだ》,「ためらう者は破滅する」.

hesitation /hèzətéɪʃən/ 名 ***without hesitation*** ちゅうちょしないで, すぐにきっぱりと ▪ He said so *without hesitation*. 彼はきっぱりとそう言った.

het /het/ 動 **(*get*) *het up*** 《口》〚通例 get を伴って〛怒る, かっとなる ▪ I don't (*get*) *het up* easy. 私はかんたんには怒らない.

hew /hjuː/ 動 ***hew a way through*** …を切り開いて通る, 切り抜ける ▪ The pioneers *hewed a way through* the forest. 開拓者たちはその森を切り開いて通った.

hew* (*close*) *to the line 《米口》(丸太などを)目印線に沿って切る; (ある基準に従って)注意深く[つましく]行動する ▪ I know the importance of *hewing to the line*. 私は注意深く行動する重要性を知っている.

hew … to* [*in*] *pieces …を寸断する, めった切りにする ▪ Agag *was hewed to pieces* by Samuel. アガグはサムエルに切り殺された (《聖》*1 Sam.* 15. 33).

hew to the ground 切り倒す; 切り殺す ▪ He *hewed* the giant *to the ground*. 彼は巨人を切り倒した.

hew one's* [*a*] *way 進路を切り開く ▪ He determined to *hew his way* to distinction through the ranks. 彼は低い身分から栄達への道を切り開こうと決心した.

hewer /hjúːər/ 名 ***hewers of wood and drawers of water*** たきぎを切り水をくむ人々; 苦役をする人々 (《聖》*Josh.* 9. 21) ▪ Being but *a hewer of wood and drawer of water*, she is rheumatic. 下層労働者にすぎないので, 彼女はリューマ

チにかかっている.

hex /heks/ 名 ***put the*** [***a***] ***hex on*** 《主に米》…に魔法をかける, 呪いをかける ▪ She's *put a hex on* me. 彼女は私に呪いをかけた ▪ These products are sure to *put the hex on* wrinkles. この製品を使えば魔法をかけたようにしわが消えます.

hey /heɪ/ 間名 ***Hey for…!*** …はうまいぞ, でかした; …へ行くべし; はありがたや ▪ Breakfast at nine, and then—*hey for* the covers. 9時に朝食で, そのとき食器が揃ってありがたい.

Hey presto! →PRESTO.

What the hey! 《米口》かまわない, 気にしない, 平気だ ▪ Yes, it's kinda weird but *what the hey!* 確かにちょっぴり奇妙だが, なに, かまうもんか.

hey-day /héɪdèɪ/ 名 ***in the hey-day of*** …の全盛期に, まっ盛りに ▪ The teachers are *in the hey-day of* their youth. 先生がたは若い盛りである.

hiccup /híkʌp/ 名 ***only a hiccup/a mere hiccup*** (進歩の)小さな妨げ, 単に一時的な頓挫(とんざ) ▪ This halt in construction is *a mere hiccup*. 今回の建設工事の中止は一時的なものにすぎない.

hide[1] /haɪd/ 名 ***a hide like a rhinoceros*** →have a hide like a RHINOCEROS.

dress [***tan***] *a person's* ***hide*** 人をむちでひっぱたく, 《俗》人(主に子供)をひっぱたく ▪ I'll *tan your hide* for you. お前をむちでひっぱたいてやるぞ ▪ I'll *tan that boy's hide* if he touches my computer again. あの子が今度またコンピューターにさわったらひっぱたいてやる.

have a thick hide 《口》つらの皮が厚い, 無神経な ▪ Writers must *have a thick hide* to criticism. 作家は批評に対して無神経でなければならない.

have *a person's* ***hide*** 《口》人をきびしく罰する ▪ I'll *have your hide* if you tell a lie. 嘘をついたら厳罰に処するぞ.

hide or hair 《口》〚主に否定文・疑問文で〛毛も皮も[全く] ▪ I haven't seen *hide or hair* of him since. それ以来彼の姿は全く見かけない.

(***in***) ***hide and hair*** 毛も皮も; すっかり, 全く ▪ He will exhibit the goods *in hide and hair* at a certain place. 彼はある場所にその品をすっかり陳列するだろう.

neither hide nor hair of 何も…ない ▪ I have seen *neither hide nor hair of* the piece ever since. それ以来それをちっとも見ません.

not see hide nor hair of 《口》…を全く見かけない ▪ I have*n't seen hide nor hair of* him for several weeks. この数週間彼をさっぱり見かけない.

save *one's* ***hide*** =save one's (own) SKIN.

hide[2] /haɪd/ 動 ***hide*** *oneself* 隠れる ▪ Tigers have a wonderful knack of *hiding themselves*. トラは身を隠すすばらしいこつを知っている.

hide *one's* ***face from*** …を見捨てる, 無視する ▪ I'll *hide my face from* them. 彼らを見捨てよう.

Hide fox and all after. 隠れよ, キツネ, みんなで捜そう《隠れんぼのとき一人が隠れて, みんなで捜すときのかけ声》.

hide *one's* ***head*** [***face***] **1** (非難を恐れて)黙っている ▪ The pessimists *hid their heads* then. 悲観論者たちはそのとき沈黙していた.
2 頭を隠す; (恥ずかしさなどで)身を隠す ▪ I *hid my head* in shame. 私は恥ずかしさで隠れた.

hide *one's* ***light*** [***candle***] ***under a bushel*** 自分の善行や才能を世間に隠す(《聖》*Matt*. 5. 15) ▪ He has the virtue of *hiding his light under a bushel*. 彼は謙遜(けんそん)して自分の才能を隠す美徳をもっている.

hide the switch 《米》木の枝捜し(ゲーム) ▪ Let us play "*Hide the switch.*" 「木の枝捜し」をしよう.

hide-and-seek /hàɪdənsíːk/ 名 ***play*** (***at***) ***hide-and-seek*** (***with***) (…と)隠れんぼをする; (の)追跡を逃れようとする ▪ The children *played hide-and-seek* for two hours. 子供たちは2時間隠れんぼをした ▪ The sun *played hide-and-seek with* me. 太陽は照ったりかげったりした《私と隠れんぼをした》.

hideaway /háɪdəwèɪ/ 名 (人目を避ける)隠れ場所 ▪ He wrote his latest novel at a *hideaway* by the sea. 彼は最新作の小説を海辺の隠れ家で書いた.

hiding[1] /háɪdɪŋ/ 名 ***be in hiding*** 隠れている, 世をしのんでいる, もぐっている ▪ The Popish priests *were in hiding*. カトリックの司祭たちは地下にもぐっていた.

be on a hiding to nothing 成功の見込みが全くない ▪ The Canadian batsmen *were on a hiding to nothing*. カナダの(クリケット)打者陣は好打の見込みは全くなかった.

come out of hiding (人が)隠れ家から出てくる[現れる] ▪ The criminal *came out of hiding*. 犯人は隠れ家から出てきた.

go into hiding 隠れる, 地下にもぐる ▪ The King was forced to *go into hiding*. 国王はやむなく地下にもぐらねばならなかった.

hiding[2] /háɪdɪŋ/ 名 ***get a good hiding*** 《口》ひどくひっぱたかれる ▪ He *got a good hiding* from his dad. 彼は父親からひどくたたかれた.

give *a person* ***a good hiding*** 《口》人をひどくひっぱたく ▪ You must *give* the boy *a good hiding*. その少年をうんとひっぱたいてやらねばなりませんよ.

hie /haɪ/ 動 ***hie*** *one* [*oneself*] 《詩》急いで行く ▪ He *hied him(self)*. 彼は急いで行った.

high /haɪ/ 形副名 ***a high five*** 《主に米》ハイタッチ《スポーツなどで(祝福のために)片手を挙げて手のひらを互いにパチンと合わせる動作》 ▪ His teammates cheered and gave him *a high five*. チームメイトは喝采し, 彼に片手でハイタッチをした.

a high-flyer あっという間に成功した人物, 高い望みを抱く人 ▪ He was *a high-flyer* in the banking industry. 彼は銀行業界で一躍トップに立った.

(***as***) ***high as a kite*** [***the sky***] 非常に高い; (酒・麻薬で)ひどく酔っぱらって, 非常に興奮して ▪ The redwoods have grown *as high as the sky*. アメリカ杉は天に届くほど高く生長した ▪ The young fellows were *high as kites* on drugs. 若者たちは麻薬をやってハイになっていた ▪ She drank whiskey until she got *as high as a kite*. 彼女はウィスキーを飲んだあげくへべれけになった.

at high pressure →PRESSURE.

be* [*get*] *high on 《口》 **1** …で浮き浮きしている[する] ▪ The kids *are high on* video games. 子供たちはビデオゲームに夢中になっている ▪ The guy *is high on* himself for no reason whatsoever. あいつは全くわけもなく自分に浮かれている.

2 …に酔っている[酔う] ▪ You can *get high on* this stuff. 君はこれで酔えるよ.

carry things off with a high hand →with a high HAND.

fly high →FLY[3].

flying high 《俗》非常にうれしい ▪ She was *flying high* after she won the first prize. 彼女は優勝して大喜びだった.

from on high 天から, 高所から ▪ Our souls are lighted with wisdom *from on high*. 我々の魂は天からの知恵の明かりをともされている.

give the high sign 《米俗》身ぶりで信号する ▪ We waited for Henry to *give* us *the high sign*. 我々はヘンリーが信号するのを待った.

go up on high 《米》急坂をハイギアで登る ▪ They were able to *go up* Pikes Peak *on high*. 彼らはパイクスピークをハイギアで登ることができた.

have a high tea →take (a) HIGH tea.

have a high time 愉快に過ごす ▪ We *had a high time* at her birthday party. 我々は彼女の誕生日パーティーで十分に楽しんだ.

high and dry **1**《海》(船が)水の外へ乗り上げて, 打ち上げられて ▪ Another surf cast the boat up *high and dry* on the beach. 寄せ波がもうひとつやって来てボートを浜辺に打ち上げた.

2 時流からはずされて, 時勢に置き忘れられて; 捨てられて; 一人立ち往生して ▪ They were not so *high and dry*. 彼らはそんなに時勢に遅れてはいなかった ▪ He was left *high and dry* in a deserted room. 彼は人のいない部屋に一人取り残された.

3 古い高教会(派)の《19世紀のオックスフォード運動と区別して》 ▪ The *high and dry* aristocrats looked on him as a tradesman. 古い高教会派の貴族たちは彼を商売人とみなした.

4 面倒に巻き込まれないで, 安全で, 無傷で ▪ There was an explosion on the street, but she was *high and dry* in her apartment. 通りで爆発があったが彼女はアパートにいて無事だった.

high and low **1** (高所・低所の区別なく)あらゆる所に[を, で]; あちらこちら ▪ The detectives looked *high and low* for the missing jewels. 探偵たちは紛失した宝石をくまなく捜した.

2 (上下貴賤の別なく)あらゆる階級(の) ▪ Men and women, *high and low*, gathered there. 上下の別なくあらゆる男女がそこへ集まった.

high and mightiness **1** 殿下, 閣下《尊称, または戯れの尊称》 ▪ His serene *high and mightiness* has never ridden in a haywaggon in his life. 殿下は生まれて以来干し草車に乗られたことはない.

2 尊大なこと, ごう慢なこと ▪ He is not loved for this *high-and-mightiness*. この尊大な性質のため彼は人に愛されない.

high and mighty **1**《古》地位高く権勢ある《威厳を形容する句》 ▪ You think you are one of the *high and mighty*. あなたは地位高く権威ある者の一人であると考えている.

2《口》ごう慢な, 尊大な ▪ Some of those bankers are as *high and mighty* as the oldest families. それらの銀行家のうちには最も古い家柄の者と同じくらい尊大な者もいる.

high fashion/high style 流行のスタイル, 最新ファッション ▪ She was dressed from head to toe in *high fashion*. 彼女は頭のてっぺんからつま先まで流行スタイルを身にまとっていた ▪ This is a guide to where to buy the best *high styles*. これは最高の最新ファッションをお求めになれる店舗のガイドブックです.

high-handed 横暴な, 高圧的な ▪ He was criticized for his *high-handed* attitude. 彼は高飛車な態度をとるといって非難された.

high up 高い所に, 高く ▪ *High up* on the hill, we could see the whole of the valley. 小山の上高く登ると盆地の全体が見えた ▪ The family is now *high up* in society. その家は今は社会的地位が高い.

high up* (*in*) *the stirrups →STIRRUP.

high, wide, and handsome きわめて印象的[感銘的]な[に] ▪ Tom could talk *high, wide, and handsome* when he set out to. トムはやりだしたら, きわめて感動的に話をすることができた.

hit the high lights やり過ぎる; 高水準に達する ▪ There is no *hitting the high lights* when he is not in training. 彼はコンディションが良くないときは高水準に達することはできない.

***hit* [*touch*] *the high spots* [*points*]** 《口》 **1** (放とう・浮かれ騒ぎで)度を過ごす, 過度になる; 夜遊びをする ▪ We'll *hit the high spots* when you come to town. 君が町に来たとき夜遊びをしよう.

2 非常に高い水準[場所]に達する; 全速力で行く ▪ The standard of racing is going to *hit the high spots*. 競走の標準は非常に高くなろうとしている ▪ Here comes the Shinkansen—*hitting the high spots*. さあ新幹線がやって来たぞ—猛スピードで走って.

3 重要点にだけ触れる ▪ With only 3 days in town the best we could do was *hit the high spots*. 町には3日しかいなかったので, 要所を訪ねるだけが精いっぱいだった.

How is that for high? 《口》すてきじゃないか《すばらしい話をしたあとで言う》 ▪ "*How is that for high*, boys?" concluded the narrator. 「少年諸君, すてきじゃないか」と語り手は言葉を結んだ. ☞もと, high-low-jack というトランプ遊びの high と呼ばれる札について言われた文句.

***it is high time* (*that*)** →it is (high) TIME.

live* [*eat*] *high off* [*on*] *the hog →HOG[1].

Mister* [*Miss,* etc.] *High and Mighty/mister* [*miss,* etc.] *high and mighty 尊大ぶった

[思い上がった, 横柄な]人 ▪ I'm disgusted with *Miss High and Mighty*. お高くとまった娘は鼻もちならない ▪ *Mister high and mighty* will never be interested in a commoner like you. 尊大ぶった男が君のような庶民に関心をもつわけがない.

on a high 《口》至福の状態で, うっとりして, 恍惚(こう)感に浸って ▪ The soccer team is *on a high* following the Asian Cup victory. サッカーチームはアジアカップで優勝した感激の余韻に浸っている.

on high **1** 高いところの[に] ▪ The runner was holding her flag *on high*. 走者は旗を高く掲げていた ▪ Monkeys chatter at you from *on high*. サルたちがはるか梢からキャッキャッと声をかける.

2 天の[に, へ] ▪ Lord our God, who dwells *on high*! 天にましますわれらの神よ! ▪ If it comes from *on high*, why fret and fume? もしそれが天から来るものなら, どうしてぷりぷり怒るのか.

3 《戯》最高幹部の ▪ We carried out the orders from those *on high*. 上からの命令を遂行した.

(*on*) *high days and holidays* お祭りや遊びの日(に) ▪ We always spend *high days and holidays* in our cottage by the sea. 我々はいつもお祭りや遊びの日を海辺の田舎家で過ごす.

on the* (*high*) *road to →ROAD.

on the high ropes →ROPE[1].

pile it* [*them*] *high and sell it* [*them*] *cheap 《主に英》(商品を)大量に生産して安価で売る; 安く大量に売る ▪ The shop has survived by *piling it high and selling it cheap*. その店は薄利多売で持ちこたえてきた.

play high **1** 大ばくちを打つ (↔ play LOW) ▪ They are *playing high*. 彼らは大ばくちを打っている.

2 高点の札を出す ▪ By *playing high* you waste a good card. 高点の札を出せば, 良い札をむだ使いすることになる.

ride high **1** (月が)空高く浮かぶ ▪ The moon was *riding high* in the heavens. 月が空高く浮かんでいた.

2 〚主に進行形で〛意気揚々としている ▪ The actor *is* seventy and still *riding high*. その俳優は70だが, まだ意気揚々としている.

3 →FLY high.

run high →RUN[2].

stake high →play HIGH 1.

stand high 高い位置を占める; 受けがよい (*with*) ▪ He *stands high* in our estimation. 彼は我々に尊重されている ▪ I *stood* very *high with* him. 私は彼にとても受けがよい.

stand a person high 《まれ》人に高くつく ▪ Carlos's War *stood* him uncommonly *high*. カルロスの戦争は異常に高くついた.

take* [*have*] (*a*) *high tea (お茶がわりに)実(み)のある食事をする ▪ We had better *have a high tea*. 我々は実のある食事をしたほうがいい.

***take the high hand* (*with*)** →HAND[1].

***take the high road* (*in*)** 《米》(…で)正道を行う (↔take the low ROAD) ▪ I *take the high road in* my campaign. 選挙運動は正々堂々と行うつもりだ.

the high ground 優位[有利]な立場 ▪ This company holds *the high ground* in the area of DVDs. この会社は DVD の分野で優位に立っている.

***the high point* [*spot*] (*of*)** (…の)最もよい[楽しい]部分 ▪ *The high spot of* this trip was the visit to Naples. 今回の旅のハイライトはナポリの探訪だった.

***touch the high spots* [*points*]** → hit the HIGH spots.

highest /háɪɪst, -əst/ 形名 ***at one's highest*** 最高で ▪ Prices are *at their highest*. 物価は最高値である.

at the highest 最高の位置に; いくら高くても, せいぜい ▪ It will be no more than five dollars *at the highest*. それはいくら高くても5ドルはしないだろう.

in the highest **1** 最高所に; 天上に (《聖》*Luke* 2. 14) ▪ Glory to God *in the highest*. 天の神に栄光がありますように.

2 最高度に ▪ He praised the book *in the highest*. 彼はその本を口をきわめて賞賛した.

highly /háɪli/ 副 ***give highly colored details*** 効果をねらって誇張する ▪ The journalist *gave highly colored details* of the boxing contest. その新聞記者はボクシングの試合を紛飾誇張した.

speak highly of …のことをほめそやす ▪ We *spoke highly of* his talents. 我々は彼の才能をほめそやした.

think highly of →THINK[2].

highness /háɪnəs/ 名 ***His* [*Her, Your*] (*Royal, Serene, Imperial*) *Highness*** 殿下《皇族の敬称》 ▪ *Her Royal Highness* Princess Victoria of Sweden visited four Asian countries. スウェーデンのビクトリア王女殿下はアジア4カ国を歴訪された.

hightail /háɪtèɪl/ 動 ***hightail it*** 《口》素早く去る[行く] ▪ The thief *hightailed it* out of town. 賊は素早く町から逃走した.

highway /háɪwèɪ/ 名 ***be on the highway to*** …への大道(どう)上にある, に近うきつつある ▪ He *is on the highway to* success. 彼は成功への途上にある.

go on* [*take* (*to*)] *the highway 追いはぎになる ▪ They were obliged to *take to the highway*. 彼らは追いはぎになるしかなかった.

go out into the highways and hedges 道やまがきのほとりに出る, (人を集めるためなどで)あちこち歩き回る (《聖》*Luke* 14. 23) ▪ They *went out into the highways and hedges* seeking the dead and wounded. 彼らは死者やけが人を探してあちこち歩き回った.

highway robbery **1** 白昼の強盗 ▪ *Highway robbery* was not uncommon in those days. 当時は白昼強盗が日常茶飯事だった.

2 法外な値段 ▪ Fifty thousand dollars is *highway robbery* for a 3-year-old car. 3年目の中古車の値段が5万ドルとはぼったくりだ.

H

highways and byways 《古風》公道と脇道, 大路小路(すべて) ▪ I've travelled all the *highways and byways* of Scotland. 私はスコットランドのすべての大路小路を旅した. ☞単数で every [each] highway and byway とも言う.

hike /haɪk/ 名 ***go on a hike*** 《口》徒歩旅行をする ▪ We *went on a hike* for exercise. 運動のため徒歩旅行をした.

on the hike 《米》長い放浪に出て ▪ Of course that put him *on the hike* again. もちろんそのため彼はまた長い放浪の旅に出た.

Take a hike! 《米口》あっちへ行け, 失せろ ▪ I've had enough of your impudence. *Take a hike!* 図々しいにもほどがある. とっとと失せろ!

hill /hɪl/ 名 ***a hill of beans*** →BEAN.

(as) old as the hills →(as) OLD as Adam.

go down hill **1** (からだが)衰える ▪ He is *going down hill* rapidly. 彼はからだが急速に衰えている.

2 堕落する ▪ The boy is *going down hill.* その少年は堕落しつつある.

go over the hill **1** 《軍》無断外出する ▪ They would *go over the hill* on their first shore leave. 彼らは最初の上陸許可を得ないで部隊を離れようとした.

2 黙って姿を消す ▪ He *went over the hill* with the money. 彼はその金を持って黙って姿を消した.

head for the hills 《口》[[しばしば命令文で]] 急いで逃げる; 逃走して隠れる ▪ The ruffian is coming. *Head for the hills!* 悪漢がやって来るぞ. 早く逃げろ.

If the hill won't [will not] come to Muhammad, Muhammad will go to the hill. →If the MOUNTAIN won't come to Muhammad, Muhammad will go to the mountain.

not amount to [《米口》not be worth] a hill of beans ほとんど[全]く値打ちがない ▪ Just because you are famous does *not amount to a hill of beans.* 名が売れているというだけでは何の足しにもならない ▪ *None* of those data *is worth a hill of beans.* あのデータのうち一つとして価値のあるものはない.

on the Hill 《米》議会で ▪ It happened *on the Hill* today. それはきょう議会であったことだ ▪ He is a gentleman *on the Hill.* 彼は国会議員だ. ☞Hill＝Capitol Hill.

over the hill **1** 《口》(年齢・能力・肉体美が)峠を越して ▪ I was *over the hill* as far as moneymaking was concerned. 金儲けに関するかぎり峠を越していた ▪ Miss Smith was a beauty, but now she is *over the hill.* スミス嬢は美人であったが, 今はもう峠を越している.

2 (病気などが)峠を越す ▪ He was seriously ill, but is *over the hill* now. 彼は重病だったが, 今はもう峠を越した.

3 《口》(兵士が)脱走して, (囚人が)脱獄して ▪ Two prisoners went *over the hill* last night. 二人の囚人が昨夜脱獄した.

take to the hills 逃げてかくれる ▪ Many soldiers *took to the hills* during the fighting. 戦闘中多くの兵が脱走してかくれた.

up hill and down dale/over hill and dale **1** 山越え谷越えて; 高くまた低く, くまなく ▪ We've searched *up hill and down dale,* and still we cannot find the fox. 我々は山越え谷越えて捜したがそれでもまだキツネは見つからない.

2 根気よく, 猛烈に ▪ Behind my smiling lips I cursed him *up hill and down dale.* 微笑のかげで内心では彼を猛烈にののしった.

hilt /hɪlt/ 名 ***hilt to hilt*** 一騎打ちで ▪ They fought *hilt to hilt.* 彼らは一騎打ちをした.

(up) to the hilt **1** (刀の)つか元まで, ずぶりと ▪ I stabbed him *up to the hilt* of the knife. 彼をナイフでずぶりと刺した.

2 徹底的に, 完全に ▪ The estate was mortgaged *up to the hilt.* その地所は完全に抵当に入っていた ▪ The charge of forgery was proved *to the hilt.* 文書偽造の罪は十分に証明された.

hinder /híndər/ 動 ***nothing shall hinder but (that)...*** 万難を排して…する ▪ *Nothing shall hinder but (that)* I will go. 私は万難を排して行きます.

What hinders but ...? …ないとはかぎるまい ▪ *What hinders but* he will come? 彼は来ないとはかぎるまい.

hind-leg, hind leg /háɪndlèg/ 名 ***could eat the hind leg off a donkey*** 《口》非常に腹がへっている ▪ Right now I *could eat the hind leg off a donkey.* ちょうど今私はおなかがぺこぺこだ.

get (up) on one's hind legs (馬が)激怒する; 《戯》(人が)激怒する ▪ "Don't *get on your hind legs,*" returned Betty. 「そんなにひどく怒らないでください」とベティーは答えた.

talk the hind leg(s) off a donkey [horse]/talk a horse's [a dog's] hind leg off 《口》のべつ幕なしにしゃべりまくる; おしゃべりである ▪ Mr. Lloyd George could *talk the hind leg(s) off a donkey.* ロイド・ジョージ氏はのべつ幕なしにしゃべり立てることができた ▪ By George, you'd *talk a dog's hind leg off.* ほんとに, 君はのべつ幕なしにしゃべるだろう ▪ They could *talk a horse's hind leg off* and I wouldn't send a single line to the papers. 彼らがいくら盛んにまくしたてたって, 新聞には1行も書き送ってはやらんのだ.

hindmost /háɪndmòʊst/ 名 ***The Devil [Satan, hell] take [catch] the hindmost.*** 遅れた者は鬼に食われろ; 早い者勝ち ▪ They all run away and cry, "*The Devil take the hindmost.*" 彼らはみな走り去って「遅れたやつは鬼に食われろ」と叫ぶ.

hindrance /híndrəns/ 名 ***without hindrance*** 支障なく, 無事 ▪ May you attain this aspiration *without hindrance.* あなたがこの大望を無事達成なさいますように.

hindsight /háɪndsàɪt/ 名 ***hindsight is 20-20*** 《口》あとの知恵は完璧だ, 悪いことが起きた後でこうすれば避けられたと言うのはたやすい ▪ *Hindsight is 20-20.* I never knew there was a clue. あと知恵に

簡単だ. 予知できる手がかりなんてあったとは思えない. ☞視力が20-20とは, 完璧な視力ということ.

knock [***kick***] ***the hindsights out*** [***off***] 《米口》完全にやっつける; 完全に打ちこわす, 粉砕する ▪ They *kicked the hindsights off* the man. 彼らはその男を完全にやっつけた ▪ He *knocked* the creature's *hindsights out*. 彼はその動物をすっかりやっつけた. ☞hindsights「ライフル銃の照尺」.

with the wisdom [***benefit, clarity***] ***of hindsight/ with*** (***twenty-twenty***) ***hindsight*** 後知恵で考えると, 今だから分かることだが, 後の祭りだが ▪ *With the benefit of hindsight*, clearly we should have done it earlier. もう後の祭りだが, やはりもっと早くやっておけばよかった ▪ *With twenty-twenty hindsight*, I shouldn't have bought this huge desk. 今思えば, こんなに大きな机を買うんじゃなかった.

hinge /hɪndʒ/ 名 ***off the*** [*one's*] ***hinges*** **1** 蝶番(ちょうつがい)がはずれて ▪ The door is *off its hinges*. その戸は蝶番がはずれている.

2 《口》(体・精神が)調子が狂って; (秩序が)乱れて ▪ Since his death she has been quite *off the hinges*. 彼が死んでから彼女は全く気が変になっている.

on the [*one's*] ***hinges*** 蝶番(ちょうつがい)によって ▪ The door slowly revolved *on its hinges*. 戸は蝶番によってゆっくり回転した.

hint /hɪnt/ 名 ***drop*** [***give, let fall***] ***a hint*** ほのめかす, 示唆する, ヒントを出す ▪ I *dropped* him *a hint* that I wanted to leave. 私は出て行きたいと彼にほのめかした.

give no hint (***of, that***) (…の)気配がない ▪ The calm sea *gave no hint of* an approaching storm. 海は穏やかで近づくあらしの気配は感じられなかった ▪ She *gave no hint that* she was in pain. 彼女は痛いそぶりも見せなかった.

take a [***the***] ***hint*** (ちょっと言われて)すぐにその意を悟る; (ほのめかされて)それと感づく[気をきかせる] ▪ He *took the hint* and went out of the room. 彼はそれと感づいて部屋から出て行った ▪ OK, I can *take a hint*. I'll go now. わかった, もう失せろということだな. では消えるとしよう.

hip[1] /hɪp/ 名 ***catch*** *a person* ***on the hip*** 人の急所を捕える ▪ I just managed to *catch* him *on the hip*. 彼の急所をかろうじて捕えた.

down in the hip(***s***) **1** (馬の)しり骨が傷ついて ▪ The horse is *down in the hip*. その馬はしり骨が傷ついている.

2 かげんが悪く; 元気がなく ▪ The doctor was *down in the hips*. 医師はかげんが悪かった.

fire [***shoot***] ***from the hip*** 《口》 **1** 銃を腰に当てて撃つ ▪ Uncle Joe taught me to *shoot from the hip*. ジョーおじさんに腰だめ撃ちの仕方を教わった.

2 後先考えずにしゃべる; よく考えずに素早く対応する ▪ He tends to *fire from the hip* without thinking. 彼はとっさに行動しがちである. ☞カウボーイの早撃ちのイメージ.

have [***get, take***] *a person* ***on the hip*** 人を(のっぴきならぬように)押さえこむ; 優位に立つ, 勝つ, 支配する ▪ He had once *had* me *on the hip*. 彼はかつて私を支配していたことがあった ▪ At last I *got* him *on the hip*, for he had slept with his daughter-in-law. とうとう彼のしっぽをつかんだ. 義理の娘と寝たのだから. ☞レスリングの腰投げから.

hip and thigh 容赦なく (《聖》*Judges* 15. 8) ▪ We smote them *hip and thigh*. 彼らをさんざんにやっつけた.

joined at the hip 《戯》 **1** 二人がいつもいっしょにいて, 親密になって, 膝と膝を突き合わせて ▪ Those two are constantly *joined at the hip*. あの二人はいつもべったりひっついている.

2 密接に関連して ▪ Although astronomy isn't physics, they are *joined at the hip*. 天文学は物理学とは異なるが, 両者には深い関連性がある.

hip[2] /hɪp/ 形 ***be*** [***get***] ***hip to*** 《俗》…に通じている[に精通する] ▪ He's *got hip to* modern jazz. 彼はモダンジャズに精通している.

hip[3] /hɪp/ 間 ***Hip! hip! hurrah!*** 万歳! ▪ *Hip! hip! hurrah!* Some good news has emerged! 万歳! よい知らせが明らかになった.

hip[4] /hɪp/ 動 ***be hipped on*** 《米俗》…に熱中している; に取りつかれている ▪ He *is hipped on* socialism. 彼は社会主義に熱中している.

feel hipped 《米》気がふさいでいる ▪ He *felt hipped* because no one cared about him. 彼は誰も問題にしてくれないので気がふさいでいた.

hire[1] /háɪər/ 名 ***for*** [***on***] ***hire*** 貸すための ▪ The boat plies *for hire*. それは貸しボートとして通っている ▪ This car is *for hire*. この自動車はレンタル用です ▪ He has horses *on hire*. 彼は貸し馬を持っている ▪ These bicycles are *on hire*. これらは貸し自転車である.

hire and fire 臨時雇い入れ ▪ "*Hire and fire*" is associated with the construction industry. 臨時雇い入れと言えば建設産業が連想される.

let out on hire …を賃貸しする ▪ He *let out* horses *on hire*. 彼は馬を賃貸しした.

hire[2] /háɪər/ 動 ***a hired hand*** [***man or girl***] (農場の)短期肉体労働者[家政婦] ▪ They needed extra *hired hands* during the harvest. 彼らは取り入れ期に臨時農場労働者を必要とした ▪ The farm is looking for *a hired girl* to do the laundry. 農場主は洗濯をしてくれるお手伝いさんを探している.

hire and fire 臨時に雇い入れる ▪ The villagers can *be hired and fired* at a moment's notice. 村人たちを即座に臨時に雇うことができる.

history /hístəri/ 名 ***airbrush*** *a person* ***out of history*** (記憶に残らないように)人の行状を塗りつぶす[拭い去る] ▪ We should never *airbrush* war crimes *out of history*. 決して戦争犯罪を隠蔽してはならない.

ancient history ずっと昔のため完全に忘れられた[もはや重要でなくなった]人[物]《誇張表現》 ▪ I never think about Tim anymore. He's *ancient histo-*

ry. もうティムのことは全然頭に浮かびません. とっくに忘れられた人です.

... (and) the rest is history あとのことは言うまでもなかろう ▪ It all started with this *and the rest is history*. ことの発端はこれで, あとの成り行きは知っての通りだ.

be history 《口》 **1** もはや現在に関わりがない, もう重要でなくなる, 歴史に[昔のことに]なる ▪ Karl Marx *is history* nowadays. 今日ではカール・マルクスは過去の人だ.

2 死ぬ, いなくなる, 終わる; もうじき出ていく, 退散する ▪ Make one mistake and you *are history*. 一つでも間違えたら命はないと思え.

become history 歴史に残る; じきに死ぬ ▪ The pioneers *became history*. 開拓者たちは歴史に残った ▪ Within the next several years, tigers will *become history* in the country. あと数年しないうちにその国のトラは絶滅するだろう.

H

go down in history 歴史に残る《永久に記憶される》 ▪ Babe Ruth *went down in history* as baseball's "home run King". ベーブ・ルースはホームラン王として歴史に残った.

Happy is the country [nation] which [that] has no history. 《諺》 歴史を持たざる国は幸福なるかな《歴史は暴力・悲惨さ・騒乱の出来事のみを記録しがち. よって歴史なき国はそんな不幸にあわずにすんだ幸運な国ということになる》.

History repeats itself. 《諺》 歴史は繰り返す.

make history 歴史(の流れ)を作る; 歴史に残るほどのことをする ▪ We are *making history*. 我々は歴史に残るほどのことをしているのだ ▪ *History is made* by the average man. 歴史は普通の人によって作られる.

pass into history 歴史[過去のこと]となる ▪ Other clans have *passed into history*. 他の一族は過去のものとなった.

rewrite history 過去の出来事を自分の目的[都合]に合うように解釈する ▪ We should not *rewrite history* to suit our own convenience. 当方の都合に合うように史実を曲げてはならない.

That's ancient history. 《口》 それは古くさい話だ ▪ He's talking about his world trip, but *that's ancient history*. 彼は世界旅行のことを話しているがそれは遠い昔の話だ.

hit[1] /hɪt/ 名 **a (*person's*) hit list** 《口》 **1** 削除[削減]対象リスト, 解雇予定者リスト ▪ The accountant general drew up *a hit list* for spending cuts. 経理局長が支出経費切り詰め対象リストを作成した ▪ The airline drafted *a hit list* of 20 pilots they considered for sacking. 航空会社は解雇予定のパイロット20名のリストを起草した.

2 暗殺[攻撃]対象者リスト, 殺人予告リスト ▪ He was at the top of *the terrorists' hit list*. 彼はテロリストの暗殺対象者リストの筆頭だった.

a hit man 殺し屋 ▪ They hired *a* professional *hit man*. 彼らはプロの殺し屋を雇った.

look to [mind] *one's* hits 成功の機会に気をつける ▪ If I *mind my hits* on this trip, I shall be rich. もしこの旅で成功の機会に気をつけたら, 私は金持ちになるだろう.

make a (...) hit **1** 大成功を収める, 大当たりを取る ▪ His first book *made a* tremendous *hit*. 彼の処女作はすごい大当たりを取った ▪ Mary *made a hit* at the Christmas party. メアリーはクリスマスパーティーで大成功を収めた.

2 《米俗》 (人に)非常に気に入る, 大いに喜ばれる (*with*) ▪ The special dessert *made a hit with* everyone. その特別のデザートはすべての人に非常に喜ばれた ▪ The new electric vehicles are *making a* great *hit with* the public. 新型電気自動車は大衆の大好評を博しつつある.

3 《俗》 殺人を犯す ▪ The criminal was about to *make* his third *hit*. 殺人犯はまさに3人目をやろうとしていた.

make [be] a lucky hit うまく当てる; 偶然に手がらを立てる ▪ Your advice *was a lucky hit*. 君の助言はみごとに的中した.

take a hit 打撃[悪影響]を受ける ▪ The auto industry *took a hit* last year. 去年自動車業界は大損害をこうむった.

hit[2] /hɪt/ 動 **be hard hit** →HIT ... hard.

before *a person* **knows what hit** *him* いつの間にか, 瞬く間に ▪ We'll have the handcuffs on them *before* they *know what*'s *hit* them. あっという間に彼らに手錠をかけてやる.

hit a blot **1** (バックギャモンで)油断して一つだけ放ってある敵のこまを取る(ような数を振り出す).

2 弱点[欠点]をあばく ▪ Mr. Morley has *hit a blot* in our policy. モーリー氏は我々の政策の弱点を見つけた.

hit *a person* **a blow** 人を打つ ▪ I *hit* him *another blow*. 私は彼にもう一撃をくわせた.

hit a clip 《米口》 ある速度で進む ▪ You'll never finish your book at the *clip* you're *hitting* now. あなたが今やっている速度ではとてもあなたの本は仕上がらないだろう.

hit bottom →BOTTOM[1].

hit ... for six →knock ... for SIX.

hit ... hard [heavily, badly] ...に大打撃を与える ▪ Everybody *is hard hit* by the coal strike. 石炭ストライキで大打撃を受けていない者はない ▪ The advent of television *hit* the cinema very *hard*. テレビの到来で映画は大打撃を受けた.

hit *a person* **hard** 人にひどい打撃を与える ▪ The taunt *hit* him *hard*. その侮辱は彼にひどくこたえた.

hit hard on ...を力説[強調]する ▪ He *hit hard on* the need for it. 彼はその必要を力説した.

hit *a person* **home [where** *he* **lives]** 人の急所をつく, 人の胸に徹せしめる ▪ You have *hit* me *home*. あなたは私の急所をついた ▪ It'll *hit* them *where* they *live*. それは彼らにひどくこたえるだろう.

hit *a person* **in the pocket [wallet]** 人を経済的に苦しめる ▪ Rising oil prices *hit* consumers *in the pocket*. 原油価格高騰のため消費者の生活が苦し

くなった ▪ The rising cost of barley has *hit* beer drinkers *in the wallet*. 大麦の価格が上昇しビール愛飲者の懐がさみしくなった.

hit it **1** 的に当てる; うまく答える; (秘密などを)うまく言い当てる ▪ You've *hit it*. ご名答.

2 (問題を)解く ▪ The problem took three weeks before I *hit it*. その問題は私が解くのに3週間要した.

3《米口》急行する, 疾走する ▪ We were *hitting it* at 50 miles an hour. 我々は1時間50マイルの速力で急行していた.

hit (***it***) ***big***《口》大成功する ▪ The band has *hit it big* in Hong Kong. そのバンドは香港で大当たりをとった.

hit it off **1**《口》調和する, うまく一致する, 仲よくやる, そりが合う (*together, with*) ▪ He *hit it off* well *with* the new boss. 彼は新社長とうまくそりが合った ▪ The couple cannot *hit it off together*. その夫婦は仲よくやっていけない.

2 素早くうまく描写する[まねる] ▪ The child noticed the singer's idiosyncrasies, and *hit it off*. その子供は歌手の特徴に気づいてそれをうまくまねた.

hit it right (***on the head***) **1** うまく打つ.

2 そのものずばりを当てる; 適評をする ▪ A Japanese Dickens—you have *hit it right*. 日本のディケンズとはけだし適評ですね ▪ You *hit it right on the head*. 実にうまく当てましたね. ☞head「くぎの頭」.

hit it up **1**《米口》急行[疾走]する; がんばる ▪ He is off *hitting it up* again. 彼はまた疾走して去った ▪ The band was *hitting it up* when we arrived. 我々が到着したとき, 楽隊は盛んにやっていた.

2 馬力をかける ▪ When you are doing better than three miles an hour, you are *hitting it up* pretty well. 1時間に3マイル以上行っているときは, かなり馬力をかけていることになります.

hit on all four [***six***] (***cylinders***)《口》**1** (内燃機関が)調子よく運転する ▪ The engine is *hitting on all six cylinders*. エンジンは調子よく運転している.

2 調子よくいく; うまくやる; 立派に演じる ▪ The best infielder takes time to have the infield *hit on all four cylinders* again. 最もすぐれた内野手でも内野を再び調子よくいかせるには時間がかかる.

3 (体・機関などが)調子がよい ▪ It will keep you *hitting on all six*—every minute of the day. それは四六時中体の調子をよくしておくだろう. ☞調子のよいエンジンは全部のシリンダー中のピストンがうまく打っていることから.

hit *a person* ***on the head*** [etc.] 人の頭[など]をなぐる ▪ He *hit* me *on the head*. 彼は私の頭をなぐった.

hit or miss **1** あてもなく, いきあたりばったりに, 無計画に, 無鉄砲に ▪ He is a *hit-or-miss* type of workman. 彼はいきあたりばったりの労働者である.

2 のるかそるか運に任せて, 当たっても当たらなくてもかまわず ▪ Let us do it, *hit or miss*. のるかそるか運に任せてそれをやろうではないか.

hit pay dirt =strike PAY dirt.

hit *a person's* ***pocketbook*** 人の財布に響く ▪ The new tax law *hits the nation's pocketbook*. 新税法は国民の財布に響く.

hit right うまくいく ▪ If matters *hit right*, we shall make a fortune. 事がうまくいけば, 我々は大金を手に入れるだろう.

hit *a person* ***right*** 人の気に入る ▪ Take whatever *hits* you *right*. あなたの気に入るものは何でもお取りなさい.

hit *one's* ***stride*** →STRIDE.

hit the books →BOOK[1].

hit the booze [***bottle, hooch, jug, pot, red-eye, sauce***]《俗》(習慣的に)大酒を飲む ▪ He is *hitting the booze*. 彼は酒をがぶがぶ飲んでいる ▪ He'll start to *hit the bottle* again. 彼はまた鯨飲し始めるだろう. ☞通例 begin [start] to hit ...の形, または進行形.

hit the buffers《口》行き詰まる ▪ His plans for expanding the business *hit the buffers*. 事業を拡大しようという彼の計画は暗礁に乗り上げた.

hit the ceiling/ go through the ceiling [***roof***] **1**《口》怒髪天をつく, 激怒する ▪ He has been *hitting the ceiling* over something or other ever since he arrived. 彼はやってきてからずっと何かのことで激怒している ▪ She saw what I had done and *went through the ceiling*. 彼女は私の所業を知ると激怒した ▪ My boss *goes through the roof* when he finds a tiny mistake. 上司は些細なミスで頭にくる.

2 (物価などが)急騰する, 天井知らずである ▪ Income tax rates *went through the ceiling*. 所得税率が急上昇した ▪ The crime rate in our city has *gone through the roof*. 当市の犯罪率が急増した.

hit the deck《口》**1** 突然倒れる, 急いで身を伏せる ▪ When we heard the shot, we *hit the deck*. 銃声を聞いてさっと身を伏せた ▪ The challenger *hit the deck* for the third time. 挑戦者はこれで3度マットに沈んだ.

2《米》起床する ▪ Come on! It's time to *hit the deck*. さあ, 起きる時間よ.

hit the flat《米》草原 (prairie) に出て行く ▪ The cowboy *hit the flat*. カウボーイは草原に出て行った.

hit the ground running《口》さっと新しいことを始める ▪ We need someone who will *hit the ground running*. 直ちに仕事にかかる人物が必要だ.

hit the high spots [***points***] →HIGH.

hit the mark →MARK[1].

hit the needle [***the pin***] 的に当てる; 図星をさす ▪ She had *hit the needle* in that way. 彼女はそのようにして的に当てたのだった.

hit the park《米》公園へ行く ▪ We'll be *hitting the park*. 我々は公園へ行きましょう.

hit the pike《米口》道を行く, 旅する ▪ They were ordered to *hit the pike*. 彼らは旅をするよう命ぜられた.

hit the sod《米》芝生を歩いて行く ▪ I *hit the sod* in the direction of the show. 私は芝生を歩い

て見世物の方へ行った.

hit the streets [***shops, stores***]《口》売り出される ▪ A new games console *hits the streets* tomorrow. 新型コンピューター・ゲーム機が明日発売になる.

hit the ties →count the TIEs.

hit the tone **1** 語気よろしきを得る ▪ It is hard to *hit the tone*. 語気よろしきを得ることはむずかしい.
2 語気をうまくまねる ▪ He has skillfully *hit the tone* of Kipling. 彼はキプリングの語気を巧みにまねた.
3 (...の)呼吸をのみこむ ▪ He *hits the tone* of society. 彼は社交界の呼吸をのみこんでいる.

hit the trail《米口》道を行く, 旅に出る, 旅をする ▪ Have you ever *hit the trail*? 君は旅をしたことがありますか.

hit the upgrade《米口》昇進する, 目的を達し始める ▪ The climber *hit the upgrade* in his 20th year. 野心家は20歳のとき昇進した.

hit town《米》町に着く ▪ The American delegation have just *hit town*. アメリカの代表団がちょうど今町に着いた.

hit** a person **when he is down 倒れた相手を打つ; ひきょうな行いをする ▪ Never *hit* a man *when he is down*. 決して倒れた相手を打つな《ボクサーの心得》.

hit** a person **where it hurts《口》人の痛い所をつく; 人の感情を害する ▪ You certainly *hit* him *where it hurt* that time. ほんとに, あの時は彼の痛いところをついたね.

hit** a person **where** he **lives →HIT a person home.

***not know what hit** one* (突然[不意に]予期せぬことが起きて)驚く[どぎまぎする] ▪ The poor man stood there *not knowing what* had *hit* him. 気の毒にその男は当惑してその場に立ち尽くした.

hitch[1] /hɪtʃ/ 名 ***in a clove hitch*** 窮境に陥って ▪ You are all *in a clove hitch*. あなたがたはみな窮地に陥っている. ☞clove-hitch「巻き結び」(丸太などを索で結ぶ結び方); このように結ばれると動きが取れなくなることから.

make a hitch of it《米口》仲よくやっていく ▪ I thought we were *making a hitch of it*. 我々は仲よくやっていっていると私は思っていた.

this hitch《米》今度は, このたびは ▪ We shall win *this hitch*. 今度は勝つだろう.

without a hitch すらすらと, 滞りなく ▪ The ceremony passed off *without a hitch*. 式は滞りなく行われた.

hitch[2] /hɪtʃ/ 動 ***get hitched***《口》結婚する ▪ They finally *got hitched* after a long period of dating. 二人は長い交際期間の末やっとゴールインした.

hitch a ride with ...の車に乗せてもらう ▪ I *hitched a ride with* the farmer. 私は農場主の車に乗せてもらった.

hitch horses together →draw HORSEs together.

***hitch** one's **wagon to** a person* 人のコネを利用して成功しようとする, にお裾分けしてもらう ▪ You can't *hitch your wagon to* people you like. 自分の好きな人のおこぼれを頂戴するわけにはいかない.

hitch** one's **wagon to a star **1** ひどく高い理想や目的を持つ ▪ It is dangerous to *hitch your wagon to a star*. 非常に高い望みをいだくのは危険だ.
2 俗事を超越する ▪ We are told to *hitch our wagon to a star*. 我々は俗事を超越せよと言われている. ☞R. W. Emerson, *Civilization* から.

hither /híðər/ 副形 ***hither and thither***《雅》あちらこちらへ ▪ It moves us *hither and thither*. それは我々をあちらこちらへ動かす.

hither and yon《米・雅》あちらこちらへ ▪ The birds were singing merrily *hither and yon*. 鳥はあちこちで楽しげにさえずっていた.

on the hither side of →on the right SIDE of.

hitter /hítər/ 名 ***a heavy hitter*** (実業界・政界の)重要人物[組織] ▪ AT&T is *a heavy hitter* in the telecommunication industry. AT&Tは通信業界の大手会社である.

hive /haɪv/ 名 ***a hive of activity*** 人が忙しく働いている場所 ▪ The hotel lobby is *a hive of activity* every morning. ホテルのロビーは毎朝立ち働く人々で活気に満ちている.

hoarse /hɔːrs/ 形 ***(as) hoarse as a*** [***an old***] ***crow*** カラスのようなしゃがれ声の ▪ He was *as hoarse as a crow*. 彼はひどくしゃがれ声だった.

shout [***talk***] *oneself* ***hoarse*** 声をからして叫ぶ; 声がかれるまで話す ▪ He waved his hat and *shouted himself hoarse*. 彼は帽子をふり声をからして叫んだ ▪ She *talked herself hoarse* answering queries over the phone. 彼女は電話で質問に答えていて声がかれてしまった.

hob[1] /hɑb|hɔb/ 名 ***play (the) hob with*** ...に害を与える; をぶちこわす, 勝手に変える ▪ He won't risk losing votes by *playing hob with* us. 彼は我々に害を与えて票を失うようなことはしないだろう ▪ The mother is *playing hob with* the children. 母親は子供たちをすっかりだめにしてしまっている.

raise hob《米口》**1** 荒らす, こわす, じゃまする (*with*) ▪ The war *raised hob with* international trade. 戦争が国際貿易をだめにした.
2 騒動を起こす, いきり立つ; がなり立てる (*with*) ▪ He has been *raising hob* because of it. 彼はそのため騒ぎ立てていた ▪ She *raised hob with* him for being late. 彼女は遅れたと言って彼にがなり立てた.
3 飲み騒ぐ ▪ Let's *raise hob* tonight. 今夜は飲み騒ごうではないか.

hob[2] /hɑb|hɔb/ 動形 ***hob a*** [***and, or***] ***nob*** **1**《古》(酒を飲んでいる二人が)さしつさされつする, 乾杯し合う ▪ With Whig or with Tory he'll drink *hob a nob*. ホイッグ党員とでもトーリー党員とでも, 彼は互いに酒をくみ交わす ▪ Here is to your friends.—*Hob or nob*. 友人諸君に乾杯—お互いさま.
2 (二人が)親しく寄り合う, 親しみ合う (*with*) ▪ I am *hob and nob with* him in the dungeon. 私は牢屋で彼と親しくしている.

hobby /hάbi|hɔ́bi/ 名 ***make a hobby of*** …を道楽にする ▪ He *makes a hobby of* his work. 彼は仕事を道楽にしている.

ride [***mount***] *one's* [***a***] ***hobby*** (***to death***) (周囲があきあきするほど)おはこを出す ▪ Some women *ride hobbies* with considerable persistence. 相当しつこくおはこを出す女性もいる.

hock /hαk|hɔk/ 名 ***from soda*** (***card***) ***to hock*** →SODA.

go in hock 《俗》借金する ▪ Daddy will never *go in hock*. 父ちゃんは絶対に借金をしない.

in hock 《俗》 **1** (トランプ・賭博に負けて)困窮して ▪ When one gambler is beat by another, then he is *in hock*. あるばくち打ちが別のに負けたら, 彼は負けて窮しているわけである.

2 (賭博の)現行犯で ▪ If the fellow should be caught *in* the *hock*, he won't snickle. もし奴が万一賭博の現行犯で押さえられても, しゃべりはすまい.

3 借金して; 恩を受けて ▪ I was *in hock* to several friends. 私は数人の友人に借金していた.

4 質に入れて ▪ They left all their stuff *in hock*. 彼らは所有物全部を質に入れたままにした.

5 監獄に入って ▪ I was *in hock* for the next three years. 私は次の3年間は監獄に入っていた.

out of hock **1** 質から出して ▪ I have to get my bicycle *out of hock* by next Sunday. 次の日曜までに自転車を質から出さなくてはならない.

2 借金を返して[せずに] ▪ How can I keep myself *out of hock*? どうすれば借金せずにすむだろうか.

hoe /hoʊ/ 動 ***have a hard*** [***long, tough***] ***row to hoe*** →ROW[1].

hoe (***it***) ***down*** [***off***] 《米口》ホウダウン式にダンスをする ▪ He *hoed it down* at a terrible rate. 彼はすごい勢いでホウダウン式のダンスをした. ☞hoedown「昔の活発奔放なダンス」.

hoe *one's* ***own row*** →ROW[1].

hog[1] /hɔːg|hɔg/ 名 ***a hog in armor*** **1** (よろいを着たブタのように)無骨で不格好な人, 美装が身についていない人 ▪ He looks like *a hog in armor*. 彼はまるでよろいを着たブタのように美装が身についていない ▪ He carried his finery like *a hog in armor*. 彼は美装を着ていかにも不格好で窮屈そうだった. ☞hog はおそらく hodge のなまり.

2 人前で不安な[落ち着かない]人 ▪ I really felt like *a hog in armor* on stage. 私はステージに立つと実に不安に感じた.

a road hog 《口》(センターラインを暴走する)乱暴な運転者; 暴走者 ▪ I have often been honked at by *road hogs*. 二車線をまたいで走る暴走族によく警笛を鳴らされる.

as a hog on ice →like a HOG on ice.

(***as***) ***independent as a hog on ice*** 《米口》 **1** 全くの独立で ▪ He cares nothing for anybody—he is *as independent as a hog on ice*. 彼は誰のことも少しもかまわない. 彼は全くの独立である.

2 きわめて自信に満ちた; うぬぼれた ▪ They are a proud people, *as independent as a hog on ice*, as their saying goes. 彼らは高慢な民で, その言い習わしにあるとおり実にうぬぼれている.

behave [***act***] ***like a hog*** ブタのように無作法にふるまう ▪ He *acted like a hog* in taking more than his share. 彼は無作法に自分の分け前以上を取った.

bring *one's* ***hogs to a bad market*** →bring one's eggs to a bad MARKET.

bring *one's* ***hogs to a fair*** [***fine***] ***market*** 《俗》面倒を起こす, 困った事態を引き起こす ▪ You've *brought your hogs to a fine market*. 困った事をしてくれたね.

drive *one's* ***hogs to market*** 《口》ブタの群れを市場へ追い立てて行く; 大いびきをかく ▪ He snored so loud that we thought he was *driving his hogs to market*. 彼はひどくいびきをかいたので, ブタの群れを市場へ追って行っているのかと思った.

eat high off [***on***] ***the hog*** =live high off the HOG.

go hog-wild [***hog wild***] 《米口》ひどく興奮する, 制しきれなくなる, 夢中になる ▪ I *went hog wild* at the sale and bought five sweaters. バーゲンセールですっかり舞い上がりセーターを5枚も買ってしまった.

go (***the***) ***whole hog*** 《口》 **1** 徹底的にやる ▪ Once he had made up his mind, he *went the whole hog*. 一度決心したら, 彼はとことんまでやった.

2 (人より)高値をつける ▪ He has offered £100. —I'll *go the whole hog* then and offer £120. 彼は100ポンドの値をつけた—それでは彼より高値をつけて120ポンド出そう.

like [***as***] ***a hog on ice*** 《米口》ぎこちないまたはあぶなっかしい格好で ▪ He went about it *like a hog on ice*. 彼はあぶなっかしい格好でそれをやった.

live [***eat***] ***high off*** [***on***] ***the hog*** 《米口》安楽[贅沢]に暮らす ▪ I would like to *live high off the hog*. 贅沢な暮らしがしてみたいものだ ▪ They've been *living high on the hog* since then. それ以来彼らは安楽に暮らしている. ☞最高級の豚肉は腹上部から得られることから.

on the hog 《米俗》歩き回って, 放浪して; 全く窮乏して, 破産して; こわれて ▪ The railroader is *on the hog*. 鉄道従業員が歩き回っている ▪ This road is *on the hog*. この道はこわれている.

hog[2] /hɔːg|hɔg/ 動 ***hog the ether*** ラジオのトークショーで話を独り占めする ▪ I'm sick of listening to environmentalists *hogging the ether* on every talk show. どのトークショーでも環境保護論者たちが我が物顔でしゃべっているのを聞いてうんざりする.

hog the phone [***the road***] 《米》電話[道路]を独占する ▪ A person who *hogs the phone* is as bad as someone who *hogs the road*. 電話を独占する人は道路を独占する人と同じほど無作法だ.

hoist[1] /hɔɪst/ 名 ***give*** *a person* ***a hoist*** 《口》(塀などに登るのに)人を下から押し上げてやる ▪ I *gave* him *a hoist* up the fence. 彼を塀の上に押し上げてやった.

hoist[2] /hɔɪst/ 動 ***hoist sail*** →SAIL[1].

hoist with [***by***] *one's* ***own petard*** → PETARD.

hold[1] /hoʊld/ 名 ***be in holds*** (レスリング・ボクシングで)つかみ合っている, 組みついている ▪ They closed again, and *were* still *in holds* when time was called. 彼らは再び取り組んで, 時間切れが宣せられたときもまだ組みついていた.

catch [***seize***] ***hold of*** …をつかむ, つかまえる ▪ He *caught hold of* a rope and saved himself. 彼はロープをつかんで助かった.

cop hold of 《英俗》…をつかむ ▪ The police officer promptly *copped hold of* the criminal's sleeve. 警官はとっさに犯人の袖をつかんだ. ☞cop 《俗》(＝catch); 北部イングランドの方言から.

get (***a***) ***hold of*** *oneself* 冷静になる ▪ *Get hold of yourself* and stop yelling. 落ち着いて, わめくのはやめろ.

get hold of 《口》 **1** …をつかまえる; (人など)を見つける ▪ If the cat *gets hold of* that bird, he will kill it. 猫がその鳥をつかまえたら殺すだろう ▪ Can you *get hold of* the manager? 支配人をつかまえることができますか(見つけることができますか).
2 …を理解する ▪ You'll soon *get hold of* the idea. あなたはじきにその考えがわかるでしょう.
3 …を手に入れる ▪ Where did you *get hold of* this picture? この絵をどこで手に入れられましたか.

get (***hold of***) ***the wrong end of the stick*** →STICK[1].

grab [***grasp***] ***hold of*** …をつかむ, しっかり握る, ひったくる ▪ She *grabbed hold of* the dog by its collar. 彼女は犬の首輪をしっかりつかんだ ▪ He managed to *grasp hold of* the rope. 彼はなんとかロープをつかめた.

have a hold on [***upon, over***] **1** …の急所を握っている, を支配している ▪ He *has a hold on* her. 彼は彼女の急所を握っている ▪ Evil passions *have a* strong *hold upon* him. 情欲が彼を強く支配している.
2 …に対して(思いどおりにさせる)勢力や威力を持つ ▪ The old religion *has* no great *hold on* the common people. 古い宗教は民衆に対してたいした勢力を持っていない.

have hold of **1** …をつかまえている, つかんでいる ▪ He *had hold of* the horse. 彼は馬を捕まえていた.
2 …を理解している, 知っている ▪ I don't know whether you *have* any *hold of* the subject. あなたがその問題を理解しておられるかどうかわかりません.

have hold on [***upon***] (人の)心をとらえる, (人の)心にくっついている ▪ Religion *had* considerable *hold on* her. 宗教は彼女の心を強くとらえていた.

keep a firm [***tight***] ***hold of*** [***on***] **1** …にしっかりつかまっている; をじっとつかんで放さない ▪ We must *keep a tight hold of* this privilege. この特権をしっかりつかまえていなければならない.
2 …をしっかりと握っている[統制, 掌握している] ▪ We must *keep a firm hold on* the boys. 我々はその少年たちをしっかりと掌握していなければならない.

keep a good hold of …をしっかり支配している[つかんでいる] ▪ He *keeps a good hold of* the land. 彼はその土地をしっかりつかんでいる.

keep hold of …を握って放さない ▪ I can't *keep hold of* it. それをじっと握っていることができない.

lay hold of [***on, upon***] **1** …をつかまえる; をつかむ; を手に入れる ▪ We must *lay hold of* the robber. 我々は盗賊を捕えなければならない ▪ Where can I *lay hold on* a good car? どこで良い車を手に入れられるかね ▪ The creditors *laid hold on* his property. 債権者たちは彼の財産を差し押さえた.
2 (相手の弱点など)に乗じる, を利用する ▪ She *laid hold of* his absence to make a breach between them. 彼女は彼の留守に乗じて彼らの仲を裂いた.

leave *one's* ***hold*** 手を放す ▪ A few who *left their hold* were drowned. 手を放した数名の人が溺死した.

leave hold (***of***) 《口》…を放す ▪ He suddenly *left hold of* me. 彼は急に私を放した.

let go *one's* ***hold*** (***of***) (つかまえている手を)放す ▪ Don't *let go your hold of* it. それを放すな.

lose hold of …を放す; の支配力を失う; の手がかりがなくなる ▪ I was slowly *losing hold of* my original self. 私は徐々にもとの自己に対する支配力を失っていた ▪ I've *lost hold of* it. 私はそれを放してしまった.

lose *one's* ***hold on*** …に対する理解力[支配力]を失う ▪ He *lost his hold on* reality. 彼は現実を理解する力を失った ▪ He *lost his hold on* public opinion. 彼は意見を支配する力を失った.

maintain *one's* ***hold over*** …に対する支配力を維持する ▪ The government *maintained its hold over* the district. 政府はその地方に対する支配力を維持していた.

on hold **1** 電話口で待たされて, 電話を切らずに待って ▪ I called the customer service and was kept *on hold* for five minutes. アフターサービス係に電話したら5分も待たされた.
2 一時保留となって, 待機して, 延期して ▪ The space launch is *on hold* until the weather clears up. 天候が晴れるまで宇宙ロケットの打ち上げは延期されている.

out of *a person's* ***hold*** つかんでいる手から放れて ▪ The jar slipped *out of my hold*. そのつぼは私の手からすべり落ちた.

put … on hold [***be put on hold***] …を延期する[される], 保留する[される] ▪ *Put* your wedding plans *on hold* until you finish school. 卒業するまで結婚の計画を延ばしなさい ▪ The expansion of the airport *was put on hold* when the residents objected. 空港の拡張は住民の反対にあって保留された. ☞受話器を持ったままオペレーターが相手と繋ぐのを待っている状態から.

relinquish *one's* ***hold of*** [***over***] …に対する支配を棄てる ▪ She has at last *relinquished her hold over* her son. 彼女は遂に息子に対する支配を棄てた.

seize hold of →catch HOLD of.

take a* (*firm*) *hold on *oneself* =take a (firm) GRIP on oneself.

take hold 定着する ▪ It is hard for him to *take hold* in the new place. 彼が新しい所に定着するのはむずかしい.

take hold of [***on***] (有形・無形のもの)をつかむ; をつかまえる; を牛耳る ▪ There was no railing to *take hold of*. つかまるための手すりは全然なかった.

(***with***) ***no holds barred*** 制限なしで, 手段を選ばず ▪ Jane and Emily tried to get him *with no holds barred*. ジェインとエミリーは手段を選ばず彼を得ようとした. ☞レスリングで「ある種のホールドが反則なのにそれが禁止 (barred) されずに」が原義.

hold[2] /hoʊld/ 動 ***be held at*** (品物が)...の相場である ▪ Those goods *are held at* high prices. それらの品は相場が高い ▪ In those days, a genuine Masamune sword *was held at* 300,000 yen. その当時, 本物の正宗の名刀は30万円の相場であった.

can't hold *one's* ***drink*** [***liquor***] (わずかな酒で)すぐ酔っ払う ▪ He *can't hold his drink*; that's his problem. 彼はじきに酔ってしまう. 困ったものだ.

hold *oneself* **1** 身のこなしをする, おのれを持す, ふるまう ▪ She *held herself* like a queen. 彼女は女王のような身のこなしをした ▪ The man *holds himself* proudly. その男はごう慢な態度を取る.
2 ...の姿勢をとる ▪ He *held himself* ready to start. 彼はいつでも出発できる姿勢をとった.

hold all the aces 決定権を握っている, すべてに有利である (→hold (all the) TRUMPs) ▪ Our president *holds all the aces* at the moment. 今のところ社長がすべての決定権を握っている.

hold (***an***) ***office*** →OFFICE.

hold (***directly***) ***of*** ...から直接租借する ▪ His imagination *holds directly of* nature. 彼の想像力は生まれながらのものである.

hold down (***a claim, a homestead***) 《米豪・口》(自作農場法により)所有権が得られるまで長くある土地に居住する ▪ He did not *hold down*, and the place was eventually deserted. 彼は所有権が得られるまで長くそこに居住しなかったので, そこはついにさびれてしまった ▪ She was a lone woman "*holding down a claim.*" 彼女は一定期間居住して土地の所有権を得ようとしている一人暮らしの女性だった.

hold everything =HOLD it.

hold fast [***firm***] (***to***) **1** (...に)しっかりとつかまる ▪ He was *holding fast to* the railing. 彼は手すりにしっかりとつかまっていた ▪ We *hold firm to* the works of God. 我々は神のみわざ(自然)にしかとつかまる.
2 (...を)固守する ▪ He *held fast to* his creed. 彼は自分の主義を固守した ▪ The sellers *held firm*. 売手はなかなか負けなかった.

hold good →GOOD.

hold hard 《口》 **1** 手綱を強く引いて馬を止める ▪ But I must *hold hard* here. しかし私はここで馬を止めなければならない. ☞《狩》より.
2 〚主に命令文で〛 止まれ, ちょっと待て, ゆっくり行け ▪ *Hold hard*! I'll be ready in a moment. ちょっとお待ちください. すぐ用意しますから.

hold *one's* ***head high*** →HEAD[1].

hold it 《口》〚主に命令文で〛 待って!; そのまま動かないで! ▪ *Hold it*, friend. I'll put your wife on the line. 君, ちょっと待ってくれ, 奥さんを電話に出すから ▪ OK, say cheese. *Hold it*! さ, 笑って. はい, そのまま!

hold it down 《米口》 待つ ▪ Can we *hold it down* a minute? 少し待つわけにはいきませんか.

hold *one's* ***noise*** [***row, jaw***] 騒がない, 黙っている ▪ *Hold your jaw*! 黙っていろ!

hold on by the eyebrows → hang on by one's EYEBROWs.

hold on like (***grim***) ***death*** → hang on like (grim) DEATH.

hold ... over *a person's* ***head*** (おどしなど)を人にふりかざす ▪ He *held* the threat of disclosure *over my head*. 彼は暴露してやると言って私をおどした ▪ He knew of our past and was *holding* it *over our heads*. 彼は我々の過去を知っていたのでそれで我々をおどしていた.

hold *one's* ***own*** **1** 地歩を維持する[守る] ▪ He is quite capable and can *hold his own*. 彼は全く有能で地歩を守ることができる ▪ The patient is *holding his own*. その患者は小康を保っている.
2 (...に)負けない, 譲らない (*against*) ▪ Japan can *hold her own against* any power. 日本はいかなる列強にも負けない.
3 屈しない; 退かない; (競争などで)負けずにやる ▪ He *held his own* like an Englishman. 彼はイギリス人らしく屈しなかった ▪ I think he is *holding his own* well in the election. 彼は選挙に負けずにうまく戦っていると私は思う.
4 《海》(どんな暴風にも)進路を変えずに走る ▪ The ship can *hold her own*. その船は進路を変えずに走れる.

hold *oneself* ***together*** 冷静さを失わない, 正気を保つ ▪ She managed to *hold herself together* till the end of the meeting. 彼女は会が終わるまでなんとか平静を保った.

hold true →TRUE.

hold up *one's* ***head*** (***high***) → hold *one's* HEAD up (high).

I'll hold you to that. 《口》(招待を先延ばしで受けて)そのうちにね ▪ Why don't we have dinner together sometime?—*I'll hold you to that.* 今度いっしょに食事でもどうだい?—いつかぜひ.

leave *a person* ***holding the baby*** [《米》***bag***] →leave a person holding the BAG.

neither to hold nor to bind 《口》 手のつけられないほど興奮[激怒]して ▪ He was *neither to hold nor to bind*, because something had been said about his wife. 彼は妻のことを何か言われたというので, 手のつけられないほど荒れまくっていた.

there's no holding [***stopping***] *a person* ... は手に負えない, を止めようがない ▪ *There is no*

H

holding her once she starts talking. 彼女が一度口を開いたらもうお手上げだ ▪ When he sets his mind on something, *there's no stopping* him. 彼があることを固く心に決めたら止めようがない.

too hot to hold *one* (自分の過去の不始末などでその場所が)居づらい, いたたまれない ▪ The cook will find this kitchen *too hot to hold* him. そのコックにはこの調理場が居づらくなるだろう.

hole[1] /hoʊl/ 名 ***a black hole*** **1** 地下牢, 営舎, 独房 ▪ He has completed 13 years in the *black hole*. 彼は13年間の独房での刑を終えたところだ.

2 巨大な無の空間, 深淵(しんえん), (すべてが)吸い込まれるように消える場所[状況] ▪ We shouldn't throw money into *a black hole*. 際限なく金のかかる事業につぎ込んではだめだ ▪ Our debt is *a black hole* we see no way out of. 我々の負債は出口の見えない底なし沼だ.

a hole card 《主に米》切り札, 隠し玉 ▪ You should never show your *hole card* until the last moment of negotiations. 交渉の大詰めまで切り札を決して見せてはならない. ☞ポーカーのルールから.

a hole in *one's* ***coat*** [***character***] (人格などの)欠点, 玉にきず ▪ She is looking for *holes in his character*. 彼女は彼の欠点を捜している.

a hole in one **1** 《ゴルフ》ホールインワン (→make a HOLE in one).

2 完璧な学業成績 ▪ She scored *a hole in one* on that test. 彼女はそのテストで満点を取った.

a hole in the air エアポケット ▪ The plane suddenly dropped into *a hole in the air*. 飛行機は突然エアポケットに落ちこんだ.

a hole in the wall/a hole-in-the-wall **1** 《主に米》不法に酒を売る小さな薄汚い店, 密売酒場 ▪ His favorite place was *a hole in the wall*. 彼のお気に入りの場所は密売酒場だった ▪ We went into *a* little *hole in the wall* bar, where they served some moonshine. 小さな違法バーに入ったら密造酒が出された.

2 現金自動支払機, ATM ▪ The elderly lady said she hated using *a hole-in-the-wall*. 老婦人は ATM を使うのはまっぴらだと言った.

3 トンネル ▪ You take the wheel after we get through this *hole in the wall*. このトンネルを抜けたら運転を代わってくれ.

a round peg in a square hole/a square peg in a round hole →PEG[1].

be full of holes 欠陥だらけである ▪ This plan of yours *is* so *full of holes* that it won't work. 君のこの計画は欠陥だらけで実行はおぼつかない.

blow a hole in →make a HOLE in.

burn a hole in *a person's* ***pocket*** (金が)じきに使われてしまう ▪ Whenever you have any money, it *burns a hole in your pocket*. あなたは金を持っているときはいつも, じきに使ってしまう.

dig *oneself* ***into a hole/dig a hole for*** *oneself* 《英口》困難な状況に陥る, 自ら状況をさらに悪化させる ▪ Stop talking or you'll *dig yourself into a deeper hole*. しゃべるのをやめないと立場をいっそう悪くする羽目になる.

dig [***get***] *a person* [*oneself*] ***out of a hole*** 《英口》人を窮地から救う[窮地を脱する] ▪ He *got* me *out of a hole* by lending me some money. 彼は金を貸して私を窮地から救ってくれた ▪ I have somehow managed to *dig myself out of a hole*. 何とか窮地を脱することができた.

every hole and corner すみずみまで, くまなく ▪ I looked for it in *every hole and corner*. 私はそれをくまなく捜した.

find holes in *a person's* ***coat*** =pick HOLEs in a person's coat.

go into a black hole **1** 跡形もなく消える ▪ All that money didn't *go into a black hole* to be lost forever. あのお金が全部消えてすっかり無くなってしまったわけではない.

2 意気消沈する, 落ち込む ▪ She *goes into a black hole* at least once a week. 彼女は少なくとも週に1度はふさぎの虫に取り憑(つ)かれる.

have holes in *one's* ***head*** 頭がおかしい, 愚かである ▪ He *has holes in his head* if he thinks it will never happen again. それが二度と起きないと考えているとしたら彼はどうかしている.

hole and corner, hole-and-corner/ 《英》 ***hole-in-the-corner*** 〚限定的〛秘密のうしろ暗い; 人目を忍んだ, 陰に隠れた ▪ I don't like *hole and corner* government. 私は秘密のうしろ暗い政府は嫌いだ ▪ They treated us in a rather *hole-and-corner* fashion. 我々はかなり人目を避けて応待された ▪ We have had enough of *hole-in-the-corner* deals. 陰でこそこそやる取引はもううんざりだ.

I'll bet you the hole of a doughnut …だが責任はもたない, だが自信はない ▪ *I'll bet you the hole of a doughnut* that he'll win. 彼が勝つと思うが外れたらごめんよ.

in a (***deep, tight***) ***hole*** 《英口・古風》窮地に陥って《特に財政上》; 苦境に立って ▪ That puts me *in a hole* all right. それじゃ僕が全く困ってしまう ▪ I'm *in a hole* right now. ちょうど今は金に窮している ▪ He found himself *in a hole* with little hope of escape. 彼は抜け出せる望みもほとんどなく追い詰められていた.

in holes (靴下などに)穴があいて ▪ The old towels were *in holes*. 古タオルは穴があいていた.

in the hole **1** 《米》借金して; 赤字になって ▪ It put the Dominion of Canada 900 million dollars *in the hole*. そのためカナダ自治領は9億ドル借金した ▪ I am fifty dollars *in the hole* this month. 私はこの月は50ドルの赤字である.

2 《野球》苦境に立つ; (打球が)内野の間げきを抜く ▪ He had the batters *in the hole* all the time. 彼は打者たちを始終苦境に立たせた ▪ At no balls and two strikes, the batter's *in the hole*. バッターはノーボールツーストライクに追い込まれた.

3 (単線列車が)待避線に ▪ The freighters had to spend a lot of time *in the hole*. 貨物列車は多くの

時間を待避線で過ごさねばならなかった.

4《主に米》(ポーカーで)札の表を下にして, 伏せて; (シンチなどで)マイナス点を取って.

like the Black Hole of Calcutta 暑苦しく空気が入らない ▪ It's *like the Black Hole of Calcutta* in here. ここは暑苦しくて窒息しそうだ. ☞1756年インドのカルカッタで多数の欧州人が一夜小さな牢獄に入れられ, 大半が死んだ事件から.

make* [*blow*] *a hole in 《口》 **1** ...に大穴をあける, 資金を目減りさせる; を大方使いこむ ▪ The hospital bills have *made a* large *hole in* my savings. 入院費のため私の貯蓄に大穴があいた ▪ The trip *blew a hole in* our budget, but it was worth it. その旅行は我が家の予算を大幅に食ったが, それだけの値打ちはあった ▪ The loss will *make a* large *hole in* your army. その損失で君の軍隊は非常に小さくなろう.

2 ...に弾を打ちこむ, 負傷させる ▪ He *made a hole in* her head. 彼は彼女の頭に弾丸を打ちこんだ.

3 ...を破る; を台無しにする, に損害を与える, の効果を弱める ▪ They *made a hole in* the silence. 彼らは静かなときにやかましい音を立てた ▪ He *made a hole in* her reputation. 彼のせいで彼女の名声が落ちた.

make a hole in one 《ゴルフ》ティーからグリーンまでを1打で穴に入れる ▪ They both *made a hole in one* during their round. 彼らは二人ともラウンド中にホールインワンを達成した.

make a hole in *one's* ***pocket*** 多額の個人資金を消費する, 大金がかかる ▪ Dining at Las Vegas *made a* big *hole in my pocket*. ラスベガスで食事をしたらひどく高くついた.

make a hole in the water 《口》身投げする, 投身自殺する ▪ He *made a hole in the water*; but luckily he was pulled out. 彼は身投げしたが, 幸いにも引き上げられた.

make holes in = make a HOLE in 2.

need* [*want*]** *a thing* ***like (*one* ***needs* [*wants*]**) ***a hole in the head*** ...は全然いらない, 絶対に必要としない[欲しくない] ▪ We *need* nuclear weapons *like a hole in the head*. 核兵器は絶対に必要ない ▪ I *need* another camera *like* I *need a hole in the head*. もう1台カメラの必要は全くない.

out of a hole 窮地から脱して ▪ Thanks for your suggestion. It got me *out of a hole*. 助言をありがとう. お陰で危ないところを助かった.

out of the hole 《口》 **1**《競技》得点0を脱して ▪ It was difficult for me to get *out of the hole*. 私が0点から脱するのはむずかしかった.

2《競技》相手の点に追いつく ▪ The team could not get *out of the hole* after all. そのチームは結局相手の得点に追いつけなかった.

3 借金を脱して, 借金をしないで ▪ In the second year, Tom got *out of the hole*. 2年目にトムは借金を脱した.

pick holes* [*a hole*] *in ...のあら捜しをする, を非難する ▪ He is always *picking holes in* me. 彼は私のあら捜しばかりしている ▪ The opposition began to *pick holes in* the bill. 野党はその法案のあら捜しをし始めた.

pick* [*make*] *holes* [*a hole*] *in *a person's* ***coat*** 人のあら捜しをする, 人の非難の種を捜す ▪ You should not always be trying to *pick a hole in his coat*. いつも彼のあら捜しをしようとしてはいけない.

pull *a person* ***out of the* [*a*] *hole*** 《米》人を赤字から抜け出させる ▪ Recent gains have *pulled* me *out of the hole*. 最近実入りがあって赤字から抜け出せた.

***punch holes* (*in*)** 反ばくして(相手を)破る《相手に穴をあける》 ▪ You seem to enjoy *punching holes in* everything I say. 君は私の言うことを片っ端からけなして喜んでいるようだ.

put *a person* ***in a hole*** → in a (deep, tight) HOLE.

put *a person* ***in the hole*** 《俗》人から金[分け前など]をだまし取る ▪ They *put* him *in the hole*. 彼らは彼の取り分をだまし取った.

take ... a hole lower ...をこきおろす, へこます, はずかしめる ▪ He has *taken* my thoughts *a hole lower*. 彼は私の思想をこきおろした.

talk through a hole in *one's* **[*the*] *head*** ばかげたことを言う ▪ You are *talking through a hole in your head*. 君は愚にもつかぬことを言っている.

want *a thing* ***like*** (*one* ***needs* [*wants*]**) ***a hole in the head*** → need a thing like (one needs) a HOLE in the head.

wear ... into holes (靴下など)をはいて穴だらけにする ▪ I have *worn* my socks *into holes*. 私はその靴下をはいて穴だらけにした.

hole[2] /hoʊl/ 動 ***hole* (*out*) *in one*** 《ゴルフ》ホールインワンをする ▪ Yesterday Henry *holed out in one* at successive holes. 昨日ヘンリーは続けざまにホールインワンをした.

holiday /hάlədèɪ|hɔ́l-/ 名 ***a busman's holiday*** 専門の仕事をして過ごす休日 ▪ Last Sunday the doctor had to look after patients—quite *a busman's holiday*. 前の日曜にその医師は患者たちの世話をしなければならなかった—全く専門の仕事をして過ごした休日だった.

be home for the holidays 《主に英》休暇で帰省している ▪ The boys *are home for the holidays*. 少年たちは休暇で帰省している.

give the boys a holiday (大きな出来事などを記念して)学校を1日休みにする ▪ He replied, "*Give the boys a holiday.*" 彼は「学校を1日休みにしてやってください」と答えた.

it is all holiday with 《口》...はもうだめである《万事休す》 ▪ *It is all holiday with* him. 彼はもう見込みがない ▪ *It is all holiday with* them. 彼らの商売はもうお手上げだ ▪ When you smile at me like this, *it's all holiday with* me! 君にこう微笑みかけられると僕はいちころだ.

make a holiday of it 休業して祝う ▪ We were

invited to a friend's wedding, so we *made a holiday of it*. 友人の結婚式に招待されたので休業して祝った.

make holiday 休む; (仕事を)休んで楽しむ[祝う] ▪ You've got the first prize! We must *make holiday* over this. 君は一等賞を取ったね, 仕事を休んでそれを祝わなければならない.

on holiday 《主に英》休暇で ▪ Our typist is away *on holiday* this week. うちのタイピストは今週は休暇で来ていません ▪ He went *on holiday* for two weeks. 彼は2週間休暇を取った.

take (a) holiday 休む; 休暇を取る ▪ We ought to *take a holiday* soon. まもなく休むべきである ▪ We will *take a* month's *holiday* in summer. 夏には1か月の休暇を取ります.

Holland /hάlənd|hɔ́l-/ 名 ***when the Dutch take Holland*** 決して…ない《オランダ軍がオランダを占領するとき, などありえない》 ▪ I hope you'll come to see me; but I suppose it will be *when the Dutch take Holland*. 遊びに来てくれたらと思うが, そいつはなかなか無理だろうな.

H

hollow /hάloʊ|hɔ́l-/ 形副名 ***all hollow*** [***holler***] 《口》全く, 徹底的に ▪ She beats us young people *all hollow*. 彼女は私たち若い者をさんざんに打ち負かす. ☞hollow は wholly のなまりか.

beat ... (all) hollow 《口》…をさんざんにやっつける[負かす] (→all HOLLOW) ▪ You'll *beat* him *hollow* in the match. 君は試合で彼をさんざんに負かすだろう.

bore ... for the hollow horn 《米》(牛の角にきりで穴をあけるように)愚か者に穴をあけて知恵が通るようにする; 耳に穴をあけて聞こえるようにする ▪ He ought to *be bored for the hollow horn*. 彼はばかなことをしたものだ《頭に穴をあけて知恵が通るようにすべきである》 ▪ You haven't had your ears *bored for the hollow horn* lately. 君は近頃, さっぱり耳が聞こえないじゃないか.

have a hollow ring =RING hollow.

in the hollow of *one's* ***hand*** 全く自分の言いなりに, 人を完全に支配して ▪ He held us *in the hollow of his hand*. 彼は我々を完全に手玉に取った.

ring hollow →RING³.

sound hollow =RING hollow.

holy /hóʊli/ 形名 ***as the devil loves holy water*** →DEVIL.

holier-than-thou 他の人より善人ぶる, 信心ぶる, 独善的な ▪ I just can't stand his *holier-than-thou* attitude. 彼のお高くとまった態度はどうにもがまんがならない.

Holy kicker [***cats, cow, mackerel, Moses, moly, smoke***]***!*** 《口》〚間投詞的に〛おやおや!, まあまあ!, チェッ!《驚き・喜び・怒りの表現》 ▪ *Holy cats!* That's good pie! まあまあ! すてきなパイだ! ▪ *Holy smoke*, I didn't know you were here too. おや, 君も来ているとは知らなかった.

holy of holies **1** (シナゴーグの)奥の院; (キリスト教会内の)至聖所 ▪ That is Wilfred's room, his *holy of holies*. それはウィルフレッドの部屋で, 彼の至聖所だ.
2《戯》限られた者しか入れない場所, 家中で最も人にじゃまされない場所 ▪ The boss invited me into his *holy of holies*. 社長が誰も入れない社長室へ私を招き入れてくれた ▪ My study is a *holy of holies* in our house. 書斎が我が家での私だけの城である.
3《口》便所 ▪ I saw him go into the *Holy of Holies* a little while ago. 彼が少し前に便所へ入るのを見た.

My holy aunt! おやおや!, まあ!《驚きの表現》.

homage /hάmɪdʒ|hɔ́m-/ 名 ***do homage*** **1** 忠順を誓って臣となる, (正式に)臣従の礼を取る, 臣下として仕える ▪ He has come to *do homage*. 彼は臣従の礼を取りにやって来た.
2 敬意を表する (*to*) ▪ They have come to *do homage to* us. 彼らは我々に敬意を表しに来た.

pay homage (to) =do HOMAGE 2.

render homage =do HOMAGE 1.

home /hoʊm/ 名形副 ***a broken home*** 両親の離別[死亡]により不安定になった家庭(生活), 欠損家庭 ▪ He can't have turned to crime just because he comes from *a broken home*. 崩壊家庭の出だという理由だけで彼が犯罪に走ったはずがない.

a home away from home/《英》***a home from home*** 《米》(施設・気安さの点で)自宅のような住居; 家から離れた憩いの場 ▪ The landlady said her house was *a home from home* for all her lodgers. 下宿のおかみさんは自分の家はすべての下宿人たちにとって自宅のような気安い所であると言った ▪ The Englishman pays handsomely for his *home from home*. イギリス人は家から離れた憩いの場のためには気前よく金を出す ▪ Australia has become *a home away from home* for me. オーストラリアは私には母国のような場所になった.

a home bird 家庭的な[マイホーム型の]人 ▪ My husband is *a home bird* and likes to spend his free time in the garden. 夫は家庭的で暇があると庭いじりを楽しむ.

a home truth →TRUTH.

at home **1** 自分の家に ▪ Mr. Smith was *at home*. スミス氏は在宅でした ▪ I left my books *at home*. 私は家に本を忘れて来た.
2《口》客を受ける, 面会する (*to*); 面会の ▪ I am not *at home to* any one today. 私は今日は誰にも会いません ▪ She decided to have her "*At Home*" day on the first Thursday of the month. 彼女は毎月の第1木曜日を面会日にすることに決めた.
3 近隣で; 自国(内)で ▪ He is famous both *at home* and abroad. 彼は国の内外で有名である.
4 (遠征地 (away) に対して)本拠地で, 地元で ▪ Our team always do better *at home* than they do at away games. わがチームはいつも遠征試合より本拠地の方が成績がよい.
5 くつろいで ▪ Please make yourself *at home*. どうぞおくつろぎください.
6 十分慣れて, 精通して, 熟練して (*in, on*) ▪ He was *at home in* that kind of role. 彼はそういう種

類の演技には十分慣れていた ▪ The girl is very much *at home in* French. 少女はフランス語にとても堪能である ▪ She is *at home on* the subject. 彼女はその問題に通じている.

away from home 留守で, 外出中で, 国を離れて ▪ We shall be *away from home* tomorrow. 我々はあすは留守をします.

be home 帰宅している; 《米》在宅する ▪ He *is home* at last. 彼はとうとう帰宅した.

be nothing* (*much*) *to write home about (大して)熱中[熱狂, 自慢]するほどではない ▪ That new restaurant *was nothing to write home about.* あの新しいレストランは大騒ぎするほどのものではなかった.

bring *oneself* ***home*** (ゲーム・競馬で)損失を取り戻す; 経済的に立ち直る; 地位を回復する ▪ He has taken a very good road to *bring himself home* again. 彼は再び財政的に相当立ち直り始めている.

***bring ... home* (*to*)** **1** (人に)…を痛切に感じさせる, 深く悟らせる ▪ He *brought home to* me the importance of science. 彼は科学の重要性を私に切実に悟らせた ▪ He *brings* the truth *home to* one's heart. 彼は真理を人の心に染み込むようにわからせる.
2 …を思い出させる ▪ You've *brought* the fact *home to* me. あなたは私にその事実を思い出させた.
3 (罪などを人が)犯したと立証する, (人に罪などを)承服させる ▪ The charge *was brought home to* William. その罪はウィリアムが犯したものと立証された ▪ They *brought* a fraud *home to* him. 彼らは彼が詐欺を犯したことを立証した.

close* [*near*] *to home (発言・話題が)相手の痛いところを突いて ▪ The spectacle touched too *close to home* for the orphan. 孤児にとってその情景は辛すぎた.

come home **1** 家に帰る, 帰宅[帰国]する ▪ He has not *come home* yet. 彼はまだ帰宅していません.
2 (…に)しみじみこたえる, (の)胸に徹する (*to*) ▪ His tale *came home to* us. 彼の話は我々の胸にこたえた.
3 (人の身に)及ぶ (*to*) ▪ Losses will *come home to* the best of us. 損害は我々の中で最優秀者にも及ぶ.
4 突然…とわかる, 急に明らかになる ▪ Suddenly, it *came home* to me that she thought I was Nancy. 彼女が私をナンシーと人違いしているとふと気づいた.
5 《海》(いかりが止まらないで)船の方へ引かれる ▪ The anchor *came home* slowly. いかりは止まらず徐々に船の方へ引かれた.
6 =hit (close to) HOME.

come home to roost →ROOST.

come home with the milk →MILK[1].

***drive ... home* (*to*)** **1** (議論・事実など)を十分論じて納得させる, 徹底させる ▪ He *drove* his thought *home to* the readers. 彼は十分論じて, 自分の思想を読者によく理解させた ▪ By citing specific examples, the orator *drove home* his points. 明確な例をあげて弁士は自分の論旨を徹底させた.
2 (くぎ)を深く打ちこむ ▪ With one blow he *drove* the nail *home*. 一撃で彼はくぎを深く打ちこんだ.

feel at home **1** くつろいだ気持ちになる (→at HOME 5) ▪ A sociable woman makes you *feel at home* with her. 社交的な女性は人に窮屈な思いをさせない.
2 慣れている (→at HOME 6) ▪ I *feel at home* on radio. ラジオには十分慣れている ▪ It's difficult to *feel at home* in a foreign language. 外国語がすっかり身につくということはむずかしい.

feel like home 自分の家のようにゆったりくつろげる ▪ After we had unpacked in the new tent, it *felt like home*. 新しいテントで装備を解いたあとはわが家のようにくつろげた.

from home **1** 郷里[家]から ▪ I received a letter *from home*. 私は家から手紙をもらった.
2 留守で, 家を離れて ▪ Her husband was *from home*. 彼女の夫は留守だった.

get home **1** 家に着く, 帰宅する[させる] ▪ We shall *get home* at six in the evening. 夕方の6時に家に着くだろう ▪ He's drunk. We'd better *get* him *home*. 彼は酔っている. 帰宅させたほうがよい.
2 (矢・推量などが)的中する ▪ The remark *got home*. その言は当たった.
3 ねらいが当たる ▪ The television program *got home*. そのテレビ番組は当たった.
4 (…の)注意を引く (*to*) ▪ That will *get home to* your father. それは君のお父さんの知るところとなろう.
5 目的を達する, 成功する ▪ I have been working on my book, and last night I *got home*. 私はずっと本を書いていたが, 昨夜できあがった.
6 《口》決勝点に着く, 勝つ; (すごろくなどで)あがりになる ▪ Jones *got home* by 10 yards. ジョーンズは10ヤードの差で勝った.
7 《口》一撃をくらわす ▪ He *got home* with a beautiful right to the jaw. 彼はあごへみごとな右手の一撃をくらわした.
8 損失を取り戻す, 経済的に回復する, 立ち直る; 地位を回復する ▪ I believe he *got home* on the sale of it. 彼はそれを販売して損失を取り戻したと思う.
9 (主旨など)を(…に)通じさせる, 理解させる (*to*) ▪ You *got* your point *home to* the audience. 君は君の話の主旨を聴衆に理解させた.

go home **1** 家[国]へ帰る ▪ He has *gone home* to England. 彼はイングランドへ帰った.
2 十分こたえる; 的にピタッとあたる, 所期の効果をあげる ▪ The thrust *went home*. 攻撃は十分こたえた.
3 腐る ▪ This meat's *going home*. この肉は腐りかけている.
4 すり切れる, 痛む ▪ My bag is *going home* fast. 私のかばんはどんどん痛んでいる.

go to *one's* ***long home*** 死ぬ (《聖》*Eccles*. 12. 5) ▪ He has *gone to his long home*. 彼はあの世へ行った.

hammer home *A* (***to*** *B*) Aを(Bに)銘記させる ▪ He *hammered home* the truth *to* the people. 彼はその事実を国民に銘記させた.

hit a home run 非常にうまくいく, 成功する

H

▪ Their band seems to have *hit a home run* that night. 彼らのバンドはその夜大当たりを取ったようだ. ☞野球の本塁打から.

hit* [*strike, be*] (*close to*) *home 的中する; 急所をつく, ひどくこたえる ▪ His remarks *hit home* when he referred to those people. その人々の事を言ったとき彼の言葉は急所をついた ▪ Her criticism of my hairdo *hit close to home*. 私の髪型を彼女にとやかく言われたのがぐさりときた.

home and dry 《主に英》(苦闘の後)無事成功して ▪ Bush was *home and dry*. ブッシュ氏は何とか当選した ▪ I just need to finish this and I'll be *home and dry*. これをすませたら万事めでたく終了だ.

home free 《米》 **1** 首尾よく目的を達成して, 勝利[成功] 疑いなしの ▪ Three more hours of work and I'm *home free*. あと3時間で間違いなく仕上がる ▪ Just another week on antibiotics and I'm *home free*! もう1週間抗生物質を飲めば完治するぞ!
2 あとは簡単[朝飯前] である ▪ Once you get past the hardest part, you're *home free*. 一番難しいところを乗り切ったらあとは楽勝だ.

home in one 一発で的中して ▪ Does this contain vegetable protein?—That's right. *Home in one*. これは植物性タンパク質が入っていますか?—そうだ. 一発で当たったね.

Home is where the heart is. 《諺》 家は心の宿る場所《家庭こそが最も心の安まる場所だ》.

Home, James* (*and don't spare the horses*)*! (運転手に)自宅まで急いで運転してくれ ▪ Mr. Brown said to his chauffeur, "*Home, James!*" 「家まで急いでやってくれ」とブラウン氏はお抱え運転手に言った. ☞F. Hillebrand のポピュラーソング(1934)の題名から. 馬車時代の御者に対する指示表現のパロディー.

home sweet home 《しばしば皮肉》 家に帰ってほっとする ▪ Hey, I'm back! *Home, sweet home*. やぁ, ただいま! 戻ってほっとするよ ▪ *Home sweet home*! I hate it here. こんな家なんか, 大嫌いだ.

keep the home fires burning → HOME(-)FIRE.

knock ... home (くぎなど)をしっかり打ち込む; (議論など)を徹底的に打ち破る ▪ He *knocked* the nail *home*. 彼はそのくぎをしっかり打ち込んだ ▪ His argument *was knocked home* by his opponent. 彼の議論は論敵によって徹底的にやっつけられた.

leave* (...) *for home 家[故国]に向かって発つ ▪ He *left* England *for home*. 彼は故国に向けてイングランドを発った ▪ She *left for home* the next morning. 彼女は翌朝家に向けて発った.

one's ***long* [*last*] *home*** 墓場, 埋葬地 ▪ They laid him in *his long home*. 彼らは彼を墓場に寝かせた ▪ He went to *his long home*. 彼は死んだ.

make *oneself* ***at home*** **1** 楽にする, くつろぐ《日本語の「お楽に」よりもっと楽にする》 ▪ Take your coat off, and *make yourself at home*. コートを脱いでお楽になさい.
2 不遠慮にふるまう ▪ He *makes himself at home* everywhere. 彼は至る所で不遠慮である.

make *one's* ***home*** 自分の住居(同様)にする ▪ Please *make your home* here with us. ここへお泊まりになって, ご自宅同様にお考えください.

My home is my castle. 《諺》 わが家は城である《プライバシーへの他人の侵害は許さない》.

nearer home **1** 自分の家[環境, 国]により近く ▪ Look for a job *nearer home*. もっとわが家に近いところで職を探しなさい ▪ There are whole countries too, such as India, or *nearer home*, Ireland. ちょうどインドのような, あるいはもっとわが国に近い所ではアイルランドのような国家もある.
2 もっと密接に; もっと感銘して ▪ He ought to look *nearer home*. 彼はもっと感銘した顔をすべきである.

nobody home 《俗》 **1** 上の空だ ▪ She is "*nobody home*." あの子は「上の空」だ.
2 頭が変である《狂気・知能の遅れ》 ▪ He tapped his head and said, "*Nobody home*." 彼は自分の頭をたたいて「(あの人は)ここがおかしくなっている」と言った.

play away from home 《英口》 伴侶以外の者と情を通じる ▪ Her husband was *playing away from home*. 彼女の夫は外で不倫をしていた.

press home (攻撃など)を徹底的にやる; (主張など)を徹底させる ▪ They *pressed home* attacks in spite of strong resistance. 彼らは強い抵抗をものともせず攻撃を強行した.

press ... right home ...を徹底的に力説する ▪ I *pressed* the point *right home*. 私はその点を徹底的に力説した.

ram home (意見など)を反復して十分会得させる (*to*) ▪ He *rammed home* the reality *to* the people. 彼は反復してその真実を人々に会得させた.

romp home 《口》 楽々と勝つ, 楽勝する ▪ The runner *romped home* in the easiest possible manner. その走者はいとも楽々と優勝した.

scrape home かろうじて地位[結果]を手に入れる ▪ At the last election Mr. Blythe *scraped home* in Monaghan. この前の選挙でブライス氏はかろうじてモナハンで当選した.

see *a person* ***home*** →SEE.

send home (打撃)をうんとくらわせる ▪ He *sent home* half-a-dozen smashing blows. 彼は猛烈なパンチを数発くらわせた.

sheet home **1** 《海》 帆脚索(ほあしつな)で(帆)を張る ▪ *Sheet* the sails *home*. 帆脚索で帆を張れ.
2 《米》 (必要性など)を痛感させる ▪ Their failure *sheeted home* the need for proper preparation. 彼らの失敗で十分に準備する必要を痛感させられた.

slope home 《口》 家へ帰って行く ▪ What can we do but *slope home* again! 我々にはまた家へ帰って行くより仕方がないではないか.

stay in the home (仕事に出ないで)家にいる ▪ He *stayed in the home* yesterday. 彼は昨日は仕事に出なかった.

strike home **1** (言葉などが)急所を突く, きく ▪ Her words *struck home* upon his conscience. 彼女の言葉は彼の良心にぐさりとこたえた ▪ The title "Satan-

ic School" *struck home*.「悪魔派」という呼称は急所を突いていた.
2 (人・武器が)急所を突く, 命中する ▪ He who strikes a lion must be sure to *strike home*. ライオンを突く者は必ず急所を突かなければならない ▪ The arrow *struck home*. 矢は命中した.
3 …をぐさりと突き刺す, 深く打ち込む ▪ *Strike* the nail *homer* yet. くぎをなおいっそう深く打ち込め.

take home …を家に連れて[持って]帰る; 手取りで…の給料をもらう ▪ After taxes he *takes* £500 *home* a week. 税金を差し引いて, 彼は手取りで週給500ポンドもらっている.

take home to *oneself* →TAKE[2].

the last home 最後の休息地, 終(つい)の住処(すみか), 墓 ▪ Only half a mile from here is *the last home* of a great poet. ここからほんの半マイルのところにさる偉大な詩人の墓地がある.

thrust home (主張など)を徹底させる ▪ He *thrust home* his point. 彼は自分の論旨を徹底させた.

to home 《米》家に (＝at HOME 1) ▪ Martha is *to home* now. マーサは今在宅です.

touch (*a person*) ***home*** (批評が人の)痛いところをつく ▪ There was much in her wild words that *touched* me *home*. 彼女の粗暴な言葉には大いに私の胸にぐさりとくるものがあった.

What is … when it's at home? 《英口・戯》…とは一体何ですか ▪ *What's* fagging *when it's at home?* ファギングとは一体どんなことなの.

Who is … when he's [***she's***] ***at home?*** 《英口・戯》…って一体誰ですか ▪ Susan White wants to meet you.—*Who's* she *when she's at home?* スーザン・ホワイトが君に会いたいそうだ—それって一体誰だ.

worth writing home about 自慢するほどの; とてもすばらしい ▪ My trip was certainly *worth writing home about*. 私の旅はとてもすばらしかった.

home(-)fire /hóʊmfàɪər/ 名 ***keep the home fires burning*** (戦時中などに)家を守る; 家庭の生活を続ける ▪ When they were fighting in France, he was *keeping the home-fires burning*, snug and comfortable. 彼らがフランスで戦っているときに, 彼は安楽に家で暮らしていた ▪ She *kept the home fires burning* while her husband was in jail. 夫の服役中, 彼女が家を守った. ☞Lena Guilbert Ford (1870–1918)が作り第1次大戦中流行した歌の1節.

home-keeping /hóʊmkìːpɪŋ/ 形 ***Home-keeping youths have ever homely wits.*** 《諺》家に引っ込んでばかりいる若者は素朴な考え方しかしない,「井の中の蛙(かわず)大海を知らず, わがうちのかまど料簡」(cf. Sh., *Two Gent*. 1. 1. 2).

Homer /hóʊmər/ 名 (***Even***) ***Homer sometimes nods.*** →NOD[2].

homesteading /hóʊmstèdɪŋ/ 名 ***urban homesteading*** 《口》都市定住奨励《荒廃した建物への入居奨励》 ▪ *Urban homesteading* is on the rise in many big cities. 大都市では都市定住奨励化が進んでいる.

home stretch /hóʊmstrètʃ/, 《英》 **home straight** /hòʊmstréɪt/ 名 ***in*** [***on***] ***the home stretch*** [***straight***] 競走の最終コースに; 仕事の最後の部分[時間, 段階]に, ほとんど終わって, 峠を越して; 3塁から本塁までの間に ▪ Negotiations on the plan are now *in the home stretch*. その計画についての交渉は今や最終段階にきている ▪ The work is *on the home stretch*. その仕事はほとんど終わった ▪ The campaign is now *in the home stretch*. その運動は今や最後の追い込みにきている.

homework /hóʊmwə̀ːrk/ 名 ***do*** *one's* ***homework*** (***on***) (…の)事前準備をする, (ある問題を)詳しく下調べする ▪ You should *do* some *homework on* your speech beforehand. スピーチの準備に下調べをしたほうがよい ▪ You should *do your homework* before you go to interview him. 彼を訪問インタビューする前によく下調べをしておくべきだ.

honest /ɑ́nəst|ɔ́nɪst/ 形 (***as***) ***honest as the day is long*** 非常に正直で ▪ This gentleman is *as honest as the day is long*. この紳士はとても正直です.

be honest with …と正しく交わる; に誠実である ▪ He has *been honest with* his customers. 彼は客に対して誠実であった.

honest Injun →INJUN.

honest to God [***goodness, Pete***] 《口》 **1**〚副詞的に〛全く, 本当に ▪ I was *honest to goodness* off and away. 私は本当に留守にしていたのです.
2〚形容詞的に〛(強調して)本当の, 正真正銘の, 純粋の ▪ This is an *honest-to-goodness* music magazine. これは本格的な音楽雑誌だ ▪ They serve an *honest-to-goodness* steak at that restaurant. あのレストランは本物のステーキを出す ▪ He used to be an *honest-to-God* cowboy. 元はといえば彼は生粋のカウボーイだった.

make an honest woman of 《戯》→WOMAN.

to be honest with you [***about it***] ありていに言うと, 正直に申しますと ▪ *To be honest with you*, I get a little fed up with the media. 実を言うとマスコミには辟易(へきえき)しているんだ.

turn [***earn***] ***an honest penny*** →PENNY.

honesty /ɑ́nəsti|ɔ́n-/ 名 ***Honesty is the best policy.*** 《諺》正直は最良の方策である.

in (***all***) ***honesty*** (全く)正直なところ, 正直言って ▪ He cannot *in honesty* refuse to pay the money. 正直言って彼はその金を払うのがいやだと言えた義理ではない ▪ I can't *in all honesty* recommend this movie. 全く正直なところ, この映画はお勧めしかねる.

honey /hʌ́ni/ 名 (***as***) ***sweet as honey*** 蜜のように甘い, きわめて優しい ▪ Her looks are *sweet as honey*, but her words are sour. 彼女の顔つきはいかにも優しいが, 言葉はひねくれている.

honeymoon /hʌ́nimùːn/ 名 ***a*** [***the***] ***honeymoon period*** 蜜月期間, 幸福な期間 ▪ I'm still in *the honeymoon period* with this laptop. このノート型パソコンをまだ愛用している.

H

the honeymoon is over 蜜月期間[よい関係の時期]は終わった, お楽しみはおしまいだ ▪ *The honeymoon was over* and they started to criticize each other. 二人の友好関係は終わり, 互いに批判しあうようになった ▪ Okay, *the honeymoon is over*. It's time to start hard training again. よし, お楽しみはこれまで. さあ, 猛練習再開だ.

honey-pot /hʌ́nipɑ̀t|-pɔ̀t/ 名 ***a honey-pot area*** 田園の景勝の地 ▪ The Lake District is known as *a honey-pot area*. 湖水地方は景勝の地として知られている.

honor[1], 《英》**honour**[1] /ɑ́nər|ɔ́nə/ 名 ***a debt of honor*** 賭博[賭け事]の借金《無証文で法律上は取り立てえないもので, 支払い義務は面目上のこと》 ▪ I owe him *a debt of honor*. 彼に賭博の借金がある.

a man of honor 恥を知る人, 君子 ▪ *A man of honor* would never do anything so disreputable. 恥を知る者ならそんないかがわしいことは断じてしないだろう.

a point of honor (しなければ)体面にかかわること, 面目にかかわる務め ▪ It is *a point of honor* with me that I should help them. 私が彼らを助けるのは面目上の務めである ▪ It is *a point of honor* with me. それは私の面目にかかわることだ. ☞フランス語法.

All honor to ...! …に敬意を尽くせ! ▪ *All honor to* the brave! 勇者たちに敬意を尽くせ!

be bound in honor to *do*/***be*** (***in***) ***honor bound to*** *do* 義理上…しなければならない; 名誉にかけて…する義務がある ▪ I *am bound in honor to* succeed. 私は義理にも成功しなくてはならない ▪ I said I would go, so I feel *honor bound to* do as I promised. 行くと言ったのだから, 私は紳士として約束は守らないとならない ▪ Every student shall *be in honor bound to* refrain from cheating. すべて学生は名誉にかけてカンニングを慎むこと.

be on [***upon***] *one's* ***honor to*** *do* 面目にかけて…しなければならない ▪ They *were upon their honor to* help him. 彼らは面目にかけても彼を助けねばならなかった.

be to *a person's* ***honor*** 人の名誉である ▪ Your conduct *is to your honor*. あなたの行為はあなたの名誉である.

compromise *one's* ***honor*** 名誉にかかわる失策をする, 名誉をきずつける ▪ I must not *compromise my honor*. 私は自分の名誉を傷つけるようなことをしてはいけない《李下にかんむりを正さず》.

do *a person* ***honor***/***do honor to*** *a person* **1** 人の名誉である ▪ Your conduct *does* you *honor*. あなたの行為はあなたの名誉である.
2 人に敬意を表す ▪ People strove with each other to *do honor to* the hero. 人々は互いに競ってその英雄に敬意を表した.

do *a person* ***the honor of*** *doing* [***to*** *do*] 《雅・主に戯》人に…する光栄を与える, 人に…してやる ▪ Will you *do* me *the honor of accepting* this trifling present? どうぞこのささやかな贈り物をお受けくださいませんか ▪ You *did* me *the honor to* dine with me. あなたはかたじけなくも私と食事を共にしてくださった.

do *oneself* ***the honor of*** *doing* …いたします ▪ I will *do myself the honor of calling* on you in person. 私自身でお訪ね申しあげます.

do the honors (***of***) (…の)主人となって接待する ▪ She *did the honors of* the house to them. 彼女は主人役をして彼らの接待をした ▪ The Duchess *did the honors of* the table. 公爵夫人が食卓の主人役をした.

do [***pay, render***] ***the last*** [***funeral***] ***honors to*** …の葬儀を営む ▪ He *paid the last honors to* his father. 彼は父の葬儀を営んだ ▪ They *did the last honors to* his remains. 彼らは彼の葬儀を営んだ.

for (***the***) ***honor of*** **1**《商》…の信用上 ▪ Any third party may accept *for the honor of* the bill. 第三者がその手形を参加引き受けしてもよい.
2 …の名誉のため ▪ We must settle that matter *for the honor of* the firm. 我々は会社の名誉のためその問題を解決せねばならない.

give [***pay***] ***honor to*** …に敬意を表する; を尊重する ▪ We should *pay honor to* law. 我々は法律を尊重すべきだ.

give *one's* ***word of honor*** かたく約束する[誓う] ▪ I *gave my word of honor* on it. 私はそれをかたく約束した.

have honor 尊敬される (《聖》*John* 4. 44) ▪ He *had honor* in the land. 彼はその国で尊敬されていた.

have [***hold***] *a person* ***in honor*** 人を尊敬する ▪ I *hold* Smith *in* great *honor*. 私はスミスを非常に尊敬している.

have the honor of …の光栄を得る ▪ May I *have the honor of* your company at dinner? 晩餐会にご出席の栄を得たく存じます ▪ May I *have the honor of* asking you? あなたにお尋ね申し上げたく存じます.

have the honor to *do* …する光栄を得る, 慎んで…します ▪ I *have the honor to* inform you that your son has graduated with honors. 御令息が優等で卒業されたことを慎んでお知らせいたします.

His Honor →Your HONOR.

honor bright 《口》**1** 名誉にかけて, きっと ▪ I will do it, *honor bright*. 私はきっとそれをする.
2 〚疑問文で〛まちがいないか; きっとやるか ▪ I don't mean to marry Mr. Jacob.—No! *Honor bright*? 私はジェイコブさんと結婚するつもりはありません—そうですか, まちがいありませんか.
3 不正なことをするな! ▪ *Honor bright*! 不正なことをするな!

honors (***are***) ***easy*** [***even***] 《口》双方あいこである; 勝ち負けなしである ▪ The quarrel finally faded away with *honors easy*. 口論は遂に勝負なしでやんだ.

in honor 体面上; 徳義上《時に, 法律上は義務なしの意味を含むことがある》 ▪ Young ladies are *in honor* obliged to blush. 淑女たちは体面上どうしても

顔を赤らめなければならない ▪ I cannot *in honor* accept this money. この金は受け取れた義理ではない.
in honor of …の記念に; に敬意を表して; を祝して, のために ▪ This monument was built *in honor of* the founder. この記念碑は創立者を記念して建てられた ▪ A farewell meeting was held *in honor of* Mr. K. K君のために送別会が催された ▪ A banquet was held *in his honor*. 彼のために宴が催された.
lay claim to the honor of …の勲功を争う ▪ Several men *laid claim to the honor of* the affair. 数人がその事柄の勲功を争った.
(***may it***) ***please your honor*** 恐れながら申しあげますが《判事または市長に向かって》 ▪ *Please your honor*, have pity on a poor orphan. 恐れながら申しあげますが, 哀れな孤児をお哀れみください.
no honor among thieves (犯罪者が)平気で仲間を警察に売る ▪ They say there can be *no honor among thieves*. ときに強欲は仁義に勝るとされる.
on [***upon***] *one's* ***honor*** **1** 名誉にかけて《特に英上院議員が法廷において用いる文句》 ▪ I certify *on my honor* that he is innocent. 私は名誉にかけて彼の潔白を保証する.
2 誓って; きっと ▪ She promised, *upon her honor*, to return within six weeks. 彼女は6週間以内に帰ると堅く約束した.
on [***upon***] *one's* ***word of honor*** 紳士の一言, 誓って ▪ He assured me *on his word of honor* that it was true. 彼はそれは誓って本当だと言った.
pay honor to →give HONOR to.
pay [***render***] ***the last*** [***funeral***] ***honors to*** →do the last HONORs to.
pledge *one's* ***honor*** →PLEDGE[2].
put [***place***] *a person* ***on*** [***upon***] *his* ***honor*** (***to*** *do*) 人に体面[面目]にかけてやらせる ▪ I *was put on my honor* not *to* tell. 私は面目にかけて絶対口外してはならないと言われた.
save *one's* [*a person's*] ***honor*** 体面を保つ[人の顔を立てる] ▪ He *saved his honor* by achieving an impossible quest. 彼は不可能な探求を成し遂げて体面を保った ▪ You *saved my honor*, now I'll save yours. 以前君が私の顔を立ててくれたから今度は私が立ててやろう.
show honor to …を敬う ▪ One should *show honor to* one's parents. 両親を敬うべきである.
the honors rest with 勝利[成功]は…に帰する ▪ *The honors* of the evening would have *rested with* him. その晩の勝利は彼に帰したであろうに.
the soul of honor 節操の鑑(かがみ) ▪ He is *the soul of honor* in every business transaction. あらゆる商取引で彼は節操の鑑である.
(***There is***) ***honor among thieves.*** 《諺》泥棒仲間にも仁義がある《犯罪者は相互に犯罪を仕掛けることはしない》,「盗人にも仁義」.
to *a person's* ***honor be it said that*** …したのはあっぱれである ▪ *To his honor be it said that* he kept to his cause. 彼が自己の主義を守ったのは立派だ.
trust to *a person's* ***honor*** 人の徳義心を信頼する《束縛しないこと》 ▪ I will *trust to your honor*. 私は君の徳義心を信頼する.
with honor **1** 立派に ▪ He played his part *with honor*. 彼は自分の役目を立派に果たした.
2 礼をもって ▪ He received his guest *with honor*. 彼は客を礼をもって迎えた.
with honors 優等で ▪ He graduated *with honors*. 彼は優等で卒業した ▪ He passed *with honors* in history. 彼は歴史(の試験)に優等でパスした.
with military honors 軍隊の礼をもって ▪ He was buried *with* full *military honors*. 彼は十分な軍隊の礼をもって埋葬された.
with musical honors 賛歌とともに ▪ We drank a toast *with musical honors*. 我々は賛歌とともに祝杯をあげた.
Your [***His***] ***Honor*** 閣下《市長・判事など》 ▪ *Your Honor* was pleased to grant it. 閣下はそれを許可された ▪ *His Honor* is going to resign. 閣下は辞任しようとしておられる.

honor[2], 《英》 **honour**[2] /ɑ́nər|ɔ́nə/ 動 ***more honored in the breach than in the observance*** 守るより破ったほうがましな (cf. Sh., *Haml.* 1. 4. 16) ▪ Such a custom is *more honored in the breach than in the observance*. そんな習慣は守るより破ったほうがましだ.

honorable, 《英》 **honourable** /ɑ́nərəbəl|ɔ́n-/ 形 *One's* ***intentions are honorable.*** 正式の結婚が目的である ▪ He assured her that *his intentions were honorable*. 彼は正式に結婚するつもりだと彼女に断言した.
with honorable intentions 正式結婚の目的で ▪ He courted a lady *with honorable intentions*. 彼は正式に結婚する目的である女性をくどいた.

honorably, 《英》 **honourably** /ɑ́nərəbli|ɔ́n-/ 副 ***be honorably discharged*** (満期・病気などのため)除隊になる; 円満退職する ▪ He *was honorably discharged* from the marine corps. 彼は海兵隊を除隊した.

honor-bound, 《英》 **honour-bound** /ɑ́nərbàʊnd|ɔ́nə-/ 形 ***be*** [***feel***] ***honor-bound to*** *do* 名誉にかけて…する義務がある ▪ I *feel honor-bound to* do as I promised. 名誉にかけて約束どおりしなくてはならないと思う.

hoof[1] /hu:f, hʊf/ 名 ***be on*** [***upon***] ***the hoof*** 《俗・戯》歩いている ▪ A man that *is on the hoof* like this can scarce find leisure for diversion. このように歩いている人は気晴らしをする暇はまず見つからない.
beat the hoof 《俗・戯》歩いて行く, てくる ▪ We *beat the hoof* as pilgrims. 巡礼として歩いて行った.
on the hoof **1** (家畜が)生きて, 殺されないで (↔on the BLOCK 2) ▪ Many cattle are sold *on the hoof*. 多くの牛が生きたままで売られる.
2 →be on the HOOF.
3 《英口》あまり準備せずに, よく考えもせずに ▪ He

tends to make decisions *on the hoof.* 彼にはどうも余り考えずにことを決めるところがある.

pad the hoof 《俗・戯》歩いて行く, てくる ▪ We must *pad the hoof* home. 歩いて家に帰らねばならん.

recognize [***see***] *a person's* ***hoof in*** 《口》…に人の勢力[干渉]のあとを認める ▪ I think I *recognize your hoof in* it. その中にあなたの関与の痕跡が認められるように思う.

sell corn on the hoof 《米》トウモロコシで家畜を飼いその家畜を売(って金にす)る ▪ The best way to *sell* his *corn* is *on the hoof.* トウモロコシを売る最良の方法はそれで家畜を飼いその家畜を売ることである.

show the cloven hoof →CLOVEN.

the cloven hoof 悪魔の本性 ▪ Just then *the cloven hoof* of imperialism revealed itself. そのとき帝国主義の魔性が頭をもたげた.

under the hoof (***of***) (…に)踏みつけられて, (に)圧迫されて ▪ You are *under my hoof.* 君は私に踏みつけられている ▪ He taunted the Canadians while they were *under the hoof.* 彼はカナダ人たちが抑圧されているときあざけった.

H

hoof[2] /huːf, hʊf/ 動 ***hoof it*** =LEG it.

hook[1] /hʊk/ 名 ***by hook or*** [***and***] ***by crook*** 《口》何としてでも; 何とかして《通例取得するときの困難の意を含む》 ▪ She determined to get hold of the jewels *by hook or by crook.* 彼女は何としてでもその宝石を手に入れようと決心した. ☞昔の荘園で借地人はたきぎを生けがきから bill-hook (なたがま)で取れるだけ, また羊飼の crook (柄の曲がった杖)の届く程度の木材は取ってよいという習慣があったことからであろう.

drop [***pop, slip***] ***off the hooks*** 《英俗》(ぽっくり)死ぬ; 職をやめる ▪ He was eighty when he *slipped off the hooks.* ぽっくりいったとき彼は80歳であった ▪ Brown *dropped off the hooks* years ago. ブラウンは何年も前に職をやめた.

fall for *a person* ***hook, line and sinker*** **1** 人を非常に好きになる ▪ I *fell for* the pretty girl *hook, line and sinker.* 私はそのかわいい女の子にぞっこんほれ込んだ.

2 嘘をすっかり信じる ▪ It was an April Fool joke and I *fell for* it *hook, line, and sinker.* エイプリルフールのジョークだったのにまんまとかつがれた. ☞→HOOK, line, and sinker

get *one's* ***hooks into*** [***on***] 《口》(男)に取り入る; (男)の心を捕える, をとりこにする ▪ She tried hard to *get her hooks into* the president. 彼女は社長に取り入ろうと一生懸命だった.

get off the hook **1** 責任から解放される; 苦境[危険, 罰]から逃れる ▪ Tom may *get off the hook.* トムは苦境を脱するかもしれない ▪ We don't know how the smugglers *got off the hook.* 密輸者がどうやって罪を逃れたのかわからない. ☞釣り針にかかった魚がもがいて逃れることから.

2 →take ... off the HOOK.

get [***give***] ***the hook*** = get the (grand) BOUNCE 1.

go off the hooks 《俗》(ぽっくり)死ぬ ▪ I may *go off the hooks* at any moment. 私は今にもぽっくり死ぬかもしれない.

hook and eye **1** (服の)ホック《掛ける方, 受ける方の両方》 ▪ The ends are united by a small steel *hook and eye.* 両端は小さい鋼鉄のホックでつなぎ合わされている.

2 〚否定文で〛少しも(かまわないなど) ▪ She did not care a *hook and eye* about it. 彼女はそのことはちっともかまわなかった.

hook, line, and sinker 《俗》すっかり, 全く ▪ He accepted our story *hook, line, and sinker.* 彼は我々の話をすっかり信じてしまった. ☞釣りから.

let *a person* ***off the hook*** 《口》(責任・罰などから)人を免除する, 放免する; 人に勝利し損なう ▪ When they found the real culprit, they *let* him *off the hook.* 真犯人が見つかって彼を釈放した ▪ The boxing champ *let* his opponent *off the hook.* チャンピオンは相手のボクサーを倒せなかった.

off the hook →get off the HOOK.

off the hooks **1** 《俗》死んで ▪ Poor old Bill is dead—went *off the hooks* rather suddenly a month ago. ビルじいさんは死んでいる. ひと月前に急にぽっくりいったのだ.

2 《口》てっとり早く, 簡単に ▪ Baronets cannot be married *off the hooks.* 準男爵たちは手軽に結婚するわけにはいかない.

on [***upon***] *one's* ***own hook*** 《口》 **1** 独力で ▪ The boy did it *on his own hook.* その少年は独力でそれをやった.

2 独立して, 自前で ▪ I am going to do business *on my own hook.* 私は独立して商売をやろう.

3 自分の責任で; 自ら進んで; 自分のために ▪ Go ahead, just do it *on your own hook.* 先へ進めろ. 自分の責任でやるんだな ▪ He went *on his own hook.* 彼は自分から進んで行った ▪ He planned it *on his own hook.* 彼は自分のためにそれを計画した. ☞釣りから.

on the hook 《米》窮地におかれて; 常に心配で, 気がもめて ▪ He was kept *on the hook* for months. 彼は何か月も気をもまされていた.

on the hook for 《米口》(金融の場面で) …に対して責任があって ▪ You are *on the hook for* the loss. 赤字の責任は君にある.

pop [***slip***] ***off the hooks*** → drop off the HOOKs.

put *a person* ***on the hook*** 《米》人を窮地に立たせる; 人に責任を持たせる ▪ That *puts* you *on the hook* again. そのためあなたはまた窮地に立つことになる.

ring off the hook 《米口》(電話が)殺到する, ジャンジャン鳴り続ける, ひっきりなしに鳴る ▪ The phone has been *ringing off the hook* all day. 朝からずっと電話が鳴りっぱなしだ.

sling [***take***] *one's* ***hook*** 《口》走り去る, こっそり去る, 急いで去る ▪ They *slung their hook* and fled to Switzerland. 彼らは逃亡してスイスへ逃れた ▪ The train had already *taken its hook* into the gloom of a tunnel. 列車はすでに暗いトンネルの中へ

入っていた.

take* [*get*] *... off the* [*a*] *hook 《口》(責任・罰などから)…を解放する, 免除する; を(窮地・危険から)逃れさせる, 救い出す ▪ His brother paid all his bills and *took* him *off the hook*. 兄が請求書を全部払って彼を窮地から救ってくれた ▪ Thanks for *getting* me *off the hook*. 私を責任から解放してくださってありがとう.

take* [*leave*] *the* (*tele*)*phone off the hook (電話の受話器を)取り上げる[外したままにする] ▪ He *took the phone off the hook* to stop it ringing incessantly. 鳴り続けるのを止めようと彼は受話器を取り上げた ▪ Someone had *left the phone off the hook*. 受話器が外れたままになっていた.

with a hook at the end しぶしぶ, 気乗りせぬままに ▪ My assent is given *with a hook at the end*. 私の承諾はしぶしぶ与えたものである.

hook[2] /hʊk/ 動 (***be***) ***hooked on*** 《口》 **1** (習慣性の薬など)に頼っている ▪ My mother got *hooked on* a pain-killing drug. 私の母は鎮痛剤に頼るようになった.

2 …にぞっこんほれている; を非常に好きになる ▪ She *is* really *hooked on* that boy. 彼女はほんとにあの少年にほれこんでいる ▪ *Are* you *hooked on* collecting stamps? あなたは切手集めが大好きですか.

hook one's fish ねらった人をうまく釣る; 人をうまく説得する ▪ The girl tried to *hook her fish*. その娘はねらった男を釣ろうとした.

hook it 《英口》走り去る, 逃走する, 急いで去る ▪ He *hooked it* when he saw a police officer. 彼は警察官を見かけると走って逃げた ▪ What are you doing here? *Hook it*, at once. ここで何をしているのか, さっさとあっちへ行け.

hook Jack 《米口》(学校などを)ずる休みする ▪ The boy *hooked Jack* for a whole day. その少年はまる1日ずる休みした.

hook oneself on to …にあくまでもついて来る ▪ Our cousins *hook themselves on to* us. いとこたちがあくまでも我々について来る.

hook(**e**)**y** /hóki/ 名 ***play hooky*** 《学俗》(学校を)ずる休みする ▪ I sorta feel like *playing hooky* myself. 僕もずる休みしたいような気がちょっとする.

hoop /hu:p/ 名 ***go through the hoop*(*s*)** 《口》きびしい試錬を受ける, つらい目にあう ▪ Let them *go through the hoops* as much as they like. 彼らには好きなだけきびしい試錬を受けさせたらよい. ☞サーカスから.

***jump through a hoop* [*hoops*]** 《口》命ぜられたことは何でもする, どんな命令にも従う ▪ Tom would *jump through a hoop* for Jane. トムはジェインのためなら何でもするのだった.

make a person* (*jump* [*go*]) *through* (*the*) *hoops 人に試練を味わわせる ▪ They *made* me *jump through hoops* just to get a boarding pass. 搭乗券を買うだけのためにひどく手間をかけさせられた ▪ His boss *made* him *go through hoops* all day. 彼は上司に一日中こっぴどく働かされた.

***put ... through the hoop*(*s*)** 《口》(人)をきびしく罰する[責める, 尋問する]; をつらい目にあわせる ▪ He got hold of his sergeant and *put* him *through the hoop*. 彼は部下の軍曹をつかまえてひどい目にあわせた. ☞サーカスから.

shoot some hoop/shoot hoops (特にバスケットボールの)練習をする, 非公式な試合をする ▪ Let's go to the gym after school and *shoot* some *hoops*. 放課後ジムへ行ってちょっとバスケの練習しようか.

hoot[1] /hu:t/ 名 ***not care a* [*one*] *hoot* [*two hoots*] (*in Hell*)** 《俗》少しも問題にしない ▪ I do*n't care one* single *hoot* what you say. 君の言うことなんかちっとも問題にしない ▪ I do*n't care two hoots in Hell* for anything you do. あなたが何をしてもちっともかまわない.

***not give a* [*one*] *hoot* [*two hoots*]** 《俗》少しも問題にしない ▪ I do*n't give a hoot* whether you come to church or not. あなたが教会に来ようが来まいがちっともかまわない.

***not matter a hoot* [*two hoots*]** 《俗》全く問題でない ▪ It does *not matter two hoots* how much you like it. それがいかに好きかは全然問題でない.

not worth a hoot 《俗》一文の値うちもない ▪ The best transmitter is *not worth a hoot* without a good antenna. 最高の送信機もよいアンテナがないと一文の値うちもない.

hoot[2] /hu:t/ 動 ***hoot and holler*** はやしたてる, やじる ▪ The fans were *hooting and hollering* at everything he did. ファンが彼のプレーの一挙手一投足に歓声を上げていた.

hop[1] /hɑp|hɔp/ 名 ***a hop, step* [*skip*], *and* (*a*) *jump* [*leap*]** **1** 三段飛び ▪ It seems *a hop, skip, and a jump*, from one shelf of crags to the other. それは一つの岩だなから他の岩だなへと三段飛びをするようなものだ.

2 ほんの近距離 ▪ It's just *a hop, skip and jump* from my house to yours. 僕の家からは君の家までつい目と鼻の先だ.

(*as*) *fast as hops* 非常に早く ▪ It must be answered *as fast as hops*. それは非常に早く答えなければならない.

catch* [*keep, have*] *a person on the hop 《口》人の去ろうとするところを捕える; 人の不意を襲う; 人の不意をついて驚かす ▪ We didn't expect you. You've *caught* us *on the hop*. あなたがおいでになるとは思っていませんでした. 全く不意のご訪問ですね ▪ The police *caught* him *on the hop*. 警察は彼が高飛びするところを取り押さえた ▪ The patient *kept* the psychiatrist *on the hop* with suicide threats. 患者は自殺すると脅して精神科医を慌てさせた.

on the hop 《口》 **1** 不意に, だしぬけに ▪ I went to see Aunt Jane *on the hop* yesterday. 私はきのうジェインおばさんを不意に訪ねて行った.

2 忙しく立ち回って ▪ He is always *on the hop*. 彼はいつも忙しく立ち回っている.

hop[2] /hɑp|hɔp/ 名 (***as***) ***mad as hops*** →

MAD.

(as) thick as hops ひどく密生して ▪ Other amusements presented themselves *as thick as hops*. 他の娯楽がきわめてたくさん出て来た. ☞hop はビールに香り•苦味をつける「ホップ」から.

hop[3] /hɑp|hɔp/ 動 ***be hopping mad*** 激怒している ▪ You are so late coming home. Daddy *is hopping mad*! ずいぶん帰るのが遅かったじゃないの. パパはかんかんよ.

get hopping 《主に英俗》立ち去る ▪ State your business and *get hopping*. 用事を言ってさっさと立ち去れ.

hop it 《口》走り去る, 逃走する, さっと立ち去る ▪ You'd better *hop it* quick before the boss catches you here. ここにいるのを親分に見つからないうちに, さっさと去ったほうがよい. ☞HOOK it よりも穏やかな言い方.

hop it along 歩いて行く ▪ I *hopped it along* with the puppy. 子犬を連れて歩いていった.

hop the perch →PERCH[1].

hop the twig [***stick***] 《俗》 **1** 去る, (債権者をまいて)逃げうせる; 急に追い出される ▪ He *hopped the twig*; he was in debt to seven merchants. 彼は借金したまま逃げた. 7 人の商人に借金していた.

2 (ぽっくり)死ぬ ▪ Giles *hopped the twig* on the fourth. ジャイルズは4日に死んだ. ☞鳥が猟人から逃げ去ることからきた.

hop the wag 《俗》(学校を)ずる休みする ▪ They often persuaded me to *hop the wag*. 彼らはたびたび私にずる休みするよう説きつけた.

hop to it **1** 《米口》急いでやる, 急ぐ ▪ We must *hop to it* if we are to catch that plane. あの飛行機に乗るのなら我々は急がなければならない.

2 《俗》仕事にとりかかる ▪ There's a lot to do today, so let's *hop to it*. 今日は仕事が山ほどあるから早速とりかかろう.

hope[1] /hoʊp/ 名 ***Abandon hope, all ye who enter here.***/***All hope abandon, ye who enter here.*** 《諺》ここから入る者はあらゆる希望を捨てよ,「入るなら最悪の場合の覚悟をせよ」. ☞(Dante, *Inferno*) の地獄の門に書かれた文字の英訳.

(be) past [***beyond***] ***all hope*** 望みが全くなくて ▪ His recovery *is beyond all hope*. 彼の回復の見込みは全くない.

build up *a person's* ***hopes*** = raise a person's HOPEs.

dash [***shatter***] *a person's* ***hopes*** (***of***) (人が…する)希望をくじく ▪ The injury *dashed his hopes of* an Olympic gold. 彼はけがをしてオリンピックでの優勝の望みがくじけた ▪ His failure in the exam *shattered his hopes of* becoming a doctor. 彼は試験に落ちて医師になる希望がついえた.

entertain (***high***) ***hopes*** 野望を抱く, 大きな期待をする ▪ He *entertained high hopes* of marrying his boss's daughter. 彼は社長令嬢との結婚という野望を抱いていた.

fasten *one's* ***hopes on*** [***upon***] → lay one's HOPEs on.

high hopes 大きな期待 ▪ The girl had *high hopes* of being named captain of the team. 彼女はチームの主将に指名されると期待に胸を膨らませていた.

hold out hope 期待させる, (困っている人を)励ます ▪ Several incidents *held out hope* that our lost son might still be alive. いくつかの出来事から行方知れずの息子は生きているのではという期待をもった.

hope chest 《米》(女性の)結婚準備用品(を入れる箱) ▪ My mother had a *hope chest* full of clothing when she married. 母には結婚したとき衣類が詰まった嫁入り箱があった. ☞(=《英》a bottom drawer).

Hope deferred maketh the heart sick. 望みを得ることが長びけば心が悩む (《聖》*Prov*. 13. 12) ▪ Caroline has lost appetite, spirits, and health. *Hope deferred maketh the heart sick.* キャロラインは食欲や元気や健康を失ってしまった. 望みを得ることが長びけば心が悩む.

Hope for the best and prepare for the worst./***Hope for the best but expect the worst.*** 《諺》最善を望み最悪に備えよ《最善を追い求めるべし, だが最悪の事態に対する備えも万全に》.

Hope is a good breakfast but a bad supper. 《諺》希望は朝抱くにはよいが夜抱くのはよくない,「一日の計は朝にあり」.

Hope springs eternal (***in the human breast***). 《諺》いつも希望を抱くのが人だ《ことがうまくいかなくても人は希望を捨てないものだ》. ☞Alexander Pope, *Essay on Man*.

in (***high***) ***hopes*** (***of, that***) (…を大いに)期待して; 望んで, (…する)つもりで《可能性の乏しい場合》 ▪ Many people undergo diet programs, *in high hopes of* losing weight. 体重減を大いに期待してダイエット計画を受ける人が多い ▪ They remained upon their guard *in hopes of* better times. 彼らは時勢のよくなるのを望んでなおも警戒し続けた ▪ I was *in hopes* you would have done so. 私はあなたはそうしただろうと期待していた ▪ I went there *in hopes of* meeting him. 彼に会えるつもりでそこへ行った.

in the hope (***of, that***) (…すると)期待して, (…)できるつもりで ▪ I went there *in the hope that* I might meet him. 彼に会えるかもしれないと期待してそこへ行った.

lay [***fasten, pin, set***] *one's* ***hopes on*** [***upon***] …に希望[期待]をかける ▪ The shopkeeper *laid his hopes upon* a revival of trade. 店主は景気の回復に望みをかけていた ▪ He *pinned his hopes on* the job, but he could not get it. 彼はその職に望みをかけていたがそれは得られなかった ▪ Don't *set your hopes on* me in the contest. 競技で僕に期待をかけないでよ.

live in hope いつか思い通りになると思う, 将来に望みをかける ▪ No luck as yet, but I *live in hope*. まだうまくいっていないが, いつか希望がかなうと期待している.

No hope!/***What a hope*** [***hopes***]***!*** 見込みは全

くない ▪ You think they will buy your pictures. *What a hope!* 君は彼らが君の絵を買ってくれると思っているが, 見込みは全くないよ.

Not a hope! 《英口》見込みは全くない ▪ Your dad will let you go, won't he?—*Not a hope.* 君の父さんが行かせてくれるだろう?—まず無理だね.

not a hope in hell →not ... in HELL.

pin *one's* ***hopes on*** =lay one's HOPEs on.

raise [***build up***] *a person's* ***hopes*** (人に)より一層の期待を抱かせる ▪ I mustn't *raise your hopes.* He may not recover. あなたにより一層の期待を持たせてはいけない. 彼は治らないかもしれない ▪ I don't want to *build up her hopes* if she doesn't have a chance. 見込みがないのなら, 彼女に一層の期待を抱かせたくない.

the (***great***) ***white hope*** (団体・チームなどに)栄誉[勝利]をもたらすと期待される人[物] ▪ He is *the white hope* of the baseball team. 彼はその野球チームのホープだ. ☞もとは「ボクシングで黒人を負かし得るような白人ボクサー」の意.

While [***Where***] ***there is life, there is hope.*** 《諺》命がある限り希望がある《命のある間は何とか望みはあるものだ》.

hope[2] /hoʊp/ 動 ***hope against hope*** 見込みのないのに望みを捨てない, 空頼みする (《聖》*Roms.* 4. 18) ▪ The parents *hoped against hope* that their son would return home. 両親は息子が帰るだろうと空頼みした.

hope and pray 切に望む ▪ All of us *hope and pray* for lasting peace. 我々はみな永遠の平和を切望する.

I hope not. 私はそうでないよう望む[と思う] ▪ Will he die?—*I hope not.* 彼は死ぬだろうか?—そんなことはないだろう.

I hope so. 私はそう望む, そうだと思う ▪ Will he live?—*I hope so.* 彼は命がもつだろうか?—もつと思うよ.

I should hope not. そうでないのは当然だ ▪ Nobody blames you.—*I should hope not*! 誰も君をとがめないよ—なくて当たり前だ.

I should hope so/so I should hope 《口》それくらいのことは当然だ ▪ You say you are sorry? *I should hope so*, indeed. 君はすまないと言うのかね. それくらいのことは当然だね, ほんとに ▪ He did apologize to you.—*So I should hope*! 彼はちゃんと君にわびを言っていたよ—言って当然だ.

hopeful /hóʊpfəl/ 形 ***be hopeful of*** [***about***] ...を期待する ▪ I *am hopeful about* the future. 私は将来を期待している ▪ He *is hopeful of* success. 彼は成功を期待している.

hopeless /hóʊpləs/ 形 ***be hopeless at*** ...がへたである, はだめである ▪ He *was hopeless at* mathematics. 彼は数学はだめであった.

be hopeless of ...をあきらめている ▪ I *am hopeless of* success. 成功はあきらめている.

hopper /hɑ́pər|hɔ́p-/ 名 ***in the hopper*** (しばしば政治で)準備中で, 処理中で ▪ There are several other projects *in the hopper.* 他にもいくつかの企画が控えている.

horizon /həráɪzən/ 名 ***above*** [***below***] ***the horizon*** 水平線より上[下]に ▪ When the sun sets, it goes *below the horizon.* 太陽が沈むと水平線下に入る.

broaden [***expand, widen***] *one's* [*a person's*] ***horizons*** 視野を広げる ▪ If you read more you can certainly *broaden your horizons.* もっと本を読めばまちがいなく広い見方ができるようになる ▪ Picture books can be used to *expand children's horizons.* 子供の視野を広げるのに絵本が役立つ ▪ We can *widen our horizons* by learning foreign languages. 外国語を学習すれば視野が広がる.

on the horizon 水平線上に; (出来事が)差し迫って ▪ A star appears *on the horizon.* 星が一つ水平線上に現れた ▪ I don't know what's *on the horizon*, but God does. 何が起きようとしているのか分からないが, それは誰にも分からない.

horn /hɔːrn/ 名 ***a horn of plenty*** → the HORN of plenty.

all horn and hide 骨と皮ばかり ▪ The cattle were *all horn and hide.* 牛どもは骨と皮ばかりだった. ☞《豪》から.

be squeezed through a horn 不首尾となる, 落ちぶれる, 負ける; (特に)大事業に大失敗をする ▪ The prodigal fool *was squeezed through a horn.* 金使いの荒いばか者は落ちぶれた.

between the horns of a dilemma →on the HORNs of a dilemma.

blow [***toot***] *one's* ***own horn*** 《米》自己吹聴をする, 自慢[自画自賛]する; ほらを吹く ▪ I have never been guilty of *blowing my own horn.* 私は自己吹聴をしたことはない ▪ He goes around *tooting his horn* merely because he's charitable. 彼は慈善家だというだけで自慢し回っている.

by the (***great***) ***horn spoon*** 《米》誓って, ほんとに ▪ I should like to shoot the gang, *by the great horn spoon.* 私はぜひギャングを撃ってやりたい.

come out at [***of***] ***the little*** [***small***] ***end of the horn*** 《米》(ある事に)不首尾になる; (特に)華々しい事業に大失敗する ▪ You didn't *come out at the little end of the horn*, did you? 君は大失敗はしなかったのだろうね.

denounce ... to the horn → put ... to the HORN.

draw [***pull, pluck, shrink***] ***in*** *one's* ***horns*** 《口》**1** 要求[意見]などを和らげる, 譲歩する ▪ The employers' representative will have to *draw in his horns* a bit. 雇い主代表は少し譲歩しなければならないだろう.

2 敵対的[威圧的]な態度を和らげる; 低姿勢となる, 軟化する ▪ When George finally arrived with our official pass, the guard *drew in his horns.* ジョージがやっと我々の公用パスを持って来ると, 車掌は態度を和らげた ▪ He *plucked in his horns*, when

Parliament was prorogued. 国会が閉会となったとき彼はほこを収めた.

3 出費を切りつめる ▪ As we grow older, so we have to *draw in our horns.* 年をとるにつれて出費を切りつめねばならない.

exalt *a person's* ***horn*** 人に勝利を与える, 人の勢力を増す (《聖》*Ps.* 89. 24) ▪ He has *exalted my horn.* 神は私に勝利を与えたもうた.

haul in *one's* ***horns*** 《米口》(のさばった人などが)こそこそ引っこむ; 譲歩する, 退く; 要求を和らげる ▪ The old man *hauled in his horns* and marched off. その老人はほこを収めて去って行った ▪ We had *hauled in our horns* considerably since our capture. 我々は捕えられてからずっと相当おとなしくしていた.

horn with [***under***] ***horn*** (牛が)角を並べて《牛の群れなどについて言う》 ▪ The herds went *horn with horn.* 牛の群れが角を並べて行った.

in a horn 《俗》あるとも思えない《不信•拒絶》 ▪ The man asserts he is a good pro-slavery man; we all think he is—*in a horn.* 自分はれっきとした奴隷制度支持者だと男は主張するが, 我々はみなそれは—ありそうもないと思う.

lift up *one's* [***the***] ***horn*** 野心満々である, 高慢である; 得意になる, いばる ▪ Don't *lift up your horn* high. そんなにごう慢であってはいけない ▪ He got full marks in English and *lifted up his horn.* 彼は英語で満点を取り得意になった. ☞聖書語法.

lock horns (***with*** *a person*) **1** (牛などが)角を交えて戦う ▪ The heifer and her mate *locked horns.* 雌牛とその相手の雄牛は角を突き合った.

2 《米口》(人が)戦う; かち合う ▪ Let them *lock horns.* 彼らを対戦させなさい ▪ I don't want to *lock horns with* the boss. 上司と諍(いさか)いを起こしたくない ▪ The two appointments *locked horns.* 二つの会合の約束がかち合った.

lower *one's* ***horn*** へりくだる; (高慢などが)へこむ ▪ Her pride *lowered its horn.* 彼女の高慢はへこんだ.

make (***the***) ***horns*** (***at***) (…に)指で角を作って見せる ▪ He *made horns at* the deceived husband. 彼は間男された夫に指で角を作って見せた. ☞妻に不貞をされる夫を軽蔑したり, または凶眼 (evil eye) をさけるしぐさ.

neither horn nor hoof 全然跡形もなく ▪ There is *neither horn nor hoof* of Antichristianity left in our church. 我々の教会には反キリスト教の跡形も残されていない.

on the horn 《米口》電話中で, 電話に出て ▪ Sorry, Joe is *on the horn* right now. Please leave a message. あいにくジョーは電話に出ておりますので, 伝言を承ります.

on [***between, in***] ***the horns of a dilemma*** 進退きわまって ▪ His argument brings him *between the horns of a dilemma.* 彼の議論は彼を進退に窮させる ▪ They put him *on the horns of a dilemma.* 彼らは彼を進退に窮させた. ☞「どちらを取っても不利な両刀論法の角に乗って」が原義.

pluck [***pull, shrink***] ***in*** *one's* ***horns*** →draw in one's HORNs.

put [***denounce***]***... to the horn*** …を法外浪人と宣言する ▪ Both of us *were put to the horn.* 我々は二人とも法外浪人と宣言された. ☞スコットランドで国王の伝令官が3度角笛を吹いて法外浪人の宣言をした習慣から.

round the horn [***Horn***] ホーン岬(みさき) (Cape Horn) を回航する ▪ The ship *rounded the Horn* in the depth of winter. その船は真冬にホーン岬を回航した.

show *one's* ***horns*** 悪魔[悪]の本性を表す; よこしまな意図を表す ▪ Last night he *showed his horns.* 昨夜彼はよこしまな意図を表した.

the [***a***] ***horn of plenty*** 《ギ神》豊穣の角《幼児の Zeus 神に授乳したと伝えられるヤギの角》; 物の豊かな象徴; 物の豊富 (cornucopia) ▪ Nature, when *the horn of plenty* is quite empty, fills it with babies. 自然は豊穣の角が全く空になると, それに赤んぼうをいっぱい入れる ▪ This book is *a horn of plenty* for after-dinner speakers. この本は食後のスピーチをやる人々にとって無尽の宝庫である.

to the horns of the altar 聖壇の角に誓って, 確かに ▪ Your friend even *to the horns of the altar.* まさしく聖壇の角に誓ってあなたの友である. ☞ユダヤの神殿の聖壇の四すみには角があって, これを握ってする誓いは破ると天罰があたると信じられていた.

toot *one's* ***own horn*** → blow one's own HORN.

wind the horn **1** 角笛を吹く ▪ The distant huntsman *winds the horn.* 遠くの猟人が角笛を吹く.

2 (昆虫が)ブンブン音を立てる ▪ There the beetle *winds* his small *horn.* そこでは甲虫がブンブンと小さな音を立てる.

hornet /hɔ́ːrnət/ 名 ***a hornets' nest/a nest of hornets*** しつこく[激しく]攻撃する敵 ▪ They dwelt as it were in *a nest of hornets.* 彼らはいわば, うるさく攻め立てる敵の中に住んでいた.

(***as***) ***mad as a hornet*** →(as) MAD as hops.

bring a hornets' nest about *one's* ***ears*** → bring the house about one's EARs.

get madder than a hornet 非常に怒る ▪ She *got madder than a hornet* and abruptly turned away from me. 彼女はかんかんになって私からぷいと顔をそむけた.

stir up [***arouse***] ***a hornets' nest*** 大勢の敵を作って騒ぎ立てられる; 騒ぎを起こす ▪ I thought my article was harmless, but I've *stirred up a hornets' nest.* 私の論説は無害だと思っていたが, 大勢の人の攻撃を受けた.

horoscope /hɔ́ːrəskòup|hɔ́r-/ 名 ***cast a*** [*a person's*] ***horoscope*** 誕生のときの星位を見て運勢を占う; 運勢図を作る ▪ To *cast a horoscope,* three essential inputs are required—time of birth, date of birth and place of birth. 天宮図を

作るには必ず出生の時刻・日付・場所の３つを入力する必要がある.

horrify /hɔ́ːrəfàɪ|hɔ́r-/ 動 ***be horrified at*** **1** …にぞっとする ▪ I *am horrified at* the bare idea. それを考えただけでもぞっとする.

2 (ひどいことをすると思って)反感を抱く ▪ We *are horrified at* the barbarity. その蛮行に反感を持つ.

horror /hɔ́ːrər|hɔ́rə/ 名 ***a little horror*** 《戯》手に負えない子供 ▪ She has three *little horrors* running round the house all day. 彼女には一日中家の中を駆け回っているいたずらっ子が３人いる ▪ What have the *little horrors* done now? 悪ガキどもは今度は何をやらかしたのか.

Chamber of Horrors (Madame Tussaud のろう人形館で犯罪者の像及び刑具など陳列した)戦慄(りつ)の間(ま); (気味の悪い物で満ちている)恐怖の室[場所] ▪ That house is a sort of *Chamber of Horrors*. あの家は一種の恐怖の家だ.

have a horror of …が大きらいである, ぞっとするほどきらいである ▪ I *have a horror of* being thanked. 私はお礼を言われるのが大きらいだ.

horror of horrors 《戯》ショックな[恐ろしい]ことに, 何としたことだ ▪ *Horror of horrors*, our old church is to be turned into a warehouse. あきれたことに我らの教会が倉庫にされてしまうことになった.

in horror ぞっとして; 恐れて ▪ I fled *in horror*. 私は恐れて逃げた.

with horror ぞっとして ▪ I viewed the scene *with horror*. 私はぞっとしてその光景を見た.

horse[1] /hɔːrs/ 名 ***a dark horse*** ダークホース《競馬で力量未知数の出走馬; 政界・競技・選挙などで思いがけない有力な競争相手》 ▪ He may gain the nomination as *a dark horse*. 彼はダークホースとして指名されるかもしれない ▪ He is quite *a dark horse*. 彼は全く未知数の人物だ.

a dead horse **1** 仕事をする前にもらう金 ▪ *A dead horse* does not appeal to me. 私は仕事賃の前払いは好かない.

2 古い借金 ▪ I paid for *a dead horse*. 古い借金を払った.

3 →flog a dead HORSE.

a horse laugh あざけるような大笑い, ばか笑い, 下品な高笑い ▪ He responded with *a horse laugh*, "Are you kidding?" 彼はげらげら笑いながら応じた. 「冗談だろう?」

a horse of another [***a different***] ***color*** 《口》全く別なこと, 全く違ったこと ▪ But if you don't want to go because you're broke, that's *a horse of a different color*. でも行きたくないのは文無しのせいだというなら, そいつは別の話だ ▪ I thought he was her boyfriend but he turned out to be her brother—that's *a horse of another color*. 彼女の男友達と思ったが実は兄で, そうなると話は別だ.

a horse of the same color 《口》同じ性質の問題[事柄] ▪ As a vice-presidential running mate, Adams would've been *a horse of the same color*. 副大統領選の下位候補にアダムズをあてがっていたとしても同じことだったろう.

a horse opera 西部劇 ▪ John Wayne starred as a hero in many *horse operas*. ジョン・ウェインは多くの西部劇映画に主演した.

a horse that was foaled of an acorn 絞首台 ▪ You'll ride on *a horse that was foaled of an acorn*. 君は絞首台にのぼるだろう.

a horse trade/horse trading **1** 馬市 ▪ How about we trade yours for mine—kind of *a horse trade*? 馬市みたいに君のを僕のと取り替えっこしない?

2 感情抜きの取引, 抜け目ない交渉 ▪ After much *horse trading*, we finally reached an agreement. 巧みな駆け引きの応酬の末やっと話がまとまった.

a horse-whisperer 馬の心が分かる人, 馬と意志の疎通ができる人 ▪ According to *a* good *horse-whisperer*, it is the horses that do the whispering. 馬とよく心を通じ合える人によれば, 語りかけるのは馬の方だという.

a horseplay 悪ふざけ ▪ There wasn't any of the usual *horseplay* that day. その日に限っていつもの悪ふざけは全くなかった.

A nod is as good as a wink to a blind horse. →NOD[1].

A short horse is soon curried. 《諺》小さい仕事はじきにできる. ☞curry「馬ぐしをかける」.

a stalking horse **1** おとり ▪ She volunteered to act as *a stalking horse* for the police. 彼女は警察のためにおとりの役を買って出た.

2 当て馬 ▪ I will not allow myself to be used as *a stalking horse* for anyone else. 自分が他の者の当て馬に使われるのはごめんだ.

3 (真実を隠す)口実, 見せかけ, だまし ▪ Dignity has often been used as *a stalking horse* for untruth. 虚偽の隠れみのとして威厳がよく使われてきた. ☞猟師が馬の陰に隠れて獲物のあとをつけることから.

a war horse/an old war horse (劇・オペラなどの)たびたび演じられて陳腐になった演目 ▪ That opera company does nothing but *old war horses*. あのオペラ団は古くさい出し物ばかり演じる.

a willing horse →WILLING.

all horse 《口》(騎手が)非常に小さい ▪ The jockey is *all horse*. その騎手は非常に小さい.

an iron horse 《口》機関車 ▪ In its early days, the roaring *iron horse* frightened many people. 初期の頃には咆哮する機関車に怯える人が多かった.

(***as***) ***holy*** [***sick, strong***] ***as a horse*** きわめて神聖で[気分が悪く, 強く] ▪ Henry, physically, is *as strong as a horse*. ヘンリーはとても体が丈夫だ.

back [***pick***] ***the wrong horse/bet on the wrong horse*** 《英口》負け馬に賭ける; 価値判断を誤る ▪ In voting for Smith, I *backed the wrong horse*. 私がスミスに投票したのは負け馬に賭けたわけだ ▪ My plan failed. I had *backed the wrong horse*. 私の計画は失敗した. 私は価値判断を誤っていたのだ ▪ Looks like you *picked the wrong horse*. 判断を誤ったようだね ▪ She *bet on the wrong horse* when she married her husband.

夫と結婚したのは彼女の眼鏡違いだった. ☞back＝bet on.

be on the [*one's*] ***high horse*** 《口》偉そうにする, 横柄にする ▪He *was* quite *on the high horse*. 彼は全く偉そうにしていた.

beat a dead horse ＝flog a dead HORSE 1.

change horses 馬を乗り換える ▪They rode all night, having twice *changed horses*. 彼らは2度馬を乗り換えて夜どおし乗って行った.

change [***swap, switch***] ***horses in midstream*** [***in the middle of a stream***] **1** 仕事の途中で人[リーダー]を変える ▪That's the danger of *changing horses in midstream*. 仕事の途中で人を変えるとそういう危険がある.

2 中途で計画を変える ▪It was very silly of you to *change horses in midstream* like that. 君がそんなふうに中途で計画を変えたのは愚の骨頂(こっちょう)だった ▪I've often heard the advice not to *switch horses in the middle of a stream*. 途中で鞍替えすべきではないという忠告をよく聞かされた. ☞リンカン大統領が1864年に行った演説の言葉から.

come [***get*** (***down***)] ***off the*** [*one's*] ***high horse*** 《口》(いばっていた者が)おとなしくなる, 高慢な態度をやめる; あいそがよくなる ▪He *came off the high horse* a little bit. 彼は少しおとなしくなった ▪The cable companies have *come off the high horse* at last. ケーブル会社側はついに低姿勢になった ▪When she discovered that he was a man of great wealth, she immediately *got down off her high horse*. 彼が大金持ちであることを知ると彼女はあわてて高慢な態度をやめた.

could choke a horse 《俗》非常に大きい, 巨大である ▪The worker pulled out a burger that *could choke a horse* and polished it off. 労働者は特大のハンバーガーを取り出してそいつを平らげた.

Don't [***Never***] ***look a gift horse in the mouth./Look not a gift*** [***given***] ***horse in the mouth.*** 《諺》もらった馬の口の中を見るな, もらい物のあらを捜すな. ☞馬の年齢[健康状態]は歯を見ればわかることから.

Don't spare the horses. 《口》〚命令文で〛急げ ▪Go and buy some flour and *don't spare the horses*. 小麦粉を買ってきてちょうだい. 早く.

draw [***hitch, set, stable***] ***horses together*** 一致する, 和合する, 仲よくやっていく ▪They *set* their *horses together* there. 彼らはそこで仲よくやっていった ▪He and Bill will not *draw horses together*. 彼とビルは和合しようとしない.

eat like a horse →EAT like a pig.

Every horse thinks its own pack heaviest. 《諺》誰でも自分が一番辛い仕事を[一番難しい問題を解決]させられると思っている.

flog [***beat***] ***a dead horse*** 《口》 **1** すんだ事をむし返す ▪Stop trying to *flog a dead horse*. I've told you you can't go to Paris. すんだ事をむし返そうとするな. パリに行ってはいけないと言ったはずだ.

2 精力を労費する, むだ骨を折る ▪It's no use *flogging a dead horse*. むだ骨を折るのはつまらない.

from the horse's mouth →(straight) from the HORSE's mouth.

gather the horse (馬に)走る用意をするようあらかじめ知らせる ▪At the first command, *gather the horse*. 最初の指令で馬に出走の準備を知らせよ.

get (***down***) ***off the*** [*one's*] ***high horse*** → come off the high HORSE.

get on [***mount, ride***] *one's* [***the***] ***high horse*** 《口》高慢な態度を取る; 偉そうにする; つけあがる ▪He at once *got on his high horse*. 彼はすぐに高慢になった ▪She was apt to *mount the high horse*. 彼女はとかく偉そうにしがちであった.

get ... straight from the horse's mouth 直接関わった当の本人から...を聞く ▪I won't believe the rumor until I *get* it *straight from the horse's mouth*. 直接本人から聞くまでは噂を信じない.

grin through a horse-collar → HORSE-COLLAR.

have a horse on *a person* 《俗》人に悪ふざけをする, 人をからかう ▪They *had a horse on* him. 彼らは彼に悪ふざけをした.

hitch horses together → draw HORSEs together.

hold *one's* ***horses*** 《口》〚主に命令文で〛もっとゆっくり...する; がまんする; はやる心を抑える; (あわてないで)落ち着く; ちょっと待つ, やめる ▪He asked us to *hold our horses* until he had finished. 彼は我々に自分の仕事がすむまでがまんしてくれと言った ▪Now *hold your horses*, Jerry. さあ, 落ち着くんだよ, ジェリー.

horse and foot (***and dragoons***) **1** 騎兵と歩兵(と竜騎兵); (昔の)全軍 ▪Then, supported by other units, Lambert's *horse and foot* rallied. 次に他の部隊の支援のもとにランバートの全軍が陣容を再び整えた.

2 〚副詞的に〛全力を出して, 誰かれの別なく ▪The Democratic party met yesterday and surrendered, *horse, foot and dragoons*, to the Republicans. 民主党は昨日集会を持ち共和党にこぞって白旗を揚げた.

horse and horse 《米口》等分されて, 五分五分で ▪It was *horse and horse* between the professors. 教授連の間には優劣はなかった ▪The match stands at *horse and horse*. 試合は今互角である.

horse sense 《口》(世俗的な)常識 ▪He is no scholar but still he has a lot of *horse sense*. 彼は学者なんかではないが, それでも実生活での知識は豊富だ.

horses for courses 《英》 **1** 馬にはそれぞれ得意の走路があるということ ▪They are followers of the *horses for courses* theory. 彼らは馬にはそれぞれ得意の走路があるという説を奉じる人々だ.

2 人それぞれに異なる向き不向き ▪Ah well, *horses for courses*. A plumber can fix your sink, but not your car. まあ, 餅は餅屋だな. 配管工に流しは直せるが, 車は無理だ.

I could eat a horse! →EAT[2].

If two* (*men*) *ride on* [*upon*] *a horse, one must sit* [*ride*] *behind. 《諺》1頭の馬に二人が乗るとしたら，一人は後ろに乗らなければならない《二人で協同するときには，リーダーは一人で，もう一人はそれに従うべき》，「両雄並び立たず」.

It is a good horse that never stumbles. 《諺》どんな名馬でもつまずくことはある，「弘法も筆の誤り」.

Lock the barn-door after the horse is stolen. 《米・諺》馬が盗まれてから馬小屋に鍵をかけよ，「あとの祭」.

mount* [*ride*] *the high horse →get on one's high HORSE.

off** one's **high horse 《口》高慢をすてて ▪ She came down *off her high horse*. 彼女は高慢でなくなった ▪ We pulled him *off his high horse*. 我々はいばっている彼をへこました.

on** one's* [the***] ***high horse*** **1**《口》ごう慢で，気取って，偉そうにして ▪ Indeed he seems to be *on his high horse*. なるほど彼はいばっているように見える ▪ Great Britain is now *on the high horse*, but it will dismount again. イギリスは今はいばっているが，また低姿勢になるだろう.

2 きげんが悪い，不きげんで ▪ The boss is *on his high horse* again. ボスはまたごきげん斜めだ.

on* (*the*) *horse of ten toes*/*on foot's horse 《戯》徒歩で，歩いて ▪ You can ride *on the horse of ten toes*. 歩いて行けばいい.

play horse 《米口》 **1** 馬乗り遊びをする ▪ His son was *playing horse* on the arm of the chair. 彼の息子はいすの腕に乗って馬乗り遊びをしていた.

2 あばれる，ばかなまねをする; あざ笑う，だます ▪ Johnson is *playing horse* again. ジョンスンはまたばかなまねをしている.

play horse with …を無作法に[そっけなく，手荒く]扱う ▪ They tried to *play horse with* you again. 彼らはまたあなたをそっけなく遇しようとした ▪ He won't *play horse with* her stake in the venture. 彼は彼女の投機の賭け金を手荒に扱いはしない.

pull** a person **off his high horse →off one's high HORSE.

pull the dead horse → work for a dead HORSE.

ride** one's* [the***] ***high horse*** →get on one's high HORSE.

***ride two horses at the same time* [*at once*]** 《英・報道》二股をかける ▪ Don't *ride two horses at the same time*. Stick to one thing only. 二股をかけたらだめだ. 一つのことだけに専念せよ.

***roll up ... horse and foot* (*and guns*)** …を完全に負かす，さんざんに負かす ▪ He made a brilliant speech, which *rolled up* the government *horse and foot*. 彼はすばらしい演説をして政府をさんざんにやっつけた.

set* [*stable*] *horses together →draw HORSEs together.

spur a willing horse →WILLING.

(straight) from* [*out of*] *the horse's mouth 直接に，確かな筋から ▪ I've got the information *from the horse's mouth*. その情報は確かな筋から得た. ☞歯を調べて馬の年齢と価値を判定することから.

swap horses in midstream → change HORSEs in midstream.

swap horses while crossing the stream →SWAP[2].

take horse 馬で行く; 馬に乗る ▪ He *took horse* to Lake Constance. 彼はコンスタンス湖へ馬で行った.

take the horse (雌馬に)種がつく ▪ Having *taken the horse* is a matter of uncertainty for three or four months. 雌馬に種がついたということは3, 4か月ははっきりしない.

talk horse 《口》 **1** 競馬用語を使う ▪ I heard the ladies *talk horse*. 私は女性たちが競馬用語を使うのを聞いた.

2 ほらを吹く ▪ He was *talking horse* to the biggest liar in Asia. 彼はアジアきっての嘘つきに向かってほらを吹いていた.

the man on the horse*/*the man on horseback 《米口》(関係)当局者，権威者 ▪ *The man on the horse* is now Lord Harlington. 権力者は今はハーリントン卿である ▪ Let Ike go as *the man on horseback*. アイクを当局者として行かせよ. ☞特に Ulysses Simpson Grant や Theodore Roosevelt のこと.

To horse! 馬に乗れ!，乗馬!《ラッパの合図・号令》 ▪ His trumpets sounded *to horse*. 彼のラッパが乗馬の合図をした.

white horses 白い波頭，白波 ▪ There were *white horses* on the sea as far as the eye could see. 見渡す限り海面に白波が立っていた. ☞泡立つ波頭が岸に打ち寄せるさまが，疾走する馬に見えることから.

***Wild horses would* [*could*] *not get* [*drag*] A *from* [*out of*] B.** 何ものもBにA(秘密)を吐かせることはできない ▪ *Wild horses wouldn't get* his address *from* me. 何ものも私に彼の住所を吐かせることはできない. ☞白状させるため，野性の馬(2頭)に人を別々の方向に引っぱらせたことから.

work for* [*off, with*] *a dead horse 前金ずみの仕事をする ▪ He had to *work for a dead horse* in the ensuing week. 彼は次の週には前金仕事をしなければならなかった. ☞この仕事はいくらしても，もう金はもらえない.

work like a horse 元気よく[忠実に]働く，がむしゃらに働く ▪ You *worked like a horse* for him. 君は彼のためにがむしゃらに働いた.

work* [*pull*] *the dead horse = work for a dead HORSE.

***You may* [*can*] *take* [*lead*] *a horse to* (*the*) *water*(*, but you can't make him* [*it*] *drink*).** 《諺》馬を水際へ連れて行くことはできても，水を飲ませることはできない《体は力で思い通りにすることができるが，心まで操ることはできない》.

horse[2] /hɔːrs/ 動 ***horse it*** 仕事ができあがらないうちに支払いを請求する，実際にした仕事以上の支払いを

要求する ▪ A workman often *horses it*. 労働者はよく実際にした仕事以上の支払いを要求する.

horseback /hɔ́ːrsbæ̀k/ 名 ***from*** [***off***] ***horseback*** 馬から(降りる, 落ちる, など) ▪ A man just alighted *from horseback*. 人が一人ちょうど馬から降りた ▪ The King fell *off horseback*. 国王は馬から落ちた.

on horseback **1** 馬に乗って (↔ on FOOT 1) ▪ They traveled *on horseback*. 彼らは騎馬旅行をした.

2 馬に ▪ I set the beggar *on horseback*. 私はその物乞いを馬に乗せてやった.

the man on horseback = the man on the HORSE.

horse-collar /hɔ́ːrskɑ̀lər|-kɔ̀lə/ 名 ***grin through a horse-collar*** おどける, 道化る ▪ He *grinned through a horse-collar* to make people laugh. 彼は人を笑わすためにおどけた. ☞ grinning match (笑いっこ)から来た; これは二人またはそれ以上の人が, 馬の首輪に頭をつっこんでやる競技で, 最も気味の悪い笑い顔をした者が勝ちとされる.

horse-marines /hɔ́ːrsmərìːnz/ 名 ***Tell that*** [***it***] ***to the horse-marines!*** → Tell that to the MARINEs.

horseshoe /hɔ́ːrsʃùː/ 名 ***Close only counts in horseshoes*** (***and hand grenades***). 《諺》近くがものを言うのは蹄鉄投げ遊び(と手投げ弾)のみである《成功が近いだけでは十分でない》.

hospital /hɑ́spɪtəl|hɔ́s-/ 名 (***be***) ***in*** (《米》 ***the***) ***hospital*** 入院して(いる) ▪ He *is in the hospital* now. 彼はいま入院している ▪ He died *in hospital*. 彼は入院中に死んだ.

be out of (《米》 ***the***) ***hospital*** 退院している ▪ I have *been out of the hospital* for only about a week. 退院してからほんの1週間です.

enter [***go into***] (***a*** [《米》 ***the***]) ***hospital*** 入院する ▪ She collapsed and had to *go* back *into hospital*. 彼女は倒れて再入院しなくてはならなかった.

rush ... to (《米》 ***the***) ***hospital*** ...を至急入院させる ▪ He got injured and *was rushed to hospital*. 彼は負傷して緊急入院させられた.

send ... to (《米》 ***the***) ***hospital*** ...を入院させる ▪ He *was* immediately *sent to hospital*. 彼はすぐ入院させられた.

walk the hospitals → WALK².

hospitality /hɑ̀spətǽləti|hɔ̀spɪ-/ 名 ***Afford me the hospitality of your columns.*** 貴紙にご掲載願います《寄稿家の依頼の言葉》.

be hospitality itself 歓待を尽くす ▪ The master *was hospitality itself*. 主人は至れり尽くせりの歓待をした.

partake of His [***Her***] ***Majesty's hospitality*** 《英口・戯》監獄に入っている ▪ He *partook of His Majesty's hospitality* then. 彼はそのとき入獄していた.

host¹ /hoʊst/ 名 ***play host to*** ...を迎える, 受け入れる ▪ Berlin *played host to* the '36 Summer Games. ベルリンは1936年夏季オリンピック大会を主催した.

reckon [***count***] ***without*** *one's* ***host*** **1** 勘定で見落としをする; 肝心の人に相談せずに[他人の見解を考慮に入れずに]自分だけで計画を立てる ▪ You are *reckoning without your host*; you've overlooked the extra item. 君は勘定で見落としをしている, 特別項目を見落としている ▪ Take care not to *reckon without your host*. 自分勝手に立案しないように気をつけなさい.

2 重要な事情を考慮に入れないで決定をする; 誤算をする ▪ Napoleon had *reckoned without his host* as regards the position. ナポレオンはその地位について誤算をしていた. ☞「宿の主人に尋ねずに宿賃を自分で計算する, 家主に相談せずに家賃を勘定する」が原義.

host² /hoʊst/ 名 ***a host in*** *oneself* (一人で大勢に匹敵する)一騎当千の人 ▪ You need not worry about entertainment, he's *a host in himself*. 余興のことで心配するに及ばない. 彼は千両役者だから.

a host of たくさんの ▪ I saw *a host of* golden daffodils. 私はたくさんの黄色いスイセンを見た.

host [***hosts***] ***of heaven*** 神に仕える無数の天使たち; 日月星辰 ▪ They worshiped all the *host of heaven*. 彼らは全天の星を拝んだ ▪ The numerous *hosts of heaven*, who are they? 無数の天使たちは誰だろう.

Lord (***God***) ***of hosts*** 万軍の主 ▪ *Lord God of hosts*, be with us. 万軍の主たる神よ, 我々とともにあらんことを.

hostage /hɑ́stɪdʒ|hɔ́s-/ 名 ***give hostages to fortune*** 《文》足手まといを背負い込む《妻子・いつ失うかもしれないものなどについて》 ▪ He had settled down and *given hostages to fortune*. 彼は定住して妻子を得た. ☞ Bacon, *Essays*, "Of Marriage and Single Life".

hold *a person* ***as a hostage*** 人を人質に取っておく ▪ Two boys *were held as hostages*. 二人の少年が人質に取っておかれた.

take [***hold***]***... hostage*** ...を人質に取る[取っている] ▪ The convicts *took* 3 guards *hostage* during their escape. 囚人らは逃亡の際3人の守衛を人質に取った ▪ Americans *were held hostage* in Tehran for more than a year. アメリカ人たちが1年以上テヘランで人質に取られていた.

hostile /hɑ́stəl|hɔ́staɪl/ 形 ***be hostile to*** [***toward***] ...に敵意を持っている ▪ At first they *were hostile to* the explorers. 初め彼らは探検家たちに敵意を持っていた.

hot /hɑt|hɔt/ 形名 ***a hot button*** 《米口》重要問題, 関心事 ▪ Gender issues were then something of *a hot button*. 当時ジェンダーの問題はちょっとした関心を呼ぶ話題だった.

a hot line (要人)への緊急用連絡電話線, ホットライン ▪ The President spoke on the *hot line* with the Prime Minister. 大統領は首相とホットラインで通話した.

a hot potato 《口》取扱いに慎重を要する問題, 難

問 ▪ The abortion issue is *a hot potato*. 中絶問題は慎重に扱うべき問題だ.

a hot spot →SPOT[1].

a hot ticket →TICKET[1].

(*all*) *hot and bothered* 《口》(急ぎ・心配などで)ひどくいらいらして ▪ Don't get *all hot and bothered*. I'll drive you to the station. そんなにいらいらしないで. 私が車で駅まで送ってあげますから.

(*as*) *hot as fire* [*blazes, hell,* 《雅》*Hades*] とても熱い, 焼けるように暑い《誇張表現》 ▪ Her cheeks turned *as hot as fire* with consternation. びっくり仰天して彼女の頬が火のようにほてった ▪ It's *hot as hell* outside. It must be nearly 100 degrees. 外は焼けるような暑さだ. きっと(華氏)100度近くあるだろう ▪ It's *hot as blazes* in here. ここはやけに暑い ▪ A puppy is trapped inside a car where it's *as hot as Hades*. 子犬が地獄のように暑い車内に閉じ込められている. ☞Hades《ギ神》「死者の国」. ただし暑い場所ではなく暗闇なので, ここでは hell の婉曲表現.

(*as*) *hot as pepper* 非常にからい ▪ Its raw root is *as hot as* a *pepper*. それの根は生ではとてもヒリヒリとからい.

be a bit hot 《口》ちょっとひどい(仕打ちだ) ▪ To dismiss the lad just because he forgot to post a letter *is a bit hot*. 手紙を投函するのを忘れただけでその若者を首にするのはちょっとひどい.

be hot at …に非常にすぐれている[精通している] ▪ She *is hot at* tennis. 彼女はテニスが非常にうまい.

be hot-blooded 情熱的である, すぐ怒り出す ▪ His son *is hot-blooded* and finds it hard to control his temper. 彼の息子はすぐかっとなり, 感情を容易に抑えられない.

be hot for …に熱心である ▪ He *is hot for* reform. 彼は改革に熱心である.

(*be*) *hot on* 《口》 **1** …に熱中して(いる), を熱愛して(いる) ▪ He *is hot on* making money. 彼は金儲けに熱中している ▪ He *was hot on* my sister. 彼は私の妹を熱愛していた.

2 …に対して[の点で]極度にきびしい ▪ She *was hot on* anyone who made the slightest mistake. 彼女は少しでもミスをする者にきびしかった.

3 =be HOT at.

be hot on the trail* [*track*] *of 捜し求めているものや人のすぐ近くまで来ている; もうすぐ捕えられそうである ▪ The police officer *is hot on the track of* the criminal. 警察官はもうすぐ犯人が捕えられそうである. ☞《狩》から.

be hot stuff **1** (男性が)すぐれている; 少し放蕩者である ▪ How is Bill getting on in his teaching job?—Oh, he *is* very *hot stuff*. ビルは教師をどんな風にやっているかい?—ああ, 彼は非常にすぐれているよ.

2 (女性が)…がすぐれている (*at*) ▪ She *is hot stuff at* the piano. 彼女はピアノがうまい.

3 《口》(女性が)セクシーである ▪ The new girl in our class *is hot stuff*. 今度転校してきた女の子はセクシーだ.

be hot under the collar →COLLAR.

be in a hot spot →in a SPOT.

catch it hot →get it HOT.

come* [*go*] *hot foot 大急ぎで来る[行く] ▪ The messenger *came hot foot* with the news. 使者は大急ぎでそのニュースを持って来た.

***drop* [*let fall*]*... like a hot potato* [*brick, chestnut*]** 《口》…を急いで捨てる, あわてて捨てる ▪ I found that he was a swindler and *dropped* him *like a hot potato*. 私は彼が詐欺師であることを知って, あわてて彼と手を切った ▪ Why did ABC *drop* the series *like a hot brick*? なぜ ABC 放送はそのシリーズを急にやめたのだろう.

***feel hot and cold* (*all over*)** =go HOT and cold (all over).

***get hot* (*and bothered*)** 《口》 **1** 熱くなる; 興奮する; 非常に熱演する; 怒る; 心配する ▪ We *got hot* over the argument. その議論に興奮した ▪ They may *get hot* and win the tournament. 熱演して試合に勝つかもしれない ▪ Everybody has *got* so *hot and bothered* about the affair. みながその事件について非常に心配している.

2 (捜したり追ったりしているものや, 当てごとに)非常に近くまで来る, もうすぐ追いつきそう[捜し当てそう]になる ▪ Not there, but you're *getting hot*. そこではない, だが君はもうちょっとで捜し当てるところだ.

get into hot water →WATER[1].

get* [*catch*] *it hot 《口》ひどくしかられる, 大目玉を食らう ▪ You'll *catch it hot*, I assure you. 君はきっと大目玉を食らうぞ.

get it hot and strong 《口》こっぴどくしかられる ▪ He *got it hot and strong* from his teacher. 彼は先生にこっぴどくしかられた. ☞→HOT and strong.

***get too hot for* [*to hold*]** *a person* 《口》(場所が)人にとっていたたまれなくなる (→make a place too HOT for a person) ▪ What with the police attention and social ostracism, the place *got too hot for* him. 警察の監視やら村八分やらで, 彼はそこにはいたたまれなくなった.

***give* [*have*] *a hot time* (*of it*)** 《口》ひどい目にあわせる[あう]; きびしくしかる[しかられる] ▪ The teacher *gave* me *a hot time of it* for not handing in an assignment. 課題を提出しなかったおかげで先生に大目玉を食らった.

give it (*a person*) ***hot* (*and heavy* [*strong*])** 《口》(人を)ひどい目にあわせる; (人を)ひどくしかりつける (→HOT and strong) ▪ I will *give it* them *hot* (*and strong*). 彼らをきびしくしかってやろう.

***go* [*feel*] *hot and cold* (*all over*)** 《英口》(恐怖のため)熱くなったり寒くなったりする ▪ The figures made me *go hot and cold*. その姿は恐ろしくて, 私は体が熱くなったり寒くなったりした.

go hot foot →come HOT foot.

go* [*sell*] *like hot cakes →CAKE[1].

have* (*got*) *the hots for *a person* 《口》異性への関心を持っている, 性的興味がある ▪ It's obvious my sister *has the hots for* the guy. 妹がそいつに熱

H

をあげているのは明らかだ ▪ Jack's really *got the hots for* you! ジャックはあなたに首ったけよ.

have hot work of it 苦しい目にあう ▪ I am afraid they are going to *have hot work of it*. 彼らは苦しい目にあうと思う.

hot and heavy 猛烈な[に], 電光石火的で[な, に], 一生懸命な[に] ▪ The resistance was *hot and heavy*. その抵抗は猛烈だった ▪ The battle was *hot and heavy* around Kabul. カブールの辺りは激戦だった ▪ I took a club and gave it to him *hot and heavy*. 私はこん棒を取って彼を猛烈になぐってやった.

hot and hot **1** (料理が)できたての, ほやほやの ▪ It was served *hot and hot*. それのできたてが出された.
2 非常に熱い ▪ The soup came in *hot and hot*. スープの非常に熱いのが出た.
3 〚名詞的に〛 できたての料理 ▪ Your job is to serve the *hot and hot*. 君の仕事はできたての料理を出すことだ.

H

hot and strong 《口》 こっぴどく, 猛烈に, 熱心に; 猛烈な ▪ My brother is going *hot and strong* at present. 弟は今のところ熱心にやっている.

Hot dog! 《米口》 〚間投詞的に〛 万歳! ▪ "*Hot dog!*" she exclaimed when she saw the birthday gift. 「万歳!」と誕生祝いを見て彼女は叫んだ.

hot dog 《米口》 **1** 〚名詞的に〛 (スキー・スケートボードで)妙技[スピード]を見せる選手, 人目を引く選手; 目立ちたがり屋 ▪ The skateboarder is such a *hot dog*! そのスケートボード選手は実に人目を引く.
2 〚動詞的に; 常に後に副詞・前置詞を伴って〛 妙技[スピード]を見せる[見せびらかす], 人目を引く ▪ He spent the day *hot dogging* down the slopes. 彼は一日中スロープを滑降して妙技を披露した.

hot from the oven →OVEN.

hot from the press →PRESS[1].

hot-headed 怒りっぽい, 短気な ▪ He is usually patient, but sometimes can be awfully *hot-headed*. 彼は普段は辛抱強いが, ときにひどくかっとなることがある.

hot off the press =hot from the PRESS.

hot off the wire (電報・電話が)今来たばかりの ▪ There it is, *hot off the wire*, ladies and gentlemen. さあみなさん, 今届いたばかりの電報です.

***hot on** a person's **tracks** [**trail**]* 《口》 …のあとにぴったりついて ▪ The burglar ran away, with the police *hot on his trail*. 賊は逃走し警察がすぐあとについて急追していた.

hot to trot/hot-to-trot 《口》 **1** (活動に参加したくて)うずうずして, 熱望して, やる気満々で ▪ My friend is really *hot to trot* about this cruise. 友人はこのクルージングに参加したくてたまらない ▪ One product that I am *hot to trot* about is this model of desktop. 欲しくてたまらない製品はこの型のデスクトップだ ▪ The two have been *hot-to-trot* to start a family. 二人はずっと第一子をもうけたいと望んできた.
2 《米卑》 セクシーで; 性的にうずうずして, 好色な ▪ That beautiful mature woman is really *hot to trot*. あの成熟した美女は実にセクシーだ ▪ He's *hot to trot* and asked her out right after he met her. 彼はナンパ好きで会ってすぐに彼女を外へ誘い出した.

hot with →WITH.

keep the wires hot (ニュースなどが)電線が熱くなるほど続いてくる ▪ War news *kept the wires hot*. [*The wires were kept hot* with war news.] 戦況ニュースが電線が熱くなるほど続いた.

let fall … like a hot potato [***chestnut***] → drop … like a HOT potato.

make it hot 《口》 **1** 多く要求しすぎる; ひどく誇張しすぎる ▪ Don't *make it hot*. あまり大げさな言い方をするな.
2 (…に)不快な[たまらない]思いをさせる (*for*) ▪ We offended them last week, and they are *making it hot for* us at the club. 先週彼らを怒らせたので, 彼らはクラブで我々に不快な思いをさせようとしている.

***make it too hot for** a person* 人に不快で耐えられなくする ▪ You are *making it too hot for* me to stay here. お前は私がここにいたたまれないようにしている. ☞次項も参照.

make** a place **too hot for [***to hold***] *a person* 《口》 ある場所を人が不愉快で[苦しくて]いたたまれないようにする (→get too HOT for a person) ▪ It *made* this city *too hot for* Ned. そのためネッドはこの市にはいたたまれなかった.

more … [***more often***] ***than** a person **has had hot dinners*** 《英口・戯》 → more … than you have had hot DINNERs.

not so [***too***] ***hot*** 《口》 (特に健康が)大してよくない, あまり満足[有効]なものでない ▪ His plan is *not so hot*. 彼の計画はあまりよくない ▪ She has *not* been *so hot* recently. 彼女は最近あまり体の具合がよくない ▪ How do you feel today?—*Not too hot*. 今日のご加減は?—あまりぱっとしません ▪ The video is hot but *not too hot* for a young audience. そのビデオはよい出来映えだが, 若い視聴者にはあまり受けない.

on the hot seat 不安[心配]の状態に; 苦しい責任の地位にあって ▪ He was *on the hot seat*, directing the gamble. 彼はその賭博の指導をして, 不安な状態にあった.

piping hot 《口》 (食物・液体がしゅーしゅー音をたてるほど)熱い, ほやほやの, 焼き[煮]たての ▪ The food was served *piping hot*. 熱々の食べ物が出された.

sell like hot cakes →go like hot CAKEs.

the hot seat 《俗》 (死刑のための)電気いす ▪ If convicted, he will get *the hot seat*. もし有罪ときまれば, 彼は電気いすで死刑になるであろう.

***too hot to handle/ too hot for** a person* 《口》 非常に危険[困難]で扱えない[かかわれない] ▪ These cases are *too hot to handle*. これらの訴訟事件はひどくあぶなくて扱えない ▪ Things got *too hot for* him and he resigned. 事態の深刻さが増して手に終えなくなり, 彼は辞職した.

hotel /hoʊtél/ 動 ***hotel it*** ホテルに宿泊する ▪ We tried *hoteling it*. ホテルに泊まろうとした.

hotfoot[1] /hάtfʊ̀t|hɔ́t-/ 名 ***give a hotfoot*** 悪

ふざけをして悩ます《人の靴の側面にこっそりマッチを入れて火を出さす》; 拍車を当てる《比喩的にも》 ▪ He *gave* the horse *a hotfoot*. 彼は馬に拍車を当てた.

hotfoot[2] /hɑ́tfʊ̀t|hɔ́t-/ 動 ***hotfoot it*** 大急ぎで行く; 素早く逃走する ▪ They were *hotfooting it* north. 彼らは北の方へ急いでいた ▪ I have to *hotfoot it* to the airport. 大急ぎで空港へ行かなくては.

hound[1] /haʊnd/ 名 ***follow*** [***ride to***] (***the***) ***hounds*** 馬に乗って一群の猟犬のあとを追って狩りをする ▪ They *follow* their *hounds* over hedges and through rivers. 彼らは馬に乗って猟犬のあとを追い, 生けがきを越えたり川を通ったりして狩りをする.

hunt with the hounds and run with the hare 二股(ふたまた)をかける (→run with the HARE and hunt with the hounds) ▪ You favor Oxford and yet you are wearing light blue; you can't *hunt with the hounds and run with the hare*. あなたはオックスフォードびいきなのにうす青のシャツ《ケンブリッジの選手・応援団の着るシャツ》を着ている. 二股をかけることはできませんよ.

hound[2] /haʊnd/ 動 ***hound*** *a person* ***to death*** 人をいじめ殺す ▪ They tried to *hound* the patrol *to death*. 彼らは巡査をいじめ殺そうとした.

hour /aʊər/ 名 ***a bad quarter of an hour*** →QUARTER[1].

a golden hour 死活の1時間《医療行為の適不適によって重傷者の生死が左右される事故発生直後からの1時間》 ▪ Within the so-called *golden hour*, surgeons have a better chance of saving life. いわゆる生死を分ける1時間以内なら, 外科医が命を救える確率は高い.

a solid hour まる1時間 ▪ We've waited for you *a solid hour*. 我々は君をたっぷり1時間待ったぞ.

after hours 規定の業務時間後に《勤務・学校・サービス業などの》 ▪ The bar served drinks *after hours*. その酒場は規定の営業時間後に酒類を出した ▪ I will work *after hours* and finish it. 私は超過勤務をしてそれを仕上げよう.

all hours 夜遅い ▪ It is dark; it must be *all hours*. まっ暗だ. 夜も遅いにちがいない.

at all hours (***of the day and night***) 《口》尋常でない時間に, 非常に朝早く[夜遅く]; いつでも, 時を選ばず; (いつまでも)ずっと(起きているなど) ▪ Please do not call *at all hours of the day and night*. 早朝や深夜に電話をしないでください ▪ He is reading some book or other *at all hours*. 彼はいつでも何かしら本を読んでいる ▪ Don't come for meals *at all hours*. 食事にくるのに早かったり遅かったりしてはいけません ▪ I was up *at all hours* trying to finish my work. 夜ずっと起きて仕事を仕上げようとした.

at an [***this***] ***unearthly*** [***ungodly***] ***hour*** 《口》むちゃくちゃに早い[遅い]時刻に ▪ She got up *at the unearthly hour* of 4 a.m. 彼女は午前4時というとんでもなく早い時刻に起きた ▪ Stop yelling at me! I don't want to get up *at this unearthly hour*! わしに向かってわめくのをやめろ! こんなに早く起こされてはたまらん ▪ He came home *at some ungodly hour* again last night. 彼はゆうべまた非常に遅く帰宅した.

at the top of the hour →TOP[1].

at this hour of the day [***the evening, the morning,*** etc.] 昼[晩, 朝, など]のこんな時刻に ▪ Leave the shop *at this hour of the night*? 夜のこんな時間に店を出るのですか.

at 0001 hours 《米》真夜中[午前0時1分]に《時刻を24時間制で表現する場合》 ▪ The assault will take place *at 0001 hours*. 攻撃は午前0時1分に開始されるだろう.

by the hour **1** 時間ぎめで, 1時間いくらで ▪ We are employed *by the hour*. 我々は時間ぎめで雇われている.

2 〚しばしば together を伴って〛 何時間も続けて ▪ I read the book *by the hour* (*together*). 私は何時間も続けてその本を読んだ.

3 〚進行形で〛 刻々と ▪ He is getting worse *by the hour*. 彼は刻々と病気が悪くなっている.

don't be half an hour 《口》ぐずぐずするな ▪ Go and put on your hat and *don't be half an hour* about it. 帽子をかぶりに行きなさい. そしてぐずぐずしないでね.

one's [*a person's*] ***finest hour*** 人生でもっとも重要なとき, 絶頂期 ▪ After receiving the trophy, he said that was *his finest hour*. トロフィーを授与されたあと彼は今が人生最高の瞬間だと語った.

for hours (***and hours***) 幾時間も(幾時間も)の間 ▪ We stood there *for hours*. 我々は幾時間もそこに立っていた.

for hours on end 何時間も, 長い間 ▪ Don't play video games *for hours on end*. 立て続けに何時間もビデオゲームをしてはいけません.

for hours together 何時間もぶっとおしに ▪ We talked *for hours together*. 何時間も続けて話した.

from hour to hour (時の経過とともに)どんどんと, 時々刻々と, 刻一刻と ▪ Each person's blood pressure changes *from hour to hour*. 誰の血圧も刻々と変化するものだ.

happy hour 《口》(酒場などの) サービスタイム《食事前にカクテルなどが安くなる時間帯》 ▪ Most bars offer reduced price drinks during *happy hour*. 大抵のバーではサービスタイムに割引価格で飲み物を提供する. ☞会社が引けてから夕食前のひとときに, バーでは料金が割引される.

hour after hour 時間が次々と; 毎時間 (every hour) ▪ *Hour after hour* passed without anyone coming to our rescue. 救助の人が来ずに時間がどんどん経っていった ▪ Announcements will be made *hour after hour*. アナウンスは毎時間されます.

hour by hour 時々刻々 ▪ The moment of death was drawing nearer *hour by hour*. 死の瞬間が刻々と迫っていた.

One's ***hour has come*** [***struck***]**.** 時節が到来した; 命数が尽きた ▪ Jesus told his disciples that *his hour had come*. イエスはわたしの命数が尽きたと

使徒たちに言われた.

One's ***hours are numbered.*** →The days of... are NUMBERed.

improve the shining hour →IMPROVE².

in a good [***happy***] ***hour*** 幸運にも ▪ He called on me *in a good hour* yesterday. 彼は運よくきのう私の所へ来た.

in an evil [***ill***] ***hour*** 運悪く, 不幸にも ▪ *In an evil hour* I changed my lodgings. 折悪しく私は下宿を変わった.

in *one's* ***hour of need*** 《主に戯》まさかのとき[一番困っているとき]に ▪ Where were you *in my hour of need?* 君の助けを一番必要としているときに, どこにいたのか.

in the hour of ...のときに ▪ Come to me *in the hour of* need. 困ったときには私の所へ来なさい.

keep bad [***late, irregular***] ***hours*** 夜ふかしする《通例この意味》; 夜遅くまで帰らない; 夜ふかし朝寝をする ▪ He is *keeping bad hours* now. 彼はこのごろは夜ふかししている ▪ Those who *keep late hours* cannot do well at school. 夜ふかし朝寝をするものは学校で良い成績は取れない.

keep good [***early, regular***] ***hours*** 夜早く寝る《通例この意味》; (夜)早く帰宅する; 夜遊びをしない; 早寝早起きする ▪ The doctor advised him to *keep good hours*. 医者は彼に夜早く寝るようにと言った ▪ Those who *keep early hours* are generally healthy. 早寝早起きする人は概して健康である.

of the hour 現時の; 刻下の, 一時的な ▪ He thinks he is the man *of the hour*. 自分は時の人だと彼は考えている ▪ The subject *of the hour* is the provision of housing for the poor. 刻下の問題は貧しい人々に住宅を与えることである ▪ All books are divisible into two classes: books *of the hour*, and books for all time. すべての本は二つの種類に分けられる――一時的な本と古今を通じて読まれる本だ.

on the half-hour ...時(じ)半きっかりに《ちょうど5時半, 6時半などに》 ▪ Buses leave here for London *on the half-hour*. ロンドン行きのバスはここを毎時30分きっかりに出発する.

on the hour ...時(じ)きっかりに, 毎正時(しょうじ) ▪ The station broadcasts the news every hour *on the hour*. 放送局は毎時きっかりにニュースを放送する.

out of hours 営業[勤務]時間外に ▪ You may smoke *out of hours*. 勤務時間外は喫煙してもよい.

rule the hour ...がその時の状態[大勢]である ▪ Madness *ruled the hour*. その時は人心狂乱の状態であった.

strike the hour 時を告げる, 時間を知らせる ▪ I heard the church bells *strike the hour* of two. 教会の鐘が2時を知らせるのを耳にした.

the early [《米》 ***wee***] ***hours/ the*** (***wee***) ***small hours*** (12時過ぎの)深更, (1時から3時ごろの)真夜中; 朝の1時から4時ごろまで ▪ They were singing and dancing till *the early hours*. 彼らは真夜中まで歌ったり踊ったりしていた ▪ She passed away in *the early hours* of Monday morning. 彼女は月曜日の早朝に亡くなった ▪ I lay awake through *the wee small hours*. 朝の2時3時ごろまでずっと寝床で目をさましていた.

the long hours 夜の11, 12時など《時計が長く打つ時間》 ▪ He was still in his office at [in] *the long hours*. 彼は深夜になってもまだオフィスにいた.

the witching hour 真夜中 ▪ He arrived just at *the witching hour*. 彼はちょうど真夜中に着いた.

There aren't enough hours in the day. することが多すぎて時間が十分ない ▪ I am far behind in my work. *There aren't enough hours in the day.* 仕事が大幅に遅れている. やることが多すぎて時間が足りない.

till [***until, to***] ***all hours*** (***of the night***) 《口》夜遅くまで ▪ He sat up *till all hours* last night. 彼は昨夜遅くまで起きていた ▪ We sat up *till all hours of the night* playing cards. 夜遅くまで起きてトランプをした.

to an hour **1** (日だけでなく)時間までも ▪ Please say *to an hour*. (日だけでなく)時間まで言ってください.

2 (1時間も違わず)ちょうど, きっかり ▪ It's only three days since she left her home—three days *to an hour*. 彼女が家を出てから3日—ちょうど3日—しか経っていない.

while away an hour 楽しく1時間過ごす ▪ Let's *while away an hour* just lying on the beach. 砂浜でただ横になって1時間ほどのんびりしよう.

within hours of ...のあとわずか数時間に ▪ *Within hours of* the quake happening, all the villagers had been rescued. 地震の発生数時間後には村人全員の救出が完了していた.

work all the hours God sends 《口》休みなく働き続ける ▪ She's been *working all the hours God sends* trying to finish her thesis. 彼女は論文を仕上げようと寸暇を惜しんで取り組んでいる.

house /haʊs/ 名 ***a clearing house*** (盗品・麻薬などの)違法売り捌(さば)き所 ▪ He used his home as *a clearing house* for the gang of robbers. 彼は自宅を強盗団の盗品売り捌き所として使った.

a fun house (遊園地のおばけ屋敷のような)仕掛け館 ▪ The children and adults all enjoyed themselves in the *fun house*. 大人も子供もみなおばけ屋敷で楽しく過ごした.

a good house 多数の聴衆 ▪ There was *a good house* at the opening. 始まりに多数の聴衆があった.

a halfway house **1** (...の間の) 妥協点 ▪ There could never be *a halfway house* between the two opposing parties. 敵対する両党間の歩み寄りはありえないだろう.

2 (ものごとの進行・発達の)中間地点 ▪ Hypnosis is *a halfway house* between being awake and being asleep. 催眠は覚醒と睡眠の中間の状態である.

3 (受刑者・精神病患者が)社会復帰するための訓練施設 ▪ He has been moved from the federal prison to *a halfway house*. 彼は連邦刑務所から更正

役務所へ移された ▪ They opened *a halfway house* for teenage Internet addicts. 10代のインターネット中毒患者のための社会復帰施設を開設した. ☞18世紀の「旅の中間地点の宿」が原義.

a house detective 警備員 ▪ He works as *a house detective* in a small hotel. 彼は小さなホテルの警備員をしている.

a house divided against itself 内部分裂した党派, または家 (《聖》*Matt.* 12. 25) ▪ She knew *a house divided against itself* must fall. 彼女は内部分裂した家はきっと倒れるということを知っていた.

a house of cards →CARD.

a house of ill [***evil***] ***fame*** [***repute***] 売春宿 ▪ She wanted to escape from the *house of ill fame* where she was. 彼女は自分のいる売春宿から逃げ出したいと思った.

a power house 精力家, 活力に満ち多大な影響力をもつ人物[企業] ▪ The delivery *power house* has moved more than 200 tons of relief shipments to needed areas. その巨大運送企業は200トン以上の救援物資を被災地に送った.

a safe house **1** (保護を要する人物を)密かに匿(かくま)う安全な場所 ▪ The witness was taken to *a safe house* by the police for his protection. 証人は身柄の保護のため警察によって安全な場所に移された.
2 (犯人の)隠れ家, アジト ▪ The gang leader was found hiding in *a safe house*. ギャングの首領はアジトに潜伏しているところを見つかってしまった.

be [***draw, have***] ***a full house*** 大入り[満員]である ▪ There *was a full house* at the theater. 劇場は大入り満員だった ▪ The new play is *drawing a full house*. 新しい劇は毎夜大入り満員である ▪ We *had a full house* with over 2,000 people at the concert. コンサートは2,000人以上の入りで大当たりを取った.

be as safe as houses (***to*** *do*) →SAFE.

be in possession of the House (議会で)発言権を持つ ▪ He *is* no longer *in possession of the House*. 彼にはもう議会発言権はない.

bring down [***carry***] ***the house*** 《口》満場をどっと笑わす; 満場の喝采を博する ▪ The comedian *brought down the house*. その喜劇役者は満場をどっと笑わせた ▪ Her performance *brought the house down*. 彼女の演技は満場をうならせた ▪ He *carried the house* last night. 彼は昨夜満場の喝采を浴びた.

Burn not your house to fright the mouse away [***fright away the mice***]. 《諺》ネズミをびっくりさせて追い払うために家を焼くな《その必要もないのに思い切ったことをするものではない》.

cast [***burn, hunt,*** etc.] *a person* ***out of house and home*** [***harbor***] 家から人を追い出す[焼け出す, 追い出す, など] ▪ They *were burnt out of house and home*. 彼らは家を焼け出された ▪ He *was hunted out of house and home*. 彼は家から追い出された ▪ He *gambled* himself *out of house and home*. 彼はばくちで家屋敷を売り払った.

clean house →CLEAN³.

eat *a person* ***out of house and home*** 《戯》 **1** →EAT².
2 長居しすぎて嫌われる ▪ After a week we started to feel he was *eating* us *out of house and home*. 1週間すると彼の長逗留に嫌気がさし始めた.

enter the House (下院)議員になる ▪ Jeannette Rankin *entered the House* in 1917 as the first woman in Congress. ジャネット・ランキンは1917年に女性議員として最初の下院議員になった.

exchange houses (...と)家を交換する[交換して休暇を過ごす] (*with*) ▪ Every summer we *exchange houses with* friends in Spain. うちは毎年夏にはスペインの友人と家を取り換えて休暇を過ごす.

from house to house 家から家へ, 戸(こ)ごとに ▪ The peddler went *from house to house* selling his wares. 行商人は商品を売りながら戸別に回った.

get a rough house (会場などで)聴衆が乱暴である ▪ We've *got a rough house* at the meeting this evening. 今晩の会では聴衆が乱暴だ.

get along [《英》***on***] ***like a house on fire*** 《米口》(人)とすぐ非常に仲良くする ▪ I *got on* with the girl *like a house on fire*. その女の子とすぐに大の仲良しになった.

go (***all***) ***round the houses*** 《英口》 **1** 回り道[遠回り]をして辿(たど)り着く ▪ He *went all round the houses* before reaching his destination. 彼は回り道をして目的地に到着した.
2 無用に長時間をかけて行く[述べる] ▪ There's no need to *go all round the houses*. 回りくどく言わなくてもよい.

house-broken/《英》***house-trained*** 《米》(家畜, 特に犬が)小用[排便]のために外へ出るようにしつけされた ▪ Is your young puppy fully *house-broken*? 子犬はちゃんとトイレのしつけができていますか?

house full 「満員」(の札) ▪ Both have practically put up the "*House Full*" sign. 両方とも実際に「満員」の札を掲げた.

house(-)***hunting*** 貸家[売家]探し ▪ I did a bit of online *house hunting* at the weekend. 週末にインターネットで少し貸家探しをした.

house to house 戸別の ▪ We had a *house to house* collection for the Fund. 我々はその基金の戸別募集を行った.

I would burn the house down but →BUT¹.

keep a good [***liberal***] ***house*** **1** 贅沢な生活をする ▪ Those who can *keep a good house* are blessed. 贅沢な生活のできる人々は幸福だ.
2 客を厚くもてなす ▪ He *kept a liberal house* to all comers. 彼は来客すべてを厚くもてなした.

keep a house 議員の出席定数を保つ ▪ We remained for the sake of *keeping a house*. 議員の出席定数を保つためにとどまった.

keep house **1** 《口》一家を構える, 所帯を持つ; 同棲する ▪ He married and *kept house* near the

H

school. 彼は結婚して学校の近くに所帯を持った ▪ Dick and Bess *keep house* these days. ディックとベスは近頃同棲している.

2 家事[家政]を(切り盛り)する ▪ When my brother was alive, I *kept house* for him. 兄が生きていたころは私が兄のために家事をしてあげた ▪ I am to *keep* his *house*. 私は彼の家事をすることになっています.

keep *one's* [***the***] ***house*** **1** 家にいる; (病気などで)家に引きこもる ▪ He could do no more, but *kept the house*. 彼はもう何もできずに, 家に引きこもっていた.

2 留守番をする ▪ Peter says he will *keep the house* until we return. ピーターは我々が帰るまで留守番をすると言っている.

keep *one's* ***house*** (***in***) (…に)住む ▪ He *kept his house in* the wood. 彼は森に住んでいた.

keep house with …と同じ家に住む, 寄合い所帯[共同生活]をする ▪ She is *keeping house with* my aunt in Kanda. 彼女は神田で私のおばと共同生活をしている.

keep open house →keep OPEN doors.

like a house afire [***on fire***] 《口》 **1** 非常に早く, どしどし, 活発に, 盛んに ▪ The truck went roaring *like a house on fire*. トラックが轟音を上げて飛ばしていった ▪ They went at it *like* 500 *houses on fire*. 彼らは猛烈な勢いでそれをやった.

2 非常にうまく[良く] ▪ The party went *like a house on fire*. パーティーは非常にうまくいった.

like the side of a house 《口》(特に女性が)非常に太って ▪ She is getting *like the side of a house*. 彼女はだんだん太っていっている.

make a house (下院で)議員の出席定員数になる (→keep a HOUSE) ▪ There were not enough members to *make a house*. 議員の出席定員数になるだけの議員がいなかった.

move house [***home***] 転宅する ▪ We must *move house* again. また転宅しなければならない ▪ I recently *moved home*. 最近引っ越ししました.

on the house 《口》(酒場などの)営業主[その家]の支払いで, ふるまいで ▪ In the main bars, the first drink Thursday was *on the house*. 主だった酒場では木曜日の最初に出す酒はふるまいであった ▪ He had it *on the house*. 彼はそれを店のおごりで飲んだ.

pack the house (劇場などを)大入満員にする ▪ "Peter Pan" still *packs houses* with kids. 「ピーターパン」は今なお劇場を子供たちで大入満員にする.

play house ままごと遊びをする ▪ They *played house* all day. 彼女らは一日中ままごと遊びをした.

pull down *one's* ***house about*** *one's* ***ears*** 自家を頭上に倒して自滅する ▪ The man who tries to destroy another's home will end by *pulling his own house down about his ears*. 他人の家庭をこわそうとする者は結局は自滅に終わるであろう.

round the houses 《英》遠回しに, もって回って ▪ She is always talking *round the houses*. 彼女はいつももって回った物言いばかりする.

set [***put, get, keep***] *one's* (***own***) ***house in order*** 家の事[財政]を整える; 秩序を回復する (《聖》 *2 Kings* 20. 1) ▪ I must *set my house in order* before leaving. 私は出発前に家の事を整えなくてはならない ▪ We told them to *put their houses in order*. 彼らに秩序を回復せよと言った ▪ You should *get your own house in order* before judging others. 他人をとやかく言うより自分の行いを正したらどうだ ▪ Our country must *get its* economic *house in order* now. わが国は今こそ経済を立て直さなければならない ▪ Stem-cell research must *keep its house in order*. 幹細胞研究は常に倫理秩序を維持しなければならない.

set up house [***home***] (***with*** *a person*, ***together***) (男女が)(…と, いっしょに)所帯を持つ《結婚・非結婚は問わない》 ▪ They have decided to *set up house together*. 彼らは所帯を持つことに決めた ▪ He *set up home with* his supermodel girlfriend. 彼はスーパーモデルのガールフレンドと暮らした.

shout the house down 大騒動をする ▪ I can't study while our little brothers are *shouting the house down*. 弟たちが大騒ぎをしている間は勉強ができない.

the big house 刑務所 ▪ The man spent twenty years in *the big house*. 男は20年間の刑務所暮らしをした.

The house meets. 議会が開かれる ▪ Does *the house meet* tomorrow? 議会はあす開かれるか.

the House of God 神の館(やかた), 教会, 礼拝堂 ▪ Sir, don't forget we are in *the House of God*. もしもし, ここは教会の中だということをお忘れなく.

the second house (劇場の)2回目上演 ▪ *The second house* starts at 9. 2回目上演は9時に始まる.

turn *a person* ***out of house and home*** → cast a person out of HOUSE and home.

household /háʊshòʊld/ 名 ***a household word*** [***name***] 日常言いなれた言葉; 人のよく知る名前[諺] (cf. Sh., *Hen. V* 4. 3. 52) ▪ The name Berwick has become *a household word*. ベリックという名は人のよく知る名前となった.

housekeeping /háʊskìːpɪŋ/ 名 ***give up housekeeping*** 所帯をたたむ ▪ They *gave up housekeeping* last year. 彼らは昨年所帯をたたんだ.

go [***set up***] ***housekeeping*** 所帯を持つ ▪ It was a good present for the young wife *setting up housekeeping*. それは所帯を持つ若妻への良い贈り物だった.

light housekeeping **1** 軽い家事 ▪ We offer *light housekeeping* services for the elderly. お年寄りのためのヘルパーを派遣します.

2 《俗》同棲 ▪ They aren't married; it's just a case of *light housekeeping*. 二人は結婚しておらず, 同棲しているだけだ.

house-room /háʊsrùːm/ 名 ***give house-room*** (人を)収容する, 泊める; (物を)受け入れる; (思想を)いれる ▪ I must trouble you to *give* this man *house-room* for a few days. ご面倒ですがこの人を2, 3日の間泊めていただかねばなりません ▪ His large genial nature *gave house-room* to ideas not easily reconciled. 彼の寛厚な性質は簡単には調和しないような思想をいれた.

would not give ... house-room (物・人)はただでもいらない, やろうと言ってもいやだ ▪I *would not give* such a chair *house-room*. そんないすはただでもいらない.

house-top /háʊstɑ̀p|-tɔ̀p/ 名 ***cry* [*declare, proclaim, shout*] *from* [*upon*] *the house-top*(*s*)** →SHOUT ... from the rooftops.

housing /háʊzɪŋ/ 名 ***a housing boom*** 家屋価格の急騰 ▪We took advantage of the *housing boom* and sold our house. 家屋価格の高騰に便乗して我が家を売り払った.

congregate housing 《口》食事つきの老人用集合住宅 ▪Our Grandma lives in a *congregate housing* facility. うちの祖母は賄いつきの老人集合住宅施設で暮らしている.

hover /hʌ́vər|hɔ́v-/ 動 ***hover on the verge of*** (ある状態)に近づいている, に瀕している ▪He *hovered on the verge of* rudeness. 彼は今にも無礼と言われそうな態度だった ▪His mind *hovered on the verge of* madness. 彼の心は狂気寸前だった.

how /haʊ/ 副名 ***And how!*** 《俗》大いに, とても; そうだとも ▪You mean it, Peggy?—*And how!* ペギー, あなたは本気なのですか?—とても本気です ▪She is spending money *and how*. 彼女は盛んに金を使っている. ☞G Und wie! のなぞり.

any* (*old*) *how 乱雑に ▪There were books thrown on the bed *any old how*. ベッドの上に本が乱雑に投げ散らされていた.

Here's how! 健康を祝して(乾杯)《親しい者同士で言う乾杯の言葉》 ▪A health to ourselves. *Here's how!* 我々自身の健康を祝して, 乾杯!

How about ...? 《口》...はどうですか; をどう思いますか ▪*How about* this dictionary? この辞書をどう思いますか ▪*How about* going on a hike? ハイキングに行かないか.

***How about that* [*it*]?** 《口》どんなもんだい; どうだい《結構なこと[嬉しい, 驚き]じゃないか, それでもいいか》 ▪My novel is going to be published. *How about that?* 僕の小説が出版されるよ. どんなもんだい? ▪Your car will be towed away if you park it here, so *how about that?* 君の車はここへ駐車すれば引っぱっていかれるよ. どうだい?《それでもいいか》.

***How are* [《俗》*How's*] *things* [*life, tricks*]?** 《口》(ごきげん)いかがですか《あいさつ》 ▪Hullo, old fellow! *How's things?* やあ, 君, ごきげんいかがです ▪*How are things* with you?—Could be worse. どうだい?—まあまあだよ ▪Hello. *How's life*, both of you? When's the baby coming? やあ. どうだい, 君たち. (出産)予定日はいつかね.

How are you?/ How* (*are*) *you doing?/ How goes it* (*with you*)?/*How's it going? **1** ごきげんいかがですか ▪*How are you*, Ed?—O.K. *How you doing?* こんにちは, エド. どう?—元気だ. そっちは ▪*How goes it?* Everything okay? どうだい? 変わりはないか ▪Nice to see you. *How's it going?* こんにちは. 調子はどう?
2 《皮肉》ほんとに!, へえ! ▪She practised the piano.—Practise? *How are you?* 彼女はピアノの練習をしました—練習ですって? へえー!

How are you fixed for ...? 《米口》...はどうなっていますか ▪*How are you fixed for* dollars? ドルの事はどうなっていますか.

***How are you off for* [*in*]...?** 《米口》...はどの程度与えられているか ▪*How are you off for* money? 金はどれくらい持っていますか.

***How came* a person *to* do?** 《英》人がどうして...するようになったか ▪*How came you to* know him? どうして彼を知るようになったのですか.

How can* [*could*] *you? 《口》君はなんてむごいことをしたのだ, よくそんなばかなことを ▪I punched him in the nose.—Oh, *how could you?* やつの鼻に一発見舞ってやった—よくもまあ, そんなひどいことを. ☞How can you behave this way? や How could you be so foolish? が短縮されたもの.

how come どういうわけか (why); 事の次第, 事情 ▪*How come* (that) Tom is not going to the movie with us? どうしてトムは私たちと映画に行かないんですか ▪They want to know *how come*. 彼らは事情を知りたがっている.

***How comes it* (*that*)?** 《口》それはどういうわけか ▪*How comes it that* you know him? どうしてあなたは彼を知っているのですか.

How crazy* [etc.] *can you get? 《口》[[crazy を強調して]] あなたってどこまで気狂いじみているんだろう ▪*How pompous can you get?* お前はいったいどこまで横柄(おうへい)なんだ.

How do? こんにちは! ▪*How do*, Mr. Rawlins? ローリンズさん, こんにちは. ☞How do you do? が短縮されたもの.

How do you do?/How d'ye do? 《古風》こんにちは; 初めまして ▪*How do you do*, Mr. Smith? スミスさん, こんにちは.

How does it* [*that*] *grab you? 《口》それをどう思うか ▪Listen, this is my idea. *How does it grab you?* いいか, 僕の考えは以上だ. 君はこれをどう思うか ▪*How does* the idea *grab you* to spend a pleasant holiday in Naples? ナポリで楽しく休日を過ごすのはどうかしら.

how d'ye do 《口》困ったはめ ▪Here is a pretty *how d'ye do*. これは困ったことになった ▪He is in a *how d'ye do*. 彼は困りきっている.

***How goes* (*it*)?** 《口》(...は)変わりはないか; (の)景気はどうだね ▪*How goes it* in your office since your new boss arrived? 新社長着任以来, 会社はどんな具合かね.

How in the world* [*a fire, on earth, the goodness, the devil, the dickens,* etc.] *...? 一体どうして...? ▪*How in the world* do you know that? 一体どうして君はそれを知っているのか ▪*How a fire* could he see this? 一体どうして彼はこれがわかったのかしら.

H

How is* [*are,* etc.]*...doing? …はいかがですか ▪ *How is* the invalid *doing?* 病人はいかがですか ▪ *How is* your business *doing?* 商売はどうですか.

How is it* (*that*)*...? **1** どういうわけで…か (why) ▪ *How is it that* he does not come? 彼はどうして来ないのか.
2 どのようにして…か ▪ *How is it that* these animals get what they need? これらの動物はどのようにして必要なものを得るのか.

How is that for ...? 《口》[[形容詞・名詞を伴って]] 何と…ではないか! ▪ *How is that for* impudence? 何と厚かましいではないか ▪ *How is that for* high? 何と高いではないか[すてきじゃないか].

How much /háʊmʌtʃ/? **1** (値段・量は)いくらか ▪ *How much* is this bag? このかばんはいくらですか ▪ *How much* (money) do you want? いくらほしいのか.
2 《口・戯》何だって? 《相手がばかに学者ぶった言葉を使ったり全く信じられない事を言ったとき》 ▪ He plays the saxtuba.—Plays the *how much?* 彼はサクスチューバを吹きます—何を吹くって?

How now? **1** それ[これ]はどうしたことか (How's that?) ▪ You have left your job on the Corn Exchange? *How now?* 穀物取引所の仕事をやめたって? それはまた, どうして?
2 《古》やあ! ▪ *How now?* What do you want with me? やあ, ぼくに何用かね.

How say you? あなたのお考えは?

How so? どういうわけか ▪ You gave me $10 this morning, and so you get $5 back.—*How so?* あなたは今朝私に10ドルくださったから, 5ドルお返しします—どうして?

how the devil →HOW in the world ...?

How then? これはどうしたことか; それではどうして.

***how to** do* どんなにすべきか, …のしかた ▪ I don't know *how to* express my thanks. 感謝の気持ちをどう言い表してよいかわかりません ▪ Teach me *how to* swim. 泳ぎ方を教えてください.

How will you ...? 《口》…してはどうですか ▪ *How will you* have it? 1杯やってはどうですか.

How would it be to** do **...? …してはどうだろうか ▪ *How would it be to* start tomorrow? あす出発してはどうだろうか.

How ya livin'?/How's it hangin'? 《俗》調子はどうかい, 元気かい ▪ Hey, pal, *how ya livin'?* よう, 相棒. 調子はどうだ?

How's about? 《主に米口》→HOW about ...?

How's that? **1** 何ですって, 何とおっしゃいましたか ▪ The house is on fire.—*How's that* again? 家が火事です—何ですって?
2 《クリケット》あれはどうです《打者はアウトか否か》 ▪ *How's that*, umpire?—Not out. 審判, あれはどうですか?—アウトではない.

that's how そういうわけで ▪ I file a report, and the company makes a report, too.—Oh, *that's how*. 私も申告書を出すし, 会社も出します—ああ, そういうわけで.

the how and why 事情や理由 ▪ He always wants to know *the how and why*. 彼はいつも事情や理由を知りたがる.

howl[1] /haʊl/ 名 ***set up a howl*** 泣きわめく ▪ The child dropped her sweets in the mud and *set up a howl*. 子供はお菓子を泥の中に落として泣きわめいた.

howl[2] /haʊl/ 動 ***howl with laughter*** 《口》長く存分に笑う ▪ I *howled with laughter* many times throughout. 始めから終わりまで何度も思う存分笑った.

howler /háʊlər/ 名 ***come a howler*** 《口》失敗する, どっと倒れる ▪ The old man *came a howler* on the Stock Exchange last week. 老人は先週株式取引所で失敗をした.

make a howler ばかげた失策をする; おかしな誤りをする ▪ Life is brightened for me when pupils *make howlers*. 生徒がおかしな誤りをするとき人生が私にとって明るくなる.

hub /hʌb/ 名 ***from hub to tire*** 《米口》全く, 完全に ▪ In the war the magazine was loyal *from hub to tire*. 戦争中その雑誌は完全に愛国的だった.

up to the hub 《米》 **1** 全く, 十分に, できるかぎり ▪ He is honest *up to the hub*. 彼は全く正直だ.
2 車輪がこしきまで泥にはまりこんで; に没頭して; に深くはまり込んで ▪ I have been *up to the hub* in business for the past month. 私はこの1か月事業に没頭していた.

huckleberry /hʌ́kəlbèri|-bəri/ 名 (***as***) ***thick as huckleberries*** 《米口》ひどく密生して, ひどくこみ合って ▪ You can see locusts *as thick as huckleberries* on the wayside. 道端にイナゴがうじゃうじゃいるのが見える.

be** a person's **huckleberry 《米口》人に特に適している ▪ If she were looking for a kind husband, you would *be her huckleberry*. もし彼女が優しい夫を探しているなら, 君が特にふさわしい人物だろう.

get the huckleberry 《米口》笑われる ▪ He got *the huckleberry* at school. 彼は学校で笑われた.

huddle[1] /hʌ́dəl/ 名 (***all***) ***in a huddle*** 乱雑に, ごたごたと ▪ Your books are (*all*) *in a huddle*. 君の本がごったがえしている.

***go* [*get*] *into a huddle* (*with*)** 《口》 **1** (…と密議するため)近く寄り合う ▪ Before resuming the game, the coach and the team *went into a huddle*. 試合を再開する前に, コーチとチームは密議のため近く寄り合った.
2 (…と)密議に入る, 密談をする ▪ The gangsters *went into a huddle* in the back room. 悪漢たちは奥の部屋で密談に入った ▪ I should like to *get into a huddle with* you. あなたと内密に相談したい.

huddle[2] /hʌ́dəl/ 動 (***be***) ***huddled up*** 体を丸くする ▪ He lay *huddled up* in bed. 彼は丸くちぢこまってベットに寝ていた.

huddle** oneself* (up***) 身を丸くちぢこめる, 体を丸くする ▪ When cold, he often *huddles himself up*

彼は寒いときはよく体を丸くちぢめる.

huddled masses 身を寄せ合う貧しい大衆 ▪ The *huddled masses* migrated to the US in search of opportunity. その貧しい人たちは成功の機会を求めて米国へ移住して行った.

hue /hju:/ 名 ***a hue and cry*** **1**《法》(被害者・警察官によってあげられる)重罪犯人追跡を求める叫喚 ▪ The old gentleman was not the only person who raised the *hue and cry*. 犯人追跡の叫喚をあげたのはその老紳士だけではなかった.

2 犯人逮捕令状, 盗品発見令状 ▪ No *hue and cry* was published for my rearrest. 私の再逮捕の令状は出されなかった.

3 犯罪者などについての情報官報 ▪ He was deeply absorbed in the interesting pages of the *Hue-and-Cry*. 彼は犯罪者情報官報のおもしろいページを読みふけっていた.

4 叫び声をあげながらの犯人追跡 ▪ There was *a hue and cry* after the villain. その悪漢に対する叫喚追跡が行われた.

5 追跡[攻撃]の叫び ▪ They pursued him with such *a hue and cry*. 彼らは大きな叫びをあげて彼を追跡した.

6 (犯人が逃げたり, 物品が盗まれたときの)警戒の叫び; 反対[非難]の叫び ▪ They raised *a hue and cry*. 彼らは泥棒, 泥棒と叫んだ ▪ When the book appeared, *a hue and cry* was raised against it. その本が出たとき, やかましい非難の声があげられた.

7 抗議[非難]の叫び声 ▪ We raised *a* great *hue and cry* about political corruption. 政治腐敗について大いに非難の声を上げた.

huff[1] /hʌf/ 名 ***get into a huff*** 不きげんになる, 怒る ▪ She *got into a huff* all of a sudden. 彼女は急に怒った.

go off in a huff 怒る ▪ She *went off in a huff* because we failed to nominate her as club president. 我々がクラブの会長に指名しなかったので彼女は怒った.

in a huff 怒って, かっとなって, むっとして ▪ She went out of the room *in a huff*. 彼女はむっとして部屋を出て行った.

take (the) huff 怒る, むっとする, 憤る ▪ He *took huff* at it. 彼はそれを怒った.

huff[2] /hʌf/ 動 ***huff and puff*** **1** ふうふう言って努力する; (困難な仕事に)ふうふう言ってまごつく ▪ He *huffed and puffed* when asked difficult questions. 彼は難しい質問をされた時はふうふう言ってまごついた. ☞「クマと3匹のブタ」という童話から.

2 口やかましく不満を言う ▪ They *huffed and puffed* about the price. 彼らは値段に不平を並べ立てた.

hug /hʌg/ 動 ***hug*** *oneself* ***at*** [***on, for***]《口》…を喜ぶ, ほくそ笑む, 得意がる ▪ He *hugged himself on* his cleverness. 彼は自分の器用さを得意がった ▪ He *hugged himself at* the idea of their failure. 彼は彼らの失敗を考えてほくそ笑んだ.

hug *one's* ***chains*** 束縛[捕われの身]を喜ぶ ▪ I *hug* these *chains* from my soul. 私は心からこの束縛を喜ぶ.

hug [***hold***] ***the road*** →ROAD.

hugger-mugger /hʌ́gərmʌ̀gər/ 名 ***be*** (***all***) ***hugger-mugger*** 乱雑で, 混乱して ▪ The dining room *was all hugger-mugger*. 食堂はすっかり乱雑になっていた.

in hugger-mugger 秘密に, こっそりと ▪ There was no way but to clap up the marriage *in hugger-mugger*. その結婚を秘密にさっさと取り決めるよりほかなかった.

keep ... on the hugger-mugger …を秘密にしておく ▪ I refuse to *keep* it *on the hugger-mugger*. それを秘密にしておくわけにはいかない.

hullabaloo /hʌ́ləbəlù:|hʌ̀ləbəlú:/ 名 ***kick up*** [***make, raise***] ***a hullabaloo*** 大さわぎを起こす, 騒動を起こす ▪ They *made* such *a hullabaloo* about the publications. 彼らはその出版物について大騒ぎをした.

hum /hʌm/ 動 ***hum and haw*** [***ha, hah***]《英》口ごもる, (返答に窮して)えーとかあーとか言う; ためらう; 咳払いする ▪ Don't stand *humming and hawing*, but speak out. 口ごもりながら立っていないで, 思いきって言いなさい ▪ What are you *humming and hawing* about now? 今何をぐずぐずためらっているんだ ▪ The boy *hummed and hawed* and said he had broken the vase. 少年は口ごもったあと花びんを割ったのは僕だと言った.

humming and hawing《英》咳払い, 口ごもり, ためらい ▪ After much *humming and hawing* he finally admitted taking the money. さんざんためらったあげく彼はその金を盗んだことをやっと認めた.

make things hum《口》事を盛んにやる; 景気づける ▪ Our manager began to *make things hum*. 我々の支配人は万事を活気づけ始めた.

human /hjú:mən/ 形 ***only human*** やはり普通の人間 ▪ After all he is *only human*. 彼だってやはり人間だからね.

***To err is human*(*, to forgive divine*).** →ERR.

humanity /hjumǽnəti/ 名 ***with humanity*** 優しい心をもって, やさしく ▪ He treated animals *with humanity*. 彼は動物を優しく扱った.

humanly /hjú:mənli/ 副 ***humanly speaking*** 人間の立場では; 人知[人力]の限りでは ▪ Is Sunday, *humanly speaking*, a blessing? 日曜日は人間の立場から言って, ありがたいものか.

humble[1] /hʌ́mbəl/ 形 ***eat humble pie*** **1** 平あやまりにあやまる ▪ He had to *eat humble pie*. 彼は平あやまりにあやまらねばならなかった.

2 前言を取り消す, まちがっていたと白状する ▪ He was forced to *eat humble pie*. 彼はやむなく前言を取り消さねばならなかった.

3 屈辱をなめる, 恥ずかしい思いをする ▪ Our savings are gone and we must *eat humble pie* for the future. 我々の貯蓄はなくなってしまったからこれから先は恥ずかしい思いをしなければならない. ☞humble pie は umble pie との地口; 貴族の家では, 高座にはシカ肉のパイが出されたが, 下座の猟人たちは臓もつをパイにしたものを食べたという昔の習慣から.

in a humble measure 及ばずながら ▪I will help you, if only *in a humble measure*. 及ばずながらではあるがお助けしましょう.

your humble servant 敬具《公式の手紙の結びの文句》;《戯》私 ▪I have the honor to be, Dear Sir, *your humble servant*, Will Pinkney. ウィル・ピンクニー敬白.

humble[2] /hʌ́mbəl/ 動 ***humble*** *oneself* へりくだる; 敬意を表する, おじぎする ▪They *humbled themselves* meekly before the cross. 彼らは十字架の前におとなしく頭を下げた.

humble ... to the dust 屈辱を与える, はずかしめる ▪He *was humbled to the dust* by the many ill things he had done. 彼は自分のした多くの悪事で恥ずかしく思った.

H

humor,《英》**humour** /hjúːmər/ 名 ***be in*** (***a***) ***humor to*** *do* [***for***] ...したい気持ちである ▪I *am in a* pretty *humor to* dance. 私はかなりダンスをしたい気持ちである ▪I *am in* no *humor for* talking. 私は全然話をする気がしない.

be in the humor to *do* [***for***] ...したい気持ちである, する気になっている ▪I *am in the humor for* joking. 私は冗談も言いたい気持ちである.

Every man has his humor.《諺》人の気持ちはさまざま,「十人十色」.

Every man in his humor.《諺》なくて七癖,「十人十色」.

have a sense of humor →SENSE.

in (***a***) ***good*** [***bad***] ***humor*** 上きげん[不きげん]で ▪You were *in good humor* yesterday. 君はきのうは上きげんだった ▪She is always *in a bad humor*. 彼女はいつも不きげんである.

in ill humor 不きげんで ▪He is *in* slightly *ill humor* today. 彼は今日は少しきげんが悪い.

out of humor (***with***)《古風》(...に)不きげんで, 怒って; (に)あいそをつかして ▪What has made you so *out of humor*? どうしてそんなに不きげんなのですか ▪He is *out of humor with* himself. 彼は自分にあいそをつかしている.

please *a person's* ***humor*** 人のきげんを取る ▪It's tough to *please his humor*. 彼のきげんを取るのはむずかしい.

when the humor takes *a person* 気が向くと ▪I go out for a walk *when the humor takes* me. 私は気が向くと散歩に出る.

hump[1] /hʌmp/ 名 ***bust*** *one's* ***hump***《俗》懸命にしようと努める, 骨を折る ▪I *busted my hump* trying to help them. 彼らを助けようと必死に努めた.

get a hump on《俗》急ぐ; 出発する, 仕事にかかる; 奮起する ▪Let's *get a hump on*. 急ぎましょう ▪Nowadays even ministers know how to *get a hump on*. 今日では牧師さんでもせわしく働くことを知っている.

get the hump《英口》しょげる, 憂鬱になる; 不きげんになる, いらいらする ▪I've *got the hump* now. 私は今しょげている ▪He *gets the hump* when you don't listen to him. 話を聞いてやらないと彼は不きげんになる.

give *a person* ***the hump***《英口》人をしょげさせる, 憂鬱にする; 人を不きげんにする ▪What *gave* me *the hump* were the staff and their attitude. 私のしゃくにさわったのは職員たちとその態度だった.

have the hump《俗》しょげている, 憂鬱になっている; 不きげんである ▪Andrew seems to *have the hump* this morning. アンドルーは今朝はきげんが悪いようだ.

live on *one's* ***hump*** 自給自足する, 外部の資源に頼らない ▪For nearly three weeks I have *lived on my* own *hump*. ほとんど3週間の間私は自給自足してきた. ☞ラクダが自分のこぶ(hump)で栄養を取ることから.

on the hump 忙しく努力して ▪My duties keep me *on the hump*. 私は勤めのためいつもせわしく働いている.

over the hump **1** 難関を越して; 危機を脱して ▪In food production Russia is *over the hump*. 食量生産ではロシアは危機を脱した.

2 麻薬でハイになって ▪He can't answer. He is *over the hump* now. 彼は電話に出られないよ. 今, 薬(ヤク)でラリっているから.

push *a person* ***over the hump*** 難関を越させる, 危機から脱出させる ▪This win is going to *push* us *over the hump*. この勝利で危機を脱することができるだろう.

hump[2] /hʌmp/ 動 ***hump*** *oneself*《米俗》急ぐ; 元気を出す; 努力する ▪We must *hump ourselves* if we are to be there in time. 間に合うようにそこへ行こうと思えば急がねばならない.

hump (***up***) ***the*** [*one's*] ***back*** **1** 背を丸くする ▪John *humped up his back* and was comfortable. ジョンは背を丸くして気楽にしていた.

2 怒る; 不きげんな顔をする ▪The dog got into a dark corner, growling and *humping its back*. 犬はうなって怒りながら暗いかたすみに入った.

Humpty Dumpty /hʌ̀mptidʌ́mpti/ 名 ***go Humpty Dumpty*** 落っこちて粉々に砕ける ▪The minister's plans all *went Humpty Dumpty*. その閣僚の計画はことごとく失敗に終わった ☞Mother Goose から.

hunch /hʌntʃ/ 名 ***have a hunch*** (***that***)《米口》(...という)予感がする; (と)強く感じる; (という)疑いを持つ ▪I *have a hunch that* something is going to happen. 何か起こりそうだという予感がする ▪I *have a hunch that* I am being tricked. 私はだまされているのではないかという気がする.

play a [*one's*] ***hunch*** 直感的に選択する, 勘に頼って行う ▪He *played a hunch* and hit the jackpot. 彼は勘を働かせて大当たりをとった.

hundred /hʌ́ndrəd/ 名形 (***a***) ***hundred and one***《口》非常に多くの; 種々さまざまの ▪I have *hundred and one* things to do. 私には非常にたくさんの仕事がある.

a* [*one*] *hundred percent 《米口》完全に，完全な ▪ He is *a hundred percent* patriot. 彼は全くの愛国者である.

be 100 not out 100歳になってなお生きている ▪ My granddad will *be 100 not out* in July this year. おじいちゃんはこの7月に100歳を迎えるが，まだかくしゃくとしている.

by hundreds* [*the hundred*]/《主に米》*by the hundreds 何百となく，百をもって数えるほどに ▪ People are flocking *by hundreds* to visit the place. そこを訪れるため何百人となく集まっている.

by the hundred **1** 百単位で ▪ They are sold *by the hundred*. それらは百単位で売られる.
2 =by HUNDREDs.

give a hundred* (*and ten*) *percent 全力を尽くす ▪ We'll *give a hundred and ten percent* effort each and every day. 日々全力を挙げて精一杯努力します.

9 ***hundred hours*** (午前)9時 ▪ Breakfast is at seven *hundred hours*. 朝食は午前7時からである ▪ Take the TGV to Geneva at seventeen *hundred hours* twenty. 17時(午後5時)20分のジュネーブ行き TGV に乗車しなさい.

hundreds and thousands ケーキの装飾に用いる非常に小さいこんぺいとう ▪ My favorite sweet is the little cake with *hundreds and thonsands* on top. 私が一番好きなスウィーツはてっぺんにこんぺいとうをのせた小さいケーキです.

in the hundred 100につき，100分の ▪ The stock will probably achieve 5 *in the hundred* in dividend. 株はおそらく100分の5(5パーセント)の配当金を達成するだろう. ☞利子などについて言うが，今は percent のほうが普通.

It will be all the same a hundred years hence. 《諺》100年後にはみな同じになる; 何が起ころうともたいした問題ではない《あきらめの叫び》.

(***it's***) ***a hundred to one*** (***that***) (…は)ほとんど確かで(ある) ▪ *A hundred to one* it will be a failure. おそらくきっとそれは失敗するだろう ▪ *It's a hundred to one that* the bus will be late. バスが遅れるのはまず間違いない.

long* [*great*] *hundred 120 ▪ Fresh herrings are sold by the *long hundred*. 新鮮なニシンは120匹いくらで売られる.

***not a hundred miles away* [*off, from*]** 《口・戯》…からすぐ近くに《明言すると悪いか危険な場所・人について》; つい最近の(出来事など) ▪ This retreat was *not a hundred miles from* the spot. この隠れ家(ᵍᵃ)はそこのすぐ近くであった ▪ Arthur was *not a hundred miles away* from an awkward situation. アーサーは危うく困った立場に立つところだった.

one hundred percent →a HUNDRED percent.

within a hundred miles of 《口・戯》…のすぐ近くに ▪ It is *within a hundred miles of* the shop. それはその店のすぐ近くにある.

hundredth /hʌ́ndrədθ/ 形名 ***a hundredth part*** (***of***) 100分の1 ▪ We will not need to use the *hundredth part of* that time. その時間の100分の1も使う必要はない.

hunger /hʌ́ŋɡər/ 名 ***from hunger*** 飢えのため ▪ He is ill *from hunger*. 彼は飢えのため病気になっている.

Hunger is the best sauce. 《諺》空腹は最高のソースである，「すき腹にまずいものなし」.

hungry /hʌ́ŋɡri/ 形 (***as***) ***hungry as a hawk* [*a hunter, a wolf*]** 《口》腹がぺこぺこで ▪ He says he is *as hungry as a hawk*. 彼は腹がぺこぺこだと言っている.

be hungry for …をひどくほしがる ▪ I *am hungry for* a good steak. おいしいステーキがひどくほしい.

feel hungry 空腹を覚える ▪ Why do I *feel hungry* soon after a meal? 食事をしたばかりなのになぜ空腹を覚えるのだろう.

go hungry 食べないでいる，食べずにすます; 飢える ▪ We shall have to *go hungry*. 我々は食べずにいなければならないだろう.

Nothing comes amiss to a hungry man. 《諺》ひもじい人には何がきても不都合ではない，「空腹にまずいものなし」.

hunkers /hʌ́ŋkərz/ 名 ***on*** *one's* ***hunkers*** うずくまって ▪ He was *on his hunkers*. 彼はうずくまっていた.

squat* [*get down*] *on *one's* ***hunkers*** うずくまる ▪ People were *squatting on their hunkers*. 人々はうずくまっていた.

hunky /hʌ́ŋki/ 形 ***all hunky*** 《米俗》立派で，壮健で ▪ Everything is *all hunky*. 何もかもすてきだ ▪ We are *all hunky*. 我々は壮健だ.

be hunky dory 《米俗》申し分がない ▪ Everything *is hunky dory*. 万事けっこうだ.

hunt[1] /hʌnt/ 名 ***be on a hunt for*** …を探している ▪ I *am on a hunt for* lodgings. 私は下宿を探している.

***have* [*make*] *a hunt* (*for*)** **1** (…の)猟をする ▪ We *had a hunt for* mule deer in Texas. テキサスでミュールジカ狩りをした.
2 (…を)探し求める ▪ I am *having a hunt for* a job. 職探しをやっている.

hunt and peck (タイプライターの)タイプを探して打つこと ▪ He does his typing by *hunt and peck*. 彼はタイプを目で探して打つ《打つのが遅い》.

The hunt is up. 狩り[追跡]が始まった ▪ *The hunt is up* and three men are after you. 追跡が始まった. そして3人の男があなたを追っている.

hunt[2] /hʌnt/ 動 ***He who hunts two hares leaves one and loses the other.*** →HARE.

hunt a pack of hounds (40, 50頭の)猟犬を使ってキツネ狩りをする ▪ He *hunted a pack of hounds*. 猟犬を多数使ってキツネ狩りをした.

hunt *one's* ***bed* [*blanket*]** 《米口》床につく ▪ They all *hunted their beds* early. みんなは早く床についた.

hunt counter →COUNTER.

hunt in couples →go in COUPLEs.

hunting /hʌ́ntɪŋ/ 名 ***a happy hunting ground*** **1** あの世，天国 ▪ They believe in the *happy hunting ground* after death. 彼らは死後にはあの世があると信じている.

2 (狩猟者・収集家にとって)獲物が楽に見つかる場所，欲しい物がいくらでも手に入る場所 ▪ The old city is *a happy hunting ground* for antique collectors. その古都は骨董収集家にとって宝の山である. ☞北米先住民が名付けた「死後の生活」.

in hunting trim 猟の服装で ▪ He looked gallant *in hunting trim.* 彼は猟の服装でさっそうとしていた.

hurdle /hə́ːrdəl/ 名 ***clear a hurdle*** ハードルを越える，問題を首尾よく処理する ▪ The bill *cleared a hurdle* when the committee voted for the plan. 委員会が計画に賛成を票決したので議案は一つハードルを越えた.

the first hurdle 最初の障害，第一関門 ▪ *The first hurdle* was to obtain permission from the mayor. 最初の関門は市長の許可をもらうことだった.

hurl /həːrl/ 動 ***hurl abuse*** [***insults***] ***at*** 人を侮辱して怒声を浴びせる ▪ Several boys were *hurling abuse at* her. 数人の男の子が彼女に悪態をついていた.

hurl** oneself **against [***at, upon***] **1** …に飛びかかる，を猛烈に攻撃する ▪ He *hurled himself against* me suddenly. 彼は急に私に飛びかかって来た ▪ They *hurled themselves at* the enemy. 彼らは敵に猛烈に襲いかかった.

2《口》…に猛烈に求愛する ▪ She *hurled herself at* the boy very openly. 彼女はその少年に公然と猛烈に求愛した.

hurl** oneself **into ＝THROW oneself into.

hurrah /hərɑ́ː, -rɔ́ː/ 間名 ***a hurrah's nest*** 《米》ごたごたしたかたまり; 混乱 ▪ It was *a* complete *hurrah's nest.* 全くの乱雑状態であった ▪ He had a head like *a hurrah's nest.* 彼はボサボサ頭だった.

Hurrah for …! …万歳! ▪ *Hurrah for* the holidays! 休暇万歳!

hurry[1] /hə́ːri|hʌ́ri/ 名 ***be in no hurry to** do* [***for***] 《口》 **1** …を急いではいない ▪ *I'm in no hurry for* marriage. 結婚を別に急いではいない.

2 なかなか…(しようと)しない ▪ He *is in no hurry to* pay me the money. 彼はなかなかその金を私に払わない.

Everything is hurry and confusion. てんやわんやの騒ぎである ▪ Just now *everything is hurry and confusion.* 目下てんやわんやの大騒動である.

in a hurry **1** 急いで ▪ John is *in a hurry* to catch the train. ジョンはその電車に乗ろうと急いでいる ▪ I drew it up *in a hurry.* それを急いで起草した.

2 あせって ▪ He is *in a hurry* to be rich. 彼は金持になろうとあせっている.

3 あわてて ▪ I am always in haste, but never *in a hurry.* 私はいつも急いでいるが，決してあわててはいない.

4《口》［否定文で］楽々と，簡単に ▪ You will not beat that *in a hurry.* 君はそれにはちょっとかなわないだろう ▪ You won't find a better specimen *in a hurry.* これほどよい標本は簡単には見つかるまい.

5《口》［否定文で］進んで，喜んで ▪ I won't ask him to dinner again *in a hurry.* あの人を進んで食事に招待するようなことはまたとありますまい.

6《口》［否定文で］そう早くは ▪ We shall not see his like again *in a hurry.* 彼のような人はそう早くはまたと見られないだろう.

in** one's **hurry 急いだあまりに ▪ I forgot it *in my hurry.* 急いだあまりにそれを忘れた.

(***There's***) ***no hurry.*** 急ぐ必要はない，急がなくてもよい ▪ Take your time. *There's no hurry.* ゆっくりやりなさい. 何も急ぐことはないから.

What's the hurry? 《口》なぜ急ぐんだ?; 急ぐ必要はない ▪ Let's finish it.—Finish it? *What's the hurry?* それをしてしまおうよ—してしまうって? そんなに急がなくてもいいよ.

hurry[2] /hə́ːri|hʌ́ri/ 動 ***hurry up and wait*** 急いでやってあとは待つ ▪ Everything is ready, now I just *hurry up and wait.* 準備は整った. 急いでやってあとはひたすら待つのみだ ▪ Now I *hurry up and wait* for their arrival. 急いでやったが，これから彼らが着くのを待たねばならない ▪ Better to *hurry up and wait* than to hurry up and be late. あわてててやっても間に合わないよりは急いでやってあとは待つだけの方がましだ.

hurt /həːrt/ 動 ***feel hurt*** 不快に思う，気を悪くする ▪ She seems to have *felt hurt* by what you said. 彼女はあなたの言ったことで気を悪くしたらしい.

get hurt けがをする ▪ I *got hurt* in the accident. 私はその事故でけがをした.

***hurt** oneself* けがをする ▪ Be careful not to *hurt yourself.* けがをしないように気をつけなさい.

It hurts. 《口》痛い.

It won't hurt. 別にさしさわりはない.

it won't [***wouldn't***] ***hurt** a person **to** do* … してても損はしないだろう ▪ *It wouldn't hurt* you to be more generous. もっと気前よくしてくれてもよさそうなものだが.

Nobody hurt. →NOBODY.

one more won't hurt 《口》(食物・酒を勧めて)もう一つ[1杯]くらいはだいじょうぶだろう ▪ *One more* drink *won't hurt,* will it? もう1杯くらいならいけるでしょう?

This will hurt me more than it hurts you. このことは君よりも僕のほうが辛いんだ《人を罰したりするときの文句》.

You cry before you are hurt. 《諺》けがをしないうちに泣く《理由もないのに恐れるな，の意》.

husband /hʌ́zbənd/ 名 ***a hen-pecked husband*** 女房のしりに敷かれた夫，恐妻家 ▪ He is said to be *an* obedient *hen-pecked husband.* 彼は従順で妻に頭が上がらないといわれている.

hush /hʌʃ/ 名形 ***hush money*** 口止め料 ▪ H[illegible] was sacked for taking *hush money.* 彼は口止[illegible]

料を受け取った廉(かど)で解雇された.

husk /hʌsk/ 名 ***separate the husk from the grain*** 《雅》悪(あ)しきものと良きものとを分かつ ▪ It is very difficult to *separate the husk from the grain*. 悪いものと良いものとを分けるのは非常に難しい.

hustle[1] /hʌ́səl/ 名 ***get a hustle on*** →get a HUMP on.

hustle and bustle 押し合いへし合い; (商売の)大景気 ▪ There was *hustle and bustle* all day at the market. 市場では一日中ごった返しの大にぎわいだった.

hustle[2] /hʌ́səl/ 動 ***hustle ... out of the way*** (じゃまもの)を押しのける ▪ He *hustled* them *out of the way*. 彼はそれらを押しのけた.

hymn /hɪm/ 名 ***be singing from the same hymn book*** [***sheet***] (ある事について)集団の誰に聞いても同じ意見である ▪ I think we*'re* all *singing from the same hymn book*. このグループの誰に聞いても答えは変わらないと思う.

hype /haɪp/ 動 (***be***) ***hyped up*** 《俗》(薬により, 薬によるかのように)興奮して ▪ The committee members *were hyped up*. 委員会の委員たちはみな興奮していた ▪ We *were* all *hyped up* after the movie. 映画のあとはみな興奮して大変だった. ☞hype<hypodermic.

hypocrite /hípəkrɪt/ 名 ***play the hypocrite*** 猫をかぶる ▪ I hate when people *play the hypocrite*. 人が猫をかぶると胸くそが悪くなる.

hysteric /hɪstérɪk/ 名 ***get*** [***fall into, go*** (***off***) ***into***] ***hysterics*** ヒステリーを起こす ▪ The woman *went into hysterics*. 女性はヒステリーを起こした.

in hysterics ヒステリーを起こして ▪ She was taken out of the coach *in hysterics*. 彼女はヒステリーを起こして駅馬車からおろされた.

I

i /aɪ/ 名 ***dot the*** [*one's*] ***i's and cross the*** [*one's*] ***t's*** 細かに説明する; (仕事をするのに)細かいところまで注意する ▪ He *dotted our i's and crossed our t's* about the lack of men in the Navy. 彼は海軍の人手不足について細かに説明した ▪ While he is spending his time *dotting the i's and crossing the t's*, other people get ahead of him. 彼が細かいところまで注意して時間を費やしている間に, 他の人々が彼より先へ進む.

ice /aɪs/ 名 ***break*** [《米口》 ***crack***] ***the ice*** 《口》 **1** 氷を砕いて道を開く ▪ He attempted to *break the ice* to make the passage easy for his countrymen. 彼は同国人の通行を易しくするため, 氷を砕いて道を開こうとした.

2 (やりにくい事などの)糸口を切る, 露払いをする ▪ He has *cracked the ice*, and other people are now following his courageous action. 彼は露払いをした. そして他の人々が今は彼の勇敢な行為にならっている.

3 (言いにくい)話を切り出す, (話を切りだして)気まずい沈黙[空気]を除く ▪ I have to *break the ice*, as he always keeps silence. 彼はいつも黙っているから私のほうから話を切り出さねばならない ▪ *The ice being* thus *broken*, another will utter her mind on the same matter. このように気まずい沈黙が破れたので, もう一人の者が同じ問題について考えを述べるでしょう.

4 堅苦しさ[気まずい空気]をほぐす; 打ち解ける ▪ The President threw back his head and laughed. That *broke the ice* and everyone laughed. 大統領はのけぞって笑った. それで堅苦しさがほぐれ, みなが笑った.

5 先制点をあげる ▪ The Rockets *broke the ice* with a touchdown. ロケッツがタッチダウンで先取点をとった. ☞ 海峡に張った氷を砕いて船が通れるようにすることから.

chop *one's* ***own ice*** 《米口》 自分の利益を図る ▪ The politician is *chopping his own ice*. その政治家は私利を図っている.

cut ice (***with***) 《口》 〚否定文・疑問文・条件文で〛 (…に)効果がある[役に立つ, 重要である] ▪ Does his opinion *cut* any *ice with* them? 彼の意見は彼らに重要なものであるか ▪ That excuse *cuts* no *ice*. その言い訳は通らない. ☞ フィギュア・スケートから.

have *one's* ***brains on ice*** 《口》 非常に冷静にしている ▪ If we want to be successful, we must *have our brains on ice* the whole time. 成功したいなら, 我々はいつも冷静にしていなければならない.

keep … on ice 《口》 …を使わずに取っておく; をそのままにしておく ▪ Why were these airplanes *being kept on ice*? これらの飛行機はなぜ使わずに取っておかれたのか ▪ She has never been able to find a man good enough for her, and so she is *keeping* herself *on ice*. 彼女は自分にちょうどよい人が見つからないので, 結婚せずにいる ▪ They *kept* the measures *on ice*. 彼らはその法案を議決せずにおいた.

not cut (***much, any***) ***ice*** (たいして, 全く)役に立たない, 効果がない, 問題でない ▪ His forces haven't been *cutting much ice* over that way. 彼の軍隊はその方面ではたいした働きをしていなかった ▪ Mere promises do *not cut any ice*. 単なる約束は全然役に立たない.

on ice **1** 《口》 (勝利・達成が)確かで ▪ They had the game *on ice*. 彼らが試合に勝つのは確かだった.

2 氷詰めになって; 保留されて, そのままにされて ▪ These measures are *on ice*. これらの法案はたな上げされている.

3 《俗》 入獄して ▪ He's been *on ice* for five years. 彼は5年前から入獄している.

4 (ショーが) スケートリンクでの, アイススケーターたちが演じる ▪ She will be here for Superstars *on Ice* next week. 彼女は来週当地のスーパースターアイスショーに出演する.

5 (ワインなどが)氷で冷やされて ▪ The champagne is *on ice*. シャンパンは氷で冷やしてある.

on thin ice 薄氷を踏むようで, はれものにさわるようで ▪ He may succeed, but he's now *on thin ice*. 彼は成功するかもしれないが, 今は薄氷を踏む思いをしている.

put … on ice **1** (計画など)を保留する, たな上げする ▪ The committee promptly *put* the measure *on ice*. 委員会は即座に議案をたな上げした.

2 《米口》 …を確保する, 決定的にする ▪ They *put* the game *on ice*. 彼らはその試合の勝利を確保した.

skate over [***on***] ***thin ice*** (談話で)薄氷を踏む思いをする; (危険な題目を)きわめて穏やかにそっと扱う ▪ He asked me many questions, so I found myself *skating over thin ice*. 彼がいろいろ質問したので, 私は薄氷を踏む思いだった.

straight off the ice (食物が)直接に[新鮮なものを]得られて; すぐに, 間をおかず ▪ I gave him three hours of it, *straight off the ice*. 私はすぐに彼にそのための3時間を与えた.

the black ice 道路上に薄く張り黒く見える氷, ブラックアイスバーン ▪ I hurried along the road, slipping on *the black ice*. 路面に張った氷に足を取られながら道を急いだ. ☞ 固くて滑りやすくしかも普段の路面にしか見えないため運転のとき危険.

the blue ice 氷河で生成された最も純度と密度の高い淡青色の氷 ▪ The skeleton of a mammal was buried in *the blue ice* of the Arctic. その哺乳類の骨格は北極の青い氷に閉じ込められていた.

iceberg /áɪsbɚ:rg/ 名 ***the tip of the iceberg*** 《口》 氷山の一角 ▪ The frauds that come to light are only *the tip of the iceberg*. 明るみに出る詐欺行為はほんの氷山の一角にすぎない.

icebreaker /áisbrèikər/ 名 ***an icebreaker*** 場の緊張を解きほぐす冗談 ▪ Our boss always uses *an icebreaker* in a formal situation. うちの社長はいつも冗談で公式の場を和ませる.

ice-leg /áislèg/ 名 ***get*** [***find***] *one's* ***ice-legs*** 《戯》氷の上を平気で歩けるようになる; スケートがうまくなる ▪ They are *getting their ice-legs*. 彼らはスケートがうまくなっている. ☞find one's SEA-LEGs にちなんで作られた句.

icicle /áisikəl/ 名 ***not an icicle's chance in Hades*** 《口》少しも見込み[機会]がない ▪ There is *not an icicle's chance in Hades* of getting her here. 彼女にここへ来てもらえる見込みは全くない. ☞Hades 《ギ神》「黄泉(よみ)の国」.

icing /áisiŋ/ 名 ***the icing on the cake*** → CAKE.

icy /áisi/ 形 ***give*** *a person* ***the icy mitt*** → give a person the frozen MITT.

idea /aidí:ə|-díə/ 名 ***a moth-eaten idea*** 時代遅れの考え, 古くさい見方 ▪ He has such *moth-eaten ideas* that he would have been happier 100 years ago. 彼の考えはとても古く, 今が100年前ならもっと幸せでいられただろうに.

at the idea of …と思うと ▪ The lion was tickled *at the idea of* the mouse being able to help him. ライオンはネズミが自分を助けることができるという考えに失笑した.

bounce an idea off *a person* 《口》人にある考えをぶつけてその反応をみる ▪ I decided to *bounce the idea off* one of my friends. その考えを友人の一人に当たってみることにした.

catch *a person's* ***idea*** 人の考えを了解する ▪ I could not *catch his idea*. 彼の考えを了解することができなかった.

float an idea 考えを持ち出してみる ▪ Who *floated the idea* of God the very first time? 誰がそもそも最初に神という考えを持ち出したのか.

form an idea (***of***) (…を)心に描く, 想像する ▪ You can *form* no *idea of* what it is like. あなたはそれがどんな物か想像できない.

get an idea **1** ある考えを考えつく ▪ He *got a* splendid *idea*. 彼はすばらしいことを思いついた.
2 …を理解する ▪ You can *get an idea* what the place is like. あなたはそこがどんな所か理解できる.

get [***have***] ***ideas*** (***into*** [***in***] *one's* ***head***) 妄想を抱く, 誤った[危険な, 実現できそうもない, 途方もない]考えを抱く ▪ Don't *get ideas into your head*, mother. I haven't lost my job. お母さん, 誤解しないでください. 僕は失業してはいないのです ▪ He *got the idea into his head* that May was in love with him. 彼はメイが自分に恋しているという妄想を抱いた.

get the idea (人の説明などが)飲み込める, わかる ▪ I think I've *got the idea*. やり方が飲み込めたと思う.

give *a person* ***an idea of*** **1** 人に…と思わせる ▪ He does not *give* us *an idea of* being in earnest. 彼は我々にまじめであると思わせない.
2 人に…を悟らせる[わからせる] ▪ I will *give* you *a* general *idea of* my scheme. 私の計画のあらましをお話ししましょう ▪ It will *give* you some *idea of* what it is like. それによってそれがどんなものかがいくらかおわかりでしょう.

give *a person* ***ideas*** = put an IDEA in a person's head.

have a great [***poor***] ***idea of*** …を偉い[つまらない]と考えている ▪ He *has a great idea of* himself. 彼は自分を偉いと思っている ▪ I *have a poor idea of* his abilities. 彼の才能を大したものとは思っていない.

have an idea 考えを思いつく ▪ Oh, I say! I *have an idea*. ああ, あのね, ある考えを思いついたよ.

have an idea of **1** …の標準[理想]を持つ, 観念を持っている ▪ They *have a* strange *idea of* female beauty. 彼らの美人観はおかしい.
2 …を知っている ▪ I *have a* rough *idea of* it. 私はその事をざっと知っている.

have an idea that …という気がする; と思う ▪ I *have an idea* somehow *that* he will come today. 何となく今日彼が来るような気がする.

have an idea who [***what***, etc.] 誰[何]が…かを知っている ▪ Do you *have* any *idea who* did it? 誰がそれをしたか君は知っているか.

have no idea わからない; 知らない; 思わない ▪ I *have no idea* what you mean. 君の言うことがさっぱりわからない ▪ I *have no idea* of what it is like. それがどんなものであるか知らない ▪ I *had no idea* that you were coming. 君が来るとは思わなかった.

have the right idea 的確な考えをもっている ▪ The senator *had the right idea* about how to fight racial discrimination. その上院議員はいかに人種差別と戦うかに関して的確な考えをもっていた.

in idea 観念[想像]において(の); 心の中で (↔in REALITY) ▪ The policy is excellent *in idea*, but in reality it won't work. その政策はアイデアとしては優れているが現実にはうまくいくまい ▪ Men talk of things *in idea*. 人間は想像上のいろいろな事を話す.

not have the first [***the least, the slightest, the vaguest***] ***idea*** (…を) 全く知らない ▪ I *haven't got the first idea* about cars. 車のことはからっきし知らない.

(***not***) *one's* ***idea of*** 《口》(人の)考える…(ではない) ▪ That is*n't my idea of* heaven. これは私の考える天国じゃない.

put an idea [***ideas***] ***in*** [***into***] *a person's* ***head*** 人に誤まった[危険な, 実現できそうもない]考えを吹き込む ▪ It has *put ideas into her head*. そのため彼女は妄想を抱くようになった.

run away with the idea [***notion***] 《口》(…と) 誤解する ▪ Don't *run away with the idea* that you're going to make it fine. うまくいくと早合点してはいけない.

That's an idea! 《口》それはよい思いつきだ ▪ Hey, *that's an idea!* We'll do it. ああ, そいつはいい. そう

しよう.

That's the idea! 《口》その調子で ▪ *That's the idea!* You're doing just fine. その調子! それでいいのだ.

The very idea! とんでもない, ばかな ▪ Women cannot understand football.—*The very idea!* 女性にはフットボールはわからない—とんでもない.

The (very) idea of (*doing*) ***…!*** …(する)なんて(考えてもばからしい, など) ▪ *The idea of his doing* such a thing! 彼がそんなことをするなんて(あきれる) ▪ *The idea of* such a thing! なんてばかなことを.

the young idea 幼い[若い]人々, (特に)生徒(の心) ▪ To teach and instruct *the young idea* is the aim of most clerics. 若い人々を教育することがたいていの牧師の目的である. ☞単数扱い. 代名詞は it.

toy with an [the] idea 特に決めるでもなく漠然と考える ▪ I'm *toying with the idea* of traveling abroad some day. いつか海外旅行をしたいと何となく考えている.

What an idea! まあ驚いた! ▪ *What an idea!* However did you imagine we could afford to send you abroad? まあ驚いた! 一体どうして, 我々にお前を外国へやる余裕があると想像したのか.

What's the (***big*** [***great***]) ***idea?*** 《口・反語》どんなばかな事をもくろんでいるのか; 何を言って[して]いるのだ ばかばかしい ▪ I sold them to the junkman today. —*What's the big idea?* それらを廃品業者に売りました—何てばかなことをするんだ. ☞the big idea「案, 計画」.

Where did you get that idea? どうしてそんなふうに思ったんだ?《全然まちがっている》 ▪ I marry Ella! *Where did you get that idea?* 僕がエラと結婚するって! どうしてそんなふうに思ったんだ?

with the idea of [that] …と思って, のつもりで ▪ *With the idea that* I was doing right, I informed him of it. 私は正しい事をしているつもりで彼にそれを知らせた ▪ I studied English *with the idea of* becoming a diplomat. 外交官になるつもりで英語を勉強した.

identify /aɪdéntəfàɪ/ 動 ***identify*** *oneself* 身分を証明する ▪ The man *identified himself* as the criminal. その男は自分が犯人だと名のった.

identify *oneself* ***with*** (運動・党派など)の同志となる, に関与する, 加盟する ▪ He *identified himself with* the party. 彼はその党に加盟した ▪ He refused to *identify himself with* such a policy. 彼はそのような政策に関与することを拒絶した.

identity /aɪdéntəti/ 名 ***establish the identity of*** …の身元を確かめる; (物が)それに相違ないことを確かめる ▪ The police *established her identity.* 警察は彼女の身元を確かめた ▪ He *established the identity of* the stolen goods. 彼は盗まれた品がそれに相違ないことを確かめた.

prove the identity of …の正体[身元]を明らかにする ▪ Passports are serviceable in *proving the identity of* the traveler. パスポートは旅行者の身元証明の役に立つ.

idle /áɪdəl/ 形 ***at an idle end*** →at a loose END.

eat idle bread 徒食する, 怠けて暮らす ▪ She does not like to *eat idle bread.* 彼女は徒食するのを好まない.

have *one's* ***hands idle*** 何もせずにいる, する事がない ▪ I *have my hands idle* now. 今は手があいている.

idle worms →WORM[1].

lie idle (人が)何もせずに寝ている; (機械・仕事場・金が)使われないでいる, 遊んでいる ▪ Don't let money *lie idle.* 金を遊ばせておくな.

run idle (機械が)から回りする ▪ The engine is *running idle.* エンジンが空転している.

idleness /áɪdəlnəs/ 名 ***eat the bread of idleness*** 徒食する, 怠けて暮らす (《聖》*Prov.* 31. 27) ▪ You cannot *eat the bread of idleness* on board a man of war. 軍艦の上では怠けて暮らすわけにはいかない.

Idleness is the root [mother, nurse] of all evil. 《諺》怠惰は諸悪の元《有益な仕事がなければ, 快楽を求めて悪いことを考えるものだ》,「小人閑居して不善を為(な)す」.

in idleness 無為に, のらくらして ▪ A man, like a sword, rusts *in idleness.* 人は剣と同じく怠けておればさびる.

idly /áɪdli/ 副 ***sit [stand] idly by*** (手を貸さずに) ぼんやり座って[立って] いる ▪ I'm not going to *stand idly by* when my pupils need my help. 生徒たちが私の助けを求めているのに, ただぼんやりしているつもりはない.

idol /áɪdəl/ 名 ***a fallen idol*** 堕ちた偶像, 崇拝者を落胆させる人, 人気の落ちた人 ▪ The actress is already *a fallen idol* in my eyes. 私にはその女優の人気はもう落ち目と映る.

make an idol of …を偶像視する, 崇拝する ▪ You *make an idol of* money. 君は金を崇拝する.

treat *a person* ***like an idol*** 心から人を崇(あが)める, 人に心酔する ▪ But not I—I don't like to be *treated like an idol.* わたしはいやよ. ちやほやされたくないの.

idolatry /aɪdɑ́lətri|-dɔ́l-/ 名 (***on***) ***this side*** (***of***) ***idolatry*** 偶像視に近い程度に ▪ I came to respect Dill *this side of idolatry.* 私はディルを偶像視に近いほど尊敬するようになった.

if /ɪf/ 接名 ***and it's a big if*** そんなことはありそうにないが ▪ If—*and it's a big if*—I meet the Mayor of London, what should I ask him? 仮に—まずありえないが—ロンドン市長に会ったら, 何を聞けばいいんだ.

as if →AS.

Dash these ifs! 「もしも」の連発はしゃくだ.

few, if any たとえあるとしても少ない, まずない ▪ There are *few, if any,* such men. そのような人はたとえいるとしても少ない ▪ *Few, if any,* of the candidates can pass the examination. 志願者のうち試験にパスできる者はまずいない.

if a day [***a man, a yard***] 1日, 一人, 1ヤードでもありとすれば; 確かに, 少なくとも ▪ He is seventy, *if a day*. 彼は確かに70歳だ ▪ I've come three miles, *if a yard*. 私は確かに3マイルは来た ▪ The enemy is 2,000 strong, *if a man*. 敵は確かに2,000人はくだらない.

if and only if もし…であり, なおかつその場合に限り ▪ Madison will eat pudding *if and only if* the pudding is custard. カスタードなら, そしてカスタードの場合に限って, マディスンはプディングを食べる.

if and when もしも《if の強調形》 ▪ I'll do it *if and when* I like. 気に入ったらの話だがそれをするよ.

if any **1** もしあれば ▪ Correct errors *if any*. 誤りがあれば訂正しなさい.
2 たとえあっても ▪ There are few trees, *if any*. 木はたとえあっても少ない ▪ There is little water, *if any*. 水はまずない.

if anybody もし誰かが…である[する]とすれば ▪ He was a hero *if anybody* was. 彼こそ英雄であった ▪ Smith can do it *if anybody* (can). スミスこそそれができる.

if anything **1** どちらかと言えば ▪ Today he is better, *if anything*. きょう彼はどちらかと言えば良い方だ ▪ *If anything*, touch the grass first. どちらかと言えば草の方に先に触れなさい.
2 もし(何かが)あるとすれば[しても] ▪ What, *if anything*, did Nixon bring back from Beijing? ニクソンが北京から持ち帰ったものは, もしあるとすれば何であったか ▪ I don't remember what, *if anything*, he said. 彼が何か言ったとしても, 何だったか覚えていません.

if at all いやしくも…するなら ▪ Troops should be sent, *if at all*, speedily. 軍隊を送るほどなら速やかに送るべきだ.

If at first you don't succeed, try, try again. 1回の失敗であきらめてはいけない ▪ I know it's hard to do, but *if at first you don't succeed, try, try again*. 確かにてごわいが, 一度うまくいかなくてもへこたれるな.

If ever I heard the like of that! こんな話が一体あるだろうか ▪ "Well, *if ever I heard the like of that!*" exclaimed John. 「さあ, 一体こんな話があるだろうか」とジョンは叫んだ.

if ever one is [***does***] もしあるとしたら[するとしたら], …こそ ▪ He is a fine English scholar, *if ever one was*. 彼こそ立派な英語学者だ ▪ He has succeeded *if ever one did*. 彼こそ本当に成功した.

if ever there is [***was***] ***one*** …こそ ▪ He is a scholar, *if ever there was one*. 彼こそ学者である.

If *one* ***has not*** *done!* しまった[ちくしょう]…した《驚き・怒り・嫌悪を含む》 ▪ *If* I *have not* lost my watch! しまった. 時計をなくした ▪ The wretch! *If* he *has not* smashed the window! ちくしょう! 奴が窓をこわしやがった. ☞前へ I'm blessed などを補う.

if I were you, I would(***n't***) *do* 私なら…する[しない]けど, (助言して)…する(しない)ほうがいい ▪ *If I were you, I wouldn't* buy that car. 私ならあの車は買わないね《あの車を買うのはやめた方がいいよ》.

If ifs and ans were pots and pans, there'd be no work for tinkers. 「もし」というのがつぼやなべであったら, いかけ職人の仕事はなくなるだろう《仮定を事実に変えることができたら, どんな貧乏人でも金持になれるだろう》 ▪ If only I were a little younger. —*If ifs and ans were pots and pans*. もうちょっと若かったらなあ—叶いっこないね. ☞前半だけがよく用いられる; *If Wishes Were Horses* という童謡から. an = if.

if *one* ***is to*** *do* →BE to do 4.

if it ain't broke don't fix it 順調なことがらに干渉するな, いらぬおせっかいを焼くな ▪ Let's not change it; *if it ain't broke don't fix it*. 変更しないでおこう. 余計なことはしないに限る.

if it had not been for もし…がなかったなら《過去の事実の反対の仮定》 ▪ *If it had not been for* your help, I should have failed. 君の援助がなかったら, 私は失敗したであろうに.

If it is not …! …ではないか!《驚きを表す》 ▪ Why, *if it is not* my uncle! おや, おじさんじゃありませんか!

if it were [***was***] ***not for*** もし…がないなら《現在の事実と反対の仮定》 ▪ *If it were not for* water, no one could live on earth. もし水がなければ, 誰も地球上に住むことはできないだろう.

if not **1** もし…でなければ (↔IF so) ▪ Where should I go, *if not* to your house? 君の家でなかったら私は他にどこへ行ったらいいのか.
2 たとえ…でなくとも ▪ He has spent more than half the money, *if not* all. 彼は金を全部とは言わないまでも半分以上使った.

if not for = IF it were not for; IF it had not been for.

if only →ONLY.

if so もしそうなら, もしそれが事実なら (↔IF not 1) ▪ Is "ditto" an English word? *If so*, what does it mean? "ditto" って英単語? もしそうだったら, どういう意味だい.

if the worst comes to the worst →WORST.

if *one* ***were to*** *do* もし…するとしたら《現在・未来の不可能なこと, またはする意志のないことの仮定》 ▪ *If* I *were to* die tomorrow, what would you say to me today? もし私が明日死ぬとしたら, 君は今日どう言うだろうか? ▪ *If* the sun *were to* rise in the west, I would never do such a thing. 太陽が西から昇るようなことがあっても, 私は決してそんなことはしない.

if you come [***go***] ***to that*** その段になれば ▪ They look a deal prettier, *if you go to that*. 彼らはきれいという段になれば, ずっときれいだ.

if you like →LIKE[2].

if you will 《口》言うならば, と言ってよければ ▪ He isn't a very honest person, a liar *if you will*. 彼はあまり正直な人間ではない, 言うならば嘘つきだ.

ifs and [***or***] ***buts***/《主に米》***ifs, ands, or buts*** 言い訳や理屈; 要求; 不平 ▪ Finish this work by 8 this evening. I'll have no *ifs or buts* from you. 今晩8時までにこの仕事を終えなさい. 君からの言い訳はいっさい聞かないよ ▪ You'd better be

I

there tomorrow, and no *ifs, ands, or buts* about it. あすそこへ行ったほうがいい，そのことでつべこべ言うな．

it's a big if 大きな疑問だが，大いに疑わしいが ▪ If (and *it's a big if*) Owen gets fired, who's our next coach? 万一(大いに疑わしいことだが)オーウェンが首になったら，我々の次のコーチは誰がなるのか《独立文で使われることもある》 ▪ If we win.—*It's a big if.* もしも我々が勝ったなら—大いに疑わしいがね．

little, if any (あるとしても)少ない《little が形容詞の場合》 ▪ There is *little, if any*, hope of his recovery. 彼の回復の見込みはまずない．

little, if anything (あるとしても)少ない《little が代名詞の場合》 ▪ He will have *little, if anything*, to eat there. 彼はそこでは食べるものはまずないだろう ▪ He has *little, if anything*, to do with us. 彼は我々とはほとんど関係はない．

little, if at all (あるとしても)ほとんどない《little が副詞の場合》 ▪ He is *little, if at all*, better than a beggar. 彼はほとんど物乞い同然だ．

no ifs and buts/《主に米》***no ifs, ands, or buts (about it)*** **1** まちがいなく，確かに ▪ Are you sure, Doctor?—*No ifs, ands, or buts about it!* 確かですか，先生—まちがいありません．
2 議論[反対，弁解]の余地なく ▪ *No ifs, ands or buts*, you're going up to bed now! つべこべ言わずに，さっさと2階で寝るんだ．

seldom, if ever →SELDOM.

ignorance /ígnərəns/ 名 ***be in ignorance of*** …を知らない ▪ I *am in* complete *ignorance of* his intentions. 私は彼の意図を全然知らない．

Ignorance is bliss. 《諺》無知は至福である，「知らぬが仏」．

Ignorance of the law is no excuse [excuses no one [man]]. 《諺》法律は知らなかったと言っても言い訳にはならない．

keep** a person **in ignorance 人に知らせずにおく; 人を無知のままにしておく ▪ The Church *kept* the people *in ignorance*. 教会は民衆を無知のままにしておいた．

sin from [through] ignorance 無知のため罪を犯す ▪ He *sinned* rather *from ignorance* than from actual wickedness. 彼は実際邪悪な心からというよりも，むしろ無知のために罪を犯した．

Where ignorance is bliss, 'tis folly to be wise. 知らないで幸福である場合には知らせて不幸にするのはばかげている《知らぬが仏だ》(T. Gray, *On a Distant Prospect of Eton College* 10).

ignorant /ígnərənt/ 形 ***be ignorant of*** …を知らない; に気うかない ▪ He *is ignorant of* the world. 彼は世間を知らない ▪ I *was ignorant of* the time. 私は時刻を忘れていた．

ill /ɪl/ 形副名 ***as ill luck would have it*** →as LUCK would have it.

be ill at …がへたである ▪ I *am ill at* making excuses. 私は言い訳がへたです．

be ill off →be badly OFF.

be ill with …で病んでいる ▪ I have *been ill with* influenza. 私はインフルエンザにかかっていた．

be taken ill 病気になる ▪ A girl aged seven died after *being taken ill* during class. 7歳の少女が授業中病気になったあと亡くなった．

do ill 悪事を働く ▪ You should not *do ill* to others. 他人に悪いことをしてはいけない．

for good or ill/for ill or well よかれあしかれ ▪ *For ill or well*, we have to employ him. よかれあしかれ彼を雇わねばならない．

get [fall] ill 病気になる ▪ She suddenly *got ill*. 彼女は突然病気になった．

go ill with →it goes ILL with.

ill at ease →EASE[1].

Ill got, ill spent. 《諺》悪銭身につかず．

***ill to** do* …しにくい ▪ He is *ill to* please. 彼は気むずかしい．

it goes ill with …がひどい目にあう，うまくいかない ▪ *It* would have *gone ill with* him. 彼はひどい目にあうところだった ▪ I am afraid *it* will *go ill with* him at the trial. 彼は裁判で負けるのではないかと思う．

***It ill becomes** a person **to** do.* →BECOME.

it is ill with →IT is well with.

not speak ill of the dead 死者の悪口を言わない ▪ You should*n't speak ill of the dead*. 死者の悪口を言うもんじゃない． ☞Solon の法律の一つ De mortuis nil nisi bonum "Of the dead (say) nothing but good." の自由訳から．

take it ill →TAKE[2].

use** a person **ill 人を虐待する ▪ His chef *used* him *ill*. 彼の頭(かしら)は彼を虐待した．

work ill =do ILL.

ill-gotten /ìlgɑ́tən|-gɔ́tən/ 形 ***ill-gotten gains [wealth]*** 不正手段で得た富 ▪ He is now enjoying his *ill-gotten gains*. 彼はいま不正利得を享受している ▪ I would rather die than batten on *ill-gotten wealth*. 不正手段で得た富で栄えるよりむしろ死んだほうがよい《渇しても盗泉の水を飲まず》．

Ill-gotten wealth seldom descends [thrives not] to the third generation. 《諺》不正の富は三代までは続かない．

illness /ílnəs/ 名 ***a diplomatic illness*** (パーティー・行事を)欠席する口実になる仮(け)病 ▪ Is this a real illness or *a diplomatic illness*? 本当に病気なのか，それとも仮病だろうか．

illusion /ɪlúːʒən/ 名 ***be under no illusion [illusions]*** 真の状態が十分わかっている，思い違いはしていない ▪ I *was under no illusion* about the difficulty of my new job. 今度の仕事の難しさは充分にわきまえていた．

be [labor] under the illusion that …という妄想を抱いている，と勘違いしている ▪ He *is under the illusion that* he is a genius. 彼は自分は天才だと勘違いしている．

illustration /ìləstréɪʃən/ 名 ***by way of illustration*** 例証として ▪ Let me quote a passage *by way of illustration*. 例証として1箇所を引用しましょう．

in illustration of …を例証するために, の例証として ▪ This may be cited *in illustration of* a principle. 原理の例証としてこれをあげることができる.

illustrative /ɪlʌ́strətɪv/ 形 ***(be) illustrative of*** …を例証する ▪ This fact *is illustrative of* the principle. この事実はその原理を例証する.

ill-will /ìlwíl/ 名 ***provoke [harbor] ill-will*** 遺恨(いこん)[悪意, 敵意]を抱かせる ▪ A slight misunderstanding *provoked* long-lasting *ill-will* between them. ちょっとした誤解がもとで二人の間に積年の恨みが生じた.

image[1] /ímɪdʒ/ 名 ***a graven image*** (崇拝の対象として用いる)神の彫像 ▪ The Bible forbids us to even bow to *a graven image.* 聖書は私たちが神の彫像に頭を下げることさえ禁じている. ☞モーゼの十戒の第2項(《聖》*Exod.* 20. 4)から.

be the very image of …に生き写しである ▪ He *is the very image of* his father. 彼は父親に生き写しである.

change** one's **image 以前とは異なる自分の印象を作り上げる ▪ You really must *change your image* if you want to be more popular. もっと人気を上げたければイメージチェンジをしなくてはだめだ.

dent an image 評判を傷つける ▪ The charges against him were aimed to *dent his image.* 彼への非難は彼のイメージを傷つけることを狙ったものだった.

erase an image ある印象を払拭する ▪ The teacher wanted to *erase the image* of being a strict disciplinarian. その教師はしつけが厳しいというイメージを消したいと思った.

the spitting [the spit and] image of →the very SPIT of.

image[2] /ímɪdʒ/ 動 ***image** oneself* 姿を写す ▪ The mountains *imaged themselves* in the lake. 山々は湖に姿を映していた.

***image ... to** oneself* …を心に描く ▪ *Image to yourselves* the scenery of rivers and lakes. 川や湖水の風景を心に描いてみなさい.

imagination /ɪmæ̀dʒənéɪʃən/ 名 ***beyond all imagination*** 全く想像もつかぬほど ▪ It is vital *beyond all imagination.* それは全く想像以上に重要である.

by no [not ... by any] stretch of (the) imagination どんなに想像をたくましくしても…しない ▪ *By no stretch of imagination* can I see Williams as a scientist. いくら想像をたくましくしても, ウィリアムズを科学者と見ることはできない.

catch [capture, seize, grip] the imagination of (あるグループ)の心を捕える ▪ Socialism had *caught the imagination of* the young. 社会主義は青年たちの心を捕えていた.

draw on imagination 工夫を凝らす; 嘘をでっちあげる ▪ When facts fail, they *draw on imagination.* 事実がなくなると嘘をでっちあげる.

not have enough imagination to come in from [out of] the rain →not have enough sense to come in from the RAIN.

The imagination boggles. → The mind BOGGLEs.

imagine /ɪmǽdʒən/ 動 ***Can you imagine!*** 驚くじゃないか! ▪ John migrated to Finland! *Can you imagine!* ジョンがフィンランドへ移住したって! 驚くじゃないか!

I can imagine. 私もそう思います ▪ Jenny's story is very funny.—*I can imagine.* ジェニーの話は非常におもしろい—同感です.

imagine things いろいろ妄想する; 思い違いをする ▪ I successfully fought my fear, convinced that I was only *imagining things.* 私はいろいろ妄想していたのだと悟って心配しなくなった ▪ That policeman's not after you. Don't *imagine things.* あの警察官は君を追跡しているのではない. 思い違いをしてはいけない.

imitation /ìmətéɪʃən/ 名 ***Imitation is the sincerest (form of) flattery.*** 《諺》模倣は最も心からなるへつらい(の形)である.

in imitation of …をまねて ▪ He wrote poems *in imitation of* Tennyson. 彼はテニスンをまねて詩を作った.

imitative /ímətèɪtɪv|ímətətɪv/ 形 ***be imitative of*** …をまねている ▪ The temple *was imitative of* the first in Thrace. この神殿はトラキアの最初のものをまねたものである.

immemorial /ìməmɔ́:riəl/ 形 ***(from) time immemorial*** →TIME[1].

immerse /ɪmɔ́:rs/ 動 ***be immersed in/immerse** oneself **in*** **1** …にひたる, ふける ▪ He *was immersed in* mathematics. 彼は数学に没頭していた.

2 …に陥っている ▪ He *was immersed in* difficulties. 彼は窮境に陥っていた ▪ They *immersed themselves in* debt to the company. 彼らはその会社に首が回らぬほど借金していた.

immune /ɪmjú:n/ 形 ***(be) immune against*** …を免れている ▪ The fort *was immune against* attack from the sea. その要塞(さい)は海からの攻撃を受ける恐れはなかった.

be immune from **1** …に対して免疫がある ▪ He *is immune from* smallpox as the result of vaccination. 彼は予防接種の結果, 天然痘への免疫がある.

2 …を免除されている; (悪・有害物)から逃れている ▪ They *are immune from* taxation. それらは免税になっている ▪ Ireland has *been immune from* snakes. アイルランドにはこれまでヘビはずっといない.

(be) immune to …に免疫が(ある) ▪ An animal *was* thus rendered *immune to* subsequent attacks. 動物はこのようにして, それから後の発病に対して免疫ができた.

immure /ɪmjʊ́ər/ 動 ***immure** oneself **in*** **1** …に閉じこもる ▪ He *immured himself* for three years *in* a German university. 彼はあるドイツの大学に3年間籠城した.

2 …に没頭する ▪ He *was immured in* his work. 彼は仕事に没頭していた.

imp /ɪmp/ 動 ***imp a wing* [*a bird*] *with* (*feathers*)** 翼[鳥]に羽をついで強化する ▪ The falconer *imped* his broken *wings with* better plumes. タカ匠は折れた翼によりよい羽をついで強化した.

***imp the wings* (*of*)** (…の)飛行力を(羽を補って)強化する ▪ *The wings of* Wordsworth's muse *were imped* with religious doctrine. ワーズワスの詩の飛翔力は宗教的教理によって強化された ▪ My spirit *imped the wings* for stronger flight. 私の精神はもっと強く飛ぶために翼を強化した.

impact /ímpækt/ 名 ***have an impact on*** …に対して衝撃となる ▪ His return will *have an impact on* the public. 彼の帰還は世間に対して衝撃となるであろう.

on impact 衝撃で, 衝突したはずみで, ぶつかった瞬間に ▪ The two planes caught fire *on impact*. 衝突するや2機とも火を噴いた.

impaired /ɪmpéərd/ 形 ***hearing-impaired*** 《婉曲》聴覚障害をもつ, 難聴の ▪ The program was closed-captioned for *hearing-impaired* viewers. その番組は耳の不自由な視聴者のために字幕表示になっていた.

visually impaired 《婉曲》視力障害をもつ ▪ The fever left her *visually impaired*. その熱病のために彼女は目が不自由になった.

impatience /ɪmpéɪʃəns/ 名 ***have an impatience of*** …をがまんしていられない ▪ I *have an impatience of* oppression. 圧制にがまんがならない.

with impatience もどかしがって; 待ち遠しく ▪ I was waiting *with impatience* for your return. あなたの帰りを今か今かと待ちかねていた.

impatient /ɪmpéɪʃənt/ 形 ***impatient at*** …にいらいらして ▪ He was *impatient at* the slow, tedious narrative of the old man. 彼は老人ののろく退屈な話を聞きあぐんでいた.

impatient for …を待ちかねて; をもどかしがって ▪ He was *impatient for* the news of my success. 彼は私の成功の知らせを待ちかねていた.

impatient of …をがまんできないで; が大きらいで ▪ The students went on strike, being *impatient of* control. 生徒たちは, 束縛に耐えかねてストライキをした ▪ He is *impatient of* poverty. 彼は貧乏が大きらいだ.

***impatient to** do* …したくてたまらない ▪ I am *impatient to* see the curiosities of the city. その市の名物を見たくてたまらない.

impatient with …に腹をたてて ▪ The teacher was *impatient with* the idle fellow. 先生はその怠け者に腹をたてていた.

impeachment /ɪmpíːtʃmənt/ 名 ***deny* [*own, admit*] *the soft impeachment*** 《戯》(穏やかな)問責をはねつける[受けいれる] (Sheridan, *The Rivals* 5. 3. 12) ▪ He *owned the soft impeachment*, and relented at once. 彼は問責を受けいれてすぐ態度を和らげた.

without impeachment of waste 《法》毀損を問われることなく《終身借地人が土地を毀損しても告発されることがないことを保証する文句》 ▪ Under your marriage settlement you are tenant for life, *without impeachment of waste*. 結婚財産贈与契約に基づき, あなたは土地毀損を問われることのない終身の借地人である.

impel /ɪmpél/ 動 ***impel … to** (do)* 強いて[心を駆って]…させる ▪ He *was impelled to* crime by poverty. 彼は貧に迫られて罪を犯した ▪ I felt *impelled to* take sides in the quarrel. 私はそのけんかに加勢しないではいられなかった.

imperative /ɪmpérətɪv/ 形 ***be imperative on … to** do* …が…することは最も必要だ ▪ It *was imperative on* Japan *to* be a democracy. 日本が民主主義国になることが最も必要だった.

imperfection /ìmpərfékʃən/ 名 ***with all** one's **imperfections on** one's **head*** いろいろな欠点[罪悪のかずかず]を持ったままで[持っているにもかかわらず] (cf. Sh., *Haml.* 1. 4. 79) ▪ He was sent to his account *with all his imperfections on his head*. 彼は多くの罪悪を身に負いながらあの世へ送られた.

impermeable /ɪmpə́ːrmiəbəl/ 形 ***be impermeable to*** (水・空気など)を通さない ▪ The waterproof *is impermeable to* water. 防水服は水を通さない.

impertinence /ɪmpə́ːrtənəns/ 名 ***have the impertinence to** do* 失敬にも…する ▪ He *had the impertinence to* write me such a letter. 彼は無礼にも私にそんな手紙をよこした.

impertinent /ɪmpə́ːrtənənt/ 形 ***impertinent to*** …に無礼で; に不適切な, 無関係の ▪ He is *impertinent to* his master. 彼は主人に無礼だ ▪ That is a point *impertinent to* the matter. それはその問題に関係のない点だ.

impervious /ɪmpə́ːrviəs/ 形 ***impervious to***

1 (水など)を通さないで ▪ Rubber boots are *impervious to* water. ゴム長ぐつは水を通さない.

2 (心が)…に感じない, がわからない ▪ He is *impervious to* criticism. 彼は批評を何とも思わない ▪ She is *impervious to* reason. 彼女は道理がわからない.

impetus /ímpətəs/ 名 ***give* [*lend*] (*an*) *impetus to*** …を促進する, に刺激を与える ▪ It *gave an* enormous *impetus to* the movement. それはその運動に莫大な刺激を与えた ▪ It will *lend* some *impetus to* the movement. それはその運動をいくぶん促進するであろう.

with impetus 非常な勢いで ▪ The two trains came into collision *with* great *impetus*. 両列車は非常に猛烈な勢いで衝突した.

implication /ìmpləkéɪʃən/ 名 ***by implication*** 暗黙のうちに ▪ They agreed with each other *by implication*. 彼らは暗黙裏に意見が一致した.

implore /ɪmplɔ́ːr/ 動 ***implore* (*of*)** *a person* ***to** do* 人に…してくれと嘆願する ▪ I *implored* (*of*) him *to* let us leave the place. 我々にそこを去らせてくれと, 彼に嘆願した.

import[1] /ímpɔ:rt/ 名 ***of* (*great*) *import*** (きわめて)重大な ▪ It is a matter *of great import.* それは重大な事柄だ. ☞import=importance.

import[2] /ɪmpɔ́:rt/ 動 ***it imports*** *a person* ***to*** *do* …することは人に重要である ▪ *It imports* us *to* know what will result. どんな結果になるかを知るのは我々にとって重要である.

importance /ɪmpɔ́:rtəns/ 名 ***attach importance to*** …を重視する ▪ Orientals *attach importance to* poetry. 東洋人は詩を重視する.

(***be***) ***full of*** *one's* ***own importance*** 《軽蔑》自分を偉いと思って(いる) ▪ The boss *is* too *full of his own importance.* 社長は自分を偉いと思いすぎている.

know [***be conscious of, have a good idea of***] *one's* ***own importance*** うぬぼれている; もったいぶっている ▪ The boy seemed to *be conscious of his own importance.* その少年はうぬぼれているようだった.

of* (*great*) *importance (非常に)重要な ▪ He is a person *of importance.* 彼は重要人物である.

of no importance とるに足らぬ ▪ It is *of no importance* who does it. 誰がそれをするかは問題でない.

set [***put***] ***importance on*** …を重要視する ▪ Don't *put* too much *importance on* theory. 理論を重んじすぎてはいけない.

with an air of importance 偉そうに, もったいぶって; 仰々しく ▪ He spoke *with an air of importance.* 彼は偉そうにして話した.

impose /ɪmpóʊz/ 動 ***impose*** *one's* ***company on*** …に押しかける ▪ I don't want to *impose my company on* other people. 他の人たちの所へ押しかけて行きたくない.

impose *oneself* ***on*** …に押しかけて行く ▪ You should not *impose yourself on* people who don't want you. あなたを求めもしない人々の所へ押しかけて行くべきではない.

impossible /ɪmpásəbəl|-pɔ́s-/ 形 ***be impossible of*** …ができない ▪ Certitude *is impossible of* attainment. 確実性は達成できない.

impress[1] /ímpres/ 名 ***leave an impress upon*** …に足跡[影響]を残す ▪ He *left an impress upon* his age. 彼は彼の時代に足跡を残した.

impress[2] /ɪmprés/ 動 ***impress*** *a person* ***in*** *one's* ***favor*** →FAVOR[1].

impression /ɪmpréʃən/ 名 ***be under the impression that*** …と思っている ▪ I *was under the impression that* you were out of town. あなたは町にいないと思っていた.

First impressions are the most lasting. 《諺》初めて会ったときの君の様子を相手はよく覚えているものだ《初対面のときは, よい身なりと行動を心がけることが大切》.

give [***create, get, have***] ***a false impression of*** …について誤った印象を与える[作りだす, 得る, 持っている] ▪ Some parents *have a false impression of* their child's ability. 自分の子供の能力に関して間違った印象を持っている親もいる.

give an impression of …の感じ[印象]を与える ▪ It *gave* me *an impression of* cruelty. それは私に残酷な感じを与えた.

give *one's* ***impression*(*s*) *of*** …に関する印象を述べる ▪ He *gave his impressions of* Europe. 彼はヨーロッパの印象を述べた.

have an impression that …という気[感じ]がする ▪ I *have an impression that* I have met him somewhere before. 私は彼に以前にどこかで会ったような気がする.

leave an impression upon …に印象を残す ▪ The event has *left a* deep *impression upon* my memory. その事件は私の心に深い印象を残した.

make an impression on **1** …に感動[感銘]を与える; に印象を与える ▪ He tried to *make an impression on* her. 彼は彼女に感銘を与えようとした ▪ Try to *make a* good *impression on* your girlfriend's parents. ガールフレンドの両親によい印象を与えるように心がけなさい.

2 …に影響[効果]を及ぼす ▪ The bombardment *made* no *impression on* the fort. 爆撃はその要塞には効き目がなかった.

improve[1] /ɪmprú:v/ 名 ***on the improve*** 《主に豪口》良くなりつつあって ▪ Conditions are *on the improve.* 事情が好転している.

improve[2] /ɪmprú:v/ 動 ***improve*** *oneself* 進歩する; 向上する ▪ I am just trying to *improve myself.* 私は今向上しようと努めています ▪ I wish to *improve myself* in English. 英語を上達させたい.

improve ... out of existence 改良を施して…をなくす ▪ The native breed of boar *was improved out of existence.* 在来種のイノシシは品種改良されて絶滅した.

improve the occasion [***the opportunity***] **1** 機会を利用する ▪ He *improved the occasion* to urge the necessity of economy. 彼はその機会を利用して, 節約の必要を力説した.

2 機会を捕えて説教する ▪ He *improved the occasion* by telling how important punctuality was. 彼はその機会を捕えて, 時間厳守がいかに大切であるかを説教した.

3 出来事から道徳的教訓を引き出す; その機を自分の教訓とする ▪ I shall never fail to *improve the occasion.* 私はその機を自分の教訓とします.

improve the [***each***] ***shining hour*** 好機を利用する (Isaac Watts, *Divine Songs for Children* 20) ▪ You *improved the shining hour* to great purpose. 君はきわめてうまく好機を利用した.

improvement /ɪmprú:vmənt/ 名 ***be an improvement on*** …よりも上出来である; より一段の進歩である ▪ This composition *is an improvement on* your last. この作文はあなたのこの前の作文よりもずっとよい.

imprudence /ɪmprú:dəns/ 名 ***have the imprudence to*** *do* うかつにも…する ▪ He *had the* *imprudence to* run into debt. 彼はうかつにも借金した.

impudence /ímpjədəns/ 名 ***have the impudence to*** *do* ずうずうしくも[厚かましくも]…する ▪ He *had the impudence to* say so in my presence. 彼は私の前で厚かましくもそう言った.

impulse /ímpʌls/ 名 ***feel*** [***be seized with***] ***an impulse to*** *do* …しようという衝動を感じる[にかられる] ▪ I *was seized with an impulse to* kill him. 彼を殺してやろうという衝動にかられた.

from impulse =on (an) IMPULSE.

give an impulse to …を促進する, に刺激を与える ▪ Rivalry *gives an impulse to* trade. 競争は商売に刺激を与える.

on (***an***) ***impulse*** 衝動的に, 考えずに, 出来心で ▪ She often acts *on impulse*. 彼女はよく出来心で動く ▪ The door was open, and *on an impulse* he went into the room. 戸が開いていた. そして彼は衝動的にその部屋に入って行った.

I

on the impulse of the moment その時[その場]のはずみで, 出来心で ▪ He did a very foolish thing *on the impulse of the moment*. 彼はその場のはずみで非常にばかなことをした.

under the impulse of …にかられて ▪ She opened the box *under the impulse of* curiosity. 彼女は好奇心にかられてその箱をあけた.

impunity /ɪmpjúːnəti/ 名 ***with impunity*** 罰を受けないで, 無難に ▪ You cannot violate the laws of nature *with impunity*. 人は自然の法則にそむけば罰を受けないわけにはいかない.

imputation /ìmpjətéɪʃən/ 名 ***cast an imputation on*** …に傷をつける, 汚名をきせる ▪ They *cast an imputation on* his character. 彼らは彼の人格に傷をつけた.

make an imputation against …を傷つける ▪ They *made an imputation against* his good name. 彼らは彼の名声を傷つけた.

in[1] /ɪn/ 名 ***get*** [***have***] ***an in*** 《主に米口》コネをつける[がある]; 後ろ盾を得る, わたりをつける[がついている] (*with*) ▪ In business, it helps to *have an in*. ビジネスではコネがあるのは役に立つ ▪ I had a chance to *get an "in" with* the director. 私は映画監督とコネをつける機会がありました ▪ He was chosen because he *had an in with* many of the party leaders. 彼が選ばれたのは党首の多くとわたりがついていたためだった. ☞in「手づる, コネ」.

give *a person* ***an in with*** 《主に米口》コネ[わたり]をつけてやる ▪ It *gave* him *an in with* the future first lady. それによって彼は未来の大統領夫人とコネができた.

the ins and outs of …の裏表, 一部始終 ▪ I am still learning *the ins and outs of* the foreign market. 私はまだ外国市場の裏表を勉強中だ.

in[2] /ɪn/ 前副 ***all in*** →ALL.

be in and out of 《口》…にしばしば出入りしている; の常連である ▪ He's *in and out of* jail all the time. 彼は刑務所にしょっちゅう出たり入ったりしている.

be in for it 《口》 **1** (罰・叱責は)免れない ▪ I shall *be in for it* when the boss hears about it. 社長がそれを聞いたら, 私はきっとしかられるだろう.

2 すっかりはまりこんでいる ▪ I *am in for it* now, over head and ears. 私は今は首ったけでほれている ▪ The speaker called my name. I *was in for it* and advanced to the table. 議長は私の名を呼んだ. 私は引くに引かれぬことになったので, テーブルの方へ進んだ.

be in it (***up to the neck***) 《口》 **1** (ひどく)困ってる ▪ He *is in it up to the neck*. 彼はひどく困窮している.

2 (深く)入っている[はまりこんでいる] ▪ They had a good time, but I *was* not *in it*. 彼らは楽しく過ごしたが私はそれに加わらなかった.

be in there 《英口》好感を持たれる, 魅力がある ▪ See how that girl is looking at you? You*'re in there*! 君を見ているあの娘の目つきといったら. 君にぞっこんだ.

(***be***) ***well in*** **1** 《競馬》(ハンディキャップ係に)有利な条件を与えられて(いる) ▪ The handicapper considerately classed the horse among the middle ones. He *was well in*. ハンディキャップ係は馬を思いやり深く中級の中へ入れた. その馬は恵まれていた.

2 《口》安楽に暮らして(いる) ▪ You want to *be well in* all the time. 君はいつも安楽に暮らしたいのだ.

3 《口》投機がうまくいって(いる) ▪ My brother has *been well in*. 兄はこのところ有利な投機をやっている.

for all there's in it 《口》全能力をあげて ▪ You've got to play *for all there's in it*. 精一杯プレーしなくてはいけない.

have it in *one* ***to*** *do* →HAVE[2].

in *oneself* →ONESELF.

in and in 内へ内へと ▪ He went *in and in* deeply. 彼はどんどん奥深くへ入って行った.

in and out **1** 見えたり隠れたり; 出たり入ったり, うねりくねって ▪ Her feet beneath her petticoat stole *in and out*. ペチコートの下の彼女の足がちらちらと見えたり隠れたりした ▪ Their affections were not so *in and out*. 彼らの愛情にはたいした消長はなかった ▪ The coat has been *in and out* five times. そのコートは5度も裏返しされた.

2 内も外もすっかり ▪ The woman knows a man *in and out*. その女は男の内も外もすっかり知っている.

in and out family (昔の)救貧院に出入り頻繁な家庭 ▪ One notable "*In and Out*" *family* entered and discharged itself 62 times. 救貧院への出入りが実に頻繁なある家族は62回入ったり出たりした.

in and out work 続かない仕事 ▪ This summer I have *in and out work*. この夏は一時的な仕事をしている.

in as much as →INASMUCH as.

In for a penny, in for a pound. 《諺》やりかけたことは終わりまでやり通せ; 乗りかけた船は後へひくな.

in here [***there***] (中をさして)ここ[あそこ]で ▪ Brr! It's freezing cold *in here*. ブルブルッ! ここの中は凍えるように寒いや.

in so far as →SO.

in so much that [***as***] →INSOMUCH that.

in that 《雅》…という点において; なのだから ▪ Men differ from brutes *in that* they can think and speak. 人間は考えたり話したりすることができるという点において, けだものと異なる ▪ *In that* he killed Abel he was a murderer. 彼はアベルを殺したがゆえに人殺しであった.

in their hundreds [***thousands***] 何百[何千]となく, 非常にたくさん ▪ Midges were out *in their thousands*. ブヨが何千となく出ていた.

in toto 全体として, 全部, 全面的に ▪ The store refused our suggestion *in toto*. その店は我々の提案を全面的に拒絶した.

In with...! 〚命令文で〛…を入れよ!; 入れ! ▪ *In with* fortune! 福は内 ▪ *In with* you! 入りなさい.

it is not in *a person* [*a thing*] ***to*** *do* 人[物]は性質上…することはできない ▪ *It is not in* mortals *to* command success. 人間は性質上, 成功を左右することはできない ▪ *It is not in* him *to* tell a lie. 彼は性質上, 嘘は言えない.

marry in and in →MARRY².

not in it (***with***) 《口》(…には)とてもかなわない; (に)劣る ▪ This work is *not in it with* that. この作品はあの作品にとても及ばない ▪ His rivals are *not in it with* him. 彼のライバルたちはとても彼にはかなわない. ☞競走用語から.

one in ten 一割; 十中の一 ▪ The losses were *one in ten*. 損害は一割であった《多い》 ▪ Not *one in ten* can do it. それのできる人は10人中一人もない.

(***there's***) ***nothing*** [***little, not much***] ***in it*** (二者の間に)全く[たいした]違い[優劣]はない ▪ Is it nearer to go by Broad Street or High Street?—*There is not much in it*. ブロード通りとハイ通りとどちらを通って行くのが近いか?—たいした違いはない. ☞競走用語から.

inadequate /ɪnǽdɪkwət/ 形 ***inadequate to*** [***to*** *do*] …に[するに]不適当で, 不十分で ▪ His revenues were *inadequate to* his expenses [*to* meet the expenses]. 彼の収入は彼の支出[その経費をまかなう]に足らなかった.

inappreciative /ìnəpríːʃətɪv|-ʃiə-/ 形 ***inappreciative of*** …の真価を認めないで, 鑑賞力がなくて ▪ He is *inappreciative of* a work of art. 彼は美術品の鑑賞力がない.

inapt /ɪnǽpt/ 形 ***be inapt at*** …がへたである ▪ A man may *be inapt at* horticulture. 園芸のへたな人もいる.

(***be***) ***inapt for*** …に不適当である ▪ These persons *are* considered *inapt for* driving. このような人たちは運転には向いていないと考えられる.

inasmuch /ìnəzmʌ́tʃ/ 副 ***inasmuch as*** …だから ▪ He knows it *inasmuch as* I have told him. 私が話したから彼はそれを知っている.

incapable /ɪnkéɪpəbəl/ 形 ***drunk and incapable*** →DRUNK and disorderly.

incapable of **1** (物・事が)…されるのを許さない; されるに耐えない ▪ The plan is *incapable of* improvement [being improved]. その計画は改善の余地がない ▪ These shoes are *incapable of* repair. この靴は修繕に耐えない.

2 (人が)…する能力がない ▪ I am still *incapable of* much exertion. 私はまだたいした活動はできない.

3 (人格的に)とてもできない ▪ He is *incapable of* telling a lie. 彼はとても嘘はつけない ▪ I am *incapable of* fear. 私は恐れを知らぬ.

4 《法》…する資格がない ▪ He is *incapable of* being elected a member. 彼は会員に選ばれる資格がない.

incapacious /ɪnkəpéɪʃəs/ 形 ***incapacious of*** (知的に)…に無能な ▪ He was *incapacious of* comprehending a law. 彼は法律を理解する能力がなかった.

incarnation /ìnkɑːrnéɪʃən/ 名 ***look*** [***be***] ***the incarnation of*** …の権化のように見える[である] ▪ She *looked the incarnation of* health. 彼女は健康そのものに見えた.

incense¹ /ínsens/ 名 ***burn incense*** 香をたく; (人に)へつらう ▪ He *burns* the *incense* of flattery beneath his master's nostrils. 彼は主人の目の前でおべっかを言う.

incense² /ɪnséns/ 動 ***be incensed at*** (あること)に激怒している ▪ He *was incensed at* her conduct. 彼は彼女の行為に激怒していた.

be incensed with [***against***] (人)に対して激怒している ▪ Why *is* he so *incensed against* us? 彼はなぜ我々に対してそんなに激怒しているのか.

inch¹ /ɪntʃ/ 名 ***an inch of cold iron*** [***steel***] (短)剣の一突き ▪ *An inch of cold iron* brought this wonderful career to a close. 剣の一突きでこのすばらしい生涯が終わりを告げた.

by inches **1** 徐々に; 少しずつ ▪ He died *by inches*. 彼は徐々に息を引き取った ▪ The ship was sailing *by inches*. 船は少しずつ進んでいた.

2 わずかのところで ▪ The car missed me *by inches*. その車はすんでのところで私にぶつかるところだった.

contest [***dispute, fight***] ***every inch of the ground*** 寸土も譲らじと奮戦する ▪ Although the enemy outnumbered us, we *disputed every inch of the ground*. 敵は数において我々に勝っていたが, 我々は一歩も譲らずに奮戦した.

every inch 全く; あらゆる点で; すみからすみまで ▪ He is a gentleman, *every inch* of him. 彼は全くの紳士だ ▪ I know *every inch* of this town. 私はこの町はすみからすみまで知っている ▪ He is *every inch* a king. 彼はどう見ても国王である ▪ I trembled *every inch* of me. 私は体中ふるえた.

every inch of the way 途中ずっと ▪ I'm going to walk *every inch of the way* from here to town. ここから町までずっと歩いて行くつもりだ.

give an inch on (人の意見)に一歩譲る[賛成する] ▪ He never *gave an inch on* that. 彼はそのことを少しでも認めなかった ▪ Our boss never *gave an inch on* what we said. 我々の上司は我々の意見に一歩も譲らなかった ☞Give him an inch and he'll take a mile という諺から.

Give him an inch (***and he'll take a yard*** [***a mile, an ell***]). 《諺》寸を与えれば尺を望む《少し譲ればつけあがってさらに要求する》. ☞昔の尺度の ell は英国では45インチ.

if (*one* ***is***) ***an inch*** 1インチでもあるとすれば; (身長などが)立派に, 確かに ▪ He stands six feet, *if* he *is an inch*. 彼は確かに6フィートある.

inch by inch 近く接して; 徐々に, 少しずつ; 入念に ▪ Follow him *inch by inch*. 彼にくっついて行きなさい ▪ He crawled *inch by inch* along the rails. 彼は手すりに沿って, 少しずつ進んだ ▪ The water will get shallower *inch by inch*. 水は徐々に浅くなるであろう ▪ I have examined that cloth *inch by inch*. 私はその服地を入念に調べた.

one's ***inches*** 人の身長 ▪ His legs are too long for *his inches*. 彼の脚は身長の割りに長すぎる.

not budge [***give, move***] ***an inch*** 一歩も譲らない ▪ I'm ready to compromise, but he wo*n't budge an inch*. こっちは歩み寄ろうとしているのに彼は頑として譲ろうとしない.

I

not trust *a person* ***an inch*** 《英》ほんの少しも人を信頼しない ▪ He's smart, but I would*n't trust* him *an inch*. 頭は切れるが, 彼のことはこれっぽっちも信用しないね.

of *a person's* ***inches*** (だれだれ)くらいの背たけの ▪ He is a fellow *of your inches*. 彼はあなたぐらいの身長の男だ.

to an inch 寸分たがわず, ぴたりと ▪ He told the height *to an inch*. 彼はその高さをぴたりと言い当てた.

within an inch of …にきわめて近く; 危うく…するところで[ところまで] ▪ They came *within an inch of* us and stood there. 彼らは我々の鼻先まで来てそこに立った ▪ He was *within an inch of* falling into the pond. 彼は危うくその池に落ちるところだった.

within an inch of *one's* ***life*** 死ぬ一歩手前まで ▪ They flogged him *within an inch of his life*. 奴らは彼をなぐって半殺しにした.

inch[2] /ɪntʃ/ 動 ***inch*** *one's* ***way along*** [***across, back***] 少しずつ苦労して進む ▪ Our troops *inched their way along* the road. わが軍はその道路を少しずつ苦労して進んだ.

inchmeal /íntʃmìːl/ 副 ***by inchmeal*** じりじりと, 徐々に (= INCH by inch) ▪ He must die *by inchmeal*. 彼はじりじりと死んでいくにちがいない.

incidence /ínsədəns/ 名 ***the incidence of the tax*** 税の帰着 ▪ What's *the incidence of the tax*? この税は誰にかかるのか.

incident /ínsədənt/ 形 ***incident on*** [***upon***] …に投射して ▪ Rays of light were *incident upon* a mirror. 光線が鏡面に投射していた.

incident to **1** …にありがちな; に伴いやすい, つきものの ▪ These diseases are *incident to* childhood. これらの病気は幼年時代にありがちだ.

2《法》付帯の ▪ The trustee exercised the rights *incident to* the legal estate. 受託者は法定不動産に付帯する権利を行使した.

incidental /ìnsədéntəl/ 形 ***incidental to*** **1** …につきものの ▪ The trials are *incidental to* married life. その苦労は結婚生活につきものだ.

2 付帯の ▪ Health insurance is one of the benefits *incidental to* employment. 健康保険は雇用に付帯する福利の一つである.

incite /ɪnsáɪt/ 動 ***incite*** *a person* ***to*** *do* 人を励まして…させる, そそのかして…させる ▪ We *incited* him *to* work harder. 我々は彼を励ましてもっと一生懸命働かせた.

inclinable /ɪnkláɪnəbəl/ 形 ***inclinable to*** [***to*** *do*] **1** …したい気持ちである, に気がある ▪ His master was *inclinable to* keep him. 彼の主人は彼を雇っておきたい気持ちであった ▪ He is *inclinable to* mercy. 彼には慈悲心がある.

2 …に好意があって; に好都合で ▪ I am rather *inclinable to* Germans. 私はドイツ人にむしろ好意を持っている ▪ These circumstances are *inclinable to* Japanese interests. これらの事情は日本の利益に好都合だ.

inclination /ìnklənéɪʃən/ 名 ***against*** *one's* ***inclination*** 不本意ながら, 心ならずも ▪ *Against my inclination* I tried to punish him. 私は心ならずも彼を罰しようとした.

follow *one's* (***own***) ***inclination*** 自分の好きなようにする ▪ Kings are not always free to *follow their own inclinations*. 国王たちも必ずしも自由に自分の望みどおりにできるとはかぎらない.

force *a person's* ***inclinations*** 人のいやなことを無理にさせる ▪ I will not *force your inclinations*. あなたのいやなことを無理にさせようとは思わない.

have an inclination for [***to, to*** *do*] **1** …が好きである ▪ He *has a* strong *inclination for* sports. 彼はスポーツが大好きだ.

2 …する気がある ▪ I don't *have* time nor *inclination for* letter-writing. 私は手紙を書く時間も気もない ▪ I *have an inclination to* print the letters. その手紙類を印刷したい気がある.

incline /ɪnkláɪn/ 動 ***be*** [***feel***] ***inclined for*** 心が…に向く; がしたい ▪ I don't *feel* much *inclined for* work. 私はあまり仕事がしたくない ▪ I know you *are* not *inclined for* company. 君が人付き合いに気が進まないのはわかっている.

be [***feel***] ***inclined to*** *do* **1** …したく思っている, したい気がある ▪ I *am inclined to* depart. 私は出て行きたいと思っている.

2 …するほうに傾いている, まあ…したいほうだ ▪ I *am inclined to* believe that. 私はまあそう思う ▪ I *am inclined to* dislike it. 私はそれはまあきらいなほうだ.

3 …する傾きがある ▪ I *am inclined to* fall asleep after a heavy meal. 私は大食後寝入る癖がある.

incline *one's* ***ear***(***s***) (***to***) …に耳を傾ける, を(好意を持って)聞いてやる (《聖》*Is*. 97. 17) ▪ It was unwise that he should *incline his ear to* them. 彼らの言に耳を傾けるとは彼は愚かだった.

incline *one's* [*a person's*] ***heart*** [***mind***] ***to*** *do* …する気になる[する気にならせる] ▪ *Incline your* *hearts to* keep this law. この法律を守る気になりなさい ▪ *Incline our hearts to* keep your laws. 我々をあなたのおきてを守る気にならせてください.

***incline to** do* **1** (生まれつき)...の傾きがある, しがちである ▪ I *incline to* run to fat. 太り癖がついている. **2** ...したいと思う, するのを好む ▪ I *incline to* think so. 私にはどうもそう思われる.

Right incline! 《号令》斜め右へ進め!

inclusive /ɪnklúːsɪv/ 形 ***inclusive of*** ...を含めて (↔EXCLUSIVE of) ▪ It is a party of ten *inclusive of* the host. 主催者を入れて10人の集まりだ.

incognito /ìnkɑgníːtoʊ|ìnkɔg-/ 名 ***drop** one's **incognito*** (匿名をやめて)本当の身分を名のる ▪ His Highness was pleased to *drop his incognito* the next morning. 殿下は翌朝本当の身分を名のられました.

income /ínkʌm/ 名 ***beyond*** [***within***] *one's* ***income*** 収入以上の[以内で] ▪ He lives *beyond his income*. 彼は収入以上の生活をしている.

incommensurable /ɪnkəménsərəbəl|-ʃərəbəl/ 形 (***be***) ***incommensurable with*** ...とは同一の基準で計れない, 比較すべくもない ▪ Companionship *is incommensurable with* money. 交わりと金銭とは比較の基準が違う.

incommensurate /ɪnkəménsərət|-ʃərət/ 形 (***be***) ***incommensurate with*** [***to***] ...と不釣合で; に不十分で, 耐えない ▪ Our means *are incommensurate with* our desires. 我々の資金は我々の願望に不十分である ▪ His abilities *are incommensurate to* the task. 彼の能力はその仕事に耐えない.

incommunicado /ìnkəmjùːnəkáːdoʊ/ 形 ***hold** a person **incommunicado*** 《米》人が外部と連絡するのを絶つ; 人を監禁する ▪ I *was held incommunicado* for 10 days. 10日間監禁された.

incomparable /ɪnkámpərəbəl/ 形 ***be incomparable with*** [***to***] ...と比較できない, 比較にならない ▪ The British patent system *is incomparable with* that of Germany. イギリスの特許制度はドイツのそれとは比較にならない.

incompatible /ìnkəmpǽtəbəl/ 形 ***be incompatible with*** ...と両立しない, 矛盾する ▪ Excessive drinking *is incompatible with* health. 飲みすぎは健康と両立しない ▪ Your argument *is incompatible with* logic. 君の議論は論理に合わない.

incongruous /ɪnkáŋgruəs|-kɔ́ŋ-/ 形 (***be***) ***incongruous with*** [***to***] ...と調和しない, つじつまの合わない ▪ His conduct *is incongruous with* his principles. 彼の行為は彼の主義と矛盾している ▪ These measures of capacity *are incongruous to* the new system. 容積を量るこれらの容器は, 新方式に合わない.

inconsiderable /ìnkənsídərəbəl/ 形 ***not inconsiderable*** 《文》かなり大きい ▪ He spends a *not inconsiderable* amount of money on entertainment. 彼は相当額を遊興費に使う.

inconsistent /ìnkənsístənt/ 形 ***be inconsistent with*** ...に一致しない, と矛盾する ▪ His actions *are inconsistent with* his principles. 彼の行為は彼の主義と矛盾している.

inconvenience[1] /ìnkənvíːniəns/ 名 ***at inconvenience*** 不便をしのんで; 万障繰り合わせて ▪ He attended the meeting *at* great *inconvenience*. 彼は万障繰り合わせて会に出席した ▪ I did it *at* some *inconvenience* to myself. 私にはいくらか迷惑であったが, それをやった.

cause inconvenience to** a person*/ ***put** a person **to inconvenience 人に不便[迷惑]をかける; 不愉快な思いをさせる ▪ I *was put to* great *inconvenience*. 私は非常に迷惑した.

inconvenience[2] /ìnkənvíːniəns/ 動 ***inconvenience** oneself* 苦労をする, 不自由をする ▪ Don't *inconvenience yourself* for my sake. どうぞ私にはおかまいなく.

incorporate /ɪnkɔ́ːrpərət/ 形 ***incorporate into*** [***in, with***] ...に解け込んで; と合体して ▪ This science is *incorporate in* these books. この学問はこれらの著書に詳しく述べられている ▪ I seem to grow *incorporate into* thee. 私はそなたと一体となっていくように思われる ▪ He found it hard to be *incorporate with* others. 彼は他人と打ち解けあうのが難しいとわかった.

increase[1] /ínkriːs/ 名 ***on the increase*** 増加して, 増大して ▪ The use of the equipment is generally *on the increase*. その機器の使用は概して増加しつつある.

increase[2] /ɪnkríːs/ 動 ***increase and multiply*** 産み増やす (《聖》*Gen.* 1. 28) ▪ Her highest purpose is to *increase, multiply* and replenish the earth. 彼女の最大の目的は産み, 増やし, 地を満たすことである.

incredulous /ɪnkrédʒələs|-krédjʊləs/ 形 ***be incredulous of*** ...を信じない ▪ They *were incredulous of* the rapid change. 彼らは急速な変化を信じなかった.

incriminate /ɪnkrímənèɪt/ 動 ***incriminate** oneself* (反証を承認することなどによって)自ら罪に陥る, 服罪する ▪ He feared *incriminating himself*. 彼は自ら罪に陥るのを恐れた.

inculcate /ɪnkʌ́lkeɪt|ínkʌlkèɪt/ 動 ***inculcate ... on*** [***in***] *a person's* ***mind*** (事実・思想・習慣など)を人の心に教えこむ, 植えつける ▪ Her tutor *inculcated* the idea *in her mind*. 家庭教師がその考えを彼女に教え込んだ ▪ The principles of book keeping *were* at last *inculcated upon his mind*. 簿記の原理がついに彼の心に教えこまれた.

incumbent /ɪnkʌ́mbənt/ 形 ***be incumbent on*** [***upon***] *a person* (***to*** *do*) (...するのが)人の義務である ▪ It *is incumbent on* you *to* warn them. 彼らに警告するのが君の義務だ ▪ It *is incumbent upon* me *to* mention that. それを述べるのが私の義務です.

incursion /ɪnkə́ːrʒən|-ʃən/ 名 ***make incur-***

I

sions into [***on***] …に侵入する, を襲撃する ▪ They *made incursions into* the enemy's country. 彼らは敵国に侵入した.

indebted /ɪndétəd/ 形 ***be*** [***stand***] ***indebted to*** *a person* **1** (…だけ)人に対して負債がある (*for, in*) ▪ I *am indebted to* him *for* a large sum. 私は彼に多額の負債がある ▪ I *stand indebted to* you *in* the amount of $10,000. 私はあなたに1万ドルの借金がある.

2 (…については)人に恩を受けている, 恩がある (*for*) ▪ I *am indebted to* you *for* your kindness. ご親切にありがとうございました ▪ *To* what business *am* I *indebted for* the honor of your visit? どのようなご用事でご来訪くださったのでしょうか.

indecision /ìndɪsíʒən/ 名 ***Hamlet-like indecision*** 煮え切らず[ハムレットのように]決断力がないこと ▪ After months of *Hamlet-like indecision*, he decided not to run for President the next spring. 何か月もうじうじと迷ったあげく彼は来春の大統領選には出馬しないことに決めた. ☞cf. Sh., *Haml.*

I

indeed /ɪndíːd/ 副 ***indeed ..., but*** なるほど…であるが ▪ *Indeed* he is young, *but* he is prudent. なるほど彼は若いが思慮深い.

indenture /ɪndéntʃər/ 名 ***take up*** [***be out of***] *one's* ***indentures*** 年季奉公をすませて主人から契約書を返してもらう, 年季を終える ▪ He is now entitled to *take up his indentures*. 彼はもう年季奉公を終える資格がある. ☞indenture「年季奉公契約書」.

independent /ìndɪpéndənt/ 形 (***as***) ***independent as a wood sawyer*** →WOOD SAWYER.

independent of **1** …から独立して ▪ The colonies became *independent of* the mother country. 植民地は母国から独立した.

2 …に無関係で, とは別で ▪ They do what they like quite *independent of* others' feelings. 彼らは他人の感情には全くおかまいなしに, 自分の好きにする.

3 …に依存しないで ▪ If you earn a good salary, you can be *independent of* your parents. 良い給料を取れば両親の世話にならずにすむ. ☞しばしば INDEPENDENTLY of の意に用いられる.

independently /ìndɪpéndəntli/ 副 ***independently of*** …から独立して; とは無関係に ▪ He will work at his canvas *independently of* his model. 彼はモデルを離れて絵をかくことがよくある ▪ He wrote it *independently of* others' help. 彼は他の人々に手伝ってもらわないでそれを書いた.

Indian /índiən/ 形 ***an Indian giver*** 《米》お返し目当てで贈り物をする人 ▪ He gave the fountain pen to you and he's not *an Indian giver*. 彼はその万年筆を君に本当にくれたのだ, 見返りをよこせなんて言わないよ.

hang [***put***] ***the Indian sign on*** 《米口》…に勝つ; に戦闘のあとを残す ▪ Paul *put the Indian sign on* them. ポールは彼らに勝った.

in Indian file →FILE.

Indian summer (晩秋の)小春日和; (末期の)幸福[平安, 繁栄]の状態 ▪ We had a brief cold spell, followed by an *Indian summer*. ちょっと寒い日が続いて, それから小春日和が来た ▪ It came out during the *Indian summer* of wartime literature. それは戦時文学の末期の隆盛期に出版された.

play Indian 《米》(子供が)北米先住民ごっこをする ▪ Boys delight in dressing up and *playing Indian*. 男の子らは北米先住民の服装をして遊ぶのを喜ぶ.

indicate /índəkèɪt/ 動 ***indicate the door*** (出て行けという意味で)ドアを指さす ▪ He *indicated the door* with a jerk of his head. 彼は頭をぐいと引いて出て行けと促した.

indication /ìndəkéɪʃən/ 名 ***give indication of*** (…の徴候)を示す ▪ A thermometer *gives indication of* changes in temperature. 寒暖計は温度の変化を示す.

indicative /ɪndíkətɪv/ 形 ***be indicative of*** …を示す ▪ His forehead *is indicative of* great mental power. 彼の額は知力のすぐれていることを示している.

indict /ɪndáɪt/ 動 ***indict*** *a person* ***on the charge of*** 人を…のかどで起訴する ▪ The offender *was indicted on the charge of* rape. 犯人は強姦罪で起訴された.

indictment /ɪndáɪtmənt/ 名 ***bring in*** [***lay***] ***an indictment*** (大陪審により)…の正式告発をする (*against*) ▪ Who dares *bring in* such *an indictment against* the divine law? 神のおきてに対してそのような大陪審による正式告発をする勇気のある者があろうか ▪ I have never *laid an indictment against* you. 私はあなたを告発したことはない.

draw (***up***) ***an indictment*** 告発状を起草する ▪ *The indictment was drawn up*. 告発状は起草された.

find an indictment (大陪審が)告発状を査定する ▪ The grand jury *found the indictment*. 大陪審はその告発状を査定した.

indifference /ɪndífərəns/ 名 ***of indifference*** 些細な; どうでもよい ▪ Success or failure is a matter *of indifference* to me. 成功するか失敗するかは私にとってはどうでもよいことです.

with indifference **1** よそよそしく, 冷淡に ▪ She treats my request *with indifference*. 彼女は私の頼みを冷淡に扱う.

2 無頓着に ▪ He looks upon wealth *with indifference*. 彼は富をまるで塵芥(じんかい)のように思っている.

3 虚心に, 平気で ▪ A judge should decide a case *with indifference*. 判事は事件を虚心に判決すべきである.

indifferent /ɪndífərənt/ 形 ***indifferent about*** …に冷淡な; に平気な ▪ He is *indifferent about* success or failure. 彼は成功失敗に無頓着である ▪ He is *indifferent about* my welfare. 彼は私の幸福に冷淡である.

indifferent to **1** …に重要でなく, どうでもよく; に無関係で ▪ Success or failure is *indifferent to* him. 成功失敗は彼には問題ではない ▪ She is *indifferent to* him. 彼女は彼の眼中にない.

2 …を感じない ▪ He is *indifferent to* pain. 彼は苦痛を感じない.

3 …に虚心[平気]で ▪ The judge was *indifferent to* the appeal. 判事はその訴えに動かされなかった.

4 …に無関心な, 冷淡な ▪ He is *indifferent to* politics. 彼は政治に無関心である ▪ She is *indifferent to* him. 彼女は彼に冷淡である.

indigent /índɪdʒənt/ 形 ***indigent of*** …が欠けて ▪ They are *indigent of* money. 彼らは金欠だ.

indignant /ɪndígnənt/ 形 ***indignant at*** (こと)に憤慨して ▪ He was *indignant at* injustice. 彼は非道にいきどおっていた.

indignant over …について憤慨して ▪ He is *indignant over* the matter. 彼はその問題について憤慨している.

indignant with [***against***] (人)に対して憤慨して ▪ He was *indignant with* the cruel man. 彼はその残酷な男に腹を立てていた.

indignation /ìndɪgnéɪʃən/ 名 ***in indignation*** 憤慨して ▪ He ran out of the room *in indignation.* 彼は憤慨して部屋から走り出た.

indignity /ɪndígnəti/ 名 ***put an indignity upon*/*subject ... to indignities*** …に侮辱を加える ▪ The bandits *subjected* us *to* all sorts of *indignities.* 山賊は我々にあらゆる侮辱を加えた.

indirection /ìndərékʃən|-daɪ-/ 名 ***by indirection(s)*** 遠回しに, 回りくどく (cf. Sh., *Haml.* 2. 1. 66) ▪ He usurped the executive *by indirections.* 彼は回りくどい方法で行政権を奪った.

indiscretion /ìndɪskréʃən/ 名 ***commit an indiscretion*** 失策をする《特に男女関係の》 ▪ He admits he has *committed an indiscretion* by seducing her. 彼は彼女を誘惑して過ちを犯したと認めている.

have the indiscretion to *do* 無分別にも[うかつにも]…する ▪ She *had the indiscretion to* forget her prudent carriage. 彼女はうかつにも慎重な立ち居ふるまいが頭になかった.

indispensable /ìndɪspénsəbəl/ 形 ***indispensable to*** [***for***] …に欠くことのできない, 絶対必要な ▪ Physical exercises were *indispensable to* young soldiers. 運動は若い兵には絶対必要だった.

indispose /ìndɪspóʊz/ 動 ***be indisposed for*** …する気にならない, 気がすすまない ▪ I *am indisposed for* cricket this morning. 今朝はクリケットをする気にならない.

be indisposed to *do* …する気にならない, 気がすすまない ▪ They *are indisposed to* accept the offer. 彼らはその申し出を受ける気がしない.

indispose *a person* ***to*** *do* 人に…する気をなくさせる ▪ The heat *indisposes* me *to* take exercise. 暑さのため私は運動するのがいやになる ▪ I *am indisposed to* work today. きょうは働く気がしない.

indoors /ìndɔ́ːrz/ 副 名 ***go indoors*** 屋内へ入る ▪ So saying, he *went indoors.* そう言って, 彼は家の中へ入った.

her indoors 《英口・戯》家内, 恋人, うちの奥さん; 恐妻 ▪ *Her indoors* and I often enjoy a glass of wine. うちのかみさんとよくワインを軽くやる ▪ He habitually refers to his wife as "*her indoors*". 彼は日頃から妻のことを「うちの奥さん」と言っている.

keep [***stay***] ***indoors*** 家にじっといる, 外出しない ▪ When the weather is fine, don't *keep indoors.* 天気のいいときには, 家にじっとしていてはいけません.

stick indoors 家の中にばかりいる ▪ The boy *sticks indoors* too much. その男の子はあんまり家の中にばかりいすぎる.

induce /ɪndjúːs/ 動 ***induce*** *a person* ***to*** *do* 人を説いて…させる; 人を誘導して…させる ▪ Nothing can *induce* him *to* stay. 彼は何と言ってもとどまってくれない.

Nothing shall induce me to *do.* 私は決して…しない ▪ *Nothing shall induce me to* go there. 私は絶対にそこへは行かない.

inducement /ɪndjúːsmənt/ 名 ***on any inducement*** どんな誘いがあっても ▪ I would not do such a thing *on any inducement.* 私はどんなに誘惑されてもそんなことはしたくない.

indulge /ɪndʌ́ldʒ/ 動 ***indulge*** *oneself* 気ままにする ▪ Don't *indulge yourself* too much. あまり気ままにしてはいけない.

indulge *oneself* ***in*** …にふける ▪ They *indulge themselves in* idle speculations. 彼らはつまらない憶測にふける.

indulge *oneself* ***with*** (好きなもの)を飲む, 食べる ▪ I *indulged myself with* a glass of wine. 私は好きなワインを1杯飲んだ.

something must be indulged to …はいくらか大目に見るべきだ ▪ *Something must be indulged to* the extravagance of Nature. 自然の力の行き過ぎはいくらか大目に見るべきだ.

indulgent /ɪndʌ́ldʒənt/ 形 ***indulgent to*** …に甘く, を大目に見る ▪ He is *indulgent to* his children. 彼は自分の子供たちに甘い.

indulgent with …に甘く ▪ He is *indulgent with* women. 彼は女性に甘い.

infallibility /ɪnfæ̀ləbíləti/ 名 ***His Infallibility*** ローマ教皇猊下(げいか); 《戯》閣下 ▪ *His Infallibility* is critically ill. ローマ教皇猊下は危篤である.

infancy /ínfənsi/ 名 ***in*** *one's* ***infancy*** **1** 幼時に, 子供のころ ▪ He lost his parents *in his infancy.* 彼は子供の時に両親をなくした.

2 初期に, 揺籃(ようらん)期に, 幼稚な状態に ▪ The invention is still *in its infancy.* その発明はまだ揺籃期にある.

infatuate /ɪnfǽtʃuèɪt|-fǽtju-/ 動 ***be infatuated with*** (女性)にのぼせている, 迷っている; (うぬぼれなど)でのぼせ上がっている ▪ He *is infatuated with* the woman. 彼はその女性にのぼせている ▪ He *is* now *infatuated with* pride. 彼は今うぬぼれてのぼせ上がっている.

infection /ɪnfékʃən/ 名 ***by infection*** 伝染して

I

▪ Hepatitis spread *by infection.* 肝炎は伝染して広まった.

inferior /ɪnfíəriər/ 形名 ***be*** *a person's* ***inferior (in)*** (...において)人に劣る ▪ I *am his inferior in* English. 私は英語においては彼に劣る.

(*be*) *inferior to* **1** ...に劣る ▪ She *is inferior to* her younger sister in beauty. 彼女は美しさにおいて妹に劣る.

2 (任)に耐えない ▪ I feel myself *inferior to* the task. 私はその任に耐えない気がする.

infest /ɪnfést/ 動 ***be infested with*** (害虫・海賊など)が横行している, はびこっている ▪ That sea-route *is infested with* pirates. その海路には海賊が横行している ▪ The back of our house *is infested with* ants. わが家の裏はアリだらけだ.

infiltrate /ɪnfíltreɪt|ínfɪltrèɪt/ 動 **(*be*) *infiltrated with*** [《まれ》 ***by***] ...が浸透している ▪ Carbonized remains *are* often *infiltrated with* mineral matter. 炭化した残物にはしばしば鉱物質が浸透している.

infiltration /ìnfɪltréɪʃən/ 名 ***advance by infiltration*** 各個前進する ▪ The troops *advanced by infiltration.* その軍隊は各個前進した.

infinite /ínfənət/ 形名 ***an infinite of*** 無数の, 無量の ▪ *An infinite of* books are written upon the subject. その問題については無数の本が書かれている ▪ That Calais tower has *an infinite of* symbolism in it. あのカレーの塔は無量の象徴性を持っている.

infinity /ɪnfínəti/ 名 ***to infinity*** 無限に ▪ Loving him *to infinity,* I almost died at the first news of his sickness. 彼を無限に愛していたので, 彼の病気の知らせを初めて聞いて死にそうな思いだった.

infirm /ɪnfə́ːrm/ 形 ***be infirm of purpose*** 意志薄弱である ▪ Like Macbeth he *is infirm of purpose.* マクベスのように彼は薄志弱行である.

old and infirm 老衰して ▪ Allowance must be made for *old and infirm* persons. 老衰した人々は酌量されなければならない.

inflame /ɪnfléɪm/ 動 ***be inflamed with*** **1** ...で燃えている ▪ The hills *were inflamed with* autumnal tints. 満山の紅葉は燃えるようだった.

2 ...に燃えている; で興奮している ▪ He *is inflamed with* lustful desire. 彼は情火を燃やしている ▪ He *was inflamed with* rage. 彼は真っ赤になって怒っていた.

influence /ínfluəns/ 名 ***exercise*** *one's* ***influence*** (...のために)尽力する (*in favor* [*behalf*] *of*) ▪ He *exercised his influence in favor of* peace [*in her behalf*]. 彼は平和[彼女]のために尽力した.

exercise [***exert***] ***influence on*** [***upon***] ...に影響感化を及ぼす ▪ The mind *exercises* great *influence on* the functioning of our organs. 精神は我々の諸器官の活動に大きな影響を及ぼす.

exercise [***exert***] ***influence over*** ...に勢力をふるう; 力を加える ▪ Japanese parents *exercise* great *influence over* their children. 日本の親は子供に大きな威力を及ぼす ▪ In England it is a misdemeanor to *exercise* undue *influence over* voters. イングランドでは投票者に不当な圧迫を加えるのは軽罪である.

fall beneath the influence of ...の影響を受ける ▪ The students *fell beneath the influence of* the teacher. 学生たちはその先生の影響を受けた.

have influence on [***upon, in***] ...に影響を及ぼす, 感化を与える ▪ Do earthquakes *have* any *influence on* the weather? 地震は天候に影響があるか ▪ The land tax would *have influence in* preventing improvements. 土地税は改良を妨げることに影響があるだろう.

have influence over [***with***] ...に対して影響力がある, 幅がきく ▪ He *has* great *influence over* the people. 彼は国民に大きな影響力がある ▪ Do you *have* any *influence with* the electors? あなたは選挙人たちを動かす力があるか.

through the influence of ...のつてで, 尽力により ▪ He has risen *through the influence of* his uncle. 彼はおじのつてで出世した.

under the influence アルコール[麻薬]に酔って ▪ He was caught for speeding *under the influence.* 彼は酔ってスピード違反をしたかどで捕まった.

under the influence of **1** ...の感化[影響]を受けて; の勢いで ▪ The blossoms expand *under the influence of* the weather. 花は天候のせいで開く ▪ He committed the crime *under the influence of* drink. 彼は酔った勢いで罪を犯した.

2 (酒など)がきいている, をきこしめしている ▪ He was *under the influence of* drink. 彼は一杯きげんであった.

use *one's* ***influence*** (...のために)運動する, 尽力する (*with a person for* [*in behalf of*]) ▪ Please *use your influence with* the minister *in my behalf.* 私のために, どうぞ大臣に運動してください ▪ He *used his influence for* peace. 彼は平和のために尽力した.

inform /ɪnfɔ́ːrm/ 動 **(*be*) *informed on*** [***about***] ...について知って(いる) ▪ He *was informed about* the Frenchman. 彼はそのフランス人について知っていた ▪ Keep him *informed on* current events. 日常の出来事をいつも彼に心得させておけ.

inform *oneself* ***of*** ...を調べる; を(調べて)知る, 知るようになる ▪ I am *informing myself of* the truth of the report. その報道の真相を調べている ▪ He *informed himself of* her character and disposition. 彼は彼女の性格と性質を知るようになった.

keep *a person* ***informed of*** 人に...のことを絶えず知らせておく ▪ *Keep* us *informed of* European and American progress. 我々に欧米の進歩を常に知らせておいてください.

information /ìnfərméɪʃən/ 名 ***for*** (*a person's*) ***information*** (人の)参考までに ▪ I enclose *for your information* a copy of the letter. ご参考までにその手紙の写しを同封します.

lay [***lodge***] (***an***) ***information against*** …を密告する ▪ He *laid information against* his friend. 彼は友人を密告した.

the information highway 《電算》情報ハイウェイ, インターネット ▪ Have you heard of *the Information* Super*highway*? It's another name for the Internet. 高速情報ネットワークって聞いたことある? インターネットのことだよ.

informer /ɪnfɔ́ːrmər/ 名 ***turn informer on*** …を密告する ▪ He *turned informer on* his friend. 彼は友人を密告した.

infuse /ɪnfjúːz/ 動 ***infuse*** *a person's* ***mind with*** 人の心に…を吹きこむ, 満たす ▪ He *infused her mind with* suspicion. 彼は彼女の心に疑惑の念を抱かせた.

ingrain /ɪngréɪn/ 動 ***be ingrained in*** (心)に染みこんでいる ▪ Some vices *are ingrained in* the children of the poor. 悪習が貧しい人々の子供に染みこんでいる.

ingratiate /ɪngréɪʃièɪt/ 動 ***ingratiate*** *oneself* ***into*** *a person's* ***favor*** …に取り入る, の気に入る ▪ He abolished the tax to *ingratiate himself into the people's favor.* 彼は人民のきげんを取ろうとしてその税を廃止した.

ingratiate *oneself* ***to*** …に愛想よくする ▪ He did his best to *ingratiate himself to* the people. 彼は人民に愛想よくしようと最善を尽くした.

ingratiate *oneself* ***with*** …に取り入る, のごきげん取りをする ▪ He did his best to *ingratiate himself with* the royal family. 彼は王室に取り入ろうと最善を尽くした.

inherent /ɪnhírənt|-híər-/ 形 ***inherent in*** **1** …の中に定着して, 含まれて ▪ A peculiar fluid is *inherent in* the substance of the nervous fibers. 特殊な液体が神経繊維の物質中に含まれている.
2 …に本質的な, 内在する ▪ The love of acting is *inherent in* our nature. 行動を愛好する心が我々の性質中に内在している.
3 …に付与されて ▪ The legislative authority was *inherent in* the general assembly. 立法の権能が総会に付与されていた.

inheritance /ɪnhérətəns/ 名 ***by inheritance*** 相続により ▪ The land came to him *by inheritance.* その土地は相続によって彼のものとなった.

inimical /ɪnímɪkəl/ 形 ***inimical to*** …に有害で; に敵意があって ▪ Fresh water is very *inimical to* coral. 真水はサンゴには非常に有害である ▪ They were *inimical to* one another. 彼らは互いに反目していた.

initiative /ɪníʃətɪv, -ʃiə-/ 名 ***have*** [***possess***] ***the initiative*** 率先権がある, 発議権がある ▪ He *has the initiative* in the docks. 彼は波止場では率先権がある ▪ The legislative assembly *possesses the initiative* in executive affairs. 立法議会は行政事項には発議権がある.

on *one's* ***own initiative*** 自発的に, 率先して ▪ He did it *on his own initiative.* 彼は自発的にそれをした.

take the initiative (***in***) …を率先してやる, にイニシアチブを取る, 機先を制する ▪ He can *take the initiative in* emergencies. 彼は非常時には率先して事に当ることができる.

injection /ɪndʒékʃən/ 名 ***have an injection of*** …の注射を受ける ▪ I *had an injection of* glucose. 私はグルコースの注射を受けた.

Injun /índʒən/ 名 ***honest Injun*** [***injun***] 《米俗・侮蔑》誓ってまちがいなく, ほんとうに《主に子供が使用》 ▪ I'd like to, *honest Injun.* 僕, ほんとにしたいんだ ▪ *Honest Injun,* I won't! 誓って私はしないぞ. ☞Injun<Indian「北米先住民」から.

play Injun 《米俗・侮蔑》隠れる, 逃げる ▪ Hereafter I have got to *play Injun.* 今後私は隠れねばならない.

injunction /ɪndʒʌ́ŋkʃən/ 名 ***lay injunctions upon*** *a person* ***to*** *do* 人に…するように命じる ▪ He *laid* strict *injunctions on* me *to* go there. 彼は私にそこへ行くように厳命した.

injurious /ɪndʒʊ́əriəs/ 形 ***injurious to*** …に有害な ▪ The habit is *injurious to* health. その習慣は健康に害がある.

injury /índʒəri/ 名 ***do*** *a person* [*oneself*] ***an injury*** 《口・戯》人に害を与える[受ける], けがをさせる[する] ▪ They *did* him *an injury.* 彼らは彼に害を加えた ▪ Be quiet, if you don't wish to *do yourself an injury.* けがをしたくなければおとなしくしていろ.

injustice /ɪndʒʌ́stəs/ 名 ***do*** *a person* [*oneself*] (***an***) ***injustice*** 人[自ら]を不当に扱う, を誤解する ▪ You *do* me great *injustice.* あなたは私を非常に誤解しておられる ▪ The movie industry *did* him *an injustice.* 映画業界は彼を不当に扱った.

without injustice to …に不公平なことなく ▪ The case was settled *without injustice to* the parties concerned. その事件は関係の人々に不公平なく片づいた.

ink /ɪŋk/ 名 (***as***) ***black as ink*** →(as) BLACK as a crow.

bleed red ink 《報道》赤字を出す ▪ Even large companies have been *bleeding red ink* since then. それ以来, 大企業でさえも赤字を出している.

in (***pen and***) ***ink*** インクで ▪ The letter was written *in ink.* その手紙はインクで書かれていた.

much ink has been spilled (***on*** [***over***]) …について多く書かれてきた ▪ *Much ink has been spilled on* the life of Shakespeare. シェイクスピアの生涯をこれまで多くの人が著わしてきた.

sling ink →SLING[2].

write with pen and ink →WRITE.

inkling /íŋklɪŋ/ 名 ***get an inkling*** (***of***) (…を)うすうす知る[感うく] ▪ I've *got an inkling of* what is happening. 私は起ころうとしていることをうすうす知っている.

give *a person* ***an inkling*** (***of***) 人に(…を)ほのめかす, それとなくヒントを与える ▪ I *gave* him *an inkling of* it. 私は彼にそれをほのめかした ▪ The remark *gave* me *an inkling*. その言葉に私はヒントを得た.

have an inkling うすうす知っている[感づいている] (*of, that*) ▪ The government has begun to *have an inkling of* the matter. 政府はその事件をうすうす感うき始めた ▪ I didn't *have an inkling that* you were so much of an authority on the subject. 君がその問題についてそれほどの権威だとは少しも知らなかった.

inner /ínər/ 形 ***the inner man*** [***woman***] **1** (肉体に対して)霊魂, 心 (《聖》*Ephes*. 3. 16) ▪ The Spirit of Christ governed *the inner man*. キリストの神霊がわが霊魂を支配した.

2 《戯》胃袋, 腹 ▪ His *inner man* now began to make himself heard. 空腹が今やこたえてきだした ▪ I must entertain [refresh] *the inner man*. 腹ごしらえをせねばならない. ☞ ↔OUTER man.

inning /ínɪŋ/, 《英》**innings** /ínɪŋz/ 名 ***have a good innings*** 《英口》 **1** 《クリケット》いい点を得る ▪ He *had a good innings*; he scored 72. 彼はいい点を取った. 72点取ったのだ.

2 幸運である, 幸運続きである《特に金銭上》 ▪ We *had a good innings* in the boom after the war. 我々は戦後景気で幸運であった.

3 長生きする, 長く職にある ▪ My grandmother *had a good innings*. 祖母は長生きした.

have a good long innings 《英》 **1** 《クリケット》打撃期間が長い ▪ The last batsman *had a good long innings*. 最終打者は打撃期間が長かった.

2 幸運続きである ▪ I've *had a good long innings* professionally. 私はこのところ商売で運がついている.

3 長生きする, 長く職にある, 長く仕事をする ▪ He has *had a good long innings* at 87. 彼は87歳の長命である ▪ She *had a good long innings* as manager. 彼女は長く部長の職にあった.

have a long innings 《口》=have a good long INNINGS 2, 3.

have an innings **1** 《クリケット》打番に立つ ▪ Walter will *have an innings* next. ウォルターは次に打番に立つ.

2 (あることに)参加する, 参与する ▪ It is time we *had an innings*. もう我々が関与するときだ.

have *one's* ***innings*** 好運にめぐり会っている; 権力を握っている ▪ Romance has *had its innings*. ロマンスの盛りは過ぎた.

have the inning(***s***) 政権担当期間を持つ, 政権を取る ▪ The Conservatives will *have the innings*. 保守党が政権を取るだろう.

innocence /ínəsəns/ 名 ***in all innocence*** ことの重大さを少しもわきまえず, 全く無邪気に ▪ The mother of Oedipus, *in all innocence*, married her own son. オイディプスの母親はそれとは全く知らずにわが息子と結婚した.

innocent /ínəsənt/ 形名 ***as innocent as a*** (***new-born***) ***babe*** とても無邪気[単純]な; 全く潔白で ▪ Jane was *as innocent as a babe*. ジェインはとても無邪気であった.

(***be***) ***innocent of*** **1** 《口》…がない ▪ This swimming pool *is* now *innocent of* water. このプールには今は水が張ってない.

2 …を犯していない ▪ He *is innocent of* the crime. 彼はその犯罪を犯してはいない.

the massacre [***slaughter***] ***of the innocents*** 《英・議会俗》時間不足での議案の切り捨て, 閉会まぎわの議案握りつぶし ▪ The leader of the House would have to go through *the massacre of the innocents*. 議長は時間不足による議案切り捨てを行わねばならないだろう.

inquest /íŋkwest/ 名 ***hold an inquest on*** [***over***] …の検死を行う, について査問会を開く ▪ *An inquest was held on* the body. 死体の検死が行われた.

inquiry /íŋkwəri|ɪnkwáɪəri/ 名 ***bear inquiry*** →BEAR[2].

make inquiries (***about, into***) (…について)問い合わせる, (を)調査する ▪ He *made* searching *inquiries into* the matter. 彼はその事件を厳重に調査した.

on inquiry 調査[問い合わせ]の結果 ▪ *On inquiry* the report proved false. 調べてみるとその報道は誤りであるとわかった.

inquisition /ìŋkwɪzíʃən/ 名 ***be an inquisition*** 目が飛び出るほど高い ▪ The prices at that shop *are an inquisition*. あの店の値段は目玉が飛び出すほど高い.

inquisitive /ɪnkwízətɪv/ 形 ***be inquisitive about*** [***after***] …についてしきりに聞きたがる ▪ My friend *was inquisitive about* the lodgers. 友人は下宿人たちのことをしきりに聞きたがった.

be inquisitive of [***for, into***] …をしきりに聞きたがる, 調べたがる ▪ Foreigners *were* very *inquisitive of* them. 外国人たちはしきりにそれらを聞きたがった ▪ He *was inquisitive into* the history of poetry. 彼は詩歌の歴史をしきりに調べていた.

be inquisitive to *do* しきりに…したがる ▪ I *am inquisitive to* know what lies for me in future. 私の将来がどうなるか知りたくてたまらない.

inroad /ínròʊd/ 名 ***make an inroad on*** [***upon***] (国)に侵入する ▪ They *made an inroad upon* Mexico. 彼らはメキシコに侵入した.

make inroads into **1** …に進出する ▪ Japanese goods *made inroads into* the British market. 日本製品はイギリス市場に進出した.

2 →make INROADs upon.

make inroads upon [***into***] …を侵食する; に食い込む, を侵害する ▪ English *makes* steady *inroads upon* French as the language of diplomacy. 英語は外交語としてフランス語を着々と侵食している ▪ Repairs to the whole house *made* deep *inroads into* our savings. 全家屋の修理費が我が家の蓄えに大きく食い込んだ.

insect /ínsekt/ 名 ***look like a stick insect*** ひどくやせて, やせ衰えて ▪ He went hitch-hiking around India and came back *looking like a stick insect.* 彼はインドへのヒッチハイク旅行に行き，骨と皮になって帰ってきた.

insensible /ɪnsénsəbəl/ 形 ***insensible of* [*to*] 1** …に無感覚で，を感じないで ▪ Swift was totally *insensible of* pain. スウィフトは苦痛を全く感じなかった ▪ He is *insensible to* wounds. 彼は傷を感じない.

2 …に鈍感で，平気で ▪ He is *insensible to* the beauty of art. 彼は芸術の美がわからない ▪ He is *insensible of* his danger. 彼は自分の危険に気がつかない.

inseparable /ɪnsépərəbəl/ 形 ***be inseparable from*** …から離しえない ▪ Charles *is inseparable from* his father. チャールズを父親から離すことはできない.

inshore /ìnʃɔ́ːr/ 副 ***inshore of*** …より海岸寄りを; と海岸との間に ▪ The ship was anchored *inshore of* the largest iceberg. 船は最大の氷山と海岸との間にいかりをおろしていた.

inside /ɪnsáɪd, ínsaɪd/ 名形副 ***be* (*on the*) *inside*** 《米口》内情に通じている ▪ The gentleman *is inside* on all these matters. その紳士はこれらの事については内情に通じている.

from the inside 内側から ▪ He knows the business *from the inside.* 彼はその事業の内情に通じている.

have the inside 《俗》内情を知っている ▪ He *has the inside* on what happened at the convention. 彼はその会議の経緯についての内情を知っている.

have* [*be on*] *the inside track →TRACK.

in* [*for*] *the inside of 《口》…以内に，足らずで ▪ They must come to London *for the inside of* a week. 彼らは1週間以内にロンドンへ来なければならない.

inside and out ＝INSIDE out 2.

inside of 《口》…以内に，足らずで ▪ I shall be in town again *inside of* a week. 1週間以内にまた町に来ます.

***inside out* 1** 裏返しにして ▪ He had one of his socks on *inside out.* 彼はソックスの片方を裏表にはいていた ▪ Turn the bag *inside out.* 袋を裏返せ.

2 何から何まで ▪ I know the business *inside out.* その事は何から何まで知っている.

the inside of a week 《英》週の中ほど《月曜から金曜まで》 ▪ We stayed in London for *the inside of a week.* 月曜から金曜までロンドンに滞在した.

turn ... inside out …を完全に変える，一変させる (→ turn ... UPSIDE(-)DOWN) ▪ U.S. labor law has *been turned inside out.* 米国の労働法はすっかり変えられた.

insight /ínsaɪt/ 名 ***gain* [*get, have*] *an insight into*** …を見抜く，洞察する ▪ He *gained an insight into* her mind. 彼は彼女の心を見抜いた ▪ I managed to *get an insight into* the main facts. 私はどうにか主な事実を洞察することができた.

give** a person **an insight into 人に…を洞察させる，見通させる ▪ This book will *give* you *an insight into* the genius of English. この本はあなたに英語の特性を洞察させるでしょう.

insignificance /ìnsɪgnífəkəns/ 名 ***fade* [*pale*] *into insignificance*** (他と比較して)重要性[価値]を失う ▪ All other issues *pale into insignificance* compared with the struggle for survival. 生存競争と比べると，それ以外の問題は影が薄くなる.

insinuate /ɪnsínjuèɪt/ 動 ***insinuate** oneself **into* 1** 巧みに[曲りくねって，知らぬまに]…に入りこむ ▪ The water has *insinuated itself into* the crevices of the rock. 水は回りくねって岩の割れ目に入りこんだ ▪ He *insinuated himself into* good society. 彼は上流社会に巧みに入りこんだ.

2 …に巧みに取り入る ▪ He has *insinuated himself into* their favor [their good graces]. 彼は巧みに彼らに取り入った.

insist /ɪnsíst/ 動 ***I insist.*** (押し問答で)それは譲れません ▪ After you.—No, after you, *I insist.* お先にどうぞ—いえ，あなたこそどうぞお先に.

insofar /ìnsoʊfɑ́ːr/ 副 ***insofar as*** …する限りでは ▪ We learn our lessons only *insofar as* we keep studying them. 学び続ける限りにおいてのみ学課は身につく.

insolence /ínsələns/ 名 ***have the insolence to** do* 生意気にも[無礼にも]…する ▪ He *had the insolence to* say such a thing. 彼は無礼にもそんなことを言った.

insomuch /ìnsoʊmʌ́tʃ/ 副 ***insomuch as*** …だから ▪ *Insomuch as* I am not French by birth, I am not well acquainted with France. 生まれがフランス人でないので，フランスのことはあまり知らないのです.

insomuch that …するほどにも ▪ The rain fell in torrents, *insomuch that* the soldiers were ankle-deep in water. 雨は滝のように降ったので，兵隊たちは足首まで水につかるほどだった.

inspection /ɪnspékʃən/ 名 ***Inspection declined* [*free*].** 縦覧謝絶[随意]《掲示》.

make an inspection of …を検分する，視察する ▪ I *made a* careful *inspection of* the apartment. 私はその部屋を入念に検分した.

on inspection 検査の結果，調べた結果 ▪ *On* close *inspection*, it was found to be a forgery. よく調べたらそれはにせものであることがわかった.

inspire /ɪnspáɪər/ 動 ***inspire** a person **to** do* 人を励まして…させる ▪ His kindness *inspired* me *to* write a poem. 彼の親切に鼓舞されて詩を書いた.

install /ɪnstɔ́ːl/ 動 ***install** oneself **in*** (席・地位など)につく ▪ He *installed himself in* the big chair before the fire. 彼は暖炉の前の大きないすに腰かけた ▪ He *is installed in* his new house. 彼は新宅に落ち着いた.

installment, 《英》**instalment** /ɪnstɔ́ːlmənt/ 名 ***in* [*by*] *installments* 1** 分割払いで ▪ He paid *in* five months' *installments.* 彼は5か月の

分割払いで支払った ▪ It was paid *by* yearly *installments* over the course of 20 years. それは年賦で20年間に払われた.

2 何回にも分けて ▪ The work appeared *in installments.* その作品は分冊で出た.

instance /ínstəns/ 名 ***at the instance of*** …の勧め[頼み, 発議]により ▪ I come here *at the instance of* Dr. Jekyll. 私はジキル博士の勧めでここへ来たのです.

for instance たとえば ▪ He will earn, *for instance*, about twice as much as I earn. 彼はたとえば, 私のおよそ2倍も儲けるだろう.

in the first instance まず第一に, 手始めに;《法》一審で ▪ There was a debate *in the first instance.* 一審では討論があった ▪ I thought so too *in the first instance.* 私も一番にそう思った.

in the last instance 最後に;《法》終審で ▪ It was a pity that he was beaten *in the last instance.* 彼が最後に負けたのは残念であった.

I

in this [that] instance この[その]場合に ▪ *In this instance* we have an example of modification. この場合は我々に修正例が一つある.

take ... for instance …を例にとる ▪ *Take* John *for instance.* ジョンを例にとってみよう.

instant /ínstənt/ 名 ***at that (very) instant*** ちょうどその時に ▪ She appeared *at that instant.* 彼女はちょうどその時に現れた.

for an instant ちょっとの間, 一瞬の間 ▪ I did not lose my presence of mind *for an instant.* 私は一瞬たりとも心を乱さなかった.

in an instant 瞬く間に, たちまち ▪ He was back with us *in an instant.* 彼はたちまち我々の所へ戻って来た.

***in the instant of** doing* …しようとする瞬間に ▪ I was struck *in the instant of crossing* the threshold. 私は敷居をまたごうとした瞬間になぐられた.

on [upon] the instant ただちに, 即座に ▪ He expired *on the instant.* 彼は即死した.

the instant (that) …するとすぐ ▪ *The instant* we met, we quarreled. 我々は出会うとすぐ口論をした.

this instant 今すぐに, 今この場で ▪ Come here *this instant.* 今すぐここへ来なさい.

instead /ɪnstéd/ 副 ***instead of*** **1** …の代わりに; でなく ▪ I gave him advice *instead of* money. 金の代わりに助言を彼に与えた ▪ I found it on the floor *instead of* in the drawer. 私はそれを引き出しの中でなく床の上に見つけた.

2 …する代わりに, しないで (*doing*) ▪ *Instead of going* myself, I sent a messenger. 私は自分で行く代わりに使いの者をやった.

instigate /ínstəgèɪt/ 動 ***instigate** a person **to** do* 人をそそのかして…させる ▪ He *instigated* workers *to* go out on strike. 彼は労働者たちをそそのかしてストライキをさせた.

instigation /ɪnstəgéɪʃən/ 名 ***at [by] the instigation of*** …にそそのかされて ▪ The riot broke out *at the instigation of* a politician. 暴動はある政治家の扇動から起こった.

instinct[1] /ínstɪŋkt/ 名 ***by [from] instinct*** 本能で, 本能的に ▪ I knew it *from instinct.* 私は本能的にそれを知った ▪ He did it *by instinct.* 彼は本能でそれをした.

have an instinct for …の才[天性]がある ▪ He *has an instinct for* field sports. 彼は野外運動に妙を得ている.

on instinct 本能のままに ▪ We sometimes act *on instinct.* 我々はときどき本能のままに行動する.

instinct[2] /ɪnstíŋkt/ 形 ***(be) instinct with*** …に満ち満ちて(いる) ▪ This is a poem *instinct with* beauty. これは美しさのあふれた詩である.

instruct /ɪnstrʌ́kt/ 動 ***be instructed in*** …に明るい, 通じている ▪ He *is instructed in* chemistry. 彼は化学に通じている.

***instruct** a person **to** do* 人に…するよう指令する, 命じる ▪ He *instructed* us *to* march at once. 彼は我々にすぐ進軍せよと命じた.

instruction /ɪnstrʌ́kʃən/ 名 ***give instruction in*** …を教授する ▪ He *gave* us *instruction in* mathematics. 彼は我々に数学を教授した.

give instructions to …に訓令する; に指図を与える ▪ He *gave* explicit *instructions to* us on this point. 彼はこの点について明白な指図を我々に与えた.

receive instruction in …の教授を受ける ▪ We *received instruction in* English. 我々は英語の教授を受けた.

instrument /ínstrəmənt/ 名 ***be an instrument for** (doing)* …する道具である; …するのに役立つ ▪ It *is an instrument for boring* holes. それは穴をあける道具である ▪ The United Nations *is an instrument for* the maintenance of peace. 国連は平和を維持するのに役立つ.

instrumental /ìnstrəméntəl/ 形 ***be instrumental in [to]*** **1** …に役立つ ▪ It *is instrumental in* clearing up the matter. それは問題を解決するのに役立つ ▪ Prayer *is instrumental to* everything. 祈りはすべての事に役立つ.

2 …に尽力する ▪ I *was instrumental in* finding work for him. 私は彼に職を見つけてやるのに尽力した.

instrumentality /ìnstrəmentǽləti/ 名 ***by [through] the instrumentality of*** …の助け[手段, 尽力]により ▪ I got it chiefly *through the instrumentality of* a skillful agent. 主として巧みな代理人によってそれを得た.

insult /ínsʌlt/ 名 ***add insult to injury*** 傷つけた上で侮辱を加える, 踏んだりけったりする ▪ To dismiss me was unjust, but to do it publicly was to *add insult to injury.* 私を解雇するのは不当であったが, 公然と解雇するのは踏んだりけったりであった.

pile insult on insult 侮辱に侮辱を加える ▪ He kept *piling insult on insult* upon me. 彼は私に侮辱に侮辱を加え続けた.

insurance /ɪnʃóərəns, -ʃɔ́:r-/ 名 ***take out insurance on*** …に保険をかける ▪ I'll *take out* fire *insurance on* my house. 家に火災保険をかけよう.

insure /ɪnʃʊ́ər, -ʃɔ́ː/ 動 ***insure** oneself* [*one's* ***life***] (***for*** *a sum*) (ある金額の)生命保険に入る ▪I have *insured myself* for 100,000,000 yen. 私は1億円の生命保険に入っている.

insurrection /ìnsərékʃən/ 名 ***rise in insurrection*** 暴動を起こす ▪We *rose* at last *in insurrection.* 我々はついに暴動を起こした.

insusceptible /ìnsəséptəbəl/ 形 ***insusceptible of*** **1** …され得ない ▪The subject is *insusceptible of* being treated otherwise. その問題はそれ以外の方法では扱うことができない.

2 …をいれない ▪My heart is *insusceptible of* pity. 私にはあわれみの心はない.

insusceptible to …を感じない; を感受しない; に動かされない ▪He is *insusceptible to* flattery. 彼はへつらいに動かされない ▪They are *insusceptible to* infection by smallpox. 彼らは天然痘には感染しない.

intake /íntèɪk/ 名 ***an intake of breath*** (驚いて)はっと息を飲むこと ▪His response drew *a* sharp *intake of breath* from most of the people around. 彼の応答に周りの大半の人ははっと息を飲んだ.

integrate /íntəgrèɪt/ 動 ***be integrated with*** …と統合[統一]される ▪The French zone should *be integrated with* the Anglo-American zones. フランス地域は英米地域と統合されるべきだ.

integrity /ɪntégrəti/ 名 ***in*** *one's* ***integrity*** そっくりそのままで, 元のままで ▪We adopted it *in its integrity.* それをそっくりそのまま採用した.

intelligence /ɪntélədʒəns/ 名 ***bring intelligence of*** …の報をもたらす ▪He *brought intelligence of* their victory. 彼は彼らの勝利の報をもたらした.

intend /ɪnténd/ 動 ***be intended for*** **1** …にするつもり[されるはず]である; に与えるつもりである; にあてられたものである ▪He *is intended for* a physician. 彼は医者にされるはずである ▪The gift *was intended for* you. その贈り物はあなたにあげるつもりだった ▪His remark *was intended for* me. 彼の言葉は私にあてられたものだった.

2 …のつもりである, を描いたものである ▪This daub *is intended for* me. このへたな絵は私の(肖像の)つもりだ.

be intended for the sea [***the army, the bar,*** etc.] 船乗り[軍人, 弁護士など]にされるはずである ▪His son *was intended for the church.* 彼の息子は牧師にされるはずだった.

intend *a person* ***to*** *do* 人に…させるつもりである ▪I *intended* him *to* go. 彼に行かせるつもりだった ▪I *intend* my son *to* be a physician. 息子を医者にするつもりだ.

intended to have *done* …するつもりだった《非実現を表す》 ▪I *intended to have* climbed Mt. Fuji. 富士山に登るつもりだったのだが.

intensity /ɪnténsəti/ 名 ***at the intensity of*** …の激しさのあまり ▪He went mad *at the intensity of* his grief. 彼は激しい悲嘆のあまりに気が狂った.

intent[1] /ɪntént/ 形 ***intent on*** [***upon***] …に一心で, 没頭して ▪He is *intent on* his task [winning the prize]. 彼は仕事に余念がない[その賞を得ようとやっきになっている].

intent[2] /ɪntént/ 名 ***to*** [***for***] ***all intents and purposes*** 《米》事実上, 実際上, ほとんど ▪The revised edition is *to all intents and purposes* a new book. 改訂版は実際上新著である ▪The nation consists, *for all intents and purposes*, of one immense class. その国民は大体一つの巨大な階級からなっている.

with good [***bad, evil, malicious***] ***intent*** 善意[悪意]をもって ▪They were rushing upon the peasant *with malicious intent.* 彼らはその農民に悪意をもって襲いかかっていた.

with intent to *do* 《法》…する意図をもって, しようと思って ▪He who wounds *with intent to* kill shall be tried as if he had succeeded. 殺意をもって人を傷つける者は殺人を果たしたかのように裁判される.

intention /ɪnténʃən/ 名 ***by*** (***deliberate***) ***intention*** 故意に ▪He did it *by intention.* 彼は故意にそうした.

by the first intention (傷・骨折などが)直接に, うまずに(治る) ▪The wound healed *by the first intention.* その傷は直接癒合(ゆごう)した《うまずに治った》.

by the second intention (傷・骨折などが)間接に, うんだあと肉がもり上がって(治る) ▪The wound was left to recover *by the second intention.* その傷はうんだあと自然に治るに任された.

have an intention of *doing* …するつもりがある ▪He *has* some [no] *intention of going* there. 彼はそこへ行くつもりがいくらかある[つもりはない].

Hell is paved with good intentions. 《諺》地獄(の道)は善意で敷きつめられている《善行をしようと思いながらも, つい悪行によって地獄へ落ちる人が多い[実行しなければ何にもならない]》. ☞Boswell の *The Life of Johnson* 中に Johnson の言葉として出ているが実際はそれよりずっと古い.

nothing is farther from my intention than to *do* …する考えは毛頭ない ▪*Nothing is farther from my intention than to* say a word against him. 彼の悪口を一言でも言う考えは毛頭ない.

The road [***path***] ***to hell is paved with good intentions.*** 《諺》地獄への道は善意で敷きつめられている《善意があってもそれを実行しなければ何にもならない》.

with good [***the best of***] ***intentions*** 善意をもって, 善意でありながら《特に結果がよくなかった場合を示す》 ▪It was done *with good intentions.* それは善意をもってなされた ▪*With the best of intentions* he has gone wrong. 彼は善意でありながら邪道に入った.

with the intention of *doing* …するつもりで ▪I went there *with the intention of seeing* him. 私は彼に会うつもりでそこへ行った.

without intention 何心なく ▪It was done *without intention.* それはなにげなくしたことだ.

intercede /ìntərsí:d/ 動 ***intercede with*** *a person* ***on behalf of*** …のため人に取りなす, 仲に入る ▪ He *interceded with* police *on behalf of* the arrested students. 彼は逮捕された学生のために仲に入って警察に取りなした.

intercept /ìntərsépt/ 動 ***intercept*** *a person* ***to*** *do* 人が…するのを妨げる ▪ He *intercepted* me *to* pull out the pistol. 彼は私がピストルを抜くのをさえぎった.

intercession /ìntərséʃən/ 名 ***make intercession to*** *A* ***for*** *B* BのためAに取りなす ▪ Dead people were said to *make intercession to* God *for* living people. 死者が生者のために神への取りなしをすると言われていた.

intercourse /íntərkɔ̀:rs/ 名 ***have*** [***hold***] ***intercourse with*** …と交際する, 交わる ▪ These countries *have* intimate *intercourse with* one another. これらの国々は互いに密接に交わっている.

interdiction /ìntərdíkʃən/ 名 ***interdiction of fire and water*** (追放して)水火その他の生活品給与禁止 ▪ Citizenship was lost by *interdiction of fire and water*. 市民の身分は追放による生活品給与禁止によって失われた.

interest[1] /íntərəst/ 名 ***against the interests of*** …の利益に反して ▪ It is *against the interests of* the people. それは国民の利益に反する.

arouse [***awake***] ***interest in*** …に興味を起こさせる ▪ It *aroused interest in* naval affairs on the part of the people. それは国民の海事に対する興味を起こさせた.

at interest 利息をつけて ▪ He lends money *at* high *interest*. 彼は高利で金を貸す.

bear [***draw***] ***interest*** 利子がつく ▪ The bonds *bear* 5% *interest*. その公債は5分の利子がつく.

buy an interest in …の株を買う ▪ He *bought a* controlling *interest in* the enterprise. 彼はその事業を左右するだけの株を買った.

feel (***an***) ***interest in*** → take (an) INTEREST in.

for *one's* ***interests*** …の利益に(なるよう) ▪ I will do the best I can *for your interests*. 私はあなたのために最善を尽くします.

go by interest 利害で決まる ▪ Everything *goes by interest* nowadays. 当世は万事が利害で決まる.

have a vested interest (***in***) →VESTED.

have (***an***) ***interest in*** **1** …に興味を持っている ▪ I *have* no *interest in* politics. 政治には何の興味も持たない.

2 …に利害関係[権益]を持つ ▪ You *have an interest in* the business. あなたはこの事業に利害関係がある《株主である》 ▪ He *has an interest in* the estate. 彼はその地所に一部の権利を持っている.

have interest (***with***) (…に)信用[勢力, つて]がある, 顔がきく ▪ He *has interest with* the minister. 彼は大臣に信用がある ▪ He *has interest* at court. 彼は宮廷に顔がきく.

have the best interests of … at heart 心から…のためを思っている ▪ I *had the best interests of* my brother *at heart*. 心から弟のためを思っていた.

in *one's* ***own interests*** 自分自身の利益のために ▪ He is always acting *in his own interests*. 彼はいつも自分の利益のために動いている.

in the interest(***s***) ***of*** …のために, のためを思って ▪ I say this *in your interest*. あなたのためを思ってこう言うのです ▪ I would do anything *in the interests of* humanity. 私は人類のためなら何でもしたい.

it is (***to***) *one's* ***interest***(***s***) ***to*** *do* …するのは人のためだ, 利益だ ▪ *It is to your interest to* remain silent. 黙っているのが君のためだ.

(***just***) ***out of interest***/(***just***) ***as a matter of interest*** 興味本位で聞くんだけど, ただ知りたいだけなんだが ▪ *Just out of interest*, how much did they offer you? 好奇心から聞くんだけど, 彼らはいくら出すと言ったのかい ▪ *Just as a matter of interest*, where did you get it? ちょっと知りたいんだけど, それ, どこで買ったの.

look to [***after***] ***the interests of*** …の利益を図る ▪ We must *look to the interests of* our country. 我々はわが国の利益を図らねばならない ▪ He *looks after his* own *interests*. 彼は自己の利益を図る.

lose (***an***) ***interest in*** …に興味を失う ▪ People are *losing interest in* politics. 人々は政治に興味を失いつつある.

lose *one's* ***interest with*** …に対する勢力[信用]を失う ▪ He has *lost his interest with* the farming population. 彼は農民に対する勢力を失った.

make for [***against***] *a person's* ***interests*** 人のため[害]になる ▪ Such arguments do not *make for*, but *against*, *your interests*. そのような議論はあなたのためにならず, 害になる.

make interest with …に運動する, に対して勢力をふるう ▪ They *made interest with* Elizabeth for the continuance of the old religion. 彼らは古い宗教を続けるようエリザベスに働きかけた.

of interest 興味ある ▪ This book is *of* great *interest* to me. この本は私には非常におもしろい.

pay *a person* ***back with interest***/***return*** *a person* ***with interest*** 人におまけをつけて仕返しをする ▪ If you hurt me, I'll *pay* you *back with interest*. 俺にけがでもさせてみろ, 倍にして返してやるから.

put … to interest …の利殖を図る ▪ They do not *put* their ideas *to interest*. 彼らは自分らの思いつきの利殖を図らない.

take [***feel***] (***an***) ***interest in*** **1** …に興味を持つ ▪ He *takes a* great *interest in* history. 彼は歴史に大いに興味を持っている.

2 …に関心を持つ; の世話をする ▪ He *takes* great *interest in* the question of physical education. 彼は体育の問題に非常に熱心である ▪ He *took an interest in* the boy. 彼はその少年の世話をした.

through interest (***with***) (…の)つてで, 縁故で ▪ He obtained his position *through interest* *with* Johnson. 彼はジョンスンのつてで今の地位を得た.

use** one's **interest with …に運動する, 働きかける ▪ Please *use your interest with* the minister in my behalf. 私のために大臣に運動してください.

with breathless* [*intense*] *interest かたずを飲んで, 手に汗を握って ▪ We watched the contest *with breathless interest*. 我々はかたずを飲んで競技を見まもった.

with interest **1** 興味をもって ▪ He examined the machine *with* great *interest*. 彼は非常な興味をもってその機械を調べた.
2 利息をつけて ▪ He returned the blows *with interest*. 彼はおまけをつけてなぐり返した.

interest[2] /íntərəst/ 動 ***be interested in*** **1** …に興味を持っている ▪ He *is interested in* the study of English. 彼は英語の研究に興味をもっている.
2 …に利害関係がある; の株を持っている ▪ I *am interested in* his proceedings. 私は彼の処置に利害関係がある ▪ He *is interested in* an automobile company. 彼は自動車会社の株を持っている.

Can* [*Could*] *I interest you in…? (商品を勧めて)…はいかがですか ▪ *Can I interest you in* some assorted nuts? ナッツの詰め合わせはいかがですか.

interest** oneself **in …に興味[関心]を持つ; にあずかる; に尽力する ▪ I do not *interest myself in* politics. 私は政治には興味を持たない ▪ He *interested himself in* the enterprise. 彼はその事業に関与した《投資した》.

interesting /íntərəstɪŋ/ 形 ***an interesting event*** 《英》子供の出生 ▪ No woman thought of going to a hospital for *an interesting event*. 出産のために病院へ行くなどと考える女性は皆無だった.

***be in an interesting condition* [*situation, state*]** 《英》妊娠している, 身重である ▪ Mrs. Davis *is in an interesting condition*. デイヴィス夫人は身重です.

interference /ìntərfíərəns/ 名 ***run interference* (*for*)** **1** 《アメフト》…のために選手の通り道を体でじゃまする ▪ He *ran interference for* the quarterback. 彼はクォーターバックのために敵のじゃまをした.
2 《口》注意をそらす ▪ He *ran interference for* me with the press. 彼は私のために新聞記者たちの注意をそらしてくれた.
3 《米口》(当人に代わって)先回りして面倒を処理しておく ▪ The press secretary *runs interference for* the President. 報道官が前もって大統領のお膳立てをする.

interim /íntərəm/ 名 ***in the interim*** その間に[は] ▪ *In the interim*, this society will take the responsibility. その間は本会が責任を引き受ける.

intermediary /ìntərmí:dièri|-diəri/ 名 ***through the intermediary of*** …の手[仲介]を経て ▪ I communicated it to him *through the intermediary of* a third. 私は第三者の手を経てそれを彼に伝えた.

intermission /ìntərmíʃən/ 名 ***without intermission*** 絶え間なく ▪ We work from 8 a.m. till 5 p.m. *without intermission*. 我々は午前8時から午後5時まで休みなく働く.

internal /ɪntə́:rnəl/ 形 ***for internal use*** 内服用の ▪ This medicine is *for internal use*. これは内服薬です.

Internot /íntərnɑ̀t|-nɔ̀t/ 名 ***an Internot*** 《電算》インターネットに全く関心のない人 ▪ Grandpa is indifferent to the Internet. He is *an Internot*. おじいちゃんはインターネットには興味がないから使わないよ.

interpretation /ɪntə̀:rprətéɪʃən/ 名 ***put a favorable interpretation on*** …をよい意味に解釈する ▪ I *put a favorable interpretation on* his act. 彼の行為をよい意味に解釈した.

interrogation /ɪntèrəgéɪʃən/ 名 ***be a walking interrogation point*** 《米俗》いつもものを尋ねたがる, 詮索好きである ▪ A girl in her middle teens *is* often *a walking interrogation point*. 10代半ばの女の子はとかく詮索好きである.

interruption /ìntərʌ́pʃən/ 名 ***without interruption*** 間断なく, 休まずに ▪ He worked 6 hours *without interruption*. 彼は6時間休まずに働いた.

interval /íntərvəl/ 名 ***after an interval of*/ *after…'s interval*** …ぶりに, 目に ▪ I saw him *after an interval of* 3 years [*after* three years' *interval*]. 私は3年ぶりに彼に会った.

at intervals **1** あちこちに; 少し間隔をおいて ▪ The spearmen took their posts *at intervals* in the shallows. やり使いたちは浅瀬に間隔をおいて陣取った.
2 ときおり ▪ A drizzling rain fell *at intervals*. ぬか雨がときどき降った.

at intervals of (距離・時間)の間隔をおいて ▪ On this line cars run *at intervals of* ten minutes. この路線では電車が10分おきに通る.

at long intervals 時たま, 長い間をおいて ▪ I see him *at long intervals*. 私は時たま彼に会う.

at regular intervals 一定の時間[距離]をおき, 定期的に ▪ This fountain plays *at regular intervals*. この噴水は定期的に噴出する.

at short intervals しばしば, しきりに ▪ Thomas called on me *at short intervals*. トマスはしばしば私を尋ねて来た.

in the interval その間に ▪ We had to call on the lawyer *in the interval*. 我々はその間に弁護士を訪ねなければならなかった.

in the intervals of …の合い間に, ひまを見て ▪ We met *in the intervals of* business. 我々は仕事の合い間に顔を合わせた.

interview /íntərvjù:/ 名 ***grant* [*give*] *an interview to*** …に会見を許す ▪ The President *granted an interview to* the journalists. 大統領は記者会見を許した.

have* [*hold*] *an interview with …と会見する, 会談する ▪ I *had* the first *interview with* the minister. 私は大臣に初めて面会した.

intimate /íntəmət/ 形 ***be intimate with*** 《婉

I

曲》(女性)と親密[深い仲]である, 懇意である ▪ I *am intimate with* Ellen. 私はエレンと懇意にしている.

be on intimate terms with …と親しい間柄である ▪ He *is on intimate terms with* my father. 彼は私の父と懇意である.

into /íntu:/ 前 *A* ***into*** *B* ***goes*** *C* ***times*** BをAで割るとCになる ▪ Two *into* six *goes* three *times*. 6÷2=3.

intolerant /ɪntálərənt|-tɔ́l-/ 形 ***intolerant of***
1 …に耐えられない ▪ The plant is *intolerant of* direct sunlight. その植物は直射日光に耐えられない ▪ We are *intolerant of* oppression. 我々は圧制にはがまんができない.
2 (異説など)を受けいれない《特に宗教上の》 ▪ He is *intolerant of* Protestantism. 彼は新教を受容しない.

intrigue /ɪntrí:g/ 動 (***be***) ***intrigued with*** [***by***] …に興味[好奇心]をいだく ▪ I *was intrigued with* his unusual speech. 彼の特異な演説に興味を持った.

I

introduce /ìntrədjú:s/ 動 ***introduce*** *oneself* (***into***) (…に)入りこむ ▪ He *introduced himself into* society. 彼は社交界に入りこんだ.

introduce *oneself* ***to*** …に名乗る, 自己紹介する ▪ They *introduced themselves to* each other. 彼らは互いに名乗り合った.

intrude /ɪntrú:d/ 動 ***intrude*** *oneself* ***into*** **1** …に押し入る, 出しゃばる ▪ Why do you *intrude yourself into* their company? なぜ君は彼らの中へ出しゃばるのか.
2 …に干渉する, 口出しする ▪ Don't *intrude yourself into* his business. 彼の事に干渉するな.

intrude *oneself* ***on*** [***upon***] (押しかけて)…のじゃまをする ▪ Will you *intrude yourself on* the patience of the public? 君は出しゃばって民衆の堪忍(かん にん)袋の緒を切ろうというのか.

intrude on [***upon***] *a person's* ***time*** [***privacy, leisure***] 人の時間[一人でいるところ, 暇なとき]のじゃまをする ▪ May I *intrude upon your time*? おじゃましてよろしいですか.

inundate /ínʌndèɪt/ 動 ***be inundated with***
1 (水)浸しになる ▪ The place *was inundated with* water. そこは水浸しになった.
2 …で混雑する; が殺到する ▪ Sapporo *is inundated with* tourists in summer. 札幌は夏場には旅行客で混雑する ▪ He *was inundated with* invitations. 彼に招待状が殺到した.

inure /ɪnjʊ́ər/ 動 ***inure*** *oneself* ***to*** …に身を慣らす ▪ He must *inure himself to* cold. 彼は寒さに身を慣らさねばならない.

inure *oneself* ***to*** *do* …することに身を慣らす, 自らを鍛える ▪ He must *inure himself to* bear sudden changes. 彼は急変化に耐えるよう身を慣らす必要がある.

invalid /ínvələd|ínvəlì:d/ 動 ***invalid*** *a person* ***home*** 人を傷病兵として送還する ▪ He has *been invalided home* from India as a result of sunstroke. 彼は日射病の結果, 傷病兵としてインドから送還された.

invalid *a person* ***out of the army*** 人を傷病兵として兵役を免除する[除隊する] ▪ His limp from the war wound *invalided* him *out of the army*. 戦傷で彼は足を引きずるようになり, そのため免役された.

invasion /ɪnvéɪʒən/ 名 ***make an invasion on*** …に侵入する, を襲う ▪ The Spaniards *made an invasion on* the colony of Georgia. スペイン軍はジョージア植民地に侵入した.

inventive /ɪnvéntɪv/ 形 ***inventive of*** …の発明の才に富む ▪ The young man was *inventive of* excuses. その若者は言い訳を考え出すのがうまかった.

inventory /ínvəntɔ̀:ri|-təri/ 名 ***make*** [***take, draw up***] ***an inventory of*** (家財・商品など)の目録を作る; …を調べる ▪ The clerk *made an inventory of* the goods. 店員は商品の目録を作った ▪ We *made an inventory of* his characteristics. 我々は彼の特徴をいちいち調べあげた.

inverse /ìnvə́:rs/ 形 ***in inverse proportion*** [***ratio***] ***to*** …に反比例して ▪ Temperature is *in inverse ratio to* altitude. 気温は高度に反比例する.

invert /ɪnvə́:rt/ 動 ***in inverted commas*** 《英》引用符つきの, かっこつきの《実際は逆に「その名に値しない」を含意する》 ▪ We were served a "meal", *in inverted commas*. かっこつきのご馳走(=ひどい料理)を出された.

investigation /ɪnvèstəgéɪʃən/ 名 ***on investigation*** 調査の結果 ▪ *On* close *investigation* it was found to be untrue. 詳しく調査した結果, それは嘘であることがわかった.

under investigation 調査中で ▪ The matter is *under investigation*. その問題は調査中である.

investment /ɪnvéstmənt/ 名 ***make an investment in*** …に投資する ▪ He *made a* huge *investment in* the enterprise. 彼はその事業に莫大な投資をした.

inviolate /ɪnváɪələt/ 形 ***keep … inviolate*** (信仰・約束など)を堅く守る ▪ I will *keep* my promise *inviolate*. 私は約束を堅く守ります.

invisible /ɪnvízəbəl/ 形 ***Good will is an invisible asset.*** 《諺》のれんは隠れた資産.

remain invisible 人に会わない ▪ He *remains invisible* when out of spirits. 彼は意気消沈しているときは人に会わない.

invitation /ìnvətéɪʃən/ 名 ***accept*** [***decline***] ***an invitation*** 招待に応じる[を断る] ▪ I shall be glad to *accept your invitation*. 喜んでご招待をお受けします.

at [***on***] ***the invitation of*** …の招きにより, に招待されて ▪ He came to the party *at my invitation*. 彼は私の招きによって, そのパーティーに来た.

invite /ɪnváɪt/ 動 ***invite*** *oneself* 来るつもりであると言う, (喜んで)出席いたしますと言う ▪ He sent us a very kind message, *inviting himself* aboard our ship. 彼は我々の船に参上いたしますという非常に好意

的な書信をよこした.

invite *a person* ***to*** *do* 人に…するよう勧める[請う] ▪I *invite* you *to* consider. あなたのご考慮をお願いします ▪They *invited* Edward *to* ascend the throne. 彼らはエドワードに王位につくよう勧めた.

involve /ɪnválv|-vɔ́lv/ 動 ***be*** [***get***] ***involved in*** **1** …に包まれている[包まれる] ▪The origin of the Japanese *is involved in* mystery. 日本人の起源は謎に包まれている.

2 …に巻きこまれている[こまれる]; かかり合いになる[合う] ▪Britain will *be involved in* the war. イギリスはその戦争に巻きこまれるであろう ▪Many people *got involved in* the scandal. その疑獄にかかり合った者が多い.

3 (借金など)に深くはまっている[はまる] ▪He *is* deeply *involved in* debt. 彼は借金で首が回らない.

4 …に没頭する, 夢中になる ▪He *is involved in* working out a puzzle. 彼は謎解きに没頭している.

be [***get***] ***involved with*** …とからみ合う; と連座する; に関係する ▪It *got involved with* the fishing line. それは釣糸とからみ合った ▪No person *was involved with* him in the crime. その犯罪に彼と連座する者は一人もいなかった ▪He *got involved with* the firm. 彼はその会社に関係した.

inward /ínwərd/ 形 ***in an inward voice*** はっきりしない[こもった]声で ▪He spoke *in an inward voice*. 彼はこもった声で話した.

inwrought /ɪnrɔ́ːt/ 形 ***inwrought on*** [***in***] …に織りこんだ, 打ちこんだ ▪Myriads of angels are *inwrought on* the curtains of the temple. 教会堂のカーテンには無数の天使の姿が織りこまれている.

inwrought with …を織りこんだ; と混合した, 密接した ▪The fabric looks as if it were *inwrought with* genuine gold. その布はまるで本物の金を織りこんだように見える.

iota /aɪóʊtə/ 名 ***not an*** [***one***] ***iota*** (***of***) (…が)少しもない ▪There is *not an iota of* truth in his story. 彼の話には本当のところはちっともない ▪I got *not one iota of* thanks for my efforts. いろいろ力を尽くしたのに, これっぽっちも感謝されなかった. ☞ギリシャ文字 ι は最小なところから「微小」の意.

Irish /áɪrɪʃ/ 形 (***as***) ***black as an Irish spinning wheel*** 《米》全く黒く ▪Pine logs looked *as black as an Irish spinning wheel*. マツの丸太は真っ黒に見えた.

get *one's* ***Irish up*** 《口》= get one's DANDER up.

One's ***Irish gets up.*** 《口》= One's DANDER is up.

weep Irish 《口》そら涙を流す ▪Surely the Egyptians *wept Irish*. 確かにエジプト人らはそら涙を流した. ☞アイルランドでお通夜に雇われた泣き男のように.

iron /áɪərn/ 名 ***a man of iron*** 強い人, 鉄人《精神または体の》 ▪His muscles show him to be *a man of iron* physically. 彼の筋肉を見れば, 彼が肉体的に強い人であることがわかる.

an iron hand [***fist***] ***in the velvet glove*** → the iron hand in the VELVET glove.

(***as***) ***hard as iron*** 鉄のように堅く; きわめて冷酷な, 厳格な ▪Our boss is *as hard as iron*. 我々のボスはきわめて厳格だ.

fresh [***new***] ***off the irons*** 学校出たての, 研究したばかりの; 新調の ▪They are young and inexperienced, *fresh off the irons*. 彼らは学校出たてで, 若く未熟である.

have [***keep***] ***many*** [***several, too many,*** etc.] ***irons in the fire*** 同時に多くの[いくつかの, 多すぎる, など]仕事[可能性]を用意しておく; 多くの仕事に手を出す[出しすぎる] ▪He *had too many irons in the fire* to find time for original research. 彼はあまりに多くの仕事に手を出しているので独創的な研究をする時間がなかった ▪I *have more irons in the fire* than one. 私は一つと言わずいろんな仕事に手を出している ▪I totally agree about *keeping several irons in the fire*. いくつかの仕事を用意しておくことに全面的に賛成だ.

in irons **1** 手かせ[足かせ]をかけられて; 束縛されて, 捕われの身となって ▪That saves the trouble of putting him *in irons*. それで彼に手かせをかける手数が省ける ▪A prisoner should not plead *in irons*. いかなる囚人にも自由に弁明させるべきだ.

2 《海》上手回しのときけたが回らないで船が金縛りの状態になって ▪The yards would not swing round, and the ship was *in irons*. 帆げたがどうしても回らないので, 船は金縛りの状態であった.

new off the irons →fresh off the IRONs.

pump [***push, throw***] ***iron*** 《口》(筋肉を鍛えるために)重量挙げをする ▪I've been *pumping iron* to try to keep in shape. このところ健康維持のためバーベル挙げをしている ▪Is *pumping iron* really necessary? 重量挙げは本当に必要か?

put [***lay***] ***every iron*** [***all irons***] ***in the fire*** あらゆる手段を試みる ▪He had begun to canvass and was *putting every iron in the fire*. 彼は選挙運動を始めていてあらゆる手段を講じていた.

put (***too***) ***many irons in the fire*** = have many IRONs in the fire.

rule with a rod of iron →ROD.

Strike while the iron is hot [***at its highest heat***]. 《諺》鉄は熱いうちに打て《好機を逸するな》.

the iron curtain 鉄のカーテン ▪There was no knowing what was happening behind *the iron curtain*. 鉄のカーテンの背後で起こっていることはわかりはしなかった. ☞鉄のカーテンとは, 1946年3月5日イギリス首相 Churchill の演説中の句で, 西ヨーロッパに接する旧ソ連勢力圏をさして言った.

the iron entered into *a person's* ***soul*** ひどい虐待を受けた; (捕われの苦悩・酷使のため)気力が打ちひしがれた ▪He gave a deep sigh; I saw *the iron enter into his soul*. 彼は深いため息をついた. 彼の気力が苦悩のため打ちひしがれているのを知った. ☞《聖》*Ps.* 105. 18のラテン語 ferrum pertransiit anima

I

ejus 'His person entered into the iron' (=he was placed in fetters) の誤訳.

with an iron hand 冷酷に ▪ He ruled the company *with an iron hand.* 彼は会社を厳しく統制した.

irreconcilable /ɪrèkənsáɪləbəl/ 形 ***irreconcilable to*** **1** (人・心が)…と和解[融和]できない ▪ He was *irreconcilable to* his father. 彼は父と和解できなかった ▪ Their minds were *irreconcilable to* the dominion of France. 彼らの心はフランスの統治とは融和しがたかった.

2 (言葉・思想が)…と調和しない, 両立しない ▪ That expression is *irreconcilable to* grammar. その表現は文法にかなっていない.

irreconcilable with (言葉・思想が)…と調和しない, 両立しない(=IRRECONCILABLE to 2) ▪ Their creeds were *irreconcilable with* salvation. 彼らの信条は救済と両立しなかった.

irregardless /ɪrɪgáːrdləs/ 形 ***irregardless of*** 《米口》…に構わず, にもかかわらず, に関係なく ▪ I don't think children should be hit, *irregardless of* what they've done wrong. 子供が悪いことをしたとしても, 子供をぶつべきではないと思う ☞非標準語法; irrespective と regardless との混交.

irrespective /ìrɪspéktɪv/ 形副 ***irrespective of*** **1** …にかかわりない, 関係ない ▪ Marriage registration should be *irrespective of* religion. 結婚登録は宗教とは無関係であって然るべきだ.

2 …にかかわりなく, を問わずに《現在の主な用法》 ▪ The posts were filled *irrespective of* nationality. それらの地位は国籍にかかわりなく振り当てられた.

irrespectively /ìrɪspéktɪvli/ 副 ***irrespectively of*** …にかかわりなく(=IRRESPECTIVE of 2) ▪ Anyone can apply for this post *irrespectively of* nationality, race or religion. 国籍, 人種, 信教の如何を問わず誰でもこの職に応募できる.

irresponsible /ìrɪspánsəbəl|-spɔ́n-/ 形 ***irresponsible for*** …に責任がなくて ▪ I am *irresponsible for* it. 私はそれには責任はない.

irresponsive /ìrɪspánsɪv|-spɔ́n-/ 形 ***irresponsive to*** …に反応なく ▪ He is *irresponsive to* exhortation. 彼は訓戒しても反応がない.

irritate /írətèɪt/ 動 ***be irritated against* [*by, with*]** *a person* 人に腹をたてる ▪ They *are irritated against* us. 彼らは我々に腹をたてている ▪ *Irritated with* her, he walked out of the house. 彼女に腹をたてて, 彼は家を出て行った.

be irritated at …にいやになる; に困る; にいらいらする ▪ He *was irritated at* the very thought of the long journey before him. 彼はこれから先の長旅を考えるだけでもいやになった.

isle /aɪl/ 名 ***the Emerald Isle*** エメラルドの島《アイルランドの愛称》 ▪ We've been exploring *the Emerald Isle* since we flew to Dublin. 空路ダブリン入りして以来ずっとアイルランド各地を探訪している.

isolate /áɪsəlèɪt/ 動 ***isolate*** *oneself* ***from*** … から離れる ▪ He *isolated himself from* all society. 彼はいっさいの交際を絶った《世を捨てた》.

issue /íʃuː, ísjuː/ 名 ***abide the issue*** 結果[成り行き]を待つ ▪ You must *abide the issue.* 君は結果を待たなければならない.

at issue **1** 論争中で[の]; 問題となっている《物が主語》 ▪ The question now *at issue* is whether the majority desire it or not. 今論争中の問題は大多数の者がそれを望むかどうかということである.

2 (人が)不和で, 意見が合わないで; (事が)調和しないで, 矛盾して ▪ We were *at issue* on the point. 我々はその点で意見が合わなかった ▪ The authority of the crown and that of the parliament are fairly *at issue.* 国王の権威と国会の権威とは全く衝突する.

bread-and-butter issues (健康・教育・雇用など)国民生活に関する重要な課題 ▪ The voters are worried about *bread-and-butter issues* like unemployment and taxes. 有権者たちは雇用や税などの国民生活に関わる諸問題を懸念している.

bring ... to an issue (事)に決着をつける ▪ He *brought* the matter *to a* successful *issue.* 彼はその事件にうまく決着をつけた.

dodge* [*duck*] *the issue 問題の対処を避ける; はっきりした返事を避ける ▪ He accused the delegates of *ducking* all *the issues.* 彼は代表団がすべての問題の対処を避けたと非難した.

force the issue 無理やり決着をつける ▪ I'm sorry to *force the issue* here, but we have to act now. ここで強引に即決してすまないが今動かないといけないのだ.

fudge the issue 問題をはぐらかす ▪ When Grandpa died, my parents *fudged the issue* by telling me he had gone away. おじいちゃんはよそへ行ったと言って両親は祖父の死をごまかした.

green issues 自然環境保護, エコロジー ▪ People's interest in *green issues* has started to grow. 環境問題に対する人々の関心が高まり始めた.

in the issue 帰するところは, 結局は ▪ They come to the same thing *in the issue.* それらは結局同じことに帰着する.

join issue **1** (訴訟・問題において…に)反対の意見を持つ, 反対の側に立つ (*with*) ▪ I will *join issue with* him upon it. 私はそれについて彼に反対します.

2 (訴訟において)双方が共同して訴訟の裁決を法廷に請う; 反対側の提起する論争点を受けいれる ▪ The plaintiff by his reply may *join issue* upon the defence. 原告はその返事によって, 相手の弁訴を受けいれることもある.

3 (問題について…と)論争する (*with*) ▪ We are ready to *join issue with* them upon this point. 我々はこの点についていつでも彼らと論争する用意がある.

4 (…と)折り合う, 意見が一致する; (と)団結する (*with*)《誤用》 ▪ Every believer will here *join issue with* David. 信者はみなこの点においてはダビデと同意見であろう ▪ He *joined issue with* his old enemy to lay waste his native country. 彼は昔の敵と協力して, 自分の故国を荒廃に帰させた.

join issues (双方が折り合わぬため)共同して訴訟の裁決を法廷に願う; (ある事柄を)法廷の決裁に任せる

▪ The plaintiff *joined issues* and the trial was set down for the next assizes. 原告は法廷の決裁に任せたので，裁判は次の巡回裁判のときと決まった.

make an issue of …を討議題とする ▪ They want to *make an issue of* everything. 彼らはすべてを討議題にしたがっている.

put … to issue (問題)を決着点まで持っていく ▪ While it is hot, I'll *put* it *to issue*. 問題がさめないうちに，それを決着させよう.

***take issue* (*with*)** **1** (…と)反対の意見を持つ; (に)反対する ▪ We *take issue* on the main point of the question. 我々はその問題の大きな点について意見を異にする ▪ I must *take issue with* his conclusions. 彼の結論に異議を唱えねばならない.

2 (…と)論争する ▪ He *took issue with* those people. 彼はその人々と論争した.

What's the big issue? 全く問題ではない ▪ *What's the big issue?* I'm 46 and I'm pretty sure I can play till I'm 50. 全然問題ないじゃないか. 僕は今46で，50までプレーできる自信があるんだから ▪ *What's the big issue* of screening to get on a plane? 飛行機に搭乗するのに所持品検査を行うことに問題なんかないだろ.

without issue 子がなくて ▪ He died *without issue*. 彼は子なくして死んだ.

it /ɪt/ 代 ***be it*** 《口》第一人者だ ▪ As a teacher he *is it*. 先生としては彼が第一人者だ ▪ Among biologists he *is it*. 生物学者の中では彼は一流だ.

have done it →DO².

have got it in one 《口》理解が早い ▪ That is true, Mr Wood; you *have got it in one*. おっしゃる通りです，ウッドさん. あなたは呑みこみが早いですね.

have got it in *one* ***to*** *do* …する才能がある ▪ I believe you'*ve got it in* you *to* write novels. 君は小説を書く才能があると信じているよ.

it is for *a person* ***to*** *do* →FOR.

it is … for *one* ***to*** *do* **1** …するのは人にとって…である ▪ *It is* bad *for* him *to* smoke. タバコを吸うのは彼には毒だ.

2 人が…するのは…である ▪ *It is* necessary *for* him *to* apologize. 彼はわびを言う必要がある.

it is kind* [*foolish,* etc.] *of *one* ***to*** *do* …するなんて(人は)親切である[ばかげている，など] ▪ *It is kind of* you *to* say so. そう言ってくださってありがとうございます ▪ *It is foolish of* him *to* go there. そこへ行くなんて彼はばかだ.

it is not for *a person* ***to*** *do* →FOR.

***it is only* [*just*] (*that*)** それは，ただ…だけである ▪ *It is just that* he doesn't have a great deal of imagination. それは，ただ，彼には想像力があまりないということにすぎない.

it is … since →SINCE.

it is … that …のは…である《it is … that の強調構文だが，…のところへ副詞・副詞句・副詞節がくる》 ▪ *It was* on Monday *that* I met him. 私が彼に会ったのは月曜であった ▪ *It was* here *that* he was born. 彼が生まれたのはここである ▪ *It is* but seldom *that* he comes this way. 彼がこちらの方へ来ることはめったにない.

***it is … that* [*who, which*]** …するのは…である《that, who, which は関係代名詞; 先行詞は it》 ▪ *It is* I *that* [*who*] am to blame. 悪いのは私です ▪ *It was* they *that* were wrong, not we. まちがっていたのは彼らであって，我々ではない ▪ *It was* this house *that* [*which*] Jack built. ジャックが建てたのはこの家であった.

it is well* [*ill*] *with …は無事[病気]である ▪ *It is well with* him. 彼は無事です.

***It's been* (*real*).** 《口》(あなたといっしょで)とても楽しかった ▪ *It's been*. Really it has. Bye. 楽しかったわ，ほんとに. じゃあね. ☞親友同士の間で言う言葉.

Italian /ɪtǽljən/ 形 ***fine Italian hand*** 手練の巧妙さ ▪ I see his *fine Italian hand* in this. この件に彼の手練の巧妙さが見える. ☞Italian hand とはもとキリストの使徒の秘書などが用いた優美な特色のある文字の書き方.

italic /ɪtǽlɪk/ 名 ***in italics*** イタリック体になって; イタリック体で ▪ The prologue is printed *in italics*. 序詞はイタリック体で印刷されている.

the italics are mine イタリック体にしたのは私である ▪ I quote the passage; *the italics are mine.* 私はその箇所を引用する. イタリック体にしたのは私である.

itch¹ /ɪtʃ/ 名 ***have an itch for*** **1** …をたまらなくほしがる，熱望する ▪ He *has an itch for* money. 彼は金をたまらなくほしがっている.

2 …したくてむずむずする ▪ I *have an itch for* seeing the sights of Paris. パリ見物がしたくてたまらない.

have an itch to *do* …したくてたまらない ▪ He *has an itch to* tour Mexico this winter. 彼はこの冬メキシコを旅行しようと熱望している.

the seven-year itch 性的倦怠[焦燥]期《結婚7年後に来るとされる》 ▪ There was the time we all had *the seven-year itch*. 誰しも結婚7年後に倦怠期に見舞われるときがあった.

itch² /ɪtʃ/ 動 *one's* ***fingers itch to*** *do* **[*for*]** …したくて手がむずむずする ▪ *The men's fingers* are *itching for* a fight. 兵士たちは一戦を交えたくて手がむずむずしている ▪ *His fingers itched to* give Nic a good slap on the chops. 彼はニックのあごにピシャリと一つやりたくて手がむずむずした ▪ *My fingers* were *itching to* hit Jim in the face. ジムの面をぶん殴ってやりたくてうずうずしていた. ☞昔体のある部分がかゆいのはある事の予兆であると思われた.

it itches むずがゆい ▪ Scratch where *it itches*. むずがゆいところをかきなさい.

itch to *do* 〚主に進行形で〛…したくてむずむずする ▪ I *am itching to* travel abroad. 海外旅行をしたくてたまらない.

itching /ítʃɪŋ/, **itchy** /ítʃi/ 形名 ***an itching palm*** →PALM¹.

***have* [*get*] *an itching foot* [*itchy feet*]** 《英口》**1** 旅行したくてたまらない ▪ He *had an itching foot* and could never stay put. 彼は大の旅行好きで少しもじっとしていられなかった.

2 別のことをしたがる ▪ He's tired of the same job and he's *getting itchy feet*. 彼は同じ仕事に飽きがきて別のことをしたいと思っている.

have an itching [***itching feet***] ***for*** …を非常にほしがる, がほしくてたまらない ▪ She *has an itching for* a television set. 彼女はテレビを非常にほしがっている.

have an itching palm [***itching fingers***] 《口》非常に強欲である; 金銭欲が深い, 賄賂をほしがる ▪ The rascal *has an itching palm*. その悪党は非常にどん欲である ▪ He *has itching fingers* and ten pounds will be enough. 彼は賄賂をほしがっているが, 10ポンドやれば十分だろう.

have itching ears ニュースや新しい事を聞きたがる (《聖》*2 Tim*. 4. 3) ▪ She *has itching ears* for something new and exciting. 彼女は新しいわくわくする話をしきりに聞きたがる.

item /áɪtəm/ 名 ***be an item*** 男女がカップルになっている, (男女関係が)できあがっている ▪ It is generally recognized that they *are an item*. あの二人がいい仲だということは衆目の一致するところだ.

item by item 一項目ごとに, 逐条的に ▪ The regulations were examined *item by item*. その規則は逐条的に調べられた.

itself /ɪtsélf/ 代 ***in and of itself*** それ自体で[は], それだけ取り上げたら ▪ Graffiti *in and of itself* is just a message. 壁の落書きそれ自体は一種のメッセージにすぎない ▪ His statement is interesting *in and of itself*. 彼の言明それ自体は興味がある ▪ The weather was not, *in and of itself*, the cause of the traffic delays. 天気それ自体は交通渋滞の原因ではなかった.

ivory /áɪvəri/ 名形 ***an ivory tower*** 象牙の塔《実社会から離れた, 夢想・思索・純理の場》 ▪ He views college as *an ivory tower*. 彼は大学を象牙の塔と見ている. ☞現代的意味は Sainte-Beuve がその著 *Pensées d'Août 3* に用いた; 《聖》*Solom*. 7. 4.

chip the ivories 《俗》話す ▪ They were *chipping the ivories*. 彼らは話をしていた.

live in an ivory tower 象牙の塔に住む, 現実を見ていない ▪ The professor *lives in an ivory tower* and has no idea of the cost of living. その教授は学究の世界に住んでいて生活費には疎い.

show one's ivories 《俗》歯をむき出す ▪ The wide grin *showed* all *his ivories*. 大きなにたにた笑いで彼の歯はみな見えた. ☞ivory《俗》=tooth.

tickle the ivories 《口・戯》ピアノをひく ▪ He sat down and began to *tickle the ivories*. 彼は腰かけてピアノをひき始めた. ☞ivory「(ピアノの)鍵」.

touch ivory 《俗》さいころ遊びをする ▪ I won't *touch ivory* tonight. 今夜はさいころ遊びをしない.

ivy /áɪvi/ 形 ***Ivy League*** アイビーリーグ《アメリカ東部の名門大学グループ》 ▪ Several *Ivy League* teams play one another regularly each year. アイビーリーグ校同士の対抗試合が例年きまって行われる.

izzard /ízərd/ 名 ***from A to izzard*** AからZまで; 初めから終わりまで; すっかり ▪ He knew his Bible *from A to* izzard. 彼は聖書を知り尽くしている. ☞izzard《古》=Zの文字.

not know A from Izzard AとZの区別がわからない, 全く文字が読めない ▪ In those days *not* a soul *knew A from Izzard*. その時代は文字のわかる者は一人もいなかった.

J

jack /dʒæk/ 名 ***A good Jack makes a good Gill* [*Jill*].** 《諺》夫がよければ妻もよくなる《妻は夫次第》.

a Jack* [*jack*] *in office いばる小役人 ▪ I hate *a Jack in office*. 私はいばる小役人は大きらいだ.

a Jack in the box*/*a jack-in-the-box びっくり箱(から飛び出す人形) ▪ He is *a* veritable *Jack in the box*. 彼はほんとにびっくり箱みたいだ《絶えず現れたり消えたりする》 ▪ He jumped to his feet like *a jack-in-the-box* at the loud noise. 大きな物音に彼はびっくり箱の飛び出し人形のように飛び上がった.

a Jack of all trades **1** 万能屋 ▪ Our gardener is *a Jack of all trades*. 我々の庭師は万能屋だ. **2** 何でも屋, よろず屋《色々なことをして生活する人》 ▪ Those boys will go through the world as *Jacks of all trades*. それらの少年は便利屋として世を渡るだろう.

a Jack of* [*on, o'*] *both sides 双方に味方する人, どっちつかず, 内股膏薬(うちまたこうやく) ▪ The bat is portrayed as *a Jack of both sides*. コウモリは内股膏薬として描かれている.

a Jack Sprat 小柄な少年[男性] ▪ He is *a Jack Sprat* and hates fat on any meat. 彼は小男でどんな肉の脂肪も大嫌いだった. ☞＜sprat「非常に小さな魚」; Mother Goose から.

a Jack Tar 船乗り[水夫]の愛称 ▪ That *Jack Tar* has just returned from sea. あの水夫は海からちょうど今戻ってきたところだ.

ball the jack 《米俗》疾走する, 急ぐ ▪ The car certainly *balled the jack*. その車はたしかに疾走した.

***be a Cheap Jack* [*cheap(-)jack*]** 安物売りをする, 汚い手を使ってまがい物を売る ▪ Bill *is a cheap-jack*, selling rubbish through the strength of his patter. ビルはぺらぺら口上を述べたてまがい物を売りつける安物売りだ.

be full of jack 《米口》いたずらっ気たっぷりである ▪ They *were full of jack*, chaffing each other. 彼らは互いにひやかし合っていたずらっ気たっぷりだった.

before* [*quicker than*] *you can* [*could*] *say Jack Robinson 《口・古風》あっという間に; 急に (→before one can say KNIFE) ▪ I'll be back *before you can say Jack Robinson*. 私はじきに帰って来ます.

climb like a steeple jack あぶなげなく高い所へ登る ▪ That boy can *climb like a steeple jack*. あの少年は全くあぶなげなく高い所へ登ることができる.

every Jack 《口》〚every を強調して〛どれもこれも ▪ *Every Jack* window was open. 窓という窓は一つ残らずあいていた.

***Every Jack has* [*must have, shall have, will have*] *his Gill* [*Jill*].** どの男にも似合いの女があるものだ; 《諺》若い男は誰でも恋人がある ▪ You'll find a partner all right; *every Jack has his Jill*. 必ず相手が見つかるよ. どの男にも似合いの女があるものだ.

every man jack 《口》〚every man を強調して〛誰もかれも, 一人残らず ▪ I'm going to get rid of *every man jack* of them. 彼らのうち一人残らず追い払うつもりだ.

I'm all right, Jack 《口》自分だけ元気であればいい ▪ "*I'm all right, Jack*" may not be all right. 「自分だけ元気ならばいい」ではよくあるまい.

Jack among the maids 女好きのする男, 女にもてる男 ▪ The Mayor was a pleasant man and *Jack among the maids*. 市長はおもしろい人で女性にもてた.

Jack ashore (陸に上った水夫, とは)水を離れた魚 ▪ You're *Jack ashore*, you know. 君はまるで水を離れた魚だね.

Jack at a pinch **1** 急場の手伝い人, 臨時雇い ▪ The Major took her to wife "*Jack at a pinch*". 少佐は彼女を急場の間に合わせとして妻にした. **2** 貧しい雇われ牧師《管轄教区がなく, 手伝いの要る教会へ雇われて行く牧師》 ▪ He was *Jack at a pinch*. 彼は貧しい雇われ牧師だった.

Jack in the* (*low*) *cellar まだ生まれないおなかの子, 胎児 ▪ His companions drank to *Jack in the low cellar*. 彼の仲間はお腹の子を祝って乾杯した.

Jack is as good as his master. 《諺》使用人も主人も同じ人間だ.

Jack of all trades and master of none. 《諺》多芸は無芸.

make* one's *jack 《俗》努力して成功する, 金持ちになる ▪ Now is the time for them to *make their jack*. 今こそ彼らが金持ちになる時だ. ☞木球遊びから.

not a Jack 《口》ただの一つも…ない ▪ *Not a Jack* window was open. 窓は一つも開いていなかった.

not ... jack* (*shit*)/*not ... jack diddly 《俗》全く…ない ▪ I don't like this job; I'm *not* earning *jack*. この仕事はいやだ, 少しも稼ぎになっていないから.

***on* one's *Jack Jones* [*jack jones*]** 《英口》独力で, 人手を借りずに (= on one's OWN (= alone)) ▪ Diet pills don't provide miracle weight loss *on their jack jones* without doing any exercise. 運動もせずにダイエット錠剤だけで奇跡的に体重は落とせない. ☞Jack Jones は 'alone' の不完全な押韻連語.

raise* [*tear up*] *jack 《米口》大騒ぎをする; 騒動を起こす ▪ The girls always *tear up jack* in my absence. 娘たちは私の留守にはいつも大騒ぎする.

jacket /dʒǽkət/ 名 ***dust* [*swinge, thrash, trim, warm*] *a person's jacket*** 《口・古風》人をぶんなぐる; 人を(むち・棒などで)さんざんに打ちすえる ▪ I will *dust the boy's jacket* if I find him in my orchard again. こんどうちの果樹園で見つけたらその少年をさんざんに打ちすえてやる.

in** one's **jacket (イモなど)皮のまま ▪ Potatoes were boiled *in their jackets*. ジャガイモは皮のままゆでられた.

jack pot, jackpot /dʒǽkpɑ̀t|-pɔ̀t/ 名 ***(be) in a jack pot*** 《米口》窮地に陥って(いる) ▪ I *am in a jack pot* now. 私は今窮地に陥っている.

get into a jack pot 《米口》窮地に陥る ▪ He finally *got into a jackpot*. 彼はついに進退窮まった.

hit the jack pot 《口》運よく勝つ, 大成功する; 急に大金にありつく ▪ Years later he *hit the* literary *jack pot*. 何年ものち, 彼は文学で大成功した ▪ When oil was discovered on his land, he *hit the jack pot*. 自分の土地に石油が発見されたとき, 彼は急に大金にありついた. ☞jack pot「ポーカーの積み立て掛け金」.

Jacob /dʒéɪkəb/ 名 ***a Jacob's ladder*** 非常に急なはしご[階段], 縄ばしご ▪ I had to climb up *a Jacob's ladder* to get to the top of the tower. 塔のてっぺんへは急な階段を登らねばならなかった. ☞(《聖》*Gen*. 28. 12); ヤコブが夢に見た天まで届くはしごから.

jag /dʒæg/ 名 ***have a jag (on)/fetch a jag*** 《米俗》酔っぱらう; 酔っぱらうほど飲む ▪ He *fetched a* complete *jag* to the festival. 彼はその祭りですっかり酔っぱらった ▪ We all *had a jag (on)*. みんなで酔っぱらうほど飲んだ.

jail /dʒeɪl/ 名 ***a jail bird [a jailbird]*** 《口》監獄の出入りを繰り返す前科者, 囚人 ▪ *The jail bird* was arrested for drunken driving again. その常習犯はまた酒気帯び運転で捕まった.

a jailbait 《俗》(性行為の)承諾年齢未満の少女[少年] ▪ Stay away from that girl; she is *a jailbait*. あの娘に近づいちゃいけない, まだ年齢が満たないから.

break jail 脱獄する ▪ Three inmates *broke jail* last night. 昨夜3人の在監者が脱獄した.

get out of jail 《英・報道》(スポーツの試合で)ピンチを逃れる, 敗北を避ける ▪ They *got out of jail* thanks to late goals. 終盤にゴールを重ねて, 彼らは敗北を免れた.

in jail 入獄して ▪ He is *in jail* for stealing now. 彼は今盗みのかどで入獄している.

send [put]...to jail …を投獄する ▪ He has *been sent to jail* twice. 彼は2回投獄されたことがある.

jam[1] /dʒæm/ 名 ***a bit of jam*** 愉快な[楽な]こと; 《俗》非常に美しい娘 ▪ That bonus is *a bit of jam*. その特別賞与は愉快なしろものだ.

a jam sandwich (英国の)警察車《パトカー》 ▪ We slowed down when we saw *a jam sandwich* in our rear-view mirrors. バックミラーにパトカーが映ったのでスピードを落とした. ☞白い車体に赤い横線が一本入っていることから.

a traffic jam 交通渋滞 ▪ We got stuck in *a traffic jam* for over an hour and missed our plane. 1時間以上交通渋滞に巻き込まれて飛行機に乗り遅れた.

all jam 《主に英》〚否定文で〛ごちそう[愉快なこと, 良いこと]ばかり ▪ This job is not *all jam*; it has its headaches. この仕事は良いことばかりではない. 頭の痛いこともある.

be money for jam →MONEY.

get in [into] (a) jam **1** 窮地に陥れる, もんちゃくを起こさせる, しからせる ▪ It *got* him *in a jam* with his girlfriend. そのため彼はガールフレンドともめた.
2 もんちゃくを起こす《警察に呼ばれる, 処罰される, しかられる》 ▪ You will *get into a jam* with the police. あなたは警察に呼ばれるだろう ▪ He *got in a jam* when he left without permission. 彼は無断で去って, 処罰された.

get out of a jam もんちゃく[窮境]から逃れる, 処罰を逃れる ▪ The country can *get out of its jam* by finding new foreign markets for its products. その国はその産物の新しい外国市場を見つけて窮境を逃れることができる.

have a bit of jam 《英俗》性交をする ▪ She *had a bit of jam* with a few locals. 彼女は2, 3人の地元の男と関係をもった.

have jam on [all over] one's face = have EGG on one's face.

have [like, want] jam on it 《口》十分以上のものを持つ[好む, 望む] ▪ I've given you everything you wanted. Do you *want jam on it*? 君にはほしいものはみなやった. これ以上まだほしいのか. ☞「パンにバターだけでなくジャムもつけて」が原義.

in a jam 《口》困って; 窮地にあって ▪ He is *in a jam* for money. 彼は金に困っている.

jam and fritters 《俗》ごちそう, 愉快なこと, 喜び[満足]を与えるもの ▪ To cheat them would be *jam and fritters* to him. 彼らをだますことは彼には実に愉快なことだろう.

jam tomorrow 《主に英口》(期待される)あすの楽しみ (Lewis Carroll, *Through the Looking-Glass*) ▪ He is concerned only with *jam tomorrow*. 彼はあすの楽しみだけにかかずらっている.

real jam =JAM and fritters.

jam[2] /dʒæm/ 動 ***be jammed up (with)*** …が(…で)ふさがれる, いっぱいになる ▪ The road *was jammed up with* motor vehicles. 道路は自動車ですっかりふさがれていた ▪ I got *jammed up with* the thought of it. そのことを考えて頭が一杯になった.

be jammed with …で雑踏する ▪ The street *was jammed with* traffic. その通りは人や車の往来で雑踏していた.

jam on one's [the] brakes/jam one's [the] brakes on 《口》急にブレーキをかける ▪ He *jammed on his brakes* but was unable to stop in time. 彼は急にブレーキをかけたが間に合わなかった.

jam up the works 《口》事をだめにする ▪ The chairman's action *jammed up the works*. 議長の行動が事をだめにした.

jam[3] /dʒæm/ 副 形 ***jam up*** 〚副詞的に〛 **1** ぴたりと接して; 十分に (*against*) ▪ Stand *jam up* *against* the wall. 壁にぴたりと寄りそって立ちなさい.

2 非常に近く, 接近して ▪ I rode *jam up* fifty miles. 私はほとんど50マイル馬で行った.

3 完全な, 徹底した ▪ In Paradise connubial bliss was really *jam up*. 楽園では結婚の幸福はほんとに完全であった.

jar[1] /dʒɑːr/ 名 ***(be) at (a) jar*** 仲たがいして(いる); 一致しない ▪ The German princes *were at a jar* about the choice of their Emperor. ドイツの諸侯は彼らの皇帝の選挙について意見が合わなかった.

jar[2] /dʒɑːr/ 名 ***on the jar*** 半開きになって, ちょっと開いて ▪ The door is *on the jar*. 戸はちょっと開いている.

jaundiced /dʒɔ́ːndəst/ 形 ***All looks yellow to the jaundiced eye.*** 《諺》黄疸(だん)にかかった人の目にはすべてが黄色く見える《ひがんで見ればどうにでも見える》(Pope, *An Essay on Criticism* 2. 359).

have [take] a jaundiced view of (ねたみ・競争心から)...をひがんで見る, に偏見を持つ ▪ He *takes a jaundiced view of* our affairs because our firm is larger than his. 我々の会社のほうが彼のより大きいので, 彼は我々の営業をひがんで見ている.

jaw /dʒɔː/ 名 ***all jaw (like a sheep's head)*** 《口》おしゃべりばっかり ▪ What was the party like? —*All jaw, jaw, jaw*! パーティーはどんなだったかい?—全くおしゃべりばっかりだった.

between the jaws of death 死地の間を, 風前のともしびで (→the JAWs of death) ▪ They are sailing *between the* very *jaws of death*. 彼らは一歩誤れば命のない状態で航海している.

get one's jaws tight 《口》怒る, 緊張する ▪ Why is she *getting her jaws* so *tight*? どうして彼女はあんなに怒っているのだろう.

have a jaw 会話する, 会談する ▪ Come with me now and let's *have a jaw* over some supper. わしについて来い, 晩飯を食いながらしゃべろう.

hold [stop, stow] one's jaw 黙っている; 黙る ▪ Please *hold your jaw* for a bit. ちょっと黙っていてください.

in the jaws of death 死地[危地]に陥って (→the JAWs of death) ▪ He is *in the jaws of death* and yet worries about her. 彼は死に瀕しているのに彼女のことを心配している.

one's jaw drops (驚き・失望で)口をあんぐり開ける ▪ *His jaw dropped* when he read the letter. その手紙を読んで彼は(驚いて)口をあんぐり開けた.

None of your jaw! 黙れ!, 生意気言うな! ▪ "*None of your jaw*," said the farmer angrily. 「黙れ」と農夫は怒って言った.

set one's jaw (あごを引きしめて)固い決意を示す, くじけない ▪ When she failed her test, she *set her jaw* and decided to try again. 彼女はテストに失敗したとき, くじけないでもう一度受ける決心をした.

shut one's jaw 《口》話をやめる; 黙る ▪ "Oh! *Shut your jaw*," said the boy. 「ああ, 文句を言うな」と少年が言った.

the jaws of death 死地 ▪ He rode into *the jaws of death*. 彼は死地におもむいた.

wag one's jaw(s) →WAG one's chin.

jawbone /dʒɔ́ːbòʊn/ 名 ***live on jawbone/call one's jawbone*** 《軍俗》信用借りで暮らす ▪ His ready money gone, he has to *live on jawbone*. 彼は現金がなくなったので, 信用借りで生活しなければならない. ☞jawbone＝credit.

jay /dʒeɪ/ 名 ***be a jay walker*** 《米》(交通規則を無視して)ふらふら街路を横切る ▪ Do you persist in *being a jay walker*? 君はあくまで交通規則を無視して街路を横切るのか.

jaybird /dʒéɪbərd/ 名 ***(as) naked as a jaybird*** →NAKED.

jazz /dʒæz/ 名 ***and all that jazz*** 《口》(それに)そういったもの, などなど ▪ We were talking about life, love, *and all that jazz*. 我々は人生, 恋愛その他もろもろのことを話題にしていた.

jealous /dʒéləs/ 形 ***be jealous of*** **1** ...を失うまいと必死である, 油断なく[大事に]守る ▪ He *is jealous of* his position. 彼は地位を失うまいと必死だ ▪ England *is jealous of* her rights. イングランドは自国の権利を油断なく守っている.

2 (人・成功など)をねたむ ▪ She *was jealous of* the newcomer. 彼女は新来者をねたんだ.

keep a jealous eye on ...を油断なく見守る ▪ He *kept a jealous eye on* my movements. 彼は私の行動を油断なく注視していた.

jee /dʒiː/ 間 ***Jee whizz!*** おやまあ《驚きを表す》 ▪ *Jee whizz*, I need a B in math this year. ちくしょう! 今年は数学でBを取らなきゃならないんだ. ☞jee＝Jesus.

Jekyll /dʒíːkɪl/ 名 ***a Jekyll and Hyde*** 二重人格者 ▪ She didn't know that he was *a Jekyll and Hyde*. 彼が二重人格者であることを彼女は知らなかった. ☞R. L. Stevenson 作の二重人格を取り扱った小説 *The Strange Case of Dr. Jekyll and Mr. Hyde* から.

jelly /dʒéli/ 名 ***be a jelly fish*** 気骨がない, ぐにゃぐにゃしている, 意志が弱い ▪ Don't *be a jelly fish*, just sitting there. そこにただ座って煮えきらないのではいけない.

beat [pound]... to [into] a jelly ...をボコボコに打ちのめす ▪ I'll *pound* you *to a jelly*. おまえをボコボコに打ちのめしてやるぞ.

shake [tremble, quiver] like a jelly 〚主に進行形で〛(恐怖・心配などで)ぶるぶる震える ▪ He *was trembling like a jelly*. 彼はぶるぶる震えていた.

turn to jelly/feel like jelly (体などが)不安[恐れ, 疲れなど]で力が入らなくなる ▪ Each time she looks into Harry's eyes, her legs *turn to jelly*. 彼女はハリーの目を見るたびに膝から力が抜けていく.

jeopardy /dʒépərdi/ 名 ***put [place]... in jeopardy*** ...をおびやかす, 危険にさらす ▪ The stoppage in the supply of fuel *put* our industry *in jeopardy*. 燃料の供給停止はわが国の産業をおびやかした.

Jericho /dʒérəkòʊ/ 名 ***go to Jericho*** 《口》失

J

せてしまう; くたばる《命令文になると go to HELL より穏やか; 拒絶などを表す》 ▪ *Go to Jericho!* Don't talk such nonsense. くたばっちまえ. そんなばか話をするな ▪ He may *go to Jericho* for all I care. あいつがどこへ失せたって, 私はいっこうにかまわない. ☞Jericho (《聖》 *2 Sam.* 10. 5)はパレスチナ (Palestine) の古都, 遠い所.

wish ... at Jericho …が(そこに)いなければよいと思う ▪ They began to *wish* the dance *at Jericho*. 彼らはダンスがなければよいのにと思い始めた ▪ I *wished* the Smiths *at Jericho*. 私はスミス夫妻がいなければよいのにと思った.

would see *a person* ***in Jericho before*** 絶対に…するものか ▪ I *would see* him *in Jericho before* I would go to him for help. あいつなんかに絶対に援助を求めるものか.

jerk /dʒəːrk/ 名 ***give ... a jerk*** …をぐいっと引く ▪ I *gave* the rope *a jerk*. 私は縄をぐいっと引いた.

put a jerk in it 《俗》機敏[活発]にやる; 急いでやる ▪ *Put a jerk in it*, can't you? しっかり機敏にやれよ. ☞体育から.

with a jerk ぐいっと ▪ He pulled the rope *with a jerk*. 彼はその縄をぐいっと引っぱった.

jerry /dʒéri/ 形 ***be jerry on*** 《俗》…に注意を集中している ▪ He *is jerry on* the job. 彼はその仕事に注意を集中している.

Jerusalem /dʒərúːsələm/ 名 ***Go to Jerusalem!*** くたばってしまえ!, ちくしょう!

the Jerusalem syndrome エルサレム症候群《エルサレムを訪れる人が自分も予言者になったような錯覚を覚える妄想》 ▪ Only one of them was diagnosed with true *Jerusalem syndrome*. 彼らのうち真性のエルサレム症候群と診断されたのは一人だけだった.

jest /dʒest/ 名 ***break [cut, drop] a jest*** 冗談を言う, しゃれをとばす ▪ He *broke an* unmannerly *jest* on me. 彼は私に対して無礼な冗談を言った.

in jest 冗談に, ふざけて ▪ Many a true word is spoken *in jest*. 冗談で言われる言葉に真実が多い.

make a jest of (人)をばかにする ▪ We *made a jest of* him. 我々は彼をばかにした.

no idle jest 冗談ではない《本気だ》 ▪ This threat to take your life is *no idle jest*. おまえの命をもらうというこの脅しは冗談ではないぞ. ☞しばしば脅しに用いる.

pass from jest to earnest 冗談からまじめに帰る, 冗談はさておく ▪ Now I'm going to *pass from jest to earnest*. Tell me why you refuse to go. 冗談はさておき, どうして行こうとしないのか聞かせてくれ.

Jesus /dʒíːzəs/ 名 ***a creeping Jesus*** 《口・軽蔑》偽善的な信心ぶる男 ▪ Tom called John *a creeping Jesus* behind his back. トムは陰ではジョンを偽善的な信心ぶる男と呼んでいた.

Jesus boots [shoes] 《俗》(ヒッピーなどの)男性用サンダル ▪ I dig your *Jesus shoes*, man, they look real cool. お前のサンダル気に入ったぜ. 超カッコいいじゃん.

Jesus wept! 〚驚き・怒りを表して〛なんということだ, ちくしょう ▪ Oh, *Jesus wept*, what am I going to do with you? ああ, なんてこった. お前をどうしてくれようか.

jet /dʒet/ 名 ***at a single jet*** 一気に ▪ It must be comprehended *at a single jet*. それは一気に理解しなければならない.

at the first jet 最初の発想により ▪ All work done *at the first jet* has a certain spontaneity. 最初の発想によって書かれたすべての作品はみなある種の自然性がある.

the jet set [jet-setter] ジェット(機)族, 贅(ぜい)を尽くし専用ジェット機で世界中を飛び回る有閑上流階級[大富豪] ▪ She is a member of *the jet set*, shopping in New York and dining in Paris. 彼女はジェット族で, ニューヨークで買い物をしパリで夕食をとる.

Jew /dʒuː/ 名 ***a perfect Jew*** 《口》欲の深い人 ▪ He is *a perfect Jew* when money is concerned. 彼は金に関するかぎり, 全くどん欲だ.

be a Jew boy 取引のすご腕である ▪ The seller *is a Jew boy*. 売り手は取引の辣腕(らつわん)家だ.

go to the Jews 《俗》金貸し[高利貸し]の所へ行く ▪ However hard up you may be, never *go to the Jews*. どんなにひどく金に困っていても, 高利貸しの所へは行くな.

Tell that to the Jews! 嘘を言え, まさか.

worth a Jew's eye きわめて貴重な ▪ The pictures are *worth a Jew's eye*. それらの絵はきわめて貴重である. ☞中世にユダヤ人に金を出させるために拷問として目をえぐり取ったことから.

jewel /dʒúːəl/ 名 ***a jewel of a*** 大切な ▪ He is *a jewel of a* boy. 彼は大切な少年です.

like a jewel [jewels] 非常に貴重に(で) ▪ Everything Romeo said was filed away *like jewels* in Juliet's heart. ロミオの言葉がすべてジュリエットの心に大切にしまい込まれた.

the jewel in the [*a person's*] ***crown*** 《米口》全ての(所持品の)中で最も貴重な物, (グループの中の)最良のもの, あることの最も魅力的な部分, 白眉, 最高の出来 (*of*) ▪ Sydney's Opera House is *the jewel in the crown of* modern Australian architecture. シドニーのオペラハウスは現代のオーストラリア建築のなかでぴかいちです ▪ St. Paul's Cathedral is *the jewel in the crown of* the City of London. セントポール大聖堂はロンドンのシティー区内で最高傑作の建造物だ. ☞1966年に出版された Paul Scott の小説名から. Jewel はインド, the crown は大英帝国をなぞらえたもの.

jib /dʒɪb/ 名 ***the cut of*** *one's* ***jib*** 風采, 容貌, 身なり ▪ I like *the cut of her jib*. 彼女の容貌が好きだ ▪ I know him for a person by *the cut of his jib*. 服装で彼が牧師であることがわかる. ☞もと水夫の使った比喩的表現; 船は三角帆の様子で見分けがつくことから.

jiffy /dʒífi/ 名 ***half a jiffy*** ちょっと(の間) ▪ Wait *half a jiffy*. ちょっと待て.

in a jiffy 《口》すぐ, 瞬く間に ▪ I'll be ready *in a jiffy*. すぐ用意します.

jig[1] /dʒɪg/ 名 ***in jig time*** 《口》非常に早く; すぐ

に ▪ They do everything *in jig time* there. そこでは何事もすぐにする.

on the jig 《口》じたばたして, そわそわして ▪ The sight of the white steam set him *on the jig* to get to the machinery. 白い蒸気を見ると彼はその機械の所に行こうとそわそわした.

(*the*) *jig is up* [*over*] 《俗》万事休す, もうだめだ (*with*) ▪ I began to think *the jig was up with* me. もう自分はだめだと私は思い始めた. ☞jig《古・俗》=trick.

jig[2] /dʒɪɡ/ 動 ***jig it*** **1** ジグ(軽快敏速なダンス)をする ▪ We are to *jig it* together again. 私たちはまたいっしょにジグをすることになっています.

2 敏活にバイオリンをひく ▪ He *jigged it* far better. 彼はずっとじょうずにバイオリンをひいた.

jigger /dʒíɡər/ 名 ***not worth a jigger*** 《口》少しの値うちもない ▪ The church is*n't worth a jigger*. その教会は三文の値うちもない.

jiggered /dʒíɡərd/ 形 ***be jiggered up*** 《俗》疲れはてる ▪ I'*m* quite *jiggered up* this evening. 私は今晩すっかり疲れはてた.

I am jiggered! 《口》おやおや!, これは驚いた! ▪ Well, *I'm jiggered*, there is good old Jim over there. おやおや, ジムのやつがあそこにいるぞ.

I'm jiggered if …なら首をかけてもよい; とんでもない ▪ *I'm jiggered if* it is true. それが本当であってたまるものか. ☞jiggered=damned.

jingbang /dʒíŋbæŋ/ 名 ***the whole jingbang*** 《口》堆積, (うずたかく積み上げた)山 ▪ The teddy bear was the only item of *the whole jingbang* that I liked. 山ほどの玩具の中でそのクマのぬいぐるみだけがお気に入りだった.

jingo /dʒíŋɡoʊ/ 名 ***by*** (***the living***) ***jingo*** ほんとに, 実際《強い断言の句》 ▪ *By jingo*, there's not a pond within five miles of the place. ほんとに, そこから5マイル以内には池は一つもない. ☞クリミア戦争(1853–1856)当時流行の愛国的俗歌のコーラス中の句から.

jink /dʒɪŋk/ 名 ***give the jink*** 計略を用いて[だまして]逃げる ▪ They have *given* us *the jink*. 彼らは我々をだまして逃げた.

jinks /dʒɪŋks/ 名 ***high jinks*** 《口》 **1** 騒々しいスポーツ, はね回り遊戯 ▪ All sorts of *high jinks* go on at the grass plot. あらゆる種類のはね回り遊戯が草地で行われる.

2 浮かれ騒ぎ, 飲み騒ぎ ▪ We always have *high jinks* at our annual picnic. 例年のピクニックでいつも浮かれ騒ぎをやる. ☞もと宴席などでの game の名.

jinx /dʒɪŋks/ 名 ***break*** [***smash***] ***the jinx*** 《俗》(競技で)連敗のあとに勝つ; ジンクスを破る ▪ He has *broken the jinx* that kept him from achieving fame. 彼は名声の獲得を妨げていたジンクスを破った.

put a jinx on =put the HEX on.

jitter /dʒítər/ 名 ***get the jitters*** 《口》非常に不安になる; 興奮する ▪ I always *get the jitters* as I sit in an airplane just before takeoff. 機内に座っていて離陸直前にはいつも不安になる.

give [***have***] ***the jitters*** 《口》ひどくいらいらさせる[する]; びくびくさせる[する] ▪ His scream *gave* the crowd *the jitters*. 彼の悲鳴は群衆を実にいらつかせた.

jive /dʒaɪv/ 名 ***collar*** [***latch***] ***the*** [*one's*] ***jive*** 《米俗》主旨を理解する ▪ Do you *collar my jive*? 主旨はわかりましたか.

job[1] /dʒɑb|dʒɔb/ 名 ***a bad job*** **1** 望みのないこと, むだ骨折り ▪ He gave up the pursuit of us as *a bad job*. 彼は我々を追うのを望みなしとあきらめた.

2《主に英》不幸な[困った]こと《出来事・事実・状態など》 ▪ She would make the best of *a bad job*. 彼女は逆境に極力善処したいと思った.

a (***bloody, jolly, very***) ***good job*** 幸運なこと ▪ It is *a jolly good job* the old woman is not dead. その老婆が死ななかったのは大変おめでたい.

a dead-end job 行き詰まった[先行きの暗い]仕事 ▪ Right now I'm working in *a dead-end job* with no hope of further progress. 今のところ更に発展の見込みもなく将来性のない仕事をしている.

a full-time job 時間と労力を目一杯要求されること ▪ Looking after three kids and an elderly man is *a full-time job*. 3人の子供と老人一人の世話をすることはかかりきりの大仕事だ.

a job lot/job lots **1** こみで安く売買する品, 一山いくらの品 ▪ They're good glasses; I bought them as *a job lot*. それは良いグラスです. こみで安く買いました.

2 雑多なもの[人々]の集まり ▪ He saw two cows belonging to Kidd among *a job lot* of cattle. 彼は雑多な牛の群れの中にキッド所有の2頭の雌牛を見つけた.

a job of work 《英》(むずかしい, 重要な)仕事 ▪ Tramps will not do *an* honest *job of work*. 浮浪者たちはまじめな仕事はしないものだ.

a man-sized job むずかしい仕事, 難事 ▪ It's *a man-sized job* to work out the timetable for a big railway. 大きな鉄道の時刻表を作るのは大仕事だ.

a put-up job 八百長; あらかじめたくらんだ仕業 ▪ The burglary was *a put-up job* by the former window-cleaner. 押し込みは元窓拭きの事前の内偵によるものだった.

an inside job 内部者(の手引き)による犯行 ▪ It must have been *an inside job*, thought the inspector. それは内部の手引きによる犯行にまずまちがいない, と警部補はにらんだ.

(***and a***) ***good job*** (***too***) 《口》よかったね ▪ I've got the first prize.—*Good job too*. 僕は一等賞をもらったよ—よかったね!

ax a job (経営維持のために)ある部門[経費, 人員]を削減する ▪ The bank is to *ax* 6,000 *jobs* across the world this year. その銀行は今年世界各地で6,000人の削減をする予定だ.

be out of (***a***) ***job*** 失業している ▪ He *is out of job* at the moment. 彼は今失業している.

by the job (時間決めでなく)一仕事いくらで, (常雇い

J

でなく)手間取りで ▪ He was paid *by the job*. 彼は一仕事いくらで給料をもらった.

do a bad job 仕事をへたにやる ▪ He *did a bad job* because he was too busy. 彼は忙しすぎてまずい仕事をした.

do a good job **1** 仕事をうまくやる; 有用な仕事をする ▪ He *does a good job* at his Youth Club. 彼は青年クラブですぐれた活動をしている.
2 (…を)立派にやる (*on, of doing*) ▪ She *did a good job of playing* the piano. 彼女はみごとにピアノを弾いた ▪ You *did a good job on* your composition. 君は作文を立派に書いた.

do a good job of it なかなかうまくやる ▪ The students are *doing a good job of it*. 学生たちはなかなかうまくやっている.

do a job on …をすっかりぶちこわす, やっつける ▪ The collision *did a job on* his car. その衝突で彼の車はめちゃめちゃになった ▪ He *did a job on* his rival in the third round. 彼は第3回戦で相手をすっかりやっつけた.

do** one's **job 割り当ての仕事をする ▪ I've *done my job* and now I am free for the rest of the day. 私は割り当ての仕事を終えたから, きょうはもうこのあとは暇です.

***do** a person's **job** (**for him**)/**do the job for** a person* **1**《口》人をやっつける[殺す] ▪ One attack of fever will *do the job for* him. 一度熱病にかかったら, 彼は往生してしまうだろう.
2 人の仕事をしてやる ▪ I'll *do the job for* you. 私があなたの仕事をしてあげましょう.

do odd jobs 雑役をする ▪ The boy was quite good at *doing odd jobs*. その少年は雑役をするのがとてもうまかった.

do the job 《口》(物が)望み通りの結果を出す, 目的を果たす (→do the TRICK) ▪ This hotel *did the job* perfectly for a one night stay. このホテルは一晩の宿のために完璧に目的を果たした.

don't quit [***give up***] *one's* ***day job*** まっとうな仕事をやめてはいけない ▪ Just because you sold a car *doesn't* mean you should *quit your day job*. 車が1台売れたからと言って, このまともな仕事をやめてよいというわけにはいかない. ☞新しい仕事にまだ慣れていない人の未熟さをからかうのに使われる.

fall [《俗》***lie***] ***down on the job*** 責任[仕事]を果たさない; 仕事を怠ける ▪ We relied on him to blow up the bridge and he *fell down on the job*. 我々は彼が橋を爆破するのを頼みにしていたが, 彼はその仕事を果たさなかった.

from job to job 職から職へ(移る, など) ▪ He drifted *from job to job*. 彼は職を転々と移った.

get a job 《俗》〚命令文で〛馬鹿な真似をやめろ, しゃきっとしろ ▪ You sat in line overnight to get a ticket to a rock concert? *Get a job*! ロックコンサートのチケットのために一晩中座って順番を取ったんだって? しゃきっとしろよ.

give it up as a bad job 《口》見切りをつける ▪ After several attempts to ride a bike I *gave it up as a bad job*. 自転車に乗る練習を数回やってみたが見込みがないと諦めた.

Good job! 《米口》すごい, よくやった ▪ Have you finished already? *Good job!* もう済ませたのかい. 大したものだ.

Good job too! いい気味だ! ▪ He's lost a lot of money in speculation. *Good job too!* 彼は投機で多額の金を失った. いい気味だ!

have a hard [***difficult***] ***job to*** do [*doing*]/***have no end of a job to*** do [*doing*] …することが非常にむずかしい ▪ I *had a hard job making* myself understood. 意図を相手に伝えるのがひと苦労だった ▪ We *had no end of a job to* persuade him to go away. 我々は彼を説いて去らせるのに非常に骨が折れた.

have a job 《口》(…することが)むずかしい ▪ As it was very dark, I *had a job* to find my key. 真っ暗だったので鍵を見つけるのがむずかしかった.

have a soft job 《口》楽な仕事をしている ▪ He *has a soft job* testing feather beds. 彼は羽根ぶとん検査という楽な仕事をしている.

in job lots 大量に, 十把一からげに ▪ His pictures were marketed *in job lots*. 彼の絵は大量に売りに出された.

it is a job… 《口》…は困難な仕事である ▪ *It is a job* for a poor man to give his children a good education. 貧しい人が子供たちに立派な教育を施すのは困難な仕事である.

***It is more than** one's **job is worth** (**to** do).* 《英口》…すると(人の)首がとぶ ▪ *It's more than my job is worth to* let you in without a pass. パスなしで君を入場させると僕の首がとぶ.

(***it's*** [***it is***] ***a***) ***good job*** (***that***) …とは大したものだ, 幸運[好都合]だ ▪ *Good job* you speak Arabic this well. 君がアラビア語をこんなにうまく話せるとはありがたい.

job lots →a JOB lot.

jobs for the boys 《口》(仲間向け, またはコネによる)楽な職 ▪ It's no longer soft *jobs for the boys*. それはもはやコネによる楽な職ではない.

just the job 《俗》まさしく欲しているもの ▪ Career change is *just the job*. 今こそ転職のチャンスだ.

know** one's **job 有能である ▪ He *knows his job* all right. 彼は確かに有能だ.

land [***be offered***] ***a plum job*** 運よくあこがれの職に就く[を勧められる] ▪ I *was offered a plum job* in a leading securities firm. あこがれの一流証券会社に職を与えられた.

lie down on the job →fall down on the JOB.

lose** one's **job 失業する ▪ He *lost his job* last week. 彼は先週失業した.

make a bad [***poor***] ***job of*** …をへたにやる ▪ You *make a poor job of* washing the windows. 君の窓の洗い方はまずいよ.

make a clean job of it 《口》十分[完全]にやり遂げる ▪ She finished inputting the data, having *made a clean job of it* as usual. 彼女はいつもどお

り完璧にデータ入力の仕事を終えた.

make a* (*good*) *job of it 《口》 **1** うまく[立派に]やる, やってのける ▪ Leave it to him. He'll *make a job of it*. それを彼に任せておけばうまくやり遂げるだろう. **2** うまいことをする, 儲ける ▪ He must have *made a good job of it*. やつはうまいことをしたに違いない.

make the best of a bad job →a bad JOB 2.

on the job **1** (人・機械が)活動して; 機敏で抜け目なく ▪ He is constantly *on the job*. 彼は絶えず活動している. **2** (仕事・務めに)精出して ▪ So long as they are *on the job*, they are sober workmen. 彼らは仕事に精出している間はまじめな労働者である ▪ The company does not allow smoking *on the job*. その会社は仕事中は禁煙である. **3** 就業して; (事務でなく)現業について ▪ I have been *on the job* since 1998. 私は1998年から現業にある. **4** 現場で, 職場で ▪ What do you want *on the job*? 職場では何を望みますか. **5** 《競馬》 (乗り手もよく)勝とうと一生懸命で ▪ The horse is *on the job*. 馬は勝とうと本気になっている. **6** 《戯》 性交中で ▪ Her parents caught them *on the job*. 彼女の両親は二人が交っているのを見つけた.

That job's jobbed. 《俗》 その仕事は終わった ▪ This is the last page. *That job's jobbed*. これが最後のページだ. これでとうとう終わりだ.

the job of* one's *life 今までにした最善の仕事 ▪ When you made that wireless set, you did *the job of your life*. あなたがあのラジオを作ったのは, 今までの最善の仕事でした.

job[2] /dʒɑb|dʒɔb/ 動 ***job it*** (ある仕事・ある期間のため)馬[車]を借りる ▪ Some were forced to *job it*. 馬を借りねばならない者もあった.

jockey /dʒɑ́ki|dʒɔ́ki/ 動 ***jockey for position*** **1** (ヨット競走・競馬などで巧みな策動によって)有利な位置を得ようとする ▪ After *jockeying for position*, the horse has now taken the lead. 策を用いて有利な位置を得た後, その馬は今や先頭に立った. **2** (策略によって)不当に有利な地歩を得ようとする, 人をだしぬこうとする ▪ The politicians are *jockeying for position*. 政治屋たちは(選挙に)有利な地位を得ようと策している.

Joe /dʒoʊ/ 名 ***an honest Joe*** 《口》 平凡正直な男 ▪ He's only *an honest Joe*. 彼は平凡正直な男にすぎない.

Joe Blow/《英口》 ***Joe Bloggs*** 《米口・戯》 普通の人 ▪ I would like to get *Joe Bloggs* to buy my books. 一般の人に私の著書を買ってもらいたい.

Joe Public* [*Schmoe*]**/《英口》 ***John Q. Public 一般市民, 公衆; 普通の人 ▪ If he was *Joe Schmoe* from nowhere, he'd be in jail. 彼がもし無名の市井人だったら今頃は獄中だろう ▪ Will *John Q. Public* buy the new product? 一般大衆はその新製品を買うだろうか.

not for Joe 《英口》 断じて...ない ▪ Go to a theatre on a hot night like this? *Not for Joe*. こんな暑い夜に劇場へ行くって? まっぴらごめんだよ. ☞ Joe = me.

jog[1] /dʒɑg|dʒɔg/ 名 ***give* a person's *memory a jog*** 人に思い出させる ▪ The book *gave his memory a jog*. その本が彼に思い出させた.

jog[2] /dʒɑg|dʒɔg/ 動 ***jog* a person's *arm* [*elbow*] *to* do** 腕[ひじ]をつついて...させる; 人を説得して[に思い出させて, うるさく迫って]...させる ▪ She *jogged his arm to* answer the question. 彼女は彼の腕をつついてその質問に答えさせた.

jog* a person's [one's] *memory 人の[自分の]記憶を呼び起こす ▪ Please *jog my memory* about that book. 私にその本を思い出させてくださいよ ▪ I failed to *jog my memory* of the event. 私はその出来事を思い出すことができなかった.

John /dʒɑn|dʒɔn/ 名 ***a dear John letter*** (特に兵役中の夫[男性]に宛てた)妻[女性]からの離縁状 ▪ His wife left him without a word, leaving only *a dear John letter* on the bed. 彼の妻はベッドに離縁状だけを残して口も利かずに彼の許を去った.

a John Bull 英国(人)を擬人化した呼び名 (→ UNCLE Sam) ▪ He is a fine specimen of *a John Bull*. 彼はまさに典型的な英国人だ.

John* [*Jane*] *Doe 《米》 (警察・病院で)本名が不明または名前を伏せているときに使う男性[女性]の仮名 ▪ The victim is still identified only as *John Doe*. 犠牲者の男性はまだ身元不詳だ ▪ That patient was referred to as *John Doe*. 患者は仮に無名氏とされた.

(one's) ***John Hancock/John Henry*** 《米口》 (直筆の)署名 ▪ Please put your *John Hancock* on this paper. この用紙にご署名をお願いします.

John Q. Public →JOE Public.

john /dʒɑn|dʒɔn/ 名 ***long johns*** 防寒用の長い下穿き[ズボン下], ももひき ▪ I am looking for blue flannel *long johns* for my son. 息子用の青いネルのズボン下を探しているのだけど.

Johnny /dʒɑ́ni|dʒɔ́ni/ 名 ***Johnny-come-lately*** 新入り, 新米, 新参者, 新鋭; (流行などに)遅れた人 ▪ A *Johnny-come-lately* beat the old favorite in the tennis match. テニスの試合で新入りの選手が優勝候補をやっつけた ▪ "Dent-de-lion" is a *Johnny-come-lately* in linguistic history. "dent-de-lion" (フランス語「タンポポ」) は言語史においては新語だ ▪ The prime minister is a *Johnny-come-lately* to the issue. 総理はその問題への取り組みが遅い. ☞ かつて米海軍で新兵につけられた名前.

Johnny-on-the-spot 《米口》 ここぞという時に直ちに駆けつける人 ▪ A good lifeguard is always a real *Johnny-on-the-spot*. 優れたライフガードはいざという時すぐに現場に急行する.

join /dʒɔɪn/ 動 ***If you can't beat* [*lick*] *'em, join 'em.*** 《口・諺》 反対できなきゃ同調せよ.

I'll join you in that. 同感です; ごいっしょしましょう ▪ Mary is the cleverest girl in the class.—*I'll join you in that*. メアリーはクラスの中で一番賢い—同感です ▪ I'll go to the pool for a swim.—*I'll join you in that*. プールへひと泳ぎしに行きたい—ごいっしょしましょう.

J

***join forces* (*with*)** →FORCE[1].

join** oneself **to …に加わる ▪ He *joined himself to* the opposite party. 彼は反対の党に入党した.

joint /dʒɔɪnt/ 名 ***case the joint*** 《俗》(盗み, その他の目的で)場所の下見をする ▪ John went in to *case the joint* for us. ジョンは我々のため下見をしに入って行った.

out of joint **1** 関節がはずれて, 脱臼して ▪ He had his shoulder put *out of joint*. 彼は肩を脱臼した. **2** 乱れて, 狂って ▪ All things here are *out of joint*. ここでは万事が乱れている ▪ The time is *out of joint*. 世の中が狂っている (cf. Sh., *Haml*. 1. 5. 189; しばしば The times are out of joint. として引用される).

put** a person's **nose out of joint →NOSE[1].

set … in joint (はずれた)…の関節を整復する ▪ Please *set* my knee *in joint*. 私のひざの関節を整復してください.

joke[1] /dʒoʊk/ 名 ***a black joke*** 愚弄(ぐろう)して笑われるべきこと ▪ Law and order have become *a black joke* nowadays. 近頃は法と秩序が鼻で笑われるようになってきた.

a corny joke 古くさいジョーク, 陳腐な冗談 ▪ I know it's *a corny joke*—I heard it somewhere before. 古い冗談だ—前にどこかで聞いたことがある.

a practical joke (人を困らせて笑う)悪ふざけ ▪ Well, I'm wet through as the result of his *practical joke*. やれやれ, あいつの悪ふざけのおかげでずぶぬれになった.

be* [*get*] *beyond* [*past*] *a joke →BEYOND.

be the* (*standing*) *joke of …の(相変わらずの)笑いものである ▪ I *am the joke of* the road wherever I go. どこへ行っても, 路上の笑い草になる.

carry* [*push*] *the* [**one's**] *joke too far 冗談の度が過ぎる ▪ You are *carrying your joke too far*. 君は冗談の度が過ぎるよ.

come a joke on …にいたずらする ▪ The rascal *came a joke on* me. その悪党は私にいたずらをした.

cut* [*break, crack, make*] *a joke 冗談を言う, しゃれをとばす; おかしい話をする ▪ He was in the habit of *cracking jokes*. 彼はしゃれを言う癖があった.

for a joke 冗談に, 冗談として ▪ I said it *for a joke*. 私は冗談にそう言った.

in joke 冗談(半分)に ▪ What I said *in joke* was taken in earnest. 私が冗談半分に言ったことがまじめに取られた.

(*It's*) *no joke.* 笑い事ではない; 重大な事だ ▪ An Irish faction fight is evidently *no joke*. アイルランドの派閥争いは明らかに重大事だ ▪ *It's no joke*, my cellphone broke. 大変! 私のケータイが壊れちゃった.

make a joke of (深刻なこと)を笑い飛ばす, からかう ▪ Don't *make a joke of* his innocence. 彼の純真さを茶化してはいけない.

play a joke on …をからかう, ひやかす ▪ Let's *play a joke on* the teacher. 先生をからかってやろうじゃないか.

push the* [**one's**] *joke too far → carry the JOKE too far.

see* [*not see*] *the joke 冗談がわかる[わからない] ▪ She does [can] *not see the joke*. 彼女は冗談がわからない.

take a joke 冗談[ひやかし, からかい]を笑って受ける ▪ Frank isn't able to *take a joke* on himself. フランクは自分に向けられたひやかしを笑ってすませられない.

***the joke is on** a person* 《口》(人をからかおうとして)かえって自分の方が笑われる羽目になる ▪ What if *the joke is on* you? かえってこっちの方がからかわれているとしたら?

turn … into a joke (あること)を茶化す ▪ You should not *turn* such a thing *into a joke*. そのような事を茶化してはいけない.

joke[2] /dʒoʊk/ 動 **(*all*) *joking apart* [*aside*]** 《口》冗談抜きで, まじめに言って (=(all) KIDding apart) ▪ *Joking apart*, what do you mean to do? 冗談はぬきにして, 君はどうしようというのか ▪ *Joking aside*, let us turn to serious matters now. 冗談はさておき, 深刻な問題に取りかかろう.

You have* (*got*) *to be* [*must be*] *joking.*/ *You're joking! =You're KIDding!

joker /dʒóʊkər/ 名 ***the joker in the pack*** 《主に英》**1** 異端児, 厄介者 ▪ He is described as *the joker in the pack* of French fashion. 彼はフランスのファッション業界では異端児とみなされている. **2** 将来予測できない影響力を持つ人[事柄] ▪ *The joker in the pack* is the political situation. 予測不能の要因は政治情勢である. ☞トランプのジョーカーから.

jolly /dʒáli|dʒɔ́li/ 副 動 ***be jolly hockey sticks*** 《英戯》(女性が)自意識過剰である, 上流階級ぶる ▪ She's okay, but a little *jolly hockey sticks*. 彼女はまあまあだが少し上品ぶっている.

Jolly good! 《英口》非常によい ▪ You're getting along fine? *Jolly good!* うまくやっているって? そいつはいい.

jolly well 《英》〚動詞・副詞を伴って〛全く, 本当に《怒って言う》 ▪ If so, you can *jolly well* walk home! そうだと言うなら, 勝手に歩いて帰るがいい.

Jordan /dʒɔ́ːrdən/ 名 ***cross the Jordan*** 死ぬ ▪ "*Crossing the Jordan*" symbolically refers to death. 「ヨルダン川を渡る」という句は象徴的に死を指す. ☞Jordan 川はこの世の荒野から the promised land (約束の国)へ行く所にあるとされ, Christian Styx (キリスト教上の三途の川)とほとんど同じに考えられた.

wish** a person **the other side of Jordan 人がどこかへ行ってしまえばよいと思う ▪ At the moment Dick *wished* her *the other side of Jordan*. その時ディックは彼女がどこかへ行ってしまえばよいのにと思った.

jostle /dʒásəl|dʒɔ́səl/ 動 ***cross and* [*or*] *jostle*** 《競走》相手の走者をじゃまして遅らせる《比喩的にも》 ▪ A thousand intrigues *crossed and jostled* one another in the forum. 法廷において多数の陰謀が互いにけん制し合った.

jostle** one's **way 押し分けて進む ▪ He is destined to *jostle his way* in the world. 彼は奮闘して出世する運命になっている.

jot /dʒɑt|dʒɔt/ 名 ***not* [*never*] *a* [*one*] *jot*** 《口》少しも…しない ▪ Solomon was *not a jot* less a tyrant. ソロモンの暴君ぶりは少しも劣らなかった ▪ He *never* abated *one jot* of his claim. 彼は自分の要求はちっとも譲らなかった.

not care a jot 《口》少しもかまわない ▪ I *don't care a jot* where you are going. 君がどこへ行こうと私はちっともかまわない.

journey /dʒə́ːrni/ 名 ***a day's* [*two days', three days',* etc.] *journey*** 1日[2日, 3日など]旅行の距離 ▪ It is *a day's journey* from here. ここから1日旅行の所にある ▪ How many *days' journey* distant? 旅行して何日くらいの距離ですか.

break** one's **journey (***at***) 旅行の途中で(…に)泊まる ▪ We *broke our journey at* Naples. 我々は途中ナポリに泊まった.

do a good journey 道がはかどる ▪ We have *done a good journey*. 我々は道がはかどった.

go* [*start, set out*] *on a journey 旅に出かける ▪ The Smiths have *gone on a journey* to Rome. スミス夫妻はローマへの旅に出かけている.

go on** one's **last journey 死出の旅路につく ▪ She *went on her last journey* yesterday. 彼女は昨日亡くなった.

(***I wish you***) ***a good* [*happy*] *journey!*** ごきげんよく行ってらっしゃい! ▪ *Wish you a happy journey!* Take care! 行ってらっしゃい! 気をつけて!

one's ***journey's end*** 旅路の果て; 人生行路の終わり ▪ I got to *my journey's end* before dark. 私は日の暮れないうちに目的地に着いた.

make* [*take, undertake*] *a journey 旅行をする (*to*) ▪ Father is *making a journey to* Rome. 父はローマへ旅行中だ.

on a* [*one's*] *journey 旅行して, 旅行中に ▪ We had capital fun *on our journey*. 我々は旅行中非常におもしろかった ▪ He is away *on a journey*. 彼は旅行に出ている.

start* [*set out*] *on a journey → go on a JOURNEY.

Jove /dʒoʊv/ 名 ***by Jove!*** 《英》おやまあ; 誓って ▪ *By Jove!* Here comes the coroner. おや, 検死官がやって来るぞ ▪ Never *by Jove!* 断じていたしません. ☞by Jove は by Jesus/by God の婉曲表現. Jove は Jupiter「ローマ神話の神々の王(ギリシャ神話の Zeus に相当)」の別名.

joy[1] /dʒɔɪ/ 名 ***Any joy?*** 《英口》うまくいった? (Any luck?) ▪ I've been looking for the missing book all afternoon.—*Any joy?* 昼からずっと行方不明の本を探していたんだ—見つかったかい?

***burst with joy* [*pride*]** 喜び[誇り]に満ちている ▪ She *burst with joy* as he smiled at her. 彼がにっこりすると彼女はうれしさで胸がはち切れそうになった.

for* [*with*] *joy うれしさのあまり ▪ She cried *for joy* at the news. 彼女はそのニュースを聞いてうれし泣きに泣いた.

full of the joys of spring 《口》とてもうれしそうに ▪ The boys came home from school *full of the joys of spring*. 少年たちはとてもうれしそうに学校から帰ってきた.

get* [*have*] *no joy 《英口》 **1** うまくいかない ▪ I tried to find that CD but *got no joy*. あの CD を探したが, うまく見つからなかった.
2 (人から) 援助をもらえない (*from*) ▪ I asked many people for help, but *got no joy from* them. 多くの人に援助を依頼したが得られなかった.

God give you joy! お幸せでありますように!

God give you joy of …の喜びが得られますように ▪ *God give you joy of* your child. お子さんをもつ喜びに恵まれますように.

in joy うれしいときに; 喜んで ▪ He was my companion *in joy* and sorrow. 彼はうれしいときも悲しいときも私の友であった.

Joy go with you* [*her,* etc.]*! あなた[彼女, など]が幸せでありますように ▪ We leave her here: *joy go with her!* 我々はここで彼女と別れる. 彼女が幸福でありますように!

to** one's **joy …が喜んだことには ▪ *To the joy of* his friends he won a lot of money. 友人たちが喜んだことには, 彼は多額の金をかち取った.

wish** a person **joy (***of, in***) 人の(…)を祝う, 人に(…の)喜びを言う; 人が(…を)喜べばよいと思う《しばしば皮肉》 ▪ I *wish* you *joy of* your success. ご成功おめでとう ▪ I *wish* him *joy of* her. 彼が彼女を気に入ればよいが ▪ The minister *wished* the couple *joy in* their marriage. 牧師はその夫婦の結婚を祝福した.

with joy →for JOY.

joy[2] /dʒɔɪ/ 動 ***joy to** do* …してうれしい ▪ I *joy to* see you. あなたに会えてうれしい ▪ Anne *joyed to* be here! アンはここにいるのを喜んだ!

joyride[1], **joy-ride**[1] /dʒɔ́ɪràɪd/ 名 ***take* [*be on*] *a joyride*** 《口》(遊山)ドライブをする ▪ They *were* off *on a joy-ride* to an unknown location. 彼らは初めての土地へドライブに出ていた.

joyride[2], **joy-ride**[2] /dʒɔ́ɪràɪd/ 動 ***go joyriding*** 盗んだ車でドライブに出かける ▪ They stole a car and *went joyriding* in town. 彼らは車を盗んで町を乗り回した.

Judas /dʒúːdəs/ 名 ***a Judas kiss*** ユダの接吻, うわべだけの好意; 裏切り行為 (《聖》*Matt*. 26. 48) ▪ He kissed her forehead—*a Judas kiss*. 彼は彼女の額にキスした—偽りのキスを. ☞Judas Iscariot がキリストにキスしてキリストを売ったことから.

play the Judas 裏切る ▪ He *played the Judas* and turned on his partner. 彼は裏切って, 自分の相棒を攻撃した.

judge[1] /dʒʌdʒ/ 名 (***as***) ***grave* [*solemn*] *as a judge*** (裁判官のように)きわめていかめしく, 厳粛で; まじめくさった ▪ He looked *as grave as a judge* when he met her penetrating glance. 彼女の刺すような視線をちらりと受けて彼は神妙な顔をしていた.

be a good* [*no*] *judge of …の鑑定がうまい[できない] ▪ He *is a good judge of* swords. 彼は刀剣の鑑別がうまい.

be judge 判断[判定]する ▪ Lady Macmillan *is judge* of her husband's speeches. レディー・マクミランは夫のスピーチを判定する ▪ Oh Heaven, *be judge* how I love Valentine. おお天よ, 私がいかにバレンタインを愛しているかご判定ください.

Let me* [*I'll*] *be the judge of that. 決めるのは私だ, それは私が判断する ▪ I'm the only one who ever loved you.—*I'll be the judge of that.* 君を愛したのは僕しかいない—それがどうかを決めるのは私よ ▪ *Let me be the judge of* what you've done. 君の実績の評価は私がする.

judge[2] /dʒʌdʒ/ 動 ***It's not for me to judge./Who am I to judge?*** 私には判断する[意見を言う]権利はない ▪ *It's not for me to judge*, but something just isn't right. 私が言うのもおこがましいが, どうもどこかがおかしい ▪ *Who am I to judge* who has value and who doesn't? 誰が有用で誰がそうでないかを私が判断するわけにはいかない.

Judge not, lest ye be* [*that ye be not*] *judged. 《諺》人を裁くな, あなたがたも裁かれないようにするためである(《聖》*Matt.* 7. 1).

You can judge* [*tell*] *a man by the company he keeps. 《諺》友を見れば人柄がわかる(→A man is known by the COMPANY he keeps).

You can't* [*Don't*] *judge a book by its cover. →BOOK[1].

judgement, 《主に英》**judgment** /dʒʌ́dʒmənt/ 名 ***a judgment call*** 《米》(法によらない)個人的判断 ▪ It's *a judgment call*, but that's what we are expected to do. 個人的な見解だが, 我々がそうすることが求められている.

a snap judgment 即座の判断 ▪ He is known for making *snap judgments*. 彼は即決することで知られている.

against** a person's **better judgment 人が好ましくないと言うのに ▪ I persuaded my son, *against his better judgment*, to be a doctor. 私は息子が好ましくないと言うのに医者になれと説得した.

cloud** one's **judgment 正しく判断する能力をあいまいにさせる ▪ Alcohol and drugs can *cloud your judgment*. 酒や薬物は正常な判断を狂わすことがある.

***form a judgment* (*on*)** (…に基づいて)判断する ▪ We must *form a judgement on* facts. 我々は事実に基づいて判断せねばならない.

in** one's **judgment …の意見[判断]では ▪ *In his judgment* they had no occasion to bow down to any one. 彼の考えでは, 彼らは誰にも頭を下げる必要はなかったのだ.

on** one's **own judgment 自分だけの判断で, 独断で ▪ He acted *on his own judgment*. 彼は自分だけの判断で行動した.

pass* [*give*] *judgment 判定[判決, 批判]を下す (*on, upon*) ▪ We'll *pass* no *judgment on* that. それには判定を下したくない.

***sit in judgment* (*on, upon, over*)** **1** (…を)裁判する ▪ The King himself *sat in judgment upon* the offenders. 国王自ら犯人たちを裁判された. **2** (…を)裁く, (を)批判[批評]する ▪ We must not *sit in judgment upon* other folks. 我々は他人を批判してはならない.

to the best of** one's **judgment →to the BEST of one's belief.

with judgment 思慮をもって ▪ He acted *with judgment*. 彼は思慮ある行動をした.

Judy /dʒú:di/ 名 ***make a Judy of** oneself* 《俗》(特に女性が)ばかなまねをする, 笑いものになる ▪ Don't *make a Judy of yourself* any more. これ以上ばかなまねはやめなさい.

jug /dʒʌg/ 名 ***in jug*** 《口》入獄して ▪ The old tramp's *in jug* right now. 老浮浪者は今入獄中だ.

jugful /dʒʌ́gfòl/ 名 ***by a jugful*** 《米口》〚主に否定文で〛大いに ▪ You have not been having all the fun, not *by a jugful*. あなたはいろいろと楽しんでばかりきたのではない. 全くそうではない.

jugular /dʒʌ́gjələr/ 名 ***go for the jugular*** 《口》(人)の最大の弱点をつく, 相手の最も弱いところを容赦なく攻めたてる ▪ I *went for the jugular* and criticized his poor English ability. 最大の弱点をついて彼のお粗末な英語力をこきおろした ▪ As a lawmaker, I always *went* straight *for the jugular*. 政治家の頃, 私は常に政敵の弱点を真っ向から攻撃した. ☞jugular「頸(けい)静脈」; 最大の弱点.

juice /dʒu:s/ 名 ***a juice dealer*** 《俗》(もぐりの)高利貸し ▪ Never go to *a juice dealer* however broke you are. いかに窮しても, 高利貸しには絶対に関わるな.

juice and cookies 代わり映えのしない[お定まりの]軽食と飲み物 ▪ The party was a disappointment—nothing but *juice and cookies*. パーティーはがっかりだったよ—ありきたりのスナックと飲み物だけでね.

let** a person **stew* [*leave** a person **to stew*] *in** his **own juice 人を自業自得で苦しませる ▪ He ignored my e-mail, so I'll *let* him *stew in his own juice* this time. 彼はぼくのメールを無視したから今度はこっちが無視してやろう.

stew in** one's **own juice →STEW[2].

tread* [*step*] *on the juice (車の)速度を速める ▪ *Tread on the juice*, old man. 君, スピードを上げろよ.

jump[1] /dʒʌmp/ 名 ***all of a jump*** 《口》びくびくして, いらいらして ▪ What's the matter with you—*all of a jump*? どうしたの? そんなにいらいらして.

(*at a*) *full jump* 《米口》全速力で ▪ The angry animal made for us (*at a*) *full jump*. 怒った動物は全速力で我々に向かって来た.

at a jump 一足飛びに, 一躍して ▪ He came to the conclusion *at a jump*. 彼は一足飛びにその結論に達した.

at the jump 初めに ▪ I put up a hallo *at the jump*. 私はしょっぱなに大声をあげた.

(*be*) *for the* (*high*) *jump*(*s*) 《口》違反者記録に

載せられて(いる); とがめ[裁判]を受け(ようとしている) ▪ Jim'll *be for the high jump* when his mother finds out he's been smoking. 喫煙しているところを母親に見つかったら, ジムは罰を受けることになるだろう. ☞乗馬が危険な柵を越えようとすることから.

***be* [*keep, stay*] *one jump ahead* (*of* a person)** (人に) 一歩先んじて(有利な立場に)いる, 人の言動の一歩先を読んでいる, 一枚上手である ▪ You have to *stay one jump ahead of* others to succeed in business. 業界で成功するには他に一歩先んじていなければならぬ ▪ We should *keep one jump ahead of* our competitors. 我々は常に競争相手の一歩先を読んでいるべきだ.

from the jump 初めから ▪ They have supported him *from the jump*. 彼らは初めから彼を支持した.

get a jump on *one* 《米俗》急ぐ ▪ You'll have to *get a jump on* you. 君は急がねばならないだろう.

get* [*have*] *the* [*a*] *jump on 《主に米口》…より先に出発する, に勝る; の先手を打つ ▪ Joyce *got a jump on* us by seeing the manager before we did. ジョイスは先手を打って, 我々より先に支配人に会った ▪ We *got the jump on* the enemy. 我々は敵より優勢になった.

give *a person* ***the jumps*** (驚き・興奮などで)人をびくっとさせる, ぎょっとさせる ▪ It *gives* me *the* most fearful *jumps* to think of it. それを思い出すと私はひどくぎょっとする.

(*go*) *take a jump* =JUMP in the lake.

have the jump on 《米口》…より先に出発して[始めて]いる; に勝っている, より優勢である ▪ U.S. students *had the jump on* their British counterparts. アメリカの学生はイギリスの学生より勝っていた.

have the jumps 《俗》(驚き・興奮で)びくっとする, ぎょっとする ▪ I just *got the jumps*. 私はちょっとぎょっとしたのです.

on the jump 《口》 **1** あちこち忙しく動いて, 忙しく ▪ My chipmunk is *on the jump* most of the time. ぼくのシマリスはたいていいつも忙しく動いている. **2** びくびく[いらいら]して ▪ The gentleman was exceedingly *on the jump*. 紳士はひどくいらついていた. **3** 全速力で ▪ John went out of the door *on the jump*. ジョンはすばやく戸外へ飛び出していった. **4** =on the keen JUMP.

on the keen jump 《米口》すぐに, 急に ▪ I met Bill *on the keen jump*. 私はビルにすぐ会った.

put *a person* ***over the big jump*** 《口》人を殺す ▪ He *put* this rascal *over the big jump*. 彼はこのならず者を殺した.

take a running jump 《口》〚主に命令文で〛立ち去る, 出て行く ▪ Oh, go and *take a running jump*! やい! とっとと立ち去れ!

take the high jump 絞首刑になる ▪ The young highwayman *took the high jump*. 若い追いはぎは絞首刑になった.

jump[2] /dʒʌmp/ 動 ***Go* (*and*) *jump in the lake.*** →LAKE.

one's ***heart jumps at*** …で心臓がどきんとする ▪ *My heart jumped at* the sound. その音を聞いて私の心臓がどきんとした.

jump a bounty 《米》入隊金目あてに軍隊に入ってすぐ脱走する ▪ He broke his leg attempting to *jump a bounty*. 彼は入隊金をもらってすぐ脱走しようとして足を折った.

jump a house 《俗》家のものを奪う; あき家を占領する ▪ They sometimes *jump houses*. 彼らはときどきあき家を乗っ取ることがある.

jump* (*a*) *ship 《米》(水夫が)船を捨てる, 船から脱走する ▪ He was detected in an attempt to *jump ship*. 彼は船から脱走しようとしているところを見つかった.

***jump at an opportunity* [*the chance, the bait*]** ある機会を進んで受け入れる ▪ You should never *jump at an opportunity* without a bit of thought. ろくに考えもせずにチャンスに飛びついてはならない ▪ He said he would pay for my vacation and I *jumped at the bait*. 彼が休暇旅行費用を出すという餌に私は飛びついた.

***jump at* [*to*] *conclusions* [*a conclusion*]** 結論[決心, 決定]を早まる, 早合点する ▪ I don't like to *jump to conclusions* and say he is wrong. 私は早合点して彼がまちがっていると言いたくない.

jump awry 一致しない; 意見を異にする ▪ The two have *jumped awry*. 二人は意見が一致していない.

jump* (*one's*) *bail 《俗》保釈中に逃亡する ▪ He *jumped bail* on a bigamy indictment. 重婚罪で起訴されて, 保釈中に逃亡した.

jump before being pushed 解雇される前に辞表を提出する ▪ His colleagues hoped that he would agree to *jump before being pushed*. 同僚たちは彼が解任される前に進んで辞職すればと思った.

jump *one's* ***bill*** 《俗》勘定を払わないで去る ▪ He rose early and *jumped his bill*. 彼は早く起きて, 勘定を払わないで逃げた.

jump *one's* ***board*** 《俗》食費を払わないで去る ▪ He *jumped his board* wherever he went. 彼はどこへ行っても食費を踏み倒した.

jump *a person's* ***claim*** 《口》 **1** (鉱山師が)他人の鉱区を横取りする ▪ Although a neighbor may *jump your claim*, don't be alarmed. 隣人が君の鉱区を不法占拠するかもしれないが, 驚いてはいけない. **2** 人の職[権利など]を横取りする ▪ A man *jumped my claim* when I was ill in hospital. 私が病気で入院中にある人が私の職を横取りした.

jump clear of 急いで…を避ける, に当たらないうちに跳びのく ▪ I *jumped clear of* the ball as it came my way. ボールがこっちに飛んできたので急いで避けた.

jump down *a person's* ***throat*** 人の言葉を激しくさえぎる; 人につっけんどんに返事する; 人を激しく攻撃する ▪ He tried in vain to *jump down her throat*. 彼は彼女の言葉を激しくさえぎろうとしたがだめだった ▪ Whatever I say, he *jumps down my throat*. 私が何を言っても, 彼は私を激しく非難する.

jump for joy 小躍りして喜ぶ ▪ He *jumped for*

J

joy when I told the news. そのニュースを知らせると, 彼は小躍りして喜んだ.

jump in at the deep end →go in at the DEEP end.

jump in the lake 《口》〚主に命令文で〛立ち去ってじゃまにならないようにする ▪ *Jump in the lake*, you nuisance! このやっかい者め, 消えうせろ.

jump in with both feet (事を)はりきって始める; (提案などに)飛びつく ▪ As soon as permission to attack arrived, the soldiers *jumped in with both feet*. 攻撃の許可が届くやいなや兵たちは勇んで攻撃を始めた.

jump into bed with 知り合ったばかりの相手と情交する ▪ She is ready to *jump into bed with* a total stranger. 彼女は見ず知らずの者と進んでベッドを共にする.

jump into the ring =JUMP in with both feet.

jump off the deep end 《米俗》大胆な[猪突猛進的な]挙に出る ▪ I *jumped off the deep end* and married again. 私は大胆にも再婚した.

jump off the page 真っ先に目に留まる ▪ The words just *jumped off the page* at me. その文字がさっと目に飛び込んできた.

jump on board [***aboard***] (活動などに)途中から参加する ▪ That's why I *jumped aboard* the program. そんなわけでその計画に途中から加わった.

jump out of harm's way 飛びのいて危険を避ける ▪ The man instinctively *jumped out of harm's way*. 男はとっさに飛びのいて危険を逃れた.

jump out of *one's* ***skin*** →fly out of one's SKIN.

jump rope 縄跳びをする ▪ With proper practice, anyone can *jump rope*. ちゃんと練習すれば誰でも縄跳びができるようになる.

jump smooth 《米俗》更正する, 堅気になる; おだやかになる ▪ He told me why he decided to *jump smooth*. 彼は足を洗おうと決めたわけを話してくれた.

jump the gun →GUN.

jump the lights 《口》信号を無視して運転し続ける ▪ A police officer stopped me for *jumping the lights*. 警察官に信号無視で止められた.

jump the queue →QUEUE.

jump the rails **1** (車が)急に脱線する ▪ A train *jumped the rails* on the line yesterday. 昨日その路線で列車が脱線した.

2 《英・報道》突然軌道がそれる, 急に歯車が狂う ▪ This is an example of how life in this modern society has *jumped the rails*. これは現代社会での生活の歯車が突然狂ってしまった状況を示す一例である.

jump the shark 《米》(テレビ番組が)低俗になる ▪ I don't think the program has *jumped the shark*. その番組の質が落ちたとは思わない.

jump the traces **1** (馬が)引き革をけりのける ▪ The horse *jumped the traces* in order to make the turn. 馬は向きを変えようと引き革をけりのけた.

2 束縛を振り切る, 反抗的[反逆的]になる ▪ I'm not telling you to *jump the traces* from your boss. 上司にたてを突けと言っているのではない.

jump the track →TRACK.

jump to conclusions →JUMP at conclusions.

jump to it 《口》素早く取りかかる; 機敏に行動する ▪ *Jump to it*, my lads! さあ若い諸君, さっさと取りかかりなさい ▪ He is ready to *jump to it*, whatever happens. 彼は何が起きても, すぐ機敏に行動ができる.

jump up and down 投げあげたりおろしたりする ▪ The child *jumped* the toy *up and down*. その子供はおもちゃを投げあげたりおろしたりした.

jumper /dʒʌ́mpər/ 名 ***stuff ... up*** *one's* ***jumper*** =shove ... up your ARSE.

juncture /dʒʌ́ŋktʃər/ 名 ***at this juncture*** **1** この時に ▪ The terrible plague advanced *at this juncture* from the East. 恐ろしい疫病がこの時東方からやって来た.

2 この重大な局面で ▪ Don't just act on impulse *at this juncture*. この重大な時に衝動的に行動しないこと.

jungle /dʒʌ́ŋgəl/ 名 ***the concrete jungle*** コンクリートジャングル《ビルが立ち並ぶ, 緑のない大都会》 ▪ I was born and raised in *the concrete jungle*. 私はビルの立ち並ぶ都会で生まれ育った.

junk /dʒʌŋk/ 動 ***(be) junked up*** 《俗》麻薬(特にヘロイン)中毒で(ある) ▪ Tom's all *junked up*. トムはすっかりヘロイン中毒だ.

junkyard /dʒʌ́ŋkjɑ̀ːrd/ 名 ***(as) mean as a junkyard dog*** 品行の悪い ▪ He was *mean as a junkyard dog* at first, tame as a kitten at the end. はじめ彼は行儀悪かったが, 終わりには実におとなしくなった.

jurisdiction /dʒùərəsdíkʃən/ 名 ***fall beyond*** [***within***] ***the jurisdiction*** ...の管轄外[内]である ▪ Such cases *fall beyond the jurisdiction* of a court. そのような事件は裁判所の管轄外である.

have jurisdiction over ...を管轄する ▪ The office *has jurisdiction over* the district. その役所はその地方を管轄する.

outside the jurisdiction of ...の管轄外で ▪ It is *outside the jurisdiction of* the office. それはその役所の管轄外である.

under the jurisdiction of ...の所轄で ▪ The Personnel Board is *under the jurisdiction of* the Cabinet. 人事院は内閣の所轄だ.

within the jurisdiction of ...の管轄内である ▪ The business is *within the jurisdiction of* this office. その事務は当所の管轄内だ.

jury /dʒʊ́əri/ 名 ***on a jury*** 陪審(団の一)員として ▪ I'm summoned *on a jury*. 私は陪審員として呼び出されている ▪ He wouldn't sit *on a jury*. 彼はどうしても陪審員を務めようとしなかった.

the jury is [***are***] ***(still) out (on)*** 《口》陪審はまだ討議中である; (...については)まだ結論[判決]が出ていない ▪ *The jury is still out on* the question of building a new parking lot. 新しい駐車場を造る問題については陪審はまだ討議中である ▪ *The jury's* *still out* regarding another increase in taxes. また増税するかに関してはまだ意見がまとまっていない. ☞裁判制度から.

just /dʒʌst/ 形副 ***Be just before you are generous.*** 《諺》寛大である前に公正であれ《金を他人にくれてやる前に借金を払え》.

be just the ticket [***thing***] (特定の状況に)おあつらえ向きのものだ, うってつけのものだ ▪ This compact car could *be just the ticket* for a small family. この小型車なら少人数家族にまさにぴったりです.

It's just one of those things. これもあきらめるより仕方のないものだ ▪ *It's just one of those things.* You'll have to get over it. あきらめるよりほかはない. 乗り越えなければならないのさ.

just a moment →Just a MINUTE.

Just a second. →SECOND[1].

just about 《口》 **1** かろうじて ▪ He will *just about* win. 彼はかろうじて勝てるところだ.
2 〚強意的に〛まさに, 全く ▪ I've had *just about* enough of you. 君には全くうんざりした.
3 ほとんど ▪ John is *just about* the fastest runner. ジョンはほとんど最速の走者である.

just another 平凡な ▪ This is *just another* political trick. これはありきたりの政治的策略にすぎぬ.

just anybody 〚否定文で〛絶対に誰(に)も ▪ They don't give this post to *just anybody*. 彼らはこの地位を絶対に誰にも譲らない.

just as **1** ちょうど…するとき ▪ *Just as* I was about to go out, he came to see me. 私がちょうど出かけようとしていたとき, 彼が会いに来た.
2 ちょうど…ように ▪ I will do *just as* you advise. ご忠告の通りにいたします.

just by すぐ近くに ▪ The house is *just by* the school. その家は学校のすぐ近くにある.

just come up 《俗》未熟の, 愚鈍な ▪ Our new guard is *just come up*. 今度雇った守衛は未熟である. ☞「植物の芽や花などが今出かけたばかり」が原義.

just in case 万一の場合に備えて, ただもしもの場合のために ▪ They should be told what is going on *just in case*. 万一の場合に備えて今起きていることを彼らに知らせねばならない ▪ Why do you ask the phone number?—Oh, *just in case*. なぜ電話番号を聞くのか?—そりゃもしもってことがあるからだよ.

just like ちょうど…のような; いかにも…のやりそうな ▪ It is *just like* a rose. それはちょうどバラの花のようです ▪ It is *just like* him to say so. それはいかにも彼の言いそうなことだ.

Just (***like***) ***my luck!*** や, またしくじった! ▪ "*Just my luck*," he said with a laugh.「あ, またやってしまった!」と彼は笑いながら言った.

just like that →THAT.

just now →NOW.

just on (数量が)ちょうど…きっかりで; ほとんど…, ほぼ… ▪ *Just on* nine o'clock, we arrived at Weilheim. 9時きっかりにワイルハイムに到着した.

just so **1** 完全で, 申し分のない状態で ▪ His new jacket was *just so*. 彼の新しいジャケットは完璧だった.
2 全くその通りで (→Just [Quite] SO) ▪ It is *just so*. いかにもその通りです.
3 端正に ▪ People did not behave *just so*. 人々は礼儀正しくしなかった.
4 申し分なく ▪ Everything passed *just so*. 万事申し分なく運んだ.
5 ちょうど(…と)同じ (just as (... as))《as ... as を強調して》 ▪ He gave them *just so* much work as they could do in a day. 彼はちょうど1日でできる分量の仕事を彼らに与えた.
6 〚接続詞的に〛であるかぎり (so long as) ▪ Take as much food as you want, *just so* you don't overeat yourself. 食べすぎない限りほしいだけ食べなさい.
7 とても (very) ▪ Life is *just so* beautiful. 人生はとても美しい.

just the job [***ticket***] 《口》まさしくうってつけの人[もの] ▪ Thanks for lending me your lawnmower—it was *just the ticket*. 芝刈り機を貸してくれてありがとう—ちょうどうってつけのものだったよ ▪ For a certain type of patients, the doctor is *just the job*. ある種の患者には, その医者こそうってつけだ.

not just 厳密には[全くは]…でない ▪ The runway was *not just* in sight. 滑走路が十分には見えていなかった ▪ I was *not just* so well. 私はあまり丈夫でなかった.

not just yet 今のところはまだ…ない ▪ I *can't* give you the money *just yet*. お金は今は無理だ(がもうすぐ渡してあげる). ☞もうすぐ起きることを暗示.

only just enough まずどうやら ▪ Things have been picking up, but *only just enough*. 景気は上向いているものの, まずまずのところだ ▪ I had *only just enough* money for the ticket. ようやく切符が買えるだけの持ち合わせだった.

That's just it [***the trouble***]. 《口》まさにそれが問題だ ▪ Are you wanted by the police?—*That's just the trouble*. 警察に追われているのか?—それがまさに頭の痛いところだ ▪ Don't ever lend the lawnmower to him.—*That's just it*. We are neighbors. 彼に芝刈り機を絶対に貸すな—そいつが問題だ. 隣同士だからね.

justice /dʒʌ́stɪs/ 名 ***bring*** *a person* ***to justice*** 人を裁判して罰する ▪ The criminal *was brought to justice* at last. 犯人はついに裁かれた末に処罰された.

deny *a person* ***justice*** 人を公平に扱わない, 人の価値を認めない ▪ They *denied* him *justice*. 彼らは彼を公平に扱わなかった.

do *oneself* ***justice*** 自分の能力を十分発揮する ▪ He *did himself justice* in the examination. 彼は試験に十分能力を発揮した.

do justice to/***do ... justice*** **1** (認めるべきを認めて)…を公平[正当]に扱う[評する] ▪ I should like to *do* full *justice to* both sides. 私は双方を正当に扱いたい ▪ To *do* her *justice*, she was a good-natured woman. 公平に言えば彼女は気立ての良い女性だった.
2 (実物)をよく[十分]表している ▪ This photograph

J

does justice to you. この写真のあなたはよく撮れている ▪ Art can *do* full *justice to* a sunset. 美術は日没を十分に描き出すことができる.

3(食物)を十分[たらふく]食べる ▪ We have *done* ample *justice to* the dinner. 食事をたらふく食べた.

4(問題など)を十分に論じる[扱う] ▪ It is impossible to *do justice to* the subject in a short article. 短い論文ではその問題を十分に扱うことはできない.

5…の真価を知る; を十分に理解する ▪ He never *did justice to* his son's ability. 彼は息子の才能が全くわからなかった.

***do … the justice to say* [*of saying*]** …を公平に評して…と言う ▪ I must *do* him *the justice to say* that he was a good man. 公平に言って彼は良い人でした.

***in justice* (*to*)** (…を)公平に言って[扱って] ▪ I must say, *in justice* (*to* him), that he is sincere. 公平に言って, 彼はまじめであると言わねばならない.

it is bare* [*mere*] *justice to say …と言うのは当然の評にすぎない《お世辞ではない》 ▪ *It is* but *bare justice to say* that he has acted honorably. 彼が立派な行動をしたというのは当然の評にすぎない.

J

poetic justice 詩的正義《勧善懲悪・因果応報などの理想的正義観》 ▪ I believe there's some form of *poetic justice* at work in real life as well. 私は(文学のみならず)実生活にも詩的正義が働いていると信じている ▪ It was *poetic justice* that I neglected my family for my work and then lost both. 仕事で家族を省みなかったところ, 次に仕事も家族も失ったのは自業自得だった. ☞Pope, *The Dunciad* 1.52.

rough justice **1** まずまずの公平な処理[処罰] ▪ I saw it as *rough justice* when I got very sick from overdrinking. 飲みすぎてひどい吐き気がしたのはまず当然の報いだと思った.

2(法に則らない)不公平な処理[不当な処罰] ▪ The youngsters were given *rough justice*. 若者たちは不当な処罰を受けた.

with justice 公正に ▪ All men should be treated *with justice*. 人はみな公正に扱われねばならない.

justification /dʒʌ̀stəfəkéɪʃən/ 名 ***in justification of*** **1**…を正当とするため ▪ Nothing can with reason be urged *in justification of* revenge. 復しゅうを正しいと主張しうる理由は何一つない.

2…を弁護して ▪ She could plead so much *in her* own *justification*. 彼女は自己弁護として大いに弁ずるところがあった.

***there is no justification of* [*for*]** …をしても正当化できるわけがない ▪ *There is no justification of* a war. 戦争は正当化できない.

justify /dʒʌ́stəfàɪ/ 動 ***be justified in*** …してもよいとされる; しても正当であるとされる ▪ He *was justified in* saying that the odds were largely in his favor. 彼は勝算が大いに自分にあると言ってもよかった ▪ The Germans *are justified in* their fear of Russia. ドイツ人がロシアを恐れるのはもっともである.

justify *oneself* 自分の行為[主張]を正当化する, (堂々と言い訳をして)身のあかしを立てる; 自分が正しい[望ましい, 保証つきである, 有用である]ことを証明する ▪ She tried to *justify herself* for her conduct. 彼女は自分の行為を弁明しようとした ▪ Science *justifies itself* when it contributes to the desire to know. 科学は知識欲に貢献するとき, 自らが有用であることを証明する.

justify* (*as*) *bail 保釈金支払い後も十分財力ありと宣誓する ▪ They *justified bail* for considerable sums. 彼らは相当多額の保釈金支払い後も十分財力があると宣誓した.

The end justifies the means. 《諺》目的がよければどんな手段でも正当となる, 目的は手段を正当化する.

K

kangaroo /kæ̀ŋgərúː/ 名 ***a kangaroo court*** 吊るし上げ, 人民裁判, リンチ《開拓地や囚人仲間で行われる》 ▪ He was tried by *a kangaroo court* and found guilty. 彼は私的裁判にかけられ有罪となった. ☞裁判の進行がカンガルーの動きのように飛躍的なことから.

keel /kiːl/ 名 ***(back) on an even keel*** 船首[船尾]の喫水が一様で, 水平に《比喩的にも》 ▪ The frigate was *on an even keel.* フリゲート艦は船首から船尾までが水平であった ▪ Everything got *on an even keel.* 万事は平静になった.

lay down a keel 船を起工する ▪ The shipyard *laid down* 10 *keels* in a year. 造船所は1年に10隻の船を起工した.

keen /kiːn/ 形 ***(as) keen as a razor*** (頭が)かみそりのように鋭い ▪ The child is *as keen as a razor.* その子供は非常に明敏だ.

(as) keen as mustard 《英口》きわめて熱心で, 熱望して ▪ He is *as keen as mustard* about going to France. 彼はしきりにフランスへ行きたがっている ▪ The clerk is *keen as mustard* in his business. その店員はきわめて仕事熱心だ. ☞商品名 Keene's mustard との語呂合わせ.

be keen about [at, for] …に熱心である, 熱中している ▪ He *is keen at* this sport. 彼はこのスポーツに熱中している ▪ They *are* very *keen about* money. 彼らは金儲けに夢中である.

(be) keen of …が鋭敏で(ある) ▪ The dog *is keen of* scent and swift of foot. 犬は嗅覚が鋭敏で足が速い.

be keen of a job 《俗》仕事好きである ▪ If you offer to take charge of those brats, you *are keen of a job.* 君がそのガキどもの世話を申し出るなら, 君はよほどの仕事好きだ.

be keen on 《口》 **1** …が大好きである; にほれている ▪ I'*m* very *keen on* dancing. 私はダンスが大好きだ.

2 …に熱心である; を熱望している ▪ They *are keen on* outdoor sports. 彼らは戸外スポーツに熱心である ▪ Why *are* you so *keen on* saving money? なぜあなたはそんなに金をためることに一生懸命なのですか.

***be keen to** do* …したがっている ▪ I *am keen to* go abroad. 私は外国へ行きたくてたまらない.

keep[1] /kiːp/ 名 ***be worth** one's **keep*** 養いがいがある ▪ Pigs *are* now *worth their keep.* 今は養豚が引き合う ▪ You *are* not *worth your keep.* おまえはごくつぶしだ.

earn** one's **keep 食っていくだけをかせぐ; 雇い[養い]がいのあるだけの仕事をする ▪ You must *earn your keep.* 君は食うだけはかせがなければならない ▪ He does not *earn his keep.* 彼はごくつぶしだ ▪ I had to *earn my keep* as a sidewalk vendor and was able to finish high school. 私は露天商をして生活費をかせがざるを得なかったが, 高校を終えることができた.

for keeps 《口》 **1** (おはじき遊びなどで)取ったら返さない取り決めで ▪ We promise not to play marbles *for keeps.* 取り上げルールでおはじき遊びはしないことを約束します.

2 永久に, きっぱりと ▪ I'm coming into the business *for keeps* next fall. 次の秋にいよいよきっぱりと実業界に入ります ▪ Sure, I'm yours *for keeps.* もちろん私は永久にあなたのものです.

3 永久に自分のものとして ▪ You can have that pen *for keeps.* そのペンはあなたに差しあげます ▪ She thought the ring was *for keeps.* 彼女はその指輪はもらったものと思っていた.

4 全く, 完全に; 本気で, まじめに ▪ He is hitting the ball *for keeps.* 彼は全くよく働いている ▪ They're separating *for keeps.* 彼らは本気で別れようとしている.

in bad [low] keep 保存が悪く, 手入れが悪く; 悪い状態で ▪ Many of them were exceedingly good horses, but *in low keep.* それらの多くはきわめて良い馬だが, 手入れが悪かった.

in good [high] keep 保存がよく, 手入れが行き届いて; 良い状態で ▪ The furniture was *in good keep.* 家具は手入れが行き届いていた.

No keeps! 《児童》取りっぱなしはなしだよ!《おはじき遊びなどで, 取っても終わったら返す遊び方》.

play (for) keeps **1** 《児童》おはじき遊びを取ったら返さない取り決めの上でやる ▪ He and I *played for keeps* and I won all his. 彼と私はおはじき遊びを取り上げルールでやって, 私は彼のをみな取ってしまった.

2 《クリケット》アウトになるまいと守勢を取る ▪ They were obliged to *play for keeps* for so long. 彼らはやむなく非常に長い間守勢を取らねばならなかった.

keep[2] /kiːp/ 動 ***How are you keeping?*** 《口・古風》→HOW are you? 1.

***keep** doing* **1** (…に)…させておく ▪ I am sorry to have *kept* you *waiting* so long. 大変長くお待たせしてすみません.

2 …し続ける ▪ He *kept working* at the problem. 彼はその問題をやり続けた.

***keep** oneself* **1** 自活する, 自分一人を養っていく ▪ I cannot *keep myself* yet, but am dependent on my parents. 私はまだ自活できないで, 両親に頼っている.

2 ある状態にじっといる ▪ The prince *kept himself* in his seat. 殿下はじっと着席しておられた.

3 (自己を)押さえる; 控える (*from*) ▪ He could not *keep himself from* laughing. 彼は笑わずにはいられなかった.

4 (…のために)精力をたくわえておく ▪ He seems to

K

keep himself for great occasions. 彼は大事に備えて精力をたくわえているようである.

keep alive **1** 人の命をつなぐ ▪ The doctor *kept* him *alive* by a blood transfusion. 医師は輸血によって彼の命をつないだ.

2 油断なく警戒する ▪ They *kept alive* and caught the two burglars. 彼らは油断なく警戒して二人の夜盗を捕えた.

keep at it やり続ける, がんばる, やり通す ▪ By *keeping at it* all day he is able to get over two acres. 一日中働き続ければ, 彼は2エーカーを耕せる.

keep *one's* ***bed*** [***room, chamber***] 病気でベッド[部屋]に引きこもっている ▪ My mother is ill and *keeps her room*. 母は病気で自室に引きこもっている.

keep body and soul together →BODY.

keep *a person* ***dangling*** 人をあいまいな状況のままにしておく, 求婚者の男性を心待ちに待たせる ▪ You shouldn't *keep* him *dangling* like this. こんな風に彼に待ちぼうけを食わせてはだめじゃないか.

keep fit [***well***] 元気である, 健康である ▪ Grandfather *keeps fit*. 祖父は元気です.

keep going 《口》(激励して)しっかり続けなさい ▪ *Keep going*. You're nearly there. がんばって続けろ. あと一息だ.

K

keep *a person* ***going*** **1** 人の命をつなぐ ▪ The medicine he gave me *kept* me *going*. 彼のくれた薬で命をつないだ.

2 人に財政的援助をする ▪ I will *keep* him *going*. 彼を財政的に援助してやろう.

3 人を楽しませる ▪ They're lively girls and will *keep* you *going*. 彼女らは元気な娘たちで, あなたを楽しませるでしょう.

keep *a thing* ***going*** 物を維持していく, 続けさせる ▪ He *keeps* the club *going*. 彼はクラブを維持している.

keep *a person* ***guessing*** →GUESS[2].

keep hard at it いつもしきりに勉強している ▪ That student *keeps hard at it*. あの学生はいつもよく勉強している.

keep *oneself* ***in*** ...を自給する ▪ He *kept himself in* clothes. 彼の衣類は自前だった.

Keep in there! 《口》がんばれ, 努力を続けろ ▪ Don't give up. *Keep in there!* あきらめたらだめだ. がんばれ!

keep it 《口》持っている, あげる, もらう ▪ Do you want this lighter back or can I *keep it*? このライター, 返そうか, それとももらっていいかな.

keep it down 静かにする ▪ Can't you *keep it down*, boys? 静かにできないのかね, 君たち?

keep it hot [***warm***] 《俗》(討論・企てなどを)やめないで続ける ▪ Though the scheme seemed hopeless, he *kept it hot*. その計画は見込みがないように見えたが, 彼はやめずに続けた.

keep it up **1** (今までどおり)続ける ▪ I pretended to be angry with her, but I could not *keep it up*. 彼女に怒っているようなふりをしたが, あまり続かなかった.

2 仕事ぶりを続ける, 努力をゆるめない; 水準を維持する ▪ He works too hard; he'll never be able to *keep it up*. 彼はあまりにひどく働きすぎる, 決してこの調子を続けてはいけないだろう ▪ I hope the firm will *keep it up* to standard. その会社には水準を維持してほしい.

3 《口》遊興を続ける ▪ I *kept it up* too long. 私はあまりにも飲み騒ぎを続けすぎた.

4 関係を続ける ▪ He *kept it up* with her. 彼は彼女との関係を続けた.

keep left [***right***] 左側[右側]通行する (＝KEEP to the left [the right]) ▪ Traffic in Britain *keeps left*. 英本国では左側通行である.

keep on keeping on 《口》努力を続ける, 手がけていることを継続する ▪ Do your best. Just *keep on keeping on*. ベストを尽くせ. 今やっていることをひたすらやり続けろ.

keep on truckin' いつも通りやっていく, 普通に続ける ▪ OK, gang, I know this is tiring, but let's *keep on truckin'*. いいか, みんな. こいつはやっかいな代物だが, まあいつも通りやろうぜ.

keep out of college 大学の寮に入らないでいる ▪ He decided to *keep out of college*. 彼は大学の寮に入らないでいることにした.

keep plugging along 《口》こつこつ取り組む ▪ He *kept plugging along* for years, and eventually became president. 彼は長年たたき上げて遂には社長になった.

keep *a person* ***posted*** →keep a person POSTed (up).

keep quiet [***still***] **1** 黙っている ▪ *Keep quiet* about the surprise party. サプライズパーティーのことは誰にも言わないこと.

2 じっとしている ▪ It's hard for children to *keep still* unless they're sleeping. 子供は眠っていない限りじっとしていられない.

keep *one's* ***shirt***(***s***) ***on***/《英口》***keep*** *one's* ***hair on*** (***one's head***) 《口》→SHIRT; HAIR.

keep time and tune 調子を合わせる ▪ If you are in a society of any sort, you must try to *keep time and tune*. どんな会にでも入っているなら, 歩調を合わせるようにしなければならない.

keep to *oneself* **1** 人に知らせない ▪ He *kept* the news *to himself*. 彼はそのニュースを人にもらさなかった.

2 自分のものとしておく[ものに取っておく] ▪ He *kept* the money *to himself*. 彼はその金を着服した.

3 人と交わらない ▪ He is a moody man, and prefers to *keep to himself*. 彼はむっつりした人間で, 人と交わらないほうが好きだ.

keep *oneself* ***to*** *oneself* 《口》人と交際しない, 一人でいる ▪ He *keeps himself to himself* too much. 彼はあまりにも交際を避けすぎる.

keep to *one's* ***bed*** ＝KEEP one's bed.

keep to *one's* ***own company*** →COMPANY.

keep to the left [***the right***] 左側[右側]通行をする (＝KEEP left[right]) ▪ Instead of *keeping to the left*, they tend to stay in the middle of the road. 左側通行をしないで，彼らは道のまん中を通る傾向がある.

keep up the good work 《俗》 続ける ▪ I want you to *keep up the good work*. あなたに続けてやってもらいたいのです.

keep up with the Joneses 自分より身分の高い人[収入の多い人]と同じ生活をする，友人や隣人と同じ生活をする ▪ Andrei was *keeping up with the* capitalistic *Joneses*. アンドレイは資本家たちと同じ生活をしていた.

keep well →KEEP fit.

Keep well! お元気で，お達者で《別れるときのあいさつ》 ▪ *Keep well* and fit, John! —Best wishes, Jack. 元気で，ジョン!—君もな，ジャック!

Keep your shop, and your shop will keep you. 《諺》 かせぐに追いつく貧乏なし.

not care whether school keeps or not → SCHOOL[1].

will keep …はあとで話してもよい，今話す必要はない ▪ That news *will keep*. そのニュースはあと回しでよい.

you can keep ... 《口》 **1** 私はもう結構です《いりません》 ▪ Shall I give you this book? —No, *you can keep* it. この本をあげようか?—いや，結構だ.
2 私はいや[きらい]です ▪ *You can keep* the country life. 私は田舎の生活はきらいです.

You can't keep a good man [woman] down. 《諺》 才能がある人は必ず頭角を現す.

keeper /kíːpər/ 名 ***not be a person's [one's brother's] keeper*** 誰かのお目つけ役[お守り役]でない ▪ Part of me wants to help my brother, but part of me realizes I *can't be his keeper*. 弟を助けたい気持ちも少しはあるが，彼のお守りなんかできないとも思う. ☞聖書中のカインとアベルの物語(《聖》 *Gen*. 4. 9)から.

keeping /kíːpɪŋ/ 名 ***have the keeping of*** … を預かっている ▪ I *have the keeping of* the papers. 私はその書類を保管している.

in a person's keeping 人が保管して ▪ The papers are *in my keeping*. 書類は私が保管している ▪ We are safe *in God's keeping*. 我々は神に護られて安全である.

in keeping with …と調和して; と一致して ▪ The carpet is *in keeping with* the rest of the room. その敷物は部屋の他の部分と調和している ▪ Your expenses should be *in keeping with* your income. あなたの支出は収入に相応しなければならない.

in safe [fine, good] keeping 安全に[立派に]保管されて，しまわれて，預けられて ▪ When I go away, I leave my papers *in safe keeping* in the bank. よそへ行くときは，書類を銀行へ安全に預けておく.

out of keeping with …と調和しないで，一致しないで ▪ The furniture is *out of keeping with* the room. その家具は部屋と調和しない.

place ... in the keeping of …を(人)に預ける ▪ I *placed* the valuables *in the keeping of* the captain. 私は貴重品を船長に預けた.

ken /ken/ 名 ***beyond [outside, out of] one's ken*** …の視界外に; の知識の範囲外に ▪ The island was *beyond our ken*. その島は我々には見えなかった ▪ That subject is quite *out of my ken*. その問題は私には全くわかりません.

in [within] one's ken …の視界内に，の知識の範囲内に ▪ The ship came *within our ken*. 船は我々に見えてきた.

swim into one's ken 見えてくる; 発見される ▪ Then a new star *swam into my ken*. そのとき新星が私に見えて来た. ☞Keats, *On First Looking into Chapman's Homer* 9–10.

kennel /kénəl/ 名 ***go to kennel*** (犬が)小屋に入る; 隠れる; 逃げこむ ▪ The dog can "sit", "lie down", "stay", and "*go to kennel*". その犬は「お座り」「伏せ」「待て」それに「(小屋に)入れ」ができる.

Kentish /kéntɪʃ/ 形 ***(a round of) Kentish fire*** 《英》 (ひとしきりの)長く熱狂的な拍手喝采 ▪ The audience gave the speaker *a round of Kentish fire*. 聴衆は弁士にひとしきり長く熱狂的な拍手喝采を送った. ☞Kent 州において1828–29年に反カトリック主義の弁士に与えられた長い喝采から.

kerb /kəːrb/ 名 ***on the kerb*** 《英》 (株式取引が)街上で行われて《特にその日の取引が終わった後》 ▪ Later in the day the trading was slow, and *on the kerb* cash was done at £40. その日遅くなると取引は緩慢で，街上で現物が40ポンドで取引された.

kernel /kə́ːrnəl/ 名 ***He that would eat the kernel must crack the nut.*** 《諺》 何かよいものを手に入れたければ働かなくてはだめだ.

kettle /kétəl/ 名 ***a kettle of fish*** **1** (遊山・川船遊びなどで)その場で料理する魚料理 ▪ They go to the water-side to eat *a kettle of fish*. 彼らは川辺へ行って即席魚料理を食べる.
2 川遊び，遊山 ▪ They had *a kettle of fish*. 彼らは遊山をした. ☞kettle<kittle<kiddle「川魚を取るかご」.

a nice [fine, pretty] kettle of fish 《主に米》 大混乱; 困った状態 ▪ Here's *a pretty kettle of fish* you have brought upon us. 君は全く困った事をしでかしてくれたな.

another [a different] kettle of fish 別のもの，別の人 ▪ It's *a different kettle of fish* altogether. それは全く別の事だ.

keep the kettle boiling =keep the POT boiling.

The pot calls the kettle black. →POT.

key[1] /kiː/ 名 ***(as) cold as a key*** →(as) COLD as fish.

find a key to …の手がかりを見つける ▪ The police have *found a key to* the mystery. 警察はその謎の手がかりを見つけた.

get [have] the key of the street 《戯》 (夜帰りが遅くて)締め出しを食う，宿なしになる ▪ It is too late now; you*'ve the key of the street*. もう遅すぎる. 君は締め出されたのだよ.

give a person the key of the street 《戯》 (夜

帰りが遅いので)人に締め出しを食わせる ▪ His father *gave* him *the key of the street* by bolting the front door. 彼の父は表の戸にかんぬきをかけて彼を締め出した.

have* (*got*) *the key of the cellar 食料を管理している ▪ *I've got the key of the cellar.* 私は食料を管理している. ☞cellar「地下食糧庫」.

have the key of the door **1** (ある場所に)自由に出入りできる ▪ There are only two persons who *have the key of the door* to the house. その家に自由に出入りできるのは二人しかいない.

2 《口》18 歳になる, 成人する ▪ Happy 18th birthday! Now you *have the key of the door*! 18 歳の誕生日おめでとう! これでお前も大人の仲間入りだな.

have* [*hold*] *the key to …の解決のかぎを握っている ▪ Now I *have the key to* the whole difficulty. さあこれでその難問もすっかり解決がつく.

hold* (*in hand*) *the keys of …のかぎ[急所]を握る, を支配する ▪ He *holds the key of* the casket. 彼はその小箱のかぎを握っている ▪ She always *holds the keys of* her own situation. 彼女はいつも自分で自分の立場を思いのままにする.

in a minor key →MINOR.

in key (…と)調子が合って; (と)調和して (*with*) ▪ The color of the curtain is *in key with* the rest of the furniture. カーテンの色は他の家具と調和している. ☞key「(音楽の) 調子」.

lay* [*put*] *the key under the door (ドアの下にかぎを置く, とは)家をたたんで去る ▪ The tenant *laid the key under the door.* 借家人は家をたたんで出た.

off key 調子が狂って ▪ My letter may sound a little *off key*. 私の手紙は少し調子が狂っているように聞こえるかもしれません.

on key 調子が整って; 整とんされて ▪ Keep the cuisine *on key*. 調理場を整とんしておきなさい.

out of key 調子はずれで ▪ His voice is *out of key*. 彼の声は調子はずれだ.

***play a key part* [*role*]** 主要な役割を演じる, 肝要である ▪ Migration will *play a key role* for population growth in Europe. 欧州の人口増加のためには移民が肝要であろう.

(*the*) *golden* [*silver*] *key* 賄賂 ▪ Every door opens to *golden keys*. 賄賂で開かない戸はない ▪ *The silver key* will open the gates of the monastery. 賄賂ならその修道院の門は開くだろう.

the key to the problem 問題解決の必須手段 ▪ *The key to the problem* of violence among our youth is education. 現代の若者の暴力問題解決のかぎは教育だ.

turn the key in …にかぎをかける ▪ He *turned the key in* the safe. 彼は金庫にかぎをかけた.

turn the key on *a person* ドアにかぎをかけて人を閉じ込める[閉め出す] ▪ The guard threw the prisoner into a cell and *turned the key on* him. 監視人は囚人を独房に放り込み, かぎをかけて閉じ込めた.

under lock and key 錠をおろし(かぎをかけ)て ▪ I keep my money *under lock and key*. 私は自分の金を厳重保管しています.

key[2] /kiː/ 動 ***key*** *one's* ***talk to*** …に話の調子を合わせる ▪ He always *keys his talk to* the occasion. 彼はいつもその場に話の調子を合わせる.

keynote /kíːnòʊt/ 名 ***give the keynote to*** …の大方針を定める ▪ You must *give the keynote to* the study of English. あなたは英語研究の基本方針を定めなければならない.

***strike* [*sound*] *the keynote* (*of*)** (…の)基調をかなでる, に触れる ▪ He *struck*, at the commencement, *the keynote of* his oration. 彼は最初に自分の演説の基調に触れた.

khaki /kǽki|kɑ́ːki/ 名 ***get into khaki*** 陸軍に入る ▪ He has *got into khaki*. 彼は陸軍に入った.

in khaki (カーキー色の)陸軍服を着て ▪ He was *in khaki*. 彼は軍服を着ていた.

kibe /kaɪb/ 名 ***follow* [*tread*] *on the kibes of*** …のすぐあとについて来る ▪ Suicide *follows* closely *on the kibes of* extravagance. 贅沢のすぐあとに自殺がやって来る.

tread on* [*gall*]** *a person's* ***kibes **1** 人にしつこく迫って怒らせる ▪ The peasant *galled the kibes of* the gentleman. 農夫はあまりしつこく迫って, その紳士を怒らせた.

2 強いて人の感情を害する, 人の痛いところに触れる ▪ All *tread on the kibes of* one another. みんながお互いの痛いところにさわっている.

kibosh /káɪbɑʃ|-bɔʃ/ 名 ***put the kibosh on*** 《口》やっつける, 阻止する, だめにする ▪ It finally *put the kibosh on* me. それはとうとう私をくたばらせた ▪ That'll *put the kibosh on* his extravagance. そうすれば彼の贅沢はやむだろう ▪ It might *put the kibosh on* the plan. それはその計画をぶちこわすかもしれない.

kick[1] /kɪk/ 名 ***a kick in the pants* [*butt, ass*]**/《英卑》***a kick up the backside* [*arse*]** 《米口・卑》**1** みじめな敗北[逆転]; スリル; こっけい; おもしろい人 ▪ It takes *a* terrific *kick in the pants* to get the citizens out of the house. 市民たちを家から出させるには, すごいスリルがいる.

2 (励ましとなる)批判[叱責, 活]を入れること ▪ The coach gave the players *a* good *kick in the butt*. そのコーチは選手たちに耳の痛い苦言を呈した ▪ I hope this will give him the *kick up the backside* he needs. これで彼の目が覚めればいいが.

***a kick in the teeth* [*the guts, the stomach,* etc.]** 急な激しい逆転[阻止, 敗北, 失望] ▪ The pleased delegation got *a* delayed *kick in the teeth*. 喜んでいた代表団はおそまきの急激な敗北を喫した ▪ My dismissal as coach was *a kick in the guts*. だしぬけにコーチをクビにされてがっかりした.

better than a kick in the teeth 《口》ないよりはましで ▪ It may not bring in much money, but still it is *better than a kick in the teeth*. 大した実入りにはならないだろうが, それでもないよりはましだ.

for kicks 《口》楽しみに, おもしろくて ▪ We play

for kicks, not money. 我々は楽しみにやるのであって, 金がほしいからではない ▪ My sister is keen to have a go at bungee-jumping—just *for kicks*. 妹はしきりにバンジージャンプに挑戦したがっている, ただスリルを求めて.

get a kick (*doing*) (…して)非常にスリル[愉悦]を感じる ▪ I *get a kick water-skiing*. 私は水上スキーには非常にスリルを感じる.

get a kick from [***out of***] 《口》…に非常なスリル[愉悦]を感じる ▪ He used to *get a kick out of* seeing such a thing. 彼はそんなものを見てとても興奮を覚えたものだ. ☞kick「食物などのぴりっとしたところ」. Cole Porter の有名な曲 "I Get a Kick Out of You"「おまえにはしびれるぜ」(1934)がある.

get *one's* ***kicks from …*** 《口》楽しみに何か(危険なこと)をする ▪ Those kids *get their kicks from* racing stolen cars. あのガキどもは盗難車をぶっとばして悦に入っている.

(***get***) ***more kicks than halfpence*** 《口・古風》賞賛よりも非難(を受ける); 報酬よりも虐待(を受ける); 利益よりも苦労(を得る) ▪ In fact I *got more kicks than halfpence*. 事実私はほめられるどころか非難された ▪ There are *more kicks than ha'pence* in his new job. 彼の新しい仕事は骨折損のくたびれもうけだ. ☞サルが芸をするとき, 集めた半ペニー貨は主人のものとなり, 芸が悪ければ主人に叱られるだけであることから.

get the kick (***out***) 《口》解雇される, 首になる ▪ She soon *got the kick*. 彼女はじき解雇された.

give *a person* ***a kick*** 人を非常にうれしがらせる, 愉快がらせる ▪ The article *gave* me *a kick*. その品は私を非常に喜ばせた.

give a kick at …をひとけりする ▪ I *gave a kick at* the ball. 私はボールをひとけりした.

give (*a person*) ***the kick*** (***out***) 《口》解雇する, 首にする ▪ They will *give* him *the kick*. 彼らは彼を首にするだろう.

have a kick in *one* 《口》 **1** (ものが)おもしろくてたまらない; 刺激性がある; (酒などが)はっきりこたえる ▪ The story *has a kick in* it. その話はとてもおもしろい ▪ This whisky *has a kick in* it. このウィスキーははっきりこたえる.

2 (馬が)ける力[癖]がある ▪ The horse *had a kick in* him. その馬にはける癖があった.

have a kick like a mule 《口》= have a KICK in one 1.

have a kick to it 強いスパイスが利いている, 刺激性がある ▪ I love that salsa. It *has a kick to it*. あのチリソース大好きよ. ピリッとして.

have (***got***) ***no kick left in*** *one* 《口》すっかり抵抗力がなくなった, すっかり参ってしまった ▪ After the fifth round he *had no* more *kick left in* him. 第5回戦が終わると彼はすっかり参ってしまっていた. ☞ボクシングから.

kick[2] /kɪk/ 動 ***be*** [***lie***] ***kicking about*** 《口》あちこち散らかっている ▪ The doctor's instruments *lie kicking about*. 医療器具があちこちに散乱している.

kick a goal 《サッカー・ラグビー・アメフト》ゴールを決める《ゴールにけり込んで1点を得る》 ▪ It is all Lombard street to a China orange that they will *kick a goal*. 彼らが1点を取ることはほとんど確かだ.

kick against the pricks [***spur, goad***] **1** 鋭くとがった武器を足でける ▪ It is mere folly to *kick against the spur* that pricks you. 足に刺さる武器をけるなんて愚の骨頂だ.

2 (かなわない敵に)強情に反抗して傷つく (《聖》*Acts*. 9. 5) ▪ My father *kicked against the pricks* determinedly. 父は断固としてかなわぬ敵に反抗して傷ついた. ☞「牛が怒って突き棒をける」が原義.

kick *oneself* (***all over the house*** [***place***]) 《口》自分がいやになって自分を責める; くやしがる ▪ I went home *kicking myself*. 私はくやしがりながら帰宅した.

kick an addiction [***the habit***] 麻薬[アルコール, タバコ]の依存症を克服する ▪ He used to smoke a lot, but now he's trying to *kick the habit*. 彼は以前へビースモーカーだったが今は禁煙しようと努めている.

kick and scream 《口》激しく不平を言う ▪ Producers *kick and scream* over free trade. 生産業者は自由貿易に大いに不満をもっている.

kick (*a person's*) ***ass*** [***butt***] 《主に米俗》(人に)高圧的な態度をとる, 無理やり従わせる, 牛耳る; (を)罰する, たたきのめす, 打ち負かす ▪ He has really been *kicking ass* lately, harassing everybody. 彼は最近とても高飛車になっていて, みなに嫌がらせをしている ▪ He'll *kick your ass* until you don't even have an ass anymore. 彼はあんたの尻がなくなるぐらいまでたたきのめすだろう.

kick ass [***butt***] ***at*** (*doing*) 《俗》(物事が)とてもよい, (人が…するのが)大変上手だ ▪ Your service real *kicks butt*! こいつは大サービスだな ▪ Those guys *kick ass at* voice-activated video games. あいつらは音声操作のビデオゲームが実にうまいな.

kick … down the ladder (***by which*** *one* ***rose***) →LADDER.

kick … downstairs 階下へけって追いやる, 家から追い出す; 格下げ[左遷]する ▪ The cat *was kicked downstairs* by the children. 猫は子供たちによって階下へけおとされた ▪ He *was kicked downstairs* to a job in Accounts. 彼は会計係に格下げされた.

kick *one's* ***heels*** →HEEL[1].

kick *a person* ***in the head*** 人の頭をける ▪ He *kicked* me *in the head*. 彼は私の頭をけった.

kick … in the teeth →TOOTH.

kick … into the long grass 《英》…をはねつける, 引き伸ばす (→kick … into TOUCH) ▪ He dealt with disputes by *kicking* them *into the long grass*. 彼は論争を引き伸ばしてそれに対処した. ☞ラグビーなどで touch「タッチラインの外側」にボールがけり出されると試合が中断することから.

kick it 《俗》 **1** 死ぬ ▪ He *kicked it* yesterday at the age of 86. 彼は昨日86歳で死んだ.

2 悪習をやめる ▪ James was a heavy drinker, but he finally *kicked it*. ジェイムズは大酒飲みだったが,

結局その悪習をやめた.

kick over the traces 《英》 **1** (馬が)引き革をけりのける, けって足をひき革の外へ出す ▪ The horse *kicked over the traces.* 馬はひき革をけりのけてあばれだした.

2 《口》 あばれて反抗的になる, 束縛を脱ぎ捨てる; 常道をはずれたことをする ▪ You must not *kick over the traces* in this town. この町では常道を破ったことをしてはいけない ▪ A genius often *kicks over the traces* of respectability. 天才は世間体という束縛をふり捨てることがよくある.

kick the habit [***drug, booze***]/ ***kick it*** → HABIT.

kick the tires [《英》 ***tyres***] 《主に米》 ざっと調べる ▪ They *kicked the tires* before investing in new companies. 彼らは新会社に投資する前にざっと当たった.

kick up a dust [***a fuss, a hullabaloo, a noise, a racket, a riot, a row, a rumpus, a shindy, a stink, a voice, hail Columbia, hell, hell's delight, the deuce, the devil, the devil's delight, the dickens***] 《口》 大騒ぎする, あばれる; 騒動を起こす ▪ They *kick up* such *a shindy.* 彼らはたいへんな騒ぎをする.

kick up *one's* ***heels*** →HEEL.

kick *one's* ***way*** けって前進する ▪ She *kicked her way* northward through the warm water. 温かい水の中を北の方へ平泳ぎで進んだ.

kick *a person* ***when he's down*** →hit a person who is DOWN.

lie kicking about →be KICKing about.

kid[1] /kɪd/ 名 ***a new kid on the block*** 《米口》 特定の場所[活動の場]への新参者, (特にスポーツ界の)新人; 新製品 ▪ Nobody calls him *a new kid on the block* anymore. 彼を新入りと呼ぶ者はもういないよ ▪ The University of Ontario Institute of Technology is *a new kid on the block.* オンタリオ工科大学は新設校である ▪ This brand is *a new kid on the block.* この銘柄は新製品です ▪ It's rare *the new kid on the block* is 56 years old. 新人が56歳というのは珍しい.

kid stuff/《英》 ***kid's*** [***kids'***] ***stuff*** 《米口》 ごく簡単なこと, 実にわけないこと ▪ Solving this problem is *kid's stuff.* この問題を解くのはわけないよ.

like a kid in a candy store/《英》 ***like a child in a sweet shop*** 《主に米》 何でもしたい放題で, 欲望を抑えきれずに, わくわくして, 大喜びで ▪ He reached to fame *like the kid in a candy store.* 彼は何でもやりたい放題で名声を手に入れた ▪ My son was *like a kid in a candy store* when his cousins arrived. 息子は従兄弟(いとこ)たちが着くと有頂天になった.

seethe a kid in its mother's milk 子ヤギをその母の乳で煮る (《聖》 *Exod.* 23. 19) ▪ God's people should not *seethe a kid in its mother's milk.* 神の民は子ヤギをその母の乳で煮てはならない.

treat [***handle***] *a person* ***with kid gloves*** とても注意深く扱う (→with KID gloves) ▪ She can be a very difficult woman, so you have to *treat* her *with kid gloves.* 時に気難しくなるので彼女の扱いは慎重にね ▪ We have *handled* them *with kid gloves* so to speak. 彼らを言うなれば優しく扱ってきた.

with kid gloves 《口》 優しく, 如才なく, 慎重に ▪ European politics are worked *with kid gloves.* ヨーロッパの政治は慎重に行われている.

kid[2] /kɪd/ 動 (***all***) ***kidding apart*** [***aside***] 《口》 冗談抜きで, まじめに言って (=(all) JOKING apart) ▪ *All kidding aside,* I hate to lose at croquet. まじめな話, クローケーで負けるのはいやだ.

Are you kidding (***me***)***?*** 冗談でしょう! ▪ Me, a liar? *Are you kidding?* この私が嘘つきだって? 何言ってるのよ?

I kid you not. =No KIDding!

kid *oneself* 《俗》 自己をあざむく, 信じこむ; うぬぼれる; 感違いする ▪ Anybody who thinks he's an expert is *kidding himself.* 自分は名人だと思う人はみなうぬぼれているのだ ▪ Don't *kid yourself* that you will ever come into a fortune. 財産にありつくことがあるだろうと思い違いしてはいけない.

No kidding! 《俗》 冗談言うな!, 全くだよ! ▪ *No kidding.* I appreciate it. 冗談ではありません. かたじけなく思っています.

Who are you kidding?/***Who do you think you are kidding?*** 《口》 (理由, 言いわけなどが)信じられない, まさか ▪ The earth is flat? *Who are you kidding?* 地球が平たいだって? そんなばかな.

Who is *a person* ***kidding*** [***trying to kid***]***?*** (言葉とは裏腹に)何を考えているのか ▪ Aw, c'mon, *who are* you *kidding?* おいおい, いったい何をたくらんでいるんだ ▪ You call me beautiful, but really, *who are* you *trying to kid?* 私がきれいだと言うけど, ほんとはどういう魂胆なの?

You have (***got***) ***to be*** [***must be***] ***kidding*** 《口》 =You're KIDding!

You're kidding! 《口》 冗談でしょう! ▪ I've got £10,000.—*You're kidding!* ぼくは1万ポンド儲けた—ご冗談でしょう.

kidney /kídni/ 名 ***of that*** [***this,*** etc.] ***kidney*** 《古風》 そんな[こんな, など]気質の ▪ Mr. Wales is a man *of another kidney* from Mr. Scott. ウェールズ氏はスコット氏とは別の気質の人だ.

kill[1] /kɪl/ 名 ***be in at the kill*** **1** 《狩》 (獲物の)殺されるのを見とどける ▪ It was a custom for hunters to *be in at the kill.* 獲物が殺されるのを見とどけるのが狩猟者の習慣だった.

2 《口》 (試合の)勝利[(事態の)クライマックス]の瞬間にその場に居合わせる, 最後を見とどける ▪ I *was in at the kill* when he was caught red-handed. 僕は彼の現行犯逮捕の場に居合わせた.

go [***move, close***] ***in for the kill*** (議論などで)最後のとどめを刺す[刺して状況を有利にする], 敵[相手]に致命傷を与える ▪ The next time they got the ball, they *went* in *for the kill.* 次にボールを奪ったと

K

きに彼らはダメ押し点をあげた.

in for the kill 絶滅させようとして ▪ Communities throughout the nation are moving *in for the kill* on polio. 国中の共同社会がポリオを絶滅するために立ち上がっている.

on the kill **1** (食用にするため)殺すつもりの[で] ▪ They were intent *on the kill*. 彼らは一心に殺すつもりだった.

2 目的を達するためには何事をも辞さないつもりで ▪ Politicians are *on the kill* in an election year. 政治家たちは選挙年には勝つためには何事をも辞さないつもりだ.

kill[2] /kɪl/ 動 ***dressed to kill*** 魅惑的[悩殺的]な身なりをして (→to KILL) ▪ She is one of the James Bond girls *dressed to kill*. 彼女は悩殺的な衣装をまとったボンドガールの一人だ.

(*even*) *if it kills* *one* 《口》どんな問題[困難]を伴おうとも, いかに困難でも ▪ Don't worry. I will take care of it *even if it kills* me. ご心配なく. どんなに難しくても処理してみせるから.

One's ***feet*** [etc.] ***are killing*** *one*. 足[など]がひどく痛む ▪ *My head is killing* me. 頭がひどく痛い.

kill *oneself doing* [***to*** *do*] 《口》無理な努力をして…する ▪ Don't *kill yourself to* get here in time. ここへ間に合うように来るために無理な努力はしなくてよい.

kill a ball **1** 《テニス》打ち返しできないようにボールを強打する ▪ Posting himself close to the net, he *killed the ball*. ネットの近くに位置して, 彼は打ち返されないように, ボールを激しく打ちおろした.

2 《サッカー》ボールを止めて殺す ▪ He *killed the ball* and shot a goal. 彼はボールの勢いを殺し, ゴールを決めた.

kill a bill 《国会》法案を完全につぶす ▪ He is confident of *killing the bill*. 彼はその法案をつぶす自信がある.

kill *a person's* ***affection*** 人にあいそを尽かされる ▪ He *killed her affection*. 彼は彼女にあいそを尽かされた.

kill ... by kindness →KILL ... with kindness.

kill ... dead [***to death***] …を完全に殺す ▪ Are you sure you *killed* him *dead*? 確かに完全に彼の息の根を止めたのか.

kill *oneself* (***laughing***) 《英口》笑い転げる ▪ This comedy movie will make you *kill yourself laughing*. この喜劇映画を見たら腹を抱えるぞ.

kill *one's* ***man*** 《口》決闘で相手を殺す ▪ He had *killed his man* before he came of age. 彼は成年にならないうちに決闘で相手を殺したことがあった.

kill or cure 《英》(治療に関して)のるかそるか; 一か八か ▪ I have some liniment that'll *kill or cure* you. 私は塗り薬を持っているが治るか命とりになるかわからないよ ▪ It is a "*kill or cure*" method. それは一か八かの方法だ ▪ I was determined to take his powder, *kill or cure*. 私は治るか死ぬかわからないが, 彼の散薬を飲む決心であった. ☞よく名詞句, 形容詞句, 独立句として用いられる.

kill *a thing* ***stone dead*** 《口》事をすっかり消す[滅ぼす, なくする] ▪ The fall of the Cabinet *killed* any such plan *stone dead*. 内閣の倒壊でそのような計画はすっかりおじゃんになった.

kill the goods 溶けた脂を部分的石けん化によって乳化する ▪ In English it is called "*killing the goods*." 英語では, それは「溶けた脂の部分的石けん化による乳化」と呼ばれる.

kill ... to death →KILL ... dead.

kill well [***badly***] 肉が厚く切り取れる[肉があまり取れない] ▪ Pigs *kill well* at that age. ブタはその年齢では肉が厚く切り取れる.

kill ... with [***by***] ***kindness*** …を甘やかしてだめにする; をひいきの引き倒しする ▪ She spoils him and will *kill* him *with kindness*. 彼女は彼を甘やかしているが, だめにしてしまうだろう.

kill *oneself* ***with laughter*** [***mirth***] 〚進行形で〛非常におもしろがっている ▪ The boys *are killing themselves with laughter*. 少年たちは非常におもしろがっている.

to kill 《口》極度に, すばらしく, ひどく ▪ She danced *to kill*. 彼女はほれぼれするほどじょうずに踊った ▪ A young fellow, dressed [got up] *to kill*, came in. すばらしく着飾った若者が入って来た. ☞「人を悩殺するほど」が原義.

killing /kílɪŋ/ 名 ***make a killing*** (***on***) 《口》(…で)急に大儲けする ▪ He *made a killing on* the stock market. 彼は株で大儲けした. ☞競馬の賭けから.

kiln /kɪln, kɪl/ 名 ***set the kiln on fire/fire the kiln*** 大騒動[大騒ぎ]を起こす ▪ He continued to *set the kiln on fire*. 彼は大騒動を起こし続けた.

The kiln's on fire. 大騒動が起こっている.

kilter /kíltər/ 名 ***be*** [***get***] ***out of kilter*** 混乱している[する]; (調子などが)狂っている[狂う]; 体が悪い[を悪くする] ▪ The seats *are out of kilter*. 座席は混乱している ▪ I *am* miserably *out of kilter*. ひどく体の調子が悪い ▪ The machine has *got out of kilter*. 機械の調子が狂った.

put ... out of kilter **1** …を混乱させる; をめちゃくちゃにする ▪ Don't *put* the papers *out of kilter*. 書類をめちゃくちゃにしないでください.

2 (…との)調子を狂わせる (*with*) ▪ That would *put* Britain *out of kilter with* the rest of Europe. そうなったら英国は他の欧州諸国との関係がぎくしゃくしてくるだろう.

kin /kɪn/ 名形 ***be*** (***of***) ***kin to*** …の親類である; に類似している, 近い ▪ They *are* (*of*) *kin to* each other. 彼らは互いに親類である ▪ It *is* next *kin to* an impossibility to do so. そうすることはきわめて不可能に近い.

(***come***) ***of good kin*** 家柄がよい ▪ I'm sure she *comes of good kin*. 彼女は家柄がよいにちがいない.

kith and kin →KITH.

more kin than kind 親類ではあるが情愛のない (cf. Sh., *Haml.* 1. 2. 65) ▪ This frequent visitor is *more kin than kind*. よく来るこのお客は親類ではあるが情愛はない.

K

near of kin (***to***) (…の)近親で ▪ He is *near of kin to* me. 彼は私の近親です.

next of kin (***to***) **1** (…の)最近親(で)《遺産にあずかる資格がある》 ▪ He is *next of kin to* Lord Halifax. 彼はハリファックス卿の最近親である ▪ They left their crowns to the *next of kin*. 彼らは王冠を最近親に残し与えた.

2 (…に)もっとも近く ▪ Lying is *next of kin to* perjury. 虚言は偽証にもっとも近い.

One touch of nature makes the whole world kin. →NATURE.

kind[1] /kaɪnd/ 形 ***be kind enough*** [***so kind as***] ***to*** *do* 親切にも…する;〚命令文で〛どうぞ…してください ▪ He *was kind enough to* lend me £100. 彼は親切にも私に100ポンド貸してくれた ▪ *Be so kind as to* tell me the way to the station. どうぞ駅へ行く道を教えてください.

it is kind of you to *do* ご親切に…してくださってありがとう ▪ *It is* very *kind of you to* give me the book. 本をくださってほんとにありがとうございます.

Your kind attention will oblige. どうぞよろしくお願い致します.

kind[2] /kaɪnd/ 名 ***a kind of*** まあ…のようなもの《その種に入れてよいが, その種の全特質は持っていない》 ▪ He is *a kind of* gentleman. 彼はまず紳士といえる人である ▪ This is *a kind of* china. これはまあ陶器のようなものだ.

after (*one's*) ***kind*** 自然の本能に従って; その種類に従って; その性質[流儀]に従って ▪ A cat catches mice *after its kind*. 猫はその本能に従ってネズミを取る ▪ The seed brings forth a crop *after its kind*. 種子はその種類に従って作物を生じる.

all kinds of **1** あらゆる種類の ▪ This bookstore sells *all kinds of* books. この書店ではあらゆる種類の本を売っている.

2《口》多数[多量]の, たくさんの ▪ The widow has *all kinds of* money. その未亡人はうなるほど金がある.

and that kind of thing [***stuff***]/***and those kinds of things*** …とかそういったもの[こと] ▪ There are many psychological causes like depression, anxiety, *and that kind of stuff*. 鬱(うつ)とか不安とかいった心理的要因がいろいろある ▪ He likes video games, simulations, *and those kinds of things*. 彼はビデオゲームやシミュレーションなどのたぐいを好む.

in a kind いくぶん, いわば ▪ He is a philosopher *in a kind*. 彼はいくぶんか哲学者である.

in kind **1** 性質において, 本質的に ▪ Our afflictions are the same with those of others *in kind*, though not in degree. 我々の苦悩は他の人々の苦悩と程度は違うが, 性質は同じである.

2 (金銭でなく)物品で ▪ They pay taxes *in kind*. 彼らは租税を物納する ▪ His food was provided *in kind*. 彼の食糧は現物で支給された.

3 (返報に)同種のもので ▪ He repaid their insolence *in kind*. 彼は彼らの無礼に報いるに無礼をもってした.

in one kind [***both kinds***]《宗》パンとブドウ酒の一種[両種]において ▪ The Church of Rome gives the communion *in one kind*. ローマ教会は一種において聖餐(さん)式を行う ▪ He received *in both kinds*. 彼はパンとブドウ酒との両種の聖餐を拝受した.

it takes all kinds (***to make a world***)《口》人さまざまだ, 十人十色だ ▪ That's crazy, but I guess *it takes all kinds*. 正気の沙汰ではないが, まあ人さまざまだな.

kind of **1** …の種類の ▪ He is a different *kind of* writer. 彼は違った種類の作家だ.

2《口》〚くずれて kind o', kind a', kinder (発音はいずれも /káɪndə/) で〛いくぶん…のようで, いわば ▪ It's *kind of* chilly tonight. 今夜は少し冷えこむ ▪ He *kind o'* laughed. 彼はちょっと笑った.

Kind [***Sort***] ***of.*** はい, ちょっとだけは ▪ Did you like it there?—*Kind* [*Sort*] *of.* あそこ, 気に入ったかい?—うん, まあな.

nothing [***not anything***] ***of the kind*** **1** 全くそのようなものはない ▪ There was *nothing of the kind* before. そのようなものは今まで全然なかった.

2 そんなことは決して…しない ▪ I'll do *nothing of the kind*. 決してそんなことはしない.

of a kind **1** 同一種の ▪ They are all *of a kind*. それらはみな同一種である.

2《軽蔑》いいかげんの, いかさまの (→a KIND of) ▪ He is a gentleman *of a kind*. 彼はいかさまの紳士だ ▪ We had coffee *of a kind*. まずいコーヒーを飲んだ.

one of a kind 特定のタイプの唯一の[ユニークな]人[もの] ▪ He's extremely generous, *one of a kind*. 彼は他に類を見ないきわめて寛大な人物だ ▪ These lamps are absolutely *one of a kind*! これらのランプはこの種の中でも全くユニークなものです.

something of the kind 何かそのようなもの ▪ *Something of the kind* had been done. 何かそのようなことがなされていた.

the kind of thing …のようなもの ▪ It is *the kind of thing* I wanted. それは私がほしがっていたようなものだ.

(***the***) ***worst kind*** →WORST.

these [***those, what***] ***kind of things*** [etc.]《口》〚複数動詞を伴って〛この[あの, 何の]種類のもの (things of this [that, what] kind) ▪ *These kind of things* have their use. この種のものにも用途はある ▪ *Those kind of pamphlets* work wonders. その種のパンフレットは奇跡を行う.

two of a kind →be TWO of a kind.

What kind of (***a***) ***man*** [etc.] ***…?*** どんな人[など]か ▪ *What kind of* (*a*) *man* is he? 彼はどんな人か. ☞a のつく形は《米》に多い.

kindle /kíndəl/ 動 ***kindle … to*** *do* …を扇動して…させる ▪ The movie has *kindled* me *to* watch it again and again. その映画に感動して何度も繰り返して見た ▪ Her email *kindled* me *to* express my anguish too. 彼女のEメールで心をかき立てられて私も悩みを吐き出した.

kindly /káɪndli/ 副形 ***kindly for*** (ある作物に)好適の ▪ The country is *kindly for* rice. その国は米作に適している.

look kindly on [***upon***] 《文》…に賛成する ▪ I hope they will *look kindly on* my request. 彼らに私の要請に賛同してもらえるといいが.

take it kindly (***of***) …を有難く思う ▪ I would *take it kindly of* you to post this letter. すみませんがこの手紙をポストに入れてくださいませんか.

take kindly to …を好む, 愛する; になつく ▪ The boy seems to *take kindly to* his books. その少年は学問が好きらしい ▪ They don't *take kindly to* me. 彼らは私になついてこない.

think kindly of *a person* (人・こと)を好む, (人)に好意を抱く ▪ If you *think kindly of* others, they will *think kindly of* you. 人に好意を抱けば向こうも好意をもってくれる.

kindness /káɪndnəs/ 名 ***do*** *a person* ***a kindness*** 人に親切を尽くす ▪ Will you *do* me *a kindness*? お願いがあるのですが.

have [***entertain***] ***a kindness for*** …への愛情[好意, 敬慕]を持つ ▪ He had once *entertained a* sneaking *kindness for* her. 彼はかつて彼女に対してひそかな愛情を抱いたことがあった ▪ He *has a kindness for* you. 彼は君を敬慕している.

have the kindness to *do* **1** 親切にも…する ▪ He *had the kindness to* tell me the right time. 彼は親切にも私に正確な時間を教えてくれた.
2〚主に命令文で〛どうぞ…してください ▪ *Have the kindness to* send it to me. どうぞそれを私に送ってください.

kill ... with kindness →KILL[2].

out of kindness 親切心から ▪ I say this *out of kindness*. 私は親切心からこう言うのだ.

king[1] /kɪŋ/ 名 ***All the king's horses*** (***and all the king's men***) ***cannot*** [***couldn't***]***...*** いかに有力な人をもってしても…できない ▪ *All the king's horses couldn't* get me out. 誰が来たって私は出て行かない. ☞Mother Goose から.

be king (人に)多大な影響力をもつ ▪ I can't help but wonder if cash really *is king*. 金が本当にものをいうかどうか疑わざるを得ない.

be unwilling [etc.] ***to call the king*** *one's* ***cousin*** 《口》全く満足した状態にある ▪ He would*n't condescend to call the king his cousin* at this present time. 彼は現在は成功しご満悦だ.

fit for a king 上品な, 贅沢な, 高価な ▪ The new condominium they bought is *fit for a king*. 彼らが買ったマンションは豪華だ.

in the king's name (国王の名において, とは)御用だ ▪ Open, *in the king's name*! あけろ, 御用だ!

King or Kaiser 世俗的な権力支配者 ▪ The tribal chieftain called the explorer *King or Kaiser*. 族長は探険家を支配者と呼んだ.

Kings have long arms [***hands***]. 《諺》国王の権威は国のすみずみまで及ぶ《国王と争ったり, 国王の目を盗んだりはできない》.

live like a king 王様気取りの贅沢な暮らしをする ▪ He *lived like a king* for five months, until the money finally ran out. 彼は贅沢三昧の生活を5か月続けたあげく, やがて金が尽きた.

take the King's shilling →SHILLING.

the king of beasts 百獣の王, ライオン ▪ Do you think *the king of beasts* can be copied? ライオンのクローンはできると思いますか.

the king of birds 鳥類の王, ワシ ▪ Throughout North America *this king of birds* is revered as divine. 北米全土でこのワシは聖鳥として崇められている.

the King of Kings **1** 王の王たる神キリスト, 上帝 ▪ Why is Jesus called *the King of Kings*? なぜイエスは王の王と呼ばれるのか ▪ We dedicate ourselves to serve *the King of Kings*. 私たちは神に仕えるためにこの身を捧げます.
2 王者の中の大王, 皇帝《昔, 東方諸国の王が用いた称号》 ▪ The Ethiopian Emperor was known as *the King of Kings*. そのエチオピアの皇帝は王の王の名で知られた ▪ Mithridates VI was *the King of Kings* who ruled over many small kingdoms. ミトリダテス6世は多くの小王国を治める大王だった.

the king of the hill/《英》***the king of the castle*** 《米》その地で最も重要な[権力のある]人物 ▪ The sheriff is *the king of the castle* around here. 保安官がこのあたりのお山の大将だ. ☞子供の同名の遊び「お城の王様[お山の大将]ごっこ」から.

turn King's evidence →EVIDENCE.

king[2] /kɪŋ/ 動 ***king it*** (***over***) (…に対して)王者気取りで臨む, 王のようにふるまう; (同僚などに対して)尊大ぶる ▪ He *kings it over* his colleagues. 彼は同僚に対して偉そうにする.

kingdom /kíŋdəm/ 名 ***come into*** *one's* ***kingdom*** 権威[権力, 魅力]を得る ▪ That woman has *come into her kingdom*. その女性は権力を得た.

kingdom come /kìŋdəmkʌ́m/ 名 ***go to kingdom come*** 《口》あの世へ行く, 天国へ行く ▪ Many of them *went to kingdom come*. 彼らの多くは天国へ行った. ☞kingdom come「来世, 天国」(《聖》*Matt.* 6. 10).

knock ... to kingdom come …をなぐって失神させる ▪ He *knocked* his opponent *to kingdom come*. 彼は相手をなぐって失神させた. ☞kingdom come「あの世」.

send [***blow, blast***]***... to kingdom come*** 《口》(爆薬などを用いて)…を殺す ▪ Cromwell *sent* him *to kingdom come*. クロムウェルは彼を殺した ▪ Nine soldiers *were blown to kingdom come* in the attack. その攻撃で9名の兵士が戦死した.

till [***until***] ***kingdom come*** いつまでも ▪ You may blow through your nostrils here *till kingdom come*. 君はここでいつまでも鼻を鳴らしておればよい. ☞「いつまで…してもむだだ」の意味のことが多い.

kink /kɪŋk/ 名 ***come*** [***work, get,*** 《主に米》***iron***] ***out the kinks***/ ***get the kinks*** (***ironed***) ***out*** 問題をうまく解決する, 処理する, 問題

K

点を取り除く ▪ We are still trying to *iron out the kinks.* 我々はまだ問題解決に努めている最中である ▪ It will be a nice car if you *get the kinks ironed out* in the engine. エンジンの問題が解決すればすてきな車になるだろう.

have a kink 特徴[奇癖]を持っている ▪ The boy seems to *have a kink.* 少年には奇癖があるようだ.

kiss[1] /kɪs/ 名 ***blow*** [***throw***] ***a kiss*** (***to***) (…に)投げキスをする, キスを送る ▪ She *blew a kiss to* me. 彼女は私にキスを送った.

sealed with a kiss/SWAK キスで封をして, 愛を込めて ▪ All her letters come *SWAK* [*sealed with a kiss*]. 彼女からの手紙はすべて愛を込めて書かれている.

the kiss of death 《口・主に戯》死の接吻, (物・事を)だめにするもの, 呪い ▪ Having sex with an acquaintance can often be *the kiss of death.* 知人と懇(ねんご)ろになると身の破滅を招くことが多い. ☞ゲッセマネの園でイスカリオテのユダがイエスにした裏切りの接吻より. (《聖》*Matt.* 26. 48–49; *Mark* 14. 44–45).

the kiss of life **1**《英》口移し式の人工呼吸 ▪ She saved her son's life by giving him *the kiss of life.* 彼女はマウストゥマウスの人工呼吸をして息子の命を救った.

K

2 倒産しかけた企業を立て直すための活動, 回復策 ▪ It's no good giving *the kiss of life* to the doomed enterprise. 先の見えたその企業に再生策を講じてもむだだ.

kiss[2] /kɪs/ 動 ***as easy*** [etc.] ***as kiss my*** [***your***] ***hand*** [***finger***] 極めてたやすい ▪ The work was *as easy as kiss your hand.* その仕事は極めてたやすかった.

kiss and be friends 《口》キスして仲直りする ▪ We'll *kiss and be friends.* キスして仲直りしよう.

kiss and make up 《戯》(キスして)仲直りする; 論争のあと再び友好的になる ▪ They often bicker but always manage to *kiss and make up.* 彼らはよくけんかするが, いつもなんとか仲直りする ▪ Will the EU *kiss and make up* with Belarus' despotic President? EU はベラルーシの独裁的な大統領と論争のあと友好的になるだろうか?

kiss and tell 《米口》(復しゅう・金儲けのために有名人との)秘め事[ゴシップ, スキャンダルなど]を暴露する ▪ Don't worry. She'll never *kiss and tell.* 心配ご無用. 彼女は絶対表ざたにはしないから ▪ Linda is gonna *kiss and tell* about her relationship with the minister in her memoir. リンダは回想録の中で大臣との秘め事を暴露しようとしている.

kiss (*a person's*) ***ass*** [《英卑》***arse***] 《米卑》(人の)きげん取りをする, (人に)へつらう, ぺこぺこする ▪ I am not going to *kiss ass* to get a pay raise. 昇給のためにごまをすったりするものか.

kiss ... good-by(***e***) **1** …にお別れのキスをする, にいとまごいをする ▪ I *kissed* him *good-by.* 私は彼にお別れのキスをした ▪ He *kissed* the old dump *good-by* tonight. 彼は今夜古いあばら家にいとまごいをした.

2《皮肉》…をあきらめる, 断念する ▪ Our son was sick, so we had to *kiss* our vacation *good-bye.* 息子が病気になったので休暇旅行をあきらめた.

kiss *one's* ***hand to*** (手で)…に投げキスをする ▪ He *kissed his hand to* me. 彼は私に投げキスをした.

kiss (*a person's*) ***hands/ kiss*** *a person's* ***hand*** **1**(任官・あいさつ・いとまごいの公式の敬礼として)国王[上官]の手にキスする ▪ He had this day the honor of *kissing Her Majesty's hand.* 彼は今日任官されて女王陛下の手にキスの礼をした ▪ He was received by the king and *kissed hands.* 彼は国王に接見され, 陛下の手にキスの礼をした.

2《古》(あいさつの言葉・手紙において)ごあいさつ申しあげます; おいとまします ▪ My son will *kiss your hands* in a letter of his own. 息子は自分自身の手紙であなたにごあいさつ申しあげます ▪ I *kiss your hands.* ではさようなら.

kiss it better (子供に)キスして打ちこぶ[傷]を治す ▪ Come here and I'll *kiss it better.* こちらへおいで. キスして(たんこぶを)治してあげるから.

kiss the book [***the Bible***] (宣誓のため)聖書にキスする ▪ The witness was told to *kiss the book.* 証人は聖書にキスせよと言われた.

kiss the cup アルコールを(ちびりちびり)飲む ▪ The bride *kissed the cup.* 花嫁は酒にちょっと口をつけた.

kiss the dust 倒される, 一敗地にまみれる, はずかしめられる; 破滅させられる, 殺される; みじめに屈服する, 屈辱をなめる (《聖》*Ps.* 72. 9) ▪ He will make all his enemies *kiss the dust.* 彼はすべての敵を倒すであろう ▪ At last he was forced to *kiss the dust.* ついに彼はやむなく屈服しなければならなかった ▪ She had yielded and *kissed the dust.* 彼女は屈して屈辱をなめたのであった.

kiss the ground **1**(敬意を表して)地に平伏する ▪ He went again to the King and *kissed the ground* before him. 彼は再び国王の所に行き, 王の前にひれ伏した.

2 地上に倒れる; 打ち倒される; 屈服する, 屈辱をなめる ▪ The driver was forced to *kiss the ground.* 御者は地上にねじり倒された ▪ Her pride shall *kiss the ground.* 彼女の高慢をたたきつぶしてやる.

kissing /kísɪŋ/ 形名 ***a kissing cousin*** 非常によく似た人[物] ▪ Your car and mine are *kissing cousins.* 僕たちの車はそっくりだね.

be kissing kind 非常に仲がよい ▪ You guys *are kissing kind.* 君たち二人は非常に仲がよい.

be on kissing terms (***with***) (…と)会えばキスするほどの親しい間柄である ▪ I *am on kissing terms with* him. 私は彼と非常に親しい間柄である.

Kissing goes by favor. キスは好きな人にだけする; 授賞[任官]はひいき次第.

kit /kɪt/ 名 ***get*** *one's* ***kit off*** 《英口》着衣を(全部)脱ぐ ▪ She doesn't hesitate to *get her kit off.* 彼女はためらわずに脱ぐ.

kit with the canstick 鬼火 ▪ They frighten us with *kit with the canstick.* 彼らは鬼火で我々をびっくりさせる. ☞canstick《廃》「ろうそく立て」.

the whole kit (***and boodle*** [***caboodle, biling, tuck***]) 《口》いっさい, 全部 ▪ We tipped *the whole kit and boodle* onto plates and started eating. 我々はすべての料理を皿に取って食べ始めた ▪ The man packed up all his gear, *the whole kit and caboodle*, and rushed out. 男はいっさいの用具を詰めこむと飛び出していった ▪ There was good reason to fear that *the whole kit and biling* would be swept away. いっさいが流し去られはしないかと心配する理由が十分あった ▪ He will beat *the whole kit and tuck* of them. 彼は彼らを一人残らず打ち負かすだろう.

kitchen /kítʃən/ 名 ***a kitchen cabinet*** 私設顧問団 ▪ He was supported by *an* infamous *kitchen cabinet*. 彼は悪名高い私設顧問団の支援を受けていた.

a kitchen talk ゴシップやたわいのないおしゃべり ▪ We used to get together for *a* little *kitchen talk* after lunch. お昼をとったあと, よく井戸端会議をしたものだった.

kitchen-sink /kìtʃənsíŋk/ 名形 ***a kitchen-sink play*** [***drama, film***] 《英》日常の家庭生活を描いた劇[映画] ▪ *Kitchen-sink drama* came into fashion in the 50s. 1950年代に家族ドラマが流行した.

everything [***all***] ***but*** [***bar, except***] ***the kitchen sink*** 《口・戯》→SINK[1].

kite /kaɪt/ 名 (***as***) ***high as a kite*** **1** 非常に興奮して, 舞い上がって, 至福の気分で ▪ When he won the lottery he was *high as a kite*. 彼は宝くじが当たって有頂天になった.

2 (酒・麻薬などで)すっかり酔っぱらって, 酩酊(めいてい)して, 高揚して ▪ He was *as high as a kite* on drugs for some time. 彼は麻薬でしばらくの間非常にハイな気分でいた.

draw in a kite たこをおろす ▪ The boy *drew in the kite*. 少年はそのたこを引きおろした.

fly [***send up***] ***a kite*** **1** たこをあげる ▪ The boy is *flying a kite*. 少年はたこをあげている.

2 世論に探りを入れる, 形勢を探る ▪ The King of Sweden *flew a kite* at us for the Garter. スウェーデン王はガーター勲章を求めて我々の意向を探った.

3 《商俗》融通手形をふり出す, 融通手形で資金を調達する ▪ *Flying a kite* is not advisable now. 融通手形で金を調達するのは今は好ましくない.

fly *one's* ***own kite*** 《米口》私利を図る ▪ He was determined to *fly his own kite* through life. 彼は生涯かけて私利を図ろうと心に決めていた.

Go fly a kite! 《主に米口》立ち去れ, うせろ, くたばれ ▪ *Go fly a kite*, you bother me. じゃまだ, あっちへ行け.

higher than a kite [***Gilderoy's kite***] 《米口》非常に高く; こっぴどく ▪ They have thrown him *higher than a kite*. 彼らは彼を非常に高く投げ上げた ▪ This theory is often knocked *higher than Gilderoy's kite* when put to the test of practice. この理論は実際の試練にあうとこっぴどく崩されることが多い. ☞Gilderoy (?–1638)はスコットランド Perthshire の有名な海賊.

send up a kite →fly a KITE.

kith /kɪθ/ 名 ***kith and kin*** 親族, 親類《比喩的にも》 ▪ They are strange to all our *kith and kin*. それらは我々の親族のすべてに見なれないものだ ▪ Greek and Latin are of the same *kith and kin*. ギリシャ語とラテン語は同族である. ☞kith = friends.

kitten /kítən/ 名 ***have*** (***a litter of***) ***kittens*** **1** 《英口》(怒り・心配・恐れ・驚き・笑いなどの)感情を激しく表す ▪ He *had a* nice *litter of kittens* when he found me. 私を見つけたとき彼は驚いて大騒ぎした.

2 (知らせを待ちながら)心配する, やきもきする ▪ I'm *having kittens*. I haven't heard anything from him for a month. 心配している. 彼から1か月も音さたがないんだ.

kittle /kítəl/ 形 ***kittle cattle to shoe*** 手に負えないあばれ牛; 扱いにくい[厄介な]人 ▪ My colleague is *kittle cattle to shoe*. 同僚は扱いにくい人物だ.

kitty /kíti/ 名 ***feed the kitty*** 寄付する, 金を出し合う ▪ Please *feed the kitty* to help sick children. 病気の子供たちのための寄付をお願いいたします.

in the kitty (勝負ごとの)賭け金入れに入って ▪ There was a total of £200 *in the kitty* for the lucky winner. 幸運な勝者に与える総計200ポンドの金が賭け金入れに入っていた.

scoop the kitty 大成功を収める, (賭け金などの)全てを獲得する ▪ The winner *scoops the kitty* at a game of poker. ポーカーでは勝った者が賭け金の山を手に入れる. ☞kitty「賭け金の山」.

knack /næk/ 名 ***have a knack of*** [***for***] ...のこつを知っている, に妙を得ている; 《皮肉》...する癖がある ▪ He *had an* admirable *knack for* teaching arithmetic. 彼は算術を教えるのにすばらしく妙を得ていた ▪ He *has a knack of* rubbing people up the wrong way. 彼は人を怒らせる癖がある.

lose *one's* [***the***] ***knack*** 効率的にできなくなる, こつを忘れる ▪ Great-grandma's *lost the knack* of sewing now—it must be her age. 曾祖母はもう裁縫のこつを忘れちゃった—きっと年のせいだ.

there is a knack in ...にはこつがある ▪ *There is a knack in* landing a fish. (食いついた)魚を釣り上げる[取り込む]にはこつがある.

knacker /nǽkər/ 名 ***be fit only for the knacker's yard*** (馬が)つぶすよりほかない ▪ The old horse *is fit only for the knacker's yard*. その老馬はつぶすよりほかはない.

go [***be sent***] ***to the knackers*** (馬が)つぶしにされる《比喩的にも》 ▪ The old horse had better *be sent to the knackers*. その老馬はつぶしたほうがよい ▪ The sooner these old carpets *go to the knackers*, the better. これらの古い敷物は廃棄されるのが早ければ早いほどよい.

knave /neɪv/ 名 ***play*** [《俗》***act***] ***the knave*** 悪人ぶる ▪ An honest man sometimes *plays the knave*. 正直者もときに悪者のふりをすることがある.

knee /niː/ 名 ***at*** *one's* ***mother's knee*** 母のひざもとで; 子供の時に ▪ He learned [was taught] it *at his mother's knee.* 彼は子供の時にそれを学んだ[教わった].

be the bee's knees 《英》最良[最適]の人[物]である ▪ His idea seems to *be the bee's knees.* 彼の案は最良だと思われる.

beat ... to the knees …を完全に負かす ▪ The King *beat* his subjects *to the knees.* 国王は人民を完全に負かした.

bow [***bend, drop***] ***the*** [*one's*] ***knee*** 《文》(礼拝・嘆願のため)ひざまずく; ひざを屈する (*to, before*) (《聖》*2 Kings* 19. 18) ▪ He *bent the knee* in worship. 彼はひざまずいて礼拝した ▪ Those Frenchmen refused to *bow the knee before* the Second Empire. そのフランス人たちは第二帝国にひざを屈しようとしなかった.

bring *a person* ***to his knees*** 人を屈服[服従]させる ▪ I took a great deal of trouble to *bring* him *to his knees.* 彼を屈服させるのに実に骨を折った.

Down on your knees! ひざまずけ《悔いてあやまれ》!

fall [***drop, go***] (***down***) ***on*** *one's* [***the***] ***knees*** (***to***) (…に対して)ひざまずく《礼拝・嘆願のため》 ▪ The elephant *fell on his knees.* ゾウはひざまずいた ▪ She *dropped to her knees* in prayer. 彼女はひざまずいて祈った.

give [***offer***] ***a knee*** ひざを貸して人を休ませる ▪ He *gave a knee* to the boxer. 彼はそのボクサーにひざを貸して休ませた.

go [***fall***] ***on one knee*** 片ひざをつく ▪ They *fell on one knee* and raised their guns. 彼らは片ひざをついて銃をかまえた.

go weak at the knees →WEAK.

knee by knee ぴったり並んで ▪ Sit down *knee by knee.* 並んで座りなさい.

knee to knee **1** =KNEE by knee.
2 向き合ってひざを接して ▪ Another old woman was sitting *knee to knee* with her. もう一人の老婦人が彼女と向き合いひざを接して座っていた.

one's [*a person's*] ***knees knock*** (***together***) 《口》〚主に進行形で〛(恐怖で)ひざがガタガタ打ち合う ▪ *My knees were knocking together* when I took the money out of the drawer. 金を引き出しから取り出した時, 私のひざは恐ろしくてガタガタ震えた.

on bended knee(***s***) 《文》 = on the [one's] KNEEs 1.

on [***upon***] ***the*** [*one's*] ***knees*** **1** ひざまずいて《嘆願・屈服する場合》 ▪ They desired *on their knees* to have their lives saved. 彼らはひざまずいて, 命乞いをした ▪ You will be *on your knees* to this Buonaparte. あなたはこのボナパルトに服従するであろう.
2 大敗北をして, 大失敗をして ▪ The nation was economically *on its knees.* その国は経済的に大いにまいっていた.
3 まさに崩れようとして, 崩壊寸前で ▪ The auto industry seems to be *on its knees* now. 自動車産業は目下崩壊寸前の様相である.

on the knees of the gods **1** 神々[運命]の手にゆだねられて, 人力の及ばない ▪ The whole affair is *on the knees of the gods.* いっさいは神々の手にゆだねられている.
2 まだ不確かで, 未定で; 人知の及ばぬ, 未来のことで ▪ Whether I shall succeed or not is *on the knees of the gods.* 私が成功するかどうかはわからない. ☞ Gk theon en gounasi (Homer) のなぞり.

over in [***at***] ***the knees*** (馬の)ひざが曲がって突き出て ▪ The horse stands *over in the knees.* その馬は立つとひざが曲がって突き出る.

owe *a person* ***a knee*** 人を崇敬[崇拝]する義務がある ▪ I *owe* him *a knee.* 私はあの人を崇敬しなければならないのです.

put *a person* ***over*** *one's* ***knee*** 子供をひざに乗せてしりをたたく ▪ My father would often *put* me *over his knee.* よく父のひざに乗せられてしりをひっぱたかれたものだ.

to *one's* ***knees*** 屈服して, 敗北して ▪ He was forced *to his knees* by competition. 彼は競争で敗北せざるをえなかった.

knee-deep /nìːdíːp/ 形 ***be knee-deep in*** …をあり余るほど持っている ▪ *I'm knee-deep in* work at the moment. 当面, 山ほど仕事を抱え込んでいる.

knee-high /nìːháɪ/ 形 ***knee-high to a grasshopper*** [***a duck, a frog, a humble-bee, a mosquito, a splinter, a toad***] 《口戯》非常に小さい, 背が低い, 非常に幼い ▪ I have known him since he was *knee-high to a duck* [*a mosquito*]. 私は彼を非常に小さかった時分から知っている ▪ His father died when he was *knee-high to a toad.* 彼は非常に幼いとき父親を失った. ☞ 通例, 身長について言う.

knell /nel/ 名 ***sound*** [***ring*** (***out***), ***toll***] ***the*** (***death***) ***knell of*** [***for***] …を葬る鐘を鳴らす; の消滅を告げる ▪ The opening of the ports *sounded the knell of* the ancient regime. 開港は旧政体の消滅を告げた ▪ It *rang the knell for* the old era. それは旧時代を葬る鐘を鳴らした.

knickers /níkərz/ 名 ***get*** [***have***] *one's* ***knickers in a twist*** [《豪》***a knot***] 《英口》取り乱す[している], 怒る[怒っている]; 心配する[している] ▪ He *gets his knickers in a twist* about the smallest thing. 彼はごくささいな事にくよくよする ▪ Let me explain the situation before you *get your knickers in a twist.* ご心配なさらないうちに状況をご説明します.

knife /naɪf/ 名 ***a knife and fork*** 食事; 食べる人 ▪ I'm glad to see you over to *a knife and fork.* お食事によくおいでくださいました ▪ He is *a* capital *knife and fork.* 彼はすばらしくよく食べる.

be afraid of the knife →have a horror of the KNIFE.

before *one* ***can*** [***could***] ***say knife*** 《口》あっと言う間に, 瞬く間; 突然, にわかに (→before you can say JACK Robinson) ▪ I'll be ready *before you can say knife.* すぐ用意します.

cut like a knife (風が)身を切るように冷たい ▪ A cold north wind *cut like a knife.* 冷たい北風が身を切るようだった.

get* [*have*] *one's* *knife into 《英口》...に対して恨みをいだく, 悪意を持つ; をひどくしいたげる, ひどくけなす ▪ The manager has *had his knife into* me from the first day I started. 支配人は私が入社した最初の日から私に悪意を持っていた.

go* [*cut*] *through ... like a* (*hot*) *knife through butter 簡単に切る, 何の苦労もなく進む (→like a (hot) KNIFE through butter) ▪ A laser beam *cuts through* metal *like a hot knife through butter.* レーザー光線はいとも簡単に金属を切断する.

go under the knife/ submit to the knife 《米口》手術を受ける (→under the KNIFE 1) ▪ He *went under the knife* for acute appendicitis. 彼は急性虫垂炎の手術を受けた.

have a horror* [*be afraid*] *of the knife 手術をこわがる, 手術が大きらいである ▪ Mom *has a horror of the knife* and anesthetics. ママは手術と麻酔をこわがる.

like a* (*hot*) *knife through butter 何の抵抗も苦労もなく, いとも簡単に ▪ The icebreaker broke ice *like a hot knife through butter.* 砕氷船はやすやすと氷を割った.

play a good* [*capital*] *knife and fork たらふく食う, 十分に食う ▪ After *playing a good knife and fork*, he took himself off. たらふく食べた後, 彼は出て行った.

***put* [*stick*] *the knife in* [*into* a person]** 《英口》(人に)致命的な打撃を与える, 敵意をぶつける, ののしる ▪ He often *puts the knife in* by saying such cruel things. 彼はよくそんなひどいことを言って人を傷つける.

the knives are out* (*for* a person)/ *have the knives out 《主に英口》相手が敵意むき出しの状態である, 険悪な状況である ▪ *The knives are out for* me at the moment. 現在, 私にとって事態は険悪である.

(*the night of*) *the long knives* 裏切りの大虐殺《比喩的にも》 ▪ The consequence was "*the night of the long knives.*" その結果は「裏切りの大虐殺」であった. ☞Hitler の Nazis の進軍歌から取った句.

***twist* [*turn*] *the knife* (*in the wound*)** (すでに苦しんでいる人を)さらに苦しめる, 追い討ちをかける ▪ He made her cry, and *twisted the knife* by saying she was too weak. 彼は彼女を泣かせた上に弱虫だと言った.

under the knife 《口》 **1** 手術を受けて, 手術中に ▪ He is [died] *under the knife.* 彼は手術を受けている[手術中に死んだ].

2 滅ぼされて ▪ Many of their plans came *under the knife.* 彼らの計画の多くがつぶされた.

war to the knife 血戦, 死戦, 苛烈な戦い ▪ It will be *war to the knife* if those two powers come into conflict. もしこの2強国が戦えば血戦になるだろう ▪ Catholicism declared *war to the knife* against modern culture. カトリックは現代文化に対して死戦を宣した.

You could* (*have*) *cut the air* [*atmosphere, it*] *with a knife. **1** 部屋(の人々)の(特によそよそしい)雰囲気が感じ取れる[れた] ▪ When I went into the room *you could have cut the air with a knife.* 私が部屋へ入って行ったとき, そこの人々のよそよそしい空気が感じ取れた.

2 (空気が)ひどくじめじめしている, (煙などが)濃く立ち込めている ▪ The smoke was so thick in there *you could cut it with a knife.* 中にはひどい煙が充満していた.

knife-edge /náɪfèdʒ/ 名 ***be* [*walk*] *on a knife-edge*** 予断を許さない, どっちに転ぶか分からない, 争っている両者のかたをもつ ▪ Dairy farming *is on a knife-edge* as rising costs force many farms to close. 物価上昇で多くの農場が破綻し酪農業の今後は予断を許さない ▪ I had to *walk on a knife-edge* between the two quarreling men. 口論中の二人の間に入って両方を立てなくてはならなかった.

knight /naɪt/ 名 ***a knight in shining armor*** 《雅・戯》輝くよろいの騎士《特に女性に献身的な頼もしい紳士》 ▪ Lord Brockway is *a knight in shining armor.* ブロックウェイ卿は輝くよろいの騎士だ. ☞中世のロマンスから.

a knight of the road (トラック[タクシー]運転手・放浪者などの)道路を頻繁に使用する人 ▪ *The knight of the road* came to the aid of another lorry driver in an accident. トラック運転手は事故にあった仲間を助けにきた ▪ He was *a knight of the road* without fixed address. 彼は住所不定の浮浪者だった ▪ *A knight of the road* was attacked by two men. タクシー運転手が二人組に襲われた. ☞17世紀中頃には「追いはぎ」を指して皮肉に用いられた.

a white knight 乗っ取りに直面した会社に入札して救済する会社, 白馬の騎士 ▪ They acted as *a white knight* and prevented it from being taken over. 彼らは白馬の騎士役を講じそれが乗っ取られるのを防いだ.

knit /nɪt/ 動 ***knit* *one's* *brows*** →BROW.

knitting /nítɪŋ/ 名 ***get down* [*stick close, attend*] *to* *one's* *knitting*** 《米口》仕事に専念する, がんばり努める ▪ The house *attended to its knitting* and passed the bill. 議会は審議に専念し, その法案を通過させた.

knob /nɑb|nɔb/ 名 ***with* (*brass*) *knobs on*** **1** 《英口・戯》(相手の言葉を承認して)おまけに, おまけをつけて ▪ You are nothing.—And so are you, *with knobs on.* 君はつまらぬ人間だ—君だってそうじゃないか, しかもよけいに ▪ I am waiting for Marquis Ferdinand.—*With knobs on.* 私はフェルディナンド侯爵を待っているのです—私だって, しかもずっと.

2 〚強調的に〛とびきりの ▪ He became an earl and

K

finally a KG too—an earl *with knobs on* in short. 彼は伯爵になり，最後にはガーター勲爵士にもなった—つまりとびきりの伯爵だ. ☞knob「こぶ」.

knock[1] /nɑk|nɔk/ 名 ***get a knock*** 打たれる ▪ He *got a* nasty *knock* on the head when he fell. 彼は倒れたとき，頭をしたたか打った.

get the knock 《口》 解雇される; (俳優などが)見捨てられる，人気を落とす ▪ He's *got the knock* at last. 彼はついに首になった.

hard knocks (そこから教訓を学ぶ)困難[不快]な人生経験 ▪ He's had a year of *hard knocks* since last year. 彼は去年からずっと苦しい1年間を過ごしてきた. ☞→the SCHOOL of hard knocks「つらい経験」.

on the knock 《口》 分割払いで ▪ We got a new television *on the knock*. 新しいテレビを分割払いで買った.

take a (hard, nasty, etc.***) knock/take the knock*** 《俗》 悪影響を受ける，ひどく損なわれる; (特に経済的な)打撃を受ける ▪ His reputation has *taken* quite *a knock*. 彼の名声ががた落ちになってしまった ▪ The backer of horses has *taken the knock*. 馬に金をかけた人は大損をした.

K

knock[2] /nɑk|nɔk/ 動 ***(be) knocked out*** 《俗》 (酒に)酔って(いる); 麻薬中毒で(ある) ▪ He is reeling. He must *be knocked out*. 彼はよろめいている. 酔っているに違いない.

don't knock it 批判したり文句を言わない ▪ *Don't knock it*—at least the food's free. 文句を言うなよ—ともかく食費はただだし.

have it knocked 《米俗》 うまくいく，成功間違いない ▪ With the job, he thought he *had it knocked*. その仕事はきっとうまくいくと彼は思った.

knock a hole 穴をぶちあける ▪ He *knocked a hole* in the ceiling. 彼は天井に穴をぶちあけた.

knock ... all of a heap →HEAP.

knock at an open door (開いた戸をたたくように)むだな事をする ▪ The discussion may *knock at an open door*. 話し合いはむだだろう.

knock** a person's **block [head] off 《英口》 人をひどく打つ，ひどく罰する ▪ I will *knock his block off*. 彼をこっぴどくやっつけてやる. ☞block＝head.

knock** a person **cold 《口》 **1** 人を打って気絶[失神]させる ▪ The blow on the chin *knocked* Bill *cold*. あごをなぐられてビルは気絶した.

2 人をあっと言わせる ▪ *Knock*'em *cold*. 彼らをあっと言わせてやれ. ☞ボクシングから.

knock** a person **dead 人を感嘆させる; 《俗》 (美しさなど)で人を悩殺する ▪ The comedian really *knocked* them *dead*. その喜劇役者は彼らをすっかり感嘆させた ▪ She *knocks* people *dead*. 彼女はまことに美しい.

knock down and drag out 《米口》 完全に打ち負かす ▪ He *knocked down and dragged out* a fellow citizen. 彼は仲間の市民を完全に打ち負かした.

knock ... down cheap …を大安売りする ▪ A friend *knocked* his television set *down cheap*. 友人が自分のテレビを大安売りした.

knock ... down for a song 《口》 二束三文で売る ▪ Family heirlooms *were knocked down for a song*. 先祖伝来の家宝が二束三文で売り払われた.

knock** a person's **eyes out 《俗》 人を目が飛び出るほどなぐる; 人に目をみはらせる《非常に美しくて》 ▪ She *knocks your eyes out*. 彼女は非常に美しい.

knock ... for a loop **1** …を完全に打ち負かす ▪ He *knocked* his opponent *for a loop*. 彼は相手を完全に打ち負かした.

2 …をさっさと片づける; を追っ払う; を破壊する ▪ It *knocked* his faith in human nature *for a loop*. それは彼の人間性に対する信頼を打ちこわしてしまった.

3 …をあ然とさせる ▪ The news *knocked* him *for a loop*. そのニュースは彼をびっくり仰天させた.

knock for admittance ドアをたたいて入室許可を求める ▪ There is no need to *knock for admittance*. ノックせずに入ってよろしい.

knock ... for six **1** 《クリケット》 (人)から一挙に6点取る; に大打撃を与える ▪ The bowler *was knocked for six*. 投手は一挙に6点取られた.

2 《口》 …を徹底的にやっつける，打倒[撃滅]する; をすっかり困らせる ▪ His troops *knocked* Rommel *for six*. 彼の軍勢はロンメルに大打撃を与えた ▪ Our product will *knock* the competition *for six*. わが社の製品はライバルを一蹴するであろう.

knock** one's **head against **1** …に頭をぶつける ▪ I *knocked my head against* the post. 私は柱に頭をぶつけた.

2 強い反対[抵抗]にぶつかる[ぶつかって傷つく] ▪ I'm *knocking my head against* his stubborn conservatism. 私は彼の頑固な保守主義にぶつかってはばまれている ▪ I *knocked my head against* a disagreeable truth. 私は不愉快な事実にぶつかった[直面した].

knock** one's **head against a brick wall → beat one's HEAD against a (stone, brick) wall.

knock** a person's **head off 人を頭が取れるくらいなぐる; 人を楽に負かす ▪ He *knocked John's head off* in Greek iambics. 彼はギリシャ語の短長格の詩ではジョンを苦もなく負かした.

knock ... in pieces →KNOCK ... to pieces.

knock ... into a cocked hat →COCKED HAT.

knock ... into** a person's **head …を人の頭にたたきこむ ▪ He *knocked* the proverb *into the head of* the student. 彼はその諺を生徒の頭にたたきこんだ.

knock ... into one 《英》 〚主に受身で〛 (間の壁)を取り払って1室にする ▪ The two rooms have *been knocked into one*. その2室は壁をぶち抜いて1室に改装された.

knock ... into shape 《口》 **1** (人)をたたき上げる ▪ He'll *be knocked into shape* in that firm. 彼はあの会社でたたき上げられるだろう.

2 まとめ上げる ▪ I will try to *knock* these ideas *into shape*. 私はこれらの思想をまとめ上げてみましょう.

knock** a person **into the middle of next week →WEEK.

knock it off 《口》〚主に命令文で〛(いやな事を)する[言う]のをやめる ▪ *Knock it off*, Tom! You know we want to forget it. トム, その話はやめろ! 我々がそれを忘れたがっていることは知っているじゃないか.

knock it out of …をすっかり疲れさせる; をきびしく罰する ▪ The uphill struggles soon *knocked it* all *out of* him. やっとこさ坂を登っているうちにまもなく彼はくたくたになった.

knock *a person's* ***legs from under*** *him* 人の足[すね]を払う ▪ The waves *knocked my legs from under* me. 波に足をさらわれた.

knock off *a person's* ***head*** = KNOCK a person's head off.

knock *a person* ***off*** *his* ***perch*** →PERCH[1].

knock off *a person's* ***pins*** 《口》人をびっくり仰天させる, ショックを与える ▪ The news of his death *knocked* me *off my pins*. 彼の死の知らせは私をびっくり仰天させた.

knock … on the head 《英口》 **1** …の頭を打って気絶させる[殺す]; を素早く殺す, 片づける ▪ He *knocked* me *on the head*. 彼は私の頭を打って気絶させた ▪ *Knock* the horse *on the head*. その馬を殺してしまえ.
2 (理論など)を打ち破る, つぶす ▪ I *knocked* the theory *on the head*. 私はその理論を打ち破った.
3 《口》(計画など)を打ちこわす, 終わらせる ▪ That's *knocked* things *on the head*. それで万事が終わった.

knock *oneself* ***out*** **1** 《口》激しく働く, 大いに努力する ▪ I am *knocking myself out* to get promoted. 昇進するため激しく働いている.
2 《口》(できるものなら)やってみよ ▪ If you think you can do it yourself, *knock yourself out*. 自分でできると思うなら, やってみろ.

knock … out (***of the box***) 《野球》打ちまくって(投手)を退かせる ▪ They *knocked* the pitcher *out* (*of the box* [game]). 打ちまくって投手を退かせた.

knock out (***of time***) 《ボクシング》ノックアウトする《相手を打ち倒して, 10 秒数えても立ち上がれないようにする》; やっつける, 再び立てなくする ▪ He *was knocked out of time* by an adversary. 彼は相手にノックアウトされた.

knock *a person* ***sideways*** **1** 《口》人の裏をかく; 人を狼狽させる ▪ Tom *knocked* me *sideways*. トムは私の裏をかいた.
2 《英》回復できないほどに痛めつける, 致命傷を与える ▪ The news of his mother's death *knocked* him *sideways*. 母の死の知らせに彼は悲嘆にくれた.

knock *a person* ***silly*** 人をぼうっとさせる, あ然とさせる ▪ Her blamed queer talk *knocked* me *silly*. 彼女がひどくへんてこな話をしたので私はぼう然となった.

knock the bottom [***filling, inside, lining, stuffing, wadding***] ***out of*** 《口》 **1** (箱など)の底を打ち抜く; (議論・証拠・計画など)を打ち破る, だめにする ▪ Your objection *knocked the bottom out of* my original plan. あなたの反対があったので, 私は元の計画をすっかりあきらめました ▪ This explanation *knocks the inside out of* many theories. この説明は多くの学説を立たなくしてしまう.
2 …を打ち負かす, へこます ▪ Let's *knock the stuffing out of* that snob. あの俗物の鼻をへし折ってやろう.

knock the socks off 《米俗》…を決定的に打ち負かす ▪ He will *knock the socks off* them. 彼は彼らを決定的に負かすだろう.

knock the spirit out of 《口》…の士気を挫(くじ)く ▪ Continuous bombardment *knocked the spirit out of* the soldiers. 連続爆撃が兵士の士気を挫いた.

knock (***the***) ***spots off*** [***out of***] →SPOT[1].

knock their heads together →HEAD[1].

knock them dead 《米口》(俳優が)観客に大いに受ける ▪ The actor *knocked them dead* in New York. その俳優はニューヨークの観客に大いに受けた.

knock … to [***in***] ***pieces*** **1** …をめちゃめちゃに打ちこわす ▪ The car *was knocked to pieces* by the impact. 自動車はその衝突でめちゃめちゃにぶち壊された.
2 (議論など)を徹底的に論破する ▪ His contention *was knocked to pieces*. 彼の主張は徹底的に論破された.

knock up copy (新聞などの)原稿を(印刷に回すために)整理する ▪ Can you *knock up copy*? 君は原稿整理ができるか.

knock-down, knockdown /nάkdàʊn|nɔ́k-/ 名形 ***a knock-down and drag-out*** 《米口》乱闘 ▪ I never saw *a* prettier *knock-down and drag-out* in my life. 私はこれほど派手な乱闘は生まれてこのかた見たことがない.

knocker /nάkər|nɔ́k-/ 名 ***on the knocker*** 《英》戸別訪問の; クレジットで, つけで ▪ It was an old-fashioned campaign, just getting out *on the knocker*. 昔ながらの選挙運動で, ただ戸別訪問に出かけるだけだった.

up to the knocker 《英俗》至極体の調子がよく; 流行の粋を集めて; 申し分なく, きわめてよく, 立派に ▪ How do you feel? —Not quite *up to the knocker*. 気分はどうかね?—どうもあまり調子がよくない ▪ We are dressed *up to the knocker*. 我々は流行の粋を集めた服装をしている ▪ I was prepared *up to the knocker*. 私は立派に覚悟していた.

knock-out /nάkàʊt|nɔ́k-/ 名形 ***a knock-out competition*** 勝ち抜き方式の競技会, トーナメント ▪ Our club won *the knock-out competition*. わがクラブが勝ち抜き戦で優勝した.

a knock-out dose of medicine 1 回分の睡眠剤 ▪ *A knock-out dose of medicine* made me fall asleep. 眠り薬 1 服で昏睡した.

knot[1] /nɑt|nɔt/ 名 ***at the*** [***a***] ***rate of knots*** 《英口》非常に速く ▪ The yacht sailed *at the rate of knots*. ヨットは猛スピードで帆走した.

cut a [***the, the Gordian***] ***knot*** 快刀乱麻を断つ; 難問を英断をもって解決する; 短兵急に事を処断する (→cut the GORDIAN knot) ▪ He soon *cut the knot* by dismissing them all. 彼はまもなく彼ら全員を首にして, 難題を一刀両断に解決した ▪ Never *cut*

K

a knot which can be untied. 解きうる結びを切断してはいけない.

get into knots 混乱[苦境]に陥る ▪ We *got into knots* about the problem. 我々はその問題で混乱に陥った.

in knots 三々五々(群れをなして) ▪ People were standing *in knots* waiting for news. 人々は三々五々群れをなして立ったまま知らせを待っていた.

make ... knots 毎時…海里で走る ▪ The ship is *making* 15 *knots*. 船は毎時15ノットで走っている.

of a knot 団結して, 結合して; 合同して ▪ People conclude Coventry, Pett, and me to be *of a knot*. 人々はコベントリーとペットと私が組んでいると決めている.

tie the knot →TIE².

tie** a person* (up***) ***in*** [***into***] ***knots*** 《英》 **1** 人を苦境[紛糾]に巻きこむ ▪ Jane would often *tie* us *in knots* with many questions. ジェインはたくさん質問して我々をしばしば困らせるのだった ▪ He *tied* himself *up in knots* trying to solve the problem. 彼はその問題を解こうとして非常に困った.
2 (説明しようとして)混乱に陥らせる ▪ I tried to explain the problem, but soon *tied* myself *up in knots*. 問題を説明しようとしたが, じきに頭がこんがらかってしまった.
3 腹が痛くなるほど大笑いさせる ▪ We *were tied up in knots* while listening to his funny experience. 彼の滑稽な体験談にみな腹を抱えて笑った.

knot² /nɑt|nɔt/ 動 ***get knotted*** 《英口》〚主に命令文で〛(人の言ったことに軽蔑・不承知・不信を表して)うるさい; ばか言え; うそ言え ▪ Go down to the shops for me.—*Get knotted*! 店へ行ってくれないか—まっぴらだよ! ▪ Oh, *get knotted*. I'm trying to work! うるさいな, あっちへ行け. こっちは仕事をしようとしているのだ.

know¹ /noʊ/ 名 ***in*** (***on***) ***the know*** 《口》消息通で, 機密[内情]に通じて ▪ He has been *in on the know* from the beginning. 彼は初めから内情に通じていた.

know² /noʊ/ 動 ***all** one **knows*** 《口》 **1**〚名詞的に〛できるかぎりのこと, 全力 ▪ I did *all* I *knew*. 私は全力を尽くした.
2〚副詞的に〛できるだけ, 全力を尽くして ▪ They will be running back *all* they *know*. 彼らは全速力で走って帰っているであろう.

as I know on 《米口》私の知っているかぎりでは ▪ I don't know what you mean, *as I know on*. どう考えても, あなたがどういうつもりなのかわからない.

... as we know it よく知られた, おなじみの ▪ This is the end of TV *as we know it*. なじみのテレビはこれで終わる.

be known as …として知られている, で通っている ▪ He *is known as* Abe [a successful lawyer]. 彼はエイブという名で通っている[弁護士として成功したとして名が知られている].

be known for …で知られている ▪ He *is known for* his good humor. 彼は上機嫌なことで知られている.

be known to **1** …に知られている ▪ The fact *is known to* them. その事実は彼らに知られている.
2 …に名前が記録されている ▪ He *is known to* the police. 彼は警察に名が記録されている《札つきである》.

before** one **knows it たちまち, あっという間に, いつの間にか ▪ I'll get it through *before* you *know it*. すぐにそれを片づけてみせます.

before we [***you***] ***know where we*** [***you***] ***are*** いつの間にか ▪ He will be a minister *before we know where we are*. 彼はまもなく大臣になるだろう.

a person ***didn't know what hit** him* 《口》(何に出くわしたかわからず)とてもびっくりする ▪ The poor man *didn't know what hit* him. 気の毒にその男はひどくショックを受けた.

Do you know where I'm coming from? 私の言っていることがわかりますか? ▪ Wow! *You* both *know where I am coming from*! やった! 君たち二人には僕の言うことがわかるんだ!

Don't I [***they***] ***know it!***/***Doesn't he*** [***she***] ***know it!*** そんなことは先刻承知です! ▪ He is her son.—*Don't I know it!* 彼は彼女の息子だ—そんなことは先刻承知だ.

don't [***do***] ***you know*** 《口》ご存じの通り; …ですよ ▪ My wife is such a nervous woman, *don't you know*. 妻はあの通り神経質な女性でしてね ▪ *Do you know*, I saw the prettiest hat you can imagine. あのね, この上もなく美しい帽子を見たのですよ. ☞話の切り出しの文句. 特に多少驚くべき話の場合.

for all I know →FOR all one knows.

for all** one **knows =for all one CAREs.

God [***goodness, Heaven, Christ, hell,*** (***the***) ***Lord***] ***knows*** **1** 神に誓って…である (*that*) ▪ *God knows that* it is true. それは天地神明に誓ってほんとうである ▪ *God knows*: I don't. 神かけて私はそうではない.
2 神だけが知る, 誰も知らない (*who, where,* etc.) ▪ *God knows where* he fled. 彼がどこへ逃げたか誰も知らない.

God knows how many 非常にたくさんの (= I don't KNOW how many) ▪ He has had *God knows how many* wives. 彼は何人妻をめとってきたかわからない.

God [***goodness, Heaven,*** (***the***) ***Lord, nobody***] ***knows what*** [***who, where,*** etc.] 何かあるもの[誰かある人, どこか, など] ▪ He is always busy with *God knows what*. 彼はいつも何かで忙しい ▪ He is in love with *God knows who*. 彼は誰かにほれている ▪ He has gone *nobody knows where*. 彼はどこかへ行ってしまった.

***have known ...** do* …が…するのを経験して知っている《受身になれば to do となる》 ▪ I *have known* it happen before. 以前にそんなことがあったのを知っている ▪ Criminals have *been known* to jest even upon the scaffold. 罪人が断頭台上でさえ冗談を言ったと知られている.

I don't know about that. それはどうだかね(疑わしい) ▪ They say snakes are intelligent.—*I don't know about that.* ヘビは賢いそうだね—どうだかね.

I don't know how many 非常にたくさんの (= God KNOWs how many) ▪ They were partners for *I don't know how many* years. 彼らは非常に長い年月の間, 共同経営者であった.

I don't know that... 《口》…ないことはかなり確かである ▪ *I don't know that* he likes this. 彼がこれを好まないことはまず確かだ.

I knew it. そんなことだと思ったよ, きっとそうなるとわかっていた ▪ He failed again.—*I knew it*, I just knew it. 彼, またしくじった—やっぱりね, どうせそんなことだろうと思っていたよ.

I know not what その他いろいろ[たくさん] ▪ He was interested in collecting eggs, skeletons, beetles, and *I know not what.* 彼は卵やがいこつや甲虫その他いろいろのものを集めることに興味を持っていた.

I know what →WHAT.

I want [***'d like***] ***to know!*** 《米口》おやおや!, ほんとかい! 《驚きなどを示す》 ▪ She said she would be delighted!—*I want to know!* 彼女は喜んでしますと言ったよ—ほんとかい.

I wouldn't know. 《口》 知っているわけがない ▪ How old is she?—*I wouldn't know.* 彼女って何歳なんだ?—知るわけないじゃないか. ☞答えたくない場合にも.

if you must know 《口》そんなに知りたければ ▪ *If you must know*, Mr. Smith is here. ぜひにとおっしゃるなら, スミス氏は来ていらっしゃいますよ.

It is a wise father that knows his own child. 《諺》 **1** いくら賢明な父親でも自分の子かどうかはわからない《母親だけが知っている》.
2 いくら賢明な父親でも自分の子のことはわからない《親ばか》.

It takes one to know one. 《口》→TAKE[2].

It's... (***Jim***), ***but not as we know it.*** 《口》(見慣れないもの, 期待していないことを指して)大した…ではない ▪ *It's* a chapel, *Jim, but not as we know it.* 礼拝堂というほどのものではないけど, 一応は.

know *oneself* おのれを知る ▪ We must *know ourselves.* 我々はおのれを知らなければならない.

know a thing [***a move***] ***or two*** 《口》世故にたけている; 抜け目がない, 如才がない ▪ Don't worry about him. He *knows a thing or two.* 彼のことはご心配にはおよびません. 彼に抜かりはありませんから ▪ He seems to *know a move or two.* 彼は世故にたけているようだ ▪ I have shown him that we in Virginia *know a thing or two.* 我々バージニアの者は抜け目がないことを彼に見せてやった.

know a trick or two/know a trick worth two of that = KNOW a thing or two.

know *a person* ***and his kind*** ある人のようなタイプの人をよく知っている ▪ I *know* Jane *and her kind.* 私はジェインのようなタイプの女性はよく知っている.

know any better 〚主に否定文・疑問文で〛まともな行動をする; 行儀よくする ▪ They sometimes don't *know any better.* 彼らはときにまともな行動ができない.

know best →BEST.

know better →BETTER[1].

know better than to *do* …するようなばかはしない ▪ You *knew better than to* expect a kindness from an enemy. あなたは敵から親切を期待するようなばかなことはしなかった.

know black from white 物事の見分けがつく, 良否がわかる ▪ Things are so mixed up that we don't *know black from white.* 事情が込み入って良否の判断がつかない.

know *a person* ***by sight*** →by SIGHT 1.

know different [***otherwise***] 《口》反対の証拠[情報, 意見]を知っている ▪ People say he will stand down and make way for a younger man. But we *know different.* 彼は立候補しないで, 若い人に譲るだろうと言われているが, 我々は反対の情報を得ている. ☞この表現を非文法的とする人もある.

know enough to come in out of the rain = know enough to go in when it RAINs.

know fine 《スコ》よく知っている ▪ I *know fine* that he is honest. 彼が正直なことはよく知っている.

know from nothing (***about***) 《米口》(…について)何も知らない ▪ Why, you don't *know from anything*! あれ, 何も分かっちゃいないんだな, お前は ▪ He *knows from nothing about* music. 彼は音楽のことは全く何も知らない.

know...full [***perfectly***] ***well*** …を熟知している ▪ You *know full well* that smoking is forbidden in here. ここでは禁煙なのはよくご存じでしょう.

know how many days go to the week [***how many go to a dozen***] = KNOW a thing or two.

know how (***to*** *do*) (…の)しかたを知っている ▪ She *knows how to* write for children. 彼女は児童読物の書き方を知っている ▪ He does not *know how.* 彼は方法を知らない.

know...inside out →INSIDE out 2.

know...like the back [***palm***] ***of*** *one's* ***hand*** →BACK; PALM.

know little [***nothing***] ***and care less*** 知りもしなければ関心もない ▪ Some people *know little and care less* about science fiction. SF を知りもしなければ関心もない人もいる.

know *one's* ***own mind*** →MIND[1].

know the ropes →ROPE[1].

know the time of day →TIME[1].

know through and through →THROUGH and through 2.

know...to be …が(…で)あることを知る ▪ I *know* him *to be* a friend. 私は彼が友人であることを知っている ▪ The stars *were known to be* bodies congruous with our sun. 星はわが太陽と同じような天体であると知られていた.

know *a person* ***to speak to*** 会えば声をかける程度に知り合っている ▪ I *know* him *to speak to.* 私

は会えば声をかける程度に彼を知っている.

know what** one **is about [*doing*]《口》万事心得ている; 抜け目がない ▪ They were a musical family and *knew what* they *were about*. その一家は音楽好きで, 音楽によく通じていた ▪ You don't *know what* you *are doing*. 君にはぬかりがある.

know what** one **is talking about 《口》(経験・教育から)主題を熟知[に精通]して話す ▪ He hardly *knows what* he's *talking about*. 彼は自分が話していることがまるでわかっていない ▪ You can trust him. He *knows what* he *is talking about*. 彼は信用していい. 経験からちゃんとわかってしゃべっているんだ.

know what it is to be [***do***] …を体験して(わかって)いる ▪ I *know what it is to be* a mother. 母親がどんな(に大変な)ものか身に覚えがある.

know what o'clock it is →O'CLOCK.

know what's what →WHAT.

know where** one **is going (人生・職業で)何を達成したいかはっきりわかっている ▪ I *know* exactly *where* I'*m going*. I want to be a doctor. 自分が何になりたいかちゃんとわかっている. 医者だ.

know where** one **stands **1** 自分がどう思われているを悟る ▪ My girlfriend wants to end us. I am seen as a burden to my parents and now I *know where* I *stand*. 僕のガールフレンドは僕と別れたいと思い, 親からは重荷だと見られている. いま自分がどう思われているかよくわかった.

2 自分の身分をわきまえる, 自分の立場を把握している ▪ Our boss believes employees always need to *know where* they *stand*. 雇用者は常に自分の身分をわきまえている必要がある, と我々の上司は信じている ▪ I just want to *know where* I *stand*, that's all. 自分の立場をはっきり知りたい, それだけだ.

know which way the wind blows →know how the WIND blows.

let it be known that/make it known that 《文》…ということを他の人々に(それとなく)知らせる, みなに周知徹底させる ▪ The mayor has *let it be known that* he won't run for election again. 市長はもう選挙に立候補しないと公表させた ▪ He *let it be known that* he wanted to resign. 彼は辞職したいということを知らせた.

like, you know 《口》あのー, そのー, えーと, 何というか ▪ That's, well, *like, you know*, too much! そいつは, えーと, その, つまり, あんまりだ!

make ... known …を発表する, 知らせる ▪ He *made* it *known* to the public. 彼はそれを世間に発表した.

make** oneself **known (***to***) (…に)名を名のる, 自己紹介する ▪ Why don't you *make yourself known to* him? 君は彼に自己紹介をしてはどうか.

never knew ... *do* …がするのを経験したことがない, したためしがない ▪ I *never knew* him tell a lie. 彼が嘘を言ったためしがない.

nobody knows what [***who, where,*** etc.] →God KNOWs what.

not if I know it 《口》もちろん…でない ▪ After that do you think I could marry you?—*Not if I know it*. あんなことがあってから, あなたと結婚できると思って?—もちろんできませんね.

not know (***a***) ***B from a bull's foot*** →B.

not know** one's **arse [《米俗》 ***ass***] ***from** one's **elbow*** 《英口》→ARSE[1].

not know** one **is born 《英口》(昔にくらべて)楽な生活をする ▪ The young people today do*n't know* they *are born*. 今日の若者たちは楽な生活をしている.

not know what [***who, where,*** etc.] 何か(わからないこと)[誰か(わからない人), どこか(わからないところへ), など] ▪ She said she *knew not what*. 彼女は何やらわからないことを言った ▪ He has gone I do*n't know where*. 彼はどこかへ行ってしまった.

***not know what hit** one* 《口》非常に驚く ▪ She did*n't know what* had *hit* her. 彼女はとてもびっくりした.

***not know what to do with** oneself* どうして時を過ごしてよいかわからない; 不愉快に感じる, 困惑を感じる ▪ I do*n't know what to do with myself* if I stay at home all day. 一日中家にいるとどうして時を過ごしてよいかわからない.

not know what to make of …を解読できない, の正体がつかめない ▪ I do*n't know what to make of* his request. 彼の要請の真意がつかめない.

not know where to put** oneself* [*one's* ***face] 《口》きまり悪く感じる ▪ When he praised me in public, I did*n't know where to put myself*. 彼が私を人前でほめたとき私は非常にきまりが悪かった.

not know whether** one's **going or coming →not know whether one is coming or going (→COME[2]).

not ... that I know of 《口》私の知るところでは…でない ▪ Is there any such book?—*Not that I know of*. そのような本がありますか?—(私の知るかぎりでは)どうもないようですね.

not that you know of 《口》そんなこと誰がするものか ▪ As Mr. B offered to take his hand, he put them both behind him.—*Not that you know of*. B氏が彼の手を取ろうとしたので, 彼は両手を後ろへ回した—握手など誰がするものか(と言わんばかりに).

One never knows. 何とも言えない (= Who KNOWs? 2) ▪ I doubt this is the same person. Still, *one never knows*. 同一人物ではなさそうだが何とも言えない.

What do you know (***about that***)***!*** 《口》→(Well,) WHAT do you know about that!

What you don't know won't [***can't***] ***hurt you.*** 《諺》知らなければ心配する[悲しむ]こともない.

Who knows? **1** 誰にもわからない ▪ I'm not sure I can make it, but *who knows?* うまくいくか自信がない, でも誰にもわからない.

2 …かもしれない, 何とも言えない (= you never KNOW) ▪ I may be the president of the company some day.—*Who knows?* 私はいつかその会社の社長になるかもしれない—そうかもしれないね.

Who knows but that …? …かもしれない ▪ *Who knows but that* he may succeed? 彼は成功するかもしれない.

a person ***wouldn't know … if it jumped up and bit*** *him/a person* ***wouldn't know … if*** *he* ***tripped over it*** (物・事が)明白な(見てすぐわかる)場合でも気がつかない ▪ I *wouldn't know* it was marijuana *if it jumped up and bit* me. マリファナだとはっきり見て取れても私はそれと気がつかないだろう.

Wouldn't you like to know? (聞かれて)誰が教えるもんか, 話すつもりはない ▪ "*Wouldn't you like to know?*" he said with a grin when she asked. 彼女に聞かれて「教えてなんかやるもんか」と彼はニヤリとして言った.

you know 《口》 **1** 〚know は降昇調〛ご承知の通り ▪ He cannot help that, *you know*. ご存知の通り, 彼はそれをどうしようもないのです.
2 〚文頭または文尾で, 低い語調で〛(人に知らせる場合)…ですよ ▪ He's such a bore, *you know*. 彼にはほんとにうんざりするんだよ.
3 〚文頭または文尾で, 低い語調で〛(意見を述べる場合)あのね; …と思うね ▪ She ought to have piano lessons, *you know*. 彼女はピアノのレッスンを受けるべきだと思うね.
4 〚通例文尾で, know は下降調〛(訂正・反対する場合)いいえ ▪ She is a good wife.—She isn't, *you know*. 彼女は良妻だよ—いいえ, ちがいます.

you know as well as I do (***that***) よくわかっていると思うが ▪ *You know as well as I do that* we can't afford that car. わかっているな. とてもあの車には手が出せないんだ.

You know best. あなたが一番良く心得ている; 私の口出しすることではありません ▪ I don't think so, but *you know best*. 私はそうは思いませんが, 私の口出しすることではありません.

you know better than that そんな事をする[言う]ものではない ▪ Let's go there.—*You know better than that*. そこへ行きましょう—そんな事を言うものじゃないよ.

You know something? →SOMETHING.

you know what [***who***] 《口》 例のこと[人] ▪ Let's talk about *you know what*. 例のことについて話そうではないか ▪ Is *you know who* still speaking ill of you? 誰かさんは相変わらず君の悪口を言っているかい.

you know what I mean [***think***] 私の言うことがおわかりでしょう; こう言っては何ですが ▪ We're like two halves of one thing. *You know what I mean*? 僕らは互いに分身といったところだ, わかるだろう?

you know what you can do (***with***) 《口》 私は(…は)欲しくない, (と)かかわりたくない, (を)もらいたくない ▪ *You know what you can do with* your typescript. 私はあなたのタイプ原稿はいりません. ☞三人称について言う場合には主語は he, she, they となる.

you know where you can put … 《口》 私は…に関心[興味]はない, …は絶対に受け入れたくない ▪ *You know where you can put* that idea. 私はその考えはいただきたくない. ☞三人称について言う場合には主語は he, she, they となる.

you never know 《口》 たぶんね; かもしれない (= Who KNOWs? 2) ▪ Do you think he will come?—*You never know*. 彼は来ると思うかい?—たぶんね.

You never know (***what you can do***) ***till you try.*** 《諺》 やってみてはじめて(自分の能力が)わかる, 「ものは試し」.

knowing /nóʊɪŋ/ 形 名 ***be knowing in*** …に精通している, に長じている ▪ Helen *was knowing in* such drugs. ヘレンはそのような薬に精通していた.

there is no knowing …はわかりはしない ▪ *There is no knowing* what may happen. 何が起こるかわかったものではない.

knowledge /nάlɪdʒ|nɔ́l-/ 名 ***A little knowledge is a dangerous thing.*** = A little LEARNING is a dangerous thing.

be common [***public***] ***knowledge*** 誰でも知っている, 周知の事実[公知]である ▪ It *is common knowledge* that he is looking for another job. 彼が別の仕事を探していることは誰だって知っている.

bring … to *a person's* ***knowledge*** …を人の耳に入れる, 人に知らせる ▪ He *brought* the fact *to his father's knowledge*. 彼はその事実を父の耳に入れた.

come to *a person's* ***knowledge*** 人の耳に入る ▪ The fact has *come to his knowledge*. その事実は彼の耳に入った.

in the full knowledge of …を十分承知の上 ▪ He declined it *in the full knowledge of* her good-will. 彼は彼女の好意を十分承知の上でそれを断った.

it is within *one's* ***knowledge that*** …は人の知るところだ ▪ *It is within my knowledge that* Keats died very young. キーツが非常に若死にをしたことは私の知るところだ.

Knowledge is power. 《諺》 知識は力なり. ☞ L Scientia est patentia のなぞり.

not to *one's* ***knowledge*** …の知るところでは…でない, …でないようだ ▪ Has he been abroad?—*Not to my knowledge*. 彼は外国に行ったことがありますか?—どうもないようです.

of *a person's* ***knowledge*** …が知っているように ▪ *Of my knowledge* five hundred friars are kept in one cloister. 私の知っているように, 500 人の修道士が一つの修道院に入れられている.

out of all knowledge 《古風》 全くわからない ▪ The number of books in this library is *out of all knowledge*. この図書館の本の数は全くわからない.

to *one's* (***certain***) ***knowledge*** 確かに, 知っているところでは ▪ He has done so *to my* (*certain*) *knowledge*. 彼は確かにそうした.

to the best of *one's* ***knowledge*** → to the BEST of one's belief.

with the knowledge and consent of 《文》 …の承知の上で ▪ The decision was taken *with the knowledge and consent of* the US authori-

K

ties. その議決はアメリカ当局の承知の上でなされた.

without the knowledge of …に知られずに, に無断で ▪ He married *without the knowledge of* his parents. 彼は両親に無断で結婚した.

knuckle /nʌ́kəl/ 名 ***a white knuckle ride*** (テーマパークの)手に汗握るジェットコースター ▪ Many people were queuing up for the thrill of *a white-knuckle ride*. 大勢の人がジェットコースターのスリルを求めて並んで順番を待っていた. ☞恐怖のあまり安全レールを強く握りしめ拳が白くなることから.

down on *one's* ***knuckles*** 《口》(金に)困って ▪ He is *down on his knuckles*. 彼は金に困っている.

give a rap on the knuckles →RAP[1].

near the knuckle 《英口》(風紀上)きわどいところまで《風紀取締りの制限にやっと触れない程度まで》 ▪ She goes pretty *near the knuckle* sometimes, but she never jumps over the fence. 彼女はときどきかなりきわどいところまで行くが, 決して一線を越えない.

rap *a person's* ***knuckles*** →RAP[3].

too close to the knuckle 生々しすぎて楽しめない, 当惑させる ▪ These films are all *too close to the knuckle*. これらの映画はみなきわどすぎる.

knuckle-bone /nʌ́kəlbòʊn/ 名 ***down on the knuckle-bone*** 《俗》困窮して, 金に窮して ▪ He has been *down on the knuckle-bone* since. 彼はそのあと金に窮している.

kudos /kjúːdoʊs|-dɔs/ 名 ***win*** [***get, gain, receive***] ***kudos*** 名声[賞賛]を得る ▪ His sole ambition is to *get kudos* without exertion. 彼のただ一つの大望は努力しないで名声を得ることである.

K

L

labor[1]**,** 《英》 **labour**[1] /léɪbər/ 名 ***a labor of love*** (報酬目あてでなく)好きで[楽しんで]する仕事; 篤志事業 (《聖》 *1 Thess.* 1. 3) ▪ Enthusiasm has rendered this biographical task *a labor of love.* 熱意を持って当たったのでこの伝記を書く仕事は楽しみの仕事となった.

(be) in labor 産みの苦しみをして(いる); (山などが)鳴動して(いる) ▪ She *was in labor* for ten hours. 彼女は10時間産みの苦しみをした ▪ We beheld the mountain incessantly *in labor.* 山が絶えず鳴動するのを見た.

withdraw** one's **labor 労働ストライキをする ▪ Workers have threatened to *withdraw their labor.* 労働者たちはストを打つぞと言っておどしている.

labor[2]**,** 《英》 **labour**[2] /léɪbər/ 動 ***labor on the way*** やっと進む, こつこつ進む ▪ He *labored on the way* up. 彼は坂を骨折って登って行った.

labor the point (すでに分かっている)その点をくだくだと言う ▪ That's so obvious that you needn't *labor the point.* そんなことは分かりきっているので, その点をくどくど言う必要はないよ.

labor** one's **way 苦心して進んで行く ▪ We *labored our way* with great difficulty upon the ice-belt. 氷帯の上を苦心して, やっと進んで行った.

labor with child 産みの苦しみをする ▪ The woman was *laboring with child.* その女性は産みの苦しみをしていた.

laborer, 《英》 **labourer** /léɪbərər/ 名 ***The laborer is worthy of his hire.*** 働く人がその報いを得るのは当然である (《聖》 *Luke* 10. 7) ▪ If *the laborer is worthy of his hire,* no protest will be uttered. 働く者が報酬を得るのが当然ならば, 抗議の声は上がらないだろう.

laboring, 《英》 **labouring** /léɪbərɪŋ/ 形 ***pull [have, ply, tug] the laboring oar*** (最も)骨の折れる役を引き受ける ▪ They willingly *plied the laboring oar.* 彼らは最も辛い役割を快く引き受けた.

lace /leɪs/ 動 ***lace** a person's **jacket [coat] (for** him**)*** 《俗》 人をむちで打つ, 打ちのめす ▪ I'll *lace your jacket for* you. お前を打ちのめすぞ. ☞おそらく lace と lash とのしゃれであろう.

lack[1] /læk/ 名 ***for lack of*** ...の不足のために, 欠乏のために ▪ The plants died *for lack of* water. 植物は水不足のため枯死した.

no lack (of) 十分(の), たくさん(の) ▪ There is *no lack of* loyalty among our people. わが国民には忠誠心は十分にある.

lack[2] /læk/ 動 ***be lacking in*** (ある性質)を欠く ▪ He *is* sadly *lacking in* common sense. 彼はあまりにも常識がない.

lad /læd/ 名 ***a bit of a lad*** 《軽蔑》 ちょっとだらしのない男 ▪ He was *a bit of a lad* till he settled down. 彼は身を固めるまでは少しだらしのない男だった.

one of the lads =one of the BOYs.

ladder /lǽdər/ 名 ***at the top of the ladder*** 最高位について ▪ He's *at the top of the ladder* after a long career. 長い職歴を経て彼は最高の地位についている.

get** one's **foot on the ladder →FOOT[1].

He who would climb the ladder must begin at the bottom. 《諺》 梯子(はしご)に登りたい者は一段目から始めなければならない《高い地位を得たいと望むなら, 低い地位から始めてゆっくりと昇らねばならない》,「千里の道も一歩より」.

kick ... down [away] the ladder (by which** one **rose) 出世の道を開いてくれた人や職業などを捨てる ▪ She pitilessly *kicked* (people) *down the ladder* as she advanced by degrees. 彼女は昇進していくにつれ, 出世を助けてくれた人を容赦なく見捨てた.

kick over the ladder 出世の助けになってくれた人を捨てる; 以前の友人や援助者を軽蔑する ▪ Now that he has risen to being manager, he has *kicked over the ladder.* 彼は支配人に昇進したので今までの友人や援助者を軽蔑した.

see through a ladder 《口》 たやすく[明白に]わかる ▪ He was so drunk that he could not *see* a hole *through a ladder.* 彼は非常に酔っていたので穴も簡単にわからなかった.

take a step up the ladder/move up the ladder 昇進する ▪ *Taking one* more *step up the ladder,* he will be director. あと一段登れば彼は社長になるだろう.

the corporate ladder 出世の梯子(はしご) ▪ My brother successfully climbed *the corporate ladder.* 兄は首尾よく出世の階段を登った.

lade /leɪd/ 動 ***be laden with*** **1** ...を(どっしり)のせられている; 負わされている, 詰められている ▪ The cart *was laden with* hay. その荷車には干し草がうんと積まれていた ▪ Her eyes *were laden with* tears. 彼女の目には涙がいっぱいたまっていた ▪ The air *was laden with* a delicious aroma. 空気は馥郁(ふくいく)たる芳香に満ちていた.

2 (苦悩など)を重く負わされている, で苦しみ悩んでいる ▪ His heart *was laden with* sorrow. 彼の心は悲しみにうちひしがれていた.

ladida(h), lah-di-dah /lɑ̀ːdɪdɑ́ː/ 形名 ***come [do] the ladidah*** 《俗》 おしゃれをする ▪ The lad goes to music-halls and *does the ladidah.* その若者は演芸場へ行きおしゃれをする.

in a ladidah sort of way 気取って, しゃれて ▪ He talks *in a ladidah sort of way.* 彼は気取った話し方をする.

lady[1] /léɪdi/ 名 ***a lady friend*** 1 女友達 ▪ She stays with *a lady friend* in Hawaii during the winter. 彼女は冬の間女友達とハワイで過ごす.
2 (女性の) 恋人 ▪ He took his *lady friend* to dinner. 彼は恋人を夕食に連れて行った.

a lady in waiting 女官 ▪ A day at court was hard work for *a lady in waiting*. 女官にとって宮廷での1日は激務であった.

a lady's man/ladies' man 女性と交際するのが好きな男性, 女に優しい男 (↔a MAN's man) ▪ The vicar is *a lady's man*. 牧師は女性に非常に親切だ.

do the lady's man (夜会などで)女性の接待をする ▪ He's always ready to *do the lady's man*. 彼はいつも進んで女性の接待をする.

it isn't over till [***until***] ***the fat lady sings*** 《口》勝負は下駄を履くまで[最後まで]わからない, 最後まであきらめてはならない ▪ Tony's only two games behind. And as they say, *it's not over until the fat lady sings*. トニーは2ゲーム負けているだけだ. よく言われるように, 勝負は下駄を履くまでわからない ▪ Relax. *It won't be over till the fat lady sings*. 気楽になさい. ことは土壇場まで決まらないから. ☞1970年代の米国の諺 The opera isn't over till the fat lady sings.「太った女性が歌うまでオペラは終わらない[ことは最後の最後までわからない]」から.

Ladies and gentlemen! 紳士淑女諸君!, みなさん!《演説などの呼びかけ》 ▪ Good evening, *ladies and gentlemen*. Welcome to SDA Late Nite Radio. 今晩は, みなさん. SDA 深夜ラジオ放送へようこそ.

ladies first レディーファースト《しばしば反語・戯》 ▪ After you, please. It's *ladies first*. どうぞお先に. レディーファーストですから.

ladies who lunch 《口》金持ちの有閑夫人たち, 社交や高級レストランでの食事などに暇を潰す裕福な女性 ▪ This club isn't just for *ladies who lunch*. このクラブは有閑マダムたちの専用ではない.

Lady Bountiful 恵み深い婦人, 婦人慈善家 ▪ His wife likes to see herself as *Lady Bountiful*. 彼の妻は自分が恵み深い婦人だと思いたがっている. ☞Farquhar 作の喜劇 *The Beaux' Stratagem* (1707)中の金持ちで慈悲深い女主人公から.

Lady Luck (擬人化された)幸運 ▪ *Lady Luck* was against them and they lost the match. 幸運の女神に見放されて彼らは試合に敗れた.

Lady Muck 《英戯》→Lord MUCK.

the lady of the house 女主人; 主婦 ▪ Would you like to speak to *the lady of the house*? この家の奥さまにお話ししたいですか.

the Old Lady of Threadneedle Street → OLD.

There is a lady in the case. この事件には女性がいる《女性がこの事件を解く鍵だ》 ▪ They suspect that *there is a lady in the case*. この事件の鍵は女性が握っているとにらんでいる.

your [***his***] ***good lady*** 《主に戯》奥さん ▪ There's Bob Fischer with *his good lady*. あそこにボブ・フィッシャーが奥さんといっしょにいる.

lady[2] /léɪdi/ 動 ***lady it*** いばる, 女王然とする (→LORD it (over)) ▪ She *ladies it* over her kitchen staff. 彼女は厨房職員に大きな顔をしている ▪ That great seven-hilled city still *ladies it* over the nations of the earth. 偉大な7つの丘のある都市は今なお世界の全ての国の上に女王然として君臨している.

lager[1] /lɑ́ːgər/ 名 ***lager louts*** 《英》〚主に複数形で〛ビールで酔っぱらって乱暴を働く若者たち ▪ Some *lager louts* were smashing shop windows. 酔っぱらいのちんぴら連中が店のショーウィンドウを叩き壊していた.

lager[2] /lɑ́ːgər/ 動 ***be*** [***get***] ***lagered up*** 《英口》ビールを多量に飲んで酔っ払っている[酔っ払う] ▪ Most of them *were* already well *lagered up*. 彼らのほとんどはもうすっかりできあがっていた.

lake /leɪk/ 名 ***Go*** (***and***) ***jump in the lake.*** 《口》行って溺れてしまえ《うるさくするな》.

lam /læm/ 名 ***on the lam*** 《主に米口》逃走中で ▪ He is *on the lam* from Boston. 彼はボストンから逃走中だ.

take it on the lam 《米俗》一目散に逃げる ▪ After the accident he *took it on the lam*. 事故の後, 彼は逃亡した.

lamb /læm/ 名 ***a wolf*** [***a fox***] ***in a lamb's skin*** 猫かぶり, 偽善者 ▪ The Pope was *a wolf in a lamb's skin*. 法王は偽善者であった.

as a lamb to the slaughter 屠(と)場に引かれて行く子羊のように(危険を知らず従順に) (《聖》*Isa*. 53. 7) ▪ You must go *as a lamb to the slaughter*. 屠場に引かれて行く子羊のように, 従順に行かなければならない.

like a lamb 1 おとなしく, 従順に, 小心に ▪ He's *like a lamb* and does everything you tell him. 彼は非常に従順で言われたことは何でもする ▪ He took it *like a lamb*. 彼はそれをおとなしく受けいれた.
2 純真でだまされやすく ▪ She looks so innocent, *like a lamb*. 彼女は純真で, とても無邪気に見える.

My lamb! よい子, 坊や《子供を呼ぶ言葉》.

One may as well be hanged for a sheep as (***for***) ***a lamb.*** →SHEEP.

lame /leɪm/ 形 ***be lame of*** [***in***] ...が不自由である; が不完全である ▪ He *was lame of* one leg. 彼は片足が不自由だった ▪ Their course *was lame in* many parts. 彼らの道は多くの所が不完全だった.

come by the lame post (ニュースなどが)遅い, 遅れる ▪ The news had the misfortune to *come by the lame post*. 運悪くそのニュースは遅れた.

go [***fall***] ***lame*** 足が不自由になる ▪ The horse *went lame*. 馬は足が悪くなった.

help a lame dog (***over a stile***) →HELP[2].

walk lame 足を引きずって歩く ▪ He was *walking lame*. 彼は足を引きずって歩いていた.

lament /ləmént/ 動 ***the*** [*one's*] ***late lamented...*** 故人(となった...); 今はなくなった人[物] ▪ My new car isn't nearly as comfortable as *my late* *lamented* Austin. 今度の新車は以前のオースティンほど乗り心地がよくない.

lamp /læmp/ 名 ***a lamp of* (*the*) *night* [*the world*]** 星, 天体 ▪ Then we saw *the lamps of* (*the*) *night*. そのとき星が見えた.

burn the midnight lamp 夜遅くまで勉強する ▪ During the exam he really *burned the midnight lamp*. 試験中に彼は本当に真夜中まで勉強した.

of the lamp 苦心の研究による; 自然でなく凝りすぎた ▪ It is a theory born *of the lamp*. それは苦心さんたんの後生まれた理論である.

pass* [*hand*] *on the lamp (人知などの)進歩に自分の分を尽くす (→hand on the TORCH) ▪ It is one's duty to *hand on the lamp* of freedom. 自由の発達に分を尽くすのは人の義務だ. ☞古代ギリシャ人のたいまつ競走で, たいまつを次の走者に渡したことから.

smell of the lamp →SMELL of the candle.

lamp-lighter /lǽmplàɪtər/ 名 ***like a lamp-lighter*** 速く ▪ He ran *like a lamp-lighter*. 彼は速く走った. ☞lamp-lighter「昔街路を走って街灯に点火した人」.

lance /læns|lɑːns/ 名 ***break a lance* (*with*)** 《古風》(...と)競争する; (と) 論争をする ▪ Turner entered classical ground to *break a lance with* Claude. ターナーは古典の分野に入って, クロードと腕を競った ▪ He *broke a lance with* visitors on the subject of socialism. 彼は訪問客と社会主義の問題について論争した. ☞中世の騎士の槍(やり)試合から.

land[1] /lænd/ 名 ***a land fit for heroes* (*to live in*)** 英雄が住むのにふさわしい国 ▪ Great Britain today is hardly *a land fit for heroes to live in*. 英国は今日英雄が住むのにふさわしい国とはとても言えない. ☞1918年, 時の首相 Lloyd George の言葉から.

a* [*the*] *land of milk and honey (移民にとって)実り豊かな地, 安楽の地 ▪ The immigrants naturally expected *a land of milk and honey*. 入植者たちが豊穣(ほうじょう)の地を期待していたのも無理からぬ. ☞聖書にある神がイスラエルに与えた豊穣の地より.

back to the land 土[田園]に帰って ▪ *Back to the land*, young men! 若者よ, 田園に帰れ!

***be in the land of nod* [*Nod*]** 《戯》(子供が[に向かって]) 眠っている ▪ Harry *is in the land of nod* at last. ハリーちゃんがやっと眠ったよ ▪ You'll *be in the land of nod* long before Dad gets home. パパが帰るずっと前に坊やはもうねんねしてるわよ.

bring* ... (*safe*) *to land (人など)を海から無事に救い上げる ▪ We *brought* the crew *safe to land*. 我々は乗組員を無事救い上げた.

by land 陸路を(通って) ▪ He always traveled *by land*. 彼はいつも陸路を行った.

clear the land →CLEAR[2].

come to land 港に着く ▪ The lifeboat *came* safe *to land*. 救命艇が無事港に着いた.

find out* [*see*] *how the land lies 情勢を判断する ▪ Let's *find out how the land lies* before we decide. 決める前によく情勢を見きわめようよ ▪ I'd better *see how the land lies* before accepting the offer. 申し出を受ける前に情勢を判断した方がよさそうだ. ☞軍の地形調べから.

(*for*) *land's sake*/ *land sakes*/ *my land* 《米口》まあ, ほんとに; 後生だから ▪ *For land's sake*, don't tell him. どうぞお願いですから, 彼に言わないでください ▪ "*My land*!" exclaimed he. 「おやまあ」と彼は叫んだ. ☞land＝Lord.

go on the land 農夫になる ▪ He *went on the land*, plowing, planting, and harvesting. 彼は農夫になって耕し栽培し収穫した.

go on to a better land 《婉曲》死ぬ ▪ Grandpa *went on to a better land* after a long illness. 長患いの末じいちゃんは死んだ.

Good land! 《米》(強い感情・驚きを表して)おお神よ, おやまあ, ほんとに ▪ *Good land!* A man can't do such a thing. ほんとにまあ! 人にはそんなことなどできはしない. ☞land＝Lord.

in the land of the living →LIVING.

La-La Land*/*la-la land (魅力的な)ロサンジェルス, 現実から逃避した空想の世界 ▪ We have lived in *La-La Land* for twenty years. 我々はロサンジェルスに20年住んでいる ▪ Another ballpark in this little town? That's *la-la land* stuff. この小さな町に球場をもう一つだって? そいつは夢の国の代物だ.

Land of Lincoln リンカンの国《イリノイ州の愛称》 ▪ From Illinois? It says "*Land of Lincoln*" on your license plate. イリノイ州のお方? 車のナンバープレートに Land of Lincoln とあるけど.

land sakes →(for) LAND's sake.

live off the land その土地のものを食べてやっていく; 食物を現地調達する ▪ The army was forced to *live off the land*. 軍隊は食物を現地調達せざるを得なかった.

my land →(for) LAND's sake.

no man's land →NO.

on land (海上[空中]ではなく) 陸上で ▪ I feel more relaxed at sea than when I'm *on land*. 私は海に出ていると陸にいるときよりもほっとする.

reach land 岸に到着する, 航海の終わりに達する ▪ I shall *reach land* again. 再び岸に着くでしょう.

see land 見当がつく ▪ I now begin to *see land*. やっと見当がついてきた.

set* (*the*) *land 陸地の方位を測る ▪ I *set the land* the next morning. 翌朝陸地の方位を測った.

spy out the land →SPY[2].

take a land tack*/*take* (*one's*) *land tacks on board 《米口》陸路を旅する ▪ I *took a land tack* with them in a wagon. 彼らと荷馬車に乗って陸路を旅した ▪ We *took our land tacks on board* and quitted the boat. 我々は陸路を旅し, 船を捨てた.

The land knows. 《米》神に誓って; 誰も知らない ▪ *The land knows*; I don't. 神に誓って, 私は知らない. ☞land＝Lord.

the land of cakes スコットランド ▪ She's from

the land of cakes or Scotland. 彼女はthe land of cakesつまりスコットランドの出身だ.

the lie [《米》 ***lay***] ***of the land*** 地勢; 情勢 ▪ We had better find out [see] *the lie of the land.* 情勢を見きわめた方がよい.

work on the land 農業をやる ▪ The businessman had *worked on the land* in his youth. その実業家は若いころ農業をやっていた.

land[2] /lænd/ 動 ***be properly*** [***nicely***] ***landed*** 《英口》ひどい目にあう ▪ If the car breaks down on the way, we shall *be nicely landed.* 車が途中で故障したらひどい目にあうぞ.

land a fish 成功する, うまいことをする ▪ We have *landed a fish* this morning. Smith has bought up our sheep. 今朝はうまいことをした. スミスがうちの羊を全部買い取ってくれたんだ. ☞「魚を捕える」が原義.

land *oneself* ***in*** ...に乗り上げる, 陥る ▪ He *landed himself in* great difficulties. 彼は大変な苦境に陥った.

land like a cat (落ちても)けがをせずに立つ ▪ She *landed like a cat* falling out of a tree. 彼女は木から落ちたがけがをせずにうまく降り立った.

land on *one's* ***feet*** **1** 落ちてころばずに立つ ▪ He fell off the tree and *landed on his feet.* 彼は木から落ちて, ころばずに立った.
2 (恐れられた)困難[危険]を逃れる ▪ Whatever fix he is in, he always *lands on his feet.* 彼はどんな苦境にあってもいつも運よく切り抜ける.

land on *one's* ***head*** 頭を地面にぶつける ▪ He fell off the porch and *landed on his head.* 彼は縁側から落ちて頭を地面にぶつけた.

land *a person* ***one*** [***a blow***] (***in*** [***on***]***...***)/ ***land a blow*** [***punch***] (***in*** [***on***]***...***) 《英俗》(人の目・鼻など)に一撃をくらわす ▪ The drunkard *landed* a policeman *one in* the eye. 酔っ払いは警官の目に一撃をくらわした ▪ I *landed a punch on* his chin. 彼のあごへ一発見舞ってやった.

land the net 魚を引き上げる ▪ They were engaged in *landing the net.* 彼らは魚を引き上げることに従事していた.

landing /lǽndɪŋ/ 名 ***Happy landings!*** **1** (飛行機に乗る人に)行ってらっしゃい ▪ Good luck and *happy landings!* ごきげんよう, 行ってらっしゃい!
2 ご幸運を祈って《主に航空関係者の乾杯の言葉》 ▪ Here's to you and your crew, *happy landings!* 君とクルーのみなさんに, 幸運を祈って, 乾杯!

make a landing 着陸する ▪ *The landing* will *be made* at one of the poles of the moon. 月の極の一つに着陸させることになるだろう.

landmark /lǽndmɑːrk/ 名 ***reach a landmark*** ある大切な段階に至る, 重要な地点に達する ▪ He finally *reached a landmark* late in life. 彼は晩年に至ってやっと大事な目標を一つ達成した.

landslide /lǽndslàɪd/ 名 ***in a landslide*** 圧倒的大勝利で ▪ He won Republican nomination for the Senate *in a landslide.* 圧倒的大勝利で彼は共和党の上院議員に指名推薦された ▪ She won the primary election *in a landslide.* 彼女は予備選挙で圧勝した.

landward /lǽndwərd/ 名 ***to*** (***the***) ***landward*** 陸地の方に; (の)陸側に[へ] ▪ They examined the vegetation *to the landward* of the mangrove. 彼らはマングローブの陸地側の植物相を調べた.

lane /leɪn/ 名 (***a trip***) ***down memory lane*** 思い出の小道(をさかのぼること), 昔の楽しかった日々(をなつかしむこと) ▪ He took *a trip down memory lane* to his childhood. 彼は昔の楽しかった幼年時代をなつかしんだ.

down the little red lane (特に子供の)のどを通って, 飲み込まれて ▪ This tasty medicine surely goes *down the little red lane.* これはおいしいお薬でお子さまがきっと喜んでお飲みになります.

It's a long lane that has no turning. → TURNING.

life in the fast lane **1** 《口》はらはらする生活, 食うか食われるかの生きざま ▪ Tired of *life in the fast lane,* he decided to quit the job. 緊張の続く生活がいやになって, 彼は仕事をやめようと決心した.
2 出世コース(の人生) ▪ I'm tired of *life in the fast lane.* I wish I could slow down. 私は出世コースの人生に疲れた. もっと速度を落とせたらなあ. ☞ fast lane「高速[追い越し]車線」.

live in the fast lane 《口》 **1** 成功を求めてめまぐるしい生活を送る ▪ We have been *living in the fast lane* since we came to New York. ニューヨークに来てからずっと激しい生存競争を生き抜いてきた.
2 パーティー続き[酒浸り, 麻薬浸け]の生活をする ▪ She has been *living in the fast lane* far too long, and now she is in a clinic. 彼女は酒と麻薬漬けの生活を長く続けてきたせいで今は入院中だ.

the slow lane 活気に欠け退屈な状態, 緊張もなく穏やかな状況 ▪ Take a rest and enjoy traveling in *the slow lane* of life for a while. ひと休みしてしばらくの間はのんびりと旅でも楽しみなさい.

up a lane 路地の突き当たりに ▪ The house is *up a lane.* その家は路地の突き当たりにある.

language /lǽŋgwɪdʒ/ 名 ***a global language*** 地球言語, 世界中で理解される共通語 ▪ English has become the dominant *global language.* 英語は最も有力な地球言語になってきている.

have a great command [***flow***] ***of language*** 言葉が非常に達者[雄弁]である ▪ He *has a great command of language* and uses it precisely. 彼は言葉が非常に達者でそれを正確に使う.

in plain language 率直に言って ▪ *In plain language,* I prefer your room to your company. 率直に言って, 私はあなたがいっしょにいないほうがよい.

in strong language 激しい言葉で ▪ He objected *in strong language.* 彼は激しい言葉で反対した.

in the language of ...の言葉を借りて言えば ▪ Brevity is the soul of wit *in the language of* Shakespeare. シェイクスピアの言葉を借りて言えば, 言は簡を尊ぶ.

L

mind *one's* ***language*** = WATCH one's language.

pick up *a language* 母語話者が話すのを聞いて言語を身につける ▪ You speak good English. Where did you *pick* it *up*? 英語がうまいね. どこで覚えたの?

speak [***talk***] ***a different language*** (***from*** *a person*) (人とは)違った言葉を話す, 共通点が少ない ▪ He *speaks a different language from* any of us. 彼は我々の誰とも共通項が少ない.

speak [***talk***] ***the same language***/ ***speak*** [***talk***] *a person's* ***language*** 共通の言葉を話す, 思想・価値観などが同じである, 同じ関心・考えを持っている ▪ It's as if we didn't *speak the same language*. 僕たち, まるで価値観が違うみたいだね ▪ We really *speak the same language* about almost everything. 僕らは何についてもたいてい意見が一致する ▪ Why don't we eat out? —You are *speaking my language* today! 外で食事しない?—今日は意見が合うな.

the language of clothes 着衣によってどのような人物かがわかること ▪ He is well-versed in *the language of clothes*. 彼は着衣による人物判断に精通している.

use bad language to …を口ぎたなくののしる ▪ She has never *used bad language to* anyone. 彼女は誰かを口ぎたなくののしったためしがない.

use language to 《英俗》…をののしる ▪ He *used language to* her. 彼は彼女をののしった.

use the language of violence 脅しという言葉の暴力に訴える ▪ To write threatening letters is to *use the language of violence*. 脅迫状を書いたら暴言の実力行使になる.

watch *one's* ***language*** →WATCH[2].

languaged /lǽŋgwɪdʒd/ 形 ***be well languaged*** 言語に秀でている[堪能である] ▪ He *is well languaged* in French. 彼はフランス語が堪能だ.

lap[1] /læp/ 名 ***be thrown into*** *a person's* ***lap*** 人のふところに転がり込む ▪ A large sum of money *was thrown into his lap*. 多額の金が彼のふところに転がり込んだ.

bred [***brought up***] ***in the lap of*** …の中に育てられて ▪ He was *brought up in the lap of* luxury. 彼は贅沢三昧に育てられた.

drop [***dump***]***... in*** *a person's* ***lap*** (問題)を人に押しつける ▪ He *dumped* all this work *in my lap* while he was away. 彼は留守中この仕事をすっかり私に押しつけた.

fall [***drop***] ***into*** *a person's* ***lap*** **1** (幸運などが)人の所に転がり込んでくる ▪ Everything *fell into his lap*. 万事彼の思う通りになった ▪ There are people who don't work and expect money to *drop into their laps*. 仕事をせずに金が転がり込んでくることを当てにしている人々がいる.
2 (責任などを)人に転嫁する ▪ I'll *drop* this work *into his lap*. この仕事を彼に転嫁してやろう.

in Fortune's lap/in the lap of Fortune 幸運に恵まれて ▪ He was once *in the lap of Fortune*. 彼は以前幸運に恵まれていたことがあった.

in Nature's lap 自然にいだかれて ▪ I found myself *in Nature's lap*. 気がつくと自然の懐に抱かれていた.

in the lap of …のふところに ▪ A green lake was sparkling *in the lap of* a pine-clad mountain. 緑の湖が松山のふところに輝いていた.

in the lap of luxury 贅沢三昧をして ▪ She lives *in the lap of luxury*. 彼女は贅沢三昧に暮らしている.

in the lap of the gods 人間にはどうにもならない[わからない] ▪ Whether I shall succeed or not lies *in the lap of the gods*. 私が成功するかどうかは人間にはどうにもならない.

land in *a person's* ***lap*** 人に無理やり押しつける, (責任など)を取らせる ▪ They have had this responsibility *land in my lap*. 私は無理やりこの責任を取らされた.

Make a lap! 《俗》座りなさい! ▪ Pull up a chair and *make a lap!* いすを引き寄せて座れよ!

nursed in the lap of =bred in the LAP of.

repose on the lap of ignorance 無知に甘んじる ▪ He will no longer *repose on the lap of ignorance*. 彼はもはや無知に甘んじることはないだろう.

the last lap 最後の1周; (旅行・事業の)最後の段階 ▪ We were on *the last lap* of our long journey. 我々は長い旅がようやく終わろうとしていた ▪ He failed at *the last lap*. 彼は最後の段階で失敗した.

lap[2] /læp/ 動 ***be lapped in luxury*** 贅沢三昧に暮らす ▪ Moses had *been lapped in luxury* from his infancy. モーゼは幼時から贅沢三昧に暮らしてきた.

lapdog /lǽpdɑ̀ːg|-dɔ̀g/ 名 ***be a lap-dog*** 大事にしすぎる, 過保護にする ▪ You sure *are* your Mom's little *lap dog*! 君ってほんとにママに甘やかされているなあ.

make a lapdog of …をちやほやしてかわいがる ▪ She is *making a lapdog of* her boy. 彼女は息子をちやほやかわいがっている. ☞lapdog「(ひざに乗せられる)ペット犬」.

lapse /læps/ 名 ***a lapse of memory*** 記憶違い, ど忘れ ▪ This discrepancy is evidently caused by *a lapse of memory*. この食い違いは明らかに記憶違いによって生じたものだ.

a lapse of the tongue [***the pen***] 言い[書き]そこない ▪ It is unmanly to snarl at little *lapses of the pen*. 小さな書きそこないをがみがみ言うのは男らしくない.

with the lapse of time 時が経つにつれて ▪ We forgot it *with the lapse of time*. 我々は時が経つにつれて, それを忘れた.

lares /lǽriːz|lɑ́ːreɪz/ 名 ***lares and penates*** 家庭の守護神, 家庭, 家財 ▪ The *lares and penates* are worshiped at household shrines. 家庭の守護神が神棚に祀(まつ)られている ▪ His family, along with his *lares and penates*, moved out of here. 彼の一家は家財道具ぐるみ当地から移住していった.

L

large[1] /lɑːrdʒ/ 形副名 ***all very fine and large*** →FINE[1].

(*as*) ***large as life*** (*and twice as natural*) →LIFE.

at large **1** 一般の[に], 全体的の[に] ▪ Baseball is popular with the nation *at large*. 野球は国民一般に人気がある ▪ He was the poet of England *at large*. 彼はイギリス全体の詩人であった ▪ They are promises made *at large*. それらは一般的になされた約束である.

2 自由で; つかまらないで, 束縛されないで ▪ The culprit is still *at large*. 犯人はまだつかまっていない ▪ The dog roamed *at large* through the grounds. 犬は構内を自由に歩き回った.

3《米》特定の任務のない ▪ He is an ambassador *at large*. 彼は無任所大使である.

4《米》(分割された選挙区からでなく)全州[郡]から出された ▪ He is a representative *at large*. 彼は全州選出議員である ▪ The members were elected *at large*. その議員たちは全州選出であった.

5 未定で ▪ We left the matter *at large*. 我々はその問題を未定のままにしておいた.

6 詳細に ▪ He told me the story *at large*. 彼はその話を詳細に私に話した.

7 でたらめに; あてどもなく; ぼんやりと ▪ He scatters imputations *at large*. 彼はむやみに非難を浴びせる.

by and large《口》概して, 全般的に見ると ▪ *By and large*, legal proceedings work well. 概して訴訟はうまくいく. ☞《海》「風に向かったり離れたりして」が原義.

in (***the***) ***large*** 大規模に (↔in SMALL); (縮小しない)大きいままで[の]; 一般に ▪ I have made trial of this method, both in small and *in large*. 私はこの方法を小規模にも, 大規模にも試してみた.

large of limb 手足の大きい ▪ He was *large of limb*. 彼は手足が大きかった.

larger [***bigger***《米》] ***than life*** (人・話などが)人目を引く; 実物[実際]よりも大きく, 誇張して; 普通よりもおもしろくはらはらする ▪ The statesman, it seemed, was painted *larger than life*. その政治家は実際よりも大物に描かれていると思われた ▪ The musician is *bigger than life* in the eyes of his fans. そのミュージシャンはファンの目には実力以上に映っている ▪ All performances have to be *bigger than life*. 全ての演技は普通よりもおもしろくはらはらするものが求められる.

on the large side かなり大きく ▪ My family, for the most part, is *on the large side*. うちの家族は概して大柄である.

set ... at large …を解放する ▪ He *was* at last *set at large*. 彼はついに放免された.

talk large →TALK big.

large[2] /lɑːrdʒ/ 動 ***be larging it up***《口》楽しく大騒ぎしている ▪ They *are larging it up* in there. 彼らは中でごきげんに騒いでいる.

lark[1] /lɑːrk/ 名 (***as***) ***gay as a lark*** ヒバリのように[ひどく]陽気で ▪ He went to work *gay as a lark*. 彼はひどく陽気な気分で仕事に出かけた.

(***as***) ***happy as a lark*** きわめて楽しく ▪ Tim is *as happy as a lark*. ティムはとても楽しそうだ.

catch the larks《米俗》繁昌する ▪ Your farm must not be limited to one product, if you would *catch the larks*. 繁昌しようと思うなら, 農場は1種類の産物に制限されてはならない.

If [***When***] ***the sky fall***(***s***) ***we shall catch larks.*** →SKY.

rise [***get up***] ***with the lark*** 朝早く起きる ▪ Old men are fond of *getting up with the lark*. 老人は朝早く起きるのが好きだ.

up with the lark 朝早く起きて ▪ We shall have to be *up with the lark*. 朝早く起きなければなるまい.

lark[2] /lɑːrk/ 名 ***blow*** [***sod***] ***that for a lark***《英俗》これでたくさんだ, もうごめんだ ▪ *Sod that for a lark*! I'm not doing any more. もういやだ. これ以上はやらないぞ.

for a lark 冗談に ▪ He only did it *for a lark*. 彼はただ戯れにそれをしただけだ.

have [***take, go on***] ***a lark*** [***larks***]《口》ふざけ騒ぐ, 浮かれ騒ぐ; (を)からかう, ふざける (*with*) ▪ I *had larks* when a boy. 私は少年の時分にはふざけ騒いだ ▪ He was *having a lark with* the gentleman. 彼はその紳士にふざけていた.

on a lark 冗談半分で ▪ If an officer comes to make inspection, he is usually *on a lark*. 役人が視察に来るときは通常冗談半分だ.

up to *one's* ***lark*** 悪ふざけをして; 戯れに夢中で ▪ The boy was *up to his lark*. その少年は悪ふざけをやっていた.

What a lark! これはおもしろい! ▪ He thinks he is clever. *What a lark!* 彼は自分が賢いと思っている. おもしろいじゃないか.

laser /léɪzər/ 名 ***focus like a laser beam on*** ひとつのことに完全に集中する ▪ The governor promised to *focus like a laser beam on* education. 知事は教育問題一本に絞ると約束した.

lash[1] /læʃ/ 名 ***give a lash with*** *one's* ***tongue*** 非難攻撃する ▪ I *gave* him *another lash with my tongue*. 私は彼をまた非難攻撃した.

under the lash むち打ちの刑[体刑]を受けて; 衝撃を受けて ▪ He expired *under the lash*. 彼はむち打ちの刑を受けて死んだ.

under the lash of competition 激しい競争の衝撃を受けて ▪ Many powerful corporations have to hustle *under the lash of competition*. 激しい競争のあおりで多くの有力会社も力こぶを入れねばならない.

use the lash on …をむち打つ ▪ He *used the lash on* kids who trespassed on his property. 彼は自分の所有地に侵入した子供たちをむち打った.

lash[2] /læʃ/ 動 ***lash*** *oneself* ***into a fury*** [***a rage, anger***] 激怒する, 憤激する ▪ At this he *lashed himself into anger*. これを聞くと彼は激怒した.

lash *a person* ***with*** *one's* ***tongue*** ―

TONGUE.

lashings /lǽʃɪŋz/ 名 ***lashings of*** たくさんの ▪ I love homemade bread with *lashings of* butter. バターをたっぷり使った自家製のパンが大好きだ.

last[1] /læst|lɑːst/ 名 ***go beyond*** *one's* ***last*** 自分の領域外のことに口出しする ▪ Sorry I have *gone beyond my last*. 領域外のことに口出ししてすみません. ☞last「(靴職人が使う)靴型」.

stick to *one's* ***last*** 知らぬ事に手を出さぬ; 自分の本分[本業]を守る (→Let the COBBLER stick to his last.) ▪ If he'd only *stick to his last*, he'd be a jolly good fellow. 彼が自分の職分を守りさえすれば, 彼は好漢なのだが ▪ You must remember that a shoemaker should *stick to his last*.「知らぬ事に手を出すな」ということを覚えていなければならない.

last[2] /læst|lɑːst/ 形副名 ***a last hurrah*** 《主に米》(仕事・活動を辞める前の)最後の試み[行動] ▪ This tournament may be my *last hurrah*. このトーナメントが私の最後の試合になるだろう.

(***and***) ***last but not least*** 《戯》最後ではあるが決して最小[軽んずべき]ではない; 大事なことを最後に言うが (cf. Sh., *Jul. Caes*. 3. 1. 189) ▪ *Last but not least*, you must keep out of debt. 大事なことを最後に言うが, 借金してはいけない ▪ *And last but not least* is the arrangement of flowers. 最後になったが決しておろそかにしてはならないのが生け花である.

at last とうとう ▪ He has finished that work *at last*. 彼はついにその仕事を仕上げた.

at long last ついに, やっとのことで ▪ *At long last* he consented. 彼はやっとのことで承諾した. ☞at LAST よりはいくぶん強い言い方.

at the last 最後に ▪ *At the last*, however, the fire died. しかし, おしまいには火は消えてしまった.

at the last moment →MOMENT.

breathe *one's* ***last*** →BREATHE.

every last 《口》一つも残さずすべての ▪ He spent *every last* penny. 彼は1ペニーも残さず全部の金を使った.

for the last time →for the first TIME.

for the last week [***month,*** etc.] この1週間[1か月, など] ▪ He has been ill *for the last month*. 彼はこの1か月間[1か月前から]病気だ.

from first to last →FIRST.

have heard the last account of …は死んだ ▪ I *have heard the last account of* him. 彼は死んだ.

have seen the last of …を見なくなった, がいなくなった ▪ I *have seen the last of* that dismal creature. あの陰気なやつがいなくなった.

have the last word →have the final WORD.

hear the last of …の聞き納めをする ▪ I shall never *hear the last of* the story. その話はいつまでもうるさく聞かされるだろう.

if it's the last thing *one* ***does*** どうあっても(…したい) ▪ I want to kill him *if it's the last thing* I *do*. どうあってもあいつを殺してやりたい.

in *one's* ***last moment*** 死にぎわに, 末期に ▪ He repented *in his last moment*. 彼は死にぎわに悔い改めた.

in the last place →in the first PLACE.

last across 近づく車の前を最後に横切るのを競う遊戯《子供の遊戯》 ▪ Lawmakers are playing a game of *last across* with Mr. Speaker. 議員らは質問時間に議長に対して誰が最後に発言するかを競っている.

last but not least →(and) LAST but not least.

Last come, last served. 《諺》応対[配膳]は入来の順.

last in, first out 最後に入った[雇われた]者が最初に出る[解雇される] ▪ Texas may be "*last in, first out*" among states battling the recession. 不況と闘う州の中でテキサスが「最後に陥って最初に脱する」かもしれない.

last of all 一番最後に ▪ And *last of all*, I'd like to wish you all good luck. 終わりに臨みみなさんのご多幸をお祈りいたします.

one's ***last penny*** [***dime***] 最後の1文(もん) ▪ The suit cost him *his last penny*. その訴訟で彼は最後の1文まで使い果たした.

last thing (***at night***) (夜)寝る直前に; 最後に ▪ I always have a hot cup of cocoa *last thing at night*. 就寝前にいつも熱いココアを1杯飲む ▪ I take my dog for a short walk *last thing at night*. 夜寝る前に犬をちょっと散歩に連れて行く ▪ I wear contact lenses from first thing in the morning to *last thing at night*. 私は朝一番から夜寝る前までコンタクト・レンズをつけています.

look *one's* ***last*** 見納めする ▪ I was *looking my last* on the old house and lingered. 私はその古い家の見納めをしていた, そして去りやらずにいた.

put the last hand to …を仕上げる, 完成する ▪ He *put the last hand to* his work. 彼は仕事を仕上げた.

put the last touch to …を仕上げる ▪ The artist *put the last touch to* his picture. その画家は絵の仕上げをした.

say the last word **1** 議論を決着させる, 議論にとどめをさす ▪ *The last word* has *been said* on the matter. その問題については議論が決着している ▪ He *said the last word* when he put it thus. 彼は次のように言って議論にとどめをさした.

2 決定的[結論的]なことを言う ▪ I have *said the last word* on the matter. 私はこの件については決定的な意見を述べた. ☞→the last WORD.

see the last of …の見納めをする, が見えなくなる ▪ You will know that you have *seen the last of* Henry Jekyll. あなたはヘンリー・ジキルがいなくなったことを知るでしょう ▪ I *saw the last of* her on the screen. 私は銀幕上での彼女の見納めをした.

the last but one [***two,*** etc.] 終わりから2番目[3番目, など] ▪ We shall begin at *the last* line *but two*. 終わりから3行目から始めましょう ▪ He was *the last but one* to arrive. 彼は終わりから2番目にやって来た.

the last day [***time***] 最後の審判の日 ▪ I should lose nothing at *the last day*. 私は最後の審判の日が来ても何も失わないであろう ▪ It will be revealed in *the last time*. 最後の審判の日に啓示されるであろう.

the last days [***times***] 晩年, 終わりの時期・時代 ▪ She spent *the last days* of her life doing what she enjoyed most. 彼女は一番楽しいことをして晩年を過ごした ▪ *The last days* of Pompeii have often been made into films. ポンペイの末期はこれまで何度も映画化された.

The last drop makes the cup run over. 《諺》最後の一滴であふれる《およそのほどを知れ》.

the [*one's*] ***last gasp*** (***of***) 《雅》(ある期間・課程の)最後に ▪ We'll discuss the decline and *last gasp of* the Roman Empire. ローマ帝国の衰亡について論じよう.

the last I heard 《口》最後に聞いた情報によると ▪ *The last I heard* she was still working at the bookstore. 最近聞いたところでは彼女はまだその書店で働いていた.

the last of pea time(***s***) →PEA.

the last of the big spenders 《戯》大金を使わない人, 金遣いの細かい人《自分や他人が非常に少額を払っているときに用いる》 ▪ Just an orange juice and some chips, please. *The last of the big spenders*! オレンジジュースとポテトチップだけください. 倹約家でしょ, 私って.

the last of the Mohicans モヒカン族最後の一人, (部族・世代・廃れゆく伝統工芸職人などの)最後の一人 ▪ The skilled artisan says he is, in fact, *the last of the Mohicans*. 実は自分を継ぐ者がいないのだと老練な職人は言っている. ☞James Fenimore Cooper, *The Last of the Mohicans* (1826).

The last shall be first (***and the first, last***). 後の者が先(になり, 前の者が後)になるであろう《あなどられている者が彼らよりもすぐれていると思われていた人々を追い抜くことがある》(《聖》*Matt*. 19. 30).

the last thing in 最新式の…, 最新流行の… ▪ This is *the last thing in* hats. これは最新流行の帽子だ.

(***the***) ***last time*** (***that***) この前…したときは ▪ *The last time* I saw him, he was not aware of it. この前会ったときは, 彼はそれを知らなかった.

the last person [***thing,*** etc.] (***to*** *do*, ***that, where,*** etc.) **1** 最も…しそうにない人[物], 決して…する人[物]ではない ▪ He is *the last person to* be accused of theft. 彼は決して盗みのかどで訴えられるような人ではない ▪ He was *the last person* (*that, whom*) I expected to see. 彼に会うとは夢にも思わなかった ▪ This is *the last place where* I expected to have met you. 君にここで出会うとは全く思わなかった.

2 最後に…する人[物] ▪ He was *the last man to* come. 彼は最後にやって来た ▪ The captain is always *the last man to* leave the ship. 船長はいつも最後に船からおりる.

the last word →WORD.

the year [***month, week, day, night, evening,*** etc.] ***before last*** 一昨年[先々月, 先々週, 一昨日, 一昨夜, 一昨晩, など](に) ▪ I met him *the night before last*. 私は一昨夜彼に会った ▪ He came to England *the year before last*. 彼は一昨年イギリスへ来た ▪ *The night before last*, a sleepwalker died in the cold. 一昨夜夢遊病者が寒さの中で亡くなった.

to [***till***] ***the last*** 最後まで, どこまでも; 死ぬまで, 負けるまで ▪ We stayed *to the last* of the concert. 音楽会の最後までいた ▪ They were determined to resist *till the last*. 彼らは死ぬまで抵抗する決心だった.

to the last cent [***man, drop,*** etc.] 最後の1セント[一人, 一滴, など]にいたるまで ▪ He paid his debts *to the last cent*. 彼は1セントも残さず借金を払った ▪ They fought *to the last man*. 彼らは一人残らず戦った.

to the last degree →DEGREE.

last[3] /læst|lɑːst/ 動 ***last through time*** 長もちする ▪ A true friendship will *last through time*. 真の友情は長もちするものである.

last *a person's* ***time*** 人の一生もつ[間に合う] ▪ This carpet will *last our time*. このカーペットは私たちが生きている間もつだろう.

latch /lætʃ/ 名 ***off the latch*** 掛け金をはずして ▪ The door was *off the latch*. 戸は掛け金がはずしてあった《半開きであった》.

on the latch 《英》(錠をおろさずに)掛け金だけ掛けて ▪ I'll leave the door *on the latch*. 戸に掛け金を掛けておくだけにしておきます.

latchkey, latch-key /lǽtʃkìː/ 名 ***a latch-key child*** [***kid***] 《主に米》鍵っ子 ▪ Most of *the latch-key children* have become addicted to television. 鍵っ子の大半はテレビ浸けになっている.

latchstring /lǽtʃstrìŋ/ 名 ***draw in the latchstring*** (***for***) 《米》(…に)家へ自由に出入りすることを許さない ▪ She closed the door and *drew in the latchstring*. 彼女は扉を閉め出入りを禁じた.

have *one's* ***latchstring out for*** 《米》…に家へ自由に出入りすることを許す ▪ They *have their latchstring out for* everyone who comes. 彼らは誰が来ても歓迎する.

one's ***latchstring is out to*** 《米》…に家へ自由に出入りすることを許している ▪ *Their latchstring was* always *out to* strangers. 彼らは見知らぬ人々に家へ自由に出入りすることを許していた.

late /leɪt/ 形副 ***as late as*** ほんの…ほど最近 ▪ I saw him *as late as* last March. ついこの3月に彼に会った.

at this late date (こんな遅い)今頃になって ▪ I wonder whether, *at this late date*, there is a chance of even minimal success. 今となっては, ほんのかすかでも成功が期待できるか疑わしい.

be late for …に(乗り)おくれる ▪ Don't *be late for* the first train. 一番の列車におくれないようにしなさい.

be late (***in***) *doing* …するのがおくれる ▪ We'll *be*

a day *late arriving* in London. 我々はロンドン到着が1日おくれるだろう.

***be too late to** do* …するには遅すぎる ▪ It *is* never *too late to* mend. あやまちを改めるに遅すぎることは決してない.

before it is too late 手遅れになる前に, まだ間に合ううちに ▪ Take drastic measures *before it's too late*. 手遅れにならないうちに思い切った措置をとれ.

Better late than never. →(but) BETTER late than never.

early and late →EARLY.

early or late →EARLY.

early* [*soon*] *or late =SOONer or later.

keep late hours →keep bad HOURs.

late in the day 《口》 遅すぎて; 手後れで (↔EARLY in the day) ▪ Rather *late in the day* to object now, isn't it? 今になって反対するなんて, 遅すぎるではないか ▪ He began it too *late in the day*. 彼はそれを始めたが手後れだった.

late of 《文》 最近まで…にいた ▪ We're having a lecture by Professor Rice, *late of* Yale University next week. ライス元イェール大学教授の講演会を来週開く.

of late 最近 ▪ He has been working very hard *of late*. 彼は最近非常によく勉強している.

of late years →YEAR.

run late (行き当たりばったりのせいで)いつものようにのろい ▪ He keeps *running late* at the firm. 彼は会社では相変わらずののろさだ.

till late at night 夜遅くまで ▪ Don't sit up *till late at night*. 夜ふかししてはいけません.

later /léɪtər/ 形副 ***It's later than you think.*** 思っているほど時間[機会]はない (R. W. Service, *Spring*) ▪ The years go by us quickly as a wink. Enjoy yourself, *it's later than you think*. 年月は瞬く間に過ぎ去るから今のうちに楽しく過ごせ. 案外時間はないから.

later on 後ほど; あとで (↔earlier on (→EARLY)) ▪ I shall explain it *later on*. それは後ほど説明します ▪ This happened *later on*. これはあとで起こった.

no* [*not*] *later than (遅くとも)…までに, …までには ▪ Please complete and return this form *no later than* 31st January. この申し込み書に必要事項を記入して遅くとも1月31日までに返送してください ▪ Facilities will be established *not later than* 6 months from the agreement. 契約から半年以内に施設が開設されるだろう.

see you later あなたにあとで会う《ちょっと別れるときに使う句》 ▪ *See you later*! あとでお目にかかりましょう ▪ I shall be *seeing you later*. あとでお目にかかりましょう.

sooner or later →SOON.

latest /léɪtəst/ 形副 ***at* (*the*) *latest*** 遅くとも ▪ We must be there by ten *at the latest*. 我々は遅くとも10時までにはそこに行かねばならない.

lath /læθ|lɑːθ/ 名 (***as***) ***thin as a lath*** →THIN.

lath and plaster 木舞としっくい ▪ It was a house built with *lath and plaster*. それは木舞としっくいでできた家であった.

lather /lǽðər|lɑ́ːð-/ 名 (***all***) ***in a lather*** 汗びっしょりになって; 《口》 興奮して, あせって ▪ He got *all in a lather*. 彼はびっしょり汗をかいた ▪ He is *in a lather* to get money. 彼は金を得ようとあせっている ▪ She is *in a lather* of nervous apprehension. 彼女はひどく心配してびくびくしている.

***get* (*oneself*) *in* [*into*] *a lather* (*over*)** 《英口》 (…について)ひどく興奮する, 怒る ▪ There's no point *getting yourself into a lather over* such trifles. そんなつまらないことで腹を立てても意味がない.

work** oneself **up into a lather 興奮する, いらいらする ▪ Don't *work yourself up into a lather* over that. そんなことでいらいらしない方がいい.

latitude /lǽtətjùːd/ 名 ***a wide latitude*** (行動の)十分な自由 ▪ You have *a wide latitude* to act as you think best. あなたは最善と思う通りに行動する自由を十分に与えられている.

out of** one's **latitude 自分の本領外で, がらになく ▪ He is a little *out of his latitude* this time. 彼は今回やや不得意なことをしている.

plenty of latitude =a wide LATITUDE.

latter /lǽtər/ 形名 ***in these latter days*** 近来は, 当今は ▪ The court has lost its authority *in these latter days*. 昨今では法廷はその権威を失ってしまった.

one's [***the***] ***latter end*** **1** 晩年, 死 ▪ God blessed *the latter end* of Job. 神はヨブの晩年を祝福し給うた ▪ A man should not play with *his latter end*. 人は自分の死をもてあそんではならない.

2 (ある期間などの)終わりの部分, 末期 ▪ At *the latter end* of the summer of 1625, the plague raged in this town. 1625年の夏の終わりごろにペストがこの町で猛威を振るった ▪ *The latter end* of the Rhine is not so romantic. ライン川の終わりの部分はたいしてロマンチックではない.

3 後部, おしり ▪ It seems as if *your latter end* were made of India rubber. 君のおしりはゴムでできているかのようだ.

laud /lɔːd/ 動 ***laud ... to the skies*** →praise ... to the skies (→SKY).

laugh[1] /læf|lɑːf/ 名 ***a laugh a minute*** 《口》 とてもおもしろい, 陽気な; 《戯・反語》 つまらない, 陰気な ▪ The new comedy show was *a laugh a minute*. 今度のコメディーショーは実におもしろかった ▪ "That was *a laugh-a-minute* show!" rapped Meg. 「つまらないショーだったわ!」とメグはわめいた ▪ A one-hour meeting with the mayor was *a laugh a minute* as expected. 市長との1時間の面会は案の定つまらなかった.

an infectious laugh その場にいる人に素早く広がる笑い, 人にうつる笑い ▪ His was such *an infectious laugh* that we all joined in. 彼の笑いについつり込まれて我々はみなげらげらと笑った.

be a barrel* [*bundle*] *of laughs 《口・主に皮

肉》非常におもしろい ▪ Life hasn't *been a barrel of laughs* lately. 近頃では生活は大しておもしろくない.

break* (*out*) [*burst*] *into a laugh わっと笑いだす ▪ They *broke out into a laugh* at his joke. 彼らは彼のしゃれにどっと笑いだした.

for laughs 《俗》おもしろ半分に ▪ They throw things out of the window just *for laughs*. 彼らはただおもしろ半分に窓から物を投げる.

get a laugh out of *a person* 《米口》人を笑わせる ▪ The boy tried on a false beard to *get a laugh out of* his mother. 男の子は母親を笑わせるためにつけひげをつけてみた.

get the laugh of →have the LAUGH of.

get the laugh on [***over***] →have the LAUGH on.

get the laugh on *one's* ***side*** →have the LAUGH on one's side.

give a laugh 笑う, 笑い声を立てる ▪ He *gave a* good *laugh* when he saw it. 彼はそれを見て大いに笑った.

give the* (*horse*) *laugh 《俗》あざける, 嘲笑する ▪ They *gave* him *the laugh*. 彼らは彼をあざけった.

good for a laugh 《口》おもしろい ▪ His stories are always *good for a laugh*. 彼の話はいつでもおもしろい.

L

have a good [***a hearty***] ***laugh*** (***at, about, over***) (...を)大いに笑う ▪ We *had a good laugh at* the joke. 我々は冗談を聞いて大いに笑った.

have [***get***] ***the last laugh*** 最後に笑う《負けそうであって結局勝つ・成功する》 ▪ It was Jim who *had the last laugh* in the competition. その競走で最後に笑ったのはジムだった.

have the [*one's*] ***laugh at*** ...を笑う ▪ I have *had my laugh at* them. 私は彼らを笑ってやった.

have [***get***] ***the laugh of*** 《口》 **1** ...を笑う ▪ He *had the laugh of* me. 彼は私を笑った.
2 (意外な成功で笑っていた者)を笑い返すことになる ▪ I have succeeded in the examination and shall *have the laugh of* my uncle. 私は試験に合格したので, おじさんを笑い返してやります.
3 (人)を出し抜く, を負かす ▪ They tried hard to *get the laugh of* us. 彼らは我々を出し抜こうと大いに努めた.

have [***get***] ***the laugh on*** [***over***] =have the LAUGH of 2, 3.

have [***get***] ***the laugh on*** *one's* ***side*** (今度は)こちらが笑う番になる; 優位に立つ; (取引・競争に)勝つ, 成功する ▪ You've beat us and *have the laugh on your side* now. 我々を負かしたから今度は君たちが笑う番だ ▪ He singled out a weak adversary and *got the laugh on his side*. 彼は弱い相手を選び出してそれに勝った.

join in the laugh (特にからかわれた人が)みなといっしょになって笑う ▪ He felt ashamed to have *joined in the laugh*. 彼は自分もいっしょに笑ったのが恥ずかしかった.

on the laugh 笑って (laughing) ▪ He was still *on the laugh*. 彼はまだ笑っていた.

raise a laugh (人を)笑わせる ▪ His remark *raised a laugh*. 彼の言葉は人を笑わせた.

raise the laugh against ...を嘲笑の種にする, 笑いものにする ▪ This *raised the laugh against* Moses. このためモーゼは笑いものになった.

That's a laugh. そいつはお笑い草だ ▪ The world's funniest joke? *That's a laugh.* 世界で一番おかしい冗談だって? とんだお笑い草だ.

the laugh is on *a person* 人が出し抜かれる ▪ *The laugh was on* the mob, not on the mayor. 出し抜かれたのは暴徒の方で, 市長ではなかった.

the laugh is on *one's* ***side*** ...の方が笑う番だ, の側が勝ちである ▪ *The laugh is on my side* anyway. どのみち私の方が勝ちである.

turn the laugh against あべこべに...を笑う ▪ Jones had been leading the laughter against Smith, but *the laugh was turned against* him. ジョーンズは先頭に立ってスミスを笑っていたが, あべこべに彼が笑われるようになった.

with a laugh 笑って, 一笑に付して ▪ He dismissed the matter *with a laugh*. 彼はその件を一笑に付した.

laugh[2] /læf|lɑːf/ 動 ***be laughing*** 《口》笑いが止まらない ▪ He's got a good job. He's *laughing*. 彼はいい仕事口についたので, 笑いが止まらないのだ.

be laughing all the way to the bank 《口》羽振りがよい, まんまと大金をせしめている ▪ Take this opportunity, or your competitors will *be laughing all the way to the bank*. このチャンスを生かさないと競争相手が難なく大儲けをすることになろう.

Don't make me laugh! 《口》(相手の意外な発言に)笑わせるな, そんなはずはない ▪ Brown earns £1,000 a week? *Don't make me laugh!* ブラウンが1週に1,000ポンド儲けるって? 笑わすなよ ▪ You never know, Jane might help you.—Jane? Help me? *Don't make me laugh!* ひょっとしたらジェインが君を手伝ってくれるかもしれない—ジェインが? 僕を手伝ってくれる? 冗談じゃない.

He laughs best who laughs last [***longest***]***.*** / ***He who laughs last laughs longest*** [***loudest, best***]***.*** 《諺》早まって喜ぶな《あまり早まって喜んでは後悔するぞ》.

it makes you laugh **1** それはばかげている; 笑わせるね ▪ He thinks no end of himself. *It makes you laugh.* 彼はひどく偉いと思っている. 笑わせるね.
2 非常におもしろい ▪ *It makes you laugh* to see our cat pretending to die. 猫が死んだふりをするのを見るのは非常におかしい.

It's to laugh! 《俗》ばかな!, 笑わすな! ▪ *It's to laugh.* Take a look at this. 何をばかな. ちょっとこれを見ろよ.

Laugh and grow [***be***] ***fat.*** 《諺》笑う者は太る《いつもほがらかな心を持てと教えたもの》.

Laugh and the world will laugh with you. 笑えば人も共に笑う《人は陰気な相手を好まない》. ☞E. W. Wilcox (1855–1919)の詩 *Solitude*

から.

***laugh at** oneself* 自分(のすること)に神経質にならない, 真剣になりすぎない ▪ It is important to be able to *laugh at yourself.* 自分のことを気にしすぎずにいられるのは大切なことだ.

laugh** one's **head off 《口》(特に人のさまを見て)のべつにげらげら笑う ▪ Watching the clown's antics, the audience were *laughing their heads off.* 道化役のおどけた身ぶりに, 観客はのべつげらげら笑っていた.

Laugh! I thought I'd die. おかしくって, 死にそうだった ▪ *Laugh, laugh, I thought I'd die* if I didn't. おかしくておかしくて, 笑わないと死ぬかと思った.

laugh in** a person's **face 《口》笑って取り合わない ▪ When I made my suggestion, they just *laughed in my face.* 私が提案すると, みんなは笑って取り合わなかった.

laugh in** one's **sleeve →in one's SLEEVE.

laugh** oneself **into 笑って...(の状態)になる ▪ At this joke, he *laughed himself into* convulsions. この冗談を聞くと, 彼は身をよじらせて笑いころげた.

laugh like a drain 《英口》げらげら笑う ▪ The play was very funny; my sister *laughed like a drain.* 劇は非常にこっけいだったので, 妹は大笑いした.

laugh like a hyena 狂おしく(ヒステリー風に)笑う ▪ The boy *laughed like a hyena* at this. その少年はこれを聞くとヒステリー患者のように笑った.

laugh ... off the stage 嘲笑して...を舞台から降ろす ▪ The poor actor *was laughed off the stage.* その大根役者は嘲笑されて舞台から降ろされた.

laugh on the other side of** one's **face/ laugh on the wrong side of** one's **mouth 《口》得意の笑いから転じて泣く[怒る] ▪ We were made to *laugh on the other side of our faces* by an unforeseen occurrence. 我々は予見しなかった出来事のため, 得意の絶頂から急に失意のどん底に落とされた.

laugh ... out of court →COURT.

laugh out of the other [wrong] side [corner] of the mouth = LAUGH on the other side of one's face.

laugh** oneself **silly [sick] 押さえきれずに[長い間]笑う ▪ I *laughed myself silly* when I heard of his confusion. 彼の慌てぶりを聞いて大笑いした.

laugh till [until]** one **cries/ laugh until the tears run down** one's **face [cheeks] 涙が出るほど笑う ▪ At his joke we *laughed until* we *cried.* 彼の冗談で私たちは涙が出るほど笑った ▪ Last night I *laughed until the tears ran down my cheeks.* ゆうべ涙が出るほど笑いこけた.

laugh** oneself **to death 死ぬほど笑いこける; あまりに笑って死ぬ ▪ He *laughed himself to death.* 彼は笑い死にした.

laugh ... to scorn 《雅》...をあざける (《聖》*Job* 22. 19) ▪ He *laughed* the doctrine of nonresistance *to scorn.* 彼は無抵抗主義をあざけった.

laugh under** one's **breath くすくす笑う ▪ He always *laughs under his breath.* 彼はいつもくすくす笑う.

laugh up** one's **sleeve →in one's SLEEVE.

laugh with alien jaws [lips] 無理して笑う, 作り笑いをする ▪ We *laughed with alien jaws* at the tedious horse play. 我々は退屈なばか騒ぎに無理して笑った. ☞ギリシャ語法.

Love laughs at locksmiths. 《諺》恋は錠前師をものともせぬ《恋人同士を隔離しておこうとするのは無理だ》.

you have (got) to laugh 《口》物事のこっけいな[明るい]面を見なくては ▪ I'm sorry you've lost your wig, but *you've got to laugh*, haven't you? 君がカツラを失くしたのは気の毒だ. でも笑っちゃうね.

You make me laugh! = Don't make me LAUGH!

You're [You'll be] laughing. 《口》もう心配いらないよ ▪ If you pass the test, *you're laughing.* その試験に受かれば, もうしめたものさ.

laughing /lǽfɪŋ|lɑ́:fɪŋ/ 名形 ***be no laughing matter*** 笑いごとでない ▪ The blow he had received *was no laughing matter.* 彼が受けた打撃は笑いごとではなかった.

burst out laughing どっと笑いだす ▪ The audience *burst out laughing* at the joke. 聴衆はその冗談にどっと笑いだした.

hold** one's **laughing 笑いをこらえる ▪ I could not *hold my laughing.* 私は笑いをこらえられなかった.

hold [split]** one's **sides with laughing 腹をかかえて笑う, 抱腹絶倒する (→split one's SIDEs) ▪ She leaned against the wall and *held her sides with laughing.* 彼女は壁に寄りかかり, お腹をかかえて笑った.

make ... a laughing stock/make a laughing stock of ...を笑いものにする ▪ They *made a laughing stock of* me [the institution]. 彼らは私[その制度]を笑い物にした.

laughter /lǽftər|lɑ́:f-/ 名 ***burst (out) into laughter/ break (out) into (fits of) laughter*** どっと笑いだす ▪ When I see such behavior, I cannot but *burst out into laughter.* 私はそのようなふるまいを見ると, 吹き出さずにはおれない.

canned laughter 《口》(テレビなどで)効果のために録音された笑い声 ▪ Where does all this laughter come from?—Why, it's *canned laughter* you're hearing. みんなどこで笑っているの?—ああ, 今聞こえている笑い声は録音だよ.

die [split] with laughter 死ぬほど笑う ▪ The joke made us *split with laughter.* その冗談は我々を死ぬほど笑わせた.

dissolve into laughter = burst (out) into LAUGHTER.

laughter and tears 笑いと涙(の交錯) ▪ The drama was full of *laughter and tears.* そのドラマは笑いと涙にみちあふれていた.

Laughter is the best medicine. 《諺》(悩みを忘れるには)笑いが一番の薬.

L

launch[1] /lɔːntʃ, lɑːntʃ/ 名 ***the launch window*** 《口》 **1** 宇宙船[人工衛星]などの打ち上げ時間帯, 太陽や月の位置などが打ち上げに最適な時間帯 ▪ Due to a malfunction during *the launch window*, the mission was postponed. 打ち上げ時間帯内に機器が故障したため, 宇宙飛行任務は延期された.
2 思い切ったことを始める好機 ▪ When is your next *launch window* for a hitchhiking trip in Africa? 今度アフリカへヒッチハイク旅行に行くチャンスはいつだい?

launch[2] /lɔːntʃ, lɑːntʃ/ 動 ***launch into eternity*** **1** 死ぬ ▪ His soul will *launch into eternity*. 彼の霊魂は死滅するだろう.
2 殺す《受身になれば死ぬの意にもなる》 ▪ He will soon *be launched into eternity*. 彼はまもなく死ぬ[殺される]だろう.

launch** oneself **on …に乗り出す, 着手する ▪ She *launched herself on* her nursing career. 彼女は看護師の仕事に乗り出した.

laundry /lɔ́ːndri, lɑ́ːn-/ 名 ***a laundry list*** (***of***) 《主に米》(買う物・用事の)大量のリスト ▪ My nephew came up with *a* whole *laundry list of* hoped-for presents. 甥(おい)っ子は欲しいプレゼントを山ほど書いた表を持ってやってきた.

***air* [*do*] *one's* dirty laundry in public** 内輪の話を公の場で話す[公開する] ▪ My father used to tell me never to *air my dirty laundry in public*. 父は内輪話を一切口外してはならないと口癖のように言っていた.

laurel /lɔ́ːrəl|lɔ́r-/ 名 ***look to** one's **laurels*** 選手権[名声]を奪われないよう気をつける ▪ The new boy seems very brilliant, and my son will have to *look to his laurels*. 今度の生徒は非常に聡明らしいから, 私の息子は首席を奪われないよう気をつけねばならないだろう. ☞laurel「古代ギリシャ人が勝利者に与えた月桂冠」.

***reap* [*gain, win*] *one's* laurels [*the laurel*]** 名声を博する, 称賛を博する ▪ Here he *reaped his* first *laurels*. ここで彼は最初の名声を博した ▪ He *won his laurels* during the Varsity boat race of 1990. 彼は1990年の大学ボートレースで栄冠をかち得た.

***rest* [*repose, retire*] *on one's* laurels** すでに得た名誉に甘んじる, それ以上名をあげようとしない ▪ He wrote one more book and then *retired on his laurels*. 彼は本をもう1冊書いて, それ以上名をあげようとはしなかった.

lavatory /lǽvətɔ̀ːri|-təri/ 名 ***go to the lavatory*** 《婉曲》トイレに行く, 用を足す, 小用に立つ ▪ Stop the car, will you? I have to *go to the lavatory*. 車を止めてくれない? 用足しをしたいから.

lavender /lǽvəndər/ 名 ***lay out in lavender*** 《口》(人を)しかる ▪ He *was laid out in lavender* for being late. 彼は遅刻してお目玉を食った.

lay* (*up*) *in lavender **1** あとで使うため大切に取っておく ▪ We must *lay* those lengths of silk (*up*) *in lavender*. 我々はその数反の絹物を大切に取っておかなければならない.
2 (人が害をせぬよう)封じ込める, 投獄する ▪ It is the duty of the State to *lay* him *up in lavender*. 彼を獄中に封じ込めるのは国家の義務である.
3 《俗》質に入れる ▪ I have *laid up* my overcoat *in lavender*. 私はコートを質に入れた. ☞乾燥させたラベンダーがしみよけに使われることから.

lie up in lavender 大事にしまわれている; 安全に監禁[保管]されている ▪ My fur coat *lies up in lavender* to keep off moths. 毛皮のコートは虫がつかないようにちゃんと保管してある ▪ Alas! the gentleman *lies up in lavender* himself. 悲しいかな, その紳士自身が厳重な監禁の身である.

put in lavender =lay (up) in LAVENDER.

lavish /lǽvɪʃ/ 形 (***be***) ***lavish of*** [***in***] …を気前よく使う, 気前よく与える, 惜しまない ▪ A liar *is* proverbially *lavish of* his oaths. 嘘つきが盛んに誓言をするとは諺の通りだ ▪ They *were* the most *lavish in* gifts to holy places. 彼らは聖所へ最も気前よく供物をした.

law /lɔː, lɑː/ 名 ***above the law*** (法が適用されないほど)自分は偉いと思って; 法[規則]に従わなくてもよい ▪ My husband has never considered himself *above the law*. 夫は自分が偉いなどと思ったことは一度もありません ▪ The emperor is *above the law*. 皇帝は法を超越する.

allow* (*fair*) *law →give (fair) LAW.

an unwritten law 慣習法, 不文律 ▪ It's *an unwritten law* that you lock the gate when leaving the swimming pool. プールを去るときには入り口に施錠するのが暗黙の了解事項になっている.

at* [*in*] *law 法的には ▪ They will get their equality *at law*. 彼らは法的には平等をつかむだろう.

***be a law unto** oneself* (慣習・忠告を無視して)自分の思う通りにする(《聖》*Rom.* 2. 14) ▪ All through his life he has always *been a law unto himself*. 彼はこれまでずっと常に自分の思う通りをしてきた.

be at law 訴訟[裁判]中である ▪ He *is at law* with his neighbors. 彼は隣人を訴訟している.

be bred to the law 弁護士[裁判官]になるための教育を受ける ▪ He *was bred to the law* and practiced as an attorney. 彼は弁護士となる教育を受けて開業した.

be good* [*bad*] *law (意見・判決などが)法律にかなう[かなわない] ▪ Such a sentence *is bad law*. そのような判決は法律にかなわない.

beyond the law 法律の届かないところへ[に] ▪ By morning he was *beyond the law*; he had died in the night. 朝までには彼は法律の届かない所へ行っていた. 夜のうちに死んだのだった.

by law 法律により ▪ People are not compelled *by law* to wear a bicycle helmet. 自転車のヘルメット着用は法律で強制されてはいない.

call in the law 警察を呼ぶ ▪ Get out of here, or I'll *call in the law*! 出て行かないと警察を呼ぶぞ!

follow the law 弁護士となる ▪ They expect their son to *follow the law*. 彼らは息子が弁護士に

なってほしいと思っている.

get (fair) law (of) →have (fair) LAW (of).

give [allow] (fair) law **1** (競技で弱い者を)時間的または距離的に先発させる; (猟でキツネなどを)猟犬より時間的または距離的に先に逃げさせる ▪ They *gave* the deer *law* for twenty minutes. 彼らはシカを(猟犬が追い始めるより)20分前に逃げさせた ▪ A hare *is allowed law*. ウサギは(猟犬が追うより)時間的に先に逃がしてもらう.
2 猶予[慈悲]を与える ▪ God will *give* them *fair law*. 神は彼らに慈悲を施すであろう ▪ You must come back by next Christmas. I can't *give* you greater *law*. あなたは次のクリスマスまでには帰って来なければならない. 私はそれ以上の猶予は与えられない. ☞→have (fair) LAW (of).

give (the) law to …に対して絶対的勢力をふるう, を支配する; を意に従わせる; をしかりつける ▪ Portugal has *given the law to* these princes. ポルトガルはこれらの君主に絶対的勢力をふるってきた ▪ In literature Greece *gave the law to* the world. 文学ではギリシャは世界を支配した.

go beyond the law 不法行為をする ▪ To thrash the man yourself is to *go beyond the law*. その男をあなた自身でむち打つことは不法行為をすることになる.

go in for the law →read LAW.

go to law (against, with) 《英》(…を相手どって)訴訟を起こす; (を)起訴する ▪ I *went to law against* him. 私は彼を起訴した.

have [get, obtain] (fair) law (of) **1** (競技で弱い者が…より)時間的または距離的に先発する, 先発させてもらう; (猟においてキツネなどが猟犬より)時間的または距離的に先に逃げる, 逃がしてもらう (*of*) ▪ The fox *obtained* a little *law of* us pursuers. キツネは我々追跡者より少し時間的に先に逃がしてもらった ▪ The silly hare, *having* good *law*, sat down to rest herself. 愚かなウサギは, 十分距離的に先へ出ていたので座って休んだ.
2 猶予[慈悲]を得ている[得る] ▪ He *has* ten days more *law*. 彼はもう10日間の猶予を得ている. ☞→give (fair) LAW.

have the law in one's own hands 勝手に成敗ができる; 局面を巧みに切り抜けうる ▪ They *have the law in their own hands*. They need not ask me. 彼らは自分で勝手に成敗ができる. 私に相談しなくてもよい.

have [take] the law of [on] 《英口》…を訴える ▪ I'll *have the law of* you. あなたを訴えます.

in law →at LAW.

in the law 法律家[弁護士]で ▪ Three of his brothers are *in the law*. 彼の兄弟のうち3人は弁護士である.

law and order 治安 ▪ Is *law and order* maintained in that city? その都市では治安が維持されていますか.

lay down the law →LAY².

Necessity has [knows] no law. →NECESSITY knows no law.

New lords, new laws. 領主が変われば掟も変わる.

obtain (fair) law (of) →have (fair) LAW (of).

One law for the rich and another for the poor. 《諺》金持ち向けの法と貧乏人向けの法は異なる《金持ちは罪を犯しても罰を逃れることがあるが, 貧乏人は必ず罰を受ける》,「富める者には法は甘く貧しき者には厳しい」.

read [study, go in for the] law 弁護士になる勉強をする ▪ My cousin is *studying law*. いとこは法律家になる準備をしている.

stand law 有効である, 通用する ▪ That charge of murder will not *stand law*. その殺人罪は成り立たないだろう.

take the law into one's own hands (法律の力を借りずに)勝手に制裁を加える, 私刑を加える ▪ These days one can't *take the law into one's own hands*. 今日では勝手に制裁を加えられない.

take the law of →have the LAW of.

The law is an ass. 法はばかげた[不当な]ものだ ▪ We've always known *the law is an ass*. 法は不当なものだと昔からわかっている. ☞Dickens, *Oliver Twist* から.

the law of averages 平均法則, ずっと勝ちっぱなし[負けっぱなし]はありえないという考え ▪ It's been raining every day this week, but by *the law of averages* it will clear up soon. 今週ずっと雨続きだけど, 降りっぱなしはないからそのうち晴れるさ.

the law of diminishing returns 《経》収穫逓減の法則 ▪ *The law of diminishing returns* becomes operative in old age. 収穫逓減の法則は老齢期に働き始める.

the law of the jungle ジャングルの掟《弱肉強食》 ▪ Now this is *the law of the jungle*, where the strong prey on the weak. さて, これがジャングルの掟で, 弱肉強食というわけだ.

the law(s) of the land 国法 ▪ You're up against *the law of the land*. 君は国法に背いている.

the letter [spirit] of the law 法文の字義[精神] ▪ You ought not to go by *the letter of the law*; it is the spirit that matters. 法文の字義にのっとっていくべきでない, 大切なのはその精神である.

the long arm of the law →ARM¹

There should be a law against it. 《口》そんなことは法律で禁止すべきだ ▪ If it causes harm against someone, *there should be a law against it*. 人に害を及ぼすようであれば, それを取り締まる法律があってしかるべきだ.

There's no law against it. 《口》それを禁止する法律はない, それは許されている ▪ I can talk to him: *there's no law against it*. 彼に口を利いてやってもよい. それを禁止する法律はないぞ.

under the law 法律によれば[により] ▪ He is authorized to act *under the law*. 彼は法律により行動する権能を与えられている.

lawyer /lɔ́ːjər, lɔ́ɪər/ 名 ***be no lawyer*** …には法律はわからない ▪ He *is no lawyer*, as far as I know. 私の知る限り, 彼には法律はわからない.

lay[1] /leɪ/ 名形 ***come into lay*** 卵を産むようになる ▪ The hen has *come into lay*. めんどりは卵を産むようになった.

in full lay 産卵の盛りで ▪ The hen is *in full lay* now. めんどりは今産卵の盛りだ.

on a lay 《俗》ある職について, ある方針で ▪ I shall be *on that lay*. その方針でいきます ▪ I first set them *on the lay*. 私は初めて彼らをその職につけた.

on* [*at*] *a... lay 《米》...の購入[収入]の条件で; の値段で ▪ I bought the articles *at a* good *lay*. 私はその品を良い条件で買った ▪ I am engaged to go out to Africa *on a* good *lay*. 良い条件でアフリカへ出て行く契約をしている.

the lay of the land **1** 地勢 ▪ The general sent out several scouts to get *the lay of the land*. 将軍は地勢を探るため数人の偵察を出した.

2 (計画・会話の)大体の様子 ▪ You only gave me some hint as to *the lay of the land*. あなたは大体の様子について私にちょっとほのめかしただけだ.

lay[2] /leɪ/ 動 ***be laid back*** 穏やかで何の心配もいらない, くつろいだ ▪ The negotiations went well. Everyone *was* quite *laid back* and friendly. 交渉は順調に運び, みながごく穏やかで友好的だった.

be laid in ...に埋葬される ▪ He *was laid in* the little church at Beaconsfield. 彼はビーコンズフィールドの小さな教会に埋葬された.

be laid on one's back 病床にふす ▪ The patient *was laid on his back* with his face looking upwards. 患者は仰向(あおむ)きで床にふしていた.

be laid up with ...で寝ている ▪ He *is laid up with* illness. 彼は病気で寝ている.

I'll lay you a bet* [*wager*] *that ...ということをあなたと賭けをしよう; きっと...だよ ▪ *I'll lay you a bet that* he has forgotten. きっと彼は忘れてしまったのだよ.

laid out 酒に酔って, (麻薬で)ラリって ▪ He is too *laid out* to go to work today. 彼は酔いつぶれて今日は仕事に行けない.

lay... asleep →ASLEEP.

lay... at a person's feet →FOOT[1].

lay... at the door of a person →DOOR.

lay bare **1** 裸にする, あらわにする ▪ He *laid* his chest *bare*. 彼は胸をむき出しにした ▪ A space of dry clay *was laid bare*. 乾いた粘土の土地が露出した.

2 示す, 現す ▪ The marks of toil *are laid bare* over the whole of both palms. 労苦の印が両の手のひらの全体に現れている.

3 (人)に明かす, 漏らす, 口外する ▪ He *laid bare* his inner feelings. 彼は意中を明かした.

4 あばく, 暴露する; 明るみに出す ▪ We *laid bare* the designs of the enemy. 我々は敵の計略をあばいた ▪ His kindliness *was laid bare* after his death. 彼の温情は彼の死後明るみに出た.

lay blows on →LAY it on.

lay... by the heels →HEEL.

lay claim to →CLAIM[1].

lay oneself down 寝ころぶ; 病臥する ▪ She *laid herself down* never to rise again. 彼女は病床に臥したまま二度と起き上がれなかった.

lay down the law **1** (あることに関し)法律はかくかくであると言明する, 法律を規定する ▪ The judge *laid down the law* on the point. 裁判官はその点について法律はこうであると言明した ▪ We may be allowed to *lay down the law* of redress against public oppression. 我々は民衆の抑圧に対する補償の法規を制定してもよかろう.

2 《口》(議論において)独断的な物言いをする, 権威者のように断言する ▪ What a fellow you are for *laying down the law*! 独断的な物の言い方をするとは, 君は何というやつだ.

3 《口》高飛車に指図する, 権ぺいずくで命令する ▪ She *laid down the law* about her husband's conduct. 彼女は夫の行為について高飛車に指図した.

4 《口》どなりつける, しかりつける ▪ When I arrived home at 2 in the morning, my dad *laid down the law*. 午前2時に帰宅したら父はひどくしかりつけた.

lay down to =LAY (oneself) down to.

lay* (*oneself*) *down to (仕事)に全力を出す ▪ The mare understood the signal and *laid down to* her work. 雌馬は合図を理解し全力を出して走った.

lay... even with the dust →LAY... level with the dust.

lay... in ruins →RUIN[1].

***lay in store*(*s*)** 品物を買い込む, 仕入れてたくわえる ▪ We must *lay in stores* for the winter. 冬の用意に品物を買い込まねばならない ▪ *Lay* them *in stores* for next year. それらを来年の用意に仕入れてたくわえなさい.

lay in the* [*one's*] *oars オールを(オール受けから)はずしてボートの中へ縦におく ▪ Soon they *laid in the oars*. やがて彼らはオールをはずしボートの中に縦においた.

lay it all over a person 《米俗》人よりすぐれる [勝る] ▪ Nobody could *lay it all over* you. 誰もあなたに勝ることはできないだろう.

lay it on 《口》 **1** 法外な代金を要求する[値をつける] ▪ The art dealer really *laid it on* thick. 画商は実に法外な代金を要求した.

2 あまりにもきびしく打つ, 懲らしめる, 非難攻撃する《目的語を取ることもある》 ▪ He didn't half *lay it on*. 彼はひどく打ちのめした ▪ I have *laid it on* Walpole unsparingly. 私は容赦なくウォールポールを攻撃した.

3 過度に誇張する; 過度にほめる ▪ Now you are *laying it on*; he could not get so high a salary. 君は今誇張しすぎている. 彼がそんな高給を得るはずがない.

4 猛烈に[過度に]やる ▪ All that money spent! My word, how you've *laid it on*! その金を全部使ったって! まあ, 何という法外な. ☞lay on「うわ塗りする」.

***lay it on thick* [*with a trowel*]** **1** 過度にほめる, お世辞を言う (cf. Sh., *A. Y. L.* 1. 2. 112) ▪ Everybody *laid it on thick*. 誰もかれもひどくほめすぎた ▪ She *laid it on with a trowel* to the Dean's

wife. 彼女は首席牧師夫人に極端なお世辞を言った.
2 大風呂敷を広げる, (少し)大げさに言う ▪ He had injured his finger slightly but *laid it on* a bit *thick*. 彼は指にかすり傷を負ったがそれをちょっと大げさに言った.

lay (land) under (土地に)...をまく[植える] ▪ *Lay* these meadows *under* grass. この牧草地に草の種をまきなさい.

lay ... level [even] with the dust ...を焼き払う ▪ They *laid* the city *level with the dust*. 彼らはその都市を焼き払った.

lay odds →give ODDS.

lay** a person **off work ⟦主に受身で⟧ 人を一時的に解雇する ▪ 30 men *were laid off work*. 30人が一時的に解雇された.

lay open →OPEN[1].

lay** a person **open to 人を...にさらす, 人に...を受けさせる ▪ It *laid* us *open to* many troubles. そのため我々は多くの災いを受けた ▪ His comment *laid* him *open to* criticism. 所見を発表して彼は非難を招いた.

lay** oneself **out (for, to** do**) 《英口》 **1** (...を得ようと, しようと)大いに骨を折る ▪ She *laid herself out for* every prize. 彼女はすべての賞を得ようと大いに努力した ▪ He *laid himself out to* amuse me. 彼は私を楽しませようと大いに骨を折った.
2 (世話など)を喜んで引き受ける, 乗り出す ▪ The lawyer must *lay himself out for* a hopeless case. 弁護士は見込みのない事件も喜んで引き受けなければならない.

lay the case →LAY type.

lay the grain 《写真》原版に粒子を塗る ▪ "*Laying the grain*" must be effected by hand. 原版に粒子を塗るのは手でしなくてはならない.

lay** oneself **to ...に精出す ▪ When he *laid himself to* engineering, he did it well. 工学に精出したとき, 彼は好成績をあげた.

lay ... to rest →REST[1].

lay type/lay the case 新活字をケースに整置する ▪ He *laid the case* neatly. 彼は活字ケースに新しいそろいの活字をきちんと詰めた.

***lay up for** oneself* (面倒などを)自ら招く ▪ Why are you *laying up* trouble *for yourself*? なぜ自ら面倒を招くようなことをするのか.

lay wait for →lie in WAIT for.

lay** oneself **wide open 非難を浴びる, 笑いものになる ▪ Comedians are always *laying themselves wide open*. 喜劇役者はいつも笑いものになっている.

lay** oneself **(wide) open to (...を)招く, に身をさらす ▪ You may *lay yourself open to* criticism from certain groups. 君はある方面からの非難を招くかもしれない ▪ He *laid himself open to* attack. 彼は攻撃に身をさらした.

let it lay 《俗》⟦命令文で⟧ 放っておく ▪ Don't quarrel with Jim. Just *let it lay*. ジムとけんかするな. 放っておけばよい.

layout /léɪàʊt/ 名 ***the layout (of)*** ⟦主に単数形で⟧ (...の) 配置[設計, 計画] ▪ *The layout of* the hotel overlooking the lake was strikingly unusual. 湖を臨むホテルの地取りは他に類を見ないものであった.

Lazarus /lǽzərəs/ 名 ***(as) poor as Lazarus*** →as POOR as a church mouse.

Lazarus and Dives 貧者と富者 (《聖》*Luke* 16. 19–31) ▪ Ruskin comments on the distinction between *Lazarus and Dives*. ラスキンは貧者と富者の区別について触れている.

lazy /léɪzi/ 形 ***be a lazy bones/be bone lazy*** 怠け者である ▪ Don't *be a lazy bones*, get moving! 怠けないで, さっさとやれ.

do the lazy 《口》怠惰なふるまいをする ▪ He indulges in *doing the lazy*. 彼は怠惰なふるまいにふけっている.

lead[1] /led/ 名 ***arm the lead*** (海底の砂泥の見本を付着させるため)測鉛の凹所に獣脂を詰める ▪ They *armed the lead* in order to discover the nature of the bottom. 海底の性質を調べるため測鉛に獣脂を詰めた.

(as) dull as lead 鉛のようなにび色の; 《俗》非常に間の抜けた, とんまな ▪ He pretended to be *dull as lead*. 彼は大間抜けのふりをした.

(as) heavy as lead 鉛のように重い[重苦しい] ▪ This box is *heavy as lead*. この箱はすごく重い ▪ His heart was *heavy as lead*. 彼の心は鉛のように重かった.

***get some lead in** one* 弾丸に撃たれる[当たる] ▪ I was afraid he would *get some lead in* him. 彼は弾丸に当たるのではないかと私は心配した. ☞lead = bullet.

get the lead 弾丸に撃たれる[当たる] ▪ We moved on our hands and knees to avoid *getting the lead*. 弾丸にあたらないように匍匐(ほふく)前進をした.

get [shake] the lead out 《米口》急ぐ, もっと速く動く, 急いで仕事をする ▪ O.K., boys. *Get the lead out*! さあ, 君たち. 急ぐんだ!

get the lead out of** one's **pants 《俗》さっさと仕事に取りかかる ▪ *Get the lead out of your pants*, kids, or you'll be late. 君たち, さっさと取りかからないと遅れるよ.

go down like a lead balloon 《口・戯》全く使い物にならず人気がない, 全然うまくいかず不評を買う ▪ The bank notes had *gone down like a lead balloon*. 紙幣が反故(ほご)同然になってしまった ▪ My joke about the drunkard *went down like a lead balloon*. 酔っ払いについての僕のジョークはまるっきり受けなかった.

have lead in** one's **pencil 《英戯》精力がある ▪ My 65-year-old uncle still *has* plenty of *lead in his pencil*. 65歳になる伯父はまだ精力絶倫である. ☞lead「鉛筆の芯」; pencil = penis.

put lead in** a person's **pencil 《英口・戯》(食べ物・飲み物が)男性の精力をつける ▪ Drink this. It'll *put lead in your pencil*. これを飲みたまえ. 精力がつくぞ.

swing the lead 《英俗》 **1** 《まれ》ほらを吹く, 嘘を

つく ▪ He was *swinging the lead* to get a permanent pension. 彼は終身年金をもらうため嘘をついていた.

2 仮病を使ってさぼる ▪ I'm certain he is *swinging the lead*. 彼はきっと仮病を使ってさぼっているのだ. ☞時折船員はさぼって浅瀬の海深を測る lead「重り」を垂らすだけで実際には測量しなかったことから.

lead[2] /liːd/ 名 ***be in the lead*** リードしている, 先頭である ▪ English *is* far and away *in the lead* as a global language. 英語は世界語として断然他をリードしている.

follow the lead (of) **1**《トランプ》(最初に出す人)について札を出す.

2 (...の)手本に従う, 例にならう ▪ The early Christians, in interpreting the Old Testament, *followed the lead of* the Jews. 初期のキリスト教徒は旧約聖書を解釈するとき, ユダヤ人の手本に従った ▪ Japan *followed the* British *lead* in naval matters. 日本は海軍の事では英国の範にならった.

gain the lead (競走で)先頭に出る; (競技で)リードを奪う ▪ She *gained the lead* on the backstretch. 彼女はバックストレッチで先頭に出た.

give** a person **a lead **1**《猟》まっ先にかきを越えて人を励ます ▪ I *gave* him *a lead*. 私はまっ先にかきを越えて彼を先導した.

2 人を誘導する ▪ I *gave* him *a lead* in solving the problem. 私は彼を誘導してその問題を解かせた.

3 範を示(して人を励ま)す ▪ I will *give* you *a lead*. 私が手本を示して励ましてあげます.

have a lead of ...だけ先んじる ▪ The horse *had a lead of* two yards. 馬は2ヤードだけ先んじていた.

have a long lead on ...をはるかにリードする ▪ I *had a long lead on* him. 彼をはるかにリードした.

have the lead **1** (競走で)先頭になる; (競技で)リードする ▪ He *had the lead* in the race. 彼はその競走で先頭になった.

2 主役を務める ▪ Grace *has the lead* in the school play. グレイスは学校の劇で主役を務める.

lose the lead (競走で)先頭を奪われる; (競技で)リードを失う ▪ He *lost the lead* when he double-bogeyed the 18th. 彼は18番でダブルボギーをたたいてトップを譲った.

on the lead ひもにつながれて ▪ The dog was *on the lead*. その犬はひもにつながれていた.

play the lead **1** 主役を務める ▪ Olivia is *playing the lead*. オリビアは主役を務めている.

2 首謀者となる ▪ He *played the lead* in the disturbance. 彼はその騒動の首謀者となった.

return** a person's [one's **partner's**] **lead 《トランプ》受け札を出す, 相手が出したのと同じ組の札で応じる ▪ You made a mistake by not *returning my lead*; I had asked for spades. あなたが受け札を出さなかったのは誤りだった, 私はスペードを要求したのに.

take a lead off third base 《野球》三塁からリードする, (投手が投球に入るとき)走者が本塁へ向けて数歩進む ▪ Sure enough, he *took a lead off third base*. 案の定, 彼は三塁からリードをとった.

take the lead **1** 先頭を切る; 率先する ▪ The gray horse *took the lead*. 灰色の馬が先頭を切った ▪ The Mayor *took the lead* and subscribed £20. 市長が率先して20ポンド寄付した.

2 さきがける; 牛耳をとる; (動物の)引き綱を取る[持つ] ▪ Germany has *taken the lead* of other nations in it. ドイツはその点において他国にさきがけている ▪ Will you *take the lead*, while I light my pipe? 私がパイプに火をつける間, 引き綱を持ってくれないか.

lead[3] /liːd/ 動 ***be easier led than driven*** ...は強制するよりも説得して導くほうが易しい ▪ Boys *are easier led than driven*. 男の子は強制するよりも説得して導くほうが易しい.

lead (a congregation) in prayer 信者たちの祈りの音頭を取る ▪ The pastor himself *led in prayer*. 司祭が自ら祈りの音頭を取った.

lead** a person **a life →LIFE.

lead** a person **a long race (追っ手)にひどく苦心させる (→lead a person a (hard) CHASE) ▪ He *led* his pursuers *a long race* before he allowed himself to be caught. 彼は神妙に縄につくまでに追っ手たちをひどく苦労させた.

lead** a person **astray →lead ... ASTRAY.

Lead me to it! 《口》それはおやすいことだ; 喜んで ▪ Can you ride a motor-bike?—*Lead me to it*, guv'nor. おまえはオートバイに乗れるか—おやすいことです, だんな.

lead** a person **nowhere →NOWHERE.

lead** a person **on to think [believe] 人に誤って思わせる ▪ We *led* him *on to believe* she was angry. 我々は彼女が怒っていると彼に思わせた.

lead the way **1** 先に立って行く, 先に立って案内する ▪ Please *lead the way* as we are strangers here. 当地は不案内なので, 先に立って案内してください.

2 率先する, 先達となる ▪ The boroughs *led the way* in self-government and free speech. 自治と言論の自由において, 自治都市が先達となった.

lead** a person **to believe 人に思い込ませる ▪ So I had *been led to believe*. そのように私は思い込まされてきた. ☞だます意志のないときにも使える.

lead ... to the altar [church] ...と結婚する ▪ He *led* her *to the* village *altar*. 彼は村の教会で彼女と結婚した.

lead (up) the ball →BALL[2].

lead** a person **up [down] the garden path →GARDEN.

lead with** one's **chin 《口》自ら災難を招く ▪ Don't go *leading with your chin*, Jim. 自ら災難を招くようなまねをするものじゃないよ, ジム. ☞ボクシングであごをガードしないことから.

leader /líːdər/ 名 ***follow the leader*** 各人が前の人のする通りをする子供の遊戯 ▪ The children were playing *follow the leader*. 子供らは「まね遊び」をしていた.

leadership /líːdərʃìp/ 名 ***take [assume] the leadership of*** ...を指揮する, 司会する ▪ He consented to *take the leadership of* the meeting. 彼は会を司会することを承諾した.

under the leadership of …の指揮を受けて ▪ They fought bravely *under his leadership*. 彼らは彼の指揮のもとに勇敢に戦った.

leading /líːdɪŋ/ 名形 ***a leading light*** 有力者 ▪ He is among *the leading lights* of the society. 彼はその協会の有力者の一人だ.

a leading question 誘導尋問 ▪ That barrister always asks *leading questions*. あの法廷弁護士はいつも誘導尋問をする.

a man of light and leading →LIGHT[1].

leading strings /líːdɪŋstrìŋz/ 名 ***in*** (*one's*) ***leading strings*** まだ子供であって; 一本立ちできないで; (特に親に)監督されて, あやつられて ▪ In this country philosophy is still *in its leading strings*. この国では哲学はまだ幼稚な状態にある ▪ My mother still wants to keep me *in leading strings*. 母はまだ私を監督したいと思っている ▪ He has been *in leading strings* all his life. 彼は一生の間人に左右されてきた.

out of (*one's*) ***leading strings*** 一本立ちになって, 独立して ▪ He is a lad of spirit, and *out of his leading strings*. 彼は気概のある青年で, 一本立ちしている.

leaf /liːf/ 名 ***come*** [***spring***] ***into leaf*** 葉(の芽)を出す ▪ The trees have *come into leaf*. 木々は葉を出した.

in leaf 葉をつけて, 葉が繁って ▪ The trees are now *in* full *leaf*. 木々は今では青葉が繁っている.

in the leaf (タバコが)葉のままで ▪ Tobacco is mostly imported *in the leaf* and prepared here. タバコはほとんど葉のままで輸入されてわが国で加工される.

in the sear and yellow leaf 老齢[老境]において (cf. Sh., *Macb*. 5. 3. 23) ▪ I'm *in the sear and yellow leaf*. 私は老境にある.

leaves without figs 実がなく葉ばかりのイチジク; 果たされない約束, (行為がともなわず)口先ばかり (《聖》 *Luke* 13. 6 ff.) ▪ Most of his promises are *leaves without figs*. 彼の約束はたいてい口先ばかりだ.

spring into leaf →come into LEAF.

take a leaf out of [***from***] *a person's* ***book*** 人の先例[手本]にならう ▪ I'll *take a leaf out of your book* and do my shopping earlier. 私はあなたにならって, 買い物をもっと早くしましょう ▪ I have decided to *take a leaf from Ann's book* and start jogging. アンに見習ってジョギングを始めることにした. ☞leaf「本のページ」.

the fall of the leaf 《古》落葉時, 秋 ▪ In *the fall of the leaf* we shall resume our studies. 秋になったら, 我々はまた研究を始めましょう.

turn over a new leaf 新しいページをめくる; 心を入れ替える; 生活を一新する ▪ I'll *turn over a new leaf* and write to you. 私は心を改めて, あなたに手紙を書きます ▪ You had better *turn over a new leaf* and stop gadding about. あなたは生活を一新し, 遊び歩くことはやめたほうがよい.

leafless /líːfləs/ 形 ***a leafless tree*** 《俗》絞首台 ▪ There was a leap from *a leafless tree*. 一人の絞首刑が執行された.

league /liːg/ 名 ***be*** (***way***) ***out of*** *one's* [*a person's*] ***league*** (ある物・人に)資金[能力]が(はるかに)及ばない ▪ A limousine *is way out of our league*. リムジン車なんてわが家には全く手が出せない ▪ That salesperson *is way out of my league*. 私はあの販売員には全然歯が立たない.

in league with …と同盟[連合, 結託]して ▪ The rebels were *in league with* a foreign government. 謀反人らは外国の政府と結託していた.

not in the same league as [***with***]/***be in a different league from*** [***with***] …にはとても及ばない, と同日の談ではない, 比べものにならない ▪ The painter was *not in the same league as* Picasso. その画家はピカソの比ではなかった ▪ She is a good pianist, but she's *not in the same league as* Ellen is. 彼女はピアノがうまいがエレンにはとても及ばない ▪ My book *is not in the same league as* his. 私の本は彼のとは比べものにならないよ.

out of *one's* ***league*** **1** 準備していない[…の能力の及ばない]ことをして ▪ What a lousy talk, the speaker was right *out of his league*! 何とお粗末なトークだったことか. 話し手は自分の力量がはるかに及ばないことをしていたのだ.

2 向いていない, ふさわしくない ▪ She's just too *out of his league*. 彼女はあまりにも彼に向いていない.

leaguer /líːgər/ 名 ***in leaguer*** 《古》野営において; 包囲陣をしいて ▪ We sat *in leaguer* there, accomplishing many adventures. 我々はそこの野営に座り, 多くの冒険を成し遂げた ▪ They were *in leaguer* before a town. 彼らは町の前に包囲陣をしいていた.

leak /liːk/ 名 ***spring*** [***start***] ***a leak*** (船に)穴があいて水が漏るようになる; 情報を漏らす ▪ One small boat suddenly *sprang a leak*. 1隻の小船に急に穴があいて水が漏れだした ▪ He might *spring a leak* if we put him under arrest. 彼を逮捕すれば情報を漏らすかもしれない.

take a leak 《俗》小便をする ▪ I stopped to *take a leak*. 小用をたすために止まった.

lean[1] /liːn/ 形 (***as***) ***lean as a rake*** → RAKE[1].

lean and mean ひどく乗り気で, すっかりその気になって ▪ He got himself *lean and mean* and was practicing very hard. 彼はやる気満々で, 猛練習に励んでいた.

lean[2] /liːn/ 名 ***have a lean*** 傾斜している ▪ The wall *has a* decided *lean* to the right. 壁ははっきり右へ傾いている.

on the lean 傾斜して ▪ Coffins were *on the lean* from their own weight. 棺はその重みのため傾いていた.

lean[3] /liːn/ 動 ***lean over backward*** →bend over BACKWARD(s) (to do).

leaning /líːnɪŋ/ 名 ***have a leaning toward(s)*** [***to***] **1** …が好きである ▪ He has *had a leaning to* mechanics since he was a boy. 彼は子供の時分から機械いじりが好きだった.

2 …への傾向がある ▪ He *has a leaning towards* pacifism. 彼は平和主義の傾向がある.

leap[1] /liːp/ 名 ***a leap in the dark*** 《口》暗やみへ飛び込むこと; 向こう見ずの行動 ▪ Hobbes said that death was *a leap in the dark*. 死は暗やみへ飛び込むことであるとホッブズは言った ▪ It is *a leap in the dark* to go into partnership with them. 彼らと協力するのは向こう見ずの冒険だ.

at a leap 一足飛びで ▪ It cannot be reached *at a leap*. それは一足飛びには到達されない.

by [***in***] ***leaps and bounds*** ずんずん, とんとん拍子に ▪ Their business has grown *by leaps and bounds*. 彼らの事業はずんずん発展した ▪ He has made progress in English *by leaps and bounds*. 彼はとんとん拍子に英語が進歩した.

take a flying leap 《口》あっちへ行って, もうやめて ▪ If this is an intrusion, feel free to tell me to *take a flying leap*. もしじゃまだったら遠慮なくあっちへ行けと言ってくれ ▪ Oh, *take a flying leap*. Just stop it, please. おい, やめろ. もうやめてくれ, 頼むから.

take a leap in the dark 暗やみに飛び込む; 向こう見ずの企てをする ▪ I have never asked you to *take a leap in the dark*. 向こう見ずの企画をするよう君に頼んだ覚えはない.

with a leap 一足飛びに ▪ His income went up *with a leap*. 彼の収入は一足飛びに増した.

leap[2] /liːp/ 動 ***leap bounds*** 限界を飛びこえる ▪ Be clamorous and *leap* all civil *bounds*. 騒いで, はめをはずしてしまえ.

leap off the page (書かれた文字などが)直ちに注意を引く, すぐに目につく ▪ The ad *leapt off the page* at me. その広告がぱっと目に入った.

leap on *one's* ***feet*** →LEAP to one's feet.

leap out of *one's* ***skin*** → fly out of one's SKIN.

leap to a conclusion 一足飛びに結論に達する ▪ He *leapt to the conclusion* that he could eat whatever he wanted. 彼は好きなものが何でも食べられるという結論に一足飛びに達した.

leap to (*one's*) ***death*** 飛び降りて死ぬ ▪ He *leapt to his death* from the roof. 彼は屋根から飛び降りて死んだ.

leap to [***on***] *one's* ***feet*** さっと立ち上がる ▪ I *leapt to my feet* and cheered. 私はさっと立ち上がって歓声を上げた ▪ He *leapt on his feet* vigorously. 彼は元気よく立ち上がった.

leap to (*a person's*) ***mind*** すぐ頭に浮かぶ ▪ That was the first thing that *leapt to mind*. それが真っ先に心に浮かんだことだった.

leap to the eye すぐ目につく, すぐわかる ▪ His name *leaped to the eye* from the newspaper. 彼の名がその新聞ですぐ目についた.

Look before you leap. →LOOK[2].

learn /ləːrn/ 動 ***be*** [***have***] (***yet***) ***to learn*** まだ知らない《通例不信の意を含んで》 ▪ Then the world *was yet to learn* of nuclear weapons. その当時世界は核兵器のことをまだ知らなかった ▪ We *have yet to learn* the truth of it. 我々はまだそれの真相を知らない. ☞今は have が普通.

I'll learn you (***how***) ***to*** *do.* 《俗》= I'll TEACH you (how) to do.

learn ... by heart [***by rote***] →by HEART; by ROTE.

learn (***how***) ***to*** *do* **1** (…のしかた)を学ぶ[習う] ▪ He will soon *learn to* speak English. 彼はまもなく英語が話せるようになるだろう ▪ He *learned how to* ride a bicycle. 彼は自転車の乗り方を習った.

2 《俗》…のしかたを教える ▪ My mother *learned* me *how to* drive. 母は私に車の運転を教えてくれた.

learn *one's* ***part*** せりふを覚える ▪ He could *learn his part* in two days. 彼は2日でせりふを覚えることができた.

learn the hard way →the HARD way.

learn ... to *one's* ***sorrow*** …を知る憂き目を見る ▪ Many a father has *learnt to his sorrow* what it is to have his boy idle. 息子を怠けさせるとは一体どういうことかを知る憂き目を見た父親は世間に多い.

Never too old [***late***] ***to learn.*** 《諺》年をとりすぎて学べないということはない,「八十の手習い」.

That'll learn you. どうだ身にしみたか, …するとどうなるか思い知るだろう (*to do*) ▪ *That will learn you to* mess with me. 私に口出しするとどうなるか今に思い知るだろう.

We must learn to walk before we can run. 《諺》走る前に歩くことを学ばなくてはならない《さらに複雑なことができる前に基本技術をマスターしなくてはならない》.

learned /lə́ːrnəd/ 形 ***be learned in*** …に通じている ▪ He *is learned in* the English tongue. 彼は英語に通じている.

learning /lə́ːrnɪŋ/ 名 ***A little learning is a dangerous thing.*** 《諺》生兵法(なまびょうほう)は大けがの元 (Pope, *An Essay on Criticism* 215).

lease /liːs/ 名 ***a new lease of*** [《米》***on***] ***life*** (病気・地位の回復, 心配の除去により)寿命が延びること, 立ち直ること ▪ After the treatment the doctor gave her, she took (on) *a new lease of life*. 医師が彼女を治療してから彼女は寿命が延びた ▪ The committee will be granted *a new lease on life*. 委員会は任期が延長されるだろう.

by [***on***] ***lease*** 貸借契約により ▪ The house is offered *on lease*. その家は貸家になっている ▪ We took the land *by lease*. 我々はその土地を賃借した.

have a lease of …を契約で借りている ▪ I *have a* long *lease of* the house. 私はその家を長期に借りている.

hold ... by [***on***] ***lease*** …を賃借している ▪ We *hold* the land *on lease*. その土地を賃借している.

hold ... under lease …を借りている ▪ Hong Kong *was held under lease* for 99 years from the Chinese government. 香港は中国政府から99年間租借されていた.

let ... on lease …を賃貸する ▪ The house *was let on lease* for five years. 家は5年間賃貸された.

on lease →by LEASE.

put* (*out*)*... to* [*on*] *lease …を貸しつける ▪ A young gentleman *put out* the best part of his land *to lease*. 若い紳士が自分の土地の大部分を貸しつけた.

take a lease of …を賃借する ▪ He *took a lease of* the building. 彼はその建物を借りた.

take ... on a lease of …を(何)年契約で借りる ▪ I have *taken* the farm *on a lease of* seven years. 私はその農場を7年契約で借りた.

take* (*on*) *a new lease of life → a new LEASE of life.

take ... on lease …を賃借する ▪ I have *taken* the house *on lease*. 私はその家を賃借した.

leash /liːʃ/ 名 ***a longer leash*** かなりの自由 ▪ If you give students *a longer leash*, things will turn out better. 学生たちをもっと自由にさせたら事態は好転するだろう. ☞leash「犬の鎖, 革紐」.

have* [*keep*] *a person* on a short [*tight*] *leash 人の自由を拘束している ▪ She does not *keep* her workers *on a short leash*. 彼女は従業員を拘束しないでいる ▪ He doesn't go out so much these days. His wife *keeps* him *on a tight leash*. 彼は最近あまり外出しない. 奥さんに縛られているんだ.

hold* [*have, keep*]*... in* [*on*] (*a*) *leash (猟犬など)を綱でつないでおく; …を束縛する, 制御する ▪ He always *keeps* his dog *on a leash*. 彼はいつも犬をつないでおく ▪ The soldiers *were* long *held in the leash*. 兵たちは長い間押さえられていた.

on* [*in*] (*the, a*) *leash ひもにつないで; 束縛して, 制御して ▪ She led three hounds *in a leash*. 彼女は3匹の猟犬をひもにつないで連れて行った ▪ The hounds hunted *on leash*. 猟犬どもはひもにつながれたまま獲物を追った.

strain at the leash 束縛を脱しようともがく, 自由に行動しようとはやる ▪ He *strained* hard *at the leash* to earn his own money. 彼は自分でかせぐ自由を得たいと激しくもがいた. ☞(猟犬が)あせって革ひもを引っぱることから.

least /liːst/ 形副 ***at least*** **1** 少なくとも; せめて ▪ Every student should spend *at least* two hours on his homework. 学生はみな少なくとも2時間は宿題に使うべきである.

2 とにかく ▪ It isn't far; *at least*, that's what this guidebook says. そこは遠くない. とにかく, この案内書にはそう書いてある.

at the* (*very*) *least =at LEAST 1.

in the least ⟦主に否定文・疑問文・条件文で⟧ 少しでも; 少しも(ない) ▪ Did he *in the least* change his habit of biting his nails? 彼はつめを噛む癖を少しでも改めましたか ▪ I wasn't *in the least* afraid. ちっとも怖くなかった ▪ I never *in the least* expected to find him there. 彼をそこで見つけようとは少しも予期しなかった.

least of all とりわけ…ない, 最も…ない ▪ I like it *least of all*. 私はそれが最もきらいだ ▪ *Least of all* should boys smoke. 少年たちはとりわけタバコをすってはいけない.

not least 特に ▪ Trade has been bad, *not least* because of the increased cost of oil. 特に石油の値段が上がったため, このところ商売はよくない.

not the least **1** ⟦least に強勢を置いて⟧ ちっとも…ない ▪ There is*n't the least* danger. 危険は少しもない.

2 ⟦not に強勢を置いて⟧ 少なからぬ ▪ There is *not the least* danger. 少なからぬ危険がある.

take the line* [*path*] *of least resistance →choose the line of least RESISTANCE.

That's the least of it. それは最もつまらぬことだ ▪ There is a comma missing, but *that's the least of it*. カンマが一つ抜けているが, それは大したことではない.

(*The*) *least said,* (*the*) *soonest mended* [*forgotten*]. 《諺》何も言わないほどよい《ものを言えばよけい事態が悪化する》.

the* (*very*) *least one can* [*could*] *do せいぜい(人が)できること, せめてできること ▪ *The least* you *can do* is to apologize. あなたにせめてできることは, あやまることだ ▪ Thank you for helping me.—Well, it was *the least* I *could do*. 手伝ってくれてありがとう—いや, あれで精一杯でね.

***to say the* (*very*) *least* (*of it*)** →SAY[2].

leather /léðər/ 名 ***give a person a leather*** 人をひとつなぐる ▪ I will *give* him *a leather*. 彼をひとつなぐってやろう.

go* [*ride*] *hell for leather →HELL for leather.

leather and prunella どうでもよいこと ▪ All the rest is *leather and prunella*. 他はみなとるに足らないことだ. ☞A. Pope の *Essay on Man* 4. 204にある句で「靴職人と牧師との身分の違い」の意味だが, これを誤解したもの.

lose leather 《俗》皮膚をすりむく ▪ I've *lost leather* while riding on horseback. 馬に乗っていてくらずれを起こした.

pull leather 《米口》(はねる馬から落ちまいとして)両手でくらにしがみつく ▪ I manage to stick on the job by *pulling leather*. 私は両手でくらにしがみついて何とか馬から落ちないようにする.

(*There is*) *nothing like leather.* 《諺》自分の物が一番良い; 自分の利益が最もたいせつ.

leathering /léðərɪŋ/ 名 ***give a person a leathering*** 人を革帯でひっぱたく; 人をなぐる ▪ I'll *give* you *a leathering*. きさまをひっぱたくぞ.

leave[1] /liːv/ 名 ***absent without leave*** (***AWOL***) 無断欠勤の, (軍隊で)無断外出の ▪ The private was punished for going *AWOL*. その兵卒は無断外出をしたため処罰を受けた.

by* [*with*] *a person's leave 失礼ながら《不快なことを言うときのしばしば皮肉の言葉》; ごめんください《荷

物運搬人が人に道をあけてくれと頼むときの文句》; ごめんをこうむって ▪ I'm off duty now, *by your leave*. 失礼ながら私は今は非番なのです ▪ *With your leave*, I'll shut this window. ごめんをこうむってこの窓を締めましょう ▪ But *by their leaves* these reasons are very weak. しかし彼らには失礼だが, これらの理由は非常に薄弱だ.

get* [*have, obtain*] *leave 休暇を取る ▪ I'll try to *get leave* for six months. 私は6か月の休暇を取るようにしましょう.

***get* [*have, obtain*] *leave to* do** …する許しを得る ▪ He *got leave to* visit the new world. 彼は新世界を訪ねる許しを得た.

***give* [*grant*] *a person* *leave to* do** 人に…する許可を与える; 〚命令文で〛失礼ながら…いたします ▪ I pray you will *give* me *leave to* go from here. どうぞ私にここを去るお許しをください ▪ *Give* me *leave to* say that it is impossible. はばかりながら, それは不可能でございます.

have leave →get LEAVE.

***I ask* [*beg*] *leave to* do** …する許しを請う, …いたします ▪ *I beg leave to* inform you of it. そのことをお知らせいたします.

neither with your leave nor by your leave あなたの気に入ろうが入るまいが (whether you like it or not) ▪ I will call him *neither with your leave nor by your leave*. 君が賛成しようとするまいと彼に電話するつもりだ.

obtain leave →get LEAVE.

***on leave* (*of absence*)** (軍隊・官庁・学校の)休暇で ▪ He was going *on leave* to see his uncle at Beverly Hills. 彼は休暇でビバリーヒルズのおじに会いに行くところだった ▪ He is home *on leave of absence*. 彼は賜暇(しか)で帰省中である.

take French leave →FRENCH.

take* one's *leave 立ち去る; いとまを告げる ▪ He suddenly got up and *took his leave*. 彼は突然立ち上がって立ち去った ▪ I must *take my leave*. 私はおいとましなければなりません.

take* (one's) *leave of …にいとまごいをする, に別れを告げる; (仕事など)と別れる ▪ He *took* a polite *leave of* the company. 彼は一座の人々に丁寧にいとまごいをした ▪ I now *took leave of* printing for ever. 私はもう印刷業をきっぱりやめました ▪ We *took our leaves of* one another. 我々は互いに別れを告げた.

take leave of* one's *senses 正気を失う, 血迷う, 気が狂(ったようにふるま)う ▪ He behaved as if he'd *taken leave of his senses*. 彼は正気を失ったようなふるまいをした ▪ I've decided I will quit my job. —What, have you *taken leave of your senses*? 仕事をやめることにしたよ—何だって? 気は確かか.

***take leave to* do** 勝手ながら…する ▪ I *take leave to* consider the matter settled. 私は勝手ながらその問題は解決したものと考えます.

with* a person's *leave →by a person's LEAVE.

without a "with your leave" or "by your leave" 《口》許可も得ずに, 全く無断で ▪ *Without a "with your leave" or "by your leave"* she sat down in the comfortable armchair. 彼女は許可も得ないで心地よいひじ掛けいすに腰かけた.

without leave 許可なく, みだりに ▪ You have no right to take it *without leave*. あなたは無断でそれを持って行く権利はない.

leave[2] /liːv/ 動 ***be left over*** **1** (金・食物が)残されて[余って]いる ▪ There is some ham *left over* from lunch. お昼ごはんのハムが残っている.
2 (過去から)現在も存在している ▪ These views *are left over* from the war. このような考え方が戦時中から今も残っている.

be well left (遺族が)十分に遺産が残されている ▪ His family *is well left*. 彼の遺族は十分に遺産が残されている.

get* [*be*] (*nicely*) *left 《口》(窮地に)見捨てられる; 失敗する; だまされる; 負かされる ▪ She went after him, and that's how I *got left*. 彼女は彼のあとを追って去った. そうやって僕は見捨てられたのだ ▪ He opened his shop there and he has *got nicely left*. 彼はそこへ店を開いたが, 大失敗だった.

leave a lot* [*a great deal*] *to be desired →LEAVE much to be desired.

leave ... alone →ALONE.

***leave* a thing *as it is* [*as you found it*]** 物をそのままにしておく, 元のままにしておく ▪ We might as well *leave* everything *as it is*. 万事そのままにしておくほうがよかろう.

leave* a person *be 人をうっちゃっておく, かまわない ▪ "*Leave* me *be*," she squeaked. 「私にかまわないでください」と彼女はキーキー声で叫んだ.

***leave* a person *cold* [*cool*]** 人を興奮させない; (見ても, 聞いても)おもしろくない ▪ The play *left* us *cold*. その芝居は少しもおもしろくなかった ▪ He is saying all sorts of beastly things about me, but it *leaves* me *cold*. 彼は私のことをさんざん悪く言っているが, 私はなんともない.

***leave go* (*of*)** 《英口》(…を)放す (let go) ▪ *Leave go of* me, you are drunk! 放してよ, あなた酔っているのね.

***leave ... hanging* (*in the air* [*in midair*])** →HANG[2].

leave* a person *high and dry →HIGH and dry.

***leave hold* (*of*)** →HOLD[1].

***leave* a person *holding the bag* [《英》*baby*]** →BAG[1].

leave it at that 《口》(議論・批評・行為などを)それくらいにしておく, それ以上に出ないでおく ▪ Our opinions are quite opposed, but let's *leave it at that*. 我々の意見は全く反対ですが, もうそのくらいにしておきましょう ▪ He had looked at her, and *left it at that*. 彼は彼女を見たが, それ以上には出ないでおいた.

leave it be それを放っておく; 触れないでおく ▪ They want to *leave it be*. 彼らはそれをそっとしておきたいと思っている. ☞let it be と leave it alone との混合し

たもの.

leave it out 《英口》[[主に命令文で]] (不平・小言などを)やめる ▪ I've had enough of your complaining. *Leave it out*, will you? 君の不平にはうんざりした. いいかげんにしてくれないか.

leave it to *a person* ***to*** *do* 人に任せて…させる ▪ I shall *leave it to* specialists *to* discuss the matter. 私はその問題の討論は専門家だけに任せます.

leave it (***up***) ***to*** それを…の決定に任せる《特に勘定・給料などを》 ▪ I'll *leave it to* you, sir. 勘定[給料]はあなたのおぼしめしにお任せします.

leave loose (***of***) 《口》= leave HOLD (of).

leave much [***a lot, something, a great deal***] ***to be desired*** 遺憾な点が多い ▪ Your composition *leaves much to be desired.* あなたの作文は遺憾な点が多い ▪ Apparently, his wife's cooking still *leaves a lot to be desired.* どうも彼の奥方の料理の腕前はまだ大いに改善の余地があるようだ.

leave nothing [***little***] ***to be desired*** 全く[ほとんど]申し分がない ▪ His essay on peace *leaves nothing to be desired.* 彼の平和に関する論文は全く非の打ち所がない.

leave ... open →OPEN[1].

leave *a person* ***out in the cold*** →COLD.

leave ... severely alone →SEVERELY.

leave something to be desired → LEAVE much to be desired.

leave ... standing →STAND[2].

leave the path of right 正道を離れる ▪ He *left the path of right* and fell headlong into evil. 彼は正道を踏み外し, まっさかさまに悪の世界に落ちた.

leave *a person* ***to*** *do* 人に…するに任せる ▪ You had better *leave* the students *to* find out for themselves. 学生たちに自分で発見させたほうがよい ▪ The door *was left to* keep itself. その戸には番人はなかった.

leave *a person* ***to*** *himself* [*his* ***own devices,*** *his* ***own resources***] (助言など与えないで)人を放任して思うようにさせる ▪ I *was left to my own devices.* 私は相談相手もなく一人残された ▪ The children *were left to themselves* during the holidays. 子供らは休暇の間放任された.

leave *a person* ***to it*** 《口》人に一人であることをさせておく ▪ Having shown him how the machine worked, I *left* him *to it.* その機械の使い方を教えたあと, 彼に一人でやらせておいた.

leave ... undone [***unsaid,*** etc.] …をせずに[言わずに, など]おく ▪ We have *left undone* those things which we ought to have done. 我々はすべきであったことをしないでおいた ▪ These must not *be left unnoticed.* これらを見のがしておいてはならない.

leave well (***enough***) ***alone*** → let WELL (enough) alone.

leave *oneself* ***wide open*** 相手[敵]のかっこうの標的になる ▪ To say you approve of violence is to *leave yourself wide open* to attack. 暴力を肯定するなどと言おうものなら, 暴力でしっぺ返しされることになる.

leave word for (人)への伝言を残す ▪ I will *leave word for* you. 君への伝言を残しておきます.

leave word with …に伝言を頼む, 言いおく ▪ He *left word with* his secretary that he would be back at 5. 彼は5時に帰る, と秘書に言っておいた.

To be left till called for. 郵便局留め置き ▪ The letter was directed *to be left till called for.* その書簡は郵便局留めになっていた.

what is left of …の残り ▪ This is *what is left of* her birthday cake. これは彼女のバースデーケーキの残りだ.

leaven /lévən/ 名 ***of the same leaven*** 同じ種類[性質]の ▪ These specimens are all *of the same leaven.* この標本はすべて同種のものだ.

the old leaven 抜きがたい旧弊 (《聖》*1 Cor.* 5. 6-7) ▪ He was raised in *the old leaven* of the hatred of Protestants. 彼は国教を憎悪する抜きがたい旧弊の中に育てられた.

lecture /lékt∫ər/ 名 ***read a lecture*** **1** 読んで講義する ▪ He *read a lecture* to the Society on the beauties of Shakespeare. 彼はシェイクスピアのさまざまなよさを読み上げその協会に講義をした.

2 説論する, しかる ▪ His mother *read* him *a* severe *lecture* on his manners. 彼の母は彼の無作法をきびしくしかった.

lee /liː/ 名 ***beneath the lee*** (***of***) = under (the) LEE (of).

make up lee way 失われた時間[地位]を取り返す ▪ We must *make up* a lot of *lee way* since the office was closed for two days. 会社は2日間閉鎖されたから, 多くの時間を取り返さねばならない.

under (***the***) ***lee*** (***of***) **1** 《海》(…の)風下の方に ▪ We saw a fleet *under the lee.* 我々は風下の方に艦隊を見た.

2 (…の)陰に(隠れて, 風を避けて) ▪ We had better get *under the lee of* the hedge until the rain ceases. 我々は雨がやむまで生け垣の陰に入った方がよい.

leech /liːt∫/ 名 ***stick*** [***cling***] ***to ... like a leech*** …に吸いついて離れない ▪ He *stuck to* his father *like a leech.* 彼はお父さんにくっついて離れなかった. ☞昔ヒルに悪血を吸わせたことから.

leek /liːk/ 名 ***eat*** [***swallow***] ***the leek*** 屈辱を忍ぶ; 高言を取り消す (cf. Sh., *Hen. V* 5:1) ▪ They very humbly *ate their leek.* 彼らはひどくへりくだって高言を取り消した ▪ He will have to *swallow* a large *leek.* 彼はひどい屈辱を忍ばなければならないだろう.

not worth a leek 三文の価値もない ▪ What he did is *not worth a leek.* 彼のしたことはとるに足らぬ.

leery /líəri/ 形 ***be leery of*** 《俗》…を警戒する ▪ He *is leery of* a proposal. 彼は提案にうっかり乗らない.

lees /liːz/ 名 ***drain*** [***drink***] ***the lees*** 飲み干す; (苦労などを)なめ尽くす ▪ They *drank the lees* of humiliation. 彼らは屈辱をなめ尽くした.

L

drain* [*drink*]*... to the lees …を飲み干す; (労苦・辛酸)をなめ尽くす ▪ He *drained* life's troubles *to the lees.* 彼は人生の苦労をなめ尽くした ▪ I hope you will *drink* your torments *to the lees.* 君には辛酸をなめ尽くしてもらいたい.

settle on* [*upon*] *the lees 悪条件にできるだけ善処する; (使ってしまった)残りの財産でやっていく ▪ People were content to *settle* down *on their lees.* 人々は悪条件にできるだけ善処することで満足していた.

leeward /líːwərd, 《海》 lúːərd/ 名副 ***get to leeward of*** 《海口》…に衝突する《比喩的にも》 ▪ Saucy Britishers won't *get to leeward of* such a smart coon. 生意気なイギリス人もあんなずるいやつには衝突しないだろう.

go* [*drop*] *to leeward 《海口》風下の方へ落ちていく; 不利な立場になる ▪ The ship was *going* fast *to leeward.* 船はどんどん風下の方へ流されていった ▪ His friend *dropped to leeward* in the conversation. 彼の友人は会話でふるわなくなった.

leeway /líːwèɪ/ 名 ***catch up on*** (*one's*) ***leeway*** →make up (one's) LEEWAY.

have* [*enjoy*] *leeway (行動・判断・選択の)余地をもつ ▪ Academics *enjoy* more *leeway* than salaried employees. 大学人はサラリーマンより活動の範囲が広い.

have much* [*a great deal of*] *leeway to make up (取り戻すのが困難なほど)非常に遅れている; (挽回に苦しむほど)非常な劣勢にある ▪ We *have much leeway to make up* in that area. 我々はその領域の仕事が非常に遅れている ▪ We *have a great deal of leeway to make up* with the enemy troops. 我が軍は敵軍に対して非常に劣勢である.

make leeway 風下に流される; それて行く ▪ The ship always *made* more *leeway* than anything else. その船はいつも他の船より風下に流される程度が大きかった ▪ He *made leeway* towards the empty seat behind me. 彼は途中でそれて私の後の空席の方に向かってきた.

make up* [*catch up on*] (*one's*) *leeway 《英》遅れを取り戻す; もがいて苦境を切り抜ける ▪ The country is rapidly *making up its leeway.* その国はどんどん遅れを取り戻している ▪ Men had to *catch up on* a dreadful *leeway* of ignorance. 人々は無学という恐ろしい短所を償わねばならなかった. ☞「船が風圧を取り戻す」が原義.

left /left/ 形名 ***a wife of the left hand*** 自分より身分の低い妻 ▪ She is only my *wife of the left hand.* 彼女は私より身分の低い妻にすぎません.

(***be***) ***left of*** …の左に(ある) ▪ The greater part of the town *is left of* the railway. 町の大部分は鉄道の左にある.

by the left hand 身分の低い妻の産んだ; 庶出の ▪ His daughter *by the left hand* married a duke. 彼の庶出の娘が公爵と結婚した.

Eyes left! 左へならえ! ▪ "*Eyes left!*", shouted the sergeant-major. 「左へならえ!」と軍曹が叫んだ.

***hang a left* [*right*]** 《米口》(主に車を運転して)左[右]に曲がる ▪ *Hang a left* at the next corner and then drive straight ahead for two miles. 次の角を左折してから2マイルほど直進しなさい.

***have two left hands* [*feet*]** 無器用である ▪ Both of my brothers *have two left hands.* 私の弟は二人とも無器用だ ▪ That dancer *has got two left feet.* あのダンサーは踊りがへただ.

keep to the left*/*keep on* one's *left 左側を通行する ▪ We *keep to the left* in England. イングランドでは左側通行だ.

left and right →RIGHT and left.

left, right and center 《口》至る所に; あらゆる点で ▪ The lower classes were sacrificed *left, right and center.* 下層階級はあらゆる面で犠牲にされていた.

marry with the left hand →MARRY[2].

on the left hand **1** 左手に ▪ *On the left hand* is the low hill of Golgotha. 左手に低いゴルゴタの丘がある.

2《口》庶出で ▪ The girl had Medici blood in her if *on the left hand.* その少女には庶系ではあるがメディチ家の血が流れていた.

on the left of …の左側に ▪ *On the left of* this picture may be seen a cottage. この絵の左側に田舎家が見える.

over the left (***shoulder***) 《俗》さかさまから《この句がつくと前に言ったことは反対の意味に取るべきことを示す》 ▪ He is a clever fellow—*over the left.* 彼は賢い人だ—さかさまからね. ☞右の親指で左肩越しに指せば, 今言ったことの「反対」を意味した.

right and left →RIGHT[1].

take the left hand (***of***) (…の)左側に身を置く ▪ He will *take the left hand* at feasts. 彼は宴会で左側に着席する.

to the left hand (***of***) (…の)左手の方向に ▪ You may find painted numbers *to the left hand of* the door. ドアの左手に数字がペンキで書いてあるだろう.

with* one's *left 《ボクシング》左手で ▪ He got in one *with his left.* 彼は左手で一発入れた.

left field /léftfíːld/ 名 ***come out in* [*out of*] *left field*** 《口》(問題が)意外なところから生じる, 突然に[予期しないところから, どこからともなく]現れる ▪ What a surprise! This new problem *came out of left field.* ああ, 驚いた. こんな問題が新たに起きるとは思わなかった ▪ His remarks *came out of left field.* 彼の言葉はだしぬけに出てきた.

play* [*fill*] *left field 《野球》左翼手を務める ▪ He will probably *play left field.* 彼はおそらく左翼手を務めるだろう.

(***way***) ***out in left field*** 《米口》 **1** (答えが)全く間違って, 大間違いで ▪ He tried to guess, but he was *way out in left field.* 彼は推測しようとしたが, まるで見当違いだった ▪ He was *way out in left field.* 彼の答えは大間違いだった.

2 (話・行動が)変な; 発狂して ▪ The old man was *out in left field.* その老人は気が狂っていた ▪ He

L

was *out in left field* and went into a hospital. 彼は発狂していて入院した. ☞野球の「レフト」から.

left-hand /lέfthæ̀nd/ 形 ***on the left-hand side*** 左手に, 左側に ▪ There was a house *on the left-hand side* of the street. その通りの左側に家が1軒あった.

leftward /lέftwərd/ 名 ***to* (*the*) *leftward* (*of*)** (...の)左手(の方)に ▪ You will see a farm-house *to the leftward of* the village church. 村の教会の左手に農家が見えるでしょう ▪ A sign appeared *to leftward of* the astonished crowd. あっけにとられている群衆の左手の方角に, ある兆しが現れた.

leg[1] /leg/ 名 ***a leg man*** **1**《口》使い走りをする助手, 雑用係 ▪ We hired *a leg man* for our office. わが社に雑用係を一人雇った.

2《俗》特に足の綺麗な女性を好む男性 ▪ Her boyfriend refers to himself as *a leg man*. 彼女のボーイフレンドは女性の美しい足に惹かれるという.

***all legs* (*and wings*)** (特に青年が)成長しすぎて(不格好な, 細長い) ▪ I met a young fellow, *all legs and wings*, at the party. パーティーで手足のひょろ長い青年に出会った.

as fast as *one's* ***legs would carry*** *one* 全速力で ▪ I ran *as fast as my legs would carry* me. 私は全速力で走った.

be tied by the leg (ある事情で)動きが取れない ▪ We *were tied by the leg* all day. 我々は一日中動きが取れなかった.

betake *oneself* ***to*** *one's* ***legs*** 走る, 逃走する ▪ They *betook themselves to their legs* in surprise. 彼らは驚いて逃走した.

Break a leg! 《口》〚主に命令文で〛がんばれ!, 幸運を祈る!, よい旅を! ▪ I've never spoken in public before. —Don't worry, you'll be fine. *Break a leg!* 人前で話したことがないのだけど—大丈夫だよ. がんばれ ▪ The greeting sent by fax before the show said, "*Break a leg* and enjoy yourself." ショーの前に受け取ったファックスには「成功を祈る. 楽しく演じろよ」と書いてあった ▪ "*Break a leg*, Betty!" Jack said as she was leaving for China by plane. 空路中国へ向かうベティーに「いい旅をね!」とジャックが言った. ☞これから舞台に立つ人に逆に不運を祈って励ますという慣習から. Fall through the trapdoor! などとも言う.

dance *a person* ***off*** *his* ***legs*** 人をダンスさせてへとへとにさせる ▪ They will *dance* him *off his legs*. 彼らは彼を踊らせてへとへとにさせるだろう.

fall on *one's* ***legs*** **1** (猫が)高い所から落ちてもうまく立つ ▪ The cat *fell* squarely *on* all four *legs*. 猫は落ちたがうまく四足ですっくと降り立った.

2 幸運である, 成功する, うまく難を逃れる ▪ A wise man generally *falls on his legs*. 賢い人は概して成功する.

feel *one's* ***legs*** 自己の能力を自覚する; 独力で行動できる ▪ Now that the firm has opened its own office, I think it is *feeling its legs*. その会社は自分の事務所を開いたから, 事業に自信がついてきていると思う.

find *one's* ***legs*** →FIND one's feet.

find *one's* ***sea legs*** →SEA LEGS.

get a leg in 《俗》取り入って信頼を得る ▪ If I could *get a leg in*, I could persuade him. 彼に取り入ってその信頼が得られたら, 彼を説得することができるのだが.

get a [*one's*] ***leg over*** 《英卑》(男性が) ...と性交する.

get a leg up 《口》人に助けられて困難を切り抜ける ▪ He doesn't want to *get a leg up*. 彼は人に助けられて困難を切り抜けたいとは思っていない.

get *a person's* ***leg*** =pull a person's LEG.

get on *one's* ***legs*** →GET on one's feet.

get *one's* ***sea legs*** →have one's SEA LEGS (on).

get* (*up*) *on *one's* ***hind legs*** →HIND-LEG.

give *a person* ***a leg up*** **1** 人が馬に乗るのを助ける; 人が登る[障害を越える]のを助ける ▪ His friend *gave* him *a leg up*. 彼の友だちが彼を助けて馬に乗せた ▪ If you will *give* me *a leg up*, I can get over the wall. 君が私を押し上げてくれれば, この塀を越えることができる.

2《口》人を助けて困難を切り抜けさせる ▪ When things were at their worst, he came along and *gave* me *a leg up*. 最悪の事態になったとき, 彼がやって来て私を助けて窮地を切り抜けさせてくれた.

***give legs* (*for it*)** 走(り去)る ▪ The best way is to *give legs for it*. 一番よい方法は, 逃走することだ.

hang a leg →HANG[2].

have a bone in *one's* ***leg*** →BONE.

have* [*get*] *a leg up on *a person* 《米》人より有利である[になる] ▪ I practiced judo very hard until at last I *got a leg up on* our captain. 柔道の猛練習をしてついに主将に勝てるようになった.

have ... by the leg 《米俗》...に不意打ちを食わせる ▪ The banks *have got* the country *by the leg*. 銀行は国に不意打ちを食わせた.

have* (*got*) *hollow legs 《戯》ひどく食欲がある ▪ Those old ladies *have hollow legs*. あの老婦人たちは食欲旺盛だ.

have *a person's* ***leg*** =pull a person's LEG.

have *one's* ***leg over the harrows*** 手に負えない, 押さえきれない ▪ She *has her leg over the harrows* now. 彼女は今は手に負えない.

have legs 《主に米》 **1** 長引く; 関心[興味]を失わない ▪ I'm sure this latest scandal *has legs*. 最近のこのスキャンダルはきっとすぐにはおさまらないだろう ▪ The phone-tapping scandal will *have legs* for a long time. その電話盗聴事件はいつまでも話題になるだろう.

2 (アイディア・計画が)うまくいきそうである, (話が)真実味を帯びてくる ▪ I'm not sure if my innovation program *has legs*. 僕の刷新計画がうまく行くかどうか自信がない ▪ Does the rumor *have legs* this time? 今度こそ噂は本当だろうな.

have no legs 《口》(ゴルフボールなどが)球足がない ▪ The golf-ball *had no legs*. そのゴルフボールには球

足がなかった.

have *one's* ***sea legs*** →find one's SEA LEGS.

have the legs of (競走などで)…より速く走る ▪ He will *have the legs of* all the other competitors. 彼は他の競走者の誰よりも速く走るだろう.

heave (***up***) *one's* [***the***] ***leg*** →lift (up) one's LEG.

in high leg 上きげんで, 大得意で ▪ The morale of our troop was *in high leg*. わが部隊の士気は大いに上がっていた.

keep *one's* ***legs*** 立っている, 歩いている; 倒れない ▪ They could scarcely *keep their legs*. 彼らは立っていられないくらいだった.

one's ***last legs*** 瀕死の状態, 破産の一歩手前, 廃用[廃止, 失敗]の一歩手前 ▪ You were pretty near *your last legs*. あなたは瀕死の状態だった ▪ He has brought me to *my last legs*. 彼は私を破産寸前に追いやった.

leg and leg (競走などで)五分五分で, 双方1点で ▪ How goes it?—*Leg and leg*, and my throw! どんな具合だ?—双方1点ずつだ. そして次はおれの番だ.

leg work 《口》よく歩いて体力を使う仕事, 刑事事件の地取り捜査活動 ▪ He is my research assistant and does a lot of *leg work* for me. 彼は私の調査助手で歩き回ってしっかり取材してきてくれる.

lift [***heave***] (***up***) *one's* [***the***] ***leg*** (犬が)足を上げて小便をする ▪ Any dog loves poles and trees he can *lift his leg* against. どの犬も小便をかけられる電信柱や木が大のお気に入りだ.

lose *one's* ***legs*** 《俗》酒に酔う ▪ He is said to have *lost his legs*. 彼は酒に酔ったそうだ.

not have a leg to stand on 《口》支え[成功の見込み, 言い訳, もっともな理由]がない ▪ The country *won't have a leg to stand on*. その国は支えがなくなるだろう《滅びるだろう》 ▪ *No* system but this *had a leg to stand on*. これ以外の方式は成功する見込みがなかった ▪ You *don't have a leg to stand on* for your behavior. 君は自分の行為に対して弁解の余地はない.

off *one's* ***legs*** 足を休めて, 休息して ▪ She was *off her legs* and just sat there alone. 彼女は休息をとってただそこにぽつんと座っていた.

on *one's* ***last legs*** 《口》 **1** (テーブルなどが)古くて使えなくなりそうで ▪ This teapot is about *on its last legs*. このティーポットは古くて使えなくなりそうだ.

2 (制度・事業などが)失敗しそうで, すたれそうで ▪ As he is against the tax, it must be *on its last legs*. 彼がその税に反対だから, それは廃止されるにちがいない ▪ The firm is *on its last legs*. その会社は倒れそうだ.

3 (人が)破産しそうで; 死にそうで ▪ He has lost a lot of money. He is about *on his last legs*. 彼は多額の金を失い, 破産に瀕している.

on [***upon***] *one's* ***legs***/《戯》***on*** *one's* ***hind legs*** 《口》 **1** 立っていて, 休まずにいて ▪ I have been *on my legs* all day and I am tired out. 私は一日中立ちっ放しだったのですっかり疲れた.

2 演説するため(演壇に)立って ▪ Mr. Smith was *on his hind legs* arguing with force. スミス氏は演壇に立って強力に議論していた.

3 (病後)歩けるようになって; 達者になって ▪ He will have been *upon his legs* by next month. 彼は来月までには歩けるようになっているだろう.

4 確立されて, 繁昌して ▪ The firm is *on its legs*. その会社は基礎が固まった.

on the leg (犬が)足が長い ▪ The dog is a trifle *on the leg*. その犬は少し足が長すぎる.

pull *a person's* ***leg*** 《口》(戯れに)人をからかう, かつぐ ▪ He *pulled my leg* by telling me how rich I was. 彼は私を大金持だと言ってからかった ▪ He's always *pulling people's legs*. 彼は人をかついでばかりいる.

Pull the other leg [***one***]***, it's got bells on it.*** →PULL[2].

put [***set***] *one's* ***best leg foremost*** →BEST.

put *one's* ***legs under the table*** 食卓につく ▪ She asked him to *put his legs under the table*. 食卓についてくださいと彼女は彼に言った.

recover *one's* ***legs*** →RECOVER.

run *one's* ***legs to jelly*** 走り回ってへとへとになる ▪ I *ran my legs to jelly* trying to get everything for the party. パーティー用品一切を買いそろえようと走り回ってバテてしまった.

run [***rush***] *a person* ***off*** *his* ***legs*** 《口》人をくたくたになるまで働かせる ▪ The children *run* me *off my legs*. 子供たちの世話でくたくただ.

run off *one's* ***legs*** 仕事[任務]が多くてへとへとになる ▪ I have no intention of *running off my legs* looking after your children. あなたの子供の世話をしてへとへとになるまで働くつもりは少しもない.

set *a person* ***on*** *his* ***legs*** 人を(健康上・経済上)立ち直らせる, 繁昌[確立]させる ▪ A pound will *set* him *on his legs*. 1ポンドあれば彼は立ち直るだろう.

shake a leg →SHAKE[2].

shake a loose [***free***] ***leg*** だらしない[気ままな]生活をする ▪ While luck lasts, the highwayman *shakes a loose leg*. 幸運の続くかぎり, 追いはぎはだらしない生活をする.

show a leg 《口》 **1** 現れる ▪ They haven't *shown a leg* yet, so I'll rouse 'em up. 彼らはまだ顔を見せないから, 私が起こしてやろう.

2 《英口》〚主に命令文で〛起きなさい ▪ *Show a leg*! It's past 10 o'clock 起きろ. 10時過ぎだ. ☞海語から.

show leg 《米俗》逃走する ▪ I will fight for you or *show leg* for you. 私は君のためなら戦いもし, また逃走もしよう.

stand on [***upon***] *one's* ***own legs*** 独力でやる, 自力で立つ, 独立する ▪ You should learn to *stand on your own legs*. 君は独力でやることを覚えるべきだ.

stretch *one's* ***legs*** 足を伸ばす; (足をほぐすために)散歩する ▪ I got down at almost every stage to *stretch my legs*. 私はほとんどどの宿場でも馬車を降り

て散歩した.

take leg 走(り去)る ▪ Her chastity *took leg.* 彼女の貞節は逃げ去った.

take to *one's* ***legs*** 走る, 逃走する ▪ He *took to his legs* when he saw someone approaching. 誰かが近づいてくるのを見て, 彼は逃げ去った.

talk the hind leg(***s***) ***off a donkey*** →HIND-LEG.

the first leg (旅行の)最初の行程 ▪ *The first leg* of the journey got me to Paris. 旅行の最初の行程でパリに行った.

the last leg (旅行の)最後の行程 ▪ *The last leg* of our round-the-world trip was London to New York. 世界一周の最後の旅程はロンドンからニューヨークだった.

walk *a person* ***off his legs*** →WALK[2].

walk off *one's* ***legs*** 歩いて疲れ果てる ▪ He *walked off his legs.* 彼は歩いてへとへとに疲れた.

leg[2] /leg/ 動 ***leg it*** 《主に英口》 **1** 歩く; 一生懸命歩く[走る] ▪ Let us *leg it* a little. 少し歩きましょう. **2** 走り去る, 急いで去る ▪ The shoplifter *legged it* down a side street. 万引きした人はわき道を大急ぎで逃げ去った.

legal /líːgəl/ 形 ***make it legal*** 結婚する (＝get married) ▪ The couple finally *made it legal.* 二人はやっと結婚した.

leg bail /légbéɪl/ 名 ***give leg bail*** 《口》 逃亡する; 脱獄する ▪ He was *giving* them *leg bail* as hard as he could foot it. 彼は一生懸命彼らから逃走していた.

legend /lédʒənd/ 名 ***a living legend/a legend in*** *one's* ***own lifetime*** 生きている伝説的な人物 ▪ His 35-year study of turtles made him *a living legend.* 35年に及ぶウミガメの研究で彼は生存中に伝説的人物になった.

become a legend in *one's* ***own*** (***life***)***time*** 生きているうちに非常に有名な[悪名が高い]人物になる ▪ Not many men build *a legend* and *become* one *in their own time.* 後世に残る業績を残し, かつ生存中に伝説的な人物になる者はそう多くない.

legion /líːdʒən/ 名 ***Their*** [***My,*** etc.] ***name*** [***number***] ***is legion.*** 彼らは多勢である; その数は無数である (《聖》 *Mark* 5. 9) ▪ The Kennedy family? My dear, *their name is legion.* ケネディー家ですか? それは多勢ですよ ▪ *The number* of such sayings *is legion.* そのようなことわざは無数である.

legit /lɪdʒít/ 形 ***go legit*** 《口》 (犯罪から)足を洗ってまともになる, 更生する ▪ He's just emerged from three years in prison and is determined to *go legit.* 彼は3年の刑期を終えて出所したばかりで, 足を洗おうと心に決めている. ☞legit＝legitimate.

leisure /líːʒər|léʒə/ 名 ***a lady*** [***woman***] ***of leisure*** 有閑夫人 ▪ She's no longer *a lady of leisure.* 彼女はもはや有閑夫人ではない.

at leisure **1** 暇で ▪ We are *at leisure* now. 我々は今は暇です. **2** ゆっくりと, 急がずに ▪ I will debate this matter *at leisure.* 私はこの問題をゆっくりと論じましょう.

at *one's* ***leisure*** 暇なときに; 都合のよいときに; 楽なときに ▪ He would go to town *at his leisure.* 彼は暇なときに町へよく行ったものだ ▪ You can take both good and evil and throw away the evil *at your leisure.* 善悪の両方をまず受入れ, 都合のよいときに悪を捨てればよい.

at leisure (***to*** *do*) 《文》 (…する)暇がある ▪ I am not *at leisure to* read such a book. 私はそのような本を読む暇がない.

Idle people [***folk***(***s***)] ***have the least leisure.*** 《諺》 ぶらぶらしている連中には一番暇な時間がない 《勤勉でなければ暇は全くできない. だらだらと仕事をすればそれを終えるのに一日中かかるからである》, 「学ぶに暇あらずという者は暇ありといえども また学ぶ能(あた)わず」.

wait (***upon***) *a person's* ***leisure*** 人が暇になるまで待つ; 都合がつくまで待つ ▪ Don't hurry with what you are doing, I can *wait your leisure.* 今している事を急がなくてもいいよ. 暇になるまで待てるから.

lemon /lémən/ 名 ***hand*** *a person* ***a lemon*** (取引で)人をだます, ぺてんにかける ▪ I felt that he had *handed* me *a lemon.* 彼にだまされたと感じた.

it's a lemon 《口》 欠陥品である ▪ My new cell phone *is a lemon.* It won't work properly. 今度買った携帯電話は欠陥商品だ. どうしてもうまく動かない.

The answer is a lemon! →ANSWER[1].

lend /lend/ 動 ***lend a*** (***helping***) ***hand*** → lend a (helping) HAND (in, at, to do).

lend oneself to 《文》 **1** (人が主として好ましからぬこと)に力を貸す, 尽くす; に身を入れる ▪ Don't *lend yourself to* such dishonest schemes. そのような不正な計画に力を貸してはいけません ▪ He *lent himself to* the concealment of the facts. 彼はその事実を隠すことに骨折った.

2 (物が誤用・乱用など)を受けやすい, に陥りやすい ▪ Free enterprise often *lends itself to* misuse. 自由企業はよく誤用されやすい.

3 (物が) …に適する ▪ This room *lends itself to* study. この部屋は勉強するのに適している.

lend wings →WING[1].

length /leŋkθ/ 名 ***all*** *one's* ***length*** 頭のてっぺんから足の先までの全長, 体全体を伸べて ▪ He laid *all his length* under a tree. 彼は1本の木の下に長々と全身を伸ばして寝ていた.

at arm's length →ARM[1].

at full length **1** 大の字なりに, 体を十分伸ばして, 長々と ▪ He was lying *at full length* at the corner of the street. 彼は通りの角で大の字になって寝ていた.

2 詳細に, 十分に ▪ We discussed the matter *at full length.* 我々はその問題を詳しく討議した.

at *one's* ***full length*** ＝at full LENGTH 1.

at great length 大変詳しく; 長たらしく, くどくどと ▪ I have explained to you *at great length* why I travel on foot. 私はなぜ徒歩旅行するかを大変詳しくあなたに説明した.

at length **1** ついに ▪ *At length,* when we were

L

tired of waiting, he came in. 我々が待ちあぐんでいたとき，ようやく彼が入って来た.
2 詳しく，十分に ▪ He discoursed *at length* on the theory of gravitation. 彼は重力説について詳しく語った.
3 長たらしく，くどくどと ▪ He spoke *at length*. 彼はくどくどと話した.

at some length 相当長く; かなり詳しく ▪ He spoke *at some length* on the other question. 彼はもう一方の問題についてかなり詳しく話した.

by a length [***three lengths,*** etc.] 1身長・1艇身[3身長・3艇身，など]だけ ▪ The horse won *by a length*. その馬は1馬身差で勝った.

fall all *one's* ***length/fall at full length*** ぱったり[大の字に]倒れる ▪ He *fell all his length* on his side. 彼はぱったり横に倒れた.

find [***get, have, know***] ***the length of*** *a person's* ***foot*** →FOOT[1].

for a length of time しばらくの間 ▪ He kept silent *for a length of time*. 彼はしばらく黙っていた.

for any length of time **1** いくらかの間だけでも ▪ When you leave your computer *for any length of time*, log off. ちょっとでもコンピューターから離れるときはログオフしなさい.
2 〚否定文で〛 あまり長く(…ない) ▪ He wasn't left alone *for any length of time*. 彼は大して長いこと一人でおきざりにはされなかった.

go a great length towards …に大いに役立つ ▪ This money will *go a great length towards* the object. この金はその目的に大いに役立つだろう.

go all lengths どこまでも行く; どんなことでもする ▪ He would *go all lengths* to gain his end. 彼は目的を達するためにはどんなことでもやる.

go *one's* ***length for*** …を得るために全力を尽くす ▪ He will *go his length for* the prize. 彼はその賞を得るためには全力を尽くすだろう.

go the same length (***as***) (…と)同じくらいの事をする ▪ I will *go the same length as* you will. 私はあなたがするだけの事はする覚悟です.

go the whole length of …を(臆面もなく)しまいまでやる，存分にやる ▪ He *went the whole length of* the expression. 彼は遠慮もなくそれをしまいまで言った.

go (***to***) ***any length***(***s***) どんなことでもする ▪ They will *go to any lengths* to get their revenge. 彼らは報復するためにはどんなことでもするつもりだ.

go to great [***extraordinary, huge, considerable,*** etc.] ***lengths to*** *do* …するためにずいぶん骨折る; 極端なことをする ▪ The father *went to great lengths to* see his son in the profession. 父は息子がその専門職につくためには，大いに骨を折った ▪ We have *gone to extraordinary lengths to* find our missing dog. いなくなった我が家の犬を探すために八方手を尽くした.

go (***to***) ***the length of*** (*doing*) …までもする，さえもする ▪ They do not *go the length of denying* that. 彼らはそれを否定することまではしなかった ▪ I *went to the length of seeing* him off. 私は彼を見送りさえもした.

in length of time 時が経つにつれて ▪ They became intimate *in length of time*. 彼らは時が経つにつれて，親しくなった.

keep ... at arm's length →ARM[1].

measure *one's* ***length*** → MEASURE (out) one's length.

slip *a woman* ***a length*** 《俗》 女性と性交する ▪ Has he *slipped* you *a length*? あいつお前さんと寝たかい. ☞length＝penis.

the length and breadth of …の全体をくまなく ▪ We searched *the length and breadth of* the city but never found him. その市をくまなく捜したが，彼は見つからなかった ▪ His knowledge ranges over *the length and breadth of* English literature. 彼の知識は英文学の全般に亘(わた)っている.

the length of *one's* ***days***/ *one's* ***length of days*** (人の)長寿，長命 ▪ He had lived *the length of his days*. 彼は長寿を全うしたのだった.

There are no lengths to which *one* ***would not go.*** 何をすることも辞さない ▪ *There are no lengths to which* he *would not go* to gain his end. 彼は目的を達するためには何をすることも辞さない.

lenient /lí:niənt/ 形 ***be lenient with*** [***on***] …に対して寛大な ▪ He *is* too *lenient with* his children about their bad manners. 彼は子供たちの無作法にあまり寛大すぎる.

leopard /lépərd/ 名 ***A leopard never changes its spots./ A leopard cannot change its spots.*** 《諺》 ヒョウは斑点を変え(られ)ない《性格[本性]は変わらないものだ》(《聖》 *Jer.* 13. 23).

leper /lépər/ 名 ***avoid ... like a leper*** 《侮蔑》 …を忌み嫌って避ける ▪ Ever since he was convicted of larceny, his brother *avoids* him *like a leper*. 彼が窃盗罪を宣告されて以来，彼の弟は彼を忌避している.

less /les/ 形 副 代 ***anything less than*** → something LESS than.

couldn't care less →CARE[2].

in less than no time →TIME[1].

less and less 次第に減って，だんだん…でなくなって，ますます…ない ▪ He found the job *less and less* attractive. 彼はその仕事にだんだん飽きてきた ▪ She phoned me *less and less* after that. その後彼女は次第に電話してこなくなった.

Less is more. 小さい[少ない]方がよい，少ないほど効果がある《陳腐な表現》 ▪ Yes, *less is more* when you buy your new house or car. そう，家や車を買うなら小さい方がいい.

Less of ...! 〚命令文で〛 …はよせ! ▪ *Less of* your nonsense! ばかも休み休み言え.

less than **1** 決して…でない (not at all) ▪ Your apology was *less than* frank. あなたのわびは全然率直でなかった ▪ It was *less than* perfectly understood. それは完全には理解されなかった.
2 …足らず ▪ He came home in *less than* an

hour. 彼は1時間足らずで帰宅した.
***less** A **than** B* AよりもむしろBで ▪ He is *less* my teacher *than* my friend. 彼は私の師というよりもむしろ友だ.
little less than →LITTLE.
more or less **1** およそ ▪ This will cost you fifty pounds *more or less*. この費用はおよそ50ポンドほどかかるだろう.
2 多かれ少なかれ; いくぶん, 多少 ▪ A lawsuit would involve *more or less* expense. 訴訟すれば, 多かれ少なかれ費用がかかるだろう ▪ It is now *more or less* settled. それは今はいくぶん解決した.
much* [*still, even*] *less [[否定的語句を伴って]] なおさら…ない (→much MORE) ▪ He does not know English, *still less* German. 彼は英語を知らない, ドイツ語はなおさらだ ▪ I don't want to see him, *much less* speak to him. 彼には会いたくない, まして話しかけるのはなおさらいやだ.
no less **1** 同様に ▪ It is *no less* important. それも同様に重要である.
2 しかも ▪ He has bought her a new fur coat.—A mink *no less*, I bet. 彼は彼女に新しい毛皮のコートを買ってやった—しかもミンクのだろうね, きっと.
3 まさしく, 本当に ▪ It was the Queen, *no less*. それはまさしく女王だった.
no less than **1** …も《数量の大きいことを表す》 ▪ He gave me *no less than* £50. 彼は私に50ポンドもくれた ▪ There were *no less than* 50 people present. 50人も出席していた.
2 …と同様に; …にほかならない ▪ She *no less than* he was guilty of the crime. 彼女は彼と同様にその罪を犯した ▪ His illness was *no less than* want of sleep. 彼の病気は睡眠不足にほかならなかった.
no less...than **1** まさしく…にほかならない; …ほどの(人) ▪ It was *no less* a person *than* the prime minister. それはまさしく総理大臣その人であった ▪ It requires *no less* a person *than* the governor to settle the problem. その問題を解決するには知事級の人が必要である.
2 …に劣らず ▪ She is *no less* beautiful *than* her sister. 彼女は姉に劣らず美しい.
no less than often 非常にしばしば ▪ They were cheerful *no less than often*. 彼らは朗らかなことが非常に多かった.
none the less それでもやはり, それにもかかわらず ▪ He has many faults, but I love him *none the less*. 彼には欠点が多いが, それでもやはり彼が好きだ.
***not...*(*any*) *the less for* [*because*]/ *none the less for* [*because*]** …にもかかわらずやはり…だ ▪ I don't think *any the less* of him *for* that. そうであっても彼を重んじる心は少しも変わらない ▪ I respect him *none the less because* he is so simple. 彼は非常に素朴だけれど私はやはり彼を尊敬する.
not less than **1** …に勝るとも劣らない ▪ She is *not less* beautiful *than* her sister. 彼女の美しさは姉に勝るとも劣らない.
2 …より多くとも少なくはない; 少なくとも ▪ He has *not less than* a million. 彼は少なくとも100万は持っている.
nothing less than **1** 少なくとも…くらいは; まさに…を ▪ We expected *nothing less than* a revolution. 我々は少なくとも革命くらいは予期していた.
2 …にほかならない ▪ It is *nothing less than* madness. それは全く狂気の沙汰だ.
something* [*anything*] *less than …でないもの ▪ February is *something less than* nature's darling. 2月は自然の寵児ではない ▪ If you drive with *anything less than* good caution, you're risking your life. よく用心して運転しないと, 生命にかかわるよ.
still less →much LESS.

lesser /lésər/ 形 ***the lesser of* (*the*) *two evils*** 二つの悪のうちの小さい方 ▪ This action seemed *the lesser of the two evils*. この行動が二つの悪のうちのましな方に思えた.
***to a lesser extent* [*degree*]** [[and のあとで挿入句として]] それには及ばないものの, それ程ではないが ▪ She was encouraged by her mother *and, to a lesser extent*, her father. 彼女は母親から, そしてやや劣るが父親からも激励を受けた ▪ Television, *and to a lesser degree* radio, is my main source of entertainment. 私は主にテレビそしてたまにラジオを視聴して楽しむ.

lesson[1] /lésən/ 名 ***be a lesson to*** …への教訓である ▪ Let her patience *be a lesson to* you. 彼女の忍耐を見て, あなたの教訓としなさい.
do** one's **lessons 学課の勉強をする ▪ I must *do my lessons* before I go to bed. 寝る前に学課を勉強しなければならない.
give** a person **a lesson = teach a person a LESSON.
***give a lesson* [*lessons*] *in* [*on*]** …を教授する ▪ I'll *give* you *a lesson in* boxing. 君にボクシングを教えてやろう ▪ He *gave* private *lessons on* the fiddle. 彼はバイオリンの個人教授をした.
have a severe lesson ひどくしかられる ▪ You will *have a severe lesson* if you are late again. 今度遅れたら, こっぴどくしかられるぞ.
have lessons in …のけいこをする ▪ She *had* daily *lessons in* dancing. 彼女は毎日ダンスのけいこをした.
have lessons with …の授業を受ける ▪ We shall *have* two *lessons with* Mr. Harris tomorrow. あすはハリス先生の授業が2回ある.
learn a* [*one's*] *lesson 教訓を得る, 経験で悟る ▪ I'm sure he has *learned a* painful *lesson*. きっと彼は苦しい経験で悟ったにちがいない.
read** a person **a lesson →READ[2].
***take lessons* (*in*)** (…の)けいこを受ける, を習う ▪ He *took* no French *lessons* on Sunday. 彼は日曜にフランス語の授業を受けなかった.
***take lessons of* [*from*]** …の授業を受ける, に習う ▪ I shall soon *take lessons of* Mr. Green. 私はまもなくグリーン先生に習うでしょう.

L

***teach** a person **a lesson/teach a lesson to** a person* 人にとって戒めとなる, 人に思い知らせる ▪ This accident will *teach* him *a* useful *lesson.* この事故は彼には役に立つ戒めとなろう ▪ British Airways *taught a lesson to* a racist passenger. 英国航空は人種差別の乗客に思い知らせた.

***teach a lesson** [**lessons**] (**in**)* = give a LESSON in.

lesson[2] /lésən/ 動 ***lesson** a person **to** do* 人に教えて[訓戒して]...させる ▪ You *lessoned* me *to* find that trouble is no trouble. あなたは私に訓戒して, 苦難は苦難でないことを知らせた.

lest /lest/ 接 ***lest ... should** do*/《米》***lest ...** do*

1 ...しないように; するといけないから ▪ Work hard *lest* you (*should*) fail. 落第しないように一生懸命勉強しなさい ▪ Take an umbrella with you *lest* it (*should*) rain. 降るといけないから, かさを持って行け.

2 ⟦fear, danger などを伴って⟧ ...しはしないかと(いう) ▪ There was *danger lest* he (*should*) be murdered. 彼が殺害されはしないかという危険があった ▪ I *fear lest* he *should* die. 彼が死にはしないかと心配だ.

let[1] /let/ 名 ***get a let for*** 《英口》...の借り手が見つかる ▪ I cannot *get a let for* the house. その家の借り手が見つからない.

without let or hindrance 何の故障[障害]もなく ▪ You will be able to make your arrangements *without let or hindrance.* あなたは何の故障もなく手はずを整えることができるでしょう. ☞法律用語から.

let[2] /let/ 動 ***be let down*** **1** (猟犬のかぎつめが)地面に触れている ▪ The dog is a pretty large hound, all her claws *are let down* of one of her forefeet. その犬はかなり大きい猟犬で, 片方の前足のかぎつめはみな地面についている.

2 (馬の腱が)くじかれている ▪ If the horse *is let down* in the sinew, he can never be made strong in that part. 馬の腱がくじかれていれば, その部分は決して強くすることはできない.

be well let down in the girth (馬・犬が)腹帯を深くはめている ▪ When a horse *is well let down in the girth,* he is a goodwinded nag. 馬が腹帯を深くはめている場合は, その馬は息の長く続く馬である.

***Don't let's** [**Let's not,** 《米口》 **Let's don't**] do.* 《英口》...するのはよしましょう ▪ *Don't let's* talk about it. そのことについて話すのはよそう ▪ *Let's not* waste our time on that. それで時間をむだにすまい.

let alone →ALONE.

***let ... alone to** do* →leave ... ALONE to do.

let be **1** 放っておく, かまわない; じゃましない ▪ The farmer *let* the plowing *be* till the next week. 農夫は耕作を次の週まで放っておいた ▪ We soon learned to *let* him *be.* 我々はまもなく彼にかまわないでおくことを覚えた.

2 《口》何ともない, どうでもよい (no matter) 《命令法》 ▪ *Let be, let be!* 何でもない, 何でもない!

3 放っておく ▪ He was about to talk to her when he was told to *let be.* 彼女に声をかけようとしたとたんに, 彼は「放っておいてよ」と言われた.

let blood 手術で血を取る, 放血する《昔の療法》 ▪ In olden times, in the case of fevers, the physician always *let blood* from the patient. 昔は熱病の場合は, 医者はいつも患者から血を取った.

let** oneself **down 評判を落とす ▪ If you did that, you would be *letting yourself down.* そんなことをすれば評判を落とすことになるよ.

***let** a person **down gently** [**softly, easily, easy**]* 《口》人の自尊心を傷つけぬよう配慮して知らせる, 体よく話す[断る] ▪ In view of the fellow's long service with the firm, the chief will *let* him *down gently.* 彼が会社に長年勤務したことにかんがみて, 社長は彼に配慮して話すだろう ▪ Bob *let* the applicant *down easy.* ボブは志願者に丁重に断った.

let fly →FLY[3].

let fly with →FLY[3].

let go →GO[2].

let** oneself **go **1** (特に一時的に)思いのままにふるまう, はめをはずす, 夢中になる ▪ They *let themselves go* and cheered wildly. 彼らは熱狂して狂気のように喝采した ▪ I *let myself go* on this subject. 私はこの題目に夢中になった.

2 なりふりをかまわない, 自堕落にする ▪ Though extremely poor, she tries not to *let herself go.* 彼女はひどく貧乏だけれど, 自堕落にしないようにしている.

let** a person **have it 《口》 **1** 人をひどくなぐる[罰する, しかる] ▪ We *let* him *have it* on the head. 彼の頭をぶんなぐってやった ▪ She really *let* him *have it.* 彼女はほんとに猛烈に彼をののしった.

2 人を撃つ ▪ I took careful aim and *let* him *have it* between the eyes. 私は入念にねらいを定めて, 彼の目と目の間を撃った.

let her** [**it**] **rip →RIP[2].

Let it roll! 《口》猛スピードでとばせ! さあ, 始めろ!

let** oneself **in (表戸のかぎで)戸を開けて入る ▪ I have a latch-key and *let myself in.* 私は表戸のかぎを持っていて, それで戸を開けて入ります.

let** a person **in for 《口》 **1** 人を知らずに...する[支払う]はめに追い込む ▪ Don't *let* yourself *in for* so much work. そんな大仕事に巻き込まれないようになさい ▪ He *was let in for* a good hundred pounds by his son's bankruptcy. 彼は息子の破産で知らぬ間にまるまる100ポンド払わされるはめになった.

2 人を...に巻き込む, 人に...させる ▪ They were *letting* him *in for* a legal wrangle. 彼らは法律上の紛争に彼を巻き込んでいた.

let** oneself **in for 《口》(知らぬ間に)...する[支払う]はめに追いこまれる ▪ I *let myself in for* £1,000. 私は1,000ポンド払わされるはめになった ▪ I've *let myself in for* all the work. 私はその仕事全部をするはめに追い込まれた.

let** a person **in for something 人を窮地に追い込む ▪ You've *let* me *in for something.* 君のおかげで私は窮地に追い込まれてしまった.

let it all hang out →HANG[2].

let it be so それならそれでよい, 仕方がない; ままよ《あ

きらめ・承諾》(＝SO be it.) ▪ If you can't change the reservation, *let it be so*. 予約の変更ができないのなら仕方がない.

let it go at that →GO².

let it spread 《俗》(もっと太っても)大丈夫だ ▪ I'm afraid I can't eat any cake.—*Let it spread*. You aren't that overweight. ケーキは食べられないのよ—平気, 平気. そんなに太ってなんかいないから.

let ... know [***hear***] ...に知らせる ▪ *Let* me *know* as soon as you arrive in Washington. ワシントンに着きしだいお知らせください ▪ We must *let* him *hear* the news. 彼にそのニュースを知らせなければならない.

let loose **1** (危険なもの)を放す, 自由にする ▪ It is unwise to *let* a sick pet *loose*. 病気のペットを放すのは賢明でない.

2 (抑えていた感情など)を存分に発する, ほしいままにする ▪ He will *let loose* fierce wrath on this nation. 彼はこの国民に対して激しい憤怒を存分に発するだろう.

3 (...を)自由にさせる (*on*) ▪ I can't *let* him *loose on* that class. 彼にあのクラスを自由にさせておくことはできない.

4 手を離す ▪ The boy picked up a coin and would not *let loose*. 男の子はコインを拾い上げ, どうしても離さなかった.

5 ずけずけ言う (*at*) ▪ He *let loose at* her. 彼は彼女にずけずけ言った.

let *oneself* ***loose*** 勝手放題に話す[行動する] ▪ He is apt to *let himself loose*. 彼は勝手放題に行動しがちである.

let me [***us***] ***have it*** 教えてくれ, 話せよ ▪ Come, come, *let's have it* from the beginning. さあさあ, 始めから話してくれ.

let me [***us***] ***see*** →SEE.

let *a person* ***off lightly*** [***easy***]/***be let off lightly*** [***get off lightly***] 人をたやすく釈放する[(人が)たやすく釈放される] ▪ The judge *let* me *off lightly*. 裁判官は軽い罰で私を赦してくれた ▪ Although caught in the act, he has *been let off lightly*. 彼は現行犯逮捕されたのにたやすく釈放された ▪ You can't commit a major crime and *get off lightly*. 大罪を犯して軽い刑で済ませてはもらえない.

let off (***the***) ***steam*** →STEAM¹.

let *oneself* ***out*** 自分で出て行く; 日雇いに雇われる ▪ Without a word he *let himself out*. 彼は一言も言わずに勝手に出て行った.

let out a reef 《口》食べすぎてバンドをゆるめる[ボタンをはずす] ▪ If I don't *let out a reef*, I think I shall burst. バンドをゆるめないと, おなかが破裂しそうだ. ☞《海》「帆を広げる」が原義.

let ... out of *one's* ***sight*** →SIGHT.

let ... over *a place* ...を場所に通す ▪ The proprietor *let* me *over* the factory. 経営者は私を工場に通した.

let ... pass ...を見のがす, 容赦する ▪ I heard what he said about me, but decided to *let* it *pass*. 彼が私について言ったことは聞いたが, それを見逃すことにした.

let slide →let ... SLIDE.

let slip →SLIP².

let the side down 味方[身内]を裏切る(ようなことをする) ▪ He *let the side down* when he let the secret out. 彼は秘密を漏らして味方を裏切ることとなった.

let us say たとえば...としよう ▪ You succeed, *let us say*, in lowering the infant death rate. たとえば, 君が幼児死亡率を下げることに成功するとしよう.

Let us [***Let's***] *do*(***, shall we?***) ...しようではないか ▪ *Let's* have a drink, *shall we?* 1杯やろうではないか.

let well (家などの)借り手がある ▪ The house does not *let well*. その家は借り手がない.

let well (***enough***) ***alone*** →WELL².

Let'em all come! →COME².

Let's do so. そうしようじゃないか ▪ That's OK, *let's do so*. それでいいよ, そうしよう.

Let's have it. →HAVE it.

let's not/《米口》***let's don't*** →Don't LET's do.

let's roll 試合[競技, 戦闘]を始めよう ▪ Are you guys ready? *Let's roll*. みんな, 用意はいいか? では, 始めよう.

to let 《英》(部屋・家などを)貸すための (＝《米》for RENT) ▪ We are looking for a house *to let* in Manchester. マンチェスターに貸家を探している ▪ *To let*. 貸家《張り札・広告》.

letter /létər/ 名 ***a bread-and-butter letter*** (訪問のあと出される)歓待のお礼の手紙, およばれの礼状 ▪ I got *a bread-and-butter letter* from my nephew. 甥っ子からおもてなしの礼状がとどいた.

a chain letter (同じ文面の手紙を次々に書き送る)連鎖の手紙, 幸運[不幸]の手紙 ▪ I received *a chain letter* asking me to mail $1 in cash to six people. 私は幸運の手紙を受けとったが, それは6人に現金で1ドル郵送することを要求するものだった.

a dead letter (住所不明などで)配達不能の手紙; 空文, 死文 ▪ *The dead letter* was opened to see if there was an address inside. その配達不能の封書は中に宛て先の住所が書いていないか開封して調べられた ▪ The Constitution of his country has become *a dead letter*. 彼の国の憲法は死文と化している.

a French letter 避妊用具, コンドーム ▪ *A French letter* will help protect you against AIDS. コンドームを使えばエイズの予防に役立つ.

a man of letters 学者; (今は通例)文学者 ▪ He is *a man of letters* teaching at Queens College. 彼はクイーンズ・カレッジで教えている学者だ ▪ Like his father and grandfather, he was *a man of letters*. 父や祖父と同じく, 彼も文学者であった.

according to the letter 字句どおりに ▪ He interpreted it *according to the letter*. 彼はそれを字句どおりに解釈した.

an open letter (要人への)公開状, 公開質問状 ▪ There was *an open letter* to the government in today's morning paper. 今朝の朝刊に政府への公開状が載っていた ▪ I read *an open letter* to the

President in the paper. 紙上で大統領への公開抗議文を読んだ.

be slow at** one's **letters (学問の)覚えが悪い ▪ He *is* very *slow at his letters*. 彼は学問の覚えが非常に悪い.

by letter 手紙で ▪ He let me know *by letter* that he had passed the examination. 彼は試験にパスしたと手紙で私に知らせてきた.

follow* [*hold to, keep to*] *the letter of the law 法文の字義に従う ▪ *Holding to the letter of the law*, the judge sentenced the prisoner to the maximum penalty. 法文の字義に従って, 裁判官は囚人に最大限の罰を宣告した.

in letter and in spirit/in spirit as well as in letter 形式実質ともに ▪ The two countries were actually allies *in letter and in spirit*. 両国は実は名実ともに同盟国であった.

keep within the letter of the law 文字通りに法に従う ▪ I have been very careful to *keep within the letter of the law*. きちんと法に従うように細心の注意を払ってきた.

The letter killeth, but the spirit giveth life. 文字は人を殺し霊は人を生かす (《聖》*2 Cor.* 3. 6) ▪ If it be said that *the letter killeth*, it is also true that the sound *giveth life*. 文字が人を殺すと言われているとすれば, 音は人を生かすというのもまた真である. ☞ 句の前半だけのこともある.

to the letter 字義どおりに, 厳密に ▪ Few motorists follow these rules *to the letter*. ドライバーのうちでこれらの規則を厳守する者はほとんどいない.

lettuce /létəs/ 名 ***as limp as last week's lettuce*** とても退屈な, 非常に不活発な ▪ Her male colleagues were all *as limp as last week's lettuce*. 彼女の男性の同僚は誰もみなまるで活気がない.

levant /ləvǽnt/ 名 ***come the levant/ run* [*throw*] *a levant*** 負けたら逃げるつもりでかけごとをする (*upon*) ▪ He has ventured to *come the levant upon* gentlemen. 彼は負けたら逃げるつもりで, 紳士たちに対して思い切ってかけをした ▪ Boldly *run a levant*. 負けたら逃げるつもりで思い切ってかけたまえ.

level[1] /lévəl/ 名形 ***(as) level as a die*** まっすぐな, 非常に正直な ▪ He is *as level as a die* and very reliable. 彼は実にまっすぐで頼りがいのある人だ.

***be laid level with the ground* [*in the dust*]** すっかり倒される, 焼きはらわれる ▪ The city *was laid level with the ground*. その市は焼き払われた.

***do* [*try*] *one's level best* (*to do*)** 《口》(…するために)できるだけの骨を折る, 最善を尽くす ▪ I'll *do my level best* during that time. その間にできるかぎり骨を折りましょう ▪ I'll *do my level best to* get you a ticket. 精一杯がんばってチケットを手に入れてあげよう.

drag* [*pull*] *a person down to one's level 人の(知的・道徳的)水準を自分の水準に下げる ▪ Never let them *drag* you *down to their level*. 決してあの連中に流されて自分を彼らのレベルに落としてはならない.

***draw level* (*with*)** (競争で…と)五分五分になる, 同点になる ▪ We *drew level with* them. 我々は彼らと同点になった ▪ They could not *draw level*, and were beaten by two to one. 彼らは同点になることができなくて, 1対2で負けた.

find one's (own) level 最も自分に適した地位[場所]に落ち着く ▪ Water *finds its (own) level*. 水は低きに流れて自然に落ち着く ▪ It was in vain to fret about it; and I soon *found my level*. それについてやきもきしてもむだだったので, 私はまもなく落ち着く所に落ち着いた.

have one's head level/have* [*keep*] *a level head 《口》(困難の際に)平然としている, 分別がある, 思慮を失わない ▪ He found it hard to *keep a level head* when his wife was nagging at him. 彼は妻ががみがみ言っているときに平然としているのは難しいと分かった.

level to …にとってとりつきやすい, にわかりやすい ▪ The task is *level to* our capacities. その仕事は我々の力量にかなっている ▪ Lincoln's English was *level to* his countrymen. リンカンの英語は彼の国の人々にわかりやすかった.

level with **1** …と水平に, と同じ高さに ▪ I filled the basin *level with* the brim. 私は洗面器になみなみとついだ ▪ The uprooted trees are lying *level with* the earth. 根こそぎにされた木々が地上に倒れている.

2 …と対等で, と肩を並べて ▪ I have done my best to keep *level with* the person next to me. 隣の人とずっと肩を並べられるよう最善を尽くした.

on a level playing field 公平な立場で, 同じ条件で ▪ We want to compete with others *on a level playing field*. 他と同じ土俵で公平に競いたい.

***on a level* (*with*)** **1** (…と)同一平面上に, と同じ高さに ▪ The water rose until it was *on a level with* the banks of the river. 川の堤と同じ高さになるまで増水した.

2 (…と)同等で, と対等で《社会的・知的・道徳的問題について》 ▪ Japan is *on a level with* Europe in civilization. 日本は文明においてはヨーロッパと対等だ.

on the level **1** 《口》公明正大な[に], 正直な[に] ▪ He is perfectly *on the level*. 彼は全く正直だ ▪ Are you kidding?—No, I'm *on the level*. あなた冗談なの?—いや, 僕は本気だよ ▪ The business is quite *on the level*. その取引は全く公正なものだ ▪ He made money completely *on the level*. 彼は全くまっとうに金を儲けた.

2 《口》公正に言って, 正直に言って ▪ *On the level*, I'm surprised at it. 正直に言って, 私はそれを聞いて驚いた.

3 穏健な, 適度の ▪ They formed a style more *on the level*. 彼らはもっと穏健な文体を作り出した. ☞ ↔on the CROSS.

on the same level 同じ水準に; 同じような位置に ▪ The opposite banks are not *on the same level*. 相対する堤防は同じ高さでない ▪ Their civil rights were not *on the same level*. 彼らの公民権

は同じ水準になかった.

sink to** a person's **level 人と同じように柄の悪いふるまいをする ▪ You will *sink to their level* when you get drunk. 君も酔っ払ったら彼ら並みに柄が悪くなるさ.

take a level **1**(水準儀による2点間の)高低測量をする ▪ We *took a level* and drew a line connecting the 2 marks. 水準儀による高低測量をし, 2点間を直線で結んだ.

2《通信・俗》(放送に先立って, 音量などの)レベルを決める ▪ There was no time to *take a level*. We started broadcasting live right away. 音量レベル調整の時間もなく, 直ちに生放送を開始した.

level[2] /lévəl/ 動 ***level** one's **aim** (**at, against**)* (…に)ねらいをつける, 照準を合わせる ▪ He *leveled his aim at* the bear's head. 彼はクマの頭にねらいを定めた.

level ... in the dust …を倒す, くずす ▪ The building *was leveled in the dust*. その建物は倒されてしまった ▪ His designs were to *level* some city *in the dust*. 彼の計画はある都市をこわしてしまうことだった.

level the playing field 機会を均等にする ▪ We should introduce new restrictions to *level the playing field*. 新しい機会均等法を採用すべきだ.

level ... to* [*with*] *the ground = LEVEL ... in the dust.

lever /lévər|lí:və/ 動 ***lever** oneself **out*** 努力[苦労]して立ち上がる ▪ The stout old woman *levered herself out* of the armchair. でっぷりした老婦人はどっこいしょと肘掛けいすから身を起こした.

lever** oneself **up 努力[苦労]して起き上がる ▪ The wounded man *levered himself up* from the floor. 負傷した男はやっとのことで床から立ち上がった.

levy[1] /lévi/ 名 ***the levy in mass*** (国・地方の)壮健な男子全員召集 ▪ *The levy in mass*, the telegraph, and the income tax are all from France. 壮健な男子の全員召集や電信機や所得税はみなフランスから来たものである.

levy[2] /lévi/ 動 ***levy execution for*** (金額など)を押収する ▪ He *levied execution for* £1,000. 彼は1,000ポンド押収した.

***levy service on* [*upon*]** …を徴用する, に奉仕を課す ▪ They willingly undertook the service which *was levied upon* them. 彼らは自分らに課された奉仕を進んで引き受けた.

***levy war on* [*upon*]** →make WAR on.

liability /làɪəbíləti/ 名 ***assume liability for*** …を支払う責任を負う ▪ My parents *assume liability for* all damage caused by me to others. 私が原因で他人に与えた損傷に対する賠償責任は両親が負う.

meet** one's **liabilities 負債を弁済する ▪ The company fully *met its liabilities* of loan repayment. その会社はローンの返済をいっさい弁済した.

liable /láɪəbəl/ 形 ***(be) liable for*** …に対して責任[義務]がある ▪ The employer *is liable for* the mistakes of his employees. 雇用主は従業員の過失に対して責任がある.

be liable to **1**(法律上)受けるべき[服すべき]である ▪ If you do such a thing, you will *be liable to* a fine. そんなことをすれば, あなたは罰金を払わねばならなくなる ▪ Everybody *is liable to* the law. 人はみな法律に服すべきである.

2(悪い事・不快な事を)受けがちである, かかりやすい, 陥りやすい ▪ This method *is liable to* an objection. このやり方をすれば反対を招きがちだ ▪ He *is liable to* malaria. 彼はマラリアにかかりやすい ▪ They *are liable to* this danger. 彼らはこのような危険に陥りやすい.

***be liable to** do* **1**(法律上)…する義務がある ▪ All Japanese youths *are liable to* serve in this movement. 全ての日本青年はこの運動に奉仕すべきだ.

2(好ましくないことを)しがちである ▪ All men *are liable to* err. 人はみな誤りをしがちである ▪ Difficulties *are liable to* occur. 困難は生じやすいものである.

3《米》…しそうである ▪ He *is liable to* call on me tonight. 彼は今夜私を訪ねて来そうだ.

liar /láɪər/ 名 ***A liar is not believed* (*even*) *when he tells* [*speaks*] (*the*) *truth.*** 《諺》嘘つきは本当のことを言っても信用されない, 「常が大事」. ☞イソップ寓話のオオカミが来たと言って人を騙した少年の話から.

I'm a liar. 《口》違った ▪ Last winter, was it? No, *I'm a liar*. This spring. 去年の冬だったかな. いや違った. この春だ.

Liars should have good memories. 《諺》嘘つきは記憶がよくなくてはならない《でなければ, 話のつじつまが合わなくなる》.

Show me a liar and I will show you a thief. 《諺》嘘は泥棒の始まり.

libel /láɪbəl/ 名 ***be a libel on*** …をはずかしめるものである, を誹謗するものである; の冒とくとなる ▪ This portrait *is a libel on* him. この肖像は彼を侮辱している《実物よりひどく悪い》 ▪ The book *is a libel on* human nature. その本は人間性を冒とくするものである.

liberal /líbərəl/ 形名 ***a bleeding-heart liberal*** 社会的弱者にやたらに同情する人物 ▪ The guy is very proud to be *a bleeding-heart liberal*. やつは弱者の味方だといって鼻高々だ.

***be liberal of* [*with*]** …を惜しまない, 気前よく出す ▪ He *is liberal of* his money for pleasure. 彼は楽しみのためには金を惜しまない ▪ He *is liberal with* his advice. 彼は助言を惜しまない.

liberty /líbərti/ 名 ***at liberty*** **1**(人が)暇で, 何もしていないで ▪ I shall be *at liberty* after midday. 正午以降は暇になります ▪ I have no doubt they will call; so be *at liberty* after twelve. 彼らはきっと来るから, 12時以降は何もせずにいなさい.

2(物が)使われないで, あいて ▪ There was a basin *at liberty*. 洗面器が一つあいていた.

3 解放されて, 禁固されて[捕われて]いないで ▪ He was not *at liberty* then. 彼はそのときは捕われていた.

***be at liberty to** do* 自由に…してよい, …することを

許されている ▪ You *are* quite *at liberty to* make use of this room. あなたはこの部屋を自由に使ってよい ▪ I'*m* not *at liberty to* tell you. 私はあなたにお話しすることは許されていません.

Liberty Hall 《主に戯》自由の館《勝手気ままにふるまえる場所》 ▪ This is *Liberty Hall.* ここでは無礼講ですよ. ☞無冠詞, 大文字で書く.

set ... at liberty …を解放[釈放]する; を自由にしてやる ▪ They *set* the prisoner *at liberty.* 彼らは囚人を釈放した.

***take liberties* (*with*)** **1** (…に)あまりになれなれしくする; 無礼なことをする; 《婉曲》(女性に)戯れる ▪ You must not *take liberties with* older people. あなたは年上の人々に失礼をしてはいけない ▪ Don't *take liberties* in this house. この家で勝手なふるまいをしてはならない ▪ He *took liberties with* my wife. 彼は私の妻にけしからぬふるまいをした.
2 (規則・事実を)勝手にいじくる[変える] ▪ He *takes* great *liberties with* the authors he translates. 彼は自分の翻訳する作家の作品を勝手にひどく変える.
3 (名声などを)傷つける ▪ He *took liberties with* my reputation. 彼は私の名声を傷つけた.

***take the liberty of* [*to* do]** 失礼ながら…する ▪ He *took the liberty to* call the nobleman bastard. 彼は失礼にもその貴族をこの野郎と呼んだ ▪ I *take the liberty of* addressing you. 失礼を顧みず一書を呈します. ☞動名詞が普通.

What a liberty! 《口》何て失礼な! ▪ *What a liberty!* He's taken my bike without asking my permission. 何て失礼なやつだ. あいつめ, 無断で僕の自転車に乗っていった.

license, licence /láɪsəns/ 名 ***a licence to print money*** 《主に英》(紙幣の印刷を許可されたように)大して努力せずに儲(もう)かる商売, ちょろい儲け話 ▪ Criminal activity cannot be *a licence to print money.* 犯罪行為がぼろ儲けになるはずがない.

artistic* [*poetic*] *license 《しばしば皮肉》芸術的自由, 詩的許容 ▪ A fair amount of *artistic license* has been taken in the book. その本ではかなり事実を曲げて扱っている ▪ A certain amount of *poetic license* is expected and required in scientific fiction. ある程度の詩的破格が空想科学小説にも期待され要求されている.

marry by license 許可証で結婚する ▪ Will you *marry by license*? あなたは許可証で結婚しますか.

under license 許可[認可]を受けて ▪ He did it *under license.* 彼は免許を受けてそれをした.

lick[1] /lɪk/ 名 ***a lick of paint*** (当座しのぎの)ペンキのひと塗り ▪ This door needs *a lick of paint.* このドアにはペンキをひと塗りする必要がある.

at a* (*fair*) *lick 《口》速いスピードで ▪ This dishwasher cleans plates *at a lick.* この食器洗い機ならあっという間にお皿がきれいになります.

at full* [*a great, quite a*] *lick 全速力で, 大急ぎで ▪ The ferry came down the river *at full lick.* 渡し船は全速力で川を下って来た ▪ He started off *at a great lick.* 彼は大急ぎで出発した.

get in a* [*one's*] *lick 《米口》大いに努力する, 活発に働く; 大いに作用する ▪ Her husband *got in his lick* and won the Senate seat. 彼女の夫は大いに努力して, 上院の議席を得た.

not ... a lick 《米口》ちっとも…しない ▪ He *can't* read *a lick.* 彼はちっとも字が読めない.

put in big* [*best, hard*] *licks 《米口》最大の努力をする; たゆまぬ努力をする ▪ It's a time for us to *put in big licks.* 我々が最大の努力をすべき時だ ▪ My dog came running to me *putting in* his *best licks.* 愛犬が全速力で私のところへとんできた.

lick[2] /lɪk/ 動 ***as hard as one could lick*** できるかぎり早く, できるかぎり急いで ▪ He ran down the road *as hard as* he *could lick.* 彼はできるかぎり速く走って道路を下って行った.

have* (*got*)*... licked 《口》困難な問題などをうまく解決する ▪ I think I'*ve* finally *got* this cold *licked.* やっとこの風邪が治ったようだ.

It licks me. →This LICKs me.

It's got me licked. 《俗》これには参った ▪ I've never seen anything like this. *It's got me licked.* こんなのは見たことがない. こいつは参った.

***lick a person's boots* [*shoe*]** 《口》人に屈従する; 人にぺこぺこする ▪ He'll have to *lick my boots.* 彼は私に屈従しなければならないだろう ▪ If you are a man of honor, do not *lick his boots.* 面目を重んじるなら, 彼にぺこぺこしてはいけません. ☞boots の代わりの arse は《卑》, spittle は《古風》.

***lick one's chops* [*fingers, lips*]** 《口》 **1** (食べたくて)舌なめずりをする ▪ I *licked my fingers* in anticipation of fine food. おいしいものが食べられると思って舌なめずりをした.
2 (おいしくて)舌鼓を打つ ▪ He was *licking his chops* over the novel. 彼は舌鼓を打つようにしてその小説を読んでいた.
3 将来のことを楽しみに待つ ▪ The kids, *licking their lips,* watched their mother cutting the cake. 子供たちは母親がケーキを切っているのをわくわくしながら見守った.

***lick creation* [*everything*]** 《口》何ものにも勝る, 比類がない ▪ The plan *licks creation.* その設計は比類のないものだ.

lick ... into fits …を完全に[さんざんに]負かす ▪ We shall *lick* our opponents *into fits.* 我々は相手をさんざんにやっつけるだろう.

lick ... into shape 《口》…を一人前に鍛える; を立派に仕上げる ▪ His indulgent parents will never *lick* him *into shape.* 彼の甘い両親では彼は決して一人前に鍛えられないだろう ▪ I'll *lick* your article *into shape* for you. 君の記事は僕がきれいに仕上げてあげるよ. ☞動物が子をなめてきれいにすることから.

lick the cub into shape 無作法者をしつける, 行儀を教える ▪ Send the boy to his school. He's the right man to *lick the cub into shape.* その少年を彼の学校へやりなさい. 彼こそ行儀を教える適任者だ.

lick the dust →bite the DUST.

lick the fat from* (*a person's*) *beard (人)の

利得をだまし取る ▪ They abhorred him for *licking the fat from their beards.* 自分らの利得をだまし取ったので, 彼らは彼を憎悪した.

lick the ground ひれ伏して屈従する ▪ Often he *licked the ground* whereon she trod. しばしば彼は彼女の歩いた地面をなめた《彼女にぺこぺこした》.

lick** one's **wounds 傷口をなめる; 敗北の痛みをかみしめる ▪ The boxer is *licking his wounds* now. そのボクサーは今敗北の痛みをかみしめている.

This* [*It*] *licks me. 《俗》これは私にはわからない ▪ *It licks me* how he did it. 彼がどうやってそれをしたのか私にはわからない.

licking /líkɪŋ/ 名 ***get* [*take*] *a licking*** 《米口》 **1** なぐられる; (ゲームに)負ける ▪ I *got* [*took*] *a* good *licking.* 私はさんざんなぐられた.

2 酷評される ▪ His latest novel *took a licking* from the critics, but it's selling well. 彼の最近の小説は批評家にはたたかれたが売れ行きは上々だ.

give** a person **a licking 《口》人をなぐる; (ゲームで)人を負かす ▪ I *gave* him *a* good *licking* at billiards. 私はビリヤードで彼をさんざん負かした.

lick-log /líklɔ̀ːg|-lɔ̀g/ 名 ***stand* (*up*) *to** one's **lick-log*** 《米口》(不愉快な義務などに)勇敢に堂々と立ち向かう ▪ I was determined to *stand up to my lick-log.* 私は勇敢に堂々と立ち向かう決心をした.

lid /lɪd/ 名 ***blow* [*take*] *the lid off*** **1** (...の)内幕を暴露する; (芝居の)幕をあける ▪ He is threatening to *blow the lid off* the city. 彼はその市の内幕を暴露するとおどしている ▪ Now the crowd *blew the lid off.* 今や群衆が幕をあけたのだ.

2 問題に直面する ▪ The best way to settle your feuds is to *take the lid off* of it. 君たちの反目を鎮める最良の方法はその根源と向き合うことだ.

clamp the* [*a*] *lid on ...を統制する, の取り締まりを厳にする ▪ They *clamped a lid on* information about military contracts. 彼らは軍需契約についての情報を統制した.

flip** one's **lid 《米俗》激怒する, 狂気になる, 爆発する ▪ Don't go *flipping your lid.* カッカしてはだめだ.

***put* [*keep*] *the* [*a*] *lid on* (*it*)** 《英口》 **1** (...を)終わらせる, (活動・計画を)中止する; (を)だめにする ▪ That'll *put the lid on* any chance of discussion. それで討議の機会はもうなくなるだろう ▪ The rain *put a lid on* fishing on Saturday. 雨のせいで土曜日の魚釣りはおじゃんになった ▪ That's *put the lid on* (*it*). それで万事終わりだ.

2 (...に)とどめをさす; (の)絶頂である; (の)すべてをしのぐ, 傑作をしでかす ▪ You *put the lid on it* when you asked her where her husband was. He's been in prison. 君が彼女に, ご主人はどこかと尋ねたときは傑作だった. ずっと刑務所なのだから.

3 《米》(...の)取締り(を)厳にする, (を)禁止する ▪ *The lid* has *been put on* gambling. とばくの取締りは厳にされている.

4 状況が悪くならないように(を)制御する, (情緒)を抑制する ▪ I've been trying to *keep a lid on* my emotions. このところ感情に流されないように努めている.

5 ...を秘密にする, (秘密を知られないように)ふたをする ▪ It's a surprise party, so try to *keep a lid on it.* サプライズパーティーだから誰にもしゃべったらだめだよ.

put the tin lid on =put the LID on (it) 1.

raise* [*lift*] *the lid on ...の統制[取締り]をはずす ▪ The government *raised the lid on* the newsprint ration. 政府は新聞用紙割当の統制をはずした.

take* [*lift*] *the lid off **1** ...を暴露する ▪ He *took the lid off* a nasty scandal. 彼はひどい汚職を暴露した.

2 ...の統制[取締り]をはずす ▪ *The lid was taken off* newsprint last year. 新聞用紙の統制は昨年はずされた.

The lid is* [*comes,* etc.] *off. 《米口》(...の)統制がはずれている[はずれる], (...の)取締りがゆるんでいる[ゆるむ] ▪ The Office of Price Administration's *lid came off* then. 物価管理局の統制がそのときはずれた ▪ *The lid was* constantly *getting off* her temper. 彼女は絶えずかんしゃくを起こしていた.

with the lid off 《口》 **1** 統制をはずして ▪ I'll back that opinion *with the lid off.* 私はその意見を無条件に支持する.

2 内幕[いやな点, 欠点など]をさらけ出したままで ▪ Writing about life *with the lid off* is much more interesting than otherwise. 赤裸々な生活を書くほうが, そうでない場合よりもはるかにおもしろい.

lie[1] /laɪ/ 名 ***a big lie*** 《口》事実を偽って伝えること, (政治団体などの)デマ宣伝, はったり ▪ *A big lie* is said to work if it is repeated often enough. デマ宣伝も数打てば効果があがるといわれている.

A lie hath no feet. 《諺》嘘は一人では立てない《多数の嘘に支えられねばならない》.

a lie with a latchet 全くの嘘, 真っ赤な嘘 ▪ I hate you. Nope, that's *a lie with a latchet.* おまえなんか大嫌い. いや, そいつは真っ赤な嘘だ.

a whacking* [*thumping, whopping*] *lie 真っ赤な嘘, 大ぼら ▪ Joe tried to win Jill's heart with *one whopping lie* after another. ジョーは次々に大嘘を並べてジルのハートを射止めようと努めた.

a white lie 悪意のない[方便の]嘘 ▪ I told her you were not at home; it was *a white lie.* 私は彼女にあなたは留守だと言った, それは方便の嘘だったのだ.

act a lie (口でなく)行為で人をだます ▪ Did he tell a lie or *act a lie*? 彼は嘘を言ったのか, それとも行為でだましたのか.

give** a person **the lie =give the LIE to 1.

give the lie to **1** 嘘を言ったと...を面責する ▪ They *gave the lie to* each other. 彼らは互いに嘘を言ったと言って面責し合った.

2 (事実・行為などが)...の偽りであることを証明する; (事実などが)...にそむいている ▪ His replies *gave the lie to* his pretended superior knowledge. 彼の返事は彼のふれこみの博学が嘘であることを証明した ▪ His acts *give the lie to* his words. 彼の行為は言葉と矛盾している.

I tell a lie. =I'm a LIAR.

L

live a lie 虚偽の生活をする ▪ As she no longer loved her husband, she felt that she was *living a lie*. 彼女はもう夫を愛していなかったので, 偽りの生活をしているような気がした.

nail a lie 《英・報道》誤りだという証拠を突きつける, 嘘だと暴く ▪ This is how you definitely *nail a lie*. 誤りの証拠をはっきり突きつけるには次のようにする ▪ That's *a lie* the witness told which we have *nailed*. それは目撃者がついた嘘で我々が暴いたものだ.

peddle lies 虚偽の噂を吹聴する, 嘘を言いふらす ▪ They distorted facts and *peddled lies* about asylum seekers. 彼らは亡命者たちについて事実に反する噂を流した.

take the lie 嘘を言ったという非難をそのまま受ける ▪ He would not *take the lie*. 彼は嘘を言ったという非難を受け入れようとしなかった.

tell a lie [***lies***] 嘘を言う ▪ I think she *told a lie*. 彼女は嘘を言ったのだと思う ▪ It's wrong to *tell lies*. 嘘を言うのはよくない. ☞1回の嘘にも lies を使うことがある.

lie[2] /laɪ/ 名 ***have a lie down*** 横になる, 寝ころがる ▪ I think I'll go and *have a lie down*. 私は行って寝ころがろうと思う.

the lie of the land →LAND[1].

lie[3] /laɪ/ 動 ***lie*** *one's* ***head off*** 盛んに嘘をつく ▪ I've seen him *lie his head off*. 彼が盛んに嘘をつくのを見てきた.

lie in [***through***] *one's* ***teeth***/ ***lie in*** *one's* ***throat*** 白々しい嘘をつく ▪ He was *lying in his teeth* when he told me he didn't know you. 君のことを知らないと彼が言ったのは, 白々しい嘘だった.

lie like a gamester [***a lawyer***] 全くの嘘を言う ▪ Don't pay attention to anything he says; he *lies like a gamester*. 彼の言うことを何も聞いてはいけません. 彼は真っ赤な嘘を言うから.

lie like a gas-meter とてつもない嘘を言う ▪ I don't believe you; you *lie like a gas-meter*. おまえの言うことなんか信じるものか, この大嘘つきめ. ☞ガスメーターはとかく不正確なことから.

lie *oneself* ***out of*** 嘘を言って...を脱する ▪ He *lied himself out of* a difficulty. 彼は嘘を言って難局を逃れた ▪ He managed to *lie himself out of* trouble. 彼は何とか嘘を言ってうまく罰を逃れた.

lie[4] /laɪ/ 動 ***all that in*** *one* ***lies***/ ***all that lies in*** *one's* ***power*** 力の及ぶかぎり ▪ Napoleon did *all that lay in his power* to prosper. ナポレオンは栄えるため力の及ぶかぎりを尽くした.

as far as in *one* ***lies*** 力の及ぶかぎり ▪ He resolved, *as far as in* him *lay*, to root out the Christian faith. 彼は力の及ぶかぎり, キリスト教を根絶しようと決心した.

lie around loose 《米》散らかった[ほったらかされた]状態にある ▪ Don't make things *lie around loose*. ものを散らかしてはいけない.

lie close 隠れている; 寄りかたまっている ▪ *Lie close* here. ここに隠れていなさい.

lie down on the job 《口》仕事を怠ける ▪ They are deliberately *lying down on the job*. 彼らは故意に仕事を怠けているのだ.

lie heavy on →HEAVY.

lie low [《英口》***doggo***] →LOW; DOGGO.

lie out of *one's* ***money*** [***due***] 金を支払われないでいる[受くべきものを受けないでいる] ▪ I can't *lie out of my money* any longer. 私はもうこれ以上金を払ってもらわずにはいられない.

take ... lying down 〚主に否定文で〛おとなしく(罰など)を受ける, (屈辱など)を甘んじて受ける ▪ They *took* every inconvenience *lying down*. 彼らはあらゆる不便をおとなしく受けた ▪ I won't *take* such treatment *lying down*. そんな仕打ちをされて黙っているものか.

lief /liːf/ 副 ***had*** [***have***] ***as lief*** *do* (***as***)/ ***had liefer*** *do* (***than***)/ ***would as lief*** *do* (***as***)/ ***would liefer*** *do* (***than***) (より)...したほうがましだ(と思う) ▪ I *had as lief* go to town tomorrow *as* stay here. ここへとどまるよりはむしろあす町へ行ったほうがましだ.

lie-in /láɪìn/ 名 ***have a lie-in*** 《英口》朝寝坊する ▪ I haven't *had a lie-in* since I had my child. この子ができてからは朝寝坊もできない.

lieu /ljuː/ 名 ***in lieu*** その代わりに ▪ God will not give us the thing we desire, but a better *in lieu*. 神は我々の望むものを与え給わず, その代わりにもっとよいものを与え給う.

in lieu of **1** ...の代わりに ▪ They had a durable stone building *in lieu of* a perishable wooden one. 彼らはこわれやすい木造の代わりに長もちのする石造の建物を建てた.

2 (支払いなどで)...と交換に, の返礼[返報]として ▪ £7 should be paid to Jane Watson *in lieu of* her money and clothes. 金と衣服の返礼としてジェイン・ワトスンに7ポンド支払うべきである.

life /laɪf/ 名 ***a bad life*** 《保険》長命の見込みのない人 (→a good LIFE) ▪ The insurance company regarded him as *a bad life*. 保険会社は彼を長命の見込みのない人物とみなした.

a Bohemian life (作家・画家に多い)陋習(ろうしゅう)に囚われない自由奔放な生活様式 ▪ He missed his *Bohemian life* in Vienna. 彼はウィーンでの奔放な生活を懐かしんだ.

a charmed life いつもついている人生, 不死身 ▪ Dick got off without a scratch; he seems to lead *a charmed life*. ディックはかすり傷ひとつ負わなかった. よほどついているようだ.

a cushy life 安楽な生き方, 贅沢な生活 ▪ He enjoys *a cushy life* with parents as rich as that. あれほど大金持ちの親のおかげで彼は贅沢に暮らしている.

a good life 《保険》(危険がなく)少なくとも平均余命は生きる見込みの人 (→a bad LIFE) ▪ He believes himself to be *a good life*. 彼は自分は少なくとも平均余命は生きる見込みがあると信じている.

a high-profile life 世人の注目を集める生活 ▪ His *high-profile life* is getting me down, honest! 彼の派手な生き方にはうんざりだ, まったく!

(*a matter of*) *life and* [*or*] *death* 生きるか死ぬかの問題; きわめて重大な問題 ▪ The decision of the judge will be *a matter of life and death* to the prisoner. 裁判官の判決は被告にとっては死活問題であろう ▪ It's *life or death* to me. それは私にとって死活問題なんです.

a short life and a merry (***one***) 短くても楽しい人生 ▪ I would prefer *a short life and a merry one*. 僕は太く短い人生の方がいい.

a still life (絵画の)静物 ▪ Claude Monet's most famous *still lifes* are his Water Lilies series. クロード・モネの最も有名な静物画は睡蓮(すいれん)の連作である.

after [***from***] ***the life*** 生きたモデルにより, 写生の ▪ He was drawing a figure *after the life*. 彼は人物を写生していた.

all *one's* ***life*** 一生涯, 終生; 今までずっと ▪ He lived *all his life* in London. 彼は終生ロンドンに住んだ ▪ He has been studying English *all his life*. 彼は今までずっと英語を研究してきた.

another of life's little ironies →(one of) LIFE's little ironies.

as I have life 確かに (surely) ▪ *As I have life*, it's all a trick. そいつは間違いなく全くのぺてんだ.

(***as***) ***large*** [《米》***big***] ***as life*** (***and twice as natural***) **1** 実物大で ▪ The statue of the late mayor is *big as life*. 故市長の銅像は等身大である ▪ The projection TV is almost *as big as life*. その投影型テレビはほとんど実物大に映し出す.
2 《戯》正真正銘の, まごうかたなき…そのもの ▪ Here he is, *as large as life*. 彼が自らやって来ている ▪ He marched up and down like a peacock, *as large as life and twice as natural*. 彼は全くのクジャクそのもののように行ったり来たりした. ☞and twice as natural をつけた形は強意.

attempt [***seek***] ***the life of*** …の暗殺を企てる, 命をねらう ▪ He *attempted the life of* the Prime Minister. 彼は首相の暗殺を企てた.

be all life 生き生きしている, 元気いっぱいである ▪ She *is all life* and gladness. 彼女は非常に快活でにこにこしている.

be *a person's* ***life*** 人の最も大切な人物[物, 事] ▪ My children *are my life*. 子供たちが私の命です ▪ Gardening *is his life*. 庭いじりが彼の生きがいだ.

be tried for *one's* ***life*** 死刑犯として裁判を受ける ▪ The man was *being tried for his life*. その男は死刑犯として裁判を受けていた.

begin [***enter***] ***life*** 実社会に出る ▪ The disadvantage of *entering life* without money is great. 一文なしで実社会に出るのは非常に不利である.

between life and death 生死の境で ▪ The child lay all night *between life and death*. その子は一晩中生死の間をさまよった.

breathe life into …に生気を吹き込む, を活発にする ▪ He'll *breathe life into* the party. 彼はパーティーに花を咲かせてくれるだろう.

bring ...(***back***) ***to life*** **1** …を生き返らせる ▪ They used artificial respiration to *bring* the swimmer *back to life*. 彼らはその溺れた人を生き返らせるため人工呼吸を用いた.
2 (人・物)を活気づかせる ▪ His direction *brought* the play *to life*. 彼の監督でそのドラマは生き生きしたものとなった.

burst into life 突然復活する ▪ The desert suddenly *burst into life* after the recent shower. 最近の降雨のあと砂漠に再び生命があふれた.

cannot ...for the life of *one* どうしても…できない ▪ I *cannot for the life of* me remember where it was. それがどこであったかどうしても思い出せない. ☞「命を取ると言われても」が原義.

can't [***won't***] *do* ***to save*** *one's* ***life*** 《口》全く…できない[しない] ▪ I *can't* remember her name *to save my life*. どうしても彼女の名前を思い出せない ▪ He *won't* touch liver *to save his life*. 彼は全くレバーを食べようとしない.

carry [***take***] *one's* ***life in*** *one's* ***hands*** 命がけの冒険生活をする, あぶない綱渡りをする ▪ We can imagine how he *carried his life in his hands*. 彼がいかに命がけの冒険生活をしたかを想像することができる ▪ The railway man must at times *take his life in his hands*. 鉄道員は時にはあぶない綱渡りをしなければならない.

choke the life out of →CHOKE.

cling to life 生き続けようと八方手を尽くす ▪ She was rushed to hospital with serious injuries and is still *clinging to life*. 彼女は重傷を負って病院に急送され, 生きようとまだ必死に闘っている.

come back to life =come to LIFE 1.

come into *a person's* ***life*** 人にとって重要な人物になる ▪ Offer up this prayer right now and Our Lord will *come into your life*. 今この祈りを捧げれば主キリストが今後あなたに大切な存在となるでしょう.

come to life **1** 生き返る ▪ Everyone thought he was drowned, but he *came to life*. みんな彼は溺死したと思ったが息を吹き返した.
2 (人・物が)生き生きしてくる, 活気づいてくる ▪ She *came to life* at a dance. 彼女はダンスパーティーで生き生きするのだった.

depart (***from***) ***this life*** この世を去る ▪ He has *departed from this life* at last. 彼はついにこの世を去った. ☞特に, 墓碑銘に用いられる.

end *one's* ***life*** **1** (…の状態で)晩年を過ごす (*in*) ▪ He lost popular support and *ended his life in* poverty. 彼はみなから見放されて晩年を赤貧で過ごした.
2 自殺する ▪ He *ended his life* after posting his will. 彼は遺書を投函してから自殺した.

enter life →begin LIFE.

eternal life 《婉曲》永遠の生命, 死後の生活 ▪ Granny is at rest in *eternal life*. おばあちゃんはあの世で安らかに眠っている.

fight for *one's* ***life*** 生死をさまよう ▪ The boy was *fighting for his life* last night but is out of danger now. 少年は昨夜生死をさまよっていたが今は峠を越している.

follow a double life [***two lives***] → lead a

L

double LIFE.

do ***for dear life*** 必死で…する ▪ I saw a man hanging on to a suspension bridge *for dear life*. 男の人が必死で吊り橋にしがみついているのが目にとまった.

for life **1** 終身の, 一生の ▪ They granted him a pension *for life*. 彼らは彼に終身年金を与えた ▪ He has become a cripple *for life*. 彼は一生身体が不自由になった.

2 =for one's LIFE 1.

for *one's* [***dear, very***] ***life*** 命がけで, 必死になって, 命を救うために ▪ They ran *for dear life*. 彼らは命からがら逃げた ▪ I worked *for my life*. 私は必死になって働いた.

for [***of***] ***my life*** =upon my LIFE.

for the life of *one* 〚否定文で〛どうしても(…ない) ▪ I can't *for the life of* me recall his name. どうしても彼の名前が思い出せない.

for two [***three,*** etc.] ***lives*** 2人[3人, など]のうち最長生者の一生涯にわたって ▪ We obtained a pension of five thousand pounds a year *for two lives*. 夫婦のうち長命する方の年額5,000ポンドの終身年金が認められた.

frighten [***scare***] ***the life out of*** *a person* 人を驚愕させる[怖がらせる] ▪ She *frightened the life out of* me, shouting all of a sudden. 彼女が急に叫んだのでぎょっとした.

from the life →after the LIFE.

full of life 生き生きして, 張り切って; 元気で ▪ Why is he so *full of life* today? 彼はなぜ今日はあんなに張り切っているのか.

Get a life! 《口》まじめに生きろ, 夢からさめよ ▪ Don't just sit around here all day and complain. *Get a life!* 一日中ここにただ座ってぶつぶつ言ってはだめじゃないか. しっかりしろ!

get a life 《口》 **1** 楽しむ, もっと充実した生活を始める ▪ You can *get a life*—in spite of everything. 君は楽しむことができる—いろんなことがあるにしても ▪ Too bad my husband is dead, but at long last I can try to *get a life*. 夫が亡くなったのは残念だけど, これでやっと自分のために生きられるわ.

2 違った生活[こと]をする, 自分の殻から出る, 誰かの言いなりにならない ▪ I need to leave home and *get a life*. 家を出て違った生活をする必要がある.

get *one's* ***life back*** (嫌な仕事をやめて)全く新しい楽しいことをする ▪ I've *got my life back* at last and I'm so happy! やっと楽しい仕事が見つかってとてもうれしい.

give life to …に活気をつける ▪ He *gave life to* the enterprise. 彼はその事業に活気を添えた.

give *a person* ***the time of*** *his* ***life*** 人にこの上なく楽しく過ごさせる ▪ We had a great time and *gave* them *the time of their life*. 我々も大いに楽しみ, 彼らにもこの上なく楽しく過ごさせた.

God's life. =upon my LIFE.

hang on to life かろうじて生きて[命を取り留めて]いる ▪ After that terrible accident, she is still *hanging on to life*. あの大事故のあと彼女は依然として危篤状態である.

have a good life →lead a good LIFE.

have a life of its own (物が)ひとりでに動く(→take on a LIFE of its own) ▪ Jumping beans seem to *have a life of their own*. トビマメはひとりでに動くみたいだ《中にいる蛾の幼虫の動きで踊る》.

have the life of Riley →live the LIFE of Riley.

have the time of *one's* ***life*** →TIME[1].

How has life been treating you? 調子はどうだ? ▪ *How has life been treating you?*—Fine, thanks, and how's the world treating you? 元気かい?—ありがとう, 元気だ. そっちはどうだい?

How's life? いかがですか ▪ *How's life?*—Not too bad. 元気かい—まあまあだよ.

in early [***later***] ***life*** 若いころに[晩年に] ▪ His father came to Canada *in early life*. 彼の父親は若いころにカナダに来た ▪ Does domestic violence lessen *in later life*? 晩年には家庭内暴力は減るか.

in life **1** 存命中, 生前; 生涯中 ▪ He was a Buddhist *in life*. 彼は生前仏教徒であった ▪ He married early *in life*. 彼は早く結婚した.

2 この世で[の] ▪ He has got a chance *in life*. 彼は出世の機会を得た ▪ I owe you everything *in life*. 私の今日あるは何から何まであなたのおかげです.

3 〚all, no などを強調して〛全く, ほんとに ▪ I will come with *all* the pleasure *in life*. 私は大喜びで参ります ▪ He owns *nothing in life*. 彼は全く何も持っていない.

in *one's* ***life*** **1** 〚否定文で〛生まれてから, 一生のうち ▪ I have never seen an elephant *in my life*. 生まれてからまだゾウを見たことがない.

2 一生のうちで ▪ It was the happiest time *in his life*. それは彼の一生のうちで最も幸福な時であった.

in real life (小説・映画の中ではない)現実では, 実生活では ▪ No women wear such hats *in real life*. 現実ではそんな帽子をかぶる女性はいない.

It's a great life (***if you don't weaken***). 《皮肉》(へこたれなければ)立派な人生だ《これは困ったことになった》 ▪ She said, "*It's a great life if you don't weaken*," and was determined not to. 「へこたれなければ立派な人生だわ」と彼女は言い, へこたれまいと意を固めていた.

know life **1** 世故に長(た)けている《社交・礼儀などに通じている》 ▪ With thirty years of experience in the business world, he *knows life* very well. 実業界で30年の経験があり, 彼は実に世故に長けている.

2 世の中を知る《世間のずるさ, せちがらさを》 ▪ He may learn to *know life* a bit. 彼は少し世の中を知るようになるかもしれない.

larger than life →LARGE[1].

lay down *one's* ***life for*** …のために命を捨てる (《聖》*John*. 15. 13) ▪ I'll *lay down my life for* the country. 私は国のために命を捨てよう.

lead a bad life 不品行である, 罪悪を事とする ▪ He is still *leading a bad life*. 彼はまだ品行の悪い生活をしている.

***lead* [*live, follow*] *a double life* [*two lives*]** (特に秘かに)二重生活をする ▪ It was almost unimaginable that the respectable man was *leading a double life.* あの立派な人が二重生活をしていたということは想像もつかないくらいだった.

lead* [*have*] *a good life 品行方正である; 幸福である ▪ Can I look back on my deathbed and say I *led a good life*? 今わの際に振り返って, 品行方正な人生を歩んだと言えるだろうか ▪ I think I have *had a good life.* 私はこれまで幸福であったと思う.

lead *a person* ***a life*** 人に心配をかける, 人を苦しめる ▪ The boy *leads* one *a life* with his stupid tricks. その少年はばかないたずらをして人に心配をかける.

lead* [*live*] *a ... life 〚life の前に形容詞を伴って〛...な生活をする ▪ He *lives an* idle *life.* 彼は何もせずのらくらして暮らしている.

life after death 来世 ▪ Do you believe in *life after death*? 来世の存在を信じますか.

life and limb 生命身体 ▪ Fire fighters risk *life and limb* to put out a fire. 消防士は生命身体をかけて消火に当たる ▪ It was a risk [danger, threat] to *life and limb.* それは生命身体を脅かすものであった. ☞無冠詞.

***Life begins at forty* [*sixty,* etc.].** 人生は40 [60, など]から始まる ▪ Maybe it's true that *life begins at 60.* 真の人生は60から始まるというのは本当だろう.

life for life 命には命を ▪ Should we give *life for life* if we cause a person to die? 自分のせいで人が死んだら, おのれの命で償わなくてはならないだろうか.

Life goes on. (悲しい出来事に)それでも人生は続く ▪ In face of death and despair, *life goes on.* 死と絶望に直面しても人生は続いていく.

life in a goldfish* [*fish*] *bowl プライバシーが全く保証されない境遇 ▪ The movie star says she is used to her *life in the goldfish bowl.* その映画スターは衆人環視のもとにさらされたような生活にも慣れたと言っている.

life in the fast lane →LANE.

life is cheap 人の命が重要でない, 人命を軽んじる ▪ *Life is cheap* in those areas. あの一帯では人が殺されても平気でいる.

Life is hell. 人生は地獄だ《特定の不愉快な事件について言う》 ▪ *Life is hell* on wet Sundays. 雨降りの日曜日は人生地獄だね.

Life is* (*just*) *a bowl of cherries. 《諺》人生は万事うまくいく,「人生は良いことずくめ」. ☞反語的に使われることがあり, Life isn't (just) a bowl of cherries.「人生は楽しいことばかりではない」という諺もある.

One ***life is lost.*** 死者は一人である ▪ Two *lives were lost.* 死者は二人だった.

Life is short and time is swift. 《諺》人生は長くは続かないので, できる限りそれを享受すべきだ.

life is too short (そんなくだらないことをするには)人生は短すぎる (*for, to do*) ▪ *Life is too short for* vain regrets [*to* find fault with others]. むなしく後悔するには[人のあら捜しをするには]人生は短すぎる.

life is worth living 人生は生きる値打ちがある ▪ I don't think *life is worth living* without music. 音楽がなければ人生は生きる値打ちがないと思う.

Life with a capital L 人生の機微 ▪ Studying philosophy will tell you something about *Life with a capital L.* 哲学の研究は人生の何たるかを教えてくれるだろう.

live *one's* **(*own*) *life*** 自分勝手に生きる ▪ At home you can't *live your own life.* 家庭では自分勝手に生きるなんてできない.

live* [*have, lead*] *the life of Riley 《口》金や仕事の心配をせず楽しく過ごす, 極楽トンボの生活を送る ▪ It was like paradise. It was just like *living the life of Riley.* 天国みたいな, つまり贅沢で気ままな暮らしだった. ☞1919年の流行歌から.

lose *one's* ***life*** 命を落とす, 死ぬ ▪ He *lost his life* in the accident. 彼はその事故で命を落とした.

make a life 自活する ▪ It must be hard to *make a life* in Los Angeles. ロサンジェルスで自活するのはきっと大変だろう.

make (*a person's*) ***life a misery*** 《主に英》(人の)生活を苦痛の日々にする; (人の)人生をみじめにする ▪ My husband has *made my life a misery.* 夫のために私の人生はみじめになった ▪ She was a very naughty girl and *made her mother's life a misery.* 彼女は極端に行儀の悪い子で母親の生活を悲惨なものにした.

make life difficult* (*for *a person*) (人の)悩みの種になる, やっかいごとを起こす ▪ His son *makes life difficult for* him. 彼の息子は親の悩みの種になっている.

make life hell for *a person* 人の人生を地獄にする, 人をひどい目にあわせる ▪ I'm determined to *make life hell for* him. 彼をひどい目にあわせてやるつもりだ.

Never in my life! **1** 今までに一度もない ▪ Did I ever see the like of it? *Never in my life.* そんなのを見たことがあるかって? これまで一度もないよ.
2 二度といやだ, とんでもない ▪ Never will I go to that restaurant again! *Never in my life.* あのレストランにはもう行くものか. 二度とごめんだ.

not ... on your* (*sweet*) *life 《口》全く...ない, 決して...ない ▪ Has there been any gambling during the trip?—*Not on your life.* 旅行中ギャンブルしたか?—とんでもない ▪ *Not on your life* will I foot the bill. おれは絶対に勘定は払わないぞ.

not ... to save *one's* ***life*** 《口》どうしても...できない ▪ I could *not* help laughing *to save my life.* どうしても笑わずにはいられなかった.

of *one's* ***life*** 生まれてこの方経験したことのないような, 大変な ▪ He had the shock *of his life.* 彼は大変なショックを受けた.

(*one* [*another*] *of*) *life's little ironies* 人生の小さな皮肉(の一つ) ▪ It is *one of life's little ironies* that vegetarians take in more calcium than meat eaters. 菜食者の方が肉食者よりもカルシウムの摂取量が多いというのは, 人生の小さな皮肉の一つだ.

pay with** one's **life 何かのために命を落とす ▪ I am happy to *pay with my life* for my sins. 自分が犯した罪を喜んで私の命で償います.

pick up** one's **life まともな生活に戻る ▪ He got out of prison and started to *pick up his life* again. 彼は出獄し, また元のちゃんとした生活を始めた.

put** one's **life in** a person's **hands 人に自分の命を預ける ▪ Once you get into hospital, you *put your life in the hands of* strangers. 一旦入院したら生かすも殺すも他人任せになる.

put** one's **life on hold 万事がうまくいくのを待つ ▪ Accept this job. It's no use *putting your life on hold*. この仕事を受けろよ. すべてがうまくいくのを待っていてもむだだから.

***put** one's **life on the line** (**for**)* (...のために)命を賭ける ▪ Firefighters often *put their lives on the line* trying to save others. 消防士は人を救助しようとして自分の命を危険にさらすことが多い ▪ Of course I would *put my life on the line for* my family. もちろん私の家族のためなら命を賭けよう.

put some life into it 《口》もっと精力的に活動する ▪ You must *put some life into it*. 君はもっと精力的に活動しなければならない.

risk life and limb 危険を冒す, 命を賭ける ▪ He has been *risking life and limb* as a race car driver. 彼はカーレーサーとして危険と隣り合わせの生活を送ってきた ▪ Fire-fighters *risk life and limb* in their work. 消防士は命がけで消火に当たる.

safe in life and limb 生命身体に別条なく ▪ He got home *safe in life and limb*. 彼は生命身体に別条なく帰宅した.

save** one's **life 生命を全うする ▪ You have *saved your life*. あなたは生命を全うした.

scare the life out of (人を)ぎょっとさせる, 怖がらせる ▪ She *scared the life out of* me when she shouted in my ear from behind. 彼女が後ろから耳元にワッと叫んだので心臓が止まるかと思った.

see life **1** 世間を知る ▪ He has *seen* nothing of *life*. 彼は世間をちっとも知らない ▪ I was dying to *see* a little of *life*. 世間を少し見たくてたまらなかった. **2** 遊楽の世界に出入する ▪ Do you want to *see life* in Phuket's best spas? プーケットの最高級の温泉で遊蕩にひたりたいと思うか.

see life whole 人生を全体的に見る ▪ The duty of the artist is to *see life whole*. 芸術家の務めは人生をまるごと見ることにある.

seek the life of →attempt the LIFE of.

***sell** one's **life dear** [**dearly**]* →SELL².

set for life 残りの生涯を食うに困らない, 一生左うちわで暮らせる ▪ If only I win the lottery, I will be *set for life*. 宝くじが当たりさえすれば, 死ぬまで遊んで暮らせるが.

spring to life →SPRING².

Such is life. →SUCH.

take life 活気[生気]を呈する ▪ When the band struck up, the party *took life*. バンドが演奏を始めると, パーティーは活気を呈してきた.

take** a person's **life 《文》...を殺す ▪ No one has the right to *take another's life*. 人を殺す権利は誰にもない ▪ You have no right to *take the life of* another. あなたに他人を殺す権利はない.

take** one's **life in** [**into**] one's (**own**) **hands 《口》(愚かにも)危険なまねをする ▪ If he drives, you'll be *taking your life in your hands*. 彼が運転するのなら, こっちはいつ死ぬやらわからないぜ.

take on a life of its own (事柄・機械が)ひとりでに[勝手に]動き始める; もはや誰にも制御できない ▪ Part of what I said got picked up by the media and *took on a life of its own*. 私の発言の一部がマスコミに取り上げられて独り歩きした ▪ The sport soon *took on a life of its own* there. そのスポーツはやがて自然にその地に普及していった ▪ Once a rumor starts, it *takes on a life of its own*. いったんうわさが立つと, もはや誰にも制御できない ▪ When he is painting, the brush *takes on a life of its own*. 彼が描いているときは絵筆が勝手に動く.

take** one's **own life 自殺する ▪ He *took his own life* in the woods. 彼は森で自殺した.

That's life./Life's like that. 人生ってそういうものだ《軽いあきらめの言葉》 ▪ The struggles and pain, *that's life*. 苦闘と苦痛, それが人生というものだ ▪ Your children soon grow up and they don't need you. Yes, *life's like that*. 子供たちはじきに大きくなって親なんかいらなくなる. そう, それが人生さ. ☞F C'est la vie! のなぞり.

the high life 上流社会の贅を尽くした生活 ▪ She has been living *the high life* in Beverly Hills since she retired. 彼女は引退後ずっとビバリーヒルズで贅沢な生活をしている.

the life and soul of 《口》...の活気の源 ▪ He is always *the life and soul of* any gathering he is in. 彼はいつも彼の加わる集会の活気の源である ▪ Ballets incidental to the piece are *the* very *life and soul of* the play. 劇に付随するバレエがその劇の花だ.

the life (《英口》 ***and soul***) ***of the party*** 《米口》(持ち前の明るさと愛想の良さで)パーティーを盛り上げる人, 一座の花, 一行の花形 (→the LIFE and soul of) ▪ He was having a good time and was clearly *the life and soul of the party*. 彼は楽しいひとときを過ごしており, 明らかに場の盛り上げ役だった ▪ Bob was always *the life of the party* in college. ボブは大学時代ずっと仲間内の花形だった.

the low life 下層の人たちの卑しい暮らしぶり ▪ I can't stand such *a low life* any more. もうこれ以上こんな卑しい暮らしには耐えられない.

the man [***woman***] ***in** one's **life*** 《口》自分の結婚[交際]相手の男性[女性] ▪ Mike is going to be *the man in my life*. 私はマイクと結婚します.

the power [***right***] ***of life and*** [***or***] ***death*** 生殺与奪の権 ▪ Ancient kings held *the power of life and death* over their people. 古代の王は人民に対して生殺与奪の権を握っていた.

the struggle for life →the STRUGGLE for existence.

L

There's life in the old dog yet. 老骨, まだくたばってはいないぞ《老人にはとてもできないと他人[自分]が思っていたことをしたとき使う》 ▪ "I'm an old man now," says Tom, but it's clear *there's life in the old dog yet.* 「もう年だから」とトムは言うが, どうみても, まだくたばってはいない.

This is the life. これこそ人生だ《満足の言葉》 ▪ Everyone you know agrees. *This is the life.* 君の知人は賛成してくれている. これが人生というものだ.

through (***the whole course of*** *one's*) ***life*** 生涯(を通じて), 終生 ▪ He was a bachelor *through life.* 彼は生涯独身であった.

to the life 生き写しに, 真に迫って, 寸分たがわず ▪ That portrait is you *to the life.* その肖像画は全くあなたにそっくりだ ▪ A murder was acted *to the life* in the tragedy. その悲劇で殺人が真に迫って演ぜられた.

true to life →TRUE.

turn *one's* ***life upside down*** 生活を180度変える ▪ A big win on the lottery will *turn their lives upside down.* 宝くじで大当たりすれば彼らの生活は一変するだろう.

upon *one's* ***life*** 殺人罪に問われて ▪ He is in the court *upon his life.* 彼は殺人罪に問われて裁判を受けている.

upon [***on, 'pon***] ***my life*** 誓って, ほんとに; きっと; これは驚いた ▪ *Upon my life*, you are an amazing person. ほんとに, 君はすばらしい人物だ ▪ *Upon my life*, it is true. 誓ってそれは本当だ.

What a life! なんたる人生ぞ《やれやれ, 情けない》 ▪ Not much hope for business now. Boy, *what a life!* 商売はまずお先真っ暗だ. いやはや, なんとも情けない.

While there is life, there is hope. 《諺》命さえあれば望みもある,「命あっての物種」. ☞[L] dum spiro, spero のなぞり.

with bare life 命からがら ▪ He escaped *with bare life.* 彼は命からがら逃れた.

with *one's* ***life*** **1** 命からがら ▪ He escaped *with his life.* 彼は命からがら逃げた.
2 命をかけて, きっと ▪ I will answer for it *with my life.* それは命をかけて保証します.

with life and limb 生命身体に別条なく, たいした傷害を受けずに ▪ They escaped *with life and limb.* 彼らはたいした傷害も受けずに逃れた.

with life (***and spirit***) きびきびと, 元気よく ▪ He does everything *with life and spirit.* 彼は万事をきびきびとやる.

you (***can***) ***bet your*** (***sweet***) ***life*** 《口》確かに ▪ *You can bet your life* (that) he will come. きっと彼は来るよ.

lifeblood /láɪfblʌ̀d/ [名] ***squeeze the lifeblood out of*** …の生き血を絞り出す, 最も重要なものを壊す ▪ A tight money system will eventually *squeeze the lifeblood out of* our economy. 金融引き締め政策をとればいずれわが国の経済は成り立たなくなるだろう.

lifeline /láɪflàɪn/ [名] ***throw a lifeline to***/***throw*** *a person* ***a lifeline*** 人が危機を脱する手段を提供する, 人の頼みの綱になる, 困っている人を助ける ▪ Post offices should *be thrown a lifeline* by their local authority. 郵便局に自治体の援助の手が差し伸べられるべきだ.

lifetime /láɪftàɪm/ [名] ***all in a*** [*one's*] ***lifetime*** 何事も運命だ《あきらめの句》 ▪ My consolation is that it is *all in my lifetime.* 私の慰めはそれもみな運命だということにある.

not in this lifetime 《口》決して…ない (never) ▪ I will not be joining the club, at least *not in this lifetime.* そのクラブには入会しないぞ, とにかく絶対に.

the … of a lifetime 一生にまたとない, 最高の… ▪ It was *the* chance *of a lifetime.* それは一生にまたとないチャンスだった.

lift[1] /lɪft/ [名] ***a good hand at a dead lift*** まさかの時に頼りになる人 ▪ My teacher is truly *a good hand at a dead lift.* 私の先生は本当にまさかの時に頼りになる人だ.

a lift in life (一般的)援助 ▪ They gave *a lift in life* to unfortunate people. 彼らは不幸な人々に援助を与えた.

beg a lift (車に)乗せてくれと言う ▪ I *begged a lift* from him. 私は彼に車に乗せてくれと頼んだ.

Could I have a lift? 車に乗せていただけませんか ▪ *Could I have a lift?*—Sure. Hop in. 乗せてもらえませんか—いいですとも. どうぞ(乗ってください).

give *a person* ***a lift*** **1** (途中で)人を乗せてやる ▪ He *gave* me *a lift* home in his car. 彼は私を家まで車に乗せて帰ってくれた.
2 人を助ける; 人を引き上げる ▪ I *gave* him *a lift* when he started business. 彼が商売を始めたとき, 私は彼を援助した ▪ Take a drink with us. It may *give* you *a lift.* 我々と1杯やりなさい. 気分が引きたつかもしれませんよ ▪ His knowledge of languages *gave* him *a* great *lift* in his career. 語学の知識が彼を大いに出世させた.

have *a person* ***at a lift*** 人を掌中に握る ▪ Now I *have* you *at a lift.* 今や私は掌中にあなたを握っている. ☞《レスリング》「相手を両手でかかえて持ち上げる」が原義.

thumb [***hitch***] ***a lift*** 道端で親指を立てて乗せてくれるように頼む ▪ I tried to *hitch a lift*, but nobody stopped to pick me up. ヒッチハイクしようとしたが誰も車を止めて拾ってくれなかった.

What a lift (***up***) ***for …!*** …は何という出世だろう ▪ Fancy his being taken on as private secretary to a millionaire. *What a lift up for* him! 彼が億万長者の秘書に採用されたなんて, 何という出世だろう!

lift[2] /lɪft/ [動] ***be lifted up with pride*** 高慢になる (《聖》*1 Tim.* 3. 6) ▪ Such a person is apt to *be lifted up with pride.* そんな人はとかく天狗になりがちだ.

lift a finger (***to*** *do*) →FINGER[1].

lift *one's* ***elbow*** [***hand, little finger***] 《口》

L

酒を飲む《特に鯨飲する》 ▪ He *lifts his elbow* too often. 彼はしょっちゅう飲みすぎる ▪ I *lifted my little finger* again last night. ゆうべまた飲みすぎてしまった.

lift** one's **face **1** 手術して顔を美しくする ▪ She had *her face lifted*. 彼女は美顔手術をしてもらった. **2** すっかり改善[改良]する ▪ The town needs *its* whole *face lifted*. 町はすっかり改良する必要がある.

***lift** one's **hand to** [**against**]* →lift a HAND to.

lift** one's **hat 帽子をちょっと持ち上げてあいさつする《国王・女性に対するあいさつ》 ▪ The King *lifted his hat* to the lady. 国王はその婦人に帽子をちょっと持ち上げてあいさつした.

lift up a cry 叫び声をあげる ▪ He *lifted up a cry* in surprise. 彼は驚いて叫び声をあげた.

lift* (*up*) *a* [*one's*] *voice →VOICE.

***lift* (*up*) *one's* *eyes* [*brow, face, visage*]** 見上げる, 仰ぎ見る ▪ You will *lift up your face* unto God. あなたは神を仰ぎ見るだろう ▪ He *lifted his brow* to the glowing sun. 彼は白熱して輝く太陽を見上げた. ☞聖書語法.

***lift* (*up*) *one's* [*the*] *hand*(*s*)** **1** 手を上げる ▪ He *lifted up his hands* with astonishment. 彼はびっくり仰天して両手を上げた. **2** (祈り・感謝などに)手を上げる ▪ In praying it was customary to *lift up the hands* toward heaven. 祈るときには, 天の方へ向けて両手を上げる習慣であった. **3** (宣誓に)手を上げる ▪ He *lifted his hands* and calling God to witness, swore it. 彼は両手を上げて, 神も照覧あれと言って, それを誓った. **4** (...を)打とうとする, (を)打つ (*against*) ▪ He *lifted up his hands against* them. 彼は彼らを打った. **5** =lift a FINGER (to do).

lift up** one's **head **1** 頭角を現す ▪ He *lifted up his head* by studying atomic power. 彼は原子力の研究によって頭角を現した. **2** 元気[勇気]を回復する; 努力を新たにする ▪ The city had begun to *lift up her head* again. その都市はまた台頭し始めていた. **3** 勝ち誇る; 誇り[自尊心]を回復する ▪ Now shall *my head be lifted up* above mine enemies. 今や私は敵に対して勝ち誇る.

***lift up** one's **heart** [**mind, soul**]* 思想や願望を高くする; 意気を高くする ▪ *His heart was lifted up* in the ways of the Lord. 彼は意気高く主の道に勤しんだ.

lift up** one's [**the**] **horn →HORN.

lift up the head of ...に自由[権威]を回復させる (《聖》 *Gen.* 40. 13) ▪ The king *lifted up his head* out of prison. 王は彼を獄舎から自由にしてやった. ☞聖書語法.

lift* (*up*) *the* [*one's*] *heel against →HEEL.

ligature /lígətʃuər|-tʃə/ 名 ***in ligature*** 一活字に結合して ▪ The two initials are *in ligature*. 語頭の頭字二つが連字になっている.

light[1] /laɪt/ 名 ***a bright and shining light*** すぐれた[傑出した]人物 ▪ Payne is *a bright and shining light* of the chapel. ペインは英国非国教会の傑出した人物である.

a man of light and leading 世を啓発指導しうる人, 識者, 権威者 (E. Burke, *Reflections on the Revolution in France*) ▪ I am not *a man of light and leading*, but a humble member of the commonality. 私は識者ではなく, つまらぬ庶民の一人です.

a window of five* [etc.] *lights 5つ[など]の縦仕切りのある窓 ▪ There was *a window of four lights*. 4つの縦仕切りのある窓があった.

according to** one's **lights 自分の主義[見解]に従って ▪ Each interprets the Bible *according to his lights*. 人はおのおの自分の見解に従って聖書を解釈する ▪ Let each man do his best *according to his lights*. 各々は自己の主義に従い最善を尽くすべきだ.

at first light 明け方に ▪ The party started *at first light*. 一行は明け方に出発した.

be exposed to the light of day →emerge into the LIGHT of day.

be in a person's light =stand in a person's LIGHT 1.

be light years away **1** はるか未来のことである ▪ A cure for all kinds of cancer *is* still *light years away*. あらゆるがんの治療ができるようになるのは, まだずっと先のことだ. **2** (進歩して...とは)全く異なる, 月とスッポンである (*from*) ▪ Modern TV sets *are light years away from* the huge machines of old days. 現代のテレビは昔のばかでかい代物とは比べものにならない.

be out like a light →go out like a LIGHT.

between two lights 《米口》日没から日の出までの間に; 夜陰にまぎれて ▪ The fellow disappeared *between two lights* shortly afterwards. その男はその後まもなく夜陰にまぎれて姿を消した.

***bring light* (*to*)** (...を)明らかにする ▪ The scientists will *bring light to* the subject. 科学者がその問題を明らかにするだろう.

bring ... to light ...を明るみに出す; を暴露する ▪ Many cases of his dishonest transactions have *been brought to light*. 彼の不正取引の事実がたくさん発覚した ▪ The excavations have *brought* many ancient tombs *to light*. その発掘でたくさんの古墳が出てきた.

by all lights 昼も夜も ▪ *By all lights* he was to be found there. 昼となく夜となく彼の姿はそこに見られた.

by the light of ...に導かれて, に助けられて ▪ You must decide *by the light of* conscience what to do. 君は良心に問うてどうすべきかを決めなければならない.

by this* (*good*) [*God's*] *light 誓って ▪ *By this light*, Anthony, you are mad. アンソニーよ, 確かに君は頭がおかしくなっている.

carry light 明らかである ▪ These arguments *carry light*. これらの議論は明らかである.

cast (a) light on [upon] →throw (a) (new) LIGHT on.
catch light (…に)火がつく ▪The spilt oil *caught light*. こぼれた油に火がついた.
catch the light 光を受けて輝く ▪The rotor blades of a helicopter *caught the light* from below. ヘリコプターの水平回転翼が下からの光を受けて輝いていた.
come to light (秘密などが)知れる, 明らかになる; 見つかる, 発覚する ▪His suicide *came to light* at last. 彼の自殺はついに知れた ▪The document *came to light* in an old trunk. その書類は古トランクの中に見つかった.
emerge into [be exposed to] the light of day (秘密などが)白日の下にさらされる, 明らかになる ▪The truth has only begun to *emerge into the light of day*. 真相は今やっと明らかになり始めたところだ.
get a light 火を借りる ▪I *got a light* for my pipe. 私はパイプにつける火を借りた.
get in** a person's **light 人の明かり先に立つ, じゃまをする ▪Don't *get in my light*. 私のじゃまをしないでください.
get [receive] light 啓発[説明]を受ける, 解釈のかぎを得る ▪I have *received* great *light* from him. 私は彼から大いに啓発を受けた ▪Can we *get* any *light* on this extraordinary event? 我々はこの異常な事件について, 何らかの説明が得られるか.
get out of** a person's **light 人の明かり先に立たないようよける, 人のじゃまにならないようよける ▪Whoever you are, *get out of my light*. 誰であろうと, 私のじゃまをするな.
get the green light 進行を許可される ▪He *got the green light* to put the plan into operation. 彼はその計画を実行することを許可された.
give** a person **a light 人に(タバコなどの)火を貸す ▪Can you *give* me *a light* for my pipe? パイプにつける火を貸してくださいませんか. ☞この場合 fire は使わない.
give light (into** a subject**) (ある問題を)明らかにする ▪*Give* me some *light into* these matters. これらのことを私に明らかにしてください.
give light on [upon] …を明らかにする ▪He will *give light on* the mystery of life. 彼は人生の謎を解き明かしてくれるだろう.
give the green [red] light 《口》進行を許す[禁止する] ▪He *was given the green light* to go ahead with the plan. 彼はその計画を進めることを許可された.
go [be] out like a light **1** (すぐに)ぐっすりと眠る ▪He hit the pillow and *went out like a light*. 彼は床についたとたんに寝入った ▪She *was out like a light*, so I threw a blanket on her. 彼女は熟睡していたので毛布を掛けてやった.
2 無意識になる, 気を失う ▪He hit his head against the floor and *went out like a light*. 彼は床に頭を打ちつけて気を失ってしまった.
hide** one's **light under a bushel つつましく暮らす; 自分の美点を隠す (《聖》 *Matt*. 5. 15) ▪He made it a matter of principle to *hide his light under a bushel*. 彼は自分の美点を隠す主義だった.
in a good [bad] light よく見える[見えない]所に ▪Hang the picture *in a good light*. その絵をよく見える所へ掛けなさい ▪The picture was *in a bad light*. その絵はよく見えない所にあった.
in different lights/in a different light 異なった見地から ▪The matter may be viewed *in different lights*. その問題はいろいろ異なった見地から見ることができる.
in light 光を受けて, 照らされて ▪Her face was half *in light* and half in shadow. 彼女の顔は半分光を受け, 半分が陰になっていた.
in light of =in the LIGHT of 2.
in the cold light of day [dawn, reason] 頭を冷やして考えてみると ▪All my dreams disappeared *in the cold light of day*. 頭を冷やして考えてみると私の夢はすべてついえてしまった.
in the light 明るい所に ▪Don't leave your CDs *in the light*. CD を明るい所に放置してはいけない.
in the light of **1** …として, のように, の姿で (*as*) ▪I now view my action *in the light of* a crime. 今は自分の行為を犯罪と(して)見る ▪He appeared *in the light of* a scoundrel. 彼は悪党に見えた.
2 《英》 …の見地から ▪Viewed *in this light*, the matter is very important. この見地から見れば, その問題は非常に重要である.
3 …に照らして, にかんがみて ▪You must study the present *in the light of* the past. 現在は過去に照らして研究せねばならない.
in** one's **true light 真の姿において(は) ▪The matter was placed *in its true light*. そのことの真相が明らかにされた.
jump the lights 《口》赤信号を無視して運転を続ける ▪A police officer stopped me for *jumping the lights*. 警察官が信号無視で私の車を止めた.
light and shade →SHADE.
light or leading 啓発または指導 ▪I owe no *light or leading* from any man in the discovery of this truth. 私はこの真理の発見には誰からも啓発または指導を受けていない.
look at … in a … light →view … in a … LIGHT.
not worth a light 《口》三文の価値もない, 少しも役に立たない ▪The painting was a fake and *not worth a light*. その絵画は贋作で三文の値打ちもなかった.
place … in a false light …を誤解させる ▪It *placed* his conduct *in a false light*. そのため彼の行為は誤解された.
place [put, set, show,** etc.**] … in a … light …を…の見地から見せる, の相に見せる ▪His mother tries to *show* his conduct *in a* good *light*. 彼の母は彼の行為をよく見せようとする ▪You have *placed* the matter *in a* new *light*. あなたはその問題の新見解を示した.

L

punch *a person's* ***lights out*** [***up***] 《口》人をひどくなぐる, なぐって気絶させる, たたきのめす ▪ He threatened to *punch my lights up*. 彼は私をなぐり倒すぞと脅した ▪ I could've *punched his lights out* at his insulting remark. 失礼な言い草を聞いて彼をぶんなぐってやろうかと思った.

put a light to …に火をともす, 点火する ▪ *Put a light to* the lamp. ランプに火をともせ.

put out [***quench***] *a person's* [***the***] ***light*** 人を殺す ▪ *Quench his light*! 彼を殺せ ▪ Put out the light and then *put out the light*. (Sh., *Oth*. 5. 2.7) ともし火を消し, それから生命のともし火を消すのだ.

receive light →get LIGHT.

regard [***see***] ***... in a ... light*** → view ... in a ... LIGHT.

see light =see DAYLIGHT.

see the light **1** 生まれる, 出版される, 日の目を見る ▪ It was here that I first *saw the light*. 私が生まれたのはここです ▪ But for him my poems would never have *seen the light*. 彼がいなかったら, 私の詩は日の目を見なかっただろう.

2 理解[納得]する, 悟る ▪ A few months ago he was opposed to it, but now he has *seen the light*. 彼は数か月前はそれに反対だったが, 今はそれをよく理解している.

3《米》(神の)霊光を見る, キリスト教に帰依する ▪ I *saw the light* at the age of 16. 16歳の時分にキリスト教に帰依した.

see the light of day =see the LIGHT 1.

see the red light 赤信号に気づく《将来の危険を予知する》 ▪ I *saw the red light* when I had a dull pain in the stomach. 私は胃に鈍痛を覚えたとき赤信号に気づいた.

set light to 《主に英》…に火をつける ▪ A spark from the fire *set light to* the curtain. 暖炉から火花が散ってカーテンに燃え移った.

shed light on [***upon***] → throw (a) (new) LIGHT on.

shoot the (***traffic***) ***lights*** 赤[黄]信号なのに車を進める, 信号無視で運転する ▪ He had to *shoot the traffic lights* to make the plane. 彼は飛行機に間に合うようにやむなく信号無視で車を飛ばした.

show *a person* ***in*** *his* ***true light*** ある人物の真の姿が現れる ▪ She refused to help her friend in need, and so *showed* herself *in her true light*. 彼女は困っている友人を助けなかった. それで彼女の本性が知れた ▪ These pictures of our daughter *show* her *in her true light*. うちの娘のこれらの写真には彼女らしさがよく撮れている.

stand in *a person's* ***light*** **1** 人の明かり先に立つ, 人の陰になる ▪ Please move a little farther that way; you are *standing in my light*. もう少しそちらへ体をずらしてください. こちらが陰になりますので.

2 人の(利益・出世の)じゃまになる, じゃまをする ▪ Your own sister will not *stand in your light*. あなた自身の姉さんがあなたのじゃまはしないでしょう.

stand in *one's* ***own light*** **1** 自分の仕事[読書]の陰をする ▪ If you read at this side of the room, you'll be *standing in your own light*. 部屋のこちら側で読書すれば, 自分の明かり先に立つことになるよ.

2 (愚行によって)自分の(出世・利益の)じゃまをする ▪ If you are so obstinate, you will *stand in your own light*. そんなに強情だと君は自分で損をするよ.

Strike a light! →STRIKE me pink!

strike a light **1** (マッチなどで)火をつける; 火を出す ▪ He *struck a light* as we entered the house. 我々が家に入ると, 彼はマッチをすって火をともした.

2 〚感嘆文で〛 おや! ▪ *Strike a light*! Here comes Edgar. おや, エドガーがやって来る.

the bright lights 大都市の華やかで刺激に満ちた生活 ▪ She went in search of *the bright lights* of Tokyo. 彼女は華やかな生活を求めて上京した.

the [***some***] ***light at the end of the tunnel***/***light on the horizon*** ようやく見えた明るい光, 長い困難のあとの希望の光 ▪ We're finally at the point where we can see the *light at the end of the tunnel*. やっと希望の光が見えるところまできたぞ ▪ We're not at a solution yet but there is *light on the horizon* for the first time. まだ決着には到っていないが初めて明るい見通しが立ってきた.

(***the***) ***light dawns*** (***on*** *a person*) (人に)やっと分かる, やっと気づく ▪ She was lying to me, but it was days before *the light dawned*. 彼女は嘘をついていたが, それに気づいたのは何日も経ってからだ ▪ *The light* finally *dawned on* her. "Oh! I'm on the wrong floor," she said. 彼女はやっと気づいて言った. 「あら, 階を間違えちゃったわ」

The light is bad. なかなか見にくい ▪ *The light is bad* even at midday when it's cloudy. 曇っていると真昼でも暗くてよく見えない.

the light of *one's* ***countenance*** 愛顧, 好意; 《しばしば皮肉》賛助, 賛助の出席 (《聖》*Ps*. 4. 6) ▪ He gave the celebration *the light of his countenance*. 彼はその式典に賛助の臨席をした.

the light of *a person's* ***eyes*** 人の最愛のもの ▪ She was *the light of my eyes*, and comfort of my old age. 彼女は私の最もいとしいものであり, 私の老齢の慰めであった.

the light of *one's* ***life*** 人生の光《愛情・希望の主な対象》 ▪ His wife was *the light of his life*. 彼の妻は彼の人生の光であった.

the light of nature 直観 ▪ We can see this by *the light of nature*. 我々は直観でこの事がわかる.

The lights are going out all over Europe. ヨーロッパの文明[文化]は滅びかけている ▪ *The lights are going out all over Europe*. We shall not see them lit again in our lifetime. ヨーロッパの文明は滅びかけており, 我々の存命中に復活することはあるまい.

the lights are on but nobody [***no one***] ***is*** (***at***) ***home*** 一見まともだが実はその逆だ, 精神的に障害がある, うわべだけで内容がない ▪ She seemed to have her *lights on but nobody was at home*. 彼女はまともではないようだった ▪ *The lights are on* *but nobody is at home*; no fresh ideas about settling eco issues. 形式だけで中身がない. 環境諸問題を解決する新しい考えは盛られていない.

the shining light of …の達人, 権威 ▪ He is *the shining light of* philosophy. 彼は哲学の権威である.

throw [***cast, shed***] (***a***) (***new***) ***light on*** [***upon***] …(の謎)を解明する; に(解決の)光明を投じる ▪ Can you *throw light upon* this mystery? あなたはこの謎を解明することができるか ▪ This fact *sheds* (*a*) *new light upon* it. この事実はその解明に新しい光を投じる.

trip the light fantastic →TRIP[2].

view … in a false light …を誤解する ▪ He *viewed* your conduct *in a false light*. 彼は君の行為を誤解した.

view [***look at, regard, see***] ***… in a … light*** …を…の見地から見る, の様相において見る ▪ He *saw* the picture *in a* good *light*. 彼は絵を良く見える所で見た ▪ You must *look at* things *in the* right *light*. 物事は正しい見地から見なければならない.

white light (病人を活気づける) 霊的治癒力 ▪ I visited a local faith healer, who gave me *white light* exercises. 私は地元の信仰療法師を訪ね霊的治癒の祈祷を受けた.

with the light 《口》(信号が) 青色になったら ▪ Let's cross *with the light*. 青色になったら渡りましょう.

light[2] /laɪt/ 形副 ***a light touch*** 巧みなやりかた, さりげない手法 ▪ He handled the difficult subject with *a light touch*. 彼はその難題を巧みに処理した.

(***as***) ***light as air*** [***a feather, thistledown***] きわめて軽い ▪ This box is *as light as a feather*. この箱は羽根のように軽い.

be light on …がかなり不足している ▪ Your summary *is light on* arguments and heavy on historical facts. 君の要約文は史実が過剰で論証が足りない.

fly light **1** (船・航空機が)空荷で走る ▪ The ship is *flying light*, sitting on top of the water like a paper bag. 船は空荷で走っている, 紙袋のように波に乗って.

2 《俗》空腹である, 食事を抜いている ▪ I didn't have time for breakfast so I'm *flying light* right now. 朝食をとる時間がなかったので, 今空腹だ.

give light weight (商品の)重量をごまかす ▪ The dealer often *gives light weight* or short measure. その商人はよく重量や寸法をごまかす.

have a light hand [***touch***] 手先が器用である, 手際がよい; 手腕がある ▪ She *has a light hand* with pastry. 彼女はケーキ作りが得意である.

Light come, light go. →COME light, go light.

Light gains make a heavy purse. 《諺》小利も積もれば財布は重い,「ちりも積もれば山となる」.

light in hand →HAND[1].

light in the head 《英》気[頭]が変で; めまいがして; 愚かな ▪ I felt *light in the head* at the news. その知らせを聞いてめまいがした.

light in the mouth (馬が)はみに敏感な, 御しやすい ▪ The beginner should be mounted on a horse that is *light in the mouth*. 初心者は御しやすくおとなしい馬に乗るべきである.

light of carriage 《口》不身持ちで, しりが軽く ▪ She was said to be rather *light of carriage*. 彼女は少し自堕落であると言われていた.

light of ear 信じやすく ▪ The old lady was *light of ear*. その老婦人は信じやすい人だった.

light of finger 手くせが悪く ▪ The boy is a bit *light of finger*. その子は少し手くせが悪い.

light of foot 足が速く ▪ The soldier was very *light of foot*. その兵士は非常に足が速かった.

light relief 緊張をほぐす[退屈をしのぐ]もの ▪ A lively argument provided a bit of *light relief* in an otherwise dull conference. 活発な討論のおかげで, そうでなければ退屈な会議が少し楽しくなった.

make light of (物・人を)軽視する, (問題などを)軽く見る ▪ He *made light of* my worry. 彼は私の心配を軽んじた ▪ You should never *make light of* your illness. 決して病気を甘く見てはいけません.

set light by →SET little by.

travel light 軽装で旅行する ▪ I make it a rule to *travel light*. 私は軽装で旅行することにしている.

with a light heart **1** にこにこと, 喜び勇んで ▪ The student left the examination room *with a light heart*. その生徒はにこにこして試験場を出た ▪ Do everything *with a light heart*. 何事も喜んでやりなさい.

2 軽率に ▪ Don't say these things *with a light heart*. うかつにこんなことを言ってはいけない.

light[3] /laɪt/ 動 ***be lit up*** (***like a Christmas tree, like Broadway***) 《口》(ひどく)酔っている ▪ Jack *was lit up like Broadway* last night. ジャックはゆうべひどく酔っていた.

light *a person* ***on*** *his* [*her*] ***way*** 明かりで人を導く ▪ It's getting dark. I'll *light* you *on your way*. 暗くなっているので, 明かりで道案内してあげよう.

light the [***a***] ***fuse*** [***touchpaper***] 緊迫事態を招くことをする, 危なっかしいことをする ▪ She *lit the touchpaper* for a governorship challenge by resigning from the bank. 彼女は銀行を辞めて思い切って知事職への挑戦に賭けた. ☞火薬の導火線に点火するイメージ.

light[4] /laɪt/ 動 ***light on*** *one's* ***feet*** [***legs***] (落ちたときなど)倒れないで両足で立つ; 幸運である, 成功する ▪ I have *lighted on my legs* as usual. 私はいつものようにうまくいった.

lighten /láɪtən/ 動 ***lighten*** *a person's* [***the***] ***load*** →LOAD[1].

lightening /láɪtənɪŋ/ 名 ***a lightening before death*** 死ぬ前のはしゃぎ[小康] ▪ This only proved *a lightening before death*. これは死ぬ前の小康にすぎなかった.

light-headed /láɪthédəd/ 形 ***be*** [***feel***] ***light-headed*** 目まいがする ▪ I *feel* a bit *light-headed* this morning. 今朝は少し目まいがする.

lightly /láɪtli/ 副 ***get off*** [***be let off***] ***lightly*** 《口》(けが・罰・面倒から)うまく逃れる ▪ Only one year in prison? I think he *got off* very *lightly*. たった1年の刑だって? やつは実にうまく逃れたものだ.

Lightly come, lightly go. →COME[2].

speak lightly of …をけなす ▪ He *spoke lightly of* its value. 彼はその価値をけなした.

take lightly **1** あまりこたえない ▪ He *took* his dismissal *lightly*. 彼は解雇されてもあまりこたえなかった. **2** 軽く受け取る ▪ His threat should not *be taken lightly*. 彼のおどしを甘く見てはいけない.

think lightly of →THINK[2].

tread lightly **1** そっと歩く ▪ I *trod lightly* because the sod might not be firmly rooted in some places. 所によって芝がしっかり根づいていないかもしれないのでそっと歩いた **2**《口》慎重にやる ▪ We shall have to *tread lightly*. 慎重にやらねばなるまい.

lightness /láɪtnəs/ 名 ***lightness of heart*** 元気, 快活, 歓喜 ▪ I can pursue my work with my usual *lightness of heart*. 私はいつものように快活に仕事をすることができる.

lightning /láɪtnɪŋ/ 名 ***a lightning rod*** 《主に米》責任者に代わって当然矢面に立つ人, (責任がないのに)非難のまとになる人 (*for*) ▪ The sales chief has become *a lightning rod for* all complaints. ずっと販売課長が苦情を一手に引き受けている. ☞a lightning rod「避雷針」.

be struck by lightning …に雷が落ちる ▪ The house *was struck by lightning*. その家に落雷した.

catch [***capture***] ***lightning in a bottle*** 《主に米》困難ながらも成功する ▪ We *caught lightning in a bottle* with this store. 私たちはこの小売店できわめて困難ながらも成功した.

Lightning never strikes in the same place twice [***twice in the same place***]. 《諺》雷は二度は同じ所に落ちない《異常な事件は同じ状況で再発することはない》.

like (***a streak of***) ***lightning*** 《口》電光石火, 素早く ▪ Our hero ran *like lightning* to the scene. われらが勇士は飛ぶようにその場へ駆けつけた.

like [(***as***) ***quick as***] ***greased lightning*** 《口》電光石火, 素早く, たちまち ▪ She picked it up *like greased lightning*. 彼女は素早くそれを拾い上げた.

with [***at***] ***lightning speed*** =like (a streak of) LIGHTNING.

like[1] /laɪk/ 形副前接名 ***and such like*** そのような ▪ I like fishing, shooting, *and such like* sports. 私は魚釣り, 銃猟やそのような戸外遊びが好きだ.

and [***or***] ***the like*** …など, …の類 ▪ He studies music, painting, *and the like*. 彼は音楽, 絵画などを研究する. ☞AND so forth よりも形式ばった言い方.

and your [***his,*** etc.] ***like*** あなた[彼, など]のような人々《賞賛にも非難にも用いられる》 ▪ Your aunt *and her like* are the salt of the earth. 君のおばさんや同類の人々が地の塩なのだ.

anything like →ANYTHING.

(***as***) ***like as not*** 《口》おそらく, たぶん ▪ It was *as like as not* that they would kill him. 彼らは彼を殺さないものでもなかった[あるいは殺すかもしれなかった].

(***as***) ***like as two peas*** [***blocks, eggs***] 非常によく似て, ウリ二つで ▪ These sisters are *as like as two peas*. この姉妹は全くウリ二つだ.

be (***just***) ***like…*** (***to do***) (…するのは全く)…らしい ▪ It *was like* him *to* think of himself last. 自分の事などいっこうに考えないのは彼らしいことだった ▪ That's *just like* your impudence. 全く君らしい厚かましさだ.

(***be***) ***like to*** *did*/***like to have*** *done* 《米口》…しそうだった ▪ I *like to* died a-laughing. 笑って死にそうだった ▪ I *like to have* got killed. 危うく殺されるところだった. ☞非文法的な表現.

be like to *do* 《口》…しそうである, する見込みがある ▪ Men who know the truth *are like to* go mad. その真相を知る人々はおそらく気が狂うだろう.

be of (***a***) ***like mind*** 同じ意見[趣味]である, 同じ考え方をする ▪ Jim and I *are* seldom *of a like mind* on the issue. その問題に関してジムと意見が合うことは滅多にない.

in like manner [***wise***] 同じように(して) ▪ Other playback devices can be used *in like manner*. 他の再生機器も同じように使用できる.

I've never seen [***heard***] ***the like.*** こんなふるまいは見た[聞いた]ことがない《あきれた》 ▪ That's outrageous. *I've never heard the like*. そいつはひどい. 聞いたことがないや.

(***just***) ***like that*** 無造作に, 簡単に ▪ He asked her for some money and she gave it to him *just like that*. 彼が金をねだると彼女はあっさりと与えた.

like a good one 殊勝らしく, 感心に ▪ He works *like a good one*. 彼は殊勝に働く.

like a little man 《米口》男らしく率直な態度で ▪ Are you going to endorse this draft *like a little man*? 君はこの手形に堂々と裏書きするつもりか.

like a (***raving***) ***lunatic***/***like a loon*** 全く気が狂ったように ▪ He grinned *like a loon* when he saw my pet frog. 彼は私のペットのカエルを見るとまるで気が触れたようにニヤニヤした.

like all get out 《米口》うんと, 大いに ▪ We both chattered *like all get out*. 我々二人は大いにしゃべった.

like anything [***a bird, a cartload of bricks, beans, boots, fun, hot cakes, old boots***] 《口》激しく, 猛烈に, ひどく ▪ He ran *like anything*. 彼は猛烈に走った.

like as we lie 《口》(ゴルフで)同点で《ゴルフのメダルプレー (medal play) で両者が同じストローク数で進んでいる場合》 ▪ One of the golfers calls out, "*Like as we lie*, sir." ゴルファーの一人が「同点です」と叫んだ. ☞lie「ゴルフボールが打たれて, コースの fairway また

は rough にある状態」.

Like attracts [***draws to, calls to***] ***like.*** 《諺》同気相求む, 類は友を呼ぶ.

Like begets like./(***The***) ***Like breeds*** (***the***) ***like.*** 《諺》「同類は同類を生む, 子は親に似る, ウリのつるにはナスビはならぬ」《似たもの同士は集まりがちだ》.

like blazes [***hell, the devil***] 《口》激しく, 猛烈に ▪ We rowed *like blazes*. 我々は猛烈にこいだ.

Like cures like. 《諺》毒をもって毒を制する.

like enough 《口》大いにありそうなことで ▪ *Like enough*. It may be so in London. 大いにありそうなことです. ロンドンではそうかもしれませんね.

like everything 《米口》どんどん, 早く ▪ The banks are caving *like everything*. 両方の土手はどんどんえぐれてきている.

Like for like. 《諺》恩には恩, 恨みには恨み.

Like knows like. 《諺》英雄相知る ▪ Only *like* can *know like*. 英雄のみが英雄を知る.

like mad [***crazy***] 《口》一生懸命に ▪ They tried [danced] *like mad*. 彼らは一生懸命に努力した[ダンスした].

Like master, like man. 《諺》主が主なら家来も家来,「似た者主従」.

like nothing on earth →NOTHING.

like so many →as so MANY.

like the ... that *one* ***is*** さすが...だけあって ▪ *Like the* samurai *that* he *was*, he remained calm on the occasion. さすがに侍(さむらい)だけあって, 彼はそのとき泰然としていた.

one's ***likes and dislikes*** (自分の)好ききらい ▪ *Your likes and dislikes* don't count in this matter. この件では君の好ききらいは問題にならない.

make like 《口》...のまね[ふり]をする ▪ The clown *made like* a bear. 道化師はクマのまねをした.

more like →MORE.

more like it 《口》...の方がいい ▪ You don't like tea? Then how about coffee?—That's *more like it*. 紅茶はいやだって? じゃコーヒーはどうだ—その方がいい.

most like =very LIKE.

no ... like/ none like **1** ...に及ぶものはなく ▪ There is *no* country *like* Japan. 日本ほどよい国はない ▪ There is *none like* our teacher. 我々の先生ほどの先生はいない.

2 ...に似ているものはなく ▪ I can find *no* plant *like* this. 私はこのような植物は見つけることができない.

not look upon his [***her,*** etc.] ***like again*** 彼[彼女, など]のような人はまたとないだろう (cf. Sh., *Haml*. 1. 2. 188) ▪ We shall *not look upon her like again*. 彼女のような人はまたとあるまい.

nothing like **1** ...に及ぶものはなく ▪ There is *nothing like* traveling by air. 空の旅に及ぶものはない.

2 ...に似ているものはなく ▪ I can find *nothing like* this piece of china. このような陶器は見つからない.

3 少しも ...のようでなく; 少しも...なく ▪ The place was *nothing like* home. そこはまるっきり家庭らしくなかった ▪ Her face was *nothing like* so clean kept. 彼女の顔は決してそうきれいにされてはいなかった.

nothing like as good とても(それに)及ばない ▪ His English is *nothing like as good*. 彼の英語はとても(それに)及ばない.

or the like →and the LIKE.

something like →SOMETHING.

somewhat like かなり(に) ▪ He will sell it *somewhat like*. 彼はそれを相当売るだろう.

That's [***This is***] ***more like it.*** (今までより)いい, よくなっている ▪ Here's your order. Sorry about the mix-up.—*That's more like it*. ご注文の料理です. 手違いがありまして申しわけありません—これなら結構.

the like(***s***) ***of*** **1** ...のようなもの[人] ▪ Did you ever see *the likes of* it? そんなものを見たことがあるかい?

2 《口》...のような(立派な, つまらぬ)者[連中] ▪ It is not for me to sit with *the likes of* you. あなたのような(偉い)人と同席するのはもったいない ▪ This is the best school that *the like of* me was ever put to. これは私ごとき者が行かされた学校では最良の学校である.

very like 《口》十中八九そうだろう ▪ I was much deceived in them.—*Very like*. 私は彼らを大いに買いかぶっていた—どうもそうらしいね.

like[2] /laɪk/ 動 *do* ***and like it*** 文句を言わずに...する, 快く...する ▪ It's Mary's birthday. You'll have a drink *and like it*. 今日はメアリーの誕生日だ. 君も快く1杯やりたまえ.

as ... as you like 〚副詞・形容詞を強調して〛ひどく ▪ He can fight *as* boldly *as you like*. 彼はすごく大胆に戦うことができる.

as you like お好きなように ▪ You may do *as you like*. お好きなようにしてよろしい.

How do you like ...? ...をどう思いますか ▪ *How do you like* my dress? 私のドレスどう思いますか.

How would you like ...? ...はいかがですか, が好きですか ▪ *How would you like* the work? その仕事はいかがですか.

How would you like it? (好ましくない目にあって)どう思うか, ひどいと思わないか ▪ *How would you like it* if someone called you a liar? 人に嘘つきと言われたとしたらどう思いますか.

I like it, but it does not like me. 《口・戯》(飲食物について)私はそれが好きだが, 私に合わない ▪ I eat anything except liver: *I like it, but it does not like me*. レバー以外は何でも食べる. レバーは嫌いではないが合わないんだ.

I like that! 《口》〚that に強勢を置いて〛そんな[あんな]のないよ, そりゃないでしょう《相手が言ったりしたりしたことに対する驚きをこめた抗議》 ▪ *I like that!* Bob smashes up my car and then expects me to pay for the repairs. あんなのないよ. ボブは僕の車をぶっこわしておいて, 修繕代は僕に払わそうと言うんだから.

I like your cheek. =I LIKE your impudence.

I like your impudence. 《皮肉》その生意気が気に入った《何を生意気な》 ▪ *I like your impudence*!—I like it too, it's my best asset. 生意気を言うな!—おあいにくさま, それだけがこっちの取り柄でね.

I never liked it, anyway. (負け惜しみで)大したことないよ ▪ I lost my digital camera, but that's okay, *I never liked it anyway.* デジカメを失くしちゃったけど, いいんだ, 大したことない.

I* [*we*] *should* [*would*] *like …がほしいものだ ▪ *I should like* a cup of tea. お茶を1杯飲みたいものだ ▪ *I would like* time to consider it. それを考慮する時間が欲しいものだ.

I* [*we*] *should* [*would*] *like to *do* [***to have*** *done*] …したいものだ[したかった] ▪ *I should* [*would*] *like to* climb the mountain this summer. この夏はその山に登りたいものです ▪ *I should like to have* met him. 彼に会いたかったのだが.

I* [*we*] *should* [*would*] *like … to *do* …に…してもらいたい ▪ *I should like* you *to* post the letter. その手紙をポストに入れてもらいたいのです.

***I* [*we*] *should* [*would*] *like to know* [*see*]** 《皮肉》知りたい[見たい]ものだ《「知らせる, または見せることはできないだろう」の意》 ▪ What, *we should like to know*, is the difference between the two operations? その二つの作用はどう違うか知りたいものだ ▪ *I should like to see* you do it, sir! あなたがそれをなさるのが見たいものですな.

if you like **1** よろしかったら ▪ You may come *if you like.* よろしかったら, おいでなさい.
2 そう言いたければ ▪ I am shy *if you like.* 〖shyを強調して〗私はまあはにかみやとは言えましょう《だが人間ぎらいとか, 憶病などではない》 ▪ I am shy *if you like.* 〖Iを強調して〗私ならまあはにかみやでしょう《他の人はそうでないが》.

***like … hot* [*cold*]** 熱い[冷たい]のがよい ▪ I *like* my tea *hot.* お茶は熱いのがよい.

like it or lump it 《口》好きでもきらいでも ▪ You may *like it or lump it*, but Aunt Cissie is going to live here in future. おまえが好きでもきらいでも, シシーおばさんは将来はここへ住むんだよ.

like … to *do* …に…してもらいたい ▪ I *like* her *to* be within reach. 私は彼女に近くにいてもらいたい.

like well …を愛する ▪ I may *like* him *well.* 私は彼を愛するかもしれない.

liked to have *done* 《俗》危うく…しそうだった ▪ I *liked to have* been killed. 私は危うく殺されるところだった.

we should* [*would*] *like →I should LIKE.

(*whether you* [*we*]) *like it or not* [*no*] 好きでもきらいでも; どうしても ▪ You must go there, *like it or not.* 君はどうしてもそこへ行かねばならない.

would like to *do* 〖特に2人称・3人称について〗…したいと思っている ▪ He *would like to* come here. 彼はここへ来たいと思っている.

likelihood /láɪklihòd/ 名 ***in all likelihood*** たぶん, 十中八九 ▪ *In all likelihood* we shall be away for a week. たぶん1週間留守をするでしょう.

likely /láɪkli/ 形 ***as likely as not*** おそらく…だろう, まあ…だろう ▪ He'll forget all about it *as likely as not.* 彼はおそらくそのことはすっかり忘れるだろう. ☞as not＝as not likely.

be likely to *do* …しそうである, おそらく…するだろう ▪ It *is likely to* rain. 雨になりそうだ ▪ You *are likely to* succeed. 君はおそらく成功するだろう.

likely enough おそらく, 十中八九 ▪ It is *likely enough* that he will succeed. 彼は十中八九成功するだろう.

more than likely おそらく ▪ Our train is *more than likely* to be late. 我々の乗る列車はたぶん遅れる.

most* [*very*] *likely たぶん ▪ *Very likely* I shall visit Europe next spring. たぶん私は来春ヨーロッパを訪問するだろう.

Not likely! 《口》とんでもない ▪ Would you go, too?—*Not likely!* 君も行くのですか?—とんでもない.

(*That's*) *a likely story.* 《皮肉》(そいつは)信じられない話だね ▪ Jim marry Ann? *A likely story*! ジムがアンと結婚する? ちょっと信じられないね.

likeness /láɪknəs/ 名 ***bear a likeness to*** …に似ている ▪ He *bears a* striking *likeness to* his father. 彼は父親にそっくりだ.

catch a likeness to …に似たところを認める ▪ I can *catch a likeness to* your father in your face. お顔におとうさんに似たところがありますね.

in the likeness of …の姿をした ▪ He is an enemy *in the likeness of* a friend. 彼は味方と見せかけた敵である.

take *a person's* ***likeness*** 人の肖像を描く, 人の写真をとる ▪ He *took the likeness of* his brother. 彼は兄の肖像を描いた.

liking /láɪkɪŋ/ 名 ***have a liking for*** …が好きである ▪ I *have a* great *liking for* physics. 私は物理学が大好きだ.

have no liking for …を好かない ▪ I *have no liking for* flattery. 私はおせじは好かない.

***take a liking for* [*to*]** …が気に入る ▪ He has *taken a liking to* philosophy. 彼は哲学が好きになった.

to *one's* ***liking*** 気に入って, 好みに合って ▪ The style is much *to my liking.* その文体は大いに私の気に入った.

too … for *one's* ***liking*** 人の好み(に合う)には…すぎる, もっと…でない方が好みに合う ▪ The climate here is *too* hot *for my liking.* 当地の気候は暑すぎて私の好みには合わない.

lily /líli/ 名 **(*as*) *fair* [*pure*] *as a lily*** ユリのように白い[純潔で] ▪ The maiden was *as fair as a lily.* その乙女はユリのように色白だった.

Consider the lilies. 《諺》野の花を思え《物欲を捨てて, 神意に任せよ》(《聖》*Matt.* 6. 28).

lilies and roses 白く美しい顔色 ▪ A face of *lilies and roses* is out of favor now. 色白の美貌は当節流行らない.

paint* [*gild*] *the lily しつこい飾り立てをする, よけいな手を加える (cf. Sh., *John* 4. 2. 11) ▪ She wears too many jewels because she will *gild the lily.* 彼女は飾り立てたがり, いやというほど宝石をつけている.

limb /lɪm/ 名 ***a limb of the devil* [*Satan*,**

hell] 悪魔の手先; いたずらないじわる, 手に負えないいたずらっ子 ▪ *A limb of Satan* may be made a member of Christ. 悪魔の手先がキリスト教徒にされることもある ▪ That boy is *a limb of Satan*. あの少年は手に負えないいたずらっ子だ.

a limb of the law 《軽蔑》法律適用に関係ある人《弁護士・警察官》 ▪ He is *a limb of the law* and will be here at our assizes. 彼は弁護士で我々の巡回裁判にここへ来るだろう.

limb and wind 五体の働き[力] ▪ They are young men, strong of *limb and wind*. 彼らは五体の力の強い若者たちだ.

out on a limb **1** 《口》 [[しばしば go, climb, leave を伴って]] (引くに引けない)不利な[不安定な, 危ない]立場に; 危ない橋を渡って ▪ No one is prepared to *go out on a limb*. 誰も危ない立場になる覚悟はできていない ▪ He was way *out on a limb*. 彼は引くに引けない危ないはめになっていた ▪ The company climbed *out on a limb*. その会社は危ない橋を渡りはじめた.
2 孤立して, 行き詰まって ▪ The supporters suddenly left me *out on a limb*. 支持してくれていた人たちが急に私を独り残して去っていった.
3 支持されないで ▪ He was pretty far *out on a limb* when he proposed a new plan. 彼は新しい計画を提唱したが全く支持されなかった. ☞limb「小枝」にしがみついているところから.

tear* [*pull, rip*]*... limb from limb 《戯》 **1** ...の手足を八つ裂きに裂く ▪ I will *tear* him *limb from limb*. あいつの手足を八つ裂きにしてやる ▪ I'll *rip limb from limb* the person who killed my pet dog. うちの犬を殺したやつを八つ裂きにしてやる.
2 (人を)痛烈に攻撃する ▪ She got so angry that she *tore* her brother *limb from limb*. 彼女はとても怒って弟をこっぴどくやっつけた.

with life and limb →LIFE.

limbo /límbou/ 名 ***be in limbo*** 不安定な状態にある ▪ I'*m in limbo* waiting for the result. 結果待ちで不安定な状態にある.

consign ... to limbo ...を忘れる ▪ Just *consign* the whole affair *to limbo*. いっさいの事を忘れてくれ.

limelight /láımlàıt/ 名 ***in* [*into*] *the limelight*** (舞台で)集中照明を受けて; 脚光を浴びて ▪ There are many people who love to be *in the limelight*. 脚光を浴びるのが好きな人は多い ▪ Asian directors have recently begun to step *into the limelight*. 最近アジア系の映画監督が脚光を浴び始めた.

keep out of the limelight 人目を避けて生活する ▪ He will do well to *keep out of the limelight* for some time. 彼はしばらく陰でひっそりと生活するのがよいだろう.

out of the limelight 目立たないで, 人目につかないで ▪ I've decided to stay *out of the limelight* after my retirement. 退職後は地味に生活しようと決めた.

push* [*thrust*]*... into the limelight ...をまっただ中へ追いこむ ▪ The country *was pushed into the limelight* of a racial conflict. その国は民族紛争のまっただ中に追いこまれた.

limit /límət/ 名 ***Ain't that the limit?*** これぐらいにしておくか ▪ I miss everybody at home, friends, family, and my kitty, *ain't that the limit?* 故郷のみんなが恋しい—友だちに家族に猫に—ああ, もうよそう.

***at* (*one's*) *limit*(*s*)** 指し値で ▪ The goods are not to be had *at your limit*. その品は指し値では手に入りません.

be over* [*below*] *the limit (運転者が)法定飲酒量を越えている[いない] ▪ He was arrested for *being over the limit*. 彼は(限度を越えた)飲酒運転で捕まった.

be the* (*absolute*) *limit 《口》忍耐の極限である, がまんがならない ▪ The buses *are the limit*. They are never on time. バスにはうんざりだ. 定刻に来たためしがない ▪ He lied again. This *is the absolute limit*! 彼がまた嘘をついた. もうどうにも我慢ならん!

fix a limit* [*limits*] *to =set a LIMIT to.

go the limit 《口》とことんまでやる; 《ボクシング》最終ラウンドまで戦う; (女が)最後の一線を越える《性交を許す》 ▪ I've made the plunge. I'll *go the limit*. 思い切った手をうったぞ. とことんまでやってやる ▪ Some schoolgirls were talking about *going the limit*. 女子学生たちが最後の一線を越える話をしていた. ☞イギリス英語では go to the limit を使う人がいる.

go to any limits =go (to) any LENGTH(s).

Here are limits./There are limits. 物事には限度がある ▪ I love music as much as the next guy but *there are limits*. 私の音楽好きは誰にも負けないが, やはり程度問題だ.

know no limits 際限がない ▪ His greed *knows no limits*. 彼の貪欲には際限がない.

***off limits* (*to, for*)** 《米》(...の)立入禁止(区域)[で] ▪ These beer halls are *off limits to* athletes in training. これらのビヤホールには練習中の運動選手は立入禁止である.

***on limits* (*to*)** (...の)立入自由(区域)[で] ▪ These exhibit rooms are *on-limits to* visitors. 入場者はこれらの展示会場に立入自由である.

over the limit 境界[限界]を越えて ▪ You've gone *over the limit*; you've made it cost £80. あなたは限界を越えた. 80ポンドも経費をかからせた.

***reach the limit*(*s*)** **1** 極限に達する ▪ Those shares have *reached the limit*. それらの株はもう極限に達している.
2 ...が尽きる ▪ We *reached the limit* of our patience with him. 彼に対する堪忍袋の緒が切れた.

set a limit* [*limits*] *to ...を制限する ▪ It is impossible to *set limits to* a man's desires. 人間の欲望を制限することは不可能である.

That's the limit. 《口》それはがまんできない ▪ *That's the limit.* Go this minute! もうがまんならない. 今すぐ, うせろ.

the frozen limit 《口》いやな[耐えられない]極限 ▪ The hotel is *the frozen limit*. そのホテルはいやで

L

たまらない.

The sky is the limit. →SKY.

there is a [***no***] ***limit to*** …には限りがある[ない] ▪ *There is a limit to* a man's energy. 人の精力には限りがある ▪ *There is no limit to* human progress. 人間の進歩には限りがない.

to the limit 《米》極端に, 十分に ▪ He can be trusted *to the limit*. 彼は十分に信頼できる.

within limits 控え目に, 適度に ▪ I have to keep my activities *within limits*. 活動は控え目にしておかねばなりません ▪ I'm willing to help you, *within limits*. 喜んで適度にお助けします.

within (*one's*) ***limits*** 指し値以内で ▪ We have a fair lot *within your limits*. お指し値以内でかなりの品がございます.

within the limits of …の範囲内に[で] ▪ It is not *within the limits of* human intelligence to discover the reasom. その理由を発見するのは人知の及ぶところでない.

without limit 際限なく, いくらでも ▪ They will supply funds *without limit*. 彼らはいくらでも資金を供給するだろう.

limitation /lìmətéɪʃən/ 名 ***have*** *one's* ***limitations*** 万能ではない, 弱点もある ▪ Every human being *has his limitations*. 人は誰しも万能ではない.

know *one's* ***limitations*** 自分の能力のほどを心得ている ▪ It's a wise man who *knows his limitations*. 自分の力のほどを心得ている者は賢明である.

without limitation 無制限に ▪ They can use the stream water *without limitation*. 彼らは川の水をふんだんに使える.

limn /lɪm/ 動 ***limn the water*** 水に描く《役に立たない事, はかない事について言う》 ▪ All he had done was but a kind of *limning the water* to them. 彼のしたことはみな彼らにとっては水に描くような徒労にすぎなかった.

limp[1] /lɪmp/ 形 (***as***) ***limp as a doll*** [***a rag***] 疲れ果てて, くたくたになって ▪ He was *as limp as a doll* after a long day at work. 彼は一日中働いて疲れ果てていた.

feel limp 体具合が悪い; 疲れ果てた感じがする ▪ I've been *feeling* a bit *limp* lately. 近ごろ少し体具合が悪い.

limp[2] /lɪmp/ 名 ***with a limp*** 足を引きずって ▪ He walks *with a limp*. 彼は足を引きずって歩く.

limpet /límpət/ 名 ***cling*** [***stick***] ***like a limpet*** (カサガイのように)しっかりとすがりつく[くっつく] ▪ The dog *clung like a limpet* to us. 犬は我々にしっかりとくっついて離れなかった.

line[1] /laɪn/ 名 ***a fine*** [***thin, narrow***] ***line*** (***between two things*** [***between*** *A* ***and*** *B*]) (両者の[AとBとの])紙一重のわずかな違い, 微妙な差 ▪ There is *a fine line* separating genius from insanity. 天才と狂気の差は紙一重である ▪ There is only *a fine line between* determination *and* obstinacy. 固い決意と頑固さとの間にはほとんど明確な違いはない.

a line of thought →one's LINE of thought.

a long line of 代々の…の家系 ▪ He comes from *a long line of* teachers [doctors]. 彼は代々の教師[医者]の家系の人だ.

above [***below***] ***the line*** **1**《ブリッジ》(スコア表の)上欄[下欄]に, 勝負に直結しない[する] ▪ My partner scored six hundred *below the line*. 私のパートナーは下欄に600点を取った.

2《経》借方[貸方]に, 経常[臨時]支出の ▪ These items are *above the line*. この項目は経常支出だ.

all along the line/all (***the way***) ***down the line*** 戦線の至る所で; あらゆる点で; 全面的に ▪ God will be victorious *all along the line* in the present battle. 神はこの戦闘では全線にわたって勝利を得給う ▪ He was successful *all down the line*. 彼は全面的に成功した.

along the lines of →on the LINEs of.

along [***on***] ***the same lines*** 同じような[に] ▪ It's strange how we both always seem to be thinking *along the same lines*. 僕たち二人はいつも同じ考え方をしているようだが, 不思議なことだ.

along [***on***] ***those*** [***these***] ***lines*** (性質・タイプ)がそれに似た, そういった類の, 前述した路線に従って ▪ I want to buy an SUV or something *along those lines*. スポーツ用多目的車とかそういった車種のものを買いたい ▪ It will be impossible to deal with the problem *on these lines*. その問題をこの方向で処理するのは無理だろう ▪ Do I have OCD or something *along those lines*? 私は強迫性障害またはこれに類した病気に罹っているのでしょうか.

(***as***) ***straight as a line*** きわめてまっすぐに ▪ Go *as straight as a line*. まっすぐに行きなさい.

be going along [***on***] ***the right lines*** 適切な方法で行っている ▪ I'm not sure whether I'*m going along the right lines* or not. 自分が正しいやり方でやっているかどうか自信がない.

be in … line …商売である, を(職として)やっている ▪ What *line are* you *in*? あなたは商売は何をやっていますか ▪ I *am in* the grocery *line*. 私は食料雑貨商です.

be (***in***) *one's* (***own***) ***line*** (***of country***) 《英》十八番[おはこ, お手のもの]である ▪ Cooking light meals *is in his line*. 軽食を作るのは彼のお手のものだ ▪ Get-togethers *are* not altogether *in my line of country*. 私は懇親会はどうも苦手である.

behind the line 銃後の[で] ▪ He fought battles *behind the line* as well as in front of it. 彼は前線だけでなく銃後でも戦った.

below the line (***cost***) 実際の生産費以下で[に] ▪ Producers sometimes attempt to reduce *below the line*. 生産者はときに実際の生産費以下に価格を下げようとすることがある.

blow [***fluff***] *one's* ***lines*** 《口》せりふを忘れる ▪ Suddenly he *blew his lines* on the stage. 突然彼は舞台でせりふを忘れてしまった.

bring … into line **1** …を整列させる, 一列にそろえる ▪ It is difficult to *bring* them at once *into line*.

彼らをすぐに整列させるのはむずかしい.

2 …を一致[結束, 同調]させる (*with*) ▪ We must *bring* workers' earnings *into line with* increased living costs. 労働者の所得を増大した生活費に合わせなければならない ▪ A spanking *brought* him *into line*. 平手打ちを一発見舞うと彼は同調した.

by line (and level) 測線(と水準器)で; きちんと正確に(測って) ▪ A garden is made *by line and level*. 庭園はきちんと測って作られる.

by rule and line →RULE[1].

by the lines of the palm 手相で ▪ He tells fortunes *by the lines of the palm*. 彼は手相で運勢を見る.

come down to the line (競走が)最後まで接戦になる ▪ I believe this game will *come down to the line*. この試合は最後までどっちに転ぶか分からんぞ.

come into line **1** 一列に並ぶ, 列につく ▪ We *came into line* side by side. 横一列に並んだ.

2《口》(…と)一致する, 同意[同調]する (*with*) ▪ They refused to *come* completely *into line*. 彼らは完全に同調しようとはしなかった.

come of a good line よい血統を引いている ▪ The girl you see over there *comes of a good line*. あそこにいる少女はよい血統の出だ.

come off the line (流れ作業で)仕上がる, 完成する ▪ Cars were *coming off the line*. 自動車が次々と仕上がっていた.

come on line (しばしばビジネスで)作動する, 軌道に乗る ▪ A new power plant is due to *come on line* by the end of this year. 新しい発電所が年末までに稼動を始める予定である.

cross [pass] the line (航海中)赤道を横切る ▪ The ship was about to *cross the line*. その船はちょうど赤道を横切ろうとしていた.

cut in line《米》列に割り込む ▪ He tried to *cut in line* to get a PlayStation 4. 彼は PlayStation 4を手に入れようと列に割り込もうとした ▪ One thing we can't stand is people who *cut in line*. がまんできないのは列に割り込む連中だ.

down the line **1** 町の中心部(の方)へ ▪ It's always raining somewhere *down the line*. 都心ではいつもどこかで雨が降っている.

2 ずっと, 完全に, 全く ▪ We are prepared to back the president *down the line*. 我々はあくまで大統領を支持する覚悟である.

3《口》将来 (→down the ROAD) ▪ Larger group sessions will be useful *down the line*. より大きなグループ会議は将来有益になるだろう.

drag A into line with B AをBと一致させる ▪ They will do anything to *drag* people *into line with* their ideology. 彼らは自らのイデオロギーに人民を染まらせるには手段を選ばないだろう.

draw a line under… (繰り返しを避けるため)済んだことに印をつける, けりをつけて忘れる ▪ We should *draw a line under* the past and try to make a fresh start. つらい過去のことは忘れて, 新しい一歩を踏み出そう.

draw the [a] line between …を区別する ▪ We must *draw a line between* public and private affairs. 公事と私事を区別しなければならない.

draw the [a] line (in the sand) **1**《口》(…までは)やらない, 以上はやらない (*at*) ▪ I don't mind lending him my razor but I *draw the line at* lending him my tooth-brush. 彼にかみそりを貸してやるのはかまわないが, 歯ブラシを貸すことまではしない ▪ I *draw the line at* poker. 私は勝負事はポーカーを限りとしてその他はやりません.

2 (行動の)限界線を引く, 一線を画す ▪ This noisy behavior cannot be allowed; we must *draw the line* somewhere. この騒々しいふるまいは許せない. どこかでけじめをつけなければならない.

3 明確に言明する ▪ Scientists *draw a line in the sand* on climate change. 科学者たちは気候変動について明確に言明している.

draw … up in (a) line …を一列に整列させる ▪ The drill-teacher *drew* the boys *up in a line*. 訓練係教師は少年たちを一列に並ばせた.

dress the line →TOE the line.

drop [send] a line [a few lines]《口》一筆書き送る ▪ *Drop* me *a line* to that effect. その旨一筆お知らせください.

fall in [into] line **1** 一列に並ぶ, 列につく ▪ At daybreak they *fell in line* once more. 夜明けに彼らはもう一度隊伍を組んだ.

2 (…と)一致する, (…に)同意[同調]する (*with*) ▪ They didn't *fall in line with* the cease-fire order. 彼らは停戦命令に従わなかった ▪ The smaller operators *fell into line*. 小規模経営者たちは同調した.

3 結束[団結]する ▪ The publications quickly *fell in line*. 新聞雑誌はすぐに結束した.

fall out of the line《軍》列を離れる ▪ *Fall out of the line* and wait here. 列を離れてここで待て.

feed** a person **a line《口》(人に)調子のいい話をする, 嘘をつく, はめる ▪ I discovered that I was *being fed a line* when he gave the job to someone else. 彼がその勤め口を他の人にまわしたので, 私はだまされていたとわかった.

fluff** one's **lines →blow one's LINEs.

get a line on《口》…についての知識[情報, 手がかり]を得る, について知るようになる ▪ He *got a* straight *line on* it. 彼はそれについて正しい知識を得た ▪ I am *getting a line on* England. 私はイギリスのことがだんだん分かってきている.

get into line =fall in LINE.

get** a person **into line 人を同調[結束]させる ▪ It was difficult to *get* all the owners *into line*. すべての所有主を結束させることはむずかしかった.

get [step] out of line **1** 列を離れる;《口》まちがい[問題]を起こす ▪ Many young men *get out of line* these days. この頃はまちがいを起こす若者が多い.

2 言われた[期待された]ように行動しない ▪ If I *stepped out of line* again I'd be out of a job. も

う一度指示に従わなかったら首にされるだろう.

get the [*one's*] ***lines crossed*** 《口》混線して通じない; 頭がこんがらがる ▪ They *got their lines crossed* and took this to be an order. 彼らは頭がこんがらがってこれを命令と取った.

give *a person* ***a line on*** 《口》...について人に知らせる ▪ *Give* me *a line on* these birds. これらの鳥について私に教えてください.

give line (***enough***) (楽に捕えるため)一時自由にさせておく, あめをしゃぶらせておく ▪ *Give* him *line enough*, and we shall find out what he is doing. しばらく勝手に泳がせておけば彼のしていることがわかるだろう. ☞「針にかかった魚に十分糸を繰り出してやる」が原義.

go down the line (***for***) (...を)心から[全面的に]支持する ▪ He *went down the line for* the federal government. 彼は連邦政府を心から支持した.

go into the line 戦列に加わる ▪ The 4th Battalion *went into the line* at Santa Maria. 第4大隊はサンタマリアの戦列に加わった.

go on wrong lines まちがった方法を採る ▪ The earlier missionaries had *gone on wrong lines*. 比較的初期の宣教師は誤った伝道方法を採っていた.

go over the line 限度を越える ▪ He *went over the line* when he shot the unarmed robber five times in the chest. 彼が丸腰の盗賊の胸を5回も撃ったのは行き過ぎだった.

L

go up on *one's* ***lines*** 《米口》せりふを忘れる, 絶句する ▪ The actor *went up on his lines* in one scene on opening night. その役者は初演の夜にある場面でせりふを忘れてしまった.

go up the line 基地から前線に出る ▪ The vicar at the front expects to *go up the line* very soon. 従軍牧師はもうすぐ基地から前線に出ることになっている.

go up the lines 塹壕(ざんごう)まで出る ▪ We *go up the lines* tomorrow to relieve them. 我々は彼らと交代するため, 明日塹壕へ出る.

hard line 強硬路線(の) ▪ The dictator has always taken a *hard line* policy. 独裁者はずっと強硬政策をとってきた.

hard lines (***on, for***) 《俗》(...に対する)不運, 苦境, ひどい仕打ち ▪ It is *hard lines on* [*for*] you to have him promoted over your head. 彼があなたを飛び越えて昇進するとはあなたは運が悪い ▪ *Hard lines*, Jim! ついてなかったね, ジム.

have a line on 《口》...についての知識[情報, 手がかり]を得る, 得ている ▪ The investigators *had a line on* the ringleader. 調査官たちは首謀者について手がかりを得た.

have *a person* ***on a line*** (話などで)人をかつぐ; 人の気をもませる ▪ He was just *having* you *on a line*. 彼はただあなたをかついでいたにすぎない.

hit the line **1** 《アメフト》球を持って敵側のラインを通り抜けようとする ▪ Don't flinch, don't fall; *hit the line* hard. ひるまず倒れず, ラインを突破せよ.

2 断固として試みる ▪ Once you determine to *hit the line*, you can do anything. 断固としてやると決めたら, 何だってできる.

hold [***keep***]... ***in line*** ...を順序よく並ばせておく; を一致[団結]させておく ▪ *Keep* the crowd *in line*. 群衆を順序よく並ばせておけ ▪ The leader must *keep* the members *in line* behind a single program. 指導者は団員たちに一つの計画を一致して支持させねばならない.

hold the line **1** (電話の)受話器を持ったまま待つ; 通話が切れないようにする ▪ *Hold the line*, please. そのままでしばらくお待ちください.

2 立場を堅く守る; 現状を維持する ▪ We must *hold the line* in the Galapagos. ガラパゴス諸島では現状を維持しなければならない ▪ It is absolutely necessary to *hold the* price *line* now. 今物価を安定させることが絶対に必要である.

3 《米》戦線を結集する, 団結する ▪ Management *held the line* against wage increases. 経営者側は賃上げに反対して団結した.

in line **1** (横)列をなして ▪ The students were drawn up *in line*. 学生たちは整列していた.

2 (意見が)一致して; 同調して ▪ They are politically *in line*. 彼らは政治上は意見が一致している.

in *one's* ***line*** **1** ...の専門[商売]で(は); ...流では ▪ To write a novel is not *in my line*. 小説を書くのは私の専門ではありません ▪ You are a good boy *in your line*. 君は君流ではよい少年だ.

2 ...の性[能力]に合って; の得意で ▪ It is not *in my line* to interfere. 口出しするのは私の柄ではない ▪ Storekeeping was not *in my line*. 商店経営は私の性に合わなかった.

3 ...の好きな, 趣味に合う ▪ Have you got anything *in my line*? 私の好きなものが何かありますか. ☞↔ out of one's LINE.

in line for [***to*** *do*] ...を得る[する]見込みがあって; の候補になって ▪ He will be *in line for* the post of chief justice. 彼は大審院長の地位を得る見込みがあるだろう ▪ He was first [second, etc.] *in line for* the governor. 彼は知事候補の最有力[第二有力, など]者だった.

in line with **1** ...と一直線に[で] ▪ If your feet are pointing at a door, then your bed is *in line with* the door. 足がドアを向いていれば, ベッドはドアと一直線になっている.

2 ...と一致[調和]して, に順応して ▪ That is *in line with* our family tradition. それは我が家の家風と一致する ▪ You must work *in line with* the progress of time. 君は時の進展に従って働かねばならない.

in [***on***] ***the front line*** **1** 第一線で, 最前線で ▪ This laboratory is *on the front line* of medical research. 当実験所は医療研究の最前線に立っている.

2 最も困難[不快, 危険]な場所で ▪ As a police officer, Jim is *in the front line* every day. ジムは警察官として毎日最も危険な任務についている. ☞「(戦場における)最前線」が原義.

in the line その道に明るく ▪ I'm poor at history, but my sister is *in the line*. 私は歴史に弱いが, 姉

はその道に精通している.

in* (*the*) *line of duty 職務中に; 公用[職務]で ▪ He has given his life *in line of duty.* 彼は殉職した ▪ *In line of duty* I visited many factories. 私は公用でたくさんの工場を訪ねた.

in the line of fire 射程内に; 攻撃にさらされて (→ in the FIRING line) ▪ You are *in the line of fire* between the two sides. あなたは両陣営からの攻撃にさらされている.

in the male* [*female*] *line 男系[女系]の[で] ▪ The succession to the throne is *in the* direct *male line.* 王位継承は直系の男子によって行われる.

jump in line 《米》列に割り込む (= jump the QUEUE); 先取りする ▪ One of the customers *jumped in line* ahead of us. 客の一人が並んでいる我々の先に割り込みをした.

keep in line 割り当てられた位置を守る[守らせる]; 規則を守る[守らせる] ▪ Everyone must *keep in line.* 人はみな規則を守らなければならない ▪ The president *kept* the members of his party *in line.* 総裁は全党員に党則を守らせた.

keep to** one's **own line 自分の専門[商売]をあくまで続ける ▪ I will *keep to my own line* of grocery. 食料雑貨商という自分の商売をあくまで続けよう.

lay it on the line 率直に言う ▪ Dad really *laid it on the line* with a lot of his comments. 父は本当に率直に, いろいろとコメントした.

lay* [*put*]** *one's* ***job* [*life, future, reputation, neck,* 《米卑》 *ass, etc.] ***on the line*/** *one's* ***job* [*life, future, reputation, neck,* 《米卑》 *ass,*** etc.] ***is on the line*** (経歴・命・将来・名誉・首などを)賭ける ▪ You will *lay your job on the line* if you tell the boss that he is wrong. 社長に間違っているなんて言ったら首を賭けることになるぞ ▪ *His neck was on the line*, but he didn't care. 彼の命運がかかっていたが, 彼は気にも留めなかった.

lay … on the dotted line (点線上に打ち出す, とは)…を表明する; 明るみに出す ▪ The professor *laid* the problem *on the dotted line.* 教授はその問題を明るみに出した.

lay … on the line 《主に米》 **1** (全額)を前払いにする[出す] ▪ A million dollars had to *be laid on the line.* 百万ドルを全額先払いしなければならなかった.
2 (命令・おどし・意見など)をきっぱりと述べる ▪ The court *laid* the proposition *on the line.* 法廷はきっぱりとその提議を主張した.
3 …を危険にさらす ▪ The boxer is *laying* his title *on the line* in the fight. そのボクサーはその試合でタイトルを奪われそうだ.

one's [*a*] ***line of thought*** 考え方, 推理の仕方 ▪ *My line of thought* is this. 私の考え方はこうだ ▪ He can take *an* independent *line of thought.* 彼は独自の考え方をすることができる.

one's ***line of work*** (人の)職業 ▪ What's *your sister's line of work*? お姉さんのお仕事は何ですか.

line upon line **1** 着々と《進むなど》 ▪ They went on, *line upon line*, with their work. 彼らは着々と仕事を続けていった.
2 繰り返し繰り返し; 諄々と; 連続して ▪ God reveals Himself *line upon line*, precept upon precept. 神は繰り返し繰り返し教えを重ねてお姿を現し給う ▪ They ranged the volumes *line upon line.* 彼らはその書物を連続的に並べた.

one's ***lines are cast* [*are set, have fallen*] (*to*** *one*) ***in … places* [*in a … place*]** 人が運命によって…な所に住むことになる, …な境遇に置かれる (《聖》 *Ps.* 16. 6) ▪ *Her lines were cast in* pleasant *places.* 彼女は運命によって愉快な境遇に置かれた ▪ *My brother's lines have fallen to* him *in an* unpleasant *place.* 兄は運命によってきわめて不快な所に住むようになった. ☞土地に線を引いて居住地を割り当てることから.

Line('s) busy. 《米》(電話が)話し中 (= 《英》 NUMBER('s) engaged) ▪ The *line's busy.*—OK, I'll call back later. お話し中ですが—わかりました, 後ほどかけ直します.

next in line (後継順で)ある地位(王位・大統領職など)の次期後継者である, 継承[相続]順位第1位の ▪ The king had no heir and his brother was *next in line* to the throne. 国王には世継ぎがおらず王の弟が王位継承順位第1位だった ▪ Who is *next in line* to become Queen of England? 誰がイギリス女王の次期後継者になるのか?

not** one's **line 自分の専門[得意]とするところではない ▪ Women were*n't my line.* 女性は私の専門とするところではなかった.

on a line 同じ平面に; 同等に[の] ▪ Place parentheses around words *on a line.* 高さをそろえて語句をかっこで囲みなさい.

on* [*off*] *line 《口》 **1** (機械が)オンライン[オフライン]で ▪ Ensure that the printer is *on line.* プリンターがオンラインになっていることを確かめなさい.
2 (人が)働いて[休んで], (機械が)動いて[止まって] ▪ He's back *on line* after a short illness. 彼はしばらく病気で休んだあとまた働いている.

on … lines …の方針[計画, 方法]で ▪ You must study the subject *on* sound *lines.* あなたは健全な方法でその問題を研究せねばならない.

on the dotted line 点線の所に《署名すべき所を言う》 ▪ The only thing lacking is Smith's signature *on the dotted line.* 不備は点線の所にスミス氏の署名がないだけである.

on* [*in*] *the firing line →FIRING.

on the line **1** 境界[分岐]線上に; はっきりどちらともつかないで ▪ His fate is still *on the line.* 彼の運命はまだどっちに転ぶかわからない.
2 (絵などが)目の高さにかけられて《優待を示す》 ▪ The picture was hung *on the line* at the Academy. その絵は王立美術院で優待されていた ▪ I was *on the line* in the big room. 私はその大きな部屋で優待席につかされていた.
3 まる見えにして, 危うくして ▪ It put his future *on the line* when he backed this policy. この政策を支持したとき, 彼の将来は明らかに危うくなった.

L

4 即座に ▪ He paid cash *on the line.* 彼は現金を即座に払った.
5 売春するように ▪ She lost her job and went *on the line.* 彼女は職を失って売春婦になった.
6 電話に出て ▪ Your party is *on the line.* 先方が電話にお出になりました.

on* [*along*] *the lines of ...の方法で, をまねて, に似た ▪ The hotel was built *on the lines of* a Swiss pension. このホテルはスイスのペンション式に造られた ▪ We want a design *along the lines of* my parents' house but smaller. 両親の家に似せてそれを小さめにしたデザインにしてほしい.

on top line 最も効率よく動いて ▪ A lot of money is needed to keep the machine *on top line.* その機械を最も効率よく動かすには大金がいる.

out of line **1** 一列にならないで, 列を乱して ▪ One of the pupils is *out of line.* 生徒の一人が列を乱している.
2 まっすぐでなく, 垂直でなく (*with*) ▪ That wall is *out of line.* その塀はまっすぐでない ▪ The tower is *out of line with* the ground. その塔は地面と垂直でない.
3 (...と)調和[一致]しないで, 釣り合わないで (*with*) ▪ Prices and wages were badly *out of line.* 物価と賃金がひどく釣り合いがとれていなかった.
4 変な; 異常な, 狂った ▪ Something is *out of line* with that man. あの男にはどこか変なところがある.
5 まちがった; 無礼をして ▪ I don't know if I am *out of line.* 私はまちがっているかどうかわからない.
6 (価格が)法外で ▪ The prices have been *out of line.* このところ物価は法外である.

out of* one's *line 性に合わないで; きらいで; 不得意[苦手]で (↔ in one's LINE) ▪ Cards are *out of my line.* 私はトランプは苦手だ ▪ It is *out of my line* to advise. 助言などするのは私のがらではない.

over the line 必要生産費以上で[を使って] ▪ They tend to be *over the line.* 彼らは必要生産費以上の費用を使いがちである.

one's (***own***) ***line of country*** 〚主に否定文で〛...の得意の[専門の, 興味をもつ]事がら ▪ That is not *my line of country.* それは私の得意とするところではない. ☞キツネ狩りで各狩猟家にはそれぞれ特定の活動範囲があることから.

pass the line →cross the LINE.

put ... on the line ...を賭ける ▪ The lawyer *put* his reputation *on the line* when he decided to defend this woman. 弁護士はこの女性を弁護することを決めたとき自分の評判を賭けた.

put* [*place*] *... on the line = lay ... on the LINE.

read between the lines →READ².

ride the line **1** 《狩》猟場で馬をまっすぐに進める ▪ He always *rode the line.* 彼はいつも猟場で馬をまっすぐに進めた.
2 《米》動く家畜[牛]の群れの周囲を馬で回って群れを離れるものを追い込む ▪ They *ride the line* day in day out. 彼らは毎日毎日牛の群れの回りを馬で乗り回して追い込みをする.

right along* [*down*] *the line = all along the LINE.

***send a line* [*a few lines*]** →drop a LINE.

shoot (*a person*) ***a line*** →SHOOT a line.

sign on the dotted line (寸分たがわず)指図に従う; 出された条件を文句なくのむ ▪ Though their demand was unreasonable, we had to *sign on the dotted line.* 彼らの要求は無茶なものだったが, 我々はそれをのむほかなかった. ☞「点線の所に署名する」が原義.

somewhere along* [*down*] *the line 《口》成長[発達, 製作]のある段階で ▪ *Somewhere along the line* I could have been a different person. 成長のある段階で私は違った人間になれただろうに ▪ *Somewhere down the line* they stopped loving each other. 交際中のある時点で互いに愛がさめた.

spin (*a person*) ***a line*** = SHOOT a line.

step out of line = get out of LINE.

strike out a line for *oneself* →STRIKE².

take a clear line はっきりした政策をとる ▪ We should *take a clear line* of action to prevent the spread of bird flu. 鳥インフルエンザ蔓延防止の明確な具体策をとるべきだ.

take a strong* [*firm*] *line 強力な行動をとる ▪ He *took a strong line* with the enemy. 彼は敵に対して強力な行動をした.

***take* [*keep* (*to*)] *one's* own line** **1** 自分の道をまっすぐに進む ▪ Every one should *keep his own line.* 人はみな自分の道をまっすぐに進むべきである.
2 (他人とは)独立の行動をとる ▪ The youth would *take his own line* rather than follow suit. その若者は他人に倣うよりは独自の行動を取る.

the line of beauty 美の線, 波状[〜形の]線 ▪ A wavy line is a line more productive of beauty, for which reason we call it *the line of beauty.* 波状線は他の線より美を多く生じる線であるから, 我々はそれを美の線と呼ぶ. ☞18世紀イギリスの風俗画家 Hogarth によれば〜形があらゆる美の形の必須要素であるという.

the thin red line 多勢に対する無勢の勇ましい抵抗 ▪ The miracle of *the thin red line* did occur. 多勢に無勢の勇敢な抵抗の奇跡がまさに起きた. ☞クリミア戦争中の赤い上着を着ていたスコットランド歩兵隊を評して W. H. Russell (1820–1907) が that thin red streak と言ったことから.

throw a good line 魚釣りがうまい ▪ Although he hasn't been fishing for long, he can *throw a good line.* 彼の釣り歴は長くないが, なかなか腕がよい.

toe* [*dress*] *the line →TOE².

***tread* [*walk*] *a fine* [*thin*] *line* (*between* A *and* B)** **1** A(好ましいこと)とB(好ましくないこと)の間でかろうじてAをする ▪ He was *walking a fine line between* being funny *and* being rude. 彼はこっけいと見られるか無礼とされるかのすれすれの行動をとっていた.
2 (成功か失敗)いずれか紙一重の道を歩んでいる

L

▪ Closers *walk a thin line between* failure *and* success. 押さえの切り札投手は失敗か成功いずれか紙一重の道を歩んでいる.

under the line 赤道(直下)に ▪ The Strait of Malacca is *under the line*. マラッカ海峡は赤道にある.

way out of line 《口》全く不適切で, 全く受け入れられない ▪ The teacher was *way out of line* when he hit you. その教師が君をなぐったのは完全に間違っていた ▪ The price of the house is *way out of line* for this part of town. その家の値段は町のこの地域にしては実に法外である.

wet** one's **line →WET[2].

with all** one's **line 一族もろとも ▪ He perished *with all his line*. 彼は一族もろとも滅亡した.

with rod and line 釣りざおで; 魚釣りに ▪ He is clever *with rod and line*. 彼は魚釣りがうまい.

line[2] /laɪn/ 動 ***line up ... in** one's **sights*** (...を)まっすぐにねらう ▪ He *lined up* the deer *in his sights*. 彼はそのシカを(銃で)まっすぐにねらった.

line[3] /laɪn/ 動 ***line** one's **(own) pockets [purse]*** たくさん金を儲ける; 私腹を肥やす ▪ The mayor *lined his pockets* with bribes. 市長は賄賂で私腹を肥やした.

line** one's **stomach 《口》腹ごしらえをする ▪ *Line your stomach* before you start. 出発前に腹ごしらえをしなさい.

linen /línən/ 名 ***wash [air]** one's **dirty linen at home [in public]*** 《口》内輪の恥を外へ出さない[出す] ▪ People ought to *wash their dirty linen at home*. 人々は内輪の恥は外へ出さないようにすべきである ▪ It is not seemly to *wash one's dirty linen in public*. 内輪の恥を外へさらけ出すのはみっともない. ☞linen「下着類」.

lingo /líŋgoʊ/ 名 ***crack the lingo*** (団体・専門用の)人にわからない言葉を話す ▪ They *cracked the lingo* of modern psychotherapy. 彼らは近代心理療法のちんぷんかんぷんの言葉を話した.

talk a lingo 《口》外国語を話す ▪ Those people cannot speak English but *talk a lingo*. あの人たちは英語が話せないで, 外国語を話す.

lining /láɪnɪŋ/ 名 ***a silver lining*** (暗い状況での)明るい見通し, (逆境の中の)希望の光 ▪ Automakers hoped for *a silver lining* with the popularity of hybrids. 自動車メーカーはハイブリッド車の好評に期待をかけた.

link[1] /lɪŋk/ 名 ***a [the] weak link (in the chain)*** 弱点, 弁慶の泣き所, (チームなど団体・組織の)一番もろい個所 ▪ That night I was *an* obvious *weak link in the chain* on this team. その夜の試合では明らかに僕がチームの足を引っ張った.

break links 繋がりを断つ, 関係を解消する ▪ I do feel inclined to *break links* with the past. ぜひとも過去のしがらみを絶ちたいと思う.

let out the links 大力を出す; もっと思い切ってやる ▪ The horse *let out the links* and trotted it in 3 minutes. 馬は大いに馬力を出して速歩でそこを3分で走った.

link[2] /lɪŋk/ 動 ***link** one's **arm in [through]*** 腕を...と組み合わせる ▪ He *linked his arm in* hers. 彼は彼女と腕を組み合った.

link hands 手を取り合う ▪ They *linked hands* before they parted. 彼らは別れ際に手を取り合った.

lion /láɪən/ 名 ***a lion in the way [path]*** (特に想像上の)前途に横たわる困難[障害]《ある行動をしない口実に使われる》(《聖》*Prov*. 26. 13) ▪ You have always *lions in the path*. 君はいつも前途に危険を想像しているんだね.

a lion's skin →the LION's skin.

(as) brave as a lion 非常に勇敢で ▪ The captain is *brave as a lion*. 船長は非常に勇敢だ.

beard the lion in his den →BEARD[2].

fight [battle, defend] like a lion 勇ましく戦う ▪ The father *fought like a lion* to protect his family. 父親は家族を守るために勇猛果敢に戦った.

in the lion's den 危険な場所に (→the LION's den) ▪ He is now *in the lion's den*—that is, the boss's room. 彼は今恐ろしい場所—つまり社長室にいる. ☞《聖》*Dan*. の話から.

in the lion's paws 大きな危険に陥って ▪ The detective found himself *in the lion's paws*. 探偵は自分が絶体絶命の危険に陥っているのを知った.

make a lion of (人)をもてはやす, (人)に大騒ぎする ▪ He *is made a lion* (*of*) among young ladies. 彼は若い女性たちの間でもてはやされている.

put [place]** one's **head in the lion's mouth ことさらに危険を求める ▪ If you deliberately offend him, it is *putting your head in the lion's mouth*. わざと彼を怒らせるなら, ことさらに危険を求めることになる.

see [show] the lions (市の)名所を見物する[案内する] ▪ He went to *see the lions*. 彼は名所見物に行った ▪ I will *show* you *the lions* of the city. 市の名所をご案内いたします. ☞ロンドン塔に昔ライオンが飼ってあって, 田舎から来た人を案内して見せたことから.

the British Lion 英国の紋章のライオン像, 英国の象徴 ▪ *The British Lion* is used in the Arms of Canada as well. 英国のライオン像はカナダの紋章にも使われている.

The lion lies down with the lamb. ライオンが子羊と共に伏す《敵同士が仲直りする》(《聖》*Isa*. 11. 6) ▪ When *the lion lies down with the lamb*, the lamb doesn't get much sleep. 敵同士が仲直りをしても, 弱い方は気を抜くことができない.

the lion's den 非常に危険な場所 ▪ They rescued me out of *the lion's den*. 彼らは私を窮地から救い出してくれた.

the lion's mouth 非常に危険な所 (《聖》*Ps*. 22. 21) ▪ It is better to die than to run into *the lion's mouth*. 非常に危ない所へ飛び込むよりは, 死んだほうがよい.

the lion's provider ジャッカル; 下働き; 手先を務める人 ▪ She is his cook and general *lion's provider*. 彼女は彼の料理人でよろず下働きだ. ☞ジャッ

L

カルはライオンが獲物をあさるときその手伝いをすると言われたことから.

the lion's share (***of***) 《英》(…の)一番大きい[主な]部分, うまい汁 ▪ You want *the lion's share of* the profit. あなたはその利益の一番大きな分け前が欲しいのだ ▪ He is ready to take *the lion's share of* responsibility. 彼はいつでも進んで責任の大半を負う. ☞他の動物とともに仕留めた獲物を分けるのを拒んだイソップ物語のライオンの話から.

the [***a***] ***lion's skin*** こけおどし; から元気 ▪ *A lion's skin* was never bought cheap. こけおどしが安くついたことはない. ☞イソップ物語のライオンの皮を着たロバの話から.

throw [***feed***]***… to the lions*** 人身御供にする ▪ I really felt I'd *been fed to the lions*. 実に人身御供にされた気分だった ▪ He is not a man to *throw* you *to the lions* if anything goes wrong. 彼は何かうまく行かないような場合, 君を人身御供にするような人ではない.

twist the lion's tail 《新聞》イギリスの悪口を書く[言う]; イギリスの権利を侵す ▪ Foreigners cannot *twist the lion's tail* with impunity. 外国人がイギリスの悪口を書くとただではすまない. ☞ライオンはイギリス王室の紋章でイギリスの象徴.

walk into the lion's den 自ら死中に入る (→the LION's den) ▪ He was so bold as to *walk into the lion's den*. 彼は勇敢にも自ら危地に立った.

L

lip /lɪp/ 名 ***be steeped*** [***immersed***] ***in … to the lips*** (悪徳など)にすっかりはまり込んでいる ▪ He *was steeped in* infamy *to the lips*. 彼は不名誉にすっかり陥っていた.

bite *one's* ***lip***(***s***) **1** (くやしさ・腹立たしさで)くちびるをかむ ▪ She *bit her lip* with annoyance at their remarks. 彼女は彼らの言葉に腹を立ててくちびるをかんだ ▪ He was furious, but *bit his lips*. 彼は激怒したが, じっと怒りを抑えた.

2 (笑いなどの感情を抑えるため)くちびるをかむ ▪ I had to *bite my lips* to keep from laughter. 私は笑いをこらえるため, くちびるをかまなければならなかった.

button [***zip***] *one's* ***lip***(***s***) 《俗》〖主に命令文で〗黙る ▪ *Button your lip*, or else! 黙れ, さもないと(ひどい目にあうぞ)!

carry [***have, keep***] ***a stiff upper lip*** 《口》 **1** がんばる, くじけない ▪ *Keep a stiff upper lip*; no bones broken. 元気を出せ. 骨はどこも折れてはいない ▪ He always *carries a stiff upper lip* and comes up smiling. 彼はいつもくじけないで, 逆境から元気よく立ち直る.

2 かたくなである ▪ She used to *carry* [*keep*] *a stiff upper lip*. 彼女は以前はがんこだった.

curl *one's* ***lip*** 《雅》上くちびるを少しあげる[曲げる]《軽蔑の表情》 ▪ You *curled your lip* when they were mentioned. 彼らの話が出たとき, あなたは口をゆがめた《軽蔑の表情をした》.

Don't give me any of your lip. 口答えをしてはいけません ▪ Do as I tell you and *don't give me any of your lip*. 私の言う通りにして, 口答えはだめよ.

drop from *one's* ***lips*** (言葉などが)口から出る ▪ The final word *dropped from his lips*. 決定的な言葉が彼の口から漏れた.

escape *one's* ***lips*** (言葉などが)つい[不用意に]もれる ▪ Not a word *escaped her lips* about her son's whereabouts. 彼女は息子の居所については一言も言わなかった.

from *one's* ***lips*** …が言うと ▪ This sounds strange *from your lips*. これは君が言えば妙に響く.

give lip 《俗》生意気である, 厚かましい ▪ A boy *gave* me some *lip* the other day. ある少年が先日私に生意気なことを言った.

give *one's* ***lips*** キスを許す ▪ She *gave her lips* to me. 彼女は僕にキスをさせてくれた.

hang *one's* ***lip*** (屈辱のため)べそをかく ▪ The boy *hung his lip* and ran away. 少年はべそをかいて走り去った.

hang on *a person's* ***lips*** →HANG².

have [***keep***] ***a stiff upper lip*** →carry a stiff upper LIP.

lay *one's* ***finger to*** *one's* ***lips*** →put one's finger to one's LIPs.

lick [***smack***] *one's* ***lips*** →LICK one's chops.

lip service 口先だけのおじょうず[同意] ▪ That's just *lip service*. あれはほんの口先だけのおじょうずさ.

one's ***lips are sealed*** 《戯》誰にも話さない ▪ Don't tell anyone about it. —*My lips are sealed*. それは誰にも言わないでくれ—誰にも話さないよ.

Loose lips sink ships. 《諺》しゃべりすぎるとこちらが不利になる.

make (***up***) ***a lip*** 口をとがらす《不きげん・侮蔑の表情》 ▪ The girl *made a lip* at her teacher. その女の子は先生に向かって口をとがらせた.

None of your lip! 《俗》生意気言うな! ▪ Never again, *none of your lip!* 二度と生意気を言うんじゃないぞ.

on everyone's lips 誰もが話して, 興味を持って ▪ The question *on everyone's lips* now is: will they win or not? 今衆目の関心を集めているのは, 彼らが勝つかどうかだ.

on *one's* [*a person's*] ***lips*** **1** 口にのぼって, よく口にして ▪ His name is often *on our lips*. 彼の名はよく我々が口にする ▪ They moved about with songs *on their lips*. 彼らは歌いながら歩き回った.

2 口から出かかって ▪ A question was *on my lips*, but I dared not ask it. ある疑問が口から出かかっていたがあえて尋ねなかった.

open *one's* ***lips*** (口を開いて)ものを言う ▪ She never *opened her lips*. 彼女は全然口をきかなかった.

pass *one's* ***lips*** **1** (言葉が)口からもれる ▪ No complaint ever *passes her lips*. 彼女は不平は一言ももらさない.

2 人に食べられる[飲まれる, 話される] ▪ No food has *passed his lips* since then. あれから彼は何も食べていない ▪ Have you ever heard a bad word about him *pass anyone's lips*? 誰かが彼の悪口を言うのを聞いたことがあるかい?

purse *one's* ***lips*** くちびるをすぼめる《非難・疑い・考えの集中などを表す》 ▪ The princess *pursed her lips* and frowned. 王女はくちびるをすぼめて顔をしかめた ▪ She was doing sums, *her lips* a little *pursed*. 彼女はくちびるを少しすぼめて計算をしていた.

put [***lay***] *one's* ***finger to*** *one's* ***lips*** くちびるに指を当てる《沈黙せよとの合図》 ▪ When I began to talk, she *put her finger to her lips*. 私が話を始めようとすると, 彼女はくちびるに指を当てた.

read by the lips (耳の不自由な人が)くちびるの動きで読み取る ▪ My deaf aunt learned to *read by the lips*. 耳が聞こえない私のおばさんは読唇術を学んだ.

Read my lips. 《米口》(私の言うことを) 注意して聞きなさい, 私の言葉を信じなさい ▪ *Read my lips.* You're not having any more chocolate. よくお聞き. これ以上チョコレートはだめよ. ☞元米国大統領 George Herbert Walker Bush が選挙のキャンペーンに用いた "Read my lips: no new taxes."「信じてほしい. 新税は導入しない」から.

seal *a person's* ***lips*** →SEAL².

shoot out the lip →SHOOT².

stop *one's* ***lip*** 《口》生意気言うのをやめる ▪ I told him to *stop his lip*. 彼に生意気言うのはよせと言った.

zip *one's* ***lip***(***s***) →button one's LIP(s).

lip service /lípsə̀ːrvəs/ 名 ***pay*** [***give, offer***] ***lip service to*** …に対して口先だけのことを言う, 口先だけ賛成する, お世辞を言う (《聖》*Matt.* 15. 8ほか) (→LIP service) ▪ He always *pays lip service to* his wife's wishes. 彼はいつも妻の願いに口先だけいい返事をする ▪ The firm *gives lip service to* the notion of sexual equality but you see only males around you. 会社は口先だけ男女平等を唱えるが周りには男性ばかりだ ▪ He is prone to *offer lip service*. 彼は口先だけのおじょうずを言いがちである.

liquid /líkwəd/ 名 ***a liquid lunch*** 《戯》(食事より)アルコール飲料が主体の昼食 ▪ He had *a liquid lunch* and fell asleep at his desk in the afternoon. 彼は昼食代わりに飲んで午後デスクで眠り込んだ.

liquid assets 流動資産 ▪ Unlike fixed assets, most *liquid assets* are intangible. 固定資産と違って流動資産はほとんど無形である.

liquid refreshment 《戯》飲み物, アルコール飲料 ▪ I'm in need of some *liquid refreshment*. 1杯ひっかけなくては.

liquidation /lìkwədéɪʃən/ 名 ***go into liquidation*** (会社など)店をたたむ, 破産する ▪ The company has *gone into* voluntary *liquidation*. その会社は自発的に店をたたんだ.

liquor¹ /líkər/ 名 (***be***) ***in liquor*** **1** きこしめして(いる), 一杯きげんで(ある), 酔って(いる) ▪ The moment he *is in liquor*, he starts quarreling. 彼は一杯きげんになるとすぐ口げんかを始める.

2 せんじ汁の状態で[の] ▪ The pekoe's strength *in liquor* is very great. せんじ汁の状態の[湯を加えて出された]ペコーの力は非常に強い《高級紅茶は濃く出る》.

carry [***hold***] *one's* ***liquor*** 酒に酔わない ▪ He can *carry his liquor* like a sailor. 彼は水夫みたいに酒に酔わない.

the worse for liquor →the WORSE for drink.

liquor² /líkər/ 動 ***liquor*** *a person's* ***boots*** 夫に不義をする, 人の妻を寝取る ▪ He had an underhand design of *liquoring John's boots* for him. 彼はジョンの妻を寝取ろうという悪巧みを持っていた.

liquor *one's* ***boots*** 酒を飲む; 《カトリック》終油の秘蹟を行う ▪ He *liquors his boots* every evening. 彼は毎晩酒を飲む ▪ As Isaac lay on his deathbed the priest *liquored his boots*. アイザックが死の床についていると司祭は終油の秘蹟を行なった.

list /lɪst/ 名 ***a list*** [***record,*** etc.] ***as long as*** *one's* ***arm*** 長ったらしいリスト[記録, など] ▪ Here is a guy with *a* criminal *record as long as his arm*. この男には延々と続く犯罪記録がある.

close the list(***s***) 募集を締め切る ▪ *The lists were closed* yesterday. 募集は昨日締め切られた.

compile [***draw up***] ***a list of*** →make a LIST of.

enter (***the***) ***lists*** 《古風》 **1** (…に対して)挑戦する; (の)挑戦に応じる《主に論戦について》(*against*) ▪ Few were capable of *entering the lists against* their assailants. 攻撃者たちに応戦できる人が少なかった.

2 戦列[競争]に加わる ▪ We have to *enter the lists* for the company. 会社のために競争に加わらねばならない. ☞lists「(中世騎士のやり試合の)試合場」.

first on the list 一番で, 筆頭で ▪ His name stands *first on the list*. 彼の名は筆頭にある《彼は一番である》.

in the list →on the LIST.

lead [***head***] ***the list*** 首位にある ▪ He *heads the list* of pro-Japanese men of prominence. 彼は知名な親日家たちのトップにいる.

make [***draw up, compile***] ***a list of*** …の表を作る ▪ She *made a list of* things to buy. 彼女は買い物のリストを作った.

on the active [***reserve, retired***] ***list*** 現役[予備役, 退役]で ▪ He is an officer *on the active list*. 彼は現役の将校だ.

on [***in***] ***the list*** 名簿に載って ▪ We did not find the name *in the list*. 名簿にその名は見あたらなかった.

on the short list 《英》(最終選考のための)候補者リストに載って ▪ You are *on the short list* for the job. 君はその仕事の候補者の一人だ.

on the sick list →SICK.

listen /lísən/ 動 ***Don't listen to him*** [***her,*** etc.]. 彼[彼女, など]の言うことを信じるな ▪ *Don't listen to him*. He's going to fool you. 彼の言うことを信じてはだめだ. だまそうとしているんだから.

listen good (***to***) →look GOOD (to).

listen (***in***) ***to the radio*** →RADIO.

listen with half an ear いいかげんに聞く ▪I was *listening with* only *half an ear* to what she was telling me. 彼女が言っていることを生半可にしか聞いていなかった.

listener /lísənər/ 名 ***a good [bad] listener*** 聞き上手[下手] ▪I found him *a good listener.* 彼は聞き上手だった.

Listeners hear no good [never hear good] of themselves. 《諺》立ち聞きして自分の良い噂を聞く者はない《立ち聞きすればしゃくの種》.

literature /lítərətʃər/ 名 ***gray literature*** 非営利目的で出版される政府広報誌 ▪*Gray literature* is freely available on many Web sites. 政府広報誌は多くのウェブサイトで自由に入手できる.

lithe /laɪð/ 形 ***(as) lithe as a panther*** 動作がきわめてしなやかで ▪That dancer is *as lithe as a panther.* あのダンサーは動作がきわめてしなやかである.

litter[1] /lítər/ 名 ***a litter bug*** 《口》道路, 公共の場にゴミを落とす人, ゴミをどこにでも捨てる人 ▪Don't be *a litter bug* and pick up your pet's waste. 道路にゴミを落とさずペットの糞も残さないこと.

at a [one] litter (ブタなど)一はらで[に] ▪The sow had ten little pigs *at a litter.* 雌ブタは一はらで子ブタを10匹産んだ.

in a (state of) litter (部屋などが)ちらかって ▪His room was *in* such *a litter.* 彼の部屋は非常にちらかっていた.

in litter (犬・ブタなどが)子をはらんで ▪The doe was *in litter* at the time of purchase. 買ったとき雌ジカは子をはらんでいた.

make a litter of ...をちらかす ▪He *made a litter of* torn paper on the floor. 彼は床の上にちぎれた紙を散らかした.

litter[2] /lítər/ 動 ***be littered with*** 〚受身で〛...で散らかって[汚れて]いる ▪The room *is littered with* broken glass. 部屋には割れたガラスが飛び散っている ▪This book *is littered with* printing errors. この本は誤植だらけだ.

little /lítəl/ 形名副 ***a little*** 少し; 少しの間 ▪I can speak English *a little.* 英語は少し話せます ▪He came after *a little.* 彼はしばらく経ってから来た.

a little goes a long way ちょっとしたことが大いに役に立つ[効力がある] ▪*A little* kindness *goes a long way* sometimes. ちょっとした親切が時に大いにものを言う.

a little thing of mine ささやかな私の作品, 拙作 ▪He spoke highly of *a little thing of mine.* 彼は拙作をほめてくれた.

after a little →AFTER.

as little 同じくあまり...ない ▪He knows the world *as little.* 彼も同じくあまり世間を知らない.

be a little ... to *do* 《米口》あまり...だから...しない[できない] ▪He *is a little* poor *to* go to college. 彼は非常に貧乏なので大学へ行けない. ☞a little = too.

but little ほんのわずかしか...ない ▪Man wants *but little* here below. 人はこの世ではほんの少しの物しかいらない ▪Though you know *but little*, yet that little you do know counts. ほんのわずかしか知らなくても, その身についたわずかな知識が重要だ.

by little and little 少しずつ ▪We knew this *by little and little.* このことが少しずつ分かった.

come to little ほとんど物にならない ▪His efforts *came to little.* 彼の努力はほとんど物にならなかった.

Every little (bit) helps. 《諺》どんなに少しのものでもみな役に立つ; ごく少しずつが力になる,「一寸の糸三寸の縄」.

have little to do with →HAVE much to do with.

in little 《文》小規模[小型]に[の] ▪The temple was an imitation *in little* of that at Olympia. その神殿はオリンピアの神殿を小型に模造したものであった.

little as *one does* ほとんど...しないけれども ▪*Little as* I liked the idea, I couldn't do otherwise than adopt it. その考えはあまり好まなかったが, 採用するより仕方がなかった.

little better than ほとんど...にすぎないで, と同様で ▪He is *little better than* a beggar. 彼はほとんど物乞い同様である ▪Life is *little better than* a dream. 人生はほとんど夢のようなものでしかない.

little by little 少しずつ ▪The face of the earth began to change *little by little.* 地表は少しずつ変わり始めた.

little does *one* ***think*** 思いもよらない ▪*Little did* I *think* that sewing machines would become automatic. ミシンが電動になるなど思いもよらなかった.

little folk [people] 妖精 ▪*Little people* are called Menehune in Hawaii. ハワイでは妖精はメネフネと呼ばれる.

little green men 《戯》緑の小人《地球外生物》 ▪He was convinced that he had seen the *little green men.* 彼はその緑の小人を見たと思い込んでいた.

little less than ほとんど...同然[同数, 同量]で《程度・数量の大きい場合に言う》 ▪It is *little less than* robbery. それはほとんど強奪も同然である ▪He has *little less than* a million. 彼はほとんど100万(ポンド)の資産がある.

little more than →MORE.

little one(s) 子供《人・クマなどの》 ▪My wife! My *little ones*! わが妻よ! わが子たちよ!

little or no ほとんど...ない, まずないと言ってもよいくらい ▪He had *little or no* money with him. 彼は金の持ち合わせがほとんどなかった.

little or nothing ほとんど何も ...ない ▪We know *little or nothing* about the matter. 我々はその事についてはほとんど何も知らない.

Little things please little men. 《諺》小人は小事を喜ぶ《子供のようなふるまいをしている人を軽蔑して使う》.

little though *one* ***does*** = LITTLE as one does.

make a little go a long way 節約する ▪We

must learn to *make a little go a long way.* 我々は節約することを学ばなければならない.

make little of …を軽んじる, 侮る; …することなどを何とも思わない (→THINK little of) ▪ He *made little of* difficulties. 彼は困難を問題にしなかった.

more than a little excited [***shocked,*** etc.] 大いに興奮して[ショックを受けて, など] ▪ I was *more than a little surprised* to receive a telegram. 電報を受け取って少なからず驚いた.

my little man [***woman***] 少年[少女]《呼びかけ》 ▪ Well, *my little man*! ねえ, 君.

no little 少なからぬ, 実に多くの《量・程度を表す》 ▪ He took *no little* pains over it. 彼はそのことで少なからず骨を折った.

not a little 少なからず, 大いに; 極度に ▪ I lost *not a little* over cards. 私はトランプで莫大な金を失った ▪ He was *not a little* surprised. 彼は大いに驚いた.

quite a little →QUITE.

set little by →SET[2].

the little man しがない人間, "負け犬" ▪ In cartoons, the hero is *the little man.* 漫画では, しがない人間が主人公だ.

think little of →THINK[2].

too little (***and***) ***too late*** (援助などが)あまりにも少なくあまりにも遅い ▪ This endowment was *too little and too late.* この寄付金はあまりにも少なくあまりにも遅かった.

what little (…) *one* ***has*** →WHAT little.

live[1] /laɪv/ 形 ***a live certainty*** 絶対確かなこと ▪ She will be with them to *a live certainty.* 彼女はきっと彼らといっしょになるだろう. ☞a dead CERTAINTY をもじったもの.

a live wire →WIRE.

a real live 《口》本物の ▪ I had never seen *a real live* manatee before. それまで本物の[生きた]マナティーを見たことがなかった.

go live 《電算》(システムが)作動し始める ▪ Our website is *going live* tomorrow. 我々のウェブサイトが明日立ち上がる ▪ Sony's video-on-demand system *went live* Tuesday. ソニーのビデオオンデマンドが火曜日から始動し始める.

live[2] /lɪv/ 動 ***as I live*** (***and breathe***) 《口》確かに ▪ Christmas is a humbug, *as I live.* 確かにクリスマスはばかげている ▪ Why, it's Jim, *as I live and breathe*! おや, まぎれもなくジムじゃないか.

(***as***) ***sure as I live*** →(as) SURE as death.

Excuse [***Pardon***] ***me for living*** [***breathing***]***!*** 《口》それは悪かったね, おあいにくさま《自分の方に非はないという含意》 ▪ Be more quiet, I'm studying.—Well, *excuse me for breathing!* もっと静かにしてよ, 勉強中なんだから—そいつはお気の毒さま.

have not long to live 先が短い ▪ I fear the old lady *has not long to live.* その老婦人は老い先が長くないと思う.

He lives long who [***that***] ***lives well.*** 《諺》よい生き方をする者は長く生きる《廉直な生き方をする人は長生きする. そうでない者は人生を無為に過ごして終わる》.

I'll [***He'll, She'll,*** etc.] ***live.*** 心配ご無用; 大丈夫ですよ ▪ How do you feel?—*I'll live.* 気分はどうですか?—大丈夫です.

I'll never live it down! (恥ずべきことなどを)時が過ぎても忘れない, 胸に刻みつけておく ▪ I fluffed my lines on stage today. *I'll never live it down.* 今日舞台で台詞(せりふ)を忘れた. 絶対いつまでも忘れられまい.

live a lie →LIE[1].

live and breathe (主題・活動)に熱中する, 没頭する ▪ My son *lives and breathes* football. 息子はフットボールに夢中になっている ▪ I don't *live and breathe* movies like you do. 私は君みたいに映画に熱中していない.

Live and learn. 《諺》長生きはするもの; 長生きすれば色々の事を見聞する《新しい知識などに接しての感嘆》.

live and let live 互いにじゃませずにやっていく ▪ Our idea is to *live and let live.* 我々の考えは, 互いにじゃませずにやっていくことである.

live apart 別居生活をする (*from*) ▪ They are *living apart* for the moment. 二人は目下別居中だ ▪ She's been *living apart from* her husband for a year. 彼女は1年前から夫と別居生活をしている.

live beyond [***above***] *one's* ***income*** [***means***] 収入以上の贅沢な暮らしをする ▪ Look out you don't *live beyond your income.* 収入以上の生活をしないように気をつけなさい.

live by *oneself* 独居する ▪ I can't bear *living by myself.* 私は一人暮らしには耐えられない.

live by *one's* ***hands*** [*one's* ***fingers' ends***] 手仕事で生活する, 労働して暮らす ▪ My grandparents used to *live by their hands.* 祖父母は昔手仕事をして生活していた ▪ He had no choice but to *live by his fingers' ends.* 彼は肉体労働をして暮らすしかなかった.

live dangerously (いつも)危険な生活をする ▪ Spies have to *live dangerously.* スパイは危険な生活をしなければならない.

live (***from***) ***hand to mouth*** →HAND[1].

live happily ever after(***wards***) その後ずっと幸せに暮らす ▪ So they married and *lived happily ever after.* そこで二人は結婚し, その後ずっと幸せに暮らしましたとさ. おしまい. ☞おとぎ話の末尾の言葉.

live hard **1** 放逸な生活をする ▪ The rascal *lived hard*, and died young. そのならず者は放逸な生活をして若死にした.

2 苦難に耐える ▪ He *lived hard* and died harder. 彼はよく苦難に耐え, さらに容易に屈しなかった.

live high 《米口》贅沢な生活をする ▪ His wife likes to *live high.* 彼の妻は贅沢な生活をするのが好きだ.

live high off the hog →HOG[1].

live in [***within***] *oneself* 一人で暮らす; 自分自身に立てこもる; 自分自身の活動に余念がない (↔LIVE in society) ▪ *Living* much *within himself*, he found his chief amusement in reading. たいてい一人で暮らしていたから, 彼は読書がおもな道楽であった.

live in close quarters →QUARTER[1].

live in hope いつか希望がかなうと信じる ▪ We *live in hope* that one day our son will come back. いつか息子が戻ってくると願っている.

live in society 人と交わって生活する (↔LIVE in oneself) ▪ Why do we *live in society* when we can live alone? 人は一人で生きられるのに, どうして集団生活をするのだろうか.

live in style →in STYLE.

live in the past [***future***] 昔[将来]のことばかり考えて暮らす ▪ Most elderly people *live in the past*. たいていのお年寄りは過去に生きている ▪ Why do some people *live in the future*? なかには将来のことばかり考えて暮らす人がいるのはなぜだろう.

live in the present 現代に生きる《現代にふさわしい生き方をする》 ▪ Grandfather is quite unable to *live in the present*. おじいさんは現代に生きることがまるでできない.

live it up 《口》 **1** 楽しく過ごす ▪ He's *living it up* in Bali right now. 彼は今バリ島で楽しく過ごしている.

2 愉快な放蕩(ﾄｳ)生活をする ▪ He *lived it up* with wine and song. 彼は酒や歌で愉快な放蕩生活をした.

live it (***with***) (競走で…に)ついて行く, おくれないでいく ▪ The Italian could not *live it with* the gallant finish of the Briton. そのイタリア選手はイギリス選手の果敢なラストスパートについていけなかった.

live large 《俗》 贅沢な生活をする, 豪華に過ごす ▪ My father has been *living large* since retiring at the age of 60. 父は60歳で退職してから悠々自適に暮らしている.

live like a king 贅沢な暮らしをする ▪ We wish we'd *live like kings* one day. いつの日か豪華な生活ができたらいいのに.

live off the country (軍隊が)戦線で現地から食糧を徴発してやっていく; 国を食い荒らす ▪ In his marches he was obliged to *live off the country*. 進軍のときは彼はやむなく現地から食糧を徴発してやっていかなければならなかった ▪ They did not *live off the country* they occupied. 彼らは占領した国を食い荒らしはしなかった.

live off the fat out of the land →live on the FAT of the land.

live off the land 自分で育てた[獲った, 見つけた]ものを食べて生活する ▪ It's easy to *live off the land* in this region. この辺では自ら食物を楽に調達できる.

live on borrowed time **1** 予想より長生き[長持ち]している ▪ He has been *living on borrowed time* since his operation. 彼は手術以来, 予想よりも長生きしている.

2 もう長く生きる見込みがない, 死を間近にしている ▪ He's got cancer. He's *living on borrowed time*. 彼はガンで余命いくばくもない.

live on *one's* ***name*** [***reputation***] (過去の)名声で生活する, 地位を保つ ▪ The poet is only *living on his reputation*. その詩人は名声で地位を保っているにすぎない.

live on *one's* ***own*** 一人で暮らす ▪ I make no bones of *living on my own*. 私は一人で暮らすのを何とも思わない.

live on sixpence a day 《英》 倹約な暮らしをする ▪ I'll *live on sixpence a day* till I am out of debt. 借金がなくなるまで切り詰めて生活しよう.

live on the fat of the land →FAT[1].

live on the streets →STREET.

live out *one's* ***days*** [***life***] 一生を送る ▪ They *lived out their lives* as peasants. 彼らは小作人として一生を送った.

live out *one's* ***dreams*** [***fantasies***] 夢[空想]を実現する ▪ The inheritance allowed her to *live out her dreams*. 遺産を相続して彼女の夢がかなった ▪ He wanted to *live out his* childhood *fantasy* of being a cowboy some day. 彼はカウボーイになるという子供の頃の空想をいつか実現したかった.

live out of a suitcase トランク1個の仮住まいをする ▪ The student was *living out of a suitcase* a year ago. その学生は1年前はトランク1個の仮住まいをしていた.

live out of tins [***cans***] 《口》 かんづめを食べて暮らす ▪ The explorers *lived out of tins*. 探検家たちはかんづめを食べて過ごした.

live rough 苦しい生活をする ▪ Some people are *living rough* because they have no income. 収入がないために苦しい生活をしている人もいる.

live to *oneself* (人とつき合わずに)一人で暮らす ▪ I prefer *living to myself* in the country. 私は田舎で一人で暮らす方が好きだ.

live to see the day 生きてその日の来るのを見る ▪ May I never *live to see the day*! 生きてその日が来るのを見ることがありませんように.

live to tell the tale 《口・戯》 苦しい経験に耐える, 困難な状況を乗り切る ▪ I expect you'll *live to tell the tale*. 君なら苦境を乗り切れると思う.

live with *oneself* 自尊心を保つ ▪ He'll find it difficult to *live with himself* if he gets fired from this job. 彼はこの仕事を首になったら, 自尊心を保つことはむずかしいだろう.

live within *oneself* →LIVE in oneself.

live within *one's* ***income*** [***means***] 収入の範囲内で生活する ▪ Nowadays we find it difficult to *live within our means*. 今日収入の範囲内で生活するのはむずかしい.

Long live (*the King*)*!* (国王)万歳! ▪ *Long live* the Emperor! 皇帝万歳!

not (***...***) ***if*** [***though***] *one* ***lives to be a hundred*** たとえ百歳まで生きても …でない ▪ You would *never* see such a specimen again *though* you *live to be a hundred*. たとえ百歳まで生きてもこんな標本には二度とお目にかかることはありますまい ▪ You will not forget this day—*not if* you *live to be a hundred*. 君は今日のことは忘れないだろう, たとえ百まで生きても.

To live long is to outlive much. 《諺》 長生きすれば恥が多い.

where *one* ***lives*** 《米俗》 急所(を) ▪ This hurt

him—right *where* he *lives*. これがちょうど彼の急所を傷つけた.

You [***We***] ***only live once.*** 人は1回しか生きられない《楽しめる間に楽しめ》 ▪ *We only live once*, so let's enjoy it. 人生は1回きりだから, 楽しくやろうよ.

you've [***he's,*** etc.] ***not*** [***never***] ***lived*** 《口》本当に生きたとは言えない ▪ *You've not lived* until you've seen Naples. ナポリを見るまでは本当に生きたとは言えない.

livelihood /láɪvlihòd/ 名 ***earn*** [***gain, get, make, obtain, seek***] ***a*** [*one's*] ***livelihood*** 生計を立てる ▪ He *earned his livelihood* by teaching. 彼は教師をして暮らしを立てた ▪ They *made a livelihood* of trapping animals for their furs. 毛皮をとるため動物をわなにかけて生計を立てた.

earn an honest livelihood 正直に稼いで生活する ▪ We are trying to *earn an honest livelihood*. 正直に稼いでやっていこうとがんばっている.

means of livelihood 暮らしを立てる手段, 生業 ▪ Her husband has no *means of livelihood*. 彼女の夫には生業がない.

pick up a scanty [***bare***] ***livelihood*** やっと生活をする, ようやく食べていく ▪ He has been *picking up a scanty livelihood*. 彼はこれまでやっと食いつないできた.

rob *a person* ***of*** *his* ***livelihood*** 生活費を稼げなくする ▪ Discrimination *robs* people *of their livelihoods*. 差別があると人は生活費が得られなくなる.

lively /láɪvli/ 形 ***have a lively time of it*** 《婉曲》大活躍をする; はらはらする, 苦しい目にあう ▪ The police *had a lively time of it* putting down the riot. 警察は暴動を鎮めるのに非常にてこずった ▪ I *had a lively time of it* with the trains shaking the house all night. 一晩中列車で家が揺れてひどい目にあった.

look lively **1** =LOOK alive 1.
2《英口》〚主に命令文で〛急ぐ ▪ *Look lively*. We have to be there in half an hour! 急げ. 30分で着かないといけない.

make things [***it***] ***lively for*** ...を困らせる ▪ The Diet *made things lively for* the Cabinet. 議会は内閣をひどい目にあわせた.

livery /lívəri/ 名 ***at livery*** (馬が)料金で飼養されて ▪ We placed the horse at the stable to remain *at livery* at 50 shillings a day. 1日50シリングで飼養されるよう, 馬をあずけた.

give livery 《法》財産の引き渡しをする ▪ The King *gave* him *livery* of his brother's lands. 王は彼に兄の土地を引き渡した.

have [***take***] ***livery*** 《法》財産の引き渡しを受ける ▪ I *took livery* of all his lands. 彼のすべての土地を引き渡された.

in livery (下働きの男などが)お仕着せを着て (↔out of LIVERY) ▪ Servants *in livery* served wine. お仕着せを着た使用人たちがワインを出した.

in the livery of ...を借り着して ▪ He is *in the livery of* other men's opinions. 彼は他人の意見を借用している.

keep a horse at livery 料金をもらって馬をあずかって養う; 料金を払って馬をあずけておく ▪ I would never ever *keep a horse at livery* again. 二度と再び料金を払って馬をあずけたりするものか.

out of livery (下働きの男などが)平服を着て (↔in LIVERY) ▪ A servant *out of livery* came out. 平服の下働きが出て来た.

put on the livery of ...の下働きをする; のお仕着せを着る ▪ Now you have *put on the livery of* medicine. 君は医学の使徒となったのだ ▪ She has *put on the livery of* grief. 彼女は喪服を着ている.

stand at livery (馬が)料金であずかり飼養されている ▪ The horse *stood at livery*. その馬は料金であずかり飼養されていた.

sue (***for***) *one's* ***livery*** (成年に達した被後見人として)土地所有の引き渡しを法廷に訴え出る ▪ The heir *sued for his livery*. 相続人は土地の引き渡しを訴え出た.

take livery →have LIVERY.

take up *one's* ***livery*** (ロンドン市の)同業組合員となる ▪ He *took up his livery* in the Stationers' Company early in life. 彼は若い頃にロンドン市書籍出版業組合員となった.

living /lívɪŋ/ 形名 ***a living legend*** →LEGEND.

be living proof of [***that***] ...を身をもって示す ▪ He's *living proof that* a heart attack doesn't mean the end of life. 彼は心臓発作が必ず死には至らないことを身をもって示している.

beat the (***living***) ***daylights out of*** *a person* →DAYLIGHT.

do for a living 生計を立てる ▪ What do you *do for a living*?—I am a dentist. お仕事は何をしていらっしゃいますか?—歯科医です.

earn [***make***] ***a*** [*one's*] ***living*** 生計を立てる ▪ He *earns his living* as a licensed victualler. 彼は酒類販売免許飲食店主として生計を立てている ▪ He can't *make a living* out of writing. 彼は文筆では暮らしが立てられない.

get a living **1** =earn a LIVING.
2 (牧師が)聖職の禄を得る ▪ The curate was fortunate enough to *get a living* in the country. その牧師補は幸運にも田舎に聖職の禄を得た.

in the land of the living 《主に戯》生きて, 現存して (《聖》*Ps.* 27. 13) ▪ He is still *in the land of the living*. 彼はまだ生きている.

living death 生きているとも言えぬほど悲惨[不幸]な状態 ▪ He lived a *living death*. 彼は生きているとも言えぬほど悲惨な生活をした.

make a living →earn a LIVING.

make *one's* ***living off*** ...で生計を立てる ▪ He *makes his living off* odd jobs. 彼は臨時雇いの仕事で食っている.

plain living and high thinking 質素なそして哲学的な生活 (Wordsworth, *National Independence* 13) ▪ The Scottish people used to be credited with *plain living and high thinking.* スコットランド人は暮らしは質素で思索は高いと以前よく言われたものだ.

scrape out a living 何とか生計を立てる, どうにか食べていく ▪ He *scraped out a living* by writing articles for a local newspaper. 彼は地元の新聞に記事を書いてどうにか食べていた ▪ He *scraped a living* as a mechanic. 彼は工員をして何とか食っていた.

the living end 《米》 **1** とてもすばらしい人[物] ▪ His aunt is *the living end*, always helping the poor. 彼のおばさんは全くすばらしい人で, いつも貧しい人々を助けている.

2 とても困った人[物] ▪ Jim is late again. He really is *the living end.* ジムはまた遅刻した. 実にいまいましいやつだ.

within* [*in*] *living memory →MEMORY.

lo /loʊ/ 間 ***Lo and behold!*** 《戯》こはそもいかに! 《驚くべきことを言う場合》 ▪ *Lo and behold*, he won the day. 驚くじゃないか, 彼が勝ったんだよ.

load[1] /loʊd/ 名 ***a load of*** 《口》たくさんの ▪ He has *a load of* money. 彼は金をどっさり持っている.

a load of* (*old*) *rubbish* [*cobblers, nonsense*]/*a load of dingo's kidneys 《口》全くのたわごと ▪ His book is *a load of old rubbish.* 彼の本は全くのたわごとだ.

a load off *one's* ***mind*** →a weight off one's MIND.

get a load of 《俗》…を聞く; を見る, 吟味する ▪ Hey, *get a load of* my new car. まあ僕の新車を見てくれ ▪ *Get a load of* this! これをごらん; この話を聞けよ.

have a load on 《米俗》酔っている ▪ He *has a load on* every time I see him at a party. パーティーで彼を見かけると, きまって酔っている.

have a load on *one's* ***mind* [*conscience*]** 気にかかることがある, 気のとがめることがある ▪ May I no longer *have that load on my conscience*! もうこれ以上あのことで私が気をとがめなくてすみますように!

lighten *a person's* **[*the*] *load*** 負担を軽くする ▪ These measures should *lighten your load.* この処置で君の負担は軽減するはずだ.

loads of 《口》たくさんの(数・量) ▪ I had *loads of* letters. たくさん手紙をもらった ▪ He had *loads of* talk with her all morning. 彼は午前中ずっと彼女と大いに語った.

make *three* ***loads of it*** それを3回で運ぶ ▪ We *made* two *loads of* refugees over the border. 難民を国境を越えて2回で運んだ.

shoot *one's* ***load*** 《卑》射精する.

take a* [*the*] *load off *one's* ***feet*** 《俗》座る, 腰かける; くつろぐ ▪ I asked him to *take the load off his feet.* 彼におかけくださいと言った.

take a load off *a person's* ***mind* [*heart*]** 人の心配を取り除く, 人をほっと安心させる ▪ His arrival *took a load off my mind.* 彼が到着したので私はほっと安心した.

with a load on 《米俗》酔って ▪ I went home *with a load on.* 私は酔って家に帰った.

load[2] /loʊd/ 動 ***be loaded down with*** **1** …の重荷で押し曲[押し下]げられている; を満載している ▪ The old man *was loaded down with* the weight of his pack on his back. 老人は背に負った包みの重みで腰が押し曲げられていた.

2 (責任・苦労など)で苦しんでいる ▪ He seems to *be loaded down with* his worries. 彼は心配事で苦しんでいるように見える.

be* [*get*] *loaded up 《米口》酔っ払っている[酔っ払う] ▪ After three glasses of wine she *got loaded up.* ワインを3杯飲むと彼女は酔っ払った.

(*be*) *loaded up with* **1** …を満載して(いる) ▪ The barge *was loaded up with* timber. はしけは材木を満載していた.

2 …を担保としてたくさん背負いこんで(いる) ▪ The bank *is loaded up with* frozen assets. その銀行は凍結資産を担保として山ほど背負わされている.

(*be*) *loaded with* **1** (果実)が枝もたわむほどなって(いる); …がぎしぎしいうほど満載されて(いる) ▪ The trees *were* plentifully *loaded with* fruits. 木々には果実が枝もたわわにたくさんなっていた ▪ The table *was loaded with* food. 食卓には食物が山ほど置かれていた.

2 …に圧倒されて(いる); やっかい物[じゃまもの]を負わされて(いる) ▪ Oaks bowed their necks, *loaded with* stormy blasts. カシの木は烈風に圧倒されてうなだれた ▪ This book *is* not *loaded with* trigonometric equations. この本には三角方程式というやっかいなものは載っていない.

3 (病気)を負わされて苦しめられて(いる) ▪ I have *been loaded with* a cold for three weeks. 私は3週間前からずっと風邪で悩んでいる.

4 《口》(金)をうなるほど持って(いる) ▪ His father *is loaded with* money. 彼の父親は金がうなるほどある.

load *one's* ***memory with*** …を詰め込んで覚える ▪ You need not *load your memory with* details. こまかい事は詰め込んで覚えなくてよろしい.

load *oneself* ***with*** …を背負う, で苦しむ ▪ He is *loading himself with* perpetual evils. 彼はひっきりなしの災害で苦しんでいる.

loaded for bear 《米俗》十分準備ができて, てぐすねをひいて ▪ Let them come; we're *loaded for bear.* 来るなら来てみろ, こっちは十分準備ができている.

loaf[1] /loʊf/ 名 ***Half a loaf is better than none* [*no bread*].** 《諺》半分のパンでもないよりはまし.

have an eye to* [*look after*] *the loaves and fishes (ある事の)物質的利益だけを目あてにする ▪ I think he *had an eye to the loaves and fishes.* 彼は物質的利益だけを目あてにしていたのだと思う. ☞下の句から.

loaves and fishes 聖職の禄; (僧職・奉公の動機としての)現世的利得 (《聖》*John* 6. 26) ▪ The clergyman's *loaves and fishes* are scanty. 牧師の禄は乏しいものである ▪ He thinks a lot of *loaves and fishes.* 彼は現世的利得を重んじる.

use** one's **loaf 《英口》頭を働かす《特に難局を切り抜けるとき》 ▪ You are going to be a useful boy, so long as you *use your loaf*. 君は頭を働かせさえすれば役に立つ少年になるよ. ☞loaf (of bread) = head との押韻俗語.

loaf[2] /loʊf/ 名 ***go* [*be*] *on the loaf*** ぶらぶらする ▪ He got tired of reading, and decided to *go on the loaf*. 彼は読書に飽きたのでぶらついてくることにした.

have a loaf ぶらぶらする ▪ I'm going to *have a loaf*. ちょっとぶらついてきます.

loan /loʊn/ 名 ***ask for the loan of*** …の借り入れを頼む ▪ He *asked* me *for the loan of* £1,000. 彼は私に1,000ポンド貸してくれと言った.

call in a loan 貸した金を返金するよう頼む ▪ Any bank or investor can *call in a loan*. いかなる銀行も投資家も出資金の返済を要求できる.

favor** a person **with the loan of 人に…を貸してやる ▪ Will you *favor* me *with the loan of* this book? この本をお貸しくださいませんか.

give** a person **the loan of 人に…を貸す ▪ I *gave* him *the loan of* £1,000. 私は彼に1,000ポンド貸した.

have ... on loan …を借りている ▪ I *have* £1,000 *on loan*. 私は1,000ポンド借りている.

have the loan of …を借りる ▪ Can I *have the loan of* this book? この本が借りられますか.

on* [*upon*] *loan 借りて; 貸付けて ▪ The man pressed for a large sum of money *on loan*. その男は多額の借用を迫った ▪ The sword is *on loan* at the museum. その剣は博物館に貸し出している.

take out a loan (銀行から)借金する ▪ He *took out a loan* to buy a new house. 彼は家を買うために銀行から融資を受けた.

loath, loth /loʊθ/ 形 ***be loath for** a person **to** do* 人が…するのをいやがる ▪ He *is loath for* his daughter *to* marry me. 彼は自分の娘が私と結婚するのをきらっている.

***be loath to** do* …するのをいやがる ▪ The company *was loath to* put people out of work. 会社は人々を失業させるのをいやがった.

lobby[1] /lábi|lɔ́bi/ 名 ***cross the lobbies*** 《英》(議案が)下院から上院へ送られる ▪ The bill promptly *crossed the lobbies*. その議案はさっそく下院から上院へ送られた.

lobby[2] /lábi|lɔ́bi/ 動 ***lobby a bill through*** ロビー活動で議案を通す ▪ They *lobbied the bill through* the Senate. 彼らはその議案をロビー活動で上院を通過させた.

lobster /lábstər|lɔ́b-/ 名 ***(as) red as a lobster*** エビのように真っ赤な《酔った顔など》 ▪ He was drunk and his face was *red as a lobster*. 彼は酔って真っ赤な顔をしていた.

localize /lóʊkəlàɪz/ 動 ***localize (attention) upon*** (注意を)…に集中する ▪ We *localized* our *attention upon* the point sufficiently. 我々はその点に十分注意を集中した.

locate /lóʊkeɪt|loʊkéɪt/ 動 ***be located in*** 《主に米》…に落ち着いている; に位置している ▪ I *am* now *located in* the suburbs of Genoa. 今はジェノバの郊外に落ち着いています ▪ The company *is located in* the town of Salem. その会社はセイラムの町にある.

***locate** oneself* 落ち着く, 居を構える ▪ He *located himself* behind the screen. 彼はスクリーンの後ろに位置を占めた.

location /loʊkéɪʃən/ 名 ***(be) on location*** ロケ中で(ある) ▪ Many actors *are on location*. 多くの俳優がロケ中だ.

lock[1] /lɑk|lɔk/ 名 ***(be) off the lock*** 錠がかかってない ▪ Make sure your holster *is off the lock*. ピストルの革ケースに錠をかけていない[ピストルをすぐ取り出せる]のを確かめろ.

(be) on the lock **1** 錠がかかって(いる) ▪ The house *is on the lock*. その家は錠がおろしてある.

2 独房に錠をおろす仕事をして(いる) ▪ Will you go and see if Bob *is on the lock*? ボブが独房の錠おろしをしているか行って見てください.

have a lock on 《米口》…をしっかり掴んでいる, 完全に支配している ▪ The mother *had a lock on* her child and wouldn't let him go. 母親はわが子を抱きしめて離そうとしなかった ▪ Our party *has a lock on* that Senate seat. あの上院の議席はわが党が確実に獲得するだろう. ☞lock《レスリング》「相手の動きを封じる組み手」.

lock, stock, and barrel →STOCK, lock, and barrel.

pick a* [*the*] *lock 錠をこじ開ける; 不法侵入する ▪ They got into the apartment by *picking the lock*. 彼らは錠をこじ開けてそのアパートへ侵入した.

under lock and key **1** 厳重に錠をおろして(しまっておく, など)《比喩的にも》 ▪ I'll put all these documents *under lock and key* in the bank. 私はこの証書類をみな銀行に厳重に保管してもらいます ▪ With great care they kept their wives *under lock and key*. 彼らは非常に注意して妻たちを外へ出さないようにした.

2 投獄されて, 服役中で ▪ The notorious train robber is now *under lock and key* in a local jail. 名うての列車強盗はいま地方刑務所に投獄されている.

(walk) lock and lock 腕を組んで(歩く) ▪ He *walked lock and lock* with her. 彼は彼女と腕を組んで歩いた.

lock[2] /lɑk|lɔk/ 動 ***be locked in each other's arms*** 互いに抱きついて離れない ▪ The lovers *were locked in each other's arms*. 恋人同士は抱きあって離れなかった.

lock** oneself **away (じゃまされないように)閉じこもる, (仕事のために)一人になる ▪ He *locked himself away* in his room and wouldn't come out. 彼は自室に閉じこもって出てこようとしなかった.

lock into each other 互いに組み合う ▪ All the parts of a jigsaw puzzle *lock into each other*. ジグソーパズルのすべてのパーツは互いに組み合う.

lock** oneself **out (鍵を中に忘れたまま)自動錠をかけ

て(家・部屋に)入れなくなる ▪ Oh, no! I've *locked myself out* of the car again! ああ, どうしよう. また車のキーを中に入れたままロックしてしまった ▪ She found *herself locked out*. 彼女は家の中に鍵を忘れて閉め出されたことに気づいた.

***lock the stable door after the horse has bolted* [*is stolen*]** →shut the STABLE door after the horse is stolen.

lock** oneself **up 自分のからに閉じこもって人に会わない ▪ He *locked himself up* and avoided the society of other people. 彼は自分のからに閉じこもって, 人とつき合おうとしなかった.

locker /lákər|lɔ́k-/ 名 ***a shot in the* [*one's*] *locker*** →SHOT[1].

(*be*) *laid in the lockers* 《古》死んで(いる) ▪ Brown's shot—*laid in the lockers*. ブラウンは撃たれて—死んだ.

lockstep /lákstèp|lɔ́k-/ 名 ***move in lockstep*** 《主に米》密着している, 相互に依存している ▪ Politicians should always *move in lockstep* with the party line. 政治家は常に党の政策に従って行動すべきである ▪ Bond prices don't *move in lockstep* with stock prices. 債権価格は株価に左右されることはない. ☞lockstep「(前の間隔をつめて歩調をとる)密接行進法」.

lockup /lákʌ̀p|lɔ́k-/ 名形 ***a lock up shop* [*garage*]** 《英》(住居部分のない)貸し店舗[ガレージ] ▪ There's a row of *lock up garages* on this street. この通りには貸しガレージが並んでいる.

locomotive /lòʊkəmóʊtɪv/ 名 ***use** one's **locomotives*** 《戯》足を使う, 歩く ▪ *Use your locomotives* a bit quicker! もう少しさっさと歩け.

locust /lóʊkəst/ 名 ***swarm like locusts*** 非常な数をなして現れる ▪ Campers *swarmed like locusts* around the big campfire. 大きなキャンプファイアーの周りにキャンプ中の人たちが大勢集まった.

lodge /lɑdʒ|lɔdʒ/ 動 ***be well-* [*ill-*] *lodged*** 部屋が良い[悪い] ▪ The hotel *is well-lodged*. そのホテルは部屋が良い.

Lodge arms! 《号令》立て銃(つつ)!

lodgment, lodgement /ládʒmənt|lɔ́dʒ-/ 名 ***make* [*effect, find*] *a lodgment*** 確固たる足場を得る; 上陸する ▪ The Second Regiment attempted to *make a lodgment* in the city. 第二連隊はその都市に拠点を置こうとした ▪ They *effected a lodgment* on the coast. 彼らは海岸に上陸した.

lodging /ládʒɪŋ|lɔ́dʒ-/ 名 ***ask for a night's lodging*** 一夜の宿を請う ▪ I *asked for a night's lodging* at a Buddhist temple. 私はある仏教寺院に一夜の宿を請うた.

find* (*a*) *lodging for the night 一夜の宿を見つける ▪ Where can we *find (a) lodging for the night*? どこに一夜の宿が見つかるか.

live* [*be*] *in lodgings 間借りしている, 下宿している ▪ Some of the students *live in lodgings*. 学生の中には下宿している者もある.

take lodgings 下宿する ▪ I *took lodgings* with a widow. 私はある未亡人宅に下宿した.

take up** one's **lodgings 宿を取る ▪ He *took up his lodgings* under our roof. 彼は私たちの家に宿を取った.

log /lɔːg|lɔg/ 名 ***a bump on a log*** →BUMP[1].

(*as*) *easy* [*simple*] *as falling* [*rolling*] *off a log* 《口》きわめて易しい[簡単な] ▪ Don't you understand that? It's *as simple as falling off a log*! そんなことが分からないのか. 簡単至極じゃないか.

be like a log (丸太のように)無力で動かない ▪ He *is like a log* or stone in his death bed. 今わの際で彼は身動き一つしていない.

(*be*) *a person's* ***log roller*** 人の計画を助ける ▪ John *became my log roller*. ジョンは私の計画を助けてくれた.

float* [*lie, fall*] *like a log (丸太のように)無力で動かないで浮かぶ[横たわる, 倒れる] ▪ He *lay like a log* on the pavement. 彼は死んだようになって舗道に倒れていた ▪ He *fell like a log* on the ground. 彼は地面にどさりと倒れた.

have a* [*one's*] *log to roll (人をほめるのも, 助けるのも)当てにするところがあるのだ ▪ They may *have a log to roll* and an axe to grind. 彼らには何か当てにするところがあるのだろう.

in the log 《口》(切らずに)丸太のままで ▪ The pine was worth 500 dollars *in the log*. そのマツは丸太のままで500ドルの値段であった.

keep the log rolling 《米口》物事を運転[活動]させておく ▪ The project will *keep the log rolling*. その事業のお陰で事が盛んに活動を続けるだろう.

roll logs for (仲間)のために骨を折る, (仲間)をほめる ▪ These writers are often accused of *rolling logs for* each other. この作家たちは馴れ合いで互い(の作品)をほめあうとしてよく非難される.

sleep like a log →SLEEP[2].

split the log 《米口》事情を説明する ▪ Well then, I'll *split the log* for you. よし, それでは事情を説明してあげましょう.

(*You*) *roll my log and I'll roll yours.* お互いに助け合おう ▪ *Roll my leg and I'll roll yours*—it's a matter of give-and-take. 互いに助け合って, ここはもちつもたれつでいこう. ☞政治家が結託して助け合う場合, 作家が互いに作品をほめ合う場合に用いる.

loggerheads /lɔ́ːgərhèd|lɔ́g-/ 名 **(*be*) *at loggerheads* (*with*)** 《口》(...と)論争して(いる); (と)けんかして(いる) ▪ They *are at loggerheads* over military bases. 彼らは軍事基地に関して意見が違って論争している ▪ They *are* always *at loggerheads with* each other. 彼らはいつも互いにけんかしている. ☞「どちらの頭が堅いか試してみる」という考えから.

fall* [*get, go*] *to loggerheads なぐり合いを始める; けんかを始める ▪ We finally *went to loggerheads* with those guys. 僕たちはとうとう, そいつらとなぐり合いを始めた.

join* [*lay*] *loggerheads together 額を集めて協議する ▪ These two often *join loggerheads together*. この二人はしばしば額を集めて相談する.

logic /lɑ́dʒɪk|lɔ́dʒ-/ 名 ***chop logic*** →CHOP².

stand logic on its head 論じ方が合理的でない，筋が通らない ▪ To call this movement radical is to *stand logic on its head.* この運動を急進的と呼ぶなんて理屈に合わない．

with logic 筋を立てて ▪ He argues *with logic.* 彼は筋の立った議論をする．

loin /lɔɪn/ 名 ***a fruit*** [***a child***] ***of*** *one's* ***loins*** 自分の子供 ▪ I hugged *the fruit of my loins.* 私は自分の子供を抱き締めた．☞ 聖書語法．

come [***spring***] ***from*** *a person's* ***loins*** 人の子として生まれる (《聖》*Gen.* 35. 11) ▪ The prince *sprang from his loins.* 王子は彼の子に生まれた．

gird (***up***) *one's* ***loins*** 《戯》(…しようと)腰をすえてかかる，ふんどしを締める (*for, to, to do*) (《聖》*Job* 38. 3) ▪ She *girded up her loins for* the fray. 彼女はけんかをしようと身構えた ▪ I will *gird up my loins* and go out to battle. 私はふんどしを締めて出征します．☞ ヘブライ人は普段ゆるい衣を着，仕事・旅行のときは腰回りを締める習慣であったことから．

loiter /lɔ́ɪtər/ 動 ***loiter with intent*** 《英・法》犯意をもって徘徊する ▪ The man was arrested on a charge of *loitering with intent.* その男は犯意をもって徘徊したかどで逮捕された．

loll /lɑl|lɔl/ 動 ***loll it*** だらりともたれる ▪ They *lolled it* away to the opera in a magnificent carriage. 彼らは壮麗な馬車にゆったり乗って，オペラを見に行った．

lollipop /lɑ́lipɑ̀p|lɔ́lipɔ̀p/ 名 ***a lollipop man*** [***lady***] 《英口》交通指導のおじさん[おばさん] ▪ *A lollipop lady* is escorting schoolchildren across a busy road. 監視係のおばさんが学童たちにつき添って交通の激しい道路を渡らせている．☞ 通学児童が道路を横断するのを補佐する交通監視員のニックネーム．

London /lʌ́ndən/ 名 ***a London particular*** (かつて住民を悩ませた)ロンドンの濃霧 ▪ *A London particular*, the thick blankets of yellow fog, used to engulf London. 濃い黄色の霧がかつてはロンドンに立ち込めていた．☞ Charles Dickens, *Bleak House* (1853)から．

lone /loʊn/ 形名 ***a lone wolf*** [***bird***] 単独行動を好む人，一匹狼 ▪ He's a bit of *a lone wolf.* 彼はちょっと一匹狼的なところがある．

play [***fight, hold***] ***a lone hand*** 《トランプ》(味方の助けなしに)一人で相手全員と戦う; (他の援助・支持なしに)一人でやる ▪ He likes to *hold a lone hand* in everything. 彼は何事においても好んでみなを敵に回して孤軍奮闘する．

lonely /lóʊnli/ 形 ***lonely hearts*** 心寂しき人々《恋人・友人を求める人々》 ▪ She always reads the *lonely hearts* column. 彼女は(新聞などの)心寂しき人の交際申し込み欄をいつも読む．

lonesome /lóʊnsəm/ 形名 ***by*** [***on***] *one's* ***lonesome*** 《口》ただ一人; 独力で ▪ I lifted it all *by my lonesome.* 私はそれを全く独力で持ち上げた ▪ When you leave for Rome next week, I shall be *on my lonesome.* 君が来週ローマへ発つと，私はひとりぼっちになる ▪ I will hit the trail *by my lonesome.* 私は一人で旅に出よう．

feel lonesome for …に思いこがれる ▪ She's *feeling* a bit *lonesome for* the young man. 彼女はその青年に少し思いこがれている．

long /lɔːŋ|lɔŋ/ 形 ***a long date*** [***day***] 遠い日付[期日] ▪ It is a bond due in October 2020, which is *a long date.* それは2020年10月支払いの債券だが，それは遠い先の日付である ▪ *A long day* will not be permitted me. 遠い期限は私には許されないでしょう．

a long face →FACE¹.

a long haul 《口》 **1** 長距離，長距離の旅 ▪ It is *a long haul* to drive across the continent. 大陸を車で横断するのは長旅である．

2 (仕事など)長い期間，(努力など)長い道のり ▪ The injured boy will be able to walk again, but it may be *a long haul.* けがをした少年は多分また歩けるようになるが日数は相当かかるだろう．

a long head 普通より長い頭; 利発(な人)，先見の明 ▪ I'm sure he has [is] *a long head.* 彼は間違いなく利発な人である．

a long word 長い時を示す語 ▪ I have never seen him since then and that's saying *a long word.* それ以来，と言えば長いことなのだが，彼に会ったことがない．

(***as***) ***broad as it is long*** →BROAD.

as long as **1** …だけ長く ▪ You may stay here *as long as* you like. あなたはお好きなだけいつまでもここにいてよろしい．

2 …する限り，ならば (＝so LONG as) ▪ You can go out *as long as* you're back before dark. 暗くならないうちに帰ってくるなら外出してもいい．

3 《米》…のだから (since) ▪ *As long as* you're going, I'll go too. 君が行くのだから，僕も行く．

at long weapons 離れて戦って ▪ We were *at long weapons* and fighting in the dark. 我々は離れて，暗やみの中で戦っていた．

at (***the***) ***longest*** どう長くみても，せいぜい，遅くとも ▪ A man's life is short *at the longest.* 人の命はいくら長くても短いものである ▪ It will take two hours *at the longest.* これはせいぜい2時間しかかかるまい．

be a long time (***in***) *doing* →be LONG (in) doing.

be long about [***in***] …に時間がかかる，が遅い ▪ He *was long in* the explanation of the particulars. 彼はこれら詳細の点の説明に時間がかかった ▪ He *is long about* his work. 彼は仕事が遅い．

be long [***a long time***] (***in***) *doing* …するのが遅い，なかなか…しない ▪ He *was long* (*in*) *finding* it out. 彼はそれを発見するのに時間がかかった ▪ Spring *is a long time coming.* 春の来るのが遅い ▪ The opportunity *was* not *long in coming.* その機会はまもなくやって来た．

be long in oil 油の比率が普通より高い ▪ This varnish *is long in oil.* このニスは含まれる油の比率が高い．

L

be long on 《俗》…をたくさん持っている ▪ He *is long on* human understanding. 彼には人間に対する理解はたっぷりある.

be long on A but short on B/be short on B but long on A 一方には事欠かないが他方には事欠く, 帯に短く襷(たすき)に長い ▪ The soccer player *is long on* skill *but short on* personality. そのサッカー選手は, 技量は充分だが人柄に欠ける.

be* [*go*] (*on the*) *long* (*side*) *of the market 《商》強気である, 強気買いに出る ▪ These investors are still anxious to *be on the long side of the market*. この投資家らはまだ強気買いに出たがっている.

before long やがて, まもなく ▪ He will be here *before long*. 彼はほどなくここへ来るだろう.

***by a long way* [*long odds*]** はるかに (→by a long CHALK) ▪ This is superior *by a long way*. この方がはるかにすぐれている.

Don't be long! ぐずぐずするな! ▪ Please *don't be long*. Or I may be asleep. 早く帰ってね. でないと寝てしまうかもしれないから.

(*for*) *a long time* [*while*] 長い間 ▪ I have not seen him *for a long while*. 長い間彼に会わない.

for long (***together***) **1** 長い間 ▪ The children had been restless *for long*. 子供らは長い間そわそわしていた.

2 〚叙述的〛長く続くらしく ▪ Well, it mayn't be *for long*. そうですね, 長くは続かないかもしれませんね.

go back a long way →go WAY back.

go* (*on the*) *long* (*side*) *of the market →be (on the) LONG (side) of the market.

have a long arm 遠くまで勢力をふるうことができる, 遠くまで届く ▪ The King *has a long arm*. 国王の統治力は遠くまで及ぶ.

have a long way to go さらにかなりの時間を要する ▪ He still *has a long way to go* before he's fully fit. 彼が全快するのはずっと先だ.

have come a long way (***since***) (から)ずいぶん進歩[出世]した ▪ He *has come a long way since* he was a mechanic. 彼は機械工のころからずいぶん出世したものだ.

have not long to live →LIVE[2].

How long ...? どれくらい長く ▪ *How long* will you stay here? いつまでここに滞在しますか ▪ *How long* is it since he died? 彼が死んでからどれくらいになるか.

How long is a piece of string? 《英口》〚How long ...? の疑問文に対する答えで(長さ・時間を尋ねられて)〛そんなことは分からない ▪ How long do you think it will take? —*How long's a piece of string?* それはどのくらいかかると思う?—分かるわけないだろ, そんなこと ▪ How long does it take to get a printer repaired? —*How long is a piece of string?* プリンターの修理にどのくらい時間がかかるの?—そんなことは分かりっこない.

in* [*over*] *the long haul →HAUL[1].

It's a long story. →STORY.

long as …する限り (= as LONG as) ▪ It's all right *long as* you're here. 君がここにいる限り大丈夫だ.

long in the tooth →TOOTH.

Long time no see. 《口》お久しぶり ▪ Hi, Peter! *Long time no see*. やあピーター! お久しぶり. ☞ふざけて非標準英語をまねたもの.

make short of long 手短に言う ▪ There, to *make short of long*, was he waylaid by many knights. 手短に言うと, そこで彼は多くの騎士に待ち伏せされた.

one ***may*** *do* ***long enough*** (***before*** *one does*) 《口》いくら…してもだめだろう; いくら…しても…はおぼつかない《before ...のある場合》 ▪ You *may* cry *long enough*. 君はいくら泣いてもむだだろう ▪ You *may* look *long enough before* you come to Hervé Riel. いくら捜してもエルヴェ・リエルは見つからないだろう.

no longer/not ... any longer もはや…しない ▪ I will stay here *no longer*. 私はもうここにはとどまらない ▪ You can*not* stay here *any longer*. 君はもうここにはいられない.

not be long for this world 先が長くない, 余命いくばくもない ▪ I can*not be long for this world*. 私はこの先長くは生きられない.

not by a long shot/《英》***not by a long chalk*** →SHOT[1]; CHALK[1].

Now, we shan't be long! 《俗》さあ決まった; ほんとにけっこうだ《取り決め, 事態に対する満足の意を表す; しばしば皮肉》 ▪ *Now we shan't be long!* We are all going back to the hotel. これで決まった. みんなホテルへ戻るとしよう.

So long! 《口》さようなら(また会うときまで) ▪ Well, I must be off now; *so long*, old pal! さて, もうおいとましなくてはなりません, では君, さようなら.

so long as 《主に英》…する限りは, さえすれば ▪ The world always will be the same, *so long as* men are men. 人間が変わらない限り, 世界はいつも同じだろう ▪ You may borrow the book *so long as* you keep it clean. あなたはその本を汚しさえしなければ, 借りてよろしい.

take long 長くかかる ▪ Don't *take* very *long* about it. そのことにあまり暇をかけないでください ▪ It will *take long* to finish the work. その仕事を終えるのは長くかかろう.

that long 《口》それだけの時間 ▪ It will take at least ten times *that long* to go there on foot. 歩いてそこへ行くには, 少なくともその時間の10倍はかかるだろう.

the long and (***the***) ***short of it*** 《口》 **1** つまるところは, 要するに ▪ *The long and the short of it* is that you must pay me the money. 要するに君は私にその金を払わなくてはならないということだ.

2 全体, 一部始終 ▪ He knows *the long and short of it* now. 彼はもうその一部始終を知っている.

the longest day …するかぎり ▪ I shall never forget it *the longest day* I have to live. 私は生きているかぎり, それを忘れません.

think long and hard (***about***) (…について)じっ

くり考える ▪I *thought long and hard about* what to do. 何をすべきかを熟考した.

this long time [***while***] 今まで長い間ずっと ▪What have you been doing *this long time*? あなたは今までずっと何をしていましたか.

longbow /lɔ́ːŋbòʊ|lɔ́ŋ/ 名 ***draw*** [***pull***] ***the longbow*** →BOW[1].

longed-for /lɔ́ːŋdfɔ̀ːr|lɔ́ŋd-/ 形 待ちこがれた, 待望の, 切望している ▪The *longed-for* letter arrived at last. 待ちに待った手紙がやっと届いた.

longing /lɔ́ːŋɪŋ|lɔ́ŋ-/ 名 ***have a longing for*** [***after, to*** *do*] …にあこがれる, を[することを]切望する ▪I *have a longing for* home. 私は故郷を恋しく思っている ▪They *have a* fierce *longing after* gold and silver. 彼らは金銀を激しく渇望している.

look[1] /lʊk/ 名 ***be in good looks*** 丈夫[健康]に見える ▪Catherine *was in* very *good looks*. キャサリンは非常に元気そうに見えた.

for the look of the thing 体裁上, 体面上 ▪I voted for them just *for the look of the thing*. 私はただ体裁上彼らに投票したにすぎない.

from [***by***] ***the look***(***s***) (***of***) …の様子から(見て) ▪*From his looks* you might suppose him to be strong. 彼の様子から見て彼を強健だと思うかもしれない ▪*By the looks of* the sky, it will be rainy tomorrow. 空模様から見てあすは雨だろう.

get a look in 《英口》〚主に否定文で〛ことがうまくいく見込みがある ▪Their team were far better. We didn't *get a look in*. 彼らのチームの方がはるかに優勢で我々に勝ち目はなかった.

give *a person* ***a black*** [《口》 ***dirty, filthy***] ***look*** 人を不きげんな顔をして見る ▪The boss *gave* me *a black look* when I asked for a holiday. 休暇をくださいと言ったら, 課長が不きげんな顔をして僕を見た ▪An elderly woman with a small dog *gave* him *a filthy look*. 子犬を連れた老婦人がむっつりとして彼を見た.

give *a person* ***a blank look*** (相手の意図が分からなくて, またはとぼけて)人をぽかんとした顔で見る ▪When I asked her about that, she *gave* me *a blank look*. 彼女にそれを聞くと, ぽかんとした顔をした.

give *a person* ***a look*** **1** 人を意味ありげに見る ▪She *gave* her husband *a look* and he said no more. 彼女が意味ありげに目配せしたので, 夫は口をつぐんだ.
2 人を怒って見る ▪The woman behind the counter *gave* me such *a look*. 売場の女性はひどく怒った顔をして私を見た.

give *a person* ***a pained look*** 腹を立てて[怒った顔をして]人を見る ▪Oh, don't *give* me that *pained look*. そんなに怒った顔をして見ないでよ.

have [***take***] ***a look at*** 《口》(調べるため)…をちょっと見る, にちょっと目を通す ▪I *have a look at* the papers before breakfast. 私は朝食前に新聞にちょっと目を通す.

have a look of …にぼんやり似ている; 外観が…に似ている ▪This picture *has a look of* you. この写真は何となくあなたに似ている.

have an ugly look うさん臭い; 険悪である ▪If he had taken the money, his conduct would *have an ugly look*. 彼がその金を取ったのなら, 彼の行為はうさん臭いはずだが ▪That cloud *has an ugly look*. あの雲は雨にでもなりそうだ.

if looks could kill [***slay***] 人をにらんで殺せるものなら《敵意にみちた目つきに言う》 ▪*If looks could kill*, Jones would have had short shrift. 人をにらんで殺せるものなら, ジョーンズはあっさり死んでいただろうに.

like the look(***s***) ***of*** …の様子が気に入る ▪I *liked the look of* this car and bought it. この車の外観が気に入ったので買った ▪I don't *like the look of* that sky. あの空模様が心配だ.

lose [***keep***] *one's* ***looks*** (…が)元の美しさを失う[保っている] ▪The actress has *lost her looks*. その女優は昔の美しさを失ってしまった ▪His armchair still *kept its looks*. 彼の肘かけいすはまだ元のように美しかった.

take a long, hard look at (問題解決のため)よく調べる, 慎重に考える, しっかり見直す ▪Step back and *take a long, hard look at* yourself. 一歩下がってじっくり自分を見つめなおしてみなさい.

take on an ugly look 険悪な様相を帯びる ▪Affairs *took on an ugly look*. 事態は険悪な様相を帯びてきた.

take one look ひと目見る (*at*) ▪You have to *take one look at* Mary to see that she is a nice girl. メアリーをひと目見るだけでいい娘(こ)だと分かるよ.

upon the look (***for***) (…を)捜して ▪Her father's ship put out to sea, *upon the look for* certain merchantmen. 彼女の父の船はある商船団を捜すため出港した.

look[2] /lʊk/ 動 ***be fair*** [***pretty,*** etc.] ***to look at*** [***on***] 外見が美しい[など] ▪The girl *is pretty to look at*. その少女は器量が良い ▪He *is* not *much to look at*. 彼はあまり見ばえがしない.

be just looking (店員に対して)ただ見ているだけである, まだ決めていない ▪Can I help you?—I'*m just looking*, thank you. 何かお探しですか—どうも. 見ているだけですから.

be looking up 見通しが明るくなる, 景気がよくなる, 上向きになる ▪Things *are looking up* for our company at long last. やっとのことでわが社の景気がよくなってきた.

cannot look at 《口》…に対して勝ち目がない ▪The batsmen *could not look at* him. 打者たちは彼に勝つ見込みがなかった.

a person (***has***) ***never looked back*** それ以来ずっと幸せである, その後成功し続けている ▪Since the day I picked up this bike, I *have never looked back*. この自転車を手に入れてからずっと僕は気分がいい ▪I quit my former job to become a lawyer, and *have never looked back*. 前の仕事をやめて弁護士になって以来はとんとん拍子である.

Let each man look at home. 《諺》各自自分の家を見よ《おのれの頭のハエを追え》.

L

look abroad **1** 外[国外]を見る ▪ He *looks abroad* into the varied field of nature. 彼は外を見て自然の多彩な野原を調べる ▪ He *looked abroad* for more business. 彼は事業拡大を目指して海外に目を向けた.
2 広く見る ▪ The young men *look abroad* for a wife. 青年たちは広く妻となる人を探す.

look after *oneself* 自分で自分の面倒を見る, 一人でやっていける ▪ She can *look after herself*. 彼女は一人でやっていける.

Look after yourself! 《英口》お大事に《別れのあいさつ》 ▪ Bye, *look after yourself*.—Take care. さようなら, 元気でね―お前も達者でな.

look *oneself* **again** (病気が)全快している, 元どおり元気になっている ▪ You *look yourself again*. あなたはまたすっかり元気になったようですね.

look *one's* **age** 年齢相応に見える ▪ He assuredly did not *look his age*. 彼は確かに年齢ほどには見えなかった.

look alive **1** 《口》〚主に命令文で〛急ぐ, 敏速に活動する ▪ Tell him to *look alive*, or he will be late. 彼に急ぐように言ってくれ, でないとおくれるから ▪ *Look alive* there. おい, てきぱきやれ.
2 生きているようだ ▪ The stuffed bird *looked alive*. その剥製の鳥は生きているようだった.

look another way よそ見する ▪ I was *looking another way* then. 私はそのときよそ見をしていた.

look as if [**though**] …のようである ▪ It *looks as if* that firm were going to fail. その会社はつぶれかけているようである ▪ It *looks as if* it's going to rain. 今にも雨が降りそうだ.

look as if [**though**] *one* **has been dragged** [*a person* **has been dragging** *one*] **through a hedge backwards** 《口》ひどくだらしない様子をしている ▪ You *look as if* you *have been dragged through a hedge backwards*. 君はひどくだらしない格好をしているね.

look as if [**though**] *one* **has been sleeping in it for a week** まるで1週間もそれを着たまま寝ていたように見える《ひどくだらしない》 ▪ Your suit is so crumpled that it *looks as if* you *have been sleeping in it for a week*. 君の服はしわだらけで, まるで1週間もそれを着て寝ていたみたいだよ.

look as if [**though**]**… has been stirred with a stick** 《口》まるで棒でかき回したように見える《ひどく汚い, 乱雑である》 ▪ This room *looks as if* it's *been stirred with a stick*. この部屋はひどく取り散らかされている.

look askance (**at**) →ASKANCE.

Look at that! 《口》〚命令文で〛(驚くべき・異常な・珍しいものを指して)…を見よ ▪ *Look at that!* Someone's broken my flower pot! 見ろよ. 誰かが植木鉢を壊してしまった.

look at the bottom of the glass 《米口》酒杯を飲み干す ▪ He often *looked at the bottom of the glass*. 彼は何度も酒杯を飲み干した.

Look at you. 《口》〚命令文で〛(相手の状態に対して)これは驚いた ▪ *Look at you!* It's almost noon and you're still in bed. こいつはたまげた. もうすぐ昼なのにまだ寝ているのか.

look bad 世間体[聞こえ]が悪い ▪ It would *look bad* not to attend the funeral. 葬式に行かないと世間体が悪いだろうな.

look bad (**for** *a person*) (人にとって)幸先がよくない, 険悪だ ▪ Things *looked bad for* them. 彼らにとって事態はよろしくなかった.

look badly [**meanly, tolerably**] 外観が悪く[みすぼらしく, かなりに]見える ▪ Things began to *look badly* for them. 形勢が彼らにとっては悪くなり始めた ▪ Do I *look meanly* in her eyes? 私は彼女の目にはみすぼらしく見えるのだろうか.

Look before you leap. 《諺》実行する前に熟慮せよ,「転ばぬ先のつえ」.

look … between the eyes …に面と向う, 対抗する ▪ Not a man *looked* me *between the eyes*. 私に対抗したものは一人もなかった.

look beyond the grave 死後のことまで考える ▪ Few people *look beyond the grave*. 死後のことまで考える人はあまりない.

look black **1** (先行きが)暗い, 険悪である ▪ Japan's economy *looks black* at the moment. 目下のところ日本の経済の先行きは暗い.
2 怒った顔をしている ▪ The boss is *looking* very *black* this morning. 社長は今朝とてもこわい顔をしている.

look *oneself* **blind** 目が見えなくなるほど見る ▪ You may *look yourself blind*, but you will never find a flaw in it. 君は穴のあくほど見ても, それには一つのきずも見つからないだろう.

look blue →BLUE.

look *one's* **consent** 目で承諾の意を表す ▪ She said nothing, but *looked her consent*. 彼女は何も言わないで目で承諾の意を表した.

look down *one's* **nose** (**at**) →NOSE[1].

look down through the ages (現代まで)時代を通観する ▪ We knew this to be true as we *looked down through the ages*. 現代まで歴史を通観してみて, これが正しいことがわかった.

look good (**to**) →GOOD.

Look here! 《口》〚間投詞的に〛いいかね; あのねえ(こうなんだよ)《こちらの苦情・提案などに相手の注意を促す》 ▪ Now, *look here!* I'll have no feelings here. さて, いいかね. わしはここでは情け容赦はしないぞ.

look … in the face [**eye**(**s**)] **1** (臆せずに)…の顔をまともに見る ▪ A speaker should *look* his audience *in the face*. 演説者は聴衆の顔をまともに見なければならない ▪ I can't *look* Bill *in the face* any more. (不義理をしたので)もうビルに顔向けできない.
2 (大胆に)…に直面する, 向かう ▪ He has *looked* death *in the face* many times. 彼は何度も死に直面したことがある ▪ He *looked* the danger *in the face*. 彼は大胆に危険に立ち向かった.
3 (事実を)直視する ▪ You must *look* your financial affairs *in the face*. あなたは財政状態を直視した

ければならない.

look it そう見える ▪ She is forty but she doesn't *look it*. 彼女は40歳だがそうは見えない ▪ He was frightened and *looked it*. 彼はびっくりした, そしてそれを顔に表した.

look like **1** …のようである, に似ている ▪ What does it *look like*? それはどのようなものですか ▪ He *looks* just *like* his mother. 彼は全く母親そっくりだ.
2 …しそうである; がありそうである ▪ It *looks like* rain. 雨になりそうだ ▪ He *looks like* winning. 彼は勝ちそうだ.
3 …らしいことである ▪ That *looks* just *like* him. それはいかにも彼らしいことだ.
4《口》おそらく…だろう ▪ Your cook kidnapped the child, *looks like* to me. お宅の料理人が子供を誘拐したものらしい.

look like a plucked chicken [***hen***] 髪の毛を思い切って切りすぎている ▪ Mom returned from the beauty parlor *looking like a plucked chicken*. 母は羽毛をむしられたニワトリみたいな頭で美容院から帰ってきた.

look like *oneself* ***again*** = LOOK oneself again.

look lively = LOOK alive 1.

look love [***hope,*** etc.] 目に愛情[希望, など]を表す ▪ Her eyes *looked love* at her child. 彼女の目はわが子に対する愛情をたたえていた.

Look, no hands. 《口》ね, うまいもんだろう ▪ *Look, no hands.* I'm on autopilot now! ほら, じょうずでしょ. もう手放しで乗れるよ. ☞子供が手放しで自転車に乗ることを自慢する言葉から.

look on [***upon***] ***the … side of*** …の…の面を見る ▪ You *look upon* one *side of* the question. 君は問題の一面だけを見ている ▪ He *looks on the* sunny [dark, black] *side of* things. 彼はものごとを楽観的[悲観的]に見る.

look one way and row another 目の方向とこぐ方向が違う, ある目的を追求すると見せかけて実際は別の目的を追求する ▪ He *looks one way, and rows another*; he pretends public profit, but intends private. 彼は言うこととすることが食い違う. うわべは公共の利益を装うが実は私利をもくろむ.

look out for squalls →SQUALL.

look *a person* ***out of countenance*** 人をじろじろ見てきまり悪がらせる ▪ He held the girl's hand a little, and *looked* her *out of countenance*. 彼はその娘の手をちょっと握って, じろじろ見てきまり悪がらせた.

look out (***of***) ***the window*** 窓からのぞく[外を見る] ▪ Don't *look out of the window*. 窓から外を見てはいけない. ☞《米》ではよく of を略す.

look right [***straight***] ***through*** *a person* 人を見て見ぬふりをする, わざと無視する ▪ Mary *looked right through* the poor woman. メアリーはその貧しい女性を見て見ぬふりをした.

look round the corner 角を曲がって探す ▪ *Look round the corner* and see if anyone is coming. 角を曲がってみて, 誰か来ているか見なさい.

look seven ways for Sunday → look nine WAYs (for Sunday, at once).

look sharp **1** 厳重警戒する, うかうかしない ▪ You must *look sharp* about you. あなたは厳重に警戒しなければなりません. ☞sharp = sharply.
2《口》素早くやる, てきぱきやる; 急ぐ ▪ You had better *look sharp*; they're all ready and waiting. 早くしなさい, 彼らはみんな用意して待っていますから.

look sharp after …を注意深く見守る ▪ I had to *look sharp after* her. 彼女を厳重に見守らねばならなかった.

look slimy [《主に米俗》 ***slippy, slippery***] 《口》素早くやる, てきぱきやる ▪ You'll have to *look slimy*. てきぱきやらなくてはだめだ.

look *one's* ***thanks*** 目で感謝の意を表す ▪ He *looked the thanks* he could not express. 彼は口で言えぬ感謝の意を目で表した.

look the other way →WAY.

look … through and through (人の思惑など)をすっかり見抜く, (人)を余す所なく調べる ▪ He *looked* me *through and through*. 彼は私の心をすっかり見抜いた.

look … through colored spectacles [***blue glasses***] …を色めがねで見る ▪ They are apt to *look* at things *through colored spectacles*. 彼らは物事を色めがねで見がちである.

look … through rose-colored spectacles → see … through ROSE-COLORED spectacles.

look to be …であるようだ ▪ The Queen *looks to be* in good health. 女王はご壮健のようだ ▪ The hat *looked to be* made of beaver. その帽子はビーバーの毛皮でできているらしかった.

look to it that 〚主に命令文で〛…するよう注意する ▪ *Look to it that* this does not happen again. こんな事が二度と起こらぬよう注意しなさい.

look to *a person* ***to*** *do* …することを人に頼る[仰ぐ, 期待する, 当てにする] ▪ We must *look to* you *to* deal with the situation. この時局の収拾はあなたに頼むよりほかはありません ▪ I *look to* him *to* make the arrangement. 彼がその取り決めをするものと思っている.

look unutterable things 言うに言われぬ[感慨無量の]顔つきをする ▪ The man *looked unutterable things* at me. 男はなんともいえない顔をして私を見た.

look … up and down **1** (人)を頭のてっぺんから足の先までじろじろ見る ▪ People *looked* her *up and down*. 人々は彼女の頭のてっぺんから足の先までじろじろ見た.
2 …をくまなく検査する ▪ We *looked* it *up and down*. 私たちはそれをくまなく検査した.

look *a person's* ***way*** 人の方を(ちらっと)見る ▪ He never *looked my way* while he talked. 彼は話をしているとき私の方を一度も見なかった.

Look within your heart! わが心中を探れ!

Look you!/《卑》***Look'ee!*** 《口》よいかね!, ねえ君! ▪ *Look you*, the matter is important. いいか, 事は重大なのだぞ.

looking at …を判断すれば ▪ *Looking at* the

matter calmly, I should say it is a very good idea. その事を落ち着いて判断すると，非常に良い考えのようだな.

looking the other way また一方を見れば ▪ There is another possibility, *looking the other way.* また一方を見れば，もう一つの可能性がある.

not know which way* [*where*] *to look (当惑して)どちらを向いていいかわからない ▪ He was so ashamed that he did*n't know which way to look.* 彼はとても恥じ入って，どちらを向いていいかわからなかった.

***not* [*never*] *look back* [*behind* one]** 《口》とんとん拍子で進む，どんどんよくなる ▪ He did *not look behind* him, but got better and better. 彼は少しの停滞もなく，どんどんよくなった.

not look good =LOOK bad.

not look twice at …に全く興味がない ▪ I would*n't look twice at* someone like him. 彼のような人物には全然関心がわかない.

not much to look at →MUCH.

to look at **1** 見れば，様子は ▪ She's not much *to look at.* 彼女はそれほど美人ではない.

2 《口》一見したところでは; 様子から判断すれば ▪ No one would think him thirty-six, *to look at.* 誰も一見したところでは，彼が36歳だとは思わないだろう.

would* [*will*] do *as soon as look you 《口》すぐさま(いやなことを)する ▪ Don't go near him. He *would* hit you *as soon as look you.* 彼のそばへ近づかない方がいい. すぐ殴るから.

looker-on /lʊ̀kərɑ́ːn|-ɔ́n/ 名 ***Lookers-on see most of the game.*** 《諺》ゲームははたから見ている者に一番よく見える，「岡目八目」.

look-in /lʊ́kɪ̀n/ 名 ***give** a person **a look-in*** 《口》〚主に否定文で〛 **1** 人に勝利[成功]の見込みを与える ▪ The home team never *gave* the visitors *a look-in.* 地元のチームは来訪チームに少しも勝利の見込みを与えなかった.

2 人に分け前を与える，参与させる ▪ They don't *give* anyone else *a look-in.* 彼らは他の者は誰も参与させない.

have* [*get*] *a look-in 《口》〚主に否定文で〛 **1** 勝利[成功]の見込みがある ▪ I shan't *have a look-in.* 私の成功の見込みはないだろう.

2 少し分け前にあずかる，参与する ▪ They don't *have a look-in.* 彼らは少しも分け前にあずからない.

look-out /lʊ́kàʊt/ 名 ***be on the look-out* (*for, to* do)** 警戒する; 見張る; (を得ようと，しようと)気をつけている ▪ They *were on the look-out for* a storm. 彼らは暴風を警戒していた ▪ I *was on the look-out for* a good used car. 私は良い中古自動車を手に入れようと気をつけていた. ☞海事用語から.

be** a person's* (*own*) *look-out 《英口》人のすべきことである，人の責任である ▪ That *is his look-out.* それは彼のすべきことだ《私の知ったことではない》 ▪ If he loses, that *is his look-out.* 彼が損をしても，それは彼の勝手だ.

keep a sharp look-out 警戒する，見張る; (を得ようと，しようと)気をつける (*for, to do*) ▪ *Keep a sharp look-out for* pickpockets. すりを厳重警戒しなさい. ☞海事用語から.

place* [*put*]... *on the look-out …に警戒させる，を見張らせる; を(得ようと，しようと)気をつけさせる (*for, to do*) ▪ He *was placed on the look-out.* 彼は見張りに立たされていた ▪ Anything new *puts* us *on the look-out to* detect a possible absurdity. 何でも新しいものが出ると，我々はなにか欠点を探そうとする.

loom /luːm/ 動 ***loom large*** ぼうっと大きく見える; 気味悪く迫る ▪ The tree *loomed large* in the twilight. その木は薄明かりの中でぼうっと大きく見えた ▪ The dangers of the international situation *loomed large* in our minds. 国際情勢の危険が我々の心に大きく写った.

loom the web たて糸を織機にかける ▪ They have begun to *loom the web.* 彼らはたて糸を織機にかけ始めた.

loon /luːn/ 名 **(*as*) *crazy as a loon*** ひどく狂って ▪ The next morning he was *as crazy as a loon.* 翌朝彼はひどく狂ったようになっていた. ☞loon(アビ)が危険を逃れるときの行動とその陰気な叫び声から.

(*as*) *drunk as a loon* ひどく酔って ▪ He has been *drunk as a loon* the last two hours. 彼は2時間前から，べろんべろんになっている.

hunt the loon 愛する人を失って悲しむ ▪ She was *hunting the loon* with a handnet. 彼女は手網でアビを狩っていた《愛する人を失って悲しんでいた》.

loop[1] /luːp/ 名 ***in the loop*** 《主に米口》機密情報を知って，(グループ・組織・会社などの)中枢にいる，関わって ▪ She is *in the loop* on all the big decisions at the company. 彼女は会社の重要な決定に関わる中枢のポストについている.

on the loop モーターが並列するように制御器を調節して.

out of the loop 《主に米口》機密情報を知らずに，(グループ・組織・会社などの)中枢から外れて，関わらずに ▪ I think that the vice president was *out of the loop.* 副大統領は蚊帳(かや)の外に置かれていたと思う.

throw* [*knock*]...*for a loop 《米》 **1** 人を驚き[興奮]または狼狽の状態に陥れる ▪ They *were thrown for a loop* when they caught sight of him. 彼らは彼を見てすっかりめんくらった.

2 人を不意の逆運[災難]に陥れる ▪ Any such attempt would *knock* our whole economy *for a loop.* そんな試みをすれば，我々の経済全体が困窮に陥るだろう.

loop[2] /luːp/ 動 ***loop the loop*** 宙返りをする; (自転車の)宙乗りをする ▪ He *looped the loop* with the powerful airplane. 彼は馬力のある飛行機で宙返りをやった.

loophole /lúːphòʊl/ 名 ***a loophole in the law*** 法の文言のあいまいさによる法令の抜け穴 ▪ He made a fortune by taking advantage of *a loophole in the law.* 彼は法の抜け穴に乗じて一財産築いた.

loose[1] /luːs/ 形名 ***at* [*after, on*] *a loose***

end/《米》***at loose ends*** 《英口》 **1** 定職がなく; ぶらぶらして ▪ I found myself *at a loose end*. 私は自分が失業したのを知った ▪ He liked to be *after a loose end*. 彼はぶらぶらしているのが好きだった.

2 何をするという当てもなく; 未定のままで ▪ He was a stranger there, and was *at a loose end*. 彼はそこではよそ者で何をする当てもなかった ▪ You must not leave the matter *at a loose end*. その件を未解決のままにしておいてはいけない.

3 混乱して, 当惑して ▪ She has been *at loose ends* since her maid left. お手伝いが去ってから彼女はずっと途方にくれている.

break loose 束縛を振り切る, 脱出する ▪ One of the tigers in the zoo has *broken loose*. 動物園のトラが1頭おりから出た ▪ The youth *broke loose* from his father's control. その若者は父の監督の目から抜け出した.

cast loose 解き放つ ▪ We *cast* the boat *loose*. 我々はそのボートを解き放った.

come loose ほどける, 離れる ▪ Some of the pages have *come loose*. 数ページが取れた.

cut loose →CUT².

get loose **1** 逃げる ▪ One of the cows *got loose* from the stake. 牛の一頭が縛られていた杭から逃げた.

2 振り放す, 解く ▪ He struggled until he *got* one hand *loose*. 彼はもがいてやっと片手を振りほどいた.

give (***a***) ***loose to*** **1** (人)を自由気ままにさせる ▪ *Give a loose to* your children for a while. しばらく子供たちを自由にさせてごらん.

2 (感情・言葉など)を自由に表出する, (想像など)をほしいままにする ▪ He *gave loose to* his feelings. 彼は感情を存分に表した ▪ The poets *give a loose to* their imagination in the description of angels. 詩人たちは天使の描写には想像をたくましくする.

go loose やたらに動き回る ▪ The angry mobs *went loose* on the streets. 怒った暴徒が通りをうろつき回った.

hang [***stay***] ***loose*** 《主に米口》 平静でいる, 落ち着いている, のんびりしている ▪ Just *hang loose*. Everything will be all right. 気楽に行こうぜ. 何もかもうまくいくからさ ▪ He just told me to *stay loose* and be prepared. 彼は私に落ち着いて準備をするように言った.

hold loose 冷淡[無関心]である ▪ The sales clerk was *holding loose* and not in earnest. その店員はよそよそしく本気ではなかった.

in the loose 一定の形に作らないで ▪ Those cigar ends were sold *in the loose*. その葉巻の先はそのままで売られた.

let loose **1** (…に)放す, 解き放す (*on*) ▪ It is dangerous to *let loose* such men *on* society. そのような者たちを世に放しておくのは危険である.

2 爆発させる ▪ He *let loose* his indignation. 彼は怒りを爆発させた.

3 遊離させる ▪ Chlorine *is let loose* by the process. 塩素はその方法で遊離させられる.

4 離れる[自由になる]に任せる ▪ She *let* her hair *loose* to the wind. 彼女は髪を風にほつれるに任せた ▪ Every evil *was let loose* to wander over the land. あらゆる害悪が国中を自由に横行するに任された.

let *oneself* ***loose*** 言行に締まりがなくなる ▪ Don't *let yourself loose* more than what you can afford. 度を越して締まりのない言動をとってはならない.

lie loose 散らばっている ▪ He took some coins that were *lying loose*. 彼は散らばっている2, 3枚の貨幣を手に取った.

live on the loose →on the LOOSE 2.

on a loose end →at a LOOSE end.

on the loose **1** 自由気ままな, 解放されて ▪ They roamed the streets shouting like a bunch of schoolboys *on the loose*. 彼らははめをはずした子供たちの集団のように叫びながら街路をうろつき回った.

2 《口》 放蕩(とう)をして; 浮かれ騒いで ▪ He has been living *on the loose*. 彼はずっと放蕩な生活をしてきた ▪ He often goes out *on the loose* with his friends. 彼はよく友人と浮かれ騒ぐ.

play loose →PLAY².

set loose 放す, 逃がす ▪ We *set* the canary *loose* from her cage. カナリアをかごから逃がしてやった.

shake loose from …と手を切る; を手放す ▪ He *shook loose from* the organization. 彼はその団体と手を切った ▪ I *shook loose from* a dollar. 私は1ドル手放した.

sit loose **1** 冷淡である ▪ He *sat loose* with the king. 彼は国王に無関心であった.

2 いいかげんに奉じる[守る] ▪ He simply *sat loose* to the theories. 彼はでたらめにその学説を奉じただけだった.

3 …にとらわれない, の奴隷にはならない ▪ You should *sit loose* to all these comforts. これらすべての慰楽にとらわれてはいけない.

tear loose =break LOOSE.

tie [***tidy***] ***up the loose ends*** [***threads***] (仕事などの)未解決の部分を処理する ▪ He is *tying* [*tidying*] *up the* few *loose ends*. 彼は2, 3の懸案を処理しているところだ.

turn loose **1** 放つ ▪ He *turned loose* the tied horse. 彼は繋いでいた馬を解き放った.

2 自由にさせる ▪ He *turned* the suspects *loose*. 彼は容疑者たちを自由にさせた.

3 発射する; 砲火を開く ▪ Everything on board *turned loose* on him. 船上のすべてのものが彼に対して砲火を開いた ▪ Someone *turned* his gun *loose* into the air. 誰かが空中に発砲した ▪ Several guns *were turned loose* on him and he was taken to the hospital. 数丁の銃に撃たれて, 彼は病院へ運ばれた.

4 とうとうと述べる ▪ He *turned loose* (a torrent of words) on me. 彼は私に対してとうとうとまくしたてた.

5 《米口》 放らつにふるまう ▪ The cowboys *turned loose* and started a bedlam on the plains. そのカウボーイたちは放らつにふるまい, 平原で大騒ぎを始めた.

turn ... loose on …を(あること)に着手させる, 働かせる ▪ He *turned* her *loose on* the activities of

L

microbes. 彼は彼女に細菌の活動について研究させた ▪ They *turned* a new tractor *loose on* the land. 彼らは新しいトラクターを使ってその土地を耕作した.

work loose →WORK[2].

loose[2] /luːs/ 動 ***loose*** *one's* ***hold of*** (つかんでいるもの)を放す ▪ *Loose your hold of* my bag. 私のかばんから手を放しなさい.

loosen /lúːsən/ 動 ***loosen*** *a person's* ***hide*** 人をむち打つ, 打ち懲らす ▪ Their master *loosened their hides*. 彼らの主人は彼らを打ち懲らした.

loosen the [*one's*] ***purse strings*** →PURSE STRING.

loosen *a person's* ***tongue*** 人をしゃべり出させる ▪ Wine *loosened his tongue*. 酒が回って彼はしゃべり出した.

lop /lɑp|lɔp/ 名 ***lop and top*** [***crop***] (材木にならない)切り枝, そだ ▪ The purchaser took the timber tree with the *lop and crop*. 買い手はその立ち木を小枝ごと買った.

lord[1] /lɔːrd/ 名 ***a lord of creation*** 《戯》男性 ▪ I had rather be a woman than one of those *lords of creation*. 私はそんな男性の一人になるよりはむしろ女性であったほうがましだ.

act the lord 《口》殿様のようにふるまう ▪ We hated it when he *acted the lord*. 彼が主人づらをするのをみなきらった.

(***as***) ***drunk as a lord*** →(as) DRUNK as a fiddler.

be lord of …を領有する, 所有する ▪ He *was lord of* a fair domain. 彼は良い国土を領有していた ▪ A true gentleman *is lord of* a great heart. 真の紳士は大きい心を持つ.

(***Good***) ***Lord!/Oh Lord!*** ああ, おお《驚き・心配を表す》 ▪ *Oh Lord*, what have you done to your hair! まあ, その頭, どうしたの.

in the year of our Lord →in the YEAR of grace.

live like a lord 贅沢に暮らす ▪ He *lives like a lord* without any worries. 彼は何の心配もなく贅沢に暮らしている.

one's [***the***] ***lord and master*** 主人; 《戯》夫 ▪ Humans are not *the lords and masters* of everything. 人は万物の主というわけではない ▪ Does a wife welcome the criticism of *her lord and master*? 妻は夫の批評を歓迎しますか.

Lord bless me [***us, my soul, you***]***!*** おやおや!, これはこれは! ▪ *Lord bless me!* I saw it two months ago. これは驚いた! それを2か月前に見たぞ.

Lord have mercy! **1** 神様, お慈悲を垂れ給え《昔祈りとして疫病の家の戸にチョークで書いたもの》(*on*) ▪ *Lord have mercy on* those three. 神様, その3人の者にお慈悲を垂れてください.

2《卑》〖Lord-a-mercy で〗おやおや! ▪ *Lord-a-mercy*, is that how she talks? おやまあ, あの女性はひどいしゃべり方だね.

Lord willing = GOD willing (and the creek don't rise).

swear like a lord →SWEAR like a trooper.

The English [***They,*** etc.] ***dearly love a lord.*** 《諺》イギリス人[彼ら, など]は貴族が好き.

(***The***) ***Lord knows.*** →God KNOWs.

the lord of creation 《皮肉・戯》万物の霊長(《聖》*Gen.* 1. 26) ▪ Man is *the lord of creation*. 人間は万物の霊長である.

the Lord of the Flies ハエの王《魔王 Beelzebub のあだ名》(《聖》*Matt.* 12. 24) ▪ Who do you think is *the Lord of the Flies*? Satan or God? ハエの王とは誰だと思うか. 悪魔か, それとも神か.

(***the***) ***Lord*** (***only***) ***knows what*** [***who, where,*** etc.] 《口》→God KNOWs what.

treat like a lord **1** 贅をきわめて歓待する, 大尽ふるまいをする ▪ They *treated* him *like a lord* at the palace. 彼らは宮殿で彼を大いに歓待した.

2 深い敬意をもって遇する, うやうやしく応待する ▪ We will *treat* him *like a lord* and let him do anything he pleases. 深い敬意をもって彼を処遇し, 何でも望みどおりにさせよう.

lord[2] /lɔːrd/ 動 ***lord it*** (***over***) (…に)いばりちらす; (に)君臨する; (を)威圧する ▪ The dictator has *lorded it over* his people for many years. その独裁者は長い間人民に君臨してきた ▪ A bull seal *lords it over* a herd of cows. 1頭の雄アザラシが雌たちのハーレムを支配する ▪ The ship seems to be *lording it over* the deep. その船は大海を威圧する観がある.

lordship /lɔ́ːrdʃìp/ 名 ***have the lordship over*** …を支配する ▪ God *has the lordship over* the universe. 神は宇宙を支配し給う.

Your [***His***] ***Lordship*** 閣下《大監督・公爵を除く貴族および裁判官に対する敬称, 戯言的にはその他の人・動物にも用いる; 複数は… Lordships》 ▪ These papers were written by *your lordship*. これらの論文は閣下の書かれたものです ▪ *Their Lordships* adjourned until the following Sunday. 諸卿は次の日曜まで休会した ▪ *His Lordship* observed that it was impossible. その方はそれは不可能だと言われた.

lorry /lɔ́ːri|lɔ́ri/ 名 ***fall off*** (***the back of***) ***a lorry*** →FALL[2].

lose /luːz/ 動 ***have*** (***got***) ***something*** [***much,*** etc.] ***to lose by*** …によって失うものが少々[たくさん, など]ある ▪ You may *have much to lose by* such precipitate action. そんなせっかちな行動をすれば多くのものを失うかもしれないぞ ▪ Poor people *have little to lose by* believing in luck. 貧しい人々は幸運を信じているからと言って失うものはほとんどない.

lose *oneself* **1** 道に迷う ▪ The little girl *lost herself* in a big building. その幼い少女は大きな建物で迷子になった.

2 没入する, 夢中になる; 眠る ▪ I longed to *lose myself* in books all alone. 私は一人っきりで本の中に没入したいと願った ▪ I *lost myself* for a few minutes during the sermon. 私は説教中に数分間眠ってしまった.

3 (驚いて)目を回す, ぼう然自失する; 取り乱す ▪ He *lost himself*, as many eyes were turned towards him. 大勢の人が彼の方を見たので彼は取り乱した.

***lose belief* [*confidence, faith, trust*] *in* …** を信じなくなる ▪ He *lost confidence in* his abilities. 彼は自分の能力に自信がなくなった.

lose** oneself **in **1** …に夢中になる; にふける, に(ふけって)我を忘れる ▪ He *lost himself in* the book. 彼はその本に夢中になった ▪ I *lost myself in* melancholy musing. 私は憂鬱な物思いにふけった ▪ I *lost myself in* joy to see him. 私は彼に会って有頂天になって喜んだ.

2 …におのれを没する; に没入する ▪ I like to *lose myself in* my own mind. 物思いにふけるのが好きだ.

3 (驚きなどで)ぼう然自失する, 目を回す ▪ We *lost ourselves in* wonder at his feats. 我々は彼の妙技に驚嘆して目を回した.

4 …に隠れて見えなくなる ▪ A vast ocean of tillage *lost itself in* the vapor. 海のように広大な耕地がもやに隠れて見えなくなった ▪ Rills *lost themselves* at length *in* matted grass. 細い流れはついに一面に密生する草に隠れた.

lose it 《口》 自制心を失う, かんしゃくを起こす ▪ He just *lost it* when he looked out into the audience. 彼は観客を見渡すと頭の中が真っ白になった ▪ Apparently he's *lost it* now. どうやら彼は今かんしゃくを起こしているようだ ▪ When he saw a scratch on his new car, he almost *lost it*. 自分の新車に引っかき傷がついているのを見て彼はキレそうになった.

***lose no time* (*in*)** *doing* →TIME[1].

lose** one's **patient (医者が)病人を殺す; 病人に逃げられる ▪ The doctor *lost his patient*. その医者は患者に逃げられた.

lose the thread of** one's **discourse/ lose** one's **train of thought 何を話(そうと)していたのかわからなくなる ▪ Where was I? I am afraid I *lost my train of thought*. どこまで話したんだっけ? どうもわからなくなったようだ.

The* [*A*] *story does not lose in the telling. 話はとかくしているうちに誇張されがちだ.

(There is) no time* [*not a moment*] *to lose. 一刻もぐずぐずしていられない ▪ *There was not a moment to lose*. 一刻の猶予もなかった.

What** one **loses on the swings** one **makes up on the roundabouts. →SWING[1].

You cannot lose what you never had. 《諺》 持っていなかったものはなくせない, 「裸で物を落とす例(ためし)しなし」.

loser /lúːzər/ 名 ***a bad* [*good*] *loser*** 負けてぶつぶつ言う人[負けて悪びれない人] ▪ He is such *a good loser*. 彼は負けても全く悪びれない[実に潔い].

be on* [*on to*] *a loser 結局失敗することになっている ▪ We knew we *were on to a loser* from the start. 我々が必ず失敗することは始めからわかっていた.

Losers are always in the wrong. 《諺》 負けたほうがいつも悪いとされる《勝てば官軍》.

losing /lúːzɪŋ/ 形 ***a losing chase*** 追いつく[勝つ]見込みのないこと ▪ I'm sure this is *a losing chase*. 追いつける見込みはまずない.

fight a losing battle →BATTLE[1].

play a losing game →GAME.

loss /lɔːs|lɒs/ 名 ***at a loss*** **1** (猟犬が)臭跡を失って ▪ The hound was *at a loss*. 猟犬は臭跡を失っていた.

2 (…できないで, わからないで)困って, 途方にくれて (*what, how, to do, whether*) ▪ I am *at a loss what* to do. 私はどうしてよいか困っている ▪ I stood utterly *at a loss how* to behave myself. 私はどういう態度を取ったらよいか全く途方にくれて立っていた ▪ I am *at a loss to* explain the reason. 私はその理由を説明するのに困っている ▪ He was *at a loss whether* he should show it to the police. 彼はそれを警察に見せるべきかどうか途方にくれた.

3 (発見できないで, 得られないで)困って, 窮して (*for*) ▪ I was *at a loss for* an answer. 私は答えに窮した ▪ She was completely *at a loss for* words. 彼女は全く言葉に窮した.

4 損をして ▪ He sold the business *at a loss*. 彼は損をしてのれんを売った.

be a dead loss 《口》 **1** 全くの損, 丸損, 全損 ▪ The government have changed the currency, so these old coins *are a dead loss*. 政府が通貨を切り替えたので, これらの旧貨幣は全くの損失だ.

2 《口》 てんでだめな人[物]である; 全くの時間の浪費である ▪ The film *was a dead loss*. その映画はてんでだめだった ▪ It rained every day, so their week at the beach *was a dead loss*. 毎日雨が降ったので彼らがビーチに滞在した1週間は完全な時間のむだだった.

be a loss* [*no loss*] *to …にとっての損失である[でない] ▪ He *is a* great *loss to* the school. 彼は学校の大損失である ▪ Such a man *is no loss to* the state. そのような者は国家にとって何の損失にもならない.

cut** one's **loss(es) 損な取引を中止する ▪ They should *cut their losses* and bring the whole matter to an end. 彼らは損な取引を打ち切っていっさいを終わらせるべきだ.

***have a (great) loss in* [*of*]** (通例, 人)を失って(非常に)困る ▪ I shall *have a great loss in* her. 私は彼女を失ったら非常に困るだろう.

make a loss 損をする ▪ The firm has *made a loss*. その会社は損をした.

One person's loss is another person's gain. 《諺》 甲の損は乙の得.

throw … for a loss **1** 《フットボール》 …にタックルして後退させる ▪ Our end *threw* him *for a loss*. わがチームのエンドが彼にタックルして後退させた.

2 (人)をがっかりさせる, 疲労困ぱいさせる ▪ When Jim failed the test, it *threw* him *for a loss*. テストに失敗したとき, ジムはがっかりした.

3 驚かせる, うろたえさせる, 心配させる ▪ I *was thrown for a loss* at what he said. 彼が言うことを聞いてどぎまぎした.

without loss of time 時を移さず, さっそく ▪ He called on the boss *without loss of time*. 彼はさっそく社長を訪問した.

lost /lɔːst, lɑst|lɒst/ 形 ***a lost cause*** 成功の見

込みのない企画[運動] ▪ The development of the electric car seemed to be *a lost cause*. 電気自動車の開発は失敗に終わりそうな企画に思えた.

All is lost. 万事休す; もうだめだ ▪ *All is* not *lost*; you still have your family. まだ見込みがあるぞ. 君にはまだ家族がいるではないか.

be lost for words 驚きで言葉が出ない ▪ I found myself completely *lost for words*. 私は驚きのあまり言葉も出てこなかった.

be lost in **1** (音・声が)…に飲まれてしまう ▪ Words *were lost in* the tumult. 言葉は騒音に消された ▪ His voice *was lost in* tears. 彼の声は涙に曇った.
2 (驚きなどに)ぼう然自失する, 目を回す ▪ He *was lost in* wonder and admiration. 彼は驚嘆と感嘆に目を回した.
3 …に隠れてしまう, 隠れて見えなくなる ▪ The thief *was lost in* the crowd. 泥棒は人ごみにまぎれて見えなくなった.
4 …に夢中になる, にふけって我を忘れる ▪ The scientist *was lost in* silent meditation. 科学者は黙想にふけっていた.

be lost on [***upon***] *a person* **1** …に効果がない, に気づいて[認めて]もらえない ▪ All his jokes *were lost on* me. 彼の冗談はどれもちっともおもしろくなかった ▪ Your kindness *is* not *lost upon* me. ご親切は決して無にはいたしません ▪ These facts seem to *be lost on* most people. ほとんどの人はこの事実に気うかないようだ.
2 …に理解できない ▪ His lecture on the economic crisis *was* totally *lost on* us. 経済危機に関する彼の講演は我々にはちんぷんかんぷんだった.

be lost to **1** (堕落して, ある観念・感情)がなくなっている ▪ He *is lost to* all sense of duty. 彼は義務の念がすっかりなくなっている.
2 …から取り去られる, もぎ取られる ▪ Joy *was lost to* me. 喜びは私から取り去られた ▪ My parents would have *been lost to* me. うちの両親は連れ去られていただろう.
3 …にはもう得られない ▪ The opportunity *is lost to* me. 機会はもう私には来ない.

be lost to sight [***view***] 見えなくなる ▪ The airplane *was lost to sight*. 飛行機は見えなくなった.

be lost to the world 世に忘れられる ▪ His works would *be lost to the world*. 彼の作品は世に忘れられるであろう.

be [***feel***] ***lost without*** 《口》…が(い)ないと困ってしまう ▪ He is an inveterate smoker; he'd *be lost without* tobacco. 彼は常習的な喫煙者で, タバコがなければ困ってしまうだろう ▪ He left his watch at home and he *felt lost without* it. 家に忘れてきたので, 彼は時計がなくて困った.

get lost **1** 道に迷う; 行方不明になる; 途方にくれる ▪ The dog *got lost* in a world of smells. 犬はたくさんのにおいがする中で途方にくれた.
2 《口》(いやな人・からむ人に向かって)あっちへ行け, 失せろ; よせやい ▪ Stop bothering me. *Get lost*! じゃまをするな. とっとと失せろ.

give lost =give up for LOST.

give up [***over***] ***for lost*** 死んだものとあきらめる, だめだとあきらめる ▪ His friends *gave* him *up* [*over*] *for lost*. 友人たちは彼は助からぬものとあきらめた.

like a lost soul 途方に暮れて, あてもなく ▪ He was wandering aimlessly about *like a lost soul*. 彼は放心したようにふらふらとさまよっていた.

lost and gone forever 失われたままで, ずっと行方不明になって ▪ My poor doggy is *lost and gone forever*. かわいそうに僕のワンちゃんがいなくなっちゃった.

lost in the mists of time 時(という霧)のかなたにまぎれて ▪ The original purpose has been *lost in the mists of time*. 本来の目的がはるか過去のものとして忘れられてきた.

lost in the shuffle 《米》混乱で見落とされて, 相応の注目をうけずに ▪ Children in the big refugee camps tend to get *lost in the shuffle*. 大規模な難民キャンプでは混乱のため子供たちが見落とされがちだ.

lost-and-found /lɔ́:stənfáund, lást-|lɔ́st-/ 名
a lost-and-found (***office***) 遺失物取扱所 ▪ When you have lost something, please contact *the lost-and-found office*. 落し物をしたら遺失物取扱所にお問い合わせください.

lot /lɑt|lɔt/ 名 ***a bad lot*** 《英口》悪党, ろくでなし ▪ I think he is *a bad lot*. 彼は悪党だと思う.

a [*one's*] ***common lot*** 共通の宿命 ▪ We all die some day. That's *our common lot*. 我々はみないつか死ぬが, そいつは避けられない.

a good [***great***] ***lot*** (***of***) 非常にたくさん(の)(数・量) ▪ He has read *a great lot of* books. 彼は非常にたくさん本を読んでいる.

a lot 大いに ▪ He works *a lot* at home. 彼は家で大いに働く.

a lot (***of***)/***lots*** (***of***) たくさん(の)(数・量) ▪ He has *a lot* [*lots*] *of* books. 彼は本をたくさん持っている ▪ They have *a lot of* money. 彼らは金持ちだ ▪ I want *a lot* more. 私はまだどっさりほしい.

a lot riding on/lot riding on/lots riding on 多くを頼っている, …次第である ▪ The game was very intense with *a lot riding on* every pitch. 試合は一投ごとに勝敗のかかった大接戦だった.

A lot you care! 《皮肉》大変なご心配ですね《何も心配しないのに》 ▪ *A lot you care!*—Don't try to pick a fight. ずいぶん心配なことだな!—けんかをふっかけるのはよせ.

across [***cross***] ***lots*** 《米口》(野原を横切って)近道をして; まっすぐに ▪ They went *across lots* to the bar. 彼らは居酒屋へ近道をして行った ▪ You may go to the devil *across lots* for all I care. お前がまっすぐに地獄へ落ちたってちっともかまやしない.

all over the lot 《米口》広範囲に広がって, 散らかって, 混乱状態で ▪ His books and magazines are scattered *all over the lot*. 彼の本や雑誌があたり一面に散乱している.

an awful lot 《口》非常に ▪ I like him *an awful lot*. 彼が大好きだ.

an awful lot of 《口》ひどくたくさんの ▪ He

spends *an awful lot of* money on books. 彼は本にひどくたくさんの金を使う.

by lot くじで ▪ Election *by lot* is the most democratic. くじで選ぶのが最も民主的だ.

by* [*in*] *lots (商品を)幾口かに分けて ▪ They sell goods *by lots*. 彼らは商品を幾口かに分けて売る ▪ We shipped goods *in lots*. 商品を分送した.

cast in *one's* ***lot with* [*among*]** …と[に加わって]運命をともにする (《聖》 *Prov*. 1. 14) ▪ He has *cast in his lot among* us. 彼は我々に加わって進退をともにした ▪ She has *cast in her lot with* me. 彼女は私と夫婦のちぎりを結んだ.

cast* [*draw*] *lots (事を決めたり, 物を得るため)くじを引く ▪ The competitors *cast lots* for the prize. 競争者たちはその賞を得るためくじを引いた ▪ The regiments *cast lots* which of them should go on shore first. どの連隊が一番に上陸するかでくじを引いた.

cross lots →across LOTs.

fall to the lot of …に当たる, の分け前となる, に割り当てられる ▪ Such good fortune *falls to the lot of* few men. そんな幸運の当たる人は少ない ▪ The revenues of a cathedral *fell to the lot of* a monastery. 主教座聖堂の収入が修道院の分け前となった.

have a lot on the ball 《口》有能である, 手腕がある ▪ He will do well in this work because he *has a lot on the ball*. 彼は有能だから, この仕事を立派にやるだろう.

have a lot to answer for 《口》(人・事が)…に大いに責任がある ▪ The man who was caught selling drugs *has a lot to answer for*. 麻薬販売の現行犯で捕まった男は大いに責めを負わねばならない ▪ The financial markets are reeling and the Republicans in general *have a lot to answer for*. 金融市場はぐらついている. 概して共和党員は責任がある.

in lots →by LOTs.

it falls to *a person's* ***lot to*** *do* 人が…する運命になる ▪ *It fell to my lot to* save the country. 私は国を救う運命になった.

one's ***lot is … cast*** …なくじを引いた ▪ *His lot is* happily *cast*. 彼は良いくじを引いた《幸運児だ》.

***lots and lots* (*of*)** 非常にたくさん(の)(数・量) ▪ We saw *lots and lots of* wild animals in Kenya. ケニアでは非常にたくさんの野生動物を見た.

pay* (*off*) *scot and lot →SCOT.

quite a lot **1** ほんとにたくさん(数・量) ▪ I bought *quite a lot* for my daughter. 娘にどっさり買い物をした.
2 大いに ▪ I like him *quite a lot*. 私は彼が非常に好きだ.

That's the lot. 《口》それで全部だ ▪ Are there any more books to pack?—No, *that's the lot*. 梱包する本はまだあるかい.—いや, それで全部だ.

***the lot falls on* [*to*]** くじが…に当たる ▪ We cast lots, and *the lot fell on* me. くじを引いたら私に当たった.

the lot falls to *a person* ***to*** *do* 人が…する運命になる, 人に…する白羽の矢が立つ ▪ *The lot fell to* him *to* save his benefactor. 彼は恩人を救う運命になった ▪ *The lot* will *fall to* her *to* negotiate on their behalf. みなを代表して交渉する役の白羽の矢が彼女に立つだろう.

The* [*One's*] *lot is cast. さいころはすでに振られた《決定的手段がとられた》 ▪ Calmly she said that *her lot was cast*. 「賽(さい)は投げられた」と彼女は落ち着いて言った.

the* (*whole*) *lot すべて; 何もかもすべて ▪ He has eaten *the whole lot*. 彼は全部食べてしまった ▪ That's *the lot*. それだけだ《それで全部だ》.

think a lot of →THINK[2].

loud /laʊd/ 形 ***be loud in*** *a person's* ***praise*** →PRAISE[1].

loud and clear はっきりと, 明瞭に ▪ He gave the message *loud and clear*. 彼はその伝言をはっきりと伝えた.

loud with …でけばけばしく飾って ▪ Mary was *loud with* cheap jewelry. メアリーは安物の宝石でけばけばしく飾っていた.

out loud →OUT[1].

lounge /laʊndʒ/ 名 《主に米》 ***a lounge lizard*** カモを求めて金持ちの女性に近づく男 ▪ He has a reputation of being *a lounge lizard*. 彼は金満女性漁りだという評判である. ☞高級ホテルのラウンジで会うことから.

louse /laʊs/ 名 ***not care* (*three skips of*) *a louse*** ちっともかまわない ▪ I do*n't care a louse* if I never see his face again. 彼の顔を二度と見なくても少しもかまいません ▪ I do*n't care three skips of a louse* for the money. その金はちっともかまいません.

not worth a louse 一文の値うちもない ▪ Such advice is*n't worth a louse*. そんな助言は一文の値うちもない.

lousy /láʊzi/ 形 ***be lousy with*** 《米俗》…がいっぱいある[いる], たんまりある ▪ The bed of the river *is lousy with* gold. 川床には金がいっぱいある ▪ The town *is lousy with* stray dogs. その町には野良犬がいっぱいいる.

love[1] /lʌv/ 名 ***a labor of love*** →LABOR[1].

a love affair 情事, 恋愛関係, 不倫 ▪ He entered into *a love affair* with his friend's wife. 彼は友人の妻と懇ろになった.

a love child 私生児, 隠し子, 庶子 ▪ The pop star has *a* secret 16-year-old *love child*. そのポップスターには16歳になる隠し子がいる.

a love nest 恋人同士が同棲する家, 愛の巣 ▪ Apparently, they had *a love nest* in Montmartre. どうも二人はモンマルトルに愛の巣を営んでいたようだ.

a love of a 愛らしい, 美しい, ほれぼれするような ▪ She is *a* little *love of a* child. 彼女は小さく愛らしい子だ.

a love rat 女性に対して極めて節制のない夫[ボーイフレンド] ▪ He has been branded *a love rat* by his estranged wife. 彼は別居中の妻から女癖の悪い夫という烙印を押された.

(*a*) *platonic love* 精神的恋愛, プラトニックラブ《性的な関係のない男女間の純粋な愛》 ▪ He says their relationship is just *a platonic love*. 彼によれば二人の関係はただの純愛にすぎないという.

be a love and *do* 《英口》〚主に命令文で〛(特に子供・家族に対して)お願いだから…して ▪ *Be a love and* carry this inside for me, would you? お願いだからこれを中に運んでくれない?

be out of love with …が非常にいやである, にあいそが尽きる ▪ I *am out of love with* life. 私は人生が全くいやになった.

fall in love **(*with*)** **1** (…に)恋する, (に)ほれる ▪ Richard has *fallen in love with* a girl half his age. リチャードは自分の半分の年齢の少女に恋した.
2 (…が)非常に好きになる ▪ They *fell in love with* his pleasantness. 彼らは彼のあいそのよさがすっかり気に入った.

fall out of love **(*with*)** (恋人などが)好きでなくなる, 熱がさめる ▪ Why has he *fallen out of love with* Mary? なぜ彼はメアリーを愛さなくなったのか.

for love 好きで; (勝負事など)かけをしないで, ただ楽しみで ▪ It is commonly a weak man who marries *for love*. 好きで結婚するのは普通弱い男である ▪ Let's play *for love*. かけないで勝負しよう.

for the love of God **[*Heaven,*** 《口》 ***Mike*]** お願いだから, 後生だから ▪ I begged them, *for the love of God*, to take care of the child. 私は彼らに, 後生だから, その子の面倒をみてくれと頼んだ ▪ *For the love of Mike*, do stop rattling those spoons. お願いだから, スプーンをカチャカチャいわせるのをやめてよ.

(*give*) (*my*) *love to* …によろしく ▪ *Give my love to* Kitty. キティーによろしく ▪ *My love to* all your family. おうちのみなさんによろしく.

have a love of …が好きである ▪ He *has a love of* learning. 彼は学問が好きである.

in love **(*with*)** **1** (…に)恋して, ほれて ▪ Jack and Jill were *in love*. ジャックとジルは相思相愛の仲だった ▪ I was *in love with* you. 私はあなたにほれていた.
2 (…が)大好きで ▪ I was *in love with* my bed. 私は自分のベッドがとても気に入っていた.

It's love that makes the world go round. 《諺》世の中を動かすのは愛だ.

(*just*) *for love/for the love of it* 無料で, 損得なしで, ただ働きで ▪ These folks are working *for the love of it*. この人たちは無報酬で働いている.

lots of love 〚女性の手紙文の結語として〛心から愛をこめて, さようなら ▪ *Lots of love*, Katie かしこ, ケイティーより.

love all 《スポーツ》双方ゼロ《得点なし》 ▪ The umpire called, "*Love all*—play," and the game started. アンパイアが「0対0, 試合開始」と言って, 試合が始まった.

Love and reason don't go together. 《諺》恋は思案のほか.

love at first sight 一目ぼれ ▪ Theirs was *love at first sight*. 彼らのは一目ぼれだった.

Love begets love. 《諺》愛は愛の父親となる《愛情をもって接すれば, 相手も愛情をもって応じるものだ》,「愛は愛を生む」.

love from …から愛をこめて《手紙の結語》 ▪ *Love from* Neil. ニールより愛をこめて.

love handles 《戯》腹の周りについた余分の脂肪 ▪ She'd like me to lose my *love handles*. 彼女は私の腹のぜい肉を落としてほしいと思っている.

love in a cottage 《雅》貧しい結婚(生活), 貧しい愛の巣 ▪ They are both poor, so marriage for them will mean *love in a cottage*. ともに貧乏だから, 二人の結婚は貧しい愛の巣となるだろう. ☞無冠詞.

Love is blind. 《諺》恋には目がない,「(ほれた目には)あばたもえくぼ」.

Love laughs at locksmiths. 《諺》想う念力は岩をも通す.

Love will find a way **[*out the way*].** 《諺》恋は道を見つける《愛し合っている者は, いっしょにいるためならどんな障害でも乗り越える》.

love's young dream 若い恋人(同士) (T. Moore, *Love's Young Dream*) ▪ She's wrapped in *love's young dream*. 彼女は若い恋人に夢中だ.

make love **(*to*)** **1** (女性と)性交[情交]する ▪ He *made love to* her and she had a baby. 彼はその女性と寝て, 彼女に子供ができた.
2 《古》(女性を)くどく, (女性に)言い寄る, 求愛する ▪ You are *making love to* her, aren't you? 君は彼女をくどいているのだね.

not for love or **[*nor*]** ***money*** 《口》義理ずくでも金ずくでも…ない, どうしても…ない ▪ He will *not* tell me *for love or money* what he intends to do. 彼は自分のしようと思っていることをどうしても私に言おうとしない ▪ We could*n't* get a ticket *for love nor money*. チケットがどうしても手に入らなかった.

off with the old love, on with the new 愛情を移して ▪ They are *off with the old love*, and *on with the new* half a dozen times a year. 彼らは1年に数回愛情を移す.

out of love 愛情から, 好んで ▪ He did it *out of love*. 彼は好きでそれをした.

play for love →for LOVE.

puppy love 《口》幼な恋 ▪ We were always together, but of course it was just *puppy love*. 私たちはいつもいっしょだったが, もちろんほんの幼な恋だった.

send *one's* [*a person's*] ***love*** **(*to*)** (…に)よろしくと言ってやる ▪ *Send* her *my love*. 彼女によろしくと伝えてください ▪ Kitty *sends her love to* you. キティーがあなたによろしくと言っています.

show love towards …に好意を持つ; を喜んで援励する気がある ▪ He *shows love towards* his neighbors. 彼は隣人たちに好意を持っている.

the love of *one's* ***life*** 《戯》生涯を通じて最愛の人 ▪ She watched *the love of her life* walk away from her. 彼女は最愛の人が自分のもとから歩み去るのをじっと見つめた.

(*The love of*) *money is the root of all evil.* 《諺》金銭(を愛すること)は諸悪の根源 (《聖》*1 Tim.* 6. 10).

(there is) no love lost between …は互いに憎み合っている ▪ *There is* really *no love lost between* my father and our next door neighbor. 父と隣の人は互いにひどく憎み合っている. ☞もとは「互いの愛情は変わらない」の意.

love[2] /lʌv/ 動 ***a loved one*** 愛する人《恋人・家族》 ▪ Here's to us and our *loved ones*. 我々と愛する家族のために乾杯.

(get [be]) loved up 《口》(麻薬・音楽に)酔って, 麻薬で仲良くなって ▪ The use of Ecstasy made us so *loved up*. 幻覚剤の「エクスタシー」をやってみなとてもいい気分で仲良くなった.

(Lord) love you [your heart]! まあ, おや, ほんとに!《人がまちがったことを言ったときなどの感嘆》 ▪ Oh, *lord love you!* Why should I do that? おやまあ(かわいい事を言う)! どうして私がそんなことをしなければならないのよ ▪ *Lord love you*, I'm not surprised at any one wanting to marry you. なるほど, 人があなたと結婚したがるのも不思議はないな.

Love me little, love me long. 細く長く愛してください ▪ *Love me little, love me long*, you see? No extreme will last long. 細く愛して, 長く愛してと言うだろ. 極端は長続きしないということさ.

Love me, love my dog. →DOG[1].

love not wisely but too well 賢明にではないが十二分に愛する (cf. Sh., *Oth.* 5. 2. 344) ▪ It is easy to *love not wisely but too well*. 賢明にではないが十二分に愛することは易しい.

love them and leave them 女性を誘惑しては捨てる ▪ His idea was *love 'em and leave 'em*. 彼の考えは女性を誘惑しては捨てるというのであった.

love you and leave you 残念ながら別れる《別れのきまり文句》 ▪ I have to *love you and leave you*. I'm supposed to be on duty. 残念ながら今日はこれで. 勤務中ということになっているのでね.

should [would] love to *do* 《口》…したいものだ ▪ I *should love to* come to dinner. ごちそうにあずかりたいものです ▪ Would you go to the movies with me?—I'*d love to*. 僕と映画を見に行きませんか—まあうれしい(喜んで行くわ)! ☞女性の好む表現法.

the *person one* ***(most) loves to hate*** (最も)好んできらう人 ▪ He is *the* politician the public *most loves to hate*. 彼は世間が最も好んできらう政治家だ.

lovely /lʌ́vli/ 形 ***lovely and*** 《英口》ほんとに, とても (= NICE and) ▪ It is *lovely and* warm today. きょうはほんとに暖かい日です.

lover /lʌ́vər/ 名 ***a lover's lane*** 恋人たちが二人きりになれる道 ▪ The holdup men went for a parked car in *a* lonely *lover's lane*. 車強盗が恋人通りに停めてあった車を襲った.

low /loʊ/ 形副名 ***as low as*** …という最近に ▪ We find it *as low as* the 20th century. 我々はそれをつい最近の20世紀に見いだす.

at low water [tide] →in LOW water.

at (the) lowest 少なくとも, 最も低くとも ▪ It will cost a hundred pounds *at the lowest*. それは安くとも100ポンドはするだろう.

be low in (one's) pocket ふところが乏しい, 金がほとんどない ▪ You talk of *being low in your pocket*. 君はふところが乏しいなどと言う.

bring low **1** (健康・力を)衰えさす, (地位・境遇を)下げる, (富・財産を)へらす ▪ Remorse *brought* her *low*. 悔恨のあまり彼女は健康を損ねた ▪ The nobles of Savoy *were brought low*. サボイの貴族は落ちぶれた.

2 (高慢を)くじく, へこます ▪ He *was brought low*. 彼はへこまされた.

3 倒す ▪ At one blow I *brought* him *low*. 私は彼を一撃のもとに倒した.

carry low (馬などが)頭を垂れている.

collar low 《サッカー》腰のところまたはそれより下を捕える.

fall low 落ちぶれる, 堕落する ▪ I hope I shall never *fall* as *low* as that. そこまで落ちぶれたくないものだ.

feel low 気分がすぐれない, 気がめいっている ▪ I have been *feeling low* all day today. きょうは一日中気分がすぐれなかった.

get (down) low 低い声を出す ▪ I cannot *get* so *low*. 私はそんなに低い声は出せない.

hit a [its] new low 《米株式》新最低値になる ▪ Many issues *hit* (*their*) *new lows*. 多くの証券が新最低値になった.

in [at] low water [tide] **1** 金が欠乏して, 金に困って ▪ She is *in low water* now. 彼女は今金に困っている.

2 貧乏に ▪ He was born *in low water*. 彼は貧乏に生まれた. ☞「干潮で」が原義.

lay low **1** 倒す; 殺す ▪ The tree *was laid low* at a single blow. 木は一撃で切り倒された ▪ The shaft *laid* my benefactor *low*. その矢が私の恩人を殺した.

2 埋葬する ▪ I wish I *were* now *laid low* in my grave. 私は今墓に埋められていたらよいのに.

3 (病気・傷などで)臥床させる ▪ He *is laid low* with illness. 彼は病気でふせっている.

4 (高慢を)くじく, へこます ▪ I will *lay low* their haughtiness. 私は彼らの高慢をくじいてやる ▪ God will *lay* our haters *low*. 神は我々を憎む者どもをへこますであろう.

5 うずくまる; 《俗》じっと待ちかまえる ▪ He *laid low* for the first passer-by. 彼は最初の通行人をじっと待ちかまえた.

lie low **1** うずくまる, 地に伏す ▪ She *lay low* beside a bubbling fountain. 彼女はわき出る泉のそばにうずくまっていた.

2 (人が)倒れている; 死んでいる, 埋められている; (建物が)くずれている, 崩壊している ▪ Priam *lay low* by the sword. プライアムは剣にかかって倒れた ▪ Our house *lies low*. 我々の家は崩壊している.

3 (高慢な人が)へこまされている, くじかれている ▪ He now *lies low* after losing his whole estate. 彼は地所をすっかり失ってへこんでいる.

4《口》身や意図を隠す; 黙っている; (注目されないよう, 何もせず)じっとしている; 雌伏している ▪ You'd better *lie low* for a few weeks. あなたは数週間身を隠していたほうがよい ▪ Royalists who had *lain low* were showing signs of life. 雌伏していた王党派が動き出す徴候を見せていた.

live low 粗食で暮らす ▪ You had better *live low* for a time. しばらく粗食したほうがよい.

low life 社会の下層の人たち[犯罪者]の生態[生きざま] ▪ He wrote a novel about *low life* in New York during the 1930s. 彼は1930年代ニューヨークの下層社会での実態を小説に書いた.

play it low (down) on (人)に卑劣なことをする; にひどい仕打ちをする ▪ He *played it low on* me. 彼は私をひどい目にあわせた.

play low 少額の金でばくちをやる (↔play HIGH 1) ▪ I would rather *play low*. 安く張りたい.

put it in low (自動車の)第1ギアを入れる ▪ *Put it in low* when you come up a steep hill. 急な坂を上るときにはギアをローに入れなさい.

run low (on) (…が)乏しくなる, 尽きそうになる ▪ The funds are *running low*. 手持金が乏しくなっている ▪ We're *running low on* fuel. 燃料が乏しくなっている.

sing low (負けて)大口をたたかなくなる ▪ This defeat will make him *sing low*. この敗北で彼も大口をたたかなくなるだろう.

talk low 低い声で話す ▪ She *talked low* to avoid curious ears. 立ち聞きされないように, 彼女は低い声で話した.

the lower orders 《戯》下層階級 ▪ A high entrance fee keeps out *the lower orders*. 高い入場料のため下層階級は締め出されている.

the lowest common denominator 普通の人々, 大衆 ▪ Too many TV programs aim at *the lowest common denominator*. 一般大衆受けを狙ったテレビ番組が多すぎる.

the lowest of the low 最低のやつ; 最も不道徳[社会的に低俗]な人々; 倫理基準のない人[団体] ▪ He regards anyone who deceives poor people as *the lowest of the low*. 彼は貧しい人をだます者は最も道義に悖(もと)ると考える ▪ Killers, drug addicts, wife-beaters, they are *the lowest of the low*. 人殺し, ヤク中, 妻をなぐる人, 彼らは最低のやつらだ.

lowdown /lóʊdàʊn, lòʊdáʊn/ 名形 ***get the lowdown on*** 《米口》…の真相[内情]を知る ▪ The police are trying to *get the lowdown on* it. 警察はそれの真相を知ろうとしている.

give the lowdown on 《米俗》…についての内情を知らせる ▪ The book *gives the lowdown on* American life. その本はアメリカの生活の内情を知らせている.

play a lowdown trick on 《口》卑劣なことをして…をだます ▪ I never thought he'd *play* such *a lowdown trick on* her. 彼があんな卑劣なことをして彼女をだまそうとは思わなかった.

play it lowdown on [upon] …に卑劣な仕打ちをする ▪ He *played it lowdown on* his benefactor. 彼は恩人に卑劣な仕打ちをした.

lower /lóʊər/ 動 ***lower oneself*** **1** 降りる ▪ He *lowered himself* down the cliff by a rope. 彼はロープを伝って崖を降りた.

2 品位を落とす ▪ He *lowered himself* by taking bribes. 彼は収賄で品位を落とした.

3 我を折る, 身を屈する ▪ He *lowered himself* to ask her pardon. 彼は身を屈して彼女の許しを請うた.

lower the tone (of) …の風格[気風]を下げる ▪ A fast-food restaurant would *lower the tone of* this street. ファストフードのレストランが開店するとこの通りの風格が下がるだろう.

lowman /lóʊmən/ 名 ***lowman on the totem pole*** 《米俗》最下位の階級の者, 権力のない人, 小者 ▪ I don't think I can be of any help. I'm *lowman on the totem pole*. 私はお役に立てないと思います. 下っ端ですから. ☞米国の喜劇俳優 Fred Allen の造語(1940年ごろ)とされる.

L.[£.]s.d. /èlesdíː/ 名 ***a matter of L.s.d.*** 金の問題《金さえあればかたうくこと》 ▪ It is *a matter of £.s.d.* それは金でかたうく問題だ. ☞ L libra, solid, denarii の略. それぞれ pound (ポンド), shilling (シリング), pence (ペンス)を表し, 1971年まで英国の通貨単位だった.

lubricate /lúːbrəkèɪt/ 動 ***lubricate** a person's **tongue*** 人の舌に油をさす《飲ませたり, 金をやったりしてしゃべらせる》 ▪ The liquor had well *lubricated his tongue*. リキュールがよく利いて彼はべらべらしゃべった.

luck[1] /lʌk/ 名 ***a breeze of luck*** 《米口》好運続き ▪ We struck *a breeze of luck*. 我々は好運続きであった.

and one (more) for luck それにもうひとつ, もうひとつおまけに ▪ Take another sip, *and one more for luck*. ひと口飲みなさい. そしておまけにもうひと口.

Any luck (with)? 《口》(…は)うまくいったか ▪ *Any luck with* job-hunting?—No, not at all. 職探しはうまくいったか?—いや, 全然.

as luck would have it 運よく; 運悪く《luck の前に good または bad [ill] を伴うこともある》 ▪ *As luck would have it*, a friend of mine gave me a lift. 運よく友だちが私を車に乗せてくれた ▪ *As (ill) luck would have it*, there was none in the room. あいにく部屋には誰もいなかった.

bad luck →tough LUCK.

Bad luck to ...! …のちくしょうめ!《野卑な呪いで, 嫌悪・悪意・失望を表す》 ▪ He has done it, *bad luck to* him! あいつがやりやがったんだ, ちくしょうめ!

Best [The best] of luck! = good LUCK to you.

better luck another [next] time 次はもっと運が良いように《落胆している人を励ます表現》 ▪ Oh, don't worry; *better luck next time*. ああ, 心配いらないよ. 次はうまくいくといいね.

by (good) luck 幸運にも ▪ *By good luck* I jumped into the train at the last moment. 運よく

ぎりぎりで列車に飛び乗った ▪ *By good luck* I drew a capital prize last week. 幸運にも先週私はすばらしい賞を引き当てた.

chance** one's **luck =try one's LUCK (at).

crowd** one's **luck =push one's LUCK.

Don't push your luck! 悪のりするな, 調子に乗るな, 無茶をすると元も子もなくなるぞ ▪ You've been okay so far, but *don't push your luck.* これまでのところはよくやっている, だが図に乗ってはいけない.

down on** one's **luck 《口》(一時的に)運が悪く, 金に窮して ▪ The gentleman was *down on his luck.* その紳士は金がなくて困っていた.

for luck **1** 縁起を担いで, 縁起に ▪ I'll take just a cup *for luck.* 縁起に1杯だけいただきます. **2** とくに(これという)理由もなく ▪ He scratched his head *for luck.* 彼は何とはなしに頭をかいた.

Give a man luck and throw him into the sea. 《諺》運のよいものは海へ投げ込まれても助かる.

***good luck to you** [**him,** etc.]* 幸運を祈ります; ごきげんよう ▪ Best wishes and *good luck to you.* —*Good luck to you* too! ご多幸を祈ります, ごきげんよう—さようなら, あなたもね.

***good luck** (**with**)* 《口》(…が)うまくいきますように ▪ *Good luck with* your exams. 試験がうまくいくといいね.

hard luck →tough LUCK.

have** (**got**) **the devil's own luck 《口》すこぶる幸運である ▪ He seems to *have the devil's own luck*—he has won a big stake in the public lottery. 彼はすごく幸運に恵まれているようだ. 宝くじで大金が当たったのだ.

have hard luck →HARD.

have luck うまくいく, 上首尾である ▪ I *had luck* when I went fishing yesterday. きのう魚釣りに行って大漁だった.

***have the luck of the devil** [**the Irish**]* 非常な幸運に恵まれている, めちゃくちゃについている ▪ That man won $5,000 on the lottery. He *has the luck of the devil!* あの人は宝くじで5,000ドル当たった. よっぽどついているんだ!

***have the luck to** do* 幸いにも…する ▪ I *had the luck to* find him at home. 幸いにも彼は在宅だった.

in luck 運が良く, 運が向いて ▪ She was *in luck* when she called me tonight. 今夜私に電話してきたとき彼女はついていた.

in luck's way 運が向いて, 運が良く; ついていて《意外な幸運にあった人など》 ▪ You are *in luck's way.* 君はついているぞ.

it is good** [**bad**] **luck 吉兆[凶兆]である, 縁起が良い[悪い] ▪ You should never put boots on the table; *it's bad luck.* 靴をテーブルの上に決して置いてはなりません, 縁起が悪いから.

(It is) just (like) my (usual) luck! 相変わらず運の悪いことだ!, またか, いまいましい! ▪ *Just my luck!* I suppose I'll have to go by train. またか, いまいましい, 列車で行かなきゃならんかな ▪ *It is just my luck* to have come all the way only to find him out. はるばるやって来たのに彼が留守とは, 相変わらず運の悪いことだなあ.

(just [all]) the luck of the game (単に)ゲームの運 ▪ It was *just the luck of the game* that he beat me. 彼に負けたのは, ついていなかっただけのことだ. ☞負け惜しみ, または自分の成功を卑下するときに用いられる.

Luck has turned in** a person's **favor. 人に運が向いて来た ▪ *Luck has turned in my favor* at last. とうとう私に運が向いてきた.

*One's **luck holds.*** 幸運が続く ▪ Let's hope *your luck holds* forever. ご幸運がいつまでも続きますように.

*One's **luck is in** [**out**].* 運が良い[悪い] ▪ I really do believe *my luck is in.* 私はついていると, つくづく思う.

***Luck is in** a person's **favor** [**on** a person's **side**].* 人に運が向いてきた ▪ *Luck is in his favor* now. こんどは彼に運が向いてきた.

more by good luck than (by) good management [judg(e)ment] かけ引き[判断]というよりも運が良くて ▪ He succeeded *more by good luck than good judgment.* 彼が成功したのは, 判断が良かったというより運が良かったからだ.

no such (good) luck 《口》(残念ながら)そうはうまくはいかない[かった], そうは問屋が卸さない ▪ She'll marry you.—*No such luck,* John. 彼女, 君と結婚するよ—そうは問屋が卸さないよ, ジョン ▪ We thought a trainer could help our dog, but *no such luck.* 訓練師がうちの犬を手助けしてくれるだろうと思っていたのに, そううまくはいかなかった.

out of luck/off luck 運が悪く, うまくいかないで ▪ He is quite *out of luck.* 彼は全く運が悪い ▪ He tried to cut it, but he was *off luck.* 彼はそれを切ろうとしたが, だめだった.

push** [**press**] one's **luck 幸運の波に続けて乗る ▪ Let's *push our luck,* now that things are coming our way. せっかくことがうまく運んでいるのだから, もっと幸運の波に乗ってみよう.

ride** one's **luck 好調の波に乗る, 望ましい成り行きに任す ▪ Mind you, you can't *ride your luck* forever! いいか, いつまでも好調の波には乗れないのだからな!

rotten luck 不運, ツキのなさ ▪ I've had nothing but *rotten luck* all day. きょうは一日中何もかもうまくいかなかった.

run for** (one's) **luck →RUN^2.

the devil's (own) luck/ the luck of the devil [the Irish] **1** すばらしい幸運 ▪ He has *the devil's own luck* in everything. 彼はすべてのことに非常に運がよい ▪ But this year *the luck of the Irish* deserted Mr. Rooney. しかし, 今年はすばらしい幸運はルーニー氏(サッカー選手)を見離した. **2** ひどい悪運 ▪ Absolutely *the devil's own luck.* Every horse I backed lost. 全くひどい悪運だ. かけた馬がみな負けた.

the luck of the draw くじ運 ▪ Is it *the luck of the draw* that some people are rich and others are not? 金持ちもいればそうでない人もいるのはくじ運だろうか.

There is luck in leisure. 《諺》果報は寝て待て.

tough* [*bad*] *luck 《英口》運悪く, (人の問題を気にかけずに)あいにくで, それは気の毒で (→a TOUGH break) ▪ So you failed again, eh? *Tough luck.* また不合格かい? それは残念だったね ▪ *Tough luck,* but that's the way the cookie crumbles. ついてないね, でも世の中ってそんなものさ ▪ She murnured "*tough luck,*" and gave a beggar a few coins. 彼女は小声で「気の毒に」と言って, 物乞いにコインを2, 3枚与えた.

try *one's* ***luck* (*at*)** (…を)のるかそるかやってみる; (で)運試しをする ▪ He *tried his luck at* the gambling tables. 彼はとばく台で運試しをやった.

wish *a person* ***good luck*** 人の幸福を祈る; 人にごきげんようと言う ▪ I went to the quay to *wish* them *good luck.* 私は彼らに幸運を祈って見送るため波止場へ行った.

with* [*knowing*]** *a person's* ***luck …の運の悪さから考えると ▪ *With her luck,* she may fall down the stairs on her way out. 彼女のつきのなさからすると, 出がけに階段から転げ落ちるかもしれない ▪ *Knowing his luck,* he'll probably get injured doing that. 彼はいつも運が悪いので多分それをしていて怪我をするだろう.

L

worse luck 《口》〖主に挿入句で〗なおさら困ったことには, 運悪く; よけい残念だ ▪ And then, *worse luck,* the teacher came into the classroom. それから, なおさら運の悪いことには, 先生が教室に入って来た ▪ I, *worse luck,* was not one of the recipients. 私は, 残念なことには, 受賞者の中に含まれていなかった.

you never know your luck ひょっとすると運がいいかもしれないよ ▪ We can't answer every problem we're asked, but *you never know your luck.* 尋ねられた疑問のすべてには答えられまいが, あるいは運よくいくかもしれない.

luck[2] /lʌk/ 動 ***luck it through*** 運に任せてやる ▪ We've just *lucked it through* to this point. ここまでただ運任せでやってきただけだ.

lucky /lʌ́ki/ 形名 ***a lucky break*** 《口》幸運 ▪ In fact it turned out to be *an* awfully *lucky break.* 実際それはすごい幸運であることがわかった.

***a lucky hit* [*shot, guess*]** まぐれ当たり ▪ I made *a lucky hit.* まぐれ当たりをやった.

cut* [*make*]** *one's* ***lucky 《俗》逃げる, 逃亡する ▪ You had better *cut your lucky.* 君は逃げたほうがよい. ☞lucky = chance.

Lucky at cards, unlucky in love. 《諺》トランプでつきがあれば, 恋愛ではつきがない.

***lucky you* [*him,* etc.]** 君[彼, など]がうらやましいな ▪ Congratulations on being pregnant! *Lucky you.* おめでたなんですって, よかったわね. うらやましいわ.

strike* (*it*) *lucky →STRIKE it rich.

take a dip in the lucky bag 良いものを得るチャンスをつかむ ▪ When Tom married Mary, he *took a dip in the lucky bag.* トムはメアリーと結婚してすばらしい幸運をつかんだ.

You* [*He,* etc.] *should be so lucky! そりゃついていますね ▪ *You should be so lucky* to encounter such a rare animal! こんな希少動物に遭遇するとは, 君は全くついているね.

lucre /lú:kər/ 名 ***filthy lucre*** 不正利得 (《聖》*Titus* 1. 7); 《戯》金銭 ▪ George would do anything for *filthy lucre.* ジョージは金のためなら何でもする ▪ He reeks with *filthy lucre.* 彼は金がたんまりある.

luff /lʌf/ 名 ***hold*** *one's* ***luff*** (船が)風下にならないようにして走る; 目的を変えない ▪ You must *hold your luff.* 目的を変えてはなりません.

lug /lʌg/ 名 ***drop the lug on*** 《米俗》…に金をねだる ▪ I'd like to *drop the lug on* you for $30. 君に30ドル無心したい.

in lug 《俗》質に入って ▪ My fiddle is *in lug* now. 私のバイオリンは今質に入っている.

put* [*pile*] *on lugs 《米俗》気取る ▪ Dr. Hall *puts on* no *lugs.* ホール博士は少しも気取らない.

put the lug on 《米俗》…から金を強制的に取立てる; に党費割付をする ▪ They *put the lug on* state employees. 彼らは国家公務員から金を強制的に取立てた.

lull /lʌl/ 動 ***lull … to sleep*** →SLEEP[1].

lumber[1] /lʌ́mbər/ 名 ***get*** *a person* ***into* (*dead*) *lumber*** 《口》人を窮境に立たせる ▪ You've *got* him *into lumber* with his boss. 君のために彼は社長ににらまれる羽目になった.

in* (*dead*) *lumber 《口》(人の不興を買うような)窮境に置かれて ▪ He is really *in dead lumber* because he was found shoplifting. 彼は万引きの現場を押さえられたので全く苦しい立場に置かれている.

lumber[2] /lʌ́mbər/ 動 ***be lumbered with*** 《口》(不要な物)を押しつけられる ▪ He *was lumbered with* his wife's mother. 彼は妻の母親を押しつけられた.

lump[1] /lʌmp/ 名 ***A lump comes* [*rises*] *into*** *a person's* ***throat.*** 人が感動して胸が詰まる ▪ *A lump* always *comes into my throat* when I think of it. それを思い出すと私はいつも感動して胸が詰まる ▪ *A lump rose into his throat* and he collapsed on the snow. 彼は感動がこみ上げてきて, 雪に崩れ落ちた.

a lump in *one's* **[*the*] *throat*** **1** のどのはれあがり ▪ She felt *a lump in her throat,* which obstructed her swallowing. 彼女はのどがはれあがっていて, ものが飲み込めなかった.

2 感動して胸が詰まること, 感情がこみあげること ▪ She felt *a lump in her throat* at his speech. 彼女は彼の演説を聞いて, 感動して胸が詰まるようだった.

a lump of …のかたまり ▪ He is *a lump of* selfishness. 彼は利己心のかたまりである.

a lump of clay 粘土のかたまり; 人間の肉体, 土くれ ▪ Being freed from these *lumps of clay,* we shall be made like the glorious angels. これらの肉体から抜け出て, 我々は輝かしい天使のようになるであろう.

☞聖書語法.

a lump sum 総額, 一括払いの金 ▪ Would you like *a lump-sum* payment or a pension scheme? 退職一時金払いがいいですか, それとも年金払いにしましょうか.

all of a lump **1** ひっくるめて, ひとかたまりになって; どさりと ▪ Answer them by the lump, for they are *all of a lump*. それらを一括してお答えください, それらはひとまとめになっていますから ▪ They fell down *all of a lump* when it blew a gale. 大風が吹いたとき, それらはどさりと倒れた.
2 一面にはれあがって ▪ Her head is *all of a lump*. 彼女の頭部は一面にはれあがっていた.

bring a lump to *one's* ***throat*** 感動して胸を詰まらせる ▪ A glimpse of her was enough to *bring a lump to his throat*. 彼女の姿をちらと見ただけで彼は胸がいっぱいになった.

by the lump =in the LUMP.

get [***take***] *one's* [***the***] ***lumps*** 《主に米口》ひどくののしられる, ひどい攻撃[罰]を受ける, 甘んじて当然の報いを受ける ▪ I *got my lumps* for disobeying my parents. 両親の言うことをきかなかったので, ひどくしかられた ▪ Quit crying and *take your lumps* like a man. 泣くのはよして潔く罰を受けよ.

in a lump 全体をいっしょに, まとめて ▪ I received two months' pay *in a lump*. 私は2か月分の給料をまとめてもらった ▪ The chair and table went over *in a lump*. いすとテーブルは一度にひっくり返った.

in the lump ひっくるめて, 総括して, 全体的に ▪ The goods were valued *in the lump*. その品はひっくるめて評価された ▪ I am heartily sorry for them, severally and *in the lump*. 私は彼らの一人一人に対してもまた全体的にも心からお気の毒に思います.

leaven the (***whole***) ***lump*** 粉のかたまり(全体)をふくらませる (《聖》*1 Cor.* 5. 6) ▪ A few bright minds can *leaven the whole lump*. ひと握りの頭のよい者がクラス全体を活気づけることがある.

take *one's* ***lumps*** =get one's LUMPs.

lump[2] /lʌmp/ 動 ***If you don't like it, you can*** [***may***] ***lump it.*** 《諺》あなたはそれがいやでもがまんしなければならない.

like it or lump it →LIKE[2].

lump it 《口》いやいやながらがまんする ▪ If he does not like what I say, he can *lump it*. 私の言うことがいやでも, 彼はがまんせねばならない.

lump large 大きく見える; 堂々としている ▪ He *lumped large* in the public imagination. 大衆の目には彼は堂々として映った.

lunar /lúːnər/ 名 ***take a lunar*** (上方を)鋭く見る ▪ I *took a lunar* at some flying grouse. 私は飛んで行くウズラを険しい目つきで見上げた. ☞lunar=lunar observation.

lunatic /lúːnətɪk/ 形 ***the lunatic fringe*** 少数狂信派 ▪ *The lunatic fringe* of the ALF smashed the windows of a butcher's shop. 動物解放戦線の過激派が肉屋の窓ガラスをたたき割った.

lunch /lʌntʃ/ 名 ***a free lunch*** 無料で得られる価値あるもの ▪ The guy will do anything to get *a free lunch*. あいつはただで貴重なものが手に入るならどんなことだってする.

do lunch 《主に米口》昼食のときに会う, いっしょに昼食をとる ▪ Let's all get together and *do lunch* sometime this week. 今週のいつかみなで集まっていっしょに昼飯を食べないか.

out to lunch **1**《米俗》気が狂って; ばかで ▪ I think he's *out to lunch*. 彼は発狂していると思う.
2《口》うわの空で, 放心して ▪ Sorry, I haven't heard a word you said. I was *out to lunch*. ごめん, 君の話, 全く耳に入っていなかったんだ. つい, ボーっとして.

there's no (***such thing as a***) ***free lunch*** ただより高いものはない, ただ飯はない ▪ The moral of the fable is *there is no such thing as a free lunch*. その寓話の教訓は「ただ飯はない」である.

lung /lʌŋ/ 名 ***at the top of*** *one's* ***lungs*** 声を張り上げて, 声を限りに ▪ The lad shouted *at the top of his lungs*. 若者は声を限りに叫んだ.

have good lungs 声が大きい ▪ He is small, but he *has good lungs*. 彼は体は小さいが, 声は大きい.

try *one's* ***lungs*** 声をいっぱいに張り上げる, 声を限りに叫ぶ ▪ I heard old Kit *try his lungs* in the open air. キット老人が戸外で声を限りに叫ぶのを私は聞いた.

lurch[1] /ləːrtʃ/ 名 ***give a lurch*** 急に一方に傾く ▪ Here the ship *gave a lurch*, and he grew seasick. ここで船が急に一方に傾いて, 彼は船酔いになった. ☞海語から.

leave *a person* ***in the lurch*** 《口》人を逆境に見捨てる; 人を窮地に置き去りにする ▪ I will not *leave* you *in the lurch*. 私はあなたを窮地に置き去りにはしません. ☞lurch《トランプ》「敗者と勝者の得点が非常に開いている状態」.

lie at [***on, upon***] ***lurch*** 潜伏している; 待ち伏せする ▪ The enemy of human happiness is always *lying at lurch*. 人間の幸福の敵はいつも待ち伏せしている.

lurch[2] /ləːrtʃ/ 動 *one's* ***heart*** [***stomach***] ***lurches*** (突然の驚き・恐怖で)心臓が飛びあがる[胃袋が飛び出す]ほどの思いをする ▪ *My heart lurched*. Was it friend or foe? 心臓が飛びあがるほどギョッとした. あれは敵か味方か ▪ *His stomach lurched* from the fear of being lost in the blinding snowstorm. 彼はその猛吹雪の中で道に迷うのではと恐れて胃袋が飛び出しそうだった.

lure /lʊər|ljʊə/ 名 ***bring*** [***call***]***... to the lure*** ...をおとりで呼び戻す, 引き寄せる ▪ He *brought* the guy *to the lure*. 彼はそいつを好餌でおびき寄せた.

come [***stoop***] ***to*** (***the,*** *a person's*) ***lure*** 呼び寄せのおとりに引かれて降りてくる ▪ Time *stoops to no man's lure*. 時は誰が呼び戻そうとしても戻らない.

lurid /lʊ́rəd|ljʊ́ərɪd/ 形 ***cast*** [***throw***] ***a lurid light on*** (事実・性格)をすごく見せる, にすごみを与える ▪ This fact *casts a lurid light on* the annals of the persecution. この事実は迫害の歴史にすごみを与

える.

lurk /ləːrk/ 名 ***on the lurk*** こそこそ偵察して ▪ A fox was sneaking *on the lurk*. キツネがこそこそかぎ回っていた.

luster, 《英》 **lustre** /lʌ́stər/ 名 ***add luster to*** …に光輝[光彩]を添える ▪ Her articles *added luster to* Life magazine. 彼女の記事がライフ誌に錦上花を添えた.

shed [***throw***] ***luster on*** …に光輝を与える ▪ Her presence *shed luster on* the assembly. 彼女の臨席がその集会に彩りを添えた.

lute /luːt/ 名 ***a*** (***little***) ***rift within*** [***in***] ***the lute*** →a RIFT in the lute.

luxury /lʌ́gʒəri|lʌ́kʃəri/ 名 ***in luxury*** 贅沢に ▪ He has been living *in luxury* since the end of the war. 彼は戦後ずっと贅沢に暮らしてきた.

lyrical /lírɪkəl/ 形 ***wax lyrical about*** [***over***] …のことを熱心に話す ▪ Frank Sinatra *waxed lyrical about* Chicago. フランク・シナトラはシカゴのことを熱心に語った.

M

mace /meɪs/ 名 ***on mace*** 《俗》掛けで, 信用で ▪ Let them have it *on mace*. それを彼らに掛けで売ってやれ.

mad /mæd/ 形名 **(*as*) *mad as a hatter*** すっかり気が狂って ▪ He's a very good fellow but *as mad as a hatter*. 彼はなかなかよいやつだが, すっかり気が狂っている. ☞帽子屋はよく狂人になると昔信じられていたことから, または as mad as an adder (マムシ)のなまりから.

(*as*) *mad as a March hare* (3月の交尾期のウサギのように)狂気じみた ▪ They were chafing him until he was *as mad as a March hare*. みんなでいら立たせたので, とうとう彼は逆上してしまった.

(*as*) *mad as hops* [*a wet hen, a hornet*] 《米口》非常に怒って ▪ Everybody that was not invited was *mad as a wet hen*. 招かれなかった連中はみなかんかんになった ▪ He was *as mad as a hornet* when he heard what you said about him. 彼は自分についての君の話を聞いて激怒した.

(*as*) *mad as mud* 《口》すっかり怒って ▪ Joan will be *as mad as mud* with me for telling. ジョーンは私が口を割ったと言ってかんかんになるだろう.

be mad about 《口》 **1** …に熱中している ▪ He *is mad about* the stage. 彼は演劇に夢中だ.
2 …のことでひどく怒っている ▪ He's just *mad about* something this morning. 今朝は何が気にくわないのか, 彼はひどくおかんむりだ.

be mad after =be MAD about 1.

be mad at 《口》…にひどく怒っている ▪ The chief *was mad at* me because I bungled the telephone call. 電話口でへまをやり, 所長にひどく叱られた.

***be mad enough to bite nails* [*a tenpenny nail in two*]** 《米口》ひどく怒っている ▪ The Colonel *was mad enough to bite nails*. 大佐はかんかんだった.

be mad for 《口》…がほしくてたまらない ▪ The dog *was mad for* water. 犬はむしょうに水をほしがった.

***be mad keen* (*on*)** 《口》(…に)熱中している ▪ Our kids *are mad keen on* computer games. うちの子たちはコンピューターゲームに熱中している.

be mad on **1** 《米俗》=be MAD at.
2 《米俗》…を憎む, きらう ▪ He's quite *mad on* me. 彼はすっかり僕をきらっている.
3 =be MAD about 1.

be mad with =be MAD at.

don't get mad, get even 《口》怒る代わりにやり返せ, 腹を立てたりせずに仕返しをせよ ▪ This is just a case of "*don't get mad, get even*". これこそまさに怒らないでやり返すべき状況だ. ☞John F. Kennedy の父 Joseph P. Kennedy の言葉から.

drive *a person* ***mad*** 《口》人を発狂させる; ひどく怒らせる ▪ Her daughter's conduct *drove* the mother *mad*. 娘のふるまいで母親はひどく怒った.

get *one's* ***mad up*** 《米口》かんしゃくを起こす ▪ The boss has *got his mad up*. 社長はかんしゃくを起こしている.

get over *one's* ***mad*** 《米口》かんしゃくを抑える ▪ I've got to *get over my mad*. 私はかんしゃくの虫を抑えなくてはいけない.

go* [*run*] *mad 発狂する ▪ Well! I shall *run mad*. いやはや, 気が変になりそうだ.

go* [*run*] *mad after 《口》…にのぼせ上がる, に熱中する ▪ The whole civilized world is *running mad after* jazz. 文明世界はこぞってジャズにのぼせ上がっている.

have a mad on 《米口》…に怒っている ▪ He *has*n't *got a mad on* anything in this world. 彼は何にも腹を立ててはいないよ.

hopping mad 《口》ひどく怒って ▪ Dad is *hopping mad* this morning. おやじは今朝かんかんだ.

like a mad thing 狂ったように ▪ He cried *like a mad thing*. 彼は激しく泣いた.

like mad 《口》猛烈に, あわてふためいて ▪ We heard them cheering *like mad*. 彼らがさかんに喝采しているのが聞こえた ▪ Though he ran *like mad*, he couldn't catch his train. 彼は死にもの狂いに走ったが, 電車に間に合わなかった.

mean mad 《米俗》怒っている ▪ He doesn't really *mean mad*. 彼は本当は怒っていない.

run mad →go MAD.

send *a person* ***mad*** =drive a person MAD.

stark raving* [*staring*] *mad 《口》完全に発狂して ▪ He must be *stark raving mad*, if he said so. そんなことを言ったのなら, 彼は完全におかしくなっているにちがいない.

madding /mǽdɪŋ/ 形 ***far from the madding crowd*** 遠く俗世間を離れて (Gray, *Elegy* 19) ▪ He is a poet who lives *far from the madding crowd*. 彼は俗世間をはるか離れて生きている詩人である.

madness /mǽdnəs/ 名 ***There's* (*a*) *method in*** *a person's* ***madness.*** →METHOD.

maggot /mǽgət/ 名 ***have a maggot* [*maggots*] *in*** *one's* **[*the*] *head* [*brain*]** 《口》気まぐれな考えをいだく ▪ He *has got a maggot in his head* on everything connected with art. 彼はこと芸術に関するかぎり奇妙な考えをいだいている. ☞気まぐれな人の脳にはウジ (maggot) がいるという古い考えから.

when the maggot bites 気が向いたときに ▪ I shall do it, *when the maggot bites*. 気が向いたときにそうしよう.

magic /mǽdʒɪk/ 形名 ***a magic carpet*** **1** 空

飛ぶ絨毯(じゅうたん) ▪ How I wish I had *a magic carpet*! 魔法の絨毯があればなあ!

2 簡単で快適な移動手段 ▪ My new motorcycle is real *magic carpet* stuff. 今度買ったバイクは実に軽快に走る代物だ.

like magic/as if by magic たちどころに, 不思議に ▪ The medicine is supposed to work *like magic*. その薬はたちどころに効くはずだ.

What's the magic word? 《英》魔法の言葉は?, …でしょ? 《子供の言葉うかいのしつけで丁寧に Please …や Thank you. と言わせるときの決まり文句》 ▪ Can I have some candy, mom?—*What's the magic word?*—Please. ママ, キャンディーくれない?—くださいでしょ?—ください.

white magic (天使などの助けにより治療・祈祷などの善を行う)白魔術 ▪ She has lost the ability to perform *white magic*. 彼女は白魔術を施す能力を失ってしまった.

magnify /mǽgnəfàɪ/ 動 ***magnify*** *oneself* ***against*** *a person* 人に対していばる (《聖》*Job* 19. 5) ▪ Don't *magnify yourself against* your inferiors. 目下の者に大きな顔をしてはいけない.

magnitude /mǽgnətjùːd/ 名 ***of the first magnitude*** (星の光度が一等の, から)最も重要な ▪ To do this would be a blunder *of the first magnitude*. こんなことをしたら, この上もなくゆゆしい誤りになるだろう.

magpie /mǽgpàɪ/ 名 ***chatter like a magpie*** ぺちゃくちゃしゃべりまくる ▪ She *chatters like a magpie* all the time. 彼女は始終ぺらぺらとしゃべる.

mahogany /məhɑ́gəni|-hɔ́g-/ 名 ***have*** *one's* ***feet under*** *a person's* ***mahogany*** 《口》

1 人と食事を共にする ▪ I shall *have my feet under Brown's mahogany* tonight. 今晩ブラウンといっしょに食事をします.

2 人に寄食する ▪ His object in life is to *have his feet under another's mahogany*. 彼の人生の目的は他人に寄食することだ.

put [***stretch***] *one's* ***feet*** [***legs***] ***under*** *a person's* ***mahogany*** 《口》人のもてなしを受ける ▪ I *put my feet under his mahogany* with the greatest satisfaction. 私はこの上もなく満足して彼のもてなしを受けた.

put [***with***] *one's* ***knees*** [***legs***] ***under the mahogany*** 《口》食卓につく[ついて] ▪ I had hoped to see you *with your legs under the mahogany* in my humble parlor. あなたが拙宅で食事してくださることを望んでいたのでしたが ▪ You'll feel better when you've *put your knees under the mahogany*. 食事をすれば気分がよくなるでしょう.

Mahomet /məhɑ́mət|-hɔ́m-/ 名 ***like Mahomet's coffin*** ムハンマドの柩(ひつぎ)のように(ぐらぐらして, 不安定で) ▪ The situation was, *like Mahomet's coffin*, still suspended in midair. 状況はムハンマドの柩のように, まだ虚空に浮いたままだった. ☞ムハンマドの柩は Medina に中空から吊るされているという伝説から.

Mahomet must go to the mountain. (向こうが来ないなら)こちらが出かけて行かなければならない《やむをえない事情のため方針を変えなくてはならない場合によく使う言葉》 ▪ The telegram says he can't come. —So *Mahomet must go to the mountain.* 電報によると, 彼は来られないそうだ—じゃあ, こっちが出かけて行かなくてはならないのだね. ☞ムハンマドが奇跡を求められ, 山を呼び寄せようとしたが, 山が動かないのを見て,「私のほうが山へ出かけていこう」と言ったという話から.

maid /meɪd/ 名 ***an old maid*** 結婚適齢期をはるかに過ぎた女性, 婚期を逸した未婚女性 ▪ She decided she would remain *an old maid* for ever. 彼女は一生独身を通そうと決めた.

(***as***) ***meek*** [***modest***] ***as a maid*** 処女のようにおとなしい ▪ The lad looked *as meek as a maid*. その若者は処女のようにおとなしそうな顔つきをしていた.

maiden /méɪdən/ 名 ***an answer to a maiden's prayer*** →ANSWER[1].

mail /meɪl/ 名 ***by mail*** 《主に米》(手段として)郵便で ▪ Order them *by mail* from Andy's Orchard. それらの注文はアンディー果樹園に郵便でお申し込みください.

hate mail (匿名の)強迫状《抗議の手紙》 ▪ I have been getting a lot of *hate mail* recently. 最近いやがらせのメールが山ほど届く.

in the mail 《主に米》郵便で, 郵便物に同封されて ▪ I received a letter *in the mail*. 郵便で手紙を受け取った ▪ I put a money order *in the mail* to you. 郵便為替を君宛の郵便物に同封した.

mail order 通信販売, メールオーダー ▪ Why don't you make a purchase by *mail order* for a change? たまには通販で買い物をしてはどうか.

pay the mail 罰金を払う ▪ The rascal has roundly *paid the mail*. 悪党は相当の罰金を払った.

mailed /meɪld/ 形 ***mailed fist*** 鉄拳制裁, 武力 ▪ Up and at him with your *mailed fist*. 断固として彼に鉄拳制裁を加えよ. ☞1897年 The Times に載ったドイツ皇帝 Wilhelm II の演説の翻訳 (Ⓖ *gepanzerte Faust*) から.

main /meɪn/ 形名 ***by main force*** 《文》全力をふるって; 力ずくで ▪ The police stopped the rioters *by main force*. 警察は全力で暴徒を引き止めた.

in the main 大部分は, 概して ▪ He is *in the main* a good-natured man. 彼は概して気立てのよい人間だ.

a person's ***main squeeze*** → a main SQUEEZE.

the main drag 《米》本通り ▪ He walked up and down *the* town's *main drag*. 彼は町の本通りを行ったり来たりして歩いた.

the main squeeze 《米俗》(ある集団の)ボス, 親分 ▪ Vance is *the main squeeze* of the works. バンスがその工場のボスだ.

turn on the main 《戯》涙の雨を降らす ▪ You've no idea how she *turned on the main*! あの女性がどんなに涙の雨を降らせたか君には見当もつかないだろう. ☞main「水道の本管」.

with (***all*** *one's*) ***might and main*** →MIGHT[1].

main-brace /mèɪnbréɪs/ 名 ***splice the main-brace*** **1**《海俗》(船員に)火酒をふるまう ▪ It was customary to *splice the main-brace* to reward a ship's crew. 水夫たちの労をねぎらうために火酒をふるまうのが習わしだった.
2《口・戯》ひどく飲む ▪ He came home with *the main-brace* well *spliced*. 彼はひどく酔って帰ってきた. ☞「大檣(しょう)転桁(こう)索をより継ぎする」を酒が元気をつけてくれることにかけたもの.

main chance /mèɪntʃǽns|-tʃɑ́:ns/ 名 ***have* [*keep*] *an eye to* [*for,*《英》*on*] *the main chance*/ *be careful of* [*mind*] *the main chance*** 自分の利益を図る ▪ Most people don't *have an eye to the main chance* in circumstances like that. 大抵の人はそんな状況では自分の利益を図りはしない ▪ He always *has an eye for the main chance*, however risky. 彼はどんなに危険を伴っても常に私利を追う ▪ The old man never seemed to *have an eye on the main chance*. その老人は金儲けの絶好のチャンスにも全く食指が動かないようだった.

with an eye to the main chance 儲けの機会をねらって ▪ He accepted the invitation *with an eye to the main chance*. 彼は儲けの機会をねらってその招待を受けた.

majesty /mǽdʒəsti/ 名 ***at Her* [*His*] *Majesty's pleasure*** (英国の)監獄に拘留されて ▪ The murderer was imprisoned *at Her Majesty's pleasure*. 殺人犯は監獄に拘留された.

majority /mədʒɔ́:rəti|-dʒɔ́r-/ 名 ***attain* [*reach*] *one's majority*** 成年に達する ▪ He will *reach* [*attain*] *his majority* next month. 彼は来月成年に達する.

be in the majority 過半数を占めている ▪ Women *are in the majority* and are very active. 女性が過半数を占め, 活発に活動している.

***by a majority of* A *against* B** B対Aの多数で ▪ The bill was carried *by a majority of* 50 *against* 30. 議案は30票対50票の多数で通過した.

join* [*go over to, pass over to*] *the* (*great, silent*) *majority なき数に入る, 死ぬ ▪ He, too, has *joined the majority*. 彼もまたあの世の人となってしまった.

the silent majority **1** 死者 ▪ Her parents went over to *the silent majority*, leaving her without a relative in the world. 両親が鬼籍に入り, 彼女は天涯孤独になった.
2 声なき一般大衆 (↔ the chattering CLASSes) ▪ Politicians ought to listen to the opinions of *the silent majority*. 政治家は声なき一般大衆の意見に耳を傾けるべきだ. ☞Richard Nixon (1913–1994)の言葉から.

make[1] /meɪk/ 名 ***get* [*do, run*] *a make on* ...** 《米俗》(...の身元など)を割り出す ▪ Did you *get a make on* the thief? 泥棒の身元を割り出せたのか?

make-believe 見せかけの, 偽りの ▪ Most creatures of Star Wars are *make-believe*. スターウォーズに出ている生き物はたいてい実在しない.

makeover 改善, イメージチェンジ ▪ The department store is getting a complete *makeover*. そのデパートは全館改装中です.

of ... make ...製の; ...作りの ▪ This car is *of* American *make*. この車はアメリカ製です ▪ He is a man *of* slender *make*. 彼はきゃしゃな作りの男だ.

on the make **1**《口》成功[昇進, 金儲け]に熱心で ▪ The factory manager was *on the make* and worked his men hard. 工場長は成功に熱心で従業員を酷使した.
2《米俗》恋人を得ようと努めて ▪ My sister has been (going) *on the make*. 妹は恋人を得ようとずっと努めている.

put the make on 《米口》人に言い寄る, 情を通じようとする ▪ I think he was trying to *put the make on* me. 彼は私にしきりに言い寄ろうとしていたと思う.

make[2] /meɪk/ 動 ***as good* [*clever,* etc.] *as they make them*** 《俗》この上もなく親切な[賢い, など] ▪ These ladies are *as good as they make them*. この女性たちはこの上もなく親切です ▪ He's *as cute as they make 'em*. あいつはこの上なくきざな奴だ.

be made for 《口》...に最適である, うってつけだ ▪ You *are made for* a teacher. あなたは教師にうってつけです ▪ Sue and Ken *are made for* each other. スーとケンはお似合いのカップルだ.

***be made* (*for life*)**《口》一生遊んで暮らせる ▪ If you marry a rich man you *are made for life*. 金持ちといっしょになると一生左うちわだよ.

***be made up* (*about, with*)**《英口》...に満足している, を喜んでいる ▪ I'*m* really *made up with* the new job. 今度の仕事が大いに気に入っている.

have* (*got*) *it made 《口》成功間違いなしだ ▪ With this fund I'*ve got it made*. これだけの資金があれば成功間違いなしだ.

How do you make that out? どうしてそういうこと[結論]になるのか ▪ *How do you make that out?* —Because I love you, honey. なぜそんなことになるの?—愛しているからさ.

made up strong 《口》厚化粧をして, めかして ▪ The young lady was *made up strong*. その若い女性はこってりと厚化粧をしていた.

***make a bundle* [*pile*]** →make one's PILE.

make a day* [*night, weekend* etc.] *of it →DAY; NIGHT; WEEKEND.

make a go of →GO[1].

make a long day →MAKE long hours.

make a quick* [*fast*] *buck*/*make a quick pound 早く金を作る ▪ Can I *make a fast buck* by investing in these shares? この株に投資したら早くお金になりますか?

make all even →EVEN.

make anything of 〚否定文で〛...を理解する ▪ I can't *make anything of* it. それは全く理解できない.

***make as if* [*as though*]** ...かのようにふるまう

M

▪ He *made as if* to strike me. 彼は私を打つようなそぶりをした ▪ He *made as though* he were tipsy. 彼は酔ったふりをした.

***make away with** oneself* 自殺する ▪ She *made away with herself* by hanging. 彼女は首つり自殺をした.

make change 《米》お金をくずす ▪ Can you *make change* for a ten dollar bill? 10ドル, くずしてもらえませんか.

make** a thing **do →DO².

make do and mend 《英》→DO².

make do with →DO².

make do without... …なしで済ます ▪ We'll have to *make do without* sugar for the tea. 私たちは紅茶を砂糖なしで済まさなければならない.

make** (...) **fly 動かす, 実行可能にする, 機能させる ▪ He may have terrific ideas, but he can't *make* them *fly*. 彼にはすばらしい考えがあるとしても, それを実行はできまい.

make it **1** 《口》〚命令文で〛…にしておけ ▪ *Make it* tomorrow. あすのことにしておけ ▪ *Make it* malted milk. 麦芽ミルクにしておきなさい.

2 《口》うまく達成する, 成功する; 到着する; 間に合う; (病気が)治る ▪ I managed to *make it* over into the bathroom on all fours. 何とかトイレまで這ってたどりつけた ▪ She *made it* as a dancer. 彼女はダンサーとして成功した ▪ We've just *made it*. やっと間に合ったぞ.

3 生命を取り留める ▪ He was losing so much blood I thought he wasn't going to *make it*. 彼の出血がひどいので命が危ないのではないかと思った.

make it back 《米口》うまく戻って来る ▪ He could not *make it back*. 彼はうまく戻って来ることができなかった.

make it fly 《口》金をばらまく, 浮かれ騒ぐ ▪ You'd better not *make it fly*. 金をばらまくのはやめたほうが身のためだ.

***make it good upon** a person* →GOOD.

make it out 《主に米》どうにかうまくやっていく ▪ I don't know whether I shall *make it out*. どうにかうまくやっていけるかどうかわからない.

make it up 合計…になる (*to*) ▪ I put in 1GB of memory, which *made it up to* 3GB of RAM. 1GB のメモリーを入れたから, 合計してラムが3GB になった.

***make it up to** a person* 人に弁償する, 埋め合わせをする ▪ We must *make it up to* him somehow. なんとかして彼に弁償しなければならない.

make it up with …と仲直りする ▪ Oh, how she longed to *make it up with* him! ああ, 彼と仲直りしたいと, どんなに彼女は望んだことか.

make it with 《俗》 **1** …の仲間にしてもらう ▪ He *made it with* the in-group. 彼はその内集団に受け入れられた.

2 …と性交する ▪ Have you *made it with* Jane? ジェインとあれしたのかい.

make like 《口》…をまねる, のまね[ふり]をする ▪ The clown *made like* a bear and frightened the little girls. 道化役者はクマのまねをして, 小さな女の子たちを怖がらせた.

make like a banana [***atom and split***] 《俗》(おどけて)立ち去る ▪ Well, folks, I'm going to have to *make like a banana*. それでは, みなさん, おいとまします.

make long hours [***a long day***] 長時間働く ▪ I *made a* very *long day* last Friday. この前の金曜日はずいぶん長いこと働きました.

make ... look foolish [***silly, a fool***] …を笑い物にする, ばかな事をさせる ▪ He was annoyed that he'd *been made to look a fool*. 彼は笑い物にされて腹を立てた.

make** oneself **look silly [***a fool***] ばかな事をする, 笑い物になる ▪ I hope you don't *make yourself look a fool* by wasting your money. 金をむだ使いして笑い物にならないといいね.

make much of →MUCH.

***make off with** oneself* 急いで去る ▪ He had successfully *made off with himself*. 彼は首尾よく逃げおおせた.

make one of …に加わる ▪ Will you *make one of* the party? 君も一行に加わりませんか.

make or break [***mar***] (…を)完全にやり遂げるかしくじるか, のるかそるか《諺的な文で》 ▪ A man *is made or marred* by his wife. 男を生かすも殺すも妻次第 ▪ She felt that her son's work would either *make or break*. 彼女は息子の仕事はのるかそるかだと思った.

make or mend →MEND².

make out a [*one's*] ***case*** 主張する, 論証する (*for, against, that*) ▪ The speaker *made out an* excellent *case*. 演説者は実に立派な主張をした ▪ He has *made out a* strong *case for* [*against*] the bill. 彼はその法案に対して強い賛成論[反対論]をぶった ▪ The lawyer *made out his case that* the prisoner was not guilty. 弁護士は被告が無罪であることを主張した.

***make something of** oneself* 《口》世の中で成功する ▪ She has enough brains and talent to really *make something of herself*. 彼女は社会で成功するだけの知力と才能を備えている.

make something out of 《米俗》…のことでごたごた言う ▪ You want to *make something out of* it? そのことでごたごた言いたいのかね.

***make the most of** oneself* 自分を最もよく見せる, できる限り魅力的に見せる ▪ That girl is pretty but she doesn't *make the most of herself*. あの少女は美しいが化粧や身なりにはかまわない.

make up a four (***at bridge***) 《トランプ》1人加わって4人でブリッジをする ▪ Okay, I'll *make up a four*. よろしい, 私が加わって4人でブリッジをしましょう.

make up the numbers 頭数をそろえる ▪ They invited me to dinner, just to *make up the numbers*. 彼らは人数をそろえるためだけに私を夕食に招いた.

not so bad as you make it 君の言うほど悪くな

い ▪ The climate is *not so bad as you make it.* 気候は君が言うほど悪くない.

see* [*find out*] *what** a person **is** (**really**) **made of 人の真価が分かる ▪ We'll *find out what* we*'re made of* in the next game. 次の試合でわがチームの真価が問われるだろう.

show** a person **what** one **is** (**really**) **made of 自分の真価を分からせる ▪ Go on. *Show* them *what* you*'re made of.* さあ, 連中に君の真価を見せてやれ.

they don't make 'em like they used to [***like that anymore***] 《口》昔と比べると品質が落ちる ▪ With the high divorce rate, *they don't* seem to *make* marriages *like they used to.* こう離婚率が高いところを見ると, 結婚は以前ほど真剣にみなされていないようだ.

what** one **is made of 《口》自分の才能[腕前] ▪ Let me do it. I'll show you *what* I*'m made of.* 私にやらせてください. 腕前をお見せしましょう.

maker /méɪkər/ 名 ***go to*** [***meet***] *one's* ***Maker*** 《しばしば戯》死ぬ ▪ That miser *went to his Maker* at last. あのけちんぼうも, とうとう死んだ.

making /méɪkɪŋ/ 名 ***be the making of*** (人)の成功[発展]の元になる ▪ This failure *was the making of* him. この失敗が彼の成功の元になった.

have the makings of …の素質がある ▪ He *has* all *the makings of* a first-class salesman. 彼には一流のセールスマンの素質がある.

in the making 発達過程の, 未完成状態の ▪ The reporter has seen history *in the making.* その記者は歴史に残るできごとを目撃したのだ ▪ The child of today is the man of the future *in the making.* 現在の子供は発育中の未来のおとなである.

of** one's (**own**) **making 自分が作った ▪ These thoughts were not *of his own making.* この考えは彼が考えたものではなかった.

male /meɪl/ 形 ***a male chauvinist*** (***pig*** [***swine***]) 男性優越主義者 ▪ I don't like to be dubbed *a male chauvinist pig.* 私は男性優越主義者と言われたくない.

malice /mǽləs/ 名 ***with malice aforethought*** 《法》予謀の悪意をもって, 故意に ▪ It wasn't an accident; he injured her *with malice aforethought.* 事故による怪我ではなかった. 彼が彼女を故意に傷つけたのだ.

malt /mɔːlt/ 名 ***The malt is above the meal*** [***wheat, water***]**.** 《口》酔っている ▪ *The malt is above the meal* with him. 彼は酔っている.

mama, mamma /mɑ́ːmə|məmɑ́ː/ 名 ***a mama's*** [***mamma's***] ***boy*** = a MOTHER's boy.

man[1] /mæn/ 名 ***a big man on campus*** 花形学生 ▪ He was *a big man on campus*, and he was at the top of the class. 彼は大学でリーダー格の学生で成績も抜群だった.

a company man 経営者側につく男性従業員 ▪ He's *a company man* and never joins in a strike. 彼は会社側のイヌでストには決して加わらない.

a dirty old man 《口》すけべおやじ ▪ Let me go, you *dirty old man*! 放してよ, このすけべおやじ.

a fancy man 愛人, 情夫, 間男(まおとこ) ▪ Her *fancy man* always slips in through the back door. 彼女の愛人はいつも裏口からこっそり入ってくる.

a [***the***] ***grand old man*** (***of…***) 老大人, (ある分野で)長く尊敬された男性, (…界の)大立者 ▪ Louis Armstrong was *the grand old man of* jazz. ルイ・アームストロングはジャズ界の大御所であった. ☞一般に GOM と略称される. 1892年に83歳で最後の当選を果たした英国の政治家 William Ewart Gladstone (1809–98)の愛称でもある.

a hired man (家・農場の)雇い人 ▪ The *hired man* was sick, and the whole house was a mess. 家事をしてくれる人が病気で, 家中が散らかっていた.

a [*one's*] ***little man*** 《戯》男の子 ▪ I hope you will be kind to *my little man.* どうかうちの息子に優しくしてやってください.

a man about town →TOWN.

a man and a brother 同胞, 対等の人間 (a fellow man) ▪ I wonder if Frankenstein's monster was *a man and a brother.* フランケンシュタインの怪物は我々と同じ人間だったのだろうか. ☞奴隷反対運動の標語 "Am I not a man and a brother?" から.

a man born of woman 人間 (《聖》*Job* 14. 1) ▪ No *man born of woman* has ever succeeded in doing so. 誰もこれまで首尾よくそうしたためしがない.

A man can die but once. 《諺》人は一度しか死ねない. ☞危険に直面した人を励ます言葉.

a man-eater 《口》男性をもてあそぶ女性 ▪ She has a reputation as *a man-eater.* 彼女は男をたぶらかすという評判だ.

a man for all seasons 《口》どんな状況にも順応する人物 ▪ He's well-known for being really *a man for all seasons.* 彼はさまざまな活動を実に見事にこなすことで名が知られている.

a man for breakfast 《米口》(朝刊新聞に出る)殺人記事 ▪ We had *a man for breakfast* nearly every day. ほとんど毎日のように殺人記事が出た.

a man Friday 忠実な従僕 ▪ He asked our *man Friday*'s name. 彼はうちの忠実な使用人の名前を尋ねた. ☞Robinson Crusoe の従僕の名から.

a man of action 行動派の活動家, 言葉や頭より体を使った活動が顕著な人 ▪ He's *a man of action*, not a scholar. 彼は学者ではなく, 行動家なのだ ▪ My brother is *a man of action* rather than words. 兄は能弁というよりは行動派だ.

a man of Belial ろくでなし, 悪人 (《聖》*1 Sam.* 25. 25) ▪ This Lefty is *a man of Belial.* このレフティーというやつは悪人だ.

a man of blood 人殺しをした人 ▪ Go out, thou *man of blood.* 出て行け, この人殺しめ. ☞ヘブライ語法.

a man of few words 口数の少ない人, 無駄口をきかない人 ▪ The principal is *a man of few words* and is loved by all the pupils. 校長先生は

M

口数が少なく生徒みんなに慕われている.

a man of god **1** 聖徒 ▪ St. Francis was *a* meek *man of god.* 聖フランチェスコはおとなしい聖徒であった.

2 聖職者 ▪ We were greeted by *a* little, fat *man of God.* 小さな太った牧師が我々を迎えてくれた.

a man of letters 《文》→LETTER.

a man of* (*many*) *parts →PART[1].

a man of men 男の中の男, 抜群の人物 ▪ He truly was *a man of men* for honesty. 正直さにかけては, 彼はまさしく男の中の男だった.

a man of straw [《米》 ***a straw man***] 《英》 **1** わら人形 ▪ He put *a man of straw* in his bed to trick the demon that came for revenge. 復しゅうに来る悪魔をだますために, 彼はわら人形をベッドに入れた.

2 仮想の敵 ▪ He was looking for *a man of straw* to attack. 彼は攻撃する仮想の敵を捜していた.

3 わらの男《つまらない男, 文無し》 ▪ If the defendant is *a man of straw,* who is to pay the costs? 被告が文無しの場合は費用を誰が出すのか.

a man of the cloth [***God***] 《文》 牧師, 聖職者 ▪ Father Adams is *a man of the cloth* in our parish. アダムズ神父は私たちの教区の牧師さんだ.

a man of the people 庶民出の人《低い身分から国家の要職についた人》 ▪ He's really *a man of the people.* 彼は実を言うと庶民出の人だ.

a man of the world →WORLD.

a man-of-war **1** メキシコ湾のクラゲ ▪ The sign says, "No swimming today, as we have a *man-of-war* alert."「クラゲ発生警告のため本日水泳禁止」と看板にある.

2 (国旗を掲げている)軍艦 ▪ The shipwreck victims were picked up by *a* British *man-of-war.* 海難事故遭難者は英国軍艦に救助された.

3 アホウドリ ▪ Some *men-of-war* were majestically sailing through the skies. 数羽のアホウドリが悠々と大空を飛翔していた.

a man or a mouse 立派な男かだめ人間か ▪ A man must be either *a man or a mouse.* 男性は立派な男になるか, だめ人間になるかのどっちかだ.

a man-to-man talk 腹蔵のない[差しの]話し合い ▪ I decided it was time for *a man-to-man talk.* いよいよ腹を割って話すべき頃合いだと決断した.

a man's gotta [***got to***] ***do what a man's gotta*** [***got to***] ***do*** 《口・戯》 したくなくてもしなければならない ▪ Sometimes *a man's gotta do what a man's gotta do.* いやでもしなくてはならないときがある.

a man's life 男の人生[仕事]《英国陸軍の新兵募集のスローガンの一部》 ▪ Join the Army. It's *a Man's Life*! 陸軍に入隊しよう. これこそ男の仕事だ.

a man's man 男性とつき合うのが好きな男性 (↔a LADY's man) ▪ I think of Bill as *a man's man.* ビルは男とつき合うのが好きな男だと思う.

a marked man [***woman***] (復しゅう・仕返しの目的で)命を狙われている男[女]性 ▪ I know I am *a marked man.* 私が狙われているのは分かっている ▪ She felt she was *a marked woman* as a witness to the robbery. 彼女は強盗の目撃者として狙われている気がした.

a rich man's hobby (名声だけを求める)金持ちの道楽 ▪ Being explorers is just *a rich man's hobby.* 探検するのは名声を得るための金持ちの道楽にすぎない.

A rich man's joke is always funny. 《諺》 金持ちの冗談はいつもおかしい《誰もが金持ちのきげんを取りたがり, その冗談を聞くと必ず笑う》.

a right-hand man 片腕, 頼りになる人 ▪ Mr. Hill has long been the Director's *right-hand man.* ヒル氏がこれまでずっと理事の片腕だった.

a self-made man 自らの努力で名を成した人, たたき上げの人物 ▪ He's the best example of *a self-made man.* 彼は自力で出世したお手本みたいな人だ.

a wise man of Gotham ゴタムの賢人, 愚か者 ▪ He's *a wise man of Gotham.* Ask someone else. 彼は何も分からないから他の人に聞け.

(***all***) ***good men and true*** →TRUE.

an angry young man 怒れる若者《1950年代に保守的な社会に対する不満を示した英国の若い作家たちの一員. Leslie Paul に同名の書(1951)がある》.

as a man (学識・地位とは別の)一個の男子として, 一個人として ▪ He is highly estimated both *as* a scholar and *a man.* 彼は学者としても一個人としても高く評価されている.

(***as***) ***man to man*** 《口》 正直率直に ▪ May I speak to you *as man to man*? 正直率直に申し上げてよろしいでしょうか.

as one man 《文》 満場一致して, 一斉に (《聖》 *Judges* 20. 8) ▪ All the people got up *as one man.* すべての人々は一斉に立ち上がった.

as one man to another 同格の人間同士として ▪ My father spoke to me *as one man to another.* 父は同格の人間同士として私に話した.

be a man/play the man 男らしくふるまう ▪ *Be a man*! 勇気を出せ ▪ He *played the man* in the time of great troubles. 彼は非常に困難な時に男らしくふるまった.

be *a person's* ***man*** [***woman***] (特定の職に)最適任の男性[女性] ▪ If you need a driver, he'*s your man.* 運転手がほしいなら彼がうってつけだ ▪ If you need a good babysitter, she'*s your woman.* よいベビーシッターを探しているなら彼女がぴったりだ.

be man enough (***to*** *do*) 男らしい(らしく…する), する勇気がある ▪ He *was man enough to* admit it. 彼は男らしくそれを認めた.

be no good [***use***] ***to man or beast*** 《口・戯》 全く役に立たない ▪ This car has two flat tires—it'*s no use to man or beast.* この車はタイヤが二つパンクしていて全然使いものにならない.

be *one's* ***own man*** **1** 気力が確かである ▪ I slept a bit at dawn and I *am* almost *my own man* now. 夜明けにうとうとして, もうほとんど気力が戻った.

2 他人の支配を受けない, 自由に行動できる ▪ Pardon

me for not being quite frank towards you; I *am* not now *my own man.* 君にすっかり打ち明けないのを許してくれ. 今は自由に行動できないのだ.

be twice the man [***woman***] (***that*** *a person* ***is***) →TWICE.

Better be an old man's darling than a young man's slave. 《諺》(若い女性は)こき使う青年よりも溺愛してくれる年配の男性と結婚した方がよい.

between man and man 男同士として(の) ▪ This is a promise *between man and man.* これは男同士の約束だ.

Call [***Count***] ***no man happy till he dies*** [***is dead***]***.*** 《諺》死ぬまでは幸福者呼ばわりをするな《人は死ぬまで, その人生が幸福だったかどうかわからぬ》.

dead men tell no tales 死人に口無し ▪ Surely he did it on purpose, thinking that *dead men tell no tales.* 死人に口無しと考えて, 彼はきっと故意にやったのだろう.

dead men's shoes [***man's shoe***] 《英》上司の死[退職]後でないと得られない地位, 退職した上役の後任 ▪ We're sick and tired of waiting to step into *dead men's shoes.* 誰かが辞めるまで昇進できないなんて全くうんざりだ.

every last man 誰もかれも, 一人残らず ▪ I'd like *every last man* to be here on time tomorrow. 全員あすは時間通りに来ていただきたい.

every [***each***] ***man for himself*** 自分のことは自分で面倒を見なければならない状況 ▪ It is (a case of) *every man for himself.* 今は自分のことは自分で面倒を見なければならない状況だ.

Every man is the architect [***artificer***] ***of his own fortune.*** 《諺》人はみな自分の運命の建設者である《君自身の決定や行動で, 君の将来の生活がどんなものになるかが決まる》,「善敗おのれによる」.

every man jack →JACK.

Every man to his taste. 《諺》人はみな好みが違う(だから好みを理由として人を咎めてはならない),「蓼(たで)食う虫も好きずき」.

every man, woman and child すべての人間, 猫もしゃくしも ▪ In a nuclear war, *every man, woman and child* would meet their deaths. 核戦争が起きればすべての人間は死ぬだろう.

every (***possible***)***... known to man and beast*** ありとあらゆる... ▪ We must exhaust *every possible* means *known to man and beast.* 我々はありとあらゆる手段を尽くさなければならない.

faceless men 無名の人; 感情を表に出さない人 ▪ I knew I was being followed by *a faceless man.* 知らない男につけられていると気づいていた.

feel *one's* ***own man*** 《口》気分がよい ▪ I don't *feel my own man* today. 今日はどうも気分が変だ.

go out and see a man 《俗》1杯やる ▪ I must *go out and see a man* tonight. 今夜人に会う用があってね.《今夜は1杯やるぞ》. ☞1杯やりたいときの「人に会いに出かける」という口実から.

gray [***grey***] ***men*** (大きな組織の)裏舞台で働く無名の人々 ▪ They are *grey men* who control gossip about the Royal Family. 彼らの役割は英国王室のゴシップを陰で抑えることだ.

have to (***go and***) ***see a man about a horse*** [***dog***] ちょっと他に用事がある; トイレに行きたい (→see a MAN about a dog) ▪ Excuse me. I *have to go and see a man about a dog.* 失礼, ちょっと用足しに《トイレに行ってきます》.

He'll be a man among the geese when the gander is gone. 《諺》彼は鳥なき里のコウモリにはなれるだろう《人の才能をあざけって言う言葉》.

high man on the totem pole 権力のある人, 大物 ▪ Who's *high man on the totem pole* around here? ここのボスは誰だ?

I'm your [***his,*** etc.] ***man*** 《口》よろしい; 引き受けた ▪ If you want to sell, *I'm your man.* 売りたいと言うのなら, 私が買おう ▪ Let any man come, *I'm his man.* 誰でも来い, おれが相手だ.

Let every man skin his own skunk. 《諺》各自は自分のスカンクの皮をはぐがよい《自分の仕事だけをして, 他人の仕事に口を挟むな》,「おのれの頭の蠅(はえ)を追え」.

like a man 男らしく, 雄々しく ▪ He bore it *like a man.* 彼は雄々しくそれに耐えた.

like painting a dead man's face red 真実を隠すように ▪ Giving the impression that I'm not willing is *like painting a dead man's face red.* 私が乗り気でないという印象を与えると, 事実を曲げることになる.

make *a person* ***a man*** 人を成功[繁栄]させる ▪ They set him upon his legs, and *made* him *a man* for ever. 彼らは彼を一本立ちさせて, いつまでも繁栄させてやった.

make a man (***out***) ***of*** *a person* 人を(一人前の)男にする ▪ There's no doubt that it has *made a man of* him. それが彼を男にしたことはまちがいない.

man alive 《俗》〚間投詞的に〛おいおい, ねえ君《驚いて呼び掛けるための》 ▪ Haul quick, Ed! or you will drown them, *man alive.* おい, 早く引っぱるのだ, エド, さもないとみんなおぼれてしまうぞ.

man and boy 少年時代から (cf. Sh., *Haml.* 5. 1. 176) ▪ I've lived here, *man and boy,* in this same parish. 私は少年時代から同じこの教区に住んでいる.

man and wife 夫婦 ▪ I'll make them *man and wife.* 二人を連れ添わせてやろう.

man bites dog (特に三流新聞の)異常な興味本位のニュース ▪ Such news is only for *man bites dog* journalism. そんなニュースは異常な興味本位の記事を載せる新聞にしか向かない.

man by man 一人ずつ ▪ They will come *man by man.* 彼らは一人ずつやって来るだろう.

Man does not live by bread alone. 《諺》人はパンだけで生きるものではない. (《聖》*Matt.* 4. 4).

man for [***to***] ***man*** **1** 一対一で(は) ▪ *Man for man* he beat me hollow. 一対一で彼はさんざんに私

M

を打ち負かした ▪ The prisoners must be exchanged *man for man.* 捕虜は一人ずつ交換しなくてはならない.

2 率直に(言って) ▪ We talked *man-to-man* about the issue. 我々はその問題について腹蔵なく語り合った.

man of sin キリストの敵, 悪魔 (《聖》 *2 Thess.* 2. 3) ▪ Is Judas Iscariot supposed to be the *man of sin?* イスカリオテのユダはキリストの敵とされているのか ▪ I wish she was choked with her *Man of Sin.* 彼女が悪魔のために窒息すればいいのに.

Man proposes, but God disposes. 《諺》ことを図るは人, 成敗を決めるは天; 人は計画し, 神は成否を決める《ヘブライ・ギリシャ・ラテンの諺》. ☞[L] Homo proponit, sed deus disponit のなぞり.

man's best friend (しばしば新聞・テレビニュースで) 人間の最良の友《犬のこと》 ▪ Look! *Man's best friend* just peed all over my shoes! 見ろ. 犬のやつ, おれの靴におしっこをかけやがった!

Men are blind in their own cause. 《諺》人は自分自身の利益のためには無分別になる《あるものを盲信すると, その欠陥やそれにまつわる危険に気づかなくなる》.

men in white coats 《戯》精神科医, 精神科医院勤務者 ▪ She was escorted by *men in white coats* to a psychiatrist. 彼女は助手たちにつき添われて精神科医のところへ行った.

Men make houses, women make homes. 《諺》夫は家を作り妻は家庭を作る.

mistake *one's* ***man*** 相手を見そこなう[見くびる] ▪ If he supposes I'm afraid, he has much *mistaken his man.* 僕がびくびくしていると思っているのなら, 彼は相手をひどく見そこなっている.

No man can serve two masters. 《諺》人は二人の主人に仕えることはできない.

No man is an island. 人間は孤島ではない《完全に孤独に生きることはできない》(Donne, *Meditation* 17) ▪ *No man is an island.* Every man is a piece of the continent. 人は孤島ではない. それぞれが陸地の一部なのだ.

no man's land →NO.

old man! →OLD.

one's ***old man*** 《口》父; 夫 ▪ *My old man* never went to college. おやじは全く大学へ行かなかった.

One man's trash is another man's treasure. 《諺》甲のがらくたは乙の宝物《ある人にとって価値のないものが, 別の人には貴重なもののことがある》.

our man 《口》(警官が容疑者を指して)ホシ ▪ We'll make an arrest, and we'll get *our man.* 逮捕するぞ, ホシをあげるんだ.

our man in Paris [***Havana,*** etc.] パリ [ハバナ, など]に駐在しているうちの者《大使・諜報部員・新聞社の特派員など》 ▪ We have got this information from *our man in Tokyo.* この情報は東京の特派員から入手した.

play the man →be a MAN.

rise as one man 一斉に立ち上がる ▪ The audience *rose as one man* clapping their hands in applause. 聴衆は一斉に立ち上がって拍手した.

see a man about a dog [***horse***] 《口・戯》お手洗いに立つ ▪ Excuse me, but I have to go *see a man about a dog.* すみません, お手洗いへ行きたいのですが ▪ Excuse me a moment—I'm going to *see a man about a horse.* 失礼, ちょっと用足しに.

tell [***separate, sort out***] ***the men from the boys*** 《口》力と勇気のある者とない者を区別する[の違いがわかる]; 本当に勇気[力量]のある人を選りわける ▪ Running a marathon *separates the men from the boys.* マラソンは力がないと走れない ▪ The final part of the race will *sort out the men from the boys.* そのレースの最後の部分で強い者と弱い者の違いが出る. ☞男女の別なく使われる.

That's what the man said. (真偽はともかく)そういう話だ ▪ Are they plainclothes officers?—Yeah, *that's what the man said.* 彼らは私服刑事なのか?—ああ, なんでもそういう話だ.

The best man wins. 一番すぐれた人が勝つ ▪ The promise that *the best man wins* will be fulfilled. 最もすぐれた者が勝つという見込みが当たるだろう.

The busiest men have the most leisure [***find the most time***]. 《諺》最も忙しい人こそ最も暇が多い《勤勉な人は仕事を手際よくするので自分がしたいことをする暇がもてる》.

the inner man →INNER.

the man at the top 最高の地位の人 ▪ Get *the man at the top* on the phone. 最高の地位の人を電話に出してくれ.

the man for me 私にうってつけの人, 願ったりかなったりの人 ▪ Such a man is *the man for me.* そのような人こそ私にうってつけの人だ.

the man for the job その仕事にうってつけの人 ▪ We take on *the* best *man for the job.* わが社では仕事に最適の人を雇い入れる.

the man in the moon 月の中の人《月面の斑点》; 架空の人 ▪ She doesn't know it any more than *the man in the moon.* 彼女はそのことは全く知らない.

the man [***woman***] ***in*** [***on***] ***the street***/《米口》***the man in the cars*** 普通の人 ▪ It is *the man in the cars* who will decide which of the candidates shall be President. その候補者の誰を大統領にするかを決めるのは一般人なのだ.

the man of the [***his***] ***day*** 今注目されている人, 時の人 ▪ John D. Rockefeller was *the* richest *man of the day.* ジョン D. ロックフェラーは大富豪の時の人だった.

the man of the house 《古》家長, 大黒柱 ▪ You'll have to be *the man of the house* now and help your mother. これからはあなたが家長になってお母さんを助けなければならない.

the man of the match 《英・スポーツ》(フットボール・クリケットなどの試合の) 最高殊勲選手 [MVP] ▪ His goal earned him the title of *man of the match.* 彼がゴールを決めてMVPに輝いた.

M

the man of the year その年に最も話題にのぼった人物 ▪ This year's *Man of the Year* goes to actor Tom Smith. 今年の「時の人」は俳優のトム・スミスに授与されます.

the man on the Clapham omnibus 《英》平均的な[一般の]人, ごく普通の人々 ▪ *The man on the Clapham omnibus* often has little interest in politics. 市井の人々は, 往々にして政治にはむとんちゃくである. ☞Clapham「ロンドンの一地域名」; omnibus「バス (bus) の古い形」.

the man upstairs 神 ▪ It was a close shave—a warning from *the man upstairs*. それは危機一髪で, まさに神の警告だった.

the men in (gray) suits ある組織内で隠然たる権力をもつ大物たち, スーツ族《重役・上役・官僚などのエリート》 ▪ *Those men in gray suits* are working in the shadows. あの黒幕らが陰で糸を引いているんだ.

the old man 《口》 **1** =one's old MAN.
2 おやじ《社長・部長など》 ▪ If you're late, *the old man* will take you to task. 遅刻したらボスにしかられるぜ.

the strong, silent man 強くて無口な男《女流小説家の愛用した句》 ▪ It is useless to model ourselves now on *the strong, silent man* of the novel. 今時小説に出るたくましく無口な男をまねてもむだだ.

the white man's burden 白人の義務《植民地の先住民に西洋文明を教化すべきと白人が信じた責務》 ▪ It seems that *the white man's burden* is still with us in the 21st century. 白人の義務は21世紀になってもまだ生きているようだ. ☞Rudyard Kipling, *The White Man's Burden* (1899)に由来. 元来は特にフィリピンにおける米国の役割に関連して用いられた.

to a man **1** 最後の一人まで ▪ They will fight it out *to a man*. 彼らは最後の一人まで戦い抜くだろう.
2 一人残らず, 満場一致で ▪ They all answered "Yes" *to a man*. 彼らは満場一致で「賛成」と言った.

to the last man 最後の一人まで (=to a MAN 1) ▪ They were killed *to the last man*. 彼らは一人残らず殺された.

You can't keep a good man down. → KEEP[2].

You'll be a man before your mother. 《口》おかあさんより早く男になれるよ《若者を励ますふざけた言い方》 ▪ Mind your business well and *you'll be a man before your mother* yet. しっかり仕事をやれば, まだ相当なことができるよ.

Young men may die, (but) old men must die. 《諺》若者は死ぬこともあるが, 年寄りは必ず死ぬ.

man[2] /mæn/ 動 ***man*** *oneself* 奮起する, がんばる ▪ He *manned himself* with a dauntless air. 彼はひるむ様子もなくがんばった.

manage /mǽnɪdʒ/ 動 ***manage it*** 《口》(女性が)男性を見つける, 結婚する ▪ Mary *managed it* somehow. メアリーはなんとかして結婚した.

mandrake /mǽndreɪk/ 名 ***eat mandrake*** 惰眠をむさぼる ▪ My cousin Joe has *eaten mandrake*. いとこのジョーは怠け者のぐうたらだ. ☞mandrake (マンダラゲ)が催眠薬として用いられたところから.

mane /meɪn/ 名 ***make neither mane nor tail of*** ...がとんとわからない (→make HEAD or tail of) ▪ I could *make neither mane nor tail of* what they were talking about. 彼らが何のことを話しているのかさっぱりわからなかった.

manes /má:nèɪs/ 名 ***appease the manes*** (遺志を果たして)霊を慰める ▪ *The manes* of the fallen soldier *were* finally *appeased*. 戦死した兵士の霊はやっと慰められた.

maneuver, 《英》 **manoeuvre** /mənú:vər/ 名 ***freedom of [room for] maneuver*** 術策の自由; (決定後の)再考の余地 ▪ Small enterprises have limited *room for maneuver*. 小企業には駆け引きの自由は限られている.

manifest /mǽnəfèst/ 動 ***manifest*** *oneself* 現れる ▪ No disease *manifested itself* during the long voyage. 長い船旅の間に何の病気も現れなかった.

manna /mǽnə/ 名 ***manna from heaven*** 天の恵み (《聖》*Exod*. 16. 15) ▪ His timely help was like *manna from heaven*. 彼の時を得た援助は天の恵みのようだった.

manner /mǽnər/ 名 ***after a manner*** どうにか ▪ He is kind *after a manner*. 彼はまあまあ親切だ.

after *one's* ***own manner*** 自分流に ▪ He is religious *after his own manner*. 彼なりに信心深い.

all manner of あらゆる種類の ▪ He healed *all manner of* diseases. 彼は多様な種類の病気を治した.

be bad manners 不作法である, 失礼である ▪ It *is bad manners* to stare at people. 人をじろじろ見るのはぶしつけだ.

by all manner of means →MEANS.

by any (manner of) means →MEANS.

by no manner どうあっても...でない ▪ He saw the battle would be ended *by no manner*. 戦闘はどうしても終わらないと彼は見てとった.

company manners 社交のエチケット, 丁重なふるまい ▪ His 5-year-old son has fine *company manners*. 彼の5歳の息子は来客の前でとてもお行儀がよい.

have no manners 行儀作法を知らない ▪ He *has no manners* at all. 彼は全く礼儀知らずだ.

in a manner ある意味では, 幾分か ▪ He is great *in a manner*. 彼には偉大なところがある.

in a manner of speaking いわば (=SO to say) ▪ The cattle have been, *in a manner of speaking*, neglected. 家畜はいわばほったらかしにされてきた.

in the manner →with the MANNER.

in the manner of 《文》...風の ▪ This is a painting *in the manner of* Raphael. これはラファエル風の絵だ.

mind *one's* ***manners*** 礼儀正しくする ▪ She told her children to *mind their manners*. 彼女は子供たちに礼儀正しくしなさいと言った.

no manner of 少しの...もない ▪ *No manner of* thing can hurt him. どんなことも彼を傷つけることはで

きない ▪There can be *no manner of* doubt about it. それについては一点の疑いもない.

to the manner born 生来熟知の, 生来…に適して[慣れて]いる (cf. Sh., *Haml.* 1. 4. 15) ▪He does it as (if) *to the manner born.* 彼は生来熟知しているかのようにそれをやる ▪He is an American expert *to the manner born.* 彼は生まれながらのアメリカ専門家だ. ☞「その習わしに生まれついた」が原義.

What manner of ...? 《古》どのような種類の… (《聖》*Matt.* 8. 27) ▪*What manner of* man is he? 彼はどういう人間なのか.

with* [*in*] *the manner 現行中に ▪He was taken *with* [*in*] *the manner.* 彼は現行犯で捕えられた.

manse /mæns/ 名 ***a child of the manse*** (スコットランド長老教会の)牧師の子供 ▪Alec was *a child of the manse.* アレックは牧師の子だった.

mantle /mǽntəl/ 名 *One's* ***mantle falls on*** [***descends to***] *a person.* 甲の衣鉢(いはつ)が乙に伝わる (《聖》*2 Kings* 2. 13) ▪The largest portion of *Goethe's mantle fell on* Heine. ゲーテの衣鉢の大部分はハイネに伝えられた.

take up *a person's* ***mantle*** 人の弟子になる ▪Mussolini *took up the mantle of* Mazzini. ムッソリーニはマッツィーニの弟子となった.

many /méni/ 形名 ***a good many*** かなり多く(の) ▪It's *a good many* years since I saw him last. この前彼に会ってからかなりの年がたつ ▪There are *a good many* of them. そういうのがかなりいる[ある].

a great many 非常にたくさん(の) ▪*A great many* (people) stayed away. 大勢の人が欠席した.

as many 同数の ▪He made six mistakes in about *as many* lines. 彼は6行に6つの誤りを犯した.

as many again 2倍の(数) ▪I have ten copies but I shall need *as many again.* 10部あるが, その倍ほしいところだ.

as many as …ほど多くの ▪*As many as* ten people saw it. 10人もの人がそれを見た.

as* [*like*] *so many 同数の…のように, さながら…のように ▪The boys climbed *like so many* monkeys. 少年たちはさながらサルのようによじ登った.

have one too many 《口》酔っ払うほど飲む ▪He looks as if he's *had one too many.* 彼は酔っ払うほど飲んだように見える ▪Apparently he had *had one too many* drinks [*one* drink *too many*]. どうやら彼は酔っているらしかった.

in so many words はっきり, まさしく(言うなど) ▪He told me *in so many words* that he did not like it. 彼はそれがきらいだとはっきり言った.

many a 《詩》〚単数名詞を伴って〛あまたの ▪I know *many a* one who would be glad of the chance. そんな機会を喜ぶ人を何人も知っている ▪*Many a* pickle makes a muckle. 《諺》ちりも積もれば山となる.

many and many a 《雅・詩》かずかずの《MANY a の強調形》 ▪I have wanted to meet you *many and many a* year. 何年も何年も前からお目にかかりたいと思っていました.

Many are called but few are chosen. 《諺》招かれる者は多いが選ばれる者は少ない (《聖》*Matt.* 22. 14).

many is* [*was*] *the ... …は多い[多かった] ▪*Many's the* time he and I went fishing together. 何度も彼と私はいっしょに魚釣りに行ったものだった.

one too many 《口》一つ[一人]だけ余計で; じゃまで ▪I have *one* card *too many.* 手札が1枚余計だ ▪The youth found himself *one too many.* その若者は自分がじゃま者だと思った.

(*one*) *too many for* 《口》…に勝る, の手に余る ▪Those boys are *too many for* us. あの子たちは私たちの手に余る ▪You can't rob me; I am *one too many for* you. 君なんかにゆすられるものか. 君も僕には歯が立たないからね. ☞正式には複数主語だが戯言的には単数主語にも用いる.

so many **1** 同数(の), それだけの数(の) ▪*So many* men, *so many* minds. 《諺》十人十色.
2 いくつか(の), ある数の ▪We pack *so many* apples in *so many* boxes. いくつの箱にいくつのリンゴを, というふうに詰めます.
3 そんなに多く(の) ▪Do you need *so many*? そんなにたくさんいるのですか.
4 いくらかの ▪This hall will hold only *so many* people. このホールにはそれほど多くの人は収容できない.

***so many words* [*names,* etc.]** 単語[名前, など]にすぎない ▪All those politicians were just *so many names* to him. そういう政治家たちはすべて彼にはただの名前でしかなかった.

two* [*three,* etc.] *too many 2つ[3つ, など]余計で ▪I have *two* books *too many.* 本を2冊余計に持っている.

many-headed /ménihédəd/ 形 ***the many-headed beast* [*monster*]** 《軽蔑》多頭の怪物; 民衆 (Horace, *Ep.* 1. 1. 76) ▪One loves *the many-headed beast* for a thousand reasons. 人が民衆を愛する理由は無数にある.

map /mæp/ 名 ***blow* [*bomb*] *... off the map*** (特に爆弾で)…を完全に破壊する ▪At least three enemy warships *were blown off the map.* 少なくとも3隻の敵艦が撃破された.

Do I have to draw you a map? 《口》長々と説明しなくてはならないのか ▪You want me to explain again? *Do I have to draw you a map?* もう一度説明してくれだって? また一から説明しなくてはいけないのか?

not on the map **1** 《軍口》ほとんど信じられない, ありえない ▪Your story *won't* be *on the map.* 君の話はまず信じられないね.
2 物の数に入らない ▪Why, I'm *not on the map,* my boy. だって私なんか物の数に入らないんだよ, 君.

off the map 《口》**1** 重要でない ▪Don't forget we've been *off the map* so far. 我々がこれまでずっと歯牙にもかけられなかったことを忘れてはいけない.
2 すたれた, 忘れられた ▪Cochineal insects are

practically *off the map* today. エンジムシは今日ほとんどいなくなっている.
3 (場所が)へんぴな ▪ His house is rather *off the map*. 彼の家はかなりへんぴな所にある.

put ... on the map 《口》(人・場所)をきわ立たせる, 名うてのものにする ▪ Well, this will *put* him *on the map*. やれやれ, これであいつも有名になるだろうよ.

smear** a person **all over the map 《米俗》人に乱暴[暴行]を加える ▪ A band of gangsters *smeared* him *all over the map*. ギャングの一団が彼をさんざんな目にあわせた.

survey the map 《米俗》(相手の)顔をよく見る, つらを拝む ▪ Let's *survey the map*. ひとつつらを拝ませてもらおうじゃないか.

throw a map 《米俗》吐く ▪ Somebody has *thrown a map* on the sidewalk. 誰かが歩道にげろを吐いている.

wipe ... off the map 《口》...を絶滅させる; を殺す ▪ The flood of 2005 almost *wiped* the town *off the map*. 2005年の洪水でその町はほぼ壊滅状態になった ▪ They wanted to *wipe* him *off the map*. 彼らは彼を消してしまいたいと思った.

mar /mɑːr/ 動 ***make** [**mend**] **or mar*** 成功または失敗させる (→MAKE or break) ▪ That will either *mend or mar* matters. それで事態は改善するか, 台なしになるかのどちらかだ.

marathon /mǽrəθɑ̀n|-θən/ 名 ***a marathon, not a sprint*** 勝負は長い, がまんが必要だ ▪ This issue is *a marathon, not a sprint*. この問題には忍耐がいる. ☞「短距離走ではなく, マラソン」が原義.

marble /mɑ́ːrbəl/ 名 ***(as) hard** [**cold**] **as a marble*** 石のように堅い[冷たい]; 冷酷無情な ▪ The miser was *as cold as a marble*. そのけちんぼうは石のように冷たかった.

(as) sharp as a marble 《米俗》退屈な, おもしろくない ▪ His witticism was *as sharp as a marble*. 彼のジョークは少しもおもしろくなかった.

have all** one's **marbles 《俗》頭がきれる ▪ He *has all his marbles* about him. 彼はなかなか頭がきれる. ☞marbles＝brains.

lose** one's **marbles 《英俗》発狂する ▪ The man ranted and raved as if he'd *lost his marbles*. 男は気が狂ったみたいにどなりちらした.

pick up** one's **marbles (and go home** [**leave**]**) 《主に米口》荷物をまとめてさっさと帰る; (ビジネス・政治で)負けたあと不きげんに手を引く ▪ If you don't talk to him, he will *pick up his marbles and go home*. 彼に声をかけないと, きげんを損ねて手を引くだろう. ☞「ビー玉遊びで負けそうな者が残ったビー玉を集めて持ち帰る」が原義.

March /mɑːrtʃ/ 名 ***March comes in like a lion and goes out like a lamb.*** 《諺》3月はライオンのように来て子羊のように去る《上旬は寒さが厳しく, 下旬には陽春になる》.

march[1] /mɑːrtʃ/ 名 ***line of march*** **1** 《軍》行進路 ▪ Scouts were sent out to discover the enemy's *line of march*. 敵の行進路を見つけるために斥候が出された.
2 旅路, 道 ▪ A deer crossed the *line of* our *march* without perceiving us. 1頭のシカが我々に気づかずに我々の進んで行く道を横切った.

on the march **1** 行進中で, 前進中で ▪ The regiment was *on the march*. 連隊は行進していた ▪ Industrial improvement was *on the march*. 産業改革が進行していた.
2 (危険・不快な思想等が)広く普及して ▪ Fascism might be *on the march* again in Europe. 欧州ではファシズムが再び広まるかもしれない.

***steal a march on** [**upon**]* ...よりも1日の行程をひそかに追い越す; の機先を制する, を出し抜く ▪ We must be off early and *steal a* long *march upon* them. 早めに出発して連中をうんと出し抜かなくてはならない.

march[2] /mɑːrtʃ/ 動 ***march** oneself* 《米俗》立ち去る ▪ He *marched himself* out of the room. 彼は部屋から出て行った.

march to (the beat of) a different drum** [**drummer**]*/《英》march to a different tune*** **1** 《英》周囲とは違った行動をとる, わが道を行く, 型にはまらない ▪ Most private schools *march to the beat of a different drummer*. たいていの私立学校は独自の路線を歩んでいる ▪ Never forget that Chinese companies *march to a different drummer* than American companies. 中国企業は米国企業とは異なる行動をとることを決して忘れるな.
2 人とは異なる意見をもっている ▪ Carl is *marching to a different drummer*, and he doesn't associate with us anymore. カールは人とは異なる意見の持ち主なので, もう我々とはつき合わない.

Quick march! 《号令》前へ進め ▪ You! Get out of here, *quick march!* 貴様, 出て行け, 速足進め!

marching /mɑ́ːrtʃɪŋ/ 形 ***get** one's **marching orders*** 《口》解雇される, 首になる ▪ He was absent without leave so often that he *got his marching orders*. 彼は何度も無断欠勤をしたので首になった. ☞「進発令を受ける」が原義.

give** a person his **marching orders 《口》人を首にする ▪ He is so careless that I shall be forced to *give* him *his marching orders*. 彼はとても不注意なので, やむなく首にしなければなるまい. ☞次項も参照.

marching orders **1** 《英》解雇通知, 退場処分
2 《米》指示書, 覚書 ▪ We were still waiting for our *marching orders*. 我々はその時なお指示を待っていた. ☞軍隊用語で歩兵隊に与えられる行進の距離と目的地の指令から.

mare /meər/ 名 ***a mare's nest*** (自慢していたが実は)つまらない[架空の]大発見 ▪ The scientist's discovery was *a* mere *mare's nest*. その科学者の発見は絵空ごとにすぎなかった. ☞雌馬は巣を作らないことから.

Money makes the mare to go. 《諺》地獄のさたも金次第. ☞おそらく mare /meər/ と mayor /meər/ の語呂合わせから.

M

on Shanks' mare →SHANK.

One ***shall*** [***must***] ***have*** *one's* ***mare again.*** 《諺》結局はうまく納まるだろう ▪ No news of him yet! But he *must have his mare again.* まだ彼の消息がないようだが, とどのつまりはまたうまく納まるだろう.

the gray mare 《口》亭主をしりに敷く妻 ▪ *The gray mare* is the better horse. 《諺》かかあ天下 ▪ *The gray mare* is ill to live with. 夫より偉い妻はいっしょに暮らし難い. ☞Flanders の gray mare はイギリスの最良の馬車馬よりすぐれていると考えられたことから.

Whose mare's dead? どうしたんだ (cf. Sh., *2 Hen. IV* 2. 1. 48) ▪ How now! *Whose mare's dead?* これはどういうことだ. どうしたのだ.

win the mare or lose the halter 一か八かやってみる ▪ It was a case of *win the mare or lose the halter.* それは一か八かの場合だった.

margin /mɑ́ːrdʒən/ 名 ***by a narrow margin*** かろうじて ▪ He escaped defeat *by a narrow margin.* 彼はかろうじて敗北を免れた.

go near the margin (道徳上)きわどいことをする, 危うきに近寄る ▪ A timid man, he never *goes near the margin.* 小心な男なので彼は決して危うきに近寄らない.

on the margins of ...の周辺に, に少し関わって ▪ Those needy people were *on the margins of* their society. その貧しい人々は社会の端に属していた.

Maria /mərí:ə, -ráɪə/ 名 ***a Black Maria*** 《俗》囚人護送車《容疑者を警察署へ輸送する黒塗りのバン》 ▪ The man was taken to the prison in *a Black Maria.* 男は黒塗りの護送車で刑務所へ連行された.

marine /məríːn/ 名 ***a dead marine*** 《俗》からびん ▪ We filled *a dead marine* at the watering-place. 給水所でからびんに水を詰めた.

kill a marine 《米》1本飲み干す ▪ Let's *kill a marine.* 1本空けようじゃないか.

Tell that [***it***] ***to the marines*** [《米》***horse-marines***]***!/That will do for the marines!*** 《口》そんなことを誰が信じるものか, 嘘をつけ ▪ You may *tell it to the marines!* そんな話を信じるものか ▪ Go and *tell it to the horse-marines!* 嘘ばっかり言うな! ☞horse-marines「騎馬水兵」; そんなことを信じる者は存在しない「騎馬水兵」だけだという意味から.

marjoram /mɑ́ːrdʒərəm/ 名 ***as a pig loves marjoram*** 少しも好まない ▪ How did you like him?—Well, *as a pig loves marjoram.* あの男はどうだった?—うん, 全くいやなやつだったね. ☞ブタは香草のマジョラムがきらいだという古い考えから.

mark[1] /mɑːrk/ 名 ***a black mark*** (***against*** *one*) (自分に対する)罰点, 黒星 ▪ The teacher will make *a black mark against* me for being late. 遅刻したので先生が罰点をつけるだろう.

a good [***bad***] ***mark*** 善行[悪行]点; 美[汚]点 ▪ If you don't clean the shoes before tomorrow, you'll earn *a bad mark.* あすまでに靴を磨いておかないと, 悪い点をつけられるよ.

a soft [***an easy***] ***mark*** 《口》かつがれやすい人, いいカモ ▪ The man is known to everyone around here as *an easy mark.* その男はこの辺りのみんなにいいカモだと知られている ▪ He was too *easy a mark* to succeed in Wall Street. 彼はウォール街で成功するにはおめでたすぎた.

above [***below***] ***the mark*** 標準以上[以下]で ▪ It is, if anything, rather *below* than *above the mark.* それはどちらかと言えば, 標準以上というよりも以下だ.

be a mark at 《口》...がじょうずだ ▪ He *was a mark at* A. B. C., and read me Grimm's fairy tales. 彼は本を読むのがうまく, 私にグリム童話を読んでくれた.

be first off the mark 《主に英》まっ先に行動する ▪ Dad *was first off the mark* when the Internet started. インターネットが始まったときパパはまっ先に飛びついた. ☞mark「スタートライン」.

beside [***far from, wide of***] ***the mark*** 的はずれで, 見当違いで ▪ Your comments are entirely *beside the mark.* 君の批評は全く見当違いだ ▪ You're rather *wide of the mark* there. その点は少し見当はずれですよ. ☞弓術から.

close to the mark =near the MARK.

full marks 満点, 最高の賛辞 ▪ *Full marks*! 満点だ ▪ I'll give him *full marks* for courage. 彼の勇気には満点をやりたい.

get [***be***] ***off the mark*** **1** (競走で)スタートを切る; (物事を)始める ▪ The car *got off the mark* in an inspiriting manner. 車は威勢よく発進した ▪ Ned *was off the mark* at once. ネッドはすぐ始めた.

2 《英》最初の得点をあげる ▪ They *got off the mark* with a blinding goal. 彼らは目の覚めるようなゴールで初得点をあげた. ☞mark「スタートラインの印」.

give a bad mark [***bad marks***] 酷評する, 責める ▪ You kept us waiting for an hour. We'll have to *give* you *a bad mark* for that! 我々を1時間待たせたりして, だめじゃないか!

(***God***) ***bless*** [***save***] ***the mark!*** **1** これは失礼《ひどいことを言ったときの謝罪》 ▪ My father had no more nose (*bless the mark*) than there is upon the back of my hand. 父には私の手の甲に鼻がないくらい(これは失礼)鼻というものがなかった.

2 よくもまあ, いやはや《じれったさ・軽蔑を表す》 ▪ His salary was 120 pounds a month, and, *bless the mark*, he thought it was enough to marry on. 彼の給料は月に120ポンドだったが, いやはや, それで結婚するのに十分だと思っていたのだ.

have (***got***) ***all the marks of*** ...の跡が歴然としている, であることがありありとわかる ▪ This book *has all the marks of* having been written in haste. この本は急いで書かれた跡が歴然としている.

hit [***miss***] ***the mark*** **1** 的中する[的をはずす]; (所期の)目的を達する[逸する] ▪ Many preachers *miss the mark* because they do not know men. 説教者には人間を知らないために所期の目的を達しないものが多い ▪ It was adopted as luckily *hitting the mark.* それは幸い目的を達するものとして採用された.

2 成功する ▪ She has a good voice, but her songs don't quite *hit the mark.* 彼女はよい声をしているが歌は大してうまくない. ☞弓術から.

keep *a person* ***up to the mark*** 人をよく働かせる ▪ He pledged himself to *keep* Joseph *up to the mark.* 彼はジョーゼフをよく働かせる約束をした.

leave *one's* ***mark*** 重大な影響を残す (*on, upon*) ▪ He *left his mark upon* the course of 19th century fiction writing. 彼は19世紀小説の流れに重大な影響を及ぼした.

make *one's* ***mark*** **1** 名をあげる ▪ Those verses have *made their mark.* その詩は有名になった ▪ They will surely *make their mark* in the world. 彼らはきっと世に名をあげるにちがいない.

2 (字の書けない人が)十字を書いて署名する ▪ My grandfather could not write; he *made his mark.* 祖父は字が書けないので, 十字を書いて署名した.

miss the mark →hit the MARK.

near the mark **1** 正鵠(ʼ)を得るに近い ▪ Five or six pounds per week would be *near the mark.* 週に5, 6ポンドと言えばほぼ当たっているでしょう. ☞弓術から.

2 (冗談などが)度が過ぎて ▪ She got angry because his joke came too *near the mark.* 彼の冗談は度が過ぎたので, 彼女は怒った.

of mark 〚主に限定的〛有名な, 重要な ▪ He still held a place *of* great *mark* in literature. 彼は依然として文壇で非常に重要な地位を保っていた.

off the mark **1** 全くまちがっている ▪ Whoever told you that is right *off the mark.* 誰がそれを言ったにしても全く的はずれだ.

2 《口》すぐさま ▪ He does it straight *off the mark.* 彼はたちどころにそれをやってのける.

on the [*a person's*] ***mark*** 《米俗》 **1** 用意して, 準備して ▪ He was already *on the mark.* 彼はすでに支度を調えていた.

2 きっちり目盛り通りで, 正確に ▪ It's exactly one quart, right *on the mark.* ちょうど1クォート, 目盛りきっかりだ ▪ *On your marks,* get set, go! 位置について, 用意, ドン!《競走の合図》.

over the mark **1** 高く見積もりすぎて ▪ The estimate is *over the mark.* その概算は高く見積もりすぎだ.

2 度を過ごして ▪ You've gone a bit *over the mark.* 君は少しやり過ぎたよ.

overshoot [***overstep***] ***the*** [*one's*] ***mark*** 《口》度を過ごす, 誇張する ▪ Your cunning has *overshot its mark.* 君のずるさも度が過ぎたよ ▪ He *overstepped the mark* when he said so. 彼がそう言ったのは大げさだった.

quick [***slow***] ***off the mark*** 行動するのが速い[遅い] ▪ He was very *quick off the mark* when he heard the news. 彼はそのニュースを聞くとすぐ行動を起こした. ☞競走でスタートが速い[遅い]ことから.

set *one's* ***mark on*** ...に所有の印をつける ▪ Disease *set its mark on* his wasted face. 彼のやつれた顔には病気に取りつかれている印がありありと見えた.

short of the mark 的[標準]に達しないで ▪ Gilbert's efforts to amuse her fell *short of the mark.* 彼女を楽しませせようというギルバートの努力は的に届かなかった.

the mark of Cain →the brand of CAIN.

the mark of mouth **1** (馬の年齢を示す)門歯のくぼみ ▪ The horse has lost *the mark of mouth.* その馬は門歯のくぼみがなくなっている.

2 年少の印 ▪ People often tell me I have lost *the mark of mouth.* 私は若さの印を失っているとよく言われる.

the mark of the beast 悪[異端]の印 (《聖》*Rev.* 16. 2) ▪ Anyhow you bear *the Mark of the Beast.* とにかくあなたには悪の印がついている.

toe the mark →TOE the line.

up to the mark **1** 〚主に否定文で〛標準に達して ▪ The story does not step *up to the mark.* この小説は標準以下だ.

2 〚主に否定文で〛《口》至極元気で ▪ I'm not feeling *up to the mark.* どうも元気が出ないんだ.

3 《米俗》準備[支度]ができて ▪ Bob was *up to the mark* and ready for action. ボブは準備ができていてすぐにも行動することができた. ☞弓術から.

way [《英》***well***] ***off the mark*** 的はずれで (→beside the MARK). ☞way, well は強調.

wide of the mark →beside the MARK.

within the mark 見当違いでない ▪ John was well *within the mark* at that. ジョンはそれに関してあまり見当違いではなかった.

mark[2] /mɑːrk/ 動 ***a marked man*** 敵にねらわれている人 ▪ I found myself *a marked man.* 自分が敵にねらわれているとわかった.

be marked for (結果)を保証されているようだ ▪ So far he has *been marked for* success. これまでは彼は成功を保証されてきたようだ.

mark *a person* ***for life*** 人に一生跡の残るような傷を負わせる ▪ I'll *mark* him *for life* if he betrays me. 彼がわしを裏切ったら一生傷が残るようにしてやる.

mark time **1** 《軍》足踏みをする ▪ My troops had to *mark time* while his men passed by. 彼の隊が通過する間, わが隊は待機していなくてはならなかった.

2 一時停頓する, ぐずぐずしている ▪ The U.N. Assembly *marked time* on Palestine. 国連総会はパレスチナ問題について態度をはっきりさせなかった.

mark with a white stone →mark ... with a WHITE stone.

Mark you! いいかい; でもね ▪ He's very rich. *Mark you,* he's stingy. 彼は大金持ちだよ. でもね, けちなんだ. ☞you は主語.

(***You***) ***mark my words.*** さあよくお聞き《強意的予言》 ▪ *Mark my words,* he will never be appointed to that position. いいかね, 彼は決してその地位に任命されはしないさ.

marker /mάːrkər/ 名 ***not a marker to*** [***on***] 《米俗》...とは比較にならない ▪ What I've told you *isn't a marker to* other things he said. 私が教えてあげたことは彼が言ったほかのこととは比較になりませんよ.

M

put down a marker 自分の能力や将来の目標を明確に示す ▪ You've got a chance to *put down a marker* in the next game. 君は次の試合で実力を発揮するチャンスがある.

market /mɑ́ːrkət/ 名 ***a buyer's [seller's] market*** 買い手[売り手]市場 ▪ In *a buyer's market* prices are low, while in *a seller's market* prices are high. 買い手市場では価格は安く, 売り手市場では価格は高い ▪ I can't afford to buy a house at the moment. It's *a seller's market*. いまは家を買う余裕はないよ. だって売り手市場なんだもの.

a meat [《英》***cattle***] ***market*** 《米》女性が美しさのみで品定めされる状況, セックスの相手を探す場 ▪ The parade of beautiful girls was rightly called *a cattle market*. 美少女のパレードはまさしく商品展示会といった風情だった ▪ That nightclub is a real *meat market*. あのナイトクラブはまさにセックスパートナー探しの場だ.

at the market 《株式》市価で《仲買人が委託された株を求める場合に言う》 ▪ They sold those warrants *at the market*. 彼らはその債権を市価で売った.

be back on the market 《米俗》(女性が)もはや決まった恋人を持っていない ▪ I'*m back on the market*, boys! 君たち! 私はもう前の恋人とは別れているのよ.

bring *one's* ***eggs*** [***hogs***] ***to a bad*** [***the wrong***] ***market*** 見込み違いをする ▪ He'd be *bringing his eggs to a bad market* if he came to us. 彼が我々のところへ来るなら, 見込み違いだろうよ.

bring *one's* ***hogs to a fair*** [***fine***] ***market*** →HOG[1].

bring ... to market ...を市場[売物]に出す《比喩的にも》 ▪ They seldom wait to mature a proposition, but *bring* it *to market* in the green ear. 彼らはめったに計画の熟するのを待たないで, 未熟なままで提出する.

come into [***onto***] ***the market*** 市場に出る, 販売される ▪ These new products will *come into the market* soon. この新製品はじき市販される予定だ.

corner the market 株[商品]を買い占める ▪ Some speculators *cornered the market*. 何人かの相場師が株を買い占めた.

drive *one's* ***hogs to market*** →HOG[1].

engross [***forestall***] ***the market*** (高く売るために)買い占めをやる ▪ Edicts were issued against *engrossing the market*. 買い占めを禁ずる布告が公布された.

feed ... to market (家畜)を市場に出すために飼育する ▪ These sheep *are* specially *fed to market*. これらの羊は特に市場に出すために飼育されている.

find a market はけ口がある ▪ British makes would probably *find a market*. イギリス製品はたぶんはけ口があるだろう.

flood the market (商品が)市場を氾濫させる ▪ Nowadays cars *flood the market*. 現在, 車が市場にあふれている.

go badly to market 買い損をする ▪ They had finally *gone badly to market*. 彼らはとうとう買い損をしてしまった.

go to a good [***bad***] ***market*** うまく行く[行かない] ▪ We went on a boat trip over to an island and we *went to a good market*. 我々は船である島に渡ってうまく行った.

go to market **1** (市場へ)買い物に行く ▪ Mother has *gone to market*. 母は買い物に行っています.
2 《口》事を企てる, やってみる ▪ The horse mightn't have *gone to market* at all. その馬は全く何もしなかったかもしれない.

hold the market (買い占めなどで)市場を左右する ▪ They *hold the market* by offering goods cheaply. 彼らは品を安く提供して市場を左右している.

in the market for (人が)...の買い方で ▪ He is *in the market for* some cattle. 彼は牛を数頭求めている.

lose *one's* ***market*** 売買の機を逸する ▪ He did not want to *lose his market* by sticking to the market price. 彼はそれを市価で買うことに固執して買う機会を失いたくなかった.

make a market 《株式》(ほぼ同じ値で売り手と買い手の2役を務めて)から景気をつける, (競売などによって)人気をあおる ▪ The next question will relate to the old abuse of *making a market*. 次の問題はから景気をつけるという古くからの悪弊にかかわりがある.

make *one's* ***market*** 在荷をさばく, 取引をすます《比喩的にも》 ▪ I *made my market* long before it was night. 夜になるずっと前に私は在荷をさばいた.

mar *a person's* [*one's*] ***market*** 人[自分]の商売を台なしにする《比喩的にも》 ▪ If they had not tried to eliminate his bad habit, he would have *marred his* own *market*. 彼らが彼の悪癖を除こうと努めなかったら, 彼は自分を台なしにしてしまっただろう.

mend *one's* ***market*** 取引を有利にする ▪ If she should marry Tom, she would *mend her market*. 万一トムと結婚すれば, 彼女はよい取引をすることになるだろう.

miss *one's* ***market*** (娘が)婚期を逸する ▪ She warned her daughter that she would *miss her market*. 彼女は娘に婚期を逸してしまうと注意した.

off the market 《米俗》婚約して ▪ She is already *off the market*. 彼女はもう婚約している.

on the market (物が)売買されて ▪ His estate is now *on the market*. 彼の地所はいま売りに出ている.

on the open market (自由に)市販されて, 売りに出されて, 誰でも入手できる ▪ Farmers are selling their crops *on the open market* at record prices. 農場主たちは作物を記録的な高値で売っている ▪ These items are freely available *on the open market*. これらの品目は誰でも自由に求められる.

overstand *one's* ***market*** 値段を譲らずに売りそこなう ▪ What madman *overstands his market* twice? どこのばかが二度も値段を譲らずに売りそこなうようなことをするものか.

play the market 相場をやる ▪ Pleasant manner and intelligence are necessary in *playing the market*. あいそのよい態度と頭のよさが相場をやるのには必要だ.

price** A **out of the market →PRICE oneself out of the market.

put ... back on the market 《米俗》(恋人)を捨てる, 振る ▪ He coldly *put* her *back on the market*. 彼は冷たく彼女を捨てた.

put* [*place*]*... in* [*on*] *the market …を売り物に出す ▪ He *placed* his house *on the market*. 彼は家を売り物に出した.

put ... into market …を売買の問題にする ▪ The good and the evil of trade is that it would *put* everything *into market*. あらゆる物を売った買ったですませるのが, 商売のよいところでもあり悪いところでもある.

raid the market 相場を狂わせる ▪ Automated online trading *raided the market* that day. その日はオートメーション化されたオンライン取引が相場を狂わせた.

raise the market upon …に高値を吹っかける ▪ He had gone too far in *raising the market upon* Jim. 彼はジムにあまりにも極端に高値を吹っかけすぎた.

rig the market 《俗》(人為的に)相場を操る ▪ We must *rig the market*. Buy up every share that's offered. 相場を操らなければならない. 売りに出されている株を全部買い占めてこい.

the pink market とくに同性愛者の男女向けの市場[商品] ▪ *The pink market* focuses on the needs of gay and lesbian customers. ピンク市場はゲイやレズの顧客のニーズに的を絞っている.

marking /mɑ́ːrkɪŋ/ 名 ***blind marking*** 所属がわからない試験官による答案の採点 ▪ Using double-*blind marking* is a more objective and reliable system. 所属不詳の試験官による二重採点方式の方が客観性があり信頼がおける.

marriage /mǽrɪdʒ/ 名 ***a broken marriage*** 夫婦が離婚[離別]した結婚, 破綻(はたん)した結婚生活 ▪ She has two young children from *a broken marriage*. 彼女は別れた夫との間にできた二人の幼子を抱えている.

a marriage of convenience (愛情によらない)政略結婚 ▪ Love can result from *a marriage of convenience*. 政略結婚からでも愛が生じることはある. ☞ F mariage de convenance のなぞり.

an open marriage 配偶者以外との肉体関係が認められた結婚生活, 自由結婚 ▪ *The open marriage* arrangement they had didn't work out too well. 彼らの自由結婚協定はあまりうまくいかなかった ▪ Do they have *an open marriage*? Who are her other lovers? あの夫婦は自由結婚だって? 彼女のほかの相手は誰だ.

defile* [*violate*] *the marriage-bed 不倫をする ▪ He has never *defiled the marriage-bed*. 彼は一度も不倫をしたことがない.

give* [*take*]*... in marriage (人)を嫁または夫にやる[迎える] ▪ He *gave* his daughter *in marriage* to a foreigner. 彼は外国人に娘を嫁がせた ▪ He *took* her *in marriage*. 彼は彼女を妻にめとった.

in the marriage market 《俗》結婚にふさわしい ▪ The girl was *in the marriage market* by virtue of her father's wealth. その娘は父親の財産のおかげで売れ口があった.

marriage lines 結婚証明書 ▪ You can open up accounts with a copy of the *marriage lines*. 結婚証明書の写しがあれば口座を開くことができる.

Marriages are made in heaven. 《諺》誰が誰と結婚することになるかは誰にも予想できない.

violate the marriage-bed → defile the MARRIAGE-bed.

marrow /mǽroʊ/ 名 ***chill** a person's **marrow*** =freeze a person's BLOOD.

the pith and marrow of →PITH.

***to the marrow* (*of* one's *bones*)** 骨の髄まで, 徹底的に ▪ I'm chilled *to the marrow* waiting on this platform. このプラットホームで待っていて骨の髄まで冷えてしまった ▪ He is an aristocrat *to the very marrow of his bones*. 彼は生粋の貴族だ.

marrowbone /mǽroʊbòʊn/ 名 ***bring** a person **to his marrowbones*** 《口・戯》人を打ちすえる, 屈服させる ▪ We should *bring* the guy *to his marrowbones*. あんなやつはやっつけてやるべきだ.

get* [*go*] *down to* one's *marrowbones 《口・戯》ひざまずく; わびを言う ▪ You'll have to *go down to your marrowbones* before he'll forgive you. 彼が赦してくれる前にわびを入れねばなるまい.

marry[1] /mǽri, méri/ 名 ***be on the marry*** 《米俗》配偶者を探す ▪ She's intently *on the marry*. 彼女は一生懸命に配偶者を探している.

off the marry 《米俗》離婚して ▪ He is *off the marry* again. 彼はまた離婚した.

marry[2] /mǽri, méri/ 動 ***be* [*get*] *married to*** …と結婚している[する] ▪ I *got married to* Sally. 私はサリーと結婚した.

be married with …と結びついている ▪ The author's intellect *is married with* sensibility. その作家の知性は感性と結びついている.

married but not churched 《俗》(結婚しないで)同棲して ▪ The young couple are *married but not churched*. その若い二人は同棲している.

marry a fortune 金持ちの妻をもらう ▪ I wish I could *marry a fortune*. 金持ちの女性と結婚できたらなあ.

marry a woman from off the street 街の女と結婚する ▪ He *married a woman from off the street* out of pity. 彼はあわれみから街の女と結婚した.

marry above** one* [*oneself, one's **station] 《文》(自分より)身分の高い者と結婚する ▪ He wanted to *marry above his station*. 彼は自分より身分の高い人との結婚を望んだ.

marry beneath** one* [*oneself, one's **station] 《文》身分の下の者と結婚する ▪ My daughter wants to *marry beneath* her. 娘は身分の下の者と結婚したがっている ▪ The Duke *married beneath*

M

himself. 公爵は身分の下の者と結婚した.

marry for convenience (愛情からではなく)政略結婚をする ▪ In those days people often *married for convenience.* 当時はよく政略結婚をした.

marry in and in 血族結婚する ▪ The *marrying in and in* of the same family tends to mental or functional disorder. 同じ一族内で近親結婚をすると, 心身機能障害が生じがちだ.

marry out of meeting 《米口》(クェーカー教徒が)信徒でない者と結婚する ▪ The Quaker is not permitted to *marry out of meeting.* クェーカー教徒は信徒でない者と結婚することを許されていない.

marry over the broomstick → BROOMSTICK.

marry with the left hand 身分の低い女性と結婚する ▪ He chose to *marry with the left hand.* 彼は身分の低い女性と結婚することにした. ☞a left-handed marriage (身分違いの結婚)の式で男が左手を出すドイツの風習から.

not be the marrying kind 《戯》結婚しそうにない[したがらない]タイプである ▪ He has a girlfriend, but he's *not the marrying kind.* 彼にはガールフレンドはいるが結婚したがらないタイプだ.

marry[3] /mǽri/ 間 ***Marry come up!*** 〚間投詞的に〛まさか, 何だと《不賛成・不信を表す》 ▪ *Marry come up*, you saucy jade! 何だと, この生意気なあばずれめ.

martial /mɑ́ːrʃəl/ 形 ***under martial law*** 戒厳令下に ▪ The city is now *under martial law.* その市は今戒厳令下にある.

Martin /mɑ́ːrtən|-tɪn/ 名 ***Martin drunk*** 泥酔して ▪ He is *Martin drunk* at this moment. 彼は今泥酔している.

martyr /mɑ́ːrtər/ 名 ***be a martyr to*** 《戯》(痛風など)に絶えず苦しんでいる ▪ He has *been a martyr to* his wife's appalling temper for the past ten years. 彼はここ10年来妻の恐ろしいかんしゃくに絶えず苦しんできた.

make a martyr of …を犠牲にする, 苦しめる ▪ He means to *make a martyr of* this man. 彼はこの男を犠牲にするつもりでいる.

***make a martyr of** oneself* 《しばしば戯》(信用を得るために)殉教者ぶる, 犠牲的なふるまいをする ▪ Please don't *make a martyr of yourself* for my sake. どうか私のために殉教者ぶるのはよしてくれ.

marvel /mɑ́ːrvəl/ 名 ***be a marvel of*** 驚くべき…である ▪ He *is a marvel of* learning. 彼は驚くべき学者だ ▪ The house *was a marvel of* neatness. その家は驚くほどこざっぱりしていた.

work marvels (薬などが)驚くほどよく効く ▪ These injections *work marvels.* この注射は驚くほどよく効く.

Mary /méəri/ 名 ***little Mary*** 《口》腹, おなか ▪ My *little Mary* is feeling uncommonly empty. おなかがものすごくすいてしまった. ☞J. M. Barrie の戯曲 *Little Mary* (1903)から.

mash[1] /mæʃ/ 名 ***have a mash on*** 《俗》…にほれている ▪ I certainly *have a mash on* her. 私は確かに彼女にほれている.

make a mash on 《俗》…に言い寄る ▪ He tried to *make a mash on* me. 彼は私に言い寄ろうとした.

make** one's **mash 《俗》恋人ができる, 首ったけにほれられる ▪ Don't be so particular about your dress. You have *made your mash.* そう服装に凝らなくていい. もう首ったけにほれられているのだから.

on the mash 《俗》いつも女性に言い寄って ▪ That fellow was always *on the mash.* その男はいつも女をくどいてばかりいた.

mash[2] /mæʃ/ 名 ***to*** [***in***] ***mash*** ぐたぐたになるまで ▪ She has beaten me *to mash.* 彼女は私をふらふらになるまで打った.

mash[3] /mæʃ/ 動 ***be*** [***get***] ***mashed on*** 《俗》…にほれている[ほれる] ▪ I'*m* not one bit *mashed on* her. 僕はこれっぽっちも彼女にほれてはいない.

mask /mæsk|mɑːsk/ 名 ***let the mask slip*** ちらっと偽らざる感情を見せる, うっかり本心を覗(のぞ)かせる ▪ When her rival failed, she *let the mask slip* and gave a little smile. ライバルが失敗すると, 彼女はつい本心を覗かせて, ちらと笑みをこぼした.

put on [***assume, wear***] ***the mask*** (***of***) (…の)仮面をかぶる, 正体や本心を隠す ▪ Successful politicians have to train themselves to *put on the mask.* 政治家として成功するには本心を隠すように修養しなくてはならない.

throw off [***drop, pull off***] ***the mask*** (***of***) (…の)仮面を脱ぐ, 正体を表す ▪ Last night he *threw off the mask.* ゆうべ彼は正体を表した.

under the mask of …の仮面をかぶって, にかこつけて ▪ He has undone me *under the mask of* friendship. 彼は友情にかこつけて私を零落させた.

mass[1] /mæs/ 名 ***by the mass*** 神かけて, 確かに ▪ I did not do it, *by the mass.* 私は誓ってそんなことはしなかった.

say masses for** a person's **soul 人の霊のためにミサを行う ▪ *Masses were said for my father's soul.* 父の霊のためにミサが行われた.

serve mass 《カトリック》ミサで伴僧を務める ▪ He *served mass* on Sunday. 彼は日曜日にはミサで伴僧を務めた.

mass[2] /mæs/ 名 ***be a mass of*** …だらけだ《誇張表現》 ▪ He *is a mass of* bruises. 彼は打ち身だらけだ ▪ This model *is a mass of* faults. この型は欠点だらけだ.

in a mass ひとまとめにして ▪ I prefer to receive any sum *in a mass.* 私はどんな金額でも耳をそろえてもらうほうが好きだ ▪ They interview *in a mass,* not one person at a time. 面接は個別ではなく集団で行われる.

in the mass ひっくるめて; 総体で ▪ We shouldn't condemn millions *in the mass* as cruel. 何百万という人を十把一からげに残忍だと決めつけてはならない.

the (***great***) ***mass of*** …の大部分 ▪ We cannot expect *the mass of* mankind to become disinterested. 我々は人間の大部分が公平になることを期待

することはできない.

massage /məsɑ́ːʒ|mǽsɑːʒ/ 動 ***massage*** *a person's* ***ego*** 人の自尊心をくすぐる, をおだてる ▪ Do not *massage another person's ego*. 他人の自尊心はくすぐらないことだ.

mast /mæst|mɑːst/ 名 (***at***) ***half mast*** → HALF-MAST.

before [***afore***] ***the mast*** 《海》平水夫として ▪ Once an earl became a sailor *before the mast*. かつて伯爵が平水夫になったことがあった ▪ He served *before the mast* in his youth. 彼は若いときに水夫として働いた. ☞水夫は前檣の前の forecastle に起居するところから.

nail *one's* ***colors to the mast*** →COLOR.

master /mǽstər|mɑ́ːs-/ 名 ***a master of ceremonies/an M.C./an emcee*** 司会者, 進行役 ▪ He was the *M.C.* of many memorable shows. 彼は多くの著名なショーの司会役を務めた.

a past master 大家, 名人 (*in, of*) ▪ He was *a past master in* the art. 彼はその技術の大家であった ▪ He is *a past master of* irony. 彼は皮肉の名人だ.

be master 好きなようにふるまえる ▪ Would you join us at the party? You *are master*. パーティーにいっしょに行きませんか. お好きなようになさって結構です. ☞Ⓕ être maître のなぞり.

(***be***) ***master in*** *one's* ***own house*** 他人に干渉されずに自分のことをやる ▪ He makes clear to us that he remains *master in his own house*. 彼は相変わらず干渉されずに自分のことをやるということを我々にはっきりさせている.

be master of **1** …を所有している ▪ I *was master of* more than twenty pounds. 20ポンド以上の金を持っていました.

2 …を自由にしうる ▪ He *is master of* the situation. 彼が局面を左右している.

3 …に通じている ▪ He *is master of* several languages. 彼は数か国語に通じている.

be master of *oneself* おのれに勝つ, 落ち着いている ▪ He *was* absolute *master of himself* under fire. 彼は砲火を受けても泰然としていた.

be *one's* ***own master*** 思う通りにできる ▪ He *is* not *his own master*. 彼は思い通りにはできていない.

get [***be***] ***the master of*** 《口》…を支配する ▪ You cannot *be the master of* your fate. 君は運命を支配することはできない.

his [***her,*** etc.] ***master's voice*** 主人・権力者の声 ▪ The girl came running at *her master's voice*. その少女は主人の声を聞くと走ってやってきた. ☞ロンドンのレコード会社の商標から.

make *oneself* ***master of*** …に熟達する ▪ He has *made himself master of* an art. 彼は一芸をきわめている.

serve two masters 二君に仕える《金と神など》(《聖》*Matt.* 6. 24); 異なる二つの考えに従う ▪ Can you *serve two masters* at the same time? 同時に二君に仕えることができますか ▪ One cannot efficiently *serve two masters*. 人はうまく二人の主人に仕えることはできない.

mastery /mǽstəri|mɑ́ːs-/ 名 ***get*** [***have***] ***mastery of*** [***over***] …を支配する ▪ He *got mastery of* the wild horse. 彼はそのあばれ馬をうまく乗りこなした ▪ He *has mastery over* the laborers. 彼は労働者たちを掌握している.

get [***gain, obtain***] ***the mastery*** 覇権を握る; 勝つ ▪ We *gained the mastery* of the enemy. 我々は敵に打ち勝った.

mat /mæt/ 名 ***go to the mat*** 《米俗》議論する, あげつらう ▪ I *went to the mat* with them. 私は彼らと議論した.

leave *a person* ***on the mat*** 人に玄関払いをくわせる ▪ I hated the sight of him, and *left* him *on the mat*. 私は彼の顔を見るのもいやだったので, 玄関払いをくわせてやった.

on the mat 罰せられて, 審問を受けて ▪ I expect I'm *on the mat* for something or other. どうやら何かで罰をくわされるらしい. ☞《軍俗》告発された兵士が中隊事務室のマットの中央に立たされたことから; →on the CARPET.

take ... to the mat 《米口》…と論争する ▪ I *took* him *to the mat* on that issue. その問題で彼と論争した. ☞レスリングから.

match[1] /mætʃ/ 名 ***a shouting match*** 怒鳴り合い ▪ The debate turned into *a shouting match*. 討論は怒鳴り合いに進展した.

a slanging [***slinging***] ***match*** 《英》大声での喧嘩, 怒鳴り合い, 中傷合戦 ▪ Two young women went into *a* sharp *slanging match*. 二人の若い女性が罵(のの)しり合いの激論をやりはじめた ▪ The debate deteriorated into *a* most furious *slinging match*. 論争が悪化して実にひどい口論になった.

be a good match よい配偶者である ▪ He [She] will *be a good match*. 彼[彼女]はよい配偶者になるだろう.

be a [***no***] ***match for*** …と匹敵できる[できない] ▪ He will *be a match for* them and all their tricks. 彼は彼らやそのたくらみのすべてに対抗できるだろう ▪ I *am no match for* you. 君にはとてもかなわない.

be more than a match for …よりうわ手だ ▪ Cromwell *was more than a match for* his foes. クロムウェルは彼の敵より強かった.

get into a pissing match (***with***) 《口》(…と)競り合う ▪ I never wanted to *get into a pissing match with* you. 君と張り合う気は全くなかったのだが.

into matches こっぱみじんに ▪ The big mirror in the hall was shattered *into matches* by a bullet. 広間の大鏡は弾丸で粉みじんに砕けた.

make a match **1** 結婚を成立させる ▪ He *made a* good *match* for his daughter. 彼は娘に良縁を得させた.

2 結婚をする ▪ Both her daughters *made* good *matches*. 彼女の娘は二人とも良縁を得た.

make a match of it (二人が)結婚する ▪ At last

M

they *made a match of it.* とうとう二人は結婚した.

meet [***find***] *one's* ***match*** 好敵手に会う ▪ He never *met his match.* 彼はまだ誰にも負けたことがない.

put [***place***] ***a match to*** …にマッチで火をつける ▪ *Put a match to* the firewood. 薪(まき)にマッチで火をつけなさい.

the (***whole***) ***shooting match*** 《口》一切がっさい, 何もかも ▪ The manager runs *the whole shooting match.* 支配人が一切がっさいを取りしきっている. ☞shooting match「射撃競技会」.

match[2] /mætʃ/ 動 ***to match*** よく似合う, 調和する ▪ She wore a dress trimmed with braid *to match.* 彼女は釣り合うモールで飾ったドレスを着ていた.

matchwood /mǽtʃwòd/ 名 ***into matchwood*** 粉みじんに ▪ The huts tumbled *into matchwood.* 小屋は崩れてこっぱみじんになった.

make matchwood of/ reduce … to matchwood (物)をこっぱみじんにする ▪ The thunderbolt *reduced* the hut *to matchwood.* 落雷で小屋はこっぱみじんになった.

mate /meɪt/ 名 ***give*** (***the***) ***mate to*** …を王手詰めにする ▪ I *give* you *mate to* your white king. あなたの白のキングを王手詰めにしますよ.

go mates with …の仲間になる, と組み合う ▪ I will accept his proposal to *go mates with* him. 私は彼と手を組もうという提案を受けいれるつもりだ.

matter[1] /mǽtər/ 名 ***a matter of*** **1** …の問題; に左右されて ▪ It's only *a matter of* time before he dies. 彼が死ぬのはもう時間の問題だ ▪ Doing anything well is all *a matter of* practice. 何事をこなすのも全く練習次第だ.

2 [[数詞を伴って]] およそ… ▪ We traded for *a matter of* ten years. 約10年間商売した.

3 わずかな… ▪ It only cost us *a matter of* a few pounds. それはほんの2, 3ポンドほどしかかからなかった ▪ She got well in *a matter of* days. 彼女はわずか2, 3日でよくなった.

a matter of concern [***interest***] 関心事 ▪ Education is *a matter of* national *concern.* 教育は国家的関心事だ.

(***a matter of***) ***life and*** [***or***] ***death*** →LIFE.

a matter of record 《法》(法廷における)記録事項, 明らかな事実, 動かせない事実 ▪ All that is *a matter of record.* それらすべては明白な事実だった ▪ It then became *a matter of record*, and could not be impeached. それはやがて動かせない事実となったので疑うことはできなかった.

as a matter of course もちろん, 当然 ▪ The innocents were acquitted *as a matter of course.* 罪のない人々はもちろん放免された.

(***as a*** [***in***]) ***matter of fact*** (とは言うものの)実際のところ, 実は ▪ *As a matter of fact*, you are quite right. 実は全く君の言う通りだ ▪ *Matter of fact*, you've hit it. 実際その通りだ.

as a matter of form →FORM[1]

as near as no matter 《口》すんでのところで ▪ My brother was killed *as near as no matter.* 兄はすんでのところで命を落とすところだった.

be only a matter of time いずれ確実に起こる, もうまもなくだ (→a MATTER of) ▪ It's *only a matter of time* before we start to take a trip to the moon. 月世界旅行ももう時間の問題だ.

be the matter 問題である, 困ったことだ, 誤っている ▪ What *is the matter*? You don't look well—Nothing. I'm just a little under the weather. どうしたの? 顔色がさえないけど—いや, ちょっと二日酔い気味でね.

for that matter その事では, それについては ▪ Few students, or adults, *for that matter*, have ever thought of it. それに考えを向けた学生は, いや, その点ではおとなも, 少ししかいなかった.

in the matter of …の件については, に関しては ▪ He is strict *in the matter of* discipline. 彼はしつけに関しては厳格だ.

Is (***there***) ***anything the matter with …?*** …はどうかしたのか ▪ *Is* (*there*) *anything the matter with* the engine? エンジンがどうかしたのですか.

it is [***makes***] ***no matter*** 何でもない, どうでもよい ▪ *It's no matter* whether they get married or not. 二人が結婚しようがしまいが, そんなことはどうでもよい ▪ *It is* [*makes*] *no matter* what happens. 何が起ころうとかまわない.

it's boloney [***bologna, baloney***], ***no matter how thin you slice it*** 《口》どう考えてみても全く理屈に合わない ▪ This religious belief *is baloney, no matter how thin you slice it.* どう見てもこの宗教的信念はナンセンスだ. ☞bologna「ボローニャソーセージ」から.

let the matter drop [***rest***] その問題を打ち切る ▪ We had better *let the matter rest.* この件は打ち切った方がいい.

make a matter から騒ぎする ▪ It is a pity that you should *make* such *a matter.* 君がそんなに大騒ぎするとは残念だ.

matter-of-fact **1** 事実だけ, 感情をはさまず割り切った ▪ She told us the bad news in a very *matter-of-fact* way. 彼女はその悪い知らせを感情抜きで伝えた.

2 冷静な, 感情を見せない ▪ My uncle was a very *matter-of-fact* person. 叔父は実に冷静な人だった.

no matter 《文》気にするな ▪ It's raining, but *no matter.* I'll go for a walk anyway. 雨が降っているが大したことはない. どっちみち散歩に出かけるよ.

no matter who [***what,*** etc.] たとえ…でも ▪ It is not true, *no matter who* may say so. たとえ誰がそう言おうと本当ではない ▪ She goes out jogging *no matter what* the weather is like. 彼女はどんな天候でもジョギングに出かける ▪ I'll do it, *no matter how.* どんな方法ででもそうしてみせる. ☞it doesn't matter の短縮された形式.

something [***nothing***] ***is the matter with/ there is*** [*one* ***has***] ***something*** [***nothing***] ***the matter with*** …はどうかしている[どうもしていな

い] ▪ *Something* must *be the matter with* him. 彼はどうかしているのにちがいない ▪ *There is nothing the matter with* his throat. 彼ののどはどうもなっていない ▪ He must *have something the matter with* his feet. 彼は足をどうかしているのにちがいない.

take matters into *one's* ***own hands*** (責任者が対応してくれないので)自分で事を運ぶ ▪ He likes to *take matters into his own hands* without consulting his chief. 彼は上司と相談しないで自分で事を運びたがる.

the crux [***heart***] ***of the matter*** 問題の核心 ▪ The bloodstains represent *the crux of the matter* in this trial. この公判では血痕が問題の核心になっている.

the fact [***truth***] (***of the matter***) ***is...*** → FACT; the TRUTH is (that).

the gray matter 脳みそ, 頭脳, 知力 ▪ Use your *gray matter* and think what will happen next. 頭を使って次はどうなるか考えなさい.

the matter in [《米》***at***] ***hand*** 《文》当面の問題 ▪ It has nothing to do with *the matter in hand.* それは当面の問題には何の関わり合いもない.

the small [***little***] ***matter of...*** 《口・戯》ちょっとした..., 小さからぬ...《反語的な強調》 ▪ It could be *the small matter of* your kid not being able to tie his own shoes. それはあなたのお子さんが自分の靴ひもも結べないという小さからぬ問題かもしれません.

What is the matter with...? **1** ...はどうしたのか ▪ *What is the matter with* your finger? 君は指をどうしたのですか ▪ I don't know *what is the matter with* me. 自分がどうなったのかわからない.
2《戯》...でかまわないではないか ▪ You don't like that book? *What is the matter with* it? その本がいやだって. それでいいじゃないか.

What matter...? かまわないではないか ▪ But *what matter* from whom I heard this? しかし, この話を誰から聞いたとしてもいいじゃないか.

What's the matter with you? お前はどうしたんだ《強いいらだち》 ▪ *What's the matter with you?* Have you lost your mind? お前はどうしたんだ. 気は確かか.

matter[2] /mǽtər/ 動 ***it matters much*** 大いに重大である ▪ *It matters much* to character where a man is born. 出生地は性格にとって大いに重要だ.

it matters nothing [***little***] 全然[ほとんど]重大でない ▪ *It matters little* [*nothing*] to me who is elected. 誰が当選しても私にはあまり[全然]問題ではない.

not matter a damn [《卑》***bugger, fuck***] てんで問題ではない ▪ It does*n't matter a damn* whether he admits it or not. 彼がそのことを認めようと認めまいと, てんで問題ではない.

Not that it matters [***mattered***]. (前述の内容を受けて)だからといって大したことではない[なかった] ▪ Made in Russia? *Not that it matters*—just curious. ロシア製だって? だからといって大したことではないが, ただ珍しい.

What does it matter (...)? それがどうしたというのだ《大したことではない》 ▪ *What does it matter* how old musicians are? 音楽家が何歳であろうとそれがどうしたというのだ ▪ *What does it matter* what they say? 彼らが何を言おうとどうでもいいじゃないか ▪ I'm only one person. *What does it matter* if I help the poor? 私は一人の人に過ぎない. 私一人が貧乏な人々を助けてどうなるというのか. ☞What は副詞.

What matters? かまわないではないか ▪ *What matters* if we are late? 遅れたってかまわんじゃないか.

mature /mətʊ́ər|-tʃʊ́ə, -tjʊə/ 形 ***on mature reflection*** [***consideration***] 《文》熟考した上で, じっくり考えて ▪ He wanted to run for governor, but *on mature reflection* he decided not to. 彼は知事に立候補したかったが, よく考えてからよすことにした.

max /mæks/ 名 ***grody to the max*** 《米》全くひどい, ひどく悪い ▪ Ugh! This burger is *grody to the max.* ゲッ! このハンバーガーはひどいや. ☞grody は恐らく grotesque「異様な」を, to the max は to the maximum「最高の程度まで」をもじったものである.

to the max 《米口》最高に, 完璧に, 徹底的に ▪ The restaurant was packed *to the max.* レストランは満員の入りだった.

maximum /mǽksəməm/ 名 ***to the maximum*** 最大限に ▪ Most surface-water resources are used *to the maximum.* 地表水資源のほとんどは極限まで使われている.

May /meɪ/ 名 ***May and January*** [***December***] 若い女と年とった男の結婚 ▪ Does nothing good ever happen when *January* weds *May*? 老人が若い女性と結婚すると, 何も良いことは起こらないのか.

may /meɪ/ 助 ***as best*** *one* ***may*** できるだけ, どうかこうか ▪ I will try to deserve that happiness *as best* I *may.* できるだけその幸福に値するように努めよう.

do ***as*** *one* ***may*** どんなに...しても ▪ Run *as* I *might* I could not overtake him. どんなに走っても, 彼に追いつけなかった.

be that as [***what***] ***it may*** 《文》いずれにせよ, それはとにかく (however that may be) ▪ *Be that as it may,* always speak the truth. いずれにせよ, いつも本当のことを言いなさい.

come what may 何事があろうとも ▪ *Come what may,* I shall never change my mind. どんな事があっても, 決心は変えないぞ.

I may say [***add***]... ...と言える[つけ加えられる]でしょう ▪ Of course, *I may say* that nobody likes separatists, nowhere. もちろん, どこにも分離主義者が好きな人はいないと言えるでしょう ▪ We are, *I may add,* old settlers here. 付言しますが, 我々は当地に昔から住んでいる者です.

if I may 《文》もしよろしければ ▪ Let me just continue then, *if I may.* それで, もしよければ, 続けさせてください.

if I may say so/if I may be so bold 《文》

このような言い方をお許しいただければ ▪ Engineers, *if I may say so*, have their own way of working. 技師たちは，こう言っては何ですが，好きなように仕事を進めます ▪ What was your cup size, *if I may be so bold*? 胸のサイズはいくらでしたかしら，失礼でなければ．

may as well** do* (as not***) →WELL[2].

(***so***) ***that*** *one* ***may*** →(so, in order) THAT one may.

That's as (***it***) ***may be.*** それはそうかもしれない ▪ I'm told he has resigned.—*That's as may be.* 彼は辞職したそうだ—そうかもしれない(がまだはっきりせぬ)．

maybe /méɪbi/ 副 ***and I don't mean maybe*** 《口》これは本気だぞ ▪ You'd better go to bed, *and I don't mean maybe*! 寝た方がいい，これは本気だぞ．

as soon as maybe 《口》できるだけ早く ▪ I'll be back *as soon as maybe*. できるだけ早く戻ってくるよ．

may-day /méɪdèɪ/ 名 ***a may-day warning*** 国際無線救難信号 ▪ In the cockpit sounded *a may-day warning* over the radio. 無線を通じて SOS が操縦席に響いた．☞may-day は May「5月」には関係なく，Help me を意味するフランス語の国際信号 M'aider の英語なまり．

maze /meɪz/ 名 ***be in a maze*** 途方にくれている ▪ His mind *was in a maze*. 彼の心は途方にくれていた．

me /mi, miː/ 代 ***Me***(,) ***too.*** 《口》(相手の言葉に対して)私も(そうです) ▪ "I'll pray for you," Mom said. "*Me too,*" I said.「あなたのために祈るわ」とママが言った.「私も」と私は言った ▪ I love you.—*Me too.* 愛しているわ—ぼくもだ．☞否定形は Me, neither ▪ I'm not cold.—*Me neither.* 寒くはない—私もよ．

Not me. 《口》(相手の質問に答えて)私はしません ▪ Who's going to talk?—*Not me.* They know my voice. 誰が話すのかい?—私はだめです．声が知られているから．

meal[1] /miːl/ 名 ***a*** [*one's*] ***meal ticket*** **1**《俗》食べさせてくれている人 ▪ My uncle was *my meal ticket*. 叔父が私を食べさせてくれていた．

2 収入源，家計のよりどころ ▪ A university degree is no longer *a meal ticket* for life. 大学の卒業資格はもはや生涯の生活を保障してくれない．

a square meal 健康的で十分な食事，多量のバランスのとれた食事，質も量も充実した食事 ▪ He needs *a* good *square meal* every day. 彼には毎日しっかりと充実した食事が必要だ ▪ The refugees looked as if they hadn't had *a square meal* in months. 難民たちはまともな食事を何か月もとれなかった様子だった．☞かつて船員が四角の木製プレートで食事をしたことから．

in meal or in malt どっちみち ▪ Some profit will be sure to accrue either *in meal or in malt*. きっとどっちみち多少の利益が生じてくるだろう．

make a meal (***out***) ***of*** **1** …を食事にして食べる; を貪(むさぼ)り食う ▪ I *made a meal of* an apple. 私は食事としてリンゴを1個食べた ▪ Slander *made* most hellish *meals of* good men's names. 中傷のために立派な人たちの名声がひどく食い荒らされてしまった．

2《口》…の度を過ごす，をやり過ぎる ▪ You can drink tonight, but don't *make a meal of* it. 今夜は飲んでもいいが，度を過ごしてはいけない．

3《主に英口》(他人の過失を)おおげさに騒ぎ立てる ▪ Don't *make* such *a meal out of* a slight mistake in the report. 報告書の些細な過ちに大騒ぎをするな．

One's ***meal is dough.*** = One's CAKE is dough.

meals on wheels (自炊ができない老人・身体障害者向けの)ボランティア給食宅配サービス ▪ *Meals on wheels* are an enormous help to the homebound elderly. 家から出られないお年寄りは給食宅配サービスでとても助かっている．

not know [***be sure***] ***where*** *one's* ***next meal is coming from*** どこで今度の食事にありつけるかわからない《ひどく貧乏である》 ▪ There are some people who do *not know where their next meal is coming from*. 世の中にはその日の食事に困るような人々もいる．

with a good meal under *one's* ***belt*** たくさん食べて ▪ He felt sleepy *with a good meal under his belt*. 彼は食物をたらふく詰め込んで眠くなった．

meal[2] /miːl/ 動 ***meal*** *one's* ***mouth*** やさしく遠回しに言う，当たらずさわらずに話す ▪ I have never *mealed my mouth* or minced my words. 私は一度も遠回しにものを言ったり控え目にものを言ったりしたことはない．

mean[1] /miːn/ 形 (***as***) ***mean as a Christian*** 《口》ひどくけちな ▪ That man is *as mean as a Christian*. あの男は恐ろしくけちだ《ユダヤ人が使うという文句》．

feel mean 《米口》気がひける ▪ She mothered me so good I *felt mean*. 彼女はとても親切に世話をしてくれたので，私は気がひけてしまった．

One ***is so mean*** *one* ***wouldn't give anyone a fright.*** 《口》ひどくけちだ ▪ Incredibly mean, *so mean* he *wouldn't give anyone a fright*. 彼は信じられないほどしみったれで，ものすごくけちん坊だ．

no mean なかなか立派な ▪ He himself was *no mean* scholar. 彼自身もなかなか立派な学者だった．

mean[2] /miːn/ 動 ***be meant to*** *do* 《英》…しなければならない，することになっている ▪ You *are meant to* take off your shoes here. ここでは靴を脱ぐことになっている．

I mean いや(つまり)《前に言ったことを訂正する》 ▪ Will you come too?—No—yes, *I mean*. あなたも来ますか?—いえ—いやつまり，はいということです．

I mean to say 《口》はっきり言えば; つまり…ということですよ《前言を補足する》 ▪ I'm afraid he is not coming. *I mean to say*, his wife is ill in bed. 彼は来ないんじゃないか，つまりその，奥さんが病気で寝ているんだよ．

mean a lot [***great deal***] ***to*** →MEAN much to.

mean a thing 《口》〚否定文・疑問文で〛重要である ▪ Her promise doesn't *mean a thing*. 彼女の

約束は何でもない.

mean business →BUSINESS.

mean mischief →MISCHIEF.

mean much [***a lot, a great deal***] ***to*** …にとって非常に意味・重要性がある ▪ Your friendship *means a great deal to* me. あなたの友情は私には非常に尊いものです.

mean no harm →HARM.

mean nothing to … (言葉などが)…(人)になじみがない, 理解できない ▪ I want to see the facts. Words *mean nothing to* me anymore. 私は事実が知りたい. 言葉はもはや私には理解できない.

mean something [***anything***] ***to*** … (名前・言葉などが)…(人)になじみがある, よく知られている ▪ This brand name *means something to* people. このブランド名は人々によく知られている ▪ Does the name Mary King *mean anything to* you? メアリー・キングという名前にあなたはなじみがありますか.

mean well 善意である, 悪気はない ▪ Perhaps she *means well*, but she is terribly interfering. 悪気はないのかもしれないが, 彼女はひどく干渉がましい.

mean well [***ill***] ***to*** [***by***] …に好意[悪意]をいだいている ▪ I don't think your cousin *means well by* you. 君のいとこが君に好意をいだいているとは思わないね.

What do you mean, …? 《口》 …だなんてどういうことかね《異議あり》 ▪ *What do you mean,* lazy? どういうことかな, 怠け者だなんて.

What do you mean by …? **1** …とはどういう意味ですか ▪ *What do you mean by* "passion"? パッションとはどういう意味ですか.
2 …はどういうことか《よくもへんなまねができるものだ》 ▪ *What do you mean by* that? それはどういうことだ ▪ *What do you mean by* calling me so late at night? こんなに夜遅く電話してくるとはどういうつもりだ.

You don't mean to say so! まさか(ご冗談でしょう) ▪ You must get to sleep early tonight.—*You don't mean to say so!* 今夜は早く寝なさい—まさか, 冗談でしょう.

You mean …ということですか ▪ I'm going to bed early tonight. —*You mean* you're not feeling well? 今夜は早く寝るわ—ということは気分が悪いのか.

meaning /míːnɪŋ/ 名 ***bear a meaning*** 意味がある ▪ This sentence does not *bear* such *a meaning*. この文にはそのような意味はない.

not know the meaning of word その言葉の意味を知らない, その経験がない ▪ War—the young generation do *not know the meaning of* the *word*. 戦争—若者たちはその意味を知らない.

take [***get***] *a person's* ***meaning*** 人の言わんとすることが分かる ▪ I *get your meaning* now. やっと君の言わんとすることが分かったよ.

meanly /míːnli/ 副 ***not meanly*** 少なからず ▪ He was *not meanly* offended. 彼は一方(ひとかた)ならず立腹していた.

think [***believe***] ***meanly of*** …をさげすむ, 軽んじる ▪ Can Olivia *think* so *meanly of* my honor? オリビアが私の名誉をそんなに軽んじることがあろうか.

means /miːnz/ 名 ***a means to an end*** 〚the は不可〛目的(達成)のための手段 ▪ For him, work was just *a means to an end*. 彼にとって仕事は目的達成の手段にすぎなかった.

a person of your means あなたのような資産家 ▪ 100,000 US dollars may be mere peanuts to *a person of your means*. あなたのような資産家には 10 万米ドルはほんのはした金にすぎないでしょう.

be the means of …の手段[助け]である ▪ He has *been the means of* my escape. 彼は私の逃走の手先になってくれた.

beyond *one's* ***means*** 収入を越えて, 身分不相応に ▪ That car is *beyond my means*. あの車は私の収入では買えない.

by all means/《古風》***by all manner of means*** **1** どうしても, ぜひとも ▪ Try *by all means* to come. ぜひ来るようにしてください.
2 よろしいとも, ぜひどうぞ《承諾の意を強調して》 ▪ Shall I ask him to come in?—*By all means*. 彼に入って来るように言いましょうか?—ぜひどうぞ.

by any (***manner of***) ***means*** 〚否定文で〛どうしても (in any way); 〚肯定文で〛何とかして, 何としても (in any possible way) ▪ None of them can *by any means* redeem my brother. 彼らのうち一人として, どうしても私の弟を救うことができない ▪ I have to get there *by any means*. 私は何としてもそこへ行かなければならない.

by fair means or foul 是が非でも ▪ They did it in the hope of making money *by fair means or foul*. 彼らは是が非でも金を儲けようと思ってそうした.

by [***through***] ***means of*** …で, によって ▪ Thoughts are expressed *by means of* words. 思想は言葉で表現される ▪ They lifted the stone *by means of* a lever. 彼らはてこを使って石を持ち上げた.

by no (***manner of***) ***means*** 決して…でない ▪ She was *by no means* happy. 彼女は決して幸福ではなかった ▪ I will *by no manner of means* consent. 決して同意しないぞ.

by some means or other なんとかして ▪ We are getting along *by some means or other*. 我々は何とかやっています.

by this [***that***] ***means*** この[その]ようにして ▪ *By this means*, they will accomplish their main design. このようにして彼らは主な目的を遂げるだろう.

by what means どのように ▪ *By what means* are you going to travel this time? 今度は何に乗って旅行しようと思っているのか?

find (***the***) ***means to*** *do* …する道を講ずる, どうにか…する ▪ We *found means to* enter the cave. 我々はどうにかしてその洞穴の中へ入った.

leave no means untried →leave nothing UNTRIED.

of means 資産のある ▪ He is a man *of means*. 彼は資産家だ.

take every means (***in*** *one's* ***power***) あらゆる手段を尽くす ▪ Though I *took every means*, I did not succeed. 私はあらゆる手段を尽くしたが成功しなかった.

***the golden* [*happy*] *mean* [*medium*]** 中庸 (Horace, *Odes* 2. 10. 5) ▪ In everything he observed *the golden mean*. 万事において彼は中庸を守った ▪ Courage is a *happy medium* between cowardice and foolhardiness. 勇気は臆病と無謀の中道を行く.

through means of →by MEANS of.

within** one's **means 身分相応に ▪ It is good for a man to live *within his means*. 人が身分相応に暮らすことは良いことだ.

meantime /mí:ntàɪm/ 名 ***for the meantime***
1 その間は ▪ When he is reading, he forgets all other things *for the meantime*. 彼は読書しているとき, その間はほかのことは一切忘れてしまう.
2 〚補語として〛 一時的な ▪ This order was *for the meantime*. この命令は一時的なものであった.

in the meantime とかくするうちに, さて話変わって ▪ *In the meanwhile* the King pursued the enemy's army. とかくするうちに王は敵軍を追跡した.

meanwhile /mí:nhwàɪl/ 名 ***for the meanwhile*** =for the MEANTIME.

in the meanwhile =in the MEANTIME.

measles /mí:zəlz/ 名 ***like the measles*** はしかのようで[に], 誰もが体験するもので ▪ Love is *like the measles*. The older you get it, the worse the attack. 恋愛ははしかのようなもので, 大きくなって罹るほど症状が重くなる. ☞Rainer Maria Rilke の言葉.

M

measurable /méʒərəbəl/ 形 ***come* [*be*] *within* (*a*) *measurable distance of*** ...の域内に来る, に近づく ▪ I have once known myself to *be within a measurable distance of* death. かつて自分が死に瀕したことがあるのを覚えている.

measure[1] /méʒər/ 名 ***above* [*beyond*] (*all*) *measure*** 法外に, 非常に ▪ He loved his son *beyond measure*. 彼は息子を猫かわいがりした ▪ The air was hot *above measure*. 大気はめっぽう暑かった.

adopt measures →take MEASUREs.

be** a person's **measure 《口》 人にあつらえ向きの人物である ▪ He's *our measure*. 彼こそあつらえ向きの人物だ.

be the measure of ...の尺度である ▪ In philosophy, time *is the measure of* motion. 哲学では時間が運動の尺度である.

by measure **1** =in MEASURE.
2 (ます・物差しで) 寸法を取って ▪ It is sold *by measure*, and not by weight. それは目方ではなくて, 寸法を計って売られる.

fill up the measure of (不正など)をぎりぎりまでやり通す, (不幸など)をなめ尽くす (《聖》 *Matt*. 23. 32) ▪ The church *filled up the measure of* her offences for many years. その教会は長年にわたってその不正をぎりぎりまでやり通した ▪ He *filled up the measure of* his misfortunes. 彼はその不幸をなめ尽くした.

find the measure of** a person's **foot → know the MEASURE of a person's foot.

for good measure 余分に, おまけに ▪ He added another illustration *for good measure*. 彼は余分にもう1例をつけ加えた.

full* [*short*] *measure 盛りだくさん[より少ない分量, 程度], たっぷりの目盛り[不足する計り] ▪ I experienced the *full measure* of their hospitality. 彼らから手厚いもてなしを受けた ▪ The concert only lasted an hour. They felt they were getting *short measure*. コンサートはわずか1時間だけだった. 彼らは期待したほどでもないと感じた.

get the measure of =take the MEASURE of a person.

give* [*show*] *the measure of ...の程度または力量を示す ▪ Words do not always *give the measure of* one's feelings. 言葉は必ずしも人の感情の度合いを表さない ▪ This book *shows the measure of* the author's intelligence. この本を読むと著者の知力の程度がわかる.

have hard measure 虐待される ▪ The man thought he *had hard measure*. その男性は虐待されたと思った.

***have** a person's **measure* (*to an inch*)** 人の人物をすっかり見抜いている ▪ She soon *had his measure to an inch*. 彼女はやがて彼の人物をすっかり見抜いてしまった.

***have the measure of** a person* 人や物を熟知している ▪ Kate is the only person I know who *has the measure of* James. 私が知る中ではケイトしかジェイムズの人柄をよく知る者はいない.

in* (*a*) *great* [*large*] *measure 大いに, 大部分 ▪ Louis was *in a large measure* responsible for the horrors of the Revolution. ルイは革命の惨事に対して大いに責任があった.

in a* [*some*] *measure 《文》 多少, いくぶん ▪ Goodness *in some measure* implies wisdom. 善にはある程度英知が含まれる.

in full measure 十分に, ふんだんに ▪ They enjoyed happiness *in full measure*. 彼らは幸福を満喫した.

in measure ある程度, いくぶん (《聖》 *Jer*. 30. 11) ▪ I will correct thee *in measure*. わたしはある程度お前を懲らしめてやる.

in measure as ...に比例して (=in PROPORTION as) ▪ His irritability increased *in measure as* he perceived the medicine was doing him no good. 薬が一向に効いていないと分かるにつれて, 彼のいらだちが募ってきた. ☞F à mesure que のなぞり.

in the same measure 同一程度に, 同様に ▪ Cider cannot be unwholesome *in the same measure* that stummed wine is so. リンゴ酒は未発酵のブドウ酒と同じ程度に体に悪いはずがない.

keep measure 拍子をとる ▪ The crew *kept measure* with their oars. 乗組員はオールで拍子をとった.

keep [***observe***] ***measure***(***s***) 中庸を守る ▪ She *keeps* no *measure* in her contempt for him. 彼女は途方もなく彼をさげすんでいる.

know no measure 際限がない ▪ Fond love *knows no measure*. 溺愛は際限というものを知らぬ.

know [***find***] ***the measure of*** *a person's* ***foot*** 人の弱点をつかんでいる ▪ Don't I *know the measure of his foot*? 私が彼の弱点をつかんでいないとでも言うのか.

made to measure 《英》 **1** (服が)寸法に合わせて作られて, あつらえで ▪ This suit is *made to measure*. この服はあつらえだ.

2 あつらえ向きで ▪ This kitchen is *made to measure* for the modern housewife. この台所は現代の主婦にとってあつらえ向きだ.

measure for measure しっぺ返し (=TIT for tat) (cf. Sh., *Meas. for M.*) ▪ The answer was *measure for measure*. その返事はしっぺ返しだった.

measures, not men 人ではなくて法令 ▪ I have opposed *measures, not men*. 私は人ではなく法令に反対したのだ.

observe measure(***s***) →keep MEASURE(s).

out of all measure =above (all) MEASURE.

pay in full measure (労苦などに)十二分に報いる ▪ I have *been paid in full measure* for the time I spent on my children. 子供のために割いた時間に対して私は十二分に報いられた.

set measures to …を制限する ▪ What *measures* can we *set to* that grief? その悲しみをどんなにして抑えることができようか.

show the measure of →give the MEASURE of.

take [***adopt, pursue***] ***measures*** 手段をとる, 策を講じる ▪ He lost no time in *taking measures* for its reduction. 彼は時を移さずそれを削減する策を講じた.

take the measure of *a person* **1** 人の服の寸法をとる ▪ The man *took my measure*, and departed. その男の人は私の服の寸法をとって帰っていった.
2 《文》 人の人物[力量]を見積もる ▪ She quietly observed him and *took the measure of* the man. 彼女はその男性をそっと観察し, その力量を見積もった.

take the measure of *a person's* ***foot*** 人の人物[力量]を見積もる ▪ We had pretty well *taken the measure of John's foot* by this time. 我々はこのときまでにはもうジョンの人物をかなり見積もってしまっていた.

trip [***tread***] ***a measure*** 舞踏する ▪ Now let us *tread a measure*. さあダンスをしよう.

measure[2] /méʒər/ 動 ***be measured for a funeral sermon*** 《米俗》 死に瀕している ▪ He had *been measured for a funeral sermon* three times. 彼はもう3度も死に瀕したことがあった.

measure *oneself* ***against*** …に対抗する, と戦う ▪ He was not afraid to *measure himself against* a dangerous enemy. 彼は危険な敵と戦うのを恐れていなかった.

measure (***out***) *one's* ***length*** 大の字なりに倒れる ▪ He lost his balance, and *measured his length* on the ground. 彼は体の均衡を失って, 地面に大の字になって倒れた.

measure *one's* ***strength*** 戦う ▪ The two factions had an opportunity of *measuring their strength*. 二つの徒党は相戦う機会があった.

measure swords 剣を交える, 戦う (*with*) ▪ And so we *measured swords*, and parted. そこで我々は剣を交えただけで別れた ▪ You wanted to *measure swords with* Esmond, did you? 君はエズモンドと戦いたかったのだね. ☞決闘の前にお互いの剣の長さが同じであるかどうかを測ることから.

measure *oneself* (***with …***) (…と)勝負[比較]する ▪ I never *measured myself with* anyone, but I sort of have a small penis. 誰とも比べてみたことはないが, 私の一物は小さいみたいだ.

measure *a person* ***with*** *one's* ***eye*** 人を頭から足の先までじろじろ見る ▪ For a moment the man *measured* me *with his eye*. しばらくその男は私を頭から足の先までじろじろ見た.

meat /miːt/ 名 ***a meat ax*** 《米口》 お粗末な方法[手段] ▪ He edited it with *a meat ax*. 彼のそれの校訂ぶりはずさんだった.

as a meat ax 《米口》 ひどく ▪ He is as savage [wicked, sharp] *as a meat ax*. 彼は恐ろしく怒っている[意地が悪い, 抜け目がない] ▪ Why, you are *as a meat ax*. だって君はひどいよ.

at [***before, after***] ***meat*** 《古》 食事[食前, 食後]に ▪ She always sat long *at meat*. 彼女はいつも長いこと食卓についていた.

be dead meat 《口》 **1** (脅迫に用いて)瀕死の状態である, 死んだも同然である, もうおしまいだ ▪ Touch that safe and you*'re dead meat*! あの金庫に触ろうものなら命はないものと思え.
2 救いようのない状況である, 困ったことになる, お手上げである ▪ Those who remember her say she *was dead meat*. 彼女を覚えている人によれば彼女はお手上げの状態だったと言う.

be meat and drink to *one* …にとって何よりの楽しみである ▪ It *is meat and drink to* me to see a clown. 道化を見るのは私には何よりの楽しみです. ☞meat 《古》 =food.

be meat for *a person's* ***master*** 人にはよすぎる (cf. Sh., *2 Hen. IV* 2. 4. 135) ▪ You don't know I *am meat for your master*. 私があなたにはもったいないことをご存じない.

be the meat in the sandwich 《英》 間にはさまれて困った立場にいること ▪ My parents were always yelling at each other so I *was the meat in the sandwich*. 両親がいつも怒鳴りあってばかりいたので私は板ばさみだった.

beat the meat 《卑》 (男性が)自慰行為をする. ☞meat=penis.

carry off meat from the graves きわめて貧しい ▪ He was so poor that he could *carry off meat from the graves*. 彼は恐ろしく貧しかった.

M

easy meat いいカモ ▪ He seemed to think of me as *easy meat*. 彼は私をいいカモだと思ったらしい.

feed** a person **meat 《口》人に滋養物を与える ▪ Someone's been *feeding* you *meat*! 誰かが君に滋養物をずっと食べさせてくれたのだな.

make* (*cold*) *meat of 《口》…を殺す ▪ Those rogues *made meat of* him. あの悪党どもが彼を殺してしまった. ☞cold meat「死体」.

meat-and-potatoes 《米口》 **1**〚限定的〛最も基本的な, 最も重要な ▪ This is how we provide *meat-and-potatoes* services to customers. お客への基本的サービスは次のようにして提供する.
2 (仕事などの)基本的な部分, 基礎的要素 (*of*) ▪ Successful negotiation is the *meat and potatoes of* mediation. 折衝の成就が調停成立の鍵だ.

meat and two veg 《英口・戯》 **1** (肉と2種類の野菜だけから成る)イギリスの伝統的な食事 ▪ The food is very much *meat and two veg* here. 当地での食事は質素な伝統料理である.
2〚one's を伴って〛男性性器.

***One man's meat* (*is another man's poison*).** 《諺》甲の薬は乙の毒. ☞しばしば省略して使われる.

strong meat 理解しにくい教義 (《聖》*Heb*. 5. 12) (↔MILK for babes) ▪ This book is too *strong meat* for a boy. 少年にはこの本はむずかしすぎる. ☞「消化しにくい食物」が原義.

there is not much meat in …にはあまり実質がない ▪ *There's not much meat in* this argument. この議論にはあまり実質がない.

medal /médəl/ 名 ***both sides* [*the reverse*] *of the medal*** 問題の両面[裏面] ▪ It is right to take *both sides of the medal*. 問題の両面を考えるのは正しいことだ ▪ Don't you want to be shown *the reverse of the medal*? 君は問題の裏面を知りたくないのか.

***deserve a medal* (*for*)** 《戯》(…とは) 勲章ものだ ▪ She *deserves a medal for* singing at the Olympics. オリンピックで歌うとは彼女は大したものだ.

medallion /mədǽljən|-liən/ 名 ***a medallion man*** 《英戯》装身具をつけシャツの胸をはだけて若く見られようとする年配の男性 ▪ *The medallion man* looked as if he had just stepped out of a time machine. その若作りな年配の男性はまるでタイムマシンから降り立ったところといった風情だった.

meddle /médəl/ 動 ***neither make nor meddle*** 《俗》(…と)いっさい関係[干渉]しない (*with*) ▪ I will *neither make nor meddle with* them further. これ以上彼らとはいっさい関係しない.

medication /mèdɪkéɪʃən/ 名 ***on medication*** 薬物治療中で, 投薬を受けて ▪ He is *on medication* and hopes to get well soon. 彼は薬を服用中で早くよくなればと願っている.

medicine /médəsən/ 名 ***administer the medicine*** →ADMINISTER.

get* [*take*] *a dose* [*taste*] *of* one's *own* [*the same*] *medicine 《口》同じ手で報復される ▪ The revolutionary leaders *got a dose of the same medicine*. 革命のリーダーたちは同じ手で報復された.

give** a person **a dose* [*a taste, some*] *of* his *own* [*the same*] *medicine 《口》同じ手で人に報復する, 同じやり方でやり返す ▪ In snubbing Bob she only *gave* him *a dose of his own medicine*. ボブを冷たくあしらったといっても, 結局彼女が同じ手で仕返ししただけのことだ ▪ If you hit me, my brother will *give* you *some of your own medicine*. 僕を殴ってみろ, 兄ちゃんがお前を仕返しに殴るからな.

make medicine 《米》(北米先住民が超自然力を祈って)まじない[祈り]をする ▪ They *make medicine* to ensure a successful season. 彼らはある季節が上首尾に終わるようにと祈る.

take** one's **medicine 《口》苦い薬を飲む; いやなことを忍ぶ ▪ I *took my medicine* like a man. 私は男らしくそれを忍んだ.

the best medicine (気持ちなどをよくする)最善の方法 ▪ Laughter really is *the best medicine*. 笑いは本当に最高の良薬である.

The medicine* [*cure*] *could be worse than the illness. 干渉せずに傍観した方がよいことがある ▪ The enterprise is fraught with danger and *the medicine could be worse than the illness*. その事業は危険をはらんでいるので手を出さず傍観した方がいいだろう.

meditate /médətèɪt/ 動 ***meditate the Muse*** 詩作に励む (Milton, *Lycidas* 66) ▪ What boots it to *meditate the Muse*? 詩作に励んで何になるのか.

medium /míːdiəm/ 名 ***by* [*through*] *the medium of*** …の媒介で, を通して ▪ Vacant positions can be made known *through the medium of* the press. 求人は新聞を通して知らせることができる.

stick to a happy medium 中庸を守る; 極端を避ける ▪ *Stick to a happy medium* in discipline. しつけでは中庸を守れ.

strike the* [*a*] *happy medium うまく中間を取る ▪ She is neither too friendly nor formal, but *strikes the happy medium*. 彼女はなれなれしすぎず, また堅苦しすぎず, ちょうどいいかげんだ.

***the golden* [*happy*] *medium* [*mean*]** →MEANS.

meek /miːk/ 形 ***(as) meek as a lamb* [*a maid, Moses*]** きわめておとなしい ▪ Though kind, he is not *as meek as a lamb*. 彼は親切だが, 子羊のようにおとなしくはない.

meek and mild おとなしい; 不平を言う勇気がない ▪ She is always rapping her husband, who is *meek and mild*. 彼女はおとなしい亭主をしかりつけてばかりいる.

meet /miːt/ 動 ***(be) well* [*happily*] *met*** いい所で会う ▪ Well, we *are happily met*. やあ, いい所で会いましたね ▪ Hi, Tom, *well met*! やあトム, いい所で会ったね.

make* (*two, both*) *ends meet →END[1].

***meet** a person's **eyes** [**gaze**]* **1** 人の目につく ▪ A newly-cut inscription *met my eyes*. 新しく刻まれた碑銘が私の目に留まった.
2 人が自分を見ているのに気がつく; (視線をそらさずに)人を見返す ▪ As she turned her head she *met his eyes*. 彼女はふり向いたとき, 彼と目が合った ▪ I dare not *meet your eyes*. あなたのお顔を見返すことはとてもできません.

meet** a person **halfway →HALFWAY.

meet the case 全くあつらえ向きである ▪ That will *meet the case* admirably. それは全くうってつけだろう.

meet the ear 《雅》聞こえる ▪ A cry was all that *met the ear*. ただ叫び声が一声聞こえただけだった.

meet the eye(s) of たまたま…の目に留まる ▪ If this should *meet the eye of* Brown, he would be extremely sad. もしこれがブラウンの目に留まろうものなら, 彼はひどく悲しむだろう.

meet trouble halfway →borrow TROUBLE.

meet well 温かく迎える ▪ They *met* us *well* and were most friendly. 彼らは私たちを温かく迎えてくれ, とても愛想がよかった.

meet with it しかられる, 罰せられる ▪ If you don't behave yourself, Tom, you will *meet with it*. トム, 行儀よくしないとしかられますよ.

more in ... than meet the eye …には目に見える以上のものがある ▪ There is *more in* most things *than meets the eye*. たいていの物には目に見える以上のものがある.

Nice meeting you. (別れ際に, または初対面の相手に対して)お目にかかれてうれしかったです ▪ I must go now. *Nice meeting you*. そろそろ行かなくては. 君に会えてよかったよ.

Well met! →(be) well met (→MEET).

meeting /míːtɪŋ/ 名 ***a meeting of (the) minds*** 《文》(特に政治で)意見の一致, 同意 ▪ There has been no *meeting of the minds* between the parties. これまでのところ政党間で意見の一致は見られない.

at a first meeting 初対面の時は ▪ It is impolite to ask personal questions *at a first meeting*. 初対面で私事にわたることを尋ねるのは失礼だ.

marry out of meeting →MARRY².

speak out in meeting 《米口》はっきりと[率直に]意見を述べる ▪ One of the villagers *spoke out in meeting*. 村人の一人がはっきりと意見を述べた.

megillah /məgílə/ 名 ***the whole megillah*** 《米口》長々とした話のすべて, 複雑な説明全体 ▪ Ted insists on giving us *the whole megillah*. テッドは退屈な話を全部聞かせると言ってきかない. ☞megillah「ユダヤ教の祝祭日に延々と朗読される巻物5書のひとつ」.

mell /mel/ 名 ***a mell of a hess*** 《口》ひどく散乱した状態 ▪ I've never seen such *a mell of a hess*. こんなひどい取り散らかしようは見たことがない. ☞a hell of a mess というところを頭音転換 (spoonerism＝2語以上の語頭の音が互いに入れ替わること)によって言い間違えたもの. Oxford 大学 New College の学長 W. A. Spooner (1844–1930)がこの種の誤りをよくしたことから.

melon /mélən/ 名 ***carve a melon/cut (up) a melon*** 《俗》(会社が株主へ)余剰利益を配当する; (株主が)特別配当金を受ける ▪ The express companies can annually "*cut a melon*" of enormous dividends. 急配運送会社は毎年巨額の特別配当金という「余剰利益を分配」できる ▪ The shareholders *cut a melon* of nearly a million dollars. 株主は100万ドルに近い余剰利益の配当を受ける.

cut the melon 問題にけりをつける ▪ The boss as usual *cut the melon* with a word. 社長が例によって一言でその問題にけりをつけた.

melt /melt/ 動 ***One's heart melts.*** 心が和らぐ (《聖》*Josh*. 2. 11; 7. 5; *Ps*. 119. 28, etc.) ▪ In that bitter cry, *the lad's heart melted* (down) again. そうして激しく泣いたために, 少年の心はまた和んだ. ☞ヘブライ語法; down を付加するのは《米俗》.

in the [a] melting mood ほろりとした気分になって (cf. Sh., *Oth*. 5. 2. 349) ▪ She was *in a melting mood*, and allowed him to kiss her. 彼女はとろんとした気分になっていたので, 彼がキスするままにした.

melt in the [one's] mouth 《口》(菓子などが)口の中でとろける, とてもおいしい ▪ This candy really *melts in the mouth*. このキャンディーはとてもおいしい ▪ They serve steaks that *melt in your mouth*. あの店ではおいしいステーキを出す.

melt into tears とめどなく涙を流す ▪ She *melted into tears* as she embraced her son. 彼女は息子を抱きしめながらとめどもなく涙を流した.

meltdown /méltdàʊn/ 名 ***a financial meltdown*** 財政的溶解, 金融事情での危機的な災難[失敗] ▪ The NHS will be facing *a financial meltdown* without more money. もっと資金がないと国家医療制度は今に財政危機に直面する. ☞meltdown は「(原発事故のあと危険なレベルの放射線が放出されたときに起こる)溶融」が原義.

melting pot /méltɪŋpɑ̀t|-pɔ̀t/ 名 ***go into the melting pot*** 改変される ▪ Everything connected with the old regime has *gone into the melting pot*. 旧制度に関係のあるものはいっさい改変された.

in the melting pot るつぼの中に《新しいものを生み出す準備として混乱状態で》 ▪ Everything is *in the melting pot* at present. すべてのものが目下混沌とした状態にある.

put [cast, throw] ... into the melting pot (制度など)を全く改造する ▪ He *threw* his original hypothesis *into the melting pot*. 彼は元の仮説を全く改造した.

member /mémbər/ 名 ***a member of Christ*** キリスト教徒 ▪ At that place I was made *a member of Christ*. そこで私はキリスト教徒になりました.

the [an] unruly member 制しにくい器官《舌》(《聖》*Jas* 3. 5–8) ▪ But the tongue can no man tame; it is *an unruly member* full of deadly poison. 誰にも舌を思い通りにはできない. 舌は猛毒を含

M

んだ手に負えない器官である ▪ It is this to have *an unruly member*! 舌を持っていると, こんなことになるのだ.

memorandum /mèmərǽndəm/ 名 ***make a memorandum of*** …をメモに取る ▪ We *made a memorandum of* his lecture. 我々は彼の講義をメモに取った.

memory /méməri/ 名 ***(a trip) down memory lane*** →take a trip down MEMORY lane; LANE.

bear [have, hold, keep]… in memory …をよく覚えている, 忘れずにいる ▪ *Keep in memory* what I said to you. 私の言ったことをよく覚えておけ.

beyond [within] the memory (of man) 人間の記憶にない[に残っている], 有史以前[以後]の ▪ The guild was begun at a time *beyond the memory of man*. ギルドは有史以前から始められた.

burden** a person's **memory 人の記憶に負担をかける ▪ I don't want to *burden your memory* with too many instructions. あんまりたくさん指図をして, 君の記憶に負担をかけたくないのです.

come to** one's **memory 胸に浮かぶ, 思い起こされる ▪ A scene from my childhood *came* suddenly *to my memory*. 子供の頃のある情景が突然思い出された.

commit … to memory 《文》…を記憶[暗記]する ▪ *Commit* these words *to memory*. この言葉を暗記しておきなさい. ☞今日では主に memorize を用いる.

from memory 記憶を頼りに, そらで (→speaking from MEMORY) ▪ The portrait was painted *from memory*. この肖像画は記憶を頼りに描かれた.

have a good [bad, poor] memory 覚えが良い[悪い] ▪ I *have a bad memory* for dates. 私は日付の覚えが悪い.

have a memory like an elephant/ have the memory of an elephant 記憶力がすぐれている ▪ My grandmother *has a memory like an elephant*. うちのおばあちゃんの記憶力は抜群だ. ☞ゾウは物覚えがよいとされている.

have [hold, keep]… in memory →bear … in MEMORY.

if my memory serves me well [correctly, etc.]/ if memory serves 私の記憶が正しければ ▪ I first went to Italy in July 1978, *if my memory serves me right*. 私の記憶が正しかったら初めてイタリアへ行ったのは1978年7月だった ▪ It was 1964, *if memory serves*. もし記憶に間違いがなければそれは1964年のことだった.

in living memory →within living MEMORY.

in memory of …の記念に ▪ This monument is *in memory of* a general. この碑はある将軍を記念したものである.

jog** a person's **memory 人に思い出させる ▪ This snapshot might *jog your memory*. この写真で思い出すかもしれないよ.

one's ***memory is green.*** …は記憶に生々しい ▪ Mother died ten years ago, but *her memory is green*. 母は10年前に死んだが, その記憶は今も生々しい.

of blessed [famous, glorious, happy] memory 誉れの高い《王候・偉人などの死後その名に添えて用いる称えの句》 ▪ This was given and granted by the late King Charles *of blessed memory*. これは誉れ高き故チャールズ王から賜ったものである.

slip (out of)** a person's **memory うっかり忘れられる ▪ The fact had quite *slipped out of her memory*. そのことを彼女はすっかり忘れてしまっていた ▪ It *slipped my memory* that he was away. 彼が留守だということをうっかり忘れていた.

speaking from memory 《口》記憶によれば[よって話しながら] ▪ *Speaking from memory*, I think Paul's haiku is more successful. 記憶によれば, ポールの俳句のほうが良くできていると思う ▪ *Speaking from memory*, Glen summarized the results of the study. 記憶に基づいて話しながら, グレンは研究の結果をまとめた.

take a trip [a stroll] down memory lane/ go [take** a person**] down memory lane 思い出の小道をたどる, 昔の楽しかったことを懐かしむ ▪ She went back to her birthplace and *took a stroll down memory lane*. 彼女は生まれ故郷へ戻り往時を懐かしんだ ▪ Reading the old letter *took* me *down memory lane*. その古い手紙を読んで昔の思い出に浸った.

to the best of** one's **memory …の記憶する限りでは ▪ The book was not published, *to the best of my memory*. 私の記憶する限りでは, その本は出版されなかったと思う.

to the memory of …の霊に捧げて ▪ *To the memory of* my wife. 亡き妻に捧ぐ《著者の献辞》 ▪ They erected a plaque (dedicated) *to the memory of* the late mayor. 故市長に捧げる記念銘板が建立された.

within [in] living memory 現在の人々に記憶されて ▪ It is still *within living memory*. それはまだ現在世人の記憶するところである.

within the memory (of man) →beyond the MEMORY (of man).

mend[1] /mend/ 名 ***be on the mend*** **1** (病気が)快方に向かっている ▪ The doctor says Jim *is* definitely *on the mend*. ジムは確かに快方に向かっていると医師は言っています.

2 (事態が)好転している ▪ Conditions *are* now perhaps *on the mend*. 事態は今たぶん好転しているのでしょう.

mend[2] /mend/ 動 ***(It is) never too late to mend.*** 《諺》行いを改めるのに遅すぎることはない,「あやまちて改むるにはばかることなかれ」.

Least said soonest mended. 《諺》口を慎めば言禍が少ない,「口は災いの元」.

make or mend 仕立てたり繕ったりする ▪ They must *make or mend* very cheaply. 彼らはひどく安く仕立てたり繕ったりしなければならない.

M

***mend** oneself* 出世する ▪ He tried his best to *mend himself.* 彼は出世するために最善を尽くした.
mend a** [one's] **pen 羽ペン (quill pen) の先をけずり直す ▪ We all sat *mending our pens.* 我々はみな腰かけて羽ペンの先をけずっていた.
mend** a person's **cheer 人にましな食べ物を作る ▪ I'll try if I can *mend your cheer.* ましな料理を作ってあげられるかどうか試しにやってみましょう.
mend** one's **fences →FENCE.
***mend** one's **manners** [**ways**]* 《英》行状を改める ▪ That wild fellow had *mended his ways.* あの放らつ男も行状を改めていた.
***mend matters** [**the matter**]* 《しばしば皮肉》事態を改める ▪ That will do something towards *mending the matter.* そうすれば多少事態を改めるのに役立つだろう ▪ To *mend matters,* it continued snowing. ありがたいことに, 雪は降り続いた.
mend or end 改善するか廃止するか ▪ They discussed the question of *mending or ending* the House of Lords. 上院を改善するか廃止するかという問題が話し合われた.
mend** one's **pace 急ぐ, 足を速める ▪ Your ass will not *mend his pace* with beating. 君のロバはたたいたところで足を速めはしないよ.

mental /méntəl/ 形 ***go mental*** 《英口》激怒する ▪ My mom will *go mental* when she sees what we've done! 僕たちがやらかしたことを見たらママはかんかんになるだろう.
***make a mental note of** [**to** do, **that**]* → NOTE.

mention[1] /ménʃən/ 名 ***(an) honorable mention*** 褒状 ▪ She received *Honorable Mention* for her work as a teaching assistant. 彼女は教育助手としての業績に対して褒状を受けた.
make mention of 《文》...のことに言及する, をあげる ▪ The book does not *make* any *mention of* the fact. その本はこの事実に少しも言及していない ▪ *Mention* has already *been made of* the importance of time. 時間の大切さについては既に触れた.

mention[2] /ménʃən/ 動 ***Don't mention it.*** 《口》どういたしまして《お礼・わびなどに対する返答》 ▪ I'm sorry to have troubled you. —Oh, *don't mention it.* ご迷惑をおかけしてすみません—いいえ, どういたしまして.
mention** A **and** B **in the same breath BとA(別のはるかに優れた人[物])とを同類として比較する ▪ How can you *mention* the Beatles *and* this group *in the same breath?* このグループとビートルズとを比べることなどできっこない.
not to mention/without mentioning ...は言うまでもなく ▪ I can't boil eggs, *not to mention* cook a meal. 私は食事の調理はおろか卵もゆでられない.

merchant /mə́ːrtʃənt/ 名 ***a Merchant of Death*** 《米俗》「死の商人」《戦争を食い物にする者》, 戦争屋 ▪ He was publicly condemned as *a merchant of death.* 彼は戦争屋だと公の場で非難された.
a merchant of doom 《口》悲観的な人 ▪ They accused me of being *a merchant of doom.* 彼らは私が悲観的だと言って責めた.

mercury /mə́ːrkjəri|-kjuəri/ 名 ***The mercury is rising.*** **1** 水銀柱が上がって行く《(気圧計では)気温の上昇は天気の好転を示す》 ▪ Summer is here and *the mercury is rising.* 夏が来て水銀柱が上昇中だ.
2 景気[きげん]がよくなっていく ▪ *The mercury is rising* for our song bird. わが歌姫の人気が高まっている.
3 ますます興奮する ▪ *The mercury was rising* in the stadium as the game neared its end. 試合が終盤に近づくと球場はますます熱気を帯びてきた.

mercy /mə́ːrsi/ 名 ***at the mercy of*** ...のなすがままに, に左右されて ▪ They found themselves *at the mercy of* their enemies. 彼らは気がついてみると敵のなすがままになっていた ▪ The ship is *at the mercy of* the waves. 船は波にもてあそばれている ▪ I throw myself *at your mercy.* わしのことは煮て食おうと焼いて食おうと好きにせよ.
be thankful for small mercies せめてもの幸いとありがたく思う ▪ It might have been worse. We should *be thankful for small mercies.* あれくらいですんでよかった. せめてもの幸いとありがたく思うべきだ.
cast** [**throw**] oneself **on** a person's **mercy 《文》人の情けにすがる ▪ I can only *cast myself on your mercy.* あなたさまのご慈悲にすがるのみです ▪ He *threw himself on the mercy of* the court. 彼は法廷の情けに訴えた.
for mercy's sake 後生だから ▪ Tell me, Helen, *for mercy's sake.* ヘレン, 後生だから話しておくれ.
have** [**take**] **mercy on ...に哀れをかける ▪ Lord, *have mercy on* me, please. 主よ, どうか私に哀れみをかけてください.
***in mercy** (**to**)* (...を)哀れんで, (に)免じて ▪ *In mercy to* him, let's drop the subject. 彼に免じて, この話はやめよう.
***it's a mercy** (**that**)* ...はありがたいことだ ▪ *It's a mercy* he wasn't killed in the accident. 彼があの事故で死ななかったのはありがたいことだ.
***leave** [**trust**] A **to the mercy of** B* AをBの意のままに任す ▪ The ship *was left to the mercy of* the waves. 船は波のまにまに捨ておかれた.
***leave** [**trust**] A **to the tender mercies of** B* 《戯・反語》AをBの手でひどい目にあわせる (《聖》*Prov.* 12. 10) ▪ He *was left to the tender mercies of* his master. 彼は主人の手でひどい目にあわされた.
mercy killing 安楽死 ▪ *Mercy killing* of humans is illegal in most countries. ほとんどの国で人の安楽死は違法とされている.
Mercy on** [**upon**] **us! おや, まあ《驚き・恐怖を表す》 ▪ Oh, *mercy upon us!* What's that over there? こいつはたまげた. あそこにあるのは何だ.
of** one's **mercy 慈悲心から ▪ God *of his mercy* gives you patience to endure. 神は慈悲心から辛抱強く耐える力を与えてくださる.
show mercy 哀れみを示す ▪ The enemy *showed*

them no *mercy.* 敵は彼らに少しも容赦をしなかった.

take mercy on →have MERCY on.

That's a mercy. そいつはありがたい ▪ You won't be asked to work overtime. —Well, *that's a mercy.* 残業しろとは言われないだろう—いや, そいつはありがたい.

works of mercy 慈善行為 ▪ The care of the elderly was one of the *works of mercy.* お年寄りの介護は慈善行為の一つだった.

merge /mə:rdʒ/ 動 ***merge into the background*** 背景に溶け込む, 目立たないように静かに振舞う ▪ He desperately tried to *merge into the background.* 彼は必死になって目立たぬように努めた.

meridian /mərídiən/ 名 ***calculated to [for] the meridian of*** …の趣味[習慣, 能力]などに適した ▪ These newspaper articles were *calculated to the meridian of* the multitude. こういった新聞記事は一般庶民の好みにあった.

merit /mérət/ 名 ***according to*** *one's* ***merits*** =on its MERITs.

make a merit of (自分の行為)を誇る, 手柄顔をする ▪ He *made a merit of* remaining at his work. 彼は仕事にとどまったことに手柄顔をした.

merits and demerits (人の)長所と短所; 損得; 功罪 ▪ Every situation must be looked at on its *merits and demerits.* あらゆる事態は長所と短所から検討されなければならない. ☞demerits /di:mérəts/ は対比強調のためにしばしば /dí:merəts/ となる.

on its [his, her, etc.***] merits/according to*** *one's* ***merits*** その真価によって ▪ Read and evaluate this book *on its* own *merits.* この本を読み, その真価によってそれを評価せよ ▪ The agency wants to hire candidates *according to their merits.* 代理店は応募者をその長所で採用したいと考えている.

merry /méri/ 形 ***(as) merry as a cricket [grig, lark]*** 《口》非常に陽気で ▪ We were all *as merry as a cricket* and had no end of fun. 私たちはみんなひどく陽気でこの上もなく楽しみました.

(as) merry as the day is long 非常に楽しい (cf. Sh., *Much Ado* 2. 1. 51) ▪ I'm sure we'll be *as merry as the day is long.* 私たちはきっととても楽しく過ごすことになるでしょう.

make merry 《文》浮かれ騒ぐ ▪ The children *made merry* in the rock garden. 子供たちは築山の庭で陽気にはしゃいだ.

make merry at …をあざわらう ▪ The boys *made merry at* the old man's queer clothes. 男の子たちはその老人の風変わりな服をあざわらった.

make merry over …をひやかす, からかう ▪ He *makes merry over* their shortcomings. 彼は彼らの欠点をからかう.

The more the merrier. 《諺》大勢になるほど陽気になる《多ければ多いほど楽しい》 ▪ Come with us on the hike; *the more the merrier.* いっしょにハイキングに行こうよ. 仲間は多いほど楽しいから.

mess[1] /mes/ 名 ***a mess of*** **1** 取り散らかした ▪ There was *a mess of* clothes on the floor. 床には衣類が散乱していた.

2 《米口》多くの ▪ She picked up *a mess of* keys and handed me one. 彼女はたくさんの鍵を取り上げ, 1本を手渡してくれた.

a mess of pottage 一椀(わん)の羹(あつもの)《高価なものを犠牲にして得る物質的慰安》(《聖》*Gen.* 25. 29–34) ▪ No one would sell the everlasting inheritance of heaven for *a mess of pottage.* 一椀の羹と引き替えに永遠に天国を継ぐ権利を売る者は誰もいないだろう. ☞Esau が1杯の羹と引き替えに家督相続権を弟の Jacob に譲った故事から.

clear up the mess 《口》整とんする ▪ I'm supposed to *clear up the mess.* 私が整とんすることになっている.

cook up a (fine) mess 不適切な行為でまわりを混乱させる ▪ He *cooked up a fine mess* when he invited a drunkard to stay overnight. 彼が酔っ払いに一晩泊まれと言ったので家中が大騒ぎになった.

get into a mess 《口》困ったことになる, ごたごたに巻きこまれる ▪ He *got into a* terrible *mess* over some girl or other. 彼はある女性のことなどでひどく困ったことになった.

in a mess **1** めちゃくちゃにして ▪ They left the whole room *in a mess.* 彼らは部屋全体をめちゃくちゃにしたままにした.

2 《口》困ったことになって ▪ He's *in a* nice *mess,* now he's been caught stealing. 彼は盗みの現場を押さえられたので, 大変困ったことになっている.

make a mess of 《口》(企てなど)を台なしにする ▪ He has *made a* precious *mess of* the whole performance. 彼はその演技全体をすっかり台なしにしてしまった.

make a mess of it 《口》へまをやる ▪ She has *made a* fine [*a* pretty] *mess of it* again. 彼女はまたひどいへまをやってしまった.

mess-up へま, ごたごた, 混乱状態 ▪ There was some *mess-up* over the car payment. 車の支払いに関してちょっとしたごたごたがあった.

mess[2] /mes/ 動 ***and no messing*** 《英口》しかもわけなく, 易々と ▪ She solved the math problem in half a minute *and no messing.* 彼女は数学の問題を30秒でしかも軽々と解いた.

mess with *a person's* ***head*** 《口》人をひどく面食らわせる, まごつかせる ▪ Don't *mess with my head.* Are you kidding or not? 面食らうじゃないか. 冗談か, それとも本気か.

no messing 《口》本当である ▪ Are you sure? *No messing*? 間違いないか. 本当か.

message /mésidʒ/ 名 ***get the message*** 《口》(言わんとすることが)わかる (→get the PICTURE) ▪ Contact me at ten tomorrow. *Got the message*? あす10時に会いに来てくれ. わかったかい.

go on [run] a message 使いに行く ▪ Will you *run a message* for me? 使いに行ってくれますか.

keep to the message (政治家が)党の狙い[考え]を強調する[はっきり打ち出す] ▪ We want to see the congressman *keep to the message.* その下院議員

が党の狙いをはっきりと打ち出すのを見たいものだ.

on* [*off*] *message (政治家が)政党の公式見解を述べて[述べずに] ▪ Obama went *off message* in last night's speech. オバマ氏は昨夜のスピーチでは党の公式見解に触れなかった ▪ Don't worry—what I say to the press will be right *on message*. 心配ご無用. 報道陣への発表はちゃんと党の公式見解に沿っているから.

send a message **1** 求愛のサインを送る ▪ The smell of the rutting does *sent a* strong *message* to the bucks. 発情期の雌ジカの匂いが雄ジカに強い受け入れのサインを送った.

2 それとなく伝える ▪ They did nothing to help the homeless, which *sent a message* that they didn't care. 彼らはホームレスの救済に何の手も打たず, その関心のなさが知れた.

messenger /mésəndʒər/ 名 ***Don't shoot the messenger.*** 《諺》悪いことを知らせてくれた人に八つ当たりをしてはいけない. ☞次項も参照.

shoot* [*kill*] *the messenger 《戯》(張本人でなく)悪い知らせをもたらした人を責める, 八つ当たりする ▪ It's no use *shooting the messenger*. The mailman only delivered it. 郵便配達員を責めても仕方がない. 彼はその手紙をもってきただけだから.

metal /métəl/ 名 ***metal more attractive*** もっと心を引くもの, いっそう美しいもの (cf. Sh., *Haml.* 3. 2. 116) ▪ Here's *metal more attractive*, a Corona from Havana! ここにもっとすてきなものがあるよ, ハバナ産のコロナ(高級葉巻)だ.

meter /mí:tər/ 名 ***in short meter*** 《米俗》すぐ ▪ I'll do it *in short meter*. すぐやります.

the meter is running メーターが動いている, 料金がかさんで[結果が累積して]いる ▪ Let's make a decision soon, for *the meter is running*. 急いで結論を出そう. こうしている間にも事態が動いているから.

method /méθəd/ 名 ***the Socratic method*** ソクラテス式問答法《古代ギリシャの哲学者ソクラテスがあらゆる問題に適用した厳格な論理分析》 ▪ *The Socratic method* is primarily used in Cognitive Therapy. ソクラテス式問答法は主として認知療法で用いられている.

there's* (*a*) *method in* [《米》 *to*] *a person's madness 人は狂気の割りには筋道が立っている; 《戯》人のふるまい[提案]は見かけほど狂人じみたものではない (cf. Sh., *Haml.* 2. 2. 208) ▪ I think *there's method in his madness*. 彼の行動は見かけほど常軌を逸したものではないと思う ▪ He's rather odd looking, but *there's a method to his madness*. 彼はずいぶんおかしな風采だが, 言動には筋道が立っている.

mettle /métl/ 名 ***be on* [*upon*] *one's mettle*** 《やや文》張り切っている ▪ He's right *on his mettle* for a world championship. 彼は世界選手権を取ろうとして大いに張り切っている.

of mettle 気概のある ▪ He is a man *of mettle*. 彼は気概のある男だ.

put* [*set*] *a person on* [*upon, to*] *his mettle 人を発奮させる, 激励する ▪ His sarcasm *set* me *on my mettle*. 彼の皮肉が私に何くそという気持ちを起こさせた ▪ The soldiers *were put to their mettle* at the sight of their old enemies. 兵士たちは旧敵を見て武者ぶるいした.

show* [*prove*] *one's mettle 《文》気概を示す ▪ He was glad to have a chance to *prove his mettle*. 彼は気概を示す機会ができたことを喜んだ.

try* [*test*] *a person's mettle 人の力量をためす ▪ The peak will *try their mettle*. その峰は彼らの力量をためすことになるだろう ▪ The training exercise will *test the mettle of* the new firefighters. その訓練で新任消防士の根性が試される.

mickey, micky /míki/ 名 ***Mickey Mouse*** 《米口》つまらない, くだらない ▪ His music is all *Mickey Mouse*. 彼の音楽は全くつまらない. ☞Walt Disney (1901–66)の漫画映画の主人公のネズミの名前から.

take the mick*(*e*)*y* [*mick*] *out of 《主に英》(人)をからかう, 愚弄する ▪ He often *takes the mickey out of* the Establishment. 彼はよく体制側を愚弄する ▪ The comedy *takes the mick out of* an absent-minded professor. その喜劇は世事にうとい大学教授をからかったものだ.

mickle /míkəl/ 名 ***Many a little* [*pickle*] *makes a mickle.*/*Many a mickle makes a muckle.*** 《諺》ちりも積もれば山となる.

microcosm /máɪkrəkὰzəm|-kɔ̀zəm/ 名 ***in microcosm*** 小規模の[に] ▪ These works represent *in microcosm* his compositional talent. この作品群には彼の作曲の才能の片鱗が表れている ▪ The treatment rooms were spas *in microcosm*. 治療室は小規模な温泉といったものだった.

microscope /máɪkrəskòʊp/ 名 ***be put under the microscope*** 詮索される ▪ Everything I did *was put under the microscope*. 自分がすることをいちいち調べられた.

midair /mìdéər/ 名 ***in midair*** = up in the AIR 1.

midchannel /mídtʃǽnəl/ 名 ***in midchannel*** 中途で ▪ The plan was wrecked *in midchannel*. その計画は中途で挫折した.

middle /mídəl/ 名 ***a middle-age*(*d*) *spread*** 中年太り《腹の周りについた脂肪》 ▪ The loose shirt worn outside his trousers concealed his *middle-aged spread*. ゆったりしたシャツの裾をズボンの外に出して着ていたので彼の中年腹が隠れた.

a middleman 仲買人, 媒介者 ▪ He serves as *a middleman* between the manufacturer and the retailer. 彼は製造業者と小売商人との仲立ちをしている.

a pig in the middle 《口》→PIG[1].

caught in the middle 板ばさみになって ▪ My parents are always arguing and I find myself *caught in the middle*. 両親が言い合いばかりするので私は間にはさまれて身動きできない.

down the middle **1** (道の)まん中を[に] ▪ She waved and walked away *down the middle* of

the street. 彼女は手を振り道のまん中を歩いていった.
2 半分に, 2 等分に, まっ二つに ▪ Slice bread *down the middle* lengthwise and gently pry it open. パンの縦半分にナイフを入れ, ていねいに押し開きなさい.

follow* [*steer, take*] *a middle course*/*find a* [*the*] *middle way 中道を探る, 妥協する ▪ We often have to *steer a middle course.* 互いに歩み寄らなければならないことがよくある.

in the middle 《俗》困った[危険な]立場に置かれて (*with*) ▪ That blunder put him *in the middle with* the boss. そのへまで彼は社長ににらまれるはめになった ▪ The man *in the middle* was much maligned. 窮地に陥ったその男性はいろいろと中傷された.

in the middle of **1** ...のまん中に ▪ The FBI stormed into his house *in the middle of* the night. 連邦捜査局が真夜中に彼の自宅に突入した ▪ Don't stand right *in the middle of* the road. 道のどまん中に立つんじゃない.
2 ...の最中で ▪ I have often stopped *in the middle of* a speech. 私は話の最中でよく立往生した.

knock* [*send*] *a person into the middle of next week →WEEK.

middle of the road*/ *middle-of-the-road
1 中道, 中庸 ▪ He chooses *middle of the road* to describe his political views. 彼は政治に関する意見を述べるのに中道を選ぶ.
2 過激で偏った思想を持たない, 無難な, 中庸の ▪ He is a moderate, *middle-of-the-road* kind of person. 彼は穏やかな中道派の人物である.

(*out*) *in the middle of nowhere* → in the middle of NOWHERE.

the middle ground 折衷案 ▪ The two parties failed to find *the middle ground* between them. 当事者たちは相互の妥協点が見つけられなかった.

middle name /mìdəlnéɪm/ 名 ***be** a person's* [*one's*] ***middle name*** 《口》...がその人[自分]の特徴である, ...はいかにもその人[自分]らしい, ...には目がない ▪ Trouble *is my middle name*, OK? 僕はすぐに面倒を起こすからね ▪ Fun and games *are his middle name.* 彼はお祭り騒ぎが大好きだ.

midnight /mídnàɪt/ 名 ***burn* [*waste, consume*] *the midnight oil*** →OIL[1].

smell of the midnight oil (文学作品が)苦心の跡が見える, 労作である ▪ There are few books that *smell of the midnight oil.* 労作はあまりないものだ.

midst /mɪdst/ 名副 ***first, midst, and last*** →FIRST.

in our* [*your, their*] *midst 《主に新聞》我々[君たち, 彼ら]のまん中に ▪ His form was seen *in their midst.* 彼の姿が彼らのまん中に見られた.

in the midst of **1** ...のまん中に ▪ Crete lies *in the midst of* the waters. クレタ島は大海原のまっただ中にある.
2 (仕事・苦労など)の最中に ▪ *In the midst of* his enormous labors, he wrote a book of poetry. 彼は大仕事をしている最中に 1 巻の詩集を書いた.

midstream /mídstríːm/ 名 ***in midstream***
1 流れの中ほどで ▪ The boat was quietly gliding *in midstream.* ボートは中流を静かに滑るように進んでいた.
2 話の途中で; 工程が未完成で ▪ He interrupted the guide *in midstream.* 彼はガイドの話の途中で口をはさんだ ▪ Those accidents forced us to abandon the project *in midstream.* その事故のために我々は企画を半ばで中止せざるを得なかった.

midsummer /mídsʌ́mər/ 名 ***midsummer madness*** 狂乱の極み (cf. Sh., *Twel. N.* 3. 4. 61) ▪ To think of flying alone to the North Pole is sheer *midsummer madness.* 北極への単独飛行を考えるなんて, いやはや全くの狂乱ざたというものだ. ☞この狂気は「真夏」の満月と暑さによると信じられた.

midsummer noon 狂気 ▪ It's *midsummer noon* with you. 君は頭がおかしくなっているのだ.

midway /mídwèɪ/ 副 ***midway of*** 《米口》...の途中で ▪ She stopped *midway of* her sentence. 彼女は文の途中で口ごもった ▪ He died *midway of* his 70th year. 彼は 70 歳の半ばで亡くなった.

mien /miːn/ 名 ***make* (*a*) *mien to*** *do* [***of*** *doing*] 《雅》...のふりをする, と見せかける ▪ They *made a mien to* oppose us. 彼らは我々に反対すると見せかけた ▪ We *made mien of holding* out *to* the last. 我々は最後までがんばるふりをした.

miff /mɪf/ 名 ***get* [*have, take*] *a miff*** 《口》むっとする, むかっぱらを立てる ▪ If she should *get another miff*, we'd never be able to appease her. もし彼女がもう一度むっとしようものなら, 二度となだめることはできまい.

in a miff 《口》むっとして, しゃくにさわって ▪ When she is *in a miff*, she never speaks a word. 彼女はむっとしているときには, ひと言も口をきかない.

might[1] /maɪt/ 名 ***might and main*** 激しく, 元気よく ▪ They called out *might and main* for our help. 彼らは大声をはりあげて我々の助けを求めた.

Might is* [*makes*] *right. 《諺》力が正義である, 「勝てば官軍」.

with all** one's **might*/ *with* (*all** one's*) *might and main 《古風》力[精]いっぱい, 全力を尽くして ▪ We set to work *with all our might and main.* 我々は全力を尽くして仕事にかかった. ☞main《古》「体力」.

might[2] /maɪt/ 助 ***I might have known* [*guessed*]...** 《口》(...と)知っていたよ[思っていたよ], 案の定...だ ▪ *I might have known* it would be a waste of time asking. 聞いても無駄だと分かっていたよ ▪ Oh there goes the door bell—Oh it's you! *I might have guessed.* おっ, 玄関のベルが鳴った—なんだ君か, そうだと思っていたよ.

mighty /máɪti/ 形 ***How the mighty have fallen.*** 《諺》権力者が失墜してこのざまだ. ☞当人が以前は蔑んだことを今している人物についてふざけて用いる.

mighty works 力あるわざ, 奇跡 (《聖》 *Matt.* 13. 54, 11. 21, etc.) ▪ Most of his *mighty works* were done there. 彼のかずかずの奇跡がほとんどそこで行われた. ☞聖書語法.

mike /maɪk/ 名 ***do*** [***have***] ***a mike*** 《英俗》のらくら時を過ごす ▪ He's *doing a mike* as usual. 彼は例によってのらくらしている.

take a mike (***at***) 《俗》(...を)見る ▪ Just *take a mike at* that picture. ちょっとあの絵を見てごらん.

take the mike out of = take the MICK(E)Y out of.

milch /mɪltʃ/ 形 ***a milch cow*** **1** 乳牛 ▪ The employees wished to keep their own *milch cows* some day. 従業員たちはいつか自分の乳牛を飼える日を夢見ていた.

2 《口》ドル箱 ▪ To him his son has been *a* good *milch cow*. 彼にとって息子は大したドル箱だった.

mild /maɪld/ 形 (***as***) ***mild as a dove*** [***a lamb, May, milk***] 非常に柔和で ▪ Even when he is angry, I can make him *as mild as a lamb*. 彼が怒っているときでも, 私は彼を猫のようにおとなしくさせることができる ▪ His temper was *as mild as milk*. 彼の気質はきわめて柔和だった.

draw it mild →DRAW[2].

mildly /máɪldli/ 副 ***put it mildly*** 穏やかに[穏便に, 柔らかく]言う ▪ He was annoyed, to *put it mildly* (i.e. he was very angry). 彼は控え目に言うと不愉快に思っていた(つまり, かんかんに怒っていた).

mile /maɪl/ 名 ***a mile a minute*** 《米》素早く, 止まらずに一気に ▪ She talked *a mile a minute* about her trip to Asia. 彼女はアジア旅行のことを息もつかずにしゃべった.

a mile away [***off***] 《口》〚see, hear, smell, spot; know, tell などを修飾して〛遠く離れていても, はっきりと ▪ He's American. You can see that *a mile off*. 彼はアメリカ人だ. それははっきりと分かる ▪ I knew it was you. I'd know your laugh *a mile away*. 君だと分かったよ. 君の笑い声を聞けばすぐに分かるさ ▪ I knew she could spot a lie *a mile away*. 彼女は嘘にちゃんと気づくと私には分かっていた.

(***a million***) ***miles away*** 《口》ぼんやりして, 上の空で, 深く考えごとをして, 茫然自失して ▪ Are you listening?—Sorry, I was *miles away*. ちゃんと聞いているの?—ごめん, つい, ぼーっとしていて ▪ I was *a million miles away* during the whole lecture. 講義の間ずっともの思いにふけっていた.

be miles apart 全く同意に至っていない, かけ離れている ▪ The two sides *are* still *miles apart* in this dispute. この争議で当事者間の主張はまだかけ離れている.

(***be***) ***miles off*** [《英》***out***] 《口》(推測・計算などが)まるっきり間違っている ▪ I thought that it would fit my wife, but I *was miles off*. それが妻にぴったりだと思ったが, まるで間違っていた ▪ It turned out the forecast *was miles out*. 天気予報が大幅にずれていたことがわかった.

by a mile ... から大きく外れて ▪ You missed the target *by a mile* again. 君はまた的を大きく外した.

go the [***that***] ***extra mile*** (***for***) 特別にひと頑張りする, 一層の努力をする, もうひと押しする (《聖》*Matt.* 5. 41) ▪ The mayor is determined to *go the extra mile for* peace. 市長は平和のためにもうひと踏ん張りすることに決めた.

one's ***jaw drops a mile*** 口をあんぐり開ける ▪ The kid's eyes widened and *his jaw dropped a mile*. その子は目を見張り口をぽかんと開けた.

like five [***ten,*** etc.] ***miles of bad road*** 《口》楽しくない, よくない ▪ I feel *like ten miles of bad road* this morning. けさはひどい気分だ.

mile markers 《俗》(州間ハイウェイ沿いにある)番号つきの小さな標識 ▪ *A mile marker* on the National Road gives distances from many places. 国道の番号標識はさまざまな地点からの距離を示す.

miles and miles 相当な距離, かなりの間; はるかに ▪ I drove for *miles and miles* before we saw a gas station. かなり走ってやっとガソリンスタンドが見えた ▪ She is *miles and miles* a better pianist than I. 彼女は私よりもはるかにピアノがうまい.

miles from anywhere 辺鄙(へんぴ)な ▪ We live in the country, *miles from anywhere*. 我々は辺鄙な田舎に住んでいる.

miles from nowhere →NOWHERE.

not a hundred [***thousand, million***] ***miles away*** [***off, from***] →HUNDRED.

run a mile 《口》 **1** さっさと逃げる ▪ When he saw a police officer, he *ran a mile*. 警察官を見ると彼はさっさと逃げていった.

2 (いやな人・ことを)極力避ける (*from*) ▪ I'd *run a mile from* such a job. そういう仕事は敬遠したいね.

stand [***stick***] ***out a mile*** →STICK out a mile.

there's no one within miles of *a person* ***as*** ...としては人の右に出る者がない ▪ *There's no one within miles of* him *as* a tennis player. テニス選手として彼の右に出る者はいない.

win by a mile 楽勝する ▪ She's going to *win* the competition *by a mile*. この大会では彼女の楽勝だろう.

within a hundred miles of →HUNDRED.

mileage /máɪlɪdʒ/ 名 ***get a lot of mileage out of*** ...をまだ長く使える ▪ He *got a lot of mileage out of* his TV before it broke down. 彼のテレビはだめになるまでずいぶん長く使えた.

mile-high /máɪlháɪ/ 形 ***join the mile-high club*** 《口》飛行機内でセックスする ▪ Did Ralph *join the mile-high club* with a stewardess? ラルフは客室乗務員と機内でやったのか.

milk[1] /mílk/ 名 ***as like as milk to milk*** そっくりその通りで ▪ The twins are *as like as milk to milk*. その双子は全くうり二つだ. ☞ラテン語法.

(***as***) ***white as milk*** 真っ白い ▪ Her arms were *as white as milk*. 彼女の腕は雪のように白かった.

bring *a person* ***to his milk*** 《米口》人にその義務を悟らせる, 分際を思い知らせる ▪ A good thrashing will *bring* you *to your milk*. したたかぶちのめせばお前も分際を思い知るだろう.

brought to milk 乳が出るようにされた ▪ We have an account of a wether *brought to milk* by the sucking of a lamb. 小羊に乳を吸われて乳が出るように

M

なった去勢羊の話がある.

come [***get***] ***home with the milk*** 《英口》朝早く帰宅する，朝帰りをする ▪ He usually *comes home with the milk* after a party. 彼はパーティーの後ではたいてい朝帰りする.

cry over spilt [***spilled***] ***milk*** 済んだことを後悔する ▪ My cousin is always *crying over spilt milk*. いとこは済んだことをくよくよしてばかりいる.

drink in ... with *one's* ***mother's milk*** →suck in ... with one's mother's MILK.

have no milk in the coconut 《俗》狂気である，気が狂っている ▪ He does*n't* seem to *have* much *milk in the coconut* these days. 彼はこのごろ少し気が変になっているらしい.

in milk (雌牛が)乳を出す ▪ The heifer will be *in milk* at the time of show. この子牛は品評会のころには乳を出すだろう.

in [***out of***] ***the milk*** (穀粒が)熟していない[熟しかけて] ▪ The corn was then *in the milk*. そのころ小麦はまだ熟れていなかった ▪ The wheat was just *out of the milk*. 小麦がやっと熟れかけた. ☞穀粒が熟れていないときには乳のような汁が残っているところから.

It is no use [***good***] ***crying over spilt milk.*** 《諺》こぼれた牛乳のことで泣いてもむだだ，「覆水盆に返らず」.

milk and cider 《米口》(毛並みの)あし毛 ▪ He was a *milk and cider* steer 3 years old. それは3歳のあし毛の雄の子牛だった.

milk and honey 豊かな生活の糧(かて) (《聖》*Exod*. 3. 8; *Num*. 16. 13, etc.) ▪ America was then the fancied land of *milk and honey*. 当時アメリカは生活の糧に富んだ国だと思われていた. ☞聖書語法.

milk and roses (顔色が)美しい桜色 ▪ She was pretty, with a face all *milk and roses*. 彼女はすっかり桜色の顔をしてきれいだった.

milk and water 水を割った牛乳; 気の抜けた談義，ふやけた感傷 ▪ The conversation had plenty of *milk and water* in its composition. その会話は気の抜けた談義のみに終始した.

milk for babes (書物・説教・意見などが)子供向け[初歩]のもの (《聖》*1 Cor*. 3. 2) (↔strong MEAT) ▪ All his poems are *milk for babes*. 彼の詩はすべて子供向けのものだ.

mother's milk 母乳; なくてはならないもの (*to*) ▪ Whisky is *mother's milk to* old John. ウィスキーはジョン爺さんには欠かせないものだ.

out of the milk →in the MILK.

suck [***drink, take***] ***in ... with*** *one's* ***mother's milk*** 生まれついたときから…を身につけている ▪ Many Christians have *sucked in* their religion *with their mother's milk*. 多くのキリスト教信者は物心ついた頃から自らの宗教を身につけている.

the milk in the coconut 《口》(問題・事情の)要点，秘密 (crux) ▪ That accounts for *the milk in the coconut*. 《戯》なるほどそれで合点がいった ▪ To get to *the milk in the coconut*, where were you last night? 要するに，君はゆうべどこにいたの?

the milk of human kindness 自然の人情 (cf. Sh., *Macb*. 1. 5. 18) ▪ *The milk of human kindness* was not cradled in her bosom. 自然の人情などというものは彼女の胸にははぐくまれていなかった.

milk[2] /mílk/ 動 ***milk ... dry*** (人・物)から搾れるだけ搾る ▪ Her husband *milked* her *dry* and left her. 夫は彼女が一文なしになるまで搾ってから去った.

milk ... for all it is [***it's***] ***worth*** 《主に米》(事・物)をとことん利用する ▪ I urge you to *milk* the fact *for all it's worth*. 君がその事実をとことん利用することを強くお勧めする.

milk over the fence 〚主に動名詞形で〛隣の牛の乳を盗む ▪ That would be *milking over the fence*. そんなことをすれば隣の牛の乳を盗むようなものだ.

milk the bull [***ram***] 望みのない仕事をやる ▪ While the one *milks the ram*, the other holds under the sieve. 《諺》甲が雄ヒツジの乳をしぼる間，乙はふるいを下で受けている，「木によって魚を求める」.

milk the market [***street***] 《米俗》株式市場を操って甘い汁を吸う ▪ To use the slang of the financial quarter, they "*milk the street*." 経済界の俗語を使えば，彼らは「株式市場を操って甘い汁を吸っている」のだ.

mill[1] /mɪl/ 名 ***All*** [***Everything***] ***is grist that comes to*** *one's* ***mill.*** →GRIST.

be through the mill →go through the MILL.

bring more sacks to the mill →SACK[1].

burn *a person's* ***mill*** 人を破産させる ▪ She feared it would *burn her mill*. 彼女はそれが自分を破産させはしないかと心配した. ☞ひく小麦がなくて石臼が焼けることから.

draw water to *one's* (***own***) ***mill*** 我田引水する ▪ He well knew how to *draw water to his own mill*. 彼は我田引水する術をよく心得ていた.

go [***pass, be***] ***through the mill*** 《口》苦しい経験を積む，辛酸をなめる ▪ He has certainly *gone through the mill*, poor chap! かわいそうに，あの男は確かに苦しい経験を積んできたのだ.

in the mill 審議中で ▪ The bill is *in the mill* right now. その法案は目下，審議中だ.

Much water runs by the mill that the miller knows not of. 《諺》粉屋が知らない水がたくさん水車場のそばを流れ過ぎる，「灯台もと暗し」.

No mill, no meal. 《諺》ひき臼がなければ粉は得られない，「まかぬ種ははえぬ」.

put *a person* ***through the mill*** 《口》人に苦しい経験を積ませる，辛酸をなめさせる ▪ Frank *put* her *through the mill*. フランクは彼女に辛酸をなめさせた. ☞小麦を粉にすることから.

run of the mill 普通の，ありふれた ▪ Those singers are just *run of the mill*. 彼らは並みの歌手にすぎない.

run through the mill 許可される，具体化される ▪ The request will soon *run through the mill*. その要求はまもなくいれられるだろう ▪ The proposed stories are *running through the mill*. 企画された物語は出版されようとしている.

The mill cannot grind with water that is past. 《諺》好機逸すべからず.

The mills of God grind slowly (but surely [they grind exceedingly small]). 《諺》天罰は来るのが遅い(が確かである),「天網恢々(かいかい)疎にしてもらさず」.

mill[2] /mɪl/ 動 ***mill doll [dolly]*** 《俗》獄舎で亜麻をたたく ▪ How happy I was, sitting with Nancy, but now she *mills doll*. ナンシーといっしょに座って実に幸福だった. だが今, 彼女は獄舎で亜麻をたたいている.

miller /mílər/ 名 ***drown the miller*** 《口》(火酒・こね粉に)水を割り[加え]すぎる ▪ This punch is not worth drinking; you've *drowned the miller*. このパンチはとても飲めたものではない, 水の割りすぎだよ, 君. ☞《諺》Too much water drowned the MILLER. から.

Every miller draws water to his own mill. 《諺》粉屋はみな, 自分の粉ひき場へ水を引く,「我田引水」.

put the miller's eye out 《口》= drown the MILLER.

Too much water drowned the miller. 《諺》水が多すぎると粉屋も溺れ死にする,「過ぎたるは及ばざるがごとし」.

milling /mílɪŋ/ 名 ***milling in the darkness*** 《俗》夜の殺人 ▪ Men fought in the open field then, and there was no *milling in the darkness*. 当時男たちは広々とした原っぱで戦い, 夜の殺人というものはなかった.

million /míljən/ 名 ***a million and one*** =(a) HUNDRED and one.

a million-to-one chance 100万に一つの[ごくわずかの]見込み ▪ This work hasn't *a million-to-one chance* of being finished today. この仕事は今日中に終わる見込みが100万に一つもない.

feel [look] like a million (dollars) 《口》 **1** きわめて健康に感じる[見える] ▪ He went home *feeling like a million dollars*. 彼はきわめて元気に感じながら家へ帰った ▪ I *feel like a million* this morning. 今朝は気分がすこぶるよい.
2 (女が)とても魅力的な気がする[に見える] ▪ She *looked like a million dollars*. 彼女はとても魅力的に見えた. ☞dollars は略されることがある.

... in a million 100万に一人[一つ]の..., ごくまれな[類のない, すばらしい]... ▪ Your mother is one *in a million*. 君のお母さんは類のないすばらしい人だ ▪ Emily is a girl *in a million*. エミリーは100万人に一人の素敵な女の子だ.

Thanks a million! 《口》= THANKs a lot.

the dumb millions (政治に発言権をもたない)民衆, (無言の)一般大衆 ▪ Mahatma Gandhi organized the power of *our dumb millions*. マハトマ・ガンジーはわが民衆の総力を結集した.

there is [a person has] a chance in a million 万が一の可能性[千載一遇の機会]がある ▪ Amazingly, he *had a chance in a million* of surviving. 驚くべきことに彼は万が一で生き残った.

millpond /mílpɑ̀nd|-pɔ̀nd/ 名 ***like a millpond/(as) calm as a millpond*** (海が)鏡のように静かで ▪ The sea was *calm as a millpond*. 海は鏡のように静かだった. ☞millpond「水車用貯水池」.

millstone /mílstòʊn/ 名 ***(as) hard as the nether millstone*** 冷酷無情で(《聖》*Job* 41. 24) ▪ Where his employees are concerned, the man is *as hard as the nether millstone*. 使用人に関することでは, あの男は冷酷無情だ.

between the upper and the nether millstone(s) 《口》絶体絶命で, 窮地に陥って ▪ He found himself *between the upper and the nether millstone*. 彼は絶体絶命の危機に瀕していることがわかった ▪ Let's see how the peasant lay *between the upper and the nether millstone*. 小作農がいかに窮していたかを見てみよう.

one's ***eyes drop millstones*** (冷酷で)とんと泣かない, 血も涙もない ▪ *Your eyes drop millstones*, when fools' eyes let fall tears. 愚者が涙を流すときも, あなたはとんと泣かない.

(have [fix]) a millstone about [(a)round] *one's* ***neck*** (特に結婚の)重荷(を負わされる)(《聖》*Matt.* 18. 6) ▪ If ever a man *fixed a millstone about his neck*, he did when he married. 人が重荷を背負ったとすれば, それは結婚したときだ ▪ The mortgage on his house had become *a millstone around his neck*. 家を抵当にしたことが彼の重荷になっていた.

see far in [into, through] a millstone/look into [through] a millstone/dive into a millstone 《主に皮肉》視力・洞察力が恐ろしく鋭い, 目から鼻へつき抜けている ▪ Your eyes are so sharp that you can *look through a millstone*. 目から鼻へつき抜けるほど君の目は鋭い ▪ Your learning helps you to *see through a millstone*. 君は学があるから, 物事の見通しがとても鋭い.

Milton /míltən/ 名 ***mute inglorious Milton*** 名もなく, もの言わぬ大詩人[天才](Gray, *Elegy* 8) ▪ Some people believe in the *mute inglorious Milton*. 一部の人々は名もなく, もの言わぬ大詩人がいると信じている.

mince /mɪns/ 動 ***not mince matters [one's words]*** 歯にきぬを着せないでずばりと言う ▪ I told him, *without mincing matters*, that I never wished to see him again. 私は歯にきぬを着せないで, 二度と君にはお目にかかりたくないと彼に言ってやった.

mincemeat /mínsmì:t/ 名 ***make mincemeat [hamburger] (out) of*** 《口》(人)をさんざんにやっつける; (議論など)をめちゃめちゃに打ち破る ▪ That bully *made mincemeat of* my son. あのいじめっ子がうちの息子をひどく痛めつけた ▪ Their team will *make hamburger out of* us. 我々は彼らのチームには惨敗するだろう.

mind[1] /maɪnd/ 名 ***a butterfly [grasshopper] mind*** 関心が次々に移って落ち着かないこと

M

▪ Her *grasshopper mind* leapt on to a completely different subject. 彼女の移り気な心は全く別なことに跳んでいった.

A contented mind is a perpetual* [*continual*] *feast. 《諺》満ち足りた心は絶えず饗宴[悦楽]である.

a load* [*weight*] *off *a person's* ***mind*** →a weight off one's MIND.

a mind reader 人の心が読める人 ▪ That's just what I was going to say. You must be *a mind reader*. ちょうどそう言おうとしていたんだ. 君はきっと人の心が読めるのだね ▪ If you don't like it, then tell me. I'm not *a mind reader*. いやならいやとはっきり言ってくれないと分からないよ.

a one-track* [*single-track*] *mind 融通のきかない頭, 偏狭な心 ▪ She could talk only about her son's success; she had *a single-track mind*. 彼女の頭は融通がきかず, 話せたのは息子の成功のことだけだった ▪ All he thinks about is sex—he has *a one-track mind*. 彼はセックスのことしか考えない偏狭な心の持ち主だ. ☞one-track「鉄道の単線」.

a weight* [*load*] *off *one's* ***mind*** 心の重荷をおろすこと ▪ To have cleared my debt is *a load off my mind*. 借金をすっかり返済して心の重荷がおりた.

after *one's* ***mind*** →to one's MIND.

(All) great minds think alike. 《諺》大人物は同じことを考える.

alter *one's* ***mind*** →change one's MIND.

apply *one's* ***mind to*** →bend one's MIND to.

at* [*in*] *the back of *one's* ***mind*** 心の奥に ▪ Money worries have always been *at the back of my mind*. 心の奥には常に金の心配事がある.

be bored* [*frightened, worried*] *out of *one's* ***mind*** 退屈で[怖くて, 心配で]おかしくなりそうになる (→out of one's MIND 2) ▪ He looked *bored out of his mind*. 彼は退屈でおかしくなった様子だった ▪ I have *been worried out of my mind* about you! あなたのことが心配で気が変になりそうだったのよ.

be in* [《米》 *of*] *two* [*twenty*] *minds*/ *have two minds 心がぐらついている, 心が迷っている (*about, as to, whether*) ▪ I *was in two minds whether* to do it or not. 私はそれをすべきかどうかで心がぐらついていた ▪ I *was of two minds as to* what I should do next. 次にどうしようかと戸惑っていた ▪ I'*m in twenty minds about* where to go. どこへ行こうか迷っている.

be of a ... mind ...の意見である ▪ Your husband will not *be of* that *mind*. あなたのご主人はそういう意見ではないでしょう.

be of *a person's* ***mind*** 人と同意見である ▪ I don't doubt you'll *be of my mind*. きっとあなたは私と同意見だと思う.

be of* [*in*] *one* [*a*] *mind 意見が一致している (*with*) (《聖》 *2 Cor*. 13. 11) ▪ Most of the electors seemed to *be of one mind*. 選挙人はたいてい意見が一致しているらしかった.

be of sound* [*unsound*] *mind 精神が正常である[に異常がある] ▪ I'*m of sound mind* and I'm whole emotionally. 私は正気だし情緒も安定している ▪ She has *been of unsound mind* since the death of her father. 父を亡くして以来彼女は正常な精神状態ではない.

be of the same mind **1** (何人かの人が)意見が一致している ▪ I'*m of the same mind* as my wife. 妻と同意見だ.

2 (一人が)心が変わらないでいる ▪ *Is* she still *of the same mind*? 彼女はまだ心が変わらないでいるのか.

be* [*go, pass*] *out of* [*from*] *mind 忘れられてしまう ▪ When a man is out of sight, soon he *passes out of mind*. 人は去ると, すぐに忘れられる.

be the last thing on *a person's* ***mind*** 最も人が考えそうにないことである ▪ Surrender *was the last thing on Hussein's mind*. 降伏などはフセインが考えもしないことだった.

bear* [*keep*]... *in mind ...を心に留める, 覚えている ▪ *Bear in mind* that neither success nor failure is ever final. 成功も失敗もこれでおしまいとはならないことを心に留めておきなさい ▪ Will you *keep in mind* that we have got to be better friends? 我々がもっと仲よしにならなければだめだということを覚えていてくださいよ.

bend* [*apply*]** *one's* ***mind to ...に心を傾ける, に苦心する ▪ She will never succeed until she *bends her mind to* her work. 彼女は仕事に心を傾けないかぎり決して成功しないだろう.

blow *a person's* ***mind*** 《俗》人を恍惚(こう)とさせる, 心をしびれさせる ▪ The film has really *blown my mind*. その映画には全くうっとりとしてしまった. ☞麻薬の効果から.

boggle the* [*a person's*] *mind 《口》動転させられる, (人が)圧倒される, 肝を潰す, 想像できない ▪ The immense size of the pyramid *boggled his mind*. そのピラミッドの大きさに彼は肝を潰した.

bring* [*call*]... *to mind ...を思い出す, 思い出させる ▪ He *called* these things *to mind* strolling along the river banks. 彼は川岸をぶらぶらしながらこれらのことを思い出していた ▪ Your story *brings* the event *to mind*. 君の話でその事件を思い出した.

broaden the mind 新しい興味が湧く ▪ Traveling abroad will *broaden your mind*. 海外旅行をしたら視野が広がるよ.

cast *one's* ***mind back*** 過去を思い出す ▪ *Cast your mind back* to your schooldays. 君の学校時代のことを思い出してごらん.

change* [*alter*]** *one's* ***mind 考えを変える ▪ I have *changed my mind* and decided not to go. 気が変わって行かないことにした.

clear *one's* ***mind of*** ...を頭からなくす ▪ You must *clear your mind of* any prejudice. 頭からいかなる偏見も捨てなければならない.

close *one's* ***mind*** (人が可能性などを)考えないようにする (*to*) ▪ In his later years, Edison *closed his mind to* constructive criticism from his assistants. 晩年にエジソンは助手たちからの建設的な批判を

考えないようになった.

come into* [*cross, enter*] *one's* *mind 心に浮かぶ, 思いつく ▪ The same idea *came* often *into my mind.* その同じ考えがしばしば心に浮かんできた.

come* [*spring*] *to mind (ある考えが)ふと頭に浮かぶ, 思いつく, 心をよぎる ▪ A wonderful idea *came to mind.* すばらしい考えがふと浮かんだ ▪ I'd like to get her a gift, but nothing *springs to mind.* 彼女へのプレゼントを買いたいのだが何も思いつかない.

disclose *one's* (***own***) ***mind*** → speak one's (own) MIND.

drive *a person* ***out of*** *his* ***mind*** (人・事が)A(人)を激怒させる ▪ His wife *drove* him *out of his mind* with her spending. 彼の妻は浪費で彼を激怒させた.

drunk* [*stoned, pissed*] *out of *one's* ***mind*** 《俗》酔いつぶれて ▪ He got home, *drunk out of his mind.* 彼は酔いつぶれて帰宅した.

ease *a person's* ***mind*** =ease a person's CONSCIENCE.

fix ... in *one's* ***mind*** (事)をしっかりと心に留める ▪ Her image *was fixed in my mind.* 彼女の面影が私の心に焼きついた.

fix *one's* ***mind on* [*upon*]** ...に心を向ける ▪ He carries out whatever he *fixes his mind on* doing. 彼はやろうと決めたことは何でも実行する.

get *one's* ***mind around* [*round*]** (困難・奇妙なもの)を理解する ▪ I still can't *get my mind around* the strange things you said. 君が言った妙なことがまだ分からない.

get ... off *one's* ***mind*** (人・事)を忘れる ▪ I can't *get* that girl *off my mind.* あの娘のことが忘れられぬ.

get ... out of *one's* ***mind*** ...を考えないようにする ▪ I suffered a complete defeat and now I can't *get* it *out of my mind.* 惨敗を喫してしまってそれがどうにも頭から離れないんだ.

give* [*tell*]** *a person* ***a piece* [*bit*] *of *one's* ***mind*** 《口》人に目の前で直言する; 人を頭ごなしにしかりつける ▪ I must *give* him *a piece of my mind* when I see him. 彼に会ったら, はっきり言ってやらなければならない.

give *one's* (***whole***) ***mind to*** ...に専念する ▪ I'll *give my mind to* you, Lord, next Sunday. 主よ, 今度の日曜日にはあなたのことだけを思います.

go out of* [*from*] *mind →be out of MIND.

go out of *a person's* ***mind*** 人に忘れられる ▪ The appointment *went* right [clean] *out of my mind.* その約束をとんと忘れてしまった ▪ It *went* right *out of her mind.* 彼女はそれをすっかり忘れた.

go out of *one's* ***mind*** 気が狂う ▪ I was *going out of my mind* with worry. 心配で気が変になりそうだった.

go over ... in *one's* ***mind*** ...を熟慮する ▪ I *go over* that terrible experience *in my mind* every day. あのひどい体験のことを毎日じっくり考えている.

***Great minds think alike* [*run in the same gutter*]**. 《諺》偉大な精神の持ち主は似たような考え方をする[同じみぞを流れる]. ☞天才の考えることはいっしょだと言って, 自分と同じことを思いついた人物をおどけてほめるのに多く用いられる.

have a closed mind かたくなである, 了見が狭い ▪ He *has a closed mind* on the subject. 彼はその問題についてはかたくなだ.

have a great* [*good*] *mind to *do* ...したい気が大いにある ▪ I *have a great mind to* write to my lawyer. 私の弁護士に手紙を出したい気が大いにある.

have a meeting of the minds 意見が一致する, 同意する ▪ We *had a meeting of the minds* regarding the project. そのプロジェクトについて意見の一致をみた.

have a mind for ...をほしいと思う, におぼしめしがある ▪ I*'ve a* great *mind for* the beautiful little house I saw last week. 先週見たあの美しい小さい家がほしくてたまらない.

have a mind like a steel trap 頭が切れる, すばらしく頭の回転が速い ▪ Dr. Smith *has a mind like a steel trap.* スミス博士は実に頭の回転が速い.

have a mind of its own (機械・車など)が思う通りに動かない ▪ My DVD player seems to *have a mind of its own.* 私の DVD プレーヤーはどうも思うように動かない.

have a mind of *one's* ***own*** 自分の意見を持つ ▪ He is old enough to *have a mind of his own.* 彼はもう自分の意見を持っていい年齢だ.

have a mind to *do* ...を(達成)したい ▪ I *have a mind to* find out the truth behind this. この裏にある真相を知りたい.

have half a mind to *do* ...しようかと思っている ▪ I*'ve half a mind to* resign unless there's a marked improvement. 著しい改善がないかぎり辞任しようかと思っています.

have ... in mind **1** =bear ... in MIND.
2 ...のことを考えている, を意図する ▪ I don't know whom he *has in mind* for the job. 彼がその仕事を誰にさせようと思っているのかわからない.

have it in mind to *do* ...しようと考えている ▪ I *have it in mind to* warn him. 彼に警告しようかと思っている.

have *one's* ***mind on*** 気[関心]が...に向いている ▪ He's made a few mistakes today. He*'s got his mind on* other things. 彼は今日少々ミスを重ねた. ほかのことに気が散っていたせいだ.

have no* [*little*] *mind to *do* ...する気が少しも[あまり]ない ▪ He *has little mind to* be a martyr. 彼は殉教者になる気はあまりない.

have ... on *one's* ***mind*** →off one's MIND.

have two minds →be in two MINDs.

if* [*when*]** *one* ***puts *one's* ***mind to it*** それに専念すれば, その気になれば(できる) ▪ You could do well in math *if* you *put your mind to it.* 君はやる気になれば数学ができるようになる.

in *one's* **[*the*] *mind's eye*** →EYE.

in *one's* ***right mind*** 〚主に否定文で〛 正気で (↔

M

out of one's MIND 1, 2) ▪ John couldn't have been *in his right mind* when he struck his wife. ジョンは妻に手を上げたとき正気であったはずがない.

It is* (*a case* [*a victory*] *of*) *mind over matter. 精神が肉体に勝つ[病気に意志の力[勇気]が打ち勝つ]かどうか(の場合[勝負])である ▪ I had a very bad cold but I worked on. *It was* (*a case of*) *mind over matter.* 私はひどい風邪を引いていたが, 働き続けた. 精神が肉体に勝つかどうか(の状況)だった ▪ Concentrate harder. *This is a case of mind over matter.* もっと集中しろ. 周囲の状況に打ち勝つ精神力が問われている.

It's all* [*only*] *in the [*a person's*] ***mind.*** (病気も勇気も)すべて心の持ち方のいかんによる ▪ He's not really ill—*it's only in the mind.* 実は彼は病気ではなく, 思い過ごしにすぎない ▪ I don't feel pain because *it's all in the mind.* 全く気の持ちようだから私は痛みを感じない.

***keep* [*have*] *an open mind* (*on ...*)** ...について決定しないでいる, 状況がわかるまで考えをまとめず待つ ▪ He *keeps an open mind on* the matter. 彼はその件については決定しないでいる ▪ You should *have an open mind* until you know the facts. 事実が分かるまでは結論を出さない方がいいだろう.

keep ... in mind →bear ... in MIND.

keep *one's* ***mind on*** ...に絶えず注意する ▪ *Keep your mind on* what you are doing. 自分が今していることに絶えず気を配りなさい.

know *one's* ***own mind*** 意思がはっきりしている, 決心を変えない ▪ Mary always *knows her own mind.* メアリーはいつでも意思がはっきりしている ▪ He does not always *know his own mind.* 彼はときとして心がぐらつく.

leap to mind (連想で)すぐ頭に思い浮かぶ ▪ Nothing has *leapt to mind* as yet. 今のところまだ何も思い浮かばない.

let *a person* ***know* [*tell*** *a person*] *one's* ***mind*** 人に自分の気持ちをはっきりと言う ▪ If I see him again, I shall *let* him *know my mind.* もう一度彼に会ったら, 私の気持ちをはっきり言ってやろう.

lose* [*go out of*]** *one's* ***mind 気が狂う ▪ She still feared that I should *lose my mind.* 彼女は私が発狂しはしないかとまだ心配していた.

***make the mind boggle/the mind boggles* (*at*)** 《口》(...に) びっくりする, そんなことは信じられない ▪ Magnitude 9.0? *The mind boggles.* マグニチュード 9.0 だって? そんなの信じられない ▪ *The mind boggles at* his stupidity. 彼の愚かさ加減にはあきれかえる ▪ The number of unsolved mysteries about Easter Island *makes the mind boggle.* イースター島についての未解決の謎の多さに舌を巻く. ☞boggle は bogey「《古風》お化け」から派生.

make up *one's* ***mind*** 決心する; 腹を決める (*to do, that, about, for, to*) ▪ I like both. I can't *make up my mind.* どちらも気に入っていて, 決められないや ▪ He has *made up his mind to* go to Mexico for his vacation. 彼は休暇にメキシコへ行こうと決心した ▪ They have *made up their mind(s) that* it is more important. 彼らはそのほうが重要だと決めている. ☞複数主語で minds としない例は多い.

make up *a person's* ***mind* (*for*** *him*) 人に腹を決めさせる ▪ Since he can't decide what to do, we will have to *make up his mind for him.* 彼がどうしてよいか自分で決められない以上, 我々が腹を決めさせてやらねばならないだろう.

mind-boggling 驚くべき ▪ There is nothing more *mind-boggling* or interesting than space. 宇宙ほど圧倒的で興味をそそるものはない.

one's ***mind goes blank*** 言葉が出ない, 言うべきことが思い浮かばない ▪ When I looked at the large audience, *my mind went blank.* 大勢の聴衆を見ると頭の中が真っ白になった.

one's ***mind is buzzing*** (人)の頭に(考えなどが)かけめぐっている ▪ *Her mind was buzzing* with questions. 彼女の頭の中を様々な疑問が去来していた.

a person's ***mind is in the gutter*** 《口》人がいやがる話題(特にセックス)を口にしたがる ▪ I don't like Jack. *His mind is* always *in the gutter.* ジャックってきらいよ, すぐいやらしいことを言うんだから.

one's ***mind is made up*** 決心がついている ▪ If *your mind is made up*, let's go. 決心がついたのなら行こう.

one's ***mind is* [*runs*] *on*** ...を意図している, 考えている, に関心を持っている ▪ *His mind runs on* something else. 彼は何かほかのことをもくろんでいる ▪ It was selfish to let *my mind run on* my own distress so much. 私の悩みのことばかりあんなに考えていたのはわがままだった.

mind over matter 体力より精神力(の問題だ) ▪ *Mind over matter*, as with everything else in life. 人生のあらゆる問題と同様, 体力よりも精神力だ.

***nobody in his right mind could* [*would*]** *do* 正気な人なら誰一人...しないだろう ▪ *Nobody in his right mind would* drive in the heavy snow storm. 正気な人なら誰もこのひどい吹雪の中で車を運転しないだろう.

off* [*on*]** *one's* ***mind 念頭を離れて[去らないで], 忘れられて[気にかかって] ▪ He has the matter *off his mind.* 彼はそのことを忘れてしまっている ▪ He has nothing but girls *on his mind.* 彼は女の子のことしか考えていない ▪ What's *on your mind?* 何が気にかかっているのか; 何を考えているのか.

open *one's* **(*own*) *mind*** →speak one's (own) MIND.

out of *one's* ***mind*** **1** 気が狂って (↔in one's right MIND) ▪ He was drunk or *out of his mind* when he was dismissed. 彼が首になったときには酔っていたか気が狂っていたかどっちかだ ▪ You paid 1,000 dollars for that junk! Are you *out of your mind?* あのがらくたに 1,000 ドル払ったって? 気は確かか.

2 狂気のようになって, (心配・退屈で)気が変になりそうで (*with*) (↔in one's right MIND) ▪ He was *out of his mind with* worry. 彼は心配のあまり狂気のよう

になっていた.
3《口》=drunk out of one's MIND.
pass out of [***from***] ***mind*** →be out of MIND.
pass through *one's* ***mind*** 心に浮かぶ, 思いつく ▪Many terrible fears *passed through her mind.* さまざまな恐怖が彼女の心中を駆け巡った.
pay no mind/not pay any mind《方》注意しない; 気にしない ▪I do*n't pay* her *any mind.* 彼女のことなんか少しも心に留めていない ▪*Pay no mind* to what they say. 彼らの言うことは少しも気にするな.
pissed out of *one's* ***mind*** →drunk out of one's MIND.
prey on *a person's* ***mind*** 人の心を悩ます ▪Remorse *preyed on his mind.* 悔恨の念が彼の心を悩ませた.
push ... to the back of *one's* ***mind*** =put ... out of one's MIND.
put *a person* ***in mind*** 人に…を思い出させる (*of, how, that, to do*) ▪You *put* me *in mind of* an old story. 君の話で私は昔の話を思い出した ▪*Put* Ralf *in mind that* he promised me a visit tonight. ラルフに今晩来ると約束したことを思い出させてください.
put [***set***] *a person's* ***mind at rest*** →set ... at REST.
put *one's* ***mind on*** …に心を集中する ▪Please turn off the radio. I can't *put my mind on* my work. ラジオを消していただきたい. 仕事に集中することができないから.
put [***give, set***] *one's* ***mind to*** …に専念する ▪*Put your mind to* your studies. 研究に専念せよ.
put ... out of *one's* ***mind*** …を(わざと)忘れる ▪I tried to *put* my past suffering *out of my mind.* 私は過去の苦しみを忘れようとした.
read *a person's* ***mind***《戯》人の心を読みとる ▪He can *read his father's mind.* 彼は父の考えを読みとることができる.
right in *one's* ***mind*** =in one's right MIND.
set [***put***] *one's* ***mind on*** **1** …に一心になる, を熱望する ▪I've *set my mind on* your joining the party. 君が一行に加わることを熱望しています.
2 …することを決意する ▪He has *set his mind on* studying French harder. 彼はもっとまじめにフランス語を勉強しようと心に決めた.
slip *a person's* ***mind*** うっかり忘れる ▪I meant to mail the letter, but it entirely *slipped my mind.* 手紙を投函しようと思っていたのに, ついうっかり忘れてしまった.
So many men, so many minds.《諺》十人十色.
speak [***say, tell, disclose, open***] *one's* (***own***) ***mind*** 考えを打ち明ける; 思うことをはっきり言う ▪In these sorts of cases, it's better to *speak one's mind.* このような場合には, 思うことをはっきり言うほうがよい.
stick in *one's* [***the***] ***mind*** →STICK[2].
stoned out of *one's* ***mind*** →drunk out of one's MIND.
take *one's* ***mind off*** …から思いをそらせる, のことを忘れる ▪He could never *take his mind off* the work. 彼はその仕事のことがどうしても忘れられなかった.
tell *a person* ***a piece*** [***bit***] ***of*** *one's* ***mind*** →give a person a piece of one's MIND.
tell *a person one's* ***mind*** →let a person know one's MIND.
time out of mind →TIME[1].
to [***after***] *one's* ***mind*** 心にかなって, 好みに合って ▪It was some time before we could get a yacht *to our mind.* 好みに合ったヨットを手に入れるまでにはかなり時間がかかった ▪If you have a wife *after your mind*, do not forsake her. 心にかなった妻がいるなら, 見捨ててはいけない.
to my mind 自分の考えでは ▪*To my mind* the action was premature. 私に言わせればその行動は早計だった.
turn *one's* ***mind to*** …に心[注意]を向ける ▪They *turned their minds to* its consideration. 彼らはその件を考慮し始めた.
turn ... over in *one's* ***mind*** …を熟考する ▪*Turn* it *over in your mind* whether to accept the offer or not. その申し出を受けるかどうかじっくり考えなさい.
weigh on *a person's* ***mind*** =prey on a person's MIND.
with ... in mind …を念頭において ▪He went out for a drive *with* no particular destination *in mind.* 彼は特に行く当てもなくドライブに出かけた.

mind[2] /maɪnd/ 動 ***Do you mind!*** やめてくれ, いやだよ; 君の知ったことではない ▪"Here, *do you mind!*" the boy said when the girl tried to touch his hand.「おい, やめてくれよ」と男の子は女の子が彼の手にさわろうとしたときに言った ▪She simply told me, "*Do you mind!*" 彼女は私に「放っといてよ」とだけ言った.
Do you mind *doing* [***my*** *doing*]***?*** →Would you MIND doing ...?, Would you MIND my doing ...?
Don't mind me.《しばしば皮肉》私のことなんか気にしなくてもいい《放っといてくれ》▪*Don't mind me.* I'm just killing time. 僕のことなら放っといてくれ. ただ時間つぶしをしているだけだから.
I don't mind admitting [***telling you***] (照れかくしに)白状すると ▪I was scared, *I don't mind telling you.* 怖かったよ, 実を言うと.
I don't mind if I do. けっこうですね, ええどうぞ《飲み物などを勧められたときの返事》▪Won't you have a glass of iced beer?—*I don't mind if I do.* 冷やしたビールを1杯いかがですか?—けっこうですね. ☞"Yes, Please" や "Thank you" の方が素直な言い方.
I don't mind (***which***)***.***《英口》(物を選ぶように言われて)どれでも結構です ▪You can call me Bill or

Billy. *I don't mind which.* 僕のことをビルと呼んでもビリーと呼んでも，どちらでもいいよ．

I should* [*would*] *not mind 《口》…しても悪くない，したいものだ ▪ *I shouldn't mind* a cup of tea myself. 私はお茶をいただきたいと思います ▪ *I wouldn't mind* living here for a while. しばらくここに住むのも悪くないな．

if you don't* [*won't, wouldn't*] *mind **1** さしつかえなければ ▪ I will sit here *if you don't mind.* さしつかえなければ私はここに座っています ▪ I'd like to ask you a few questions, *if you wouldn't mind.* さしつかえなければ2, 3お尋ねしたいのですが．

2《口》気をつけないと ▪ They'll see you, *if you don't mind.* 気をつけないと彼らに見られるよ．

3 ＝Do you MIND! 1.

4〚相手の言動に反対して皮肉に〛こう言ってはなんですが ▪ I give the orders around here, *if you don't mind.* こう言ってはなんですが，ここで指令を出すのは私なのですがね．

if you don't mind me* [*my*] *saying so 《口》こういっては失礼ですが ▪ This color doesn't really suit you, *if you don't mind my saying so.* 失礼ですが，この色はあまりあなたにお似合いになりません．

mind and do 《口》きっと…しなさい ▪ *Mind and do* what you're told. きっと言われた通りにするのだよ．

mind *one's* ***business*** 仕事に精出す ▪ He went back to Samaria and *minded his business.* 彼はサマリアへ帰って行って，仕事に精出した．

mind *one's* ***eye*** 《口》〚主に命令文で〛気をつける ▪ Hold your tongue, and *mind your eye.* おしゃべりはやめて，注意しなさい ▪ I recommended him to *mind his eye* for the future. 私は彼に将来に向けて気を配ったほうがいいぞと言ってやった．

Mind how you go. 《口》 **1** 気をつけて ▪ *Mind how you go* with this knife. このナイフを使うときは気をつけろよ．

2《別れの挨拶に》さようなら ▪ Goodbye then. *Mind how you go!* では，これで．さようなら．

mind out of the way 道をあける ▪ *Mind out of the way,* will you? 道をあけてくれませんか．

mind *one's* ***own business*** 自分の仕事に精出して他人におせっかいしない ▪ *Mind your own business!*—I was only trying to help. いらぬお世話だ—手を貸してやろうとしただけなんだがね．

mind *one's* ***P's and Q's*** →P.

mind the shop [《米》***store***]《英》留守をあずかる ▪ He's *minding the shop* while the boss is abroad. 社長が海外にいるときは彼が取り仕切っている ▪ Dad's *minding the store* while Mom's away. ママの留守中はパパが家事をしている．

Mind you! 《口》いいかい; よく聞きたまえよ《話者が言っていることに注意を促したり，強調したいときの挿入句》 ▪ But I have no objection, *mind you!* とは言っても，こちらには何も異存はないんだよ，いいね．

mind you *do* 《口》必ず…してください ▪ Never mind your handwriting, but *mind you* write. 字の上手下手なんかどうでもいい，だが必ず書いてくれよ．

Never mind! 《口》 **1** 心配するな，何でもない ▪ *Never mind!* I can do this by myself. なあにいいさ．これは僕一人でやれるから．

2 君の知ったことではない ▪ Do you call yourself a gentleman, sir?—*Never mind,* sir. あなたは紳士のつもりですか?—大きなお世話ですよ．

never mind **1**《口》…は言うまでもなく (＝let ALONE) ▪ I can't speak French, *never mind* Russian. 私はフランス語は話せない，ロシア語は言うまでもない．

2〚命令文で〛…などやめなさい ▪ *Never mind* worrying about that. そんなことを心配するのはやめなさい．

never you mind… 《口》…はお前の知ったことじゃない(から教えない) ▪ *Never you mind* what we're talking about. 私たちの話はお前の知ったことじゃない．

Would* [*Do*] *you mind *doing* ***…?*** どうか…してくださいませんか ▪ *Would* [*Do*] *you mind opening* the window? 窓を開けてくださいませんか． ☞Would you…? のほうが普通; 答えは次の成句の場合と同じ．

Would* [*Do*] *you mind my *doing* ***…?*** 私が…してもかまいませんか ▪ *Do you mind my shutting* the door? ドアを閉めてもかまいませんか ▪ *Would you mind my asking* you what part of the country you come from? どのあたりのご出身かお尋ねしてよろしいですか． ☞「いいですよ」と応じるときの答えは "No, not at all." または "Certainly not."

mine[1] /maɪn/ 名 ***a mine of information*** 知識の宝庫 ▪ This book is *a mine of* useful *information.* この本は役に立つ知識の宝庫である．

Back to the salt mines. 《戯》(いやだが)また仕事に戻ろう ▪ Vacation is over. *Back to the salt mines.* 休暇は終わった．また仕事だ． ☞昔ロシアで囚人をシベリアの岩塩坑で働かせたことから．

salt a mine 《口》(鉱山の鉱石・帳簿などをごまかして)経営を実際よりもよく見せかける ▪ They would *salt a mine* to deceive prospective customers. 彼らは帳簿を改ざんして手応えのある顧客の目を欺いたものだった．

mine[2] /maɪn/ 代 ***make mine…*** (食物の調味・衣服のサイズなど)私のは…にしてください ▪ I'd like an apple pie.—*Make mine* cherry. アップルパイをもらおうか—僕にはチェリーパイを．

miniature /míniətʃər|-nə-/ 名 ***in miniature*** 小規模の ▪ He is a Hercules *in miniature.* 彼はヘラクレスを小型にしたようなものだ．

minimum /mínəməm/ 名 ***at the* [*a*] *minimum*** 最低でも，最小でも ▪ *At the minimum,* he needs an apology. 最低でも彼は謝罪しなければならない ▪ The doctors wanted to keep him there a month, *at the minimum.* 医者たちは最低でもひと月は彼がそこにとどまるように求めた．

keep…to a minimum …を最低限に抑える ▪ We must *keep* our expenditure *to a minimum.* 出費を最低限に抑えなければならない．

minion /mínjən/ 名 ***a minion of fortune*** 《軽蔑》運命の寵児，幸運児 ▪ His son suddenly became *a minion of fortune.* 彼の息子は一躍幸

運児となった.

the minions of the law 《軽蔑》警察官, 獄吏 ▪ I had a most painful morning with *the minions of the law*. けさは警察官を相手にひどくつらい目にあった.

ministering /mínəstərɪŋ/ 形 ***a ministering angel*** 守護天使《親切な看護師など》 ▪ She was good and kind, *a ministering angel*. 彼女は優しく親切で, まさに守護天使だった.

minnow /mínoʊ/ 名 ***a Triton of*** [***among***] ***the minnows*** →TRITON.

minor /máɪnər/ 形名 ***in a minor key*** 《楽》短調で; 《口》陰気な気分で, 低い調子で ▪ The conversation was pitched *in a minor key*. その会話は陰気な調子で行われた.

send to the minors 解雇する, 関係を絶つ ▪ My girlfriend has *sent* me *to the minors*. ガールフレンドにふられてしまった.

minority /mənɔ́:rəti|maɪnɔ́r-/ 名 ***be in a minority of one*** 支持者が一人もない ▪ I'*m in a minority of one* on that point. その点に関して私の支持者は一人もいない.

be in the minority 少数派である ▪ Judging by the cheers, we'*re in the minority*. 拍手の数からして我々のほうが劣勢だ.

mint[1] /mɪnt/ 名 ***a mint of*** 《口》山ほどの, 多大の ▪ There are *a mint of* reasons to choose a BMW. BMW を選ぶ理由は山ほどある ▪ He has *a mint of* money. 彼には巨万の富がある.

in mint state [***condition***] (貨幣・切手・書籍などが)真新しい ▪ The stamp was unused and *in mint state*. その切手は未使用で真新しかった.

mint[2] /mɪnt/ 動 ***be minting it*** [《米》***money***] 《英口》楽々と大金を儲ける ▪ Hollywood films *were minting it* every year. ハリウッド映画は毎年悠々と巨額を稼いでいた.

minus /máɪnəs/ 名 ***an x-double minus*** 《口》(演技など)きわめて下手な, お粗末な ▪ She gave *an x-double minus* performance at the audition. 彼女はオーディションでひどい演技をしてしまった.

minute /mínət/ 名 ***a minute*** ちょっと ▪ Wait *a minute*. ちょっと待って.

(***at***) ***any minute*** [***moment***] (***now***) いつでも, いつなんどき; 今すぐにも, 今にも ▪ Hurry up! She'll be back *any minute now*. 急げ. 彼女が今に戻ってくる ▪ It may occur *at any moment*. それはいつなんどき起こるかもしれない.

at the last minute まぎわ[いよいよという時]になって ▪ Don't say such dreadful things just *at the last minute*! 土壇場になってそんなひどいことを言わないでくれ.

by the minute 刻一刻《一分ごとに》 ▪ The grass was growing greener *by the minute*. 草地は刻一刻と緑の色を増していった.

Do you have [《英》***Have you got***] ***a minute?*** ちょっと時間がありますか ▪ Hi. *Do you have a minute?* Let me ask you a question. やあ, ちょっといいですか. ひとつ質問させてください.

every [***any***] ***minute*** 今か今かと ▪ I'm expecting her *every* [*any*] *minute*. 彼女を今か今かと待ち受けているのです.

Every minute [***moment***] ***counts.*** 一秒を争う ▪ *Every minute counts* in performing surgery. 執刀の際は一刻を争う.

every minute of... **1** (事)の一瞬一瞬[すべて] ▪ Alan loved *every minute of* that trip. アランはその旅行の間ずっと楽しかった.

2 〚副詞的に〛 ...の間中ずっと ▪ Failure is there *every minute of* your life. 人生には失敗がつきものさ.

famous for fifteen minutes (一般人が)つかの間有名になって ▪ His art made him *famous for fifteen minutes*. 彼は持ち前の技で一時名が売れた.

for a minute ちょっとの間 ▪ I must go downstairs *for a minute*. ちょっと階下へ降りてきます.

hang [***hold***] ***on a minute*** 《俗》〚命令文で〛待て; (今していることを)少しの間やめろ ▪ *Hang on a minute*, wait a minute. ちょっと, ちょっと待って ▪ Honey, wait a minute. *Hold on a minute*. あなた, ちょっと, 少し待って.

in a minute すぐに ▪ The train will be starting *in a minute*. 電車はすぐに出るだろう.

Just a minute [***a moment, a second***]. 《口》ちょっと待ってくれ ▪ *Just a moment*, I was here first. ちょっと待って. 僕が一番に来たんだ ▪ *Just a second*, please. I'll check. しばらくお待ちを. 調べてみます.

make a minute of = make a MEMORANDUM of.

not for a minute →for a MOMENT 3.

Now just a minute! 何だって ▪ You are a fool. —*Now just a minute!* お前はばかだ—何だと.

one minute **1** ちょっと待って (→Wait a MINUTE.) ▪ "*One minute*," said the stage manager. 「ちょっと待て」と舞台監督が言った.

2 ある時には(...だったかと思うと)《the next (minute) と相関的に使われて》 ▪ *One minute* his eyes are open, and *the next* they're shut. ほんの一瞬彼の目が開いたかと思ったら次の瞬間には閉じている.

one minute to midnight 《口》最後の瞬間, ラストチャンス ▪ It's *one minute to midnight*, one minute to go. これがラストチャンスだ, もう時間がない.

the minute (***that***) ...するとすぐ ▪ I'll tell him *the minute* he gets here. 彼がここへ来たらすぐ伝えましょう.

the minutes of the meeting 会議の議事録 ▪ *The* secretary read the *minutes of the* last *meeting*. 書記官が前回の議事録を読み上げた.

the next minute 次の瞬間には (→one MINUTE) ▪ *The next minute* Steve had vanished. 次の瞬間にはスティーブの姿は消えていた.

There's one born every minute. 《諺》だまされやすい人はいつもいる.

this (***very***) ***minute*** 今すぐ ▪ Come here *this*

minute! 今すぐここへ来てください.

to [***on***] ***the minute*** 1分もたがわずに, きっかり ▪ The train left at five o'clock *to the minute*. 電車は5時きっかりに出た ▪ He arrived *on the minute*. 彼は1分もたがわずに到着した.

up to the minute 《米口》ごく最新の, ごく最近まで ▪ This machine is absolutely *up to the minute*. この機械は全く最新式のものだ ▪ He is *up to the minute* on world developments. 彼は世界情勢の進展について最新の知識を持っている.

Wait a minute. **1** 少し待ってください ▪ *Wait a minute*. I'll be with you soon. 少し待って. すぐ行くから.

2 ちょっと待て《相手の話をさえぎって・驚いて》 ▪ *Wait a minute*! Was it you who started the rumor? ちょっと待て. その噂を流したのはお前か.

within minutes 数分もしないうちに; すぐに ▪ There was enough cyanide in each pill to kill a person *within minutes*. 数分以内に人を殺すのに十分な量のシアン化物が各々の丸薬の中に含まれていた ▪ *Within minutes* she fell into a snoring sleep. すぐに彼女はいびきをかいて眠り始めた.

miracle /mírəkəl/ 名 ***perform a miracle*** = work MIRACLEs.

to a miracle 驚くほど立派に ▪ Things went on *to a miracle*. 事態は驚くほどうまく運んだ.

work [***do, perform***] ***miracles*** 《口》奇跡を行う; 驚くほどうまくいく, (薬などが)非常によく効く (= work WONDERs) ▪ This washing powder will *work miracles* on difficult stains. この洗剤なら頑固な汚れが見事に落ちる.

M

mire /maɪər/ 名 ***bring*** [***lay, leave***] *a person* ***in the mire*** 人を苦境に陥れる ▪ The lie *brought* him *in the mire*. その嘘のため彼は苦境に陥った.

drag ... into the mire **1** ...をはずかしめる, 中傷する ▪ How could you *drag* our family name *into the mire*? よくも我が家の家名に泥を塗ったな!

2 ...を落ちぶれさせる ▪ Those bad guys will *drag* you *into the mire*, right where they are. あの不良たちとつき合ったら, あそこまで堕落するぞ.

drag ... through the mire [***mud, dirt, filth***] ...に恥をさらさせる, をはずかしめる ▪ They *dragged* his name *through the mire*. 彼らは彼の名をはずかしめた ▪ The media are willing to *drag* people in power *through the dirt*. マスメディアは権力者を好んで愚弄する ▪ Memories can *drag* you *through the filth*. 昔のことを思い出して恥じることもある.

find *oneself* [***stick***] ***in the mire*** 苦境に陥る ▪ He *found himself in the mire* after he wrote the article. 彼はその記事を書いたあと苦境に陥った ▪ I am *stuck* fast *in a* deep *mire*. 私は非常な苦境に身動きもできないほど陥っています.

wallow in the mire (酒などの)快楽におぼれる ▪ He spent all of his time *wallowing in the mire*. 彼は四六時中, 快楽にふけって過ごした.

mirror /mírər/ 名 (***all***) ***done with mirrors*** 魔術を使って達成された, 錯覚して, 当てにならない ▪ This trick isn't *done with mirrors*. この奇術は錯覚ではない ▪ Life is magic, and it's *all done with mirrors*. 人生は魔術で, 全く当てにならない.

hold the mirror up to nature **1** 自然を鏡に写す, 自然のままを写す (cf. Sh., *Haml*. 3. 2. 24) ▪ Is it a poet's function to *hold the mirror up to nature*? 自然のままを写すのが詩人の役目だろうか.

2 舞台に立つ ▪ It seems my only resort to *hold the mirror up to nature*. 私としては舞台に立つより仕方がないように思われる.

misapprehension /mìsæprəhénʃən/ 名 ***under a misapprehension*** 誤解して, 勘違いして ▪ He gave her the sack *under a misapprehension*. 彼は勘違いして彼女を首にしてしまった.

miscarriage /mìskærɪdʒ/ 名 ***a miscarriage of justice*** 誤審 ▪ The district court's sentence proved to be *a miscarriage of justice*. 地方裁判所の判決は誤審だと分かった.

have a miscarriage 流産する ▪ Unluckily she *had a miscarriage*. 彼女はあいにく流産した.

mischief /místʃɪf/ 名 ***do*** *a person* ***a mischief*** 《英口》人に傷を負わせる, 人を殺す ▪ That rascal may *do* you *a mischief* in the wood. あの悪党が森の中であなたに傷を負わせるかもしれません.

do *oneself* ***a mischief*** 《英口》けがをする ▪ Take care you don't *do yourself a mischief*, Bill. ビルや, けがをしないように気をつけなさいよ.

do mischief いたずらをする, 人を困らせる ▪ Children like to *do mischief*. 子供はいたずら好きだ.

full of mischief 茶目っ気たっぷりで ▪ Her eyes were *full of mischief*. 彼女の目は茶目っ気たっぷりだった.

get into [***keep out of***] ***mischief*** (子供が)いたずらをする[しないでいる] ▪ He's always *getting into mischief*. 彼はいつもいたずらばかりしている ▪ Tell the children to *keep out of mischief*. 子供たちにいたずらをしないように言ってください.

get up to mischief = get into MISCHIEF.

go to the mischief 《口》堕落する ▪ If girls *go to the mischief*, they're good for nothing I know of. 娘が堕落したら, 全くろくでなしになる. ☞the mischief = the devil.

How the mischief...? → What the MISCHIEF ...?

like mischief 《米俗》素早く ▪ He did it *like mischief*. 彼はそれを素早くやってのけた.

make mischief いたずらをする; (特に告げ口して)水をさす, 不和の種をまく (*between*) ▪ She was always *making mischief between* the two lovers. 彼女はその二人の恋人の間に水をさしてばかりいた.

mean mischief 害意をいだく, 胸に一物を持つ ▪ He invariably *means mischief*. 彼はいつでも胸に一物を持っている.

One mischief comes on the neck of another. 《諺》不幸は続いてやって来る,「泣きっつらには

ち」.

out of pure mischief ほんのいたずら半分に ▪ Don't scold the boy; he did it *out of pure mischief*. その子をしからないでください. ほんのいたずら半分にしたのですから.

play the mischief with 《口》(健康・機械・整とんした物など)を台なしにする, めちゃくちゃにする ▪ It's *playing the* very *mischief with* his health. それは恐ろしく彼の健康をそこなっている ▪ The wind has *played the mischief with* my papers. 風で書類がめちゃくちゃになった.

the mischief in person 悪魔の化身 ▪ Why, this is *the mischief in person*. なにしろ, これは悪魔の化身というべきものだ.

the mischief (of it) is that 困る点は…だ ▪ *The mischief is that* I have left my purse at home. 困ったことに財布をうちへ忘れてきた.

up to mischief 悪さをたくらんで ▪ The boy is *up to mischief* again. あの男児はまた悪さをたくらんでいる.

What [How, When, etc.] ***the mischief...?*** 《口》一体何が[どうして, いつ, など]…? ▪ *What the mischief* have you done with my book? 僕の本を一体どうしたのだ ▪ *Where the mischief* have you been? 君は一体どこへ行っていたのだ.

misconduct /mɪskάndʌkt|-kɔ́n-/ 動 ***misconduct** oneself* 《文》不品行をする; 不倫をする (*with*) ▪ He found that his wife had *misconducted herself with* his friend. 彼は妻が彼の友人と不倫をしたことに気づいた.

misery /mízəri/ 名 ***(a) misery guts*** 《口》いつも不満を言う人 ▪ He turned into *an* old *misery guts*. 彼は不平ばかり鳴らすやつになった.

be in misery **1** 困窮している ▪ He *is in* the depth of *misery*. 彼は困窮のどん底にある.
2 (肉体的に)苦しんでいる ▪ He *is in misery* from the toothache. 彼は歯痛で苦しんでいる.

have a misery 《米俗》痛みに苦しむ ▪ I *have* such *a misery* in my back. 背中がうずいてたまらん.

make** (a person's) **life a misery →LIFE.

Misery loves company. 《諺》同病相憐れむ.

put...out of** his [its] **misery **1** (動物)を殺して楽にしてやる ▪ Shall we *put* the injured animal *out of its misery*? このけがをした動物を殺して楽にしてやりましょうか.
2 《口》(人)の不安を取り除く ▪ The good news *put* me *out of my misery*. その吉報で私の不安は取り除かれた.

wallow in misery 苦悩に溺れる, 不幸[惨めさ]に浸かる ▪ Stop *wallowing in* your *misery*. 自分の涙に溺れるのはよせ.

misfortune /mɪsfɔ́ːrtʃən/ 名 ***Misfortunes never come single [singly].*** 《諺》不幸は続いてやって来る,「泣きっつらにはち」.

misgive /mɪ̀sgív/ 動 *one's* ***heart [mind] misgives** one* 心配している (*about, that*) ▪ *My mind misgives* me he is in deep waters. 彼がひどい苦境に陥っているのではないかと心配だ.

miss[1] /mɪs/ 名 ***A miss is as good as a mile.*** 《諺》少しでも失敗は失敗.

a near miss **1** 《空》ニアミス ▪ A passenger jet had *a near miss* with a jet fighter. ジェット旅客機がジェット戦闘機と危うく衝突するところだった.
2 いま一歩 ▪ Your answer is such *a near miss*. 君の答えはいま一歩というところだ.
3 危機一髪, きわどいこと ▪ I was almost hit by a car yesterday. It really was *a near miss*. きのう危うく車にはねられるところだった. 全く危機一髪だった.

give...a miss 《英口》…を避ける, 放っておく ▪ I shall *give* the party *a miss*. そのパーティーには出ないでおこう. ☞上の give a MISS から派生した用法.

miss[2] /mɪs/ 動 ***miss** one's **aim [mark]/ miss the mark*** ねらいがはずれる, 目的を逸す ▪ He threw the dart, but *missed his aim* on purpose. 彼はダーツを投げたが, わざと狙いをはずした ▪ His irony is so profound that it has *missed its aim*. 彼の皮肉は難しすぎて, 相手には効き目がなかった.

miss by a mile 《米》**1** (的から)遠くはずれる, てんで的はずれである ▪ All my answers *missed by a mile*. 私の答えはすべててんで的はずれだった.
2 《口》大失敗をする ▪ He *missed by a mile* in the mayoral election. 市長選で彼は惨敗した.

miss fire →FIRE[1].

miss** one's **footing →lose one's FOOTING.

miss the bus [boat] 機会をとり逃がす, チャンスをのがす ▪ Don't *miss the bus*. Get it while it's available 今がチャンスです. 売り切れないうちにお求めください ▪ I'm afraid you *missed the boat*. I just sold that car. 残念ですが一歩違いで, あの車はたった今売れました.

miss the mark →MISS one's aim.

miss** one's **tip →TIP[2].

miss** one's **way 道に迷う ▪ Take which path you will, you cannot *miss your way*. どっちの道を行っても, 道に迷うはずはない.

not know what** one **is missing 失っているものの良さを知らない ▪ I have never played tennis. —Then you do*n't know what* you *are missing*. 僕はテニスをしたことがない—では, 失っているものの良さを知らないわけだ.

not [never] miss a trick [move] 《口・軽蔑》やることにそつがない; 必ずチャンスをものにする, どんなミスも逃さない ▪ The conductor *never misses a trick*. あの指導者はやることにそつがない ▪ He *never misses a trick* in doing business. 彼は商売をするとき好機を決して逃さない.

not [never] miss much 《口》必ずチャンスをものにする ▪ He's a clever chap—does*n't miss much*. 彼は利口な男で, 必ずチャンスをものにする.

without missing a beat 《米》間をおかずに, ためらわずに ▪ "No way," he replied *without missing a beat*.「とんでもない」と彼は即座に答えた.

missing /mísɪŋ/ 形 ***be among the missing*** **1** (戦争などで)行方不明で ▪ My brother *is among*

M

the missing at this horrific battle. 兄はこの激戦での行方不明者の一人に数えられている.

2《米口》欠席[欠勤]する ▪He chose to *be among the missing.* 彼は欠席することにした.

come [***turn***] ***up missing*** 《米口》姿を見せない, 欠席する, 欠勤する ▪The young man *came up missing* at the party. 青年はパーティーに姿を現さなかった ▪He has a trick of *turning up missing.* 彼は欠席する名人だ.

missing in action 戦闘中行方不明になった, 戦場から帰還しない ▪Private Jones was reported *missing in action* and is presumed dead. ジョーンズ一等兵は戦闘中行方不明になったと報告され, 戦死したものとみなされている.

the missing link **1**(系列上)欠けている要素 ▪The identity of the victim was *the missing link* in the investigation. 被害者の身元が捜査上欠けている要素だった.

2《生物》失われた環《人間と類人猿との中間にあったと仮想される動物》 ▪If mankind sees you, it will think you are *the missing link.* もし人間があんたを見れば, あんたを失われた環だと思うだろうよ《君は猿みたいに醜い男だ》.

mission /míʃən/ 名 ***Mission accomplished!*** 《口》使命を果たしたね, お役目ご苦労《ある使命を果たした人に向かって言う言葉》.

... with a mission 意志の固い… ▪When Jackie arrived in Walford she was a woman *with a mission.* ウォルフォードに着いたときジャッキーは意志の強い女性だった.

M

missionary /míʃənèri|-ʃənəri/ 名形 ***the missionary position*** (性交の)正常位.

mist /mɪst/ 名 ***cast*** [***throw***] ***a mist before*** *a person's* ***eyes*** 人の目をくらます ▪He was a juggler, who *threw mists before your eyes.* 彼は人の目をくらませるぺてん師だった.

Scotch mist 《戯》こぬか雨 ▪We got into a *Scotch mist.* 我々はこぬか雨の中へ出ていった.

mistake[1] /mɪstéɪk/ 名 ***And no mistake!*** 《主に英》(前言を強めて)しかもまちがいなしだ, 確かに ▪He's a real old devil, *and no mistake.* あいつは極悪人だ, しかもまちがいなしにだ.

by mistake まちがって ▪I took your umbrella *by mistake.* まちがって君の傘を持っていってしまった.

If you don't make mistakes, you don't make anything. 《諺》誤りを犯さなければ何もできない《何かをしようとすれば誤りは避けられない》. ☞間違いをしでかした人を慰めるのに用いられる.

in mistake for …とまちがえて ▪I gave the driver a ten-dollar bill *in mistake for* a five-dollar bill. 運転手に5ドルとまちがえて10ドル札を渡しちゃった.

make no mistake (***about it***) (それは)絶対に嘘ではない《発言を強めて》 ▪If you don't behave, you'll be punished. *Make no mistake about it.* 行儀よくしなければ, 罰だぞ. きっと本当なんだからな.

make the mistake of *doing* …するというへまをやる ▪I *made the mistake of deleting* an e-mail from my boss without reading it. 上司からのEメールを読まずに消してしまうというへまをやった.

Now no mistake. さあ誤解しないで(聞いて)くださいよ ▪*Now no mistake.* It was indeed so. さあ誤解しないでくださいよ. それは本当にそうだったのです.

there must be some mistake 何かの間違いに違いない《他人の誤りを暗示》 ▪Diabetes? *There must be some mistake.* 糖尿病だって? 何かの間違いに違いない.

there's no mistake about it 確かに, 疑いなく ▪*There's no mistake about it,* he's a tyrant. 確かに, 彼は暴君だ.

we all make mistakes 《口》誰にでも間違いはある.《慰めの言葉》 ▪*We all make mistakes* from time to time. 人はみな, 時には間違いをしますよ.

mistake[2] /mɪstéɪk/ 動 ***mistake the way*** [***road***] 道を間違える ▪My son has *mistaken the way.* 息子は道を間違えた.

there's no mistaking *a thing* …はすぐにそれと分かる, 間違えようがない ▪*There's no mistaking* his voice—he's got a strong Southern accent. 彼の声はすぐ分かるよ. 強い南部訛りがあるから ▪*There is no mistaking* his house; it's next to the church. 彼の家は間違えっこない. 教会の隣だから.

mistaken /mɪstéɪkən/ 形 ***be mistaken about*** …のことで勘違いしている ▪I *was mistaken about* her. 彼女のことを誤解していた.

be much mistaken 大間違いである ▪You would *be much mistaken* if you thought so. そう考えるなら大間違いだぜ.

mistress /místrəs/ 名 (***be***) ***mistress in*** *one's* ***own house*** (女性が)家長で他人に干渉されない ▪Mind you, I *am mistress in my own house.* いいですか, 私が家長だから他人の干渉は受けませんからね.

mite /maɪt/ 名 *one's* ***mite*** 貧者の一灯, 微力(《聖》*Mark* 12. 43) ▪He subscribed *his mite* for the erection of the statue. 彼はその像の建立のためにわずかながらも寄付をした.

not a mite 《口》少しも…でない (not at all) ▪He has *never* suspected it *a mite.* 彼は一度もそれを疑ったことがなかった.

mitt /mɪt/ 名 ***get*** *one's* ***mitts on*** 《口》…を自分のものにする, 手に入れる ▪I can't wait to *get my mitts on* a Blu-ray player! ブルーレイ・プレーヤーが早くほしくてたまらない.

give [***hand***] *a person* ***the frozen*** [***icy***] ***mitt*** 《俗》人によそよそしくする, 冷たく当たる ▪I just *gave* him *the frozen mitt.* 私は彼にただよそよそしくしてやった. ☞人と冷淡な握手を交わすことから.

tip *one's* ***mitt*** 《米俗》手のうち[意向]を見せる; 密告する (→show one's HAND) ▪That would be *tipping her mitt* too much. そんなことをしたら, あまりにも彼女の手のうちを見せることになるだろう ▪He *tipped his mitt* to the town marshal. 彼は市警察署長に密告した.

mitten /mítən/ 名 ***cast*** *one's* ***mittens*** 挑戦す

る ▪ I *cast* him *my mittens* upon the quarrel. 私はそのけんかのことで彼に挑戦した.

get* [*give*] *the mitten 《口》 **1** (恋人などが)ひじ鉄をくう[くわせる] ▪ Young gentlemen who have *got the mitten* always sigh. 恋人にふられた青年たちはいつもため息をつく ▪ Susan *gave* her young man *the mitten*. スーザンは恋人にひじ鉄をくわせた.

2 (一般的に)解雇される[する] ▪ The youngster, who's always causing trouble, will *get the mitten*. その若者は面倒ばかり起こしているので, 首だろう.

handle without mittens 容赦なく取り扱う ▪ He *handled* the young writers *without mittens*. 彼は若い作家たちを容赦なく取り扱った.

mittimus /mítəməs/ 名 ***get** one's **mittimus*** 《口》 **1** 解雇される, 首になる ▪ He *got his mittimus* again. 彼はまた首になった.

2 死ぬ, とどめを刺される (= get one's QUIETUS) ▪ He *got his mittimus* by one of the enemy's bullets. 彼は敵軍の弾丸のうちの一発に当たって死んだ.

mix[1] /mɪks/ 名 ***in a mix*** まごついて, 困惑して ▪ I was more *in a mix* than ever. 私はますます困惑してしまった.

mix-up (誤解・混乱による)誤り, 過失 ▪ Our luggage was put on a different plane due to some *mix-up*. 手違いで我々の手荷物は別の便に乗せられた.

mix[2] /mɪks/ 動 ***be* [*get*] *mixed up in*** (特に不正な事件)にかかわり合っている[合う] ▪ He *got mixed up in* the scandal. 彼はそのスキャンダルにかかわり合った.

be mixed up with (不良など)と交わる ▪ His son *was mixed up with* hoodlums. 彼の息子は非行少年たちと交わっていた.

mix and match 種々雑多なものをうまく組み合わせる, 衣服やアクセサリーなどをコーディネートする ▪ It's fun to *mix and match* my skirts and blouses on a limited budget. 限られた予算でブラウスとスカートをうまく組み合わせるのは楽しい.

mix** one's **drink 《口》 色々な酒をちゃんぽんに飲む ▪ I *mixed my drinks* too much last night. ゆうべ色んな酒をちゃんぽんに飲み過ぎた.

mix it 《口》 激しく戦う ▪ The referee told the challenger to *mix it*. レフェリーは挑戦者にファイトと言った.

***mix it up* (*with** a person*)** **1** 《米口》 (訴訟・ボクシングなどで)八百長をやる.

2 競争する, 口論する, 激しく戦う ▪ Some guys were in the mood to *mix it up with* someone. 何人かの男たちが誰かとけんかしそうな様子だった.

3 …と交際する ▪ She loved *mixing it up with* the rich and famous. 彼女は金持ちや有名人と好んで付き合った.

4 《口》 …との仲を裂く ▪ He *mixed it up* for me *with* Joe. 彼は私とジョーとの仲を裂いてくれた.

mixed /mɪkst/ 形 ***a mixed bag* [*lot, bunch*]** 《口》 ごたまぜ ▪ This book is *a mixed bag* of prose and poetry. この本は散文と詩のごたまぜだ ▪ The students in this class are rather *a mixed bunch*. このクラスにはかなり成績に差のある学生がごたまぜになっている.

a mixed blessing 利害相半ばするもの ▪ The introduction of Western influences may prove *a mixed blessing*. 西洋の影響を受け入れたことは利害相半ばするものとなるかもしれない.

have mixed feelings (うれしくもあり悲しくもあり, など) 相反する感情を同時に抱く ▪ They *had mixed feelings* of sadness and pleasure. 彼らは悲喜こもごもの思いを抱いた.

mixed(-)up /mìkstʌ́p/ 形 **1** 《口》 頭が混乱した, 情緒不安定な ▪ She's been all *mixed up* after the accident. 彼女はその事故以来全く動転している.

2 散らかった ▪ The papers on her desk are *mixed up*. 彼女の机の上は書類が散乱している.

3 《口》 (悪事・不正に)関わって, (悪友)と交わって ▪ The youth got *mixed up* in a group of bad boys. その若者は不良少年グループと交わった.

a* (*crazy*) *mixed-up kid (狂気じみた)頭の混乱した若者 ▪ Why is Tom such *a crazy, mixed-up kid*? なぜトムはあんなに頭の混乱した若者になったのか.

mixer /míksər/ 名 ***a good* [*bad*] *mixer*** 《口》 人うき合いの良い[悪い]人 ▪ He's *a* very *good mixer*. 彼は人うき合いが非常に良い.

mixture /míkstʃər/ 名 ***the mixture as before*** 《口》 従来と変わりばえのしないもの ▪ Too many books of short stories these days are *the mixture as before*. 最近の短篇集には従来と変わりばえがしないものがあまりにも多い. ☞以前, 薬瓶に「従来通りの処方」というラベルを貼ったことから.

mo /moʊ/ 名 ***Half* [*Just*] *a mo./Hang on a mo.*** 《口》 **1** ちょっと待ってくれ ▪ *Half a mo*, my boy. ちょっと待ってくれよ, 君 ▪ If you *hang on a mo*, I'll just check if it's true. ちょっと待ってくれたら本当かどうか調べてみる.

2 ちょっとの間 ▪ I shan't be *half a mo*. すぐ帰って来ます. ☞mo = moment.

moan[1] /moʊn/ 名 ***make* (*one's*) *moan*** 《古・詩》 嘆く, 不平をかこつ (*of, that*) ▪ I *make my moan of* love. 私は愛を嘆いている ▪ The people *made their moan that* they were ground down. 人々はしいたげられていると不平をかこった.

moan[2] /moʊn/ 動 ***moan and groan*** ぶつくさ言う, 不平をこぼす ▪ He's always *moaning and groaning* about his wife. 彼はいつもぶつくさ妻のことをこぼしてばかりいる.

mob /mɑb|mɔb/ 動 ***mob it*** (暴徒が)なだれ寄ってくる ▪ They *mobbed it* about the door of the house. 彼らは群れをなしてその家の戸口付近に集まった.

mobile /móʊbəl, -biːl|-baɪl/ 形 ***downwardly* [*upwardly*] *mobile*** 社会的地位がより下位に落ちて[上位にのぼって], 富や地位を失って[得て] ▪ The divorced woman was *upwardly mobile* in age, *downwardly mobile* in income. その離婚した女性は, 年齢は上がり収入は下がっていた.

mock /mɑk|mɔk/ 名 ***make a mock of*** …をなぶりものにする ▪ I could never forgive him for *making a mock of* me. 私をなぶりものにしたので断じて彼を赦せなかった. ☞make a mock at は《廃》.

make mock of 《文》…をからかう ▪ Never *make mock of* a foreigner. 外国人をからかってはならない.

mocker /mάkər|mɔ́k-/ 名 ***put the mockers on*** **1**《英俗》…を台なしにする ▪ The rain *put the mockers on* our picnic. 雨のためピクニックがおじゃんになった.

2 …に不運をもたらす ▪ I was afraid my return would *put the mockers on* this good progress. 私が復帰してこのよい流れに水を差さねばよいがと思った.

mockery /mάkəri|mɔ́k-/ 名 ***hold ... up to mockery*** …をなぶりものにする, あざける ▪ He *held* the Government *up to mockery*. 彼は政府をあざけった.

make a mockery of **1** …をあざ笑う, ばかにする ▪ She *made a mockery of* his husky voice. 彼女は彼のしゃがれ声をあざ笑った.

2 …をこっけい化する ▪ Buying votes *makes a mockery of* free elections. 票を買ったりすれば, 自由選挙がこっけいになってしまう.

3 …がごまかしだということを示す ▪ He sent his son to private school, which *made a mockery of* his socialist principles. 息子を私学へ通わせたので彼の社会主義信条はまやかしだとわかった.

mod /mɑd|mɔd/ 形 ***(with) all mod cons*** 《英口》最新式の便利な設備がそろった ▪ They want a flat *with all mod cons*. 彼らは近代機器完備のアパートを求めている. ☞mod con＜modern conveniences.

mode /moʊd/ 名 ***all [much] the mode*** 大流行で ▪ Some time ago, a man of forty was *all the mode*. 少し以前は40歳の男性が大モテだった.

in [out of] (the) mode 流行して[すたれて] ▪ These clothes are now *out of mode*. これらの服はもうすたれている.

model /mάdəl|mɔ́dəl/ 名 ***be a model of*** …の典型[手本]である ▪ He *is a model of* industry. 彼は勤勉さの典型だ.

on [after] the model of …を模範として, にならって ▪ Make yours *on the model of* your brother's. お兄さんのものにならって君のを作りなさい.

stand model モデルになる ▪ She *stood model* for the nudes. 彼女は裸体画のモデルになった.

the (very) model of/ a perfect model of 《口》…とうり二つ ▪ He is *the very model of* his father. 彼は父親とうり二つだ.

moderation /mὰdəréɪʃən|mɔ̀d-/ 名 ***in moderation*** 適度に, ほどよく ▪ He drinks *in moderation*. 彼はほどほどに酒を飲む.

Moderation in all things. 《諺》何事をするにも多すぎず少なすぎず,「何事もほどほどに」.

modesty /mάdəsti|mɔ́d-/ 名 ***in all modesty*** 自慢する気は毛頭ないが ▪ I think I can say, *in all modesty*, that I am the highest authority on human rights. 自慢する気はさらさらないが, 人権に関する最高権威は私だと言えるのではないか.

module /mάdʒuːl|mɔ́djuːl/ 名 ***a command module*** **1**《宇宙》アポロ宇宙船の司令室 ▪ The astronauts operated the LM from *the command module*. 宇宙飛行士たちは司令室から月着陸船を操作した.

2《口》司令室, 司令塔 ▪ The president's desk is her *command module*. 彼女は社長室にいながらそこから一切の指令を出す.

a lunar module 《宇宙》月着陸船 ▪ *The lunar module* successfully landed on the moon. 着陸船は無事月面に着地した.

Mohammed /moʊhǽməd|məʊ-/ 名 ***If the mountain won't come to Mohammed, Mohammed will go to the mountain.*** → MOUNTAIN.

Mohammed must go to the mountain. → MAHOMET must go to the mountain.

moil /mɔɪl/ 動 ***toil and moil*** →TOIL².

moisten /mɔ́ɪsən/ 動 ***moisten*** *one's* ***clay*** → wet one's CLAY.

moisten *one's* ***lips [throat]*** (飲料水・酒類で)くちびる[のど]を潤す ▪ They *moistened their lips* with the sweet grapejuice. 彼らは甘いグレープジュースでくちびるを潤した.

mojo /móʊdʒoʊ/ 名 ***put [work] a mojo on*** *a person*/ ***put the whammy on*** *a person* 《口》…に魔法をかける ▪ I'm sure she *put a mojo on* me. I'd never said such things to a girl before. きっと彼女が僕に魔法をかけたのだろう. 女の子にあんなことを言ったのは初めてだ ▪ The witch waved a magic wand, and *worked a mojo on* the prince. 魔女は杖を振って王子に魔法をかけた ▪ A witch doctor was hired to *put the whammy on* the feudal lord. 領主に呪いをかけようと祈祷師が雇われた.

molasses /məlǽsəz/ 名 ***(as) slow as molasses in winter*** [《米》***January***] 《口》ひどくのろくさい, とんまな ▪ Can't you get dressed any faster? You're *as slow as molasses in January*. もっとさっさと身支度できないか. ひどくのろくさいな, お前は. ☞冬には「糖みつ」が固くなっていることから.

mold¹, 《英》**mould**¹ /moʊld/ 名 ***be cast from [《英》 in] the same [a different] mold*** 全く同じ[違う]性格をしている ▪ My mother *was cast from the same mold* as his mother. 僕の母は彼の母と全く同じ性格をしていた ▪ His detective stories *are* all *cast in the same mold*. 彼の推理小説はどれもワンパターンである ▪ He's *cast in a* very *different mold* from his brother. 彼は兄とは非常に違った性格だ.

be cast in a ... mold …のたち[肌]にできている ▪ His son *was cast in a* truly heroic *mold*. 彼の息子は真に英雄肌にできていた.

break the mold …の型を破る (*of*), 同じ型の物を複製できないようにする ▪ He *broke the mold* in every way. 彼はどの点から見ても旧来の陋(ろう)習を破ったのだ ▪ Now is the time to *break the mold of* the old ways of thinking. 今こそ昔ながらのものの考

え方の型を破る時期だ ▪ A counsel in heaven will *break the mold of* all contrary counsels on the earth. 天にある一つの意向が, それに反対の地上の意向を全て二度と作れないようにするだろう.

***from the same mold* (*as*)** (…と)同じタイプで ▪ The twin baseball players were *from the same mold*. 双子の野球選手は甲乙つけられなかった.

They broke the mold when they made a person. (型にはまらない人を褒めて)ユニークな人物である ▪ She is terrific! *They* sure *broke the mold when they made* her. 彼女はすごい! 実に型破りの女性だ.

mold[2], 《英》 **mould**[2] /moʊld/ 名 ***mold-breaking*** 大変革をもたらす ▪ These *mold-breaking* tennis shoes are ultra-lightweight. この画期的なテニスシューズは超軽量である. ☞mold「鋳型」.

on* (*the*) *mold 《詩》この世に[の] ▪ Our time *on mold* is three score and ten. この世の人の寿命は70歳である.

mole /moʊl/ 名 **(*as*) *blind as a mole*** →(as) BLIND as a beetle.

molehill /móʊlhìl/ 名 ***make a mountain* (*out*) *of a molehill*** →MOUNTAIN.

molt, 《英》 **moult** /moʊlt/ 名 ***in molt*** (犬・猫が)毛が生えかわって ▪ Our dog is *in molt*. うちの犬は毛が生えかわっている.

moment /móʊmənt/ 名 ***a moment*** ちょっと ▪ Wait [Just] *a moment*. ちょっと待ってください.

(*at*) *any moment* [*minute*] (*now*) →(at) any MINUTE (now).

(*at*) *every moment* 絶えず, 今か今かと ▪ We are expecting him *every moment*. 我々は彼を今か今かと待ちもうけているのです.

at odd moments →ODD.

at one moment 一度に ▪ All the doors opened *at one moment*. すべてのドアが一斉に開いた.

at the last moment いよいよという時になって ▪ He arrived *at the last moment*. 彼はいよいよという時になってやって来た.

at the moment ちょうど今は, そのときは ▪ I am busy *at the moment*. ちょうど今は忙しい ▪ I could not recall his name *at the moment*. ちょうどそのときは彼の名前が思い出せなかった.

***at this moment* (*in time*)** 《英》現時点で ▪ What can we actually do *at this moment in time*? 現時点で実際何ができるのか.

a person's ***big moment*** 人の力を発揮すべき[できる]場面, 見せ場 ▪ *Reynolds' big moment* comes at the end of the banquet. レイノルズの見せ場は宴会の終わりにやって来る.

for a moment **1**〖補語として〗当座だけの ▪ A lying tongue is but *for a moment*. 偽りを言う舌はただいっときのものである.
2〖副詞句として〗ちょっとの間 ▪ He was silent *for a moment*. 彼はちょっと黙っていた.
3〖not を伴って〗決して…でない (never) ▪ Have you ever thought of having plastic surgery?—*Not for a moment*! あなたは整形手術を受けてみようと思ったことがありますか?—とんでもない!

for the moment 差し当たり ▪ This will do *for the moment*. これで当座は間に合うだろう.

from one moment to the next 刻一刻, 次々と ▪ Our plans were being changed *from one moment to the next*. 我々の計画は目まぐるしく変更されていた.

give a bad moment 《米俗》びっくり[ぎょっと]させる ▪ He *gave* me quite *a bad moment*. 彼は私をひどくびっくりさせた.

half a moment ちょっとの間 ▪ Can't you wait *half a moment*? ちょっと待ってくれないか.

have* one's [*its*] *moments 《口》楽しい時もある ▪ Even an unsuccessful dramatist *has his moments*. 売れない劇作家にだって楽しい時もある.

in a moment すぐに ▪ It was all done *in a moment*. それはすべてすぐに終わってしまった.

in a weak moment 気が弱くなっている時に ▪ She was afraid that *in a weak moment* she would give in to the temptation. 彼女は気弱になっている時に誘惑に負けてしまうのではないかと恐れた.

in an unguarded moment うっかりしていた瞬間に ▪ *In an unguarded moment* he admitted that he had been to prison. 刑務所へ入っていたことがあると, 彼はうっかり言ってしまった.

in* one's *last moment →LAST[2].

live for* [*in*] *the moment 将来のこと考えずに生活する ▪ Pet animals *live for the moment*. ペットの動物は将来のことなど考えずに生きている.

never a dull moment いつも並はずれたことが起きている, 常に何かが変化している ▪ First he sneezes, then he coughs, then he hiccups. *Never a dull moment* with this baby. くしゃみのあとは咳で, 次はしゃっくりと, それは忙しいのよ, この子ったら.

not a moment too soon ほとんど遅すぎて; 後の祭りとなったころに ▪ His help came *not a moment too soon*. 彼の援助は来るのが遅すぎた.

of* (*great*) *moment (非常に)重要な ▪ This is an affair *of great moment*. これは重大事件だ.

of no* [*little*] *moment 少しも[ほとんど]重要でない ▪ Oh, it's *of no moment* at all. いや, これは少しも重要なことではない ▪ The matter appeared at first view to be *of little moment*. 問題はさして重要ではないように最初は見えた.

of the moment 現在最も重要な ▪ He is the man *of the moment*. 彼は時の人だ ▪ The issue *of the moment* is dealing with the fuel price hike. 現下の最重要課題は燃料価格上昇への対応だ.

on* [*upon*] *the spur of the moment → SPUR[1].

One moment. ちょっとお待ち[お聞き]ください ▪ *One moment*, please. I'll go get it. どうかちょっとお待ちを. 私が取ってきます.

one moment A, the next B Aかと思えば次の瞬間にはB《A, Bは節や句》(= one MINUTE 2)

▪ *One moment* the UFO was there; *the next* it was careening toward the northern horizon. UFO がそこにいたかと思えば, 次の瞬間には北の水平線にむけて疾走していた ▪ In war, *one moment* you're alive, *the next moment*, you're dead. 戦争では生きているかと思えば次の瞬間には死んでいる.

pick* [*choose*] *one's* *moment **1** 最もふさわしいときを選ぶ ▪ I *picked my moment*, when she was in a good mood. 絶好の瞬間, つまり彼女がきげんのよいときを選んだ.

2《皮肉》最もふさわしくないときを選ぶ ▪ That's too bad. You really *chose your moment*. そいつは気の毒に. ちょうどタイミングが悪かったな.

the moment of truth (闘牛で)とどめの一突き(の瞬間); (のるかそるかの)正念場, 決定的瞬間 ▪ He knew that *the moment of truth* was approaching. 彼は正念場が近づいていることを知った. ☞ Sp el momento de la verdad のなぞり; Ernest Hemingway, *Death in the Afternoon* (1932).

the next moment 〚主に文頭で; 副詞的に〛いきなり, 突然; 次の瞬間には ▪ *The next moment*, the hallway door opened and a dark-haired woman walked in. 突然, 広間のドアが開いて一人の黒髪の女性が歩いて入ってきた ▪ *The next moment*, Scrooge found himself standing outside his old schoolroom. 次の瞬間, スクルージは自分が昔の教室の外に立っているのに気がついた.

the* (*very*) *moment 〚接続詞的に〛...するとすぐ ▪ I came *the very moment* I heard of it. それを聞いてすぐやって来ました.

There's never a dull moment. (色々なことがあって)退屈な時なんてない ▪ *There's never a dull moment* with this job. この仕事をしていると全く退屈しない.

this* (*very*) *moment **1** ただちに ▪ Go to bed *this* (*very*) *moment*! 今すぐさっさと寝なさい.

2 たったいま ▪ I received your letter (just, only) *this moment*. たったいまお手紙を受け取りました.

to the* (*very*) *moment 1分もたがえずに, きっかり ▪ The clock is timed *to the moment*. 時計はきっかり合わせてある.

momentum /moʊméntəm/ 名 ***lose* [*gather*, *gain*] *momentum*** 勢いがなくなる[勢いがつく, はずみがつく] ▪ The movement *gathered momentum* in recent decades. ここ数十年間にその運動にはずみがついた.

monarch /mάnərk|mɔ́n-/ 名 ***be monarch of all one surveys*** 見渡すものすべての君主である (Cowper, *Verses Supposed to be Written by Alexander Selkirk*) ▪ With those things, you *are monarch of all* you *survey*. そういったものがそろえば, 君は見渡すものすべての君主というわけである.

Monday /mʌ́ndeɪ/ 名 ***blue Monday*** 楽しい週末の後に仕事をする月曜日, ブルーマンデー ▪ It was *blue Monday* and I nodded over my papers. 憂鬱な月曜日で書類に目を通しながらうとうとした.

Monday* (*morning*) *feeling 《口》日曜日のあとの仕事をしたくない気分 ▪ Anything wrong?—No; only that *Monday feeling*. どうかしたの?—いや, 例の月曜日気分というだけのことさ ▪ I like my new job. I never have that awful *Monday morning feeling*. 今度の仕事は気に入っている. 例の月曜朝のいやな気分は全くない.

Monday morning quarterback **1**〚名詞的に〛《米》事後になってとやかく批評をする人 ▪ It's easy to be a *Monday morning quarterback*. 後知恵をするのはたやすい ▪ Doris was a *Monday morning quarterback* about all the personal changes in her department. ドリスは自分の部局のあらゆる人事異動についてあとからあれこれと批評する.

2〚動詞的に〛《米》結果論で他人を批判する ▪ I don't like to *Monday morning quarterback* any work someone else has done. 他の人のやった仕事を後知恵で批判するのは好まない. ☞ 日曜日に行われたアメフトの試合結果について月曜日の朝にあれこれ批判することから.

Monday's child is fair of face. 《諺》月曜日に生まれた子は容姿が美しい《この句で始まる童唄(子供は生まれた曜日に従ってどんな子になるかが決まるという内容)から》.

play* (*the*) *Monday morning quarterback 結果論からあれこれ批判する, 後知恵を働かせる (→ MONDAY morning quarterback) ▪ Fans will get to *play Monday morning quarterback*. とかくファンは試合後にあれこれ批評するようになるものだ.

money /mʌ́ni/ 名 ***a money-spinner*** 《英》金儲けになるもの, 利益をあげるもの ▪ This project is becoming *a* real *money-spinner* for the city. この事業は市にかなりの収益をもたらしつつある.

a pot* [*pots*] *of money →POT.

a run for one's money 接戦 ▪ Let's give them *a run for their money*. 彼らに互角の勝負を挑もう.

a tight money policy 金融引き締め政策 ▪ The government has adopted *tight money policies* to bring down inflation. インフレ抑制のため政府は金融引き締め政策をとった.

after the big money 大金を儲けようとして ▪ He spent his life going *after the big money*. 彼は一攫千金を夢見て生涯を送った.

at the money →for the MONEY.

Bad money drives out good. 《諺》悪貨は良貨を駆逐する《価値のない物は貴重な物を流通から追い出す》. ☞ この原理は Gresham's Law「グレシャムの法則」としても知られている.

be a money spinner 金儲けになる (→ a MONEY-spinner). ▪ Wastepaper *is* no longer waste but *a money-spinner*. 紙くずは今では廃物ではなく商売になる.

be any man's money 金を出せば誰にでも買える ▪ In those days they *were any man's money*. 当時それらは金を出せば誰でも買えた.

be bad* [*good*] *money (投資して)儲けにならない[なる] ▪ That firm used to *be good money*, bu now it's as bad as the rest of them. あの会社は以前は儲かったが, いまは他の例にもれず儲けにならない.

be everybody's [***every man's***] ***money*** 《口》〚主に否定文で〛全ての人に価値がある(とはかぎらない), 万人向きの(とはいかない) ▪ The case is valuable, but it is so ugly that it *is* not *everybody's money*. その箱は値うちはあるが, 見てくれが悪いから誰もが買いたいと思うとはかぎらない ▪ Though she is a beauty, she *is* not *every man's money*. 彼女は美人だけれど, 万人向きとはいかない.

be made of money 《口》〚主に否定文・疑問文で〛うなるほど金を持っている ▪ Do you think I'*m made of money*? 僕がうなるほど金持ちだと思うかね ▪ I'*m* not *made of money*, you know. 私にはうなるほどの金はないのでね.

be money for jam [***old rope***] 《英口》 **1** 確実に儲かる; (一般的に)楽に儲かる ▪ He won 5 million dollars in the lottery. It *was money for jam*. 彼は宝くじで500万ドル当てた. 朝飯前の儲けだった. ☞かつて船乗りが古いロープを解きほぐし板の隙間をふさぐ紐として造船所に売ったことから.

2 わけない, 造作ない ▪ Persuade him to pay for it? That'*s money for jam*. 彼を口説いて払わせるだって? そんなこと, わけないさ.

be (***right***) ***on the money*** →(right) on the MONEY.

bet [***lay***] ***money on*** 《米俗》…は確かである ▪ I can *bet money on* it. そいつは確かだ.

black money 不正に使われる内緒の金 ▪ A *black money* scandal erupted around the former president. 元大統領の周辺にヤミ資金疑獄がもちあがった.

blow *one's* ***money on...*** …に金をまとめて使う, 金を無駄遣いする ▪ He *blew* the large sum of *money* he had inherited all *on* a cabin cruiser. 彼は相続した多額の金をそっくり豪華ヨットの購入にはたいた.

blue *one's* ***money*** 金を派手に浪費する ▪ He has *blued* all the *money* I lent him on gambling and drink. 彼は僕が貸した金を全て酒と博打(ばくち)につぎこんだ.

coin [***mint***] ***money*** 《口》金をどんどん儲ける ▪ He has been *coining money* ever since he went into that business. 彼はあの商売をやり出してからというものは, どんどん金を儲けている.

easy money 《口》苦労せずに得た金, あぶく銭 ▪ This is how to make *easy money*. こうすれば楽にかせげる.

electronic money 電子マネー ▪ *Electronic money* is easiest to hide from pickpockets. スリにやられないようにするにはまず電子マネーが一番だ.

even money 五分五分の見込み ▪ It's *even money* that he'll get a promotion. 彼が昇進する見込みは五分五分だ.

for love or money →not for LOVE or money.

for money **1** 金のために, 金と引き替えに ▪ I won't do it *for money*. 私は金のためにそんなことはしません.

2 《英・商》直(じき)取引で (for cash) ▪ A copy is not to be had *for money*. その本は直取引では買えない.

for my money 《口》 **1** あつらえ向きの, 願ったりかなったりの ▪ He is the very man *for my money*. 彼こそ願ったりかなったりの人物だ.

2 私の意見では ▪ *For my money*, the best candidate is Senator Williams. 私としては, 一番よい候補者はウィリアムズ上院議員だ.

for [***at***] ***the money*** その値にしては ▪ It is a bargain, *for the money*. その値にしては掘り出しものだ.

fork over a lot of money (いやいや)法外な金額を払う ▪ We have to *fork over a lot of money* for living expenses. 生活費に多額の出費が必要だ.

funny money 詐欺で得た不正な金 ▪ He has the reputation of dealing in *funny money*. 彼はやばい金を扱っているともっぱらの噂だ.

get *one's* ***money's worth*** →WORTH.

good money 良質; 高い金額, 高賃金 ▪ He earns *good money*. 彼は高賃金をもらっている.

have money on (*one*) 金の持ち合わせがある ▪ I didn't *have* any *money on* me. 私は少しも金を持ち合わせていなかった.

have [***got***] ***more money than sense*** 《口》むだ遣いをする ▪ My wife *has got more money than sense*. 妻はむだ遣いをする.

have too much money for *one's* ***own good*** 金を持ちすぎてためにならない ▪ Nowadays children *have too much money for their own good*. 近ごろの子供はためにならないほどの大金を持っている.

hush money 口止め料 ▪ He is said to have received *hush money* from the firm. 彼は会社から口止め料を受け取ったとのことだ.

I'll bet you any money that …ということにいくらでも賭けてもよい ▪ *I'll bet you any money that* he won't win. いくら賭けてもいいさ, 彼は勝てないよ.

in the money **1** 《口》金のある ▪ That explains why he is *in the money*. それで彼が金持ちである説明がつく.

2 《俗》(試合・興業などで)賞金を獲得して, 入賞して ▪ One of them is today a champion, the other three *in the money*. その一人が今日の優勝者で, ほかの3人が入賞者だ.

It takes money to make money. 《諺》金儲けをしようと思えば, まず投資する幾ばくかの金が要る.

It's like eating money. 《口》これは恐ろしく金がかかる ▪ We rarely eat caviar. *It's like eating money*. キャビアはめったに口にしない. 目玉が飛び出るほど高いからね.

knock some money off 価格の値下げをする ▪ I got the seller to *knock some money off*. 店の人に少し安くしてもらった.

launder money (麻薬などでかせいだ)不正な金を銀行に預ける ▪ The man was accused of *money laundering*. その男は資金洗浄罪で告発された.

lay money on →bet MONEY on.

lose money (***over***) (…で)損をする ▪ Don't *lose money over* long distance calls. 長距離電話で損をしないで《宣伝用文句》.

make money 金を儲ける ▪ It is I who am [is] *making money*. 金を儲けているのは私だ ▪ You'll never *make* any *money*. 金は少しも儲かりませんよ.
make** one's **money 金持ちになる ▪ How does the CEO of Facebook *make his money*? どうやってフェイスブックの最高経営責任者は金持ちになるのか.
make* [*lose*] *money hand over fist 《口》あっという間に大金をかせぐ[失う] ▪ The golfer is *making money hand over fist*. そのゴルファーはどんどん金を儲けている ▪ He *lost money hand over fist* in gambling. 彼はばくちであっという間に大金を失った.
***make money off** a person* 《米口》(弱みなどにつけこんで)人から金を巻き上げる[儲ける] ▪ I'm trying to *make money off* them. 彼らから金を巻き上げようとしているところだ.
make money* (*out*) *of …を金にする, で儲ける ▪ The War Office ought not to *make money out of* the rifle clubs. 陸軍省はライフル・クラブで金儲けをすべきではない.
make the money fly 札びらをきる ▪ My mother told me not to *make the money fly*. 金を湯水のように使ってはだめだと母に言われた.
marry money 金持ちと結婚する ▪ She will *marry money* when she accepts him. 彼を受けいれると彼女は金持ちと結婚することになる.
mint money →coin MONEY.
Money begets money. 《諺》金は金を生む.
money burns* (*a hole*) *in** one's **pocket 金などが使いたくてしょうがない[うずうずしている] ▪ His lottery win was *burning a hole in his pocket*. 彼は宝くじで当たった金を使いたくて仕方がなかった ▪ I am always broke because *money burns in my pockets*. 金を使いたくてうずうずしているから, 僕はいつもおけらだ.
Money doesn't grow on trees. 《諺》金は木になるものではない《楽には儲からない》.
***money down* [*out of hand*]** 現金(で) ▪ I paid *money down*. 私は現金で払った ▪ He would buy that land if he had the *money down*. 彼は現金があればその土地を買うのだが.
money down the drain →down the DRAIN.
money from home 《卑》楽に儲けた金, 労せずして手に入った金 ▪ This is like taking candy from a baby. It's *money from home*. こいつは赤んぼうから飴を取り上げるようなものだ. ちょろい儲けさ.
Money is a good servant, but a bad master. 《諺》金は使うべくして, 仕えるべきにあらず.
money* (*is*) *no object 価格は問題にしない ▪ Show me your best mink coat; *money* (*is*) *no object*. この店で一番のミンクのコートを見せてほしい. 値段は問わない.
Money is power. 《諺》お金があれば何でも手に入り何でもできる,「金は力なり」.
Money is the root of all evil. =(The LOVE of) money is the root of all evil.
Money is the sinews of war. 《諺》金はいくさの元手 (Cicero, *Phil*. 5. 2. 5).
Money makes the mare to go. →MARE.
Money makes the world go round. 《諺》世の中はお金でうまく回っている.
Money marries money. 《諺》金持ちは金持ちと結婚する.
Money talks. 《諺》金はものを言う.
money to burn 燃やすほどの金, 大金 ▪ The old lady has *money to burn*. その老婦人は大金持ちだ ▪ His aunt left him *money to burn*. 彼のおばは彼に大金を残してくれた.
***my money's on** a person* 《口》(私の見るところ)…が成功する[勝つ]だろう ▪ *My money's on* Brazil to win the next World Cup. 次のワールドカップではブラジルが勝つと思う.
new money 成金の人々 ▪ He has won a lottery and his family are *new money*. 宝くじが当たり, 彼の一家は一躍して財を成した.
out of money **1** 金に困って ▪ Too bad he is almost *out of money*. 彼が相当金に困っていて残念だ. **2** (…だけ)損をして (*by*) ▪ I found myself *out of money by* one thousand yen at yesterday's horserace. きのうの競馬で1,000円だけ損をした.
out of the money 《米俗》=out of MONEY 1.
***pay good money* (*for*)** 《口》(…に)大金を払う ▪ I *paid good money for* this stereo. このステレオは大金を出して買ったんだ.
pay** one's **money and take** one's **choice 《米口》正当なやり方をする, きちんとやっていく ▪ Well, sir, you *pay your money and take your choice*. さあ, きちんと事を運んでいただきますよ.
pin money 《口》(妻への, または予備の)こうかい銭 ▪ She earns extra *pin money* by selling Christmas cards. 彼女はクリスマスカードを売って余分のこうかい銭をかせぐ.
pocket money =spending MONEY.
pour money down the drain 金をドブに捨てる, 金をむだに使う ▪ Buying that old house is just *pouring money down the drain*. あのおんぼろ家屋を買うなんて金を捨てるようなものだ.
put money into …に投資する ▪ He was willing to *put* a large sum of *money into* his friend's business. 彼は喜んで友人の事業に大金を投資した.
put* (*one's*) *money on **1** …に賭ける ▪ *Put your money on* that horse I told you of. 僕が話していたあの馬に賭けろ. **2** …の真実性[成功]を確信する[請け合う] ▪ I *put my money on* Alice to win the match this time. 今回はアリスが試合に勝つこと請け合いだ ▪ I'd *put money on* it that he did it on purpose. 彼がわざとそうしたのは間違いない.
put** one's **money on a scratched horse 《米口》勝ち目のないのに賭ける ▪ You *put your money on a scratched horse* when you bet on the Reds. 君がレッズに賭けたのは勝ち目がないのに賭けたことになる. ☞scratch「競走馬で出走を取り消す」.
put** one's **money where** one's **mouth is 《米》**1** 約束した通りに金を出す ▪ I hope the firm

will *put its money where its mouth is* for our research. 我々の研究のために会社が約束した通りに金を出してほしい.

2 自分が言ったことを行動で裏打ちする ▪ I wish he'd *put his money where his mouth is* by voting against it. 彼が約束通りに反対票を投じてくれればいいが.

raise money 金を調達[工面]する ▪ Our church is trying to *raise money* for a new organ. 我々の教会は新しいオルガンを買う金の調達に努めている.

raise money on …を売って[質に入れて]金をつくる ▪ How much *money* can I *raise on* this gold watch? この金時計でどれほど金がつくれるだろうか.

ready money 手持ちの金, 即金 ▪ I want to be paid in *ready money*, not by cheque. 小切手ではなく現金で支払ってもらいたい.

(*right*) *on the money* 《米口》ちょうどぴったりで, 正確な, きっかりで ▪ She was *right on the money* with her prediction. 彼女の予測はぴたりと当たった ▪ When you said he'd be all right, you were *right on the money*. 彼は大丈夫と君は言ったが, 全くその通りだった. ☞元々ぴったり当たる賭けを指した.

run for *one's* ***money*** 《米俗》生計のためにせっせと働く ▪ He is a day laborer, and must *run for his money*. 彼は日雇いの労働者だから, 食うためにせっせと働かなくてはならない.

run into money どっさり金が入る ▪ He *ran into money* when his aunt died. おばが死んだとき, 彼にはどっさり金が入った.

see the color of *a person's* ***money*** →COLOR.

seed money 事業の元手, 着手資金 ▪ All you need is some *seed money* and you can start your own business. 幾らかの元手さえあれば君は自分の事業を興せる.

serious money 多額の金, 大金 ▪ It needs *serious money* to carry out such a program. このような計画を実行するには大金がいる.

spend money like water **[*a sailor*]/*spend money like it's going out of fashion*** 金を湯水のように使う ▪ Our prodigal son *spends money like water*. うちのどら息子は湯水のように金を使う.

spending money/pocket money こうかい ▪ I was given $20 in *spending money*. 20ドルのおこうかいをもらった ▪ I'm out of all my *pocket money*. こうかいがすっかりなくなってしまった.

take money from blind beggars 弱みにつけ入る, 無防備な人を食い物にする ▪ You should never *take money from blind beggars*. 決して人の弱みにつけ入ってはならない.

take the money and run (しばしばビジネス・政治で)もらえるものはもらっておく ▪ Shareholders *took the money and ran* before the situation became worse. 事態が悪化しないうちに株主は出資金を引き上げた.

the smart money **1** 《報道》専門家たち, 金儲けのことについてよく知っている人々, 投資のプロたち ▪ A lot of *the smart money* is turning to bonds these days. 最近, 投資プロの多くが債権に目を転じている ▪ *The smart money* says that the company will go bankrupt. 専門家たちによれば, その会社は破産するとのことだ.

2 儲けになる投資, 勝ちそうな賭け ▪ *Smart money* is pouring into New York right now. 情報通の投資家による出資金が今ニューヨークに大量に流れ込んでいる ▪ *The smart money* is on the Tigers. タイガーズに賭けるのは利口だよ.

the smart money is on 専門家の見るところではそうなる[うまくいく]ようだ (→the smart MONEY) ▪ *The smart money is on* the defending champion in the title match. タイトルマッチは現チャンピオンの勝ちと専門家は見ている.

there is money in …は儲かる ▪ *There is* undoubtedly *money in* fur farming. 毛皮獣の飼育は確かに儲かるぞ.

throw good money after bad 儲からない事業になお金をつぎこむ, 泥棒に追い銭をやる ▪ You must stop *throwing good money after bad*. 泥棒に追い銭をやるようなまねはやめなくてはいけない.

throw **[*toss*]** *one's* ***money about*** **[*around*]** 《口》散財する, 金をはでに使う ▪ He likes to *throw his money about*. 彼は散財が好きだ.

throw money at **1** よく考えずに(問題などを)金で解決する[片づける] ▪ The government is trying to *throw money at* the problem. 政府はその問題を金で解決しようとしている.

2 (ふつう公費を)赤字になっている事業に融資する, むだ金を使う ▪ I don't want to *throw money at* a lost cause. 失敗しそうな企画にむだ金を使いたくない.

throw *one's* ***money away*** 《米俗》金を湯水のように使う ▪ In his younger days he was *throwing his money away*. 彼は若いころには金を湯水のように使っていたものだ.

What's the money? (値段は)いくらですか.

You pays your money and you takes your chance(s) **[*choice*]**. 《諺》自分の金を出すのだから自分の好きなものを選んでよい《大して変わりはないから好きな方を選べ》. ☞pays, takes という文法上の誤りは意図的なもの.

Your money or your life. 金を出さなければ命はないぞ《追いはぎのきまり文句》 ▪ "*Your money or your life*," yelled the highwayman, holding me at gunpoint. 「命が惜しければ金をだせ」と追いはぎが銃でおどしながらどなった.

monkey /mʌ́ŋki/ 名 ***a monkey up*** **[*on*]** ***a stick*** 棒につけたおサルさん《ぴくぴく動いてみせるおもちゃ》 ▪ Willie had *a monkey on a* yellow *stick*. ウィリーは黄色い棒につけたサルのおもちゃを持っていた.

(*as*) *artful* **[*clever, crafty, cunning*]** ***as a barrel*** **[*cartload, barrel load, wagonload*]** ***of monkeys*** 《英》とても狡猾で ▪ That guy is *as crafty as a barrel of monkeys*. あいつはとても狡猾だ ▪ Those merchants are *cunning*

M

as a cartload of monkeys. あの商人たちはとてもずる賢い.

(*as*) *mischievous as a monkey* とてもいたずらっぽい ▪ The boy is *as mischievous as a monkey.* その男の子はひどくいたずらっぽい.

get a* [*the*] *monkey off *one's* ***back*** (人)のやっかいな問題を取り除く ▪ The guy fell victim to heroin addiction and then tried to *get the monkey off his back.* その男はヘロインのとりこになったが麻薬中毒問題を絶とうと努力した.

get *a person's* ***monkey up*** →put a person's MONKEY up.

get* [*have*]** *one's* ***monkey up 《英口》かんしゃくを起こす ▪ The mare is clean out of her senses when she *gets her monkey up.* その雌馬はかんしゃくを起こすと, すっかり正気を失ってしまう. ☞サルのかんしゃくから.

have a monkey on *one's* ***back*** 《主に米俗》 **1** 麻薬常用者である ▪ He has *had a monkey on his back.* 彼は以前からの麻薬常用者だ.
2 つらい重荷を背負っている.

I'll be* [*I am*] *a monkey's uncle! 《口》驚いたなあ ▪ Your wife gave birth to triplets? Well, *I'll be a monkey's uncle.* お宅の奥さんが三つ子を生んだって? 驚いたなあ, もう.

make a monkey* (*out*) *of 《口》…をばかにする, ちゃかす, 笑いものにする ▪ He *makes a monkey of* all religions. 彼は宗教という宗教をばかにする ▪ I don't mind *making a monkey out of* myself at parties. パーティーでばかなまねをしたって平気だよ.

One's ***monkey is up.*** 《英口》かんしゃくを起こしている ▪ Be very careful when *the man's monkey is up.* あの男がかんしゃくを起こしているときは, 充分気をつけろよ.

monkey love 甘やかしてむやみやたらにかわいがること ▪ They showered their children with *monkey love.* 彼らは子供たちを猫かわいがりした.

monkey on *one's* **[*the*] *house*/*monkey on* [*up*] *the chimney*** 家の抵当 ▪ He has a *monkey on his house* alone. 彼は自分だけの名義で家を抵当に入れている. ☞monkey と mortgage との連想から.

Monkey see, monkey do. 《諺》サルは見たらそのまねをする《子供はほかの人がするのを見てそのまねをする》, 「サルのものまね」 ▪ It's *monkey see, monkey do* with that kid. あの子ったら, 人のまねばかりして.

monkey suits 《戯》フォーマルウェア, 礼服, 男子用夜会服《タキシード》 ▪ All men are supposed to wear *monkey suits* at dinner on the cruise. クルーズの夕食へは男性はみなタキシードを着て出る習わしだ.

monkey tricks 《口》悪ふざけ ▪ Don't you try to get up to any of your *monkey tricks.* 例の悪ふざけをやろうとしてはだめだよ.

monkey's allowance 《口》とんだ虐待 ▪ You fellows worked like bricks and got a *monkey's allowance.* 君たちは猛烈に働いて, とんだ虐待を受けたものだ. ☞猿回しがサルが働いても報酬をやらずにけとばすことから.

more fun than a barrel of monkeys 非常に愉快な, おもしろい ▪ This video game is *more fun than a barrel of monkeys.* このビデオゲームは実に楽しい.

not give* [*care*] *a monkey's (《俗》***fart,*** etc.) 《英》てんで気にしない, 全くむとんちゃくである ▪ I don't *give a monkey's* if you drop down dead. お前がばったり死んだところでてんで気にしないね ▪ I don't *give a monkey's fart* whether you go or not. お前が行こうが行くまいがおれの知ったことか.

put* [*get*]** *a person's* ***monkey up 《英口》人を怒らせる ▪ You'll *put his monkey up* directly. 君はすぐに彼を怒らせることになるよ.

Take the monkey off your back. 《英俗》まあ落ち着きたまえ ▪ Do *take the monkey off your back* and don't put so much pressure on yourself. どうか落ち着いて, 自分をそう追い込むのはやめろよ.

the three* (*wise*) *monkeys 三猿(さんえん)《見ざる・聞かざる・言わざるの三態を表す》 ▪ A Chinese Buddhist monk introduced *the three wise monkeys* to Japan. 中国の仏教僧が三猿を日本に伝えた.

throw a monkey wrench into the works 《米》=throw a SPANNER into the works.

monopoly /mənápəli|-nɔ́p-/ 名 ***get a monopoly on*** 《米俗》…と結婚する ▪ John will *get a monopoly on* his girl very soon. ジョンはじき恋人と結婚するだろう.

monster /mánstər|mɔ́n-/ 名 ***the greeneyed monster*** →GREEN-EYED.

month /mʌnθ/ 名 ***a month's mind*** 《カトリック》(死後1か月後に行う)死者追悼ミサ ▪ They held *a month's mind* in honour of the late mayor last Sunday. この前の日曜日に故市長のための追悼ミサが行われた.

by the month 月ぎめで《支払うなど》 ▪ I needed a car for a short while, so I rented one *by the month.* 短期間必要だったので, 月ぎめで車を借りた.

from the month (産婦の)枕直しの日から《枕直しはイギリスでは産後1か月》 ▪ A widow wanted to take care of the child *from the month.* ある未亡人がその子を枕直しの日から世話をしたいと言った.

month after* [*by*] *month*/*from month to month 毎月毎月 ▪ So he waited *month after month.* そこで彼は毎月毎月待ち続けた.

month by month 月ごとに ▪ Every parent must have some knowledge about infant development *month by month.* すべての親は幼児の月ごとの発育について知っていなければならない.

month in, month out 来る月も来る月も ▪ I work in the Middle East on a rotation *month in, month out.* 私は来る月も来る月も中東でローテーションで働いています.

not ...for* [*in*] *a month of Sundays 《口》非常に長い間…ない ▪ We haven't seen you *for* [*in*] *a month of Sundays.* ずいぶん長いこと会わなかったね.

M

...of the Month 月間最高[最良]の ▪ In addition, there's a wine *of the Month*. 加えて, 月間最高のワインも出されます.

this day month 来月[先月]の今日 ▪ We have put off the meeting to *this day month*. 我々は会合を来月の今日に延ばした.

Monty /mánti|mɔ́nti/ 名 ***do the full Monty*** 《英口》素っ裸になる ▪ Bingo boys will *do the full Monty*. 酔っ払いたちは素っ裸になるだろう. ☞Monty の語源は不明.

go the full Monty **1** (舞台で)素っ裸になる ▪ Are you actually brave enough to *go the full Monty*? 本当に君は舞台でヌードになる勇気があるのか.

2 必要なことをすべてしようと固く決意する ▪ Teachers should *go the full Monty* and get test scores up. 教師は決意も新たに手を尽くして学業成績を向上させるべきだ.

mooch /mu:tʃ/ 名 ***do a mooch*** 《俗》ぶらつく ▪ Why are you just *doing a mooch* round the town? 君はなぜ町をただぶらつき回っているんだね.

on the mooch 《俗》ぶらぶらして ▪ He was often *on the mooch*. 彼はよくぶらぶらしていた.

mood /mu:d/ 名 ***a man of moods*** 気分のよく変わる人 ▪ He's *a man of moods*, but we like him. 彼はお天気屋だが, 我々は彼が好きだ.

change *one's* ***mood*** 気分を変える ▪ Nothing shall *change my mood*. どんなことがあっても私の気分は変わらない.

in a mood 《口》不きげんで ▪ Why are you *in a mood*? なぜ不きげんなのですか.

in a mood for ...する気になって ▪ She was not *in a mood for* sleep. 彼女は眠る気分ではなかった.

in no mood for [***to*** *do*] ...する気がしない ▪ I am *in no mood for* joking [*to* work]. 私は冗談を言う[仕事をする]気がしない.

in the [***a***] ***melting mood*** →MELT.

in the mood for [***to*** *do*] ...する気になって ▪ You see I'm not *in the mood for* joking [*to* joke]. ね, 僕は冗談など言う気がしないんだよ.

mood food ムード・フード《気分をよくする効力のある化学エンドルフィンを発生させる食物; 例えば, 生イチゴ(とくに砂糖・クリームをかけた), チョコレート, アイスクリームなど》 ▪ Chocolate is the most popular ideal *mood food* that boosts endorphins. チョコレートはエンドルフィンを発生させる一番人気の理想的なムード・フードだ.

moon /mu:n/ 名 ***aim*** [***level***] ***at the moon*** 途方もない野心をいだく ▪ He's just *aiming at the moon*. 彼は途方もない野心をいだいているだけだ.

bark [***howl***] ***at*** [***against***] ***the moon*** → BARK[3].

bay (***at***) ***the moon*** →BAY[3].

believe [***think***] ***that the moon is made of green*** [***cream***] ***cheese*** ばかげたことを信じる《諺的な句》 ▪ You would have me *believe that the moon is made of green cheese*. あなたはばかげたことを私に信じさせたいのですね.

cry [***ask, beg, wish***] ***for the moon*** 《英口》得られないものをほしがる, できないことを望む ▪ You're like a child *crying for the moon*. 君はお月さんがほしいと言って泣いている子供みたいだ《かなわぬ望みを抱いている》 ▪ I'm not *asking for the moon*. ないものねだりをしているのではない ▪ Don't *beg for the moon*. Be more reasonable! 無茶を言ってはいかん. もっと道理をわきまえろ!

find an elephant in the moon 実はつまらない大発見をする ▪ You have *found an elephant in the moon*. 君は大発見をしたと思っているが実はつまらないことなのだ. ☞Sir Paul Neal が望遠鏡の中にいたネズミをゾウだと思ったことから.

for a blue moon 《米俗》長い間 ▪ I haven't seen him *for a blue moon*. 長いこと彼に会ってない.

Go climb over the moon! いらぬおせっかいはよせ.

jump over the moon 有頂天になる ▪ I could have *jumped over the moon* for delight. うれしくて月を飛び越えられるくらいだった. ☞Nursery Rhyme から.

level at the moon →aim at the MOON.

live on the moon 日常生活からかけ離れている ▪ If you haven't heard of IT, you must be *living on the moon*! IT を聞いたこともないだって? 君はずいぶん浮世離れしているなあ!

make *a person* ***believe*** [***persuade*** *a person*] ***that moon is made of green cheese*** ばかげたことを人に信じさせる, 人をばかにする ▪ You cannot *make* me *believe that* the *moon is made of green cheese*. 私をばかにしようとしても, そうはいかない.

Make rye while the moon shines. 《米俗》好機を逃がすな.

many moons ago ずっと以前 ▪ I met her *many moons ago*. 彼女と会ったのはずっと前のことだ.

once in a blue moon 《口》ごくまれに ▪ I'm a teetotaller, but *once in a blue moon* I may take a little champagne. 私は禁酒家だが, たまにはシャンパンを少し飲むこともある. ☞「青い月」は空気中の微粒子によって起こる, まれな現象であるところから.

over the moon 有頂天で; ひどく興奮して ▪ He was *over the moon* about his new car. 彼は新車のことで有頂天になっていた.

promise *a person* ***the moon*** (***and stars***) → PROMISE the earth.

reach for the moon [***the stars***] 不可能なことをしようとする ▪ She's always *reaching for the moon* and getting disappointed. 彼女はいつも不可能なことをしようとしては失望している ▪ This is not the time for me to *reach for the stars*. 今は途方もないことを望む場合ではない.

shoot the moon **1**《口》夜逃げする ▪ He wished to gammon the landlord and *shoot the moon*. 彼は家主をだまして夜逃げしたいと願った.

2《米俗》ズボンなどを下げてしりを見せる ▪ The protesters lined up and *shot the moon* at City Hall. 抗議行動の参加者たちは一列に並び市役所に向かってお

しりを出して見せた.

shootings of moons 《俗》夜逃げ ▪ I warned him when *shootings of moons* seemed likely. 彼は夜逃げをしそうに見えたとき, 私は彼に警告した.

the man in the moon →MAN[1].

the old moon in the new moon's arms [***lap***] 新月の角(つの)の間に月の暗黒面が(地球の反射光のために)かすかに見えるもの ▪ It was *the new moon with the old moon in her arms*. その夜は新月で, その角の間に月の暗黒面がかすかに見えていた.

There is a [***no***] ***moon.*** 月が出ている[いない] ▪ *Is there a moon* tonight? 今夜は月が出ていますか.

think that the moon is made of green [***cream***] ***cheese*** →believe that the MOON is made of green cheese.

throw a moon 《英俗》=shoot the MOON 2.

wish for the moon →cry for the MOON.

moonlight /múːnlàɪt/ 名 ***a moonlight wanderer*** 《口》夜逃げする人 ▪ *A moonlight wanderer* is someone who cheats his landlord and runs away by night. 夜逃げ人というのは家主をだまして夜逃げる人のことである.

do [***take***] ***a moonlight*** (***flit*** [***flitting***]) 《英口》夜逃げする ▪ They *took a moonlight flit* soon after. 彼らはその後間もなく夜逃げした.

let moonlight into *a person* 《米俗》人を撃ち殺す ▪ I'll *let moonlight into* the captain. おれは隊長を撃ち殺してやる.

not be all moonlight and roses 常にバラ色とは限らない ▪ Marriage *isn't all moonlight and roses*. 結婚は楽しいことや幸せなことばかりではない.

mooring /mʊ́ərɪŋ/ 名 ***lose*** *one's* ***moorings*** 行動のより所を失う ▪ He felt as if he had *lost his moorings* when his mother died. 彼は母が死んだとき行動のより所を失ったような気がした.

slip *one's* ***moorings*** **1** (船が)係留が解けて[切れて]ただよい出る ▪ A typical Black Sea storm caused one of the tankers to *slip its moorings*. 典型的な黒海のあらしのためにタンカーの一隻の係留が解けて漂流を始めた.

2 (人が)自制心を失う; 破目をはずす ▪ Ross has certainly *slipped his moorings* then. ロスはその時確かに自制心を失っていた.

moot /muːt/ 形 ***a moot question*** [***point***] 未決定の[論争の余地がある]問題[論点] ▪ It is *a moot question* what might have happened. 何が起こったかは, まだはっきりしない ▪ It's *a moot point* whether the chicken or the egg came first. ニワトリと卵はどちらが先かはどちらとも決められない論点だ.

mop[1] /mɑp|mɔp/ 名 ***a Mrs. Mop*** 《侮蔑・戯》掃除おばさん ▪ Those people call charwomen *Mrs Mops*. その人らは雑役婦を掃除おばさんと呼んでいる. ☞第二次大戦中の BBC ラジオドラマの人物名から.

mops and brooms 《俗》ほろ酔いで ▪ I am not drunk, I'm only *mops and brooms*. 私は酔っ払ってはいない. ただほろ酔い気分なのだ. ☞お手伝いを雇う市(娘たちはぞうきんやほうきをもって集まってきた)で酒が飲まれたことから.

mop[2] /mɑp|mɔp/ 名 ***mops and mows*** (特にサルの)しかめつら ▪ We saw him make *mops and mows* at her. 我々は彼がその女性にしかめつらをするのを見た. ☞mop はおそらく唇の動きの擬声語; D moppen 'to pout'.

mop[3] /mɑp|mɔp/ 動 ***mop the floor*** [***ground***] (***up***) ***with*** →wipe the FLOOR with; mop the GROUND (up) with a person.

mop[4] /mɑp|mɔp/ 動 ***mop and mow*** しかめつらをする ▪ He *mops and mows* and shakes his head. 彼はしかめつらをしてかぶりを振る.

mope[1] /moʊp/ 名 ***have*** (***got***) (***a fit of***) ***the mopes*** ふさぎ込む, しょげる ▪ I *have got the mopes* today. 私はきょう気がふさいでいる.

in the mopes ふさぎこんで ▪ Master is still *in the mopes*. 主人はまだふさぎこんでいる.

mope[2] /moʊp/ 動 ***mope*** *oneself* ふさぎこむ ▪ He urged her not to *mope herself* at home. 彼は家の中でふさぎこまないようにしなさいと彼女に言った.

mop-up /mɑ́pʌ̀p|mɔ́p-/ 名 ***mop-up operation*** (残った敵の)掃討(作戦) ▪ Some soldiers continued the *mop-up operations* in the area. 兵士の一部は一帯の敗残兵の掃討を続けた.

moral /mɔ́ːrəl|mɔ́r-/ 名形 ***a moral certainty*** →CERTAINTY.

a moral victory 当然勝てる試合での敗北, 精神的勝利 ▪ We played better football but lost the game. Still, it was *a moral victory* for our side. フットボールの試合でわがチームの方が優勢だったが勝負には負けた. でも, 我々の方が試合には勝っていた.

draw a [*one's*] ***moral*** (実例から)教訓を引き出す ▪ You may *draw your* own *moral* from this. この事からあなた自身の教訓を引き出しなさい.

have the morals of an alley-cat ふしだらで品行が悪い ▪ Keep away from those girls, who *have the morals of alley-cats*. あの娘らに近づくなよ. 身持ちが悪いからな.

moral support 精神的ささえ ▪ My two brothers came along to provide *moral support*. 二人の兄が来てくれて元気づけられたよ.

point a moral (適切な話などを引き合いに出して)教訓に力を添える, 強調する (S. Johnson, *Vanity of Human Wishes* 222) ▪ Napoleon's death *points a moral* to those who would sacrifice everything for power. ナポレオンの死は, 権力のために一切を犠牲にしようとする人々への教訓を強調している.

take [***claim, seize,*** etc.] ***the moral high ground*** 自分の側が道徳的に優れていると主張する ▪ How dare you *take the moral high ground* with me! 私よりも品行方正だとはよく言えたものだ.

more /mɔːr/ 形副名 ***a little more*** もう少し ▪ Would you like *a little more* of this excellent beef? このけっこうな牛肉をもう少し召しあがりませんか.

all the more なおさら, かえって ▪ That made the task *all the more* difficult. それで仕事がかえってむずかしくなった.

and more →nay MORE.

and no more …だけのこと, にすぎない ▪ It's a sound *and no more*. ただの物音にすぎないよ.

as many more 2倍の数 ▪ I should like *as many more*. その2倍ほしいところです.

couldn't be more… この上もなく… ▪ You *couldn't be more* mistaken. それはとんでもない間違いだよ ▪ I *couldn't be more* sorry. これ以上ないくらい残念です.

(*even*) *more so* もっと[なおさら]そうだ ▪ An already heated debate got *even more so*. すでに白熱していた議論がなおさらそうなった ▪ Diesel cars are quite popular in Europe, certainly *more so* than in the United States. ディーゼル車はヨーロッパでは本当に人気がある, 米国においてよりも確かにそうだ.

little more than ほとんど…と同様 ▪ The village was *little more than* a collection of huts. その村はあばら屋の集合にすぎなかった.

many* [*far*] *more 〚複数名詞を伴って〛ずっと多くの ▪ There are *many more* books than I expected. 思っていたよりもずっと多くの本がある ▪ There are *far more* "Mary"s than "Violet"s. バイオレットという名の女性よりメアリーの方がはるかに多い.

more and more ますます ▪ The story got *more and more* exciting. 話はいよいよおもしろくなった ▪ The crowd is growing *more and more*. 人出はますます多くなってきた.

more like 《口》(特定の数・量)に近い ▪ The door opened ten minutes later—it felt *more like* ten hours to me. ドアは10分後に開いたが, 私には10時間近くに感じられた.

More means worse. (大学教育などで)人がふえれば質が低下する ▪ Nowadays there are fewer enough qualified students. *More means worse.* 今日では質の高い学生が減っている. 定員増は質の低下を招く. ☞Kingsley Amis の言葉から.

more of a (…よりは)むしろ…(*than*) ▪ It's *more of a* euro weakness *than* a dollar strength. それはドルの強みと言うよりはむしろユーロの弱さだ ▪ I'm not good with street names. I'm *more of a* visual person. 通りの名前を覚えるのは得意でない. 僕はどちらかと言うと視覚型人間だ.

more or less **1** 多少, いくらか ▪ He was *more or less* excited. 彼は多少興奮していた.

2 大体, …くらい ▪ The trip will take ten days, *more or less*. 旅行は10日ぐらいかかるだろう.

3 多かれ少なかれ ▪ All crowns are *more or less* crowns of thorn. 総じて王冠というものは多かれ少なかれ荊(いばら)の冠である.

4〚否定文で〛少しも(…ない) ▪ I could not afford to ride, *more or less*. 馬車に乗れるゆとりは全然なかった.

more than **1** (いくら)以上に[の] ▪ He died *more than* ten years ago. 彼は10年以上も前に死んだ.

2〚形容詞・副詞・動詞・名詞などを後に伴って〛…をしのぐ, どころではない ▪ He was *more than* glad to help me. 彼は大喜びで助けてくれた ▪ He has *more than* repaid my kindness. 彼は私の親切に十二分に報いた ▪ He is *more than* a father to her. 彼は彼女にとっては父親以上だ.

more than a bit [《文》***a little***] かなり, 相当 ▪ He was *more than a bit* drunk. 彼はかなり酔っていた ▪ When he heard the news, he was *more than a little* angry. 彼はそのニュースを聞くとひどく怒った.

more than all とりわけ ▪ I like this poem *more than all*. 私はとりわけこの詩が好きです.

more than anything (***else***) (***in the world***) 何にもまして ▪ I dislike smoking *more than anything else*. 私は何よりもタバコがきらいだ.

more than** one **can say [***tell***] 言葉で言い表せないくらい ▪ I love her *more than* I *can tell*. 口で言えないくらい彼女を愛している.

more than enough 十分すぎるくらい ▪ You have done *more than enough* for me. あなたは私に十分すぎるくらいよくしてくださいました.

more than ever (***before***) いよいよ多く ▪ Father loved me *more than ever*. 父はいよいよ私をかわいがってくれた.

more than one 一つ[一人]ならず ▪ *More than one* has found it so. 一人ならずそうだと思った. ☞普通単数動詞で呼応する.

more than one can say for [***of***]/ ***more than one can claim for*** …については当てはまらない ▪ Bill is a hardworking boy, and that's *more than one can say for* your friends. ビルは勉強家だが, お前の友だちについてはそうは言えないね.

much* [*still*] *more **1** ずっと多く(の) ▪ He has *much more* money than I. 彼は私よりもずっと多くの金を持っている.

2 なおさら, まして(…だ) (→much LESS) ▪ You have a right to your property, *still more* to your life. 君には財産の権利がある, 生命の権利はなおさらのことだ ▪ They rob, *much more* cheat each other. 彼らは互いに盗み合いをする, ましてだまし合うくらいはいうまでもない.

nay* [*and*] *more のみならず ▪ He was industrious, *nay more*, he was handsome. 彼は勤勉家で, のみならず, 美男子だった.

neither more nor less than **1** ちょうど… ▪ There were *neither more nor less than* sixty sheep. ちょうど60頭の羊がいた.

2 てっきり…, にほかならない ▪ It is *neither more nor less than* absurd. それはばからしいと言うほかない ▪ It was *neither more nor less than* the enemy's ship. それはまさしく敵艦だった.

never* [*not*] *more もう…しない, 今後…しない ▪ We shall see him *never more*. もう彼に会えまい.

no more **1** もはや…しない ▪ I saw her *no more*. もう彼女には会わなかった ▪ There are *no more* new continents to explore. 今ではもう探検する新大陸というものはない.

2 もはや(い)ない, 死んだ ▪ Troy is *no more*. トロイはもはや滅びた.

M

3 …もまた…でない ▪ You did not come, *no more* did he. 君も来なかったが，彼もだ.

no* [*nothing*] *more than わずかに…にすぎない (→not MORE than) ▪ I have *no more than* five dollars with me. たった5ドルしか持ち合わせがない ▪ He is *no* [*nothing*] *more than* a puppet. 彼は傀儡(かいらい)にすぎない.

no more* A *than* B/**《口》not* A *any more than* B** AでないのはBでないのと同じ，Bと同様Aでない (→not MORE…than) ▪ A whale is *no more* a fish *than* a horse is. = A whale is *not* a fish *any more than* a horse is. クジラが魚でないのは馬が魚でないのと同じだ ▪ I am *no more* mad *than* you (are). = I am *not* mad *any more than* you (are). 君と同様僕は正気である.

No more than I have to. 相変わらず元気です ▪ How have you been doing?—*No more than I have to.* 最近どうだい?—まあまあさ. ☞How are you doing? に対する返答.

not… any more もはや…しない (= no MORE 1) ▪ I can*not* walk *any more*. もうこれ以上歩けない.

not more than せいぜい (→no MORE than) ▪ I have *not more than* five dollars. 僕の持っているのはせいぜい5ドルだ.

not more… than ほど…でない (→no MORE A than B) ▪ I am *not more* generous *than* you are. 私は君ほど寛大ではない.

***not* [*none*] *the more for* [*because*]** …とはいえそれでもなお…しない ▪ I do *not* love him *the more for* his abilities. 彼は才能はあるがやはりきらいだ ▪ I am *not the more* inclined to help him *because* he is poor. 彼が貧乏でもやはり助ける気持ちはしない.

once more →ONCE.

one* [*two,* etc.] *more もう一つ[二つ，など] ▪ Read *one more* passage. もう一節読みなさい.

or more あるいはそれ以上，少なくとも ▪ She is a girl of ten *or more*. その子は少なくとも10歳ぐらいの少女だ.

some more もう少し(の) ▪ Help yourself to *some more* cake. ケーキをもう少し召しあがれ.

still more →much MORE.

That's more like it!《口》(より望ましい応答に対して)今度はずっとよくなった ▪ Turn it up louder! *That's more like it!* もっとボリュームを上げて. うん，それでいいよ ▪ In that case I can move my date and help you.—Now, *that's more like it*. だったらデートをほかの日に変えてお手伝いしてもいいです—いや，そいつはよかった.

***the more…for* [*because, as*]** …だからますます ▪ I like him *the more for* his honesty [*because* he is honest]. 彼は正直だから余計好きだ.

***the more so because* [*in that*]** …だからなおさらで ▪ I was excited, *the more so because* I was the only one who solved the problem. その問題を解いたのは私一人だったのでなおさら興奮した. ☞more に強勢を置く.

The more the merrier. 多ければ多いほど楽しい ▪ Mind if she comes?—Not at all. *The more the merrier.* 彼女が来てもいいかい?—かまわないとも. 多いほど楽しいから.

the more… the more …すればするほどますます ▪ *The more* one has, *the more* one wants. 多く持てば持つほどますますほしくなる ▪ *The more* he cried, *the more* we laughed. 彼が泣けば泣くほど，我々はますます笑った.

(*the*) *more's the pity* →PITY.

what is more →WHAT.

morgue /mɔːrg/ 名 **(*as*) *still as a morgue*** 無気味なほど静かで ▪ The whole town was *still as a morgue*. 町全体が無気味なほど静まりかえっていた.

morn /mɔːrn/ 名 ***at morn and* (*at*) *even*/*eve and morn*** 《詩》朝な夕な ▪ The birds came *at morn and even*. 小鳥たちは朝な夕なやって来た.

from morn to* [*till*] *night 《詩》朝から夕べにいたるまで，一日中 (→from MORNING till evening) ▪ He would fight, yes, *from morn till night*. 彼は戦うだろう，そう，朝から晩までも.

morn by morn 《詩》朝ごとに ▪ *Morn by morn* the lark shot up. 朝ごとにヒバリがさっと舞い上がった.

morning /mɔ́ːrnɪŋ/ 名 ***all* (*the*) *morning*** 朝じゅう ▪ *All morning* she dreamt of her husband. 朝じゅう彼女は夫のことを思い続けた.

***from morning till* [*to*] *evening* [*night*]** 朝から晩まで (→from MORN to night) ▪ He works hard *from morning till night*. 彼は朝から晩まで精出して働く.

in the gray of the morning →GRAY[1].

in the morning **1** 朝(に) ▪ I get up early *in the morning*. 私は早起きだ.

2《時刻につけて》午前 (a.m.) ▪ School begins at eight o'clock *in the morning*. 学校は午前8時から始まります.

3 あした ▪ I'll see you again *in the morning*. あしたもう一度お目にかかります.

morning and evening 朝晩 ▪ Take a spoonful of it *morning and evening*. それを朝晩スプーンに1杯お飲みなさい.

morning breath 起きがけ[目覚め時]の口臭 ▪ My wife complains that I have *morning breath*. 起きがけの口臭がひどいと家内がこぼすんだ.

Morning dreams come* [*are*] *true. 《諺》朝方に夢を見たら，見た通りのことが起きる，「朝夢は正(まさ)夢」.

morning, noon, and night 一日中，始終 ▪ *Morning, noon, and night* I hear nothing else. 四六時中そのことばかり聞かされる.

of* [*in*] *a morning*/*of mornings いつも朝に ▪ He takes a walk in the High Street *of a morning*. 彼はいつも朝に本通りを散歩する.

one fine morning ある朝《次に何事かが起こる場合によく用いる句》 ▪ *One fine morning* he called on me. ある朝彼がやって来た. ☞フランス語法.

***the morning after* (*the night before*)** 《口》

二日酔い ▪ I've got a bad case of *the morning after*. 僕はひどい二日酔いだ.

morocco /mərɑ́koʊ|-rɔ́k-/ 名 ***in morocco*** 裸で ▪ There you are *in* your *morocco*! それ君は裸になっているじゃないか. ☞Longfellow が *The Spanish Student* 3. 5で用いたロマの俗語表現.

morrow /mɔ́:roʊ|mɔ́r-/ 名 ***on the morrow of*** 《雅》(事件)の直後に ▪ *On the morrow of* a long war, the whole country was in some measure pauperized. 長い戦争の直後で, 国全体がある程度貧しかった.

mortal /mɔ́:rtəl/ 形 ***mortal remains*** 死がい ▪ His *mortal remains* were laid in St. Paul's Churchyard. 彼の遺体は聖ポール寺院の境内に葬られた.

this mortal coil 《戯》この世のわずらわしさ (cf. Sh., *Haml*. 3. 1. 67) ▪ I have thrown off *the mortal coils* of shore affairs. 私は陸上のことのわずらわしさはかなぐり捨ててしまった.

mortar /mɔ́:rtər/ 名 ***bricks*** [***stone***] ***and mortar*** 《口》家屋; 家財 ▪ Business will be confined to *brick and mortar* investments. 取引は家屋投資に限られるだろう.

mortify /mɔ́:rtəfàɪ/ 動 ***be*** [***feel***] ***mortified at*** [***by***] …にくやしがる ▪ He *felt mortified at* his failure. 彼は失敗をくやしがった.

mortify the flesh 情欲を克服する ▪ They *mortify the flesh* by fasting. 彼らは断食をして情欲を克服する.

moss /mɔ:s|mɔs/ 名 ***A rolling stone gathers no moss.*** →STONE[1].

most /moʊst/ 形名副 ***at*** (***the***) ***most/at the very most*** せいぜい, 多くて ▪ I can only pay £10 *at the most*. 多くて10ポンドしか払えません ▪ This is *at most* a makeshift. これはせいぜい一時の間に合わせというものだ.

(***for***) ***the most part*** →PART[1].

get the most out of = get the BEST out of.

make the most of **1** …をできるだけ利用する ▪ He *made the most of* his opportunity. 彼は自分の機会をできるだけ利用した ▪ She *makes the most of* her looks. 彼女は顔が最も引きたつようにする. **2** …をこの上もなく大事にする ▪ I always *make the most of* the youngest son. 私はいつも末の息子をこの上もなく大事にする. **3** …を精いっぱいほめたてる[悪く言う] ▪ He *makes the most of* her beauty. 彼は彼女の美しさを絶賛する[くそみそに言う].

most and least 《詩》一人残らず, ことごとく ▪ Pan fought in the ranks with you *most and least*. パンの神はあなた方みなといっしょに一兵卒として戦った. ☞「最も位の高い人たちも最も低い人たちも」が原義.

most of 大抵の, 大部分の ▪ *Most of* the students know it. 大抵の学生はそれを知っている ▪ He has been ill *most of* this winter. 彼はこの冬はほとんどずっと病気だった.

most of all とりわけ ▪ I miss you, mother dear, *most of all*. おかあさん, あなたがいないのが一番寂しいわ.

the most (***that***) ***one say for*** [***of***]/***the most*** (***that***) ***one can claim for*** …の取り柄はせいぜい ▪ *The most one* can *say for* this novel is that it is very long. この小説の取り柄はせいぜい, とても長いということだ.

mot /moʊ/ 名 ***mot juste*** /mòʊʒú:st/ 《文》至言, 適語, 的確な表現 ▪ I'm searching for the *mot juste* to describe her. 彼女の特徴を述べるぴったりの言葉を探しているのだが. ☞F 'just or right word'.

mote /moʊt/ 名 ***the mote in*** *a person's* ***eye*** 他人の目にあるほこり《自分の大きな欠点を忘れて他人に見いだす小さな欠点》(《聖》*Matt*. 7. 3) ▪ It's easier to see *the mote in our neighbor's eye* than in our own. 自分のより隣人の目にあるほこりの方が見えやすい ▪ Whilst we can see *the mote in our neighbor's eye* it is often difficult to discover the beam in our own. 隣人の目にあるほこり(他人の小さな欠点)は見えても, 自分の目の梁(はり)(自分の大きな欠点)は見つけにくいことが多い.

moth /mɔ:θ|mɔθ/ 名 ***like a moth*** (***that flies***) ***round a light/ like a moth to a*** [***the***] ***flame*** 《雅》素敵な魅力[誘惑]に負けて, 抗しがたく惹きつけられて ▪ The kids gathered around the pile of candies, *like moths around a light*. 子供たちは山と積まれたキャンディーに惹き寄せられてその周りに集まった.

moth(**-**)**ball** /mɔ́:θbɔ̀:l|mɔ́θ-/ 名 ***bring ... out of mothballs*** …を貯蔵所から取り出して使う, 現役に復帰させる ▪ To *bring* our old lawnmower *out of mothballs* would cost much less. 古い芝刈り機を出して使う方がずっと安上がりだろう.

in moth-balls (船・飛行機など)しまい込んで, 予備役に入れて ▪ The ceremony was also attended by two admirals *in mothballs*. 儀式には予備役の提督二人も出席した ▪ After ten years *in mothballs* the destroyers were sent to be broken up. その駆逐艦は10年間予備役に入れられたのち解体にやられた.

put ... in mothballs (計画・考えなど)を一時中断[たな上げに]する, あとで使うためにとっておく (→in MOTH-BALLs) ▪ They *put* the plans for a new library *in mothballs*. 新図書館の建設計画はたな上げになった ▪ Most fighters *were put in mothballs* after the war. 戦後ほとんどの戦闘機は後日に備えて保管され[予備役に入れられ]ていた. ☞羊毛類をナフタリンなどの防虫剤を使って収納することから.

mother /mʌ́ðər/ 名 ***a mother lode*** 《米》主要な供給源 ▪ This site is *a mother lode* of information on folklore and legends. この地は民間伝承と伝説に関する情報の宝庫である.

a mother's [***mama's***] ***boy*** 《軽蔑》(母親に異常な愛情を示す)お母さんっ子, マザコンの男 ▪ Many young men today are *mother's boys*. 今日の若者

M

はお母さんっ子が多い ▪ You're such *a mama's boy*. Grow up! お前はひどいマザコンだな. 大人になれよ!

an expectant mother 妊婦 ▪ The clinic was filled with *expectant mothers*. 診療所は妊婦で溢れんばかりだった.

As is the mother, so is her daughter. 《諺》「この母にしてこの娘あり」.

be mother 《英口・戯》食べ物[飲み物]を出す, (特に)紅茶を入れる ▪ We'll go and have tea and you *be mother*. 行ってお茶にしよう. 君が入れてくれるんだ ▪ Here comes the tea. Shall I *be mother*? さあ, お茶が来た. 私がついであげようか.

become a mother 母となる ▪ I am glad I have *become a mother*. 母になれてうれしいわ.

Does your mother know you're out? 《俗》おふくろさんは君が外へ出ているのを知ってるのかい《母の目付を要するようなぼんやり者に言う文句》 ▪ Sir, *does your mother know you're out* at this unearthly hour? ねえ君, おふくろさんは君がこんな時刻に外へ出ているのを知ってるのかい.

every mother's son 《口》誰もかれも ▪ The bandits massacred them all, *every mother's son* of them. 山賊どもは彼らを一人残らずみな殺しにした. ☞この句の出典としてよく Sh., *Mids. N. D.* 3. 1. 74 の "Come, sit down, every mother's son" が引かれるが, この句はすでに 14 世紀ごろから用いられている.

have too much of his mother's blessing (青年が)途方もなく取りすましている, 几帳面である ▪ That young man *had too much of his mother's blessing*. その若者は度外れて取りすましていた.

kiss** one's **mother earth 《戯》地面に倒れる ▪ He *kissed his mother earth* with bloody mouth. 彼は口から血を流して地面に倒れた.

Like mother, like daughter [child]. 《諺》娘は母親に似てくる, 「子は親に似る」(《聖》*Ezek*. 16. 44).

like mother makes it 《口》大変うまい ▪ Umph! not *like mother makes it*. ははん, そううまくないな.

meet** one's **mother 《俗》生まれる ▪ He wished he had never *met his mother*. 彼は生まれてこなければよかったと思った.

mother country **1** 母国 ▪ Japan is my *mother country*. 日本が私の母国です.

2 (植民地から見た)本国 ▪ These colonies separated from the *mother country* after the war. 戦後これらの植民地は本国から分離した.

mother earth = an EARTH Mother 1.

Mother Nature 母なる自然, 自然の摂理 ▪ *Mother Nature* combines the latest science to create environment-friendly products. 大自然が最新科学と結びついて環境に優しい製品を作る.

mother tongue **1** 母国語 ▪ English is his *mother tongue*. 英語が彼の母国語だ.

2 《言》母語, 祖語 ▪ American English was separated from the *mother tongue* at an early period. アメリカ英語は早い時期に祖語と分離した.

mother wit 生来の才知; 常識 ▪ It is extempore, from my *mother wit*. これは即興で, 僕の生来の才知でやったのだ.

mother's milk →MILK[1].

mother's son 《口》甘えっ子 ▪ He's never been allowed to shift for himself; he's his *mother's son*. 彼はまだ自分でやっていくことを許されたことがない, 母親っ子だから.

Oh, mother, look at Dick! まあ, あの様子を見てごらんよ《人が知識・腕を見せびらかしているのをあざけって言う文句》.

the mother and father of (all)... 《口》...の最上[最悪]の見本, 親玉 ▪ It was *the mother and father of all* roses. それは全くみごとなバラだった ▪ I'm suffering from *the mother and father of all* headaches. 今すごい頭痛がしている.

the Mother of Parliaments 議会の母, 世界最古の議会《ウエストミンスターの議会[英国議会], マン島, スイスのカントンがそれぞれ主張しているが, 英国では多くの議会の規範として専らウエストミンスターの議会を指す》.

tied to mother's apron-strings → cling to the APRON-STRINGS (of).

Who's she, the cat's mother? 《主に英口》she とは誰のことかね, 猫のお母さんのことかい《同席する女性本人の面前で名前を使わずに she を使った人の無礼さをたしなめていう》 ▪ Whenever we referred to Mom as "she", my Dad would snap, "*Who's 'she'? The cat's mother?*" 私たちが母さんのことを「彼女」と言うと, 父さんは「"彼女" とは誰のことだね, 猫のお母さんのことかい」ときつく言ったものだった.

You'll be a man before your mother. → MAN[1].

motion[1] /móʊʃən/ 名 ***go through the motions*** **1** (...の)様子[しぐさ]をする (*of*) ▪ With this she *went through the motions of* drinking tea. そう言って, 彼女はお茶を飲むようなしぐさをしてみせた.

2 本気ではなく形だけやる, お義理でやる ▪ His heart isn't in the game—he is just *going through the motions*. 彼は試合に集中していない. お義理でやっているだけだ.

in motion **1** 動いて, 運転中の (↔ at REST 1) ▪ The machine was *in motion*. 機械は運転中だった.

2 活動[興奮]して (↔ at REST 2) ▪ The inhabitants were *in* great *motion*. 住民たちは非常に興奮していた.

in slow motion **1** (映像に関して)スローモーションで ▪ Let's watch this scene one more time *in slow motion*. もう一度今度はスローモーションでこのシーンを見てみよう.

2 (動作に関して)ゆっくりと[で] ▪ Very, very gently, as if *in slow motion*, I put the phone back in its cradle. この上なくゆっくりと, まるでスローモーションのように, 受話器を受け台においた.

make a motion 提案する ▪ I'd like to *make a motion* that the meeting be adjourned. 延会の動議を提出します.

make a motion [***motions***] ***to*** *do* …するように身ぶりで合図する ▪ He *made motions* to me *to* lend him his sword. 彼は自分の剣を貸してくれるように私に身ぶりで合図した.

put [***set***] ***… in motion*** …を動き出させる; の運転を開始させる ▪ The wind *puts* the mill *in motion*. 風が水車を回す ▪ They *set* a revolution *in motion*. 彼らは革命を動き出させた.

motion[2] /móʊʃən/ 動 ***motion for*** [***to***] *a person* ***to*** *do* 人に…するよう合図する ▪ The teacher *motioned for* the boys *to* run. 先生は少年たちに走れと合図した.

motive /móʊtɪv/ 名 ***have mixed motives*** 動機が不純である ▪ He *had mixed motives* in taking on the job. その仕事を引き受けたときの彼の動機はいろいろ雑多であった.

motley /mátli|mɔ́t-/ 名 ***wear*** [***put on***] ***motley*** 道化師の役を務める; ばかなことをする, おどけたことを言う ▪ His wit is so exuberant that his very wisdom *wears motley*. 彼の機知はあふれるばかりで, 彼の知恵までがおどけて聞こえるほどだ.

mount /maʊnt/ 動 ***mount guard*** 番兵に立つ ▪ I have seen them *mounting guard*. 私は彼らが番兵に立っているのを見た.

mount guard over [***upon***] …の番をする ▪ The chief's son *mounted guard over* the bungalow, while we slept. 我々が眠っている間, 族長の息子がバンガローの見張りをしてくれた.

mount the breach 城壁の破れ口に登る; 先頭を切る ▪ The man *mounted the breach* first, and they took the city. その男がまず先頭を切り, 彼らはその町を占拠した.

mountain /máʊntən|-tɪn/ 名 ***a mountain*** [***mountains***] ***of*** 山のような, 膨大な ▪ Her father died leaving *a mountain of* debts. 彼女の父親は借金の山を残して他界した ▪ There were *mountains of* potatoes. ジャガイモが山ほどあった.

a mountain to climb 《主に英》目の前に立ちはだかる困難 ▪ Winning every year must be *a mountain to climb*. 毎年勝ち続けるのは至難の業にちがいない. ☞次項も参照.

have a mountain to climb 非常な困難に直面して[が目の前に立ちはだかって]いる ▪ The government *has an* economic *mountain to climb*. 政府は重大な経済問題を抱えている.

If the mountain won't [***will not***] ***come to Muhammad, Muhammad will*** [***must***] ***go to the mountain.*** 《諺》山がムハンマドの所へ来ないなら, ムハンマドが山へ行く[行かねばならない]《やむをえない事情のため方針を変えなくてはならない》. ☞イスラムの教祖 Muhammad (Mohammed, Mahomet とも言う)にまつわる話から.

make a mountain (***out***) ***of a molehill*** (特に困難・苦情などの)小さなことを大仰に言う, 針小棒大に言う ▪ He *made a mountain out of a molehill* in describing his quarrel with Smith. 彼はスミスとのけんかを針小棒大に言った.

move [***remove***] ***mountains*** **1** 山をも動かす(ような奇跡を行う), 不可能を可能にする ▪ With that belief, you can *move mountains*. その信念があれば何だってできる ▪ He had that faith which *removes mountains*. 彼には山をも動かすような信仰があった.
2 あらゆる努力を傾ける ▪ I will *move mountains* to win a gold medal in the speech contest. スピーチコンテストでの優勝目指して精一杯の努力をするつもりだ. ☞《諺》Faith will move mountains.「信仰は山をも動かす」から; 《聖》*Matt*. 17. 20; *1 Cor*. 13. 2.

the mountain in labor 労多くして効少ないこと, 「泰山鳴動してネズミ一匹」 ▪ This would certainly look like *the mountain in labor*. これはきっと労多くして効少ないことのように思えるだろう. ☞イソップ寓話の "*The Mountain in Labor*" から.

mourner /mɔ́ːrnər/ 名 ***crowd the mourners*** 《米口》 **1** 無理をする, 不当に圧迫する ▪ He rather *crowds the mourners* in his historical illustrations. 彼はその歴史の例証で少々無理をしている.
2 あわてふためく, 早まる ▪ Keep calm now, and don't *crowd the mourners*. さあ落ち着いて, あわてふためくんじゃないぞ.

mourning /mɔ́ːrnɪŋ/ 名 ***be out of mourning*** 喪があける ▪ She *was* already *out of mourning*. 彼女はもう喪があけていた.

deep [***half, second***] ***mourning*** 正式[略式]喪服 ▪ She was in *deep mourning*. 彼女は正式な喪服を着けていた.

go into [***put on, take to***] ***mourning*** 喪に服する, 喪服を着る ▪ I must *go into mourning* for my aunt. おばの喪に服さなければならない ▪ The whole community *put on mourning* for the dead priest. 地域全体が亡くなった神父の喪に服した.

in mourning **1** 喪服を着て ▪ One of the ladies was *in mourning*. 女性の一人は喪服を着ていた.
2 《俗・戯》(目が打たれて)黒あざができて ▪ Jim had his eyes *in mourning*. ジムは目に黒あざをこしらえていた.
3 《俗・戯》(爪が)黒くよごれた ▪ His finger nails were *in mourning*. 彼の爪は黒くよごれていた.

leave off [***go out of***] ***mourning*** 喪があける; 喪服を脱ぐ ▪ He will soon *go out of mourning*. 彼はまもなく喪があけるだろう ▪ She perceived that her father had *left off mourning*. 彼女は父が喪服を脱いでいるのに気づいた.

put … into mourning …を喪に服させる ▪ She *put* even her servants *into mourning*. 彼女は使用人たちまでも喪に服させた.

second mourning →deep MOURNING.

mouse /maʊs/ 名 ***a little mouse*** 非常にはにかみやで目立たない人, 引っ込み思案の人物 ▪ She won't accept his offer. She is such *a little mouse*! 彼女は彼の申し出を受けはしないさ. ひどいはにかみ屋だから.

a mouse click [***mouse clicks***] ***away*** (パソコンのマウスをクリックするだけで) 簡単にアクセスできる ▪ Help is only *a mouse click away*. マウスを

ちょっとクリックするだけで支援が得られます ▪ Dinner reservations are just a few *mouse clicks away*. お宅のパソコンからわけなく当レストランのディナーの予約ができます.

a mouse potato マウス・ポテト, 長時間コンピューターゲームをして楽しむ人, パソコンゲームおたく ▪ The Internet has turned couch potatoes into *mouse potatoes*. インターネットによってカウチ・ポテトがマウス・ポテトに変わった. ☞a couch potato をもじったもの.

(as) drunk as a mouse 泥酔して ▪ He came home *as drunk as a mouse*. 彼はへべれけになって帰宅した.

(as) mum [mute, quiet, silent, still] as a mouse ごく静かに ▪ She looked *as quiet as a mouse*. 彼女はこの上もなくもの静かに見えた ▪ I stood there, listening, *as silent as a mouse*. 私はそこに立って, こっそり聞き耳を立てていた.

(as) poor as a church mouse ひどく貧乏で ▪ He's *as poor as a church mouse* and never has any money to spend. 彼はひどく貧しく, 使えるお金は全くない. ☞教会のネズミは何も食物がないので.

like a drowned mouse 情けないはめに陥って, しょんぼりして ▪ He looked piteous, *like a drowned mouse*. 彼はひどくしょんぼりして, 哀れに見えた.

mouse and man 生きとし生けるもの ▪ The ship sank in the West Indies, *mouse and man*. 船は西インド諸島であらゆる生きものを乗せたまま沈没した.

neither man nor mouse 生きたものは一つも…しない ▪ Nobody—*neither man nor mouse*—could survive long without water. 水なしでは誰も—どんな生き物も—長くは生き延びられまい ▪ Can't you see any audience?—*Neither man nor mouse*. 聴衆は一人も見えないか—人っ子一人いませんよ.

The mountains have brought forth a mouse. 《諺》泰山鳴動してネズミ一匹 ☞イソップ寓話中の "*The Mountain in Labor*" から.

The mouse that has but one hole is quickly [easily] taken. 《諺》穴を一つしか持たぬネズミはたちまち捕らえられる《常に一つのものだけに依存するのは危険である》,「狡兎(こうと)の三穴」.

mousetrap /máʊstræ̀p/ 名 ***a better mousetrap*** 人気商品の改良型, すでによいものを更に改良すること ▪ The need for *a better mousetrap* will soon arise. 今に改良型を求める声が上がるだろう.

make [build] a better mousetrap and the world will beat a path to *one's* ***door*** (ネズミ捕り器のように)簡単な日用品の改良型を作れば人がわっと押し寄せる ▪ It has long been said that if you *build a better mousetrap, the world will beat a path to your door*. 日用品を改良して売るとみなが飛びつくと昔から言われている.

mouth[1] /maʊθ/ 名 ***a big [loud] mouth*** 《米口》おしゃべり(の人) ▪ He is such *a big mouth*. 彼はひどいおしゃべりだ ▪ Keep your *big mouth* shut! おしゃべりをやめろ ▪ He is *a loud mouth* and cannot be trusted with secrets. 彼はおしゃべりだから秘密は打ち明けられない.

a loose mouth 軽率な人, 無分別な人物 ▪ He is such *a loose mouth* he always creates trouble. 彼はとても軽はずみで面倒ばかり起こしている.

a mouth to feed 養われるべき人, 被扶養者 ▪ I have three *mouths to feed*. 扶養家族が3人いる.

a useless mouth 穀つぶし ▪ They got rid of the *useless mouths* in this way. 彼らはこうして穀つぶしどもを厄介払いした.

be all mouth and trousers 《口》口先ばかりで実行が伴わない ▪ The trouble with him is he *is all mouth and trousers*. 彼の欠点は口先ばかりで実行が伴わないことだ.

be in *a person's* ***mouth*** 人の噂になって, 人に言われて ▪ His death *is in every man's mouth*. 彼の死はみんなの噂になっている ▪ The actor's name *was in* many *mouths*. その俳優の名は多くの人の口にのぼっていた.

by the mouth of *a person* 人に代弁させて, 人を通じて (《聖》*Luke* 1. 70) ▪ He sent an excuse for absence *by the mouth of* his son. 彼は息子を通じて欠席の言い訳をした.

by word of mouth 口上で, 口頭で (↔by WRITING) ▪ The message was given *by word of mouth*; it was not written. その伝言は口頭で与えられた. 文書でではなかった. ☞by mouth は《廃》.

close [shut] *one's* ***mouth*** 黙っている ▪ *Shut your mouth*, or I'll slap you! 黙ってろ, さもないとひっぱたくぞ.

come out of *a person's* ***mouth*** 《口》(言葉・発言が)人の口から出る, 人が言う ▪ During the late '60s the words "peace" and "Vietnam" rarely *came out of the president's mouth* in the same sentence. 60年代の後半には「平和」と「ベトナム」という語が同一文内で大統領の口から発せられることはめったになかった.

condemn *a person* ***out of*** *his* ***own mouth*** 人の言った言葉で人を非難する (《聖》*Luke* 19. 22) ▪ The sinner *was condemned out of his own mouth*. その罪人は自分の言った言葉で自分を非難するはめになった.

down in [at] the mouth 《口》しょげて, がっかりして ▪ Poor lad! He will be most horribly *down in the mouth*. かわいそうに, その若者はひどくがっかりするだろう. ☞がっかりしたとき, 口の端を下げることから.

from hand to mouth →HAND[1].

from *a person's* ***mouth*** 人の口から ▪ He won't hear any advice coming *from my mouth*. 彼は私の口から出た忠告など聞かないだろう.

from mouth to mouth 口から口へ; (大勢の人が話すときに)順次に ▪ The news spread quickly *from mouth to mouth*. そのニュースは人から人へと速やかに広まった.

get down in the mouth →GET down in the dumps.

give it mouth 〚命令文で〛熱をこめて言う ▪ What I say in respect to the speeches is, "*Give it mouth*." 私が演説について言っているのは,「熱をこめて

言え」ということだ.

give mouth **1** (猟犬が)激しくほえ立てる ▪ The watch-dog on the distant shore *gave mouth.* はるかかなたの岸辺の番犬が激しくほえ立てた.

2 (人が)話し始める ▪ Jones, thus challenged, solemnly *gave mouth.* ジョーンズはこのようにいどまれたので, 重々しく話し始めた.

give mouth to …を口に出す ▪ It is not easy to *give mouth to* my opinion of you. 私があなたをどう思っているかを口に出すのは容易ではありません.

have a big mouth 《米俗》大声で話す, べらべらとしゃべる ▪ Why did you have to *have* such *a big mouth*? どうして君はあんなにべらべらとしゃべる必要があったのかね.

have a good* [*bad, hard, no*] *mouth (馬が)はみがきく[きかない] ▪ He has a horse that *has no mouth.* 彼ははみがきかない馬を所有している.

***have a mouth like the bottom of a parrot's cage* [*birdcage*]** 《口》(酒・タバコをやりすぎて)舌がざらざらしている ▪ This morning I *have got a mouth like the bottom of a parrot's cage.* 今朝は舌がざらざらしている.

have *one's* ***heart in*** *one's* ***mouth*** →HEART.

have marbles* [*a plum*] *in *one's* ***mouth*** 上流階級のような言葉うかいをする ▪ She speaks as if she *had a plum in her mouth.* 彼女はまるで上流階級のような言葉うかいをする.

have *one's* ***mouth made up for*** 《米口》…を待ち受けている ▪ She *had her mouth made up for* a laugh. 彼女は今にも笑い出しそうだった.

in* [*with*] *a French* [*an English, etc.] ***mouth*** フランス語[英語, など]流の発音で ▪ It is intolerable to smatter Latin *in an English mouth.* 英語流の発音でたどたどしくラテン語をしゃべるのはがまんできない.

in *a person's* ***mouth*** 人が言えば ▪ It sounds strange *in your mouth.* それは君が言うとおかしく聞こえる ▪ Your blamelessness will be accounted blame *in the mouths of* base interpreters. あなたの潔白も口うるさい連中に言わせると罪とみなされるだろう.

it does not lie in *a person's* ***mouth to*** *do* …するのは人に似つかわしくない ▪ *It did not lie in his mouth to* be curious on the subject. 彼がその問題を知りたがるのは似つかわしくなかった.

keep *one's* ***mouth shut*** 《口》黙っている ▪ He *kept his mouth shut* all the while. 彼はその間じゅう黙っていた.

laugh out of* [《英》 *on*] *the other* [*the wrong*] *side of *one's* ***mouth*** 《口》→LAUGH on the other side of one's face.

look down in the mouth がっかりした顔をする, ふさぎこんでいる ▪ She was *looking* very *down in the mouth* this morning. 彼女は今朝ひどくしょげた顔をしていた.

make* [*put on*] *a poor mouth (支払いを逃れるために)貧乏だからと言い訳する ▪ He wanted to *make a poor mouth* to her. 彼は彼女に貧乏だからと言い訳したいと思った.

***make a* (*wry, ugly, hard*) *mouth* [*mouths*]** (不賛成・嘲笑などを示すために)口をゆがめる, 顔をしかめる (*at, upon*) ▪ He shook his head, and *made a wry mouth.* 彼はかぶりを振って顔をしかめてみせた ▪ He doesn't care to *be made mouths at.* 彼は人に顔をしかめられるのをいやがる.

make *a person's* ***mouth water*** **1** よだれを出させる ▪ The smell of the soup *made my mouth water.* スープのにおいでよだれが出てきた ▪ The sight of this chocolate cake *makes my mouth water.* このチョコレートケーキを見ているとよだれが出てくる.

2 非常に魅力的である, 気をそそる ▪ The beautiful picture *made his mouth water.* その美しい絵は彼には垂涎(すいせん)の的だった ▪ The boots in the window *made my mouth water.* ショーウィンドウに飾られたブーツはほんとうに素敵だった ▪ Those travel folders about Venice *made her mouth water.* そのベネチアの旅行パンフレットは彼女の気をそそった.

make up *one's* ***mouth to*** 《米口》…を受けいれることに決める ▪ To save my life I couldn't *make up my mouth to* it. 命を助かるためでも, それを受けいれる気にはなれなかった.

me* [*you, him, her*] *and my* [*your, his, her*] *big mouth 《口》言ってはならないことを言ってしまった, 秘密をしゃべってしまった ▪ Oh, I shouldn't have said such a thing. *Me and my big mouth.* ああ, あんなこと言わねばよかった. まずいことを言ってしまった.

one's ***mouth is made up for*** 《米口》…を待ち受けている ▪ *His mouth is made up for* a chicken salad. 彼はチキンサラダを待ち構えている.

one's ***mouth was made*** (馬がはみに慣らされているように)服従するようにしつけられた[仕向けられた] ▪ At first, the man resisted, but in the end *his mouth was made.* 最初, 男は抵抗したが, しまいには服従するように仕向けられた.

one's ***mouth waters*** 口からよだれが出る, 渇望する (*after, at, for*) ▪ Never did *my mouth water* so much *for* a pipe in my life. 私は生まれてこのかたあれほどタバコを吸いたいと思ったことはなかった.

open *one's* ***mouth*** **1** (食べたり話したりするために)口を開く ▪ He *opened his mouth* and said no. 彼は口を開いてノーと言った.

2 《口》ものを言う ▪ I was afraid to *open my mouth* about it. 私は怖くてそのことを言えなかった.

open *one's* ***mouth* (*too*) *wide*** 《口》法外な値をふっかける ▪ He did not *open his mouth* so *wide* as the others. 彼は他の連中ほど高値をふっかけなかった.

out of *a person's* ***own mouth*** 人の言葉そのままを使って ▪ The maid delivered the message *out of her mistress's own mouth.* お手伝いは奥さんの言葉そのままを使って伝言を伝えた.

out of the mouth(s) of babes and sucklings 《雅》みどり児(ご)の口から (《聖》 *Ps.* 8. 2) ▪ Shrewd questions can come *out of the* *mouths of babes and sucklings*. みどり児の口から鋭い質問が出ることもある.

put (***a speech***) ***into*** *a person's* ***mouth*** 人が(言いもしないことを)言ったことにする ▪ Many *speeches* have *been put into the mouths of* the wrong persons. 多くの話が言いもしない人が言ったことにされてきた.

put on a poor mouth → make a poor MOUTH.

put the mouth on *a person* 《英俗》ある人が成功していると他人に知らせてその人を失敗させる ▪ I failed because you *put the mouth on* me. 僕が失敗したのは, 僕が好調だと君が人に言いふらしたせいだ.

put the words into *a person's* ***mouth*** 言うべきことを人に教える(《聖》*2 Sam*. 14. 3) ▪ I have *put the words into the mouths of* various characters of my invention. 私はその言葉を私が創造したさまざまの登場人物に言わせてきた.

run off at the mouth 《米口》余計なことをしゃべる, 口をすべらす ▪ That politician is always *running off at the mouth*. あの政治家は失言ばかりしている.

shoot off *one's* ***mouth***/***shoot*** *one's* ***mouth off*** 《口》(自慢顔に)べらべらまくし立てる ▪ He's always *shooting off his mouth* about his attractiveness to woman. 彼はいつも女性を惹き付ける自分の魅力についてべらべらまくし立てている.

shut *one's* ***mouth*** →close one's MOUTH.

spend *one's* ***mouth*** **1**(猟犬が)激しくほえ立てる ▪ The hounds *spent their mouths* very lustily. 猟犬たちが実に盛んにほえ立てた.

2(人が)話し始める ▪ They *spent their mouths* freely against the boss again. 彼らはまた上司の悪口を盛んに言い始めた.

stop *a person's* ***mouth*** **1** 人に猿ぐつわをはめる; 人を黙らせる; 人の口止めをする ▪ I *stopped his mouth* by shouting. 私は大声でどなって彼を黙らせた ▪ We *stopped his mouth* with a share of the money. 私たちはその金の分け前を与えて彼の口止めをした ▪ I just said so by way of *stopping their mouths*. 私は彼らに口止めするためにそう言っただけだ.

2 人を殺す ▪ He threatened to *stop my mouth*. 彼は殺すぞとおどした.

take the words (***right***) ***out of*** *a person's* ***mouth*** →WORD.

watch *one's* ***mouth*** 《口》言葉に気をつける ▪ Your thoughts and words decide your future. So *watch your mouth*. あなたの考えと言葉があなたの将来を決めます. だから言葉には気をつけなさい.

with a French [***an English,*** etc.] ***mouth*** → in a French MOUTH.

M

mouth[2] /maʊð/ 動 ***mouth it*** **1** 壮語する ▪ You've *mouthed it* bravely. 君は勇敢に大言壮語しましたね.

2(闘鶏が)くちばしで戦う ▪ The cocks came to *mouth it*. 雄鶏たちはくちばしで戦い始めた.

mouthful /máʊθfʊ̀l/ 名 ***at a mouthful*** ひと口で ▪ He consumed it *at a mouthful*. 彼はひと口でそれを飲み込んだ.

give *a person* ***a mouthful*** 《英口》毒舌を吐く, 悪態をつく ▪ She asked him to help her and he *gave* her *a mouthful*. 彼女が手を貸してくれるように頼むと彼は悪態をついた.

say a mouthful 《口・しばしば皮肉》重要な[うまい]ことを言う ▪ He *said a mouthful* when he asked her to marry him. 彼があの女性に結婚してくださいと頼んだのは, 大事なことを言ったわけだ ▪ Wow! You *said a mouthful* and I agree with you 100%. わぁ! うまいことを言ったな. 僕も君の意見に諸手を挙げて賛成だ. ☞通例, 過去時制.

What a mouthful! 《口》なんと長ったらしい[言い難い]語(句)だ ▪ Malva Sylvestra Zebrina? *What a mouthful* for such a pretty flower! Malva Sylvestra Zebrina だって? こんなかわいらしい花の名前なのに, 舌を噛みそうだ!

movable /múːvəbəl/ 形 ***a movable feast*** 開催の日(付)が一定していないこと ▪ They have a party every summer but it's something of *a movable feast*. 彼らは毎年夏にパーティーを開くがその日は年によってあまり一定していない.

move[1] /muːv/ 名 ***a good*** [***bad***] ***move*** 良い[まずい]手・措置 ▪ Traveling about always isn't *a good move*. 始終あちこち旅行するのはいい手ではないね.

bust a move [***bust some moves***] 人目を惹く目覚しい動きをする ▪ The score is tied, but if he really does *bust a move*, they can still win. 同点だが, もし彼が華麗なプレーを見せればまだ勝てる ▪ The man dancing over there really *busts a move*. あそこで踊っている人は見事な動きでみなの注目をしっかり集めている.

one's [*a person's*] ***every move*** 自分の[人の]あらゆる動き ▪ *Your every move* has been recorded. 君のすべての動きは記録されている.

get a move on 《口》 **1**〚しばしば命令文で〛急ぐ, 出かける ▪ *Get a move on* if you want to get there in time. そこに間に合うように着きたければ急げ.

2〚しばしば命令文で〛急いで始める ▪ For Heaven's sake, *get a move on*! 頼むから, すぐに始めてくれ.

3 進捗する ▪ The business may *get a move on* at last. あの仕事もいよいよ進むかもしれない.

get on the move 動き始める; 動き出させる ▪ The traffic *got on the move* again. 渋滞がまた流れ始めた ▪ The captain could not *get* his men *on the move*. 船長は船員を働き始めさせられなかった.

have all the moves 《米俗》(スポーツなどが)抜群の腕前である ▪ Anthony *has all the moves*. アンソニーの運動能力は抜群である ▪ Paul *had all the moves* of a great craftsman. ポールは偉大な工芸家らしく抜群の技量を備えていた.

know [***be up to***] ***a move or two***/***be up to every move on the board***/***be down to every move*** 抜け目がない, 如才がない, くえない ▪ They plume themeslves on *knowing a move* *or two.* 彼らは抜け目がないのを自慢にしている ▪ The old loan shark *was up to every move on the board.* その老獪な高利貸しはなかなかくえないやつだった. ☞チェスから.

make a move **1** 動く ▪ If any of you *make a move*, I will shoot. 一人でも動いたら, ぶっぱなすぞ.

2《英口》立ち去る ▪ I really must *make a move* now and go home. 本当にもうおいとまして帰宅しなくてはなりません.

3 出かける ▪ The first holiday makers are *making a move* to the seaside. 最初の観光客が海へ出かけているところです.

4 (ある)行動をする, 措置を講じる ▪ The boss *made* quite *a* good *move* when he decided to open a branch of the business in Paris. 社長がパリに支店を置くことに決めたのは全くいい手を打ったものだ.

5《チェス》こまを動かす ▪ Smith *made a move*, and his opponent's position became hopeless. スミスがこまを動かすと相手の形勢は絶望的になった.

make* [*put*] *a move on 《口》 **1** (人)を口説く, 誘惑する ▪ Nick is known for *making a move on* any young woman. ニックは若い女性と見れば誰でも口説くことで知られている ▪ He *put the moves on* my sister when she was only 16. 彼は僕の妹がまだ16歳のときに誘惑しようとした.

2《スポーツ》(レースで)前の走者を追い抜く ▪ He *made a move on* Tom just before breaking the finish line. 彼はゴール直前にトムを抜き去った.

make no move to *do* …するための行動を何ら起こさない, …しようとしない ▪ He said he would clean the counter, but *made no move to* do so. 彼はカウンターを片づけると言ったがその気配を見せなかった.

make the first move (好いた者同士のうちで)はじめに行動を起こす ▪ Most women are still too embarrassed to *make the first move.* 大抵の女性はまだ先に手を出すのはきまりが悪いのです.

never miss a move = not MISS a trick.

on the move **1** あちこち動いて ▪ Everybody seemed to be busy, humming, and *on the move.* 誰もが鼻歌を歌ったり, あちこち動いたりして忙しそうだった.

2 旅行して ▪ John likes selling because it keeps him *on the move.* ジョンはいつもあちこち旅行していられるので, 販売することが好きだ.

3 (物事が)進行[発展]して ▪ It does not follow from this that civilization is always *on the move.* このことから文明が始終進歩しているということにはならない.

put the moves on = make a MOVE on 1.

move[2] /muːv/ 動 *one* ***can't move*** (***for …***) 《口》身動きできないほど(人で)ごった返している[いっぱいである] ▪ The disco place started to get packed so that you *couldn't move* in the place. ディスコ会場は込み始めたので身動きできないほどであった.

get moving **1** 働き始める[始めさせる], 動き始める[始めさせる] ▪ Can you *get* the car *moving*? 車を動かせるかね ▪ It's time to *get moving.* もう働いてもいいころだ.

2《口》…を進展させる ▪ The new management *got* the business *moving.* 新経営陣は取引を進展させた.

move *a person's* ***blood*** 人の血をかき立てる, 人を興奮させる ▪ No youthful spirits *move his blood* now. もう若々しい元気が彼の血をかき立てることもない.

move heaven and earth to *do* 《口》…するためありとあらゆる努力をする ▪ The police are *moving heaven and earth to* track him down. 警察は彼の居所を突き止めようとして八方手を尽くしている.

move house →HOUSE.

move it 《口》〚主に命令文で〛急ぐ ▪ I yelled at her to hurry, "*Move it*, Princess." 彼女に急ぐように大声で言った.「姫, 急ぐのです」.

move up in the world 昇進する ▪ She hoped she would *move up in the world.* 彼女は昇進したいと思った.

move with the times →TIME[1].

movement /múːvmənt/ 名 ***in the movement*** 時勢におくれずに, 風潮に乗じて (= in the SWIM (of things)) ▪ To make life vivid, to be *in the movement*, this was his desire. 人生を生き生きとさせ, 時勢におくれないこと, これが彼の願いだった.

mover /múːvər/ 名 ***a mover and shaker*** 中心人物, 実力者, 大物 ▪ Her father quit banking, but is still *a mover and shaker.* 彼女の父は銀行から身を引いたが, 今も影響力は健在である ▪ Who exactly are *the movers and shakers* here in this firm? この会社のお偉方にはどういった面々が名を連ねているか? ☞Arthur O'Shaughnessy, *Ode* (1874)の一節から.

movie /múːvi/ 名 ***go to* [*see*] *a movie*** 《米口》映画を見に行く[見る] ▪ He has *gone to a movie.* 彼は映画を見に行っている ▪ I *saw a movie* after supper. 夕食後映画を見た.

go to the movies 《口》映画を見に行く ▪ How often do you *go to the movies* in a month? ひと月に何回映画を見に行きますか.

moving /múːvɪŋ/ 名形 ***a moving of the waters*** 騒ぎ, 興奮; (事件進行中の)変化, 妨害 (《聖》*John* 5. 3) ▪ Once in a while there is *a moving of the waters.* 時折変化が見られる.

the moving spirit 《雅》主導者, 主唱者 ▪ He was *the moving spirit* in the affair. 彼がその事件の主導者だった.

Mr. /místər/ 名 ***Mr. Big*** 《口》あるグループ[地域](とくに犯罪組織)の頭(かしら), 大ボス; 実力者 ▪ The man is believed to be the *Mr. Big* of the criminal underworld. 男は犯罪組織のボスと目される人物だ ▪ He allegedly became Washington's "*Mr Big*". 彼はワシントンの実力者になったと言われている.

Mr. Clean 清廉潔白の士, 清く正しい政治家 ▪ The lawmaker has always been known as *Mr. Clean.* その政治家はずっと清廉潔白の士ということで知られてきた.

Mr. Nobody. 《口》誰でもない《返事》 ▪ Who has

gone and broken it?—*Mr. Nobody.* 誰がそれをこわしたりなどしたのか?—誰でもありませんよ.

Mr. Right →RIGHT[1].

No more Mr. Nice Guy! 《口》お人好しでいるのはもうごめんだ, 優しいまねはもうおしまいだ ▪ *No more Mr. Nice Guy.* It doesn't pay. 人に親切はもうやめだ. 割に合わん.

much /mʌtʃ/ 形名副 ***a bit much*** = a bit THICK.

amount to much →come to MUCH.

as much ちょうどそれだけ, 等しく ▪ I thought *as much.* そんなことだと思ったよ ▪ Can you do *as much*? 君も同じだけのことができますか.

as much as 《米》 **1** =MUCH as 2.

2 …も同然で ▪ He *as much as* promised to marry her. 彼は彼女と結婚すると約束したようなものだった.

as much* (…) *as …ほど, だけ ▪ Take *as much as* you like. 好きなだけ取りなさい ▪ I have half [twice, three times] *as much as* you. 私は君の半分[2倍, 3倍]持っています ▪ Give me half *as much* again *as* that. その1倍半ください ▪ It was *as much as* I could do not to cry. 泣くまいとするので精いっぱいだった.

as much as to say …と言わんばかりに ▪ He shook his head *as much as to say* "Impossible." 彼は「あり得ない」と言わんばかりに首を横に振った.

be not much of a one for… …はあまり好きではない ▪ I *am not much of a one for* modern art. 私は現代美術にはあまり気が向きません.

by much 大いに, ずっと ▪ She is younger than I *by much.* 彼女は私よりずっと年下だ.

come* [*amount, lead*] *to much 〚否定文・疑問文で〛たいしたことになる, 役立つ ▪ I don't think this evidence *amounts to* very *much.* この証言がたいして役立つとは思えない ▪ Does all this *come to much*?—No! こんなことが役に立つでしょうか?—いいえ!

have much to do to *do* →HAVE[2].

How much? →HOW.

in as much as →INASMUCH as.

***it is not too much to say* (*that*)** (…と)言っても過言ではない ▪ *It is not too much to say that* he is a genius. 彼は天才だと言っても過言ではない.

make much of **1** …を重んじる, 重視する ▪ They *made much of* me in those days. あのころはみんな私を重んじてくれたんですよ.

2 …をもてはやす, 甘やかす ▪ The mother *made* too *much of* her youngest son. 母親は末の息子を甘やかしすぎた ▪ He *was made much of* on that account. 彼はそのためにもてはやされた.

3 〚主に否定文で〛…をよく理解する ▪ I didn't *make much of* that lecture. その講義はよくわからなかった.

much about **1** ほぼ…ごろ ▪ It was *much about* that time. ほぼその頃だった.

2 《口》ほとんど ▪ I was *much about* exhausted. 私はほとんど疲れきっていた.

much as **1** …とほぼ同じように ▪ He values a woman's personality, *much as* he does with looks. 彼は女性の容姿と同程度にその人格を重視する.

2 非常に…だけれども ▪ *Much as* I should like to go, I can't. とても行きたいのですが, 行けないのです.

much good at 〚主に否定文で〛あまり得意で ▪ I'm not very *much good at* this sort of work. こんな仕事はあまり得意なほうではない.

***Much good may it do** a person!* 《皮肉》大いにためになりますように ▪ Here's the money you earned from the races. *Much good may it do you!* あなたが競馬で儲けた金がここにある. たんとあなたのお役に立ちますように.

much less →LESS.

much more →MORE.

much of a ほぼ同じの ▪ We are *much of an* age. 我々はほぼ同じ年齢だ ▪ They are *much of a* size. それらはほぼ同じ大きさだ.

much of a muchness 《口》似たりよったり, 大同小異 ▪ Men are men; they're *much of a muchness.* 男は男さ, いずれも似たりよったりだ ▪ Our football players are all too *much of a muchness.* わがフットボールチームの選手たちはどれもドングリの背比べだ.

much though =MUCH as 2.

Much will have more. 《諺》あるが上にもほしがるもの.

not anything much =NOTHING much.

***not go* [*be*] *much on* [*for*]** 《口》 **1** …はおもしろくない; はあまり好きではない ▪ I do*n't go much on* a big spider running up my bare arms. 素肌の腕を大きなクモが這い上がるのって, 心地よくはないね ▪ I'*m not much on* poems. 詩はあまり好きではない.

2 …は大したもの[上手]ではない ▪ He *is not much on* conversation. 彼は会話は得意ではない.

Not much! 《口》 **1** とんでもない ▪ Do you think he'd be any good as secretary?—*Not much!* あの男が秘書として役に立つと思うかね?—とんでもない.

2 《皮肉》確かに ▪ Is he dead?—*Not much* he isn't. 彼は死んだのか?—むろん死んだrange.

not much in it ほとんど違いがない ▪ He won, but there was*n't much in it.* 彼が勝つには勝ったが僅差だった.

not much of a 《口》たいした…ではない ▪ He's *not much of a* scholar. あいつはたいした学者じゃない ▪ It was*n't much of a* dinner. たいしたごちそうじゃなかった.

not much to look at 見ばえがしない ▪ She was *not much to look at.* 彼女は見ばえがしなかった.

not much to speak of とり立てて言うほどでない ▪ *None* of the candidates are *much to speak of.* 候補者の中でとり立てて言うほどの人物は誰もいない ▪ My French study was *not much to speak of.* 私のフランス語の勉強はとくに言うほどのものではなかった.

not so much A as B **1** BほどAでない ▪ I am *not so much* fond of jazz *as* you are. 僕は君ほどジャズが好きではない.

2 AよりはむしろB ▪ He is *not so much* a scholar *as* a writer. 彼は学者というよりはむしろ文士だ

M

▪ The engineer seeks *not so much* to know nature *as* to use her. エンジニアは自然を知ろうというよりはむしろそれを利用しようとする.

not* [*never*] *so much as *do* …すら(し)ない ▪ He can*not so much as* write his own name. 彼は自分の名前を書くことさえできない ▪ He *never so much as* spoke. 彼は口もきかなかった.

not up to much →UP[1].

pretty much ほとんど ▪ Her homework was *pretty much* finished. 彼女の宿題はほとんど終わっていた.

see much of *a person* →SEE.

so much **1** それほど ▪ Don't worry *so much.* そんなにくよくよするな.
2 全くの; それだけ(の) ▪ It is only *so much* rubbish. それは全くのがらくたにすぎない ▪ If that is the case, *so much* the better for us. そういう事情なら, 我々にとってますます結構だ ▪ Australia is *so much* the better for being a true multicultural society. オーストラリアは真の多文化社会であるのでそれだけよい国だ.
3 いくらの ▪ They work for *so much* a week. 彼らは1週間いくらで働く.
4 大いに ▪ I do want *so much* to help you. 君を助けたいのは山々だ.

so much as 〚主に否定文で〛…だけで, 少しでも…; さえ(しないで) ▪ She'll inform your wife if you *so much as* look cross-eyed at her. 君が流し目をしただけで, 彼女は君の奥さんに言いつけるぞ ▪ He departed without *so much as* a goodbye. 彼はさよならも言わずに立ち去った.

so much for **1** …のことはそれだけ, それでおしまい ▪ Anyway, *so much for* today. それはともかく, 今日はこれでおしまい ▪ *So much for* roses, now about lilies. バラはそれくらいとして, さて次はユリです.
2 …とはそんなもの; …するとそんな目にあう ▪ *So much for* his learning on the job. その仕事に関する彼の知識なんてそんな程度さ ▪ *So much for* being in debt, heigh-ho! 借金するとこんな目にあう, やれやれだ.

so much so that 非常にそうなので ▪ He is rich—*so much so that* he does not know what he is worth. 彼は金持ちだ—大金持ちなのでいくら財産があるのかわからないほどだ.

***so much the better* [*worse*] (*for …*)** → so MUCH 2.

that much そこまで, それだけ ▪ I have only done *that much* so far. これまででそれだけしかやっていない.

there is nothing* [*not*] *much in …にはさしておもしろい[値うちのある]ところはない ▪ *There was nothing much in* the first round. 第1ラウンドにはさしてめぼしい展開はなかった.

think it much* (*to *do*) (…するのを)大変なことだと思う; (…するのを)いやがる ▪ I *thought it much to* be so long confined. それほど長く監禁されるのはひどく辛いことだと思った.

think much of →THINK[2].

this* [*thus*] *much これだけは, ここまでは ▪ *This much* is certain. これだけは確かだ ▪ I only know *thus much.* これだけしか知りません.

too much **1** あまりたくさん ▪ You work *too much.* 君は働きすぎる.
2 =TOO much (of a good thing).
3 《米俗》すてきな, すごい ▪ The music was just *too much.* その音楽は全くすごかった.

too much for 《口》…の手に負えない ▪ That young lady is *too much for* me. あの娘さんにはかなわない ▪ This poem is *too much for* me. この詩は僕の手に負えない.

very much 非常に ▪ Thank you *very much.* どうもありがとう. ☞much だけの代わりに普通用いる.

very much so 〚yes を強調して〛まさにその通り ▪ I understand you are interested in economics. —*Yes, very much so.* 君は経済に関心があると聞いているが—そう, まさにその通りだ.

without so much as …すらせずに, さえしないで (→not so MUCH as do) ▪ He went out *without so much as* saying goodbye. 彼はさよならとも言わずに立ち去った.

muck /mʌk/ 名 **(*as*) *sick as muck*** 《口》ひどくしょげて ▪ Poor coach was *as sick as muck.* かわいそうにコーチはすっかりしょげてしまった.

(*as*) *wet as muck* ずぶぬれになって ▪ I was *wet as muck* when I got home. 家に着いたときずぶぬれになっていた.

be in* [*all of*] *a muck of 《口》(よごれ・汗・苦労など)にまみれる, 埋まる ▪ She *was all of a muck of* sweat. 彼女は汗みどろになっていた ▪ The old man *was in* such *a muck of* trouble. 老人は苦労の山に埋もれていた.

be in a muck-sweat 《俗》狼狽している, 面くらっている ▪ He *was* obviously *in a muck-sweat* to hear it. それを聞いて彼は明らかに泡をくっていた. ☞muck-sweat=perspiration.

in a muck 《英口》乱雑な[に] ▪ The kitchen is *in a muck*! 台所が散らかっている.

Lord* [*Lady*] *Muck 《戯》偉ぶろうとする男[女] ▪ She was acting like *Lady Muck.* 彼女は偉い女性を気取っていた.

make a muck of 《口》…を台なしにする ▪ She *made a muck of* her speech by crying. 彼女は泣き出してスピーチを台なしにしてしまった.

muck and truck 《商俗》雑貨 ▪ Miscellaneous items are commonly spoken of as "*muck and truck.*" 雑多な品は「雑貨品」と一般に呼ばれている.

rake muck (個人・政界の)醜聞をあさって暴露する ▪ Journalists usually *rake muck.* 記者はたいてい醜聞をあさって暴露する. ☞muck raking から.

treat *a person* ***like muck*** 《口》人をぞんざいに扱う ▪ She *treats* him *like muck*, but he's crazy about her. 彼女は彼にぞんざいに接するが彼の方はぞっこんだ.

***Where there is muck, there is brass* [*money*].** 《諺》糞のあるところに富がある《手を汚さずに大金は得られない》. ☞brass《古風》=money.

mucker /mʌ́kər/ 名 ***come a mucker***《俗》
1 ひどく倒れる ▪ He *came a* most awful *mucker* in that motor-bike race last week. 彼は先週のあのオートバイ競走でひどく転倒した.
2 ひどい目にあう, 身をつぶす ▪ They *came a mucker* in the Wall Street crash. ウォール街での相場暴落で彼らは大打撃をうけた. ☞mucker「牛馬ふん(muck)で足をすべらせてころぶこと」.

muck(-)rake[1] /mʌ́krèɪk/ 名 ***the man with the muck(-)rake*** 醜事件をかぎ回る人 (Bunyan, *Pilgrim's Progress*) ▪ We must not be like *the man with the muck rake*. 我々はスキャンダルをかぎ回るやつのまねをしてはならない.

muck-rake[2] /mʌ́krèɪk/ 動 ***muck-raking***《口》スキャンダルをあばくこと ▪ The reports were nothing but *muck-raking*. その報告書は全くの醜聞あばきだった.

mud /mʌd/ 名 ***(as) clear as mud*** [《米》***blue mud***]《皮肉》あいまいきわまる ▪ The nature of the case is *as clear as mud*. その事件の正体はあいまいきわまる.

(as) mad as mud →MAD.

(as) sick as mud《口》しょげて; 怒って ▪ He was *as sick as mud* about it. 彼はそのことでしょげて[怒って]いた.

(as) sure as mud《学俗》ごく確かな[に] ▪ I shall die *as sure as mud*. 僕はきっと死ぬ.

drag ... through the mud = drag ... through the MIRE.

fling [***sling, throw***] ***mud at*** …の顔に泥を塗る, をそしる ▪ He spends his whole life *slinging mud at* people ten times better than himself. 彼はいつも自分より10倍も優れた人々のことをそしっている.

(here's) mud in your eye《口》ご幸運を祝して《乾杯のときの文句》▪ Each time John raised his glass he would say, "Well, *here's mud in your eye*." ジョンはグラスをあげるたびに,「さて, 君の幸運を祝して」と言うのだった.

mud sticks《英》(体面などについた)泥がなかなか落ちない ▪ He's blanketed the scandal, but some *mud sticks*. 彼はスキャンダルをもみ消したが, ついた泥はなかなか落ちない.

One's ***name is mud.***《口》(特に不道徳のために)…の名[信用]は地に落ちている ▪ You probably agree that *his name is mud*. 彼の信用が地に落ちていることに君も異論あるまい. ☞リンカン大統領の暗殺者 John Wilkes Booth が逃走中に折った足を治療したため投獄された Samuel Mudd 医師の名から.

pull mud《米俗》旅行する ▪ We began to *pull mud*. 我々は旅行し始めた.

sell for the mud《米》二束三文で売る ▪ His holding *was sold for the mud*. 彼の持ち株は二束三文で売られた.

sling mud at →fling MUD at.

stick in the mud **1** 泥の中にはまり込んで動かない ▪ The wheels have *stuck in the mud*. 車輪が泥にはまりこんで動かない.
2 保守的[旧弊]である ▪ They just *stuck in the mud*. They moved against the times. 彼らはまさに保守的だった. 時勢に逆行した.
3 卑しい境遇に甘んじる ▪ He is content to *stick in the mud*. 彼は卑しい境遇に平気で甘んじている.

throw mud at →fling MUD at.

treat *a person* ***as mud*** [***as the mud beneath*** *one's* ***feet***] 人をつちくれのように扱う ▪ It is not proper to *treat* a person *as mud*. 人をつちくれのように扱うのはよくない.

muddle /mʌ́dəl/ 名 ***in a muddle*** 雑然と, めちゃめちゃで; ぼうっとして, まごついて ▪ We both grubbed on *in a muddle*. 我々は二人ともめちゃめちゃに働き続けた.

make a muddle of …をめちゃめちゃにする ▪ The court has *made a muddle of* this question. 法廷がこの問題をすっかりめちゃめちゃにしてしまった.

muff[1] /mʌf/ 名 ***make a muff of***《口》…をやりそこなう ▪ Unfortunately he *made a muff of* the whole business. あいにく彼が事をすっかりやりそこなってしまった.

make a muff of *oneself*《口》(ばかなことをして)笑いものになる ▪ Both sides have succeeded in *making muffs of themselves*. 双方ともまんまと笑いものになってしまった.

make a muff of it《口》へまをやる, どじを踏む ▪ I know I shall *make a muff of it*. 僕はへまをやるに決まっているんだ.

muff[2] /mʌf/ 動 ***muff it*** へまをやる, どじを踏む ▪ When I make speeches in public, I always *muff it*. 人前で講演するといつもへまをしてしまう.

muffle /mʌ́fəl/ 動 ***muffle*** *oneself* ***up*** くるまる ▪ I *muffled myself up* in furs. 毛皮にくるまった.

mufti /mʌ́fti/ 名 ***in mufti*** 平服を着て[た] ▪ I met an amiable police officer *in mufti*. 私は私服を着た愛想のよい警察官に会った.

mug /mʌg/ 名 ***a mug shot*** 逮捕者の顔写真 ▪ Go over these *mug shots* and tell me if you see the one who robbed you. この顔写真をざっと見て, あなたを襲った者がいるか教えてください.

a mug's game《英口》割に合わない仕事 ▪ It's *a mug's game* to kidnap a child. 子供を誘拐するのは割に合わない仕事だ. ☞mug = fool.

make a mug at《英口》…に向かってしかめつらをする ▪ The boy *made a mug at* me. 少年は私にしかめつらをしてみせた. ☞mug = grimace.

make a mug of *oneself*《英口》ばかなまねをする ▪ Don't *make a mug of yourself*. ばかなまねはよせ. ☞mug = fool.

muggins /mʌ́gɪnz/ 名 ***talk muggins***《俗》ばかなことを言う ▪ He is always *talking muggins*. 彼はいつもばかなことばかり言っている.

mule /mjuːl/ 名 ***(as) obstinate*** [***stubborn***] ***as a mule*** ひどく強情な ▪ She was *as obstinate as a mule* on that point. 彼女はその点ではひどく頑固だった.

M

mull /mʌl/ 名 ***make a mull of*** 《英口》…を台なしにする ▪ On a second attempt I nearly *made a mull of* the business. 2度目の試みで，危うく事を台なしにしてしまうところだった.

make a mull of it 《英口》へまをやる，みそをつける ▪ There's where I always *make a mull of it.* そこのところで僕はいつもへまをやるんだ.

multitude /mʌ́ltətjùːd/ 名 ***cover* [*hide*] *a multitude of sins*** 《戯》 色々とぼろが隠せる (《聖》*1 Pet.* 4. 8) ▪ I'll say I was ill. That will *cover a multitude of sins.* 病気だったと言ってやろう. そうすれば色々とぼろが隠せる.

mum /mʌm/ 名形 **(*as*) *mum as a mouse*** →MOUSE.

keep mum 《口》黙って[内緒にして]いる ▪ *Keep mum* till it is over. それがすむまで黙っていてくれ.

Mum's the word. 《口》黙っているんだよ; 他言無用 ▪ Remember, *mum's the word.* いいかね，他言無用だよ.

play mum 《古》黙っている ▪ Yet he would *play mum.* しかし彼は黙っているだろう.

stand mum 《古》黙って立っている ▪ Don't *stand* there *mum.* そこで黙って立っていてはだめだ.

mummy /mʌ́mi/ 名 ***to a mummy*** ぐにゃぐにゃになるまで ▪ I beat him *to a mummy.* 彼を打って打って打ちのめしてやった ▪ Don't boil the rice *to a mummy.* 米をべとべとになるまで煮るな.

mumps /mʌmps/ 名 ***have mumps above the ears*** 《米俗》うぬぼれている，気取っている ▪ I can't stand him. He *has mumps above the ears.* 彼にはがまんできない. 気取ってやがるから.

have the mumps すねている，ふくれている ▪ Don't go near Jim. He *has the mumps.* ジムには近づくな. 不きげんだから.

munchies /mʌ́ntʃɪz/ 名 ***get* [*have*] *the munchies*** 《口》ちょっと小腹がすく[すいている]，急に空腹になる[なっている] ▪ I've been *getting the munchies* all the time. このところ小腹がすきっぱなしだ ▪ I *have the munchies* and I don't have any money. 腹はへったが金はない. ☞動詞 munch「むしゃむしゃ食う」から.

murder[1] /mə́ːrdər/ 名 ***cry* [*scream, yell*] (*blue* [《英》*bloody*]) *murder*** 《口》(まるで殺されるときのように)大げさな叫び声をあげる，大声を張り上げる ▪ Our baby always *screams bloody murder* when we give him a bath. うちの赤んぼうはお風呂に入れるときまって大泣きをする. ☞blue murder はフランス語の誓いの言葉 morbleu<mort Dieu の翻訳借用(＝blue death). bleu(＝blue) は Dieu(＝God) の婉曲的表現.

get away* [*by*] *with* (*blue*) *murder →GET.

it's murder on 《口》(体の一部)が痛くなる; …に対して害がある ▪ Watch that gingerbread, *it's murder on* the teeth! あのジンジャーブレッドをご覧，歯が痛くなるよ ▪ Wine is great with dinner—but *it's murder on* your good linens. ワインはディナーにはいい取り合わせですが，上等のリネンには害があります《こぼしたらしみが取れない》.

like blue murder 全速力で ▪ They were off down the road *like blue murder.* 彼らは全速力で道路を下って去った.

***Murder will out* [*cannot be hid*].** 《諺》悪事は必ずばれるもの.

The murder is out. 《口》秘密がばれた，謎が解けた ▪ So at last *the murder is out.* では，とうとう秘密がばれたのだな. ☞上の諺から.

murder[2] /mə́ːrdər/ 動 ***I could murder a thing*** 《口》…が食べ[飲み]たくてたまらない ▪ *I could murder* some coffee. コーヒーを飲みたくてしかたがない.

murder the King's English → the King's ENGLISH.

A person ***will murder*** *one*. 《口》人が話し相手にひどく怒るだろう ▪ Tom *will murder* you when he finds out what you've done to his car! トムの車に君がやったことを知ったら彼はかんかんになるぞ.

murmur /mə́ːrmər/ 名 ***without a murmur*** 不平も[ぶつぶつ]言わずに ▪ She paid the surcharge for the trip *without a murmur.* 彼女は愚痴一つこぼさず旅行の追加料金を支払った.

muscle /mʌ́səl/ 名 ***control* [*govern*]** *one's* ***muscle*** おかしさ[笑い]をこらえる ▪ I could scarcely *control my muscles.* 笑いをこらえきれないほどだった.

flex *one's* ***muscles*** 《口》 **1** 肩ならしする ▪ I am just *flexing my muscles* so that I can write a best-seller some day. いつかベストセラーが書けるように肩ならしをしているだけだ.

2 (腕)力があることを誇示する，威力を示す ▪ The terrorists *flexed their muscles* with a suicide bombing attack. テロリストらは自爆攻撃で実力誇示をした.

not move a muscle びくりともしない，身動きもしない ▪ He stayed quite still and *never moved a muscle.* 彼は全くじっとしたままで，びくりともしなかった.

pull a muscle 筋肉を痛める，肉離れを起こす ▪ I *pulled a muscle* in my back and can't work today. 私は背中の筋を痛めたのできょうは仕事ができない.

put some muscle into it 《口》もっと力を入れる，もっと頑張る ▪ You have to *put some muscle into it* to incorporate the eggs fully. 卵をよくかき混ぜるにはもっと力を入れなければなりません.

use *one's* ***muscle*** とびきりの腕力をふるう ▪ He would *use his muscle* rather than his limited intellect. 彼は乏しい知力よりむしろ腕力をふるったものだ.

museum /mjuːzíːəm/ 名 ***a museum piece*** 時代遅れの人[物]，使い古しの物 ▪ Uncle Jim is *a* real *museum piece.* ジムおじさんは全く時代遅れだ ▪ We can't go to Boston in that *museum piece* of a car. あの博物館行きのポンコツ車でボストンへは行けやしないよ.

mush /mʌʃ/ 名 ***make a mush of*** 《口》…をめちゃめちゃにする ▪ The storm *made a mush of* the

M

garden-flowers. あらしで庭の花がめちゃめちゃになった.

mushroom /mʌ́ʃru:m|-rʊm/ 名 ***like mushrooms*** 急にものすごい数で, 雨後の筍(たけのこ)のように ▪ Many skyscrapers have sprung up *like mushrooms* in Dubai. ドバイでは摩天楼があっという間に林立した.

music /mjú:zɪk/ 名 ***be (like) music to*** *a person's* ***ears*** 《口》(音楽のように)快く響く ▪ Her scoldings *were music to my ears.* 彼女の小言も私には快く響いた ▪ The news of his resignation *was like music to my ears.* 彼の辞任のニュースは私の耳には快く響いた.

face the music 《口》 **1** ひるまずに難局に当たる ▪ He *faced the music* like a man. 彼は男らしくひるまずに難局に当たった.

2 報いを甘んじて受ける ▪ He had made a mistake and now had to *face the music.* 彼はまちがいを犯したので, その報いを甘んじて受けねばならなかった. ☞music は皮肉に "unpleasant noise" の意味.

make (beautiful) music (together) 《口》性交する ▪ I think we should *make music together.* 二人で音楽を奏でようよ.

rough music (隣人へのいやがらせになべ・かまなどをたたいて立てる)やかましい音, 大騒ぎ ▪ A number of boys came out with shovels, playing the *rough music.* 大勢の子供たちがシャベルを持って出てきて, やかましい音を立てていた.

set ... to music (詩など)を楽曲に合わせる, 節づけする ▪ The poem *was set to music.* 詩は節づけされた.

Stop the music. 動くな; ちょっと待て.

the music of the spheres →SPHERE.

musical /mjú:zɪkəl/ 形 ***play musical chairs*** たらい回し[ドミノ式]にポストを引き継がせる ▪ Our boss loves to *play musical chairs* with the staff. 社長は好んで社員の役職を順々に変える. ☞「いす取りゲーム」から.

musketeer /mʌ̀skətíər/ 名 ***three musketeers*** 3人の親密な仲間[親友] ▪ These gentlemen are known as the *three musketeers.* この紳士たちは親友トリオとして知られている. ☞Alexandre Dumas の Three Musketeers「三銃士」(1844)より.

muslin /mʌ́zlɪn/ 名 ***a bit of muslin*** 《英俗》婦人, 少女 ▪ That was *a* pretty *bit of muslin* hanging on your arm, who was she? 君の腕にすがっていたあの女の子はきれいな子だったね, 誰だったの.

musquash /mʌ́skwɑ̀ʃ|-wɔʃ/ 名 ***talk musquash*** 《米》毛皮の商談をする ▪ They were endlessly *talking musquash.* 彼らは果てしもなく毛皮の商談をしていた.

must[1] /mʌst/ 形 ***go must*** **1** (交尾期のゾウ・ラクダの雄が)さかりがついてあばれる ▪ The elephant had suddenly *gone must.* ゾウが突然さかりがついてあばれだした.

2 (人が)かんしゃくを起こしてあばれる ▪ He *went must* on the business. 彼はその問題でかんしゃくを起こしてあばれ回った.

must[2] /mʌst/ 名 ***be a must for*** *a person* 人がぜひ…しなければならないもの[こと]である ▪ This novel *is a must for* all lovers of fiction. この小説はすべての小説愛好家の必読書である.

must[3] /məst, mʌst/ 助 ***if you must*** ぜひそうしたいとおっしゃるなら(よろしい) ▪ May I smoke here? —*If you must.* ここでタバコを吸ってもいいですか?—どうしてもと言うならね.

if you must know 言いたくはないが ▪ *If you must know*, you've got dirty nails, haven't you? 言いたくはないんだけど, きたない爪をしているね, 君.

must have *done* **1** …したにちがいない《過去の強い推定》 ▪ He *must have* been wise. 彼は賢かったにちがいない ▪ How you *must have* hated me! さぞ僕を憎んだことだろう.

2 …したにちがいないのに《過去の事実に反する仮定》 ▪ You *must have* caught the train if you had hurried. もし急いでいたら, 君はその電車にきっと間に合っただろうに.

3 …していなければならない《必要》 ▪ Applicants *must have* finished high school. 志願者は高等学校を卒業していなければならない.

must needs/needs must →NEEDS.

mustard /mʌ́stərd/ 名 ***a grain of mustard seed*** ひと粒のからしだね《将来の大発展を蔵している小さなもの》(《聖》*Matt.* 13. 31-32) ▪ This hope had grown up again like *a grain of mustard seed.* この希望はひと粒のからしだねのようにまた大きくなっていた.

(as) keen as mustard →KEEN.

(as) strong as mustard きわめて激しい ▪ My passion is *strong as mustard.* 私の情熱はきわめて激しいものだ.

be all [so much] to the mustard 《米俗》 **1** 申し分がない ▪ Why don't you invite him if he *is so much to the mustard?* もし彼がそんなに申し分がないのなら, 招いてはどうだ.

2 丈夫である ▪ I'*m all to the mustard* these days. 私はこのごろはとても丈夫なんだ.

be mustard at 《俗》…がじょうずだ ▪ She's *mustard at* the piano. 彼女はピアノの名手だ.

be the (proper) mustard 《米俗》本物である, 重要な人[物]である ▪ *Are* the pearls *the proper mustard?* その真珠は本物なのかい.

cut the mustard 《米俗》目的にかなう, 基準に達する, 期待に沿う, 成功する ▪ This *cuts the mustard* exactly. これでちょうど間に合う ▪ Even though he studied hard, he just couldn't *cut the mustard.* 熱心に勉強したのに彼はどうしても合格できなかった.

muster[1] /mʌ́stər/ 名 ***in muster*** 召集されて, 呼び集められて ▪ Are all the people of our house *in muster?* うちの者はみんな集まっているか ▪ All the old silver was *in muster* on the table. 古い銀器が食卓の上に総動員されていた.

pass muster **1** 検閲を通過する ▪ The new regiment has *passed muster.* 新連隊は検閲を通過した.

2 標準に達する, 合格する, 目的にかなう (*as, for*) ▪ Oh, he will *pass muster* all right. いや大丈夫,

M

あの男は物になるでしょう ▪ Such a ship might well *pass muster for* a man of war. そのような船舶が戦艦として通るのは当然だろう.

muster[2] /mʌ́stər/ 動 ***muster into (the) service*** 《米》入隊させる (↔MUSTER out of service) ▪ He *was mustered into the service* as a private. 彼は兵卒として入隊した.

muster out of service 《米》除隊させる (↔MUSTER into (the) service) ▪ The remaining soldiers *were* all *mustered out of service*. 残りの兵士たちはみな除隊させられた.

muster up support for …の支持者を集める ▪ He's been *mustering up support for* his political views. 彼は自分の政見の支持者を集めてきた.

mute /mju:t/ 名 ***(as) mute as a fish*** 《口》黙りこくって ▪ She suddenly became *as mute as a fish* at the sight of a pistol. 彼女はピストルを見て突然黙りこくってしまった.

stand mute (of malice) 《法》(故意に)黙秘権を行使する ▪ The jury realized the man was *standing mute of malice*. その男性が黙秘権を行使していることが陪審員たちに分かった.

mutton /mʌ́tən/ 名 ***(as) dead as mutton*** 《口》全く死んで; すたれて ▪ I shot a swan *as dead as mutton*. 私は1羽のハクチョウを撃ち殺してしまった ▪ Some of the popular songs are now *as dead as mutton*. その流行歌のいくつかは今は全く廃れている.

eat [take] one's [a bit of] mutton with 《口》…と食事を共にする ▪ Will you *eat your mutton with* me today? きょういっしょに食事をしないか.

mutton dressed (up) as lamb 《英口》小羊の服を着た羊《若うくりをした中年女性》 ▪ Look at her, *mutton dressed as lamb*. あの女の人をごらんよ, 小羊のなりをした羊だね. ☞mutton「成長した羊の肉」, lamb「子羊の肉」.

to return to [resume] our muttons 《戯》さて本題に立ち戻って ▪ But let us *return to our muttons*. でも, 本題に立ち戻りましょう. ☞F Revenons à nos moutons のなぞり.

mutual /mjú:tʃuəl/ 形 ***a mutual congratulation(s) society*** 《戯》互いにお世辞を言い合っている人々 ▪ We sang in turn and made *a* sort of *mutual congratulation society*. 我々は順番に歌を歌い, 互いにお世辞を言い合う成り行きとなった.

my /maɪ/ 間 ***My backside [arse]!*** 《卑》→MY foot!

My foot [eye, aunt Fanny]! 《口》ばかばかしい ▪ Culture, *my foot*! 教養だって, ばかばかしい.

Oh, my! 《口》まあ, あら, これはしたり ▪ *Oh, my!* ain't I hungry! ああ, ひどく腹がへった! ☞Oh, my God! の God の省略から.

mystery /místəri/ 名 ***be lost in mystery*** 不明のままである ▪ The origin of this tribe *is lost in mystery*. この種族の起原は不明のままである.

make a mystery of (何でもないこと)を神秘化する, 内緒にしておく ▪ He did not *make a mystery of* his knowledge, but publicly boasted. 彼は自分の知識を秘密にしないで, おおっぴらに自慢した ▪ They *made* no *mystery of* this matter. 彼らはこの問題を少しも内緒にしなかった.

N

nadir /néɪdɪər/ 名 ***be at its nadir*** そのどん底に達している ▪ His fortune *was at its nadir.* 彼の運命はどん底に達していた.

from the zenith to the nadir てっぺんからどん底まで, とことんまで ▪ You shall command me *from the zenith to the nadir.* 私にとことんまで命令してください.

in the nadir しょげきって ▪ I can see him *in the nadir,* in the deepest dejection. 私には彼がしょげこんで実に意気消沈しているのがわかる.

nail[1] /neɪl/ 名 ***a nail/a nail's breath*** 〚主に否定文で〛少し, いささか ▪ The sea ebbs and flows and does not vary *a nail.* 海は潮が満ち引きし, いささかも変わらない ▪ He may not swerve *a nail's breath.* 彼はいささかも迷わないだろう. ☞Ⓛ transversum unguem のなぞり.

a nail in *one's* [*a person's*] ***coffin/another nail in the coffin/the last*** [***final***] ***nail in the coffin*** **1** (人・物の)命取りになるもの ▪ Every glass of spirits you take is *a nail in your coffin.* 君が飲む酒が1杯ごとに君の命取りになっている ▪ The quarrel was *the final nail in the coffin* of our friendship. あの口論のために我々の友情は取り返しがつかなくなった.

2 《俗》1杯の酒 ▪ Here's *another nail in your coffin.* さあもう1杯やれよ. ☞「棺おけに打ち込むくぎ」が原義.

add a nail in *a person's* ***coffin*** →drive a NAIL in a person's coffin.

(***as***) ***deaf as a nail*** 少しも耳が聞こえない ▪ She was *deaf as a nail*; you could not hammer a meaning into her. 彼女は耳が全く不自由で, どんなにがなり立ててもからっきし通じなかった.

(***as***) ***hard*** [***tough***] ***as nails*** [《英》***old boots***] **1** 全く頑健な ▪ Thank you, I'm *as hard as nails.* おかげさまで私はぴんぴんしています.

2 きわめて冷酷な ▪ They are merciless, with hearts *as hard as nails.* 彼らは無慈悲で氷のように冷酷な心をしている.

3 精神的に強くて自立している ▪ She is *tough as old boots* and keeps her husband under her thumb. 彼女はしっかり者で夫を尻に敷いている.

(***as***) ***right as nails*** 全く強健な ▪ In a fortnight I shall be *as right as nails.* 2週間もすればすっかり元気になれるでしょう.

bite *one's* ***nails*** 爪をかんでくやしがる; (することがなくて)指をくわえる ▪ This caused the Cardinal to *bite his nails.* これが枢機卿をくやしがらせた ▪ He sat all day in the private room, *biting his nails.* 彼は一日中私室に引っ込んで何もせずに暮らした.

Don't take any wooden nails! 《米俗》うっかりするなよ, つかまされちゃだめだぞ.

drive a nail くぎを打つ, 急所を突く ▪ To gain success, we must proceed with discretion, *driving the nail* that will go. 成功するためには効くくぎを打ちながら慎重に行動しなくてはいけない ▪ Every cough *drove a nail* into her skull. せきをするたびに彼女の頭がずきずき痛んだ ▪ A mischievous wind from the wrong quarter *drives a nail* into the very head of the expedition. 反対方向から意地悪い風が吹いてくると, 探検隊は全く急所を突かれてしまう.

drive [***add, pound, put***] ***a nail in*** *a person's* ***coffin*** 人の命取りになる, 寿命を縮める ▪ What you have told me will help to *put a nail in their coffin.* 君が僕に教えてくれたことは, 連中の寿命を縮めるのを早めることになる.

Drive a nail where it will go in. くぎの入りそうな所へ打ち込め, すきがあったら進出せよ《英国主義の標語》.

drive the nail home/drive the nail (***up***) ***to the head*** **1** くぎを頭まで打ち込む ▪ He *drove the nail up to the head* by repeated blows of a hammer. 彼は何度もハンマーでたたいてくぎを頭まで打ち込んだ.

2 とことんまで論じつめる, 徹底させる ▪ You must *drive the nail* right *home* by leaving no doubt in their minds. 君は彼らの心に疑惑を少しも残さないようにして, とことんまで論じつめなければだめだ ▪ He will be sure to *drive the nails* of his exhortations *to the head.* 彼は必ず訓戒を徹底させるだろう.

from the tender nail ごく幼いころから (Horace, *Odes* 3. 6. 24) ▪ He has loved them inwardly *from their tender nails.* 彼らがごく幼いころから彼はひそかに愛してきた.

gnaw *one's* ***nails*** つめをかむ《手持ちぶさたの表現》 ▪ He sat all day over the fire, *gnawing his nails.* 彼は一日中火にあたりながら, 所在なく暮らした.

hit the (***right***) ***nail on the head*** 図星をさす, 肯綮(こうけい)に当たったことをする[言う] ▪ He *hit the right nail on the head* when he said that my chief fault was vanity. 彼が私のおもな欠点はうぬぼれだと言ったのは図星だった. ☞head「くぎの頭」.

on the nail 《英口》**1** 少しの狂いもなく, ぴったり正確に, (支払いが)遅れずに ▪ She arrived here at five o'clock, just *on the nail.* 彼女はちょうど5時きっかりに着いた. ☞中世商人が金銭を乗せて正確な金額を示すのに使用した nail と呼ばれる円柱状の秤の目盛から.

2 即座に; 即金で ▪ Answer me that *on the nail*! 今すぐそのことを返事してくれ ▪ He paid for them *on the nail* with other people's money. 彼は他人の金で即座にその支払いをした. ☞ブリストル取引所ではくぎ (nail) と称する, テーブルのように頂部の広がった柱があり，この「くぎの上で」昔の商人たちは契約の手付け金を払ったことから; =《米》on the barrel (head).

3 まんまと捕らえられて ▪ "We shall have the rogue *on the nail* yet," cried he.「いまにあの悪党をまんまと捕らえてやるぞ」と彼は大声で言った.

4 用意して ▪ He had never a word *on the nail*. 彼は一言も言うことができなかった.

5 問題となって ▪ Theosophy is at present very much *on the nail*. 神智学は今大いに問題にされている.

One nail drives out another. 《諺》くぎを打ってくぎを抜く,「毒をもって毒を制す」.

pound* [*put*] *a nail in* a person's *coffin → drive a NAIL in a person's coffin.

to the* [*a*] *nail 徹底的に (Horace, *Satires* 1. 5. 32) ▪ The man knew that rude sport *to the nail*. 男はその荒っぽいスポーツを完全に知り尽くしていた ▪ My speech was always polished *to a nail*. 私の演説はいつも徹底的に推敲されていた.

tooth and nail →TOOTH.

nail[2] /neɪl/ 動 ***nail*** one's ***colors to the mast*** →COLOR.

nail it 《米俗》及第する; 成功する ▪ At last he *nailed it*. とうとう彼は及第した.

nail ... shut …をくぎうけして締める ▪ He *nailed* them *shut*, with long spikes. 彼はそれらを大くぎを打ちつけて締めた.

nail ... to the barn-door …を見せしめ[さらしもの]にする ▪ They used to *nail* vermin *to the barn door* as a warning. かつては見せしめに害獣をさらしものにしたものだった.

nail ... to the counter (虚偽)をあばく ▪ I *nailed* that lie *to the counter* at once. 私はその嘘をすぐあばいてみせた. ☞店主がにせ金を帳場にくぎうけにして戒告した昔の習慣から.

nail a person ***to the wall*** 《口》…を厳しく罰する ▪ We *nailed* him *to the wall* for what he'd done. その行為に対して彼を厳罰に処した.

nailer /néɪlər/ 名 (***as***) ***busy as a nailer*** 《口》非常に忙しい ▪ Tom is being kept *as busy as a nailer*. トムは忙しくててんてこ舞いしている.

(***be***) ***a nailer at*** 《俗》…の名人(である) ▪ He *is a nailer at* golf. 彼はゴルフの名手だ.

like a nailer 《口》頑として ▪ He stuck to it *like a nailer*. 彼は頑としてそれを固執した.

naked /néɪkəd/ 形 (***as***) ***naked as a jaybird*** 一糸まとわず，真っ裸で ▪ He came out of the shower, *naked as a jaybird*. 彼はシャワーをすませて素っ裸で出てきた.

(***as***) ***naked as*** one's ***mother bore*** one/(***as***) ***naked as the day*** one ***was born*** 生まれたままのまる裸で ▪ We were walking around *as naked as the day* we *were born*. 我々は生まれたままのまる裸で歩き回っていた.

go naked 裸でいる ▪ The natives always *go naked*. 先住民たちはいつも裸でいる.

***naked heart* [*soul*]** 赤心，真心 ▪ I show you this so you may read my *naked heart*. これをお見せすれば私の真心がおわかりいただけましょう.

naked of …のない，欠けている ▪ They are *naked of* comfort. 彼らには慰安がない ▪ How infinitely *naked* Covent Garden is *of* people today! きょうはコベント・ガーデンには全く人っ子一人いないじゃないか.

the naked ape はだかのサル《動物としての人間》 ▪ *The naked ape* may destroy himself. はだかのサルは自らを滅ぼすかもしれない. ☞英国の人類学者 D. Morris の著書 *The Naked Ape* (1967) から.

***the naked eye* [*sight*]** 肉眼 ▪ I can see the star with *the naked eye*. その星は肉眼で見えます.

the naked truth ありのままの真実 ▪ His wife is a vixen. That is *the naked truth*. 彼の細君は意地悪女だ. それがありのままの真相さ.

nakedness /néɪkədnəs/ 名 ***the nakedness of the land*** 国の無防備状態; 無防備，赤貧 (《聖》*Gen*. 42. 9) ▪ They sent spies to discover *the nakedness of the land*. 彼らはスパイを送ってその国が無防備なのを発見した ▪ When my uncle saw *the nakedness of the land*, he felt he ought to send me some money. おじは僕の赤貧ぶりを見たとき，金を送ってやらねばならないと思った.

name[1] /neɪm/ 名 ***a maiden name*** 女性の結婚前の姓，(既婚女性の)旧姓 ▪ We only remember her by her *maiden name*, Kate Jones. 私たちは彼女のことを旧姓のケイト・ジョーンズとしか憶えていない.

a name day 霊名の日《自分の洗礼名となっている聖人の祝日》 ▪ John's *name day* is December 27, the feast of St. John. ジョンの聖名祝日は聖ヨハネの祝日の12月27日である.

a name to conjure with →CONJURE[1].

a nice name to go to bed with 《口》いやな名前 ▪ Creakle! What *a nice name to go to bed with*! クリークルだって，なんていやな名前だろう.

another name for …の別名 ▪ Larva is *another name for* caterpillar. 幼虫はイモムシの別名だ.

answer to the name of …と呼ばれて返事をする，という名である ▪ The dog *answers to the name of* Flush. その犬はフラッシュという名だ ▪ May I ask what *name* he *answers to*? あの人の名前は何というのですか.

blacken a person's ***name*** 人に汚名を着せる ▪ *His name was blackened* in sensational weeklies. 彼は煽情的な週刊誌で汚名を着せられた.

by name **1** 名指して，名前で ▪ I'll tell you them all *by* their *names*. あの人たちの名前をいちいち教えてあげよう ▪ She did not mention you *by name*. 彼女は君を名指しては言わなかった.

2 名前は ▪ I know a detective, Philo Vance *by name*. 私はファイロ・バンスという名前の探偵を知っている.

by the name of **1** …という名の ▪ There was a captain *by the name of* Clark. クラークという名の船長がいた.

2 …の名で ▪ In Europe that spy went [passed] *by the name of* Block. ヨーロッパではそのスパイはブ

N

ロックという名で通っていた.

call *a person* **(*hard, bad*)** ***names*** 人の悪口を言う, ののしる ▪ He *called* me all kinds of *names*. 彼は僕にかずかずの悪口を言った ▪ They *called* each other *hard names*. 彼らは互いにののしり合った.

call *a person* ***out of*** *his* ***name*** 人の名を間違えて呼ぶ ▪ He *called* me *out of my name*. 彼は私の名を間違えて呼んだ.

clear *one's* [*a person's*] ***name*** 自分[人]の汚名をそそぐ ▪ He is determined to *clear his name*. 彼は自分の汚名をそそごうと決心している.

drag *a person's* ***name through the mire*** [***mud***] 人の名声を公然と汚して傷つける ▪ *Her* good *name was dragged through the mud* for political reasons. 政治がらみで彼女の名声が傷ついた.

drop names 《口》有名人の名をあげる; 専門語を連発する ▪ He likes to *drop names* to make himself look important. 彼は自分を偉く見せるために有名人の名をあげたがる.

enter *one's* ***name for*** = put one's NAME down for.

get a **(*bad*)** ***name*** 《口》悪名を得る ▪ Their beloved house would be *getting a name*. 彼らの愛する家が悪名を得ることになるだろう.

get *a person* ***a name*** →make a person a NAME.

get [***make***] *oneself* ***a name*** 名をあげる (《聖》*2 Sam*. 8. 13) ▪ I am sure you will *make yourself a name*. あなたはきっと名をおあげになりますよ.

get *one's* ***name in the pot*** 《米俗》できあいの食事をする ▪ Well, I must *get my name in the pot* this evening. やれやれ, 今晩はできあいの料理でがまんしなくてはなるまい.

give a bad [***an ill***] ***name*** 悪名をつける, …の評判を落とす ▪ That would *give* him *a bad name*. そんなことをしたら彼の評判が悪くなる ▪ Mine accidents *gave* the company *a bad name*. たび重なる炭鉱事故で会社の評判が落ちた.

Give a dog a bad name and hang him. →DOG[1].

give it a hard name and →GIVE.

Give it a name. 《口》ほしいものを言いたまえ《特に人に飲み物をおごるとき》 ▪ Well, boys, the drinks are on me. *Give it a name*! さあ君たち, 酒は僕がおごる. ほしいものを言いたまえ.

give *one's* ***name*** 名前を言う ▪ The caller went away without *giving his name*. 訪問者は名も名乗らずに立ち去った.

give *one's* ***name to*** …を発明[発見]する ▪ She *gave her name to* a chemical element. 彼女はある化学元素を発見した ▪ He *gave his name to* a new make of bicycle. 彼は新型の自転車を創作した.

a person's ***good name*** 《古風》良い評判, 名声 ▪ You have saved *my good name*. あなたのおかげで私の評判が傷つかずにすんだ.

have a name for …で評判になっている ▪ He *has a name for* honesty. 彼は正直で評判になっている.

have *a person's* ***name*** **(*and number*)** ***on it*** 《口》 **1** (弾丸などが)特定の人を殺す運命になっている ▪ The bomb *had his name on it*. その爆弾は彼を殺す運命になっていた.

2 大好物[大のお気に入り]なのでとってある ▪ There's a piece of cake left and it's *got your name on it*. あなたの好きなケーキがひと切れ残してあるから, どうぞ ▪ I'm sure there's a job somewhere with *your name on it*. 君を待っているうってつけの仕事がきっとどこかにあるよ.

have *one's* ***name in lights*** **1** (俳優が有名になって劇場の外に)名前を電灯で出してもらう ▪ He was determined to top the bill and *have his name in lights*. 彼は主役になって, 名前を電灯で出してもらおうと決心していた.

2 (芸能界で)有名になっている ▪ She has *had her name in lights* as a brilliant actress. 彼女は名女優として名を上げている.

have *one's* ***name inscribed in the book of life*** 《婉曲》鬼籍に入る, 死ぬ ▪ They had all *had their names inscribed in the book of life* by then. それまでに彼らはみな死んでしまっていた.

have *one's* ***name up*** 有名になる ▪ There are ill effects of *having one's name up*. 有名になることの悪い結果がいろいろある.

have *a person's* ***name written all over it*** 《口》(仕事に)求められる全ての資質を備えている, まさに適任である ▪ Apply for that job. It's *got your name written all over it*. あの仕事に応募しろよ. 君ならぴったりだ.

have the name of …だとの評判だ ▪ He *has the name of* an eccentric. 彼は変人で通っている.

have … to *one's* ***name*** …を所有している, 自分のものにしている ▪ At this rate you'll never *have* a penny *to your name*. この割で行くと君は一文も持てなくなる.

in all but name →ALL but 1.

in God's [***heaven's, hell's, Christ's***] ***name*** 《口》一体《驚き・いらだちを表す》 ▪ What, *in heaven's name*, do you want? 一体どんな用事なのか.

in name 名義上 (↔ in REALITY) ▪ He is a scholar only *in name*. 彼は名ばかりの学者だ. ☞次項も参照.

in name only ただ名目上の (= only in NAME) ▪ She was his wife *in name only*. 彼女は彼の名目上の妻にすぎなかった.

in *one's* ***own name*** 自分の名義で, 独立で ▪ He started the business *in his own name*. 彼は自分の名義でその仕事を始めた.

in the name of **1** …のみ名にかけて, に誓って ▪ I charge you, *in the name of* God, to desist. 後生だからやめてくれ ▪ This, *in the name of* Heaven, I promise here. これを神に誓って私はここに約束する.

2 …の名において, の権威をもって ▪ Open! *In the King's name* [*in the name of* the State]. 御用だ, あけろ!

3 …の名義で; の代表として, に代わって ▪ I deposited the money *in the name of* my son. 息子の名義で貯金した ▪ Thank him *in my name*. 私に代わって彼にお礼を申しあげてください.

keep** one's **name on (学校・クラブなどの名簿)に名前をそのままにしておく, の会員でいる (↔take one's NAME off) ▪ I should like to *keep my name on* the list for the present. 当分会員のままでいたい.

know ... by name **1** ...の名前を知っている ▪ I *know* her only *by name*. 彼女は名前しか知らない. **2** ...をひとつひとつ[別々に]知っている ▪ He *knows* all the stars *by name*. 彼はすべての星を個々に知っている.

lend** one's **name to (企業など)に名義を貸す ▪ He *lent his name to* the undertaking. 彼はその企業に名義を貸した.

make* [*get*]** *a person* ***a name 人に名をあげさせる (《聖》 *Zeph*. 3. 20) ▪ I will *get* you *a name* among all the peoples of the earth. 私は地のすべての民の中であなたがたに名を得させよう.

make** oneself **a name →get oneself a NAME.

make a name* (*for *oneself*) 《口》 名をあげる ▪ He *made a name for himself* writing children's books. 彼は児童書を書いて名をあげた ▪ He *made a name* in literature. 彼は文学で名をなした.

One's ***name is mud.*** →MUD.

***no name* (*for*)** (...は)名状しがたい ▪ Hot? That's *no name for* it. 暑いかって, 暑いどころの騒ぎじゃないよ ▪ It is a balm that has *no name*. えもいわれぬ芳しい香りだ.

No names, no pack-drill. 責任者の名が出ていなければ, 誰も罰せられない. ☞pack-drill「懲罰軍装行進」.

of* (*great, high*) *name 有名な ▪ Authors *of great name* are prone to quarrel. 高名な作家たちは口論をしがちだ.

of no name/ without* (*a*) *name 無名の ▪ They were men *of no name* [*without a name*]. 彼らは無名の人間だった.

of the name of 《口》 ...という名の ▪ I met a man *of the name of* Tom Brown. 私はトム・ブラウンという名の男と会った.

only in name =in NAME only.

or my name is not *Smith* [etc.] 《口》 確かに ▪ I'll do it, *or my name is not* Smith. きっとそういたします ▪ He's skipped, *or my name is not* Pinkerton. やつは確かにずらかったのだ.

over** one's **own name (匿名でなく)自分の姓名を署して ▪ He has published a book *over his own name*. 彼は自分の姓名を署して本を出版した.

pass by the name of ...と名乗る ▪ Norman *passes by the name of* Norny among his pals. ノーマンは仲間内ではノーニーという名で通っている.

put a name to 《口》 [[cannot, could not を伴って]] ...の名前を言う ▪ I once met him, but I *can't put a name to* him. 彼とは一度会ったことがあるが, 名前が言えない.

Put a name to it. =Give it a NAME.

put* [*write*]** *one's* ***name down for (参加者・入会者として)...の記名をする ▪ *Put my name down for* two tickets. 切符を2枚, 私の名につけてください ▪ What shall I *put your name down for*? ご寄付はいくらとつけましょうか.

put** one's **name on the line 名誉を賭ける ▪ I'm not afraid to *put my name on the line* for impeachment. 弾劾に自分の名誉を賭ける勇気はある.

put* [*set*]** *one's* ***name to ...に署名する ▪ I *put my name to* the document. その書類に署名した.

take a name in vain → take (*a person's* name) in VAIN.

take** one's **name off (学校・クラブなどの名簿)から名を削除する (↔keep one's NAME on) ▪ Please *take my name off* your lists. 名簿から私の名を削ってください.

the name of the game 《口》 肝心な点, 眼目 ▪ In driving, carefulness is *the name of the game*. 車の運転では慎重が肝心だ.

to** one's **name 《口》 [[主に否定文で]] 自分のものと言うべき ▪ He doesn't have a penny *to his name*. 彼は自分の金はびた一文も持っていない.

trade on** one's **name ビジネスに自分の名門の姓を利用する ▪ He was accused of *trading on his name*. 彼は身分を濫用したとして訴えられた.

under** one's **own name 自分の名前[名義]で ▪ I wrote *under my own name*. 私は署名して文を書いた ▪ He carried the business on *under his own name* till 2008. 彼は2008年まで自分の名義で商売をやっていた.

under the name of **1** ...の名称の下に, という名の[で] ▪ He fled *under the name of* Abe. 彼はエイブという名前で逃亡した ▪ He cheated me *under the name of* friendship. 彼は友情と称して私をだました. **2** ...の名義で ▪ The business continued *under the name of* Brown & Co. その商売はブラウン商会という名義で続いた.

What was the name again? お名前をもう一度お願いします ▪ *What was the name again?* —Jack. お名前は何とおっしゃいましたか?—ジャックだ.

What's in a name? 名前なんか何だ《ただの符丁ではないか》(cf. Sh., *Rom. & Jul*. 2. 2. 43).

win a name* (*for *oneself*) = make a NAME (for oneself).

without* (*a*) *name →of no NAME.

write** one's **name down for → put one's NAME down for.

name[2] /neɪm/ 動 ***name and shame*** (恥じて品行を改めるように) 非行者の名前を公表する ▪ We'll *name and shame* employers not paying the minimum wage. 最低賃金を出さない雇い主の名前を懲らしめに公表してやる.

***Name it* [*yours*].** 《米俗》 飲みたいものを言いたまえ《酒をおごるとき》 ▪ Next treat on me. You *name it*. 次は私のおごりだ. 飲みたいものを言ってくれ.

N

name names (関係者などの)名をあげる ▪ The spokesman refused to *name names.* スポークスマンは名をあげるのを拒んだ.

name no names (悪事などの)関係者の名を公表しない[明かさない] ▪ One of them (I *name no names*) looked suspicious. 名前は明かさないが, 中の一人が怪しかった.

name the day →DAY.

name the name of Christ キリスト教徒たることを公言する (《聖》*2 Tim.* 2. 19) ▪ There are many denominations that *name the name of Christ.* キリスト教を標榜(ひょうぼう)する多くの宗派がある.

not be named on [***in***] ***the same day*** (***with***) →DAY.

to name (***but*** [***only, just***]) ***a few*** (ごく)少数の名をあげるなら ▪ Attending the party were John, Bill, Mary, Sally, *to name a few.* そのパーティーの出席者は, 少数の名をあげるなら, ジョン, ビル, メアリー, サリーなどであった.

You name it, *a person* ***has got it.*** 《口》何を言っても…は持っている, …は何だって持っている ▪ He's got a large collection of coins—*you name it,* he's *got it.* 彼はコインをたくさん集めており, 何でもみな持っている. ☞次項も参照.

You name it, *a person does* [***has*** *done*] ***it.*** 《口》何を言っても…する[している] ▪ Bill is a great traveller—*you name it,* he's seen *it.* ビルは大変な旅行家だ—どこを取り上げても, 彼はもう行っているんだ.

nameless /néɪmləs/ 形 ***shall be*** [***remain***] ***nameless*** 《戯》名前は伏せておく ▪ My informant *shall be nameless.* 情報提供者の名前は伏せておきたい.

nanny /næni/ 名 ***a nanny state*** (保護すると見せかけて)政府が国民生活を管理する国家 ▪ Let's guard against being turned into *a nanny state.* 政府による管理社会に陥らないように目を光らそう.

get *a person's* ***nanny*** 《米俗》人を怒らせる, いやがらせる ▪ Such a fellow *gets my nanny.* ああいう男には全く腹が立つ. ☞get a person's (nanny) GOAT から.

play the nanny goat 《口》ばかなまねをする ▪ Don't be *playing the nanny goat* in that fashion. そんなばかなまねをするのはよしてくれ.

nap[1] /næp/ 名 ***bring*** [***get***] ***up*** *a person's* ***nap*** 《米口》人を怒らせる ▪ This information *brought our nap* right *up.* この知らせは我々をすっかり立腹させた. ☞nap「ラシャなどのけば」.

nap[2] /næp/ 名 ***a nap hand*** 冒険すれば勝てる持ち札[手] ▪ He showed me the way to deal myself *a nap hand.* 彼は冒険すれば勝てる持ち札を自分に配る方法を僕に教えてくれた.

go nap **1**《トランプ》nap 遊戯で5回全勝を企てる.
2 いっさいを賭ける, 大ばくちを打つ (*on, over*) ▪ Look here, you *go nap on* that horse. いいかい, あの馬に全部賭けるんだぞ ▪ He'll *go nap over* this deal. He stands to win handsomely. 彼はこの配り札にいっさいを賭けるだろう. 見事に勝てる見込みがあるのだ.
3 自分の名を賭けて保証する (*on*) ▪ I'd *go nap on* his getting that appointment. 彼がその職につくことは太鼓判を押してもいいよ. ☞nap＝napoleon「トランプ遊びの一種」.

nap[3] /næp/ 名 ***give*** [***take***] ***the nap*** 《劇俗》なぐる[なぐられた]ふりをする ▪ I *give* him *the nap* and knock him on his back. おれはなぐるまねをして相手の背中を打つ ▪ I shall not be able to *take the nap* any longer. 私はなぐられたふりをもうこれ以上はできまい. ☞nap＜knap「カチンという音」からか.

nap[4] /næp/ 名 ***fall*** [***drop***] ***into a nap*** うたた寝する ▪ He *fell into a* short *nap* during the sermon. 彼は説教のときに少しだけうとうとした.

play nap 仮眠する ▪ We *played nap* to keep our minds off the discomfort. 我々は不愉快を忘れるため仮眠した.

take [***catch, get, have***] ***a nap*** うたた寝する ▪ He usually *takes a nap* after dinner. 彼はたいてい夕食後にうとうとする.

tumble out of a nap あわててうたた寝から目をさます ▪ He may have *tumbled out of a nap.* 彼はあわてて仮眠から目をさましたのかもしれない.

nap[5] /næp/ 動 ***catch*** [***take***] *a person* ***napping*** **1** 眠っているのを見つける ▪ He came in very quietly and you *were* nearly *caught napping.* 彼はとても静かに入ってきたので, 君はすんでのところで寝込みを襲われるところだった.
2 人の油断に乗じる, 不意打ちをくわせる ▪ He's a clever swindler, but the police will *catch* him *napping* sooner or later. 彼は抜け目のないペテン師だが警察はそのうちに不意打ちをくわすだろう.

nap[6] /næp/ 動 ***nap it*** 《俗》(特にボクシングで)ひどくぶたれる ▪ Josh as usual *napped it* in the first part of the round. ジョシュは例によってそのラウンドの最初からひどく打ち込まれた.

napkin /næpkən/ 名 ***hide*** [***keep, lay up, wrap,*** etc.]***... in a napkin*** …を使わずにしまっておく, 持ち腐れにする (《聖》*Luke* 19. 20) ▪ He's a lazy devil and *keeps* his talent *in a napkin.* 彼は怠け者で, あたら才能を持ち腐れにしている.

stick a napkin under *one's* ***chin*** 食事する ▪ Even here I may *stick a napkin under my chin.* ここでも私は食事することができる.

Naples /néɪpəlz/ 名 ***See Naples and*** (***then***) ***die.*** 《諺》ナポリを見てから死ね,「日光を見ずにけっこうと言うな」. ☞[It] 'Vedi Napoli, e poi mori' のなぞり.

nark[1] /nɑːrk/ 名 ***a copper's nark*** 《英俗》警察の手先[犬] ▪ That man's *a copper's nark,* and you've been telling him everything. あの男はサツの犬なのに, 君は何もかもばらしてきたんだぞ.

nark[2] /nɑːrk/ 動 ***nark it*** 《英俗》〚主に命令文で〛やめる ▪ *Nark it* for God's sake! お願いだから, やめてくれ.

narrow /næroʊ/ 形 ***by a narrow majority*** (選挙などで)わずかの多数で ▪ He was elected *by a narrow majority.* 彼はわずかの差でやっと当選した.

by a narrow margin すれすれで ▪ John passed the examination *by a narrow margin*. ジョンはすれすれで試験にパスした.

in narrow means [***circumstances***] 窮乏して ▪ The family is *in* very *narrow circumstances*. その一家は非常に窮乏している.

make [***have***] ***a narrow escape*** [***shave, squeak***] 危いところを助かる ▪ He had *made a narrow escape*; the bullet had grazed his head. 彼は危機一髪で助かったのだ. 弾丸は彼の頭をかすっていた.

one's ***narrow house*** [***bed, cell***] 墓 ▪ She now lies in *her narrow house*. 彼女は今, 墓の中で安らかに眠っている.

the narrow way [***path***] 狭くて困難な道, 正道 (《聖》 *Matt*. 7. 14) ▪ He was himself a wanderer from *the narrow way*. 彼自身も正道を踏みはずしていた.

nary /néəri/ 形 ***nary a*** 少しも…ない ▪ *Nary a* soul could be seen on the street. 通りには人っ子一人見られなかった. ☞ne'er a (=never a) の転化.

nasty /nǽsti|nɑ́:s-/ 形名 ***a nasty cut*** [***jar***] ひどい仕打ち ▪ The boss invited all his staff except me.—My word! That's *a nasty jar*! 所長は部下全員を招待したんだよ, 僕を除いてね—おや, そいつはひどい仕打ちだね.

a nasty one **1** ひじ鉄, ひどい一打ち[目] ▪ It would be funny if she got a few "*nasty ones*," as the boys say. あの女が男の子たちのいう「ひじ鉄」を2, 3発くらえばおもしろいだろうに.
2 急所を突いた文句 ▪ That's *a nasty one*, Sam. Your hair is red, and she called it Ginger! そいつはまさに適評だよ, サム. 君の髪は赤いから彼女は赤毛と言ったのさ.

a nasty piece [***bit***] ***of work*** [***goods***] 《英口》いやな人物 ▪ He's really *a* rather *nasty piece of work*. 彼は実にいやな奴だ.

cheap and nasty →CHEAP.

cut up nasty =CUT up rough.

do the nasty 《俗》 セックスをする ▪ Do you think they are *doing the nasty*? 二人は男女の関係だと思うかい?

leave a nasty taste in the mouth →leave a bad TASTE in the mouth.

nasty, brutish, and short (人生が)危険で, 残酷で, 短い (Hobbes, *Leviathan*) ▪ The way to death is *nasty* and *brutish and* often not *short*. 死に至る道は危険で残酷で, しばしば短くない.

something nasty in the woodshed →SOMETHING.

turn [***get***] ***nasty*** 怒る, 意地悪くなる ▪ She *got* quite *nasty* at his words. 彼の言葉を聞いて彼女はすっかり腹を立てた.

nation /néɪʃən/ 名 ***a nation of poets and thinkers*** 詩人と思想家の国民, ドイツ人 《Lytton の呼称》.

the [***a***] ***nation of shopkeepers*** 商人国, イギリス ▪ But for such men, we might really become *a* mere *nation of shopkeepers*. そのような人たちがいなければ, 我々は本当に単なる商人国になるかもしれない. ☞通俗には Napoleon Iの悪罵と言われるが, 実は A. Smith の *The Wealth of Nations* 4. 7. 3にある句.

native /néɪtɪv/ 形名 ***astonish the natives*** 世間をあっと言わせる ▪ She made a party gown with which to *astonish the natives*. 彼女は世間をあっと言わせるようなパーティー用のガウンを作った.

go native 《戯》 (特に西洋人が)土地の人と同じ生活をする; 異端に陥る ▪ In Japan he wanted to *go native*. 日本では彼は日本人と同じ生活をしたいと思った ▪ Christianity in South America had *gone native*. 南米のキリスト教は異端に陥ってしまっていた.

native and foreign 内外の ▪ There were delicious fruits *native and foreign*. 内外のおいしい果物が出ていた.

one's ***native language*** [***tongue***] 自国語, 母語 ▪ German is *his native language*. ドイツ語が彼の母語です.

native to (動植物が)…に生まれつきの, 原産の ▪ One of the animals *native to* India is the tiger. インド固有種の動物の一つはトラである ▪ Tobacco is *native to* the American continent. タバコはアメリカ大陸原産である.

The natives are restless. 《諺》 彼らは不穏な動きをしている. ☞植民地時代にアフリカの現地人が英国人に反逆したことから.

nativity /nətívəti/ 名 ***calculate*** *a person's* ***nativity*** (星占いをして)運勢を見る ▪ The king ordered the astrologer to *calculate the nativity of* his child. 王はその占星術師に王子の運勢を見るよう命じた.

natural /nǽtʃərəl/ 形名 ***a natural man*** (天啓を受けずに動物的に行動する)自然人 ▪ *Natural men* are as wolves to each other. 自然人はお互いにオオカミのごとき存在だ.

a natural son [***daughter***] 庶出の息子[娘], 私生児 ▪ She is widely rumored to be *an* allegedly *natural daughter* of the landlord. 彼女は地主の私生児ではないかともっぱらの噂だ.

be a natural for 《口》 …にはまり役[適役]である ▪ You *are a natural for* the job. あなたはその仕事にはまり役である.

come natural to *a person* 《口》 人にはたやすい, 楽だ ▪ Writing *comes natural to* him. 書くことは彼には楽なものだ.

die a natural death 自然に死ぬ[絶える] ▪ My father *died a natural death* at age 92. 父は92歳の天寿を全うした ▪ The conversation *died a natural death*. 話は自然に尽きた.

for [***in***] ***all*** *one's* ***natural*** 《口》 生まれてこの方 ▪ I've never seen such a man *in all my natural*. 生まれてこの方そんな男性にお目にかかったことがない. ☞natural<natural life.

one's ***natural life*** この世の寿命 ▪ The old woman was happy for the remainder of *her nat-*

ural life. そのお婆さんはその後亡くなるまで幸せだった.

naturally /nǽtʃərəli/ 副 ***come naturally to a person*** 人にはたやすい, 楽だ ▪ It *comes naturally to* him to write in verse. 彼には詩を書くのはたやすい.

nature /néɪtʃər/ 名 ***against [contrary to] nature*** **1** 自然にもとった, 不道徳な, 非道な ▪ It is *against nature* for a mother to kill her baby. 母親がわが子を殺すのは非道である ▪ You cannot go *against nature.* 人情にはそむけない.

2 奇跡的な ▪ If the man lives, it would appear to be *contrary to nature.* その男が命を取りとめれば奇跡的に思えるだろう.

all nature **1** 万物 ▪ *All nature* looks gay. 万物が歓喜にあふれている.

2《米口》誰もかれも, 何もかも ▪ I have just returned from the balloon; *all nature* was there. いま気球のところから帰ってきたところだ. 猫もしゃくしもあそこに行っていたよ.

answer [obey] a call of nature →CALL[1].

be (in) the nature of the beast 避けられない本性である ▪ We rarely reach perfection because imperfection *is in the nature of the beast.* 滅多に完璧にできないのは人が生まれつき不完全なせいだ.

beat all nature《米口》すべてをしのぐ, かなうものがない ▪ Hurrah for you; that *beats all nature*! でかしたぞ, そいつは最高の出来映えだ ▪ I know something about pottery. This piece here *beats all nature.* 私は焼き物のことはいささか知っている. この品はとびきり上等だ.

one's ***better nature*** 人柄のよりよい面, 良心 ▪ I appealed to *his better nature.* 彼の良心に訴えた.

N

by nature 生まれつき, 本来 ▪ Man is *by nature* a social animal. 人間は本来社会的動物である ▪ He is reserved *by nature.* 彼は生まれつき内気だ.

by [from] the nature of things [the case] →in the NATURE of things.

by *one's* ***(very) nature*** 性質上, 本質的に ▪ I am, *by my very nature*, a peaceful man. 私は本質的に穏やかな人間である.

contrary to nature →against NATURE.

ease [relieve] nature 大小便する ▪ Her dog *eased nature* on the grass. 彼女の犬が芝生の上で糞をした.

from nature 実物から ▪ He drew it *from nature.* 彼はそれを写生した.

get [go] back to nature 自然と調和した昔の生活様式に戻る, (文明世界から離れて)自然に帰る ▪ We couldn't tolerate city life and *went back to nature.* 我が家は都会生活に耐えられず自然の懐に抱かれた生活に戻った.

go the way of nature →go the WAY of all flesh.

Habit is second nature. →second NATURE.

human nature 人間性 ▪ *Human nature* forbids. 人情において忍びない.

in a state of nature **1**《神》(神の恩寵に浴さない)精神的未更生の状態で (↔a STATE of grace) ▪ It is man's own fault, if he is *in a state of nature.* 人が精神的未更生の状態にあるとすれば, それは人に責任がある.

2 (人間が)未開[野蛮]状態で; (動植物が)野生のままの状態で ▪ The true civet is found *in a state of nature* in most parts of Africa. 本物のジャコウネコはアフリカのほぼ全土に野生のままの状態で生息している.

3 まっ裸で ▪ The natives go about their work *in a state of nature.* 先住民たちはまっ裸で仕事をする.

in nature **1** 事実上 ▪ There is really, *in nature*, such a thing as high life. 世には高潔な生活というものが実際にある.

2〚最上級・否定・疑問を強調して〛世にも; 全然; 一体 ▪ It was one of the strangest things *in nature.* それは世にも不思議なものだった ▪ It had no effect *in nature.* それは全然効きめがなかった ▪ What *in nature* do you mean? 一体何のことだ.

in [by] the (normal, ordinary) course of nature →COURSE.

in [of] the nature of …の性質を帯びて, に似た ▪ Your request is *in the nature of* a command. 君の依頼はまるで命令だ ▪ He shows nothing *of the nature of* genius. 彼は天才的なところは全く示さない.

in [by, from] the nature of things [the case] 物の道理として, 道理上 ▪ *By the nature of things*, you can't be so definite in advance. 事の性質上前もってそんなにはっきり言うことはできないよ ▪ It was not *in the nature of things* that such popularity should be permanent. そんな人気が永続的であるなどということは物の道理としてありえなかった.

it is (not) in *one's* ***nature to*** *do* 性質として…する(ことはできない) ▪ *It is not in my nature to* do such cruel things. 私の性質としてそんな残酷なことはできない ▪ *It was in his nature to* look after others. 他人の面倒を見るのは彼の天性であった.

let nature take its course《口》自然の成り行きに任せる ▪ They will fall in love all right. *Let nature take its course.* 二人はきっと恋に落ちるよ. 自然の成り行きに任せたらいい.

like all nature《米口》全く, 完全に ▪ The poor creature would have been dragged off *like all nature.* その哀れな生き物はすっかり引きずり出されてしまっていただろう.

nature, red in tooth and claw 残忍な自然, 激烈な競争 (Tennyson, *In Memoriam* 56) ▪ Life can't be really solved by admirable maxims. *Nature's red in tooth and claw*, you know. 人生は立派な金言で実際に解決できるものではない. 自然は残忍なものなのだよ.

nature's engineering 造化の巧み ▪ How can we take advantage of *nature's engineering*? 造化の巧みを利用するにはどうすればよいか.

of a … nature …の性質をした ▪ She is *of a* quiet *nature.* 彼女は天性温和だ ▪ The injury is *of a* permanent *nature.* その傷害はずっと尾を引く性質の

ものである.

of the nature of →in the NATURE of.

one of Nature's gentlemen 生まれは卑しいが本性気高く思いやりのある人;《反語》無教養な無作法者 ▪ Hopper is *one of Nature's gentlemen*, the worst type of gentleman I know. ホッパーは無教養な無作法者だ. 私の知っているうちで一番ひどい紳士だよ.

One touch of nature makes the whole world kin. 人情は東西変わりなし (cf. Sh., *Tr. & Cr.* 3. 3. 175) ▪ An earthquake, a flood, some disaster, and then we see how *one touch of nature makes the whole world kin.* 地震, 洪水その他の災害にあうといかに人情は東西変わりないものであるかがわかる.

pay the debt of [*one's* ***debt to***] ***nature*** → DEBT.

relieve nature →ease NATURE.

second nature 第二の天性 ▪ Habit is *second nature.*《諺》習慣は第二の天性だ. ☞無冠詞.

the nature of the beast《戯》(人の)当然の特質 ▪ For a boy to be dirty and noisy is *the nature of the beast.* 男児が汚れて騒々しいのは当然の特質だ.

true to nature 実物通りで, 真に迫って ▪ His portrayal is admittedly *true to nature.* 彼の描写は真に迫っているという定評がある.

naught /nɔːt/ 名 ***all for naught*** むだに, いたずらに ▪ We had all our trouble *all for naught.* すべてが骨折り損だった.

bring ... to naught (計画など)をぶちこわす, 無効にする ▪ You have *brought* all my labors *to naught.* 君のおかげで僕の苦心はすっかり徒労になった.

care naught for ...を少しも愛さない[欲しない] ▪ He *cares naught for* renown and applause. 彼は名声や称賛は少しも望まない.

come to [***go for***] ***naught***《雅》(計画などが)むだになる, 失敗に終わる ▪ All his ideas *came to naught.* 彼の考えはすべて水の泡になった.

of naught つまらない ▪ He is a man *of naught.* 彼はつまらぬ男だ.

set ... at naught/set naught by ...を軽蔑する, 無視する ▪ He *set* my advice *at naught.* 彼は僕の忠告を無視した.

think [***make***] ***naught of*** ...をものともしない, など眼中にない ▪ He *thinks naught of* his illness [making a few mistakes]. 彼は自分の病気のこと[少しくらい誤りをすること]などなんとも思っていない.

naughty /nɔ́ːti/ 形名 ***do the naughty/ go naughty***《俗》(特に女性が)ふしだらをする ▪ Some girls *do the naughty* for their clothes. 女の子の中には服がほしくてふしだらをする者もいる.

navel /néɪvəl/ 名 ***contemplate*** [***gaze at, stare at, regard***] *one's* (***own***) ***navel*** 黙想にふける ▪ He sits *contemplating his navel* by the hour. 彼は何時間も座って黙想にふける.

navy /néɪvi/ 名 ***be in the navy*** 海軍にいる ▪ My son *is in the navy*, stationed in Virginia. 息子は海軍で, バージニア州に駐屯している.

Go join the navy! いらぬおせっかいはよせ ▪ *Go join the Navy*, you puke. Disappear! いらぬお世話だ, お前を見ていると反吐(へど)が出る. とっとと失せろ.

nay /neɪ/ 名 ***Let your yea be yea and your nay be nay.*** 賛否をはっきり言え (《聖》*Jas.* 5. 12) ▪ You need to at least *let your yea be yea and your nay be nay.* 君は少なくともイエスかノーかをはっきり言わなくてはならない.

say nay 否と言う, 拒絶する (*to*) ▪ I cannot *say nay to* him. 彼には否とは言えない ▪ Do not *say* me *nay.* いやとは言ってくださるな.

The nays have it! (議会で)反対者多数です《議案否決の宣言》.

will not take nay 否と言わせない ▪ I *will not take nay* for an answer. 人にノーとは答えさせない.

yea and nay はいと言ったり, いいえと言ったり ▪ They were at *yea and nay* and sharp contradiction. 彼らははいと言ったり, いいえと言ったりとひどく矛盾していた ▪ You say *yea and nay*, but what do you really think? 君ははいと言ったり, いいえと言ったりしているが, 本当はどう思うのかね.

near /nɪər/ 形前副 ***a near escape*** [***go, miss, shave, squeak, thing, touch***] 危ういところを逃れること ▪ It was *a near go.* The car missed the streetcar by inches. 危機一髪のところだった. 自動車は数インチの差で路面電車と衝突しないですんだ ▪ I caught the train, but it was *a near touch.* 電車に乗れたが, 危ういところだった ▪ I managed to stop short just in time, but it was *a near miss.* 何とか急停車して避けられたが, 間一髪だった.

as near as *one* ***can*** できるかぎり ▪ *As near as* I *can* guess, he is an honest man. 察しうるかぎりでは, 彼は正直な人だ ▪ We will follow nature's steps *as near as* we *can.* 我々はできるだけ自然の例に倣(なら)おう.

as near as dammit (***to***)《口》すんでのところで ▪ He *as near as dammit* missed his train. 彼はもう少しで列車に乗り遅れるところだった ▪ I was *as near as dammit to* letting out the whole thing. 私はすんでのところで一部始終をしゃべりそうだった. ☞dammit = damn it.

as near ... as makes no difference [***matter, odds***]《口》ほとんど... ▪ She was *as near* sixty *as makes no difference.* 彼女はほとんど60歳に近かった.

be as near as can be to 今少しで...するところである ▪ He *was as near as could be to* being knocked down by a bus. 彼は危うくバスにはねられるところだった.

come [***go***] ***near*** **1** 近く来る[行く], 近寄る ▪ *Nearer* and *nearer* he *came.* 彼はだんだん近づいてきた.

2 ...に匹敵する ▪ Nobody can *come near* him. 誰も彼と肩を並べる者はいない.

come [***go***] ***near to*** *do* [*doing*] 今少しで...するところ ▪ The loss *went near to* ruin [*ruining*]

N

him. この損失で彼は危うく破産するところだった.

draw near **1** …が近寄る ▪ The ship was now *drawing near(er)* to us. 船は今やこちらへ近づきつつあった.
2 (時が…に)近づく ▪ It's *drawing near* Easter. もうすぐイースターだ.

far and near 遠くにも近くにも, いたる所に ▪ The people came from *far and near.* 人々はいたる所からやって来た.

***get* [*go*] *near* (*to*)** (…に)近づく, 近寄る ▪ *Get near* (*to*) the fire, you look cold. 火のそばへ近寄りなさい, 寒そうな顔をしておられます ▪ I never seem to *go near* (*to*) winning. 私が勝利に近づけるようには思えない.

go near to *do* [*doing*] →come NEAR to do.

lie near to *do* …するのは自然[当然]である ▪ It *lies near to* suppose that he went there himself. 彼が自分でそこへ行ったと考えるのは当然だ.

***near about*(*s*)** 近くに ▪ There was no soul *near abouts.* 近くには誰もいなかった.

near and dear 近しく大事な (*to*) ▪ They were those persons so *near and dear to* him. 彼らは彼には近しく大事な人々であった.

near at hand **1** (場所が)手近に ▪ I once saw it *near at hand.* 私は一度それを手近に見たことがある.
2 (時が)間近に, 近々に ▪ With my vacation *near at hand,* I decided to get some new clothes. 休みが近づいてきたので, 服を新調することに決めた.

near by すぐ近くに[の] (→HARD by) ▪ He rushed to a drugstore *near by.* 彼はすぐ近くの薬局へ駆けつけた.

N

near enough 《英口》ほとんど, …も同然で, ほぼ間違いなく ▪ We've been here for thirty years, *near enough.* ここに30年住んでいる. ほぼそれくらいだ

***near here* [*there*]** この[あの]近くに ▪ Her house is somewhere *near here.* 彼女の家はどこかこの近くだ.

***near on* [*upon*]** ほとんど…, 今少しで… ▪ It is *near upon* six o'clock. もう少しで6時だ ▪ The old man is *near upon* eighty years of age. その老人はかれこれ80歳だ.

near to …の近くに ▪ I live *nearer to* the school than you. 君の家より僕の家のほうが学校に近い.

one's ***nearest and dearest*** 《戯》自分の家族[夫, 妻], 一番近い人たち[親友, 血縁者など]《皮肉にも》 ▪ One never does know much about *one's nearest and dearest.* 人は自分の家族について, 実はあまりよく知らない.

not near so まだまだ…でない, …とは大違いで ▪ He is *not near so* rich. 彼はとてもそんな金持ちではない.

nowhere* [*not anywhere*] *near 決して…ではない ▪ That's *nowhere near* enough. それではまだまだ不十分だ ▪ The train is *nowhere near* as dear as the plane. 列車は飛行機よりもはるかに安い.

or near it あるいはそれに近い ▪ It is the same *or near it.* それと同じものか, あるいはそれに近いものだ.

pretty near to ほとんど… ▪ The scheme is *pretty near to* achievement. その計画は成就しかかっている.

so near and yet so far …が近くて遠い(ので近づけない, 入手できない) (Tennyson, *In Memoriam* 97) ▪ The bird in the cage seemed *so near and yet so far* to the cat. かごの鳥は猫には近くて遠い存在のように思われた.

to the nearest… 〚数詞を伴って〛…の位まで ▪ The cost, rounded up *to the nearest* $100, was $2,800. 100ドル未満を切り上げると, 費用は2,800ドルだった.

nearly /níərli/ 副 ***not nearly*** 決して…でない ▪ It is *not nearly* so important as you think. それは君が考えているほど大事なものでは決してない.

neat /niːt/ 形 **(*as*) *neat as a bandbox* [*new pin*]** 《口》きわめてこざっぱりした, すごくこぎれいな ▪ Everything was *as neat as a new pin* in the house. 家の中のものは何もかもきわめてこざっぱりしていた.

make a neat job of …を手際よく仕上げる ▪ You've *made a neat job of* that darn; it is almost invisible. そのかがりを手際よく仕上げたものだね. ほとんど目につかないよ.

neat and trim (服装・様子が)きれいさっぱりした ▪ He looked so *neat and trim* at dinner. 夕食時に彼はとてもこざっぱりとした身なりだった.

neat but not gaudy こざっぱりときれいな ▪ It was a little flowery border *neat but not gaudy.* こざっぱりときれいな花壇であった.

necessarily /nèsəsérəli/ 副 ***not necessarily*** 必ずしも…でない ▪ The good will *not necessarily* prosper. 善人が必ずしも成功するとは限らない.

necessary /nésəsèri|nésəsəri/ 形名 ***a necessary evil*** 必要悪 (Paine, *Common Sense*) ▪ Is the army *a necessary evil*? 軍隊は必要悪か.

do the necessary 《口》必要なことをする ▪ I want a taxi. Will you *do the necessary*? タクシーに乗りたいのだが, 必要な手配をしてくれないか.

find* [*provide*] *the necessary 《口》先立つ物(金)を工面(くめん)する ▪ I must *find* [*provide*] *the necessary.* 先立つ物を工面せねばならない.

if necessary 必要ならば ▪ Let him go, *if necessary.* 必要なら彼を行かせなさい.

it is necessary that *one* ***should* [*for*** *one* ***to*** *do*] …しなければならない ▪ *It is necessary that* you *should* go [*for* you *to* go]. 君は行かねばならぬ.

the necessaries of life 生活必需品 ▪ Our income allows only *the* bare *necessaries of life.* 我々の収入ではやっと暮らしていけるだけの生活必需品しか買えない.

necessity /nəsésəti/ 名 **(*a*) *work of necessity*** (安息日でもしなければならない)必要な仕事 ▪ He had to do it; it was *a work of necessity.* 彼はそれをしなければならなかった. それは必要な仕事だった.

as a necessity 必然的に ▪ Such a conclusion follows *as a necessity* from the premises. その前提からは必然的にこのような結論が生まれる.

bare necessities 最低限の必要品 ▪ The room is furnished with the *bare necessities.* その部屋は必要最低限の家具つきである.

(*be*) *in necessity* 貧乏である ▪ He *is in* extreme *necessity.* 彼は極めて金に困っている.

be under the necessity of *doing* …しなければならない必要に迫られている ▪ I *am under the necessity of selling* my house. 私は余儀なく家を売らなければならない.

from* [*by, out of*] *necessity 必要に迫られて, やむをえずに ▪ He stole it *out of* sheer *necessity.* 彼はやむをえずそれを盗んだのだ.

in case of necessity 必要な場合には ▪ They seldom do it except *in case of necessity.* 彼らは必要な場合のほか, そんなことはめったにしない.

lay* [*put*]** *a person* ***under the necessity of *doing* 人を…しなければならないようにする ▪ It *laid* him *under the necessity of leaving* the village. それで彼は村を出て行かねばならなくなった ▪ My promise *puts* me *under the necessity of doing* so. 約束したからにはそうしなくてはならない.

make a virtue of necessity →VIRTUE.

Necessity is the mother of invention. 《諺》必要は発明の母.

Necessity knows* [*has*] *no law. 《諺》必要の前に法律はない,「背に腹は代えられず」.

of necessity ぜひとも, やむをえず ▪ It must *of necessity* be so. 当然そうあるべきだ ▪ I went there *of necessity.* 私はやむをえずそこへ行ったのだ.

out of necessity →from NECESSITY.

there is no necessity to *do* …する必要はない ▪ *There is no necessity* for you *to* go. 君が行くには及ばない.

neck /nek/ 名 ***be dead* [《俗》 *bone-headed*] *from the neck up*** 《口》頭が悪い ▪ He's *dead from the neck up.* He can't even do sums. 彼は頭が悪い. 計算もできないんだ.

be neck-deep in (困難など)に首まではまっている ▪ I *was neck-deep in* trouble. 私は苦境にどっぷり浸かっていた.

bow the neck to →BOW[4].

break *a person's* ***neck*** 人の首をへし折る ▪ I'll *break your neck* if you bully my sister again. 今度妹をいじめたら首をへし折るぞ.

break *one's* ***neck*** **1** 首の骨を折る[折って死ぬ] ▪ The old lady fell down a flight of stairs and *broke her neck.* 老婦人は階段から落ち, 首の骨を折って死んだ.
2 《口》大いに骨を折る ▪ I *broke my neck* trying to get there on time. そこへ時間きっかりに着こうと思って精一杯努力した.
3 〚almost, nearly, practically などを伴って〛大急ぎする ▪ He *nearly broke his neck* to get there in time. 彼は間に合うようにとそこへ急行した.

break the neck of (仕事・旅行の)とうげを越す ▪ He has *broken the neck of* his day's work. 彼は1日の仕事をあらかた片うけてしまった ▪ The days knew how to be hot, although *the neck of* the summer *was broken.* 夏の盛りは過ぎたのに毎日ひどく暑かった. ☞動物の首の骨を折って殺すことから.

breathe down *a person's* ***neck*** 《俗》 **1** (競争などで)人の背後に迫る; つきまとう, 後にぴったりつく ▪ Although Jim was taking the lead, Tom was *breathing down his neck.* ジムがトップを切っていたものの, トムがその背後に迫っていた ▪ Never *breathe down the neck of* someone using the ATM. ATM を使っている人のすぐ後に決してついてはならない.
2 人を厳しく監視する, 常に人の一挙一動を調べる ▪ I don't like to have the boss *breathing down my neck* all the time. 上役に始終監視されるのはいやだ.
3 締め切りが間近に迫る ▪ The due date for the paper was *breathing down his neck.* 彼がその書類を提出する期限が迫っていた.

down on *a person's* ***neck*** 《口》人をとっちめて, 罰して ▪ He had the police *down on his neck* for overspeeding. 彼はスピード違反で警察に罰せられた.

fall neck-deep into (困難など)に首まではまり込む ▪ He *fell neck-deep into* difficulties. 彼は困難に首まではまり込んだ.

fall on *a person's* ***neck*** 人の首に抱きつく ▪ The girl *fell on her mother's neck.* 少女は母親の首に抱きついた.

get* [*catch, take*] *it in the neck 《英口》 **1** ひどい打撃を受ける ▪ He's *got it in the neck* all right; his creditors were pressing him for money. 彼はまちがいなくひどい打撃を受けたのだ. 債権者たちが返金を催促していたのだから.
2 ひどく罰せられる, しかられる ▪ The boy will *get it in the neck* this time. その少年も今度はひどくしかられるだろう.
3 ひどい目にあう ▪ In the final analysis it's the little fellow who really *gets it in the neck.* とどのつまりはひどい目にあうのは弱者なのだ. ☞昔罪人が首を斬られた習慣から.

give it *a person* ***in the neck*** 《口》人を厳しく攻撃する[しかる] ▪ The old man will *give it* you *in the neck* if you aren't careful. 気をつけていないとおやじに大目玉をくらうぞ.

(*hang*) *around* [*round*] *a person's* ***neck*** 人の首のまわりに(掛ける); 旧悪を執拗に思い出させる, (難局などが)人に重荷[責任]として(のしかかる) ▪ The Ancient Mariner is obliged to carry the burden of the albatross *hung around his neck.* 老水夫は首のまわりに掛けた重いアホウドリを運ばなければならない(＝罪の烙印に一生苦しまねばならない) ▪ Will the cross *hanging around someone's neck* save them from Hell? 人の首につるした十字架は地獄から彼らを救ってくれるだろうか. ☞→an ALBATROSS (a)round [about] one's neck.

have a lot of neck 《口》ひどく厚かましい ▪ He must *have an* awful *lot of neck*, to do such a thing. あんなことをするなんて, 彼はひどく厚かましいやつにちがいない.

have a stiff neck 首がこわばっている; リューマチで首が動かせない ▪ I *have a stiff neck* from looking upward. ずっと上を見ていて首がこわばっている ▪ My grandfather *has a stiff neck.* 祖父はリューマチで首が動かせない.

have (got) a [the] neck 《口》厚かましい, ずうずうしい ▪ You*'ve got a neck* to suggest such a thing. 君は厚かましいねえ, そんなことを言いだすなんて.

in the neck of →on the NECK of.

lose by a neck →win by a NECK.

make a long neck 首を伸ばす ▪ He *made a long neck* to see the procession. 彼は行進を見ようと首を伸ばした.

neck and crop 《古風》**1** 身ぐるみ; いきなり ▪ If he comes here again, I shall have him thrown out *neck and crop.* 彼がもう一度ここへ来たら, 直ちにつまみ出させてやるぞ.

2 そっくり, 完全に ▪ The cabinet was thrown out, *neck and crop.* 内閣は総辞職させられた. ☞crop は croup (馬などのしり)のくずれで「首からしりまで」の意からか.

neck and heels しっかりと ▪ They tied him up *neck and heels.* 彼らは彼をしっかりと縛り上げた.

neck and [by, to] neck **1** (競馬で)相並んで ▪ The horses will reach the fence *neck and neck.* 馬は首を並べて柵に着くだろう.

2 (競走・競技などで)負けず劣らず ▪ At present the two candidates are running absolutely *neck and neck.* 目下のところ二人の候補者は全く互角だ.

neck of the woods 《米俗》界わい ▪ I haven't been in that *neck of the woods* for a long time. 久しくその界わいへ行ったことがありません.

neck or nothing 命がけで, のるかそるかで ▪ It is *neck or nothing* on my side. 私の方はのるかそるかだ. ☞競馬で「首の差で勝つか負けるか」, または「絞首刑になっても」という意味から.

nip ... by the neck ...をねじ伏せる, 手も足も出ないようにする ▪ He *nipped* the burglar *by the neck.* 彼は強盗をねじ伏せた. ☞nip「切り取る」.

on [upon, in] the neck of ...のすぐあとに, にくびすを接して ▪ One temptation followed *in the neck of* another. 誘惑が次から次へとやって来た ▪ A dozen more of such expressions poured *on the neck of* one another. そのような言い回しがさらに1ダースばかり次から次へと出てきた.

put** one's **neck in a noose 《口》自ら招いて危地に陥る ▪ For him to go there as a spy is simply *putting his neck in a noose.* 彼がスパイとしてそこへ行けば, 自ら招いて危地に陥ることになる.

put** one's **neck on the line 一か八かやる ▪ I don't want to *put my neck on the line* and take a risk. 危険を覚悟で一か八かやるのは気が進まぬ.

risk** one's **neck 命を賭ける ▪ The way the young motorists *risk their necks* is simply extraordinary. 若い暴走族が命を賭けている様子ときたら全く驚くばかりだ.

save** one's **neck 絞首刑を免れる; 命拾いする ▪ He revealed his accomplices to *save his own neck.* 彼は自分が絞首刑を免れるために共犯者のことをばらした.

shot in the neck 《米俗》ほろ酔いで ▪ He was only *shot in the neck.* 彼はいささかきこしめしていたに過ぎない.

speak [talk] through [out of] (the back of)** one's **neck 《口》**1** ほらを吹く, 大げさなことを言う ▪ He *talked through his neck* when we missed our shots. 我々が当てそこなうと彼は大げさにはやし立てた.

2 わけのわからないことを言う ▪ I wish you would not *talk through the back of your neck.* 君が愚にもつかぬことを言わないでくれたらと思うよ.

stick** one's **neck out 《口》自ら危ない目にあう ▪ He avoids *sticking his neck out* politically. 彼は政治的に自分から危ない目にあうようなことは避ける. ☞ボクシングであごをガードしないことから.

stiff neck 強情, がんこ (《聖》*Ps.* 75. 5) ▪ Speak not with *stiff neck.* 強情な口をきいてはならない.

take it in the neck →get it in the NECK.

the same neck of the woods 同じ狭い地域[共同社会] ▪ I've lived in *the same neck of the woods* all my life. 生まれてからずっとこの狭い社会に住んでいる.

throw** a person **out on** his **neck 《口》人を急に首にする ▪ When he got too much of a nuisance, I *threw* him *out on his neck.* 彼があまりうるさくなったので, ぽいと首にしてやった.

tie neck and heels →NECK and heels.

up to the [**one's**] neck in ...に深くはまり込んで, 没頭して ▪ I am *up to my neck in* work. 僕は仕事に忙殺されている ▪ He was *up to his neck in* debt. 彼は借金で首が回らなかった.

win [lose] by a neck **1** (競馬で)首の差で勝つ[負ける] ▪ He *won* the race *by a neck.* レースを首の差で勝った.

2 辛勝[惜敗]する ▪ The worst of it is that I only *lost by a neck.* 一番いけないのは惜敗したことだ.

wring** a person's **neck 《口》懲らしめてやる ▪ I'll *wring his neck* if he cheats again. 彼がまたズルをしたらただでは置かないから.

necktie /néktàɪ/ 名 ***a necktie party [sociable]*** 《米俗》絞首(刑), リンチ ▪ He won't stand for any *necktie party.* 彼はどんなリンチにも我慢はしないだろう.

throw a necktie party 《米俗》(リンチで木などに)つるし上げる ▪ We're going to *throw a necktie party* this morning. 我々は今朝つるし上げをすることになっている. ☞necktie が絞首刑執行人のロープを意味するところから.

Ned /ned/ 名 ***By Ned!*** 《米口》確かに, きっと《穏やかな誓言》 ▪ *By Ned!* If it ain't Miss Mash. 確かに, あれはマッシュ嬢にちげえねえ.

make** one's **ned out of 《俗》...で金をこしらえる, 金儲けする ▪ They have *made their ned out of* the Blue-noses. 彼らはノバスコシア産のジャガイモで金

N

儲けをした. ☞ned＝a guinea.

raise (***promiscuous, merry***) ***Ned*** 《米俗》わいわい騒ぐ, 大騒ぎを起こす (＝raise CAIN) ▪ Your factory girls go to work *raising promiscuous Ned*. 君の工場の女子工員さんたちはわいわい騒ぎながら仕事に行くんだね.

need[1] /ni:d/ 名 ***A friend in need is a friend indeed.*** 《諺》困ったときの友こそ真の友.

as the need arises →when the NEED arises.

at need まさかの時に (＝in case of NEED) ▪ Brandy is good *at need*. ブランデーはまさかの時に役に立つ.

be [***stand***] ***in need of*** …を必要としている ▪ He *is* badly *in need of* a hair-cut. 彼はとても髪がのびている《散髪の必要がある》 ▪ This ship *stands in need of* repairs. この船は修理が必要である.

fail *a person* ***in*** *his* ***need*** 人がいよいよ困るときになってその人を見捨てる ▪ Never have I *failed* him *in his need*. 私は彼が困っているときに彼を見捨てたことは一切ない.

had need (***to***) *do* 《雅》…すべきである (ought to do) ▪ Women *had need to* be very careful. 女性はよくよく気をつけていなければならない ▪ If you wish to succeed, you *had need* work harder. 成功したければもっと一生懸命に働かなくてはならない.

have need of [***for***] 《文》(物)を必要とする ▪ I *have need of* a good cook. 良いコックが必要だ ▪ He *has need for* further study of commercial subjects. 彼はさらに商業問題を研究する必要がある.

have need to *do* …しなければならない (must do) ▪ We *have* no *need to* be proud of such a thing. そんなことは自慢するに足らない.

if need be [***were, require***] もし必要とあらば ▪ *If need be*, I can come early tomorrow. 必要なら, あす早く来てもよろしい ▪ I would shed my blood, *if need were*. 必要とあらば, 私の血を流してもよろしい ▪ Repeat this *if need require*. 必要ならこれを繰り返しなさい.

in case [***time, the hour***] ***of need*** まさかの時に ▪ *In case of need*, I will help him. まさかの時は彼を助けてやります ▪ He helped me *in my hour of need*. 彼は私が困っている時に助けてくれた.

in (***great***) ***need*** (非常に)困窮している ▪ My friend is *in great need* right now. 私の友人が今ひどく困っています.

stand in need of →be in NEED of.

there is need of [***for, to*** *do*, ***that***] 〚what, little, no などを伴って〛…の必要がある ▪ *There is no need of* your hurrying [*for* you *to* hurry, *that* you should hurry]. 君は急ぐには及ばない ▪ *There is no need for* further analysis. これ以上分析するには及ばない ▪ *What need is there to* go? 行く必要がどこにあるのか.

when [***as, if***] ***the need arises*** 必要な時に ▪ You can take money from the bank *when the need arises*. 必要な時に銀行から金をおろせる.

Your need is greater than mine. 私よりもあなたの方がそれを必要としている ▪ Keep it—I'm sure *your need is greater than mine*. 取っておきなさい—間違いなく僕より君の方にそれが必要だ. ☞Sir Philip Sidney の言葉から.

need[2] /ni:d/ 動 ***did not need to*** *do* …するには及ばなかった ▪ We *didn't need to* hurry. 急ぐには及ばなかった(ので急がなかった).

I don't need this! 《口》(トラブル続きで) いまいましい, 腹が立つ ▪ The printer has stopped working again. *I don't need this!* プリンターがまた止まってしまった. いやになってしまう.

it needs …が必要である ▪ *It needs* heaven-sent moments for this skill. この技巧のためには天与の瞬間[絶好の機会]が必要である.

need not [《口》***do not need*** (***to***)] *do* …するには及ばない ▪ He *need not* [*does not need* (*to*)] go. 彼は行くには及ばない.

need not have *done* …するには及ばなかった(のにしてしまった) ▪ We *needn't have* hurried. 我々は急ぐには及ばなかったのに.

not need any telling 人にあれこれ言う必要はない ▪ He did*n't need any telling*, he was so willing. 彼にあれこれ言う必要はなかった. 大乗り気になっていたから.

that's all *one* ***needs*** 《反語》それは一番ほしくないものだ, それだけはごめんだ ▪ Another train strike? *That's all* I *need*! また鉄道ストかい? 勘弁してくれよ ▪ Stop mentioning my ex-girlfriend. *That's all* I *need* now. 僕の元カノのことに触れるのはやめろ. そいつは今一番聞きたくないことだ.

there needs …が必要である ▪ *There needs* no such apology. そんな弁解はいらない.

Who needs it [***them***]***?*** 《口》そんなものはお呼びでない ▪ Euthanasia: *Who needs it*? 安楽死か. そんなもの, お呼びじゃないな.

needful /ní:dfəl/ 形 ***do the needful*** **1**《ラグビー》トライをゴールに換える.

2 必要なことをする ▪ Aunt Agatha wants a taxi; will you *do the needful*? アガサおばさんがタクシーに乗りたいと言っている. 手配をよろしく頼めないか.

send [***supply, have***] ***the needful*** 《口》(必要な)現金を送る[出す, 持つ] ▪ I will *send the needful* pretty soon. じきに必要な金をお送りします ▪ To live I must *have the needful*. 生きるには金がいる.

needle[1] /ní:dəl/ 名 ***a needle fight*** 《俗》 **1** (ボクシングなどで)お互いに個人的な恨みをもった試合, 因縁試合 ▪ It's likely to be a bit of *a needle fight*. 試合はちょっとした因縁試合になりそうだ.

2 個人的な感情の入った競争 ▪ This election is *a needle fight* all right. こんどの選挙は確かに遺恨競争というやつだ.

a needle's eye **1** 針のめど[目] ▪ I found it hard to get the thread through *the needle's eye*. 針(の目)に糸をなかなか通せなかった.

2 ごく小さいすきま (《聖》*Matt*. 19. 24) ▪ The lane was as narrow as *a needle's eye*. その小道は針のめどみたいに狭かった.

(*as*) ***sharp as a needle*** 目から鼻へ抜けるように鋭い ▪ Our new boss is *as sharp as a needle*. 今度の上司は目から鼻へ抜けるような人だ.

as the needle is true to the pole 磁針がまちがいなく極を示すように; 確実に (Barton Booth, *Song*) ▪ It is true *as the needle is true to the pole*. それは磁針がまちがいなく極を示すように確実だ.

get the (***dead***) ***needle*** 《俗》いらいらする, 怒る (*with, to*) ▪ Take care lest he should *get the needle with* you. 彼に怒られないように気をつけろよ.

give *a person* ***the needle*** 人をいらいらさせる, 怒らせる ▪ It will *give* him *the needle* being left in the lurch this way. こんなふうに見殺しにされると彼もいらいらするだろう. ☞仕立師が指を針でつくと, いらいらすることから.

have (***got***) ***the needle*** 《俗》いらいらしている ▪ Mom *has got the needle* this morning. 母は今朝いらいらしている.

hit the needle →HIT[2].

look for [***seek***] ***a needle in a bottle*** [***truss, bundle***] ***of hay***/***look for*** [***seek***] ***a needle in a meadow*** [***haystack***] 見つかる当てのないものを探す, 至難なことを企てる, むだ骨を折る ▪ The coach seemed to have lost its way, by *looking for a needle in a bottle of hay*. 馬車は見つかる当てのないものを探して道に迷ったようだ ▪ But it's bad to be *looking for a needle in a haystack*. だが, むだ骨を折っているのはまずい.

on the needle 《俗》麻薬常習で ▪ Who put him *on the needle* and supplied him? 誰が彼に麻薬を常習させ, ブツを与えたのか.

pass through the eye of a needle きわめて狭い所を通り過ぎる《企ての不可能である場合に言う》(《聖》*Matt*. 19. 24) ▪ God can even make the camel *pass through the eye of a needle*. 神はどんな不可能なことをも可能とさせ給う.

pins and needles/***needles and pins*** (しびれが直りかけて)ちくちくする感じ ▪ I've got *pins and needles* in my foot. 足がしびれてちくちくする.

take the needle 《俗》怒る, むっとする ▪ He will *take the needle* if you persist in bantering him. いつまでも彼をからかっていれば彼もむっとするだろう.

thread the needle 困難な課題をなし遂げる ▪ The committee will *thread the needle*. 委員会は困難な課題をなし遂げるだろう.

use the needle 《俗》麻薬を常用する ▪ He has two habits—playing the fiddle and *using the needle*. 彼には二つの癖がある—バイオリンをひくことと麻薬を常用することだ.

needle[2] /níːdəl/ 動 ***needle*** *one's* ***way*** 縫うように進む ▪ We *needled our way* through the woods. 我々は森の中を縫うように進んだ.

needless /níːdləs/ 形 (***it is***) ***needless to say*** [***to add***] 言う[つけ加える]までもなく ▪ *Needless to say*, they were not at home when he called for the money. 言うまでもないが, 彼がその金を取りに行ったとき彼らは家にいなかった.

needs /niːdz/ 副 ***must needs*** 《文》 **1** きっと…にちがいない ▪ It *must needs* be a great evil. それはきっと大きな罪悪にちがいない.

2 ぜひ…ねばならない ▪ He *must needs* think of her once more, how in the grave she lies. 彼は妻が草葉の陰で眠っているさまを再び思い起こさずにはいられない.

3 ぜひ…すると主張する ▪ He *must needs* go away just when I want him. 私がちょうど彼に用事があるときに, 彼は出かけると言ってきかない.

needs must 《文》…せざるをえない ▪ A man *needs must* lie down when he sleeps. 人間, 寝るときにはいやでも横にならねばならない. ☞ = must NEEDS 2.

Needs must when the devil drives. 《諺》必要ならいやでもそうせざるをえない.

ne'er /neər/ 副 ***a ne'er-do-well*** やくざ者, ごくつぶし ▪ He's one of those *ne'er-do-wells* that simply won't work. 彼は全然働こうとしないごくつぶしの一人だ.

ne'er the less 《主に詩》それにもかかわらず, やはり (nevertheless) ▪ *Ne'er the less* I must have three. やはり3つなくてはいけない. ☞ne'er = never.

negative /négətɪv/ 名 ***in the negative*** **1** 拒否的な ▪ His answer is *in the negative*. 彼の返事はノーだ.

2 否定して, 否定的に ▪ The question was decided *in the negative*. その問題は否決された ▪ He answered *in the negative*. 彼は「いいえ」と答えた.

return a negative ノーと答える ▪ He *returned a negative* to my question. 彼は私の質問にノーと答えた.

neglect /nɪglékt/ 名 ***for*** [***from, out of, through***] ***neglect*** 怠慢のため (*of*) ▪ He was dismissed *for neglect of* duty. 彼は職務怠慢のため首になった ▪ It was *through* your *neglect* that we were late. 我々が遅れたのは君の怠慢のせいだ.

in neglect なおざりにして ▪ He left his children *in* utter *neglect*. 彼は子供たちをすっかりほったらかしにしておいた.

neglectful /nɪgléktfəl/ 形 (***be***) ***neglectful of*** [***to do***] …を投げやりにする ▪ He *is neglectful of* his duties. 彼は職務を投げやりにする ▪ They *were neglectful to* implore that heavenly aid. 彼らはその天の助けを請うのを怠った.

negligent /néglɪdʒənt/ 形 (***be***) ***negligent in*** …の点で投げやり[むとんちゃく]である ▪ He *is negligent in* his work. 彼は仕事が投げやりだ ▪ She *is negligent in* dress. 彼女は服装にむとんちゃくだ.

(***be***) ***negligent of*** …を怠る ▪ He *was negligent of* his duties. 彼は職務を怠った.

negotiation /nɪgòʊʃiéɪʃən/ 名 ***be in negotiation with*** …と交渉中である ▪ We *are in negotiation with* the management. 我々は経営者側と交渉中だ.

(***be***) ***under negotiation*** 交渉中で ▪ The proposal *is* now *under negotiation*. その提議は目下

N

交渉中だ.

enter into* [*upon*] *negotiations with …と交渉を開始する ▪ They *entered into negotiations with* the Government. 彼らは政府と交渉を始めた.

neighbor, 《英》 **neighbour** /néɪbər/ 名 ***Love thy neighbor as thyself.*** 隣人を自分のように愛しなさい (《聖》 *Matt.* 19. 19) ▪ It is not easy to *love one's neighbor as oneself.* 隣人を自分のように愛するのはやさしくない.

neighbors from hell けんか腰で暴言を吐く隣人 ▪ The hell with such *neighbors from hell*! 隣のごろつきみたいなやつらなんか糞くらえだ.

next door neighbors 隣り同士 ▪ The Browns are our *next door neighbors.* ブラウン家と私どもは隣り同士です.

neighborhood, 《英》 **neighbourhood** /néɪbərhòd/ 名 ***in the neighborhood of*** **1** …の近所に ▪ He wants to live *in the neighborhood of* London. 彼はロンドンの近郊に住みたがっている.

2 《口》 およそ ▪ The skyscraper cost *in the neighborhood of* 25 million dollars. その摩天楼は約2,500万ドルかかった.

in this* [*that*] *neighborhood この[その]近所には ▪ There is no park *in this neighborhood.* この界わいには公園はない.

neither /ní:ðər, náɪ-/ 副 ***neither fish nor fowl* [*flesh*]/*neither fish, flesh, nor fowl*** とらえどころのない人 ▪ I felt he was *neither fish nor fowl.* 彼は得体の知れない人物だと思った. ☞《諺》 Neither fish nor flesh (nor good red herring). 魚肉でも獣肉でも(上等の燻製ニシンでも)ない, 「どっちつかずのもの」より.

neither here nor there →HERE.

neither more nor less than まさに…にほかならない ▪ History is *neither more nor less than* biography on a large scale. 歴史は大規模な伝記にほかならない.

***neither** A **nor** B* AもBも…ない ▪ *Neither* you *nor* I know. 君も私も知らない ▪ He will *neither* eat *nor* drink. 彼は食べも飲みもしないだろう. ☞neither A or Bも英米ともに用いられるが, 誤用.

neither one thing nor the other*/*neither* (*the*) *one nor the other どっちつかずの ▪ The book is *neither one thing nor the other.* それはどっちつかずの本だ.

Neptune /néptju:n/ 名 ***a son of Neptune*** 船乗り ▪ The young man looked every inch *a son of Neptune.* その若者は紛れもない船乗りに見えた. ☞Neptune「ローマ神話の海の神」.

nerve[1] /nə:rv/ 名 ***a bundle* [《英》 *bag*] *of nerves*** 《口》 非常に神経質の人 ▪ She was *a bundle of nerves* before school started. 学校が始まるまでは, 彼女は非常に神経質だった.

a man of nerve 気の強い[精力的な]男性 ▪ He is *a man of nerve* and sinew. 彼は気が強く筋骨たくましい男だ.

a war* [*battle*] *of nerves 神経戦, (威嚇などによる) 精神的な戦い ▪ He kept himself cool and won in *a battle of nerves.* 彼は冷静さを保って神経戦に勝った.

be all nerves 極度に神経過敏である ▪ She *is all nerves* over the upcoming school play. 彼女は今度の学校の劇で神経をとがらせている.

be in a state of nerves 興奮している, いらいらしている ▪ She *was in a state of nerves* then. 彼女はそのときいらいらしていた.

brace** one's **nerves 勇を鼓する, 気を引き締める ▪ They *braced their nerves* for the danger. 彼らはその危険に備えて勇を鼓した.

first-night nerves 初めての公式行事前の緊張[神経過敏] ▪ I always suffer from *first-night nerves* before an important speech. 重要な演説の直前にはきまってひどく緊張する.

get** one's **nerves back 平静を取り戻す ▪ He will *get his nerves back* in a minute. 彼はすぐに平静を取り戻すでしょう.

get* [*grate*] *on** a person's **nerves*/*give** a person **the nerves 人の神経にさわる, 癇(かん)にさわる, 人をいらいらさせる ▪ His continual sniffing *gets on my nerves.* 彼がしきりに鼻をすするのでいらいらしてくる ▪ That music really *grates on my nerves.* あの音楽, 実に耳ざわりだな.

get up the nerve 勇気を奮い起こす ▪ I *got up the nerve* to ask Jane to marry me. 僕は勇気を出してジェインに結婚を申し込んだ.

have a fit of nerves 神経過敏になる ▪ When I saw them coming, I *had a fit of nerves.* 私は彼らがやって来るのを見るとそわそわしてきた.

have a* [*some*] *nerve ずうずうしい ▪ You *have a nerve* telling me what to do! 《口》 僕に指図して, 君はずうずうしいねえ ▪ You*'ve got some nerve*! 君は相当厚かましいな.

***have nerves of iron* [*steel*]** 豪胆である ▪ He *has nerves of iron* and a cool head. 彼は度胸が据わっており冷静でもある.

***have the* [*a*] *nerve* (*to** do*)** **1** (…する)勇気がある ▪ You can try to run the business yourself, if you *have the nerve.* 君にそれだけの勇気があれば, 自分でその事業を経営してもいい.

2 《口》 厚かましくも(…する) ▪ He *had the nerve to* ask for another rise. 彼は厚かましくももう一度昇給を要求した.

hit* [*touch, strike*] *a* (*raw*) *nerve **1** (人の)つらい話題に触れる ▪ I'm afraid I *hit a nerve* when I mentioned her dead daughter, and she began to cry. 死んだ娘のことを口に出したのはつらい話題に触れたらしく, 彼女は泣き出してしまった.

2 人を狼狽させる, 怒らせる ▪ I *struck a nerve* when I asked him about his past life. 彼に過去を尋ねて怒らせてしまった.

hold* [*keep*] one's *nerve 平静を保つ, 冷静沈着である ▪ It' hard to *keep my nerve* when my boyfriend keeps in touch with his ex-girlfriends. 私

の彼が元カノたちと連絡を取り合っているとなれば私は冷静ではいられない.

I like your nerve! 《米俗》ずうずうしいにもほどがある ▪ *I like your nerve* coming here and telling me what to do! ここへ乗り込んできてあれこれ指図するとは, ずうずうしいにもほどがある.

jar on *one's* ***nerves*** 神経にさわる ▪ His creaky voice *jars on my nerves*. 彼のキーキー声は僕の神経にさわる.

live on *one's* ***nerves*** [***nerve ends***] 《英》神経をすり減らすような生活をする, 常にびくびくして過ごす ▪ Rose was a woman who *lived on her nerves*. ローズは神経をすり減らすような生活をしている女性だった ▪ She must be really *living on her nerve ends*. 実は彼女, きっと心配が絶えないのだろう. ☞F vivre sur les nerfs のなぞり.

lose *one's* ***nerve*** 《口》気おくれする, 度を失う ▪ He *lost his nerve* at the sight. その光景を見て彼は気おくれしてしまった.

my nerves will crack 神経が参ってしまう ▪ *My nerves will crack* if you nag at me much longer. これ以上君にがみがみ言われると神経が参ってしまう.

one's ***nerve is on edge*** 神経がいらだっている ▪ Don't speak to him now. *His nerve is on edge*. いま彼に口をきいてはいけない. 神経がいらだっているから.

not know what nerves are 泰然自若としている ▪ He's a cool-headed fellow. I think he does*n't know what nerves are*. 彼は冷静な男だ. そわそわするということは少しもない.

Of all the nerve! 《口》なんて心臓だろう ▪ *Of all the nerve!* Get back where you belong. なんて心臓だ. 元の場所へ帰れ.

regain *one's* ***nerve*** 勇気を取り戻す ▪ Soon I *regained my nerve*. やがて私は勇気を取り戻した.

strain every nerve (***to*** *do*) (…しようと)極力(肉体的)努力をする ▪ We *strained every nerve to* reach the top. 頂上に着くために力を出し尽くした.

The nerve of…! …はなんて心臓だろう ▪ *The nerve of* her stealing my jewelry and coming back to see me! 私の宝石を盗んでおいて会いに舞い戻ってくるなんて, 彼女はなんて心臓だろう.

touch a nerve →hit a (raw) NERVE.

What a nerve!/You've got your nerve! まあずうずうしい ▪ *What a nerve* you have got to say so! そんなことを言うなんて, なんてずうずうしいのだろう.

nerve[2] /nəːrv/ 動 ***nerve*** *oneself* 元気[勇気]を出す (*to, to do, doing, for*) ▪ The man *nerved himself to* the ordeal. その男は勇気を出してその試練に当たった ▪ *Nerve yourself for* another attempt. 元気を出してもう一度やってみなさい ▪ She cannot *nerve herself to* accept [*accepting*] his offer. 彼女は元気を出して彼の申し込みを受けいれることができない.

nervous /nə́ːrvəs/ 形 ***a nervous wreck*** 《口》神経のすっかり参った人 ▪ He became *a nervous wreck* from shell shock. 彼は砲弾ショックのため神経がすっかり参ってしまった.

(***as***) ***nervous as a cat*** [***kitten***] ひどくびくびくして ▪ I felt *as nervous as a cat* about letting him go alone. 彼を一人で行かせるのが実に心配だった.

be [***feel, get***] ***nervous*** 心配する; 気おくれする (*about*) ▪ He *is nervous about* the result. 彼は結果を心配している ▪ I *felt nervous* in his presence. 彼の前で私は気おくれした.

be nervous of *doing* 《英》…するのに気おくれを感じる ▪ We *were nervous of broaching* the subject. 我々はその話題を持ち出すのに気おくれを感じた.

nest /nest/ 名 ***an empty nest*** 子供が独立して出て行った家庭 ▪ Now that we have *an empty nest*, we'll open a little tea shop. 子供も出たことだし, 小さな喫茶店でも開くとするか.

an empty nester 《口》子供が成長し家を出ていった家庭の親 ▪ We are *empty nesters* in our fifties. 私たちは50代で, 子供たちはみな独立している.

be on *one's* ***nest*** 《英俗》(新婚の)新床の喜びを味わう ▪ The newly-weds spent a whole week *on their nest* in a hotel room. 新婚カップルはホテルの部屋で新床の喜びを味わってまる1週間過ごした.

bring a hornet's nest about *one's* ***ears*** → bring the house about one's EARs.

feather *one's* ***nest*** →FEATHER[2].

fly [***leave***] ***the nest*** 巣立つ, 独立する, 一人立ちする ▪ Our children have recently *flown the nest*. うちの子供たちは最近親元を離れて暮らすようになった. ☞「飛べるようになった小鳥の雛が巣立ちをする」が原義.

foul *one's* ***own nest*** 家名を汚すようなことをする, 自家の悪口を言う ▪ It is disgraceful to *foul one's own nest*. 自家の悪口を言うのはみっともない ▪ It is an ill bird that *fouls its own nest*. 《諺》どんな鳥でも自分の巣はよごさない《内の恥は外に出さない》.

one's [***a***] ***nest egg*** (将来のための)貯え ▪ I have *my nest egg* in the bank. 私は銀行に預金がある.

on a nest 巣についている ▪ A female blackbird is *on a nest*. 雌のツグミが巣ごもっている.

stir up [***arouse***] ***a hornets' nest*** →HORNET.

net /net/ 名 ***a Net junkie*** 《電算》ネットサーフィンやコンピューターギャンブルの中毒者 ▪ I'm afraid you've turned into *a Net junkie*. 君はネット中毒に罹っていると思うよ.

All is fish that comes to *one's* ***net.*** → FISH[1].

cast [***throw***] ***a net*** 網を打つ ▪ He *cast a net* widely. 彼は広く網を打った.

cast *one's* ***net wide*** [***widely, farther***] 網を広く打つ, 探索の範囲を広げる ▪ The editors have *cast their net*(s) *wide*. 編集者たちは探索網を広げている.

slip [***fall***] ***through the net*** 《英》置き去りにされる, 見落とされる, 逃れる (→ fall through the CRACKs) ▪ Bad people are apt to *slip through the net*. とかく悪いやつが見逃されがちだ ▪ Patients *fell through the net* under the new system. 患

者たちは新制度のもとで置き去りにされた.

spread *one's* **[*a*]** ***net for*** …に網[わな]をかける (《聖》 *Prov.* 29. 5) ▪ The police *spread their net* very widely *for* him. 警察は彼を捕えるため非常に広範囲な捜査網を張った.

surf the Net **[*net*]** 《電算》(インターネットで)サーフィンをする, サイトをあちこち見て回る ▪ I spend at least an hour a day *surfing the Net*. 1日に少なくとも1時間ネットサーフィンをして過ごす.

the old boy net ＝the old boy NETWORK.

tighten the net より強力な手段を講じる ▪ The police have started to *tighten the net* on speeding motorists. 警察は暴走族対策を強化し始めた.

walk **[*fall*]** ***into the net*** 《口》わなにかかる ▪ He *walked into the net* himself. 彼のほうからわなにかかった.

nether /néðər/ 形 *one's* ***nether garments*** 《戯》ズボン ▪ The old porter could not pull his legs through *his nether garments*. 老人の門番はズボンから足を抜くことができなかった.

one's ***nether man*** **[*person*]** 《戯》足 ▪ He warmed *his nether man* on the hearth rug. 彼は暖炉の前に敷かれた敷物の上で足を暖めた.

nettle[1] /nétəl/ 名 ***cast*** **[*throw*]** *one's* ***frock to the nettles*** 牧師をやめる ▪ Young parsons *threw their frocks to the nettles* and put on the full panoply of war. 若い牧師たちは聖職を捨てて, よろいかぶとで身を固めた. ☞F jeter le froc aux orties のなぞり.

grasp **[*seize*]** ***the nettle*** 《英古風》進んで困難と戦う, 決然としていやな仕事を引き受ける ▪ *Grasp the nettle* like a man of mettle. 気概のある人間らしく進んで困難と戦え.

have pissed upon a nettle 《俗》非常にそわそわしている, 非常に不きげんである ▪ He *has pissed upon a nettle* this morning. 今朝彼は非常に不きげんだ.

on nettles いらいら[そわそわ]して ▪ Some of them were *on nettles* till they learned your name was Dickson. 彼らの中のあるものは君の名前がディクスンだとわかるまでそわそわしていた.

nettle[2] /nétəl/ 動 ***nettle*** *oneself* イラクサに刺される ▪ He *nettled himself* badly. 彼はイラクサにひどく刺された.

network /nétwə̀:rk/ 名 ***a network of lies*** 嘘八百 ▪ His story is *a network of lies*. 彼の話は嘘八百だ.

the old boy network 《英》同窓関係のコネ ▪ He got a good job through *the old boy network*. 彼は同窓のコネで良い仕事についた.

neuter /njú:tər/ 形 ***stand neuter*** 中立する, 局外に立つ ▪ Those who had *stood neuter* took this occasion to declare against them. それまで中立していた人々もこの機会に彼らに戦いを宣した.

neutral /njú:trəl/ 形 ***on neutral ground*** **[*territory*]** どちらの側にも立たずに ▪ We decided to meet *on neutral ground*. 中立の立場で会うことにした.

never /névər/ 副名 ***as never before*** かつてなかったほど ▪ Unemployment has hit Japan *as never before*. 失業が日本に未曾有の打撃を与えている.

Better late than never. 《諺》遅くともしないよりはまし.

I never did!/Well, I never! まさか!, これは驚いた! 《女性がよく使う》 ▪ "*I never did!*" exclaimed Eliza when her brother had read the letter aloud. 「まあ驚いた」とイライザは弟がその手紙を音読したとき大きな声で言った ▪ "*Well, I never!*" ejaculated the young lady. 「まあ, あきれた」と若い婦人が叫んだ.

make no nevermind to 《米俗》…にはどうでもよい, 少しも重要ではない ▪ That *makes no nevermind to* me. 私にはそんなことはどうでもいい.

never a word [etc.] 《文》一言[など]も…しない ▪ He spoke *never a word*. 彼は一言も言わなかった ▪ He spent all his money with *never a thought* for tomorrow. 彼は明日のことは少しも考えないで金を使い果たした.

Never again! 《口》(あんないやなことは)二度とごめんだ ▪ He muttered "*Never again*" to his wife. 彼は妻に「あんなことは二度とごめんだな」とささやいた.

never cease to *do* いつまでも…する ▪ I *never cease to* marvel at his eloquence. 彼の雄弁にはいつまでも驚嘆せずにはおられない.

never ever 《口》絶対にない《never の強調形》 ▪ Everytime my mum goes driving she *never ever* wears her seat belt. ママはドライブへ行くときいつも絶対シートベルトを着用しない.

Never is a long day **[*word*].** 《諺》「もう決して」などとはうっかり言わぬこと.

never let it be said **(*that*)** 《口・戯》…などと言ってほしくない ▪ *Never let it be said that* I make light of women. 私が女性を軽く見るなどと言ってほしくない.

never-never land 夢の国 ▪ She visited the *never-never land* of Oz—a place very far away, and populated by exotic beings. 彼女は夢の国オズ—とても遠く, 別世界の生き物たちの住む国—を訪ねた.

Never say die! 《俗》弱音を吐くな, 悲観するな (Dickens, *Pickwick Papers*) ▪ *Never say die!* You'll eventually persuade her to marry you. 悲観しちゃいかん. 結局は彼女を説き伏せて結婚させることができるから.

never say never 不可能なことはない, 何が起きないとも限らない (Dickens, *Pickwick Papers*) ▪ She will never call me again.—*Never say never*. 彼女はもう僕に電話をくれないよ—そんなこと, 分かるものか.

never so 《古》〚譲歩節中で〛いくら…でも (＝EVER so) ▪ She would not marry Jim though he were *never so* rich. 彼女はジムがいくら金持ちでも彼と結婚するのはいやだろう.

Never tell me! →TELL.

never the wiser **[*better*,** etc.] (…なのに)少しも

賢く[よく，など]ない ▪ I am *never the wiser* for it. それでも少しもわからない ▪ The patient's condition was *never the better*. 病人の容態は少しもよくならなかった．

never ... yet まだ一度も…ない ▪ I have *never* found a fault in him *yet*. まだ一度も彼の欠点を見つけたことがない．

now or never →NOW.

on the never(-never) 《俗》掛けで ▪ I bought this chair *on the never-never*. このいすを掛けで買った．

pay no nevermind 《米俗》少しも注意を払わない ▪ He *pays* it *no nevermind*. 彼はそれには少しも注意を払わない．

Well, I never! →I NEVER did!

You never did. 《主に英》まさか; うそでしょう ▪ Ah, you're making it up; *you never did*. ああ，でっち上げてるんだね．うそだろ．

you never know/you never can tell → KNOW²; TELL.

new /nuː, njuː|njuː/ 形 ***a new boy*** [***girl***] 新入生; (ある社会の)新入り ▪ I am *a new boy* in the team. 私はそのチームの新入りです．

a new broom 改革に熱心な新任の指導者 ▪ What is needed right now is *a new broom*. 今こそ新しいリーダーが必要だ．☞A new broom sweeps clean. 《諺》新しいほうきはきれいに掃ける《新任の役員はいろいろ変革を行う》より．

a new man/a New Man 《英》男女平等意識の強い男性，家事・育児を進んでする男性，新男性 ▪ Her husband is very much *a New Man*. 彼女の夫は進んで家事をしてくれる．

as new 《米》新品同様で ▪ The clothes offered for sale were all *as new*. 売りに出された衣類はすべて新品同様であった．

be a new one on *a person* 人にとって初めてのものである ▪ This joke *is a new one on* me. こんな冗談は初めてだ．

become a new man 生まれ変わったようになる ▪ He has *become a new man* since then. 彼はその時以来生まれ変わったようだ．

buy *a thing* ***new*** 物を新調する ▪ Darling, look at the hat I *bought new*. あなた，私の新調した帽子を見てちょうだい．

feel (like) a new man [***woman***] 生まれ変わったような気がする ▪ I *feel* quite *a new man*. 全く生まれ変わったような気持ちだ．

lead a new life 新生活に入る ▪ I'm going to try to *lead a new life* from now on. 僕はきょうから生活を一新するつもりだ．

make a new man [***woman***] ***of*** *a person* 人の品性・素行を改めさせる; 人を健康に復させる ▪ Well, this will *make a new man of* my son. やれやれ，これで息子の素行も改まるだろう．

make ... (look [***seem***]***) like new*** …が新品に見えるようにする ▪ They *make* your clothes *like new*. あそこでは衣類を新品のようにきれいにしてくれる．

new from …から出た[来た]ばかりの ▪ He is *new from* school. 彼は学校を出たばかりだ ▪ The servant is quite *new from* the country. その使用人は田舎から出たばかりだ．

New lord, new laws. 《諺》地頭が変われば掟も変わる．

new to **1** …には初めて ▪ That is *new to* me. それは私には初耳だ．

2 …の経験のない，に新参の ▪ He is *new to* the business. 彼はその仕事には慣れていない ▪ I am *new to* this town. この町は初めてだ．

put on the new man 回心して宗教に帰依する (《聖》*Col*. 3. 10) ▪ He has been in a desperate hurry to *put on the new man*. 彼は回心して宗教に帰依しようとひどくあせってきた．

Tell us something new!/That's nothing new! 《口》その話は古い ▪ Oh, *tell us something new!* We all knew that a month ago. なあ，古い話はよしてくれよ．そんなことはみなひと月も前に知っているぜ．

That's a new one on me! 《口》それは初耳である ▪ And you eat sea cucumber raw? *That's a new one on me!* それに，ナマコを生で食べるんだって? 初めて聞いたよ．

the new poor 最近おちぶれた人たち，斜陽族 ▪ We of *the new poor* cannot afford a villa. 我々斜陽族は別荘などを持つ余裕はない．

the new rich 成り金(連中) ▪ *The new rich* are like men drunk with new wine. 成り金連中は新しい酒で酔っている人のようなものだ．☞F nouveaux riches のなぞり．

There is no new thing under the sun. (《聖》*Eccles*. 1. 9) 日の下に新しいものはない ▪ One cannot quite say that *there is no new thing under the sun* in language. 言葉に関しては日の下に新しいものはないとは言いかねる．

What's new (with you)? 《口》お変わりありませんか ▪ *What's new?*—Nothing in particular. お変わりありませんか?—ええ，特には．

Newcastle /njúːkæsəl|-kàːs-/ 名 ***carry coals to Newcastle*** →COAL.

Newgate /njúːgeɪt/ 名 ***be in Newgate*** 《口》罪人である ▪ No doubt he ought to *be in Newgate*. もちろん彼は罪人でなければならない．☞昔ロンドンにあった有名な監獄から．

news /njuːz/ 名 ***be all the news*** …のニュースでもちきりである ▪ The election *is all the news*. 選挙のニュースでもちきりだ．

be good [***bad***] ***news*** 《口》(人が…に)福[災い]である (*to, for*) ▪ Jesus Christ *is good news to* the humble but he *is bad news to* the arrogant. イエス・キリストは謙虚な人には福だが，傲慢な人には災いだ．

be news to (人)には初耳だ，思いがけない知らせだ ▪ It *is news to* me that they have got divorced. 彼らが離婚していたとは聞いて驚く．

break the news to 《口》(人)に最初に(よくない)ニュースを伝える，(通例，騒ぎを引き起こすような) 新しい情報を伝える ▪ You had better *break the news* gently *to* her. 彼女にそのニュースをお手柔らかに伝える方がいい ▪ I hate to *break the news to* you that you failed in the exam. 言いにくいのだけど，君の試験，だめだったよ.

come as news to …にとって初耳だ ▪ That *came as news to* me. それは私には初耳だった.

Good news goes on crutches. 《諺》好事門を出でず.

***Ill* [*Bad*] *news travels* [*flies, runs*] *fast* [*apace*].** 《諺》悪事千里を走る.

in the news (新聞などに)発表されて ▪ Last week Seaborg and his associates were *in the news* again. 先週シーボーグとその一味はまた新聞種になった.

news from nowhere 周知の事実 ▪ That's *news from nowhere*. そんなことは周知の事実だ. ☞William Morris の書名から.

No news is good news. 《諺》たよりのないのは良いたより.

Tell me news! そんな話は古くさいよ ▪ *Tell me news*. What else is new? そんな話は古くさいよ. 他に新しいのはないのかい.

***that is news* [*no news*] *to*…** それは…には初耳だ[珍しくもない] ▪ Adams married! *That's* quite *news to* me. アダムズが結婚したって. そいつは初耳だ.

newt /njuːt/ 名 ***(as) pissed as a newt*** 《卑》ひどく酔って ▪ He looks *as pissed as a newt*. 彼はひどく酔っているようだった.

New York /njùːjɔ́ːrk/ 名 ***a New York minute*** 《米口》ほんのつかの間，一瞬 ▪ The tickets for the concert were sold out in *a New York minute*. コンサートのチケットはまたたく間に売り切れた.

next /nekst/ 形副前名 ***as… as the next fellow* [*guy, person, man, woman*]** 誰にも劣らず ▪ I am *as* brave *as the next fellow*. 私は誰にも劣らず勇気がある ▪ I like parties *as* much *as the next guy*. パーティーは誰にも負けず好きだ ▪ Mr. Bryan knows this *as* well *as the next man*. ブライアン氏はこのことを誰にも劣らずよく知っている. ☞次項も参照.

***as… as the next* (*one*)** (物が)何[どれ]にも劣らず ▪ This car is *as* good *as the next one*. この車のすばらしさはどの車にも劣らない.

be next in line →next in LINE.

come next 次にくる ▪ This one *comes next*. 次はこれだ ▪ What *comes next*? 次は何だ.

get next 《米俗》賢くなる，感うく ▪ I hope he doesn't *get next* before we get out of town. 我々が町から出ないうちに彼が感うかなければいいが.

get next to 《米俗》 **1** (親しくなるため，きげんをとるために)…に近うく ▪ *Get next to* him and get his ear. 彼に近ういて，君の意見を聞いてもらえ.

2 …を知る，知るようになる ▪ They are *getting next to* Dowie. 彼らはダウイーと知りあいになりつつある.

3 (特に女性)と親密になる ▪ You look likely to *get next to* that girl. お前はあの女の子と深い仲になってしまいそうだ.

4 …を取る，着服する ▪ She *got next to* all my small change. 彼女は私の小銭をかっさらってしまった.

get next to oneself 《米俗》現実的に[賢く]なる ▪ The boy is *getting next to himself*. あの少年は賢くなりつつある.

in my next 次便で ▪ I will tell you *in my next*. 次便でお知らせしよう.

in the next place (順次に話して)次に(は) (→in the first PLACE) ▪ *In the next place*, the chairs should be dusted. 次にいすのちりを払わなければならない.

let a person next to →put a person NEXT to.

next after **1** …の次に位する，より一段下の ▪ The duke was *next* in dignity *after* the king. 公爵は威厳にかけては王に次いでいた.

2 …の一つ次の ▪ It happened on the Sunday *next after* his arrival. それは彼の到着後最初の日曜日に起こった.

3 …に次いで ▪ He was, *next after* Lucy, by far the best newsgatherer in the area. 彼はその近所界わいではルーシーに次いで断然情報集めの名手だった.

next before **1** すぐ前の，一段上の ▪ He had spoken of it in the verse *next before*. 彼はそのことを直前の詩で詠(うた)っていた.

2 …の一つ前の ▪ It was the day *next before* his death. それは彼が死んだ前の日だった.

***next… but one* [*two*]** 2[3]番目の… ▪ Her letter reached me the *next* day *but one*. 彼女からの手紙は翌々日[2日後]に届いた ▪ The grocer's is *next* door *but one*. 食料品店は一軒おいて隣りだ.

next door to →DOOR.

next one's hand 一番手近の ▪ I take anything that is *next my hand*. 一番手近のものを手に取る.

next one's heart 非常になつかしい ▪ They talked of the subject that lay *next their hearts*. 彼らは自分たちになつかしい話題について話した.

Next, please! **1** お次は ▪ *Next, please!* I've heard that story before. 次のを聞かせてくれ，その話は前に聞いたことがある.

2 お次の方どうぞ ▪ "*Next, please!*" said the hairdresser. 「お次の方どうぞ」と理髪師が言った.

next thing to ほとんど…と同じ (＝next DOOR to) ▪ Anybody who can put up with him is *next thing to* a saint. 彼にがまんできる人は誰でも，ほとんど聖人なみだ.

next to **1** …の次に位する，の次の ▪ His poems are *next to* Milton's. 彼の詩はミルトンの詩の次に位する ▪ In English he is *next to* none in the class. 英語にかけては，彼はクラスの誰にも引けを取らない ▪ I saw her at the shop *next to* the corner. 彼女を角から2軒目の店で見かけた.

2 ほとんど ▪ It is *next to* a miracle. それは奇跡に近い ▪ He *next to* adored his mother. 彼は母親をほとんど崇拝せんばかりだった ▪ It is *next to* impossible. それはまず不可能だ.

next to nothing ごくわずか(しかない) ▪ We know *next to nothing* of ancient Greek music. 古代ギリシャ音楽についてはほとんど何も分かっていない ▪ I bought it for *next to nothing*. それをただ同然で買った.

Not till the next time. この次まではやめていよう《禁酒・禁煙の冗談約束》.

put* [*let*] *a person* *next to 《米俗》人に…を知らせる ▪ He will *put* you *next to* the rules. 彼が君に礼法を教えてくれるだろう.

the next best thing 次に最もよいもの, 次善の策 ▪ *The next best thing* would be to tell him the truth. 次善の策は彼に真相を話すことであろう.

the next of* one's *blood* [*kin*]/one's *next of kin 《文》自分の最近親 ▪ My cousin is *the next of my kin*. いとこが私の最近親だ ▪ This form must be signed by *your next of kin*. この申し込み書には近親者のサインがいる.

***the next thing* (one *knew*)** 《口》いつのまにか ▪ He was walking alone at night and *the next thing* he *knew* someone was following him. 彼は夜一人で歩いていて, ふと気がつくと誰かにあとをつけられていた.

(*the*) *next to last* 終わりから2番目の[で] ▪ What is *the next to last* Greek letter?—It's Ψ. ギリシャ語の最後から2番目の文字は何ですか?—Ψ(プシー)です.

***To be concluded* [*continued*] *in our next* (*issue*).** 次号完結[に続く] ▪ Well, that's all for this time; suppose we say *to be continued in our next*. さて, このたびはこれでおしまいです. 以下次号に続くとしておきましょうかね.

What is the next article? 次に何を差しあげましょうか《商人用語》.

What next? **1** [[間投詞的に]] (こういうことになると)お次はなんだろう; あきれたことだ《驚きを表す》 ▪ As old ladies say, *what next?* お婆さん連の言い草じゃないが, あきれたことだ ▪ Well, I'm sure! *What next*, I wonder! いやはや全く. お次はなんだろう.

2 お次に何を差しあげましょう ▪ "*What next*, Madam?" asked the shop assistant. 「次は何にいたしましょうか, 奥さま」と店員が尋ねた.

Niagara /naɪǽgərə/ 名 ***put on the Niagara act*** 《米俗》さめざめと泣く ▪ And then the old woman *put on the Niagara act*. それから老婦人はさめざめと泣いた.

shoot Niagara 大冒険を試みる ▪ Maryland "*shot Niagara*" in 1809 by adopting manhood suffrage. メリーランド州は1809年に成年男子参政権を採用して「大冒険を試み」た.

nib /nɪb/ 名 ***his* [*her*] *nibs*** 《英口》いばった親分, もったいぶった御仁 ▪ *His nibs* wants fresh oysters in July. 大将は7月なのに生きのよいカキをご所望だ.

nice /naɪs/ 形 ***a nice little earner*** 《英口》儲かる商品, 収入のよい商売 ▪ That plumbing job is *a nice little earner*. 配管工事の仕事は実入りがよい仕事だ.

(*as*) *nice as a nun's hen* 気むずかしい, 好ききらいが多い ▪ I know a priest *as nice as a nun's hen*. 私はひどく気むずかしやの牧師と知り合っている.

(*as*) *nice as* (*a*) *pie* **1** 《口》(人が)この上もなくいんぎんな ▪ His aunt is *as nice as a pie*. 彼のおばさんはとてもいんぎんだ.

2 (予想に反して)とても愛想がよい, (意外にも)非常に丁寧な ▪ I had been very nervous, but they were all *as nice as pie*. 私はひどくおどおどしていたが, 案に相違して彼らはみんな愛想がよかった. ☞主語が they の場合は a pie の a が落ちる.

as nice as* (*nice*) *can be **1** この上もなく親切で ▪ The villagers were *as nice as could be*. 村人たちはこの上もなく親切だった.

2 この上もなくすばらしい ▪ Everything's *as nice as can be*. 何もかもこの上なくすばらしい.

***be nice about* [*in*]** …について(好みが)やかましい ▪ He *is nice about* the choice of words. 彼は言葉うかいについて口うるさい.

Have a nice day! 《主に米口》よい1日を, またおいでください《客へのくだけた別れの挨拶》 ▪ Thanks.—Thank you, sir. *Have a nice day*. どうも—ありがとうございました. またのお越しを.

have a nice time おもしろく時を過ごす ▪ We *had a* very *nice time* at the party. パーティーではとても愉快だった.

Here is* [*We are in*] *a nice mess. 《口》これは困ったことになった ▪ Now *we are in* such *a nice mess*. さてこいつはひどく困ったことになったな.

***it is nice* doing** …するのは愉快だ ▪ *It'll be nice working* together again. またいっしょに働くのは楽しいだろう.

look nice きれいな[愛嬌のある]顔つきをしている ▪ She was desirous of *looking* as *nice* as possible. 彼女はできるだけ感じのよい顔をしたいと願っていた.

***make nice* [*nice-nice*]** 《米口》偽善的に[うわべだけ]愛想よく丁寧にする, ちやほやする ▪ He has been trying to *make nice-nice* with me. 彼はこのところやけに私にちやほやしている.

nice and /naɪsənd/ 《口》 **1** ほどよく, …でよい ▪ The house is *nice and* high. この家は高くて申し分ない ▪ It is *nice and* warm today. きょうは暖かくてよい.

2 《皮肉》非常に ▪ Let's walk *nice and* quiet down to the station house. さあおとなしく本署まで来るんだ ▪ You'll be *nice and* ill in the morning. 君はあしたにはひどく具合が悪くなっているだろう.

Nice going! 《口》いい調子《ほめ言葉》 ▪ The coach said to the pitcher, "*Nice going*, kid." コーチは投手に「よし, いい調子」と言った.

***Nice one*(*, Cyril*).** 《英口》でかしたぞ, よくやった ▪ You have passed the entrance examination? *Nice one, Cyril*. 入学試験にパスしたんだって, よくやったね. ☞フットボールの名選手 Cyril Knowles を歌ったレコードの歌詞(1973年)の一節.

Nice to meet* [*see*] *you. お会いできてうれしいです《通例 meet は初対面, see は既知の人に用いる丁寧なあいさつ》.

***Nice work* (*if you can get it*)!** 《主に英口》なかなかお見事《いい仕事に対する賛辞》 ▪ Good for you—*nice work if you can get it!* でかしたぞ—なかなかお見事. ☞Gershwin の歌(1937年)の題名から.

not nice to know 《口・戯》(人が)気にくわない, 不らちな ▪ That friend of yours is *not nice to know*. 君のあの友人は気にくわないやつさ.

nicely /náɪsli/ 副 ***do nicely*** **1**《口》[[主に進行形で]] 無事である; 快方に向かう ▪ How is Mary?—She's *doing nicely*. メアリーはどうですか?—元気でいます ▪ The patient *is doing nicely*. 病人は快方に向かっている.

2 ふさわしい, 都合がよい ▪ Tomorrow at three will *do nicely*. 明日の3時で結構です.

nicety /náɪsəti/ 名 ***to a nicety*** きちんと, 精密に (→to a T) ▪ The coat will fit you *to a nicety*. その上着は君にぴったり合うでしょう ▪ The lawyer described the position *to a nicety*. 弁護士はその立場を精密に説明した.

niche /nɪtʃ|niːʃ/ 名 ***carve (out) a niche (for** oneself**)*** 職場に自分の居場所を見つける, 仕事で成功する, 最適の地位を得る ▪ The firm is *carving out a niche* in the international market. その会社は国際市場で繁栄する地位を占めつつある. ☞niche「(彫像などの展示用に作られた)壁のくぼみ」.

have [be worthy of] a niche in the temple of Fame 名を後世に残すに値する ▪ He *has a niche in the temple of Fame* as a general. 彼は将軍として名を後世に残すだけの功績がある.

Nick /nɪk/ 名 ***full of the old Nick*** 《米俗》いたずらな ▪ That son of his is *full of the old Nick*. 彼のあの息子はとてもいたずらっ子だ. ☞the Old Nick「悪魔」.

nick[1] /nɪk/ 名 ***hit the nick*** 的に当たる ▪ My rejoinder *hit the nick*. 私の答弁が的を射た.

in good nick 《英口》(人が)健康で, (物が)良好な状態で ▪ The ground was *in good nick*. グラウンドのコンディションは良かった.

in the nick **1** ちょうどよい時に ▪ *In the* very *nick* he entered. ちょうどよい時に彼が入って来た.

2《英俗》刑務所に入って ▪ The man was put *in the nick*. その男は刑務所へ入れられた.

in the nick of ちょうど...したときに ▪ He was rescued *in the nick of* being drowned. 彼はまさにおぼれようとしたときに助けられた.

in [at] the nick of time きわどい時に, ちょうどよい時に (→the NICK of time) ▪ The letter reached his hands *in the* very *nick of time*. その手紙はきわどい時に彼の手に届いた. ☞勘定などを示すため長い棒に刻み目 (nick) をつけた古い習慣から.

out of all nick 非常に, なんとも言いようのないほど ▪ He loved her *out of all nick*. 彼はその女性をいたく愛した.

the nick of time きわどい[ちょうどよい]時 ▪ Something must be done and now is *the nick of time*. 何か手を打たなければならない, 今がその潮時だ.

nick[2] /nɪk/ 動 ***nick it*** うまく的に当てる; うまく言いあてる ▪ At every ball how prettily you *nick it*! 一球一球ごとになんとうまく当てるのでしょう ▪ You've *nicked it*; the fact is, you must turn missionary. 君はうまく言いあてたよ. 実はね, 君は宣教師にならなくちゃいけないんだ.

nick** a person **with nay 人にいやだと言う ▪ I trust you will not *nick* me *with nay*. あなたはきっといやだとはおっしゃいますまい.

nickel /níkəl/ 名 ***accept a wooden nickel*** 《米》全く価値のないものをつかまされる, だまし取られる ▪ He is too smart to *accept a wooden nickel*. 彼は目利きに優れていて偽物をつかまされはしない.

double nickel 《俗》制限速度《高速道路で時速55マイル》 ▪ We'd better not go over *double nickel*. 55マイルの制限速度を超えない方が身のためだ.

not be worth a wooden [plug(ged)] nickel/ wouldn't give a wooden [plug(ged)] nickel for 《米》取るに足らない, 全く価値がない, 一銭の値打ちもない ▪ My advice may *not be worth a wooden nickel*, though. 私の助言なんか取るに足らないだろうけど ▪ This old horse *isn't worth a plugged nickel*. この老いた馬は全然役に立たない. ☞質の悪い nickel「米国5セント白銅貨」ほどの価値もないから; a plugged coin「劣位金属を混ぜた偽造硬貨」.

not take any wooden nickels 《米俗》油断しない ▪ He's a smart boy, he does*n't take any wooden nickels*. 彼は抜け目のないやつだ. なかなか油断しない.

nifty /nífti/ 名 ***pull a nifty*** 《米俗》気のきいた文句をはく ▪ He's always trying to *pull a nifty*. 彼はいつも気のきいた文句を言おうとする.

niggardly /nígərdli/ 形 ***be niggardly of*** ... をけちけちする, 惜しむ ▪ Father has *been niggardly* to me *of* his money. 父はこれまで私に金をくれるのを惜しんだ.

nigger[1] /nígər/ 名 ***a nigger in the woodpile [fence]*** 《侮蔑》隠れた目的, 隠れた魂胆 ▪ He said he wanted to study art in Paris, but I guessed that Mary was *the nigger in the woodpile*. 彼はパリで美術を研究したいと言ったが, 私の想像ではメアリーが隠れた目的だったのだ ▪ There's *a nigger in that fence*! あれには何か隠された魂胆がある.

let off a little nigger 《米口・侮蔑》黒人のようなふるまいをする ▪ He was only *letting off a little nigger* when he said so. 彼はそう言ったときただ黒人みたいなまねをしていただけだ.

work like a nigger 《侮蔑》あくせく働く ▪ I have toiled night and day, I've *worked like a nigger*. 夜も昼も働いた, あくせくと働いた.

nigger[2] /nígər/ 動 ***nigger** oneself* 《侮蔑》(顔を黒くして)黒人のように見せかける ▪ Jim was *niggering himself* by adorning his rosy cheeks with black. ジムは紅顔を黒くぬって黒人のように見せかけていた.

nigger it 《米・侮蔑》貧乏暮らしをする ▪ These better-dressed fellows were obliged to *nigger it* as well as ourselves. このましな身なりの連中も我々と同様に貧乏暮らしをしなければなかった.

night /naɪt/ 名 ***a night letter*** (料金が安く翌朝配達される)夜間取り扱い電報 ▪ We can say more for the same price in *a night letter.* 夜間取り扱い電報なら同じ料金で中身が多く打てる.

a [*one's*] ***night off*** 仕事のない夜, 非番の夜 ▪ *His night off* occurred on a Friday. 金曜日が彼の非番の夜になった.

a night on the town →a night (out) on the TOWN.

a [*one's*] ***night out*** 外で浮かれ騒ぐ夜 ▪ I go to the theater on *my night out.* 外で遊ぶ夜には芝居を見に行く.

a night out of ten thousand 千載一遇の夜 ▪ It was *a night out of ten thousand* for my purpose. それは私の目的には千載一遇の夜であった.

a night person 夜型人間, 昼間より夜に活力が出る人 ▪ I am more awake after sunset. I am *a night person.* 私は日が沈まないと頭がはっきりしないのです. 夜型人間ですから.

all [***the whole***] ***night*** (***long***)/***all the night through***/ (***all***) ***the long night*** 夜どおし ▪ The doctor watched by the patient *all night long.* 医師は徹夜で病人のそばにつき添っていた ▪ He continued *the whole night* without a wink of sleep. 彼は夜どおしまんじりともしなかった.

(***as***) ***dark*** [***black***] ***as night*** 真っ暗[黒]で ▪ The chamber was *as dark as night.* その部屋は真っ暗だった ▪ Her hair was *as black as night.* 彼女の髪は真っ黒だった.

(***as***) ***different as night and day*** 《陳腐》全く異なる, 全然違う ▪ The twins look exactly alike, but their characters are *different as night and day.* その双子は見た目にはそっくりだが, 性格はまるきり違う.

at [***in the***] ***dead of night*** →at [in the] DEAD of.

at night 日暮れに, 宵に; 夜間に《午後6時から真夜中までの時刻についても使う》 ▪ He went to bed early *at night.* 彼は夜早く寝た ▪ There came two gentlemen at twelve o'clock *at night.* 夜の12時に二人の紳士がやって来た.

at nights 夜な夜な, 夜は ▪ *At nights* they had the shelter of a barn. 夜は彼らには納屋という隠れ家があった.

at this time of night/***at this hour of the night*** 夜分こんな(遅い)時間に ▪ It's a shame for you to call on her *at this time of night.* 夜分こんな時間に彼女を訪ねるなんてお前にもあきれたものだ.

be like night and day 夜と昼ほどの違いがある, 二つのこと(人)が全く違う ▪ The difference in performance between the two *is like night and day.* 両者の性能の違いは月とスッポンほどもある.

bid *a person* ***good night*** 人におやすみを言う ▪ Soon I *bade* her *good night.* やがて私は彼女におやすみなさいを言った.

by night 《文》 **1** 夜分 (↔by DAY) ▪ Bats come out *by night.* コウモリは夜出てくる ▪ The City is the busiest part of London by day and the quietest *by night.* ロンドン旧市内は昼間はロンドンで一番にぎやかで, 夜分は一番静かな区域だ.

2 夜にまぎれて ▪ The enemy attacked us *by night.* 敵は夜陰に乗じて攻撃して来た.

by night and day 昼夜の別なく, いつも ▪ Time comes stealing on *by night and day.* 時は昼夜の別なくそっと忍び寄ってくる.

call it a night 《口》今夜はこれで打ち上げる (→call it a DAY) ▪ It's ten. Let's *call it a night.* もう10時だ. 今夜はこれで切り上げよう.

day and night →NIGHT and day.

during the night 夜間に ▪ It snowed *during the night.* 夜中に雪が降った.

far into the night 夜ふけまで ▪ He always sits up *far into the night* and studies. 彼はいつも夜ふかしして勉強する.

for the night **1** 寝るために ▪ He retired *for the night.* 彼は寝室に引き下がった.

2 その晩は ▪ Could you put me up *for the night*? 今晩泊めていただけますか.

Good night! **1** おやすみ! ▪ *Good night!* I am off to bed. おやすみ. 私は寝ます.

2 《米》 =Good GRIEF!

have [***pass***] ***a good*** [***bad***] ***night*** よく眠れる[眠れない] ▪ Have you *had a good night*? よく眠れましたか.

have a night on the tiles →on the TILEs.

have a [***the***] ***night out*** 一夜を外で遊び明かす ▪ Let's *have a night out* for a change. ひとつ気分を変えて, 今晩は外で遊び明かそうじゃないか.

have an early [***a late***] ***night*** (いつもより)早寝する[遅く寝る] ▪ He's *had* a lot of *late nights* recently. 彼は最近夜更かしが多い.

in a night 一晩に ▪ I awoke three times *in a night.* 一晩に3回も目をさました ▪ It was built *in a* single *night.* それはたった一夜で作られた.

in the night 夜中に ▪ *In the night* it started raining. 夜中に雨が降りだした.

into the night **1** 暗がりの中へ ▪ I don't like your going out *into the night* without a lantern. 君にカンテラを持たずに暗がりの中へ出て行ってほしくない.

2 世に埋もれて ▪ That was the last we ever heard of him. I fear he went *into the night.* それ以来彼の噂は全然ない. 世に埋もれてしまったのではないか.

(***it will be***) ***all right on the night*** (リハーサルはよくないが)初演の夜にはうまくいくだろう《比喩的にも》 ▪ They hoped that the Atlantic Pact would turn out *all right on the night.* 大西洋条約もいよいよ実施されればうまくいくだろうと彼らは考えていた.

last night 昨晩 ▪ I had a queer dream *last night.* 昨夜妙な夢を見た.

make a night of it 《口》一晩遊び明かす ▪ Come on, we'll get some fellows together and *make a night of it.* さあ数人集まって, 一晩遊び明かそうじゃないか.

make *one's* ***good nights*** おやすみを言う ▪ She

promptly *made her good nights* and vanished. 彼女は素早くおやすみを言って姿を消した.

make night hideous やかましく騒いで他人を寝かせない (cf. Sh., *Haml.* 1. 4. 54) ▪ The people who live next door to me *make night hideous* with their jazz. 隣りに住んでいる一家は夜にジャズでやかましく騒いで人を寝かせない.

night after [***by***] ***night*** 毎晩 ▪ The strange star was seen *night after night.* その見なれぬ星は毎夜のように見られた.

night and day/day and night 《口》昼夜の別なく, いつも ▪ They rowed *night and day.* 彼らは昼夜の別なくこぎ続けた.

night in, night out 夜な夜な, 毎晩 ▪ Day in, day out, *night in, night out* he sat at home dictating his account of the day. 毎日, 毎晩, 彼は家に座って昼間の記録を口述していた.

night life 夜の娯楽 ▪ We can find more *night life* in town than in the country. 田舎より都会の方が夜の娯楽が多い.

Night night./Nighty night. 〚間投詞的に〛おやすみ《子供が[子供に対して]用いる》 ▪ *Night night,* sleep tight! おやすみ. よくねんねするのよ.

one's ***night off*** →a NIGHT off.

night or day 夜も昼も ▪ He never rested *night or day,* till he came to Dover. 彼はドーバーに着くまでは夜も昼も少しも休まなかった.

one's ***night out*** **1** (使用人が)外出してよい晩 ▪ It was one of *her nights out.* その晩は彼女が外出してよい晩だった.

2 お祭り騒ぎする夜 ▪ For these people the fair was, as they put it, *their "night out".* この人々にとっては, その市はいわゆる「お祭り騒ぎの夜」なのだった.

of a night/of [《口》***o'***] ***nights*** 夜分 ▪ I can't sleep *of a night* thinking of that. そのことを考えて夜も眠れない ▪ He slept soundly *of nights* without a dream. 彼は夜夢もみずにぐっすり眠った.

over night **1** 一晩 ▪ Stay with us *over night.* 一晩うちへお泊まりなさい ▪ The fish will not keep *over night.* この魚は朝までもつまい.

2 一夜にして《ごく短い時間で》 ▪ The writer became famous *over night.* その作家は一夜にして有名になった.

pass a good [***bad***] ***night*** → have a good NIGHT.

pass a night at …に1泊する, で夜を明かす ▪ We *passed a night at* the hotel. 我々はそのホテルに1泊した.

sit the night out 徹夜する ▪ I *sat the night out* reading a novel. 徹夜して小説を読んだ.

sit up at night 夜寝ずにいる ▪ The boy *sat up* late *at night.* その少年は夜遅くまで起きていた.

spend the night with *a person* 人の家に泊まる ▪ Please come and *spend the night with* us. どうかうちへ泊まりに来てください.

last thing (***at night***) →LAST².

the night before last → the year before LAST.

the whole night (***long***) →all NIGHT (long).

turn night into day 昼間すべきことを夜する ▪ It's sheer folly *turning night into day* as you're doing. 君のように昼間すべきことを夜しているのは愚の骨頂だよ.

under (***the***) ***cover of night*** → under (the) COVER of 2.

nightmare /náɪtmèər/ 名 ***live*** (***in***) ***a nightmare*** 非常な恐れと心配の状況の中で生活する ▪ The people in the war-torn city *lived in a nightmare.* 戦禍を被ったその街の人々は恐れおののいて日々を送っていた.

nighttime /náɪttàɪm/ 名 ***in the nighttime*** 夜分に ▪ We assailed the enemy *in the nighttime* unawares. 我々は夜分に敵を奇襲した.

night watch /náɪtwɑ̀tʃ|-wɔ̀tʃ/ 名 ***in the night watches*** →WATCH¹.

nihility /naɪhíləti/ 名 ***become a nihility*** 消えてなくなる, 無に帰してしまう ▪ All he did *became a nihility.* 彼のしたことはすべて水の泡になってしまった.

nimble /nímbəl/ 形 (***as***) ***nimble as a goat*** 非常にすばしこい ▪ The boy is *nimble as a goat.* その少年はとてもすばしこい.

the nimble ninepence [***shilling, sixpence***] 《古》流通の速い金 ▪ *The nimble ninepence* is better than the slow shilling. 《諺》足の速い9ペンス銀貨の方が足の遅いシリングよりもよい,「薄利多売」,「商いは数でこなせ」. ☞1971年まで用いられた英国の旧通貨単位で 1 shilling＝12 pence.

NIMBY /nímbi/ 名 →Not In My BACKYARD!

nine /naɪn/ 形名 ***a nine days'*** [***day***] ***wonder/a one-day wonder*** じきに騒がれなくなる事件,「人の噂も75日」(Chaucer, *Troilus and Criseyde* 4. 588) ▪ The Duke's marriage to the milkmaid was *a nine days' wonder* in the country. 公爵と乳しぼり女の結婚は田舎では「人の噂も75日」というやつだった ▪ The storm was *a one-day wonder* bringing lots of wind and rain. あらしは風雨が強かったがあっという間に通り過ぎた. ☞犬や猫の子は生後9日ほどは目があかないので, それまではいつあくかと好奇の目を向けていることから. また, カトリックの Novena「九日間の祈り」の祭からとも.

a nine to five job (朝9時から午後5時までの)サラリーマンの仕事 ▪ He was getting tired of *a nine to five job.* 彼はサラリーマンの仕事にあきかけていた.

get [***put***] ***in the nine hole***(***s***) 《米俗》窮地に陥る[陥れる] ▪ He *got in the nine holes* and sold his slave to the general. 彼は困窮して自分の奴隷を将軍に売った ▪ We have *put* the gentleman *in the nine holes.* 我々はその紳士を窮地に陥れた.

go the whole nine yards 《米口》(危険[困難]なことを)最後までやり通す ▪ We *went the whole nine yards* in terrible weather and got to the top of the mountain. 荒天をついて山頂をきわめた.

have nine lives なかなか死なない, 運よく危機を脱する ▪ The old man seemed to *have nine lives,* and soon made a complete recovery. その老人はそのたびに窮地を脱してやがて全快した. ☞《諺》A cat has nine lives.「猫に九生あり」から.

look nine ways (***for Sunday, at once***) →WAY.

nine in ten =NINE times out of ten.

nine times [***cases***] ***out of ten*** 十中八九, たいてい ▪ In *nine cases out of ten*, you will not find your confidence misplaced. 十中八九信頼を裏切られることはないでしょう.

Possession is nine points of the law. →POSSESSION.

the whole nine yards 《主に米口》あらゆるもの, すべて, 全体, 一切合財 ▪ He sells fake watches, bags, jeans, and *the whole nine yards*. 彼は偽ブランドの時計, かばん, ジーンズ, その他あらゆる偽物を売っている ▪ I got dysentery: chills, fever, hallucinations, *the whole nine yards*. 赤痢にかかり, 悪寒, 高熱, 幻覚その他あらゆる症状を覚えた.

(***up***) ***to the nines*** [《まれ》***nine***] 《英口》申し分なく, 極度に ▪ That would please me *to the nines*. それは全く申し分ありません ▪ Here comes Ms Green, dressed *up to the nines* for the ball. そら舞踏会のために盛装をこらしてグリーン嬢がやって来るぞ. ☞9が完成を含意する神秘的な数であるところから.

ninepins /náɪnpìnz/ 名 ***be knocked*** [***fall***] ***over like*** (***a lot of***) ***ninepins*** 将棋倒しに倒される[ころぶ] ▪ The little urchins *fell over like ninepins*. いたずらっ子たちは将棋倒しにころんだ.

go down [***fall***] ***like ninepins*** **1**《英》楽に片づく ▪ The problems *went down* before me *like ninepins*. その問題はばたばたと片づいていった.
2 (多くの人が)バタバタと倒れる ▪ People were *going down like ninepins* near me. すぐそばで人が次々に倒れていた.

nineteen /nàɪntíːn/ 名 ***nineteen to the dozen*** →DOZEN.

nineteenth /nàɪntíːnθ/ 形 ***the nineteenth hole*** 《戯》ゴルフ場内のバー ▪ Most courses have been completely unplayable, except at *the nineteenth hole*! たいていのコースは全然プレーできなくなっている, ただし場内のバーは別だ. ☞18 holes からなるゲーム終了後やって来る場所の意から.

ninety /náɪnti/ 名 ***in*** *one's* ***nineties*** 90歳代で ▪ The old man may be *in his nineties*. その老人は90歳代かもしれない.

in ninety-nine cases out of a hundred 100のうち99まで ▪ *In ninety-nine cases out of a hundred* she is better. ほぼ間違いなく彼女は具合が良くなっている.

ninety-nine times out of a hundred ほとんどいつも ▪ The boy is late for school *ninety-nine times out of a hundred*. その男の子はほとんどいつも遅刻する.

the Naughty Nineties 奔放の90年代, 奢侈(しゃし)の悪名が高い1890年代 ▪ She found herself in a room decorated in *the Naughty Nineties* style. 気がつくと彼女は奔放の90年代様式に装飾された部屋にいた. ☞1890年から世紀末まで英国で一世を風靡したダンディズム[はいから好み]とデカダンス[退廃]の風潮.

ninth /naɪnθ/ 形 ***the ninth part of a man*** 仕立屋 ▪ That ninny is but *the ninth part of a man*. あの愚か者は仕立屋にすぎない《半人前以下だ》. ☞Nine TAILORs make a man.「仕立屋は9人で一人前」という諺から.

nip[1] /nɪp/ 名 ***a nip and*** (***a***) ***tuck*** 《米口》**1** 美容整形 ▪ These days it doesn't cost much to get yourself *a nip and tuck*. 近頃では美容整形を受けるのに大して費用はかからない.
2 少しずつの変化[削減] ▪ *A nip* here *and a tuck* there in our household would give us the extra money we need. 家計をあれこれと少しずつ切り詰めていけば, 必要な余剰金が浮くだろう.

a nip in the air 肌を刺すような寒さ ▪ There's quite *a nip in the air* this evening. 今夜は実に肌を刺すような寒さだ.

freshen the nip →FRESHEN.

give *a person* ***a nip*** 人をつねる ▪ She *gave* me *a nip* on the arm. 彼女は私の腕をつねった.

nip and tuck 《米口》**1** 負けず劣らず(の), 互角に[の] (= NECK and neck) ▪ The game was *nip and tuck* all the way. その試合は終始互角だった.
2 きわどい[危うい]ところで ▪ It was *nip and tuck*, but we made it just in time. きわどかったが, なんとか間に合った.

nip[2] /nɪp/ 動 ***nip ... in the bud*** →BUD.

nip on ahead 追い越そうと走る ▪ One of them *nipped on ahead*. その中の一人が走って追い越そうとした.

nit /nɪt/ 名 ***pick nits*** あら探しをする, 難癖をつける, 揚げ足を取る, 重箱の隅を突っつく ▪ Excuse me for *picking nits* with you like this. このように君のあら探しをして申しわけない. ☞nits「アタマジラミの卵」.

nitty-gritty /nìtigríti/ 名 ***get down to the nitty-gritty of*** 《俗》...の核心に触れる ▪ He's not afraid to *get down to the nitty-gritty of* unpleasant problems. 彼は不愉快な問題の核心に触れるのを恐れていない.

nix /nɪks/ 名 ***keep nix*** 警戒する ▪ "*Keeping nix*" was, in other words, keeping a look-out that no person might catch us.「警戒する」というのは, つまり, 誰にもつかまらないように気を配ることだった.

nix cum arous 《米口》どうにもしようがない ▪ We were dying for a smoke, but it was *nix cum arous*. 一服ふかしたくてたまらなかったが, どうにもならなかった. ☞Ⓖ nichts kommt heraus のなぞり.

Nix my dolly! 心配するな ▪ *Nix my dolly*, pals, go away. 心配するな, みんな, 帰ってくれ. ☞Ainsworth が使い, 他の作家がまねた句.

nix on 《口》...はもう十分だ, よせよ ▪ *Nix on* the conversation game. おしゃべり競争はもうよせ ▪ *Nix on* that kid stuff! そんな子供っぽいまねはよせ. ☞Ⓖ nichts 'nothing'.

no /noʊ/ 形副名 ***be no deal/ be no sale***

《俗》だめだ，失敗だ ▪ He wanted me to join his team, but I said it *was no deal*. 彼のチームに入ってくれと言われたが，だめだと断った.

be no go 《口》むだだ，だめだ ▪ It's *no go*, folks. The manager says no. だめだよ君たち. マネージャーがいけないと言うんだ.

no can do 《口》(そんなことは)だめだ，できない ▪ Sorry, *no can do*—not today. 申し訳ないが，だめだ—きょうのところは.

no duh 《口》(子供が自分の知っていることを言われて)ばかだなあ ▪ Well, *no duh*. Who did you think she was? ばかだなあ. 彼女が誰だと思ったんだ.

no man's land **1** 荒地；持主のない土地 ▪ The country is not a *no man's land*. その土地は持主のない土地ではない.
2《軍》(対抗した敵・味方陣地の)中間空地 ▪ It is perilous work repairing wires in the *No Man's Land* between trenches. 塹壕(ざんごう)間の中間空地で鉄条網を修理するのは危険な仕事だ.
3 はっきりしない地域；不安定な状態 ▪ They lived in a *no-man's-land* between slavery and freedom. 彼らは奴隷状態とも自由の状態ともわからないような状態で暮らしていた.

no A, no B AがないならBもない ▪ *No* work, *no* food. 働かないなら食べられないよ ▪ *No* dollars, *no* imports from the States. ドルがなければ米国からの輸入もできない.

no one **1** /nóʊwʌn/ 誰も…ない ▪ *No one* can do it. 誰もできない.
2 /nóʊwʌ́n/ 誰も一人では…ない ▪ *No one* man can do it. 誰でも一人ではできない.

no way →WAY.

... or no …であろうとなかろうと ▪ Cold *or no*, you must go today. 寒かろうとなかろうと君はきょう行かなければならない ▪ Whether *or no*, I will go. どっちにしても僕は行くよ.

say no 「ノー」と言う ▪ I *say no*, once for all. 私は断然いやです.

The noes have it. 反対投票が多数だ ▪ *The noes* in the former question *had it*. 先の問題では反対投票が多数だった.

***There is no** doing.* →THERE.

will not take no for an answer 否とは言わせない ▪ You must come and see us. No, I *won't take no for an answer*. ぜひ遊びにおいでください. いや，否とは言わせませんよ. ☞W. Churchill, *My Early Life* (1930)から.

nob[1] /nɑb|nɔb/ 名 ***get ... into*** [***through***] *one's* ***nob*** 《米俗》…を理解する ▪ He is a dull boy and cannot *get* it *into his nob*. 彼は頭の鈍い子で，それがどうしてものみ込めない. ☞nob＝head.

one for his nob **1**《トランプ》(cribbage (2人でするトランプゲーム)でめくり札と同じ組の)ジャック (knave) で取れる1点 ▪ Yes, you get "*one for his nob*" by having the Knave of Trumps. そうです，切り札のジャックを持っていれば1点取れます.
2 頭への一撃 ▪ I gave him *one for his nob* and he fell senseless. やつの頭に一撃加えると，気絶して倒れた.

nob[2] /nɑb|nɔb/ 名 ***a nob of the first water*** 《俗》一流の人物 ▪ I see *nobs of the first water* are looking with a fatherly eye into our affairs. お歴々が好意的な目で我々の事件を調べてくれているのがわかる.

noble /nóʊbəl/ 形 ***the noble art*** [***science***] (***of defence***) ボクシング(のような護身術) ▪ Tom was much his superior at *the noble art of defence*. トムはボクシングでは彼よりもずっと優れていた. ☞"Might is right." (力は正義なり)が支配していた時代には，護身術を知らない者は下品 (ignoble) だと考えられていたことから.

nobody /nóʊbədi/ 名代 ***a mere nobody*** 名もない人 ▪ They are *mere nobodies*. 彼らは名もない人たちだ.

be nobody's fool →be no FOOL.

like nobody's business →BUSINESS.

Mr. Nobody. →MR..

nobody home →HOME.

Nobody hurt. 《米俗》(事件が)大したことはない ▪ It was nobody's fault, *nobody hurt*. 誰のせいでもないし大したこともなかった.

no-brainer /nòʊbréɪnər/ 名 ***be a no-brainer*** 《口》明白である，わかりやすい ▪ Protecting the environment *is a no-brainer*. 環境を保護しなければならないのは言うまでもない.

nod[1] /nɑd|nɔd/ 名 ***a nod and a wink*** 《英》ほのめかし，合図 ▪ Everything was done by *a nod and a wink* from the captain. 主将の合図ひとつで万事が運んだ.

A nod is as good as a wink (***to a blind horse***). 《諺》(目の見えぬ馬には)うなずいても目くばせしても同じこと《むだである》，「馬の耳に念仏」 ▪ I will say no more at present, *a nod is as good as a wink*. 今はもうこれ以上言うまい. いくら言って聞かせてもむだだからな.

be at** a person's **nod 人にあごで使われる，勝手にされる ▪ The whole empire *was at his nod*. 全帝国が彼の意のままに左右された.

collar a nod 《米俗》眠る ▪ You can't *collar nods* all day. 一日中眠るわけにいきませんよ.

get the nod 《米口》 **1** 口が見つかる ▪ He has *gotten the nod* at last. 彼はとうとう勤め口を見つけた. ☞「採用の承諾をもらう」が原義.
2《ボクシング》判定で勝つ ▪ The prizefighter *got the nod*. そのボクサーは判定で勝った.
3《英口》承認を得る ▪ He *got the nod* as a poet. 彼は詩人として認められた.

give** a person **a nod 人に黙礼する ▪ He *gave* me *a nod* as he passed. 彼は通りすがりに私に黙礼した.

give ... the nod 《口》 **1** …を是認する ▪ Industry has at last *given* literature *the nod*. 産業界もついに文学を是認した.
2 (人)に同意する，許可を出す ▪ They *gave* us *the*

N

nod. Now we can start building. 許可が下りた. さあ, これで建設に取りかかれる.

have** a person **at** one's **nod 人をあごで使っている ▪ You *have* multitudes of men *at your nod*. あなたはたくさんの人々をあごで使っておいでです.

on the nod 《英口》 **1** 信用で, 顔で ▪ We went into a shop and wanted to be served *on the nod*. 我々はとある店へ入って行って, 顔で売ってもらいたいと言った.

2 票決によらずに, 満場一致で ▪ The agenda was accepted *on the nod*. その会議事項は票決によらずに承認された.

3 《俗》 (麻薬で)うとうとして ▪ I gave him half a grain of LSD and he went *on the nod*. 彼に LSD をちょっぴり与えると, うとうとし始めた.

the land of Nod 《古風》 眠りの国 ▪ I'm going to *the land of Nod*. 僕は寝るつもりだ. ☞《聖》 *Gen*. 4. 16に現れる地名との地口から.

nod[2] /nɑd|nɔd/ 動 ***be on nodding terms with*** …とは会釈を交わす程度の知り合いである ▪ I'*m on nodding terms with* him. 彼とは会えば会釈をする程度の間柄だ.

catch** a person **nodding 人のへまを見つける ▪ There is hardly an author but *is caught nodding*. へまを見つけられない作家はほとんどいない.

(Even) Homer sometimes nods. 《諺》 ホメロスのような大詩人でもときどきへまをやる,「弘法も筆の誤り」(Horace, *Ars Poetica* 359) ▪ Scientific reason, like *Homer, sometimes nods*. 科学的理性も, ホメロスのようにときには誤ることがある.

have a nodding acquaintance **1** 会えば会釈する程度の間柄だ ▪ I can't say I know him well, but we *have a nodding acquaintance*. 彼をよく知っているとは言えないが, 会えば会釈する程度には知っている.

2 皮相の知識を持っている (*with*) ▪ He *has* more than *a nodding acquaintance with* art and literature. 彼は美術と文学に対して皮相の知識以上のものを持っている.

nod** one's **head →HEAD[1].

nod** one's **head off 無性にこくりこくりする ▪ He is *nodding his head off*. 彼はさかんにこくりこくりやっている.

nod like a mandolin しきりにうなずく ▪ At that the child began to *nod like a mandolin*. それを聞くと子供はしきりにうなずき始めた.

nod to its fall **1** 今にも倒れそうに傾く ▪ The house is *nodding to its fall*. 家は今にも倒れそうに傾いている.

2 今にも滅亡しそうになっている ▪ This vast and ill-founded empire seems indeed *nodding to its fall*. この広大な, 基盤のしっかりしていない帝国は確かに今にも滅亡しそうに見える.

noggin /nɑ́gɪn|nɔ́g-/ 名 ***use the (old) noggin*** 《米俗》 考える ▪ That's *using the old noggin*. それこそ頭を働かせるというものだ.

no-go /nóʊgóʊ/ 形 ***a no-go area*** 《主に英》 **1** 立入禁止区域, 無法地帯 ▪ This part of the city has become *a no-go area*. 市のこのあたりは無法地帯と化している.

2 議論しない話題 ▪ This subject is *a* definite *no-go area*. この話題は絶対に話し合わないこと.

nohow /nóʊhàʊ/ 形 副 ***feel [look] nohow*** 気分がすぐれない[様子をしている] ▪ I *feel* all *nohow* today. きょうは全然気分がすぐれない ▪ I dare say I *looked nohow*. たぶん私は気分のすぐれない顔つきをしていたのだろう.

nohow you [they] can fix it どんなにしても ▪ I couldn't read a chapter in the Bible *nohow you could fix it*. 私はどんなにしても聖書の一章が読めなかった ▪ They would have nothing to do with that affair, *nohow they could fix it*. 彼らはどうしてもその事件に巻きこまれたくなかった.

noise[1] /nɔɪz/ 名 ***a [the] big noise*** 《俗》 名士, 顔役 ▪ She thinks she's *the big noise* in Great-White Alley. あの女は自分はグレート・ホワイト街の花形だと思っている.

have a noise under** one's **hood 《英俗》 気が違っている ▪ That man over there *has a noise under his hood*. 向こうにいる男は気が違っている.

have noises in the ears 耳鳴りがする ▪ Sometimes I *have noises in the ears*. ときどき耳鳴りがする.

hold** one's **noise 〚主に命令文で〛 黙る ▪ *Hold your noise*! 黙れ.

make a noise **1** 騒ぐ ▪ Don't *make* such *a noise*! そんなに騒ぐんじゃない.

2 ぶうぶう言う, 不平をもらす (*about*) ▪ She had a toothache and she was *making a noise about* it. 彼女は歯が痛くて, そのことをぶうぶう言っていた.

3 自慢する (*about*) ▪ He is *making a noise about* his new car. 彼は新しく買った自動車のことをぺちゃくちゃ自慢している.

make a noise in the world 世間の評判になる, 有名になる《良い意味でも悪い意味でも使う》 ▪ Such persons have *made a noise in the world*. そのような人々が世間の評判になった ▪ This scandal will *make a noise in the world*. このスキャンダルは世間の評判になるだろう.

make a noise like a hoop [drum, tree] and roll away [beat it, leave] 《戯》 急いで立ち去る ▪ And now we'll just *make a noise like a hoop and roll away*. それでは急いで立ち去ることにしよう.

make (all) the right noises お世辞に人の意に沿うことを言う, うわべだけ熱意を示す ▪ He *made all the right noises* about my presentation. 彼は私の発表について一応好意的な口ぶりだった.

make ... noises (about) 《口》 **1** (…に対して)関心[意図]をほのめかす ▪ He has been *making noises about* changing his job. 彼はそれとなく仕事を変えたいと匂わせている.

2 〚形容詞を伴って〛 …のように発言する ▪ You should *make* more friendly *noises*. もっと友好的

N

に言うべきだ.

white noise 白色ノイズ[騒音にかぶせる音] ▪ He tried to tune the radio, but all he got was *white noise*. 彼はラジオのダイヤルを合わせようとしたが聞こえてくるのはホワイトノイズだけだった.

noise[2] /nɔɪz/ 動 ***noise abroad*** [***about***] …を盛んに言い広める ▪ The end of war soon *was noised abroad*. 戦争の終結がやがて盛んに噂された ▪ It *was noised about* that he had been arrested. 彼が捕えられたというもっぱらの評判だった.

nomination /nɑ̀mənéɪʃən|nɔ̀m-/ 名 ***place*** *a person's* ***name in nomination for*** 《口》人を…の候補者に指名する ▪ We *placed your name in nomination for* the office of president. あなたを社長候補者に指名しました.

nonage /nɑ́nɪdʒ|nóʊnɪdʒ/ 名 ***be still in*** *one's* ***nonage*** まだ未成年である ▪ My son *is still in his nonage*. 息子はまだ未成年だ.

nonce /nɑns|nɔns/ 名 ***at the very nonce*** ちょうどこの瞬間に ▪ *At the very nonce* the lift stopped and the light went off. ちょうどその瞬間にエレベーターが止まり明かりも消えた.

for the nonce 《雅》さし当たって, 当分 ▪ You can use the little room for a studio *for the nonce*. 当分その小部屋をスタジオに使っていい.

none /nʌn/ 代 ***be none of*** **1** 決して…の一人ではない ▪ He *is none of* the party. 彼は決してその一行の一人ではない.

2 決して…でない ▪ It *is none of* my business. それは僕の知ったことではない ▪ This marriage *was none of* her own choosing. この結婚は決して彼女が自ら選んだものではなかった.

3 〚最上級を伴って〛全然…でない ▪ His English *is none of* the best. 彼の英語は全然よくない ▪ His pronunciation *is none of* the clearest. 彼の発音は決して明瞭でない.

be second to none →SECOND[2].

have [***want***] ***none of it*** [***that***] 《口》…はごめんだ; それを認めない[拒否する] ▪ We told him all about our plan, but he would *have none of it*. 我々は自分たちの計画のことを彼に全部話したが, 彼はそんなことはごめんだと言った ▪ Let me *have none of* your chat. もうおしゃべりはよしてくれ ▪ The management had offered a 5% pay rise but the workers *wanted none of it*. 経営者側は5%の賃上げを提示したが労組はそれを突っぱねた.

none better (***than*** *one*) (自分が)誰よりもよく ▪ He is aware, *none better* (*than* he), that it is not perfect. 彼は誰よりもよくそれが完全でないことを知っている.

none but 《文》…の他の誰も…ない ▪ *None but* the brave deserve the fair. 勇者でなくては美女を得るに値しない ▪ They chose *none but* the best. 一番すぐれた人しか選ばれなかった.

none of *one's* ***beeswax*** 《戯》= NONE of one's business.

none of *one's* ***business*** →BUSINESS.

None of (***your***)***…!*** …はごめんだ ▪ *None of your* lip! 生意気言うな ▪ *None of your* tricks! いたずらはごめんだ.

none other than …にほかならない ▪ This is *none other than* the house of God. これは神の宮にほかならない ▪ This was *none other than* the general. これは将軍その人だった.

none so あまり…でない ▪ They are *none so* fond of him. 彼らはあまり彼を好いてはいない.

none so … as ほど…な人はない ▪ There are *none so* deaf *as* those who won't hear. 聞こうとしない人々ほど耳の聞こえない人はいない.

none the 〚比較級を伴って〛決して…でない (*for*) ▪ He is *none the* happier *for* his wealth. 彼は金があっても少しも幸福ではない ▪ I am *none the* worse *for* a single failure. たった1回失敗したところで少しもへこたれてはいない.

none the less →LESS.

none too あまり…ではない (not very) ▪ He is *none too* clever. 彼はあまり利口ではない ▪ The pay is *none too* high. 給料はあまり高くはない.

none too soon [***early***] だいぶ遅れて, 遅すぎて ▪ He arrived *none too early*. 彼はだいぶ遅れて到着した.

non-linear /nɑ̀nlíniər|nɔ̀n-/ 形 ***go non-linear*** 《口》(ある特定の妄想で)非常に興奮する[怒り狂う] ▪ Age seems to make us *go non-linear* easily. 年をとると怒りっぽくなるようだ.

nonplus /nɑ̀nplʌ́s|nɔ̀n-/ 名 ***at a nonplus*** 途方にくれて, 閉口して ▪ Prophets are never *at a nonplus* and never surprised by a question. 予言者というものは決して途方にくれたり質問にまごついたりしない.

put [***bring, drive, reduce***] *a person* ***to a nonplus*** 人を困惑させる ▪ Hasty speech often *drives* a man either *to a nonplus* or to stammering. 急いで話そうとすると往々にして行きうまるか, さもなければどもってしまう.

take *a person* ***at a nonplus*** 人に不意打ちをくわせる ▪ As I *took* you *at a nonplus*, it did very well. 不意打ちだったので非常にうまくいった.

nonsense /nɑ́nsens|nɔ́nsəns/ 名 ***knock the nonsense out of*** →take the NONSENSE out of.

make nonsense 意味をなさない ▪ This passage *makes nonsense*. この一節は意味をなさない.

make nonsense of …を無意味なものにする ▪ This *makes nonsense of* the policy. これではその政策は無意味なものになってしまう. ☞《英》では make a nonsense of とも言う.

make sense out of nonsense →make SENSE (out) of.

None of your nonsense! ばかなことはよせ ▪ Come, *none of your nonsense*, give me back my clothes. さあ, ばかはよして僕の着るものを返せ.

stand no nonsense/not stand any nonsense ばかなまねは許さない ▪ I won't *stand any*

N

nonsense from people working in my firm. 私は自分の会社で働いている人々にばかなまねは許さない ▪ Mr. Mills will *stand no nonsense* about coming late to school. ミルズ先生は学校に遅刻するなどというばかなまねは許さない.

stuff and nonsense →STUFF[1].

take* [*knock*] *the nonsense out of …の気ままを直す ▪ Contact with other boys will *take the nonsense out of* the boy. 他の子供に接するとあの子の気ままが直りましょう.

talk* [*speak*] *nonsense たわごとを言う ▪ Don't *talk nonsense*! Shame on you. ばかを言うな! 恥を知れ ▪ If they *speak nonsense*, they believe they are talking humor. 彼らはたわごとを言っているくせに, ユーモアをとばしていると思いこんでいる.

nook /nʊk/ 名 ***every nook and corner* [*cranny*]/*nooks and crannies*** すみずみ, いたる所 ▪ I looked in *every nook and corner* of the room. 私は部屋の中をくまなく捜した.

noon[1] /nuːn/ 名 ***it's high noon* (*for*)** 《新聞・報道》今が(…の)対決の時である ▪ *It's high noon* now and the showdown is about to begin. いよいよ決着の時で, まさに対決が始まろうとしている.

noon[2] /nuːn/ 動 ***noon it*** 《米口》正午の時を過ごす ▪ We *nooned it* just above the entrance of a large river. 大きな河口の少し上手で正午を過ごした.

noonday /núːndèɪ/ 名 ***as clear as noonday*** きわめて明らかで (Coverdale, *Job* 11. 17) ▪ It is *as clear as noonday* that crying will not mend matters. 泣いたところで事態が回復しないのは明白だ.

(*as*) *clear* [*plain*] *as the sun at noonday* 白日のごとく明々白々で ▪ That he was not a thief was *as clear* to her *as the sun at noonday*. 彼が泥棒でないことは彼女には白日のごとく明白だった.

at the noonday of …の盛り[絶頂]で ▪ He was *at the noonday of* his prosperity. 彼は繁栄の絶頂に達していた.

noose /nuːs/ 名 ***have the noose round one's neck*** 首つりなわを首に巻かれている《必ず処刑される》 ▪ The evidence is dead against him. He's as good as *got the noose round his neck*. 証拠は彼にとって断然不利だ. 彼は首つりなわを首に巻かれているようなものだ.

put one's neck* [*head*] *into the noose*/*be caught in one's own noose 自ら危地に陥る, わなにかかる ▪ I have *put my neck into the noose* like a pigeon. ハトみたいに私は自らわなにかかってしまった ▪ Am I tricked now? *Caught in my own noose*. 今度はだまされたのかな. 自縄自縛だ.

The noose is hanging. 《米俗》万事用意ができた ▪ *The noose is hanging*; each man will attempt to outdo the others. 用意はすべて整った. めいめいが相手を出し抜こうと努めるだろう.

noplace /nóʊplèɪs/ 副 ***get noplace*** → GET nowhere.

Norfolk /nɔ́ːrfək/ 名 ***a Norfolk dumpling*** ノーフォーク風蒸しだんご, 愚鈍な人 ▪ He is *a Norfolk dumpling* through and through. 彼は骨の髄までのろまな男である.

normal /nɔ́ːrməl/ 名 ***above normal*** 平均[標準]以上で ▪ He weighs two pounds *above normal*. 彼は体重が平均より2ポンド重い.

below normal 平均[標準]以下で ▪ The temperature is three degrees *below normal*. 気温は平均より3度低い.

Norman /nɔ́ːrmən/ 形 ***have Norman blood in one's veins* [*blood*]** ノルマン貴族の出である ▪ They claim to *have Norman blood in their blood*. 彼らはノルマン貴族の出だと称している.

north /nɔːrθ/ 名副 ***a little more north*** 《俗》(酒を)ややきつく ▪ An old salt delights to order his steward to make his grog "*a little more north*." 老水夫はボーイに火酒を「ややきつく」してくれとよく好んで言う.

by north 微北 ▪ This leaves me fronting south *by north*. これで私は南微北に向かっていることになる.

in the north of …(内)の北部に ▪ Russia is *in the north of* Europe. ロシアはヨーロッパの北部にある.

north and south **1** 南北に長く ▪ This bay lies *north and south*. この湾は南北に長く横たわっている ▪ They buried him in the churchyard, *north and south*. 彼は教会の墓地に南北に寝せて埋葬された《異端者の印》.

2《英俗》口 ▪ Dust floating in the air gets in your *north and south*. 空気中を浮遊しているほこりが口に入ってくる. ☞mouth の押韻俗語.

north of …の北方に ▪ The hill stands three miles *north of* the city. その丘は町の3マイル北方にある.

on the north of …の北に接して ▪ Kawaguchi is *on the north of* Tokyo. 川口は東京の北に接している.

to the north of …の北方に(当たって) ▪ Omiya lies *to the north of* Tokyo. 大宮は東京の北方にある.

too far north 《俗》利口すぎる, 悪賢い ▪ You will find me *too far north* for you. 君よりも僕のほうが役者が一枚も二枚も上なんだからな ▪ She is what I call *too far north* for that. 彼女は私にいわせれば悪賢い女性でその手はくわない. ☞イングランド北部の Yorkshire の住民が値切るとき悪賢いところから.

up north 《口》北へ[に], 北部で ▪ What's happening *up north*? 北部で何が起こっているか?

northing /nɔ́ːrθɪŋ, nɔ́ːrðɪŋ/ 名 ***have northing*** (天体が)北進する ▪ When the moon *has northing* or southing the shade is elliptical. 月が北進または南進するときには影が楕円形である.

nose[1] /noʊz/ 名 ***a Greek nose*** 鼻梁の高い鉤(かぎ)鼻 ▪ She complained of her *Greek nose*, before having plastic surgery to correct it. 彼女は整形外科で矯正手術を受けるまでは高い鉤鼻を愚痴っていた.

a nose dive **1** 飛行機の急降下 ▪ He got out of *a nose dive*. 彼は急降下を避けた.

2（物価・証券の）暴落 ▪ The stock market took *a nose dive* last week. 株式市場は先週暴落した.

a nose job 鼻の（美容）整形（手術） ▪ Dad wouldn't allow me to get *a nose job*. パパはどうしても私に鼻の整形を受けさせてくれなかった.

a nose of wax 他人の言いなりになる人，思い通りになるもの ▪ He was *a nose of wax* with this woman. 彼はこの女性に対しては全く言いなりだった ▪ You may turn and set as you please oral tradition, *that nose of wax*. あのどうにでもなる口承というものは，好きなように変え整えることができる.

a political nose 政治に対する直感，民衆の欲求を本能的に察知する才 ▪ The minister is possessed of *a political nose* which rarely fails him. 大臣は滅多に外れない政治勘を備えている.

a Roman nose かなり大きく肉太の鼻 ▪ I had *a* really *Roman nose*, so I booked myself in to a plastic surgeon. ひどく大きい鼻だったので整形外科医の予約をとった.

a white nose 小さな白い波がしら ▪ Many *a* "*white nose*" is chequering the blueness of the open water.「小さな白い波がしら」の数々が広い水面の青さに変化を与えている.

(*as*) *plain as the nose on* [***in***] *one's* ***face*** 《口・皮肉》きわめて明白で ▪ That he's the most suitable of all the candidates is *as plain as the nose on your face*. 彼が全候補者の中で一番適任だということは至って明白だ.

before *one's* ***nose*** 自分の真正面に［を］ ▪ I ran straight *before my nose*, till I could run no longer. 私はまっすぐに前方へ走っていって，しまいにはもう走れなくなってしまった.

bite [***snap***] *a person's* ***nose off*** （人の言い分を聞かないで）がみがみ言う，つっけんどんな返事をする ▪ He *bit my nose off*, "Don't annoy me." 彼はつっけんどんに「うるさい」と言った ▪ I asked him if he was free in the afternoon, but he *snapped my nose off*. 午後から暇かと尋ねたが，彼はけんもほろろに答えた.

bloody *a person's* ***nose*** 人の（自慢の）鼻をへし折る ▪ I'll *bloody his nose* for him. やつの天狗の鼻をへし折ってやろう.

blow *one's* ***nose*** 鼻をかむ《ときに涙を隠すため》 ▪ He *blows his nose* with a handkerchief. 彼はハンカチで鼻をかむ.

blow *one's* ***own nose*** 《米俗》自分でやっていける ▪ He can *blow his own nose* all right. 彼はけっこう自分でやっていける.

blow through *one's* ***nose*** 鼻を鳴らす ▪ The captain would *blow through his nose*. 船長は鼻を鳴らすのだった.

by a nose 《競馬》鼻の差で; わずかの差で ▪ The horse won the race *by a nose*. その馬が鼻の差で勝った ▪ He won the election *by a nose*. 彼はわずかの差で選挙に勝った.

cannot see further [***can see no further***] ***than*** (***the end of***) *one's* ***nose*** （他の可能性や自分の行動の結果を）予測できない，目先が利かない，洞察力がない ▪ He is so selfish he *can't see further than his nose*. 彼はとても自分本位だから相手の立場に立てない.

cock (***up***) ***the*** [*one's*] ***nose*** 鼻をつんと上へ向ける《冷淡・軽蔑の表情》 ▪ He *cocks his nose* upon disgrace. 彼は恥辱に対しても鼻をそらして平気だ.

count [***tell***] ***noses*** （出席者・賛成者などの）人数を数える ▪ Keep still, everyone. I'm *counting noses*. みんな，じっとしていなさい. 人数を数えているから.

cut off *one's* ***nose*** わが身を傷つける ▪ Do it if you wish, but you'll *cut off your nose*. やりたければやってごらん，でもわが身を傷つけることになりますよ.

cut off *one's* ***nose to spite*** [***to be revenged of***] *one's* ***face*** 人が憎さにかえってわが身を傷つける ▪ Don't *cut off your nose to spite your face*! 短気は損気だ ▪ To annoy his mother, Bill married that stupid widow, *cutting off his nose to spite his face*. 母親を困らせるためにビルはあの愚かな後家さんと結婚して，かえってわが身を傷つけた. ☞「自分が醜いので鼻を切り取ってかえって醜さが増す」が原義.

find *one's* ***nose out of joint*** 寵愛などを横取りされる，鼻をあかされる（→put a person's NOSE out of joint） ▪ Now that there is a baby boy in the family, Mary will *find her nose out of joint*. こんど家に男の子が生まれたから，メアリーは寵愛を横取りされるだろう.

follow *one's* ***nose*** 《口》 **1**（鼻の向いた方向に）まっすぐに行く ▪ Turn sharp to the right and *follow your nose*. 急に右へ曲がってまっすぐに行きなさい.

2（意の向く所に）まっしぐらに［本能のままに］進む ▪ Juan *followed* honor and *his nose*. フアンは名誉と本能の導くままに進んだ.

get [***have, receive***] ***a bloody nose*** （競争に負けて）鼻をへし折られる ▪ Mary argued so cleverly that I *got a bloody nose*. メアリーはとても巧みに論じたので，僕は鼻をへし折られてしまった. ☞「鼻血を出す」が原義.

get it up *one's* ***nose*** のぼせ上がる ▪ He has *got it up his nose* and doesn't object to being bossed. 彼はのぼせ上がっていて，こき使われても平気だ.

get *one's* ***nose down to*** 身を入れて（仕事）をする ▪ He is really *getting his nose down to* business. 彼は本当に身を入れて商売をやっている.

get (***right***) ***up*** *a person's* ***nose*** 《英口》人を怒らせる，いらいらさせる ▪ His sneer *got up my nose*. 彼のせせら笑いは頭にきた.

give *a person* ***a bloody nose***/《英》***bloody*** *a person's* ***nose*** 決定的な打撃を与える，窮地に追い込む ▪ We *gave* our opponents *a bloody nose* in the debate. ディベートで相手チームに決定打を浴びせた.

Go blow your own nose! 《米俗》大きなお世話だ ▪ Keep your mouth shut and *go blow your own nose!* 黙れ，大きなお世話だ.

have a clean nose 《米俗》非の打ちようがない，罪がない ▪ Thank goodness he *has a clean nose*! ありがたい. 彼は非の打ちようがない.

have a good [***bad***] ***nose*** (特に犬が)かぎつけるのがうまい[へただ] ▪ The dog *has a* wonderfully *good nose*. その犬はすばらしく鼻がよくきく.

have a nose for 《口》…をかぎつけるのがうまい ▪ Those correspondents *have the* proverbial *nose for* news. その通信員たちはニュースをかぎつけるのがうまいので有名だ.

have a nose (***round***) 《英口》辺りを見回す ▪ He left the room for a minute, so I *had a nose round*. 彼がちょっと部屋を出たので中を見回した.

have *one's* ***nose*** (***buried*** [***stuck***]) ***in a book*** 読書に熱中している ▪ My son always *has his nose in a book*. せがれはいつも読書に熱中している.

have [***stick***] *one's* ***nose in the air*** 傲(ごう)慢な態度をとる ▪ Our next-door neighbor always *has her nose in the air*. 隣に住む女性はいつもお高くとまっている.

have *one's* ***nose out of joint*** (鼻を明かされて)イライラしている, 欲求不満である ▪ He's *had his nose out of joint* since she got promoted. 彼女が昇進して以来彼はイライラしている.

hold *one's* ***nose*** **1** (悪臭・非道などに)鼻をつまむ ▪ It's stinking! *Hold your nose*, sir. ああ臭い. 鼻をつまみたまえ.
2 不快な[違法な, いやな]ことを無視しようと努める ▪ I hated doing it, but I *held my nose* and signed the contract. ほんとうはいやだったけれど, 私はしぶしぶ契約に署名した.

keep *one's* ***nose clean*** 《口》ごたごたに巻き込まれないようにする ▪ If you only *keep your nose clean*, I'll let you have it. ごたごたに巻き込まれるようなことさえしなければ, それをあげるよ.

keep *one's* ***nose out of*** 《口》…に口を出さない, 干渉しない ▪ *Keep your nose out of* this! このことに口を出さないでくれ.

keep [***put, hold***] *a person's* [*one's*] ***nose to the grindstone*** →hold a person's nose to the GRINDSTONE.

lead *a person* ***by the nose*** 人を意のままに使う, あごで使う (cf. Sh., *Oth.* 1. 3. 407) ▪ The terrible Mrs. Juggins *leads* her husband *by the nose*. おっかないジャギンス夫人は夫をあごで使っている. ☞牛・馬・クマなどを鼻につけたひもでひっぱるところから.

look down *one's* ***nose*** (***at***) (…を)じろりと見下す, 軽蔑する ▪ He *looked down his nose at* the offer. 彼はその申し出を鼻であしらった.

make a bridge of *a person's* ***nose*** (飲酒などで)人を負かす, だしぬく ▪ Pray, my Lord, don't *make a bridge of my nose*. お願いですから御前さま, 私をだしぬかないでください.

make a long nose 《俗》(鼻先に親指をあて他の4本の指を扇形に広げて)人をばかにした格好をする (*at*) ▪ He *made a long nose* in the direction of her house. 彼は彼女の家に向かってばかにした格好をした.

make *a person's* ***nose swell*** 人をうらやましがらせる ▪ That will *make my* brother's *nose swell*. それには弟もうらやましがるだろう.

measure noses 《口》出くわす ▪ We *measured noses* at the crossroads. 我々は十字路で出くわした.

One's ***nose can light a candle.*** 1杯やって赤い鼻をしている ▪ *Their noses* will *be able to light a candle*. 彼らは1杯やって赤い鼻をしている.

One's ***nose is out of joint.*** 鼻をあかされている ▪ I guess *her nose is out of joint*. 彼女は鼻をあかされたのではないかと思う.

nose to nose 顔をつき合わせて ▪ The two parties would often meet *nose to nose* in the same street. 両派の人々はよく同じ通りで鉢合わせをした.

nose to tail 《英》(車が)前の車につくほど接近して, くびすを接して ▪ Traffic was *nose to tail* on Route 18 this morning. 今朝国道18号線は数珠(じゅず)つなぎの渋滞だった.

not see an inch beyond *one's* ***nose*** 1寸先も見えない, 洞察力がない ▪ The trouble with you lawyers is that you *never see an inch beyond your noses*. 君たち弁護士の困ったところは, 1寸先も見えないということだ.

on the nose **1** 《口》寸分違わず, きっかり ▪ You said you would be home at six, and you were right *on the nose*. 君は6時に帰ると言って, 6時きっかりだったね.
2 〚形容詞的に〛(馬・犬のレースで)1着を予想される ▪ He bet $10 on the favorite *on the nose*. 彼は1着を予想される人気馬(本命馬)に10ドル賭けた.

pay through the nose 《口》法外な代価を取られる ▪ You'll have to *pay through the nose* if you stay at that hotel. あのホテルに泊まったら目が飛び出るほどぼられますよ. ☞「不満の鼻を鳴らしながら払う」の意から.

poke [***push, thrust, stick***] *one's* ***nose into*** (他人のこと)に口を出す, 干渉する ▪ You're always *sticking your nose into* my affairs. 君はいつも僕のことに口を出してばかりいる.

powder *one's* ***nose*** 《戯》(女性が)トイレにいく ▪ She disappeared to *powder her nose*. 彼女は座をはずしてお手洗いに行った.

put *a person's* ***nose out of joint*** **1** 人を押しのけて愛顧を得る, (愛顧を得ている)人に取って代わる ▪ I hope the new baby won't *put young Peter's nose out of joint*. こんどの赤ちゃんがピーター坊やが受けている愛情を横取りしてしまわなければいいが.
2 人の計画をくつがえす, 人の鼻をあかす ▪ This method of proceeding *put their noses* quite *out of joint*. こうした事の運び方がすっかり彼らの鼻をあかした. ☞→find one's NOSE out of joint.

rub [***push***] *a person's* ***nose in it*** [***the dirt***] 《口》人のした失敗のことをしつこく言う; 遠慮なく注意する, ずけずけ言う ▪ I let you down badly, but don't *rub my nose in it* now. 僕は君をひどい目にあわせたが, そのことをしつこく言わないでくれ ▪ He made another mistake, so I *rubbed his nose in it*. 彼がまた間違えたので, やかましく言った.

see beyond (***the end*** [***length***] ***of***) *one's* ***nose***/ ***see farther than the end of*** *one's* ***nose*** 洞察力がある ▪ If anyone can *see beyond the end of his nose*, Phil can. 誰かに洞察力があるとすればフィルこそその人だ ▪ He's ignorant and can't *see farther than the end of his nose*. 彼は無知で先も読めない.

show *one's* ***nose in*** …に顔を出す ▪ He seldom *shows his nose in* his shop. 彼はめったに店に顔を出さない.

snap *a person's* ***nose off*** →bite a person's NOSE off.

speak through the nose 鼻声で言う ▪ The Puritans *spoke through the nose* and were spoken of as snuffling saints. 清教徒は鼻声で話したので鼻声の聖徒とあだ名された.

stick [***thrust***] *one's* ***nose into*** →poke one's NOSE into.

tell noses →count NOSEs.

thumb *one's* ***nose at*** →THUMB[2].

turn up *one's* ***nose*** (***at***)/***turn*** *one's* ***nose up*** (***at***) 《口》 **1** (提供されたもの)を軽蔑する, 鼻であしらう ▪ He *turned up his nose at* my offer. 彼は私の申し出を鼻であしらった.
2 (ばかにして…)を拒絶する ▪ He *turns up his nose at* hamburger. 彼はハンバーグなんか, と言って見向きもしない.

under *a person's* [*one's*] (***very***) ***nose*** **1** (気づかれずに)すぐ目の前で ▪ You fail to observe things passing *under your nose*. 君はすぐ目の前を過ぎていく事柄が見えないのです ▪ Look! There it is, right *under your nose*. ほら! 君の目の前にあるじゃないか.
2 (人を無視して)人の目の前で ▪ The cat ate it up *under my very nose*. 猫が僕の目の前でそいつを平らげてしまった ▪ The armed robber walked out of the bank right *under the nose of* the customers. 武装した強盗は客たちのつい目の先を歩いて銀行から出て行った.

with *one's* ***nose at the grindstone*** あくせくと ▪ The clerks, *with their noses at the grindstone*, were in the dingy room. 事務員たちはむさくるしい部屋の中であくせく働いていた.

(***with*** *one's*) ***nose in*** (***the***) ***air*** 鼻をつんと上げて; 傲(ごう)慢な態度で ▪ He walked off, *nose in air*. 彼は鼻をつんと上げてすたすた行ってしまった ▪ He always walks past *with his nose in the air*. 彼はいつもいばりくさって通り過ぎる.

nose[2] /noʊz/ 動 ***nose a job in everything*** 何からでも自分の利益になることをかぎ出す, 何でも物にしようとする ▪ He *noses a job in everything*. 彼は何でも物にしようとする.

nose *one's* ***way*** 前進する ▪ The plane *nosed its way* through the fog. 飛行機は霧の中を突き進んだ.

nose-bag /nóʊzbæɡ/ 名 ***put*** [***get***] ***on the nose-bag*** 《俗》(急いで)食事をする ▪ I haven't *put on the nose-bag* yet. まだめしを食っていない. ☞nose-bag「食べ物」.

nose dive /nóʊzdàɪv/ 名 ***go into a nose dive*** 《口》挫折する; がっくりくる ▪ The man *went into a nose dive* after his wife died. その男は妻が死ぬとがっくりきてしまった.

nosey, nosy /nóʊzi/ 形 ***a Nos***(***e***)***y Parker***/ ***a nos***(***e***)***y parker*** 《英口》おせっかいやき, ほじくり屋 ▪ I've never met such *a Nosy Parker* as he is. 彼みたいなおせっかいやきにお目にかかったことがない. ☞16世紀のカンタベリー大主教 Matthew Parker は他人事に口を挟むので有名だったことから.

nostril /nástrəl|nɔ́s-/ 名 ***stink in the nostrils of*** …にとってとてもいやなものだ, 鼻もちならない (《聖》*Amos* 9. 10) ▪ That makes religion *stink in the nostrils of* many. それで宗教が多くの人々にとって鼻もちならなく思えるのだ.

the breath of *one's* ***nostrils*** →BREATH.

not /nɑt|nɔt/ 副 ***as … as not*** どちらかと言えば ▪ He'll be at home *as* likely *as not*. 彼はおそらく家にいるだろう ▪ I would *as* soon do it *as not*. どちらかと言えばやってみたい.

if not →IF.

more often than not →OFTEN.

not a single ただ一つ[一人]も…ない ▪ There was *not a single* word of gratitude from him. 彼からはひとことも感謝の言葉はなかった.

not all that … 格別に…ではない ▪ How was the movie?—*Not all that* good. 映画どうだった?—特にどうってことなかったよ.

not *A*, ***but*** *B* AではなくてB ▪ He is *not* my son, *but* my nephew. 彼は私の息子ではなくておいだ.

not but that →BUT[1].

not one [***a man, the man***] ***to*** *do* …するような人間ではない ▪ He is *not one to* steal. 彼は盗みをするような人間ではない.

not only [***simply, merely***] *A* ***but*** (***also***) *B* AばかりでなくBも ▪ He *not only* reads, *but* writes poetry. 彼は詩を読むばかりでなく書く ▪ *Not only* he *but also* I am invited. 彼ばかりではなく私も招かれている.

not so そうではない ▪ You will apologize?—*Not so*. 謝罪しますか?—いいえ.

not that →THAT.

not that …, but that …というのではなくて…というのである ▪ *Not that* you resemble a monkey, *but that* the monkey resembles you. 君がサルに似ているというのではなくて, サルが君に似ているのだ ▪ *Not that* I loved Caesar less *but that* I loved Rome more. カエサルを愛する心が浅かったのではない, ローマを愛する心がさらに深かったためである.

not tonight, Josephine 《戯》今夜はだめだよ, ジョゼフィーヌ ▪ Care for a drink?—*Not tonight, Josephine*. 1杯やるかい?—いや, 今夜はけっこうだ. ☞Napoleon 1世が最初の妻 Josephine に言ったとされる言葉. 妻・恋人などの誘いを断るときに用いるが, 最近はこの例のようにそれ以外の場合にも用いられる.

notch /nɑtʃ|nɔtʃ/ 名 ***be a notch*** [***notches***]

***above* [*higher than*]** 《口》…より一段[数段]上だ ▪ He *is a notch higher than* the others. 彼は他の者よりひとけた上だ ▪ This book *is notches above* the usual product. この本は普通の本よりも数段勝っている.

***come down a notch* (*or two*)** 《口》名を落とす ▪ He *came down a notch or two* through his mistake. 彼はその失敗のため名を落とした.

***take** a person **down a notch* (*or two*)** 少し人の高慢の鼻を折ってやる ▪ He *was taken down a notch or two* in his self-conceit. 彼はうぬぼれの鼻をへし折られた.

note /noʊt/ 名 ***a note of hand*** 約束手形 ▪ This *note of hand* is priceless. この約束手形は貴重なものだ.

change** one's **note 《口》話しぶり[態度]を一変する ▪ When he found the police knew it, he very quickly *changed his note*. 警察がそのことを知っているのがわかると, 彼はたちまち態度を一変した. ☞F changer de note のなぞり.

compare notes (…と)情報[意見]を交換する (*with*) ▪ He was *comparing notes with* a friend. 彼は友人と情報を交換していた.

from notes 草稿[メモ]を見て(↔without a NOTE) ▪ He made a speech *from notes*. 彼はメモを見て演説した.

***make a mental note of* [*to* do, *that*]** …をよく覚えておく ▪ I *made a mental note of* the phrase. その句をよく覚えておいた ▪ I must *make a mental note to* call my mother. 母に電話をすることを覚えておかなくては ▪ She *made a mental note that* he didn't like fish. 彼女は彼が魚嫌いだということを覚えておいた.

***make a note* (*of,* 《米》 *on*)** (…を)筆記する; (に)注目する ▪ I shall *make a note of* your statement. あなたの声明を筆記しましょう ▪ I *made notes on* the lecture. その講義のノートを取った.

of* (…) *note 知名の, 注目すべき ▪ They were all men *of note* and weight. 彼らはみな知名の有力者だった ▪ He was *of* the first *note* in his age as a philosopher. 彼は当時哲学者として一番有名だった.

on an optimistic* [*cheerful,* etc.] *note 楽観的な[陽気な, など]調子で ▪ His speech ended *on an optimistic note*. 彼のスピーチは楽観的な調子で終わった.

sound the* [*a*] *note of …を通告する, 唱える ▪ Roger Lestrange *sounded the note of* war in the "Observer". ロジャー・レストレインジはオブザーバー紙で主戦論を唱えた ▪ He *sounded a note of* warning on the vice. 彼はその悪徳に対して警告を発した.

strike* [*sound*] *a false* [*wrong*] *note 見当はずれのことをする, または言う ▪ His statement *strikes a wrong note*. 彼の説は見当はずれだ.

strike a new note 新機軸を出す ▪ This author *strikes a new note* in modern "Western" fiction. この作家は現代の「西部」小説で新機軸を出している.

strike* [*hit*] *a sour note 悪い知らせで場の空気を湿らせる ▪ The news of her sudden illness *struck a sour note* during the party. 彼女が急病との知らせでパーティーの雰囲気が曇った.

strike the right note **1** 適切な意見を述べる; 適切な[好ましい]ことをする ▪ Your editorial today *strikes the right note*. 君のきょうの社説はもっともな説を述べている ▪ He *struck the right note* when he wore a suit and tie to the conference. 彼が会議に正装して出かけたのは適切だった.
2 望んだ結果を達成する ▪ His speech failed to *strike the right note* with the audience. 彼のスピーチは聴衆に受けなかった.

***take a note* [*notes*] (*of*)** =make a NOTE (of).

take note of …に注意する; を考察する ▪ No one *took note of* me. 誰も私に注意しなかった ▪ We *took* careful *note of* his request. 彼の依頼を慎重に考えてみた.

There's a child among you taking notes. 《口》誰かが目を光らせている, 監視している ▪ I shall say no more now, for I fancy *there's a child among you taking notes*. 今はこれ以上言うまい, どうも誰かが目を光らせているような気がするから.

***without a note* [*notes*]** 草稿[メモ]なしで (↔from NOTEs) ▪ The governor spoke for an hour *without a note*. 知事は草稿なしで1時間演説をした.

noted /nóʊtəd/ 形 ***be noted for*** …で有名である ▪ This island *is noted for* its fine sunsets. この島は美しい日没で有名である.

nothing /nʌ́θɪŋ/ 名副 ***a mere nothing*** 取るに足らないもの ▪ Was it a bad accident?—No, no, *a mere nothing*. ひどい事故だったのかい?—いやいや, たいしたことはなかったよ ▪ He is *a mere nothing*. 彼は吹けば飛ぶような男だ.

all to nothing **1** この上もなく; とことんまで ▪ Is a voyage to India *all to nothing* a better venture than marriage? インドへの航海が結婚よりも断然ましな冒険なのだろうか ▪ He has carried his point *all to nothing*. 彼はとことんまで主張を通した.
2 (成功の)見込み十分 ▪ It is *all to nothing* that he will succeed. 彼の成功の見込みは十分だ.

be all for nothing →ALL.

be as nothing to …に比べれば取るに足らない, ゼロに等しい ▪ What we know *is as nothing to* what we do not know. 我々の知っていることは, 知らないことに比べればゼロに等しい.

be at nothing 何もしていない ▪ I *am at nothing*, I am only reading. 私は何もしていない. 本を読んでいるだけだ.

be nothing どの宗派にも属さない; 無神論者 ▪ My uncle doesn't believe in God. He *is nothing*. 伯父は神の存在を信じない. 彼は無神論者だ.

be nothing if not …なのが一番のとりえだ (cf. Sh., *Oth.* 2. 1. 120) ▪ He *is nothing if not* kind. 彼は親切なのが何よりのとりえだ ▪ Christianity *is nothing if not* spiritual. キリスト教は霊的なのが一番のと

N

りえだ.

be nothing of 少しも…らしいところがない ▪ He *is nothing of* a poet. 彼は少しも詩人らしいところがない.

be nothing to **1** …には何でもない ▪ A hundred dollars *is nothing to* you. 100ドルなんか君には何でもない.

2 (お粗末で)…と比較にならない ▪ Why, this job *is nothing to* the one we did last week. なんだ, この仕事は先週したのとは比べ物にならないじゃないか.

beat** a person* **(*all*)** ***to nothing 人を完全に打ち負かす ▪ Christians *beat* us *all to nothing* in honor and humanity. キリスト教徒は名誉と人情にかけては我々を完全に打ち負かす.

Believe nothing of what you hear, and only half of what you see. 《諺》噂はたいてい誤りで, 目に見えるものにも騙されることがある《証拠が見つかるまでは疑え, の意》.

Blessed is he who expects nothing, for he shall never be disappointed. 《諺》何も期待しない人は幸せである. 失望することがないからである, 「無いが極楽知らぬが仏」.

can make nothing of **1** …を理解できない ▪ I *can make nothing of* what he says. 彼の言うことは少しもわからない.

2 …をしくじる, 利用できない ▪ He *could make nothing of* the job. 彼はその仕事をやりおおせることができなかった ▪ He *could make nothing of* his talents. 彼は才能を発揮しえなかった.

care nothing for →CARE².

Civility* [*Courtesy, Politeness*] *costs nothing. 《諺》(人に)丁寧(にしてやること)には金は一文もかからない, 「男は辞儀に余れ, 女は会釈に余れ」.

come to nothing 何にもならない, むだに終わる ▪ This voyage *came to nothing.* その航海は何にもならなかった ▪ His falling in love with Julia had *come to nothing.* 彼のジュリアへの恋愛は実を結ばなかった.

do nothing but *do* …ばかりする ▪ She *does nothing but* cry all day. 彼女は一日中泣いてばかりいる.

(*don't*) ***know from nothing*** 《米俗》少しも知らない ▪ If they ask you anything, you *don't know from nothing.* もし連中が何か聞いたら, 君は何も知らないことにするんだよ ▪ I *know from nothing* about the crime. 犯罪のことはさっぱり知らない. ☞New York の Yiddish 語法から; 現在は don't のつかない方が多用.

for nothing **1** 無益に ▪ He did not go to Oxford *for nothing.* 彼はオックスフォードへ行ってむだではなかった.

2 理由なく ▪ They quarreled *for nothing.* 彼らはいわれもなくけんかをした.

3 無料で ▪ I got it *for nothing.* ただでそれを手に入れた ▪ I cannot give instruction *for nothing.* 私は無料で教えるわけにいかない.

good for nothing →GOOD.

have nothing against …に反感[恨み]はない ▪ I *have nothing against* immigrants from abroad. 私は外国からの移民に含むところはない.

have nothing between the ears →EAR.

have nothing in *one* 何のとりえもない ▪ He *has nothing in* him. 彼は能なしだ.

have nothing of **1** …とかかり合わない, を相手にしない ▪ He will *have nothing of* it. 彼はそれにはかかり合おうとしない.

2 …らしさが少しもない ▪ She *has nothing of* the lady in her. 彼女は少しも淑女らしいところがない.

have nothing on →HAVE².

have nothing to do with **1** …に少しも関係がない ▪ I *have nothing to do with* you. 僕は君には何のかかわりもない ▪ That *has nothing to do with* the matter. それはこの事に少しも関係がない.

2 …と交際しない ▪ Take my advice and *have nothing to do with* him. 私の忠言をいれてあの男と交際するな.

Here goes nothing! 《米口》どうせだめだがさあやるぞ ▪ I'm running a race. *Here goes nothing!* これからレースが始まる. とても無理だががんばるぞ.

if nothing else 少なくとも ▪ Your time-keeping, *if nothing else*, is perfect. 少なくとも君の時間厳守は完璧だよ.

in nothing flat 《口》あっと言う間に ▪ The rain swallowed up the tail light *in nothing flat.* 雨は瞬く間にテールライトを包み隠してしまった.

it's nothing =not at ALL.

know from nothing **(*about*)** →KNOW².

leave nothing to the imagination 想像の余地がない《露骨にセクシーで感心しない》 ▪ The salesperson came up with a swimsuit for her that *leaves nothing to the imagination.* 店員が彼女に出してきた水着ときたら, 露骨にセクシーなものだった.

like nothing on earth この上もなく, またとなく(変な, 醜い, みじめな, など) ▪ I feel *like nothing on earth.* またとなくみじめな気持ちだ ▪ His hat looked *like nothing on earth.* 彼の帽子はこの上もなく不格好に見えた.

little or nothing →LITTLE.

make nothing of **1**〚主に動名詞を伴って〛…を何とも思わない ▪ He *makes nothing of* making a few mistakes. 彼は誤りを少しくらいするのは何とも思っていない ▪ He *made nothing of* hardship. 彼は苦難を何とも思わなかった.

2 …が少しもわからない ▪ I could *make nothing of* his words. 彼の言葉がさっぱりわからなかった.

next to nothing →NEXT.

no nothing 《口》…も何もかもない ▪ There is no bread, no butter, no cheese, *no nothing.* パンもバターもチーズも何もかもない.

not for nothing **1** 理由[いわれ]のないことではない ▪ It was *not for nothing* that he protested. 彼が抗議したのはいわれのないことではない.

2 無益ではない ▪ I did*n't* learn English *for nothing.* だてには英語を勉強していない.

***nothing but* [*except*]** ただ…だけ (only) ▪ *Noth-*

ing but peace can save the world. 平和しか世界を救うことはできない ▪ He is *nothing but* a student. 彼は学生にすぎない.

Nothing comes from nothing./ Out of nothing, nothing comes. 《諺》無からは何も生じない,「まかぬ種は生(は)えぬ」.

nothing comes of …はものにならない ▪ *Nothing came of* the matter. それはものにならなかった ▪ I have done my best for his sake, but *nothing comes of* it. 彼のためにできるだけのことはしてやったが, どうにもならない.

nothing doing →DOING.

***nothing else but* [*than*]** …にほかならない ▪ Sin is *nothing else than* moral evil. 罪とは道徳的悪にほかならない ▪ Newton says that this power is *nothing else but* that of attraction. この力は引力にほかならないとニュートンは言う.

nothing except →NOTHING but.

***Nothing is certain but death and quarter day* [(*the*) *taxes*].** 《諺》確実なことは死ぬことと四季支払日[税金]だけ,「死ぬるばかりはまこと」.

Nothing is certain but the unforeseen. 《諺》予見されないこと以外に確実なことは何もない《これから起きることを前もって知ることはできない, の意》,「当てごとと褌(ふんどし)は向こうからはずれる」.

***nothing is* [*can be*] *farther from* one's *mind* [*thoughts*] (*than* ...)** (…などは)毛頭考えていない ▪ *Nothing is farther from my mind than* the idea of marrying her. 彼女と結婚しようなどとはさらさら考えていない.

Nothing is given so freely as advice. 《諺》助言ほど進んで人がくれるものは他にはない.

***nothing is so* [*more*] ... *as* [*than*]** ほど…なものはない ▪ *Nothing is so* precious *as* time. = *Nothing is more* precious *than* time. 時間ほど貴重なものはない.

nothing less than →LESS.

nothing like →LIKE[1].

nothing like* [*near*] *so* [*as*] ... *as とても…に及ばない ▪ This poem is *nothing like so* excellent *as* that. この詩はあの詩の秀逸さに遠く及ばない ▪ This is *nothing near so* large *as* the other. これはもう一つの大きさにはとてもかなわない.

nothing more or less than 全く…にほかならない ▪ The affair was *nothing more or less than* an insult. その事件は全くの侮辱だった.

nothing more than …にすぎない ▪ He is *nothing more than* a dreamer. 彼は夢想家にすぎない.

nothing* [*not anything*] *much 《口》大したことはない ▪ How goes it with your business?—*Nothing much*. 商売はどうかね?—大したことはないよ ▪ The smell is good but the texture is *not anything much*. 香りはいいが口当たりは大したことはない.

nothing of 少しも…ない (→be NOTHING of) ▪ I know *nothing of* it. そのことは少しも知らない ▪ I see *nothing of* him lately. 最近彼にちっとも会わない ▪ There is *nothing of* the lady in her behavior. 彼女のふるまいには淑女らしいところは少しもない.

***nothing of the kind* [*sort*]** 決してそんなわけではない ▪ Did he apologize?—*Nothing of the kind*. 彼は謝ったのか?—いいや, 全く ▪ Did you see the comet?—I saw *nothing of the sort*. 彗星を見たかい?—そんなものは見やしないよ.

nothing short of →SHORT.

nothing so **1** 決して…(ほど)そうではない ▪ He is *nothing so* as his brother. 彼は決して兄ほどそうではない.

2 決してそうではない ▪ He is believed to be a fool, but it is *nothing so*. 彼は愚かだと思われているが, 決してそうではない.

Nothing so bad but* (*it*) *might have been worse. 《諺》どんなに悪いことでもそれ以上悪くはならなかっただろう,「上見ろ下見ろ」.

Nothing succeeds like success. → SUCCESS.

nothing to it →There is NOTHING to it.

nothing to nobody 《米俗》言葉で言いようがない ▪ The way those women love punch is *nothing to nobody*! その女性たちがパンチを好むことといったら何とも言いようがない.

nothing to speak of 言うに足らない, ささいな ▪ It's just a slight cold, I think—*nothing to speak of*. ほんの鼻風邪だと思う—大したことはない.

nothing to wire home about = nothing to WRITE home about.

nothing to write home about →WRITE.

Nothing venture, nothing have* [*gain, win*]./*Nothing ventured, nothing gained. →VENTURE[2].

Out of nothing, nothing comes. →NOTHING comes from nothing.

set ... at nothing …を何とも思わない ▪ They *set* their lives *at nothing*. 彼らは命を何とも思わなかった.

soft nothings 《口》たわいもない恋の言葉, (恋人同士が交わす)甘いささやき (→SWEET nothing) ▪ My brother and his fiancée spend the whole day whispering *soft nothings* to each other. 兄とその許婚者は一日中たわいもない恋をささやき交わしている ▪ He whispered *soft nothings* in her ear. 彼は彼女の耳許に愛の言葉をささやいた.

stop at nothing →STOP[2].

There is nothing doing. 何もなされていない, 何の結果も生じていない ▪ *There is nothing doing* around here now of any importance. このところこの辺りでは何も重要なことはなされていない.

There is nothing else for it. それより仕方がない ▪ You walked back? —*There was nothing else for it*. 歩いて帰ったのですか?—それより仕方がなかったのです.

there is* [*one has*] *nothing for it but 〚不定詞・動作名詞を伴って〛…より仕方がない ▪ *There is nothing for it but* extraction; that tooth must come out. 抜くより仕方がない. その歯は抜かねばならな

い ▪ *There was nothing for it but* to obey. 従うより仕方なかった.

there is nothing in **1** …は取るに足らないことだ ▪ The rumor was all over the place, but *there was nothing in* it. その噂はそのあたり一帯に広まっていたが, 取るに足らないことだった ▪ *There is nothing in* him and no girl wants to marry him. 彼はとりえのない男で, 彼との結婚を望む娘はいない.

2 …はまるで嘘だ ▪ He made a great promise of help, but *there was nothing in* it at all. 彼は助けてやると大きなことを約束したが, それはまるで嘘だった.

3 勝目は五分五分 ▪ As far as their respective experiences go, *there is nothing in* it. 彼らそれぞれの経験に関するかぎりでは, 勝つ見込みは五分五分だ.

there is nothing like …に及ぶものはない ▪ *There's nothing like* going to the bottom of things. 物事の奥義を窮めるに越したことはない ▪ *There is nothing like* a good lunch on a picnic. ピクニックにはおいしい弁当に勝るものはない.

There is nothing to it. 《口》 **1** (それは)造作ないことだ ▪ Driving a car is not difficult. *There is* really *nothing to it.* 車を運転するのはむずかしくない. 全くわけないよ.

2 大したことではない ▪ It is all probably a misunderstanding. *There is* surely *nothing to it.* それは恐らくすべて誤解なのだろう. 確かに大したことじゃない.

think nothing of →THINK[2].

to nothing 跡かたもなく ▪ The parapet dwarfed down *to nothing.* 欄干(らんかん)は小さくなって見えなくなった ▪ The conversation fell and dropped *to nothing.* 会話がだれてぱったりやんでしまった.

to say nothing of →SAY[2].

want nothing to do with …とは関わりたくないと思う ▪ I *want nothing to do with* him. 彼とは関わりを持ちたくない.

with nothing on 何も着ないで, 裸で ▪ He always swims *with nothing on.* 彼はいつも裸で泳ぐ.

with nothing to *one's* ***name*** 全く財産なしに, 丸裸で ▪ The refugee came to the U.K. *with nothing to his name.* 難民は裸一貫で英国に来た.

nothingness /nʌ́θɪŋnəs/ 名 ***fade*** [***pass, sink***] ***into nothingness*** 無に帰してしまう, 消えうせてしまう ▪ A thing of beauty is a joy for ever; it will never *pass into nothingness.* 美しいものは永久に喜びである. それが無に帰することは決してないだろう.

out of nothing 無から ▪ God created the world *out of nothing.* 神は無から世界を創造した.

notice[1] /nóʊtəs/ 名 ***at a minute's notice*** 通知のあり次第 ▪ Be ready to start *at a minute's notice.* 通知のあり次第出発できる準備をしておけ.

at [***on***] ***a moment's notice*** 即刻に ▪ We cannot have it ready *at* [*on*] *a moment's notice.* それを即座に準備することはできない.

at [***on***] ***short notice*** 急に, すぐに ▪ We have to leave for America *at short notice.* 我々は急にアメリカへ立たなくてはならない ▪ We serve meals to guests at any time *on short notice.* お客様にはいつでもすぐにお食事が出せます.

at [***on***] ***ten days'*** [etc.] ***notice*** 10日[など]の予告[猶予]で ▪ Special trains can be arranged *at two or three hours' notice.* 特別列車は2, 3時間の猶予で仕立てられる ▪ He may be dismissed *at a month's notice.* ひと月前に予告すれば彼を解雇してもよい.

be under notice (***to leave***) 暇を取ることになっている ▪ My servant *is under notice* (*to leave*) at the end of the month. うちの使用人は月末に暇を取ることになっている.

beneath (*a person's*) ***notice*** 取るに足らない, 卑しむべき ▪ Pretty though she is, she is *beneath your lordship's notice.* 彼女は美人ではありますが, 閣下の注目するに足らない女です.

bring ... to [***under***] *a person's* ***notice*** …を人の目に留めさせる, に注目させる ▪ The late occurrence *brought* this fact *to* [*under*] *my notice.* 今度の事件でこの事実が私の注意を引いた.

come into notice 注目を引くようになる ▪ The author is beginning to *come into notice.* その作家は注目を引くようになってきた.

come to the notice of *a person*/***come to*** *a person's* ***notice*** …に知られる, 認められる ▪ The fact *came to the notice of* the world. その事実は世間に知られた ▪ The issue *came to my notice* this morning. その問題に今朝気づきました.

come [***fall***] ***under*** *one's* ***notice*** …の注意を引く, 目に留まる ▪ This is the most practical English grammar which has *come under my notice.* これは私の目に留まった最も実用的な英文法書だ.

commend ... to *a person's* ***notice*** …を人に見知りおくように頼む ▪ I *commend* her *to your notice.* 彼女をお見知りおきください.

give a week's [***a month's,*** etc.] ***notice*** 1週間[1か月, など]前に(特に解雇・家の明け渡しなどの)予告をする ▪ The landlord *gave a week's notice* from next Friday. 家主は来週の金曜日から1週間目に明け渡しを申し入れた ▪ He *gave a month's notice* to the servants. 彼は使用人たちに1か月前に解雇の予告をした.

give [***serve***] ***notice of*** [***that***] …の通知をする, 知らせる ▪ I *gave notice of* inability to attend. 欠席届を出した ▪ The whistle *gave notice that* the boat was about to leave. 汽笛が鳴ってまもなく船が出ることを知らせた.

give notice to …に届け出る ▪ He *gave notice to* the authorities. 彼は当局へ届け出た.

have [***receive***] ***notice of*** …の通知を受ける ▪ We have *received notice of* a storm. あらしの警告を受けた.

have [***receive***] ***notice to quit*** **1** 解雇を予告されている[される] ▪ You won't be troubled with him much longer; he *has notice to quit* next week. あの男にこれ以上煩わされずにすむだろう. 来週解雇を予告されているから.

N

2《口》(病気で)いよいよおさらばだということを悟る ▪ I wonder why he can be so cheerful when he knows he *has notice to quit*. 彼はいよいよだとわかっているのに, なぜあんなに明るくしていられるのだろう.

on a moment's notice →at a moment's NOTICE.

on notice 通告されて ▪ They are *on notice* that their house is no longer theirs. 彼らは家がもう自分のものでないということを通告されている.

on short notice →at short NOTICE.

put *a person* ***on notice*** 人に通告する ▪ We *put* them *on notice* that fundamental rights are to be observed. 我々は基本的権利は守らねばならないと彼らに通告した.

serve notice of [***that***] →give NOTICE of.

sit up and take notice《戯》 **1** 快方に向かう ▪ The patient is *sitting up and taking notice*. 病人は快方に向かっています.

2 急に関心を示す, はっとする ▪ When they eloped, people *sat up and took notice*. 二人が駆け落ちすると人々は急に関心を示した.

take notice **1** 注意する, 目を留める (*of, that, how*) ▪ I warned him, but he *took* little *notice of* it. 警告したが, 彼はあまり心に留めなかった ▪ He *took* no *notice that* she was so near. 彼は彼女がそんなに近くにいることは少しも顧みなかった.

2 (赤んぼうが)ものの見分けがつく, 知恵がつく ▪ He is beginning to *take notice*. 坊やも知恵がつき始めた.

take notice that **1** ...するように注意する ▪ *Take notice that* nothing is omitted. ぬかりのないように頼むよ.

2 →take NOTICE 1.

till [***until***] ***further notice***《文》追って通知があるまで ▪ Remain here *till further notice*. 追って知らせがあるまでここにいるように.

without notice 無断で ▪ He was absent from school *without notice*. 彼は無断で学校を欠席した.

without previous notice 予告なしで ▪ The dismissal came *without previous notice*. 解雇は予告なしに行われた.

notice[2] /nóʊtəs/ 動 ***be noticed to quit*** 立ち退きの通告を受ける ▪ He *was noticed to quit* a week ago. 彼は1週間前に立ち退きの通告を受けた.

not so as [***so's***] ***you'd notice***《口》ひどく...ではない《しばしば「全然...でない」を含意する》 ▪ Was he angry?—*Not so as you'd notice*. 彼は怒っていたか?—いや, 別に.

notify /nóʊtəfàɪ/ 動 ***notify*** *a person* ***that*** 人に...ということを通知する ▪ He *was notified that* he must depart at once. 彼はすぐ出て行けという通知を受けた.

notion /nóʊʃən/ 名 ***as the notion goes*** 世間で言う ▪ He is not a learned man, *as the notion goes*. 彼は世間で言う学者ではない.

form a true [***wrong***] ***notion of*** ...について正しい[まちがった]考えをいだく ▪ You have *formed a wrong notion of* my worldly circumstances. あなたは私の財産について考えちがいをしておられる.

have a good notion to *do* ...したくてたまらない ▪ I*'ve a good notion to* take it out on you. お前を懲らしめてやりたくてたまらない.

have a notion (***that***) ...と考えている ▪ She *has a notion* he is going to propose. 彼女は彼がプロポーズするつもりだと考えている.

have [***take***] ***a notion to*** *do* ...しようかと思う ▪ I *have a notion to* travel abroad and see the world. 私は外国を旅行して世界を見ようと思っている ▪ I changed my mind, and *took a notion to* go. 私は気が変わって行ってみるつもりになった.

have half a notion to *do* = have half a MIND to do.

have no notion of **1** ...する気は全然ない (*doing*) ▪ I *have no notion of being* made a fool of. 私はばかにされるつもりは少しもない ▪ He *has no notion of risking* his money. 彼は金を危ない投資に回す気は毛頭ない.

2 ...を少しも解さない ▪ The natives *have no notion of* discipline. 先住民は規律の何たるかを少しも解さない ▪ They *have no notion of* honor. 彼らは名誉がどういうものか少しもわかっていない.

have no notion to *do* ...するつもりは少しもない ▪ The Indian *had no notion to* cross the mountains with us. 北米先住民は我々といっしょに山を越えるつもりは少しもなかった.

have not the first notion about ...のことは少しも知らない ▪ I *haven't the first notion about* it. そのことは少しも知らない.

take a notion to *do* 急に...する気になる ▪ I *took a notion to* go with them. 急に彼らと同行する気になった.

under the notion of ...の概念[項目, 名称]のもとに ▪ Goals have been set *under the notion of* sustainable development. 持続可能な開発の名目で目標が設定された.

notorious /noʊtɔ́:riəs/ 形 ***be notorious for*** ...で評判だ《悪い意味で》 ▪ The ship *is notorious for* her ill luck. この船は運の悪いので評判だ ▪ The neighborhood *is notorious for* robbery. その辺は強盗が出るので有名だ.

it is notorious that ...は周知のことである《悪い意味を含まない》 ▪ *It is notorious that* they knew nothing of agriculture. 彼らが農業のことは少しも知らなかったということは周知の通りだ.

nought /nɔ:t/ 名 ***bring*** [***come, go***] ***to nought***《雅》無に帰させる[帰する] ▪ Zeal and courage have *been brought to nought* by cowardice. 熱意も勇気も, 臆病のために無に帰してしまった ▪ All human plans *came to nought*. 人間の計画はことごとく無に帰してしまった.

noughts and crosses ○×遊び《○×を五目ならべのように3つ連なるように並べ合う子供の遊戯》 ▪ They indulged in *noughts and crosses*. 彼らは○×遊びにふけった.

set ... at nought =set ... at NAUGHT.

nourishment /nə́ːrɪʃmənt|nʌ́r-/ 名 ***sit up and take nourishment*** 《戯》(無関心のあと)敏活になる; (病後)元気になる ▪ The patient is *sitting up and taking nourishment.* 病人は元気になりつつある. ☞sit up and take NOTICE の類推によって生じた言い方.

novel /nάvəl|nɔ́v-/ 名 ***read like a novel*** 《口》小説のようにおもしろい ▪ His adventures *read like a novel.* 彼の冒険談はすごくおもしろい.

novice /nάvəs|nɔ́v-/ 名 ***be a novice in*** [***at***] …はしろうとである ▪ He *was a novice at* the art. 彼はその技術にはしろうとだった ▪ I *am* no *novice in* affairs of this sort. 私はこのような事柄にはしろうとなんかではない.

now /naʊ/ 副接名 ***any*** [***minute, moment, day, week,*** etc.] ***now*** すぐに, まもなく (very soon) ▪ *Any day now,* I shall obtain my visa. まもなくビザが手に入るさ.

as of now 今[本日]から ▪ The bus fare is going up by 15 percent *as of now.* バス代は本日から15パーセント上がります.

before now これまでに ▪ I have told you about this *before now.* このことは君にこれまでにも言ったことがある.

between now and then 今からそれまでに ▪ I shall see you *between now and then.* 今後それまでにお会いしましょう.

by now 今ごろはもう ▪ He will have arrived *by now.* 彼は今ごろはもう着いているだろう.

Come now! **1** (人を誘い促して)さあさあ ▪ *Come now,* tell me everything. さあ, 一部始終を話すんだ. **2** (驚き・非難などを表して)まあ, これ, さあ ▪ Oh, *come now!* Give him a break. まあ, まあ! 彼にひと息入れさせてやれよ.

(***every***) ***now and then*** [***again***] ときどき ▪ These gypsies *now and then* foretold very strange things. これらのジプシーはときどききわめて不思議な事柄を予言した ▪ The database should be updated *every now and then.* データベースは折に触れ更新しなくてはいけない. ☞every は ever のなまり.

for now **1** さしあたり ▪ Thank you; that will do *for now.* ありがとう. それでさしあたり間に合う. **2** 今すぐ《未来》 ▪ I will do it *for now.* 今すぐそうします.

from now on [***onwards, forth, forthward, forward***] これから先, 今後 ▪ *From now on* Henry will work in another office. 今後ヘンリーは別の事務所で働くのだ ▪ *From now forth* you must put your back into your work. これからは君も仕事に身を入れなければならない.

from now till doomsday 今から世の終わりまで ▪ I could very well live *from now till doomsday* without a priest. 牧師がいなくても今から世の終わりまでけっこう暮らすことができよう.

here and now →HERE.

just now **1** 今しがた ▪ He was here *just now,* reading a book in the corner. 彼は今しがたまでここにいて隅で読書をしていた ▪ I saw him *just now* in the street. たった今通りで彼に会った. ☞過去時制とともに用いられる. **2** 今のところ, ただ今 ▪ I'm busy *just now.* ちょうど今忙しいところだ ▪ He is engaged with a client *just now.* 彼は目下依頼人と話し合っている. **3** 今すぐ ▪ I will do it *just now.* すぐいたします.

now … and again →NOW … now.

Do ***now and pay later.*** 《口》代金は後でよいから, 今…しなさい ▪ Talk *now and pay later.* 代金は後払いで, 今通話してください《電話の宣伝》.

now and then [***again***] →(every) NOW and then.

now for [***as to***] さて次は… ▪ *Now for* the second question. さて次は第二の問題です ▪ And *now as to* Dr. White. I owe him a great deal. さて次にホワイト博士だが, あの方には大変恩恵を受けている.

now if ever 今こそ(…である) ▪ *Now if ever* is the time to fight. 今こそ戦うべき時だ.

Now I've seen everything. もう(世の中の)ありとあらゆる物を見た《今後は何を見ても驚かない》 ▪ Fake notes? I'd say *now I've seen everything.* 偽札だって? そんなことでは驚かないね.

now now/there now これこれ, こらこら《親しみをもって抗議・注意などするとき》 ▪ *Now now,* you mustn't do that here! これこれ, ここでそんなことをしてはいかん ▪ *There now,* none of your nonsense. こらこら, もうばかを言うのはよせ.

now … now/now … then/now … and again 時には…また時には ▪ The kite is gliding through the sky, *now* rising, *now* falling. トンビが上がったり下がったりして滑空している ▪ The weather was quite unstable, *now* wet, *then* fine. 降ったり照ったりと天候がかなり不安定だった ▪ His walk was *now* quick, *and again* slow. 彼の歩き方は速かったり遅かったりした.

now of 《米口》現在…に勤めている ▪ He is Dr. Keys, lately of M.I.T., *now of* Hebrew University. 彼は以前 M.I.T. に, 現在はヘブライ大学に勤めているキーズ博士です.

now or never 今…しなければまたと機会がない, 今こそ ▪ We must strive for peace; it's *now or never.* 我々は平和のために努力すべきだ. 今を逃すともうチャンスはない ▪ *Now* is the time, *or never.* 今こそ好機逸すべからずだ.

now (***that***) もう…だから ▪ *Now that* I am a man, I think otherwise. 僕はもうおとなになったので, 考え方がちがってきた ▪ *Now that* you mention it, I remember. そう言われると思い出した.

now then **1** =NOW now. **2** さあどうだ, わかったか《挑戦的な言葉の後に用いる》 ▪ I will refuse, *now then.* 断るつもりだ, わかったな.

Now you tell me! 今になって言うなんて ▪ *Now you tell me* he ain't even here! 彼はここにもいないなんて今になって言うなんて!

only now やっと今 ▪ It is *only now* that he is beginning to understand. やっと今になって彼はわかり

かけたのだ.

Really now!/Now really! へえー!, まさか!, 驚いたね! ▪ He has failed in the examination.—*Really now!* 彼は試験をしくじったよ—へえー!

right now →RIGHT[1].

there now →NOW now.

till [up to] now 今まで, 今日にいたるまで ▪ I have heard nothing from him *up to now.* 今日まで彼から何のたよりもない ▪ *Till now* he has always been very friendly. 今まで彼はいつもとても親しくしてくれた.

What now? 《口》→WHAT.

nowhere /nóʊhwèər/ 副名 ***be nowhere***
1《俗》さんざんに打ち負かされる, 大失敗する, 全然ものにならない ▪ Many men *were nowhere* at the end. 多くの人々が終わりにはさんざんに負けた ▪ In fiction, Italy *is nowhere.* 小説ではイタリアは全然お話にならない ▪ He *was nowhere* in the examination. 彼は試験で大失敗した.
2《米俗》途方にくれてしまう ▪ When he began to ask me questions about surgery, I *was* just *nowhere.* 彼に外科手術についていろいろ尋ねられ始めたとき, ほんとに途方にくれた.

come in nowhere =be NOWHERE 1.

from (out of) nowhere/out of nowhere どこからともなく; 不意に ▪ He came *from nowhere.* 彼はどこからともなくやって来た.

get nowhere →GET.

in the middle of nowhere 《口》辺ぴな所に ▪ The hotel was located *in the middle of nowhere.* そのホテルは辺ぴな所にあった.

lead [get] *a person* ***nowhere*** 人に効果がない, 何にもならない ▪ All my efforts *led* us *nowhere.* 私のすべての努力も何の効果もなかった.

leave *a person* ***nowhere*** 人を顔色なからしめる ▪ Her beauty *left* her rivals *nowhere.* 彼女の美しさに競争相手たちは顔色を失った.

miles from nowhere 《口》辺ぴな ▪ His house is *miles from nowhere.* 彼の家は辺ぴな所にある.

nowhere near 《口》...どころではない ▪ This is *nowhere near* so [as] good as that. これはあれには遠く及ばない.

out of nowhere =from (out of) NOWHERE.

nth /enθ/ 形 ***for the nth time*** 《口》何回か分からないほど, これまで幾度となく ▪ I've told him, *for the nth time*, to tidy his room but he won't listen. 部屋を片うけるように口をすっぱくして言ってきたが, 彼は聞こうとしない.

to the nth/ to the nth degree [power]
1《数学》n 次 [n 乗]まで ▪ The value can be raised *to the nth degree*, as long as n represents a natural number. n が自然数の時のみ, その数値は n 次まで累乗され得る[を n 乗することができる].
2《口》極度に; あくまでも ▪ I'll support him *to the nth.* 私はとことんまで彼を支持する ▪ The play was boring *to the nth degree.* 演劇はこの上なく退屈だった ▪ Poetry is ordinary language raised *to the nth power.* 詩は日常の言葉が極度にまで高められたものである.

nuclear /njú:kliər/ 形 ***go nuclear [ballistic]***
1 核武装する ▪ I think Japan should not *go nuclear.* 日本は核武装すべきではないと思う.
2 激怒して手に負えないふるまいを始める ▪ He *went nuclear* when he found his new bike stolen. 彼は買ったばかりの自転車が盗まれたのを知り, 怒り狂って暴挙に出た. ☞a ballistic missile「弾道ミサイル」が炸裂すること.

nude[1] /nju:d/ 名 ***in the nude*** 裸体で ▪ He is painting her *in the nude* this time. 彼は今度は裸体の彼女を描いている.

nude[2] /nju:d/ 動 ***nude it*** 《米俗》裸体になる; 裸体主義を実行する ▪ Don't go *nuding it* in my presence. 僕の前で裸体になったりしないでくれ.

nudge /nʌdʒ/ 名 ***a nudge and a wink/ nudge-nudge, wink-wink*** 《口》 **1**(性的な意味を暗示して)ほら, あれ[例のこと] ▪ *Nudge-nudge*, know what I mean? あれさ, あれ, 分かるだろ ▪ We spent a lot of time together, *nudge nudge, wink wink.* 僕たちはずっとあれをして過ごした.
2 なにげなくなされる激励, 内緒の支持 ▪ I'm tired of all *the nudges and the winks.* あれだけの陰の支援にはもううんざりだ. ☞1970 年代英国の TV コメディーシリーズ “Monty Python's Flying Circus” の登場人物の台詞から.

nuf(f), 'nuf(f) /nʌf/ 代 ***nuf(f) ['nuf(f)] said*** 《口》それでよし, けっこう ▪ *'Nuff said*, old chap! There's no need for explanations. もういいよ, 君. 言い訳するには及ばない. ☞nuff = enough.

nuisance /njú:səns/ 名 ***abate a nuisance*** 《法》(被害者が自力で不法)妨害を除去する ▪ He repaired the drain so as to *abate the nuisance* complained of. 彼は不平の種になっている妨害を除去するために下水溝を修理した.

Commit no nuisance. 迷惑無用《小便無用; ごみ捨てるべからず》.

have (a) nuisance value いやがらせの効果がある ▪ Intestinal worms don't cause any serious disease but *have a nuisance value.* 回虫は重病の原因とはならないが, 厄介の種にはなる.

make a nuisance of *oneself*/***make*** *oneself* ***a nuisance*** 人の迷惑[じゃま]になる ▪ Tommy, stop that now. You're *making a* thorough *nuisance of yourself.* トミー, もうそんなことはよしなさい. ほんとに人の迷惑になっているんですよ.

What a nuisance! まあうるさい! ▪ *What a nuisance* that child is! あの子のまあうるさいこと.

null /nʌl/ 形 ***null and void*** 《法》(契約などが)無効で ▪ Any votes given to him are *null and void.* 彼に入れられた票はすべて無効だ.

numb /nʌm/ 形 ***a numb hand*** 《俗》不器用者 ▪ The writer is really *a numb hand.* その作家は実に不器用者だ.

number[1] /nʌ́mbər/ 名 ***a back number*** 《口》時代おくれの人[物] ▪ He was once a great leader, but now he is *a back number.* 彼はかつては偉大な

指導者だったが，今では時代おくれだ ▪ The sewing machine was quite *a back number.* ミシンは相当時代遅れの代物だった．☞「雑誌の旧号」の意味から．

a good number of 相当たくさんの ▪ There were *a good number of* people present. かなり多数の人が出席していた．

a great* [*large*] *number of 大勢の，たくさんの ▪ This is true in *a great number of* cases. これは多くの場合当たっている ▪ He has *a large number of* hangers-on. 彼は大勢の食客をくわせている．

a hot number 《俗》いま旬の人(物)，とても人気のある人(物) ▪ She has invented a new peeler that is *a hot number* in the stores. 彼女はいま店で大人気の皮むき器を考案した．

a number cruncher 《戯》 **1** 計算屋，複雑な暗算を楽にやってのける人 ▪ *A number cruncher* like you would find a job pretty soon. 君のように込み入った計算の得意な人ならすぐ就職口が見つかるだろう．
2 複雑な計算をこなせるコンピューター ▪ They use their *number cruncher* on election night. 選挙当夜は高性能コンピューターを使う．

a number of **1** いくらかの (some) ▪ *A number of* books are missing from the library. 蔵書がいくらか紛失している ▪ Only *a* small *number of* errors were made. 誤りはほんの少ししかなかった．
2 多数の ▪ He kept himself by keeping *a number of* bees. 彼は多くのミツバチを飼って自活している．

a* [*the*] *numbers game (人を惑わす)数字のトリック ▪ *The numbers game* did not tell the whole story. 数字に騙されて全容がつかめなかった．☞米国では numbers game「数当てゲーム」は違法な賭博を指す．

among the number その数の中に ▪ There are many persons, myself *among the number,* who saw it. それを見た人は多くいるが，私もその一人だ．

among the number of the dead 亡き数に入って ▪ He is *among the number of the dead.* 彼は亡き者の数に入った．

any number of →ANY amount (of).

be added to the number of …の仲間に入る ▪ He *is* now *added to the number of* my enemies. 彼は今は僕の敵の仲間だ．

beyond number →without NUMBER.

by* (*force* [*weight*] *of*) *numbers 人数(の優勢)で ▪ They were overwhelmed *by numbers.* 彼らは数で圧倒された ▪ The enemy won *by force of numbers.* 敵は数の優勢で勝った．

by the numbers 《米俗》ひとつひとつ着実に，順序通りに; 機械的に ▪ Writing music is not something you can do *by the numbers.* 作曲は順番にこつこつ積み上げてできる代物ではない．

***do a number on** a person* 《主に米口》…をわざと騙して[恥をかかせて]ひどい扱いをする，試合で一方的に負かして痛めつける ▪ My colleagues really *did a number on* me at work. 職場で同僚たちが私にひどくつらく当たった．

get* [*take, have*]** *a person's* ***number 《口》相手の正体を知る，人の本心を見抜く ▪ To hurt Bolshevism you need at least to *get its number.* 過激主義をやっつけるためには，少なくともその正体を知る必要がある ▪ I saw one policeman trying to *take my number.* 一人の警官が私の正体を探ろうとしているのが目に留まった ▪ She knew I *had her number.* 彼女は私が彼女の正体をつかんでいることを知っていた ▪ You can't fool me. I've *got your number.* 僕をだまそうとしても，そうはいかない．そっちの手の内は分かっている．☞電話から．

have** a person's **number on it =have a person's NAME (and number) on it.

in great numbers 大勢で ▪ Chinese students used to come *in great numbers.* 中国の学生が昔は大勢やって来た．

in number **1** 全部で ▪ They were ten *in number.* 全部で10あった[10人いた]．
2 数で言えば ▪ They exceed us *in number.* 彼らは数の上で我々に勝っている．

in numbers **1** (雑誌など)分冊で，何回にも分けて ▪ The novel came out *in numbers.* その小説は何回にも分けて出た．
2 韻文で ▪ I lisp'd *in numbers,* for the numbers came. 片ことで詩句を唱えた．詩句の浮かぶままに．
3 大勢で，たくさん ▪ They are found here *in numbers.* それは当地にはたくさんある ▪ They came *in numbers.* 彼らは大勢でやって来た．

in round numbers 概算で，概数で ▪ The list gives it *in round numbers.* 表は概数でそれを示している．

in small numbers 少数で ▪ They now come only *in small numbers.* 彼らは今は少数しか来ない．

look after* [*take care of*] *number one*/*look out for number one 《口》自分のことばかり考える ▪ I've got to *look after number one* first. 僕はまず自分のことを考えなければならない ▪ You have to *look out for number one* in this business. この商売では自分のことをまず考えないといけない．

lose the number of** one's **mess 死ぬ ▪ I have an idea that some of us will *lose the number of our mess.* 我々のうちの何人かが死ぬのではないかと考えている．

One's (***lucky***) ***number comes up.*** 《口》(競争などで)つきが回って来る ▪ One of these days *my number* will *come up.* 今につきが回ってくるぞ．

make** one's **number 《口》顔出しする，出頭する (*at*); あいさつをする (*with*) ▪ I *made my number at* his office. 彼の事務所に顔出しした ▪ *Make your number with* the Browns. ブラウン夫妻にあいさつをしなさい．

not of our* [*the*] *number **1** 我々の[その]仲間ではない ▪ The man over there is *not of our number.* あそこの男の人は我々の仲間ではない．
2 我々[その連中]といっしょにいない ▪ Jenkins here! No, he's *not of our number.* ジェンキンズがここかって! いや，ここにはいないよ．

***One's* number is [has gone] up.** 《口》 **1** 命数が尽きた ▪ I fear *his number is up*; the doctor says he is a hopeless case. 彼の命数は尽きたのではないか. 医師の話ではとても助かるまいとのことだ.
2 運がつきた ▪ *His number is up* at last. The Chief has decided to get rid of him. 彼の運もとうとう尽きた. 社長は彼をお払い箱にすることに決めたのだ.

number one/No.1 **1**《口》自己(の利害) ▪ I am tired of *No.1*. 僕は自分に飽きてしまった.
2《幼児》おしっこ ▪ I want to do *number one*. おしっこがしたい.
3〚形容詞的に〛《口》第一の, 第一級の ▪ As an ornament it is not *number one*. それは飾りとして第一級ではない ▪ She is America's *number one* woman golfer. 彼女はアメリカ第一の女流ゴルファーだ.

Number Ten/No. 10 (Downing 街10番地の)英国首相の官邸; 首相の意見[影響力] ▪ He is now about to enter *Number Ten* after his general election triumph. 彼は総選挙の勝利をうけて今まさに首相になろうとしている ▪ Academic opinion differs from *No.10*. 学者の意見は首相のものとは異なる.

number two **1**《口》(団体・部局の)次長 ▪ My *number two* is on leave. 次長は休暇をとっている.
2《幼児》うんち ▪ I want to do *number two*. うんちがしたい.

number('s) engaged 《英》話し中《電話で》 ▪ *Number engaged*. Ring again, please. 話し中です. またおかけ直しください.

numbers of 多数の ▪ I saw *numbers of* fish swimming in the pond. 池の中にたくさんの魚が泳いでいるのが見えた.

one's ***opposite number*** →OPPOSITE.

out of number →without NUMBER.

pluck a number out of the air ある数を適当に選び出す ▪ *Pluck a number out of the air* and multiply it by five. 任意の数に5を掛けなさい.

quite a number of かなり多数の… ▪ *Quite a number of* paintings have been sold. かなり多数の絵が売られた.

rely on numbers 数をたのむ ▪ The enemy *relied on numbers*. 敵は数をたのんだ.

settle the number of *a person's* ***mess*** 人を死なす, 命を取る ▪ The blow on my skull would have *settled the number of my mess* but for my helmet. ヘルメットがなかったら, 頭への打撃で私は命を取られていたことだろう.

take care of number one →look after NUMBER one.

take *a person's* ***number*** → get a person's NUMBER.

the great [large] number of 多数の ▪ *The great number of* people are affected by mass psychology. 多数の人々が群集心理に影響される ▪ *The large number of* writers seem to think so. 多数の作家がそう考えているようだ. ☞複数で呼応する.

there are numbers who …の者が多い ▪ *There are numbers who* are superstitious. 迷信を信じる人がたくさんいる.

to the number of …だけ, まで ▪ Books, *to the number of* not more than eight at one time, may be taken out of the Library. 本は一度に8冊までは館外へ借出しできる ▪ They volunteered *to the number of* 10,000. 志願者は1万人にも達した.

without [beyond, out of] number 無数の ▪ We have been told these things times *without number*. これらのことは今まで何度も何度も聞かされてきた ▪ Examples *beyond number* could be quoted. 無数の例を引用することもできる.

number[2] /nʌ́mbər/ 動 ***The days [years, hours] of ... are numbered.*** …の余命いくばくもない (《聖》*Ps*. 90. 12) ▪ Poor fellow, *his days are numbered*. かわいそうに, 彼の余命はいくばくもない ▪ *The days of* Spanish rule *were* already *numbered*. スペインによる支配の命数はもう尽きていた.

nurse[1] /nəːrs/ 名 ***a visiting nurse*** 訪問看護師 ▪ *A visiting nurse* comes round once a week to check his health. 訪問看護師が週に一度, 彼の健康チェックにやってくる.

at nurse 乳母(うば)に預けて ▪ The baby is now *at nurse*. 赤んぼうは今乳母に預けてある ▪ He had a child *at nurse* in the country. 彼は田舎に乳母に預けた子供があった.

go to nurse (地所が)管財人の手にゆだねられる ▪ His estate of £1,200 a year *went to nurse*. 年1,200ポンドの彼の地所が管財人の手にゆだねられた.

put (out)... to nurse **1** …を里子に出す ▪ She has *put out* the child *to nurse*. 彼女は子供を里子に出した.
2 (地所)を管財人の手にゆだねる ▪ He has *put* his estate *to nurse*. 彼は自分の地所を管財人の手にゆだねた.

take in ... at nurse …を里子に預かる ▪ The woman *took in* children *at nurse*. その女性は子供たちを里子に預かった.

nurse[2] /nəːrs/ 動 ***be nursed in*** …の状態に育つ ▪ He has *been nursed in* luxury. 彼は贅沢に育った.

nurse a drink →DRINK[1].

nurse *one's* ***constituency*** 《英》(政治家が)選挙区の面倒を見る ▪ Politicians are eager to *nurse their constituency* especially before an election. 政治家も特に選挙の前には熱心に選挙区の面倒を見ようとする.

nut[1] /nʌt/ 名 ***a hard [tough] nut (to crack)/a nut to crack*** **1** 難問, 難題 ▪ The third question was rather *a hard nut to crack*. 第3問はいささか難問だった ▪ It was *a nut to crack* for many, what these two could see in each other. この二人がお互いにどんなところを認め合ったのかは, 多くの人にとって難問だった.
2 難物, 扱いにくい人 ▪ Fortified towns are *hard nuts to crack*. 要塞化した町は攻めにくい ▪ You will find him *a hard nut to crack*. 彼は扱いにくい

N

人間だということがわかるだろうよ.

a nut case 発狂した人, 愚かな人, 奇人 ▪I am going to be *a nut case* if I don't take a rest a while. ちょっとひと休みしないと頭がおかしくなりそうだ.

a nut house [《まれ》 ***college, factory, farm***] 《米俗》精神病院 ▪He went away to *the nut house*. 彼はあの精神病院へ行った.

be a nut at 《俗》(ゲーム)がひどくうまい ▪He *is a nut at* bridge. 彼はブリッジの名手だ.

be* (*dead*) *nuts on [***upon, about, over***] 《俗》 **1** …に熱中している, が大好きだ, 大いに気に入っている ▪He'*s dead nuts on* netsurfing. 彼はネットサーフィンにすっかり熱中している ▪He'*s nuts about* Natalie Portman. 彼はナタリー・ポートマンが大好きだ ▪I *am* quite *nuts upon* myself. 全くごきげんだよ.

2 …がじょうずだ ▪Get Merlin on our side; he'*s nuts on* this game. マーリンを味方につけよう. 彼はこのゲームがじょうずなんだ.

be nuts to *a person* 《俗》人の大好物である ▪Mischief is said to *be nuts to* some people. いたずらが大好きな人もいると言われている ▪To see me here would *be* simply *nuts to* her. ここで私に会うのは彼女にはほんとにうれしいことだろう.

do *one's* ***nut*(*s*)** 《英口》かんかんに怒る; 狂的に努める ▪They are *doing their nuts* to get themselves out of the red. 彼らは赤字から脱出しようと狂奔している.

don't care a* (*rotten*) *nut ちっともかまわない ▪I *don't care a nut* whether he will come or not. 彼が来ようが来まいがちっともかまわない.

drive *a person* ***nuts*** 《米俗》人を悩ます ▪The story *drove* him *nuts*. その話は彼を悩ました.

for nuts 《英口》 **1** 〚否定語を伴って〛どうしても ▪He can't play golf *for nuts*. 彼はゴルフはてんでだめだ. ☞昔は nuts はずいぶん高価だったが, 「その nuts をもらっても」の意から.

2 おもしろ半分に (for fun) ▪Why don't you sink a shaft, just *for nuts*? ほんの慰みに, たて坑を掘り下げてみないかね.

go nuts 《俗》気が狂う ▪I'll *go nuts* if he doesn't turn off that radio soon. 彼があのラジオをすぐ消さなければ僕は頭がおかしくなってしまう.

go off *one's* ***nut*** 《俗》気が狂う ▪He *went off his nut* and killed himself. 彼は気が変になって自殺した.

have a loose nut 《米俗》気が狂っている ▪Don't you see he *has a loose nut*? 彼が正気でないことがわからないのか.

have a nut to crack with …と議論すべきことがある ▪I *have a nut to crack with* him. 彼と議論すべきことがある.

off *one's* ***nut*** 《英口》 **1** 発狂して ▪He has been *off his nut* for years. 彼はもう何年もおかしくなっているのだ ▪He is getting every day more *off his nut*. 彼は日ましに気がふれてきている.

2 酔って ▪The old woman was a bit *off her nut*. 老婆は少し酔っていた. ☞nut＝head.

prove that a nut has no shell 不可能なことを証明する ▪It would be like trying to *prove that a nut has no shell*. それはクルミに殻がないと証明しようとするようなものだ.

talk like a nut つまらぬことを言う, 愚かなことをしゃべる ▪Don't *talk like a nut*! We can't afford another car! ばかを言っちゃいけない. 車をもう1台買えるわけがないじゃないか.

the nuts and bolts (***of***) 《口》 **1** (…の)基本, 土台 ▪He learned *the nuts and bolts of* journalism with the "Herald." 彼はジャーナリズムの基本を「ヘラルド」紙で学んだ.

2 実際的な事柄, 実際面 ▪It's time to consider *the nuts and bolts*, not theory. 今は理論ではなく実際面を考えるべきときだ.

use a sledgehammer [***hammer***] ***to crack a nut*** 《英》小さなことにむだな労力を使う, 必要以上に強力な手段を用いる (→take a SLEDGEHAMMER to crack a walnut) ▪You are always *using a sledgehammer to crack a nut*. 君はいつだって些細な事柄にむだ骨を折ってばかりいる.

nut[2] /nʌt/ 動 ***go* (*a-*)*nutting*** 木の実拾いに行く ▪He and I used to *go nutting* in the wood. 彼と私はいつも森へ木の実拾いに行ったものだ.

nutmeg /nʌ́tmèg/ 名 ***a wooden nutmeg*** 《米》偽物, 紛(まが)い物 ▪We are sick and tired of those *wooden nutmeg* venders. あの偽物売りには全くうんざりする.

like [***as***] ***a nutmeg-grater*** (表面が)おろし金みたいにざらざらして ▪Her hands were rough *like a nutmeg-grater*. 彼女の手はおろし金みたいにざらざらしていた.

nutshell /nʌ́tʃèl/ 名 ***in a nutshell*** 簡単に言えば, ほんの一言で ▪You have my history *in a nutshell*. かいつまんで言えばこれが私の身の上話です. ☞小さいクルミの殻が仁(じん)をきちんと入れていることから.

lie in a nutshell きわめて簡単なことだ, 議論の余地がない ▪The whole matter *lies in a nutshell*. 事のすべてはきわめて簡単だ.

put in a nutshell 一言で言う ▪I can *put* the matter *in a nutshell*. そのことはたった一言で言える.

nutty /nʌ́ti/ 形 (***as***) ***nutty as a fruitcake*** 《口》ひどく狂気じみた ▪He's *nutty as a fruitcake*. 彼は全くどうかしている. ☞nutty＝insane. フルーツケーキとの類似点はケーキに nut が入っている点.

be nutty on [***upon***] 《俗》…にほれている, 熱中している ▪Tom *is* quite *nutty on* Mary. トムはメアリーに首ったけだ.

nuzzle /nʌ́zəl/ 動 ***nuzzle*** *oneself* 寄り添う ▪Wisdom *nuzzles herself* in his bosom. 知恵が彼の胸に寄り添っている.

O

O, Oh /oʊ/ 間 ***O for ...!*** ああ…がほしいなあ(I wish to have) ▪ *O for* a draught of vintage! (Keats, *Ode to a Nightingale*) ああ1杯の美酒がほしいなあ!

Oh that ...! ああ…であったらなあ(I wish) ▪ *Oh that* I had never seen it! ああ, あんなものを見なければよかったのに!

oh, to be in ああ…にいたいなあ(I wish to be) ▪ *Oh, to be in* England/Now that April's there. (Browning, *Home Thoughts from Abroad*) ああイギリスにいたいなあ/いま4月が来ているのに.

oh well まあ仕方がないか《あきらめを表す》 ▪ I can't go out to the movies tonight.—*Oh well.* 今晩は映画に行けないよ—まあ仕方がないか.

oh, yeah? え, 本当かい《不信を表す》 ▪ This sauce tastes bad.—*Oh, yeah?* What makes you think so? このソースはまずいよ—え, 本当かい? どうしてそう思うの?

oak /oʊk/ 名 (*a*) ***heart of oak*** →HEART.

Great [***Mighty***] ***oaks from little acorns grow.*** 《諺》大きなオークの木も小さなドングリから,「千里の道も一歩から, ちりも積もれば山となる」. ☞acorns「ドングリ(オークの実)」.

sport (*one's*) ***oak*** →SPORT[2].

oakum /óʊkəm/ 名 ***pick oakum*** まいはだを作る《昔罪人・貧民に普通の仕事》 ▪ I shall make you *pick oakum* from now until your dying day. 今後お前が死ぬまでまいはだを作らせてやるぞ《牢にぶち込むぞ, の意》.

oar[1] /ɔːr/ 名 ***a pair of oars*** 二人でこぐ船 ▪ He went into *a pair of oars* that was ready. 彼は待ちかまえている二人こぎの船に乗った.

chain [***condemn***] *a person* ***to the oar*** (奴隷・罪人)にガレー船をこぐことをしいる; 苦役をしいる ▪ He *condemns* criminals *to the oar.* 彼は罪人にガレー船をこがせる ▪ The anguish that flows from your sins *chains* you *to the oar.* お前の罪から生じる苦悩によって苦役をしいられるのだ. ☞ガレー船の奴隷が鎖でかいに縛られていたことから.

first oars (ボートの)整調手; 主要人物 ▪ He was always *first oars* at a party. 彼はパーティーではいつも主要人物だった.

have an oar in every man's boat [***barge***] 何事にも口を出す, ちょっかいを出す ▪ He's sure to *have an oar in every man's boat.* あの男は必ず何事にも口を出す.

have *one's* ***oar in*** *a person's* ***boat*** →put one's OAR in a person's boat.

have [***take, pull, ply,*** etc.] ***the laboring oar*** →pull the LABORING oar.

lay in the oars →LAY[2].

lie on *one's* ***oar*** →rest on one's OARs.

pull a lone oar 一人だけ調子はずれにこぐ; (協力者なしで)一人でやっていく ▪ Despite offers of assistance, he insists on *pulling a lone oar.* 援助の申し出があるのに彼はどうしても一人でやると言っている.

put [***thrust, shove, stick***] ***in*** *one's* ***oar*** 《口》いらぬ世話をやく, くちばしを入れる ▪ I am settling the matter—you need not *put in your oar.* 僕が問題を処理しているのだ, 君はくちばしを入れなくていい.

put [***have***] *one's* ***oar in*** *a person's* ***boat*** いらぬ世話をやく ▪ I *put my oar in no man's boat.* 私は誰にもおせっかいはしない.

rest [***lie***] ***on*** [***upon***] *one's* ***oars*** **1** オールを上げてこぐのを休む ▪ He ordered the boats to *lie upon their oars.* 彼は各ボートにオールを上げてこぐのを休むよう命じた.

2 《英》(仕事・努力を)ひと休みする ▪ If we expect to finish in time, we can't *rest on our oars.* 間に合うように終えたければ, ひと休みしてはいられない. ☞オールを水から水平に上げオールの柄上で休むことから.

shove [***stick, thrust***] ***in*** *one's* ***oar*** →put in one's OAR.

oar[2] /ɔːr/ 動 ***oar it*** 泳ぐ ▪ I *oared it* in translucent waters. 私は半透明な水中を泳いだ.

oar *one's* ***way*** こぐように進む ▪ Stately white swans were *oaring their way* with rosy feet. 見事なハクチョウがバラ色の足を動かして泳ぎ進んでいた.

oasis /oʊéɪsəs/ 名 ***an oasis in the desert*** 砂漠のオアシス《寂しい[単調な]生活の中の憩いの場所[時]》 ▪ His little sanctum is *an oasis* of art *in the* howling *desert* of London. 彼の小さな私室はロンドンという寂しい砂漠の中の芸術的なオアシスである.

oat /oʊt/ 名 ***feel*** *one's* ***oats*** 《口》 **1** (馬が)元気がよくてはねかえる ▪ The pony *felt his oats,* and took a frightful canter. 小馬は元気よくはねかえり, がむしゃらにかけ出した.

2 (人が)うぬぼれる, いい気になる ▪ My father installed me as clerk in this country store. Of course I *felt my oats.* おやじが僕をこの日用雑貨店の店員にしてくれた. もちろん僕はいい気になった.

get [***have***] *one's* ***oats*** 《英口》性交する ▪ She wouldn't let him *have his oats.* 彼女は彼に性交を許さなかった.

have *one's* ***wild oats*** →sow one's wild OATs.

off *one's* ***oats*** →OFF one's feed.

smell *one's* ***oats*** (終わりが近づいて)勇み立つ ▪ *Smelling his oats,* he took heart. 彼は勇み立って, 気を取り直した. ☞馬がうまやに近づくのに気がついて急ぎ出すことから.

sow [《俗》***have***] *one's* ***wild oats*** 若気のいたりから道楽をする《通例のちの改心を暗示する》 ▪ He's very young and I suppose he's *sowing his wild* *oats.* 彼はとても若いのだから，たぶん道楽をしているのだろう．☞良い種の代わりに愚かにも野生のカラスムギ (wild oats) をまくことから．

oath /oʊθ/ 名 ***make (an) oath/swear an oath*** 誓いを立てる，宣誓する ▪ Rose *made oath* to her soul she would rescue him. ローズは彼を救おうと心に誓った ▪ I *swear an oath* on the Bible. 聖書に誓って断言する．

on [upon] (one's) oath 誓って ▪ He made the statement *on oath.* 彼は誓いを立てて供述した ▪ You swear that?—*On my oath.* 誓ってか?—誓ってです．

place [put] a person under oath 《法》人に宣誓させる ▪ The witness *was placed under oath.* 証人は宣誓させられた．

put [place] a person on (his) oath 人に誓わせる ▪ I *put* him *on his oath* before handing over the letter. 手紙を手渡す前に彼に誓いを立てさせた．

take (an, one's) oath 誓う，宣誓する (*that, on*) ▪ I'll *take my oath* it was him that I saw. 誓って言いますが，私が見たのはあの男でした ▪ I will go before a lawyer and *take my oath on* that matter. 私が弁護士の前へ行って，その問題について宣誓しよう．

under oath =on (one's) OATH.

obedience /oʊbíːdiəns|əb-/ 名 ***hold a person in obedience*** 人を心服させている ▪ He *held* his servants *in* complete *obedience.* 彼は使用人を完全に心服させていた．

in obedience to …に服従して，に従って ▪ A heavy body falls to the ground *in obedience to* the law of gravitation. 重い物体は引力の法則に従って地面に落ちる．

obeisance /oʊbéɪsəns/ 名 ***do [make, pay] (an, one's) obeisance*** 《文》 **1** …に会釈する，敬礼する ▪ The foreign representative *did obeisance* before the sovereign. 外国代表は元首の前で敬礼した ▪ He *paid* her *his obeisance.* 彼は女性に会釈した．

2 …に敬意を表す，服従する ▪ He *did obeisance* to the king. 彼は王に敬意を表した．

obey /oʊbéɪ|əb-/ 動 ***He that cannot obey cannot command.*** 《諺》服従することのできない人は命令することもできない《リーダーになろうと思うなら，まず誰かに従う術を身につけるべきだ》．

object[1] /ábdʒekt|ɔ́b-/ 名 ***an object lesson*** 実地[実物]教育，(あることをすべき(でない)という教訓となる)実例 ▪ Let that be *an object lesson* to your son. それを君の息子が学ぶ教訓とせよ．

(be) no object …は問題[支障]とならない; (特に広告文句で)…は問わない，どうでもよい ▪ With him distance *is no object.* 彼にとって距離など問題ではない ▪ Every convenience is obtainable there and expense *no object.* そこではあらゆる便宜が得られ，しかも費用はいくらかかってもよい ▪ Salary will *be no object.* 月給に対しては特別の要求なし．

with the object of …という目的をもって ▪ He is working hard *with the object of* earning money. 彼は金儲けの目的で懸命に働いている．

object[2] /əbdʒékt/ 動 ***I object.*** 《英》異議あり《下院議場用文句》 ▪ "*I object!*" he shouted, jumping to his feet. 「異義あり!」と彼は叫んで，さっと立ち上がった．

if you don't object ご異議がなければ ▪ I think I'll have a smoke, *if you don't object.* おさしつかえなければ一服やりたい．

object against a person that …の理由で人に反対する ▪ I *object against* him *that* he is too young for the position. 彼がその地位には若すぎるという理由で反対だ．

objection /əbdʒékʃən/ 名 ***feel an objection to doing*** …するのにいや気を感じる ▪ I *felt an objection to* his *leaving.* 私は彼が去るのをいやだと思った．

have an [no] objection to …に異議がある[ない] ▪ I *have a* strong *objection to* him. 彼には大いに文句がある ▪ I *have no objection to* join [joining] with you in the enquiry. 君といっしょになってそれを調べることに異存はない．

make [raise] an objection to/take objection to …に異議を唱える，反対する ▪ He will *make an objection to* the match. 彼はその結婚に異議を唱えるだろう ▪ He has *taken objection to* the proposal. 彼はその提案に反対した．

see [there is] no objection to …に別に異議はない ▪ I *see no objection to* doing so. そうすることに別に異議はない ▪ *There is no objection to* your leaving at once. 君はすぐ立ち去ってもさしつかえない．

objective /əbdʒéktɪv/ 形 ***an objective point*** **1** 《軍》目標地点 ▪ Atlanta was *the objective point* of the Federals. アトランタは北部連邦軍の目標地点であった．

2 (一般に)目的地，ねらい ▪ No light as to his next "*objective point*" has yet been gained. 彼の次の「ねらい」についてはまだなんの情報も得られない．

obligation /àbləgéɪʃən|ɔ̀b-/ 名 ***be [lie] under an obligation to*** …に義務[義理]がある ▪ I *lie under an obligation to* him. 彼には義理がある ▪ I'*m under* many *obligations to* you for my son. 息子の件で君にはいろいろご厄介になっています．

discharge one's obligations 債務を果たす[払う] ▪ He *discharged his obligations* at the inn, and journeyed on. 彼は宿で勘定をすませ，旅を続けた．

of obligation 義務上当然の，義務的な ▪ There is only one Muslim pilgrimage *of obligation,* that to Mecca. ムスリムの義務的な巡礼は一つしかない，メッカへの巡礼である．

put [place, lay] a person under an obligation 人に義理を負わせる ▪ Your kindness *puts* me *under an obligation.* ご親切にしていただいて恩義を感じています ▪ He once *laid* me *under an obligation.* 彼には一度厄介になったことがある．

without obligation 代金無用で (for free); 義務なしの ▪ This book will be sent *without obliga-*

tion to any university student personally requesting it. 本書は個人で要求されるいかなる大学生にも無料でお送りします ▪ Freedom *without obligation* is anarchy. 義務なしの自由はアナーキーである.

oblige /əbláɪdʒ/ 動 ***be obliged to*** …をしなければならない ▪ The people *were obliged to* these severities by self-preservation. 人々は自己保存のために, これらのきびしい道を講じなければならなかった.

***be obliged to** do* …しなければならない ▪ We *are obliged to* yield to the times. 時節には従わねばならない.

***be obliged to** A **for** B* BのことでAに恩義を受けている, BはAのおかげである ▪ I *am* very much *obliged to* you *for* your help. お助けいただいてどうもありがとうございます ▪ *To* those hills we *are obliged for* all our metals. 我々の使うすべての金属があるのはこれらの山のおかげである.

oblivion /əblíviən/ 名 ***be buried in oblivion*** 忘れられてしまう ▪ The question ought to have *been buried in oblivion*. その問題は忘れられてしまうべきものだった.

consign … to oblivion …を忘れてしまう ▪ It would have *been consigned to* lasting *oblivion*. それは永久に忘れられていたことだろう.

fall [sink, go, pass] into oblivion (世に)忘れられる ▪ In England this doctrine has *sunk into* complete *oblivion*. イギリスではこの教理はすっかり忘れられてしまっている.

oblivious /əblíviəs/ 形 ***(be) oblivious of [to]*** **1** …を忘れがちで《to は誤用》 ▪ They are playing, *oblivious of* all care. すべての苦労を忘れて彼らは遊んでいる.

2 …に気がつかずに《誤用》 ▪ Lovers *are oblivious to* anything but themselves. 恋人同士は自分たち以外のことは何にも気がつかない.

obscure /əbskjʊ́ər/ 形 ***(be) of obscure origin [birth]*** 素性が卑しい ▪ His face indicates that he *is of obscure birth*. 彼の顔は素性が卑しいことを示している.

obscurity /əbskjʊ́ərəti/ 名 ***live in obscurity*** 世に埋もれて暮らす ▪ He is content to *live in obscurity*. 彼は世に埋もれた生活に甘んじている.

rise [spring, emerge] from obscurity 無名から身を起こす ▪ The man has *risen from obscurity* to fame. その男は無名から身を起こして名を成した.

sink [lapse] into obscurity 世に埋もれる ▪ His works have *sunk into obscurity*. 彼の作品は世に埋もれてしまった.

observant /əbzə́ːrvənt/ 形 ***be observant of*** **1** (法律・習慣など)を守る ▪ He *is* always *observant of* his duty. 彼はいつも義務を守る.

2 …に注意している ▪ He *was* cautiously *observant of* all that passed. 彼は通り過ぎるすべての人を用心深く注意していた.

observation /ɑ̀bzərvéɪʃən|ɔ̀b-/ 名 ***come [fall] under** a person's **observation*** 人の目に留まる ▪ A fact has *come under my observation*. ある事実が私の目に留まった.

escape observation 見られないですむ ▪ Fortunately he *escaped observation*. 幸い彼は見られないですんだ.

place … under observation (犯罪者・病人を)監視[観察]下に置く (→ under OBSERVATION) ▪ The police *placed* him *under observation*. 警察は彼を監視下に置いた.

take an** [one's] **observation = work an OBSERVATION.

under observation 監視[観察]中の ▪ They kept the prisoner *under observation*. 彼らは囚人をずっと監視し続けた.

work an** [one's] **observation 天測の結果を計算して緯度・経度を確かめる ▪ I have shown you how to *work your observation*. 私は君に天測の結果を計算して経緯を確かめる方法を教えた.

observe /əbzə́ːrv/ 動 ***the observed of all observers*** 衆目の的 (cf. Sh., *Haml.* 3. 1. 162) ▪ He was, indeed, *the observed of all observers* about town. 彼は確かに町中の衆目の的であった.

obsess /əbsés/ 動 ***be obsessed by [with]*** (ある考え)につかれている ▪ He *is obsessed by* the idea of his own importance. 彼は自分が大物だという考えに取りつかれている.

obstructive /əbstrʌ́ktɪv/ 形 ***be obstructive of [to]*** …の妨げになる ▪ This angry haste might some day *be obstructive of* his own work. こんなに怒って急いでいると, いつか彼の仕事の妨げになるかもしれない ▪ Academies may *be obstructive to* inventive genius. アカデミーは創造的才能の妨げになるかもしれない.

obtrude /əbtrúːd/ 動 ***obtrude** oneself* 出しゃばる (*on, upon, into*) ▪ That woman will *obtrude herself on* our notice. あの女性は我々の目につくように出しゃばろうとしている ▪ He *obtruded himself into* matters beyond his office. 彼は自分の職権外の事柄に出しゃばった.

occasion /əkéɪʒən/ 名 ***a sense of occasion*** →SENSE.

as occasion arises [offers, requires, may require] 必要があれば ▪ He will help us *as occasion arises*. 彼は必要なら我々を助けてくれるだろう.

equal to the occasion 事にあたって動じない, 事に立派に対拠しうる ▪ A great man is *equal to any occasion*. 偉い人は事にあたって動じない ▪ Young as he was, he was *equal to the occasion*. 彼は若かったが事に臨んで立派に対拠することができた.

for [on, upon]** a person's **occasion 人のために ▪ Had he not come only *upon [for] their occasion*? 彼はただ彼らのために来てくれたのではなかったか.

for the occasion 臨時に ▪ He is engaged *for the occasion*. 彼は臨時雇いだ.

give occasion to …を引き起こす ▪ That gave *occasion to* a burst of laughter. それでどっと笑いが

まき起こった.

***have* [*have no*] *occasion for* [*to* do]** …の必要がある[ない] ▪ Captain Brown is dismissed from the Army, his Majesty *having no* further *occasion for* his services. ブラウン大尉は除隊された，王はもはや彼の奉仕を必要としないからだ ▪ I have *had* frequent *occasion to* make use of enamel. 私はしばしばエナメルを使う必要があった.

improve the occasion →IMPROVE[2].

in honor of the occasion 祝意を表して ▪ Let's make a night of it *in honor of the occasion*. ひとつ祝意を表して一晩飲み明かそう.

***on every occasion* [*all occasions*]** あらゆる場合に ▪ That will serve you *on every occasion*. それはあらゆる機会に役に立ちましょう.

on* [*upon*]** *a person's* ***occasion →for a person's OCCASION.

on* [*upon*] *occasion(s) 折に触れて，時おり ▪ I meet him *on occasion* at the club. 彼とは時たまクラブで会う.

on the first occasion 機会のあり次第 ▪ I'll speak to him *on the first occasion*. 機会があり次第彼に話してみよう.

on* [*upon*] (*the*) *occasion of …のついでに，にあたって ▪ *Upon occasion of* the mention of the battle, I could not help adding a few remarks. その戦いのことが言われた際，私は二言三言，言い添えないではおられなかった.

rise to the occasion 難局に対処する，臨機の策をとる ▪ He will *rise to the occasion* all right when the time comes. その時が来れば，彼は必ず臨機の策をとるだろうよ.

***take occasion by the forelock* [*hair, hand*]** 機会をのがさず捕える ▪ We can escape just now, if we *take occasion by the forelock*. 機会をのがさず捕えればちょうど今なら逃げられる ▪ He *took occasion by the hand*, and when he saw the queen, presented a book to her. 彼は機会をのがさず捕えて，女王を見ると1冊の本を差し上げた. ☞好機が後頭部のはげた女性として擬人化されるところから.

take occasion to *do* 機会を利用して…する ▪ I'll *take occasion to* talk to him about it. 機会を捕えて彼にそのことを話してみよう.

take this* [*that*] *occasion to *do* この[その]機会を利用して…する ▪ I should like to *take this occasion to* ask your favor. この機会を利用してお願い申し上げます.

***there is no occasion for* [*to* do]** …の必要はない ▪ *There* will *be no occasion for* apology. 陳謝の必要はないだろう ▪ *There is no occasion to* call in magicians. 魔術師を呼び入れる必要はない.

whenever* [*wherever*] *an occasion offers 機会があり次第[ある所はどこでも] ▪ He distinguished himself *wherever an occasion offered*. 彼は機会のある所ではどこでも頭角を表した.

occupy /ɑ́kjəpàɪ|ɔ́kju-/ 動 ***be occupied in* [*with*]** …に従事している，で多忙だ ▪ He *was occupied with* his work. 彼は仕事で忙しかった ▪ I *was* deeply *occupied in* thinking of the matter. 私はそのことを深く考えこんでいた.

***occupy oneself in* [*with*]** …に従事する，で多忙だ ▪ Having retired from business, he now *occupies himself with* his garden. 退職したので彼は今は庭仕事に精を出している ▪ He *occupies himself in* the study of philosophy. 彼は哲学の研究に没頭している.

occurrence /əkə́ːrəns|əkʌ́r-/ 名 ***of frequent* [*rare,* etc.] *occurrence*** しばしば[まれに，など]起こる ▪ Snow is *of frequent occurrence*. 雪はしばしば降る ▪ Such an accident is *of rare occurrence*. そんな事故はめったに起こらない ▪ Conflicts were *of daily occurrence*. 衝突は毎日のように起こった.

ocean /óʊʃən/ 名 ***an ocean of/oceans of*** たくさんの《誇張表現》 ▪ I am now plunged into *an ocean of* troubles. 私は今苦難の海の中に飛び込んでいる ▪ In her letter she sent him *oceans of* love. 彼女は手紙の中で彼におびただしい愛情の言葉を送った.

be oceans apart =be POLEs asunder.

o'clock /əklɑ́k|əklɔ́k/ 副 ***know* [*find*] *what o'clock it is*** 真相を知っている[見抜く] ▪ He *knows what o'clock it is*. 彼は真相を知っている ▪ You've *found what o'clock it is*, haven't you? 君は真相を見抜いたな.

lie at nine o'clock 南東から北西に横たわる ▪ The veins *lie at nine o'clock*. 鉱脈は南東から北西に横たわっている.

like one o'clock 《俗》猛烈に ▪ Though he ran *like one o'clock*, he couldn't catch his train. 彼は猛烈に走ったが，電車に間に合わなかった ▪ They found him still sleeping *like one o'clock*. 彼らが行ってみると，彼はまだぐっすり寝こんでいた.

odd /ɑd|ɔd/ 形 ***an odd corner* [*angle*]** 人目につかない片すみ ▪ He was constrained to seek *odd corners* for his safety. 彼は身の安全のため人目につかない片すみを探さねばならなかった.

***an odd fish* [*bird*]** 《口》変人，変わり者 ▪ He seems *an odd fish*. 彼は変人みたいだ.

an odd-job man 《主に英》雑用係，便利屋 ▪ *The odd-job man* fixes everything in and around the office. 現業職員は社内外のすべての補修をする.

***an odd man* [*lad, hand*]** 片手間仕事をする人，臨時雇い ▪ A chambermaid and *a* nondescript *odd man* constituted her staff of assistants. 小間使いと得体の知れぬ臨時雇いだけが彼女を手助けした.

an odd pair **1** (二つ一組の)片方 ▪ I've got on *an odd pair* of socks. 靴下の片方だけをはいている. **2** 余分の一組 ▪ When he played rugby he always took *an odd pair* of shorts with him. 彼はラグビーをするときにはいつも余分のパンツを持って行った.

and odd …とはしたの ▪ He had two hundred *and odd* pounds. 彼は200ポンドとなにがしの金を持っていた.

at odd moments [***times***] 折に触れて，ときどき ▪ He wanders in here *at odd times*. 彼はときどきぶらぶらここへやって来る.

do odd jobs →JOB[1].

even or odd =ODD and even.

evenly odd 偶数の奇数倍の ▪ 14 is an *evenly odd* number. 14は偶数の奇数倍の数だ.

odd and [***or***] ***even*** 丁か半か《手に何か小さいものを一つか二つか握って，相手にその数を当てさせる子供の遊戯》 ▪ The children played at *odd and even*. 子供たちは数の当てっこをして遊んだ.

odd man out **1** はんぱ除き《銭投げなどによって３人(以上)の中の１人をある事の当事者に選び出す方法・遊戯》 ▪ Here, we'll toss and it shall be the *odd man out*. さあ銭投げをして１人を選び出すことにしよう. **2** (ダンスの)パートナーのいない人; 仲間はずれの人 ▪ I was *odd man out* all evening. 僕は一晩中パートナーがいなかった.

3 他とはっきり異なる人[物] ▪ He is the *odd man out* among the criminals. 彼は犯罪者の中で異色だ.

the odd man (調停者・委員会の３番目・５番目などの人で議論が賛否相半ばしたとき)決裁投票をする人 ▪ The fifth was *the odd man* whose casting vote would turn the scale. ５番目の人が裁決権を握っていて，局面を一変させる決裁投票者だった.

the odd one out 他とは異なる人，はみ出し者 ▪ She sure is *the odd one out*. She never fits in socially. 彼女は社交にとけ込めず，確かにはみ出し者だ.

the odd trick 《トランプ》(whist で双方が６回ずつ勝ったあと)勝負を決する13回目 ▪ The party got *the odd trick*. その組は13回目で勝負を決めた.

odd-come-shortly /ɑ́dkʌ̀mʃɔ́ːrtli|ɔ́d-/ 名 ***one of these odd-come-shortlies*** 《口》近いうちに ▪ I will write her a long letter *one of these odd-come-shortlies*. 近いうちに彼女に長い手紙を書くことにしよう.

oddly /ɑ́dli|ɔ́d-/ 副 ***oddly enough*** 妙な話だが ▪ *Oddly enough*, I couldn't recall his name. 妙なことに彼の名前が思い出せなかった.

oddly even [***odd***] 偶数[奇数]の奇数倍の ▪ *Oddly even* numbers may be parted into equal halves. 偶数の奇数倍の数は２等分することができる.

odds /ɑdz|ɔdz/ 名 ***against all*** (***the***) ***odds***/***against the odds*** 大変な困難にもめげずに ▪ I finished my work well *against all the odds*. 大変な困難にもめげずに私は仕事を立派にやってのけた ▪ I have struggled *against the odds* to keep my business going. 取引を続けるため困難に負けず尽力してきた.

against long [***fearful, heavy, terrible,*** etc.] ***odds*** 強敵に対して ▪ We have fought *against longer odds*. 我々はもっと強敵と戦ったことがある ▪ There is no fighting *against such odds*. そんな大敵に立ち向かうことなどできない.

ask no odds 《米》恩恵を求めない ▪ I *ask no odds* of them. 私は彼らに恩恵を求めない ▪ I *ask no* man any *odds* further than civility. 私は誰にも丁寧さの他何の恩恵も求めない.

(***at***) ***long*** [***short***] ***odds*** 勝算の低い[高い]賭け率(で) ▪ Everyone was surprised when Success won the race, *at* very *long odds*. 勝算がひどく低いのに，サクセス号が優勝したときには誰もがびっくりした.

at odds with the world [*oneself*] 何も手につかず，困惑して，不満で ▪ I've been more and more *at odds with the world* lately. 近頃ますます憂鬱がつのっている.

be at odds (***with***) **1** (...と)争っている，不和である ▪ They *are* always *at odds* about something. 彼らはいつも何かのことで争っている ▪ He'*s at odds with* his wife over money. 彼は金のことで奥さんと不和になっている.

2 ...と食い違っている，異なっている ▪ Washington *is at odds with* the EU over drug strategies. 麻薬政策に関して米国は EU と食い違いがある.

be no odds of 《俗》...の知ったことではない ▪ It'*s no odds of* mine. それは私の知ったことじゃない.

by (***long, all***) ***odds*** 〚比較級・最上級を強調して〛はるかに，断然 ▪ He is *by long odds* the ablest of the candidates. 彼は候補者中でずばぬけて有能だ ▪ Of course the American was *by all odds* the stronger man. もちろんアメリカ人の方がずっと強かった.

defy the odds 可能性に挑戦する ▪ Norman Douglas, an adventurer and explorer, lived a lifetime of *defying the odds*. 冒険家で探検家のノーマン・ダグラスは可能性に挑戦する生涯を過ごした.

give [***lay***] ***odds*** (試合・賭けなどで)有利条件を与える，歩(ぶ)をつける ▪ I beat Jones in billiards because he *gave* me tremendous *odds*. ビリヤードでジョーンズに勝ったのは，ひどく歩をつけてくれたからだ ▪ What *odds* will you *lay* against him? 彼にどれだけの歩を与えるのか ▪ I will *give odds* of 7 to 3. 7対3の歩をつけよう.

have the odds on *one's* ***side*** 自分の側に勝ち目がある ▪ As far as I can judge, we *have the odds on our side*. 僕の判断では，勝ち目は我々の側にある.

it is even odds that ...の見込みは五分五分だ ▪ *It's even odds that* he will come. 彼が来るか来ないか，見込みは五分五分だ.

it is long odds against [***that***] ...の見込みはほとんどない ▪ *It is long odds against* his getting the managership. 彼が支配人の職につく見込みはほとんどない ▪ *It is long odds that* you'll ever see your umbrella again. 君の傘が見つかる見込みはまずないね. ☞競馬の賭けから.

it is no odds 《口》少しも差がない，何の影響も与えない ▪ But there, *it's no odds*. しかしまあ，問題ではないじゃないか.

it is odds (***on***) (***that***) たぶん...だ ▪ *It's odds on* she did it. たぶん彼女がそうしたのだ ▪ *It is odds that* he will fall asleep. 彼はたぶん寝込んでしまうだろう.

lay odds →give ODDS.

lay [***give***] ***odds on*** [***that***] ...に賭ける，推量する ▪ I'll *lay odds on* his coming [*that* he wil come]. 彼はきっと来ると思う.

make no [***little***] ***odds*** 《英口》少しも[ほとんど]差がない, 全然[ほとんど]重要ではない ▪ You can come this week or next, it *makes no odds* to us. 君は今週来ても来週来てもいい, 私たちにはどちらでもよい ▪ It *makes no odds* whether a man has a thousand pounds or nothing. 人が1,000ポンド持っていようが無一文であろうが同じことだ.

make odds even 不平均をならす, 優劣をなくす ▪ Death *makes* these *odds* all *even*. 死はこれらの不均衡をすべてならしてしまう.

no odds 《口》たいしたことはない ▪ I have lost my hat.—*No odds*. Come without one. 帽子をなくしたんだよ—かまわないよ. 帽子なしで来たまえ.

odds and ends [《英俗》***sods***] 《口》残り物, がらくた ▪ The *odds and ends* are in this box. がらくたはこの箱の中にあります ▪ He has picked up several *odds and ends* of free thought. 彼は自由思想をあれこれとかじっている.

over the odds 《英口》定価より高く; 法外な ▪ He refuses to pay? That's a bit *over the odds*. 彼は払わないと言うのか. そいつはちょっとひどいな ▪ Some people try to buy rationed articles by paying a bit *over the odds*. 中には少し高く金を払って配給品を手に入れようとする者もいる. ☞競馬から.

set *a person* ***at odds*** 人を争わせる, 不和にさせる (*with*) ▪ That *set* him *at odds with* his wife. それが彼と妻とを不和にさせた.

shout the odds 自分のことばかりしゃべる, 自慢する ▪ No one *shouts the odds* quite so much as he does. 彼ほど自慢する者はいない. ☞競馬から.

stack the odds against = STACK the cards against.

take [***receive***] ***the odds*** (競技・賭けなどで)有利な条件・歩(ぶ)をつけた申し込みに応じる, 歩をつけてもらう ▪ There's no great honor in getting a victory when *the odds are taken*. 歩をつけてもらって勝ったところで, さして名誉ではない.

the odds are against *one* [***in*** *one's* ***favor***] 自分のほうに勝ち目がない[ある] ▪ In this game of chance *the odds are* a hundred to one *against* you. この一六勝負では百中九十九まで君に勝ち目はないでしょう ▪ *The odds are* now greatly *in his favor*. 今は大いに彼のほうに勝ち目がある.

the odds are even that …の見込みは五分五分だ ▪ *The odds are even that* he will win. 彼が勝つか負けるか, 見込みは五分五分だ.

the odds are that たぶん…だろう ▪ *The odds are that* Jim will be able to come. たぶんジムは来られるだろう.

What's the odds? 《英口》どうでもいいじゃないか ▪ Let him come if he wants to. *What's the odds?* あの男が来たいと言うのなら来させたらいい. どうでもいいじゃないか. ☞odds=difference.

within the odds 《口》どうやら見込みのある ▪ The cards you have been dealt are *within the odds*. 君に配られたカードにどうやら見込みがあるようだ.

odor, 《英》**odour** /óʊdər/ 名 ***be in bad*** [***ill***] ***odor*** 《文》(人が)評判がよくない ▪ He's *in* pretty *bad odor* among his colleagues. 彼は同僚の間で評判がよくない.

be in good odor 《文》(人が)評判がよい ▪ He *is in good odor* with his students. 彼は学生間に受けがいい.

the [***an***] ***odor of sanctity*** 《まれに皮肉》聖者のおもかげ, 高徳の誉れ; 圧倒される敬虔な雰囲気 ▪ My respected grandmother died in *the odor of sanctity*. 私の尊敬する祖母は高徳の誉れを残して死んだ ▪ He carried *the odor of sanctity* about him. 彼にはどことなく聖者のおもかげがある ▪ There was *an odor of sanctity* about the vicarage. 牧師館には何となく息の詰まるような敬虔な雰囲気があった. ☞聖者が死ぬときやその遺骸が掘り出されたときには, 芳香を放つという伝説から.

Oedipus /édəpəs|íːdɪ-/ 名 ***the*** [***an***] ***Oedipus complex*** エディプス・コンプレックス《息子が無意識に父親に反発し母親に対して性的思慕の情を抱くこと》 ▪ Hamlet could be read as a tale of a boy with *an Oedipus complex*. ハムレットをエディプス・コンプレックスの青年の物語として読むことも可能だろう. ☞フロイト学派の概念で, 古代ギリシャ伝説に基づく. オイディプスはそうとは全く知らずに父親を殺害し母親と結婚した.

of /əv, ɑv|ɔv/ 前 ***of a Sunday*** [***night, morning, an afternoon,*** etc.] 日曜日[夜, 朝, 午後, など]はいつも ▪ He takes a nap *of an afternoon*. 彼は午後はいつも昼寝をする.

off[1] /ɔːf|ɔf/ 副前形名 ***a bit off*** (ふるまいが)少々無礼な[いただけない] ▪ Her childish behavior was *a bit off*. 彼女の子供じみたふるまいは少々無礼だった.

a [*one's*] ***day*** [***night, week, year,*** etc.] ***off*** 1日[1晩, 1週間, 1年, など]の休暇 ▪ He asked for *a week off*. 彼は1週間の休暇を願い出た ▪ It was *his night off*. それは彼の非番の夜だった.

be a bit off 《英俗》(行為が)卑劣だ; いかがわしい ▪ By Jove! It's *a bit off*, isn't it? 全くそいつは卑劣じゃないか.

be all off 《米俗》死んでいる; おしまいだ ▪ Sorry but it's *all off*. 悪いがその話はそれでおしまいだ.

be badly [《口》***bad, ill, miserably, poorly***] ***off*** 暮らし向きが悪い, 困っている ▪ He *is badly off* for money. 彼は金に窮している ▪ They *are* very *miserably off*. 彼らはひどく困っている.

be better off (暮らし向き・事態が)前よりもよくなっている ▪ He *is* far *better off* than he was ten years ago. 彼は10年前よりもずっと暮らし向きがよくなっている ▪ He might well *be better off* without her. 彼はたぶん彼女がいない方が幸せだろう.

be neither off nor on **1** …と関係のない (*to*) ▪ It *was neither off nor on to* what Paul said. それはポールの言ったことと関係がなかった.
2 どっちつかずで, 優柔不断で ▪ He's *neither off nor on*. 彼はどっちつかずの男だ.

be off and running 《口》とんとん拍子で進んでいる ▪ We're *off and running* again for another year. 私たちは今年もまたとんとん拍子で進んでいる.

be well [***comfortably***] ***off*** 暮らし向きがいい ▪ He *is* not *well* enough *off* to marry. 彼は結婚できるほど暮らし向きがよくない.

be well [***badly,*** etc.] ***off for*** 《口》…が豊かである[乏しい, など] ▪ *How are* you *off for* money? ふところ具合はどうかね ▪ They *are well off for* food and drink. 彼らには飲食物はたっぷりある.

one's ***day off*** →a day OFF.

first off →FIRST.

from off →FROM.

get off *a person's* ***back*** [***case***] →BACK[1].

off and on **1** ときどき ▪ I see him *off and on* at the Club. 彼にはときどきクラブで会う.

2 断続して, したりやめたり ▪ It has been raining *off and on*. 雨が降ったりやんだりしている ▪ I slept *off and on* all the way to Crewe. 私はクルーまでずっと眠ったり起きたりして行った.

3 (陸に)離れたり近づいたりして ▪ The ship has been beating *off and on* all day. 船は一日中沖を縫航した ▪ We lay *off and on* the shore all day yesterday. きのう終日陸に離れたり近づいたりして航行した.

off color **1** 普段より顔色が悪い ▪ He looked rather *off color*. 彼はどちらかと言えば, いつもより顔色が悪かった.

2 不十分な, 調子が狂って ▪ My English was still *off color*. 私の英語はまだ不十分だった ▪ Even the flute was *off color*. フルートさえ調子が狂っていた.

3 《米俗》いかがわしい, 下卑た, きわどい ▪ Everybody considered her a little *off color*. 誰もが彼女をちょっと下卑ていると考えた.

4 (ダイヤモンドなどが)色の悪い ▪ He purchased *off color* diamonds. 彼は色の悪いダイヤを買った.

O

off *one's* ***feed*** [***oats***] 《口》(病気などで)食欲がない, 気分がすぐれない ▪ Poor old Joe seems *off his feed* [*oats*] today. かわいそうにジョー爺さんはきょうは食欲がないように見える. ☞馬がものを食べないことから.

off for …に出発[乗り出]して ▪ He is *off for* some big game hunting in East Africa. 彼は東部アフリカの猛獣狩りに出発している ▪ Liberia is *off for* a jet-propelled ride into the 20th century. リベリアはジェット機のように20世紀に突進している.

off (*one's*) ***form*** =(be) out of FORM.

off of 《口》…を離れて, から (off) ▪ I could not keep my eyes *off of* her. 彼女から目を離すことができなかった ▪ That takes the beauty *off of* it. そのためにその美が失われてしまう.

off the peg [《米》***hook***] 《英》吊るしで, 出来合いで ▪ I usually buy a suit *off the peg*. 私はたいてい既製服を買う.

off to a good [***slow***] ***start*** 《米》すべり出しがよい[遅い] ▪ The race was *off to a slow start*. 競技はすべり出しが遅かった ▪ The party campaign got *off to a good start*. 党の選挙運動はすべり出しよくいった.

off with 《口》〖主に命令文で〗(帽子・服など)を脱ぐ, 取る ▪ *Off with* your hats! 脱帽!《掲示》 ▪ *Off with* his head! 彼の首をはねよ.

Off with you! 《口》行ってしまえ ▪ *Off with you!* and do not return. 失せろ, そして戻って来るな.

play off and on with... をはずしたりつけたりする ▪ Sarah, in deep confusion, *played off and on with* her ring. セアラはひどくどぎまぎして, 指輪を抜いたりはめたりした.

ready for the off 《口》(人・乗り物が)いつでも出発できる準備ができて ▪ On that morning we were up at 4 and *ready for the off* at 5. その朝我々は4時に起き5時には出発の準備が整っていた.

right [***straight***] ***off*** → RIGHT away; STRAIGHT off.

off[2] /ɔːf|ɔf/ 動 ***off it*** 立ち去る;《俗》死ぬ ▪ He has *offed it* abroad. 彼は外国に行ってしまった.

off-chance /ɔ́ːftʃæ̀ns|ɔ́ftʃɑ̀ːns/ 名 ***on the off-chance*** 《口》万一を頼みに ▪ He will not be at home, but I'll go round *on the off-chance*. 彼は不在だろうが, 万一を頼みにして行ってみよう.

on the off-chance of [***that***] 《口》…の万一を頼みに ▪ I dropped in *on the off-chance of* a cup of tea. あわよくばお茶を1杯飲ませてもらえることを当てにして立ち寄ったのです ▪ I phoned *on the off-chance that* he would help us. ひょっとしたら彼が助けてくれることを頼みに電話した.

offcut /ɔ́ːfkʌ̀t|ɔ́f/ 名 ***an offcut*** 木の切れ端, 木材のくず ▪ His father made his toys from workshop *offcuts*. 彼の父親は作業場から出た木片でおもちゃを作ってくれた.

offense, 《英》**offence** /əféns/ 名 ***a hanging offense*** (絞首刑に処されるほどの)重罪 ▪ Piracy on the high seas is *a hanging offense*. 公海での海賊行為は大罪である.

commit an offense against (法・慣習・作法など)を犯す; (人)に非行を働く ▪ You have *committed an offense against* decency. あなたは無作法なことをしましたね ▪ We have never seen him *commit* any *offense against* you. 我々は彼があなたに非行を働いたのを見たことがない.

give [***cause***] ***offense to*** …の気を悪くさせる, 怒らせる ▪ This will *give offense to* the most scrupulous. これにはごく慎重な人々でも気を悪くするだろう.

mean offense 悪気でする[言う] ▪ No *offense was meant*. 悪気があってした[言った]のではありません.

No offense. 悪気はなかった ▪ *No offense*, sir, I dropped my stick by accident. 悪気はなかったのです, 誤ってステッキを落としたのです.

No offense meant. 君の気分を害するつもりはなかった ▪ Excuse that remark. *No offense meant.* あんなことを言ってごめん. 悪気はなかったんだ.

No offense taken. 平気だ, なんとも思っていない ▪ Excuse that last remark.—It's okay. *No offense taken.* 最後に言った言葉, ごめんね—大丈夫, どうもないよ.

take offense 気を悪くする, 怒る (*at*) ▪ He is too quick to *take offense*. 彼は何かというとすぐ怒る ▪ I hope you will not *take* any *offense at* my words.

私の言葉に気を悪くしないでください.

without offense 気を悪くさせないで[しないで] ▪ One cannot hear such a remark *without offense*. こんなことを言われたのでは怒らずにはいられない ▪ It cannot be done *without offense*. そんなことをすれば人の気を悪くさせるにきまっている.

offend /əfénd/ 動 ***be offended*** **1** 気を悪くしている ▪ I hope you *are* not *offended*. お気を悪くなさっていなければいいですが.

2 立腹する (*at* [*by*] *a thing, with a person for his act, that*) ▪ I *was offended at* his remark and told him so. 私は彼の言葉に腹が立ったのでそう言ってやった ▪ I *am* deeply *offended by* his conduct. 彼の行為には非常に腹が立つ ▪ Why *are* you *offended with* us? どうして私たちに腹を立てているのですか ▪ Some people *are offended that* I have turned these tales into modern English. 私がこの物語を現代英語に訳したので気を悪くしている人もいる.

offend the ear [***eye***] 耳[目]ざわりになる ▪ Avoid using words that *offend the ear*. 耳ざわりになる言葉は使わないようにしなさい.

offensive /əfénsɪv/ 名 ***act on*** [***go on, take, assume***] ***the offensive*** 攻勢を取る, 攻勢に出る (*against*) ▪ The council felt itself now strong enough to *act on the offensive against* him. 評議会は彼に対して攻勢に出るほど強くなったと感じた.

on the offensive 攻勢に出て ▪ Troops are *on the offensive*. 隊は攻勢に出ている ▪ He kept himself *on the offensive*. 彼は攻勢を維持した.

offer[1] /ɔ́:fər|ɔ́fə/ 名 (***be***) ***open to offer***(***s***) (売り手が)客の言い値を考慮する ▪ The president stands firm, but *open to offers*. 社長は毅然としてがんばったが, 客の言い値も考慮していた.

make an offer **1** 提議する, 申し出る ▪ He will *make a* definite *offer*. 彼ははっきりと申し出るだろう.

2 (結婚の)申し入れをする ▪ Catherine thought he would *make an offer* that evening. キャサリンは彼が今晩プロポーズするだろうと思っていた.

3 つけ値する ▪ He intends to *make an offer* of £15 for the carpet. 彼はそのじゅうたんに15ポンドのつけ値をするつもりだ.

on offer **1** 売り物に出て ▪ There is only inferior quality *on offer*. 劣等品しか売り物に出ていない.

2 《主に英》 値引きされて ▪ Flour is *on* special *offer* this week. 小麦粉が今週特売になっている.

the nearest offer (言い値に)一番近いつけ値 ▪ I'll take £50 or *the nearest offer*. 50ポンドか, それに一番近いつけ値で売りましょう.

under offer 《英》 (家を買う)申し込みを受けて ▪ We are *under offer* with option of refusal. 断ることもある条件で家を買う申し込みを受けている.

offer[2] /ɔ́:fər|ɔ́fə/ 動 ***have something*** [***nothing***] ***to offer*** 提供すべきものがある[ない] ▪ We *had nothing to offer* in return for his money. 彼が金をくれたお返しに差し出すものが何もなかった.

offer** oneself **as …として名乗り出る ▪ He *offered himself as* candidate. 彼は候補に立った ▪ I will *offer myself as* a peacemaker between them. 私が彼らの仲裁役を買って出よう.

offer** oneself **for …に申し込む ▪ He *offered himself for* the post. 彼はその口に申し込んだ.

offer** one's **hand **1** (握手しようと)手を差し出す ▪ The champion *offered his hand* to his opponent. 優勝者は相手に握手を求めて手を差し出した.

2 (女性に)結婚を申し込む ▪ Jack *offered* her *his hand*. ジャックは彼女に結婚を申し込んだ.

offer itself [***themselves***] 現れる ▪ I shall wait till a better chance *offers itself*. もっと良い機会が到来するまで待とう.

offer** oneself **to …に身をささげる ▪ Christ *offered Himself to* His Father for our sins. キリストは我々の罪を被って父なる神に献身した.

office /ɔ́:fəs|ɔ́fɪs/ 名 ***by*** [***through***] ***the good offices of*** …の世話で, 斡旋(あっせん)で ▪ He was able to get a good position *by the good offices of* the governor. 彼は知事の世話で良い地位に就けた ▪ I got the job *through the good offices of* my uncle. 私は叔父の口利きでこの職に就いた.

come into office →take OFFICE.

do [***exercise***] ***the office of*** …の役目をする ▪ They *exercise the offices of* the judge, the priest, the counsellor. 彼らは裁判官, 僧侶, 相談役の役目をする.

fill (***an***) ***office*** →hold (an) OFFICE.

give [***take***] ***the office*** 《俗》暗示や合図を与える[受ける] ▪ Ride about the country till I *give* you *the office*. 君に合図をするまでこの界わいを馬で回っていなさい ▪ He *took the office*. 彼はヒントを悟った.

go out of [***leave, resign***] (*one's*) ***office*** (特に大臣が)政権を離れる, 辞任する ▪ Feeling himself overtaken by age, he *resigned his office*. 彼は自分はもう年だと思って辞任した.

good [***kind***] ***office/office of kindness*** 好意, 世話 ▪ He did me many *good offices*. 彼は私にいろいろと好意を尽くしてくれた ▪ He desired my friend's *good offices* to introduce him to me. 彼は私に紹介してくれるように私の友人の斡旋を頼んだ.

hold [***fill***] (***an***) ***office*** 職にある, 在職する ▪ In France the President *holds office* for seven years. フランスでは大統領は7年間在職する ▪ He *filled* several *offices* under Sir Robert Walpole. 彼はサー・ロバート・ウォルポールのもとにいろいろな職に就いた.

ill office あだ, 害 ▪ He suspects that she has done him some *ill office*. 彼は彼女が自分に何かあだをしたのではないかと疑っている.

in office **1** 職にあって ▪ He died *in office*. 彼は職にあって死んだ ▪ He is no longer *in office*. 彼はもう在職していない.

2 政権をとって (↔in OPPOSITION) ▪ The Conservative Party is *in office*. 保守党が政権をとっている.

last office(***s***) 葬式 ▪ They showed their love to a dead friend in that *last office*. 彼らは亡き友

への愛をその葬式において示した.

leave [***resign***] (*one's*) ***office*** → go out of (one's) OFFICE.

office of kindness →good OFFICE.

out of office **1** 職を離れて ▪ He is now *out of office*. 彼は今職を離れている.
2 政権を離れて ▪ The Labor Party is now *out of office*. 労働党は今野党である.

perform the last offices to [***for***] …の葬儀を行う ▪ He *performed the last offices to* his father. 彼は父の葬儀を行った.

run for the office of 候補者として政治レースに参戦する ▪ He decided to *run for the office of* mayor. 彼は市長選に出馬することにした.

say office 《宗》日課を唱える《祈りや聖句》 ▪ She *said* the great *office* in the breviary every day. 彼女は毎日聖務日課書にあるありがたい聖句を唱えた.

take [***come into***] ***office*** 就任する ▪ The elected governor died before *taking office*. 当選した知事は就任しないうちに死んだ ▪ He had *come into office* at the head of the party. 彼はその党の党首に就任した.

take the office →give the OFFICE.

the front office 《口》首脳陣, 経営陣 ▪ *The front office* decides how long the workers work. 労働時間を決めるのは経営陣だ.

through the good offices of →by the good OFFICEs of.

officer /ɔ́:fəsər|ɔ́fɪ-/ 图 (***an***) ***officer and*** (***a***) ***gentleman*** 軍人にして紳士《古い英国軍人の理想像》 ▪ His grandfather was *an officer and a gentleman*. 彼の祖父は軍人でもあり紳士でもあった.

offing /ɔ́:fɪŋ|ɔ́f-/ 图 ***gain*** [***get, make, take***] ***an offing*** 沖合へ出る ▪ By noon we had *gained an offing* of near twenty leagues. 正午までに我々は20リーグほど沖合に出ていた.

in the offing **1** 沖合に ▪ We could see the ships *in the offing*. 沖合に船が見えた.
2 あたりに, 近くに ▪ Whenever he goes to see his girl, her mother is *in the offing*. 彼が恋人に会いに行くといつでも母親があたりにいる.
3 今にも起こりそうで ▪ A new war is *in the offing*. 新しい戦争が今にも起こりそうだ.

keep an offing 引き続き沖合を航行する ▪ My father had *kept a* wide *offing*. 父は引き続きずっと沖合を航行した.

often /ɔ́:fən|ɔ́fən/ 副 ***all*** [***only***] ***too often*** (よくないことが)あまりにもしばしば ▪ Is medical science *all too often* wrong? 医学はあまりにもしばしば誤っているか?

as often as… のたびごとに ▪ *As often as* he sees me, he asks for money. 彼は会うたびに金をねだる.

(***as***) ***often as not*** たいていの場合 ▪ *As often as not*, that is the case. たいていそうなのだ.

every so often ときどき ▪ I go to the movies *every so often*. 私はときどき映画へ行く.

how often 何回 ▪ *How often* do the buses run? バスは何回出ますか.

more often than not しばしば, たいてい ▪ *More often than not*, we lay awake all night. 我々は夜どおしまんじりともしないことが多かった.

often and often (***again***) 幾度も幾度も ▪ I have seen it *often and often*. それは幾度も幾度も見たことがある.

often as 何度も…するけれども ▪ *Often as* I asked him to, he never helped me. 何度頼んでも彼は一度も助けてくれなかった.

once too often またぞろしでかして, ついに《まずい結果を招く》 ▪ He exceeded the speed limit *once too often* and was fined £10. 彼はまたぞろスピード制限を越えて, ついに10ポンドの罰金を課せられた.

oil[1] /ɔɪl/ 图 ***add*** [***put, pour***] ***oil to*** [***on***] ***the fire*** [***flames,*** etc.] 火に油を注ぐ, 激情[怒り]をあおる ▪ There were also certain other malicious persons who *added oil to the flames*. 他にも火に油を注いだ意地悪い連中がいた ▪ As the common saying is, his words *poured oil upon the fire* [*flames*]. 俗に言う通り, 彼の言葉は火に油を注いだ.

be no oil painting 《英戯》→PAINTING.

burn [***waste, consume***] ***the midnight oil*** 深夜まで勉強する ▪ I trimmed my lamp, *consumed the midnight oil*. 私はランプの芯をつんで深夜まで勉強した ▪ He may have *wasted the midnight oil* in preparing his lessons. 彼は教える準備をして夜遅くまで勉強したのかもしれない.

oil and vinegar (油と酢のように)互いに相いれないもの, 「油に水」 ▪ We might as well try to blend *oil and vinegar* as do it. そんなことをするのは, 水と油を混ぜ合わせようとするようなものだ《不可能だ》.

oil and water 水と油《全く違う二つのこと[二人]》 ▪ He and I are basically like *oil and water*. 彼と私はまるっきり違う.

Oil and water (***do not mix***)**.** 《諺》油に水(の混じるごとし).

paint in oils 油絵をかく ▪ I sometimes *paint in oils* as a pastime. 私は趣味でときどき油絵をかく.

pour [***put***] ***oil on the fire*** [***flames***] →add OIL to the fire.

pour [***throw***] ***oil on the waters*** [***troubled waters***] 風波を静める, 丸く収める ▪ The two men were shouting abuse, but she did her best to *pour oil on troubled waters*. 二人の男は大声でののしっていたが, 彼女は丸く収めようとして精いっぱい努力した. ☞古代ローマ時代に水夫が波立つ水面に油を投じて波を静めたということから.

put oil to the fire [***flames,*** etc.] →add OIL to the fire.

smell of oil (文章などが)苦心のあとが見える ▪ A work of this nature should *smell of oil*. この種の作品は苦心のあとが見えるはずだ.

strike oil **1** 油脈を掘り当てる ▪ The company at last *struck oil*. 会社はついに油脈を掘り当てた.
2 《口》うまいもうけにありつく, やまを当てる ▪ I really

believe I've *struck oil* at last! 私はとうとうほんとにやまを当てたと思う.

waste the midnight oil →burn the midnight OIL.

oil[2] /ɔɪl/ 動 ***have a well-oiled tongue*** おしゃべりだ ▪The old woman *had a well-oiled tongue*. その老婆はおしゃべりだった.

oil *a person's* ***hand*** [***fist, palm***] 《口》人にそっと金をつかませる, チップをやる ▪He was speaking in private to the same official *whose hand* he had already *oiled*. 彼は既に金をつかませておいた同じ官吏にこっそり話しかけていた ▪There's a porter still hanging about. I suppose I must *oil his palm*. ポーターがまだうろうろしている. チップをやらねばなるまい.

oil the wheels →grease the WHEELs.

oil *one's* [***the***] ***tongue*** ぺらぺらおべっかを使う ▪They *oil the tongue*, and bow the knee. 彼らはぺらぺらおべっかを使い, 小腰をかがめる.

oiled up 《米俗》酔って ▪He was pretty *oiled up*. 彼は相当酔っていた.

ointment /ɔ́ɪntmənt/ 名 ***a fly in the ointment*** →FLY[1].

OK, okay /òʊkéɪ/ 形名 ***be doing OK*** [***okay***] 《口》うまくいっている, 儲かっている ▪How's business?—We*'re doing OK*, thanks. 商売はどう?—お陰で順調だ.

be OK [***okay***] **1**《米口》けっこうだ ▪He *is* quite *OK*. 彼は全く申し分がない.

2 承知だ ▪It's *OK* by me. 僕は同意するよ. ☞1840年の大統領選挙戦の民主党の標語 OK《M. V. Buren を支持する一派が彼の生地 Kinderhook, N.Y. にちなんで命名した Democratic OK [Old Kinderhook] Club の略語》から.

get [***receive***] ***an OK*** [***okay***] 《口》承諾を得る ▪He *got an OK* on the proposal. 彼はその提案に承諾を得た.

give the OK [***okay***] 《口》承諾を与える ▪His plan has *been given the okay*. 彼の計画は OK をもらった.

put the OK on 《米口》...を承認する ▪Will he *put the OK on* this plan? 彼はこの案を承認してくれるかしら.

... rule OK! ...が一番, ...万歳《みんなに承認されている》 ▪Kids *rule OK!* 子供たちが一番! ▪Westies *rule OK!* (ウェストハイランド)ホワイトテリアが一番! ☞rule は動詞.

old /oʊld/ 形 ***A man is as old as he feels, and a woman*** (***is***) ***as old as she looks.*** 《諺》男の年は気(持通り), 女の年は顔(つき通り).

an old bag [***bat***] →BAG[1]; BAT[2].

an old boy [***girl***] 《口》 **1** 年配の男性[女性] ▪There's *a* nice *old girl* living next door. お隣に素敵なおばあさんが住んでいる.

2 男子[女子]卒業生 ▪We have an *old boys'* reunion every ten years. 僕たちは10年ごとに同窓会を開いている.

an [***that***] ***old chestnut*** →CHESTNUT.

an old dear 《口》(慇懃無礼に)ご婦人, おばさま ▪And then *this old dear* came up and jumped in line. すると例のおばさまがやってきて列に割り込んだ.

an old flame →FLAME.

an old fogey [***fogy***] (主に年配の)旧式な人, 古風な人物 ▪My grandfather is not such *an old fogey*. うちの祖父はそんな古い人間ではない.

an old hand →HAND[1].

an old maid もう若くない未婚女性, オールドミス ▪She was terrified of becoming *an old maid*. 彼女は結婚できないかもしれないと恐れた.

an old woman 口やかましい人《男女ともに》 ▪My boss is *a* real *old woman*. He easily gets annoyed at trifles. ボスは実に口やかましく, 些細なことですぐ腹を立てる.

any [***every***] ***old*** 《口》何でも, どれでも ▪Take *any old* hat. どの帽子でも取りなさい ▪Try *every old* thing. 何でもやってごらん.

any (***old***) ***how*** →HOW.

any old place [***where***] 《口》どこででも ▪You can buy one *any old where*. それはどこででも買えるよ.

any old time 《口》いつでも ▪Call in *any old time*. いつでも遊びにいらっしゃい.

any old way →WAY.

as of old 昔のように, 昔と変わらず ▪He was talking loudly, *as of old*. 彼は昔と変わらず大声でしゃべっていた.

(***as***) ***old as Adam*** [***the hills, the world, time***] 実に古い, ひどく年取って (《聖》*Job* 15. 7) ▪I can't wear that hat—it's *as old as the hills*. その帽子はとてもかぶれない—ひどく古いんだもの.

for old sake's sake →SAKE.

from of old 昔から ▪The custom has been known *from of old*. その習わしは昔から知られている.

give ... the old one two 《俗》...に色目を使う ▪Jim *gave* the girl *the old one two*. ジムはその娘に色目を使った. ☞今は古くさい表現.

have a high old time →TIME[1].

have an old head on young shoulders →HEAD[1].

in days of old 昔は, 以前は ▪*In days of old* people believed in giants and fairies. 昔人々は巨人や妖精がいると信じていた.

like old boots [***Billy***] 《俗》猛烈に, 勢いよく, 徹底的に ▪They ate *like old boots*. 彼らはもりもり食べた ▪I will stick to you *like old boots*. 私は徹頭徹尾あなたに忠節を尽くします ▪The man was out of sight *like old boots*. その男は猛烈な速さで見えなくなった ▪The balls did whistle round *like old Billy*. 弾丸が猛烈にあたりをビュンビュン飛んだ. ☞old boots [Billy] = the devil.

of old 《文》 **1**〚形容詞的に〛昔の ▪Then I remembered the times *of old*. そのとき私は往時を思い出した.

2〚副詞的に〛昔は, 古くは; 古くから ▪I know you *of old*. 昔から君のことは知っている.

old and young/young and old 老いも若きも ▪ He flattered rich and poor, *old and young.* 彼は貧富老若の別なく誰にもおべっかを言った.
old before** one's **time →TIME[1].
old beyond** one's **years →YEAR.
old enough to be** a person's **father [***mother***] 父親[母親]になれるくらいの年で ▪ You want to marry John? Why, he's *old enough to be your father.* ジョンと結婚したいって? でも, あなたの父親になれるくらいの年だよ. ☞結婚などで年齢が不相応に違いすぎる時に用いる.
old familiar faces 昔なじみの人々 (Lamb, *The Old Familiar Faces* 1) ▪ The countryside was nothing to me without my *old familiar faces.* 昔なじみの人々がいなければ, 田舎も私には無意味だった.
old hat 《口》流行おくれの; 平凡な ▪ For that matter, it is now *old hat.* そのことなら, それはもう流行おくれだ. ☞女性が帽子をかぶる習慣だった頃, その流行が目まぐるしく変わったことから.
old man [***chap, fellow, boy, girl, thing***] 《口》(おい)君《親しい間柄の呼びかけ》 ▪ Never mind, *old man.* 気にするなよ, 君 ▪ Take another cup, *old chap.* もう1杯やれよ, 君 ▪ I say, *old boy.* おい君.
the old country [***home***] 《米》(植民地人から見て)英本国; 母国, 祖国《とくにヨーロッパ》 ▪ His wife was born here, but he is from *the old country.* 彼の妻は当地生まれだが彼は英本国出身だ ▪ Many Americans tour *the old country* every year. 毎年多くのアメリカ人がヨーロッパを観光旅行する.
the old guard [***brigade***] 《口》(組織体の中の)古株連; 保守派, 守旧派 ▪ *The old guard* don't like change. 古株連は変化を好まない ▪ They admit they are waging a private war against *the* Stalinist *old guard.* 彼らはスターリン主義の守旧派に対して私的な戦いをしかけていることを認めている.
the Old Lady [***Woman***] ***of*** [***in***] ***Threadneedle Street*** イングランド銀行 (the Bank of England) のニックネーム ▪ *The Old Lady of Threadneedle Street* was 300 years old in 1994. イングランド銀行は1994年に創業三百周年を迎えた ▪ People often jocularly refer to *the Old Lady of Threadneedle Street.* 人々はよくふざけて「スレッドニードル街の老婦人」と言う. ☞イングランド銀行がロンドンのシティー区の Threadneedle Street にあって手堅いやり方をするところから.
the Old Man of the Sea つきまとって離れないやっかい者 ▪ He's been round me like *the Old Man of the Sea* ever since I left home. 彼は僕が家を出てからずっとまとわりついて離れないんだ. ☞アラビア夜話で Sindbad の背にしがみついた恐ろしい老人の話から.
the old one/the old gentleman (***in black***)/***old Billy*** [***Harry, Nick, Scratch***] 《戯》悪魔 ▪ He must have sold himself to *Old Scratch.* 彼は悪魔に身を売ったのにちがいない.
(***the***) ***old school tie*** 《英》→TIE[1].

olde-worlde /óʊldiwə́ːrldi/ 形 《英》(場所が)古風な ▪ We stopped at a sweet little village, full of *olde-worlde* charm. 我々は古風な魅力に溢れたすてきな小村に立ち寄った.

olive /ɑ́lɪv|ɔ́l-/ 名 ***the*** [***an***] ***olive***(-)***branch*** ⟦bring, hold out, extend, tender, accept などを伴って⟧ 和平, 和解 (《聖》*Gen.* 8. 11) ▪ After a long war, the exhausted enemy *held out the olive branch.* 長い戦争のあげく疲弊した敵は和平を申し出た. ☞「オリーブの枝」が平和・和解の象徴であるところから.

omega /oʊméɪgə|óʊmɪgə/ 名 ***from Alpha to Omega*** →ALPHA.
the Alpha and Omega →ALPHA.

omelet, omelette /ɑ́mlət|ɔ́m-/ 名 ***You*** [***One***] ***cannot make omelettes*** [***an omelette***] ***without breaking eggs.*** 《諺》まかぬ種は生(は)えぬ ☞[F] On ne saurait faire une omelette sans casser des œufs のなぞり.

omen /óʊmən|óʊmen/ 名 ***be of good*** [***bad***] ***omen*** 幸先(さいさき)が良い[悪い] ▪ I trust your visit to my house *is of good omen.* あなたがお訪ねくださったのは, きっと幸先が良いのだと思います.

on /ɑn, ɔːn|ɔn/ 前 副 形 ***be a bit on*** 《口》ほろ酔いである ▪ He's *a bit on* now. 彼は今ほろ酔いだ.
be neither off nor on →OFF[1].
be not on 《口》許されない ▪ That *was* simply *not on.* そんなことは絶対にだめだった.
***be on** one* …の支払いで, おごりで ▪ This lunch *is on* me, pal. 君, この昼飯は僕がおごるよ.
be on it 《米俗》 **1** じょうずだ ▪ You bet he could cook. He *was* just *on it.* ほんとに彼は料理ができた. まさに名手だった.
2 やる気がある ▪ He took his coat off, and inquired, *Are* you *on it?* 彼は上着を脱いで「やる気があるかい」と聞いた.
3 わかった ▪ Okay. I'*m on it.* よし, わかった.
be on the in 内情に通じている ▪ I'm too new to the firm to *be on the in* yet. 入社したばかりでまだ内情に明るくない.
be on to a good thing 《俗》うまいもうけ[こと]を見いだした ▪ I like this new process; I think we'*re on to a good thing.* この新しい方法はいいな. うまいことに気がついたと思うよ.
be well on in [***into***] (時)が遅い, (年)を取って ▪ It *was well on in* the afternoon. 午後も遅くなっていた ▪ He *is well on into* his fifties. 彼はもう十分50の坂を越えている.
have nothing on →HAVE[2].
have [***get***] ***something on** a person* →SOMETHING.
I'm on. 《口》賛成だ.
(***just***) ***not on*** 《口》許されない; 不可能だ ▪ The thing is *just not on.* そんなことは不可能だ.
keep on and on 話し続ける, 小言を言い続ける (*at*) ▪ He *kept on and on at* me. 彼は私に小言を言い続けた.
on again, off again/off again, on again

=OFF and on.

on and off =OFF and on.

on and on 引き続き, どんどんと ▪ She talked *on and on.* 彼女はどんどん話し続けた ▪ He went *on and on* till he came to a river. 彼は川の所へ出るまでどんどん歩き続けた.

on with …を着なさい ▪ *On with* your coat. 上着を着なさい.

You are on. 《口》その賭け[取引]承知した.

once /wʌns/ 副 ***A man can die but once.*** 《諺》人は一度だけしか死ねない.

all at once **1** たちまち, にわかに ▪ *All at once* I saw a host of golden daffodils. たちまち私はラッパズイセンの大群を見た.

2 みんな一度に ▪ The three boys answered *all at once.* 3人の少年はみんないっしょに答えた.

at once **1** 同時に ▪ Don't all talk *at once.* 口々に話してはいけない.

2 ただちに, すぐ ▪ Do it *at once,* please. どうかすぐそうしてください.

at once A and B AでもありBでもある ▪ He is *at once* stern *and* tender. 彼は厳しくもあり優しくもある.

every once in a while [***way***] ときどき ▪ He visits us *every once in a way.* 彼はときどき遊びに来ます.

every once in so often 《米》しょっちゅう (very often) ▪ They forgot it *every once in so often.* 彼らはそれをしょっちゅう忘れた.

for once =(for) this ONCE.

for once and all =ONCE (and) for all.

(***for***) ***once and away*** →ONCE (and) for all.

(***for***) ***once in a way***/ ***once in a*** [***every***] ***while*** まれに, たまに ▪ *Once in a while* we visit the theater. たまに芝居を見に行きます.

for once in one's life 生まれてから今度だけ ▪ He has succeeded *for once in his life.* 彼は生まれてから今度だけ成功した.

(***for***) ***this*** [***that***] ***once*** この[あの]時だけ ▪ Listen to me *for this once.* 今度だけ僕の言うことを聞いてくれ ▪ He departed from his principles *for that once.* 彼はその時だけ主義をまげた.

if once/when once いったん…なら, 一度…すると ▪ *When once* virtue is lost, all is lost. いったん美徳がなくなったら何もかもおしまいだ ▪ *If once* we lose sight of him, we shall never set eyes on him again. 一度彼の姿を見失えば二度と再び見つからないだろう.

in once 《俗》一度で ▪ You've guessed it *in once,* pop. 一度で当たったよ, おとうさん.

more than once 一度ならず, 再三 ▪ I have seen him *more than once.* 彼に会ったのは一度や二度ではない.

not once 一度も[決して]…しない ▪ He shall *not once* be received into the kingdom of heaven. 彼は決して天国へは入れまい ▪ *Not once* have you done as I have asked! ただの一度も君は僕の言う通りにしてくれたことはない.

once a ..., always a ... 一度…ならば生涯…だ ▪ *Once a* beggar, *always a* beggar. 《諺》「乞食を3日すればやめられぬ」 ▪ *Once a* parson, *always a* parson. 《諺》「一度牧師になると生涯牧師でいる」.

once and again **1** 再三 ▪ The affair has been *once and again* maturely considered by this Board. その問題は一度ならず本委員会で慎重に審議された.

2 《米》たびたび ▪ I have told you *once and again* that you must not smoke in this room. この部屋でタバコを吸ってはいけないとたびたび言ったはずだ.

once (***and***) ***for all*** [***always, altogether, ever***]/(***for***) ***once and away*** これを最後に; きっぱり ▪ She told him, *once for all,* that she would not marry him. 彼女は彼とは結婚しませんときっぱりと言った ▪ The judges have cleared the question *once for ever.* 判事たちはその問題をきっぱりと解決した ▪ He has just *once and away* made up his mind to self-sacrifice. 彼は自分を犠牲にしようときっぱりと腹を決めた.

Once bit [***bitten***], ***twice shy.*** →BITE[2].

once in a blue moon →MOON.

once in a lifetime 一生に一度 ▪ One can have such an experience only *once in a lifetime.* そのような経験は一生に一度しかすることはできない.

once in a [***every***] ***while*** →(for) ONCE in a way.

once more [***again***] もう一度 ▪ I should like to see him *once more.* もう一度彼に会いたい ▪ Let me hear you sing *once again.* もう一度歌って聞かせてください.

once or twice →TWICE.

once removed **1** 一親等だけへだたった ▪ He is my (first) cousin *once removed.* 彼はいとこの子だ.

2 (…と)あまり変わらない (*from*) ▪ The condition was only *once removed from* that of the lower animals. その状態は下等動物のとへだたること紙一重だった.

Once seen [***heard***], ***never forgotten.*** 《諺》一度見たら[聞いたら]もう忘れられない《人や物の目立った特徴について, しばしば皮肉に用いる》.

once too often →OFTEN.

once upon a time **1** 昔々; ある時 ▪ *Once upon a time* there were gods only, and no mortal creatures. 昔々神さましかいなくて人間はいなかった. ☞おとぎ話のおきまりの書き出し; →LIVE happily ever after(wards).

2 《文》(古きよき時代を偲んで)昔は ▪ *Once upon a time,* nobody bothered locking their doors. 昔は, わざわざ戸締まりをする者なんか一人もいなかった.

when once →if ONCE.

once-over /wʌ́nsòʊvər/ 名 ***get the once-over*** 《口》ちらっと見て品定めされる ▪ He didn't want to *get the once-over* from her parents. 彼は彼女の両親にちらっと見て品定めされたくなかった.

give ... a once-over [***a once-over-lightly***]

《口》 **1** …を手早く［おざなりに］する，いい加減にする ▪ She *gave* her room *a* quick *once-over-lightly*. 彼女は部屋をざっと掃除した.
2 …を素早くざっと調べる ▪ My sister *gave* my essay *the once-over* before I handed it in. レポートの提出前に姉がざっと目を通してくれた.

give … the once-over 《口》 …をちらっと［ざっと］見る ▪ They came to *give* Europe *the once-over*. 彼らはヨーロッパをざっと見るために来た.

one /wʌn/ 形名代 ***a hot one*** 《口》 ひどく変わった人(物)，並外れた［すばらしい］物 ▪ Joe's joke sure was *a hot one*. 彼のジョークは実におかしかった.

a hundred* [*thousand, million*] *and one … (数の多さを強調して)何百［何千，何百万］もの…，無数の… ▪ I've got *a hundred and one* things to do. 私は仕事が山ほどある ▪ There are *a thousand and one* ways to save the Earth. 地球を救う方法は無数にある.

a right one 《英口》 愚か者 ▪ We have *a right one* here. ばかなやつだな，こいつ.

all in one 一つでみんな兼ねて ▪ He is teacher, principal, treasurer, custodian, *all in one*. 彼は教師，校長，会計，守衛を一人で兼ねている.

(*all*) *rolled into one* 何人かの性格が一人に集約されて，別々のものが一つに合体して ▪ He was producer, director, and writer of the film *all rolled into one*. 彼はその映画の製作，監督，脚本の三役を一人でこなした.

an old one 聞き慣れたジョーク，いつもの冗談 ▪ Here is *an old one*. おなじみのジョークを一つ.

***as one/as one man* [*woman*]** →MAN[1].

be* (*a*) *one for 《口》 …の熱心家［熱狂者］である ▪ She *was one for* football. 彼女はフットボールに熱中していた ▪ She *is* (*a* great) *one for* wearing bright colors. 彼女は派手な服を着るのが好きだ.

be all one **1** (意見などが)一致している ▪ We *are all one* on that point. 我々はその点では一致している.
2 (…には)全く同じことだ，大した違いはない (*to*) ▪ Wealth or poverty *is all one to* him. 金があっても貧乏でも彼には全く同じことだ ▪ It'*s all one to* me whether you go or stay. 君が行こうが残ろうが僕には一向に変わりはない.

(*be*) *at one* 一致［同意］している (*with*) ▪ I *am at one with* Chester in his belief. 私もチェスターと同じことを信じている ▪ All the accounts *are at one* on that point. その点ではみなの話が一致している.

be one of a kind 他に類例をみない［ユニークな］人 ▪ As a female truck driver, she *was one of a kind* in those days. 当時女性のトラック運転手として彼女は異彩を放っていた.

be* [*have*] *one over the eight 《英俗》 少し酔っている［酔う］ ▪ He seemed to *be one over the eight*. 彼は少し酔っているみたいだった ▪ He was wild when he *had one over the eight*. 少し酔ったときには彼は乱暴者だった. ☞もと軍隊で許されている8杯より1杯だけ飲みすぎるの意から; また8杯を越えると酔っ払うという俗信から.

***be* [*get, have*] *one up on** a person* 《口》 人より有利になる，勝る，リードする (→ONE up on a person) ▪ She *is one up on* me because she already passed geometry. 彼女は幾何に合格しているから私を一歩リードしている ▪ I *got one up on* my other competitors. 他の競争相手よりも一歩先んじた.

be* [*be made*] *one with 《文》 …と一体である［となる］ ▪ He *was made one with* Nature. 彼は自然と一体になった ▪ We *are one with* Christ. 我々はキリストと一体だ.

become* [*be made*] *one 一体となる，(特に)夫婦になる ▪ They *were made one*. 彼らは夫婦になった.

bite the big one 《米口》 死ぬ ▪ I hope to travel abroad before I *bite the big one*. 死ぬまでに海外旅行ができるといいけど.

bring … at one →set … at ONE.

buy the big one 《婉曲》 死ぬ ▪ He *bought the big one* hanging from the ceiling. 彼は天井から首を吊って死んだ.

by ones and twos 一つ二つずつ，ぽつぽつ ▪ They came *by ones and twos*. 彼らはぽつぽつやって来た.

for one 少なくとも自分は，自分としては ▪ I, *for one*, do not believe his story. 私としては彼の話を信じていない.

for one thing →THING.

get it in one 《口》 初めての試みで成功する ▪ He *got it in one*. 彼は初めての試みで成功した.

go (*a person*) ***one better*** →BETTER[1].

Have a good one! 《米口》 (別れ際に)ごきげんよう (Have a nice day!).

have had one too many 《口》 酔っ払っている ▪ You'*ve had one too many*. You can hardly stand up. 酔っているな. ろくに立てないじゃないか.

***have* (*got*) *one on** a person* 《米俗》 人をやりこめる種がある ▪ I'*ve got* a good *one on* her. 彼女をやりこめるすてきな種があるのです.

in one 一体［いっしょ］になって ▪ They gathered up *in one*. 彼らはいっしょに集まった ▪ Why do not your words and deeds agree *in one*? なぜ君の言行は一致しないのか.

in ones ひとつひとつで ▪ The goods are sold *in ones*. この商品はばら売りされる.

in ones and twos 《英》 =by ONEs and twos.

(*in*) *the year one* [*1*] →in the YEAR dot.

It is only a little one. ほんのちっちゃなものだから《理由にならない言い訳に用いる》. ☞Marryat, *Mr Midshipman Easy* の中で私生児を産んだ娘の弁解の言葉.

It takes one to know one. →TAKE[2].

(*it's*) *a hundred to one* (*that*) →HUNDRED.

(*just*) *one of those things* 《口》 どうしようもないこと; (訳は分からないが)よくあることだ ▪ A love affair? Well, it's *just one of those things*. 恋愛事件だって? まあまあ，それはよくあることだ.

land** a person* ***one 《口》 =SOCK a person one.

Let's have one. 《米俗》1杯やろうじゃないか《酒を飲むのを誘うときの言葉》.

like a good one →GOOD.

little [young] ones 《口》(幼い)子供たち ▪ I am pregnant and have two *little ones.* 私は身ごもっていてさらに子供が二人いるの.

make ... at one →set ... at ONE.

no one →NO.

No one is indispensable. 《諺》誰でも用なしになりうる《みんな職を失う可能性がある》.

one above the other →ABOVE.

one after another (三つ以上のものについて)次々に, 順々に ▪ *One after another* all his plans have failed. 次々と彼の計画はすべて失敗した ▪ *One* thing went *after another.* 一つ二つと消えていった.

one after one →ONE by one.

one after the other (通例二つのものについて)相続けて, 交互に ▪ He lifted *one* of his feet *after the other.* 彼は両足を交互に上げた ▪ Four of his sons came to the throne *one after the other.* 彼の4人の息子は相続いて王位を継いだ. ☞このように三者以上のものに用いることもあるが, あくまでも「交互に」という意味に重点が置かれている.

one and all 《口》誰もかれも ▪ The entertainment was greatly enjoyed by *one and all.* その娯楽は誰もかれもが大いに楽しんだ.

one and another 甲も乙も ▪ I have heard it from *one and another* during the week. 今週そのことを甲からも乙からも耳にした.

one and indivisible 一つに結びついている ▪ The Republic was *one and indivisible.* その共和国は一つに結びついていた.

one and only 《口》 **1** ただ一つ[一人]の ▪ This was his *one and only* chance. これは彼にとって唯一無二のチャンスだった.

2 恋人; 一人子 ▪ Their *one and only* was ten. 彼らの一人子は10歳だった ▪ Jimmy was her *one and only.* ジミーは彼女の恋人だった.

one and the same 同一の ▪ Mark Twain and Samuel Clemens were *one and the same* person. マーク・トウェインとサミュエル・クレメンズとは同一の人物だった.

one another (二者またはそれ以上について)お互い (→each OTHER) ▪ They met *one another.* 彼らはお互いに会った ▪ They spoke to *one another.* 彼らはお互いに話し合った.

one ... another 甲は[の]...乙は[の] ▪ *One* man's meat is *another*'s poison. 《諺》「甲の薬は乙の毒」.

one by [after] one 一つずつ, 一人ずつ《順次に》 ▪ The jury filed back into the courtroom *one by one.* 陪審員は法廷へ列をなして一人ずつ戻って行った.

One cannot be in two places at once. 《諺》同時に二つ以上の場所にいたり二つ以上のことをすることはできない.

One cannot love and be wise. 《諺》恋に落ちるとばかなまねをすることが多い.

one for you and two for himself 《俗》人のためより自分のためを考えている ▪ Don't trust his favors; it's generally *one for you and two for himself.* 彼の親切など当てにしてはいけない. たいてい人のためより自分のためを考えているんだから.

one in a thousand [million, billion] 千[百万, 十億]人に一人[わずかの...] ▪ Jack, not *one* man *in a thousand* would have forgiven you as he has done. ジャック, 千人中の一人だって彼のように君を赦してはくれなかっただろうよ ▪ This ring is *one in a billion.* この指輪は実に稀少品である.

one in ten →IN².

one in the eye 《口》目への一撃; けんつく, 侮辱 (*for*) ▪ He gave me *one in the eye.* 彼から目に一発くらわされた ▪ It was "*one in the eye*" *for* his aunt. それは彼のおばにとっては「けんつく」だった.

one (more) for the road 《口》(店を出る前の)最後の1杯 ▪ Give me *one for the road,* big boy. 最後の1杯をくれよ, 君.

one of the boys [girls, 《英》 ***lads]*** 《米口》気の合った仲間 ▪ Jim is really *one of the lads* here. ジムはここでは実にいい仲間だ ▪ She's never been *one of the girls.* 彼女は女の子の仲間に加わったことがない.

one of these days **1** いつか, そのうち ▪ I will visit him *one of these days.* そのうち彼の所へ行ってみよう.

2 厄日, 災難続きの日 ▪ So it's going to be *one of these days.* Okay. ではきょうは厄日になるというわけか. まあいいさ.

one of those ホモ ▪ I'm sure he's *one of those.* きっと彼はホモだ.

one of those days =ONE of these days.

one of us 仲間; 《口》ホモ ▪ You are *one of us,* so you can act like one. 君は仲間なんだから, 仲間のようにふるまってください.

one on the city →CITY.

one ... or another 《口》何やかや ▪ I am busy *one* way *or another.* あれやこれやで忙しい ▪ We must repay him in *one* thing *or another.* 彼に何やかやで報いなければならない.

one or other of ...のうちのどれか[誰か] ▪ All clients receive *one or other of* the main services. すべてのクライアントは主要なサービスのどれかを受ける.

one or two 2, 3の (a few) ▪ I shall be away only *one or two* days. 私は2, 3日留守にするだけだ.

one ... the other (二者の前後を問わず)一方は...他方は ▪ We have two dogs; *one* is white, and *the other* is black. うちには犬が2匹います. 1匹は白犬でもう1匹は黒犬です.

one thing, ... another (thing) 甲と乙とは別だ ▪ To know is *one thing,* to teach *another.* 知っていることと教えることとは別問題だ ▪ If he said *one thing,* she was sure to say *another.* 彼が白と言うと, 彼女がきまって黒と言った.

One up for [to] *a person.* 《口》...はあっぱれだ, よくやった ▪ *One up for* the team. そのチームはよくやった.

one up on *a person* 《口》〚be, get, put などの動詞を伴って〛人よりも1点勝ち越して; 一段勝って, に差をつけて (→be ONE up on a person) ▪ I like to *be one up on* my neighbors. 近所の人に差をつけているのが好きだ.

one with another 平均して, 概して ▪ The same person spends *one with another* about two pounds per day. 同じ人が1日に平均2ポンド費やす ▪ They contribute *one* year *with another* eight million pounds to the society. 彼らは毎年平均してその協会に800万ポンドの寄付をする.

owe *a person* ***one*** **1**《口》(人に)負うところがある, 恩に着る ▪ I *owe* you *one*. すまないね[恩に着るよ]. **2** 人に恨みがある ▪ I *owe* you *one* for the last trick you played on me. この前僕にいたずらをしたからお前には恨みがある.

pull [***put over***] ***a fast one*** 《口》まんまとだます, さっとだしぬく, 一杯食わす, インチキをする (*on, with*) ▪ He tried to *pull a fast one with* me. 彼はとっさに私を騙そうとした ▪ I paid him for six bottles of champagne, but he *pulled a fast one on* me and gave me six bottles of cheap wine. 私は彼にシャンパン6本分払ったが, 彼は私をだまくらかして私に渡したのは安もののワイン6本だった ▪ He has *pulled a fast one on* the Legislature and the people. 彼は議会と国民をペテンにかけた.

put one over *a person* 《口》人よりも一段勝る ▪ I can *put one over* you there. その点では僕の方が一歩勝っているね.

put one over on *a person* (人を)かつぐ, だます ▪ It's no use trying to *put one over on* me! その手には乗らないよ.

set [***bring, make***]***... at one*** 《古》…を仲直りさせる ▪ They that are at odds must *be set at one*. 不和の者は仲直りさせねばならない.

such a one そんなもの, 人 ▪ I want a book, but I don't want *such a one*. 本がほしいがそんなやつはほしくない.

ten [***six, seven***] ***to one*** 〚主に否定文で〛きっと…だ, 十中八九, たぶん ▪ I'd bet *ten to one* against it. 十中八九そうはならないよ ▪ *Six to one* he will arrive late. たぶん彼は遅れて来るだろう.

That's one on him [***you,*** etc.]***!*** 《口》それで彼[君, など]は一点負けだ.

the one about …についての(冗談)話 ▪ You know *the one about* a young salesman who allegedly murdered his wife? 妻を殺したとされる若いセールスマンの話を知ってるかい?

the one... of all others とりわけ ▪ *The one* person *of all others* I wish to see is Jane. 私がわけても会いたい人はジェインです ▪ *The one* thing *of all others* I detest is hypocrisy. 私がとりわけきらいなのは偽善だ.

the one that got away 《口》逃げた[逃がした]魚《比喩的にも》 ▪ He thought of his former girlfriend as *the one that got away*. 彼には昔の女友達が逃がした魚のように思われた.

the one thing needful 必要なただ一つのもの[こと] (《聖》*Luke* 10. 42) ▪ Silver is *the one thing needful*. 銀がただ一つ必要なものだ.

there's always one 《英口》必ず…する人がいる ▪ *There's always one* who loves a lot. And one who loves just a little. たくさん愛する人とほんの少ししか愛さない人とが必ずいる.

tie one on *a person* 《口》飲み代をおごってやる ▪ If you take me to a nice bar, I'll *tie one on* you. 素敵なバーへ連れて行ってくれたら, 飲み代は僕がもつ.

When you've seen [***heard,*** etc.] ***one, you've seen*** [***heard,*** etc.] ***them all.*** 《諺》一つ見ればあとをすべて見たのと同じだ,「一時が万事」.

(***You've***) ***Got it in one!*** 《口》(相手の推測が的中して)その通りだ, お察しの通りだ ▪ Are you pregnant again?—*Got it in one!* またおめでたなの?—当たりよ ▪ Are you thinking of leaving?—Yes, *you've got it in one*. 辞めようと考えているのか—その通りだ.

one-hit /wʌ́nhít/ 形 ***a one-hit wonder*** →WONDER[1].

one-horse /wʌ́nhɔ́ːrs/ 形 ***a one-horse race*** ぶっちぎりの楽勝, 独走; 勝利が明らかな選挙 ▪ This election has been *a one-horse race*. 今回の選挙は圧勝だった.

a one-horse town 《米口》過疎の小さくて退屈な町, さびれた町 ▪ I grew up in *a* small *one-horse town* in Texas. 私はテキサス州のさびれた町で育った.

one-man /wʌ́nmǽn/ 形 ***a one-man*** [***one-woman***] ***band*** [***show***] 単独行動・独演をする人, 何でも自分だけでする人 ▪ A doctor is *a one-man band*. 医師は一人で仕事をする.

oner /wʌ́nər/ 名 ***be a oner at*** [***for***] 《俗》…の名人である ▪ She *is* such *a oner at* eating. 彼女はすばらしい大食だ.

give *a person* ***a oner*** 《俗》人を強打する ▪ I *gave* him *a oner* on his ears. 彼の耳をいやというほどぶってやった.

oneself /wʌnsélf/ 代 (***all***) ***by*** *oneself* **1** 自分だけで, 一人ぼっちで ▪ He lives (*all*) *by himself*. 彼は一人(ぼっち)で暮らしている. **2** 一人で ▪ Did you do this *by yourself* or did someone help you? これはあなた一人でしましたか, それとも誰か手伝いましたか. ☞この意味では for ONESELF と似ているが, by oneself は「自分のために」という意味を含まない.

all over *oneself* 《口》 **1** 大喜びで ▪ He's got engaged, and he's *all over himself*. 彼は婚約したので, 大喜びだ. **2** うぬぼれて, 傲慢で ▪ Since he has come into money, he's *all over himself*. 彼は金ができたため傲慢だ.

be *oneself* **1** 自然にふるまう ▪ If she would only *be herself*, she would be more liked by the other girls. 彼女が自然にふるまいさえしたら, 他の女の子にもっと好かれるだろうに. **2** 正常である ▪ I'*m* not *myself* today. きょうは調子

が悪い ▪ Now I *am myself* again. もうよくなった.

***beside** oneself* (**with**) →BESIDE.

***come to** oneself* 正気に返る, 正気づく ▪ She swooned, but *came to herself* soon. 彼女は気絶したが, すぐ正気づいた.

***feel** oneself* →FEEL[2].

***for** oneself* **1** 自分のために ▪ He has built a new house *for himself.* 彼は自分のために新居を建てた ▪ This one I shall keep *for myself.* これは私の分に取っておきましょう.

2 自分で, 独力で ▪ There are some things one can't do *for oneself.* 自分でしかねることもあるものだ《そんなことは他人がすべきだ》 ▪ You must find it out *for yourself.* 君は自分でそれを解かなければならない.

3 そのもののために ▪ I love her *for herself.* 彼女を彼女そのもののために愛しているのだ《財産などが目的ではない》.

***have ... to** oneself* →to ONESELF 2.

***in** oneself* 本来, それだけで ▪ A fine courtesy is a fortune *in itself.* 立派な礼儀はそれだけで財産だ ▪ These substances are not poisonous *in themselves.* これらの物質は本来は有毒でない.

***keep** oneself **to** oneself* →KEEP[2].

***leave to** oneself* →to ONESELF 2.

***of** oneself* **1** (他に原因なく)ひとりでに ▪ He awoke *of himself.* 彼はひとりでに目をさました ▪ The door opened *of itself.* ドアがひとりでに開いた.

2 (他の問題と関係なく)それだけで ▪ The league can do nothing *of itself.* 連盟はそれだけでは何ひとつできない ▪ London seems like a world *of itself.* ロンドンはそれだけで一つの世界のように思われる.

***to** oneself* **1** (他人にではなく)自分自身に ▪ I had kept the secret *to myself.* 私はその秘密を自分の胸に秘めていた ▪ I chuckled *to myself.* 私は一人でくつくつ笑った.

2 自分だけに ▪ I had the large room *to myself.* 私はその大きな部屋を独り占めした ▪ Left *to himself*, he got up and began to wander round the room. 一人きりになると彼は立ち上がって, 室内をぶらぶらし始めた.

one-track /wʌ́ntræ̀k/ 形 ***have a one-track mind*** 一つのこと(とくにセックス)だけを考えている, 心が狭い ▪ He always brings sex into a conversation. He's *got a one-track mind.* 彼はいつもセックスを話題にする. そればかり考えているんだ.

one-two /wʌ́ntúː/ 名 ***a one-two*** **1** 《ボクシング》ワンツーパンチ, 左右2連打 ▪ The boxer gave his opponent *a one-two.* ボクサーは相手にワンツーを食らわした.

2 (不意打ちの)素早い決定的な行動 ▪ You can't give them the old *one-two* and win the game. 彼らに決定攻撃を加えて負かすことはできないよ.

a one-two punch 《米》 **1** =a ONE-TWO 1.

2 二つの災難が続いて生じること ▪ The weather delivered *a one-two punch* to us with unseasonal snowfalls and strong winds. 天候に季節はずれの降雪と強風のダブルパンチを見舞われた.

one-way /wʌ́nwéɪ/ 形 ***be a one-way ticket*** (***to***) (...が)確実に起きる, (から)逃れられない ▪ Experimenting with drugs *is a one-way ticket to* addiction. 麻薬を試せば間違いなく中毒になる.

onion /ʌ́njən/ 名 ***know** one's **onions*** 《口》能力がある, やり手だ ▪ Leave it to him; he *knows his onions.* 彼に任しておけよ, ちゃんとやるさ.

off** one's **onion 《主に英俗》気が変になって ▪ He went right *off his onion.* 彼はすっかり気が変になってしまった ▪ After four glasses of beer I am properly *off my onion.* ビールを4杯も飲むと, すっかり前後不覚になってしまう. ☞ onion＝head.

onlooker /ɑ́nlʊ̀kər|ɔ́n-/ 名 ***an onlooker*** 傍観者, 見物人 ▪ *The onlooker* sees most of the game. 《諺》勝負はそばで見ている人の方がよくわかる, 「岡目八目(おかめはちもく)」.

only /óʊnli/ 副形接 ***if only*** **1** たとえ...でも ▪ You should attend the meeting, *if only* half an hour. たとえ30分でも会合に出席すべきだ.

2 ...さえしたらなあ ▪ *If only* he would stop talking! 彼がおしゃべりをやめてさえくれたらなあ ▪ *If* I had *only* known! あの時わかってさえいたらなあ.

3 ...しさえすれば ▪ You will succeed *if only* you do your best. 一生懸命働きさえすれば成功するよ.

if only for [***because***] ただ...のためだとしても ▪ You must respect him *if only for* his honesty [*because* he is honest]. ただ彼の正直さのためだけでも彼を尊敬しなければならない.

not only** A **but (***also***) *B* →NOT.

only fair [***right, natural,*** etc.] 全く正当で[自然で, など] ▪ It's *only natural* to favor one's own kin, isn't it? 親類の者をひいきにするのはごく自然なことでしょう. ☞ 言い訳・警告に用いられる.

only if ...する場合に限って ▪ *Only if* I have given permission are you allowed to leave the room. 私の許可がない限り退室は許されない.

only just かろうじて; たった今...したばかり ▪ We were *only just* in time for the train. やっとその電車に間に合った ▪ We got by, but *only just.* どうにか切り抜けたが, 危いところだった ▪ I have *only just* arrived. たった今着いたばかりです.

only not ほとんど ▪ I was *only not* a boy. 私は少年と言ってよいくらいだった ▪ The fort was *only not* abandoned to the enemy. とりではほとんど敵の手中にあったと言ってよかった.

only that ...ということさえなければ (but for the fact that) ▪ He is a good student, *only that* he is a little idle. 彼はいい学生だ, ただ少し怠けるだけだ ▪ *Only that* I know you don't love bustle, I should wish you here. あなたがやかましいのがおきらいでなければ, こちらへおいで願うところなのですが.

***only to** do* 結局[あいにく]...する《意外な, またはかんばしくない結果》 ▪ He went to America *only to* die. 彼はアメリカへ行ったが結局死んでしまった ▪ I went all the way to see him *only to* find him absent. はるばる訪ねて行ったが, あいにく彼は留守だった.

only too **1** 《口》〖glad, happy などを伴って〗この上

なく ▪ I shall be *only too* pleased to come. それはもう喜んで参ります ▪ I shall be *only too* thankful if you accept my invitation. 招待を受けていただければこの上なくありがたく存じます.

2 残念ながら, 遺憾ながら ▪ It is *only too* true. それは遺憾ながら本当だ ▪ He knew *only too* well. 彼は知りすぎるほど知っていた. ☞1 の意味では only too pléased と形容詞に強勢を置き, 2 の意味では ónly too true と only に強勢を置く.

***the only thing is* (*that*)** ただ…である ▪ *The only thing is* it is rather expensive. ただそれは少し高いのだ.

onset /ánset|ɔ́n-/ 名 ***at the first* [*very*] *onset*** 手始めに ▪ She kissed the girl a dozen times *at the first onset*, and called her dear heart. 彼女は手始めにその少女に何度も何度もキスして, かわいい子と言った.

give* [*make*] *an onset …を攻撃する ▪ We *made an onset* on the fort. 我々はとりでを攻撃した.

onwards /ánwərdz|ɔ́n-/ 副 ***onward*(*s*) *and upward*(*s*)** **1** とんとん拍子で ▪ Our team are moving *onwards and upwards*. わがチームは連戦連勝中だ.

2 (不運にあった人を励まして) 希望を持って進め ▪ It's not the end of the world. *Onwards and upwards*! またいいこともあるさ. 元気を出せよ.

ooze /uːz/ 動 ***ooze its way*** じくじく流れ出る ▪ A small creek *oozed its way* through a wilderness of reeds and slime. 小さな湧き水がアシと泥からなる荒野をじくじくと流れ出ていた.

open[1] /óʊpən/ 形名 ***an open invitation* (*to*)** …しやすい状況 ▪ Leaving your bag on the bench is *an open invitation to* thieves. ベンチにかばんを置きっぱなしにしては, 盗んでくれと言うようなものだ.

an open letter →LETTER.

an open marriage →MARRIAGE.

an open sesame →SESAME.

be open with* a person *about …について人に隠し立てしない ▪ I will *be open with* you *about* it. それについて腹臓なくお話ししましょう.

***be* (*wide*) *open to abuse* [*criticism, attack,* etc.]** 虐待[非難, 攻撃など]に(大いに)身をさらす ▪ This position *is wide open to criticism*. この立場にいると非難の矢おもてに立たされそうだ.

bring ... into the open …を明るみに出す, 公表する ▪ We must *bring* this matter *into the open*. 我々はこの件を公表せねばならない.

come* (*out*) *in* [*into*] *the open **1** 隠し立てをしない, 真意を表明する ▪ We have been trying for months to get them to *come out into the open*. ここ何か月も彼らに真意を表明させようと努めてきた.

2 公表される, 公然と知らされる ▪ The whole scandal *came into the open*. スキャンダルがすっかり明るみに出た ▪ Everything needs to *come out in the open*. 万事が公表される必要がある.

fly open ぱっと開く ▪ The door *flew open*. ドアが急に開いた.

have an open hand 気前がよい ▪ He *has an open hand*; you will get a good subscription from him. 彼は気前がよい. たんまり寄付してもらえるよ.

hold ... open **1** = keep ... OPEN 1.

2 (職)をあけておく ▪ His firm will *hold* his job *open* for him while he is abroad. 彼が外国にいる間会社は彼のポストをあけたままにしておくだろう.

in the open 戸外で, 野外で; (立木・建物などのない)広々とした所に ▪ The house stands *in the open*, outside the woods. その家は森を離れて樹木のない所にある ▪ The soldier is taught how to attack *in the open*. 兵士は野外での攻撃の仕方を教えられる.

in the open air 戸[野]外で ▪ We have exercise *in the open air*. 僕らは戸外で運動する.

in the open court 公の法廷で ▪ He has refused it *in the open court*. 彼は公の法廷でそれを拒んだ.

keep an open mind あらゆる意見をいれる ▪ We are *keeping an open mind* as to that. その件についてはあらゆる意見をいれる用意がある.

keep ... open **1** …をあけたままにしておく ▪ He *kept* the door *open* to let some air in. 彼は風を入れるためにドアをあけっ放しにしておいた.

2 = hold ... OPEN 2.

***keep open doors* [*house, table*]** 誰でも来客を歓迎する ▪ A chief must *keep open doors* and entertain. 上に立つ者は来客を歓迎してもてなさねばならない ▪ Sir Roger always *keeps open house* at Christmas. サー・ロジャーはいつもクリスマスには誰でも来客を歓迎する.

lay open **1** 裸にする, あらわにする ▪ The land *was laid open*. その土地の木が切りはらわれた ▪ He *laid open* the wound. 彼は傷をむき出しにした.

2 切開する, (ぶつけるなどして)切る ▪ He *laid* his cheek *open*. 彼はけがでほおを切った.

3 あばく, 説明する ▪ They *laid open* to him the whole scheme of Mr. Astor. 彼らはアスター氏の陰謀をすっかり彼にあばいてみせた ▪ He tried to *lay open* the general principles of civic laws. 彼は民法の一般原理を説明しようとした.

lay* oneself *open to →LAY oneself (wide) open to.

leave ... open **1** …を未決定のままにする ▪ The matter of salary *was left open*. 月給の件は未決定のままにしておかれた.

2 = keep ... OPEN 1.

on the open market →MARKET.

***open and above-board* [*aboveboard*]** 公明率直で, 隠し立てをいっさいしない ▪ He was entirely *open and above-board* in his statements. 彼の申し立ては全く公明率直だった. ☞open [above-board] = honest. aboveboard はトランプの賭けで不正をしないようテーブル (board) の上に手を置いたことから.

open and shut **1** 〚名詞的に〛 確かなこと ▪ It was a dead *open and shut* that we've got to stay

with them. 我々が彼らの所にいなければならないということは全く確かなことだった.
2〚形容詞的に〛(結果の)明白な ▪ It was an *open and shut* case in favor of his client. それは彼の依頼人に明らかに有利な事件だった.
open as the day 公明正大な, 包み隠さない ▪ *Open as the day*, he made no secret of the fact. 彼は公明正大に, そのことを隠し立てしなかった ▪ Her life was *open as the day*. 彼女の生活は包み隠すところがなかった.
open ear (注意深い)聞き耳 ▪ The King gave *open ear* to his request. 王は彼の願いに耳を傾けた.
open to **1** …をいれる ▪ The evidence is *open to* doubt. その証拠は疑いをはさむ余地がある ▪ His heart is *open to* pity. 彼の心はあわれみに容易に動かされる ▪ I am *open to* conviction. 理には服する.
2 (人)に利用できる ▪ It is *open to* anyone to reject both stories. どちらの話をもはねつけることが誰にでもできる ▪ There are three courses *open to* us. 我々には取りうる道が3つある.
push at an open door (多くの支持を得て)わけなく目的を達成する, 楽々と仕事をやり遂げる ▪ Everyone supported our campaign, so we were *pushing at an open door*. みなが我々の運動を支持してくれたので, 楽に活動を進めていた.
the great [***wide***] ***open spaces*** 広々とした平野地域 ▪ He lives somewhere out there in *the great open spaces*. 彼はどこかあちらの広々とした平野地域に住んでいる.
the open door 門戸開放; (通商上の)機会均等 ▪ She is of *the open door*. 彼女は誰でも快くむかえてくれる.
with (***an***) ***open hand*** 気前よく ▪ He gives *with open hand*. 彼は気前よく物を与える.
with open arms →ARM[1].
with open doors 門戸を解放して; 傍聴を許して ▪ The court sits *with open doors*. 法廷は傍聴を許して開かれている.
with open mouth (言おうとして)口を開いて; あっけにとられて; がつがつして ▪ I saw him swallowing the news *with open mouth*. 私は彼が口をあんぐり開けてその知らせを聞いているのを見た.

open[2] /óʊpən/ 動 ***open sesame*** →SESAME.
open the floodgates of (***to***) →open FLOODGATEs of.
open to *one's* ***mind*** わかってくる ▪ The mysteries of the universe *opened to my mind*. 宇宙の神秘が私にわかってきた.
open up *one's* ***mind*** 心を打ち明ける ▪ He *opened up his mind* freely. 彼はわだかまりなく心を打ち明けた.

opener /óʊpənər/ 名 ***for openers*** 《主に米口》手始めに, まず第一に, 最初に ▪ *For openers*, they played the national anthem. まず初めに国歌が演奏された.

opening /óʊpənɪŋ/ 名 ***make an opening for*** *a person* 人に仕事の口を見つけてやる ▪ He *made an opening for* me in this business. 彼がこの仕事の口を見つけてくれたのです.
see an [*one's*] ***opening*** 機会を見つける ▪ I *saw an opening* and quickly explained my purpose to him. 私は機会を見つけて, 早速私の決意を彼に話して聞かせた.

operation /ɑ̀pəréɪʃən|ɔ̀p-/ 名 ***a Caesarean operation*** 帝王切開(術) ▪ She was delivered of a baby boy by *Caesarean operation*. 彼女は帝王切開で男の子を出産した.
a domino-type operation ドミノ(式)移植《立て続けに二人(以上)の患者に対して行われる二重(以上)移植手術》 ▪ The kidney transplants were performed in *a domino-type operation*. 腎臓移植はドミノ式移植手術で行われた.
a mom-and-dad operation/ ***a mom-and-pop operation*** 家族経営, 夫婦だけによる自営業 ▪ Tom and Ann's small bookshop is a typical *mom-and-dad operation*. トムとアンの小さな本屋は典型的な夫婦営業だ.
bring … into operation →put … into OPERATION.
come into operation 実施[施行]される ▪ The new regulations will *come into operation* next Tuesday. 新規則は来週火曜日に施行される.
do an operation on [***for***] (体の部分・病気)の手術をする ▪ He can *do* difficult *operations on* the abdomen. 彼はむずかしい腹部手術ができる.
in operation **1** 運[活]動中 ▪ The machine is now *in operation*. その機械は今運転中だ ▪ The plant is *in* full *operation*. その工場は全能力をあげて操業している.
2 効力を有する ▪ At present the old regulations are *in operation*. 今はまだ古い規則が効力を有する.
put [***bring***] ***… into operation*** …を実施[施行]する ▪ The provisions will *be brought into operation* on 1st April. 規定は4月1日から施行される ▪ The law has *been put into operation*. その法律はもう施行されている.
undergo an operation 手術を受ける ▪ He *underwent an operation* for liver trouble. 彼は肝臓病の手術を受けた.

operator /ɑ́pərèɪtər|ɔ́p-/ 名 ***a fly-by-night operator*** 夜逃げ操業者, 借金をして夜逃げをする人 ▪ *The fly-by-night operator* was running away to escape debts. その夜逃げ商人は借金を踏み倒して逃走中だった.
a smooth operator やり手, 策士, 口先のうまい人 ▪ You can't be *a smooth operator* without developing your empathy skills. 如才なく振舞うには感情移入の技を磨かねばならない.

opinion /əpínjən/ 名 ***a matter of opinion*** 各自が意見を持ちうる問題 ▪ I suppose it's *a matter of opinion*; you have your views and I have mine. 見解上の問題だと思うな. 君には君の考えがあり, 僕には僕の考えがあるわけだ.
a second [***another***] ***opinion*** もう一人の医者の

意見《比喩的にも》 ▪ If you want *another opinion*, why not get it? セカンド・オピニオンがほしければ，もらったらどうですか．

act up to** one's **opinions 信じるところを行う ▪ I like to see a man *act up to his opinions*. 私は人が信じるところを行うのを見るのが好きだ．

be of ... opinion …の意見を持っている ▪ I *am* not *of* their *opinion*. 私は彼らの意見に賛成しない ▪ They *are of* the same *opinion*. 彼らは同意見だ．

be of* (*the*) *opinion that …と考える ▪ I *am of opinion that* there will be no kings or queens a hundred years hence. 今から100年後には王とか女王というものはいないだろうと思う ▪ He *was* strongly *of the opinion that* they were both wrong. 彼は彼らが二人とも間違っていると確信していた．

buy golden opinions → win golden OPINIONs.

entertain golden opinion*(*s*) *of …に非常に敬服する ▪ I *entertain golden opinions of* him. 彼に非常に敬服している．

halt between two opinions →HALT².

have* [*form*] *a bad* [*low, poor, mean*] *opinion of …を悪く思う，見下げる ▪ I *have a poor opinion of* him. 私は彼をあまり買っていない ▪ You *have* too *mean an opinion of* yourself. 君はあまり自分を卑下しすぎる．

have* [*form*] *a good* [*high, favorable*] *opinion of …をよく思う，信用する ▪ The Head Master seems to *have a good opinion of* your son. 校長はあなたの息子さんをよく思っているようだ ▪ I *have a high opinion of* his scholarship. 彼の学識を高く買っている．

have no opinion of …をあまりよく思わない ▪ I *have no opinion of* the new method of teaching. その新教授法はあまり感心しない．

have the courage of** one's **opinions 大胆に自説を述べる[実行する] ▪ One must *have the courage of one's opinions*. 人は大胆に自説を述べるようでなくてはいけない．

in the opinion of …の意見では ▪ *In my opinion* the step is wrong. 私に言わせればその方法はまちがいだ ▪ *In the opinion of* the doctor the invalid will recover. 医師の意見では患者はよくなるそうだ．

offer an* [*one's*] *opinion (…について)意見を述べる (*to, on*) ▪ He is well qualified to *offer an opinion to* this sort of thing. 彼はこういうことに意見を述べる資格が十分ある ▪ We are not inclined to *offer* any *opinion on* that point. 我々はその点についても何も意見を述べたくない．

pass an opinion on …に評価を下す ▪ I don't know enough about paintings to *pass an opinion on* this landscape. 私はこの風景画に評価を下せるほど絵のことを知らない．

win* [*buy*] *golden opinions 絶賛を博する (cf. Sh., *Macb*. 1. 7. 31) ▪ The new President has already *won golden opinions*, even from his political opponents. 新大統領はすでにその政敵からさえ絶賛を博している．

opium /óʊpiəm/ 名 ***the opium of the people*** 民衆のアヘン《宗教を指す》 ▪ Religion is *the opium of the people*. 宗教は民衆のアヘンだ．☞Marx の言葉 das Opium des Volks から．

opportunity /àpərtjúːnəti | ɔ̀p-/ 名 ***at* [*on*] *the first opportunity*** 機会があり次第 ▪ The death penalty should be abolished *at the first opportunity*. 死刑は機会のあり次第廃止すべきだ ▪ I will speak to him *on the first opportunity*. 機会があり次第彼に話しましょう．

have an* [*the*] *opportunity of* [*for*]** *doing* [to** do*] …する機会がある ▪ I will examine the statement as soon as I *have an opportunity of doing* so. その機会があり次第例の申し立てを調べてみよう ▪ I *have* much *opportunity for hearing* good music. 私はよい音楽を聞く機会が大いにある ▪ He *had* no *opportunity to* display his genius. 彼は自分の才能を示す機会に恵まれなかった．

lose* [*miss, neglect*] *no opportunity of* [*for*]** *doing* [to** do*] …する機会をのがさない ▪ He *loses no opportunity to* express his antagonism. 彼は自分の敵意を表す機会をのがさない ▪ She *never missed an opportunity of being* kind to him. 彼女は機会あるごとに彼に親切にした．

Opportunity knocks but once. 《諺》機会は一度しか訪れない．

Opportunity makes the thief. 《諺》すきを与えると魔がさす．

take* [*seize*] *an* [*the*] *opportunity of* [*for*]** *doing* [to** do*] 機会をとらえて…する ▪ May I *take this opportunity to* express my gratitude for your kindness? この機会にご親切のお礼を申し述べさせてください．

oppose /əpóʊz/ 動 ***as opposed to*** …と対照した(場合の) ▪ I mean letters *as opposed to* life. 私が言っているのは人生と対照した文学のことです．

be opposed to …に反対である ▪ From the first he *was* much *opposed to* the plan. 初めから彼はその計画にひどく反対していた ▪ The two characters *are opposed to* each other. 二人は反対の性質だ ▪ We *are opposed to* naming the new school after the governor. 新設校の校名を知事に因んでつけるのには反対だ．

oppose** oneself **to …に反対する ▪ He *opposed himself to* the scheme with all his might. 彼は全力を尽くしてその企てに反対した．

opposite /ápəzɪt | ɔ́pəzɪt/ 形副名 ***one's opposite number*** 《主に英》(他の職場などで)対等の地位にいる人，同役 ▪ Jackson is *my opposite number*. Both are chief clerks. ジャクスンは僕の同役で，二人とも事務長だ．

***Opposites attract* (*each other*).** 《諺》逆は引き合うものだ．

play opposite …の相手役を務める ▪ She *played opposite* Irving. 彼女はアービングの相手役を務めた．

the opposite sex 異性 ▪ She is too shy to talk to members of *the opposite sex*. 彼女は恥ずかしがりやで男性会員には声をかけられない.

opposition /àpəzíʃən|ɔ̀p-/ 名 ***have an opposition to*** …に反対である ▪ He *has an opposition to* my doing so. 彼は私がそうすることに反対だ.

in opposition 在野の (↔in OFFICE 2) ▪ They are *in opposition* and not in office. 彼らは与党ではなく, 野党なのだ.

in opposition to **1** …に反対して ▪ I did it *in opposition to* public opinion. 私は世論に反対してそうしたのだ.

2 …に向かい合って ▪ The houses are *in opposition to* each other. その家は向かい合っている.

in opposition with《天》…に対して衝にある《惑星が太陽に対して正反対の方向に来ること》 ▪ The moon when she is eclipsed is always *in opposition with* the sun. 月は月食のときには常に太陽に対して衝にある.

meet (***with***) ***opposition*** 反対を受ける ▪ Any attempt to tax bachelors would *meet with* strong *opposition*. 独身者に課税しようとする企てはどれでも強い反対を受けるだろう.

offer [***set up***] ***opposition to*** …に反対する ▪ They *offered* no *opposition to* our scheme. 彼らは我々の計画に少しも反対しなかった.

oppress /əprés/ 動 ***be oppressed with*** …で苦しめられている ▪ My mind *is oppressed with* doubts and anxieties. 不安と心配でいても立ってもいられない.

opt /ɑpt|ɔpt/ 動 ***opt in favor of*** …を選ぶ ▪ I have *opted in favor of* electronic payment since then. それ以来は電子マネーでの支払いを選んでいる.

optimistic /ɑ̀ptəmístɪk|ɔ̀p-/ 形 ***be optimistic about*** [***of***] …を楽観している ▪ He *was optimistic about* the future of Taiwan. 彼は台湾の将来を楽観していた ▪ He still *was optimistic of* a cease-fire agreement. 彼はまだ停戦協定を楽観していた.

option /ɑ́pʃən|ɔ́p-/ 名 ***a*** [***the***] ***soft option*** (二つのうちで)安易な道 ▪ I don't like to take *the soft option* in this case. この場合, 安易な道を選びたくない.

an [***the***] ***easy option*** =a soft OPTION.

at [***in, to***] *one's* ***option*** 随意に ▪ It is left *at the option of* the student to study French or German. フランス語とドイツ語のいずれを学ぶかは学生の随意に任されている.

have no option but to *do* …するよりほかはない ▪ You *have no option but to* talk with each other. 君たちは互いに話し合うほかない.

keep [***leave***] *one's* ***option***(***s***) ***open*** 選択の自由を保留しておく ▪ You had better *keep your option open*. 選択の自由を保留しておく方がよい.

make *one's* ***option*** 選択する ▪ They seem to have *made their option*. 彼らは選択をしたらしい.

with [***without***] ***the option of a fine*** 罰金をもって代えうる[代ええない] ▪ He was sentenced to two years' imprisonment *with the option of a fine*. 彼は罰金をもって代えうる禁固2年の刑を宣告された ▪ Two were given thirty days *without the option of a fine*. 二人は罰金をもって代えられない30日の刑を申し渡された.

or /ər|ɔ:/ 接 ***or else*** さもないと《しばしばおどしの文句》 ▪ Make haste, *or else* you will be late. 急がないと遅れますよ ▪ Pay up, *or else*. すっかり支払わないと承知しない[大変なことになる]ぞ.

or *A* ***or*** *B* 《詩》AかBか ▪ To love is the one way to know *or* God *or* man. 愛することは神か人かを知る唯一の道である.

or rather →RATHER.

or so **1** …かそこいら ▪ He will stay a week *or so*. 彼は1週間くらいここにいるでしょう.

2 …のようなもの, みたいなもの ▪ It must have been a ghost *or so*. それは幽霊か何かだったにちがいない.

or something [***somewhere***] …か何か[どこか] ▪ He is sick *or something*. 彼は病気か何かだ ▪ I put it in the cupboard *or somewhere*. それを戸だなかどこかへ入れた.

or whatever あるいは何かそんなもの[人] ▪ I hear he died of cancer *or whatever*. 彼はがんか何かそんなもので死んだそうだ.

oracle /ɔ́:rəkəl|ɔ́r-/ 名 ***work the oracle*** **1**(陰で策略して)有利な証言[結果]を得る ▪ How did you manage to persuade your father to let you go?—It was my uncle who *worked the oracle*. どうやっておとうさんを説きつけて行かしてもらったのかね?—事をうまく運んでくれたのはおじさんなんだよ.

2《俗》金策をする, 金を作る ▪ How did you manage to *work the oracle*? どうやって金を工面したのか. ☞神託僧を買収して希望通りの託宣を得ることから.

orange /ɔ́:rɪndʒ|ɔ́r-/ 名 ***a squeezed*** [***sucked***] ***orange*** (汁をしぼり取ったオレンジのように)利用価値のなくなったもの, しぼりかす ▪ By this time Dibdin was *a sucked orange*; his brain was dry. この時にはディブディンはしぼりかすみたいになっていた. 彼の頭はからっぽだった.

gather orange-blossoms 花嫁をもらう ▪ What has he come to this lovely retreat for? To *gather orange-blossoms*? 彼は何のためにこの美しい隠れがへ来たのか. 花嫁をもらうためか. ☞オレンジの花を花嫁が結婚式に髪に飾ったり花束にして持ったりする習慣(1820–30年ごろにフランスからイギリスに入った)から.

"Oranges and Lemons" 「オレンジとレモン」《この句で始まるイギリスの童謡・遊技歌》 ▪ Someone started singing "*Oranges and Lemons*", and everybody joined in. 誰かが「オレンジとレモン」を歌い始めると, みんなが唱和した.

squeeze [***suck***] ***an*** [***the***] ***orange*** **1** オレンジの汁を全部しぼり取る ▪ As soon as *the orange is squeezed*, it is thrown upon the ground. オレンジは, 汁を全部しぼり取るとすぐ地面に投げ捨てられる.

2 甘い汁をしぼり取る, よい所を全部取り去る ▪ His

father *sucked the orange*, and the boy has merely inherited the skin. 父親が甘い汁をしぼり取ってしまい, 息子はただ皮のところをもらっただけだ.

squeeze the orange until the pips squeak (相手がくたびれ果てるまで質問をして)情報を絞り出す ▪ I'll *squeeze the orange until the pips squeak* at the meeting. 会合で情報を搾り取ってこよう.

oration /əréɪʃən/ 名 ***make an oration*** **1** 演説をする ▪ He *made an oration* to the people. 彼は人々に向かって演説した.

2《英・方》わいわい言う ▪ He *makes* such *an oration* about anything. 彼は何事につけ大騒ぎする.

orb /ɔːrb/ 名 ***the orb of day*** 《詩・雅》日輪 (Gray, *The Bard* 136) ▪ They worshiped the elements and *the orb of day*. 彼らは四大と日輪を崇拝した.

orbit /ɔ́ːrbət/ 名 ***go into orbit*** 《米俗》 **1** 軌道に乗る, 成功する ▪ Our firm has *gone into orbit*. わが社は軌道に乗った.

2 逆上する, かっとなる ▪ He *went into orbit* when I teased him. からかったら彼はかっとなった.

in* [*into*] *orbit **1** 軌道に乗って ▪ The earth is *in orbit* round the sun. 地球は太陽を回る軌道に乗っている.

2 恍惚(こう)として, うっとりとなって ▪ Dad went right *into orbit* when he won the lottery. パパは宝くじが当たって有頂天になった.

3《口》(酒・麻薬に)酔って ▪ She was *in orbit* after drinking too much. 彼女は飲みすぎて酔っ払ってしまった.

ordeal /ɔːrdíːl/ 名 ***weather an ordeal*** 苦い経験に耐える, 厳しい試練を乗り切る ▪ He gave me strength to *weather the ordeal*. 厳しい難局を切り抜ける力を彼が与えてくれた.

O

order[1] /ɔ́ːrdər/ 名 ***a large* [*tall*] *order*** 《口》不当な要求[提案]; できない相談, むずかしい仕事 ▪ Exchange all the beautiful things I've got inside? It's *a large order*. 中にある美しい物をみな交換しろだって? それは不当な注文だよ ▪ It's *a tall order*, but it's worth trying, isn't it? これはむずかしい仕事だが, やりがいはありますね.

a* [*the*] *pecking order 序列, 上下関係 ▪ The astronauts need to have *a* definite *pecking order*. 宇宙飛行士の間には厳格な序列が必要だ. ☞ニワトリがつついて序列を決めることから.

a short order 即席料理(の注文) ▪ The diner serves *short orders* exclusively. その安レストランではもっぱら即席料理を出す.

a take-out order テイクアウト[持ち帰り料理](の注文) ▪ We were sitting down to wait for our *take-out order*. そのとき我々は座って持ち帰り料理を待っていた.

an order to view 《英》(売家・貸家の)下見許可書, 家屋などを買うための検分許可 ▪ It's to let. I have *an order to view*. これは貸し家だ. 私は下見許可書を持っている ▪ The house-agents gave me *an order to view*. 家屋周旋人は検分許可をくれた.

at short order →in short ORDER.

by order of …の命令によって ▪ It was done *by order of* the governor. それは知事の命令でなされた.

call ... to order **1** (議長が弁士)に不謹慎を注意する ▪ Here Mr. Speaker *called* Sir Francis *to order*. ここで議長がサー・フランシスに不謹慎を注意した.

2《米》...の開会を宣言する ▪ The chairman *called* the meeting *to order*. 議長は開会を宣言した.

come to order 開会する ▪ Will the meeting please *come to order*? どうか開会してくれませんか.

get one's marching orders **1** 推進するように命じられる ▪ The sales force *got their marching orders* today. 販売部員は今日, 発売開始の指令を受けた.

2 解雇される ▪ He *got his marching orders* only yesterday. 彼はつい昨日首になったばかりだ.

give an order for …を注文する ▪ I *gave an order* to a steward *for* coffee. 私は客室乗務員にコーヒーを注文した.

give a person his marching orders → MARCHING.

give* [*issue*] *orders 命令する ▪ He has *given orders* that it should be done. 彼はそれをするようにと命令した.

go* [*get*] *into orders 聖職につく ▪ My brother John is to *go into orders* this Lent. 兄のジョンはこの四旬節に聖職につきます.

in bad order 不健康な状態で; 使えない状態で ▪ The land is *in bad order*. この土地は荒れている.

in good order **1** 健康な[使える]状態で ▪ The goods arrived *in good order*. 商品は無傷で届いた ▪ The land is *in good order*. その土地は整備してある《草などがはえていない》.

2《戯》ごきげんで, 酔って ▪ Being *in good order*, he did not notice it. ごきげんだったので彼はそれに気がつかなかった.

in* (*holy*) *orders 聖職について ▪ My brother is *in orders*. 兄は聖職についている ▪ Persons, even *in holy orders*, have stood unconcerned. 聖職についている人々でさえ我関せずといった顔をしてきた.

in open* [*close*] *order 散開[密集]隊形で ▪ The troops advanced *in close order*. 部隊は密集隊形で前進した.

in order **1** 順を追って, 順序正しく ▪ It is important to take things *in order*. 物事を順に取り上げるのは重要だ ▪ Are the letters *in order*? 手紙は順にしてありますか.

2 整然として, きちんとして ▪ He always keeps things *in order*. 彼はいつも物事をきちんとしておく.

3 規則にかなって, 当を得て ▪ You will be *in order* if you speak after the chair. 議長のあとから話すと規則にかなうのです ▪ Therefore the following suggestions may be *in order*. そこで次のような提案をするのも当を得たことかもしれない.

4 望ましい ▪ Any gossip of that kind would not be *in order*. その種のゴシップは望ましいことではない

▪ We dispatched the goods today and charged them to your credit card, trusting this will be *in order*. 本日，商品を急ぎ発送いたし，お客様のクレジットカード払いとさせていただきました．以上，貴意に添うものと信じつつ．

5 はやりの，流行の ▪ A quotation from Professor James on any subject is always *in order*. どんな話題であれ，ジェイムズ教授からの引用はいつでもはやりだ．

in order of …の順に ▪ The candidates will be interviewed *in order of* arrival. 志願者は到着順に面接する ▪ Who is next *in order of* application? 申し込み順では，次はどなたですか．

in order that *one* ***may*** *do* 《文》…するために ▪ He worked hard *in order that* he *might* get the prize. 彼は賞を得るために熱心に勉強した． ☞文語的な in ORDER to よりもさらに形式ばった言い方．

in order to 〚不定詞を伴って〛…するために，しようとして ▪ He works hard *in order to* keep his family in comfort. 彼は家族を安楽にさせておくために精出して働く． ☞in order to は so as to よりも文語的で，いっそう目的の気持ちが強い．

in [***at, on***] ***short*** [***quick***] ***order*** すぐさま，てっとり早く ▪ I was so comfortable that I went to sleep *in short order*. とても心地よかったので，すぐさま寝入ってしまった．

keep … in order …を統御する ▪ The new teacher *kept* her class *in order*. 新任の先生はクラスをうまく統制した．

keep order 秩序を保つ ▪ The police officer *keeps order*. 警官が秩序を保つ．

leave *one's* ***affairs in order*** →put one's affairs in ORDER.

made to order ちょうどふさわしい ▪ The weather was *made to order* for the picnic. ピクニックにおあつらえ向きの天気だった．

make … to order →to ORDER.

of the highest order/of the first order 最もすぐれた[劣った]，最高[最低]水準の; 極端な ▪ That was a scandal *of the first order*. きわめつけの大スキャンダルだった．

of [***in***] ***the order of*** 《英》(数量・重要性などが)ほぼ…ほどの，約… ▪ The loss is *of the order of* thousands a month. 損失は1か月数千ドルに及ぶ．

on order 注文して ▪ The curtains are *on order* but they have not yet been delivered. カーテンは注文してあるが，まだ配達されていない ▪ It can be secured *on order*. それは注文すれば得られる．

on the order of **1** 《米》…に属して，似かよって ▪ It was something *on the order of* a state park. それはやや州立公園に似かよっていた．

2 ＝of the ORDER of.

Orders are orders. 命令は命令だ《従わなければならない》 ▪ *Orders are orders*, not requests. 命令だから従うほかない．要請ではないのだ．

out of order **1** 順が狂って，乱れて ▪ You are speaking *out of order*. 君が今しゃべる番ではないでしょう ▪ The room was *out of order*. 部屋は乱雑になっている．

2 調子が狂って，体の具合が悪くて ▪ Our refrigerator is *out of order*. うちの冷蔵庫は故障している ▪ The machine gets *out of order* again very soon. その機械はじきにまた狂う ▪ Since I came here I have been *out of order*. ここに来てからというもの体調が悪い．

3 規則にそむいて，違法で ▪ You will be *out of order* if you interrupt the Chairman. 議長のじゃまをするのは違法である ▪ His motion was ruled *out of order*. 彼の動議は定例にそむくものとして却下された．

4 《口》(言動が)適切でない，場違いで ▪ His behavior in the ceremony was completely *out of order*. 式の最中の彼の行動は全く場にふさわしくなかった．

place an [*one's*] ***order*** [***orders***] 注文する (*with*) ▪ We are going to *place an order with* the firm for a new machine. 新しい機械をその企業へ注文するつもりだ ▪ To avoid disappointment please *place your orders* early. 品切れにならないうちに早めにご注文ください．

put [***set, leave***] *one's* ***affairs in order*** (死ぬ前に)私事を整理しておく ▪ He had already *put his affairs in order*. 彼はすでに私事を整理していた．

put [***set***] ***… in order*** …を整理する，整とんする ▪ You must *put* [*set*] things *in order*. 物を整とんしておかねばならない．

reduce … to order …を整理[整とん]する ▪ He *reduced* my money affairs *to order*. 彼は私の会計を整理した．

rise to (***a point of***) ***order*** (議員が)起立して議事[発言]の違法を議長に抗議する ▪ Mr. Chairman, I *rise to a point of order*. 議長，私は発言の違法に抗議します．

take (***holy***) ***orders*** 聖職につく，牧師になる ▪ The new Bishop *took orders* thirty years ago. 新主教は30年前に牧師になった ▪ My brother has just *taken holy orders*. 兄がただいま牧師に叙任された．

take order 手段をとる; 取り決めをする ▪ No *order was taken* by the Spanish authorities for this necessity. この必要に対してスペイン当局はなんの手段もとらなかった ▪ They *took order* to meet there at 8. 彼らは8時にそこで会うように取り決めた．

take orders from *a person*/***take*** *a person's* ***orders*** 人の指図を受ける，人の風下に立つ ▪ You will *take orders from* Mr. Sullivan, the manager. 君は支配人のサリバンさんの指図を受けるのです．

the order of the day **1** 日程，(特に議会の)議事日程 ▪ He made a motion that they should read *the order of the day*. 彼は議事日程を読もうという動議を出した．

2 《口》慣行; 流行 ▪ Books and games are *the order of the day*. 読書と競技が毎日の行事である ▪ Fires seem to be *the order of the day* just now. 火事は目下の流行のようである．

to order 注文によって ▪ He has all his suits made *to order*. 彼は全部の服をあつらえて作る ▪ We make hand-made shoes *to order*. 当店ではご注文に応じて手作りの靴をお作りします.

under orders 命令を受けて ▪ The regiment is now *under orders* for the front. その連隊は今前線へ行く命令を受けている.

under sailing orders **1** 出帆命令を受けて ▪ The ship is *under sailing orders* and will soon set sail. 船は出帆命令を受けていて, まもなく出航する.

2《米俗》死にかかっている ▪ He is *under sailing orders*. あの男ももうすぐおさらばだ.

under the orders of (人)の部下で; の命のもとに ▪ He has good men *under his orders*. 彼はよい部下を持っている ▪ These expeditions were made *under the orders of* the Russian Government. この遠征はロシア政府の命のもとになされた.

order[2] /ɔ́ːrdər/ 動 ***order abroad*** [***away, back,*** etc.] 〚主に受身で〛 …に洋行せよ[去れ, 下がれ, など]と命じる ▪ He has *been ordered abroad*. 彼は洋行を命じられた ▪ He *was ordered away* for health. 彼は保養に行かされた ▪ He *was ordered back* to Japan. 彼は日本へ帰国を命じられた.

Order arms [***a gun***]***!***《号令》立て銃(つつ) ▪ The commanding officer directed the men to *Order Arms*. 指揮官が隊員に「立て銃」を命じた.

order off (***the field***)《スポーツ》(選手)を退場させる ▪ He *was ordered off* in the second half. 彼は後半戦で退場させられた.

They order things better in *France*. (フランスなど)では諸般の事情がうまくいっている. ☞ L. Sterne, *A Sentimental Journey* 冒頭の文から.

O

ordinary /ɔ́ːrdənèri|-nəri, -nèri/ 形名 ***above*** [***out of***] ***the ordinary***《口》普通以上の, 異常な ▪ He has brains *above the ordinary*. 彼は普通以上の頭を持っている ▪ Something *out of the ordinary* was anticipated. 何か異常なことが予期された.

in ordinary《英》(職員が)常任[直属]の ▪ He was chaplain *in ordinary* to His Majesty. 彼は陛下常任の礼拝堂牧師だった.

in the ordinary run of things [***course of events***] 通例 ▪ *In the ordinary run of things* I go home nearly every weekend. 通例, 私はほとんど毎週のように週末には家に帰ります.

in the ordinary way《英》いつもの通り(なら) ▪ *In the ordinary way* I should refuse. いつもだったら断るのだが.

ore /ɔːr/ 名 ***in ore*** 原鉱のままの, 磨かれない ▪ A good yeoman is a gentleman *in ore*. 良き郷士は磨かれざる紳士である.

organ /ɔ́ːrgən/ 名 ***the organ grinder's monkey***《英》権力者に追従する人, 小間使い ▪ He looks majestic but actually he's *an organ grinder's monkey*. 彼は堂々としているが実は小者である. ☞かつて大道音楽師が手回しオルガンの音楽に合わせてサルに芸をさせていたことから.

orient /ɔ́ːriənt/, 《英》**orientate** /ɔ́ːriəntèɪt/ 動 ***orient*** [***orientate***] *oneself* 自分を正しい立場・関係に置く; 自分の立場を見定める ▪ You might, in this way, *orient yourself* before the public. 君はこうすれば一般大衆に対して自分を正しい立場に置くことができる ▪ Men must *orient themselves* before they can expect to go right. 人は道を間違わないようにする前に自分の立場を見定めなければならない.

origin /ɔ́ːrədʒən|ɔ́r-/ 名 ***by origin*** 生まれは ▪ He is a Frenchman *by origin*. 彼は生まれはフランス人だ ▪ He belonged *by origin* to the rural gentry. 彼は地方の素封家の出であった.

ornament /ɔ́ːrnəmənt/ 名 ***be an ornament to*** …の誉れ[飾り]である ▪ He *is an ornament to* his country. 彼は国の誉れだ ▪ He *is a* mere *ornament to* the board of directors. 彼は重役会の飾りにすぎない.

for ornament 装飾(用)に ▪ Many years ago tomatoes were principally cultivated *for ornament*. 昔トマトは主として装飾用に栽培されていた.

ostrich /ɑ́strɪtʃ|ɔ́s-/ 名 ***bury*** *one's* ***head in the sand like an ostrich***/***play ostrich*** 頭を隠してしりを隠さないような間抜けなことをする ▪ This would mean *burying one's head in the sand like an ostrich*. こんなことをすれば頭隠してしり隠さずというような間抜けをすることになる ▪ He tried to *play ostrich*. 彼は頭を隠してしりを隠さないようなまねをしようとした. ☞ダチョウは追われると砂の中に頭を埋めて姿を隠したつもりになると言われるところから.

have the digestion of an ostrich/***have a stomach like an ostrich*** 非常に胃袋が強い ▪ Those rustics *have stomachs like ostriches*. その田舎者たちはすこぶる胃袋が強い. ☞ダチョウが消化を助けるために小石などを丸飲みにするところから.

ostrich belief [***policy***] 頭隠してしり隠さぬ浅知恵[政策] ▪ He pursues an *ostrich policy*. 彼はまだ頭隠してしり隠さぬ政策をやっている.

play ostrich → bury one's head in the sand like an OSTRICH.

Othello /əθéloʊ/ 名 ***the Othello***('***s***) ***syndrome*** オセロ症候群《自分の妻に関心を寄せる者に異常なまでの嫉妬心を抱く夫の精神病的心理状態》 ▪ Many ancient warriors harbored *the Othello's syndrome* about the chastity of their wives. 多くの古代の戦士たちは自分の妻の貞操について妄想的な疑念を抱いた. ☞ cf. Sh., *Oth*.

other /ʌ́ðər/ 形代副 ***among other things*** その中でも, なかんずく ▪ *Among other things*, he had a long bamboo spear. 他にもあるが, 彼は長い竹やりを持っていた.

among others …もその一人[一つ] ▪ Ten of us have passed the examination, myself *among others*. 我々のうち10人が試験にパスした, 私もその一人だ ▪ He had many vices, and *among others*, that of drinking to excess. 彼にはたくさん悪癖があったが, 飲みすぎることもそのひとつだった.

any other 何か他の(もの) ▪ Do you have *any other* question(s)? 何か他に質問がありますか ▪ This wool is too dark; do you have *any other*? この毛糸は黒っぽすぎる. 何か他のはありませんか.

do the other thing →THING.

Do unto others as you would have them do unto you./Do as you would be done by. 《諺》人々にしてもらいたいと思うことを, 人にもしなさい. ☞"The Golden Rule (黄金律)" として知られている (《聖》*Matt*. 7. 12; *Luke* 6. 31).

each other お互い (→ONE another) ▪ The two love *each other*. 二人は互いに愛し合っている ▪ We know *each other*'s weak point. 我々はお互いの弱点を知っている. ☞通例二者について用いるが, 三者以上について用いる場合も多い.

every other **1** 一つおきの ▪ The doctor visits her *every other* day. 医師は1日おきに彼女を見に来てくれる.
2 他のすべての ▪ John is stupid; *every other* boy in the class knows the answer. ジョンは愚かだ. クラスの他のすべての生徒は答えがわかっている.

no other 他の何も…ない ▪ I have *no other* son(s). 私には他にはもう息子はいない ▪ Use this soap once, and you will use *no other*. この石けんを一度使ったら他のは使えませんよ.

no [none] other than …にほかならない ▪ It was *no* [*none*] *other than* the King. それはほかならぬ王様だった.

no [not,** etc.**] (…) other than …よりほか(…)ない ▪ I have *no other* friend *than* you. 私には君しか友人がいない ▪ They were given *nothing other than* dry bread and water. 彼らはバターのついていないパンと水しか与えられなかった ▪ I could *not* read *other than* cursorily. ざっとしか読めなかった ▪ I can do *no other than* accept. 受けるよりほかない.

of all others すべての中で特に ▪ Why is the typhoon coming here on that day *of all others*? よりにもよって, どうしてその日に台風が来るのだろう ▪ Why, you are the one *of all others* I have wanted to see. だって君にとりわけ会いたかったんだよ.

other than [from] …とは違った ▪ I couldn't wish him *other than* what he is. 彼はあのままで申し分ない ▪ They live in a world *other from* ours. 彼らは我々とは別な世界に住んでいる.

other than that …ということを除けば ▪ *Other than that* the nearest store is six miles away, it is a perfect location. 最寄りの店が6マイル離れている以外は申し分ない場所だ.

other things being equal 他のことが同じであれば《二つの人や物を比べて》 ▪ *Other things being equal*, Alice would marry Tom, not Jim. 他のことが同じであれば, アリスはジムとではなくトムと結婚するだろう. ☞[L] ceteris paribus のなぞり.

Other times, other manners. 《諺》時代が違えば風習も違う, 「移れば変わる世の習い」. ☞[F] Autres temps, autres moeurs のなぞり.

some ... or other 何かしら ▪ *Some* time *or other* we may be at leisure. いつか暇になるだろう ▪ *Some* idiots *or other* have done it. どこかのまぬけどもがそれをしたのだ.

some other 他のいくつかの ▪ I have *some other* questions. 他にいくつかの質問があります.

somewhere [sometime, somehow, someone] or other どこか[いつか, どうにか, 誰か] ▪ The wrench is *somewhere or other* in the garage. スパナは車庫のどこかにある ▪ *Somehow or other* I managed to make it there. どうにかこうにかそこへ行き着いた ▪ I lent my pen to *someone or other* at work. ペンを職場の誰かに貸した.

the other day 先日, この間 ▪ I met Tom on the street *the other day*. この前トムと通りで会った.

the other end (電話の)先方 ▪ The girl's voice at *the other end* was fruity. 先方の女の子の声は甘ったるいものだった.

the other man [woman] (男 [女] の) 愛人 ▪ *The other woman* is always a problem. 愛人というのはいつも問題だ.

the other morning [evening] 先日の朝[夕方] ▪ We got together *the other evening*. 我々はほんの2, 3日前の夜集まった.

the other night 先夜, この間の晩 ▪ I dreamed of you *the other night*. この間の晩, 君のことを夢に見た.

the other [wrong] way about [(a)round] →WAY.

this, that, and the other →THIS.

otherwise /ʌ́ðərwàɪz/ 副形 ***and otherwise*** その他 ▪ I have succeeded by friendly help *and otherwise*. 私は好意ある援助や何やで成功した ▪ He helped me with advice *and otherwise*. 彼は助言やら何やらで援助してくれた.

do no otherwise (than** do**) (…するより)ほかない ▪ I could *do no otherwise than* laugh. 私は笑わずにはおれなかった ▪ He could *do* it *no otherwise*. 彼はそれをそうするほかなかった.

or otherwise **1** あるいはその逆 ▪ Let's discuss the merits *or otherwise* of his paintings. 彼の絵の美点あるいは欠点について話し合って見よう ▪ I am not concerned with its accuracy *or otherwise*. それが正確であるかないかは私の関知するところではない.
2 あるいは別の方法で ▪ You can get there by train *or otherwise*. そこへは列車か別な方法で行ける.

otherwise than **1**〚形容詞的に〛…とは別の ▪ He is *otherwise than* I thought. 彼は思ったとは違う人だ ▪ How can it be *otherwise than* fatal? 致命的ならざるをえようか.
2〚副詞的に〛…とは別なふうに ▪ How can I do *otherwise than* laugh? どうして笑わずにいられようか ▪ I don't know him *otherwise than* in business. 私は商売の上でしかあの男を知らない.

ought /ɔːt/ 助 ***be no better than** one **ought to be*** 行いが正しくない, いかがわしい人物だ ▪ She *is no better than* she *ought to be*. 彼女は行いの正しくない女性だ.

O

***ought to** do* …すべきである; するのは当然である ▪ I think you *ought to* go. 君は行くべきであると思う ▪ Such a man *ought to* succeed. そのような人は成功するのが当然だ.

***ought to have** done* **1** …すべきであった《しなかったのは残念だ》 ▪ You *ought to have* known such a thing. そんなことは知っておくべきだったのに ▪ You *ought to have* seen it. 君に見せたかったよ.

2 …しているはずだ ▪ He *ought to have* arrived at Kyoto by now. 彼は今ごろは京都に着いているはずだ.

ounce /aʊns/ 名 ***An ounce of discretion is worth a pound of wit.*** 《諺》1オンスの思慮分別は1ポンドの才知の値打ちがある,「落ちた後で高みを恐る」.

An ounce of practice is worth a pound of theory. 《諺》理論より実行, 百の説法より一つの行い.

An ounce of prevention (is worth a pound of cure). 《諺》ほんのわずかな予防は山ほどの治療に値する,「転ばぬ先の杖」.

out[1] /aʊt/ 副形前間名 ***a long way out*** すっかりまちがって ▪ You're *a long way out* in your idea of what happened. 君は今度の事件についてすっかり考えちがいをしている.

all out 《俗》〚副詞的に〛 **1** 全く, 完全に ▪ It is seven *all out*. もうすっかり7時です.

2 〚通例 go all out として〛 全力をあげて (*for, to do*); 全速力で ▪ They are *going all out for* production. 彼らは生産に全力をあげている ▪ He *went all out to* entertain his guest. 彼は全力をあげて客をもてなした ▪ My car does 80 miles an hour when it's *going all out*. 私の車は全速力で走るときには時速80マイル出す. ☞all-out effort「渾身の努力」のように形容詞にも.

3 《米》 交替, 乗り換え ▪ *All out!* みなさん, お乗り換えです (= 《英》(All) CHANGE (here)!).

be at [on the] outs (with) 《口》(…と)不和だ, 仲たがいしている ▪ She *was at outs with* her parents because of her marriage. 彼女は結婚したため両親とそりが合わなかった ▪ They have *been on the outs* ever since they had that dispute. 彼らはあの口論をしたとき以来ずっと仲たがいしている.

be out **1** 不人気になる, 流行ではなくなる ▪ Loose jeans are in again, and tight ones *are out* nowadays. 近頃はゆるいジーンズがまたはやりで, きついのはすたれている.

2 仕事や家から離れる ▪ I'm sorry, Ms. Hill *is out* at the moment. 申し訳ありません, ヒルはただいま出かけております.

be out and about 《英》(病後など)ぶらぶら出歩いている; 外出できる ▪ Ellen *was* already *out and about*. エレンはもうぶらぶら出歩いている.

***be out to** do* 《口》…しようと努める ▪ He *was* really *out to* comfort her. 彼は彼女を慰めようとやっきになっていた.

be well out of it [that] 《口》 運よくそれを逃れる ▪ You didn't take the job? Well, you*'re well out of it*. 君はその職につかなかったって. そりゃ, 君, つかなくて良かったね.

***beat [knock, whale] the (living) daylights [the carp, the tar] out of** a person* →DAYLIGHT; knock the TAR out of a person.

from out 《雅》…から ▪ It arose *from out* the azure main. それは青海原から現れた.

from out to out (幅・長さの)端から端までで, 外法(そとのり)で ▪ The diameter is near 20 inches *from out to out*. 直径は外法で20インチ近くある ▪ The chapel was 52 feet wide *from out to out*. 礼拝堂は端から端までで52フィートの幅がある.

from that out 《主に米》その時以来 ▪ *From that out* his health began to decline. その時以来彼の健康は衰えはじめた.

from this out/from here (on) out 《主に米》今後は ▪ I will think of you as a man *from this out*. 今後は君のことを大人として考えよう.

have an out 逃げ道がある, (逃れる)口実[言い訳]がある ▪ I'm supposed to attend the meeting, but I *have an out*. その会に出席することになっているが, さぼるうまい口実があるぞ.

make a good [poor] out うまくいく[いかない] ▪ He *made a good out* of his speech. 彼はスピーチを立派にやってのけた ▪ Warren actually tried to pray; but he *made a poor out*. ウォレンは実際に祈ろうとしたが, うまくいかなかった.

on the outs (with) →be at OUTs (with).

out and away 〚最上級を強調して〛 特にすぐれて, 断然 ▪ This is *out and away* the funniest book I've ever read. これは今まで読んだ本のうちで断然一番おもしろい本だ.

out and home **1** (遠方への)往復とも; 往復の ▪ They trade at all parts *out and home*. 彼らは各地で往復とも交易する.

2 (競技が)味方のグラウンドと敵のグラウンドとで交互に行われる ▪ They played 8 *out and home* cricket matches with each other. 敵味方のグラウンドで交互に8回のクリケット対抗試合を行った.

out and in **1** →IN and out.

2 外も内も ▪ It was full *out and in*. そこは外も内もいっぱいだった.

out and out 完全に[な], 徹底的に[な] ▪ He knows English *out and out*. 彼の英語の知識は完璧だ ▪ He is a scoundrel *out and out* [an *out and out* scoundrel]. 彼はよくよくの悪党だ.

out cold →COLD.

out from under 《口》〚be, get を伴って〛 心配事がなくなって; 窮地から脱して; 終わって ▪ I have so much to do, I feel as though I can never *get out from under*. 仕事がひどくたくさんあるので, とても終わりそうにない.

out loud 声を立てて, 声高に ▪ He laughed *out loud* when I read the letter. 私がその手紙を読むと, 彼は声を立てて笑った.

out of **1** (町など)から離れて ▪ My house is a little *out of* the road. 私の家は道から少しはずれています.

2 (ある数)の中から; のうちで ▪ We must choose *out of* these. この中から選ばなければならない ▪ We shut up the shops one day *out of* the seven. 我々は7日のうち1日店を閉めます.
3 (ある行為・機能)の届かない所に ▪ He is placed quite *out of* their hearing. 彼のいる所は彼らから全然聞こえない所だ ▪ He went *out of* sight. 彼の姿が見えなくなった.
4 (ある場所・源)から ▪ The wind blew *out of* the east. 風は東から吹いた ▪ The idea came *out of* my own brain. その考えは私のこの頭から出たのです ▪ He came *out of* a base stock. 彼は卑しい家系の出だ.
5 (ある材料)から, …で (of) ▪ We make many things *out of* paper. 我々は紙でいろいろな物を作る.
6 (ある動機)から ▪ He did it *out of* kindness. 彼は親切心からそうした.
7 (持っていたもの)が不足して, なくなって ▪ The grocer is *out of* coffee. あの食料品屋はコーヒーを切らしている ▪ I am *out of* patience with him. あの男には勘忍袋の緒(お)が切れた ▪ He returned *out of* money. 彼は無一文になって帰ってきた.
8 (以前からの状態・性質・仕事)を失って ▪ She was *out of* her mind. 彼女は気が狂っていた ▪ My horse is *out of* condition. 私の馬は調子が悪い ▪ Many people are now *out of* work. 職を失っている人々が多い.
9 (所有物)を奪われて ▪ He cheated me *out of* my money. 彼は僕をだまして金を巻き上げた.
10 (ある状態)を越えて ▪ That is *out of* doubt true. それは疑いもなく本当だ ▪ The meeting will be a little *out of* the ordinary. その会は少し並みはずれたものになるだろう.
11 (正常)からそれて, はずれて ▪ I was perfectly *out of* my duty. 私はすっかり義務からそれていた ▪ Some characters are *out of* drawing. ある文字は不正確に書かれている.

***out of** one's **box** [**head**]* 《英口》酔っ払って, (麻薬で)ハイになって, はめをはずして ▪ I'm sure the guy was seriously *out of his box*. あの男は相当酔っ払っていたにちがいない. ☞box＝head.

out of it **1** (行為)をしていない; (事件)に加わっていない ▪ I was jolly clean *out of it*. 僕はこれっぽちもそれに関係がなかった.
2 まちがって, 真相を誤って ▪ You're absolutely *out of it*. 君は全くまちがっているよ.
3 《口》成功の見込みがない ▪ It was soon obvious that he was *out of it*. 彼が成功する見込みがないということがすぐはっきりしてきた.
4 (パーティーなどに)招かれていない, のけ者にされて ▪ She felt *out of it* as she watched the others set out on the picnic. 彼女はほかの者がピクニックへ出かけるのを見ながら, 自分はのけ者だという気がした.
5 《口》疲れ切って ▪ Dad works so hard that he is *out of it* in the evening. パパはよく働いて夕方にはへとへとになる.
6 《口》(酒・麻薬で)ひどく酔っぱらって ▪ He was totally *out of it*. 彼はぐでんぐでんの状態だった.

***out of** one's **mind** [**head, tree, skull,** etc.]* →MIND[1]; HEAD[1]; TREE.

out of things ＝OUT of it 4.

out on** one's **feet 立ってはいるが気絶しそうになって ▪ You are ill. You may not know it but you are *out on your feet*. 君は病気なんだ. 気づいていないかもしれないが, 今にも気絶して倒れそうになっているぞ. ☞ボクシングから.

Out, please. (エレベーターから) 出させてください ▪ *Out, please.* This is my floor. 出してください. この階で降りますから.

out there →THERE.

out with 〚主に命令文で〛…を追い出す, 取り出す ▪ *Out with* him! 彼をたたき出せ ▪ *Out with* your cambric, dear ladies. ご婦人がた, 白麻ハンカチをお出しなさい.

Out with it. (思っている事を)言ってみなさい ▪ What's the matter? Come on, now. *Out with it.* どうしたんだ. さあさあ, 言ってみなさい.

Out you go! 出て行け.

straight* [*right*] *out はっきりと包み隠さずに ▪ I told him the truth *right out*. 彼にはっきりと真相を話した.

the best* [*worst,* etc.]*… out 世に出ているうちで一番良い[悪い, など] ▪ This is *the best* book *out*. これは出版されているうちで一番良い本だ ▪ He is *the worst* [*cleverest*] teacher *out*. 彼は世の先生のうちで最低だ[最高に賢い].

the ins and outs of →IN[1].

out[2] /aʊt/ 動 ***out it*** 《口》遊びに出る, (特に)ハイキングに行く ▪ We met dozens of pleasure-boats *outing it* for the afternoon. たくさんの遊覧船がその日の午後出ているのに出会った.

outdo /àʊtdúː/ 動 ***not to be outdone*** 人に負けないように ▪ *Not to be outdone*, he studied even harder. 人に負けないように彼は一層猛勉強した.

outdoors /àʊtdɔ́ːrz/ 名 ***all outdoors*** 《米口》誰もかも ▪ I was going to tell the news to *all outdoors*. 私は誰もかもにそのニュースを話してやるつもりだった.

as … as all outdoors 《米口》この上もなく…, すこぶる… ▪ His letter was *as* long *as all outdoors*. 彼の手紙はものすごく長かった.

the great outdoors 《口》屋外, 野外生活 ▪ I enjoy getting out on my mountain bike into *the great outdoors*. マウンテンバイクで野外に出るのは楽しい.

outer /áʊtər/ 形 ***outer man*** **1** 〚the を伴って〛肉体 ▪ He regards it not only with the eye of *the outer man*, but the eye of law and order. 彼はそれを肉眼で見るばかりでなく, 法と秩序の目でも見る.
2 《戯》風さい, 身なり ▪ A woman must be good inside to present such an *outer man* to her fellows. 女性は仲間にそんな風さいを示すためには心が立派でなければならない. ☞↔the INNER man.

outfit /áʊtfìt/ 動 ***outfit*** *oneself* 支度をする ▪ He *outfitted himself* for the journey. 彼は旅支度をした.

outgoing /àʊtgóʊɪŋ/ 形 ***an outgoing letter*** [***phone call***] 発信書簡[通話] ▪ Affix the correct postage to *outgoing letters* [*mail*]. 差し出す郵便物に適正額面の切手を貼ってください.

an outgoing plane [***passenger***] 出発機[客] ▪ The airport was full of incoming and *outgoing passengers*. 空港は出発客と到着客とでごったがえしていた.

outing /áʊtɪŋ/ 名 ***go for an outing*** 遠足に行く ▪ Let's *go for an outing* next Sunday. 今度の日曜に遠足に行きましょう.

outlet /áʊtlèt/ 名 ***find an outlet*** (***for*** *A*) ***in*** *B* (Aの)はけ口をBに見いだす ▪ He *found an outlet for* his anger *in* shouting at the top of his voice. 彼は腹立ちまぎれに大声で叫んだ.

outline /áʊtlàɪn/ 名 ***give an outline of*** …の大体を述べる ▪ I will *give* you *a* very brief *outline of* the story. 君にその話のごく簡単なあらましだけをお話ししよう.

in outline **1** 輪郭を描いて ▪ The mountain stood *in* bold *outline* against the sky. 山は空を背景にくっきりした輪郭を見せていた.

2 あらましの[を] ▪ He treated the subject *in* brief *outline*. 彼はその問題を簡単に概説した.

3 体つきが ▪ She was masculine *in outline*. 彼女は男のような体つきだった.

outlook /áʊtlʊ̀k/ 名 ***on the outlook*** 警戒して, 待ちかまえて (*for*) ▪ You seem *on the outlook*, eh? 君は警戒しているらしいね, え ▪ The crows were *on the outlook for* plunder. カラスどもは掠め取ろうと待ちかまえていた.

O

outreach /áʊtrìːtʃ/ 形 ***an outreach worker*** 福祉[社会事業]職員 ▪ We have a vacancy for *an outreach worker*. 福祉職員に1名欠員がある.

outset /áʊtsèt/ 名 ***at the outset*** 最初に ▪ Do not trouble yourself much about this matter *at the outset*. この件に最初はあまり気をもんではいけない.

from the outset 最初から ▪ The story fascinates the reader *from the outset*. その物語は最初から読者を魅了する.

outside /àʊtsáɪd, áʊtsaɪd/ 名形副前 ***an outside chance*** 万一の機会 ▪ They see *an outside chance* for their candidates in New Mexico. ニューメキシコで彼らの立候補者たちがひょっとしたら当選するかもしれないと彼らは見ている.

at the (***very***) ***outside*** 《口》せいぜい ▪ He will return in a few weeks *at the outside*. 彼はせいぜい2, 3週間もしたら帰って来る.

on the outside **1** 外見は, 見た目には ▪ He may seem calm *on the outside*, but he is quite worried on the inside. 彼はうわべこそ冷静だが内心ではひどく心配している.

2 (刑務所の)外界の ▪ Life *on the outside* took him some time to get used to again. 彼がまた娑婆(しゃば)での生活に慣れるのにしばらくかかった.

on the outside (***of…***) ***looking in*** (人が)グループ[活動]から除外されて, のけ者になって ▪ I am *on the outside of* the rotation *looking in* now. 僕は今ローテーションからはずされている.

outside of **1** …の外側へ[に]; 以外の ▪ His grave lay *outside of* the city. 彼の墓は町の外にあった ▪ His object of interest *outside of* his special work is sports. 彼の専門の研究以外の興味の対象はスポーツだ.

2 《米口》…以外には ▪ *Outside of* the merchants there was no one at the meeting. 商人以外にはその集いには誰もいなかった.

outside of a horse 《口》馬に乗って ▪ He looked better *outside of a horse* than on his own legs. 彼は立ち姿より馬上姿のほうが立派だった.

the outside edge 《俗》(悪いものの)極限 ▪ Why, as a miser, he's quite *the outside edge*! 何しろ, けちんぼうとしてはあの男の右に出る者はいない.

the outside world/***the world outside*** 外の世界 ▪ The nun decided to get a job in *the outside world*. 修道女は俗世間の職に就こうと決心した.

turn outside in 裏返しにする ▪ A keeper is only a poacher *turned outside in*. 番人とは密猟者を裏返しにしたものにすぎない.

outskirt /áʊtskə̀ːrts/ 名 ***on*** [***at, in***] ***the outskirts of*** …のはずれに ▪ The Gobi Desert is just *at the outskirts of* China proper. ゴビ砂漠は中国本土のちょうどはずれにある.

outstanding /àʊtstǽndɪŋ/ 形 ***leave … outstanding*** …をそのまま[未払い]にしておく ▪ He *left* the work still *outstanding*. 彼はその仕事をまだそのままにしておいた.

outstrip /àʊtstríp/ 動 ***outstrip*** *oneself* 前例のないほどうまくやる ▪ You have *outstripped yourself*. ほんとうに上できだった.

outward /áʊtwərd/ 形 *one's* ***outward man*** =OUTER man.

the outward eye 肉眼 ▪ The vision was not visible to *the outward eye*. その姿は肉眼で見えるものではなかった.

to outward appearance [***seeming***] 見たところ ▪ The church, *to outward appearance*, stood more securely than ever. 教会は見たところますます堅固に建っているもののようだった.

ovation /oʊvéɪʃən/ 名 ***get*** [***receive***] ***a standing ovation*** 一斉に立ち上がっての万雷の拍手を受ける ▪ The speaker *received a standing ovation*. 講師はスタンディング・オベーションを送られた.

oven /ʌ́vən/ 名 (***as***) ***warm as an oven*** 蒸すように暑い ▪ I preached in a house *as warm as an oven*. 私は蒸すような暑い家で説教した.

have [***there's***] ***something in the oven*** 《口》妊娠している ▪ She knew definitely she *had something in the oven*. 彼女は自分が妊娠していることをはっきりと知った. ☞ oven=womb.

hot from the oven 焼き立ての ▪ The bread is

hot from the oven. そのパンは焼き立てだ.

in [***into***] ***the same oven*** 《俗》同じはめ•境遇に ▪ I've been and gone *into the same oven* like a fool. 僕は愚か者みたいに同じはめに陥ってしまった.

over /óʊvər/ 前副名 ***all over*** →ALL.

(***all***) ***over again*** **1** もう一度 ▪ Please do it *over again.* どうかもう一度そうしてください.

2 繰り返した, そっくりの ▪ He is his father *all over again.* 彼は父親にそっくりだ.

all over with →ALL.

be all over 《口》 **1** (人)を大げさに迎える, に深い愛情を示す ▪ The hostess *was all over* us. 女主人は我々を大げさに迎えてくれた.

2 《スポーツ》…を制圧する ▪ The team *were all over* us to the end. そのチームは最後まで我々を制圧した.

be all over *oneself* 《口》大得意である ▪ Now he is promoted, he *is all over himself.* 昇進したので彼は大得意である.

It's not over until it's over. 完全に終わるまで結論がわからない.

over against **1** …の真向こうに ▪ His house is *over against* the school. 彼の家は学校の真向かいにある ▪ He sat *over against* the temple. 彼は寺の真向かいに座っていた.

2 …と対照して ▪ It exhibits the vain tumults of men, and *over against* them, the calm supremacy of God. それは人間のむなしい激情と, それと対照して神の静かな優越性をあらわにする.

over and above **1** 《文》…に加えて ▪ I gave the cabman fifty pence *over and above* his legal fare. 私はタクシーの運転手にきまった料金のほかに50ペンスやった.

2 〚副詞的に〛 なおその上 ▪ He not only forgave the affront but gave the poor fellow his freedom *over and above.* 彼はその侮辱を許したばかりか, なおその上にそのかわいそうな男を自由にしてやった.

over and done with すっかり終わって, けりがついて ▪ Now that the war is *over and done with,* we may return to normality. もう戦争が終わったのだから平常に復してもいい ▪ His homework was *over and done with* by then. そのときにはもう彼の宿題は片づいていた.

Over and out. 交信終わり ▪ Mike Hill, *over and out.* 交信終了. こちらマイク•ヒル.

over and over (***again***) 何度も何度も ▪ I've told you *over and over* (*again*) to close the door. ドアを閉めるように何度も何度も言ったはずだ.

over easy [***medium, hard***] 《米》目玉焼きの黄身側も軽く[中位に, しっかり]焼いて ▪ Two eggs *over easy* and a cup of coffee, please. 卵2個を両面焼きにして, それとコーヒーを一つ ▪ Naturally OE means *over easy*: "The egg is flipped once, the yoke is runny." もちろん, OE は「両面半熟焼き」のことだ.「卵を一回裏返し, 黄身は半熟」だ.

over here [***there***] こちら[向こう]の方に; こちら[あちら]では《イギリスとアメリカ•フランス, アメリカとヨーロッパなどの関係で用いられる》 ▪ It has been warm *over here.* こちらでは暖かかった.

over or under 多かれ少なかれ ▪ To come near to it *over or under* is commendable. 多少ともそれに近づくことはほめていいことだ.

Over to you. 《口》(今度は)そちらに任せる. ☞交信の Over (to you) (応答どうぞ)から ▪ *Over to you.* I've been really busy. そっちに任すよ. このところこっちは目が回るほど忙しいから.

overbalance /òʊvərbǽləns/ 動 ***overbalance*** *oneself* 体の平衡を失う ▪ He *overbalanced himself,* and the next moment, he was in the water. 彼は体のバランスを失い, あっという間に水の中へ落ちていた.

overboard /óʊvərbɔ̀ːrd/ 副 ***fall overboard*** **1** (船から)海中へ落ちる ▪ He *fell overboard* and was drowned. 彼は船から海中へ落ちて溺れ死んだ.

2 =go OVERBOARD.

go overboard 極端に走る; やっきになる, (特に)過度にほめる (*on, for, about*) ▪ The critics *went overboard for* his novel. 批評家たちは彼の小説をやたらにほめそやした ▪ They tend to *go overboard on* this subject. 彼らはこの問題については極端に走りがちだ.

throw overboard **1** 海中に捨てる ▪ The cargo *was thrown overboard.* 船荷は海中に捨てられた.

2 《口》捨てる, 放棄する ▪ They *threw overboard* all their loyalty. 彼らは忠誠をすっかり捨て去った.

overcome /òʊvərkʌ́m/ 動 ***be overcome by*** [***with***] …に圧倒される, 参る ▪ She *was overcome by* shyness. 彼女はすっかり内気になってしまった ▪ He *was overcome with* liquor. 彼は酒に酔いつぶれた.

overcrowd /òʊvərkráʊd/ 動 ***be overcrowded with*** (人)でひどく混んでいる, (物)が詰め込まれすぎている ▪ The boat *was overcrowded with* tourists. 船は観光客でひどく混んでいた.

overdo /òʊvərdúː/ 動 ***overdo*** *oneself* 体を使いすぎる, 無理をする ▪ I ran down too fast and *overdid myself.* あまりに早く駆けおりて無理をした.

overdo it [***things***] **1** 体を酷使する ▪ You may work hard, but don't *overdo it.* 懸命に働くのはよいが, 過労になってはいけないよ ▪ He's been *overdoing things* recently. 彼は最近働きすぎだ.

2 誇張する; 度を過ごす ▪ He showed sympathy, but *overdid it* a little. 彼は同情を示したが, 少し大げさ過ぎた.

overdress /òʊvərdrés/ 動 ***overdress*** *oneself* 身なりを飾りすぎる ▪ He never *overdresses himself.* 彼は決して身なりを飾りすぎない.

overdrink /òʊvərdríŋk/ 動 ***overdrink*** *oneself* 飲みすぎる ▪ He often *overdrinks himself.* 彼はよく飲みすぎる.

overdrive /óʊvərdràɪv/ 名 ***be*** [***go, move***] ***into overdrive/be in overdrive*** 全力で働いている[働き始める], 非常に行動的である[になる], 過度に興奮している[する] ▪ The whole cast of the show

O

is in overdrive rehearsing. ショーの出演者全員が懸命にリハーサル中だ ▪ He often *goes into overdrive*, risking his health. 彼はよく健康を賭して仕事に打ち込む ▪ The media *went into overdrive* at the big news. その重大ニュースにマスコミは一気に加熱した. ☞overdrive「車の高速専用ギア」.

Mexican overdrive 《米口》坂を降りるときのニュートラルのギア位置; ギアをニュートラルにして坂を下ること ▪ He coasted down in *Mexican overdrive*. 彼はギアをニュートラルにして坂を下った.

overeat /òʊvərí:t|əʊvərí:t/ 動 ***overeat** oneself* 食べすぎる ▪ She has only *overeaten herself*. 彼女はただ食べすぎただけです.

over-egg /òʊvərég/ 動 ***over-egg the*** [*one's*] ***pudding*** 《主に英》誇張する ▪ He has made the mistake of *over-egging the pudding*. 彼は誇張するという誤りを犯した.

overflow /òʊvərflóʊ/ 動 ***fill to overflowing*** あふれるほど一杯にする ▪ The boys *were filled to overflowing* with the excitement of the hour. 少年たちはその折の興奮で胸一杯になっていた.

full to overflowing あふれるほど一杯の ▪ The hall was *full to overflowing*. ホールは超満員だった.

overgrow /òʊvərgróʊ/ 動 ***overgrow** oneself* 大きくなりすぎる ▪ The plant has *overgrown itself*. この植物は大きくなりすぎた.

overleap /òʊvərlí:p/ 動 ***overleap** oneself* あまり遠くまで飛びすぎる; やりすぎてしくじる ▪ Ambition sometimes *overleaps itself*. 野心はときどきやりすぎてしくじる.

overnight /òʊvərnáɪt/ 副 ***keep overnight*** (飲食物などが)朝までもつ ▪ The meat will *keep overnight*. 肉は朝までもつでしょう.

overpass /óʊvərpæ̀s|-pɑ̀:s/ 名 ***an overpass*** 《主に米》高架道路 (《英》flyover) ▪ The new *overpass* was designed by a noted architect. 新高架道路は著名建築家のデザインによるものである.

overplay /òʊvərpléɪ/ 動 ***overplay** one's **hand*** 自分の実力を過信する ▪ We *overplayed our hand*, so that our competitors were awarded the contract. 我々は実力を過信し, そのために競争者が請負を許された. ☞トランプで自分の手の強さを過信して欲張ることから.

overreach /òʊvərrí:tʃ/ 動 ***overreach** oneself*
1 手足を無理に伸ばす ▪ Yesterday I *overreached myself* in getting a book from the shelves and strained myself badly. きのう本だなから本を取るときに手を無理に伸ばして, ひどく筋をたがえた.
2 無理をしてしくじる, (策士が)策に溺れる ▪ The man is far too presuming, one of these days he will *overreach himself*. あの男はあまりにも生意気すぎる. そのうちに無理をしてしくじることだろう.

override /òʊvərráɪd/ 動 ***override** one's **commission*** 職権を濫用する ▪ Such difficulties occur only when one *overrides one's commission*. そんな面倒は職権を濫用したときに起こるだけだ.

overrun /òʊvərrʌ́n/ 動 ***be overrun with*** **1** (雑草・害虫など)がはびこる, 一面にはえる ▪ The small room *was overrun with* mice. その小部屋にはネズミがはびこっていた.
2 (良くないもの)で一杯である ▪ I have *been overrun with* invitation cards. 招待状責めにあっている.

***overrun** oneself* 走り[働き]すぎて疲れる ▪ He *overran himself* and fell. 彼は走りすぎて疲れて倒れた ▪ He has *overrun himself*, and may never be at his best again. 彼は働きすぎて疲れてもう元気一杯にならないかもしれない.

overrun the constable → outrun the CONSTABLE.

oversea(s) /òʊvərsí:z/ 副 ***go oversea(s)*** 海外へ行く ▪ He *went overseas* for (a) change. 彼は気分を変えるために海外へ行った.

overshoot /òʊvərʃú:t/ 動 ***overshoot** oneself* やりすぎる, 度を過ごす, 大げさに過ぎる ▪ I never saw wise men *overshoot themselves* thus sorely. 賢い人がこんなにひどく度を過ごすのを見たことがない ▪ His irony has *overshot itself*. 彼の皮肉は大げさ過ぎた.

overshoot the [*one's*] ***mark*** →MARK[1].

oversleep /òʊvərslí:p/ 動 ***oversleep** oneself* 寝過ごす ▪ I missed my train by *oversleeping myself*. 寝過ごして電車に乗れなかった.

overspend /òʊvərspénd/ 動 ***overspend** oneself* 資力以上に金を使う ▪ Italy has not *overspent herself* like France. イタリアはフランスほど資力以上に金を使わなかった.

overstep /òʊvərstép/ 動 ***overstep the mark*** →overshoot the MARK.

overtake /òʊvərtéɪk/ 動 ***be overtaken*** (***in drink***) 酔っ払っている ▪ To be sure he *was overtaken* (*in drink*) a little. 確かに彼は少し酔っ払っていた.

overtime /óʊvərtàɪm/ 副 ***work overtime to** do* 《口》…しようと一生懸命に努力する ▪ I'm *working overtime to* master Japanese. 日本語をマスターしようと一生懸命に努力しているところだ.

overture /óʊvərtʃər|-tjʊə/ 名 ***make overtures*** (***to***) (…に)提議する, 申し込む ▪ They are *making overtures to* the authorities for a free-trade agreement. 当局に自由貿易協定を提議中だ.

overwalk /òʊvərwɔ́:k/ 動 ***overwalk** oneself* 歩きすぎて疲れる ▪ I rather *overwalked myself* yesterday. きのうちょっと歩き疲れた.

overwhelm /òʊvərhwélm/ 動 (***be***) ***overwhelmed by*** [***with, at***] …によって[のために, を見て]圧倒される, 感きわまる ▪ He *was overwhelmed by* grief. 彼は悲しみに打ちひしがれていた ▪ I *was overwhelmed at* the change in the baby. 私はその幼児に起こった変化を見て衝撃を受けた.

overwork /òʊvərwɔ́:rk/ 動 ***overwork** oneself* 働きすぎる ▪ He got sick by *overworking himself*. 彼は働きすぎて病気になった.

overwrite /òʊvərráɪt/ 動 ***overwrite** oneself* (作家などが)多作して体をこわす ▪ It is a pity that many young authors of promise *overwrite* *themselves*. 多くの有望な作家が多作して体をこわすのは遺憾である.

owe /oʊ/ 動 ***I owe you one*** 《口》借りが一つできましたね (→owe a person ONE) ▪ Thanks, babe, *I owe you one*. ありがとう, かわい子ちゃん, これで借りが一つできたね.

owe it to *a person* ***to*** *do* 人に対して…する義務がある ▪ I *owe it to* him *to* be faithful. 彼に対しては忠誠を誓う義理がある.

you owe me one 《口・戯》あなたに貸しが一つできたね ▪ Helen, *you owe me one* now. ヘレン, これで一つ貸しができたよ.

owing /óʊɪŋ/ 形 ***be owing to*** …のためである ▪ His failure *was owing* mainly *to* ill health. 彼の失敗は主として体調不良のせいだった ▪ The effect *is owing to* the presence of light. その効果は光があるためだ.

owing to …のために (= on (the) ACCOUNT of (a person)) ▪ *Owing to* the drought, the crop was short. 日照りのために不作だった.

owl /aʊl/ 名 ***a night owl*** 《口》宵っ張り, 夜型人間 ▪ Call me at midnight. I'm *a night owl*. 午前0時に電話してくれ. こっちは夜型だから.

a solemn owl 《軽蔑》(ユーモアに欠ける)ひどくまじめくさった人物 ▪ Oh, my. What *a solemn owl* you are tonight! おや, まあ, 今夜はやけにすましているね, 君.

(*as*) *drunk as an owl* ぐでんぐでんに酔っぱらって ▪ The men are *as drunk as owls*. あの連中はぐでんぐでんに酔っている.

(*as*) *solemn as an owl* (人・表情が)ひどく生まじめ[真剣]で ▪ She looked *as solemn as an owl*. 彼女はひどく生まじめな顔をしていた.

carry* [*send*] *owls to Athens 余計なことをする, 蛇足を加える (Aristophanes, *Birds* 301) ▪ I may be thought to *carry owls to Athens*. あるいは私は蛇足を加えると思われるかもしれない. ☞フクロウがアテネの守護女神 Pallas Athene の象徴であるところから.

fly with the owl 夜歩き[夜遊び]の癖がある ▪ Those who go abroad after sunset are said to *fly with the owl* by a common proverb. 日暮れから出歩く人々は下世話に夜歩きの癖があると言われる.

make an owl of *oneself* ばかなまねをする ▪ It vexes me to see so fine a poet *make* such *an owl of himself*. あんな立派な詩人がそのようなばかなまねをしているのを見ると腹が立つ.

take owl 《俗》立腹する, むっとする ▪ He *takes owl* easily. 彼はすぐむっとする.

own /oʊn/ 形 ***a moment* [*minute, second*] *to call*** *one's* ***own*** 自分の時間 ▪ I don't have *a moment to call my own* this week. 今週は自分の時間が少しもない.

all *one's* ***own*** 独特の ▪ The orange has a scent *all its own*. オレンジは独特のにおいがある.

be on *one's* ***own*** 一本立ちしている ▪ I left the firm, because I wanted to *be on my own*. その会社を出たのは一本立ちしたかったからだ.

(*be*) *one's* ***own man* [*woman*]** →MAN[1]; one's own WOMAN.

come into *one's* ***own*** →COME[2].

each to each his own/《米》***to each his own*** →EACH.

for *one's* **(*very*) *own*** 自分一人のものとして ▪ May I have it *for my very own*? それをもらって僕だけのものにしていいですか.

hold *one's* ***own*** →HOLD[2].

make ... *one's* ***own*** …を自分ならではのものにする ▪ *Make* your products *your own*. あなたの制作物を独創的なものにしなさい.

of *one's* ***own*** 自分所有の ▪ He has no house *of his own*. 彼には自分の家というものがない ▪ He is a great friend *of my own*. 彼は私の親友だ.

of *one's* **(*own*)** *doing* 自ら…した ▪ There is a picture *of his own painting*. 彼が自分で描いた絵がある ▪ The dinner was *of aunt's own cooking*. そのごちそうはおばさんのお手製だった.

on *one's* ***own*** 《口》 **1**〚副詞的に〛自分で, 独立して, 自分の責任で, 自前で ▪ He did the work *on his own*. 彼はその仕事を自分でした ▪ I've been living *on my own* since February. 2月以来独立して生活している ▪ The Times appears to have inserted the notice *on their own*. タイムズ紙はその広告を自らの責任で挿入したらしい.
2〚形容詞的に〛一人ぼっちで ▪ I am (all) *on my own* today. きょうは(たった)一人ぼっちだ.

on *one's* ***own ground* [*home ground, turf, patch*]** 自分の得意の問題で; 慣れた立場で; 自分の家で ▪ A man is strong *on his own ground*. 人は自分の得意の問題では強い.

ox /ɑks|ɔks/ 名 **(*as*) *strong as an ox*** →(as) STRONG as a horse.

the black ox 苦労; 老齢 ▪ *The black ox* has trod on his foot. 《諺》彼は苦労の味を知った; 老いの身となった. ☞黒牛が「不幸・老齢」の象徴とされているところから.

oyster /ɔ́ɪstər/ 名 ***an oyster of a man*** 無口な人 ▪ He is *an oyster of a man*. 彼は寡黙だ.

(*as*) *close as an oyster* 非常に口が堅い ▪ You can trust him with anything. He's *as close as an oyster*. あの男にはなんでも打ち明けられるよ. とても口が堅いんだ.

as like as an apple to an oyster 月とスッポンで ▪ They are *as like as an apple to an oyster*. 彼らは月とスッポンほど違う.

(*as*) *tight as oyster* 《米口》ひどくきっちりと ▪ Every place was shut *as tight as oyster*. どの家もきっちりと戸締まりがしてあった.

like an oyster in the mud 《米口》この上もなく満足に ▪ I found Alf well, enjoying himself *like an oyster in the mud*. 行ってみるとアルフは元気で, この上もなく上きげんで楽しんでいた.

The world is *one's* ***oyster.*** 世界は儲けの種だ, この世はもう自分のものだ (cf. Sh., *Merry W.* 2. 2. 2) ▪ I feel like *the world is my oyster* today. この世は自分の思うままだという感じが今日はする.

P

P, p /piː/ 名 ***mind*** [***watch***] *one's* ***P's and Q's*** [***p's and q's, peas and cues***] 言行を慎む ▪ You must *mind your P's and Q's* with him, I can tell you. あの男には言行を慎まなくてはいけないよ，ほんとに. ☞(1)子供の手習いや印刷工に p, q の混同を戒めることから，(2)居酒屋のつけではP (pint) と Q (quart) とを混同してはいけないことから.

one's ***P's and Q's*** 文字，「いろは」 ▪ Almost all of you have learned *your P's and Q's* from me. 諸君の大半は私からいろはを習ったわけです. ☞子供が p と q とをまちがいやすいことから.

pace[1] /péɪs/ 名 ***at a good pace*** 相当の速さで，活発に ▪ He walked *at a good pace.* 彼はかなりの速度で歩いた.

at a snail's pace のろのろと ▪ The party traveled *at a snail's pace.* 一行はのろのろと旅をした.

at *one's* **(*own*)** ***pace*** 自分のペースで ▪ I want to go at it *at my own pace.* それを自分のペースでやってみたいのです.

go the pace **1** 大速力で進む ▪ The hounds *went the pace* over the heath towards Lymington. 猟犬どもは大速力でヒースを越えてリミントンの方へ進んでいった.

2 放蕩(とう)な生活をする ▪ He *went the pace* as other young men do. 彼は若い者のご多分にもれず放蕩な生活を送った.

go through *one's* ***paces*** 力量を示す，腕前を見せる (→ show one's PACEs) ▪ The competition began—we *went through our paces.* 競技が始まった—我々は器量を発揮した.

It is the pace that kills. 《諺》命取りになるのは速度である，「親が死んでも食休み」. ☞あまりに多くのことをあまりに速くしようとすると体に悪い，の意.

keep pace with …と歩調をそろえる，について行く《比喩的にも》 ▪ He walked so fast that they could hardly *keep pace with* him. 彼はひどく足早に歩いたので，彼らはついて行くこともできないくらいだった ▪ I can't *keep pace with* your plans. 君の計画にはついていけない.

mend *one's* ***pace*** 速度を速める ▪ While we stood there, the ship *mended her pace.* 我々がそこに立っているうちに，船は速度を速めた.

off the pace 先頭(グループ)に遅れて ▪ Mark Spitz finished last, four seconds *off the pace* in his first 100-meter butterfly race. マーク・スピッツは4秒遅れで初の100メートルバタフライでびりになった.

put … through his [***its,*** etc.] ***paces*** **1**（馬）の足並みをためす ▪ The trainer *put* the young racehorse *through its paces.* 調教師は若い競走馬の足並みをためした.

2《口》（人）の力量をためす，…の技量[能力，性能]をためす ▪ We will give the lad some work that will *put* him *through his paces.* あの青年の技量をためすような仕事をさせてみよう ▪ We *put* the car *through its paces.* 私たちはその車の性能を試した.

set [***make***] ***the pace*** 歩調を示す，整調する (*for*) ▪ He was accustomed to hiking and had *set the pace* which none of the rest could follow. 彼は山歩きに慣れていて，他の者についていけないような歩調を定めていた ▪ Jones rode ahead on his bicycle, and *made the pace for* the remainder of the club. ジョーンズは自転車に乗って先頭に立ち，クラブの他の者のペースメーカーになった.

show *one's* ***paces*** 力量を示す，腕前を見せる ▪ I'm going there tomorrow to *show my paces.* 自分の腕前を見せにあすそこへ行くつもりだ. ☞乗馬から.

stand [***stay***] ***the pace*** 他の足取りについて行く；耐えることができる ▪ I couldn't *stand the pace*: it was too fast for me. そのペースについて行くことができなかった. あまりにも速すぎたのだ ▪ We are a little concerned about whether he will be able to *stand the pace* at this factory. 彼がこの工場での仕事に耐えられるかどうかちょっと心配だ.

the pace is [***find the pace***] ***too hot for*** ペースが速すぎて…にはついていけない ▪ I was last in the race because *the pace was too hot for* me. ペースがあまりにも速いので私はそのレースでびりだった.

try *a person's* ***paces*** 人の力量をためす，人物を見る ▪ We hired him at first on trial for a week, to *try his paces.* その男の人物を見るために最初1週間は臨時に雇った.

pace[2] /péɪs/ 動 ***pace it*** ゆっくりやる[話す] ▪ Charles instead of *pacing it* ran violently to destroy his subjects. チャールズはゆっくりやらずに，急激にことを運んで臣民を破滅に追いやった.

pace to and fro (通例悩んで)行ったり来たりする ▪ He *paced to and fro*, worrying about his missing friends. 彼は行方不明の友人たちを案じて行ったり来たりしていた.

pace up and down (通例悩んで)行ったり来たりする ▪ He *paced up and down* in the waiting room. 彼は待合室の中を行ったり来たりした.

pack[1] /pæk/ 名 ***a pack of*** 《軽蔑》たくさんの《嘘・たわけたことなど》 ▪ In my opinion the current Cabinet is *a pack of* fools. 私に言わせれば今の内閣は愚者どもの群だ ▪ That girl told me *a pack of* lies. あの女の子は僕に嘘八百を言った.

ahead of the pack ライバルに先んじて，群を抜いて ▪ Nick's record puts him three strokes *ahead of the pack* going into today's final. ニックは今日の決勝に進むライバルたちより3打差の記録で先に立った. ☞pack はオオカミなどの群れを指す.

in packs (オオカミなどが)群をなして ▪ Wolves hunt *in packs*. オオカミは群をなして獲物をあさる.

Joe Six-pack 中流階級の下の男性 ▪ *Joe Six-pack* would prefer a rock concert to opera. 中流階級の下の男ならオペラよりロックのコンサートのほうが好きだろう. ☞工事現場用のヘルメットをつけシャツ姿で,仕事のあとに1ケース6本入りのビールを飲み干す男の連想から.

pack[2] /pæk/ 動 ***be packed to the limit*** [***to capacity***] 満員である ▪ The movie-house *was packed to the limit*. 映画館は満員だった.

be packing 立ち去る ▪ Now, *be packing*; I don't wish to see you again. さあ,とっとと出て行け. お前の顔など二度と見たくないのだ.

pack a punch [***wallop***]《口》強打を加える; すごい効きめがある ▪ These severe thunderstorms still *packed a punch* when they moved into Louisiana. これらの激しい雷雨はルイジアナに移動しても猛威を振るった ▪ Vodka really *packs a punch*. ウォッカはほんとに強い効きめがある.

pack cards with《古》(人)をだます ▪ The poor King tried to *pack cards with* fortune. 哀れな王は運をぺてんにかけようとした. ☞トランプで札をごまかして切ることから.

pack heat《米俗》ピストルを持ち回る ▪ If you *pack heat*, you got to know what you're doing. はじきを持ち回るなら,自分が何をしているか知ってなくちゃいけないよ.

pack it in **1**《米俗》敗北[失敗]を認める ▪ If the show isn't funny, I'm ready to *pack it in*. あのショーがおもしろくなければ,僕は潔く失敗を認めるよ.
2《口》(仕事・活動などを)やめる ▪ Let's *pack it in* for the day. これで今日の仕事は終わりだ.
3 寝る,床に就く ▪ Well, it's time for me to *pack it in*. さて,僕は寝る時間だ.
4 ＝PACK it up.

pack it up 〚主に命令文で〛《口》(おしゃべり・仕事を)やめる ▪ For Heaven's sake *pack it up*! 後生だから黙ってくれ.

pack *oneself* ***off*** 立ち去る ▪ I hope you'd *pack yourself off*. 向こうへ行ってくださいな.

pack the house →HOUSE.

pack them in 多くの人々を引き寄せる ▪ That comic book convention really *packed them in*. そのコミック誌大会は実に多くの客を集めた.

send *a person* ***packing*** 人を追いやる,さっさとお払い箱にする ▪ Sure as fate, we'll *send* you *packing*. きっとお前をお払い箱にしてやるぞ.

packet /pǽkət/ 名 ***make*** [***cost, lose, spend***] ***a packet***《口》多額のお金を儲ける[要する,失う,使う] ▪ Some people *make a packet* out of selling baseball souvenirs. 野球の記念品を売って大儲けをする人もいる ▪ We *spent a packet* on our weekend—everything was so expensive. 週末に大散財した,すべての物の値段が高かったから.

sell *a person* ***a packet***《口》人に嘘を言う ▪ It never crossed my mind that the man was *selling* me *a packet*. その男が私に嘘を言っているとは思いもよらなかった. ☞'a packet of lies'から.

stop [***catch, get***] ***a packet***《英口》**1** 弾丸に当たる ▪ She'll *stop a packet* if she's not careful. 彼女は気をつけていないと弾丸に当たるぞ.
2 不意に難儀[不幸]に見舞われる ▪ The poor old fellow is absolutely ruined. He has *got a packet* all right. かわいそうにあいつは全く破産してしまった. 確かに一発くらったわけだ.

pad /pæd/ 動 ***pad it***《俗》(特に浮浪者・求職者が)ぶらつく,とぼとぼ歩く ▪ Why are you *padding it* at this time of the morning? なぜこんなに朝早くからぶらついているのか.

pad the hoof →HOOF[1].

paddle[1] /pǽdəl/ 名 ***at the paddle*** 静かにこぎながら ▪ We came back *at the paddle* to Putney. 静かにこぎながらパトニーへ帰った.

paddle[2] /pǽdəl/ 動 ***paddle the filling out of*** *a person*《米口》人をひどくぶつ ▪ He caught hold of his stick and *paddled the filling out of* them. 彼は杖をつかんで彼らをぶちのめした.

paddle[3] /pǽdəl/ 動 ***paddle*** *one's* ***own canoe*** →CANOE[1].

paddy /pǽdi/ 名 ***come the paddy over***《俗》(人)をだます,かつぐ ▪ They fairly *came the paddy over* him. 彼らはまんまと彼をかついだ. ☞アイルランド人 (Paddy) がよく人をかつぐという評判から.

paddyw(h)ack /pǽdi*h*wæk/ 名 ***in a paddywack***《英口》かんかんに怒って ▪ He was *in a* raving *paddywack*. 彼はかんかんに怒っていた.

page /peɪdʒ/ 名 ***be*** [***get***] ***on the same page*** (***with***)《米》二人,二つのグループの意見・目標が一致している,目指すものが同じ ▪ They*'re* all *on* about *the same page* in their careers. 彼らはみな,経歴がほぼ一致している.

have a few pages stuck together 何が起きたのかわからない,何も知らない ▪ She must have *had a few pages stuck together* because she told me that I was ugly. 彼女は何も知らないのにちがいなかった,なにしろ私が醜いと言ったのだから.

turn the page 難局を乗り越えて再スタートする ▪ Russia has *turned the page* toward something new. ロシアがなにか新しいものに向かって新たなスタートを切った.

pagoda /pəgóʊdə/ 名 ***shake the pagoda tree***《英》(インドへ行って)楽々と大金を儲ける ▪ The amusing pursuit of "*shaking the pagoda tree*" was once so popular.「インドで大金を儲ける」というおもしろい仕事がかつて大いにはやった. ☞pagoda tree に戯言的に「金のなる木」の意味があるところから.

paid /peɪd/ 動 ***not if you paid me*** どんなことがあっても…ない,いくら金を積まれても ▪ I wouldn't do a bungee jump, *not if you paid me*. 何があっても決してバンジージャンプはしないよ.

pain /peɪn/ 名 ***a pain in the neck*** [《英俗》***arse,***《米》***ass,***《米》***butt***]《口》いやな人,うるさい人,迷惑者 ▪ The boss's son is in the office

P

today. Oh, he is *a pain in the neck*. 社長の息子がきょう会社にいる. とてもいやなやつさ ▪ Jane told her sister to stop being *a pain in the ass*. ジェインは妹に困らせるようなことはしないでと言った. ☞「首すじの痛み」が原義.

be at* [*go to*] *the pains of *doing*/ ***be at pains to*** *do* …しようと骨を折る ▪ The university was *at the pains of publishing* a Latin paper to justify itself. その大学は自分の立場を正当化するためにラテン語の論文を公にしようと骨を折った ▪ I *was at* great *pains to* make the dinner a success. 晩餐会を成功させようと大いに骨を折った.

feel no pain 《米俗》酔っぱらう ▪ He was *feeling no pain* then. 彼はその時酔っぱらっていた.

for *one's* ***pains*** 《しばしば反語》骨折り賃に, 骨折りがいもなく ▪ All he got *for his pains* was ingratitude and suspicion. 骨折りの報いとして得たものは忘恩と疑いのみであった.

give *a person* ***a pain*** (***in the neck*** [《英俗》***arse,*** 《米》***ass,*** 《米》***butt***]) 《口》人をいらいらさせる, じりじりさせる ▪ He *gives* me *a pain* (*in the neck*). あの男にはいらいらさせられる.

growing pains **1** 成長期の脚の痛み ▪ The little boy's legs hurt, and his mother told him he had *growing pains*. 少年の脚が痛んだ. すると母親は息子に成長痛だと言った.
2 (新しい事が始まる際の)初期の苦しみ ▪ Change comes with *growing pains*. 変化には産みの苦しみが伴う.

***No pain*(*s*), *no gain*(*s*).** 《諺》苦労なしにはもうけもない,「たなからぼたもちは落ちてこない」.

on* [*upon, under*] (*the*) *pain of 違反したら…するとして ▪ Return to your houses, *on pain of* life. 家に帰れ, 違反すれば命はないぞ ▪ He ordered the tribes to join him *under pain of* death. 彼は部族の者たちに違反すれば死刑に処するという条件で, 彼に加わるように命じた. ☞pain《廃》= penalty.

pains and penalties 刑罰 ▪ The courtiers talked of a bill of *pains and penalties*. 廷臣たちは刑罰法の噂をしていた. ☞pain《廃》= penalty.

put … out of (*his*) ***pain*** (傷ついた人・動物)を殺して楽にしてやる ▪ She gave the dying dog a cup of poison to *put* him *out of his pain*. 彼女は瀕死の犬を楽にしてやるために毒を1杯飲ませた.

spare no pains to *do* 骨を惜しまずに…する ▪ He *spares no pains to* apologize. 彼はしきりに弁解に努める.

spare *a person* ***pain*** 人を動揺させる話題を避ける ▪ Don't let's talk about the car accident in which her brother died. We want to *spare* her the *pain* of remembering. 彼女の弟が死んだ自動車事故を話題にしないようにしよう. 彼女にそれを思い出させる話は避けたい.

take pains 骨を折る, 気を配る (*to do, with, over*) ▪ He *takes* great *pains* in educating his children. 彼は子供の教育に大いに骨を折る ▪ He has *taken pains to* show me how to do the work. 彼は骨折ってその仕事の仕方を私に教えてくれた.

under* (*the*) *pain of →on (the) PAIN of.

paint[1] /peɪnt/ 名 (***as***) ***smart*** [***pretty, clever,*** etc.] ***as paint*** この上もなくスマートな[きれい, 賢い, など] ▪ You're *as smart as paint*. 君はすごくスマートだよ ▪ Those rustic buildings were all *as pretty as paint*. この田舎風の建物はどれもすごくきれいだった ▪ My hounds are *as handsome as paint*. 私の猟犬はすばらしく見事だ.

be like watching paint dry*/*be* (*as*) *exciting [***interesting,*** etc.] ***as watching* (*the*) *paint dry*** 《皮肉》(活動・経験が)ひどく退屈な ▪ Watching golf on television *is like watching paint dry*. テレビでゴルフをみても全然楽しくない. ☞ペンキが乾くのを見るのと同じようにつまらないことから.

paint[2] /peɪnt/ 動 ***a painted sepulcher*** →a whited SEPULCHER.

(***as***) ***painted as a picture*** 厚化粧して ▪ She's (*as*) *painted as a picture*. 彼女は厚化粧している.

paint *a person* ***black*** 人をあしざまに言う ▪ *Paint* an angel *black*, and that is enough to make him pass for a Devil. 天使をあしざまに言えば, それでたちまち悪魔として通るようになる ▪ He's not so *black* as he's *been painted*. やつは言われているほど悪いやつではない. ☞悪魔を黒く描いたことから; 主に否定文脈で使われる; →so BLACK as one is painted.

paint … in bright* [*high*] *colors →COLOR.

paint … in dark colors →COLOR.

paint *oneself* ***into a corner*** 抜き差しならない状況に追い込まれる ▪ The President has *painted himself into a corner*. 大統領は自分の落ち度で困った立場に陥ってしまった. ☞「床にペンキを塗って行き自分が立つところだけが塗り残される」が原義.

paint it red 《米俗》扇情的に書き立てる ▪ The writer seems to have *painted it red*. その作家は扇情的に書き立てたらしい.

paint the lily →LILY.

***paint the town* (*red*)** お祭り騒ぎ[底抜け騒ぎ]をする ▪ The boys *painted the town red* with fire crackers. 男の子たちは爆竹でどんちゃん騒ぎをした ▪ Let's *paint the town red* tonight. 今夜はひとつお祭り騒ぎをしようじゃないか. ☞たぶん, 酔ったカウボーイたちがピストルを撃ちながら町を駆け回ったことから. red を火事と関連づけたり, 漠然と暴力との連想とする説もある.

so* [*as*] *black as *one* ***is painted*** →BLACK[1].

painter /péɪntər/ 名 ***cut* [*slip*] *the*** [*one's*] ***painter*** 手を切る, (植民地が)独立する ▪ I can see signs of his *cutting the painter* before long. そのうちに彼が手を切るきざしが見える ▪ The sooner we *cut the painter*, the better it would be for Englishmen. 我々が関係を絶つのが早ければ早いほど, 英国人にとってはけっこうなことだろう. ☞painter「もやい綱」.

painting /péɪntɪŋ/ 名 ***be like painting the Forth Bridge*** → like painting the Forth BRIDGE.

be no oil painting 《英》美人[男前]ではない

P

▪ Mary *is no oil painting*, but nice. メアリーは美人じゃないが優しい. ☞「とても油絵にはならない」が原義.

pair /peər/ 名 ***a pair of hands*** 《口》仕事が出来る一人 ▪ What we need, frankly, is *a pair of hands*. 率直に言って, 欲しいのは仕事が出来るやつだ.

a pair of lawn sleeves 《口》監督 (bishop) ▪ At every levee, appeared eighteen *pair of lawn sleeves*. 接見のたびに18人の監督が姿を見せた. ☞英国教会の bishop の法衣のそでがローンでできているところから.

another [a fresh] pair of eyes さらにもう一人加わる検査[調査]員 ▪ You want *a fresh pair of eyes* on the problem. You want a second opinion. その問題の検査にはもう一人必要だ. セカンドオピニオンを要する.

another [a different] pair of shoes [boots] 《口》別問題 ▪ That is quite *another pair of shoes*. それは全く別問題です.

have a [fine, good, etc.***] pair of lungs*** 《戯》声がでかい ▪ The baby*'s got a good pair of lungs*. あの赤ちゃんは泣き声が大きい.

have only got one pair of hands 《口》これ以上速くは働けない ▪ I can't look after the children and cook the dinner at the same time; I*'ve only got one pair of hands*. 子供の世話と料理を同時にはできないわ. 腕は二本しかないのだから.

in pairs 二つ一組になって ▪ The company then went off *in pairs*. 一行はその後二人ずつ立ち去った.

make a pair **1** 結婚する ▪ They'll *make a* good *pair*—those two. いい夫婦になるだろうよ, あの二人は.

2 一対になる ▪ Those two jugs will *make a pair*; they are alike in every way. あの二つの花びんは一対になるでしょう. どこから見ても同じだ.

two [three, etc.***] pair front [back]*** 《英》3階[4階, など]の表[裏] ▪ She was living in a spacious room on the *two pair front*. 彼女は3階の表の広々とした部屋に住んでいた ▪ He is lodging on the *three pair back*. 彼は4階の裏に下宿している.

pal /pæl/ 名 ***the old pals act*** 《口》ひどくあいそのよい態度 ▪ The man started *the old pals act* with me when he discovered that I was his son's teacher. その男は私が彼の息子の先生であることを知ると, ひどくあいそのよい態度をとりはじめた.

palate /pǽlət/ 名 ***suit** a person's **palate*** 《口》人の口[好み]に合う ▪ The dish *suited his palate*. その料理は彼の口に合った ▪ A job like that does not quite *suit my palate*. そのような仕事はどうも僕の好みに合いません.

tickle** a person's **palate **1** 人の味覚をそそる ▪ Her mince pie will *tickle your palate*. 彼女のミンスパイはあなたの味覚をそそるでしょう.

2 人の気に入る ▪ The style of this new author *tickles my palate*. この新人作家の文体は僕にはぐっとくる.

pale[1] /peɪl/ 名 ***beyond [out of, outside] the pale*** **1** 範囲外に (*of*) ▪ There is no salvation to be expected *outside the pale of* the Church. 教会という枠の外ではいかなる救済も期待できない ▪ She is *out of the pale of* all theories. 彼女はあらゆる説にとらわれていない.

2 (社会から)見捨てられて ▪ His cruelty puts him *beyond the pale*. 彼は残酷なので社会から見捨てられている ▪ Socially she is *outside the pale*. 社会的には彼女は見捨てられている.

3 ひどい ▪ His swearing is *beyond the pale*. 彼ののしり言葉はひどいものだ. ☞pale は柵を作るための杭, 杭で出来た柵の意. そこから発展して囲まれた場所の意. ここでは pale＝the English Pale (イングランドに支配されたアイルランドの一地域).

within [inside] the pale 範囲内に (*of*) ▪ He is *within the pale of* good society. 彼は上流社会に属する ▪ Do you think you can act in that manner and yet remain *inside the pale*? そんな態度をとって, しかも「則(のり)を越えず」にいられるとでも思うのか?

pale[2] /peɪl/ 形 ***(as) pale as a ghost [a wax doll]*** 真っ青な, ろうのように青白い ▪ She came into the room, *as pale as a ghost*. 彼女は真っ青になって部屋に入ってきた.

as pale as a lily [pastry] 真っ青で, ひどく青白い肌色で ▪ The Marquis is *as pale as a lily* because the bats drained his blood. 侯爵はコウモリに血を吸われて真っ青な顔色をしている ▪ She was in bed with flu and looked *as pale as pastry*. 彼女はインフルエンザで寝ていてひどく青白い顔をしていた.

(as) pale as ashes →ASH.

(as) pale as death 真っ青で ▪ You look *as pale as death*. 君は顔が真っ青だよ.

look pale 顔色が悪い ▪ What's the matter with you? You *look pale*. どうした. 顔色が悪いじゃないか.

turn pale **1** 青くなる ▪ He *turned pale* with fright. 彼は驚いて青くなった.

2 (色が)薄くなる ▪ The writing in the old letter had *turned* very *pale*. 古い手紙の文字がひどく薄れてきた.

pall /pɔːl/ 名 ***cast a pall over [on]*** (しばしば新聞・テレビニュースで)…に暗い影を落とす ▪ The death of five students in a car accident has *cast a pall over* the high school's graduation ceremonies. 交通事故で5人もの生徒が亡くなったので, 高校の卒業式は暗いものとなった.

palm[1] /pɑːm/ 名 ***an itching [itchy] palm*** 強欲, 金銭欲 ▪ Fees were always welcome to his *itching palm*. 金銭欲の深い彼には報酬はいつもうれしいものだった.

grease [gild, oil, tickle, 《米俗》 ***cross] the palms of*** …に賄賂を使う ▪ He obtained that road contract by *greasing the palms of* a few officials. 彼は何人かの役人に賄賂を使ってあの道路契約を手に入れた.

have an itching [itchy] palm 欲が深い, 賄賂をほしがる (cf. Sh., *Jul. Caes.* 4. 3. 9–10) (→an itching PALM) ▪ They say he *has an itching palm*. あの男は欲張りだそうだ. ☞手の平がむずむずするときには賄賂が入ってくるという古い迷信から.

have* [*hold*]... *in the palm* [*hollow*] *of one's hand ...を完全に掌握する; (観客など)を掌中におさめる ▪ He *had* the organization *in the palm of his hand*. 彼はその組織を完全に掌握していた ▪ She's *got* the audience *in the palm of her hand*. 彼女は聴衆を意のままに操っている.

know... like* [*as* one *knows*] *the palm of* one's *hand ...をよく承知している ▪ I *know* the village *like the palm of my hand*. その村のことは手に取るように知っている.

oil* [*tickle*] *the palms of →grease the PALMs of.

palm oil/oil of palms 賄賂 ▪ *Palm oil* plays its part more or less in the conduct of daily life here. 賄賂というものは当地で日常生活を送るにあたって多少とも役割を果たしている.

palm[2] /pɑːm/ 名 ***bear* [*carry off*] *the palm*** **1**《古風》勝つ, 優勝者になる ▪ He *bore the palm* in the contest. 彼はその試合で優勝した ▪ He will *carry off the palm* from all his rivals. 彼はあらゆる競争者に勝つだろう.

2 卓絶する ▪ For sheer beauty, the view from Naples *bears the palm*. 純粋な美にかけてはナポリからのながめは卓絶している. ☞シュロの木の葉が勝利の象徴であるところから.

give the palm to ...に軍配をあげる ▪ He *gives the palm* without hesitation *to* American love. 彼は迷わずアメリカ人の愛情に軍配をあげる.

hold the palm among ...の中で首位を占めている ▪ *Among* the electrical achievements of the British Empire, Canada now *holds the palm*. 大英帝国の電気関係の業績面ではカナダが現在首位を占めている.

win the palm 賞[勝利]を得る ▪ *The palm was won* by a boy of fourteen whose paper contained no mistakes at all. その賞は論文に誤りが全然なかった14歳の少年が得た.

yield the palm to ...に勝ちを譲る, 参ったと言う ▪ I *yielded the palm to* her as a superior athlete. 格上のアスリートだとして彼女に参りましたと言った.

palm[3] /pɑːm/ 動 ***palm* oneself *off*** 《口》...であるようなふりをする (*as*) ▪ He *palmed himself off as* a Colonel. 彼は陸軍大佐であるようなふりをした.

palmy /pɑ́ːmi/ 形 ***palmy days*** (過去の)全盛時代 ▪ In the *palmy days* of goldmining, many rough men became millionaires. 金鉱の全盛時代には, 多くの粗野な連中が百万長者になった.

palmy state 黄金時代 (cf. Sh., *Haml.* 1. 1. 113) ▪ Rome was in her *palmy state* then. 当時ローマは黄金時代であった.

pan /pæn/ 名 ***go down the pan* [*toilet*]** 《英俗》役に立たなくなる, 哀れな落伍者になる, 無用の長物と化す ▪ After the drugs scandal, the actor's career *went down the toilet*. 薬物スキャンダルがあってからその俳優はだめになった. ☞pan はトイレットの便器(ball)の略式語.

(*jump, leap*) *out of the frying pan into the fire* →FRYING-PAN.

leap* [*fall*] *out of the pan into the fire 小難を逃れて大難にあう ▪ This would be only to *leap out of the pan into the fire*. これは小難を逃れて大難にあうことにしかなるまい.

on the pan 《米口》こきおろされて ▪ A professor who wasn't there was *on the pan*. そこにいなかった教授がこきおろされた.

pan gravy 煮詰めていない味つけ肉汁 ▪ My wife liked cream gravy, but I preferred *pan gravy*. 妻はクリームグレービーを好んだが, 私はパングレービーの方が好きだった.

put... on the pan 《米口》...を酷評する, こきおろす ▪ The boss *put* him *on the pan* for being late. 社長は遅れたと言って彼をこきおろした.

savor of the pan お里が知れる, 地金を現す ▪ There are many things that *savor of the pan* in his work. あの男の作品にはお里の知れるような箇所がたくさんある.

shut* one's *pan 《俗》口をつぐむ, 黙っている ▪ *Shut your pan*, you! 黙れ, こら.

pancake /pǽnkèɪk/ 名 **(*as*) *flat as a pancake*** →FLAT.

Pandora /pændɔ́ːrə/ 名 ***open* (*a*) *Pandora's box*** (意図せずに)いろいろな災いを招く ▪ Some Communist party leaders warned that free elections would *open a Pandora's box*. 共産党指導者のなかには自由選挙はパンドラの箱を開けることになろうと警告する者もいた ▪ Europe's expansion had *opened a Pandora's box* of diseases. ヨーロッパの拡大はさまざまな病気というパンドラの箱を開けてしまった. ☞次項も参照.

Pandora's box パンドラの箱,「玉手箱」(→a CAN of worms) ▪ There may be some hope left in the bottom of this *Pandora's box* of calamities. この災難の玉手箱の底には何か希望が残っているかもしれない. ☞《ギ神》Zeus が Pandora に与えた箱を, 禁を犯して夫が開くと, 中から人類の諸悪が地上に広がり, 希望だけが底に残ったという話から.

panel /pǽnəl/ 名 ***go* [*be*] *on the panel*** 《英》健康保健医の診察を受ける[ている] ▪ I *am on the panel* now. 今健康保健医の診察を受けている.

on the panel **1** 陪審名簿に登録されて ▪ Your name is down *on the panel* of jurors. あなたの名は陪審員の名簿に載っています.

2《英》保険医名簿に登録されて ▪ Dr. Hibberton is *on the panel* of local doctors. ヒバートン博士は地方保健医だ.

panic /pǽnɪk/ 名 ***hit* [*press, push*] *the panic button*** 《英口》ひどくあわてふためく, 周章狼狽する ▪ The boss *hit the panic button* and just went to pieces. 頭取はあわてふためき, すっかり取り乱してしまった. ☞a panic button「緊急警報装置」.

P

panic stations 《英口》危機的状態，不安状態 ▪ One hour before the show started, it was *panic stations.* ショーの始まる1時間前は，パニック状態であった. ☞海軍の action stations (戦闘配置)に倣ったおどけた表現.

pannikin /pǽnɪkən/ 名 ***off*** *one's* ***pannikin*** 《俗》気がふれて; ぼうっとして ▪ He's clean *off his pannikin.* 彼はすっかり気が狂っている ▪ I'm *off my pannikin* with sitting in the sun. 僕は日なたで座っていたためにぼうっとしている. ☞pannikin「頭」.

pants /pænts/ 名 ***a kick in the pants*** →KICK[1].

be caught with *one's* ***pants down*** 《口》不意をつかれる，まずいところを見られる (→with one's PANTS down) ▪ Have you ever *been caught with your pants down?* 今まで不意をつかれて弱みを握られたことがありますか.

beat [***ride, act***] ***the pants off*** *a person* 《口》人をこてんぱんにやっつける，完全に打ち負かす (→beat...(all) HOLLOW) ▪ The last time we played the Smiths, they *beat the pants off* us. この前スミスさんちとプレーしたとき，こてんぱんにやられた ▪ Don't worry about us—we can *ride the pants off* any of those Ivy League guys. 心配するなよ—あんなアイビーリーグ野郎たちなんかみな完全にやっつけてやるさ.

catch *a person* ***with*** *a person's* ***pants off*** 人の不意をつく，狼狽させる ▪ They had *caught* me *with my pants off.* 彼らは私をあたふたさせたのだった.

fancy pants 《米俗》にやけた男 ▪ We need no *fancy pants.* にやけた男はごめんこうむりたい.

put (*one's*) ***pants on one leg at a time*** 《諺》一度に片足ずつズボンをはく,「みなと同じ普通の人間である」 ▪ The rich are no different than anybody else. They eat, they *put pants on one leg at a time.* 金持ちはみなとちっとも変わらないよ，ご飯も食べるし，ズボンも片方ずつはくよ. ☞「有名人も同じ人間である」というときに使われる.

scare [***frighten, shock, bore, talk, kid, charm***] ***the pants off*** *a person* 《口》人を大いに[とことん]怖がらせる[ショックを与える，退屈させる，しゃべってうんざりさせる，からかう，魅了する] ▪ I tell you, you *scared the pants off* him. 本当に，やつはビビッてたぜ ▪ The ending of the movie *shocked the pants off* me. 映画の結末には本当にショックを受けた ▪ He *bored the pants off* us with his long speech. 彼が長いスピーチをしたので私たちはすっかり退屈してしまった ▪ You just *talked the pants off* of me. 君のおしゃべりにはもううんざりだ ▪ I bet your friends at school *kidded the pants off* you. きっと君は学校の友だちにすっかりからかわれているのさ ▪ Sam is the sort of person who loves rushing around, *charming the pants off* everyone he meets. サムは大騒ぎするのが大好きなタイプの男で，会う人みなをとことん魅了してしまう. ☞the pants off は動詞の意味を強調するために使われている.

smarty pants (大人が子供に向けて)利口ぶるので嫌われる人《しばしば子供が使う》 ▪ See, I told you so!—Yeah, all right *smarty pants.* そら，言った通りでしょう—うん，分かってるよ，知ったかぶり屋さん.

wear the pants (女が)夫をしりに敷いている ▪ She's older than he is and she *wears the pants.* 彼女は夫よりも年上で，夫をしりに敷いている.

wearing [***in***] ***short pants*** 《口》とても幼い，成熟していない ▪ It's too bad that I couldn't visit him like I did when I was *wearing short pants.* 残念ながら私が幼い頃のようには彼の家へ遊びに行けなかった ▪ His father continued to treat him as if he were still *in short pants.* 父親はまるで彼がまだ青二才であるかのような扱いを続けた.

with *one's* ***pants down*** 《口》まずいところを，不意のところを ▪ After that the camp was caught *with its pants down* by the surprise attack. その後で野営地は不意のところを奇襲された.

panty /pǽnti/ 名 ***get*** *one's* ***panties in a bunch*** 《口》ささいなこと[くだらないこと]を心配する; イライラする ▪ It's just two blocks away, man—don't *get your panties in a bunch!* ほんの2ブロック先だよ，心配するなってことよ.

pap /pæp/ 名 *One's* ***mouth is full of pap.*** まだ乳臭い《子供っぽい人を評して》 ▪ Though a full-grown youth, *his mouth is full of pap.* 成長した青年のくせに，彼はまだ乳臭い.

paper[1] /péɪpər/ 名 ***bad paper*** 《米俗》不渡り小切手; にせ札 ▪ I was passed off some *bad paper.* 私はにせ札をつかまされた.

be in the papers 新聞に出ている ▪ His name *is* continually *in the papers.* 彼の名前は絶えず新聞に出ている.

be on a paper 新聞記者だ ▪ He *is on a paper.* 彼は新聞記者だ.

brown paper bag 《俗》覆面パトカー ▪ She got a Christmas card because she didn't notice the *brown paper bag* following her. 覆面パトカーが後ろにつけているのに気がつかなかったので彼女はスピード違反切符を切られた.

commit ... to paper →COMMIT.

couldn't ... *one's* ***way out of a*** (***wet***) ***paper bag*** 無能である，無気力である ▪ Kevin *couldn't* teach *his way out of a paper bag.* ケビンには教育しようとする気概がない ▪ He *couldn't* write [fight] *his way out of a paper bag* right. 彼はちゃんとものを書く[戦う]能力がない.

get into papers 新聞に載る，新聞種になる ▪ The accident *got into papers.* その事件は新聞に出た.

get *one's* ***walking papers*** →WALKING.

give *a person his* ***walking papers*** →WALKING.

light the touch paper 導火紙に点火する，災害を起こす要因になる ▪ Blair *lit the touch paper* when he encouraged devolution in Scotland and Wales. ブレア首相がスコットランドとウェールズに自治権移譲を奨励したことが論争の火種となった.

make the papers (新聞に)書き立てられる，注目を

集める ▪ That handwritten letter from jail by Saddam *made the papers*. 獄中からのサダム・フセインの肉筆の手紙が紙面をにぎわした.

not worth the paper it's [***they're***] ***written*** [***printed***] ***on*** (書類が正式の文書に見えて実は)何の役にも立たない ▪ That contract is*n't worth the paper it's written on*. All the signatures are forged. あの契約書は全くの反故(ほご)だ. 署名が全部偽物だから.

on paper (事実はともかく)机上では, 書いた物の上では; 理屈の上では ▪ Problems of any sort are easily worked out *on paper*. どんな問題でも机上では容易に解決される ▪ It is all right *on paper*. それは理屈の上では申し分ない.

paper chase 《米》(面倒な)書類作成 ▪ The *paper chase* trying to get visas was frustrating and time-consuming. 査証をもらうための書類作成はいらいらして時間がかかった.

paper tiger 張り子の虎, こけおどし ▪ They are *paper tigers*, weak and indecisive. やつらは軟弱で優柔不断な張り子の虎だ ▪ Imperialists are *paper tigers*. 帝国主義者なんて張り子の虎だ. ☞人・おどし・思想などに用いる.

paper trail 《米》(しばしばビジネス・政治で)人の行動の証拠となる文書 ▪ Police are following a *paper trail*, checking credit cards and criminal records. 警察がクレジットカードと犯罪記録を調べながら, 文書足跡を追跡中である.

peddle (*one's*) ***papers*** 《米俗》〚命令文で〛おせっかいするな; 行ってしまえ ▪ I told him to go *peddle his papers*. 彼にあっちへ行けと言った.

push paper 《口》つまらない管理事務の仕事をする ▪ I don't want to *push paper* like my father. 父のようにつまらない事務処理で終わりたくない.

put ... on paper ...を書きつける ▪ I should prefer you to *put* it *on paper*. それを書きつけておいてくれたほうがいいね.

put pen to paper 筆をとる →PEN.

send in *one's* ***papers*** (特に将校が)辞表を提出する ▪ I *sent in my papers*, and here I am. 私は辞表を提出して, ここに来ているわけです.

paper[2] /péɪpər/ 動 ***paper over the cracks*** →CRACK[1].

par /pɑːr/ 名 ***above par*** **1**《商》額面[平価]以上で ▪ This stock is *above par*. この株は額面以上だ ▪ The rate of exchange for dollars is *above par*. ドルの為替相場は平価以上だ.

2 標準以上で ▪ You will soon find out if they are *above par*. あの人たちが標準以上であるかどうか, じきにわかるでしょう.

at par 額面価格で, 平価で ▪ The stock is *at par*. その株は額面通りだ ▪ Foreign coins do not pass *at par*. 外国硬貨は平価では通用しない.

be (***about***) ***par for the course*** (ほぼ)並みの出来ばえで, 当たり前で ▪ A bit of bugging *is about par for the* political *course*. 政治では少々の盗聴はほぼ当たり前である. ☞ゴルフ用語から.

be on [***upon***] ***a par*** (...と)同様である, 同等である (*with*) ▪ The gains and losses *are* about *on a par*. 損益はほぼ同様だ ▪ He *is* quite *on a par with* his brother in brains. 彼は頭では兄と全く同等だ.

below [***under***] ***par*** **1**《商》額面[平価]以下で ▪ The insurance shares you mentioned are *under par*. 君の言った保険の株は額面以下だ.

2 標準以下で; 体の具合が悪い ▪ He is mentally *below par*. 彼は知的にはコンマ以下だ ▪ I'm feeling a good deal *below par* this morning. けさはひどく調子が悪い.

on a par 平均して ▪ The farms contain *on a par* about ninety acres. 農場は平均90エーカーある.

par excellence 〚名詞に伴って〛特に優れた, ...の好例 ▪ They went up to Troy, which was the tourist site *par excellence*. 彼らはトロイへ行った. そこは格好の観光名所だった. ☞F 'by EXCELLENCE'.

up to par 標準に達して; 体がふだんの状態で ▪ The crops are *up to par*. 作物は平作に達した ▪ I am not feeling *up to par*. 体の調子がよくない.

parable /pǽrəbəl/ 名 ***speak in parables*** たとえ話で話す ▪ You can please some people by *speaking in parables*. 人によってはたとえ話で話すのが気に入るかもしれない.

parachute /pǽrəʃùːt/ 名 ***a golden parachute*** →GOLDEN.

parade /pəréɪd/ 名 ***hit parade*** 《俗》**1** ヒットパレード, (歌・曲の)売上げ人気番付 ▪ Paul was overjoyed when his new song was named on the *hit parade*. ポールは新曲がヒットパレードに出ると狂喜した.

2 (人の)お気に入り番付表 ▪ John is no longer number one on Elsie's *hit parade*. ジョンはエルシーのヒットパレードでもはやトップではない.

make a parade of ...を見せびらかす ▪ He *makes a* fine *parade of* his own good qualities. 彼は自分のすぐれた能力を仰々しく見せびらかす.

on parade **1** 行列を作って ▪ The soldiers marched *on parade*. 兵士らは隊列を作って行進した.

2 (俳優・踊り子などが)総出で ▪ I wanted to find people *on parade*. 私は人々が総出のところを見たいと思った.

rain on *a person's* ***parade*** 《主に米口・報道》行事の楽しさをぶち壊しにする, 人の計画を台なしにする, 水を差す ▪ He enjoys *raining on other people's parades*. 彼は他人の楽しい行事にけちをつけて喜ぶ.

paradise /pǽrədàɪs/ 名 ***live in a fool's paradise*** →FOOL[1].

paragon /pǽrəgɑ̀n|-gən/ 名 ***a paragon of virtue*** 美徳の化身[鑑(かがみ)] ▪ Few men are *paragons of virtue*. 美徳の化身であるような人は少ない.

parallel /pǽrəlèl/ 形名 ***draw a parallel between*** (二者)の相似点を比較する ▪ We can *draw a parallel between* the fate of the Kaiser and that of Napoleon. 我々はドイツ皇帝の運命とナポレオンのそれとの相似点を比較することができる.

in parallel 平行して;《電》並列式で (↔in SERIES 2) ▪ Several generators are operated *in parallel.* 数個の発電機が並列式で動かされている.

in parallel with …と平行して, 同時に ▪ Negotiations for a peace were going slowly on *in parallel with* the languishing war. 平和交渉が苦しい戦いと平行してゆっくりと行われていた.

run parallel with [***to***] …と平行する ▪ The river *runs parallel with* the main street. 川は本通りと平行して流れている.

without (***a***) ***parallel*** 比類のない ▪ The complete success of Helen Keller's life is *without parallel* in history. ヘレン・ケラーの生涯の完全な成功は歴史上比類がない.

paramount /pǽrəmàʊnt/ 形 ***paramount to*** …に勝る ▪ This duty is *paramount to* all the others. この義務は他のすべてに優先する.

parcel /pɑ́ːrsəl/ 名 ***a parcel of*** 《軽蔑》一群の ▪ The directors of this company are *a parcel of* blockheads. この会社の重役連中ときたら揃いも揃ってばかどもだ ▪ I'm not going to be lectured by *a parcel of* girls. 僕は小娘連中に説教などされないぞ.

by parcel post 小包郵便で ▪ The book has been sent to me *by parcel post.* その本は小包郵便で送られて来た.

drop a parcel 《俗》(賭けで)大金を失う ▪ He has *dropped a parcel* over the race. 彼はそのレースの賭けで大金を失った.

pass the parcel (責任をとらず)次々に他に押しつける, (たらい回しにして)他に責任を転嫁する ▪ Various countries have been playing *pass the parcel* with this war criminal. この戦犯はさまざまな国でたらい回しにされている. ☞pass the parcel は子供の遊び. 音楽に合わせて包みを順に手渡しで送り, 音楽が止まったときに手にしている子がそれを開ける.

win a parcel 《俗》(賭けで)大金を儲ける ▪ I can put you in the way of *winning a parcel* on the race. 君にそのレースで大金を儲けさせてあげられるよ.

parchment /pɑ́ːrtʃmənt/ 名 ***in the parchment*** 《米》(皮を)なめしてない ▪ He had one elk skin *in the parchment.* 彼はなめしてないヘラジカの皮を1枚持っていた.

pardon[1] /pɑ́ːrdən/ 名 ***beg pardon of*** *a person* →BEG.

begging [***asking***] *a person's* ***pardon*** 失礼ながら ▪ *Asking your pardon,* Mr. Trelawney, the secret has been told. トリローニーさん, 失礼ですが, 秘密は漏れていますよ.

(***I***) ***beg your pardon.*** **1** すみません《思わず犯した小さな過失などに対するわび言葉》 ▪ *I beg your pardon.* I did wrong. すみません. 悪いことをしました.

2 失礼ですが《相手の意見に反対したり, または見知らぬ人に声をかけるとき》 ▪ *I beg your pardon,* but that is my coat. 失礼ですが, それは私の上着です ▪ *I beg your pardon,* is this your handbag? 失礼ですが, これはあなたのハンドバッグですか.

3 〚上昇調で〛何とおっしゃいました《問い返すときの決まり文句》 ▪ "*I beg your pardon*?" said Alice. 「何とおっしゃいましたか?」とアリスが言った.

Never ask pardon before you are accused. 《諺》とがめられるまでは謝るな. ☞謝ると自分が過ちを犯したと認めることになるから自分の方からは謝らないこと, の意.

pardon[2] /pɑ́ːrdən/ 動 ***Pardon me*** [***us***]. ごめんください; 恐れ入ります ▪ *Pardon me,* may I disturb you a minute? 恐れ入りますが, ちょっとおじゃましてもよろしいでしょうか.

Pardon me [***us***]***?*** 〚上昇調で〛何とおっしゃいましたか ▪ Do you know anyone here?—*Pardon me?* ここにいる人を誰か知っていますか?—え, 何ですって?

Pardon me for breathing [***living***]***!*** 《口》(いつもぶつぶつ言っている相手に対して, 怒って)悪かったね, 悪うございました ▪ Oh, *pardon me for breathing,* I'm sure*!* いや, 悪かったわねー, 本当に.

pare /peər/ 動 ***pare and burn*** (灰肥を造るために芝生を2, 3インチに刈り込んで)野焼きする ▪ Seventeen acres *were pared and burned.* 17エーカーの土地が野焼きされた.

pare to [***beyond***] ***the quick/pare too close*** [***near***] **1** 深うめを切る ▪ His nails *were pared to the quick.* 彼は深うめを切った.

2 痛手を負わす, 酷使する ▪ Great fines *pared* me *too near.* 高い罰金でひどい目にあった ▪ They *pared* the people *to the quick,* to raise their revenues. 歳入を工面するため人民を酷使した.

parent /péərənt/ 名 ***our first parents*** アダムとイブ ▪ God's hands had written in the hearts of *our first parents* all the rules of good. 神の手はアダムとイブの心に善のすべての規則を書きつけていた.

parenthesis /pərénθəsəs/ 名 ***by way of parenthesis*** ちなみに, ついでながら ▪ He quoted it, *by way of parenthesis.* 彼はついでにそれを引用した.

in parentheses **1** かっこに入れて ▪ English equivalents are given *in parentheses* after Japanese words. 英訳は日本語の後にかっこに入れてある.

2 ちなみに ▪ It might also be remarked *in parentheses* that he is still living there. またちなみに言うが, 彼はまだそこに住んでいる.

parish /pǽrɪʃ/ 名 ***be sent to the parish*** 教区の世話に任される ▪ The boy will certainly *be sent to the parish,* if you don't pay for him. その少年は君が金を出してやらなければ, きっと教区のやっかいになるだろう.

go [***come***] ***on*** [***upon***] ***the parish*** 教区のやっかいになる《poor law (1947年廃止)の時代》 ▪ He will either *go upon the parish* or starve. 彼は教区のやっかいになるか, 飢え死にするかのいずれかだ.

on the parish 教区のやっかいになって ▪ The man was obliged to leave his children *on the parish* through unthriftiness. その男は浪費をしたために子供を教区に任せなければならなかった.

parity /pǽrəti/ 名 ***by parity of reasoning*** 類推によって ▪ *By parity of reasoning* that house is in no danger of falling. 類推によればあの

P

家も倒れる危険はない.

on a parity with …と同等に ▪ Music should be established as a major subject *on a parity with* other studies. 音楽は他の学科と同等に主要科目と定められるべきである.

parity of esteem (学校制度などの)平等な尊重 ▪ There should be *parity of esteem* for all forms of secondary education. すべての中等学校制度は平等に尊重されなければならない.

park[1] /pɑːrk/ 名 ***a walk in the park*** →WALK[1].

hit the park →HIT[2].

in park (オートマチック車の駐車ギア)をパーキングに入れて ▪ The driver stopped the car and placed it *in park*. 運転者は車を停め, ギアをパーキングに入れた.

industrial park 工場団地, 美化された都市郊外の工業地域 ▪ The nearest supermarket that sells car tires is at the *industrial park* twenty miles from downtown. 車のタイヤを売っている最寄りのスーパーは町の中心街から20マイルも離れた工業団地にある.

park[2] /pɑːrk/ 動 ***No parking (here)./Parking prohibited.*** 駐車お断り《掲示》.

***park** oneself* 《米口》みこしをすえる ▪ His mother-in-law *parked herself* on him. 彼の奥さんの母親が彼の家にいすわった.

park it 《口》座る, 座ってじゃまにならないようにする ▪ Dennis, *park it* over there in the corner. Stop pacing around. デニス, あそこの隅に座って. 歩き回るのはよしなさい.

parlance /pɑ́ːrləns/ 名 ***in legal [common,** etc.**] parlance*** 《文》法律用語[俗な言葉, など]では ▪ It's cardiac arrest—*in common parlance*, his heart has stopped beating. これは心拍停止—俗な言葉で言えば, 彼の心臓が打つのをやめたのですな.

parley /pɑ́ːrli/ 名 ***in parley*** 談判して ▪ We had been *in parley* for an hour. 我々は1時間前から談判していた.

Parliament /pɑ́ːrləmənt/ 名 ***a hung parliament*** 絶対多数の政党がない議会《1党で絶対多数を占められず政府が連立によってのみ維持成立する議会》 ▪ They say the final result will be *a hung parliament*. 最終的には連立による議会に落ち着くだろうと言われている.

be before Parliament 下院で審議中だ ▪ The Bill *is* now *before Parliament*. その法案は今下院で審議中だ.

enter [go into] Parliament 下院議員になる ▪ He first *entered Parliament* in 1911 as a Conservative member. 彼は保守党議員として1911年に初めて下院入りをした.

open Parliament 議会の開会を宣する ▪ *Parliament was opened* by the King. 王が議会の開会を宣した.

parlor, 《英》**parlour** /pɑ́ːrlər/ 名 ***parlor tricks*** 《口》隠し芸 ▪ I don't possess any *parlor tricks*. 私には隠し芸というものがない.

parole /pəróʊl/ 名 ***break** one's **parole*** 仮釈放中に逃げる ▪ They had *broken their parole* and fled. 彼らは仮釈放中に逃げた.

(out) on parole **1** 宣誓釈放されて[た] ▪ A good many French prisoners of war had been living *on parole* in Melrose. 大勢のフランス人の捕虜がメルローズで宣誓釈放されて暮らしていた.

2 (罪人が)仮釈放中で[の] ▪ The criminal is *on parole*. その罪人は仮釈放中だ ▪ Although Harry is *out on parole* he must watch his step very carefully. ハリーは仮釈放中だが, 特別に用心して行動しなくてはならない.

parrot /pǽrət/ 名 ***(as) sick as a parrot*** 《英戯》とてもがっかりして ▪ David was *sick as a parrot* when he heard Manchester had lost the match. デイビッドはマンチェスターが試合に負けたと聞いてこの上なくがっかりした.

like a parrot オウムのように《訳もわからずに》 ▪ He talks *like a parrot* and just repeats what he heard. 彼はオウムのようにしゃべり, 人に聞いたことを繰り返すだけだ.

parrot fashion オウム返しに ▪ The boy repeats his prayers *parrot fashion*. その少年はオウム返しに祈りを繰り返す.

parsnip /pɑ́ːrsnɪp/ 名 ***Fine [Fair, Soft] words butter no parsnips.*** 《諺》口先ばかりの優しい言葉ではなんの足しにもならない.

part[1] /pɑːrt/ 名 ***(a) great part of*** …の大部分 ▪ I stay in London for (a) *great part of* the year. 1年の大半はロンドンにいます. ☞しばしば慣用的に a を落とす.

a man [woman] of (many) parts 有能の士, 多才な人 ▪ Some of them were indeed *men of parts*. 彼らのうちのある者は確かに有能の士だった ▪ My father was *a man of many parts*: a talented painter, a good cook and not a bad musician. 父は多芸な人だった. 絵画に長けていたし, 料理も上手だし, 音楽もなかなかのものだった.

(a) part of …の一部分 ▪ (*A*) *part of* the work was done. その仕事の一部はすんだ ▪ *Part of* the pupils are idle. その生徒らの一部は怠け者だ. ☞しばしば慣用的に a を落とす.

act a part →play a PART.

act [do, play]** one's **part 本分を尽くす (→do one's BIT) ▪ I will try to *act my part* for world peace. 世界平和のために本分を尽くそう ▪ He *played his part* worthily. 彼は立派に本分を尽くした.

act the part 《口》あることを極度に誇示する ▪ Now that he is rich, he certainly *acts the part*. 彼は金ができて, 確かにひどく金持ち風を吹かす.

act the part of →play the PART of.

be (all) part of life's rich pageant [tapestry, fabric, pattern] 《雅》(辛いことがあろうともそれも避けることが出来ない)多彩な[豊かな]人生模様の一部 ▪ Having kids certainly causes problems, but it's *all part of life's rich pageant*. 子供がいるといろいろ面倒が起きるが, それも人生模様の一コマだ.

P

☞tapestry とは物語を織り込んだ一枚の大きな布.

bear a part in …に加わる ▪The king himself *bore a part in* it. 王までがそれに加わった.

dress the part/be dressed for the part 役割にふさわしい服装をする ▪His solicitor came in, *dressed for the part.* 彼の事務弁護士が役にふさわしい服装をして入って来た.

feel the part それらしく感じる ▪I felt young. A leotard makes you *feel the part.* 私は若々しい気分になった. レオタードを身につけるとそれらしく感じるのだ.

for** one's **part …としては ▪*For my part* I prefer to stay at home. 私としては家にいるほうがいい ▪The Japanese, *for their part,* consider themselves affronted by the use of the word "Jap." 日本人としては「ジャップ」という言葉が使われると侮辱されたように感じる.

(for) the most part 大部分は, 大体は ▪They ride *the most part* without saddles. 彼らは大体くらをつけずに馬に乗る ▪The shops were *for the most part* closed. 大方の店は閉まっていた.

have a part in …にあずかる, かかわりをもつ ▪Everyone must *have a part in* changing the company. 各人が会社の改革に関与しなければならない.

have a part to play in …を助けることが出来る, 責任がある ▪We all *have a part to play in* the fight against global warming. みなが地球温暖化防止において果たす役割がある.

have neither part nor lot in …に少しも関係がない (《聖》 *Acts* 8. 21) ▪She declared that she would *have neither part nor lot in* his dishonest career. 彼女は彼の不正直な生活には少しも関係しません, と言い放った.

have [play, take, want] no part in [of] …と[に]関係しない, かかわりたくない ▪He *had no part in* the planning. 彼はその計画立案にはかかわらなかった ▪I *want no part of* this dirty business. こんな汚い商売にはかかわりたくない.

in good part 主に, 大部分 (→(for) the most PART) ▪The company's failure is *in good part* the result of poor management. 会社が失敗したのは主に下手な経営のせいだ.

in good [ill, evil] part 《英》〚主に take などの動詞を伴って〛善意[悪意]に ▪I am sure he will *take* it *in good part.* きっと彼はそれを善意に解して[怒らないで聞き入れて]くれるだろうと思う ▪The man *took* this remonstrance *in ill part.* その男はこの抗議を悪意に取った. ☞<[L] in bonam partem accipere.

in large [small] part 主に, 大部分[少しは, わずか] ▪The White House was constructed about 200 years ago *in large part* by slaves. ホワイトハウスは約 200 年前に主に奴隷によって建てられた ▪Tom was the one to blame, *in large part* because he was the one who hired the consultant. トムが責められるべきだ, 主としてコンサルタントを雇ったのはトムだから ▪His mother was *in small part* responsible for his divorce. 母親が多少は彼の離婚に責任があった.

in part 一部分, いくぶん (↔in (the) WHOLE 1) ▪His success was *in part* owing to luck. 彼の成功はいくぶん運がよかったためだ ▪He reformed the laws *in part.* 彼はその法律を一部分改正した.

in parts 分けて; 一部分ずつ ▪The story appeared *in parts.* その物語は数回に分載された.

in [round] these parts このあたりに, この界わいで ▪I am a stranger *in these parts.* 私はこのあたりは初めてです ▪We don't see many foreigners *round these parts.* この界隈ではあまり外国人は目にしない.

look the part **1** その通りの人物に見える ▪He may not be a teacher, but he certainly *looks the part.* 彼は教師ではないけれど, 確かに教師らしく見える. **2** 《主に英》うってつけに見える ▪Peter has done well in football training and really *looks the part.* ピーターはフットボールの練習で成果をあげ, 本当に適役に思われる.

most part of …の大半 ▪He lives there *most part of* the year. 彼は 1 年の大半をそこで暮らしている ▪*Most part of* them failed. 彼らの大半は失敗した.

not want any part of (計画・提案など)に関わりたくない ▪I *don't want any part of* this scheme. この計画には関わりたくない.

on the one part ... on the other (part) 一方…他方… ▪An agreement was reached between Jones *on the one part* and Brown *on the other.* 一方ジョーンズ他方ブラウンとの間に協定が成立した.

on the part of/on** a person's **part **1** …の方には, としては ▪It was a mistake *on our part.* それは私どもの誤りでした. **2** …のした, による《行為者》 ▪It was a crime *on the part of* the Romans. それはローマ人の犯した罪悪だった ▪It was a kindly thought *on Dr. Leidner's part.* それはライドナー博士の思いやりだった.

part and parcel 身ぐるみ[一切がっさい]抱えて ▪All right, if you won't pay the rent, out with you, *part and parcel!* よろしい, 家賃を払わないのなら出て行ってもらおう, 一切がっさいをまとめて.

part and parcel of …の肝心かなめの部分, 眼目 ▪The invitation to dinner was *part and parcel of* the villain's plans. 夕食に招くことがその悪党の計画の眼目だった. ☞parcel《古》=part.

part of →(a) PART of.

part of the furniture [furnishings] 《口》家具の一部《その存在が気うかれないくらい, 会社・学校などに長くいる人》 ▪The porter at that hospital was *part of the furniture.* あの病院の門衛は家具の一部のごとき存在だった. ☞通例無冠詞.

part ..., part 一つには…で, また一つには ▪His speech was *part* threat, *part* reassurance. 氏の演説は一つには脅しであり, また一つには元気づけであった.

play [act] a part **1** 一役を演じる (*in*) ▪These foreigners have *played a part in* the history. これらの外国人はその国の歴史において一役を演じた. **2** ふうをする, 行動を偽る ▪He was skilled to *act a part* and speak half the truth. 彼はふうを装い, 本当のことを半分しか言わないのが巧みだった.

P

play [***do***] *one's* ***part*** 役割を果たす ▪He *played his part* admirably. 彼は見事に自分の役割を果たした.

play [***act***] ***the part of*** …の役をする ▪He *played the part of* Hamlet. 彼はハムレットの役を演じた ▪He *played the part of* informer at the expense of his fellow-clansmen. 彼は一族の者を犠牲にして密告者となった.

take part in **1** …に加わる, 関与する ▪I *took part in* the debate. 私はその討論に加わった.
2 =take PART of.

take part of …にあずかる ▪Those who saw her were constrained to *take part of* her sorrow. 彼女を見た人々はその悲しみを共にしないわけにいかなかった.

take part with *a person* 人の味方をする ▪Some *took part with* him, some with Carrol. 彼に味方をする者もいれば, キャロルの味方をする者もいた.

take something in good part 《英》 → in good PART.

take the part of *a person* 人の肩をもつ ▪You are a brave boy to *take the part of* a little fellow. 小さい子供の肩をもつなんて君は勇敢な少年だね ▪He *took my part* in a quarrel. 彼はけんかで僕に加勢してくれた.

the better [***best***] ***part of*** …の大半[ほとんど全部] ▪I rode *the best part of* the way. 私は途中大部分馬で行った. ☞形容詞の better [best] は質でなく量を表す.

the greatest part (***of***) →GREAT.

throw *oneself* ***into a part*** 課された義務を喜んで引き受ける ▪Having been appointed to the Chair, Ruth *threw herself into the part* with all her energy. 議長に任命されたので, ルースはその職務に全力で没頭した.

part[2] /pɑːrt/ 動 ***be parted from*** 親しい人[者]から離される ▪*Being parted from* her family made Sue feel homesick. 家族と離れ離れになってスーはホームシックになった.

part brass rags (***with***) →BRASS.

part company **1** 絶交する, 別れる ▪He *parted company* from the vain talker. 彼はそのうぬぼれやの弁士とたもとを分かった.
2 (…と)意見を異にする (*with*) ▪At this point the scientific man is apt to *part company with* the theologian. この点で科学者はえてして神学者と意見を異にするものである.
3 (途中で)別れる (*with*) ▪The two *parted company* and traveled in a different direction. 二人は別れて違った方向に旅した.

part hence/***part out of this life*** あの世へ行く ▪After six months she *parted hence*. 半年後に彼女はみまかった.

partial /pάːrʃəl/ 形 ***be partial to*** **1** …にえこひいきする ▪The teacher *is partial to* pretty women students. あの先生はきれいな女子学生をひいきする.
2 《口》 …が好きだ ▪I *am partial to* duck and green peas. グリンピースをそえたカモ肉には目がない.

particle /pάːrtɪkəl/ 名 ***not a particle of*** みじんの…もない ▪There is *not a particle of* truth in his story. 彼の話には真実味はつめのあかほどもない.

particular /pərtíkjələr|-kjʊ-/ 形名 ***be particular about*** [***as to, in***] …にかけて気むずかしい, 几帳面だ ▪He *is particular about* money matters. 彼は金銭問題については几帳面だ ▪I *am* very *particular* (*as to*) whom I trust. 誰を信用するかということでは私はとても凝ります.

give particulars 詳述する ▪I cannot *give* any *particulars*. 私は詳述することはできません.

go [***enter***] ***into particulars*** 詳細にわたる ▪You need not *go into particulars*. 詳細にわたるに及びません.

in every particular あらゆる点において ▪The statement is correct *in every particular*. その陳述はあらゆる点においてまちがいがない.

in particular 特に (↔in GENERAL 2) ▪He talked about things in general, and his travels *in particular*. 彼は一般的なことをいろいろ話したが, 特に旅行のことを話した ▪I am going nowhere *in particular*. 私は別にどこへも行きません.

parting /pάːrtɪŋ/ 名 ***the*** [***a***] ***parting of the ways*** 道路の分かれ目; 岐路 (《聖》 *Ezek*. 21. 21) ▪Who has not stood doubtful at *the parting of the ways*? 岐路に立って迷わなかった者がどこにいるだろうか.

partner /pάːrtnər/ 名 (*one's*) ***partner***(***s***) ***in crime*** 《戯》 共犯者; 相棒 《おどけた言い方》 ▪I want you guys to do some real work today. Bill, where's your *partner in crime*? 今日はひと仕事してもらいたい. ビル, 仲間はどこだ? ▪They are as much *partners in crime*—buddies, pals—as they are family. かれらは家族であるのと同様, 仲間, ダチ, 共犯者でもある.

sleeping [《米》 ***silent***] ***partner*** 《英》 (出資はするが)業務を担当しない社員 ▪For the rest of his life, B. Franklin was a *silent partner* in the printing business. B•フランクリンは余生を印刷業の匿名社員として過ごした.

sparring partner 議論相手 ▪Jim's my best *sparring partner*. ジムは私の最高の議論仲間だ. ☞ボクシングの sparring partner から.

partnership /pάːrtnərʃìp/ 名 ***enter*** [***go***] ***into partnership with*** …と共同経営をする ▪He has *entered into partnership with* us. 彼は我々と共同経営を始めた.

in partnership with …と合名で; と共同して ▪He is doing business *in partnership with* us. 彼は私たちと共同で商売している.

party /pάːrti/ 名 ***a certain party*** 知っているが名は明かしたくない人, さる人物 ▪I spoke to *a certain party* about the matter you mentioned. 君が言ったことをある人に話してみた.

a Dutch party 参加者がそれぞれ料理•飲み物を持ち寄るパーティー ▪We had *a Dutch party* last Monday to celebrate Labor Day. この前の月曜に労働者の日を祝って料理持ち寄りパーティーを開いた.

a stag party →STAG.

a third party 第三者 ▪ They deposited a sum in the hands of *a third party*. 第三者の手に, ある金額を預けた.

bankroll a party 政党に援助資金を出す ▪ All political *parties are bankrolled* to a certain extent by rich members and unions. 全ての政党は財政豊かな個人や団体からある程度資金援助を受けている.

be (a) party to (悪事など)に関係する, 加担する ▪ He *was a party to* the affair. 彼はその事件に関係した.

bring ... to the party ...に貢献する ▪ As a Harvard M.B.A., the company's new president *brought* significant business experience *to the party*. ハーバード卒の経営学修士として, 新社長は豊富な実務経験でもって会社に貢献した.

coming out party 若い娘の社交界デビューのパーティー ▪ *Coming out parties* used to be more popular in the early twentieth century than nowadays. 社交界へのデビューパーティーは20世紀のはじめは今より盛んであった.

hearty [life and soul] of the party (集団の中で)一番活発で魅力的な人 ▪ No matter how hard she was trying, Helen could not compete with Vanessa, who once more turned out to be the *hearty of the party*. どうあがいたってヘレンはバネッサに太刀打ちできなかった. バネッサはまたもやパーティーの華であることが分かった.

make** one's **party good 自分の主張を通す, 立場を守り通す ▪ Julia has *made her party good* with him. ジュリアは彼に対して自分の立場を守り通した ▪ A man has much ado to *make his party good* against gnats. 人はブヨに対して身を防ぐためには大騒ぎせねばならない.

party animal 《俗》パーティー好きでお酒をたくさん飲む人 ▪ Liz is a real *party animal* but I wish she wouldn't drink so much. リズはパーティー大好き人間だが, あまり飲まなければいいのに.

party line 党路線, (組織・政党の)公式路線 ▪ Tom seldom has an original idea and he keeps faithfully repeating his company's *party line*. トムはめったに独創的なアイディアを出さず, 会社の方針を忠実に反復する.

one's ***[a] party piece*** 《英口》(パーティーでの)十八番(おはこ)の余興 ▪ You haven't done [given] *your party piece* yet. まだ十八番の余興を披露していないよ.

piss on** a person's **party 《英俗》何かをして人の計画を台なしにする ▪ I don't want to *piss on your party* but next week John and I won't be here. パーティーをだめにしたくはないが, ジョンも僕も来週はここにいないんだ.

The party's over. 《口》パーティー[お祭り]は終わった, 楽しいひとときはもうおしまいだ ▪ Now that he's been promoted *the party's over*. 彼は昇進したのだから, 楽しいことはもうおしまい.

throw [give] a party パーティーを催す (*for*) ▪ We'll *throw a* birthday *party for* you. あなたの誕生日のパーティーを開いてあげよう.

pas /pɑː/ 名 ***give [yield] the pas to*** ...に先を譲る, 上席を譲る ▪ Aristotle would have the latter *yield the pas to* the former. アリストテレスなら, 後者よりも前者を上席につかせることだろう. ☞F pas 'step'.

take [have] the pas (of) (...の)上席につく, (に)先んじる ▪ He *took* the *the pas* (*of* dukes). 彼は(公爵たちの)上席についた.

pash /pæʃ/ 名 ***have a pash on*** 《俗》 = have a CRUSH on. ☞pash<passion.

pass[1] /pæs|pɑːs/ 名 ***a fine [nice, pretty] pass*** 困ったこと ▪ This is *a pretty pass*. これは困ったことだ.

bring ... to pass ...をなし遂げる; を生じさせる ▪ Faith and sanctity *are brought to pass* by education. 信仰と高潔とは教育によってなし遂げられるものである ▪ He will *bring* huge wonders *to pass*. 彼は大いなる驚異をもたらすだろう.

come to a pretty [nice, fine] pass/come to such a pass 《戯》困ったことになる; 《米・婉曲》大変なことになる ▪ Things have *come to a pretty pass* when a husband has to ask his wife for sixpence! 夫が女房に6ペンス貸してくれと頼まねばならないとは, 困ったことになったものだ ▪ Things have *come to such a pass*. 事態はたいへん困ったことになった.

come to pass (事が)起こる; (予想などが)実現する ▪ No one knows for sure how the accident *came to pass*. その事件がどういうふうに起こったか, 誰もはっきりとは知らない ▪ What the prophet foretold did not *come to pass*. その予言者の予言したことは実現しなかった.

come to this pass こういう事態になる ▪ That things should have *come to this pass*! こうした事態になろうとは.

head [cut]** a person **off at the pass 《口》他に先んずる, (人の)機先を制す ▪ Bill is going to the boss's office—let's *head* him *off at the pass*. ビルが社長室に行こうとしている. 先回りして阻止しよう.

it comes to pass that ...ということになる ▪ And *it came to pass* after these things *that* God did tempt Abraham. これらのことのあとで, 神はアブラハムを試されることになった (《聖》*Gen.* 22. 1). ☞聖書語法.

make a pass at **1** 《フェンシング》(剣で)...に突きかかる ▪ He drew his sword and *made a pass at* John. 彼は剣を抜いてジョンに突きかかった.

2 ...を手で突く[にかみつく]ようなふりをする ▪ The dog *made a pass at* the man. 犬は男にかみつくそぶりをした.

3 《俗》(女)に言い寄る ▪ I never *made a pass at* Sally. サリーに言い寄ったことは一度もない ▪ Men seldom *make passes at* girls who wear glasses. 男はめがねをかけた娘にはめったに言い寄らない.

4 《口》やってみる, ためしてみる ⟦take a pass at ともいう]] ▪ I've *made a pass at* opening it. それを開けてみようとした ▪ Will you *take a pass at* changing the oil? オイルを換えてみてくれないか. ☞pass「フェンシングの突き」.

pass[2] /pæs|pɑːs/ 名 ***hold* [*keep*] *the pass*** 主義・利益を守る ▪ They would be able to *keep the pass*. 彼らは主義を守ることができるだろう ▪ They *held the pass* of the laborer. 彼らは労働者の利益を守った. ☞「他国へ入る山道を守る」が原義.

sell the pass 主義を売る[にそむく] ▪ I wouldn't *sell the pass* for a thousand pounds. 僕は1,000ポンドもらっても主義は売らないぞ.

pass[3] /pæs|pɑːs/ 動 ***let ... pass*** …を大目に見る ▪ I don't like it, but I'll *let* it *pass*. これは好かないが, 大目に見よう.

pass a remark **1** 一言言う ▪ He *passed a remark* about the weather. 彼は天気について一言言った.
2 けなすようなことを言う ▪ He *passed a remark* about Bill's religious affiliations. 彼はビルの宗教関係をけなすようなことを言った.

pass by on the other side 困っている人を助けようとしない ▪ When I learned that my sister was in difficulties, I could not *pass by on the other side*. 妹が困っていることを知ったとき, 知らぬ顔をしていることはできなかった. ☞《聖》*Luke* 10. 30-35にある「よきサマリア人」の話から.

pass one's eyes over …にざっと目を通す ▪ He *passed his eyes over* the letter. 彼は手紙にざっと目を通した.

pass from among us 死ぬ ▪ There *passed from among us* a man who held a high position in English literature. 英文学において高い地位を占めていた人物が亡くなってしまった.

pass hence →go HENCE.

pass in one's checks 《俗》死ぬ ▪ I see that young John has *passed in his checks*. どうやらジョン青年も死んでしまったと見える.

pass ... in review **1**《軍》…を閲兵する, 分列式を行わせる ▪ The general *passed* the army *in review*. 将軍は軍隊を閲兵した.
2 …を検閲[検討]する ▪ Their works might also *be passed in review*. 彼らの著作も検閲してもよい ▪ We will *pass in review* these conditions. これらの条件を検討してみよう.
3 …を次々と回想する ▪ He *passed* his life *in review*. 彼は自分の一生を回想した.

***pass the buck* (*to*)** →BUCK[2].

pass the chair (議長・会長・市長などの)任期を終える ▪ The mayor has *passed the chair*. 市長は任期を終えた.

pass* [《口》*make up*] *the hat →HAT.

passage /pǽsɪdʒ/ 名 ***a bird of passage*** →BIRD.

a passage of* [*at*] *arms なぐり合い, けんか; 口論; 痴話げんか ▪ Luther had not forgotten his early *passage at arms* with the English King. ルターは以前のイギリス王との論争を忘れていなかった ▪ We don't want *a passage of arms* over this matter. この件についてけんかはしたくない.

***book one's passage* (*to*)** (…までの)乗船券を買う ▪ He *booked his passage to* Lisbon. 彼はリスボンまでの乗船券を買った.

force* [*fight*] *a passage through …を押し分けて進む ▪ He *forced a passage through* the crowd. 彼は人ごみを押し分けて進んだ.

give ... a rough* [*smooth*] *passage …に対して海が荒れる[静かである]; に骨を折らせる[折らせない] ▪ The storm *gave* the boat *a rough passage*. そのあらしで船の航海は楽ではなかった ▪ The bill *was given a smooth passage* through the Lower House. 法案は下院を楽に通過した.

***have angry passages* (*with*)** (…と)口論する ▪ She *had angry passages with* her husband. 彼女は夫と口論した.

work one's passage 働いて船賃を稼ぐ ▪ He *worked his passage* to England as a cabin boy. 彼は船賃代わりに船室ボーイとして働いて英国へ渡った.

passing /pǽsɪŋ|pɑ́ːs-/ 名 ***in passing*** ついでに, ちなみに ▪ It may be remarked *in passing* that his story was untrue. ついでに言わせてもらえれば, 彼の話は本当ではなかった. ☞F en passant のなぞり.

passion /pǽʃən/ 名 ***be one's passion*** …は大好きなものである (↔ be one's ABHORRENCE) ▪ Pictures *are his* sole *passion*. 彼は絵だけが大好きだ.

break* [*burst*] *into a passion 急にかっとなる, 急に怒りだす ▪ He *broke into a* violent *passion* and threw a book at my head. 彼は激しく怒りだして私の頭に本を投げつけた ▪ She suddenly *burst into a passion* of crying. 彼女は不意にわっと泣きだした.

fall* [*get*] *into a passion かんしゃくを起こす, かっとなる ▪ He *got into a* violent *passion*. 彼はひどくかんしゃくを起こした.

fly into a passion 急にかっと怒りだす ▪ At this the woman *flew into a passion*. これを聞くとその女性は急にかっと怒りだした.

have a passion for …が大好きだ ▪ He *has a passion for* fishing. 彼は魚釣りが大好きだ.

in a passion かんしゃくを起こして, かっとなって ▪ He struck me *in a passion*. 彼はかっとなって私をなぐった.

put a person in a passion 人をかっと怒らせる ▪ This *put* the woman *in a passion*. これでその女性はかっとなった.

ruling* [*master*] *passion 主情, ひたむきの感情 ▪ Collecting curios is the *master passion* with him. 骨とう収集は彼の道楽だ.

the tender passion →TENDER[2].

passport /pǽspɔːrt|pɑ́ːs-/ 名 ***be the passport to*** …に必ず入っていける ▪ Flattery *is the* sole *passport to* his favor. 彼に取り入るにはへつらう

ほかない.

past /pæst|pɑːst/ 形名前 ***be* [*look*] *past it*/ *be getting past it*** 《英口》以前していたことができなくなっている, 年取っている, くたびれている ▪ I don't dance any more. I *am past it*. 私はもうダンスはしない. もう年だ ▪ The car we've got at the moment *is getting* a bit *past it*. 今持っている車は少しがたがきている.

be past praying for 《口》 **1** (人が)とても改心の見込みがない ▪ The man is a brutal murderer; he *is past praying for*. その男は残忍な人殺しだ. とても改心の見込みはない.
2 (物が)とても直る見込みがない ▪ The old shoes *were past praying for*. その古靴はとても直せる見込みがなかった.

cannot undo the past 過去のことは取り返しがつかない ▪ Let us think of the future as we *cannot undo the past*. 過去のことは取り返しがつかないのだから, 将来のことを考えよう.

get* [*go*] *past caring …を気にしなくなる ▪ I've *got past caring* about clothes. 服装のことは気にしなくなった.

not put it past *a person* 《口》人があることをやりかねないと思う (*to do, that*) ▪ I would*n't put it past* him even *to* knock at the front door. あの男なら玄関の戸をノックしかねないと思う ▪ I would*n't put it past* him *that* he had kicked old Jerry on purpose! あの男ならジェリー爺さんをわざとけったということもありかねないと思う.

past *a person* ***to*** *do* 《口》…するのは人の力に余る ▪ It's *past* parsons *to* console us. 我々を慰めることは牧師にはとてもできない.

with a past (いかがわしい)過去のある ▪ I prefer a woman *with a past*. 僕は過去のある女のほうがいい.

paste /peɪst/ 名 ***scissors and paste*** →SCISSORS.

pasting /péɪstɪŋ/ 名 ***give* [*get*] *a pasting*** 《主に英口》人をぼこぼこにやっつける[やられる]; 酷評する[される] ▪ The Republicans *got a* real *pasting* at the local elections. 共和党は地方選挙で惨敗した ▪ He *gave* me *a* real *pasting* for handing in my paper a week late. レポート提出が1週間遅れて彼にこっぴどく言われた.

pasture /pǽstʃər|pάːs-/ 名 ***pastures new* [*fresh, greener*]** / 《米》***new* [*fresh, greener*] *pastures*** 《英》新しく違った状況, (特に)よりよい仕事, 青く見える隣の芝生 ▪ Mike decided he wanted to move on to *pastures new* for financial reasons. マイクは経済的な理由から新しい環境に移ることに決めた. ☞Milton "fresh woods, and pastures new" (*Lycidas* (1637))から.

put* [*turn, send*]*...* (*out*) *to pasture = put (out)...to GRASS.

pat[1] /pæt/ 名 ***give* [*get, receive, deserve*] *a pat on the back*** ほめる[ほめられる] (*for*) ▪ The General *gave* the soldiers *a* verbal *pat on the back*. 将軍は兵士をほめたたえた ▪ Students at the school have *received an* official *pat on the back for* achieving a high academic standard. その学校の生徒たちは勉学で高水準を達成したので公式にほめられた.

pat[2] /pæt/ 形副 ***come* [*fall*] *pat*** (…に)ぴったりと合う (*to*) ▪ It will *fall pat* as I told you. それは僕の言った通りになるだろう ▪ The dancer's feet *fell pat to* the music. 踊り子の足は音楽にぴったり合った.

get* [*know, have, learn*]*... off pat …をすっかり暗記する ▪ He *got* a New York accent *off pat* for the role. 彼はその役を演じるためにニューヨークなまりをものにした.

have* [*know, learn*]*... down pat 《米》…をすっかり知っている, 暗記している ▪ Everyone except Tim *had* his part *down pat*. ティムの他は誰も自分の役割をすっかり心得ていた.

stand pat 《米》 **1** (ポーカーなどで)初手を変えない ▪ He *stood pat* because he'd already got a good hand. もうよい手がきていたので彼は初めに配られたカードを変えなかった.
2 (主張・意見などを)固守する, まげない (*on*) ▪ The newspaper *stood pat on* its stated policy. その新聞は既述のポリシーを固守した.

pat[3] /pæt/ 動 ***pat*** *a person* ***on the back*** (激励・称賛のため)人の背中をポンとたたく ▪ I *patted* him *on the back*, and told him what a priceless fellow he was. 私は彼の背中をポンとたたいて, とてもすばらしいやつだと言った.

pat *oneself* ***on the back*** 自分で自分をほめる, 自画自賛する ▪ He *patted himself on the back* for having done it. 彼はそれをやったので一人悦に入った.

patch /pætʃ/ 名 ***be a cross patch*** ひどく怒りっぽい ▪ The old servant *was a cross patch*. その年取った使用人はすぐに腹を立てた.

be not a patch on 《英口》…の足もとへも寄りつけない ▪ He *is not a patch on* you for looks. 彼は容貌では君の足もとにも及ばない.

go through* [*hit*] *a bad* [*difficult, rough, sticky*] *patch (多くの問題を抱えて)つらい時期を経験する ▪ One of Tom's strengths as a manager has been his ability to calm the team when they *hit a rough patch*. トムの管理者としての強みの一つは不運なときに仲間を落ち着かせる力であった.

in patches 所々 ▪ This poem is good *in patches*. この詩は所々いいところがある.

lay a patch =burn RUBBER 1.

strike* [*have*] *a bad patch 《英口》不運な目にあう, 芽が出ない ▪ They *had a* month's *bad patch*. 彼らは1か月間芽が出なかった.

patching /pǽtʃɪŋ/ 名 ***not a patching to*** 《米口》…とは比べものにならない《ひどく劣っている》 ▪ Your dog is*n't a patching to* mine. 君の犬は僕のとは比べものにならない.

smell the patching 《米口》危険の迫っているのに感づく ▪ It finally made the federal party *smell the patching*. それでついに連邦党は危険の迫っているのに気づいた.

P

patent /pǽtənt|péɪt-/ 名 ***take*** (***out***) [***get***] ***a patent*** 特許を取る ▪ He *took out a patent* for his new invention. 彼は新発明の特許を取った.

paternal /pətə́:rnəl/ 形 ***be related on the paternal side*** 父方の親類である ▪ He and I *are related on the paternal side*. 彼と私は父方の親類同士だ.

paternoster /pǽtərnɑ́stər|-nɔ́st-/ 名 ***say an ape's paternoster*** →APE[1].

the devil's paternoster ぶつぶつ祈る言葉; ぶつぶつ独り言を言うこと ▪ He was pattering *the devil's paternoster* to himself. 彼は早口にぶつぶつ独り言を言っていた.

path /pæθ|pɑ:θ/ 名 ***beat a path to*** *a person's* ***door*** (有名な)人の所に大勢で押しかける, 殺到する ▪ The writer has become so famous that all the newspaper reporters in the city are *beating a path to his door*. その作家は非常に有名になったので, その市のすべての新聞記者で門前は市をなしている.

cross *a person's* ***path*** **1** 人に偶然出会う ▪ Surprisingly, I *crossed Jack's path* in Hibiya Park one afternoon. 驚いたことに, ある日の午後日比谷公園でジャックにばったり会った.
2 人に出会う, 人とかかり合う; 人の前を横切る[行く手のじゃまをする]; 人の計画などを妨害する ▪ I hope I shall never *cross his path* again. 二度と彼に出会わないだろうと思う ▪ Let him again *cross my path* at his peril. もう一度あいつが私の行く手をじゃましてみろ, ただではおかぬぞ ▪ *His path was crossed* by a woman. 彼の生涯はある女性によって妨げられた.

cross paths with *a person* 偶然出会う, ひょっこり出くわす ▪ Martin was surprised to *cross paths with* a childhood friend in London. マーティンはロンドンで昔なじみとばったり出会ってびっくりした.

one's ***paths cross*** (偶然)出会う ▪ Goodbye. I hope *our paths cross* again soon. さようなら, またお会いできますように.

the beaten path →the BEATEN track.

patience /péɪʃəns/ 名 ***be out of patience with*** …に愛想を尽かす ▪ I *am out of patience with* him. あの男には愛想が尽きた ▪ He *was out of* all *patience with* himself. 彼は自分自身にほとほと愛想を尽かした.

have no patience with 《口》…にはがまんがならない ▪ I *have no patience with* the Colonel. あの大佐にはがまんがならない.

Have patience! 辛抱しなさい ▪ *Have patience* for another day or two. もう一両日辛抱してくれ.

lose patience がまんができなくなる (*with*) ▪ I *lost* all *patience with* him. あの男には全くがまんできなくなった.

My patience! 《口》おやおや! これはしたり! 《驚きの叫び》 ▪ *My patience*, that beats me*!* おやおや, これには閉口した.

Patience is a virtue. 《諺》忍耐は美徳である, 「堪忍は身の宝」.

put *a person* ***out of patience*** 人を怒らせる ▪ That *put* him *out of patience*. それで彼は勘忍袋の緒を切らした.

the patience of Job [***a saint***] ヨブ[聖人]のような強靭な忍耐力 ▪ You need *the patience of a saint* to be a kindergarten teacher. 幼稚園の先生になるには大変な忍耐力がいる. ☞Job は聖書に登場する人物; 家族, 家, 財産, 健康を失うという絶望の中でなお神を見捨てなかった.

try *a person's* ***patience*** 人を(がまんできないほど)いらいらさせる ▪ Little Teddy's constant bombarding me with "why?" "why?" "why?" and more "whys," really *tried my patience*. テディー坊やの矢継ぎ早の「どうして」の質問攻めには本当に閉口した ▪ His wife's constant complaining was beginning to *try his patience*. 妻に始終愚痴を言われて彼のいらいらも限界に達しかけていた.

try [***provoke***] ***the patience of Job*** どんな忍耐強い人をも怒らせる (→enough to provoke a SAINT) ▪ You are enough to *try the patience of Job*. あなたはどんな忍耐強い人でも怒らせるに十分だ.

wear *a person's* ***patience threadbare*** [***thin***] 忍耐がすり減る[尽きる] ▪ After two months, Dennis has *worn my patience threadbare*. 2か月経ち, デニスには私の我慢も限界に達した.

patient[1] /péɪʃənt/ 名 ***a heartsick patient*** 医師に突き止められない病気を抱えた患者, 心の病の患者 ▪ I no longer saw her as *a heartsick patient*. もはや彼女を心を病んだ患者とはみなさなかった.

patient[2] /péɪʃənt/ 形 (***as***) ***patient as Job*** [《米》 ***Job's cat***] (ヨブのように)きわめて辛抱[忍耐]強い ▪ Still, she waited, *patient as Job*. それでも彼女は非常に忍耐強く待った ▪ You must be *as patient as Job* when teaching young children. 幼児を教えるときにはきわめて忍耐強くなければならない.

patient of **1** …に耐える ▪ Sailors are *patient of* hardships. 水夫は難儀に耐える.
2 …を許す ▪ The fact is *patient of* two interpretations. その事実は二つの解釈を許す[二様に解釈できる].

patient with …に対してがまん強い ▪ He is *patient with* others. 彼は他人に対してがまん強い.

patriotism /péɪtriətìzəm|pǽtri-/ 名 ***Patriotism is not enough.*** 《諺》愛国心だけでは足りない《1915年に負傷した捕虜を逃がしたかどで処刑される前に英国の看護師 Edith Cavell が言った言葉》.

Patriotism is the last refuge of a scoundrel. 国のためと言うのは悪党の最後の逃げ口上である (Boswell, *Life of Dr. Johnson*).

patrol /pətróʊl/ 名 ***on patrol*** 巡回中; 哨戒中 ▪ Police were *on* a twenty-four-hour *patrol*. 警官たちは24時間巡回をやっていた.

patronage /pǽtrənɪdʒ/ 名 ***have patronage in*** *one's* ***hands*** 任用権を握っている ▪ He *has* a great deal of *patronage in his hands*. 彼は絶大な任用権を握っている.

take away *one's* ***patronage*** (商店への)ひいきをやめる ▪ He *took away his patronage* because of poor service. サービスが悪いので彼は(その店の)ひいきをやめた.

under the patronage of …の保護の下に; …御用達で ▪ The art flourished *under the patronage of* the family. その芸術はその一家の保護の下に栄えた ▪ It is *under the patronage of* the Imperial Household. それは宮内省御用達だ.

patter /pǽtər/ 名 ***the patter of little [tiny] feet*** 《口》《戯》ぱたぱた走る子供 (Longfellow, *The Children's Hour*); (生まれてくる)赤んぼう ▪ She's yearning for *the patter of little feet*. 彼女は子供をほしがっている.

Paul /pɔːl/ 名 ***a Paul Pry*** 詮索好きな人 ▪ Some of the *Paul Prys* of the parish were present. 教区の詮索好きな連中の幾人かは出席していた. ☞Paul Pry は John Poole の同名の喜劇(1825)の主人公; "I hope I don't intrude!" を連発しながら人のことを聞きほじくる.

rob Peter to pay Paul →PETER.

pause /pɔːz/ 名 ***give*** (*a person*) ***pause*** (***for thought***) (人に)再考を促す, ちゅうちょさせる ▪ The orphan's remark *gave* us all *pause for thought*. その孤児の言葉に我々はみな再考を促された ▪ What *gives* me *pause* is the thought of the poor girl. 私が迷うのはあの哀れな娘のことを考えるからだ.

in [at] (a) pause 中止して, じっとして; ちゅうちょして ▪ All nature was *in a pause*. ものみなは静止していた ▪ You stand there *at pause*, and silent. 君はそこにじっとして黙って立っていろ.

make a pause 休止する, 立ち止まる ▪ He *made a pause* on the brink of the precipice. 彼は断崖のふちで立ち止まった.

put ... to a pause …をとどまらせる, ちゅうちょさせる ▪ These considerations *put* me *to a pause*. こうした考えが私をちゅうちょさせた.

pave /peɪv/ 動 ***pave the way for [to]*** …の道を開く; を容易にする, に至る ▪ One lie always *paved the way for* another. 一つ嘘を言うと, いつでも次の嘘をつくこととなった ▪ I believe this treaty will *pave the way to* peace in Europe. この条約はヨーロッパの平和への道を開いてくれると信じる.

pavement /péɪvmənt/ 名 ***on the pavement*** 通りを歩いて; 宿なしで, 捨てられて ▪ They were suffered to starve *on the pavement*. 彼らは宿なしで飢え死にするがままにされた ▪ I was left completely *on the pavement*. 私はすっかり打ち捨てられたままだった. ☞F sur le pavé 'on the street'.

pound [hit] the pavement (職を探して)歩き回る ▪ Jack *pounded the pavement* looking for a job. ジャックは職を求めて街を歩き回った.

paw /pɔː/ 名 ***give one's paw*** 《口》(人と)握手する ▪ *Give* me *your paw*, old fellow. 握手してくれよ, 君.

pawn[1] /pɔːn/ 名 ***only a pawn*** (***in the game***) 強力な他者に操られる非常に無力な人物 ▪ I was *only a pawn* on their chessboard. 彼らの土俵の上では私は使い捨ての身であった. ☞pawn はチェスで一番弱いこまで, 将棋の歩に相当する.

pawn[2] /pɔːn/ 名 ***at [in, to] pawn*** 質に入って, かたに取られて ▪ Her jewels are *at* [*in*] *pawn* for money. 彼女の宝石類は金に替えて質に入っている.

give [put] in pawn …を質に入れる, かたに入れる ▪ He *put* a watch *in pawn*. 彼は時計を質に入れた ▪ He *gives* his veracity *in pawn* to see it fully performed. 彼はそれが完全に行われることに誠実を賭けている.

pay[1] /peɪ/ 名 ***back pay*** 未払いの給料[賃金] ▪ They owe me hundreds of dollars in *back pay*. 彼らは私にまだ何百ドルもの給料を払っていない.

be good [excellent] pay **1**《口》(借金の)払いがよい ▪ He *is good pay*. 彼は払いがよい.
2 儲けになる ▪ Great men *are good pay* in the long run. 偉い人間は結局は儲けになる.

in [《米》on] pay 給料をもらって (↔out of PAY) ▪ His men were *in pay*. 彼の部下は給料をもらっていた ▪ He had a month's vacation *on pay*. 彼は1か月の有給休暇をもらった.

in the pay of *a person* (給料をもらって)人に雇われて《しばしば不名誉の意味を含む》 ▪ The murderer was *in the pay of* Sparta. その殺し屋はスパルタに雇われていた ▪ He has six men *in his pay*. 彼は給料を払って6人雇っている.

out of pay 給料をもらっていない (↔in PAY) ▪ When they were *out of pay*, they looked upon themselves as their own masters. 彼らは給料をもらっていないときには, 一本立ちしたのだと思った.

strike [hit] pay dirt [gravel] 《米口》金づるをつかむ, 掘り出し物にありつく ▪ When he invested in that property in Texas, he really *struck pay dirt*. 彼がテキサス州のあの地所に投資したとき, ほんとうに金づるをつかんだのだ ▪ They finally *hit pay dirt* in the Library of Congress. ついに米国議会図書館で掘り出し物[新事実]を見つけた. ☞"pay dirt" は探すだけの価値のある金脈が含有されている土地を指す.

without pay 無報酬で[の], 名誉的な ▪ He is working *without pay*. 彼は無給で働いている.

pay[2] /peɪ/ 動 ***it*** (***always [never]***) ***pays to*** *do* …するのは引き合う[割に合わない] ▪ *It pays to* advertise. 広告するのは損にならない ▪ *It always pays to* get professional advice. 専門的な助言をもらえることはいつも役立つ ▪ *It never pays to* cheat in exams because you will always be discovered eventually. 試験中にカンニングをすることは割に合わない, いつも結局見つかるのだから.

pay as you go (信用貸しなどせずに)現金払いでやっていく ▪ *Pay as you go* is the truest economy. 現金払いでやっていくのが一番本当に経済的だ.

pay *a person* (***back***) ***in his own coin*** → COIN[1].

pay dearly [heavily] for …で高くつく, ひどい目にあう ▪ You shall *pay dearly for* your insolence. 無礼なまねをするとひどい目にあわせてやるぞ.

pay one's dues 苦労して(今の地位)を築く ▪ Daisy had *paid her dues* in small-town shows before

P

she finally got a Broadway part. デイジーは場末のショーで下積みの苦労をしてついにブロードウェイでの役を獲得した.

pay for itself 採算が合う, 元が取れる, 割りが合う ▪ With the tax rebates, a solar roof will *pay for itself* in five to seven years. 税金が戻ってくるので, 太陽光発電は5年から7年で元が取れます.

pay home 《古》…に存分に復しゅうする ▪ If any man comes near her, she *pays* him *home*. 男がそばに来ると彼女は存分に復しゅうする.

pay in trade 《米口》商売で支払う《雇い主が給料を払わずにいろいろな店で必要品を安く買えるように取引をしておくと言って雇い人をごまかすこと》 ▪ "*Paying in trade*" often worked to the disadvantage of the workman. 「商売払い」はしばしば労働者に不利をもたらした.

pay lip service to →LIP SERVICE.

pay off an old score [***old scores***] 古い恨みを晴らす ▪ It was time to *pay off old scores* against him. あの男への古い恨みを晴らす時機だった.

pay *one's* (***own***) ***way*** **1** 借金しないでやっていく ▪ He *pays his way* as he goes. 彼は借金しないでやっていっている ▪ The school *pays its own way*. その学校は収支償っている.

2 (機械などが)元が取れて儲かる, 投資に見合う利益をあげる ▪ Their new toll bridge will *pay its way* by next year. 彼らの新しい有料橋は来年までには元が取れるようになるだろう.

pay the debt of nature →DEBT.

pay the piper →PIPER.

pay the price 報いを受ける ▪ In the long run we all have to *pay the price* of our follies. とどのつまりは我々はみな自分の愚行の報いを受けねばならない.

pay through the nose →NOSE[1].

pay *a person's* ***way*** 人の費用を持ってやる ▪ Mom offered to *pay my way* if I went to Spain with her. 母はいっしょにスペインに行ってくれるのなら費用を持とうと言った.

put paid to 《英口》…にけりをつける ▪ The new currency restrictions have *put paid to* our hopes of a Continental holiday this year. 今度の通貨制限で今年はヨーロッパで休日を過ごす夢がおじゃんになってしまった.

Something is to pay. 《米口》どこか具合の悪い[変な]ところがある ▪ *Something is to pay*; that girl acted queer. どこか変なところがある. その少女は妙なふるまいをした.

What is to pay? 《米口》どうしたのか ▪ "*What*, then, *is to pay?*" urged his mother earnestly. 「じゃあ, どうしたの?」と彼の母親は熱心な口調で促した.

payment /péɪmənt/ 名 ***in payment for*** …の報酬として ▪ He was not willing to take goods *in payment for* his services. 彼は奉仕の報酬として品物を受け取りたがらなかった.

stop payment →STOP[2].

suspend payment →SUSPEND.

payroll /péɪròʊl/ 名 ***on*** [***off***] ***the payroll of*** …に雇われて[を首になって] ▪ He has been *off Radio's payroll* ever since. 彼はその後放送局を首になっている ▪ I want to take him *on our payroll*. 彼を当社に雇いたい.

pea /piː/ 名 (***as***) ***like*** [***alike***] ***as two peas*** (***in a pod***) ウリ二つで ▪ His son is *as like* him *as two peas*. 彼の息子は彼とウリ二つだ ▪ The sisters were *as like as two peas*. その姉妹はウリ二つだった.

the last of pea time(***s***) 《米口》最後の段階, 命の終わり ▪ What's the matter with you? You look like *the last of pea times*. どうしたのかね. まるでこれでおさらばだという顔つきじゃないか.

peace /piːs/ 名 ***at peace*** **1** 仲よく, 平和に (*with*) (↔at WAR (with)) ▪ We are nominally *at peace with* the country. 我々はその国と表面上は平和状態にある.

2 安らかに, 静かで ▪ Neither heaven nor earth has been *at peace* tonight. 今夜は天も地も静かでなかった.

be [***feel***] ***at peace with the world*** (生活に満足して)心に平安を感じて ▪ Sitting on the terrace and looking out over the flower garden, she *felt at peace with the world*. テラスに腰掛けて花壇を見渡しながら, 彼女は心の平安を感じていた.

be sworn of the peace 治安判事に任命される ▪ I *am sworn of the peace*. 私は治安判事に任命されました.

bind (***over***) ***to*** (***keep***) ***the peace*** 公安を害さないように誓わせる ▪ The wrongdoer *was bound over to keep the peace*. その非行者は公安を害さないように誓わされた ▪ I'll have him *bound to the peace* instantly. あの男にすぐ謹慎を誓わせよう.

break [***disturb***] ***the peace*** 治安を乱す ▪ The man threatens to *disturb the* public *peace*. その男は公安を乱す恐れがある.

go in peace 放免される ▪ Let him *go in peace*. 彼を放免してやれ.

have peace 静かにしている ▪ Do let me *have* a little *peace*. 頼むから私を少しそっとしておいてくれ.

hold *one's* ***peace*** 沈黙を守る ▪ *Hold your peace* when a wise man is speaking. 賢い人が話をしているときには黙っていなさい.

If you want peace, (***you must***) ***prepare for war.*** 《諺》平和を欲するなら戦備を整えよ,「備えあれば憂いなし」. ☞ある国の軍備が万全なら, 敵は容易には攻めてこない, の意.

in peace 平和に, 静かに, 黙って ▪ Leave me *in peace*. 私をそっとしておいてください ▪ He died *in peace*. 彼は安らかに死んだ.

keep the peace 公安を維持する; 争いの起こらないようにする ▪ *Keep the peace* between the dog and the bear. 犬とクマとの間に争いの起こらないようにせよ.

make peace 和解する, 講和する, 仲直りさせる ▪ We persuaded the combatants to *make peace*. 我々は戦闘員らに和睦を勧めた ▪ He will *make peace* with me. あの男は僕と仲直りするだろう

▪ *Make peace* between them. 二人を仲直りさせてください.

make** a person's **peace 人を仲直りさせる (*with*) ▪ I will *make your peace with* him, if I can. できれば彼と仲直りさせてあげましょう.

make** one's **peace 仲直りする, 親しくなる (*with*) ▪ He had *made his peace with* the king. 彼は王と仲直りしていた ▪ They have *made their peace with* God. 彼らは神と親しくなった.

one's (***own***) ***peace of mind*** 心の安らぎ ▪ He confessed his theft for *his own peace of mind*. 彼は心の安らぎを得るために盗みを自白した.

peace and goodwill 平和と善意 (《聖》*Luke* 2. 14) ▪ Christmas is the season of *peace and goodwill*. クリスマスは平和と善意の季節である.

peace and quiet (騒音・けんかの後の)安らぎと静けさ ▪ Let's have a bit of *peace and quiet* instead of quarrelling. けんかをやめて, 少しほっと静かにしよう.

peace at any price 絶対平和(主義) ▪ He wanted to purchase *peace at any price*. 彼は何を犠牲にしても平和がほしいと思った.

Peace be with** a person**! 人の安らかならんことを; 人の無事を祈る (《聖》*John* 20. 19) ▪ *Peace be with* her. She is dead. 彼女の安らかならんことを. もう亡くなってしまった ▪ Farewell! And *peace be with* you. さようなら! 君のご無事を祈ります.

peace dividend (政府が武器調達を止めて貯めた)平和のための配当金 ▪ The child-support programs should benefit from the *peace dividend*. 子育て支援計画は平和の配当金で援助されるべきだ.

peace of mind 心の平静 ▪ He found *peace of mind* in the last few weeks of his life. 人生の最晩年の数週間に彼は心の平安を感じた.

peace offering (特にけんかのあとの)和睦のための贈物 ▪ He took Liz some flowers as a *peace offering*. 彼はリズに和解のための贈物として花束を持参した.

Peace to** a person's **ashes [***memory, soul***]***!*** 願わくは人の霊安からんことを ▪ Rare Ben Jonson! Long *peace to thy ashes!* 類いまれなるベン・ジョンスンよ, なんじの霊のいつまでも安からんことを.

peace with honor (双方とも体面を汚さない)名誉ある平和[和睦] ▪ The people continued to enjoy *peace with honor*. 人民は依然として名誉ある平和を享受した.

***swear the peace against** a person* (ある人に危害を加えられる恐れがあるので)その人を謹慎させてもらいたいと宣誓する ▪ They may *swear the peace against* us. あの連中は我々を謹慎させてもらいたいと宣誓するかもしれない.

peach /piːtʃ/ 名 ***a peach of a ...*** すばらしい… ▪ She is *a peach of a* cook. 彼女は料理が見事だ.

peaches and cream **1** (少女の顔色の)うすもも色 ▪ Nothing could be more delightful than the *peaches and cream* complexion of young English girls. 若いイギリス娘のうすもも色の顔色くらい見て楽しいものはない.
2 《俗》いい[楽しい]ことずくめ ▪ Life isn't all *peaches and cream*. 人生は楽しいことずくめではない.

peacock /píːkɑ̀k|-kɔ̀k/ 名 ***a peacock in his pride*** →in one's PRIDE.

(***as***) ***proud as a peacock*** これ見よがしにいばって[得意になって] ▪ The fellow is *proud as a peacock* because his vegetable marrow took first prize at the show. あいつは自分のペポカボチャが共進会で1等になったものだから, これ見よがしにいばっている.

play the peacock 得意顔にふるまう ▪ Don't *play the peacock*, looking everywhere about you. あちこち見回して得意顔にふるまうものではない.

peak[1] /piːk/ 名 ***at the peak*** 絶頂で ▪ Prices are *at the peak*. 物価は今が絶頂期だ.

past** one's **peak 盛りを過ぎた ▪ He used to be a terrific baseball player but we're afraid he is *past his peak*. 彼はその昔はすごい野球選手だったが, もう盛りが過ぎたな.

peak[2] /piːk/ 動 ***peak and pine*** (恋わずらいなどで)うつうつとして日を送る (cf. Sh., *Macb*. 1. 3. 23) ▪ She died after *peaking and pining* away twelve or fourteen years of her best-looking days. 彼女は一番器量のよい時代を12年か14年かうつうつとして過ごしたあげく亡くなった. ☞この句では特に pine の意味を強調している.

peal /piːl/ 名 ***in peal*** (鐘声が)調子を合わせて ▪ The bells of the churches rang *in peal*. 教会の鐘が調子を合わせて鳴った.

peanut /píːnʌ̀t/ 名 ***If you pay peanuts, you get monkeys.*** 《英口》低賃金では優秀なスタッフは雇えない ▪ We have no hope of attracting the best applicants; *if you pay peanuts, you get monkeys*. 優秀な応募者は来てくれそうもない; 安月給ではよい人材は雇えない. ☞peanuts「少額の金」.

pearl /pəːrl/ 名 ***a pearl of great price*** 非常に価値あるもの (《聖》*Matt*. 13. 46) ▪ In their virginity girls possess *a pearl of great price*. 少女には処女性という非常に価値あるものがある.

a pearl of wisdom 《皮肉・戯》ごもっともな意見 ▪ Never be afraid of failure; just be afraid of not trying.—Another *pearl of wisdom*. 失敗を恐れちゃだめだ. 何もしようとしないことを恐れよ—全くごもっともな意見です.

cast [***throw***] (*one's*) ***pearls before swine*** ブタに真珠を投げ与える,「猫に小判」(《聖》*Matt*. 7. 6) ▪ Give them the advice if you like. It will only be *casting pearls before swine*. なんならあの連中にその忠告をしてやってごらん.「猫に小判」ということになるのが落ちだよ.

pearls of wisdom 類(たぐ)いまれな英知・体験から生まれた言葉, 文殊の知恵 ▪ If you listen to his comments attentively, you may catch some *pearls of wisdom*. 注意して彼のコメントに耳を傾けると, いろいろと賢明な忠告が聞けるかもしれないよ.

pear-shaped /péərʃèɪpt/ 形 ***go pear-shaped*** 《英口》事態が狂い始める, まずいことが起こり始める, おじゃんになる ▪ Everything was absolutely marvelous. Then it all *went pear-shaped*. 万

事絶好調だった. それから調子が全く狂い始めた. ☞一説に, 英空軍の俗語; 曲芸飛行できれいな円を描くはずがいびつな円になることから.

pebble /pébəl/ 名 ***a pebble on the beach*** 多数の中の一人 ▪ You aren't the only *pebble on the beach.* 大勢の中で君だけが人間じゃありませんよ《相手のうぬぼれをくじくとき》 ▪ There's more than *one pebble on the beach.* 大勢の中には他にも人はいるんですよ《君だけに頼っているわけではない》.

There are plenty of other pebbles on the beach [shore]. 《諺》浜辺には小石は他にもたくさんある《通例失恋した人を慰めるときに用いる》.

peccavi /pekɑ́ːviː/ 名 ***cry peccavi*** 悪かったと言う, 謝罪する ▪ My letter to him made him *cry peccavi* all right. 彼宛ての手紙を読んで彼はほんとに謝罪した. ☞Ⓛ peccavi 'I have sinned.'

peck[1] /pek/ 名 ***a peck of*** 《口》たくさんの, 大変な(面倒など) ▪ You'll get into *a* pretty *peck of* troubles. 君はすごくたくさんの苦労に陥ることだろうよ.

One has to eat a peck of dirt [dust] before one dies. 《諺》死ぬまでにだいぶ(空気中の)ほこりを食べなければならない《一生の間にはいろいろな侮辱を受け忍ばなければならない》. ☞peck「約 7.2 リットル」.

peck[2] /pek/ 動 ***a peck(ing) order*** 《口》つつき序列《鳥の社会で, 自分よりも弱い者はつつくが, 強い者からはつつかれるという序列をなすこと, 動物・人間社会についても言う》; 人間社会における上下関係 ▪ Boys settle their *pecking orders* by fighting. 男の子はけんかによってつつき序列を決める ▪ Our natural tendency is to establish *a pecking order.* 我々人間は自然の傾向として序列を作るものである.

pecker /pékər/ 名 ***keep** one's **pecker up*** 《口》元気を出す, しょげない ▪ *Keep your pecker up*; you will be all right soon. 元気を出せよ. すぐよくなるさ. ☞pecker = nose.

put [get] up** a person's **pecker 《口》人をいらだたせる, 怒らせる ▪ I am not quite sure of that, if he *puts my pecker up.* 僕を怒らせたら, そうは問屋がおろすかどうかわからんぞ.

pedal /pédəl/ 名 ***dead pedal*** とろとろ走っている車 ▪ Better pass that eighteen wheeler, Tom; it's a *dead pedal.* トム, あのトレーラートラック, 抜いた方がいいよ. のろのろ運転だから.

get [have]** one's **foot on the loud pedal 大声を上げてしゃべる ▪ She's worth listening to when she's *got her foot on the loud pedal.* 彼女が大声を上げてしゃべっているときには聞きがいがある. ☞the loud pedal「ピアノの強音器を上げるペダル」.

press [push, put] the pedal to the metal/with the pedal to the metal 《米口》アクセルを踏み込む, 全速力で車を運転する; 一生懸命取り組む ▪ Mick *put the pedal to the metal* and drove his car. ミックはアクセルを目いっぱい踏み込み猛スピードで車を走らせた ▪ Suzy *pushed the pedal to the metal* and finished writing her essay a day early. スージーは大急ぎで仕上げ, 随筆を1日早く書き終えた.

put [tread] on the soft pedal 黙る ▪ Hey, *put on the soft pedal.* おい, 黙らないか. ☞the soft pedal「ピアノの弱音器のペダル」.

take** one's **foot off the pedal 《口》努力を緩めリラックスする ▪ At Yale, she never *took her foot off the pedal.* イェール大学で彼女が手を緩めることは決してなかった.

pedestal /pédəstəl/ 名 ***come [climb] down from the pedestal*** 一人舞台から降りる, 自分が一番だという考え方を捨てる ▪ She had to *come down from the pedestal* where she had placed herself as the heroine of democracy. 彼女は自分を民主主義のヒロインと位置づけていた立場から身を引かざるを得なかった. ☞pedestal「胸像などをのせる台」.

knock [force, take]** a person **off** his **pedestal 人を尊敬されている立場から引きずり降ろす ▪ The scandal *knocked* the superstar *off his pedestal.* そのスキャンダルでスーパースターは祭り上げられていた地位を失墜してしまった.

place [put, seat, set]... on a pedestal …に重要な位置を与える, を祭り上げる ▪ In the United States we have *placed* work *on a pedestal.* アメリカでは我々は仕事というものを祭り上げてきた.

pee'd /piːd/ 形 ***pee'd off*** 《口》腹を立てて, かんしゃくを起こして ▪ The soccer superstars are *pee'd off*—they're being forced to provide a urine sample every day. サッカーのスーパースター選手たちはかんかんだ. 尿検査のサンプル提出を毎日強制されているのだから. ☞pissed の婉曲語法.

peel /piːl/ 動 ***keep** one's **eyes peeled*** →keep one's EYEs open.

peel** one's **eyes 《米口》目を見開いている, 注意を怠らない ▪ *Peel your eyes,* Mike. I have a surprise for you. 目を見開いていろよ, マイク. びっくりさせる物があるんだ.

peel it 《米俗》全速力で走る ▪ *Peel it* now, or you'll be late. さあ, 全力で走って行かないと遅れるぞ.

scattered and peeled 苦しめしいたげられて (《聖》*Isa.* 18. 2) ▪ The harmless servants were then *scattered and peeled,* and mercilessly killed. 罪のない使用人たちはそれから苦しめしいたげられ, 情け容赦なく殺された.

peep[1] /piːp/ 名 ***as drunk [tight] as a peep*** 《米口》すっかり酔っ払って ▪ The old man was *as drunk as a peep.* 老人はへべれけに酔っ払っていた. ☞peep「イソシギの類」.

hear a peep out of 〚主に否定文で〛…から何らかの反応がある, 小声を耳にする ▪ I didn't know they were around. I didn't *hear a peep out of* them. 彼らが近くにいたとは知らなかった. 彼らの小声一つ聞こえなかったし.

peep[2] /piːp/ 名 ***take [get, have] a peep at*** …をちらっと見る ▪ Let's *take a peep at* the picture. あの映画をちょっとのぞいて見ようじゃないか.

the peep of day [dawn, the morning] 夜明け ▪ We have often seen him at *the peep of dawn.* 我々はよく夜明けに彼と会った.

peep[3] /piːp/ 動 ***a Peeping Tom*** (他人の寝室内・家庭内を)のぞき見する男 ▪ Several women have complained to the police about the presence of *a Peeping Tom.* 数人の女性がのぞき見する男がいると言って警察に訴えた. ☞Lady Godiva が夫に減税訴願のため Coventry を裸体乗馬姿で通るのをのぞき見して目がつぶれたという仕立て屋の名から.

peer /pɪər/ 名 ***have*** [***find***] *one's* ***peer*** 匹敵する者を持っている[見つける] ▪ In song he never *had his peer.* 歌では彼に匹敵する者がいなかった ▪ You will not easily *find his peer.* 彼に匹敵する者は容易に見つからないでしょう.

peer (***group***) ***pressure*** 仲間(集団)の圧力, 仲間意識による強制力, 仲間と同じ行動を取らせる集団内での強制観念 ▪ Bill was forced to commit crime under *peer pressure.* ビルは仲間の圧力に屈してやむなく罪を犯した.

without a peer 無比の ▪ It is *without a peer* in the world. それは天下一品だ.

peerage /píərɪdʒ/ 名 ***raise*** *a person* ***to the peerage*** 人を貴族に列する ▪ Mr. Brown *was raised to the peerage* last year. ブラウン氏は昨年貴族に列せられた.

peg[1] /peg/ 名 ***a peg to hang … on*** [***upon***] (議論など)を持ち出すきっかけ[口実] ▪ I have not *a peg to hang* such a theory *upon.* こんな理屈を持ち出す口実は僕にはない.

a peg too low 《俗》 **1** ほろ酔いで ▪ I am *a peg too low.* 私はほろ酔いだ.
2 しょげて ▪ He is *a peg too low.* 彼はしょげている.

a round peg in a square hole*/*a square peg (***in a round hole***) 不適任者, 不適当なもの ▪ I've used a thick wad of paper to stuff up that gap in the wall; it's *a square peg in a round hole.* あの壁のすき間をふさぐために厚い紙の詰め物をしてみたが, どうもぴったりこない ▪ I think he is *a square peg* for accounts. 彼は計算には不向きだと思う.

bring [***let***] *a person* ***down a peg*** (***or two***) [***a peg lower***] →take a person down a PEG (or two).

buy … off the peg [《米》 ***off the rack***] 《英》 (衣服)を既製のを買う ▪ They *bought* what they could *off the peg.* 彼らは買える服は既製のを買った.

come down a peg (***or two***) 面目を失う, 鼻柱を折られる ▪ He has *come down a peg or two,* and he doesn't like it. あの男は鼻柱を折られ, それが気に入らないのだ.

start [***stir, move***] ***a peg*** 行動する ▪ You've got to fork over fifty dollars, or I don't *start a peg.* 50ドル支払ってくれなければ, 僕は動かないぞ.

strip a peg →STRIP[2].

take [***bring, let***] *a person* ***down a peg*** (***or two***) [***a peg lower***] 人の鼻柱を折る, 人をへこませる ▪ I must *take* that proud girl *down a peg.* あの高慢ちきな娘をへこませてやらなければならない. ☞昔軍船旗を木くぎ (peg) を使って上げ下げしていて, 高く上がるほど名誉であるが, 一段下げることはそれだけ体面を落とすことであったところから.

peg[2] /peg/ 動 ***have*** *a person* [*a thing*] ***pegged*** 《主に米》(ある人[もの]が)どんな人[もの]かよく知っている ▪ The woman thinks we're all taken in by her charm, but I*'ve got* her *pegged.* あの女は我々みながその魅力にまんまと引っかかったと思っているが, 僕はだまされないよ.

peg it into 《口》 …を激しく攻撃する[しかる] ▪ *Peg it into* him, and don't spare him. あの男をこてんこてんにやっつけて容赦するな.

pelt[1] /pelt/ 名 (***at***) ***full pelt*** 全速力で ▪ The others ran on (*at*) *full pelt* behind him. 他の連中も彼の後から全速力で走り続けた.

go full pelt at (仕事)をせっせとやる ▪ He *went full pelt at* it. 彼はそれをせっせとやった.

pelt[2] /pelt/ 動 ***be pelting with*** (雨)がひどく降っている ▪ It *was pelting with* rain. どしゃ降りだった.

pen /pen/ 名 ***a slip of the pen*** →SLIP[1].

dip *one's* ***pen in gall*** →GALL.

draw *one's* ***pen against*** [***for***] →DRAW[2].

drive a [*one's*] ***pen*** ペンを駆る ▪ He *drove his pen* afresh. 彼は再びペンを駆った.

from pen to knife 初診を受けてから手術のため外科医に照会されるまで ▪ "At last my operation is behind me," she said happily. "It has taken one whole year *from pen to knife.*" 「やっと手術が受けられるわ」と彼女はうれしそうに言った.「初診から手術までまる1年かかったの」

pen and ink 文筆 ▪ What meager profits spring from *pen and ink*! 文筆からの収入はいかに乏しいことか.

pen pal [《英》 ***pen***(-)***friend***] ペンパル, 文通友達 ▪ Ben's *pen pal* writes him letters about school in Finland. ベンのペンフレンドはフィンランドの学校生活について書いてよこす.

push a pen 《米俗》 事務員の仕事をする ▪ I *push a pen* in an office. 私はある事務所で事務をしている.

put *one's* ***pen through*** ペンで(文字)を消す ▪ He *put his pen through* the word. 彼はその語をペンで消した.

put [***set***] ***pen to paper*** 筆をとる, 書き始める ▪ I am not in the mood to *put pen to paper* today. きょうは筆をとる気がしない.

The pen is mightier than the sword. 《諺》 文は武よりも強し.

touch the pen (文字の書けない人が)ペンに手を添えてもらって署名する ▪ He told me to *touch the pen,* while he ingeniously wrote my name for me. 彼は私にペンに手を添えるように言って, じょうずに私の名前を書いてくれた.

wield a [*one's*] ***pen*** 筆をふるう ▪ He *wields a pen* with the hand of a master. 彼は達人の腕前で筆をふるう.

write with pen and ink →WRITE.

penalty /pénəlti/ 名 ***on*** [***upon, under***] (***the***) ***penalty of*** 違反すれば…の刑に処する条件で

P

▪ They are responsible for the work, *under penalty of* losing their positions. 彼らはその仕事の責任を果たさなければ免職になる.

pay the penalty of …の報いを受ける ▪ He had to *pay the penalty of* his foolishness. 彼は愚行の報いを受けねばならなかった.

penalty box 《ホッケー》ペナルティーボックス ▪ Two players came to blows and were sent to the *penalty box* for two minutes. 二人の選手がなぐり合いになり2分間のペナルティーボックス入りを食らった.

penance /pénəns/ 名 ***do penance*** 罪の償いをする ▪ He *did penance* in sackcloth and ashes. 彼は深く後悔して罪の償いをした.

penchant /péntʃənt|pɑ́:ŋʃɑ:ŋ/ 名 ***have a penchant for*** …を偏愛する, の傾向がある ▪ You *have a penchant for* stating the obvious. 君は分かりきったことを言う傾向がある.

pencil[1] /pénsəl/ 名 ***in pencil*** 鉛筆(書き)で (with a pencil) ▪ You can't sign a check *in pencil*! 小切手に署名するのは鉛筆ではだめよ.

pencil[2] /pénsəl/ 動 ***blue-pencil*** 検閲する ▪ Most of my report *was blue-pencilled* by the authorities. 私の報告書の大半は当局の検閲を受けた.

pendent /péndənt/ 形 ***pendent with*** …が下がっている ▪ Their roofs were often *pendent with* icicles. 屋根にはよくつららがぶら下がっていた.

pendulum /péndʒələm|-djʊ-/ 名 ***play pendulum*** (人・物・意見などが)振り子のようにぐらぐらする ▪ Great rollers make vessels *play pendulum*. 波の大うねりで船は振り子のように動揺する ▪ He is *playing pendulum* between two opinions. 彼は二つの意見に挟まれてぐらついている.

the swing of the pendulum (人心・世論などの)浮動; (政党間の)勢力の推移 ▪ The Socialists have won the last six by-elections. I suppose it's *the swing of the pendulum*. 社会党は過去6回の補欠選挙に勝ってきた. 勢力の推移というものだと思う.

penetrate /pénətrèɪt/ 動 ***be penetrated with*** (感情など)が染み込んでいる ▪ He *is* thoroughly *penetrated with* Communism. 彼は骨まで共産主義が染み込んでいる.

penny /péni/ 名 ***a bad penny*** つまらないやつ, くず野郎 ▪ Willy is *a bad penny*. Someday he'll end up in jail. ウィリーはろくでなしだ. いずれは刑務所送りになるだろう.

A bad penny [shilling] always comes back [turns up] (again). 《諺》偽造銅貨はいつも戻って来る《家出した放蕩息子は必ず帰って来るものである》. ☞いやな人物ほど思いがけず姿を現すものだ, の意.

(a) penny for your thoughts [for them] 《口》(黙って考えている人にふざけて)何をぼんやり考えているのか ▪ Come, *a penny for your thoughts*. さあ, 何をぼんやり考えているのか. ☞"I'll give you a penny if you tell me your thoughts" の意.

a penny plain and twopence colored 色なし1ペンスで色つき2ペンス《安ぴか物に対する冷やかし言葉》 ▪ Having been all her life so very "*twopence colored*" she wants the "*penny plain*" for a change. これまでずっととても「色つき2ペンス」(派手で目立つ)にしてきたので, 彼女は気分転換に「色なし1ペンス」(じみで目立たない)になりたがっている. ☞おもちゃの芝居から; 風景や人物を切り抜くボール紙が色なしは1ペンス, 色つきは2ペンスであった.

A penny saved is a penny gained [got, earned]. 《諺》1ペンスの節約は1ペンスの儲け.

A penny soul never came to twopence. 《諺》けちな了見の者は成功しない.

a pretty [fine, fair] penny 大金 ▪ Good wine costs *a pretty penny* these days. いいワインは今ではかなりの金がかかる ▪ The soldiers made *a pretty penny*. 兵士たちは大金を儲けた.

(be) two [ten] (for) a penny 《英》安い, いくらでも手に入る (=《米》a DIME a dozen) ▪ Here apples *are two a penny*. ここではリンゴはいくらでも手に入る ▪ TV cookery shows seem to *be ten a penny* these days. テレビの料理番組は今どきどの局でもやっているようだ.

count the pennies 《口》銅貨を数える, けちけちする ▪ He had learnt to *count the pennies*. 彼はけちけちするようになっていた.

earn an honest penny → turn an honest PENNY.

for a penny =for a SONG.

have not a penny to bless** oneself **with → to BLESS oneself with.

In for a penny, in for a pound [dollar]. 《諺》 **1** 手を出した以上はとことんまでやれ; 乗り出した船はあとへは引けない ▪ If we're *in for a penny* we must be *in for a pound*. 手を出した以上はとことんまでやり通さねばならない.
2 毒を食らわば皿まで ▪ We're already over an hour late, so I'm certainly not going to hurry now. *In for a penny, in for a pound*! 我々は1時間以上も遅刻している. だから僕は断然もう急ぐつもりはないね. 毒を食らわば皿まで, さ.

in penny numbers 一度に少しずつ ▪ They sold only *in penny numbers*. 一度に少しずつしか売らなかった. ☞penny number「1ペンスで買える探偵小説の定期刊行1回分」.

not … a penny the better [worse, etc.] そのためにちっとも良く[悪く, など]ならないで ▪ *No*body was *a penny the better*. 誰もそれで少しも良くならなかった.

not have one penny [two pennies, 《米》 two nickels] to rub against another [together] 《口》一文もない ▪ You can gamble until you *haven't one penny to rub against another*. 人間一文なしになるまでギャンブルをすることがある ▪ The family sounded as if they *hadn't two pennies to rub together*. その家族はまるで極貧生活を送っていたかのように聞こえた.

not know [be sure] where** one's **next penny is coming from = not know where one's next MEAL is coming from.

not worth a penny 一文の価値もない ▪ It is *not worth a penny*. それは一文の価値もない.

pennies from heaven 《口》思いがけない幸い,「たなからぼたもち」 ▪ All he hopes for is *pennies from heaven*. 彼はただたなからぼたもちを期待しているだけだ. ☞同名の映画(1936)で Bing Crosby が歌う歌に由来.

penny ante 《米》小額の, 取るに足りない ▪ We were burgled but they took just *penny ante* stuff in the front office. 店が泥棒に入られたが, 営業部門のつまらぬものを取られただけだ.

penny dreadful (扇情的な)かすとり雑誌 ▪ Older children like to read *penny dreadful* comics. 年かさの子供はかすとり雑誌の漫画を読みたがる.

penny wise and pound foolish/ penny-wise and pound-foolish 《諺》《主に英》一文惜しみの百知らず.

pinch pennies 《米》極端にけちけちする ▪ She *pinched pennies* whenever she could. 彼女はできるときはいつでも極端にけちけちした.

spend a penny 《英口》(有料)トイレに行く ▪ Wait a moment while I go and *spend a penny*. 用足しして来るからちょっと待っててくれ.

Take care of* [*Look after*] *the pence, and the pounds will take care of* [*look after*] *themselves. 《諺》小銭を大事にすればひとりでに大金ができる; 小事をゆるがせにせねば大事は自らうまくいく.

the penny drops 《口》うまくいく; 合点がいく ▪ I'm glad that *the penny dropped*. 言うことがわかってもらえてうれしい. ☞自動販売機に「1ペンスが入った」が原義.

turn* [*earn*] *an honest penny 律気に働いて金を儲ける ▪ I have tried to *turn an honest penny*; but I have been unsuccessful. 私は律義に働いて金を儲けようと努めてきたが, うまくいかなかった. ☞honest＝legitimate.

turn up like a bad penny 《口》うるさくやって来る《いやな客について, またはユーモラスな訪問約束として》 ▪ He's always *turning up like a bad penny*. 彼はいつもうるさくやって来てばかりいる ▪ I shall be *turning up like a bad penny* till you get sick of me. 君がうんざりするまで, うるさくやって来るよ.

pennyworth /péniwə̀ːrθ|pénəθ/ 名 ***a bad* [*dear*] *pennyworth*** 損な買い物 ▪ You will not find it *a dear pennyworth*. お買いになって損なことはないでしょう.

a good* [*great, fair, rich, cheap*] *pennyworth 得な買い物; 掘り出し物 ▪ The armor is undoubtedly *a great pennyworth*. そのよろいは確かに掘り出し物だ.

get** one's **pennyworth 《口》 **1** 金だけのものを手に入れる ▪ Mr. Cataway makes sure he *gets his pennyworth* of work from those assistants. キャタウェイ氏はその助手から必ず金を出しただけの仕事をしてもらうようにしている.

2 したたかぶたれる ▪ He'll *get his pennyworth* all right. 彼は確かにぶちのめされるだろう.

not a pennyworth of 少しも…でない ▪ There will *not* be *a pennyworth of* grudging in her welcome. 彼女の歓迎ぶりには少しもいやいやなところがなかろう.

pension /pénʃən/ 名 ***on pension*** 年金を受けている ▪ The old man was an ex-official *on pension*. その老人は年金を受けている前官吏だった.

retire on a pension 年金をもらって退職する ▪ He *retires on a pension* after forty years' service. 彼は40年勤続後年金をもらって引退する.

pent /pent/ 形 ***be pent up* (*in*)** (…に)閉じ込められている ▪ He has *been pent up in* prison. 彼は牢獄に閉じ込められてきた.

peony /píːəni/ 名 **(*as*) *red as a peony*** 真っ赤で ▪ Her mouth was *as red as a peony*. 彼女の口は真っ赤だった. ☞peony「シャクヤク, ボタン」.

blush like a peony 顔を真っ赤にする ▪ The maiden *blushed like a peony*. 娘は顔を真っ赤にした.

people /píːpəl/ 名 ***as people go*** 世間並みから言えば ▪ He is a nice fellow *as people go*. 彼は世間並みから言えばいい男だ.

of all people 人もあろうに ▪ The boss promoted Jack, *of all people*. 所長は人もあろうにジャックを昇進させた.

the beautiful people **1** (流行の先端を行く)うっとりさせる特権階級の人々 ▪ A lot of *the Beautiful People* were at the party, even on the front lawn. たくさんの社交界の人々がパーティーに出席して前庭の芝生の上まであふれていた.

2 (1960年代の)美しい人々《ヒッピーの人たち》 ▪ *The beautiful people* believed in peace and love, opposed the accepted ideas and often lived in groups. ヒッピーたちは平和と愛を信じ, 既成の考えに反対し, しばしば集団で生活した.

the best people 《口》上流社会の人々 ▪ People collect works of art because *the best people* do it. 人々が美術品を収集するのは上流社会の人々がそうするからだ.

the People's Princess 民衆の皇太子妃《Diana, the Princess of Wales (1961–97)のニックネーム》 ▪ Diana was often called *the People's Princess*, as she devoted much of her time to the public. ダイアナ妃はよく「民衆の皇太子妃」と称された. 多くの時間を大衆に捧げたからだ. ☞晩年は慈善事業や人道主義に基づく活動にいそしみ, その事故死は全世界からいたまれた.

pep[1] /pep/ 名 ***full of pep*** 《米俗》元気いっぱいの ▪ He's young, clever, and *full of pep*. 彼は若くて賢くて元気いっぱいだ.

give** a person **a pep talk 《口》人を励ます, 勇気づける ▪ Our teacher *gave* us all *a pep talk* before our math exam. 数学の試験の前に先生ががんばれと励ましてくださった. ☞pep talk は「激励の言葉, 檄(げき)」の意.

lose** one's **pep 《米俗》元気をなくす ▪ The paper

may be *losing its pep.* あの新聞は元気をなくしているのかもしれない.

pep rally 壮行会, 激励会 ▪ There is a *pep rally* today. 本日壮行会があります.

take the pep out of …から元気[精気]を奪う ▪ That *took* all *the pep out of* him. それで彼はすっかり元気をなくしてしまった.

pep[2] /pep/ 動 ***pepped out*** 《米俗》へたばって ▪ I'm tired and *pepped out.* 僕は疲れてへたばった.

pepper /pépər/ 名 ***full of pepper*** 《米》元気いっぱいの ▪ The paper is *full of pepper.* あの新聞は元気いっぱいだ.

lose *one's* ***pepper*** 《米》元気をなくす ▪ He accused me of having *lost my pepper.* 彼は私が元気をなくしたと言って非難した.

per /pər, pəːr/ 前 ***as per*** 《商》…により ▪ Would you please pay us *as per* enclosed account. 同封の勘定書によりお支払いください.

(as) per usual [normal] 《口》いつものように, いつも通りに ▪ *As per usual,* the rain was our constant companion. 例によって, またしても雨にたたられた ▪ Is Dad in a bad mood this morning?—Yes, *as per normal.* 今朝は父さんきげんが悪いの?—うん, いつもの通りね.

percentage /pərséntɪdʒ/ 名 ***no percentage*** 何の得にもならない ▪ There's *no percentage* in bullying your inferiors. 弱い者いじめをしても何にもならない.

play the percentages [percentage game] 《口》勝率を計算して安全[確実]な行動をとる, 先を見越して行動する ▪ When in doubt, *play the percentages.* 疑わしいときは先を見越して行動せよ.

perch[1] /pəːrtʃ/ 名 ***cannot flutter above the perch*** (ひなが)とまり木の上で羽ばたきできない; (無経験・無知な人が)独り歩きができない ▪ As yet some *cannot flutter above the perch.* 今のところ独り歩きのできない者もいくらかいる.

come off *one's* ***perch*** 《口》お高く止まるのをやめる ▪ *Come off your perch* and stop bragging. お高く止まって自慢するのはよせよ.

drop [fall, topple] off *one's* ***perch/hop the perch/tip [pitch] (over) the perch*** 《英口》 **1** 落ちぶれる, 敗れる ▪ I never thought him such an idiot as to *hop the perch* so sillily. 彼があんなに愚かにも敗れるようなまぬけとは思っていなかった.

2 くたばる, おさらばする ▪ The drug must have made him *pitch over the perch.* その薬がその男をくたばらせたにちがいない ▪ You never know when he's going to *drop off his perch.* 彼がいつくたばるかは分かったものじゃない.

knock [take] *a person* ***off*** *his* ***perch/throw [turn]*** *a person* ***over the perch*** 《口》人を負かす, 破滅させる; 人をやっつける, 殺す ▪ Russell *took* the Dean *off his perch.* ラッセルは司祭長をやっつけた ▪ If we should be caught, we shall *be thrown over the perch.* 万一つかまったら, 我々は殺されてしまうだろう.

take *one's* ***perch*** (鳥などが)止まる, 降りる ▪ A falcon flew to the elm to *take her perch.* タカがニレの木まで飛んで行って止まった ▪ The sea-nymph *took her perch* on the raft. その海の精はいかだの上に乗り移った.

perch[2] /pəːrtʃ/ 動 ***(be) perched on*** (狭い場所)の上に位している ▪ The old town *is perched on* a hill. その古い町は丘の上にちょこんと乗っている.

perch *oneself* ***on*** …に止まる, 座る ▪ Crows *perch themselves on* the top of loaded camels. カラスは荷物を積んだラクダの上に止まる.

perfect /pəːrfékt/ 動 ***perfect*** *oneself* ***in*** (技術)に熟達する ▪ It will take some years to *perfect yourself in* that language. その言語に熟達するには数年かかりましょう.

perfection /pərfékʃən/ 名 ***be the perfection of*** …の極致である ▪ This would *be the* very *perfection of* a dress for you. これこそまさにあなたには申し分のないドレスになりましょう.

bring ... to perfection **1** …を完成させる ▪ At last he *brought* the work *to perfection.* ついに彼はその仕事を完成させた.

2 …を成熟させる ▪ They *brought* no fruit *to perfection.* 彼らはどんな果実も成熟させなかった.

come to perfection 完成する, 円熟[成熟]する ▪ That girl will never *come to perfection.* あの娘は決して成熟しないだろう.

to perfection 完全に, 完ぺきに ▪ She cooks *to perfection.* 彼女の料理は完ぺきだ ▪ The dress fitted her *to perfection.* そのドレスは彼女にぴったり合った.

perforce /pərfɔ́ːrs/ 名 ***by perforce*** 力ずくで, むりやりに ▪ Now *by perforce* they cause the cardinals to choose a pope. 今やむりやりに枢機卿たちは教皇を選ぶように仕向けられるのだ.

of perforce やむをえず ▪ *Of perforce* he is an authority on the subject. やむをえず彼はその問題に関しては権威となっている.

perfume /pə́ːrfjuːm/ 名 ***acoustic perfume*** 《俗》「音の香水」《建設現場などでの耳障りな騒音をかき消してくれる音》 ▪ The park is famous for the *acoustic perfume* of its waterfall. その公園は滝の音の香水で有名である.

peril /pérəl/ 名 ***at*** *one's* ***peril*** (無視・不服従の場合は)身に危険があるものと思って《特に命令・警告などに用いる》 ▪ Do such a thing *at your peril.* そんな事をしたらどんな目にあっても知らないぞ ▪ We bade them to keep off *at their peril.* 我々は彼らにあぶないから近寄るなと警告した.

at the peril of (特に生命)を賭けて ▪ He acquitted himself of this commission *at the peril of* his life. 彼は命を賭けてこの任務を果たした.

in peril of (特に生命)の危険にさらされて ▪ You were never *in* such *peril of* your life as you have been within these few moments. 君はこの数分くらい生命の危険にさらされていたことはなかったのだ.

period /píəriəd/ 名 ***a period piece*** (小説・劇・

P

映画・家具・衣裳などの)時代物 ▪ The film is *a period piece*. その映画は時代物だ.

at stated periods 一定の時期に ▪ The floodgate was opened *at stated periods*. 水門は一定の時期に開かれた.

grace period/ period of grace 猶予期間 ▪ The teacher gave him a week's *period of grace* to complete the assignment. 先生は彼に課題をやってしまうために1週間の猶予を与えた.

perish /périʃ/ 動 ***be perishing for*** 《口》…したくてたまらない ▪ I'*m perishing for* a glass of beer. ビールが1杯飲みたくてたまらない.

be perishing with 《口》…で死にそうだ ▪ I'*m perishing with* cold. 寒くて死にそうだ.

Perish the thought! 《口》よしてくれ!, とんでもない!《激しい不賛成を表す句》 ▪ I, a friend of a fellow like that? *Perish the thought!* 僕があんな男の友人だって. とんでもないよ! ☞「そんな考えはなくなってしまえ」が原義.

perjure /pə́ːrdʒər/ 動 ***perjure*** *oneself* 偽誓[偽証]する ▪ A person who has *perjured himself* is the bane of society. 偽誓した人は社会の害毒である.

perk /pəːrk/ 動 ***perk it*** いばる, 出しゃばる ▪ The girl *perked it* in his face. 少女は彼の面前でいばった.

perk *oneself* ***out*** **1** めかす, いきに作る ▪ The girl *perked herself out* daintily. 娘は粋にめかしこんだ.
2 = PERK oneself up.

perk *oneself* ***up*** そり身になる, つんとする ▪ "Dear me!" ejaculated her mother, pretending to *perk herself up*. 「あらまあ!」と彼女の母親はつんとするようなふりをして叫んだ.

permeate /pə́ːrmièɪt/ 動 ***be permeated with*** …が満ちあふれている ▪ The air *is permeated with* the fragrance. 大気はその芳香に満ちあふれていた.

permission /pərmíʃən/ 名 ***give permission to*** *do* …する許可を与える ▪ He has *given* me *permission to* use his library. 彼は私に蔵書を利用する許可を与えてくれた.

with your permission ごめんをこうむって ▪ I should prefer—*with your permission*—to do that myself. 私は—おさしつかえなければ—自分でそれをやってみたいのです.

without permission 許可を受けずに, 無断で ▪ The tourists entered the grounds *without permission*. 旅行者たちは無断で構内に入った.

permit /pərmít/ 動 ***permit*** *oneself* ***in*** …にふける, 任せる ▪ Don't *permit yourself in* dissipation. 身を持ちくずしてはいけない ▪ They will *permit themselves in* ugliness. 彼らはかまわず醜いことにふけるだろう.

permit me to *do* どうか…させていただきたい ▪ *Permit me to* explain. どうかわけを聞いてください.

perpendicular /pə̀ːrpəndíkjələr/ 名 ***out of the perpendicular*** 傾斜して ▪ The wall is a little *out of the perpendicular*. この壁は少し傾いている.

perpetuity /pə̀ːrpətjúːəti/ 名 ***in*** [***to, for***] ***perpetuity*** 永久に ▪ We have here a plant which is self-fertilized *for perpetuity*. ここに永久に自花受精する植物がある.

perplexity /pərpléksəti/ 名 ***in perplexity*** 当惑して ▪ He looked at us *in perplexity*. 彼は当惑して我々の方を見た.

persimmon /pəːrsímən/ 名 ***a huckleberry to a*** [*one's*] ***persimmon*** 《米口》全く比較にならないもの, ほんとにつまらぬもの ▪ My learning is *a huckleberry to your persimmon*. 私の学識はあなたのと比較になりません ▪ I wouldn't risk *a huckleberry to a persimmon* that we don't sink to the bottom. 我々が水底まで沈まないとは私にはこれっぽちも請け合えない.

be a [***come***] ***huckleberry over*** [***above***] *a person's* [*one's*] ***persimmon*** 《米口》(才能などが)人[自分]をはるかにしのぐ ▪ You can *come huckleberry over my persimmon* today. 君はきょうは僕よりもはるかにじょうずだよ ▪ But to do this *was* at least *a huckleberry over my persimmon*. でもこれをするのは少なくとも私の手に余ることだった.

be a jump above *one's* ***tallest persimmons*** 《米口》すぐには理解できない, 合点がいかない ▪ Well, this *is a jump above my tallest persimmons*. どうも, これは僕にはすぐには合点がいかない.

bring down the persimmon 《米口》賞を獲る ▪ The lad is the one that *brings down the persimmon*. あの若者が賞を獲る若者なのだ.

rake up [***walk off with***] ***the persimmon***(***s***) 《米口》(賭けの)賞金をかっさらう; 賞を獲る ▪ He must *rake up the persimmons*. 彼は賞金をかっさらうにちがいない ▪ The elevator company *walked off with the persimmon*. そのエレベーター会社が賞をかっさらった.

the longest [***tallest***] ***pole knocks the persimmon*** 《米口》最優秀の者が勝つ ▪ Let both parties meet where there will be no interruption, and *the longest pole* will *knock the persimmon*. 両者をじゃまの入らない場所で合わせるがよい, そうすればもっと優秀な者が勝つということになる.

person /pə́ːrsən/ 名 ***a young person*** 若い男[女]; (現在では特に)若い女《話者が "girl," "woman," "lady" のように相手の身分をはっきりさせたくないときに用いる》 ▪ There is *a young person* to see you. 若い女の人がご面会です.

accept [***respect***] ***persons*** えこひいきする ▪ God is no *respecter of persons*. 神はえこひいきしない. ☞St. Peter の言葉 (《聖》*Acts* 10. 34); 聖書語法.

be *one's* ***own person*** 一人で責任がもてる (→be one's own MAN) ▪ We can't tell Sue what to do—she's *her own person*. スーに指図は出せない—彼女は自分の思い通りにするから.

be the last person to *do* 最も…しそうでない, 決して…しそうもない, …することはまずない, まさか…しないと思われる ▪ Jayne *is the last person* I want to talk to. ジェインとは決して話をしたくない.

feel like a different person 全く別人のように回復する，生まれ変わったかのように感じる（→FEEL like a new person） ▪ After she finally got a divorce from her alcoholic husband, Nell *felt like a different person*. アル中の亭主とやっと離婚して，ネルは生まれ変わったような感じがした.

get* [*hit*] *a person where he lives → WHERE[1].

***hit* [*get*] *a person home* [*where he lives*]** →HIT[2].

in one's (own) person/ in (one's) proper person （代表でなく）個人の資格で ▪ The poet is speaking *in his own person*. 詩人は個人の資格で話しているのだ.

in person **1** 自ら，親しく（↔ by ATTORNEY） ▪ You had better go and speak to him *in person*. 行ってじかにあの人に話したほうがよい.
2 容姿は ▪ *In person* he was handsome, strong, and healthy. 彼の容姿は立派で強壮そうだった.

in the person of **1** …の資格で，を代表して ▪ I had always written *in the person of* the Spectator. 私はいつもスペクテイター紙を代表して書いていた.
2 …に扮して，という人として ▪ The actor appeared *in the person of* King Lear. その俳優はリア王に扮して現れた ▪ A great scholar passed away *in the person of* Dr. Jones. ジョーンズ博士という大学者が亡くなった.

on* [*about*] *one's person 《戯》身につけて，携帯して ▪ He had a chisel *on his person* at the time of arrest. 彼は逮捕されたとき，のみを所持していた ▪ You don't happen to have a lighter *about your person*, do you? ひょっとしてライターお持ちではないでしょうか.

person of color 有色人；黒人，白人でない人 ▪ Tiger Woods was the first *person of color* ever to win the Masters. タイガー・ウッズはマスターズを制した最初の有色人だった.

respect persons →accept PERSONs.

personage /pə́ːrsənɪdʒ/ 名 ***in the personage of*** …という人に ▪ She found a friend *in the personage of* her brother. 彼女は弟という友だちができた.

represent the personage of …の役を演じる ▪ You have hitherto *represented the personage of* my benefactor. あなたはこれまで私の恩人の役を演じてきたのです.

take upon* [*put on, play, assume*] *the personage of …の役を演じる ▪ Every one of us *played* so well *his personage* in this comedy. 我々はみなこの喜劇で立派にそれぞれの役を演じた.

personally /pə́ːrsənəli/ 副 ***take ... personally*** （一般論なのに）自分のこととして話を受け取る[腹を立てる] ▪ She showed no anger, no sign that she *took* it *personally*. 彼女は，怒りも，またそれが自分に向けられたものと受け取った様子も，見せなかった.

perspective /pərspéktɪv/ 名 ***in its* [*their*] *right perspective*** 正しい釣り合いで，正しく ▪ You must see things *in their right perspective*. 物ごとを正しい釣り合いで見なければならない.

in perspective **1** 遠近法によって（描かれて） ▪ The painter must put it *in perspective*. 画家はそれを遠近法によって描かなければならない.
2 遠近に配置されて《比喩的に時間にも言う》 ▪ The tops of the trees receded *in perspective* into the distance. こずえが遠近に配置されて遠くへ退いていた ▪ The events of old times were unfolded *in* just *perspective* to the view. その昔の事件が正しく遠近に配置されて現れてきた.

out of perspective 遠近法をまちがえて ▪ The picture is *out of perspective*. その絵は遠近法が狂っている.

put ... into perspective 釣り合いのとれた見方をする ▪ You should *put* your losses *into perspective* before complaining. 不平を言う前に損失を正しい釣り合いで見るべきだ.

perspiration /pə̀ːrspəréɪʃən/ 名 ***be in (a) perspiration*** 汗をかいている ▪ He *was in* profuse *perspiration*. 彼は汗びっしょりだった.

persuade /pərswéɪd/ 動 ***be persuaded of* [*that*]** …を[と]信じる ▪ I *am* firmly *persuaded of* his innocence [*that* he is innocent]. 私はその人の無罪を堅く信じている.

***persuade a person of* [*that*]** …を[と]人に確信させる ▪ I *persuaded* him *of* his being mistaken [*that* he was mistaken]. 私は彼に自分がまちがっていることを納得させた.

***persuade oneself of* [*that*]** …を[と]信じる ▪ I cannot *persuade myself of* his being dead [*that* he is dead]. 私は彼が死んだとは信じられない.

persuade a person to do 勧めて人に…させる ▪ I *was persuaded to* give up the attempt. 私は勧められてその企てをあきらめた.

persuasion /pərswéɪʒən/ 名 ***it is my persuasion that*** 私は…と確信している ▪ *It is my persuasion that* he is mad. 彼は気が狂っていると私は確信している.

of the ... persuasion **1** …の宗派の ▪ They are both *of the* same *persuasion*. 二人とも同じ宗派だ.
2 《戯》…の種類[国籍，性別]の ▪ He is a man *of the* French *persuasion*. 彼はフランス人だ ▪ No one *of the* male *persuasion* was there. 男は誰もそこにいなかった.

Peru /pərúː/ 名 ***from China to Peru*** →CHINA.

pervade /pərvéɪd/ 動 ***be pervaded with*** …が充満している ▪ The air *is pervaded with* the scents of flowers. 大気は花の香りでみちあふれている.

pervert /pərvə́ːrt/ 動 ***pervert the course of justice*** 《法律》正義の道をゆがめる，検察[司法]の妨害をする ▪ He stood trial on charges of conspiracy to *pervert the course of justice* after a car crash. 彼は，衝突事故のあと司法妨害の陰謀を企てた容疑で裁判を受けた.

pest /pest/ 名 ***Pest on*** [***upon***] *a person!* 人が疫病にでもとっつかれろ! ▪ "*Pest on* them!" answered Clarence.「やつら疫病にでもとっつかれるがいい!」とクラレンスは答えた.

pester /péstər/ 動 ***pester the life out of*** 《口》...をたまらないほど悩ます[苦しめる] ▪ Girls *pestered the life out of* the actor by asking for his autograph. 少女たちは実にうるさく俳優にサインを求めた.

pet[1] /pet/ 名 ***make a pet of*** (子供・動物)をかわいがる ▪ He *made a pet of* the monkey. 彼はそのサルをかわいがった.

one's ***pet aversion*** 《戯・皮肉》特に虫の好かないもの ▪ She's *my pet aversion*. 私は彼女が特に虫が好かん.

pet name 親しみを込めた呼び名, 愛称 ▪ He never calls his wife by her real name, "Tatiana," but only such *pet names* as "honey," "honey bunch," "sweetheart," and "sugar." 彼は妻を本名でタティアナとは決して呼ばず, ハニー, ハニーバンチ, スウィートハート, シュガーなどという愛称で呼んだ.

pet peeve/《英》***pet hate*** 《米》とりわけいやなこと[もの] ▪ The grunting noise Tim makes with his stuffed-up nose is a *pet peeve* of the people about him. ティムが鼻詰まりで発するブーブー音は周りの人にとって全くいやなものである ▪ Cleaning the toilet is my *pet hate*. トイレ掃除は実にいやなことだ.

teacher's pet 先生のお気に入り; 上司に気に入られる人 ▪ Meg was *teacher's pet* because she was smart. メグは賢かったので先生のお気に入りの生徒だった ▪ Joel has managed to be *teacher's pet* in any workplace. ジョエルはどこの職場でもうまく上役からかわいがられてきた.

pet[2] /pet/ 名 ***get into a pet*** すねる, むくれる ▪ The child *got into a pet* at my refusal. その子供は私が断るとむくれた.

in a pet (子供みたいに)すねて, むくれて ▪ Mother's *in a pet* this morning. おかあさんはけさはごきげんななめなんだ ▪ He went back to the house *in a pet*. 彼はむくれて家へ帰っていった.

take (***the***) ***pet*** むっとして不きげんになる[すねる] ▪ About a year ago I *took the pet* at my diary. 1年ほど前自分の日記を読んで不きげんになってしまった.

petal /pétəl/ 名 ***rose-petal skin***/***petal-soft cheeks*** 非常に柔らかくデリケートな肌[頬] ▪ Her creamy, *rose-petal skin* was flecked with faint freckles. 彼女の柔らかい, バラの花びらのような肌には, うっすらとそばかす模様があった ▪ The mother kissed her sleeping child on her *petal-soft cheek*. 母親は眠っている子の柔らかいほっぺにキスをした.

petard /pətá:rd/ 名 ***hoist with*** [***by***] *one's* ***own petard*** 自分のわなにかかって, 自縄自縛で (cf. Sh., *Haml.* 3. 4. 207) ▪ It's too disastrous a victory. I'm *hoist with my own petard*. あまりにも悲惨な勝利だ. 私は自分のわなにかかったのだ ▪ They saw through his stratagem, and determined to *hoist* him *with his own petard*. 彼らは彼の計略を見抜き, 彼を自縄自縛にさせてやろうと決心した. ☞「自分が仕掛けた爆発物にふっとばされて」が原義; petard は Sh. では petar だが, 普通 petard と誤って引用される. また, hoist は hoise《廃》の過去分詞であるが, 第2例のように不定詞として使われることもある.

Pete /pi:t/ 名 ***for Pete's sake*** 《英》後生だから, 頼むから ▪ Well, *for Pete's sake*, Janet, just use your brain for a second. ねえ, ジャネット, 頼むからちょっと頭を使ってよ. ☞《聖》Peter (ペテロ)の愛称.

Peter /pí:tər/ 名 ***be a Peter Pan*** (成人男性が)精神的に少年期に留まっている ▪ Ever since then, I have wanted to *be a Peter Pan*. それ以来ずっと少年のままでいられたらなあと思ってきた.

rob Peter to pay Paul 甲から借りて乙に返す; 借金を返すために借金をする ▪ You may make a shift by *robbing Peter to pay Paul*. 甲から借りて乙に返せば何とかなるかもしれない.

petrel /pétrəl/ 名 ***a stormy petrel*** 紛争をもたらす人 ▪ Smith is *a stormy petrel*. There is likely to be some kind of trouble. スミスは紛争屋だから, きっと何かごたごたが起こるぞ.

petrify /pétrəfài/ 動 ***be petrified with*** ...で茫(ぼう)然自失する, 立ちすくむ ▪ He *was petrified with* fear. 彼は恐ろしさで立ちすくんだ.

petticoat /pétikoʊt/ 名 ***in petticoats*** **1** (男の子が)まだ子供で ▪ I have known him ever since he was *in petticoats*. 彼が子供の頃から知っている.
2 女の ▪ She was a Nero *in petticoats*. 彼女は女性版暴君ネロだった.

petticoat government かかあ天下; 女性による政治 ▪ He was under strict *petticoat government*. 彼はきびしいかかあ天下のもとにあった ▪ Then *petticoat government* would prevail. そうすれば女性による政治がはばをきかすことになるだろう.

run [***be***] ***after a petticoat*** 《口》女のしりを追い回す[している] ▪ He *is* always *after a petticoat*. 彼はいつも女を追い回している.

wear [***be in***] ***petticoats*** 女である, 女らしくふるまう ▪ Since she *wears petticoats*, I will answer for her protection. 彼女は女なのだから, 彼女の保護には私が責任をもつ.

petto /pétoʊ/ 名 ***in petto*** 胸中に, 秘密にして ▪ It should yet remain *in petto*. それはまだ秘密にしておかねばならない. ☞ It 'in one's own breast'.

pew /pju:/ 名 ***find*** [***take, grab***] ***a pew*** 《英口》《戯》席を見つける[座る] ▪ *Take a pew*, please. どうかお座りください. ☞ pew「木製で背もたれのついたベンチ形をした教会の長い座席」.

phase /feɪz/ 名 ***go*** [***pass***] ***through a phase*** (青春期の男女が)困難な段階を通過する ▪ Young girls often *go through a phase*. 若い女の子はよく困難な段階を通りかかることがある.

in [***out of***] ***phase*** 《英》 **1** 同位相で[位相を異にして] ▪ The current and voltage are *in phase*. 電流と電圧は同位相である.
2 一致して[不一致で] (*with*) (→in SYNC (with), out of SYNC) ▪ We should keep the supply *in*

P

phase with productive capacity. 供給を生産力と一致させねばならない.

philosopher /fəlɑ́səfər|-lɔ́s-/ 名 ***be a philosopher*** 悟っている, あきらめがよい ▪ He *was* too great *a philosopher* to be disturbed by this incident. 彼は大いに悟っていたので, この事件で心を乱さなかった.

philosophers' stone 錬金石; 仙丹(せんたん)《昔, 錬金術師がすべての金属を金・銀に変える性能をもつと信じていた固体; またある時代には不老長寿の薬とも信じられていた》 ▪ He was in search of the *philosophers' stone*. 彼は錬金石を捜していた ▪ He declared that the true *philosophers' stone* was the new life in Jesus Christ. 彼は真の仙丹はイエス・キリストにおいて新しい生命を得ることだと断言した. ☞philosopher《廃》＝alchemist; philosopher's とするのは誤用.

phone /foʊn/ 名 ***be on the phone*** **1** 電話に出ている ▪ Who *is on the phone*? 誰が電話に出ているのか.

2 電話を引いている ▪ We *are on the phone* now. もう電話を引いている.

get on the phone **1** 電話口に呼び出す ▪ Truman *got* Lucas *on the phone*. トルーマンはルーカスを電話口へ呼び出した.

2 電話をかける ▪ Once in a while I had to *get on the phone*. ときどき私は電話をかけねばならなかった.

hold the phone 《口》〚主に命令文で〛 **1** ちょっと待つ ▪ *Hold the phone*! I've already paid for the room rent—I don't owe anything. ちょっと待って. 部屋代はすでに払った. だからなんら借りはない.

2 やっていることをやめる ▪ *Hold the phone*! There's no sense in complaining to her. やめろ. 彼女に不平を言っても意味がない. ☞→HOLD it!

off the phone 話し終わって ▪ Let me know when you're *off the phone*, please. 電話が終わったら知らせてくれ.

P

phone-in /fóʊnìn/ 名形 ***phone-in*** (***programme***) 《英》視聴者が電話で参加する形式の(番組), 電話注文の ▪ There was a *phone-in* about it. そのことに関して視聴者電話参加番組があった ▪ Kipling's "If" was voted Britain's favorite poem in a *phone-in* vote conducted by the BBC. キプリングの「もしも」が BBC 実施の視聴者電話参加番組の投票でイギリスの愛唱詩に決まった ▪ The restaurants offer walk-in, fax-in or *phone-in* orders. そのレストランは, 来店でも, ファックスでも, 電話でも注文できる.

photo /fóʊtoʊ/ 名 ***a photo finish*** (競争などでの)写真判定; 大接戦, きわどい勝負 ▪ *A photo finish* is predicted by the opinion polls. 世論調査によれば大接戦が予想されている.

a photo op (カメラマンに許す)写真撮影の機会 ▪ All the photographers rushed toward *a photo op* with the president. カメラマンたちは一斉に大統領の写真撮影に殺到した. ☞op＜opportunity.

photograph /fóʊtəgræ̀f|-grɑ̀:f/ 名 ***have*** [***get***] *one's* ***photograph taken*** 写真をとってもらう ▪ I wish to *have my photograph taken*. 写真をとってもらいたい.

sit for a photograph 写真をとってもらう ▪ The man was *sitting for a photograph*. その男は写真をとってもらっていた.

take a photograph of …の写真をとる ▪ I *took a photograph of* my friends at the seaside. 海岸で友人の写真をとった.

phrase /freɪz/ 名 ***as the phrase goes*** よく言われるように ▪ *As the phrase goes*, flattery will get you nowhere. よく言われるように, おべっかを使っても何にもなるまい.

to coin a phrase 《口》新しい言い方をすると《常套句をおどけて言う場合に使用する》 ▪ Stunned Steve was, *to coin a phrase*, "sick as a parrot." 呆然としたスティーブは, 変わった言い方をすると, オウムのように気分が悪かった《ひどく失望していた》. ☞通常 "coin a phrase" は新語をつくることを意味するが, ここでは皮肉的に使われている.

phut /fʌt/ 名 ***go phut*** 《口》(機械が)止まる; ひどい目にあう, おじゃんになる ▪ The hospital has all *gone phut*. その病院はすっかりつぶれてしまった.

phylactery /fəlǽktəri/ 名 ***make broad*** *one's* ***phylactery*** [***phylacteries***]/ ***wear*** *one's* ***broad phylacteries*** 正義風を吹かせる (《聖》*Matt.* 23. 5) ▪ Russell has *worn his broadest phylacteries*. ラッセルはこの上もなく正義風を吹かせた. ☞phylactery は羊皮紙に旧約聖書からの文句を記したものを納めた皮の小箱で, ユダヤ人が朝の祈りのとき身につけるもの.

physical /fízɪkəl/ 形 ***get physical*** 《口》 **1** 攻撃的になる, 凶暴になる ▪ Stop pushing; there's no need to *get physical*. ごり押しするな, カッカする必要はない.

2 ねんごろになる, 肉体関係をもつ ▪ Thirteen is too young to *get physical* in that way. 13歳でそこまでの関係になるのは早すぎる.

3 体を動かす, 運動する ▪ *Get physical*; take a brisk walk, and scrub the kitchen floor. 体を動かしなさい; 急ぎ足で歩き, 台所の床を磨きなさい.

physician /fəzíʃən/ 名 ***Physician, heal thyself.*** 《諺》医師よ, 自分の病気を治せ,「医者の不養生」.

picayune /pìkəjú:n/ 名 ***not worth a picayune*** 《米》全くつまらない ▪ Our chance would*n't* be *worth a picayune*. 我々のチャンスは全くとるに足らないものだろう.

pick[1] /pɪk/ 名 ***break*** *one's* ***pick*** →BREAK[2].

pick and shovel つるはしとシャベル《重労働のシンボル》 ▪ They work with *pick and shovel*. 彼らはつるはしとシャベルで働く[重労働者だ].

take [***have, get***] ***the*** [*one's*] ***pick*** 自由に選ぶ (*of, from*) ▪ I was the first to arrive at the inn and *got the pick of* rooms. 私が一番に旅館に着いたので, 部屋の選択ができた ▪ The plane was fairly empty, so they *had their pick of* the seats. 飛行機はかなり空いていたので, 彼らは自由に席を取った.

the pick of the crop [***basket, bunch, litter***]（あるまとまった物，人の中で)最善のもの，ずば抜けているもの(人) ▪ Shoppers who want *the pick of the crop* will want to arrive early for this market. 掘り出し物を御所望の方は早めに本市場に来られたし ▪ The Blue Course is *the pick of the litter*. ブルーコースが最高のゴルフコースだ. ☞litter「動物の一腹の子」.

pick[2] /pɪk/ 動 ***have a bone to pick with*** *a person* →BONE.

pick a brand《米》(ナイフで)毛をむしり取って烙印が見えるようにする ▪ At their leisure they *picked a brand*. 暇な時に毛をむしって烙印が見えるようにした.

pick a [*one's*] ***flint*** **1**《米》(燧(ひ)発銃の)火打ち石の面をざらざらにする ▪ Boone, *picking the flint of* his rifle, took aim at the panther. ブーンはライフル銃の火打ち石の面をざらざらにして，ヒョウに狙いを定めた.

2《米口》改めてひと奮発する ▪ The baseball club should *pick their flints* and try again. その野球部は改めてひと奮発して，もう一度やってみたらいい.

pick a lock →LOCK[1].

pick a quarrel [***fight, an argument***] けんかを吹っかける (*with*) ▪ The men began to *pick quarrels*. その男たちはけんかを吹っかけ始めた ▪ He *picks a quarrel with* whoever is at hand. 彼は誰であろうとそばにいる人にからんでくる.

pick and choose より[えり]すぐる，丹念に選ぶ ▪ Take them as they come; you must not *pick and choose*. 出てくる順に取るんだ. よりすぐってはいけない ▪ You may *pick and choose* what you like best out of those. その中から一番好きなものをえりすぐってよろしい. ☞主に自動詞.

pick and steal こそこそ盗む ▪ Keep your hands from *picking and stealing*. その手でこそこそ盗みを働かないようにしなさい.

pick ... apart = PICK ... to pieces; → pick HOLEs in.

pick *a person's* ***brains*** →BRAIN.

pick ... clean (骨)から肉をきれいにしゃぶり取る ▪ The dog *picked* the bone *clean*. 犬は骨から肉をきれいにしゃぶり取った.

pick holes [***a hole***] ***in*** →HOLE[1].

pick *one's* ***men*** 人を精選する，人選に気をつける ▪ He always *picks his men*. 彼はいつも気をつけて人選する.

pick *one's* ***nose*** 鼻をほじくる ▪ The child must be made to stop *picking his nose*. その子供に鼻をほじくることをやめさせなくてはいけない.

pick on *a person* ***your own size***《口》弱い者いじめをしない，自分と同等の者をいじめる ▪ *Pick on* someone *your own size*. She's not your size, Peter. 弱い者いじめはよせ. あの子は相手じゃないぞ，ピーター ▪ America should have *picked on* someone *their own size*. アメリカは自分と同等の国に当たるべきだった.

pick over the bones (***of***) (価値あるもの[こと]を見つけて自分のものにするために) 細心の注意で調べ上げる ▪ The newspapers *picked over the bones of* the split between the Prince and his girlfriend. 新聞は皇太子とガールフレンドとの不和についてあれこれ調べ上げた.

pick *a person's* ***pocket*** [***purse***] 人の懐中物をする ▪ I had my *pocket picked*. 懐中物をすられた.

pick ... to pieces **1** ...をばらばらにする，ずたずたに裂く ▪ The coat *was picked to pieces*. 上着はずたずたに裂かれた.

2 ...を酷評する，のあら捜しをする ▪ As soon as she left the room, the other girls began to *pick* her *to pieces*. 彼女が部屋から出て行くとすぐ，他の少女たちは彼女をこきおろし始めた.

pick oneself up **1** (ころんで)はね起きる ▪ Tom *picked himself up*, and settled himself on his bench again. トムははね起き，またベンチに腰をおろした.

2 元気を出す ▪ *Pick youself up*, my man. 元気を出せよ，君.

pick up *one's* ***feet*** →FOOT[1].

pick up flesh (病後など)肉が元のようについてくる ▪ He has *picked up flesh*. 彼は肉が元のようについてきた.

pick up speed [***momentum***] スピードを上げる ▪ You'll have to *pick up speed* if you want to finish this job. この仕事を終らせたければ急がないと.

pick up (*one's*) ***spirits*** [***courage***] 元気を出す; (気付薬などが)元気を回復させる ▪ She had so far *picked up her spirits*. 彼女はこれまでは元気を出してきた ▪ I *picked up courage* and spoke without trepidation. 私は元気を出して狼狽せずに言った.

pick up the bill [***tab, check***]《口》他人の分を支払う; (勘定の)支払いを引き受ける (*for*) ▪ When we eat out it's always John who *picks up the bill*. 食べに出るときおごるのはいつもジョンだ ▪ I cannot *pick up the bill for* the damage. その損害の請求書の支払いを引き受けることはできない ▪ The American taxpayer may have to *pick up the bill for* reconstructing Kosovo. アメリカの納税者がコソボ再建のつけを払わされることになるかもしれない.

pick *one's* ***way*** [***steps***] (危険な道などを)気をつけて進む，道を拾って歩く ▪ She *picked her way* between the heather and bracken. 彼女はヒースとワラビの間を道を拾って歩いた ▪ He *picked his steps* among the rocks. 彼は岩の間を気をつけて進んだ.

pick *one's* ***words*** 言葉を精選する，言葉づかいに気をつける ▪ You had better *pick your words* carefully. 言葉づかいに気をつけたほうがいい.

picket /píkət/ 名 ***from picket***《米》歩哨(の役目)から ▪ I have just returned *from picket*. 私は歩哨から帰ってきたばかりだ.

on picket 歩哨に立って ▪ You were *on picket*. 君が歩哨に立っていたんだ.

pickle /píkəl/ 名 ***be in a*** (***sad*** [***sorry, nice, pretty,*** etc.]) ***pickle***《口》取り散らかしている; 困っている ▪ The house *was in* such *a pickle*. その家はひどく乱雑になっていた ▪ I *was* certainly *in a*

P

pickle when my front tire blew out. 前のタイヤがパンクしたときにはほんとに困ってしまった.

***have a rod in pickle for** a person* →ROD.

in pickle 用意して ▪ He has a million dollars now *in pickle* in the English funds. 彼は今イギリスの国債で100万ドル用意している.

picnic /píknɪk/ 名 ***be no picnic*** 《口》遊びごと[生やさしいこと]じゃない ▪ An escape *is no picnic*. 逃亡は生やさしいことじゃない.

go on* [*for*] *a picnic/have a picnic ピクニックに行く ▪ I am *going on a picnic* with my sisters. 妹たちといっしょにピクニックに行くつもりです ▪ It wasn't raining when they *went for a picnic*. 彼らがピクニックに出かけたときは(雨が)降ってはいなかった.

have a picnic with 《米》…を嘲笑する ▪ The Spanish *had a picnic with* the explanation. スペイン人はその説明を嘲笑した.

make ... seem like a picnic …を気楽に思わせる ▪ We have to avert a catastrophe that will *make* the Gulf War *seem like a picnic*. 我々は湾岸戦争をなんでもないと思わせるような破局は避けねばならない.

picnicking /píknɪkɪŋ/ 名 ***take** a person **picnicking*** 人をピクニックに連れて行く ▪ I *took* him *picnicking* on the island. 彼を島にピクニックに連れて行ってやった.

picture[1] /píktʃər/ 名 ***a perfect picture*** **1** 正確で充実した内容 ▪ The author has given us *a perfect picture* of Haiti. 著者はハイチについて正確無比に描写している.

2 美しい眺め ▪ The bride was *a perfect picture*. 新婦は実に美しかった.

A* [*One*] *picture is worth a thousand words. 《諺》一枚の絵[写真]は千個の言葉の価値がある,「百聞は一見に如(し)かず」. ☞目で見るほうが耳で聞くよりも効果的に情報が伝わる, の意.

be* [*look*] *a picture (絵のように)美しい, きれいな ▪ The bride *looked a picture* in the gown. 花嫁はガウンを身に着けて絵のようにきれいだった.

(*be*) *in the picture* **1** 姿を現して(いる), 目立って(いる) ▪ At that time Blenheim *was* not *in the picture* at all. その当時ブレンハイムは全然目立っていなかった.

2 目につく, 重要である ▪ He was getting too high up *in the picture* anyhow. 彼はどうしてかひどく偉くなりかけていた.

3 《口》最新情報を得ている, 十分知っている ▪ He *is* fully *in the picture* about the case. 彼はその件については十分承知している.

(*be*) *the* (*very*) *picture of* **1** …の権化で(ある) ▪ He looks *the picture of* health. 彼は健康そのもののように見える.

2 …にそっくり[生き写し]で(ある) ▪ The sons *were the very picture of* their father. 息子たちは父親にそっくりだった.

blacken the picture (…を)実際よりも悪く言う ▪ No wonder he tries to *blacken the picture*. He is jealous of me. 彼が僕のことを悪く言うのは不思議ではない. ねたんでいるんだよ.

break into pictures 《米俗》(特に俳優として)映画界へ入る ▪ While there, I tried to *break into pictures* in Hollywood. そこにいる間に私はハリウッドの映画界へ入ろうと努めた.

come into* [*enter*] *the picture かかわりを持つ, 登場する ▪ I don't think you *come into the picture* at all. 君の出る幕じゃないと思う ▪ The dress *entered the* fashion *picture*. そのドレスが流行界へ登場した.

Consarn* [*Blast, Drat,* etc.] *your* [*his,* etc.] *picture! 《米俗》こん[あん]ちくしょう! ▪ Young Bob's dad—*consarn his picture!* ボブ少年のおやじ—あんちくしょうめ! ▪ *Blast your picture*, see what you've done. こんちくしょう, とんでもないことをしでかしたじゃないか.

get the* [*a*] *picture 《口》(状況を)理解する; 〚疑問文で〛分かる (→get the MESSAGE) ▪ We should *get a* clear *picture* of what has happened. 事件をはっきりと理解すべきだ ▪ We need everyone's cooperation. *Get the picture*? みんなの協力が必要なんだ. わかったかい?

give a picture of …を描写する ▪ It *gives* us *a* vivid *picture of* English life at the period. それは当時の英国人の生活を生き生きと描写してみせてくれる.

look at the big picture 大局を理解する ▪ Jim should *look at the big picture* before he starts criticizing the firm. ジムは批判する前に会社の全体像を把握すべきである.

out of the picture **1** おかど違いで ▪ Her resolution is admirable, but a trifle *out of the picture*. 彼女の決心はあっぱれなものだが, ちとおかど違いだ.

2 《米》勝てる見込みがない ▪ The tall girl is *out of the picture*, and Joan will win the prize. あの背の高い少女に勝算はなく, ジョーンが賞を得るだろう.

3 《米俗》死んで ▪ He had passed *out of the picture* long since. 彼はとっくの昔にくたばっていた.

4 退場して; 手を引いて ▪ They wanted him *out of the picture*. 彼らは彼が退陣することを望んだ ▪ Willkie bowed *out of the picture*. ウィルキーはおじぎをして退場した.

5 事情を知らないで ▪ He must be kept *out of the picture*. 彼には事情を知らせてはならない.

6 かかわりがなくなって ▪ He simply went *out of the picture*. 彼はもう全くかかわりがなくなった.

paint a rosy* [*gloomy, bleak, dark,* etc.] *picture of …について楽観的[悲観的]な見方をする ▪ Betty *painted a rosy picture of* family life. ベティーはバラ色の家庭生活を夢見た ▪ He *painted a gloomy picture of* East-West relations. 彼は東西陣営関係について悲観的な見方をした.

picture perfect/picture-perfect 絵に描いたように完璧な, 非の打ちどころのない ▪ The forecasters are predicting *picture perfect* weather for New Year's Day. 気象予報士はこの元旦は申しぶんのない天気であると予想している ▪ It was a *picture perfect* wedding. それは非の打ち所のない結婚式であった.

P

push ... out of the picture …を駆逐する, すたれさす ▪ Hillbilly music is just about *pushing* jazz *out of the picture*. カントリーミュージックがジャズをすたれさせようとしている.

put [***keep***] *a person* ***in the picture*** 人に最新情報[進捗状況]を知らせる ▪ Please *put* me *in the picture* about the matter. その件について私に最新情報を知らせてください.

see pictures in the fire ぼんやりと炎のゆらめきを見つめる ▪ The old man sat on the hearth *seeing pictures in the fire*. 老人は炉辺に座ってぼんやりと炎のゆらめきを見つめていた.

see [***look at***] ***the whole picture*** 全体像を見る, 大局を見通す ▪ It's important for the kids to *see the whole picture*. 子供たちが全体像を見ることが大切です.

sit for a picture 肖像を描いてもらう ▪ The beggar was *sitting for a picture*. その物乞いは肖像を描いてもらっていた.

spoil *a person's* ***picture*** 《米俗》(けんかなどで)人の顔をめちゃめちゃにする ▪ If I catch him, I'll *spoil his picture*! あの男をつかまえたら, 顔をめちゃめちゃにしてやるから.

take a picture 写真を撮る ▪ *Take a picture* of me with my new friends. 新しい友だちといっしょの写真を撮ってよ.

take *oneself* ***out of the picture*** (選挙運動などから)手を引く ▪ The general *took himself out of the* Presidential *picture*. 将軍は大統領選挙戦から手を引いた.

taking pictures 《俗》スピード違反取り締まりにレーダーを使用中; カメラ作動中 ▪ The traffic police are *taking pictures*! 交通警察がレーダーで速度チェック中だよ.

the picture of (***good***) ***health*** [***innocence,*** etc.] 非常に健康的な人, よい健康状態[全くの無邪気, 無垢] ▪ The doctor says I am *the picture of good health*. 医者によれば私は健康そのものだという ▪ Dora was *the picture of innocence*. ドーラは純真無垢そのものだった.

picture[2] /píktʃər/ 動 ***picture to*** *oneself* …を想像する ▪ *Picture to yourself* an open common. 広々とした共有地を想像しなさい.

pidgin /pídʒən/ 名 ***Pidgin English*** ピジン英語《中国語・マレー語などが混合した商取引用の英語》 ▪ The whole business was done in *pidgin English*. 商談は一切ピジン英語で行われた. ☞business の転化.

that's [***this is***] ***my pidgin*** 《口》それ[これ]は私のする事だ ▪ *This is my pidgin*. None of yours at all. これは私のする事だ. 君の知ったことでない.

pie /paɪ/ 名 ***a piece*** [***slice***] ***of the pie*** (金銭・取引の) 分け前, 取り分 ▪ I maintained a relationship with him so I could get *a piece of the pie*. 分け前にあずかれるように彼との関係を続けた.

(***as***) ***easy as pie*** →EASY.

(***as***) ***nice*** [***good***] ***as pie*** 《米口》ひどくきげんがいい, あいそがいい ▪ He is *as nice as pie* this afternoon. 彼はきょうの午後はひどくきげんがいい.

cut a pie 《米口》おせっかいする ▪ By gosh, you had better not *cut that pie*. いや全く, それにはおせっかいしないほうがいいですよ.

eat humble pie →HUMBLE[1].

finger in *a person's* ***pie*** →FINGER[2].

go to pie めちゃめちゃになる ▪ Your arrangements are *going* all rapidly *to pie*. 君の手筈はすべてめちゃめちゃになっている.

have a finger in the pie →FINGER[1].

have enough pie 《米口》だめになる, 使い古される ▪ The house I was born in *has* sure *gotten enough pie*. 私が生まれた家は長年住んですっかりくたびれてしまっている.

pie in the sky 《口》当てにならない先の楽しみ[幸福] ▪ Good, solid government is more palatable than *pie in the sky*. 立派な, しっかりした政府のほうが当てにならない先の幸福よりもありがたい. ☞Joe Hill の歌 *The Preacher and the Slave* (1906年ごろ)の "You'll get pie in the sky when you die." から.

piece[1] /piːs/ 名 ***a nasty piece of work*** →NASTY.

a piece of ass [***tail***] 《卑》性交 ▪ Jack was out for *a piece of ass*. ジャックは一発やりに町へ出た.

a piece of change 《俗》かなりの額の金 ▪ For *a* nice *piece of change*, you can take home a handcrafted wooden dining table. かなりの金を払えば, 手作りの木製食卓テーブルを持ち帰ることができるよ.

a piece of goods 《口・戯》人, (特に)女 ▪ She seemed *a* pretty *piece of goods* enough. 彼女はなかなかの美形のようだった.

a piece of *one's* ***mind*** →give a person a piece of one's MIND.

a piece of skirt 《俗》若い女 ▪ How come guys look at me like *a piece of skirt*? 男の人ってどうして私を若くもないのにじろじろ見るのかしら.

a piece of the action 《俗》(活動・利益の)分け前, 取り分, おこぼれ ▪ You want more than *a piece of the action*. 君は割り当て以上を望んでいる.

a piece of work **1** 作品 ▪ What *a piece of work* is a man! 人間とはなんという傑作なのだろう!
2 仕事; 困難な仕事 ▪ It would be *a* long *piece of work*. それは長い仕事になるだろう ▪ It's such *a piece of work* to make you shake hands. 君に握手させるのはなかなか骨の折れる仕事だ.
3《口》騒ぎ ▪ What are you making all this *piece of work* for? 何だってこんなに大騒ぎしているの?
4《米》とんでもなくすごいやつ ▪ Son of a bitch, Bob was thinking as he said that, this guy's *a piece of work*. ちくしょう, ボブはそう言いながらこの男はとんでもないやつだと考えていたんだ.

(***all***) ***in one piece*** (全く)無事に, 無傷で ▪ Come back in a hurry, but *in one piece*. 急いで, しかし無事に帰って来なさい ▪ John's son was sent to war as a pilot and came home *all in one piece*.

P

ジョンの息子はパイロットとして参戦し無傷で帰国した.

(all) of a piece 同種類[性質]の; 首尾一貫した; 調和した ▪ Odd how *all of a piece* taste is! 味というものがどれも同じとは妙だ ▪ He does not always write *all of a piece*. 彼はいつも首尾一貫した書き方をしているわけではない ▪ He and his horse were *of a piece*. 彼と馬とはぴったり呼吸が合っていた. ☞F tout d'une pièce のなぞり.

all to pieces 《俗》十分に, すっかり ▪ I know him *all to pieces*. 彼のことは何もかも知っている.

be cut off the same piece of goods 《米口》同類である ▪ He *wasn't cut off the same piece of goods* as the other watermen. 彼は他の船頭たちとは同類ではなかった.

by the piece **1** (支払いなどが)仕事の出来高に応じて ▪ Most pottery workers are paid *by the piece*. たいていの陶器製造人は出来高で支払いを受ける.

2 1反ずつで ▪ This cloth is sold only *by the piece*. この布は1反ずつでないと売らない.

cut ... in [to] pieces →CUT[2].

fall [come] to pieces ばらばらになる, ぼろぼろになる ▪ My clothes are *falling to pieces*. 私の服はぼろぼろになりかけている.

go (all) to pieces **1** ばらばら[めちゃめちゃ]になる; 突然崩れる ▪ A large ship had *gone to pieces* on the reef. 大きな船が暗礁に乗り上げてばらばらになってしまった ▪ Losing our competitive position abroad, our financial system has *gone to pieces*. 海外での競争力を失いわが国の経済体制は急に瓦解した.

2 (健康・精神が)参ってしまう, すさんでしまう ▪ Since his wife's death, Jones has *gone all to pieces*. 妻に死なれてからジョーンズはすっかり参ってしまった.

huff** a person **to pieces 人を徹底的にいじめる ▪ She has *huffed* him all *to pieces*. 彼女は彼をぼろぼろになるまでいじめてきた.

P

in [of] one piece ひとかたまりに; 渾然として (*with*) ▪ The whole was cast *in one piece* in bell metal. 全部が鐘青銅でひとかたまりに鋳造された ▪ I must have the part all *of one piece with* the rest. その部分を他のものと渾然たるものにしなければならない.

in pieces **1** ばらばらで, こなみじんになって ▪ The dish lay *in pieces* on the floor. 皿はこなごなになって床に散らばっていた.

2 分裂して, 不和で ▪ We are all *in pieces*. 我々はみんな仲たがいしている.

knock ... to [in] pieces →KNOCK[2].

like a piece of chewed string 《英口》くたくたに疲れて ▪ After a long walk I felt *like a piece of chewed string*. 遠道を歩いた後くたくたに疲れた.

of a piece with ...と一致[調和]して ▪ It is *of a piece with* the rest of his character. それは彼の性格の他の面と調和している.

on the piece 出来高仕事をして ▪ There is no constant work for a man *on the piece*. 出来高仕事をしている人間には一定の仕事はない.

pick [pull] ... to pieces ...をぼろくそに言う, 酷評する (→TEAR to pieces) ▪ The papers *pulled* his new novel *to pieces*. 新聞は彼の今度の小説をぼろくそに批評した.

pick up the pieces (不首尾などの)しりぬぐいをする, 後始末をする; 事態を収拾する ▪ If anything goes wrong, he always *picks up the pieces*. 何かまずいことが起こると, 彼がいつもしりぬぐいをする ▪ Della and her mom were left to *pick up the pieces*. デラと彼女の母親は生活を立て直すべく残された.

piece by piece ひとつひとつ; 少しずつ ▪ Bring it out *piece by piece*. それをひとつひとつ持ち出しなさい. ☞F pièce à pièce のなぞり.

puzzle** a person **to pieces 人をひどく途方にくれさす ▪ I *am puzzled to pieces* about it. 私はそのことでほとほと途方にくれている.

speak a piece 《米口》(詩などを)暗誦する ▪ I would rather hunt rabbits than *speak pieces*. 暗誦するよりウサギを捕えるほうがいい.

speak [say]** one's **piece 《口》意見を率直に述べる ▪ Don't you want to hear me *speak my piece*? 君は僕が自分の意見を率直に述べるのを聞きたくないのか.

take ... to [in] pieces ...をばらばらにする, 分解する ▪ The watch will have to *be taken* all *to pieces*. その時計はすっかり分解しなければならないだろう.

think piece →a THINK piece.

to pieces 《口》 **1** 故障して動かない ▪ After 100,000 miles my car went *to pieces*. 10万マイルを超えたので私の車はお釈迦になった.

2 ひどく, 非常に ▪ Della was thrilled *to pieces* to see Ann. デラはアンに会えるというので大喜びした.

to [in, into] pieces きれぎれに, ばらばらに ▪ They pulled the old building *to pieces*. その古い建物は倒されてばらばらになった ▪ The glass fell and was smashed *into pieces*. グラスが落ちて粉々に砕けた.

***want a piece of** a person* 《米俗》...に会って話をしたい ▪ I *want a piece of* Lee Byung-hun. 私, イ・ビョンホンに会って話がしてみたいわ.

piece[2] /piːs/ 動 ***piece** oneself **to [with]*** ...といっしょになる, 合体する ▪ When the Romans became so significant, he *pieced himself with* them. ローマ人がそれほど重要になってくると彼はそれと合体した.

piecemeal /píːsmìːl/ 名 ***by piecemeal*** 少しずつ ▪ I am forced to write *by piecemeal*. 私はやむなく少しずつ書かねばならない.

piecrust /páɪkrʌst/ 名 ***(as) short as piecrust*** 《米口》非常にじりじりして, 怒りっぽくて ▪ I feel *as short as piecrust*. 僕は実にじりじりしている.

Promises are, like piecrust, made to be broken. 《諺》約束とパイの皮は破れるもの.

pig[1] /pɪg/ 名 ***a pig in the middle*** まん中のブタ《二人に挟まれて身動きできない人》(＝the PIGGY in the middle) ▪ He doesn't know which side he's on. He is *a pig in the middle*. 彼はどちらの陣営に属しているのか分かっていない. まん中のブタといったところだ.

a pig of a… 《英口》きつくておもしろくない… ▪ I've had *a pig of a* day. 大変な一日だった.
a pig's eye 《口》不手際, へま ▪ Your composition is *a* real *pig's eye*. 君の作文は全く不出来だ.
(as) common as pig tracks 《米口》全く平凡な[月並みな] ▪ The girl was *as common as pig tracks*. その娘は全く平凡な女だった.
(as) happy as a pig in mud 《英口》この上なく幸せな ▪ Tom was *as happy as a pig in mud*. トムはこの上なく幸せだった.
(as) happy as a pig in shit 《卑》とても楽しい ▪ Grandpa is just *as happy as a pig in shit* when his grandson shows up. おじいちゃんは孫息子が来るとうれしくて仕方がない.
(as) sick as a pig 《英》いらいらした ▪ She's *as sick as a pig* today. 今日は彼女, いらいらしてるね.
bleed like a (stuck) pig 多量に出血する ▪ He *bled like a pig*. 彼は多量に出血した.
bring [drive] *one's* ***pigs to a fine [a pretty, the wrong] market*** 《主に皮肉》売り損をする; やまがはずれる ▪ We *brought our pigs to a fine market*. 我々はやまがはずれた ▪ He never could have *brought his pigs to a worse market*. 彼はそれ以上売り損をすることはできないほどだった.
buy [sell] a pig in a poke [bag] 見もしないで[価値も知らずに]買う[売る] ▪ He does not like *buying a pig in a bag*. 彼は品物を見もしないで買うのを好まない. ☞昔, 袋(poke)にブタを入れて売買したが, 悪徳業者はブタの代わりに猫を入れたことから. "Let the cats out of the bag." (秘密をもらす)も同じ慣習から.
carry *one's* ***pigs to market*** 商売をしようとする ▪ Roger may *carry his pigs to* another *market*. ロジャーは別な所で商売をしようとするかもしれない.
drive *one's* ***pigs to market*** いびきをかく ▪ The sleeping men went on *driving their pigs to market*. 眠っている連中はいびきをかき続けた.
eat like a pig →EAT[2].
in a [the] pig's eye 《米俗》〚肯定文のあとで〛決して…ない; …なんかじゃない ▪ Yeah, we'll get it back. *In the pig's eye*. いいや, 決して取り戻せやせんよ ▪ You think she's efficient? *In a pig's eye*! 君は彼女が有能だっていうの, とんでもない. ☞"in a pig's ass" の婉曲語法; 強い否定に使われる.
in a pig's whisper **1**《俗》すぐに, あっという間に ▪ The boy was back *in a pig's whisper*. その男の子はすぐに帰ってきた.
2《方》ひどく小声で ▪ He spoke *in a pig's whisper*. 彼はひどく小さな声で話した.
in less than a pig's whistle 《米口》あっという間に ▪ I'll do so *in less than a pig's whistle*. あっという間にそうしてやるさ.
in pig (雌ブタが)子をはらんで ▪ The sow is *in pig*. その雌ブタは子をはらんでいる.
like a greased pig 《主に米》誰にも捕まえられないくらい素早く ▪ True love is actually more *like a greased pig*! You have to chase after it and pursue it. 真実の愛とは本当に素早く逃げるものだ. 追いかけて捕まえなければならない. ☞油まみれの子ブタを捕まえて競い合うという昔の競争から.
live (like pigs) in clover →CLOVER.
look [stare] like a stuck pig (驚き・恐怖で)硬直する, 目と口を大きく開けて立ちすくむ ▪ Paul *looked like a stuck pig*, bleeding out of every spot on his face. ポールは顔面のいたるところから血を流し, 恐怖におののいていた.
make a pig's ear (out) of →EAR.
make a (real) pig of *oneself* 《口》(ブタのように)大食する; 食い過ぎる ▪ He *made a pig of himself* at the party. 彼はそのパーティーで大食いをした.
pigs in clover クローバーのブタ《板を傾けてマーブルを板の穴に入れる遊戯》 ▪ "*Pigs in clover*" was the rage at that time. 「クローバーのブタ」という遊びは当時大流行だった.
Pigs might fly (if they had wings)./《米》***when pigs fly*** 《英・皮肉》奇跡が起こらぬともかぎらない, そんなことありえない ▪ My uncle give me money! *Pigs might fly if they had wings*. 僕のおじさんが金をくれるって! 奇跡が起こりかねないよ ▪ That will happen *when pigs fly*! まさかそんなことは起こらないよ.
please the pigs 《戯》都合よくいけば ▪ *Please the pigs*, I'll marry her to her cousin George. 都合よくいけば彼女をいとこのジョージと結婚させよう. ☞"PLEASE God" のふざけた代用.
sell a pig in a poke [bag] →buy a PIG in a poke.
squeal [scream, sound, yell] like a stuck pig 《口》大声でわめく, やかましくキーキーと叫ぶ, 金切り声を立てる《a stuck pig は「畜殺のためナイフで喉を突かれたブタ」の意》 ▪ The wound is nothing, and you're *screaming like a stuck pig*! 傷はなんともないのにぎゃーぎゃーわめいたりして, 君は ▪ It was only a scratch, but my daughter started *squealing like a stuck dog*. ほんのかすり傷だったのに, うちの娘ときたら, 大声でわめき始めたの.
sweat like a pig →SWEAT[2].

pig[2] /pɪg/ 動 ***be pigged off*** 《英口》ひどくいらいらする, とても動揺する ▪ Erick *was pigged off* by Jane's apparent indifference. エリックはジェインに明らかに無視されて不愉快だった.
pig it [together] 《主に英》(ブタのように)ごちゃごちゃ住む ▪ You'd have to *pig it* with the goats and the cattle. 君はヤギや牛といっしょにごちゃごちゃ住まねばならんだろう.

pigeon /pídʒən/ 名 ***a clay pigeon*** 《俗》カモ; たやすい仕事 ▪ The test was *a clay pigeon*. テストはやさしかった. ☞射撃の「クレー(ピジョン)」から.
be *a person's* ***pigeon/not be*** *a person's* ***pigeon*** 《英》…の責任[仕事]だ/…に関わりのないことだ, …の知ったことではない ▪ That's *your pigeon*, Tina. それはあなたがやることよ, ティナ ▪ It's *not my pigeon*—ask Bill. それはおれの知ったことじゃない—ビルに頼むんだな. ☞元は "not a person's pidgin." "pidg-

P

in" は17世紀の中国式発音で "business" のこと.

pigeon's milk **1** ハト乳 ▪ The young of the pigeon are fed with so-called "*pigeon's milk.*" ハトのひなは, いわゆる「ハト乳」で養われる.

2《英戯》(All Fools' Day に)子供をだまして取りにやらせるありもしない物 ▪ Boys are frequently sent on the first of April to buy *pigeon's milk.* 少年たちは4月1日によくありもしない「ハトの乳」を買いにやらされる.

pluck a pigeon《俗》のろまの金をだまし取る ▪ "Here comes *a* nice *pigeon* to *pluck,*" said one of the thieves. 「金をだまし取るのにうってつけのムクドリがやって来るぞ」と泥棒の一人が言った. ☞pigeon「だまされやすい人」.

stool pigeon 通報者; おとり; (特に警察の)スパイ, 犬 ▪ He was a *stool pigeon* for the Justice Department. 彼は米国司法省のスパイだった.

That's *one's* ***pigeon.*** それは…自身の問題だ ▪ Don't start talking about expenses now, because *that's my pigeon.* 費用の話など今さら出さないでくれ, それは僕自身の問題なんだから.

piggy /pígi/ 名 ***the piggy in the middle***《英》板ばさみ状態にある人 (＝a PIG in the middle) ▪ The thing is I seem to be *the piggy in the middle.* 問題は自分が板ばさみになっているように思われることだ. ☞子供のボール投げ遊び, 真ん中の人に捕られないように二人がボールを投げ合う.

pike /paɪk/ 名 ***come down the pike***《米口》起こり始める, その場に姿を現す, 使えるようになる ▪ Malnourished children are apt to catch any disease to *come down the pike.* 栄養不足の子供たちははやりの病気に感染しがちである. ☞有料高速道路を使って移動している人の連想から; pike＝turnpike.

down the pike《米》ある期間がたって, 時が流れて ▪ Five years *down the pike,* the couple will have a kid or two. 5年もすれば, あの夫婦に子供の一人や二人はいるだろう.

hit the pike →HIT[2].

trail a pike 軍務に服する ▪ He *trailed a pike* in Germany in the 1940s. 彼は1940年代にドイツで軍務に服した.

pikestaff /páɪkstæ̀f|-stɑ̀ːf/ 名 ***(as) plain as a pikestaff*** **1** きわめて明白で ▪ The evidence against him was *as plain as a pikestaff.* 証拠が彼に不利であることはきわめて明白だった.

2 (男・女が)ひどく見てくれが悪くて ▪ He's *as plain as a pikestaff,* poor boy. かわいそうに彼はいかにも醜男だ. ☞古形は packstaff (負い荷支えづえ)で, それが無装飾 (plain) であるところから.

(as) stiff as a pikestaff しゃちこばって ▪ He sat up in bed *stiff as a pikestaff.* 彼はしゃちこばってベッドに座り直した.

call a pikestaff a pikestaff 言葉を飾らない, あからさまに言う (＝call a SPADE a spade) ▪ When will you *call a pikestaff a pikestaff*? いつ君は言葉を飾らないようにするつもりなのか.

pile[1] /paɪl/ 名 ***a pile of junk*** がらくた[くずもの]の山 ▪ On the left-hand balcony there was *a pile of junk* covered with a gray cloth. 左手のバルコニーに灰色の布に覆われたがらくたの山があった.

at the bottom [top] of the pile《口》(組織・社会などの中で)低く弱い[高く強い]立場にある ▪ They had always been *at the bottom of the pile* in this company. 彼らはこの会社でいつも低く弱い立場にずっと置かれていた.

bet [stake] *one's* ***pile on***《口》…に大金を賭ける ▪ He *bet his pile on* it. 彼はそれに大金を賭けた.

make *one's* ***[a] pile***《口》身代を作る ▪ He *made his pile* in stock-market investments. 彼は株式投資で身代を作った.

pile[2] /paɪl/ 名 ***cross and [or] pile*** → CROSS[1].

pile[3] /paɪl/ 動 ***pile it on***《口》大げさに言う ▪ The visitors *piled it on* very heavily. 訪問客らはひどく大げさに言った.

pile on [up] the agony →AGONY.

pilgrimage /pílgrəmɪdʒ/ 名 ***go on a pilgrimage to*** …に巡礼に出かける ▪ He *went on a pilgrimage to* Mecca last year. 彼は去年メッカに巡礼に出かけた.

make *one's* ***[a] pilgrimage to*** …に参詣(さんけい)する ▪ The custom of *making pilgrimages to* sacred peaks is an ancient one in Japan. お山参りのしきたりは日本では古いものだ.

pill /pɪl/ 名 ***a bitter [hard] pill to swallow*** (がまんをしなければならない)いやなもの[こと] ▪ It's *a bitter pill to swallow,* but there's no other way out of it. それはいやなことだが, それを免れる他の手がないのだ ▪ It's *a* pretty *hard pill to swallow* when the world turns on you. 世間が君に刃向かっているときは, 事態はがまんしなければならないものだ.

a pill to cure an earthquake その場逃れの手段,「二階から目薬」 ▪ He thought it was like "prescribing *a pill to cure an earthquake.*" それはまるで「二階から目薬をさす」ようなものだと彼は考えた.

be on the pill (女性が)ピル[経口避妊薬]を服用している ▪ Kate got pregnant despite *being on the pill.* ケイトはピルを常用していたのに妊娠してしまった.

pill popper 麻薬の常用者; ピル[経口避妊薬]の常用者 ▪ We really must try and help that *pill popper.* 麻薬を常用するあの友だちに是非手を貸してやらないといけない.

pill popping ピルを常用すること; 麻薬を常用すること ▪ *Pill popping* isn't the only way to head off period pain. ピルを服用することだけが生理痛を回避する方法ではない.

pop pills 〚主に進行形で〛錠剤をのみすぎる ▪ She'd spend all day *popping pills.* 彼女は終日たくさんヤクをやっていたものだ.

sugar [《英》***sweeten,*** 《米》***sugar(-)coat, gild***] ***the pill*** いやなものをうまそうに見せる ▪ I will *sugar* and *gild the pill* so as to make it pretty to look at and easy to swallow. 見た目にきれいで飲みやすいようにするために, 私がそのいやなものをうまそうに見

せてやろう ▪ Because *the pill was sugar-coated*, Lennon's "Imagine" was accepted. レノンの「イマジン」は不快さを和らげるように書かれていたので受け入れられた. ☞錠剤に糖衣をかけることから.

pillar /pílər/ 名 ***a pillar of cloud*** [***fire***] 雲[火]の柱, 神の指導 (《聖》*Exod.* 13. 21; *Ps.* 105. 39) ▪ The Scripture, like *the pillar of cloud*, is light to the true Israelite. 聖書はかの火の柱のごとく真のイスラエル人にとって光である.

a pillar of society [***community***] 社会の柱石, 社会の要(かなめ)となる人物 ▪ The older generation used to be *an* important *pillar of society*. 以前はお年寄りが社会の重要な柱石だった.

a pillar of strength →STRENGTH.

from pillar to post/from post to pillar (拒絶されて)あちこちへ, 次から次へ ▪ Life seems to drive me *from pillar to post*. 人生は私をあちこちへ追いやるように思われる ▪ Here I have been knocking about *from pillar to post*. ここであちこちほっつき回っている. ☞古いやり方のテニスから来た比喩.

pillion /píljən/ 名 ***ride pillion*** (馬・オートバイで)人の後ろに乗る ▪ She was *riding pillion* on the clerk's machine. 彼女はその事務員のバイクの後ろに乗っていた.

pillow /píloʊ/ 名 ***consult*** (***with***) [***take counsel of, advise with***] *one's* [***the***] ***pillow*** 一晩寝てじっくり考える,「ひざとも談合」 ▪ They *took counsel of the pillow*, and concluded to make a treaty. 彼らは一晩寝てじっくり考えて, 条約を結ぶことに決定した ▪ He *consulted with his pillow* upon it. 彼はそのことを一晩寝てじっくり考えた.

sew pillows under people's elbows (偽って)高枕をしていられるという感じを人にいだかせる ▪ No, you cannot *sew pillows under people's elbows*. いいえ, 高枕をしていられるという感じを人にいだかせるわけにはいきません.

pilot /páɪlət/ 名 ***drop the pilot*** 良い助言者を退ける ▪ The king decided to *drop the pilot*. 王は良い助言者を退けることに決めた. ☞Wilhelm II が Bismarck (水先案内の姿に画かれている)を解任した場面を描いた漫画 (*Punch*, Mar. 20, 1890)から.

on automatic pilot/on autopilot 《口》自動操縦で, 自動で, 惰性で, 無意識的に ▪ Investors go *on automatic pilot*. 投資家は惰性で行っている ▪ During your regular commute, your brain, *on automatic pilot*, gets little stimulation. 普段の通勤時に人の頭は惰性で働いており刺激を受けることはほとんどない ▪ The airplane was *on autopilot* and nobody was actively flying the airplane. 飛行機は自動操縦で, 誰も実際には操縦していなかった. ☞automatic pilot「自動操縦」; 飛行機の自動操縦装置から.

pin[1] /pɪn/ 名 ***A pin might have been heard to drop./You could have heard*** [***could hear***] ***a pin drop.*** ピンの落ちる音も聞こえるほどの静けさであった[ある] ▪ It was so still that *you could have heard a pin drop*. とても静かでピンの落ちる音も聞こえるほどだった ▪ Barack Obama was talking. Everyone was watching. It was quiet. *You could have heard a pin drop*. バラク・オバマ氏が語った. みなが耳を傾けた. 静かであった. 咳ばらい一つ聞こえなかった.

a pin's head [***point***] ピンの先; わずか ▪ Aquinas asked how many angels could dance on *the head of a pin*. アクィナスはピンの先で天使が何人踊れるか尋ねた ▪ We did not lose the value of *a pin's head*. 我々はわずかの価値も失わなかった.

(***as***) ***clean as a new pin*** →CLEAN[1].

at a pin's fee →FEE.

be quick [***firm, steady, strong, weak***] ***on*** *one's* ***pins*** 《口》足が速い[しっかりしている, 強い, がくがくしている] ▪ He *is* wonderfully *strong* and *quick on his pins*. 彼はすばらしく足が強くて速い ▪ The messenger *was weak on his pins*. 使者は足ががくがくしていた.

for two pins わけなく; すぐに ▪ *For two pins* I would box his ears. わけなく彼の耳をぶってやれる.

hit the pin →HIT the needle.

in (***a***) ***merry pin*** 上きげんで ▪ He was glad to find his friend *in merry pin*. 彼は友人が上きげんでいるのを見て喜んだ.

keep in the pin 《口》禁酒している ▪ He had determined to *keep in the pin* for a year. 彼は1年間禁酒していようと決心していた.

like pulling the pin from a grenade 悲惨な結果を生む出来事を引き起こすような ▪ If the peacekeeping troops were to leave the area, it would be *like pulling the pin from a grenade*. 万一, 平和維持部隊がその地域から撤退するようなことがあれば, 惨事の引き金になるだろう.

not care a pin [***two pins***] ちっともかまわない; 少しも好かない ▪ It is evident you *never cared a pin* for me. 君が私をちっとも好いてくれなかったことは明らかだ ▪ My elephant did *not care two pins* for a tiger. 私のゾウはトラなどちっとも問題にしなかった.

not worth a pin ちっとも価値がない ▪ Yet he is *not worth a pin*. それにしても, あの男にはちっとも値打ちがないね.

on *one's* ***last pins*** 《口》死にかかって; 疲れ果てて ▪ Poor old chap, he's *on his last pins*. かわいそうに, 彼は疲れ果てている[棺桶に片足突っ込んでいる].

on pins and needles 《米》ひどくそわそわ[ひやひや]して ▪ He was plainly *on pins and needles* while awaiting the doctor's verdict. 医者の診断を待っている間, 彼は明らかにひどくそわそわしていた.

pin curl ヘアピンなどで留めて作ったカール[巻き毛] ▪ Alice put her own hair in *pin curls*. アリスは自分の髪をピンカールで渦巻状にした.

pin money →MONEY.

pins and needles →NEEDLE[1].

put in the pin 《口》(悪習などを)やめる; (特に)禁酒する ▪ He had once resolved to better himself, and had *put in the pin*. 彼は一度改心しようと決心して酒を絶ったことがあった. ☞水漏れなどを目くぎ

(pin) で止めることから.

stick pins into *a person* 《米口》人を刺激する, 悩ませる ▪ This is meant to *stick pins into* you. これは君を悩ませるつもりのものだ.

there is not a pin to choose 選ぶところがない, 大差がない ▪ *There's not a pin to choose* between them. 両者に大差はない.

You could have heard [***could hear***] ***a pin drop.*** →A PIN might have been heard to drop.

pin[2] /pɪn/ 動 ***pin*** *one's* ***faith to*** (*a person's* ***sleeve***) →FAITH.

pin *one's* ***soul*** [***hope, knowledge, faith,*** etc.] ***upon*** [***on, to***] …に魂[希望, 知識, 信頼, など]を託す ▪ No man is to *pin his soul to* another man's sleeve. 誰も自分の魂を他人に託すべきではない ▪ We *pinned our hopes on* his returning in time. 我々は彼が間に合うように帰ってくることに希望を託した ▪ I wouldn't want to *pin my faith on* them. どうしても彼らを信用したくなかった.

pincer /pínsər/ 名 ***pincer(s) movement*** 相対する二方向からの働きかけ, 挟み撃ち作戦 ▪ A powerful *pincer movement* is vital to forcing the enemy general to array the military to fight on two fronts. 敵将が自軍を2方面に展開させざるを得ないように仕向けるには強力な挟撃戦が絶対に必要である ▪ Let's make a *pincer movement* on Mother about our winter holidays. 冬休みの計画についてお母さんに二人で挟撃作戦を張りましょう.

pinch[1] /pɪntʃ/ 名 ***a narrow pinch*** 危ういところ, 危機一髪 ▪ The news came in time, but it was *a narrow pinch*. その知らせは間に合うように届いたが, 危機一髪というところだった.

at [***on,*** 《米》 ***in***] ***a pinch*** 《英口》危急の場合には, せっぱ詰まれば ▪ They'll stand by me *at a pinch*. まさかの時には彼らが助けてくれるだろう ▪ *On a pinch* my father could walk ten miles in a day. せっぱ詰まれば父は1日に10マイル歩くことができた.

feel the pinch 金が無くてつらい思いをする ▪ He is out of work and is *feeling the pinch*. 彼は失業していてきゅうきゅう言っている.

give *a person* ***a pinch*** 人をつねる ▪ He *gave* her *a* spiteful *pinch*. 彼は女を意地悪くつねった.

when [***if***] ***it comes to the pinch*** まさかの時には ▪ But that apprehension seemed groundless *when it came to the pinch*. が, まさかの時にはその心配は根拠のないものに見えた.

pinch[2] /pɪntʃ/ 動 ***be pinched for*** …に窮する, 困る ▪ I *am pinched for* time at this moment. 私は目下時間がなくて困っている.

be pinched with (寒さ・貧乏など)に苦しむ ▪ I *am pinched with* cold. 私は寒さで縮み上がっている ▪ He *was pinched with* poverty. 彼は貧乏に苦しんでいた.

pinch and scrape →SCRAPE[2].

pinch pennies →PENNY.

where the shoe pinches →SHOE[1].

pinch hitter /píntʃhítər/ 名 ピンチヒッター, 代打; (緊急時の)代役 ▪ The only question is who will be the *pinch hitter*. 問題は誰を代打に出すかだけだ.

pink /pɪŋk/ 名形 ***in the pink*** 《口》とても元気[健康]で ▪ He says that he is *in the pink*. 彼はとても元気だと言っている. ☞競走馬が in the pink of condition「最上の調子で」の意から.

in the pink of …の極致で ▪ He seems to be *in the pink of* health once more. 彼はまたこの上もなく健康であるらしい ▪ He got himself up *in the* very *pink of* fashion. 彼は流行の粋な服装に整えた.

pink slip 《米》解雇通知 ▪ The *pink slip* came in November 2008. その解雇予告は2008年の11月に届いた.

see pink elephants [***spiders, snakes***] 《口》(譫妄(せんもう)症に伴う)幻覚を見る, 幻覚症状を呈する ▪ At last I got to the point of *seeing pink elephants*. とうとう私は幻覚を見るに至った ▪ I shall worry when I start *seeing pink elephants*. 幻覚を見るようになったら私は心配するだろう.

the pink dollar [《英》 ***pound***] 同性愛者の集団としての購買力 ▪ Further proof of the strength of *the pink dollar* can be seen in San Francisco, where there are numerous successful gay clubs. ゲイの落とす金の力のさらなる証明はサンフランシスコに見られる. そこには多くの成功したゲイクラブがある.

the pink of perfection 完璧な状態, 完全さの極み ▪ Her performance was marvelous—graceful, elegant and stylish—*the pink of perfection*! 彼女の演技はすばらしく—優雅で上品でしかもスマートで—まさに完璧だった!

pinprick /pínprìk/ 名 ***a policy of pinpricks*** いやがらせ政策 ▪ Russian provocation is at present but *a policy of pinpricks*. ロシアの挑発は目下のところいやがらせ政策にすぎない.

pint-size(d) /páintsàiz(d)/ 形 《口》非常に小さい ▪ Much of this *pint-size* technology is based on silicon, the main ingredient in computer chips. この極小技術の大半はコンピューターチップの主要素であるシリコンに依存している.

pip[1] /pɪp/ 名 ***give*** *a person* ***the pip*** 《俗》人をうんざり[いらいら]させる ▪ His later works *gave* her *the* pure *pip*. 彼の後期の作品は全く彼女をうんざりさせてしまった. ☞pip「ヒヨコの舌病」.

have [***get***] ***the pip*** 《俗》かげんが悪い[悪くなる], ふさいでいる[ふさぐ] ▪ Don't worry your sister; she's *got the pip* now. 姉さんにかまうんじゃない. 今は気分がすぐれないんだから.

pip[2] /pɪp/ 名 ***squeeze … until*** [***till***] ***the pips squeak*** 《口》相手が音(ね)をあげるまで絞り取る ▪ The new taxes will *squeeze* rich people *until the pips squeak*. 新税によって金持ちは音をあげるまで絞り取られるだろう. ☞Sir Eric Geddes (1875–1937)の演説(1918)の言葉から.

pip[3] /pɪp/ 動 ***pip*** (*a person*) ***at*** [***on, to***] ***the post*** 《英口》最後になって(相手に)勝つ ▪ The runner *pipped at the post*. その走者は土壇場で勝った ▪ Paul came up behind me and *pipped* me *to*

P

the post. ポールは後ろから迫り私に僅差で勝った. ☞競馬から.

pipe[1] /paɪp/ 名 ***a pipe dream*** (実現不可能な)はかない希望[計画] ▪ You're holding on to *a pipe dream.* 君ははかない夢にしがみついているのだ. ☞パイプをふかしながら夢を追うことから.

fill *one's* ***pipe*** →FILL[2].

have [***smoke***] ***a pipe*** 一服やる ▪ I *smoked a pipe* after supper. 私は夕食後一服やった.

hit the pipe 《米俗》アヘンを吸う ▪ The man was seen *hitting the pipe.* その男はアヘンを吸っているところを見つかった.

knock *one's* ***pipe out*** パイプをたたいて灰を出す ▪ He *knocked his pipe out* against the grate. 彼は炉格子でパイプをたたいて灰を出した.

lay pipe [***pipes***] 《米》やみ票を集める (*for*) ▪ They charged him with *laying pipes for* the Presidency. 彼らは彼が大統領選のためにやみ票を集めたと言って告発した. ☞「水道・ガスのパイプを敷設(ふせつ)する」が原義.

light a pipe 一服つける ▪ I *lit a pipe* to cheer me. 私は元気を出すために一服つけた.

pull at *one's* ***pipe*** パイプをふかす ▪ John sat calmly *pulling at his pipe.* ジョンは静かにすわってパイプをふかしていた.

put *a person's* ***pipe out*** 人の成功のじゃまをする, 人を顔色なからしめる ▪ You're jealous of the girl, and want me to *put her pipe out.* あなたはあの娘をねたんでいるので, 私に彼女の成功をじゃまさせたいのですね ▪ *His pipe is put out.* 彼は成功を妨げられた. ☞「他人のタバコの火を消す」が原義.

Put that in your pipe and smoke it. そのことをよく考えてごらん《通例小言を言ったあとで》 ▪ Well, I think you are really wasting your talent. *Put that in your pipe and smoke it.* いいか, 君はあたら才能をむだにしていると私は思う. そのことをよく考えてごらん. ☞喫煙は反省を誘うので.

smoke a pipe →have a PIPE.

smoke the pipe of peace (北米先住民が)和親の印にきせるを吸い合う; 仲直りする ▪ Let's drop our enmity and *smoke the pipe of peace.* お互いに敵意を捨てて仲直りしようじゃないか.

pipe[2] /paɪp/ 動 ***pipe*** *one's* ***eye*** [***eyes, the eye***] 涙を流す, 泣く ▪ Lucy and he must have *piped their eyes* enough by this time. ルーシーと彼はもう十分涙を流したにちがいない ▪ The smoke kept us *piping the eye.* 煙で涙が出続けた.

We have piped to you and ye have not danced. 私たちは笛を吹いたのに, あなたたちは踊ってくれなかった(《聖》*Matt.* 11. 17).

pipeline /páɪplàɪn/ 名 ***in the pipeline*** **1**(品物が)輸送されて ▪ The goods are at present *in the pipeline.* その商品は目下輸送中だ.

2《口》準備[考慮]中で ▪ New series are now *in the pipeline.* 新しいシリーズが目下準備中だ.

3《口》予算がついているがまだ消化されていない ▪ There's $5 million more *in the pipeline* for emergencies. 緊急事態に備えての予算がまだ500万ドル余使われていない.

piper /páɪpər/ 名 (***as***) ***drunk as a piper*** すっかり酔っぱらって ▪ There he was on the floor, *drunk as a piper.* そこの床の上に彼がすっかり泥酔して倒れていた.

pay the piper 笛吹きに金を払う; 費用[損失]を負担する ▪ He [The man] who *pays the piper* calls the tune. 《諺》笛吹きに金を払う者が曲を注文する権利がある《費用をかぶる者がほしい物を手に入れる権利がある》 ▪ Mary's unfortunate husband has to *pay the piper.* メアリーの不幸な夫が出費をかぶらねばならない. ☞17世紀以来, 祭りや婚礼で旅回りの楽団を雇う習慣から; →call the TUNE.

piping /páɪpɪŋ/ 形 (***the***) ***piping time***(***s***) ***of peace*** 平和な時 (cf. Sh., *Rich. III* 1. 1. 24) ▪ In *piping times of peace,* the national debts loom large. 平和な時には国家の借金は大きく見える. ☞「軍楽の代わりに牧歌的な笛の聞こえる時」の意.

pique[1] /piːk/ 名 ***in a*** (***fit of***) ***pique*** かっとして, 腹を立てて ▪ He went out *in a pique.* 彼はかっとして出て行った ▪ The bishop turned monk *in a* momentary *fit of pique.* その司教は一時の腹立ちまぎれに修道士になった.

out of pique 腹立ちまぎれに ▪ He did it *out of pique.* 彼は腹立ちまぎれにそれをした.

take [***have, bear***] ***a pique at*** [***against***] ...に腹を立てる[立てている], 気を悪くする[している] ▪ *Take* no *pique at* it. それに腹を立てないでください ▪ He *had a pique against* his uncle. 彼はおじさんに腹を立てていた.

pique[2] /piːk/ 動 ***be piqued at*** [***by***] ...に腹を立てる, にいらいらする ▪ He *was piqued at* her refusal. 彼は彼女に拒絶されて憤慨した ▪ She *was* a little *piqued by* the excess of his mirth. 彼女は彼があまりはしゃぎすぎるので少しいらいらした.

pique *a person's* ***interest*** [***curiosity***] 《米》人の関心[興味]を引く ▪ Lucy wanted to *pique his interest* another way. ルーシーは別のやり方で彼の気を引こうとした.

pique *oneself* ***on*** [***upon***] ...を自慢する ▪ He *piques himself on* his wit [being punctual]. 彼は自分の機知[時間厳守]を自慢にしている.

piss[1] /pɪs/ 名 ***a piece of piss*** 《口》造作なくできる仕事 ▪ This job is *a piece of piss.* こんな仕事はお茶の子だ.

be (***out***) ***on the piss/go*** (***out***) ***on the piss*** 《英卑》パブやクラブに繰り出し大酒を飲む ▪ Bob *was out on the piss* with his mates last night. ボブは昨晩仲間と外で鯨飲した.

frighten [***scare***] ***the piss*** [***hell***] ***out of*** ひどく...をおびえさせる ▪ The film *frightened the piss out of* children. その映画で子供たちはひどくおびえた.

full of piss and vinegar 《米俗》元気いっぱいで ▪ We went out into the warm Miami night, *full of piss and vinegar,* ready for an evening of fun. 我々は楽しい夜を過ごそうと元気いっぱいでマイアミ

の暑き夜に繰り出した ▪ Why were these musicians so *full of piss and vinegar*? これらの音楽家たちはどうしてそんなに元気いっぱいだったのだろうか?

piss[2] /pɪs/ 動 (***as***) ***pissed as a newt*** → NEWT.

piss against [***into***] ***the wind*** 《卑》(時流に抗して)成功の見込みのないことをする ▪ He's always *pissing against the wind*. 彼は成功の見込みがないことをしてばかりいる.

piss and moan 《口》ぶつぶつ文句ばかり言う ▪ Why do people *piss and moan* about people breaking the law? どうして人は法律違反をする人にぶつぶつ文句を言うのか. ☞"piss" は良い言葉ではないので "piss and moan" の代わりに "whine" を使う人がいる: Why don't you stop whining and ask for a raise? (ぶつぶつ不平を言うのをやめて, 昇給を請求したら).

piss it down 《英卑》雨が激しく降る ▪ It's still *pissing it down* out there. 外ではまだ雨が激しく降っている.

piss *oneself* (***laughing***) 《英俗》ちびるほど大笑いする ▪ We were all *pissing ourselves laughing*. 我々はみな笑い転げていた.

pissed /pɪst/ 形 ***as pissed as a fart*** [《英》***newt***] 《英俗》ぐでんぐでんに酔った ▪ You're *as pissed as a fart*! べろんべろんに酔ってるね!

pisser /písər/ 名 ***That's*** [***it's***] ***a*** (***real***) ***pisser!*** [***What a pisser!***] 《俗》嫌な状況, なんてこった ▪ *What a pisser!* To lose my job just before Christmas! やだやだ! クリスマスをすぐ前にして職を失うなんて! ☞"That's [It's] a bummer." も同種の意味を表し, かつ無礼な表現ではない.

piss-take /pístèɪk/ 名 《英卑》おちょくり, からかい ▪ Have I really won or is this a *piss-take*? 本当に勝ったのかな, それともおちょくられているのかな?

pistol /pístəl/ 名 ***hold a pistol to*** *a person's* ***head*** ＝hold a GUN to a person's head.

pit[1] /pɪt/ 名 ***be the pits*** 《口》(事態が)最悪[最低]だ ▪ Steve got into an accident and ruined his new car. *Is*n't that *the pits*? スティーブは事故を起こして新車をだめにした. それって最悪じゃないか?

bottomless pit 底なしの穴; 大食漢 ▪ My teenage son's a *bottomless pit*. うちの10代の息子は大飯食らいだ ▪ The problem is so big it's like a *bottomless pit*. 問題はとても大きくて際限がない.

dig a pit for …を陥れようとする (《聖》*Eccles*. 10. 8) ▪ He who *digs a pit for* others falls in himself. 人を陥れようとする者は自分が落ちる.

fly [***shoot***] ***the pit*** (臆病風を吹かして)逃げ出す ▪ He *shot the pit* a month ago. 彼はひと月前に逃亡した. ☞臆病な闘鶏が pit (囲い)から逃げ出すことから.

the pit (***of hell***)/ ***the bottomless pit*** 地獄 ▪ Such a one might take the path that leads to *the pit of hell*. そのような人間は地獄に通じる道を選ぶかもしれない.

the pit of *one's* [***the***] ***stomach*** みぞおち ▪ I had a sinking feeling in *the pit of the stomach*, but that didn't last long. みぞおち辺りに虚脱感を感じたがそれは長くは続かなかった. ☞恐怖や不安を感じるところと考えられた.

pit[2] /pɪt/ 動 ***be pitted with*** …でくぼみ[あばた]が出来ている ▪ His face *is pitted with* smallpox. 彼の顔は天然痘であばたになっている.

pit *one's* ***wits*** (***against …***) (人・者と)知識などを競う ▪ She's *pitting her wits against* a skillful computer opponent. 彼女は巧みなコンピューターを相手に知恵比べをしている.

pit-a-pat /pítəpǽt/ 副 ***go pit-a-pat*** (足が)パタパタと動く, (胸が)どきどきする ▪ Her feet *went pit-a-pat*. 彼女はパタパタと走った ▪ His heart *went pit-a-pat* at the news. その知らせを聞いて彼の胸はどきどきした.

pitch[1] /pɪtʃ/ 名 (***as***) ***black*** [***dark***] ***as pitch*** 真っ黒[暗]な ▪ It is growing *dark as pitch*. 真っ暗になりかけている.

You [***One***] ***cannot touch pitch without being defiled.***/ ***He who touches pitch shall be defiled therewith.*** 《諺》朱に交われば赤くなる (《聖》*Eccles*. 13. 1).

pitch[2] /pɪtʃ/ 名 ***at the pitch of*** *one's* ***voice*** 声を限りに ▪ The boy was singing *at the pitch of his voice*. 男の子は声を限りに歌っていた.

fly (***to***) ***a high pitch*** ある高さに達する ▪ Another comedy *flies a* much *higher pitch*. もう一つの喜劇のほうがずっと高い水準に達している ▪ Their proud presumption *flies to* so *high a pitch*. 彼らの高慢な出しゃばりはとても鼻もちならない. ☞タカが獲物をめがけて降りてくる前にある高さに飛び上がることから.

full pitch まっすぐに ▪ The stone came *full pitch* at my head. 石はまっすぐ私の頭をめがけて飛んできた.

make a pitch **1** 称賛して人に支援させる[物を買わせる] ▪ The Brazilian President *made a pitch* for Rio de Janeiro to become the first South American country to host the Olympics. ブラジル大統領はリオデジャネイロを南米で最初のオリンピック開催地にするように訴えた.

2 手に入れようとする ▪ When we first opened the hotel, we *made a pitch* for Japanese guests. ホテルを最初に開いたとき, 日本人客を呼び込もうとした.

make *one's* ***pitch*** 《米口》住居を定める ▪ He *made his pitch* at the foot of the hill. 彼はその丘のふもとに居を定めた.

play pitch and toss 投げ銭遊びをする《銭を投げて表面の出た分が自分の物になる》; 一か八かやってみる ▪ I'd *play pitch and toss* with my life. 私は命をもてあそんでみたい.

queer the pitch for *a person*/***queer*** *a person's* ***pitch*** (評判を落とさせて)人の計画や仕事をぶちこわす ▪ I'm going to let his firm know about his past, and that'll *queer his pitch* for him. 彼の会社に彼の過去を知らせてやるんだ, それで彼の仕事はぶちこわしさ. ☞pitch「(露店商などの)店を出す場所」.

reach the pitch of excellence [***the highest***

pitch] 最高水準に達する ▪ In that work you have *reached the pitch of excellence*. あの作品では君は最高水準に達している.
sales pitch 《俗》売り込み文句[口上] ▪ Let's hear your latest *sales pitch* for solar energy generation. 太陽光発電売り込みの最新の宣伝文句を聞こうじゃないか.
slink *one's* ***pitch*** 《米口》おとなしくなる ▪ The witness *slunk his pitch* mightily when old Kasm put him through on the cross-examination. その証人は老キャズムの反対訊問を受けるとひどくしゅんとしてしまった.
take the pitch out of 《米口》(カウボーイの乗る小馬)を勝手にあばれて疲れるに任せておとなしくさせる ▪ They led the animals out to the sand to *take the pitch out of* them. 彼らは馬を砂地に連れ出し，勝手にあばれて疲れるのに任せてならそうとした.
wild pitch 不注意な発言[行動] ▪ Calling comic books great literature—is that a *wild pitch*! 漫画を偉大な文学と呼ぶのは暴言だろうか. ☞野球の暴投から.

pitch[3] /pɪtʃ/ 動 ***be in there pitching*** 《米口》精いっぱい努力している ▪ Whenever I feel I can help I'll *be in there pitching*. いつでもお手伝いできると思ったときには，私は精いっぱい骨を折りましょう. ☞野球で投球することから.
pitch a curve 《米》カーブを投げる ▪ I can *pitch a curve* and catch a fly. 僕はカーブが投げられ，フライが取れます.
pitch a [*one's*] ***yarn*** [***line, story***] 《口》ほら話をする ▪ The skipper *pitches his yarns* with gusto. 船長はいかにもおもしろそうにほら話をする.
pitch and toss (船などが)あちこちに揺れる ▪ The ship was *pitching and tossing* in the storm. 船はあらしの中であちこちに揺れていた.
pitch it in (武器・言葉で)攻撃する，やっつける ▪ We were *pitching it in* red hot. 我々は猛烈にやっつけていた.
pitch it strong 《口》大げさに言う，話に尾ひれをつける ▪ Don't forget about my foreign languages when you meet him. You'll *pitch it strong*, won't you? あの人に会ったら忘れずに僕の語学を吹聴してくれ. 話に尾ひれをつけてくれ.
pitch woo 《米俗》いちゃつく; ペッティングをする ▪ And she *pitched* some more *woo* with Jan. そして彼女はジャンともう少しいちゃついた.

pitcher /pítʃər/ 名 ***Little*** [***Small***] ***pitchers have long*** [***wide***] ***ears.*** 《諺》子供は早耳.
Pitchers have ears. 《諺》壁に耳あり (＝WALLs have ears.).
The pitcher goes often to the well, but it is broken at last. 《諺》水差しはしばしば井戸に行くが，ついには割れてしまう《調子に乗りすぎるとついに失敗する》.

pitchfork /pítʃfɔ̀ːrk/ 名 ***rain pitchforks*** どしゃ降りに降る ▪ It is *raining pitchforks*. 雨がどしゃ降りに降っている.

pith /pɪθ/ 名 ***of*** (***great***) ***pith and moment*** 至極重大な (cf. Sh., *Haml*. 3. 1. 86) ▪ I have a secret to communicate, a secret *of great pith and moment*. 私はお伝えしたい秘密がある，至極重大な秘密なのだ.
the pith and marrow of …の最も重要な部分; の精髄 ▪ This is *the pith and marrow of* his views. これが彼の見解の精髄だ.
the pith and substance of →SUBSTANCE.

pit stop /pítstɑ̀p|-stɔ̀p/ 名 ***make a pit stop*** 《主に米口》(給油などのために)途中で停車する ▪ I have to use the bathroom—can we *make a pit stop* at the next service station? お手洗いに行きたいわ—次のサービスステーションで止まってもらっていい? ☞カーレースの pit stop (ピットイン)から.

pity /píti/ 名 ***feel pity for*** …を哀れむ，気の毒に思う ▪ I *feel* no *pity for* you at all. 君なんかちっとも気の毒とは思わない.
for pity's sake 後生だから ▪ *For pity's sake*, do be quiet! 後生だから，静かにしてくれ.
have [***take***] ***pity on*** [***upon***] …を哀れむ，気の毒に思う ▪ *Have pity on* me then. では私を哀れんでください.
in pity of …を気の毒に思って ▪ She wept *in pity of* his sad fate. 彼女は彼の悲しい運命を気の毒に思って泣いた.
it is a pity to *do* [***that***] …するのは[とは]残念だ ▪ *It* would *be a pity to* alter it. それを変更するのは残念だ ▪ *It is a* great *pity* [a thousand *pities*] *that* we should not be friends. 仲良しになれないとは非常に残念だ.
out of pity 気の毒に思って (*for*) ▪ I saved him *out of pity for* his children. 子供たちがかわいそうだから彼を救ってやった.
take pity on [***upon***] →have PITY on.
(***the***) ***more's the pity*** 《口》それは(ますます)残念だ ▪ *More's the pity* that we cannot adopt it. それを採用できないのは返すがえすも残念だ.
The pity of it! 残念なこと! ▪ But yet *the pity of it*, Iago! しかし残念だわい，イアゴー!
What a pity! なんと気の毒[残念]なことだろう (*that*) ▪ *What a pity* it is I was not born in the golden age. 黄金時代に生まれなかったとはなんて残念なことだろう ▪ *What a pity that* she can't come! 彼女が来られないなんてなんと気の毒なことだろう!

place[1] /pleɪs/ 名 ***a high place*** 高い地位 ▪ Ted reached *a high place* in the government at Washington. テッドはワシントンの政府高官になった.
A place for everything, and everything in its place. 《諺》しかるべき所にしかるべき物を《何もかもがきちんと整理され，あるべき場所に収まっている》.
a place in the sun →SUN[1].
a place of arms **1** 軍隊集合場 ▪ I was posted upon *a place of arms*. 軍隊集合場に配置された. **2** (火薬庫・退却地として用いられた)要さい(都市) ▪ Dunkirk was prized as *a place of arms*. ダンケルクは要さい都市として重要視された.

all over the place **1** 四方八方に ▪ His work took him *all over the place*. 彼は仕事のため四方八方へ行った.
2 《口》乱れて; 取り散らかして ▪ Her hair was *all over the place*. 彼女の髪は乱れていた ▪ The shavings were *all over the place*. かんなくずが一面に散らばっていた.
3 《口》ひどく取り乱して ▪ She was *all over the place* when her husband had an accident. 彼女は夫が事故にあったときひどく取り乱した.
4 《口》(計算などが)めちゃくちゃで ▪ When I run, my calculations are *all over the place*. 走ると, 私は計算がむちゃくちゃになる.

another place 上院 ▪ He had been called "a heaven-born minister" in *another place*. 彼は上院では「天国生まれの大臣」と呼ばれていた. ☞英国の下院用語.

as if [***like***] *one* ***owns the place*** 《口》わがもの顔で, 無遠慮に, 横柄に ▪ Mr. Hamilton walked around *as if* he *owns the place*. ハミルトン氏が遠慮会釈もなく歩き回っていた ▪ He prances around *as if* he *owns the place*. 彼はわがもの顔に大いばりで闊歩する.

be in the right [***wrong***] ***place at the right*** [***wrong***] ***time*** ちょうどよい[まずい]時にちょうどよい[まずい]場所に居合わせる ▪ Like all heroes, he *was in the right place at the right time*. あらゆるヒーローと同様, 彼はちょうどよい時代にちょうどよい場所に居合わせたものだ.

be no place for …のいる[来る]場所ではない ▪ This *is no place for* a young man. ここは若者の来る所ではない.

be *one's* ***place to*** *do* …するのは人の義務である ▪ It *is her place to* keep me company. 私の相手をするのは彼女の義務だ.

change places with *a person* 人と席[地位]を交換する ▪ I would not *change places with* anyone in the world. 私は世界中の誰とも地位を交換しはしない.

come to the right place (助言・援助を求めて)最適任者に近づく ▪ You've *come to the right place*, dear. We've all had similar experiences. あなたは良い所においでくださいました. 我々はみな同じ経験をしていますから.

Don't spend it all in one place. 《諺》一箇所で全部使ってはいけない,「大事に使え」. ☞人にお金, 特に少額の金をあげたあとに言われる文句.

fall [***click, drop, fit***] ***into place*** **1** つじつまが合う; 急にはっきりしてくる, 突然分かる ▪ It was all *fitting into place*. それは全て腑に落ちた ▪ Everything *clicked into place*! 全容が突然わかってきた.
2 望み通りに事が運ぶ ▪ If we use this as a guide, everything should *fall into place*. もしこれを指針にすれば, 万事うまく運ぶはずだ.
3 適当な場所[位置]に納まる[つく] ▪ When he told me his story, all the facts I had known before *fell into place*. 彼が事情を話してくれて, 私が前に知っていた事実がみな適当なところに納まった.

fill the place of →take the PLACE of.

find (***a***) ***place*** (位置を)占める, 宿る (*in*) ▪ His name has *found a place in* history. 彼の名は歴史に残った ▪ Can discontent *find place* within that breast? 不満があの胸中に宿ることがあろうか.

from place to place あちらこちらと ▪ Nomads roam *from place to place* in search of pasture for their cattle. 遊牧の民は家畜の牧草地を求めてあちこちと流浪する.

give place to **1** …に席[地位]を譲る; に取って代わられる ▪ Winter sped by, *giving place to* spring. 冬がすみやかに去って, 春に取って代わられた ▪ Wonder *gave place to* admiration. 驚きが感嘆に変わった.
2 …をさせるようになる ▪ His resignation *gave place to* a regular house-cleaning of cabinet officers. 彼が辞任したので, 内閣の職員の本格的な整理が行われることとなった.

go places 《口》 **1** 方々へ行く, 遊び歩く ▪ *Go places* and see things. 方々へ行って色々な物を見よ.
2 成功する ▪ That new movie star is *going places* and will soon be in the front ranks in Hollywood. あの新人映画スターは成功していて, じきにハリウッドの第一線に立つだろう.

go to *one's* ***place*** →GO^2.

have a … place in …の位置を占める ▪ English *has an* important *place in* Japanese universities. 日本の大学では英語は重要な位置を占める.

have a soft place in *one's* ***heart for*** = have a soft SPOT (in one's heart) for.

have place 存在する余地がある; 存在する (*in, among*) ▪ Vague assertions *have* no *place in* scientific discussion. ばく然とした言説は科学上の議論には無用だ ▪ The same law *had place in* Thebes. それと同じ法律がテーベにあった.

in its place あるべき場所に ▪ I wish you would keep everything *in its place*. 万事をきちっとしておいてくれたらいいのに.

in place **1** きまった[適当な]場所に; きちっとしていて (= in POSITION) ▪ Everything was *in place*. 万事きちっとしていた.
2 適当な (↔out of PLACE 2) ▪ Your suggestion is quite *in place*. ご注意は全く当を得ています.
3 同じ場所で ▪ Warm up by marching *in place* 100 times as you swing your arms. 腕を振りながら同じ場所で100回足踏みをして体を温めなさい.

in a person's place 他人の立場に ▪ Put yourself *in his place*. 彼の立場になってみなさい ▪ If I were *in your place*, I would not do so. 僕が君の立場にあったら, そうはしないね.

in places 所々に ▪ I found the book absorbing *in places*. その本は所々とてもおもしろかった.

in the first [***second, last,*** etc.] ***place*** 第一[第二, 最後, など]に ▪ *In the first place*, frost strikes deeper and *in the second place*, the streets are more often disturbed. 第一に霜はより

深く染み込み，第二に往来はより頻繁にかき乱される．

in **(*the*)** ***place of*** …の代わりに ▪ Plant a willow tree *in* (*the*) *place of* this dead pine. この枯れたマツの木の代わりにヤナギの木を植えなさい ▪ Mr. Jones is sick and Mr. Brown teaches *in his place* today. ジョーンズ先生が病気なので，きょうはブラウン先生が代わって教える．

into place 適当な所へ ▪ Hoist the tent poles *into place*. テントの柱を適当な所へ立てなさい．

keep *a person* ***in*** *his* ***place*** 人をつけ上がらせない ▪ She gave them a cold look in order to *keep* such people *in their place*. 彼女はそのような人々をつけ上がらせないように冷ややかな視線を送った．

keep *one's* ***place*** **1** 読んでいる所をはっきりさせておく ▪ Use a book-mark to *keep your place*. 読んでいる所をはっきりさせておくためしおりを用いなさい．
2 身のほどを忘れない ▪ The servant should *keep his place*. 使用人は身のほどを忘れてはならない．

know *a person* ***in high places*** 有力者と面識がある ▪ Ted's grandfather was the mayor of Chicago so he *knows* people *in high places*. 祖父がシカゴ市長だったので，テッドはお歴々と懇意である．

know *one's* ***place*** 身のほどを知る ▪ Someone ought to teach him to *know his place*. 誰か身のほどを知ることを彼に教えてやらねばならない．

one's ***last resting place*** 《婉曲》永眠の場所，墓場 ▪ A true brave soldier, a loving father has gone to *his last resting place*. 真の勇者，愛する父上はお墓に入ってしまわれた．

lose *one's* ***place*** **1** 自分の場所[位置]を失う ▪ He *lost his place* in the class. 彼は席次が下がった．
2 読んでいた所がわからなくなる ▪ I've *lost my place* in the book. この本の読んでいた所がわからなくなった．

make place for …に席をあける ▪ Please *make place for* the ladies. ご婦人がたに席をおあけください．

Nice place you have here. 素敵なお住まいですね ▪ *Nice place you have here.*—Thanks. We like it. 素敵なお住まいね—ありがとう．気に入ってるんだ．

not *one's* ***place to*** *do* 《古風》…するのは自分の分際ではない[僭越である] ▪ It's *not my place to* give orders. 命令するなんて私の分際ではありません．

of all places (驚きを強調して)よりによって，あろうことか，なんと ▪ Austin was born in Austin, *of all places*. オースティンはよりによってオースティンで生まれた．

out of place **1** 適所を得ていないで，置き違えて ▪ The two verses are evidently *out of place*. その二つの詩は明らかに置き違えられている．
2 場違いで，不適当で (↔in PLACE 2) ▪ It may not be *out of place* to examine it here. それをここで吟味するのも場違いではないだろう ▪ Your conduct is quite *out of place*. 君の行為は全く当を得ていない．
3 失職して[した] ▪ They are domestic servants *out of place*. 彼らは勤め口のない使用人だ．

put *a person* ***in*** *his* ***place*** ＝keep a person in his PLACE.

put *oneself* ***in*** *a person's* ***place*** ＝put oneself into a person's SHOEs.

run in place (努力するが)進歩がない (→in PLACE 3) ▪ I've worked on this plan for months but feel I'm *running in place*. この計画に数か月尽力してきたが，進歩がないと感じている．

scream the place down 大声で叫ぶ，絶叫する ▪ Mum would *scream the place down* if she saw a dead mouse. お母さんは死んだネズミを見たら絶叫するだろう．

supply the place of …の代用になる ▪ It *supplies the place of* a dictionary. それは辞書の代用になる．

take place 起きる; 催される ▪ The police were informed of what had *taken place*. 警察は起こったことを知らされた ▪ When does the concert *take place*? 音楽会はいつあるの?

take *one's* ***place*** 位置を占める ▪ He has *taken his place* among the writers of this age. 彼は当代の作家の間に伍するようになった ▪ His name has *taken its place* in history. 彼の名は歴史に載った．

take second place **(*to …*)** 優先順位が(…の次に)くる，後回しにされる，二の次で ▪ Golf has to *take second place to* his work. ゴルフは二の次で本業が優先されなければならない ▪ Once every four years, Wimbledon has to *take second place to* the World Cup. 4年に1度ウィンブルドンはワールドカップがあるため二の次の扱いを受ける．

take **[*fill*]** ***the place of*** …に代わる，の代理をする ▪ A torii *takes the place of* an arch in Japan. 日本では鳥居がアーチの代わりをする ▪ I *took his place* as judge. 私が審判として彼の代理をした．

teach *a person his* ***place*** 人に身のほどを知らせる，分際をわきまえさせる ▪ He should *teach* his servants *their place*. 彼は召し使いに分際をわきまえさせるべきだ．☞place は常に単数．

the other place 別な場所; あちらさん《Oxford 大学から見ての Cambridge 大学，またはその逆》; (天国に対して)地獄 ▪ Shall I go to heaven for doing that, or to *the other place*? そんなことをしたら天国行きだろうか，地獄行きだろうか．

There's no place like home. 《諺・陳腐》わが家に勝る場所はない (J. H. Payne, *Home, Sweet Home*).

place[2] /pleɪs/ 動 ***be well*** **[*better, ideally,*** etc.**]** ***placed for*** **[*to*** *do***]** **1** (…するよう[…に])好都合[理想的]な立場にある ▪ Graduates *are well placed for* a wide career choice. 本学卒業生はさまざまな職種につく機会に恵まれています．
2 いい立地にある ▪ The hotel *is ideally placed for* those who wish to visit the Vatican while staying in Rome. 当ホテルはローマ滞在中にバチカン宮殿を訪問なさりたいお客様に理想的な立地にございます．

place first 第一位に置く ▪ Of many factors this may *be placed first*. 多くの要因のうちでもこれが第一のものだろう．

plague[1] /pleɪg/ 名 ***A plague on both your houses!*** (けんかばかりする両者にうんざりして)どっちもく

P

たばるがいい, いい加減によさないか (cf. Sh., *Rom. & Jul.* 3. 1. 96) ▪ I am hurt: *A plague on both your houses!* やられてしまった. 両家ともくたばってしまえ!

A plague take ...!/(A) plague on* [*upon, of*] *...! ...はいまいましい!, ちくしょう! ▪ *A plague take* him! あんちくしょうめ! ▪ There he is come back—*plague on* him! あそこへ彼がまた帰って来ている—いまいましい!

avoid ... like the plague ...を疫病のようにきらって近寄らない ▪ I *avoid* controversy *like the plague*. 私は論争を疫病のように避けている.

What the* [*a*] *plague!/How the plague! 一体; まあ ▪ *What the plague* do you send me on your fool's errand for? 一体なんのために僕をむだな使い走りにやるのか.

plague[2] /pleɪg/ 動 ***plague the life out of*** *a person* 《口》人をひどくいじめる[悩ます] ▪ You are so odd that you would *plague the life out of* her. 君はとても変人だから彼女をひどく悩ませるだろう.

plague *a person* ***to death*** 人をひどく困らせる[悩ませる] ▪ I *am plagued to death* by his everlasting begging. 彼にしょっちゅう金の無心をされるのでほとほと困っている.

plain /pleɪn/ 形 ***a plain Jane*** 不器量な少女[女性] ▪ She has always thought herself *a plain Jane*. 彼女は常に自分は不器量だと思っていた.

***(as) plain as a packsaddle* [*as print, as day(light), as the sun at noonday, as Salisbury, as the way to parish-church*]** 《口》きわめて明白で, 明々白々な ▪ Why, it's *as plain as Salisbury*. いや, それはきわめて明白だよ《Salisbury Plain との地口》 ▪ Her look said *as plain as print*, "Have you not had enough?" 彼女の目つきはきわめて明瞭に「もう十分食べたでしょ」と言っていた ▪ I can see every detail *plain as day* even without my reading glasses! 眼鏡をかけなくてもどんな細かな点までもはっきり見えるぞ!

(as) plain as a pikestaff →PIKESTAFF.

(as) plain as the nose on* [*in*]** *one's* ***face →NOSE[1].

in plain clothes 私服[平服]の ▪ He turned out to be a policeman *in plain clothes*. 彼は私服の警官であることがわかった.

***in plain English* [*words*]** 平たく言えば, はっきり言えば ▪ The outside will be, *in plain English*, nearly useless. 外側は平たく言えばほとんど無価値になるだろう.

make plain =make CLEAR.

plain and simple =PURE and simple.

plain dealing 率直(なやり方) ▪ He was a lover of ingenuity and *plain dealing*. 彼は創意と率直さを愛していた.

plain sailing とんとん拍子に運ぶこと ▪ For a man of his ability, that assignment was *plain sailing*. 彼のように才能のある人間にはそんな仕事は朝めし前だった. ☞PLANE sailing「平面航法」の通俗用法から.

to be plain with you 率直に言えば ▪ *To be plain with you*, we do not consider your work entirely satisfactory. 率直に言えば, 我々は君の仕事をすっかり満足すべきものとは考えていないのだ.

plan[1] /plæn/ 名 ***according to plan*** 計画通りに ▪ Everything went *according to plan*. 万事計画通りにいった.

in plan 平面図として (↔in SECTION) ▪ We see the planets' evolution, not *in plan*, but in section. 我々は惑星の運行を平面図として見るのではなくて, 断面図として見る.

lay-away plan 商品予約購入法《代金を払い終わるまで店が品物を取り置きしておく》 ▪ Unable to pay for the coat all at once, she used the *lay-away plan*. 彼女はコート代金を一度に払う余裕がなかったので, 商品予約購入法を利用した ▪ We now offer a *lay-away plan* for our customers. 当店ではお客様に商品予約購入法を提供しております.

make plans for ...の計画を立てる ▪ I'm *making plans for* the holidays. 休暇の計画を立てています.

on* [*under*] *a plan ある案・計画に従って ▪ I shall be able to finish this work *on the plan* I have commenced. 初めの計画通りにこの著作を完成できるだろう.

plan B 代替案, 代わりの戦略 ▪ "I'll have a back-up plan." She always had a *plan B*. 「私には代替策があります」彼女はいつも代案を用意していた.

the best-laid plans この上もなく慎重に練り上げた計画 (→the best-laid SCHEMEs of mice and men) ▪ *The best-laid plans* go astray. どんなに練り上げられた計画でも誤ることがある.

plan[2] /plæn/ 動 ***plan ahead*** 前もって計画する ▪ I always *plan ahead*. 私は常に前もって計画する.

plane /pleɪn/ 名形 ***be on another plane from*** ...とは趣を異にする ▪ They *are on* altogether *another plane from* Jesus. 彼らはイエスとは全く趣を異にしている.

by plane/in* [*on*] *a plane 飛行機で, 空路 ▪ He traveled to Paris *by plane*. 彼は空路パリへ旅行した.

on the same plane as ...と同列[同格]で ▪ The superstitious man is *on the same plane as* the savage. 迷信家は野蛮人と同列にある.

planet /plǽnət/ 名 ***(live) on another planet*** 《口》現実離れしている, 現実を認識できていない ▪ What a foolish idea! I think she's *living on another planet*. なんてばかげた考えだ! 彼女の考えは実現不可能だと思う.

What planet are you on? 《口》何をぼんやりしているの? 現実がわかっているのか? ▪ Mr. President, *what planet are you on?* (Why war?) 大統領閣下, 現実がおわかりですか. (どうして戦争を?)

plank[1] /plæŋk/ 名 ***a plank in a* [*one's*] *platform*** 政綱の一項目 ▪ They will make temperance *a plank in their platform*. 彼らは禁酒を

P

政綱の一項目にするだろう.

burn the planks 長らく座っている ▪ He sat obstinately *burning the planks*. 彼は頑固に長らくじっと座っていた.

have the plank 《米戯》発言権を持っている ▪ "Silence," said Ned, "Mr. Walker *has the plank*."「静かに」とネッドが言った.「ウォーカーさんが発言しているのです」.

walk the plank [***gangplank***] **1** 舷側から突き出した板を目隠しして歩かされる《板がはねて海中におぼれて死ぬ; 17 世紀ごろ海賊が捕虜を殺すのに用いた方法》 ▪ I had to take it, or *walk the plank*. 私はそれを受けいれるか, 舷側から突き出した板を目隠しして歩かされるかどっちかしなければならなかった.

2《口》(強制的に)辞職させられる, クビになる ▪ I was made to *walk the plank*. 私は無理に退職させられた ▪ When a new owner bought the supermarket, the manager had to *walk the plank*. そのスーパーのオーナーが代わったとき, 支配人は辞めねばならなかった.

plank[2] /plæŋk/ 動 ***plank*** *oneself* ***down*** どっかり座る ▪ He *planked himself down* on a sofa. 彼はソファにどっかと座った.

plank it 板の間[地べた]に寝る ▪ We'll *plank it* at night. 夜は地べたに寝ることにしよう.

plant[1] /plænt|plɑːnt/ 名 ***in plant*** 生長して; 葉をつけて ▪ Clover is now *in plant*. クローバーが今や葉をつけている.

lose plant 枯れる ▪ The wheat often *loses plant* in spring. 小麦は春枯れることが多い.

miss [***fail in***] ***plant*** はえそこなう ▪ Clover, if sown oftener, is apt to *fail in plant*. クローバーはたびたび蒔(ま)くとはえそこないがちだ.

plant[2] /plænt|plɑːnt/ 動 ***plant*** *oneself* **1** 陣取る, 腰をおろす ▪ The dog *planted himself* close by the door. 犬はドアの間近に陣取っていた.

2 身を落ち着ける ▪ They invited him to come and *plant himself* in Sicily. 彼らは彼にシチリア島に来て落ち着くように招いた.

plaster[1] /plǽstər|plɑ́ːs-/ 名 ***use as a sticking plaster*** 応急修理をする ▪ If you are *using* gambling *as a sticking plaster* for other difficulties in your life, just stopping gambling will automatically solve everything else. もし賭け事を他の人生の問題解決の応急措置として使っているのなら, 賭け事を止めさえすればすべて自動的に解決します. ☞sticking plaster「テープばんそうこう」.

plaster[2] /plǽstər|plɑ́ːs-/ 動 ***be plastered*** (***over***) ***with*** …を(一面に)貼りつけている, 塗り立てている ▪ The old trunk *was plastered* (*over*) *with* hotel labels. その古トランクにはホテルのラベルがべたべた貼りつけてあった.

plate /pleɪt/ 名 ***a full plate*** 予定表のぎっしりの仕事, 多くのやらなくてはならないこと ▪ I have got *a full plate* this weekend but I will have more time this summer! この週末はとても忙しいが, この夏はゆったりと時間が取れるだろう.

a selling plate 勝馬を予定価格で売る条件で入場を許された競馬 ▪ Success was a good horse for *a selling plate*. サクセス号は勝馬を予め定めた値で売却する競馬用としてはいい馬だった.

have enough [***a lot,*** etc.] ***on*** *one's* ***plate*** 《口》すべき仕事が十分[たくさん, など]ある ▪ Nowadays I *have too much on my plate*. 近ごろは仕事が多すぎる.

have [***hand, give, serve up***]***... on a plate*** 《口》…(貴重なもの)を労せずして手に入れる[与える] ▪ The car factories of Japan will *have* a new market *on a plate*. 日本の自動車工場は据え膳で新市場を得るだろう ▪ Just ask him—he'll *serve up* the data *on a plate*. 彼にちょっと頼んだら簡単にデータをくれるだろう.

home plate 《野球》本塁, ホームベース ▪ Felix slid headfirst across *home plate*. フィーリックスはヘッドスライディングで本塁を落とし入れた.

put up *one's* ***plate*** (医院などを)開業する ▪ He *put up his plate* in London. 彼はロンドンで医院を開業した. ☞plate「医者の看板」.

spin the plate 《米口》皿回し《家の中での遊び》 ▪ We played the old-fashioned games like "*spin the plate*." 我々は「皿回し」のような古いゲームをした.

step up to the plate 《米》責任を負う, 困難に立ち向かう ▪ The administration said they were going to *step up to the plate*. 本部は自分たちが責任を取るといった. ☞plate《野球》「打者が立つホームベース」.

platinum /plǽtənəm|plǽtɪ-/ 名 ***go platinum*** (レコード・CD が)プラチナディスクに値する販売実績を挙げる ▪ Their albums *go platinum* almost instantly. 彼らのアルバムはリリースとほぼ同時に 100 万枚売れる.

platter /plǽtər/ 名 ***hand*** [***give***]***... to*** *a person* ***on a*** (***silver***) ***platter*** 人に(貴重な)物をやすやすと[据え膳で, 労せずに]与える ▪ No one is going to *hand* you democracy *on a silver platter*; you have to fight for it. 誰も民主主義を労せずに与えてくれはしない. 闘い取らなければならないのだ ▪ He *was handed* the job *on a silver platter*. 彼は労せずしてその職を与えられた ▪ She expected to *be handed* everything *on a silver platter*. 彼女は何でも簡単にもらえるものと期待していた.

play[1] /pleɪ/ 名 ***All work and no play makes Jack a dull boy.*** 《諺》休みなしの勉強や仕事は人をだめにする,「よく学び, よく遊べ」.

as good as a play 芝居のように[非常に]おもしろい ▪ The tale that he told was *as good as a play*. 彼がした話は芝居のようにおもしろかった ▪ It was *as good as a play* to see it. それを見るのはとてもおもしろかった.

at play 遊んでいる ▪ He was *at play* while the rest were at work. 彼は他の人がみな仕事をしているときに遊んでいた.

bring [***call, put***]***... into play*** …を活動させる, 活用する ▪ He knows how to *bring into play* all the experience he has accumulated. 彼は身につけ

た経験をすっかり活用する方法を知っている ▪ Those impressions *called* his brain *into play*. それらの印象が彼の頭を働かせ始めた.

child's* [*boy's*] *play 児戯に類すること, 朝めし前のこと ▪ This crossword is mere *boy's play*. このクロスワードはほんの朝めし前の仕事だ.

come into play 活動し始める; 影響を及ぼし始める, 効果が現れる ▪ The muscular fibers of the stomach next *come into play*. 胃の筋肉組織が次に働き始める ▪ Market forces might *come into play* that could hold gasoline prices down. 市場動向がガソリン価格を引き下げかねない影響を及ぼし始めよう.

give full* [*free, more*] *play (...を)十分[存分に, もっと]働かせる (*to*); (に)ゆとりを持たせる ▪ *Give full play to* your imagination. 君の想像力を十分に発揮しなさい ▪ He *gave free play to* his imagination. 彼は思う存分に想像力を働かせた ▪ *Give* the rope *more play*. ロープをもっとゆるめなさい.

go out of play 《スポーツ》(ボールが)線外に出る ▪ The ball *went out of play*. ボールが線外に出た.

go to the play 芝居を見に行く ▪ Let's *go to the play* this evening. 今晩芝居を見に行こう.

have play (機械の部品が)遊び[ゆるみ]がある ▪ The tenon *has* too much *play* in its mortise. そのほぞはほぞ穴の中で遊びがありすぎる.

hold* [*keep*]*... in play ...を働かせておく, に仕事をさせておく ▪ A struggling faction *held* them continually *in play*. あがいている徒党のため彼らは絶えず仕事があった ▪ I *keep* my devotion *in play* by the rehearsal of an anthem or two. 賛美歌を一つ二つ復誦して私の信仰心を働かせておく.

in full play 盛んに活動[運転]中で ▪ The usual bustle was *in full play*. いつものようにひどく雑踏していた ▪ The engine was *in full play*. エンジンは盛んに動いていた.

in play **1** 冗談に (↔in EARNEST) ▪ Don't be offended; I only said it *in play*. 気を悪くしないでください. 冗談に言っただけですから. ☞in FUN のほうが普通の言い方.

2 (試合中のボールが)生きて (↔out of PLAY) ▪ The striker touched the ball while *in play*. 打者はボールが生きているうちに手を触れた.

3 働いて, 作動して, 影響を及ぼして ▪ Powerful political forces were *in play* here. ここには強力な政治力が働いていた.

4 《商・口》会社を乗っ取る状況にある, 会社買収の可能性がある ▪ The world was aware that the company was *in play*. 世間はその会社が他社を乗っ取ろうとしていることを知っていた.

make a play for 《口》 **1** あの手この手で...を手に入れようとする ▪ Both parties are *making a play for* the agricultural vote. 両党とも農民票を得ようとやっきになっている.

2 ...に言い寄る ▪ When she *made a play for* the lad, her husband got mad. 彼女がその若者に言い寄ったとき, 夫はかんかんに怒った.

***make great* [*much, a good deal of, a big*] *play with* [*of, about*]** (手柄・苦しみ・数字など)を大げさに言う; (金時計など)をこれ見よがしにいじくり回す ▪ He *made great play with* his sufferings. 彼は自分の苦しみを大げさに言った ▪ She *made much play with* her diamond ring. 彼女はダイヤの指輪をこれ見よがしにいじくり回した ▪ The press has *made great play of* the massive rise in wages in South Korea over the past ten years. 新聞は, 過去10年にわたる韓国の大幅な賃金上昇をことさら強調してきた.

make play **1** 《競馬・狩》追っ手を悩ます[じらす] ▪ The fox *made play* for no less than nine-and-twenty dogs. そのキツネは29頭もの犬をじらした.

2 《ボクシング》敵を猛撃する ▪ Gully *made play*, and planted two other blows on his adversary's head. ガリーは猛攻して相手の頭にもう2発見舞った.

3 (一般的に)どしどしやる; 急ぐ ▪ They *made play* in the New World. 彼らは新世界で盛んに働いた ▪ I'm too late, and therefore must *make play*. 私は遅れているので急がねばなりません.

4 (...を)効果的に[華々しく]利用する (*with*) ▪ He *made play with* political issues in comedy. 彼は喜劇に政治問題を効果的に利用した.

out of play (ボールが)死んで (↔in PLAY 2) ▪ The ball is *out of play*. ボールは死んでいる[ボールデッドだ].

part of the play しなければならないこと ▪ He ordered you to do it. Surely that's *part of the play*. 彼は君にそれをしろと言ったのだ. 確かにそれはしなければならないことだよ.

play on* [*upon*] *words しゃれ, 地口 ▪ It was a childish *play on words*. それは幼稚なしゃれであった.

play[2] /pleɪ/ 動 ***a level playing field*** → FIELD.

be played out 《口》 **1** へとへとになる ▪ I'*m* absolutely *played out*. すっかりへとへとだ.

2 使いものにならない; 時代おくれだ ▪ The poor old car *is played out*. この古車はおんぼろになってしまった ▪ That old plot *is* completely *played out*. その古いプロットはすっかり時代おくれだ. ☞「芝居が終わって」が原義.

have* (*money, time,* etc.) *to play with 《口》余るほど(金, 時間, など)がある ▪ We won't waste any time, because we *have*n't *got* much *time to play with*. 一刻の猶予もない, なぜならもてあそぶような時間はないのだから.

How does it play? どうやって遊ぶの?; どう反応するのか?; どう見極めるのか? ▪ Sure the game looks nice, but *how does it play?* ゲームは確かにおもしろそうだけど, どうやって遊ぶの ▪ *How is* our attempt at liberating Iraq *playing* in the Arab streets, now that Baghdad has fallen? バグダッドが陥落した現在, イラクを自由にしようとするわれらの試みはアラブの町でどう受け入れられるのであろうか.

play a good stick フェンシングがうまい ▪ If he is a tolerably good boxer, he can *play a good stick*. 彼はボクシングはまあまあだとしても, フェンシングはうまい.

play a straight bat まっとうに全力を尽くす

▪ You're entering upon life, my boy; always try to *play a straight bat*. お前は世の中へ出て行くわけだが, いつもまっとうに全力を尽くすんだよ.

play a town 《米口》ある町での公演をする ▪ A troupe of barnstormers are *playing* the smaller *towns* in this vicinity. へぼ役者の一座がこの付近の小さい町々で巡業している.

play big luck 《米口》運がいい ▪ You're *playing big luck*. 君はついているんだよ.

play both ends against the middle 《米口》両者を張り合わせて漁夫の利を得ようとする ▪ Do you always *play both ends against the middle*? 君はいつも両者を張り合わせて漁夫の利を得ようとするのかね. ☞faro という賭けトランプから.

play dead 死んだふりをする ▪ Ted dropped down and *played dead*, just to avoid that strike. テッドはその一撃を避けるためばったり倒れて死んだふりをした.

play** a person **dirt →DIRT.

play dirty 《口》ずるい[不正な, 汚い]やり方でする, いかさま[いんちき]をする ▪ We don't *play dirty*, but we play serious. えげつないことはせず, まじめにやります.

play even 《米》損[破産]をしないようにする ▪ He resorted to ways that are dark in order to *play even*. 彼は破産をしないようにするためによからぬ手段に訴えた.

play fair (***with***) →FAIR.

play false [***foul, foully***] (人)をだます, 裏切る ▪ You *played false* with us. あなたは私たちをあざむいた ▪ His memory *played* him *false* in this matter. これはあの人の記憶ちがいだ.

play fast and loose →FAST.

play favorites 《米口》えこひいきをする ▪ I mustn't "*play favorites*," as those slangy nephews of mine put it. 私はあの俗語をよく使う甥っ子たちの言う「えこひいきをし」てはいけない.

play for safety やまをかけない, 大事をとる ▪ The firm *played for safety* and refused to take on any new commitments. その会社は大事をとって新しい売買契約は絶対にしなかった.

play for time 時をかせぐ ▪ Our only hope is to *play for time* until help arrives. 我々の望みは助けが来るまで時をかせぐことだけだ.

play freeze-out 窓[扉]を開け放ったり冷房を下げたりする[下げて人に凍える思いをさせる] ▪ It's very cold in here! Who's *playing freeze-out*? この中はとても寒いや! 冷房を下げているのは誰だ?

play** one's **hand for all it is worth → HAND[1].

play hard to get →HARD.

play hardball (***with** a person*) → HARDBALL.

play ignorant [***dumb***] 知らないふりをする, しらばっくれる ▪ I *played ignorant* as to the letter he spoke of. 彼が話した手紙のことは知らないふりをした ▪ The press *played dumb*. 新聞・雑誌はだんまりを決め込んだ.

play** oneself **in (スポーツ, 特にクリケットで)体を慣らして徐々に調子を上げる ▪ The batman *played himself in* carefully. 打者は注意深く体を慣らして調子を上げていった.

play in hard luck →PLAY to hard luck.

play it alone 《米》相棒なしにやっていく ▪ He concluded that he would *play it alone*. 彼は相棒なしでやっていくことに決めた.

play it cool 《口》冷静に構える, 言質(げんち)を与えない ▪ We asked for a price and the agent *played it cool*. 値段を聞いたが, 外交員は言質を与えなかった.

play it (***low***) ***on** a person* 《俗》人をだます ▪ He *played it on* William in a way I despise. 彼は見下げたやり方でウィリアムをだました.

play it right うまく立ち回る ▪ If you *play it right*, you will get promotion. うまく立ち回れば昇進するだろう.

play (***it***) ***safe*** 万全を期す, 慎重に行動する ▪ He seldom *plays it safe*. 彼はめったに慎重に行動しない.

play it straight 事実をありのままに扱う[話す] ▪ Newspapers should *play it straight*. 新聞は事実をありのままに伝えるべきだ.

play itself out 終わる, すたれる ▪ This burlesque gradually *played itself out*. この低俗な笑劇は次第にすたれた ▪ The style *played itself out* completely. その様式はすっかりすたれてしまった.

play kissy (-) ***face*** [***kissy-kissy***] 《口》人目も憚(はばか)らずキスし合う; やたらといちゃつき合う ▪ John and Mary *played kissy face*. ジョンとメアリーはいちゃつきまくった.

play loose 《フェンシング》攻撃を加える ▪ Making the assault and *playing loose* are synonymous. 「攻撃を加える」と "play loose" とは同じ意味である.

play on [***upon***] ***words*** しゃれを言う ▪ He has a habit of *playing on words*. 彼はしゃれを言う癖がある.

play out time (守勢のチームが得点を許さずに)ゲームの最後まで持ちこたえる ▪ There's no hope of victory but at least we can *play out time*. 勝つ見込みはないが, 少なくともゲームの最後までは持ちこたえられる.

play politics 私利を図る, 私欲にふける ▪ We're tired of you guys *playing politics* with this issue. おまえたちがこの件で私腹を肥やしているのにはうんざりする.

play safe 危険は犯さない, 大事をとる ▪ The tendency in Europe is to *play safe*. ヨーロッパにおける傾向は危険は犯さないということだ.

play second 下っ端役を務める (*to*) ▪ I refuse to *play second to* young Simpson. 若造のシンプスンの下っ端役を務めるのはごめんだ.

***play sharp on** a person* 《米口》人を抜け目なくだます ▪ I *played sharp on* the coach, by pretending to be ill. 僕は仮病を使って抜け目なくコーチをだましてやった.

play smash with 《米口》…をぶちこわす, ぺしゃんこにする ▪ That *played smash with* a passenger train. それが客車をぶちこわした.

play straight (***with***) (…に対して)公正にふるまう

▪ I have always *played straight with* everyone. 私はいつも誰にも公正にふるまってきた.

play the game →GAME.

play the heavy line →HEAVY.

play to* [*in*] *hard luck 《米口》つらい目にあう ▪ These young people have been *playing to hard luck* in the southwest. この若者たちは南西部でつらい目にあってきた.

***play well* [*badly*]** 《クリケット》(グラウンドが)試合のやれる[やれない]状態である ▪ The pitch *plays well*. 三柱門の中間の場所は試合のやれる状態だ.

play with *oneself* 《俗》自慰する ▪ I didn't feel the urge to *play with myself*. 僕は自慰したい衝動は感じなかった.

What are you playing at? 《口》何をふざけたことをしているのか《危険な, あるいはばかげたことをしている人への叱責の言葉》.

playful /pléɪfəl/ 形 **(*as*) *playful as a kitten*** 子猫のようにふざけたがる ▪ The little girl is *as playful as a kitten*. その女の子は子猫みたいにふざけたがる.

playhouse /pléɪhàʊs/ 名 ***upset*** *a person's* ***playhouse*** 《米口》人の計画をぶちこわす ▪ It certainly would *upset my playhouse*. それできっと私の計画はぶちこわされてしまうだろう. ☞playhouse「(子供の)おもちゃ遊びの家」.

plea /pliː/ 名 ***cop a plea*** 《米俗》 **1** (罪を軽くしてもらうため)口を割る ▪ The prisoner *copped a plea* of guilty. 被告は口を割って罪を認めた.

2 許しを請う, 言い訳をする ▪ The man is refusing to *cop a plea* for his latest charge. 男は先の告発に対して許しを請おうとはしないでいる ▪ He tried to "*cop a plea*" about missing a test. 彼は試験を欠席した「口実を述べ」立てようとした.

on* [*under*] *the plea of …を口実に ▪ He resigned *under the plea of* ill-health. 彼は病気を口実に辞職した.

P

plead /pliːd/ 動 ***plead guilty* [*not guilty*] (*to*)** (被告人が)自分の罪を認める[認めない];《口》身に覚えがある[ない]と言う ▪ *To* this I must *plead guilty*. このことに私は身に覚えがあると言わねばならない ▪ I can *plead not guilty to* a fondness for gossip. 私はゴシップ好きだなんて身に覚えがない.

pleasant /plézənt/ 形 ***make*** *oneself* ***pleasant*** あいそよくする (*to*) ▪ She *made herself* particularly *pleasant to* the visitors. 彼女はお客に特にあいそよくした.

please /pliːz/ 動 ***as … as you please*** 《口》とても… ▪ She was dressed for the wedding and she looked *as* pretty *as you please*. 婚礼衣装を身につけたら彼女はこの上なくきれいに見えた.

(*as*) *pleased* [*proud*] *as Punch* →PUNCH.

be pleased at …を喜んでいる ▪ I *am pleased at* your coming. ようこそおいでくださいました.

be pleased to *do* **1** …してうれしい ▪ We*'re* very *pleased to* see you here. ここでお目にかかれて大変うれしい.

2 喜んで…する ▪ He *is* quite *pleased to* be leaving. 彼は喜んで去ろうとしている ▪ I shall [will] *be pleased to* help you. 喜んでお助けいたしましょう.

3 …したもう, してくださる ▪ His Majesty *was* graciously *pleased to* pay a visit. 陛下はかしこくも行幸したもうた.

4 《皮肉》気まぐれに…する ▪ My dear Sir! You *are pleased to* be amusing this morning. まあ, あなた, けさはどういう風の吹き回しか, おもしろいことをおっしゃるんですね.

be pleased with …が気に入っている, に満足している ▪ I *am pleased with* my new servant. 今度の使用人に満足している.

be pleased with *oneself* 自分一人で満足している, 一人悦に入っている《しばしば非難をこめて》 ▪ Paul's glance at me showed he *was* very *pleased with himself*. ポールが私をチラッと見たことで彼が自己満足していることが分かった.

do what* [*as*]** *one* ***pleases 好きなようにする, 勝手にする ▪ You may *do what* you *please*. 好きなようになさい ▪ I will *do* exactly *as* I *please*. 思う通りにします.

hard to please 気むずかしい, 喜ばしにくい ▪ He is *hard to please*. 彼は気むずかしやだ.

if you please **1** どうぞ ▪ Do so, *if you please*. どうかそうしてください ▪ Will you have another cup?—*If you please*. もう1杯いかがですか?—よろしければ.

2 ごめんこうむって ▪ I will wash my hands, *if you please*. 失礼して手を洗わしてもらいます.

3 《皮肉》どうでしょう, 驚いたことには《驚くべき事柄を挿入的に強調して》 ▪ He must travel first class, *if you please*, like his betters. あの男はどうでしょう, 目上の者と同様にファーストクラスで行くと言ってきかないんですよ ▪ And then *if you please* he blamed me for it! それからどうだろう, 彼はそのことで私を責めたんだ.

I'm* (*very*) *pleased to meet you. 《文》お会いできてうれしゅうございます; はじめまして ▪ Richard, this is Dr Leech.—*I'm pleased to meet you*. リチャード, こちらはリーチ博士だ—はじめまして. ☞初対面のときのしばしば握手をしながらの挨拶.

it pleases *one* ***to*** *do* 人が…する気になる ▪ *It* has never *pleased* him *to* explain it. 彼はいつもその説明をしたがらなかった.

more than pleased 非常にうれしい (→MORE than 2) ▪ The pen arrived today and I am *more than pleased*. ペンが今日届いたよ, とてもうれしいです.

none too pleased むっとして, いらだって ▪ Jo was *none too pleased* at the news of his girlfriend's pregnancy! ジョーはガールフレンドが妊娠したという知らせを聞いてむっとした.

only too pleased* (*to *do*) この上なくうれしい, 進んで[喜んで]…する (→ONLY too 1) ▪ We're *only too pleased to* help in any way we can. 喜んでできる限りお手伝いをさせていただきます ▪ Robinson was *only too pleased to* have someone to talk to. ロビンスンは話相手ができてとてつもなくうれしかった.

please *oneself* **1** 満足する (*with*) ▪ I dress to

please myself. 私は楽しみに身うくろいするのです ▪ He *pleased himself with* the notice of his superiors. 彼は上長の目に留まったことで満足した.
2《口》好きなようにする ▪ I am going home; you can *please yourself.* 僕は帰る. 君は勝手にしたまえ.

please God 神の御意ならば, うまくいけば ▪ Tomorrow night, *please God*, we will then have a snug party. うまくいけばあすの晩, 水いらずのパーティーを開くことにしよう.

please the eye →EYE.

please your honor →(may it) please your HONOR.

You cannot please everyone.《諺・陳腐》何をしようと, それを好まない者が必ずいるものだ.

pleasure /pléʒər/ 名 ***a man*** [***woman***] ***of pleasure*** 道楽男[女] ▪ Kirk was also *a man of pleasure.* カークもまた道楽者だった.

at (*one's*) ***pleasure*** 好きなときに, 随意に ▪ We are free to go *at our pleasure.* 我々は好きなときに自由に行ってよい ▪ You may come or go *at pleasure.* 来るも行くもご随意だ.

consult *a person's* ***pleasure*** 人の意向[都合]を聞く ▪ It is etiquette to *consult a person's pleasure* when you want to call on him. 人を訪問したいときにはその都合を聞くのが礼儀である.

do *a person* (***a***) ***pleasure*** 人の気に入るようにする, 喜ばせる ▪ But you *do* your friend no *pleasure* in the act. しかしそんな事をすればお友だちは喜びますまい ▪ *Do* me the *pleasure* of dining with me. ご会食いただければ幸甚です.

during (*one's*) ***pleasure*** (人の)気の向いている間 ▪ He can hold office *during His Majesty's pleasure.* 陛下のきげんがななめにならぬ間は彼は在職していられる.

find pleasure in …に喜びを見いだす ▪ He *finds pleasure in* looking at a crowd. 彼は人ごみを見ることに喜びを見いだす.

for pleasure 楽しみに ▪ I read the book half *for pleasure.* その本を慰み半分に読んだ.

have the pleasure of …の光栄に浴す (*doing*)《敬語表現》 ▪ May I *have the pleasure of taking* a glass of wine with you? 1杯おつき合いくださいませんか ▪ I once *had the pleasure of* your company for dinner. 一度あなたさまと夕食を共にする栄に浴しました.

it gives *one* ***pleasure to*** *do* …することを喜ばしく思う ▪ *It gives* me *pleasure to* inform you of the news. このニュースをお知らせできるのがうれしいです.

it is our pleasure to *do* …することを望む《国王の言葉》; …するのはうれしいことだ ▪ *It is our pleasure to* see each project concluded. それぞれの企画の完了を見るのはうれしいことです.

It's a [***my***] ***pleasure.*** (相手の感謝の言葉に対して)どういたしまして ▪ Thanks for the ride.—*It's a pleasure.* 乗せていただいてありがとう—どういたしまして.

My pleasure. どういたしまして, こちらこそ ▪ Thank you for bringing this up here.—*My pleasure.* わざわざ持ってきてくださってありがとう—どういたしまして.

show pleasure うれしい顔をする ▪ He *showed* no *pleasure* at my offer. 彼は私の申し出を聞いても少しもうれしい顔をしなかった.

take (***a***) ***pleasure in*** …を[することを]好む, 喜ぶ ▪ Children *take pleasure in* making and breaking toys. 子供たちはおもちゃを作ったりこわしたりすることを喜ぶ.

take *one's* ***pleasure*** 楽しむ ▪ I'm going to *take my pleasure* for a time. これからしばらくの間楽しむつもりだ.

The pleasure is mine. どういたしまして; こちらこそです ▪ Thank you very much.—*The pleasure is mine.* どうもありがとうございます—どういたしまして ▪ I'm so glad to meet you.—*The pleasure is mine.* お目にかかれてうれしく存じます—こちらこそです.

There is no pleasure without pain.《諺》苦のない楽はない,「楽(ら)は苦の種(た)苦は楽の種」.

What is your pleasure? 何をお見せしましょうか《お客に》.

with pleasure 喜んで ▪ I will do it *with pleasure.* 喜んでそういたしましょう.

pledge[1] /pledʒ/ 名 ***be*** [***lie***] ***in pledge*** 質に入れてある; 担保にしてある ▪ My watch *is in pledge.* 私の時計は質に入れてある.

be under a pledge 誓いをしている ▪ I *am under a pledge* of secrecy. 私は秘密を守る誓いを立てている.

break the pledge《口》禁酒の誓いを破る ▪ He *broke the pledge* and began to drink again. 彼は禁酒の誓いを破ってまた飲みはじめた.

give [***have, lay, put***]***... to*** [***in***] ***pledge*** …を担保に入れる; を質に入れる ▪ He *gave* himself *to pledge.* 彼は自分の命を担保にした ▪ He *put to pledge* most of his own household stuff. 彼は家具の大半を質入れした.

hold ... in pledge …を担保に取っておく ▪ The land *was held in pledge.* その土地は担保に取っておかれた.

keep the pledge《口》禁酒の誓いを守る ▪ I find many men still *keeping the pledge.* 多くの人がまだ禁酒の誓いを守っているのがわかった.

lie in pledge →be in PLEDGE.

redeem *one's* ***pledge*** 約束を果たす ▪ Clive *redeemed his pledge.* クライブは約束を果たした.

sign [***take***] ***the pledge***《口》禁酒の誓いをする ▪ Many people *sign the pledge* in youth and break it in later years. 若いときに禁酒の誓いをし, 後年にそれを破る人が多い.

take a pledge 誓う ▪ He *took a* lifelong *pledge* to abstain from drinking whisky. 彼は一生涯ウィスキーを飲まないと誓った.

take ... out of pledge …を質受けする ▪ He *took* his clothes *out of pledge.* 自分の服を質受けした.

pledge[2] /pledʒ/ 動 ***pledge*** *oneself* 誓約する (*to, to do*) ▪ I here *pledge myself to* secrecy. 私はここに堅く秘密を誓います ▪ I *pledge myself to* serve the King faithfully. 私は国王に忠誠を尽くすことを誓約します.

pledge *one's* ***honor*** [***word, life,*** etc.] 自分の名誉[言葉, 生命, など]を賭けて誓う ▪ To this I *pledge my honor*. このことを私は名誉を賭けて誓います ▪ I now *pledge my word* that Ellen is innocent. 私の言葉に賭けて誓うが, エレンは無実だ.

plentiful /pléntɪfəl/ 形 (***as***) ***plentiful as blackberries*** 非常に豊富で (cf. Sh., *1 Hen. IV* 2. 4. 267) ▪ Ideas seem *as plentiful as blackberries* in autumn. 秋には着想がふんだんにわいてくるような気がする.

plenty /plénti/ 名形副 ***a plenty of*** 《主に米》多数の, 多量の ▪ This soil produces *a plenty of* wood. この土地からは材木がたくさん出る ▪ He had *a plenty of* things to do. 彼は仕事がたくさんあった.

as plenty as blackberries 非常に豊富で (cf. Sh., *1 Hen. IV* 2. 4. 267) ▪ Excuses are *as plenty as blackberries*. 口実は掃いて捨てるほどある. ☞この形でしばしば使われているけれども, Sh. の正しい形は plentiful.

in plenty たくさんに; 豊かに ▪ He possesses money *in plenty*. 彼は金をたくさん持っている ▪ He lived *in plenty* the rest of his days. 彼は豊かに余生を送った.

in plenty of time じゅうぶん間に合って ▪ They arrived *in plenty of time*. 彼らはじゅうぶん間に合って到着した.

plenty large enough 《口》大きさはたっぷりで ▪ The gown is *plenty large enough*. このガウンは大きさはたっぷりだ.

plenty more (***of***) まだたくさん(の) ▪ There's *plenty more* (*of* it) in the kitchen. それはまだ台所にたくさんある.

plenty of 多数の, 多量の ▪ This article contains *plenty of* errors. この論文にはたくさんの誤りがある ▪ We have *plenty of* sunlight. 日ざしが十分ある.

There are plenty more where they [***that***] ***came from.*** 別のもの[人]がたくさんある[いる] ▪ These are just a few examples of work sold in the past—but don't worry ... *There are plenty more where they came from*! これらは今まで売れた商品のほんの数例です, でも心配御無用…まだまだたくさんございますので.

plight[1] /plaɪt/ 名 ***in a miserable*** [***piteous, terrible, woeful,*** etc.] ***plight*** 目も当てられない有様で ▪ He found himself *in a miserable plight*. 気がついたら彼は目も当てられない有様になっていた ▪ What *a plight* you are *in*! なんという有様だ.

plight[2] /plaɪt/ 動 ***plight*** *oneself* (…に)誓う (*to*) ▪ You *plighted yourself to* me in the cloisters. 君は回廊で私に誓った.

plod /plɑd|plɔd/ 動 ***plod*** *one's* ***way*** とぼとぼ歩いていく ▪ The plowman homewards *plods his* weary *way*. 農夫は疲れてとぼとぼと家路をたどる.

plop /plɑp|plɔp/ 動 ***plop*** (*oneself*) ***down*** 《口》どすんと座る ▪ Emma *plopped down* on the living room couch. エマは居間のソファにすとんと座った ▪ Jack *plopped himself down* on the edge of the bed. ジャックはベッドの端にどすんと座った.

plot[1] /plɑt|plɔt/ 名 ***foil*** *one's* ***plot*** 計画をくじく, …の裏をかく ▪ The marines managed to *foil the terrorists' plot*. 海兵隊はなんとかテロリストの陰謀をくじいた.

lose the plot 《報道・口》混乱して前後の見境がつかなくなる, 状況判断ができなくなる ▪ I had *lost the plot* entirely. 話の筋が完全に追えなくなっていた.

The plot thickens. 《口・戯》筋がますます込み入ってきた (G. Villiers, *The Rehearsal*).

plot[2] /plɑt|plɔt/ 動 ***plot it*** 計画を立てる ▪ I'll *plot it* from now on. 今後は僕が計画を立てる.

plow[1], 《英》**plough**[1] /plaʊ/ 名 ***be at*** [***follow, hold***] ***the plow*** 農業をやっている ▪ The famous doctor *followed the plow* till he was twenty-eight. あの有名な医者は28歳まで農業をやっていた.

put [***lay, set***] *one's* ***hand to the plow*** → HAND[1].

under the plow 耕作されて ▪ There are actually 800 acres *under the plow*. 実際に800エーカーの土地が耕作してある.

plow[2], 《英》**plough**[2] /plaʊ/ 動 ***plow a lonely furrow*** 一人で仕事をやる ▪ Since his wife's death he has been *plowing a lonely furrow*. 妻が死んでからは彼は一人で仕事をやっている.

plow ... into the land 土地に(肥料・植物など)をすき込む; 土地に(資本)を注ぎ込む ▪ He *plowed* his capital *into the land*, and it never came out. 彼は土地に資本を注ぎ込んだが, 戻って来なかった.

plow *one's* ***own furrow*** = PLOW a lonely furrow.

plow the sand(***s***) [***air***] → SAND.

plow *one's* ***way*** **1** 波を切って進む ▪ The steamer *plowed her way* across the blue waters. 汽船が青海原を波を切って進んだ.

2 骨折って進む ▪ We *plowed our way* through the mud. 泥の中を骨折って進んだ.

3 入り込む ▪ The bullet *plowed its way* through his bones. 弾丸が彼の骨を貫いた.

plow with *a person's* ***heifer*** [***ox***] 将を得んとしてまず馬を射る (《聖》*Judges* 14. 18) ▪ He will not be contented that other men *plow with his oxen*. 彼は他人が将を得んとしてまず馬を射るのに満足しないだろう.

plowtail, 《英》**ploughtail** /pláʊtèɪl/ 名 ***at the plowtail*** 耕作[農業]に従事して ▪ There was a Roman dictator *at the plowtail*. 農業に従事しているローマの独裁者がいた.

from [***to***] ***the plowtail*** 農場から[農業に] ▪ The men were all *from the plowtail*. その男たちはいずれも農場の出だった ▪ They returned home *to the plowtail*. 彼らは国へ帰って農業に従事した.

pluck[1] /plʌk/ 名 ***give a pluck*** ぐいと引く (*at*) ▪ I *gave a pluck at* his hair. = I *gave* his hair *a* *pluck*. 彼の髪の毛をぐいと引っぱった.

pluck[2] /plʌk/ 動 ***be* [*get*] *plucked*** 《英》試験にしくじる, 落第する ▪He *was plucked* for his declamation. 彼は朗読法で落第した.

pluck** a person's **goose (***for** him*) →GOOSE.

pluck ... out of the air →AIR[1].

pluck up (*one's*) ***courage*** [***spirits, heart***] 勇気[元気]を奮い起こす ▪I *plucked up my spirits* as well as I could. 私は精いっぱい元気を奮い起こした.

plug[1] /plʌg/ 名 ***make*** [***put in***] ***a plug for*** …をお願いする, 推薦する ▪Vice President Al Gore *made a plug for* the human rights of Malaysians in his speech at Mahathir's official dinner. アル・ゴア副大統領はマハティール主催の公式晩餐会でのスピーチでマレーシア人の人権促進を要請した.

pull the plug on **1** (たいてい資金を打ち切ることによって計画・仕事)を打ち切る《しばしばビジネス・政治で》 ▪The new president decided to *pull the plug on* the space program. 新大統領は宇宙計画から手を引くことを決定した.

2 (植物状態の人)の延命装置をはずして安楽死させる (*on a person*): ▪Eleanor would *pull the plug on* her daddy and let him die. エリナーは父さんの生命維持装置をはずして, 安楽死させるだろう.

3 《俗》(人)の秘密を暴く ▪The citizen's organization *pulled the plug on* the lady mayor, and she lost her election. 市民団体が女性市長の秘密を暴露したので彼女は選挙で破れた.

4 《俗》自殺する ▪He reached behind the bed and tried to *pull the plug on* himself. 彼はベッドの後ろに手を伸ばして自殺しようとした.

plug[2] /plʌg/ 動 ***be plugged in to*** 《口》〚受身で〛(思想など)に深い関心を抱いている ▪He *is plugged in to* anarchism. 彼は無政府主義に深い関心を持っている.

plughole /plʌ́ghòʊl/ 名 ***go down the plughole*** 《英》失敗する, 敗れる, むだになる ▪A lot of my plans *went down the plughole*. 私の計画の大半が水の泡となった.

plum /plʌm/ 名 ***a plum role*** [***job, post,*** etc.] 非常に好ましい役割[収入のとてもよい職, きわめてよい地位, など] ▪Actress Samantha Seager has landed *a plum role* in a West End show. 女優のサマンサ・シーガーがウェストエンドの劇場でおいしい役を手に入れた.

have a plum in** one's **mouth →have marbles in one's MOUTH.

like a ripe plum [***ripe plums***] 容易に(入手できる), わけなく[やすやすと](手に入る) ▪The election victory fell in their lap *like a ripe plum*. 彼らはたやすく選挙の勝利を手中にした.

speak with a plum in** one's **mouth 《英》社会的身分の非常に高い出身を示す話し方をする ▪Wilson *spoke with a plum in his mouth*. ウィルスンは上流気取りの話し方をした.

take all the plums 一番よいものは自分のために残しておく ▪You give each a part to play, but you *take all the plums* yourself. 君はみんなに役割を与えるが, 一番いいのは自分のために残しておくのだね.

wait for the plums to fall in** one's **mouth たなからぼたもちが落ちてくるのを待つ.

plumb /plʌm/ 名 ***off*** [***out of***] ***plumb*** 垂直でない ▪The column is seriously *off plumb*. その柱はひどくゆがんでいる ▪That wall is *out of plumb*. その壁は垂直ではない.

plumbing /plʌ́mɪŋ/ 名 ***check out the plumbing*** 《婉曲》トイレに行く, 用足しに[化粧を直しに]行く ▪You'd better *check out the plumbing* before we get on the interstate. 州間高速自動車道に乗る前にトイレを済ませておいた方がいいよ.

visit the plumbing 《婉曲》トイレに行く ▪I need to *visit the plumbing* once more. もう一度トイレに行かなきゃ.

plume[1] /plu:m/ 名 ***borrowed plumes*** 借り着; 受け売りの知識 ▪Some people do not care to appear in *borrowed plumes*. 借り着を着て人前に出たがらない人もいる ▪In the process of his examination, he was stripped of his *borrowed plumes*. 彼は試験されているうちに, 受け売りの知識をひっぱがされてしまった. ☞小ガラスがクジャクの羽をつけて笑われたイソップ寓話から.

plume[2] /plu:m/ 動 ***plume** oneself **on*** [***upon***] …のことで得意になる ▪He *plumes himself on* being able to speak every European language. 彼はヨーロッパのどの言語でも話せるというので天狗になっている.

plump /plʌmp/ 動 ***plump*** (*oneself*) ***down*** ドシンと落ちる[落とす] ▪He *plumped* (*himself*) *down* into a chair. 彼はドシンといすに腰をおろした ▪The man *plumped down* the bags in a corner. その男は袋をすみっこにドシンと落とした.

plunge[1] /plʌndʒ/ 名 ***take the plunge*** (ちゅうちょしていたこと, または冒険的に新しいことを)思いきってやる ▪I've been warned against matrimony, but I'll *take the plunge*. 僕は結婚するなと言われていたが, 思いきってやるつもりだ.

plunge[2] /plʌndʒ/ 動 ***be plunged in thought*** 考え事に没頭している ▪He won't hear you; he's *plunged in thought*. 彼には君の言葉が聞こえない. 考え事に没頭しているから.

plus /plʌs/ 前 ***plus or minus*** プラスマイナスの範囲, 上下幅 ▪The sampling error is *plus or minus* 2.8%. サンプリング誤差は上下幅2.8%である.

plush /plʌʃ/ 名 ***be on plush*** 有利な立場にある ▪He *was*, to all appearances, *on plush*. 彼はどう見ても立場が有利のようであった.

ply[1] /plaɪ/ 名 ***take a*** [***the,** one's*] ***ply*** 癖がつく ▪England *took a ply* which she has never wholly lost. イギリスはある癖がついて, それをまだ完全になくしてはいない.

ply[2] /plaɪ/ 動 ***ply for hire*** [***trade, business***] 《英》客待ちをする ▪The driver was fined £250 for illegally *plying for hire*. 運転手は違法

に客待ちをしたかどで250ポンドの罰金を取られた.

ply** one's **trade →TRADE.

poach /poʊtʃ/ 動 ***poach on* [*upon*] *a person's* *preserves*** 人の縄張りを荒らす ▪ The poet *poaches upon a novelist's preserves*. その詩人は小説家の領域を侵している.

poacher /póʊtʃər/ 名 ***a poacher turned gamekeeper*** 《英》密猟者転じて猟場番 ▪ Ben used to be the union rep but now he's in management—a case of *poacher turned gamekeeper*. ベンはもと労組の代表だったが, いまは経営者の一人だ—まさに密猟者転じて猟場番のケースだね. ☞次項も参照.

An old poacher makes the best gamekeeper. 《諺》老密猟者は一番優れた猟場番人になる《警備の最適任者は, それの盗み方を熟知している者だ》, 「蛇(じゃ)の道は蛇(へび)」.

pocket /pάkət|pɔ́kɪt/ 名 ***be ... in pocket*** **1** (金)を手元に持っている ▪ He happened to *be* somewhat *in pocket*. 彼はたまたまいささか金の持ち合わせがあった.

2 (金)を儲けている ▪ I *am* ten shillings *in pocket* by the transaction. その取引で10シリング儲けた.

be* (...) *out of pocket (取引で)損をしている ▪ I *am* $10 *out of pocket* for my expenses. 僕は出費が多くて10ドル赤字だ.

dig into** one's **pocket ...に寄付をする, 金を使う ▪ How many Americans would *dig into their pocket* and give to the group voluntarily? どれ位の米国人がその団体に進んで寄付をするのだろうか.

dip** one's **hand in** one's **pocket = put one's hand into one's POCKET.

dip* (*one's* *hand*) *into* *one's* *pocket 支払いをする(*for*), 自腹を切る ▪ The father of a family is always *dipping into his pocket for* something. 子供の父親はいつも何かの支払いをしてばかりいる ▪ What this club needs is for the directors to *dip their hands into their pockets*. このクラブに必要なのは監督たちが身銭を切って払うことだ.

easy* [*hard*] *on the* [*a person's*] *pocket ふところがいたまない[いたむ] ▪ Foreign trips are no longer *hard on the pocket*. 海外旅行はもはやふところがいたむものではない.

have deep pockets 《口》十分な富[資力]がある ▪ They *have deep pockets* to buy off legislators. 彼らには国会議員を買収するだけの財力がある.

have** one's **hand in** one's **pocket いつも金を使っている ▪ He always *has his hand in his pocket*. 彼はいつも金を使っている.

have* [*carry*] ... *in* *one's* *pocket ...を完全に支配している ▪ She *has* him *in her pocket*. 彼女は彼をしりに敷いている.

hit the pocket 人に支払いをさせる ▪ Insurance problems *hit the pocket* more than any other sector. 保険の問題には他の分野よりも支払いがかさむ.

***in one another's pocket* [*pockets*]** (二人が)相互に依存し合って ▪ You can't invite Jan without inviting Susan as well. They are *in one another's pocket*. ジャンを招待するならスーザンも招待しないわけにはいかない. 二人は一心同体だから.

in a person's pocket **1** 人のすぐ近くに, 腰ぎんちゃくになって ▪ He sat *in her pocket* all the evening. 彼は宵じゅう彼女の腰ぎんちゃくになっていた.

2 完全に人のものになって, 思う通りになって ▪ He was sitting with the family seat *in his pocket*. 彼は家族席を完全に自分のものにして座っていた.

keep** one's **hands in** one's **pockets ふところ手をしている; 働かずにいる ▪ Mr. Obama *kept his hands in his pockets* to ward off the chill. オバマ氏は寒さを防ぐためポケットに手を突っ込んだままだった.

line** one's (**own**) **pockets →LINE[3].

live* [*be*] *in each other's pockets 《英》人とべったりと共同生活をする ▪ They *lived in each other's pockets* for two weeks. 彼らは2週間いつもいっしょに生活をした.

live* [*be*] *in a person's pocket 人の費用で生活する ▪ At Taplow last summer you *lived in his pocket*. 去年の夏タプローで君は彼の費用で生活した.

money burns* (*a hole*) *in* *one's* *pocket → MONEY.

pay out of* [*from*] *one's* *own pocket 自腹を切る ▪ He *paid* for it *out of his own pocket*. 彼は自腹を切ってその代を払った.

pick a* [*a person's*] *pocket →PICK *a person's* pocket.

pockets of resistance 軍事孤立地帯 ▪ Their revolution may be over, but they certainly still have small *pockets of resistance*. 彼らの革命は終わったかもしれないが, 少数ながら依然として軍事孤立地帯が残っているのは確かだ.

put** one's **hand into** one's **pocket 金を出す, 慈悲心から金を与える ▪ The father of a family often has to *put his hand into his pocket*. 子供の父親というものは金を出さねばならないことが多い.

put** one's **tongue in** one's **pocket 言葉を抑える ▪ You had better *put your tongue in your pocket*. 君は言葉を抑えた方がいいぞ.

suffer in** one's **pocket 損をする ▪ He will *suffer in his pocket*. 彼は損をするだろう.

pocketbook /pάkətbʊ̀k|pɔ́kɪt-/ 名 ***vote with** one's **pocketbook*** [《英》***wallet***] →VOTE[2].

pod /pɑd|pɔd/ 名 ***in pod*** 《口》妊娠して ▪ She's *in pod* and now in her third month. 彼女は妊娠していて, いま4か月目だ. ☞日本では妊娠した時点で「妊娠1か月」とされるが, 欧米では妊娠した時点では「0か月」である. 例文の third month は, 日本流に言えば「4か月」を指している.

poet /póʊət/ 名 ***Poets are born, not made.*** 《諺》詩人は作られるのではなく生まれるもの. ☞[L] Poeta nascitur, non fit. のなぞり.

poetic /poʊétɪk/ 形 ***poetic justice*** → JUSTICE.

poetic license →artistic LICENSE.

po-faced /póʊfèɪst/ 形 ***be po-faced*** 全くユーモ

アを解さない，まじめくさった ▪ Both women remained *po-faced* in response to my truly joyful tale. 二人の女性は私の実に陽気な話にもまじめくさったままだった．

point[1] /pɔɪnt/ 名 ***a case in point*** 適例，問題になっている点 ▪ Many politicians owe much to their wives; he was *a case in point*. 夫人に非常なおかげを被っている政治家は多い．彼はその適例だった．

a point of honor →HONOR[1].

a point of view 見地，観点；視点 ▪ From *a* literary *point of view*, they are beneath criticism. 文学的見地からすれば，それらは批評に値しない．☞Ｆ point de vue のなぞり．

a sticking point (問題解決の)障害，(一連の議論・交渉における)行き詰まりの原因，膠着点 ▪ Money had never been *a sticking point*. 金の問題で行き詰まっているわけではなかった ▪ It has been *a* major *sticking point* in the negotiation. それが交渉において主に障害となる点だ．

at all points 〚主に armed に伴って〛どの点においても，完全に ▪ They were *armed at all points*. 彼らは完全に武装していた ▪ We are safe-guarded *at all points*. 我々は完ぺきに守りを固めている．

at that point (in time) その時には，その時点に ▪ *At that point in time*, that was the happiest day of my life. その時点ではそれがわが人生の最高の日だった．

at the point of …の間際で，まさに…しようとして ▪ The man was *at the point of* death. その男は死に瀕していた ▪ They were *at the point of* going. 彼らはこれから出かけるところだった．

at the point of the bayonet [sword] 銃剣[刀]を突きつけて，武力で；ひどく不和の状態で ▪ The troops carried the position *at the point of the bayonet*. その軍は武力で陣地を占領した ▪ The two men conducted their business *at the point of the sword*. 二人の男はひどく不和の状態で仕事を進めた．

at this point (in time) この点で，ここの所で，今は，現時点で(は) ▪ *At this point* he was interrupted. この時彼は話の腰を折られた ▪ *At this point in time* we don't need a new washing machine. 今のところは新しい洗濯機は必要ない．

away from the point →beside the POINT.

be close to breaking point 神経衰弱になる寸前である；持ちこたえられる限界に達している ▪ Madonna *was close to breaking point* following her former nanny's tell-all threat. マドンナは元住み込み家政婦の暴露話のあともう少しで神経がいかれそうになった ▪ A lot of companies may *be close to breaking point*. 多くの会社は倒産の限界に達しているだろう．

beat [defeat, win] on points 《ボクシング》判定で勝つ (↔lose on POINTs) ▪ Tom *beat* William *on points*. トムはウィリアムを判定で破った．

belabor the point (必要もなく)くどくど(と)述べる ▪ I don't want to *belabor the point*, but do you think he is breaking the law? くどくど言いたくはないが，あなたは彼が違法活動をしていると思いますか．

beside [away from] the point [mark, question] 要点をはずれて ▪ All that is *beside the point*. それはまるきり不得要領だ ▪ He argued *away from the point*. 彼は要点を外れた議論をした．

beyond a certain point/once a certain point is reached 一定の段階[時点]を過ぎると ▪ The medicine becomes ineffective *beyond a certain point*. この薬は一定の段階を過ぎると効き目がなくなる．

brownie points →get brownie POINTs.

carry [gain] *one's* ***point*** 言い分を通す ▪ George wanted Mary to marry him, and *carried his point*. ジョージはメアリーと結婚したいと思い，自分の言い分を通した．☞弓術から．

come (straight) to the point 要点に触れる ▪ Let us now *come to the point* in hand. もう目下の要点に触れようじゃないか ▪ Now, to *come to the point*, will you go yourself, or send a representative? さて要点に触れれば，君が行ってくれるのか，それとも代理人を送ってくれるのか．

come to points 剣を交える ▪ They would have *come to points* immediately. 彼らはすぐ剣を交えたことだろう．

defeat on points →beat on POINTs.

gain a point/get points 《口》点をかせぐ，優勢になる ▪ I *got points* on her for the time being. 私はさしあたり彼女より優勢になった．☞ゲームで点をかせぐことから．

gain *one's* ***point*** →carry one's POINT.

get [earn, score, win, etc.***] brownie points*** 善行に対する評価，(評価を高める)点数，得点 ▪ John definitely *scored* some *brownie points* last night after cooking me a fantastic gourmet dinner. ジョンは昨夜とてもおいしい食事を作ってくれた後で確かに点数を上げた．☞brownie と呼ばれるガールスカウトの最年少組が諸活動で獲得した得点から．

get *a person's* ***point*** →take a person's POINT.

get (straight) to the point ＝come (straight) to the POINT.

get the point of …の意図を理解する，言いたいことが分かる ▪ Watch Part 1 first in order to *get the point of* the movie. その映画の意味が分かるためには，まず第一部を見なさい ▪ I don't really *get the point of* this article. 僕にはこの記事の意味があまり分かりません．

give a point to …をとがらせる ▪ He *gave a point to* a pencil. 彼は鉛筆をとがらせた．

give points to **1** (相手)に分(ぶ)を与える ▪ She could *give points to* many younger women and beat them. 彼女は多くの若い女たちに分を与えてしかも負かすことができた．

2 《口》…に勝る ▪ Any average Eton boy could *give points to* His Holiness in the matter of Latin verses. 普通のイートン校の生徒なら誰でもラテン詩にかけては教皇に勝ることができた．☞Ｆ donner [rendre] des points のなぞり．

P

have (***got***) ***a point*** (***there***) 《口》(その点は)もっともである ▪ You*'ve got a point there*. その点はごもっともです.

have (***got***) *one's* ***good*** [***plus***] ***points*** 長所, 良い点がある ▪ Everyone craves to meet someone, but being single *has its good points*. 誰もがよい人に出会えることを望むが, 独身にもいいところがある.

hit the high points →hit the HIGH spots.

if it comes to the point →when it comes to the POINT.

in every point すべての点で ▪ He is right *in every point*. 彼はすべての点で正しい.

in point 適切な ▪ They are *in point* to the present subject. それらは当面の問題に適切である.

in point of …に関して ▪ *In point of* learning and ability my friend is superior. 学識と才能にかけては私の友人のほうが勝っている.

in point of fact 実際のところは, 実は ▪ But *in point of fact*, he has never been near India in his life. しかし実のところは, 彼は生まれてこのかたインドの近くへ行ったことはないのだ.

keep [***stick***] ***to the point*** 要点をはずさない ▪ Do *keep to the point*, my excursive friends. どうか要点をはずさないでくれ, とりとめもない話をする諸君.

labor the point (わかりきったことなどを)くどくど述べる ▪ My granddad always *labors the point*. 私のおじいちゃんはいつもくどくど話します.

lose on points 《ボクシング》判定で負ける (→beat on POINTs) ▪ Campolo will retire if he *loses on points*. キャンポロは判定負けしたら引退するだろう.

make a point of **1** …を重視する ▪ Her husband *made a point of* his tea. 彼女の夫はお茶を非常に重視していた.

2 必ず…するように心がける (*doing*) ▪ He *makes a point of attending* such meetings. 彼はそのような会には必ず出席するように心がけている.

make it a point to *do* …することにしている ▪ I always *make it a point to* paint things as they are. 私はいつも物事をあるがままに描くことにしている.

make [***score***] (*one's*) ***point***(***s***) **1** 主張の正しいことを立証する; 目的を果たす ▪ I saw by their faces that he had *made his point*. 彼が目的を果たしたことは彼らの顔でわかった.

2 好印象を与える, 株を上げる ▪ He was *scoring points* with the judges and their cheerleaders. 彼は裁判官と熱心な支持者に気に入られた ▪ Did the President really think he was *making points* with the public? 大統領は大衆に好印象を与えていると本当に思っていたのか.

miss [***see***] ***the point*** 要点がわからない[わかる] ▪ He *missed the point* of my joke. 彼は私の冗談のやまがわからなかった.

more to the point 一層重要な[適切な]ことで ▪ It is wrong, and (what is) *more to the point*, dangerous. それはまちがっており, 更に重要なことに, 危険だ.

not to put too fine a point upon it 《英》あからさまに言えば, 有り体に言えば ▪ He was—*not to put too fine a point upon it*—hard up! 彼は一率直に言うと—金につまっていた.

off the point 要点をはずれて ▪ Your remark is *off the point*. 君の言葉は要点をはずれている.

on [***upon***] ***the point of*** 〖動名詞・動作名詞を伴って〗まさに…しようとして ▪ She was *on the point of* swooning. 彼女はいまにも気絶しそうだった ▪ Everything seemed *on the point of* moving. 何もかもが今にも動き出しそうに見えた.

on this [***that***] ***point*** この[その]点で ▪ I am with you *on this point*. この点では同感です.

once a certain point is reached →beyond a certain POINT.

point by point 一々, 逐一 ▪ He asked questions *point by point*. 彼は一つ一つ細かに質問した.

point for point 一々, 正確に ▪ They correspond *point for point*. それらは一々符合する.

point of contact 接点; 連絡先 ▪ Bush's main *point of contact* inside of Moscow was Yeltsin. ブッシュ氏のモスクワ内部での主な接触先はエリツィン氏であった.

point of departure **1** 出発地点, 起点 ▪ She'll return to her *point of departure*, Chicago. 彼女は出発地のシカゴへ戻るだろう.

2 (議論・理論の)出発点 ▪ As my *point of departure*, let me cite two extensive but significant passages. 議論の手始めとして, 長いけれど重要な二つの節をひこう.

press the point その点を言い張る ▪ He *pressed the point* at today's meeting. 彼は今日の会合でその点を言い張った.

ride (***at***) ***point*** 《米》馬に乗って先に立って牛群を導く ▪ You see a herd drifting before a storm, with your pal *riding point*. 牛群があらしに追いまくられ, 君の友が馬に乗って先導しているのが見えるだろう.

score a point [***points***] ***off*** [***over, against***] 《主に英》(議論で人)をやりこめる ▪ I won't let him *score a point off* me. 彼に1本取られるようなことをさせるものか ▪ I don't like Rick. He's always trying to *score points off* people. リックは好きじゃない. いつも人をやっつけようとするから.

score *one's* ***point***(***s***) →make (one's) POINT(s).

score points (***with*** *a person*) (人に認めてもらう[好かれる]ために)点数をかせぐ ▪ The airline *scored points with* passengers by banning smoking on all domestic flights. その航空会社はすべての国内便を禁煙にして乗客の点数をかせいだ.

see *a person's* ***point*** 人の言わんとすることを理解する ▪ I *see your point*, but I can't agree with you. 言おうとしていることは分かるが, 同意できない.

see point in *doing* …するのは意味があると考える ▪ He *saw* no *point in complying*. 彼は同意するのは無意味だと考えた.

see the point →miss the POINT.

shave off points 八百長で負ける ▪ The FBI is currently investigating Tim Donaghy for *shav-*

ing off points during a game. FBI は現在ティム・ドナフィーを試合中に八百長審判を働いたかどで取り調べ中である.

stand upon points 細かいところにこだわる ▪ You *stand upon points* so, we shall never move ahead. 君がひどく細かいところにこだわるので我々は少しも前進しやしない.

stick to the point →keep to the POINT.

strain* [*stretch*] *a point 一歩を譲る, 特別扱いにする ▪ Well, I'll *strain a point* and reduce the price by a pound. じゃあ一歩譲って1ポンドだけ値引きしましょう ▪ The landlord is willing to *stretch a point*, and allow us to stay another week. 宿の主人は喜んで特別扱いして, 我々をもう1週間泊まらせてやると言っている.

one's ***strong* [*weak*] *point*** 得意[不得意]な点, 強み[弱み] ▪ Modesty is not one of *her strong points*. 謙虚にするのは彼女の得意とするところではない.

take* [*get, see*]** *a person's* ***point 人の言い分がわかる, 人の意見に賛成する ▪ I can *see your point*. 君の言い分はわかるよ.

talking point 売込みに有利な点, 長所; 話題 ▪ The streamlined shape of the train was one of its *talking points*. 流線型がその電車の強みのひとつだ ▪ I think that's going to be a *talking point* over the next couple of days. それは今後数日間話題になるだろうと思う.

the finer points of …の微妙な[詳しい]点, 極意 ▪ This school teaches *the finer points of* maple syrup. 本校ではメイプルシロップの奥義をお教えします.

the point of no return 帰還不能点《航空機が出発点へ戻るのに必要な燃料のなくなる地点》; もはや後ろに引けない段階 ▪ The matter had reached *the point of no return*. 事態はもはや後ろに引けない段階に到達していた.

there's no* [*not much*] *point in doing …しても少しも[あまり]意味がない ▪ *There's no point in doing* that. そんなことをしても少しも意味がない.

to a* (*fine*) *point 完全に ▪ I had been polished right off *to a point*. 私は完全にやっつけられていた.

to the point 要領を得て, 適切な ▪ He speaks *to the point*. 彼は要領を得た話をする ▪ Let us be brief but *to the point*. 手短に要領よく話をしよう.

to the point of …と言ってもいい程度まで ▪ He is modest *to the point of* ridicule. 彼はこっけいなくらい腰が低い.

up to a* (*certain*) *point ある点までは, ある程度まで ▪ I agree with you only *up to a point*, but no further. 君にある程度までは賛成だけど, その先はそうでない.

when* [*if*] *it comes to the point いざという時になると ▪ Her father, *when it came to the point*, little liked her going. 彼女の父親は, いざとなると彼女が行くことには気が進まなかった.

win on points =beat on POINTs.

point[2] /pɔɪnt/ 動 ***point a moral*** →MORAL.

***point the way* (*to* [*towards*])** (…への)進路[方向]を示す ▪ Hybrid vehicles are *pointing the way to* a new age of world transportation. ハイブリッド車は新時代の世界の交通手段の方向を示している.

point-blank /pɔ́ɪntblǽŋk/ 副 ***ask* [*tell,* etc.]** *a person* ***point-blank*** ずばりと尋ねる[言う, など] ▪ Sue *asked* the doctor *point-blank* why she could not recover. スーは医師にどうして治らないのかと単刀直入に尋ねた.

poise[1] /pɔɪz/ 名 ***hang at poise*** (問題が)懸案になっている ▪ The question *hangs at poise*. その問題は懸案になっている.

on the poise 未決定のままで ▪ The event was long *on the poise*. 事件は長い間未解決のままだった.

poise[2] /pɔɪz/ 動 ***poise*** *oneself* **1** 体のつり合いを取る ▪ He *poised himself* on his toes. 彼はつま先で体のつり合いを取った.

2 奮起する ▪ He *poised himself* for the ordeal. 彼はその試練に備えて奮起した.

poison /pɔ́ɪzən/ 名 ***a poison-pen letter*** 匿名の脅迫状, 中傷の手紙 ▪ Whatever was said in the *poison-pen letter* was all false. その中傷の書状に書かれた事はすべて嘘だった.

hate *a person* ***like poison*** 《口》人をひどくいみきらう ▪ They *hate* each other *like poison*. 彼らは犬猿の間柄だ.

look like poison at *a person* ひどく嫌って…を見る ▪ Mrs. Moore *looked like poison at* her husband's mistress. モア夫人は夫の愛人に憎悪の眼を向けた.

Name your poison. 《戯》(パブで)飲み物は何になさいますか (=What's your POISON?).

spit poison 相手を傷つける言葉[非難]を投げかける ▪ Joe and Kat can't help but *spit poison* at each other. ジョーとキャットは互いに毒舌をふるわざるを得ない.

What's your poison? 《口》飲み物は何にするかね (=Name your POISON.).

poisoned /pɔ́ɪzənd/ 形 ***a poisoned chalice*** →CHALICE.

poke[1] /poʊk/ 名 ***have a poke around*** 《口》注意深く見回る ▪ You could *have a poke around* in the Flea Market for something rare. 何か珍しいものを求めてノミの市を見回ることができますよ.

take a poke at 《口》 **1** …を(こぶしで)なぐる ▪ Stop talking like that, or I'll *take a poke at* you. そんな言い方はやめろ, でないとなぐるぞ.

2 …を批判する; をからかう ▪ He *took a poke at* President Obama in his speech. 彼は演説の中でオバマ大統領を批判した ▪ My roommate *took a poke at* my hairstyle, telling me I looked like a scarecrow! ルームメートがかかしのようだと言って私の髪型をからかった.

poke[2] /poʊk/ 動 ***poke and pry*** あれこれ詮索する ▪ His lawyer *poked and pried* into his accounts. 彼の弁護士は彼の口座をあれこれ詮索した.

poke fun at →FUN.

poke *one's* ***nose into*** →NOSE[1].

poke *oneself* ***up*** 《口》(窮屈な場所に)閉じこもる ▪ He must be bored *poking himself up* in a dull town. 活気のない町でくすぶっているので彼はうんざりしているにちがいない.

poker /póʊkər/ 名 ***(as) stiff as a poker*** → STIFF.

by the holy poker 《戯》誓って, 確かに ▪ *By the holy poker*, the old fellow now is out there. 確かにあの老人はいまあそこに出ている. ☞アイルランド起源の誓言で, はっきりした意味はない.

look as if *one* ***had swallowed a poker*** 《口》この上もなく堅苦しい顔つきをしている ▪ He *looks as if* he *had swallowed a poker*. 彼はひどく堅苦しい顔つきをしている.

pole[1] /poʊl/ 名 ***be in pole position*** 《主に英》勝利や成功に最も近い位置に ▪ The Giants *are in pole position* to win the championship this year. ジャイアンツが今年優勝までの最短距離にいる. ☞自動車レースの用語から.

have [***take***] ***the pole*** 《米》(競馬・競走などで)走路の内側を走る; 有利の地歩にある ▪ Success *had the pole*. サクセス号が走路の内側を走った.

not touch ... with a ten-foot pole [《英》***a barge pole***] (ある人・事柄を)好まずそれに巻き込まれたくない, 実にいやである; (いやで)手も触れたくない ▪ I would *not touch* the game *with a barge pole*. その競技はまっぴらごめんだ ▪ I would*n't touch* him *with the end of a barge pole*. やつには手も触れたくない ▪ Some people wo*n't touch* pimento *with a ten-foot pole*. ピーマンがどうしてもだめな人がままいる ▪ His direction was: "Do*n't touch* this guy *with a barge pole*." 彼からの指令は「この男には関わるな」というものだった. ☞"a barge pole" は屋形船用の長いさおを指す.

the greasy pole 成功するための難所 ▪ Walsh joined the company, moving up *the greasy pole* over the years until he took over as CEO in 2001. ウォルシュは入社後何年も難しい仕事をこなして2001年に最高経営責任者としての仕事を受け継いだ. ☞かつてあった油棒をよじ登って景品を獲る競争から.

under [***with***] (***bare***) ***poles*** **1** 《海》(船が暴風雨などで)帆を張らずに ▪ The ship was allowed to drive before the tempest *under bare poles*. 船は帆を張らずにあらしに追いまくられるに任された.

2 困り果てて, 赤貧で ▪ He is drifting *under bare poles*. 彼は困り果ててぶらぶらしている.

up the pole 《口》 **1** 気が狂って; 酔っ払って ▪ He came home *up the pole* at one a.m. 彼は酔っ払って午前1時に帰ってきた.

2 進退きわまって, 困却して ▪ It was so difficult that I was practically *up the pole* with it. それはとてもむずかしかったので, それでほとんどにっちもさっちもいかなくなってしまった ▪ His action has put us *up the pole*. 彼の行動は我々を困ったはめに陥れた.

pole[2] /poʊl/ 名 ***be poles asunder*** [***apart***]/ ***be as far apart as the poles*** 天地の隔たりがある ▪ In thought and ideas they*'re poles asunder*. 二人は思うことも考えることも天地の隔たりがある.

from pole to pole 北極から南極まで; 世界中で ▪ Sleep is a gentle thing beloved *from pole to pole*. 眠りは世界中で愛されている優しいものだ.

police /pəlíːs/ 名 ***go to the police*** 警察に訴える ▪ He *went to the police* at once. 彼はすぐに警察に訴えた.

policeman /pəlíːsmən/ 名 ***A*** [***The***] ***policeman's lot is not a happy one.*** 警察官の巡り合わせは幸せなものではない《いろいろいやな仕事をしなければならない》(W. S. Gilbert, *Pirates of Penzance*).

a sleeping policeman 眠れるお巡り, スピード抑止帯《一連の道路の隆起や一部を道路に突き出して作られた花壇など》 ▪ The *sleeping policemen* slow down the traffic. スピード抑止帯は車の往来を遅くしてくれる.

policy /pɑ́ləsi|pɔ́l-/ 名 ***a scorched-earth policy*** 焦土作戦 ▪ Saddam has launched *a scorched-earth policy* in Kuwait. サダムはクウェートで焦土作戦を開始した.

play (***in the***) ***policy*** 《米》数当てくじをやる ▪ He used to *play in the policy*. 彼は数当てくじをやるのが常だった.

take out a policy on ...に保険をつける ▪ He *took out a policy on* his life. 彼は生命保険に入った.

the policy of the big stick 棍棒政策, 武力による脅迫 ▪ Now is the time when schools need *the policy of the big stick* to beat bullies. 今こそ学校はいじめ撲滅のために断固たる態度を示すべきだ. ☞古い諺に因む "speak softly and carry a big stick"「優しく話し棍棒を携える」という Theodore Roosevelt の高圧的な外交政策演説中の引用から.

polite /pəláɪt/ 形 ***do the polite*** 《口》(骨折って)上品にふるまう ▪ He is only *doing the polite*. 彼は上品にふるまっているだけだ.

political /pəlítɪkəl/ 形 ***political football*** 政争の具, 政治上の駆け引き ▪ Education in this country has become a *political football*. わが国の教育は政争の道具になってしまった.

politically /pəlítɪkəli/ 副 ***politically correct*** →CORRECT[1].

politics /pɑ́lətìks|pɔ́l-/ 名 ***be not practical politics*** 縁遠くて討議の価値がない ▪ The matter *is not practical politics*. その件は縁遠いので討議の価値がない.

play politics 《軽蔑》(主義よりは)党利[私利]を図る, 策を弄する ▪ I don't think this politician is fair—he's *playing politics*. この政治家は公正ではないと思う—私利を図っている.

Politics makes strange bedfellows. 《諺》政治のかけひきが縁で奇妙な友情が生まれる (→a strange BEDFELLOW).

poll[1] /poʊl/ 名 ***at the head of the poll*** 最高得票で ▪ He stood *at the head of the poll*. 彼は最高得票であった.

be successful at the poll 当選する ▪ Mr.

Smith *was successful at the poll.* スミス氏は当選した.

declare the poll 投票の結果を発表する ▪ *The poll* will *be declared* by evening. 晩までに投票の結果が発表されるだろう.

go to the polls 投票に行く ▪ I *went to the polls* and cast my vote. 私は投票に行って投票した.

head the poll 最高得票をする ▪ Mr. Brown will probably *head the poll.* たぶんブラウン氏が最高票を獲得するだろう.

take a poll 投票を行う ▪ *The poll* will *be taken* on Sunday. 投票は日曜日に行われる.

poll[2] /poʊl/ 名 ***go out in the poll*** 普通で卒業する ▪ He modestly *went out in the poll* in January, 1930. 彼は1930年1月に欲張らずに普通で卒業した. ☞Cambridge 大学の俗語; the poll「普通学位卒業者」.

pomp /pɑmp|pɔmp/ 名 ***with pomp and circumstance*** 仰々しい盛儀をもって, ものものしく (cf. Sh., *Oth.* 3. 3. 354) ▪ Their wedding was celebrated *with pomp and circumstance.* 彼らの結婚はものものしく祝われた.

pond /pɑnd|pɔnd/ 名 ***across the pond/on the other side of the pond*** 《主に英口》大西洋の向こう側で ▪ *Across the pond* in the U.S., no one was surprised either. 海の向こうの合衆国でも, 誰も驚かなかった.

poor /pʊər|pɔː, pʊə/ 形 ***a poor second*** [***third***] 大差がついて2位[3位]の人 ▪ The Internet poll gave Maradona 53.6% of the votes; Pele came *a poor second* with 18.5% of the votes. インターネットの投票ではマラドーナが53.6%を取り, ペレは大きく離された18.5%で2位だった.

as poor as a church mouse [***a church-mouse, a rat, Job, Lazarus,*** 《米》***Job's cat***] きわめて貧しい ▪ The young couple are *as poor as church mice.* その若夫婦は赤貧だ.

be poor at ...がへたである ▪ I *am poor at* mathematics. 私は数学が苦手だ.

be poor in ...が貧弱である, に乏しい ▪ Japan *is poor in* minerals. 日本は鉱物に乏しい.

poor little rich girl [***boy***] 金はあるのに不満だらけの不幸な若者 ▪ I'm not a *poor little rich girl,* any more than you are. あなた(がそうでない)と同様お金はあるが不平たらたらの娘ではない.

poor old... かわいそうな... ▪ The *poor old* chap was killed in an accident. かわいそうにあの男は事故で死んだ. ☞年寄りでない人・古くない物にも用いられる.

Poor thing [***fellow***]***!*** かわいそうに ▪ The dog sank into the water in a moment. *Poor thing!* 犬はたちまち水の中に沈んでしまった. かわいそうに!

take a poor view of →VIEW[1].

The poor are always with us. 《諺》貧しい人たちはいつも我々と共にいる《援助を必要としている》(《聖》*John* 12. 8).

the [***a***] ***poor man's...*** 貧乏人の..., ...の安価な代用品; ...もどき ▪ In those days English was *the poor man's* classical language. 当時, 英語は貧乏人の古典語であった ▪ In recent years, chemical weapons have become *the poor man's* nukes. 最近, 化学兵器が核兵器の廉価版になった ▪ They were looked upon as *a poor man's* Beatles. 彼らはビートルズもどきとみなされた.

poorly /pʊ́ərli|pɔ́ː-, pʊə-/ 副形 ***be poorly off*** →be badly OFF.

think poorly of ...をつまらなく思う, 感心しない ▪ He *thinks* very *poorly of* my new novel. 彼は私の今度の小説をひどくつまらなく思っている.

pop[1] /pɑp|pɔp/ 名副 ***go pop*** ポンと鳴る[取れる] ▪ I heard it *go pop.* それがポンと鳴るのが聞こえた ▪ *Pop went* the cork! コルクがポンと取れた.

have [***take***] ***a pop at*** 《英口・報道》 **1** ...を狙って一発撃つ, なぐる ▪ The guy *took a pop at* Jim. そいつがジムを小突いた.

2 ...を言葉で攻撃する, 批判する ▪ He can never resist *taking a pop at* the opposition candidates. 彼は反対党の立候補者を批判せずにはおかない.

in pop 《俗》質に入って ▪ My watch is *in pop.* 私の時計は質に入っている.

Pop goes the weasel. イタチがぴょんと飛び出る《6人で踊る英国の田舎踊り》 ▪ "*Pop goes the weasel*" met with a good reception. 「イタチがぴょんと飛び出る」は評判がよかった. ☞Mother Goose から.

pop[2] /pɑp|pɔp/ 動 ***pop*** *one's* ***clogs*** 《英戯》死ぬ ▪ Which meal would you have just before you *popped your clogs*? あなたは死ぬ直前には何が食べたいですか.

pop off the hooks →drop off the HOOKs.

pop (***the***) ***corn*** 《米》トウモロコシをはじけるまで炒る ▪ "I *popped the corn*!" he cried. 「トウモロコシが(はじけるまで)炒れたぞ!」と彼が大声で言った.

pop the question 《口》(女性に)結婚を申し込む ▪ Mary has managed to get Bertie to *pop the question* at last. メアリーは工夫してとうとうバーティーに結婚の申し込みをさせた.

pop up a question 急に質問する ▪ After a brief walk, Jack suddenly *popped up a question.* しばらく歩いた後で, ジャックが突然質問して来た.

Pope /poʊp/ 名 ***Is the Pope*** (***a***) ***Catholic?*** 《口》当たり前じゃないか, 答はわかっている[明白]だろ? ▪ Are you sure about that?—*Is the Pope Catholic?* Of course I'm sure. 確かか?—当たり前だろう, もちろん確かだ. ☞類例に次のようなものがあるが, 親しい友人間以外で使うと, 失礼になる. 類例: Does a bear shit in the woods? 《卑》クマは森で糞(ふん)をするの? Is the Earth round? 地球は丸いの? Is a frog's ass watertight? 《卑》カエルのおけつは防水か?

more Catholic than the pope → CATHOLIC.

pope /poʊp/, **poop** /puːp/ 名 ***take*** *a person's* ***pope*** 人のももの急所を打つ ▪ He struck at me and *took my pope.* 彼は私に打ちかかって, 私のももの急所をなぐった.

poppy /pɑ́pi|pɔ́pi/ 名 ***a tall poppy*** 特権階級

の[著名な]人 ▪ *A tall poppy* is someone who stands above the crowd because of his achievements.「背の高いケシ」とはその業績のために一段抜け出た人のことをいう.

popular /pápjələr|pɔ́pjʊ-/ 形 ***be popular with*** [***among***] ...に人気のある, 受けがよい ▪ He *was popular with* the teachers. 彼は先生がたの受けがよかった.

pore[1] /pɔːr/ 名 ***at every pore*** **1** すべての毛穴から ▪ He was sweating *at every pore*. 彼は毛穴という毛穴から汗を吹き出していた.

2 体中で, 全身で ▪ He sees *at every pore*. 彼は体中で見る.

pore[2] /pɔːr/ 動 ***pore*** *oneself* ***blind*** 過度の読書で盲目になる ▪ He *pored himself blind*. 彼は本の読みすぎで目が不自由になった.

pore *one's* ***eyes out*** 過度の読書で目を台なしにする, 目を疲れさせる ▪ I'll *pore my eyes out* rather than lose her. 彼女を失うくらいなら読書で目を台なしにするほうがましだ.

porridge /pɔ́ːrɪdʒ|pɔ́r-/ 名 ***do porridge***《英》刑期を務める, 懲役に服する ▪ The singer *did porridge* in 1999 for a drug-related crime. その歌手は1999年に麻薬関連の犯罪で服役した.

keep [***save***] *one's* ***breath to cool*** *one's* ***porridge*** →BREATH.

not earn salt to *one's* ***porridge*** →SALT[1].

port /pɔːrt/ 名 ***a port of call*** (船の)寄港地; よく訪れる場所 ▪ For me, our first *port of call* was the highlight of the trip. 私にとって最初の寄港地が旅の山場だった ▪ The pub was *a* regular *port of call* for him. そのパブは彼の行きつけの場所だった.

any port in a storm 窮余の策, おぼれる者へのわら ▪ The hotel was a matter of *any port in a storm*. そのホテルはおぼれる者へのわらというところだった.

clear (***a***) ***port***/***leave port*** 出港する ▪ The steamer has just *left port*. 汽船は出港したところだ.

in port 入港して ▪ Many vessels are *in port*. 多くの船が入港している.

make (***a***) ***port***/***come*** [***get***] ***into port***/***arrive in port*** 入港する ▪ The ship is *coming into port*. 船は入港しているところだ ▪ The ship has *arrived in port*. 船は入港した.

portage /pɔ́ːrtɪdʒ/ 名 ***make a*** [*one's*] ***portage***《米》カヌー・食料などを陸うたいに運ぶ ▪ We were obliged to *make a portage* up three sharp hills. 我々は3つのけわしい丘の上へカヌーなどを運び上げなければならなかった.

porter /pɔ́ːrtər/ 名 ***swear like a porter*** どなりちらす ▪ The drunken man *swore like a porter*. 酔っ払いはどなりちらした.

portfolio /pɔ̀ːrtfóʊlioʊ/ 名 ***resign*** [***deliver up***] *one's* ***portfolio*** 大臣をやめる ▪ The ministers all *delivered up their portfolios*. 大臣たちは総辞職した.

without portfolio 無任所の ▪ Mr. Johnson is minister *without portfolio*. ジョンスン氏は無任所大臣だ.

pose /poʊz/ 名 ***strike a pose*** 気取った態度をする ▪ My purpose was to achieve results, not to *strike a pose*. 私の目的は成果をあげることで, 気取った態度をすることではなかった.

posh /pɑʃ|pɔʃ/ 動 ***be poshed up***《英口》めかしこんでいる ▪ What *are* you all *poshed-up* for? 君は何のためにすっかりめかしこんでいるのかい?

posh *oneself* ***up***《英口》めかす ▪ He *poshed himself up* for the party. 彼はパーティーのためにめかしこんだ.

position /pəzíʃən/ 名 ***be in a position to*** *do* ...する立場にある, することができる ▪ We *are* now *in a position to* discuss it. これでその問題を論じることができる ▪ I'm sorry I'*m* not *in a position to* assist you in any way. 残念ですがどうにもお手伝いすることができません.

in [***out of***] ***position*** 正しい[まちがった]位置に ▪ Place it *in position*. それを定位置に置け.

in scoring position《野球》(ランナーが)スコアリング・ポジションにいて; もう少しで成功する ▪ The Yankees are hitting 259 with runners *in scoring position*. ヤンキースの得点圏打率は2割5分9厘である ▪ The publisher is *in scoring position* with that photographic collection of the actress. その出版社はその女優の写真集で成功寸前のところだ.

of position 高い地位の ▪ He is a man *of position*. 彼は高い地位の人だ.

put [***place***] *oneself* ***in*** *a person's* ***position*** 人の立場になって考える ▪ Just *put yourself in my position*. まあ私の身にもなってみてください.

take up a position **1** 陣取る ▪ The detective *took up a position* near the station. 刑事は駅の近くに張り込んだ.

2 立場をとる[明らかにする] ▪ What *position* is he *taking up* on this matter? この件につき彼はどんな立場をとっているのか.

positive /pázətɪv|pɔ́z-/ 形 ***be positive about*** [***of, on***] ...を確信している ▪ He *is positive of* his facts. 彼は事実を確信している ▪ I *am* quite *positive on* that point. 私はその点は全く確信している.

be positive that ...と確信している ▪ I *am positive that* he will win. 彼が優勝すると確信している.

possess /pəzés/ 動 ***be possessed by*** (悪霊など)に取りつかれている ▪ She *is possessed by* a devil. 彼女は悪魔に取りつかれている.

be possessed of ...を所有している ▪ He *is possessed of* a copious vocabulary. 彼は豊富な語彙を持っている.

be possessed with **1** (ある考えなど)に取りつかれている ▪ He *is possessed with* a sense of being in danger. 彼は自分が危険な立場に陥っているという意識に取りつかれている.

2 (悪霊など)に取りつかれている (＝be POSSESSed by) ▪ I *am possessed with* the devil and cannot sleep. 私は悪魔に取りつかれていて眠れない.

like all possessed《米》張り切って, 夢中になって

■ That old minister is fiddling away *like all possessed* at the dance. あの老牧師はダンスパーティーで張り切ってバイオリンをひいている.

like one* [*a man, a woman*] *possessed 悪魔に取りつかれた人間のように ■ He fought *like one possessed.* 彼は悪魔に取りつかれた人間のように戦った ■ She spoke *like a woman possessed.* 彼女は何かに取りつかれたようにしゃべった.

***possess** oneself* 自制する ■ He cannot *possess himself* enough. 彼はそれほど自制できない.

possess** oneself **of 《文》…を自分のものにする ■ He *possessed himself of* the lands. 彼はその土地を手に入れた.

possess** one's **soul in patience じっとがまんしている (《聖》*Luke* 21. 19) ■ All Christians are obliged to *possess their souls in patience.* すべてのキリスト教信者はじっとがまんしていなければならない.

***What possessed** a person **to** do?* 人がどういう気で…したのか ■ *What possessed* you *to* do that? どういう気でそんなことをしたのか.

possession /pəzéʃən/ 名 ***be in possession of** a thing* 物を所有している ■ The widow *is in possession of* a large fortune. その未亡人は莫大な財産を持っている.

***be in the possession of** a person* 人の所有になっている ■ A large fortune *is in the possession of* the widow. 莫大な財産がその未亡人の所有になっている ■ The keys *are in his possession.* かぎは彼が持っている.

***come* [*enter*] *into possession of** a thing* 物を手に入れる; にありつく ■ He *came into possession of* a fortune. 彼はひと財産にありついた.

come* [*pass*] *into the possession of 人の手に渡る ■ The land *passed into the possession of* the firm. 土地はその企業の手に渡った.

get* [*take*] *possession of …を手に入れる, 占有する, 占領する ■ For a few shillings I *got possession of* a good one. 2, 3シリングで良いのを手に入れた ■ He *took possession of* the islands in the name of the King of Spain. 彼はスペイン王の名のもとにその島を占有した.

Possession is nine points* [*parts*] *of the law. 《諺》所有は九分の強み,「預り主は九分の主」.

put** a person **in possession of 人に…を所有させる ■ This move *put* them *in possession of* the village. この手段で彼らはその村を手に入れた.

rejoice in the possession of 幸いにも…を持っている ■ He *rejoices in the possession of* great wealth. 彼は幸いにも大きな財産を持っている.

take possession of →get POSSESSION of.

possibility /pɑ̀səbíləti|pɔ̀s-/ 名 ***beyond a possibility of*** …の可能性がないまでに ■ I can prove it *beyond a possibility of* doubt. 疑いを入れる余地がないまでにそれを証明することができる.

by any possibility 万が一にも ■ If I could *by any possibility* manage to do it, I would. 万が一にも何とかしてそれがやれるものなら, やるのだが.

it is out of* [*within*] *the bounds* [*range*] *of possibility that …はありえない[うる]ことで ■ *It is* quite *within the bounds of possibility that* he will succeed in his enterprise. 彼の企業はまずうまくいきそうだ.

there is no possibility of …の見込みは少しもない ■ *There is no possibility of* my going there [*of* success]. 私がそこへ行ける[成功する]見込みは少しもない.

possible /pɑ́səbəl|pɔ́s-/ 形名 ***as* [*so*]... *as possible*** できるだけ… ■ Make the room *as* dark *as possible.* 部屋をできるだけ暗くせよ ■ Read *as* much *as possible.* できるだけ多く読め ■ We want to argue the point *so* far *as possible.* その点についてできる限り論じたい.

do** one's **possible できるだけのことをする, 全力を尽くす ■ I had *done my possible* to gratify you. あなたの意にかなうようにできるだけのことはしました. ☞F faire son possible のなぞり.

if possible できれば ■ Call on me, *if possible.* できればお訪ねください.

possum /pɑ́səm|pɔ́s-/ 名 ***come the possum over*** 《米口》(人)をだます ■ I believe he's *coming the possum over* his mother. 彼はきっと母親をだましているのだと思う.

grin like a possum 《米口》フクロネズミのような顔つきをする ■ I went to sleep *grinning like a possum.* 僕はフクロネズミのような顔つきをして眠った.

play* [*act*] *possum 死んだふりをする, 仮病を使う, しらばくれる ■ All that time he had been *playing possum.* その間じゅう彼は仮病を使っていたのだった ■ I will *play possum* with these folks. この連中に対してしらばくれてやろう. ☞フクロネズミは攻撃されると死んだふりをすることから.

post[1] /poʊst/ 名 ***(as) deaf as a post*** 全然耳が聞こえない ■ She was *deaf as a post.* 彼女は全然耳が聞こえなかった.

(as) stiff as a post しゃちこばって ■ There he stood, *stiff as a post.* そこに彼はしゃちこばって突っ立っていた.

(as) stupid as a post 全くの大ばかで ■ The fellow, *stupid as a post*, believed it was a ghost. その男は全くの大ばかなのでそれが幽霊だと思いこんだ.

beat** a person **on the post (競争で)ごくわずかの差で人を負かす ■ He just got his nose in front and *beat* me *on the post.* 彼がちょっと鼻を前につき出してわずかの差で僕を負かした. ☞post「競馬の決勝点の標柱」.

between you and me and the post →BETWEEN you and me and the bedpost.

first past the post 《英》 **1** (競馬などで)1位でゴールインして ■ *First past the post* was Team Agni's bike, ridden by Rob Barber. 最初にゴールしたのはロブ・バーバーが運転するチーム・アグニのバイクだった. **2** (選挙制度の)多数票方式で選出されて; 小選挙区制で ■ The electoral system used for UK general elections is commonly known as *first past the*

P

post. イギリスの総選挙で採られている投票様式は普通多数票方式として知られています. ☞"the post" は競馬場のゴールポストを指し, しばしば選挙戦で用いられる.

from pillar to post →PILLAR.

left at the post 競争相手に全く負かされて ▪ Poor old Bill is always *left at the post.* かわいそうにビルのやつはいつも他人に先を越されてばかりいる. ☞競馬から.

make a hack in the post 大金を費やす ▪ One horse *made a* sad *hack in the post.* 1頭の馬がひどく大金を食った.

on the right [wrong] side of the post **1** (競争で)コースをまちがえずに[まちがえて] ▪ At length his horse ran *on the wrong side of the post*, and was distanced. とうとう彼の馬はコースをまちがえて走って引き離された.

2 方針・行動を誤らないで[誤って] ▪ I find I am *on the wrong side of the post.* 私は方針を誤っているのがわかった.

pip** a person **at [to] the post 《英》人にかろうじて勝つ, 辛勝(しんしょう)する ▪ Arsenal *pipped* us *to the post*, again by just one point. アーセナルがまたもやわずか1点差で我々に勝った.

run** one's **head against a post →beat one's HEAD against a (stone, brick) wall.

post[2] /poʊst/ 名 ***at** one's **post*** 持ち場で ▪ He was accused of sleeping *at his post.* 彼は持ち場で居眠りをしたという問責を受けた.

on post 歩哨に立って; 巡回中で ▪ It was a policeman *on post.* それは巡回中の警官だった.

remain [stay] at** one's **post/stand to** one's **post 持ち場にとどまる ▪ The guard was determined to *remain at his post.* 歩哨は持ち場にとどまる決心をしていた.

take post 陣取る ▪ They *took post* at the bridge. 彼らは橋の所に陣取った.

post[3] /poʊst/ 名 ***by post*** 郵便で ▪ He sent me a package *by post.* 彼は小包を郵送してくれた.

by return of post 折り返し ▪ Please send me an answer *by return of post.* 折り返しご返事を請う. ☞F par retour du courrier のなぞり.

have a heavy post 郵便がたくさん来る ▪ I have *had a heavy post* today. 今日は郵便がたくさん来た.

in (the) post 郵送中に ▪ The letter has been lost *in the post.* 手紙は郵送中に紛失した.

miss [catch] the post 集配に間に合わない[間に合う] ▪ I *missed the* morning *post.* 朝の集配に間に合わなかった ▪ Those letters *caught the post.* それらの手紙は集配に間に合った.

through the post 郵便で ▪ These are the inquiries received *through the post.* これらは郵便で受けた問い合わせです.

post[4] /poʊst/ 動 ***be well posted (up) in*** …に通じている ▪ He *is well posted up in* the question. 彼はその問題に通じている.

keep** a person **posted (up) 人を常に…に通じさせておく, 状況を絶えず知らせる (*on*) ▪ My secretary *keeps* me *posted on* everything that goes on at the office. 秘書が事務所の出来事は逐一報告してくれる ▪ I hope you *keep* me *posted* about my son's condition. 息子の容態を絶えずお知らせください.

post[5] /poʊst/ 動 ***Post no bills.*** 貼り紙お断り《掲示》.

postal /póʊstəl/ 形 ***go postal (on** a person**)*** 《米口》…に対して急に凶暴になる[怒り出す], キレる ▪ I'm just sitting here and all of a sudden you *go postal on* me. ここにただ座っているだけなのに, 突然あなたがキレるんだもの ▪ An employee got so angry and *went postal on* his boss. 一人の雇い人がひどく怒って社長に食ってかかった. ☞米国の郵便局員が怒って他の従業員を撃ち殺した事件から.

poster /póʊstər/ 名 ***poster child [boy, girl]*** 《米・報道》イメージキャラクター; 典型例 ▪ Mary is the *poster girl* of this year's fair. メアリーは今年の祭りのイメージキャラクターです ▪ Our boss is a *poster child* for militant vegetarianism. 我々のボスは活動的な菜食主義唱道者です.

pot /pɑt|pɔt/ 名 ***a big pot*** 大物 ▪ Dick pointed out some of the *big pots* of the day. ディックは当代の大物を幾人か指摘した.

A little pot is soon hot. 《諺》小人(しょうじん)は怒りやすい.

a pot (of money)/pots of money 《口》大金 ▪ He went to India and came back with *a pot of money.* 彼はインドへ行って大金を持って戻ってきた ▪ I don't earn *pots of money.* 大金を稼いではいない.

A watched pot never boils. 《諺》待つ身は長い; あせってはだめ.

be pot luck 事前の計画や特別な食べ物を準備しないで ▪ "We'll just be casual and eat in the kitchen. It's just *pot luck*," Maria said. 「普段の通りにして台所で食事しましょう. ほんのあり合わせよ」とマリアは言った.

boil the pot **1** 暮らしを立てる ▪ I have just enough money to *boil the pot.* 私はやっと暮らしを立てられるほどの金しかない.

2 生計のために作品を書く ▪ He now simply *boils the pot.* 彼は今生活のために作品を書いているだけだ.

call each other pot and kettle お互いに自分のことはたなに上げて相手を責める ▪ They are *calling each other pot and kettle.* 彼らはお互いに自分のことはたなに上げて相手を責めている.

for the pot 食用に ▪ This herb is *for the pot.* この草は食用にされている.

get a pot at →take a POT at.

go to pot 《口》落ちぶれる, 破滅する ▪ They will smile to see him *go to pot.* 彼らは彼が落ちぶれるのを見て笑うだろう. ☞悪い肉はこまぎれにしてなべに入れることから.

in (**one's**) pots 酔っ払って (→in one's CUPs) ▪ *In his pots* he always brags. 彼は酔っ払うといつもほらを吹く.

keep the pot boiling **1** (特に文筆などで)暮らしを立てていく ▪ He is so poor that he is hardly able to *keep the pot boiling*. 彼はとても貧しいので暮らしを立てていくこともできないくらいだ.
2 景気よく[盛んに]続けていく ▪ His lieutenants *keep the* rebellion *pot boiling* in Ireland. 彼の中尉たちはアイルランドで盛んに反逆を続けている.

make the pot boil 暮らしを立てる ▪ Glory is excellent, but it will not *make the* national *pot boil*. 栄光はすばらしいが, それでは国家は立ちゆかない.

not have a pot to piss in 《卑》とても貧乏で ▪ Ken still did*n't have a pot to piss in*. ケンはいまだにひどい貧乏であった. ☞"not have two CENTs to rub together" がより丁寧な言い方.

pee in the same pot 《卑》同じ穴のムジナである ▪ The two of them *pee in the same pot*. あの二人は同じ穴のムジナだ.

pots and pans なべとかま, 炊事道具 ▪ Boiled meats involve an apparatus of *pots and pans*. ゆで肉にはなべかまなどの道具がいる.

pots of money →a POT (of money).

put on the pot/put the pot on 《俗》大金を賭ける ▪ He solaced himself by *putting on the pot* at cards. 彼はトランプで大金を賭けて自らを慰めた.

put the big pot in the little one 《米口》とても念入りにやる ▪ The town proposes to *put the big pot in the little one* to make an occasion of the day. その町はその日を祝って盛大にやろうと提案している. ☞[F] mettre les petits plats dans les grands のなぞり.

shit or get off the pot 《米卑》さっさとどちらかに決めろ; きちんとやれ, できないなら他人にまかせろ ▪ Son, it's time to *shit or get off the pot*. 息子よ, やるかまかせるか, どちらかにすべき時だな. ☞"FISH or cut bait" がより丁寧な言い方.

sweeten the pot 賭け金を増す ▪ "Five dollars," he said, *sweetening the pot*. 「5ドル」と彼は賭け金を増して言った.

take* [*get*] *a pot at …をねらい撃ちする ▪ He *took* [*got*] *a* cool *pot at* the bear with a revolver. 彼は連発銃でクマをじっとねらい撃ちした. ☞pot＝pot-shot (ねらい撃ち).

take a pot shot at/take a potshot* [*potshots*] *at 《口》 **1** …をねらい撃ちする, 近距離射撃をする ▪ He *took a pot shot at* the bird, but missed. 彼はその鳥をねらい撃ちしたが, 当たらなかった ▪ The soldiers were *taking potshots at* each other on the battlefield. 兵士たちは戦場でお互いを狙って乱射を続けた.
2 急に批判[中傷]する, やたらに批判する ▪ The professor *took a pot shot at* the student's jump of logic. 教授は突然に学生の論理の飛躍を批判した ▪ Some Americans like to *take potshots at* our country. アメリカ人の中にはわが国を批判するのが好きな人がいる.

The pot calls the kettle black./the pot calling the kettle black 《諺》自分のことをたなに上げて人を責める,「目くそ鼻くそを笑う」 ▪ How about yourself? It's a case of *the pot calling the kettle black*. そういう君はどうなんだい? それは「目くそ鼻くそを笑う」というもんだよ.

The pot goes so long* [*often*] *to the water* [*well*] *that it is broken at last. 《諺》かめはあまり長いこと[しばしば]水場[井戸]に行くのでついに割れてしまう《あまり調子に乗るとやりしくじる》.

the top of the pot 《米口》抜群の地位[物] ▪ Indeed, among our ministers he is actually at *the top of the pot*. 全く我々の牧師の中では彼はまさに抜群の地位にある.

throw ... into the pot 議論の材料を提供する ▪ Anyone else have suggestions they want to *throw into the pot*? 他に誰か提案希望者はいないか.

potato /pətéɪtoʊ/ 名 ***a hot potato*** 《口》多くの人々が議論している問題, 関わりたくない難問題《しばしば政治で》 ▪ When it comes to *a* political *hot potato* such as abortion or tightening the gun laws, it's beyond my power. 中絶や銃規制などの政治的難問だと私はお手上げだ ▪ Many school boards found segregation *a hot potato* in the 1960s. 多くの教育委員会は60年代に差別の問題で悩んだ.

drop* [*let fall*] *... like a hot potato →HOT.

hold** one's **potato 《米口》待つ, 辛抱する ▪ Now let me beg of the gentleman to *hold his potato*. さてその紳士が辛抱してくださることをお願いする.

quite the potato 《口》あつらえ向きのもの, 本物 ▪ His first two volumes are not *quite the potato*. 彼の最初の2巻はどうも本物とは言えない ▪ Larry is *quite the potato*. ラリーはまさにうってつけの人物だ.

***shut* (*up*) *one's potato-trap* [*box*]** 《俗》黙る ▪ *Shut your potato-trap*! 黙れ!

***small potatoes* (*and few of* [*in*] *a hill*)** 《口》つまらない物[人] ▪ This is what I call *small potatoes and few of a hill*. これが私の言ういわゆるつまらないものだ ▪ They are very *small potatoes*. 彼らはとてもつまらない連中だ.

***thinks no small potatoes of** oneself* 《口》自分を相当のもの[大物]だと思う ▪ He *thinks no small potatoes of himself*. 彼は自分を大物だと思っている.

pother /pɑ́ðər|pɔ́ð-/ 名 ***in a pother*** うろたえて, 心配して ▪ He cried out all *in a pother*. 彼はすっかりうろたえて大声で叫んだ.

kick up a pother ほこりをもうもうと立てる ▪ What *a pother* she *kicks up* with her broom! 彼女はほうきでやけにほこりをもうもうと立てるじゃないか!

make* [*raise*] *a pother わいわい騒ぐ (*about*) ▪ He *made a pother about* it. 彼はそのことで大騒ぎした.

potluck /pɑ́tlʌ̀k|pɔ́t-/ 名 ***take potluck*** **1** あり合わせの食事をする ▪ Do come along and *take potluck* at my place. うちに来てあり合わせの食事をしてください.
2 知らないことでも運任せで選ぶ ▪ We'd *take potluck* at whatever restaurants might still be

open. どんなレストランがまだ営業中かは運任せにしよう.

potty /páti|pɔ́ti/ 形 ***be potty about*** [***on***] 《俗》...に参っている, 首ったけだ ▪ I'*m potty about* her. 僕はあの子に首ったけだ.

potty little 《俗》(人・物が)ちっぽけな, つまらない ▪ It is such a *potty little* town. 実にちっぽけな町だ.

pounce /paʊns/ 名 ***be on the pounce*** 今にも飛びつこうとしている, 虎視たんたんとしている ▪ His enemies *were on the pounce* to belittle his efforts. 敵は彼の努力をけなそうと虎視たんたんとしていた.

make a pounce (動物などに)さっと飛びつく (*on, upon*) ▪ He will *make a pounce upon* me with his collected force. 彼は全身の力をふりしぼって私に飛びかかってくるだろう.

pound[1] /paʊnd/ 名 ***by the pound*** 1ポンド幾らで ▪ Sugar is sold *by the pound*. 砂糖は1ポンド幾らで売られる.

exact [***claim, demand, have, insist on, take, want***] *one's* ***pound of flesh*** 約束通りの支払いを要求する, 非道な取り立てをする (cf. Sh., *Merch. V.* 4. 1. 99, 308) ▪ He's just the type to *insist on his pound of flesh*. あの男はまさに約束通りの支払いを要求してやまないといったタイプだ. ☞高利貸しのシャイロックが借金のかたとしてアントニオの胸の肉を1ポンド求めたことから.

in the pound 1ポンドにつき ▪ He is a usurer and takes four shillings *in the pound*. 彼は高利貸で1ポンドにつき4シリング取り立てる.

(***it is***) ***a pound to a penny*** (***that***) 《口》たぶん...だろう ▪ *A pound to a penny* he will succeed. たぶん彼は成功するだろう.

pile on the pounds 体重が非常に増える ▪ People *pile on the pounds* when they eat too much and when they exercise too little. 食べ過ぎて運動をしないと人は体重がぐんと増える.

P

pound and [***for***] ***pound*** 同じ割合で ▪ All creditors had *pound and pound* alike. すべての債権者は等しく同じ割合で取った.

pounds, shillings, and pence 金銭; 金銭上の; 現実的な《《口》で £.s.d. ともいう》(→L.S.D.) ▪ It is a question of *pounds, shillings, and pence* [*£. s.d.*] それは金の問題だ ▪ They are a *pounds-shillings-and-pence* people. 彼らは現実的な国民だ.

the gray dollar [《英》***grey pound***] 《米》子供たちが家を離れたのち年輩の夫婦が自分たちのために金を使うこと; そのお金の総称 ▪ Some businesses have already realised the potential of *the grey pound*. 中にはすでに年配者の購買力の可能性に気がついている企業がいる.

pound[2] /paʊnd/ 名 ***bring ... into a pound*** (敵など)を進退きわまらせる ▪ We *brought* the enemy *into a pound* by this means. 我々はこの手段で敵を進退きわまらせた.

pound[3] /paʊnd/ 動 ***pound it*** 《英俗》請け合う ▪ I'll *pound it*, that Barney's managing properly. 確かにバーニーはきちんと事を処理していますよ ▪ I'll *pound it* to be so. そうだということは請け合うよ. ☞ポンドを賭けることから.

pound[4] /paʊnd/ 動 ***pound*** *one's* ***ear*** 《俗》眠る ▪ He came while I was *pounding my ear*. 彼は私が眠っているときにやって来た.

pour /pɔːr/ 動 ***be pouring with*** (涙・汗などが大量に)流れ出る ▪ During the judo practise, you *are pouring with* sweat. 柔道の稽古中は汗だくになる.

it is pouring with (雨)がどしゃぶりに降っている ▪ *It's pouring with* rain outside. 外はどしゃぶりだ.

It never rains but it pours. →RAIN[2].

pour cold water on [***upon***] ...にけちをつける, 水をさす ▪ He was obliged to *pour cold water on* the zeal of his friends. 彼は友人たちの熱心さに水をささねばならなかった.

pour *oneself* ***into*** **1** ...に深く関わる, 没頭する ▪ She coped with the loss of her husband by *pouring herself into* her young son. 彼女は自分の幼い息子に没頭することで夫の死を乗り越えた.

2《戯》窮屈な衣服を何とかして着る ▪ Marilyn *poured herself into* a dress which fit like a second skin. マリリンは第二の皮膚のようにぴったりの服を苦労して身につけた.

pour it on 《米》 **1** 最大限の力を出す, 全速力で走る ▪ Allied bombers began really to *pour it on*. 連合軍の爆撃機はほんとに最大限に攻撃し始めた ▪ When he ran he *poured it on*. 彼は走るときには全速力で走った.

2 最大限に誇張する ▪ He really *poured it on* in the ten-minute talk. その10分間の演説で彼は最大限に誇張した.

pour itself into (川が)...に注ぐ ▪ The river *pours itself into* the sea. その川は海へ注いでいる.

pour on the coal(***s***) 《俗》(車などの)スピードを上げる ▪ India was *pouring on the coal* to use nuclear energy in the 21st century. インドは21世紀に核エネルギー利用をするために急いでいた ▪ Christmas is coming so let's *pour on the coals* and wrap all the presents. クリスマスが近づいたのでスピードを上げてプレゼントの包装をしよう.

pour scorn [***contempt***] ***on*** 非難[嘲笑]する ▪ China *poured scorn on* the Dalai Lama on Sunday. 中国は日曜日にダライ・ラマを非難した.

pout /paʊt/ 名 ***have the pouts*** ふくれっつらをしている ▪ My sister *has the pouts* this morning. 姉は今朝はふくれっつらをしている.

in the pouts ふくれっつらをして ▪ That put him *in the pouts*. それで彼はふくれっつらをした.

poverty /pávərti|pɔ́v-/ 名 ***fall*** [***sink***] ***into poverty*** 貧乏になる ▪ He has *fallen into* abject *poverty*. 彼は極貧に陥った.

in poverty 貧乏して; 貧乏の中で ▪ He is *in poverty*. 彼は貧乏している ▪ He died *in poverty*. 彼は赤貧の中で亡くなった.

Poverty is not a crime [***no sin***]. 《諺》貧しいということで人を咎(とが)めてはならない.

When poverty comes in at the door, love flies out at the window. 《諺》貧乏が戸口から入ってくると愛が窓から飛び出して行く.

powder[1] /páʊdər/ 名 ***burn powder*** 《米口》弾丸を発射する ▪ The soldiers *burned powder* to no purpose. 兵士たちは銃撃したがむだだった.

food for powder →FOOD.

powder and shot **1** 弾薬, 軍需品 ▪ We have spent all our *powder and shot*. 我々は弾薬を使い果たしてしまった.

2 費用, 労力 ▪ These fellows are not worth *powder and shot*. この連中は骨折りがいがない.

sit on a powder keg 非常に危険な状況に置かれている ▪ Herod knew that he was *sitting on a powder keg*. ヘロデ王はいつでも爆発しかねない火種を抱えていることを知っていた. ☞a powder keg「火薬保存用の小さな木製の樽」.

smell the powder 実戦を経験する ▪ They were *smelling the powder* for the first time. 彼らは初めて実戦を経験していた.

take a powder **1** 散薬[粉薬]を飲む ▪ He *takes a powder* every morning. 彼は毎朝散薬を飲む.

2《米口》姿をくらます, ずらかる ▪ The witness suddenly *took a powder*. 証人は突然姿をくらました.

powder[2] /páʊdər/ 動 ***powder*** *one's* ***nose*** [***face***]《戯》(女性が)お手洗いに立つ[行く] ▪ Excuse me, I have to *powder my nose*. 失礼してお化粧を直しに行かなくっちゃ.

power /páʊər/ 名 ***a power couple*** [***partnership***] パワーカップル, どちらも幹部役員で同等の社会的地位にある若いカップル ▪ Any two people who work in powerful partnership can be *a power couple*. 強固な協力関係で働く二人なら誰でも力強いカップルになれる ▪ We believe Alex and Simon have *a power partnership* in their new world. アレックスとサイモンは新たな業界でともに重責を果たすことを我々は信じている.

a power house →HOUSE.

a power nap パワーナップ, 権力者の午睡《ビジネス業界で幹部が重要な会議の合間にとる英気を養うための仮眠》 ▪ Max is taking *a power nap* right now, saving up his energy. マックスは力を蓄えるために仮眠中です.

a power of 《俗》たくさんの (= a LOT (of)) ▪ They had left *a power of* servants at their master's. 彼らは主人の所に使用人を大勢残しておいた ▪ He knows *a power of* botany. 彼は植物学のことをずいぶん知っている.

Absolute power corrupts absolutely. 《諺》絶対[独裁的]権力は絶対腐敗する. ☞英国の歴史家 Lord Acton の "Power tends to corrupt and absolute power corrupts absolutely." から.

beyond *one's* ***power*** =out of one's POWER.

bring ... under *one's* ***power*** (町など)を支配下に入れる ▪ The king *brought* the town *under his power*. 王はその町を支配下に入れた.

by (***all***) ***the powers*** 誓って, きっと ▪ No, I won't do so, *by all the powers*! いいや, 誓ってそんなことはしない. ☞powers という複数形はもと異教の神々をさしたもの.

come into power 権力[政権]を握る ▪ The party *came into power* in 1930. その党は1930年に政権を握った.

(***do*** *a person*) ***a power*** [***world***] ***of good*** 《口》とてもためになるもの, とても効き目があるもの, 大変役に立つもの ▪ That holiday *did* me *a power of good*. その休暇は私に大いにためになった.

fall into [***put*** *oneself* ***in***] *a person's* ***power*** 人に支配されるようになる ▪ The minds of men *fell into the power of* the orator. 人々の心はその弁士に支配されてしまった ▪ You have *put yourself in their power*. あなたは彼らに支配されるようになった.

gray power 老人パワー《退職して悠々自適の生活をしている富裕な年寄りが行使する力》 ▪ The elderly now exercise "*gray power*" in this country. この国では年配の人たちが今「老人パワー」を発揮している.

have *a person* ***in*** *one's* ***power/have power over*** *a person* 人を思いのままにしている ▪ I *have* the man *in my power*. その男を意のままにしている.

in [***out of***] ***power*** 政権を握って[離れて] ▪ The party is at present *in power*. その党が現在政権を握っている ▪ The party went *out of power*. その党は政権から離れた.

in [***within***] *one's* ***power*** …にできる ▪ It lies *in your power* to refuse the proposal. 君はその申し出を拒否することができる ▪ I will do everything *in my power* for you. できることは何でもしてあげます.

Merciful powers! ありがたや!, あら! ▪ *Merciful powers!* I remember. ああ, 思い出したぞ.

More [***all***] ***power to your elbow*** [***you***]***!*** 《英》ますますご健闘を祈る!, ご成功を祈る! ▪ So you've decided to be a farmer in Canada? Well, *more power to your elbow!* ではカナダで農夫になる決心をされたのですね. とにかくご成功を祈ります ▪ He's decided to climb Mount Everest—Well, *more power to* him. 彼はエベレスト登頂を決心した—そうか, 成功を祈る. ☞ユーモラスな乾杯の文句で「ひじが強くてもっと火酒を口へ持っていけるように」が原義.

out of power →in POWER.

out of *one's* ***power*** …にできない ▪ It is *out of my power* to help him. 彼を助けることは私にはできない.

put *oneself* ***in*** *a person's* ***power*** →fall into a person's POWER.

put ... into power …に政権をとらせる ▪ The party *was put into power* at the election. その党が選挙で政権をとった.

staying power 持続力, 耐久力, スタミナ ▪ Do you think this guy has *staying power*? この男は長持ちすると思うか.

the power behind the throne (国家・会社・家などの)陰の実力者 ▪ In that firm, Mr. Wilson is *the power behind the throne*. その会社ではウィルソン氏が陰の実力者だ.

the powers that be 《戯》当局者; 幹部 (《聖》 *Roms*. 13. 1) ▪ There is in the masses of this country a great principle of submission to *the powers that be*. この国の大衆の間には当局者には服従するという大原則がある.

to the best [***utmost***] ***of*** *one's* ***power*** 力の及ぶかぎり, できるだけ ▪ They defended him *to the best of their powers*. 彼らは力のかぎり彼を守った.

under its own power (車などが)自力で ▪ The car came in *under its own power*. その車は自力で入って来た.

within *one's* ***power*** →in one's POWER.

powerful /páʊərfəl/ 形 ***a powerful lot of*** 《俗》たくさんの, おびただしい ▪ It costs *a powerful lot of* money to go there. そこへ行くにはべらぼうな金がかかる ▪ I have *a powerful lot of* trouble. 私にはたくさんの悩みがある.

practical /prǽktɪkəl/ 形 ***a practical joke*** →JOKE[1].

for (***all***) ***practical purposes*** 実際的には ▪ It is useless *for practical purposes*. それは実際の役には立たない.

practice[1] /prǽktəs/ 名 ***bring*** [***carry***] ***... in*** [***into***] ***practice*** →put ... in PRACTICE.

get out of practice (練習不足で)へたになる ▪ She *got out of practice* on the piano. 彼女は練習不足でピアノの腕がにぶった.

have an extensive [***a large***] ***practice*** (医者・弁護士が)手広くやっている, はやっている ▪ The lawyer *has an extensive practice*. あの弁護士は手広くやっている.

in practice **1** 事実[実際]上 ▪ *In practice* it has but little changed. 実際上はごくわずかしか変わっていない ▪ It is not so easy *in practice* as in theory. それは理論で言うほど実際には容易ではない.
2 (へたにならないように)練習を積んで (↔out of PRACTICE) ▪ He always kept his hand *in practice*. 彼はいつも練習して手を慣らしていた.
3 (弁護士・医者が)開業して ▪ He is a physician *in practice*. 彼は開業医だ.

make a practice of ...を習慣的に行う, 常習する ▪ He *makes a practice of* traveling abroad. 彼はいつもよく海外旅行をする ▪ You must not *make a practice of* it. 君はそれを常習としてはいけない.

make it a [*one's*] ***practice to*** *do* ...することを習慣[常習]とする ▪ I *make it a practice to* have an early morning walk. 私は早朝に散歩するのを習慣にしている.

out of practice 練習不足で, へたになって (↔in PRACTICE 2) ▪ He played a very poor game, he was plainly *out of practice*. 彼はひどくへたな試合をやった. 明らかに練習不足だったのだ.

Practice makes perfect. 《諺》習うより慣れよ ▪ I do this for two hours every day. *Practice makes perfect*, you know. これを毎日2時間やっています.「習うより慣れよ」ですから.

put [***bring, carry***] ***... in*** [***into***] ***practice*** ...を実行に移す, 実行する ▪ He *put* the idea *into practice*. 彼はその考えを実行に移した.

with practice 練習すれば ▪ *With practice* anyone can learn to play golf. 練習すれば誰でもゴルフができるようになる.

practice[2], 《英》 **practise** /prǽktəs/ 動 ***practice at*** [***on, with***] ...の練習をする ▪ She is *practicing at* [*on*] the piano. 彼女はピアノの練習をしている ▪ I am *practicing with* the rifle. 私は射撃の練習をしている.

practice *a person* ***in*** 人に...を教え込む ▪ The captain *practices* his company *in* all the phases of war. 隊長は自分の部隊に戦争のあらゆる面を教え込んでいる.

practice religion 信仰生活を実践する ▪ Out of forty thousand inhabitants, four thousand *practiced religion*. 4万人の住民のうち4千人が信仰生活を実践していた. ☞F practiquer la religion のなぞり.

Practice what you preach. 《諺》自分の説くところを実行せよ.

praise[1] /preɪz/ 名 ***be beyond*** [***above***] ***all praise*** 賞賛する言葉がない ▪ His heroism *is beyond all praise*. 彼の勇ましい行為はほめきれない.

be loud [***warm***] ***in*** *a person's* ***praise*** 人を大いに[熱心に]ほめる ▪ All *were loud in his praise*. 万人が口をきわめて彼をほめそやした.

be loud [***warm***] ***in*** *one's* ***praise of*** ...を大いに[熱心に]ほめそやす ▪ They *are loud in their praises of* the work. 人々は口をきわめてその作品をほめそやしている.

damn with [***by***] ***faint praise*** →DAMN[2].

in praise of ...をほめて ▪ Much was written *in praise of* him. 彼をほめて多くの記事が書かれた.

Praise be (***to God***)***!*** ありがたや!

sound [***sing***] *one's* ***own praises*** 自画自賛する ▪ The boy was *singing his own praises* after the award. 少年は受賞したあと自画自賛していた.

sound [***sing***] ***the praises of*** ...をほめたたえる ▪ All *sang the praises of* his valor. 万人が彼の勇気をほめたたえた.

praise[2] /preɪz/ 動 ***God be praised!*** ありがたや!

praise ... to the skies →SKY.

prank[1] /præŋk/ 名 ***play pranks on*** [***upon***] ...にいたずらをする ▪ Boys are fond of *playing pranks on* girls. 男子は女子にいたずらをするのを好む.

prank[2] /præŋk/ 動 ***prank*** *oneself* ***out*** [***up***] めかしこむ ▪ She spent half a day in *pranking herself out*. 彼女は半日かけてめかしこんだ.

pray /preɪ/ 動 ***be past praying for*** →PAST.

pray to the porcelain god 《俗》酔ってトイレに吐く, もどす ▪ Unfortunately, I was *praying to the porcelain god* most of last night. 不幸なことに私は飲みすぎて昨晩の大半を吐きまくっていた.

pray to [***for***] ***... to*** *do* (神など)に...するよう祈る ▪ We *prayed to* God *to* save us. 我々は神にお救い

P

くださいと祈った.

prayer /preər/ 名 ***be at*** (*one's*) ***prayers*** お祈りをしている ▪ They *were at prayers* in the chapel. 彼らは礼拝堂でお祈りをしていた.

in prayer お祈りをして ▪ I found her *in prayer*. 彼女はお祈りをあげていた.

not have a prayer (***of*** *doing* ...) 《口》(…する)成功の望み[見込み]は全くない ▪ He did *not* seem to *have a prayer of winning* the U.S. Open golf tournament. 彼が全米オープンで勝てるという望みは皆目ないようだった.

say [***give***] *one's* ***prayers*** 祈りを上げる ▪ He did not get it *saying his prayers*. 彼は祈りを上げてそれを得たのではない《自分の努力で得たのだ》.

preach /pri:tʃ/ 動 ***preach*** [***talk, speak***] ***to the converted*** 改宗者に説教する, 釈迦に説法をする ▪ If you only talk to your supporters, you will be *preaching to the converted*. 自分の支持者とだけ話をしたら, 改宗者に説教するようなことになるよ.

preach to the saved [***the choir***] 救済された人たちに[聖歌隊に]説教する ▪ You are *preaching to the saved*! 余計な世話というものだ.

precaution /prɪkɔ́:ʃən/ 名 ***by way of precaution/as a*** (***means of***) ***precaution*** 用心に, 念のため ▪ Take an umbrella *as a precaution*. 念のため雨がさを持って行きなさい.

take (*one's*) ***precautions*** 警戒する, 用心する (*against, to do*) ▪ *Take precautions against* fire. 火の用心 ▪ I will *take precautions to* guard against such incidents. そのような事件が起こらないように用心しよう.

precedence /présədəns/ 名 ***give*** *a person* ***precedence*** 人に上位[上席]を与える ▪ His great insight has *given* him *precedence* over all the poets. すぐれた洞察力によって彼はすべての詩人よりも上位を占めている.

take [***have***] (***the***) ***precedence of*** [***over***] …に優先する, の上位に立つ ▪ The question of expense *takes precedence of* all others. 費用の問題が何より先だ ▪ Government messages *take precedence over* all others. 政府の通達は何よりも優先する.

precedent /présədənt/ 名 ***beyond all precedents*** 全く先例がない ▪ His valor is *beyond all precedents*. 彼の勇気は全く先例がない.

set [***create***] ***a precedent*** 先例となる (*for*) ▪ The French Revolution *created a precedent for* it. フランス革命がその先例となった.

without precedent 先例のない ▪ It is *without precedent* in history. それは歴史に先例がない.

precept /prí:sept/ 名 ***Practice*** [***Example***] ***is better than precept.*** 《諺》実行[実例]は教訓に勝る.

precious[1] /préʃəs/ 名 ***My precious!*** 私の大事な人《呼びかけ》 ▪ How are you, *my precious*? どうかね, 私の大事な人よ.

precious[2] /préʃəs/ 形 ***precious few*** [***little***] 《口》極めて少数の[少量の], ほとんどない ▪ There were *precious few* places to sit to have lunch. 座ってお昼を食べられる場所が極めて少なかった ▪ As it turned out, I got *precious little* sleep. あとで分かったことだが, 私はほとんど寝ていなかった.

precipitate /prɪsípətèɪt/ 動 ***precipitate*** *oneself* ***into*** **1** …にまっさかさまに落ちる ▪ He was obliged to *precipitate himself into* the sea. 彼はやむをえず海の中へまっさかさまに飛び込んだ.

2 (良くない状態)に急に陥る ▪ The youth *precipitated himself into* debt. 若者は急に借金をつくった.

precipitate (*oneself*) ***upon*** (攻撃の対象)にぶち当たる, を猛攻する ▪ He *precipitated himself* once more *upon* his task. 彼はまた仕事に立ち向かった.

precise /prɪsáɪs/ 形 ***prim and precise*** 几帳面で ▪ He is *prim and precise* in his manner. 彼は態度が几帳面だ.

to be (***more***) ***precise*** [(***more***) ***precisely***] (もっと)はっきり言うと, (もっと)正確に言うと ▪ It was forty years ago—July 3, 1965, *to be more precise*. 40年前—より正確には1965年の7月3日—のことであった.

preen /pri:n/ 動 ***preen*** *oneself* おしゃれをする ▪ I hate to see a man *preening himself* before a mirror. 男性が鏡の前でおしゃれをしているのを見るのはきらいです.

preen *oneself* ***on*** …を誇る, に満悦する ▪ He *preened himself on* his cleverness. 彼は自分の知恵を誇った.

prefer /prɪfə́:r/ 動 ***prefer to*** *do* ***rather than*** *do* …するよりもむしろ…するのを好む[選ぶ] ▪ He *preferred to* die *rather than* pay. 彼は支払うよりはむしろ死ぬほうを選んだ.

preference /préfərəns/ 名 ***by*** [***for***] ***preference*** 好んで, 第一に ▪ In science, read *by preference* the newest works. 科学においてはまず最新の著作を読むがいい.

give (***a***) ***preference to*** ... …を優先する ▪ *Preference* will *be given to* students with a physical disability. 身体障害を持つ学生が優先されます.

give preference over …よりも優先する ▪ He *was given preference over* everyone else. 彼は他の誰よりも優先された.

have a preference for [***to***] …のほうを好む, を選ぶ ▪ I *have a preference for* town life. 僕は都会生活のほうが好きだ.

in preference to …に優先して ▪ It was chosen *in preference to* several others. 他のいくつかに優先してそれが選ばれた.

pregnant /prégnənt/ 形 ***a pregnant pause*** [***silence***] 意味ありげな間, 意味深長な沈黙, 話の中断 ▪ After *a pregnant pause*, Ann said, "Rome. By all means Rome." 意味ありげに少し沈黙した後, アンは「ローマ. 間違いなくローマです」と言った.

one ***can't be half pregnant*** 積極的に参加しなければならず, 途中でやめることはできない ▪ Just as you

P

can't be half pregnant, you can't be half innocent. 半分の妊娠がないのと同様に半分の無罪はない.

pregnant by (男)のたねを宿して ▪ She is *pregnant by* the former husband. 彼女は先夫のたねを宿している.

pregnant of (子)をみごもって ▪ She is *pregnant of* her first child. 彼女は初めての子をみごもっている.

pregnant with **1** =PREGNANT of.
2 …の充満した ▪ His poems are *pregnant with* metaphors. 彼の詩は隠喩にみちあふれている.

prejudice[1] /prédʒədəs|-dʒudɪs/ 名 ***have a prejudice against*** …を毛ぎらいする ▪ He *has a prejudice against* foreigners. 彼は外国人を毛ぎらいしている.

have a prejudice in favor of …をえこひいきする ▪ He *has a prejudice in our favor*. 彼は我々をひいき目に見てくれる.

in prejudice of …を害するようにもくろんで, の損害となるように ▪ The mother advanced the younger son, *in prejudice of* the eldest. 母親は長男の損になるように次男を昇進させた.

to the prejudice of …の損害に帰するように ▪ People will talk *to your prejudice*. 人々はあなたの害になるように噂をするでしょう.

without prejudice …を害さずに, の権利を侵害せずに; 権利を侵されずに ▪ It may be swept off by a tax *without prejudice* to the interests of any class. それはいかなる階級の権利も侵さずに税金でかたをつけることができるだろう ▪ He was relieved of his duty *without prejudice*. 彼は権利を侵されずに義務を免れた.

prejudice[2] /prédʒədəs|-dʒudɪs/ 動 ***prejudice*** *A* ***in favor of*** *B* Bに対してAに好感をいだかせる ▪ You *are prejudiced in favor of* him. 君は彼にえこひいきしている ▪ These facts *prejudiced* us *in his favor*. これで我々は彼をひいき目に見るようになった.

preliminary /prɪlímənèri|-mɪnəri/ 名 ***without preliminaries*** 単刀直入に ▪ Their talk began *without preliminaries*. 彼らの話はやぶから棒に始まった.

premise /préməs/ 名 ***off the premises*** 店外へ, 邸外へ ▪ I showed him *off the premises*. 彼を屋敷から送り出した.

on the premises 店内で; 邸内で ▪ He retails wine and beer to be consumed *on the premises*. 彼は店内で飲用すべき酒やビールを小売りしている.

premium /príːmiəm/ 名 ***at a premium*** **1** プレミアムつきで, 額面以上で ▪ These shares are now *at a premium*. この株はいま額面以上だ ▪ The tickets were sold *at a premium* of 5 percent. その切符は5パーセントのプレミアムつきで売られた.
2 大需要があって; 珍重されて ▪ The goods will be *at a premium*. その品物は大いに需要があるだろう ▪ In a ship every inch of space is (placed) *at a premium*. 船ではわずかのスペースでも貴重だ.

put [***place***] ***a premium on*** …を奨励する, 尊重する ▪ Merely giving money will *put a premium on* idleness. 金をやるだけでは怠けることを奨励するばかりだ.

put *a person* ***at a premium*** 人を尊重させる ▪ Her good knowledge of English *put* her *at a premium* in her new job. 英語がよくできたので彼女は新しい仕事で高く評価された.

prentice /préntəs/ 名形 ***try*** *one's* ***prentice hand at*** …に未熟ながら手を出してみる ▪ I will *try my prentice hand at* it. 未熟ながらやってみましょう. ☞apprentice の頭音消失.

preoccupy /priákjəpàɪ|-ɔ́kju-/ 動 ***be preoccupied with*** …で頭がいっぱいである, に夢中である ▪ He *is* always *preoccupied with* his work. 彼はいつも仕事に夢中である.

preparation /prèpəréɪʃən/ 名 ***be in preparation*** 準備中で ▪ The meal *is in preparation*. 食事は仕度中だ ▪ The book *is in preparation*. その本は出版準備中だ.

for preparation 準備に ▪ What time will be required *for preparation*? 準備にどれだけかかるか.

in preparation for …の用意に ▪ We are getting things together *in preparation for* the journey. 旅行の支度に荷物をまとめています.

make preparations for …の準備をする ▪ I *made* mighty *preparations for* the feast. 私は大わらわでごちそうの準備をした.

preparatory /prɪpǽrətɔ̀ːri|-təri/ 形 ***preparatory to*** 〚副詞的に〛…の準備として; に先んじて ▪ I am packing it up *preparatory to* my journey. 旅行の用意に荷づくりをしています ▪ He made his will *preparatory to* his voyage. 彼は渡航に先立って遺言状を書いた.

prepare /prɪpéər/ 動 ***be prepared for*** …の用意[覚悟]ができている ▪ I *am prepared for* the worst. まさかの時の覚悟ができている ▪ We *were* not *prepared for* rain. まさか雨になろうとは思わなかった.

be prepared to *do* 進んで[潔く]…する ▪ I'*m prepared to* admit my fault. 私は自分の誤りは潔く認める.

prepare *oneself* ***for*** …の用意[覚悟]をする ▪ He *prepared himself for* the examination for Harvard. 彼はハーバードの入学試験の準備をした ▪ He *prepared himself for* the bad news. 彼は悪い知らせの覚悟をした.

prepare the ground for …の基礎をつくる, 下準備をする ▪ The meeting was to *prepare the ground for* future co-operation between the two companies. 会議は両社の将来の提携の下準備をするためのものだった.

prepare the way 道を開く (*for, to*) ▪ They were *preparing the way for* his victory. 彼らは彼の勝利への道を開いていた ▪ Luxury *prepares the way to* poverty. 贅沢は貧乏の元になる.

prepense /prɪpéns/ 形 ***of*** [***with***] ***malice prepense*** **1** 《法》予謀の悪意をもって, 計画的犯意があって ▪ To kill a man *of malice prepense* is

murder. 予謀の悪意をもって人を殺すことは殺人である.
2《戯》故意に ▪I have put in this chapter on fighting *of malice prepense*. 私はけんかを扱ったこの章を故意に挿入したのである.

presage /présɪdʒ/ 名 ***of evil presage*** 不吉な, 縁起の悪い ▪They looked upon it as *of evil presage*. 彼らはそれを不吉なものと考えた.

presence /prézəns/ 名 ***be admitted to** a person's **presence*** 人に目通りを許される ▪At last I *was admitted to his presence*. ついに私は彼に目通りを許された.

from** a person's **presence 人の面前から ▪He retired *from the Imperial presence*. 彼は陛下の御前から引き下がった.

grace** a person **with** one's **presence 《口・皮肉》(人)に臨席の栄誉を与える ▪It's so good of you to *grace* us *with your presence*. ご臨席を賜りますことに恐縮に存じます.

in the presence of …の面前で; に直面して ▪He feels shy *in the presence of* the opposite sex. 彼は異性の前に出ると恥ずかしがる ▪He was discouraged *in the presence of* failure. 彼は失敗に直面してがっかりした.

make** one's **presence felt 自分の存在[重要性]を認めさせる ▪The democratic way of *making your presence felt* is to speak. 自分の存在を認めさせる民主主義的な方法は話すことである.

presence of mind (危急の際の)沈着, 落着き (↔ ABSENCE of mind) ▪He had the *presence of mind* to throw a rug over the burning basket. 彼は少しも騒がず燃えているかごに毛布をかぶせた ▪I lost my *presence of mind*. 私はあわててしまった. ☞[L] præsentia animi のなぞり.

saving your presence →SAVING.

present[1] /prézənt/ 形名 ***all present and accounted for***/《英》***all present and correct*** 《口》総員準備完了, 全員問題なし ▪Is everyone ready to board the ship?—*All present and accounted for*. みな乗船の準備は完了したか—全員異常なし.

at present 目下, 今は ▪I myself am a busy man *at present*. 私も自身目下忙しいのです.

at the present time 現在のところ ▪*At the present time* the head of the Church is Makarios. 現時点では当教会の代表はマカリオスが務めている.

by these presents 《法》本書類により ▪Know all men *by these presents*, that I John Griffin make the aforesaid my last will. 本書類により私ジョン・グリフィンは上記を私の遺言とすると承知されたい.

for the present 当分, さし当たり ▪That will do *for the present*. さし当たりそれでよい ▪The work is suspended *for the present*. その仕事は当分中止だ. ☞[F] pour le présent のなぞり.

on present form →on ... FORM.

present company excepted [《米》***excluded***]《戯》ここにおられる方々は別として ▪"Teachers are so stupid," she said, "*present company excepted!*"「ここにいる人は別だけど先生って本当にばかなんだから」と彼女は言った. ☞批判が目の前の人には当てはまらないことを言う表現.

the present day 現代[今日](の) ▪She continues to *the present day* to devote herself to women's education. 彼女は今日に至るまで女性教育に献身し続けてきた ▪Knowledge is the most important resource of *the present day* global economy. 知識が現代の地球経済を救う最重要資源である.

the present volume [***writer***] 本書[筆者, 著者] ▪*The present writer* has been unable to verify this. 筆者はこれをまだ確かめられていない.

up to [***until***] ***the present*** 今にいたるまで ▪*Up to the present* they have not been brought into collision. 今までは彼らは衝突していない. ☞[F] dès à présent のなぞり.

present[2] /prézənt/ 名 ***at the present*** ささげ銃(つつ)をして (→PRESENT arms) ▪A soldier stood on guard, his rifle *at the present*. 一人の兵士がささげ銃をして歩哨に立っていた.

make [***give***] ***a present*** (***of***) (人に物を)贈る ▪He *made* her *a present of* a new dress. 彼は彼女に新しい服をプレゼントした.

present[3] /prɪzént/ 動 ***present** oneself* **1** (人が正式に)出頭する, 出席する ▪He *presented himself* before the king. 彼は王の前に伺候した ▪He *presented himself* at the meeting. 彼はその会に出席した.
2 (物が)現れる ▪An awful sight *presented itself* before me. 恐ろしい光景が目の前に現れた.

present arms 《軍》ささげ銃(つつ)をする ▪*Present arms*! ささげ銃! ▪*Arms were presented*. ささげ銃をした.

presentation /prèzəntéɪʃən/ 名 ***on*** [***at***] ***presentation*** (書類など)呈示次第 ▪The check is payable *on presentation*. その小切手は呈示次第支払われる.

preserve /prɪzə́ːrv/ 動 ***be well preserved*** (初老の人が)若々しい ▪My father *is well preserved* for his age. 父は年の割には若々しい.

God [(***the***) ***Lord, Saints***] ***preserve us!*** おやおや, やれやれ《驚き・不信・じれったさなどを表す》 ▪You want more money? *Saints preserve us!* まだ金がいるのかい. やれやれ.

***preserve** oneself* いつも若々しくする ▪She has *preserved herself* carefully. 彼女は注意していつも若々しくしてきた.

preside /prɪzáɪd/ 動 ***preside at the organ*** [***piano***] (ある式で)オルガン[ピアノ]弾奏の役をする ▪A hymn was then sung by the congregation, Mr. Brown *presiding at the organ*. それから賛美歌を会衆が歌い, ブラウン氏がオルガンひきの役をした.

press[1] /pres/ 名 ***a full-court press*** 《米》マンツーマン戦法, 総動員, 全力対応 ▪Clinton engaged in *a full-court press* on peace talks in the final months of his presidency. クリントン氏は大統領職

P

の最後の数か月間和平交渉に全力で当たった. ☞《バスケ》ディフェンス側がバスケット・ゴールの前ではなくコート全面に広がって相手選手に張りつく戦術から.

a press campaign (ニュースの報道よりも)新聞で世論を喚起する宣伝活動 ▪The *press campaign* against the university continued to increase in violence. 大学当局に対するプレスキャンペーンは攻撃の度合いがますますひどくなった.

be in [***at***] (***the***) ***press*** 印刷中である ▪A second impression *is* now *at press*. 目下第2刷を印刷中である ▪The book *is* now *in the press*. その本は今印刷中だ.

be off the press 印刷を終わっている; 発行されている ▪We will send you the book as soon as it *is off the press*. 印刷でき上がり次第本をお送りします ▪The book *is* just *off the press*. その本はちょうど発行されたところだ.

bring [***put, commit, send, submit***]***... to the press*** ...を印刷に回す ▪It will *be put to the press* in the course of the next month. それは来月中に印刷に回されるだろう.

carry [***see***] ***through the press*** 印刷に付する ▪A translation is now *being carried through the press*. ある翻訳書が目下印刷されている.

come [***go***] ***to*** (***the***) ***press*** 印刷に付される ▪I had seen the manuscript before it *came to the press*. 印刷に回される前にその原稿を見た.

correct the press 校正する ▪My father *corrected the press* himself. 父は自ら校正の筆をとった.

get [***have,*** etc.] ***a good*** [***bad***] ***press*** (新聞雑誌から)好評[悪評]を受ける ▪The play *got a good press*. その劇は好評を受けた.

give a good [***bad***] ***press*** (新聞雑誌が)好評[悪評]する ▪Newspapers have *given* him *a good press*. 新聞が彼に好評を与えた.

go through the press → pass through the PRESS.

have [***receive***] ***a good*** [***bad***] ***press*** 新聞雑誌で好評を博する[悪評を招く] ▪Mr. Leaf has *had a good press* lately. リーフ氏はこのところ新聞雑誌で好評を博している ▪England has always *had a bad press* in every country—except in Spain. イギリスはスペインを除くすべての国でいつも悪評を招いてきた.

hot from [***off***] ***the press*** (本・ニュースなどが)出たばかりの, 活字になりたての, 最も新しい ▪I've got his book here, *hot off the press*. 彼の刷りたてほやほやの本がここにあります ▪This is the news *hot from the press*. これは最も新しいニュースだ.

on the press 新聞記者で ▪He's *on the press*. 彼は新聞記者だ.

on the presses 《米》印刷中で ▪6,500 copies are *on the presses* in Manhattan. 6,500部がマンハッタンで印刷中である.

pass [***undergo***] (***the***) ***press*** 印刷に回される ▪My book has *passed the press*. 私の本は印刷に回された.

pass [***go***] ***through the press*** 印刷される ▪The new book is *passing through the press*. その新刊書は目下印刷中である.

press box (球場の高い位置にある)記者席 ▪I was in the *press box* at Dodger Stadium. 私はドジャー・スタジアムの記者席にいた.

press conference 記者会見 ▪The reporters questioned the actor about his present feelings at the *press conference*. 記者会見でレポーターは俳優に今の気持ちを聞いた.

put [***send, submit***]***... to the press*** →bring ... to the PRESS.

receive a good [***bad***] ***press*** →have a good PRESS.

see through the press →carry through the PRESS.

write for the press 新聞に寄稿する ▪My father *writes for the press*. 父は新聞に寄稿します.

press[2] /pres/ 動 ***be hard pressed*** →HARD.

be pressed for (金・暇など)が無くて困っている ▪I *am pressed for* money. 私は金に困っている ▪I *am* rather *pressed for* time today. きょうはちょっと忙しくて暇がない.

press *a person* ***hard*** 《口》人をひどくいじめる ▪Don't *press* him too *hard*. 彼をあまりひどくいじめるな.

press home an [*one's*] ***advantage*** →ADVANTAGE[1].

press ... into service ...を利用する ▪We must *press* science *into* its *service*. 我々は科学をこれに利用しなければならない.

press on *one's* ***way*** 道を急ぐ ▪We *pressed on our way*, for the light was going fast. 我々は道を急いだ. 日が急速に暮れかかっていたからだ.

press ... right home →HOME.

press the button →BUTTON[1].

pressure /préʃər/ 名 ***at high pressure*** 大車輪で ▪He is working *at high pressure*. 彼は大車輪で働いている.

bring pressure to bear upon *a person* 人に圧迫を加える ▪Great *pressure was brought to bear upon* him to accept it. 彼にそれを受諾させようとして大いに圧力が加えられた.

pile the pressure on 圧力を加える, はっぱをかける ▪The new teacher *piled the pressure on* from the beginning. 今度の教師は初めからはっぱをかけた.

pressure cooker 圧力がま[なべ]; プレッシャーのかかるつらい立場 ▪He is in the *pressure cooker* of soccer management. 彼はサッカーの監督というつらい立場にいる.

pressure group 圧力団体 ▪There are few *pressure groups* to influence the government here. 政府に影響を与える圧力団体は当地には少ない.

put [***place***] ***pressure on*** *a person* 人に圧迫を加える ▪If he doesn't sign the paper, we'll *put pressure on* him by threatening to inform the police. 彼がその書類にサインしなければ警察に知らせると

おどして圧力を加えてやろう.

snap under the pressure 神経衰弱になる ▪ Once Mary wants more kids after the twins, Tom will *snap under the pressure*. メアリーが双子の上にさらに子供が欲しいといったら, トムは神経が参ってしまうよ.

take** a person's* [*one's*] ***blood pressure (人・自分)の血圧を計る ▪ Kate *takes her blood pressure* at home every day. ケイトは毎日自宅で血圧を計る.

under pressure (事情に)迫られて ▪ The book was written hastily and *under pressure*. その本は大急ぎで事情に迫られて書かれた.

under the pressure of …に迫られて ▪ He commited the crime *under the pressure of* poverty. 彼は貧に迫られてその罪を犯した.

presto /préstoʊ/ 副 ***Hey presto!*** そうれ《奇術師のかけ声》 ▪ *Hey presto*, be gone—'Tis here again. そうれ, なくなれ—また出てきました.

presume /prɪzjúːm/ 動 ***You presume.*** 差し出がましい; 生意気だよ.

presumption /prɪzʌ́mpʃən/ 名 ***on the presumption*** (***that***) …と推定して ▪ He acted *on the presumption that* the firm would go bankrupt. 彼はその会社は破産すると推定して行動した.

the presumption is that 恐らく…だろう ▪ *The presumption is that* he had lost it. 恐らく彼はそれをなくしたのだろう.

pretense, 《英》 **pretence** /príːtens|prɪténs/ 名 ***by*** [***on, under***] ***false pretences*** 《法》詐欺によって; 真実を偽って, 偽りの仮面をかぶって ▪ He obtained the money *by false pretences*. 彼は詐欺によってその金を得た ▪ You obtained entrance to my house *under false pretences*. あなたは偽りの口実を設けて私の家に入った.

make a pretence of …のふりをする ▪ He *made* but *a pretence of* eating. 彼は食べるまねをしただけだった.

make [***have***] ***a pretence to*** [***at***] …があると主張する, があるようなふりをする ▪ The book *makes* no *pretence at* being exhaustive. この本に遺漏がないなどとは言っていない ▪ He *makes* no *pretence to* profound learning. 彼は深い学識があるというふりは少しもしない.

on [***under***] ***false pretences*** →by false PRETENCEs.

on [***under***] (***the***) ***pretence of*** **1** …にことよせて, かこつけて ▪ He cheated me *under* (*the*) *pretence of* friendship. 彼は友情にかこつけて僕を欺いた. **2** …という口実で ▪ He declined *on pretence of* an important engagement. 彼は大事な約束があると口実をつけて断った.

on the pretence that …という口実で ▪ He called *on the pretence that* he wanted my advice. 彼は私に助言してほしいという口実で訪ねてきた.

on the slightest [***smallest***] ***pretence*** ほんのちょっとした口実で ▪ He rings for the servants *on the smallest pretence*. 彼はほんのちょっとしたことでベルを鳴らして使用人を呼ぶ.

pretension /prɪténʃən/ 名 ***have pretensions to*** …と自負する, うぬぼれる ▪ He *has pretensions to* being a pop star. 彼にはポップスター気取りのところがある ▪ She *has* no *pretensions to* learning. 彼女は学者ぶらない.

make no pretensions to …があると主張しない ▪ She *makes no pretensions to* beauty. 彼女は美人だなどとは思っていない.

pretext /príːtekst/ 名 ***on*** [***upon***] ***some pretext or other*** 何とかかこつけて ▪ He declined *on some pretext or other*. 彼は何とかかこつけて断った.

on [***upon, under***] (***the***) ***pretext of*** [***that***] …を[ということを]口実として ▪ She did not come *on the pretext of* ill health. 彼女は健康がすぐれないのを口実にして来なかった ▪ She came here *under the pretext that* she was collecting for the Christmas fund for the poor. 彼女は貧しい人々へのクリスマス基金を集めているということを口実にここにやって来た.

pretty /príti/ 形名副 ***a pretty how d'you do*** 《口》困ったこと ▪ That's *a pretty how d'you do*, with a vengeance! そいつは全く困ったことだね.

(***as***) ***pretty as a picture*** 絵のように美しい ▪ His youngest daughter is *as pretty as a picture*. 彼の末の娘は絵のように美しい.

do the pretty 《口》丁寧にふるまう ▪ John was *doing the pretty*. ジョンは丁寧にふるまっていた.

have a pretty time of it 《口》ひどい目にあう ▪ He *had a pretty time of it* yesterday. 彼はきのうひどい目にあった.

make** oneself **pretty 身ぎれいにする ▪ Go and *make yourself pretty*. 身ぎれいにして来なさい.

My pretty [***pretties***]***!*** (妻・子などに呼びかけて)ねえお前[お前たち] ▪ If you would only understand me, *my pretty*. ねえお前, 私の言うことをわかってくれさえしたらなあ.

not a pretty sight →SIGHT.

Pretty is as pretty does. 《諺》美しい容貌よりは他人に親切にする方が大切《美しいからといってよい人物とは限らない》.

pretty near 《米口》ほとんど ▪ It's *pretty near* impossible for us to define middle class. 中流階級を定義することはほとんど不可能だ.

pretty nearly 《英口》ほとんど ▪ The car is new or *pretty nearly* so. この車は新車同様だ.

pretty please (***with sugar*** [***a cherry***] ***on top***) 《口》ねえ, お願いだから《子供が物をもらえそうにないときの懇願の言葉》 ▪ Mom, can I have a piece of cake? —No, you'll spoil your dinner. —Oh, please, *pretty please*? ママ, ケーキちょうだい—だめ, 晩御飯が食べられなくなるから—ねえ, 頼むからお願い.

pretty well [***much***] 《口》ほとんど, あらかた ▪ We have *pretty well* finished the work. その仕事はあらかた片づいた ▪ I think everybody is *pretty much* the same. みな大体似たものだと思うよ.

sit pretty 《口》楽な立場にある, 裕福である ▪ With all those government contracts, the firm can *sit pretty* for a long time. あのように政府との契約があるのであの会社は今後長いこと楽にやれるだろう ▪ He is *sitting prettier* today than before. 彼は今では前より裕福だ.

up to the pretty コップのみぞ飾りのところまで, 約3分の1くらいまで ▪ Don't fill the glass full; just *up to the pretty* will be sufficient. グラスにいっぱい入れないでください, 約3分の1くらいまでで十分です. ☞pretty《英》「グラスに彫った縦みぞ飾り」.

prevention /prɪvénʃən/ 名 ***(An ounce of) prevention is better than (a pound of) cure.*** →An OUNCE of prevention (is worth a pound of cure).

preview /príːvjùː/ 名 ***sneak preview*** 非公式の試写会《予告された映画に加えて上映される》; 前もってされる催し ▪ I saw the film in 1997 at a *sneak preview*. その映画を1997年に試写会で見た ▪ Do you want a *sneak preview* of our food? あなたは私たちの料理を試食してみたいですか.

previous /príːviəs/ 形 ***previous to*** …に先立って (before) ▪ He died *previous to* my arrival. 彼は私が着く前に死んだ.

too previous 《米口》早まりすぎた, せっかちな ▪ The grumbling in this matter has been *too previous*. この問題で不平を言うのは早まりすぎていた.

prey[1] /preɪ/ 名 ***a beast [bird, fish] of prey*** 猛獣[猛禽, 食肉魚] ▪ A falcon is *a bird of prey*. タカは猛禽である.

be [become, fall] (a) prey to 《文》…のえじき[犠牲]になっている[なる] ▪ The deer *fell a prey to* the lion. そのシカはライオンのえじきになった ▪ She has *been a prey to* melancholy ever since. 彼女はそれ以来憂鬱に取りつかれている ▪ Today more and more kids are *falling prey to* sports-related injuries. 今日ますます多くの子供がスポーツ関連のけがの犠牲になっている.

make a prey of …をえじき[食い物]にする ▪ He *was made an* easy *prey of* by the gamesters. 彼はまんまとばく師の食い物にされた.

prey[2] /preɪ/ 動 ***The strong prey upon the weak.*** 《諺》「弱肉強食」.

price[1] /praɪs/ 名 ***above [beyond, without] price*** (価値の知れないほど)高価な, 価値のある ▪ Sincerity is *above* all *price*. 誠実はこの上もなく価値がある.

at a (considerable) price 相当の値段[代価]で ▪ He will dispose of it *at a price*. 彼はそれを相当の代価で手放すだろう.

at any price **1** どんな代価を払っても; ぜひとも ▪ Experience is cheap *at any price*. 経験というものはどんな代価を払っても安いものだ ▪ He determined to carry it out *at any price*. 彼はどうあってもそれをやってのける決心をした.
2 [[否定文で]] いくら金を積まれても…ない, どうあっても…ない ▪ My boy, I won't have this late homecoming *at any price*. ねえお前, 私はどうあってもこんなに遅く帰ってこられるのはごめんだよ.

at cut prices =at cut RATEs.

cheap at the price その代価を払っても安い ▪ I lent Jim five dollars, but if he keeps out of my way, it'll be *cheap at the price*. ジムに5ドル貸してやったが, それで僕に近うかないならそれでも安いものだ.

cheap at twice the price 倍の値段でも安い, とてもお買い得な ▪ Ben got a $3,000 rebate on his new car—it was *cheap at twice the price*. ベンは3,000ドルの割引で新車を購入したが, ものすごく安い買い物だった.

Every man has his price. 《諺》どんな人でも金で買える.

of price 貴重な ▪ She had many things *of price*. 彼女は貴重品をたくさん持っていた.

pay a (heavy [small]) price (高い[少しの])代価を払う (*for*) ▪ He had to *pay a heavy price for* his treason. 彼は反逆罪を犯したために高い代価を払わねばならなかった.

pay the price 報いを受ける (*for, of*) ▪ Let drunk drivers *pay the price for* their crime. 飲酒運転手にその罪の報いを受けさせよう.

price on *a person's* ***head*** (犯罪者などを捕まえるための)人の首にかけられた懸賞金 ▪ James got mistaken for a murderer with a *price on his head*. ジェイムズは懸賞金つきの殺人犯に間違えられた.

put a price on …に値段をつける ▪ He refused to *put a price on* the Rubens painting. 彼はそのルーベンスの絵に値段をつけるのを断った.

set [put] a price on the head of *a person* 人の首・捕縛に賞金をかける ▪ *A price was set on the head of* every Jesuit. すべてのイエズス会士の首に賞金がかけられた.

slash prices 思い切って価格を下げる ▪ Oil firms have already *slashed prices* of gasoline and diesel products. 石油会社はすでにガソリンと重油製品の大幅値下げを行ったところだ.

the price is right 値段は手頃だ ▪ The food is good and *the price is right*. 食べ物はおいしかったし値段も手頃だった.

What is the price of...?/What price is...? …(の値段)はいくらですか ▪ *What is the price of* [*What price is*] that article? あの品はいくらですか.

What price...? **1**《競馬》(人気馬の)勝ち目はどうか ▪ *What price* the favourite? 人気馬の勝ち目はどうか.
2《口》…をどう思うか ▪ *What price* fine weather tomorrow? あすの天気はどんなものかね.
3《口》…はなんてざまだ《特に野心的な企てが失敗したのを軽蔑して》 ▪ *What price* the Big Four talk? 四大国会談はなんてざまだい ▪ *What price* glory? 栄光何するものぞ.
4《英口》ありそうにない, 見込みがない ▪ *What price* Japan winning the World Cup? 日本がワールドカップで勝てる見込みはない.

without price →above PRICE.

price[2] /praɪs/ 動 ***price*** *oneself* [*one's* ***goods***] ***out of the market*** けたはずれな高値をつけて売れが落ちる ▪They *priced themselves out of the* world *market*. 彼らはけたはずれの高値をつけて世界の市場で売れが落ちた ▪They *priced* coal *out of the market*. 彼らは石炭にけたはずれの高値をつけて売れが落ちてしまった.

prick[1] /prɪk/ 名 ***kick against the pricks*** →KICK[2].

prick of conscience 良心のとがめ ▪I feel no *prick of conscience* whatever. 私は少しも心にやましいところがない.

prick[2] /prɪk/ 動 ***a pricking in*** *one's* ***thumbs*** 前兆, 予感, 虫の知らせ ▪I feel *a pricking in my thumbs*, something wicked this way comes. 何かよからぬことが起こりそうな予感がする.

by the pricking of *one's* ***thumbs*** (確かな知識ではなく)親指のちくちくする感じで (cf. Sh., *Macb*. 4. 1. 44) ▪*By the pricking of my thumbs* I knew that something unpleasant was going to happen. 親指のちくちくする感じで何か不愉快なことが起こりそうだということが分かった.

prick a [***the***] ***bladder*** =prick the BUBBLE.

prick *a person's* ***conscience***/ *one's* ***conscience pricks*** *one* 人の良心を悩ます, 良心に悩まされる ▪The guilt of his action *pricked his conscience*. 自分のとった行動に対する罪悪感が彼の良心を悩ませた ▪*Her conscience pricked* her as she told the lie. 嘘をついたとき, 彼女は良心がとがめた.

prick up *one's* ***ears*** (犬・馬などが)耳をそばだてる; (人が)聞き耳を立てる ▪At this the lawyer *pricked up his ears*. これを聞くと弁護士は聞き耳を立てた.

pride[1] /praɪd/ 名 ***in*** *one's* ***pride*** **1** 《紋章》(クジャクが)羽を広げて ▪His standard was of yellow and blue, with a peacock *in his pride*. 彼の旗は黄色と青色からなり, 羽を広げたクジャクをつけていた. **2** たけなわで ▪May was *in its pride*. 5月はたけなわだった.

in the pride of ...の絶頂で ▪He is *in the* full *pride of* manhood. 彼は今男盛りだ.

out of pride 誇りから ▪It's just *out of pride* that she refuses. 彼女はただ誇りから断っているのだ.

one's ***pride and joy*** 喜びと自慢の種 ▪His eldest son is *his pride and joy*. 彼の長男は彼の喜びと自慢の種である.

Pride goes [***comes***] ***before a fall.***/ ***Pride will*** [***must***] ***have a fall.*** 《諺》おごるもの久しからず (《聖》*Prov*. 16. 18).

Pride must take a pinch./ ***Pride must be pinched.*** 《諺》思い上がりは締めつけられなければならない《かわいくしてもらっている間は少々の苦痛に耐えねばならない》, 「おごりは長ずべからず」.

pride of place 最高位; 高慢 (cf. Sh., *Macb*. 2. 4. 12) ▪I gave "The Tempest" *pride of place* for this reason. 私は次の理由で「あらし」に最高位を与えた ▪Yorkshire pudding took [had] *pride of place* on the lunch menu. ヨークシャー・プディングがランチメニューで一番を取った ▪*Pride of place* spurred him on. 高慢が彼をかりたてた.

put *one's* ***pride in*** *one's* ***pocket***/ ***pocket*** [***swallow***] *one's* ***pride*** 自尊心を抑える, 恥を忍んでする ▪I *swallowed my pride* and asked him for a loan. 私は恥を忍んで彼に借金を申し込んだ.

take (***a***) ***pride in*** ...を誇りとする, 自慢する ▪The man *takes a* real *pride in* his garden. その男は自分の庭園を心から自慢している.

the pride of the morning 早朝のにわか雨《晴天の前兆》 ▪This is only *the pride of the morning*. これは早朝のにわか雨にすぎないのだ.

pride[2] /praɪd/ 動 ***pride*** *oneself* ***on*** [***upon, in, that***] ...を自慢する, 誇る ▪He *prided himself on* his punctuality. 彼は時間を厳守することを自慢した.

priest /priːst/ 名 ***high priest*** 理論[教義]の指導的代表者 ▪Stanley Fish was once described as "the *high priest* of political correctness." スタンリー・フィッシュはかつて「政治的公正運動の領袖(りょうしゅう)」と呼ばれた.

Once a priest, always a priest [***Once a whore, always a whore***]. 《諺》牧師[売春婦]を3日すればやめられない. ☞職業気質はやめたあともついてくる, の意.

unfrock a priest (非行・義務不履行・不道徳により)牧師を追放する ▪The Russian Orthodox Church has *unfrocked a priest* for marrying two homosexual men. ロシア正教会は同性愛男性同士の結婚式を行ったかどで一人の司祭を追放した.

prim[1] /prɪm/ 形 ***prim and proper*** 上品でつんとした, 取り澄ました ▪Rose was very *prim and proper*. ローズはとても堅苦しくて淑女ぶっていた.

prim[2] /prɪm/ 動 ***prim it*** つんと澄ます ▪A lady will *prim it*. 女性はよくつんと澄ます.

prim *oneself* (***up***) 飾り立てる ▪So she *primmed herself up* and went out. そこで彼女は飾り立てて出て行った.

prim (***up***) *one's* ***mouth*** [***lips***] (澄まして)口をきゅっと結ぶ ▪She *primmed her lips* after every mouthful of tea. 彼女はお茶を一口飲み終わるたびに口をきゅっと結んだ.

prime /praɪm/ 名形 ***be cut off in*** *one's* ***prime*** (人が)若盛りで死ぬ; (計画などが)早い段階でつぶれる ▪His idea *was cut off in its prime*. 彼の考えは早い段階でつぶれてしまった.

in *one's* ***prime*** 若盛りで ▪She was *in her prime*, and pretty as a lamb. 彼女は若盛りでとてもきれいだった.

in the prime of life 人生の盛りで ▪He seems to be *in the* very *prime of life*. 彼はまさに男盛りのようだ.

past *one's* ***prime*** 盛りを過ぎて, 全盛期を過ぎて (→over the HILL) ▪He is well *past his prime*. 彼はとうに盛りを過ぎている ▪Kate was a wonderful tennis player, but she's *past her prime* now. ケ

イトはすばらしいテニスの選手だったが今はもう盛りを過ぎている ▪ Our voting system is *past its prime*. わが国の選挙制度はガタが来ている.

prime mover 原動力, 主導者 ▪ Thomas Jefferson was a *prime mover* in the creation of the Library of Congress. トマス・ジェファスンは議会図書館創設の主導者だった.

primp /prɪmp/ 動 ***primp*** *oneself* ***up*** (通例女性が)めかす ▪ She *primped herself up* before going out. 彼女は外出する前におしゃれをした.

primrose /prímròʊz/ 名 ***the primrose path*** [***way***] 歓楽の道; 快楽の追求 (cf. Sh., *Haml*. 1. 3. 50; Sh., *Macb*. 2. 3. 21) ▪ He sold his soul by traveling *the primrose path* to wealth and distinction. 彼は富と栄誉への歓楽の道を辿って魂を売った.

prince /prɪns/ 名 ***a prince of the blood*** 王族 ▪ Next to the *princes of the blood*, the eyes of all are fixed on you. 王族に次いで万人の目はあなたに注がれています.

Prince Charming 《戯》(おとぎ話のシンデレラに現れるような)理想の男性 ▪ She's still waiting for her *Prince Charming*. 彼女はいまだに理想の男性が現れるのを待っている.

the prince of liars 嘘つきの中の大嘘つき ▪ The first European to visit Japan was unjustly called *the "Prince of Liars."* 日本に始めてやってきたヨーロッパ人は不当にも「大ほら吹き」と呼ばれた.

the prince of peace 平和の君《キリスト》(《聖》*Isa*. 9. 6) ▪ Peace on earth! *The Prince of Peace* is born. 地に平和あれ. 平和の君, 生まれ給えり.

the prince of the air [***darkness, evil, fiends, the world***] 悪魔, サタン ▪ They are so misguided by *the prince of the air*. 彼らは悪魔のためにひどく道を迷わされる.

P

princely /prínsli/ 形 ***a princely gift*** [***sum***] 実に気前のよい贈物[多額のお金] ▪ The Queen gave him *a princely sum* of money. 王妃は彼に莫大なお金を与えた.

principle /prínsəpəl/ 名 ***in principle*** 原則として, 大体において ▪ He has admitted *in principle* liability for the accident. 彼はその事故に対する責任を大筋で認めた ▪ I agree with you *in principle*. 大体において君と同意見です.

of high [***no***] ***principle*** 節操の高い[ない] ▪ He is a man *of high* [*no*] *principle*. 彼は節操の高い[ない]人だ.

on general principle 特別の理由なしに, 一般に ▪ Hippies oppose the military *on general principle*. ヒッピーは一般に軍隊に反対である.

on principle/as a matter of principle 主義として; 道徳的見地から ▪ I don't smoke *on principle*. 私は主義としてタバコを吸いません ▪ I disliked Harley *on principle*. 私は道義的見地からハーリーが嫌いだった.

on the principle of [***that***] …という主義・信念に基づいて ▪ We shouldn't carry on foreign trade *on the principle of* protection. 保護主義に基づいて貿易を行うべきではない ▪ I am against war *on the principle that* the taking of life is always wrong. 私は生命を奪うのは常にまちがいであるという信念に基づいて戦争に反対だ.

prink /prɪŋk/ 動 ***prink*** *oneself* (***up***) 《口》飾り立てる ▪ She *prinked herself up* in her best. 彼女は晴れ着を装って着飾った.

print[1] /prɪnt/ 名 ***get into print*** 印刷に付す, 印刷して出版する ▪ Over the years we have helped a number of authors *get into print*. 長年にわたって当社は多くの方々の出版のお手伝いをしてきました.

in cold print 印刷物になって; 変更の余地がなくなって ▪ These speeches are not very interesting *in cold print*. この演説は活字になるとあまり魅力がない.

in print **1** 印刷になって ▪ The book is now *in print*. その本は目下印刷中だ ▪ It appeared *in print* in magazines. それは雑誌に活字になって載せられた.

2 (本が)発売されて ▪ These books are still *in print* and available. それらの本はまだ絶版になっていないから手に入る.

3 活字体で ▪ Please write your name and address *in print*. 住所氏名を活字体で書いてください.

out of print 絶版で ▪ It's impossible to get one, for the book is *out of print*. 一部手に入れることはできない, その本は絶版だから.

put (***forth***) ***into print*** 印刷に付する ▪ The book has of late *been put into print*. その本は近ごろ印刷に付された.

rush into print (大急ぎで)書いたものを活字にする; やたらに新聞に書く ▪ Many people are anxious to *rush into print*. 書いたものを活字にしたがる人が多い.

the small [***fine***] ***print*** 細字部分《契約者に不利な所を細かい字で印刷した注意事項》 ▪ You shouldn't buy a house without reading *the small print*. (契約書の)細字部分を読まずに家を買うべきでない.

print[2] /prɪnt/ 動 ***print*** *itself* ***on*** (心)に焼きつく ▪ The incidents *printed themselves on* her mind. その事件は彼女の心に焼きついた.

printed word [***page***] 活字になった言葉[ページ] ▪ I got so homesick for the *printed word* that I reread the six-page menu. 活字に触れたくてたまらなかったので6ページのメニューを何度も読んだ.

prior /práɪər/ 形副 ***prior to*** **1** …の前の[先の] ▪ The sin is *prior to* and independent of the action. 罪は行為に先立つものであって行為とは関係がない.

2 …の前に ▪ I called on him *prior to* my departure. 私は出発前に彼を訪ねた.

priority /praɪɔ́:rəti|-ɔ́r-/ 名 ***according to priority*** 順位によって ▪ The proceeds of the sale will be distributed *according to priority*. 売却した収益は順位によって分配されるだろう.

get *one's* [***the***] ***priorities wrong*** [***right, straight***] 最も大事なことを第一にしない[する] ▪ You should *get your priorities straight.* 君は最も大事なことを第一になすべきだ.

give priority to …を優先する ▪ The Headquarters will *give priority to* bombarding the capital. 司令部は首都の空襲を優先するだろう.

have priority over *a person* 人よりも優先権がある ▪ I *have priority over* you in my claim. 要求ではあなたより私に優先権があります.

prism /prízəm/ 名 ***through the prism of*** …の視点で見ると ▪ The event is interesting *through the prism of* European history. その出来事はヨーロッパの歴史の視点を通して見ると興味深い.

prison /prízən/ 名 ***be*** [***lie***] ***in prison*** 在監・拘留中である ▪ The convict *is* safely *in prison.* 囚人は拘留されて危険がなくなっている.

break prison 脱獄する ▪ The convict *broke prison.* 囚人は脱獄した.

cast [***put, set***]***... in prison*** …を投獄する ▪ The man *was put in prison.* 男は投獄された.

find [***go to***] ***prison*** 収監される ▪ He *found prison* at last. 彼はついに収監された.

let [***come***] ***out of prison*** 出所させる[する] ▪ He *was let out of prison.* 彼は出所を許された.

send [***take***]***... to prison*** …を刑務所に入れる ▪ He *was sent to prison* for theft. 彼は窃盗罪で刑務所に入れられた ▪ *Take* the thief *to prison.* 泥棒を刑務所に入れよ.

prisoner /prízənər/ 名 ***be a prisoner to*** (病人などが)…から離れられない ▪ He has *been a prisoner to* his sofa lately. 彼は近頃はソファに寝たきりだ.

keep *a person* ***a prisoner*** 人をとりこにしておく ▪ Flu *kept* me *a prisoner* in my room. インフルエンザのため部屋から一歩も出ることができなかった.

make [***take***]***...*** (***a***) ***prisoner*** …をとりこにする ▪ She *took* his hand *prisoner.* 彼女は彼の手をしっかり握って離さなかった.

prisoner of conscience 政治犯, 国事犯, 宗教犯 ▪ He is no longer a *prisoner of conscience,* but the conscience of his nation remains imprisoned. 彼はもはや政治犯ではなかったが, 自国の良心は牢獄につながれたままである.

take no prisoners **1** 敵を(捕虜にしないで)みな殺しにする ▪ Orders were to *take no prisoners.* 命令は敵を殲滅(せんめつ)せよだった.
2 《報道》極端に無情[冷酷, 残忍]である, 全く容赦しない ▪ The new dean *takes no prisoners.* 新任の学部長は一切の妥協を許さない.

take *a person* ***prisoner*** (特に戦争で)人を捕虜にする ▪ He *took* ten thousand men *prisoner.* 彼は1万の兵を捕虜にした. ☞prisoner は常に無冠詞, 単数形.

privacy /práɪvəsi|prí-/ 名 ***in privacy*** ひそかに; 隠れて ▪ They were married *in* strict *privacy.* 二人はごくひそかに結婚した ▪ He was living *in* absolute *privacy.* 彼は完全な隠とん生活を送っていた.

in the privacy of …に隠れて, の奥底で ▪ She wept *in the privacy of* her own room. 彼女は自分の部屋に一人隠れて泣いた.

private /práɪvət/ 名 ***for*** *a person's* ***private ear*** 内密で ▪ This is *for your private ear.* これは内密の話ですよ.

in private 内緒で, こっそりと, 私生活において (↔in PUBLIC) ▪ I wish to speak to you *in private.* 内々でお話ししたい ▪ She observed him *in* public and *private.* 彼女は彼を公的にも私的にも観察した.

keep ... private …を内密にしておく ▪ It *was kept private.* それは秘密にしておかれた.

private eye 私立探偵 ▪ He even hired a *private eye* in the early '80s. 彼は80年代の初めに私立探偵を雇ってさえいた.

private parts 《口・婉曲》陰部 ▪ His hands covered up his *private parts.* 彼は自分の手で陰部を覆った.

privilege /prívəlɪdʒ/ 名 ***enjoy*** [***have***] ***the privilege of*** …という特権を享有する ▪ They *enjoyed the privilege of* married life. 彼らは結婚生活の特権を享有した.

It is a woman's privilege to change her mind. 《諺》考えを変えるのは女性の特権.

privity /prívəti/ 名 ***with*** [***without***] ***the privity of*** …の承知の上で[に知らせずに] ▪ It was done *with the privity of* his chiefs. それは彼の上役の承知の上でなされた ▪ All the doors were laid open for his departure, *without the privity of* the Duke. 公爵に知らせずに彼が立ち去るために戸が全部あけられた.

privy /prívi/ 形 ***be privy to*** …に内々関与[関知]している ▪ Many persons *were privy to* the plot. 多くの人が内々この陰謀にあずかっていた.

make *a person* ***privy to*** 人に…を内々知らせる ▪ I *was made privy to* it. 内々それを明かされた.

prize[1] /praɪz/ 名 ***booby prize*** 最下位賞, ブービー賞 ▪ Tom should get the *booby prize* for the worst showing in the race. トムはレースでの最悪のプレーに対してブービー賞を受けて当然だ. ☞日本語では最下位から2番目の意だが, 英語での本来の意は最下位.

carry away [***off***] ***a prize/ gain*** [***win***] ***a prize*** 賞を得る ▪ He *carried off every prize* that was open to him. 彼は得られる賞はすべてかっさらった ▪ He failed to *win a prize* at all. 彼は全然賞が得られなかった.

make prize of …を捕獲する ▪ We resolved to *make prize of* it, as in a time of war. 我々は戦時のようにそれを分捕ろうと決心した.

play a prize (特にフェンシングの)試合をする ▪ He can *play a prize* in all weapons. 彼はどんな武器ででも試合をすることができる.

play *one's* ***prize*** **1** (立派に)自分の役割を果たす ▪ You have *played your prize.* 君は君の役割を果たしたのだ ▪ The darkness *played its prize.* 暗や

P

みは役割を果たした.

2 =play a PRIZE.

play [***fight***] (*one's*) ***prizes*** (賞を得るために)試合をする ▪They came there to see the fencers *play their prizes*. 彼らは剣士が試合をするのを見るためにそこへやって来た.

run (*one's*) ***prizes*** (賞を得るために)競走する ▪The horses and their chariots are let forth when they *run their prizes*. 彼らが競走するときには馬や戦車が出される.

(***there are***) ***no prizes for guessing...*** 《口》 [[主に疑問詞を伴って]] ...は見当をつけやすい ▪*No prizes for guessing* who will finish first! 誰がまっ先に終える[1着でゴールする]かは明白だった.

win a prize →carry away a PRIZE.

prize[2], 《主に英》**prise** /praɪz/ 動 ***prize... open*** 《英》(戸・ふたなど)をこじあける ▪He *prized* the box *open*. 彼はその箱をこじあけた.

pro /proʊ/ 名副 ***pro and con*** [[副詞的に]] 賛成反対して ▪They debated it *pro and con*. 彼らはそれに賛成反対の討論をした.

pro(***s***) ***and con***(***s***) 賛否両論, 長所短所 ▪We must listen to the *pros and cons* of a matter. 我々はある問題の賛否両論に耳を傾けなければならない ▪The House rocked with *pro and con*. 下院は賛否両論でごった返した ▪Consider the *pros and cons* of a diesel. ディーゼルエンジンの良い点悪い点を考えてごらん.

probability /prɑ̀bəbíləti|prɔ̀b-/ 名 ***in all probability*** たぶん ▪*In all probability* the money will not be paid. たぶん金は払ってもらえまい.

the probability is that たぶん...だろう ▪*The probability is that* he will come. たぶん彼は来るだろう.

there is every probability of [***that***] ...はきわめてありそうなことだ ▪*There is every probability of* his being arrested. どうも彼は逮捕されるらしい.

there is no [***little, not much***] ***probability of*** [***that***] ...は全然[あまり]ありそうもないことだ ▪*There is no probability of* his coming. 彼はどうも来そうもない.

probation /proʊbéɪʃən/ 名 ***on probation*** **1** 試験のため, 見習いで; 仮入学で ▪He is engaged *on probation*. 彼は仮採用だ ▪He was admitted to college *on probation*. 彼は仮入学を許された.

2 《法》執行猶予で ▪They placed the offender *on probation*. 彼らは犯罪者を執行猶予にした.

3 《米》(学生が)仮及第で ▪The next day the office put Billy *on probation*. その翌日事務局はビリーを仮及第させた.

place [***put***]***... on*** [***under***] ***probation*** (犯罪者)を保護観察に付す ▪He has *been put under* a year's *probation*. 彼は1年間の保護観察に付された.

problem /prɑ́bləm|prɔ́b-/ 名 ***a chicken-and-egg problem*** →a CHICKEN and egg situation.

Do you have a problem with that? 《口》(異を唱える人に対して)何か問題があるというのですか.

have an alcoholic [***a drinking***] ***problem*** 《婉曲》アルコール中毒である ▪If you *have a drinking problem*, please consult your doctor. 飲酒問題をかかえているなら先生に診察してもらいなさい.

It's [***That's***] ***not my problem.*** 《口》私の知ったことではない.

knotty problem 難問, 難題 ▪"That is a *knotty problem*, Ted," said Claire. 「テッド, それは困ったことね」とクレアは言った.

No problem. 《口》問題ない, 何でもないこと(さ); どういたしまして ▪But I don't have an evening dress. —*No problem.* My wife can lend you one. でも私夜会服なんて持っていないわ—何でもないことさ. 家内が貸してくれるよ ▪Thanks very much for the call. —Oh, *no problem.* 電話ありがとう—どういたしまして.

That's your [***his***] ***problem.*** 《口》それは君[彼]の問題だ.

What's your [***his***] ***problem?*** 《口》君[彼]はいったい何を考えているんだ.

probs /prɑbs|prɔbs/ 名 ***no probs/no problems/There is no problem.*** 全く問題ない ▪*No probs*, just follow the guidelines. 全く問題ありません. ただ指針に従ってください.

proceeding /prəsíːdɪŋ/ 名 ***take*** [***institute***] (***legal***) ***proceedings*** (***against***) (...を相手に)訴訟を起こす ▪She *took* divorce *proceedings against* her husband. 彼女は夫を相手に離婚訴訟を起こした.

process /práses|próʊses/ 名 ***in process*** 進行中で ▪The work of construction is still *in process*. 建築工事は今なお進行中である.

in process of ...中で ▪The bridge is *in process of* construction. 橋は今建造中だ ▪The project is *in process of* realization. その企画は実現されつつある.

in process of time 時が経つにつれて ▪She grew *in process of time* into a beautiful girl. 彼女は時が経つにつれて美少女になっていった.

in the process (***of*** *doing*) ...の一方で; の最中で ▪A magazine can lose its old audience *in the process of trying* to get a new one. 雑誌は新しい読者を獲得しようとして古くからの読者を失うことがある ▪They were *in the process of cleaning* out asbestos. 彼らはアスベストの除去作業中であった.

serve process upon *a person* 人に(召喚)令状を発する ▪The town *served process upon* him. 市は彼に令状を発した.

procession /prəséʃən/ 名 ***in procession*** 行列を作って ▪They were walking *in procession* through the streets. 彼らは行列を作って通りを歩いていた.

proclaim /prəkléɪm/ 動 ***proclaim peace*** 休戦を布告する ▪A French gentleman there *proclaimed peace*. そこのあるフランス紳士が休戦を布告した.

proclaim war 宣戦を布告する (*against*) ▪Sebastian *proclaimed war against* the Duke. セバ

P

スティアンは公爵に対し宣戦を布告した.

procrastination /prəkræstənéɪʃən/ 名 ***Procrastination is the thief of time.*** 《諺》遅延は時間の盗人である.

procuration /prɑ̀kjəréɪʃən|prɔ̀k-/ 名 ***by procuration*** 代理で《略 p.p., per proc.》 ▪ They wish to do it *by procuration.* 彼らはそれを代理でやらせたがっている.

procure /prəkjúər/ 動 ***procure** a person's **death*** (自ら手を下さずに)人を死に至らしめる ▪ Hamlet's uncle soon *procured the king's death* by means of a poisoned drink. ハムレットのおじはまもなく毒を飲ませて王を死に至らしめた.

prod /prɑd|prɔd/ 名 ***on the prod*** 《米口》面倒を探し求めて, けんかを売って, 抗争を招いて ▪ I thought they were *on the prod* for you. 彼らは君にけんか腰になっていると思った.

prodigal /prɑ́dɪgəl|prɔ́d-/ 形名 ***a* [*the*] *prodigal son*** 放蕩(ほう)息子《長い放浪の後悔い改めた息子》(《聖》*Luke* 15. 11-32) ▪ Thousands turned out to welcome home *the prodigal son.* 何千もの人々が放蕩息子を出迎えた ▪ Are you going to kill the fatted calf for *the prodigal son*? 久しぶりに息子さんが帰省するのかい? ☞肥えた子牛を屠って放蕩息子の帰りを迎えた父親の話から.

play the prodigal 惜しげもなく使う; 道楽をする ▪ The water overflowed; then dashed away, *playing the prodigal.* 水はあふれ, それから惜しげもなくこぼれながら, 勢いよく流れ去っていった.

prodigal of …を惜しげもなく使う, ふんだんに与える ▪ He is *prodigal of* time. 彼は時間を浪費する ▪ Nature had been *prodigal* to him *of* her gifts. 造化は賜物を彼に惜しげもなく与えていた.

produce /prɑ́dju:s|prɔ́d-/ 名 ***brought to produce*** (銃砲・軍需品が)分解され処分しうるようにされて ▪ A gun carriage *brought to produce* is disposed of as so much metal. 分解され処分しうるようになった砲架はただ同量の金属として処分される.

production /prədʌ́kʃən/ 名 ***make a production* (*out*) *of*** …をやたらに手の込んだ複雑なやり方でする, 騒ぎ立てる ▪ She *made a production of* lighting the cigar and blew a cloud of smoke. 彼女は仰々しくタバコに火をつけて煙を一服ふかした. ☞production「芝居・ミュージカルなどの作品」.

on production of 《文》…の提示によって ▪ Discounts will be given *on production of* your student ID card. 学生証を提示すれば割引になります.

productive /prədʌ́ktɪv/ 形 ***be productive of*** …を生じる ▪ Their discussions *are productive of* quarrels. 彼らの議論はけんかを生む.

profess /prəfés/ 動 ***profess** oneself* 公言する, 告白する (*to be*) ▪ He *professed himself* satisfied. 彼は満足している旨を公言した ▪ He *professes himself* (*to be*) a socialist. 彼は社会主義者だと公言している.

profession /prəféʃən/ 名 ***by profession*** 職業は ▪ He was a writer *by profession.* 彼は作家を業(わざ)としていた.

in profession 口先では ▪ He is an atheist in fact if not *in profession.* 彼は口先ではともかく実際は無神論者だ.

make** one's **profession (修道会の)聖職者になる誓いを立てる ▪ The novice kneeling before him *made her profession.* 彼の前にひざまずいている修練女が誓義を立てた.

make profession of …を公言[告白]する ▪ He *makes profession of* his friendship for me. 彼は私に友情をいだいていると公言する ▪ He *made profession of* his faith in Christianity. 彼はキリスト教への信仰を告白した.

the oldest profession 最古の職業《売春》 ▪ *The oldest profession* is alive in big cities. 大都市では売春はすたれていない.

professional /prəféʃənəl/ 形 ***turn professional*** (スポーツ選手などが)プロになる ▪ That tennis player has recently *turned professional.* あのテニス選手は最近プロになった.

proficient /prəfíʃənt/ 形 ***proficient in* [*at*]** …に熟達した, 堪能な ▪ He is *proficient in* English. 彼は英語に熟達している ▪ He is *proficient at* repartee. 彼は返答が当意即妙だ.

profile /próʊfaɪl/ 名 ***in profile*** 横顔の[で] ▪ She is fine *in profile.* 彼女は横顔が美しい ▪ Roman emperors always appear *in profile.* ローマ皇帝はいつも横顔で現れている.

keep* [*maintain*] *a low* [*high*] *profile 低[高]姿勢を保つ ▪ We'd better *keep a low profile* until the trouble is over. このもめごとが終わるまで低姿勢を保つ方がよい.

raise** one's **profile 自分のイメージをもっと好ましいものにする ▪ Oliver Wilson once again *raised his profile* in the golfing world. オリバー・ウィルスンは再びゴルフ界で注目を浴びた.

P

profit /prɑ́fət|prɔ́f-/ 名 ***at a profit*** 儲けて ▪ He works the mine *at a profit.* 彼はその鉱山をやって儲けている.

for profit 営利[利欲]のために ▪ The college is not operated *for profit.* この大学は営利目的で経営されてはいない.

***make* [*have*] *a profit on* [*out of*]** …でひと儲けする ▪ He *made a profit on* the transaction. 彼はその取引でひと儲けした ▪ He *has a profit on* everything he sells. 彼は何を売ってもひと儲けする.

make** one's **profit of …を利用する ▪ We *made our profit of* his learning. 彼の学識を利用した.

to** one's **profit 利益になるように ▪ I have done it *to my profit.* 私はそれをやって儲けた.

turn ... to profit (物)を利用する ▪ He *turns* anything *to profit.* 彼は何でも利用する.

with profit 利益を得て ▪ I have read it *with profit.* 私はそれを読んで利益を得た.

profuse /prəfjú:s/ 形 ***be profuse in* [*of*]** …を惜しげもなく使う ▪ He *is profuse in* his hospitality. 彼は惜しみなく人をもてなす ▪ He *is profuse of* his money. 彼は金ばなれがいい.

profusion /prəfjú:ʒən/ 名 ***a profusion of*** たくさんの ▪ He received *a profusion of* gifts. 彼はたくさんの贈り物をもらった.

in profusion 豊富に, ふんだんに ▪ Wheat was growing *in profusion*. 小麦が豊かに生長していた.

program, 《英》 **programme** /próʊgræm/ 名 ***get with the program*** 《口》 予定[取決め, きまり]を守る, 仕事をきちんとこなす ▪ Come on, *get with the program*. さあ, やるべきことをやるんだ.

What's the program for ...? 《口》 ...はどうすることになっているのか ▪ *What's the program for* tomorrow? あすはどうすることになっているのか.

progress /prágrəs|próʊgres/ 名 ***in progress*** 進行中で[の] ▪ The inquiry is now *in progress*. その調査は目下進行中だ ▪ There are no auctions *in progress* at present. 今競売はどこもやっていない.

in progress of time 時が経つにつれて ▪ This virtue decays *in progress of time*. この効力は時が経つにつれて薄れていく.

make progress 進行[進歩, 上達]する (*in*) ▪ He is *making progress in* his studies. 彼は学業が進歩している ▪ The patient is *making* good *progress*. 病人はどんどんよくなっています.

progression /prəgréʃən/ 名 ***in geometrical progression*** 幾何級数的に, 加速度的に, どしどしと ▪ Human beings tend to increase *in geometrical progression*. 人口は加速度的に増える傾向だ.

in progression 順次に; 次第に ▪ The experiment was extended to all the others *in progression*. その実験は順次に他のすべてにも及ぼされた.

project /prədʒékt/ 動 ***project*** *oneself* ***into*** ...に身を置いて考える ▪ He tried to *project himself into* the heroine's situation. 彼はヒロインの身になって考えてみようとした.

project *oneself* ***into the past*** [***future***] 《口》 過去[未来]に身を置いてみる ▪ Can we not *project ourselves* far *into the future*? 遠い未来に身を置いてみることはできないものだろうか.

project *oneself* ***to*** *a person* (霊媒術で)遠方の人に自分の姿を見せる ▪ The man has the power to *project himself to* some percipient in the distance. その男は遠くにいて見ている人に自分の姿を見せる力がある.

prolong /prəlɔ́:ŋ|prəʊlɔ́ŋ/ 動 ***prolong the agony*** →AGONY.

prominence /prámənəns|prɔ́m-/, **prominency** /prámɪnənsi|prɔ́m-/ 名 ***bring ... into prominence*** ...を目立たせる ▪ Luther *brought* his new ideas *into* splendid *prominence*. ルターはその新しい思想をすばらしく目立つものにした.

come into prominence (人が)有名になる, (物が)目立ってくる ▪ He had *come into prominence* as an orator. 彼は雄弁家として有名になっていた ▪ Its importance *comes into* historical *prominence*. その重要性は歴史的に目立ってくる.

give ... prominence = bring ... into PROMINENCE.

promise[1] /práməs|prɔ́m-/ 名 ***a bow of promise*** 虹 (rainbow) (《聖》 *Gen*. 9. 13) ▪ A father's love beams, like *a bow of promise*, through the cloud. 父親の愛は雲間を通して虹のように輝く.

A promise is a promise. 約束は約束だ《守らねばならない》.

be as good as *one's* ***promise*** = be as good as one's WORD.

break *one's* ***promise*** 約束を破る ▪ He has never *broken his promise*. 彼は一度も約束を破ったことがない.

full of promise 前途有望な ▪ He was a child *full of promise*. 彼は前途有望な子供だった.

give [***afford, show***] ***promise*** (***of***) (...の)見込みがある ▪ The sky *gives promise of* fine weather. 空模様では天気になりそうだ ▪ The author *shows promise of* better things. その作家はもっといい仕事をする見込みがある.

keep *one's* ***promise*** 約束を守る ▪ We should always *keep our promise*. 我々はいつも約束を守らねばならない.

make a promise 約束をする ▪ He *made a promise* to come here tomorrow. 彼はあすここへ来る約束をした.

of promise 有望な ▪ I know a young writer *of promise*. 私は有望な青年作家を知っている.

on a promise of ...の約束で ▪ He told me *on a promise of* secrecy. 彼は他言しない約束で私に話した.

on the promise that ...という約束で ▪ He surrendered *on the promise that* his life would be spared. 彼は命を助けてもらうという約束で降服した.

Promises, promises! またいつもの「約束する」かい?《約束ばかりで守ったこともないくせに!》 ▪ "I'll marry you." he said to her. "*Promises, promises!*" she answered with a flirtatious smile. 「君と結婚するよ」と彼は言ったが, 彼女は軽薄な笑みを浮かべて「いつもの約束ばっかりね! (守ったこともないくせに)」と応じた.

show promise 見込みがある, 将来性がある ▪ He *showed promise* as a poet. 彼は詩人として将来性がある.

the land of promise 約束の地; あこがれの土地; 天国 (《聖》 *Gen*. 1 2. 7) ▪ To them America was *the land of promise*. 彼らにとってアメリカはあこがれの土地であった.

promise[2] /práməs|prɔ́m-/ 動 ***a*** [***the***] ***promised land*** = the land of PROMISE.

be promised to 《古》 ...と婚約している ▪ Mary *was promised to* King Charles. メアリーはチャールズ王と婚約していた.

I promise you. **1** 《口》 確かに, ほんとに《未来について》 ▪ *I promise you*. I'll be back soon. 請け合うよ. すぐ帰ってくる.

2 《口》 確かに, ほんとに《現在について》 ▪ *I promise*

you I'm preciously tired already. 確かに私はもうひどく疲れているんですよ.

promise *oneself a thing* あることを期待する ▪I *promise myself* a pleasant evening. 私は楽しい一晩を期待している.

promise fair [***well***] 見込みがある, 頼もしい ▪The crops *promise well.* 豊作らしい ▪The weather *promises fair.* 天気はいいらしい.

promise *oneself* ***that*** …と決心する ▪She ran out, *promising herself that* she would be back in ten minutes. 彼女は10分もしたら戻ってこようと決心して駆け出していった.

promise the earth [***moon*** (***and stars***)] 果たせそうもない途方もない約束をする ▪Communism seemed to him to be *promising the moon.* 共産主義は果たせそうもない途方もない約束をしているように彼には思えた ▪He wrote her many love letters and *promised* her *the moon and stars.* 彼は彼女にせっせとラブレターを書き, できもしない約束をした.

promise to be …になりそうだ, なる見込みがある ▪It *promises to be* fine in the afternoon. 午後は晴れになりそうだ.

promise well →PROMISE fair.

promotion /prəmóʊʃən/ 图 ***be on*** *one's* ***promotion*** **1** 昇進を目当てにして身を慎む ▪The little kitchenmaid *was on her promotion.* その台所お手伝いの小娘は昇進を目当てにして身を慎んでいた.

2《口》結婚話があるので身を慎む ▪She *was* apparently *on her promotion.* 彼女はどうも結婚話があるので身を慎んでいるらしかった.

on promotion 昇進の途中にある; 試験中で ▪It was a square, squat room—a cellar *on promotion.* そこは四角いひっそりとした部屋で, 地下室が昇格しているようなものだった.

prompt /prɑmpt|prɔmpt/ 形 ***be prompt to*** *do* すぐ[喜んで]…する ▪He *is prompt to* obey. 彼はてきぱきと言うことをきく.

prone /proʊn/ 形 ***be prone to*** [***to*** *do*] …の傾向がある, しがちである ▪He *is prone to* idleness. 彼は怠けがちだ ▪All *are* by nature *prone to* err. 誰しも生まれつき誤りを犯しがちである.

lie [***fall***] ***prone*** うつ伏せに横たわる[倒れる] ▪The man *lay prone* on the ground. その男は地面にうつ伏せに横たわっていた.

proof /pruːf/ 图形 ***above proof*** → below PROOF.

as (***a***) ***proof of*** …の印に ▪They gave him a gold watch *as* (*a*) *proof of* their regard. 彼らは尊敬の印に彼に金時計を贈った.

be proof against [***to***] **1** …のきかない ▪He *is proof against* flattery. 彼はおべっかには乗らない ▪His skin *is proof to* wounds. 彼の皮膚は傷など受けない.

2 …に耐える ▪The building *is proof against* fire. その建物は耐火である.

be proof positive of [***that***] …の[ということの]確証である ▪This *is proof positive of* his intention. これが彼の意図の確証である.

below [***above***] ***proof*** (蒸留酒が)標準強度以下[以上]で ▪This rum is 30 percent *below proof.* このラム酒は標準強度より3割低い.

bring [***put, set***]***... to*** [***in, on***] (***the***) ***proof*** …をためす, 吟味する ▪I should like to *put* their loyalty *to the proof.* 彼らの忠誠をためしてみたい.

correct proofs →read PROOFs.

give proof of [***that***] …を[と]証明する ▪He has *given proof of* his honesty. 彼は自分の正直なことを証明した ▪Can you *give proof that* you are British? あなたはイギリス人であることを証明できますか.

in proof 校正刷で ▪I am correcting my book *in proof.* 私は自分の本の校正をしているところです.

in proof of [***that***] …を[ということを]立証するために ▪He produced papers *in proof of* the justice of his claims. 彼は自分の要求の正当さを立証するために書類を提出した ▪I will take it *in proof that* his commands had been obeyed. 彼の命令通りにしたという証拠にこれを持って行こう.

make proof of …をためす ▪They *made proof of* his courage. 彼らは彼の勇気をためしてみた.

pass the proofs for press 校了にする ▪I have *passed the proofs for press.* 校了にした.

put ... to the proof …をためす, テストする ▪He *put* the chemical *to the proof.* 彼はその化学薬品をテストした.

read [***correct, revise***] ***proofs*** 校正する ▪We found him *correcting proofs.* 我々が行ってみると彼は校正していた.

show proof of …の印を示す ▪He *showed proof of* good will. 彼は善意の印を見せた.

stand the proof テストに合格する ▪It has *stood the proof.* それはテストに合格している.

The proof of the pudding is in the eating.《諺》プディングの味は食べてから《実際やってみなければ善し悪しはわからない》 ▪I think they are foolish to get married, but *the proof of the pudding is the eating.* あの二人が結婚したのはばかなことだと思うが, でもプディングの味は食べてからというからね.

prop /prɑp|prɔp/ 動 ***prop ... open*** (ドアなど)をつっぱりをして開けておく ▪He *propped* the door *open* with a thick book. 彼はぶあつい本でつっぱりをしてドアを開けておいた.

propagate /prɑ́pəgèɪt|prɔ́p-/ 動 ***propagate*** *oneself* 繁殖する ▪Weeds *propagate themselves* rapidly. 雑草は繁殖が早い.

proper /prɑ́pər|prɔ́p-/ 形 ***as you think proper*** 然るべく ▪Do *as you think proper.* 然るべくやってください.

do the proper thing by *a person* 人に公平[誠実]にする ▪We must *do the proper thing by* him. 彼に公平にしてやらねばならない.

good and proper《英口》完全に ▪They got beaten *good and proper.* 彼らは完敗した.

one's (***own***) ***proper*** 自分自身の ▪I saw it with *my* (*own*) *proper* eyes. それをこの目で見ました.

P

proper for …にふさわしい ▪It was *proper for* the occasion. それは時宜(じぎ)を得ていた.

proper to **1** …に特有の ▪Ferocity is *proper to* tigers. 残忍性はトラの本性である.

2 …にふさわしい ▪He behaved himself with dignity *proper to* his high rank. 彼は高位にふさわしい威厳をもってふるまった.

properly /prάpərli|prɔ́pəli/ 副 ***properly speaking/to speak properly*** 正確に言えば ▪Virtue is not virtue, *properly speaking*, when it is constrained. 美徳は強制されたときには, 正確に言えば美徳ではない.

property /prάpərti|prɔ́p-/ 名 ***a man of property*** 資産家 ▪Mr. Forsyte is *a man of property*. フォーサイト氏は資産家だ.

be common property (ニュースなどを)みんな知っている ▪The news *is common property*. そのニュースはみんな知っている.

prophet /prάfət|prɔ́fɪt/ 名 ***A prophet is without honor in his own country.*** 《諺》予言者は自分の郷里では敬われない,「所の神様ありがたからず」(《聖》*Matt.* 13. 57).

a prophet of doom いつも最悪の事態が起こると予想している人 ▪He thinks he will fail; he's such *a prophet of doom*. 彼は自分は失敗すると思っている. いつも最悪の事態を予期しているのだ.

prophetic /prəfétɪk|prəʊ-/ 形 ***be prophetic of*** …を予言する ▪Those deeds *were prophetic of* his future greatness. その行為は彼の将来の偉大さを予言するものだった.

propitious /prəpíʃəs/ 形 ***propitious for*** (天気・場合などが)…に好都合の ▪The weather was *propitious for* our enterprise. 天気は我々の企てに好都合だった.

propitious to **1** (特に神が)…に好意を有する, 親切な ▪The fates were *propitious to* them. 運命は彼らに好意を寄せていた.

2 =PROPITIOUS for.

proportion /prəpɔ́ːrʃən/ 名 ***a large [considerable, fair] proportion of*** …の大部分[かなりの部分] ▪*A large proportion of* the earth's surface is water. 地球の表面の大部分は水だ ▪It is true in *a considerable proportion of* cases. それは相当多くの場合において正しい.

a proportion of …の一部分 ▪*A proportion of* the apples proved rotten. その数あるリンゴの一部は腐っていた.

bear no proportion to …とつり合いがとれない ▪His duties *bear no proportion to* his abilities. 彼の職務は能力とつり合っていない.

get out of (all) proportion …をつり合いを取れなくする ▪You've *got* the head *out of proportion*; it's too big. 君の頭はつり合いが取れていない. 大きすぎるんだ.

in proportion 比例して ▪He has a great taste for art, but his critical ability is not *in proportion*. 彼は美術の趣味は大いにあるが, 批評の才はそれに伴わない.

in proportion as 〚節を伴って〛…するに比例して ▪A man will not always succeed *in proportion as* he exerts himself. 人は必ずしも努力に比例して成功するものではない.

in proportion to …に比例して ▪The camel possesses strength *in proportion to* its size. ラクダは大きさに比例して力がある.

out of (all) proportion つり合いがとれてなくて (*to*) ▪The building is *out of proportion*. その建物はつり合いがとれていない ▪His extravagance *was out of proportion to* his means. 彼の贅沢は収入につり合わない.

proportional /prəpɔ́ːrʃənəl/ 形 ***be directly [inversely] proportional to*** …に正[反]比例する ▪The weight *is directly proportional to* the volume. 重さは量に正比例する.

proposal /prəpóʊzəl/ 名 ***make [offer] a proposal of [for]*** …を申し込む ▪He *made a proposal of* marriage to her. 彼は彼女に結婚を申し込んだ.

make a proposal to …に申し入れる ▪I am going to *make a proposal to* the meeting. 私はこの会に申し入れをするつもりだ.

propose /prəpóʊz/ 動 ***propose a toast to*** …のために乾杯を発議する ▪I *propose a toast to* the future of our club. わがクラブの未来のために乾杯の音頭を取ります.

propose (marriage) to (女性)に結婚を申し込む ▪Did he *propose marriage to* you? 彼は君に結婚を申し込みましたか.

propose the toast [health] of (健康・幸福を祝って人)のために乾杯を発議する ▪He *proposed the toast of* Miss Nancy. 彼はナンシー嬢のために乾杯しましょうと言った.

propriety /prəpráɪəti/ 名 ***observe [keep] the proprieties*** 礼儀を守る ▪It is important to *keep the proprieties*. 礼儀を守ることは大切だ.

offend [sin] against the proprieties 礼儀にはずれる ▪At the risk of *offending against the proprieties*, we may state another defect. 礼儀にはずれるが敢えて, もう一つの欠点を指摘しよう.

play propriety for …のつき添いをする ▪Her aunt will *play propriety for* her. おばさんが彼女のつき添いをするだろう.

with propriety 正しく, 適当に ▪It is important to speak and write *with propriety*. 正しく話しかつ書くことは大切だ.

prospect /prάspekt|prɔ́s-/ 名 ***command [afford, give, have] a ... prospect (of)*** (…の)見晴らしが…だ ▪The hill *commands a* fine *prospect*. その山は見晴らしがよい ▪It *affords a* broad *prospect of* the sea. そこは海が広く見晴らせる.

have ... in prospect …を予期する, もくろんでいる ▪I *have* nothing *in prospect* at present. 今のところ何の計画もない.

in prospect 予期されて, 見込みがあって ▪Some

relief to the taxpayers is *in prospect.* 多少の減税が予期されている.

in prospect of …を見込んで, 予想して ▪ Men plow and sow *in prospect of* the coming harvest. 人はきたる収穫を見込んで耕作する.

prosper /prάspər|prɔ́s-/ 動 ***Cheats*** [***Cheaters***] ***never prosper.*** 《諺》人を欺く人は決して成功しない《相手が取引を打ち切るので事業に失敗する》.

prosperity /prɑspérəti|prɔs-/ 名 ***in prosperity*** 裕福に ▪ He is living *in prosperity.* 彼は裕福に暮らしている.

Prosperity makes friends, adversity tries them. 《諺》繁栄は友を作り, 逆境は友を試す.

prostrate[1] /prάstreɪt|prɔ́s-/ 形 ***fall prostrate*** **1** ばったり倒れる, 腹ばいになる ▪ He *fell prostrate* upon the ground and died. 彼は地べたにばったり倒れて死んだ.

2 地にひれ伏す ▪ He *fell prostrate* at the feet of the king. 彼は王の足もとにひれ伏した.

lay prostrate 屈服させる ▪ They *laid* the Republic *prostrate.* 彼らは共和党を屈服させた.

prostrate[2] /prάstreɪt|prɔ́s-/ 動 ***prostrate** oneself* 平伏する; 平身低頭する ▪ He had to *prostrate himself* in apology. 彼は平身低頭して謝罪しなければならなかった.

protection /prətékʃən/ 名 ***live under*** (*a person's*) ***protection*** 《婉曲》(女性が)男性の世話になって暮らす《めかけになること》 ▪ She was *living under his lordship's protection.* 彼女は閣下の世話になって暮らしていた.

under the protection of …に保護されて ▪ He traveled *under the protection of* soldiers. 彼は兵に守られて旅行した.

protest /próʊtest/ 名 ***enter*** [***lodge, make***] ***a protest against*** [***with***] …に抗議を申し込む ▪ I must *enter a protest against* the verdict. 私はその評決に対して抗議を申し込まねばならない ▪ He *lodged a protest with* the committee. 彼は委員会に抗議を申し込んだ.

in protest 抗議して ▪ He wrote to The Times *in protest.* タイムズ紙に抗議文を送った.

under protest 不承不承 ▪ He paid the amount claimed *under protest.* 彼は要求額を渋々払った.

without protest 文句を言わずに ▪ He gave way *without protest.* 彼は文句を言わずに折れた.

proud /praʊd/ 形 (***as***) ***proud as Lucifer*** ひどく傲慢で ▪ He's *as proud as Lucifer* and won't accept advice. 彼はひどく傲慢で助言など受けつけまい. ☞Lucifer「魔王」.

(***as***) ***proud as Punch*** [***a hen, a peacock, a turkey, Hell***] →(as) pleased as PUNCH.

be proud of …を誇る ▪ England may well *be proud of* her poets. イングランドがその詩人を誇るのは無理もない.

do** a person **proud →DO[2].

do** oneself **proud →DO[2].

prove /pru:v/ 動 *One* ***has something*** [***a lot***] ***to prove.*** 頑張ってやれるということを証明する ▪ I *had a lot to prove* by fighting him. 彼と争って頑張ったらやれるということを証明した.

not proven 《法》証拠不十分 ▪ A verdict of "*not proven*" is common in Scotland. 「証拠不十分」という判決はスコットランドでは普通である.

prove** one's* [the***] ***case*** [***point***] 自分の[その]主張の正しさを証明する ▪ Can you *prove the point?* その主張の正しさを証明できますか.

prove** oneself* (to be***) …であることを証明してみせる ▪ He *proved himself to be* a capable general. 彼は立派な将軍となってみせた.

proverb /prάvə:rb|prɔ́v-/ 名 ***as the proverb is*** [***says, goes, runs***] 諺に言う通り ▪ *As the proverb is,* time is money. 諺に言う通り, 時は金なりだ.

be a proverb for …の点で有名である ▪ He *is a proverb for* stinginess. 彼のけちんぼうぶりは有名だ.

pass into a proverb 諺になる; 評判[笑い草]になる ▪ His ignorance *passed into a proverb.* 彼のもの知らずは笑い草になった.

to a proverb 諺になるほど ▪ The country is swampy even *to a proverb.* その地方は沼地が多いので諺になっているくらいだ.

provide /prəvάɪd/ 動 ***be poorly*** [***well, amply***] ***provided for*** 生活に困っている[困らないでいる] ▪ They *are poorly provided for.* 彼らは生活に困っている ▪ His sons *were well provided for.* 彼の息子たちは生活に何不足なかった.

be provided with …の設備がある, を持つ ▪ The building *is provided with* fire escapes. このビルには非常口の設備がある ▪ I *am provided with* all I need. 私は必要なものはいっさい持っている.

providence /prάvədəns|prɔ́v-/ 名 ***fly in the face of Providence*** 天意にそむく; 向こう見ずなことをする ▪ To row a boat in a storm is to *fly in the face of Providence.* あらしにボートをこぐのはむちゃだ.

provider /prəvάɪdər/ 名 ***a universal provider*** 《英》よろず屋, 何でも売る店 ▪ He is well known as *a universal provider.* 彼はよろず屋としてよく知られていた.

the lion's provider →LION.

province /prάvəns|prɔ́v-/ 名 ***fall outside the province of*** …の領域をはずれる ▪ Doesn't your question *fall outside the province of* science? 君の質問は科学の領域をはずれてはいませんか.

within [***outside***] *one's* ***province*** 自分の本分内[外]で ▪ To treat a case of typhoid is not *within my province.* チフス患者の治療は私の本分外のことです.

provision /prəvíʒən/ 名 ***make provision against*** (危険など)に備える ▪ We must *make provision against* rainy days. 我々は不慮に備えておかねばならない.

make provision for …の準備をする, に備える ▪ We must *make provision for* our children.

我々は子供のために備えてやらねばならない ▪ He has *made* little *provision for* the future. 彼は将来の備えをほとんどしていない.

proviso /prəváɪzoʊ/ 名 ***subject to this proviso*** この条件をつけて ▪ *Subject to this proviso* I agree with you. この条件をつけて同意します.

with the proviso that …という条件つきで ▪ Jim was admitted to the eighth grade *with the proviso that* he was to be put back if he failed in any subject. ジムはひとつでも学科ができなかったら落第させるという条件つきで8学年に入れられた.

provocation /prɑ̀vəkéɪʃən|prɔ̀v-/ 名 ***on*** [***at***] ***the slightest*** [***least***] ***provocation*** ほんのちょっとしたことで ▪ She blushes *at the slightest provocation.* 彼女はすぐ赤くなる ▪ He resorts to force *on the least provocation.* 彼はちょっとしたことで暴力に訴える.

under provocation 気にさわることをされて ▪ He did not lose his composure *under provocation.* 彼は気にさわることをされても落着きを失わなかった.

provoke /prəvóʊk/ 動 ***provoke*** *a person* ***to*** [***to*** *do*, ***into*** *doing*] 人を刺激して…させる ▪ An insult *provokes* a person *to* anger. 侮辱は人を怒らせる ▪ His impudence *provoked* her *into slapping* him on the face. 彼の生意気な態度にかっとなって彼女は相手の顔を平手打ちした.

prowl /praʊl/ 名 ***on*** [***upon***] ***the prowl*** (盗み・女漁りで)うろつき回って ▪ A poor miserable thief had been all night *upon the prowl.* 哀れでみじめな盗人が一晩中うろついていたのだった.

proximity /prɑksímәti|prɔk-/ 名 ***in close*** [***immediate***] ***proximity to*** …にきわめて接近して ▪ His house is *in close proximity to* the park. 彼の家は公園のすぐ近くにある.

in the proximity of …の近くに ▪ The ground lies *in the proximity of* the town. そのグラウンドは町の近くにある.

proxy /prɑ́ksi|prɔ́k-/ 名 ***be*** [***stand***] ***proxy for*** …の代理となる, 代わりとなる ▪ I'll *stand proxy for* you. 君の代理になってあげます.

by proxy 代人をもって, 代理で ▪ The address was read *by proxy.* その講演は代読された.

prude /pru:d/ 名 ***act the prude*** 淑女ぶる ▪ She was *acting the prude* as usual. 彼女は例によって淑女ぶっていた.

prune /pru:n/ 名 ***Facts*** [***Dates,*** etc.] ***go through*** *one* ***like prunes.*** 事実[日付, など]がなかなか覚えられない ▪ You needn't tell me your birthday. I'm sorry to say that *dates go through* me *like prunes.* 君の誕生日を僕に言う必要はないよ. 悪いけど, どうせ聞いてもなかなか覚えられないから.

full of prunes =full of BEANs.

prunes and prism(***s***) 気取った言葉うかい; 上品なふるまい ▪ He has none of the "*prunes and prism*" style, and is addicted to strong language. 彼は上品な文体は少しもなく, 激しい言葉ばかり使いたがる. ☞Dickens の *Little Dorrit* 2. 5. である父親が "prunes and prism" という言葉がほとんど無意味だが語呂がよいので上品だと思っているところから.

pry /praɪ/ 動 ***pry loose*** (てこで)こねてゆるめる ▪ I *pried* a board *loose.* 板を1枚こねてゆるめた.

pry open (てこで)こじ開ける ▪ The box had *been pried open.* 箱はこじ開けられていた.

pub /pʌb/ 名 ***a pub crawl*** 《口》(パブからパブへの)はしご酒 ▪ He formed a habit of going on *pub crawls.* 彼ははしご酒の癖がついた.

puberty /pjú:bərti/ 名 ***reach*** [***arrive at, attain***] ***puberty*** 年ごろになる, 色気づく ▪ In towns, women *reach puberty* sooner than they do in the country. 都会では田舎よりも早く女性が色気づく.

public /pʌ́blɪk/ 形名 ***go public*** **1** (株を)公開する ▪ The next year the company *went public.* 翌年その会社は株を公開した.

2 (秘密を)公にする ▪ He has *gone public* about being gay. 彼はゲイであることを公にした.

in public 人前で; 公然と (↔ in PRIVATE) ▪ Though praised *in public*, he was abused behind. 彼は人前でほめられたが, 陰では悪口を言われた.

in the public eye 世間の注目を浴びて, 衆人環視の中で ▪ He is now "a man *in the public eye.*" 彼は今「注目の人」となっている.

make public 〚主に受身で〛公表[公刊]する ▪ The first of his books has never *been made public.* 彼の最初の本はついに公刊されなかった.

public property (万人)周知の事実 ▪ His bankruptcy is *public property.* 彼の破産は周知の事実だ.

sell ... to the public …に対して一般大衆の支持[承認]を得る ▪ Our plan will be difficult to *sell to the public.* 我々の計画に一般の支持を取りつけるのは難しいだろう.

publicity /pʌblísəti/ 名 ***give publicity*** 公表する; 広告する (*to*) ▪ They will *give publicity to* the fact. 彼らはその事実を公表するだろう.

in the full blaze of publicity 衆目を浴びて ▪ Royal personages live *in the full blaze of publicity.* 皇族は衆目を浴びて生活している.

publish /pʌ́blɪʃ/ 動 ***Publish or perish.*** 発表するか死ぬか. ☞米国の大学教授が研究を次々に発表しなければ職を失いかねない, という立場を表す文句.

Publish(***ed***) ***and be damned.*** (スキャンダルなどを)公表したければ勝手にしたらいい. ☞Wellington (1769–1852)公爵の言葉とされる.

pucker /pʌ́kər/ 名 ***in a pucker*** 《口》そわそわして, 狼狽して ▪ She seemed *in a* great *pucker.* 彼女はひどくそわそわしている様子だった.

in puckers しわ[ひだ]になって ▪ His brow was *in* deep *puckers.* 彼の額は深いしわがよっていた.

put *a person* ***into a pucker*** 《口》人を狼狽させる ▪ Those few things *put* her *into a pucker.* それらわずかの事柄が彼女をそわそわさせた.

pudding /pʊ́dɪŋ/ 名 ***more praise than pudding*** 実の伴わない世辞, から世辞 ▪ Writers get

P

more praise than pudding here. ここでは物書きは実の伴わないお世辞をもらう.

pudding rather than praise/prefer pudding to praise 「花より団子」 ▪ He turned, *preferring pudding to praise.* 彼は花より団子とそっぽを向いた.

puff[1] /pʌf/ 名 ***a puff piece*** 《口》 大げさな称賛文, 誇大広告 ▪ That's *a puff piece* about the boss, written by one of his people. それは部下の一人が書いた上司に関するヨイショ記事だ.

be out of puff 《口》 息切れがしている ▪ I *am out of puff* with running. 私は走って息切れがしている.

give* [*get*] *a puff 褒めそやす[される] ▪ For a little money any person can *be given a puff* in some newspaper. わずかな金を出せばどんな人でも何かの新聞で褒めそやしてもらえる ▪ He has *got a* good *puff* of his book. 彼は著書をうんと褒めそやされた.

have* [*take*] *a puff at (パイプ)を吹かす ▪ He *took a puff at* his pipe. 彼はパイプを吹かした.

in all** one's **puff 《主に英口》 全生涯で, 一生のうちに ▪ We have a lot of things to do *in all our puff.* 一生のうちにしなければならないことがたくさんある.

puff[2] /pʌf/ 動 ***puff and blow*** ハーハーあえぐ; ぶうぶう文句を言う ▪ He was *puffing and blowing* as if very much out of breath. 彼はひどく息切れがしてでもいるようにハーハーあえいでいた.

puff* (*and blow*) *like a grampus ひどく(ハーハー)あえぐ ▪ He was *puffing* (*and blowing*) *like a grampus.* 彼はひどく(ハーハー)あえいでいた.

pull[1] /pʊl/ 名 ***give a pull at*** …を引っ張る ▪ He *gave a pull at* the rope. 彼はロープを引っ張った.

go for a pull ボートこぎに行く (*on*) ▪ We *went for a* short *pull on* the lake. 我々は湖にちょっとボートこぎに行った.

have a pull **1** ひとこぎする ▪ We *had a* hard *pull* with our oars. 我々はオールを一生懸命にこいだ. **2** 《口》 手うるがある (*with*) ▪ He got the job because his father *has a* lot of *pull* in that company. 彼がその職につけたのは父親があの会社によい手うるがあるからだ ▪ He *has a* strong *pull with* the manager. 彼は支配人にとても顔がきく. **3** ぐっと1杯やる (*at*) ▪ He *had a pull at* the mug. 彼はコップでぐっとひっかけた. **4** 《卑》 自慰をする.

***have a* [*the*] *pull of* [*on, upon, over*]** *a person* 人より有利である, 分がいい ▪ I think, on the whole, I *have the pull of* [*over*] him. 私は概してあの男より分がいいと思う.

long pull (居酒屋での, 通例ビールの)おまけ ▪ They had the power to prohibit what was called the "*long pull.*" 彼らはいわゆる酒の「おまけ」を禁止する権限を持っていた. ☞ビールサーバーを「余計に押すこと」が原義.

take a pull at …で1杯[一服]やる ▪ He *took a pull at* his pipe. パイプを一服吹かした.

the pull of the table (とばくで)親の持つ利点 ▪ The dealer has *the pull of the table.* トランプの配り手には親の利点がある.

pull[2] /pʊl/ 動 ***Don't pull that crap* [*shit*].** ばかなことを言う[する]な ▪ Come on, you, *don't pull that shit* with me! 頼むよ, 君, 僕にばかなことを言わないでくれ!

***pull a face* [*faces*]** しかめつらをする ▪ When she heard that she had lost, she *pulled a face.* 彼女は自分が負けたと聞くとしかめつらをした.

pull a fast one →ONE.

pull a long face →draw a long FACE.

pull a sanctimonious face 信心うらをする ▪ I *pull* no solemn *sanctimonious face.* 私はしかつめらしい信心うらはしない.

***pull caps* [*wigs*]** つかみ合いする, けんかをする ▪ They were like a pair of Amazons *pulling caps.* 彼女らはまさにつかみ合いするアマゾン族の女といったありさまだった. ☞お互いの帽子を取り合うことから.

Pull devil, pull baker!/Pull dog, pull cat! どっちも負けるな ▪ "*Pull devil, pull baker!*" cried the women. 「どっちも負けるな!」と女性たちが叫んだ ▪ It's *pull dog, pull cat* with man and woman, ever since the days of the apple. アダムとイブの昔から男と女はどっちも負けるな, である. ☞綱引きから.

pull even with …に接近する ▪ Box-office receipts are *pulling even with* a year ago. 映画界の収入は1年前に接近している.

***pull foot* [*it*]** 《口》 逃げ去る; 精いっぱい走る ▪ She flew out of sight as fast as she could *pull it.* 彼女は一目散に走って見えない所へ逃げて行った ▪ You'll have to *pull foot* to overtake them. あの連中に追いつくためには大急ぎで走らねばなりません.

pull** oneself **in 〚主に命令文で〛 腹を引いて背筋を伸ばす ▪ *Pull yourselves in* there. あなたたち, 腹を引いて背筋を伸ばしなさい.

pull ... in pieces →PULL ... to pieces.

pull it →PULL foot.

pull it over** a person's **eyes = draw the WOOL over a person's eyes.

pull** a person's **leg →LEG[1].

pull off** one's **hat to 帽子を脱いで…にあいさつする ▪ They *pulled off their hats to* one another with great civility. 彼らはとてもいんぎんにお互いに帽子を取ってあいさつした.

pull out from behind (車)を追い越すために後ろから出てくる ▪ The driver of the car *pulled out from behind* the lorry. 車の運転手はトラックを追い抜こうとして後ろから出てきた.

pull out something big 特別に奮発する ▪ If you're going to get through this, you'll have to *pull out something big.* これをすますつもりなら, 特にひと奮発しなければいけない.

pull* (one's) *punches →PUNCH[1].

***pull something on** a person* 人に悪事を行う, 人をだます[ひっかける] ▪ Who *pulled something on* that old woman? 誰があのばあさんをだましたんだ?

Pull the other leg* [*one*], *it's got bells on

it. もっとましな嘘を言えよ《そんな話，誰が信じるものか》.

pull (***the***) ***strings*** [***wires***] 陰で策動する; 内密に運動する ▪ The men who *pull the strings* are down in the Cape. 陰で策動している連中はケープにいる ▪ His uncle *pulled* all sorts of *wires* to get John placed with that organization. ジョンのおじはジョンをその会社に入れようと八方内密に運動をした. ☞ 人形劇から.

pull ... to [***in***] ***pieces*** **1** …をずたずたにする; をぶちこわす ▪ The boy *pulled* his toy *to pieces*. 男の子はおもちゃをばらばらにした.

2 …を酷評する, こきおろす ▪ I showed him my work, but he *pulled* it *to pieces*. 彼に作品を見せたら, ぼろくそに言った.

pull *oneself* ***together*** **1**《口》元気を取り戻す; 気を静める; 立ち直る ▪ I realized this in a moment, and *pulled myself together* with an effort. 私はこのことがすぐわかってやっとのことで気を静めた ▪ *Pull yourself together* and face up to life. 立ち直って人生に立ち向かうんだ.

2 所持品[身の回りのもの]を寄せ集める ▪ Let's leave as soon as we *pull ourselves together*. 所持品をとりまとめ次第, 出かけよう.

pull *oneself* ***up*** **1** 自制する, 急にやめる ▪ He *pulled himself up* short. 彼は急に口をつぐんだ.

2 背すじを伸ばして立つ ▪ He *pulled himself up* to his full height. 彼は背すじを伸ばしてまっすぐに立った.

pull up *one's* ***socks*** [***stockings***]《口》ふんどしを締めてかかる ▪ It's time you *pulled up your socks*. 君はふんどしを締めてかかっていいころだよ.

pull (*one's*) ***weight*** (ボートで)体重に比例したこぎ方をする; 一人前の働きをする, 務めを果たす ▪ We will be able to succeed only if each *pulls his weight*. 我々はめいめいが務めを果たして初めて成功することができるだろう ▪ No member of the climbing party *pulled* more *weight* than these two men. 登山隊のメンバーのうちでこの二人の男くらい務めを果たした者はいなかった.

pull wigs →PULL caps.

pulp /pʌlp/ 名 ***to*** (***a***) ***pulp*** ぐしゃぐしゃに;《口》こてんぱんに ▪ His arm was caught in the machinery and crushed *to pulp*. 彼は腕を機械にはさまれてぐしゃぐしゃに砕かれた ▪ I reduced him *to a pulp*. 彼をこてんぱんにやっつけてやった.

pulse /pʌls/ 名 ***feel*** *a person's* ***pulse*** 人の脈を見る ▪ Give me your hand, and let me *feel your pulse*. 手を出して脈を見せてください.

feel the pulse of …の意向[大勢]を探る, に探りを入れる ▪ Only he who has *felt the pulse of* an age can tell us that. 時代の大勢を打診した人だけがそのことを教えることができる.

stir *a person's* ***pulses*** 人を興奮させる ▪ The idea of becoming a Director *stirred my pulses*. 重役になると思うと私は興奮した.

pump[1] /pʌmp/ 名 ***fetch the pump*** ポンプに迎え水を差す ▪ This process is vulgarly called *fetching the pump*. このやり方が俗にポンプで迎え水を差すと呼ばれる.

on the pump ポンプでくみ上げられて ▪ The wells will be *on the pump* in two years. その(石油)井戸は2年すればポンプでくみ上げられるだろう.

parish pump《英》村の共同井戸(的な)田舎政治(的な); 視野の狭い ▪ His speech smelt a little of the *parish pump*. 彼の演説は少し偏狭なところがあった ▪ He is a *parish pump* politician. 彼は田舎政治家だ.

prime the pump (***for***) (…の)迎え水とする ▪ The U.S. granted great sums to *prime the pump for* European recovery. アメリカはヨーロッパ復興の迎え水とするため多額の金を供与した.

pump[2] /pʌmp/ 動 ***be pumped out*** 息ぎれがしてしまう ▪ I *am* perfectly *pumped out*. すっかり息ぎれがしてしまった.

be [***get***] ***pumped up*** (***about*** [***for***]) (…に)非常に興奮する ▪ They *were* really *pumped up about* the game. 彼らはその試合に全く興奮していた.

pump a ship 船のあかをポンプでくみ出す ▪ They *pumped a* leaky *ship*. 彼らは水漏れ穴のある船のあかをくみ出した.

pumpkin /pʌ́mpkən/ 名 ***The pumpkin has not turned into a coach.*** 先の約束はかなえられず魔法が解けてしまった. ☞ 12時までに帰らないと王宮の舞踏会に行くために魔法使いがつくってくれた馬車がもとのカボチャになってしまうと注意されたシンデレラの童話から.

Punch /pʌntʃ/ 名 (***as***) ***pleased*** [***proud***] ***as Punch***《主に英》大喜び[大得意]で ▪ I am *as pleased as Punch* at the thought. 私はそのことを考えるとうれしくてたまらない ▪ I was *as proud as Punch*, for I was trusted to make a journey by myself. 私は大得意だった. 一人で旅行することを任されたからだ. ☞ 英国の人形劇 *Punch and Judy* に出る鼻が長く曲がった Punch という人物の表情から.

play Punch and Judy over (二人が)…について互いに口論[議論]し合う ▪ They *played Punch and Judy over* how to spend the summer vacation. 彼らは夏休みの過ごし方について互いに議論し合った. ☞ Punch は妻の Judy をいじめ殺す.

punch[1] /pʌntʃ/ 名 ***beat*** *a person* ***to the punch***《口》人を先に打つ, 人の機先を制する ▪ He will *beat* you *to the punch* by having his say first. 彼は先に自分の言いたいことを言って君の機先を制するだろう. ☞ ボクシングから.

get a punch in =get a BLOW in.

give [***get***] ***a punch on*** …をぶんなぐる[なぐられる] ▪ I *gave* him *a punch on* the chin. その男のあごをぶんなぐってやった.

pull no punches (攻撃・批評などで)手心を加えない ▪ She *pulled no punches* in doing so. 彼女は容赦なくそうした.

pull (*one's*) ***punches*** (ボクシングで)わざと効き目のないパンチを加える; (攻撃・批評などで)手心を加える ▪ Ask him his opinion. He never *pulls his punches*. あの男の意見を質(ただ)してみろ. 決して手心は

加えないから.

roll with the punches **1**(ボクサーが出されたパンチと同方向に身を引いて)相手のパンチをかわす; 柔軟な態度で衝撃を和らげる ▪ It looked like a deprived black child was urged to "*roll with the punches*." それはまるで貧しい黒人の子が「相手のパンチをかわす」ようにせきたてられているようだった ▪ When you suffer a calamity, it's better to *roll with the punch* than try to fight it. 災難にあったら, それと戦うよりも柔軟な態度で衝撃を和らげる方がいい.

2 逆境に慣れる, 困難な状況に耐える ▪ He has *rolled with the punches* since his childhood. 彼は子供のころから困難な状況に耐えてきた.

sucker punch 不意打ち, いきなりくらわすパンチ ▪ The rise in price was a *sucker punch* to the citizens. 物価の値上げは市民には不意打ちだった.

throw [***take***] ***a punch*** 一発くらわす ▪ I *threw a punch* at him. 彼に一発くらわした.

punch[2] /pʌntʃ/ 動 ***cannot punch*** *one's* ***way out of a paper bag*** 《口》ひどく軟弱だ ▪ He is so weak-hearted that he *can't punch his way out of a paper bag*. 彼は気が弱くてひどく軟弱だ.

punch *a person's* ***lights out*** [***up***] →LIGHT[1].

punctillio /pʌŋktíliou/ 名 ***stand on*** [***upon***] (*one's*) ***punctillios*** (つまらぬことに)儀式張りすぎる ▪ The Bishop *stood upon his punctillios*. 監督は儀式張りすぎた.

punctual /pʌ́ŋktʃuəl/ 形 (***as***) ***punctual as the clock*** きわめて時刻厳守で ▪ Morris came up to the door, *punctual as the clock*. モリスは時間を厳守して玄関口へやって来た.

punctual to the [***a***] ***minute*** 1分もたがえない ▪ He was *punctual to a minute*. 彼は1分もたがえなかった.

punctuality /pʌ̀ŋktʃuǽləti/ 名 ***Punctuality is the politeness of kings.*** 《諺》時間厳守は王者の礼節.

Punctuality is the soul [***hinge***] ***of business.*** 《諺》几帳面は仕事の極意である.

pup /pʌp/ 名 ***buy a pup*** 《口》儲けにならないことに手を出す ▪ He advised a brother officer to *buy a pup*. 彼は仲間の士官に儲けにならないことに手を出すように勧めた. ☞pup「小犬」.

in [***with***] ***pup*** (雌犬が)はらんでいる ▪ He can discover whether a bitch is *in pup*. 彼は雌犬がはらんでいるかどうか知ることができる.

sell *a person* ***a pup*** 《口》人に値うち以下のものを売りつける, つかませる ▪ You can see at a glance that the builder *sold* him *a pup*. 彼が建築屋につかまされたことはひと目でわかるだろう.

purchase /pə́ːrtʃəs/ 名 ***at ... years' purchase*** ...年間の土地収入に相当する値で ▪ He was ordered to sell these lands *at* nine *years' purchase*. 彼はその土地を9年間の土地収入に相当する値で売るように命じられた.

get [***secure***] ***a purchase on*** ...をしっかりと握る ▪ I cannot *get* any *purchase on* it. それがしっかり握れない.

make a purchase 買い物をする ▪ She *made* some *purchases* in Paris. 彼女はパリで少し買い物をした.

not worth a day's [***an hour's,*** etc.] ***purchase*** (重体で)1日[1時間, など]ももちそうにない ▪ The doctor says that his life is *not worth an hour's purchase*. 医師の話では彼の命は1時間ももちそうにないとのことだ. ☞purchase「土地からの年々のあがり高」.

pure /pjuər/ 形 (***as***) ***pure*** [***clean***] ***as*** (***the***) ***driven snow*** 《しばしば反語》(人柄が)清らかで ▪ I'm sure she's *pure as the driven snow*. She goes out with any rich man. 彼女はさぞ清らかだろうさ. 金持ちなら誰とでもデートするのだからね.

pure and simple 〚名詞の後に伴って〛純然たる, 単なる ▪ What we are speaking of is knowledge *pure and simple*. 我々が話題にしているのは純然たる知識のことなのだ.

purely /pjúərli/ 副 ***purely and simply*** かけ値なしに, 全く ▪ It was *purely and simply* for show. それは全く見せびらかしであった.

purge /pəːrdʒ/ 動 ***purge*** *oneself* ***of*** [***from***] (疑いなど)を晴らす ▪ He had to *purge himself of* [*from*] a like suspicion. 彼は同様の疑いを晴らさねばならなかった.

purler /pə́ːrlər/ 名 ***come*** [***take***] ***a purler*** 《英口》まっさかさまに倒れる ▪ He *came a purler* on the slippery road. 彼はすべりやすい道路で転倒した.

purple /pə́ːrpəl/ 名形 ***a purple passage*** [***patch***] (文章・音楽などの中で特に)華麗な一節 ▪ Some teachers encourage children to produce the *purple passage*. 教師の中には生徒が華麗な一節を書くことを励ますものがいる.

be raised to the purple 枢機卿に任ぜられる ▪ He *was raised to the purple*. 彼は枢機卿に任ぜられた. ☞purple「枢機卿 (cardinal) の用いる深紅色の衣」.

born [***cradled***] ***in*** (***the***) ***purple*** 帝王の家に生まれる; 王侯貴族の家に生まれる ▪ The old Whig party reserved the highest places for those *cradled in the purple*. 古いホイッグ党は王侯貴族の家に生まれた人々に最高の地位を確保していた. ☞紫衣 (purple) はローマ皇帝だけが着用していたことから.

go purple (***in the face***) 《口》(怒って)赤黒い顔になる ▪ He *went purple* with anger. 彼は怒って赤黒い顔になった.

lay aside the purple 王位を捨てる ▪ Constantine *laid aside the purple* and became a priest. コンスタンティヌスは帝位を捨てて司祭となった.

marry into the purple (女性が氏なくして)玉のこしに乗る ▪ My dear Helena *married into the purple*. かわいいヘレナは玉のこしに乗った.

purpose /pə́ːrpəs/ 名 ***accidentally on purpose*** →ACCIDENTALLY.

answer [***serve, suit***] ***the*** [*one's*] ***purpose***

目的にかなう, 間に合う ▪ Either will *answer our purpose*. どちらでも我々の目的にかなう ▪ A knife will *serve my purpose*. ナイフで間に合う.

attain* [*accomplish, achieve*] *one's* *pur-pose →gain one's PURPOSE.

(***be, play,*** etc.) ***at cross purposes*** → CROSS[1].

for medicinal purposes 《戯》薬用目的で; 健康のために ▪ What parts of the aloe plant are used *for medicinal purposes*? アロエのどの部分が薬用に使われるの ▪ Under the kitchen sink Bill kept a bottle of bourbon *for medicinal purposes*. ビルは台所の流しの下に健康のためと言ってバーボンのビンを保管していた.

for* [*with*] *the purpose of *doing* …するために ▪ He bought the land *for the purpose of building* on it. 彼はそこに建物を建てようとその土地を買った.

for this* [*that*] *purpose この[その]ために ▪ I have sufficient cash *for that purpose*. そのための現金は十分ある.

from the purpose 《古》要点をはずれて ▪ He answered her far *from the purpose*. 彼は彼女に要点をひどくはずれた答えをした.

gain* [*accomplish, achieve, attain, effect*]** *one's* ***purpose 目的を達する ▪ The regulation *achieved its purpose*. その規則は目的を達した.

on purpose 故意に, わざと (↔by a mere ACCIDENT) ▪ He has come *on purpose* to ask after my health. 彼はわざわざ見舞いに来てくれた ▪ Then she did it *on purpose*. では彼女はわざとそうしたのだ.

on purpose to *do* [***that***] …するために[の目的で] ▪ He did so *on purpose to* be sent to prison with them. 彼はその連中といっしょに投獄されるためにそうしたのだ ▪ I am placed here *on purpose that* I may render essential help to the cause of God. 私は神のために重要な助力をする目的でこの世に置かれているのだ.

serve* [*suit*] *the [*one's*] ***purpose*** → answer the PURPOSE.

to all intents and purposes →INTENT[2].

to little* [*no*] *purpose ほとんど[全く]むだに ▪ In his opinion, a general council is *to little purpose*. 彼の意見では教務総会などほとんど無益なものだ ▪ We spoke *to no purpose*. 我々はしゃべったが何にもならなかった.

to *one's* ***purpose*** 自分の目的にかなう ▪ I found some books *to my purpose*. 読んでみたら何冊かは目的にかなうものだった.

to some* [*good, great,* etc.] *purpose かなり[よく]成功して, かなり[十分に]効果をあげて ▪ We must live *to some purpose*. 我々は何か意義ある生活をしなければならない ▪ I wrote a letter *to the best purpose* I could. 私はできるだけ効果的に手紙を書いた ▪ He would have roared *to lusty purpose*. 彼は十分に大声をあげてどなったことだろう.

to* (*the*) *purpose **1** 適切に[で] ▪ I will tell you a story *to the purpose*. 君に一つ適切なお話をしてあげよう.
2 効果的に ▪ He lessoned me *to purpose*. 彼は私に効果的にお説教をした.

with the purpose of *doing* → for the PURPOSE of doing.

purse /pəːrs/ 名 ***A heavy purse makes a light heart.*** 《諺》財布が重いと心は軽い.

A light purse makes a heavy heart. 《諺》財布が軽いと心は重い,「貧ほどつらいものはない」.

a well-lined purse たくさんの金 ▪ One needs *a well-lined purse* to stay at the Ritz Hotel. リッツホテルに泊まるには金がたくさんいる.

beyond *a person's* ***purse*** …には買えない ▪ That big car is *beyond my purse*. あの大きな車は私には買えない.

close *one's* ***purse*** →open one's PURSE.

dig into *one's* ***purse*** →DIG[2].

give a purse →put up a PURSE.

have a common purse 資産を共有している ▪ They *have a common purse*. 彼らは資産を共有している.

He that hath a full purse never wanted a friend. 《諺》金持ちになると決して友人に事欠かない.

hold* [*control*] *the purse strings →PURSE STRING.

line *one's* ***purse*** →LINE *one's* (own) pockets.

Little and often fills the purse. 《諺》小金でもたびたび入れば財布はいっぱいになる,「塵(ちり)も積もれば山となる」.

make* (*up*) *a purse for …のために寄付金を募る ▪ His friends *made a purse for* him when he was to travel in Egypt. 彼がエジプト旅行をすることになったとき友人たちが寄付金を募ってやった.

open* [*close*]** *one's* ***purse 金を出す[出ししぶる] ▪ The old man *opened his purse*, and gave all its contents to his pupil. 老人は財布をあけて中身をそっくり弟子に与えた.

put up* [*give*] *a purse (競技などで)賞金を出す ▪ The Committee decided to *put up a purse* for competition. 委員会は競争に賞金を出すことに決定した.

Who holds the purse rules the house. 《諺》財布の主が家の主.

within *one's* ***purse*** 収入の範囲で ▪ I make it a point to live *within my purse*. 私は収入の範囲で生活することにしている.

You cannot make a silk purse out of a sow's ear. 《諺》ブタの耳からシルクの財布は作れない,「ウリのつるにはナスはならぬ」.

purse string /pə́ːrsstrìŋ/ 名 ***hold* [*control*] *the purse strings*** 財布のひもを握っている ▪ My wife *holds the purse strings* in our family. わが家では家内が財布のひもを握っている ▪ These days women *control the purse strings* in their families. 近頃は女性が家庭内で財布のひもを握っている.

keep a tight hold on the purse strings 財

P

布のひもをしっかり締めている, ひどくけちだ ▪ Cleon *keeps a* very *tight hold on the purse strings*. クレオンはひどくけちだ.

loosen [***tighten***] ***the*** [*one's*] ***purse strings*** 財布のひもをゆるめる[締める], 気前がよい[けちだ] ▪ He refused to *loosen his purse strings* any further. 彼はそれ以上財布のひもをゆるめるのを断った.

pursuance /pərsjúːəns/ 名 ***in pursuance of*** **1** …に従って ▪ I wrote to him *in pursuance of* your instruction. ご教示に従って彼に手紙を書きました.

2 …を履行して ▪ They reached London *in pursuance of* their little plan. 彼らはそのささやかな計画を履行してロンドンに着いた.

pursuant /pərsjúːənt/ 形 ***pursuant to*** 《文》 …に応じて, 従って ▪ We acted *pursuant to* their agreement. 彼らの同意に従って行動した.

pursuit /pərsjúːt/ 名 ***in*** (***hot***) ***pursuit*** (***of***) **1** …を(激しく)追って ▪ They were like children *in pursuit of* butterflies. 彼らはチョウを追っている子供のようだった ▪ The gang fled from the scene with the police *in hot pursuit*. ギャングが犯行現場から逃走し, そのあとを警察が必死に追っていた.

2 …を求めて ▪ I am *in* daily *pursuit of* happiness. 私は毎日幸福を求めている.

in pursuit 追跡して ▪ He set out *in pursuit*. 彼は追跡を始めた.

purview /pə́ːrvjuː/ 名 ***fall within the purview of*** 《法》 …の条項に該当する ▪ It *falls within the purview of* Art. 1. それは第1条に該当する.

within [***outside***] ***the purview of*** …の範囲内[外]に ▪ These questions lie *outside* [do not come *within*] *the purview of* our inquiry. これらの問題は我々の調査の範囲外にある[範囲に入らない].

push[1] /pʊʃ/ 名 ***at a push*** うまく行けば; いざという時には ▪ We can sleep seven or eight people in the house *at a push*. いざという時には7, 8人の人を泊めることができる.

at one push **1** 一気に ▪ Many men do not pay their debts *at one push*. 借金を一気に払わない人が多い.

2 =with one PUSH.

at the first push 最初のひと押しで ▪ Exact reformation is not perfected *at the first push*. 正確な改革は最初のひと押しでは完成しない.

come [***bring, put***] ***to the*** [***a***] ***push*** 苦境に陥る[陥らせる] ▪ It *came to the* solemn *push*. それはひどい苦境に陥った ▪ He was a subtle disputant, and would several times *put* the professor *to a push*. 彼は巧妙な議論家で何回もその教授を苦境に陥らせたものだった.

give a push **1** ひと押しする ▪ She *gave* him *a push* and threw him into the pond. 彼女は彼をひと押しして池の中へ落とした.

2 (人の)あと押しをする ▪ Will you *give* me *a push* in this? このことで私の後援をしてくださいますか.

give [***get***] ***the push*** 《英口》 首にする[される]; 絶交[絶縁]する[される] ▪ They'd be thinking of *giving* me *the push*. 彼らは僕を首にしようかと考えるだろう ▪ If you don't improve, you will *get the push*. 精勤しなければ首になるぞ ▪ Ellie's a bit upset—she *got the push* from Warner last night. エリーは少し気落ちしている, 昨夜ウォーナーに絶交を食らったから.

make a [*one's*] ***push*** **1** どんどん進んで行く (*at, for*) ▪ We *made a push for* the lake. 我々は湖に向かってどんどん進んで行った ▪ Matt *made a push at* the finish but it wasn't enough. マットは決勝に向かってつき進んだが, それだけでは十分ではなかった.

2 総攻撃する ▪ The enemy *made a push* on the western front. 敵は西部戦線を総攻撃してきた.

push and go がんばり ▪ He has plenty of *push and go*. 彼はひどくがんばりやだ.

put to the [***a***] ***push*** →come to the PUSH.

when [***until***] ***it comes to the push***/***when*** [***if***] ***push comes to shove*** いざという時になると[なるまで] ▪ He seemed a satisfactory man *until it came to the push*. 彼はいざという時になるまでは申し分のない男のように見えた.

with one push ひと押しで ▪ He opened the gate *with one push*. 彼はひと押しで木戸を開けた.

push[2] /pʊʃ/ 動 ***be pushed for*** …に窮している (=be PRESSed for) ▪ I *am* a little *pushed for* time [money]. 私は少し時間[金]に窮している.

be pushing 40 [***50,*** etc.] 《口》 そろそろ40 [50, など]歳に手が届く ▪ He *is pushing* 65. 彼はそろそろ65歳だ. ☞通例40歳以上について言う.

must [***should***] ***be pushing along*** 《英口》 そろそろ帰らなくては ▪ It's getting late. I think I *should be pushing along*. 遅くなってきた. そろそろ帰らなくちゃ.

push *oneself* **1** 自分を売り込む ▪ You have to *push yourself* if you want to be a success. 成功したければ自分を売り込む必要がある.

2 努力する, がんばる ▪ Don't *push yourself* too hard. あんまりがんばりすぎないように.

push and shove 押し合いへし合いする ▪ I had to *push and shove* to get onto a train. 電車に乗るために押し合いへし合いしなければならなかった.

push back the limits [***frontiers, boundaries***] 新しい発見をする, より良い方法を見つける ▪ They're trying to *push back the limits* of science and technology. 彼らは科学技術に関する新しい発見に努めているところだ. ☞境界[限界]を押し戻すとは, 最先端を押し進めることになる.

push *a person's* ***buttons*** →press a person's BUTTONs.

push *one's* ***fortune*** せっせと財産をつくる ▪ It is high time for you to *push your fortune* in the world. 君はもう世へ出て財産作りに励んでいい頃だ.

push *oneself* ***forward*** 出しゃばる ▪ He never *pushes himself forward*. 彼は決して出しゃばらない.

push it 《口》 しつこくせがむ ▪ They say Tom's *pushing it* strong there. トムはあそこでしつこくせがん

でいるという話だ.

push** one's **luck →LUCK[1].

push open 押し開く ▪ She turned the key and *pushed open* the door. 彼女はかぎを回してドアを押し開いた.

push paper →PAPER[1].

push the bottle ボトルを回す ▪ Thomson could *push the bottle* like a regular bon vivant. トムスンは本式の美食家のようにボトルを回すことができた.

push the envelope →push (the edge of) the ENVELOPE.

push the panic button →hit the PANIC button.

***push things* [*it*]** 《口》やりすぎる, 言い過ぎる, 図に乗って無茶をする ▪ You certainly did not *push things* too far. 君がやりすぎてはいなかったのは確かだ.

push** a person **to* [*to** do*]/*push** a person **into 人をせき立ててさせる ▪ He *pushed* me *to* its completion [*to* complete it]. 彼は私をせき立ててそれを完成させた ▪ He *was pushed into* shoplifting. 彼はむりやりに万引きをやらされた.

push ... to the back of** one's **mind 何かいやなことを忘れようとする ▪ I tried to *push* the thought *to the back of my mind* and concentrated on swimming. それは考えないようにして泳ぎに集中した.

push* (*up*) *daisies →DAISY.

push** one's **wares 品物を押し売りする ▪ You must *push your wares* if you want better sales. 販売を更に伸ばしたければ品物を押し売りしないとだめだ.

push** one's **way (じゃま物を)押しのけて進む ▪ He *pushed his way* to the front of the crowd. 彼は人ごみを押しのけて先頭に進み出た.

push** one's **way forward 人を押しのけて前へ出る ▪ He got to the front by *pushing his way forward*. 彼は人を押しのけて前へ出た.

push** one's **way through (...を)押し分けて進む ▪ He *pushed his way through* (the crowd). 彼は(人込みを)押し分けて進んだ.

pussl(e)y /pʌ́sli/ 名 ***meaner than* [*as mean as*] *pussley*** 《米口》ひどく卑劣で ▪ They are *meaner than pussley*. 彼らはひどく卑劣だ ▪ He treated her *as mean as pussley*. 彼は彼女をひどく卑劣に取り扱った.

put /pʊt/ 動 ***be* (*hard, sore*(*ly*), *sadly, greatly*) *put to it*** 《口》(ひどく)困却する ▪ We *were hard put to it* to get it done in so short a time. 我々はそれをそんなに短時間にし終えるのにひどく困ってしまった.

can't put ... down (本)が下におけないほどおもしろい ▪ He *couldn't put* her latest book *down*. 彼は彼女の最新作がおもしろくて読み出したらやめられなかった.

***not know where to put** oneself* 気づまりである, 窮屈である ▪ I don't *know where to put myself* in the presence of the headmaster. 私は校長先生の前へ出ると気づまりです.

***not put it past** a person* →PAST.

put* (*a*) *spin on ...にある意味[解釈]を与える ▪ Arab leaders *put* positive *spin on* the UN resolution. アラブ諸国の指導者たちは国連決議を前向きに解釈している ▪ The chef has *put a* new *spin on* seafood dishes. そのシェフはシーフード料理に新しい趣向を凝らした.

put** oneself **about **1** (有名になるために)社交的[友好的]である ▪ She is always *putting herself about* at parties. 彼女はパーティーではいつも社交的に振舞っている.
2 《英口》(スポーツなどで)精力的である[精力的にプレーする] ▪ He *puts himself about* and is popular with the fans. 彼は果敢にプレーするのでファンに人気がある.
3 ＝PUT it about.

put** oneself **across (*to** a person*) 《英》(人)に理解させる, 分からせる ▪ He *put himself across* well at the meeting. 彼は会議の席で自分の考えを理解してもらった.

put ... down to experience (失敗などの経験)を今後にいかす ▪ You don't have to worry about it. Just *put* it *down to experience*. そのことは心配しなくていい. 今後の教訓にすればいいんだ.

put in a hard day 1日しっかり働く ▪ I *put in a hard day* and I'm very tired. 1日しっかり働いたので, とても疲れた.

put in an appearance (会合などに)ちょっと顔を出す ▪ I think you should at least *put in an appearance*. 君はせめてちょっとだけでも顔を出すべきだと思うが.

***put** oneself **in** a person's **place* [*shoes, position*]** 他人の身になってみる ▪ Try to *put yourself in his place* to feel his pain. 彼の痛みを感じるために彼の身になってみなさい.

put it 言う ▪ I don't know how to *put it*. どう言ってよいかわからない.

put it about しり軽である ▪ She is always *putting it about*. 彼女はいつもしり軽に振舞っている.

***put it across** a person* **1** 人をひどく非難する, とっちめる ▪ The boss *put it across* him properly. 社長は彼をしっかりとっちめた.
2 人をわけなく負かす ▪ We *put it across* them. 我々は彼らをわけなく負かしてやった.
3 人をだます; 人に仕返しをする ▪ You can't *put it across* me. 君は僕をだますことはできないよ.

***put it all over** a person* 《米口》人を断然しのぐ[負かす] ▪ There was one boy who could *put it all over* the other members. 他の連中を断然負かせる少年が一人いた.

***put it differently* [*another way*]** 別な言い方をする ▪ Or, to *put it another way*, what goes around, comes around. あるいは別な言い方をするなら, なるようにしかならないということだ ▪ Only one of them *puts it differently*. 彼らのうち一人だけが別な言い方をしている.

***put it into** a person* 《米口》人を懲らしめる, ののしる ▪ I *put it into* them about lying. 私は彼らが嘘をついたことで懲らしめてやった.

put it mildly 控え目な言い方をする ▪ That's *putting it* very *mildly*. それはとても控え目な言い方だね.

put it on 《口》 **1** 法外な値段を吹っかける, ぼる ▪ 200 dollars for that job! They know how to *put it on*! その仕事に200ドル出せって! ぼり方を心得ているもんだな!

2 (感情・苦悩を)誇張する, ほらを吹く ▪ It wasn't as hard as you claim; you're *putting it on*. 君が言うほど苦しいものじゃなかった. 君は大げさに言っているんだ.

3 ふりをする ▪ He is *putting it on*. 彼はふりをしている[ぶっている].

4 太る ▪ You're *putting it on* a bit, aren't you? 君は少し太ってきたじゃないか.

put it there 《口》(完全に同意した印に)握手する ▪ "*Put it there*, partner," and he held out a grimy hand. 「握手しよう, 相棒」と言って, 彼はよごれた手を差し出した.

put it to *a person* **1** (意見を促したり懇請をするために)人に質問する; に意見を述べる (*if, that*) ▪ He *put it to* me *if* I should like to read Spenser. 彼は私にスペンサーを読んでみたいかと質問した ▪ I *put it to* you *that* you were not there at the time. あなたは当時そこにいなかったと申しあげたい《弁護士の反対尋問》.

2 《米口》人を懲らしめる, ののしる (= PUT it into a person) ▪ The man has *put it to* daddy very hard. その男は父をこっぴどくののしった.

3 人に過度の負担をかける ▪ They *put it to* me, expecting me to do all the packing, loading and hauling. 社は私に過重労働をさせ, 荷造りから荷積み, 運搬まですべてが求められた.

4 人に非難を押しつける ▪ My parents didn't know who ate the pie so they *put it to* me. 両親は誰がパイを食べたかわからなかったので僕になすりつけた.

5 人をだます, ぺてんにかける; から不正な利益を得る ▪ The used-car dealer *put it to* the old couple. 中古車業者は老夫婦をだまして暴利をむさぼった.

put it up to *a person* 《米口》(責任・行動などを)人にすっかり任せる ▪ Let us *put it* all *up to* the governor. 知事にすっかり任せようではないか.

put *a person* **off** *his* **stride** [**stroke**] 《口》人の仕事の進捗(しんちょく)を乱す; 人を面くらわす, 狼狽させる ▪ He *was put off his stride* by telephone calls. 電話が度々かかってきて彼の仕事は進まなかった ▪ She *was put off her stroke* by his question. 彼女は彼の質問に面くらった.

put off the evil day [**hour**] いやなことを先に延ばす ▪ You'll gain nothing by *putting off the evil day*. いやなことを先に延ばしたってなんの得にもならない.

put *a person* **off the track** [**the trail**] = put a person off the SCENT.

put ... on one side →SIDE.

put one [**that**] **across** *a person* = PUT it across a person 3.

put [**get**] **one** [**a fast one, it, something**] **over on** *a person* 人をだます[かつぐ]; 人よりも一歩先んじる ▪ He is very shrewd; you can't *put one over on* him. 彼は抜け目がないので一杯くわせることはできない ▪ I couldn't *put anything over on* Richard. リチャードは全然だませなかった ▪ He tried to *put it over on* us, letting on he was just puzzled. 彼は全く見当がつかないようなふりをして, 我々をかつごうとした ▪ Looks to me like they tried to *get a fast one over on* me. どうも彼らは俺をかつごうとしたように思える.

put *oneself* **out** (他人のために)骨を折る (*to do*) ▪ He was willing to *put himself out to* help people. 彼は人を助けるために骨を惜しまなかった.

put *oneself* **over** (**to** *a person*) (人に)うまく伝える, 理解させる ▪ He *put himself over* at the interview. 彼は面接でわかってもらえた.

put paid to →PAY[2].

put the joke [**laugh**] **on** [**upon**] *a person* 《米口》人を笑いものにする ▪ They have come back and *put the laugh on* him. 彼らは戻ってきて彼を笑いものにした.

put the law on *a person* 《米口》人に訴訟を起こす ▪ If he dares to open a package of mine, I'll *put the law on* him! 彼が僕の荷物を開くようなまねをしたら, 訴訟を起こしてやる.

put the make on ...に言い寄る ▪ He *put the make on* one of his wife's friends. 彼は妻の友人の一人をくどいた.

put the phone down 受話器を置く, 電話を切る ▪ As soon as she heard his voice, she *put the phone down*. 彼の声が聞こえてきた途端に彼女は電話を切った.

put the phone down on *a person* ...が話している途中で受話器をおく ▪ Whenever I call, she *puts the phone down on* me. 僕が電話するといつも彼女は話の途中で電話を切る.

put the run on *a person* 《米口》人を追っ払う ▪ I was hopeful of *putting the run on* the fellow by telling him ghost stories. 私はその男に怪談をして追っ払ってやろうと考えていた.

put the word out 《口》噂[ニュース]を広める ▪ *Put the word out* that the meeting has been called off. 会合は中止になったとみんなに伝えてくれ.

put this [**that**] **and that together/put two and two together** あれこれ考え合わせて結論を出す ▪ Young as I was, I also could *put that and that together*. 青二才だったが, 私もあれこれを考え合わせて結論を出すことはできた.

put *a person* **through it** 《口》人をひどく扱う ▪ Our sergeant *put* us all *through it*. 軍曹は我々全員をひどく扱った.

put *a person* **through school** [**university, college,** etc.] 人を助けて学校[大学, など]を卒業させる ▪ Many parents are wondering how they're going to *put* their children *through college*. 多くの親が子供を援助して大学を卒業させるにはどうすればよいかと思案している.

put *a person* **through the wringer** 〚主に受身で〛...を苦境におく ▪ The victim's family *was*

P

once again *put through the wringer*. 犠牲者の家族は再び苦境に追い込まれていた.

put *oneself* ***to*** [***into***] …に身を入れる, に打ちこむ ▪ He *put himself to* [*into*] the study of law. 彼は法律の勉強に身を入れた.

put *oneself* ***up*** 立候補する (*for*) ▪ He decided to *put himself up for* that seat. 彼はその議席を求めて立候補することにした.

put up a fight [***struggle***] ***against*** …と戦う ▪ She was the first to *put up a fight against* the ironclad rules of the Board. 彼女が委員会の厳しい規則に戦いをいどんだ最初の人間だった.

put up or shut up 《口》金を出すかそれとも黙っているか; はっきり言うか文句を言わないか ▪ The time will come when we shall have to *put up or shut up*. 我々がはっきり言うか文句を言わないかのどちらかにしなければならない時がやって来よう.

Put 'em up! 《口》両手をあげろ《銃でおどす言葉》.

stay put →STAY[2].

to put it no higher 誇張せずに言って, 掛け値なしに ▪ He is a remarkable novelist, *to put it no higher*. 彼は掛け値なしに, すばらしい小説家だ.

would not put it past *a person* ***to…*** 《口》人が…をやりかねないと思う ▪ I *wouldn't put it past* him *to* do that. 彼ならそうしかねないと思う ▪ I *wouldn't put it past* him *to* give all his money away. 彼なら自分の金を全部人にやってしまいかねないと思う.

putty /pʌ́ti/ 名 ***as soft as putty in*** *a person's* ***hands*** 人に非常に従順な, 進んで希望をかなえる ▪ He'll be *as soft as putty in your hands* if you give him a ticket for a concert. 彼にコンサートのチケットをやれば, なんでも言うことを聞いてくれるよ.

deserve a putty medal パテの勲章に値する《わずかな奉仕に対する皮肉なねぎらい言葉》 ▪ Really, you *deserve a putty medal* for your thoughtfulness. 全く君のご配慮にはパテの勲章でも差し上げないといかんな.

like putty in *a person's* ***hands*** (人の)全く言いなりになって ▪ He's *like* so much *putty in their hands*. 彼らの手中では彼は全くの言いなりだ.

put-up /pʊ́tʌ̀p/ 形 ***a put-up job*** 《英口》予定のたくらみ, 作りごと, 八百長 ▪ The whole thing was *a put-up job*. 何から何まで仕組まれたたくらみだった.

puzzle[1] /pʌ́zəl/ 名 ***be in a puzzle*** 当惑している ▪ I *am in a puzzle* about his sudden death. 彼が突然死んだことで当惑しています.

like a (***jigsaw***) ***puzzle***/ ***like piecing together a puzzle*** 謎を解くようで ▪ Answering this question is *like piecing together a puzzle*. この問題を解くのは謎解きのようなものだ.

puzzle[2] /pʌ́zəl/ 動 ***puzzle*** *one's* ***way*** 迷いながら進む ▪ He *puzzled his way* through geometry. 彼は迷いながら幾何学を勉強していった.

Q

Q, q /kjuː/ 名 ***mind*** *one's* ***P's and Q's*** →P.

Q.T., q.t. /kjuːtíː/ 名 ***on the*** (***strict***) ***Q.T.*** [***q.t.***] 《俗》(ごく)内緒で ▪I told you *on the strict Q.T.* ごく内緒で教えてあげたのです ▪They have met several times *on the q.t.* 彼らは数回こっそり会った. ☞Q.T. は "quiet" の略.

quack /kwæk/ 名 ***a cyber quack*** (インターネット上で診断料をだまし取る)にせ医師 ▪Lots of Americans have gone to the so-called *cyber quacks* for healthcare advice. 大勢のアメリカ人が健康管理の助言を求めていわゆるネット上のにせ医師を訪れた.

quadruple /kwɑdrúːpəl|kwɔ́drʊpəl/ 形 ***quadruple*** (***of*** [***to***]) …の4倍の ▪The value of silver was *quadruple* what it is now. 銀の価値は現在の4倍だった.

quadruplicate /kwɑdrúːplɪkət|kwɔd-/ 名 ***in quadruplicate*** (同一文書を)4通にして ▪The letter was written *in quadruplicate.* その手紙は4通書かれていた.

quaff /kwɑf, kwæf|kwɔf/ 動 ***quaff*** *oneself* ***into*** ぐいぐい酒をあおって…の状態になる ▪He *quaffed himself into* drowsiness. 彼はぐいぐい酒をあおって眠くなった.

quagmire /kwǽgmàɪər|kwɔ́gmàɪə/ 名 ***in a quagmire*** 泥沼に陥って《比喩的にも》 ▪He is *in a quagmire*, and he knows it well. 彼は苦境に陥っていてしかもそのことをよく知っている.

quake /kweɪk/ 動 ***make*** *a person* ***quake in*** *his* ***boots*** [***shoes***] 人をおびえさせる, 身震いさせる ▪His thriller *made* me *quake in my boots.* 彼のスリラー小説は僕を身震いさせた.

quake in *one's* ***boots*** [***shoes***] (***like a leaf***) (木の葉のように)ひどくおびえる, 身震いする ▪The manager's angry voice had me *quaking in my boots.* 監督の怒った声で僕はひどくおびえてしまった.

qualification /kwɑ̀ləfəkéɪʃən|kwɔ̀l-/ 名 ***have one qualification*** 一つ欠けるものがある ▪His delight *had one qualification.* 彼の喜びには欠けるものが一つあった.

with qualifications 手かげんして ▪You must accept it *with* certain *qualifications.* それは多少手かげんして受けいれてくれなくてはいけない.

without (***any***) ***qualification*** 何の制限[条件, 手かげん]もなしに ▪You can accept his statement *without qualification.* 彼の言うことは無条件に受けいれてよい.

qualify /kwɑ́ləfàɪ|kwɔ́l-/ 動 ***qualify*** *oneself* ***for*** [***to*** *do*] …の[する]資格を身につける ▪I am *qualifying myself for* my new calling. 私は自分の新しい職業への資格を身につけつつある ▪He is *qualifying himself to* give lessons. 彼は教授をする資格を身につけているところだ.

qualify *a person* ***to*** *do* 人に…する資格がある ▪His experience *qualifies* him *to* become a section chief. 彼が課長の資格を得るのにこれまでの経験がものを言っている.

quality /kwɑ́ləti|kwɔ́l-/ 名 ***give a taste*** [***touch***] ***of*** *one's* ***quality*** 人に手腕・能力をちらと示す (cf. Sh., *Haml.* 2. 2. 452) ▪He *gave* me *a touch of his quality* by spearing a bird on the wing. 彼は飛ぶ鳥をやりで突いて手腕をちらと示した.

have quality すぐれている; 気品がある ▪The wine *has quality.* その酒はすぐれている ▪She *has quality* in every movement. 彼女の一つ一つの動きには気品がある.

have the defects of *one's* ***qualities*** →DEFECT.

qualm /kwɑːm/ 名 ***have no qualms about*** …に何のためらいも感じない ▪I *had no qualms about* asking him to do that for me. 彼にそれをしてくれるように頼むのに何のためらいも感じなかった.

have qualms about …に不安をいだく ▪I *had qualms about* letting her go there alone. 彼女を一人でそこへ行かせるのを不安に感じた.

quandary /kwɑ́ndəri|kwɔ́n-/ 名 ***in a quandary*** 《口》困惑して ▪I'm *in a quandary.* 私は困惑している ▪I was put *in a quandary.* 私は途方にくれてしまった.

quantity /kwɑ́ntəti|kwɔ́n-/ 名 ***a negligible quantity*** 数に入らない人[物], つまらない人[物] ▪Her husband is *a negligible quantity.* 彼女の夫はつまらない人物だ.

a quantity of 多量の, 多数の ▪There were *a quantity of* people in the room. 部屋にはかなりの数の人がいた.

an imaginary quantity 実在しない人[物] ▪This Holy Roman Empire was becoming *an imaginary quantity.* この神聖ローマ帝国は実在しないものになりつつあった. ☞「虚量」が原義.

an unknown quantity 未知数の人[物] ▪His bravery is *an unknown quantity.* 彼の勇気は未知数だ. ☞「未知量[数]」が原義.

any quantity (***of***) (…の)いくらでも ▪I have *any quantity of* them. それはいくらでも持っている.

in quantities [***quantity***] たくさんに, 多量に ▪Fish are caught *in* great [large] *quantities.* 魚は大量に取れる.

quantities of 多数の, 多量の ▪We've had *quantities of* rain this summer. この夏には雨がたくさん降った ▪There were *quantities of* girls. 少女たちが大勢いた.

quantum /kwɑ́ntəm|kwɔ́n-/ 名 ***quantum***

leap/《米》***quantum jump*** (知識・方法の)劇的な進歩 (*forward, from*) ▪ The election of a female president is a *quantum leap forward* for sexual equality. 女性の大統領を選ぶことは，男女平等への劇的な前進である ▪ Every creative act requires a *quantum jump from* one pattern of thinking to an entirely new one. 何にせよ創造的な行為をしようとすると一つのものの考え方から全く新しいものの考え方への劇的な進歩が必要である.

quarantine /kwɔ́:rəntì:n|kwɔ́r-/ 名 ***in*** [***out of***] ***quarantine*** (悪疫流行防止のため)隔離されて[隔離を解かれて] ▪ The children with measles were *in quarantine* for a week. はしかの子供たちは一週間隔離されていた.

quarrel[1] /kwɑ́rəl|kwɔ́rəl/ 名 ***fasten*** [***fix***] ***a quarrel on*** [***upon***] *a person* 人にけんかを吹っかける ▪ He *fastened a quarrel on* me one day. ある日彼は私にけんかを吹っかけてきた.

fight in a good quarrel 正義の争いをする ▪ We are *fighting in a good quarrel*. 我々は正義の争いをやっているのだ.

fight *a person's* ***quarrel*** (***for*** *him*)/ ***espouse*** *a person's* ***quarrel*** 人のけんかに加勢する ▪ He's always *fighting other people's quarrels*. 彼はいつも人のけんかに加勢してばかりいる.

find quarrel in a straw ちょっとしたことにもとがめ立てする (cf. Sh., *Haml*. 4. 4. 55) ▪ He is not one to *find quarrel in a straw*. 彼はちょっとしたことでとがめ立てするような人間ではない. ☞「わらしべ1本にけんかの種を見いだす」が原義.

have a quarrel against [***with***] ...に苦情がある ▪ I *have* no *quarrel against* [*with*] him. 彼に何も苦情はない.

have a quarrel with *a person* 人とけんかをする (*about*) ▪ I *had a quarrel with* him *about* a matter. あることで彼とけんかをした.

make up *one's* [***a***] ***quarrel*** 仲直りする ▪ They *made up their quarrel*. 彼らは仲直りした.

pick a quarrel →PICK[2].

take up *a person's* ***quarrel*** 人のけんかを買って出る ▪ He *takes up no man's quarrel* but his own. 彼は人のけんかは買って出ない.

quarrel[2] /kwɑ́rəl|kwɔ́rəl/ 動 ***A bad workman quarrels with his tools.*** 《諺》へたな職人は道具に難癖をつける,「能書は筆を選ばず」.

quarrel with *one's* ***bread and butter*** (腹立ちまぎれに)自分の職業を捨てる ▪ It's not wise to *quarrel with your bread and butter*. 自分の職業を捨てるのは賢明ではない.

quart /kwɔ:rt/ 名 ***put a quart into a pint pot*** (大きい物を小さい器に入れるような)無理なことをする ▪ It is no use sending that stupid boy to another school. One cannot *put a quart into a pint pot*. あの愚かな少年を別の学校へやってもむだです. 無理なことはできませんからね.

quarter[1] /kwɔ́:rtər/ 名 ***a bad*** [***nasty,*** etc.] ***quarter of an hour*** 不愉快なひと時，気まずい思い ▪ I hope he will have *a* rather *nasty quarter of an hour*. あの男が少々気まずい思いをすればいいと思う. ☞ F un mauvais quart d'heure のなぞり.

ask [***beg***] ***for quarter***/***cry quarter*** (戦敗者・捕虜が)命ごいする ▪ The beaten enemy *asked for quarter*, and were well treated. 負けた敵は命ごいをして，良いあしらいを受けた. ☞「捕虜が宿所を求める」が原義.

at close quarters 接近して，肉薄して ▪ They fought *at close quarters*. 彼らは白兵戦を行なった.

at the first quarter [***at three quarters***] (月が)上[下]弦で ▪ The moon is *at the first quarter*. 月は上弦だ ▪ There was a moon *at three quarters*. 下弦の月が出ていた.

beat up the quarters of →BEAT[2].

cry quarter →ask for QUARTER.

do [***win***] ***the quarter*** 4分の1マイルを走る[で優勝する] ▪ He has *done the quarter* in 50 seconds. 彼は4分の1マイルを50秒で走った.

from a good [***reliable***] ***quarter*** 確かな筋から ▪ I had the news *from a good quarter*. そのニュースは確かな筋から聞いた.

from every quarter/***from all quarters*** 四方八方から ▪ People gathered *from all quarters*. 各方面から人が集まった.

give [***show***] ***quarter*** 助命する，情け容赦する ▪ I'll *give* no *quarter* and take none. 私は情け容赦しないし，してももらわない. ☞「捕虜に宿所を与える」が原義.

go into [***take up***] ***winter quarters*** 冬期の宿泊をする ▪ This year we shall *take up winter quarters* in Cairo. 今年はカイロで冬期の宿泊をする.

go the quarter (時計が)15分を打つ ▪ It has *gone the quarter*. 時計が15分を打った.

in every quarter/***in all quarters*** 至る所で ▪ I hear the same complaint *in every quarter*. 至る所で同じ苦情が聞かれる.

in its last quarter (月が)かけ始めて ▪ The moon was *in its last quarter*. 月はかけ始めていた.

in (***the***) ***high***(***est***) ***quarters*** (最)上層部では ▪ The suggestion did not find favor *in the highest quarters*. 提案は最上層部に歓迎されなかった.

live in close quarters 狭苦しい所にごちゃごちゃと住む ▪ They were *living in close quarters*. 彼らは狭苦しい所にごちゃごちゃと住んでいた.

show quarter →give QUARTER.

take up *one's* ***quarters*** **1** (ある場所に)落ち着く，滞在する (*at, in, with*) ▪ He *took up his quarters at* a hotel. 彼はホテルに落ち着いた.

2 《海》部署につく ▪ Officers and men at once *took up their quarters*. 上級船員も水夫もすぐ部署についた.

take up winter quarters →go into winter QUARTERs.

What quarter is the wind in? 風向きはどうか《比喩的にも》 ▪ *What quarter is the wind in?* —It is in the right quarter. 風向きはどうですか?—

風向きはよろしい.

win the quarter →do the QUARTER.

quarter[2] /kwɔ́ːrtər/ 動 ***quarter*** *oneself* ***on*** [***with***] (人)の所に宿を取る ▪ I *quartered myself on* him. 私は彼の所に泊まった.

quarter (*soldiers*) ***on*** [***upon***] (兵)を…の所に宿営させる ▪ He *quartered* his men *on* the villagers. 彼は兵士を村人たちの家に宿営させた.

quarterback /kwɔ́ːrtərbæ̀k/ 名 ***a Monday morning quarterback*** →MONDAY.

quarter-deck /kwɔ́ːrtərdèk/ 名 ***come the quarter-deck over*** …に上役風を吹かす ▪ If he thinks he can *come the quarter-deck over* me, he's making a mistake. あの男が僕に上役風を吹かせると思っているのならそれはまちがいだ. ☞quarter-deck (後甲板)は士官のいる所.

queen[1] /kwiːn/ 名 ***fit for a queen*** 実にすばらしい ▪ My dear, you've provided a meal *fit for a queen*. お前, 実にすばらしいごちそうを作ったじゃないか.

Queen Anne is dead. 《皮肉》それは旧聞に属する ▪ Oh, *Queen Anne's dead*! Tell us something fresh. ああ, それは旧聞に属するよ. 何か新しいニュースを教えてくれ. ☞Queen Anne が1714年に死んでいるところから.

to the Queen's taste →to the King's TASTE.

turn Queen's evidence → turn King's EVIDENCE.

queen[2] /kwiːn/ 動 ***queen it*** 女王として君臨する, 女王然とふるまう ▪ Josephine was *queening it* at the party. ジョゼフィーヌはそのパーティーで女王然とふるまっていた ▪ Mary likes to *queen it* over her friends. メアリーは友だちに対してお高くとまりたがる.

queer[1] /kwɪər/ 形 ***a queer fish*** [***bird, card, cove***] 変わり者 ▪ He's *a queer cove*, and no mistake! 彼は変わり者だ, 確かに.

be queer for 《米口》…が大好きだ, に惚れている ▪ I'*m queer for* Tom. 私, トムにいかれているの.

be queer in the head 頭が少しおかしい ▪ He *is queer in the head*. 彼は頭が少しおかしい.

feel [***look***] ***queer*** 《口》気分が悪い[ように見える] ▪ I do *feel queer*. I'll sit down for a while. ほんとに気分が悪い. 少し座っていよう.

go queer 少し気が変になる ▪ He has *gone queer*. 彼は少し気が変になった.

in Queer Street 《俗》(借金・病気などで)困って ▪ I am landed *in Queer Street*. 僕は困っているんだ. ☞おそらく, 破産者の法廷のあるロンドンの Carey Street から.

on the queer 不正直で; にせ金を作って ▪ Dick may have been *on the queer* all right. ディックは確かに正直ではなかったのかもしれない.

shove (***the***) ***queer*** 《米》にせ金をつかませる ▪ We are on the lookout for those who *shove the queer*. 我々はにせ金をつかませる連中を警戒している.

queer[2] /kwɪər/ 動 ***queer*** *oneself* 信用をなくす ▪ He has *queered himself* with the professor. 彼は教授の信用をなくしてしまった.

queer *a person's* ***pitch*** → queer the PITCH for a person.

quench /kwentʃ/ 動 ***quench the smoking flax*** 才能を伸ばすのを妨げる, せっかくの発展を中途で押さえる (《聖》*Isa*. 42. 3) ▪ How many parents do you suppose *quench the smoking flax*? 才能を伸ばすのを妨げる親がどれほどいるか知っているか.

quencher /kwéntʃər/ 名 ***a modest quencher*** 《口》ちょっと1杯 ▪ I am still open to *a modest quencher*. まだちょっと1杯はやれます.

query /kwíəri/ 名 ***look a query at*** …をけげんそうに見る ▪ He *looked a query at* me. 彼は私をけげんそうに見た.

quest /kwest/ 名 ***in quest of*** …を求めて[尋ねて] ▪ They went out to Australia *in quest of* gold. 彼らは金を探しにオーストラリアへ出かけた.

question[1] /kwéstʃən/ 名 ***a burning question*** 緊急の議題[質問] ▪ Here's *a burning question* for you. Can you grow cabbage on Mars? 君に緊急に質問がある. 火星でキャベツが栽培できるかい.

a good question 難問 ▪ That's *a good question* with no clear answer. そいつは難問で明確な答えはない.

a question mark 疑わしい[不確かな]こと ▪ There's *a* big *question mark* over the future of the whole project. この企画全体の先の見通しについて大きな疑問点がある ▪ *A question mark* hangs over the government's ability to govern. 政府の統治能力について疑問符がつきまとっている.

(***and***) ***no question***(***s***) ***asked*** 無条件で, 異議なく ▪ If you don't like the coat, the shop will take it back and refund your money, *no questions asked*. コートがお気に召さなければ, 当店が無条件で返品をお受けし代金を払い戻しいたします.

Ask a silly question (***and you'll get a silly answer***)***!*** 愚問だね《分かりきったことを聞かれた場合の返事》.

Ask me no questions and I'll tell you no lies. そんなに詮索しないでほしい.

be a question of time (遅かれ早かれ必ず起きる)時間の問題である ▪ Personalizing your PC *is a question of time*. パソコンを個人の好みに合わせるようになるのは時間の問題である.

(***be***) ***an open question***/(***be***) ***open to question*** 異論が多い, 未解決である, 議論の余地のある問題(である) ▪ Whether meat is bad for you or not *is open to question*. 肉が体に悪いかどうかは異論が多い ▪ It's *an open question* whether coffee is good or bad. コーヒーがよいか悪いかは簡単には決められない ▪ Today, the cause of Type 2 diabetes *is* still *an open question*. 今日, 2型糖尿病の原因はまだ未解決の問題だ.

beg the question →BEG.

beside the question 問題をはずれて[それて] ▪ Your answer is *beside the question*. 君の答えはピントがずれている.

Q

beyond (all) question 疑いもなく, むろん ▪ *Beyond all question* you are right. むろん君の言う通りだ ▪ His honesty is *beyond question.* 彼の正直さは疑いの余地がない.

bring ... into question …に疑いをはさむ ▪ It is only natural that the system should *be brought into question.* その方式に疑義が出るのはごく当然だ.

call ... in question **1** (陳述など)に疑いをはさむ, 異議を唱える ▪ I *call in question* the magistrate's right to send that man to prison. 私は治安判事にあの男を刑務所に送る権利があるかどうか疑わしく思う ▪ His conduct *was called in question.* 彼の行為に異議が唱えられた.
2 裁く (《聖》 *Acts* 19. 40) ▪ Socrates *was called in question,* and had sentence of death pronounced against him. ソクラテスは裁かれて死刑を宣告された.

come into question 問題になる, 論議される ▪ After dinner we talked till Mr. Brown *came into question.* 夕食後おしゃべりしていてブラウン氏のことが問題になった.

in question **1** 問題になって ▪ The dates are not *in question.* 年代は問題になっていない.
2 問題の, 当の ▪ I don't think I have ever seen the lady *in question.* 私は問題の女性を見たことがないと思います.
3 疑われて ▪ His honesty is not *in question.* 彼が正直であることに疑いはない.

it is no [not a] question →there is no QUESTION.

make no question of [about, but that] …を疑わない ▪ I *make no question of* it. 私はそれを疑わない ▪ I *make no question but that* it is so. むろんそうだと思う.

out of question 疑いもなく, むろん ▪ *Out of question,* he ought to have the position. むろん彼がその地位を与えられるべきだ.

out of the question (不可能で)問題にならない, 考えられない ▪ His objection is *out of the question.* 彼の反対は問題にならない ▪ Retreat was now *out of the question.* 退却はもう考えられないことだった.

past question 疑いもなく ▪ *Past question,* this is the better piece of work. 疑いもなくこちらの方がすぐれた作品だ.

pepper** a person **with questions 矢継ぎ早に質問を浴びせる ▪ The students *peppered* him *with questions.* 学生たちは彼に矢継ぎ早に質問した.

place [have] a question mark over (特に地位・役職)に疑問を抱かせる ▪ His past behavior *places a question mark over* his international future. 彼の過去のふるまいは国際的な将来性に疑問を抱かせるものだ.

pop the question →POP².

***put a question to** a person* 人に質問する ▪ Go and *put that question to* him. 行ってそんなことは彼に聞け.

put the question (議長が)決を採る ▪ That being so, I shall *put the question.* そういう次第ですから, 決を採ります.

put ... to the question **1** (人)を拷問にかける ▪ He *was put to the question.* 彼は拷問を受けた.
2 (結論を出すために)…を討議に付す ▪ The important matter will *be put to the question.* その重要問題は討議に付されるだろう.

(That's a) good question! **1** 《口》 〚good に強勢を置いて〛 (答えに窮して)そうですねえ, どうですかねえ ▪ What's the secret of your youth?—*That's a good question!* あなたの若さの秘訣は?—そうですねえ.
2 〚question に強勢を置いて〛 いい質問ですね ▪ Why are you so energetic and active?—*That's a good question!* なぜあなたはそんなに精力的で意欲的なんですか?—いい質問だね.

the big question 重大な問題点, 大問題 ▪ *The big question* is how to use technology to enhance learning. 大問題は学術を高めるためにいかに科学技術を使うべきかということだ.

the question is 問題は…だ ▪ *The question is* who is going to be chairman. 問題は誰が議長になるかだ.

the 64,000 [sixty-four thousand] dollar question 《口》 最も重要な問題 ▪ *The 64,000 dollar question* is how and when to do it. 最も重要な問題は, いつどのようにそれをするかだ. ☞ 第二次大戦中アメリカの CBS のクイズ番組の最高の賞金が sixty-four thousand dollar question と呼ばれていたことから.

there is no question/it is no [not a] question 疑いはない (*about, that, but that*) ▪ *There is no question about* it. それには疑問の余地はない ▪ *It is no question that* he did it on purpose. 彼がそれを故意にしたことに疑いはない ▪ *There is no question but that* he will succeed. 彼が成功することは疑いがない.

with no questions asked 誰にも知られずに, とがめられずに ▪ If you're not 100% satisfied, we'll send you a complete refund *with no questions asked.* もし100%ご満足でなければ, 私どもはどなたにも知られることなく全額払い戻させていただきます.

without question 疑いなく, むろん ▪ He is *without question* a great genius. 彼は疑いもなく大天才だ ▪ He will obey *without question.* 彼はむろん従うだろう.

question² /kwéstʃən/ 動 ***I do not question that [but (that)]*** …ということを私は疑わない ▪ *I do not question but* you'll do him justice. 私は君が彼を公平に扱ってくれることを疑いません.

queue /kjuː/ 名 ***form a queue*** 列を作る ▪ People *formed a queue* for the show. 人々はそのショーを見るために列を作って並んだ.

in a queue 列をなして ▪ We stood *in a queue.* 我々は列をなしてたたずんだ.

jump the queue 《英口》 **1** 列に割り込む ▪ To attempt to *jump the queue* is to court disaster. 列に割り込もうとすると, 災難を招くことになる.

2 順番を待たずに得ようとする ▪ They are *jumping the queue* and seeking a special arrangement. 彼らは順番を待たずに特別の取り計らいを求めている.

quick /kwɪk/ 形名副 ***a quick one*** 《口》ちょっと1杯(の酒) ▪ What do you say to *a quick one*? ちょっと1杯どうだい.

(***as***) ***quick as lightning*** [***a flash, a wink, thought***] 電光石火のように, たちまち, すばやく, 瞬く間に ▪ *Quick as thought*, I grasped it. 瞬く間に私はそれをつかんだ ▪ Fire away *as quick as a wink*. 電光石火のようにどしどし射て ▪ *Quick as a wink*, the thief took her purse. 泥棒は彼女のハンドバッグをさっとひったくった.

Be quick (***about it***)***!*** 早くしろ ▪ Get your clothes on; please *be quick!* 服を着ろ. どうか急いでくれ!

be quick at (勉強など)が早い ▪ He *is quick at* figures. 彼は計算が早い.

be quick of …の点で早い ▪ He *is quick of* foot. 彼は足が速い ▪ He *is quick of* belief [understanding]. 彼はすぐ信じこむ[理解が早い].

be quick to *do* …するのが早い ▪ He *is quick to* make up his mind. 彼は決心するのが早い.

cut to the quick 人の感情をひどく傷つける ▪ He *was cut to the quick* by her malicious criticism. 彼は彼女の意地悪な非難にひどく心を傷つけられた.

have (***got***) ***a quick temper*** →TEMPER[1].

in double quick time 《口》大至急 ▪ You'll have to get there *in double quick time*. 君はそこへ大至急行かねばならないだろう.

look (***like***) ***a million quick*** = feel like a MILLION (dollars).

of quick parts 悟りの早い, 機敏な ▪ As he is a man *of* very *quick parts*, his conversation is intensely interesting. 彼はとても機敏な人だから, 会話がとてもおもしろい.

quick and dirty 《主に米口》早かろう悪かろうの, 粗製濫造の ▪ The FBI often resorts to a *quick and dirty* job that wasn't done right. FBI は往々にしてきちんとなされない早かろう悪かろうの手段に訴えたりする.

quick in [***at***] ***the uptake*** →be quick on the UPTAKE.

quick off the mark →MARK[1].

quick on the draw →DRAW[1].

(***the***) ***quick and*** (***the***) ***dead*** 生者と死者 (《聖》*Acts* 10. 42) ▪ The uproar was enough to rouse both (*the*) *quick and* (*the*) *dead*. その騒ぎときたら, 生者と死者との双方を目ざめさせるほどのものであった.

to the quick **1** 生き肉の所まで, 深く ▪ He cut his fingernails *to the quick*. 彼は深づめをした ▪ He was wounded *to the quick*. 彼は大けがをした.
2 急所[痛い所]まで ▪ His words cut [wounded, stung] me *to the quick*. 彼の言葉は痛切にこたえた.
3 徹頭徹尾 ▪ He is a Tory *to the quick*. 彼は徹頭徹尾保守派だ.
4 生きたように, 生き写しに ▪ It is painted *to the quick*. それは生き写しに描かれている.

quicksilver /kwíksìlvər/ 名 ***have quicksilver in*** *one's* ***veins*** 《口》気が早い ▪ You *have quicksilver in your veins* for a certainty. 君は確かに気の早い人だ. ☞水銀の動きが早いことから.

quid /kwɪd/ 名 ***be quids in*** 《英口》幸運だ, (思いのほか)儲かっている ▪ If he will help you, you'll *be quids in*. 彼が助けてくれれば上首尾だ ▪ Two cheeky punters thought they *were quids in* when the New Year dawned. 二人の小生意気な投機家は新年が明けて思いのほか儲かったと思った.

(***like***) ***a million*** (***dollars*** [***bucks,*** 《英》***quid***]) →feel like a MILLION (dollars).

quiet /kwáɪət/ 形名 (***as***) ***quiet as a mouse*** [***lamb***] 非常に静かな, ひどくおとなしい ▪ Rebecca's rights once obtained, we will be *as quiet as mice*. レベッカの権利がいったん得られれば, 私たちはとてもおとなしくします.

(***as***) ***quiet as the grave*** = (as) SILENT as the grave.

at quiet 平静に, 平穏に ▪ The country remained *at quiet*. その国は依然として平穏であった.

fall quiet 静かになる, 黙る ▪ They all *fell quiet*. 彼らはみな静かになった.

have a quiet dig at …を遠回しに当てつける ▪ I *had a quiet dig at* him. 彼を遠回しに当てつけた.

in quiet 平穏に ▪ He settled down there to end his days *in quiet*. 彼は余生を平穏に過ごすためにそこに落ち着いた.

in *one's* ***quiet way*** 控え目ながら ▪ *In his quiet way* he is very proud of his daughter. 控え目ながら彼は娘を大そう誇りにしている.

keep ... quiet **1** …を秘密にしておく ▪ Please *keep* it *quiet*. どうかそれは秘密にしておいてください.
2 (子供など)をおとなしくさせておく ▪ She tried to *keep* her child *quiet*. 彼女は子供をおとなしくさせておこうと努めた.

on the quiet 《口》秘密に, こっそりと (→on the (strict) Q.T.) ▪ They got married *on the quiet*. 彼らは秘かに結婚した.

quietus /kwaɪíːtəs/ 名 ***get*** [***obtain***] *one's* ***quietus*** 死ぬ ▪ Some *obtain their quietus* without any pain at all. 全く苦しまずに死ぬ人もいる.

give a [***the***] ***quietus to*** …を絶滅する ▪ This discovery *gave the quietus to* theories of common origin. この発見は一般大衆から出た諸説の根を絶った.

give *a person his* ***quietus*** **1** 人を殺す ▪ It was a blow from a dagger that *gave* him *his quietus*. 彼にとどめを刺したのは短剣の一撃だった.
2 人を厄介払いする ▪ Tell him we'll send for the police; that will *give* him *his quietus*. 警察を呼びにやると言ってやるがいい. それで彼を厄介払いできるさ.

quill /kwɪl/ 名 ***draw*** *one's* ***quill against*** → DRAW one's pen against.

drive the quill ペンを走らせる, 書く ▪ He *drives the quill* for a slender wage. 彼はわずかな賃金かせ

Q

ぎのためにもの書きをする.

the pure quill 本物, 極上物 ▪ The fine old wine was *the pure quill.* その上等の古いワインは極上物だった.

quire /kwáɪər/ 名 ***by the quire*** (紙を24枚の)一帖ずつ ▪ They sell paper *by the quire.* 紙は一帖ずつ売られている.

in quires ばらで, 製本せずに ▪ I gave my book to the office *in quires.* 私は自著を製本せずに事務所へ提出した.

quirk /kwəːrk/ 名 ***a quirk of fate*** 運命の気まぐれ, 予想外の不思議 ▪ I remarried my husband's brother. It was *a* dirty *quirk of fate.* 私は夫の弟と再婚したの. それは運命のいやないたずらだったわ.

quit[1] /kwɪt/ 形 ***be quit for*** ...だけですむ ▪ He *was quit for* a fall on the grass. 彼は芝生の上でころんだだけですんだ.

be [***get***] ***quit of*** ...を免れる ▪ We *are* well *quit of* him. あの男を厄介払いしてよかった ▪ Thank goodness I'*m quit of* my debts at last. ありがたいことにとうとう負債を完済した.

go quit 放免される ▪ The others can *go quit.* 他の者は放免だ.

quit[2] /kwɪt/ 動 ***have*** (***a***)***... that*** (***just***) ***won't quit*** 《俗》とてもすばらしい...を持っている ▪ He *has* vocabulary *that just won't quit*, and loves to tell stories. 彼はとてもすばらしい語彙を持っていて物語を語るのが大好きだ.

have [***give***] ***notice to quit*** 立ちのきの通告を受ける[する] ▪ We've *had notice to quit.* 我々は立ちのくように通告された ▪ I've *given* my driver *notice to quit.* 運転手に暇を出すと通告した.

quit hold of ...を手放す ▪ Don't *quit hold of* it. それを手放すな.

quit *oneself* ***of*** ...を厄介払いする ▪ I cannot *quit myself of* these feelings. 私はそういう感情を払いのけることができない.

quit while *one* ***is ahead*** うまくいっているものに手をつけない, すでに完成しているものを改良しようとしない (= let WELL (《米》 enough) alone) ▪ I think we should just *quit while* we *are ahead.* 我々はうまくいっているものに手をつけるべきではないと思う.

quite /kwaɪt/ 副 ***be quite the thing*** → be (all, quite) the THING.

isn't quite 《英口》あまり紳士[淑女]とは言えない ▪ He *isn't quite.* 彼はあまり紳士とは言えない.

not quite 全く...とはいえない ▪ It is *not quite* proper. それは全く適当とはいえない.

quite a bit 《口》= QUITE a little.

quite a bit of 《口》とてもたくさんの..., 相当の... ▪ We had *quite a bit of* snow last night. ゆうべ雪がとてもたくさん降った ▪ I have *quite a bit of* work to do today. 今日は仕事がたくさんある.

quite a few 《口》たくさんの ▪ There were *quite a few* students absent from class today. きょうはたくさんの学生が欠席していた.

quite a little 《口》 **1** とてもたくさん(の) ▪ He knows *quite a little* about it. 彼はそのことについてはずいぶん知っている.
2 大いに; たびたび ▪ I was drunk *quite a little* last year. 去年はよく酔っ払った.

quite a lot 《口》かなり多く, 相当量 ▪ We've had *quite a lot* of rain this year. 今年はかなりたくさん雨が降った.

Quite so. → Just SO.

quite some [***long***] ***time*** かなり長い間 ▪ *Quite some time* has passed since I last saw you. この前お会いしてから大分時間が経ちましたね.

quite something 《口》大したもの ▪ His library is *quite something.* 彼の蔵書は大したものだ.

quite the best [***the worst,*** etc.] 《口》絶対最良の[最悪の, など] ▪ It was *quite the best* film I've ever seen. 今まで見た中で実に最良の映画だった.

quite too とても; あまりにも ▪ Your offer is *quite too* low. お申し出はあまりにも安すぎます ▪ Going to his house again would have been *quite too* dismal. 彼の家へまた行くなどとても憂鬱なことだったろうね.

Where you've quite finished!/ When you are quite ready! 《口》もうおやめなさい《相手がしていることをやめさせる言葉》.

quits /kwɪts/ 形 ***be quits with*** ...と五分五分だ; に仕返しする ▪ I *am quits with* you. これで君とは五分五分だ ▪ I will *be quits with* him some day. いつかあの男に仕返ししてやる.

call it quits **1** = call it a DAY.
2 あきらめる, 勝負なしにする ▪ Neither side having a clear advantage, they decided to *call it quits.* 双方とも明確な勝ち目がないので, 引き分けにすることに決めた.

cry quits 五分五分だと言う; 勝負なしにする (*with*) ▪ On the young man making an apology, the old man had been content to *cry quits.* 若者がわびを言ったので老人は甘んじて勝ち負けなしにした.

double or quit(***s***) → DOUBLE[1].

quittance /kwítəns/ 名 ***Omittance is no quittance.*** 催促せぬのは帳消しとは別 (cf. Sh., *A. Y. L.* 3. 5. 133) ▪ We do not press for payment, but *omittance is no quittance.* 我々は支払いを督促しないが, 催促せぬのは帳消しとは別のものだ.

quiver[1] /kwívər/ 名 ***have an arrow*** [***a shaft***] ***left in*** *one's* ***quiver*** まだ手段が尽きてはいない ▪ Never say die! We *have an arrow left in our quiver.* 弱音を吐くんじゃない. まだ手段が尽きたわけではない.

quiver full of children 大家族 (《聖》 *Ps.* 127. 5) ▪ Boyce was a man who had his *quiver full of children.* ボイスは大家族をかかえた男だった.

quiver[2] /kwívər/ 名 ***all of a quiver*** = all of a TREMBLE.

quod /kwɑd|kwɔd/ 名 ***in*** [***out of***] ***quod*** 《米俗》入獄[出獄]して ▪ He has been *in quod* for a fortnight. 彼は2週間入獄していた ▪ She's grudged me a hundred pound to get me *out of quod.* 彼女は私を出獄させる100ポンドをけちった.

☞quod は恐らく quadrangle「中庭を囲む建物」から.

quote /kwoʊt/ 動 ***Don't quote me.*** 私が言ったとは言わないでください ▪ *Don't quote me*, but I wouldn't put it past him. 私が言ったと言わないでほしいが, 彼ならやりかねないと思うね.

quote a price on [***for***] ...の相場を言う ▪ Shall we *quote a price on* the cloth? その生地の値段を言いましょうか.

quote, ..., unquote [《米》 ***end quote***] かっこ, ..., かっこ閉じ《文字にして引用符でくくられることを示す》 ▪ She said, *quote*, "I'll never give up," *end quote*. 彼女は(かっこ)「私, 決してあきらめないわ」(かっこ閉じ)と言った ▪ Our teacher said *quote*, "a certain number", *unquote* of the students were absent today. 先生はきょう欠席した生徒の数を(引用ですが)「若干名」だと言った.

R

R, r /ɑːr/ 名 ***the "r"* [*R*] *months*** 9月から4月までの8か月《月名に r を含み, カキ (oyster) が旬(しゅん)である季節》 ▪ Oysters are only in season in *the R months*. カキは9月から4月までしか旬ではない.

***the three R's* [*Rs*]** 読み・書き・算数《Reading, Writing, Arithmetic》 ▪ His lessons at school were limited to *the three R's*. 彼が学校で受けた授業は読み・書き・算数に限られていた.

rabbit[1] /rǽbət/ 名 **(*as*) *timid as a rabbit*** →TIMID.

breed like rabbits 《軽蔑》たくさんの子を産む ▪ Poor people often *breed like rabbits*. 貧しい人々は子だくさんだ.

like a rabbit caught in the headlights 取り乱してどうしてよいかわからなくて ▪ In the other games he played in he looked *like a rabbit caught in the headlights* of a car. 彼がプレーした他の試合では, 取り乱してなす術を知らないようだった.

pull* [*bring, produce*] *a rabbit out of the* [*a*] *hat (不可能と思えることを)魔法のようにやすやすと生み出す ▪ He finished writing a book like a conjurer *bringing a rabbit out of a hat*. 彼は手品師が魔法のようにやすやすとなにかを生み出すがごとく1冊の本を書き上げた.

work the rabbit's foot on 《米》…をだます, ひっかける ▪ They *worked the rabbit's foot on* him and skinned him of his money. 彼らは彼をだまして金をまきあげた.

rabbit[2] /rǽbət/ 動 **(*Oh,*) *rabbit it* [*him,* etc.]*!*** ちくしょう! ▪ *Oh, rabbit it!* I've forgotten my watch again. ええちくしょう! また時計を忘れた.

race[1] /reɪs/ 名 ***a one-horse race*** 勝ちレース ▪ His team made *a one-horse race* in Formula One last year. 昨年のF1では彼のチームが一人勝ちした.

***a race against time* [*the clock*]** →TIME[1].

a* [*the*] *race to the bottom 《経営》悪化地獄, 悪化の一途 ▪ What's happening in the world today is *a race to the bottom*. 今日, 世界中で起こっているのは悪化地獄だ.

be in* [*out of*] *the race 成功する見込みがある[ない] ▪ He *is in the race* for getting that post. 彼はその職にうまくありつく見込みがある.

hold a race 競走を行う ▪ Every year we *hold a race* from London to Brighton. 毎年我々はロンドンからブライトンまでのレースを開催する.

make the race 《米》立候補する ▪ He might perhaps consider *making the* Senate *race*. 彼はひょっとすると上院に出馬することを考えるかもしれない.

play the race card 人種差別的な発言をする[ことを書く] ▪ He was accused of often *playing the race card*. 彼は人種差別的な発言をたびたびしたことで非難された.

One's ***race is run.*** 寿命が尽きた ▪ *His race is* nearly *run*. 彼の寿命はほとんど尽きた.

ride a race 競馬に出る ▪ He *rode a* winning *race*. 彼は競馬に出て優勝した.

***run a race* (*with*)** …と競走する ▪ He *ran a race with* Death to save the drowning child. 彼は死との戦いの末おぼれる子を助けた.

Slow and steady wins the race. →SLOW.

The race is not to the swift. 足の速い者が勝つとはかぎらない (《聖》*Eccles*. 9. 11) ▪ Life had not taught him that *the race is not to the swift*. 足の速い者が勝つとはかぎらないということを人生で彼は学んでいなかった.

with a strong race 激しい急流をなして ▪ The tide set *with a strong race*. 潮が激しい急流をなしていた.

race[2] /reɪs/ 動 ***race against the clock* [*time*]** 時計[時間]と競争する, 急いで仕事をする ▪ You needn't *race against the clock*. 急いで仕事をしなくてもいい.

race** a person **off** his **feet 《口》人を立てなくなるまで走らせる ▪ He used to *race* me *off my feet*. 彼は私を立てなくなるまで走らせるのが常だった.

race to stand still 懸命に頑張る ▪ I'm *racing to stand still* but I'm so behind in my work. 懸命に頑張っているのだが, 仕事はずいぶん遅れている.

rack[1] /ræk/ 名 ***a* [*the*] *rack of bones*** 《米口》 **1** (魚の)骨 ▪ I saw *the rack of bones* of a large fish. 私は大きな魚の骨を見た.

2 やせこけた人[動物] ▪ She was but *a* mere *rack of bones*. 彼女はほんの骨と皮ばかりのような女性だった.

be on the rack **1** 苦心している, 張りつめている ▪ His ingenuity *was* for ever *on the rack* to supply himself with a light. 彼は明かりを得るために絶えず工夫を凝らしていた ▪ They have both worn themselves out by *being* eternally *on the rack* to give entertainment to others. 彼らは二人とも他人をもてなそうと絶えず心が張りつめていたのでくたくたに疲れてしまった.

2 非常に心配して[苦しんで]いる ▪ I *was on the rack* until I received the doctor's report. 私は医者の報告を受け取るまで非常に心配していた. ☞「拷問台に乗せられている」が原義.

off the* [*a*] *rack つるしで (→buy ... off the PEG) ▪ His suit was *off a rack*. 彼のスーツはつるしだった.

put* [*set*]... *on* [*upon*] *the rack (頭など)を極度に働かせる, しぼる ▪ His skill *was put upon the rack*. 彼のわざが極度に働かされた ▪ Sometimes I *set* my wits *on the rack*. ときどき私は知恵をしぼるこ

とがある. ☞「拷問台に乗せる」が原義.

***stand* [*come*] *up to* one's [*the*] *rack* (*fodder or no fodder*)** 《米口》潔く運命に従う[責務を果たす] ▪ I was determined to *stand up to my rack*. 私は潔く自分の運命に従う決心をした ▪ We must strike a bargain before I *come up to the rack*. 私が潔く責務を果たす前に手を打たねばならない.

rack[2] /ræk/ 图 ***go* [*come, run*] *to rack* (*and ruin*)** 破滅する, めちゃめちゃになる ▪ The house has *gone to rack and ruin*. その家は荒れ果ててしまっている. ☞rack = wreck, wrack.

leave not a rack behind 片りんさえもとどめない (cf. Sh., *Temp*. 4. 1. 156) ▪ He had gone, *leaving not a rack behind*. 彼は立ち去って, 影も形も見えなかった. ☞rack「ちぎれ雲」.

rack[3] /ræk/ 動 ***rack* one's *brains* [*wit*]** 脳みそをしぼる ▪ She was *racking her brains* for something to say. 彼女は何か言おうとして脳みそをしぼっていた.

rack* one's *memory 懸命に思い出そうと努める ▪ I *racked my memory* in vain. 懸命に思い出そうと努めたが, だめだった.

racket /rǽkət/ 图 ***be in on a racket*** 《口》ゆすりのグループに加わっている ▪ He *was* once *in on a racket*. 彼は以前ゆすりのグループに加わっていた.

go* [*be off, be*] *on the racket 道楽をする ▪ He had *been off on the racket*, perhaps for a week at a time. 彼はおそらく一度に1週間も道楽をして過ごしていたのであった.

It isn't my racket. 《米俗》僕の知ったことじゃない.

make* [*kick up, raise, set up*] *a racket 大騒ぎを起こす, わいわい言う (*about, with*) ▪ Her father has always *made* such *a racket with* her. 父親はいつも彼女に向かってそのようにわいわい言ってきた.

stand the racket **1** 試練に耐える, 長くもつ (*of*) ▪ His work will *stand the racket of* adverse seasons. 彼の作品は不運の試練に耐えるだろう. **2** (行為の)責任を負う; 費用を負担する ▪ I shall have to *stand the racket* tomorrow morning. 僕はあすの朝責任を取らなければならない ▪ We're going to Paris, and Father has promised to *stand the racket*. 我々はパリへ行くのだが, 父が費用は出すと約束してくれた.

What's the racket? 《米口》どうしたんだ.

racy /réɪsi/ 形 ***be racy of the soil*** 本場特有の味のある, その土地特有の《主としてアイルランドについて》 ▪ This Irish superstition *is* so *racy of the soil*, that it is really deserving of a much wider publicity. このアイルランドの迷信は本場特有の味があるので, 本当はもっと広く知られる価値がある.

radar /réɪdɑːr/ 图 ***below* [*off, under*] *the radar* (*screen*)** レーダーに映らないで, 気うかれないで ▪ The tensions stayed *under the radar* because incidents between the two groups stopped showing up in police reports. 緊張は人目に触れなかったが, それは2グループ間の事件が警察の報告書に載らなくなったためだ.

by radar レーダーで ▪ We can follow the flight of an aircraft *by radar*. レーダーで飛行機の飛行をたどることができる.

***on the radar* (*screen*)** レーダーに映って, 周知[注目]されて ▪ It clearly deserves to be *on the radar screen*. 明らかにそれは注目に値する.

radio /réɪdioʊ/ 图 ***a radio ham*** アマチュア無線家 ▪ C.Q. is the code letters that *radio hams* use. C.Q. はアマチュア無線家が使うコード文字だ. ☞C.Q. = call to quarters.

by radio 無電で ▪ A strange message was sent *by radio*. 無電で奇妙な通信が送られた.

hear ... on* [*over*] *the radio ...をラジオで聞く ▪ I *heard* the news *over* [*on*] *the radio*. そのニュースはラジオで聞いた.

listen* (*in*) *to the radio*/*listen in on the radio ラジオを聞く ▪ After supper I *listen to the radio*. 夕食後ラジオを聞く. ☞listen to が最も普通な言い方.

radius /réɪdiəs/ 图 ***within a radius of*** ...の半径以内の ▪ He knows everyone *within a radius of* 20 miles. 彼は半径20マイル以内に住んでいる人はすべて知っている.

rag /ræg/ 图 **(*as*) *limp as a rag*** →(as) LIMP as a doll.

chew the rag →CHEW.

drop the rag 《米口》合図をする ▪ He *dropped the rag* and left the room. 彼は合図をして部屋から去った.

feel like a rag 《口》くたくたに疲れている ▪ I *feel like a rag* after a long journey. 長旅のあとなのでくたくたに疲れている.

***get* one's *rag out* [*up*]** 《口》怒る ▪ Why d'you *get your rag out* over a trifle like that? どうしてそんなつまらぬことで君は怒るんだい.

glad rags 《口》晴れ着, いっちょうら ▪ She went out in *glad rags*. 彼女はいっちょうらを着て出かけた.

go from rags to riches 貧乏から金持ちになる ▪ The girl became a pop singer and *went from rags to riches*. その少女は流行歌手になり, 貧乏から金持ちになった.

have not a rag to* one's *back 《口》着る服が1枚もない ▪ You see I *haven't a rag to my back*. なにしろ私は着る服が1枚もないんです.

in rags ぼろを着て; ぼろぼろで ▪ The beggar was *in rags*. その物乞いはぼろを着ていた.

knock* a person *all to rags 《米》人をなぐって気絶させる ▪ I *knocked* him *all to rags*. 私は彼をなぐって気絶させた.

like a red rag to a* [*the*] *bull →BULL.

lose* one's *rag 《英口》ひどく怒る ▪ Your mistake will make him *lose his rag*. 君の間違いで彼はひどく怒るぞ.

not a* [*no*] *rag of 少しも...のない ▪ They have *no rag of* evidence to uphold him. 彼らには彼を支持する証拠が少しもない.

***not leave a rag on* a person** 人を完膚なきまで

にこきおろす ▪ You should have heard her. She did *not leave a rag on* him. 君に彼女の言葉を聞かせたかったよ. 彼をこてんぱんにこきおろしたんだからね.

on the rag 《米口》 怒って, いらいらして ▪ Mary was *on the rag* this morning. けさメアリーはいらいらしていた.

rags and tatters ぼろぼろの服 ▪ He went about in *rags and tatters*. 彼はぼろ服を着て歩き回った.

take the rag off (the bush) 《米口》 何[誰]よりもすぐれている ▪ You *take the rag off the bush*. 君は誰よりもすぐれている ▪ Nothing was ever seen so fine since creation. It quite *takes the rag off*. こんなにすばらしいものは見たことがない. 全くもって絶品だ.

the rag trade 《口》 アパレル業, 洋服(のデザイン[製造, 販売])業 ▪ Mum worked in *the rag trade* until she was 62. 母は62歳まで服飾業界で働いた.

to rags ぼろぼろに ▪ His clothes were torn *to rags*. 彼の服はぼろぼろに裂けていた ▪ The meat is cooked *to rags*. この肉はくたくたに煮てある.

wave a red rag at a bull 雄牛に向かって赤いきれを振る《相手を激怒させる》 ▪ Don't talk about politics with him. You might as well *wave a red rag at a bull*. 彼と政治の話をしてはいけない. 雄牛に赤いきれを振って見せるようなものだよ.

rage[1] /reɪdʒ/ 名 ***be (all) the rage*** (一時的な)大流行である ▪ Quiz games *are all the rage*. クイズゲームが大流行だ ▪ That shade of blue *is* quite *the rage* this season. その青色が今シーズンは大流行だ.

fly [fall, get] into a rage かっと怒りだす ▪ He *fell into an* appalling *rage*. 彼はひどく怒りだした.

have a rage for …に熱中している ▪ He *has a rage for* collecting stamps. 彼は切手マニアだ.

in a [one's] rage かっとなって ▪ He left the room *in a rage* with me. 彼は私にかっとなって部屋を出て行った ▪ *In his rage*, he broke the vase. 彼はかっとなって花びんをこわした.

put** a person **into a rage 人をかっと怒らせる ▪ Her retort *put* him *into a rage*. 彼女の口答えに彼はかっと怒った.

R

rage[2] /reɪdʒ/ 動 ***rage and fume*** (人が)かんかんに怒る ▪ She heard him *raging and fuming* in his study. 彼女には彼が書斎でかんかんに怒っているのが聞こえた.

rage itself out (あらしなどが)大あばれにあばれてやむ ▪ The storm *raged itself out*. あらしは大あばれにあばれて収まった.

ragged /rǽgəd/ 形 ***on the ragged edge*** 《米口》 危い瀬戸ぎわに ▪ He is sometimes *on the ragged edge* of starvation [bankruptcy]. 彼はときどき餓死[破産]に瀕することがある.

run** a person **ragged 人をへとへとに疲れさせる ▪ Teachers *are run ragged* trying to individually help the exceptional child. 特別支援の児童一人一人に支援しようとして教師たちは疲れ切っている.

ragtag /rǽgtæ̀g/ 名 ***ragtag and bobtail*** **1** 社会のくず, ろくでなし (*of*) ▪ This paper cuts up the *ragtag and bobtail of* the faction. この新聞はその党派のろくでなしを散々にこきおろしている.

2 全部 ▪ He shall have them all, *ragtag and bobtail*. 彼にそれをそっくりくれてやろう.

raid /reɪd/ 名 ***make a raid on [upon]*** **1** …を襲う; に手入れする ▪ *A* stern *raid was made upon* all the gamblers. 博徒全体にきびしい手入れが行われた.

2 いつもと違った所へ買い出しに行く ▪ We *made a raid on* the neighboring shops. 近くのいつもと違う店へ買い出しに行った.

rail /reɪl/ 名 ***a [the] third rail*** **1** (電車に給電する高圧の)第三軌条 ▪ Cameramen set their tripods over *a* dead *third rail*. カメラマンたちは廃線になった第三軌条に三脚を設置した.

2 扱いにくい[危険な]問題[話題] ▪ Medicare has become *the third rail* of politics. 老人医療保障は政界のデリケートな問題になった.

(as) thin [lean] as a rail ひどくやせて ▪ I am getting *thin as a rail*. ひどくやせてきた.

back on the rails 《英口》 ふたたび軌道に戻って; 再起[復帰]して (→on the RAILs) ▪ Bill 107 was *back on the rails* and the hearings were scheduled. 議案107は再び審議されることになり, 公聴会が計画された.

beat the devil and carry a rail 《米》 完全に打ち負かす ▪ For a sample of honesty this *beats the devil and carries a rail*. 正直の見本としてこれに勝るものは断然ない. ☞競走のときハンディキャップとして足に横棒をつけて走る地方の習慣から.

by rail 電車で ▪ It may be approached *by rail*. そこへは電車で行ける.

go [run] off the rails 《英口》 脱線する; 混乱する; 常規を逸脱する ▪ His company *went off the rails* last year. 彼の会社は去年調子がおかしくなってしまった ▪ He has never *gone off the rails*. 彼は脱線的行為をしたことはない.

hunt the top rail 《米口》 大急ぎで逃げる ▪ *Hunt the top rail*, and do it quick. 大急ぎで逃げるんだ, 早く.

keep on the rails 《口》 社会常識を守る[守らせる] ▪ He *kept* his son *on the rails*. 彼は息子に常識を守らせた.

off the rails **1** 脱線して ▪ The train ran *off the rails*. 列車が脱線した.

2 調子が狂って; 狂って ▪ A sane healthy mind can get momentarily *off the rails*. 正気で健康な心の持ち主でも一時的に狂う場合がある.

on the rails **1** うまく進行して ▪ They got it *on the rails*. 彼らはそれをうまく進行させた.

2 正しい方向をたどって ▪ Weak men are kept *on the rails* by society. 意志の弱い人は社会の中で正しい方向をたどらされている.

3 (競馬で馬・騎手が)トラックの内側のフェンスに最も近い位置で ▪ He came smoothly round the retreating horses to take third place *on the rails*. 彼は後集団からスムーズにまわりこんでトラック内側フェンスに最

も近い位置で3番手につけた.

over the rails 手すりを越えて; 手すりにもたれて ▪ Bruce went *over the rails* off a cruse ship at about 9:45 p.m. ブルースが午後9時45分ごろ大型遊覧船から海へ落ちた ▪ They leaned *over the rails* and peered down into the eddying tides of Naruto. 彼らは手すりにもたれて鳴門の渦潮に目を凝らした.

put the bottom rail on top →BOTTOM[1].

ride *a person* ***on a rail*** 《米口》人を横木の上にのせて運び回る《私刑の一種》 ▪ They decided to *ride* the woman *on a rail.* 彼らはその女性を横木の上にのせて運び回ることに決めた.

ride the rails 《米》貨車に無賃乗車する ▪ The children *rode the rails* and got off at the next station. 子供たちは貨車に無賃乗車して, 次の駅で降りた.

run off the rails →go off the RAILs.

sit on the rail 《口》どちらにも加担しない ▪ Henry IV was always *sitting on the rail* between Catholics and Huguenots. アンリ4世は常にカトリック教徒とユグノーのどちらにも加担しなかった.

railroad /réɪlròʊd/ 名 ***an underground railroad*** (逃亡者をかくまったり移動させたりする)秘密組織 ▪ Fran heads *an underground railroad* for abused women. フランは虐げられた女性のための秘密組織の先頭に立っている. ☞もと奴隷解放のための秘密結社を指す.

railway /réɪlwèɪ/ 名 ***at railway speed*** 大急ぎで ▪ He made a trip to Rome *at railway speed.* 彼は大急ぎでローマへの旅をした.

What a way to run a railway! 《口》何というめちゃめちゃなやり方だ.

rain[1] /reɪn/ 名 ***(as) right as rain*** →(as) RIGHT as my glove.

come rain or (come) shine =RAIN or shine.

get out of the rain 《口》ごたごたが起きそうなときに姿を見せない ▪ He sent word that he was ill. Trust him to *get out of the rain*! 彼は病気だと言うけをしてきた. ごたごたが起きそうなときにはきまって姿を見せないんだ.

give *a person* ***a rain check*** 人にまた今度と約束する ▪ I'm sorry you can't come to dinner this evening. I'll *give* you *a rain check.* 今晩夕食によべなくてごめんね. また今度ね.

in rain 雨のように(繁く) ▪ Meteors fall *in rain.* 流星は雨のように降りおちる.

in the rain 雨の中で, 雨をついて ▪ Don't go out *in the rain.* 雨の中へ出て行ってはいけない.

not have enough sense [imagination, intelligence] to come in from [out of] the rain 《口》人並みの知恵がない ▪ Never allow him do the work by himself. He *hasn't got enough sense to come in from the rain.* 彼一人にその仕事を任せてはいけない. 人並みの知恵がないんだから.

out of the rain 雨の降っているところから ▪ Come in *out of the rain*! 雨を避けて中へ入りなさい.

rain in buckets →rain (in) BUCKETs.

rain or shine/(in) rain or fine 晴雨にかかわらず, どんな事があっても ▪ I'll be there, *rain or shine.* 降っても照ってもそこへは行きます.

take a rain check on ...を後日改めてと約束する ▪ They *took a rain check on* the game tomorrow. 明日の試合は後日改めてやると約束された.

rain[2] /reɪn/ 動 ***If it should rain porridge, he would want his dish.*** 《諺》ポリッジの雨が降っても皿がない,「好機を利用する能力がない」.

It never rains but it pours. 《諺》降ればどしゃ降り,「不幸[物事]は重なるもの」(《口》When it rains, it pours.).

it rains **1** 雨が降る ▪ *It rained* very hard. 激しく雨が降った.

2 ...が雨と降る[注ぐ] ▪ *It* has *rained* blood. 血の雨が降った ▪ *It rained* invitations. 招待状が雨と降り注いだ.

know enough to go in when it rains/can go in when it rains 《米口》〖しばしば否定文で〗少なくとも十人並みの頭はある ▪ He doesn't *know enough to go in when it rains*! 彼は十人並みの頭もない ▪ Anyone who *can go in when it rains* ought to understand it. 少なくとも十人並みの頭のある人なら当然それはわかるはずだ.

rain cats and dogs →CAT.

rain itself out 雨が降りやむ ▪ It will probably *rain itself out* before morning. たぶん朝にならないうちに雨は降りやむだろう.

rain on *a person's* ***parade*** 《米》...に冷水を浴びせる, を興ざめにする ▪ The lower demand expectations *rained on the parade of* bullish optimism. 需要は低いという予測は強気の楽観主義に冷水を浴びせた.

rainbow /réɪnbòʊ/ 名 ***all the colors of [in] the rainbow*** 《口》あらゆる種類の色, 多彩 ▪ I was myself beaten into *all the colors of the rainbow.* 私はなぐられて打ち身だらけになった ▪ The woman was dressed in *all the colors of the rainbow.* その女性は多彩な服を着ていた.

chase (after) rainbows/chase the rainbow 虹を追いかける; かなわぬ夢を追いかける ▪ He would sit there *chasing rainbows.* 彼はよくそこに座ってかなわぬ夢を追いかけたものだ.

over the rainbow =over the MOON.

the end of the rainbow/the rainbow's end 虹の果て《金の入ったかめがあるとされる》 ▪ He had found the jackpot, *the end of the rainbow.* 彼は大金を見つけた, まさに虹の果てだった.

rainy /réɪni/ 形 ***a rainy day*** **1** 雨天 ▪ Monday was *a rainy day.* 月曜日は雨降りだった.

2 困った[まさかの]時 ▪ We must provide [save] against [for] *a rainy day* while the sun shines. 機会のある内に非常時の備えをしなければならない.

a rainy day fund まさかの時[いざという時]のための蓄え[資金] ▪ The mayor said his biggest concern is that the city has no *rainy day fund.* 市長は, 最大の心配は市に困窮時の蓄えがないことだと述べた.

raise[1] /reɪz/ 名 ***get a raise*** 給料が上がる ▪ He *got a raise* because of his good work. いい仕事ぶりなので彼の給料は上がった.

make a raise 《米口》(金・貴重品などを)手に入れる, 儲ける (*of*) ▪ I've *made a raise of* a hundred dollars. 100ドル儲けた ▪ They *made* quite *a raise* in the California mines. 彼らはカリフォルニアの鉱山でしこたま儲けた.

raise[2] /reɪz/ 動 ***raise a dust*** →DUST[1].

raise a laugh [***smile***] 人を(おもしろがらせて)笑わせる[微笑させる] ▪ He was in low spirits that morning. I couldn't *raise* even *a smile.* 彼はその朝しょげていた. 僕はにっこりさせることさえできなかった.

raise ...from death [***from the dead, to life***] …をよみがえらせる ▪ Christ *raised* Lazarus *from death.* キリストはラザロをよみがえらせた ▪ He *raised* their dead bodies *to life.* 彼は彼らの死体をよみがえらせた.

raise the devil [(***merry***) ***hell, hob, the mischief, Cain, the hatchet, Ned, the roof, a stake, the yell***] 騒動を起こす; 大声で怒る, 大声で抗議する ▪ Mother'll *raise Cain* if you break those plates. その皿を割ったら母さんがぶうぶう言うぞ.

raise the market upon →MARKET.

raise the specter of 疑心暗鬼を生む ▪ The budget cuts have *raised the specter of* an increase in lunch prices. 予算削減のため昼食代が値上げされるのではないかという疑心暗鬼を生んだ.

raise the wind →WIND[1].

raise *one's* ***voice*** **1** 声をあげる, どなる ▪ Father never once *raised his voice* at any of us children. 父は私たち子供の誰をもどなりつけたことは一度もなかった.

2 話す ▪ No one *raised his voice.* 誰も口をきかなかった.

raise *one's* ***voice against*** …に反対を唱える ▪ I must *raise my voice against* such a decision. そのような決議には反対を唱えなければならない.

rake[1] /reɪk/ 名 (***as***) ***lean*** [***thin***] ***as a rake*** やせて骨と皮ばかりで ▪ His horse was *lean as a rake.* 彼の馬はやせて骨と皮ばかりだった.

R

rake[2] /reɪk/ 名 ***a rake-off*** 《口》(不正な)分け前, 取り分, リベート ▪ I have got no *rake-off* from anything. 私は何からも上前をはねてはいない.

rake's progress 放蕩者のたどる道; 間断のない堕落[悪化] ▪ The inflationary *rake's progress* is going merrily on. インフレーションの間断のない悪化が陽気に行われている. ☞Hogarth の一連の版画(1735)の題名から.

rake[3] /reɪk/ 動 ***rake*** (***it***) ***in*** 《口》大金を儲ける[かせぐ] ▪ He *raked it in* on the race. 彼は競馬で大金を儲けた.

rake over old ashes [***coals***]/***rake over the ashes*** [***past***] 《口》過去の不愉快なことを話題にする[むしかえす]《非難を表す》 ▪ Why do you *rake over old ashes*? なぜ昔の不快なことを話題にするのか.

rally /rǽli/ 動 ***rally to the support of*** …の援助にかけつける ▪ Mr. Gladstone *rallied to the support of* the Government. グラッドストン氏が政府の援助にかけつけた.

ram /ræm/ 動 ***ram ... down*** *a person's* ***throat***/***ram ... into*** *a person's* ***head*** 人に(意見など)を押しつける (→cram ... down a person's THROAT) ▪ There is no attempt to *ram* ideas *down other people's throats.* 思想を他人に押しつけようとする試みなどはなされていない.

ram ... into *a person's* ***head*** →RAM ... down a person's throat.

ram *one's* ***way*** (船が)ぶつかりながら進む ▪ The ship *rammed her way* through four miles of ice. 船は4マイルにわたる氷の間をぶつかりながら進んだ.

ramble /rǽmbəl/ 名 ***go for a ramble*** ぶらぶら歩きに行く ▪ I studied all the morning, after which I *went for a ramble.* 朝じゅう勉強して, それからぶらぶら歩きに出た.

on [***upon***] ***the ramble*** 漫歩中《比喩的にも》 ▪ I shall be *upon the ramble* for some time. しばらくぶらぶら歩いていよう ▪ I will set my imagination *on the ramble.* ひとつ想像力を働かせてみよう.

rampage /rǽmpeɪdʒ/ 名 ***be*** [***go***] ***on the*** [***a***] ***rampage*** あばれ回っている[回る] ▪ She's *been on a rampage* about five minutes. 彼女は5分ほど前からあばれ回っている ▪ The river is *going on the rampage.* 川は荒れ狂っている.

ramrod /rǽmrɑ̀d|-rɔ̀d/ 名 (***as***) ***straight*** [***stiff***] ***as a ramrod*** →(as) STIFF as a poker.

ranch /ræntʃ|rɑːntʃ/ 名 ***bet the ranch*** [***farm***] 《米口》全財産を賭ける, 全てを託す ▪ Our company is *betting the ranch* on your company. わが社は君の会社に全てを託しているところだ.

buy the ranch 《米俗》死ぬ ▪ The cat *bought the ranch* when a car hit him. 車にひかれたときその猫は死んだ.

random /rǽndəm/ 名 ***at random*** でたらめに, 出まかせに ▪ He fired a shot *at random.* 彼はでたらめに発砲した.

range[1] /reɪndʒ/ 名 ***at close range*** まのあたり, 手にとって ▪ I saw farm life *at close range.* 農村生活をまのあたりに見た. ☞range「ミサイルの射程」.

at long [***short***] ***range*** 遠[近]距離で ▪ He fired *at short range.* 彼は近距離から発砲した.

at range 《米》放牧地に放されて ▪ All horses *at range* are ordered to be branded. 放牧地に放されているすべての馬は烙印を押すように命じられている.

beyond [***outside***] ***the range of*** …の範囲外に ▪ It is *beyond the range of* my conjecture. それは私の想像に余ることだ ▪ The word is *outside the range of* a middle schoolboy's vocabulary. その単語は中学生の語彙の範囲外にあるものだ.

get out of range of (砲)の射程外に出る ▪ We had to *get out of range of* enemy fire. 敵の砲撃の射程外に出るほかなかった.

get within range of (砲)の射程内に入る

▪ They were *getting within range of* the enemy guns. 彼らは敵の砲の射程内に入りかけていた.

go* [*help*] *over the range 《米》死ぬ[殺す] ▪ The man *went over the range.* その男は死んだ ▪ There is a suspicion that she *helped* him *over the range.* 彼女が彼を殺したのではないかと疑われている.

in range with …と並んで ▪ They keep the two buoys *in range with* the lighthouse. 二つのブイが灯台と一直線にしておかれている.

on the range 《米》(牛などが)放牧地にいる ▪ Most of his hogs had been out *on the range.* 彼のブタの大部分は放牧地に出してあった.

out of** one's **range …の手が届かない; の知識の範囲外で ▪ Hebrew is *out of my range.* ヘブライ語は私には手が届かない.

outside the range of →beyond the RANGE of.

ride* (*the*) *range 《米》放牧地の家畜の世話をする ▪ She *rode the range* from that time. 彼女はその時から放牧地の家畜の世話をした.

run on the same range 《米》つき合う, いっしょに大きくなる ▪ We've been *running on the same range* since we were boys. 僕たちは子供のときからつき合ってきている.

within* [*out of*] (*the,* one's) *range 射程内[外]で; 範囲内[外]で ▪ The ship came *within the range* of guns. 船は砲火の届く所に来た ▪ The enemy is altogether *out of range.* 敵は完全に射程外にある ▪ The price is not *within my range.* その値段は私の手に届かない.

range[2] /reɪndʒ/ 動 ***range** oneself* **1** (だらしない生活のあとに結婚して)身を固める ▪ He had no intention of marrying and *ranging* himself just yet. 彼はまだ結婚して身を固めるつもりはなかった. ☞F se ranger のなぞり.

2 整列する ▪ The soldiers *ranged* themselves on each side. 兵士らは両側に整列した.

***range against* [*on the side of, with*]** 〚主に再帰的〛…と反対の側に立つ[に味方する] ▪ The Norman baronage *ranged themselves with* the king or *against* him. ノルマン貴族たちは王に味方する者もいれば反対の側に立つ者もいた ▪ I *ranged myself on the side of* the Duke of Bedford. 私はベッドフォード公爵の味方についた.

rank /ræŋk/ 名 ***all ranks*** (軍隊・団体などの)全員 ▪ He had decided to retire *all ranks* to the Base Camp. 彼は全員を基地に下げることに決めていた.

be in the ranks of …の仲間である ▪ He *is in the ranks of* the unemployed. 彼も失業者の一人だ.

break rank →keep RANK.

break ranks (所属グループ内で)異議を唱える, 造反する (*with*) ▪ Thirty-one Democrats *broke ranks with* their party. 31人の民主党員が党に造反した.

close* (*the,* one's) *ranks 隊列を詰める; (集団が)結束を固める ▪ The sergeant then *closed the ranks.* それで軍曹は隊列を詰めさせた ▪ At the approach of the enemy the British people *closed ranks.* 敵の接近にあたり英国民は一致団結した.

come up from* [*through*] *the ranks = rise from the RANKs.

fall into rank 列につく ▪ He *fell into rank* at sight of the legate. 彼は使節を見ると列についた.

in* [*into*] *rank 列を組んだ[組んで] ▪ Four men *in rank* came stepping down the plank. 横一列になった4人が板を踏んで降りてきた.

keep* [*break*] *rank 列を乱さない[乱す], 落伍しない[する] ▪ Fifty thousand could *keep rank.* 5万人の兵が列を乱さずにいることができた ▪ The horsemen had *broken rank* and were asunder. 騎兵隊は列を乱してしまってちりぢりになった.

of* (*high*) *rank 身分の高い ▪ He was a person *of* (*high*) *rank.* 彼は身分の高い人だった.

pull* (one's) *rank 地位をかさに着て命令を押しつける (*on*) ▪ The General will *pull his rank on* him. 将軍は地位をかさに着て彼に命令を押しつけるだろう.

rank and fashion 上流社会 ▪ All the *rank and fashion* will be there. すべての上流人士がそこへやって来るだろう.

rank and file **1** 隊伍 ▪ The soldiers marched in *rank and file.* 兵たちは隊伍を組んで行進した.

2 《口》兵卒と下士, 下士卒 ▪ The corps consisted of about 12,000 *rank and file* of British infantry. その軍団は約12,000のイギリス歩兵の下士卒から成り立っていた.

3 一般メンバー, 下っぱ連中 ▪ For other committees there remains only the *rank and file* of the House. 他の委員会のために残っているのは議会の一般議員にすぎない. ☞《軍》「横隊(の兵)と縦隊(の下士)」が原義.

rise from* [*through*] *the ranks **1** 一兵卒から身を起こす ▪ The officer has *risen from the ranks.* あの将校は兵卒から身を起こしたのだ.

2 低い身分から出世する ▪ He *rose from the ranks* to become president of the company. 彼は低い身分から出世してその会社の社長になった.

swell the ranks of …の数を増す ▪ Business depression *swells the ranks of* the unemployed. 不景気になると失業者の数がふえる.

take rank with …と肩を並べる ▪ He can never *take rank with* the great poets. 彼はその大詩人たちと肩を並べることはとてもできない.

take the rank of …の地位を占める ▪ He earned promotion and *took the rank of* major. 彼は昇進して少佐の位についた.

rankle /rǽŋkəl/ 動 ***rankle in** one's **mind* [*heart*]** (記憶などが)心にうずく, 胸にわだかまる ▪ This refusal *rankles in his mind.* この拒絶が彼の胸にわだかまっている.

ransom /rǽnsəm/ 名 ***a king's ransom*** 大金 ▪ I couldn't look upon his face for *a king's ransom.* 彼の顔なんかいくら金をもらっても見たくなかった.

☞「王の身の代金」の意から.

hold** a person* (up***) ***to ransom*** 人質にして身の代(しろ)金を要求する ▪ Let us *hold* him *to ransom.* 彼を人質にして身の代金を取ってやろうではないか.

rant /rænt/ 動 ***rant and rave*** [***roar***] わめき散らす ▪ They would *rant and rave* in loud voices. 彼らは大声でわめき散らすのだった.

rantan /rǽntæ̀n/ 名 ***on the rantan*** 《俗》ばか騒ぎして ▪ Some of them went *on the rantan* that night. 彼らの何人かはその晩ばか騒ぎした.

rap[1] /ræp/ 名 ***a rap sheet*** 《米口》前科[犯罪]記録 ▪ His *rap sheet* includes two incidents of violence against women. 彼の犯罪記録には女性への暴行が2件含まれている.

beat the rap 《米俗》罪を免れる ▪ The prisoner *beat the rap* and went free. 被告は罪を免れ釈放された ▪ I'd at least *beat that rap.* せめてその罰はくわずにすむだろう.

give [***get, receive***] ***a rap on the knuckles*** 《口》ひどくしかりつける[つけられる] ▪ The chief *gave* him *a rap on the knuckles.* 所長は彼をひどくしかった ▪ The servant *received a rap on the knuckles* for his carelessness. 使用人は不注意のためにひどくしかりつけられた. ☞罰として子供の指関節をぶつことから.

take [***get***] ***the rap*** 《俗》しかられる, 罰をくらう ▪ The quarrel was not of his making, but he had to *take the rap.* そのけんかは彼が始めたものではないのに, 彼がしかられねばならなかった.

rap[2] /ræp/ 名 ***not care*** [***give, matter***] ***a rap*** 少しもかまわない[問題ではない] ▪ You do*n't care a rap* for me. あなたは私のことなどちっともかまってくれない ▪ It does*n't matter a rap* whether it's rough or fine. あらしになっても上天気であっても少しも問題じゃない. ☞rap「18世紀にアイルランドで半ペニーとして通用した私鋳貨幣」.

not worth a rap 少しも価値がない ▪ His opinion is*n't worth a rap.* あの男の意見なんかなんの価値もありはしない.

without [***not***] ***a rap*** 一文もない ▪ I have seen the landowners *without a rap.* 一文なしの地主連中を見たことがある ▪ He died and left *not a rap* behind him. 彼は死んで後に一文も残さなかった.

rap[3] /ræp/ 動 ***rap** a person's **knuckles*** [***fingers***]/ ***rap** a person **on*** [***over***] ***the knuckles*** (子供の罰として)指ふしをたたく; 人をひどく叱責する ▪ The teacher *rapped the child's knuckles* for holding his pen in the wrong way. 先生は子供のペンの持ち方がまちがっていたので指ふしをたたいた ▪ Let me take the liberty of *rapping his knucles.* 失礼を顧みず彼のことは激しく叱責したい.

rapid /rǽpəd/ 名 ***shoot the rapids*** 危いことをする ▪ If you dare do that, you'll be *shooting the rapids.* あえてそんなことをすれば危い橋を渡ることになるだろう. ☞「ボートで早瀬を乗り切る」が原義.

rapidity /rəpídəti/ 名 ***with rapidity*** 迅速に ▪ He advanced towards them *with rapidity.* 彼は迅速に彼らの方へ進んで行った.

rapport /ræpɔ́ːr/ 名 ***come into*** [***on***] ***rapport with*** …と関係を持つようになる ▪ He *came into* closer *rapport with* them. 彼は彼らといっそう親密な関係を結ぶにいたった.

in [***en***] ***rapport*** (***with***) (…と)和合して, 一致して ▪ This is a proof that I have been *in rapport with* you. これは私が君とずっと気が合っているという証拠です.

rapture /rǽptʃər/ 名 ***fall*** [***go***] ***into raptures*** 夢中になる, 有頂天になる (*over, about*) ▪ She *went into raptures over* the dress. 彼女はそのドレスに夢中になった.

in rapture [***raptures***] 有頂天になって ▪ Women always speak *in rapture* when they speak of beauty. 女性は美について話すときにはいつも有頂天になって話す ▪ He was instantly *in raptures* at the news. 彼はその知らせを聞くとすぐ我を忘れて喜んだ.

with rapture 夢中になって, うっとり(と)して ▪ He gazed *with rapture* at the face of the girl. 彼は少女の顔をうっとりして見つめた.

rare /reər/ 形 ***have a rare time*** [***fun***] 非常に楽しく時を過ごす ▪ He *had a rare time* at their house last night. 彼はゆうべ彼らの家でとても楽しい時を過ごした.

rare and 《口》〚形容詞を強調して〛とても ▪ I was *rare and* hungry. 私はすごく腹がへっていた.

rarely /réərli/ 副 ***rarely ever/rarely or*** [***if***] ***ever*** めったに…しない ▪ He *rarely ever* drinks. 彼はめったに酒を飲まない ▪ Those schemes *rarely or ever* answer the end. そのような計画はめったに目的にかなわない.

raring/rarin' /réərɪŋ/ 形 ***be raring*** [***rarin'***] ***to** do* 《口》…する気は十分である; すぐにも活動したがっている ▪ The racer *was raring to* go. レーサーはやる気十分だった ▪ The dog *was raring to* fight. 犬は闘志満々だった ▪ Everyone is charged up and *raring to* go. 誰もが興奮してすぐにも活動したがっている.

raspberry /rǽzbèri|rɑ́ːzbəri/ 名 ***get*** [***give** a person*] ***the raspberry***/《英》***blow a raspberry*** 《俗》酷評される[する], 嘲笑される[する] ▪ They *gave* him *the raspberry* every time he started to speak. 彼らは彼が話そうとするたびに彼を嘲笑した.

rat /ræt/ 名 ***a pack rat*** 《米口》何でもため込んで捨てない人, がらくた収集癖のある人 ▪ He is *a pack rat*; he is unable to throw stuff away. 彼はがらくたを収集してきて, 捨てられないんだ ▪ Mom was *a pack rat.* Of course she kept letters in cans. ママは物を捨てなかった. もちろん手紙類も缶にしまっていた.

a rat fink 《米口》いけ好かないやつ; (警察への)密告者 ▪ I'm not *a rat fink* or a traitor. 私は密告者でも裏切り者でもない.

a rat pack 《俗》チンピラ集団; スキャンダルを追う記者たち ▪ Princess Diana's death is said to have been caused by *the rat pack* of reporters. ダイア

R

ナ妃の死はパパラッチ記者たちが招いたと言われている.

a rat race 《俗》がむしゃらな生存競争 ▪ Our jobs are *rat races*; the faster we work, the faster our boss wants us to work. おれたちの仕事はがむしゃらな生存競争みたいなもので, 早くやればやるだけボスはまた要求してくる.

a rat run 通り抜け道 ▪ This road is used as *a rat run*. この道路は抜け道として使われている.

(as) drunk [poor, weak] as a rat 酔いつぶれて; 無一文で; 弱り切って ▪ The man was *drunk as a rat*. その男は酔いつぶれていた ▪ He's *as poor as a rat*. 彼は無一文だ ▪ He was *weak as a rat*, and had no appetite. 彼は弱り切っていて全然食欲がなかった.

give** a person **rats 人をこっぴどくしかりつける ▪ You may write a letter and *give* the Inspector *rats*. 手紙を書いて警部をうんとしかりつけてやればよい.

go down like a rat sandwich/be as popular [welcome] as a rat sandwich 人気が下がる ▪ She's been *going down like a rat sandwich* as an actress. 彼女の女優としての人気はこのところ下がり続けている.

have rats in the attic →ATTIC.

like [as wet as] a drowned rat 《口》ぬれネズミになって ▪ I was dragged out of the river *like a drowned rat*. 私はずぶぬれで川から引き上げられた.

like a rat in the hole 追いつめられたネズミのように ▪ He died *like a rat in the hole*. 彼は追いつめられたネズミのように死んでいった.

Oh, rats! 《俗》ばかを言え ▪ A miss, by Jove. —*Oh, rats!* ほんとに当てそこねたんだ—ばか言え.

rat-assed/ 《英》 ***rat-arsed*** 《口》ぐでんぐでんの, 酩酊(めいてい)した ▪ They came home completely *rat-arsed*. 彼らは完全にぐでんぐでんに酔っぱらって帰宅した.

rats and snails and puppy-dog's tails ネズミやカタツムリや子犬の尻尾《いやな性格》 ▪ What do you think I'm made of? —*Rats and snails and puppy-dog's tails*. 僕が何でできていると思っているのかな—いろんないやな性格からだよ. ☞Mother Goose から.

Rats desert a sinking ship. 《諺》ネズミは沈む船を見捨てる.

smell a rat 《口》変だと思う, うさん臭い ▪ He'll be sure to *smell a rat* if I'm with you. 僕が君といたら彼はきっとうさん臭いと思うだろうよ.

rate[1] /reɪt/ 名 ***as sure as rates*** 《米》確かに ▪ The man is mad, *as sure as rates*. あの男は確かにおかしい.

at a ... rate …の速度[度合い]で ▪ Off they went *at a* rapid *rate*. 彼らは大急ぎで出かけて行った ▪ The dogs were panting *at a* great *rate*. 犬たちは激しくあえいでいた.

at a rate of →at the RATE of.

at a rate of knots 《英口》あっという間に ▪ He finished up a plate of food *at a rate of knots*. 彼はあっという間に一皿きれいに平らげた.

at all rates ともかく ▪ They were determined *at all rates* that all should know the fact. 彼らはみんなにその事実を知らせることをともかく決心していた.

at an easy rate 安価に; 楽に ▪ He thought to win it *at an easier rate*. 彼はそれをもっと楽に手に入れようと思った ▪ I thought myself happy in coming off *at* so *easy a rate*. そんなに苦もなく免れられたのは幸運だったと思った.

at any rate **1** ともかく, いずれにしても ▪ I'll come *at any rate*. ともかく参ります.
2 少なくとも ▪ All would be well, or *at any rate*, comfortable with her. 彼女の場合, 何もかもよくなる, いや少なくとも楽になるだろう.

at cut rates 割引価格[料金]で ▪ Students can get into the cinema *at cut rates*. 学生は割引料金で映画館へ入れる.

at that rate そんなわけなら; そんな調子では ▪ *At that rate* we shan't get any dinner. そういう具合なら夕飯にはありつけないぞ ▪ If you go on *at that rate*, you will injure your health. そんな調子でいくと体をこわすよ.

at the [a] rate of …の速さで, 割合いで ▪ The train is traveling *at the [a] rate of* 50 miles an hour. 電車は時速50マイルの速さで走っている ▪ He lends money *at the rate of* four percent. 彼は4分の割合で金を貸す.

at this rate この分では; こんなふうに ▪ *At this rate*, he won't be elected. この分では彼は当選すまい ▪ You mustn't treat me *at this rate*. こんなふうに私を扱ってはいけない.

cut the rates 《米》運賃[料金]率を下げる ▪ If one road *cuts the rates*, it will get the freight. 一つの道路が料金率を下げれば運送便の利用があろう.

go [be] on the rates 生活扶助を受ける[ている] ▪ The family will have to *go on the rates*. その家族は生活扶助を受けねばなるまい.

the going rate 時価 (*for*) ▪ *The going rate* for salmon caviar is about $100 a pound. イクラの時価は1ポンド約100ドルだ.

rate[2] /reɪt/ 動 ***be rated to*** (税など)を課されている ▪ Clergymen *are* deeply *rated to* all payments. 牧師にはあらゆる重税が課せられている.

rate high [low] 高く[低く]評価する ▪ A future age may *rate high* this poor invention. 後世ではこのしがない発明品が高く評価されるかもしれない ▪ The author *is rated low* in originality. その著者は独創性が低く評価されている.

rather /rǽðər|rɑ́ːðə/ 副 ***had [would] rather*** むしろ…したい (than) ▪ He *would rather* have died than refused. 断るなら彼は死んだほうがましだった.

or rather いやむしろ ▪ He came home last night, *or rather* very early this morning. 彼はゆうべ遅く, というよりはけさとても早く帰ってきた.

***rather than** do* …するよりむしろ ▪ I resigned *rather than* take part in such a plot. 私はそんな陰謀に加担するよりはむしろ辞職したのだ.

R

rather ... than not [***otherwise***] どちらかと言えば ▪ It is *rather* cold *than not.* どっちかと言えば寒いほうだ.

rather too 少し…すぎる ▪ It is *rather too* long. それは少し長すぎる.

rather [***sooner***] ***you*** [***her,*** etc.] ***than me*** 《英》君[彼女]の役目でよかった, 自分の仕事でなくて助かった ▪ I'm sure it'll be amazing but *rather you than me*! きっとすてきだろうよ, でも僕はやりたくないな.

the rather that [***because***] …だからなおさら ▪ I love her *the rather that* she is weak. 彼女は弱いからなおさら好きだ ▪ I am glad of it *the rather because* you will benefit by it. それであなたの利益になるのだからなおさらうれしい.

would rather →had RATHER.

ratio /réɪʃioʊ/ 名 ***in the ratio of*** …の割合で ▪ They are *in the ratio of* three to two [3:2]. それらは3対2の割合だ.

ration /ræʃən/ 名 ***be on short rations*** 配給を制限されている ▪ We *were on short rations* in wartime. 戦時中は配給を制限されていた.

draw rations 配給を受ける ▪ Go and *draw rations.* 配給をもらいに行きなさい.

put *a person* ***on rations*** 人に定額支給する ▪ He *was put on rations*. 彼は定額支給された.

rattle /rætəl/ 動 ***get rattled*** 《口》あわてる, まごまごする ▪ He *got rattled* when he saw the policeman. 彼は警官を見るとあわてた.

rattle *a person's* ***cage*** 《口》人をいらだたせる[怒らせる] ▪ Who's *rattled his cage*? 誰が彼を怒らせたの?

ratty /ræti/ 形 ***get ratty with*** 《英俗》…に腹を立てる ▪ He *got* quite *ratty with* me. 彼は私にすっかり腹を立てた.

rave /reɪv/ 動 ***rave*** *oneself* 荒れ狂って[どなって]…の状態になる ▪ He *raved himself* hoarse [to sleep]. 彼はどなり散らして声をからした[寝入った].

rave itself out (あらしが)あばれるだけあばれてやむ ▪ The storm *raved itself out.* 大しけは荒れ狂うだけ荒れてやんだ.

ravel /rævəl/ 動 ***the raveled skein of life*** 錯雑混乱した人生 ▪ Not even age can disentangle *the raveled skein of life*. 年の功でも混乱した人生のもつれをほぐすことはできない.

raving /réɪvɪŋ/ 形 (***stark***) ***raving mad*** [***bonkers***] 《口》完全に狂って, …に逆上して (*about*) ▪ The governor was *stark raving mad about* the Iraqi war. 知事はイラク戦争に猛反対だった ▪ They become calmer and more rational as you become *raving bonkers*. 君がかっかしてくるにつれて彼らのほうはより冷静で理性的になる.

raw /rɔː/ 形名 ***a raw deal*** 《口》ごまかし, ひどい仕打ち ▪ It was *a raw deal* assigning it to another salesman. それを別のセールスマンに任せたのはひどい仕打ちだった.

catch *a person* ***on the raw*** →touch a person on the RAW.

eat raw 生で食べる ▪ I like to *eat* oysters *raw*. カキを生で食べるのが好きだ.

in the raw **1** 生のままの; 未加工の ▪ We could supply you with the stuff *in the raw* tomorrow. あすには原料を供給してあげられます ▪ Look at life *in the raw*. ありのままの人生を見よ.

2《口》裸の[で] ▪ I took a bath *in the raw* in a cold mountain stream. 私は冷たい山間の小川で裸で水を浴びた.

raw at [***in***] …に無経験で, 未熟な, 不慣れで ▪ Painting is an art I am *raw in*. 絵は私には不慣れな芸術です ▪ The recruits were *raw at* drill. 新兵たちは訓練に不慣れだった.

raw-head and bloody-bones **1** (おとぎ話に出る)おばけ, 怖いもの ▪ They were ruffians and murderers, worse than *Raw-head and Bloody-bones*. その連中はおとぎ話のおばけよりも怖い悪党やら人殺したちだった.

2〚限定的に〛おばけの話のように恐ろしい ▪ He told us a *raw-head and bloody-bones* story. 彼は私たちにおばけの話のように恐ろしい話をしてくれた.

touch [***catch***] *a person* ***on the raw*** 人の痛いところ・弱味に触れる ▪ This remark *touched* Tom *on the raw*. この言葉がトムの痛いところに触れた.

ray /reɪ/ 名 ***a*** (***little***) ***ray of sunshine*** (人を元気づける)明るい人《特に若い女性》 ▪ You're *a little ray of sunshine*. 君は太陽のように明るい人だ.

a [***one***] ***ray of hope*** 一縷(いちる)の望み ▪ There is *a ray of hope* for them. 彼らには一縷の望みがある.

catch [***bag***] ***some*** [***a few***] ***rays*** 《米俗》日焼けする, 日光浴する ▪ You see I have *caught some rays*. 私少し日焼けしたでしょう.

not a ray of わずかの…もない ▪ There was *not a ray of* hope. わずかの希望もなかった.

raze /reɪz/ 動 ***raze ... to the ground*** …を完全に破壊する ▪ The school *was razed to the ground* by fire. 学校は火事で完全に破壊された.

razor /réɪzər/ 名 (***as***) ***blue as a razor*** 《米口》非常に青い ▪ The violet is always blue—*blue as a razor*. スミレはいつも青い—かみそりを研いだように青い.

(***as***) ***keen as a razor*** →KEEN.

(***as***) ***sharp as a razor*** (顔つき・頭が)かみそりのように鋭い ▪ His little wizened face was *as sharp as a razor*. 彼の小さいしわくちゃの顔はかみそりのように鋭かった ▪ The fellow is *as sharp as a razor*. あの男はかみそりのように鋭いやつだ.

cut blocks with a razor →BLOCK[1].

on the razor-edge of …の危機に臨んで, きわどい別れ目に立って ▪ They were *on the* very *razor-edge of* fate. 彼らはまさに運命の危機に臨んでいた ▪ Kant kept himself *on the razor-edge of* orthodoxy. カントは正説とのきわどい別れ目に立っていた.

on the razor's edge/on a razor-edge 危険に陥って ▪ Here am I back; we stand no more *on the razor's edge*! さあ私は戻ってきた. 我々はもう危機を脱したぞ. ☞ギリシャ語法.

razz /ræz/ 名 ***give*** [***get***] ***the razz*** 《米俗》酷評する[される], あざ笑う[われる] ▪ The mob *gave* him *the razz.* やじ馬たちは彼をあざ笑った.

razzle /rǽzəl/ 名 ***a night*** (***out***) ***on the razzle*** 《口》どんちゃん[乱ちき]騒ぎ ▪ We've had *a night on the razzle*, so I've got a bit of a hangover. 昨晩酒盛りをしたので, 二日酔い気味だ.

be [***go***] (***out***) ***on the razzle*** 《口》(酔っ払って)乱ちき騒ぎをする ▪ We're all *going on the razzle* together! みんなでいっしょに乱ちき騒ぎをしようと思っているんだ.

reach[1] /riːtʃ/ 名 (***a***) ***boardinghouse reach*** (人に頼まず)自分で手を伸ばしてテーブル上の食べ物等を取ること, 寄宿舎風手盛り ▪ Last year we all crowded around a long table, all using *boardinghouse reach* for food. 昨年は押し合いへし合いしながら長テーブルを囲み, 食べ物をとるのにみんな自分で手をのばした. ☞かつて寄宿舎の大テーブルで行われた不作法な行為.

above [***beyond, out of***] (***the***) ***reach of*** **1** …の手の届かないところに, 力の及ばないところに ▪ The tiger, seeing them *out of his reach*, began roaring. トラはそれらが自分の手の届かない所にいるとわかって見てほえ始めた.
2 …に理解できない ▪ These things were *beyond the reach of* men. そういう事柄は人間には理解できないことであった.

by a long reach ぐっと手を伸ばして ▪ He got an apple *by a long reach.* 彼はぐっと手を伸ばしてリンゴを取った.

in [***within***] ***reach*** 手が届く範囲で, 資力の及ぶ範囲に ▪ Don't price this too high; it should be *in reach* of the average customer. あまり高い値をつけないように, 平均的な顧客の手の届く範囲にしなくてはだめだ.

make a reach for …を取ろうと手を伸ばす ▪ He *made a reach for* the nearest one. 彼は一番近いのを取ろうと手を伸ばした.

within easy reach すぐ手の届く所に ▪ I like to have my dictionaries *within easy reach.* 辞書はすぐ手の届く所に置いておきたい.

within (***easy***) ***reach of*** …から(すぐ)行ける所に ▪ The hotel is *within easy reach of* the waterfront. そのホテルは海岸通りからすぐ行ける所にある.

within the reach of …の手の届く所に, 力の及ぶ所に ▪ This is the most useful dictionary ever placed *within the reach of* the public. これは一般人に買える辞書の中で一番便利なものだ ▪ This is *within your reach.* これは君にも手が届く.

reach[2] /riːtʃ/ 動 ***reach for the sky*** [***roof***] (銃をつきつけられて)両手をあげる ▪ Now *reach for the sky.* さあ, 両手をあげろ.

read[1] /riːd/ 名 ***have good*** [***quiet, short,*** etc.] ***read*** 十分[静かに, ちょっと, など]本を読む ▪ I *had* a *quiet read* in my room. 自分の部屋で静かに読書した.

read[2] /riːd/ 動 ***Do you read me?*** 私の言ってること, わかった? ▪ Clean your room immediately. *Do you read me?* すぐにお部屋の掃除をしなさい. わかった?

He that [***who***] ***runs may read.*** 走っている人にもわかる, きわめて明白である (《聖》*Hab.* 2. 2) ▪ This lesson is so clear that *he who runs may read.* この教訓はとても明らかだから走っている人にもわかるほどだ.

read *a person* ***a lesson*** [***lecture***] 人にお説教する, 小言を言う ▪ I'll be her tutor, and *read* her *another lesson.* 彼女の先生になってもう一度お説教をしてやろう.

read … aloud …を音読する ▪ *Read* the letter *aloud*, please. その手紙を音読してください.

read between the lines 行間を読む, 言外の意味を読みとる ▪ Diplomatic messages have to *be read between the lines.* 外交文書は言外の意味を読みとらねばならない ▪ I was able to *read* jealousy *between the lines.* 言外にねたみ心が読みとれた.

read *a person's* ***fortune*** 人の運命を占う ▪ He can *read men's fortunes* in their faces. 彼は人の顔を見てその運命を占うことができる.

read *a person's* ***hand*** [***palm***] 人の手相を見る ▪ She says she can *read your palm.* 彼女はあなたの手相を見ることができると言っている.

read *oneself* ***hoarse*** [***stupid, blind***] 本を読みすぎて声をからす[ばかになる, 盲目になる] ▪ Some people *read themselves stupid.* 本を読みすぎてばかになる手合いがいる.

read *oneself* ***in*** (英国国教の39箇条の信条などを公に朗読して)牧師の職につく ▪ He *read himself in* at the church. 彼はその教会で牧師の職についた.

read *oneself* ***into*** [***to***] 読書しながら…の状態になる ▪ He *read himself into* a nap. 彼は読書しながらうたた寝した ▪ I *read myself to* sleep. 私は本を読みながら寝てしまった.

read … into a [***the***] ***record*** …を読んで記録に残す ▪ The President's letter *was read into the* conference *record.* 大統領の書簡は朗読されて議会の記録に残された.

read like 読むと…のようだ ▪ This book *reads like* a novel. この本は読むと小説のようだ.

read *a person* ***like a book*** →BOOK[1].

read *a person's* ***mind*** [***thoughts***] 人の心[考え]を読む ▪ I can *read your mind* accurately. 君の心は正確に読めるよ.

read my lips 《口》〚命令文で〛よく聞きなさい, 約束します ▪ *Read my lips.* No new taxes. ご静粛に. 新税は設けません.

read round [***around***] ***the class*** [***the room***] クラス[教室]で輪読する ▪ We *read* the story *round the class.* その物語をクラスで輪読した.

read the time [***clock***] 時計を読みとる ▪ Can the child *read the time* yet? その子はもう時刻が読めますか.

read to *oneself* 黙読する ▪ I found him *reading to himself* in his study. 行ってみると彼は書斎

R

で黙読していた.

read too much into …を深読みする ▪ You had better not try to *read too much into* his comment. 彼のコメントを深読みしようとしない方がいい.

read well 読んでおもしろい ▪ The play *reads well*. その戯曲は読んでおもしろい.

read[3] /red/ 形 (***be***) ***read in*** (ある科目)に通じている ▪ He *is* deeply *read in* English literature. 彼は英文学に精通している.

take ... as read《英》…を同意した[当然の]こととする ▪ We'll *take* it all *as read*. すべて同意したことにしよう ▪ You may *take* it *as read* that your father will be angry when he hears this. このことを聞いたら当然お父さんは怒るぞ.

readiness /rédinəs/ 名 ***hold*** [***maintain***] *oneself* ***in readiness*** 待機の姿勢をとる ▪ We must *hold ourselves in readiness* against the enemy's attack. 敵の攻撃に備えて待機の姿勢をとっていなくてはならない.

in readiness 準備を整えて ▪ The car is at the door *in readiness*. 車が玄関に用意してある ▪ He had everything *in readiness* for an early start. 彼は早い出発に備えていっさいの準備を整えていた.

The readiness is all. 覚悟が肝心だ (cf. Sh., *Haml.* 5. 2. 216).

with readiness 快く, 進んで ▪ The women spoke *with* greater *readiness* than the men. 女たちは男たちよりもいっそう快く話した.

reading /rí:dıŋ/ 名 ***of immense*** [***wide, vast, extensive***] ***reading*** 博学の ▪ He is a man *of immense reading*. 彼は博学の人だ.

ready /rédi/ 形名 ***at the ready*** (銃を)構えの姿勢にして ▪ The soldiers held their rifles *at the ready*. 兵士は銃を構えの姿勢にしていた.

be ready to roll《主に米》**1** (なにかを)やり始める ▪ They gathered around the table and *were ready to roll*. 彼らはテーブルの周りに集まってなにかをやり始めた.

2 出かける, 外出[退出]する ▪ Give me a call when you*'re ready to roll*, and I'll meet you outside. 外出の用意が出来たら電話してくれ. 君とは外で会うから.

be ready with すぐ…する ▪ You *are ready with* excuses. 君はすぐ言い訳をする.

come to the ready 構えの姿勢をとる ▪ They *came to the ready*, as if to fire. 彼らはいかにも発砲するかのように構えの姿勢をとった.

get ... ready …の仕度をする ▪ I'm going to *get* dinner *ready*. 夕食の支度をしようと思います.

get ready for …の用意をする ▪ He *got ready for* a journey. 彼は旅行の用意をした.

have ... at the ready …をすぐ使えるようにしておく ▪ He *had* his gun *at the ready*. 彼は銃をいつでも撃てるようにしていた.

keep ... ready …を手近に置いておく ▪ He always *kept* a revolver *ready*. 彼はいつも拳銃を手元に置いていた.

make ... ready …を用意する (*for*) ▪ We must *make ready* the two spare bedrooms *for* our visitors. お客さん用に予備の寝室を二つ整えねばならない.

make *oneself* ***ready*** 用意[準備]する (*for*) ▪ She *made herself ready for* her ride. 彼女は乗馬の支度をした.

make ready for [***to*** *do*] …の[する]支度をする ▪ They *made ready for* a revolution. 彼らは革命の準備をした ▪ His companions *made ready to* fight. 彼の仲間は戦う用意をした.

ready and waiting すっかり準備ができて ▪ Our children were *ready and waiting* to go on a picnic. うちの子供たちはピクニックに出かける準備がすっかりできていた.

ready at …が早い, じょうずな ▪ He is *ready at* reckoning. 彼は計算が早い ▪ He is very *ready at* excuses. 彼は言い訳がとてもうまい.

ready at hand →READY to (one's) hand(s).

ready cash [***money***] 現金 ▪ He paid for everything with *ready money*. 彼は何でも現金で支払った.

ready for **1** …の用意ができた ▪ The goods are now *ready for* packing. 商品はもういつでも荷づくりできる.

2 …の覚悟がついた ▪ Be *ready for* your death tomorrow. あす死んでもいいと覚悟をしろ.

ready for anything どんなことにも対処する用意ができて ▪ He was always *ready for anything*. 彼はいつもどんなことにも対処する用意ができていた.

ready for (***the***) ***off***《口》出かける準備ができて ▪ Be *ready for the off* right away! すぐにお出かけの準備をしなさい.

Ready, steady, go! 位置について! 用意! どん!《子供の競走で》. ☞ On your mark(s) (get) set, go! とも言う (→on the MARK 2).

ready to *do* **1** …する用意の整った ▪ My nephew is *ready to* sail. おいはいつでも出帆できます.

2 喜んで[進んで]…する ▪ I am *ready to* forgive him. 喜んで彼を許します.

3 …しがちで ▪ He is too *ready to* promise. 彼は安受け合いをしすぎる ▪ He is always *ready to* apologize. 彼はいつでもなにかと弁解する.

4 今にも…しようとして ▪ The ship was *ready to* sink any time. 船は今にも沈みそうであった.

ready to (*one's*) ***hand***(***s***)/***ready at hand*** すぐ使えるようになって ▪ Help is *ready to* [*at*] *hand*. 手伝いはすぐ得られる ▪ He had an English dictionary *ready to his hands*. 彼は英語の辞書をいつでも使えるようにしておいた.

ready when you are 当方はいつでも OK, 君の準備ができしだい開始可能 ▪ When would you like me to begin?—*Ready when you are*. いつ始めたらいい?—ぼくのほうはいつでも大丈夫だよ.

ready, willing, and able《陳腐》やる気満々の ▪ He is *ready, willing, and able* to do anything we ask him. 彼はやる気満々で私たちが頼むことならなんでもやってくれる.

real /ríːəl|ríəl/ 形 ***for real*** **1**《口》本気の, 真剣な ▪ Are you *for real*? 本当かい《嘘みたいだ》.
2《非標準》本当に, 真剣に ▪ He started working *for real*. 彼は真剣に働き始めた.
get real《口》真実を受け入れる; 〚命令文で〛冗談はやめろ, まじめにやれ; 現実を見ろ ▪ You'll never win the lottery. *Get real!* 宝くじなんかに当たりっこないさ. 現実を見ろよ ▪ Then *get real* about it. じゃあそのことで現実的になりなさい.
It's been real.《俗》とても楽しかった. ☞It's been real nice (being with you). の略で, 親しい友人同士で使う.
keep it real《口》〚主に命令文で〛ありのままにふるまう ▪ Don't mind me. *Keep it real*. 私のことは気にせず, ありのままにふるまいなさい.
the real presence《宗》聖餐(さん)におけるキリストの肉と血の実在 ▪ Wyclif did not deny *the real presence* of Christ in the element. ウィクリフは聖餐に不可欠な要素としてキリストの肉と血の実在を否定したのではなかった.
the real thing [《米》***stuff***] **1** 本物, 実物 ▪ It was represented with the vividness of *the real thing*. それは実物のようにあざやかに描かれてあった.
2《俗》すばらしい人[物] ▪ He is *the real thing*, and no mistake. 彼は確かにすばらしい人物だ.

reality /riǽləti/ 名 ***a reality check*** 実態調査, 現実把握 ▪ The director general is overpaid and needs *a reality check*. 会長には給料を払いすぎなので, 実態調査が必要だ.
bring *a person* ***back to reality*** 人を(夢想・感傷から)現実に連れ戻す ▪ He tried to *bring* her *back to reality*. 彼は彼女を現実に連れ戻そうとした.
in reality 実際は; 現実には (↔in IDEA, in NAME) ▪ She gives the impression of being generous, but *in reality* she is a very selfish woman. 彼女は気前がいいような印象を与えるが, 実際はとても利己的な女性だ ▪ He was *in reality* penniless. 彼は実は無一文だった.
with reality 実物そっくりに ▪ It is described *with* extraordinary *reality*. それは驚くほど実物そっくりに描かれている.

really /ríːli|ríəli/ 副 ***Not really.*** まさか.
really and truly 実際に, 本当に ▪ And are you *really and truly* the person who sent us all those presents? で, あなたは本当にこれらすべてのプレゼントをくださった方なのですか.
Well really! いやはや《軽い非難・困惑の表現》.

realms /relmz/ 名 ***beyond*** [***within***] ***the realms of possibility*** 不可能[可能]な ▪ It is not *beyond the realms of possibility* for Howard to hang on as Prime Minister all the way through the next term. ハワードが次期任期までずっと首相として居座ることは不可能ではない.

ream /riːm/ 名 ***reams of***《口》多量の(書きもの) ▪ He has written *reams and reams of* worthless verse. 彼はおびただしい量のくだらない詩を書いた. ☞ream「連(洋紙480枚)」.

reap /riːp/ 動 ***As a man sows, so he shall reap./ Reap as*** [***what***] *one* ***has sown./ Reap the harvest of*** *one's* ***own sowing./ As you sow, so shall you reap./ You reap what you sow.*** 自分のしたことの結果を受ける,「因果応報」 ▪ How terribly ill he looks, but he's only *reaping what he sowed* in youth. あの男はひどく病気じみて見えるが, 若いときにまいた種を刈っているだけの話だ.
reap the fruit(s) of …の報いを受ける ▪ We die before we can *reap the fruit of* our labors. 我々は努力の報いを受けないうちに死ぬのだ.
reap where *one* ***has not sown*** 他人の功を横取りする (《聖》*Matt*. 25. 24) ▪ He is the man who *reaps where* he *has not sown*. 彼は他人の功を横取りするような人間だ.

rear¹ /rɪər/ 名 ***at*** [***in***] (***the***) ***rear of*** …の背後に, (家など)の裏に (↔in (the) FRONT of) ▪ The girl disappeared *in the rear of* her mother. 少女は母親の後ろに隠れた ▪ *At the rear of* the house was a barn. 家の裏に納屋があった.
close [***bring up***] ***the rear*** しんがりを務める, 最下位になる ▪ Tom was in front, while I *brought up the rear*. トムは前方にいて私がしんがりを務めた.
front and rear 前後に ▪ The enemy beset them *front and rear*. 敵は彼らを前後から包囲した.
get *one's* ***rear in gear***《米俗》急ぐ ▪ Now, let's *get our rear in gear*. さあ, 急ごうぜ.
hang on *a person's* ***rear*** (機会を見て襲いかかるために)人のあとをつけ回す ▪ A body of the enemy *hung on their rear*. 敵の一団が彼らのあとをつけ回した.
in [***on***] *one's* ***rear*** 背後に, 後ろに ▪ A huge mountain range rose *in their rear*. 大山脈が彼らの背後にそびえていた.
in the rear (敵の)背面から; 後ろから ▪ We tried to take [attack] the enemy *in the rear*. 我々は敵の背面を突こうとした ▪ She saw, far *in the rear*, a party of men looming up. 彼女はずっと後方に一団の男たちがぼうっと現れるのを見た.
send ... to the rear …を危くない所へやる ▪ The women and children *were sent* at once *to the rear*. 女性と子供はすぐ危くない所へやられた.
the rear (***end***) **1** (車の)後部 ▪ There's a large dent in *the rear end* of the car. 車の後部に大きなへこみがある.
2 おしり, 臀部 ▪ I'm afraid these pants don't fit my *rear end*. このズボンには私のお尻は入りそうにない.

rear² /rɪər/ 動 ***rear*** *oneself* **1** 立ち上がる ▪ A bear will *rear himself* upon his hind-legs. クマは後ろ足で立ち上がる.
2 そびえる ▪ The stately tree *reared itself* aloft. 堂々とした木が高くそびえていた.
rear-end《米》追突する ▪ Her car *was rear-ended* while she was stopped at the light. 彼女の車は信号で停められていたら追突された.
rear the [*one's*] ***head*** 頭を上げる; (悪心などが)

R

頭をもたげる ▪ Vice could not *rear its head*. 悪が頭をもたげることはなかった.

rearguard /ríərgɑ̀ːrd/ 名 ***fight*** [***mount***] ***a rearguard action*** 最後の抵抗をする ▪ We are *fighting a rearguard action* to protect our voting rights. 我々は投票権を守ろうと最後のあがきを見せているところだ.

rearrange /rìːəréɪndʒ/ 動 ***rearrange the deckchairs on the Titanic*** しても役に立たないことをする, 実効性に欠ける ▪ A security analyst described the decision as *rearranging the deckchairs on the Titanic*. ある証券アナリストはその決定を実効性に欠けると述べた.

rearward /ríərwərd/ 名副 ***in*** [***at***] ***the rearward*** 後部に ▪ He came behind *in the rearward*. 彼は後ろからやって来た.

in [***on***] ***the rearward of*** …の後部に ▪ He shall be *in the rearward of* the fight. 彼はこの戦闘の後部にいてもらおう.

rearward of …の後ろに ▪ There was a sewer *rearward of* the building. その建物の後ろに下水管があった.

reason[1] /ríːzən/ 名 ***a woman's*** [***the ladies'***] ***reason*** 女の理屈《好きだから好きだというような, 理由にならぬ理由》 ▪ I have no other but *a woman's reason*: I like him, because I like him. 私には女の理屈しかないの. 彼が好きだから好きなのよ.

against all reason 全く理屈に反して ▪ What he says is *against all reason*. 彼の言うことは全く理屈に反している.

as reason was 当然のことだったが ▪ I obeyed his command *as reason was*. 私は当然のことだったが, 彼の命令に服従した.

beyond (***all***) ***reason*** 途方もなく ▪ The cost of materials has advanced *beyond all reason*. 材料費が途方もなく高騰した.

bring *a person* ***to reason*** 人に道理を悟らせる, 聞き分けさせる ▪ They failed to *bring* her *to reason*. 彼らは彼女に聞き分けさせることができなかった.

by reason of 《文》…のために ▪ The arrangement was canceled *by reason of* his illness. その取り決めは彼の病気のために取り消しになった.

come to reason 正気に返る ▪ He has at last *come to reason*. 彼はやっと正気に返った.

for no other reason than [***but***] ***that*** ただ…だけの理由で ▪ He came *for no other reason than that* he wanted to. 彼が来たのは来たかったからにほかならない.

for reasons best [***only***] ***known to*** *oneself* 個人的な理由で, 他人にはわからない理由で ▪ She tried very hard to adopt me, but my father, *for reasons best known to himself*, wouldn't give me up. 彼女は一生懸命に私を養子にしようとしたが, 父は個人的な理由で私を手放そうとはしなかった.

for reasons of …の理由で, のために ▪ He resigned *for reasons of* health. 彼は健康上の理由で辞任した.

give [***yield, render***] (***a***) ***reason*** (行動などの)理由を述べる ▪ You must *give a reason* of your conduct. あなたは自らの行いの理由を述べねばならない.

give reasons for …の理由をあげる ▪ He *gave reasons for* doing so. 彼はそうする理由をあげた.

have every reason to *do* …する理由が十分ある ▪ I *have every reason to* know that. 私がそれを知っているのには十分理由がある.

have reason 正しい ▪ Both sides *had reason*. 双方正しかった. ☞F avoir raison のなぞり.

have reason for [***to*** *do*] …の[する]理由がある, は[するのは]もっともだ ▪ You *have* no *reason for* that. 君にはそんなことをする理由は少しもない ▪ I *have reason to* remember it. 私にはそれを覚えている理由があります.

hear [***listen to***] ***reason*** 道理に従う, 聞き分ける ▪ My impression is that your wife will *listen to reason*. 私の感じでは奥さんは聞き分けられるでしょう.

in (***all, any***) ***reason*** **1** 道理上, 当然 ▪ The Law could not *in reason* take notice of any such thing. その法律では当然そのような事柄を考慮することはできなかった.

2 道理にかなって, 無理でない ▪ I am willing to do anything *in reason* for him. 彼のためなら理にかなっていることは何でも喜んでする ▪ It is not *in any reason* to expect me to do so. 私にそうしろと期待するのは無理というものだ.

it stands to reason (***that***) …は理の当然だ, もっともなことだ ▪ If you go out in the rain, *it stands to reason that* you'll get wet. 雨の中へ出て行けばぬれるのは理の当然だ.

listen to reason →hear REASON.

lose *one's* ***reason*** 気が狂う ▪ She *lost her reason* after the execution of her husband. 彼女は夫の処刑後気が狂った.

no earthly reason …する理由が全然ない ▪ There's *no earthly reason* why you should do this by yourself. 君が一人でこれをすべき理由なんてこれっぽっちもない.

or you [***he, she, they***] ***will know the reason why*** 《口》さもないとひどい目にあうぞ ▪ Shut up, *or you will know the reason why*. 黙れ, さもないとひどい目にあうぞ.

out of all reason 途方もない ▪ It cost me a sum *out of all reason*. それには莫大な金がかかった.

reason of state 国家的理由《しばしば為政者の口実》 ▪ Napoleon is an incarnation of the doctrine that *reason of state* covers all. ナポレオンは国家的理由はすべてに当てはまるという教義の具現者だ.

One's ***reason returns*** [***is restored***] ***to*** *one*. 正気に返る ▪ At the same time *my reason was restored to* me. 同時に私は正気に返った.

render (***a***) ***reason*** →give (a) REASON.

see reason 道理がわかる ▪ I couldn't make him *see reason*. 彼に道理をわからせることができなかった.

speak reason 道理にかなったことを言う ▪ Why can't you *speak reason*? どうして君は理にかなったこ

とが言えないのか.

the ladies' reason →a woman's REASON.

the reason ... is that [《口》***because***] ...の理由は...だ ▪ *The reason* for my poor work in French *was that* [*because*] I didn't like the subject. フランス語の成績が悪かったのはこの科目がきらいだったからだ.

the reason why その理由 ▪ Tell me *the reason why*. その訳を話してくれ.

there is reason for [***to*** *do*] ...の[する]理由がある ▪ *There is* no *reason for* delay. 遅れる理由はない ▪ *There is reason to* believe so. そう信ずべき理由がある.

there is reason in ...には道理がある ▪ *There is reason in* what you say. 君の言うことには一理ある.

will (***want to***) ***know the reason why*** 《口》ひどく怒るだろう ▪ If I'm not home before 10 o'clock, my father'*ll want to know the reason why*. 10時前に帰らないと父が怒るだろう.

with (***good***) ***reason*** 理由をもって(...する), (...するのも)無理はない ▪ He complains *with good reason*. 彼が不平を言うのも無理はない ▪ Nothing can *with reason* be urged in justification of revenge. いかに論じても復しゅうを正当化するのは無理だ.

within reason 穏当な, 無理のない ▪ I got it for a price *within reason*. それを手頃な値で手に入れた.

without reason 理由もなく ▪ It is not altogether *without reason* to believe so. そう信じるのは全然理由のないことではない.

yield (***a***) ***reason*** →give (a) REASON.

reason[2] /ríːzən/ 動 ***Ours*** [***Yours, Theirs,*** etc.] ***not to reason why.*** 《口》我々[あなた方, 彼ら, など]には文句を言う権利はない《上司の命令は理不尽なものでも聞かねばならない》. ☞Tennyson, *The Charge of the Light Brigade* の "Theirs not to reason why./Theirs but to do and die." から.

reason *oneself* ***into*** 道理を考えて...に至る ▪ He *reasoned himself into* an error. 彼は自分勝手な理屈をつけて誤りを犯した.

Theirs not to reason why. →Ours not to REASON why.

Yours not to reason why. →Ours not to REASON why.

rebellion /rɪbéljən/ 名 ***in rebellion*** 反乱[暴動]を起こして (*against*) ▪ Every province was *in rebellion*. どの地方も暴動を起こしていた ▪ She lived *in* constant *rebellion against* the narrowness of the town. 彼女はその町の偏狭さに絶えず反抗しつつ生活した.

rise in rebellion 反乱[暴動]を起こす (*against*) ▪ The people *rose in rebellion against* tyranny. 人民は圧政に対して暴動を起こした.

rebound /ríːbàʊnd/ 名 ***catch*** [***take***] *a person* ***at*** [***on***] ***the rebound*** 感情の反動を利用して人の心をとらえる ▪ She *caught* him *on the rebound*, after he had been refused by someone else. 彼女は彼が誰か他の女にはねつけられたあとの感情の反動を利用して彼の心をとらえた.

on the rebound 失恋の痛手を受けた反動で ▪ He married Sally *on the rebound*. 彼は失恋の痛手を受けた反動でサリーと結婚した.

recall[1] /rɪkɔ́ːl/ 名 ***beyond*** [***past, without***] ***recall*** 取り返しのつかない; 思い出せない ▪ It is gone *beyond recall*. それは取り返しがつかないことになってしまった ▪ The village sank 70 years ago beneath the waves of memory *beyond recall*. その村は70年前に記憶の彼方の波の下に沈んでしまった.

recall[2] /rɪkɔ́ːl/ 動 ***recall ... to mind*** ...を思い出す ▪ I can't *recall* his name *to mind*. 彼の名前を思い出せない.

recede /rɪsíːd/ 動 ***recede into the background*** (人が)勢力を失う; (問題などが)重要でなくなる ▪ The incident *receded into the background*. その事件は世間から忘れられた.

receipt /rɪsíːt/ 名 ***be in receipt of*** ...を受け取る ▪ We *are in receipt of* your favor dated the 9th inst. 本月9日付の貴簡, まさに拝受いたしました.

on receipt of ...を受け取り次第 ▪ I will pay the money *on receipt of* the goods. 品物を受け取り次第代金を支払います.

receive /rɪsíːv/ 動 ***receive Christ in baptism*** 洗礼を受けてキリスト教徒になる ▪ We *receive Christ in baptism* once as the first beginner of our life. 我々は人生を初めて始める者として1回洗礼を受けてキリスト者になる.

receive *a person* ***into the Church*** 人を教会員と認める ▪ They have *been received* by immersion *into the Church*. 彼らは洗礼を受けて教会員と認められた.

recess /ríːses|rɪsés/ 名 ***at recess*** 休憩時間に ▪ The children play on the playground *at recess*. 子供たちは休み時間には運動場で遊ぶ.

in a recess 休会中で ▪ We are *in a* Parliamentary *recess*. 国会は休会中だ.

in the inmost [***innermost, deepest***] ***recess of*** ...の一番奥で(は) ▪ The fear had lain *in the inmost recess of* my heart. 不安が私の胸の一番奥につかえていた.

make a recess 休憩する ▪ It will be convenient to *make a recess* for a while. しばらく休憩をするのが好都合だろう.

recharge /rìːtʃɑ́ːrdʒ/ 動 ***recharge*** *one's* ***batteries*** 《米口》休養する, 元気を回復する, 浩然の気を養う ▪ They will have a couple of days off to *recharge their batteries*. 彼らは元気回復のため2, 3日休暇をとる予定だ.

recipe /résəpi/ 名 ***be a recipe for*** ...になりそうだ (→be a recipe for DISASTER) ▪ Stopping the development *is a recipe for* disaster. その開発を止めることで惨事を招きそうだ.

reckon /rékən/ 動 ***I reckon*** 〚挿入的または文尾に用いて〛...だと思う ▪ It's faith, *I reckon*, that's kept her going. 彼女をがんばらせたのは信仰だと思う

▪ He will come soon, *I reckon.* 彼はおっつけやって来るだろう.

reckon *A* ***to be*** *B* AをBであるとみなす ▪ I *reckon* her *to be* the prettiest girl in this group. 彼女はこのグループの中で一番きれいな少女だと思う.

reckon without *one's* ***host*** →HOST[1].

reckoning /rékənɪŋ/ 名 ***be out in*** [***of***] *one's* ***reckoning*** 勘定をまちがえる; 当てがはずれる ▪ The examiner *is* quite *out in his reckoning.* 試験官はすっかり勘定をまちがえている.

day of reckoning 〚a をつけて〛清算日; 〚the をつけて〛(特に)報いの来る日, 最後の審判日 ▪ There will be *a day of reckoning* sooner or later. 遅かれ早かれ清算日がやって来るだろう ▪ Remember *the Day of Reckoning.* 最後の審判日を忘れるな.

in(***to***) [***out of***] ***the reckoning*** 《英・スポーツ》勝利が計算できる[できない], 優勝候補である[ない]; 成功の見込みがある[ない] ▪ The player looks likely to come *into the reckoning* for the next game against Iceland. その選手は次のアイスランド戦では勝ち残りそうだ ▪ Frendo was *out of the reckoning* with an ankle injury. フレンドは足首の負傷のため優勝候補からはずれた.

leave ... out of (*one's* [***the***]) ***reckoning*** …を勘定に入れない ▪ Those who rule the earth are apt to *leave out of their reckoning* Him who rules the universe. 地球の支配者はえてして宇宙の支配者[神]のことを勘定に入れないものだ.

lose *one's* ***reckoning of*** …の計算がわからなくなる ▪ I should *lose my reckoning of* time. 時間のたつのがわからなくなってしまうだろう.

reclaim /rɪkléɪm/ 名 ***past*** [***beyond***] ***reclaim*** 矯正[改善, 教化]の見込みのない ▪ I see you are *past reclaim.* どうやら君は改心の見込みがないようだ.

recognition /rèkəgníʃən/ 名 ***beyond*** [***out of, past***] ***recognition*** 元のおもかげのないほど, 見る影もなく ▪ The man had changed *beyond recognition.* 男は見る影もなく変わっていた.

in recognition of …を認めて, の返礼として ▪ I gave him some money *in recognition of* his faithful services. 彼の忠勤の返礼に多少の金を与えた.

recollect /rèkəlékt/ 動 ***recollect*** *oneself* 《まれ》気を落ち着ける; (はっと気づいて)自戒する ▪ His heart beat violently, and he stopped to *recollect himself.* 胸が激しく高鳴ったので彼は気を落ち着けるために立ち止まった.

recollection /rèkəlékʃən/ 名 ***have a*** [***no***] ***recollection of*** …の記憶がある[ない] ▪ I *have a* distinct *recollection of* so doing. 私はそうしたことをはっきりと覚えている ▪ I may have said so, but I *have no recollection of* it. そう言ったかもしれないが, その覚えがない.

in [***within***] *one's* ***recollection*** **1** 覚えている ▪ The battle was well *within his recollection.* その戦いのことを彼はよく覚えていた ▪ The event is *in the recollection of* everybody. その事件はすべての人の記憶にある.
2 覚えているところでは ▪ It has never happened *within my recollection.* 私の覚えているところではそんな事は全く起きなかった.

to the best of *one's* ***recollection*** 記憶するかぎりでは ▪ Did you ever, *to the best of your recollection,* see this picture before? あなたは確かにこの絵を以前見た覚えがありますか.

recommend /rèkəménd/ 動 ***recommend*** *oneself* [*one's* ***soul***] ***to God*** わが身[魂]を神に託す ▪ He *recommended his soul to God.* 彼は神に自らの魂を託した.

recommendation /rèkəmendéɪʃən/ 名 ***in recommendation of*** …を推薦して ▪ He wrote *in recommendation of* the book. 彼はその本の推薦文を書いた.

recompense /rékəmpèns/ 名 ***in recompense for*** [***of***] …の報酬として ▪ He got renown *in recompense for* years of hard work. 彼は長年の精励の報いとして名声を得た.

reconcile /rékənsàɪl/ 動 ***be reconciled to*** …に甘んじている ▪ He *is reconciled to* living in the country. 彼は田舎暮らしに甘んじている.

reconcile *oneself* ***to*** …に甘んじる ▪ I *reconciled myself to* my fate. わが運命に甘んじた.

record /rékərd|-kɔːd/ 名 ***a matter*** [***thing***] ***of record*** →MATTER[1].

a track record →TRACK.

bear record to …を証言する ▪ I can *bear record to* his previous good conduct. 彼の以前のふるまいが立派であったことを証言できます.

beat [***break, cut***] ***the record*** 記録を破る ▪ He is out to *beat the record* for the quarter mile. 彼は4分の1マイルレースのレコードを破ろうと必死になっている.

change the record 《口》曲目を変える《同じことの繰り返しをやめる》 ▪ I wish Dad would *change the record* from time to time. おやじには同じことを繰り返すのを時々やめてもらいたいものだ.

for the record 公式の[に]; 事実を記録するために ▪ What he said was *for the record.* 彼の言ったことは公式のものであった ▪ I'd like to state, just *for the record,* that I disagree with the committee's decision. 記録に残すため発言しておきたいのだが, 私は委員会の決定には反対だ.

get ... on record with *a person* 人に…を表明する ▪ I will *get* my doubts *on record with* the boss. 自分の疑いを所長に打ち明けよう.

get the record straight →put the RECORD straight.

go down in the records 歴史に残る ▪ His achievements will *go down in the records.* 彼の業績は歴史に残るだろう.

go off the record 発表[記録]を中止する ▪ Let's *go off the record* for a moment. ちょっと記録するのをやめよう.

go [***put*** *oneself*] ***on record*** 自分の態度[意見]を

R

明らかにする ▪ He has already *gone on record* in favor of "fewer and better books." 彼はすでに「少数の良書を」に賛成だという態度を明らかにしている ▪ The association of bankers *put itself on record* as favoring government subsidies. 銀行家協会は政府助成金に賛成する旨の態度を明らかにした.

have a good* [*bad*] *record (人・馬・船などが)履歴が良い[悪い] ▪ That airline *has a bad record.* その定期航空路の履歴は良くない《事故が多発している》.

***have the record* (*for*)** (…の)記録を保持している ▪ He *has the record for* the high jump. 彼は高跳びの記録保持者だ.

just for the record →for the RECORD.

keep to the record 本筋をたどる ▪ Never mind what you longed for. *Keep to the record.* 君が何にあこがれたかなどどうでもよろしい. 本筋をたどりなさい.

off the record 《口》公表してはいけない, 非公式の, オフレコで《元来, 政治家の用いる言葉》(↔on (the) RECORD 2) ▪ The Governor emphasized the fact that everything he said was *off the record.* 知事は自分の言うことはすべてオフレコだと強調した.

on* [*upon*] (*the*) *record **1** 記録に載って ▪ It was one of the longest droughts *on record.* それは今までの記録にある一番長い干ばつの一つだった.
2《米》公表されて (↔off the RECORD) ▪ Stalin is *on record* as having said, "I, too, am an Asiatic." スターリンは「私もアジア人です」と言ったと報じられている.

put* [*place*]*… on record **1** …を記録に残す ▪ Such a case certainly deserves to *be put on record.* そんな事例は確かに記録にとどめる値うちがある.
2 …を報じる ▪ They *are put on record* as approving his campaign strategy. 彼らは彼の選挙運動の戦略を是認していると報じられている.

put oneself on record →go on RECORD.

put* [*get, set*] *the record straight 事実を正しく記録する, 誤解を正す ▪ He tried to get in touch with me to *put the record straight.* 彼は誤解を正すために私と連絡をとろうとした.

rewrite the record books (スポーツ選手が)記録を塗り替える ▪ Ichiro *rewrote the record books* year after year. イチローは毎年記録を塗り替えた.

sound like a broken record (壊れたレコードのように)しつこく同じことを繰り返して言う ▪ The elderly man *sounded like a broken record.* その老人はしつこく同じことを繰り返して言った.

travel out of the record 本題からそれる ▪ He will speak to the point and not *travel out of the record.* 彼は要領を得た話をして本題からそれはすまい.

recoup /rɪkúːp/ 動 ***recoup oneself*** 入費[損失]を取り返す ▪ He sells at a low price and *recoups himself* by large sales. 彼は安く売って損失を多売で取り返す.

recourse /ríːkɔːrs|rɪkɔ́ːs/ 名 ***have recourse to*** …に頼る, を用いる ▪ He was compelled to *have recourse to* self-tuition. 彼は独学に頼らねばならなくなった ▪ I cannot spell correctly without *having recourse to* a dictionary. 私は辞書を用いずには正しい字がつづれない.

without recourse 《法・商》支払いの義務なし《証書の裏書人などの用いる句》 ▪ The document said "*without recourse.*" その書類には「支払いの義務なし」と書かれてあった.

without recourse to …に頼らないで ▪ I can read a French novel *without recourse to* a dictionary. 私は辞書を引かずにフランス語の小説を読むことができます.

recover /rɪkʌ́vər/ 動 ***recover oneself*** **1** 平静[体のバランス]を取り戻す ▪ He almost fell, but quickly *recovered himself.* 彼は今にもころびそうになったが, すぐバランスを取り戻した ▪ He intended to *recover himself* a little with the people. 彼は民衆に対して自ら少し平静さを取り戻すつもりになった.
2 正気に返る ▪ Being stunned, it was half an hour before he *recovered himself.* 気絶して半時間たってやっと正気に返った.
3 (疲れ・病気が)治る, 元気になる ▪ He speedily *recovers himself* by taking a walk in the country. 彼は田舎を散歩すればすぐ元気になる.

***recover one's legs* [*feet*]** (倒れてから)立ち上がる ▪ He had no sooner *recovered his legs* than he ran away. 彼は立ち上がるが早いか走って逃げ去った.

recovery /rɪkʌ́vəri/ 名 ***be past recovery*** 回復の見込みがない ▪ The loss *is past recovery.* その損失は取り戻せる見込みがない.

make a good recovery うまく回復する ▪ The patient is *making a good recovery.* 病人はうまく回復している.

recreate /rékrièɪt/ 動 ***recreate oneself*** 休養する, 英気を養う (*with, by*) ▪ He was *recreating himself with* a journey in Scotland. 彼はスコットランド旅行で英気を養っていた.

recruit /rɪkrúːt/ 動 ***recruit oneself*** (飲食・旅行などで)保養する, 元気をつける ▪ He went to the seaside to *recruit himself* for some days. 彼は数日間保養するために海岸へ行った ▪ I sat down to *recruit myself* with a glass of milk. 私は腰をおろしミルクを1杯飲んで元気をつけた.

red /red/ 形名 ***a red face*** 《口》赤面, 当惑, きまり悪さ ▪ There will likely be a lot of *red faces* once the full story comes out. 話が全部明らかになればきっと多くの人がバツの悪い思いをするだろう.

a red letter day 記念日 ▪ Each time she met him was *a red letter day.* 彼女が彼と会う度にそれが記念日となった.

(*as*) *red as a rose* [*a cherry, blood, fire, a peony, a turkey-cock, a beetroot*] (恥ずかしさなどで)真っ赤になって ▪ The bride was *red as a rose.* 花嫁の顔は(恥じらいで)バラのように赤かった.

be taken* [*caught*] *red-handed → catch RED-HANDED.

burn red (恥ずかしさでほおが)真っ赤になる ▪ Her cheeks *burned redder* and *redder.* 彼女のほおはだんだん真っ赤になった.

R

go in [***into***] ***the red*** 《口》赤字になる ▪ He had *gone* $6,000 *in the red.* 彼は6,000ドルの赤字を出してしまった.

go into red ink 赤字になる ▪ The company was *going into red ink.* その会社は赤字になっていくところであった.

go red (***in the face***) 《口》(怒り・恥ずかしさ・当惑で顔が)真っ赤になる ▪ He *went red* with shame. 彼は恥ずかしさで真っ赤になった.

have a red face 当惑する ▪ He *had a red face* when he was caught stealing. 彼は盗みの現場をつかまえられて当惑した.

in the red **1** (シカが)赤い毛をして ▪ The animal is now said to be "*in the red.*" シカは今「赤い毛」の状態だと言われている.
2《口》赤字になって, 借金して (↔ (be) in the BLACK) ▪ Business is *in the red.* 商売は赤字だ. ☞簿記で, 借り方は赤インクで, 貸し方は黒インクで記入した習慣から.

not care a red cent 《米》少しもかまわない ▪ I do*n't care a red cent* what you say. 君が何と言おうと少しもかまわない.

not have a red cent 《米口》一文無しで ▪ I wish I could come with you, but I do*n't have a red cent* at the moment. 君といっしょに行けたらいいんだけど, いまお金の持ち合わせがないもんで.

on red alert 非常態勢を取って, 特別警戒体制で ▪ Military and police forces have been placed *on red alert* ahead of the Labor Day celebration. 軍隊と警察は労働者の日の祝典を前に特別警戒態勢に入っている.

out of the red 《口》赤字を脱して ▪ The business is getting *out of the red* at long last. ようやく商売は赤字を脱するところだ.

paint the town (***red***) →PAINT².

red in tooth and claw 血みどろの; 無情な, 弱肉強食の ▪ Nature is *red in tooth and claw* and its fundamental law is the survival of the fittest. 自然界は弱肉強食であり, その基本法則は適者生存だ.

red ink →go into RED ink.

red tape →TAPE¹.

reds under the bed(***s***) 《戯》(西欧民主主義にとって危険な)左翼活動家 ▪ He believes that there are *reds under the beds.* 彼は危険なアカの分子がいると思っている.

see red 激怒する, かっとなる ▪ Well, I admit I *saw red*, and didn't much know what I was doing. とにかく僕も認めるが, かっとなって自分が何をしているかよくわからなかったのだ. ☞闘牛が赤い布に興奮することから.

see the [***a***] ***red light*** 危険が近づいていることを知る ▪ If you don't *see the* [*a*] *red light*, you must be blind! 危険の近づいていることがわからないのなら, 君は何も見えていないにちがいない.

the red carpet 歓待(の) ▪ It was an unofficial visit so the guests didn't get *the* usual *red carpet* treatment. 非公式の訪問だったので客人はいつもの丁重なもてなしは受けなかった.

the red meat of …の一層強力な[粗野な]面 ▪ He was hungry for *the red meat of* pornography. 彼は一層強烈なポルノを見たがっていた.

the red, white and blue 英国の国旗の色; 英国国旗 ▪ Our careers are dedicated to *the red, white and blue.* 我々は生涯を英国国旗に捧げている.

Was my face red! ほんと恥ずかしかったなあ.

with red hand (殺人の)現行犯で ▪ A murderer was caught *with red hand.* 殺人者が現行犯で捕えられた.

redeem /rɪdíːm/ 動 ***a redeeming feature*** (他の欠点を補う)取り柄 ▪ Her eyes were the only *redeeming feature.* 彼女の目はただ一つの取り柄だった.

redeem *oneself* (償金を出して)自由の身となる ▪ He had been a slave for 9 years, then *redeemed himself.* 彼は9年間の奴隷のあと自由の身となった.

redemption /rɪdémpʃən/ 名 ***beyond*** [***past, without***] ***redemption*** 回復の見込みのない, 救いがたい ▪ Our contract is broken *past* all *redemption.* 我々の契約は修復の見込みが全くないまでに破綻した状態だ ▪ He is *beyond redemption.* 彼は救いがたい.

the year of (***our***) ***redemption*** 西暦 ▪ The king died in *the year of* (*our*) *redemption* 701. その王は西暦701年に死んだ.

red-handed /rèdhǽndəd/ 形 ***catch*** [***nab, take***] ***red-handed*** (犯罪などの)現場を押さえる, 現行犯で捕まえる ▪ I *caught* him *red-handed* going through my desk. 彼が私の机の中を捜している現場を押さえた.

redress /rɪdrés/ 動 ***redress the balance*** つり合いを取り戻す ▪ The personal greatness of the king *redressed the balance.* 王の個人的な偉大さでつり合いが取り戻せた.

reduce /rɪdjúːs/ 動 ***be reduced to*** *doing* [《まれ》***to*** *do*] (困窮して)やむなく…するはめになる ▪ He *was reduced to borrowing* [*to* borrow] clothes. 彼はやむなく借り着をした.

in reduced circumstances 困窮して ▪ He retired to the country *in reduced circumstances.* 彼は困窮して田舎に引っこんだ.

reduce ... into possession 《法》(物・権利)を手に入れる ▪ He must *reduce* the property *into possession* if he can. 彼はできればその財産を手に入れなければならない.

reduce *a person* ***to*** *doing* 人に否応なしに…させる ▪ That *reduced* him *to asserting* an absurdity. それが彼にむちゃなことを主張させた.

reduce ... to [***into***] ***practice*** [***action***] (理論など)を実施する, 実行する ▪ He *reduced* the theory *to practice.* 彼はその理論を実施に移した.

reduce *a person* ***to tears*** [***silence***] 人を泣かせる[沈黙させる] ▪ The booing *reduced* Serena *to tears.* ブーイングを受けてセレナは悔し涙を流した ▪ His rude interruption completely *reduced* me *to silence*. 彼が無作法に割り込んできたので私はやむなく黙った.

reduce ... to [into] writing …を文につうる ▪ Why *was* not the protestation *reduced into writing*? その抗議はなぜ文書にされなかったのか.

reduced circumstances → in bad CIRCUMSTANCEs.

reed /riːd/ 名 ***a broken reed*** 折れアシ; 当てにならないもの (《聖》*Isa*. 42. 3; *Matt*. 12. 20) ▪ In the emergency his brother proved to be *a broken reed*. その危急時に彼の弟は当てにならないことがわかった.

A reed before the wind lives on, while mighty oaks do fall. 《諺》無名で融通のきく者の方が有名で厳格な者よりも危機にあってもけがをしないものだ (Oaks may fall when reeds stand the storm. 「柳に雪折れなし」).

a reed shaken with [by, in] the wind 風にそよぐアシ; 定見のない人 (《聖》*Matt*. 11. 7) ▪ Man is *a* mere *reed shaken in the wind* of force. 人間は力という風にそよぐアシにすぎない.

lean on a reed 頼みにならない物[人]に頼る ▪ I only meant to show that you were *leaning on a reed*. 私はあなたが頼みにならない人に頼っているということを明らかにしたかったにすぎません.

reef /riːf/ 名 ***let out a reef*** →LET².

shake out another reef 《海》もう一つ帆を広げる; 《俗》逃げる ▪ I'll *shake out another reef*, and outwit them. おれは逃げてやつらに一杯くわしてやるんだ.

take in a reef 《海》縮帆する; (服を)小さくする; (財産などを)切りつめる ▪ She has had to *take in a reef* in her dress. 彼女は服を小さくしなければならなかった ▪ He is wasting away, and will be obliged to *take in a reef* very soon. 彼はどしどし金を使っているから, じき切りつめなければならなくなるよ.

reel¹ /riːl/ 名 ***(right) off the reel*** **1** 立て[ぶっ]続けに ▪ This story should be read *off the reel*. この物語はぶっ続けに読まねばならない ▪ He won five races *off the reel*. 彼は続けざまに5回優勝した.

2 ためらわず, 直ちに ▪ Where's my old man; tell me *right off the reel*. おやじはどこにいるんだ. すぐ教えてくれ. ☞ 糸が糸巻きからすらすらと出ることから.

(straight) off the reel ＝(right) off the REEL 1.

reel² /riːl/ 名 ***without a reel or a stagger*** よろめかずに, しっかりと ▪ He walked on *without a reel or a stagger*. 彼はしっかりと歩いて行った.

refer /rɪfə́ːr/ 動 ***refer*** *oneself* ***to*** …に依頼する, 任せる ▪ I *refer myself to* your generosity. ご寛容におすがりします.

reference /réfərəns/ 名 ***for reference*** 参考のために ▪ They have got an album, *for reference*, at all the chief police stations. すべての主要な警察署では参照用に写真帳を備えている.

have reference to …に関係がある ▪ The parts of a machine all *have reference to* each other. 機械の各部品は互いに関連している ▪ Success seems to *have* little *reference to* merit. 成功は実力とほとんど関係がないようだ.

in [with] reference to …に関して ▪ I have nothing to say *with reference to* this question. この問題に関しては何も言うことはない.

make reference to **1** …を参照する, に当たってみる, 問い合わせる ▪ Did you *make reference to* a guidebook? ガイドブックに当たってみましたか ▪ I should like to *make reference to* your last employer. あなたの前の雇用主に問い合わせたいと思います.

2 …に言及する ▪ *Reference was made to* the events in the Times. タイムズ紙ではその事件について論及されていた.

without reference to **1** …に関係なく, をかまわず ▪ This is true of all persons, *without reference to* gender. このことは男女を問わず万人に当てはまる.

2 …に相談せずに ▪ He acted *without reference to* me. 彼は私に相談せずに行動した.

reflect /rɪflékt/ 動 ***reflect credit [discredit] on [upon]*** …に名誉[不名誉]をもたらす ▪ His misdeed *reflected discredit on* the firm. 彼の非行が会社に不名誉をもたらした.

reflect favorably [well] on [upon] …をよく見せる, 名誉となる ▪ His action *reflects well on* his judgment. 彼の行為は彼の判断がよく反映されたものだ.

the reflected glory 他者の威光, (有名人の)七光り ▪ His father was a great painter, but he was not content to bask in *the reflected glory*. 彼の父親は偉大な画家であったが, 彼はその七光りに浴することに甘んじなかった.

reflection /rɪflékʃən/ 名 ***be a (sad [poor]) reflection on [upon]*** …を辱めるものである ▪ Your conduct *is a reflection on* your character. 君の行為は君の人格を辱めるものである ▪ The increase in crime *is a sad reflection on* our society today. 犯罪の増加は今日の社会を反映する悲しい事実だ.

cast reflection on [upon] …を非難する, の不名誉となる ▪ How dare you *cast reflection on* my motives? よくもまあ私の動機を非難できるものだね.

on [upon] reflection 熟考の上, よく考えてみると ▪ *On reflection* you will change your mind. よくよく考えれば君も気持ちが変わりましょう.

reform /rɪfɔ́ːrm/ 動 ***reform*** *oneself*/ ***reform*** *one's* ***heart [life]*** 改心する ▪ Go and *reform yourself*. 行って改心するがよい.

refresh /rɪfréʃ/ 動 ***feel refreshed*** 気が清々する ▪ I took a walk in the woods, and *felt* quite *refreshed*. 私は森を散歩してすっかり気分がよくなった.

refresh *oneself* **1** (休憩・飲食などして)元気をつける ▪ Is there any quiet inn, where one might rest and *refresh oneself*? 一服して元気をつけることのできる静かな宿がどこかありますか.

2 1杯飲む ▪ We stopped at a pub to *refresh*

ourselves. 我々は居酒屋へ寄って1杯やった.

refresh** one's* [*a person's*] ***memory 思い出す[思い出させる] ▪ *Refresh my memory*, will you? How many children has she got? 思い出させてくれないか. 彼女には何人子供がいたんだっけ?

refuge /réfju:dʒ/ 名 ***give refuge to*** …をかくまう, 保護する ▪ A sanctuary *gives refuge to* the wronged. 教会は虐待を受けた人々をかくまってくれる.

seek [***take***] ***refuge with** a person* 人の所に隠れる, 逃げ込む ▪ He *sought refuge with* a neighbor. 彼は隣人の家に隠れた.

take refuge at …に避難する ▪ A thunderstorm forced the King to *take refuge at* a hut. 雷雨のために王は小屋に避難しなければならなくなった.

take refuge in **1** …に避難する ▪ He *took refuge in* Switzerland. 彼はスイスに避難した.
2 …に慰安を求める ▪ He *took refuge in* a cigar. 彼は葉巻に慰安を求めた.

the last refuge 最後の逃げ口上, 奥の手 ▪ Patriotism is *the last refuge* of a scoundrel. 国のためというのは悪党の最後の逃げ口上である.

refusal /rɪfjú:zəl/ 名 ***give** a person **a flat refusal*** 人にきっぱり断る ▪ If you refer it to me, I will *give* you *a flat refusal*. 私の方へそれを持ち込まれるなら, きっぱりお断りします.

give [***have, get***] (***the***) ***first refusal*** 優先的選択権を与える[得る] ▪ I'll *give* you *first refusal* when I sell this old book. この古書を売るときには君が諾否を決めていいよ.

give [***have***] ***the refusal of*** …の取捨権を与える[がある] ▪ I will *give* you *the refusal of* my offer till the end of the month. 私の申し入れに対する諾否のご返答は月末までお待ちします ▪ Will you let me *have the refusal of* it till tomorrow? それを売らずにあすまで取っておいてもらえませんか.

take no refusal いやとは言わせない ▪ I will *take no refusal* from you; you must do exactly what I wish. いやとは言わせないよ. 僕の希望通りにしてくれ.

regale /rɪgéɪl/ 動 ***regale** oneself* (飲食物・娯楽などで)元気をつける, 楽しむ (*with*) ▪ He *regaled himself with* a cigar. 彼は葉巻をくゆらした.

R

regard[1] /rɪgá:rd/ 名 ***give** one's **regards*** よろしくと言う (*to*) ▪ *Give my regards to* your friends. 君の友人諸君によろしく.

have great [***a high***] ***regard for*** …を大いに重んじる, 尊敬する ▪ I have come to *have a high regard for* him. 私は彼を大いに尊敬するようになった.

have no [***little***] ***regard for*** …を少しも[ほとんど]重んじない, 考慮しない ▪ He *has no regard for* the feelings of others. 彼は人の感情を全く考えない.

have [***pay***] ***regard to*** …を考慮する, 尊重する ▪ You must *pay regard to* public opinion. 君は世論を尊重しなければならない.

hold ... in high [***great***] ***regard*** …を大いに尊敬する ▪ I *hold* him *in high regard* because of his sturdy independence. 彼の確固たる独立心のゆえに彼を大いに尊敬している.

hold ... in low regard …を軽く見る ▪ Mere skill *is held in low regard*. 単なる技術だけでは軽視される.

in** a person's **regard 人に関しては ▪ There was nothing to do *in his regard*. 彼については何もしてやることはなかった.

in regard of [***to***]/***with regard to*** …に関しては ▪ What have you to say *in regard to* this matter? この件について何かご意見がおありですか ▪ I speak *with regard to* sensible things only. 私はわかるものだけについて話しているのです.

in this [***that***] ***regard*** この[その]事については ▪ Have you anything to say *in this regard*? この事について何か言い分がありますか.

kind regards to …によろしく ▪ *Kindest regards to* all. みなさまにくれぐれもよろしく.

out of regard for …のことを考慮して ▪ *Out of regard for* your father, I shall not dismiss you this time. 君のおとうさんのことを考えて今回は君を解雇すまい.

pay regard to →have REGARD to.

send** one's **regards (人に)よろしくと言う ▪ We *send* her *our regards*. あの人によろしく.

with kind regards to [***from***] …に[から]よろしく ▪ *With kindest regards to* your family. お宅のみなさまにどうかよろしく ▪ *With kind regards from* the author. 謹呈, 著者より.

with regard to →in REGARD of.

without regard to [***for***] …をかまわずに; に関係なく ▪ They sent him there *without regard to* his family circumstances. 彼らは彼の家庭状況におかまいなしに彼をそこへやった.

regard[2] /rɪgá:rd/ 動 ***as regards*** …に関しては, の点では《主文が過去のときは as regarded となることがある》 ▪ I cannot agree with you *as regards* that. それについては君に同意することはできない ▪ Baths were occasionally disappointing *as regarded* hot water. 風呂は湯に関してときとして失望させられることがあった.

regardful /rɪgá:rdfəl/ 形 ***be regardful of*** …を気にかける ▪ *Be* more *regardful of* your own interests. 自分の利害をもう少し気にかけなさい.

regardless /rɪgá:rdləs/ 形 ***regardless of*** **1** …にかまわずに; を無視して ▪ I shall go *regardless of* the weather. 天候にかかわらず参ります.
2 …にかかわらず ▪ *Regardless of* his faults, I like him. 欠点はあるけれど私は彼が好きだ.

region /rí:dʒən/ 名 ***in the region of*** ほとんど…, ほぼ… ▪ The number of applicants was *in the region of* 60. 志願者の数はほぼ60であった.

register /rédʒəstər/ 動 ***register** oneself* 登録する (*as*) ▪ They *registered themselves* in the census *as* members of the Church of England. 彼らは国勢調査でイギリス国教徒として登録した.

registry /rédʒəstri/ 名 ***marry at a registry*** (***office***) 登記所で結婚する《宗教的儀式をあげない》 ▪ They are to *be married at a registry*. 二人は

登記所で結婚する予定だ.

regret[1] /rɪgrét/ 名 ***a matter for regret*** 遺憾な事柄 ▪ It is *a matter for* deep *regret*. それは非常に遺憾な事だ.

express regret at …に対して遺憾の意を表する ▪ We have to *express regret at* the inadvertence. その不注意に対して遺憾の意を表さねばならない.

express regret for …を悪かったとわびる ▪ He *expressed regret for* having done so. 彼はそうしたことは悪かったとわびた.

feel regret for …を後悔する ▪ I *felt* deep *regret for* past misdeeds. 過去の不心得を深く悔いた.

have no regrets 悔いることがない, 悪いことをしたと思わない ▪ The boy is past praying for, he *has no regrets*. あの少年は度しがたく悔いることがない.

to one's regret 残念ながら ▪ *To my* deep *regret* I cannot accept your invitation. はなはだ残念ですがご招待には応じかねます.

with regret(s) 残念に思って ▪ He heard *with regret* of the news. 彼はその知らせを聞いて残念に思った ▪ I refused it *with* much *regret* [many *regrets*]. 非常に残念ながらそれを断った.

regret[2] /rɪgrét/ 動 ***I regret to say (that)*** 遺憾ながら ▪ *I regret to say that* your letter arrived a day too late. 残念だがあなたの手紙は1日遅く届いた.

regular /régjələr/ 形 ***a regular guy [fellow]*** 《米口》いいやつ, 男 ▪ Tom is *a regular guy*. トムはいいやつだ.

(as) regular as clockwork 時計のように規則正しく ▪ He comes home every night, *regular as clockwork*. 彼は毎晩時計のようにきちんと帰宅する.

regulation /règjəléɪʃən/ 名 ***a blanket regulation*** 全てに一律に適用される規則 ▪ *The blanket regulation* will bring about the ruin of many schools. 規則の一律の適用は多くの学校で荒廃をもたらすだろう.

rehabilitate /rìːhəbílətèɪt/ 動 ***rehabilitate oneself*** 名誉[信用]を回復する ▪ He hoped to *rehabilitate himself*. 彼は名誉が回復することを願った.

reign[1] /reɪn/ 名 ***a reign of terror*** 恐怖時代[状態], 独裁体制 ▪ A lot of people became his victims during *a* ten-year *reign of terror*. 多くの人々が彼の10年に及ぶ独裁体制の犠牲になった.

in [under] the reign of …の御代(みよ)に ▪ The poem was written *in the reign of* Charles II. その詩はチャールズ2世の御代に書かれた.

reign[2] /reɪn/ 動 ***reign supreme*** 主権を握る; 行き渡る ▪ Specialists *reign supreme* in hospitals. 病院では専門家が主権を握っている ▪ Silence *reigned supreme*. あたりはしんと静まり返っていた.

rein /reɪn/ 名 ***assume [drop, resign] the reins of government*** 政権を握る[離れる] ▪ The council of state *assumed the reins of government*. 最高行政裁判所が政権を握った ▪ The Shogun *resigned the reins of government* into the hands of his son. 将軍は世子(せいし)に政権を譲った. ☞ F les rênes du gouvernement のなぞり.

draw rein 手綱を引く, 馬を止める ▪ We never *drew rein* for twenty miles. 我々は20マイルの間馬を止めなかった.

give [allow] full [free] rein (人に)自由にふるまわせる, (感情を)ほしいままにする ▪ The children *were given free rein* to do whatever they liked. 子供たちは何でもしたいことをすることを許された ▪ He *gave full rein* to his progressive views. 彼は自由に自分の進歩的な考えを述べた.

give (the) rein(s) to **1** (馬)が行きたい方に行かせる ▪ We *gave rein to* our horses. 我々は馬に行きたい方へ行かせた.

2 (想像・情欲など)をほしいままにさせる ▪ He *gave the rein(s) to* his imagination. 彼は想像をたくましくした ▪ He *gave* loose *rein to* his passions. 彼は情欲に身を持ちくずした.

have free rein やりたい放題にする ▪ The tyrant *had free rein* in his country. その暴君は自分の国でやりたい放題のことをした.

hold [keep] a tight rein on …を厳格に制御する ▪ I am *keeping a tight rein on* his activities. 私は彼の行動を厳しく制限している.

hold the reins 手綱を握っている; 政権[実権]を握っている ▪ The party still *hold the reins* of government. その党がまだ政権を握っている ▪ There is no doubt his wife *holds the reins*. 彼の細君が実権を握っていることは確かだ.

resign the reins of government → assume the REINs of government.

take (up [over]) the reins 指導[支配]する, 引き継ぐ ▪ He *took the reins* of the business in his hands. 彼がその仕事の指導権を握っていた.

throw (up) the reins to …をほしいままにさせる ▪ To do so is to *throw the reins to* his whim. そんなことをすれば彼の気まぐれを勝手にさせることになる.

with a loose [slack] rein 甘やかして, 寛大に ▪ The Sultan governs *with a loose rein*. そのスルタンは寛大な政治をする.

reinvent /rìːɪnvént/ 動 ***reinvent the wheel*** (既存の有益なものがあるのに)最初からやり直す; むだなことをする ▪ Stop *reinventing the wheel* every time you design a Web site. ウェブサイトをデザインするたびに一からやり直すのはやめなさい.

rejoice /rɪdʒɔ́ɪs/ 動 ***be rejoiced at [by, to do, that]*** …で[して, ということを]喜ぶ ▪ The King *was rejoiced at* seeing [*to* see] him. 王は彼に会って喜ばれた ▪ I *am rejoiced at* it [*that* it should be so]. 私はそのこと[それがそのようであること]を喜んでいる.

rejoice in the name [title] of …という(おもしろい)名で呼ばれている ▪ Our village *rejoices in the name of* Stokoe. わが村はストーコーと呼ばれている.

rejoinder /rɪdʒɔ́ɪndər/ 名 ***in rejoinder to*** …の返答に ▪ *In rejoinder to* your note of Sunday morning, I wrote an answer. 日曜日の朝の貴信に

R

答えて返事を書きました.

relapse /rɪlǽps/ 名 ***have a relapse*** (***of***) (病気を)ぶり返す ▪ The patient has *had a relapse of* cold. その患者は風邪をぶり返した.

relate /rɪléɪt/ 動 ***as relates to*** …に関しては ▪ Nor is he fortunate *as relates to* pronunciation. また彼は発音に関してもうまくいっていない.

be related to **1** …と関係がある ▪ The play "Twelfth Night" *is* not *related* at all *to* the day. 「十二夜」という芝居は十二夜と少しも関係がない.

2 …と親類である ▪ *Is* the man *related to* the royal family? その人は皇族と姻せき関係にあるのですか.

be related with …と関係がある ▪ These two facts *are* curiously *related with* each other. これら二つの事実は奇妙なことに互いに関連している.

curious [***strange***] ***to relate*** 妙な話だが ▪ *Curious to relate*, the giraffe has no voice. 妙な話だがキリンは声が出せない.

relate *oneself* ***to*** …に結びつく ▪ It is not fully clear how the words *relate themselves to* the context. それらの語がどのように文脈に結びついているのかあまりはっきりしない.

strange to relate →curious to RELATE.

relation /rɪléɪʃən/ 名 ***a*** [***the***] ***poor relation*** (同類の中で)劣っている[劣ると見られる]人[もの] ▪ Students at Oxbridge usually regard students at other universities as *poor relations*. オックスブリッジの学生は他大学の学生を二流と考えるのが普通だ ▪ Prostate-cancer research funding is *a poor relation* compared to the big money commanded by breast cancer. 前立腺がんの研究資金は乳がん研究に当てられる大金に比べて見劣りする.

be out of all relation to/***bear no relation to*** …と全くつり合わない ▪ The outlay *is out of all* [*bears no*] *relation to* the object aimed at. 支出は策定した目標とはまるでつり合っていない.

have no relation to …と関係がない ▪ That *has no relation to* the present situation. それは現状と関係がない.

have relation to …と関係がある, に言及している ▪ It *had relation to* horses. それは馬と関係があった ▪ These words *have relation to* his return into Flanders. これらの言葉は彼がフランドルへ戻って行ったことに言及している.

have relations with …と交渉[関係]がある ▪ The girl *has relations with* a man. その娘は男と関係をもっている.

in [***with***] ***relation to*** …に関連して, について ▪ He has become an absolute sceptic *in relation to* religion. 彼は宗教に関しては全くの懐疑主義者になってしまった.

make relation to …に言及する ▪ *Relation was made to* the affair. その件について話があった.

relationship /rɪléɪʃənʃìp/ 名 ***a love-hate relationship*** けんか友達の[愛憎]関係 ▪ The investors enjoy *a love-hate relationship* with the stocks and the dealers. 投資家たちは株とディーラーとの愛憎関係を享受しているのだ.

relative /rélətɪv/ 形 ***be relative to*** **1** …に呼応[比例]する ▪ The market value will always *be relative to* its demand. 価格は常に需要に比例する.

2 …に相対的である ▪ Beauty *is relative to* the beholder's eye. 美醜は見る人の目いかんによる.

relative to **1** …に関して[する] ▪ I wrote to the office *relative to* my health. 私は健康状態について職場に手紙を出した.

2 …に比例して, の割合いに ▪ The population of the town is large *relative to* its size. その町の人口は面積のわりに多い.

relatively /rélətɪvli/ 副 ***relatively speaking*** 相対的に言えば, それとの関連で言えば ▪ *Relatively speaking*, these were minor events. 相対的に言えば, これらはあまり重大ではない出来事だ.

relatively to **1** …と相関的に ▪ He does not put a value on himself *relatively to* others. 彼は他の人との関連において自分を評価することがない.

2 …に比較して, のわりには ▪ *Relatively to* his other novels, Dickens's "Oliver Twist" is not a great one. ディケンズの他の小説と比べれば「オリバー・ツイスト」は優れた小説ではない.

relax /rɪlǽks/ 動 ***relax*** *oneself* くつろぐ, 休養する ▪ Take a day or two off and *relax yourself*. 1, 2 日休んでくつろぎなさい.

relax *one's* ***grip*** [***hold***] ***on*** …を握っている手をゆるめる《比喩的にも》 ▪ The chancellor will *relax his hold on* the economy. 財務大臣は経済統制の手をゆるめるだろう.

relay /ríːleɪ/ 名 ***in*** [***by***] ***relays*** 交替で ▪ They were working *in relays*. 彼らは交替で働いていた.

reliance /rɪláɪəns/ 名 ***in reliance on*** …を当てにして ▪ I waited *in reliance on* your promise. お約束を当てにして待っていました.

place [***put, have***] ***reliance on*** [***upon, in***] …を信用する, 当てにする ▪ You can *place* full *reliance on* his sagacity. 彼の賢さを全面的に当てにしていい ▪ He *had* great *reliance in* her talents. 彼は彼女の才能を大いに信用していた.

reliant /rɪláɪənt/ 形 ***be reliant on*** …に頼る ▪ I *am reliant on* sleeping pills these days. このごろは睡眠薬に頼っている.

relief[1] /rɪlíːf/ 名 ***bring*** [***throw***]***...*** (***out***) ***into*** (***sharp***) ***relief*** …を目立たせる ▪ The horrors *were brought out into* full *relief* by him. その惨事が彼の手で余すところなく浮き彫りにされた.

in relief **1** 浮き彫りにして (↔in the FLAT, in the ROUND 1) ▪ It was a figure sculptured *in relief*. それは浮き彫りで彫られた像だった.

2 くっきりと, 目立って ▪ The mountains stand out *in* bold *relief* against the sky. 山々は空にくっきりと浮かび出ている.

relief[2] /rɪlíːf/ 名 ***by way of relief*** 息抜きに ▪ He introduced comic scenes into his tragedies *by way of relief*. 彼は息抜きに悲劇の中に喜劇的場

R

面を入れた.

give a relief to …の慰み[気晴らし]になる ▪ A walk will *give a relief to* the tired brain. 散歩は疲れた頭の気晴らしになる.

give [***heave***] ***a sigh of relief*** → breathe a SIGH of relief.

on relief 生活保護を受けて ▪ We were poor, but we never went *on relief*. 私たちは貧しかったが, 生活保護を受けたことは一度もなかった.

send relief to …に救援物資を送る ▪ We *sent relief to* the people made homeless by floods. 我々は洪水で家を失った人々に救援物資を送った.

to *one's* ***relief*** ほっとしたことには ▪ *To my* great *relief* the difficulties were all overcome. 困難がすべて取り除かれて大いにほっとした.

with relief ほっと[安心]して ▪ She sighed *with relief*. 彼女は安堵(ど)のため息をついた.

without relief 息抜きのない ▪ We crossed wide stretches of moorland *without relief*. 我々は広々とした荒野を休むことなく横切った.

relieve /rɪlíːv/ 動 ***be relieved against*** …を背景にして引き立つ ▪ His tall figure *was relieved against* the blue sky. 青空を背景にして彼の背の高い姿が引き立って見えた.

be relieved by [***with***] …で趣を添える ▪ The black dress *is relieved by* white lace. その黒いドレスは白いレースで変化を持たせてある.

relieve *oneself* [***nature***] 用を足す, 大小便する ▪ Children are likely to *relieve themselves* on any street. 子供はどこの通りでも用を足しがちだ.

relieve *one's* ***feelings*** (泣く・どなる・あばれるなどして)気を晴らす ▪ The girl *relieved her feelings* by shedding tears. 少女は涙を流して気を晴らした.

relievo /rɪlíːvoʊ/ 名 ***in relievo*** 浮き彫りにして[した] ▪ The walls are covered with figures sculptured *in relievo*. 周囲の壁一面に浮き彫りにした像がずらりと刻んである.

religion /rɪlídʒən/ 名 ***be in religion*** 修道者の身である ▪ His two brothers *are in religion*. 彼の二人の兄弟は修道者の身である.

enter into religion 修道生活に入る ▪ We must *enter into religion* and be made nuns by will or by force. 私たちは修道生活に入り, 自分の意志か, 力ずくで尼僧にならなければなりません.

get [***experience***] ***religion*** 《口》発心(ほっしん)する, 信仰に入る ▪ We had come here to *get religion*. 私たちは入信するためにここへ来ていた.

make (***a***) ***religion of*** *doing*/***make it a religion to*** *do* 後生大事に[必ず]…する ▪ Under the circumstances, he *makes a religion of doing* so. そういう次第で彼は後生大事にそうするんだ ▪ I *make it a religion to* obey your command. 私は必ずご命令に従うようにします.

profess a religion 宗教を信奉する ▪ What *religion* do you *profess*? どの宗教を信奉しているのか.

relish /rélɪʃ/ 名 ***have no relish for*** …に食欲がない; に興味がない ▪ I *have no relish for* my food. 食事はいらない ▪ I *have no relish for* that sort of novel. そんな小説には興味がない.

with relish **1** うまそうに ▪ He ate *with* keen *relish*. 彼はとてもうまそうに食べた.
2 おもしろ[得意]そうに ▪ He went on reading *with* great *relish*. 彼はいかにもおもしろそうに読書を続けた.

reluctance /rɪlʌ́ktəns/ 名 ***show reluctance to*** *do* …したがらない ▪ He *showed reluctance to* go. 彼は行きたがらなかった.

with reluctance いやいやながら, しぶしぶと ▪ I gave up my liberty *with* great *reluctance*. 私はきわめていやいやながら自由を捨てた.

without reluctance いやがらずに, 喜んで ▪ He consented to part with it *without reluctance*. 彼は喜んでそれを手放すことに同意した.

reluctant /rɪlʌ́ktənt/ 形 (***be***) ***reluctant to*** *do* …するのをいやがる, 気が進まない ▪ He seemed *reluctant to* join us. 彼は我々の仲間になるのをいやがっている様子だった.

rely /rɪláɪ/ 動 ***rely upon it*** 確かに, きっと ▪ *Rely upon it*, he will be here. きっと彼は来るよ.

remain /rɪméɪn/ 動 ***I remain yours truly*** [***sincerely,*** etc.]. 敬具《手紙の結び》.

it (***only***) ***remains*** (***for*** *one*) ***to*** *do* 《口》最後に…しておきたい, まだ…することが残っている ▪ *It only remains for me to* thank our host for such a lovely evening. 最後にかくも楽しい夕べを過ごさせてくださったご主人に対してお礼を申しあげておきます ▪ *It remains to* be seen if it will last. それが続くかどうかはのちのちにならないとわからない ▪ *It remains for* us *to* apply the law to the fact. まだその事実に法を適用することが残っている.

it remains to *a person* ***to*** *do* …するのは人の役目だ ▪ *It remains to* her *to* do it. それをするのは彼女の役目です.

nothing remains (***for*** *one*) ***but to*** *do* あとは…するだけだ ▪ *Nothing remains for* me *but to* draw the moral. あとはもう教訓を引き出すだけだ.

remain to be seen まだ誰にもわからない ▪ His brilliant career as a violinist *remains to be seen*. 彼のバイオリン奏者としての輝かしい経歴はまだ誰にもわかっていない.

who will [***shall***] ***remain nameless*** 《口》名前は伏せておくが《誰かが失敗・悪事をしでかした時に》 ▪ A certain woman, *who will remain nameless*, forgot to turn off the light. 名前は伏せておくが, ある女性が灯りを消し忘れたんだ.

remand[1] /rɪmǽnd|-mάːnd/ 名 ***keep … under remand*** …を再拘留しておく ▪ There was enough against him to make it my duty to *keep* him *under remand*. どうしても再拘留しておかねばならないほど彼には不利な証拠がそろっていた.

on remand 再拘留中で ▪ The prisoner appeared *on remand*. 被告が再拘留の姿を見せた.

remand[2] /rɪmǽnd|-mάːnd/ 動 ***remand a*** *person* ***in custody*** 《法》〚しばしば受身で〛人を再拘留する ▪ The prisoner *was remanded in cus-*

R

tody on the charge of murder. 被告人は殺人罪で再拘留された.

remark /rɪmάːrk/ 名 ***make* [*let fall*] *a remark*** 何か言う ▪ Did you *make a remark* on the subject? 君はそのことについて何か言ったのか.

make remarks かれこれ言う, 批評する; 演説する ▪ He *made* some *remarks* I could not catch. 彼は私には聞きとれないことをあれこれ言った.

pass a remark 所見を述べる ▪ He *passed a remark* or two on the subject. 彼はその問題について一言二言所見を述べた.

***pass remarks upon* [*at*]** …についてかれこれ言う ▪ She began to *pass remarks at* the new guy. 彼女はその新米のことをかれこれ言いだした.

pass without remark (触れないで)黙過する ▪ Let it *pass without remark*. それは黙過するがいい.

the theme of general remark 世評の種 ▪ Her marriage was *the theme of general remark*. 彼女の結婚は世評の種であった.

worthy of remark 注目に値する ▪ I have nothing *worthy of remark*. 言うほどのことは何もない.

remarkable /rɪmάːrkəbəl/ 形 ***remarkable for*** …で目立つ[著しい] ▪ He is *remarkable for* his courage. 彼は並みはずれた勇気がある.

remedy /rémədi/ 名 ***be past* [*beyond*] *remedy*** 救済の見込みがない, 矯正できない ▪ He *is past remedy*. 彼はもう手おくれだ ▪ The evil *is beyond remedy*. この害悪は矯正できない.

There is a remedy for everything* [*all things*] *but* [*except*] *death. 《諺》死を除けば全てのものに救済の道がある, 生きてさえいればなんとかなる.

there is no remedy but to *do* …するよりほかに仕方がない ▪ *There is no remedy but to* fight. 戦うよりほかに仕方がない.

remember /rɪmémbər/ 動 ***be remembered as* [*for*]** …として[の故に]記憶される ▪ Michael Jackson will forever *be remembered as* the King of Pop. マイケル・ジャクソンはポップ音楽のキングとして永遠に記憶されるだろう ▪ Edward Kennedy *is remembered for* his passion, work ethic and sense of humor. エドワード・ケネディーは情熱と労働倫理とユーモアのセンスにより記憶に残る.

Not that I remember. そういう記憶はない ▪ Have you ever met my mother?—*Not that I remember*. 母に会ったことがありますか—そういう記憶はありませんね.

remember *doing* [***to have*** *done*] …したのを覚えている ▪ I *remember seeing* him once. 彼に一度会った覚えがある ▪ I do not *remember to have* said anything of the sort. そんなことを言った覚えはない.

***Remember the Alamo* [*Pearl Harbor*].** 《諺》アラモ[真珠湾]を忘れるな,「歴史を忘れるな」.

something to remember me by 《口》プレゼント; 一撃, 一発 ▪ Here's *something to remember me by*! これ記念に差し上げます ▪ If you do that again, I'll give you *something to remember me by*. もう一度そんなことをしたら, 一発くらわすぞ.

remembrance /rɪmémbrəns/ 名 ***bear* [*have, keep*]*... in remembrance*** …を記憶にとどめている, 覚えている ▪ His name deserves to *be kept in* evergreen *remembrance*. 彼の名はいつまでも変わらぬ思い出として記憶にとどめておく価値がある.

bring* [*call*]*... to remembrance …を思い出す ▪ I cannot *bring* the deed *to remembrance*. その行為を思い出すことができない.

give *one's* ***remembrance to*** …によろしくと言う ▪ *Give my* kind *remembrance to* your parents. ご両親にどうかよろしくお伝えください.

have remembrance of …の記憶がある ▪ I *have* no *remembrance of* it. そのことは少しも覚えていない.

in remembrance of …の記念[思い出]に[の] ▪ Keep it *in remembrance of* me. 私の思い出にそれを納めておいてください ▪ It was a pillar *in remembrance of* the exploit. それはその偉業を記念する柱であった.

put* [*keep*]** *a person* ***in remembrance of 人に…を思い出させる, 記憶させておく ▪ This might *put* him *in remembrance of* the fact. これで彼もそのことを思い出すかもしれない.

to the best of my remembrance 私が覚えているかぎりでは ▪ *To the best of my remembrance*, he sat there four days together. 私が覚えているかぎりでは彼は4日間ぶっ続けでそこに座っていた.

within *one's* ***remembrance*** …の記憶するところでは ▪ It has happened more than once *within my remembrance*. 私の記憶するところではそれは何回も起こっている.

remind /rɪmáɪnd/ 動 ***Don't remind me.*** 《口・戯》(思い出したくないことを)思い出させないでくれ ▪ So baby, *don't remind me*. だから可愛こちゃん, 思い出させないでくれ.

remind *a person* ***to*** *do* [***that, how***] 人に…すること[ということ]を気づかせる ▪ Please *remind* me *to* write tomorrow. あす手紙を書くことを私に思い出させて ▪ Allow me to *remind* you *that* grass is green. ちょっとご注意しますが草は緑ですよ.

That reminds me. それで思い出した.

reminder /rɪmáɪndər/ 名 ***as a reminder of* [*that*]** …を思い出すために ▪ I've pinned a note on the notice board *as a reminder of* our meeting next week. 我々が来週会うことを思い出すように掲示板に紙きれを留めておいた.

reminiscence /rèmənísəns/ 名 ***there is a reminiscence of*** …をしのばせるものがある ▪ *There is a reminiscence of* the Greek type in her face. 彼女の顔にはギリシャ人をしのばせるものがある.

reminiscent /rèmənísənt/ 形 ***reminiscent of*** …を思い起こさせる, しのばせる ▪ It made me *reminiscent of* my young days. それは私の若い頃を思い出させた.

remorse /rɪmɔ́ːrs/ 名 ***feel remorse for*** …を

R

後悔する ▪ She *felt remorse for* her bad conduct. 彼女は自分の悪行を後悔した.

without remorse 情け容赦なく, 無慈悲に ▪ He kicked his servant out *without remorse*. 彼は使用人を情け容赦なく追い出した.

remote /rɪmóʊt/ 形 ***not the remotest*** ほんのわずかの…もない ▪ I have*n't the remotest* conception of it. それが何のことか少しもわからない ▪ He has*n't the remotest* idea where it came from. 彼はそれがどこから来たのか全然知らない.

remote from **1** …から離れた ▪ The house lies *remote from* the road. その家は道路から遠く隔っている.

2 …とは大いに異なる ▪ This is *remote from* my intentions. これは心にもないことだ.

remove[1] /rɪmú:v/ 名 ***at one remove*** 少し距離を置いて (*from*) ▪ He always stayed *at one remove from* those about him. 彼はいつも周囲の人々から一歩距離を置いていた.

be a far remove from …が遠く隔たっている ▪ A word processor *is a far remove from* a typewriter. ワープロはタイプライターとは大きく異なる.

but [***only***] ***one*** [***a***] ***remove from*** …に近い ▪ Genius is *but one remove from* insanity. 天才は狂人と紙一重だ ▪ He is *only one remove from* a fool. 彼はほとんどばかに近い.

get *one's* [***a***] ***remove*** 《英》進級する ▪ I didn't *get my remove* this term. 僕は今学期は進級しなかった.

remove[2] /rɪmú:v/ 動 (***far, further, furthest***) ***removed from*** …から(遠く, より遠く, 最も遠く)隔たって; (大きく)異なって ▪ He is only one step *removed from* a swindler. 彼はほとんどぺてん師に近い ▪ His feeling is *far removed from* love. 彼の気持ちは愛とはほど遠い.

A ***is removed by*** *B* (献立で)Aの次にBが出る ▪ Fish *was removed by* pork. 魚の次にはポークが出た.

remove *oneself* 立ちのく, 遠ざかる ▪ We can *remove ourselves* from these temptations. 我々はこういう誘惑から遠ざかることができる.

rend /rend/ 動 ***rend*** *one's* ***garment*** [***hair***] (悲しみなどで)衣服を裂く[髪をかきむしる] ▪ She *rent her hair* in grief. 彼女は悲嘆のあまり髪をかきむしった.

rend the air (音が)空気をつんざく ▪ A shout of joy *rent the air*. 喜びの叫びが空気をつんざいた.

rend … to pieces (著書など)を酷評する ▪ The reviewer *rent* her book *to pieces*. 書評家は彼女の本を酷評した.

turn and rend →TURN[2].

render /réndər/ 動 ***render*** *oneself* 降参する ▪ The rest will *render themselves* to me soon. 残りの者もやがて私に降参するだろう.

render help [(***a***) ***service***] ***to*** 《文》…を援助する ▪ We should *render help to* those in need. 我々は困っている人々を援助しなければならない.

renounce /rɪnáʊns/ 動 ***renounce the world*** (精神的生活を送るために)世を捨てる ▪ We *renounced the world* when we were baptized. 我々は洗礼を受けたときに世を捨てたのだ.

renown /rɪnáʊn/ 名 ***of*** (***great, high***) ***renown*** (非常に)名高い ▪ He was a citizen *of high renown*. 彼は非常に名高い市民だった.

rent[1] /rent/ 名 ***for rent*** 《米》貸すための (=《英》to LET) ▪ Apartments *for Rent*. 貸室あり《アパートの広告》 ▪ The houses *for rent* are all so expensive around here! この辺りでは貸家(の家賃)はみな実に高い!

rent[2] /rent/ 動 ***rent*** *a person* ***high*** [***low***] 人に高く[安く]家を貸す ▪ He *rents* his tenants *low*. 彼は借家人に安く家を貸します.

reopen /rióʊpən/ 動 ***reopen old wounds*** 古傷に触れる, 古傷を暴く[思い出させる] ▪ The photo *reopened* some *old wounds* for me. その写真を見て昔のいやなことをいろいろ思い出した.

repair /rɪpéər/ 名 ***beyond*** [***past***] ***repair*** 修理の見込みがない ▪ The ship is damaged *beyond repair*. 船は修理がきかないほど破損している.

in good [***bad, poor***] ***repair*** (建物などが)手入れが行き届いて[届かないで] ▪ The old gate is still *in good repair*. その古い門はまだ手入れが行き届いている ▪ The house was now *in* very *bad repair*. その家は今やひどく手入れが悪かった.

in [***out of***] ***repair*** (建物などが)手入れが行き届いて[届かないで] ▪ They always keep the road *in repair*. その道路はいつもよく手入れが行き届いた状態です ▪ Most of the houses are *out of repair*. その家々の大半は手入れが行き届いていない.

put … in [***into***] ***repair*** …を手入れする ▪ The house needs *putting in repair*. その家は手入れする必要がある.

under repair(***s***) 修理中 ▪ The houses are *under repairs*. その家は修理中だ.

reparation /rèpəréɪʃən/ 名 ***demand reparation for*** …の賠償を求める ▪ He was in no condition to *demand reparation for* injustice. 彼は不当な扱いの賠償を求めるどころのさわぎではなかった.

in [***as***] ***reparation for*** …の償いとして ▪ He was educated at royal expense *as reparation for* the death of his father. 彼は父親の死の償いとして王室から学資を出してもらった.

make reparation 償いをする (*for*) ▪ You must *make* your wife *reparation for* that. 君は奥さんにその償いをしなくてはいけない.

repay /rɪpéɪ/ 動 ***repay itself*** 報いがある ▪ The effort will *repay itself*. その努力は報いられるだろう.

repeat /rɪpí:t/ 動 ***Don't repeat it.*** 人に言ってはいけない ▪ I'll tell you a secret, but *don't repeat it*. 秘密を教えてあげるが, 人に言っちゃだめだよ.

No, repeat, no! 《口》断然ノーだ.

not bear repeating 人前で話せるものではない ▪ His words do*n't bear repeating*. 彼の言葉は人前で話せるものではない.

repeat *oneself* **1** 同じことを繰り返して言う ▪ He spoke more than an hour without a note—never *repeating himself*. 彼はメモを持たずに1時間以上も話したが，1回も同じことを繰り返して言わなかった.
2 (同じ姿で)再び現れる ▪ History *repeats itself*. 《諺》歴史は繰り返す.

repentant /rɪpéntənt/ 形 ***repentant of*** [***for***] …を後悔して ▪ He was heartily *repentant for* his sins. 彼は心から罪を悔いていた.

replete /rɪplíːt/ 形 ***replete with*** **1** …でいっぱいに詰まって，を十分に備えて ▪ This book is *replete with* witty remarks. この本には機知に富んだ言葉がふんだんに見られる.
2 …で満腹して ▪ She was *replete with* the good things of the table. 彼女はおいしいごちそうで満腹だった.

repletion /rɪplíːʃən/ 名 ***to repletion*** いっぱいに，飽きるまで ▪ It is wrong to eat *to repletion*. 満腹するまで食べるのはよくない.

replica /réplɪkə/ 名 ***make a replica of*** …を模写する ▪ He *made a replica of* a painting. 彼はある絵を模写した.

reply /rɪpláɪ/ 名 ***in reply*** 答えて，返事として ▪ He nodded *in reply*. 彼は返事としてうなずいた.
in reply to …に答えて ▪ I am sending this *in reply to* your letter of December 5. 12月5日付の手紙にお答えしてこれをお送りします.
make [***give***] ***reply*** 《文》答える (*to*) ▪ He *made reply to* them with a sigh. 彼はため息をついて彼らに答えた.

report[1] /rɪpɔ́ːrt/ 名 ***make report*** **1** (調査したことを)報告する ▪ When you find him, *make report* to me. 彼を見つけたら私に報告してくれ.
2 (…を)知らせる (*of*) ▪ Do not *make report of* this to any man. このことを誰にも知らせないでください.
of good [***bad, evil***] ***report*** 評判のよい[悪い] ▪ He was a man *of good report*. 彼は評判のよい人だった.
put *a person* ***on report*** (しかるために)人を呼びつける ▪ Perhaps he could *put* somebody *on report*, and get him some extra duty. ひょっとしたら彼は誰かを呼びつけて，余分の仕事を与えるかもしれない.
report has it that/the report goes [***runs***] ***that*** …との噂だ ▪ *The report goes that* you have conspired to destroy the sect of Luther. 君たちは共謀してルーテル派を滅ぼそうとしたとの噂だ.
through good and (***through***) ***evil report*** 評判のよしあしにかかわらず (《聖》*2 Cor.* 6. 8.) ▪ He held to his purpose, *through good and through evil report*. 彼は評判の如何に関係なくわが目的を通した.

report[2] /rɪpɔ́ːrt/ 動 ***move to report progress*** (下院でじゃまする目的で)討論を打ち切るように動議する ▪ He *moved to report progress* as a representative of the party. 彼は党を代表して討論を打ち切るように動議を提出した.
report *oneself* (当局に)到着[所在]を報告する ▪ Every officer on his arrival must *report himself* to the governor. すべての士官は到着すると知事に到着の報告をしなければならない.
report badly of →REPORT well of.
report for duty [***work***] 出勤する ▪ They failed to *report for duty* on the date indicated. 彼らは指定の日に出勤しなかった.
report (***in***) ***sick*** 病気だと届け出る ▪ He *reported sick* today. 彼はきょうは病気だと届け出た.
report progress (進行)経過を報告する ▪ The committee *reported progress*. 委員会は経過を報告した.
report ... to the House (第2読会と第3読会との中間に法案)の結論を出して下院に報告する ▪ The chairman of the committee *reported* the bill *to the House*. 委員会の委員長はその法案の結論を出して下院に報告した.
report well [***badly***] ***of*** …をよく[悪く]報告する ▪ He *reports well of* the prospects. 彼はその見通しを好意的に報告している ▪ He *is badly reported of* among diplomatic circles. 彼は外交部会で評判が悪い.

repose[1] /rɪpóʊz/ 名 ***in repose*** 落ち着いて ▪ Now the sea is *in repose*. 今，海は穏やかだ.
seek [***take, make***] ***repose*** 休息する ▪ He *took repose* in the shade. 彼は木陰で休息した.

repose[2] /rɪpóʊz/ 動 ***repose*** *oneself* 休息する ▪ She *reposed herself* on his breast. 彼女は彼の胸で憩うた.

repossess /rìːpəzés/ 動 ***repossess*** *oneself* ***of*** …を取り戻す，再び自分のものにする ▪ He *repossessed himself of* his former position. 彼は以前の地位を取り戻した.

represent /rèprɪzént/ 動 ***represent*** *oneself* ***as*** [***to be***] 自分は…であると称する，触れこむ ▪ She *represented herself as* his wife. 彼女は彼の妻だと触れこんだ ▪ He *represented himself to be* starving. 彼は飢えかけていると言いふらした.
represent ... to *oneself* …を心に描く，想像する ▪ Can you *represent* infinity *to yourself*? 君は無限を想像することができるか.
represent *A* ***to be*** *B* AがBであると述べる ▪ I am not what you *represent* me *to be*. 僕は君が言っているような人間ではない.

representation /rèprɪzentéɪʃən/ 名 ***make representations to*** **1** …に陳情する ▪ The tenants decided to *make representations to* the mayor. 間借り人たちは市長に陳情しようと決めた.
2 …に陳述する ▪ *Make* no false *representations to* me. 私に偽りの陳述をするのはよしなさい.

representative /rèprɪzéntətɪv/ 形 ***representative of*** **1** …を象徴する，表す ▪ It was a group of statuary *representative of* the theological virtues. それは神学上の諸徳目を象徴する群像だった.
2 …を代表する ▪ The exhibition is *representative of* modern French art. その展覧会は現代フランス美術を代表している.

R

reprisal /rɪpráɪzəl/ 名 ***by*** [***by way of, in***] ***reprisal*** (...への)報復として (*for*) ▪ He seized the effects of the Spaniard *in reprisal for* injuries he had committed. 彼はそのスペイン人が与えた被害の報復にその持ち物を取り上げた.

make reprisal(***s***) (...に)報復[仕返し]する (*on, upon, for*) ▪ He said that he must *make reprisal upon* them. 彼はあの連中に仕返ししなければならないと言った ▪ He was determined to *make reprisals for* her conduct at the ball. 彼は舞踏会での彼女のふるまいに仕返しをしてやろうと決心していた.

reprise /rɪprí:z/ 名 ***above*** [***besides, beyond***] ***reprises*** 借地料その他の支払い後に残る ▪ It was a leasehold estate of twelve pounds per annum *beyond reprises*. それは借地料その他の支払い後に年々12ポンドだけ残る借地であった.

at [***in***] ***two*** [***different, frequent***] ***reprises*** 二度に[何度もかかって] ▪ The tower fell, not all at once, but *in two reprises*. その塔は一気にでなく二度にわたって倒れた ▪ He lost it *at different reprises*. 彼は何度もかかってそれを失った.

reproach /rɪpróʊtʃ/ 名 ***above*** [***beyond, without***] ***reproach*** 一点も非難するところのない, 申し分のない ▪ His morals are *above reproach*. 彼の行状は一点も非難するところがない.

be a reproach to ...の名折れである ▪ The state of the roads *is a reproach to* civilization. その道路の状態は文明の名折れである.

bring [***draw***] ***reproach on*** [***upon***] ...の恥辱となる, の顔に泥を塗る ▪ His conduct had *brought* so much *reproach upon* his predecessor. 彼の行状は前任者の顔にひどく泥を塗っていた.

heap [***cast***] ***reproaches on*** [***upon***] ...をさんざんに非難する, に非難を浴びせかける ▪ She *heaped reproaches upon* her sister. 彼女は妹をさんざんに非難した.

reproduce /rì:prədjú:s/ 動 ***reproduce oneself*** **1** 再生する ▪ Sin perpetually *reproduces itself*. 罪は絶えず再生していく.
2 繰り返して現れる ▪ History is apt to *reproduce itself*. 歴史はとかく繰り返しがちだ.

reproof /rɪprú:f/ 名 ***in reproof of*** ...をとがめて ▪ He spoke *in reproof of* idleness. 彼は怠惰を戒める話をした.

repugnant /rɪpʌ́gnənt/ 形 ***repugnant to*** **1** ...が鼻持ちならない ▪ All food is *repugnant to* me during my illness. 病気中は食べ物は全部いやだ.
2 =REPUGNANT with.

repugnant with ...と相容れない ▪ Naturalism is *repugnant with* tragedy. 自然主義は悲劇とは相容れない.

repulse /rɪpʌ́ls/ 名 ***meet with*** [***suffer***] ***repulse*** はねつけられる ▪ His request *met with* another *repulse*. 彼の願いはまたはねつけられた. ☞meet with a repulse ともいう.

repulsion /rɪpʌ́lʃən/ 名 ***feel repulsion for*** [***towards***] *a person* 人に反感を持つ ▪ She *felt* strong physical *repulsion towards* him. 彼女は彼に激しい肉体的な嫌悪を覚えた.

reputation /rèpjətéɪʃən/ 名 ***be held in reputation*** 尊敬される ▪ The ancient sages *were held in reputation*. 古代の賢人らは尊敬されていた.

have a reputation for ...で聞こえている ▪ He *has a reputation for* swindling. 彼は人をだまして金品をまきあげることで聞こえている.

have the reputation of ...という評判だ ▪ He *has the reputation of* a good landlord. 彼は良い地主だとの評判だ.

in reputation 評判よく ▪ He passed the remainder of his life *in reputation* and justice. 彼は余生を評判をけがすことなく正直に過ごした.

live up to *one's* ***reputation*** 行いが評判通りだ ▪ He has *lived up to his reputation*. 彼の行いは評判通りだった.

of good [***bad***] ***reputation*** 評判の良い[悪い] ▪ He is a man *of good reputation*. 彼は評判がいい.

of reputation 名声のある ▪ He was a writer *of reputation* at that time. 彼は当時令名のある作家であった.

repute[1] /rɪpjú:t/ 名 ***be*** (***held***) ***in high repute*** 評判が良い, 信用がある ▪ The wine of Shiraz *is* (*held*) *in high repute*. シラーズのワインは評判が良い.

be in good [***bad***] ***repute*** (***with***) 《口》(人に)受けが良い[悪い] ▪ He *is in good repute with* everyone. 彼は誰にも受けが良い.

be of good [***bad***] ***repute*** 評判が良い[悪い] ▪ The firm *is of good repute*. その会社は評判が良い ▪ He *is of bad repute* with everyone. 彼は誰からも評判が悪い.

by repute 世評で ▪ I know him well *by repute*. 彼のことは噂でよく知っている.

in common repute 世間の評判では ▪ *In common repute* it was a victory. 世間の評判ではそれは勝利であった.

of repute 名高い, 世に聞こえた ▪ A man *of repute* will desire to avoid doing what is ludicrous. 世に聞こえた人は人の笑いものになるようなことをするのを避けたがる.

through good or ill repute 世評を意に留めないで ▪ He persevered *through good or ill repute*. 彼は世評など意に留めないでがんばった.

repute[2] /rɪpjú:t/ 動 ***be reputed as*** [***to be***] ...と[であると]の評判だ, 考えられている ▪ He *is reputed as* the best surgeon in London. 彼はロンドン切っての外科医との評判だ ▪ He *is reputed to be* very wealthy. 彼は大金持ちであるとの評判だ.

be reputed for ...で名高い ▪ He *is reputed for* his genius. 彼は天才だとの評判が高い.

request[1] /rɪkwést/ 名 ***at the request of*** ...の依頼によって ▪ A copy of our catalog will be promptly sent *at your request*. ご請求があればカタログ1部を至急お届けします ▪ We came *at the re-*

R

quest of Mr. Smith. スミス氏の依頼でやって来ました.

by request 頼みに応じて ▪ No flowers *by request*. 遺志により供花はご辞退いたします《掲示》 ▪ Buses stop here *by request*. バスは頼めばここに止まります.

come into request 需要が起こる ▪ These goods have *come into* great *request*. この品は非常に売れ出した.

in request 需要があって ▪ These goods are *in* much *request*. この品は大いに需要がある.

make a request 願う ▪ I would like to *make a request* to you. 一つお願いをしたいのですが.

on* [*upon*] *request 請求次第 ▪ A catalog will be mailed free *on request*. カタログはご請求次第無料で郵送いたします.

request[2] /rɪkwést/ 動 ***as requested*** 《商》ご要求通りに ▪ It will be sent to your address *as requested*. ご要求通りに貴名あてにお送りします.

require /rɪkwáɪər/ 動 ***require ... at*** *a person's* ***hands*** 人から…を要求する ▪ He *required* a gift *at my hands*. 彼は私に贈り物を要求した.

requirement /rɪkwáɪərmənt/ 名 ***meet the requirements*** 要求に応える, 規定された要件を満たす ▪ They did not *meet the requirements* for graduation. 彼らは卒業要件を満たさなかった.

requisition /rèkwəzíʃən/ 名 ***bring* [*call, place*] *... into requisition/put ... in requisition*** …を徴用する, 徴発する ▪ He *placed* all the horses *into requisition* for the French army. 彼はすべての馬をフランス軍のために徴発した ▪ His eldest son *was put in requisition*. 彼の長男は徴用された.

in* [*under*] *requisition 使用されて ▪ The guillotine was *in* constant *requisition*. ギロチンは絶えず使用されていた.

make a requisition on *A* ***for*** *B* (占領軍が)Aに対しBの提供を命じる ▪ The troops *made a requisition on* the citizens *for* provisions. 軍隊は市民に対し食料の供出を命じた.

R

requital /rɪkwáɪtəl/ 名 ***in requital for* [*of*]** …の仕返しに ▪ He did so *in requital for* many injuries. 彼はかずかずの被害の仕返しにそうしたのだ.

***in requital* (*of*)** (…の)お礼に, 報償として ▪ They requested a sum of money and offered *in requital* to withdraw from the province. 彼らはある金額を要求し, お返しにその地方からの撤退を申し出た ▪ *In requital of* all his former kindnesses, they basely deserted him. 彼が以前いろいろ親切にしてやったのに, 彼らは卑劣にも彼を見捨てた.

rescue[1] /réskjuː/ 名 ***come* [*go*] *to the*** [*a person's*] ***rescue*** 人の救援に来る[行く] ▪ They *came* presently *to our rescue*. 彼らはやがて我々の救援にやって来た.

rescue[2] /réskjuː/ 動 ***rescue*** *oneself* 救われる ▪ The traders of Birmingham have *rescued themselves*. バーミンガムの商人たちは救われた.

reseat /rìːsíːt/ 動 ***reseat*** *oneself* (立った人が)また座る ▪ I *reseated myself* in the bottom of the boat. 私はボートの船床にまた座った.

resemblance /rɪzémbləns/ 名 ***bear* [*have*] *a resemblance to*** …に似ている ▪ He *has a* strong *resemblance to* his father. 彼は父親にそっくりだ.

resentful /rɪzéntfəl/ 形 ***be resentful against*** …を怒っている ▪ He *was resentful against* the party. 彼はその党に腹をたてていた.

resentment /rɪzéntmənt/ 名 ***bear* [*have, harbor*] *resentment against* [*at*]** …に恨みをいだく ▪ I *bear* no *resentment against* him. 彼に恨みは少しもいだいていない.

in resentment 怒って ▪ My heart rises up *in resentment*. 腹が立って胸くそが悪くなってくる.

reservation /rèzərvéɪʃən/ 名 ***a mental reservation*** 心中留保《陳述・誓いなどをするとき言ってはまずいこと, または言う必要のないことを黙秘すること》 ▪ They did it with *a mental reservation*. 彼らは心中留保をしてそうした.

make* [*procure*] *reservations 《米》借切りの予約をする ▪ *Make reservations* for me on the Empire. エンパイア号に予約してください.

***with reservation*(*s*)** 保留つきで ▪ This fact must be taken *with* some *reservations*. この事実は少し割引きして考えねばならない.

without* (*any*) *reservation **1** 無条件で ▪ A bill of sale, *without any reservation*, was drawn up. 何の条件もつかない売渡し証が作成された. **2** 腹臓なく, 率直に ▪ The lords replied *without reservations* that they would support the crown. 貴族たちは王を支持するとはっきりと答えた.

reserve[1] /rɪzə́ːrv/ 名 ***have a reserve of*** …のたくわえがある ▪ He *has a* great *reserve of* energy. 彼は大いに精力をたくわえている.

in reserve 取っておいた, 予備の ▪ He had enough strength *in reserve* to overcome the obstacles. 彼はその障害に打ち勝つだけの力をたくわえていた ▪ I shall keep this *in reserve* until we need it. これが必要になるまで取っておこう.

put* [*place*] *a reserve* (*price*) *on …に最低価格をつける ▪ He has *put a reserve price on* his house. 彼は自分の家に最低価格をつけた.

with reserve 条件つきで, 遠慮して ▪ The report should be taken *with* all *reserve*. その報告は大いに割り引きして受けとられねばならない.

without reserve **1** 腹臓なく, 遠慮なく ▪ Tell me your ideas on the subject *without reserve*. その問題についての君の考えを遠慮なく聞かせてくれ. **2** 無条件で; (競売の際)価格無制限で ▪ I accept your statement *without reserve*. 君の申し立てを無条件で承認する ▪ The sale has been declared to be *without reserve*. その売却は価格に制限を設けないものだと発表された.

reserve[2] /rɪzə́ːrv/ 動 ***be reserved to*** …に限られている ▪ Admission to the Society *is reserved to* people over sixty. その会への入会(許可)は60歳

以上の人に限られている.

it was reserved for *a person* ***to*** *do* …することは人のために予定された運命であった ▪ *It was reserved for* Columbus *to* make the discovery. その発見をすることはコロンブスのために予定された運命だった.

reserve *oneself* ***for*** …のために精力をたくわえておく ▪ *Reserve yourself for* tomorrow. あすのために精力をたくわえておきなさい.

residence /rézədəns/ 名 ***have*** [***keep***] *one's* ***residence*** 居住する ▪ He also *had his residence* at Rome. 彼もまたローマに住んでいた.

in residence **1**(公職にある人が)官舎[公邸]に住んで ▪ I wish I was *in residence* to play the host to you. 公邸に住んでいて君を接待できたらいいんだが.

2(大学関係者が)学内に寄宿して ▪ There are about a hundred students *in residence*. 約百人の学生が学内に寄宿している.

take up (*one's*) ***residence*** 《文》居を定める ▪ He married an English woman and *took up his residence* in London. 彼はイギリス人の女性を妻としてロンドンに居を定めた.

resident /rézədənt/ 形 ***resident at*** [***in***] …に居住して ▪ He is *resident at* Thomson Hall (in Boston). 彼は(ボストンの)トムスンホールに居住している.

resign /rɪzáɪn/ 動 ***resign*** *oneself* ***to*** **1** …に身を任せる, ふける ▪ She *resigned herself* entirely *to* his will. 彼女は彼の意志にすっかり身を任せた ▪ I will *resign myself to* sleep. 眠りに身を任せよう.

2 …とあきらめる ▪ He *resigned himself to* his fate. 彼は運命に従った.

3 …を甘受する; あきらめて…する ▪ She *resigned herself to* failure. 彼女は失敗を甘受した ▪ We *resigned ourselves to* passing the night under the stars. あきらめてその夜を星の下で過ごすことにした.

resignation /rèzɪgnéɪʃən/ 名 ***give*** [***hand in, send in, tender***] *one's* ***resignation*** 辞表を出す ▪ Mr. Pole has *handed in his resignation*, I hear. ポール氏は辞表を出したそうだ.

with resignation あきらめて ▪ She bore the pain *with resignation*. 彼女は観念して苦痛に耐えた.

resist /rɪzíst/ 動 ***cannot resist*** *doing* …せざるを得ない ▪ She *could not resist kissing* him. 彼女は彼にキスしないではいられなかった.

resistance /rɪzístəns/ 名 ***a piece of resistance*** **1** 一番実(ᵐ)のある料理 ▪ Our appetite demands *a piece of resistance*. こんなに腹がへっているので一番実のある料理がほしい.

2 主要物, 主要作品 ▪ She liked *a piece of resistance*, a solid tome. 彼女は主要作品で読みごたえのある本を好んだ. ☞ F pièce de résistance のなぞり.

choose [***take, follow***] ***the line*** [***course, path***] ***of least resistance*** 最も抵抗の少ない策を採る, 最も楽な方法を採る ▪ People generally *choose the line of least resistance*. 人は通常最も楽な方法を選ぶものである.

offer [***give, make***] ***resistance*** 抵抗する; 手ごたえがある ▪ She *offered* no *resistance*. 彼女はなんの抵抗もしなかった ▪ The pavement *gives* little *resistance* to the tires. この舗道はタイヤにほとんど抵抗を与えない.

resolute /rézəlù:t/ 形 ***be resolute for*** [***against***] …に賛成[反対]の決意を固めている ▪ The Queen *was resolute for* peace. 女王は和睦の決意を固めていた.

resolution /rèzəlú:ʃən/ 名 ***come to*** [***form, make, take***] ***a resolution to*** *do* …しようと決心する, 覚悟する ▪ He *made a* firm *resolution to* give up drink. 彼は酒をやめようと堅く決心した ▪ I've *formed a resolution* never *to* go to bed later than eleven. 私は11時までには必ず寝ようと決心した.

make good resolutions 行いを改めようという決心をする ▪ We *make good resolutions* on every New Year's Day. 我々は毎年元旦に行いを改めようという決心はする.

pass a resolution (…に賛成の, 反対の)決議案を可決する (*in favor of, against*) ▪ *A resolution* of thanks *was passed* unanimously. 感謝の決議案が満場一致で可決された ▪ The conference *passed a* strong *resolution in favor of* the measure. 会議でその法案に強い賛成の決議が通された.

resolve[1] /rɪzálv|-zɔ́lv/ 名 ***form*** [***make, take***] ***a resolve*** 決心をする ▪ He *made a resolve* to do better. 彼はもっとよくやろうと決心した.

keep *one's* ***resolve*** 決心を変えない ▪ She made up her mind never to marry again, and she *kept her resolve*. 彼女は二度と結婚すまいと決心し, その決心は変えなかった.

of high [***great***] ***resolve*** 決心の堅い ▪ He is a man *of high resolve*. 彼は決心の堅い人だ.

resolve[2] /rɪzálv|-zɔ́lv/ 動 ***be resolved on*** [***upon***] …に決心している ▪ I *am resolved on* it [*on* going]. 私はそうしよう[行こう]と決心している.

be resolved to *do* …しようと決心している ▪ I *am* firmly *resolved to* do so. 私はそうしようと堅く決心している.

resolve itself into **1** …に分解する ▪ The matter *resolves itself into* three elements. その物質は三つの元素に分解する.

2 …に帰着する ▪ The problem *resolves itself into* this. その問題はつまりこういうことに帰着する.

3(審議会が委員会)になる ▪ The House of Commons *resolved itself into* a committee. 下院が全院委員会となった.

resolve *a person* ***to*** *do* [***on*** *doing*] 人に…する決心をさせる ▪ This *resolved* us *to* start [*on starting*] at once. これで我々はすぐ出る気になった.

resort /rɪzɔ́:rt/ 名 ***have resort to*** …に訴える ▪ We *had resort to* various devices for raising money. 我々は募金のため種々の手段に訴えた.

in the last resort/as a last resort 最後の手段として，結局 ▪ The delight is, *in the last resort*, quite untranslatable into so many words. その楽しさは結局言葉に尽くしがたい. ☞[F] en dernier ressort のなぞり.

make [have] (one's) resort to …によく行く ▪ People *made their resort to* the prophet. 人々はその予言者のもとへよく出かけた.

of (great, public) resort (場所が)人の多数寄り集まる ▪ There are some places *of great resort* in this town. この町には盛り場が2, 3ある.

without resort to …に頼らずに ▪ It cannot be done *without resort to* compulsion. それは強制手段に訴えなければできない.

resource /ríːsɔːrs|rɪzɔ́ːs/ [名] ***a man of no resources*** 無趣味な人; 無資力の人 ▪ Tom was universally known to be *a man of no resources*. トムは資力のない人であると一般に知れわたっていた.

at the end of *one's* ***resources*** 万策尽きて ▪ I am *at the end of my resources*. 私は万策尽きた.

be full of resource 機略縦横[臨機応変]である ▪ He *is full of resource* in any emergency. 彼は臨機応変の才に富んでいる.

have no other resource but to *do* …するよりほか仕方がない ▪ She *had no other resource but to* weep. 彼女は泣くよりほか仕方がなかった.

leave *a person* ***to his own resources*** → LEAVE a person to himself.

pool *one's* ***resources*** 資金をプール[共有]する ▪ They suggested that they should *pool their resources* for a rainy day. 彼らは万一に備えて資金をプールしておくことを提案した.

without resource 援助の当てもなく ▪ Napoleon was lost *without resource*. ナポレオンは援助の当てもなく敗れた. ☞[F] sans ressource のなぞり.

respect[1] /rɪspékt/ [名] ***give*** *one's* ***respects to*** *a person* 人によろしくと言ってやる ▪ Please *give my respects to* him. どうか彼によろしく言ってください.

have respect for **1** …を尊敬する ▪ He *has* no *respect for* age. 彼は老人を尊敬しない.

2 …を尊重する ▪ We should *have respect for* our promise. 我々は約束を尊重しなければならない.

3 …を考慮する ▪ We must *have respect for* the needs of the general reader. 我々は一般読者の欲求を考慮しなければならない.

have respect that …ということを考慮する ▪ But *having respect that* night had begun to come on, we took in our sails. しかし夜になり始めたことを考えて我々は帆を巻き上げた.

have respect to **1** …に関係がある ▪ Sanguine men *have respect to* dryness. 陽気な人と乾燥状態とは関係がある.

2 …に関心を持つ; を考慮する ▪ They have not *had respect to* anything but color. 彼らは色彩以外は何も考慮しなかった.

3 …のことを頭に置いている，考えている ▪ He *had* only *respect to* length of days. 彼はただ日数の長さということを考えていただけであった.

hold *a person* ***in respect*** 人を尊敬する ▪ The old man *was held in respect* by all. その老人は万人から尊敬されていた.

in all [many, some] respects すべての[多くの，いくつかの]点で ▪ The new house is *in all respects* better than the old one. 今度の家はあらゆる点で前のよりも良い.

in every respect あらゆる点で ▪ He was doing the duties of a good shepherd *in every respect*. 彼はあらゆる点でりっぱな羊飼いの仕事をしていた.

in no respect いかなる点でも[全然]…でない ▪ His answer is *in no respect* satisfactory. 彼の答えは全然満足すべきものでない.

in one respect 一つの点で ▪ *In one respect*, I like your work better than his. 一つの点で彼の作品より君の作品のほうが好きだ.

in respect of [to] …に関して，については ▪ He is senior to me *in respect of* service. 彼は勤めに関しては僕の先輩だ.

in this [that] respect この[その]点では ▪ People are often very thoughtless *in this respect*. 世人はしばしばこの点でははなはだ軽率である.

out of respect for …を尊重して ▪ He set the slaves free—*out of respect for* humanity. 彼は奴隷を解放した—人道を尊重して.

pay respect to …を考慮する; を尊重する ▪ We *pay respect to* wealth. 私たちは富を尊重する.

pay *one's* ***respects to*** *a person* 《しばしば反語》人の所へ行って敬意を表する ▪ I came out here yesterday to *pay my respects to* the Count. 私は伯爵の所へ行って敬意を表するためにきのうここへ参りました.

respect of persons 差別待遇，えこひいき (《聖》 *Rom.* 2. 11) ▪ Is there no *respect of persons* in you? 君には人への差別待遇の思いはありませんか.

send *one's* ***respects*** よろしくと言ってやる (*to*) ▪ My father *sends* you *his respects*. 父がよろしくと申していました.

show respect for …に敬意を表する ▪ You must *show respect for* age. 老人には敬意を表さねばならぬ.

with all (due) respect for …には大いに敬意を表するものの ▪ *With all respect for* your great learning, I still think you are mistaken. あなたの深い学識には大いに敬意を表しますが，でもやはり思い違いをしておられると思います.

with respect to …に関して，については ▪ *With respect to* this question, there are three opinions. この問題に関しては三つの意見がある.

without respect of [to] …を無視して，と無関係に ▪ Faith makes a man righteous *without respect of* works. 信仰は行(ぎょう)とは無関係に人を正す.

respect[2] /rɪspékt/ [動] ***as respects*** …に関して ▪ He is perfectly tolerant *as respects* religion. 彼は宗教に関しては全く寛容だ.

respect *oneself* 自重する，自尊心がある ▪ This

shows that he ceased to *respect himself*. これは彼に自尊心がなくなった証拠である.

respect persons →accept PERSONs.

respecter /rɪspéktər/ 名 ***be no respecter of persons*** 人を差別待遇しない (《聖》 *Acts*. 10. 34) ▪ Death *is no respecter of persons*. 死は人をわけ隔てしない《死は万人に訪れる》.

respectful /rɪspéktfəl/ 形 ***be respectful of*** …を重んじる ▪ We must *be respectful of* tradition. 我々は伝統を重んじなければならない.

be respectful to [***towards***] *a person* 人にいんぎんである ▪ He *is respectful to* age. 彼は老人に対していんぎんだ.

respite /réspət|-paɪt/ 名 ***put … in respite*** …を猶予する, 延期する ▪ The articles *were put in respite* until fuller counsel could be had. その条項はさらに十分に審議されるまで延期された.

without (***a***) ***respite*** 小休止もせずに ▪ He worked *without* (*a*) *respite*. 彼は小休止もせず働いた.

response /rɪspáns|-spɔ́ns/ 名 ***in response*** 答えて ▪ He murmured something *in response*. 彼はそれに答えて何やらつぶやいた.

in response to …に答えて, 応じて ▪ The lectures have been published in book form *in response to* numerous requests. その講演は多くの要望に答えて本の形で公にされた.

responsibility /rɪspɑ̀nsəbílətì|-spɔ̀n-/ 名 ***on one's own responsibility*** 自分の一存で, 独断で ▪ The thing was done *on his own responsibility*. そのことは彼の一存でやったのだ.

take [***assume***] ***the responsibility of*** [***for***] *doing* 責任をもって…する ▪ I'll *take the responsibility of bringing* the children home. 私が責任をもって子供たちを家へ連れて帰ります.

responsible /rɪspánsəbəl|-spɔ́n-/ 形 (***be***) ***responsible for*** (人が)…に対して責任がある (*to*); (事が)…のせいである ▪ I *am* not *responsible to* you *for* any actions. 私がどんな行動に出ても君に弁明する義務はない ▪ The weather *was responsible for* the delay. 遅れたのは天候のせいだ.

hold [***make***] *a person* ***responsible for*** 人に…の責任を負わせる ▪ He must *be held responsible for* it. 彼がその責任を負わなければならない.

rest[1] /rest/ 名 ***at rest*** **1** 休息して; 休止して (↔in MOTION 1) ▪ Are you not yet *at rest*? 君はまだ休んでいないのですか ▪ Vesuvius is not really *at rest*. ベスビオ山は本当の休火山ではない.

2 安んじて (↔in MOTION 2) ▪ My mind is *at rest* about the matter. その件については安心している.

3 解決して ▪ The question is now *at rest*. その問題はもう解決している.

4 永眠して ▪ My father is *at rest* with his ancestors. 父は祖先とともに永眠しています.

be called to *one's* ***eternal rest*** 死ぬ, 亡くなる ▪ My father *was called to his eternal rest* two years ago. 父は2年前に亡くなった.

bring … to rest (エンジンなど)を停止させる ▪ He *brought* his tractor *to rest* and lighted a cigarette. 彼はトラクターを止めてタバコに火をつけた.

come to rest (動いている物が)止まる ▪ The engine *came to rest*. エンジンが止まった.

day of rest 〚the をつけて〛安息日; 〚a をつけて〛休養日 ▪ It is *the day of rest*. きょうは安息日だ ▪ Sunday is *a day of rest* for many people. 日曜日は多くの人たちにとって休養日である.

give a rest ひと休みさせる ▪ He *gave* them *a rest* from work. 彼は彼らを仕事からひと休みさせた.

Give it a rest! 《口》やめなさい; 黙りなさい.

go to (*one's*) ***rest*** **1** 就寝する ▪ This done, they *went to* (*their*) *rest* again. これを済ませると, 彼らはまた床についた.

2 永眠する ▪ David *went to rest*. ダビデは永眠した.

have a rest →take a REST.

lay … to rest **1** (恐怖など)をすっかり静める ▪ His fears *were laid to rest*. 彼の恐怖心は全く静まった.

2 …を埋葬する ▪ He *was laid to rest* in the cemetery of Chester. 彼はチェスターの共同墓地に葬られた.

3 …を寝かしつける ▪ He *was laid to rest* on the sofa. 彼はソファの上に寝かしつけられた.

No rest for the wicked. 《諺》悪人に休息なし.

retire to rest =go to (one's) REST 1.

set [***put***] ***… at rest*** **1** (心)を安心させる ▪ But *set* [*put*] your mind *at rest*. しかしご安心ください.

2 (問題など)を解決する ▪ The question has *been set at rest*. その問題はけりがついている. ☞→at REST.

take [***have***] ***a rest*** ひと休みする ▪ Let us sit down and *take a rest*. 座ってひと休みしましょう.

take (*one's*) ***rest*** **1** 就寝する ▪ We two will watch your safety while you *take your rest*. 我々二人があなたがお休みの間あなたをお守りしていましょう.

2 永眠する ▪ The old man lay *taking his rest* after a life of hardship. その老人は苦しい生涯を終えて永眠していた.

without rest 休みなしに ▪ He ran on *without rest*. 彼は休みなしに走り続けた.

rest[2] /rest/ 名 ***among the rest*** **1** その中に加わって ▪ Ten passed; himself was *among the rest*. 10人がパスした. 彼自身もその中の一人だった.

2 なかんずく, 特に ▪ These words *among the rest* struck sharply home upon my mind. とりわけこれらの言葉が私の心にひどくこたえた.

and (***all***) ***the rest*** (***of it***) その他何もかも ▪ She is young and beautiful and rich *and all the rest of it*. 彼女は若くて美人で金があってその他何もかもいいことずくめだ.

(***as***) ***for the rest*** その他については, あとは ▪ *As for the rest*, I could not exactly make it out. その他については私にははっきりわからなかった.

as to the rest その他の点では ▪ *As to the rest*, I don't care. その他のことはどうだっていい.

R

do the rest あと(の仕事)は…がする ▪ We'll *do the rest.* あとの仕事は私たちがします.

The rest is history. あとは知っての通り ▪ He quit his job, but *the rest is history.* 彼は仕事を辞めたが, あとは知っての通りだよ.

rest[3] /rest/ 動 ***cannot rest here*** [***there***] (事件が)この[その]ままにしておけない ▪ The matter *cannot rest here.* その問題をこのままにしてはおけない.

cannot rest under …されて黙ってはいられない ▪ I *cannot rest under* an imputation. 汚名を着せられては黙っていられない.

(***God, Heaven***) ***rest his soul*** [***him***]***!*** 彼の魂[彼]が安らかに眠らんことを.

let … rest **1** …をそのままにしておく ▪ If I could *let* the matter *rest,* I would do it. 問題をそのままにしておければそうするのだが.

2 (耕地)を休ませる ▪ He *let* the land *rest.* 彼はその土地を休ませた.

rest *oneself* 休養する ▪ *Rest yourself* before the fire. 暖炉の前で休んでください.

rest *one's* ***case*** →CASE.

rest in peace 安らかに眠る ▪ May he *rest in peace.* 彼が安らかに眠らんことを.

restitution /rèstətjúːʃən/ 名 ***make restitution*** 返還[賠償]する ▪ They had wronged her, therefore they ought to *make* her *restitution.* 彼らは彼女をひどい目にあわせた. だから彼女に損害賠償しなければならない.

the times of restitution of all things 万物更新の時 (《聖》 *Acts* 3. 21) ▪ Peter's statement speaks clearly of *the times of the restitution of all things.* ペテロの言明は明確に万物更新の時を述べている.

restore /rɪstɔ́ːr/ 動 ***restore*** *oneself* **1** 健康を取り戻す ▪ There may John *restore himself.* そこでジョンも健康を取り戻せよう.

2 元の位置へ戻る ▪ A spring *restores itself* again. ばねは元の位置へ戻る.

restrain /rɪstréɪn/ 動 ***restrain*** *oneself* がまんする, 自制する ▪ I must *restrain myself* from making further discussion. これ以上の議論はさし控えなければならない.

restraint /rɪstréɪnt/ 名 ***be beyond restraint*** 抑圧できない ▪ His anger *was beyond restraint.* 彼は腹だちを押さえ切れなかった.

put a restraint on …を抑制する ▪ We have no desire to *put a restraint on* his activity. 我々は彼の行動を抑制したい気持ちなど少しもない.

under restraint (特に精神病者が)監禁[束縛]されて ▪ The lunatic was put *under restraint.* その精神病者は監禁されていた.

without restraint 自由に, たっぷり ▪ Her tears flowed *without restraint.* 彼女の涙はとめどなく流れた ▪ Let your pity spread *without restraint.* あわれみを惜しみなく広げよ.

restriction /rɪstríkʃən/ 名 ***place*** [***put***] ***restrictions on*** …に制限[束縛]を加える ▪ The Government is going to *place restrictions on* foreign trade. 政府は外国貿易を制限する予定である.

result /rɪzʌ́lt/ 名 ***as a result of*** …の結果(として) ▪ Several people were killed *as a result of* the storm. あらしの結果数人が亡くなった.

in the result 結局 ▪ Real ability will win *in the result.* 結局実力が勝つものだ.

the result was that その結果…になった ▪ *The result was that* his profits diminished. その結果彼の利益が減少した.

with little [***good***] ***result*** あまり成果なく[成果をあげて] ▪ The meeting ended *with little result.* 会合はさほど成果なく終わった.

without result 成果なく, むなしく ▪ The meeting ended *without result.* 会合は結局むだだった.

retail /ríːtèɪl/ 名 ***by*** [***at***] ***retail*** 小売りで (↔by WHOLESALE) ▪ It is ordinarily more economical to purchase supplies *at retail,* than at wholesale. 必要な品物は卸売りよりも小売りで買うほうが通常経済的である.

retaliation /rɪtæ̀liéɪʃən/ 名 ***in retaliation*** (***for***) (…の)仕返しに ▪ They, *in retaliation,* attacked the enemy fort. 彼らは仕返しに敵軍要塞を攻撃した.

retard /rɪtɑ́ːrd/ 名 ***in retard*** 遅れて, 引き留められて ▪ The rearward regiments are *in* painful *retard.* 後衛部隊はひどく遅れている.

in retard of …よりも遅れて ▪ I was far *in retard of* them in real knowledge. 私は実知識にかけては彼らよりもずっと遅れていた.

retentive /rɪténtɪv/ 形 ***retentive of*** **1** …をよく保つ ▪ These soils are *retentive of* moisture. この土壌は水をよく保つ.

2 …をよく記憶している ▪ His memory is *retentive of* details. 彼は細かいことをよく覚えている.

reticent /rétəsənt/ 形 ***reticent on*** [***about***] …について口を閉じて語らない ▪ She was *reticent on* what Tom had said. 彼女はトムが言ったことについて黙して語らなかった.

retire /rɪtáɪər/ 動 ***retire from the world*** 世を捨てる ▪ He *retired from the world* at sixty and lived alone. 彼は60歳の時に世を捨てて一人暮らしをした.

retire into *oneself* 自分の中に閉じこもる ▪ To discover truth one must *retire into oneself.* 真理を発見するには人は自分の殻に閉じこもらねばならない.

retire to rest [***bed***] 《文》 床につく, 寝る ▪ He usually *retires to bed* at eleven. 彼は通例11時に床につく.

retired /rɪtáɪərd/ 形 ***put*** [***place***] *a person* ***on the retired list*** (士官)を退役させる ▪ He had consented to *place* them *on the retired list.* 彼は彼らを退役させることに同意していた.

retirement /rɪtáɪərmənt/ 名 ***in retirement*** 隠とんして ▪ He has been living *in retirement* for ten years. 彼は10年前から隠とん生活をしている.

retort /rɪtɔ́ːrt/ 名 ***in retort*** しっぺ返しに ▪ He

R

looked at her all over *in retort*. 彼はしっぺ返しに彼女をじろじろながめ回した.

retrace /rɪtréɪs/ 動 ***retrace*** *one's* ***steps*** [***way***] **1** 後戻りする ▪ He was *retracing his way* in haste. 彼は急いで後戻りしていた.

2 やり直す ▪ I would gladly have *retraced my steps* to please you. あなたのお気に入るためなら喜んでやり直したことでしょうに.

retreat /rɪtríːt/ 名 ***beat a retreat*** **1** 退却する; 逃亡する ▪ The enemy *beat a* hasty *retreat*. 敵はあわてて退却した ▪ We had better *beat a retreat* before he sees us. 彼に見られない間に逃げた方がいい.

2 手を引く, 事業をやめる ▪ Six of his men were wounded, and the expedition was obliged to *beat a retreat*. 彼の部下のうち6人が負傷したので, その遠征はやめねばならなくなった. ☞太鼓を打って退却の合図をすることから.

beyond retreat のっぴきならない ▪ He is *beyond retreat* now, so he must go through with it. 彼はもう手が引けないから, やり通すしかない.

blow the [***a***] ***retreat*** →sound the RETREAT.

cover the retreat 退却のしんがりをする ▪ The commanders of our cavalry heroically *covered the retreat*. わが騎兵隊の指揮官たちが勇ましく退却のしんがりをつとめた.

go into retreat 《カトリック》静修に入る ▪ He *went into retreat* for a week. 彼は1週間静修に入った.

in full retreat 総退却して《比喩的にも》 ▪ Seeing him *in full retreat*, I then ventured to make the civil offer of a dinner. 彼がすっかり参っているのを見て, 私は思いきって夕食をいっしょにどうかと言ってみた.

intercept [***cut off***] ***the retreat of*** ...の退却を遮断する ▪ It requires some patience and skill to *intercept their retreat*. 彼らの退却を遮断するには多少の忍耐と技術を要する.

make a tactical retreat 戦術的撤退をする ▪ He *made a tactical retreat* to try to obtain more evidence. 彼は戦術的撤退をしてもっと多くの証拠を手に入れようとした.

make good *one's* ***retreat*** 首尾よく逃げおおせる ▪ We finally *made good our retreat*. 我々はついに首尾よく逃げおおせた.

sound [***blow***] ***the*** [***a***] ***retreat*** 退却のらっぱを吹く ▪ The general thought it prudent to *sound a retreat*. 将軍は退却のらっぱを吹くのが賢明だと考えた.

retrieval /rɪtríːvəl/ 名 ***beyond*** [***past***] ***retrieval*** 回復の見込みがない, 取り返しがつかない(ほど) ▪ The hut was ruined *beyond retrieval*. その小屋は回復の見込みがないほどこわれていた.

retrieve[1] /rɪtríːv/ 名 ***beyond*** [***past***] ***retrieve*** 回復の見込みがないほど ▪ In an unguarded hour he ruined himself *beyond retrieve*. 油断しているときに彼は取り返しがつかないほど零落してしまった.

retrieve[2] /rɪtríːv/ 動 ***retrieve*** *oneself* 面目を取り戻す ▪ He *retrieved himself* by becoming a lawyer. 彼は弁護士になって面目を取り戻した.

retrospect /rétrəspèkt/ 名 ***in retrospect*** 回想して ▪ He considered those events *in retrospect*. 彼はそれらの事件を回想した.

return[1] /rɪtə́ːrn/ 名 ***and return*** 《米》また折り返して ▪ The train ran from Waukegan to Chicago *and return* every day. その列車は毎日ウォーキガンとシカゴ間を往復していた.

by return (***of post*** [《米》***mail***]) 折り返しに ▪ He may expect an answer *by return of post*. 折り返し彼は返事がもらえるものと思っていい. ☞至急の手紙を持って来た急便に返事を持たせて帰したことから.

get a good return on ...で大儲けする ▪ He has *got a good return on* an investment. 彼は投資で大儲けした.

have a good return (クリケットなどで)うまい返球をする ▪ That fielder *has a* wonderfully *good return*. あの野手は返球がすばらしくうまい.

have a return of (病気)がぶり返す ▪ I *had a return of* my rheumatism. リューマチがぶり返した.

(***I wish you***) ***many happy returns*** (***of the day***)***!*** このめでたい日が何度も繰り返されることを祈ります《誕生日・祝日の祝詞》 ▪ *Many happy returns of this day* to you. このめでたい日があなたに何度も巡って来ますように[お誕生日おめでとうございます].

in return 返事に; お返しに ▪ I wrote to my old friend at Lisbon, who *in return* sent me a note. 私はリスボンにいる旧友に手紙を出したが彼は返事に短い手紙を寄こした ▪ He paid his fare to the conductor, and *in return* received a ticket. 彼は車掌に乗車賃を払い, かわりに切符を受け取った.

in return for ...のお返しに ▪ A present is usually given *in return for* the hospitality. そのもてなしのお返しとしてたいてい贈り物をする.

make a return of **1** (郡保安官が)...の答申をする ▪ The sheriff *made a return of* nulla bona. 保安官は無財産[不存在報告]であるとの答申をした.

2 (所得税)の申告をする ▪ He *made a* false *return of* his income. 彼は偽りの所得申告をした.

on *one's* ***return*** **1** 帰ったとき ▪ I shall see you immediately *on my return*. 帰り次第会おう.

2 帰る途中で ▪ He is *on his return*. 彼は帰る途中だ.

secure a return for (代議士が)...から選出される ▪ He *secured a return for* Manchester. 彼はマンチェスターから選出された.

small profits and quick returns 薄利多売《商店のモットー》.

return[2] /rɪtə́ːrn/ 動 ***be returned guilty*** 有罪と答申される ▪ The prisoner *was returned guilty*. 被告は有罪と答申された.

return the compliment →COMPLIMENT.

return to *oneself* 我に返る ▪ She swooned at the news, but soon *returned to herself*. 彼女はその知らせを聞いて気を失ったが, やがて我に返った.

return to life よみがえる ▪ The dying man *returned to life*. その瀕死の人は生き返った.

to return 〚独立不定詞〛それはさておき，本題に帰って ▪ But *to return* to our subject. しかし，本題に帰ろう．

returned /rɪtə́ːrnd/ 形 ***returned empties*** (送り主に)返送された空箱[空だる，など]; 《軽蔑》植民地から英本国へ帰ってきた牧師 ▪ They were Colonial Bishops—"*returned empties.*" 彼らは植民地帰りの監督―いわゆる返送された空だるだった．

reveal /rɪvíːl/ 動 ***reveal** oneself* **1** 名のる ▪ Here is Lord Angelo. *Reveal yourself* to him. ここにアンジェロ卿が来られた．この方に名を名のるがいい．

2 示す ▪ In his letters he *reveals himself* as full of kindness. 手紙を見ると彼が非常に親切な人であることがわかる．

reveal itself 現れる，知れる ▪ I'll tell you exactly how the thing *revealed itself* to me. その事がまさにどのように私に知れたかお話ししよう．

revelation /rèvəléɪʃən/ 名 ***be*** [***come as***] ***a revelation*** (…にとって)新発見[新事実]である，意表外である (*to*) ▪ The news of Rodham's involvement *was a* horrible *revelation*. ロダムが関与していたというニュースは恐るべき新事実だった ▪ The clash *came as a revelation to* many. その衝突は多くの人には晴天のへきれきだった．

revenge[1] /rɪvéndʒ/ 名 ***by one of Time's revenges*** 例の皮肉なめぐり合わせで，奇(く)しくも (cf. Sh., *Twel. N.* 5. 1. 385) ▪ They met again *by one of Time's revenges*. 彼らは奇しくも再会した．

give** a person* (*his*) ***revenge (特にトランプ・チェスなどで)負けた人に復しゅうの機会を与える，雪辱戦に応じる ▪ Well, I will *give* you *your revenge* whenever you please. ああ，いつでも好きなときに雪辱戦に応じるよ．

have [***get, take***] *one's* ***revenge*** 復しゅうする，恨みを晴らす (*on*) ▪ We shall *take our revenge on* him. あの男に恨みを晴らしてやる．

in revenge of [***for***] …の返報に，腹いせに ▪ The people killed him *in revenge for* a murder. 人々は殺人の腹いせにその男を殺した．

out of revenge 恨みから ▪ *Out of revenge* for a fancied slight the boy set fire to his master's shop. ばかにされたと思う恨みから少年は主人の店に火をつけた．

Revenge is a dish best served cold./***Revenge is a dish that should be eaten cold.*** 《諺》復しゅうは冷まして出す[食べる]べき料理である，復しゅうは冷却期間をおいて冷酷に行うべし．☞La vengeance est un plat qui se mange froid (de Laclos (1741–1803))から．

Revenge is sweet. 《諺》復しゅうは快い．

take revenge for …のあだを報いる ▪ He *took revenge* too deep *for* a transient wrong. 彼はちょっとした非行のあだをあまりにもひどい形で報いた．

revenge[2] /rɪvéndʒ/ 動 ***be revenged on*** [***upon, of***] *a person* 《文》人に復しゅうする，恨みを晴らす ▪ In this they *are* sufficiently *revenged on* us. この点で彼らは我々に十分復しゅうしている．

revenge** oneself* ***on [***upon***] *a person* 《文》人に復しゅうする，恨みを晴らす (*for*) ▪ You would not *revenge yourself upon* the parson? 君は牧師に恨みを晴らしはしないでしょうね．

reverence /révərəns/ 名 ***have*** [***hold***]***… in reverence*** …を尊敬する ▪ The man *was had in* great *reverence*. その人は非常に尊敬されていた．

have [***show, feel***] ***reverence for*** …に崇敬の念をいだく ▪ The Indians *have* great *reverence for* the tombs of their kindred. 北米先住民は彼らの親族の墓を大いに崇敬している．

make a [*one's*] ***reverence*** おじぎをする ▪ I *made my reverence* to the guest. 客に一礼した．

pay reverence to …に敬意を表する; に敬礼する ▪ *Reverence* continues to *be paid to* her memory at the present day. 今日なお彼女の霊には敬意が払われている．

saving your reverence →SAVING your presence.

show reverence for →have REVERENCE for.

under the reverence of …のごめんをこうむって ▪ *Under the reverence of* Claudius, I say this. クローディアスさまのごめんをこうむって，こう申します．

with reverence 失礼ながら ▪ *With reverence*, you don't know him. 失礼だが，君は彼をご存じない．

reverie /révəri/ 名 ***fall into*** (***a***) ***reverie*** 空想[物思い]にふける ▪ He had *fallen into a* profound *reverie*. 彼は深い夢想にふけっていた．

in (***a***) ***reverie*** 空想[物思い]にふけって ▪ He was *in a* long *reverie*. 彼は長らく空想にふけっていた．

reverse[1] /rɪvə́ːrs/ 名形副 ***in reverse*** **1**《軍》背面に ▪ Our troops were now exposed to attack *in reverse*. わが軍は今や背面からの攻撃にさらされていた．

2 常とは反対に，逆に ▪ The inedited manuscripts by da Vinci were written *in reverse*. ダ・ビンチの未刊行原稿は逆に書いてあった《鏡に映せば読める》．

3 (車が)バックして ▪ The car was *in reverse*. 車はバックしていた．

put … in reverse (自動車)を逆行させる ▪ She *put* the car *in reverse* and backed into a telephone pole. 彼女は車を逆行させて電信柱に激突した．

reverse to …にあべこべの[に] ▪ It is utterly *reverse to* true happiness. それは真の幸福に全く反するものだ ▪ Some act *reverse to* their own ideas. 考えとは逆の行動をする者もいる．

suffer a reverse 敗北する ▪ Our forces have *suffered a* slight *reverse*. わが軍はやや旗色が悪かった．

reverse[2] /rɪvə́ːrs/ 動 ***reverse** oneself* ***about*** [***over***] …について自説を翻(ひるがえ)す ▪ He *reversed himself about* the superiority of mother's cooking. 彼は母親の料理がまさっているという自説を翻した．

reverse the charge(***s***) (電話で)受信人に料金を払わせる，コレクトコールをかける ▪ Please *reverse the charge*. 料金受信人払いにしてください．

revert /rɪvə́ːrt/ 動 ***revert to*** **1** (元の状態・話題な

ど)に帰る ▪ The fields have *reverted to* moorland. 畑はまた荒れ地になってしまった.
2《法》(不動産・権利が)…に復帰[帰属]する ▪ If he dies without an heir, his property will *revert to* the State. 彼が相続人なしに死ねば, その財産は国家に帰属する.
revert to type →TYPE.

review /rɪvjúː/ 名 ***in review*** 検査[検討]されて ▪ This machine should be *in review*. この機械は検査しなければいけない.
march in review 検閲を受ける; 分列行進をする ▪ The little family *marched in review* before him. 小家族は彼の前で検閲を受けた.
pass ... in review →PASS[3].
under review 考察[調査, 論評]されて(いる) ▪ Those works came *under review*. それらの作品が論評された ▪ Let us pass *under review* the dangers of war. 戦争の危険を考察してみよう.

revolt /rɪvóʊlt/ 名 ***in revolt*** 反抗して, 反乱を起こして ▪ She will lie there *in* most innocent *revolt*. 彼女はそこに横たわってこの上もなく無邪気な反抗をするだろう ▪ The Christian tribes of Lebanon were *in revolt*. レバノンのキリスト教徒たちが反乱を起こしていた.
rise [***break out***] ***in revolt*** 反抗する, 反乱を起こす (*against*) ▪ Some of the group might *rise in revolt against* the government. そのグループの一部は政府に反抗するかもしれない.
stir up [***rouse***]***... to revolt*** …を反乱させる ▪ Who first *stirred* them *up to revolt*? 誰が最初に彼らを反乱させたのか.

revolve /rɪvάlv|-vɔ́lv/ 動 ***revolve ... in*** *one's* ***mind*** [***thoughts, breast***] …を思いめぐらす ▪ He had been *revolving* the problem *in his mind* for the last five minutes. 彼は5分間ほどその問題に思いをめぐらしていた.
think the world revolves around 《軽蔑》世界は自分を中心に回っていると思う, 他人を見下す ▪ She behaved like a little princess who *thinks the world revolves around* her. 彼女は, 世界は自分中心に回っていると思っている, 幼いお姫さまのようにふるまった.

reward /rɪwɔ́ːrd/ 名 ***gone to*** *one's* ***reward*** 昇天して ▪ He is *gone to his reward*. 彼は昇天した.
in reward for …の賞として, に報いて ▪ He was granted a pension *in reward for* his services. 彼は功労の報いに恩給を下賜された.

rhapsody /rǽpsədi/ 名 ***go into rhapsodies over*** …について熱狂的に語る[ほめる] ▪ Everyone *went into rhapsodies over* Mary's dress. メアリーのドレスのことを誰もが熱狂的にほめそやした.

rhinoceros /raɪnάsərəs|-nɔ́s-/ 名 ***have a hide*** [***skin***] ***like a rhinoceros*** 《口》(攻撃・非難などに対して)神経が図太い, 面の皮が厚い; 侮辱に対して[馬鹿にされても]鈍感である ▪ He *has a skin like a rhinoceros*, and doesn't mind asking other people for money. 彼は面の皮が厚くて, 他人にお金の無心をするのをなんとも思っていない ▪ He *has a skin like a rhinoceros* and is conceited about everything. 彼は侮辱に対しては鈍感だが何事に対してもうぬぼれている ▪ He *has a hide like a rhinoceros*. 彼は(攻撃されても)平気である.

rhyme[1] /raɪm/ 名 ***find a rhyme to*** …の同韻語を見つける ▪ Can you *find a rhyme to* "hiccups"? hiccups の同韻語が見つかりますか.
give rhymes 押韻する ▪ "Quality" and "frivolity" *give rhymes*. "Quality" と "frivolity" は押韻する.
in rhyme 韻文で ▪ The poet addressed us *in rhyme*. 詩人は韻文で私たちに語りかけた.
neither [***no***] ***rhyme nor reason*** わけも理由もない ▪ There's *neither rhyme nor reason* about it. これは全くわけがわからない ▪ There's *no rhyme nor reason* why I shouldn't go to the dance. 私がダンスへ行っていけない理由は少しもない. ☞F ni rime ni raison のなぞり.
without (***either***) ***rhyme or reason*** わけも理由もない[なく] ▪ He set upon me *without either rhyme or reason*. 彼は全くわけも理由もなしに僕に襲いかかってきた. ☞上の句から.

rhyme[2] /raɪm/ 動 ***rhyme ... to death*** **1** 呪文を唱えて(ネズミ)を絶やす ▪ No rat *is rhymed to death*. 呪文を唱えてネズミを絶やすことはできない.
2 詩を作って(人)の名声を失わせる ▪ It is pretty friendship to *rhyme* your friends *to death*. 詩を作って友人の名声を失わせるとはとんだ友情というものだ.

rib /rɪb/ 名 ***poke*** [***dig, nudge***] *a person* ***in the ribs*** (意味あり気に)そっと人の横っぱらをこづく ▪ He *poked* me *in the ribs* and winked. 彼は僕の横っぱらをこづいて目くばせしてみせた.
smite *a person* ***under the fifth rib*** →FIFTH.
stick to *one's* [***the***] ***ribs*** 《口》(食べ物などが)身につく ▪ He liked a breakfast that would *stick to his ribs*. 彼は身につくような朝食を好んだ.
tickle *a person's* ***ribs*** 《口》人をおもしろがらせる ▪ His jokes always *tickle my ribs*. 彼のジョークは僕にはいつもおもしろい.

ribbon /ríbən/ 名 ***cut a*** [***the***] ***ribbon*** (開館式・開通式などで)テープカットをする ▪ The local elders *cut the ribbon* at the opening ceremony of a new freeway. 地元のお年寄りが新しい高速道路の開通式でテープカットを行った.
hold [***handle, take***] ***the ribbons*** 手綱を取る, 馬を駆る, 馬車を駆る ▪ He *held the ribbons*, while she took the box-seat. 彼が手綱を取り, 彼女が腰かけて座った. ☞ribbons＝reins.
in ribbons ぼろぼろになって ▪ His clothes were *in ribbons*. 彼の服がぼろぼろになっていた ▪ The sails hung *in ribbons* from the yards. 帆がぼろぼろになって帆げたから下がっていた.
to a ribbon 《米口》完全に ▪ That's Judith's character *to a ribbon*. それは完全にジュディスの性格

だ.

to ribbons ぼろぼろ[ずたずた]に ▪ The coat was torn *to ribbons*. 上着はずたずたに裂けていた.

rich /rɪtʃ/ 形 ***a rich seam*** 《文》豊かな鉱脈, 利用[掘り下げ]可能な主題 ▪ Chinese shoppers are increasingly viewed as *a rich seam* of profit for fashion brands. 中国人買い物客たちはブランド品によってますます利益をもたらす豊かな鉱脈と見なされている.

filthy [***stinking***] ***rich*** 《口》(ぷんと鼻につくほど)大金持ちの ▪ Most of us are *stinking rich* compared to the average citizen in the Third World. 第三世界の平均的市民に比べれば我々の大半はどえらい金持ちだ.

get rich quick (あまり働きもせずに)すぐに大金持ちになる ▪ Can a man *get rich quick* quite honestly? とても正直なやり方ですぐに大金持ちになれるだろうか.

rich in …に富んで, がたくさんあって ▪ The museum is *rich in* fine specimens. あの博物館にはすばらしい標本がたくさんある ▪ His life has been *rich in* experiences. 彼の生涯はさまざまな経験に富んでいる.

Rich men feed, and poor men breed. 《諺》金持ちの食い道楽, 貧乏人の子だくさん.

rich with …に恵まれて ▪ The annals of Edo Castle are *rich with* incidents of interest. 江戸城の歴史は興味深い事件に富んでいる.

strike it rich →STRIKE[2].

That's rich! 《口》それはおもしろい; 《反語》そいつはこっけいだ[ばかげている].

the newly rich 成金 ▪ *The newly rich* have not yet learned to give. 成金はまだ人に与えることを知らない.

(***the***) ***rich and*** (***the***) ***poor*** 富者と貧者, 富者も貧者も ▪ Ring out the feud of *rich and poor*. 富者と貧者の反目を鐘を鳴らして送り出せ ▪ *Rich and poor* are supposed to be treated equally. 富める者も貧しき者も平等に扱われて然るべきだ.

riches /rítʃɪz/ 名 ***Riches have wings.*** 《諺》お金は羽が生えている《すぐに無くなる》.

rid /rɪd/ 動 ***get*** [***be***] ***rid of*** …を免れる, 除く, 追い払う ▪ I cannot *get rid of* my horrible cold. 私はひどい風邪を治すことができない ▪ The world *is* well *rid of* him. あんな奴が死んでいい厄介払いをした.

R

riddance /rídəns/ 名 ***a happy*** [***fair***] ***riddance*** いい厄介払い ▪ The loss of so many captives was treated as *a happy riddance*. そんなに大勢の捕虜がいなくなったことはいい厄介払いだとされた.

good riddance **1**〚間投詞的に〛いい厄介払いだ ▪ Let him go, *good riddance*! 彼を行かせたらいい, いい厄介払いだ!

2 いい厄介払い ▪ Such a girl was indeed *good riddance*. あんな娘が去ってほんといい厄介払いだった.

Good riddance to bad rubbish! (つまらぬ物がなくなって)いい厄介払いができた ▪ "*Good riddance to bad rubbish*," he muttered, using his mother's favorite phrase. 「(やっとなくなった)やれやれ」と彼は母親の口癖を使ってつぶやいた.

make (***clean***) ***riddance of*** …を(きれいに)一掃する ▪ The police tried to *make clean riddance of* street roughs. 警察は町のよた者をきれいに一掃しようとした.

riddle[1] /rídəl/ 名 ***be a riddle to*** …には解けない謎だ ▪ What he did it for *is* still *a riddle to* me. 彼がなぜあんなことをしたかはまだ私には解けない謎だ.

speak [***talk***] ***in riddles*** 《口》謎めいたことを言う ▪ You always *speak in riddles*. あなたはいつも謎めいたことを言うね.

riddle[2] /rídəl/ 名 ***make a riddle of*** …にハチの巣のように穴をあける ▪ I was to *be made a riddle of* if I attempted to escape. 私は逃げようとしたりなどすればハチの巣のように穴をあけられるはずだった. ☞riddle「粗目(あらめ)のふるい」.

riddle[3] /rídəl/ 動 ***Riddle me a*** [***my***] ***riddle.*** なぞなぞなあに ▪ *Riddle me a riddle*, what is this? なぞなぞなあに, これなあに?

Riddle me, riddle me. なぞなぞなあに ▪ *Riddle me, riddle me*, what's this? なぞなぞなあに, これなあに?

Riddle me this. この謎なあに ▪ *Riddle me this* then. じゃあ, この謎なあに?

riddle[4] /rídəl/ 動 ***be riddled with*** (欠点など)でいっぱいである, だらけである ▪ This book *is riddled with* printing mistakes. この本は誤植だらけだ.

ride[1] /raɪd/ 名 ***a rough*** [***bumpy***] ***ride*** (経済的)試練, 逆境; 乱高下 (→give a person a rough RIDE) ▪ Cameron faced *a rough ride* from right-wingers. キャメロンは保守主義者からの試練に直面した ▪ Bolivia is probably in for *a bumpy ride*. ボリビアは平坦ならざる道を経験しなければなるまい.

along [***just***] ***for the ride*** 《口》(人が)一応[おもしろ半分で]参加して, お相伴で ▪ I'm not a member of the group. I'm just (going [coming]) *along for the ride*. 僕はこの会の会員じゃない. 単にオブザーバーだ.

be opposite a smooth ride 平坦ではない ▪ If both of you get married, it'll *be opposite a smooth ride*. 君たち二人が結婚すれば, 平坦にはいかないだろう.

get a free ride ただ乗りする, 甘い汁を吸う; やりたい放題にやる ▪ That country is *getting a free ride* with a small defense budget, thanks to America. あの国はアメリカのおかげで少ない国防予算で甘い汁を吸っている ▪ That company has been *getting a free ride* for too long. あの会社はあまりにも長い間好き放題にやってきている.

get an easy ride 《口》やすやすとやってのける, 楽勝である ▪ He will *get an easy ride* in his appearances for the next election. 彼は次の選挙に向けての状況では楽勝だろう.

give *a person* ***a ride*** **1** (乗り物に)人を乗せてやる ▪ I will *give* you *a ride* in a boat. 君をボートに乗せてあげよう ▪ I *gave* the child *a ride* on my shoulders. 子供を肩車に乗せてやった.

2《米》人をかつぐ ▪ She's *giving* him *a ride*, isn't she? あの女は彼をかついでいるんだろ.

give *a person* ***a rough ride*** 人をいやな目にあわせる ▪ He *was given a rough ride* at the meeting. 彼はその会合でいやな目にあわされた.
go for a ride (馬・自転車・車で)ひと乗りしに出かける ▪ They *went for a ride* in a car. 彼らは車でひと乗りしに出かけた.
have [***take***] ***a ride*** (乗物に)一回乗る ▪ Let me *have a ride* in your car. あなたの車に一度乗せてください.
have a ride on 《俗》…とやる ▪ He reckons to *have a ride on* her. 彼は彼女とあれしようと思っている.
have a rough [***bumpy, an easy***] ***ride*** いやな目にあう[困難な目にあう, 順調に進む] (→get an easy RIDE) ▪ He is *having a rough ride* in London. 彼はロンドンでいやな目にあっている ▪ She hasn't always *had an easy ride* in her business life. 彼女はいつも仕事が順調にいったわけではない.
hitch [***thumb***] ***a ride*** 《米》(ヒッチハイクで)車に乗せてもらう ▪ So he *hitched a ride* in a fire department emergency vehicle. こうして彼は消防署の緊急車両に乗せてもらった ▪ The man *thumbed a ride* on the truck. その男はトラックを止めて乗った ▪ The girl *thumbed a ride* to New York. その女の子はヒッチハイクしてニューヨークまで行った.
take *a person* ***for a ride*** 《口》 **1** (ギャングが自動車などで)人を連れ出して殺す ▪ The police assume the victim *was taken for a ride* by some of his enemies. 警察では被害者は敵の誰かに連れ出されて殺されたと想定している.
2 人をかつぐ, だます ▪ Don't pay any attention to what he says; he's just trying to *take* you *for a* (sleigh) *ride*. 彼が言っていることなんか問題にするな. 君をただかつごうとしているだけなんだよ.
3 人を利用する ▪ She just *took* you *for a ride*. 彼女は君を利用しただけだ.

ride[2] /raɪd/ 動 ***let…ride*** 《口》…を成り行きに任せる ▪ *Let* things *ride* for a while. しばらく事態を成り行きに任せておけ.
ride a horse 馬を乗りこなす ▪ I never *rode a horse* so well in my life. 私はこれまでそんなにうまく馬を乗りこなしたことはなかった.
ride astride [***side-saddle***] 馬にまたがって[片鞍に]乗る ▪ Some women *ride astride* and some *ride side-saddle*. 馬にまたがって乗る女性もいるし, 片鞍に乗る女性もいる.
ride double (馬などに)二人乗りする ▪ Don't *ride double*; it's dangerous. 二人乗りはやめなさい. 危険だから.
ride for a [*one's*] ***fall*** (落馬するような)むちゃな乗り方をする; むちゃなことをして災いを招く ▪ He has quarreled with all his fellow workers—I'm sure he's *riding for a fall*. 彼はすべての同僚とけんかをした—いまに災難を招くことになるぞ.
ride hard [etc.] →RIDE well.
ride herd on →HERD.
ride *one's* ***horse*** 《競馬》馬をめちゃくちゃに走らせる ▪ He began to *ride his horse* too soon. 彼は馬をめちゃくちゃに走らせ始めるのが早すぎた.
ride off on side issues 枝葉の問題を持ち出して要点を避ける ▪ He had a desire to *ride off on side issues*. 彼は枝葉の問題を持ち出して要点を避けたいと願っていた.
ride on a rail [***hurdle***] (罰として)横木[すの子そり]にのせて引き回される ▪ Many a wretch has *ridden on a hurdle* who has done less mischief. それほど悪事をしなかったのにすの子そりにのせて引き回されたみじめな人間が多い.
ride *a person* ***on a rail*** →RAIL.
ride (*a child*) ***on*** *one's* ***shoulders*** [***back, knees***] (子供)を肩[背, ひざ]に乗せる ▪ He *rode his child on his shoulders*. 彼は子供を肩車してやった.
ride (***on***) ***the wind*** 風に乗って飛ぶ ▪ An albatross was *riding* (*on*) *the wind*. アホウドリが風に乗って飛んでいた.
ride shotgun 《米》護衛する; 車の助手席に乗る ▪ He offered to *ride shotgun* for Mary. 彼はメアリーの護衛を買って出た. ☞武装して駅馬車の御者の隣りに座って護衛することから.
ride side-saddle →RIDE astride.
ride the brake [***clutch***] ずっとブレーキ[クラッチ]ペダルに足をのせておく ▪ You mustn't *ride the brake*. ブレーキペダルに足をのせっ放しにしてはいけない.
ride the crest of the waves = RIDE the waves 2.
ride the lightning 《米俗》電気いすに座る ▪ He was to *ride the lightning*. 彼は電気いすに座ることになっていた.
ride the pine [***bench***] 《米口》(運動選手が)ベンチを温めている, 補欠である ▪ He still *rides the pine* in the basketball team though he is an old-timer. 彼はバスケットチームでは古参だが, いまだに補欠だ.
ride the waves **1** 波に乗って進む ▪ The ship *rode the waves* smoothly. 船は波に乗ってすべるように進んだ.
2 得意の絶頂にいる ▪ He was still *riding the waves* as a singer. 彼はまだ歌手として得意の絶頂にいた.
ride…to death …を使いすぎてだめにしてしまう ▪ Inferior imitators will *ride* such a method *to death*. 亜流の模倣者どもはそんな方法を使いすぎてだめにしてしまうだろう.
ride to (***the***) ***hounds*** →follow (the) HOUNDs.
ride well [***soft, hard,*** etc.] (土地などが)乗りごこちがよい[柔らかい, 堅い] 《通例馬に乗る場合》 ▪ The heavy rain made the course *ride soft*. 大雨のためにコースは乗りごこちが柔らかかった ▪ The ground *rode hard* after the frost. 地面は霜の後で乗りごこちが堅かった.

ridicule /rídəkjùːl/ 名 ***hold…up to ridicule*** 〚主に受身で〛…を物笑いの種にする ▪ Jack *was held up to ridicule* for his whopping lie. ジャッ

クは大ぼらを吹くので物笑いの種にされた.

lay** oneself **open to ridicule 物笑いになるようなことをする ▪ This man especially *lays himself open to ridicule* by calling himself Le Roi. この男は自分のことを王様と呼ぶので特に物笑いにされる.

pour ridicule on …をさんざんにひやかす ▪ He *poured ridicule on* our scheme. 彼は私たちの計画をさんざんにひやかした.

turn ... into* [*to*] *ridicule …をあざ笑う, ひやかす ▪ He *turns* everything *into ridicule*. 彼は何もかもひやかしてしまう.

rife /raɪf/ 形 (***be***) ***rife with*** …に満ち満ちて(いる) ▪ The country *was rife with* rumors of war. 国じゅうに戦争が起こるという噂が満ちていた.

run rife 〚主に進行形で〛(噂などが)盛んに行われている ▪ Rumors about an earthquake *are running rife* in the town. その町は地震の噂で持ちきりだ.

riffle /rífl/ 名 ***make the* [*a*] *riffle*** 《米口》早瀬を渡る; 事をうまく運ぶ ▪ I'll try if I can *make the riffle*. 事をうまく運べるかどうかやってみよう.

rifle-range /ráɪfəlrèɪndʒ/ 名 ***within* [*out of*] *rifle-range*** ライフル銃の届く[届かない]所に ▪ The deer kept feeding *out of rifle-range*. そのシカはライフル銃の届かない所で草を食べ続けた.

rift /rɪft/ 名 ***a rift in the lute*** 不和のきざし ▪ His silent departure was *the* first *rift in the lute*. 彼が黙って立ち去ったのが不和の最初のきざしであった. ☞Tennyson, *The Idylls of the King*, "Merlin and Vivien" (388–390)から.

heal the rift 亀裂を埋める, 仲直りさせる ▪ Our daughter helped to *heal the rift* between us. 娘が私たちの仲をとりもってくれた.

open up a rift 亀裂を広げる, 重大な不和[対立]を生む ▪ The question over whether to expel him from school or not *opened up a rift* in the school. 彼を退学処分にするかどうかの問題は校内に対立を生んだ.

rig[1] /rɪg/ 名 ***in full rig*** 《口》盛装して, 着飾って ▪ They all went to church *in full rig*. 彼らはみんな盛装して礼拝に出向いた.

run a* [*the*] *rig*/*run* (*one's*) *rigs 《口》ふざける, あばれる ▪ He little dreamt, when he set out, of *running* such *a rig*! 彼は出かけるとき自分がそんなにふざけるとは夢にも思っていなかった ▪ I hope you will not *run your rigs* as you have done. 君が今までのようにあばれ回らなければいいと思う.

rig[2] /rɪg/ 動 ***rig** oneself* (***out***) 《口》服を着る ▪ He *rigged himself out* in a new suit. 彼は新調のスーツを着た.

right[1] /raɪt/ 名形副 ***a bit of all right*** 《口》 **1** とてもすばらしい ▪ My new job is *a bit of all right*. 僕の今度の仕事はとてもすばらしいものです.
2 すばらしい異性《特に女性》 ▪ My girlfriend is *a bit of all right*. 僕のガールフレンドはすばらしい女性だ.

***a right-hand man* [*woman*]** 右腕, 信頼できる助力者《女性にも man を使用可》 ▪ Give it to Jill, she's my *right-hand man*. ジルに渡してくれ, 彼女は私の右腕だから.

all right →ALL.

All's right with the world. すべて世は事もなし. ☞Browning, *Pippa Passes* 1より.

***along* [*on*] *the right lines* [*track*]** 《英》軌道に乗っている, うまくいっている ▪ Don't worry because we're *on the right lines*. 私たちはうまくいっているので安心してください.

as of right 当然の権利として ▪ One third of the estate comes to you *as of right*. 財産の3分の1は当然の権利としてあなたのものになります.

(***as***) ***right as my glove* [*ninepence, a trivet, rain, the bank*]** 《口》全く達者で, 至極元気で ▪ I hope you are well, sir.—*Right as a trivet*, sir. お元気なんだろうね—至極達者ですよ ▪ We both felt *as right as the bank*. 私たちは二人とも全く元気だった.

assert** one's **rights →stand on one's RIGHTs.

bang to rights →dead to RIGHTs.

be in** one's **right mind*/*be right in** one's **mind 正気である, 気が狂っていない ▪ He's not *in his right mind*. 彼は正気ではない ▪ *Is* he *right in his mind*? 彼は正気なのだろうか.

be in the right 道理がある, 正しい (↔in the WRONG) ▪ I will not apologize because I *am in the right*. 私は正しいのだからあやまるつもりはない.

be in the right of it 道理がある, 正しい ▪ You *are* always *in the right of it*. 君はいつも正しい. ☞it は不特定の it.

be in the right place at the right time しかるべき時にしかるべき場所に, 好機をのがさないで ▪ The secret of success is *being in the right place at the right time*. 成功の秘訣は場所とタイミングをのがさないことだ.

***be within** one's **rights to** do* (人が)…する権利がある ▪ You*'re within your rights to* protest. あなたには抗議する権利がある.

bring* [*put, set*]*... to rights …をまともにする, 直す, 正す ▪ How the ill should *be brought to rights* was the difficulty. その悪をどのようにして正すかがむずかしい点であった ▪ A good sleep will *put* me *to rights*. 十分眠れば元気になると思います ▪ He sent the watch to *be set to rights*. 彼は時計を修理にだした.

by right of …の権利[権限]で; によって ▪ He did it *by right of* his office. 彼は職権でそうした ▪ The Normans ruled England *by right of* conquest. ノルマン人は征服によってイングランドを統治した.

by rights*/*by* (*good*) *right **1** 正しくは, 当然 ▪ I should not, *by rights*, speak in this tone to you. 本当はこんな調子で君に話しかけてはいけないんだ.
2 当然(の権利によって) ▪ The property should have gone to him *by rights*. その財産は当然彼のものになるべきであったのだが ▪ He affirmed the kingdom to be his *by good right*. 彼はその王国は当然自分のものだと断言した.

catch* [*have*]** *a person* ***dead* [《英》*bang*] *to

rights 人を現行犯で捕まえる, の犯行の証拠が十分にある ▪ I *was caught dead to rights* with what I had done. 私は自分のやったことで現行犯逮捕された.

come right **1** 元通りになる, 都合よくなる (→go WRONG) ▪ All will *come right* in the end. 結局は万事うまく解決するだろう.
2 (計算が)正しく出る ▪ This sum won't *come right*. この合計がどうしても正しく出ない.

dead right その通り ▪ We put this in the bank?—You are *dead right*. これを銀行に預けるのですか—その通りだ.

dead [《英》***bang***] ***to rights*** **1** 現行犯で ▪ The man was caught *dead to rights* on a charge of theft. その男は窃盗罪の現行犯で捕えられた.
2 隅々まで正確に ▪ He got me *bang to rights* somehow. なぜか彼は私のことを隅々まで知っていた.

do right (...に)正しいことをする, 丁重な態度をとる, 公平に扱う (*by*) ▪ It is our moral obligation always to *do right*. 常に正しいことをするのは我々の道徳的義務だ ▪ The House *did right by* veterans. 議会は退役軍人たちを公平に扱った.

do *a person* ***right*** 人を公平に取り扱う, 正当に評価する ▪ Who'll *do* him *right* now? 今や彼を正当に評価する者がいるだろうか.

do right to *do* →DO[2].

do the right thing →THING.

do *a person* ***to rights*** 《口》人に報いる, (特に)仕返しをする ▪ Oh! I'll *do* him *to rights*, I give you my word! ああ, あの男には仕返ししてやるとも, きっとだ.

face to the right about →go to the RIGHT about.

fly right 《米口》正しくふるまう ▪ He always *flies right* at a party. 彼はパーティーではいつも正しくふるまう.

get in right (***with***) →GET in good (with).

get on the right side of *a person* 人に取り入る ▪ He could manage to *get on the right side of* the abbot. 彼は何とかして大修道院長に取り入ることができた.

get out of bed on *one's* ***right side*** [***leg***]/ ***get out of bed the right way***/ ***rise on*** *one's* ***right side*** ベッドの右側から起きる《縁起がよいとか上きげんでいられるという迷信》 ▪ I said my prayers, and *rose on my right side*. 私は祈りを唱え, ベッドの右側から起きた.

get ... right **1** ...を正しくやる ▪ Don't mix up my silks, Lucy; I shall never *get* them *right* again. 私の絹の服をぐちゃぐちゃにしないでちょうだい, ルーシー. またきちんとすることなんかとてもできないから.
2 ...を正しく理解する ▪ Now let's *get* this *right* before we pass on to the next point. さて次の問題に移る前に, このことを正しく理解しておこうじゃないか.

give [***read***] *a person* ***his rights*** **1** 《口》(容疑者)に正当な権利を伝える ▪ The police *read* Tom *his rights* after the arrest. 警察は逮捕後, トムに正当な権利について知らせた.
2 (配偶者に)弁護士と離婚の相談をする権利があると告げて別れる ▪ She *gave* him *his rights* three months after their marriage. 彼女は結婚3か月後に文句があれば弁護士にご相談なさいと言って彼と別れた.

go right うまくいく ▪ Nothing ever *goes right* in this house. この家では何一つうまくいかない.

go [***face, turn, wheel***] ***to the right about*** 回れ右をする; 主義や政略などを変える ▪ All men rose and *turned to the right about*. すべての人は立ち上がって回れ右をした ▪ Whenever I chose, I could make them *wheel to the right about*. その気になれば私はいつでも彼らに主義を変えさせられるさ.

have a [***the***] ***right to*** **1** 〚不定詞を伴って〛...する権利がある ▪ A creditor *has the right to* demand payment. 債権者は支払いを要求する権利がある.
2 〚名詞を伴って〛...を要求する権利がある ▪ You *have a right to* my service. 私は君のために何でもする義務がある.

have the right 正しい, 道理がある ▪ I *have the right*, and he the wrong. 私が正しくて彼がまちがっている.

How right you are! 全くその通りだ《強い賛成の言葉》 ▪ Ah! Henry! *How right you are!* おお! ヘンリー! あなたの言う通りだ《Henry David Thoreau の詩の1節に感動して》

in *one's* (***own***) ***right*** 生得の権利で; 独自に; 自分名義の[で] ▪ They were entitled to the property *in their own right*. 彼らは生得の権利でその財産を所有する資格がある ▪ She has a little money *in her own right*. 彼女は自分名義の金が少しある.

in right of ...の権利[権限]で, によって ▪ He claimed the dukedom *in right of* his wife. 彼は妻の権利で公爵の位を要求した ▪ I once ruled the people *in right of* my ax. 私は自分の斧によってその連中を支配したことがあった.

in the right 正しい, もっともである ▪ In an argument between husband and wife, it is hard to say who is *in the right*. 夫婦げんかでどちらが正しいかを言うのは難しい.

It's all right. →That's all RIGHT.

(***It's***) ***all right for some.*** 《英口》うらやましいなあ, いいなあ ▪ Each guest will be treated to lunch.—*It's all right for some*. ゲストには昼食がふるまわれる—けっこうなことで.

just right for ...にぴったりで, あつらえ向きで ▪ She's *just right for* me. 彼女は僕にぴったりだ ▪ The tune was *just right for* the occasion. その曲はその場にぴったりだった.

keep to the right/***keep on*** *one's* ***right*** 右側を通行する; 正道を歩む ▪ *Keep to the right*. 右側通行《掲示》 ▪ In most countries traffic *keeps to the right*. 大抵の国で交通は右側通行である.

make (***all***) ***the right noises*** (...に)興味[熱意]を示す (*about*) ▪ The manager always *makes the right noises*, but never actually does anything about our complaints. 部長は我々の苦情にいつも興味だけは示すが実際には何一つしてくれない.

make it right 事のかたをつける ▪ We *made it*

R

right by the expenditure of half a crown. 我々は半クラウン出して事のかたをつけた.

Mr. [***Miss***] ***Right*** 《口》結婚の相手としてふさわしい人; 未来の夫[妻] ▪ I suppose I'm not the *Mr. Right* of her affection. 僕はどうも彼女の愛情にふさわしい人物ではないように思う ▪ Couldn't you live with me till *Miss Right* comes along? 未来の妻がやって来るまで僕といっしょに暮らしてくれませんか.

not be right in the head 《口》頭がおかしい, 気が触れて(いる) ▪ His brother *is not right in the head* and requires constant monitoring. 彼の兄は頭がおかしいので, いつも監視が必要だ.

of right **1** 当然の権利として ▪ He ought *of right* to have precedency. 彼は当然優先権を持つべきだ. **2** 当然の権利のある ▪ Bail in misdemeanors is *of right*. 軽罪の保釈金は支払われて当然だ.

on the right side →SIDE.

on the right side of →SIDE.

on the right side of the tracks →TRACK.

put ... right →set ... RIGHT.

put *oneself* ***right*** →set oneself RIGHT.

put *one's* ***right hand to*** ...に精を出す ▪ You must *put your right hand to* the work. 君はその仕事に精を出さねばならない.

put ... to rights →bring ... to RIGHTs.

right about 《軍》回れ右 ▪ The rear goes [turns] *right about*. 後部は回れ右をするんだ.

Right about-face[***-wheel, -turn***]***!*** 回れ右!《号令》 ▪ *Right about-turn!* 回れー右.

right along **1** 《米口》休まずに, 絶えず ▪ Public interest in hybrid cars is increasing *right along*. 大衆のハイブリッド車への関心は絶えず高まっている. **2** 《口》順調に ▪ After the engine was fixed, the train ran *right along*. 機関修理後, 列車は順調に走行した.

right and left **1** 左右の[に]; 方々から[に] ▪ The crowd divided *right and left*. 群衆は左右に分かれた ▪ He was abused *right and left*. 彼はあっちからもこっちからも悪く言われた. **2** 右から左に, 自由に ▪ He spent his money *right and left* until he didn't have a penny left. 彼は右から左に金を使って後には1ペニーも残らなかった.

right and proper 申し分のない, 当を得た ▪ His view was *right and proper*. 彼の意見は当を得たものであった.

right and wrong 正邪, 善悪 ▪ I know the difference between *right and wrong*. 私には善悪の区別がわかる.

right away [***off***] 《口》すぐさま ▪ He said that he would be back *right away*. 彼はすぐ帰ると言った ▪ I'll do the job *right off*. すぐその仕事をしよう.

right down 《口》〚分詞・形容詞を伴って〛全く ▪ He was *right down* sorry for me. 彼は僕のことを心から気の毒に思ってくれた.

right enough 《口》確かに, 疑いもなく ▪ He's coming *right enough*. 彼はきっと来るさ.

one's ***right hand*** (***man***) →the RIGHT hand (man).

right here 《主に米口》今この場で ▪ I may as well say so *right here*. 今この場でそう言う方がいい.

right in *one's* [***the***] ***head*** 《口》〚主に否定文で〛正気で ▪ He isn't exactly *right in his head*. 彼は少し正気でないところがある.

right, left, and center = LEFT, right and center.

right now 《口》今すぐ, たった今; 今のところ(は) ▪ I'll do it *right now*. 今すぐそうしましょう ▪ The prices are very high *right now*. 今のところ値段は非常に高い.

right off →RIGHT away.

right oh!/ right-o! 《英俗》よろしい, 承知した ▪ Come and see me before you go down. —*Right oh!* 帰省する前に遊びに来いよ—いいよ.

right on 《米俗》正しい; 〚間投詞的に〛その通り; 《英》公平[公正]な, 差別のない ▪ You're *right on* there. その点はおっしゃる通りだ《黒人英語に多い》 ▪ Lady Gaga is the greatest!—*Right on*! レディー・ガガは最高だ!—その通りだ!

right or wrong 正しくてもまちがっていても, どうしても ▪ We must do it *right or wrong*. それはどうしてもしなければならない.

right out **1** すぐさま, 即座に ▪ They killed him *right out*. 彼らは彼を即刻殺害した. **2** ありのままに, 率直に ▪ Why don't you say *right out* "this middle-class westernized Pakistani girl"? 「この中流階級の西洋かぶれしたパキスタン娘」って率直に言ったらどうなの.

right-side out (衣服などの)表を外にして ▪ Clothes should be turned *right-side out* before they go into the washing machine. 洗濯機に入れる前に衣類は表を外にしておかなければいけません.

right smart 《米》**1** 〚a をつけて名詞的に〛たくさん ▪ She'll leave him *a right smart* when she passes on. 彼女は亡くなるとき彼にたくさんの金を残すだろう. **2** 〚形容詞的に〛かなりの ▪ It was a *right smart* distance. それはかなりの距離だった. **3** 〚副詞的に〛非常に ▪ The hill there is *right smart* steeper than the side we were on. 向こうの小山は我々がいた側よりもずっと険しい.

right there 《主に米》ちょうどそこで ▪ He died *right there*. 彼はちょうどそこで亡くなった.

right up 《米口》すぐに ▪ I am going *right up* to do your errand. すぐにあなたのお使いに行きますから.

Right you are! 《英口》よろしい, よしきた ▪ *Right you are*; I don't think I'll go out. わかった, 外出しないでおこう.

rise on *one's* ***right side*** = get out of bed on one's RIGHT side.

see *a person* (***all***) ***right*** **1** 《英口》人に損はさせない; 人に賃金を支払う ▪ Do this and I'll *see* you *right*. これをしてくれないか. 損はさせないから. **2** 《英口》援助[支援]する ▪ If you run into a problem, speak to Lucy. She'll *see* you *right*. 困ったらルーシーに話しなさい. 助けてくれるよ.

send ... to the right about **1**《軍》...を回れ右をさせて退却させる ▪ We *sent* all these fellows *to the right about*. 我々はその連中にすべて回れ右をさせて退却させた.
2 ...を即座に解雇する; を追い払う ▪ The beggar asked for money, but I soon *sent* him *to the right about*. 物乞いは金をめぐんでくれと言ったが, すぐ追っ払ってやった.
set* [*put*] *... right **1**(物)を直す, (人)を再び健康にする ▪ Can you *put* this bicycle *right* for me? この自転車を直してくれませんか ▪ This medicine soon *put* her *right*. この薬ですぐ彼女は再び健康になった.
2(人)を矯正する, 訂正する ▪ I'll *set* you *right* in your opinion of the man. その人に対する君の意見は訂正してもらうよ.
***set* [*put*] *oneself* right** 自己を正しいと主張する, おのれの行為を弁明する ▪ He tried to *set himself right* by that means. 彼はそうすることによって自分が正しいと主張しようとした.
set ... to rights →bring ... to RIGHTs.
stand on* [*assert*] *one's rights 権利を主張する ▪ I will *stand on my rights* as a citizen. 私は市民としての自分の権利を主張するつもりだ.
That's all right. いや, いいとも ▪ I'm sorry I broke your mirror.—*That's all right.* 鏡をこわしてすみません—いえ, かまいません.
That's right. その通り ▪ Are you French?—*That's right.* あなたはフランス人ですか?—その通り.
the* [*one's*] *right hand* (*man*)/ *the* [*one's*] *right arm 右手;「右腕」,「片腕」 ▪ He is indispensable as *her right hand*. 彼は彼女の右腕として欠かすことのできない人物だ.
the right man in the right place 適材適所 ▪ We should have *the right man in the right place*. 適材を適所に配置すべきだ.
(the) right side* [*way*] *up 表[上部]を上にして, 天地無用 ▪ Have you got it *the right side up*? 表を上にしたかい? ▪ Please keep the box holding the china *right-side up*. 陶器入りの箱の上下を逆さにしないでください.
the right way **1**〚名詞的に〛(道徳・宗教から見ての)本道, 正道 ▪ She leads *the right way*. 彼女は正道を歩んでいる.
2 最も効果的な方法 ▪ He took *the right way* to offend us. 彼はまさに我々を怒らせるやり方をした.
3 真相 ▪ Nobody seems to know *the right way* of it. 誰もその真相を知らないようだ.
4〚副詞的に〛正しく, 適切に ▪ Scrub the boards *the right way* of the grain. その板をまさ目にごしごしこすりなさい.
the rights and wrongs of ...の是非 ▪ We discussed *the rights and wrongs of* corporal punishment. 我々は体罰の是非を論じた.
To the right about! 《号令》回れ右 (=RIGHT about) ▪ *To the right about!* Let us return the way we came. 回れ右! いま来た道を引き返そう.
turn* [*work*] *out all right うまくいく, 成功する ▪ Fortunately, everything *turned out all right*. 幸い, 万事うまくいった ▪ Things *worked out all right* for us. 我々にはうまくことがはこんだ.
turn ... to the right about = send ... to the RIGHT about 2.
We've got a right one here! 《英口》ばかみたい ▪ *We've got a right one here*, eh! まったくばかみたいじゃないか, そうだろ!
within one's rights ...の権限内[権利の範囲内]で; (...するのが)当然で (*to do*) ▪ They were *within their rights* in seeking to better their conditions. 彼らが条件の向上を求めたのは彼らの権限内でのことだった ▪ They were *within their rights to* change their minds. 彼らが変心したのは当然だった.

right[2] /raɪt/ 動 ***right oneself*** **1**(船が)水平に立ち直る ▪ The boat *righted herself*, and glided swiftly into the still water. ボートは水平に立ち直ってすべるように淀みへ進んで行った.
2 平衡を取り戻す, 立ち直る ▪ The pony *righted himself*, and she rode on unhurt. そのポニーは立ち直り, けがなく歩を進めた.
3 平常の状態に帰る ▪ Slowly all things *right themselves*. 徐々にすべては平常に復すのだ.
right a wrong 過ち[旧悪]を正す ▪ You can't *right a wrong* by creating another wrong. 別の悪を為すことによって悪を正すことはできない.

rightly /ráɪtli/ 副 ***rightly or wrongly*** 是非のほどはわからないが ▪ *Rightly or wrongly*, I think the man should not be punished. 是非のほどはわからないが, その男は罰すべきではないと思う.

rigor,《英》**rigour** /rígər/ 名 ***with rigor*** きびしく ▪ Parents should not use their power *with* too much *rigor*. そう厳しく親の権力はふるうべきでない.
with the utmost rigor of the law 法律をきわめてきびしく適用して ▪ They punished the man *with the utmost rigor of the law*. その男には法律を極度にきびしく適用して罰した.

rile /raɪl/ 動 ***be* [*get*] (*all*) *riled up*** 《米口》(...に)怒る, イライラする, むかつく (*about, over*) ▪ Don't *get riled up about* killing birds. 鳥の捕殺のことでかっかするのはやめなさい ▪ They *got riled up over* government regulation. 彼らは政府の規制に怒った.

ring[1] /rɪŋ/ 名 ***a brass ring*** → go for the brass RING.
be in the ring for ...の選挙に打って出ている ▪ He *is in the ring for* the governorship. 彼は知事選挙に打って出ている.
form a ring 輪をなす, 車座になる ▪ All joined hands and *formed a ring*. みなが手をつないで輪になった.
go* [*grab, reach*] *for the brass ring/ get the brass ring 最高のものを手に入れようとする ▪ I always *reach for the brass ring* in food, furniture, paintings and others. 私はいつも食べ物, 家具, 絵画など, 最高のものを手に入れるようにしている.

R

in a ring **1**(人が)車座に(なって) ▪ We sat *in a ring.* 我々は車座に座った.

2 輪になって，ぐるぐると ▪ The boys and girls danced *in a ring.* 少年少女は輪になって踊った.

keep [***hold***] ***the ring*** (けんか・論争などを)監視する ▪ The State should confine itself to *holding the ring.* 州がやるべきは監視するだけでよい.

make a ring **1** 輪状に取り巻く ▪ The soldiers *made a ring* for their officers to fight in. 兵士たちは輪状に取り巻いて士官がその中で戦うようにした.

2 同盟して市場を左右する ▪ These merchants *made a ring* on the sugar market and prices soared tremendously. こうした商人たちが同盟して砂糖市場を左右したので値段が恐ろしく高騰した.

make rings round *a person* → run RINGs round a person.

run [***ride***] ***at the ring*** (棒につるした)環を馬を走らせながらやり先で取る《昔の武技》 ▪ She egged me on to *run at the ring* for every prize. 彼女は私をそそのかしてすべての賞を得るように馬上からやり先で環を取らせようとした.

run [***make***] ***rings around*** [***round***] *a person* 《口》《競技》人をゆうゆうと負かす ▪ He would *run rings around* us in everything. 彼は何をやっても我々より役者が上だった ▪ He absolutely *made rings round* me. 彼は僕をゆうゆうと完全に負かしてしまった. ☞「競走場を何回も走り回る」が原義.

throw [***toss***] *one's* ***hat into the ring*** 立候補を宣言する ▪ He *threw his hat into the* presidential *ring.* 彼は大統領への立候補を宣言した.

ring[2] /rɪŋ/ 名 ***give ... a ring*** **1**(ベル)を押して鳴らす ▪ He *gave* the bell *a ring.* 彼はベルを押して鳴らした.

2(人)に電話をかける ▪ *Give* me *a ring* this afternoon. きょう午後にお電話をください.

have a false [***the true, the right***] ***ring*** 音が悪い[良い]; にせ物[本物]だ ▪ He does not seem to *have the right ring* about him. あの男はどうも本物のようには思えない. ☞ 硬貨・ガラス器などに本物・上物の響きがあるかどうかということから.

have a familiar [***ironical,*** etc.] ***ring*** (***about*** [***to***] ***it***) (それには)なじみ深い[皮肉な，など]響きがある ▪ The name *has a familiar ring about it.* その名にはなじみ深い響きがある.

have the ring of truth [***sincerity, madness,*** etc.] 本当[誠実，どうかしている，など]らしい ▪ His story *had the ring of truth.* 彼の話は本当らしく聞こえた.

hold the ring 中立的な立場をとる ▪ The judge needs to *hold the ring* impartially on the law. 判事は法に基づき公平に中立的な立場をとる必要がある.

ring[3] /rɪŋ/ 動 ***Don't ring us, we'll ring you.*** 電話しないでください，こちらから電話します《求職者に対する断り文句》 ▪ All left with the familiar parting shot, "*Don't ring us, we'll ring you.*" みなが「問い合わせの電話はしないように，こちらからしますから」といういつもの去り際の捨てぜりふを耳に立ち去った.

ring a bell 《口》共感を呼ぶ; 思い出させる ▪ He has a sense of the ridiculous which *rings a bell* with us. 彼はおかしみを解する心をもっていて我々の共感を呼びます ▪ The name *rings* no *bell* in your mind? その名前では何も思い出さないのですか. ☞ 頭の中にベルがあって，何か思い当たることを聞くと鳴ると想像することから.

ring *a person* ***a peal*** 人をしかりつける ▪ He *rang* his wife *a peal.* 彼は妻をしかりつけた.

ring at the door 玄関の呼び鈴を鳴らす ▪ Someone is *ringing at the door.* 誰かが玄関の呼び鈴を鳴らしている.

ring bells/《米》***ring*** *one's* ***bell*** 《口》〚否定文で〛心に訴える，ぴんとくる ▪ That doesn't *ring bells* in my heart. そいつは心にぴんとこない.

ring down (***the curtain***) ベルを鳴らして幕をおろす; (ある事件)の結末をつける (*on*) ▪ This sorry episode *rang down the curtain on* a spectacular adventure. このみじめな挿話がはなばなしい冒険譚に幕をおろした.

ring false →RING true.

ring [***sound***] ***hollow*** 嘘のように[そらぞらしく]響く ▪ The story he told us *rang* pretty *hollow.* 彼が我々にした話はかなりそらぞらしく響いた.

ring in *one's* ***ears*** [***head***] (故人の言などが)耳に残る ▪ These words *ring* constantly *in my ears.* これらの言葉は絶えず私の耳に残っている.

ring in *one's* ***fancy*** [***heart***] 心に残る ▪ The voice of God still *rang in my heart.* 神のそのお声がまだ私の心に残っていた.

ring off the hook 《米》(電話が)鳴りっぱなしである，鳴りやまない ▪ The phones *rang off the hook* with requests for tickets to his speech. 電話は彼の講演のチケットを求める依頼で鳴りっぱなしだった.

ring (***out***) ***the knell of*** → sound the (death) KNELL of.

ring the bell **1**(使用人を呼ぶために)呼び鈴を鳴らす (*for*) ▪ He *rang the bell for* the servant. 彼は呼び鈴を鳴らして使用人を呼んだ.

2《口》うまくいく，功を奏する ▪ This last advantage *rang the bell* with bankers. この最後の利点が銀行家には功を奏した. ☞ 力だめしなどでうまくいくと鐘を鳴らすことから.

3 賞を勝ち取る ▪ It was the shot that *rang the bell.* それは賞を勝ち取るためのワンショットであった.

ring the changes →CHANGE[1].

ring the curtain up ベルを鳴らして幕をあげる; (...の)幕開けとなる (*on*) ▪ They are just going to *ring the curtain up* for the first scene. ベルが鳴って第1場の幕があがるところだ ▪ With Marlowe, *the curtain was rung up on* a new epoch in English drama. マーロウと共にイギリス戯曲の新時代の幕があいた.

ring true [***false***] (硬貨が)本物の[にせ金の]音がする; 本当[嘘]らしく聞こえる ▪ The coin *rings true* [*false*]. この貨幣は本物[にせ金]の音がする ▪ His words do not *ring true* [*false*]. 彼の言葉は本当

[嘘]らしく聞こえない.

You rang, sir? 何かご用でございますか《呼び鈴に対する執事などの言葉》 ▪ *You rang, sir?*—Where have you been, Strong? 何かご用でございますか—どこに行っていたのだ, ストロング.

ringer /ríŋər/ 名 ***be a (dead, real) ringer for***《俗》…に(全く)生き写しである ▪ You *are a dead ringer for* Smith. 君はスミスに全く生き写しだ.

ringlet /ríŋlət/ 名 ***in ringlets*** 巻き毛になって ▪ She wore her hair *in ringlets*. 彼女は髪の毛を巻き毛に束ねていた.

ringside /ríŋsàɪd/ 名 ***a ringside seat [view]*** 最前列, 特等席 ▪ Visitors to the site have had *a ringside seat* for the construction. その場への訪問者たちは建設を間近に見た ▪ You can get *a ringside view* of Mt. Fuji from here. ここからは富士山を間近で見ることができます.

rink /rɪŋk/ 名 ***a skating rink***《俗》スリップしやすい道路 ▪ Watch out! There's *a skating rink* ahead. 注意して! 前方はスリップしやすい道路だから.

riot /ráɪət/ 名 ***raise [get up] a riot*** 暴動を起こす ▪ No one thought of *raising a riot*. 誰も暴動を起こそうと考えた者はなかった.

read the Riot Act《口》(特に子供を)きびしくしかりつける ▪ He *read* me *the Riot Act* for what I'd done. 彼は私のしたことをきびしくしかりつけた ▪ The pupils *were read the Riot Act* by the teacher. 生徒たちは先生に厳しく叱りつけられた. ☞「騒じょう取締り令(1715年英国で発布された)を読み聞かせる」が原義.

run riot 奔放自在にふるまう; あらゆる制限を無視する; やたらにはびこる, 咲き乱れる ▪ The sculptor seems to have let his imagination altogether *run riot*. その彫刻家は想像力を全くほしいままにしているようだ ▪ The flu *ran riot* among them. インフルエンザが彼らの間でやたらに蔓延(まんえん)した. ☞ 猟犬が違った動物の臭跡を追い回すことから.

rip[1] /rɪp/ 名 ***like rips***《米口》ひどく, すごく ▪ The captain swore *like rips* at the crew. 船長は乗組員をひどくののしった.

rip[2] /rɪp/ 動 ***let her [it] rip***《口》(船・車・機械などを)ぶっとばす; (事を)ほっておく ▪ When we get to a nice road, I'll *let her rip*. いい道に出たら, 車をぶっとばすよ ▪ You have simply to sit still and *let her rip*. 君はただじっとしてほっておきさえすればいいんだ ▪ When he said, "OK, *let her rip*," she stepped on the gas. 「よし, さあ, とばせ」と彼が言うと彼女はアクセルを踏み込んだ.

let rip **1**《口》自由[勝手]にふるまう ▪ Inflation *let rip* again. またインフレが猛威をふるった ▪ We usually *let rip* at Christmas. クリスマスにはたいていはめをはずして騒ぎます.

2 ぺらぺらしゃべる ▪ He *let rip* over her inadequacies in the past. 彼は彼女の過去の失敗をぺらぺらしゃべった.

3《英俗》放屁する, ぶっぱなす ▪ You can't just *let rip* when you're in a smart restaurant. 高級レストランでおならをするわけにはいかない.

let things rip 事態を放任する, 成り行きに任せる ▪ You had better *let things rip*. 君は事態を成り行きに任せたほうがよい.

rip and tear《米口》あばれ狂う ▪ A man doesn't want to *rip and tear* around all the time. 人間はいつもあばれ狂ってばかりいたいとは思わない.

rip in two [half] …を二つに引き裂く ▪ He *ripped* the letter *in two*. 彼は手紙を二つに引き裂いた.

rip open …を引き裂いてあける ▪ He *ripped open* an envelope. 彼は封筒を手でちぎって開いた.

rip to pieces [shreds] …を完膚なきまでに攻撃する ▪ I stood up and *ripped* his argument *to pieces*. 私は立ち上がって彼の議論を徹底的にたたいた.

rip up the rulebook 白紙に戻す ▪ We have to just *rip up the rulebook* and start again. 我々は白紙に戻してやり直さなければならない.

ripe /raɪp/ 形 ***a ripe old age*** 高齢, 熟年 ▪ He reached [lived to] *a ripe old age*. 彼は高齢に達した.

at a ripe age 高齢で ▪ He died *at a ripe age*. 彼は高齢で亡くなった.

be ripe for **1**(いたずら・反乱など)の用意がすっかりできている ▪ The mob *were* only too *ripe for* a tumult. 暴徒は騒ぎ立てる用意がすっかりできていた.

2(ある目的)の機が熟している ▪ The conspiracy *was ripe for* execution. その陰謀の実行の機が熟していた.

be ripe in [upon](仕事など)に熟達している, 円熟している ▪ He *was ripe in* wisdom. 彼の知恵は円熟していた ▪ I *am* not very *ripe upon* this subject. この問題にはあまり熟達していません.

be ripe to *do* …する準備がすっかりできている ▪ He *is ripe to* hear the truth. 彼は真相を聞く心構えがすっかりできている.

of ripe [riper] years(青年期を過ぎて)成熟した ▪ He is a man *of riper years*. 彼は成熟した大人だ.

reeling ripe《俗》ひどく酔っ払って (cf. Sh., *Temp*. 5. 1. 279) ▪ The Irish teetotaler was found *reeling ripe*. そのアイルランドの禁酒主義者はひどく酔っ払っていた.

Soon ripe, soon rotten.《諺》早熟は大成せず.

ripping /rípɪŋ/ 形 ***have a ripping time***《俗》すてきな思いをする ▪ We *had a ripping time* at the party. 我々はそのパーティーでとても楽しく過ごした.

ripple /rípəl/ 名 ***a ripple effect*** 波及効果, 連鎖反応 (*on, in*) ▪ The oil spill is having *a ripple effect on* the local economy. 原油流出事故は地元経済に連鎖的影響を及ぼしている ▪ Physical and mental ailments can create *a ripple effect in* your body. 肉体的および精神的苦痛は身体に連鎖反応を引き起こすことがある.

cause a ripple (on the surface)〖主に否定文で〗さざ波を立てる, かき乱す ▪ The change *caused*

R

hardly *a ripple* in the foreign exchange market. その変化は外国為替市場にさざ波一つ立てなかった.

make the ripple 《米口》早瀬を渡る; 事をうまく運ぶ ▪ I told him I was not able to *make the ripple*. 私にはそううまく事は運べないと彼に言った.

rise[1] /raɪz/ 名 ***a meteoric rise to fame*** [***power***] 彗星のごとく名声[権力]の座に上りつめること ▪ She began her *meteoric rise to fame* in the world of entertainment. 彼女は芸能界で彗星のごとく名を上げた.

and the rise 《米》...余り, 以上 ▪ There were a thousand *and the rise*. 1,000以上あった.

get a rise (釣りで)魚が(水面近くでエサを)食う ▪ I fished two hours without *getting a rise*. 私は2時間釣りをしたが, 魚は1匹も食わなかった.

get [***have, take***] ***a*** [***the***] ***rise out of*** **1** (人)をからかって怒らせる ▪ He's so touchy, I love to *take a rise out of* him. 彼はとても短気だから彼をからかって怒らせるのが大好きだ. ☞蚊針[毛針]を投げて魚を水面に浮かばせる (rise) ことから.

2 《卑》(...で)性的に興奮する, 勃つ ▪ He always *gets a rise out of* watching adult videos. 彼はアダルトビデオを見て性欲をかきたてるのが常だ.

give rise to ...を引き起こす, の元となる ▪ It may *give rise to* serious trouble. それはほんとうに厄介なことになるかもしれない.

have [***take***] ***a*** [***the***] ***rise out of*** = get a RISE out of 1.

have [***take***] ***its rise in*** [***among***] ...に源を発している ▪ The river *has its rise among* the hills. その川は山間に源を発している ▪ The expression *took its rise in* America. その表現はアメリカが元だ.

make a rise うまく金鉱を探し当てる ▪ You've got to work till you *make a rise* for my sake. 私のためにうまく金鉱を探し当てるまでは働いてもらうよ.

on the rise **1** 騰貴の傾向で ▪ Prices are *on the rise*. 物価は上昇してきている.

2 (鳥が)飛び立つところを ▪ He shot a bird *on the rise*. 彼は鳥が飛び立つところを射った.

take a rise out of *a person* →get a RISE out of.

the rise and fall of (価格・需要など)の上下すること; (文明・国家など)の盛衰 ▪ *The rise and fall of* prices is governed by the law of supply and demand. 物価の上下は需要供給の法則に支配されている ▪ The book's title is "*The Rise and Fall of* Civilizations". その本の書名は「文明の盛衰」である.

rise[2] /raɪz/ 動 ***rise*** (***again***) ***from the dead*** [***grave***] 死者の間からよみがえる ▪ Jesus Christ *rose* (*again*) *from the dead*. イエス・キリストは死からよみがえった.

rise and fall **1** (波・価格・需要などが)上下する; (音・音楽などが)高くなったり低くなったりする ▪ Their voices *rose and fell*. 彼らの声は高くなったり低くなったりした.

2 (国・文明などが)盛衰する ▪ He compared the way civilizations *rise and fall*. 彼は諸文明が盛衰するさまを比較した.

rise and shine 《口》起きててきぱきやる (《聖》*Isa*. 60. 1) ▪ Come on, now. *Rise and shine!* さあさあ, 起きててきぱきやりなさい.

rise in the world/rise in life 出世する ▪ He must have *risen in the world*; he's just bought a new car. 彼は出世したにちがいない. 新車を買ったところだから.

rise to the bait [***fly***] (人が)誘惑に乗る ▪ He *rose to the fly* with a charming simplicity. 彼は全く単純に誘惑に乗ってきた. ☞魚が蚊針[毛針]に食いつくことから.

rising /ráɪzɪŋ/ 前 ***rising*** (***of***) 《米口》...以上 ▪ There were *rising* (*of*) a thousand men killed at the battle. その戦闘で1,000人以上の人が死んだ.

risk[1] /rɪsk/ 名 ***a calculated risk*** 計算ずみの危険, 予測される危険[失敗] ▪ The sending of American troops to Afghanistan is *a calculated risk*. アメリカ軍のアフガニスタンへの派遣は危険が予測される.

at all risks/at any [***whatever***] ***risk*** どんな危険を冒しても, ぜひとも ▪ It must be done *at any risk*. それはぜひともやらなくてはならない.

at *one's* ***own risk*** 自分の責任において ▪ Do so *at your own risk*. 自分の責任においてそうしなさい《婉曲に「...すべからず」の意》.

at owner's risk (貨物が)損害は荷主負担で ▪ The goods were sent by rail *at owner's risk*. 商品は損害荷主負担で鉄道便で送られた.

at risk **1** 危険にさらされて, 危険な状態で[に]; (...を)危険にさらして (*to*) ▪ Children's health and lives are *at risk* from passive smoking. 子供たちの健康と生命が受動喫煙のため危険にさらされている ▪ He dived in to save the child *at* considerable *risk to* his own life. 彼は自分の生命を相当な危険にさらして子供を助けるために飛び込んだ.

2 (...の損失[損傷]に対して)法的責任がある ▪ The sponsor is *at risk* for providing such coverage. スポンサーはそのような担保を提供する法的責任がある.

at the risk of ...を犠牲にして ▪ Some of the photos have been taken *at the risk of* life and limb. その写真の中には身命をかけて撮ったものもある.

run [***take***] ***a*** [***the***] ***risk/run*** [***take***] ***risks*** 危険を冒す (*of*) ▪ He *ran a* narrow *risk of* being hanged. 彼は絞首刑にされるようなひどい危険を冒した ▪ I'll *take the risk of* being late. 遅れることを承知でやってみよう.

risk[2] /rɪsk/ 動 ***risk life and limb*** 命をかける, 命を危険にさらす (= risk one's NECK) ▪ He was on the roof *risking life and limb* to rescue the kitten. 彼は子猫を助けようと命がけで屋根の上にいた.

rite /raɪt/ 名 ***a rite of passage*** 通過儀礼 ▪ Marriage is *a rite of passage*, while it is no longer regarded as a journey without end. 結婚は一つの通過儀礼だが, 一方でもはや終わりのない旅路だとはみなされていない.

ritz /rɪts/ 名 ***put on the ritz*** 《米口》気取る ▪ Don't try to *put on the ritz*. 気取ろうとするのは

よせ. ☞the Ritz hotel から.

You are not at the Ritz! ここはリッツ・ホテルじゃないでしょ!《料理に不満を言う人への応答》 ▪ Just remember *you are not at the Ritz*. It is a nice meal for the money. ここはリッツ・ホテルではありませんが, 料金の割にはいい食事です.

rival /ráɪvəl/ 名 ***without a rival*** 匹敵するもののない, 無比の ▪ The stadium is extoled as *without a rival*. このスタジアムは無比のものとして称揚されている.

rivalry /ráɪvəlri/ 名 ***enter into rivalry with*** …と競争を始める ▪ The store *entered into rivalry with* other stores. その店は他の店と競争を始めた.

river /rívər/ 名 ***cross the river*** (***of death***) 《口》死ぬ ▪ He had at last *crossed the river*, on whose brink he had been so long waiting. 彼は死のふちを長いことさまよっていたが, とうとう亡くなった.

follow the river 《米口》川汽船で働く ▪ His occupation had been *following the river*. 彼の職は川汽船で働くことであった.

get on the river 《米》川[川汽船]での仕事を見つける ▪ Boy after boy managed to *get on the river*. 少年たちは次々と何とかして川での仕事にありついた.

go (***and***) ***jump in the river*** = Go (and) jump in the LAKE.

go down the river (奴隷がミシシッピ川の)川下に売られて行く ▪ He saved his slaves from *going down the river*. 彼は奴隷たちが川下に売られて行くのを救ってやった.

row *a person* ***up Salt River*** →ROW⁴.

run the river 《米口》川汽船に雇われる ▪ I thought I'd made a mistake to let him *run the river*. 彼が川汽船に雇われるのを許したのはまちがいだったと私は思った.

sell ... down the river 《口》…を裏切る, だます; を台なしにする ▪ He *sold* many of his old friends *down the river*. 彼は旧友の多くを裏切った ▪ Our engagement *was sold down the river*. 私たちの約束は破られてしまった. ☞奴隷を罰として Mississippi 川下流の農場に売って苦役につかせたことから.

send ... up the river 《米俗》…を刑務所にぶち込む ▪ I done it. *Send* me *up the river*. おれがやったんだ. おれを刑務所にぶち込んでくれ. ☞New York で有罪を宣告された囚人は Hudson 川上流の Sing Sing 刑務所に送られることから.

rivet /rívət/ 動 ***rivet*** *a person* ***to the ground*** [***the spot***] 人を地面[その場]にくぎうけにする ▪ The terrible news *riveted* me *to the ground*. その恐ろしいニュースを聞いて私はその場に立ちすくんだ ▪ All eyes *are riveted to the spot*. すべての目がその場にくぎうけにされた.

roach /roʊtʃ/ 名 (***as***) ***sound as a roach*** 《口》すこぶる健康で, ぴちぴちして ▪ My father is seventy but *as sound as a roach* still. 父は70歳だが, まだとても元気だ. ☞roach「ヨーロッパ産のコイ科の淡水魚」; F sain comme un gardon のなぞり.

road /roʊd/ 名 ***a fair road for stumps*** 《米口》困難な立場 ▪ I reckon he's in *a fair road for stumps*. 彼は困難な立ち場にあるのだと思う.

a road to nowhere 進歩[発展]の見通しが立たない情勢 ▪ The band is cool, but it seems like *a road to nowhere*. そのバンドはカッコいいが, 名が売れる見通しはないように思える.

a royal road →ROYAL.

down the road 将来, その[この]先 (→down the LINE) ▪ The effect of the event will show up years *down the road*. その件の結果は数年先に現れるだろう ▪ This type of test could be useful *down the road*. このタイプのテストは将来役立つかもしれない ▪ A management crisis a few years *down the road* becomes inevitable. 2, 3年後の経営危機は不可避となる.

for the road 別れの印に ▪ He gave me a final glass *for the road*. 彼は別れの印に最後の1杯を注いでくれた.

give *a person* ***the road*** 人を通行させる ▪ I *gave* them *the road*. 彼らを通らせてやった.

go down that road **1** 特定の方針に決める, 望ましくない方向に向かう ▪ If we *go down that road*, we're going to go down the road of higher taxes. その道に行けば, 重税路線を進むことになる.

2 悪い道に進む ▪ I've seen many talented kids *go down that road*. 多くの才能のある子供たちが悪の道に進むのを見てきた.

go over the road 《米口》刑に服する ▪ It's right good of you to come and see him before he *goes over the road*. 彼が刑に服する前に会いに来てくださってほんとうにありがとう.

hit the road 《口》 **1** (長い)旅に出る ▪ I'm *hitting the road* tomorrow. 私はあす旅に出ます.

2 (車で)出かける (*for*) ▪ He *hit the road for* home. 彼は車で家に向かった.

hug [***hold***] ***the road*** (車が)路面に密着して走る ▪ This car *hugs the road* well. この車は路面によく密着して走る.

in *one's* [***the***] ***road*** じゃまになって ▪ You're quite *in my road*. 君は全く足手まといだ.

It's a long road that has no turning. → It's a long lane that has no TURNING.

on the (***high***) ***road to*** …の途上[途中]にあって ▪ He is *on the high road to* recovery. 彼は快復の途上にある ▪ The jinrikisha is *on the road to* extinction. 人力車はなくなりかかっている.

on [***upon***] ***the road*** **1** 旅行していて, 旅の途中で, 巡業中で; 《米口》(セールスマン・講師として)地方を回って ▪ How long were you *on the road*? どれくらいの間旅していましたか ▪ They slept one night *upon the road*. 彼らは旅の途中で一晩眠った ▪ The company has been *on the road* for the last three years. その一座はここ3年ほど巡業している ▪ He has always been *on the road*. 彼はいつもセールスマンとして地方を回っている.

R

2《米口》放浪(生活を)して ▪ Thirty dollars won't last long *on the road*. 放浪生活では30ドルなんてすぐ消える.

one* (*more*) *for the road →ONE.

out of the common* [*general, usual*] *road 常道を逸して, かけ離れて ▪ He is altogether *out of the common road*. 彼は全く常軌を逸している.

out of the [*one's*] ***road*** 《主にスコ》 **1** 辺ぴな ▪ Britain is *out of the road* of the world. イギリスって世界の辺ぴなところにあるんだよ.

2 場ちがいの, おかどちがいの ▪ It was a question *out of my road*. それは私にはおかどちがいの問題だった ▪ It would not be *out of the road* to do so. そうしても場ちがいではないだろう.

out of the road of …の常道を逸して, とかけ離れて ▪ It is *out of the road of* common sense. それは常識とはかけ離れている.

a person's ***road to Damascus*** 《英・文》ダマスカスへの道; 人生の転機, 重要体験《限定的にも》 ▪ *His road to Damascus* is clearly imprinted in his mind. 彼の人生の転機は彼の心にはっきりと刻まれている ▪ Alec Roth recalls *his "Road to Damascus* experience" at the 1979 Music Festival. アレック・ロスは1979年の音楽祭での自分の「重要体験」を思い起こす. ☞イエスの迫害者だったサウロ(後の使徒パウロ)がダマスコ(ダマスカス)でイエスに出会い, 劇的な回心を遂げたことから.

take the low road 邪道を行く, 人の道を外れる (↔take the HIGH road (in)) ▪ The government *took the low road* on economic policies. 政府の経済政策は邪道だった.

take the road 旅立つ ▪ He *took the road* among the rest. 彼も他の者といっしょに旅立った.

take the road of …の上に立つ ▪ Most certainly, he *takes the road of* all mankind. 確かに彼はすべての人間の上に立つ男だ.

take to the road **1**(劇団などが)地方巡業に出る (→ hit the ROAD 1) ▪ The theater company *took to the road* for the summer. その劇団は夏の間地方巡業に出た.

2《英》浮浪者になる ▪ One of the effects of unemployment is the number of young men who are *taking to the road*. 失業の結果の一つに大勢の若者が浮浪者になっているという事実が見られる.

3《英》追いはぎになる ▪ So I *took to the road*, and first robbed a parson. そこで私は追いはぎになり, 最初に牧師の物を奪った.

The road to hell is paved with good intentions. = Hell is paved with good INTENTIONs.

roar[1] /rɔːr/ 名 ***go with a roar*** 《俗》とんとん拍子にいく ▪ Everything *went with a roar*. 何もかもとんとん拍子にいった.

set ... in a roar (***of laughter***) …をどっと笑わせる ▪ His jokes *set* the table [room] *in a roar*. 彼の冗談が食卓についた[部屋中の]人々をどっと笑わせた.

roar[2] /rɔːr/ 動 ***roar*** *oneself* ***hoarse*** どなってしゃがれ声になる ▪ Paulo *roared himself hoarse*. パウロはどなってしゃがれ声になった.

roar with laughter 大笑いする ▪ The whole party were *roaring with laughter*. 一座の者は全員大笑いしていた.

roaring /rɔ́ːrɪŋ/ 形 ***a roaring success*** 《口》大成功 ▪ The surgery was *a roaring success*. その手術は大成功だった.

drive* [*make, do*] *a roaring trade [《米》 ***business***] 商売が大繁昌している ▪ He is evidently *making a roaring trade*. 彼の商売は明らかに大繁昌している.

have a roaring time 《口》とても楽しい思いをする ▪ What *a roaring time* I *had*! ああ, とっても楽しかった!

in roaring* (*good*) *health 《口》はち切れそうに健康で ▪ He is *in roaring good health*. 彼ははち切れんばかりに健康だ.

roaring drunk ひどく酔って騒々しい ▪ He will come home *roaring drunk*. 彼はひどく酔って騒々しく帰って来るだろう.

roast[1] /roʊst/ 名形 ***cry roast meat*** 自分の幸運を他人に話す ▪ He cannot fare well but he must *cry roast meat*. 彼は自分の幸運を他人に話さずにはおられない.

make roast meat of …を焼き殺す; をやっつけてしまう ▪ They will *make roast meat of* the enemy. 彼らは敵をやっつけてしまうだろう.

rule the roast 事を主宰する, 支配する, 牛耳る ▪ The ladies always *rule the roast* in this part of the world. この国では女性が常に牛耳っている.

roast[2] /roʊst/ 動 ***a fire fit to roast an ox*** すこぶる大きな火 ▪ You've made *a fire fit to roast an ox*. すごく大きな火を起こしたもんだね.

roast *oneself* 暖まる ▪ *Roast yourself* in front of the fire. 火の前へ来て暖まりなさい.

roasting /róʊstɪŋ/ 名 ***get a roasting*** 《口》どやされる, 酷評される ▪ I'd better go. I'll *get a roasting* if I'm late again! 行かなくっちゃ. また遅刻したらどやされてしまう.

give *a person* ***a roasting*** 《口》人をどやす, 酷評する (*about, for, over*) ▪ The fans *gave* Fuhr *a roasting about* his problems. ファンたちは問題ありのファーをどやした ▪ His boss *gave* him *a roasting for* not finishing the job on time. 仕事を予定通り仕上げられなかったことで彼は上司にこってり油を搾られた ▪ The Australian press *gave* Sonn *a roasting over* the selection. オーストラリアのマスコミはその選抜に関してサン氏を酷評した.

rob /rɑb|rɔb/ 動 ***rob*** *a person* ***blind*** →steal a person BLIND.

rob Peter to pay Paul →PETER.

we wuz* [*was, were*] *robbed いかさまでやられた[負けた], 不当な判定だ ▪ "*We wuz robbed,*" is one of sport's most-worn statements. 「不当判定」はスポーツで最も使い古された言葉の一つだ. ☞1932年のヘビー級タイトルマッチで Max Schmeling が Sharkey

に敗れたときファイトマネージャー Joe Jacobs (1896–1940) がつぶやいた言葉から.

robbery /rάbəri|rɔ́b-/ 名 ***daylight*** [***highway***] ***robbery*** 公然の泥棒行為《法外な代金》 ▪ The charge in that bar is unbelievable—it's (plain, absolute) *daylight robbery*. あのバーの料金は信じられないほど高い—公然のぼったくりだ.

robe /roʊb/ 名 ***both robes*** 文官と武官 ▪ The council was made up of *both robes*. 審議会は文官と武官とから成り立っていた.

either robe 文官と武官のいずれか ▪ A learned man of *either robe* will do. 学識のある人なら文官でも武官でもよい.

follow the robe 弁護士をやる ▪ They *follow the robe* as a profession. 彼らは弁護士の職にある.

the long [***short***] ***robe*** 文官[軍人](の職) ▪ *The long robe* as well as *the short* have felt his fury. 軍人はもちろん文官も彼の怒りに苦しんできた.

robin /rάbən|rɔ́bɪn/ 名 (***a***) ***round robin*** **1** 総当たり戦《限定的にも》 ▪ The club always holds *a* tennis *round robin* on the weekend before the Fourth of July. そのクラブでは独立記念日前の週末にはいつもテニスの総当たり戦が行われる ▪ There can be no favorite teams in *a round robin* tournament like this. このような総当たり戦のトーナメントではひいきのチームなんてありえない.

2 円形上申書[抗議書]《発起人が特定できないように円形に署名されたことから》 ▪ The cabinet received *a round robin* from eighty-seven MPs. 内閣は87人の下院議員による抗議文書を受け取った.

roc /rɑk|rɔk/ 名 ***roc's egg*** ロックの卵; 話だけで実際にはないもの, とても手に入らない物 ▪ I might wish for the *roc's egg*. 例のロックの卵がほしいところだ. ☞roc はアラビア伝説の巨大な鳥.

rock[1] /rɑk|rɔk/ 名 ***a pocket full of rocks*** 《米俗》大金 ▪ If I had *a pocket full of rocks*, you should share them. 僕に大金があれば, 君もいっしょに使っていいんだが.

(***as***) ***firm*** [***solid, steady***] ***as a rock*** 岩のように堅固で, 確固不抜で ▪ That post is *as firm as a rock*. その地位は確固不抜だ.

between a rock and a hard place 困った状態の, どう転んでも悪い結果の, 板ばさみになって (→between the DEVIL and the deep (blue) sea ▪ I think we are caught *between a rock and a hard place*. 我々は板ばさみの状態に置かれていると思う.

built [***founded***] ***on a rock*** 基礎の堅実な ▪ The firm is sound enough—*built on a rock*, all right. あの会社はとても確実で, 確かに基礎はがっしりしている.

get *one's* ***rocks off*** スリルを味わう[楽しむ] ▪ They *got their rocks off* taking a ride on the roller coaster. 彼らはジェットコースターに乗ってスリルを味わった.

have (***got***) ***rocks in the*** [*one's*] ***head*** 《米口》頭がどうかしている《とんでもない質問に答えて》 ▪ Kid, you'*ve got rocks in your head*? 若いの, 頭がどうかしてるね.

hit the rocks 思いがけない結果になる ▪ His attempt to sell their house *hit the rocks* with his wife opposing it. 家を売りに出す彼の試みは奥さんの反対で思いがけない結果になった.

keep off the rocks 危険からのがれる ▪ We must economize to *keep off the rocks*. 危険からのがれるためには節約しなければいけない.

on the rocks 《口》 **1** 座礁して; 進退きわまって ▪ Soon their marriage went *on the rocks*. やがて彼らの結婚生活が暗礁に乗り上げた.

2 金に窮して ▪ I'm fair *on the rocks*. 僕はひどく金づまりだ.

3 (ウィスキーなど)氷の小塊を浮かせて, オンザロックの ▪ I ordered Scotch *on the rocks*. 私はスコッチのオンザロックを注文した.

reach [***be at, hit***] ***rock bottom*** (物価などが)底をつく; (気分が)落ち込む ▪ Prices have *reached rock bottom*. 物価は底をついた ▪ Then I *hit rock bottom*. My girlfriend left me. その後私は滅入ってしまった. ガールフレンドが離れて行ったからだ.

Rocks ahead! 暗礁だ!; 危いぞ! ▪ Take him away. *Rocks ahead*, sir. あの男を連れてお行きなさい. 危うございます.

run against a rock/run on the rocks 座礁する; 危険な目にあう ▪ He will not be so short-sighted as to *run against* such *a rock*. 彼はそんな危険な目にあうほど目先がきかないことはないだろう.

see rocks ahead 危険があるのがわかる ▪ I fear I *see rocks ahead*. どうも危険があるようだ.

strike [***split***] ***on a rock*** 暗礁にぶつかる ▪ It is not known to us how they *struck on these rocks*. 彼らがどのようにしてこれらの暗礁にぶつかったかはわかっていない.

There are rocks ahead. 危険が待ち受けている ▪ *There are rocks ahead*, so be careful. 危険が待ち受けているから, 気をつけたまえ.

rock[2] /rɑk|rɔk/ 動 ***Let's rock and roll!*** 《口》始めましょう! ▪ Everybody ready?—Oh yeah. —Good. *Let's rock and roll!* みんな, いいか—うん, いいよ—よし, 始めよう.

rock the boat 平穏な状態をかき乱す, 波風を立てる ▪ Trips should not be timed to *rock the boat* in countries where elections are being held. 旅行は選挙が現に行われているような国々での波風が立つような時機に合わせるべきでない.

rock ... to sleep →SLEEP[1].

rocker /rάkər|rɔ́k-/ 名 ***be*** [***go***] ***off*** *one's* ***rocker*** 《俗》気が狂っている[気が狂う] ▪ When he had swallowed the liniment, he *was off his rocker*. 塗布薬を飲み下したとき彼は乱心していたのだ.

rocket /rάkət|rɔ́k-/ 名 ***be not*** (***a***) ***rocket science*** それほど難しくない ▪ Using a PC *is not rocket science*. パソコンを使うのはそれほど難しくはない.

give *a person* ***a rocket*** 《英口》人をしかりつける,

どやす (*for doing*) ▪ My mum *gave* me *a rocket for tearing* my new jeans. 新しいジーンズを破ったことでお母さんに大目玉をくらった.

get a rocket 《英口》ひどくしかられる, どやされる (*for doing*) ▪ He *got a rocket* from his teacher *for being* late. 彼は遅刻して先生にひどくしかられた.

it doesn't take a rocket scientist ロケット科学者でなくても[誰にでも]わかる ▪ *It doesn't take a rocket scientist* to figure out how bad this problem is. これがどれほど悪質な問題かは誰でも想像がつく.

off *one's* ***rocket*** 《口》気が狂って ▪ He's quite *off his rocket*. 彼はすっかり気が狂っている.

put a rocket under *a person* 《英》人をなんとかして急がせる[せき立てる] ▪ We're going to have to *put a rocket under* Tim if we want to catch that train. その電車に乗りたいのなら, なんとかしてティムをせき立てねばならないだろう.

shoot up like a rocket (価格・株が)急騰する ▪ The stocks of our company have *shot up* in value *like a rocket*. わが社の株価は跳ね上がっている.

take off like a rocket 短期間で大成功を収める ▪ The economy at home *took off like a rocket* in the mid-1990s. 国内経済は1990年代半ば, 短期間で大いに栄えた.

rod /rɑd|rɔd/ 名 ***a hot rod*** 改造車 (hopped up) ▪ It is possible to build *a hot rod* entirely from new parts. すべて新品のパーツで改造車を組み立てることは可能だ.

grab a handful of rods →ride the RODs.

have [***keep***] ***a rod in pickle for*** *a person* (人)を懲らしめようと手ぐすねひいている ▪ He *has a rod in pickle for* the idle. 彼は怠け者に罰を用意している.

kiss the rod 神妙に罰[運命]を受ける ▪ All we can do is to *kiss the rod*. ただ神妙に運命を受けいれるのみだ. ☞rod「体罰用のむち」.

make [***pickle***] ***a rod for*** *oneself*/ ***make*** [***pickle***] ***a rod for*** *one's* ***own back*** 自ら困難を招く ▪ I fear you have *made a rod for yourself* by associating with hooligans. 君はよた者とつき合ったりして自ら困難を招いたのではないのだろうか. ☞「自ら背中をむちで打たれる」が原義.

ride [***hit***] ***the rods***/ ***grab a handful of rods*** 《米俗》(浮浪者が車両と車両とのあいだに乗って)列車にただ乗りする ▪ Then I *rode the rods* east. それから私は列車にただ乗りして東部へ行った.

rule with a rod of iron 非常にきびしく治める[しつける](《聖》*Ps*. 2. 9; *Rev*. 2. 27) ▪ Their father *ruled* the children *with a rod of iron*. 父親は子供たちを非常にきびしくしつけた.

spare the rod (人を)甘やかす ▪ My mother *spared the rod* to my brother. 母は弟を甘やかした.

Spare the rod and spoil the child. 《諺》むちを惜しめば子供をそこなう,「かわいい子には旅させよ」.

roger /rάdʒər|rɔ́dʒə/ 名 ***a ten roger*** 《俗》了解 ▪ That's *a ten roger*. 了解しました.

Roger (***wilco***)***.*** 分かりました, 合点承知しました ▪ Can you do this right now?—*Roger*. いますぐこれをやれる?—合点承知しました.

rogue /roʊg/ 名 ***a rogue's gallery*** (警察の)犯罪者写真帳 ▪ They formed *a* real *rogue's gallery*. 彼らはまさしくそろいもそろって悪人うらをしていた.

roguish /róʊgɪʃ/ 形 (***as***) ***roguish as a kitten*** とてもいたずら好きな ▪ Tom, you're *as roguish as a kitten*. トム, お前はとてもいたずら好きだな.

role /roʊl/ 名 ***cast*** *a person* ***in the role of the villain*** 人に悪事の責任を負わせる ▪ You've *cast* me *in the role of the villain*. 君のせいで私が悪人にならされたのだ.

play a role in …で役割を演じる ▪ American women *play* important *roles in* society. アメリカの女性は社会で重要な役割を演じている.

take over the role of 責任[役割]を…から引き受ける[引き継ぐ] ▪ Her brightness qualifies her to *take over the role of* the president. 彼女は聡明なので社長の役割を引き継ぐ資格はある.

roll[1] /roʊl/ 名 ***a roll in the hay*** 《戯》性交 ▪ For him, love-making was no more than *a roll in the hay*. 彼にとってセックスは交尾でしかなかった.

a roll of honor 名誉の戦死者名簿; 成績優秀者名簿 ▪ His name is in *the roll of honor* at the university. 大学の成績優秀者名簿に彼の名前がある.

call the roll 出席を取る; 指名点呼する ▪ The chairman *called the roll* on the question. 議長はその問題について(賛否を問うため)人を指名点呼した.

have rolls of fat on …が丸々太っている ▪ He *has rolls of fat on* his neck. 彼は首が丸々太っている.

on a roll 順調で, 波に乗って ▪ They were *on a roll* with the new cars being sold. 彼らは新車が売れて波に乗っていた.

on [***upon***] ***the rolls*** 《英》弁護士録に載って ▪ He was *on the rolls* but had never set up for himself. 彼は弁護士録に載っていたがまだ独立して開業したことはなかった.

strike *a person* ***off the rolls*** 《英》(不正行為などで)人を弁護士名簿から除く ▪ They've *struck* Milson *off the rolls*. ミルスンは弁護士名簿から除名された.

the roll of fame 英傑録 ▪ His name shines brightest in all *the rolls of fame*. 彼の名はすべての英傑録の中でも一番輝かしい.

roll[2] /roʊl/ 動 ***be rolling in*** 《口》…がうなるほどある; に取り巻かれている ▪ He *is rolling in* money [cash, it]. 彼には金がうなるほどある.

get (…) ***rolling*** **1**《米》始まる, (…を)始める ▪ The Junior Soccer League *got rolling* with its first two games last week. 先週ジュニアのサッカーリーグが最初の2試合で始まった ▪ She made a few light-hearted comments to *get* the conversation *rolling*. 会話を始めるために彼女は軽いおしゃべりをした. **2**《米口》立ち去る ▪ Come on, let's *get roll-*

ing—it's late. さあ，もう出よう—遅いから.
roll a big wheel 《米俗》何かをたくらむ ▪ John is always *rolling a big wheel.* ジョンはいつも何かをたくらんでばかりいる.
roll a smoke 《口》紙たばこを巻いて作る ▪ *Roll* me *a smoke.* 紙たばこを巻いておくれ.
roll *one's* ***eyes at*** 上目づかいにする，目をぎょろつかせて…を見る ▪ He *rolled his eyes at* a pretty girl. 彼はきれいな女の子を目をぎょろつかせて見た.
roll ... in *one's* ***mind*** …を心の中で思いめぐらす ▪ I came home *rolling* the matter *in my mind.* 私はそのことを心の中で思いめぐらしながら帰宅した.
roll out the red carpet for →roll out the (red) CARPET.
roll *one's* ***own*** 《米口》自分で紙たばこを巻いて作る ▪ They are old-timers who *rolled their own.* 彼らは自分で紙たばこを巻いてつくった昔かたぎなんだ.
roll *one's* ***r's*** r を巻き舌で発音する ▪ They *roll their r's* and use their noses as trombones of conversation. 彼らは r を巻き舌で発音し，鼻をトロンボーンみたいに鳴らして会話する.
roll *oneself* (***up***) **1** 丸くなる ▪ The hedgehog *rolled itself* into a ball. ハリネズミはボールのように丸くなった.
2 (夜具などに)くるまる ▪ He *rolled himself up* in the blanket. 彼は毛布にくるまった.
roll with the punches →PUNCH[1].
rolled into [***in***] ***one*** 合わせて一つにされた ▪ It is somewhat like Christmas and a birthday feast *rolled into one.* それはまあクリスマスと誕生日をいっしょにしたようなものだ.

Roman /róʊmən/ 形 ***a Roman holiday*** 他人の苦しみになる娯楽 ▪ Diplomats make *a Roman holiday* for a new President every four years. 外交官たちは4年目ごとに新しい大統領の娯楽のために犠牲になる. ☞古代ローマで大衆の娯楽のために奴隷や捕虜が武器をもって闘わされたことから.

Rome /roʊm/ 名 ***All roads lead to Rome.*** 《諺》すべての道はローマに通じる《行き方は異なっても達するところは同じ》.
Do in Rome as Rome does [***as the Romans do***]./***When*** (***you are***) ***in Rome, do as Rome does*** [***the Romans do***]. 《諺》郷に入っては郷に従え.
fiddle while Rome burns 大事をよそにして安逸にふける ▪ What! Carelessly playing billiards when your father is dying? It's *fiddling while Rome* is *burning.* おや，おとうさんが死にかけているというのにのんきにビリヤードをしているのか. まさに大事をよそにして安逸にふけるというやつだ. ☞紀元64年ローマ炎上の際，竪琴を奏しながら見物したという暴君ネロの故事から.
go over to Rome カトリックに改宗する ▪ He's thinking of *going over to Rome.* 彼はカトリックに改宗しようかと考えている.
Rome was not built in a day. 《諺》ローマは一日にして成らず《大事業は短期間ではできない》.

romp /rɑmp|rɔmp/ 名 ***in a romp*** 楽々と ▪ He will win *in a romp.* 彼は楽勝するだろう.

roof /ru:f/ 名 ***a roof over*** *a person's* ***head*** 寝るところ，住みか ▪ Unlike hundreds of thousands of our less fortunate neighbors, we still had *a roof over our heads.* 数えきれないほどの恵まれていない隣人たちと異なり，私たちはまだ雨露をしのげた.
(***be left***) ***without a roof*** (***over*** *one's* ***head***)/***have no roof over*** *one's* ***head*** 住む家がない ▪ She found herself *without a roof over her head.* 彼女は住む家がなくなった.
go through the roof 《口》 **1** ＝hit the ROOF 1.
2 (物価が)天井知らずに上昇する ▪ They must do something to stop the rates *going through the roof.* 料金が天井知らずに上昇しないように何か手を打たねばならない.
hit the roof 《口》 **1** かんかんになる，かっとなる ▪ He *hit the roof* when he heard the news. 彼はそのニュースを聞くと激怒した.
2 (物価が)天井に達する ▪ The prices have *hit the roof* recently. 最近物価が天井に達した.
live under the same roof with [***as***] …と同じ家に住む (→under one ROOF) ▪ How can you *live under the same roof with* him? 君にどうして彼と同じ家に住むことができようか.
out on the roof 《米俗》飲み騒いで ▪ I was *out on the roof* last night and I've got a hangover. ゆうべ飲み騒いだので二日酔いだ.
raise [***lift***] ***the roof*** 《口》大騒ぎをする; やかましく抗議する; 盛んに拍手喝采する ▪ She knew that her husband would *raise the roof* as soon as he saw the bills. 彼女は夫がその勘定書を見るとすぐ大騒ぎするだろうとわかっていた.
That would put the gilded roof on it! 《口》それですべてが台なしになってしまう.
the roof caves [***falls***] ***in*** 《米》屋根が落ちる; 大災害が起きる; 万事うまくいかない ▪ We had a pitfall and *the roof fell in* on us. 不足の事態が生じ，我々は不幸に見舞われた.
the roof of the world 世界の屋根《中央アジアの Pamir 高原》; (一般に)非常に高い高原 ▪ He lived in the desolate mountains at *the roof of the world.* 彼は世界の屋根の寂しい山中に住んでいた.
through the roof →go through the ROOF.
under one [***the same***] ***roof*** 《口》ひとつ[同じ]屋根の下で[に]，同一家屋で[に] ▪ There were three generations of the family living *under one roof.* 3世代が同居していた.
under *a person's* ***roof*** 人の家に泊まって; 人の世話になって ▪ Since you are now *under my roof,* I cannot refuse their proposal. あなたが私の家に泊まっておられる以上，彼らの提案を拒むわけにはいきません ▪ For about two years he lived *under the roof of* his sister. 2年ばかり彼は姉の世話になっていた.
You'll bring the roof down! 《口》いまに屋根が落ちるぞ《やかましく騒ぐな》 ▪ "*You'll bring the*

roof down crying like this", he fondly chided the baby.「こんなに泣くと屋根が落ちてくるぞ」と彼はやさしく赤ん坊をたしなめた.

rooftop /rúːftɑ̀p|-tɔ̀p/ 名 ***shoot* [*scream, shout, yell*] *from the rooftops*** 吹聴する, 触れ回る ▪ This computer excites me enough to *shoot from the rooftops*. このコンピューターは吹聴したいくらい私をわくわくさせるのだ.

room /ruːm/ 名 ***breathing room* [*space, spell, time*]** 息つくひま, 息抜き ▪ The authorities should revalue upwards to give us some *breathing room*. 当局は我々に息つくひまを与えるよう通貨の上向き再評価を行うべきだ.

give room どく; (他人)に席を譲る ▪ *Give* this man *room*. この男のためにどいてやりなさい.

in a smoke-filled room (政治上の駆け引きが)少数の政治家によって内密に行われて, 密室政治で ▪ The cabinet reshuffle was carried out *in a smoke-filled room*. 内閣改造は密室での駆け引きで行われた.

in the room of (人など)の代わりに ▪ He went *in the room of* another. 彼は他人に代わって出かけた ▪ I am now assuming the pen *in his room*. 私は今彼に代わってペンを執っています.

leave room for …の余地を残しておく ▪ That *leaves* no *room for* doubt. それで疑いを差しはさむ余地は少しもなくなる.

leave the room 《口》便所に行く ▪ Just let me *leave the room*. ちょっとトイレに行かせてください.

make room for …に場所をあける, 席を譲る ▪ Would you kindly *make room for* my friend? 私の友人のために少し寄ってやってくれませんか.

***not room* (*enough*) *to swing a cat* (*in*)** → SWING[2].

room and board まかないつき貸間 ▪ *Room and board* together run fourteen dollars a week. まかないつき貸間は1週14ドルかかる.

room* (*and*) *to spare 十分な余地 (*for*) ▪ There's *room and to spare* in that box *for* my hat. その箱には僕の帽子を入れる余地が十分ある.

R

***Room for** a person!* 人を通してやれ ▪ *Room for* Antony! アントニーを通してあげろ.

take up room 場所をとる ▪ This desk *takes up* too much *room*. この机は場所をとりすぎる.

There is always room at the top. トップにはいつも余裕がある《ある分野で一流の人は少数だから必ず成功するチャンスがある》. ☞D. Webster (1782-1852) の言葉から.

***there is room for* [*to* do]** …の[する]余地・機会がある ▪ *There is* much *room for* improvement. 改良の余地は十分ある ▪ *There is* no *room to* turn in. 体を動かす余地がない ▪ *There's* no *room for* doubt. 疑いを差しはさむ余地はない.

would* [*had*] *rather have** a person's* **room than** his* **company 人がいっしょにいるよりもいないほうがいい ▪ I must confess I'*d rather have his room than his company*. 白状するが僕はあの男がいっしょにいるよりはいないほうがいい.

roost /ruːst/ 名 ***at roost*** ねぐらについて; 《口》(人が)床について ▪ A fox spied a cock *at roost*. キツネがねぐらについている雄鶏を見つけた.

come home to roost (犯罪・誤りなどが)元[わが身]に帰る ▪ Curses, like chickens, *come home to roost*. 《諺》「人をのろわば穴二つ」 ▪ All our mistakes surely *come home to roost*. 誤りは必ずわが身へ帰ってくる.

go to roost ねぐらに帰る; 《口》(人が)床につく ▪ The birds *went to roost*. 鳥たちはねぐらについた ▪ It's time for me to *go to roost*. もう寝る時間だ.

rule the roost 主人となる, 牛耳る ▪ They say she *rules the roost*; I am vastly sorry for her husband. 彼女が牛耳っているそうだが, ご主人は非常に気の毒だと思う. ☞雄鶏 (rooster) が鶏舎を牛耳ることから.

root[1] /ruːt/ 名 ***at* (*the*) *root*** 根は, 本質的には ▪ He was, *at root*, a kind-hearted pedant. 彼は根は親切な知ったかぶり屋だった.

be at the root of …の根本をなしている ▪ Ignorance *is at the root of* a great deal of infantile mortality. 幼児の死亡の多くは世人の無知に基づく.

***by the root*(*s*)** **1** 根こそぎ ▪ The weeds must be pulled up *by the root*(*s*). その雑草は根こそぎにしなければならない.

2 根本的に ▪ We must tear out the evil *by the roots*. その弊害を根本的に根絶しなければならない.

come* (*the*) *roots over 《米俗》…を欺く ▪ He tried to *come the roots over* folks with some silly game. 彼は愚かなたくらみで人々をだまそうとした.

go to* [*find, get at, get to*] *the root of …の根本から調べる, 真相を究める ▪ He resolved to *get at the root of* the matter. 彼はその事件の真相を究めようと決心した.

grab a root 《米俗》懸命にやる ▪ One of them sang out, "*Grab a root!*" その連中の一人が「一生懸命やれ!」と大声でどなった.

have* (*its*) *root*(*s*) *in …に根底を持つ; に基づいている ▪ War *has its roots in* selfishness. 戦争の根源は私欲にある.

lay the ax to the root of →AX.

lie at the root of …の根本をなす, 原因である ▪ Wine *lies at the root of* all evils. 酒があらゆる悪の原因だ.

play roots on 《米俗》…をひどい目にあわせる ▪ He *played roots on* those guys. 彼はあいつらをひどい目にあわせた.

pull up** one's* **roots (しぶしぶ)定住地を離れる ▪ He decided to *pull up his roots* and live in London. 彼は定住地を離れてロンドンに住む決心をした.

put down* (*new*) *roots (新たに)根を下ろす; (家を構えて)落ち着く ▪ I wanted to take a wife and *put down roots*. 妻をめとって落ち着きたいと思った.

root and branch 〚副詞的に〛完全に, 徹底的に ▪ The police put an end to the smuggling, *root and branch*. 警察はその密輸を根絶した.

strike at the root of →STRIKE[2].

take* [*strike*] *root **1** 根がつく ▪ The vine *took root*. ツタは根がついた.

2 定着する; 住みつく ▪ His popularity has *struck root*. 彼の人気は定まった ▪ I have *taken root* in my new soil. 私は新しい土地に住みついてしまった.

***the root cause* (*of*)** (...の)根本原因 ▪ Poverty is *the root cause of* most of the crime in the city. 貧困がほとんどの都市犯罪の根本原因だ.

the root of the matter 事物の根底, 本質部分 (《聖》*Job* 19. 28) ▪ He has *the root of the matter* in him and that is what counts. 彼は本質的なものを持っている. それが大切なことなのだ ▪ *The root of the matter* has not been reached in this case. この件では問題の根底にはまだ到達していない.

***to the root*(*s*)** 徹底的に ▪ He was enjoying himself right down *to the roots*. 彼は徹底的に楽しんでいた.

root[2] /ruːt/ 動 ***be rooted in*** ...に根ざしている ▪ Her attachment to Hitler *is rooted in* the notion that he was leading Germany to greater prosperity. 彼女のヒットラーへの愛着は彼がドイツをより大きな繁栄へと導いていたとの考えに根ざしている.

***root** a person **to the ground* [*the spot*]** = RIVET a person to the ground.

root[3] /ruːt/ 動 ***root hog or die*** 《米》〘しばしば命令文的に〙真剣に働かねばまずいことになる ▪ They raised you in the stern tradition of "*root hog or die*!" 彼らは君を「真剣に働かねばまずいことになる」というきびしい伝統のもとに育て上げたのだ.

rope[1] /roʊp/ 名 ***a rope of sand*** 薄弱なきずな; 頼むに足りないもの ▪ Our union will become *a rope of sand*. 我々の連合は薄弱なきずなになるだろう.

at the end of the rope 万事休して, 死に瀕して ▪ It's no fun to find oneself *at the end of the rope*. 万事休してしまうのは愉快なことではない.

come* [*run*] *to the end of** one's **rope (悪事が見つかって)進退きわまる, 運が尽きる ▪ They have *come to the end of their rope*: their time is up. あの連中はもう進退きわまっている. 運の尽きだ.

Give a fool* [*one*] *rope enough and he'll hang himself. 《諺》愚か者を勝手気ままにさせておくと, 最後に身を滅ぼす.

give** a person **rope* (*enough*)/*give** a person **plenty of rope 人にしたい放題のことをさせる, 勝手気ままにさせる ▪ *Give* this man *rope*; he's doing our work splendidly. この男に勝手気ままにさせてやってください, 我々の仕事をりっぱにやっているのです.

***give** a person **rope enough* [*plenty of rope*] *to hang** himself* 人に勝手気ままにやらせて身を滅ぼさせる ▪ Evidently the best way was to *give* him *plenty of rope to hang himself*. 一番よい手は彼にしたい放題のことをさせて身を滅ぼさせることであるのは明らかであった.

give** a person **some* [*a bit of*] *rope 《口》人に多少の自由を与える ▪ You must *give* your son *some rope*. 息子さんを少しは自由にしてあげなさい.

Go piss up a rope! 《米卑》うるさい, うせろ! ▪ Oh *go piss up a rope!* I'm sick of your scolding. うせろ, お説教はたくさんだ.

hang to the ropes →HANG[2].

have the rope about* [*round*]** *one's* ***neck 絞首刑の危険に瀕している ▪ These wretches *had the rope about their necks*. この哀れな連中は絞首刑の危険に瀕していた.

know* [*learn*] *the ropes こつ・呼吸をのみ込んでいる[学ぶ] ▪ The business is new to him, but he will soon get to *learn the ropes*. その仕事は彼には初めてだが, じきにこつを覚えるようになるだろう. ☞《海》「帆綱の知識がある」が原義.

Name not a rope in his house that hanged himself. 《諺》首つりのあった家でなわとは言うな,「病人の前で死人の話をするな」.

on the high ropes 《口》得意になって; ごう慢な; 怒って ▪ She was *on the high ropes* about something. 彼女は何かに得意になっていた. ☞綱渡りで得意になって下を見おろすことから.

on the rope (登山者が)互いにロープで身を縛って ▪ The climbers were *on the rope*. 登山者たちは互いにロープで身を縛っていた.

on the ropes 《俗》全く窮して, 困って ▪ Physically and financially I was *on the ropes*. 肉体的にも財政的にも僕は参っていた. ☞ボクシングで力が尽きるとロープにつかまることから.

put** a person **up to the ropes/show** a person **the ropes 人にこつ[呼吸]を教える ▪ You've *put* me *up to the ropes*. 君は僕にこつを教えてくれた.

One's ***rope is out.*** 進退きわまった, 運が尽きた ▪ *His rope is* long *out*. 彼の運はとっくに尽きている.

run to the end of** one's **rope →come to the end of one's ROPE.

rope[2] /roʊp/ 動 ***rope it*** ロープを利用して進む ▪ He was like an Alpine climber *roping it* over a peril. 彼は危険な所をロープを利用して進んで行くアルプス登山者のようであった.

rose /roʊz/ 名 ***a path strewn with roses*** 《文》歓楽の生活 ▪ His *path* is not quite *strewn with roses*. 彼の生活はそれほど楽と言えるものではない.

A rose by any other name would smell as sweet. 《諺》バラはどんな名で呼んでもかぐわしい. (cf. Sh., *Rom. & Jul.* 2. 2. 1-2).

(*as*) *red as a rose* →RED.

be not all roses/ be not roses all the way/be not a bed of roses のんきな[楽しい]ことばかりではない ▪ Life *is not roses all the way*. 人生は楽しいことばかりではない.

come up roses 《口》〘主に進行形で〙(予想以上に)うまく行く ▪ Everything *is coming up roses*. 万事うまく行っている.

come out* [*up*] *smelling like roses 《米口》(困難などを)無事に切り抜けて名声を高める, 非難されないですむ, なんら損なわれないでのりきる[復帰する], 予想していた以上にうまくいく ▪ The desert storm came and went but Schumacher still *came up smelling like roses*. 砂漠のあらしが通過したが, シューマッハは無事にのりきった ▪ He *came out smelling like roses* and carried on working. 彼は運よく持ち直して働き続けた ▪ He *came out* of the deal *smelling like roses*. 彼はその取引をうまくこなして名を高めた.

come out* [*up*] *smelling of roses 《英口》= come out smelling like ROSEs.

***Every rose has its thorn./No rose without a thorn* [*prickle*].** 《諺》とげのないバラはない《完全な幸福はない》.

gather* (*life's*) *roses 快楽を求める ▪ He wished to *gather life's roses*, unscathed by the briar. 彼は苦しみをなめずに快楽を求めたいと願った.

Gather ye rosebuds while ye may. できる間にバラを摘め《快楽を求めよ》(Herrick, *To the Virgins*).

lose *one's* ***roses*** (病気などで)顔色が青くなる ▪ The child's *losing* all *her roses*. あの子は顔がすっかり青ざめてきている.

put* [*bring*] *the roses* (*back*) *in *a person's* ***cheeks*** 《英口》血色のよい[健康そうな]顔色にする[に戻る] ▪ There's nothing like a low-down political fight to *put the roses in the cheeks*. 卑劣な政争ほど人を元気にしてくれるものはない ▪ A week in the countryside will *put the roses back in your cheeks*. 田舎で1週間過ごせばまた顔色がよくなろう.

Rose is a rose is a rose. バラはあくまでもバラだ《それ以上でも以下でもない》(G. Stein, *Sacred Emily*). ☞しばしばA story is a story is a story. のようにもじって使用される.

under the rose 秘密に, 内緒で ▪ I speak among friends, and *under the rose*. 私は友人の間で内緒で話しているのです. ☞[L] sub rosa のなぞり; 昔はバラは秘密の象徴であった.

rose color, 《英》**rose colour** /róʊzkʌ̀lər/ [名] ***be all rose color*** 〚主に否定文で〛すべてよい時ばかりである ▪ Even a fashionable painter's life *is* not *all rose color*. 流行画家の生活でもいつもよい時ばかりではない.

paint ... in rose color …をいいことずくめに描く ▪ The farmer's office is important, but you must not try to *paint* him *in rose color*. 農場主の仕事は大切だが, 彼をいいことずくめに描こうとしてはいけない.

see ... in rose color …をいいことずくめな見方をする, 楽観的に見る ▪ He was inclined to *see* things *in rose color*. 彼は物事を楽観的に見がちだった.

rose-colored, 《英》**rose-coloured** /róʊzkʌ̀lərd/ [形] ***see* [*behold, look at*]*... through rose-colored spectacles* [*glasses*]** …を楽観的に見る, ひいき目に見る ▪ Oxford was a sort of Utopia to him. He continued to *see* Oxford *through rose-colored spectacles*. オックスフォードは彼にはユートピアのようなものだった. 彼は相変らずオックスフォードをひいき目に見ていた.

take a rose-colored view of …を楽観する ▪ It is habitual with him to *take a rose-colored view of* things. 物事を楽観するのが彼の癖だ.

roseleaf /róʊzlìːf/ [名] ***a crumpled roseleaf*** 《口》幸福の最中に起こるささいなやっかい事, 「花にあらし」 ▪ I am hypersensitive, and *a crumpled roseleaf* would irritate me. 神経が過敏すぎるので幸福に影を落とす一抹の心配をしようものならいらいらするだろう.

rosy /róʊzi/ [形] ***rosy in the garden*** 異常がない, けっこうで ▪ Everything is *rosy in the garden* once more. また何もかも異常なしになった.

rot /rɑt|rɔt/ [名] ***A* [*The*] *rot sets in* [*starts*].** **1** 失敗続きになる; 事態が傾き出す ▪ *A rot* has *set in*. We can't stop it. 失敗続きになった. それはくい止められない.

2 士気が衰えてくる, 突然何もかもうまくいかなくなりだす ▪ We must take care that *a rot* doesn't *start*. 士気が衰えないように注意しなければならない. ☞クリケットから.

stop the rot 危機を防ぐ ▪ Such pitiful economies as these could not *stop the rot*. こんな哀れな経済状態では危機を防ぐことはできないだろう. ☞クリケットから.

rotation /roʊtéɪʃən/ [名] ***by* [*in*] *rotation*** 交代制で ▪ Three members sit daily *in rotation*. 3人のメンバーが毎日交代で座る.

rote /roʊt/ [名] ***by rote*** 機械的に; そらで ▪ He did his business *by rote*. 彼は機械的に仕事をした ▪ At that school little boys learn to repeat the Koran *by rote*. あの学校では生徒たちはコーランを全部そらで言うのを学ぶ. ☞rote《廃》= mere routine.

rotten /rɑ́tən|rɔ́tən/ [形] ***feel rotten*** **1**《俗》気分がひどく悪い ▪ I'm *feeling rotten* today. きょうは気分がくさくさする.

2 (…について)申し訳なく思う (*about*) ▪ I *feel rotten about* John, who was fired from his job instead of me. 私はジョンのことで申し訳なく思っている. 私の代わりに仕事を首になったのだから.

rotten to the core 芯(しん)まで腐って ▪ The man's morals are *rotten to the core*. あの男の品行は芯まで腐っている.

Something is* [*There's something*] *rotten in the state of Denmark. どうもおもしろくない (cf. Sh., *Haml*. 1. 4. 90) ▪ I don't like their conduct. It is strange. *There's something rotten in the state of Denmark*. あの連中のやり方が気にくわない. 妙なんだ. どうもおもしろくない.

spoil *a person* ***rotten*** 《口》人を甘やかしきる, にしたいようにさせる ▪ They*'re* already *spoiled rotten* by their rich parents. 彼らはもうすでに金持ちの両親に甘やかされている ▪ She *spoiled* her own children *rotten*. 彼女はわが子を甘やかしきった.

rough[1] /rʌf/ [形][名][副] ***a diamond in the rough/a rough diamond*** →DIAMOND.

a rough house 《口》大騒ぎ; 大げんか ▪ The game became [turned into] *a rough house*. その試合は大げんかになった.

R

***be rough on** a person* **1** 人につらく当たる ▪ They're mighty *rough on* strangers. 彼らはよそ者にはすごくつらく当たる.
2 (運命などが)人に対して酷である ▪ It *was rough on* him having to live with his mother-in-law. 姑と暮らさねばならないのは彼には酷であった.
cut up rough →CUT².
face rough and smooth つらい事にも楽しい事にも直面する ▪ He *faced rough and smooth* as it came. 彼はつらい事にも楽しい事にも直面した.
feel rough 《主に英口》気分が悪い ▪ I'm *feeling* a bit *rough* today. 今日は少し気分がすぐれないんだ.
***get rough with** a person* 《米口》人を手荒く扱う, にひどい扱いをする ▪ We are going to *get rough with* him. 我々は彼をひどい目にあわせてやるつもりだ.
give** a person* **(*a lick with*) *the rough side of** one's **tongue 《英口》人をひどくしかりつける ▪ I just *gave* him *the rough side of my tongue* for five minutes. 僕はあの男を5分ほどどなってやった.
give** a person* ***a rough time 人をひどい目にあわせる, 苦労させる ▪ The boss will *give* you *a rough time* if you make any mistakes. ミスをしたら上司に大目玉をくらうぞ.
have a rough time (***of it***) ひどい[つらい]目にあう ▪ They've *had* rather *a rough time*. あの連中はかなりひどい目にあってきた.
have a rough tongue ぞんざいな言葉うかいをする ▪ Don't *have* such *a rough tongue*. そんなぞんざいな言葉うかいはするな.
in rough 《英》= in the ROUGH 1.
in the rough **1** 磨かぬままの, 未完成のままの ▪ The plan is yet *in the rough*. その案はまだ未完成のままだ ▪ He wrote out the essay *in the rough*. 彼はその論文の下書きをした.
2 だらしない; ふだんのままで ▪ We are all *in the rough* today, for I am very busy with this job. 我々はきょうはみんなだらしなくしています. 私がこの仕事でひどく忙しくしているものですから ▪ You must take her *in the rough*. ふだんのままの彼女を見ないといけないよ.
3 おおよそ, 大体 ▪ *In the rough*, it may be said so. 大体においてそう言ってよろしい.
4 《米口》困ったはめになって, 困却して ▪ We've been *in the rough* for the past six years. 私たちは過去6年間困ったはめに陥っていた.
in the rough leaf 親葉が出て ▪ The plants are *in the rough leaf*. その植物には親葉が出ている.
lie rough →sleep ROUGH.
live rough →LIVE².
look rough 《英口》(人が)だらしない ▪ My boyfriend *looks rough* but I'm fond of him. 私の彼氏, だらしないんだけど, 好きなのよね.
over rough and smooth でこぼこの所も平らな所も, いたる所に ▪ *Over rough and smooth* she trips along. 彼女はでこぼこの所も平らな所もすたすたと通って行く.
rough and ready 間に合わせの, 粗雑な; 粗野な ▪ The technology is rather *rough and ready* but it's capable. その技術はやや大ざっぱだが, 用は果たしてくれる ▪ They see him as too *rough and ready*. 彼らは彼をあまりにも粗野だと見ている.
rough and tough たくましい ▪ My husband is *rough and tough*, so I can rely on him. うちの夫, たくましくて, 頼りがいがあるの.
rough and tumble **1** 荒っぽく, 乱暴に ▪ Will you fight fair, or take it *rough and tumble*? 正々堂々と戦うのか, それとも乱暴にやるのか.
2 激しい競争 ▪ I got the first *rough and tumble* of sea life. 初めて海での生活の激しい競争を知った.
rough edges 不備, 欠点[弱点]; 不作法 (→have rough EDGEs) ▪ It's a funny family movie that has a few *rough edges*, but you'll leave with a smile on your face. それはある家族に関するおかしな映画であり, 多少の欠点もあるが, 終って出るときは顔に笑みを浮かべているだろう ▪ Despite his *rough edges*, Goldin's heart is in the right place. 礼儀知らずなところもあるが, ゴルディンは気性がよい.
rough going 《米俗》悪路, 難航, 苦戦 ▪ She had a bit of *rough going*. 彼女は少々苦戦した.
rough justice 《英》不当な扱い; 法によらない裁き ▪ *Rough justice* ruled; Hull earned the goal. 不当な扱いがまかり通り, ハルは目的を達した ▪ Price discrimination often metes out *rough justice* among buyers. 売値の違いによりバイヤーは不当な扱いを受けることがしばしばある.
rough trade 《俗》ホモ稼業, (ホモ相手の)男娼 ▪ Eddie has a hankering for *rough trade*. エディーにはホモ相手をして稼ぎたいという願望がある.
sleep [***lie***] ***rough*** (通例戸外で)ごろ寝をする ▪ You may *sleep rough* here till he calls you. 彼が呼ぶまでここでごろ寝をしていてもよろしい.
take the rough with the smooth 《英》人生の苦楽浮沈をそのまま受けいれる ▪ Don't be discouraged; you must learn to *take the rough with the smooth*. 失望しちゃいけない. 人生の苦楽をそのまま受けいれるようにならねばだめだ.
***the rough*(*s*) *and the smooth*(*s*)** 浮沈, 幸不幸 ▪ The boys must encounter *the rough and the smooth* of weather, as of life. 少年たちは人生の浮沈と同じく天候のよしあしにも遭遇しなければならない.

rough² /rʌf/ 動 ***rough it*** 《口》困難な[不自由な]生活を忍ぶ ▪ We were obliged to *rough it* the whole passage. 航海の間中不自由な生活を忍ばねばならなかった.
rough (***it***) ***out*** 困苦欠乏に耐える ▪ I determined, to use a nautical expression, to *rough it out*. 私は海語で言えば困苦欠乏に耐えようと決心した.
rough ... up the wrong way (人)を怒らせる ▪ It *roughs* them *up the wrong way*. それで彼らは怒ってしまう. ☞猫の毛を逆なでると怒ることから.

roughshod /rʌ́fʃɑ̀d|-ʃɔ̀d/ 形 ***ride roughshod over*** ...にいばり散らす; を荒く扱う ▪ We have *ridden roughshod over* neutrals in our time. 我々のころには中立国にいばり散らしていた ▪ The Chairman *rode roughshod over* all ob-

R

jections to his plans. 議長は自分の案への反対論はすべてけんもほろろに扱った. ☞馬にくぎの頭の突き出たてい鉄をはかせることから.

round /raʊnd/ 形名副前 ***a (good) round sum*** かなりの大金 ▪ Three thousand pounds is *a good round sum.* 3,000ポンドとは相当な大金だね.

all round **1** あたり中, どこにも; 全体的に ▪ *All round* the forest sweeps off. そこら中に森が広がっている.

2 …の回り中に ▪ There are service stations *all round* the city. 町のあちこちにガソリンスタンドがある.

(at) (good) round pace [trot] 迅速に, 足早に ▪ He walked *at good round pace.* 彼は足早に歩いた.

be round with *a person* 人にはっきり[あからさまに]ものを言う ▪ He resolved to *be round with* his wife. 彼は妻にはっきりものを言ってやろうと決めた.

do the rounds (of) →make the ROUNDs (of).

find [make] *one's* ***way round*** 一人で進んで行く ▪ You won't be able to *find your way round* alone. 君一人で進んで行くことはできないだろう.

go a long way round 遠回りして行く ▪ He was willing to *go a long way round* by Newgate. 彼はニューゲイトを通って遠回りして行くことをいとわなかった.

go a round →take a ROUND.

go for a good round 遠くまで一回りしに行く ▪ We *went for a good round* in the park. 私たちは公園の中を遠くまで一回りしに行った.

go *one's* ***round(s)*** →make one's ROUND(s).

go the round (of) (ニュースなどが…に)次から次へと伝わる[広まる] ▪ The anecdote is now *going the round of* the papers. その逸話は目下新聞に次から次へと載せられている.

go the rounds (of) →make the ROUNDs (of).

in a round 輪になって ▪ The girls were dancing *in a round.* 少女たちは輪になって踊っていた.

in good, round terms ずけずけと ▪ He scolded me *in good, round terms.* 彼は私をずけずけとしかりとばした.

in the round **1** 丸彫りの[で] (↔in RELIEF 1) ▪ The statue was carved *in the round.* その像は丸彫りに刻まれていた.

2 丸太のままの[で] ▪ The trees were all *in the round.* その木はすべて丸太のままだった.

3 全体的に ▪ You must see it *in the round.* それは全体的に見なければいけない.

4《劇》舞台を観客にぐるりと囲まれて ▪ We performed *in the round.* 我々は舞台を観客にぐるりと囲まれて芝居をした.

make a round →take a ROUND.

make a round of visits あちこち訪問する ▪ I had *a round of visits* to *make.* 私はあちこち訪問しなければならなかった.

make [go, take, walk] *one's* ***round(s)*** (巡査・物売りなどが)巡回する ▪ A potman was *going his rounds* with beer. 給仕がビールを持ち回っていた.

make [do, go, march, take] the rounds (of) (…を)巡回する, 歩き回る; (医療スタッフが入院患者を)診て回る ▪ In a short time we *made the rounds of* society. まもなく我々は社交界を巡回した ▪ The surgery residents *make rounds* with their chief every morning. 毎朝, 外科実習生は主任といっしょに患者の巡回をする.

make *one's* ***way round*** → find one's way ROUND.

on *one's* ***round*** 視察中で ▪ The inspector is *on his round.* 検査官が視察中だ.

out of round 丸みがひずんで ▪ A roll of newsprint got *out of round.* 一巻きの新聞印刷用紙の丸みがひずんでしまった.

round about **1**〚副詞的に〛輪になって; 回りに; 四方八方に ▪ He looked back and *round about.* 彼は後ろや回りを見回した ▪ They work in the villages *round about.* 彼らは回りの村々で働いている.

2 ぐるぐると ▪ The earth goes *round about.* 地球はぐるぐる回っている.

3 反対の側に ▪ He turned *round about* and walked off. 彼はくるりときびすを返して立ち去った.

4 回り道をして ▪ I came *round about* and slowly to these conclusions. 私は回り道をしてゆっくりとこういう結論に到達しました.

5〚前置詞的に〛…の回りを[に] ▪ They danced lightly *round about* the maypole. 彼らはメイポールの回りで軽やかに踊った.

6 およそ ▪ He died *round about* ten o'clock last night. 彼はゆうべ10時ごろに亡くなった.

round after round of (一斉射撃・歓声)の繰り返し ▪ He was welcomed with *round after round of* cheers. 彼は歓呼の繰り返しをもって迎えられた.

round and round [around and around] **1**〚副詞的に〛ぐるぐると ▪ Thus we go *round and round* in a circle and make no progress. このように我々は堂々巡りをして一向に前へ進まない.

2〚前置詞的に〛…の回りをぐるぐると ▪ The boy ran *round and round* his mother. 男の子は母親の回りをぐるぐると走り回った.

round here《英》→AROUND here.

stand a round (of drinks) 仲間全員に飲み物を買う[ふるまう, おごる] ▪ It's my turn to *stand a round*, so what are you all having? おれがおごる順番だ, みんな何を飲む?

take [go, make] a round (買物・見物などのため)一巡する, 歩き回る ▪ I *took a round* with a friend about the castle. 私は友人といっしょに城の回りを一巡した.

take ... all round …を全体から見る ▪ You're less of a fool than many, *taken all round.* 君は全体的に見て多くの人よりも利口だ.

take *one's* ***round(s)*** →make one's ROUND(s).

take the rounds (of) → make the ROUNDs

(of).

the daily round 毎日の生活 ▪ I'm now back to *the daily round*. 私はまた日々の生活に戻った.

the trivial round 平凡な日常生活 (J. Keble, *Morning* 10) ▪ Each generation repeated *the trivial round*. どの世代も平凡な日常生活を繰り返した.

this (earthy) round 地球 ▪ Let all *this round* sound thy honor. この世の人すべてにそなたの名誉を賛美させるがいい.

walk** one's **round(s) →make one's ROUND(s).

win a round ひとまず勝つ, (敵に)一時的な敗北を与える ▪ It's impossible for my robot to *win a round* of combat against your robot. ぼくのロボットが君のとの戦いで一度だって勝つことなど不可能だ.

roundup /ráʊndʌ̀p/ 名 ***head for the last roundup*** 《婉曲》生涯を閉じる; 耐用年数が尽きる ▪ My watch *is headed for the last roundup*. 私の時計はいよいよ寿命がつきた.

rouse /raʊz/ 動 ***rouse** oneself* **1** (眠り・沈思から)目ざめる ▪ I *roused myself* and looked about. 私は目をさましてあたりを見回した ▪ He *roused himself* from deep thought. 彼は沈思から我に返った.

2 奮起する ▪ He *roused himself* with zeal. 彼は熱意をもって奮起した.

want rousing 目をさまさせる必要がある, 怠け者である ▪ That son of his *wants rousing*. 彼のあの息子は怠け者だ.

rout[1] /raʊt/ 名 ***in [on] a rout*** 一団となって ▪ Many birds followed *in a rout*. 多くの鳥が一団となってあとに続いていた.

make a rout about ...でわいわい言う[騒ぐ] ▪ She needn't *make* such *a rout about* such a trifle. 彼女はそんなつまらぬことで大騒ぎするには及ばない.

rout[2] /raʊt/ 名 ***put ... to (the) rout*** (敵)を敗走させる《比喩的にも》 ▪ We instantly *put* them *to the rout*. 彼らをたちまち敗走させた ▪ Napoleon *put to rout* all these things when he inhabited the palace. ナポレオンはその宮殿に住んだとき, こういうものをすべて駆逐してしまった.

route /ruːt, raʊt/ 名 ***en** /ɑːn/ **route/on route*** (...への)途中, 旅行中に (*to*) ▪ They changed horses twice *en route*. 彼らは途中で2回馬を替えた ▪ The book was *on route to* him from England in a ship. その本はイングランドから船で彼のもとに送られている途中だった.

get [give] the route 行進命令を受ける[下す] ▪ He *got the route* for Warbrok. 彼はウォーブロックへの行進命令を受けた ▪ "I don't move till he *gives* me *the route*," said she. 「あの人が私に出て行けと言うまで動きません」と彼女は言った.

go down that route その行動方針に従う ▪ We can't *go down that route*. 私たちはその行動方針には従えない.

go the route 《米俗》(野球で投手が)完投する ▪ He *went the route* for the Braves. 彼はブレイブズ軍のために完投した.

on the route 途中に ▪ There are many stations *on the route*. 途中に駅がたくさんある.

rove /roʊv/ 名 ***a roving eye*** 色目, 浮気癖 (→ have a roving EYE).

on [upon] the rove うろついて, 漂泊して ▪ He went *upon the rove*. 彼は漂泊の旅に出た.

rover /róʊvər/ 名 ***shoot at rovers*** **1** (弓術で)遠矢を射る ▪ They *shot* remote, *at rovers*. 彼らは遠くから遠矢を射た.

2 やたらに的を射る, でたらめに射る ▪ Nature does not *shoot at rovers*. 自然はやたらに的を射ない.

row[1] /roʊ/ 名 ***be at the end of** one's **row*** 《米口》万策が尽きる; へとへとに疲れる ▪ It's my opinion he'*s at the end of his row*. 僕に言わせりゃ彼は万策尽きたんだ.

have [be] a hard [long, tough] row to hoe 《米》困難な仕事がある[である], 先が長い ▪ I've *had* a pretty *hard row to hoe* down there in New York. 僕は向こうのニューヨークじゃかなり仕事がやりにくかった ▪ I'd like to be a surgeon, but it'*s a long row to hoe*. 私は外科医になりたいんだが, 先の長い話だ.

have a new row to hoe 《米口》新しい仕事が控えている ▪ I *have a new row to hoe*, but I'll go ahead. 新しい仕事が控えている, でも前進してみせるぞ.

hoe a big row 《米口》務めをりっぱに果たす ▪ He can *hoe* as *big a row* as Bland did. 彼はブランドと同様務めをりっぱに果たせる.

hoe another row 《米口》新しい仕事を始める ▪ He was compelled to commence *hoeing another row*. 彼は新しい仕事を始めにかかるしかなかった.

hoe** one's **own row 《米口》自分で仕事をする, 一人でやっていく ▪ I'd rather *hoe my own row*. 私はむしろ一人でやっていきたい.

in a row **1** 一列に ▪ There are three houses *in a row* near the sea. 海の近くに家が3軒並んでいる.

2 引き続いて ▪ He has been late for three days *in a row*. 彼は3日続けて遅刻した.

in rows 列をなして, 幾列にも ▪ A hundred bonfires burned *in rows*. 百ものかがり火がずらりと並んで燃えていた.

not worth [amount to] a row of beans [pins] 《口》たいしたものではない, 取るに足りない ▪ He does*n't amount to a row of beans*. 彼はたいしたやつではない.

row[2] /raʊ/ 名 ***be always ready for a row*** 《口》けんか好きだ ▪ That man *is always ready for a row*. あの男はけんか好きだ.

be locked in a row 激論の途中で行き詰まる ▪ The teachers have *been locked in a row* over whether to ban the students from using their cellular phones on campus. 生徒の構内での携帯電話の使用を禁止するかどうかの激論で先生たちは途中動きが取れなくなった.

get into a row 《口》しかられる ▪ He'll *get into* a jolly old *row* when he goes home. 彼は家に帰っ

たらこっぴどくしかられるだろう.

have a row with 《口》…とやかましく口論する ▪ He *had a row with* the neighbors. 彼は近所の者とやかましく口論した.

Hold* [*Shut*] *your row! 《俗》黙れ! ▪ "*Hold your row*," said Dan in a low voice. "Don't speak."「黙れ, しゃべるでない」とダンは低い声で言った. ☞row = mouth.

make* [*kick up, raise*] *a row 《口》騒動を起こす; やかましく口論する, 抗議する ▪ Now and then he *kicked up* [*raised*] *a row* in the street. ときどき彼は通りで騒動を起こした ▪ You can do no good to yourself by *making a row*. やかましく抗議しても身のためになりませんよ.

What's the row? 一体どうしたのか ▪ Hullo, my friends! *What's the row?* やあ君たち! どうしたんだい?

row[3] /roʊ/ 名 ***go for a row*** ボートこぎに行く ▪ Let's *go for a row* after lunch. 昼食後ボートに乗りに行こう.

row[4] /roʊ/ 動 ***look one way and row another*** あることをねらうと見せて実は他のものをねらう ▪ In her Court there were persons who *looked one way and rowed another*. 彼女の宮廷には敵は本能寺といった人間どもがいた.

***row against the flood* [*the stream, wind and tide*]** 難事を企てる, 難局に当たる ▪ I am not *rowing against the stream*. I write for general amusement. 私は難事を企てているのではない. 私は一般人に楽しんでもらうために書いているのだ. ☞潮流[風]に逆らってこぐことから.

row dry (練習のため)空(から)こぎする, こぐまねをする; 水を飛ばさないようにこぐ《比喩的にも》 ▪ "Do you call this *rowing dry*?" cried he, as a sea swept over the boat.「これを水を飛ばさないこぎ方というのかい?」と彼はボートを波がどっと洗ったとき叫んだ ▪ He's *rowing dry*—only making believe. 彼は空こぎしているんです—ただまねをしてるだけなんです.

row in one* [*the same*] *boat →sail in one BOAT.

row** a person **up Salt River 《米俗》 **1** (反対党員)をやっつける ▪ He made a speech and *rowed* the Tories *up Salt River*. 彼は演説をぶって保守党をやっつけた.

2 人をひどくしかりつける ▪ We *rowed* him *up Salt River* in no time. すぐ彼をひどくしかりつけてやった.

royal /rɔ́ɪəl/ 形 ***a right royal*** (時・食事・歓迎などが)すばらしい ▪ We had *a right royal* time yesterday. きのうはすばらしく愉快だった.

a royal road 王道, 近道, 楽な手段 (*to*) ▪ There is no *royal road to* learning. 《諺》学問に王道はない. ☞Euclid がエジプト王 Ptolemy に "There is no royal road to geometry." と言ったという故事から.

royalty /rɔ́ɪəlti/ 名 ***feel like a royalty*** 威厳があると感じる ▪ I *feel like a royalty* for my boss. 私の上司は威厳があると思う.

rub[1] /rʌb/ 名 ***a rub of* [*on*] *the green*** 《ゴルフ》球が何かに当たってそれること; 幸運, ツキ ▪ It must be reckoned *a rub of the green*. それは球のそれと考えなければならない.

It is impossible to play at bowls without meeting with rubs. 《諺》球技をやっていれば必ず地面のでこぼこにぶつかる; 事を行う際には必ず困難が伴う.

There's* [*Here lies*] *the rub.*/*Therein lies the rub. そこが困ったところだ (cf. Sh., *Haml.* 3. 1. 65) ▪ But her relations are not intimate with mine. Ah, *there's the rub*. しかし彼女の親類は僕の親類と親しくしていない. ああ, そこが困ったところなのだ.

rub[2] /rʌb/ 動 ***rub** one's **hands*** 両手をもむ《満足の身ぶり》 ▪ He sighed and *rubbed his hands* with pleasure. 彼はため息をつき, 喜んで両手をもんだ.

rub it in 《俗》(いやなことを)繰り返し言う (→rub a person's NOSE in it) ▪ You needn't *rub it in* any more. もうくどくど言うには及びませんよ.

rub** a person's **nose in it →NOSE[1].

rub noses with (あいさつとして)…と鼻をこすり合わせる《マオリ族などの習慣》 ▪ Lynda enjoyed New Zealand hugely, *rubbing noses with* Maori children. リンダはマオリ族の子供らと鼻をこすり合わせたりして, ニュージーランドを大いに楽しんだ.

rub shoulders* [《米》*elbows*] *with (人)と接触する, 交際する ▪ She had *rubbed shoulders with* the great. 彼女はおえら方と交際してきていた ▪ It brought the most different people to *rub elbows with* one another. さまざまな人たちが多くそれで互いに接触するようになった.

rub through the world どうにか暮らしていく ▪ They *rub through the world* with ease and quiet. 彼らは楽々と静かに暮らしを立てていっている.

rub** a person **up the right way 《英口》人を喜ばせるように遇する ▪ She was careful to *rub* him *up the right way*. 彼女は注意して彼を喜ばせるようにあしらった.

rub** a person (**up**) **the wrong way 《英口》人を困らせる, じらす ▪ He *was* always *rubbed the wrong way* by her. 彼はいつも彼女に困らされていた. ☞猫の毛を逆なですると怒るところから.

rubber /rʌ́bər/ 名 ***a rubber check*** 《米戯》不渡り小切手 ▪ Employees of the House routinely wrote *rubber checks*. そのバーの従業員たちは日常的に不渡り小切手を書いていた.

(*a*) *rubber stamp* **1** ⟦名詞的に⟧ ゴム印; よく調べずに判を押すこと, そのような承認(をする人[機関]), すぐに同意する人 ▪ The committee is just *a rubber stamp* for the president's policies. 委員会は大統領の政策の形式的承認機関にすぎない ▪ The dean gave his *rubber stamp* to the proposal. 学部長はその申し出にすぐに賛成してくれた.

2 ⟦動詞的に⟧ よく調べずに判を押す ▪ I will not simply *rubber-stamp* this request. 私はこの要求を安易に承認する気はない.

burn rubber 《米俗》 **1** (オートバイを)急速発進させる ▪ A group of drag racers *burned rubber* in front of my house. 暴走族のグループがうちの前で急発進させた.

2 急に立ち去る ▪ I'm going to have to *burn rubber*. そろそろ急いで帰らなくちゃ.

lay rubber 《米俗》 = burn RUBBER 1.

Those* [*They*] *who play at bowls must expect* [*look for, look out*] *rubbers. 球技をやるものは三番勝負を覚悟しなければならない; 事を行うには前途の困難を覚悟しなければならない. ☞rubbers は rubs をのちに変えたもの.

where the rubber meets the road 実力が試される[真価が問われる]場 ▪ I'll make him face up to *where the rubber meets the road*. 私は彼に真価が問われる場に立ち向かわせるつもりだ.

rubbish /rʌ́bɪʃ/ 名 ***a load* [*lot*] *of* (*old*) *rubbish*** →LOAD[1].

good riddance of* [*to*] *bad rubbish 役に立たない人[物]が(い)なくなって大助かり ▪ He's gone at last. *Good riddance to bad rubbish*! 彼はやっと去った. 役に立たない者がいなくなって大助かりだ.

ruby /rúːbi/ 名 ***far above rubies*** きわめて貴重な (《聖》 *Prov.* 31. 10) ▪ My wife knows her price is *far above rubies*. 妻は自らの値うちはきわめて貴重なものだと心得ている.

ruck /rʌk/ 名 ***get out of the ruck*** 凡人だと思われないようにする ▪ He was ambitious to *get out of the ruck*. 彼は凡人だと思われないために熱心だった.

rude /ruːd/ 形 ***a rude awakening*** 《文》突然の目覚め; 不快な現実への目覚め, 突然のショック ▪ We got *a rude awakening* when we started playing with the pros. プロと対戦を始めたら, とたんに現実を思い知らされた.

rue /ruː/ 動 ***rue it*** 後悔する ▪ You will live to *rue it*. いつか後悔するよ.

***rue the day* [*hour*] *when* [*that*]** ...したのを今に後悔する ▪ You'll *rue the day when* you did it. そんなことをして今に後悔するぞ.

ruffle[1] /rʌ́fəl/ 名 ***put ... in* [*into*] *a ruffle*** ...を動揺させる, 狼狽させる ▪ This news *put* them *into a* considerable *ruffle*. その知らせは人々をかなり狼狽させた.

ruffle[2] /rʌ́fəl/ 動 ***ruffle* (*up*)** *one's* **[*a few*] *feathers* [*plumage*]** **1** (鳥が)怒って羽を逆立てる ▪ The cock *ruffled* (*up*) *his feathers* at a cat. 雄鶏が猫を見て羽を逆立てた.

2 (人が)怒る ▪ He *ruffled his plumage*, and spoke with asperity. 彼は怒って手きびしく言った.

ruffle up the wrong way = RUB a person (up) the wrong way.

rug /rʌg/ 名 ***cut the* [*a*] *rug*** ダンスする ▪ How about *cutting the rug*? ダンスはどうかね?

lie like a rug 《俗》大嘘をつく ▪ You *lie like a rug*. I never said that! おまえは大嘘をついてるね. 私はそんなことは言わなかった!

pull the rug* (*out*) *from under **1** ...の立場を失わせる ▪ His new theory *pulls the rug from under* the Marxist-Leninist. 彼の新学説はマルクス・レーニン主義者の立場を失わせるものである.

2 ...の計画をくじく ▪ We were dining out, but the child's illness *pulled the rug out from under* us. 外出の予定でいたら, 子供の病気で当てがはずれた.

sweep under the rug (恥になる事を)隠す (= SWEEP ... under the carpet) ▪ In schools, drug abuse by students *is swept under the rug*. 学校では生徒による薬物乱用をひた隠しにしている.

ruin[1] /rúːɪn/ 名 ***be the ruin of*** ...を破滅させることになる ▪ This blackout business will *be the ruin of* me. この灯火管制というやつのおかげで商売が上がったりだ.

bring* [*reduce*] ... *to ruin ...を没落させる, 失敗させる ▪ He *was brought to ruin* by drink. 彼は酒で零落した ▪ It was the Conservative party which *brought* this bill *to ruin*. この議案をお流れにさせたのは保守党だった.

fall in* [*into*] *ruins 荒廃する ▪ His palace of marble will *fall into ruins*. 彼の大理石造りの宮殿も荒廃してしまうだろう.

fall to* [*into*] *ruin*/*come* [*go, run*] *to ruin 崩壊する; 零落する ▪ Such a man is ready to *fall to ruin*. そのような人が自ら零落しようとするんだ ▪ All *goes to ruin*. いっさいは滅びる.

go to rack* [*wrack*] *and ruin 荒廃する, 廃屋になる; 破滅[破たん]する ▪ The once magnificent home *went to rack and ruin* due to poor maintenance. かつては堂々とした家屋だったが, きちんと手入れしなかったため荒れ果ててしまった ▪ Under the party's stewardship the economy has almost *gone to rack and ruin*. その政党の管理の下で経済はほとんど破たんしている.

in ruins **1** 廃虚となって(いる) ▪ Babylon *in ruins* is not so melancholy a spectacle. 荒廃しているバビロンもそう陰気ながめではない.

2 (計画などが)台なしになって ▪ All his hopes lay *in ruins*. 彼の希望はことごとくついえてしまった.

lay ... in ruins (町)を荒廃させる ▪ The enemy *laid* the town *in ruins*. 敵はその町を荒廃させた.

reduce ... to ruin →bring ... to RUIN.

ruin[2] /rúːɪn/ 動 ***ruin*** *oneself* 身を滅ぼす ▪ Men *ruin themselves* every day by their horses. 毎日のように競馬で身を滅ぼす人がいる.

rule[1] /ruːl/ 名 ***a rule of thumb*** →the RULE of thumb.

as a* (*general*) *rule*/*as the rule 概して, 一般に ▪ *As a rule*, hail falls in summer. 概してひょうは夏に降る.

bear rule 支配[統治]する, 権力を行使する ▪ Those great Celtic houses *bore rule* in Ulster. それらの偉大なケルト系の一家がアルスターを統治した.

bend* [*stretch*] *the rules 規則を(強引に)ねじ曲げる ▪ They were forced to *bend the rules* to tackle the problem. 彼らはその問題に取り組むためには強引に規則をねじ曲げざるを得なかった.

break the rules 規則を破る ▪ He keeps *breaking the school rules*. 彼は校則を破り続けている.

by rule 規定通りに[ずくめに] ▪ They speak *by rule*, though they determine by common sense. 彼らは常識で決定するが, 話すのは規定通りだ.

by rule and line [***measure***] 正確に, 厳密に ▪ The process of change had been done not rashly, but *by rule and measure*. その変化の過程は性急ではなくて厳密になされたのであった.

make it a rule to *do*/ ***make a rule of*** *doing* …することにしている ▪ I *make it a rule to* get up early. 私は早起きすることにしている ▪ She *makes a rule of going* for a walk in the morning. 彼女は朝散歩に行くことにしている.

out of rule 常例をはずれて, 慣例にそむいて ▪ His conduct was very much *out of rule*. 彼のふるまいはひどく常例をはずれていた.

play by the [*one's* (***own***)] ***rules*** 規則を厳格に守る ▪ Whatever happened, they *played by the rules*. 何が起ころうとも彼らは規則を厳格に守った.

run the rule over (修正などのため)…をざっと調べる ▪ The committee *ran the rule over* the plan. 委員会はその計画を(修正のため)ざっと調べた.

the golden rule →GOLDEN.

the rule of three 比例(算) ▪ This is your first number in *the rule of three*. これが君の比例算の最初の数字です.

the [***a***] ***rule of thumb*** 大ざっぱなやり方, 経験法 ▪ He ran the ship by *the rule of thumb*. 彼は経験に基づいて船を走らせた ▪ *The rule of thumb* has been that a retiree requires about 70 percent to 80 percent of preretirement income to cover day-to-day living expenses. 経験的概算では, 退職者は日常の生活費をカバーするのに退職前の収入の70〜80パーセントを必要とする. ☞大まかに長さを測るときに親指(thumb)を用いたことからとされる.

the rules of the game ゲームの規則, 標準的な行動原則, (特定分野での)慣例 ▪ Both sides are adhering to *the* "*rules of the game*" and attempting to avoid escalation. 両者とも「ゲームのルール」を順守しており, エスカレートするのは避けようとしている.

There is no rule without some exceptions. 《諺》例外のない規則はない.

under the rule of …の支配のもとに ▪ The Netherlands came *under the rule of* Spain. オランダはスペインに支配されるようになった.

work to rule (労働組合員が)順法闘争を行う ▪ The men decided to *work to rule*. 従業員たちは順法闘争をすることを決めた.

rule[2] /ruːl/ 動 ***be ruled by*** …の忠告[指導]に従う ▪ Listen to me, and *be ruled by* me. 私の言うことを聞いて忠告に従いなさい.

rule good (作物が)概して良好である ▪ Crops *rule good*. 農作物は概して良好である.

rule high [***low***] (物価が)高値[低値]にもち合っている ▪ Prices *rule high*. 物価は高値にもち合っている.

rule ... out of order (人・事)を違例と判定する ▪ The chairman *ruled* the motion *out of order*. 議長はその動議を違例と判定した.

rum /rʌm/ 形 ***a rum go*** [***do***] おかしなはめ[出来事] ▪ This was *the rummest go* he ever saw. これは彼がお目にかかったこともないくらいおかしな出来事だった ▪ The situation was "*a rum do*". その状況は「奇妙」だった.

a rum start 妙な事態 ▪ Come, this won't do. This is *a rum start*. ああ, これじゃだめだ. こいつは妙な具合だ.

rumor[1], 《英》**rumour**[1] /rúːmər/ 名 ***rumor has it*** [***there is a rumor***] ***that*** …という噂だ ▪ *Rumor has it* [*There is a rumor*] *that* there will be a General Election in the autumn. 秋には総選挙が行われるという噂だ.

rumor[2], 《英》**rumour**[2] /rúːmər/ 動 ***be rumored to*** *do* …するという噂だ ▪ He *is rumored to* have escaped to France. 彼はフランスへ逃れたという噂だ.

rumor abroad [***about***] 広く噂を流す ▪ It's *rumored abroad* that the Minister was resigning. その大臣は辞任するという噂が広まった.

rumpus /rʌ́mpəs/ 名 ***have a rumpus with*** *a person* 《口》人ともめごとを起こす ▪ The boy *had a rumpus with* his masters. その少年は先生たちともめごとを起こした.

kick up [***make***] ***a rumpus*** 《口》騒ぎを起こす ▪ You've *made a* fine *rumpus* in the family. あなたは家族内にとんだ騒ぎを起こしてくれましたね.

rumpy /rʌ́mpi/ 名 ***rumpy-pumpy*** 《英戯》セックス, エッチ ▪ Now she's fit enough for *rumpy-pumpy* with her husband. 今では彼女は健康になって夫とあれができる.

run[1] /rʌn/ 名 ***a dry*** [《英》***dummy***] ***run*** 予行演習, リハーサル ▪ *A dummy run* with the metric system was successful. メートル法の予行演習は成功した.

a run of (***good***) ***luck*** [***bad luck***] 一連の幸運[不幸], 幸運[不幸]続き ▪ Can't we have *a run of luck*? 私たちには幸運なんてあり得ないのだろうか? ▪ The company went bankrupt after *a run of bad luck*. 不幸が続いたのち, その会社は倒産した.

a run on the bank 銀行の取付け ▪ There was *a run on the bank*. 銀行の取付けが行われた.

a run on the red 《トランプ》(赤と黒で)赤の出続け ▪ There has been *a run on the red*. さっきから赤が出続けだ.

allow the run of →have the RUN of.

at a run 駆け足で ▪ He started off *at a run*. 彼は駆け足で出発した.

by the run **1** 《海》(水夫を雇うのに)目的地までという約束で ▪ Those seamen were engaged *by the run*. 水夫たちは目的地までという約束で雇われていた. **2** 急速に, 急落して, どっと ▪ The cab came down *by the run*. 辻馬車は急速におりて来た.

get the run of …のこつがわかる ▪ It may take him a few weeks to *get the run of* things. 彼がいろんな事のこつがわかるまで数週間かかるだろう.

get the run upon *a person* 《米口》人をなぶる,

ひやかす ▪ They *got the run upon* the poor boy. 彼らはかわいそうにその男の子をひやかした.

give *a person* ***a*** (***good***) ***run for*** *his* ***money*** **1** 人に骨折った[金を使った]だけのかいのあるようにする ▪ We must *give* him *a run for his money*. 彼に骨折りがいのあるようにしてやらねばならない.
2 人にほとんど互角の[はらはらする]競争をさせる ▪ Although the cop did not catch up with us, he certainly *gave* us *a run for our money*. 巡査は我々に追いつきはしなかったが, 確かにはらはらさせられた.

give a run (***to***) (...を)走らせる ▪ Let's *give a* good *run to* the car. 車を十分に走らせようよ.

give ... a trial run ...の試運転をする; を試しに使ってみる ▪ The assistant has *been given a trial run*. その助手は試しに使われている.

give ... the run of the house →have the RUN of.

go and have a run 《俗》とっとと去る ▪ *Go and have a run*! とっとと消えうせろ!

go on a beer [***cigarette***] ***run*** 《口》ビール[タバコ]を買いに走る ▪ I asked him to *go on a beer run*. 彼にビールの買い走りを頼んだ.

have [***get***] ***a*** (***good***) ***run for*** *one's* ***money*** 金をかけただけのかいがある, 骨折っただけのかいがある ▪ Silly backers do not always *have a run for their money*. ばかな競馬のかけ手は必ずしも金をかけただけのかいがあるとはかぎらない. ☞競馬語から.

have a great [***good***] ***run*** 非常に人気がある, 大いに求められる ▪ The play *had a* very *great run*. その芝居は非常に人気があった.

have *a person* ***on the run*** →on the RUN 3.

have [***give, allow***] ***the run of*** ...を自由に使わせてもらう[使わせてやる], に自由に出入りさせてもらう[やる] ▪ There one can *have the run of* every variety of bath. そこではあらゆる種類の風呂を自由に利用することができる ▪ He has *had the run of* the Apsly House archives. 彼はアプスリー家の記録保管所に自由に出入りさせてもらってきた.

in runs 連続的に ▪ The cases are apt to occur, as it were, *in runs*. そういう事例はいわば引き続いて生じがちだ.

in the long run 長い間には, 結局 ▪ I trust that, *in the long run*, I shall not be a loser. 私は結局損をすることにはならないと信じている.

in the short run 目先だけのことを考えると ▪ *In the short run*, this would reduce our overseas costs. 目先だけのことを考えると, これはわが国の海外での経費を削減することになろう.

keep [***lose***] ***the run of*** 《米》...と接触を保つ[失う], 遅れをとらない[とる] ▪ I shall very much wish to *keep the run of* public sentiment. 世の人心に遅れないでいたいものだ ▪ I kind of *lost the run of* the time. 僕はちょっと時勢に遅れてきた.

make a run for it 逃げ去る, 急いで逃げる ▪ He stood with the drink in his hand, deciding whether or not to *make a run for it*. 彼は逃げ去るかどうか決めかねて, 手に飲み物を持ったまま立っていた.

on the run **1** 走って, 駆け足で ▪ They came hurrying down, *on the run*. 彼らは駆け足で急いでおりてきた.
2 駆け回って, あくせく奔走して ▪ She is kept *on the run* every minute of the day. 彼女は一日中てんてこまいだ.
3 逃走して, 退却[敗走]して, 防戦一方で ▪ It was impossible to start the enemy *on the run* again. 敵を再び退却させることは不可能だった ▪ After last night's broadcast debate, he has the opposition candidate *on the run*. 昨夜の公開放送討論ののち, 彼は対立候補を防戦一方にさせた.

out of the usual [***common***] ***run*** 並みはずれた, とっぴな ▪ There will be nothing *out of the usual run*. とっぴなものは何一つないだろう ▪ The hotel was *out of the common run*. ホテルは並みはずれてりっぱだった.

put the run on *a person* →PUT.

put ... to the run ...を走らせる, 退却させる ▪ These fanatics have *put* the King's Life-Guards *to the run*. これらの狂信者たちが王の護衛兵を退却させてしまった.

take a run over (目が)...をざっと見る ▪ My eye *took a run over* the scene. その光景をざっと見た.

take a run to ...にひと旅行する ▪ He *took a run to* the city last summer. 去年の夏彼はその町へひと旅行した.

the common [***general, ordinary***] ***run of*** 普通の種類の ▪ I appeal to *the ordinary run of* readers. 私は普通の読者に訴えるのだ.

the run of *one's* ***teeth*** (通例仕事の報酬として)無料のまかない; 扶養 ▪ They frequently in turn provided him with *the run of his teeth*. 彼らはよくお返しに彼を無料でまかなった. ☞run「使用の自由」.

with a run 急速に, すらすらと; 急落して, どかっと ▪ Everything went *with a run*. 万事すらすらと運んだ ▪ Prices came down *with a run*. 相場がどかっと下がった.

run[2] /rʌn/ 動 ***run amok*** 狂ったように暴れまくる (=run RIOT) ▪ They got drunk and *ran amok* at the bar. 彼らはバーで酔っ払って暴れまくった.

run and run 《主に英》(議論などが)いつまでも続く ▪ It seems this debate really is going to *run and run*. この論争は実際いつまでも続きそうに思える.

run (***a***)***round like a scalded cat*** = run round like a blue-arsed FLY.

run at the nose [***mouth***] 鼻水[よだれ]を出す ▪ The child is *running at the nose*. その子, 鼻水をたらしてるよ.

run away on *a person* 人を置いてけぼりにする, すっぽかす ▪ I didn't mean to *run away on* you. 君をすっぽかすつもりはなかったのだ.

run before *one* ***can walk*** 《口》歩けないうちに走ろうとする; 基礎ができないうちにむずかしいことをやろうとする ▪ He's cautious about *running before* he *can walk*. 彼は基礎ができないのに難しいことをしないように気をつけた.

run** a person **close **1** (競争などで)人に肉薄する，迫る ▪ I won the race, but the nearest runner *ran* me *close*. 私はそのレースで優勝したけれど，すぐあとのランナーに肉薄された．
2 ほとんど…くらい金がかかる ▪ This dish *ran* me *close* to $10. この料理はほとんど10ドルかかった．

run counter to →COUNTER.

run cross to …に反する ▪ It seems also to *run cross to* the Holy Scriptures. それはまた聖書にも反するように思われる．☞潮流が反対に流れることから．

run dry **1** 水がかれる; 乳が出なくなる ▪ The stream of living waters will never *run dry*. 流れてやまない川の水は決してかれることはない ▪ Most cows *run dry* in about ten months. たいていの牛は約10か月で乳が出なくなる．
2 尽きてしまう ▪ His novels *ran dry* at last. 彼の小説もとうとう種切れになった．

run...fine (特に時間)をきちきちに切りつめる ▪ He had *run* things rather *fine*. 彼はいろんな事をきちきちに切りつめたのだった．

run flat (タイヤが)パンクしたままで走る ▪ These tires can *run flat* for 50 miles. このタイヤはパンクしたままで50マイル走ることができる．

run for dear** [one's] **life →for one's LIFE 1.

run for it 《口》逃げ出す，逃げ去る ▪ They were ready to stop their work and *run for it*. 彼らはいつでも仕事をやめて逃げ出したかった．☞it＝one's life.

run for** (one's) **luck 《米口》一か八かやってみる ▪ I have to *run for luck* as to horses. 僕は競馬で一か八かやってみなければならない．

run foul of →fall FOUL of.

run hard just to stand still ストレスに押し潰されそうである ▪ I feel as if I'm *running hard just to stand still* because I've got a lot of things to do. すべきことが多くてストレスで潰されそうに感じる．

run high **1** (物価が)上がる ▪ Prices for fruit are *running high*. 果物の相場が上がっている．
2 (海が)荒れる ▪ Here the waves of the sea *run high*. ここでは波が荒れる．
3 (感情が)高まる，強まる ▪ Feelings always *run high* during an election. 選挙中は常に感情が高まる．

***run in the** [one's] **family** [**in the...blood, in families**]* 血統を引く，遺伝である ▪ They say that musical talent *runs in his family*. 彼の家族は音楽の才があると言われている ▪ Cruelty *runs in the* Tartar *blood*. 残虐さがタタール人の本性だ ▪ Does cancer *run in families*? がんは遺伝するのだろうか．

run in the** [one's] **head (歌曲・考えなどが)しきりに思い出される ▪ This tune has long been *running in the head*. この調べは長い間，人が心に浮かべてきているものだ．

run into a brick wall 壁に突き当たる ▪ We *ran into a brick wall*, and couldn't do anything. 我々は壁に突き当たって，何もできなかった．

run into one (特に溶けた状態で)一つに固まる，団結する ▪ By this the wax on both *runs into one*. これによって両方のろうが一つに固まる．

run into the ground →GROUND[1].

run into the sand(s) 尽きる，無くなる ▪ English drama ended when blank verse *ran into the sands*. 無韻詩が無くなったとき英国劇は終わった．

run it/run the voyage 護送船なしで航海する ▪ We resolved to *run it*. 我々は護送船なしで航海しようと決心した．

run it down 《米俗》いきさつ[事情]を十分に説明する ▪ Write me a letter and *run it down*. 手紙を書いて事情を十分に説明してほしい．

***run it fine** [**close**]* ＝CUT it fine.

run it on 《米口》…をひやかす ▪ The members of the troop thought to *run it on* the "dough boy" captain. 騎兵中隊員らは歩兵隊長をひやかそうと思った．

run** one's **mouth 《米俗》ぺらぺらしゃべり立てる ▪ He was drunk and *running his mouth*. 彼は酔ってしゃべり続けていた．

run off at the mouth 《米俗》べらべらまくし立てる; たわごとを言う ▪ He *runs off at the mouth*, boring you to hell. 彼はべらべらまくし立てて人をうんざりさせる．

run** a person **off** his **legs →LEG[1].

run** oneself **out **1** 《クリケット》(打者が打手線間を走っていて)アウトになる ▪ Studd foolishly *ran himself out*. スタッドはへまをやってアウトになった．
2 走って疲れ果てる ▪ He *ran himself out* in the first mile. 彼は最初の1マイルで走り疲れてしまった．

***run out of gas** [《英》**steam**]* 《口》ガス欠になる，エネルギーが切れる，興味を失う ▪ I worked really well for three months of the project, then I suddenly *ran out of gas*. 私はそのプロジェクトのために一心不乱に3か月働いたが，突然やる気をなくした．

run...ragged …を疲れさせる，くたびれさせる ▪ The children were *running* her *ragged*. 子供たちのことで彼女はくたびれていた．

run riot →RIOT.

run scared →SCARED.

***run short** (**of**)* →SHORT.

run strong (潮流の)流れが激しい; (怒り・悪などが)たけり狂う，荒ら立つ ▪ The tide is *running strong*. 潮流の流れが激しい ▪ Evil and good *run strong* in me. 善と悪が私の心中でたけり狂っている．

Run that by me again! 《口》もう一度言って! ▪ Mom's pearls, they're missing!—*Run that by me again?*—The pearls. ママの真珠が無くなったの—もう一度言って—真珠だってば．

run the cutter 密輸出入する ▪ Sailors, as a rule, appreciate *running the cutter*. 水夫は概して密輸出入のうまみがわかっている．☞税関の巡視船(cutter)を避けることから．

run the line(s) 《米》境界線を定める ▪ *The lines* between the governments have *been run*. 両政府の境界線が定められた．

run the voyage →RUN it.

R

run** oneself **to death 働きすぎて死ぬ ▪ You'll *run yourself to death*, working at this rate. こんな調子で働いてると過労で死んでしまうよ.

run to seed →go to SEED.

run ... too far (比喩など)を極端に用いる ▪ I am *running* my simile *too far*. 私はこの比喩を度を超して用いている.

run wild →WILD.

runaround /rʌ́nəràʊnd/ 名 ***get a* [*the*] *runaround*** 《口》ごまかされる, だまされる ▪ All he *got* was *the runaround*. 彼はだまされただけだった.

give a* [*the*] *runaround 《口》(人)をごまかす, だます ▪ You're *giving* me *a runaround*. 君は僕をだましているんだ.

rune /ruːn/ 名 ***read the runes*** 《英》(現状から)未来を読み解く[先読みする] ▪ The Minister of Finance *read the runes* and introduced additional tax measures. 財務大臣は将来を見越して付加税措置を導入した.

rung /rʌŋ/ 名 ***on the top rung* (*of the ladder*)** (職業の)最上位にあって ▪ Mr. Blade is *on the top rung* as a surgeon. ブレイド氏は外科医としては最上位にある.

the first rung of the ladder 職業の入り口[最初の一歩] ▪ The company was *the first rung of the ladder* to him. その会社は彼にとって仕事への最初の一歩となった.

run-in /rʌ́nìn/ 名 ***have a run-in with*** 《米口》...とやり合う; と交通事故を起こす ▪ I *had a run-in with* the Administration. 私は本部とやり合った ▪ It looked as if he must have *had a run-in with* a telephone pole. 彼はまるで電柱にぶつかったにちがいないような感じだった.

runner /rʌ́nər/ 名 ***do a runner*** 《英口》ずらかる, 逃亡する ▪ The driver *did a runner* after the crash. 運転手は衝突のあと逃亡した.

running[1] /rʌ́nɪŋ/ 名 ***do* (*all*) *the running*** →make (all) the RUNNING.

(*Go*) *take a running jump!* 《口》 **1** あっちへ行け, 立ち去れ ▪ I told him to *go take a running jump*. 私は彼に引き上げるように言った.
2 いやだね, まっぴらごめんだ ▪ Joe wants to borrow your new book.—Tell him to *take a running jump*. ジョーが君の新しい本を借りたいって—お断りだ.

have the best of the running 断然トップを行く ▪ He certainly *has the best of the running* in the competition. 彼は競争で断然先頭を走っている.

in* [*out of*] *the running 競走・競争に加わって[加わらないで]; 勝算があって[なくて] ▪ He doesn't count, does he? He is *out of the running*? あの男は問題じゃないのだろう? 勝算もないのだろう?

make* [*do*] (*all*) *the running **1** 先頭に立って走る ▪ He may *make the running*, and come in first. 彼は先頭に立って走って1着になるかもしれない.
2 (馬が他の馬の)歩調を定める ▪ His horse was employed to *make the running*. 彼の馬が歩調を定めるために使われた.
3 積極的に事に当たる ▪ She seems to have *made all the running*. 彼女が何もかも積極的にやってのけたものらしい.

make good** one's **running with ...と互角に走る[勝負する] ▪ The world had esteemed him when he first *made good his running with* Lady Fanny. 世間の人は彼がファニー夫人と初めて互角に勝負したとき彼を高く評価した.

make running 先を走る ▪ He is averse to *making running*. 彼は先を走るのがきらいだ.

take up the running 先頭に立つ; 率先する ▪ I will *take up the running* in his stead. 彼の代わりに僕が率先してやる.

running[2] /rʌ́nɪŋ/ 動 (run の現在分詞) ***a running battle*** 長期戦 ▪ Dan was engaged in *a running battle* with his neighbors over parking and other problems. ダンは駐車や他の問題で隣人と長期にわたって争っていた.

be running on empty →run on EMPTY.

be up and running きちんと働く[作動する]; (出だしが好調で)軌道に乗っている ▪ The Web site *is up and running*. そのウェブサイトはちゃんと稼働している ▪ The project *was* once *up and running*, but it isn't going well now. そのプロジェクトはかつて軌道に乗っていたが, いまはさんざんだ.

come running (援助に)飛んでくる ▪ She expects her husband to *come running* every time she wants something. 彼女は何かしたいときにはいつも夫が手伝いに来てくれると思っている.

rush[1] /rʌʃ/ 名 **(*as*) *straight as a rush*** まっすぐな ▪ The larch shoots up *as straight as a rush*, to a great height. カラマツはまっすぐに伸びて非常な高さに達する.

not ... a rush 少しも...ない ▪ He did *not* mind it *a rush*. 彼はそれを少しも気にかけなかった.

not worth a rush 少しも価値のない ▪ Without money, he is *not worth a rush*. 金のない彼は少しも価値はない.

wed* [*marry*] *with a rush ring (特に女性をだますために)まねごとの結婚をする ▪ A custom appears anciently to have prevailed of *marrying with a rush ring*. 古くはまねごとの結婚をする習慣が広く行われていたらしい. ☞rush「イグサ」.

rush[2] /rʌʃ/ 名 ***a rush of brains to the head*** 《英俗》すばらしい思いつき, ひらめき ▪ Suddenly I had *a rush of brains to the head*. 突然すばらしいことを思いついた.

***a* (*sudden*) *rush of blood* (*to the head*)** → have a (sudden) RUSH of blood (to the head).

at a rush 大急ぎで ▪ Victory had to be won *at a rush*. 勝利は大急ぎで得なければならなかった.

give the bum's rush →BUM.

***have a* (*sudden*) *rush of blood* (*to the head*)** 頭に血が上る, かっとなって愚かなことをする[言う] ▪ The driver *had a rush of blood to the head* and decided to make a U-turn on the narrow country lane. 運転手は頭に血が上って, 狭い田舎道でUターンをすることにした.

in a* [*on the*] *rush 《米》急いで, あわてて ▪ He is always *in* such *a rush* that he never thinks of anything. 彼はいつもひどくあわてているので何も考えつけない ▪ Last night she was *on the rush*. ゆうべは彼女は急いでいた.

What is the rush? 《口》あわてることはない ▪ Sit down and relax. After all, *what's the rush?* お掛けになってゆっくりなさってください. だって, あわてることはありませんから.

with a rush 突撃して; 一挙に, どっと ▪ We carried the citadel *with a rush*. 我々は突撃してその要塞を攻め落とした ▪ War books are coming out *with a rush*. 戦記物がどっと出されている.

rush[3] /rʌʃ/ 動 ***be rushed for*** (時間)が足りない ▪ I'll do that tomorrow, I'*m rushed for* time now. それは明日するよ, 今は時間がない.

***Fools rush in* (*where angels fear to tread*).** →ANGEL.

rush *one's* ***fences*** 《俗》(結果を求めて)あまりにあせりすぎる ▪ Don't *rush your fences*. あまりあせりすぎないようにしなさい. ☞狩猟であわてて馬で柵を飛び越えることから.

rush into extremes 極端に走る ▪ He always *rushes into extremes*. 彼はいつも極端に走る.

rush into print 大急ぎで本を出す ▪ So many foolish persons are *rushing into print*. 非常に多くのばかな連中が大急ぎで本を出している.

rush it 《米口》張り切ってやる ▪ The old man is *rushing it* with his fiddle. その老人はバイオリンを張り切ってひいている.

rush *a person* ***off*** *his* ***legs*** →run a person off his LEGs.

rush to conclusions あわてて結論を出す ▪ Don't *rush to conclusions*. あわてて結論を出してはいけない.

rush *one's* ***way*** 大急ぎで進む ▪ This morning by dawn we were *rushing our way* along the river. けさ夜明けには我々は大急ぎで川岸を進んでいた.

Russian /rʌ́ʃən/ 形 ***play Russian roulette*** 自殺行為をする, 破滅につながる賭けをする ▪ Thousands of consumers are *playing Russian roulette* with their lives by buying prescription drugs online. 大勢の消費者がオンラインで処方薬を購入することによって自らの生命を危険にさらしている.

rust[1] /rʌst/ 名 ***in rust*** 職にあぶれて ▪ He is bent on looking out for actors *in rust*. 彼は職にあぶれている俳優をやっきになって探している.

take* [*nab*] *the rust 《口》(馬が)御しがたくなる ▪ My horse shied at a road wagon, and then *took the rust*. 私の馬が荷馬車におびえ, それから御しがたくなった.

rust[2] /rʌst/ 動 ***Better* (*to*) *wear out than* (*to*) *rust out.*** さび切ってしまうよりはすり減ったほうがよい《無為を戒める言葉》 ▪ How irksome it is to be unable to use one's faculties! *Better to wear out than to rust out*. 自分の能力を使うことができないのはなんとうんざりすることだろう. さび切ってしまうよりはすり減ったほうがましだ.

rust *oneself* ***away*** のらくらしてむだに過ごす ▪ I'm not going to *rust myself away*. 私はのらくらしてむだに過ごすつもりはない.

rustle[1] /rʌ́səl/ 名 ***get a rustle on*** 《米口》急ぐ (= get a MOVE on) ▪ It's about time for me to *get a rustle on*. 私はもうそろそろ急いでいい時機だ.

rustle[2] /rʌ́səl/ 動 ***rustle for*** *oneself* 《米口》自分で自分の面倒を見る ▪ He turns you out thinking he'll let you *rustle for yourself* awhile. あの人はしばらく自分で自分の面倒を見させてやろうと思って君を外へ出すのだ.

rusty /rʌ́sti/ 形名 ***cut rusties*** 《米口》ふざけちらす ▪ It won't do for us to be *cutting rusties* here at this time of night. 我々がここで夜今時分ふざけまわっているのはよくない.

ride* [*run*] *rusty (人・馬が)手に負えなくなる; 腹をたてる ▪ Even my wife *rides rusty* on me now and then. 妻でさえときには私の手に負えなくなることがある ▪ To add to my misery he has again *run rusty*. さらにいやなことに彼がまた腹をたててしまった.

turn* [*cut up, get*] *rusty 《口》怒る, ぷりぷりする ▪ He never said a word to make her *turn rusty*. 彼は彼女を怒らせるようなことは一言も言わなかった ▪ The people *got rusty* about it. 人々はそのことで怒った.

rut[1] /rʌt/ 名 ***at* (*the*) *rut*** (シカ・ヤギ・ヒツジなどが)さかりがついて ▪ The goats are now *at rut*. ヤギは今さかりがついている.

go to* (*the*) *rut (シカ・ヤギ・ヒツジなどが)さかりがつく ▪ Deer *go to rut* in September. シカは9月にさかりをむかえる.

rut[2] /rʌt/ 名 ***be* [*stay*] *in a rut*** 型にはまった[マンネリの]生活をしている ▪ Women like to *stay in a rut*. 女性は型にはまった生活をしたがる.

get* [*drag, lift*] *out of the rut = get out of the GROOVE.

get* (*stuck*) *in a rut 型にはまってくる ▪ He has *got in a rut*, sitting at home by himself. 彼は家で一人でいるものだから型にはまってしまった.

run in ruts (話などが)型にはまっている ▪ His conversation *runs in ruts*. 彼の談話は型にはまって[マンネリ化して]いる.

settle* [*sink*] *into the rut ありきたりの生活になる ▪ On his return to civilized life, he will *settle into the rut*. 彼が文明生活に戻ると, ありきたりの生活を送ることになるだろう.

S

Sabbath /sǽbəθ/ 名 ***a Sabbath day's journey*** 安息日に許された旅行道程《2,000 cubits, 約3分の2マイル》; (一般に)短い旅行 ▪ Leeds in those days was *a Sabbath day's journey.* リーズは当時短い道程だった.

break* [*keep, observe*] *the Sabbath 安息日を守らない[守る] ▪ The Primitive Church *kept* both *the Sabbath* and the Lord's day. 原始キリスト教会は安息日も主の日もどちらも守った.

saber, 《英》 **sabre** /séɪbər/ 名 ***rattle*** *one's* ***saber*** 怒って威嚇する ▪ He very rarely put his threats into practice. All he can do is *rattle his saber.* 彼はおどしを実行することはめったにない. ただ怒っておどすだけだ.

saber rattling (軍事的)威嚇, さや当て ▪ America's response to North Korea's *saber rattling* should emphasize military preparedness above all. 北朝鮮の威嚇に対する米国の反応は軍事的に用意ができていることを何よりも強調するはずだ.

sable /séɪbəl/ 形 ***his sable Excellency*** [***Majesty***] 色の黒い君主; (特に)悪魔大王 ▪ *His sable Excellency* is a man of great force of character. その色の黒い君主は非常に個性の強い人だ.

sack[1] /sæk/ 名 ***a sack rat*** 《俗》よく寝るやつ ▪ My roommate is a regular *sack rat.* It takes real effort to wake him up. おれのルームメイトときたら全くよく寝るやつで, 起こそうと思ったらひと苦労だ.

a sad sack 《米口》(行動・考えの)暗い人 ▪ I think Jim *a sad sack.* ジムはねくらだと思う.

bring* [*carry*] *more sacks to the mill ますます議論をしげくする; もっと重しを加える ▪ The boys would weigh me down, crying "*Bring more sacks to the mill!*" 男の子たちは「もっと重しを加えろ」と叫んで, 私を押さえつけるのだった.

get* [*have*] *the sack 《口》首になる ▪ If Bill doesn't work harder he'll *get the sack.* ビルはもっと精出して働かなければ首になるだろう.

give *a person* ***the sack*** 《口》人を首にする; (恋人)をはねつける ▪ They *gave* Phillipson *the sack* because he came late so often. フィリップスンはたびたび遅刻したので首にされた ▪ She *gave the sack* to successive suitors. 彼女は求婚者を次々とはねつけた.

hit the sack =hit the HAY.

hold* [*be left to hold*] *the sack 《米口》窮地に置き去りになる[される], 貧乏くじを引く[引かされる] ▪ It seems to me that Uncle Sam is *holding the sack* right now. 米国政府は目下貧乏くじを引いているように私には思われる.

hop* [*jump*] *in the sack 《口》誰とでもセックスする ▪ He *hops in the sack* with anybody. 彼は誰とでもセックスする.

like a sack of potatoes (体つきが)不格好で[に] ▪ The man waddled along *like a sack of potatoes.* その男は不格好によたよた歩いて行った.

sack[2] /sæk/ 名 ***put ... to sack*** …を略奪する ▪ The soldiers *put* all *to sack.* 兵士たちはあらゆるものを略奪した.

sackcloth /sǽkklɔ̀ːθ|-klɔ̀θ/ 名 ***in sackcloth and ashes*** 悲哀に沈んで, 深く後悔して(《聖》 *Matt.* 11. 21; *2 Sam.* 3. 31, etc.) ▪ While he groaned and prayed *in sackcloth and ashes,* his brother smiled at his remorse. 彼が深く後悔してうめいたり祈ったりしている間, 彼の兄は彼の悔悟の様子を見てにやにやしていた. ☞ユダヤ人が悲哀・深い後悔の表れとしてざんげ服を着て頭に灰を振りかけたことから.

sacrament /sǽkrəmənt/ 名 ***administer the sacrament*** 聖餐(さん)式を行う ▪ The priest often *administered the sacrament* to her. その牧師は彼女にしばしば聖餐式を行ってやった.

receive* [*partake of, take*] *the sacrament 聖餐を受ける ▪ They *received the sacrament* weekly. 彼らは毎週聖餐を受けた.

take* [*receive*] *the sacrament upon* [*to *do*] …を[することを]誓って聖餐を受ける ▪ They *took the sacrament to* fight it out to the last man. 彼らは最後の一人まで戦い抜くことを誓って聖餐を受けた ▪ I'll *take the sacrament upon* it. そのことを誓って聖餐を受けよう.

the last sacraments 臨終塗油の秘蹟 ▪ William had *the last sacraments.* ウィリアムは臨終塗油の秘蹟を受けた.

sacred /séɪkrəd/ 形 ***a sacred cow*** (インドの)聖牛《神聖で侵す[批判する]ことのできない人[物]》 ▪ Newspapers had a lot more *sacred cows* than they do now. 新聞には今よりずっと多くの聖牛の記事があった.

be sacred from …を免れる, 被らない ▪ No place *was sacred from* outrage. 乱暴を受けない場所はなかった.

hold ... sacred …を神聖視する; を尊重する ▪ Their persons will *be held sacred.* 彼らの身柄は尊重されるだろう.

nothing is sacred 《口》何も隠しておけない ▪ You are so nosy that *nothing is sacred* around here. 君はとても詮索好きだから, この辺には何も隠しておけないよ.

sacred to **1** (神)に捧げられた ▪ The dove is *sacred to* Venus. ハトはビーナスに捧げられたものだ.
2 (ある人・目的)に献じた; に特に適切な ▪ Lombard Street has been *sacred to* the banking interests. ロンバード街は金融業者の天地になっている ▪ The epitaph is *sacred to* the memory of Samuel Butler.

この墓碑銘はサミュエル・バトラーを記念したものである.

sacrifice /sǽkrəfàɪs/ 名 ***at a sacrifice*** 見切りで ▪I will part with the goods *at a sacrifice* for ready cash. 即金なら見切りで商品を手放そう.

at any sacrifice どんな犠牲を払っても ▪It must be done *at any sacrifice*. どんな犠牲を払ってもそれをやらなければならない.

at* [*by*] *the sacrifice of …を犠牲にして ▪He gained fame *at the sacrifice of* his principles. 彼は主義を犠牲にして名声を得た.

make a sacrifice 見切り売りをする ▪Well, madam, we'll *make a sacrifice*. では奥さん, 見切り売りをしましょう.

make a sacrifice of …を犠牲にする ▪She *made* to him *a sacrifice of* her happiness. 彼女は彼のために自分の幸福を犠牲にした.

make sacrifices 犠牲を払う ▪Parents often *make sacrifices* in educating their children. 親は子供を教育するために犠牲を払うことが多い.

make the supreme sacrifice **1** (戦争などで)命を捨てる ▪He *made the supreme sacrifice* in the war. 彼は戦争で命を捨てた.
2 《戯》(女性が)初めて最後のものを許す ▪She *made the supreme sacrifice* to him. 彼女が最後まで許したのは彼が初めてだった.

sad /sæd/ 形 ***a sadder and a wiser man*** 悲しい経験を味わって賢明になった人 (Coleridge, *The Rime of Ancient Mariner* 7. 25) ▪When he takes his way homewards, he is *a sadder and a wiser man*. 家路をたどるとき, 彼は悲しい経験を味わって賢明になっている.

in sad earnest まじめに, 真剣に ▪I began to be a Christian *in sad earnest*. 私は真剣にキリスト者になり始めた.

sad to say 残念なことに ▪*Sad to say*, the funds were exhausted. 残念なことに, 資金が尽きた.

saddle[1] /sǽdəl/ 名 ***be back in the saddle*** 日常生活に戻っている ▪The best news of all is that he may *be back in the saddle* soon. 何よりもいい知らせは彼が間もなく日常生活に戻るかもしれないということだ.

cast** a person **out of the saddle 人を免職する ▪My bare word would have *cast* him *out of the saddle*. 私が一言言えば彼は免職になっていただろう.

***either win the saddle* [*horse*] *or lose the horse* [*saddle*]** 一か八かやってみる, のるかそるかやってみる ▪We resolved *either* to *win the saddle or lose the horse*. 一か八かやってみることにした.

for the saddle 乗用の ▪He had two horses, one *for the saddle*, and the other as a packhorse. 彼は馬を2頭飼っていたが, 1頭は乗用で, 残る1頭は荷馬としてであった.

get into* [*take*] *the saddle **1** 馬に乗る ▪He *got into the saddle* again. 彼は(落馬したが)また馬に乗った.
2 職につく; 権力を握る ▪They have *got into the saddle* by the favor of fortune. 彼らは運に恵まれて権力を握った.

in the saddle **1** 馬に乗って ▪He performed the journey *in the saddle*. 彼は馬に乗ってその旅をした.
2 職に納まって, 権力を握って ▪The Presbyterians were now again *in the saddle*. 長老派が今やまた権力を握っていた.
3 仕事に精出して ▪He is *in the saddle* from seven every morning. 彼は毎朝7時から仕事に精出している.

keep* [*lose*] *the saddle 落馬しない[する] ▪He could not *keep the saddle*. 彼は落馬してしまった.

lay* [*put, set*] *the saddle upon the right* [*wrong*] *horse 《口》責めるべき[おかど違いの]人を責める ▪I'll clear myself, and *put the saddle upon the right horse*. 身のあかしを立て, 責めるべき人を責めよう ▪You have *laid the saddle upon the wrong horse*. 君は責める人を間違えている.

out of the saddle 権力を失って ▪Of course, now he's *out of the saddle*. もちろん今は彼も権力を失っている.

remain in the saddle 権威のある地位に留まる ▪The principal *remained in the saddle* despite the attempts by the teachers to remove him. 先生方による排斥工作にもかかわらず校長はその座を譲らなかった.

ride high in the saddle 意気揚々としている ▪They *rode* a little *higher in the saddle* after their victory. 彼らは勝利のあと, 少しばかり意気揚々としていた.

take the saddle →get into the SADDLE.

under saddle くらをつけて ▪The horses were worked *under saddle*. 馬はくらをつけて働かされた.

saddle[2] /sǽdəl/ 動 ***saddle and bridle*** 制御する ▪Unless the steam is *saddled and bridled*, the pump will have no pressure. 蒸気が制御されない限りポンプには圧力がかからない.

saddle** a person **with 人に(責任など)を負わせる ▪I *am saddled with* the responsibility of educating three small children. 私は小さい子供を3人教育する責任を負わされている.

safari /səfɑ́ːri/ 名 ***go on safari*** (特に狩猟の)遠征旅行に行く ▪He had *gone on safari* to Uganda. 彼はウガンダへ遠征旅行に行っていた.

on safari 遠征旅行中で ▪I am *on safari*. 私は遠征旅行中です.

safe /seɪf/ 形名 ***a safe first*** 《口》一番にまちがいのない人 ▪He is *a safe first*. 彼は疑いなく一番だ.

a safe pair of hands 《英》確実に難題をこなせる人, 手堅い人 ▪It's *a safe pair of hands* that we need now. いま我々に必要なのは確実に難題をこなせる人だ.

(*as*) *safe as houses* 《英口》全く安全で ▪This wooden bridge is *as safe as houses*. この木の橋は全く安全だ.

as safe as safe 必ず ▪He'll win it, *as safe as safe*. 彼は必ず優勝するだろう.

at safe (銃に)安全装置をかけて ▪The rifle was *at*

S

safe. ライフル銃には安全装置がしてあった.

be as safe as houses [***the Bank of England***] (***to*** *do*) (…することは)全く確実だ ▪ He *is as safe as houses to* come round. 彼がやって来ることは全くまちがいない ▪ He *is as safe as the Bank of England*. 彼は全く確実な人間だ.

be in safe hands 信頼のおける人に面倒を見てもらっている ▪ My mother *is in safe hands* at the old folks' home. 母は老人ホームに委ねて面倒を見てもらっている.

be on the safe side **1** 大事をとる ▪ *Be on the safe side*, and do not trust him too far. 大事をとってあの男をあまり信用しないようにしなさい.

2 安心できる状態である ▪ The train doesn't leave for an hour, so we *are on the safe side*. 列車はまだ1時間は出ないから大丈夫だ.

be safe to *do* 確かに…する ▪ The Liberals *are safe to* win. 自由党は勝つから大丈夫.

Better (***to be***) ***safe than sorry.*** 《諺》泣く目にあうよりも用心するほうがよい.

err on the safe side 大事をとりすぎる ▪ It is always best to *err on the safe side*. いつも十二分に大事をとるのが一番よい.

have ... safe …を安全に捕えてある ▪ We *have* him *safe* enough. 彼を十分安全に捕えてある.

it is safe to *do* …してもまちがいではない, 大丈夫だ ▪ *It is safe to* say that he will never come back again. 彼はもう二度と帰って来まいと言っても大丈夫だ.

keep ... safe …を安全にしまっておく ▪ *Keep* it *safe* till I return. 私が戻るまで安全にしまっておいてください.

play (***it***) ***safe*** →PLAY².

play safe →PLAY².

safe and sound 無事息災で (《聖》*Luke* 15. 27) ▪ I have arrived in London *safe and sound*. 私は無事ロンドンへ着きました.

safe and sure (薬・投資など)安全で効果的で ▪ This medicine is *safe and sure*. この薬は安全でよく効く.

Safe bind, safe find. =FAST bind, fast find.

safe from …の危険[心配]がない ▪ The house is *safe from* theft. その家は盗難の心配がない ▪ Nothing was *safe from* her fingers. 彼女は手癖が悪いったらなかった.

safe in the knowledge that …だと確信をもって ▪ He went out *safe in the knowledge that* he could have a fabulous weekend. 彼はすばらしい週末が過ごせると確信して出かけた.

to be on the safe side 大事をとって (→be on the SAFE side 1) ▪ We'd better be off, *to be on the safe side*. 大事をとって, もう出かけるほうがいい.

safe-conduct /sèɪfkɑ́ndʌkt|-kɔ́n-/ 名 ***in*** [***with***] ***safe-conduct/ under*** [***upon***] (***a***) ***safe-conduct*** (敵国人などが国王などから)安全通行を許されて ▪ He had come over *under a safe-conduct*, and he was not detained. 彼は安全通行を許されて来ていたので, 引き留められなかった.

safekeeping /sèɪfkíːpɪŋ/ 名 ***be in safekeeping with a person*** 人の所に保管してある ▪ The documents *are in safekeeping with* him. その文書は彼の所に保管してある.

have ... in safekeeping …を保管しておく ▪ I shall *have* your effects *in safekeeping*. あなたの動産は私が保管しておきましょう.

safety /séɪfti/ 名 ***a safety net*** 安全[防止]策, (苦境にある人に対する)セイフティーネット ▪ They provided *a safety net* for students who ran out of money. 彼らはお金に困っている学生へのセイフティーネットを提供した.

at safety 安全装置をして ▪ He put his rifle *at safety*. 彼はライフル銃に安全装置をかけた.

for safety 安全のために ▪ We deposit money in a bank *for safety*. 安全のために銀行に金を預ける.

in safety 無事に, 安全に ▪ My long errand has been completed *in safety*. 私の長い使いはつつがなく終わった.

keep ... in safety …を安全にしまっておく ▪ Please *keep* it *in safety*. 安全にしまっておいてください.

play for safety →PLAY².

safety first 安全第一《スローガン》 ▪ "*Safety first*" was a creed with him. 「安全第一」が彼の信条だった.

seek safety in flight 避難する ▪ They *sought safety in flight*. 彼らは避難した.

(***There is***) ***safety in numbers.*** 《諺》数の多いほうが安全 (《聖》*Prov*. 11. 14) ▪ We have *safety in numbers*. 我々は多数で安全だ.

with safety 危険の恐れなく, 無難に ▪ I may say it *with safety*. それを言ってもさしつかえないだろう.

safety-valve /séɪftivæ̀lv/ 名 ***act*** [***serve***] ***as a safety-valve*** 安全弁の役をする ▪ Public lotteries *acted as safety-valves* to the gambling spirit of the nation. 宝くじはその国民のとばく欲への安全弁の役をした.

open a safety-valve 安全弁を開く ▪ The appearance of the butler with the cocktails *opened a safety-valve*. 給仕頭がカクテルを持って現れたのが安全弁を開いた格好になった.

sit on the safety-valve 安全弁を押さえる; (一時の策として)抑圧手段をとる ▪ The authorities *sat on the safety-valve* against the protesters. 当局は抗議デモの参加者に抑圧手段をとった.

sail¹ /seɪl/ 名 ***at full sail***(***s***)***/full sail*** **1** 強い順風を受けて, 全速力で ▪ The vessel was *at full sail*. 船は強い順風を受けていた ▪ So the two ships sailed away *at full sail*. かくして2隻の船は全速力で走り去った.

2 まっしぐらに ▪ He often went *full sail* into controversial subjects. 彼はよくまっしぐらに論争の中へ飛びこんでいった.

carry sail 帆を揚げている ▪ The Admiral *carried* all *sail*. 提督号は帆をすべて揚げていた.

full sail →at full SAIL(s).

get under sail 出帆する, 出港する ▪ In the afternoon we *got under sail*. 午後になって我々は出

S

帆した.

go for* [*take*] *a sail 船遊びに行く ▪ We *went for a sail* upon the bay. 湾へ船遊びに行った.

haul in *one's* ***sails*** 《口》 遠慮する, さし控える ▪ If you don't *haul in your sails* a bit, you'll find yourself in the bankruptcy court. 少しさし控えないと破産のうき目を見ることになるぞ. ☞「帆をたぐり込む」が原義.

hoist sail 帆を揚げる; 《口》しりに帆を揚げる, 立ち去る ▪ How goes the time?—Time to *hoist sail* and get away home. 時間はどうかね—しりに帆を揚げて家へ帰る時間だよ.

Hoist your sail when the wind is fair. 《諺》 順風のときに帆を上げよ,「得手に帆」.

lower *one's* ***sail*** **1** 帆を降ろす.
2 恐れ入って降参する, しっぽを巻く (*to*) ▪ I will not *lower my sail to* them unresistingly. 彼らにおめおめ降参しはしないぞ.

make sail **1** 帆を揚げる, 出帆する ▪ We *made sail* the next day. 翌日我々は出帆した.
2 (速力を加えるために)帆を増す ▪ We *made sail* and caught a good wind. 帆を増してしっかり風をとらえた.
3 《口》 立ち去る ▪ The signal to *make sail* for the drawing-room was given. 応接間へ立ち去る合図が出された.

more sail than ballast 実質より見栄 ▪ Our captain was a "loud" young man, with rather *more sail than ballast.* 我々の船長は「はで」な青年で実質よりも見栄をとるといったほうだった. ☞ballast「(船を安定させるための)底荷」.

set sail 出帆する (*for*) ▪ They will *set sail for* Le Havre on Wednesday. 彼らは水曜日にルアーブルへ向けて出帆する.

shorten (*one's*) ***sails*** 《海》 速度を落とすため帆をしぼる 《比喩的にも》 ▪ As you approach the shore, *shorten your sails.* 岸に近づいたら帆をしぼれ ▪ I must *shorten sails* for you. あなたのために歩度を落とさねばなりません.

strike sail (敬礼・降伏の印に)帆を下げる ▪ The mariners *struck sail* and submitted. 水夫たちは帆を下げて降伏した.

take a sail →go for a SAIL.

take in sail **1** = shorten (one's) SAILs.
2 (欲望・活動などを)控え目にする ▪ We shall have to *take in sail* somewhat for the future. 今後は少し控え目にしなければならない.

take sail 乗船する ▪ He *took sail* in the vessel. 彼はその船に乗船した.

take the wind out of the sails of → WIND[1].

trim the [*one's*] ***sails*** (***to*** [***before***] ***the wind***) (風向きに応じて)帆を調節する; 臨機の処置をとる; 倹約する ▪ The pilot will *trim his sails to* every variation of wind. 水先案内人はいろいろと変わる風向きに応じて帆を調節するものだ ▪ They had to *trim their sails.* 彼らは倹約しなければならなかった.

under full sail 大急ぎで ▪ I saw him going *under full sail* for their house. 彼が大急ぎで彼らの家へ行っているのが見えた.

under sail 帆を揚げて; 航行中で (↔ under STEAM 1) ▪ She made for port *under* all *sail.* 船はすべての帆を張って入港をめざした ▪ The ship was *under sail*, making towards the land. 船は帆を揚げて陸に向かって航行していた.

sail[2] /seɪl/ 動 ***sail against the wind*** → against the WIND.

sail before the wind 追手に帆をかけて走る; とんとん拍子にいく, 出世する ▪ He had *sailed before the wind* with the party in power. その党が政権を握っているので彼はとんとん拍子に行っていた.

sail near [***close to***] ***the wind*** 詰開きで航行する; (法・道徳にすれすれの)きわどい事をする, 危ない世渡りをする ▪ He had *sailed* too *close to the wind* at home, and came to the colony to be whitewashed. 彼は本国であまりにも危ない世渡りをして, 体裁をごまかすために植民地へやって来た.

sailing /séɪlɪŋ/ 名 ***be smooth*** [***clear,*** 《米》 ***easy,*** 《英》 ***plain***] ***sailing*** 順風満帆[とんとん拍子, 楽勝]だ ▪ It'll *be smooth sailing* if he can go on with his present work. 彼がいまの仕事を続けられれば順風満帆だろう.

sailor /séɪlər/ 名 ***a sailor's yarn*** 大げさな[信じがたい]話 ▪ Most of his stories are *sailor's yarns.* 彼の話はたいてい信じがたい.

be a bad [***poor, wretched***] ***sailor*** 船に弱い ▪ He pleaded that he *was a wretched sailor.* 彼は船に弱いんですと訴えた.

be a good [***an excellent***] ***sailor*** 船に強い ▪ We *were excellent sailors*, and bore the voyage without inconvenience. 我々は船に強くてさし障りもなく航海に耐えた.

saint[1] /seɪnt/ 名 ***enough to provoke a saint*** この上もなく腹立たしい (→try the PATIENCE of Job) ▪ You're *enough to provoke a saint.* 君は全くこの上もなく腹立たしい人間だよ. ☞「聖徒をも怒らせるような」が原義.

play the saint 信心家ぶる ▪ That aunt of his likes *playing the saint.* 彼のあのおばさんは信心家ぶるのが好きだ.

Saints preserve me [***us***]***!*** →God PRESERVE us!

the departed saint 故人, ほとけ《特に会葬者の用語》 ▪ A prayer was given for the soul of *the departed saint.* 故人の霊のために祈りがささげられた.

Young saints, old devils [***sinners***]. 《諺》 若いうちの信心は当てにならない.

saint[2] /seɪnt/ 動 ***saint it*** 聖徒らしくふるまう, 聖人ぶる ▪ He *sainted it* and sinnered it in turns. 彼は聖人ぶったり罪人ぶったりした.

sake /seɪk/ 名 ***for both*** [***all***] ***our sakes*** 我々二人[みな]のために ▪ *For both our sakes* I would wish that the words were true. 私たち二人のためにその言葉が本当であればいいと思う.

for God's* [*goodness', Heaven's, mercy's, pity's, Christ's, Pete's*] *sake 後生(ごしょう)だから; どうぞ ▪ *For goodness' sake*, say something! 後生だから何か一言言ってください. ☞このうち for goodness' sake が最も弱く, for Christ's sake が最も強く無礼に響く.

for name sake 名前のために ▪ *For name sake* I gave a token to a beggar. 名前のために, 私は物乞いに記念品をくれてやった.

for** one's **name('s) sake …の名[名誉]のために ▪ I love you *for your name's sake*. 私はあなたの名のゆえにあなたを愛します.

for old sake's sake 昔のよしみで (= for old TIMEs' sake) ▪ I continue to take an interest in him *for old sake's sake*. 私は昔のよしみでその男にいまでも関心を持っている.

for ... 's sake …のために ▪ *For my* own *sake* I will do my very best. 私自身のために精いっぱい全力を尽くすつもりだ ▪ It is doing mischief *for* mischief's *sake*. 悪戯(いたずら)のために悪戯をすることになる.

for the sake of …のために ▪ Society exists *for the sake of* the individual. 社会は個人のためにある.

Sakes alive! 《口》こいつは驚いた ▪ *Sakes alive!* You call him clever! こいつは驚いた. あの男が賢いと言うのかい.

salad /sǽləd/ 名 ***one's salad days*** 無経験な青二才時代 (cf. Sh., *Ant. & Cl.* 1. 5. 73) ▪ But those were *my salad days*. でも当時は僕の無経験な青二才時代だった.

sale /seɪl/ 名 ***a sale of work*** 慈善市《宗教団員などの作品を売る》 ▪ *A sale of work* took place last month. 慈善市が先月行われた.

be up for sale 《米》売り物に出されている ▪ One tractor *was up for sale*. トラクターが1台売り物に出ていた.

come up for sale 売りに出される ▪ This house will *come up for sale* shortly. この家は間もなく売りに出されよう.

for sale 売り物の ▪ These articles are not *for sale*. この品物は非売品です.

No sale. だめです[いけません].

on sale 売りに出した ▪ Every article on view will be *on sale*. 展示品はすべて売り物です.

(on) sale and* [*or*] *return 《商》売れなければ返すという約束で, 委託で ▪ Those goods are *on sale or return* by next Friday week. これらの品物は来週の金曜日までに売れなければ返すことになっている.

put up ... to* [*for*] *sale …を売りに出す ▪ They *put* a house *up for sale*. 彼らは家を1軒売りに出した.

***sales are up* [*down*]** 売り上げが上がった[下がった] ▪ *Sales are up* this month. 今月は売り上げが上がった.

set ... on sale …を売りに出す ▪ She *set* her jewels *on sale*. 彼女は宝石を売りに出した.

white sale (タオル・シーツなどの売出しをする)ホワイトセール ▪ The stores have *white sales* in January. お店は1月にホワイトセールをやる.

sally /sǽli/ 名 ***make a sally*** (籠城軍が)出撃する ▪ The garrison *made a* successful *sally*. 守備隊は出撃して成功した.

saloon /səlúːn/ 名 ***be (drinking) in the last chance saloon*** 《英》土壇場にいる ▪ He *was drinking in the last chance saloon* because of the bank failure. その銀行の破綻で彼は土壇場に立たされていた.

salt[1] /sɔːlt/ 名 ***above the salt*** **1** 上席に ▪ The marshals were the lowest *above the salt*. 元帥たちが上席では一番身分が低かった.

2 貴族に属して ▪ He is definitely *above the salt*. 彼は確かに貴族に属している. ☞食卓の中央に大きな塩つぼを置き, 身分の高い者がそのかみ手に座り使用人などがそのしも手に座るという, 昔広く行われていた習慣から.

be neither sugar nor salt/be not made of sugar or salt →SUGAR[1].

be up Salt River 《米俗》酔っ払っている (→row up SALT River) ▪ He *was* quite *up Salt River*. 彼はへべれけになっていた.

below* [*beneath, under*] *the salt **1** 末席に ▪ He never drinks *below the salt*. 彼は決して末席では酒を飲まない.

2 下層階級に属して ▪ The family is certainly *below the salt*. その一家は確かに下層階級に属している.

drop* [*cast, put,* etc.] *(a pinch of) salt on the tail of …を捕える ▪ You will never *cast salt on his tail*. That is, he has clean escaped. 君は決してあの男を捕えることはできない. というのはまんまと逃げてしまったからだ. ☞鳥を捕えるには尾にひとつまみの塩を落とせと戯れに子供に教えるところから.

earn* [*make*] *one's salt 食うだけかせぐ ▪ I am going to *earn my salt*. 食うだけかせぐつもりだ.

eat a person's salt/eat salt with a person 人の客となる, 人のもてなしを受ける; 人の家の居候になる ▪ I cannot speak against a man when I have *eaten his salt*. 私は人のもてなしを受けたときには反対ができない.

full of salt (話が)機知縦横の ▪ It was a conversation *full of salt*. それは機知縦横の談話であった.

go to Salt River 《米》(特に政治的に)敗北する (→row a person up SALT River) ▪ There must be compromise, or the whole confederacy must *go to Salt River*. 妥協しなければ南部連邦全体は敗北するほかない.

in salt 塩をふりかけた, 塩うけにした ▪ Let it remain *in salt* for twenty-four hours. それをまる一日中塩うけにしておけ.

make one's salt →earn one's SALT.

not earn salt to one's porridge ほとんど何も儲けない ▪ I *never earned salt to my porridge* till then. その時までほとんど何の儲けもなかった.

put (a pinch of) salt on the tail of →drop (a pinch of) SALT on the tail of.

row up Salt River 《米俗》酔っ払う (→be up SALT River) ▪ The man was *rowing up Salt*

River with Scott. その男はスコットといっしょに酔っ払っていた.

row** a person **up Salt River 《米口》(特に政治的に)人を敗北させる(→go to SALT River) ▪ He *rowed* Stanberry *up Salt River.* 彼はスタンベリーを敗北させた. ☞おそらく Kentucky 州の小さな曲がりくねった川の名から.

rub salt in** a person's **wounds 傷口に塩を塗る, ますます人をいじめる ▪ He spoke very rudely to Mary and then, to *rub salt in her wounds*, he began to laugh at her. 彼はメアリーにひどく無礼な口をきき, さらにますます彼女をいじめるためあざ笑い始めた.

speak with salt 機知に富んだ話をする ▪ She *speaks with salt.* 彼女は機知に富んだ話をする.

spill salt 塩をこぼす《縁起が悪いとされる》 ▪ I *spilled salt*, upon which my wife started up with a scream. 塩をこぼすと妻は悲鳴をあげて飛び上がった.

take ... with a grain [***pinch***] ***of salt*** (人の話など)を少し割り引きして受け取る ▪ We must *take* this *with a grain of salt.* これは少し加減して受け取らねばならない. ☞<[L] cum grano salis.

the salt of the earth (世の腐敗を防ぐ)地の塩; 社会の健全分子, 中堅階級(《聖》*Matt.* 5. 13) ▪ Lily says that the universities of Christendom should be *the salt of the earth.* キリスト教国の大学は地の塩であるべきだとリリーは言っている.

true to** one's **salt 主人に忠実で ▪ In these modern days, it's no longer the fashion to be *true to one's salt.* 当節は主人に忠実にするなんてもうはやらない.

under the salt →below the SALT.

weep salt tears 《雅》さめざめと泣く ▪ She *wept salt tears* in her chamber. 彼女は自分の部屋でさめざめと泣いた.

worth** one's **salt 〚主に否定文で〛給料だけの働きがある, 有能な ▪ The captain is not *worth his salt.* その隊長は穀(ごく)つぶしだ ▪ Every one who is *worth his salt* has his enemies. 有能な人は誰でも敵がある. ☞ローマの兵士が給料の一部を塩代としてもらったことから; salary<[L] salarium<sal salt.

salt[2] /sɔ:lt/ [動] ***salt the cow to catch the calf*** 《米口》間接的な手段で目的を達する,「将を得るために馬を射る」 ▪ I went on the old saying of *salting the cow to catch the calf.* 私は「将を得るために馬を射る」という古いことわざに従った.

salute /səlú:t/ [名] ***exchange salutes*** 礼砲を交換する ▪ *Salutes were exchanged* on both sides. 双方で礼砲を交換した.

fire [***give***] ***a salute*** (***of ten guns,*** etc.) (10発, などの)礼砲を放つ ▪ A frigate was *firing a salute.* フリゲート艦が礼砲を放っていた.

make [***give***] ***a salute*** 敬礼する ▪ The soldier *gave a salute* to his officer. 兵士は上官に敬礼した.

return the salute 答礼する; 答砲を放つ ▪ I waved my hand, and he *returned the salute.* 私が手を振ると彼は答礼した.

stand at (***the***) ***salute*** 《軍》敬礼の姿勢をとる ▪ The soldiers *stood at salute.* 兵士たちは敬礼の姿勢をとった.

take the salute (閲兵式で)敬礼を受ける ▪ The general *took the salute* of the military review. 将軍は閲兵式の敬礼を受けた.

salvation /sælvéɪʃən/ [名] ***be the salvation of*** ...の救いとなる ▪ Sleep *is the salvation of* the nervous system. 睡眠は神経系を救ってくれるものだ.

work out** one's **own salvation 自力で救済策を講じる, 自力で問題を解決する(《聖》*Philip.* 2. 12) ▪ Bill will have to *work out his own salvation.* ビルは自力で自分の問題を解決しなければならないだろう.

Sam /sæm/ [名] ***stand Sam*** 《英俗》勘定をもつ, (特に酒を)おごる(= stand SAMMY) ▪ Landlady, serve them with a glass of gin, all round; and I'll *stand Sam.* おかみさん, みなにジンを1杯ずつ注いでおくれ. 僕がおごるから.

upon [***'pon***] ***my Sam*** 《英俗・戯》誓って, 全くもって ▪ *'Pon my Sam*, it's enough to drive a man to drink. 全くもってそれは人を酒に走らせるに足る.

what [***who,*** etc.] ***the*** [***in***] ***Sam Hill*** 《米口》一体何[誰]が ▪ *What in Sam Hill* is that fellow balling about? 一体何であの男はまごまごしているのか. ☞Sam Hill = hell.

Samaritan /səmǽrətən/ [名] ***a good Samaritan*** よきサマリアびと, 情け深い人(《聖》*Luke* 10. 33) ▪ I took leave of *the good Samaritan.* 私は情け深い人にいとまを告げた.

same /seɪm/ [形][代] ***about the same*** (以前と)ほとんど同じ[変わりがない] ▪ The patient is *about the same* as yesterday. 患者は昨日とほぼ変わりがない.

all the same **1**〚形容詞的に〛全く同じ; どうでもよい(*to*) ▪ You can go or you can remain; it's *all the same to* me. 君は行ってもいいし残っていてもいい. 私はどちらでもかまいません.

2〚副詞的に〛それでも, やはり ▪ He was punished *all the same.* それでもやはり彼は罰せられた.

at one and the same time = at the SAME time 2.

at the same time **1** 同時に ▪ She was laughing and crying *at the same time.* 彼女は同時に笑ったり泣いたりしていた.

2 ではあるが, それでも ▪ I know he is untruthful, but, *at the same time*, I must admit he is a good worker. 彼は不正直者だとは知っているが, それでもよく仕事をすることは認めなくてはならない. ☞《俗》では the を省く.

be not in the same league as →not in the same LEAGUE as.

***be the same to** a person* 人に対する態度に変わりがない ▪ She *was* always *the same to* me. 彼女は私に対する態度に変わりがなかった.

come [***amount***] ***to the same thing*** (そう言ってみたところで)結局同じ結果になる ▪ You may pay in cash or by check; it *comes to the same thing.*

S

現金払いでも小切手払いでもけっこうです．結局同じことになりますから．

feel the same of *a person* →think the SAME of a person.

I wish you the same!/(The) same to you! あなたも《A Happy New Year! とか Merry Christmas! とかに答える言葉》 ▪ Merry Christmas!—*The same to you*, Liz! メリークリスマス!—メリークリスマス，リズ!

It will all be the same in a hundred years. 《諺》百年後も世の中は変わらない《あまりくよくよするな》．

(It's) the same the whole [all the] world over. 《諺》世界中どこへ行っても同じこと《損をするのは貧しい人》．

just the same **1** =all the SAME. **2**〚副詞的に〛全く同じように ▪ When I am away things go on *just the same*. 私が留守をしても事は全く同じように運んでいく．

more of the same 似たようなもの，同類 ▪ Their latest releases are just *more of the same*. 彼らの最新作も今までのと似たようなものだ．

much the same =about the SAME.

one and the same 〚the same を強調して〛全く同一の ▪ They belong to *one and the same* class. それらは全く同一の種類に属する．

Same difference. 《口》同じことさ ▪ Have you been married for twenty years, or twenty-five years?—*Same difference*. It's a long time anyway. 君たち，結婚して20年，それとも25年?—どっちでも同じさ．とにかく長い年月だよ．

Same here./The same with me. 《口》こちらも同じだ ▪ She said she wanted a Coke and I said *same here*. 彼女がコークがほしいと言ったので，僕もだと私は言った．

same old 《口》いつもと変らない ▪ How's it going?—Oh, you know, *same old*. 元気?—ああ，知っての通り，いつもと同じさ．

sing the same tune/ 《英》***sing from the same hymnsheet [singsgeet]*** → SING the same song.

(the) same again もう1杯(飲みものの)お代わり ▪ What would you like? —I'll have *the same again*. 何になさいますか?—もう1杯お代わりをください．

(the) same as …と同じように ▪ They do not think *the same as* we do. 彼らは我々と同じような考え方はしない ▪ We like good things (*the*) *same as* you. 我々もあなたがたと同じように良い物が好きです．

the same (...) as 〚従節・従節の縮約形を伴って〛…と同じ(の) ▪ He sells at *the same* price *as* I do. 彼は私と同じ値段で売っている ▪ Your schedule is not *the same as* mine. 君の予定は僕のと同じではない ▪ He is *the same* age *as* his wife. 彼は奥さんとおない年だ ▪ I gave *the same* answer *as* before. 私は以前と同じ返事をした．☞現在最も普通の構文; また the same ... as は「同種類」, the same ... that は「同一物」を表すという学校文法の区別は絶対的なものではない: They are sold *the same* day *as* [*that*] they come in. それは入荷したその日に売れる．

the same as ever 相変わらずだ ▪ How are you getting along?—*The same as ever*. いかがお暮らしですか?—相変わらずです．

the (same) old story →STORY.

the same ... that [which, when, where] …と同じの ▪ I was *the same* sort of man *that* he was. 私は彼と同じたぐいの人間だった ▪ I found it in *the same* place *where* I had left it. それは元置いていた所にあった．☞この構文では関係詞が略される場合がある: I have *the same* Bible he gave me. 私は彼がくれたのと同じ聖書を持っている．

the same the whole [all the] world over →(It's) the SAME the whole world over.

(The) same to you. →I wish you the SAME!

the same (...) with 〚名詞・代名詞を伴って〛…と同一(の) ▪ Pen went to *the same* college *with* him. ペンは彼と同じ大学へ行った ▪ His salary is *the same with* mine. 彼の月給は僕と同額だ．

think [feel] the same of *a person* 人に対して同様の考え[気持ち]をいだく ▪ You'll never *think the same of* me again. あなたは二度と私を以前と同じようには考えてくれないでしょう．

Sammy /sǽmi/ 名 ***stand Sammy*** 《英俗》(酒などを)おごる (= stand SAM) ▪ I'll *stand Sammy* this time. 今回は僕がおごろう．

sample /sǽmpəl|sɑ́ːm-/ 名 ***be up to [below] sample*** 見本通りである[よりも劣っている] ▪ The last supply of gloves you sent us *are below sample*. この前送ってくれた手袋は見本よりも劣ってる．

buy [sell] by sample(s) 見本で買う[売る] ▪ I *bought* it *by sample*. 見本でそれを買った．

come up to sample 見本通りである ▪ The merchandise do not *come up to sample*. この商品は見本通りでない．

give [show] a sample of *one's* ***knowledge [ingenuity]*** 自分の知識[発明の才]の実例を見せる ▪ He often *shows* you *a sample of his knowledge*. 彼はよく人に自分の知識の実例を見せる．

sanction /sǽŋkʃən/ 名 ***apply [take] sanctions against*** …に制裁手段をとる ▪ The Big Four are going to *apply sanctions against* the aggressor country. 四大国は侵略国に制裁手段をとろうとしている．

give (a) sanction to …を認可[是認]する ▪ Religion *gave sanction to* that intense animosity. 宗教はあの激しい敵意を是認した．

sanctuary /sǽŋktʃuèri|-tʃuəri/ 名 ***seek sanctuary*** 避難所を求める ▪ Those who *sought sanctuary* fled to the church. 避難所を求めた人々は教会へ逃げて行った．

take sanctuary 聖域に逃げ込む; 安全な場所に逃げ込む ▪ The Queen was forced to *take sanctuary* at Westminster. 女王はやむなくウェストミンスター寺院の聖域に逃げ込んだ ▪ The gunner had *taken sanctuary* in the woods. 銃を持った男は森の中へ

逃げ込んでいた.

violate* [*break*] *sanctuary (犯人などを連れ去るために)聖域を侵す ▪ You do not *break sanctuary* in seizing him. 彼を捕えても聖域を侵すことにならない.

sand /sænd/ 名 ***be on shifting sands*** (関係などが)不安定である ▪ Conditions in the country have *been on shifting sands* since the civil war. その国の情勢は内戦以来ずっと不安定である.

built on* [*upon*] (*the*) *sand 砂上に築いた, 不安定な (《聖》*Matt.* 7. 26) ▪ It is a token that your foundation was *built upon the sand*. それはあなたの基礎が不安定であるという印です.

bury** one's **head in the sand like an ostrich →OSTRICH.

footprints on the sands of time 歴史に残る足跡 (Longfellow, *A Psalm of Life* 7) ▪ These writers left behind them *footprints on the sands of time*. 作家たちは死後歴史に足跡を残した.

***knock the sand from under** a person* 《米口》人の計画をくつがえす ▪ I never had *the sand* so *knocked from under* me before in my life. 生まれてこのかたこんなに計画をくつがえされたことがない.

like sand on the seashore for number 浜の真砂(まさご)のように無数で ▪ They were *like sand on the seashore for number*. 彼らは浜の真砂のように無数だった. ☞ 次項も参照.

***numberless* [*numerous*] *as the sand*(*s*) (*on the seashore*)** 浜の真砂のように無数で (《聖》*Gen.* 22. 17) ▪ You want your offspring to be *numberless as the sands on the seashore*. あなたは子孫が浜の真砂のように無数になることを望んでいる.

***plow* [*measure, number*] *the sand*(*s*)** 無益なことをする, むだ骨を折る (→beat the AIR) ▪ I tell you that you're just *plowing the sand*. いいかい, 君はむだ骨を折っているだけなんだよ ▪ I fear we are *plowing the sands*: we see no fruit of our labors. 我々はむだ骨を折っているのではないか. 努力の結果が少しも現れないもの.

***put* [*throw*] *sand in the wheels* [*machine*]** 事をじゃまする, 破壊する ▪ I don't mean to *put sand in the wheels*. 私は事をじゃまする気はない.

raise sand 《米口》騒ぎを起こす ▪ They were scaring horses and *raising sand*. 彼らは馬をおどしたり騒ぎを起こしたりしていた.

sand in** one's **craw 《米口》勇気, 肝ったま ▪ He has sufficient *sand in his craw* for this new position. 彼はこの新しい任務を果たすための勇気が十分ある.

One's ***sand*(*s*) *run*(*s*) *out.*** → The SAND(s) run(s) out.

sow** one's **seed in the sand 無益なことをする ▪ I might have *sown my seed in the sand*. 私はむだ骨を折ったかもしれない.

The* [*One's*] *sand*(*s*) *run*(*s*) *out. 時間[寿命]が切れる ▪ You had better confess; *the sands* are *running out*. 白状したほうがよいぞ. もうすぐ時間が切れるからな ▪ No, doctor, *my sand* has *run out*. いいや先生, 私の寿命は切れたのです. ☞ 砂時計の砂粒が少なくなることから.

sandboy /sǽndbɔ̀ɪ/ 名 ***(as) jolly* [*merry, happy*] *as a sandboy*** 非常に陽気な ▪ Thank you, I'm all right, and *as jolly as a sandboy*. おかげさまで僕は元気でとても快活です. ☞ sandboy (砂売りの小僧)はこの句にしか用いられない.

sandman /sǽndmæ̀n/ 名 ***The sandman is shaking sand in your eyes./ The sandman has come* [*is coming*].** 眠くなってきた ▪ Now, Master Alfred, I can see *the sandman is shaking sand in your eyes*. さあアルフレッド坊ちゃま, お眠くおなりのようですね. ☞ sandman「小児に眠気を催さす睡魔」.

sandwich[1] /sǽndwɪtʃ|sǽnwɪdʒ/ 名 ***a sandwich of** A **and** B* AとBとの混ぜ合わせ, 背中合わせ ▪ His talk was *a* perfect *sandwich of* oaths *and* orders. 彼の話は全くののしりと命令の混交だった.

be a* [*one*] *sandwich short of a picnic 《口》狂っている, 愚かだ ▪ If you read his novel, you'll think the author *is a sandwich short of a picnic*. その作家の小説を読めば, 作家が狂っていると思うだろう.

en sandwich 二人の間にはさまれて ▪ A young man came down the lane *en sandwich*. 青年が二人の間にはさまれて小道を下ってきた.

sandwich[2] /sǽndwɪtʃ|sǽnwɪdʒ/ 動 ***be sandwiched between*** 間にはさまれる ▪ There was a tall and narrow building *sandwiched between* two other houses. 2軒の家屋にはさまれて高くて幅の狭いビルが1棟あった.

sandwich** A **and** B **together (***with** C*) AとBを(Cで)合わせる[つなぐ] ▪ We *sandwiched* the cakes *together with* cream. ケーキ同士をクリームで合わせた.

sap /sæp/ 動 ***sap** one's **way*** ひそかに進んで行く ▪ Lies, while they *sap their way*, are safe enough. 嘘もひそかに進んで行く間は全く安全だ.

sardine /sɑ̀ːrdíːn/ 名 ***packed like sardines*** (***in a box***) すし詰めになって ▪ The steamer arrived at the quay with tourists *packed like sardines*. 汽船は観光客をすし詰めに乗せて波止場へ着いた. ☞ イワシ (sardine) はびっしり並べてかん詰めにしてあるところから.

Satan /séɪtən/ 名 ***Satan rebuking* [*reproving*] *sin*** 自分の悪いことはたなに上げて人を非難する人 ▪ It is a case of *Satan rebuking sin*. それは炭団(たどん)が炭を黒いと言って笑うというやつだ.

sate /seɪt/ 動 ***be sated with*** …に飽きている, 堪能している ▪ He *was sated with* the ordinary sights of London. 彼はロンドンの普通の景色には飽きていた.

satiety /sətáɪəti/ 名 ***to* (*the point of*) *satiety*** あきあきするほど ▪ He indulged in pleasure *to satiety*. 彼はあきあきするほど快楽にふけった.

satin /sǽtən/ 名 ***(as) smooth as satin*** (しゅすのように)非常になめらかで ▪ Her skin is shining and *as smooth as satin.* 彼女の肌はつやがあってとてもなめらかだ.

satisfaction /sætəsfǽkʃən/ 名 ***demand satisfaction*** **1** 弁解[謝罪]を要求する ▪The fleet set sail to *demand satisfaction* from the Chinese. 艦隊は中国人の不当を詰問するために出航した.

2 決闘を申し込む ▪If he thinks himself injured, he knows where to *demand satisfaction.* 彼は侮辱されたと思えば, どこへ決闘を申し込めばよいかわかっているはずだ.

enter (***up***) ***satisfaction*** 《法》(裁判所の要求する)支払いを完了したことを裁判所の記録にとどめる ▪The attorney *entered up satisfaction* on record. 代理人は支払いが完了したことを裁判所の記録にとどめた.

find satisfaction in/***feel satisfaction at*** …に満足[安心]する (*doing*) ▪He *found satisfaction in* the monastic life. 彼は修道士の生活に満足した ▪He *felt satisfaction at having* his ability recognized. 彼は才能を認められたことに満足した.

give *a person* ***satisfaction*** **1** 人に満足を与える; 人に賠償する ▪If you *give* me *satisfaction*, you shall in future have my custom. 気に入ればこれからお客になってあげよう.

2 人の決闘の申し込みに応じる ▪I was ready to *give* him *satisfaction.* 私は喜んで相手の決闘の申し込みに応じるつもりだった.

have the satisfaction of …を満足に思う ▪He *has the satisfaction of* being successful in life. 彼は出世したことを満足に思っている.

in satisfaction (***of***) 《主に法》(…の)賠償として ▪He paid $100,000 *in satisfaction of* the claim. 彼はその要求の賠償として10万ドルを払った.

make satisfaction 《主に法》(…を)賠償する, 償う (*for*) ▪I would be glad to *make* you *satisfaction.* 喜んであなたに償いをしましょう ▪He *made satisfaction for* his debt. 彼は借金を返済した.

to *one's* [*a person's*] ***satisfaction*** 自分[人]の満足のいくように ▪The paper was at last written *to my* own *satisfaction.* 論文がやっと満足がいくように書けた ▪The difficulty was settled *to the satisfaction of* everyone. 難点のかたがつきみなが満足した.

with satisfaction 満足の念をもって ▪I can say *with satisfaction* that my whole task is completed. 私は自分のすべての仕事が完了したと満足して言うことができる.

satisfy /sǽtəsfàɪ/ 動 ***be satisfied of*** …を納得している ▪I *am* fully *satisfied of* the truth of his statement. 私は彼の話が本当だと十分に納得している.

be satisfied with [***to*** *do*] …に[することに]満足する ▪*Are* you *satisfied with* my answer? 私の返事で納得がいきましたか ▪I *am satisfied to* hear from him. 彼から便りをもらって満足しています.

rest satisfied 満足している, 甘んじる (*with*) ▪We were willing to *rest satisfied with* what we saw. 我々は快く自分たちの見たもので満足していた.

satisfy *oneself* **1** 満腹するまで食べる ▪Well, have you quite *satisfied yourself*? さあ, すっかり満腹するまで食べましたか.

2 (事実・ニュースなどを)確かめる ▪I want to *satisfy myself* further about the fact. その事実についてはさらに確かめてみたいと思う.

satisfy *oneself* ***of*** [***that***] …のこと[ということ]を得心する ▪I have *satisfied myself of* the truth of the report. その報告にまちがいないことを納得した ▪He *satisfied himself that* the servant was honest. 彼は使用人が正直者だとよくわかった.

satisfy *a person* ***that*** 人に…ということを納得させる ▪I *satisfied* her *that* there was no cause for her fears. 何の心配もないということを彼女に得心させた.

satisfy the examiners 《英大学》普通の成績で試験に合格する ▪Certain students attempt only to *satisfy the examiners.* 一部の学生は普通の成績で試験に合格することのみを試みる.

saturate /sǽtʃərèɪt/ 動 ***saturate*** *oneself* ***in*** …に没頭する ▪He *saturated himself in* Greek history. 彼はギリシャ史に没頭した.

saturation /sætʃəréɪʃən/ 名 ***to saturation*** 飽和するまで ▪We made an experiment in dissolving a salt *to saturation.* 塩(えん)を飽和するまで溶解する実験をした.

sauce /sɔːs/ 名 ***Don't give me any of your sauce.*** 生意気な口をきくな[偉そうにするな].

hit the sauce 《米俗》大酒をあおる ▪He used to *hit the sauce* in his twenties. 彼は20代には大酒をあおったものだった.

Hunger is the best sauce. →HUNGER.

None of your sauce! 《口》生意気を言うな ▪Now then, *none of your sauce*, my boy. おいおい, 生意気を言うんじゃないよ, おまえ.

on the sauce 酒癖がついて, 酔っ払って ▪My secret slipped out when I was *on the sauce* the other day. 先日酔っている時に秘密を漏らしてしまった.

serve *a person* ***with the same sauce***/***give*** *a person* ***a sop of the same sauce***/***make*** *a person* ***taste of the same sauce*** 人に同じ手で仕返しをする, しっぺ返しをする ▪He thought to *give* them *a sop of the same sauce.* 彼は彼らにしっぺ返しをしてやろうと思った ▪I will *make* you *taste of the same sauce.* お前にしっぺ返しをしてやる.

Sweet meat will have sour sauce. 《諺》楽があれば苦があるもの.

The sauce is better than the fish. 添えもののほうが主要部よりもすぐれている《本文よりも挿絵がすぐれているときなど》.

What is sauce for the goose is sauce for the gander. 《諺》一方に当てはまることは他方にも当てはまる ▪*What is sauce for* the verb *is* surely *sauce for* the verbal noun. 動詞に当てはまることはもちろん動名詞にも当てはまる.

saucer /sɔ́ːsər/ 名 (***as***) ***big*** [***round***] ***as sau-***

cers (驚き・好奇心で目を)皿のように丸くして ▪ The boy's eyes grew *as big as saucers* when he saw a robot. ロボットを見ると男の子の目は皿のようになった.

saunter[1] /sɔ́:ntər/ 名 ***at a saunter*** ぶらぶら歩きで ▪ They came along *at a saunter.* 彼らはぶらぶら歩きでやって来た.

saunter[2] /sɔ́:ntər/ 動 ***saunter through life*** のんびり一生を暮らす ▪ He'll *saunter through life* just like that. 彼はあの通りのんびり一生を暮らすだろう.

sausage /sɔ́:sɪdʒ|sɔ́s-/ 名 ***not a sausage*** 全く何もない ▪ He didn't speak. *Not a sausage.* 彼は口をきかなかった. 全然.

savage /sǽvɪdʒ/ 形 ***be*** [***get***] ***savage with*** [***on***] *a person* 《口》人に対してひどく怒っている[怒る] ▪ The doctor *was* pretty *savage with* him. 医者は彼に対してひどく怒っていた.

make *a person* ***savage*** 《口》人をひどく怒らせる ▪ Her retort *made* him *savage.* 彼女の口答えが彼をかんかんに怒らせた.

save[1] /seɪv/ 前接 ***save for*** …を除いては ▪ *Save for* the slumbering fire, all was dark within the house. 消えかかっている火のほかは, 家の中はどこも暗かった.

save[2] /seɪv/ 動 ***as I hope to be saved*** 誓って, きっと ▪ *As I hope to be saved,* I will never mention a word of it. 誓ってそのことは一言も言いはしません.

(***God***) ***save me from my friends!*** 友だちごかしのおせっかいはごめんだ《時機を失したおせっかいに対する評言》 ▪ If Wilson said that of me, well, *save me from my friends!* もしウィルスンが僕のことをそんなに言ったのなら, いやはや, ひいきの引き倒しはよしてもらいたい.

God save the King [***Queen***]***!*** 国王[女王]万歳! ▪ He said to Absalom: *God save the King!* 彼はアブサロムに「国王万歳!」と言った.

save *oneself* **1** 骨惜しみをする ▪ I never *saved myself* on the stage. 舞台で骨惜しみしたことはない.
2 逃れる, 逃げる; 免れる ▪ He *saved himself* to the ship. 彼はその船に逃れた.
3 《婉曲》(結婚するまで)処女のままでいる ▪ Loyalty to her aunt and uncle made it possible to *save herself.* 叔父と叔母への義理から彼女は結婚するまで処女のままでいた.

save *one's* ***ass*** [***butt***] 《主に米卑》しりぬぐいをする; 自分の身を守る ▪ She climbed out the back of the car to *save her ass.* 彼女は身を守るため車の後ろから這い出た.

Save it. 《口》その話はやめてくれ, 口を出すな ▪ *Save it.* I'll do it the way I like. 口出しはやめてくれ. おれは好きなようにやるから.

save (***money***) ***toward*** …を買うために貯金する ▪ We've been *saving toward* a new house. 新しい家を買うために貯金しているところだ.

save *one's* (***own***) ***pocket*** 金を使わなくてすむ ▪ He may have *saved his own pocket.* 彼は自分の金は使わずにすんだかもしれなかった.

save *one's* ***strength*** 骨惜しみをする ▪ He is *saving his strength* for the heavy work. 彼はその大仕事に備えて力をたくわえている.

save the goal 《スポーツ》ゴールを守る ▪ Jack *saved the goal* well on several occasions. ジャックは数回立派にゴールを守った.

Well saved! よく落ちなかった《落馬を免れた人に》; よく守った《フットボールなどで》 ▪ *Well saved,* my lad. よく落ちなかったな, 君.

saving /séɪvɪŋ/ 前接形 ***by the saving grace of God*** 神明の加護により ▪ The ship weathered the storm *by the saving grace of God.* 船は神明の加護によりあらしを切り抜けた.

saving your presence [***reverence***] (長上者・聖職者などの前で)こう申しては失礼ですが; ごめんいただいて ▪ There's nothing I hate so much as politics—*saving your presence.* 政治くらいいやなものはないのですよ—こう申しては失礼ですが.

the saving grace of →a saving GRACE.

savor, 《英》 **savour** /séɪvər/ 名 ***have a savor of*** …の風味がする; の気味がある ▪ His political views *have a savor of* fanaticism. 彼の政見は狂信的なところがある.

saw[1] /sɔ:/ 名 ***old saw*** 格言, 古い諺; 《俗》古臭いジョーク ▪ "Haste makes waste" is an *old saw.* 「急がばまわれ」は一つの格言だ.

saw[2] /sɔ:/ 動 ***saw gourds*** 《米俗》いびきをかく ▪ In five minutes we were all *sawing gourds* together in the land of Nod. 5分もたつと我々はみんなぐっすり眠りこけていた.

saw *one's* ***hand*** のこぎりをひくような手ぶりをする(= SAW the air 2) ▪ He stood singing at church, and *sawing his hand.* 彼は教会で歌を歌い, 手を前後に動かしていた.

saw on the fiddle バイオリンをギーギーかき鳴らす ▪ She was only *sawing on the fiddle.* 彼女はバイオリンをギーギーかき鳴らしているにすぎなかった.

saw the air **1** 《野球俗》から振りする ▪ He *sawed the air* three times without hitting anything. 彼は三振して全く当たらなかった.
2 (のこぎりをひくように)手を前後に動かす ▪ With his right hand the speaker ceaselessly *sawed the air.* 演説者は右手をしきりに前後に動かした.

saw wood **1** 《米俗》人のことに干渉しない ▪ He *sawed wood* and said nothing. 彼はおせっかいをせず何も言わなかった.
2 = SAW gourds.

sawder /sɔ́:dər/ 名 ***soft sawder*** →SOFT.

sawdust /sɔ́:dʌst/ 名 ***knock*** [***let***] ***the sawdust out of*** …のぼろをさらけ出す, 高慢の鼻を折る; を台なしにする ▪ I'll *knock the sawdust out of* any man. 誰でもいいからぼろをさらけ出してやるぞ. ☞人形の中からおがくずを出すことから.

sawyer /sɔ́:jər/ 名 ***a top*** [***bottom, pit***] ***sawyer*** 《英》腕ききの[腕のきかない]人; 上役[下役] ▪ Benson is very capable and *a* real *top saw-*

S

yer. ベンスンはとても有能で本当に腕ききの男だ. ☞「木びき穴 (sawpit) の上[中]でひく木びき」が原義.

say[1] /seɪ/ 名 ***have a*** [***no, not much***] ***say in*** …に口を出す権利がある[ない, あまりない] ▪ Those who found the money wished to *have a say in* its disposal. その金を見つけた連中はその金の処分に口を出す権利を持ちたがった ▪ You *have no say in* the matter. 君はこの件については発言権がない.

have one's say (機会をとらえて)自分の意見を述べる ▪ I *had my say* on the subject before. その問題については以前自分の意見を述べたことがある.

have the say 《米》意のままにする, はぶりをきかす ▪ He *had the say* over $50 million. 彼は5千万ドルを意のままにした ▪ Somebody has to *have the say*. 誰かが指揮する必要がある.

say (***out***) ***one's say/say one's say*** (***out***) 言いたいことを言う ▪ I have done my best, and *said my say*. できるだけのことはして, 言いたいことは言った.

say[2] /seɪ/ 動 ***after all is said and done*** = when all is said (and done) (→SAY[2]).

And so say all of us. 我々はみんな同意見だ ▪ He is a jolly good fellow! *And so say all of us.* 彼らはとてもいいやつだ. 我々はみんなそう言っている.

Anything [***Whatever***] ***you say.*** 《口》(上司・妻などからの依頼に)わかりました, 承知しました ▪ Will you please take these blouses over to the cleaners?—Sure, *anything you say*. これらのブラウス, クリーニングへ持っていってくれる? ―いいとも, 承知した ▪ That's alright, girl, *whatever you say*. いいよ君, 合点承知.

as one [***you***] ***might say*** 言ってみれば ▪ He's a bit eccentric, *as you might say*. 彼は言ってみれば少々変人だからね.

as they [***people, we***] ***say*** いわゆる ▪ We were at the very neck of the bottle, *as they say*. 我々はまさにいわゆるあい路に陥っていた.

as who should say …と言いでもする(人でもある)かのように ▪ He smiled *as who should say*, "Well done!" 彼は「でかした」と言わぬばかりににっこりした. ☞F comme qui dirait のなぞり.

be not saying much あまりほめたことにならない ▪ To say that he is a genius *is not saying much*. 彼は天才だと言ってもほめすぎではない.

can't say no (気が弱くて)いやだと言えない ▪ I'm just a girl who *can't say no*. 私はいやだと言えない女の子なんです.

Easier said than done. 《諺》言うはやすく行うは難し.

have nothing [***not have anything***] ***to say for oneself*** **1** 何も弁解することがない, 何も文句がない ▪ Bishop Ken was dispossessed, but he *had nothing* special *to say for himself*. ケン主教は立ちのかされたが彼は別に文句はなかった.
2《口》(ひっ込み思案などのため)いつも黙っている ▪ He *never has anything to say for himself*. 彼はいつも黙っている.

have plenty [***something, little,*** etc.] ***to say for oneself*** 弁解することまたは言い分がたくさんある[少しある, ほとんどない] ▪ He *has plenty to say for himself*. 彼は弁解すること[言い分]がどっさりある.

have something [***nothing***] ***to say to*** [***with***] (…が)…とかかわりがある[ない] ▪ Perhaps you *have something to say with* the gentleman. たぶん君はあの紳士と何かかかわりがあるのだろう ▪ It *has nothing to say to* the origin of the word. それはその語の語源とは何のかかわりもない.

I cannot [***couldn't***] ***say.*** 私には何とも言えない ▪ What the end of it all would have been *I* really *cannot say*. そういうことの結果がどうなっただろうかは, ほんとに私には何とも言えない.

I dare say →DARE say.

I mean to say. →MEAN[2].

I must say [***admit, confess***]. 《口》確かに, 全く ▪ This news surprises me, *I must say*. この知らせは確かに驚きですね. ☞特に驚いたときに用いる.

I say! **1**《口》おい, ちょいと, あのね; まあ!, これは驚いた! (《米》Say!) ▪ *I say*, open the door. おい, ドアをあけてくれ ▪ Well, *I say!* これはこれは!
2《口》…だと言うんだよ, …なんだよ ▪ *I say!* It won't do. それはだめだと言うんだよ.

I should say so [***not***]. 確かにそうだ[そうじゃない]と思う ▪ Is he a soldier?—*I should say so* [*not*]. 彼は軍人ですか?—きっとそうだ[そうじゃない]と思いますよ.

I should say (***that***) まあ…でしょうね ▪ *I should say* (*that*) he is rather stupid. まあ彼は間抜けでしょうね.

I wouldn't [***won't***] ***say no to*** …を喜んで承知します ▪ *I wouldn't say no to* a glass of beer. ビールを1杯やるのは悪くないね.

if I say so myself 絶対に, 間違いなく ▪ *If I say so myself* her bed was more comfortable than my bed. 絶対彼女のベッドの方が私のより心地よかった.

I'll say **1**《口》全くその通り, 本当に ▪ *I'll say* this is a good book! 全くこれはいい本だ.
2《口》(相手の言葉に相うちを打って)全くね, なるほど, もちろんです ▪ I think it's terrible.—*I'll say*. ひどいもんだね—全くね.

I'll say it [***he, she,*** etc.] ***is.*** 《口》全くだよ, その通りだ ▪ She is cute.—*I'll say she is*. あの子かわいいね—全くだね.

I'm not saying. お答えはできません ▪ Why were you absent yesterday?—*I'm not saying*. なぜきのう欠席したの?—お答えできません.

(***It***) ***does*** (***exactly***) ***what it says on the tin.*** 《口》《諺》うたい文句通りだ.

(***it***) ***goes without saying*** (***that***) (…は)言うまでもない ▪ *It goes without saying that* health is above wealth. 健康が富に勝ることは言うまでもない ▪ That *goes without saying*. そんなことは言うまでもない. ☞F cela va sans dire のなぞり.

it is said [***people say***] (***that***) (…)だそうだ, と言われている ▪ *It is said that* King Alfred burned the cakes. アルフレッド王はケーキをこがしたと言われる.

it [***that***] ***is saying a great deal*** それはたいした

S

ものだ; それは大変だ ▪ He never gets into debt, and *that is saying a great deal*. 彼は決して借金をしないが, それはたいしたことだ.

it says 《口》(書物などで筆者が)言っている ▪ *It says* in the Bible that you must not steal. 「盗むべからず」と聖書に書いてある ▪ Please, *it says* so in the book. 先生, 本にそう書いてあります.

it says much [***a lot***] ***for*** [***about***] *A* ***that*** ... はAがどんな人[物]であるかをよく表している ▪ *It says much about* the high quality of this camera *that* it is still in use today. このカメラが今日まだ使われているということは, このカメラの品質の良さをよく物語っている.

let it be said ...は言っておくほうがいい ▪ John had difficulty, *let it be said*, in reading and writing. これは言っておくほうがいいが, ジョンは読み書きが困難だった.

let us [***shall I, shall we***] ***say*** **1** たとえば ▪ You may learn to play the violin in, *let us* [*shall I*] *say*, three years. バイオリンをひくようになるには, そうだな, 3年はかかるだろうね.

2 ...ということにしよう ▪ *Let us say* that we will meet here again on Sunday. ここで日曜日にもう1度会うということにしよう.

not say much for ...にあまり感心しない ▪ I can*not say much for* the style. 文体にはあまり感心しない ▪ That does*n't say much for* his intelligence. それでは彼があまり利口だとは言えないね.

not to say **1** ...と言うほどではない ▪ No, papa, not old—*not to say* old. いいえパパ, 年をとってないわ—年をとっていると言うほどじゃないわ.

2 《口》...とは言わないまでも, と言ってよいくらい ▪ He is very frugal, *not to say* stingy. 彼は非常な倹約家で, けちと言ってもいいくらいだ ▪ The facts are singular, *not to say* grotesque. その事実は奇怪と言わないまでも奇妙なものだ.

people say (***that***) →it is said (that) (→SAY^2).

say a few words 《口》簡単なあいさつをする ▪ I was suddenly called upon to *say a few words*. 私は突然簡単なあいさつをすることを求められた.

say a good word for →WORD.

say a word for **1** ...のために一言弁じる ▪ I should be glad if you'd *say a word for* my brother. 弟のために一言弁じていただければうれしいです.

2 ...の代わりに話す ▪ He asked me if I would *say a word* or two *for* him. 彼は自分の代わりに話してもらえないかと私に頼んだ.

say a word in *a person's* ***ear*** 人に一言耳うちする ▪ In the matter of those shares I should like to *say a word in your ear*. この株券のことであなたに一言耳うちしたいのですが.

say (***for*** *a person*) ***to*** *do* 《米口》(人に)...せよと命じる ▪ The teacher *says to* come early. 先生は(我々に)早く来いと言っておられる ▪ He *said* (*for* me) *to* leave at once. 彼は(私に)すぐ帰れと言った. ☞for a person は文脈で明白なので, 通例省略される.

say I =I SAY! 2.

Say it with flowers! →FLOWER.

say nay [***no***]... いやだと言う, 拒絶する (*to*) ▪ His mother never *said nay to* any request. 彼の母親はどんな頼みにもいやと言わなかった.

say no more 《口》もうこれ[それ]以上言う必要はない ▪ He is an adult, so *say no more*! 彼は大人だから, もうそれ以上言う必要なし!

say ... over and over ...を繰り返して言う ▪ He *said* it *over and over* again. 彼はそれを何度も繰り返して言った.

say *one's* ***part*** [***lessons, work***] 習ったことを復誦する ▪ The boy was *saying his lessons*. 男の子は習ったことを復誦していた.

say *one's* ***piece*** 《口》思っていることをはっきり言う ▪ I *said my piece* about my working conditions to the boss. 上司にはっきりと労働条件について私の思っていることを言った.

say the right [***wrong***] ***thing*** うまい[まずい]ことを言う, 人を喜ばせる[怒らせる]ようなことを言う ▪ Sorry, did I *say the wrong thing*? すまない, まずいことを言ったかな.

say to *oneself* **1** 心の中で考える ▪ "This fellow is certainly very conceited," I *said to myself*. 「この男は確かにひどくうぬぼれている」と私は心の中で考えた《当人の前で》.

2 ひとりごとを言う ▪ I *said* the word softly *to myself*. 私は小声でその言葉をひとりごちた.

say well もっともなことを言う ▪ You *say well* that the firm is quite unreliable. あの会社がてんで信用がおけないと君が言うのはもっともだ.

Say what? 《米口》何ですって? ▪ She's getting married.—*Say what?* 彼女, 結婚するんだって—何ですって?

say when →WHEN.

say yes 同意する, 承諾する (*to*) ▪ There is no doubt they will *say yes to* your request. むろん彼らは君の頼みを聞いてくれるよ.

Says [***Sez***] ***you*** [***who***]***!*** 《口》まさか《不信の言葉》 ▪ I've seen an ET.—*Says you!* 僕は宇宙人を見たことがある—まさか.

shall I [***we***] ***say*** →let us SAY.

so to say →SO.

So you [etc.] ***say!*** それは全くかね《しばしば疑いを表す》 ▪ He goes to the club.—*So he says!* 彼はクラブへ行く—そう言っているけどね.

that is not to say (***that***) と言って...というのではない ▪ I am very busy today. *That is not to say* (*that*) I won't come. 今日はとても忙しい. と言って来ないというのじゃないよ.

That is saying a great deal. →It is SAYing a great deal.

that is to say **1** すなわち, 換言すれば ▪ He came home three hours later, *that is to say*, about eleven o'clock. 彼はそれから3時間後, すなわち11時ごろに帰宅した.

2 (あるいは)少なくとも ▪ He's coming, *that is to say*, he promised to. 彼は来る, 少なくとも来ると約

束した.

That's* [*It's*] *easier said than done. 《口》言うだけなら簡単だ.

That's what you say. それはあなたの言い草だ ▪ I had to work late today.—*That's what you say.* きょうは遅くまで働かねばならなかったんだ—それはあなたの言い分よ.

The less said* (*about it*) *the better. 言わぬが花.

there is much to be said for …には十分な理由[とりえ]がある ▪ *There is much to be said for* beginning now. 今始めることには十分な理由がある ▪ *There is much to be said for* this invention. この発明には十分なとりえがある.

there is no saying 何ともわからない ▪ *There is no saying* what will happen. 何が起こるやら何ともわからない. ☞there is no TELLING のほうが普通の言い方.

there is something* [*much*] *to be said 言い分は少し[たくさん]ある ▪ *There was something to be said* on both sides. 双方に言い分は幾分あった.

they say …だそうだ ▪ *They say* that he is a miser. 彼はけちんぼうだそうだ.

***though I say it* [*so*] (*myself*) (*who* [*that*] *should not* [*ought not to*] *say it*)** 私の口から言うのは変だが《自慢話の前置き》 ▪ *Though I say it* I am a man of my word. 私の口から言うのは変ですが私は約束の堅い男です ▪ It is a very pretty thing, *though I say it that shouldn't say it.* それは大変きれいなものです, 私の口から言うのも変ですが.

to say nothing of …は言うまでもなく ▪ She can dance, *to say nothing of* singing. 彼女は歌はもちろんダンスもできる ▪ He has no scholarship, *to say nothing of* experience. 彼は経験はおろか学問もない.

to say* (*the*) *truth*/*truth to say 実を言えば ▪ And, *to say the truth*, we have had enough of it. それに実を言えば我々はそれにはうんざりした.

***to say the* (*very*) *least* (*of it*)** 控え目に言っても ▪ Lying is a bad habit, *to say the least of it.* 嘘を言うのは, 控え目に言ってもよくない癖だ.

What do you say to ...? →WHAT.

What* [*Whatever*] *he says goes. 《口》彼の言うことは通る《誰も反対できない》.

whatever you say 《口》何でもあなたの言う通りにします; お好きなように ▪ Do it now!—*Whatever you say.* いますぐ, それやって!—承知しました.

***when all is said* (*and done*)** 何と言っても, 結局 ▪ It must be as the woman wills, *when all is said and done.* 結局その女性の希望通りにしなくてはなるまい.

Who can say? 誰にも予言できない ▪ *Who can say* that we shall never discover the fourth dimension? 我々に第四次元が見つけられないと誰にも予言できはしない.

Who says ...? 《口》…と誰が言ってるんだ, とは言わせないぞ ▪ *Who says* I can't do that? 私にそれができっこないなんて, 誰が言ってるんだ.

Who* [*What name*] *shall I say? 《口》どなた様でしょうか《取り次ぎで》 ▪ *Who shall I say*, please? どなた様でしょうか.

Who's to say ...? 《口》…だと誰が言える?, だとは誰も言えない ▪ *Who's to say* we wouldn't be able to do such a thing? 私たちにそんなことができないなんて誰が言える?

You can say that again. 《口》全くだ, まさにその通り ▪ He is rather difficult to talk to, isn't he?—*You can say that again!* 彼はひどく話しかけにくいね—全くだね.

***You can't say fairer* (*than that*).** 《英口》これ以上はむりだよ ▪ I'll give you just three thousand yen. *You can't say fairer than that.* 君に3千円だけやるよ. これ以上はむりだよ.

***you could say* (*that*)** …と言えないことはないね ▪ *You could say* he was blackmailed into stealing. 彼はゆすられて盗みを働いたと言えなくもないね.

***You don't say!*[*?*]** 《口》まさか!, あらほんと ▪ I saw a live mouse in the subway.—*You don't say!* 正真正銘のネズミを地下鉄で見かけたよ—まさか!

***You don't say so!*[*?*]** 《口》まさか, どうだか!《人の言ったことに驚いて発する言葉》 ▪ She was graduated from college at sixteen.—*You don't say so!* 彼女は16歳で大学を出たんだ—まさか!

You said it. ほんとにそうだね ▪ We need a new car.—*You said it.* 新車がいるね—ほんとにそうね.

saying /séɪɪŋ/ 名 ***as the saying is* [*goes*]** 俗に言う(ように), ことわざに言う(ように) ▪ I can see into a millstone, *as the saying is*. 私は俗に言う目から鼻へ抜けているのだ.

it's* [*that's*] *not saying much それほど大したことではない ▪ He is very competent but *that's not saying much.* 彼はすごく有能だけれど, まあ, それはそれほど言うほどのことではない.

scab /skæb/ 動 ***scab it*** 《米俗》非組合員として働く ▪ Their business was to watch the Jews that they did not *scab it*. 彼らの仕事はユダヤ人が非組合員として働かないように注視することであった.

scabbard /skǽbərd/ 名 ***throw* [*fling*] *away the scabbard*** 和睦しようという考えをきっぱり捨てる, あくまで戦う決心をする ▪ *The scabbard* seemed to *be thrown away* on both sides. 双方とも和睦しようという考えはきっぱり捨てたようであった. ☞「刀のさやを捨てる」が原義.

scaffold /skǽfəld|-fəʊld/ 名 ***die* [*perish*] *on the scaffold*** 死刑に処せられる ▪ Noble men have *died on the scaffold*. 高貴な人々が死刑に処せられてきた.

mount* [*go to*] *the scaffold 処刑台に登る ▪ *Mounting* now *the scaffold*, she attends the fatal stroke. 彼女は今や処刑台に登って, 死の一撃を待ち受ける.

send* [*bring*] *a person to the scaffold 人を処刑台に送る ▪ The King *sent* the man *to the scaffold* on a political charge. 王はその男を政治犯として処刑台に送った.

S

scald /skɔːld/ 動 ***be scalded to death*** やけどをして死ぬ ▪ He *was scalded to death* when the boiler exploded. 彼はボイラーが爆発したときやけどをして死んだ.

***scald** oneself* やけどする ▪ He sipped it, for fear of *scalding himself.* 彼はやけどしないように, それをすすりながら飲んだ.

scale[1] /skeɪl/ 名 ***be in the scale(s)*** (生命などが)風前のともし火である ▪ His life *was in the scales.* 彼の生命は風前のともし火であった.

hang [be] in the scale どちらとも決定しない ▪ Victory *was* long *in the scale.* 勝利は長いことどちらとも決定しなかった.

hold the scales even [equally] 公平に裁く ▪ God *holds the scales even* in his hands. 神は公平に裁きたもう.

on a scale of one to ten [1 to 10]《口》10点満点で, 10段階で ▪ How was your last quiz *on a scale of one to ten?* この前の小テスト, 10点満点で何点だったの?

throw ... on [into] the scale …を討論[競技]の相手[対象]とする ▪ We *threw* the environmental destruction *on the scale.* 我々は環境破壊を討論の対象とした.

tip the scales →TIP[3].

turn the scale(s) →TURN the balance.

scale[2] /skeɪl/ 名 ***remove the scales from [take the scales off]** a person's **eyes*** 人の目のかすみを取る, 誤りを悟らせる ▪ I hope in time *the scales* will *be removed from his eyes.* 奴がそのうち誤りを悟ってくれればと思う. ☞次の句から.

The scales fall [A scale falls] from** one's **[the] eyes. 目からうろこが落ちる, 誤りを悟る (《聖》*Acts* 9. 18) ▪ One may look at a person for years and not see the reality till *a scale falls from the eyes.* 人はある人間を何年見ていても目からうろこが落ちるまでは実際の姿が見えないものだ.

scale[3] /skeɪl/ 名 ***in [out of] scale*** つり合いがとれて[を失して] (*with*) ▪ The building is *in scale with* its surroundings. このビルはその周囲のものとつり合いがとれている.

on a large [gigantic, grand, vast] scale 大規模に, 大々的に ▪ They do construction work *on a large scale.* 彼らは大規模に土建業をしている.

on a small scale 小規模に, こじんまりと ▪ She keeps house *on a small scale.* 彼女はこじんまりと家計を取りしきっている.

on the [a] scale of …の縮尺にした ▪ This is a map *on the scale of* two inches to the mile. これは1マイルを2インチに縮尺した地図です.

run [sing] up the scale 音階を奏する ▪ Let me hear you *run up the scale.* 音階を奏して聞かせてください.

sink in the scale 落ち目になる ▪ As drink gradually took a stronger hold on the man, he *sank in the scale.* 男はだんだん酒におぼれるようになるにつれて, 落ち目になっていった.

to scale 一定の比例に応じて ▪ The floor plans are drawn *to scale.* この床の設計図は比例尺に合わせて描かれている.

scalp /skælp/ 名 ***after** a person's **scalp***《主に米》人をやっつけようとして ▪ He's coming *after my scalp.* 彼は僕をやっつけようとして来ているんだ. ☞scalp「北米先住民などが倒した敵の死体から戦利品としてはぎ取った頭皮」.

call for (**a person's**) scalp (人を)やっつけようとする, 復しゅうしようとする ▪ They were *calling for (our) scalps.* 彼らは(我々に)復しゅうしようとしていた.

have** a person's **scalp 人を負かす, やっつける ▪ He said he would either *have* our votes or *our scalps.* 彼は我々に投票してもらうか我々をやっつけるかのどっちかだと言った.

out for** a person's **scalp《主に米》人に復しゅうしようとして ▪ He'll be *out for your scalp.* 彼は君に復しゅうしようとする.

scamper /skǽmpər/ 名 ***take (a) scamper through*** …を大急ぎで読む[旅行する] ▪ I *took (a) scamper through* Dickens. 私はディケンズを大急ぎで読んだ.

scandal /skǽndəl/ 名 ***a scandal sheet***《米口》スキャンダル新聞, 暴露雑誌 ▪ This magazine is *a scandal sheet* full of murders and sex. この雑誌は殺人とセックスでいっぱいの暴露雑誌だ.

create a [become] scandal 醜聞になる ▪ If she leaves her husband she will certainly *create a scandal* in the village. 彼女が夫を捨てれば, きっと村でスキャンダルになるだろう.

make a scandal out of …を種に悪評を立てる ▪ He will surely *make a scandal out of* this. 彼はきっとこのことを種に悪評を立てることだろう.

talk scandal 陰口をたたく, 中傷する ▪ The women *talked scandal* about her. 女性たちは彼女の陰口をたたいた.

scant /skænt/ 形 ***scant of*** …が足りない, 不足して ▪ He is fat, and *scant of* breath. 彼は太っているので息を切らしている.

with scant courtesy ぞんざいに ▪ He was received *with scant courtesy.* 彼は適当に迎えられた.

scar /skɑːr/ 名 ***leave a scar*** (傷・不幸などの)あとを残す ▪ Such sorrows *leave a scar.* そのような悲しみは(心に)傷あとを残す.

scarce /skeərs/ 形 ***be as scarce as hen's teeth*** →(as) scarce as HEN's teeth.

make** oneself **scarce《口》立ち去る, 隠れる ▪ When his wife began to show me that she was tired of my company, I *made myself scarce.* 彼の奥さんが私の相手にあきたようなそぶりを見せ始めると, 私は退散した ▪ Just *make yourselves scarce,* all the lot of you. さあ誰もかもとっとと消えうせてくれ.

scarcely /skéərsli/ 副 ***scarcely any*** ほとんど何もない ▪ There is [are] *scarcely any.* ほとんど何もない ▪ *Scarcely any*body believes that. それを信じる者はほとんどいない.

scarcely ever →hardly EVER.

S

scarcely ... when [***before***] …するかしないうちに ▪I had *scarcely* said the word, *when* he entered. その言葉を発するか発しないうちに彼が入って来た ▪I had *scarcely* started *before* a man came up to me. 出かけるとすぐ男が一人近寄って来た.

scare[1] /skeər/ 名 ***give*** [***get***] ***a scare*** 《口》どぎもを抜く[抜かれる] ▪You did *give* me *a scare*. 本当に君にはどぎもを抜かれたよ.

throw a scare into *a person* 《米》人のどぎもを抜く, 人をぎくっとさせる ▪We fired over their heads to *throw a scare into* them. 彼らをぎくっとさせるために頭上に発砲した.

scare[2] /skeər/ 動 ***be scared at*** …を見て[聞いて]おびえる ▪They *were scared at* the strange noise. 彼らはその妙な音を聞いておびえた.

be scared shitless/《米》***be scared shit*** すごくおびえる ▪I *was scared shitless* because someone was moving around upstairs. 誰かが2階で動き回っていてすごく怖かった.

more scared than hurt 取り越し苦労をする ▪They found themselves *more scared than hurt* by his threats. 彼らは彼のおどしで取り越し苦労をしているのに気づいた.

scare *a person* ***out of*** *his* ***life*** 極度におびえさせる ▪The sight of that fire *scared* me *out of my life*. その火事の光景は私を極度におびえさせた.

scare *a person* ***out of*** *his* ***senses*** [***wits***] 人をびっくりさせて度を失わせる ▪Such practices *scare* the multitudes *out of their wits*. そのような慣習は大衆をびっくりさせて度を失わせる.

scare *a person* ***stiff*** [***silly, to death***] 人をひどくおびやかす ▪The wild midnight ride *scared* him *stiff*. 真夜中の無謀運転は彼をひどくおびやかした.

scare the pants off *a person* →PANTS.

scare the shit [***daylights, hell***] ***out of*** …をひどく怖がらせる ▪Don't *scare the shit out of* me, putting on such a mask. そんな仮面をつけて私を怖がらせないで.

scare *a person* ***witless*** 人を非常に怖がらせる[心配させる](→be scared WITLESS) ▪She *scared* me *witless* when she talked about the exploration of a cave. 彼女は洞窟探検の話をして私を非常に怖がらせた.

scared /skeərd/ 形 ***be scared of*** 《口》…を怖がる ▪What *are* you *scared of*? 何を怖がっているのか.

run scared 《米口》[[主に進行形で]] 負けを予想している; おじけづいている ▪The game is ours; the other team *are running scared*. この試合はこっちのものだ. 相手チームはおじけづいている.

scarlet /skɑ́:rlət/ 形 ***a scarlet woman*** [***lady***] 多情な女, 売春婦 ▪She was dubbed *the scarlet lady* of the movie business. 彼女は映画界の淫婦と称せられた. ☞《聖》*Rev.* 17の「緋色の淫婦」《後にローマカトリック教会に対する蔑称》から.

blush [***flush***] ***scarlet*** (恥ずかしさなどで)真っ赤になる ▪His cheeks *flushed scarlet* with shame. 彼は恥ずかしさでほおが真っ赤になった.

scarlet fever **1** 猩(しょう)紅熱; ▪Her little son died of *scarlet fever* at age 3. 彼女の幼い息子は3歳のとき猩紅熱で死んだ.

2《俗・戯》(女性の)軍人へのあこがれ ▪Ladies who run after military society are said to have *scarlet fever*. 軍人を追い回している女性たちは軍人熱にかかっていると言われる. ☞イギリス軍隊の制服の色が赤であるところから.

scat /skæt/ 名 ***like scat/quicker than scat*** 《米口》大急ぎで ▪But the scheme fell through *like scat*. しかし企てはたちまち失敗した.

scathe /skéɪð/ 名 ***do*** [***work***] ***scathe*** 害を加える (*to*) ▪They were *doing* more *scathe to* themselves than to their enemies. 彼らは敵というよりも自分自身に害を加えていた.

without scathe 《古》害がなく, つつがなく ▪The firm came through the crisis *without scathe*. 会社はその危機を無事に切り抜けた.

scatter /skǽtər/ 動 ***scatter far and wide*** [《文》***to the*** (***four***) ***winds***] 四方八方にまき散らす; 散り散りになる ▪The family of twelve *scattered far and wide*. 12人の家族の者は四方八方に散り散りになった.

scavenger /skǽvəndʒər/ 名 ***act the scavenger*** **1** 掃除屋をする ▪Someone must *act the scavenger* and clean up this room. 誰か掃除屋をしてこの部屋をきれいにしなければならない.

2 醜聞あさりをする ▪I dislike to *act the scavenger* in the ranks of society. 私は社会の各階層で醜聞あさりをするのはいやだ.

scene /si:n/ 名 ***a change of scene*** 環境の変化; 転地 ▪He went abroad for *a change of scene*. 彼は環境の変化を求めて外国に出かけた ▪*A change of scene* would do him good. 転地をすれば彼のよい療養になるのだが.

behind the scenes **1** 舞台裏で ▪The actor spoke to a man *behind the scenes*. 俳優は舞台裏の男に話しかけた.

2 裏面に, 黒幕に, 内幕に通じて ▪She was *behind the scenes* in many fashionable families. 彼女は多くの上流家庭の内幕に通じていた ▪He knows what is going on *behind the scenes*. 彼は裏で何が行われているかを知っている.

3 秘密に ▪A decision was reached *behind the scenes*. ある決定が秘密になされた.

enter [***appear, arrive, be, come***] ***on the scene*** 舞台に現れる; 登場する; (一般に)姿を現す ▪Whereupon his solicitor *came on the scene*. そこで彼の弁護士が登場した.

have a scene (泣いたりわめいたり)大騒ぎされる ▪We *had a scene* when I scolded her. 私が彼女をしかると, 大騒ぎされた.

lay the scene 場面を設定する ▪*The scene* of the novel *is laid* in Paris. 小説の場面はパリに置かれている.

make [***create***] ***a scene*** (泣いたりわめいたり)大騒

ぎをする ▪ In her jealousy she *made a scene* before her husband. 嫉妬にかられて彼女は夫の前で大騒ぎした. ☞[F] faire une scène のなぞり.

make the scene 《米俗》出席する, そこへ行く ▪ I am eager to *make the scene.* そこへぜひ行きたい.

not** a person's* ***scene 《俗》人の好みに合わない, 人にとって関心がない ▪ Motherhood is*n't my scene.* 母性愛なんて私には関心がない.

quit the scene **1** 退場する ▪ It was clear she could not *quit the scene* of action. 彼女が活動の舞台を去ることができないのは明白だった.

2 《口》死ぬ ▪ He *quit the scene* just before his 50th birthday. 彼は50歳の誕生日の直前に死亡した.

set the scene **1** 場所[状況]について詳しく説明する ▪ The guide began to *set the scene.* ガイドが場所について詳しい説明を始めた.

2 (…への)道を開く (*for*) ▪ His support *set the scene for* the meeting. 彼の支援によって会談への道が開かれた.

steal the scene =steal the SHOW.

(this) scene of things この世 ▪ Who would enter upon this tragical *scene of things*? 悲劇的なこの世に生まれてきたい者があろうか.

scenery /síːnəri/ 名 ***chew (up) the scenery*** 《米俗》大げさにふるまう ▪ When he praised my picture, he sure was *chewing the scenery.* 彼は私の絵をほめたとき, 確かに大げさにふるまっていた.

scent[1] /sent/ 名 ***a cold scent*** (臭跡の)かすかなにおい《比喩的にも》 ▪ He is now at *a cold scent.* 彼はもう手がかりを失いそうになっている.

carry a [the] scent **1** (土地が)臭跡をとどめている ▪ The surrounding country *carrying a good scent*, a bad hunter is of little use here. あたりの土地は強い臭跡をとどめているので, へたな猟犬はここらではあまり役にたたない.

2 (猟犬が)臭跡をたどる ▪ The hound *carried the scent* to the fox's kennel. 猟犬はキツネのねぐらまで臭跡をたどって行った.

follow (up) the scent 臭跡をたどる; 手がかりを追及する ▪ The dogs are *following up the scent* of a fox. 犬どもはキツネの臭跡をたどっている ▪ I am still *following the* same *scent.* 私はまだ同じ手がかりを追及しています.

get (a, the) scent of (犬が)…をかぎつける; (人が)…に感づく, をけどる ▪ The police had *got scent of* the intended affray. 警察は騒ぎの企てをけどっていた.

have (a) scent 臭跡を追っている; 手がかりをつかんでいる ▪ He *has a scent* of it. 彼はその手がかりをつかんでいる.

have a scent for 《口》…を見つける勘がある ▪ He *has a* good *scent for* young talent. 彼は若いタレントを見つけるすぐれた勘がある.

lay … on [upon] the scent → put … on the SCENT.

lose the scent (猟犬が)臭跡を失う; (人が)手がかりを失う (*of*) ▪ You have *lost the scent of* your comrade. 君は君の同志の足どりを見失ったのだ.

off the scent 手がかりを失って ▪ I think the police are *off the scent.* 警察は手がかりを失っているのだと思う.

on the scent 臭跡を追って; かぎつけて, 手がかりを得て (*of*) ▪ The hounds are *on the scent.* 猟犬は臭跡を追っている ▪ The police are *on the scent of* a new plot. 警察は新たな陰謀をかぎつけている.

pursue (up) the scent → follow (up) the SCENT.

put** a person* ***off the scent/put** a person* ***on a false [wrong] scent 人をまく, まどわす ▪ She wished to *put* him *off the scent* by this false announcement. 彼女はこの嘘の話で彼をまどわしたいと思った.

put [lay] … on [upon] the scent (猟犬)に臭跡を追わせる; (人)に手がかりをつかませる ▪ He immediately called in the dogs, and *put* them *on the scent.* 彼はすぐ猟犬を呼び入れて臭跡を追わせた ▪ The umbrella he carried with him *put* the police *on the scent.* 彼が持っていた傘から足がついた.

recover the scent 失った臭跡[手がかり]を見つける ▪ The hounds were for some time at fault. They soon, however, *recovered the scent.* 猟犬はしばらくまごまごしていた. が, やがて失った臭跡を見つけた.

The scent has gone cold. その情報はもう役に立たない.

throw** a person* ***off the scent 人をまく, 人の追及をかわす ▪ He *threw* his pursuer *off the scent.* 彼は追跡者をまいた.

scent[2] /sent/ 動 ***scent the air*** **1** (花が)あたりに良いにおいを放つ ▪ Roses *scent the air.* バラはあたりに良いにおいを放つ.

2 あたりの空気をかぐ ▪ The dog lifted its head and *scented the air.* 犬は頭を上げてあたりの空気をかいだ.

scepter, 《英》 **sceptre** /séptər/ 名 ***sway the scepter*** →SWAY[2].

wield [hold] the scepter 君臨する, 支配する ▪ Queen Victoria *wielded the scepter* for over sixty years. ビクトリア女王は60年以上も君臨した. ☞帝王の scepter (笏(しゃく))は王位の象徴.

schedule[1] /skédʒuːl|ʃédjuːl/ 名 ***according to schedule*** 予定表通りに ▪ The work is *according to schedule.* 仕事は予定表通りに進んでいる.

behind (the) schedule 《米》予定より遅れて ▪ The train was in an hour *behind schedule.* 列車は定時より1時間遅れて入って来た.

off schedule 予定が狂って ▪ The timetable is already badly *off schedule.* 時刻表はすでに大いに予定が狂っている.

on (the) schedule/on scheduled time/up to schedule 時刻表通りに, 定時に ▪ The train was in *on schedule.* 列車は定時に入って来た ▪ Such things don't move *on scheduled time.* そのような事は時刻表通りに運びはしない.

schedule[2] /skédʒuːl|ʃédjuːl/ 動 ***be scheduled for*** 《米》 **1** …の予定である, することになってい

る ▪ He *is scheduled for* a speech. 彼は一言話すことになっている.

2 (日時が)…に予定されている ▪ The game *is scheduled for* Saturday. 試合は土曜日に予定されている.

***be scheduled to** do* 《米》…する予定である ▪ He *was scheduled to* attend the luncheon. 彼は午さん会に出る予定であった.

scheme /ski:m/ 名 ***in the*** (***grand*** [***great***]) ***scheme of things*** 物事の性質上, 当然 ▪ They will attain their rightful place *in the scheme of things.* 彼らは当然正当な地位を得るだろう.

the best-laid schemes of mice and men みなで慎重に練った案 (Burns, *To a Mouse*) ▪ *The best-laid schemes of mice and men* often go wrong. みなで慎重に練った案でも頓挫することがよくある.

schmeer /ʃmɪər/ 名 ***the whole schmeer*** 《俗》全て, あらゆる側面[要素] ▪ He did it, considering *the whole schemeer.* 彼はすべてを考慮してそうした. ☞schmeer はイディッシュ語で smear, smudge (汚れ, しみ)の意味.

scholar /skɑ́lər|skɔ́lə/ 名 ***be no scholar*** 《口》ろくに読み書きもできない ▪ He *is no scholar.* 彼はろくに読み書きもできない. ☞「彼は学者ではない」という意味ではない.

school[1] /sku:l/ 名 ***a school of thought*** 見解を同じくするグループ ▪ As to that subject, there are two *schools of thought.* その問題については二つの違った考え方の人々がいる.

after school 放課後 ▪ He was kept *after school.* 彼は放課後残された.

at school **1** 学校で, 授業中で ▪ He is clever *at school.* 彼は学校でできがよい.

2 就学中で ▪ He is *at school* in England. 彼はイギリスで教育を受けている.

be in for *one's* [***the***] ***schools*** →sit for one's SCHOOLs.

go to school 学校へ行く; 入学する ▪ She was a vixen when she *went to school.* 彼女は学校へ行っていたころは口やかましい女だった ▪ The child is old enough to *go to school.* その子は入学していい年頃だ.

go to school to [***in***] …から学ぶ ▪ Why not *go to school to* the wisdom of bees and ants? ミツバチやアリの知恵からなぜ学ばないのか ▪ In the 14th century English poetry *went to school in* French poetry. 14世紀にイギリスの詩はフランスの詩から学んだ.

have school [***no school***] 授業がある[ない] ▪ We *have school* till 4. 4時まで授業がある.

in school 学校で; 在学中で ▪ We recite lessons *in school* every day. 私たちは学校で毎日学課を暗誦します ▪ The boys are still *in school.* 子供たちはまだ在学中です.

in [***out of***] ***the schools*** 《英大学》学士試験を受けて[終えて] ▪ I am going *out of the schools.* 学士試験を終えるところだ. ☞オックスフォード大学の用語.

keep (***a***) ***school*** (私立)学校を経営する ▪ He *keeps school* at Netherdale. 彼はネザーデイルで学校を経営している ▪ The Misses Donaldson *keep* an infant *school.* ドナルドスン姉妹は幼稚園を経営している.

leave school **1** 退学する ▪ He had to *leave school* at the early age of twelve. 彼は早くも12歳のときに退学しなければならなかった.

2 卒業する ▪ He went into business on *leaving school.* 彼は学校を出るとすぐ実務についた.

not care whether school keeps or not 《米口》どうなってもかまわない ▪ I *don't care whether school keeps or not.* 私はどうなってもかまわない.

of the old school 旧式の, 旧弊の ▪ Father was definitely *of the old school.* 父は断然旧弊だった.

out of school 学校を出て, 卒業して ▪ At that time I was only a girl just *out of school.* 当時私は学校を出たばかりの一少女にすぎなかった.

out of the schools →in the SCHOOLs.

put … to school **1** (子供)を学校へ上げる ▪ My sister *was put to school* in a nunnery. 私の妹は修道院の学校へ上げられた.

2 …を学ばせる; (年長者)をおこがましくもたしなめる ▪ My child *put* his mother *to school.* 私の子供がおこがましくも母親をたしなめた.

put A to school to B AにBの教えを受けさせる, 師事させる ▪ We'll *put* you *to school to* an ant. 我々は君をアリに教えを受けさせてやろう.

send … to school (子供)を学校へ上げる ▪ My father *sent* me *to school* to Paris. 父は私をパリの学校へ上げた.

sit [***be in***] ***for*** *one's* [***the***] ***schools*** 《英大学》学位試験を受ける ▪ He is *sitting for his schools* now. 彼は今学位試験を受けている. ☞オックスフォード大学の用語.

teach (***a***) ***school*** 学校の教師をする ▪ He *taught school* for three years. 彼は3年間学校の教師をした.

tell tales out of school 秘密を外にもらす, 恥を外にさらす ▪ I made them angry with me for *telling tales out of school.* 私は秘密を外にもらしたというので彼らを怒らせてしまった.

the old [***new***] ***school*** 保守[革新]派, 旧式[新式]の人々 ▪ My father belongs to *the old school.* 父は保守派の人間です ▪ He was trained in *the new school.* 彼は新式の教育を受けた.

the school of hard knocks 《米口》いろいろな経験をなめる生活 ▪ It looks as if they are fraternity brothers in *the school of hard knocks.* 彼らはいろいろな経験をなめる生活における仲間といったふうだ.

school[2] /sku:l/ 動 ***school*** *oneself* 修養する ▪ He *schooled himself* against showing any emotion. 彼は感情を表さないように修養した.

schoolmaster /skú:lmæstər|-mɑ̀:s-/ 名 ***The schoolmaster is abroad.*** 教育は普及している; 《戯》教育は留守になっている ▪ He lived in those dark days, before *the schoolmaster was abroad*. 彼は教育がまだ普及していなかった,あの暗黒時代に住んでいた. ☞1828年1月30日の Times 紙所載の Lord Brougham の言葉から.

s(c)htum /ʃtʊm/ 名 ***keep s(c)htum*** 《英口》何も言わない ▪We'd better *keep schtum* about this. このことについては何も言わないほうがいい. ☞schtum はイディッシュ語で,ドイツ語 stumm = silent が起源.

science /sáɪəns/ 名 ***blind** a person **with science*** 人を煙に巻く《専門用語でごまかす》 ▪The doctor *blinded* her *with science* and didn't tell her the real name of her disease. 医師は彼女を専門用語で煙に巻いて本当の病名を教えなかった.

have [get]...down to a science 《米戯》...の知識[技術]が完璧である ▪She always says she *has* shopping *down to a science*. 買物知識は完璧よ,と彼女はいつも言う.

the noble science (of defence) → the NOBLE art (of defence).

scintilla /sɪntílə/ 名 ***not a scintilla of*** 少しの...もない ▪There is *not a scintilla of* truth in the story. その話には真実はみじんもない.

scissors /sízərz/ 名 ***give** a person **scissors*** 《米口》人をやっつける,しかりつける ▪He is dead bitter against us, so you must *give* him *scissors*! 彼は我々にひどく悪意を抱いているからやっつけてやれ.

scissors and paste (はさみとのりの)つぎはぎ細工《独創的でない書物など》 ▪He's a writer of a kind, but I fancy it's mostly *scissors and paste*. 彼はまあ作家ということだが,たいていはつぎはぎ細工だと思うね.

scoff /skɑf|skɔf/ 名 ***be the scoff of*** ...の物笑いになる ▪He *was the scoff of* the town. 彼は町の物笑いになった.

scold[1] /skoʊld/ 名 ***a common scold*** 近所迷惑ながみがみ女 ▪The woman was *a common scold*. その女性は近所迷惑ながみがみ女だった.

be a scold 口やかましく言う ▪Now, don't *be a scold*. さあ,口やかましく言わないでください.

scold[2] /skoʊld/ 動 ***scold** a person **out of doors*** がみがみ言って人を外へ追い出す ▪She had *scolded* her husband one day *out of doors*. 彼女はある日のことがみがみ言って夫を外へ追い出した.

scold** a person **quiet 人をしかって静かにさせる ▪The teacher *scolded* the pupils *quiet*. 先生は生徒をしかって静かにさせた.

scoop[1] /sku:p/ 名 ***at one scoop*** ひとすくいで;一挙に ▪He won £50 *at one scoop*. 彼は一挙に50ポンド得た.

get the scoop (on) 《口》(...の)特ダネを得る ▪I *got the scoop on* the new building. その新しいビルのスクープ情報を得たよ.

make a scoop **1** 特ダネをとる ▪It was *the* best *scoop* he'd ever *made*. それは彼がまだとったこともないすばらしい特ダネだった.

2《口》大儲けをする ▪We *made a scoop* over that investment. 我々はその投資で大儲けした.

on the scoop 《俗》酒を飲んで,放蕩して ▪He had gone *on the scoop* with his friends. 彼は友人といっしょに酒を飲み回った.

What's the scoop on ...? ...になにか変わったことでもあるのかい? ▪*What's the scoop on* him? Is he going to quit the job? 彼になにか変わったことでもあるの? 仕事を辞めるつもりだとか?

scoop[2] /sku:p/ 動 ***scoop the pool*** 賭け金をかっさらう;賞金を一人占めにする ▪He *scooped the pool* at the shooting match. その射撃大会で彼は賞金を一手にかっさらった.

scoot /sku:t/ 名 ***make a scoot*** 《俗》突進する ▪We *made a scoot* for the road. 我々は道の方へ突進した.

scope /skoʊp/ 名 ***beyond [out of, outside] the scope of*** ...の及ばぬところで,の範囲外で ▪Mathematics is *out of my scope*. 数学は全く私の及ばぬところだ.

give free [full] scope ...を自由[十分]に働かせる (*to*) ▪I *gave full scope to* my imagination. 私は想像力を十二分に働かせた.

give [have] scope for ...を発揮する場を与える[がある] ▪He *has* no *scope for* his abilities. 彼は手腕をふるう場がない ▪Football will *give* you *scope for* courage. フットボールは勇気を発揮する場をくれる.

within the scope of ...の及ぶところで,の範囲内で ▪It falls *within the scope of* the present article. それはこの論文の範囲内に入る.

score[1] /skɔ:r/ 名 ***by [in] scores*** たくさんに,多数 ▪They are deserting *by scores*. 彼らは群れをなして持ち場を去っている ▪People came *in scores*. 人々がたくさんやって来た.

clear [pay (off), quit, settle, wipe off, wipe out] a score [scores] 支払いをすます;恨みを晴らす (*with*) ▪You do nothing to *quit scores with* them. 君はあの連中に恨みを晴らすようなことは何もしない ▪I have *an* old *score* to *settle with* him. 彼には遺恨がある.

Death pays all scores. 《諺》死ねば勘定はすむ,「死者を恨まず」.

go off [set off, start] at score **1** (馬などが)急に全速力で走りだす ▪His horse *went off at score*. 彼の馬は急に全速力で走りだした.

2 (人が)急に威勢よくやり[話し]だす ▪He *set off at score* with a song. 彼は急に威勢よく歌を歌いだした.

go off full score (馬などが)急に全速力で走りだす ▪The bull picked himself up and *went off full score*. 雄牛は身を起こして急に全速力で走りだした.

keep on at a score 全速力で走り続ける ▪He *kept on at a score* to follow Bob. 彼はボブのあとについて行くために全速力で走り続けた.

keep the score 点数を記録する ▪Who is going to *keep the score*? 誰が点数を記録するのか.

know what the score is/know the score 《口》注意を怠らない;事情に通じている ▪In this job we need someone who *knows what the score is*. この仕事には注意を怠らない人が必要だ ▪He

S

knows the score. 彼は事情に通じている.

make a score 得点する ▪ Smith *made a score* in the second half. 後半戦でスミスが得点した.

make a score* [*scores*] *off 《俗》…をやっつける, へこます ▪ The politician is clever at *making scores off* hecklers. あの議員は見事にやじをへこます.

make a score off *one's* ***own bat*** (助力なしに)独力でやる, ひとり立ちする ▪ He *made a score off his own bat.* 彼は独力でやった.

on *a person's* ***score*** 人の勘定で ▪ We drank a pint *on his score.* 彼の勘定で1パイント飲んだ.

on that* [*this*] *score その[この]ために, その[この]点では ▪ *On that score* you need have no further worry. その点はもうご心配には及びません.

on the score of …のために; の点で ▪ It is advantageous *on the score of* economy. それは経済という点で有利だ ▪ He retired from service *on the score of* illness. 彼は病気のために引退した.

quit* [*pay* (*off*), *settle*] *a score →clear a SCORE.

run up a score 《口》借金をためる ▪ I'm not going to *run up a score* with any of them. 私は彼らの誰にも借金をためないつもりだ.

scores of 多くの ▪ I've been there *scores of* times. 私はたびたびそこへ行ったことがある.

set off* [*start*] *at score →go off at SCORE.

settle an old score 恨みを晴らす ▪ They turned on one another to *settle old scores.* 彼らは恨みを晴らそうと互いに攻撃し合った.

three score and ten →THREESCORE (years) and ten.

What's the score? 今何点?; 《口》状況はどう?

***wipe off* [*out*] *a score* [*scores*]** →clear a SCORE.

score[2] /skɔːr/ 動 ***be where*** *one* ***scores*** (主語)が得をするところである ▪ Now, I've got the sun in my eyes. That *is where* you *score.* 今僕の目に日が当たっている. そこが君にとって有利なところだ.

***score points* [*a point*] *off* [*against, over*]** *a person* (議論・応答などで)人を負かす, やりこめる ▪ I *scored points off* him in the debate. 私は討論で彼をやりこめた.

scorn[1] /skɔːrn/ 名 ***heap* [*pour*] *scorn on*** 《米》…をあざける ▪ She *poured scorn on* his dream to travel through space. 彼女は彼の宇宙旅行の夢をあざけった.

hold ... in scorn/hold ... up to scorn …を軽蔑する ▪ They *hold* him *in* high *scorn.* 彼らは彼をばかにしきっている ▪ He *holds* everybody *up to scorn.* 彼はすべての人を軽蔑する.

laugh ... to scorn …をあざ笑う ▪ He *laughed to scorn* their furious pride. 彼は彼らのすさまじい自尊心をあざ笑った.

point the finger of scorn at …をあざ笑う ▪ Let no one *point the finger of scorn at* such a woman. そのような女性を誰もあざ笑ってはいけない.

think scorn of …を軽蔑する ▪ He *thinks scorn of* wastefulness in his superiors. 彼は目上の者のむだ使いを軽蔑している.

with scorn 軽蔑して ▪ He dismissed the proposal *with scorn.* 彼はその提案を軽蔑してはねつけた.

scorn[2] /skɔːrn/ 動 ***scorn delights and live laborious days*** →DELIGHT[1].

scorner /skɔ́ːrnər/ 名 ***sit in the seat of the scorner*** 宗教をあざける(《聖》*Ps.* 1. 1) ▪ Those persons habitually *sit in the seat of the scorner.* その人たちは常に宗教をあざけっている.

scot /skɑt|skɔt/ 名 ***pay* (*for*)** (*one's, a person's*) ***scot*** 勘定を払う; 責任を果たす ▪ He was wheedled into *paying their scot.* 彼は口車に乗せられてその連中の勘定を払わされた ▪ He *paid his scot* by reciting some verses. 彼は詩をいくつか暗唱して責めをふさいだ.

pay* (*off*) *scot and lot 分相応の税を納める; 《口》皆済する ▪ The election was free to every one that *paid scot and lot.* この選挙は分相応の税を納めた者はすべて自由に行うことができた ▪ I'll *pay* you *off scot and lot* by and by. そのうちにあなたに皆済します. ☞scot and lot「昔の英国の市民税」.

scotch /skɑtʃ|skɔtʃ/ 動 ***scotch, not kill*** 生殺しで息の根を止めない (cf. Sh., *Macb.* 3. 2. 13) ▪ The snake *is scotched, not killed.* そのヘビは生殺しで息の根を止められてない.

scot-free /skɑ̀tfríː|skɔ̀t-/ 形 ***go* [*get away, get off, escape*] *scot-free*** **1** 税を逃れる ▪ Lots of people *escape scot-free.* 多くの人が税を逃れている.

2 《口》罰せられずにすむ, 無事に逃げる, 無事にすむ ▪ The notorious offender has *got off scot-free.* その名うての犯罪者は罰せられずに逃げきった.

scout /skaʊt/ 名 ***a good scout*** 《米口》理解のある人, 頼りになる人 ▪ Dad's *a good* old *scout* and he's pretty sure to do it. パパは理解のある人だから, まず大丈夫そうしてくれるさ.

in* [*on*] (*the*) *scout 偵察をして ▪ I set myself *on the scout* as often as possible. 私はできるだけしばしば偵察に出て行った.

on the scout 《米口》(警察につかまらないように)あちこち逃げ回って ▪ Ben spent some four years *on the scout,* after which he gave himself up. ベンは約4年間あちこち逃げ回っていたあとで, 自首した.

scrabble /skrǽbəl/ 動 ***scrabble a living*** どうにか暮らしていく ▪ He *scrabbled a living* as a part-time teacher. 彼は非常勤講師としてどうにか暮らしていった.

scramble /skrǽmbəl/ 動 ***scramble to*** *one's* ***feet*** 急いで立ち上がる ▪ He *scrambled to his feet* at the sound. 彼はその音を聞くとあわただしく立ち上がった.

scran /skræn/ 名 ***out on the scran*** 《俗》物乞いをして ▪ The old man was *out on the scran.* 老人は物乞いをしていた.

scrap[1] /skræp/ 名 ***a scrap of a ...*** (愛情・軽蔑をこめて)小さな, ちっちゃな ▪ He is still *a scrap of a* baby. 彼はまだちっちゃな赤んぼうだ.

a scrap of paper 《皮肉》紙くず同然の条約 ▪ He no more dreamt of honoring *his scrap of paper*. 彼はもう彼の結んだ紙くず同然の条約を履行しようとは夢にも思っていなかった. ☞1914年8月ドイツがスイスの中立を犯したときのドイツ首相の言葉から.

not a scrap 少しも…しない ▪ I don't care *a scrap*. 私はちっともかまわない ▪ *Not a scrap* of meat was left on board. 肉はひときれも食卓に残っていなかった.

throw … on the scrap heap 《口》[[主に受身で]] (物)を廃棄する, (人)をお払い箱にする ▪ They are afraid they'll *be thrown on the scrap heap*. 彼らはお払い箱になるのではと心配している.

scrap[2] /skræp/ 名 ***get into a scrap*** 《俗》けんかをする ▪ He *got into a scrap* in a barroom. 彼はバーでけんかをした.

have a (bit of) scrap with 《俗》…と争う ▪ I *had a (bit of) scrap with* a friend. 私は友人と争った.

scrape[1] /skreɪp/ 名 ***a bow and a scrape*** 右足を後ろに引いておじぎをすること ▪ I made him *a bow and a scrape*. 私は彼に右足を後ろに引いておじぎをした.

get into a scrape [scrapes] 窮地に陥る ▪ He has *got into a* great *scrape*. 彼はひどく困ったはめに陥った.

get** a person **out of** his **scrapes 《口》人を窮地から助け出す ▪ Don't expect me to *get* you *out of your scrapes*. 僕が君を窮地から助け出してやるなどと当てにしないでくれ.

in [out of] a scrape 窮地に陥って[を脱して] ▪ He is always *in a scrape* about money. 彼はいつも金のことで困っている ▪ I congratulated myself on my dexterity in getting *out of the scrape*. 私はうまくその窮地を脱したことをうれしく思った.

keep out of scrapes 窮地に陥らないようにする ▪ Take care and *keep out of scrapes*. 気をつけて窮地に陥らないようにしなさい.

scrape[2] /skreɪp/ 動 ***bow and scrape*** →BOW[4].

pinch and scrape/ scrape and screw [save] つめに火をともすように倹約する ▪ He has to *pinch and scrape* for his children. 彼は子供たちのためにつめに火をともすように倹約しなければならない.

scrape a bow ぎごちなくおじぎする ▪ The old gentleman *scraped a bow* on being introduced to the lady. 老紳士はその婦人に紹介されるとぎごちなくおじぎした.

scrape a living →scrape out a LIVING.

scrape (up) (an) acquaintance (通例紹介なしに)むりに知り合いになる(*with*) ▪ He contrived to *scrape acquaintance with* certain smugglers. 彼は取り入ってむりにある密輸業者らと近づきになった.

scrap heap /skrǽphìːp/ 名 ***on the scrap heap*** (…が)捨てられて ▪ Those torn books can go *on the scrap heap*. この破れた本はごみためにに捨ててもよい ▪ My father was thrown *on the scrap heap* because he became sixty-five. 父は65歳になったのでくずのようにお払い箱にされた.

scratch[1] /skrætʃ/ 名 ***a scratch of the pen*** 一筆, 署名 ▪ It will be yours by *a scratch of the pen*. 署名一つで君のものになります.

at scratch →from SCRATCH.

at the scratch いざという時に ▪ He was brave *at the scratch*. 彼はいざという時に勇敢だった.

bring** a person **(up) to (the) scratch 人を決然と対戦させる; 人にはっきりと決断させる ▪ He could not *bring* himself *to the scratch* for a second round. 彼は第2ラウンドは決然と対戦することができなかった ▪ She hopes to *bring* him *up to the scratch* this evening. 彼女は今晩こそは彼にはっきりした態度をとらせたいと願っている. ☞scratch「ボクシングの試合線」.

come to [toe] (the) scratch = come (up) to (the) SCRATCH 1.

come (up) to (the) scratch **1** 試合線に立つ; 定時に姿を見せる, ずるけない ▪ Finally I consented to *come up to the scratch*. とうとう私は定時に行くことに同意した.

2 期待に添う ▪ Her cooking didn't always *come up to scratch*. 彼女の料理はいつも期待に添うとは言えなかった.

from [at] scratch [[しばしば start を伴って]] 出発線から, 最初から; 無から ▪ He has won three races *from scratch*. 彼は最初から3勝した ▪ We had to *start from scratch* rebuilding our house. 我々は家の建て直しをいちから始めなければならなかった.

get [bring] … up to scratch 《英口》(物)を満足な状態にする ▪ I'll be able to *bring* those works *up to scratch* by next week. 来週までにはそれらの作品を満足のいく状態にすることができるよ.

no great scratch 《俗》あまりたいしたものじゃない ▪ They ain't *no great scratch*. 彼らはたいしたものじゃない.

up to scratch 仕事をやれる状態で; 標準に達して ▪ I've had influenza, and am still not *up to scratch*. 僕はインフルエンザにかかっていたので, まだ仕事をやれるまでになっていない ▪ Her acting was right *up to scratch*. 彼女の演技は十分標準に達していた.

when [till] it comes to the scratch いざという時になると[なるまで] ▪ He was brave *till it came to the scratch*. 彼はいざという時になるまでは勇敢だった.

scratch[2] /skrætʃ/ 動 ***scratch a hit*** 《野球》やっと1塁まで行けるヒットを放つ ▪ Another *scratched a hit*. もう一人がやっと1塁まで行けるヒットを放った.

scratch a living かろうじて生計を立てる ▪ He *scratches a living* by selling from door to door. 彼は家から家へ売り歩いてかろうじて生計を立てている.

Scratch a Russian, and you (will) find a Tartar. 《諺》文明人もひと皮むけば野蛮人.

scratch** a person's **eyes out 人の目玉をえぐり出す《嫉妬心からのおどしによく用いる》 ▪ If I meet that woman, I'll *scratch her eyes out*! あの女に会ったら，目玉をえぐり出してやる.

scratch for *oneself* 《米口》自分で自分の世話をする，自分の利益を求める ▪ Then each one had to *scratch for himself*. そこで誰もが自分で自分の世話をしなければならなかった.

scratch gravel 《米口》 **1** 大急ぎで行く，去る ▪ I *scratched gravel* for Tennessee. 大急ぎでテネシーへ向かった.
2 (生計を立てるために)熱心に働く ▪ I had to *scratch gravel* like all possessed. 私は必死になって働かねばならなかった.

scratch *one's* ***head*** 頭をかく《途方にくれたしぐさ》，知恵をしぼる ▪ The fellow *scratched his head* in bewilderment. 当惑してその男は頭をかいた.

scratch out a living ＝SCRATCH a living.

scratch the surface of …の表面をかいなでる ▪ Scientists are only as yet *scratching the surface of* the universe. 科学者は今までのところ宇宙の上っつらをなでているにすぎない.

(*You*) *scratch my back* [*me*] *and I will scratch yours* [*you*]. 《諺》お互いに助け合おう，「魚心あれば水心」.

scream[1] /skri:m/ 名 ***a perfect scream*** 《口》とてもおもしろい物《主に少女が用いる》 ▪ The new play is *a perfect scream*. その新しい劇はそりゃとてもおもしろい物なのよ.

That's a scream. そいつぁ，お笑い草だ.

scream[2] /skri:m/ 動 ***scream*** *oneself* 〚補語を伴って〛金切り声をあげて…になる ▪ The child *screamed itself* red in the face. 子供はキーキー泣いて顔を真っ赤にした.

scream blue murder →cry (blue) MURDER.

scream *one's* ***head off*** 大声でわめき立てる ▪ The child was *screaming his head off* with temper. 子供はかんしゃくを起こしてぎゃあぎゃあわめき立てていた.

scream the place down そこら中わめき立てる ▪ We could hear the woman *screaming the place down*. その女性がそこら中わめき立てている声が聞こえた.

screen[1] /skri:n/ 名 ***act as a screen for*** …をかばう ▪ He *acted as a screen for* the criminal. 彼はその犯人をかばった.

the silver screen 銀幕，映画(界) ▪ She is one of the earliest stars of *the silver screen*. 彼女は映画の初期の頃のスターの一人だ.

the small screen テレビ ▪ I watched the game on *the small screen*. その試合をテレビで見た.

under the screen of …にまぎれて; にかこつけて ▪ He discovered the art of deceiving *under the screen of* royal authority. 彼は王の権威にかこつけて人を欺くすべをおぼえた.

screen[2] /skri:n/ 動 ***screen*** *oneself* 隠れる ▪ The girl *screened herself* behind the door. 少女はドアの陰に隠れた.

screen *a person* ***for*** 人を…について調べる ▪ The doctor *screened* a patient *for* flu. 医者は患者がインフルエンザにかかっていないか調べた.

screen well [***badly***] (劇・人などが)映画に向く[向かない] ▪ She *screens well*. 彼女は映画に向く ▪ This play will *screen badly*. この劇は映画に向かないだろう.

screw[1] /skru:/ 名 ***a screw loose*** 《口》変わったところ，故障，手抜かり ▪ There is *a screw loose* in the plan. その計画には手抜かりがある ▪ He was a genius with *a screw loose*. 彼はねじが1本ゆるんでいる天才だった.

a turn of the screw ねじを1回回すこと; (困難な状態に対する)圧力，締めつけ; 思いもよらない出来事 ▪ The injury added *a turn of the screw* to the penniless youth. そのけがは一文なしの若者をさらに苦しめることとなった.

give a screw ねじる，ひねる ▪ *Give* it *another screw*. もうひとねじりしなさい.

have a screw loose 《口》頭が少し変だ; (ある事に)気が狂ったように凝っている ▪ He *has a screw loose*. 彼は頭が少し変だ ▪ He*'s got a screw loose* on religion. 彼は宗教に気が狂ったように凝っている.

put [***tighten, turn***] ***the screw*** [***screws***] ***on***/***apply the screw to*** **1** …を圧迫する，締めつける ▪ When there is plenty of work, the operatives *turn the screw on* the masters. 仕事がたくさんあるときには職人は雇い主を圧迫する.
2 借金をむりに取り立てる ▪ These creditors think now's the time to *put the screw on*. この債権者たちは今こそ借金をむりやり取り立てる時だと思っている.

screw[2] /skru:/ 動 ***have*** *one's* ***head screwed on right*** [***the right way***]/*one's* ***head is screwed on right*** [***the right way***]/***have*** *one's* ***head very well screwed on*** 《口》分別がある，抜かりがない ▪ She *has her head very well screwed on*. 彼女は抜かりのない女だ ▪ The fact is, *my head is* not *screwed on right*. 実は私は分別がないのです.

screw *one's* ***courage to the stickingplace*** →screw ... to the STICKING(-)PLACE.

screw *one's* ***head on tight*** 《口》頭が変にならないように努力する ▪ I feel it necessary to *screw my head on tight* and go my own way gently. 私は頭が変にならないように努力しておとなしくやっていかねばならないような気がする.

screw its way (船が)スクリューで進んで行く ▪ The boat rolled and *screwed its way*. 船は横揺れしながらスクリューで進んで行った.

screw up *oneself*/***screw*** *oneself* ***up*** 勇気を奮い起こす ▪ He had to *screw up himself* to face the danger. 彼はその危険に立ち向かうために勇気を奮い起こさねばならなかった ▪ He *screwed himself up* to the talking point. 彼は口がきけるようになるまで勇気を出した.

scribble /skríbəl/ 動 ***No scribbling on the wall.*** 壁に落書き無用《掲示》.

scrimp /skrɪmp/ 動 ***scrimp and save***

[***scrape***] つましく暮らす, こつこつためる ▪ We are *scrimping and scraping* so that we can buy a house. 家を買うためにつましく暮らしている.

scripture /skríptʃər/ 名 ***The devil can quote*** [***cite***] ***Scripture for his purpose.*** 悪魔も聖書の句を引用することができる,「味方の武器は敵の武器」(cf. Sh., *Merch. V.* 1. 3. 99) ▪ But he quoted Scripture to prove his point!—Don't forget that *the devil can quote Scripture for his purpose*. でも彼は自分の主張のあかしとして聖書を引用したんだよ—悪魔も聖書の句を引用することができるということを忘れちゃいけないね.

scrounge /skraʊndʒ/ 名 ***be*** [***go***] ***on the scrounge*** (***for...***) 《英口》(金品を)たかっている[たかる] ▪ He's always *on the scrounge for* whisky. 彼はいつもウィスキーをたかっている.

scrub[1] /skrʌb/ 名 ***give a*** (***good***) ***scrub*** (よく)ごしごしこする, 洗う ▪ I was *giving* the floor *a scrub*. 私は床をごしごし洗っていた.

scrub[2] /skrʌb/ 動 ***Scrub it*** [***that***]***!*** 《口》やめろ!

scrub up well 《戯》めかす ▪ He *scrubs up* pretty *well* today, doesn't he? 彼, 今日はかなりめかしてるね.

scruff /skrʌf/ 名 ***by the scruff of*** *a person's* [***the***] ***neck*** 襟首を, 首根っこを ▪ He seized Jim *by the scruff of the neck* and kicked him. 彼はジムの首根っこをつかんでけとばした.

scruple /skrú:pəl/ 名 ***a man of*** [***with***] ***no scruples*** どんなことでも平気でする人 ▪ Lime's character totally changed, and he became *a man of no scruples*. ライムの性格はすっかり変わって, どんなことでも平気でする人となった.

have little [***no***] ***scruple about*** [***in*** *doing*] ...することにほとんど[少しも]気がとがめない, ためらわない ▪ I *had little scruple about* the matter. 私はその件にはほとんど気がとがめなかった ▪ They *had no scruple in applying* to a witch. 彼らは少しもためらわずに魔法使いに頼みこんだ.

have scruples about [***in*** *doing*] ...のことで[することに]ためらう ▪ A man may *have* some strange *scruples about* a trifle. 人は小さなことに妙にためらう場合がある ▪ You need no longer *have* any *scruples in doing* it. もうそれをするのをためらう必要はない.

make no scruple to *do* [***of*** *doing*] 平気で...する, ...することをはばからない ▪ He *made no scruple to* profess it. 彼はそれを公言してはばからなかった ▪ He *makes* little or *no scruple of lying*. 彼は平気で嘘をつく.

stand on scruple 遠慮する, 気がねする ▪ He always *stands on scruple* with me. 彼はいつも僕に気がねする.

without scruple ためらわずに, 平気で ▪ He will tell lies *without scruple*. 彼は平気で嘘をつく.

scrutiny /skrú:təni/ 名 ***under scrutiny*** 精査されて ▪ The patient was kept *under scrutiny* for a while. 病人はしばらくの間厳しく監視されていた.

scum /skʌm/ 名 ***the scum of the earth*** 《口》人間のくず, ろくでなし ▪ They are *the scum of the earth*. やつらは人間のくずだ.

scupper /skʌ́pər/ 名 (***full***) ***to the scuppers***
1《海》水落としの所まで(いっぱいに) ▪ The boat was loaded *to the scuppers*. 船は水落としの所まで積荷していた.
2《口》満腹で ▪ No, thank you, I'm *full to the scuppers*. いやもうけっこうです, 満腹です.

sea /si:/ 名 ***a sea change*** 《文》大変革[変貌] (cf. Sh., *Temp.* 1. 2. 400) ▪ There was *a sea change* in the relations between East and West. 東西両陣営間の関係に大変革があった.

a sea of/ seas of 山なす... ▪ He looked wretched, as if he were overwhelmed by *a sea of* troubles. 彼はまるで山ほどの苦労に圧倒されたかのようなみじめな顔をしていた.

above (***the***) ***sea***(***-***)***level*** 海抜 ▪ I live on the top of a mountain, 5,400 feet *above sea-level*. 私は海抜5,400フィートの山の頂きに住んでいる.

all at sea →at SEA 2.

at sea **1** 海上で, 航海中で; 水夫に雇われて ▪ All my fortunes are *at sea*. 私の全財産は海上にある ▪ The ship is now *at sea*. その船は今航海中だ ▪ I have not been long *at sea*. 水夫になって長くない.
2《英》〚all, totally などで強調して〛途方にくれて, 五里霧中で ▪ He seemed *all at sea* on this case. 彼はこの件については全く五里霧中のようであった.

at the sea 海岸で ▪ I spent the summer *at the sea*. その夏は海岸で過ごした.

between the devil and the deep (***blue***) ***sea*** →DEVIL.

beyond (***the***) ***sea***(***s***) 海外へ, 外国で ▪ He may have been *beyond the seas*. 彼は外国へ行っていたのだろう ▪ He has come from *beyond the sea*. 彼は外国からやって来た.

by [***on***] ***land and sea*** 海陸で ▪ They had fought battles both *by land and sea*. 彼らは海陸で戦いを交えていた.

by sea **1** 海路で ▪ He is going *by sea* to London. 彼は海路ロンドンへ行くことになっている.
2 海上で ▪ I have been very unfortunate *by sea*. 私は海上ではとても不運だった.

follow the sea 船乗りをやる ▪ The mariner *followed the sea* for fifty years. その水夫は50年間船乗りをしていた.

from sea to shining sea 東[西]海岸から西[東]海岸まで, 国中に ▪ The viral disease spread *from sea to shining sea* in a matter of months. ウィルス性の病気がものの数か月もすると国中に広がった.

get [***lose***] *one's* ***sea legs*** 《口》船酔いしない[する] ▪ He always *gets his sea legs*. 彼はいつも船酔いしない.

go (***and***) ***jump in the sea*** =Go (and) jump in the LAKE.

go out to sea →stand out to SEA.

go to sea **1** 航海に出る ▪ He wants to *go to sea* again. 彼はまた航海に出たいと思っている.
2 船乗りになる ▪ He *went to sea* at eighteen years of age. 彼は18歳のときに船乗りになった.
half seas over →HALF-SEAS.
have** a person **all at sea 人をすっかり途方にくれさせる ▪ He *had* his opponent *all at sea*. 彼は相手をすっかり途方にくれさせた.
He that would go to sea for pleasure, would go to hell for a pastime. 《諺》船乗りは嫌な仕事なので, 道楽でなろうとする者はどうかしている.
keep the sea **1** 制海権を保つ ▪ *The sea was kept* between Middleburg and Orwell. ミドルバーグとオーウェルの間は制海権が保たれていた.
2 (船が)続航する ▪ The U-boat could *keep the sea* for three months. Uボートは3か月間続航できた.
on land and sea →by land and SEA.
on the high seas 公海[外洋]上で ▪ A big ship was built to sail *on the high seas*. 外洋航海用の大きな船が建造された.
on [***upon***] ***the sea***(***s***) **1** 海上に, 船上に ▪ She prayed to God for those in peril *on the sea*. 彼女は海上で危険に瀕している人々のために神に祈った.
2 (住居などが)海に臨んで ▪ The house faces *on the sea*. その家は海に面している.
over (***the***) ***sea*** **1** 海のかなたへ, 海外へ ▪ They take their merchandise *over the sea*. 彼らは商品を海外へ持って行く.
2 外国に ▪ I have a lot of friends *over the sea*. 私は外国に友人がたくさんいる.
put (***off, out***) ***to sea*** 出帆する ▪ The ship *put to sea* from Liverpool. 船はリバプールから出帆した.
retire from the sea 水夫をやめる ▪ He *retired from the sea* at sixty. 彼は60歳で水夫をやめた.
roll back out to sea 沿岸部の霧が晴れる ▪ None of the boats could set out until the fog *rolled back out to sea*. すべての船のうち一隻として沿岸部の霧が晴れるまで出航できなかった.
sail the Seven Seas 七つの海[全世界]を航海する ▪ The captain has *sailed the Seven Seas*. その船長は七つの海を航海してきた.
seas of →a SEA of.
ship a sea →SHIP[2].
stand [***go***] ***out to sea*** 沖に乗り出す ▪ He *stood out to sea* before a favorable wind. 彼は順風を受けて沖に乗り出した.
suffer a sea-change 奇跡的に一変する, 急変貌する (cf. Sh., *Temp*. 1. 2. 400) ▪ It must long ago have *suffered a sea-change* into something rich and strange. それはとっくの昔に奇跡的に一変して豊かで不思議なものになったにちがいない.
take the sea 乗船する; 進水[出帆]する ▪ He *took the sea* at Dover. 彼はドーバーで乗船した ▪ We saw a newly-built ship *taking the sea*. 我々は新造船が進水するのを見た.
take to the sea =go to SEA 2.
when the sea gives up its dead よみがえりの日に (《聖》*Rev*. 20. 13).
within the four seas イギリス内に ▪ He is the safest confident to be found *within the four seas*. 彼はイギリス中で見いだされる一番安心できる腹心の友だ. ☞ the four seas「イギリスを囲む四方の海」.
Worse [***Stranger***] ***things happen at sea.*** 《諺》海ではもっとひどいこともある《これくらいの不幸は耐えられる》.

seal[1] /siːl/ 名 ***give the seal to*** …を保証[証明]する ▪ These facts *gave the seal to* his theory. これらの事実は彼の理論を証明した.
have the seal of death on** one's **face/***Death has set its seal on** a person's **face.*** 顔に死相が現れている ▪ If ever a man *had the seal of death on his face*, he has. 彼の顔には確かに死相が現れている ▪ *Death had* already *set its seal on his face*. 彼の顔にもう死相が現れていた.
pass the seals 官許を受ける ▪ Their commissions are *passing the seals* accordingly. 彼らの任命はしかるべく官許を受けつつある.
put** one's **seal to =set one's SEAL to.
put the seal on =set the SEAL on.
return the seal 《主に英》(大臣が)辞任する ▪ The King ordered him to *return the seal*. 王は彼に辞任を命じた.
seal of approval →APPROVAL.
set [***put***] ***one's seal to*** [***on***] **1** (文書)に捺印する ▪ He *set his seal to* the document. 彼はその文書に捺印した.
2 …を認める, の裏書きをする ▪ He *set his seal to* this truth with eagerness. 彼はこの真理を進んで認めた.
set [***put***] ***the seal on*** …を決定的なものにする ▪ That pleasant evening *set the seal on* our friendship. あの愉快な晩が我々の友情を決定的なものにした. ☞ 法律文書に調印することから.
under** one's **hand and seal 署名捺印した ▪ This is a bond *under your hand and seal*. これはあなたが署名捺印した証文です.
under (*one's*) ***seal*** 調印されて, 押印証明された ▪ He produced a written contract *under seal*. 彼は調印した証書を取り出した.
under the seal of secrecy [***silence***] 秘密[沈黙]を守るという約束で ▪ He told me this *under the seal of secrecy*. 彼は秘密を守るという約束で私にこのことを話した.

seal[2] /siːl/ 動 ***a sealed book*** 内容不可解の書; 不可解なこと ▪ This, too, was *a sealed book* to him. これもまた彼には不可解なことだった.
one's ***eyes are sealed on*** 目が…にじっと注がれる ▪ *His eyes were sealed on* the door. 彼の目はドアにじっと注がれていた.
seal** a person's **lips 人の口を封じる ▪ I can tell you nothing. *My lips are sealed*. 何も教えてあげられない. 私は口を封じられているのです.

sea legs /síːlègz/ 名 ***find*** *one's* ***sea legs/have*** [***get***] *one's* ***sea legs*** (***on***) 《口・戯》甲板をよろけないで歩ける; 新しい仕事[状況]に慣れる ▪ I have never yet *found my sea legs*. 私はまだ甲板をよろけずに歩いたことがない. ☞F avoir le pied marin のなぞり.

seam[1] /siːm/ 名 ***burst*** [***bulge, creak, pop***] ***at the seams*** 《口》〚進行形で〛はち切れそうになる, はみ出しそうになる ▪ He ate so much that he *was bursting at the seams*. 彼はたらふく食べておなかがはち切れそうだった.

come [***fall, break***] ***apart at the seams***
1《俗》落ち着き[自信]を失う ▪ Silas felt himself *coming apart at the seams*. サイラスは落ち着きを失っている自分に気がついた.
2《口》だめになる, 失敗する; 老いぼれる ▪ His father is *coming apart at the seams*. 彼の父は老いぼれかけている.

seam[2] /siːm/ 動 ***be seamed with*** (傷跡・しわ)がついている ▪ His face *was seamed with* many a scar. 彼の顔にはたくさんの傷跡があった.

sea-mile /síːmàɪl/ 名 ***by a long sea-mile*** はるかに ▪ You are superior to me *by a long sea-mile*. あなたは私よりもはるかにすぐれている.

seamy /síːmi/ 形 ***the seamy side of*** (人生など)の暗黒面, ぱっとしない面 (cf. Sh., *Oth*. 4. 2. 146) ▪ He has seen *the seamy side of* human affairs. 彼は人事の暗黒面を見てきた. ☞「服の縫い目の出る裏面」が原義.

sear, sere /sɪər/ 形 ***the sear and yellow leaf*** →in the sear and yellow LEAF.

search[1] /səːrtʃ/ 名 ***in search of*** …を探し求めて ▪ I am at present *in search of* a house. 目下家を探している ▪ They went out to Australia *in search of* gold. 彼らは金鉱を探しに豪州へ出かけた.

in the [*one's*] ***search for*** …を探し求めて ▪ The novelist is traveling *in the search for* materials for future work. その小説家は将来の作品の資料を探し求めて旅行をしている.

make (***a***) ***search*** 探す, 捜す, 調査する (*for*) ▪ He *made a search for* his poor son. 彼はかわいそうな息子を捜した.

S

search[2] /səːrtʃ/ 動 ***search*** *a person's* ***heart*** [***conscience, soul***] 《文》人の心を探る ▪ I listened to the boss *searching his heart*. 私は社長の心を探りながら話を聞いていた.

search *one's* ***heart*** [***soul***] 内省する ▪ The teacher *searched his heart* after hitting a naughty boy. 行儀悪い子をなぐった後で先生は内省した.

search high, search low あちこちくまなく捜しても ▪ *Search high, search low*, no trace of his clothes was to be found. あちこちくまなく捜しても, 彼の衣服は影すら見つからなかった.

(***You can*** [***may***]) ***search me!*** 《口》私には少しもわからない ▪ Where is he?—*You can search me!* あの男はどこにいるのか?—知るもんか! ▪ What does he want?—*Search me*. 彼は何を求めているのか?—てんでわからんね.

searcher /sə́ːrtʃər/ 名 ***the searcher of*** (***men's***) ***hearts*** 人の心を究める者, 天の神 (《聖》*Rom*. 8. 27) ▪ It can only be known to *the Searcher of men's hearts*. それは天の神にしかわからない.

seaside /síːsàɪd/ 名 ***at*** [***by***] ***the seaside*** 海辺に[の] ▪ You were *at the seaside* last summer. この夏は海辺にいましたね ▪ He spent the summer at a cottage *by the seaside*. 彼はその夏を海の家で過ごした.

go to the seaside (保養・海水浴のために)海辺へ行く ▪ He *went to the seaside* for his summer holidays. 彼は夏休みを過ごしに海岸へ行った.

season /síːzən/ 名 ***at all seasons*** 四季を通じて; いつも ▪ These pictures represent Japanese landscapes *at all seasons* of the year. これらの絵は四季を通じての日本の風景を表している ▪ He may come and court her *at all seasons*. 彼はいつでも彼女に求婚しに来てよい.

(***for a***) ***long*** [***short***] ***season*** 久しい[しばらくの]間 ▪ He had departed from her *for a long season*. 彼が彼女から去って久しかった ▪ Be patient and wait *short season*. 当分の間辛抱して待て.

in fit [***due, proper, just***] ***season*** 適当な時期に ▪ It is important that this should be done *in proper season*. これを適当な時期にすることが大切だ.

in good season 折よく, 早目に ▪ He desired to go back again *in good season*. 彼は早目にまた戻って行くことを希望した.

in season **1** 時を得た[て], 折よい[よく] ▪ He gave me a word *in season*. 彼は私に時を得た忠告をしてくれた ▪ They arrived *in season* for the meeting. 彼らは会にちょうど間に合うように着いた.
2 (果実・魚類が)出盛り[旬]で; 猟期で; さかりの時期で ▪ Grouse are *in season* after the 12th of August. ライチョウは8月12日以後が猟期だ ▪ Strawberries are *in season* now. イチゴは今が旬だ ▪ Female cats come *in season* twice a year. 雌猫は年に2回さかりがつく.
3 (盛り場などが)たけなわで ▪ The fair of St. Lawrence is now *in season*. 聖ローレンス祭は今がたけなわだ.

in season and out of season/in and out of season いつも, のべつ幕なしに ▪ He will be repeating his folly *in season and out of season*. 彼はのべつ幕なしにばかなまねを繰り返していることだろう.

open season for [***on***] …の解禁期《比喩的にも》 ▪ It became *open season for* criticism. 今や批評の解禁期となった.

out of season **1** 時を得ない(で), 時機を失して ▪ True wit can be spoiled only by making use of it *out of season*. 本当の機知は時を得ないで使ったときしかそこなわれない.
2 季節[旬]はずれで; 禁猟期で ▪ Oysters are *out of season* when there is no R in the month. カキは

月名にRのない月は季節はずれだ.

3 はやらないで ▪ The hard-grained Muses were *out of season*. 堅苦しい詩歌ははやらなかった.

seat[1] /siːt/ 名 ***be in the driving seat*** [《米》 ***driver's seat***] ハンドル[主導権]を握っている ▪ In Congress the radicals *were in the driver's seat*. 議会ではタカ派が主導権を握っていた.

by the seat of *one's* ***pants*** 《米》(飛行機の操縦に)計器を用いないで, 勘で ▪ The pilot flew *by the seat of his pants*. パイロットは勘で操縦した.

catbird seat 有利[優位]な状況 ▪ Her promotion put Susie in the *catbird seat*. 昇進によってスージーは優位な状況に置かれた. ☞catbird (ツグミの一種)はいつも高い所に止まることから.

have a good [***firm, graceful***] ***seat*** (馬・自転車などに)じょうずに[しっかりと, 上品に]乗る ▪ The lad is only six years old, but he *has a good seat* and (good) hands already. あの子供はたった6歳だが, もう馬にしっかりと乗って手綱さばきがうまい.

hold [***have, keep***] ***a*** [*one's*] ***seat*** **1** 席についている; 落馬せずにいる ▪ Please *keep your seat*. どうか腰掛けたままでいてください ▪ The rider reeled but *kept his seat*. 騎手はよろめいたが落馬せずにいた.

2 議席・地位を保っている ▪ He *has a seat* on the executive board. 彼は幹部のいすを占めている.

in [***on***] ***the hot seat*** 《口》困難な立場[苦境]に置かれて ▪ The boss is really *in the hot seat* over this problem. 社長はこの問題で苦境に立たされている. ☞hot seat「死刑用の電気いす」.

keep *a person's* ***seat warm*** (***for him***) →WARM[1].

lose [***win***] *one's* ***seat*** 地位・議席を失う[得る] ▪ He has *lost his seat* in Parliament. 彼は国会の議席を失った.

on the anxious seat →ANXIOUS.

put bums on [《米》 ***fannies in the***] ***seats*** 《口》大勢の人がお金を払って見に行く ▪ The movie will certainly *put bums on seats*. その映画はきっと多くの人がお金を払って見に行くだろう.

take a back seat →BACK SEAT.

take a seat **1** 腰掛ける ▪ Won't you *take a seat*? お掛けになりませんか.

2 地位を占める ▪ Russia refused to *take a seat* in the commission. ロシアは委員会に属すのを拒んだ.

take *one's* ***seat*** 着席する《劇場などで》; 地位[議席]を占める ▪ The judge has *taken his seat*. 裁判官は着席した ▪ He *took his seat* in Congress. 彼は議会に議席を占めた.

the seat of the mighty 権力の座 ▪ He imagines he is sitting in *the seat of the mighty*. 彼は自分が権力の座に座っているものと思っている.

win *one's* ***seat*** →lose one's SEAT.

seat[2] /siːt/ 動 ***be deeply seated*** (病気が)根深い ▪ The disease *was* too *deeply seated* for recovery. 病気はあまりに根深く治りそうもなかった.

be seated for **1** …から選出されて議員となる ▪ Mr. Kinglake has *been seated for* Bridgewater. キングレイク氏はブリッジウォーターから選出されて議員となった.

2 (…人分)の座席がある ▪ The hall *is seated for* 1,000. その会館には1,000人分の座席がある.

seat *oneself* 座る ▪ She *seated herself* at the piano. 彼女はピアノに向かって座った.

seaway /síːwèɪ/ 名 ***in a seaway*** 荒海で ▪ The boat was both buoyant and clever *in a seaway*. ボートは荒海でも浮力があり扱いやすかった.

make seaway 進航する; 進行する (*with*) ▪ She began to *make seaway*. 船は進航し始めた ▪ We must *make seaway with* this work. この仕事を進行させなければならない.

sec /sek/ 名 ***Half a sec.*** 《口》ちょっと待ってくれ. ☞sec＝second.

secede /sɪsíːd/ 動 ***secede from the Union*** 《米》(州が)連邦から脱退する ▪ Possibly their colonies might *secede from the Union*. ひょっとすると彼らの植民地は連邦から脱退するかもしれない.

seclude /sɪklúːd/ 動 ***seclude*** *oneself* ***from*** …から隠遁(とん)[引退]する ▪ He *secluded himself from* the rest of mankind. 彼は世を捨てて隠遁した.

seclusion /sɪklúːʒən/ 名 ***in seclusion*** 隠遁して ▪ He lived *in seclusion* for the rest of his life. 彼はその後は一生隠遁生活をした.

second[1] /sékənd/ 名 ***a split second*** ほんの一瞬 ▪ The swimmer came in *a split second* before the others. その水泳選手が他の選手よりほんの一瞬早くタッチした.

finish [***come in***] ***a close second*** ほぼ互角である ▪ Both teams *come in a close second*. 両チームはほぼ互角だ.

for a second **1** 少しの間 ▪ I can't do without it *for a second*. 私は片時もそれなしではすまされない.

2 〚否定文で〛決して…ない ▪ I'm not *for a second* thinking of marrying her. 彼女と結婚しようなんてさらさら思っていない.

in a second or two/in a few seconds すぐ ▪ I shall be ready *in a second or two*. すぐ用意します.

in (***half***) ***a second*** たちまち ▪ Flames licked up the building *in a second*. 火炎はたちまちその建物をなめ尽くした.

Just a second./Wait a second. 《口》ちょっと待って ▪ *Just a second*, please. どうか少し待って.

second[2] /sékənd/ 形 ***a second opinion*** →OPINION.

be second to …に次ぐ ▪ The United States *is second to* Chile in the production of copper. 米国は銅の産出量ではチリに次ぐ.

be second to none 誰にも引けをとらない ▪ He's *second to none* in karate. 彼は空手にかけては誰にも引けをとらない.

have second thoughts (***about***) →THOUGHT.

on second thought [《主に英》 ***thoughts***] 考え直して ▪ *On second thought*, I think I'll go. 考え

S

直して行ってみようと思う. ☞＜*Second thoughts* are best.《諺》「考え直しが一番」から.

play second →PLAY[2].

one's [***a***] ***second childhood*** もうろく ▪ My grandfather is in *his second childhood*. 祖父はもうろくしている.

second nature 第二の天性 ▪ To him work is *second nature*. 彼にとって仕事は第二の天性だ.

second off 《米俗》 第二に ▪ *Second off*, it means that everyone is cheated. 第二に, それはすべての人がだまされたということだ.

second only to …以外の何[誰]にも劣らない ▪ Milton is *second only to* Shakespeare. ミルトンはシェイクスピア以外は誰にも劣らない.

second sight 千里眼 ▪ He has the gift of *second sight*. 彼には千里眼の才がある.

second[3] /sékənd/ 動 ***be seconded to*** 《英》 …に一時的に配置替えされる ▪ He *was seconded to* the section for three months. 彼は3か月間その部門に配置替えされた.

second-best /sèkəndbést/ 副 ***come off second-best*** (競争で)負ける ▪ He was *coming off second-best* in the encounter. 彼はその試合で負けていた.

second-class /sèkəndklǽs|-klɑ́:s/ 副 ***go*** [***come, travel***] ***second-class*** 2等で行く[来る, 旅行する] ▪ He says he *came second-class*. 彼は2等で来たと言っている.

secrecy /sí:krəsi/ 名 ***in*** [***with***] ***secrecy*** 秘密に, 内緒で ▪ The proceedings were conducted *in* profound *secrecy*. 議事は極秘のうちに行われた.

secret /sí:krət/ 名形 ***an open secret*** 公然の秘密 ▪ The fact is *an open secret* to the few. その事実は少数の者には公然の秘密だ.

be in the secret 秘密を握って[知って]いる ▪ He *is in the secret* of his brother's plan. 彼は兄の計画の秘密を知っている.

be top secret トップシークレットである ▪ This affair *is top secret*. この件はトップシークレットだ.

have no secret from …に何も秘密にしていない ▪ We *have no secret from* you. あなたに何も隠しだてしていません.

in secret 秘密に, こっそり ▪ She wept *in secret*. 彼女はひそかに泣いた ▪ She was his wife *in secret*. 彼女は彼の内緒の妻だった.

keep a [***the***] ***secret*** ある[その]秘密を守る ▪ He *kept the secret* to himself. 彼はその秘密を胸にたたんでいた.

keep … a secret …を秘密にする (*from*) ▪ I *keep* nothing *a secret from* you. 君に何一つ隠しだてしないよ.

keep … secret …を秘密にしておく (*from*) ▪ He *kept* it *secret from* his family. 彼はそれを家族の者に秘密にしておいた.

let *a person* ***into the*** [***a***] ***secret*** 人に秘密[秘訣]を打ち明ける (*of*) ▪ The lad *was let into the secret of* the trade. 若者は商売の秘訣を教えられた.

make a [***no***] ***secret of*** …を秘密にする[しない] ▪ He *made a* [*no*] *secret of* the matter. 彼はその件を秘密にした[しなかった].

no [***not any***] ***secret*** 周知のこと ▪ His dislike of his wife was *no secret* around here. 彼が妻をきらっていることはこのあたりでは周知の事実だった.

section /sékʃən/ 名 ***in section*** 断面にして (↔ in PLAN) ▪ The portion of the glacier is shown *in section*. 氷河のその部分は断面にして示されている.

in sections 分解して ▪ It actually took me hours to put together the bookcase built *in sections*. 組立式の本箱を組立てるのに実に何時間もかかった ▪ It was conveyed to York *in sections*. 分解してヨークに送られた.

secure[1] /sɪkjʊ́ər/ 形 ***feel secure about*** [***as to***] …について不安がない ▪ I *feel secure about* [*as to*] my future. 私は将来について不安がない.

hold … secure …をしっかりと逃げられないようにつかむ ▪ Now you've got him, *hold* him *secure*. 彼を捕えたのだから, しっかりと逃げられないようにつかんでおけ.

secure against [***from***] …の恐れがない, 危険がない ▪ The town was *secure against* the attacks of the enemy. 町は敵の攻撃を受ける恐れがなかった.

secure of **1** …を確信して ▪ He is *secure of* my honesty. 彼は私の正直さを確信している.
2 …を確保して ▪ He is *secure of* his livelihood. 彼は生活の安定を得ている.

secure[2] /sɪkjʊ́ər/ 動 ***Secure arms!*** 《号令》 (雨にぬれないよう)腕に銃(つつ)!

security /sɪkjʊ́ərəti/ 名 ***be a security against*** …に対して保護する, を防ぎ護る ▪ Pride should at least *be a security against* meanness. 自尊心があれば少なくとも卑劣なことはできないはずだ.

go [***stand***] ***security for*** …の保証人になる, を保証する ▪ He was willing to *go security for* his friend. 彼は喜んで友人の保証人になるつもりだった.

in security 安全に ▪ I crossed the street *in security*. 私は道路を安全に横切った.

in security for …の担保として ▪ He handed me the deeds of the house *in security for* the advance of this £200. 彼はこの200ポンドの前金の担保としてその家の証書を渡してくれた.

on security 抵当で ▪ He lends money *on security*. 彼は抵当を取って金を貸す.

one's ***security blanket*** 《口》ねんねタオル; 安心感を与えるもの ▪ His sister is *his security blanket*. 彼の姉が彼の心の頼りだ. ☞Schultz の漫画 *Peanuts* 中の Linus 坊やの毛布から.

sedulous /sédʒələs|-djʊ-/ 形 ***play the sedulous ape*** →APE[1].

see /si:/ 動 ***can see to read*** (明るくて)字が読める ▪ It was dark and I *could* not *see to read*. 暗かったので私は字が読めなかった.

cannot see it 《米口》その正しさ[正当さ]がわからない ▪ The fare was $3.50 and we *could not see it*. 運賃は3ドル50だったが, それが正当と思えなかった.

can't [***don't***] ***see it happening*** そういうことにな

るとは思え[思わ]ない ▪ He promised to help, but I *don't see it happening*. 彼は援助すると約束したが, そういうことにならないのではないか.

go [***come***] ***to*** [《口》***and***] ***see*** …に会いに行く[来る] ▪ *Come and see* me on Sunday. 日曜日に遊びにいらっしゃい.

go (***to***) ***see a man*** (***about a dog***)/***go to see a dog*** (***about a man***) 《米俗》1杯やりに行く (→SEE a man about a dog) ▪ We are *going to see a dog about a man*. 1杯やりに行くところだ.

have seen better [*one's* (***best***)] ***days*** よい時もあった; もはや盛りを過ぎている, 使い古されている ▪ He's an Englishman, and I guess, *has seen better days*. 彼はイングランド人で, たぶん昔はよい時代もあったのだろう ▪ He was dressed in an old coat that *had seen better days*. 彼は着古された洋服を着ていた ▪ The old housekeeper *had seen her days*. 老家政婦はもう盛りを過ぎていた.

have seen hard wear (服が)長いこと着られた ▪ This coat of mine *has seen hard wear*. 僕のこの上着は長いこと着られてきた.

have seen the day [***time***] ***when*** …の時代を知っている ▪ He *has seen the day when* there were no motor-cars on the roads. 彼は自動車が道を走っていなかった時代を知っている.

have to be seen to be believed (美しさ・汚さなどが)見なければとてもわからない ▪ The beauty of the scenery would *have to be seen to be believed*. その景色の美しさは見なければわかるまい.

I see./I see what you mean. 《口》なるほど; …ですね ▪ *I see*, it's very interesting. なるほど, なかなかおもしろいですね ▪ Mr. Brown is not in, *I see*? ブラウンさんはご在宅ではないようですね.

(***I'll***) ***be seeing you.*** 《口》じゃ, またね. (→SEE you!)

I'll (***have to***) ***see.*** 考えてみよう ▪ May John come to tea?—*I'll see*. ジョンもお茶に呼んでいいですか—さてね.

I'll see you dead before …するのはまっぴら御免だ ▪ *I'll see you dead before* I accept your terms. 君の条件を受けいれるのはまっぴら御免だね.

I'll see you hanged [***damned, blowed, further, somewhere, in hell***] ***first.*** 《口》まっぴら御免だ《強い拒絶を表す》 ▪ Let us get married on Sunday.—*I'll see you hanged first*. 日曜日に結婚しようじゃないか—まっぴら御免だわ.

let me [***us***] ***see*** ええっと, はてな《あることを思い出そうとしたり, 答える前に考えねばならないときに使う文句》 ▪ *Let me see*, has anybody heard of the story? はてな, 誰かこの話を聞いたことがありますか ▪ When shall we begin? *Let us see*, it's two o'clock now. いつ始めることにしようか. ええっと, 今2時ですね.

must be seen to be believed = have to be SEEN to be believed.

not be seen dead with 《口》…は死ぬほどいやだ ▪ *No* decent person would *be seen dead with* a man like that. 上品な人ならあんな男は絶対にいやだろう.

see a doctor 医者に見てもらう ▪ You ought to *see a doctor* about that cough. そのせきはお医者に見てもらわなければいけませんよ.

see a great deal [***a lot***] ***of*** *a person* 人にしばしば会う ▪ I have *seen a great deal of* Smith. スミスとはしばしば会った.

see little [***nothing***] ***of*** *a person* 人にあまり会わない [全然会わない] ▪ I was *seeing* very *little of* him. 私は彼とはごくまれにしか会っていなかった.

see a man [***friend***] **1**《口》1杯やる ▪ What do you say to us going to *see a friend* together? いっしょに1杯やるのはどうかね.
2 人[友人]に会う《部屋を出て行くときの口実》 ▪ Excuse me a moment; I just have to go and *see a man* about something. ちょっと失礼, あることで人に会いに行かなきゃならないので.

see a man about a dog 《戯》(婉曲的に)トイレに行く, ちょっとそこまで(行く) (→go (to) SEE a man (about a dog)) ▪ Where are you going?—I'm going to *see a man about a dog*. どこに行くの?—ちょっとそこまで.

see *a person* (***all***) ***right*** →RIGHT[1].

see and *do* 《口》心がけて…する ▪ I'll *see and* get you another. 心がけてもう一つ手に入れてやろう.

see *a person* ***back*** 人を送り届ける ▪ I'll *see* you *back* to your house. 家まで送り届けてあげよう.

see … coming (良くない[不快な]こと)を予見する ▪ I was able to *see* the company's decline *coming*. 私にはその会社の衰退が予見できた.

see *a person* ***coming*** 《口》人に法外な値段をふっかける, かたる ▪ My dear fellow, they must have *seen* you *coming*. ねえ君, 君はきっとかたられたんだ.

see fit (***to*** *do*) →SEE (it) good.

see for *oneself* 自分で確かめる ▪ You can *see for yourself*! 自分で確かめてみたらいいよ.

see … for what they (***really***) ***are*** [***it*** [***he, she***] ***is***] …が思ったほど良くないことに気づく ▪ I suddenly *saw* him *for what he was*. 私は彼が思ったほど良くない人間であることに突然気づいた.

See here. →Look HERE.

see *a person* ***home*** 人を家まで送り届ける ▪ I *saw* her safely *home*. 彼女を無事家まで送り届けた.

see … in a better [***different, new***] ***light*** …を見直す ▪ After what he had done to my son, I began to *see* him *in a better light*. 彼が息子にああいうことをしてくれたので, 彼のことを見直すようになった.

see into a brick wall [***a millstone***] →SEE through a brick wall.

see (***it***) ***good*** [***fit, proper, right***] (都合が)よいと思う (*to do*) ▪ Others may do as they *see good*. 他の連中はよいと思うとおりにすればいい ▪ I *saw* (*it*) *fit to* say something. 何か一言するほうがいいと考えた.

see much [***more***] ***of*** *a person* 人とたびたび[もっとたびたび]会う ▪ He wanted to *see more of* Mary. 彼はもっとたびたびメアリーに会いたいと思った ▪ I don't *see much of* him these days. このところ彼とはあまり会わない.

see ... off the premises (うさん臭い人)を屋敷外に送り出す ▪ Mind you *see* him *off the premises.* 必ずその男を屋敷外へ送り出すんだよ.

see ourselves as others see us 自分のことを他人が見るように[客観的に]見る (Burns, *To a Louse*) ▪ To *see ourselves as others see us* is a salutary capacity. 自分のことを他人の目で見ることは健全な能力である.

see proper [***right***] →SEE (it) good.

see red →RED.

see the last of →LAST².

see the red light →RED.

see them come and see them go 〚主に完了形で〛そういう人[事件]を何度も見る ▪ I'm not afraid of bankruptcy. I *have seen them come and* I *have seen them go.* 破産なんか怖くない. そういうものは何度も見てきた.

see through [***into***] ***a brick wall*** [***a millstone***] 目から鼻へ抜けている, 洞察力が鋭い ▪ He could *see through a brick wall.* 彼は洞察力が鋭かった.

see to it that きっと…になるようにする, 取り計らう, 配慮する ▪ *See to it that* the letter is posted without fail. 必ず手紙を投函するようにしてください.

see ... to the deuce (人)をたたき出す ▪ I should have *seen* you *to the deuce.* お前さんをたたき出していたところだ.

see ... to the door (人)を玄関まで見送る ▪ I *saw* her *to the door.* 彼女を玄関まで見送った.

see *one's* ***way*** (***clear***) →WAY.

see with half an eye [***at a glance***] すぐわかる, 訳なくわかる ▪ One could *see with half an eye* that she was very ill. 彼女が重病であることはひと目でわかった.

See you! 《口》またね ▪ *See you* on Monday! 月曜日にまたね.

So I see. そのようですね ▪ I'm afraid I'm a bit late.—*So I see.* 少し遅れたのでは—そのようですね.

We shall see what we shall see. 先のことは分からない.

S

We'll (***have to***) ***see.*** =I'll (have to) SEE.

will never see forty [***fifty,*** etc.] ***again*** 《口》もう40[50, など]の坂を越えている ▪ He *will never see forty again.* 彼は40の坂を越えている.

you see 《口》そら, (だって…)でしょう《相手の承知していることを述べ, 驚きまたは非難を避けるために文中または文尾につける文句》 ▪ We ought to have him back, *you see.* だって当然あの人に帰ってもらうべきでしょう ▪ *You see,* I've been poor all my life. 私はこれまでずっと貧乏でしたでしょう.

seed /siːd/ 名 ***go*** [***run***] ***to seed*** 花時が過ぎる; とうが立つ, 衰える; ペンペン草が生える ▪ Her looks have a little *run to seed.* 彼女の容色も少し衰えてきた.

Good seed makes a good crop. 《諺》よい材料を使って始めれば, よい結果が得られる,「陰徳あれば陽報あり」.

in seed 種ができて ▪ The onion is *in seed.* タマネギに種ができている.

in the seed 《米》(綿が)綿繰り機にかけないままで ▪ How much cotton do you have *in the seed?* 綿繰り機にかけないままの綿をいくら持っていますか.

make seed corn off *a person* 《米口》人を負かす ▪ Nobody can *make seed corn off* me at cards. トランプで僕を負かせるものはひとりもいない.

seed money (新事業の)元手, 資金 ▪ They started the shop with 5,000,000 yen in *seed money.* 彼らは500万円の資金でその店を始めた.

sow [***plant***] ***the seeds of*** …の種をまく, 原因となる ▪ This oppression *sowed the seeds of* the French Revolution. この圧制がフランス革命の種をまいた.

the seed of Abraham ユダヤ人 ▪ In many countries *the seed of Abraham* is present in great numbers. 多くの国にユダヤ人がたくさんいる.

seeing /síːɪŋ/ 名接 ***Seeing is believing.*** 《諺》論より証拠.

seeing that [***seeing as, seeing as how***] …である点から見ると; であるからには ▪ *Seeing that* he is ill, he's unlikely to come. 彼は病気なのだから, まず来ないだろう.

seek /siːk/ 動 ***be not far to seek*** 求めるにむずかしくない ▪ The reason *is not far to seek.* その理由は明白である.

be (***still, yet***) ***to seek*** まだ見つからない; 欠乏している ▪ A good maid *is yet to seek.* 良いお手伝いはまだ見つからない ▪ These kind of things *are* sadly *to seek.* こういうものがひどく不足している.

be to seek in …が不足している ▪ He *is* sadly *to seek in* grammar. 彼はひどく文法力が不足している.

not have far to seek for …を遠く捜すに及ばない, がすぐ見つかる ▪ The poet will *not have far to seek for* a subject. その詩人には主題がすぐ見つかるさ.

seek dead 〚主に命令文で〛(犬が)射落とした獲物を捜して来る ▪ The pertinacity with which some dogs will *seek dead* is really surprising. 一部の犬が射落とした獲物を捜して来るときのねばり強さは真に驚くべきものがある.

seek *one's* ***fortune*** →FORTUNE.

seeking /síːkɪŋ/ 名 ***be not*** [《口》***none***] ***of*** *one's* ***seeking*** (成功・けんかなど)自分の求めたものではない ▪ This success *is not of our seeking.* この成功は我々の求めたものではない.

be of *one's* ***own seeking*** (不幸が)自分の招いたものだ ▪ The misfortune *is* entirely *of my own seeking.* この不幸は全く私の招いたものです.

seem /siːm/ 動 ***as*** (***it***) ***seems good*** [***best***] 良い[最善]と思われるように ▪ I shall act *as* (*it*) *seems best.* 最善と思われるように行動します.

cannot seem to *do* 《口》…できるように思えない ▪ I *can't seem to* get out of that bad habit. その

悪い癖を直せないような気がする.

it seems **1** …のようだ, らしい (*that*) ▪ *It seems that* he likes study. 彼は勉強が好きらしい.

2〚挿入句として〛…ということだ ▪ He married a rich widow, *it seems*. 彼は金持ちの未亡人と結婚したということだ.

***it seems as if* [*though*]** まるで…のように思われる ▪ *It seemed as if* he would recover. 彼は回復するかと思われた.

it seems like …のように思われる ▪ *It seems like* yesterday. つい昨日のように思われる ▪ *It seems like* it's going to rain. どうやら雨になりそうだ.

It seems so./So it seems. そうらしい, そのようだ ▪ It seems that he failed.—*So it seems.* 彼は失敗したらしい—そのようだね.

it would seem どうやら…らしい《it seems よりもためらいと不確かさを表す言い方》 ▪ From all this *it would seem* that he was under fifty at that time. こういう事実から推して, どうやら彼は当時50歳以下だったように思われる.

or so it seems 少なくともそのようだ ▪ He was angry. *Or so it seemed.* 彼は怒っていた. 少なくともそのようだった.

seeming /síːmɪŋ/ 名 ***in* (*all*) *seeming*** どう見ても ▪ He is healthy *in all seeming*. 彼はどう見ても健康体だ.

seen /siːn/ 形 ***seen one, seen them all*** 一つの例で十分だ ▪ I don't like home movies—*seen one, seen them all*. ホームムービーは好きではない—1回見れば十分だ.

seesaw /síːsɔ̀ː/ 名副 ***go seesaw*** 動揺[上下]する ▪ The scales *went seesaw* until settling in equilibrium. 秤は平衡状態に落ち着くまで上がり下がりした.

play* (*at*) *seesaw シーソーをして遊ぶ ▪ The children *played at seesaw* on the pasture-gate. 子供たちは牧草地の木戸でシーソーをして遊んだ.

seethe /siːð/ 動 ***be seething with*** …で煮え立っている, 騒然としている ▪ He *is seething with* anger. 彼は怒りでかんかんになっている ▪ The country *was seething with* discontent. その国は不満で騒然としていた.

seize /siːz/ 動 ***be seized* [*seised*] *of*** **1**《法》…の法定所有者である ▪ He *was seised of* the lands. 彼はその土地の法定所有者であった.

2 …を所有している; を知っている ▪ In due time we shall *be seized of* that letter. いずれそのうちその手紙を手に入れるだろう.

be seized of…in fee/ be seized of…in one's demesne as of fee《法》…を世襲地として所有している ▪ Sir John *was seized of* the country *in fee*. ジョン卿はその土地を世襲地として所有していた ▪ He *is* lawfully *seized of* the manor *in his demesne as of fee*. 彼はその荘園を世襲地として合法的に所有している. ☞この意味では専門語では seise とつづる.

be seized with (死・病気・恐怖など)に襲われる, とりつかれる ▪ I *was seized with* terror. 私は恐怖にとりつかれた.

seize hold of …をひっつかむ, 捕える ▪ I *was seized hold of* by a hideous old woman. 私は恐ろしい老婆にひっつかまれた.

seize…into one's hands …を(領主などの)手に取り上げる, 没収する ▪ A grey horse *was seized into the Duke's hands*. あし毛の馬が公爵の手に没収された.

seize…with both hands (機会など)に飛びつく ▪ He *seized* the opportunity *with both hands*. 彼はもろ手を上げてその機会に飛びついた.

seldom /séldəm/ 副 ***not seldom*** しばしば ▪ We hear it *not seldom* said that time is money. 時は金なりということをよく耳にする.

seldom, if ever たとえ…としてもきわめてまれ, めったに…しない ▪ He *seldom, if ever*, goes to church. 彼はたとえ行くとしてもめったに教会へ行かない.

seldom or never まず…ない ▪ He *seldom or never* goes out. 彼は出かけることはまずない.

Seldom seen, soon forgotten.《諺》去る者日々にうとし.

self /self/ 名 ***be above self*** 自己に打ち勝つ ▪ Few men are great enough to *be above self*. 自己に打ち勝つほど偉い人は少ない.

one's old* [*former*] *self 以前の自分 ▪ There is no vestige of *his former self*. 彼の昔の面影はない.

our noble selves《戯》自分たち ▪ Let us drink to *our noble selves*. 我々のために乾杯しましょう.

one's own* [*very*] *self 自分自身 ▪ Ah! That's more like *your own self*. ああ, そのほうがいっそう君らしいよ.

put…before self 自分のことよりも…を先に考える ▪ They *put* service *before self*. 彼らは自分のことよりも奉仕を先に考える.

one's second self 親友; (性格・好み・容貌が)自分とそっくりな人 ▪ She met *her second self* at the bazaar. 彼女はバザーで自分とそっくりな人に出会った.

Self do, self have.《諺》自業自得, 「身から出たさび」.

sell¹ /sel/ 名 ***the hard sell***《口》執拗で強引な売り込み ▪ *His hard sell* turned off many women. 彼の執拗で強引な売り込みに多くの女性は閉口した.

sell² /sel/ 動 ***be sold on***《口》…に熱中している, ほれている ▪ After that he *was* surely *sold on* me as a pilot. それからのちは彼は水先案内人としての私に確かにほれこんでしまった.

made to sell (品質などおかまいなしに)単に売品として造られた ▪ I seized a musket *made to sell* and sallied out. 私は単に売品として造られた銃をつかんで, 勢いよく飛び出して行った.

sell oneself **1** (利のために)身を売る, 金をもらって御用を務める ▪ He was eager to *sell himself* to that court. 彼はその委員会に金で身を売ろうと必死だった.

2 自己宣伝をする ▪ He is *selling himself* for publicity. 彼は有名になるために自己宣伝をしている.

3 (悪魔に)魂を売る ▪ It is an old story that men

sell themselves to the devil. 人が悪魔に魂を売るというのは古くからある話だ.

sell *a person* ***a bill of goods*** →BILL[1].

sell *one's* ***back*** 《レスリング》金をもらってわざと負ける ▪ He *sold his back* in the match. 彼はその試合で金をもらってわざと負けた.

sell ... down the river →RIVER.

sell *one's* ***life dear*** [***dearly***] 犬死にしない, 敵に大損害を与えて死ぬ ▪ The brave soldier was doing his utmost to *sell his life dearly*. 勇敢な兵士は犬死にしないように根かぎり奮戦していた.

sell like wildfire [***hot cakes***] 飛ぶように売れる ▪ This book is *selling like wildfire*. この本は飛ぶように売れている.

sell short →SHORT.

sell *oneself* ***short*** →SHORT.

sell *one's* ***soul*** (悪魔に)魂を売る; (利のために)良心を犠牲にする ▪ Very many *sell their souls* and all for money. 金のためなら良心も何もかも犠牲にしてしまう人が非常に多い.

sell the pass →PASS[2].

sell-by date /sélbaɪdèɪt/ 名 ***be past*** *one's* ***sell-by date*** →pass one's sell-by DATE.

seller /sélər/ 名 ***a seller's market*** →a buyer's MARKET.

sell-off /sélɔ̀ːf|-ɔf/ 名 《米》(株・証券の)急落, 大量売り; 《英》(国営企業の)払い下げ, 売却 ▪ Share prices in Tokyo were knocked by New York's *sell-off*. 東京の株価がニューヨークでの大量売りで打撃を受けた.

semblance /sémbləns/ 名 ***have*** [***bear***] ***the semblance of*** …に似ている ▪ It *had the semblance of* a rapid dream. それはつかの間の夢に似ていた ▪ The country *bears the semblance of* wealth. その国は裕福そうに見える.

in semblance 外見(だけ)は ▪ His government was Roman *in semblance*. 彼の政治は外見だけがローマ様式であった.

in (***the***) ***semblance of*** …の姿をして, に似るように ▪ An angel came *in semblance of* a dove with wings outspread. 天使が羽を広げたハトの姿で現れた.

make semblance ふり[様子]をする (*of, that, as if, as though, to do*) ▪ He *made semblance of* reading [*to* read] the book. 彼はその本を読んでいるようなふりをした ▪ He *made semblance as if* he were rich. 彼は金持ちのようなふりをした.

put on a semblance of …のふりを装う ▪ She *put on a semblance of* gaiety. 彼女は陽気なふりを装った.

take the semblance of …のような様子をする ▪ He had *taken the semblance of* an old man. 彼は老人のような様子をしていた.

to the semblance of …に似るように ▪ And now the lake narrowed *to the semblance of* a tranquil river. 今や湖はせばまって静かな川の様相を呈した.

under (***the***) ***semblance of*** …のふうをして ▪ She did it *under the semblance of* an angel. 彼女は天使のような様子でそれをした.

seminal /sémənəl/ 形 ***in the*** [*one's*] ***seminal state*** 未発達(状態)の ▪ It is pleasant to see great works *in the seminal state*. 偉大な作品が萌芽の状態にあるのを見るのは楽しい.

send /send/ 動 ***be sent into the world*** (この世に)生まれる ▪ I *was sent into the world* to become a letter-carrier. 私は郵便集配人になるためにこの世に生まれてきた.

be sent to try us 我々を試そうとする神の思召でよこされて ▪ These things *are sent to try us*. こういうことは我々を試すために神がよこされたのだ.

God [***Heaven, Lord***] ***send*** **1** 願わくは神[天, 主]の…を授けたまわんことを ▪ *Heaven send* me just thoughts. 願わくはお天道さまが私に正しい考えを授けたまわらんことを.

2 神[天, 主]よ…ならしめたまえ (*that*) ▪ *God send* (*that*) he may be happy. 神よ彼を幸せにしてください.

send *a person doing* 人に…をさせる ▪ The blow *sent* him *sprawling*. その打撃を受けて彼は大の字に倒れた.

send *a person* ***about his business*** →BUSINESS.

send ... flying →FLY[3].

send *a person* ***mad*** →drive a person MAD.

send off the field (反則などで選手を)退場させる ▪ Two players *were sent off the field*. 二人の選手が退場させられた.

send *a person* ***packing*** →PACK[2].

send ... under (競争・商売で人)を負かす ▪ The player's skill *sent* his opponent *under*. その選手のわざが相手を負かした.

send word →WORD.

senior /síːnjər|síːniə/ 形名 ***be*** *a person's* ***senior*** 人より年上である ▪ He *is* two years *my senior* [my senior by two years]. 彼は私より二つ年上だ.

be senior to …よりも年上である ▪ He *is* ten years *senior to* me. 彼は私よりも10歳年上だ.

sensation /senséɪʃən/ 名 ***create*** [***cause, produce***] ***a sensation*** センセーションを巻き起こす, 大評判となる ▪ The new invention has *created a* great *sensation*. その新発明は大評判になった.

deal in sensation 扇情的なことを扱う ▪ Our popular newspapers *deal* largely *in sensation*. 大衆紙は主に扇情的なことを扱う.

sense /sens/ 名 ***a man of sense*** 分別のある人 ▪ Consult Mr. Wade; he is *a man of sense*. ウェイド氏に相談してみなさい, 分別のある人ですから.

a sense of occasion (重要な機会での)適切な感覚, 常識的行動感覚; 時を計る才; (社交での)臨機応変のセンス, 場の盛り上げ ▪ Candles in the garden gave the night *a sense of occasion*. 庭のろうそくがその夜を盛り上げた ▪ I need ambiance, *a sense of occasion*. 僕は雰囲気が必要だ, 適切な感覚が.

a sixth sense →one's sixth SENSE.

be common* [*sound*] *sense 賢明なことである ▪ It *is common sense* to practice thrift. 節約をするのは賢明なことだ.

bring *a person* ***to*** *his* ***senses*** **1** 人を正気づかせる ▪ They threw cold water on him to *bring* him *to his senses*. 彼を正気づかせるために彼らは冷たい水をぶっかけた.
2 人を本心に立ち返らせる ▪ A little adversity will *bring* him *to his senses*. 少し苦労をすればあの男も本心に立ち返ることだろう.

come to *one's* ***senses*** **1** 正気づく ▪ She *came to her senses* in the hospital. 彼女は病院で正気づいた.
2 本心に立ち返る, 分別を取り戻す ▪ I hope you'll *come to your senses* later on. 君にはあとで分別を取り戻してほしいものだね.

frighten *a person* ***out of*** *his* ***senses*** 人をびっくりさせてぼうっとさせる ▪ She *was frightened out of her senses*. 彼女はびっくりしてぼう然とした.

give* [*have*] *sense 意味をなす ▪ This is the only reading that *gives* any *sense*. これが何らかの意味をなす唯一の読み方である ▪ It *has* no *sense* at all. それでは全然意味をなさない.

have a sense of humor ユーモアがわかる ▪ He *has* a good *sense of humor*. 彼はユーモアがよくわかる.

have more sense than to *do*/ ***have too much sense to*** *do* …するような分別のない人間ではない ▪ He *has more sense than to* go where he is not wanted. 彼はお呼びでない所へ出かけて行くような分別のない男ではない.

have the sense to *do* …するだけの分別がある ▪ She *had the sense to* think of it. 彼女はそのことを考えるだけの分別があった.

in a* [*some*] *sense ある意味では; ある程度は ▪ He is *in a sense* a representative of his firm. 彼はある意味では彼の会社の一代表である.

in all senses あらゆる点で ▪ My success is owing to you *in all senses*. 私の成功はあらゆる点であなたのおかげです.

in any sense どの点から言っても ▪ He could be looked upon as *in any sense* an Englishman. 彼はどの点から言ってもイングランド人とみなすことができた.

in every sense どの意味から言っても, どう見ても ▪ Their marriage was *in every sense* a happy one. 彼らの結婚はどう見ても幸福なものであった.

in no sense*/*not in any sense どの意味でも[断じて]…でない ▪ I'm *in no sense* an Anglomaniac. 私は断じて英国心酔者ではない.

in *one's* (***right***) ***senses*** 正気で ▪ No man *in his senses* would have done so. 正気な人なら誰だってそうはしなかっただろう.

knock* [*beat, drive, talk*] (*some*) *sense into *a person* 《口》人に分別あるふるまいをさせる; 人に手荒い手段でわからせる ▪ I tried to *knock some sense into* my daughter. 私は娘に分別あるふるまいをさせようとした.

labor under a sense of (まちがって)…と考えている ▪ He is *laboring under a sense of* wrong. 彼は自分はまちがっていると考えている.

lose *one's* ***senses*** 気を失う; 気が狂う ▪ He had *lost his senses*. 彼は気が狂っていた.

make sense **1** 意味をなす ▪ It *makes* no *sense* at all. それでは全然意味をなさない.
2 分別がある, 賢明である (《英》stand to sense) ▪ It *makes sense* to have better advice. よりすぐれた助言をもらうことは賢明なことだ.

make sense* (*out*) *of …の意味をとる ▪ How can I *make sense out of* nonsense? どうしてたわごとの意味がとれようか ▪ I couldn't *make* any *sense of* his letter. 彼の手紙は少しも意味がとれなかった.

not have enough sense to come in from the rain →RAIN[1].

out of *one's* (***seven***) ***senses*** 正気を失って; 気が狂って ▪ If you gave a pound for that thing, you must be *out of your senses*. そんな物に1ポンド出したのなら, 君は気が狂っているにちがいない.

see sense 道理が分かる (=see REASON) ▪ Help him to *see sense*. 彼に道理が分かるよう助けてやれ.

one's [***a***] ***sixth sense*** 第六感, 直観 ▪ *My sixth sense* worked well that day. その日は私の第六感がよく働いた.

speak* [*talk*] *sense もののわかった話をする ▪ Now you are *talking sense*. それでこそ話がわかるというものだ.

stand to sense 《口》道理にかなう ▪ It *stands to sense* that he should sit at top of the table. 彼が食卓の上席につくのは当然だ.

take leave of *one's* ***senses*** 気が狂う ▪ The public would think that he had *taken leave of his senses*. 世間の人は彼は気が狂ったと考えるだろう.

take the sense of …の意向を確かめる ▪ He *took the sense of* the meeting. 彼は会の意向を確かめた.

there is no* [*a good deal of, a lot of*] *sense in …には分別がない[いかにももっともなところがある] ▪ *There is no sense in* doing so. そうすることは無分別だ ▪ *There's a good deal of sense in* what you say. 君の意見には至極もっともなところがある.

What is the sense of *doing* ***…?*** …して何の役にたつのか ▪ *What is the sense of inventing* such a thing? そんなものを発明して何の役にたとうか《何の役にも立たない》.

write* (*good*) *sense 分別のあることを書く ▪ He seldom *writes good sense*. 彼は分別のあることはめったに書かない.

sensible /sénsəbəl/ 形 ***be sensible of*** …に気づいている, 知っている ▪ He *is sensible of* the danger of his position. 彼は自分の立場の危うさに気づいている.

sensitive /sénsətɪv/ 形 ***sensitive about*** …を気にかけて ▪ He is very *sensitive about* his appearance. 彼は容貌を非常に気にかけている.

sensitive to **1**(刺激)を感じる ▪ The eyes are *sensitive to* light. 目は光を感じる.

2…に敏感で ▪ He is *sensitive to* dairy products. 彼は乳製品に対して敏感だ[アレルギーである] ▪ The Stock Exchange is *sensitive to* political disturbances. 株式取引所は政治的騒乱に対して敏感である.

3…を気にしやすい ▪ Children are usually *sensitive to* blame. 子供はたいてい叱られるのを気にしやすい.

sentence /séntəns/ 名 ***pass*** [***pronounce***] ***sentence*** 刑を申し渡す; 意見を述べる (*on, upon*) ▪ The judge *passed sentence upon* the prisoner. 裁判官は被告に刑を申し渡した.

serve *one's* [***a***] ***sentence*** 刑に服する ▪ He *served his sentence* of five years' penal servitude. 彼は5年間の懲役に服した.

sentiment /séntəmənt/ 名 ***These are*** [《戯》 ***Them's***] ***my sentiments.*** これが私の所感だ ▪ "*Them's my sentiments*," Jones said. 「これが私の所感です」とジョーンズが言った.

sentinel /séntənəl|-tɪn-/ 名 ***stand sentinel*** **1**歩哨に立つ ▪ He was made to *stand sentinel* four hours instead of two. 彼は2時間ではなく4時間歩哨に立たされた.

2見張る (*over*) ▪ The castle *stood sentinel over* the North Sea. 城は北海を見張っていた.

sentry /séntri/ 名 ***be on*** [***keep***] ***sentry*** 見張りをする ▪ Some *are on sentry*. 何人かが見張りをしている ▪ Can they *keep* sufficient *sentry* about it? 彼らはそれを十分張り番することができるのか.

come off [***go on***] ***sentry*** 下番[上番]する ▪ The soldier *came off sentry* at two in the morning. その兵は午前2時に下番した.

stand sentry 歩哨に立つ; 見張る (*over*) ▪ His trusty dog *stood sentry* at the gate. 彼の頼みになる犬は門の所で見張っていた ▪ We *stood sentry over* the sleepers. 眠っている人たちの見張りをした.

sentry-go /séntrigoʊ/ 名 ***do sentry-go*** 歩哨勤務をする ▪ We'll have to *do sentry-go*. 歩哨勤務をしなきゃいけない.

separate[1] /sépərət/ 形 ***go*** *one's* ***separate ways*** 別々の道を歩む, 袂を分かつ ▪ They *went their separate ways* out of school. 彼らは卒業して別々の道を歩んだ.

separate but equal 分離すれども平等の, 分離独立政策の ▪ The budget was divided up so that the girls' clubs are *separate but equal* to the boys'. 女の子のクラブと男の子のクラブは分離すれども平等という考えでその予算は分割された. ☞施設•機会の利用が平等であればアフリカ系アメリカ人は分離されてもいいという考え. 1890年のルイジアナの法律. 1954年に最高裁で違憲とされた.

separate[2] /sépərèɪt/ 動 ***separate the men from the boys*** 《口》一人前の男と少年を区別する ▪ This uphill race will really *separate the men from the boys*. この上り坂レースで一人前の男かまだほんの男の子かが実際に判別されるだろう《大人かガキかが試される》.

sepulcher, 《英》 **sepulchre** /sépəlkər/ 名 ***a whited*** [***painted***] ***sepulcher*** 偽善者 (《聖》 *Matt.* 23. 27) ▪ He was a sham—*a whited sepulcher*. 彼は詐欺師—偽善者だった.

sequel /sí:kwəl/ 名 ***in sequel to*** …の結果として, のために ▪ *In sequel to* age he is failing somewhat. 年のために彼はいささか弱っている.

in the sequel その後になって, 結局 ▪ *In the sequel* they became quite good friends. その後に至って彼らはすっかり仲よしになった.

sequence /sí:kwəns/ 名 ***in historical sequence*** 時代順に ▪ Give the facts *in historical sequence*. その事実を時代順に挙げよ.

in sequence **1**次々と ▪ Calamities fall *in* rapid *sequence*. 災難は矢つぎ早に起こる.

2順序通り ▪ Now, try to tell me the events of the day *in* strict *sequence*. さてその日の事件を正確に順序通りに話してごらんなさい.

sequester /sɪkwéstər/ 動 ***sequester*** *oneself* ***from*** …から引退する; との関係を絶つ ▪ He *sequestered himself from* his wife [the world]. 彼は妻と別居した[世間から引退した].

serene /sərí:n/ 形 ***all serene*** 《俗》けっこうだ; 異常なし ▪ Please bring me the money tonight. —*All serene*. 今夜金を持って来てください—よしきた ▪ How are affairs at home?—*All serene*. 家のことはどうかね—異常なしだよ.

series /síəri:z/ 名 ***in series*** **1**連続して ▪ We placed several pumps *in series*. 我々は数個のポンプを連続してすえた.

2《電》直列で (↔in PARALLEL) ▪ These wires are *in series*. これらの線は直列になっている.

serious /síəriəs/ 形 ***to be serious*** まじめな話だが ▪ And now *to be serious*, what will you do? さて, まじめな話ですが, あなたはどうしますか.

You can't be serious. まさか本気じゃないだろうね[冗談だろう].

seriously /síəriəsli/ 副 ***take ... seriously*** …をまじめに考える, 真に受ける ▪ It is time that you should *take* things more *seriously*. もう君が物事をもっとまじめに考えていい時だ.

to speak seriously まじめな話だが, 冗談は抜きとして ▪ *To speak seriously*, what ought I to do? 冗談はさておき, 私はどうすべきだろうか.

seriousness /síəriəsnəs/ 名 ***in all seriousness*** 本当のところ, 真面目に言うと ▪ You're not telling me, *in all seriousness*, that you can't finish the work by this evening? 君は今日の夕方までに仕事を仕上げられないという本当のところを話していないね《まさか実は仕上げられないと言うのではないだろうね》.

sermon /sə́:rmən/ 名 ***at*** [***after***] ***sermon*** 礼拝中で[礼拝がすんでから] ▪ Men were *at sermon* the Sunday afternoon. 人々はその日曜日の午後礼拝中であった ▪ He rode home with her *after ser-*

mon. 彼は礼拝がすんでから彼女といっしょに馬で帰った.

preach a sermon 説教をする ▪ The priest went to the pulpit and *preached a sermon.* 牧師は説教壇へ行って説教をした.

sermons in stones 木石の教訓 (cf. Sh., *A. Y. L.* 2. 1. 17) ▪ He preferred *sermons in stones* to sermons in churches. 彼は教会の説教よりも木石の教訓のほうがよかった.

servant /sə́ːrvənt/ 名 ***a servant of servants*** しもべのしもべ, 最も卑しいしもべ ▪ *A servant of servants* shall he be unto his brethren. 彼をしもべのしもべとしてその兄弟たちに仕えさせる. ☞ヘブライ語法.

Fire and water may be good servants, but bad masters. 《諺》火と水は便利なものだが使用を誤ると大変なことになる.

His [***Her***] ***Majesty's servants*** 国王のしもべ《大臣など》;《戯》俳優 ▪ It was a comedy acted by *His Majesty's servants.* それは俳優の演じる喜劇だった.

servant of servants of God 神の最も卑しいしもべ《ローマ教皇の自称》 ▪ The Pope calls himself *servant of servants of God.* ローマ教皇は神の最も卑しいしもべと自称する. ☞大聖グレゴリウス (Gregory the Great) が初めて用いた; Ⓛ servus servorum Dei のなぞり.

What did your last servant die of? 《口・戯》この前のお手伝いは何で死んだのかね《そんなことは自分でしたらどうだ》.

your humble servant →HUMBLE[1].

serve[1] /sə́ːrv/ 名 ***break*** *a person's* ***serve*** 人のサービスゲームを取る ▪ Tom won the match, *breaking Bill's serve.* ビルからサービスゲームを取ってトムは試合に勝った.

serve[2] /sə́ːrv/ 動 ***If you would be well served, serve yourself.*** 《諺》十分に仕えてもらいたいならば, 自らが自らに仕えよ,「人使うより胴使え」.

It serves [《口》***Serve(s)***] ***you*** [***him,*** etc.] ***right!*** いい気味だ! ▪ *It* would *serve him right* if they tossed him. 彼らが彼を放り投げたらいい気味だ.

serve a summons [***writ***] ***on***/***serve*** *a person* ***with a summons*** [***writ***] 人に召喚状を送る ▪ They *served a writ on* him for nonpayment of debt. 彼が負債を返済しないので召喚状を送った.

serve mass →MASS[1].

serve *one's* ***(own) turn*** →TURN[1].

serve *one's* ***purpose*** →answer the PURPOSE.

serve the place [***stead***] ***of*** ...の代わりになる ▪ This may *serve the place of* a candle. それはろうそくの代わりになるかもしれない.

serve the shop (店員が)お客の相手をする ▪ The baby cried whenever she *served the shop.* 赤んぼうは彼女がお客の相手をするといつも泣きだした.

serve the time 時勢のひよりを見る ▪ Be wary, and always *serve the time.* 注意深くしていていつも時勢のひよりを見るがいい.

serve time =do (one's) TIME.

serve *one's* ***time*** 年季をすませる ▪ They had *served their time* as soldiers in India. 彼らはインドで兵士としての年季をすませていた ▪ I *served my time* to trawling. 私はトロール漁業の年季をすませた.

serve *a person* ***well*** [***badly, ill***] 人を親切に扱う[虐待する] ▪ He *served* me very *badly.* 彼は私をひどく虐待した.

Serve(s) you right! →It SERVEs you right!

They also serve who only stand wait. 《諺》たとえ手助けしたくても, じっとがまんして何もしないでいなければならないこともある.

service /sə́ːrvəs/ 名 ***at*** *a person's* ***service***
1 人の命ずるがままに ▪ My name is Matthew Bramble, *at your service.* 私はマシュー・ブランブルと申す者です, どうぞよろしく ▪ I am entirely *at your service.* 私は何でもおっしゃることをいたします.
2 人の自由になって ▪ My means are *at your service.* 私の金はご自由になさってください.

bring ... into service (バスなど)を運転されるようにする ▪ The Victoria line *was brought into service.* ビクトリア路線が運転されるようになった.

Call my service. 留守番電話に(ご用を)お話しください.

do *a person* ***a service*** 人に仕える; 人に尽くす ▪ Will you *do* me *a service*? 一つ頼まれてくれないか.

do *oneself* ***a service*** 自分の役に立つことをする ▪ You are *doing yourself a service* in helping him. 彼を助ければ自分の役にも立つことになるのです.

do service **1** (馬・物などが)役に立つ ▪ The horse will *do* better *service* in his hands. 馬は彼の手にあるほうがいっそう役に立つだろう.
2 貢献する (*to*) ▪ He has *done* great *service to* the world. 彼は世のために大いに尽くした.

do *a person* ***service*** 《詩》人に仕える, の世話をする ▪ Remember I have *done* thee worthy *service.* 私があなたに立派にご奉公してきたことを忘れないでください.

go [***get***] ***into service*** **1** 運転[操作]を始める ▪ When will the cable car *go into service*? ケーブルカーの運転はいつからですか.
2 奉公する ▪ They swarm up to London in hopes of *getting into service.* 彼らは奉公することを望んでロンドンへ群がってやって来る.

go into the service 兵役に服す ▪ He *went into the service* when he graduated from college. 彼は大学を卒業すると兵役に服した.

go out of service (物が)使われなくなる ▪ The old models *went out of service.* 古いモデルは使われなくなった.

go out to service 奉公に出る ▪ She will *go out to service.* 彼女は奉公に出るだろう.

hold divine service 礼拝を行う ▪ *Divine service is held* daily in this church. この教会では毎日礼拝が行われる.

S

in active service →on active SERVICE.
in service **1** 運転[使用]中で, 利用できる ▪ Is this elevator *in service*? このエレベーター, 乗れる?
2 奉公して; 出征して ▪ My eldest girl *in service* forgot to write. 奉公している長女が手紙をよこすのを忘れた ▪ He died *in service*. 彼は戦死した.
in the service of …に仕えて ▪ I know a lieutenant *in the service of* King George. 私はジョージ国王に仕えている中尉を知っている.
make a service charge サービス料を取る ▪ Do you *make a service charge* at this hotel? このホテルではサービス料を取りますか.
of service to 〚述語的に用いて〛 …に役に立って ▪ He was *of* great *service to* me. 彼は私に非常に役に立った ▪ I found it *of service to* me. 私はそれが私に役に立つのがわかった.
on [***in***] ***active service*** 出征中に; 現役の ▪ He was disabled when *on active service*. 彼は出征中に廃兵となった.
On His [***Her***] ***Majesty's Service*** 《英》 公用 《手紙の表に書く句で, しばしば O.H.M.S. と略す》 ▪ Three letters were marked "*On Her Majesty's Service*." 3通の手紙には「公用」としるしてあった.
on service 服務して ▪ When I was a soldier we were *on service* together. 私が兵隊のころは, 私たちはいっしょに服務していました.
out of service **1** 運転[使用]停止の, 利用できない ▪ All the elevators were put *out of service* because of the blackout. 停電のためすべてのエレベーターが運転を停止していた.
2 奉公口をなくして ▪ My master turned me *out of service*. 主人は私に暇を出した.
press ... into service (物)を臨時に使う; (人)を説得して手伝わせる ▪ He *was pressed into service* as my assistant. 彼は説得されて私の助手として手伝った.
put ... into service **1** …を奉公させる ▪ He had *put* two of his daughters *into service*. 彼は娘を二人奉公させていた.
2 (バス・船など)の運転を始める, を使用する ▪ The buses will *be put into service* on the route. バスはその道筋に使用されるはずだ.
render (***a***) ***service*** 尽くす, 貢献する ▪ He has *rendered a* great *service* to his country. 彼は祖国に大いに貢献してきた.
see service **1** (兵士が)実戦の経験をする ▪ He has an ardent desire to *see service*. 彼は実戦の経験をしたいと熱望している.
2 使用される; 〚完了形で〛 (物が)だいぶ使われて[古びて]いる ▪ My coat *has seen service*. 私の上着はだいぶ着古している.
take ... into *one's* ***service*** …を雇い入れる ▪ I begged to *be taken into his service*. 私は彼に雇い入れてくれるように頼んだ.
take service **1** 兵隊になる ▪ He *took service* under Nelson. 彼はネルスンのもとで兵隊になった.
2 実戦に参加する ▪ He had gone to Spain to *take service* against the enemy. 彼は敵との実戦に参加するためにスペインへ行っていた.
3 勤める, 奉公する (*with*) ▪ He *took service with* the legation at Athens. 彼はアテネの公使館に勤めた.

sesame /sésəmi/ 名 ***an open sesame*** …を達成するうまい方法 (*to*) ▪ Education is said to be *an open sesame to* success. 教育は成功へのかぎだと言われている.
open sesame 開け, ごま; 入りにくい所へ入る[難関を切り抜ける]まじない ▪ His word is a sort of *open sesame*. 彼の口添えは「開け, ごま」のようなものだ. ☞「アラビア夜話」の *Ali Baba and the Forty Thieves* の「開け, ごま!」という開門のまじないから.

session /séʃən/ 名 ***a gross-out session*** 《俗》 (10代の若者の)口げんか ▪ My two teenage sons were engaging in *a gross-out session* when I came home. 家に戻ると10代の息子二人が口げんかしていた.
in secret session 秘密会で ▪ He read the letters to the House *in secret session*. 彼は下院の秘密会でその手紙を読んだ.
in session (議会・法廷・会議などが)開会中, 開廷中 ▪ The Diet is now *in session*. 議会は今開会中だ.

set[1] /set/ 名 ***a set of pipes*** 大きな声, みごとな歌声 ▪ She sang with *a set of pipes*. 彼女はみごとな歌声で歌った.
a set of wheels (自動)車 ▪ My son wants *a* new *set of wheels*. 息子が新車をほしがっているんだ.
at a dead set 行き詰まって ▪ What's this! He is *at a dead set*! これはどうしたことか. 彼は行き詰まっている.
make a dead set **1** 猛烈に攻撃する (*at, against*) ▪ He *made a dead set at* [*against*] me. 彼はやっきになって僕に食ってかかった.
2 (女性, まれに男性が)歓心を得ようと熱心に努力する (*at*) ▪ Women *made a dead set at* Garibaldi. 女性たちはガリバルディの歓心を得ようと必死だった.
3 《狩》 (猟犬が)獲物の方へ鼻先を向けてぴたりと立ち止まる ▪ My dog *made a dead set* seeing a fox at a distance. 犬はやや離れた所にキツネを見つけ, その方へ鼻先を向けてぴたりと立ち止まった.
make a set =make a dead SET 1, 2.
set of new threads 新しい男物のスーツ ▪ He wore a nice *set of new threads*. 彼はなかなかの新しいスーツを身にまとっていた.

set[2] /set/ 動 (***be***) ***all set*** 《口》 すっかり準備ができて(いる) (*to do, for*) ▪ Yes, I *am all set to* go. はい, すっかり行く用意ができました ▪ We*'re all set for* our holidays. 休暇の準備はすっかり整っている.
be (***dead***) ***set against*** …に(まっこうから)反対している ▪ His mother *was dead set against* his marrying so young. 母親は彼がそんなに若く結婚するのにまっこうから反対していた.
(***be***) (***dead***) ***set on*** [***upon***] …を堅く決心している (*doing*) ▪ He *is dead set upon leaving* school. 彼は学校をやめることを堅く決心している.
be hard set **1** 非常に困っている (*for, to do*)

S

▪ He *was hard set for* his excuse. 彼は言い訳に大いに窮した ▪ They *were hard set to* live. 彼らは大いに暮らしに困っていた.
2 非常に腹がへっている ▪ After that long walk we *were hard set*. その長い散歩のあと腹がぺこぺこだった.
be set round with …に取り巻かれている ▪ The small room *was set round with* velvet settees. その小部屋は四方にビロードの長いすが置いてあった.
be sharp [***keen***] ***set*** 飢えている; 鋭い ▪ I knew the lioness must *be keen set*. 雌ライオンが飢えているにちがいないのはわかっていた ▪ Wit *is sharpest set* by politeness. 機知はいんぎんさによって最も鋭くなる.
be well [***straight***] ***set up*** 体格ががっしりしている ▪ He *was* tall and *well set up*. 彼は背が高くて体格ががっしりしていた.
be (***well***) ***set up for*** [***with***] 《口》…を十分に供給されている, 十分に持っている ▪ I'*m set up with* tobacco for the week. 今週分のタバコは十分にある.
get set 《米》用意する ▪ At the words "*Get set!*" the starter braced his legs apart. 「用意!」の掛け声を聞くとスタートを切る人は足をぐっとふんばった.
have** a person **set 《口》人をだしぬく ▪ I'*ve got* him *set* all right. 確かに彼をだしぬいてやった.
set … doing …を…させる ▪ His joke *set* everyone *laughing*. 彼の冗談がみんなを笑わせた.
set a great deal by →SET much by.
set** oneself **against …に強硬に反対[反抗]する ▪ The Cardinals *set themselves against* reformation. 枢機卿らは改革に強硬に反対した.
set fair **1** (晴雨計が)晴れをはっきりと示して; 好天気が続きそうで ▪ I think the day will be fine; the glass *is set fair*. きょうは天気だと思う, 晴雨計が晴れをはっきりと示しているから.
2 見込み十分で (*for, to do*) ▪ Everything *is set fair for* success [*to* succeed]. 全て成功間違いなしだ.
set** a person **in mind of 人に…のことを思い出させる ▪ This tune always *sets* me *in mind of* my dead sister. この曲を聞くといつも亡くなった妹のことを思い出す.
set little [***light***] ***by*** …を軽視する ▪ Do not *set little by* death. 死を見くびってはいけない.
set much [***a great deal***] ***by*** …を大いに尊重する, 大事にする ▪ I shall *set much by* this book. 私はこの本を非常に大事にするだろう.
***set off to** do* …するつもりである ▪ I *set off to* write a poem, but had to give up. 詩を書くつもりだったが, あきらめざるを得なかった.
set … on the sea [***water***] …を進水させる ▪ The ship *was set on the sea*. その船は進水した.
set** oneself **out **1** 骨を折る, 努力する ▪ He is always willing to *set himself out* to help people. 彼はいつも喜んで他人を助けるために骨を折る.
2 着飾る ▪ She *set herself out* in her best dress for the theater. 彼女は観劇のため晴れ着で着飾った.
set (***out***) ***fire*** 《米》向かい火を放つ《山火事の延焼防止のため》 ▪ The inhabitants were generally opposed to *setting out fire*. 住民は大半が向かい火を放つことに反対していた.
set store by [***on***] →STORE.
set the tone →TONE.
***set** a person **to** do* 人に…させる ▪ He *set* the servant *to* chop wood. 彼は使用人にまきを割らせた.
***set** oneself **to** do* **1** …しに取りかかる ▪ He *set himself to* study it. 彼はその研究に取りかかった.
2 …しようと決心する ▪ I've *set myself to* finish the job by the end of March. その仕事を3月末までにすませようと決心した.
set to work on …を本気で始める ▪ We *set to work on* the party food. パーティーのごちそうを本腰を入れて食べ始めた.
set** oneself **up against …と競争することに決める ▪ I've *set myself up against* his company. 彼の会社と競争することに決めた.
set** oneself **up as **1** …と主張[自負]する ▪ I have never *set myself up as* a scholar. 私は学者だなどと自負したことは一度もない.
2 身を立てる ▪ He had no intention of *setting himself up as* a prophet. 彼は予言者として身を立てるつもりは少しもなかった.
***set up for** oneself* 独立で仕事をやり始める ▪ Augustus had a mind to *set up for himself*. オーガスタスは一人でやってみる気になった.
set up opposition against …に反対する ▪ They *set up* strong *opposition against* the government's plan. 彼らは政府案に強く反対した.
set** oneself **up to be …であると主張する ▪ He has never *set himself up to be* a scholar. 彼は学者だなどと主張したことは一度もない.

setout /sétàʊt/ 名 ***at the*** (***first***) ***setout*** 最初は ▪ The two were pretty equal *at the setout*. 二人は最初はかなり同等であった.

setting /sétɪŋ/ 名 ***keep your setting*** 《米口》そのまま座っていてください ▪ *Keep your setting*, Mrs. Villars. どうぞそのまま, ビラーズさん.

settle /sétəl/ 動 ***marry and settle down*** 結婚して身を固める ▪ Why don't you *marry and settle down*? どうして君は結婚して身を固めないのか.
***settle** oneself* **1** (いす・くらなどに)ゆったりと座る ▪ *Settling himself* in his saddle, he started off. 彼はくらにゆったりと座って出かけた.
2 (…することに)決心する (*to do*) ▪ He *settled himself to* marry her. 彼は彼女と結婚しようと決心した.
3 居を定める ▪ They *settled themselves* in Italy. 彼らはイタリアに居を定めた.
settle** one's **affairs [***estate***] (死後・転居・引退などを考慮して)財産などの処置を定める ▪ He made his will, and *settled his affairs*. 彼は遺言を書き, 財産などの処置を定めた.
settle** oneself **down in (ソファなど)にゆったりと座る ▪ He *settled himself down in* an armchair. 彼はゆったりとひじかけいすに座った.
settle** oneself **down to …に落ち着いて取りかかる ▪ He *settled himself down to* his pursuits. 彼は

落ち着いて仕事に取りかかった.

settle in life 結婚して身を固める ▪ Their object was to *settle in life.* 彼らの目的は結婚して身を固めることにあった.

settle ... on *a person* 《英口》(財産など)を人に譲与する ▪ He *settled* part of his estate *on* his son. 彼は地所の一部を息子に譲与した.

settle ... out of court 《法》...を示談にする ▪ It was agreed to *settle* the case *out of court.* その訴訟は示談にすることに決まった.

settle *oneself* ***to*** 落ち着いて...にとりかかる ▪ He *settled himself to* work at eight o'clock. 彼は8時に落ち着いて仕事にとりかかった.

settlement /sétəlmənt/ 名 ***in settlement of*** ...の決済として ▪ I enclose a check *in settlement of* your account. 貴勘定の決済として小切手を同封します.

make a settlement on ...に財産を贈与する ▪ He was ready to *make a* splendid *settlement on* his son. 彼は喜んで息子にすばらしい財産を贈与するつもりであった.

reach [***come to***] ***a settlement with*** ...と了解に達する ▪ The strikers have *reached a settlement with* the employers. ストをやっていた人々は雇用者側と合意に達した.

seven /sévən/ 形名 ***a twenty-four seven*** → TWENTY.

at sixes and sevens →SIX.

be more than seven 分別がある, 抜け目がない ▪ We all know that Mr. Gammon'*s more than seven.* 我々はみなギャモンさんが抜け目がないということは知っている. ☞seven = seven years of age.

two sevens 77年 ▪ He was in his *two sevens* at that time. 当時彼は77歳であった.

seventeen /sèvəntíːn/ 名 ***sweet seventeen*** かぐわしき17歳, 妙齢,「鬼も十八」 ▪ That petitionary grace of *sweet seventeen* subdued me ere she spoke. 妙齢の娘の優雅に嘆願する様子が彼女が口をきかないうちから私を征服してしまった.

seventh /sévənθ/ 形 ***commit the seventh*** 《俗》姦通する ▪ He fancied that he was *committing the seventh.* 彼は姦通しているような気になった. ☞the seventh = the seventh commandment.

seventy /sévənti/ 形名 ***in*** *one's* ***seventies*** 70歳代で ▪ The woman was *in her seventies* then. 当時その女性は70歳代だった.

in the seventies 70年代に ▪ He must have been born *in the* late *seventies.* 彼は70年代の終わりに生まれたにちがいない.

seventy times seven 7たびを70倍するまで, いくたびとなく(《聖》*Matt.* 18. 22) ▪ *Seventy times seven* did I take counsel with my soul. いくたびとなく私は自分の心に聞いてみた.

sever /sévər/ 動 ***sever*** *oneself* ***from*** ...との関係を断つ, から脱退する ▪ He should *sever himself from* them completely. 彼は彼らとの関係をすっかり断たねばならない.

several /sévərəl/ 形 ***every*** [***each***] ***several*** おのおのの ▪ I know *each several* person of them. 彼らのおのおのを知っている.

Several men, several minds. 《諺》十人十色.

severalty /sévərəlti/ 名 ***in severalty*** 別々に ▪ They are trifling when regarded *in severalty.* それらは別々に見ればささいなものだ.

severe /sɪvíər/ 形 (***be***) ***severe on*** [***upon, with***] ...に手きびしい ▪ He *is severe with* his children. 彼は子供に厳格だ.

severely /sɪvíərli/ 副 ***leave*** [***let***] ***... severely alone*** ...をわざと避ける, 無視する, 敬遠する ▪ You must show him your contempt by *leaving* him *severely alone.* 彼をわざと避けて軽蔑を見せつけてやらねばならない ▪ The question *was* regarded as quite insolvable and *severely left alone.* その問題は全く解けないものとみなされ無視された.

severity /sɪvérəti/ 名 ***with severity*** 厳格に ▪ The king punished him *with severity.* 王は彼を厳罰に処した.

sew /soʊ/ 動 ***be sewed up with*** ...で忙しい ▪ He *was sewed up* all afternoon *with* visitors. 彼は午後の間ずっとお客さんで忙しかった.

sew up *a person's* ***stocking*** 《俗》人を黙らせる, やりこめる ▪ You've *sewed up my stocking.* 僕はぐうの音も出なくなったよ.

sex /seks/ 名 ***the fair***(***er***) [***gentle***(***r***), ***soft***(***er***), ***weak***(***er***), ***devout, second***] ***sex*** 女性(women) ▪ It is much frequented by *the fair sex.* そこはよく女性が行く所だ.

the rough(***er***) [***sterner, stronger***] ***sex*** 男性(men) ▪ While *the rough sex* seek prey abroad, women keep home and spin. 男性が外で獲物を捜している間, 女性は家にいて糸を紡ぐ.

the third sex 《口》同性愛者 ▪ He is rumored to belong to *the third sex.* 彼はゲイだという噂だ.

shabby /ʃǽbi/ 形 ***Not too shabby.*** 《俗》悪くない, なかなかいいよ, まあまあだ ▪ How're you doing? —*Not too shabby.* どう, 元気かい—まあまあだ.

shackle /ʃǽkəl/ 名 ***throw*** [***knock***] ***off the shackles*** 束縛をかなぐり捨てる ▪ John *threw off the shackles* and went his own wild way. ジョンは束縛をかなぐり捨てて放らつにやった.

shade /ʃeɪd/ 名 ***a shade better*** [***more,*** etc.] 心持ちよい[多い, など] ▪ I feel *a shade better* today. きょうは少し気分がいい ▪ I drew my chair *a shade nearer* to her. いすを少し彼女の方へ寄せた.

be in the shade 隠とんしている, 世に知られずにいる ▪ How can we see a man's brilliant qualities if he *is* what we call "*in the shade*"? 人がいわゆる「隠とんして」いたら, どうしてその英才を知ることができようか.

cast [***throw, put***] ***... into*** [***in***] ***the shade*** ...を顔色なからしめる, の光彩を失わせる ▪ The flower was so pretty as to *throw* all others *into the shade.* その花は他のすべての花の光彩を失わせるほどきれいだった.

S

fall into the shade 世間から忘れられる ▪ But, finally, the original Semite *fell* more *into the shade*. しかし, ついに元のセム族はますます世間から忘れられていった.

go (***down***) [***dismiss***] ***to the shades*** 死ぬ[殺す] ▪ Then let our swords *dismiss* him *to the shades*. では我々の剣で彼を冥府へ送ってやろう.

in the shade 日陰で; 目立たない所で (↔in the SUN 2) ▪ The thermometer stood at 90°F *in the shade*. 寒暖計は日陰でカ氏90度だった ▪ He has been brought up *in the shade* from a child. 彼は子供の時から目立たない所で育て上げられた.

light and shade **1** (絵画の)明暗 ▪ The picture has a good contrast of *light and shade*. この絵は明暗のコントラストがよい.
2 (文学作品・音楽などの)明るさと暗さ ▪ You must be careful of your *light and shade* in this passage. このくだりの明るさと暗さに注意しなければならない.

put [***throw***]***... into*** [***in***] ***the shade*** →cast... into the SHADE.

remain in the shade 隠とんしている, 世間に知られていない ▪ Bacon still *remained in the shade*. ベイコンはまだ世間に知られていなかった.

shades of …の再来 ▪ They say there are *shades of* the financial panic of 1929 now. いまは1929年の大恐慌の再来だと言われている.

the shades of night [***evening***] 夜陰[夕闇] ▪ *The shades of night* had by this time fallen upon the great city. 夜陰がこの頃はもうその大都会に降りていた.

the shadow of a shade 《詩・雅》空(ᵏᵘ)の空(ᵏᵘ), 幻影 ▪ My life is *the shadow of a shade* now. 私の命は今や幻影のごときものだ.

shadow /ʃǽdoʊ/ 名 ***be a shadow of*** *one's* (***former*** [***old***]) ***self*** 変わり果てる (→the (mere) SHADOW of one's former self) ▪ The fine-looking, commanding man has *become a shadow of his former self*. かっこよく堂々とした男が変わり果ててしまった.

be afraid [***frightened, scared***] ***of*** *one's* ***own shadow*** わが影をこわがる, むやみにびくびくしている ▪ The truth is, she *was afraid of her own shadow*. 実は彼女はむやみにびくびくしていたのだ.

beyond a shadow of doubt 《法》全く疑いなく ▪ The opinion poll proves *beyond a shadow of doubt* that the conservatives will confound the nation. 世論調査では保守党員が将来国を混乱させるという結果がはっきり出ている.

cast a [*one's*] ***shadow on*** [***over***] …に影を投げる; を傷つける ▪ This scandal *cast a shadow on* his reputation. このスキャンダルが彼の名声を傷つけた.

cast *one's* ***shadow before*** 前もってその影を投げる, 前兆がある ▪ Coming events *cast their shadows before*. 事の起こるときにはその前兆がある.

catch at the [***run after a***] ***shadow*** 影をつかもうとする, むだ骨を折る ▪ He was now determined to seize the substance as well as *catch at the shadow*. 彼は今や影をつかもうとするばかりか実をもつかんでやろうと決心していた.

emerge from the shadows 表舞台に登場する ▪ The scientist *emerged from the shadows* after having studied for a long time. 長年の研究の後, その科学者は表舞台に登場した.

fight with *one's* ***own shadow*** むだ骨を折る; でたらめを話す ▪ In this argument he *fought with his own shadow*. この議論で彼はでたらめを話した.

five o'clock shadow 朝剃ってまた夕方のびてくるひげ, またのびかけたひげ ▪ He shaved away his *five o'clock shadow* before he went out. 彼は出かける前にのびかけていたひげを剃った.

in *a person's* ***shadow*** →in the SHADOW of.

in the shadow of …のすぐ近くに; の影響下に, 陰に隠れて ▪ They seem to live *in the shadow of* misfortune. 彼らは不幸と隣り合わせに住んでいるように見える ▪ He lived *in the shadow of* his brother. 彼は兄に隠れて生活した.

live in the shadow 日陰の生活をする ▪ He *lived in the shadow* after his retirement. 彼は引退してから日陰の生活をした.

May your shadow never grow [***be***] ***less!*** ますますご繁栄のほどを! ▪ "*May your shadow never grow less!*" said another. 「ますますご繁栄のほどを!」ともう一人が言った. ☞ペルシャ起源の句で,「アラビア夜話」などに出てくる.

not the [***a***] ***shadow of/no shadow of*** みじんの…もない ▪ He has*n't* really *the shadow of* a claim on us. 彼は我々に事実みじんの要求権も持っていない ▪ There is *no shadow of* doubt. みじんの疑いもない.

quarrel with *one's* ***own shadow*** 《口》自分の影とけんかをする, ごくつまらないことで怒る ▪ He'd *quarrel with his own shadow*, if he hadn't got anyone else to be angry with! 他に腹を立てる人がいなければ彼は自分の影とけんかをしかねない.

run after a shadow →catch at the SHADOW.

shadow of turning 〚主に否定文で〛ごくわずかの変転 (《聖》*Jas.* 1. 17) ▪ The human psyche knows no *shadow of turning*. 人間の心は変転ということはみじんも知らない.

the Land of the Shadow of Death 死の影の国《西アフリカの白人住民の死亡率の一番高い地域の修辞的な呼称》 ▪ *The Land of the Shadow of Death* stretches from Goree to Loanda. 死の影の国はゴリーからロアンダまで広がっている.

the (***mere***) ***shadow of*** *one's* ***former self*** (病気・悲しみ・苦労などで)見る影もなく変わり果てた姿 ▪ He is but *the mere shadow of his former self*. 彼は全く見る影もなく変わり果ててしまっている.

the shadow of a name 微かに残る名声 ▪ What he earned was but *the shadow of a name*. 彼がかち得たのは微かに残る名声にすぎなかった. ☞Ⓛ nominis umbra のなぞり.

the shadow of death 死の影, 死相 ▪ *The*

shadow of death is on his face. 死相が彼の顔に現れている.

the valley of the shadow of death 死の影の谷《病気で死に直面している状態を言う》(《聖》*Ps*. 23. 4) ▪ I have watched my child through *the valley of the shadow of death* and seen it come back to life. 私はわが子が死の影の谷をさまようのを見守り, またよみがえるのを見た.

under the shadow of **1** = in the SHADOW of.

2 …の危険があって, になりそうな様子で ▪ In old age we live *under the shadow of* death. 老年には我々は死の影のもとに暮らしている.

3 …の庇護のもとに ▪ The deed was done *under the shadow of* his name. その行為は彼の名の庇護のもとになされたのだった.

worn to a shadow 見る影もなくやせ衰えて ▪ I was *worn to a shadow* by want. 私は貧困のために影のようにやせ衰えた.

Your shadow hasn't grown any less. 少しもおやせになりませんね.

shady /ʃéɪdi/ 形 ***keep shady*** 《米口》人目を避ける[避けさせる] ▪ Don't hang around, but *keep shady*. ぶらぶらしていないで人目を避けなさい ▪ I've promised to *keep* him *shady*. 私は彼をかくまってやることを約束した.

on the shady side of →on the wrong SIDE of.

shaft /ʃæft|ʃɑːft/ 名 ***give*** [***get***] ***the shaft*** 《米俗》だます[だまされる], ぺてんにかける[かかる] ▪ If you signed that paper, you would be *getting the shaft*. その書類に署名したら, だまされることになるぞ.

shag[1] /ʃæg/ 名 ***like a shag on a rock*** 《豪口》全く一人ぼっちに ▪ My parents went out and left me *like a shag on a rock*. 両親が出かけて私を全くの一人ぼっちにした.

shag[2] /ʃæg/ 動 ***be shagged out*** 《英口》くたくたになる ▪ I'*m shagged out* after a day's work. 1日働いたのでくたくただ.

shake[1] /ʃeɪk/ 名 ***a fair shake*** 《米俗》公平なやり方 ▪ That wasn't *a fair shake*. あれは公平なやり口じゃなかったよ. ☞get a fair [good] shake で「公平に扱われる」, give a fair [good] shake で「公平に扱う」の意.

a shake of the hand 握手 ▪ Our salutations consist of many *shakes of the hand*. 我々のあいさつはたびたび握手することから成っている.

a shake of the [*one's*] ***head*** (否定・疑いなどで)首を横に振ること ▪ He observed with *a shake of his head* that he himself hadn't made it out. 彼は自分もわかっていないのだと首を横に振りながら言った.

all of a shake 《口》ぶるぶる震えて ▪ We found the boy *all of a shake*. 我々が行ってみると男の子はぶるぶる震えていた.

be no great [***some, considerable,*** etc.] ***shakes*** 《口》(才能・重要性が)たいしたものではない[である] ▪ He *is no great shakes* at learned chat. 彼は学問的なおしゃべりではたいしたものではない ▪ Ten years ago the party *was considerable shakes*. 10年前にはその党はかなりのものだった. ☞おそらくさいころを振ることから.

for a shake 《口》ちょっとの間 ▪ *For a shake* they had stood there silently. ちょっとの間彼らは黙ってそこに立っていた.

give a shake **1** (…を)ひとゆすりする ▪ We *gave* the tree *a shake*. 我々はその木をひとゆすりした ▪ It seems to have *given a shake* to memory. それは記憶をひとゆすりしたもののようだ.

2 《米俗》(いやな人・物を)追っぱらう, 避ける ▪ I want to *give* them *a shake*. 私は彼らを追っぱらいたいと思う.

give the cold shake 《米俗》(…を)追っぱらう, 避ける ▪ They all *give* him *the cold shake*. 彼らはみんな彼を避けている.

have a fit of the shakes **1** (恐怖のために)震える ▪ She *had a* terrible *fit of the shakes*. 彼女はひどくがたがた震えた.

2 悪寒[おこり]がする ▪ He *had a fit of the shakes*. 彼は急に悪寒がしてきた.

in a shake/ in half a shake/ in two [***a brace of, a couple of***] ***shakes/ in the shake of the hand*** [***a lamb's tail***] 《口》たちまち, あっと言うまに ▪ He'll be at the church *in two shakes*. 彼はあっと言うまに教会に着くだろう ▪ I'll finish this *in the shake of a lamb's tail*. これをあっと言うまにすませるよ.

shake[2] /ʃeɪk/ 動 ***Let's shake on it.*** (握手をして)これで手を打とう.

shake *oneself* **1** (人・動物が雪・ちり・しこりなどを払うために)体をぶるぶるっとする ▪ The dog *shook itself* to throw off the wet. 犬は水気を払うために体をぶるぶるっと振るった.

2 身を振るい起こす ▪ The watchman *shook himself*. 夜番は身を振るい起こした.

shake a foot [***a toe,*** *one's* ***bones, feet, heels, shanks***] 踊る ▪ I'd like to *shake a foot* with Fanny there. 僕はあそこのファニーと踊りたい.

shake a leg **1** =SHAKE a foot.

2 《口》急ぐ ▪ We'd better *shake a leg* or we'll miss the train. 急がなければ列車に遅れるぞ.

3 動き回る ▪ In my house honesty alone should *shake a leg*. 私の家では正直者だけが動き回るべきだ.

shake *one's* ***bones*** →SHAKE a foot.

shake *a person* ***by the beard*** [***ears***] 人のひげ[耳]をつかんでこうき回す ▪ He gripped me and *shook* me *by the ears*. 彼は私をぐっと握って耳をつかんでこうき回した.

shake *a person* ***cold*** 《米》人にきっぱりとひじ鉄をくわせる ▪ She *shook* him *cold* yesterday. 女はきのうきっぱりと彼にひじ鉄をくわせた.

shake *one's* ***ears*** **1** (人が)目をさます, 動き出す ▪ The thrifty villagers had long since *shaken their ears*. 倹約家の村人たちはとっくに目ざめていた.

2 冷淡[嫌悪, 喜び]の色を表す ▪ He *shook his ears*

S

as if he had drunk base wine. 彼はひどくまずいワインを飲んだかのように嫌悪の色を示した ▪ He will *shake his ears* to hear himself praised. 彼は自分がほめられるのを聞いたら喜びの色を表すことだろう. ☞動物が耳を振ることから.

***shake feet* [*heels*]** →SHAKE a foot.

shake** one's **finger at (人)に人差し指を向けてぴくぴく動かす《脅迫·叱責のしぐさ》 ▪ The master *shook his finger at* the idle boy. 先生は怠惰な少年に人差し指を向け動かしてしかった.

shake** one's **fist (怒って)こぶしを振り回す ▪ He *shook his fist* in the old man's face. 彼は老人の顔の前でこぶしを振り回した.

***shake** oneself **free* [*loose, awake, sober*]** 体を振って離れる[脱する, 目をさます, しらふになる] (*from*) ▪ The Roman Church determined to *shake itself free from* this thraldom. ローマ教会はこの束縛から身を振り離そうと決心した ▪ He *shook himself awake*. 彼は体を振って目をさました ▪ Just *shake yourself sober*, and listen. ちょっと体を振ってしらふになってこちらの言うことを聞いてくれ.

shake** a person's **hand/shake** a person **by the hand 人と握手する ▪ He *shook her hand* earnestly. 彼は熱心に彼女と握手した ▪ I *shook* him *by the hand* at the parting. 私は別れるとき彼と握手した.

shake hands (あいさつ·仲直りなどのしるしに)握手する (*on, over, with*) ▪ We *shook hands*, and parted. 我々は握手をして別れた ▪ *Shake hands with* Mr. Smith. 《米俗》スミスさんをご紹介します ▪ They *shook hands on* [*over*] the bargain. 彼らはその契約を決めたしるしに握手した.

shake** one's **head →HEAD[1].

***shake in** one's **shoes* [*boots*]** (怖くて)身震いする ▪ The boy *shook in his shoes* when he saw the cane in the master's hand. 男の子は先生の手のむちを見ると身震いした.

Shake it! 《口》急いで!

***shake like a leaf* [*jelly*]** (恐怖·不安などで)ぶるぶる震える ▪ The boy stood before the teacher, *shaking like a leaf*. その少年は教師の前にぶるぶる震えながら立っていた.

shake shanks →SHAKE a foot.

shake** one's **sides →split one's SIDEs.

shake the dust off** one's **feet →DUST[1].

shake** oneself **together 《口》気力を奮い起こす ▪ Come, *shake yourself together*. さあ, 元気を出すんだ.

sham /ʃæm/ 動 ***sham** oneself **into*** ごまかして…になる ▪ She *shammed herself into* favor at court. 彼女はごまかして宮中で愛顧を得るようになった.

shame[1] /ʃéɪm/ 名 ***a crying shame*** 実に残念なこと, 全く遺憾な話 ▪ It's *a crying shame* that they should be separated from one another. 彼らが別れ別れにされるなんて全く遺憾な話だ.

a son* [*child*] *of shame 私生児 ▪ As *a child of shame*, the people of the village did not treat her well. 村の人々は彼女を私生児としてまともに扱わなかった.

be lost* [*dead*] *to shame 恥を知らない ▪ The girl *is lost to* all sense of *shame*. あの娘は少しも恥を知らない.

bring* [*put*]*... to shame **1** …を赤面させる, 侮辱する ▪ That *puts* me *to shame*. それで私は赤面させられる.

2 …を顔色なからしめる, しのぐ ▪ That *brings to shame* even a professional singer. それでは本職の歌手も顔負けだ.

***cry shame on* [*upon*]** 恥さらしだと言って…を非難する ▪ The policy was detestable: all the citizens *cried shame upon* it. その政策はひどいものだったので, 全ての市民は恥さらしだと言ってそれを非難した.

feel shame at …を恥ずかしく思う ▪ I *feel shame at* having told a lie. 私は嘘を言ったのを恥ずかしく思っている.

Fie for shame! 恥を知れ!, みっともない! ▪ *Fie for shame!* Here is someone coming. みっともない! 誰かやって来るよ.

for shame **1** 恥ずかしいので; 恥をかかないように ▪ I cannot do it *for shame*. 恥ずかしくてそんなことはできない.

2 〚間投詞的に〛 恥ずかしい ▪ *For shame*, let me go. みっともない, 離してください.

for shame's sake 恥ずかしくて ▪ I could not *for shame's sake* take this course. 私は恥ずかしくてこの道を選ぶことができなかった.

have no shame 恥を知らない ▪ *Have* you *no shame*, boy? 恥を知らないのか, お前は.

have shame 《詩》恥じる, 恥ずかしく思う (*of, to do, that*) ▪ She *had* great *shame that* she had a child. 彼女は自分に子がいることをひどく恥じていた.

***it is a* (*real*) *shame to* do [*that ...*]** 《口》…するとは恥さらしだ[残念だ, 気の毒だ] ▪ *It is a* great *shame to* treat you like that! 君をそんなふうに扱うとはとんでもないことだ ▪ *It's a shame that* you're sick. 病気だなんてお気の毒に.

past* [*without*] *shame 恥を知らない ▪ He is *past shame*. 彼は恥知らずだ ▪ He is quite *without shame*. 彼は全く恥知らずだ.

put ... to shame →bring ... to SHAME.

Shame to* [*on*]*...! …の恥知らずめ! ▪ *Shame on* you*!* この恥知らずめ! ▪ *Shame to* them*!* あの連中の恥さらしめ!

***take shame to* [*upon*] oneself** 恥ずかしく思う; 自分が悪かったと認める (*for*) ▪ They *take shame to themselves for* the evil which is in them. 彼らは自分のうちにある悪を恥ずかしく思っている ▪ I *take shame upon myself for* this crime. この罪のことでは私は自分が悪かったことを認める.

(The) more shame for ...! …は恥の上塗りだ! ▪ *(The) more shame for* him, that he sends it me. あの男がそれを僕に送ってよこすなんて恥の上塗りだ.

think* (*it*) *shame 恥じる (*of, for, to do, that*) ▪ Don't you *think shame of* yourself? あなたは自

S

分を恥ずかしいとは思いませんか ▪I would *think shame to* do it. そんなことをするのは恥ずかしい.

to one's shame 恥ずかしいことではあるが ▪*To my shame*, I never read a line of him since. 恥ずかしいことだがその後1行も彼の作は読んでいない.

What a shame! 《口》 **1** なんてひどいことだ, けしからん! ▪*What a shame* to deceive a girl! 少女を欺くなんてけしからん.

2 気の毒[残念]だ ▪*What a shame* (that) it had to rain today! 今日雨が降るとは残念だ.

without shame →past SHAME.

shame[2] /ʃéɪm/ 動 ***(tell [say, speak] the truth and) shame the devil*** 言うまいとする心を押し切って大胆に本当のことを言う, 思いきって本当のことを話す ▪Come, *tell the truth and shame the devil*. さあ思い切って本当のことを言いなさい ▪Paul answered, boldly *shaming the devil*. ポールは答えとして大胆に本当のことを言った ▪I'll *tell the truth and shame the devil*—I've failed my exam. 思いきって本当のことを言います—僕, 試験に落ちたんです.

shank /ʃæŋk/ 名 ***on Shanks' [Shank's] mare*** [《英》***pony***] 徒歩で, ひざ栗毛で ▪I'd rather ride *on Shanks' mare*. 私はむしろ徒歩で行きたい ▪I'll start for London *on Shanks' pony*. 私は徒歩でロンドンへ立ちましょう. ☞shanks 《戯》= legs.

shape[1] /ʃeɪp/ 名 ***find a shape in*** …に実現化[具体化]する ▪His dreams *find a shape in* poetry. 彼の夢は詩に具体化する.

get [be] bent out of shape 《口》怒る, 頭にくる ▪I *get* really *bent out of shape* when he takes no notice of me. 彼が私を無視すると本当に頭にくる.

get in shape →keep in SHAPE.

get into shape まとめる; 格好がつく ▪It is time I *got* my ideas *into shape*. もう考えをまとめていい頃だ.

give shape to …に格好をつける, をまとめる ▪We are *giving shape to* a new plan. 我々は新しい案をまとめているところだ.

in all shapes and sizes 大小様々な形で ▪The plants grow *in all shapes and sizes*. その植物は大小様々な形で生えている.

in any shape (or form) どのような形でも ▪Tell me how I may be useful *in any shape*. どのような形でお手伝いできるか言ってください ▪He asks commission *in any shape or form*. 彼は何らかの形の手数料を要求する.

in good [bad, poor] shape 《口》良い[悪い]状態で ▪The business was *in* very *bad* [*good*] *shape*. 業務はひどい状態になっていた[非常にうまくいっていた].

in no shape 全く…ない ▪I am *in no shape* worthy of your care. 私はあなたに世話していただく値うちは全くありません.

in shape **1** 格好は ▪*In shape* Chesterton resembled a barrel. チェスタトンは格好がたるに似ていた.

2 体調がよい (↔out of SHAPE 2) ▪I felt relieved she looked *in shape*. 彼女の体調がよさそうでほっとした.

in the shape of **1** …に体現して ▪We found their patriotism *in the shape of* George Washington. 我々は彼らの愛国心がジョージ・ワシントンに体現しているのを見いだした.

2 …の類の ▪I had nothing *in the shape of* food. 私は食物に類するものは何ひとつなかった.

3 …の形の[で] ▪A demon appeared *in the shape of* a man. 悪魔が人間の姿で現れた ▪His services were recognized *in the shape of* a small pension. 彼の功労は僅かな年金の形で報いられた.

keep [get] in shape **1** 形がくずれないようにする ▪The box *was kept in shape* by paste. その箱はのりで形がくずれないようにしてあった.

2 良好な状態におく ▪*Get* your car *in shape* for the race. 車をレースに備えて調子をよくしておけ.

knock ... into shape →KNOCK[2].

lick ... into shape →LICK[2].

out of shape **1** 形がくずれて ▪My hat was quite *out of shape* after the rain. あの雨のあと帽子の形がすっかりくずれてしまった.

2 体の調子が悪くて (↔in SHAPE 2) ▪He is badly *out of shape*. 彼はひどく調子が悪くなっている.

put ... in shape …を調子よくする ▪A few months in the country will *put* him *in* good physical *shape* again. 田舎で数か月過ごせば彼はまた健康になるだろう.

put [throw] ... into shape (考え・計画など)を具体化させる, まとめる ▪He tried to *put* his thoughts *into shape* by talking. 彼は話すことによって自分の考えをまとめようとした.

settle into shape 形が定まる, 目鼻がつく ▪Things are *settling into shape*. 物事の目鼻がつきかけている.

show one's shapes 《口》姿を現す ▪Step forward, and *show your shapes*, man. 前へ出て来て姿を見せるんだ, おい.

take shape 形をなす, 目鼻がつく, 具体化する (*in*) ▪The building is now *taking shape*. その建物は今形をなしつつある ▪Intention *took shape in* action. 意図が行動に具体化した.

take the shape of …の形をとる ▪Their present *took the shape of* a check for £100. 彼らの贈り物は100ポンドの小切手という形になった.

the shape of things to come 未来図; 未来 (future) ▪I am going to describe to you *the shape of things to come*. 私は諸君に未来図を描いてみせようと思う. ☞H. G. Wells, *The Shape of Things to Come* (1933)から.

throw ... into shape →put ... into SHAPE.

shape[2] /ʃeɪp/ 動 ***shape an answer*** (言葉を定めて)返答する ▪He thus *shaped an answer*. 彼はこのように返答した.

shape one's course 《海》(ある場所に向けて)舵を

取る; 進んで行く (*for, to*) ▪ We now *shaped our course for* Madeira. 我々は今やマデイラへ向けて舵を取った.

Shape up, or ship out. 《口》しっかりしろ, それができなければ出て行け.

share[1] /ʃeər/ 名 ***be*** *one's* ***share*** 《口》割り前を負担する ▪ He was asked to *be his share*. 彼は割り前を負担することを求められた.

bear a [*one's*] ***share in*** →have a SHARE in.

bear *one's* ***share of*** ...を分担する ▪ He must *bear his share of* responsibility. 彼も責任を分担しなければならない.

club shares (***with***) →go SHAREs (with).

cry shares (他人が見つけたり盗んだものの)割り前を要求する ▪ When I found the money, he *cried shares*. 私がその金を見つけると, 彼は分け前を要求した.

fall to *one's* ***share*** 割り当てられる; めぐり合わせになる (*to do*) ▪ The plants *fell to his share*. その木が彼に割り当てられた ▪ It *fell to my share to* be confined to a room in the house. 私はその家の部屋に閉じ込められるめぐり合わせになった.

for *one's* ***share*** ...としては (= for one's PART) ▪ *For my share* I scorn a sycophant. 私としてはごますりは軽蔑する.

get a share of ...の分け前にあずかる ▪ I must *get a share of* the plunder. 私もその分取り品の分け前にあずからねばならない.

give a share in ...の分け前を与える, を分かち合う ▪ I want to *give* you *a share in* my happiness. 私の幸福をあなたと分かち合いたい.

go share and share alike 平等に分ける, 山分けする (*with*) (→SHARE and share alike) ▪ He *went share and share alike with* them in everything. 彼はその連中と何もかも山分けにした.

go [***run, club***] ***shares*** (***with***) (...と)共同でする, 分担する, 山分けする (*in*) ▪ I *ran shares with* a friend *in* the enterprise. 私はその仕事を友人と共同でやった ▪ If you find the treasure, we will *go shares*. 君がその宝を発見したら山分けにしよう.

have [***take***] ***a share in*** ...を分担する ▪ Let me *take a share in* the expenses. 費用を分担させてください.

have [***take, bear***] ***a*** [*one's*] ***share in*** ...にあずかる ▪ You *had a share in* our victory. あなたも我々の勝利に貢献したのだ ▪ He *took* no *share in* the business. 彼はその仕事には少しも関与しなかった.

have [***take***] *one's* (***fair***) ***share of*** ...の分け前を得る ▪ You've *had* more than *your fair share of* this cake. 君はこのケーキを分け前以上に食べた ▪ You must *take your share of* the blame. 君も同様に非難を受けねばならない.

on [***upon***] (***the***) ***shares*** (損得を)持ち合いにして (*with*) ▪ He proposed to me to go *on shares with* him. 彼は私に持ち合いにして行こうと提案した.

run shares (***with***) →go SHAREs (with).

share and share alike 平等に分けて, 山分けにして ▪ All costs should be *share and share alike*. すべての費用は平等に分けねばならない ▪ They shared the inheritance *share and share alike*. 彼らは遺産を平等に分け合った.

one's [***a***] ***share of the pie*** [《英》***cake***] 《米》利益の分け前 ▪ Workers are demanding *their share of the cake*. 労働者も利益の分け前を要求している.

take a share in →have a SHARE in.

share[2] /ʃeər/ 動 ***share alone*** ひとり占めにする《誤用》 ▪ You should not *share alone* the glory of the deed. 君はその行為の光栄を独占すべきではない.

share and share (***alike***) 平等に分ける, 山分けにする (→SHARE[1] and share alike) ▪ In Kent the sons *share and share alike*. ケント州では息子は平等に分ける.

sharp /ʃɑːrp/ 形副 (***as***) ***sharp as a needle*** [***razor,*** 《米》 ***tack, sickle***] 非常に鋭い ▪ Her words were *sharp as a needle*. 彼女の言葉はとてもしんらつだった.

(***as***) ***sharp as a serpent's tooth*** (毒舌が)とても鋭い ▪ That woman's tongue is *sharp as a serpent's tooth*. あの女性の舌はとても毒々しい.

be not the sharpest knife in the drawer/ be not the sharpest tool in the box 《戯》賢くない, 頭が切れない ▪ She's pretty, but she's *not the sharpest knife in the drawer*. 彼女, かわいいけど, 賢くはないね.

be sharp on [***upon***] (非難・批評で)...を手きびしくやっつける ▪ You *were* so *sharp upon* those ladies. 君はあの女性たちをとても手きびしくやっつけたな.

be too sharp for *a person* 人をだし抜く[だます] ▪ He *was too sharp for* me. 彼は私の裏をかいた.

have a sharp tongue 《口》口が悪い, 毒舌をふるう ▪ He's *got a sharp tongue*, so you've got to be careful of him. 彼は口が悪いので気をつけな.

look sharp →LOOK[2].

play sharp on *a person* →PLAY[2].

Sharp is the word! 早く, 早く!; 抜かりなくやれ! ▪ Are you thereabouts? Then *sharp's the word*. 君はその辺にいるのかい. だったら早く早く ▪ *Sharp's the word* and quick's the motion with him. あの男は抜かりがなく動きがすばやい.

sharp practice 抜け目のない取引 ▪ The firm is known for its *sharp practice*. その会社は抜け目のない取引で知られている.

so sharp *one'****ll cut*** *oneself* 利口すぎて失敗する ▪ He's *so sharp* he'*ll cut himself* one of these days. 彼は利口すぎるのでいずれ失敗しよう.

the sharp end 《主に英口》大変な立場, 矢面 (*of*) ▪ He is at *the sharp end of* investors. 彼は投資家たちの矢面に立たされている.

sharpen /ʃɑ́ːrpən/ 動 ***sharpen*** *one's* ***brain*** [***wits***] もっと頭を働かせる ▪ You'll need to *sharpen your wits* if you hope to get on in business. 商売で成功したければもっと頭を働かせる必要がある.

shave[1] /ʃeɪv/ 名 ***a close*** [***near, narrow***]

shave やっと逃れること, 間一髪 ▪ We passed clear, but it was *a close shave*. すっぱり通り抜けはしたものの, まさに間一髪というところだった ▪ I had *a narrow shave* of it. やっと逃れた.

have a shave ひげをそってもらう ▪ Being here, I may as well *have a shave*. ここにいるのだから, ひげをそってもらったほうがいい.

What a shave! 気の毒, 大変 ▪ I missed the train this morning.—Oh, *what a shave!* けさ列車に乗り遅れた—それはお気の毒でしたね.

shave[2] /ʃeɪv/ 動 ***shave*** *oneself* ひげをそる ▪ He seldom *shaves himself*. 彼はめったにひげをそらない.

shave a note 《米》手形を大割引きで買う ▪ He says he is making a good living in *shaving notes*. 彼は手形を大割引きで買っていい儲けをしていると言っている.

shave paper = SHAVE a note.

she /ʃi, ʃiː/ 名 ***Is it a he or a she?*** (生まれた子が)男の子か女の子か ▪ The child's born, Doctor? *Is it a he or a she?* 子供は生まれたんですか, 先生. 男の子ですか女の子ですか.

shear /ʃɪər/ 動 ***(be) shorn of*** …を奪われて(いる) ▪ I *am shorn of* my strength. 私は力を奪われている ▪ The gambler came home *shorn of* his money. ばくち打ちは金をすっかり無くして帰って来た.

shebang /ʃɪbǽŋ/ 名 ***the whole shebang*** [***enchilada***] 《米口》何もかも, 誰もかも ▪ I'm sick of *the whole shebang*. 何もかもいやになった.

shed /ʃed/ 動 ***shed*** [***spill***] ***blood*** 人を殺す ▪ They *shed blood* they had no right to shed. 彼らは殺す権利のない人を殺した.

shed much [***little***] ***blood*** 多くの[少数の]人を殺す ▪ *Much blood was shed* in the field that day. その日戦場では多くの人が殺された.

shed *one's* ***(own) blood*** (祖国・大義などのために)血を流す(*for*) ▪ They *shed* much of *their blood for* their country. 彼らは祖国のために多く血を流した.

shed the blood of *a person* 人を殺す ▪ He is a holy man; we may not *shed his blood*. 彼は聖なる人だ. 彼を殺してはなるまい.

sheep /ʃiːp/ 名 ***a black sheep*** もて余し者; 恥さらし, 面汚し ▪ There is *a black sheep* in every flock. 《諺》どこにも困り者はいる ▪ Here comes Kate, *the black sheep* of the family. ケイトが来たよ, あの一家のもて余し者が.

a lost [***stray, wandering***] ***sheep*** 迷える羊, 正道を踏みはずした人 (《聖》*Jer*. 50. 6; *Matt*. 10. 6, etc.) ▪ Many are *lost sheep* at times. 多くの人がときとして迷える羊となる.

cast [***make***] ***sheep's eyes at*** …に色目を使う, 秋波を送る ▪ He was *casting sheep's eyes at* my daughter. 彼は私の娘に色目を使った ▪ Local leaders *cast sheep's eyes at* the seat. 地方の指導者たちはその席に秋波を送っていた.

count sheep 羊の数を数える《寝入ろうとする》 ▪ I lay in bed, *counting sheep*. 私は羊の数を数えながらベッドに横たわっていた.

follow like sheep 盲従する ▪ Some men will *follow* a leader *like sheep*. 人によっては指導者に盲従する者がいる.

like being savaged by a dead sheep 効果がない, 少しもこたえない ▪ When I scold him he finds it's *like being savaged by a dead sheep*. 彼はしかっても少しもこたえない.

like sheep 《軽蔑》自主性のない, 従順な ▪ He just follows my orders *like sheep*. 彼は私の命令にただ従順に従うだけだ.

One may as well be hanged [***Just as good***] ***for a sheep as (for) a lamb.*** 《諺》毒をくらわば皿まで.

return to *one's* ***sheep*** 本題[当面の問題]に戻る ▪ But to *return to my sheep*. しかし本題に戻ろう.

separate [***divide, sort out***] ***the sheep and*** [***from***] ***the goats*** 善人と悪人とを区別する, 役に立つ人と立たない人とを区別する (《聖》*Matt*. 25. 32) ▪ We'll go through the list of members, and *separate the sheep from the goats*. 会員名簿に目を通して役に立つ人と立たない人を区別しよう.

sheep that have no shepherd/sheep without a shepherd 指導者のない群衆, 烏合の衆 (《聖》*Matt*. 9. 36) ▪ His guests were as *sheep without a shepherd*. 彼の客たちは烏合の衆のようだった.

sheese /ʃiːz/ 名 ***the whole sheese*** 《俗》一番実力のある人, 唯一偉い人 ▪ He is *the whole sheese* in the business world. 彼が財界で一番の実力者だ.

sheet[1] /ʃiːt/ 名 ***a clean sheet*** **1** 無事故の経歴 ▪ I've had *a clean sheet* ever since I've been with my present firm. 私は現在の会社に勤めてからずっと無事故で過ごしてきている.

2 《英・報道》無得点, 無失点 ▪ The pitcher kept *a clean sheet* in the game. ピッチャーはその試合で無失点に押さえた.

(as) white as a sheet →WHITE.

between the lawful sheets 正式に結婚して ▪ My daughters got *between the lawful sheets*. 娘たちは正式に結婚した.

between the sheets 《口》床について ▪ He was already lying *between the sheets*. 彼はもう床についていた.

in sheets **1** (雨などが)滝のように ▪ The rain came down *in sheets*. 雨は滝のように降ってきた.

2 (本が)製本されずに ▪ These books are all *in sheets*. この本はどれも製本していない.

put on [***wear, stand in***] ***a white sheet*** (公に)前非をざんげする, 悔い改める ▪ I don't see why I should *stand in a white sheet* for something I did not do. しなかったことを悔い改めなければならない理由がわからない. ☞罪人に白衣を着せて公衆の前に立たせたことから.

sing from the same hymn [***song***] ***sheet*** 《英》人前で同じ意見を述べる ▪ We have to show him that we are all *singing from the same hymn sheet*. 私たちはみんな同じ意見だということを彼に示す必要がある.

with a clean sheet =with a clean SLATE.

sheet[2] /ʃiːt/ 名 ***be* [*have*] *a sheet in the wind* [*wind's eye*]** ほろ酔いである ▪ We *were* all *a sheet in the wind's eye*. 我々はみんなほろ酔いかげんだった.

one's ***sheet anchor*** (困ったときの)頼みの綱 ▪ I regard him as *my sheet anchor*. 僕は彼を頼みの綱と思っている. ☞sheet anchor《海》「非常用の大いかり」.

three* [*both, four*] *sheets in* [*to*] *the wind ひどく酔って ▪ He was about *three sheets in the wind*. 彼はかなり酔いつぶれていた ▪ He came home *three sheets in the wind*. 彼はぐでんぐでんに酔って帰ってきた.

shelf /ʃelf/ 名 ***a shelf life*** つかの間の命 ▪ Most of the small businesses had *a* short *shelf life*. 中小企業はたいてい寿命が短かった.

be flying off the shelves (人気の商品が)飛ぶように売れている ▪ His various inventions have *been flying off the shelves*. 彼の数々の発明品は飛ぶように売れています.

off the shelf **1**《米》実施された ▪ Last year's plans *off the shelf* have all been failures. 昨年実施された案件はことごとく失敗に終わった.

2 既成[在庫]で[の] ▪ My casual clothes generally are *off the shelf*. 私のふだん着は普通は既製品よ.

on* [*upon*] *the shelf **1** (…が)たな上げにされて, 用いられないで; (新曲が)発売待ちで; (映画が)封切り待ちで ▪ The question was put *on the shelf*. その問題はたな上げにされた ▪ He's ever since been laid *on the shelf*. 彼はその後ずっと冷やめしを食わされている.

2 (女性が)オールドミスになって ▪ There are mothers who lay their girls *upon the shelf*. 世の中には娘をオールドミスにしてしまう母親がいる.

3《俗》質入れして ▪ My watch is *on the shelf*. 僕の時計は質に入っている.

shell[1] /ʃel/ 名 ***a shell game***《主に米》いかさま, 詐欺 ▪ We accused him of playing *a shell game*. 私たちは彼を詐欺で告訴した.

bring *a person* ***out of*** *his* ***shell*** 人を打ち解けさせる ▪ He was so shy I could not *bring* him *out of his shell*. 彼はひどく内気で打ち解けさせることができなかった.

come out of *one's* ***shell*** 殻から出てくる, 打ち解ける ▪ Under the soothing influence of coffee and tobacco, he *came out of his shell*. コーヒーやタバコの和やかな力のおかげで彼は打ち解けてきた.

creep* [*draw, go, retire, stay*] *into *one's* ***shell*** 自分の殻に閉じこもる, 無口になる ▪ I long ago *crept into my shell* for good. 私はとうの昔に永久に自分の殻に閉じこもっているのだ ▪ He speedily *retired into his shell* again. 彼はまたすぐ無口になった.

in the shell **1** (卵・ひななどが)孵化(ふか)せずに ▪ He killed a serpent's egg *in the shell*. 彼はヘビの卵を孵化しないままで殺した.

2 未完成で ▪ As a writer he is still *in the shell*. 作家としては彼はまだ未完成だ.

not out of *one's* ***shell*** 生まれていない ▪ You are *scarecely out of your shell* yet. 君にはまだ10年早い《年に不相応のことをしようとする年少者に言う文句》.

shell[2] /ʃel/ 動 ***as easy as shelling peas***《口》実にたやすい ▪ This work is *as easy as shelling peas*. この仕事は朝めし前にやってのけられる. ☞「豆の皮をむくくらい易しい」が原義.

shellacking /ʃəlǽkɪŋ/ 名 ***take a shellacking*** 完敗[大敗]する ▪ Our team *took a shellacking* last night. わがチームは昨夜は大敗した.

shelter[1] /ʃéltər/ 名 ***give shelter to*** …をかばう ▪ The branches of the cedar *gave shelter to* an eagle. 杉の枝がワシをかばっていた.

in* [*under*] *shelter かばわれて, 避難して ▪ The enemy lies *in shelter*. 敵は潜伏している.

seek* [*find, take*] *shelter 避難する, 隠れる ▪ We *took shelter* from the rain under a tree. 我々は木の下に雨宿りした ▪ He *took shelter* in silence. 彼は困って黙ってしまった.

under the shelter of …にかばわれて, 守られて ▪ The town is *under the shelter of* a fortress. 町は要さいに守られている ▪ I took him *under my shelter*. 彼をかばってやった.

shelter[2] /ʃéltər/ 動 ***shelter*** *oneself* ***under* [*behind*]** …の陰に隠れる ▪ I have no intention of *sheltering myself under* the Bishop's authority. 私は監督の威光の陰に隠れるつもりは全くない.

shield /ʃiːld/ 名 ***be the shield and buckler*** 十分な保護者である(《聖》*Ps*. 91. 4) ▪ He has *been the shield and buckler* of the family. 彼は一家の十分な保護者となってきた.

both sides of the shield たての両面, 問題の表裏 ▪ As an insider he of course knows *both sides of the shield*. 部内者として彼はもちろん問題の表裏を知っている.

the other* [*reverse*] *side of the shield たての半面, 問題の他の一面 ▪ It does appear so at first sight, but you don't know *the other side of the shield*. 確かに一見したところではそう見えるが, 君にはあとの一面がわからないのだ. ☞F le revers de la médaille のなぞり.

shift[1] /ʃɪft/ 名 ***be at*** *one's* ***last shift*(*s*)** 絶体絶命になる, 百計が尽きる ▪ They *are at their last shifts*. 彼らは百計が尽きている.

drive *a person* ***to* (*his*) *shifts* [*to a shift*]** →put a person to (*his*) SHIFTs.

full of shifts and devices 機略縦横で ▪ He is *full of shifts and devices*. 彼は機略縦横だ.

in shifts 交替で ▪ Taxi drivers work *in shifts*. タクシーの運転手は交替で働く.

one's **[*the*] *last shift*** 最後の頼みの綱 ▪ You see me now driven to *my last shift*. ご覧のように僕は

S

今せっぱつまっているんだ.

make* (*a*) *shift **1** どうにかしてする(*to do*) ▪ Now I can *make shift to* talk English a little. 今ではどうにかして英語を少しは話せます.

2 せいぜいうまくやる, 辛抱する(*with, without*) ▪ I have to *make shift with* what I have. 今あるもので辛抱しなければならない ▪ I must *make shift without* help. 援助なしで何とかやっていかねばならない.

3 いろいろ手を打つ ▪ I'd *make shift* to give you more liberty. 君をもっと自由にしてあげるようにいろいろ手を打ってみよう.

on the day* [*night*] *shift 日勤[夜勤]で ▪ He is *on the night shift* this week. 彼は今週は夜勤だ.

put* [*drive, reduce*]** *a person* ***to (*his*) ***shifts* [*to a shift*]** 人を窮地に追い込む, せっぱつまらせる ▪ Two or three bad harvests might *put* you sadly *to your shifts*. 不作が2, 3回もあればせっぱつまってしまうだろう.

put* [*drive, reduce*]** *a person* ***to the last shifts 人を絶体絶命にする ▪ The situation *drove* me *to the last shifts*. その状況で私は絶体絶命になった.

shift[2] /ʃɪft/ 動 ***shift for*** *oneself*/ ***shift for*** *one's* ***own safety*** **1** 自力でやっていく ▪ His father left him to *shift for himself*. 彼の父は彼が自力でやっていくに任せた ▪ They *shifted for their own safety*. 彼らは自力でやっていった.

2 (物が)成り行きに任せられる ▪ I concluded to let my papers *shift for themselves*. 私は自分の書類を成り行きに任せることに決めた.

shift ... onto* [(*on*) *to*]** *a person* [*a person's* ***shoulders] (責任などを)人に転嫁する ▪ He *shifted* the blame *to* me. 彼はその罪を私になすりつけた.

shilling /ʃílɪŋ/ 名 ***a shilling dreadful* [*shocker*]** 《英》扇情的な安小説 ▪ Stevenson was writing *another shilling dreadful*. スティーブンスンは扇情的な安小説をもう1冊書いていた.

cut *a person* ***off with* [*without*] *a shilling*** 1シリング与えて[も与えずに]人を勘当する ▪ I'll *cut* him *off with a shilling*. 1シリングやってあいつを勘当してやるのだ.

pay twenty shillings in the pound 全部支払う ▪ I *paid twenty shillings in the pound* on my father's liabilities. 私は父の借金を皆済した.

take the* (*King's* [*Queen's*]) *shilling 《英》兵士になる, 募兵に応じる ▪ He *took the shilling* in despair. 彼はやけになって兵士になった ▪ The silly youth *took the King's shilling* at once. ばかな若者はすぐ募兵に応じた. ☞昔募兵に応じた者が1シリングもらったことから.

turn an honest shilling = turn an honest PENNY.

want twopence in the shilling 少し抜けている ▪ He *wants twopence in the shilling*. 彼は少し足りない.

shimmy /ʃími/ 名 ***shake a shimmy*** 《米俗》シミーを踊る ▪ That music was enough to make a saint *shake a shimmy*. その音楽は聖徒でもシミーを踊りたくなるようなものだった. ☞shimmy「上半身を震わせながら踊る扇情的なジャズダンス」.

shin[1] /ʃɪn/ 名 ***break shins*** 《英俗》借金する ▪ At last he was obliged to *break shins*. とうとう彼は借金しないわけにいかなくなった.

graze the shins of もう少しで…になろうとする ▪ They were *grazing the shins of* treason by doing so. 彼らはそうすれば危うく反逆になるところだった.

shin[2] /ʃɪn/ 動 ***shin it*** 《米》速く歩く ▪ Didn't I *shin it* along the bridge pretty speedily! ねえ僕はとても速く橋を歩いてみせただろう.

shindy /ʃíndi/ 名 ***kick up a shindy***/《米》 ***cut shindies*** 大騒ぎを起こす[始める] ▪ You *cut shindies* under the broadsword of justice. 君は法の剣のもとで大騒ぎを起こした ▪ He joined in *kicking up a shindy*. 彼もいっしょになって大騒ぎを始めた.

shine[1] /ʃaɪn/ 名 ***come a shine over*** *a person* 《米俗》人をだます ▪ They could not *come a shine over* him. 彼らは彼をだますことはできなかった.

come rain or* (*come*) *shine = RAIN or shine.

cut* [*make*] *a shine **1** 異彩を放つ ▪ His name was well calculated to *cut a shine*. 彼の名前は十分異彩を放つものと思われた.

2 《米》ふざけちらす ▪ Peele gazed, Jim *cut a shine*. ピールはじっと見ていた, ジムはふざけちらした ▪ Has your skipper begun to *cut* any *shines* yet? 踊り手はもうふざけ始めたかい.

kick up* [*make*] *a shine 《口》大騒ぎを起こす ▪ He is always *kicking up a shine* about a trifle. 彼はいつもつまらぬことで大騒ぎを起こしてばかりいる.

make a shine with *a person* 《米俗》人に取り入る ▪ To *make a shine with* Sally, I sent her a parasol. サリーに取り入るために, パラソルを送った.

pull shines 《米俗》いたずらする, 悪ふざけをする ▪ You will never *pull* any *shines*. 君は悪ふざけなどしないだろう.

put a shine on …を磨く ▪ Would you *put a* good *shine on* these boots? このブーツを十分磨いてくれませんか.

rain or shine →RAIN[1].

rub the shine off …の輝き[喜び]を薄れさせる ▪ The team's recent losses have *rubbed* some of *the shine off* their earlier victories. そのチームは最近負けているので以前の勝利の輝きが少し薄れてきた.

take a shine to 《口》…にほれこむ ▪ He *took a shine to* you that night. 彼はあの晩にあなたにほれこんだのです.

***take the shine out of* [《米》 *off*]** 《口》…を顔色なからしめる; を見劣りさせる ▪ He sang so well as to *take the shine out of* a professional singer. 彼はとてもうまく歌ったので本職の歌手も顔負けするくらいだった.

shine[2] /ʃaɪn/ 動 ***it shines*** 日が照る ▪ According to his mood it rains or *it shines*. 彼の気分次

第で雨が降ったり日が照ったりする.

shingle /ʃíŋgəl/ 名 ***a shingle short*** 少し気が狂って ▪ Poets are usually *a shingle short*. 詩人はたいてい少し気がふれている.

hang out* [*up*] *one's* *shingle*/ *hoist* [*put up*] *one's* *shingle 《米口》(医師・弁護士が)開業する, 看板を出す ▪ He studied law and *hung out his shingle*. 彼は法律を修めて開業した ▪ He *hoisted his shingle* as a food consultant. 彼はフードコンサルタントの看板を出した ▪ I have decided to *hang out* a *shingle* as an environmental consultant. 環境コンサルタントの看板を掲げることにした. ☞shingle「小看板」.

shining /ʃáınıŋ/ 形 ***a shining example*** 模範, すばらしい例 ▪ John and Mary are *a shining example* of a happily married couple. ジョンとメアリーは幸福な夫婦のすばらしい例だ.

a shining light 目立つ人物[事例] ▪ He considers himself *the shining light* of our club. 彼は自分がわがクラブの花形だと考えている.

improve the shining hour →IMPROVE².

shinny /ʃíni/ 動 ***shinny on* *one's* *own side*** 《米》いらぬせっかいをしない ▪ Let them *shinny on their own side*. 彼らにいらぬせっかいをさせるな.

***shinny up* [*down*]** 《米口》よじ登る[下りる] ▪ He *shinnied down* the rope and broke into the house. 彼はロープをつたって下りて, その家に侵入した.

ship¹ /ʃıp/ 名 ***be in the same ship*** 同じ危険にさらされている ▪ We *are in the same ship*. 我々は同じ危険にさらされているのだ.

burn* *one's* *ships →BURN one's boats.

by ship 船で ▪ He also fled to Africa *by ship*. 彼も船でアフリカへ逃げた.

give up the ship 〖主に否定文で〗あきらめる, 降参する ▪ Nobody ever *gives up the ship* in parlor debate. 客間の討論で降参するような人は誰もいない.

jump* [*abandon*] *ship **1** 船から脱走する, 無断で船を去る ▪ One deckhand *jumped ship* at the last port. 一人の甲板員が最後に立ち寄った港で船から脱走した.

2 (不満などが生じて)突然仕事を辞める; (組織などから)離脱する (→JUMP (a) ship) ▪ They all *jumped ship* as soon as they got other jobs. 彼らは全員他の仕事を手に入れるとすぐにいまの仕事を辞めた.

leave* [*abandon, desert*] *a sinking ship 危険が近づいたとき持ち場[友人]を捨てる ▪ He is the last man to *leave a sinking ship*. 彼は危険が近づいたとき持ち場を捨てるような人間では決してない. ☞ネズミが沈む船を去るとされることから.

like a ship without a rudder*/*like a rudderless ship 舵のない船のように, あてどもなく ▪ The party drifted about *like a ship without a rudder*. 一行はあてどもなくさまよった.

not give up the ship 《米》断念しない ▪ My exhortation would rather be "*not* to *give up the ship*." 私が勧めたいことはむしろ「断念するな」ということだ. ☞Captain James Lawrence の臨終の言葉, "Don't give up the ship." (1813)から.

old ship 《戯》船乗りさん《呼びかけ》 ▪ Come, *old ship*, give us a yarn. さあ船乗りさん, 話を聞かせてよ.

run a tight ship (組織を)厳格な管理下で運営する, 牛耳る, 支配する, 主導権を握る ▪ My daughter always *runs a tight ship* and conducts the meeting. 娘がいつも主導権を握って会議を仕切る ▪ The crime boss *runs a tight ship* and keeps himself out of the limelight. 犯罪組織のボスは厳格な管理体制を敷き, 自分は表に出ないようにしている.

ships that pass in the night 行きずりの人 (Longfellow, *Tales of a Wayside Inn*) ▪ I only met him once—we were like *ships that pass in the night*. 彼とは1回会っただけだ—私たちは行きずりの者同士だった.

spoil the ship for a ha'porth of tar 《口》けちけちして大損をする ▪ You are just *spoiling the ship for a ha'porth of tar* in so doing. そんなことをするのはけちけちして大損をしてるにすぎないんだよ.

take ship 船に乗る ▪ He *took ship* from Hong Kong. 彼は香港から船に乗った.

the ship of state 国家 (Machiavelli, *The Prince* 9) ▪ I am needed by my country to steer *the ship of state*. 私が国務を執ることを祖国が必要としている.

the ship of the desert ラクダ ▪ We were borne on the back of *the* swift *ship of the desert*. 我々は速いラクダの背で運ばれた.

***when* *one's* *ship comes home* [*in*]** 《口》金持ちになったら ▪ One customer always says he'll pay me *when his ship comes home*. お客さんの一人は, 金持ちになったら支払いしようといつも言います.

ship² /ʃıp/ 動 ***ship a sea*** (船・人が)波を浴びる ▪ We did not *ship a sea*. 我々は波を浴びなかった.

ship water (船が)水を浴びる ▪ We were *shipping water* all the time. 船は終始水を浴びていた.

shipboard /ʃípbɔ̀ːrd/ 名 ***go on shipboard*** 乗船する ▪ He commanded his men to *go on shipboard*. 彼は部下に乗船するように命じた.

on shipboard 船上に[で] ▪ They were fellow passengers *on shipboard* back to Charleston. 彼らは船に乗ってチャールストンへ戻る相客たちだった.

shipshape /ʃípʃèıp/ 形 ***be all shipshape and seaworthy*** きちんと整っている ▪ Now the warehouse *was all shipshape and seaworthy*. 今や倉庫はきちんと整っていた.

shipwreck /ʃíprèk/ 名 ***end in shipwreck*** 台なしになる ▪ The conference nearly *ended in shipwreck*. 会議は危うく台なしになるところだった.

make shipwreck of **1** …を失う ▪ They *made shipwreck of* all they had. 彼らは持っているものをすべて失ってしまった.

2 …をぶちこわす, めちゃめちゃにする ▪ He *made shipwreck of* my happiness. 彼は私の幸福をめちゃめちゃにしてしまった.

suffer shipwreck 難破する ▪ We *suffered*

shipwreck on the same coast. 我々はその同じ海岸で難破した.

shirk /ʃəːrk/ 動 ***shirk for*** *oneself* 《米》自活する, 自分でやっていく ▪ The cows were turned into the pasture to *shirk for themselves*. 牛は自分でやっていくように放牧された.

shirk off... upon [***onto***] *a person* 《米》人に(責任など)を転嫁する ▪ He *shirked off* the work *upon* the others. 彼はその仕事を他の者に転嫁した.

shirt /ʃəːrt/ 名 ***a stuffed shirt*** 《口》堅物,「石部金吉」; 退屈な人 ▪ He is *a* terrible *stuffed shirt* with no sense of humor. 彼はユーモア感覚なんて全然ないすごい堅物だ.

bet [***lay, stake, put***] *one's* ***shirt on*** 《英》 **1** (馬)にあり金を全部かける ▪ *Put your shirt on* Success. あり金を全部サクセス号にかけなさい.
2 (全財産をかけてもよいほど)...を確かと思う ▪ I would have *laid my shirt on* his getting in. 彼の当選は全財産をかけてもよいくらい確かだと私は思った.

get *a person's* ***shirt out*** [***off***] 《俗》人を怒らせる ▪ So you have *got his shirt out*, have you? では君はあの男を怒らせてしまったのだね.

give away [***you***] ***the shirt off*** *one's* ***back*** 《口》財産全部を与えてしまう ▪ He would *give away the shirt off his back*. あの男は財産全部を与えてしまうだろうよ.

have not a shirt to *one's* ***back*** 着るシャツもない, 無一物だ ▪ He *had* neither glass to his windows, *nor a shirt to his back*. 彼は窓にはガラスがなく着るシャツもなかった.

have *one's* ***shirt out*** [***off***] 《俗》かんしゃくを起こしている ▪ Don't go near him. He *has his shirt out* now. 彼に近づくな. 今かんしゃくを起こしているんだ.

hold on to *one's* ***shirt*** 《米俗》すっからかんになるのを防ぐ ▪ He hopes to *hold on to his shirt* this winter. 彼は今年の冬は破産を防ぐことを望んでいる.

in *one's* ***shirt*** (***sleeves***) 上着を脱いで, シャツ1枚になって, くつろいだ格好で ▪ He fled *in his shirt*. 彼はシャツ1枚で逃げた ▪ He came to the door *in his shirt sleeves*. 彼は下着姿で玄関に出てきた.

keep *one's* ***shirt***(***s***) ***on*** 《口》〚主に命令文で〛怒らない, 冷静にしている ▪ I'll tell you now, if you'll *keep your shirt on*. 君が冷静にしていてくれるなら訳を話すよ.

lay *one's* ***shirt on*** →bet one's SHIRT on.

lose *one's* ***shirt*** 《口》無一文になる ▪ John *lost his shirt* when that business failed. ジョンはその事業が失敗したとき無一文になった.

Near is my shirt but nearer is my skin. 《諺》人のためよりおのがため.

put *one's* ***shirt on*** →bet one's SHIRT on.

strip to the shirt シャツ1枚になる ▪ Knowing the Chief was away, the secretary *stripped to the shirt*. 社長がいないのを知っていたので, 秘書はシャツ1枚になった.

tear *one's* ***shirt*** 《米俗》へまをやらかす ▪ Some of those guys really *tore their shirts*. あいつらの中には実にへまをやらかした者もいた.

the shirt of Nessus 破壊的な(影響)力 ▪ We have to face up to any *shirt of Nessus*. 我々はいかなる破壊的な力にも立ち向かわねばならない. ☞ギ神の Nessus から. Hercules の妻を犯そうとして毒矢で射られたが, 彼女に恋の媚薬として自分の血を与え, その血を塗った下着を着けた Hercules も死んだことから.

wave the (***bloody***) ***shirt*** 《米》北部と南部の敵意をあおる ▪ They *waved the bloody shirt* in many a political campaign. 彼らは多くの政治運動で北部と南部の敵意をあおった. ☞「血染めのシャツ」は復しゅうの象徴で敵意をあおるものであるところから.

without a shirt to *one's* ***back*** 極貧で ▪ We were *without a shirt to our back* when we were children. 私たちは子供の頃, 極貧状態だった.

shirty /ʃə́ːrti/ 形 ***get shirty*** 《俗》かっとなる ▪ He *got* very *shirty*. 彼はひどく怒った.

shit[1] /ʃɪt/ 名 ***bad shit*** 《卑》深い対立[溝] ▪ There was so much *bad shit* between the two gangs. その二つの一味の間にはかなり深い対立があった.

be in the shit/be in deep shit 《口》面倒なことになる, どつぼにはまる ▪ If you cause me any trouble, you'll *be in the shit*. もしおれの手を煩わしたら, 面倒なことになるぜ.

be on *a person's* ***shit list*** 《口》気に食わないやつのリストに載る ▪ He *was on everybody's shit list*. 彼はみんなの気に食わないやつのリストに載っていた.

be shit scared 非常に怯えている, ひどくびくびくしている ▪ I knew you *were shit scared* there. そこで君がひどくびくびくしているのがわかったよ.

feel like shit ひどく気分が悪い ▪ I woke up *feeling like shit*. 目覚めるとひどく気分が悪かった.

get *one's* ***shit together*** 《米俗》= get it TOGETHER.

give *a person* ***shit*** 《口》人を侮辱する ▪ If he *gives* me *shit*, I can get back at him. もし彼がおれを侮辱するなら, 仕返ししてやるさ.

give *a person* ***the shits*** 人を怒らせる ▪ He always *gives* me *the shits* when he makes up an excuse. 彼の口実にはいつも腹が立つ.

grip *a person's* ***shit*** 《卑》人のしゃくに障る ▪ It *grips my shit*, the way he looks big. 彼がでかい顔をしているのを見るとしゃくに障る.

have shit for brains 《米》非常にばかである ▪ You*'ve got shit for brains*. 君ってすごくばかだな.

knock (***the***) ***shit out of*** 《卑》= knock (the) HELL out of.

No shit! **1** 《口》嘘だろ[ばか言え] ▪ That gal's my sister.—*No shit!* Really? あの子, おれの妹だ—嘘だろ. ほんと?
2 ほんとだ《No shit, Sherlock! の形でも》 ▪ If it rains we'll all be late.—*No shit, Sherlock!* 雨が降れば全員遅刻だ—ほんとだ.

not give a shit かまわない, 知らない ▪ I do*n't give a shit*. かまうもんか[知るもんか] ▪ My parents do*n't give a shit* about me. 両親はおれのことなどかまうもんか.

not know shit (***from shinola***) 《口》まるで分かってない ▪ I'm not going to explain everything to him because he does*n't know shit from shinola*. 彼は味噌もくそも区別できないのですべてを彼に説明するつもりはない.

same shit, different day 《俗》いつも通り《SSDD と略す》 ▪ What's happening, Tom?—Nothing much, you know, *same shit, different day*. トム, どうかした?—いやなにも, いつも通りさ.

scare the shit out of ...を非常に驚かす, ぎょっとさせる ▪ You *scared the shit out of* me, coming in without knocking. ぎょっとするじゃないか, ノックなしで入ってくるなんて.

Shit happens. 《口》まずいこと[嫌なこと]は起こるもの.

shit hot 《卑》すばらしい ▪ His singing was *shit hot*. 彼の歌は最高だった.

Shit—or get off the pot. 《卑》さっさとしろ, ぐずぐずしてるなら他にまわせ.

shoot the shit 《卑》自分のことをぶち上げる ▪ Don't believe him. He's just *shooting the shit*. 彼の言うことなんか信じるな. 自画自賛してるだけだ.

the shit hits [***will hit***] ***the fan*** 《卑》大変なことになる ▪ Wait till the boss hears that! Then *the shit*'ll *hit the fan*! ボスがそんなことを聞いたら, 大変なことになるぞ.

Tough shit! 《卑》お気の毒!

shit[2] /ʃɪt/ 動 ***shit all over*** ...の扱いがひどい ▪ They *shit all over* us on every occasion. 彼らの我々への扱いはことあるごとにひどい.

shiver[1] /ʃívər/ 名 ***a shiver go*** [***run***] ***down*** *one's* ***back*** (恐怖・興奮で)背すじがぞくぞくっとする ▪ When I heard the news of the accident, I felt *a shiver going down my back*. その事故のニュースを聞いたとき, 背すじがぞくぞくするのを感じた.

(***all***) ***in a shiver*** 《口》(寒さなどで)ぶるぶる震えて ▪ You are cold, and *all in a shiver*. あなたは冷えきってぶるぶる震えているじゃありませんか.

get [***have***] (***the***) ***shivers*** 《口》ぞっとする ▪ I *get the shivers* every time I sit in your drawing-room. お宅の応接間に座るたびに私は寒気がしてきます.

give *a person* ***the shivers*** 人をぞくぞく[ぞっと]させる ▪ If you dip in one foot, it will *give* you *the shivers*. 一方の足をつけたらぞくぞくしますよ.

send shivers [***a shiver***] ***up*** [***down, up and down***] *a person's* ***back*** [***spine***] (恐怖・興奮で)人の背すじをぞくぞくっとさせる ▪ The strange cry *sent a shiver down my spine*. その不思議な叫び声で私の背すじがぞくぞくっとした.

shiver[2] /ʃívər/ 名 (***all***) ***to shivers*** こっぱみじんになって ▪ It blew the ship *to shivers*. それは船をこっぱみじんに吹き飛ばした.

in [***into***] ***shivers*** こなごなに ▪ The vase fell and broke *in shivers*. 花びんが落ちてこなごなになった.

shiver[3] /ʃívər/ 動 ***Shiver my timbers*** [***sides***]***!*** 《口・戯》決してそんなことはない, (もしあったら)首でもやる《水夫の誓いの文句とされる》 ▪ *Shiver my timbers* if I do so. そんなことをしたら首でもやる.

shoal /ʃoʊl/ 名 ***in shoals*** 群れをなして, どっさり ▪ He got letters *in shoals*. 彼は手紙をどっさり受け取った.

shock[1] /ʃɑk|ʃɔk/ 名 ***get a shock*** **1** ぎょっとする ▪ I *got a* great *shock* when I heard the news. その話を聞いたとき非常にびっくりした.

2 感電する ▪ If you touch that live wire you'll *get a shock*. その電気の通っている針金に手を触れると感電しますよ.

give a shock ぎょっとさせる ▪ The news *gave* me quite *a shock*. その知らせには全くぎょっとした.

shock[2] /ʃɑk|ʃɔk/ 動 ***be shocked at*** [***by, to*** *do*] ...に[によって, して]ぎょっとする, ぞっとする ▪ I *was shocked at* the news of his death. 彼が死んだという知らせを聞いてぎょっとした ▪ He *was shocked to* hear his daughter swearing. 彼は娘が悪態をついているのを聞いてぞっとした.

shoe[1] /ʃuː/ 名 ***another pair of shoes*** 〚述語的に〛全く別な問題 ▪ I'll lend you £50, but a loan of £1,000 is *another pair of shoes*. 50ポンドなら貸してあげるが, 1,000ポンド貸しつけるとなれば全く別な問題だ.

(***as***) ***comfortable as an old shoe*** 《米口》(人が)気楽な, 気の置けない ▪ My neighbor is *as comfortable as an old shoe*. 隣人はとても気さくな人だ.

(***as***) ***common*** [***easy***] ***as an old shoe*** 《口》(人が)とても控え目な ▪ The famous singer was *common as an old shoe*. その有名な歌手はとても控え目な人だった.

as fine a man [***woman***, etc.] ***as ever trod in shoe of leather*** 今までの誰にも負けない立派な男[女, など] ▪ He was *as fine a man as ever trod in shoe of leather*. 彼はかつてないほどの立派な男性だった.

be [***stand***] ***in*** *a person's* ***shoes*** 人の立場に立つ ▪ I would not do so if I *were in his shoes*. 私が彼の立場に立てばそうはしないだろうが.

blast my old shoes if 《米口》...なら首でもやる《強意表現》 ▪ I will give you a fair chance, *blast my old shoes if* I don't! お前に公平な機会を与えてやるよ, そうしなかったら首でもやるさ.

cast [***fling***] ***an old shoe after*** *a person* (結婚式などで幸運を祈って)人の後ろから古靴を投げる; 人に幸運を祈る ▪ Now for good luck, *cast an old shoe after* me. さあ幸運を祈って, 私に古靴を投げかけてください.

die in *one's* ***shoes*** →DIE in one's boots.

drop the other shoe (中途半端な状態に)決着をつける ▪ The Pentagon was compelled to *drop the other shoe* about the matter. 国防総省はその件について最終決定を余儀なくされた.

fill dead men's shoes =step into dead men's SHOEs.

fill *a person's* ***shoes*** =step into a person's SHOEs.

hope for dead men's shoes →wait for dead

S

men's SHOEs.
If the shoe fits, wear it. ＝If the CAP fits, wear it.
in** a person's **shoes 《口》…と同じ立場で，の立場に身を置いて ▪ *In your shoes* I wouldn't accept his offer. あなたの立場なら彼の申し出は受けないと思う.
in** one's **shoes **1** (身長を計るときに)靴をはいたままで ▪ I am six feet two *in my shoes*. 私は靴をはいたままで6フィート2インチある.
2 (兵士が)十分武装して ▪ I have now 60,000 men *in their shoes*. 今6万の兵を十分に武装させている.
kiss** a person's **shoe 人の靴にキスする《屈従・服従などの身ぶり》 ▪ Her every motion seemed to *kiss his shoe*. 彼女のひとつひとつの動作は彼への服従を示していた.
Old shoes are easy, old friends are best. 《諺》靴も友だちも古いが一番.
Over shoes, over boots. 《諺》毒をくらわば皿まで.
over* (*the*) *shoes/up to the shoes 没頭して (*in*) ▪ I found him *over the shoes in* love. 私は彼が恋におぼれているのを知った.
***place* [*put*]*... in the shoes of** a person* …を人の後がまに座らせる ▪ They *were placed* by him *in the shoes of* seculars. 彼らは彼によって教区牧師の後がまに座らされた.
***put** oneself **into* [*in*] *a person's* shoes* [*place*]** 人の立場になってみる，身になって考える ▪ You must *put yourself into their shoes*. 彼らの立場になってみなければならない.
put the shoe on the right* [*proper*] *foot 《俗》責めるべき人を責める，ほめるべき人をほめる ▪ Don't keep on blaming me. *Put the shoe on the right foot*. いつまでも僕を責めないでくれ．責めるべき人を責めてもらいたい.
shake in** one's **shoes →SHAKE².
stand in** a person's **shoes →be in a person's SHOEs.
step into dead men's shoes 故人の地位[遺産]を継ぐ ▪ I *stepped into dead men's shoes* to fill the vacancy. 空席を満たすために故人の地位を継いだ.
step into** a person's **shoes 人の後がまに座る ▪ What would happen if you *stepped into my shoes* after my death? 私が死んでお前が私の後がまに座ったらどんなことになるだろう.
the shoe is on the other foot 《米口》形勢は逆転している ▪ His brothers used to tease him for being so small, but now *the shoe is on the other foot*. 彼の兄たちは彼が背が低いと言ってよくいじめたが，今は形勢が逆転している.
there's an old shoe after you 幸運を祈ります ▪ With all my heart, *there's an old shoe after you*. 心からご幸運を祈ります.
too big for** one's **shoes あまり高慢で[うぬぼれて] ▪ He goes about among us *too big for his shoes*. 彼は我々の間で高慢すぎる態度をとっている.
tread the shoe awry →AWRY.
up to the shoes →over (the) SHOEs.
wait* [*hope*] *for dead men's shoes 人の遺産をねらう ▪ He stuck to the hearth, *waiting for dead men's shoes*. 彼は人の遺産をねらってその家にかじりついていた.
wait for the other shoe to drop 《米》次に起きることに心を備える ▪ We should *wait for the other shoe to drop* in everything. 私たちはなにごとにも次に起きることに対し心構えすべきだ.
waste** one's **shoes いたずらに靴をすり減らす ▪ *Wasting his shoes*, he wandered to and fro before the altar. 彼はいたずらに靴をすり減らして祭壇の前をあちこちとさまよった.
where the shoe pinches 悩み[厄介]の種 ▪ That is *where the shoe pinches*. そこが悩みの種なのだ ▪ He knows *where the shoe pinches*. 彼は厄介の種を知っている.

shoe² /ʃuː/ 動 ***shoe the goose* [*gosling*]** むだなことに時を費やす ▪ Don't *shoe the goose*. むだなことに時を費やすな.

shoestring /ʃúːstrìŋ/ 名 ***on a shoestring*** 《米俗》わずかの資金で ▪ Henry Ford started his business *on a shoestring*. ヘンリー・フォードはわずかな資金で事業を始めた.
tie** one's **own shoestrings 《米口》自分のことは自分でやる ▪ It was his habit to *tie his own shoestrings*. 自分のことは自分でやるのが彼の癖だった.
walk on** one's **shoestrings 《米口》無一物である ▪ I was literally *walking on my shoestrings*. 私は文字通り無一物だった.

shoot¹ /ʃuːt/ 名 ***go the whole shoot*** 《俗》一切をかける ▪ I *went the whole shoot* on one throw of the dice. サイコロの一投に一切をかけた.
the whole* [*entire*] *shoot 《俗》何もかも全部，誰もかもみんな ▪ He called *the whole shoot* of us "his lads." 彼は我々全員を「子供たち」と呼んでいた.

shoot² /ʃuːt/ 動 ***be shot through with*** (織物が)目立つ糸を備えている; (物語などが)特徴を終始備えている ▪ Her songs *are shot through with* bitterness. 彼女の歌には恨みが備わっている.
Don't shoot the pianist [etc.] (***, he's doing his best***). ピアニスト[など]を非難しないでほしい．一生懸命にやっているのだから.
get shot of 《口》(仕事・苦難など)を片づける，免れる ▪ I have a small problem to *get shot of*. 片づけねばならないちょっとした問題がある.
I'll be shot if 《俗》…なら首をやる，断じて…のことはない ▪ *I'll be shot if* I let you into this house. 断じてこの家へは入らせるものか.
I'll see you shot first. 《俗》くそくらえ《強い拒絶の文句》 ▪ Then let me tell you straight, *I'll* just *see you shot first*. じゃあはっきり言わせてもらうが，お前なんかくそくらえだ.
like shooting fish in a barrel ばかばかしいくらいたやすい《誇張表現》 ▪ Using a computer is *like shooting fish in a barrel*. コンピューター操作なんてすごくやさしいよ.

not shoot to kill 威嚇(ｲｶｸ)射撃する ▪ The police did *not shoot to kill*. 警官は威嚇射撃をした.

shoot a line 《俗》ほらを吹く ▪ He's always *shooting a line*. 彼はいつもほらを吹いてばかりいる.

shoot a look [***glance***] ちらと見る ▪ She *shot* him *an* indignant *look*. 彼女は彼をちらとにらんだ.

shoot a match 射撃の試合をする ▪ They *shot* two *matches* then. それで彼らは射撃試合を2回した.

shoot a sitting bird 赤子を裸にするようなことをする ▪ To cheat a commoner is like *shooting sitting birds*. 平民をだますなんて赤子の手をねじるようなものです.

shoot ahead (船が他の船を追い抜くために)急に速力を出す; (仕事などが)どんどん進んでいく ▪ We *shot ahead*. 我々は急に速力を出した ▪ The work has *shot ahead* rapidly. この仕事はどんどんはかどった.

shoot at the mouth = shoot one's MOUTH off.

shoot (*one's*) ***breakfast*** [***lunch, dinner, supper, cookies***] 《米俗》(食べたものを)もどす ▪ You're going to *shoot your cookies*. 君は今にもどすぞ.

shoot center 《米》(銃が)正確に命中する ▪ This old rifle *shoots center*. この古いライフル銃は正確に命中する.

shoot ... dead [***to death***] …を射殺する ▪ The killer *shot* him *dead* in two bullets. 殺し屋は2発でその男を射殺した.

shoot first and ask questions afterwards [***later***] 是非を考えずに撃つ ▪ The man was ruthless and would *shoot first and ask questions afterwards*. その男は冷酷でかまわず発砲するのだった.

shoot from the hip 《米口》(あと先を考えずに)やみくもにしゃべる[行動する] ▪ He's always *shooting from the hip* without thinking first. 彼はよく考えもしないでいつもやみくもにしゃべってばかりいる. ☞腰撃ちすることから.

shoot *one's* ***grandfather*** 《米俗》勘違いする ▪ You showed her she had *shot her grandfather*. 君は彼女が勘違いしていたのを教えてやったわけだ.

shoot *oneself* ***in the foot*** 《口》結局自分の首を絞める, 自ら災いを招く ▪ He *shot himself in the foot*, telling the teacher about his classmate. 彼は級友のことを先生に告げて, 結局自分の首を絞めることになった.

Shoot (***it***)***!*** 《米俗》まあ!, ちぇっ! 《驚き・不快などの発声》.

shoot it out 《米口》決着がつくまで撃つ ▪ The outlaws *shot it out* with the sheriff and his men. 無法者らは決着がつくまで保安官とその部下と撃ち合った.

shoot *one's* ***linen*** [***cuffs***] 《口》(ワイシャツの)カフスを上着のそでの外へ出す《気どりを表す》 ▪ He *shot his linen* in style. 彼は気どってカフスを上着のそでの外へ出した.

shoot *one's* ***load*** 《米俗》= SHOOT one's wad 2.

shoot *one's* ***mouth off*** →MOUTH[1].

shoot off *one's* ***mouth*** [***face, bazoo, yap***] 《口》わけ知り顔にしゃべる ▪ There you go, *shooting off your mouth* to him. そら君は彼にわけ知り顔にしゃべっているじゃないか.

shoot off the tie 射撃の決勝試合をする ▪ The two then *shot off the tie*. 二人はそこで射撃の決勝試合をした.

shoot out the lip くちびるを突き出す (《聖》*Ps.* 22. 7) ▪ He *shot out a* solemn *lip*. 彼は厳粛な表情をしてくちびるをとがらせた.

shoot questions at (人)に矢つぎばやに質問をする ▪ The reporters *shot questions at* the minister. 記者たちは大臣に矢つぎばやに質問をした.

shoot straight [***square***] 命中させる; 正直にふるまう ▪ He never *shoots straight*. 彼は決して命中させることはできない ▪ I can *shoot straight* with him. 私は彼に対しては正直にふるまえる.

Shoot that hat. 《米俗》うるさい, いまいましい ▪ Oh, *shoot that hat*! ああうるさい!

shoot the breeze →BREEZE.

shoot the cat 《俗》(飲みすぎなどで)もどす ▪ He *shot the cat* because he had too much booze in him. 彼は酒を飲みすぎたのでもどした.

shoot the chutes 《米》(トボガンぞり・ボートで)急な傾斜をすべり降りる ▪ *Shooting the chutes* is drawing large crowds. 急な傾斜をすべり降りる遊びが大勢の人々を呼び寄せている.

shoot the gulf 大胆なことをやる ▪ I have never slept since I *shot the gulf*. あの大胆なことをやってから一睡もしていない.

shoot the light 《口》信号を無視する ▪ He usually *shoots the light*. 彼はいつも信号を無視する.

shoot [***blame, kill***] ***the messenger*** 悪い知らせを伝えた人を責める ▪ Don't *shoot the messenger* because it's true. 悪い知らせを伝えたからと言って責めないで, だって事実なんだもの.

shoot the works →WORK[1].

shoot ... through and through …を撃って穴だらけにする ▪ We *shot* the ship *through and through*. 我々は何度も撃ってその船を穴だらけにした.

shoot ... to death →SHOOT ... dead.

shoot *one's* ***wad*** 《米俗》**1** 有り金をはたく ▪ I've *shot my wad* gambling. ギャンブルで有り金をはたいてしまった.

2 思っていることを洗いざらいしゃべる ▪ I'm going to *shoot my wad* at the meeting. 会合では思っていることを洗いざらいしゃべるつもりだ.

shoot *one's* ***way*** 猟をし[撃ち]ながら進んで行く ▪ The party were *shooting their way* home. 一行は猟をしながら帰りつつあった ▪ The soldiers *shot their way* back to safety. 兵たちは発砲しながら安全なところへ退いた.

Well shot! 見事!, 当たり! 《射撃の命中の称賛》 ▪ He said, "*Well shot*, my liege!" 彼は「殿(ﾄﾉ), お見事で!」と言った.

shooter /ʃúːtər/ 名 ***a straight*** [***square***]

shooter 《口》正直者, まじめな人 ▪ He is *a straight shooter* but has no sense of humor. 彼はまじめだがユーモアを解さない.

shooting /ʃúːtɪŋ/ 名 ***(as) sure as shooting*** 《米口》確かに ▪ You'll be scolded *sure as shooting*. 君は確かにしかられるぞ.

shop /ʃɑp|ʃɔp/ 名 ***all over the shop*** 《俗》どこもかしこも; 取り散らかして; しゃにむに ▪ I've looked for it *all over the shop*. そこら中それを捜してみた ▪ Things are *all over the shop*. いろんな物が取り散らかしてある ▪ They went sailing *all over the shop*. 彼らはしゃにむに船を走らせていった.

come to the right [wrong] shop 《口》(物を求めて)正しい所へ来る[おかど違いをする] ▪ They have *come to the right shop* for morals. 彼らは教訓を求めて求むべき所へ来た ▪ He's *come to the wrong shop* if he wants money. 彼が金がほしくて来たのならおかど違いだ.

give all [the best] *one* ***has in the*** [*one's*] ***shop*** 《米口》徹底的にやっつける ▪ If Thelma comes bothering you, *give* her *all* you*'ve got in your shop*. セルマが君を悩ましに来たら, 徹底的にやっつけてやるがいい.

keep shop 店を開いている; 店番をしている ▪ He first *kept shop* at the corner. 彼は最初かどの所に店を開いていた ▪ Rob was despatched for a coach, the visitors *keeping shop* meanwhile. ロブは馬車を呼びにやられ, お客がその間店番をした.

Keep your shop and your shop will keep you. 《諺》商い三年.

mind the shop (誰かの不在中に)代わって仕事をする, 留守を預かる ▪ With the president away on business, the vice-president is *minding the shop*. 社長が出張で不在なので, 副社長が留守を預かっている.

set up shop 店を出す; 仕事を始める ▪ He *set up shop* with haberdashery. 彼は小間物の店を出した ▪ He *set up shop* as the local commissar. 彼は地方人民委員として仕事を始めた.

shut [close] up shop 閉店する; 《口》仕事をやめる ▪ We may *shut up shop*, and make holiday. 我々は閉店して休みにしてもいい ▪ It's about time he *shut up shop* and took a rest. 彼はもう仕事をやめてひと休みしていいころだ.

S

Shut your shop! 《俗》黙れ! ☞shop「口」.

sink the shop 自分の商売[専門]のことを話さないようにする (↔talk SHOP) ▪ Unlike many people, I always *sink the shop* at a party. 多くの人と違って, 私はパーティーで仕事の話はしないことにしている.

smell of the shop **1** 商人かたぎを見せる ▪ Such double dealings *smell* too much *of the shop*. そのような表裏のあるやり口はあまりにも商人かたぎを示す. **2** (言葉などが)あまりに自分の商売[専門]くさい ▪ That expression of his *smells of the shop*. 彼のその表現はあまりにも専門くさい.

talk shop (時・所をかまわず)自分の商売[専門]の話をする (↔sink the SHOP) 《a talk [talking] shop は《主に英》「(会議・組織が)むだであること」》 ▪ Come, Tom, stop *talking shop* now. さあトム, もう自分の商売の話はよせよ.

the other shop 《口》商売がたき(の店・学校・病院など) ▪ We shall have to watch *the other shop*. 商売がたきを警戒しなければなるまい.

shopkeeper /ʃɑ́pkìːpər|ʃɔ́p-/ 名 ***the nation of shopkeepers*** →NATION.

shopping /ʃɑ́pɪŋ|ʃɔ́p-/ 名 ***do shopping*** 買い物をする ▪ I must *do* some *shopping*. 少し買い物をしなければならない.

go shopping 買い物に行く ▪ Men generally dislike to *go shopping*. 男性はたいてい買い物に行くのがきらいだ.

shop-window /ʃɑ́pwìndoʊ|ʃɔ́p-/ 名 ***have all*** *one's* ***goods in the shop-window*** = have all one's goods in the (front-, shop-)WINDOW.

open [shut] (*one's*) ***shop-window*** 店を開ける[閉める]; 仕事を始める[やめる] ▪ He was obliged to sell his land, and *shut shop window*. 彼はやむなく土地を売り仕事をやめた.

shore /ʃɔːr/ 名 ***in shore*** (海上から見て)岸に近く, 浅瀬に ▪ Steer *in shore* of them. その岸に近く船を走らせるがよい.

off (the) shore 岸を離れて, 沖に ▪ The ship stopped a little way *off the shore*. 船はやや海岸を離れて停泊した.

on shore 岸辺に, 岸へ; 陸(上)で ▪ He resolved to swim *on shore* as soon as it was dark. 彼は暗くなったらすぐ岸へ泳いで行こうと決心した ▪ The marines serve both at sea and *on shore*. 海兵は海でも陸でも勤務する.

short /ʃɔːrt/ 形副名 ***a short, sharp shock*** 《英》ショック療法的処罰, 短期だけれど厳しい処罰 ▪ What he needs is *a short, sharp shock*. 彼に必要なのはショック療法的処罰だ.

be caught [taken] short (of) 《口》あいにく(...が)不足している; 《英口》急に便意[尿意]を催す ▪ I *was caught short* when the milkman came for his money. 牛乳屋が集金に来たとき, あいにく持ち合わせがなかった.

be short with *a person* 人につっけんどんである ▪ He *was* very *short with* me at the party. 彼はパーティーで私にとてもつっけんどんだった.

be taken short 《口》急に便意を催す ▪ Go on, you fellows. I*'m taken short*. 先へ行ってくれたまえ, 諸君. 急に便意を催したんでね.

break [snap] short (off) ポキリと折る; ポキリと折れる ▪ This weapon will *snap short*. この武器はポキンと折れるだろう.

bring *a person* ***up short*** 人を急に止める ▪ The oil crisis *brought* us *up short*. 石油危機のために我々の仕事はばったり止まった ▪ Two astronauts who were about to embark on a spacewalk have *been brought up short* by a malfunctioning spacesuit. 宇宙遊泳に出ようとした二人の宇宙飛行士が宇宙服の不具合で急に止められた.

come* [*fall*] *short 不完全[不十分]である ▪ Beasts *come short* in the faculty. 獣はその能力が不完全である ▪ Your reputation *comes* too *short* for my daughter. 君の評判は娘をやるためには不十分すぎる.

come* [*fall*] *short of (標準)に達しえない; (性質が)…に及ばない, 劣る (*in*) ▪ They *came short of* such a triumph. 彼らはそのような勝利に達することができなかった ▪ He *comes short of* none *in* genius. 彼は天才にかけては誰にも劣らない.

come up short (支払いが)足りない ▪ I *came up short* at the store and cut them down. その店でお金が足りなくてまけてもらった.

cut short **1** (生命・経歴・行動・話などを)急に終わらせる ▪ The malady threatened to *cut short* his days. その病気は彼の生命を急に奪う恐れがあった.
2 (人の)行動[話]を急にさえぎる ▪ He *cut* her *short* with—"You may go." 彼は急に女の話をさえぎって「下がってよろしい」と言った.
3 切って短くする ▪ He had his hair *cut short*. 彼は髪を短くかっていた.
4 (特権・資産を)削って少なくする ▪ The soldiers *were cut short* of their pay. 兵士は給料を削減された.

draw short and long (長短のわらなどで)くじ引きする ▪ We shared the spoil by *drawing short and long*. 我々はくじ引きをして分取品を分け合った.

draw the short straw 《口》=get the SHORT end of the stick.

drop short **1** 《口》(ぽっくりと)死ぬ ▪ One of these days he must *drop short*. 近いうちに彼はきっと死ぬ.
2 =fall SHORT (of).

eat short 食べるとすぐ砕ける ▪ Biscuits *eat short*. ビスケットは食べるとすぐ砕ける.

***fall short* (*of*)** (…に)達しない ▪ All the shells *fell short of* the mark. 弾丸はすべて的に届かなかった ▪ The result *fell short of* our expectation. 結果は我々の期待に添わなかった.

fly short of …に達しえない ▪ They *flew short of* the spirit. 彼らはその精神に達しえなかった.

for short 略して ▪ Benjamin is called "Ben" *for short*. ベンジャミンは略してベンと呼ばれる.

***get the short end of the stick* [*it, the deal*]** 《米》貧乏くじをひく, ばかをみる ▪ He *got the short end of the stick* when he was assigned another night duty. 彼はもう1晩, 夜勤をあてがわれてばかをみた.

go short **1** 手詰まる, 困窮する ▪ So you *go short*, Tom? では手詰まりなんだな, トム?
2 《米》(証券で)空売りする ▪ He sold five million bushels, *going short*. 彼は5百万ブッシェルを空売りした.

***have* [*get*] *a person by the short hairs* [*by the short and curlies*]** 《口》→get a person by the short HAIRs.

in short 手短に言えば, 要するに ▪ The man, *in short*, is not to be trusted. その男は要するに信用できないのだ.

in short order →ORDER[1].

keep a person short 人に供給を不十分にする ▪ Under these circumstances he had to *keep* them *short*. こうした事情で彼らへの供給を切りつめねばならなかった.

little short of ほとんど…の, に近い ▪ *Little short of* £1,000 will be required. ほとんど1,000ポンド必要だろう ▪ Our escape was *little short of* miraculous. 私たちの脱出は奇跡に近かった.

make short of long →LONG.

make short work of (仕事・敵・食事など)をさっさと片づける ▪ They *made* such *short work of* the Prayer Book. 彼らは祈とう書をひどくさっさと済ませしまった ▪ We *made short work of* the enemy. 我々は敵をさっさと片づけてしまった.

not be short of a bob or two*/*not be short of a few bob 《英口》裕福である ▪ He's *not short of a bob or two*, you know. 彼って, 裕福なんだよね.

nothing short of …以外のものでは…ない, 全く…にほかならない ▪ *Nothing short of* war will avail. 戦争以外のものではだめだ ▪ The escape was *nothing short of* a miracle. その脱出は全く奇跡というほかなかった.

on short time 操業短縮をして ▪ The factory is *on short time*. その工場は操業短縮をやっている.

pull up short 急に止まる (→bring a person up SHORT) ▪ He *pulled up short* and began to discuss an entirely different matter. 彼は急に話をやめて, 全然別のことを論じ始めた.

***run short* (*of*)** (…が)不足する, (を)切らす ▪ Turnips sometimes *run short*. カブはときに不足することがある ▪ He was *running short of* supplies. 彼は商品を切らしかけていた.

sell short **1** (証券で)空売りする ▪ A speculator will *sell* stocks *short*. 山師は株を空売りする.
2 軽視する, 見くびる ▪ Don't make the mistake of *selling* the Democratic candidate *short*. あの民主党候補を見くびるという誤りを犯してはいけない.
3 だます, 裏切る ▪ He may *sell* me *short*. 彼は私を裏切るかもしれない.

sell a person short 人の要求に応えない ▪ His works are *selling* me *short* and I'm not contented. 彼の作品は私の要求に応えていないので不満だ.

sell oneself short 自分(の才能)を過少評価する, 控え目にする, 能あるタカは爪を隠す ▪ He has missed good job offers because he is always *selling himself short*. 彼は自分を過少評価してばかりいるので, いい仕事の口を逃してきた ▪ He didn't *sell himself short* or underestimate his own ability. 彼は控え目にせず, 自らの能力を過小評価することもなかった.

short and sweet **1** 短くて楽しい ▪ After-dinner speeches should be *short and sweet*. 食後のスピーチは短くて楽しいものであるべきだ.
2 《皮肉》(表現が)ひどく短い[簡単な] ▪ After a con-

versation *short and sweet*, I left the steward. ひどくそっけない会話のあとで私は執事の所を離れた.

short and to the point 簡にして要を得た ▪ His letter was *short and to the point*. 彼の手紙は簡にして要を得たものだった.

short back and sides 《英》(軍人などの)刈り上げの髪型 ▪ The British soldiers used to have the universal *short back and sides*. イギリスの軍人は以前は一様に刈り上げにしていた.

short for …の略 ▪ "Phone" is *short for* "telephone." Phone は telephone の略だ.

short of **1** …が不足[欠乏]して ▪ I am very *short of* funds. 私はとても資金不足だ.

2 (必要なもの)がなくて ▪ He might be useful to us, if we are *short of* a gun. 我々に銃がないのなら, あの男は役に立つかもしれない.

3 (ある状態・程度)に達し[及ば]ないで ▪ His age is *short of* thirty. 彼の年齢は30に達しない ▪ You are far *short of* the truth. 君はだいぶ見当はずれだ.

4 (他の…)に劣って ▪ You are far *short of* him in wit. 君は機知にかけてはあの男にはるかに劣っている.

5 (ある数・量)よりも少なくて ▪ The Spaniards were not much *short of* two hundred. スペイン人は200人をあまり下らなかった.

6 〚前置詞的に〛 …以外は, を除いて ▪ He had everything *short of* genius. 彼は天才以外は何でも備えていた ▪ *Short of* murder, he would do anything. 人殺し以外なら, あの男はどんなことでもしかねない.

short on 《口》…が足りない ▪ This book is *short on* illustrations. この本は挿し絵が不足している.

snap short (***off***) →break SHORT (off).

something short →SOMETHING damp.

stop short of (極端な行為)まではしない; …を突然止める ▪ I had *stopped short of* insulting him. 私は彼を侮辱することまではしなかった ▪ She *stopped short of* talking in amazement. 彼女は驚いて突然話を止めた.

take *a person* (***up***) ***short*** **1** 人に不意打ちをくわせる ▪ He *was taken short* after dinner, and died in his chair. 彼は夕食後に不意打ちをくわされていすに座ったまま死んだ ▪ I *was taken up* very *short* by this. 僕もこれにはひどく面くらった.

2 (言葉を返して)人の話をさえぎる ▪ But, my dear sir, you *take* me *up* so very *short*. でもあなた, そう話の腰を折らないでください ▪ The master *took* her *up short* when she mentioned his name. 彼女がその男の名を言ったときに主人は急にそれをさえぎった.

to make a long story short →STORY.

turn short (***round***) 急に(ぐるりと)向き直る ▪ After a considerable pause he *turned short round*. かなりの間立ち止まっていてから, 彼は急にくるりと向きを変えた.

win [***lose***] ***by a short head*** 僅差で勝つ[負ける] ▪ The *winner by a short head* was Davis. 勝者は僅差でデイビスだった.

work short 加工すると砕ける ▪ Sand causes it to *work short*. 砂のためそれは加工すると砕ける.

shorten /ʃɔ́ːrtən/ 動 ***shorten*** *a person's* ***arm*** [***hand***] 人の力を制限する (《聖》*Num.* 11. 23) ▪ God will *shorten your hand* of cruelty. 神はあなたの残酷さの力を制限されるでしょう.

shortness /ʃɔ́ːrtnəs/ 名 ***for shortness*** 時間[距離]を省くために ▪ They took side roads *for shortness*. 彼らは近道をするために間道を取った.

shot[1] /ʃɑt|ʃɔt/ 名 ***a big shot*** ＝a big NOISE.

a cheap shot 《米俗》不当な[悪意のある]言葉(による攻撃) (→ take a cheap SHOT at) ▪ It's *a cheap shot*, calling him an amateur. 彼のことをアマチュアと呼ぶのは悪意のある言葉だね.

a long shot **1** 成功する見込みがほとんどない試み, 大胆な企て ▪ So he went in for *a long shot*. そこで彼は大胆な企てをやりだした ▪ It's *a long shot* that Joan will actually finish the marathon. ジョアンが実際にマラソンを完走しようとするなんて大胆な試みだね.

2 当てずっぽう ▪ As *a long shot*, I'd say she's over forty. 当てずっぽうだが, 彼女は40歳を越えているのじゃないか.

3 〚比較級・最上級を強調して〛《米口》ずっと ▪ He fooled men *a long shot* keener than you are. 彼は君よりもずっと鋭い連中をだました.

a shot across the [*a person's*] ***bow***(***s***) (へさきを横断する)警告の一撃; (実行中の事柄を止めさせる)強行手段; 警告, おどし ▪ A quack doctor should regard the new law as *a shot across the bow*. いんちき医者は新法を警告とみなすべきだ ▪ A Google browser would be *a* major *shot across the bows* of Microsoft. グーグルのブラウザーはマイクロソフトへの主要な警告となるだろう. ☞18世紀には, 船長は不審な船のへさきを横断する弾丸を撃って, 停船を命じたり船旗を揚げさせたりしていたことから.

a shot between wind and water (船の)喫水線付近の命中弾《船には致命的》; とどめの一発 ▪ And then he let fly at her *a shot between wind and water*. 次に彼は女にとどめの一発をくわせた.

a shot in the arm 《口》刺激, 景気うけ ▪ The whole market needs *a shot in the arm*. 市況は景気うけが必要だ. ☞「腕の注射」が原義.

a shot [***stab***] ***in the dark*** 当てずっぽう ▪ The question was *a shot in the dark* on the part of the prosecutor. その質問は検事の当てずっぽうだった.

a shot in the eye 《口》ひどい仕打ち ▪ He has done me such *an* unscrupulous *shot in the eye*. 彼は僕にとんでもないひどい仕打ちをしてきた.

a shot in the [*one's*] ***locker*** 〚否定的に〛ポケットの中の金; ひとつの方策 ▪ As long as there is *a shot in the locker*, she shall want for nothing. ポケットに金があるかぎりは, 彼女に不自由はさせない ▪ I have not *a shot in the locker*. 私は万策尽きた[一文もない]. ☞「弾薬箱に残った一発」が原義.

as a shot 当てずっぽうで ▪ *As a shot*, I should say she's over sixty. 当てずっぽうだが, 彼女は60は越えていると思うね.

by a long shot 〚否定文で〛全く; 〚肯定文で〛ずば

ぬけて ▪ He is the best tennis player in Japan, *by a long shot*. 彼は日本ではずばぬけてうまいテニスプレイヤーだ.

call** one's **shots **1** 弾丸が的のどこに当たるか予告する ▪ An expert rifleman can *call his shot*. ライフルの名人は弾丸がどこに当たるか予告することができる.
2 結果を予見する, 先の見通しをつける ▪ He is so hard-headed that he is very poor at *calling his shots*. 彼は実に石頭で, 先を見通すのはとても苦手だ.
3 あからさまに言う ▪ When you called him a sneak, you certainly *called your shots*. 彼をこそこそ野郎と言ったのは確かにあからさまに言ったものだ.

call the shots 《口》 采配を振る ▪ The wife *calls the shots* in his house. 彼の家では妻が采配を振っている.

fire the first* [*opening*] *shot (けんか・討論などで)先手をとる, 先制攻撃をかける ▪ Obama *fired the first shot* in the election campaign. 選挙運動ではオバマ氏が先手をとった.

give ... a shot **1** 《口》 (何か難しいこと)をやろうとする ▪ Playing the violin wasn't an interest of hers, but she at least *gave* it *a shot*. バイオリンは彼女の趣味ではなかったが, いずれにしてもやろうとはした.
2 =take a SHOT at 1.

***give** a person **a shot** (**at**)* 人に(何か難しいことを)やらせてみる ▪ The director decided to *give* a young actor *a shot at* the leading role. 監督は若手の俳優に主役をやらせてみることを決めた.

give ...** one's **best shot ...にベストを尽くす ▪ Even if you don't get the job, at least you should *give* it *your best shot*. たとえ仕事につけなくても, 少なくともつけるようにベストを尽くすべきだ.

have a shot **1** やってみる (*at, for*) ▪ He is going to *have a shot at* the race. 彼はそのレースに出てみようかと思っている ▪ I'll *have a shot for* the train. その列車に乗れるかどうかひとつ急いでみよう.
2 =take a SHOT at 1.
3 注射を受ける ▪ Have you *had a* polio *shot*? あなたは小児麻痺(ひ)の注射をしましたか.

in* [*within*] *shot 射程内に ▪ They were getting well *in shot*. 彼らは十分に射程内に入ってきていた.

like a shot 《口》 **1** すぐに, 早く ▪ I went off *like a shot*. 私はすぐに飛んでいった.
2 大喜びで ▪ I'd take any chance of employment *like a shot*. どこか勤め口があれば大喜びで飛びつきます.

***make a shot* (*at*)** **1** (...を)当て推量する ▪ You've *made a* good [bad] *shot*. 君はうまく当てた[当たらなかった] ▪ "Is it a girl?" he asked, *making a shot at* the sex of the newborn baby. 「女の子ですか?」と彼は生まれたばかりの赤んぼうの性を当て推量で言った.
2 (...を)やってみる ▪ He *made a shot at* the job. 彼はその仕事をやってみた.
3 =take a SHOT at 1.

not by a long shot 《口》 全く見当はずれで; まるっきり...でない, 全然...ない ▪ Do you think he is a good businessman? —Gracious, no! *Not by a long shot*! あの男は有能な実務家かい?—いやいや, とんでもないよ ▪ The election isn't over yet, *not by a long shot*. 選挙はまだ終わっていない. 全然まだだ《勝負はこれからだ》.

out of shot 射程外に ▪ The ship went *out of shot*. 船は射程外に出ていった.

pay** one's [**the**] **shot 《口》 勘定を払う ▪ I *paid my shot*, and came away. 勘定を払って出てきた.

powder and shot →POWDER[1].

put the shot 砲丸を投げる ▪ My brother practices *putting the shot* every day. 兄は毎日砲丸投げの練習をする.

stand shot 《口》 勘定を持つ (*to*) ▪ Are you to *stand shot to* all this good liquor? 君はこのうまい酒の代金をみな持ってくれるのかい.

take a cheap shot at (人を)不当に批判する ▪ Don't *take a cheap shot at* minorities. 少数派の人々を不当に批判してはいけない.

take a shot at **1** ...をねらう, 狙撃する ▪ I *took a* good *shot at* the bird. 私はその鳥をねらい撃ちした.
2 ...をやってみる ▪ He *took a shot at* forming a Cabinet. 彼は組閣を試みた.

within shot →in SHOT.

shot[2] /ʃɑt|ʃɔt/ 形 ***(all) shot to pieces* [*hell*]** (...が)めちゃめちゃになって ▪ His health is now *shot to pieces*. 彼の体はもうめちゃめちゃになっている.

be* [*get*] *shot of 《英口》 (人)を追い払う; (物)を早急に取り除く ▪ My daughter wanted to *be shot of* me. 娘は私の存在を一刻も早く消したかったのだ.

be shot* (*through*) *with (特徴など)でいっぱいだ ▪ This novel *is shot through with* satire. この小説は風刺にみちあふれている ▪ His life *was shot with* excitement. 彼の一生は興奮にみちあふれていた.

half shot 大分酔いが回って ▪ Bill came back to the office *half shot*. ビルはだいぶ酔いが回って事務所へ帰ってきた.

shot in the neck →NECK.

shotgun /ʃátgʌ̀n|ʃɔ́t-/ 名 ***a shotgun marriage* [*wedding*]** (妊娠のため)やむをえずさせられる結婚; やむをえない合併 ▪ The two companies hastily arranged a *shotgun marriage*. その二つの会社はばたばたとやむなく合併した. ☞ 妊娠させた娘の父親に散弾銃をつきつけられてやむなく結婚することから.

should /ʃəd, ʃʊd/ 助動 ***as it should be*** → AS.

be no better than** one **should be いかがわしい, (女性が)しりが軽い ▪ He *is no better than* he *should be*, between ourselves. 彼はいかがわしい男ですよ, ここだけの話ですが ▪ Jane *is no better than* she *should be*. ジェインはしりの軽い女だ.

***I should** do* 《口》 私なら...しますね, ...したほうがいいですよ ▪ *I should* get her back as soon as I can. できるだけ早く彼女を連れ戻したほうがいいですよ.

***I should say* (*that*)** →SAY[2].

I should think →THINK[2].

***should have** done* **1** ...すべきであった(のにしなかった) ▪ You *should have* come with us. 君もいっしょに来るべきだった.

S

2 …しているはずだ ▪ He *should have* arrived by this time. 彼はもう今ごろは着いているはずだ.

3 (君に)…させたかった ▪ You *should have* seen the fight. 君にそのけんかを見せたかったよ.

***who* [*whom*] *should* A *but* B** Aしたのは他でもないBであった ▪ When I approached the table, *who should* be sitting *but* Mary. テーブルに近づいてみると, そこに座っていたのは誰あろうメアリーだった ▪ *Whom should* I meet *but* Tom! 出会ったのは誰あろうトムだった.

shoulder[1] /ʃóʊldər/ 名 ***a shoulder to cry* [*lean*] *on*** 同情と慰めを与えてくれる人[もの] ▪ I know that my husband will always provide *a shoulder to cry on*. 夫はいつも私に同情と慰めを与えてくれます.

be looking over* one's *shoulder 周りをうかがって戦々恐々としている ▪ All the employees *are looking over their shoulders*, wondering if they will be next. 従業員は次は自分の番かとみなびくびくしている.

carry* a person *shoulder high 人を肩車に乗せて歩く《歓迎・熱狂的支持の表現》 ▪ His admirers *carried* him *shoulder high* through the crowd. 彼の賛美者らは彼を肩車に乗せて群衆の中を練り歩いた.

come from the shoulder 《米口》まっこうから向かってくる, 率直で包み隠ししない ▪ He fought with men who *came from the shoulder*. 彼はまっこうから向かってくる連中と争った.

cry on* a person's *shoulder 人に悩みを打ち明ける[愚痴をこぼす] ▪ I'm sorry to *cry on your shoulder* but I've no one else to talk to. 愚痴をこぼしたりしてごめん, でも他に話す人もいないので.

do from the shoulder 《米口》助力なしにやり遂げる ▪ All of this work he had to *do from the shoulder*. この仕事を全部彼は助力なしにやり遂げなければならなかった.

fall on* a person's *shoulders 人の責任[負担]になる ▪ The Obama budget might *fall on your shoulders*. オバマ政権の予算があなたがたの負担になるかもしれない.

***give* [*get, show*] *the cold shoulder*/*turn the cold shoulder on* [*upon*]** (人)によそよそしい態度を見せる; (人)をきらう, 避ける ▪ The rich friend he had once known so well now *gave* him *the cold shoulder*. 彼がかつてよく知っていた金持ちの友人が今は彼によそよそしい態度を見せた ▪ Since then he has *turned the cold shoulder upon* me. それ以来彼は私をきらってきている.

have broad shoulders 重荷に耐えられる ▪ Fortunately, he is in a good position and *has broad shoulders*. 幸い彼はいい地位にあるから重荷に耐えられる.

have ... on* one's *shoulders (責任)を負う ▪ It is a terrible responsibility to *have on one's shoulders*. それは負うにはとても重い責任だ.

have* one's *shoulders to the collar 一生懸命に働く ▪ Have I not always *had my shoulders to the collar*? 私はいつも懸命に働いてきたではないか.

head and shoulders →HEAD[1].

lay* one's *shoulder to the wheel →put one's SHOULDER to the wheel.

lay the blame on the right* [*wrong*] *shoulders 責めるべき[責めるべきでない]人を責める ▪ I'm not going to accept responsibility; *lay the blame on the right shoulders*. 僕は責任を取るつもりはないよ. 責めるべき人を責めてもらいたいね.

look over* a person's *shoulder 振り返って見る; 迫る危険におびえる; 様子をうかがって人をいらいら[不安に]させる ▪ My dad kept *looking over my shoulder* while I was working. 仕事中親父が様子をうかがっていたのでいらいらした.

open out the shoulders 元気を出す ▪ He began to *open out the shoulders* and struck right and left. 彼は元気を出し始めて, 盛んに打ちまくった.

***over the left* (*shoulder*)** →LEFT.

over the shoulder 当てこすって[た] ▪ It may be called criticism *over the shoulder*. それは当てこすった批評と言うことができよう.

overleap* one's *shoulders 《米口》やりすぎる ▪ The pedlar had somewhat *overleaped his shoulders*. 行商人は少しやりすぎていた.

put an old head on young shoulders → HEAD[1].

put* one's *shoulder out 肩の骨をはずす ▪ The man fell from the haystack and *put his shoulder out*. 男は干し草の山から落ちて肩の骨をはずした.

put* [*set*] one's *shoulder to (仕事など)に熱心に取りかかる ▪ We must all *put our shoulders to* the work. 我々はみな気合いを入れてその仕事に取りかからねばならない.

put* [*set*] one's *shoulder to the wheel 熱心に仕事に取りかかる, ひとはだ脱ぐ ▪ They stood idle there, instead of *putting their shoulders to the wheel*. 彼らはひとはだ脱ごうともしないでそこにぼんやりと立っていた. ☞ぬかるみにはまった車を出すために車に肩を当てることから.

rest on* a person's *shoulders …の双肩にかかっている ▪ The success of the plan *rests on your shoulders*. この計画の成功いかんはあなたの双肩にかかっている.

rub shoulders with →RUB[2].

shoulder to shoulder **1** 肩と肩を触れ合って, 相並んで ▪ The houses stood *shoulder to shoulder* against the sidewalk. 家々は並んで歩道に面していた.

2 互いに協力して ▪ To succeed we must go *shoulder to shoulder*. 成功するためには我々は互いに協力していかねばならない.

show the cold shoulder → give the cold SHOULDER.

shrug* one's *shoulders →SHRUG.

(*straight*) *from the shoulder* (打撃・ののしりなどが)いやというほど, まっこうから ▪ I told that young

S

man, *straight from the shoulder*, what I thought of his conduct. 私はあの青年にそのふるまいを私がどう思っているかをまっこうから聞かせてやった. ☞ボクシングから.

stand shoulder to shoulder (***with***) …を支える, と協力する (→ SHOULDER to shoulder 2) ▪ We should *stand shoulder to shoulder with* each other. 互いに支え合うべきだ.

take a load [***weight***] ***off*** *a person's* ***shoulders*** 人の肩から重荷を降ろす ▪ She felt *a weight was taken off her shoulders* when the children went away to college. 子供が大学へ行ってしまうと, 彼女は肩から重荷が降りたような気がした.

take … on *one's* (***own***) ***shoulders*** …を一身に引き受ける ▪ I'll *take* the responsibility *on my shoulders*. 私がその責任を負おう.

turn the cold shoulder on [***upon***] → give the cold SHOULDER.

up to *one's* ***shoulders*** (仕事に)没頭して ▪ I am *up to my shoulders* in the work. 私はその仕事に没頭している.

shoulder[2] /ʃóʊldər/ 動 ***Shoulder arms!*** 《号令》になえ銃(つつ)! ▪ Sergeants will remain steady at *shoulder arms*. 軍曹は「になえ銃」の姿勢で体を動かさずにいるだろう.

shoulder *one's* [***a***] ***rifle*** 兵士になる ▪ Many a poor gentleman finds himself obliged to *shoulder a rifle*. 貧乏紳士にはやむなく兵士になるはめになる者が多い.

shoulder *one's* ***way*** [*oneself*] 肩で押しのけて進む (*through*) ▪ He *shouldered his way through* the crowd. 彼は人ごみを肩で押しのけて進んだ ▪ He designed to *shoulder himself* into notice. 彼は肩で押しのけて進んで人目につこうともくろんだ.

shout[1] /ʃaʊt/ 名 ***give*** [***make, raise, set up***] ***a shout*** 一声叫ぶ, 叫び声をあげる ▪ The boys *gave a* great *shout* at the passing train. 少年たちは通り過ぎていく列車を見て大声をあげた.

in with a shout 《口》よい機会に恵まれて ▪ When the championship tournament heated up, the players were said to be *in with a shout*. 優勝戦が過熱してきたとき, 選手たちはよい機会に恵まれていると言われた.

stand (***a***) ***shout*** みんなにおごる ▪ There is a great deal of *standing shout* in the Colonies. 植民地ではみんなにおごるということが大いに行われている.

with a shout 叫びながら ▪ He ran off *with a shout*. 彼は叫びながら走り去った.

shout[2] /ʃaʊt/ 動 ***be nothing to shout about*** 大したものではない ▪ He writes poems, but they *are nothing to shout about*. 彼は詩を書くが, 大したものじゃない.

Now you're shouting. 《米俗》それでこそ話せる ▪ Yes, I will go with you.—Well, *now you're shouting*. ええお供しましょう—いや, それでこそ話せるというものです.

shout [***cry, preach, proclaim,*** etc.] ***…from the rooftops*** [***housetops***] …を公衆に知らせる, 世間に宣伝[吹聴]する (《聖》*Matt.* 10. 27) ▪ Just because I passed the entrance exam you needn't *shout* it *from the rooftops*. 私が入試に合格したからといって, そのことを世間に吹聴する必要はないからね ▪ The Government *cried from the housetops* that they needed voluntary organizations and their cooperation. 政府はボランティア組織とその協力を必要としていると公示した. ☞Palestine 地方の家は平たい屋根を持ち, ここへ集まって雑談したり公の宣言をしたり眠ったりしたことから.

shout *one's* ***head off*** 大声でどなる ▪ The drunken man was *shouting his head off*. その酔いどれは大声でどなっていた.

shout *oneself* ***hoarse*** 大声を出して声をからす ▪ He waved his hat and *shouted himself hoarse*. 彼は帽子を振り, 大声を出して声をからした.

within shouting distance of …から大声で呼べば聞こえるくらいの所に ▪ The barber's shop is *within shouting distance of* his house. その理髪店は彼の家のすぐ近くにある.

shouting /ʃáʊtɪŋ/ 名 ***be all over but*** [《英》***bar***] ***the shouting*** 《口》もう勝利は間違いない, ほぼ勝負がついてあとは喝采だけだ ▪ Another game won by our team—it'*s all over bar the shouting*. 試合はまたわがチームが勝つ—もう勝利は間違いない.

shove[1] /ʃʌv/ 名 ***a shove in the mouth*** 《俗》(酒の)1杯 ▪ He gave me *a shove in the mouth*. 彼は僕に1杯飲ませてくれた.

get the shove 《俗》お払い箱になる ▪ Did you *get the shove* today? きょう首になったのかい.

shove[2] /ʃʌv/ 動 ***shove*** *oneself*/***shove*** *one's* ***way*** 〚副詞句を伴って〛押し進む ▪ He *shoved himself* among the thicket. 彼はやぶの中を押し進んだ ▪ He *shoved his way* to the front. 彼は押し進んで前へ出た.

Shove it! 《主に米口》くそくらえ, ふざけるんじゃねえよ, 勝手にしやがれ. ☞Shove it up one's ass! から.

shovel /ʃʌ́vəl/ 名 ***put in*** *one's* ***shovel*** 《米口》おせっかいをする ▪ She *puts in her shovel* about a thing that is none of her business. 彼女はいらぬおせっかいをする.

shovel and tongs 《米口》猛烈に ▪ Spitting on his hands, he went at it *shovel and tongs*. 両手につばをつけて, 彼は猛烈にそれに立ち向かった.

show[1] /ʃoʊ/ 名 ***a brave show*** **1** 見事な眺め ▪ The daffodils made *a brave show*. 黄水仙は見事な眺めだった.

2 (恐いくせに)大胆[平気]を装う ▪ He put on *a brave show* of indifference. 彼は平気な顔をしてむとんちゃくを装った.

a (***damned, pretty***) ***poor show*** ひどいやり方 ▪ He never even offered to help. It was *a pretty poor show*. 彼は手を貸そうとも言わなかった. かなりひどいやり方だった.

a show of hands (賛否の)挙手 ▪ It can be settled by *show of hands*. それは挙手で決められる.

a show of reason 一見もっともらしいこと ▪ The chef said, with *a show of reason*, that it was impossible to make an omelette without eggs. シェフはもっともらしく卵なしでオムレツは作れないと言った.

all over the show =all over the SHOP.

boss [run] the (whole) show 《口》采配を振る; 牛耳る ▪ They endeavored to *boss the whole show*. 彼らは牛耳ろうと努めた ▪ Ike *ran the show*. アイクが采配を振るった.

by [under a] show of ...にかこつけて ▪ They introduced novelty *by show of* antiquity. 彼らは古さにかこつけて新しさを導入した ▪ He invited her to his house *under a show of* friendship and there did kill her. 彼は友情にかこつけて彼女を自宅に招き, そこで彼女を殺害した.

for show 見せびらかしに[の], 見栄に[の] ▪ He wears glasses *for show*. 彼はだてに眼鏡をかけている.

get the show on the road 《口》(計画などを)実行する ▪ We've decided on the plan. Let's *get the show on the road*. その計画に決めた. ひとつ実行してみよう. ☞劇を巡業することから.

give** a person **a (fair) show 《口》人に力量を示す(公平な)機会を与える ▪ As he's a gentleman, he's bound to *give* you *a show*. あの人は紳士だからきっと君に力量を示す機会をくださるさ ▪ He promised to *give* each contestant *a fair show* in answering the questions. 彼は各競争者に質問に答える公平な機会を与えることを約束した.

give the show away 《俗》内幕をあかす[べらべらしゃべる] ▪ I didn't want to *give the show away*. 僕は内幕をべらべらしゃべりたくなかったのだ. ☞見せ物の種をあばくことから.

go on with the show 《米口》事を続ける ▪ It was decided to *go on with the show*. 事を続けることに決まった.

good show **1** すばらしい業績 ▪ It was a *good show* for the West Indies to beat the Australians. 西インド諸島軍がオーストラリア軍を破ったのはすばらしい成果だった.

2 《英口》すてきだ, けっこうだ ▪ So Hilda is going to marry John. *Good show*! ではヒルダはジョンと結婚するんだな. すてきだ!

S

have [stand] a show 《口》力量を示す機会がある (*of, for, to*) ▪ They *have a* fair *show* in Boston. 彼らはボストンでは力量を示すいい機会がある ▪ He *stood* no *show of* winning. 彼には勝ち目がなかった.

have a [the] show of 《口》...のふうがある, のようだ ▪ It *had the show of* wine, but was not wine. それはワインのようだったが, ワインではなかった.

in show 見かけ[うわべ]は ▪ The boy was like a merchant's prentice *in show*. その少年は見かけは商人のでっちのように見えた ▪ He is a friend only *in show*. 彼はうわべだけの友人だ.

make a fine [sorry, poor] show 立派な[みすぼらしい]外観を呈する ▪ This diamond ring *makes a fine show*. このダイヤの指輪は見ばえがいい.

make a good show **1** 立派にやる ▪ The team *made a good show*. そのチームは立派にやった.

2 美しい外観を呈する ▪ The roses in our garden will *make a good show* in June. 庭のバラは6月には美しいながめになるだろう.

make a show **1** 武力[強硬策]を示す ▪ Henry IV *made a* strong *show* against the followers of Wyclif. ヘンリー4世はウィクリフの後継者たちに強硬策を示した.

2 はなばなしい外観を呈する ▪ In May all things flourished and *made a show*. 5月にはいっさいのものが繁茂してはなばなしい外観を呈した.

make a show of **1** ...をさらしものにする ▪ He *made a show of* them openly. 彼は彼らを公にさらしものにした.

2 ...を見せびらかす ▪ He *makes a show of* his learning. 彼は自分の学問を見せびらかす.

3 ...のように見せかける ▪ Two men, who did nothing, *made a show of* doing it all. 二人の男は何もしないくせにそれを全部しているふりをした.

***make a show of** oneself* さらし者になる ▪ I don't like to *make a show of myself* before strangers. 見ず知らずの人の前でさらし者になりたくない.

make show of =make a SHOW of 3.

on show 陳列されて ▪ We proceeded to look at the tables *on show*. 我々は陳列されてあるテーブルを見にかかった.

put on a show ふりをする ▪ She's not really ill, she's just *putting on a show*. 彼女は本当は病気ではない. ふりをしているだけなのだ.

put up a good show 《口》立派にやってのける[ふるまう] ▪ He *put up a good show* when he heard the bad news. 彼はその悲報を聞いたとき, 立派にふるまった.

run the (whole) show → boss the (whole) SHOW.

show and tell 提示と説明, ショーアンドテル ▪ His class was boring just with his *show and tell* of historical facts. 彼の授業は歴史的事実の提示と説明だけで退屈だった.

stand a show →have a SHOW.

steal [walk off with, run away with] the show [spotlight] (スターより)脇役が人気をさらう ▪ He succeeded in *running away with the show*. 彼はまんまと脇役で人気をさらってしまった.

stop the show (cold) 《劇》(何度ものアンコールであとの出し物ができないくらい)大受けに受ける ▪ Carter's dancing in the third act always *stops the show*. 第3幕のカーターの踊りはいつも大受けに受ける.

the only show in town 唯一重要なこと, 最も大切なこと ▪ *The only show in town* is that we keep peace. 唯一重要なのは平和を維持することだ.

The show is over. 《米口》事は終わった ▪ *The show is over*, and the girl is my own. 事は終わった. そしてその娘は私のものだ.

The show must go on. (どんなに辛くても)義務を果たさなくてはならない ▪ I know you've been tired, but we cannot stop this job now; *the show must go on*. 君が疲れてきているのは分かるが, この仕事をここで止めるわけにはいかない, 辛いが予定通りやるしかない.

the whole show 《米口》事柄全体 ▪ I hate *the whole* blamed *show*. そのいまいましい事柄全体がきらいだ.

under a show of →by SHOW of.

show[2] /ʃoʊ/ 動 ***(...) and it shows*** 《口》(見れば)一目瞭然だ, (良し悪しは)一見してすぐわかる ▪ He's doing drugs *and it shows*. 彼, ヤクをやってるね, 一目瞭然だよ. ☞特に良くないことを指して言うときに用いられる.

go to show 証明する ▪ His new novel *goes to show* that he is talented. 彼の今度の小説は彼に才のあることを示すに足りる.

(*have*) ***something*** [***nothing, little***] ***to show for...*** …の成果を得る[は何もない, はほとんどない] ▪ They worked tirelessly all evening, but *had nothing to show for* it. 彼らはひと晩中精力的に働いたが, 努力の成果は何もなかった.

have... to show for it その証拠に…を示すことができる ▪ I *have* this watch *to show for it*. 私はその証拠にこの時計を見せることができる.

show *oneself* **1** 顔見せする; 姿を現す ▪ The King has to *show himself* to be adored. 王は姿を見せさえすれば敬慕される.

2 (物が)見える ▪ Here and there the lighter green of an oak *showed itself*. カシの木の明るい緑色がちらほら見えた.

3 [[補語を伴って]] 自分が…であることを示す ▪ He was anxious to *show himself* a patriot. 彼はしきりに自分が愛国者であることを示したがった ▪ She had *showed herself* to possess a dainty taste. 彼女は優雅な趣味を持っていることを示した.

4 (性質・状態が)現れる ▪ The same arrogant disposition *showed itself* in occasional quarrels with his friends. その同じ傲慢な性質は彼が友人とときどきけんかするときに現れた.

show a clean pair of heels →HEEL.

show *a person* ***a good time*** →TIME[1].

show daylight 光の漏れるすき間がある ▪ The man who *shows daylight* between himself and his saddle is a bad rider. 体とくらとの間に光の漏れるすき間のできるような人間は乗馬がへたなのだ.

show **(*good*)** ***cause*** …に正当な理由[十分な根拠]を示す (*for*) ▪ Can you *show good cause for* it? それに対しての十分な根拠を示せますか.

show *one's* ***head*** [***face,*** 《戯》 ***nose***] (歓迎されない所へ)顔出しする, 現れる ▪ He was ashamed to *show his head* in the streets. 彼は街に現れるのを恥じていた.

show *one's* ***heels*** →HEEL.

show leg →LEG[1].

show *one's* ***teeth*** →TOOTH.

show *a person* ***the door*** 人に出て行けと言う; 人を追い出す ▪ He was so insolent that I finally *showed* him *the door*. 彼はひどく無礼だったので私はついに出て行けと言った.

show *a person* ***the way*** 人に道を教える, 道案内する ▪ *Show* me *the* easiest *way* to your house. 君の家へ行く一番わかりやすい道を教えてください.

show the way from (競争で)…を引き離す ▪ Merry Maiden, at a good pace, *showed the way from* other horses. メリー・メイデン号はかなりの速さで他の馬を引き離した.

show *a person* ***up*** [***upstairs***] →UP[1], UPSTAIRS.

shower /ʃáʊər/ 名 ***in showers*** [***a shower***] どっと, 雨あられと ▪ Letters came *in showers*. 手紙がどっと殺到した.

send *a person* ***to the showers*** 《米》人を辞任させる, 更迭する; 選手を試合から引っ込める ▪ The team owner weighed a variety of factors before *sending* the manager *to the showers*. チームのオーナーは監督を更迭する前にさまざまな要因を考慮した.

You need a cold shower. 《戯》頭を冷やせ.

showing /ʃóʊɪŋ/ 名 ***make a good*** [***bad, sorry***] ***showing*** 《米》体裁がよい[悪い, みすぼらしい] ▪ The greyhounds *made a* very *sorry showing* in the public contests. グレイハウンド犬は公のコンテストではいかにもみすぼらしい格好だった.

on *a person's* ***own showing*** 人の言い分によれば ▪ The step is *on their own showing* a momentous one. その処置は彼らの言い分によれば重大なものだ.

on this showing 事実がこうであるとすれば ▪ *On this showing*, the notes of private banks are not money. 事実がこうであるとすれば私立銀行の紙幣はお金ではない.

shred /ʃred/ 名 ***in*** [***into***] ***shreds*** きれぎれになって ▪ The flag was *in shreds*. 旗はずたずたになっていた ▪ The curtain went *into shreds*. カーテンはきれぎれになった.

not a shred of ほんの少しの…もない ▪ There's *not a shred of* truth in anything he told you. 彼が君に言ったことは何から何まで僅かな真実性もない.

tear... shred by shred …をずたずたに裂く; を破壊する (→TEAR to pieces) ▪ He *tore* the letter *shred by shred*. 彼は手紙をびりびりに裂いた.

shrewd /ʃruːd/ 形 ***a shrewd turn*** 《雅》いたずら ▪ He may do us *a shrewd turn*. あの男は我々にいたずらをするかもしれない.

shriek[1] /ʃriːk/ 名 ***give*** [***utter***] ***a shriek*** 悲鳴をあげる ▪ He *gave a* piercing *shriek* of joy. 彼は耳をつんざくような金切り声をあげて喜んだ.

shriek[2] /ʃriːk/ 動 ***shriek*** *oneself* ***hoarse*** 金切り声を出して声がしゃがれる ▪ He *shrieked himself hoarse*, cursing it. 彼はそれを金切り声でののしって声がしゃがれた.

shrift /ʃrɪft/ 名 ***come*** [***go***] ***to shrift*** さんげに来る[行く] ▪ He's *going to shrift*. 彼はざんげに行っている.

get short shrift さっさと片づけられる, 容赦なくやっ

つけられる ▪ You'll *get short shrift* if you answer back. 口答えすると容赦なくやっつけられるぞ.

give short shrift to …をさっさと片づける, 容赦なくやっつける ▪ It is to be hoped that the House of Commons will *give short shrift to* the present measure tonight. 下院がこの議案を今晩早急に片づけることが望まれる. ☞short shrift「死刑執行前のざんげのための短い時間」.

shrink /ʃrɪŋk/ 動 ***shrink in the wetting*** 〚主に受身で〛…をだめにする ▪ His son *was shrunk in the wetting*. 彼の息子はだめになってしまった. ☞元ある北国製の布がぬれると縮むので有名であったことから.

shrink into *oneself* 《口》黙りこんでしまう, 内気になる ▪ He seemed to *shrink into himself*. 彼は黙り込んでしまうように思われた.

shroud /ʃraʊd/ 名 ***Shrouds have no pockets.*** 《諺》死人にものは不要. ☞「(死人がまとう) 経かたびらには (物を入れる) ポケットがない」が原義.

shrug /ʃrʌg/ 動 ***shrug*** *one's* ***shoulders*** (両手の手の平を上に向けて)肩をすくめる《無関心・冷笑・嫌悪などのしぐさ》 ▪ The humorist is more likely to *shrug his shoulders* than to condemn. ユーモリストは人を非難するよりも肩をすくめる場合のほうが多い.

shuck[1] /ʃʌk/ 名 ***be not worth shucks*** 《米》なんの価値もない ▪ His old dog *wasn't worth shucks*. 彼の老犬はなんの価値もなかった. ☞shuck「トウモロコシ, ピーナツの皮」.

light a shuck 《米口》急いで去る ▪ But they *lit a shuck* for the mountains. しかし彼らは山の方へ急いで去って行った.

not care shucks 《米》少しも気にしない ▪ I *don't care shucks* about it. そんなことはちっとも気にしない.

shuck[2] /ʃʌk/ 動 ***get shucked out*** 《米口》だしぬかれる, 負ける ▪ He didn't try any more to win the fight, and he *got shucked out* bad. 彼はもうけんかに勝とうとしなかったので, ひどく負けてしまった.

shudder[1] /ʃʌ́dər/ 名 ***give*** *a person* ***the shudders*** 《口》人を恐れさせる ▪ The ghost story *gave* me *the shudders*. その幽霊談に私はぞっとした.

shudder[2] /ʃʌ́dər/ 動 ***shudder to think*** …と考えるとぞっとする ▪ I *shudder to think* what he'll do to her. あの男が彼女にどんなことをするかと思うとぞっとする.

shuffle[1] /ʃʌ́fəl/ 名 ***be*** [***get***] ***lost in the shuffle*** 《米口》(混乱のなか)見落と[見過ご]される, (人ごみのなか)見失われる ▪ Safety is most important and shouldn't *be lost in the shuffle*. 安全が一番大事で見過ごされてはいけない.

shuffle[2] /ʃʌ́fəl/ 動 ***shuffle and cut*** トランプ札を切る; 事態をあやつる ▪ The princes *shuffled and cut* for the destinies of the world. 王侯たちが世界の運命を決めるために事態をあやつった.

shuffle off this mortal coil 人の世のわずらいを打ち捨てる, 死ぬ (cf. Sh., *Haml.* 3. 1. 67) ▪ We must all *shuffle off this mortal coil* sooner or later. 我々はすべて遅かれ早かれ死ななければならない.

shuffle the [*one's*] ***cards*** 事態をあやつる, 方針を変更する ▪ They had *shuffled their cards* so cunningly as to be out of the reach of the law. 彼らは事態を巧みにあやつって法網をくぐり抜けた. ☞トランプを切ることから.

shufti, shufty /ʃʌ́fti/ 名 ***have*** [***take***] ***a shufti*** (***at***) 《英口》(…を)ちらっと見る ▪ I don't mind *having a shufti at* the car, but I can't afford to buy it. その車をちょっと見るのはかまわないけど, 買う余裕はないね.

shut /ʃʌt/ 動 ***be*** [***get***] ***shut of*** 《俗》(人)と縁を切る ▪ Do what I can, I can not *get shut of* him. どんなにしてもあの男と縁を切ることができない.

shut *a person's* ***door against*** [***on, in*** *a person's* ***face***] →SHUT the door against.

shut *one's* ***eyes to*** [***against, on***] …を見て見ぬふりをする, 無視する ▪ I cannot *shut my eyes against* manifest truth. 私は明白な真相を見て見ぬふりはできない.

shut *oneself* ***in*** …に閉じこもる ▪ She *shut herself in* the attic. 彼女は屋根裏部屋に閉じこもった.

shut ... in the door …をドアにはさまれる ▪ I *shut* my fingers *in the door*. 私は指をドアにはさまれた.

shut *one's* ***lights*** (***off***) 《口》死ぬ ▪ I'll *shut my lights off* quick before it happens! そんな事が起こる前にさっさと死んでしまいたい.

shut *one's* ***mouth*** [***face, gob, trap***] 《口》黙る ▪ Whenever his father spoke to him, he *shut his mouth* at once. 父が話しかけるといつも, 彼はすぐ黙ってしまった.

shut *oneself* ***off*** 絶縁する (*from*) ▪ In the Tokugawa age Japan *shut herself off from* the rest of the world. 徳川時代に日本は世界の他の国々と絶縁した.

shut *oneself* ***out*** (***of***) (鍵を忘れたまま錠をかけて)入れない ▪ We've *shut ourselves out of* the house. 私たちは家に入れないでいる.

shut ... out of doors (人)を家から締め出す ▪ He *was shut out of doors* by his wife that night. 彼はその晩妻から締め出しをくった.

shut *one's* ***purse against*** …に金を貸さない ▪ *His purse is shut against* his friends. 彼は友人に金を貸さない.

shut the door after [***behind***] *one* 入ってから戸を閉める, 出てからドアを閉める ▪ He went out of the room and *shut the door after* him. 彼は部屋から出てからドアを閉めた.

shut the [*a person's*] ***door against*** [***on, in*** *a person's* ***face***] 人が出入りしたり近寄ったりしないように戸を閉める ▪ He found *the door shut against* him. 彼はドアが閉まっていて入れないのに気づいた ▪ She *shut her* own *door on* herself. 彼女は人が近寄れないように自分の部屋のドアを閉めた.

shut the door on [***upon***] (提議など)をはねつける, 考慮しない ▪ Why have you *shut the door upon* further negotiations? どうしてこれ以上の交渉をはねつ

けてしまったのですか.

shut** oneself **up 閉じ込もる(*in*) ▪He *shut himself up in* his room. 彼は自室に閉じ込もった.

shutter /ʃʌ́tər/ 名 ***bring* [*put*] *down the shutters*** 自分の考え[気持ち]を他人に教えない ▪She *brought down the shutters* on the image of the building. 彼女はその建物のイメージを他人には教えなかった.

put up the shutters **1** (1日が終わって)店を閉める ▪I ordered him to *put up the shutters* for the day. 今日はこれで閉店にせよと彼に言った.
2《口》店じまいにする; 店をたたむ ▪His losses are serious enough to force him to *put up the shutters*. 彼の損は店をたたまねばならないくらい大きい.

shuttle /ʃʌ́təl/ 名 ***shuttle diplomacy*** 往復外交 ▪The *shuttle diplomacy* continued between China and France. 中国とフランスの間の往復外交が続いた.

shuttlecock /ʃʌ́təlkɑ̀k|-kɔ̀k/ 名 ***like a shuttlecock*** (羽根つきの羽根のように)あちこち動いて ▪I'm sent about all over the place *like a shuttlecock*. 私は至る所へ行ったり来たりしている.

shy[1] /ʃaɪ/ 形名 ***be shy of* [*on*]**《米口》...が不足している ▪I *am* a little *shy of* money. 少し金が不足している ▪It *is shy of* a bathroom. そこには浴室がない.

***be shy of** doing* ためらって...しない ▪They *are shy of speaking* to one another. 彼らはためらってお互いに声をかけない.

***be* [*look*] *shy on* [*at*]** ...をうさんくさく思う, 疑いの目で見る ▪The two were *looking shy at* him. 二人は彼を疑いの目で見ていた.

fight shy of ...をきらう; を避ける ▪He *fights shy of* the job. 彼はその仕事をきらっている ▪Don't *fight shy of* me. 私を避けないでください.

have* [*take*] *a shy at《口》...を試みる ▪I'll *have a shy at* the task. その仕事をやってみよう.

shy[2] /ʃaɪ/ 動 ***shy off/shy clear of*** ...を避ける ▪He always *shied clear of* publicity. 彼はいつも人目に立つことを避けた.

sick /sɪk/ 形 **(*as*) *sick as a dog* [*cat, horse, cushion*]**《俗》ひどくむかついて ▪He makes me *as sick as a dog*. あの男を見るとひどくむかついてくる ▪I am *sick as a horse* already. 僕はもうひどくむかついているんだ.

(*as*) *sick as a parrot*《英戯》非常に失望して ▪He was *sick as a parrot* when he heard the news. 彼はその知らせを聞いて非常に失望した.

be in sick bay (病気で)寝こんで ▪He has *been in sick bay* with influenza. 彼はインフルエンザで寝こんでいる. ☞sick bay「船内の病室」.

be off sick 病気で欠勤[欠席]している ▪He *was off sick* for a week. 彼は1週間病欠[欠席]した.

***be sick at* [*about*]**《口》...のことで失望している ▪He *was sick at* failing to pass the examination. 彼は試験にパスしなかったのでがっかりしていた.

be* [*feel*] *sick at heart《文》心を悩ましている ▪She *was sick at heart* at the thought of that. 彼女はそのことを考えて心を悩ました.

(*be*) *sick for* ...を恋しがっている ▪He *is sick for* a sight of home. 彼は故郷を一目見たいと恋しがっている.

be sick of **1** ...に飽きはてている ▪The world *is sick of* such societies. 世間はそんな社交界にはあきあきしている ▪I *am sick of* flattery. お世辞はごめんだ.
2 (病気)にかかっている ▪He *was sick of* a fever. 彼は熱病にかかっていた. ☞聖書語法.

fall sick《米》病気になる ▪If I *fell sick* who is to carry on the business? 私が病気になったら誰が仕事を続行してくれるだろうか.

feel sick to** one's **stomach《米》気分が悪くなる, むかつく ▪Looking at the accident I *felt sick to my stomach*. その事故を見て, 気分が悪くなった.

get sick to** one's **stomach 吐く ▪My child always *gets sick to his stomach* in the car. うちの子は車に乗るといつも吐くの.

go sick **1**《米》病気になる ▪She hasn't *gone sick* once in six months. 彼女は半年の間, 1回も病気になっていない.
2《軍》病気欠勤を届ける ▪He has *gone sick* under false pretenses. 彼は口実を作って病気欠勤を届けた.

make** a person **sick《口》人を怒らせる ▪Your words *make* me *sick*. 君の言葉にはカチンとくる.

on sick leave 病気休暇中で ▪He is now *on sick leave*. 彼は今病気休暇中だ.

on the sick list 病気欠勤して ▪I cannot come. I'm *on the sick list* at the present. 私は行けません. 目下病気欠勤しているのです.

report sick =go SICK 2.

sick and tired of《口》...がつくづくいやになって, 飽き飽きして ▪I am *sick and tired of* good women. 善良な女性というやつには全くいやになった.

sick of the sight of ...を見るとうんざりする[むかむかする] ▪I get *sick of the sight of* that fellow. あの男を見るとむかむかする.

sick to death of ...が死ぬほどいやになって ▪I'm *sick to death of* kids. 子供は死ぬほどいやだ.

take sick/be taken sick《米》病気になる ▪He *took sick* while on the trip. 彼はその旅行中に病気になった.

side /saɪd/ 名 ***at* [*by*] *one's* side** わきに, わきの ▪He always has a dictionary *at his side*. 彼はいつも座右に辞書を置いている ▪I said this to a friend *by my side*. 私はわきの友人にこう言った.

***be on the good side of** a person*《米口》人に気に入られている ▪They *are on the good side of* him. 彼らは彼に気に入られている.

be on the safe side →SAFE.

burst** one's **sides →split one's SIDEs.

by the side of ...の側に, 近くに; に比べて ▪She passed five hours *by her friend's side*. 彼女は友人のそばで5時間を過ごした ▪She appeared quite a supermodel *by the side of* her companion. 彼女

は彼女の連れと比べるとまるでスーパーモデルのようだった.

choose up sides (二人の主将が)互いに選手を選んで二つのチームを作る ▪ The boys *chose up sides* for a game of baseball. 野球をするためにキャプテンが互いに少年を選んで, 二つのチームを作った.

come down on one side or the other 選択する ▪ He was a decisive person, so he would always *come down on one side or the other*. 彼は果断な人物だったので常に甲乙いずれかを選択したものだった.

err on the side of …に失する, 過ぎる ▪ His opinion *errs on the side of* optimism. 彼の意見は楽天主義に失する.

from all sides/from every side 四方から; 周到に ▪ Birds came flying *from all sides*. 鳥が四方から飛んで来た ▪ He studied the question *from every side*. 彼は周到にその問題を研究した.

from side to side 端から端に, 左右に ▪ The ship rolled *from side to side*. 船は左右に揺れた.

get on** a person's **good side 《米口》人の気に入る[きげんを取る] ▪ Janice knows how to *get on her father's good side*. ジャニスは父親のごきげんを取るすべを心得ている.

get on the wrong side of →on the wrong SIDE of.

go to [get to, reach] the other side (死んで)あの世へ行く, 天国へ行く ▪ My sister has *gone to the other side*. 妹は天国へ行った.

have much [lots of] side 《口》偉ぶる, ひどく気取る ▪ He seems to *have lots of side*. 彼はひどく気取っているようだ.

have no side 《口》気取らない ▪ I like Bill, because he *has no side*. 私はビルが好きだ, ちっとも気取らないから.

have ... on** one's **side …を有利な点として持っている ▪ You *have* youth *on your side*. 君は若さが利点なんだよ.

keep [stay] on the right side of 《口》…を怒らせないようにする, 侵さないようにする ▪ *Keep on the right side of* the manager. 支配人を怒らせないようにしなさい.

keep on the right side of the law 法を犯さない ▪ He sticks at nothing so long as he *keeps on the right side of the law*. 彼は法を犯さない限り何事もちゅうちょしない.

keep** one's **side of a [the] bargain 自分の方も約束を守る ▪ I've done everything I promised, but he's not *keeping his side of the bargain*. こっちは約束したことは全部したのに, 彼の方は約束を守っていない.

leave [put] ... on [to] one side …をしばらくたな上げにする ▪ Let's *leave* that point *to one side*. その点はしばらくたな上げにしておこう.

let the side down 《英口》友人[仲間]の足を引っ張るようなことをする, 家族に恥をかかせる ▪ If you go astray, you're just *letting the side down*. 君がぐれたりすれば家族に恥をかかせることになるよ.

like the dark side of the moon 謎に包まれて, 全く謎の ▪ What they're doing in the institute is *like the dark side of the moon*. 彼らがその研究所で何をやっているのか, 全くの謎だ.

look on the bright side (of) →BRIGHT.

No side! 《ラグビー》試合終了! ▪ At last "*no side*" was called. とうとう「試合終了」が宣された.

not leave** a person's **side 人に寄り添う, のそばから離れず面倒を見る ▪ My wife did*n't leave my side* while I was in hospital. 私が入院中, 妻は私に寄り添っていてくれた.

on all sides/on every side 四方八方に, 至る所に ▪ *On all sides* war is believed inevitable. どこでも戦争は不可避だと信じられている.

***on** a person's **bad [good] side/on the bad [good] side of** a person* 《口》人にきらわれて[気に入られて] ▪ He got *on her father's bad side* by asking her out to the dance. 彼は彼女をダンスパーティーに誘い出すので彼女の父親にきらわれていた.

on both sides 両側に, 双方に ▪ There is right and wrong *on both sides*. 双方に是非がある.

on either [each] side どちら側にも ▪ Grass grows *on either side* of the road. 草は道のどちら側にもはえる.

on** one's **side …の側[方]に ▪ We have right *on our side*. 我々の方には正義がある ▪ The fault must be *on your side*. 落ち度はきっと君の方にある.

on the other side あの世に, 天国に ▪ Mother is *on the other side*. 母さんは天国にいる.

on the right side **1** (人に)気に入られて (*of*) ▪ I see you were *on the right side of* your mother. 君はどうやらお母さんのお気に入りだったらしいね.

2 黒字で ▪ The accountant says we are £125 *on the right side*. 会計係は125ポンド黒字だと言っている.

3 たちのよい, 許せる ▪ It's a fault *on the right side*. それは許せる欠点だ.

4 有利で, 勝ち目のある ▪ We are *on the right side*; our horse is winning. 我々は勝ち目があるぞ. かけた馬がリードしている.

on the right [better, bright, green, hither sunny] side of …の坂を越えないで, より若い (↔ on the wrong SIDE of) ▪ He is still *on the sunny side of* fifty. 彼はまだ50の坂を越えていない.

on the right [wrong] side of the tracks → TRACK.

on the side **1** 《口》(定職の)ほかに, アルバイトで ▪ He makes more than his salary *on the side*. 彼はアルバイトで月給以上の金をかせいでいる ▪ He wrote *on the side*. 彼は内職で文筆をとった.

2 《米口》添えものとして ▪ They served us fried chicken with peas and corn *on the side*. フライドチキンが豆とトウモロコシを添えて出された.

3 《口》こっそりと ▪ His wife has affairs *on the side*. 彼の妻はひそかに浮気をしている.

on the ... side いくぶん…の気味で ▪ Prices are *on the* high *side*. 物価は上がり気味だ ▪ The boy is always *on the* rough *side.* その男の子はいつも荒っぽくなりがちだ.

***on the side of** a person* 人に味方して ▪ Nature is *on the side of* the man who tries to rise. 自然は立身しようとする人に味方する ▪ I am *on your side.* 僕は君の味方だ.

on the side of the angels 天使に味方して; 正統的な見方をして ▪ Fowler himself is *on the side of the angels.* ファウラー自身は正統的な見方をしている. ☞B. Disraeli が Nov. 25, 1864 にした演説から.

on the wrong [shady, other, thither] side of …の坂を越えて, より年取って (↔on the right SIDE of) ▪ The widow was *on the wrong side of* fifty. 未亡人は50の坂を越えていた.

***on the wrong side of** a person* 人にうとまれて ▪ He got *on the wrong side of* his master. 彼は主人にうとまれた.

on the wrong side of the law 法[罪]を犯して (→keep on the right SIDE of the law) ▪ I found myself *on the wrong side of the law* after hitting a child while driving. 運転中に子供をはねて法を犯した身となった.

on this side (of) (ある時間)の前に ▪ He is *on this side of* forty, I should think. 彼は40を越していないと思う ▪ All won't be completed *on this side* Christmas. クリスマス前に全部は完成すまい.

on this [that, the other] side (of) (ある場所)のこちら[あちら]側に ▪ He lives *on this side of* the river. 彼は川のこちら側に住んでいる ▪ The moon was risen *on the other side* the willows. 月はヤナギの向こう側へ上っていた.

pass by on the other side →PASS³.

play sides 組を分けてやる ▪ Let's *play sides.* 組を分けてやろうよ.

put ... on one side **1** (あとで使うため)…を取っておく; (金のない客のため品物)を取っておく ▪ I'll *put* the money *on one side* for my old age. 老後のためにその金を取っておきます.

2 …をうっちゃっておく ▪ The question *was put on one side* for the time being. その問題は当分放っておかれた.

put on side 《口》 もったいぶる ▪ I don't like him; he *puts on side* [side on]. あの男はきらいだ. もったいぶるから.

remain [stay] on the right side of the law =keep on the right SIDE of the law.

see both sides (問題などの)両面を見る《賛成・反対のどちらの立場も分かる》 ▪ A man of action cannot *see both sides* of the question. 行動家は問題の両面を見ることはできない.

see the funny side of (深刻な事態)のこっけいな面を見る ▪ He can *see the funny side of* life. 彼は人生のこっけいな面を見ることができる.

side by side 相並んで; 協力して (*with*) ▪ They sat *side by side.* 彼らは並んで座った ▪ I had to work *side by side with* them. 彼らと協力して仕事をしなければならなかった.

speak [talk] out of both sides of** one's **mouth 《米》二枚舌を使う ▪ I can't stand a fellow who *talks out of both sides of his mouth.* 私は二枚舌を使うやつにはがまんできない.

split [shake, burst]** one's **sides 腹をかかえて笑う, 腹の皮をよじる ▪ He *shook his sides* with laughing. 彼は腹をかかえて笑った ▪ He laughed ready to *split his sides.* 彼は腹の皮がよじれんばかりに笑いこけた.

stay on the right side of →keep on the right SIDE of.

take [draw]** a person **on [to] one side (注意するために)人をわきへ呼ぶ ▪ I *took* him *on one side* and gave him a piece of advice. 彼をわきへ呼んで一言注意した.

take the side of/take sides with …の味方をする, に組する ▪ He would *take my side* to the last drop of his blood. 彼は死ぬまで私の味方をしてくれるだろう ▪ I declined to *take sides with* him in the dispute. 私はその議論で彼に組するのを断った.

the other side of the coin →COIN¹.

the seamy side of →SEAMY.

(the) two [opposite] sides of the same coin 互いに関連していて切り離せないもの, 表裏一体 ▪ Ethnic cleansing and ethnic separatism are *two sides of the same coin.* 民族浄化と民族分離主義は表裏一体である ▪ Love and hate are *the opposite sides of the same coin.* 愛と憎しみは表裏一体である.

the wrong [right] side of fifty 50歳を越えて[未満で] ▪ She's married, with three sons, and now she's *the wrong side of fifty.* 彼女は結婚していて3人の息子がおり, いまは50を越えている.

the wrong side out 裏返しに ▪ He put his socks on *the wrong side out.* 彼は裏返しに靴下をはいた. ☞INSIDE out のほうが普通の言い方.

There are two sides to every question [story]. 《諺》一枚の紙にも表裏あり.

There is much to be said on both sides. 《諺》言い分は五分五分.

this [the other] side 《口》大西洋のこちら[あちら]側で ▪ The society has expanded very rapidly "on *the other side.*" その協会は「大西洋のあちら側で」急速に拡張してきた.

this side (of) …の一歩手前で ▪ He admired her just *this side of* idolatry [*of* worshipping her]. 彼は彼女を崇拝すると言っていいほど愛慕していた.

this side (of) heaven [the grave] この世では, 存命中は ▪ There is no end to anything *this side the grave.* この世では何事にも終わりがない.

turn the best side outward →BEST.

sideline /sáɪdlàɪn/ 名 ***stand [be, remain, sit, stay] on the sidelines*** 事態を傍観する ▪ In this case I am inclined to *stand on the sidelines.* この場合, 私はむしろ事態を傍観していたい. ☞サイドラインの外側でゲームを観戦することから.

sideways /sáɪdwèɪz/ 副 ***knock ... sideways***

《英口》 **1** (人)にショックを与える，当惑させる ▪ I *was knocked sideways* by the news. その知らせでショックを受けた.

2 (物事)に悪影響を与える，混乱させる ▪ The oil crisis *knocked* prices *sideways*. 石油危機で物価が混乱してしまった.

look sideways **1** けげんな顔をする; 疑いの目で見る ▪ He was spending too much, and his housekeeper began to *look sideways*. 彼がひどく金を使うので家政婦がけげんな顔をし始めた.

2 (...を)伏目使いで見る; (に)流し目を送る (*at*) ▪ He was *looking sideways at* me. 彼は私を伏目使いに見ていた ▪ She was *looking* all *sideways* and never touched her dinner. 彼女はずっと目を伏せていて食事にも全然手をつけなかった ▪ They were *looking sideways at* each other. 彼らは互いに流し目を送り合っていた.

sideswipe /sáɪdswàɪp/ 名 ***take a sideswipe at*** (人・事を)ことのついでに非難する ▪ They *took a sideswipe at* him by playing up to their boss. 彼らは彼が上司に媚びるのでことのついでに非難した.

siege /siːdʒ/ 名 ***a siege mentality*** 強迫観念 ▪ Some scholars develop *a siege mentality* because they're afraid someone will steal their ideas. 学者の中には自分の考えが盗まれるのではないかと心配して強迫観念にかられている者もいる.

be under siege **1** (軍隊・警察に)包囲されている ▪ The town has *been under siege*. 町は包囲されていた.

2 絶えず非難にさらされている ▪ The dollar has *been* coming *under siege*. ドルはずっと非難にさらされてきている.

lay siege to ...を攻囲する《比喩的にも》 ▪ The enemy will *lay siege to* the capital before long. 敵はまもなく首都を攻囲するだろう ▪ He *laid siege to* her heart and won her hand. 彼は彼女をくどいて結婚した.

raise a siege on/raise the siege of ...の包囲を解く ▪ The General gave order to *raise a siege on* the city. 将軍はその都市の包囲を解くことを命令した.

stand a siege 包囲攻撃に耐える ▪ The city *stood* many *sieges*. その都市は何度もの包囲攻撃に耐えた.

sieve /sɪv/ 名 ***(as) leaky as a sieve*** 何でも口外して，口をすべらして ▪ He is *as leaky as a sieve*. 彼は何でもすぐ口をすべらしてしまう.

draw water with a sieve/pour water into sieve/take up water in a sieve むだ骨を折る ▪ That's no better than *taking up water in a sieve*. それはざるで水をすくうのと変わりがない.

have a memory [a head, a mind] like a sieve ひどく忘れっぽい ▪ I'll write those things down. I *have a memory like a sieve*. これらを書きつけておこう. ひどい健忘症なんだから.

sigh /saɪ/ 名 ***breathe [heave, give] a sigh of relief*** 安堵のため息をつく ▪ I *breathed a sigh of relief* when I heard that my son was safe. 息子が無事だと聞いて安堵のため息をついた.

give a sigh ため息をつく ▪ The woman *gave a* deep *sigh*. その女性は深いため息をついた.

sight /saɪt/ 名 ***a (long, jolly) sight*** 《俗》はるかに ▪ You're *a sight* too clever for me to talk to. 君はあんまり利口者だから僕の話相手にならない.

a sight for sore eyes 《口》見るもうれしいもの，(特に)珍客 ▪ Come in, my dear, you're *a sight for sore eyes*. お入り，お前，よく来てくれたねえ.

a sight of 《俗》たくさんの ▪ What *a sight of* people! なんて大勢なんだ!

after sight 《商》一覧後 ▪ The bill is payable at 15 days *after sight*. 手形は一覧後15日払いだ.

at ... days' sight 一覧後...日に ▪ He drew a bill payable *at* six *days' sight*. 彼は一覧後6日払いの手形を振り出した.

at first sight →FIRST.

at [on, upon] sight **1** 見てすぐ ▪ He can play and sing *at sight*. 彼は楽譜を見るとすぐ演奏したり歌ったりできる ▪ I can tell a reporter *on sight*. 新聞記者は見るとすぐわかる.

2 《商》一覧払いの[で]，呈示払いの[で] ▪ He received a bill payable *at sight*. 彼は一覧払いの手形を受け取った ▪ These bills are payable *at sight*. これらの手形は一覧払いができる.

at [on, upon] (the) sight of ...を見て ▪ She started *at sight of* something. 彼女は何かを見てぎくっとした ▪ He ran away like a thief *at the sight of* a detective. 彼は刑事を見ると泥棒のように逃げ去った.

burst into sight 急に見えてくる，突然現れる ▪ A big bear *burst into sight* and caught him off guard. 大きなクマが突然現れて彼は不意をつかれた.

by a darned [considerable, long] sight 《米俗》[[主に否定文で]] 断然，決して ▪ These animals are slyer *by a long sight* than foxes. この動物たちはキツネよりも断然ずるい ▪ That ain't all *by a long sight*. それは決して全部ではない.

by sight **1** ただ一面識で，顔は ▪ I know him only *by sight*. 彼のことは顔だけは知っている.

2 目に頼って (《聖》*Cor*. 5. 7) ▪ He might well have doubted of success, had he walked *by sight*. 彼が目に頼って歩いたのであったら，当然成功を疑ったかもしれない.

cannot stand [bear] the sight of ...をひどくきらう ▪ They *can't stand the sight of* each other. 彼らは互いにひどくきらっている.

catch [get] sight of ...を見つける ▪ You may *catch sight of* it from the railway. それは列車から見える.

come [heave] in sight 見えてくる ▪ Land *came in sight*. 陸地が見えてきた ▪ I was glad to see you *heave in sight*, Betty. 君が現れてきたのでうれしかったよ，ベティー.

come to one's sight 目につく所へやって来る ▪ Don't *come to my sight* again. 私の目につく所へ

二度とやって来るんじゃない.

come within sight of →within SIGHT of.

do the sights →see the SIGHTs.

draw a sight upon 《米》…をねらう ▪ You must *draw a sight upon* the animal's head. 君はその動物の頭をねらわねばならない.

find* [*gain*] *favor in a person's sight 人の受けがよい ▪ I should like to *find favor in his sight*. 彼の受けがよくなりたいものだ.

get sight of →catch SIGHT of.

go out of sight 見えなくなる ▪ The land *went out of sight*. 島は見えなくなった.

have a reward in sight 報酬を当てにしている ▪ The lad worked hard as he *had a reward in sight*. 少年は報酬を当てにしていたので懸命に働いた.

have a sight of …を一目見る ▪ You should have *had a sight of* it. それを君に一目見せたかったよ.

have* [*get*]…(*lined up*) *in one's sights/ have* [*get*] *one's sights* (*lined up*) *on …を目標に設定する, に照準を定めている ▪ I*'ve got* that post (*lined up*) *in my sights*. 僕はそのポストにぴたりと照準を定めている.

have long* [*near, short*] *sight 遠視[近視]である ▪ I *have long* [*near, short*] *sight*. 私は遠視[近視]だ.

heave in sight →come in SIGHT.

in sight 見えて ▪ The bridge was full *in sight*. 橋がすっかり見えていた ▪ The end of the task is not yet *in sight*. 仕事の終わりはまだ見当がつかない.

***in a person's sight* 1** 人の面前に[で] ▪ His wife was weeping *in his sight*. 彼の妻は彼の面前で泣いていた.

2 人から見れば ▪ We are mere worms *in his sight*. 彼から見れば我々は虫けらにすぎない.

in sight of …の見える所に ▪ We passed *in sight of* an old castle. 我々は古城の見える所を通り過ぎた ▪ We came *in sight of* land. 我々は陸地の見える所へやって来た.

in the sight of …から見れば ▪ All human beings are equal *in the sight of* God. すべての人間は神から見れば平等だ.

keep… in sight/keep sight of …を見失わないようにする ▪ He managed to *keep* the car *in sight*. 彼はなんとかその車を見失わないようにした.

let… out of one's sight …から目を離す ▪ He could not *let* the money *out of his sight*. 彼はその金から目が離せなかった.

look a sight 《英》おかしく[変に]見える; 醜い, 汚い ▪ She *looks a sight* in that old dress. 彼女はあの古い服を着ているとおかしな風采だ ▪ Your room *looks a sight*. Go and tidy it. 部屋が汚いから, きれいにしてらっしゃい.

lose one's sight 失明する ▪ She *lost her sight* at the age of three. 彼女は3歳のときに失明した.

***lose sight of* 1** …を見失う ▪ He began to run as if he dreaded *losing sight of* her. 彼は彼女を見失いはしないかと心配しているかのように走りだした.

2 …を見落とす, 忘れる ▪ You've *lost sight of* the fact. 君はそのことを忘れている.

lower one's sights 照準を下げる《あまり野心的でなくなる》(↔raise one's SIGHTs) ▪ You are over-ambitious; *lower your sights*. 君はあまりにも野心的だ. 照準を下げるんだな.

make oneself a sight/ make a sight of oneself 《口》みっともないふうをする ▪ You've *made yourself a* regular *sight*. 君は全くみっともないふうをしたものだ.

not a pretty sight 《口》見られたものではない, ひどい状態[格好]で ▪ She was *not a pretty sight* soon after she woke up. 彼女の寝起き直後は見られたものでなかった.

on* [*upon*] *sight →at SIGHT.

out of* (*all*) *sight はるかに, 断然 ▪ It is *out of all sight* the best of his works. それは彼の作品中で断然一番よいものだ.

***out of sight* 1** 見えない所に ▪ *Out of sight*, out of mind. 《諺》「去る者は日々にうとし」 ▪ He was nearly *out of sight*. 彼はほとんど見えなくなっていた.

2 法外に(高い) ▪ Butter went almost *out of sight*. バターが法外と言ってよいほど高くなった.

3 《米俗》最高で ▪ His new album is *out of sight*, you bet. 彼の新しいアルバムはほんとに最高だよ.

4 空想だけの, 現実味のない ▪ Her dreams about becoming an actress are really *out of sight*. 彼女の女優になる夢は全く現実味がない.

5 《俗》酒[麻薬]にひどく酔って ▪ As he had been drinking since morning, he was *out of sight*. 彼は朝から飲んでいたので, ぐでんぐでんだった.

out of one's sight …の見えぬ(所に) ▪ Get *out of my sight*! 消えうせろ! ▪ The ship has gone *out of our sight*. 船は我々から見えなくなっていた.

put… out of sight …を見えない所へ置く, 隠す ▪ *Put* those toys *out of sight*. これらのおもちゃを見えない所へ置きなさい.

raise one's sights 照準を上げる《もっと野心的になる》(↔lower one's SIGHTs) ▪ Political leaders should *raise their sights* to match the situation. 党首たちはこの状況に合わせて照準を上げるべきだ.

see sights 見物する (*of*) ▪ You may go and *see sights of* the city the whole day. きょうは1日町見物に出て行ってもいい.

see* [*do*] *the sights 名所見物をする ▪ Three days is very little time to *see* all *the sights* of New York. ニューヨークのすべての名所見物をするには3日では短い.

set one's* [*a person's*] *sights high 高い目標を掲げる[掲げさせる] ▪ Some students *set their sights* too *high*. 学生の中にはあまりにも高い目標を掲げるものがいる ▪ My parents *set my sights high* from the beginning. 両親は初めから私に高い目標を掲げさせた. ☞sight「(銃の)照準」.

set one's sights on …を目指す, 目的とする ▪ He *set his sights on* getting a large fortune.

彼は大財産獲得を目指した.

sight unseen 《米》現物を見ないで ▪ The farmer of today has got beyond trading "*sight unseen.*" 今日の農民は「現物を見ずに」取引などしなくなっている.

take a sight **1** 《俗》親指を鼻に当てほかの指は握って小指だけを動かす《不信・軽蔑の身ぶり》 ▪ The urchin proceeded to *take a sight* at him. その小僧は小指をのばし親指を鼻に当てて彼をあざけった.

2 ねらう ▪ He *took a* careful *sight* before firing. 彼は発砲する前によくねらった.

3 (...を)測定する (*at*) ▪ We *took a sight at* the sun. 我々は太陽の位置を測定した.

to sight 目に; 見えるように ▪ The head was lost *to sight* among tall weeds. 頭は高い雑草の間で見えなくなっていた.

within sight 見えて ▪ It is, in fact, already *within sight.* それは現にもう実現しかけている.

within sight of ...の見える所に[で] ▪ He came *within sight of* the church. 彼は教会の見える所へやって来た ▪ We were every day *within sight of* death. 我々は毎日いつ死ぬかわからなかった.

sign[1] /saɪn/ 名 ***a sign of the times*** →SIGNs of the times.

at the sign of ...の看板のある店で ▪ They met *at the sign of* the griffin. 彼らはグリフィンの看板のある店で会った.

by signs 身ぶり[手まね]で ▪ The dumb man made himself understood *by signs.* その口のきけない男は手まねで意思を表明した.

cut a [*a person's*] ***sign*** 《米口》(先住民・獲物などの)形跡に出くわす ▪ He chased the Indians off his ranch whenever he *cut their sign.* 彼は先住民の形跡に出くわすたびに彼らを農場から追い払った.

in sign of [***that***] ...の[という]印に ▪ He kissed the boy *in sign of* love. 彼は愛情の印にその男の子にキスした ▪ He kissed her hand *in sign that* he respected her. 彼は尊敬の印に彼女の手にキスした.

make a sign [***signs***] (手・頭で)合図する, 身ぶりをする ▪ The moment he saw her he *made a sign* of silence. 彼は彼女を見るとすぐ黙ってという合図をした.

show [***give***] ***signs of*** ...のそぶりを見せる ▪ The poor old man *showed* no *signs of* having heard us. 哀れな老人は我々の言葉が聞こえた様子は見せなかった.

signs [***a sign***] ***of the times*** 時のきざし, 時勢 (《聖》*Matt.* 16. 3) ▪ It is *a sign of the times* that children are taken to listen to debates in Parliament. 子供たちが議会討論を聞きに連れて行かれるのも時勢というものだ.

the sign of the cross **1** Xの記号 ▪ I could not write my name, so I made *the sign of the cross.* 名前が書けなかったのでXを記した.

2 (右手で空に描く)十字の形 ▪ He made *the sign of the cross* on his breast on entering the church. 彼は教会に入ると胸の上に十字を切った.

sign[2] /saɪn/ 動 ***sign*** *oneself* 署名する ▪ The reporter *signs himself* "Victor." その通信員は「ビクター」と署名する.

sign on the dotted line →LINE[1].

signed, sealed (***and delivered***) 《口》すべての手続きを完了して, 滞りなく完了して ▪ He wished to have the agreement *signed and sealed.* 彼はその契約を滞りなく完了したいと思った.

signal /sígnəl/ 名 ***get*** *one's* ***signals crossed*** 言葉の行き違いが起こる; 電話が混線して通じない ▪ We couldn't meet for lunch because we *got our signals crossed.* 連絡ミスで私たちはいっしょに昼食を食べられなかった.

give the signal for ...の合図をする ▪ The general *gave the signal for* a retreat. 将軍は退却の合図をした.

signalize /sígnəlàɪz/ 動 ***signalize*** *oneself* 異彩を放つ ▪ He never *signalizes himself* by his wit. 彼は機知で異彩を放つようなことは決してない.

signature /sígnətʃər/ 名 ***a signature dish*** (有名シェフによる)特選料理 ▪ We had a dinner in a top restaurant with *a signature dish* by the most famous chef in town. 一流レストランで市内随一の有名シェフによる特選料理のディナーにありつけた.

over *one's* (***own***) ***signature*** (書類が)自署がしてあって ▪ As the docket was *over his own signature* he could scarcely deny having written it. 覚え書きは彼の自署がしてあるので, それを書いたことを否定することはとてもできなかった.

put *one's* ***signature to*** ...に署名する ▪ He *put his signature to* the letter. 彼は手紙に署名した.

significance /sɪgnífəkəns/ 名 ***of significance*** 重要な ▪ This is a matter *of* great *significance.* これは非常に重要な問題だ.

significant /sɪgnífəkənt/ 形 ***a significant other*** 《主に米》大事な人 ▪ I took my *significant other* to the hotel. 私の大事な人をホテルに連れて行った.

signify /sígnəfàɪ/ 動 ***What ... signify?*** ...が何であろう ▪ *What* does a little loss *signify?* 少しばかりの損失が何であろう.

silence /sáɪləns/ 名 ***a deafening silence*** 深い静寂; 当惑を物語る無言 ▪ There was *another deafening silence* between them. 彼らの間には再びばつの悪い沈黙が続いた.

break silence 沈黙を破る, 口を開く ▪ At length the Mayor *broke silence.* ついに市長が口を開いた.

break the silence 静寂を破る; (しらけた)沈黙を破る ▪ Nothing *broke the silence* of the night. 夜のしじまを破るものは何もなかった ▪ It was Jim who *broke the silence.* その場の沈黙を破ったのはジムだった.

buy *a person's* ***silence*** 人に口止め料を払う ▪ He gave the girl 30,000 yen to *buy her silence* after she had seen him crash into a parked car. 彼が停めてあった車にぶつけたのを見ていた女の子に彼は口止め料として3万円を渡した.

in silence 黙って ▪ He looked on *in* admiring

S

silence. 彼は感嘆して無言でながめ続けた.

keep silence 沈黙を守る ▪ It is impossible to *keep silence* on such an event. そのような事件について沈黙を守ることは不可能だ.

pass into silence (世の中から)忘れられる ▪ The event has already *passed into silence.* その事件はすでに忘れられてしまっている.

pass with silence/pass over in silence 言わずにおく ▪ He *passed* it *with silence.* 彼はそれを言わずにおいた.

put [***reduce***]***... to silence*** (議論などで人)を沈黙させる ▪ He *put* her *to silence* before all the people. 彼はみんなの前でその女性を沈黙させてしまった.

Silence gives consent. 《諺》沈黙は承諾の印.

Silence is golden. 《諺》沈黙は金.

Silence reigned. しんとして声がなかった; 誰も口をきかなかった.

silent /sáɪlənt/ 形 (***as***) ***silent as the grave*** [***the tomb, death***] 《文》全く静かな, 全然ものを言わない ▪ I'll be *as silent as the grave.* 私は全くものを言わないからね.

give *a person* ***the silent treatment/get the silent treatment*** 人を完全に無視する ▪ Are you going to *give* me *the silent treatment*? 僕のことを完全に無視するつもりなんだね?

silhouette /sìluét/ 名 ***in silhouette*** シルエットで, 輪郭だけで ▪ The illustrations are done *in silhouette.* そのさし絵はシルエットで描いてある ▪ They were *in silhouette* against a morning sky. 彼らは朝空を背にして輪郭だけ見えていた.

silk /sɪlk/ 名 ***carry silk*** **1** =wear SILK. **2** (馬が騎手を乗せる, から)競走に出る ▪ The horse will never *carry silk* again. その馬はもう二度と競走に出ないだろう.

fine as silk 《米口》とてもすてきだ[元気だ] ▪ That's *fine as silk.* そりゃとてもすてきだ ▪ I am *fine as silk.* 私はとても元気です.

hit the silk 《米俗》パラシュートで飛び降りる ▪ The commandos *hit the silk* over the target zone. 特殊部隊は目標地帯にパラシュート降下した.

in silk 《米》トウモロコシの毛がふさふさして ▪ Now many of the hills are *in silk.* 今や多くの丘にはトウモロコシの毛がふさふさしている ▪ By August the corn is *in silk.* 8月までにはトウモロコシの毛がふさふさしている. ☞silk「トウモロコシの毛」.

Silks and satins put out the fire in the kitchen. 《諺》着道楽はかまどの火を消す.

soft as silk 絹のように柔らかい ▪ Her skin was *soft as silk.* 彼女の肌は絹のように柔らかかった.

take [***obtain, receive***] (***the***) ***silk*** 《英》王室弁護士に任命される ▪ He *received silk* in 1868. 彼は1868年に王室弁護士に任命された. ☞絹のガウンを着ることから.

wear silk (騎手のジャケットを着る, から)騎手をする ▪ He ceased to *wear silk.* 彼は騎手をやめた.

silly /síli/ 形 ***Don't be silly.*** ばかなことを言うんじゃない《軽いたしなめ》 ▪ *Don't be silly.* Keep your money. ばかなことを言うんじゃない. 金は取っておくんだ.

drink *oneself* ***silly*** 《口》飲み過ぎでまともにふるまえない ▪ He *drank himself silly.* 彼は飲み過ぎでまともじゃなかった. ☞drink の代わりに laugh, shout も可.

go silly over (女性)にのぼせあがる ▪ He *went silly over* a woman. 彼はある女性にのぼせあがった.

the silly season 《英口》(新聞の)夏枯れ時 ▪ There's not much news and it's *the silly season.* 大したニュースもなく, 夏枯れ時だな.

silver /sílvər/ 名 ***for thirty pieces*** [***a handful***] ***of silver*** 銀貨30枚と引き換えに ▪ He would sell himself *for thirty pieces of silver.* 彼は銀貨30枚で自分を売るだろう. ☞ユダが銀貨30枚でキリストを売った故事から(《聖》*Matt.* 26. 15).

hand ... to *a person* ***on a silver platter*** →PLATTER.

silver lining 希望の光, 明るい見通し ▪ The *silver lining* is that he will help me. 明るい見通しとして, 彼が私の手助けをしてくれそうなんだ.

silver-tongued 《文》弁舌のさわやかな, 雄弁な ▪ He is a very *silver-tongued* speaker. 彼は非常に弁舌さわやかな話し手だ.

the silver screen 映画, 銀幕 ▪ All the stars of *the silver screen* gathered here. 映画界のスターたちが全員ここに集まった.

similitude /sɪmílətjù:d/ 名 ***in similitudes*** 直喩を使って ▪ He talked *in similitudes.* 彼は直喩を使って話した.

in the similitude of ...の姿で, を模して ▪ It was a devil *in the similitude of* a serpent. それはヘビの姿をした悪魔であった.

simmer /símər/ 名 ***on the simmer/at a simmer*** (湯が)ちんちんわいて《比喩的にも》 ▪ The kettle was kept *on the simmer.* やかんはちんちんわかしておかれた ▪ The feelings of the populace are *on the simmer.* 大衆の感情はわき立っていた.

simple /símpəl/ 形名 (***as***) ***simple as falling off a log*** →(as) easy as falling off a LOG.

It's as simple as that. 〚しばしば否定文で〛《口》ことはそれほど簡単だ《他の説明・理由はない》 ▪ *It's* not *as simple as that.* ことはそう簡単じゃない.

simply /símpli/ 副 ***simply and solely*** ただただ(...のみで) ▪ The loss is due *simply and solely* to the existence of a state of war. その損失はただただ戦争のある状態が存在することによるものである.

sin[1] /sɪn/ 名 ***a sin tax*** 《米口》(酒・タバコなどの)"罪悪"税 ▪ Politicians like *a sin tax* because it brings lots of revenue. 政治家は多くの歳入をもたらす"罪悪"税を好む.

(***as***) ***black as sin*** 恐ろしく黒い, 険悪な ▪ He looked *as black as sin* at them. 彼は恐ろしく険悪な顔つきをしてその連中を見た.

(***as***) ***clever as sin*** →CLEVER.

(***as***) ***ugly*** [***miserable***] ***as sin*** →UGLY.

for *one's* ***sins*** 《戯》何の因果か ▪ *For my sins,*

S

I live in a village of the plain. 僕は何の因果か平原の村に住んでいる.

like sin 《俗》非常に激しく, むきになって ▪ The man began to hit out *like sin*. 男は猛烈にこぶしを振り回した ▪ It was raining *like sin*. ひどく激しく雨が降っていた.

live in sin 同棲している ▪ Don't tell my mother I'm *living in sin*. 僕が同棲しているなんて母に言わないでくれ.

One's ***sin(s) will find*** *one* ***out.*** 《文・戯》その罪は必ず身に及ぶ(《聖》*Num.* 32. 23).

the seven deadly sins 7つの大罪《キリスト教で地獄に堕ちるとされる罪》 ▪ She is a Christian woman, with a clear view of *the seven deadly sins*. 彼女はクリスチャンで7つの大罪については明確な見方をもっている.

The sins of the fathers are visited upon the children. 《諺》父の罪は子に加えられる[前の世代の罪や誤りは次の世代を苦しめる](《聖》*Exod*. 20. 5).

the sins of the flesh 肉欲の罪 ▪ The priest resisted temptation and fought against *the sins of the flesh*. 神父は誘惑に負けることなく肉欲の罪と闘った.

sin[2] /sɪn/ 動 ***be more sinned against than sinning*** 罪を犯したというよりもむしろ他人にひどい目にあわされる (cf. Sh., *Lear* 3. 2. 60–1) ▪ You *were more sinned against than sinning*, that I admit. 君は罪を犯したというよりもむしろ他人にひどい目にあわされたのだ, それは僕も認める.

sin *one's* ***mercies*** 神の恵み[幸運]を感謝しない ▪ It would be *sinning your mercies*. それではあなたの幸運を感謝しないことになりますよ.

since /sɪns/ 副接 ***ever since*** **1** その後ずっと ▪ He has remained abroad *ever since*. 彼はその後ずっと外国にいる.

2 ...以来ずっと ▪ I have known him *ever since* he was in petticoats. 私は彼が赤んぼうの頃からずっと知っている.

it is [《主に米》***has been***] ***... since*** ...から...になる ▪ *It is* [*has been*] ten years *since* I came to this town. 私がこの町へ来てから10年になる.

S

sincerely /sɪnsíərli/ 副 ***yours sincerely*** → YOURS faithfully.

sinew /sínjuː/ 名 ***the sinews of war*** 軍資, 資金 (Cicero, *Philippica* 5. 2. 5) ▪ There was one possible method of obtaining *the sinews of war*. 資金を得ることのできる道は一つあった.

sing[1] /sɪŋ/ 名 ***on the sing*** (やかんが)しゅんしゅん鳴って ▪ Two are boiling; the others *on the sing*. 二つは沸いており, もう一つはしゅんしゅんいっている.

sing[2] /sɪŋ/ 動 ***hear a bird sing*** 内々の知らせを受ける ▪ I have *heard a bird singing* something in my ear. あることを内々に聞かされた.

sing another song/sing a different tune 調子[態度]をがらりと変える (→change one's TUNE) ▪ The Jesuits began to *sing another song*. イエズス会員たちは態度をがらりと変え始めた.

sing different 調子を変える ▪ If you come to be a bride, you'd *sing different*. あなたが花嫁になれば調子を変えることでしょう.

sing dumb →DUMB.

sing for *one's* ***supper*** →SUPPER.

sing from the same song [***hymn sheet***] 《口》(公式に)意見が一致する ▪ We finally *sang from the same hymn sheet*. 我々はついに意見の一致をみた.

sing *one's* ***heart out*** 高らかに感情をこめて歌う ▪ The birds are *singing their hearts out*. 小鳥たちは高らかに感情をこめてさえずっている.

sing one song →SING the same song.

sing small →SMALL.

sing sol-fa [***sorrow, woe***] 嘆く ▪ The very stones would *sing woe* for it. 石さえもそのために嘆くことだろう.

sing the blues 嘆いて言う, かこつ, 不平[泣き言]を言う ▪ She always *sings the blues* about her troubles. 彼女はいつも自分の苦労をかこっている.

sing the praises of →sound the PRAISEs of.

sing the same [***one***] ***song*** [***tune***] 同じ話を繰り返す; 繰りごとを言う; 同調する ▪ You will *sing the same song* as I do now. 君も今の僕と同じ話をするようになる ▪ He was always *singing one song*. 彼はいつも繰りごとを言っていた ▪ We should all *sing the same tune* and assert our rights. 我々は同調して我々の権利を主張すべきだ.

sing ... to sleep →SLEEP[1].

singe /sɪndʒ/ 動 ***singe*** *one's* ***feathers*** [***wings***] (危険に近づいて)ひどい目にあう ▪ All the young men have *singed their wings* over Miss Vane. 若者はみなベイン嬢に近づいてはひどい目にあわされた.

singe the King of Spain's beard スペインの海岸を荒らす ▪ They went down the coast to *singe the King of Spain's beard*. 彼らはスペインの海岸を荒らすために海岸を下って行った.

single /síŋɡəl/ 名形 ***in singles*** 一人ずつ, 一つずつ ▪ *In singles* or pairs men began to put in an appearance. 一人ずつまたは二人づれで人々は姿を見せ始めた.

single blessedness 《戯》(わずらわしさのない)ひとり身, 独身生活 (cf. Sh., *Mids. N. D.* 1. 1. 78) ▪ He has not yet changed his state of *single blessedness*. 彼はまだひとり身の状態を変えていない.

with a single eye 一意専心に (《聖》*Luke* 11. 34) ▪ I beg you to read the following discourse *with a single eye*. 次の話を一意専心に読んでいただきたい.

singular /síŋɡjələr/ 形名 ***all and singular*** すべての(人) ▪ *All and singular* articles shall be strictly observed. すべての条項は厳格に遵守されるべきものとする ▪ This is true of *all and singular*. これはすべての人に当てはまる.

sink[1] /sɪŋk/ 名 ***a sink of iniquity*** 悪の巣 ▪ That part of the town is *a sink of iniquity*. 町のその部分は悪の巣だ.

everything [***all***] ***but*** [***bar, except***] ***the kitchen sink*** (流しを除く)ほとんどすべてのもの; (必要・不必要は問わず)たくさんの物《誇張表現》 ▪ He went away for a holiday, taking *everything but the kitchen sink*. 彼はたくさんの物を持って休暇を過ごしに出かけた ▪ The new pocket PC has *everything but the kitchen sink*. 新しいポケット PC にはほとんどすべてのものがついている.

sink[2] /sɪŋk/ 動 ***a sinking feeling*** 《口》気のめいるような感じ ▪ I have *a sinking feeling* now. いまは気がめいってるんだ.

a sinking ship (会社が)傾きかけていること ▪ He realized he was on *a sinking ship*, seeing the company's accounts. 会社の収支を見て彼は会社が危ないとわかった.

be sinking (疲れなどで)今にも倒れそうである ▪ He *was sinking* with fatigue. 彼は疲れで今にも倒れそうだった.

I'm sunk. 万事休す ▪ Oh, *I'm sunk* then. ああ, じゃあ万事休すだ.

sink or swim **1** うまくいってもいかなくても, どうあっても; どんな事があっても ▪ *Sink or swim*, I am determined to go to London. 私はどうあってもロンドンへ行く決心だ ▪ For the rest they don't care whether they *sink or swim*. あとは彼らは浮こうが沈もうがかまわない ▪ *Sink or swim*, I won't give in. どんな事があっても, おれは降参しないぞ.

2 浮くか沈むか, のるかそるか, 一か八か ▪ It was *sink or swim* with us. 我々はのるかそるかだった. ☞魔女の容疑をかけられた女性を水に沈め, 沈まなければ無実としていた昔の習慣から.

sink so low それほどまでに落ちぶれる ▪ How could you *sink so low*? 君がそれほどまでに落ちぶれるなんて.

sink** one's **teeth into →get one's teeth into (→TOOTH).

sink to** a person's **level →LEVEL[1].

sink to rest (人が)死ぬ; (陽が)沈む ▪ The sun *sank to rest* behind the hills. 山のかなたに太陽が沈んだ.

sir /sər, səːr/ 名 ***Yes*** [***No***]***, sir*** /sə́ːr/. 《米口》そうだとも[とんでもない]《相手の性別に関係なく, Yes, No を強める》 ▪ You love her?—*Yes, sir*, I do. 彼女を愛してるの?—うん, そうだとも.

siree /sərí:|sə:rí:/ 名 ***No siree*** (***Bob***)***!*** 《米口》絶対にだめです[いやだ, 絶対に] ▪ You don't want spinach, do you?—*No siree!* ホウレンソウなんかいらないよな—いらないわ, 絶対に.

sit /sɪt/ 動 ***be sitting on a fortune*** [***gold mine***] →be sitting on a GOLD MINE.

make** a person **sit up 《口》人をびっくりさせる, こき使う ▪ The story will *make* you *sit up*. その話はあなたをびっくりさせるだろう.

sit at** one's **heart →SIT near one's heart.

sit close to** one's **heart →SIT near one's heart.

sit** oneself (down***) 《口》(ゆったりと)座る, 着席する ▪ I *sat myself* (*down*) by the fire. 炉ばたに座った.

sit it out 何もしないでいる, 傍観する ▪ So we *sat it out*, trying not to hurt his feelings. だから我々は彼の感情を傷つけまいとして何もしないでいた.

sit lightly [***heavily, heavy***] ***on*** [***upon***] ...を軽く[重く]圧する ▪ Old age *sits lightly upon* you. 年はとってもあなたはあまりこたえていない ▪ This food *sits heavy on* the stomach. この食べ物は胃にもたれる.

sit loose to ...に無関心である ▪ They *sit loose to* the responsibilities. 彼らはその責任に無関心だ.

sit loosely on **1** (服が)...にはだぶだぶである ▪ The overcoat *sat loosely on* the boy. そのオーバーは男の子にはだぶだぶだった.

2 (主語が)...をあまり拘束しない ▪ His principles *sit loosely on* him. 彼は自分の主義にあまり拘束されない.

sit near [***nigh, close to, at***] *one's* ***heart*** 深く心にかかる ▪ The misfortune *sits close to my heart*. この不幸が一番痛切に私の心にかかっている.

sit on** one's **hand 《米口》(芝居で)あまり拍手をしない ▪ They were *sitting on their hands* tonight. お客さんは今夜はあまり拍手をしなかった. ☞「手の上に座る」という意味から.

sit on the [*one's*] ***throne*** 王位についている ▪ An empress was then *sitting on the throne*. 女帝が当時帝位についていた.

sit pretty →PRETTY.

sit tight →TIGHT.

***sit to** a person* 人のモデルになる ▪ Emma *sat to* him for her portrait. エマは肖像画を描いてもらうために彼のモデルになった.

***sit up and** do* 注目して...する ▪ The music made them *sit up and* listen. その音楽に彼らは注目して耳を傾けた.

sit up and take notice →NOTICE[1].

sit up nights 《米口》一生懸命に働く, 骨身を惜しまない ▪ We will *sit up nights* to preach the Gospel. 我々は福音を説くのに骨身を惜しみません.

sit well 乗馬がうまい ▪ My father *sits well*. 父は乗馬がうまい.

sit well on ...によく似合う ▪ The suit will *sit well on* her. このスーツは彼女によく似合うだろう.

sit well [***comfortably, easily***] ***with*** 〚主に否定文で〛...の同意を得る ▪ The proposed pact didn't *sit well with* the Norwegians. 提案された条約はノルウェー人の同意を得なかった.

site /saɪt/ 名 ***a green-field site*** 未開発地 ▪ *The green-field site* was occupied by a citizens' group. 未開発地はある市民団体に占拠された.

sitting /sítɪŋ/ 名形 ***a sitting duck*** [***target***] 《口》いいカモ, 楽な目標 ▪ He seemed to be *a sitting duck* for critics. 彼は批評家にとっていいカモに思われた. ☞「飛んでいないカモ」が原義.

at a [***one***] ***sitting/at*** [***in***] ***one sitting/at a***

single sitting 一度に, 一気に ▪I read the book through *at a sitting.* 私は一気にその本を通読した ▪Turtles lay *at one sitting* a hundred eggs. ウミガメは一度に卵を100個も産む.

situation /sìtʃuéɪʃən/ 名 ***a no-win situation*** 絶望的な状況 ▪I'm now in *a no-win situation.* 私, いま, 絶望的状況なの.

save the situation 危急の場を脱する, その場を取り繕う ▪*The situation was* completely *saved.* 危急の場はすっかり脱していた ▪I did my best to *save the situation.* 私はその場を収拾するため全力を尽くした.

situations vacant [***wanted***] 求人, 求職《新聞広告の見出し》 ▪I found my new job in the "*situations vacant*" column. 「求人」欄で新しい勤め口を見つけた ▪I put an advertisement in the "*situations wanted*" column. 「求人」欄に広告を載せた.

six /sɪks/ 形名 ***at sixes and sevens*** **1** 乱雑になって ▪He has left everything *at sixes and sevens.* 彼は何もかも乱雑にしておいた.

2 不一致で ▪They are still *at sixes and sevens* about the question. 彼らはその問題ではまだ意見がまちまちだ.

knock [***hit***] ***...for six***《英口》(相手)を完全に打ち負かす; (計画など)を完全に無効にする; 開いた口がふさがらない, (不意をつかれて)ひどく驚く ▪He *knocked* his opponent *for six.* 彼は相手をこてんぱんにやっつけた ▪The wound *knocked* me *for six.* その負傷で私はすっかりまいってしまった ▪He *was knocked for six* when she left him and went out with another boy. 彼女が彼を捨てて他の男とつき合ったときは彼は開いた口がふさがらなかった. ☞クリケットで最高の6点を打つことから

six feet under →six feet under (the ground) (→FOOT[1]).

six (***of one***) ***and half-a-dozen*** (***of the other***) (いずれも)似たり寄ったりで, 五十歩百歩で ▪I never know the children. It's just *six of one and half-a-dozen of the other.* あの子供たちはどうしてもわからない. いずれも全く似たり寄ったりだ.

six of the best《英》むち[革ひも]でたたく罰 ▪The boy was given *six of the best* for being noisy. その男子生徒は騒いだためにむちでたたかれた.

six to one →ten to ONE.

sixpence /síkspəns/ 名 ***on a sixpence***《英口》(停車・方向転換が)狭い場所で(できる); 短距離間で ▪You can turn this car *on a sixpence.* この車は狭い場所でも方向転換できます.

sixty /síksti/ 名 ***a sixty percent***《口》高利貸 ▪Was he going to be *a sixty percent*? あの男は高利貸になるつもりだったのか.

like sixty《口》激しく, すさまじく ▪He kept running *like sixty* all along. 彼は途中ずっとすさまじく走りとおした.

the Swinging Sixties 進んでいる60年代, 性行動[性表現]に開かれた60年代 ▪"I grew up in *the Swinging Sixties* and I had Beatlemania," he broke in. 「おれは60年代に育ったビートルズ狂だった」と彼は口をはさんだ.

size[1] /saɪz/ 名 ***cut*** [***chop***]***...down to size***《口》(飾りなどをはぎとって)...を等身大にする, に身のほどを思い知らせる, の天狗の鼻をへし折る ▪That young man is too proud; he needs to *be cut down to size.* あの青年は生意気すぎる. 身のほどを思い知らせてやる必要がある ▪This lesson gives students permission to *cut* Shakespeare *down to size.* 本授業は学生たちにシェイクスピアを等身大にすることを認める.

for size 大きさに従って ▪These things are to be separated *for size.* これらの物は大きさに従って分けなければならない.

of a [***one***] ***size*** 同じ大きさの ▪They are much *of a size.* それはほぼ同じ大きさだ.

of all sizes 大小とりどりの ▪We have hats *of all sizes.* 大小さまざまの帽子がございます.

Pick on somebody your own size.《諺》弱い者いじめはやめろ.

this [***that***] ***is the size of***《口》これ[それ]が(事柄)の実情だ ▪*This is* about *the size of* it [this business]. この事の実情はまあそんなところだ.

try ...for size《英》=try ... on for SIZE.

try ... on [***out***] ***for size***《米》...がぴったりかどうか試してみる ▪He *tried* a dramatic role *on for size.* 彼は劇の役割がぴったりかどうか試してみた.

size[2] /saɪz/ 動 ***size*** *a person's* ***pile***《米口》人のふところ具合を見抜く ▪Doctors try to *size your pile.* 医者は君のふところ具合を見抜こうとする.

skate[1] /skeɪt/ 名 ***get*** [***put***] *one's* ***skates on***《英口》急ぐ ▪*Get your skates on* if you want to catch the 3:40. 3時40分の列車に乗りたければ急ぎなさい.

skate[2] /skeɪt/ 名 ***a cheap skate*** つまらん[けちな]やつ ▪He's *a* real *cheap skate* when it comes to checking. 勘定のこととなると彼は本当にけちだ.

skate[3] /skeɪt/ 動 ***skate over*** [***on***] ***thin ice*** →ICE.

skeleton /skélətən/ 名 ***a skeleton*** [***ghost, spectre***] ***at the feast*** [***banquet***]《英》興ざまし ▪He acted *the skeleton at the feast.* 彼は興ざましとなった.

a skeleton in the closet [《英》***cupboard, house***]/***a family skeleton*** 内輪の恥, 内輪の悩みの種 ▪Our family had *a skeleton in the cupboard.* わが家には内輪の恥があった ▪There is *a skeleton in* every *house.* どこの家にも内輪の悩みの種はあるものだ.

a skeleton key 合鍵, マスターキー ▪I forgot my office key and borrowed *a skeleton key* at the desk. 研究室の鍵を忘れて受付でマスターキーを借りた.

be reduced to a skeleton 骨と皮ばかりになっている ▪He has *been reduced to a skeleton* after a long illness. 彼は長い間の病気のあとで骨と皮である.

skeleton staff [***crew***] 最小限の職員[人員] ▪During the strike the trains ran with a *skele-*

S

ton crew. スト中列車は最小限の職員で運行した.

sketch /sketʃ/ 名 ***a thumb-nail sketch*** → THUMBNAIL.

skew /skjuː/ 名 ***on the [a] skew*** はすかいに, 曲がって ▪ The birds seemed to fly *on the skew.* 鳥ははすかいに飛んで行くように見えた.

skid /skɪd/ 名 ***be on skid row*** 《米口》ひどく落ちぶれている, 路頭に迷う ▪ He didn't want to throw himself on people's mercy even if he *was on skid row.* 彼はたとえ落ちぶれていようとも人の情けにすがりたくはなかった.

hit the skids 《口》 **1** 落ち目になる ▪ Eventually they *hit the skids.* とうとう彼らは落ち目になった. **2** 素早く立ち去る ▪ He *hit the skids* at the party. そのパーティーでは彼は早くに席を立った.

on the skids 《米俗》敗北[没落]の途上に ▪ Bix was *on the skids.* ビックスは没落の途上にあった.

put the skids under [to] *a person* **1**《口》人を失敗させる, どじを踏ませる ▪ You sure *put the skids under* me. 君には確かにどじを踏まされたよ. **2**《口》人をせき立てる ▪ *Put the skids under* him, or we'll be late. 彼をせき立てないと遅れてしまう.

skim /skɪm/ 動 ***skim the cream off*** …の一番いいところを取ってしまう ▪ The head porter *skimmed the cream off* the tips. 主任の赤帽はチップの一番いいところを取ってしまった.

skim the surface of …を皮相的に取り扱う ▪ This book only *skims the surface of* the problems. 本書はその問題を皮相的に取り扱っているだけだ.

skin[1] /skɪn/ 名 ***(be) all [only] skin and bone(s)*** 《口》(人が)骨と皮ばかりにやせて(いる) ▪ There was an old woman *all skin and bone.* 骨と皮ばかりにやせたおばあさんがいた.

be in *a person's* ***skin*** 人の身[立場]になる ▪ I would not *be in their skins.* 私はあの人たちの立場になりたくない.

by [with] the skin of *one's* ***teeth*** 《口》かろうじて, 命からがら (《聖》*Job* 19. 20) ▪ I got in *by the skin of my teeth.* 私はかろうじて乗りこんだ ▪ He escaped [came off] *with the skin of his teeth.* 彼は命からがら逃れた.

change *one's* ***skin*** うって変わった性格になる (《聖》*Jer.* 13. 23) ▪ He cannot *change his skin.* 彼はうって変わった性格になることはできない.

fit like a second skin ぴったり体に合う ▪ She wore a T-shirt which *fitted* her *like a second skin.* 彼女は体にぴったりのTシャツ姿だった.

fly [leap, jump] out of *one's* ***skin*** **1** (喜び・驚きなどで)飛び上がる ▪ I *jumped out of my skin* for terror [with joy]. 私は怖さ[喜び]のあまり飛び上がらんばかりだった. **2** 元気でぴんぴんする ▪ The horse was fit and *jumped out of his skin.* 馬は元気でぴんぴんしていた.

get into *a person's* ***skin*** 人の立ち場に立つ ▪ A writer has to *get into the skin of* his characters. 作家は作中人物の立ち場に立ってみなければならない.

get under *a person's* ***skin*** 《口》人の心を強く捕える; 人をひどく怒らせる; 人の本心を知る ▪ Several remarks he made *got under my skin.* 彼が言った二言三言が私の勘にさわった ▪ I *got under my colleagues' skin* and I was shocked. 同僚の本心を知って私はショックを受けた.

get underneath the skin of …の心を捕える ▪ He *got underneath the skin of* his audience. 彼は聴衆の心を捕えた.

give me some skin/slip me five 《俗》(手のひらをたたくようにして)握手する ▪ "*Give me some skin!*" he said to a fresh hand. 「握手してくれ」と彼は一人の新米に言った.

have a skin like a rhinoceros → have a hide like a RHINOCEROS.

have a thick [thin] skin 鈍感[敏感]である, 神経が太い[細い] ▪ It is certain Voltaire was a fool not to *have a thicker skin.* もっと神経が太くなかったとはボルテールはばかだったにちがいない.

have [put] skin in the game 《米》仕事の成否に積極的に関わる ▪ I want them to *have* a little *skin in the game.* 私は彼らに少しは積極的に仕事に関わってもらいたいと思っている.

hitting skins 《俗》性交, セックス ▪ Jim is good at nothing except for *hitting skins.* ジムはセックス以外に得意なことはない.

in a whole skin = with a whole SKIN.

in *one's* ***skin*** 裸で ▪ He stood *in his skin.* 彼は裸で立っていた.

jump [leap] out of *one's* ***skin*** → fly out of one's SKIN.

keep a whole skin → sleep in a whole SKIN.

make *a person's* ***skin crawl*** 人をぞっとさせる ▪ The sight *made her skin crawl.* その光景は彼女をぞっとさせた.

next (to) *one's* ***skin*** 肌にじかに ▪ I always wear woolens *next my skin.* 私はいつもウール製品を肌にじかに着る.

no skin off *one's* ***back [elbow, knuckles, nose]*** 《口》自分の知ったことではない ▪ That was *no skin off my elbow.* そんなことは私の知ったことじゃなかった.

no skin off *one's* ***(back) teeth*** = no SKIN off one's back.

risk *one's* ***skin*** (危険なことに)命を賭ける ▪ The firefighters have *risked their skin* to save small children and older adults. 消防隊員は小さな子供や老人を救うために命を賭けた.

save *one's* ***(own) skin*** (損失・負傷から)無事に逃れる ▪ The poltroon was considering how to *save his skin.* その卑怯者はどうやって無事に逃れようかと考えていた.

skin and bone(s) 〚しばしば nothing but を伴って〛 **1** 骨と皮ばかり ▪ He was reduced to all *skin and bone.* 彼は全く骨と皮ばかりになっていた ▪ She came home from her trip *nothing but skin and bones.* 彼女が旅から戻ったときは全くの骨と皮ばかりに

S

なっていた.

2 骨と皮ばかりの人 ▪"Heh, heh, heh," cried an old *skin and bones*.「へ, へ, へ」と骨と皮ばかりの老人が叫んだ. ☞誇張表現.

sleep in* [*keep*] *a whole skin 負傷を免れる, 傷つかずにいる ▪He took to his heels to *keep a whole skin*. 彼は負傷を免れるためにすたこらと逃げた.

to the skin **1** 肌まで ▪They were soaked [drenched] *to the skin*. 彼らはずぶ濡れになっていた.

2 すっかり, 丸裸になるまで ▪We were robbed *to the skin*. 我々は身ぐるみはがされた.

under the skin **1** こっそりと, 腹の中で ▪He laughed *under the skin*. 彼は腹の中でほくそえんだ.

2 ひと皮むけば, 内実は ▪We are brothers *under the skin*. 我々はひと皮むけばみんな兄弟だ.

with a whole skin けがなしで, 無事で, 傷一つ負わずに ▪He came off *with a whole skin*. 彼はけがなしですんだ ▪He got off *with a whole skin*. 彼は傷一つ負わずに逃れた ▪I want to die *in a whole skin*. 私は傷一つ負わずに死にたい.

with the skin of *one's* ***teeth*** →by the SKIN of one's teeth.

skin[2] /skɪn/ 動 ***have* (*got*)** *a person* ***skinned* (*a mile*)**《米俗》人を完全に打ち負かす ▪In my opinion you *have* him *skinned a mile*. 私に言わせれば君はあの男を完全に負かしている.

keep *one's* ***eyes* [*eyeteeth*] *skinned***《俗》油断なく見張る, 油断なく気を配る ▪*Keep your eyes skinned* for any chance of escape. 油断なく逃亡の機会を待ちかまえなさい ▪He *kept his eyeteeth skinned* lest he should be robbed of his purse. 彼は財布を取られないように油断なく気を配った.

***skin a flint* [*a cat, a flea for his hide and tallow*]** ひどくけちけちする,「つめに火をともす」 ▪She would *skin a flint* if she could. 彼女はできればつめに火をともすような女だ ▪He would *skin a flea for his hide and tallow*. あの男はつめに火をともすようなけちだ.

skin *a person* ***alive***《口》散々にやっつける; しかりとばす; 生皮をはぐ ▪Our team got *skinned alive*. わがチームは散々にやっつけられた ▪Mother will *skin* you *alive* when she sees your torn jacket. おまえの破れた上着を見たら母さんにとっちめられるぞ.

S

skin mules《米俗》ラバの群れを追う ▪John is *skinning mules* now. ジョンは今ラバの群れを追っている.

skin the cat《米》平行棒にぶらさがり両腕の間に足を通してくぐり抜ける; 狭い所を通り抜ける ▪He "*skinned the cat*" among the rafters. 彼はたる木の間にぶらさがり両腕の間に足を通してくぐり抜けてみせた.

skinny /skíni/ 名 ***get* [*give*] *the skinny on*** ...のとっておきの情報を手に入れる[与える] ▪She looked at the sales handbill to *get the skinny on* beef. 彼女は牛肉に関するとっておきの情報を得るために販売チラシをじっと見つめた.

skip /skɪp/ 動 ***skip*** *one's* ***bail*** →jump one's BAIL.

Skip it. もういいよ; どうだっていいよ ▪Shall I go to get more butter?—No, *skip it*. もっとバターを取って来ましょうか—いや, もういい.

skipper /skípər/ 名 ***skipper's daughters*** 高い白波 ▪Out in the open there were *skipper's daughters*. 外の広い海では高い白波が荒れていた.

skirt /skəːrt/ 名 ***clear*** *a person's* ***skirts*** 人の汚名をすすぐ ▪You cannot *clear the skirts of* your party for the treachery. あなたは党の裏切り行為の汚名をすすぐことはできない.

clear *one's* ***skirts***《米口》非難を免れる, 手を切る ▪Whether this man is to be convicted or not, I *clear my skirts*. この男が有罪になろうとなるまいと, 私は手を切る ▪He calculated to *clear his* own *skirts* anyway. 彼自身は何とかして非難を免れるつもりだった.

like a bit of skirt《俗》女性とつき合うのが好きである ▪Sam was always merry and *liked a bit of skirt*. サムはいつも陽気で女性とつき合うのが好きだった.

on the skirts of ...のはずれに ▪There is an unfenced pasture *on the skirts of* the village. 村のはずれに柵のない牧草地がある.

skittle /skítəl/ 名 **(*all*) *beer and skittles*** →BEER[1].

skull /skʌl/ 名 ***get it through*** *one's* **(*thick*) *skull how*** =get it through one's (thick) HEAD how.

have a thick skull 愚鈍である ▪He *has a thick skull*, he won't change his mind. 彼はばかだから考えを変えないだろう.

sky /skaɪ/ 名 ***A red sky at night is the shepherd's delight* [*Red sky at night, shepherd's delight*].**《諺》夕焼けは羊飼いの喜び《翌日は晴天》.

drop from the skies 空から落ちて来る, 突然現れる ▪A lame dog appeared on the scene, as if it had *dropped from the skies*. 足の具合の悪い犬がまるで空から落ちて来たかのようにその場に現れた.

If* [*When*] *the sky fall*(*s*) *we shall catch larks.《諺》空が落ちたらヒバリが取れる《取り越し苦労はしないでよい》.

in the skies 有頂天になって ▪He was *in the skies* at once. 彼はすぐ有頂天になった.

out of a clear* [*blue*] *sky 青天のへきれき, 不意に (→out of the BLUE) ▪He called upon me suddenly *out of a clear sky*. 彼は不意に私を訪ねてきた.

***praise* [*exalt, extol, laud*]*... to the skies* [*sky*]** 熱狂的にほめる, ほめちぎる ▪Italians *extol* their own things *to the sky*. イタリア人は自国の物をほめちぎる ▪He *was praised to the skies*. 彼はほめちぎられた.

Reach for the sky. 両手を上げろ《ピストルを突きつけてギャングのする命令》; 目標を高く持て.

The sky is the limit. 制限なしだ ▪Order anything you want. *The sky is the limit.* 何でもほしい物を注文しなさい. 制限なしだ.

under the* (*open*) *sky 野天で, 戸外で ▪ *Under the* wide and starry *sky*, dig the grave and let me lie. 広い星空のもとに墓を掘って私を埋めてほしい.

sky-high /skàɪháɪ/ 形副 ***blow ... sky-high*** 《俗》 **1** …を論破する ▪ We should have *been blown sky-high*. 我々は論破されていただろう.
2 …を爆発で破壊する, 吹っ飛ばす ▪ Get away fast or you'll *be blown sky-high*. 早く逃げろ, さもないと吹っ飛ばされるぞ.

go sky-high (値段が)非常に高くなる ▪ Prices *went sky-high* when there was inflation. インフレで物価が高騰した.

slack[1] /slæk/ 形名 ***cut*** *a person* ***some slack*** 《米口》人に息抜きを与える, 人をそっとしておく ▪ *Cut* me *some slack*, and you'll be able to relax. 私に息抜きをさせてくれたら君もくつろげるよ.

get slack at (仕事)を怠ける ▪ Don't *get slack at* your work. 仕事を怠けるな.

have a good slack 《口》ゆっくりひと休みする ▪ I'm going to *have a good slack* this afternoon. きょうは午後からゆっくりひと休みするつもりだ.

keep a slack hand [***rein***] ***on*** …の手綱をゆるめておく; を緩慢に治める ▪ He *keeps a slack rein on* his daughters. 彼は娘を甘やかしている.

pull up *one's* ***slacks*** 《口》元気を出す ▪ Now boys, *pull up your slacks*. さあみんな元気を出すんだ.

take up [***in***] ***the slack/pull in the slack/pick up the slack*** 沈滞している活動を活発にする 《pick, take は《米口》》 ▪ We should *take up the slack* in the economy. 沈滞している経済を活発化しないといけない. ☞たるんでいる綱をぴんと張ることから.

slack[2] /slæk/ 動 ***slack*** *one's* ***hand***(***s***) (努力の)手をゆるめる ▪ I don't *slack my hand*; I can preach and write still. 私は手をゆるめはしない. 私はまだ説教したりものを書いたりできる.

slagheap /slǽghìːp/ 名 ***on the slagheap*** ぼた山に捨てられて, もう使いものにならなくて ▪ On retiring he felt he was now put *on the slagheap*. 退職したとき彼は自分がもう使いものにならなくなった気がした.

slam[1] /slæm/ 名 ***a slam dunk*** 《主に米》本命, 勝ちが確実な人; 《バスケ》ダンクショット ▪ He was *a slam dunk* in the race. 彼はレースでの本命だった.

slam[2] /slæm/ 動 ***slam the door in*** *a person's* ***face*** 人に門前払いをくわせる; (話し合いを求める)人をはねつける ▪ They all *slammed the door in his face*. 彼らはみな彼に門前払いをくわせた.

slam the door on ＝SHUT the door on.

slang /slæŋ/ 動 ***a slanging match*** 《英口》ののしり合い ▪ The peaceful discussion eneded in a real *slanging match*. その平和的な話し合いは本物の, ののしり合いになって終わった.

slant /slænt|slɑːnt/ 名 ***on the*** [***a***] ***slant*** 傾斜して ▪ The road was quite *on the slant*. 道は全く傾斜していた.

slap[1] /slæp/ 名 (***a bit of***) ***slap and tickle*** 《主に英口・戯》(男女の)いちゃつき ▪ They were having *a bit of slap and tickle* on the bed. 彼らはベッドの上でいちゃついていた.

a slap in the face [***teeth,*** 《口》 ***kisser***] 顔への平手打ち; 失望・落胆させるもの ▪ I gave him *a slap in the face*. 私は彼の顔をぴしゃりと平手で打った ▪ It was *a slap in the face* to Cinderella to be told she was not going to the ball. 舞踏会へ行ってはいけないと言われたのでシンデレラはひどく失望した.

a slap on the back ほめ言葉 ▪ He got *a slap on the back* for working hard. 彼はよく勉強したのでほめられた.

a slap on the wrist 軽い叱責 ▪ Punishment will be just *a slap on the wrist*. 罰は軽い叱責ですむだろう.

at a slap たちまち (＝all at ONCE) ▪ He lost ten thousand pounds *at a slap*. 彼はたちまち１万ポンド失った.

slap[2] /slæp/ 動 ***slap*** *a person* ***in the face*** 人を侮辱する ▪ He *was slapped in the face* by a flat denial. 彼はすげなく拒絶されて侮辱された.

slap *a person* ***on the back*** →pat a person on the BACK.

slap *a person* ***on the wrist/slap*** *a person's* ***wrist*** 人を軽く叱責する ▪ He *was slapped on the wrist* for coming late. 彼は遅刻したので軽く叱責された.

slate[1] /sleɪt/ 名 ***a clean slate*** 立派な経歴 ▪ All the tenants have *a clean slate*. すべての借家人は立派な経歴を持っている.

break the slate 《米》(政党の)指名候補の支持を拒む ▪ Sometimes Lincoln *broke the slate* of those who were making a list of appointments. ときどきリンカンは任命名簿に載っている人々の支持を拒むことがあった.

clean the slate/wipe the slate clean 債務を果たす; 行きがかりを捨てる; 白紙に戻す ▪ Very well, we'll *clean the slate*, and forget all the past. よろしい, 行きがかりは捨てて過去はすっかり忘れよう ▪ The lunar New Year is the time for *wiping the slate clean*. 旧暦の新年は債務を果たす時期だ ▪ We wanted to *wipe the slate clean* of the long-term contract. 我々はその長期契約を白紙に戻したかった.

have a slate loose [***off***] 《主に英》頭が変になっている ▪ You must *have a slate loose* this morning. 君はけさ頭がどうかしてるにちがいない.

on the slate (パブなどで)掛けで ▪ Put it *on the slate*. それをつけといてくれ. ☞昔, 掛けはスレートに記入されていたことから.

start with a clean slate [***sheet*** (***of paper***)] 白紙に返って出直す ▪ They *started* afresh *with a clean slate*. 彼らは白紙に返って出直した.

wipe ... off the slate (問題にならぬものとして)…をすっかり忘れてしまう ▪ The rest *were wiped off the slate* days ago. 残りの者は何日も前にすっかり忘れられてしまった.

wipe the slate clean →clean the SLATE.

with a clean slate 白紙に返って ▪ An ex-convict should start a new job *with a clean slate.* 前科者も白紙に返って新しい職業につくべきだ.

slate² /sleɪt/ 動 ***be slated for*** …に予定されている ▪ My friend *is slated for* a diplomatic post abroad. 友人は外国での外交のポストに予定されている.

slaughter /slɔ́ːtər/ 名 ***like*** [***as***] ***sheep*** [***lambs***] ***to the slaughter*** 屠所に引かれる羊のように (《聖》*Acts* 8. 32) ▪ My generation flocked to the war *like sheep to the slaughter.* 私の世代は屠所に引かれる羊のようにぞろぞろ戦争に出かけて行った.

slave /sleɪv/ 名 ***a slave driver*** 部下をこき使う上司 ▪ He was such *a slave driver* that he was disliked by all the staff. 彼は部下をこき使う上司だったのでスタッフ全員からきらわれていた.

be a slave to/be the slave of …の奴隷となる ▪ He *was a slave to* drink. 彼は飲酒の奴隷となっていた.

make a slave of …をこき使う ▪ You mustn't *make a slave of* your servants. 君は使用人をこき使ってはいけない.

work like a slave 奴隷のように[あくせく]働く ▪ He *worked like a slave* from the time he was fifteen. 彼は15歳の時からあくせく働いた.

sledding /slédɪŋ/ 名 ***smooth*** [***hard, rough, tough***] ***sledding*** 《米》とんとん拍子の[思わしくない]状況 ▪ We do not always have *smooth sledding.* いつもとんとん拍子にいくとはかぎらない.

sledgehammer /slédʒhæ̀mər/ 名 ***take a sledgehammer to crack*** [***break***] ***a walnut*** [***nut***]/***crack*** [***break***] ***a walnut*** [***nut***] ***with a sledgehammer*** 《口》鶏を割(さ)くに牛刀をもってする ▪ Fancy three men spending all day mending my telly! It's like *taking a sledgehammer to crack a nut.* 3人が1日かけて僕のテレビを修理するなんて, 正に鶏を割くに牛刀をもってするようだ.

thump like a sledgehammer (心臓が)激しく打つ, 非常に興奮する ▪ When she saw an object like a UFO, her heart began to *thump like a sledgehammer.* UFOのような物体を見たとき, 彼女の心臓は激しく鼓動し始めた.

S

sleep¹ /sliːp/ 名 ***can*** [***could***] ***do ... in*** *one's* ***sleep/be able to do ... in*** *one's* ***sleep*** 《口》…は眠っていてもできる, するのはいともたやすい ▪ I've done it so many times I *could do* it *in my sleep.* 何度もやっているので, そんなのいとも簡単にやれるさ.

cry *oneself* ***to sleep*** 泣き寝入りする, 泣きながら寝入る ▪ Leave him alone, and he will *cry himself to sleep.* 放っておけば彼は泣き寝入りするだろう ▪ The baby *cried itself to sleep.* 赤んぼうは泣きながら寝入った.

drop off to sleep 覚えず寝こむ ▪ He had *dropped off to sleep* over a book. 彼は本を読んでいて覚えず寝こんでいた.

fall into a sleep 寝入る ▪ He *fell into a* deep *sleep.* 彼は深く寝入った.

fall on sleep 《古》眠る; 死ぬ ▪ Soon she *fell on sleep.* やがて彼女は眠った ▪ David *fell on sleep* and laid unto his fathers. ダビデは眠りにつき先祖たちの中に加えられた.

get a sleep 眠る ▪ I'm going to *get a sleep* this afternoon. きょうの午後眠ってみようと思う.

get off to sleep **1** 寝つく, 寝入る ▪ I can *get off to sleep* by trying to count up to 100. 私は100まで数えようとすれば寝入ることができる.

2 (子供を)寝つかせる ▪ She *got* the baby *off to sleep* at last. 彼女はやっと赤んぼうを寝つかせた.

get to sleep (何とかして)寝つく ▪ I can't *get to sleep* nowadays. 近ごろ寝つけない.

go to sleep **1** 寝入る ▪ He *went* happily *to sleep.* 彼は幸福に寝入った.

2 (手・足などが)しびれが切れる ▪ My foot has *gone to sleep.* 足がしびれた.

in sleep 眠って ▪ I found him *in sleep.* 行ってみたら彼は眠っていた.

in *one's* ***sleep*** 眠りながら ▪ He talks *in his sleep.* 彼は寝ごとを言う ▪ She was murdered *in her sleep.* 彼女は睡眠中に殺された.

lull ... to sleep …をあやして寝かせる; をもみ消す ▪ The mother *lulled* her baby *to sleep.* 母親は赤んぼうをあやして寝かせた ▪ We must *lull* his suspicion *to sleep.* 我々は彼の疑いをもみ消さねばならない.

not get a wink of sleep 一睡もしない (→not a WINK) ▪ I did*n't get a wink of sleep* last night. 昨晩は一睡もしなかった.

not lose any sleep about [***over***] 《口》…についてあまり心配しない ▪ I have*n't lost any sleep about* the matter. その件については心配しなかった.

put [***lay***] ***... to sleep*** …を寝かしつける《比喩的にも》; を退屈させる[あきあきさせる] ▪ She *put* her baby *to sleep.* 彼女は赤んぼうを寝かしつけた ▪ He *laid* his doubts *to sleep.* 彼は疑惑の念を捨てた ▪ His dull lecture *put* me *to sleep.* 彼の退屈な講話にはうんざりした.

put [***send***] *an animal* ***to sleep*** **1** 動物に麻酔をかける ▪ The dog *was put to sleep* for the operation. その犬は手術のために麻酔をかけられた.

2 (慈悲のために)動物を殺す ▪ The old dog *is* better *put to sleep.* あの老犬は眠らせるほうがよい.

read *oneself* ***to sleep*** 読みながら寝入る ▪ I have long had the custom of *reading myself to sleep.* 長いこと本を読みながら寝入る習慣がついている.

rock ... to sleep …をゆすって眠らせる ▪ She took the baby in her arms and *rocked* it *to sleep.* 彼女は赤んぼうを抱き上げ, ゆすって眠らせた.

sing ... to sleep 歌を歌って…を寝かしつける ▪ She *sang* the baby *to sleep.* 彼女は歌を歌って赤んぼうを寝かしつけた.

sob *oneself* ***to sleep*** すすり泣き[泣きじゃくり]ながら寝る ▪ The child *sobbed herself to sleep* on her father's breast. 子供は父親の胸にだかれて泣きじゃくり

ながら寝てしまった.

weep** oneself **to sleep 泣き寝入りする ▪ Phillipa *wept herself to sleep* in her sister's arms. フィリッパは姉に抱かれて泣き寝入りした.

sleep[2] /sliːp/ 動 ***sleep like a log*** [***top***] ぐっすり眠る ▪ I shall *sleep like a top*. 私はぐっすり眠るだろう.

sleep rough →ROUGH[1].

sleep** oneself **sober 眠って酔いをさます ▪ He tried to *sleep himself sober*. 彼は眠って酔いをさまそうとした.

sleep the clock round →around the CLOCK.

sleep the sleep of the just 《文》心にわだかまりのない者の安らかな眠りを眠る ▪ The old priest was *sleeping the sleep of the just*. 老司祭は心にわだかまりのない者らしく安らかに眠っていた.

Sleep tight. 《口》ぐっすりとおやすみ.

sleeve /sliːv/ 名 ***carry ... on** one's **sleeve*** …を一般に見せびらかす ▪ The poet should not *carry* his vanity *on his sleeve*. 詩人は虚栄心を一般に見せつけてはいけない.

Every man has a fool in his sleeve. →FOOL[1].

hang on** a person's **sleeve 《口》人の言うなりになっている ▪ They are always *hanging on his sleeve*. 彼らはいつも彼の言うなりになっている.

have a card [***an ace, a trick***] ***in*** [***up***] *one's* ***sleeve*** 《口》秘策[別の秘策]がある, 用意の奥の手[もう一つの奥の手]がある ▪ We're not sure if management *has another card up its sleeve*. 経営者側が別の決め手を握っているかどうかはっきりしない ▪ We can count on Bill to *have an ace up his sleeve*. ビルには奥の手があると当てにしてよい ▪ I took the precaution of *having a card up my sleeve*. 私は用心のため奥の手を用意しておいた ▪ If he *has* yet *another card up his sleeve*, he has kept it secret from me. 彼にもう一つの奥の手があるとしても, 彼はそれをずっと私に隠してきた. ☞トランプ詐欺から.

in [***up***] *one's* ***sleeve*** ひそかに, 腹の中で (↔in a person's FACE 2) ▪ He enjoyed his joke *in his sleeve*. 彼はひそかに自分の冗談を楽しんだ ▪ They laughed *up their sleeves* over his failure. 彼らは彼が失敗したのを腹の中で笑った《手で笑いを隠すしぐさから》.

pin** one's **faith [***belief***] ***on*** [***upon, to***] *a person's* ***sleeve*** 人を一から十まで信用する ▪ We may not *pin our belief upon their sleeves*. 我々は彼らを一から十まで信用することはできない.

Stretch your arm no further than your sleeve will reach. 《諺》袖の長さ以上に手を伸ばすな,「カニは甲羅に似せて穴を掘る」

turn [***roll***] ***up** one's **sleeves*** (仕事・けんかの用意に)腕をまくる ▪ She *turned up her sleeves* and set to work. 彼女は腕をまくり上げて働きだした ▪ We *rolled our sleeves up* and made a bit more effort. 我々は厳しい仕事に備えてさらに少し努力した.

wear [***pin***] *one's* ***heart on** one's **sleeve*** →HEART.

sleight /slaɪt/ 名 ***sleight of hand*** 手先の早業, 手品; 巧妙なごまかし ▪ By *sleight of hand* he made an entire pack of cards disappear. 手先の早業で彼は一組のトランプ札を全部隠した ▪ Some mathematical *sleight of hand* was required to make the accounts balance. 帳尻を合わせるためにはちょっとした数学的なごまかしが必要だった.

slice[1] /slaɪs/ 名 ***a slice of life*** 人生の一断面(を描いた作品) ▪ The documentary is *a* remarkable *slice of life*. そのドキュメンタリーは人生の一断面を描いたすばらしいものだ.

A slice off a cut cake is never missed. 《諺》切りかけのケーキからひと切れ取っても気づかれない《特に人妻との性交渉について言う》.

one's [***a***] ***slice of the cake*** [***pie***] → one's SHARE of the pie.

slice[2] /slaɪs/ 動 ***any way you slice it*** 《米口》どのように考えても ▪ He shouldn't have divorced, *any way you slice it*. どのように考えても, 彼は離婚すべきじゃなかったんだ.

slick /slɪk/ 形副 (***as***) ***slick as*** (***bear's***) ***grease***/(***as***) ***slick as molasses*** [***a whistle***] 《米俗》非常になめらかな[に] ▪ I passed *slick as grease* down the current of time. 私は時の流れをとてもなめらかに下っていった ▪ He's lost it, *slick as a whistle*. 彼はするするっとそれを失った.

slick and clean 《米口》完全に ▪ That fire wiped me out *slick and clean*. その火事で私はすっかりやっつけられた.

slide[1] /slaɪd/ 名 ***on the slide*** (精神的・肉体的に)だんだん具合が悪くなって ▪ He has been *on the slide* since his wife died. 彼は妻を亡くして以来次第に具合が悪くなっている.

slide[2] /slaɪd/ 動 ***let ... slide***/ ***allow ... to slide*** …をうっちゃって[放って]おく ▪ *Let* things *slide*. 事を成り行きに任せるがいい ▪ The question *was allowed to slide*. その問題は放っておかれた.

slight /slaɪt/ 形名 ***make slight of*** …を軽視する, 見くびる ▪ He first *made slight of* his illness. 彼は初めは自分の病気を軽く見ていた.

not ... in the slightest ちっとも…しない ▪ You did*n't* annoy me *in the slightest*. あなたはちっとも迷惑ではありませんでした.

not the slightest ほんのわずかの…もない《強意表現》 ▪ He *never* had *the slightest* liking for her. 彼はちっとも彼女を好いていなかった.

put [***pass***] ***a slight on*** …を軽蔑する ▪ He *passed an* unmeaning *slight on* them. 彼はその人たちを無意味に軽蔑した.

slime /slaɪm/ 名 ***a slime ball*** 《口》(口先だけの)いやなやつ ▪ He's such *a slime ball*. 彼って, すごくいやなやつだね.

sling[1] /slɪŋ/ 名 ***the slings and arrows*** (***of outrageous fortune***) (残酷な運命の)石投げや矢《人生の危害・損失・失望》(cf. Sh., *Haml.* 3. 1. 58) ▪ Leave him alone to face *the slings and ar-*

rows; he's so tough. 彼ならほっといても人生の苦難に立ち向かっていくさ，とてもタフなんだから. ☞通例戯言的に用いる.

sling[2] /slɪŋ/ 動 ***sling a nasty foot*** [***ankle***] 《米俗》ダンスがうまい ▪ She *slings the nastiest ankle*. 彼女が一番ダンスがうまい.

sling** one's **Daniel 《俗》立ち去る (→sling one's HOOK) ▪ *Sling your Daniel* this instant! 今すぐ立ち去ってしまえ. ☞句源不明.

sling hash 《米俗》(レストランで)給仕をする ▪ She *slings hash* on North Clark Street. 彼女はノース・クラーク街で給仕をしている.

sling ink 《俗》記事を書きなぐる ▪ You ask me to *sling ink* for your paper. あなたは私にご自分の新聞に記事を書きなぐれとおっしゃいます.

slip[1] /slɪp/ 名 ***a*** (***mere***) ***slip of a*** ほっそりした，ひょろひょろした ▪ He has but *a slip of a* daughter. 彼にはひょろひょろの娘が一人いるきりだ.

a slip of the pen [***tongue, lip***] 書き損ない[失言] ▪ It was originally *a* transcriber's *slip of the pen*. それは元は写字生の書き損ないだった ▪ It was *a slip of the tongue*. それは失言でした.

give** a person **the slip 《口》人をまく，すっぽかす ▪ He rode the whole way, having *given* them *the slip*. 彼はその連中をまいて途中ずっと馬をとばしたのだった ▪ He *gave* his creditors *the slip*. 彼は借金取りをすっぽかした.

make a slip まちがいをする ▪ He *made* just *one slip* in English. 彼は英語でたった1回まちがいをした.

One's ***slip is showing.*** スリップが見えている; ぼろが出る.

There's many a slip (***between*** [***twixt***] ***the cup and the lip***)***.*** 《諺》茶わんを口に持って行く間にもいくらもしくじりはある,「100里を行く者は99里を半ばとせよ」.

slip[2] /slɪp/ 動 ***be slipping*** 《口》(行い・やり方が)ぬけている，よくない ▪ *You're slipping*: this report is full of typing errors. 君って，ぬけてるね. このレポート，タイプミスだらけだよ.

let slip **1** (獲物を追わせるために犬の)綱を解いてやる ▪ He *let slip* the bloodhounds. 彼は猟犬の綱を解いてやった.
2 うっかり口から出す ▪ I will not *let* his name *slip* from my lips. 彼の名をうっかり口からすべらすまい.
3 失う，逸する ▪ He has *let slip* chance after chance. 彼は次から次とチャンスを逸した.

let slip the dogs of war →let loose the DOGs of war.

slip between** one's **fingers [***the net***] →SLIP through one's fingers.

slip** one's **breath [***wind***] 《口》息を引き取る，死ぬ ▪ He won't *slip his wind* this time. 彼はこのたびは死なないでしょう.

slip** one's **cable(***s***) →cut one's CABLE(s).

slip from** one's **hand [***grasp***] →SLIP out of one's hand.

***slip it over** a person* 《俗》人をだます，ごまかす ▪ I could not *slip it over* the German. そのドイツ人をごまかすことができなかった.

slip** a person's **mind [***memory***] →MIND[1]; slip (out of) a person's MEMORY.

slip off the hooks →drop off the HOOKs.

slip on a banana skin →BANANA.

slip one over 《米口》…をぺてんにかける ▪ He tried to *slip one over* the policeman. 彼はその警官をぺてんにかけようとした.

slip out of [***from***] *one's* ***hand*** [***grasp***] (人・富・権力が)手からすべり落ちる，手から失われる ▪ She *slipped out of his hand*. 彼女は彼の手から逃れてしまった ▪ Wealth *slips from the possessor's hand*. 富は所有者の手から放れる.

slip through [***between***] *one's* ***fingers*** [***the cracks, the net***] →FINGER[1]; fall through the CRACKs; slip through the NET.

slip [***fall***] ***through the net*** →NET.

slipper /slípər/ 名 ***give ... the slipper*** …を(スリッパで)打つ ▪ He *gave* me *the slipper* for climbing on the school roof. 校舎の屋根に登ったので彼にぶたれた.

hunt the slipper スリッパ捜し《遊戯》 ▪ Last of all, they sat down to *hunt the slipper*. 最後に，彼らは座ってスリッパ捜しをやった.

take** one's **slipper to (人)を打つ ▪ I should dearly like to *take my slipper to* him. あの男は本当になぐってやりたいものだ.

slippery /slípəri/ 形 ***a*** [***the***] ***slippery slope*** 危険な坂道 ▪ He may go down *the slippery slope* into debt. 彼は危険な坂道を下って借金をするかもしれない.

(***as***) ***slippery as an eel*** ぬるぬるとすべっこい; つかみどころのない ▪ This piece of alpaca is *as slippery as an eel*. このアルパカの毛皮の切れ端はつるつるとすべっこい ▪ Don't do business with him. He's *as slippery as an eel*. 彼と取引をしてはいけない. とらえどころのないやつだから.

slippy /slípi/ 形 ***be*** [***look***] ***slippy*** 《主に英俗》すばしこくやる ▪ Come, *be slippy*. さあすばしこくやるんだ ▪ You'll have to *look slippy*. すばしこくやらねばだめだ.

slog /slɑg|slɔg/ 動 ***slog*** [***slave, sweat, work***] *one's* ***guts out*** →sweat one's GUTs out.

slog it out =SLUG it out.

slot /slɑt|slɔt/ 動 ***slot into place*** →fall into PLACE.

slouch /slaʊtʃ/ 名 ***no slouch at*** 《口》…がなかなかうまい ▪ He is *no slouch at* shooting. 彼は射撃がなかなかうまい.

no slouch of 《俗》なかなかたいした ▪ It seemed to be *no slouch of* a city. それはなかなかたいした都会のように見えた.

slough /slu:|slaʊ/ 名 ***a Slough of Despond*** 失望の泥沼; 〚小文字で〛絶望のふち (Bunyan, *The Pilgrim's Progress* 1) ▪ He would raise himself out of such *a slough of despond*. 彼はそのような絶望のふちから立ち上がるだろう.

slow /slou/ 形副 ***be in the slow lane*** 遅れている ▪The economic recovery *is in the slow lane* in this country. この国の経済回復は遅れている.

do a slow down 《米口》少しずつ怒りがこみ上げる ▪As he heard the news he started *doing a slow down*. 彼はその知らせを聞いてだんだん怒りがこみ上げ始めた.

go slow ゆっくり行く[やる]; 用心する ▪Tell the driver to *go slow*er. 運転手にもっとゆっくり行くように言ってくれ ▪We had better *go slow* in this transaction. この取引では用心したほうがよい.

Slow and [but] steady [sure] wins the race. 《諺》ゆっくり着実なのが勝つ,「急がば回れ」.

slow in [of] **1**(頭)が鈍い ▪He is *slow of* understanding. 彼は物わかりが鈍い.

2(足・口など)がのろのろした, 遅い ▪He is naturally *slow in* speech. 彼は生まれつき口が重い.

slow to (*do*) **1**(…するの)をぐずぐずする ▪He is *slow to* learn his lessons. 彼は勉強するのをぐずぐずする ▪He was not *slow to* defend himself. 彼はすぐ自己弁護した.

2 なかなか…しない ▪He is *slow to* anger [*to* take offence]. 彼はなかなか怒らない.

slowly /slóʊli/ 副 ***slowly but surely*** ゆっくりと着実に ▪The town is *slowly but surely* changing. その町はゆっくりと着実に変りつつある.

slug[1] /slʌg/ 名 ***put the slug on*** 《米俗》(人)を打つ, 攻撃する ▪He was fined for *putting the slug on* a man. 彼はある男をぶんなぐったかどで罰金をくらった.

slug[2] /slʌg/ 動 ***slug it out*** 《口》最後まで戦う[議論する] ▪The two fighters *slugged it out*. 二人のボクサーは最後まで戦った.

slum /slʌm/ 動 ***go slumming*** 《軽蔑》(慈善・好奇心から)スラム街を訪れる ▪A party of young people thought they would *go slumming*. 青年たちの一行がスラム街を訪れてみようと考えた.

slum it 《口》《しばしば戯》つましく過ごす ▪Corporate directors are also having to *slum it* in economy class seats because of cutting down expenses. 重役たちも経費削減でいまはエコノミーシートでつましく過ごさなければならない.

slur /slə:r/ 名 ***cast [put, throw] a slur on [upon]*** …に汚辱を与える, 汚名をきせる ▪It would *cast a slur on* the credit of such people. それはそのような人々の信用に汚名をきせることになるだろう.

sly[1] /slaɪ/ 名 ***on [upon, under, by] the sly*** 《口》こそこそと, 内緒で ▪She likes a drop *on the sly*. 彼女は内緒で1杯やるのが好きだ ▪The business was done *by the sly*. その仕事は内緒でなされた.

sly[2] /slaɪ/ 形 ***sly as a fox*** →(as) cunning as a FOX.

smack[1] /smæk/ 名 ***a smack in the eye*** ひじ鉄, けんつく ▪A strong yen was *a* real *smack in the eye* for small companies. 円高は小さな会社にとってはまさしく打撃だった.

get a smack in the eye 《口》期待がはずれる; ひじ鉄[けんつく]をくらう ▪A naughty boy often *gets a smack in the eye*. いたずら小僧はよく小言をくらう.

give** a person **a smack on the lips [cheek] 人の口[頬]にキスする ▪The ambassador *gave* his guest *a smack on the cheek*. 大使はゲストの頬にキスした.

have a smack at 《口》…をやってみる ▪I am longing to *have a smack at* Greek. 僕はひとつギリシャ語をやってみたいと思っている.

smack[2] /smæk/ 動 ***smack** one's **lips [chops]*** =LICK one's chops.

smack-bang /smǽkbæ̀ŋ/ 副 《口》まともに, もろに ▪He lives *smack-bang* in the middle of New York. 彼はニューヨークのど真ん中に住んでいる.

small /smɔ:l/ 形副 ***a small and early*** 早く切り上げる小夜会 ▪She added *a small and early* to the dinner. 彼女は晩餐に早く切り上げる小夜会をつけ加えた.

and small blame to him それも彼が悪いのではない ▪He failed, *and small blame to him*. 彼は失敗したが, 彼のせいではない.

(and) small wonder →(and) no WONDER.

do the smalls 小さな町を旅行して回る ▪I like *doing the smalls*. 私は小さな町を旅行して回るのが好きだ.

Don't sweat the small stuff. 《米口》ささいなことは気にするな ▪*Don't sweat the small stuff*. It's just a bit of gossip. ささいなことは気にするな. それはちょっとした噂話にすぎないんだから.

feel small 肩身の狭い[恥ずかしい]思いをする ▪I *felt* very *small* at being seen in such a place. 私はそんな所にいるのを人に見られてとても恥ずかしい思いだった.

great and small/small and great 貴賤, 上下 ▪Both *great and small* praised him. 貴賤を問わず彼をほめた.

in a small way つましく, 地味に ▪They were living *in a small way*. 彼らはつましく暮らしていた ▪He was a composer *in a small way*. 彼は及ばずながら作曲家だった.

in small/in the small 小規模に (↔in (the) LARGE) ▪I have made trial of it *in small*. 私はそれを小規模に試してみた.

in small doses 短い間だけなら ▪He's all right *in small doses* but I wouldn't spend a lot of time with him. 彼とは短い間だけならいいんだけど, 長時間は過ごしたくないわ.

look small 小さくなる, 恐れ入る ▪She *looked small* after you mentioned the fact. 君が例の事実を言ってから彼女は恐れ入ったよ.

no small 少なからぬ, たいした ▪It is a matter of *no small* moment. それは非常に重要な問題だ.

on the small side 少し小さすぎて ▪This hat is *on the small side*. この帽子は少し小さすぎる.

sing small 《口》下手に出る; 大口をたたかない; 口をつぐむ ▪ I must *sing small* in her company. 私は彼女の前では下手に出なければならない ▪ He was so angry with me that I had to *sing small*. 彼は私をひどく怒ったので, 私は口をつぐまねばならなかった.

small and great →great and SMALL.

the small change 小銭; つまらないもの[事] (*of*) ▪ Sex is not *the small change of* love. セックスは愛にとって小事ではない.

smart[1] /smɑːrt/ 形 ***a right smart*** 《米》たくさん(の) ▪ It was *a right smart* distance. それはかなりの道のりだった ▪ I have read *a right smart* of that book. 私はその本はだいぶ読んだ.

a smart Alec(k) [***alec(k)***] 《米口》利口ぶる人, うぬぼれ屋, 生意気なやつ ▪ Say, you *smart Aleck*! おい, 利口ぶっているお前さん.

a smart-ass 《米口》/***a smart-arse*** 《英口》 = a SMART Alec(k).

a smart few 《米口》かなりたくさん(の) ▪ He owns *a smart few* horses. 彼は相当な数の馬を持っている.

a smart mouth 《米口》生意気なやつ, 生意気な口のきき方 ▪ Your *smart mouth* could lose you your job. 君の生意気な口のきき方で職を失うことになるかもしれないよ.

(***as***) ***smart as a steel trap*** [***a whip***] 《米口》実に機敏な, 非常に利口な ▪ He was a successful businessman, *smart as a whip*. 彼は成功した実務家で実に機敏な人だった.

(***as***) ***smart as threepence*** 実に利口な (→(as) smart as PAINT) ▪ You're a lad, but you're *as smart as threepence*. 君は若いが, とても利口だね.

get smart with (人に)生意気な口をきく ▪ My son is beginning to *get smart with* me. 息子が私に生意気な口をきき始めているの.

look smart =LOOK sharp 2.

make oneself smart 身なりを整える ▪ Go and *make yourself smart*. 身なりを整えて来なさい.

play it smart 《主に米口》てきぱきとふるまう, うまく立ち回る ▪ My secretary *plays it smart* and is popular in the office. 私の秘書はてきぱきとふるまってくれるのでオフィスで評判がいい.

smart to work 《米》働き者で ▪ The old woman was always *smart to work*. そのおばあさんはいつも働き者だった.

the smart money →MONEY.

the smart set 社交界の名士たち ▪ This restaurant is used by *the smart set*. このレストランは社交界のお歴々の御用達だ.

smart[2] /smɑːrt/ 動 ***get smarted up*** 《米口》 **1** めかしこむ ▪ She *got smarted up* to go and take a walk with me. 彼女は私と散歩に行くためにめかしこんだ.

2 利口になる ▪ He *got smarted up* a good deal. 彼はとても利口になっていた.

smarty /smɑ́ːrti/ 名 ***a smarty pants*** = a SMART Alec(k).

smash[1] /smæʃ/ 名副 (***a***) ***smash and grab*** (***raid***) ウインドー破り ▪ *Smash and grab* was his line. ウインドー破りが彼の専門だった.

a smash hit 《米》大当たり, 大成功 ▪ The play has been *a smash hit*. その芝居は大当たりだった.

break [***knock***]***... to smash*** …をぺちゃんこにする, 粉砕する ▪ The vase has *been broken to smash*. 花びんは粉々になっていた.

go [***run***] ***smash*** **1** ガチャンと砕ける, ピシャッと砕ける ▪ The dish *went smash*. 皿がガチャンと砕けた.

2 破産する ▪ The firm has *gone smash* at last. その会社はついに破産した.

go [***come***] ***to smash*** ぺちゃんこになる, 完全に失敗する, 破産する ▪ The arrangements all *went to smash*. その手筈はすっかりおじゃんになってしまった ▪ His business *went to smash*. 彼の事業はつぶれた.

play smash 《米》憂き目を見る ▪ He's already *played smash* anyway. あの男はどっちみちもう憂き目を見ているんだ.

smash[2] /smæʃ/ 動 ***be smashed on*** 《米口》…にほれこんでいる ▪ The widow *is smashed on* the Australian. あの未亡人はあのオーストラリア人にほれこんでいる.

smash *a person's* ***face*** [***head***] ***in*** 人をぶちのめす《しばしばおどしに使用される》 ▪ Get out, or I'll *smash your face in*. 出て行け, でないとぶちのめすぞ.

smasher /smǽʃər/ 名 ***come a smasher*** 《俗》大挫折(ざせつ)[大転落]をする ▪ He will *come a smasher* some day. 彼はいつか大挫折をするだろう.

smattering /smǽtərɪŋ/ 名 ***have a smattering of*** …を生かじりしている ▪ I *have a smattering of* Greek. ギリシャ語を生かじりしています.

smell[1] /smel/ 名 ***have*** [***take***] ***a smell at*** …をかぐ ▪ *Have a smell at* this egg. この卵をかいでみてください.

smell[2] /smel/ 動 ***come out*** [***up***] ***smelling like*** [***of***] ***roses*** →ROSE.

smell fishy うさんくさい, 眉唾である ▪ I *smelled* something *fishy* when he didn't give me his new address. 彼が新しい住所を教えなかったときちょっとうさんくさいと思った.

smell of the candle [***lamp, oil***] (文章などが)苦心さんたんの跡が見える (→smell of OIL) ▪ His works *smelt* all *of the candle*. 彼の作品はすべて苦心さんたんの跡が見えていた.

smell to high heaven →stink to (high) HEAVEN.

smile[1] /smaɪl/ 名 ***be all smiles*** 満面に笑みをたたえている ▪ He *was all smiles* and courtesy. 彼は喜色満面ですこぶるいんぎんだった.

crack a smile 《口》にこっとする, 笑う ▪ At first he was surprised, and then *cracked a* big, beautiful *smile*. 最初彼は驚いていたが, それから後, 破顔一笑した ▪ I met with him probably ten times and he never *cracked a smile*. 彼とはたぶん10回は会っているが, 一度も笑い顔になったことがない.

put a smile on *a person's* ***face*** 人をにこにこさ

S

せる ▪ This news will *put a smile on his face*. このニュースを聞けば, 彼もにこにこするだろう.

wipe [***take***] ***the smile off*** *a person's* ***face*** →FACE[1].

with a smile にっこりして ▪ He answered *with a smile*. 彼はにっこりして答えた.

smile[2] /smaɪl/ 動 ***come up smiling*** → COME[2].

I should smile. 《米口》なるほどね《人の考えを嘲笑して言う》 ▪ Sing for nothing? Well *I should smile*! ただで歌えって? へえ, なるほどね.

keep smiling 微笑を絶やさない, へこたれない ▪ I was penniless; it was hard to *keep smiling*. 僕は一文なしだった. へこたれないでいるのは大変だった.

smile *one's* ***approval*** [***thanks***] 微笑して是認[感謝]の意を表す ▪ Father *smiled his approval*. 父はにっこりして是認の意を表した.

smite /smaɪt/ 動 ***be smitten by*** =be smitten with 1, 2 (→SMITE).

be smitten with **1** (女性)に参る, ほれる ▪ He *is* quite *smitten with* the girl. 彼はその娘にぞっこん参っている.

2 (病気)にかかる ▪ He has *been smitten with* the plague. 彼は疫病にかかっている.

3 (ある感情)にかられる, 打たれる ▪ He *was smitten with* amazement. 彼は驚きに打たれた.

4 …に深く打たれる ▪ He *is* deeply *smitten with* her beauty. 彼は彼女の美しさに深く打たれている.

smithereens /smìðəríːnz/ 名 ***to*** [***into***] ***smithereens*** 粉みじんに ▪ The ship was blown *to smithereens*. 船はこっぱみじんに爆破された.

smoke[1] /smoʊk/ 名 ***a smoke screen*** 煙幕, 偽装 ▪ He hides his lust for power behind *a smoke screen* of modesty. 彼は謙虚さを煙幕にして権勢欲を隠している.

blow smoke (***up*** *a person's* ***ass***) 《米卑》 **1** ごまをする, へつらう ▪ He would never *blow smoke up my ass*. 彼は私にごまをすったりはしないだろう.

2 煙に巻く ▪ He was certainly up to something, but it sounded to me he was *blowing smoke*. 確かに彼は何かを企んでいたが, 私には彼が煙に巻いているように思われた.

come to [***end*** (***up***) ***in, vanish into***] ***smoke*** (計画・談判などが)水泡に帰する, 雲散霧消する ▪ This whole affair will *come to smoke*. この事件はすべてうやむやになるだろう ▪ His scheme *ended in smoke*. 彼の計画は水泡に帰した.

from the smoke into the smother 小難から大難へ ▪ They went *from the smoke into the smother*. 彼らは小難から大難に陥った.

go up in smoke **1** =come to SMOKE.

2 燃える ▪ The storehouse full of tires *went up in smoke*. タイヤがぎっしり詰まっている倉庫が燃えた.

have [***take***] ***a smoke*** 一服する ▪ Stop working and *have a smoke*. 仕事をやめて一服しなさい.

like smoke/like a smoke on fire 《俗》素早く ▪ The hounds are running *like smoke*. 猟犬たちは素早く走っている.

sell smoke 詐欺をやらかす, ごまかす ▪ I found they were only *selling smoke*. 彼らがごまかしているだけだとわかった. ☞[L] fumum vendere のなぞり.

smoke and mirrors 《米》偽装, ごまかし ▪ Our plan is free of the *smoke and mirrors* which have characterized their plan. 私たちの企画には彼らの企画のようなごまかしは一切ありません.

smoke signals (考え・計画の)ほのめかし, 兆候 ▪ Recent economic *smoke signals* suggest that the economy began to pick up. 最近の経済兆候は景気が回復し始めたことを示しています.

the (***big***) ***smoke*** [***Smoke***] 《英》(ロンドン・シドニーなどの)大都会 ▪ When were you last in *the smoke*? この前, 大都会に出てきたのはいつ?

There is no fire without smoke. →FIRE[1].

There is no smoke without fire. 《諺》火のない所に煙は立たぬ. ☞Where there's smoke, there's fire. とも言う.

Watch my smoke. 《米俗》私のやっていることを見てくれ ▪ Suspend judgment and *watch my smoke*. 判断を下すのを待って僕のすることを見ていろ.

smoke[2] /smoʊk/ 動 ***smoke*** *oneself* (***into***) タバコをふかして…になる ▪ I gradually *smoked myself into* a certain degree of acquaintance with him. 私はタバコをふかして彼とちょっとした知り合いになった ▪ He *smoked himself* sick. 彼はタバコをふかして胸がむかむかしてきた.

smoke like a chimney やたらにタバコを吸う ▪ He *smokes like a chimney*. 彼はやたらにタバコを吸う.

smoking /smóʊkɪŋ/ 名 ***a smoking gun*** 《新聞》確かな犯罪の証拠 ▪ *A smoking gun* was found in the form of a memorandum. 確かな犯罪の証拠がメモの形で発見された.

be off smoking タバコをやめている ▪ He's *been off smoking* while he's had flu. 彼はインフルエンザにかかっている間タバコをやめていた.

No smoking. 禁煙《掲示》.

smooth[1] /smuːð/ 形名 (***a***) ***smooth chance*** [***spell***] 荒海中で波の立たない区域 ▪ Seeing *a smooth spell*, he started to go forward. 荒海中の波の立たない区域を見つけて, 彼は前へ進み始めた.

(***as***) ***smooth as glass*** [***a billiard-table***] (道・床などが)とてもなめらかで ▪ The road was *as smooth as glass*. 道路はすごく平坦だった.

(***as***) ***smooth as velvet*** [***silk, a baby's bottom***] (肌・布・木などが)とても柔らかで, とてもすべすべして ▪ Her hands are *as smooth as velvet*. 彼女の手はとてもすべすべしていた.

give ... a smooth …をなでつける ▪ She *gave* her hair *a smooth*. 彼女は髪の毛をなでつけた.

make smooth 障害をなくする, 円滑にする ▪ They will *make* everything *smooth* for us. 彼らは万事円滑にしてくれるだろう.

smooth sailing 順風満帆 ▪ The system is *smooth sailing* now. そのシステムは今は問題ない.

smooth[2] /smu:ð/ 動 ***smooth** a person's* ***path*** [***way, passage***] 行く手の障害を取り除く; 事態を容易にする ▪ Ask the director yourself, I'll *smooth your way* there. 自分で社長に頼んでみたまえ. 僕が根回しをしておいてあげるよ ▪ They tried to *smooth the bill's way* through Congress. 彼らは議案がスムーズに議会を通るように尽力した.

smother /smʌ́ðər/ 名 ***from the smoke into the smother*** →SMOKE[1].

snack /snæk/ 名 ***come*** [***put***] ***in for a snack*** 分け前にあずかる ▪ He would take all if we did not *come in for snacks*. 我々が分け前にあずからなければ彼が全部取ってしまうだろう.

go snacks 山分けにする (*in*) ▪ They *went snacks in* the profits. 彼らは利益を山分けにした.

snaffle /snǽfəl/ 名 ***ride** a person* ***in*** [***on, with***] ***the snaffle*** 人を手柔らかに制御する ▪ He will never obey my command till he *is ridden in the snaffle*. あの男は手柔らかに制御しないうちは私の命令に決して従わないだろう.

snag /snæg/ 名 ***come*** [***run***] (***up***) ***against a snag/catch on*** [***hit, strike***] ***a snag*** 《口》(思わぬ)障害にぶつかる ▪ I was continually *running (up) against some snag* in the shape of an unwritten law. 私は絶えず不文律という障害にぶつかっていた. ☞snag「航行を妨げる水中の隠れ木」.

snail /sneɪl/ 名 ***at a snail's gallop*** [***pace***] 蝸牛(かぎゅう)の歩みで, のろのろした歩みで ▪ For a time they got along *at a snail's gallop*. しばらくは彼らは実にのろのろした歩みで進んで行った.

snail mail 《口・戯》郵便《電子メールと比較してのユーモラスな言い方》 ▪ These days I don't use *snail mail* but E-mail. 最近は郵便ではなく電子メールを使います.

snake /sneɪk/ 名 ***a*** [***the***] ***snake in the grass*** 見えない危険, 隠れた敵 (Virgil, *Elcogues* 3. 93) ▪ You're driving too fast; there's *a snake in the grass*. 君はあまり速く飛ばしすぎている. 見えない危険があるものだよ ▪ He's *the snake in the grass* who'll ruin you. 彼は君を滅ぼす隠れた敵だ.

(***as***) ***cold as snake in August*** 《米口》とても冷淡な ▪ He is about *as cold as* a *snake in August*. 彼はとても冷淡な人間だ.

(***as***) ***sure as snakes*** 《米口》確かに ▪ *As sure as snakes* it must be fun. 確かにそれはおもしろいにちがいない.

be above snakes 《米》生きている ▪ If a person *is "above snakes,"* he/she is still alive and kicking. 人が「生きている」とは, いまなお生き生きと楽しんでいるということだ.

have snakes in** one's* ***boots 《米俗》へべれけに酔っている ▪ He'*s got snakes in his boots* now. 彼は今へべれけに酔っている.

scotch the snake 仕事を台なしにする ▪ Whether to *scotch the snake* or not is up to you. 仕事を台なしにするかしないかは君次第だ.

see snakes アル中になっている ▪ We must not *see snakes*. 私たちはアル中にならないようにしないといけない.

snake oil 《米口》まやかし物 ▪ A lot of goods at that store are pure *snake oil*. あの店の商品の多くは全くのまやかし物だ.

the snake in the grass →a SNAKE in the grass.

wake [***raise***] ***snakes,*** (***and walk your chalks***) 《口》苦境に陥る; 素早く逃げ去る ▪ Oh, *wake snakes, and walk your chalks*! やい, とっとと逃げてしまえ.

warm [***cherish, nourish***] ***a snake in** one's* ***bosom*** 恩をあだで返される, 飼犬に手をかまれる ▪ You are *cherishing a snake in your bosom*. あなたは飼犬に手をかまれるようなことをしているのですよ. ☞イソップ寓話から.

Why in snakes ...? 《米口》一体なぜ ▪ *Why in snakes* should anybody want to be a sculptor? 一体なぜ彫刻家になりたいなどと思うんだろう.

snap[1] /snæp/ 名 ***cold snap*** [***spell***] ひとしきりの寒さ ▪ The *cold snap* continued for several days. そのひとしきりの寒さは数日間続いた.

in a snap すぐに, たちまち ▪ I'll put you to rights *in a snap*. すぐに直してあげますよ.

not care [***worth***] ***a snap*** 少しもかまわない[価値がない] ▪ I do*n't care a snap*. 僕は全くかまわない.

not give [***care***] ***a snap of** one's* ***fingers for*** ...をちっともかまわない ▪ I do*n't give a snap of my fingers for* what he says about me. 彼が僕のことを何と言おうとちっともかまわない.

take a snap at ...にかみかかる ▪ The dog *took a snap at* him. 犬が彼にかみかかった.

with a snap ポキリ[パタン]と ▪ He shut the book *with a snap*. 彼は本をパタンと閉じた.

snap[2] /snæp/ 動 ***snap** one's* ***fingers at*** ...を軽蔑する, 無視する ▪ You'll be able to *snap your fingers at* them all. 君もあの連中全部を軽蔑することができるようになるよ.

snap it up 《米》=SNAP to it.

snap** a person's* ***nose [***head***] ***off*** つっけんどんに人に話しかけるまたは返事をする ▪ He *snapped my nose off* for coming late. 彼は僕が遅刻したというのでつっけんどんな口をきいた ▪ If I had not been quite sure, he would have *snapped my head off*. 私に確信がなかったら彼はつっけんどんな返事をしていただろう.

snap ... (***off***) ***short*** いきなり(人の話)をさえぎる ▪ He *snapped* me (*off*) *short*. 彼はいきなり私の話をさえぎった.

snap out of it 《口》しっかりする, 元気を出す ▪ *Snap out of it* and get to work! しっかりして仕事にかかるんだ.

snap to attention =spring (to) ATTENTION.

snap to it 《口》〖主に命令文で〗急いで始める ▪ *Snap to it*, everybody! みんな, さっさと始めろ.

snap up (***short***) (いきなり)差出口をする ▪ He grew angry and *snapped* her *up* very *short*. 彼は腹を立てていきなり彼女に差出口をした.

snappy /snǽpi/ 形 ***make it snappy*** 《口》(話

などを)てきぱきとする, 急ぐ ▪ You had better *make it snappy*, if you want to catch that train. その列車に乗りたいのなら急いだほうがいい.

snare /sneər/ 名 ***lay* [*set*] *a snare for*** …にわなをしかける ▪ I *laid a snare for* the rabbits. 私はウサギにわなをしかけておいた.

(*the*) *snares and pitfalls* 誘惑と危険 ▪ Life is full of *snares and pitfalls*. 人生は誘惑と危険に満ちている.

snatch /snætʃ/ 名 ***by* [*in*] *snatches*** ちょいちょいと, とぎれとぎれに ▪ He has to take his victuals *by snatches*. 彼は食事をとぎれとぎれに取らねばならない ▪ I slept *in snatches*. 私はとぎれとぎれに眠った.

make a snatch at …につかみかかる ▪ He *made a snatch at* the truth. 彼は真相をつかもうとした.

put the snatch on (人)に要求する ▪ *Put the snatch on* him for a cut of the take. 彼にその売り上げの分け前を出せと言ってやれ.

sneak /sni:k/ 形 ***a sneak preview*** 《米》(映画の)覆面試写会 ▪ They gave us *a sneak preview* of the latest movie. 最新映画の覆面試写会が催された.

sneer /snɪər/ 動 ***sneer out of existence*** 冷笑してなくしてしまう ▪ We *sneered* his pride *out of existence*. 我々は冷笑して彼の高慢さをくじいた.

sneeze /sni:z/ 動 ***not* [*nothing*] *to be sneezed* [*sniffed*] *at*** 《口》ばかにならない; 軽んじられない ▪ A thousand pounds was *not* a thing *to be sneezed at*. 1,000ポンドはばかにならない金額だった ▪ He is *not* a guy *to be sneezed at*. 彼は軽くみれないやつだ. ☞not は《英》, nothing は《米》.

sneeze into a basket 《婉曲》ギロチンにかけられる ▪ The court sentenced him to *sneeze into a basket*. 法廷は彼にギロチンによる死刑の判決を下した.

sniff[1] /snɪf/ 名 ***not get a sniff of…*** 《口》…を得る気配[チャンス]もない ▪ I've *never got a sniff of* the big money. これまで大金を得る機会はなかった.

sniff[2] /snɪf/ 動 ***not to be sniffed at*** =not to be SNEEZEd at.

sniffle /snífəl/ 名 ***have* [*get*] *the sniffles*** 《口》軽い風邪をひく ▪ I *have the sniffles*. 軽い風邪なんだ.

snit /snɪt/ 名 ***be in a snit*** 《米口》(不合理だと思って)いらいらしている ▪ What *are* you *in a snit* about? 何にいらいらしてるの?

snook /snʊk|snu:k/ 名 ***cock* [*cut, make*] *a snook* [*snooks*]** 《英口》親指を鼻に当て他の指を広げてみせる《軽蔑のしぐさ》(*at*) ▪ The boy put his tongue in his cheek and *cocked a snook at* me. その男の子はほっぺたを舌でふくらませ親指を鼻に当て他の指を広げて私を軽蔑した.

snoot /snu:t/ 名 ***have* [*get*] *a snoot full*** 《米俗》酔っぱらっている[酔っぱらう] ▪ Then I *got a snoot full*. それから私は酔っぱらった.

snooze[1] /snu:z/ 名 ***take a snooze*** うたた寝する ▪ He had unbuttoned his jacket and was preparing to *take a snooze*. 彼は上着のボタンをはずしてしまっていて, うたた寝の準備をしているところだった.

snooze[2] /snu:z/ 動 ***you snooze, you lose*** 《口》自業自得だ ▪ You didn't study hard and got bad grades—*you snooze, you lose*. 君はよく勉強せずに成績が悪かった—だから, 自業自得さ.

snow[1] /snoʊ/ 名 ***a snow job*** **1** 《主に米口》嘘偽り ▪ She did *a snow job* to get him to run an errand for her. 彼女は彼をだまして使いにやらせた.
2 専門家気取り ▪ His talk was *a snow job* and I didn't like it. 彼の話は専門家気取りで嫌だった.

(*as seasonable*) *as snow in summer* 季節はずれで; 不適当[任]で(《聖》*Prov.* 26. 1) ▪ You are *as seasonable as snow in summer*. 君は不適任だ.

sell snow to the Eskimos 人がすでに持っているものを売る ▪ The new salesman said he could *sell snow to the Eskimos*. その新人セールスマンは持っている人にも売ってみせますと言った.

snow[2] /snoʊ/ 動 ***It snows.*** 雪が降る ▪ *It snowed* heavily last night. ゆうべは大雪だった.

snowball /snóʊbɔ̀:l/ 名 ***not have* (*got*) [*stand*] *a snowball's chance in hell*** → (not) have a CHANCE in hell (of doing).

snowflake /snóʊflèɪk/ 名 ***as much chance* [*hope*] *as a snowflake in hell*** →HELL.

snuff[1] /snʌf/ 名 ***a snuff movie* [*film*]** 殺人実写映画, 不法映画 ▪ He was charged with importing *snuff movies*. 彼は殺人実写映画の輸入のかどで告訴された.

beat…to snuff 《口》…をすっかり打ち負かす ▪ *Beat* all other colleges *to snuff*. 他のすべての大学を完全に打ち負かしてしまえ.

chew snuff →rub SNUFF.

give** a person **snuff 《口》人を手きびしくしかる, 懲らしめる ▪ He *gave* me *snuff* about my extravagance. 彼は僕の浪費を手きびしくしかった.

in great snuff 《米俗》派手に ▪ One of the females was dressed *in great snuff*. 女性たちの一人は派手な身なりをしていた.

in high snuff 《米俗》得意になって ▪ They were *in high snuff*. 彼らは得意になっていた.

in* (*the*) *snuff 立腹して ▪ Don't fly up *in the snuff* at me. 腹を立てて私に飛びかかってくるなよ.

rub* [*chew*] *snuff 《米》(溶かしたろうにしんをつけて)ろうそくを作る ▪ The woman sat in the corner *rubbing snuff*. その女性はすみに腰かけてろうそくを作っていた.

up to snuff **1** 《主に英口》抜け目[如才]のない ▪ You American ladies are so *up to snuff*, as you say. あなたたちアメリカ人女性はいわゆるとても抜け目がない方々ですね.
2 《主に米口》標準に達して ▪ The concert was hardly *up to snuff*. コンサートは全く標準以下だった.
3 《主に米口》体調がよい, 普通通りで ▪ I didn't feel *up to snuff* this summer. この夏は体調がよくなかった.

snuff[2] /snʌf/ 動 ***snuff it*** 《英俗》くたばる ▪ He

isn't going to *snuff it* just for a crack on the head. 彼は頭が割れたくらいで死にはしない.

snuffle /snʌ́fəl/ 名 ***have*** [***get***] ***the snuffles*** 《口》風邪をひく ▪ Be careful not to *have the snuffles*. 風邪をひかないように気をつけなさい.

snug /snʌg/ 形 ***(as) snug as a bug in a rug*** [***blanket***] 《戯》すてきに居心地よく ▪ You might sit *as snug as a bug in a rug*. 君はすてきに居心地よく座れることでしょう.

Snug's the word! 他言無用 ▪ *Snug's the word* with him. 彼には他言無用ですよ.

so /soʊ/ 代副接 ***and so*** **1**〚前言を確認または強調して〛そして確かに ▪ You are perhaps hungry. —*And so* I am. 君は多分空腹だろう—確かにそうだ.

2 また同様に ▪ I am tired, *and so* are you. 僕は疲れているが君も同様だ.

3 そこで ▪ He was ill, *and so* they were quiet. 彼は病気だった, そこでみんな静かにしていた.

4 それから ▪ The Ambassador showed him his commission, *and so* took his leave of him. 大使は彼に委任状を示し, それからいとまを告げた.

and so forth [***on***] →AND.

as ..., so →AS.

in so far as ...のかぎりでは ▪ *In so far as* my education was concerned, they spared no expense. 私の教育に関するかぎりでは彼らは出費をいとわなかった.

Just [***Quite***] ***so.*** 《口》全くそうだ, その通り ▪ Jane is a nice girl and nice girls should marry. —*Just so*. ジェインはいい娘だ. そしていい娘は結婚すべきだ—その通りだ ▪ The aliens don't obey our orders.—*Quite so*. 外国人は我々の命令を聞いてくれないよ—その通り.

or so **1**(数量が)...かそこいら ▪ It is two miles *or so*. 2マイルかそこらだ.

2 またはそんなもの ▪ He is a fool *or so*. 彼はばかみたいなもんさ ▪ My joints are somewhat stiff *or so*. 関節がややこわばっているみたいだ.

So am I. →SO do I.

so and in no other way/so and so only 方法はそれきりで ▪ It can be done *so and in no other way*. それをやる方法はただそれきりだ.

so and so **1**〚名詞的に〛某; 何々しかじか ▪ Mr. *So and so* called today. 何とかさんがきょう来られた.

2〚a を伴って〛いやなやつ ▪ He's *a* real *so and so*. 彼はほんとにいやなやつだ.

3〚副詞的に〛しかじかに; かなりに ▪ I improved it *so and so*. それをしかじかに改良した ▪ How is trade? —Just *so and so*. 商売はどうかね—ぼちぼちさ.

so as **1** ...さえすれば ▪ I care not how you come by them, *so as* they supply my wants. それが私の必要をみたしてくれさえすれば君がどうやってそれを手に入れようとかまわない.

2 ...するように ▪ He repeated aloud *so as* there'd be no chance of a mistake. 彼はまちがいの余地がないように大声で繰り返した.

so ... as **1** ...と同様に ▪ They must *so* walk, *as* he walked. 彼らは彼が歩んだ通りに歩かねばならない.

2〚否定文・疑問文で〛...と同じ程度に ▪ This is not *so* strange *as* it may appear. これはうわべほど変なことではない ▪ Who is *so* true and honest *as* he is? 彼ほど真実で正直な者がいるだろうか.

3 ...のごとき《特殊な例を引いて》 ▪ It was impossible that *so* amiable a girl *as* Emily could fail to attract attention. エミリーのような愛嬌のあるいい娘が人目をひかないなどというはずはなかった.

so as *one* ***can ...*** 《口》...できるように ▪ Leave the door open, *so as* I *can* hear if anyone comes. 誰か来たら聞こえるようにドアを開けておいてくれ.

so as not to *do* ...しないように ▪ We hurried *so as not to* be late. 私たちは遅れないように急いだ.

so as to *do* ...するように ▪ I got up early *so as to* be in time for the train. 私はその列車に間に合うように早く起きた.

so ... as to *do* 〚結果・程度〛...なので...する; ...するほどに ▪ The vase was *so* broken into small fragments *as to* be useless. 花びんは粉みじんに砕けていたので使いものにならなかった ▪ He is *so* lame *as to* be unable to walk. 彼は歩けないほど足が不自由だ.

So be it./Be it so./Let it be so. それならそれでよい, ままよ《あきらめ・承諾》 ▪ You are going to give me my dismissal. *So be it*. あなたは私を首にしようとおっしゃる. それならそれでよろしい.

So best. それなら一番よい ▪ If this be practicable, *so best*. これが実行できれば, それが一番よい.

So do [***am***] ***I.*** 私もそうです《前の発言を受けて》 ▪ He gets up early, and *so do I* /áɪ/. 彼は早起きだが, 私もそうです ▪ I am happy.—*So am I* /áɪ/. 私は幸福です—私もです.

so far →FAR.

So I do [***am***]. そうです《前の発言を受けて》 ▪ They say you like apples very much.—*So I do* /dúː/. リンゴが大層お好きだそうですが—そうなんです ▪ You look very happy.—*So I am* /ǽm/. とても楽しそうですね—そうなんですよ.

so ... it isn't true 《口》すこぶる[信じられないくらい]...だ ▪ He is *so* rich *it isn't true*. 彼は信じられないくらい金持ちだ. ☞so の後には ignorant, rich, efficient, hideous, comfortable などの形容詞がくる.

so or so あれかこれか (this or that) ▪ From her face, he sets her down in his mind as *so or so*. 彼女の顔から彼は心の中であれかこれかと品定めする.

so so 《口》まあまあで ▪ He speaks English but *so so*. 彼は英語を話すがまあまあだ ▪ How's business? —Oh, only *so so*. 景気はどうかね—ああ, まずまずさ.

so that **1**〚結果〛それで, そのため ▪ The roof had fallen in; *so that* the hut was of no use to me. 屋根は落ち込んでしまっていた. そこで小屋は私には何の役にも立たなかった.

2 ...するかぎりは, でさえあれば ▪ *So that* it be done, I don't care who does it. それをしさえすれば誰がしようとかまわない ▪ You may go anywhere, *so that* you avoid bad company. 悪い仲間を避けさえすればどこへ行ってもよい.

S

so ... that 1〚形容詞・副詞を伴って〛非常に...なので; ...ほど ▪ He was *so* angry *that* he could hardly speak. 彼はひどく腹をたてていたのでほとんど口がきけなかった ▪ No one is *so* poor *that* he cannot afford to be neat. こぎれいにする余裕のないほどの貧者はいない.

2〚動詞を伴って〛...のように ▪ The bridge is *so* made *that* it opens in the middle. その橋は中央が開くように作られている.

so that** one **may [《口》***can, shall, will***] ...するように, できるように《目的》 ▪ Turn the lantern *so that* we *may* see what it is. それが何だかわかるようにちょうちんを向けてください ▪ They sent her out of the room, *so that* they *could* talk freely. 彼らは自由に話ができるように彼女を部屋から出した ▪ My mother will call the baby Alfred *so that* we *shall* never forget you. 母は我々があなたをいつまでも忘れないように赤んぼうをアルフレッドと名づけようというのです ▪ They are hurrying *so that* they *will* not miss the train. 彼らは列車に遅れないように急いでいる.

(So) that's that. →(and) THAT's that.

so to say [***speak***] いわば ▪ The man is, *so to say* [*speak*], a grown-up boy. あの男は言うなれば大きくなった子供だ.

So what? 《口》それがどうしたというのか《反論》 ▪ He took a drink now and then.—*So what?* 彼はときどき酒を飲んだ—それがどうしたというんだ.

soak[1] /soʊk/ 名 ***in soak*** **1**(水に)つけて ▪ He laid the leathers *in soak* to supple them. 彼は革をしなやかにするために水につけた.

2《米俗》質に入って ▪ Everything we had is either gone or *in soak*. 我々の持っていたものは全部なくなったか質に入っている.

3《米俗》(人が)入獄して ▪ He was put *in soak*. 彼は投獄された.

4《米俗》準備して ▪ I have had a speech *in soak* these six months. 私はこの6か月ほどある演説を準備してきた.

soak[2] /soʊk/ 動 ***be*** [***get***] ***soaked to the skin*** ずぶぬれになる ▪ We *got soaked to the skin*. 我々はずぶぬれになった.

Go soak yourself! 《米俗》いいかげんにしろ《不信・いらだちの返答》.

soak** one's **clay →wet one's CLAY.

soak** oneself **in **1**(酒)を浴びるように飲む, (酒)びたりになる ▪ They *soaked themselves in* beer. 彼らはビールを浴びるように飲んだ.

2 ...に専心[没頭]する ▪ He *soaked himself in* the classics. 彼は古典に専心した.

***soak it to** a person* 《米俗》人をひどい目にあわせる, 罰する ▪ *Soak it to* him good! 奴をこっぴどくひどい目にあわせてやるがいい.

soak its way 染み通っていく ▪ The water *soaked its way* through the soil. 水が土に染み通っていく.

soaker /sóʊker/ 名 ***an old soaker*** **1** 老練家, 海千山千の人 ▪ *Old soakers* are hardly reclaimed. 海千山千の代物はなかなか改心させられない.

2 大酒飲み ▪ Some quiet *old soakers* were sleeping. おとなしい大酒家の中には眠っている者もいた.

soap[1] /soʊp/ 名 ***a soap opera*** **1** ソープオペラ, (ラジオ・テレビの)連続メロドラマ ▪ My grandmother watches *soap operas* all day long. 祖母は一日中テレビのメロドラマを見ている.

2(ドラマ番組にあるような)家庭内のトラブル ▪ She goes on and on about her family problems, one long *soap opera*. 彼女はテレビドラマよろしく家のごたごたを延々としゃべる. ☞ラジオのドラマが石けん会社の提供だったことから.

no soap 《米俗》だめ; 知らない ▪ I tried to persuade him, but it was *no soap*. 彼を説き伏せようとしたがだめだった ▪ Just say, "*No soap*." ただ「知らない」と言いなさい.

soft soap →SOFT sawder.

wash** one's **hands with invisible soap もみ手をする《へつらい・困惑の身ぶり》 ▪ He's always *washing his hands with invisible soap*. 彼はいつももみ手をしている.

soap[2] /soʊp/ 動 ***soap** oneself **down*** 体じゅうに石けんをすりつける ▪ I *soaped myself down* and had a shower. 私は体じゅうに石けんをすりつけてシャワーを浴びた.

soap the ways 仕事を楽にする ▪ Peggy has *soaped the ways*. ペギーが仕事を楽にしてくれた.

soapbox /sóʊpbɑ̀ks|-bɔ̀ks/ 名 ***mount a soapbox*** 街頭演説をぶつ ▪ I was so angry at the unfairness of it I was ready to *mount a soapbox*. 私はその不当さに腹が立って街頭演説をぶちたくなった.

on [***off***] ***one's soapbox*** 自分の意見を力説する[しない] ▪ If anyone mentions music, he gets *on his soapbox* and tells us that Mozart is the greatest composer. 誰かが音楽を話題にすると, 彼は自説を力説してモーツァルトが最大の作曲家だと言う. ☞石けんを入れる大きな箱を即席の演台にすることから.

soapbox oratory 即席街頭演説 ▪ I enjoy *soapbox oratory* better than anything else. 私は何よりも即席街頭演説が好きなの.

sob[1] /sɑb|sɔb/ 名 ***pull sob stuff*** 《口》泣き言を言う, 泣く ▪ Don't *pull sob stuff*. 泣き言を言うな.

sob[2] /sɑb|sɔb/ 動 ***sob** one's **heart out*** 《口》おんおん泣きじゃくる ▪ The mother left the child *sobbing his heart out*. 母親は子供がおんおん泣きじゃくるのにまかせた.

sob** oneself **into すすり泣いて...になる ▪ She *sobbed herself into* an illness. 彼女はすすり泣いて病気になった.

sob** oneself **to sleep →SLEEP[1].

sober[1] /sóʊbər/ 形 ***(as) sober as a judge*** 全くしらふで; 落ち着き払って ▪ The child sat through the sermon *as sober as a judge*. その子は説教の間中落ち着き払って座っていた.

in sober earnest →in dead EARNEST.

S

in sober fact [***truth***] 全くの話 ▪ Where *in sober fact* does he get his money from? 全くの話，彼はどこから金を得ているのか.

sober² /sóʊbər/ 動 ***a sobering thought*** そう思うとまじめ[不安]になる ▪ A baseball player can earn more money than a Cabinet Minister in a year. It's *a sobering thought*. 野球の選手は1年で大臣よりもかせぎが多いことがある. そう思うとしらけてくる.

social /sóʊʃəl/ 形 ***a social climber*** 成り上がり者 ▪ He is *a* dedicated *social climber*. 彼はすごい成り上がり者だ.

society /səsáɪəti/ 名 ***a throwaway society*** 使い捨て社会 ▪ I can't put up with today's *throwaway society*. 今日の使い捨て社会にはがまんがならない.

a walk-on-by society 犯罪を見て見ぬ振りをする人々 ▪ We have become *a walk-on-by society*, afraid of getting involved. 関わり合いになるのを恐れて，犯罪を目撃しても見て見ぬ振りをするようになっている.

avoid [***seek***] ***the society of*** ...との交際を避ける[求める] ▪ He *avoids the society of* his companions. 彼は仲間とのつき合いを避けている.

enjoy *a person's* ***society*** 人との交際を楽しむ ▪ I greatly *enjoyed his society* at sea. 海でのその人との交際は楽しかった.

go into [***move in***] ***society*** 社交界に出る[出入りする] ▪ I do not *go* much *into society*. 私はあまり世間に顔を出さない.

have no society with ...とつき合いがない ▪ He *had no society with* mankind. 彼は人とつき合いがなかった.

in the society of ...といっしょに ▪ I spent an evening *in the society of* my friends. 友人たちといっしょにある晩を過ごした.

sock¹ /sɑk|sɔk/ 名 ***beat*** [***bore, charm***] ***the socks off*** (人を)打ちのめす，(人に)圧勝する ▪ He *beats the socks off* his students with his classes. 彼は授業で生徒を打ちのめす.

blow [***knock***] *one's* ***socks off*** 《口》...をとても感心[感動]させる，に驚かされる ▪ When I listened to his lecture, it *blew my socks off*. 彼の講演を聴いてとても感動した.

give *a person* ***socks*** 《口》人をひどい目にあわせる，ひどくしかる ▪ When I catch you, I'll *give* you *socks*! つかまえたらひどい目にあわせてやるぞ.

knock the socks off →KNOCK².

pull up *one's* ***socks*** 《口》ふんどしを締めてかかる ▪ Metaphorically an Irish-American "*pulled up his socks*." 比喩的に言えば，あるアイルランド系アメリカ人が「ふんどしを締めて」かかった.

Put a sock in [***into***] ***it!*** 《英俗》黙れ!，ばかを言うな ▪ "Oh, *put a sock in it!*" she said to him scornfully. 「あら黙ってちょうだい」と女はばかにしたように彼に言った. ☞it＝your mouth.

scare the socks off ＝scare the PANTS off a person.

take a sock at (人)をげんこつでなぐる ▪ Angrily he *took a sock at* me. 彼は怒って私を拳で殴った.

the sock and buskin 喜劇と悲劇，演劇 ▪ He knew all the niceties of *the sock and buskin*. 彼は演劇のことは細かいことまで全部知っていた. ☞sock「古代ギリシャ・ローマ演劇の喜劇俳優のはいた軽い靴」; buskin「悲劇俳優のはいた底の厚い半長ぐつ」.

work [***laugh, run***] *one's* ***socks off*** 《口》一生懸命働く ▪ The lawyer I know *works his socks off* and gets a lot of money. 私の知り合いの弁護士は精一杯働いて金を稼いでいる.

sock² /sɑk|sɔk/ 動 ***be socked in*** 《米》(悪天候などのため飛行機が)飛行不能になる，(空港が)閉鎖される ▪ Our plane [The airport] *was socked in* by bad weather. 悪天候のために我々の飛行機は飛べなくなった[空港が閉鎖された].

sock it to 《主に米口》...をひどく打つ; に強烈な衝撃[印象]を与える ▪ They are waiting to hear you sing, so *sock it to* them. みんな君の歌を聞きたがっているのだから，思いきりぶちかましてやれ.

sock *a person* ***one*** 人をしたたか打つ ▪ I was tempted to *sock* him *one*. 彼をうんとぶってやりたくて仕方なかった.

sod /sɑd|sɔd/ 名 ***put ... under the sod*** ...を(殺して)埋める ▪ A lot of boys swore together to *put* him *under the sod*. 大勢の少年たちが彼を殺して埋めてやろうと誓い合った.

Sod's Law/sod's law 《英戯》マーフィーの法則，経験則 ▪ It's *Sod's Law* that she's late when he comes on time. 彼が時間通りに来ると彼女が遅れて来るというのがマーフィーの法則さ.

the old sod 故郷，祖国 ▪ He did not like to leave *the old sod*. 彼は故郷を去るのがいやだった.

under the sod 《口》死んで埋められて ▪ He has been *under the sod* these six months. 彼は半年前に死んで埋められた.

under the sod of grass 草葉の陰に ▪ We buried him *under the sod of grass*. 我々は彼を草葉の陰に葬った.

soda /sóʊdə/ 名 ***from soda*** (***card***) ***to hock*** 《米》初めから終わりまで ▪ He played the deal *from soda to hock*. 彼はその勝負を初めから終わりまでやった.

soft /sɔːft|sɔft/ 形 ***A soft answer turneth away wrath.*** →WRATH.

a soft job 楽な仕事 ▪ Teaching isn't *a soft job*. 教職は楽な仕事ではない.

(***as***) ***soft as clay*** [***butter, down***] 非常に柔らかい ▪ The unknown substance was white and *as soft as clay*. 未知の物体は白くてとても柔らかかった.

be soft on [***upon, about***] 《口》...に恋している ▪ They *were* mighty *soft upon* each other. 二人はお互いにぞっこんほれ合っていた ▪ She *is* rather *soft about* Jim. 彼女はジムにちょっとほれている.

get soft 柔弱になる ▪ The young people of this period are *getting soft*. 今の青年は柔弱化している.

go soft **1** 軟化する ▪ The national character has *gone soft*. 国民性が軟化してしまった.

S

2《口》気が変になる ▪ He's *gone soft.* 彼は気が変になってしまった.

have a soft spot [***place***] (***in*** *one's* ***heart***) ***for*** →SPOT[1].

have a soft thing on《口》朝めし前にやってのけられる, 造作ない ▪ If that's what you are after, you've *got a* pretty *soft thing on*! それが君の求めていることなら, そいつは朝めし前だよ.

soft in the head →HEAD[1].

soft sawder [***soap, corn***]《口》お世辞, おべんちゃら ▪ He's feeding me on *soft corn.* 彼は僕にお世辞ばかり使っている ▪ He knows how to use *soft soap.* 彼はおべんちゃらの使い方を知っている ▪ If she goes to cut ugly, I'll give her a dose of *soft sawder.* もしあの女が意地悪いふるまいに出るようなら, お世辞を一服もってやる.

softly /sɔ́:ftli|sɔ́ft-/ 副 ***Softly, softly catchee monkey.*** ゆっくりが肝心 (→a softly-softly APPROACH).

soil /sɔɪl/ 名 ***a son*** [***child***] ***of the soil*** 田舎の人; 耕作者 ▪ Don't be so anxious about *a* mere *child of the soil*! 一介の耕作者をそう心配なさるな.

on *one's* ***native soil*** 生まれた土地に ▪ I'm looking forward to standing once more *on my native soil.* 私はもう一度生まれた土地に立つことを待ちわびている.

solace[1] /sáləs|sɔ́l-/ 名 ***find solace in*** …に慰めを見いだす ▪ The invalid *found solace in* music. 病人は音楽に慰めを見いだした.

solace[2] /sáləs|sɔ́l-/ 動 ***solace*** *oneself* ***with*** …で自ら慰める ▪ I'm going home to *solace myself with* a pipe of tobacco. 私はパイプをふかして自らを慰めに家に帰るところだ.

soldier[1] /sóʊldʒər/ 名 ***come the old soldier*** **1** (人に)老練家ぶって指揮する; (人を)だます (*over*) ▪ You needn't try to *come the old soldier over* me. 君は僕をぺてんにかけようとしなくてもいいよ.

2 仮病を使う ▪ He *came the old soldier* to avoid doing work. 彼は仕事をさぼろうと仮病を使った.

3 貧しい旧軍人のふりをして金や酒をねだる ▪ Don't *come the old soldier* in my pub again. うちのパブでは二度と貧しい旧軍人のふりをして酒をねだらないでくれ.

go for a soldier 徴兵に応じる ▪ Bill's *going for a soldier.* ビルは徴兵に応じるつもりだ.

Old soldiers never die. 老兵は死なず. ☞第一次世界大戦中に無名の兵士の作った歌から.

play at soldiers 兵隊ごっこをする;《軽蔑》義勇兵になる ▪ The boys were *playing at soldiers* in the street. 男の子たちは通りで兵隊ごっこをしていた.

play the old soldier **1** 先輩風を吹かせる (*over*) ▪ I'm rather tired of his *playing the old soldier over* us at the Club. 彼がクラブで先輩風を吹かすのには少々うんざりだ.

2 仮病を使う ▪ He's just *playing the old soldier.* 彼はただ仮病を使っているだけだ.

soldier[2] /sóʊldʒər/ 動 ***go soldiering*** 軍人になる ▪ It does not do to *go soldiering* in these times. 当節は軍人になってもだめだ.

soldier it 軍人生活を送る ▪ I will *soldier it* with anybody, but I will not go to school. 私は誰とでも軍人生活は送るが, 学校へは行かないぞ.

sole /soʊl/ 名 ***from the soles of*** *one's* ***feet to the crown of*** *one's* ***head*** 足の先から頭のてっぺんまで ▪ I'm your loyal servant, *from the soles of my feet to the crown of my head.* 私は足の先から頭のてっぺんまであなたの忠実なるしもべです.

solicitous /səlísətəs/ 形 ***be solicitous about*** …を案じる, が心配だ ▪ I *am solicitous about* the future. 私は将来が案じられる.

be solicitous for …を念じる ▪ I *am solicitous for* her comfort. 彼女の安楽を念じている.

be solicitous of [***to*** *do*] …を[することを]熱望する ▪ You *are solicitous of* his goodwill. あなたは彼の好意を熱望していますね.

solid /sáləd|sɔ́l-/ 形 (***as***) ***solid*** [***firm, steady***] ***as a rock*** →(as) firm as a ROCK.

be solid for **1** …にこぞって賛成している ▪ We *are solid for* peace. 我々はこぞって平和に賛成している.

2《米》…に必ず投票する ▪ I *am solid for* Mr. Peck every time. 私は毎回必ずペック氏に投票する.

be solid with *a person*《米口》人に気に入られている ▪ He *is solid with* all these wealthy people. 彼はそういう金持ち連中みんなに気に入られている.

go solid for [***against***] …にこぞって賛成する[反対する] ▪ The fleet seems to have *gone* almost *solid against* him. 海軍はほとんどこぞって彼に反対したらしい.

make *oneself* ***solid with***《米口》…に気に入られる ▪ I advise you to *make yourself solid with* her. 君は彼女に気に入られるほうがいいよ.

solitude /sálətjù:d|sɔ́l-/ 名 ***in solitude*** 一人で, 孤独に ▪ He dwelt *in solitude.* 彼は一人で暮らしていた.

Solomon /sáləmən|sɔ́l-/ 名 (***as***) ***wise as Solomon*** 非常に賢い (《聖》*1 Kings* 3. 28) ▪ He was as brave as Hercules and *as wise as Solomon.* 彼は非常に勇敢だし非常に賢かった.

solution /səlú:ʃən/ 名 ***in solution*** 溶けて; (考えなどが)まとまらないで ▪ His ideas are *in solution.* 彼の考えはまとまらないでいる.

some /səm, sʌm/ 代形 ***and*** (***then***) ***some*** →AND.

(***at***) ***some time or other***/ (***at***) ***some or other time*** いつか ▪ He will be back *some time or other* tomorrow. 彼はあすのいつか戻ってくる.

be going some《米口》なかなかやっている, 相当なものだ ▪ You took an MA? That's *going some,* isn't it? 修士号を取ったって? なかなかやるじゃないか.

some certain ある ▪ *Some certain* point should finish the debate. ある点で討論は打ち切られるべきだ.

some considerable 相当の ▪ They were absent *some considerable* time. 彼らはかなりの時間席をはずしていた.

some few →FEW.

some little わずかの ▪ The bridge is *some little* distance from the main street. その橋は本通りからわずかばかり離れている.

some more もう少し多く ▪ Give me *some more* /səmɔ́ːr/. もう少しください.

some of these (***fine***) ***days*** 近いうちに ▪ He will be home *some of these fine days*. 彼は近いうちに帰って来るだろう.

some one **1** /sʌ́mwʌ́n/ 何か一つ(の), 誰か一人(の) ▪ You should follow at least *some one* path of scientific attainment. 諸君は少なくとも何か一つの科学の勉強をしなければならない ▪ *Some one* of them saw him. そのうちの誰か一人が彼を見かけた.
2 /sʌ́mwʌn/ ある人, 誰か ▪ Lead him to the guest-room, *some one*! この方を客間に案内しなさい, 誰か!

some ... or other [***another***] 何か, いつか ▪ I must go *some* day *or other*. 私はいつか行かねばならない ▪ The park is planted with trees of *some* kind *or another*. 公園には何かの木が植えてある.

some other 何か他の ▪ I wish I were *some other* country's man! 私がどこか他国人ならいいのに.

some ..., others あるものは..., またあるものは ▪ *Some* are born to command, and *others* to obey. 命令するように生まれつく者もいれば, 服従するように生まれつく者もいる.

some small わずかの ▪ *Some small* quantity of salt is needed. 塩が少量必要だ.

some ..., some ある者は..., またある者は ▪ *Some* ran; *some* did not run. 逃げた者も逃げない者もいた.

Win some, lose some. 勝つこともあれば, 負けることもある.

somebody /sʌ́mbədi/ 名 ***Somebody up there loves*** [***hates***] ***me.*** 《米口》私はついている[いない].

somehow /sʌ́mhàʊ/ 副 ***somehow or other*** [***another***] **1** 何とかして ▪ *Somehow or other* he contrived to finish the work. 何とかして彼はその仕事をやり遂げた.
2 どういうわけか ▪ But, *somehow or other* [*another*], the paper was missing. しかし, どうしたものかその書類が見当たらなかった.

somersault /sʌ́mərsɔ̀ːlt/ 名 ***turn a somersault*** とんぼ返りする ▪ All I remember is *turning a somersault* in the air. 私が覚えているのは空中をとんぼ返りしたことだけだ.

something /sʌ́mθɪŋ/ 名副 ***have a taste*** [***drop***] ***of something*** ちょっと1杯やる ▪ You must *have a drop of something*. ぜひちょっと1杯やれよ.

have (***got***) ***something going for*** *one* 《米俗》才能や美貌に恵まれている, 重要な所で顔がきく ▪ He will succeed all right, because he's *got something going for* him. 彼はきっと成功するさ, 才能があるからね.

have (***got***) ***something there*** 《口》それには一理がある ▪ His wife has made him what he is.—You *have got something there*. 今日の彼があるのは彼の妻のおかげなんだ——一理あるね.

have something about *one* →ABOUT.

have something on *a person* 《口》人の弱味を握っている ▪ His opponents *had something on* him. 彼の敵は彼の弱味を握っていた.

have something on the ball →have much on the BALL.

I will tell you something. →I('ll) TELL you what (it is).

It does something. それは何か[プラス]になる ▪ *It does something* for me. それは私にはプラスになる.

It's (***quite*** [***really***]) ***something.*** 《口》(全く)すばらしい, (全く)貴重である ▪ *It's quite something* being rich. (= Being rich *is quite something*.) 金があることは全くすばらしいことだ.

make something of ...をものにする; を活用する ▪ He hopes to *make something of* the young man. 彼はその若者をひとかどの者に仕上げようと思っている ▪ I *made something of* my relations with him. 私は彼との関係を活用した.

make something of *oneself* よい仕事を得る, 成功する ▪ I think it's our duty to *make something of ourselves* by being successful in business. 仕事でうまくやって成功するのが我々の義務と思う.

make something (***out***) ***of it*** 《口》〖主に疑問文・条件文で〗いちゃもんをつける ▪ (Do you) want to *make something out of it*? いちゃもんをつける気か.

or something ...か何か ▪ He is a lawyer *or something*. 彼は弁護士か何かだ ▪ He lost his train *or something*. 彼は列車に遅れたかどうかしたのだ.

or something of a similar type 《口》何かそのようなもの ▪ You can add pictures, texts *or something of a similar type* to your site. サイトには画像か文書などのたぐいを加えることができる.

see something of ...を少し見る ▪ I have *seen something of* Europe. 私はヨーロッパを少し見物した ▪ I hope to *see something of* you. 時にはお目にかかりたいですね.

something between *A* ***and*** *B* AとBとの中間 ▪ He is *something between* knave *and* fool. 彼は悪党とばかの中間といったところだ.

something damp [***short***] 《口》1杯の酒; 火酒 ▪ I want to take *something short*. 1杯やりたいな.

something doing 《口》おもしろい事 ▪ There's always *something doing* there. そこにはいつもおもしろい事がある.

something else **1** 何か他のもの ▪ He thought it was *something else*. 彼はそれは何か別物だと思った.
2 《俗》実にすばらしい人[もの] ▪ Mary is really *something else*. メアリーはほんとに美人だ.

something else again 別問題 ▪ I like John,

but whether or not I will lend him money is *something else again*. ジョンは好きだが，金を貸すかどうかは別問題だ．

something has (***got***) ***to give*** 緊張[圧力]が強くて耐えられない（ので妥協しなければならない） ▪ John hates Jill. Jill hates John. *Something has to give*. ジョンはジルを憎んでいる．ジルはジョンを憎んでいる．これじゃ緊張が強くてたまらない．

Something is better than nothing. 《諺》何かあるのは何もないよりまし，「枯れ木も山のにぎわい」．

Something is in the wind. 何かが起きそうだ ▪ There had been a lot of whispering going on—*something was in the wind*. それまであちこちでひそひそ話がなされていたので何か起こりそうだった．

something like **1** いくぶん…のような ▪ He is *something like* what his father was at that age. 彼はあのくらいの年ごろの父親にちょっと似ている．
2 およそ，ざっと ▪ It must be *something like* five o'clock. もうかれこれ5時にちがいない．
3《口》〚like に強勢を置いて〛たいした，すてきな ▪ This is *something like* a dinner. これはたいしたごちそうだ ▪ Now, that's *something like* /láɪk/! おや，そいつはすてきだ．
4 …のようなもの ▪ Isn't there *something like* a detective story? 推理小説のようなものはありませんか．
5〚副詞的に〛かなり，相当に ▪ I was *something like* blamed for this. 私はこのため相当とがめられた．

something nasty in the woodshed 薪小屋のいやらしいこと《人に強い永続的な印象を残すショッキングなこと》(S. Gibbons, *Cold Comfort Farm*, 1932) ▪ He has seen *something nasty in the woodshed*. 彼は薪小屋で何かいやらしいことを見たのだ．

something of a ちょっとした ▪ She is *something of a* beauty. 彼女はちょっとした美人だ．

something of the kind →KIND[2].

something or other 何か，何者か ▪ He was arrested on suspicion of being *something or other*. 彼は何者かであるという疑いで捕えられた．

something short →SOMETHING damp.

something tells me 《口》…という気がする ▪ *Something tells me* that Mary loves him. メアリーは彼を愛しているような気がする．

take something 何か飲む[食べる] ▪ She desired to *take something*. 彼女は1杯やりたいと言った．

there is something ... about *a person* 人にはどこか…なところがある ▪ *There is something* noble *about* him. 彼にはどことなく気高いところがある．

there is something in …には一理[とりえ]がある ▪ *There's something in* it. それには一理ある ▪ *There's something in* him. 彼にはとりえがある．

think something of *oneself* 自分をひとかどの人物だと考える ▪ Demmick *thinks something of himself*. デミックは自分をひとかどの人物だと考えている．

You don't get something for nothing. 《諺》ただではものは手に入らない．

You know something? あのね ▪ *You know something?*—Nope. あのね—何だ．

You've got something there. そりゃいい考えだ ▪ Why don't you take a shower?—*You've got something there*. シャワーをお浴びになったら—そりゃいい考えだ．

sometime /sʌ́mtàɪm/ 副 ***sometime or other*** いつかそのうち ▪ You may *sometime or other* come to Bath. 君もいつかそのうちバースへ来るかもね．

somewhat /sʌ́mhwʌ̀t|-wɔ̀t/ 副 ***more than somewhat*** 《口》非常に (very) ▪ He is *more than somewhat* kind. 彼は非常に親切だ．

somewhere /sʌ́mhwèər/ 副 ***Don't I know you from somewhere?*** どこかでお目にかかりましたかね《初対面の人との話の口切りに》．

get somewhere 何とかなりそうだ ▪ I think I'm *getting somewhere* with this. 何とかこれに目鼻がついてきたような気がする．

somewhere about **1** ほぼ…の頃に ▪ He is said to have been born *somewhere about* A.D. 40. 彼はほぼ西暦40年頃に生まれたと言われている．
2 およそ… ▪ He kept to his room *somewhere about* two months. 彼はおよそふた月も自分の部屋に閉じこもっていた．
3 …のあたりに ▪ He lives *somewhere about* Ely. 彼はイーリーあたりに住んでいる．

somewhere else どこかよそに ▪ We must look *somewhere else* for the cause. その原因はどこかよそに求めなければならない．

somewhere or another [***other***] どこかしらで ▪ I have heard it *somewhere or another*. それはどこかしらで聞いたことがある．

son /sʌn/ 名 ***a son of a bitch*** 《米俗》ちくしょう，野郎《ののしりの句》;《米口》やっかいなこと[もの] ▪ Make *the son of a bitch* gallop. 馬のやつにギャロップで走らせろ．

a son of a gun **1**《米口》ばか，ろくでなし ▪ You're really *a son of a gun*. お前って，ほんと，ばかだね．
2《米口》お前さん，こいつ《親しみをこめて》 ▪ The little *son of a gun* has won all his races. このチビがレースすべてに勝ったんだよ．
3《米口》やっかいなこと[もの] ▪ My computer's crashed and I don't know how to get the *son of a gun* working again. コンピューターが壊れちゃってさ，こいつをどうやって再起動させたらいいのか，わかんねえんだ．

a son of the soil →SOIL.

be one's father's [***mother's***] ***son*** 父親[母親]に似ている ▪ He *is his father's son*, he's always bragging. 彼は父親似でいつもほらを吹いてばかりいる．

every mother's son →EVERY.

one's [***the***] ***son and heir*** 跡取り息子 ▪ *His son and heir* has spent all. 彼の跡取り息子が全財産を使い果たしてしまった．

son of man **1** 人間 ▪ God rules angels and *sons of men*. 神は天使と人間を支配する．
2〚the を伴って大文字で〛キリスト ▪ They spoke of the days of *the Son of Man*. 一同はキリストのありし日のことを話した．

the prodigal son →a PRODIGAL son.

the Son of God **1** 神の子(キリスト) ▪ *The Son of God* created the world. 神の子が世を創り給うた.

2 天使 ▪ I came among *the Sons of God*. 私は天使とともにやって来た.

song /sɔːŋ|sɔŋ/ 名 ***for a song/for an old song*** 二束三文で, 捨て値で ▪ I bought it *for a song*. それを二束三文で買った ▪ The antique went *for a song*. その骨董品は二束三文で売られた. ☞古い楽譜帳は非常に安いことから.

go into a song [***the same song***] ***and dance*** 言い訳[口実]を繰り返す ▪ He is always *going into a song and dance*. 彼は言い訳を並べ立ててばかりいる.

go off song 歌うのをやめる ▪ Then she *went off song*. それから彼女は歌うのをやめた.

make a song (***and dance***) ***about*** 《英口》…のことで大騒ぎする ▪ No one *made a song about* it. 誰一人そのことで大騒ぎしなかった ▪ It was nothing to *make a song and dance about*. それはわいわい騒ぐほどのものではなかった.

No song, no supper. 《諺》働かざるもの食うべからず.

not worth an old song [***a song***] 無価値で ▪ The place is now *not worth an old song*. その場所は今では三文の値うちもない.

on song 《英口》絶好調で ▪ With the help of his teammates, he was back *on song*. チームメイトの助けがあって彼は絶好調で復帰した.

song and dance **1** 《米》歌と踊り ▪ The show is a *song and dance* about a telepathy gag. そのショーは読心術のギャグをめぐっての歌と踊りだ.

2 《米俗》言い逃れ ▪ He gave me the usual *song and dance*. 彼はいつもの言い逃れをしてみせた.

soon /suːn/ 副 ***anytime soon*** 《主に米》近いうちに; 〚否定語を伴って〛当分…ない ▪ Do you think he'll be back *anytime soon*? 彼, 近いうちに戻ってくると思う?

as soon (***as***) **1** …するとすぐ ▪ I will go *as soon as* he comes. 彼が来たらすぐ帰ります.

2 (…と)同じくらい早く ▪ We were at the gate *as soon* (*as* they). 我々は(彼らと)同じくらい早く門の所へ着いた.

as soon as look at *a person* すぐに, たちまち ▪ I'll box his ears *as soon as look at* him. 彼の横っ面をすぐさま張ってやる. ☞主文は通例未来指向的.

as soon as not むしろ喜んで ▪ I'll go there *as soon as not*. むしろ喜んでそこへ行きましょう.

as soon as possible/as soon as may be/as soon as *one* ***can*** できるだけ早く ▪ Come back *as soon as possible*. なるべく早く戻りなさい.

at (***the***) ***soonest*** いくら早くても ▪ It will take three days *at the soonest*. 早くても３日はかかる.

had [***would***] (***just***) ***as soon*** *do* (***as*** *do*) (どちらかと言えば)…のほうがいい[を好む], (…するよりも)むしろ…したい ▪ I *would* [*had*] *as soon* die (*as* surrender). (降伏するくらいなら)死んだほうがましだ ▪ I'd *just as soon* read a novel (*as* watch the TV). 僕は(テレビを見るよりも)小説を読むほうがいい.

no sooner ... than …するやいなや ▪ *No sooner* said *than* done. 言うが早いかやってのけた ▪ She had *no sooner* made an end of her speech, *than* withdrew. 彼女は話を終えたかと思うとすぐ引き下がった.

over soon →too SOON.

so soon as **1** 〚否定語のあとで〛…ほど早く ▪ He did not arrive *so soon as* I expected. 彼は予期していたほど早く着かなかった.

2 …するとすぐ《因果関係が暗示される場合》 ▪ *So soon as* there is any talk of paying, he cools down. 金を支払う話が出ると彼はすぐ冷静になる.

soon after **1** その後まもなく ▪ He married her, and *soon after* she was taken ill. 彼は彼女と結婚したがその後まもなく彼女が病気になった.

2 …の後まもなく ▪ *Soon after* he returned [his return] to his native country, he married her. 彼は故国へ帰るとまもなく彼女と結婚した.

soon as 《詩》…するやいなや ▪ She knew it, *soon as* she heard the name. 彼女はその名前を聞いたとたんそれがわかった.

Soon got(***ten***)***, soon gone*** [***spent***]***.*** 《諺》悪銭身につかず.

sooner or later 遅かれ早かれ, 早晩, いつかは ▪ The dying man is one whom, *sooner or later*, we shall certainly resemble. 死にかけている人とは我々も早晩必ず似てくる人のことだ ▪ We must all die *sooner or later*. みんないつかは死なねばならない.

sooner rather than later いますぐに ▪ Solve the problem *sooner rather than later*. 今すぐにその問題を解決してくれ.

Sooner you [***him, her, them***] ***than me.*** 《口》僕でなくてよかったよ ▪ The boss wants to see me.—Well, *sooner you than me*. 社長が僕に会いたいと言っている—やれやれ, 僕でなくてよかった.

The less said, the sooner mended. 《諺》口数が少なければ少ないほど災いは少ない.

The sooner the better. 早ければ早いほどいい.

too [***over***] ***soon*** あまりにも早く ▪ The boy died *over soon*. その男の子はあまりにも早く亡くなった.

would (***just***) ***as soon*** *do* (***as*** *do*) → had (just) as SOON do (as do).

would sooner *do* ***... than*** *do* … するよりもむしろ…したい ▪ I *would sooner* starve *than* betray him. あの人を裏切るよりむしろ飢え死にしたほうがよい.

soot /sʊt/ 名 (***as***) ***easy as juggling with soot*** 《皮肉》ほとんど不可能な, とても難しい ▪ Trying to enter the theater free will be *as easy as juggling with soot*. ただで劇場に入ろうなんてとても無理だよ.

sop /sɑp|sɔp/ 名 ***a sop in the pan*** **1** 焼き肉汁に浸したパンきれ; 一口のうまいもの ▪ This he considered as *a mere sop in the pan*. これは一口のうまいものにすぎないと彼は考えた.

S

2 贈りもの，賄賂 ▪ Take a bouquet home as *a sop in the pan* to mother. 花束をおかあさんへの贈りものとして持ち帰りなさい.

soppy /sάpi|sɔ́pi/ 形 ***be soppy on*** *a person* 《口》人にほれている ▪ I'*m soppy on* that girl. あの娘に僕はほれているんだ.

sore /sɔːr/ 形名 ***a sore place*** [***point, spot***] 痛い所，人の感情を害する点 ▪ I'm afraid I touched you on *a sore place*. あなたの痛い所に触れたのではないでしょうか.

be sore about …に苦しむ[悩む，傷つく] ▪ She *is* still *sore about* her boyfriend going out with her best girlfriend. 彼女は彼氏が彼女の親友とデートしていることに苦しんでいる.

be sore on [***over***] 《米俗》…に腹を立てている ▪ All hands *were sore on* him, but he couldn't take a hint. 従業員はみんな彼に腹を立てていたが彼にはそれが察せられなかった.

feel sore (***on***) (…を)気にしている ▪ He *feels sore on* the subject. 彼はその問題を気にしている.

get sore on [***over***] 《米俗》…に腹を立てる ▪ He *got sore over* the remark. 彼はその言葉で立腹した.

like [***as***] ***a bear with a sore head*** → BEAR[1].

reopen old sores 古傷をあばく ▪ Let's not *reopen old sores*. 古傷をあばくのはよそうよ.

sorely /sɔ́ːrli/ 副 ***sorely tempted to*** *do* いたく[非常に]…したい ▪ I was *sorely tempted to* go and see him. 私は大いに彼に会いに行きたかった. ☞行為はなされないという含みがある.

sorrow /sɔ́ːroʊ|sɔ́rəʊ/ 名 ***drown*** *one's* ***sorrows*** 《口》酒を飲んで悲しみを紛らす ▪ When I failed my examinations, I *drowned my sorrows*. 試験に落ちたとき酒を飲んで悲しさを紛らした.

more in sorrow than in anger 怒るよりも悲しんで (cf. Sh., *Haml*. 1. 2. 232) ▪ He looked at Tredwell *more in sorrow than in anger*. 彼は怒るよりも悲しんでトレッドウェルを見た.

sorry /sάri, sɔ́ːri|sɔ́ri/ 形 ***be*** [***feel***] ***sorry for*** …が気の毒[残念]である; をすまなく思う，後悔する ▪ I *am sorry for* you. お気の毒に存じます ▪ I'*m* really *sorry for* my bad behavior. あんな無礼なことをしてほんとにすみません.

(***I'm***) ***sorry to say*** 残念ながら ▪ *Sorry to say*, he was not pleased with the picture. 残念ながら彼はその絵が気に入らなかった.

sorry for *oneself* ふさぎこんで，しょげている ▪ You seem somewhat *sorry for yourself* today. きょうは少し元気がないようだね.

sort[1] /sɔːrt/ 名 ***a good*** [***bad***] ***sort*** 《口》いい[悪い]やつ ▪ Dick is *a good sort*. ディックはいいやつだ.

(***a***) ***sort of/sort o'/sort a/***《俗》***sorter*** 《口》 〚副詞的に〛多少，いくらか ▪ It's *a sort of* cold. ちょっと寒い ▪ This seemed to *sort of* lighten the boat. これでボートがいくらか軽くなったように思われた ▪ I am *sort o'* proud of him. 私は彼をちょっと自慢にしているんだ.

a sort of (***a***) (不十分ながら)一種の，…のようなもの ▪ He wore *a sort of* gaiters. 彼はゲートルのようなものを巻いていた ▪ He is but *a sort of a* gentleman. 彼はまあ紳士みたいなものだ.

after a sort まあどうやら，いくらか ▪ He loves his wife *after a sort*. 彼はいくらか妻を愛している.

after … sort …の仕方で ▪ They explained all things *after* this *sort*. 彼らはすべてのものをこんなふうに説明した ▪ She received him *after* a most friendly *sort*. 彼女はいかにも親しげに彼を迎えた.

all sorts and conditions of men あらゆる種類階級の人々 (Prayer-book, "*Prayers*") ▪ My way of life has made me acquainted with *all sorts and conditions of men*. 私の生活様式のおかげで私はあらゆる種類階級の人々と知り合いになった.

all sorts of あらゆる種類の，種々さまざまの ▪ *All sorts of* things are sold in this street. この通りではあらゆる種類の品物が売られている.

all that sort of thing そのようなもの ▪ I don't like *all that sort of thing*. 私はそんなものはきらいだ.

and all sorts 《口》その他何やかや ▪ I hope to hear about papa's visit to London, *and all sorts*. パパがロンドンへ行った話とか何かを聞きたいな.

in a sort いくらか，ある意味では ▪ I am *in a sort* sorry for him. 私は彼がいくらか気の毒だ ▪ In law the judge is *in a sort* superior to his king. 法においては裁判官はある意味では王より偉いとも言える.

in a sort of way 不完全に，不正確に ▪ He knows it *in a sort of way*. 彼はそれを完全に知っているわけではない ▪ I advised you to go back.—Yes, *in a sort of way*. 君に帰るように勧めたはずだよ—ええ，はっきりとじゃなしにね.

in some sort ある程度，いくらか ▪ She was *in some sort* related to the Abbot. 彼女はその修道院長とある程度縁続きだった.

It takes all sorts to make a world. 《諺》世の中には時には変人もいる.

no sort of なんらの…もない ▪ There is *no sort of* harmony between them. 彼らの間にはなんの調和もない.

nothing of the sort →NOTHING of the kind.

of a sort **1** 同種類の… ▪ They were men all *of a sort*. 彼らは誰も似たり寄ったりの人たちだった.

2 《口》まあ…と言える，へぼ… ▪ He could speak English *of a sort*. 彼はへたな英語が話せた.

of sorts 《口》いいかげんな，へぼ… ▪ Up to this time you have been an orator *of sorts*. 今までは君はへぼ弁士だった.

out of sorts **1** 気分がすぐれずに，いつもの元気がなく ▪ I am weary and *out of sorts* tonight. 今晩は疲れていつもの元気が出ない.

2 (物が)不ぞろいで，乱れて ▪ Something is *out of sorts* in the display. 陳列のどこかが乱れている.

3 品切れで ▪ Sometimes they may be *out of sorts*. それらはときどき品切れになる場合がある.

something of the sort 何かそのようなもの[こと]

▪ *Something of the sort* must be done. 何かそのようなことをしなければならない.

sort of [***o', a***] →(a) SORT of.

that [***this***] ***sort of thing*** その[この]ようなもの ▪ She likes pendants, and *that sort of thing*. 彼女はペンダントだとかそのたぐいのものが好きだ.

That's your sort. 《俗》その調子, そこだよ《ほめて言う言葉》 ▪ Pitch it into him, *that's your sort.* やつにうんと攻撃してやりな, その調子.

these [***those***] ***sort of*** こう[そう]いう種類の ▪ *These sort of* girls are saucy. こういうたぐいの女の子は生意気だ.

what sort of (***a***) どんな種類の ▪ *What sort of* tree is it? それはどんな種類の木ですか ▪ *What sort of a* workman is he? 彼はどういうふうな労働者なのか. ☞a をつけるのは口語体.

sort[2] /sɔːrt/ 動 ***sort*** *oneself* [*itself*] ***out*** 正常な状態になる, 落ち着く ▪ Things will *sort themselves out* in the end. 事態はおしまいには正常な状態になりますよ ▪ You can sleep here till you get *yourself sorted out*. 落ち着くまでここで寝ていなさい.

sort well [***ill***] ***with*** …に調和する[しない], ふさわしい[しくない] ▪ His action *sorts ill with* his professions. 彼の行動はその言うところと一致しない.

soul /soʊl/ 名 ***a lost soul*** 道に迷った[途方に暮れた, 日常生活に対処できない]人 ▪ He had been like *a lost soul* since his wife died. 妻を亡くして以来, 彼は腑抜けた様子であった.

at (*one's*) ***soul*** 心底では ▪ I am glad *at soul* that I have no other child. 私は他に子供がいないのを心底では喜んでいる.

bare *one's* ***soul*** ＝bare one's HEART.

be a good soul and *do* お願いだから…しておくれ ▪ *Be a good soul and* say nothing about it. お願いだからそのことは何も言わないでくれ.

be good for the soul 《戯》人にとってよい, 人のためになる ▪ Walking *is good for the soul*. ウォーキングはためになるよ.

be the soul of …の典型[権化]である ▪ Her grandmother *was the soul of* propriety. 彼女のおばあさんは礼儀正しい人の典型だった.

be the soul of discretion 非常に口が堅い, 秘密を厳守する ▪ He's *the soul of discretion* and he won't mention this to anyone. 彼は非常に口が堅いので, このことは誰にも言わないだろう.

by my soul →upon my SOUL.

cannot call *one's* ***soul*** *one's* ***own*** すっかり人に左右されている ▪ From that moment he *could not call his soul his own*. その瞬間から彼は完全に人に左右されることとなった.

Don't tell a soul. 誰にも言わないで ▪ Is your sister getting married?—Yes, but *don't tell a soul.* It's a secret. 君の姉さん, 結婚するんだって?—うん, でも, 誰にも言わないで. 内緒なんだ.

for the soul of me 〚否定文で〛どうしても ▪ I cannot *for the soul of me* conceive where he got that notion from. 彼がどこからあんな考えを仕入れたかどうしても考えつかない.

from *one's* ***soul*** 心から ▪ I do repent it *from my* very *soul*. 心の真底からそのことを悔いています.

have a soul above 《口》…よりもよい趣味を持っている, を潔しとしない ▪ Thank goodness I*'ve a soul above* that sort of art. ありがたいことに私はそんな種類の芸術よりもよい趣味を持っている.

have a soul for 《口》…に理解がある ▪ He *has a soul for* music. 彼は音楽には理解がある.

have no soul **1** 非情[冷酷]だ ▪ That man *has no soul*. あの男は非情な人間だ.
2《口》(芸術家・作品などが)センス[迫力]がない ▪ The tailor in the attic *has no soul* in him. 屋根裏べやの仕立て屋はセンスがない.

keep body and soul together →BODY.

not a (***living***) ***soul*** 人っ子一人…でない ▪ *Not a soul* was to be seen on the platform. ホームには人っ子一人見えなかった.

Poor soul! かわいそうに ▪ He knows nothing about it, *poor soul!* かわいそうにあの男はそのことは少しも知らないのだ.

possess *one's* ***soul in patience*** →POSSESS.

save *one's* [*a person's*] ***soul*** 自分[人]の魂を救済する ▪ How can I *save my soul*? いかにしてわが魂を救済することができるか.

sell *one's* ***soul*** →SELL[2].

the life and soul of …の中心人物 ▪ He was *the life and soul of* the party. 彼はそのパーティーの中心人物だった.

upon [***on, by***] ***my soul*** 誓って, 確かに ▪ *Upon my soul*, it's a wicked lie. 確かにたちの悪い嘘だ.

with all *one's* ***soul*** 真剣に, 心から ▪ I deplore his loss *with all my soul*. 心から彼の死をいたむ.

sound[1] /saʊnd/ 名 ***a sound bite*** (政治家が)繰り返し引用する発言 ▪ President Lincoln's statement "government of the people, by the people, for the people" is *a* famous *sound bite*. リンカン大統領の「人民の, 人民による, 人民のための政治」という発言は有名でしばしば引用されるものだ.

be wired (***for sound***) 密かに会話録音用の機械を身につけている ▪ He offered the policeman, who *was wired for sound*, an ounce of cocaine. 彼は録音機を装着した警官にコカイン1オンスを差し出した.

in [***within***] ***the sound of*** …の聞こえる所に ▪ I was *in the sound of* the sea. 私は海の音の聞こえる所にいた ▪ A Cockney is one born *within the sound of* Bow bells. ロンドンっ子とはボウ教会の鐘の音(ね)が聞こえる所に生まれた者のことだ.

like [***love***] ***the sound of*** *one's* ***own voice*** 《軽蔑》自分ばかりしゃべりたがる ▪ She *likes the sound of her own voice*. 彼女は自分ばかりしゃべりたがる人だ.

out of sound 聞こえない所に ▪ The lad was out of sight and *out of sound*. 少年は姿も見えず声も聞こえない所にいた.

sound and fury 騒々しいおしゃべり (cf. Sh., *Macb*. 5. 5. 27) ▪ Life may be something more

S

than *sound and fury*. 人生は騒々しいおしゃべり以上のものかもしれない.

sound[2] /saʊnd/ 形副 ***A sound mind in a sound body.*** 《諺》健全な身体に健全な精神(が宿らんことを)《教育の理想》 ▪ It is great happiness to have *a sound mind in a sound body.* 健全な身体に健全な精神が宿るのは実に幸せだ. ☞Juvenal, *Satires* 10. 356の Mens sana in corpore sano のなぞり.

(as) sound as a bell すこぶる健康で ▪ He remained *as sound as bell.* 彼は相変わらずすこぶる健康だった.

(as) sound as a dollar 《米》至極元気で; 非常に信頼がおける ▪ The physician said, "You're *as sound as a dollar.*" 医者は「あなたは至極お元気です」と言った ▪ This vaccum cleaner is *as sound as a dollar.* この掃除機は安心して使える.

(as) sound as a top →TOP[2].

be sound asleep →sleep SOUND.

be sound on …について意見がしっかりしている ▪ *Is* he *sound on* free trade? 彼は自由貿易について意見がしっかりしているか.

sleep sound ぐっすり眠る ▪ I *slept sound* last night. ゆうべはぐっすり眠った.

sound in wind and limb 《口》すこぶる健康で ▪ I am an old man, but, thank God, I am *sound in wind and limb.* 私は老人だが, ありがたいことにすこぶる健康です. ☞もと馬について言った.

sound[3] /saʊnd/ 動 ***sound like*** …のように聞こえる[思われる] ▪ The statement *sounds like* fiction. その陳述は作りもののように聞こえる ▪ (It) *sounds like* fun. (そいつは)おもしろそうだ.

(That) sounds great. それはすばらしい; 大いに結構だ ▪ How about going on a picnic?—(*That*) *sounds great.* ピクニックに行ってはどうだろう—大いに結構だね.

soup /suːp/ 名 ***from soup to nuts*** 《米俗》何から何まで ▪ Today's drugstores have everything *from soup to nuts.* 現今のドラッグストアには何から何まで一切そろっている. ☞スープに始まりナッツに終わる食事から.

in the soup 《口》苦境に陥って ▪ His failure left many persons *in the soup.* 彼の失敗が多くの人を苦境に陥れた.

soup and fish 《米口》(男子の)正装 ▪ Everyone who attended the party wore *soup and fish.* そのパーティーに出席した人はみな正装をしていた. ☞正式の dinner で出る料理から.

sour /saʊər/ 形名副 ***(as) sour as vinegar [a crab]*** ひどく酸っぱい; ひどく気むずかしい, ひどく意地悪な ▪ Her look was *as sour as a crab.* 彼女の目つきはひどく不きげんなものだった. ☞crab = crab apple《酸味の強い小粒のリンゴ》.

be sour on …に敵対している, をきらっている ▪ Unions *are sour on* the new merger. 組合は今度の合併をきらっている.

get [go, turn] sour だめになる ▪ The project *went sour.* その計画はだめになった.

look sour 渋い顔をする ▪ Mother *looked sour* on me. 母は私に渋い顔をした.

take the sweet with the sour 人生をのんきにかまえる ▪ He *takes* the good with the bad, *the sweet with the sour.* 彼は苦楽を平然と受けいれ, 人生をのんきにかまえている.

south /saʊθ/ 副名 ***by south*** 微南 ▪ The town lies east *by south* off us. その町はここから東微南にある.

down south **1** 南部へ[に] ▪ He is coming *down south* next week. 彼は来週は南部へやって来る.
2《米口》南部(諸州)へ ▪ I'm taking her *down South.* 彼女を南部へ連れて行くつもりです.

go south **1** 南に行く ▪ The swallows *go south* in winter. ツバメは冬に南へ行く.
2《米口》(状況などが)悪化[低下]する; (組織が)うまくいかない; (株が)暴落する ▪ Stock prices have *gone south.* 株価が暴落した.

in the south of …の南部に ▪ He lives *in the south of* England. 彼はイングランド南部に住んでいる.

on the south of …の南境に ▪ The city lies *on the south of* the mountain. その町は山の南にある.

south by east [west] 南微東[西]に ▪ We were steering *south by west.* 南微西に航行していた.

south of …の南に ▪ It lies thirty miles *south of* Victoria Station. そこはビクトリア駅から南へ30マイルの所にある.

to the south of …の南方に ▪ Mexico is *to the south of* the U.S.A. メキシコは米国の南方にある.

sow /saʊ/ 名 ***get [have, take] the wrong [right] sow by the ear*** おかど違いの[でない]…をつかまえる; 誤った[正しい]見解を持つ, 誤った[正しい]結論を下す ▪ When he first meddled with her, he *had the wrong sow by the ear.* 彼が最初にあの女性におせっかいをしたとき彼はおかど違いの人をつかまえたわけだった ▪ I believe you have *got the right sow by the ear.* 君は正しい見解を持っていると信じる.

You cannot make a silk purse out of a sow's ear. →PURSE.

space[1] /speɪs/ 名 ***a space cadet*** 《戯》変人, いかれたやつ ▪ He's *a* real *space cadet.* 彼って, ほんと, いかれてるよ.

(for) a space しばらくの間 ▪ Let us rest (*for*) *a space.* ちょっと休憩しよう.

in space 宇宙には ▪ Nothing is motionless *in space.* 宇宙には動かないものはない.

in the space of …の間に ▪ It revolves *in the space of* ten days. それは10日間で回転する.

invade one's space 人のプライバシーを侵す ▪ My family is large and *my space* is always *being invaded* by someone. うちは大家族なので私のプライバシーはいつも誰かに侵されている.

look [gaze, stare] into space 空を見つめる ▪ He just sat there *looking into space.* 彼は空を見つめてそこに座っているだけだった.

Watch this space. (新聞・雑誌などで)乞う, ご期

待.

space[2] /speɪs/ 動 ***be spaced out*** 《俗》(麻薬などで)ぼうっとしている ▪ He *was spaced out* and talking nonsense. 彼はぼうっとしていて, たわごとをしゃべっていた.

spade /speɪd/ 名 ***call a spade a spade*** ありのままに[あからさまに]言う (Plutarch, *Apophthegmata* 178B) ▪ I cannot say the crow is white, but must needs *call a spade a spade*. 私は黒を白と言うことはできない. どうしてもありのままに言わざるをえない.

in spades 《口》 **1** 断然, 確かに ▪ He is a bum *in spades*. 彼は断然飲んだくれだ ▪ You've got trouble—*in spades*. 君は困難に陥っている—確かに. **2** あからさまに, 率直に ▪ I am going to tell him off—*in spades*. 彼を叱りつけてやるんだ—率直にな. **3** 《主に米》極端に ▪ He has confidence for his job *in spades*. 彼は自分の仕事にすごく自信を持っている. ☞ブリッジなどではスペードが最高の組札であるところから.

spanner /spǽnər/ 名 ***throw*** [***put***] ***a spanner into the works*** 《英》計画をぶちこわす ▪ I'll *throw a spanner into the works* by refusing money. 金を出すのを断ってその計画をぶちこわしてやる. ☞《米》は throw a monkey wrench in the works.

spare[1] /speər/ 名 ***make no spare*** つましくしない ▪ He spent and *made no spare*. 彼は金を使いつましくしなかった.

make spare つましくする ▪ It is desirable to *make spare*. つましくすることは望ましい.

spare[2] /speər/ 形 ***a spare tire*** [***tyre***] → TIRE[1].

go spare 《口》怒る, 激高する ▪ My boss *went spare* when I forgot to hand in the necessary papers. 必要書類を提出し忘れたら上司は激高した.

spare[3] /speər/ 動 ***and to spare*** あり余るほどの ▪ He has money *and to spare*. 彼にはあり余るほど金がある.

enough and to spare あり余るほどの (《聖》*Luke* 5. 17) ▪ You have *enough* (money) *and to spare*. 君はあり余るほど(金を)持っている.

if I am spared もし命(いのち)があれば ▪ *If I am spared*, I will accomplish my purpose at any cost. もし命があれば私はぜひとも目的を達成したい.

***spare** oneself* 労を惜しむ, 楽をする ▪ He doesn't *spare himself*. 彼は労を惜しまない.

spare** one's **feelings …を怒らせないようにする ▪ I didn't tell him the fact because I wanted to *spare his feelings*. 彼を怒らせないようにしようと思って事実を告げなかった.

spare no pains [***expense***] 労[金]を惜しまない ▪ He *spared no expense* in educating his son. 彼は息子の教育に金を惜しまなかった ▪ He *spares no pains* to do it. 彼は労を惜しまずそれをする.

to spare 余分の ▪ I paid my bill and still had money *to spare*. 勘定を払ったがまだ余剰金があった.

sparing /spéərɪŋ/ 形 ***sparing in*** [***of***] …が控え目で; を惜しんで ▪ The ancient Romans were very *sparing in* the use of wine. 古代ローマ人は飲酒が非常に控え目であった ▪ He is *sparing of* his time. 彼は時間を惜しむ.

spark[1] /spɑːrk/ 名 ***a bright spark*** 《口》明るい人; 《皮肉》ばか ▪ What *bright spark* left the door open? どこのあほうがドアを開けっ放しにしたのか.

a spark in** one's **throat 《俗》のどのかわき ▪ Give me a Coke. I have *a spark in my throat*. コークをくれ. のどがからからだ.

as the sparks fly upward (火の粉が上へ飛ぶように)確かに, まちがいなく (《聖》*Job* 5. 7) ▪ Poor Miss Tonks is born to misfortune *as the sparks fly upward*. かわいそうにトンクス嬢はまちがいなく不幸に生まれついている.

make the sparks fly **1** 著しく活動的である ▪ He worked so hard that he fairly *made the sparks fly*. 彼はまさに火花を散らすほどとても一生懸命に働いた. **2** 議論の火花を散らせる ▪ We are determined to *make the sparks fly* at the next meeting. 我々は次の会合では議論の火花を散らせるつもりだ.

not a spark of みじんの…もない ▪ He has*n't a spark of* generosity in him. 彼はみじんの寛大さも持ち合わせていない.

***strike a spark out of** a person* 人の才気などを発揮させる ▪ His words *struck a spark out of* her. 彼の言葉が彼女の才気を発揮させることとなった.

strike sparks (火打ち石などで)火を切る ▪ I *struck sparks* out of [from] a flint. 私は火打ち石で火を切った.

strike sparks off each other [***one another***] …と互いに切磋琢磨する[火花を散らす] ▪ Tom and Richard are *striking sparks off each other*. トムとリチャードは互いに火花を散らしている.

the spark plug 《米口》中心人物 ▪ He's *the spark plug* in the circle. 彼はサークルの中心人物だ.

(***the***) ***sparks fly*** 議論[口論]の火花が散る ▪ *Sparks* will *fly* before we decide on the plan. その計画に決定する前に議論の火花が散ることだろう.

spark[2] /spɑːrk/ 動 ***spark it*** 《米》求婚する ▪ He *sparked it* with full twenty girls. 彼はたっぷり20人もの娘に求婚した.

sparking /spɑ́ːrkɪŋ/ 名 ***go a-sparking*** 《米口》(女性を)くどきに行く ▪ He *went a-sparking* among the rosy country girls. 彼はバラ色のほおをした田舎娘たちをくどきに行った.

sparkle /spɑ́ːrkəl/ 名 ***not a sparkle of*** 《口》みじんの…もない ▪ He has*n't a sparkle of* honesty in him. 彼には正直さがみじんもない.

spasm /spǽzəm/ 名 ***work in spasms*** 勤務が不規則である ▪ He *works in spasms* and his salary is low. 彼は勤務が不規則なので給料が安い.

spate /speɪt/ 名 ***a spate of*** 《英》洪水のようにたくさんの ▪ *A spate of* words poured out from the speaker's lips. 言葉が洪水のように弁士の口からあふれ出た ▪ I have *a spate of* work. 仕事が山ほどある.

in full spate ＝in full FLOOD.
in spate (河川が)はんらんして ▪ Yesterday the water was *in spate.* きのう水がはんらんしていた.

speak /spiːk/ 動 ***as they [men, we] speak*** いわゆる ▪ Many of them became petrified, *as they speak.* 彼らの多くはいわゆる茫然自失の体だった.
be spoken for **1** 婚約済みである; 要求されている ▪ She's already *spoken for.* 彼女は婚約済みだ. **2** (金などが)取っておかれている ▪ Half of my savings *are spoken for.* 私の蓄えの半分は取ってある.
(even) as we speak 《陳腐》今こうして話している間にも, たった今, まさにこの瞬間に ▪ The plane is taking off *as we speak,* I'm sorry. 申し訳ございませんが飛行機はただ今離陸中です.
generally [broadly, correctly, properly, roughly, strictly, etc.] ***speaking*** 概して[大ざっぱに, 正確に, 正しく, ざっと, 厳密に, など]言えば ▪ *Generally speaking,* girls are gentler than boys. 概して言えば女の子は男の子よりもおとなしい.
no ... to speak of これと言うほどのものではない ▪ There is *nothing* strange *to speak of.* これと言うほどの不思議なものは何もない.
not to speak of ...は言うまでもなく ▪ He can dance, *not to speak of* singing. 彼は歌はもちろんダンスもできる ▪ I cannot afford to buy a silver watch, *not to speak of* a gold one. 私は銀時計が買えない, 金時計はなおさらだ.
not (...) to speak to 口をきくほど(...)ではない ▪ I do*n't* know him *to speak to.* 彼とは口をきくほどの知り合いではない.
so to speak →SO to say.
speak as *one* ***finds*** 自分で見た通りに判断する ▪ A lot of people don't like Smith, but I *speak as* I *find.* スミスを好かない人は多いが, 私は自分で見たままに判断する.
speak *a person* ***fair*** →FAIR.
speak favorably of ...をよく言う, 好評する ▪ He has *spoken favorably of* my new work. 彼は私の新作を好評してくれた.
speak for *oneself* **1** 自分のために弁じる ▪ Take courage and *speak for yourself.* 勇気を出して自分のために弁じるがいい. **2** 自分の思うことを言う ▪ *Speaking for myself,* I feel that you were in the wrong. 僕の思うところを言えば, 君はまちがっていたような気がするよ.
speak for itself おのずから明らかだ ▪ The fact *speaks for itself.* 事実はおのずから明らかだ.
Speak for yourself! 《口》人の意見まで代弁するな; こっちの意見は違う.
speak ill [evil] of ...のことを悪く言う, をそしる (↔ speak WELL of) ▪ Never *speak ill of* men behind their backs. 陰で他人の悪口を決して言うな.
Speak now, or forever hold your peace. 今こそ口を開いて主張[抗議]すべき時だ (*Book of Common Prayer*).
speak of wisdom 賢明に思われる ▪ His advice *speaks of wisdom.* 彼の忠告は賢明に思われる.
speak small 小声で話す ▪ She *speaks small* like a woman. 彼女は女性らしく小声で話す.
speak to *oneself* ひとりごとを言う ▪ A madman will *speak to himself.* 狂人はひとりごとを言うものだ. ☞TALK to oneself のほうが普通.
speak too soon 早合点する ▪ I've *spoken too soon* about moving to London. ロンドンへの引越しについては早合点だった.
speak well [much] for ...のよいことの証明になる; のためによい ▪ Your health *speaks well for* your mode of life. 君の健康なのは君の生活様式がいい証拠だ ▪ It *speaks well for* him that he did not accept. 彼が承諾しなかったのは彼のためにはよい.
speak well of →speak WELL of.
speak without (*one's*) ***book*** 覚えで話す ▪ When I say we've made £500 on the deal, I *speak without my book.* その取引で500ポンド儲けたと言うのは覚えで話しているのです.
speaking of ...のことを言えば ▪ *Speaking of* movies, have you seen "The Road"? 映画と言えば,「ザ・ロード」を見ましたか.
speaking (quite) candidly 包み隠さず[ざっくばらんに]言えば ▪ *Speaking candidly,* I find your behavior a bit offensive. ざっくばらんに言えば, 君のふるまいにはいささか頭にくるところがあるんだ.
to speak of 〚主に否定文で〛これというほどの ▪ I have no baggage *to speak of.* これというほどの手荷物はない ▪ It is nothing *to speak of.* それはたいしたものではない.
Who's speaking, please? どなたですか《電話で》 ▪ *Who's speaking, please?*—It's me. どなたでしょうか—私ですよ.

speaking /spíːkɪŋ/ 名形 ***a speaking acquaintance*** 会えば言葉を交わすくらいの交際; 《戯》話せるくらいの知識 ▪ My acquaintance with Italian never became *a speaking acquaintance.* 私のイタリア語の知識はついに話せるほどの知識にならなかった.
at the [this] present speaking 《米》目下のところ ▪ *At the present speaking* the days are not picnic days. ただ今のところ毎日がピクニックデーとはいきません.
on speaking terms with 〚主に否定文で〛...と会えば言葉を交わすほどの間柄で ▪ He was no longer *on speaking terms with* Stephen. 彼はもうスティーブンと会っても言葉を交わす仲ではなかった.
within speaking distance of ...と話ができるほどの距離に ▪ He came *within speaking distance of* the enemy. 彼は敵と話ができるほどの距離にやって来た.

spear /spɪər/ 名 ***at spear point*** 強制的に ▪ The natives were made, *at spear point,* to work all day. 先住民らは強制的に一日中働かされた.
on the spear side 父方の, 男系の (↔on the SPINDLE side) ▪ He got those qualities from a grandfather *on the spear side.* 彼はそういう性質を父方の祖父から受け継いでいた.

spec /spek/ 名 ***on spec*** 《英口》やまかんで

▪ They have taken up the case *on spec.* 彼らはやまかんでその事件を取りあげたのだ. ☞spec = speculation.

turn out a good spec よい儲けになる ▪ The shares *turned out a good spec.* その株はよい儲けになった.

speciality /spèʃiǽləti/ 名 ***in speciality*** 特別に ▪ He took them as clients *in speciality.* 彼は特別に彼らを依頼客として受けいれた.

make a speciality of …を専門とする, 得意とする ▪ He *made a speciality of* the Japanese stage. 彼は日本の演劇を専門とした.

specie /spíːʃi/ 名 ***in specie*** 正金[硬貨]で; 同種のもので, 同じように ▪ All play-debts must be paid *in specie.* ばくちの借りはすべて正金で払わなければならない ▪ He repaid the offense *in specie.* 彼は無礼には無礼で仕返した.

species /spíːʃiːz/ 名 ***a species of*** 一種の…, …のようなもの ▪ Their gratitude is *a species of* revenge. 彼らの感謝は復しゅうのようなものだ.

spectacle /spéktəkəl/ 名 ***make a spectacle of*** *oneself* 人に笑われるようなまねをする ▪ The fishmonger *made a spectacle of himself* by that. 魚屋はそのために人の笑いものになった.

***see* [*behold, look at*]*... through rose colored* [*rose-tinted*] *spectacles* [*glasses*]** →ROSE-COLORED.

take off *one's* ***rose-colored* [*rose-tinted*] *spectacles*** 楽観的な見方をやめる ▪ It is high time he *took off his rose-tinted spectacles.* 彼はもう楽観的な見方をやめてもいいころだ.

spectator /spéktèɪtər|spektéɪtə/ 名 ***The spectator sees more of the game.*** = The outsider sees the best of the GAME.

specter, 《英》 **spectre** /spéktər/ 名 ***raise the specter of*** 《文》 …の不安を抱かせる, を騒ぎ立てる ▪ The war *raised the specter of* food shortages. その戦争は食料不足の不安をかき立てた.

speculation /spèkjəléɪʃən/ 名 ***as a* [*on*] *speculation*** 投機で, やまを張って ▪ I bought mining shares *as a speculation.* 私は鉱山株をやまを張って買った.

S

speech /spiːtʃ/ 名 ***give speech to*** …を口に出す ▪ He openly *gave speech to* his feelings. 彼はおおっぴらに感情を口に出した.

***have speech with* [*of*]** *a person* 人と話をする ▪ He has come from London to *have speech with* his sweetheart. 彼は恋人と話をするためにロンドンからやって来た ▪ None *had speech of* her. 誰も彼女と話をしなかった.

lose* [*find*]** *one's* ***speech 口がきけなく[きけるように]なる ▪ He has *found his speech* again. 彼はまた口がきけるようになった.

make a speech 演説をする (*on, about, to*) ▪ I *made a* little *speech to* them. 彼らにちょっとした演説をした.

speechless /spíːtʃləs/ 形 ***leave*** *a person* ***speechless*** (驚き・喜びなどで)人を唖然とさせる, 口をきかなくさせる ▪ Bill, you *leave* me bloody *speechless.* ビル, お前にはあきれてものが言えないよ.

speed /spiːd/ 名 ***a turn of speed*** →TURN[1].

at a speed of …の速力で ▪ The moon-ship will move *at a speed of* 5 miles a second. 月旅行宇宙船は毎秒5マイルの速力で飛ぶ.

at break-neck speed 危険きわまるスピードで ▪ The boy dashed along *at break-neck speed.* 少年は猛スピードで走って行った.

(*at*) *full* [*top*] *speed* 全速力で, フルスピードで ▪ The wagoner drove off *(at) full speed.* 荷馬車の御者はフルスピードで馬車を駆って去った.

at speed 《口》 速く, スピードを出して ▪ They went off *at speed.* 彼らは速く立ち去った ▪ It's dangerous to corner *at speed.* (車で)スピードを出して角を曲がるのは危険だ.

break the speed limit スピード違反をする ▪ You're *breaking the speed limit.* スピード違反をしているぞ.

bring *a person* ***up to speed/ get up to speed*** **1** 人に最新情報を提供する; 人が最新情報に通じている ▪ I should *bring* you *up to speed* on what's happening. 今起こっていることをもれなく知らせておいたほうがいいね.

2 最高レベル(の効力)に達する ▪ This system will be expensive to *get up to speed.* このシステムが最高レベルに達するには費用がかかるだろう.

Full speed ahead! 全速力で前進《どんどん働け》. ☞船長の命令から.

make speed 急ぐ ▪ They *made speed* with their journey. 彼らは旅を急いだ.

More haste, less speed. → (The) more HASTE, (the) less [worse] speed.

pick up speed スピードを上げる ▪ You'll have to *pick up speed* if you want to finish this job. この仕事を終らせたければ急がないと.

with* (*all*) *speed (非常に)急いで ▪ The execution was hurried on *with all speed.* その処刑は大急ぎでばたばたと行われた.

spell[1] /spel/ 名 ***break the spell*** まじないを解く; お座をさます ▪ The slightest mistake will *break the spell.* ほんのちょっとしたまちがいでもお座がさめる.

***cast* [*put*] *a spell on* [*over*]** …を魅了する ▪ This little book will *cast a spell on* the reader. この小さな本は読者を魅了することだろう.

fall under *a person's* ***spell*** 人に魅了される ▪ The audience *fell under the actor's spell.* 観客はその俳優に魅了されてしまった.

have ... in *one's* ***spell*** …を魅了する ▪ The actor *had* the audience *in his spell.* その俳優は観客を魅了した.

take spells at …を交替でやる ▪ We *took spells at* the wheel. 我々は交替でハンドルを握った. ☞wheel = steering wheel.

under a spell 魅せられて ▪ We listened to the young violinist as though we were *under a* *spell*. 我々はまるで魅せられたかのようにその若いバイオリニストに耳を傾けた.

under** a person's **spell 人に魅惑されて ▪ The novelist keeps us *under his spell* by those devices. 小説家はそういう工夫で読者を魅惑するのである.

weave a** [one's] **spell 魔法をかける, 魔法を行う ▪ Fresh air might *weave a spell*. 新鮮な空気が魔法を行ってくれるかもしれない.

spell[2] /spel/ 名 ***a cold spell*** ひどく寒い時期 (→cold SNAP) ▪ You should dress warm in *this cold spell*. この寒さでは暖かくしたほうがいいよ.

a dry spell 日照り続き, 乾期 ▪ *The dry spell* will kill the crops. 日照り続きで作物が枯れるだろう.

a spell →(for) a SPELL.

a spell ago [***back***] 《米口》ちょっと前に ▪ I got a letter from him *a spell back*. ちょっと前に彼から便りがあった.

by spells ときどき, 折々 ▪ It rained *by spells* for three days. 3日間ときどき雨が降った.

(for) a spell 暫く, 一時 ▪ He tried doctoring *for a spell*. 彼は一時医者になろうとした ▪ Wait *a spell*. ちょっと待ちなさい.

give** a person **a spell 交替して人をひと休みさせる ▪ He offered to *give* me *a spell* when I became tired. 彼は疲れたら替わって休ませようと言ってくれた.

spell and spell (about)/spell for spell 交替で, 輪番に ▪ They bailed our boat *spell and spell about*. 彼らは交替で我々の船のあかをくみ出してくれた ▪ *Spell for spell* is fair play. 輪番制が公平だ.

Spell oh! [***ho!***] (仕事を)休め! ▪ *Spell ho*, mates! The neighbors want to get past. みんな休め! 近所の人が通り抜けたいとおっしゃるんだ.

take [***keep***] ***spell*** 交替する ▪ He *takes spell* after me. 彼が私の後から交替してくれる ▪ He was *keeping spell*. 彼が交替していた.

spell[3] /spel/ 動 ***spell baker*** 《米口》難事をやってのける ▪ If an old man will marry a young wife, why then he must *spell baker*! 老人が若い女性と結婚したいというのなら, 難事をやってのけなければならない.

spell short いっそう端的な言い方をする ▪ In fact, *spelt short*, it was a bribe. 事実いっそう端的な言い方をすれば, それは賄賂だった.

spend[1] /spend/ 名 ***on*** [***upon***] ***the spend*** 金を費やして ▪ He is always *on the spend*. 彼はいつも金を使っている.

spend[2] /spend/ 動 ***spend** oneself* [***itself***] 精根が尽きる ▪ Man after man *spends himself* in this cause. 人は次々とこの大義のために働いて精根が尽きてしまう ▪ His passion had *spent itself*. 彼の情熱は尽きてしまっていた.

spend and be spent 物を費やしまた身をも費やす (《聖》*2 Cor.* 12. 15) ▪ He counted it blessedness enough so to *spend and be spent*. 彼はそのように物を費やし身をも費やすことを大変な幸福だと思った.

spender /spéndər/ 名 ***(the) last of the big spenders*** 《口》最も大金を使いそうにない人《ユーモラスな言い方》 ▪ Here comes *the last of the big spenders*. 最も金を使いそうにないやつが来たぞ.

spent /spent/ 形 ***a spent force*** 勢力をなくした人[グループ] ▪ The band is not *a spent force* yet. そのバンドはいまだに勢力をなくしていない.

spent out **1** 疲れきって ▪ After a hard game of tennis the champion was *spent out*. 激しいテニスの試合のあとでチャンピオンは疲れきっていた.

2 無一文になって ▪ We came home from our Continental holiday, *spent out*. 我々は無一文になって大陸での休暇から戻ってきた.

spent up =SPENT out 2.

sphere /sfɪər/ 名 ***out of the sphere of*** ...の範囲外に ▪ Your proposal lies *out of the sphere of* our activities. 君の提案は我々の活動範囲外にある.

the music [***harmony***] ***of the spheres*** 天球の楽音《天球回転の際に生じると考えられた快音》 ▪ Our organs are like *the music of the spheres* to them. 我々のオルガンは彼らにとっては天球の楽音のごときものだ.

within** one's **sphere 範囲[本領]内に ▪ That does not come *within my sphere*. それは私の分野に入らない.

spice /spaɪs/ 動 ***be spiced with*** **1** ...の香料を入れてある ▪ The pudding *was spiced with* cloves. あのプディングはクローブを入れてあった.

2 ...で趣味を添えてある, 味をつけてある ▪ His book *was spiced with* clever topical allusions. 彼の本は気のきいた時事問題への言及で味をつけてあった.

spick /spɪk/ 形 ***spick and span*** **1** 真新しい, 新調の ▪ His uniform was *spick and span*. 彼の制服は真新しかった.

2 きれいさっぱりとした ▪ Her house is always *spick and span*. 彼女の家はいつもきれいさっぱりとしている.

spider /spáɪdər/ 名 ***spider and fly*** わなにかける者とかけられる者 ▪ There was too much of *spider and fly* business in the arrangement. その取決めにはわなにかける者とかけられる者といった関係がありすぎた.

spike /spaɪk/ 動 ***spike** one's **drink*** (何も分からずに)飲み物にアルコール[薬物]を加える ▪ They've *spiked my drink*. 彼らは私の飲み物に薬物を加えた.

spike** a person's **guns 《英》人の計画の裏をかく ▪ He *spiked my guns* by saying, "We were married last week." 彼は「先週結婚しました」と言って私の計画の裏をかいた. ☞敵の砲の火門をふさいで使用できなくすることから.

spill[1] /spɪl/ 名 ***take a spill*** つまずく, ころぶ ▪ He *took a spill* when the sidewalk was covered with snow. 歩道が雪で覆われていて彼はころんだ.

spill[2] /spɪl/ 動 ***spill** one's **blood*** (人を)殺す, 傷つける ▪ Nothing can justify *spilling blood*. 何者も人を傷つけることを正当化することはできない.

spill** one's **guts (to) 《米口》(...に)本心をもらす ▪ I *spilled my guts to* my parents. 私は両親に本音をもらした.

S

spill the beans [***soup, works, it***] 《口》秘密をぶちまける, 秘密を漏らす ▪ *Spill the beans*, old man! 秘密をぶちまけろよ, 君!

spin[1] /spɪn/ 名 ***a spin doctor*** スポークスマン ▪ He was *a spin doctor* of the political party. 彼はその政党のスポークスマンだった.

go for a spin (自動車・自転車に)乗りに行く ▪ Jack has invited us to *go for a spin* in his new car tomorrow. ジャックはあす彼の新車でドライブに行こうと我々を誘った.

go into a (***flat***) ***spin*** (飛行機が)きりもみ状態になる; (人が)自制心を失う ▪ When her husband met an accident, she *went into a flat spin*. 夫が交通事故にあったとき彼女はすっかり取り乱してしまった.

go into a tail spin →TAILSPIN.

in a (***flat***) ***spin*** まごまごして; がっかりして ▪ He has been *in a spin* since the bankruptcy. 彼は破産して以来しょげている.

take a spin (***in***) (...に乗って)軽く[ちょっと]ドライブする ▪ How about *taking a spin in* my Porsche? (= How about *taking* my Porsche for *a spin*?) ぼくのポルシェでちょっとドライブでもどうだい?

spin[2] /spɪn/ 動 ***send ... spinning*** ...をきりきり舞いさせる ▪ The box on the ear *sent* the boy *spinning*. 耳をなぐられて少年はきりきり舞いした.

spin a yarn →YARN.

spin *one's* ***wheels*** むだな努力をする ▪ The company was *spinning its wheels* for improving the business results. その会社は業績改善に向けてのむだな努力を重ねていた.

spindle /spíndəl/ 名 ***on the spindle side*** 母方の, 女系の (↔on the SPEAR side) ▪ Such and such qualities he got from a great-uncle *on the spindle side*. しかじかの性質を彼は母方の大おじから受け継いでいた.

spine /spaɪn/ 名 ***chill*** *a person's* ***spine*** = freeze a person's BLOOD.

spirit /spírət/ 名 ***be with*** *a person* ***in spirit*** 〚主に will, shall を伴って〛心の中で[遠くから]人のことを思っている (→in the SPIRIT) ▪ I am sorry I cannot attend your wedding, but I*'ll be with* you *in spirit*. あいにく結婚式には出席できないが, 心の中で君のことを思っている.

break *a person's* ***spirit*** 人の気力をそぐ ▪ *His spirit was broken* by the torture. その拷問で彼の気力はなえてしまった.

breathe spirit into ...に活気を吹き込む ▪ His very presence *breathed spirit into* the stricken throng. 彼がいるだけで傷ついた群衆が活気づいた.

catch the spirit of ...の精神をつかむ, 空気をのみこむ ▪ His translation seems to have *caught the spirit of* the original. 彼の翻訳は原作の精神をつかんでいるようだ.

dampen *one's* ***spirits*** せっかくのいい気分をそぐ ▪ She trusted her husband to *dampen her spirits*. 夫ならいい気分をそぎかねないと彼女は信じた.

depressed in spirits しょげて ▪ He left the court *depressed in spirits*. 彼は悄(しょう)然として法廷を出た.

enter into the spirit of ...の精神[気分]にとけ込む ▪ He *entered into the spirit of* our conversation. 彼は我々の談話の気分にとけ込んだ.

get into the spirit (***of***) (...に)関心を持つ, 熱中する ▪ Listening to carols helps us *get into the spirit of* Christmas. キャロルに耳を澄ませているとクリスマスの気分が高められる.

give up the spirit 死ぬ ▪ The Patriarch *gave up the spirit* at 3 a.m. 長老は午前3時に死去した.

in good spirits 上きげんで, いそいそと ▪ He was *in* pretty *good spirits*. 彼はかなり上きげんだった.

in great [***high***] ***spirits*** 元気よく, 意気ごんで ▪ I walked home *in great spirits*. 私は元気よく歩いて家に帰った ▪ The men were *in high spirits* at the prospect of a fight. 兵士たちは戦闘が起こりそうなので意気ごんでいた.

in low [***poor***] ***spirits*** 意気消沈して, 元気なく ▪ He was *in low spirits* then. 彼は当時意気消沈していた.

in spirit **1** ひそかに ▪ He was vexed *in spirit*. 彼はひそかに悩んでいた.
2 = in the SPIRIT.

in spirits 元気よく; 意気揚々と ▪ I suppose he is quite *in spirits* at your success? たぶんあの人は君の成功で意気揚々としているのでしょうね.

in the spirit 精神では, 想像で (→be with a person in SPIRIT) ▪ I cannot attend the concert, but I shall be with you *in the spirit*. 音楽会には出席できないが, 心では君といっしょにいるよ.

keep up *one's* ***spirits*** 元気を落とさないようにする ▪ *Keep up your spirits*, old boy! 元気を出せよ, 君.

kindred spirits 気の合う物同士 ▪ We're *kindred spirits* and have the same views on everything. 我々は気の合う者同士ですべてに同じ見方をする.

knock the spirit out of →KNOCK[2].

lose all spirit 気を落とす, がっかりする ▪ If my project fails, I shall *lose all spirit*. 計画が失敗したら私はがっかりしてしまうだろう.

of spirit しっかりした, 気概のある ▪ She is a woman *of spirit*. 彼女はしっかりした女性だ.

out of spirits 元気なく, 意気消沈して ▪ Who can be *out of spirits* in such weather? こんないい天気に意気消沈する者がいるものか.

raise [***lift***] *a person's* ***spirits*** 人を元気[勇気]づける ▪ Your advice *raised his spirits* considerably. 君の助言で彼はかなり元気づけられた.

One's ***spirits rise*** [***sink***]. 元気が出る[無くなる] ▪ *My spirits rose* a little. 少し元気が出た.

take ... in the right spirit (助言・批判を快く)受け入れる, 汲み取る ▪ Thank you for having *taken* my advice *in the right spirit*. 私のアドバイスを快く受け入れてくださりありがたく思います.

That's the spirit! それでこそ元気があるというものだ

▪ You say you will try again. *That's the spirit!* もう一度やろうと言うんだね. その意気だ.

The spirit is willing, but (***the flesh is weak***). 気持ちははずんでいるが, 肉体が弱い (《聖》*Matt.* 26. 41) ▪ Will you go out with me tonight?—*The spirit is willing, but.* 今晩いっしょに出かけませんか—気持ちははずんでいるんだが, 体がね.

the spirit takes [***moves***] *one* 《戯》気が向く ▪ I work in the garden when *the spirit moves* me. 私は気が向いたときには庭いじりをする.

with some spirit 少々むきになって ▪ The maid defended herself *with some spirit.* メイドは少々むきになって弁解した.

with spirit 元気よく ▪ He conducted himself *with spirit.* 彼は元気よくふるまった.

spiritual /spírɪtʃuəl/ 形 ***be*** *a person's* ***spiritual home*** 人の心の拠り所となる場所である ▪ I think Geneva *is my spiritual home.* ジュネーブは私の心の拠り所となる場所だと思う.

spit[1] /spɪt/ 名 ***a spit and a stride*** 非常に近い所, 近距離 ▪ We are now within *a spit and a stride* of the peak. 今や頂上は目と鼻の近さにある.

spit and polish (兵士・水夫の)磨き仕事; 外見を強調すること ▪ All his energies had been expended on *spit and polish.* 彼の全精力は磨き仕事に費やされていた.

spit and sawdust 《英》掃き溜め ▪ That river is now *spit and sawdust.* あの川は今は掃き溜めだ.

the very [***dead***] ***spit of/ the very*** [***dead***] ***spit*** (***and fetch*** [***image, picture***]) ***of*** …の生き写し ▪ You are a queer fellow—*the very spit of* your father. 君はおかしな男だ—おとうさんに生き写しだ ▪ She is *the dead spit and image of* Cleopatra. 彼女はクレオパトラに生き写しだ.

spit[2] /spɪt/ 動 ***I could*** (***just***) ***spit!*** 《口》頭に来てる!

spit blood [***venom, feathers***] 《口》猛烈に怒る ▪ I was *spitting blood* by the end of the meeting. 会議の終りまでにはすごく頭に来ていた.

spit cotton [《英》***sixpences***] **1** (のどがかわいて)白いつばを吐く ▪ He was *spitting cotton,* he was that thirsty. 彼は白いつばを吐いていた. それほどのどがかわいていたのだ.

2 怒る ▪ The sheriff's *spitting cotton.* 郡保安官は怒っている.

spit in *a person's* ***face*** [***eye***] 人の顔につばを吐く, 侮蔑する ▪ You *spit in your* own *face.* 君は自分の顔につばを吐いているのだ.

spit in [***on***] *one's* ***hands*** 手につばする ▪ Before I had time to *spit in my hands,* he finished the work. 私が手につばしないうちに彼はその仕事をすませてしまった.

spit in the eye of …を軽蔑する ▪ He *spits in the eye of* commercialism with these words. 彼はこうした言葉で商業主義を軽蔑している.

spit it out 《口》〚主に命令文で〛あからさまに言う ▪ Don't be afraid, *spit it out.* 心配することはない, あからさまに言いなさい.

spit nails 《米口》ひどく怒る ▪ He *spat nails* when he saw what had happened to his car. 彼は自分の車にされた仕打ちを見て猛烈に腹を立てた.

the spitting image of …の生き写し ▪ Mary is *the spitting image of* her mother. メアリーは母親の生き写しだ.

within spitting [***shouting***] ***distance*** → within striking DISTANCE of.

spite /spaɪt/ 名 ***for*** [***from, in, out of***] ***spite*** 悪意で, 腹いせに ▪ He did it just *for spite.* 彼はただ悪意でそうやったのだ ▪ He ruined the flowers *out of* [*from*] *spite.* 彼は腹いせに花を台なしにした.

have a spite at [***against***] …に恨みをいだく ▪ The mystery is why the neighbors *had a spite at* me. 不思議なのはなぜ近所の人が私に恨みをいだいていたかということだ.

in spite →for SPITE.

in spite of **1** …を物ともせず, に逆らって ▪ They succeeded in it *in spite of* the hardships. 彼らは苦難を物ともせずにそれに成功した.

2 …にもかかわらず ▪ *In spite of* all his riches, he is never contented. あんなに金があるくせに彼は決して満足しない.

in spite of *oneself* 我知らず, 思わず ▪ The judge laughed *in spite of himself.* 裁判官は思わず吹き出してしまった.

out of spite →for SPITE.

owe *a person* ***a spite*** 人に恨みをいだく ▪ He *owes* us *a spite.* 彼は我々に恨みをいだいている.

spittle /spítəl/ 名 ***lick*** *a person's* ***spittle*** = LICK a person's boots.

splash[1] /splæʃ/ 名 ***add a splash of color to*** …によく映える, を色鮮やかにする ▪ The reddish picture on the wall *adds a splash of color to* the whitish room. 壁に架けられた赤味を帯びた絵は白っぽい部屋によく映える.

cut a splash =make a SPLASH 2.

make [***cause***] ***a splash*** **1** ザブンと音を立てる ▪ The stone fell into the pond *making a splash.* その石はドボンと音を立てて池に落ちた.

2 《口》あっと言わせる, はでにやらかす ▪ I expect our drum to *make a* great *splash.* 我々のドラムが大いにあっと言わせるものと思う.

with a splash ザブンと ▪ He jumped into the river *with a splash.* 彼はザブンと川へ飛び込んだ.

splash[2] /splæʃ/ 動 ***splash*** *one's* ***money about*** [***around***] 《俗》(人気取りに)金をばらまく ▪ He *splashed his money about* to carry the election. 彼は選挙に勝つために金をばらまいた.

splash *one's* ***way*** ザブザブ音を立てて進む ▪ We *splashed our way* into the lake. 我々はザブザブと湖の中へ入って行った.

spleen /spliːn/ 名 ***give*** [***have***] ***the spleen*** 憂鬱にする[になる] ▪ This quiet room *gives* me *the spleen.* この静かな部屋が私を憂鬱にする.

vent *one's* ***spleen on*** 《雅》…にうっぷんをもらす

▪ He *vented his spleen on* everybody around. 彼は周囲のすべての人にやつ当たりした.

splendor, 《英》 **splendour** /spléndər/ 名 ***in splendor*** 《紋章》(太陽が)光線と人面を持った ▪ The sun is always supposed to be *in splendor*. 太陽はいつも光線と人面を持っているものとされる.

splice /splaɪs/ 動 ***be*** [***get***] ***spliced*** 《俗》結婚する ▪ They are *getting spliced* next Saturday. 彼らは来週の土曜日に結婚することになっている.

splice the main-brace →MAIN-BRACE.

split[1] /splɪt/ 名 ***a split second*** ほんの一瞬 ▪ *A split second* later I was on the floor. ほんの一瞬の後, 私は床の上に倒れていた.

(***at***) ***full split/like split*** 《米》全速力で, 一目散に ▪ He was off *full split*. 彼は一目散に立ち去った ▪ They were running *like split* all over the city. 彼らは町じゅうを全速力で走り回っていた.

do the splits (アクロバットダンスの)大開脚をする ▪ I had to *do the splits* and strides. 私は大開脚や大股歩きをしなければならなかった.

split[2] /splɪt/ 動 ***split ... down the middle*** ...を真ん中で[半分に]分ける ▪ The party *was split down the middle* on the problem. 党はその問題では半分に分かれた.

split hairs [***a hair, straws, words***] ささいなことをとやかく論じる; (ことさらに)細かい区別立てをする ▪ He does not *split straws*, or bandy words. 彼は細かいことをとやかく論じたり言い合ったりなどしない ▪ Theologians will *split hairs* over the shape of a Greek letter. 神学者たちはギリシャ文字の形についても細かい区別立てをするものだ.

split in two 二つに割れる[割る] ▪ He *split* the firewood *in two*. 彼はまきを二つに割った.

Split me [***my windpipe, my sides***]***!*** 断じて(...だ), (...ならば)首をやる《誓言》 ▪ *Split me* if I sell it for less. 断じてそれより安くは売るものか ▪ *Split my windpipe*, you are a fool! 断じて君はおばかさんだよ!

split open 張り裂ける, はじける ▪ The fruit falls to the ground and *splits open*. その実は地面に落ちてはじける.

split *one's* ***sides*** [*oneself*] →SIDE.

split the difference →DIFFERENCE.

split (*one's* [***the***]) ***vote*** [《米》 ***ticket, ballot***] (2票以上を有する有権者が反対党候補者に)票を分割する ▪ I have never *split my ticket* in my life. 私はこれまで投票を分割したためしがない.

spludge /splʌdʒ/ 名 ***cut a spludge*** 《米口》見栄を張る ▪ She tries to *cut a spludge*. 彼女は見栄を張ろうとしている.

spoil[1] /spɔɪl/ 名 ***make spoil of*** ...を略奪する ▪ In this way they *made spoil of* all the countryside. このようにして彼らはその地方全体を略奪した.

spoil[2] /spɔɪl/ 動 ***be spoiling for*** 《口》(けんかなど)がしたくてたまらない ▪ He *is* chronically *spoiling for* a fight. 彼はいつもけんかがしたくてうずうずしている.

spoil all [***everything***] 何もかも台なしにする ▪ She was a very beautiful person, but her demeanor *spoiled all*. 彼女は美人だったが, 立居ふるまいで何もかもぶちこわしだった.

spoil *a person's* ***beauty*** [***face***] ***for*** *him* (目のふちに黒あざをつけたりして)人の顔を台なしにする ▪ I'll *spoil your* pretty *face for* you. お前のきれいな顔を台なしにしてやるぞ.

spoil *a person* ***rotten*** →ROTTEN.

spoke /spoʊk/ 名 ***a spoke in the*** [*one's*] ***wheel*** じゃま, 妨げになるもの ▪ So, here's *a* fresh *spoke in your wheel*. ではこれでまたじゃまが増えたわけだね. ☞次項も参照.

put a spoke in *a person's* ***wheel*** 《英口》人のじゃまをする ▪ If you were to attempt to make your escape, I should be obliged to *put a spoke in your wheel*. 君が逃げようとするようなら, いやでも君のじゃまをしなければなるまい.

put in *one's* ***spoke*** 《口》おせっかい[口出し]をする ▪ Mary, not thinking to be silent, *put in her spoke*. メアリーは黙っているつもりはなく口出しをした.

sponge /spʌndʒ/ 名 ***have a sponge bath*** ぬれたタオル[スポンジ]で体を拭く ▪ During the suspension of the water supply my family *had* only *sponge baths*. 断水の間, 家の者はぬれたタオルで体を拭くだけだった.

have a sponge down (スポンジを用いて)沐浴する ▪ I *had a sponge down*. 私はスポンジで体を洗った.

pass the (***wet***) ***sponge over*** (怒り・恨みなど)を忘れ去る, 水に流す ▪ He *passed the wet sponge over* the old spite. 彼は古い恨みを忘れ去った.

set [***lay***] ***the sponge*** パンだねを発酵させる ▪ He went to bed immediately after *laying the sponge*. 彼はパンだねを発酵させてからすぐ寝た.

soak ... up like a sponge (情報・知識など)を苦もなく吸収する ▪ He *soaked up* a lot of knowledge *like a sponge*. 彼は多くの知識を苦もなく吸収した.

throw in [***up***] ***the sponge/ chuck*** [***fling***] ***up the sponge*** 《口》闘争をやめる; 降参する ▪ He *chucked up the sponge* and cleared out for good and all. 彼は参ったと言って永久に立ち去ってしまった. ☞ボクシングで勝負の決したときスポンジを投げたことから.

spoon /spuːn/ 名 ***a greasy spoon*** →GREASY.

be born with a silver spoon in *one's* ***mouth*** 富貴の家に生まれる, 幸運に生まれつく ▪ It was a common proverb that few lawyers *were born with a silver spoon in their mouths*. 富貴の家の出の弁護士は少ないというのはありふれた諺だった.

be [***go***] ***spoons on*** [***with***] 《俗》(女性)にべたぼれしている[する] ▪ They *were* both *spoons with* Ann. 彼らは二人ともアンにべたぼれしていた ▪ He has *gone spoons on* the girl. 彼はその娘にいかれちゃった.

Gag me with a spoon! 《米俗》うんざりした, むかつきそうだ ▪ Oh my gosh, *gag me with a spoon!* Those are the ugliest shoes I've ever seen! まあひ

どい，むかつきそう! こんな不格好な靴は見たことないわ!

get* [*take, win*] *the wooden spoon 《英口》 最下位になる ▪ We went into hard training for the game to avoid *getting the wooden spoon*. 我々は最下位になるのを避けるため試合に備えて猛練習に入った ▪ We must win this match if we are to avoid *taking the wooden spoon*. ビリにならないためにはこの試合に勝たねばならない.

He should have a long spoon that sups with the Devil. → He that sups with the DEVIL must have a long spoon.; when you dine with the DEVIL, use a long spoon.

make a spoon or spoil a horn のるかそるか一番やってみる ▪ Your son will *make a spoon or spoil a horn*. 息子さんはのるかそるか一番やってみられますわい. ☞昔スコットランドで牛・羊の角でさじを作っていたことから.

need a long spoon (悪人を念頭に置いて)細心の注意がいる ▪ I *needed a long spoon* to do business with Stewart. スチュワートと取引するにはよほど注意してかかる必要があった.

put *one's* ***spoon into*** *a person's* ***broth*** 人の事におせっかいをする ▪ She was always fond of *putting her spoon into other people's broth*. 彼女は他人の事におせっかいをするのがいつも好きだった.

spoony /spúːni/ 形 ***spoony on*** [***upon***] 《口》 …にほれこんで ▪ He got *spoony upon* a gipsy girl. 彼はジプシー娘にほれこんだ.

sport[1] /spɔːrt/ 名 ***a real sport*** 喜んで協力してくれる[頼みをきいてくれる]人 ▪ I love Tom because he is *a real sport*. トムは頼みがいがあるから大好きよ.

Be a* (*good*) *sport. 《口》 スポーツマンらしくやれ ▪ Let me go, mister! *Be a sport*! 放してくださいよ，だんな! スポーツマンらしくしてくださいよ.

be the sport of …にもてあそばれる ▪ Man *is the sport of* Fortune. 人は運命にもてあそばれる.

for sport 慰みに ▪ He catches birds *for sport*, not for gain. 彼の小鳥捕りは慰みのためであって，金儲けのためではない.

have good sport 大猟をする ▪ We *had good sport* today. きょうは大猟だった.

in sport 冗談に，戯れに ▪ He said it merely *in sport*. 彼は冗談半分にそう言っただけだ ▪ Dogs fight *in sport*. 犬は戯れにかみ合う.

make sport 楽しませる ▪ It will *make* us excellent *sport* at night. それはすてきな我々の夜の楽しみになるだろう.

make sport of [***at, with***] …をからかう，笑い物にする ▪ The boys *made sport of* his stammering. 少年たちは彼のどもりをからかった ▪ Why do they *make sport at* me? なぜ彼らは私を笑い物にするのか.

show sport あばれ回って慰みになる ▪ This wild boar will *show sport*, depend upon it. このイノシシはあばれ回って慰みになるよ，ほんとに.

spoil the sport 興をそぐ ▪ He likes to act so as to *spoil the sport* of others. 彼は他人の興をそぐようなふるまいをしたがる.

the sport of kings 王者のスポーツ，競馬 ▪ I like gambling, but most of all, I enjoy *the sport of kings*. 賭け事が好きだが，とりわけ競馬にはまっている.

sport[2] /spɔːrt/ 動 ***sport it*** ふざける，戯れる ▪ She was *sporting it* with Zephyr. 彼女は西風と戯れていた.

***sport* (*it*) *at* [*over, upon*]** …をからかう ▪ He *sported at* those simple folks. 彼はそのお人好しの人たちをからかった.

sport (*one's*) ***oak*** [***timber***] 《主に英大学俗》ドアを閉め(て面会謝絶す)る ▪ He *sported his oak* for the rest of day. 彼はその日はその後ずっとドアを閉めていた ▪ I *sport my oak* when I go out or want to be quiet. ぼくは外出したり静かにしていたいときにはドアを閉めておく. ☞外出または面会謝絶のときに，私室入口のカシの外戸 (oak) を閉めることから.

sporting /spɔ́ːrtɪŋ/ 形 ***a sporting blood*** → BLOOD.

a sporting chance →CHANCE[1].

a sporting man 運動屋《三流・金銭目当てのものを言う》 ▪ He is not a sportsman, but *a sporting man*. あの男は運動家ではなくて運動屋なのさ.

spot[1] /spɑt|spɔt/ 名 ***a*** [*one's*] ***blind spot*** (網膜の)盲点，死角; 弱点 ▪ Most parents have *a blind spot* for their children. たいていの親は子供を溺愛する ▪ The social reality of Northern Ireland remained *a blind spot* for Southern Irish nationalists. 北アイルランド社会の現実は，いつまでも南アイルランド民族主義者の盲点であり続けた ▪ Mathematics is *my blind spot*. I can't find any interest in it. 数学は私の弱点だ. 全然興味がわかない.

a hot spot 《口》 **1** 政治的に不安定な地域; 危険[戦争，紛争]地域 ▪ The correspondent was sent to one *hot spot* after another. 特派員は危険地域に転々と派遣された ▪ I'm going to be off again to *another hot spot* to help the casualties of war. 死傷兵の支援に，また危険地域に出かけるつもりだ.
2 人気のある娯楽場; (女性を目当てに男性が集まる)遊興場 ▪ The club is one of the top *hot spots*. そのクラブは指折りのセクシースポットの一つである.

a spot of 《口》 少量の… ▪ What about *a spot of* whisky, old chap? ウィスキーをちょっぴりどうかね，君.

a spot of bother [***trouble***] 《口》 ちょっとしたもめごと，ちょっとしたごたごた ▪ He had *a spot of trouble* with his colleagues. 彼は同僚とちょっとしたもめごとを起こした.

a tender [***sore***] ***spot*** 痛い所 ▪ If you mention marriage, you'll touch Egbert on *a tender spot*. 結婚のことを言えばエグバートの痛い所を突くことになる.

change *one's* ***spots*** 性格を変える (《聖》 *Jer*. 13. 23) ▪ She'll never *change her spots*. 彼女の性格は決して変わるまい.

get … down to a spot 《米口》 …をすっかり覚える ▪ He has *got* everything *down to a spot*. 彼はいっさいをすっかり覚えてしまった.

have a soft [***weak***] ***spot*** (***in*** *one's* ***heart***) ***for*** …を好いている ▪ The old man *had* always *a*

S

soft spot in his heart for Jack. 老人はいつもジャックを好いていた.

hit the high spots →HIGH.

hit* [*go to*] *the spot 《口》(飲食物が)おあつらえ向きだ, 気分転換になる ▪ I was dying of thirst, and that coca-cola just *hit the spot*. 僕は死にそうにのどがかわいていたので, そのコカコーラはまさにおあつらえ向きだった ▪ It *went* right *to the spot*. それはまさに申し分なかった.

in a* (*bad* [*hot, tight, tough*]) *spot 《口》悪状態にあって, 困って ▪ I was certainly *in a hot* [*tight*] *spot* then. 私はそのころ確かにひどく困っていた.

in spots 《米俗》 **1** ときどき, 合い間合い間に ▪ I sleep *in spots*. 私は合い間合い間に眠るのです.
2 ある程度は ▪ He is clever *in spots*. 彼はある程度は利口だ.

keep off the spot 《米俗》安全策をとる, 危険を避ける ▪ We'd be rich if we could *keep off the spot* long enough. 十分長く安全策をとっていれば金は儲かるだろう.

***knock* (*the*) *spots off* [*out of*]** 《英口》…を完全に打ち負かす, よりもはるかにすぐれている ▪ She can *knock the spots off* these boys at that game. 彼女はそのゲームではこんな少年たちを完全に打ち負かせる.

make a spot for 《米》…を歓迎する ▪ Last week Manhattan concert-goers *made a spot for* Cage's music. 先週マンハッタンの音楽会の常連たちはケイジの音楽を歓迎した.

off the spot 不正確[不適切]で (↔on the SPOT 3) ▪ His books have a tendency to be *off the spot*. 彼の本は不正確の傾向がある.

on* [*upon*] *the spot **1** 即座に, ただちに ▪ He was run over and killed *on the spot*. 彼はひかれて即死した.
2 その場で, 現場で ▪ I was *upon the spot*. 私はその場にいた ▪ Mischief was brewing, and he ought to have been *on the spot* to counteract it. 悪事が企てられていたので, 彼は当然それに対処するために現場へ行かねばならなかったのだが.
3 そつがなく; 正確で (↔off the SPOT) ▪ He appears to be well *on the spot*. 彼はなかなかそつがないように見える ▪ Our ground fielding was well *on the spot*. 我々のフィールディングはなかなか正確だった.
4 《俗》窮地に陥って, 困って ▪ With the mortgage payment due and no money to meet it, he was *on the spot*. 抵当の支払い期限がきてそれに当てる金がないので, 彼は困っていた.

pay spot cash 現金払いをする ▪ We always *pay spot cash*. 我々はいつも現金払いをする.

put *a person* ***on the spot*** 《口》人を困難な状況に追い込む; 人に単刀直入に質問する ▪ Don't *put* me *on the spot*. I can't give you a ready answer. 困らさないでくれよ. 即答はできないから.

rooted* [*frozen, glued*] *to the spot その場に釘づけになって ▪ The boy *was rooted to the spot* and terrified. 少年はその場に釘づけになって怯えていた.

spot on 全く正しい[正確で] ▪ You're *spot on*. 全くおっしゃる通りです.

spots in the sun 玉にきず ▪ He candidly acknowledged the *spots in the sun*. 彼は率直にその玉にきずを認めた. ☞「太陽の黒点」が原義.

the man* [*men, people*] *on the spot 当事者(たち) ▪ Let's leave the decision to *the men on the spot*. その決定は当事者たちに任せよう.

touch the spot 《口》急所をつく; うまくいく ▪ Then percussion *touched the spot*. それから撃発が効を奏した ▪ A glass of iced lager *touches the spot* on a hot day. 冷えたビールの1杯が暑い日にはあつらえ向きだ.

without* (*a*) *spot (道徳的な)汚点のない ▪ He kept his character *without spot*. 彼は人格を汚点のないものにしておいた.

spot[2] /spɑt|spɔt/ 動 ***it spots with*** (雨が)パラパラ降る ▪ *It's spotting with* rain. 雨がパラパラ降っている.

spotlight /spɑ́tlàɪt|spɔ́t-/ 名 ***be in the spotlight*/ *hold* [*be put under, come into, steal*] *the spotlight*** 衆目を一身に集める ▪ He likes to *be in the spotlight*. 彼は衆目を一身に集めるのを好む.

spout /spaʊt/ 名 ***put* [*shove*]... *up the spout*** 《俗》…を質に入れる ▪ Please *put* that *up the spout*, ma'am. さあ奥さん, それを質に入れなさい.

up the spout 《俗》 **1** 質に入って ▪ Even my wig and gown are *up the spout* together. かつらやガウンまでもいっしょに質に入っているのです.
2 《英口》困窮[破産]して; すっかり参って ▪ I shall be *up the spout* altogether if you don't help me. 君が助けてくれないことには僕は全く困ってしまうだろう.
3 《英口》はらんで ▪ After a year's absence he found that his wife was *up the spout*. 1年家をあけていた後で彼は妻がはらんでいるのに気がついた.

sprat /spræt/ 名 ***throw* (*out*) [*fling away, give*] *a sprat to catch a herring* [*mackerel, whale*]** 「エビでタイを釣る」 ▪ It is safe only on the principle of *throwing out a sprat to catch a herring*. エビでタイを釣るという原則によった場合に限ってそれは安全だ.

sprawl[1] /sprɔːl/ 名 ***all of a sprawl*** だらしなく手足を伸ばして横たわって; だらしなく広がって ▪ The yokel lay *all of a sprawl* along the bench. その田舎者はベンチにだらしなく大の字に横たわっていた ▪ His writing was *all of a sprawl*. 彼の字はだらしなく広がっていた.

sprawl[2] /sprɔːl/ 動 ***send... sprawling*** …を大の字に倒す ▪ His kick *sent* the dog *sprawling* on the ground. 彼にけとばされて犬は地面に手足を伸ばして倒れた.

sprawl *one's* ***last*** もがいて死ぬ ▪ Sans-culottism lies *sprawling its last*. 過激主義は最期のあがきをしている.

spread /spred/ 動 ***spread*** *oneself* **1** 広がる, 延びる ▪ The clouds *spread themselves* over the tops of the hills. 雲が山の頂きの上に広がった

▪ The city *spreads itself* far beyond the river. 街(まち)は川のずっと向こうまで広がっている.
2《米》大いに努力する, 奮発する ▪ He *spread himself* in the preparation. 彼はその仕度に奮発した ▪ He *spread himself* on that contribution. その寄付では彼は大奮発した.
3《俗》見栄を張る, ほらを吹く ▪ I must be allowed to *spread myself* a little. ぜひ少々ほらを吹かせてくれ.
4 長々と寝そべる ▪ Tired from running, he *spread himself* on the ground. 走ったために疲れて, 彼は地べたに長々と寝そべった.

spread it on thick(ly) →LAY it on thick.

spread the word about …について(広く)知らせる ▪ Let's *spread the word about* the dangers of nuclear power. 原子力の危険性について周知させよう.

spread *oneself* ***(too) thin*** 《米》一時にたくさんのことをやりすぎる ▪ Aren't you *spreading yourself too thin*? 手を広げすぎてはいませんか.

spree /spriː/ 名 ***have a spree*** 《口》浮かれ騒ぐ ▪ The cook was drunk and *having a* regular *spree*. 料理人は酔っ払って全く浮かれ騒いでいた.

on a [the] spree 《口》飲み騒いで ▪ She's out *on a spree*. 彼女は飲み騒ぎに出かけている ▪ He is too fond of getting [going] *on the spree*. 彼は飲み騒ぐのを好みすぎる.

spring[1] /sprɪŋ/ 名 ***have its spring in*** …に起源がある ▪ The custom *had its spring in* another country. その習慣は別の国に起源があった.

make [take] a spring 飛ぶ ▪ I *made a spring* towards a boat. ボートの方へ飛んだ.

spring chicken 《俗》〚主に no を伴って〛若者 (→be no (spring) CHICKEN) ▪ He is *no spring chicken* and still going strong. 彼は若くはないが, まだ元気にしている.

one's ***[the] springs of action*** 行為の動機 ▪ His reactions disclosed *his springs of action*. 彼の反応で行為の動機があらわになった.

There is a spring in *a person's* ***step.*** 人の足取りが軽快だ ▪ I noticed the change in him, because *there was a* real *spring in his step*. 彼の変化に気ういたのは彼の足取りがとても軽快だったからだ.

with a spring ぱっと(立ち上がる, など) ▪ He rose *with a spring*. 彼はぱっと立ち上がった.

with a spring in *one's* ***step*** (うれしくて)うきうきして ▪ As she had passed the entrance exam, she went shopping *with a spring in her step*. 彼女は入試に合格していたので, うれしくてうきうきした気分で買物に出かけた.

spring[2] /sprɪŋ/ 動 ***Hope springs eternal (in the human breast).*** →HOPE[1].

spring a leak →LEAK.

spring a surprise on *a person* 突然人を驚かす ▪ He *sprang a surprise on* them when he suddenly withdrew his guarantee of £100. 彼は100ポンドの担保を突然引っ込めて彼らを驚かした.

spring a trap わなにひっかかる[ひっかける] ▪ The police *sprang a trap* on the burglars. 警察は強盗をわなにひっかけた.

spring on *one's* ***feet*** →SPRING to one's feet.

spring open ぱっと開く ▪ The lid *sprang open*. ふたがぱっと開いた.

spring to [on] *one's* ***feet*** ぱっと立ち上がる (→bound to one's feet (→FOOT[1])) ▪ He *sprang to his feet* at the news. 彼はその知らせを聞くとぱっと立ち上がった.

spring to [into] life [action] **1** 急に活気うく, 急に動き始める ▪ After the storm, officials *sprang into action*. あらしの後で役人は活発に動き出した ▪ Mobile phones *sprang to life* in Bagdad. バグダッドでは携帯電話が盛んに使われるようになった ▪ I did as you asked and the motor *sprang to life*. あなたの指示通りにすると, 急にモーターが動き始めた.
2 存在し始める, 生まれる ▪ The company *sprang to life* a decade ago. その会社は10年前に誕生した.

spring to *one's* ***lips*** (言葉が)急に口をついて出る ▪ A question *sprang to his lips*. 質問が彼の口をついて出た.

sprout /spraʊt/ 名 ***put ... through a course of sprouts*** 《米》…をなぐる; に猛訓練をする ▪ Let him *be put through a* regular *course of sprouts*. 彼をうんとなぐってやれ ▪ He *put* the dogs *through a course of sprouts*. 彼はその犬たちに猛訓練を施した.

spruce /spruːs/ 動 ***all spruced up*** すっかりおめかしして, ひどくしゃれた服装をして ▪ Yesterday I met him *all spruced up*, and I could hardly recognize him. きのうすっかりめかしこんだ彼に会ったが, 誰やらわからないくらいだった.

spruce *oneself* ***up*** めかしこむ ▪ Go and *spruce yourself up*. めかしこんで来なさい.

spry /spraɪ/ 形 ***look spry*** =LOOK sharp 2.

spunk /spʌŋk/ 名 ***get*** *one's* ***spunk up*** 《米口》かんしゃくを起こす; 勇気を出す ▪ I *got my spunk up* about it. 私はそのことでかんしゃくを起こした ▪ She *got her spunk up* and left the country. 彼女は勇気を出して国を出て行った.

spur[1] /spəːr/ 名 ***on [upon] the spur*** 全速力で, 大急ぎで ▪ The enemy fled *upon the spur*. 敵軍は全速力で逃げ去った.

on [upon] the spur of the moment [occasion] 時のはずみで, 一時の思いつきで; 即座に ▪ There's nothing like acting *on the spur of the moment*. 時のはずみで行動するに及ぶものはない ▪ The speaker gives us a ready reply *upon the spur of the occasion*. あの弁士は即座にちゃんと返事をする.

put [give, set] spurs to …に拍車をあてる; にはっぱをかける ▪ At the same time they *put spurs to* their horse. 同時に彼らは馬に拍車をあてた ▪ He procceded to *set spurs to* her resolution. 彼は彼

女の決心にはっぱをかけにかかった.

win [***earn, gain***] *one's* ***spurs*** 《主に英》(武勲により)ナイトに叙せられる; 偉功[手柄]を立てる; 名をあげる ▪ The painter had to *win his spurs.* その画家は名をあげねばならなかった. ☞ナイトに叙せられるとき金の拍車をもらったことから.

(***with***) ***whip*** [***switch***] ***and spur/with spur and yard*** 大急ぎで, 早急に (→(ride) WHIP and spur) ▪ He rode *whip and spur.* 彼は大急ぎで馬を飛ばした ▪ They came *with spur and yard.* 彼らは早急にやって来た.

spur[2] /spəːr/ 動 ***spur*** *a person* ***on*** [***up***] ***to*** [***to*** *do*] 人を刺激して…させる ▪ He *was spurred on* by poverty *to* commit a crime. 彼は貧困にかられて罪を犯した ▪ He has *been spurred up to* industry by ambition. 彼は野心にかられてあのように精出してきたのだ.

spurt /spəːrt/ 名 ***by spurts*** 思い出したように, 不規則に ▪ He can work hard *by spurts.* 彼は思い出したように精を出すことができる.

put on a spurt (最後の)奮闘をする ▪ I *put on an* extra *spurt.* 私は余分に奮闘した.

spy[1] /spaɪ/ 名 ***act the spy*** スパイ行為をする ▪ He moved about the office and seemed to be *acting the spy.* 彼は事務所の中を動き回ってスパイ行為をしているように見えた.

be a spy on [***upon***]***/play the spy on*** …をスパイする, 偵察する ▪ He refused to *be a spy on* her conduct. 彼は彼女の行動をスパイするのを断った.

spy[2] /spaɪ/ 動 ***spy out the land*** 形勢を見る ▪ We must send someone to *spy out the land* before buying the estate. 我々はその地所を買う前に形勢を見に誰かをやらなければならない.

squall /skwɔːl/ 名 ***look out for squalls*** 危険を警戒する ▪ *Look out for squalls,* that's all. 危険を警戒しさえすりゃいいんだ. ☞海語から.

square[1] /skweər/ 名形 ***a square deal*** 公明正大なやり方 ▪ They are getting *a square deal.* 彼らは公平な仕うちを受けている.

a square meal →MEAL[1].

a square peg (***in a round hole***) →a round PEG in a square hole.

all square **1** (ゴルフなどで)同点で ▪ They were *all square* at the 18th. 彼らは18番では同点だった.
2 万事整って, うまくいって ▪ Things will be *all square.* 万事うまくいくだろう.

back to [***at***] ***square one*** 振り出しに戻って ▪ Our plans have changed and we're *back to square one.* 計画が変わり, 我々は振り出しに戻った.

break no square(***s***) 悪いことはない, 問題ではない ▪ This fault *broke no squares* in the family. この過失は家庭内に何の影響も及ぼさなかった.

by square 定規を用いて ▪ A poet does not work *by square* as smiths do. 詩人はかじ屋のように定規を用いて仕事をするものではない.

by the square 正確に ▪ Tell us *by the square* why it is so. なぜそうなのか, きっちり教えてくれ.

call it square 《口》決済ずみとする; けりをつける ▪ He was willing to *call it square.* 彼は喜んで決済ずみとするつもりだった ▪ Why not *call it square* and have done with absurd quarrelling? どうしてけりをつけてこのばかなけんかをやめないのか.

fair and square →FAIR.

from square one 振り出しから ▪ He lost everything in the fire and had to start again *from square one.* 彼は火事で一切を失い, 再び振り出しからやり直さねばならなかった.

get square with **1** …と清算する ▪ He *got square with* his creditors. 彼は債権者と清算した.
2 …に仕返しする ▪ I'll *get square with* him for this. 彼にこの仕返しをしてやるぞ.

get things square 《俗》事をのみこむ ▪ Now I'm beginning to *get things square.* 今や事がのみこめてきた.

on [***upon***] ***the square*** **1** 正直に, 几帳面に (↔on the CROSS 2) ▪ He does not always deal *upon the square.* 彼は必ずしも正直な取引をしない.
2 《俗》[[補語句として]] 正直な, 几帳面な ▪ I've always been *on the square* with you. あなたにはいつも正直にしてきました.
3 直角に, まっすぐに ▪ This bridge is to be built under the railways *on the square.* この橋は鉄道の下にまっすぐにかけられるはずだ.
4 (体が)がっしりと ▪ The man is built *on the square.* その男はがっしりとした体格だ.
5 フリーメイソン会員で ▪ We parted *on the Square.* 我々はフリーメイソン会員であるときに別れた. ☞フリーメイソンのシンボルは四角であることから.

out of square **1** 常態でない, 乱れて ▪ How *out of square* this error of the world is! この世界の誤りはなんと常態でないことか.
2 無秩序に, 混乱して ▪ That put all things *out of square.* それで万事が支離滅裂になってしまった.
3 直角をなさないで; がっしりしていない ▪ There was nothing in him that was *out of square.* 彼はがっしりしていないところはどこもなかった.

play square 公明正大にやる ▪ Finance is a difficult game in which to *play square.* 財政は公明正大にやるのがむずかしいゲームだ.

square play [***dealing***] 公明正大なやり方 ▪ He has a reputation for integrity and *square dealing.* 彼は正直さと公明正大なやり方で評判だ.

the square thing 正直[公平]な扱い ▪ I've tried to do *the square thing* by you. 君には公平な扱いをするように努めてきました.

three squares (***a day***) 1日3回の食事, 食うに困らない暮らし ▪ I got back home to *three squares* after graduating from college. 大学卒業後1日3回の飯にありつけるわが家に戻った.

square[2] /skweər/ 動 ***square*** *one's* [***an***] ***account with/square accounts with*** →ACCOUNT[1].

square *one's* ***elbows*** [***shoulders***] ひじを張る[肩をいからせる]《けんかの身がまえ》 ▪ He stood there

S

with his head thrown back and *his shoulders squared*. 彼は頭をそらし, 肩をいからせてそこに立っていた.

square it 《米俗》正直に暮らす, 行動する ▪ Give a poor fellow a chance to *square it* for three months. かわいそうな男に3か月間正直に暮らすチャンスを与えてやるがいい.

square the circle →CIRCLE.

square** oneself **with …にわびる, と仲直りする ▪ It is better to *square yourself with* Helen. 君はヘレンと仲直りするほうがよい.

squeak /skwiːk/ 名 ***a narrow*** [***near, tight***] ***squeak*** (***for it***) 間一髪, 九死に一生 ▪ I have often had *a narrow squeak for it*. 私は何度も間一髪という目にあった.

squeaky /skwíːki/ 形 ***squeaky clean*** → CLEAN[1].

squeaky wheel 《米》ゴネ得, 声のでかい人(→The squeaking WHEEL gets the oil) ▪ The *squeaky wheel* gets the grease [oil]. 大声の人ほど注目を集める.

squeal /skwiːl/ 動 ***make** a person **squeal*** 《俗》人をゆする ▪ Yeah, I *made* him *squeal* once or twice. うん, おれはあいつを1, 2回ゆすったよ.

squeeze[1] /skwiːz/ 名 ***a main squeeze*** 《米俗》決まった恋人, 妻 ▪ His *main squeeze* is my good friend's sister. 彼のお決まりの相手はぼくの親友の妹さ ▪ Jill is Jack's *main squeeze*. ジルはジャックの奥さんだ.

a narrow [***close, tight***] ***squeeze*** 《口》間一髪, 九死に一生 ▪ He had *a* still more *narrow squeeze*. 彼はさらにきわどい間一髪という目にあった.

a squeeze play スクイズ; 圧力 ▪ Workers were caught in *a squeeze play* between union and management. 労働者たちは労使双方の圧力のもとに置かれていた.

at [***upon***] ***a squeeze*** 危急の場合は ▪ I assist as solist *at a squeeze*. 危急の場合は私は独奏者として援助するのです.

give** a person **a squeeze (***of the hand***) 人の手をぎゅうっと握りしめる ▪ She *gave* me a hug and *a squeeze*. 彼女は私を抱きしめぎゅうっと握手した.

in a tight squeeze 困った立場に陥って ▪ We shall be *in a tight squeeze* if we cannot find the £10. 例の10ポンドを見つけることができなければ困ったことになるだろう.

put the squeeze on =put the SCREW on.

squeeze[2] /skwiːz/ 動 ***squeeze** oneself* 割り込む ▪ He *squeezed himself* into a crowded bus. 彼は満員のバスの中へ割り込んだ.

squeeze a tear 無理に泣く, 悲しそうに見せかけて泣く ▪ When that woman dies I shall find it hard to *squeeze a tear*. あの女が死んでも無理には泣けまい.

squeeze ... dry …を干からびさせる ▪ The war *squeezed* the economy of this country *dry*. 戦争でこの国の経済は枯渇した.

squeeze** one's **way 押し分けて進む ▪ He *squeezed his way* through the crowd. 彼は群衆を押し分けて進んで行った.

squib /skwɪb/ 名 ***a damp squib*** →DAMP.

squint /skwɪnt/ 名 ***have a squint at*** 《口》…を見る ▪ Let's *have a squint at* the picture. その絵を見てみようじゃないか.

stab[1] /stæb/ 名 ***a stab in the back*** 背信行為; 中傷 ▪ It was the most dastardly *stab in the back* that any man could experience. それはこの上もなく卑怯な背信行為だった.

a stab in the dark あて推量 ▪ He is a criminal if I may make *a stab in the dark*. あて推量で言わせてもらうなら, 彼が犯人さ.

have [***make***] ***a stab at*** 《口》…をやってみる ▪ D'you think you'll be able to travel tomorrow? —I'll *have a* good *stab at* it. あす旅行に出られると思うかい——一つ大いにやってみましょう.

stab[2] /stæb/ 動 ***stab** a person **in the back*** →BACK[1].

stab** a person **to the heart 《口》人の心を刺す ▪ His reproach *stabbed* me *to the heart*. 彼の非難は私の心を刺した.

stable /stéɪbəl/ 名 ***go out of the stable*** (馬が)競走に出る ▪ He allowed Woodbrook to *go out of the stable*. 彼はウッドブルック号が競走に出るのを許した.

shut [***close, lock***] ***the stable door after the horse is stolen*** [***has bolted***] 《諺》馬が盗まれたあと納屋[馬小屋]のドアを閉める,「泥棒を見てなわをなう」.

smell of the stable ふるまいで仕事がわかる ▪ Of course he's a schoolmaster. All his type *smells of the stable*. もちろん彼は学校の先生だ. あのタイプはすべてふるまいで仕事がわかる.

talk stable 馬の話をする ▪ He is always *talking stable*. 彼はいつも馬の話をしてばかりいる.

stack[1] /stæk/ 名 (***as***) ***dark*** [***black***] ***as a stack of black cats*** 《米口》きわめて暗い ▪ It's pretty still, and *as black as a stack of black cats*. 辺りはかなり静かでとても暗い.

blow** one's **stack 《米口》=blow one's TOP.

stacks of/a (***whole***) ***stack of*** 《口》非常にたくさんの(much) ▪ I have *a whole stack of* work to get through. すまさねばならない仕事が山ほどある.

stack[2] /stæk/ 動 ***Stack arms!*** 組め銃(つつ)《号令》!

stack the cards [***deck***] 《米》不正な切り方でトランプの札をそろえる ▪ Fortune had *stacked the cards* against him. 運命は彼に不利になるように不正な切り方で札をそろえていたのだ.

stack the cards [***chances, chips, deck, odds***] ***against*** [***in favor of***] …が非常に不利[有利]な立場にある ▪ I doubted your success. There are too many *cards stacked against* you. 僕は君の成功を疑っていた. 君はあまりに不利な立場にあるんだもの ▪ He had *the odds stacked against*

S

him from the start. 彼は最初から非常に不利な立場にあった ▪ *The cards were stacked against* me. 状況は私にとって不利であった.

staff /stæf|stɑːf/ 名 ***beat*** *a person* ***by*** [***with***] ***his own staff*** 人をその人の論法で論破する ▪ How well have I *been beaten with my own staff*! 私は自分の論法でまんまと論破されてしまったわい. ☞staff「杖, 棒」.

break the staff of bread 食物の供給を減じる[断つ](《聖》*Ps.* 105. 16, etc.) ▪ When the famine came, *the staff of bread was broken*. 飢きんになって食物の供給が減じた.

have the better end of the staff まさっている, うわ手である ▪ Miss Byron, I *have the better end of the staff*, I believe? バイロン嬢, 私のほうがうわ手のようですね.

have the staff in *one's* ***own hand*** 牛耳っている ▪ They knew they *had the staff in their own hands*. 彼らは自分たちが牛耳っていることは承知していた.

on the staff 部員[職員]で (*of*) ▪ He is *on the staff of* the "Japan Times." 彼はジャパンタイムズの社員だ ▪ We have the right men *on the staff*. うちの部員には適任者がいる.

set up *one's* ***staff*** 定住する ▪ They *set up their staff* in London. 彼らはロンドンに定住した.

staff and staple 主要素 ▪ Events of this sort are among the *staff and staple* of history. このたぐいの事件が歴史の主要素の一部となっている.

the staff of life 《文》生命の糧(かて), 主食《パンなど》 ▪ Rice has been and is *the staff of life* in Japan. 日本では米が昔も今も主食となっている.

stag /stæg/ 名 ***a stag party*** [***night***] 《口》(結婚前夜に友人が開く新郎のための)男だけのパーティー, 女性御法度の集まり (→a HEN party) ▪ On his *stag night*, his friends threw him into the pool. 男だけのパーティーで友人たちが彼をプールに投げ込んだ ▪ We wanted to give him *a stag party* before the wedding but Mick wasn't interested. 結婚式の前にミックのためにスタッグパーティーを開きたかったが, 彼は興味がなかった. ☞stag は女性を同伴していない男性の意.

go stag 《米口》(パーティーへ)女性の同伴者なしで行く ▪ Some of his friends were *going stag*. 彼の友人の中には女性の同伴者なしで行く者もいた.

turn stag 《俗》密告する ▪ He might prattle—*turn stag*. あの男はぺらぺらしゃべる, つまり密告するかもしれない.

stage /steɪdʒ/ 名 ***at that*** [***this***] ***stage of*** ...のその[この]段階では ▪ I don't need assistants *at this stage of* the experiment. 実験のこの段階では助手はいらない.

be on the stage 俳優である ▪ His uncle *is on the stage*. 彼のおじさんは俳優だ.

bring *a person* ***on*** [***to***] ***the stage*** 人を芝居にしくむ ▪ I will *bring* them *to the stage* out of revenge. 仕返しにあの連中を芝居にしくんでやろう.

bring [***put***]***...on the stage*** (劇)を上演する ▪ A new opera will *be brought on the stage* here. 新作オペラが当地で上演されます.

by [***in***] ***easy*** [***slow***] ***stages*** 楽な[ゆっくりした]行程で ▪ We proceeded leisurely and *by easy stages*. 我々はゆっくりと楽な行程で進んで行った.

by stages 一度に一定の距離ずつ, 徐々に ▪ The traveler did the long journey *by stages*. 旅人は一度に一定の距離ずつ長旅を行っていった.

come on the stage 舞台[世の中]に出る ▪ The final band that *came on the stage* was Trapt. 最後に出たバンドはトラプトだった.

go on [***take to***] ***the stage*** 舞台に出る, 俳優になる ▪ If he had *gone on the stage*, he would have made a good actor. 彼が舞台に出ていれば, いい俳優になっていただろうが.

have stage fright 人前であがる ▪ Even veteran actors and actresses *have stage fright* before the curtain goes up. ベテランの役者でさえ幕が開く前にはあがるものだ.

hold the stage **1** 上演されて観客を引きつける ▪ The play *holds the stage* year after year. その劇は毎年のように上演されて観客を引きつけている.
2 注目の的になる, 一人舞台である ▪ He likes to *hold the stage* at any meeting. 彼はどんな会でも注目の的になるのが好きだ.

in a stage whisper →a stage WHISPER.

quit [***retire from***] ***the stage*** 舞台を退く; 引退する; 死ぬ ▪ He *quitted the stage* of politics. 彼は政界から引退した.

set the stage for ...のお膳立てをする ▪ They *set the stage for* the discussion of problems. 彼らは諸問題を討議する準備をした.

take center stage 注目を浴びる ▪ She *took center stage* at the meeting. 彼女はその会議の席で注目を浴びた.

take the stage 《劇》(感銘的なせりふを述べ終わって)ものものしく舞台を歩き去る ▪ Having said so, she *took the stage*. そう言い終わると, 彼女はものものしく舞台から歩き去った.

walk on stage and off stage again 舞台にちょっと出てすぐ引っ込む, 端役をやる ▪ He played a very small part and *walked on stage and off stage again*. 彼はほんの端役だったので舞台に出るとすぐにまた引っ込んだ.

stagger /stǽgər/ 動 ***stagger belief*** 信じられない ▪ Such a scene almost *staggers belief*. そのような光景はほとんど信じられないものである.

stagger to *one's* ***feet*** →FOOT[1].

stair /steər/ 名 ***a flight*** [***pair***] ***of stairs*** 一続きの階段 ▪ He lives up two *pair of stairs*. 彼は3階に住んでいる.

below stairs 地下室で; 使用人室で ▪ Their affairs were being discussed *below stairs*. 彼らの情事は使用人室で話し合われていた.

down stairs 階下で[へ] ▪ Let's go *down stairs* now, and have some supper. さあ階下へ行って夕食にしましょう.

S

grease the stairs わなをしかける ▪ She had *greased the stairs* and I was fool enough not to see the danger. 彼女がわなをしかけていたのだが, 私は愚かにもその危険に気づかなかった.

up stairs 階上で[へ] ▪ Will you walk *up stairs* first? まず2階へお上がりくださいますか.

stake[1] /steɪk/ 名 ***at stake*** 危なくなって, 存亡にかかわって ▪ Your honor is *at stake*. 君の名誉がかかっている.

be condemned to the stake 火刑を宣告される ▪ He *was condemned to the stake*. 彼は火刑を宣告された.

burn ... at the stake …を火刑に処する[こっぴどく責める] ▪ He *was burnt* to death *at the stake*. 彼は火刑に処せられて死んだ.

draw stakes **1**《米》くいを抜く ▪ We must *draw stakes* and remove our tents. くいを抜いてテントを取りのけなくてはならない.
2 かけ金などを引っこめる ▪ He left off and *drew stakes*. 彼はやめてかけ金を引っこめた.

drive [***set, stick*** *one's*] ***stakes*** 《米》テントを張る; 落ち着く ▪ Where he settles, there he *sticks his stakes*. 彼は落ち着く所があると, そこでテントを張る ▪ I finally *drove stakes* on the river. 私はついにその川っぷちに落ち着いた.

go to the stake 《主に英》(信念を貫くために)どんな罰[困難]をも覚悟する ▪ They would *go to the stake* in defence of their rights. 彼らはおのれの権利を守るためにはどんな困難をも辞さないだろう. ☞信仰のために火刑に処せられたことから.

have a stake in (事件•事業)に利害関係を持つ; の福祉に関心を寄せている ▪ Scotland came to *have a stake in* this struggle. スコットランドはこの争いに利害関係を持つにいたった ▪ Those who hold landed property *have a stake in* the country. 地主たちは国の繁栄に関心を寄せている.

in the ... stakes …の面で ▪ She gives us a good impression *in the* personality *stakes*. 彼女は人柄の面で好感がもてます.

make [***raise***] ***a stake*** 《米口》金を儲ける, 財産を作る ▪ They work merely long enough to *raise a stake*. 彼らは金を儲けられる間だけ働いているにすぎない.

move stakes 《米口》転居する ▪ We have to *move stakes* farther down. 我々はずっと下の方に転居せねばならない.

pluck [***pull, haul***] ***up stakes*** 《口》(長年の居住地から)立ち去る ▪ They *pulled up stakes*, and returned to Springfield. 彼らは立ち去ってスプリングフィールドへ帰って行った.

set [***stick*** *one's*] ***stakes*** →drive STAKEs.

sweep the stakes →SWEEP².

up stakes →UP².

stake[2] /steɪk/ 動 ***stake all*** [*one's* ***life***] ***on*** ... に首をかける, 太鼓判を押す ▪ I'd *stake my life on* it. そのことには太鼓判を押してもいい.

stake (***out***) ***a*** [*one's*] ***claim*** (***to*** [***for, on***]) くいを打って自分の主張をする, 土地を区画する; 権利を主張する ▪ We have done so in order to *stake a claim for* a footing in Morocco. モロッコでの足がかりへの権利を主張するためにそうした.

stake *a person* ***to*** 《米口》人に…を貸して[買って]やる, 人に…を援助する ▪ I decided to *stake* the poor fellow *to* the money he needed. 私はそのかわいそうな男に必要な金額を貸してやることに決めた.

stalking /stɔ́ːkɪŋ/ 名 ***a stalking horse*** 当て馬候補; 口実 ▪ He is just *a stalking horse*. 彼は当て馬候補にすぎない ▪ The talk was *a stalking horse* of the deal between the two parties. その話し合いは二党間の取引の口実だった.

stall[1] /stɔːl/ 名 ***set out*** *one's* ***stall*** 《英》準備万端整える ▪ We have *set out our stall* to win the game. その試合に勝つために準備万端整えている.

stall[2] /stɔːl/ 動 ***stall for time*** 《米》時をかせぐためにゆっくりやる, 引き延ばし戦術をとる ▪ I decided that I'd better *stall for time*. 私は引き延ばし戦術をとったほうがよいと思った.

stamp[1] /stæmp/ 名 ***a rubber stamp*** →(a) RUBBER stamp.

bear the stamp of …の特徴を持っている ▪ He *bears the stamp of* an honest man. 彼には正直者の特徴がある.

of *one's* ***stamp*** …のような, 式の ▪ I dislike a man *of his stamp*. 彼のような人間はきらいだ.

stamp[2] /stæmp/ 動 ***stamp ... down*** [***to the ground***] …を踏みにじる ▪ His horse *stamped down* some of the enemy. 彼の馬は敵を幾人か踏みにじった.

stamp ... flat …をぺちゃんこに踏みつぶす ▪ The crowd *stamped* his hat *flat*. 群衆は彼の帽子をぺちゃんこに踏みつぶした.

stamp (***with***) *one's* ***foot*** じだんだを踏む ▪ He furiously *stamped with his foot*. 彼は怒り狂ってじだんだを踏んだ.

stand[1] /stænd/ 名 ***at a stand*** **1** 立ち往生して, 行きうまって ▪ The wind left us *at a stand*. 風のため我々は立ち往生してしまった ▪ Public business was *at a stand*. 公務は行きうまっていた.
2 途方にくれて ▪ Here I am a little *at a stand*. この点で僕は少し当惑している.

bring ... to a stand …を立ち往生させる ▪ We *were brought to a stand* on this very plain by severe fever. 我々は激しい熱病のおかげでちょうどこの平原に立ち往生させられた.

come to a stand **1** (特に獲物を見つけた犬が)ぴたっと止まる ▪ The dogs *came to a stand* on finding a fox. 犬たちはキツネを見つけてぴたっと止まった.
2 (事が)行きうまる ▪ Vegetation has quite *come to a stand*. 植物は全く生長が止まった.

lie at a stand 立ち往生する; 行きうまる ▪ Matters *lie* a little *at a stand*. 事態は少し行きうまっている.

make a stand **1** (敵などに)踏みとどまって防戦する, 抵抗する ▪ They will *make a stand* against op-

S

pression [for their principle]. 彼らは踏みとどまって抑圧に[主義のために]抵抗するだろう.

2 立ち止まる ▪ He *made a* sudden *stand*. 彼は突然立ち止まった.

make *one's* ***stand*** =make a STAND 1.

put ... to a stand **1** …を立ち往生させる ▪ His whole army *was put to a stand* at the first pass. 彼の全軍隊は最初のとうげで立ち往生させられた.

2 (人)を当惑させる ▪ There is one point, however, that *puts* me *to a stand*. しかし私を当惑させる点が一つある.

take a (firm) stand on [over] …に対して断固とした態度をとる ▪ Teachers are now *taking a firm stand on* indiscipline. 教師たちは無規律に対して今や断固とした態度をとっている.

take *one's* ***stand***/《詩》***take stand*** **1** 立つ, 陣取る ▪ He *took his stand* near the door. 彼は戸口のそばに立った.

2 (…に)拠る, 立脚する (*on*) ▪ I *take my stand on* the exact wording of the act. 私はその法令通りの言葉に立脚しているのです.

take the stand 《米》証人席につく ▪ The judge next asked the defendant to *take the stand*. 裁判官は次に被告に証言台に立つことを求めた.

take the stand on 《米口》…を保証する ▪ I could not *take the stand on* that myself. 私自身もそのことを保証することはできなかった.

stand² /stænd/ 動 ***as ... stands*** …の現状では; のままで ▪ *As* things *stand*, we can't hope to finish the work before next month. 現状では来月までに仕事を終えるなど望むべくもない ▪ The law, *as* it now *stands*, is severe on authors. その法律は現行のままでは著者に酷だ.

Don't just stand there(, do something)! (危機・困難に際して)そこにつっ立っていないで(何かしろ)《てきぱきやれ》.

How does it stand with ...? …はどんな様子か ▪ *How does it stand with* your studies? 君の勉強はどんな様子かね.

How does *one* ***stand?*** (財政的には)どういう具合なのか ▪ Nobody quite knew *how* he *stood* financially. 彼が財政的にはどういう具合なのか誰にもはっきりはわからなかった.

S

it stands well [ill, etc.] ***with*** …はうまく[まずく, など]いっている ▪ When *it stands well with* him, *it stands ill with* her. 彼がうまくいっているときには彼女がうまくいかない.

leave ... standing …よりずっと急速な進歩をする; 《英口》をはるかにしのぐ ▪ I *left* him *standing* in the study of English. 私は英語の勉強では彼よりも急速に進歩した ▪ She is a good singer and *leaves* the others *standing*. 彼女の歌はうまくて, 他の人をはるかにしのいでいる. ☞競馬から.

let ... stand …を中止にしておく, うっちゃっておく ▪ He *let* the matter *stand* for some time. 彼はしばらくその問題をうっちゃっておいた.

not know whether *one* ***is standing on*** *one's* ***head or*** *one's* ***heels*** 全く途方にくれている ▪ At her harsh words he *scarcely knew whether* he *was standing on his head or his heels*. 彼女のきつい言葉を聞いて彼はほとんど途方にくれていた.

stand a chance [a show] (成功・残存などの)見込みがある, 有望である (*of, for*) ▪ Do you want to *stand a show* in competition with them? 君は彼らと競争して勝ちたいのか ▪ This ideal *stands a* good *chance of* realization. この理想は実現の見込みが十分にある.

Stand and deliver! 止まってあり金を渡せ!《追いはぎの文句》 ▪ The highwayman ordered him to *stand and deliver*. その追いはぎは彼に止まってあり金をよこせと命じた.

stand and fight 踏みとどまって戦う ▪ They were not willing to *stand and fight*. 彼らは踏みとどまって戦うのがいやだった.

stand clear 離れている (*from, of*) ▪ The liftman asked the people to *stand clear from* the gates. エレベーター係は客に戸口から離れていてくださいと言った.

stand corrected →CORRECT².

stand deep in (土地が作物)で豊かにおおわれている ▪ The fields *stand deep in* corn. 畑は小麦で豊かにおおわれている.

Stand easy! →EASY.

stand fair **1** 都合がよい, 見込みがある (*for, to do*) ▪ He seems to *stand fairest for* that important post. 彼がその要職には一番都合がよいように見える ▪ He *stands fair to* be elected pope. 彼は教皇に選ばれる見込みがある.

2 よごれがない; 気に入りである (*with*) ▪ The priest *stood fair with* the neighborhood. その司祭は近所の人々の受けがよかった.

stand four-square against → FOUR-SQUARE.

stand free (from) (…から)免れている ▪ He seems to have *stood free from* all suspicion. 彼はあらゆる疑いを免れてきたように思われる.

stand good →hold GOOD.

stand it out **1** あくまでもがんばる ▪ I *stood it out* obstinately. 私は頑固にがんばり通した.

2 主張する (*that*) ▪ He stoutly *stood it out that* he was a gentleman of Cumberland. 彼は自分はカンバランドの出身だと頑固に主張した.

stand on end →on END.

stand ... on *one's* ***head*** → stand ... on its HEAD.

stand on [upon] *one's* ***head*** **1** 逆立ちする ▪ A tumbler came in, and *stood on his head*. 軽業師が入って来て逆立ちした.

2 逆立ちせんばかりに喜ぶ ▪ He would have *stood on his head* with joy at the news. その知らせを聞いていたら彼は逆立ちせんばかりに喜んだことだろう.

3 (議論など)を覆す, ひっくり返す ▪ The chairman *stood* the idea *on its head* by showing its unpracticality. 議長はその考えが実務的でないことを示してそれをひっくり返した.

stand or fall (…が)生きるか死ぬか, のるかそるか, 立つか倒れるか (*with, together, by*) ▪ I know we must *stand or fall together.* 我々が生死を共にしなければならないのは私も承知している ▪ The solicitors must *stand or fall by* [*with*] the bill they have sent in. 事務弁護士たちは彼らが提出した議案によって[とともに]のるかそるかしなければならない.

stand out a mile ＝STICK out a mile.

stand pat →PAT².

stand still →STILL.

stand to it **1** 頑強に戦う; せっせと励む ▪ He encouraged his men to *stand to it.* 彼は兵士たちに頑強に戦うように励ました ▪ The peasants *stood to it* like men. 農民たちは男らしくせっせと励んだ.
2 (陳述・主張などを)主張[固執]する (*that*) ▪ He *stood to it* at first *that* he knew nothing. 彼は初めのうちは何も知らないと言い張った.

stand to win [***gain, lose***] (賭け・投機などで)勝ち[儲け, 失い]そうな形勢にある ▪ He *stands to win* either way. 彼はどっちみち勝ちそうな形勢だ ▪ He *stood to lose* twenty thousand dollars. 彼は2万ドル失いそうな形勢だった.

stand up and be counted (抵抗に負けずに)強く主張する ▪ Why weren't the delegates men enough to *stand up and be counted?* なぜ代表団は男らしく強く主張しなかったのか.

stand up for *oneself* ちゃんと自立する, 他人に左右されない ▪ He's able to *stand up for himself* in any affair. 彼は何をやらせてもちゃんと自分でできる.

stand upright 直立する ▪ My hair *stood upright* for fear. 恐ろしさのあまり髪の毛が逆立った.

stand well with *a person* 人に受けがよい ▪ He *stood well with* his aunt. 彼はおばに受けがよかった.

standing on *one's* ***head*** 楽に, 訳なく ▪ You can pass that *standing on your head.* 君はそんなものは朝めし前にパスするよ.

where *one* ***stands*** 〚know, learn, find out の目的語として〛 自分の現状[関係] (*with*) ▪ John and I have quarreled and I don't *know where* I *stand with* him. ジョンとはけんかをしたので, どういう関係になっているか分からない.

standard /stǽndərd/ 名 ***below standard*** 標準以下で ▪ The work is *below standard.* その仕事は標準以下だ.

join the standard of …の旗下にはせ参じる ▪ All the nations of southern Italy were ready to *join his standard.* 南イタリアのすべての民族は進んで彼の旗下にはせ参じようとしていた.

raise *one's* [***the***] ***standard*** 兵を起こす ▪ He *raised his standard* at once and marched to London. 彼はすぐ兵を起こしてロンドンに進軍した ▪ He *raised the standard* of revolt in his province. 彼は自分の地方で反旗を翻した.

under the standard of …の旗下に ▪ He had 2,000 men *under his standard.* 彼は2,000人の兵を旗下に集めていた.

up to (***the***) ***standard*** 標準に達して, 合格して ▪ The methods were fully *up to standard.* その方法は十分に標準に達していた ▪ He comes *up to standard.* 彼は合格だ.

standby /stǽndbàɪ/ 名 ***on standby*** キャンセル待ちで; 待機して ▪ In this country passengers often wait *on standby* for available seats. この国では乗客は座席を取るためによくキャンセル待ちをさせられる.

standing /stǽndɪŋ/ 名形 ***all standing***
1 《海》 艤装を解かずに ▪ The next morning we found the ship *all standing* as we had left it. その翌朝船は以前通り艤装を解かぬままになっていた.
2 衣服を着たままで ▪ I dined, and turned in *all standing* for the night. 私は夕食をすまし, 衣服を着たままで寝た.

be in good standing with *a person* 人の受けがよい ▪ The Duke *was in good standing with* the English king. 公爵はイギリス王の寵遇を得ていた.

in good standing (会員が)会費を全納している ▪ He is a member *in good standing.* 彼は会費を全納している会員だ.

of long standing 長い間の ▪ She was suffering from tuberculosis *of long standing.* 彼女は長い間肺結核を病んでいた.

of (…) ***standing*** 地位[名声]のある ▪ They are all men *of* high *standing.* 彼らはすべて地位の高い人々だ ▪ He is *of* no *standing.* 彼は名声など少しもない.

standstill /stǽndstɪ̀l/ 名 ***be at a standstill*** 止まっている; 行き詰まっている ▪ Many mills *are at a standstill.* 多くの工場は休業している ▪ All our plans *are at a standstill.* 我々の計画はすべて行き詰まっている.

come to [***be brought to***] ***a standstill*** 止まる; 行き詰まる ▪ The conference has *come to a standstill.* 会議は行き詰まった.

stand-up /stǽndʌ̀p/ 形 ***a stand-up comedian*** 一人演技のコメディアン ▪ He performs well as *a stand-up comedian.* 一人演技のコメディアンとしての彼はうまい.

a stand-up fight [***argument***] 正々堂々たる戦い ▪ They had *a stand-up fight.* 彼らは正々堂々と戦った.

star¹ /stɑːr/ 名 ***be born under an unlucky*** [***a lucky, a fortunate***] ***star*** 不運[幸運]の星の下に生まれる ▪ Lost that job as well? You *were born under an unlucky star.* その仕事にもあぶれたって? 君は不運の星の下に生まれたんだね.

be born under the same star 同じ星の下に生まれる, 性が合う ▪ They *were born under the same star.* 彼らは性が合う.

be through with *one's* ***star*** 運が尽きる; 人気を失う ▪ Royce *is through with his star* as far as this town is concerned. ロイスはこの町に関するかぎり人気を失っている.

bless *one's* (***lucky***) ***stars*** → thank one's (lucky) STARs.

S

curse *one's* ***stars*** 運勢の星をのろう ▪ It will be folly to *curse your stars*. 自分の運勢の星をのろうのはばかげている.

My stars!/《戯》***My stars and garters!*** これは驚いた!, おやまあ!《軽い驚きの表現》 ▪ *My stars and garters!* What sort of man is this? こいつはおったまげた! こやつは一体どういう人間なんだろう.

see stars 《口》目から火が出る ▪ He hit me so hard that it made me *see stars*. 彼にひどくぶんなぐられたので目から火が出た.

shoot [***reach***] ***for the stars*** 高望みをする ▪ One of my friends is an ambitious boy who is *shooting for the stars*. ぼくの友人の一人は高望みをする覇気に満ちたやつだ.

One's ***star has set*** [***is in the ascendant***]. 運勢の星が沈んだ[上ってきている] ▪ She was a good actress, but *her star has set*. 彼女はよい女優だったが今は落ち目になっている ▪ He considered *her star* to *be in the ascendant*. 彼女の運勢は上り坂だと彼は考えていた.

stars in *one's* ***eyes*** 大得意, 意気揚々; 夢心地 ▪ She was a young girl with *stars in her eyes*. 彼女は意気揚々としたうら若い娘だった ▪ She had *stars in her eyes* when she talked about her paintings. 彼女は絵の話となると夢心地だった.

stars in their courses 軌道を運行する星 (《聖》*Judg*. 5. 20) ▪ The *stars in their courses* are for man. 軌道を運行する星は人間のためのものだ.

thank [***bless***] *one's* (***lucky***) ***stars*** 運勢の星に感謝する ▪ I *blessed my stars* that I was a bachelor. 私は自分がひとり者であることを運勢の星に感謝した ▪ I *thank my stars* for it. 私は運勢の星にそれを感謝する.

the star of day [***noon***] 太陽 ▪ *The star of day* had reached the west. 太陽は西に傾いていた.

under the stars 星空の下で ▪ He returned home *under the stars*. 彼は星をいただいて帰宅した.

star[2] /stɑːr/ 動 ***star it*** (俳優が)主演する ▪ Fitzwilliam is *starring it* among them. フィッツウィリアムが彼らのうちで主演している.

star the provinces (俳優が)地方を主演して回る ▪ She had *starred the provinces* with great eclat. 彼女は地方を主演して回って大喝采を博した.

starch[1] /stɑːrtʃ/ 名 ***take the starch out of*** 《米口》 **1** (人)の高慢の鼻をくじく ▪ I will *take* some *starch out of* the Cheyennes. シャイアン族の高慢の鼻をちょっぴりくじいてやろう.

2 (人)を疲れさせる, 無気力にする ▪ The travel *took the starch out of* Robert's knees. その旅行はロバートの足を疲れさせてしまった.

3 …の堅苦しさを取り去る ▪ Her genial smile *took the starch out of* his manner. 彼女のにこやかなほほえみで彼の態度の堅苦しさが取れた.

starch[2] /stɑːrtʃ/ 動 ***be starched up*** 《米》着飾っている ▪ She *is starched up* for the party. 彼女はパーティーのために着飾っている.

stare[1] /steər/ 名 ***greet a person with an icy stare*** 人を冷淡に迎える ▪ They *greeted* me *with an icy stare*. 彼らは私を冷淡に迎えた.

stare[2] /steər/ 動 ***make*** *a person* ***stare*** 人をびっくりさせる ▪ Even good men like to *make* the public *stare*. 善人でも大衆の目を見張らせるのを好む.

stare *a person* ***in the face*** **1** じろじろ人の顔を見る ▪ He *stared* me *in the face* without recognizing me. 彼はじろじろ私の顔を見たが私に気がつかなかった.

2 (死・破産・滅亡などが)人の目前に迫る; (誤り・矛盾などが)人には明白である ▪ Ruin and bankruptcy were *staring* him *in the face*. 滅亡と破産が彼の目前に迫っていた ▪ The contradiction *stared* him *in the face*. その矛盾は彼には明白であった.

stare *a person* ***out of countenance*** 人をじろじろ見てきまり悪がらせる ▪ She *stared* the young man *out of countenance*. 彼女はその青年をじろじろ見てきまり悪がらせた.

stare *a person* ***up and down*** 人を頭のてっぺんからつま先までじろじろ見る ▪ They are *staring* me *up and down* like a wild animal. 彼らはまるで野生の動物でも見るように私を頭のてっぺんからつま先までじろじろ見ている.

staring /stéərɪŋ/ 副 ***stark staring mad*** すっかり気が違って ▪ He must be *stark staring mad*. 彼はすっかり気が違っているにちがいない.

stark /stɑːrk/ 副 ***stark*** [《米》***buck***] ***naked*** 素っ[真っ]裸の ▪ He was walking on the beach *stark naked*. 彼は素っ裸でビーチを歩いていた.

start[1] /stɑːrt/ 名 ***at the start*** 初めは ▪ It is difficult work *at the start*. 初めはむずかしい仕事だ.

by fits and starts →FIT[1].

for a start 手始めに; まず第一に ▪ You will work here *for a start*. 手始めにここで働きなさい ▪ *For a start* his data are wrong. まず第一に彼のデータはまちがっている.

from start to finish 初めから終わりまで, 終始一貫 ▪ The whole thing was unusual, *from start to finish*. その事はすべて初めから終わりまで異常だった.

from the start 最初から ▪ Women have voted in County Council elections *from the start*. 女性は州参事会の選挙では最初から投票してきた.

get a good start →make a good [bad] START.

get off to a flying [***running***] ***start*** 好調なすべり出しをする ▪ He *got off to a flying start* in his new job. 彼の新しい仕事は好調なすべり出しだった.

get off to a good [***bad***] ***start*** すべり出しが好調[不調]である ▪ We *got off to a good start*. すべり出しは好調だった.

get [***have***] ***the start*** (***of***) (競争相手の)先駆けをする, 機先を制する ▪ I let him *have the start of* me. 彼に私の機先を制することを許した.

give a start ぎくり[はっ]とする ▪ He *gave a start* of astonishment, and stood still. 彼ははっと驚いて立ち止まった.

give *a person* ***a start*** **1** 人をぎくり[びくっ]とさせる ▪ What *a start* you *gave* me! 君にはひどくぎくりと

させられたよ.

2 人に(…の)先発を許す ▪ The children *were given a start* of ten yards [15 seconds]. 子供たちは10ヤード[15秒]の先発を許された.

have a head start 人に先んずる, 幸先のよいスタートを切っている ▪ She *has a head start* in her class. 彼女はクラスで人に先んじている.

make a fresh start 新規まき直しをする ▪ Let's *make a fresh start*, and be friends. 新規まき直しをして友人になろうじゃないですか.

make* [*get*] *a good* [*bad*] *start 幸先よく[悪く]乗り出す ▪ There is nothing in life like *making a good start*. 人生では幸先よく乗り出すに越したことはない ▪ He *made a bad start*. 彼は手始めがまずかった.

make a start on (事)を始める ▪ I have *made a start on* my next book. 私は次の本を書き始めた.

with a start ぎくっ[はっ]として ▪ He awoke *with a start*. 彼はぎくっとして目をさました.

start[2] /stɑːrt/ 動 ***Don't* (*you*) *start!*** 《英口》文句を[ぶつくさ]言わないで.

start** a person **doing 人に…させ始める ▪ This news *started* me *thinking*. この知らせをきっかけに私は考え込んだ.

start fair (競走などで)平等にスタートする ▪ No, let's *start fair*. いや, 平等にスタートしましょう.

start in business 商売を始める ▪ He *started in business* on his own account. 彼は独力で商売を始めた.

start in life 世の中へ出る, 世渡りを始める ▪ He *started in life* very heavily handicapped. 彼はひどく不利な条件で世渡りを始めた.

start off on the right* [*wrong*] *foot = get off on the right FOOT.

***start off to** do* …するつもりで始める ▪ I *started off to* do it by myself, but in the end I had to ask for help. それを一人でするつもりで始めたが, 結局援助を頼むはめになった.

***start on* [*upon, to*] *one's* feet** ぱっと立ち上がる ▪ He *started on his feet*. 彼はぱっと立ち上がった.

start school 学校へ行き始める ▪ I *started school* on September 10th. 私は9月10日に登校を始めた.

start something 《米口》騒動を起こす ▪ The man was an agitator, seeking to *start something*. 男は騒動を起こそうとしている扇動者だった.

start* (*up*) *from cold (エンジンを)冷えているのをかける ▪ Do not race the engine when *starting up from cold*. エンジンの冷えているのをかけるときにはふかしてはいけない.

One ***started it!*** 《口》人が先に始めたんだ! ▪ Don't fight, you two—He *started it!* 二人ともけんかするな—彼が先に始めたんだ!

***starting from* [*with*]** …から始めて ▪ We will recite this poem, *starting from* Tom. トムから始めて, この詩を朗読しよう.

to start with 〚独立不定詞〛まず第一に; 初めに ▪ You have no right to be here, *to start with*. まず第一に君はここにいる資格がない ▪ We had six members *to start with*. 我々の顔ぶれは初めは6人だった.

starter /stáːrtər/ 名 ***as* [*for*] *a starter*** 《口》手始めに ▪ I'll offer you fifty a week *as a starter*. 手始めに週50ドルあげよう.

for starters 《口》= as a STARTER.

starting /stáːrtɪŋ/ 名 ***at starting*** **1** (競走・旅行の)初めに ▪ I have not taken a roundtrip ticket *at starting*. 出発のときに往復乗車券を買わなかった.

2 手始めに ▪ Let me remind you of this *at starting*. 手始めにこのことを思い出してもらいたい.

startle /stáːrtəl/ 動 ***startle** a person **out of** his **mind* [*wits*]** 人をびっくり仰天させる ▪ You *startled* me *out of my wits*. 君にはひどくびっくりしたよ.

starvation /stɑːrvéɪʃən/ 名 ***be on a starvation diet*** 飢餓食をしている ▪ During the war we *were on a starvation diet*. 戦争中我々は飢餓食をしていた.

starve /stɑːrv/ 動 ***be starved for* [*of*]** (必要物)が不足している; 《米口》腹ペコだ ▪ The engine *was starved for* fuel. エンジンは燃料が不足していた.

be starving for = be STARVEd for.

***starve … into surrender* [*submission*]** …を兵糧攻めで降服させる ▪ We tried to *starve* the garrison *into surrender*. 我々は守備隊を兵糧攻めで降服させようとした.

starve to death 飢え死にする ▪ The man *starved to death*. 男は飢え死にした.

starve with cold こごえ死にしそうにさせる ▪ The kitten mewed as though it *was starved with cold*. 子猫は凍死しかけているような声で鳴いた.

state /steɪt/ 名 ***a state of grace*** 恩寵を受けている状態; (一般に)有利な状態 (↔in a state of NATURE 1) ▪ We aspire to *a state of grace*. 我々は恩寵を受けている状態にあこがれる.

be in a state 《口》 **1** (よごれたりぬれたりして)ひどい格好をしている ▪ Just look what *a state* I *am in*! まあこのひどい格好を見てくれよ!

2 興奮[心配]している ▪ She *was in* quite *a state* about it. 彼女はそのことですっかり興奮していた.

future state 来世, 後世 ▪ It is clear evidence of a *future state*. それは来世のある明らかなあかしである.

get into a state 《口》興奮[心配]する ▪ Now don't *get into a state*. まあ興奮しないでください.

in a bad state ひどい状態で ▪ The house was *in a bad state*. 家はひどい状態になっていた.

in great* [*easy*] *state ものものしい[くつろいだ]様子で ▪ The Lord Mayor went *in great state* to the Cathedral. ロンドン市長はものものしく大聖堂へ進んだ.

in state ものものしく; 従者をたくさん従えて; 威風堂々と ▪ The king traveled *in state*. 王は従者をたくさん従えて進んだ ▪ Lamas came to the temple *in state*. ラマ僧たちはものものしく寺院へやって来た.

keep (*one's*) **state** もったいぶる, 威厳を保つ ▪ But *keep your state* with them. しかし, あの連中に対しては威厳を保つがよい.

One's **last state is worse than the first.** 《諺》最後の状態は初めよりももっと悪くなる《改良のつもりが改悪になることがある》(《聖》*Matt.* 12. 45).

lie in state (遺骸が埋葬の前に)厳かに安置されている ▪ The king's body *lay in state* for two days in the cathedral. 王の遺体は大聖堂に2日間安置された.

of state 壮麗な, 豪華な ▪ Parliament forced the King to relinquish the chair *of state*. 議会は強引に国王に王座を破棄させた ▪ He rode in his carriage *of state*. 彼は豪華な馬車に乗っていた.

the state of play (特にクリケットの)現在までの得点; (交渉・論争などの)現在までの状況 ▪ This is highly readable summary of *the state of play*. これは現在までの状況の非常におもしろい要約である.

the state of the art **1** = the STATE of play. **2** 最先端の科学技術[ハイテク] ▪ I always buy *the* latest, *state-of-the-art* personal computer. いつも最新式で最先端のハイテクによるパソコンを買うんだ《通例 state-of-the-art のように形容詞として用いられる》.

the state of the case 事情 ▪ This totally changes *the* whole *state of the case*. これで事情はすっかり変わってしまう.

the [**a**] **state of things** [**affairs**] 事態, 形勢 ▪ On the Welsh border *the state of things* was very unsettled. ウェールズの国境では事態はすこぶる不安定であった.

static /stǽtɪk/ 名 **give** *a person* **static** 人に生意気な返事をする, 口答えをする ▪ Do it at once! Don't *give* me any *static*! すぐにそれをやれ! 口答えは許さん!

station[1] /stéɪʃən/ 名 **above** *one's* **station** 自分の地位[身分]を忘れて ▪ The newcomer is getting *above his station*. あの新米は身の程を忘れかけている.

go [**make, perform**] *one's* [**the**] **stations**/ **go on** [**for**] **stations** 予定の各聖地を巡礼する ▪ They made us *perform the stations* at three altars. 彼らは我々に聖地を3か所巡礼させた ▪ He *went* to the temple *on stations*. 彼は巡礼してその寺院へ向かった.

S

in any station [**all stations**] **of life** どんな地位においても ▪ Thomas could be a great credit *in any station of life*. トマスはどんな地位についても, 大変立派にやってのけるだろう.

keep *one's* **station** 持ち場を離れない ▪ They *kept their station* for a while. 彼らはしばらくその持ち場を離れなかった.

marry beneath *one's* **station** 人より身分の下の人と結婚する ▪ She *married beneath her station* and her father refused to speak to her. 自分より身分の下の者と結婚した彼女に父親は口をきこうともしなかった.

of good [**lowly**] **station** 良い[低い]身分の ▪ The man came *of good station*. 男は良い身分の出であった ▪ The Mayor was *of lowly station*. 市長は低い身分の出だった.

one's **station in life** 社会的地位[身分] ▪ *Mr. Peel's station in life* was that of a solicitor's clerk. ピール氏の身分は事務弁護士の書記だった.

take (**up**) *one's* **station** 持ち場につく, 陣取る ▪ He *took up his station* at the mouth of the cave. 彼は洞窟の入り口に陣取った.

station[2] /stéɪʃən/ 動 **station** *oneself* (...に)陣取る ▪ The detective *stationed himself* among the bushes. 探偵は茂みの中に隠れた.

status /stéɪtəs/ 名 **status** (**in**) **quo** 現状 ▪ They are keen to maintain the *status quo*. 彼らは現状維持に懸命だ. ☞ L 'the state in which (something is)'.

stave /steɪv/ 動 **be stove up** 《米口》へとへとだ ▪ I can't walk any further. I'*m stove up*. もう歩けない. くたくただ.

stave ... to pieces ...をばらばらにこわす ▪ The ship *was staved to pieces* by the violence of the winds and waves. 船は激しい風波でばらばらに壊れた.

stay[1] /steɪ/ 名 **make** (**a**) **stay** 立ち止まる; ひと息する ▪ He *made* many *a stay* ascending up the craggy hill. ごつごつした山道を登りながら彼は何度も立ち止まった ▪ We *made stay* at the inn. その宿屋で一服した.

put a stay on ...を制御[抑制]する ▪ This will *put a stay on* his activity. これで彼の活動も抑制されるだろう.

stay[2] /steɪ/ 動 **be here** [**there, in**] **to stay** 《米》普及してきた, 基礎が固まった, 定着してきた ▪ Digital television (DTV) *is here to stay*. デジタルテレビが普及してきた ▪ The South's new industry *is there to stay*. 南部の新産業の基礎が固まってきた.

come to stay 《口》定着する; 確固たる地位を得てくる ▪ I hope peace will *come to stay*. 平和が定着すればよい ▪ Byron as a letter-writer has *come to stay*. 書簡家としてのバイロンの地位が確立した.

stay at home 家でじっとしている ▪ I hate to *stay at home* doing nothing. 何もしないで家でじっとしているのは嫌いだ.

stay *one's* [*a person's*] **hand** 《古》手を押さえる; 攻撃したり行動するのをやめる[やめさせる] ▪ My tongue is tied and *my hand is stayed*. 私は口止めされてはいるし手も押さえられている ▪ None can *stay his hand*. 誰も彼の手を押さえることができない.

stay on top **1** 優秀[健康]である ▪ *Stay on top*! 健康であれ. **2** (...を)支配[統御, 管理]する (*of*) ▪ The teacher *stayed on top of* the students. 先生は生徒を管理した.

stay one step ahead of = keep one STEP ahead (of).

stay put 《口》(...が)動かずにいる; 変わらない ▪ I'll go and fetch some tools; meanwhile, you *stay put*. 僕が道具を取りに行ってくるから, その間君はこのま

までいてくれ.

stay still じっとしている ▪ The painter asked the model to *stay still*, as she was. 画家はモデルにそのままの姿勢でじっとしていてくれと頼んだ.

stay for supper [***tea, coffee,*** etc.] 夕飯[お茶，コーヒー，など]までいる ▪ He *stayed for supper* with us. 彼はうちに夕飯までいた ▪ I asked them to *stay for tea*. 私は彼らにお茶までいてくださいと言った.

stay the night →spend the NIGHT with a person.

stay the [*one's*] ***stomach*** [***appetite***] 一時的に飢えをしのぐ ▪ The fight seemed to have *stayed the stomach* of the Lamas for fighting. その戦闘はラマ僧たちの戦闘欲を一時静めた様子だった ▪ This will *stay the appetite* when chewed. これをかめば一時飢えがしのげる.

stay up late 夜更かしする ▪ I have to *stay up late* these days because I'm preparing for the final exam. 期末試験準備でこのところ夜更かししている.

stead /sted/ 名 ***in*** *a person's* ***stead*** 《雅》人の後がまとして; 人の代わりに ▪ A new sexton was chosen *in his stead*. 彼の後がまとして新しい寺男が選ばれた ▪ I am willing to die *in his stead*. 彼の身代わりなら喜んで死ぬよ.

in the stead of 《古》…の代わりに ▪ He was elected Alderman *in the stead of* Mr. John Nangle. 彼はジョン・ナングル氏に代わって市参事会員に選出された.

stand *a person* ***in little*** [***much, good***] ***stead*** 人にほとんど役に立たない[大いに役に立つ] ▪ His early training *stood* him *in good stead*. 彼の若いころの訓練が大いに役に立った ▪ Our good intentions *stand* us *in little stead*. 我々の善意もほとんど役に立たない.

steady /stédi/ 形副 ***a steady hand*** **1** 震えない手 ▪ John has *a steady hand*. ジョンは震えない手の持ち主だ.

2 しっかりした人 ▪ He is *a steady hand*. 彼はしっかりした人物だ.

(***as***) ***steady as a rock*** →(as) firm as a ROCK.

go steady **1** いつも決まった相手とデートをする (*with*) ▪ Are you *going steady with* Alice? 君はアリスといつもデートをしているのかい.

2 慎重にやる[扱う] (*about, with*) ▪ *Go steady with* that vase. その花器は大事に扱ってくれよ.

Steady on! 《口》ばたばたするな!, 注意しろ! ☞急いでいる人に向かって言う.

steady on *one's* ***legs*** [《俗》***pins***] 《俗》足がしっかりして ▪ The baby is already *steady on his pins*. 赤んぼうはもう足がしっかりしている.

steal[1] /stiːl/ 名 ***be a steal*** 《主に米》格安だ, 掘り出し物だ ▪ I got this for 5,000 yen. It's *a steal*. これ, 5千円だったよ. 格安だろ.

What a steal! すごく安い! ▪ I paid only 30,000 yen for this antique. *What a steal!* この骨董品, たったの3万円だったよ. すごく安かっただろ!

steal[2] /stiːl/ 動 ***steal a glance at*** →GLANCE[1].

steal a kiss from 《文》…の知らぬ間にキスをする, に不意にキスをする ▪ He first *stole a kiss from* me here. 彼はここで初めて私の知らぬ間にキスしたの.

steal *a person* ***blind*** →BLIND[1].

steal *one's* ***way*** こっそり行く ▪ He *stole his way* into the midst of their camp. 彼はその連中の野営地のまっ只中へ忍び込んだ.

stealth /stelθ/ 名 ***by stealth*** こっそりと, ひそかに ▪ The two lovers had met only *by stealth*. 二人の恋人同士は人目を盗んで会うしかなかった.

steam[1] /stiːm/ 名 (***at***) ***full*** [***half***] ***steam*** 全速力[半速力]で ▪ *Full steam* ahead and we'll clear this ground by mid-day. 全速力で進めば正午までにこの土地を離れることができるぞ.

blow off steam →let off (the) STEAM.

by steam 汽船で ▪ I traveled *by steam* to Marseilles. 私は汽船でマルセイユまで旅した.

come apart at the steams たくさんの問題を抱える ▪ We *came apart at the steams* at that time. その当時私たちはたくさんの問題を抱えていた.

Full steam ahead! ＝Full SPEED ahead!

gain steam 急速に増加[活発化]する ▪ Our interest in global warming has *gained steam* recently. 最近, 地球温暖化への関心が急速に高まってきている.

get up [***put on***] (***the***) ***steam*** **1** 蒸気を立てる ▪ The steamer *got up* more *steam*. 船はいっそう蒸気を立てた.

2 馬力を出す ▪ *Put* a little more *steam on*, ma'am. 奥さん, もう少し元気を出してください.

3 怒る ▪ When the bull had *got up steam*, he came for him. 雄牛は怒ると彼に突っかかってきた.

have all [***much,*** etc.] ***steam on*** すべての[大変な, など]馬力を出している ▪ I naturally went to grass through *having* too *much steam on*. あんまりひどく馬力を出したので私がへたばったのも無理はない.

have steam coming out of *one's* ***ears*** (***at***) 《口》(…に)激怒している, 腸が煮えくり返っている ▪ I *had steam coming out of my ears*, being kept waiting so long. 長い間待たされて向かっ腹が立っていた.

in steam (蒸気機関を)動かして ▪ He set the engine wholly *in steam*. 彼は蒸気機関をフルに動かした.

let [***blow***] ***off*** (***the***) ***steam*** 《口》ガス抜きをする, うっぷんを晴らす ▪ They *let* [*blew*] *off steam* by dancing and shouting. 彼らは踊ったりどなったりしてうっぷんを晴らした.

on *one's* ***own steam*** 独力で ▪ He had got here *on his own steam*. 彼は独力でここまで来ていたのだ.

pick [***build, get***] ***up steam*** 《米》勢いを増す; スピードを上げる ▪ The economy will *pick up steam* next year. 景気は来年には勢いうくだろう.

put on (***the***) ***steam*** →get up (the) STEAM.

S

raise steam ＝get up (the) STEAM 1.

run out of steam 《口》(運動・攻撃などが)勢いが衰える, 活力を失う; (人が)気力をなくす, 息切れする ▪ The movement has *run out of steam.* その運動は勢いが衰えた ▪ They *ran out of steam* while going up the hill. 彼らは丘に登っている途中で息切れした.

shut [***turn***] ***off*** (***the***) ***steam*** 蒸気を遮断する[止める] ▪ The engineer had *turned off the steam* to prevent the boilers from exploding. 機関士はボイラーが爆発しないように蒸気を止めた.

under *one's* ***own steam*** **1** (船が)自分の力で走って ▪ The ship went down the river *under her own steam.* 船は自力で川を下っていった.
2 (人が)自分から ▪ She went out of the room *under her own steam.* 彼女は自分から退室した.

under steam **1** (船が)汽力で動いて, 汽走して (↔ under SAIL) ▪ The ship is *under steam*, and not under sail. この船は帆走ではなく汽走するものだ.
2 (蒸気機関を)動かして ▪ The ship was *under steam*, ready to make her exit. 船は出ていこうとしてエンジンを動かしていた ▪ The ship went *under* easy *steam.* 船はゆっくりした速力で航行した.

with all steam on ＝(at) full STEAM.

with steam up (蒸気機関を)動かして ▪ The fire-engine was kept in readiness *with steam up.* 消防車はエンジンを動かして出動準備態勢を整えていた.

work off steam ＝let off (the) STEAM.

work up steam **1** 蒸気を立てる ▪ It took the engineer two hours to *work up steam.* 機関士は蒸気を立てるのに2時間かかった.
2 《口》精を出す ▪ You'll have to *work up steam* if you want to be free by 4. 4時までに仕事から解放されたければ精を出さねばなるまい.

steam[2] /stiːm/ 動 ***get*** [***be***] (***all***) ***steamed up*** 《口》(...のことで)興奮する, 怒る, いらいらする (*about* [*over*]) ▪ We can get a taxi somehow. Don't *get all steamed up.* 何とかしてタクシーは拾えるさ, いらいらするな.

steam it 汽船で行く ▪ We shall *steam it* up the Rhine to Lyons. 我々はライン川を汽船でさかのぼってリヨンへ行く.

steam open (封筒など)を蒸気であける ▪ She might easily *steam open* the envelope. 彼女はわけなく封筒を蒸気であけるかもしれない.

steel[1] /stiːl/ 名 ***a heart of steel*** 冷酷な心 ▪ He has *a heart of steel.* 彼は冷酷な心の持ち主だ.

(***as***) ***hard as steel*** →(as) HARD as a bone.

(***as***) ***true as steel*** →TRUE.

give ... a taste [***an inch***] ***of cold steel*** ...を剣で傷つける ▪ He *gave* the enemy *an inch of cold steel.* 彼は敵を剣で傷つけた. ☞cold steel「剣」.

worthy of *one's* ***steel*** (敵が)相手として不足のない ▪ Warriors feel a joy in foemen *worthy of their steel.* 戦士は相手として不足のない敵にめぐり会ったときに喜びを感じる.

steel[2] /stiːl/ 動 ***steel*** *one's* ***heart*** [*oneself*] ***against*** ...に心を冷酷にして当たる ▪ We have had to *steel our hearts against* the tales of beggars. 物乞いの話を心を鬼にして聞くしかなかった.

steel *one's* ***heart*** [*oneself*] ***for*** [***to*** *do*] ...のため[するために]心を冷酷にする, 勇気を奮い起こす ▪ *Steel yourself to* withstand the attack. 勇気を奮い起こして攻撃に耐えよ.

steep[1] /stiːp/ 名 ***in steep*** 浸して ▪ Lay all these *in steep* in rose water. これらはみなバラ(香)水に浸しておけ.

steep[2] /stiːp/ 形 ***be rather*** [***a bit***] ***steep*** 《口》(値段・要求が)法外である, 高すぎである ▪ That's *a bit steep*! そいつは高すぎだ!

steep[3] /stiːp/ 動 ***be steeped*** (***to the lips***) ***in*** **1** (酒など)に(すっかり)おぼれている ▪ He *was steeped to the* very *lips in* liquor. 彼はすっかり酒びたりになっていた.
2 (研究など)に(すっかり)没頭している ▪ He *is* still *steeped to the lips in* Greek. 彼はまだギリシャ語にすっかり没頭している.
3 ...に満ちている ▪ Our university *is steeped in* tradition. 私たちの大学は伝統に満ちています.

steep *oneself* ***in*** (研究など)に没頭する ▪ The minister does well to *steep himself in* a language of devotion. 牧師は信仰の言葉に没頭するのが賢明だ.

steer /stɪər/ 動 ***steer a*** [*one's*] ***course*** **1** (航海者が)ある針路を取る (*for*) ▪ Blow east, blow west, he *steers his course* alike. 東風でも西風でも, 彼は同じように針路を取る ▪ We *steered our course for* the railway station. 私たちは駅の方へ進んで行った.
2 ある方針を取る ▪ Let us learn to *steer* the [*a*] middle *course.* 中道を歩むことを学ぼうではないか.

steer clear of ...をきれいに通り抜ける; を完全に避ける ▪ They managed to *steer clear of* torpedoes. 彼らは何とか数発の魚雷をかわして舵を取った ▪ I *steered clear of* these difficulties. 私はこれらの困難を完全に避けた.

steer *A* ***clear of*** *B* AをBから救い出す ▪ Reliable friends would *steer* you *clear of* difficult situations. 頼りになる友人なら困難な状況から救いの手を差しのべてくれるだろう.

steer *a person* ***straight*** 人を正しい方向に導く ▪ Our teacher *steered* some students *straight* by persuading them to return to school. 先生は何人かの生徒に学校に戻るように説得して正しい方向に導いてくださった.

stem /stem/ 動 ***stem the tide*** 流れをくい止める ▪ It is difficult to *stem the tide* of inflation. インフレの進行を食い止めるのは難しい.

step[1] /step/ 名 ***a giant step*** 偉大な一歩, 大偉業の始まり ▪ Landing on the moon is said to be *a giant step* for mankind. 月面着陸は人類にとって偉大な一歩だと言われている.

a pair* [*set*] *of steps 《口》段ばしご ▪ There was *a pair of* wooden *steps* in the corner. すみには木の段ばしごが一つあった.

a* [*one*] *step ahead of …より先んじて; から離れて, を免れて ▪ He always seemed to be *a step ahead of* the competition. 彼はいつも競争において一歩先んじているように思えた.

a step in the right* [*wrong*] *direction (するのに)良い[まずい]こと ▪ I see you've started to economize; that's *a step in the right direction.* 君は倹約し始めたらしいね. それはけっこうなことだよ.

at every step 一歩ごとに ▪ *At every step* he took, the sound became louder. 彼が一歩歩むごとに物音は大きくなった.

attend* [*dog*]** *a person's* ***steps 人の後(あと)につきまとう ▪ Envy and hatred *dogged his steps.* そねみと憎しみが彼の後につきまとった.

be one step ahead of the sheriff 《米》ひどく借金している ▪ They have *been* just *one step ahead of the sheriff.* 彼らはほんとにひどい借金をしている. ☞「郡保安官につかまりそうで」が原義.

bend* [*direct, turn*]** *one's* ***steps 《文》足を向ける (*to*) ▪ He *bent his steps* homewards. 彼は家路についた ▪ He *directed his steps to* the hotel. 彼はそのホテルへ足を向けた.

Change step! 《号令》踏み変え!

conduct* [*guide*]** *a person's* ***steps 人を道案内する ▪ He wielded a pine for a staff to *conduct his steps.* 彼は道案内になるようにつえの代わりにマツの枝を持っていた ▪ This will be a good rule to *guide your steps.* これは君の処世のよい手引となろう.

dog *a person's* ***steps*** → attend a person's STEPs.

fall in step with …と歩調を合わせる; に同調する ▪ Not all of us *fall in step with* the committee. 我々全員が委員会に同調しているのではない.

follow *a person's* ***steps*** **1** 人の後(あと)について行く ▪ I was obliged closely to *follow his steps.* 私はやむをえず彼の後にぴったりとついて行った.
2 人の先例にならう ▪ My daughter *followed my steps* and became a teacher. 娘は私の先例にならって教師になった.

go a step beyond *a person* →BEYOND.

in step **1** 歩調を合わせて (*with*) 《比喩的にも》 ▪ We must march *in step with* our Commonwealth. 我々はわが連邦と歩調を合わせて進んでいかねばならない ▪ She tried to keep *in step with* the fashion. 彼女は流行に歩調を合わせようとした.
2 《電》(二つもしくはそれ以上の交流が)同期になって ▪ The secondary voltages are always *in step.* 2次電圧はいつも同期になっている.

***keep* [*be, remain, stay*] *one step ahead* (*of*)** (…よりも)一歩先んずる, 一歩先を行く ▪ It's not always easy to *keep one step ahead of* others. 他よりも一歩先んずることは必ずしも容易ではない.

keep step 歩調を合わせる (*with, to music*) ▪ Two friends *kept step with* me. 二人の友人が私と歩調を合わせた ▪ *Keep step to* the *music.* 音楽に歩調を合わせよ.

make* [*take*] *a false step 足を踏みはずす; 一歩を誤る, へまをやらかす ▪ I *made a false step*, and tumbled down into the boat. 足を踏みはずしてボートの中へころげ込んだ ▪ He *took a false step* in offering the constable a bribe. 彼は警官に賄賂を使おうとするようなへまをやらかした.

make a ... step 一歩を進める ▪ He *made a* sudden *step* to the gate. 彼は突然木戸へ一歩進んだ.

make* [*take*] *but one step ひとまたぎに行く, ひと足飛びに行く (*from... to*) ▪ He *made but one step from* the door *to* the bed. 彼はドアからベッドの所までひとまたぎで行った.

mind *one's* ***steps*** =watch one's STEP.

Mind the step! 足もとにご注意!

one step forward, two steps back 《諺》一歩前進, 二歩後退.

out of step 歩調を乱して (*with*) 《比喩的にも》 ▪ You will never see the Guards marching *out of step.* 護衛兵が歩調を乱して行進しているなんて, 決して見られない ▪ He seems to be *out of step with* his colleagues. 彼は同僚とそりが合わないらしい.

pick *one's* ***steps*** →PICK one's way.

***remain one step ahead* (*of*)** → keep one STEP ahead (of).

retrace *one's* ***steps*** →RETRACE.

step by step **1** 一歩一歩; 着実に ▪ *Step by step* we gain knowledge. 一歩一歩我々は知識を身につけていく.
2 歩調を合わせて (*with*) ▪ I go *step by step with* the British Ambassador. 私はイギリス大使と歩調を合わせてやっています.

step for step 歩調を合わせて (*with*) ▪ The officer walked alongside him *step for step.* 士官は彼と並んで歩調を合わせて歩いた.

take a drastic step 思い切った行動をとる ▪ She *took the drastic step* of having her long hair cut very short. 彼女は思い切って長い髪をうんと短く切ってもらった.

take a false step →make a false STEP.

***take a step* [*steps*]** 処置をとる, 取り計らう ▪ *Take* such *steps* as you think best. 最善と思われる処置をとりなさい ▪ We must *take steps* to prevent it. それを防ぐ処置をとらねばならない.

take but one step →make but one STEP.

The first step is always the hardest. 《諺》新しい試みは最初の一歩が肝心.

turn *one's* ***steps*** →bend one's STEPs.

walk* [*tread*] *in *a person's* ***steps*** =follow a person's STEPs.

watch *one's* ***step*** 足もとに気をつける, 用心する ▪ Let this be a warning to you and *watch your step* in future. これを戒めにして, 今後は用心しなさい.

What is the next step? 次は何をするのか.

step[2] /step/ 動 ***as good* [*fine*] *a man as***

ever stepped (***in shoe-leather***) かつて見られない立派な人 ▪ He is *as fine a* young *man as ever stepped*. 彼はかつて見られない好青年だ.

step astray [***awry***] (正道から)踏み迷う ▪ My heedless youth has *stepped astray*. 私の無鉄砲な青春は道を踏み迷ってきた.

step foot in [***on***]《米》...に足を踏み入れる ▪ For the first time he *stepped foot in* the metropolis. 彼は初めて首都に足を踏み入れた.

step high [***well***] (馬が)足を高く上げる ▪ My foolish young horse *stepped high*. 私の愚かな若い馬は足を高く上げた.

step it《口》 **1** 踊る ▪ We *stepped it* for a while. 私たちはしばらく踊った.

2 立ち去る ▪ After I had been with him about three months, I *stepped it* again. 彼と3か月いっしょにいたあとで私はまた立ち去った.

step it out てきぱきと歩く ▪ The day was cool, so we *stepped it out*. その日はひんやりしていたので, 我々はてきぱきと歩いた.

step lively《口》急ぐ ▪ She was told to *step lively* on the trolley-car. 彼女はトロリーバスに急いでお乗りくださいと言われた.

step on it [***the gas***]《口》急ぐ ▪ *Step on it*, we haven't got all day, you know. 急ぐんだ. まる1日あるわけじゃないんだからね.

step short **1**《軍》歩度を縮める ▪ The length of a pace is 10 inches in "*stepping short*." 歩幅は「歩度を縮める」ときには10インチである.

2 またぎようが足りない ▪ He *stepped short* from the boat, and fell into the water. 彼は船から上がるときまたぎが足りないで水中に落ちた.

Step this way. どうぞこちらへ《店員などの文句》 ▪ Please *step this way*. どうぞこちらへ.

step up (***to the plate***)《米》援助を申し出る, 責任をとる ▪ She hoped her husband would *step up to the plate* and share the housework. 彼女は夫が援助を申し出て家事を分担してくれるよう期待した.

step upon *a person*《米俗》人を手きびしくしかりつける ▪ He has *been stepped upon*. 彼は大目玉をくらった.

step well →STEP high.

Stephen /stíːvən/ 名 ***it's even(s) Stephen(s)***《口》(競技者などが)五分と五分である (→EVEN Stephen.). ☞Stephen(s) は even(s) と押韻するために用いられたもの.

stereotype /stériətàɪp/ 動 ***be stereotyped as***《軽蔑》...として固定観念をもって見られる ▪ Feminists *are* sometimes *stereotyped as* aggressive. フェミニストは固定観念でときに攻撃的だと見られる.

sterling /stə́ːrlɪŋ/ 名 ***pass as*** [***for***] ***sterling*** 法定英貨として通用する; 本物として通用する ▪ His inconsistent speech seemed to have *passed as sterling* in the assembly. 彼のつじつまの合わない演説がその集まりでは本物として通用したらしかった.

stern /stəːrn/ 名 ***stern foremost*** 船尾を前にして; 後ろ向きに ▪ The boat drove *stern foremost* before the tide. 船は潮流に押されて船尾を前にして進んでいった ▪ The man backed out, *stern foremost*. その男は後ろ向きに後ずさって出ていった.

stew[1] /stjuː/ 名 ***get*** [***go***] ***into a stew***《口》興奮する; やきもきする; いらだつ ▪ Everyone *got into a stew* about it. そのことでみんなやきもきした.

in a stew **1**《口》気をもんで, やきもきして ▪ Mr. Allen is *in a stew* about his sermon. アレン氏は自分のする説教のことでやきもきしている.

2 怒って ▪ Don't get *in* such *a stew* about it. そのことでそう怒らないでください.

stew[2] /stjuː/ 動 ***stew*** *oneself* ひどく気をもむ ▪ The cashier was *stewing himself* over the sum of £10 which was missing. 会計係は足りない10ポンドの金額のことでひどく気をもんでいた.

stew in *one's* ***own juice*** [***grease***]《口》自業自得に苦しむ ▪ He left the hypocrite to [let the hypocrite] *stew in his own juice*. 彼はその偽善者が自業自得に苦しむままにしておいた.

stick[1] /stɪk/ 名 ***a dry old stick*** (自分の意見をほとんど持たない)退屈な人 ▪ I don't want to become *a dry old stick*. 退屈な人間にはなりたくない.

a stick or [***and***] ***stone*** 木石, 無生物 ▪ Hang it all, I'm not *a stick or stone*. ちくしょう, 俺は木石じゃないぞ.

a stick with which to beat/ ***a stick to beat with*** (人)の弱みを突く道具 ▪ They used his failure as *a stick with which to beat* him. 彼の失敗をあげて彼の弱みを突いた.

as cross as two sticks 非常に不きげんな ▪ This morning my wife was *as cross as two sticks*. 今朝は家内がとても不きげんだった.

be beat [***hit***] ***with an ugly stick***《俗》〚完了形で〛とても醜い, 見苦しい ▪ What does he look like? —Well, like he's *been hit with an ugly stick*. 彼の様子は?—そう, とても見苦しかったね.

beat [***knock***]***... all to sticks*** ...を完全に負かす ▪ I used to *knock* him *all to sticks*. 私はいつも彼をこてんぱんに負かしたものだった ▪ It *beats* Newmarket *all to sticks*. ニューマーケットもてんでそれにはかなわない.

bits of sticks《口》家具 ▪ He talked about his *bits of sticks*. 彼は自分の家具のことを話した.

carry a big stick over =wield a big STICK over.

cut *one's* ***sticks***《俗》逃げ去る ▪ It was lucky for him that he *cut his sticks* as he did. 彼があのように逃げ去ったのは幸いだった.

eat stick →EAT[2].

every stick 家の木組残らず(焼けた, など) ▪ The fire burnt up *every stick*. その火事で家の木組残らず焼けてしまった.

fire a good stick 射撃がうまい ▪ He *fired a* capital *good stick*. 彼はとても射撃がうまかった.

get [***come in for***] ***a lot of stick*** =take (a lot of) STICK.

get (hold of) the wrong [right] end of the stick 《口》(物事・話を)勘ちがいする, 完全に誤解する[正しく理解する] ▪ That shows that you have *got hold of the wrong end of the stick.* それで君が話を勘ちがいしていることがわかる ▪ I think he's *got the wrong end of the stick.* 彼は誤解していると思う.

get on the stick 《米口》仕事にとりかかる ▪ Shall we *get on the stick*? 仕事にとりかかろうか?

get the short end of the stick 《主に米》不利な立場[状況]に追いやられる ▪ It's usually the consumer who *gets the short end of the stick.* いつも不利な立場に立たされるのは消費者だ.

give** a person* ***(a lot of) stick 《英口》人をひどくしかりつける[非難する] ▪ She will *give* me *stick* if I'm late. 彼女は私が遅れたらひどくしかりつけるだろう.

give** a person* ***the stick 人をつえで打つ ▪ Come in, or I'll *give* you *the stick.* 入ってこい, さもないとつえでなぐるぞ.

go to sticks (and staves) 瓦解する; 破滅する ▪ The church was *going to sticks.* その教会は瓦解しかかっていた ▪ I hear they all *went to sticks and staves.* 彼らはみな破滅してしまったということだ.

have [get] a stick up** one's* ***ass [butt, behind] 《卑》懸命に[せっせと]働く ▪ He always *gets a stick up his ass.* 彼はいつもせっせと働くさ.

have [get] the right [wrong] end of the stick (売買競争などで)有利[不利]な地位に立つ ▪ I was convinced that I *had the right end of the stick.* 私は自分が有利な立場に立っていると確信していた ▪ He rarely *gets the wrong end of the stick* in a bargain. 彼は取引で不利な位置に立つことはめったにない.

hold the sticks to/hold sticks with (自分よりすぐれた者)と互角に競う ▪ No kitten can *hold the sticks to* the weasel. どんな子猫だってイタチと互角に競うことはできはしない.

in a cleft stick 進退きわまって, 苦境に陥って ▪ He put his friend *in a cleft stick.* 彼は友人を苦境に陥れた.

keep** a person* ***at the stick's end 人を遠ざける, によそよそしくする ▪ The captain *kept* me *at the stick's end* the most part of the time. 船長はたいてい僕によそよそしくしていた.

knock ... all to sticks →beat ... all to STICKs.

more ... than [as many ... as]** one* ***can shake a stick at 《口》数えられないほど多くの ▪ We have in Lancaster *as many* taverns *as* you *can shake a stick at.* ランカスターにはどこにも負けないくらいたくさんのパブがある ▪ There were *more* posters *than* you *could shake a stick at.* 数え切れないほどたくさんのポスターがあった.

not a stick 家の木組み1本も…しない ▪ His house was consumed with fire, and *not a stick* was left. 彼の家は焼け落ちて木組み1本残らなかった.

(out) in the sticks 《口》田舎で[に] ▪ I have lived *in the sticks* all through my high school years. 高校時代ずっと田舎で暮らしたことがある.

play a good stick **1** バイオリンをよくひく ▪ I hear he *plays a good stick.* 彼はバイオリンをじょうずにひくそうだ.

2 立派に役割を果たす ▪ The hungry travelers sat down, and "*played a good stick.*" 腹をへらした旅人たちは腰をおろし,「立派に役割を果たした」ものだ《盛んに食べたということ》.

stick and stock [stone] いっさいがっさい; 洗いざらい ▪ He sold up *stick and stock.* 彼は洗いざらい売り払った.

stick, stark, staring 全く, すっかり ▪ Aunt Hannah will be *stick, stark, staring* mad with both of us. ハンナおばさんは我々二人にすっかり腹をたてることだろうよ.

Sticks and stones will [may] break my bones but names [words] will never hurt me. 《諺》棒や石は骨を折るかもしれないが, 悪口ではけがはしない.

take (a lot of) stick 《英口》こっぴどくたたかれる[しかられる] ▪ He *took a lot of stick* at the meeting. 彼はその会でこっぴどくたたかれた.

take a stick to ...につえをくらわせる ▪ She'll want *a stick taken to* her soon, I can see. 彼女はすぐつえをくらわせてもらいたいらしいな, どうやら.

that can shake a stick at 《米口》...に比肩できる ▪ I never set eyes on anything *that could shake a stick at* that. 私はそれに比肩できるものは何ひとつ見たことがない.

the stick and the carrot →the CARROT and the stick.

up stick(s) **1** 《海俗》船のマストを立てる ▪ So we *upped stick*, and made sail. そこで我々は船のマストを立てて出帆した.

2 《英口》立ち去る ▪ Why do you not *up sticks* and off? どうして君はとっとと立ち去らないんだ.

up the stick 《口》=up the SPOUT 3.

wield a big stick over ...に強権を振るう ▪ The government *wielded a big stick over* the people. 政府は人民に強権を振るった.

with a sharp stick 《米》復しゅうしようとして ▪ He is still after me *with a sharp stick.* 彼はまだ復しゅうしようとして私を追い求めている.

with a stick in it 《米俗》(茶・コーヒーなどに)少しブランデーを入れた ▪ Have some tea—*with a stick in it*, as papa calls it. お茶を召しあがれ—パパのいわゆる少しブランデーを入れたやつを.

stick² /stɪk/ 動 ***a sticking point*** →POINT¹.

be stuck for ...が不足している ▪ I'*m stuck for* money at present. 目下金つまりだ.

be stuck full of ...がいっぱいささっている ▪ The pincushion *was stuck full of* needles. 針さしには針がいっぱいさしてあった.

be stuck on 《口》...に夢中になる, ほれこむ ▪ I *am stuck on* that picture. 僕はあの絵に夢中なのだ.

be stuck up 《俗》高ぶっている, つんと澄ましこんでいる ▪ I don't like them; they'*re* so *stuck up.* 彼ら

は好かない. とてもお高くとまっているから.

be* [*get*] *stuck with (いやなこと)を押しつけられる ▪ Why should I *be stuck with* (looking after) my mother-in-law? なぜ僕が姑(の世話)を押しつけられなければならないのか.

get stuck **1** はまり込む ▪ Our car *got stuck* in the ditch. 我々の車がみぞにはまり込んだ.

2 だまされる ▪ He certainly *got stuck* when he bought that antique. 彼はその骨董品を買ったとき確かにだまされたのだ.

get* [*be*] *stuck after 《米口》…に夢中になっている, ほれている ▪ I *am stuck after* one of the girls. 僕はその娘たちの一人にほれている.

get stuck in 《英口》真剣に仕事に取りかかる, どんどん食べ始める ▪ Come on, girls, *get stuck in*. さあみなさん, 食べて食べて.

get stuck into 《口》真剣に(仕事)に取りかかる, (食べ物)をどんどん食べ始める ▪ Now boys, *get stuck into* work. さあみんな, どんどん仕事を始めよう.

make ... stick 《口》…を証明[実証, 実行]する ▪ The charge will *be made* to *stick*. その罪は実証されよう ▪ Can he *make* his decision *stick*? 彼は自分の決心を実行できるだろうか.

***stick a pin there* [*here*]** 《米口》〚主に命令文で〛よく注意する, よく心に留める ▪ Time is money. *Stick a pin there*. 時は金なりだ. よく心に留めておけ.

stick at home =STAY at home.

stick at nothing 《口》何事にもちゅうちょしない ▪ That scoundrel *sticks at nothing* in the way of villainy. あの悪党は悪事にかけてはどんなことにもちゅうちょしない.

stick** one's **chin* [*neck*] *out →CHIN[1]; NECK.

stick in** a person's **fingers →STICK to a person's fingers.

***stick in** one's **gizzard* [*craw, crop*]** (不快なものが)のどにつかえる; 悩ませる, 困らせる ▪ The mere thought just *sticks in my gizzard*. そう思うだけでものどがつかえてくる.

stick in** one's* [*the*] ***mind 心にこびりついて離れない, なかなか忘れられない ▪ Her face *sticks in my mind*. 彼女の顔が心にこびりついて離れない.

***stick in the briers* [*clay, mire*]** 困難にまきこまれる ▪ They *stuck in the briers*, being accused of theft. 盗みを訴えられて, 彼らは困難にまきこまれた.

***stick in** one's **throat* [*gullet*]** 《口》 **1** (言葉が)のどにつかえて口に出ない ▪ Amen *stuck in my throat*. アーメンがのどにつかえて声にならなかった.

2 =STICK in one's gizzard.

***stick it/shove it* (*up** one's **ass*)** 《俗》耐えぬく; 〚Stick [Shove] it! で〛くそくらえ, ふざけんじゃねえぜ ▪ They look as if they can *stick it*. 彼らは耐えぬくことができそうに見える.

***stick it in* [*on*]** 《主に英俗》 **1** (人)に法外な値をふっかける ▪ In short, we *stick it in* him. 要するに, あの男に法外な値をふっかけるんだ.

2 大げさに話す, ほらを吹く ▪ I think he's *sticking it on*. 彼はほらを吹いているんだと思う.

stick it out 《口》最後までがまんする ▪ It would be ridiculous to fly, so she must *stick it out*. 逃げたりすればばかなことをすることになる. そこで彼女は最後までがまんしなければならない.

stick it there 《口》 **1** 握手する ▪ *Stick it there*, old man, I congratulate you. 握手しよう, 君. おめでとう.

2 〚命令文で〛がんばれよ ▪ *Stick it there*; you're winning the game. がんばれよ, 勝っているんだぞ.

***stick it to** a person* 《主に米口》人にきびしく当たる[ひどい仕打ちをする] ▪ She liked to *stick it to* me once in a while, even though she was my best friend. 彼女は親友なのに時折私にひどく当たりたがった.

***stick like a* (*sand*) *bur*(*r*) [*a limpet, a leech, glue*]** ダニのようにくっつく ▪ I'm *sticking* to the truth *like a sand bur*. 僕はその真相にダニのようにしがみついている.

stick* [*poke*] *one's oar* [*nose*] *into →put in one's OAR, poke one's NOSE into.

stick out a mile/ stick out like a sore thumb 《口》一目瞭然だ; ひどく目立つ ▪ It *sticks out a mile* that he never intended to help you. 彼が君を助けるつもりが少しもなかったのは一目瞭然だ.

stick ... to death (やり・刀などで)…を刺し[突き]殺す ▪ He *was* taken and *stuck to death*. 彼は捕えられて突き殺された.

stick to** a person's **fingers (金銭が)人に着服される ▪ One-third of the money *stuck to his fingers*. 金の3分の1は彼に着服された.

Stick to it! がんばれ!, たるむな!

stick to** one's **last →LAST[1].

stick to** one's **text →TEXT.

stick up straight (髪の毛が)まっすぐに突っ立つ ▪ His hair *stuck up straight* with fright. 彼の髪の毛は恐怖のためにまっすぐに突っ立った.

Stick up your hands! =STICK 'em up!

Stick with it. あきらめてはいけない ▪ I'm really tired of doing my homework.—*Stick with it*. 宿題, ほんといやになっちゃった—あきらめるな.

Stick 'em up! 《口》両手を上げろ《銃でおどす言葉》.

sticking(-)place /stíkɪŋplèɪs/ 名 ***screw ... to the sticking-place*** …をぎりぎりまで締めあげる (cf. Sh., *Macb*. 1. 7. 60) ▪ I've at last managed to *screw* my courage *to the sticking place*. 私はついにありったけの勇気を奮い起こした ▪ His rent has *been* already *screwed to the sticking-place*. 彼の家賃は既にぎりぎりのところまで引き上げられていた. ☞バイオリンなどのねじを「動かなくなるまで巻く」が原義.

stickler /stíklər/ 名 ***be a stickler for* [*about, over*]** …にやかましい ▪ He *is a* great *stickler for* etiquette. 彼は作法にかけては大変やかましやだ ▪ I *am* no *stickler for* precision. 私は綿密家なんかではない.

sticky /stíki/ 形 ***have sticky fingers*** →FINGER[1].

stiff /stɪf/ 形副名 ***a big stiff*** 役立たず, でくのぼ

S

う ▪ There I sat like *a big stiff* for five hours. そこに私はでくのぼうみたいに5時間座っていた.

a stiff one [**'un**] **1**《俗》死体 ▪ Ah! You'll be *a stiff one* by tomorrow. ああ! おまえはあすまでには死体になっているだろうさ.
2《競馬俗》勝ち目のない馬 ▪ I backed *a stiff 'un* with it. 私はその金で勝ち目のない馬にかけた.

(***as***) ***stiff as a poker*** [***a ramrod, buckram, a board***]《口》(態度などが)きわめて[非常にまっすぐで]堅苦しい ▪ Each walked off *stiff as pokers*. 両人ともきわめて堅苦しく歩み去った ▪ He became *as stiff as a ramrod* at my word. 彼は私の言葉を聞くとしゃきっとしゃちこばった ▪ He marched in, *as stiff as a poker*. 彼は実に厳しい態度でつかつかと入って行った. ☞poker「火かき棒」.

carry [***keep, have***] ***a stiff upper lip*** →LIP.

give it to *a person* (***pretty***) ***stiff*** 人にきびしく言う, 人をしかりつける ▪ He *gave it to* her *pretty stiff*. 彼は彼女にきびしく言った.

have a stiff neck →NECK.

keep a stiff face [***lip***] まじめくさる; 物に動じない ▪ He *kept a stiff face* under any circumstances. 彼はどんな場合にも物に動じなかった.

stiff and stark 堅くなって (cf. Sh., *Rom. &Jul.* 4. 1. 103) ▪ Poor old Tom lay *stiff and stark*, under the Union Jack. かわいそうにトムのやつは英国旗の下に死んで堅くなっていた.

stiff in the back《口》断固として ▪ You never can be *stiff in the back*, Charley. 君は断固としていられっこないよ, チャーリー.

stiff with《口》…がいっぱいあふれて ▪ The harbor was *stiff with* craft. 港には船がぎっしりあふれていた.

stile /staɪl/ 名 ***help a lame dog*** [***lamb***] ***over a stile*** →HELP[2].

still /stɪl/ 形副 ***as still as a stone*** [***the grave, death***] きわめて静かで ▪ The air was *as still as the grave*. 空気はきわめて静かだった.

as still as still《口》きわめて静かに ▪ He lay *as still as still*. 彼はきわめて静かに横たわっていた.

hold [***keep***] ***still*** じっとしている ▪ It is hard for a child to *hold still*. 子供はじっとしているのが苦手だ.

hold [***stand***] ***still for*** …をがまんする[耐える] ▪ I couldn't *hold still for* my teacher's talk. 先生の話には耐えられなかった ▪ Elizabeth could not *hold still for* such disrespect. エリザベスはそんな無礼ががまんならなかった ▪ I won't *stand still for* your threats any more. お前の脅しにはもうがまんも限界だ.

keep a still tongue in *one's* ***head*** →keep a quiet TONGUE (in one's head).

stand still じっと立ち止まる, 静止する ▪ His heart *stood still*. 彼の心臓がぱったり止まった.

still and all《米口》結局 ▪ *Still and all*, he was there on time. 結局彼は時間通りにそこに来ていた.

Still waters run deep.《諺》音なし川の水は深い《口数の少ない人はしばしば強い性格や深い感情を持っている》.

stop still ぱったり止まる ▪ The car *stopped still* in the middle of the road. 車は道路のまん中でぱったり止まった.

the [***a***] ***still small voice*** 静かな細い声《神・良心の声》(《聖》*1 Kings* 19. 12) ▪ They followed *the still small voice* that governs the painters. 彼らは画家を支配する静かな細い声に従った.

stilt /stɪlt/ 名 ***on stilts*** **1** 竹馬に乗って ▪ Tom was walking *on stilts*. トムは竹馬に乗っていた.
2 大げさに, 大言壮語して ▪ Artists talk *on stilts* about the poetry of painting. 画家は絵画の詩ということについて大言壮語する.

sting[1] /stɪŋ/ 名 ***a sting in the tail***《英》(話・手紙などの)あと味が悪いこと (《聖》*Rev.* 9. 10) ▪ Read through this letter; you will see *a sting in the tail*. この手紙を読み通してごらん. あと味が悪いのがわかるから.

have no sting in it 弱い ▪ His service *had no sting in it*. 彼のサーブは弱かった.

take the sting out of《口》…を柔らげる ▪ His smile *took the sting out of* his reproof. 彼の微笑が彼の叱責を柔らげた.

sting[2] /stɪŋ/ 動 ***be*** [***get***] ***stung for***《口》…をだまし取られる ▪ He *got stung for* 5 dollars. 彼は5ドルだまし取られた.

stingo /stíŋgoʊ/ 名 ***give*** *a person* ***stingo*** 人をひどくしかりつける ▪ I'll *give* them hot *stingo*. やつらをこっぴどく叱りつけてやる. ☞stingo「強いビール」.

stink[1] /stɪŋk/ 名 ***like stink***《俗》すさまじい勢いで ▪ If you see a Minnie coming, you have to run *like stink* sometimes. 迫撃砲弾が飛んでくるのを見たら, 命からがら逃げなければならないことも時にはある.

raise [***create, kick, make***] ***a*** (***big,*** [***real***]) ***stink***《口》悪評をかき立てる; 大声で不平を言う ▪ The newspapers had *raised a stink* before the eye and mind of the public. 新聞は大衆の面前で悪評をかき立てた. ☞kick は《英》, make, raise は《米》.

stink[2] /stɪŋk/ 動 ***stink in the nostrils of*** →NOSTRIL.

stink like a polecat/stink to high heaven《口》強い悪臭を放つ ▪ That fellow *stinks like a polecat*. あいつはひどく臭い. ☞polecat「スカンク」.

stink of money/be stinking with money/be stinking rich《口》(金が)腐るほどある ▪ He *stinks of money*. 彼には腐るほど金がある.

stink *a person* ***to death*** 死ぬほど臭い ▪ A pigsty *stinks* one *to death*. ブタ小屋は死ぬほど臭い.

stint[1] /stɪnt/ 名 ***do*** *one's* ***stint*** 仕事の割り当て量をする ▪ He is *doing his stint*. 彼は自分の仕事の割り当て量をやっている.

without stint 制限なく, 惜しみなく ▪ His wife spent money *without stint*. 彼の妻は金を惜しみなく使った.

stint[2] /stɪnt/ 動 ***stint*** *oneself* 切り詰める ▪ He *stints himself* for his children. 彼は子供らのために切り詰めている.

stipulation /stìpjəléɪʃən/ 名 ***on the stipulation that*** …という条件で ▪ We rented the house *on the stipulation that* certain rooms should be painted. いくつかの部屋にペンキを塗るという条件でその家を借りた.

stir[1] /stəːr/ 名 ***make*** [***cause, create***] ***a stir*** 大評判[大騒ぎ]になる; (人を)興奮させる; 混乱を引き起こす ▪ His arrival *made a* great *stir*. 彼の到着は大騒ぎとなった ▪ His lecture *caused a stir* in the hall. 彼の講演はホールの人々をわかせた.

stir[2] /stəːr/ 動 ***stir*** *oneself* 手足を動かす, 動き回る ▪ You had better *stir yourself*. 手足を動かすほうがいいですよ.

stir *one's* ***stumps*** →STUMP[1].

stir the [*a person's*] ***blood*** →BLOOD.

stir ... to the depths (人)を深く感動させる ▪ I *was stirred to the depths* by the news. 私はそのニュースに深く感動した.

stir up mud 不名誉な事実をすっぱ抜く ▪ He tried to destroy his opponent by *stirring up mud*. 彼は不名誉な事実をすっぱ抜いて敵を葬ろうとした.

stir up with a long pole 《戯》奮起させる, しりを突っつく ▪ Whenever the dance showed signs of flagging, he *stirred* them *up with a long pole*. ダンスがだれる気配がするたびに, 彼は彼らの尻を突いた. ☞猛獣使いが棒で突っついて獣を立たせることから.

stirrup /stə́ːrəp|stír-/ 名 ***high up*** (***in***) ***the stirrups*** 身分が高い ▪ He is proud of being *high up in the stirrups*. 彼は身分が高いのを誇りにしている.

hold the [***a***] ***stirrup*** (***for***) (…に)仕える ▪ He was so mean that he would *hold a stirrup for* the Devil. 彼は悪魔に仕えるほど卑しい男だった. ☞馬に乗る人に敬意を表して「あぶみを持つ」ことから.

stitch /stɪtʃ/ 名 ***a man of stitches*** 《戯》仕立て屋 ▪ He called his *man of stitches*. 彼は仕立て屋を呼んだ.

A stitch in time saves nine. 《諺》きょうの一針はあすの十針《手おくれを戒める》.

drop a stitch (編物などで)一針かがり落とす, 一目すき落とす ▪ She had been knitting, but she *dropped* several *stitches*. 彼女は編物をしていたが, 幾目かすき落とした.

every stitch **1** 身にまとうものいっさい ▪ *Every stitch* of his clothing is wet. 彼の衣服いっさいがぬれている.

2 帆の各部 ▪ The captain gave instant orders to lighten *every stitch* of sail. 船長は帆の各部を軽くするようにただちに命令した.

have not a dry stitch on *one's* ***back*** [***on*** *one*] 《口》全身ずぶぬれだ ▪ I *had not a dry stitch on my back*. 私は全身ずぶぬれだった.

have not a stitch (***of clothes***) ***on*** 丸裸である ▪ I did*n't have a stitch on* when he called. 彼が訪ねて[電話して]来たとき私は丸裸だった.

have not [***without***] ***a stitch on*** [***to***] *one's* ***back*** **1** 裸だ[で] ▪ We could bathe *without a stitch to our backs*. 私たちは裸で泳ぐことができた.

2 ひどく貧乏だ[で] ▪ They *have scarcely a stitch to* their backs. 彼らはひどく貧乏だ.

in stitches 笑いころげて ▪ His jokes had us *in stitches*. 彼のジョークで我々は笑いころげた.

put a stitch in …を1針縫う ▪ The doctor *put* three *stitches in* my head. 医師は私の頭の傷を3針縫った.

stitch by stitch 1針ずつ; 一つ一つ ▪ His reply in these matters has been *stitch by stitch* confuted. これらの問題についての彼の返答は一つ一つ反ばくされている.

without a stitch on [***to***] *one's* ***back*** →have not a STITCH on one's back.

stiver /stáɪvər/ 名 ***not a stiver*** 少しも…ない ▪ He has *not* done *a stiver* of work all day. 彼はまる1日少しも仕事をしなかった ▪ I do*n't* care *a stiver* if she dies. あの女が死んだってちっともかまわん.

stock /stɑk|stɔk/ 名 ***get in a good stock*** 十分に仕入れる ▪ If coal is going to be dear this winter, we had better *get in a good stock* this month. 石炭がこの冬高くなるのなら, 今月たっぷり仕入れておくほうがいい.

have ... in the stocks …を国債で持っている ▪ I *have* £5,000 *in the stocks*. 国債で5千ポンドある.

in stock 在庫して, 手持ちの (↔out of STOCK) ▪ Goods are kept *in stock*. 品物はいつも在庫しております ▪ Have you any linen sheets *in stock*? リンネルのシーツの在庫がありますか.

kiss the stocks さらし台にさらされる ▪ I will make you *kiss the stocks*. お前をさらし台にさらしてやるぞ.

lay [***get***] ***in a stock*** (***of***) (…を)仕入れる, たくわえる ▪ I am in hopes to *lay in a stock of* health. 私は健康をたくわえたいと思っています.

lock, stock, and barrel →STOCK, lock, and barrel.

make stock of …で儲ける ▪ Susie *made stock of* it in the circumstances. スージーはそういう事情でそれで儲けた.

on the stocks **1** (船が)建造中で ▪ Two ships are *on the stocks*. 船が2隻建造中だ.

2 計画し着手されて ▪ My other play is now *on the stocks*. 私のもう一方の劇は今執筆中だ.

out of stock 品切れになって, 持ち合わせがなくて (↔in STOCK) ▪ The book you write for is now *out of stock*. ご注文の本はただいま品切れでございます.

stand stock still じっと立ち止まる ▪ He *stood stock still* and listened. 彼はじっと立ち止まって耳をすました.

one's ***stock in trade*** 商売道具, 常套手段 ▪ *Her stock in trade* is flattery. 彼女の商売道具はおべんちゃらだ.

one's ***stock is high*** [***low***] 株が高い[安い], 評判が良い[悪い] ▪ *His stock is high* in college. 大学での彼の評判は良い.

stock, lock, and barrel/ lock, stock, and barrel **1** 全体, いっさいがっさい, そっくり全部(まとめて) ▪ Even the capital, *stock, lock, and barrel*, all went. 資本金までいっさいがっさいなくなった ▪ I intend to buy the business—*lock, stock, and barrel*. そののれんをそっくり全部買うつもりだ ▪ He cleared out *lock, stock, and barrel*. 彼は全部まとめて廃棄処分にした.

2〚副詞的に〛残らず, 全く ▪ He was *lock, stock, and barrel* an Irishman. 彼はどこからどこまでもアイルランド人だった ▪ I am going to sell everything, *lock, stock, and barrel*. 私は何もかもすっかり売るつもりです. ☞lock, stock, barrel で銃 (gun) の全体を構成することから.

stocks and stones 《軽蔑》偶像; 木石 (《聖》*Jer*. 3. 9) ▪ There was a worship of nature instead of *stocks and stones*. 偶像の代わりに自然を拝むということが行われた.

take no stock of …を問題にしない ▪ I *take no stock of* his absurd threats. 彼のばかげたおどしなど問題にしない.

take stock たな卸しをする《比喩的にも》 ▪ We *took stock* last night. 我々はゆうべたな卸しをした ▪ One day I *took stock* on a train, and found I possessed 80 dollars. ある日車中でふところ具合を調べてみると80ドルあった.

take stock in …に興味を持つ, を重んじる; を信用する ▪ Educated men *took stock in* the theory. 教育ある人はその理論に興味を持った ▪ I do not *take* much *stock in* such a story. 私はそういう話はあまり信用しない.

take stock of **1** …を評価する ▪ It is occasionally good to *take stock of* our mental experience. ときどき我々の内的経験を評価してみるのもいいことだ.

2《口》(興味・疑りの目で人)をつくづくながめる ▪ I spotted him when I *took stock of* the passengers. 私は乗客をつくづくながめていて彼を見つけた.

stocking /stákɪŋ|stɔ́k-/ 名 ***have wealth in*** *one's* ***stockings*** 金をしまい込んでいる ▪ Grandfather is supposed to *have wealth in his stockings*. 祖父はへそくりをためていると思われる.

in [***on***] *one's* ***stocking-feet*** 靴下ばかりで; 靴をはかずに (→stand…in one's STOCKINGs) ▪ *In his stocking-feet* he was five feet five. 靴をはかずに彼は5フィート5インチあった ▪ They entered devoutly *on their stocking-feet*. 彼らはうやうやしく靴下だけになって入った.

sew up *a person's* ***stocking*** →SEW.

stand … in *one's* ***stockings*** 靴をはかずに…の身長がある (→ in one's STOCKING-feet) ▪ He *stands* over six feet *in his stockings*. 彼は靴をはかずに6フィート以上の身長がある.

throw the stocking 靴下を投げる《結婚式の晩に花嫁の靴下を来客の間に投げ, 当たった人が次に最初に結婚するとされた古いしきたり》 ▪ They all came to dance at her wedding, and help "*throw the stocking*." 彼らはみんな彼女の結婚式に踊ったり「靴下を投げる」のを手伝ったりしようとやって来た.

stolen /stóulən/ 形 ***Stolen sweets*** [***fruits, kisses***] ***are sweeter*** [***sweetest***]. 《諺》盗んだ菓子[果物, キス]の方が[が一番]おいしい.

stomach /stʌ́mək/ 名 ***for*** *one's* ***stomach's sake*** 健康のために ▪ He used a little wine *for his stomach's sake*. 彼は健康のために酒を少々たしなんだ.

go against *one's* ***stomach*** →GO².

have a strong stomach たやすくショックを受けない; 吐き気を催さない; へっちゃらだ ▪ *Have a strong stomach* if you are going to take the initiative. 人の先頭に立つつもりなら, たやすくショックを受けたりするな ▪ He *has a strong* enough *stomach* to watch the war scenes. 彼は戦争シーンを見てもへっちゃらさ.

have no stomach for [***to*** *do*] 《文》…を好かない; の気がない ▪ I *had no stomach for* a fight. けんかはごめんだった ▪ I *have no stomach to* write. 私には筆をとる気はないね.

have the stomach for **1** …を(がまんして)食べることができる ▪ Do you *have the stomach for* Blue Cheeze? 青かびチーズは食べられますか?

2 …する勇気[決意]がある ▪ I don't *have the stomach for* entering the haunted house. お化け屋敷に入る勇気はありません.

hold *one's* ***stomach in*** 腹を引っ込める ▪ A bodice would successfully *hold your stomach in* and shape the waistline. ボディスを着ればうまくお腹が引っ込んで腰のくびれもできるだろう.

lie (***heavy***) ***on*** *one's* ***stomach*** (食物が)胃にもたれる ▪ I ate sturgeon, and it *lies heavy on my stomach*. チョウザメを食べたが, それが胃にもたれている.

on a full stomach 満腹で ▪ You must not run *on a full stomach*. 満腹のまま走ってはいけない.

on an empty stomach すき腹で ▪ He took some brandy *on an empty stomach*. 彼はすき腹でブランデーを飲んだ.

on *one's* ***stomach*** 腹ばいになって ▪ I lay *on my stomach* in bed. 私は寝床で腹ばいになっていた.

settle the stomach 吐き気を止める ▪ This herb *settles the stomach* well. この薬草で吐き気がうまく止まる.

sick to *one's* ***stomach*** **1** 吐き気がして ▪ I felt *sick to my stomach* reading that filth. その卑猥な雑誌を読んで吐き気がした.

2 うんざりして, 嫌気がして ▪ I'm *sick to my stomach* of novels because they are so fraudulent. 小説は欺瞞的なのでうんざりする.

sit (***heavy***) ***on the stomach*** (食べ物が)胃にもたれる, 消化しにくい ▪ Chinese food *sits heavy on the stomach*. 中華料理は胃にもたれる.

stay the stomach →STAY².

One's ***stomach feels like water.*** 不安[緊張]で吐き気がする ▪ *My stomach felt like water* at the thought of giving an after-dinner speech. 食後のスピーチをすることを考えると不安で胸がむかむかした.

One's ***stomach is as tight as a knot.*** 緊張

[心配]する ▪ When I heard his name, *my stomach was as tight as a knot.* 彼の名前を聞いて私は緊張した.

turn** a person's **stomach 人の胸を悪くさせる, 不快の念を起こさせる ▪ It was enough to *turn one's stomach.* それは人の胸を悪くさせるに足るものだった.

stone[1] /stoʊn/ 名 ***A rolling stone gathers no moss.*** 《諺》転石こけむさず《しばしば職業・住居を変える人は金がたまらない》. ☞《米》では「活動的な人はつねに清新である」の意味にも用いる.

a stone's throw from …のごく近くに (→within a STONE's throw of) ▪ The church is *a stone's throw from* his office. 教会は彼の事務所からごく近い.

(*as*) *blind as a stone* 全く目が見えない ▪ The man continued *as blind as a stone.* その男は相変らず全く目が見えなかった.

(*as*) *cold as a stone* 石のように冷たい ▪ All was *cold as a stone.* どこもかも石のように冷たかった.

(*as*) *dead as a stone* 完全に死んで ▪ He fell down *dead as a stone.* 彼は倒れて息絶えていた.

(*as*) *deaf as a stone* 全く耳が聞こえない ▪ She was *deaf as a stone.* 彼女は全く耳が聞こえなかった.

(*as*) *dumb as a stone* まるで口のきけない ▪ The beggar was *dumb as a stone.* その物乞いはまるで口がきけなかった.

(*as*) *firm as stone* 石のように堅い ▪ His heart is *as firm as stone.* 彼の心臓は石のように堅い.

(*as*) *hard as a stone* 石のように堅い, 無情な ▪ The seed is *as hard as a stone.* その種子は石のように堅い.

ask for bread and be given a stone パンを求めて石を与えられる《同情を求めて冷たい仕打ちを受ける》(《聖》*Matt.* 7. 9) ▪ He *asked for bread and* you *gave* him *a stone.* 彼は同情を求めたのに君は冷たい仕打ちをしたのだ.

be set [carved, cast, etched, written] in stone 【否定文で】(計画・決定・考え方などが)不変[不動]である ▪ Our plan *is* not *set in stone* and can be changed. 計画は確定ではなく変更も可能だ.

break stones (道路補修用の)砂利を砕く; 最も落ちぶれた生活をする ▪ Live with that woman! Why, I'd rather *break stones* by the roadside. あの女と暮らすだと! そんなら, むしろ道端の石を割る方がましだ.

cast stones at →throw STONEs (at, against).

cast [throw] the first stone まっ先に非難する (*at*) (《聖》*John* 8. 7) ▪ Let him who is innocent *cast the first stone.* 罪なき者がまっ先に非難せよ.

Constant dropping [dripping] wears [will wear] away a [the] stone. 《諺》絶えず滴り落ちる水は石にさえ穴をあける,「点滴石を穿つ」.

give a stone and beating to …を楽々と打ち負かす ▪ Their smoking room can *give a stone and beating to* ours. 彼らの家の喫煙室はうちのを楽々と負かしてしまえるくらいだ. ☞競馬俗語から.

leave no stone unturned (もくろんでいる結果を得るために)あらゆる手段を尽くす (*to do*) ▪ He *left no stone unturned to* do the work. 彼はその仕事をするためにあらゆる手段を尽くした.

mark with a white stone →mark ... with a WHITE stone.

run into a stone wall 暗礁に乗り上げる, 壁に突き当たる ▪ We've *run into a stone wall* in our enterprise. 我々の事業は暗礁に乗り上げてしまった.

set a stone rolling とんでもない結果を生じるようなことをし始める ▪ If you *set this* dangerous *stone rolling*, it will fall on yourselves. こんな危険なことをおっぱじめたら, あなたがた自身が傷つくことになりますよ.

sink like a stone 石のように沈む, 直ちに沈む; 人気がなくなる ▪ The diver let go his hold of the lifeline and *sank like a stone.* 潜水夫は命綱を離して, 石が沈むように沈んでいった ▪ The band has *sunk like a stone.* そのバンドの人気は失われてしまった.

The stones will cry out. 石も叫ぶべし《悪事があまりにもひどいので》(《聖》*Luke* 19. 40) ▪ If these were silent *the* very *stones would cry out.* この人たちが黙っていれば, 石ですら叫ぶだろう.

throw [cast] stones (at, against) (…を)攻撃する, 非難する ▪ Those who live in glass houses should not *throw stones.* 《諺》弱点のある者は人を非難してはいけない ▪ All the logicians *threw stones at* him. すべての論理学者が彼を非難した.

within a stone's throw [stone-cast] of …から(石を投げて届くほどの)近距離に (→a STONE's throw from) ▪ His house is *within a stone's throw of* the road. 彼の家は道路のすぐ近くにある.

stone[2] /stoʊn/ 動 ***get [be] stoned*** 《俗》(酒・麻薬で)気分が高揚する[ハイになる] ▪ He *was stoned* so she had to carry him up the stairs. 彼は酔っ払っていたので彼女が2階に運び上げねばならなかった.

stone** a person **to death 石を投げて人を殺す ▪ The Christian martyr *was stoned to death.* そのキリスト教の殉教者は投石で殺されたのだ.

stoned out of** one's **mind [head] →drunk out of one's MIND.

stone-cold /stòʊnkóʊld/ 形 ***be stone-cold sober*** 《口》全くのしらふである ▪ I *was stone-cold sober* at the party. パーティーでは私は全くのしらふだった.

stool /stu:l/ 名 ***a stool pigeon*** おとり, スパイ ▪ The police use a lot of information obtained from *stool pigeons* to solve crimes. 警察は犯罪を解決するためスパイからの多くの情報を利用している.

fall [come to the ground, sit] between two stools あぶはち取らずに終わる ▪ Truly he had *fallen between two stools.* 確かに彼はあぶはち取らずに終わっていた ▪ Alma *sits between two stools.* アルマはあぶはち取らずに終わっている ▪ Trying to be both teacher and parent, his wife *fell between two stools.* 教師と母親の二役をこなそうとして彼の妻はどっちつかずになってしまった.

stoop /stu:p/ 動 ***stoop (so low as) to** do* ... するような卑しいまねをする ▪ He never *stoops so* *low as to* eavesdrop. 彼は立ち聞きするような卑しいまねはしない.

stoop to conquer 屈辱を忍んで目的を達する ▪ Masculine dignity forbids our *stooping to conquer*. 負けるが勝ちというのは男の体面が許さない.

stop[1] /stɑp|stɔp/ 名 ***a long stop*** 頼みの綱, 最後の切り札, 奥の手 ▪ You can be *the long stop*. 君が最後の望みの綱だ.

a nature stop (ハイウェイ長距離バスツアーの)トイレ休憩 ▪ Can I have *a nature stop*? トイレ休憩できますか?

a stop street 完全停止しなければならない道路 ▪ As his car ran on *a stop street*, he was late. 車で完全停止の必要な道を走ったので彼は時間に遅れた.

at full stop すっかり行き詰まって[窮して] ▪ All persons depending on the Turkey trade were *at full stop* for many months. トルコ貿易に依存している人たちは幾月間もすっかり窮してしまった.

be at a stop 停止[休止]している ▪ Business *is at a stop*. 業務は停止している.

bring ... to a stop …をやめる, 終わらせる ▪ We must *bring* this *to a stop*. これをやめなくてはならん.

come to a stop 止まる, 終わる ▪ The story thus *comes* unexpectedly *to a* full *stop*. 物語はかくて意外に完全に終わりを告げる ▪ The car *came to a* dead *stop* in the middle of the road. 車は道のまん中でばったり止まった.

full stop (話の締めくくりを強めて)以上!, 終わり! ▪ It's time to decide which idea we should adopt, *full stop*. 我々はどちらの案を採用すべきか決める時だ, 以上.

make a stop (***and stay***) 立ち止まる, 休む ▪ Many *a stop and stay* he *made*. 彼は何度も何度も立ち止まった ▪ I *made a* full *stop*. 私はぴたりと立ち止まった.

Mind your stops. 句読点に気をつけよ《音読している子供への注意; 比喩的にも用いる》 ▪ *Mind your stops*, or I shall shy a biscuit at your head. 一点一画に気をつけるんだよ. さもないと頭にビスケットを投げつけるよ.

pull out all the stops 《口》最大限の努力をする, 全力を傾ける ▪ We'll have to *pull out all the stops* to fulfil our aim. 目的を遂げるためには全力を傾けなければならない. ☞オルガンの全音栓を使って演奏することから.

put [***give***] ***a stop to*** (活動など)を中止させる, 終わらせる ▪ Henry *put a stop to* this. ヘンリーがこれを中止させた.

put on the sentimental stop 《口》感傷にふける ▪ He is prone to *put on the sentimental stop*. 彼はともすれば感傷にふけりがちだ.

stop and go のろのろ運転 ▪ Traffic on the Metropolitan Expressway can be *stop and go* every day. 首都高速道路は毎日のろのろ運転になる.

with all the stops out 極力 ▪ He tried to win the election *with all the stops out*. 彼は極力選挙に勝とうと努めた.

without a stop 止まらずに, 絶えず ▪ The train runs from London to Crewe *without a stop*. 列車はロンドンからクルーまで止まらずに走る.

stop[2] /stɑp|stɔp/ 動 ***stop a blast*** 《俗》(上官から)お目玉をくう ▪ He *stopped a blast* from a superior. 彼は上官からお目玉をくった.

stop a bullet [***one, a packet, a shell***] 《俗》弾丸に当たって死ぬ, 傷つく ▪ He contrived to *stop a packet* from a sniper. 彼はまんまとそ撃兵の弾に当たってしまった.

Stop a moment! ちょっと待て《人の議論・批評などをさえぎるとき》 ▪ *Stop a moment*, sir. This is the way to do it. ちょっとお待ちください. こうやるのです.

stop at home =STAY at home.

stop at nothing どんな事でもやりかねない ▪ They *stopped at nothing* to obtain their favorite food. 彼らはお気に入りの食物を手に入れるためにはどんな事でもやりかねなかった.

stop dead [***cold***]/***stop in*** *one's* ***tracks*** [***on a dime***] 《口》(人・機械などが[を])ばったり止まる[止める] ▪ The horse *stopped dead*. 馬はばったり止まった ▪ He *stopped* the ball *dead*. 彼はボールをぴたりと止めた ▪ He pulled the trigger and *stopped* the bear *cold*. 彼は引き金を引いてクマを急に止まらせた.

stop it out 《口》(他のもので)節約して経費を省く (*in*) ▪ I might *stop it out in* buses. バスで節約して経費を省くこともできる.

stop *a person's* ***mouth*** →MOUTH[1].

stop payment **1** (紛失したり盗まれたりした手形などの)支払いを差し止める ▪ As the numbers of the notes were known, *payment* of them *was stopped*. 手形の番号はわかっていたのでその支払いは差し止められた.
2 (支払い不能に陥った会社などが)支払いを停止する ▪ The bank has *stopped payment*. その銀行は支払いを停止した.

stop short **1** (フェンシングなどで打撃を)受け止める ▪ I *stopped* his blade *short*. 彼の剣を受け止めた.
2 (人の話を)さえぎる, 中止させる ▪ He *stopped* me *short*. 彼は私の話をさえぎった.
3 はたと立ち止まる[やめる] ▪ He *stopped short* at the gate. 彼は門の所ではたと立ち止まった ▪ He *stopped short* in the middle of his speech. 彼は話の途中ではたとやめた.

stop short at …にとどめる ▪ He wouldn't *stop short at* theft. 彼は盗みだってやりかねない.

stop short of →SHORT.

stop stone dead =STOP dead.

stop the breath of …の息の根を止める ▪ They rushed into his tent and *stopped the breath of* all. 彼らは彼のテントの中へなだれ込んですべての人間の息の根を止めた.

stop the press (追加などのために)印刷機の運転を中止する ▪ I shall *stop the press* in this case. このケースでは印刷機の運転は中止します.

Stop thief! どろぼうだ(捕えてくれ)《追跡者の叫び声》

S

▪ I heard behind me the cry of "*Stop thief!*"「どろぼうだ!」という叫びが背後で聞こえた.

stop to think ゆっくり考える ▪ He never *stops to think.* 彼はゆっくり考えることをしない.

stop** a person's **way 人の通路のじゃまをする; 人を妨げる ▪ I went, but he *stopped my way.* 私は行ったが, 彼が私の行く手をさえぎった.

stopper /stάpər|stɔ́p-/ 名 ***put a stopper [the stoppers] on***《口》…をやめさせる ▪ The father tried to *put a stopper on* his daughter's late hours. 父親は娘の遅い帰宅をやめさせようとした.

storage /stɔ́:rɪdʒ/ 名 ***in cold storage***《口》必要な時までしまって, 保留して; 死亡して ▪ His ideas were very good, but we had to keep them *in cold storage* for a while. 彼の着想はとてもよかったが, しばらくの間温存しておくよりほかなかった ▪ My poor son is *in cold storage.* かわいそうに息子は死んでしまった. ☞cold storage「冷蔵」.

store /stɔ:r/ 名 ***a chain store*** チェーン店 ▪ When you're in *a chain store*, you don't know what city you're in. チェーン店に入るとどこの街にいるのかわからない.

a store of/stores of たくさんの ▪ He has *a store of* wit. 彼は機知に富んでいる.

in store たくわえて, 用意して ▪ Who knows what the future may hold *in store*? 将来どんなことになるか誰にわかるだろうか ▪ I have many objections *in store.* 私には文句がたくさんある.

***in store for** a person* (物が)人を待ちかまえて; (人が)人のために用意して ▪ A surprise was *in store for* me at home. 家に帰ってみるとびっくりすることが私を待ちかまえていた ▪ I have good news *in store for* you. 君に聞かせるいい知らせがある.

keep [tend] store《米口》(主人・店員が)店番をする; 店を持っている ▪ He has *kept store* in a country town. 彼は田舎町に店を持っていた.

lay in store(s) →LAY[2].

lay in stores of …を仕入れる ▪ He has *laid in stores of* coal for the winter. 彼は冬に備えて石炭を仕入れた.

lay up in store (将来使うために)大事にしまっておく ▪ We decided to *lay up in store* all the Waterford glasses. 我々はウォーターフォード製グラスを全部大事にしまっておくことに決めた.

lie in store (for** a person**) (人の身の上に出来事が)起きようとしている, (人に運命が)降りかかろうとしている ▪ I wonder what *lies in store for* me in the future. 将来どんなことが私を待ち受けているのだろうか.

mind the store《米》仕事に専念する, 仕事を取り仕切る; 問題に着目し解決しようとする ▪ We assume somebody else is paying attention to the problem, but nobody's really *minding the store.* 我々は他の誰かがその問題に注意を向けていると思っているが, ほんとうは誰もそれを解決しようとはしていないのだ.

set [lay, put] store by [on] …を重んじる ▪ I know you *set store by* your mother's letters. 君がおかあさんの手紙を大事にしているのは知っている ▪ I have *set* little *store on* it. 私はそれをほとんど重んじていない ▪ He *lays* great *store by* tradition. 彼は伝統を非常に重んじる.

Store is no sore.《諺》たくさんあるのは苦にならない.

stores of →a STORE of.

tend store →keep STORE.

stor(e)y /stɔ́:ri/ 名 ***weak [wrong, gone] in the [one's] upper story/not right with the upper story***《戯》頭がおかしい ▪ I was born *weak in the upper story.* 私は生まれつき頭がおかしかった ▪ All is *not right with his upper story.* 彼は頭が少しおかしい.

storm /stɔ:rm/ 名 ***After a storm (comes) a calm.***《諺》あらしのあとはなぎ,「雨降って地固まる」.

a storm in a spittoon 内輪もめ, 空騒ぎ ▪ The wrestling match was like *a storm in a spittoon.* そのレスリングの試合は内輪もめのようだった.

a storm in a teacup [a puddle] 内輪もめ, から騒ぎ (Cicero, *De Legibus* 3. 16. 36) ▪ Our skirmish is but *a storm in a teacup.* 我々の小ぜりあいはほんのから騒ぎにすぎない.

attack ... by storm …を強襲する ▪ The next day we *attacked* the fort *by storm.* その翌日我々はそのとりでを強襲した.

bow to the storm 世論の激しさに屈する ▪ The Town Council *bowed to the storm.* 市議会は世論の激しさに屈した.

bring a storm about** a person's **ears 自分の言動によって反感を買う ▪ His strong speech against the President *brought a storm about his ears.* 彼は大統領への強い非難演説によって激しい反感を買うこととなった.

go down a storm (観衆に)熱狂的に受け入れられる ▪ His scenarios *go down a storm.* 彼の書くシナリオは熱狂的に受け入れられる.

provoke [cause] a storm 怒号のあらしを呼ぶ ▪ The authorities *provoked a storm* when they said that they would stop the school festival. 当局が文化祭を中止すると告げると怒号のあらしが起きた.

ride the storm =ride the WHIRLWIND.

storm and stress **1** 疾風怒濤時代《18世紀後半古典派に対する反動として起こったドイツ文学のロマン主義運動》 ▪ The *Storm and Stress* period was then about to astonish Germany. 疾風怒濤時代が当時ドイツを驚がくさせようとしていた.
2 動乱, 動揺 ▪ His time of *storm and stress* was over. 彼の動乱の時代は終わっていた. ☞G Sturm und Drang のなぞり.

take ... by storm《軍》…を強襲して取る; の心を奪う; をうっとりさせる ▪ The town *was taken by storm.* 町は強襲して取られた ▪ These ideas were *taking* my spirit *by storm.* こういう考えが私の心を奪っていた.

the calm [lull] before the storm あらしの前の静けさ ▪ When things were relatively calm, it was *the calm before the storm.* 事態が比較的穏

やかであるのはあらしの前の静けさであった.

up a storm 《米口》非常に熱中して, とことん(…しまくる) ▪ They sang *up a storm.* 彼らはとことん歌いまくった.

weather* [*ride out*] *the storm 危機を切り抜ける ▪ Pitt contrived to *weather the storm.* ピットは何とかして危機を切り抜けた.

story /stɔ́:ri/ 名 ***a tall story*** →TALL.

an old story よくあること, ありふれた話 ▪ Her mood swings are *an old story.* 彼女の気分の揺れはよくあることさ.

as the story goes 人の言うところでは ▪ *As the story goes*, she left him as soon as she discovered that he had no money. 人の言うところでは, 彼女は男に金がないのがわかるとすぐ別れたとのことだ.

be a different story 話[様子]が違う ▪ Telecasting *is a different story* altogether. テレビ放送は全く様子が違う.

be all in one story/be in the same story (通例ぐるになって)みな言うことが一致している ▪ They *are all in one story*, Mr. Mann. やつらはみんな言うことが一致しているんですよ, マンさん.

break a story 特ダネ記事を他に先駆けて報じる ▪ The Yomiuri *broke the story* before other newspapers could even send reporters to the scene. 読売新聞は他社が現場に特派員を差し向ける前に特ダネ記事を報じた.

cap a story 人の話を横取りする ▪ Whenever I try to tell *a story*, my husband interrupts and *caps* it. 私が話をしようとするといつも主人が割り込んできて話を横取りするの.

for the story 筋[ストーリー]を知るために ▪ She reads only *for the story.* 彼女は筋だけを追って読む.

It's a long story. 《口》話せば長くなる ▪ Hey, what happened to you?—*It's a long story.* おい, 何があったの?—話せば長くなるさ ▪ Oh, *it's a long story*—I'll tell you some other time. 長い話になるので, またいつか話すよ.

It's* [*That's*] *the story of my life! 《戯》不運続きだ!, これが私の人生さ! ▪ It's been raining for ten straight days and I make no money. *That's the story of my life!* 10日連続の雨で稼ぎがないんだ. 私の人生こんなもんさ!

not the whole story/not the end of the story (それだけでは)話はまだ終わらない ▪ He is poet, musician and occasional actor, but that is *not the whole story.* 彼は詩人で音楽家でときには役者もする. しかもそれで話が終わったわけじゃない.

sit on a story 話の公表を遅らせる ▪ The media *sat on a story* to save a hostage's life. マスコミは人質の生命を救うため事件の公表を遅らせた.

Tell me* [*us*] *the old, old story. 《口》何度も聞いた言い訳だね(とても信じられない).

tell** one's* [its***] ***own story*** それだけで明らかだ ▪ The advertisement is too brief to *tell its own story.* その広告は短いのでそれだけでは明らかでない.

tell stories (特に子供が)つくり話をする, 嘘を言う ▪ Don't *tell stories.* 嘘を言うんじゃない.

That is another* [*a different*] *story. それは別の話だ ▪ There he met Mary. But *that is another story.* そこで彼はメアリーと会った. だがそれは別の話だ《今は述べない》.

the* (*same*) *old story 例のよくあるやつ, いつもの同じ言い訳 ▪ It's *the* (*same*) *old story.* そいつは例のよくあるやつだ ▪ You say you'll pay next week—*the same old story*! 君は来週は払うと言う—いつもの同じ言い訳じゃないか.

the story goes that …という話だ ▪ *The story goes that* the following colloquy took place. 次の会話が行われたという話だ.

to make* [《英口》 *cut*] *a long story short 《米口》かいつまんで言えば, 早い話が ▪ *To make a long story short* the man will be there next week. かいつまんで言えば, その人は来週そこへ行くのだ.

You story! 《口》この嘘つき《特に子供の言う文句》 ▪ "Oh, *you story!*" exclaimed Rhoda, with indignation. 「まあこの嘘つき!」とローダは腹を立てて叫んだ.

stout /staʊt/ 形 ***a stout fellow* [*feller*]** 《口》頼りになる人 ▪ Dad is *a stout fellow.* おやじは頼りになる人間だ. ☞女性にも用いる.

stove /stoʊv/ 名 ***slave over a hot stove*** 《戯》あくせく料理する ▪ You needn't *slave over a hot stove* so much. そんなにあくせく料理しなくていい.

stow /stoʊ/ 動 ***Stow it!*** 《俗》やめろ!, 黙れ! ▪ "*Stow it!*" he cried, vehemently. 「やめろ!」と彼はすごいけんまくで叫んだ.

straight /streɪt/ 形副名 ***a straight arrow*** 《米口》愚直な人 ▪ He is *a straight arrow* who rarely drinks and smokes. 彼はめったに酒もタバコもやらない愚直な人間だ.

a straight shooter 《米口》正直人間 ▪ Tom's *a straight shooter* and doesn't tell a lie. トムは正直人間なので嘘は言わない.

(*as*) *straight as a die* [*pin*] →DIE¹.

(*as*) *straight as an arrow* (体が)この上もなくまっすぐで; 一直線に; 正直な, まっとうな ▪ You are *as straight as an arrow* still. あなたはまだ体がしゃきっとまっすぐでいらっしゃる ▪ He's *straight as an arrow* and you can trust him with the money. 彼は正直者だからそのお金をあずけても大丈夫だよ.

as straight as straight この上もなくまっすぐな ▪ His legs are *as straight as straight.* 彼の足はこの上もなくまっすぐだ.

get … straight …をまちがいなく把握する ▪ You must *get* the facts *straight.* その事実をまちがいなく把握しなければならない ▪ Let's *get* it *straight.* このことは再確認しておこう.

get* [*put, set*] *the record straight → put the RECORD straight.

give it to** a person* ***straight 《口》人に率直に言う ▪ I asked the doctor to *give it to* me *straight.* 私は医者に率直に言ってくれと頼んだ.

go straight **1** まっすぐに行く ▪ *Go straight* to the end of the road and then turn left. この道の

S

突き当たりまでまっすぐに行ってそれから左に曲がりなさい.

2 まともにやっていく ▪ The man really did try to *go straight*. 男はまともにやっていこうと本当に努めたのだった.

have a straight eye 物の位置がまっすぐかどうか見てわかる ▪ There is no difficulty about it to anyone who *has a straight eye*. 物の位置がまっすぐかどうかが見てわかる人にとっては, それには少しも困難はない.

hit [***shoot***] ***straight*** 命中させる ▪ The arrow *hit straight* in the center of the target. 矢は的の中央に命中した ▪ Suddenly a bullet *hit* him *straight* in his head. 突然1発の弾丸が彼の頭に当たった.

keep a straight face →FACE[1].

keep straight まじめに暮らす[暮らさせる] ▪ He proved he could *keep straight*. 彼はまじめに暮らすことができることを証明してみせた ▪ They *kept* him *straight*. 彼らは彼をまじめに暮らさせた.

keep to [***stay on***] ***the straight and narrow*** 《口》終始品行方正にする(《聖》*Matt*. 7. 14) ▪ He *kept to the straight and narrow* for the rest of his life. 彼はその後は一生品行方正にした.

on the straight **1** 一直線に; ふちと並行に ▪ It is usually cut *on the straight*. それは通例ふちと並行に切られる.

2 《口》(前科者などが)曲がったことをしないで ▪ That was when Jerry's *on the straight*. それはジェリーが曲がったことをしないでいるときのことだった.

out of (***the***) ***straight*** ゆがんで, 曲がって ▪ The line got *out of the straight*. 線がゆがんでしまった.

put ... straight (部屋など)を整とんする ▪ *Put* that room *straight* as soon as you can. なるべく早くあの部屋を整とんしなさい.

run straight まっすぐに走る; 曲がったことをしない ▪ The jockeys *ran* very *straight*. 騎手たちはまっ正直にやった.

set ... straight **1** (人)の誤りを正す ▪ He *set* us *straight* with his excellent suggestion. 彼は優れた示唆で我々の誤りを正してくれた.

2 =put ... STRAIGHT.

straight away 《俗》すぐに ▪ He was paid the money *straight away*. 彼は即刻金の支払いを受けた.

S

straight from the shoulder →SHOULDER[1].

straight off 《英》ためらわずに, さっさと ▪ I am going to marry her *straight off*. 彼女とさっさと結婚するつもりだ ▪ I discovered *straight off* that he was lying. 彼が嘘を言っていることはすぐわかった.

straight out 率直に, あからさまに ▪ You're a good 'un to tell me *straight out* like this. こんなふうに率直に話してくれるなんて君はいいやつだな.

straight up 《英口》本当に; 《主に米》(お酒を)ストレートで ▪ I didn't see him, *straight up*! 彼には会わなかった, 本当だよ ▪ He ordered a whisky *straight up*. 彼はウィスキーをストレートで注文した.

tell straight はっきりと言う ▪ I *told* him *straight* what I thought. 私の考えを彼にはっきりと言ってやった.

the straight and narrow (***path*** [***way***]) 《戯》正直な暮らし方(《聖》*Matt*. 7. 14) ▪ His youngest son departed from *the straight and narrow*. 彼の末の息子は正道を踏み外してしまった.

think straight 〚主に否定文で〛きちんと[理路整然と]考える ▪ I was so tired I wasn't *thinking straight*. 疲れていたのでまともに考えがまわっていなかった ▪ I am too excited to *think straight* on the subject. とても興奮していてその件をきちんと考えられない.

vote the straight ticket 自党の公認候補者のみに投票する(→a straight TICKET) ▪ I *voted the straight* Democratic *ticket*. 私は民主党の公認候補のみに投票した.

with a straight face 《口》まじめくさった顔をして ▪ Few people can read the story *with a straight face*. その小説を笑いを堪えて読める人はまずいない.

straightforward /strèɪtfɔ́ːrwərd/ 形 ***It's as straightforward as that.*** =It's as SIMPLE as that.

strain[1] /streɪn/ 名 ***at*** (***full, utmost***) ***strain*** 全力を尽くして, 張りつめて ▪ She sat with her wide eyes *at full strain*. 彼女は目を大きく見開いて座っていた ▪ They were all laboring *at utmost strain* to try and save the ship. 彼らはみなその船を救おうとして全力を尽くして働いていた.

be a (***great***) ***strain on*** *one's* ***nerves*** ひどくいらいらする ▪ Living with other students in the dormitory *was a great strain on my nerves*. 寮での学生たちとの生活で私はひどくいらいらした.

crack under the strain 神経をすり減らす, 神経衰弱になる ▪ As I left home, mother *cracked under the strain* of worrying about me. 親元を離れていたぼくを心配して母は神経をすり減らした.

on the strain 緊張[努力]して ▪ All his faculties were *on the strain*. 彼の能力はすべて張りつめていた ▪ They are perpetually *on the strain* till nine at night. 彼らは夜の9時までいつも努力している.

put a strain on [***upon***] ...に重圧を加える ▪ The stoppage in the supply of oil *put a* sudden *strain on* us. 石油の供給停止は突然我々に重圧を加えた.

stand the strain 無理に耐える(*of*) ▪ I can't *stand the strain of* constant travel. 絶えず無理をして旅をするなんて耐えられない.

take the strain **1** (綱引きで)綱を引き締める ▪ The Referee said, "*Take the strain.*" 審判は「綱を引き締めよ」と言った.

2 (人・ロープ・経済などが)圧力に耐える ▪ Can the country *take the strain* successfully? その国はその圧力にうまく耐えられるだろうか.

under the strain 緊張[過労]のために ▪ The rope broke *under the strain*. ロープはあまり引っ張ったので切れた.

without strain 自然に, 楽に ▪ He writes *without strain*. 彼は自然な書き方をする.

strain[2] /streɪn/ 動 ***strain** oneself* **1** 精いっぱい努力する ▪ He *strained himself* to a final burst of speed. 彼は精いっぱい努力してこれを最後とばかりスピードを出した.

2 捻挫(ねんざ)する ▪ He *strained himself* by treading on a loose stone. 彼は緩んだ石を踏んで捻挫した.

strain a point やり過ぎる, 分を越えたことをする ▪ It would be *straining a point* to arrest him. あの男を逮捕するのは行き過ぎだろう.

strain at a gnat and swallow a camel 小事にこだわって大事をゆるがせにする (《聖》*Matt.* 23. 24) ▪ The trouble with the thesis is that it *strains at a gnat and swallows a camel.* その命題の困った点は小事にこだわって大事をゆるがせにしていることだ.

strain at stool/ strain down 便所でいきむ ▪ The patient was directed to *strain at stool.* その患者は便所でいきむように指示された.

strain at the leash →LEASH.

strain** one's **ear(s) 一心に聞き耳を立てる ▪ She *strained her ear* at the keyhole. 彼女はかぎ穴の所で一心に聞き耳を立てた.

strain every nerve [sinew] 《文》必死の努力をする ▪ The hotel owners *strained every nerve* to make the place a success. ホテルの所有者たちはその土地を売り出そうとして必死の努力をした.

strain** one's **eyes **1** 目をこらす ▪ If you *strain your eyes*, you can just see the church. 目をこらせばかろうじて教会が見えます.

2 目を疲らせる ▪ Don't *strain your eyes* by reading such small print. そんな小さな活字を読んで目を疲らせてはいけない.

strain ... to** one's **bosom [breast, heart] ...を胸に抱きしめる ▪ He *strained* the girl again *to his heart.* 彼は女の子をまた胸に抱きしめた.

strait /streɪt/ 名 ***in (dire) straits*** 困って, 窮境に陥って ▪ He is *in straits* financially. 彼は金銭的にひどく困っている.

reduce [put] ... to straits ...を窮境に陥らせる ▪ They *were reduced to* great *straits* by the failure of the rice crop. 彼らは稲の不作のために非常に困ってしまった.

straiten /stréɪtən/ 動 ***be straitened for*** ...に窮する ▪ We *were straitened for* provisions. 我々は食料に窮していた.

strait-jacket /stréɪtdʒækət/ 名 ***put** a person **in a strait-jacket*** 人の自由を束縛する ▪ I felt as though I *were put in a strait-jacket* at that school. あの学校ではまるで自由が束縛されているかのように感じた.

strange /streɪndʒ/ 形 ***be strange at*** ...がへたで ▪ I *am strange at* the work. その仕事は苦手だ.

be strange to **1** ...が不慣れで ▪ I *am strange to* the work. その仕事は不慣れです.

2 ...に未知の, よく知られていない ▪ This handwriting *is strange to* me. この筆跡には見覚えがない.

feel strange **1** 体の調子が変だ《目まいがするなど》 ▪ I *feel strange.* 調子が変だ.

2 勝手が違う, 妙な感じがする ▪ It *feels strange* to sleep in broad daylight. 白昼に眠るのは妙な感じだ.

strange enough 不思議なことに ▪ *Strange enough*, he was seen no more. 不思議なことに, 彼の姿はそれきり見えなかった.

strange to say [tell, relate] 不思議な話だが ▪ *Strange to say*, George took particular notice of this place. 不思議な話だが, ジョージはこの場所に限って目を留めたのだった.

the strange woman 〚総称的に〛売春婦 (《聖》*Prov.* 2. 16) ▪ There was no fear of my being tempted by *the strange woman.* 私が売春婦に誘惑される恐れはなかった.

stranger /stréɪndʒər/ 名 ***be a [no] stranger (to)*** **1** (...の)経験がない[ある], (を)知らない[知っている] ▪ He *was no stranger to* dissipation. 彼は放蕩の味は知っていた ▪ The dirty floor has long *been a stranger to* the broom. 汚い床は長いことほうきではいたことがなかった.

2 (...は)不案内です, 初めてです ▪ I *am a stranger* here [*to* this town]. 私は当地[この町]は不案内です.

I spy [see] strangers. 《英》傍聴禁止を求めます《下院で秘密会を要求して》.

make a [no] stranger of ...を他人扱いする[しない] ▪ They *make no stranger of* me. あの人たちは私を他人扱いなどしません.

the little stranger 《戯》(生まれたばかりの)赤んぼう ▪ We never talked obstetrics when *the little stranger* came. 赤んぼうが生まれたとき我々はお産についての話は少しもしていなかった.

You are quite a stranger! 《口》全く久しぶりですね.

strap[1] /stræp/ 名 ***a pennyworth of strap oil*** むち打ち ▪ The new lad was sent there for *a pennyworth of strap oil.* 新米の青年はむち打ちを受けるためにそこへよこされた.

on (the) strap 《俗》信用で, かけで ▪ It had been put *on strap.* それはかけにしてあった.

strap[2] /stræp/ 動 ***be strapped for*** 《口》(お金)に困っている ▪ He *is* always *strapped for* cash. 彼はいつもお金に困っている.

straw /strɔː/ 名 ***A drowning man will catch at a straw.*** →DROWN.

a face of straw にせの顔 ▪ Off drops the visor, and *a face of straw* appears. ぱっと仮面が取れると, にせの顔が表れる.

a man of straw →MAN[1].

a straw in the wind 《英》大勢の赴くところを示すもの ▪ The CIO action was *a straw in the wind.* 最高情報責任者のその行動は時勢の動向を示すものであった.

A straw shows which way [how] the wind blows. 《諺》わずかの兆候で大勢の赴くところがわかる.

a straw vote [poll] (非公式の)世論投票, 調査 ▪ They took *a straw poll* on the bill. 彼らはその法案について世論調査を行った.

S

catch* [*grasp, clutch*] *at a straw*/*cling to a straw (苦しまぎれに)わらのようなものにでもすがりつく ▪ Love, like despair, *catches at a straw*. 愛は絶望と同じようにわらのごときものにもすがりつく. ☞A DROWNing man will catch at a straw. という諺から.

draw straws **1** わらくじを引く ▪ They had to *draw straws* for the food they had. 彼らは手持ちの食料にありつける者を決めるわらくじを引かねばならなかった.
2 (目が)眠たくなる ▪ Their eyes all *drew straws*. 彼らの目はもうどれも眠くなっていた.

draw the short straw 貧乏くじを引く ▪ I *drew the short straw*, so I treated him to dinner. 貧乏くじを引いちゃって彼に夕食をおごった.

gather* [*pick*] *straws (目が)眠くなる ▪ My eyes are *gathering straws*. 私の目が眠くなってきた ▪ Their eyelids did not once *pick straws*. 彼らのまぶたは一度も眠くならなかった.

in the straw **1** お産の床について (↔out of the STRAW) ▪ They found the lady *in the straw*. 彼らが行ってみると夫人はお産の床についていた. ☞お産があるとき, 音がしないように家の前にわらをまく習慣が普通に行われていたことから.
2 (穀物が)まだ打穀していない ▪ I paid for two loads of oats *in the straw* 18 shillings. 私はまだ打穀していないカラスムギ2荷分に18シリング支払った.

make bricks without straw →BRICK.

***not care a straw* [*two straws, three straws*]** 少しもかまわない ▪ The British Government does *not care a straw* what religion its subjects profess. イギリス政府はその臣民がどのような宗教を信仰していても少しもかまわない.

not worth* [*matter*] *a straw 少しも価値がない[問題ではない] ▪ The whole houseful of furniture is*n't worth a straw*! 家いっぱいの家具が少しも価値がないとは! ▪ He is angry, but it does*n't matter a straw*. 彼は怒っているが, 少しもかまわない.

out of the straw お産がすんで (↔in the STRAW 1) ▪ I hope Mrs. Brown is safe *out of the straw*, and the child well. ブラウン夫人のお産が無事にすみ, お子さんも元気のことと思います.

S

pick straws →gather STRAWs.

run to straw (麦が)わらになっていく ▪ It would make corn *run* entirely *to straw*. そんなことになれば小麦はすっかりわらになっていくだろう.

***the last* [*final*] *straw* (*that breaks the camel's back*)** (負担・がまんの限度を越える)最後の一小事, もはや耐えきれない難儀 ▪ Sunstroke may act as *the last straw*. 日射病が命を奪う最後の一因になる場合もある. ☞It's the last straw that breaks the CAMEL's back. という諺から.

throw straws against the wind むだ骨を折る ▪ You will be *throwing straws against the wind* if you try to cure that youth. あの若者を矯正しようとすればむだ骨を折ることになりますよ.

streak[1] /stri:k/ 名 ***a losing streak*** (スポーツでの)連敗 (↔a winning streak) ▪ Our team has been on *a losing streak*. わがチームは連敗中だ.

a streak of ...の気味 ▪ He has *a streak of* humor in him. 彼には少しユーモアがある ▪ He has *a streak of* cowardice in him. 彼には少し憶病なところがある.

***a streak of luck* [*bad luck*]** 《口》幸運[不運]続き ▪ He happens to be in *a streak of bad luck*. 彼はたまたま不運続きだ ▪ Tom had *a* sudden *streak of luck* and kept winning steadily. トムは急についてきて, どんどん勝ち続けた.

a streak of red (北米)先住民の血統 ▪ She is suspected of *a streak of red*. 彼女は先住民の血を引いているのではないかと思われている.

a yellow streak 卑怯[憶病]なところ ▪ There is *a yellow streak* in him. 彼には卑怯なところがある.

like a* (*blue*) *streak* (*of lightning*)/ *like streaks 《口》電光石火のように ▪ He was running *like a streak of lightning*. 彼は電光石火のように走っていた ▪ We worked *like streaks*. 我々は電光石火のように仕事をした.

make a streak 《米口》急いで行く (*for*) ▪ They *made a* clean *streak for* the woods. 彼らは森をさしてすたこらと去って行った.

talk a blue streak 《口》べらべらと早口に話す ▪ He was *talking a blue streak* to her. 彼は彼女に早口にべらべらしゃべっていた.

streak[2] /stri:k/ 動 ***be streaked with*** ...のすじ[しま]がついている ▪ The sky *is streaked with* smoke. 空には煙がすじのように立ち上っている.

stream /stri:m/ 名 ***against the stream*** 流れ[時勢]に逆らって ▪ It is pointless for you to strive *against the stream*. 時勢に逆らおうとしてもむだである ▪ I have done it *against the stream* of my resolution. 私は自分の決心の流れに逆らってそうしたのだ.

be* [*come, go*] *on stream 《米》生産を始める ▪ Our plant will *go on stream* in June. わが工場は6月に生産を始めるだろう.

Cross the stream where it is shallowest. 《諺》流れを渡る時は最も浅い所を選べ,「浅い川も深く渡れ」.

down* (*the*) *stream 下流へ, 川下へ ▪ He was carried *down the stream*. 彼は川下へ流された.

go* [*drift, sail*] *with the stream 時勢に従う (→SWIM with the stream) ▪ There is hardly a man who does not *go* [*drift, sail*] *with the stream*. 時勢に従わない人はほとんどいない.

in a stream*/*in streams (血・涙などが)どくどくと ▪ Wine and ale flowed *in streams*. ワインやビールがどくどくとあふれた.

in the stream (川の)中流に ▪ The boat is *in the stream*. ボートは中流にいる.

up* (*the*) *stream 川上へ ▪ On went the salmon *up stream*. どんどんとサケは川上へ上って行った.

street /stri:t/ 名 ***a side street*** 横丁 ▪ The hotel is on *a* quiet *side street*. そのホテルは静かな

横丁にある.

a two-way street **1** 対面式道路 ▪ The two vehicles were racing side by side along the *two-way street.* 2台の車が対面式道路を並んで疾走していた.

2 相互に便益を与え合う間柄, 互恵的関係 ▪ Government-private-sector cooperation will have to be *a two-way street.* 官民協同は互恵的関係でなければなるまい ▪ Learning is *a two-way street* for students and teachers. 学習には生徒と先生にとって双方からの働きかけがいる.

be streets ahead [***better***] 《英口》はるかに先になる; はるかにまさっている ▪ As regards mechanical ingenuity, the Japanese *are streets ahead* of other nations. 機械いじりの器用さにかけては日本人は他の国民よりもはるかにまさっている.

beat the streets 町を行ったり来たりする, うろつき回る ▪ The policemen began to *beat the streets.* 警官は町を巡邏(ら)し始めた.

by long streets 《口》はるかに ▪ He is cleverer than you *by long streets.* 彼は君よりもずっと利口だ.

down street →up STREET.

from off the streets 売春婦あがりの ▪ She is a woman *from off the streets.* 彼女は売春婦あがりの女性だ ▪ He married her *from off the streets.* 彼は売春婦あがりの女性と結婚した.

get [***be***] ***on easy street*** 《米口》安楽に暮らす[暮らしている] ▪ He *is* now *on easy street.* 彼はいまは安楽に暮らしている.

get [***have***] ***the key of the street*** →KEY[1].

go on the streets 夜の女になる (→on the STREET(s)) ▪ What made those girls *go on the streets*? なぜあの娘たちは夜の女になったのか.

in Queer Street →QUEER[1].

in [***down, up***] *one's* ***street*** 《俗》関係がある, 得意で; …の好みに合って ▪ That's not *in my street.* それは僕の知ったことじゃない ▪ A great many of the books published today are right *down* [*up*] *her street.* 今日出版されている本の多くはまさに彼女のお手のものである ▪ Playing the violin is *right up my street.* バイオリン演奏はぼくのおはこさ.

in the street (株式取引所の)締め後の ▪ The tone *in the street* this evening appeared firm. 今晩の締め後の相場は手堅いように見えた.

in [《米》***on, upon***] ***the street***(***s***) 通りで ▪ I met him *in the street.* 彼と通りで会った.

live in the street 始終外出がちである ▪ He's very hard to catch at home: he seems to *live in the street.* 彼に自宅で会うのは至難の業だ. しょっちゅう外出しているらしい.

live on the streets 夜の女の生活をする (→on the STREET(s)) ▪ The two girls had to *live on the streets.* 二人の少女は夜の女の生活をしなければならなかった.

not in the same street with 《口》…とは同日の談ではない, と比べものにならない ▪ He's *not in the same street with* Tom. 彼はトムとは比較にならない.

not the length of a street 《俗》たいした隔たり[差]はない ▪ In point of beauty there is *not the length of a street* between Kitty and her sister. 美しさの点ではキティーと妹の間にたいした差はない.

on the street(***s***) **1** 売春して ▪ She is *on the streets* of London. 彼女はロンドンで売春している.

2 住む家がなくなって ▪ He found himself *on the street* when he could not pay his rent. 彼は家賃が払えなくて路頭に迷った.

(***right***) ***up*** *one's* ***street*** →in one's STREET.

street smarts 《米》(都会での)サバイバル術, 生き残りの知恵 ▪ He's not much good reading or writing, but he sure has *street smarts.* 彼の読み書きは大したことないが, 生き残る術(すべ)は確かにある.

take to the streets デモを行う, 実力誇示をする ▪ We *took to the streets* for higher wages. 我々は賃上げを要求してデモを行った.

the man [***woman***] ***in the street*** →MAN[1].

The streets are paved with gold. この町ではすぐ金持ちになれる.

up [***down***] ***street*** 通りの上手[下手]に[へ] ▪ A retired man died of dropsy *up street.* 仕事をやめた男が通りの上手で水腫で死んだ.

walk the street(***s***) **1** 通りを歩き回る ▪ When he *walks the streets*, he never condescends to look about him. 彼は通りを歩き回るときにあたりを見回しなどしない.

2 売春する ▪ I have often wept lest you should come to *walk* London *streets.* あなたがロンドンで売春をするようになりはしないかと泣いたことが幾度もあった.

strength /streŋθ/ 名 ***a pillar*** [***tower***] ***of strength*** 頼りになる人, 力強い柱, 柱石; 強力な支持者, 擁護者 (cf. Sh., *Rich. III* 5. 3. 12) ▪ Miss Brown was *a tower of strength* at the concert. ブラウン嬢はコンサートでは大いに役に立った ▪ Our uncle proved to be *a pillar of strength* after my father's death. 父の死後, 叔父が強く支えてくれた.

below strength 定員が足りない ▪ The police force is 400 *below strength.* 警察は400人定員が足りない.

by brute strength 力まかせに, 力いっぱい ▪ He moved the heavy desk *by brute strength.* 彼は力まかせにその重い机を動かした.

gather strength →GATHER.

get the strength of …を十分に了解する, の真相をつかむ ▪ Then, bit by bit, Mick *got the strength of* it. やがて少しずつミックはその真相をつかんできた.

Give me strength! 《口》これでいらいらせずにいられるか《相手の愚かさに腹を立てて言う》 ▪ Can't you even do sums? *Give me strength!* 君は足し算もできないのか. これで怒らずにいられるかね.

go (***on***) ***from strength to strength*** 新たに試みるたびに進歩していく (《聖》*Ps.* 84. 7) ▪ Having acquired self-confidence, he *went on from strength to strength.* 自信がついたので彼は新たにや

るたびに進歩していった.

in full strength **1** 全員そろって ▪ The regiment mustered *in full strength*. 連隊は全員集合した.
2 (酒が)生(き)一本の ▪ Be careful with the brandy, it is *in full strength*. そのブランデーには気をつけなさい. 生一本なんだから.

in* (*great*) *strength 大勢そろって ▪ The students of the school were present *in* (*great*) *strength*. 学校の生徒が大勢そろって出席していた. ☞strength＝large numbers.

in *one's* ***own strength*** 自力で, 神力に頼らずに ▪ She can now walk firmly *in her own strength*. 彼女はもう自分の力でしっかりと歩ける.

measure *one's* ***strength*** →MEASURE[2].

on the strength of …を種にして; に頼んで (《聖》 *1 Kings* 19. 8) ▪ I did it *on the strength of* your promise. 君の約束を当てにしてそうやったのだ ▪ Let's have a drink *on the strength of* it. それを種にして1杯やろうよ.

outgrow *one's* ***strength*** (幼年期に)体が早く大きくなって体力が追いつかない ▪ The child is apt to *outgrow his strength*. 子供はとかく体力が成長に追いつかないことがある.

play to *one's* ***strengths*** 長所を生かす[生かせる] ▪ Each member of our team has a task that *plays to their strengths*. わがチームのメンバーはそれぞれ, その長所を生かせる仕事をもっている.

Union* [*Unity*] *is strength. 《諺》 団結は力なり.

up to strength 定員に達して ▪ We must bring the police force *up to strength*. 警察隊を定員に達するようにしなければならない.

strengthen /stréŋθən/ 動 ***strengthen*** *one's* [***the***] ***hand*** →strengthen the HAND(s) of.

stress /stres/ 名 ***lay* [*place, put*] *stress on* [*upon*]** …に重きを置く; を力説する, 強調する ▪ I do not *lay* any *stress upon* these deductions. 私はこのような推論には少しも重きを置かない.

No stress. 《口》 問題ないよ ▪ Don't worry, man, *no stress*. 気にしなくていい, 大丈夫さ.

stress of weather 荒天 ▪ A frigate was driven ashore by *stress of weather*. フリゲート艦が荒天のために岸へ打ち上げられた.

under* [*driven by*] (*the*) *stress of …のために仕方なく ▪ The man stole it *driven by stress of* poverty. 男は貧にかられてそれを盗んだ ▪ He began to weep *under the stress of* excitement. 彼は興奮のあまりに泣きだした.

stretch[1] /stretʃ/ 名 ***at a* [*one*] *stretch*** 一気に, 立て続けに ▪ I read the last five books *at a stretch*. 一気に最後の5巻を読みあげた. ☞at a SITTING に比べて「一続きの時間の長さ」を強調.

at full stretch 全力操業して ▪ The workers were [The factory was] *at full stretch*. 工員たち[工場]は全力操業していた.

bring … to the stretch …をぴんと張りつめる ▪ The chains *were brought to the stretch*. その鎖はぴんと張りつめられた.

by a stretch of …を無理に使って ▪ We might, *by a stretch of* the imagination, admit his work to be a "novel". 想像をたくましくして, 彼の作品が「小説」だと認めてもよかろう ▪ It is only *by a stretch of* language that we can be said to desire that which is inconceivable. 我々が想像つかないものを求めると言えるのはただのこじつけだ.

by any stretch of the imagination →by no stretch of (the) IMAGINATION.

do *one's* [***a long***] ***stretch*** 《俗》 服役[長い間服役]する ▪ He is now *doing his stretch*. 彼は今服役している.

***for long stretches* [*a long stretch*]** 長い距離を ▪ We walked *for long stretches* without meeting anyone. 我々は長いこと歩いたが, 誰にも会わなかった.

give a stretch のびをする ▪ The cat woke and *gave a stretch*. 猫は目をさましてのびをした.

on the stretch **1** ぴんと張って ▪ The ligament was *on the stretch*. ひもはぴんと張っていた.
2 大急ぎで ▪ We are now *on the stretch* for Europe. 我々は今大急ぎでヨーロッパへ向かっています.
3 気を張りつめて, 全力をふるって ▪ His business keeps his mind *on the stretch*. 彼は仕事のためにいつも気を張りつめている ▪ He is *on the stretch* to save their souls. 彼は彼らの魂を救済するために全力をふるっている.

put* [*set*]*… upon the* (*full*) *stretch …に全力を出させる ▪ The praise of God *puts* our faculties *upon the full stretch*. 神をほめたたえれば我々は全能力を出せる.

upon* [*on*] *a stretch 一気に ▪ We always played seven hours *on a stretch*. 我々はいつも一気に7時間遊んだ.

upon the stretch ＝on the STRETCH 1.

stretch[2] /stretʃ/ 動 ***be stretched out at a gallop*** →STRETCH out into a gallop.

fully stretched 才能[能力]を最大限に伸ばして ▪ He felt that he was not *fully stretched*. 彼は自分の才能が最大限に伸ばされていないと感じた.

stretch *oneself* **1** のびをする ▪ Jim soon woke up and *stretched himself*. ジムはやがて目をさましてのびをした.
2 大の字なりに寝る ▪ He *stretched himself* on his bed. 彼はベッドに大の字なりに寝た.

stretch a point →strain a POINT.

stretch *one's* ***credit*** 信用を過度に利用する ▪ They extended their business by *stretching their credit*. 彼らは無理な算段をして事業を拡張した.

stretch *one's* ***legs*** →LEG[1].

stretch *one's* ***length*** 大の字なりに寝そべる ▪ We *stretched our length* upon the grass. 我々は草の上に大の字なりに寝そべった.

stretch *oneself* ***out*** ＝STRETCH oneself 2.

stretch out into a gallop/ be stretched out at a gallop (馬などが)力の限り疾駆する ▪ The roused animal commenced to *stretch out*

S

into a gallop. 興奮した馬は力の限り疾駆し始めた ▪ His Cossack horse *was stretched out at a gallop.* 彼のコサック馬は力の限り疾駆した.

***stretch** a person **out** (**on the ground**)* 人を(地面に)なぐり倒す ▪ The blow *stretched* him *out on the ground.* その一撃をくらって彼は地面に大の字に伸びた.

***stretch to the oar** [**stroke**]* 力漕する《比喩的にも》 ▪ They seized their oars, and *stretched to the stroke.* 彼らはオールをつかんで力漕した ▪ He must *stretch to the oar* for his own credit. 彼は自分の名誉のために力いっぱいやらねばならない.

strew /struː/ 動 ***be strewn with*** ...でいっぱいである ▪ My room *is strewn with* books. 私の部屋は本でいっぱいだ ▪ Her career *was strewn with* misfortune. 彼女のキャリアには不運がいっぱいだった.

stricken /stríkən/ 形 ***stricken with*** [***by***] (病気)にかかって, (悲しみなど)に襲われて ▪ He was *stricken by* paralysis. 彼は麻痺(まひ)にかかっていた.

strict /strɪkt/ 形 ***keep a strict hand over*** ...に対してきびしい ▪ She *keeps a strict hand over* her son. 彼女は息子に対してきびしい.

strictly /stríktli/ 副 ***strictly speaking/to speak strictly*** 厳密に言えば ▪ There is, *to speak strictly*, no American language. 厳密に言えばアメリカ語というものはない.

stricture /stríktʃər/ 名 ***lay*** [***bestow, pass***] ***strictures on*** [***upon***] ...を酷評する ▪ He *bestowed* some *strictures upon* Dr. Kennet's sermons. 彼はケネット博士の説教をかなり酷評した.

stride /straɪd/ 名 ***at*** [***in***] ***a stride*** ひとまたぎに ▪ He was running with his long legs, two yards *at a stride.* 彼は長い脚でひとまたぎに2ヤードも走っていた.

break** one's **stride 歩調を緩める ▪ I *broke my stride* and waited for him getting near to me. 私は歩調を緩めて彼が近づいて来るのを待った.

get into** [**hit, strike**] one's **stride 《英》(仕事に)調子が出る ▪ Now I am *getting into my stride.* もう調子が出てきたぞ.

hit** one's **stride 《米》本調子を出す ▪ The Yankees never really *hit their stride* until about the middle of the season. ヤンキースはシーズンの半ばごろまで全く本調子が出なかった.

lengthen** [**shorten**] one's **stride 速度を速める[ゆるめる] ▪ We *lengthened our stride* and covered 12 miles. 我々は速度を速めて12マイルの道のりを歩いた.

make great** [**rapid**] **strides/make a wide stride/take strides 長足の進歩をする ▪ Surgery has *made great strides.* 外科は長足の進歩をした ▪ His illness *made rapid strides.* 彼の病気はどんどん進んだ.

put** a person **off** his **stride = put a person off his STROKE.

put** [**throw**] a person **out of** his **stride 人を面くらわせる ▪ Your detective *threw* me *out of my stride.* 君の探偵は私を面くらわせた.

stride for stride なんとか互角に, 遅れずに ▪ They competed *stride for stride* regarding prices. 彼らは価格に関しては互角に競い合った.

strike** one's **stride →get into one's STRIDE.

take ... in** (one's) **stride **1** (馬・乗馬者が)...をひとまたぎに跳び越える ▪ Seven hunters *took* the brook *in their stride.* 7人のハンターがその小川をひとまたぎに跳び越えた.
2 (難事)を苦もなく切り抜ける ▪ He could not *take* his bad luck *in stride.* 彼は自分の不運を苦もなく切り抜けることができなかった.

with long** [**big, great**] **strides 大またに《比喩的にも》 ▪ He walked away *with long strides.* 彼は大またに歩いて去った.

without breaking stride じゃまされずに, スムーズに ▪ My work has been going well *without breaking stride.* 仕事はスムーズにいっている.

strife /straɪf/ 名 ***be at strife*** 争っている, 不和である (*with*) ▪ The two parties *are at strife.* 両党は反目している ▪ The crown of England had always *been at strife with* its own barons. イギリス王はいつも諸侯たちと争っていた.

make strife あつれきを起こす ▪ They said that he *made strife* among them. その男は彼らの間にあつれきを起こすと彼らは言った.

strike[1] /straɪk/ 名 ***go on strike/come out on strike*** ストライキをやる ▪ The workers decided to *go on strike.* 従業員はストを打つことに決めた.

***have two strikes against** [**on**] one* 2ストライク取られている; 不利な立場に立っている ▪ Any old building should be considered to *have two strikes on* it. 古い建物はどれでも不利な立場にあると考えなければならない.

make a strike at (ヘビが)...にかみかかる ▪ The snake *made a strike at* my boot. そのヘビは私のブーツにかみかかってきた.

on strike/《米》***on a strike*** ストライキをして ▪ Three hundred men *on strike* have taken a mill. スト中の300名が工場を奪った.

Three strikes and you're out. 3回チャンスを逸したらおしまいだ, 3ストライクでバッター・アウトだ ▪ After a third conviction the authorities lock you up. You know, *three strikes and you're out.* 3度目の有罪判決を受けると当局に拘束されるぞ. いいか, 3ストライクでバッター・アウトだ.

***with one strike** [**two strikes**] **on** one* 少し[非常に]不利な立場で ▪ A cripple may be said to have been born *with two strikes on* him. 手足の不自由な人は非常な不利を背負って生まれたと言える.

strike[2] /straɪk/ 動 ***be struck by*** [***on***] 《英口》(異性)にほれこむ ▪ We teased him about *being struck by* Miss Ledrook. 我々は彼がレッドルック嬢にほれこんでいることでからかった.

***be struck off the rolls** [**the Medical Register**]* 弁護士[医者]の業を営むことを拒否される ▪ He *was struck off the rolls* for unprofessional

S

conduct. 彼は職にあるまじき行為をしたので弁護士業を営むのを拒否された.

be struck up 《米口》うろたえる, 当惑する ▪I *was struck up* in a heap at seeing her in such a fix. 私は彼女がそんな苦境に陥っているのを見て全く当惑してしまった.

be struck up on 《米》(異性)にほれこむ ▪That young man *is struck up on* Irene. あの青年はアイリーンにほれこんでいる.

be struck up with 《米》(部屋など)にほれこむ ▪I *was* quite *struck up with* the room. 私はその部屋にすっかりほれこんでしまった.

be struck with **1** =be STRUCK by.
2 (強い感情)に打たれる ▪I *was struck with* wonder at the scene. その光景を見て驚きの念に打たれた.

it strikes me that 私は...という気がする ▪*It struck me that* he was telling a lie. 彼は嘘を言っているのだという気がした.

strike a bad patch →PATCH.

strike a bargain [***deal***] ***with*** ...と取引する, 手を打つ ▪They *struck a bargain with* the employer. 彼らは雇い主と取引した.

strike a [***one***] ***blow for*** →BLOW[1].

Strike a light! →STRIKE me pink!

strike a [*one's*] ***line*** [***path***] 進路をとる ▪We decided to *strike a* bee *line* across country. 我々は一直線に土地を横切って行くことに決めた ▪They *struck their path* across the fields. 彼らは畑を横切って進んで行った.

strike at the root [***foundation***] ***of*** ...を根底からくつがえそうとする, の根底を破壊しようとする ▪These principles *strike at the root of* all established Government. そういう原理はすべての確立した政府を根底からくつがえそうとするものである ▪He intended to *strike at the root of* the evil. 彼はその悪の根底を破壊しようと思った.

strike *a person's* ***average*** 《米》人を見積もる ▪I tried to *strike his average*, but failed. 私はその男を見積もろうとしたが失敗した.

strike *a person* ***blind*** **1** (雷などが)人を打って盲目にする ▪Lightning has often been known to *strike* people *blind*. 雷は人を打って盲目にするとしばしば言われてきた.
2 〚受身で〛人を突然盲目にする ▪A young fellow *was struck blind* all of a sudden. 一人の若者がにわかに盲目になった.

strike *a person* ***dead*** **1** 人を刺し[切り]殺す ▪They *struck* him *dead*. 彼らは彼を切り殺した.
2 (雷などが)人を打って殺す ▪He *was struck dead* by lightning. 彼は雷に打たれて死んだ.
3 (神が罰として雷などで)人を打ち殺す ▪Heaven *struck* him *dead* with lightning. 神は彼を雷で打ち殺した.

strike *a person* ***deaf*** (雷などが)人を打って耳を不自由にする ▪A great cold had *struck* him *deaf* of one ear. 非常な寒さが彼に当たって一方の耳が不自由になった.

strike *a person* ***dumb*** **1** (雷などが)人を打って口をきけなくする; 〚受身で〛人をにわかに口がきけなくさせる ▪They sat long confounded, as *struck dumb*. 彼らはにわかに口がきけなくなったもののように長いこと途方にくれていた.
2 (恐怖・驚きなどが)人をあ然とさせる《誇張表現》 ▪His eloquence *struck* him *dumb*. 彼の雄弁に彼はあ然とした.

strike fear [***horror, terror***] ***into*** *one's* ***heart*** 《文》...に恐怖を起こさせる ▪The crime *struck horror into people's hearts*. その犯罪は人々に恐怖心を与えた.

strike hands →HAND[1].

strike home →HOME.

strike it rich [***lucky***] 《口》豊富な鉱脈を見つける, 大儲けする, 一発当てる; 意外な幸運にあう《比喩的にも》 ▪Courage and hope are kept up by the expectation of *striking it rich*. 今に「豊富な鉱脈を見つける」という期待で勇気と希望が保たれた ▪He thinks he has *struck it rich*. 彼はすばらしい掘り出しものをしたと思っている ▪He *struck lucky* on the very day of his arrival by finding a job. 彼は来たその日に職を見つけるという意外な幸運に恵まれた ▪He *struck it rich* in the IT business. 彼は IT ビジネスで大儲けした.

strike me blind [***dead, dumb, lucky***] ***if*** [***but***] ...だったら[でなければ]首でもやる《強い誓言》 ▪*Strike me blind if* it is not true. それが嘘なら首でもやらあ.

Strike me pink!/Strike a light! 《口》ちぇっ! 《驚き・不信を表す》 ▪*Strike a light!* You might have taken the trouble to put the kettle on. ちぇっ! 湯わかしをかけてくれてもよかったのに.

strike ... off [《まれ》***out of***] (***the list***) 《英》(名前・人など)を名簿から削除する, 除名する ▪Vernon *was struck off the list* of admirals. バーノンは海軍大将の名簿から削除された.

strike out a line for *oneself* 独立独行する; 新機軸を出す ▪You must *strike out a line for yourself* to achieve something in art. 芸術の分野で何かを成就したければ新機軸を出さねばだめだ.

strike out on *one's* ***own*** 独り立ちする ▪He left the bank to *strike out on his own* as a writer. 彼は作家として独り立ちするために銀行をやめた.

strike *a person* ***speechless*** =STRIKE a person dumb 2.

strike terror into one's heart →STRIKE fear into one's heart.

strike *a person* ***to*** (***the***) ***death*** 人を刺し[切り]殺す ▪The maid-servant *struck* her mistress *to death* with an ax. 女中はおので女主人を切り殺した.

strike town 《米》野営地から町へ出ていく ▪John got a pretty warm welcome when he *struck town*. ジョンは野営地から町へ出ていったときかなり歓迎された.

strike twelve the first time [***all at once***] →TWELVE.

strike up the heels of …を倒す ▪ A strong gale *struck up the* very *heels of* our main mast. 強風が我々の主檣までも倒してしまった.

Strike while the iron is hot. →IRON.

strike work ストをやる ▪ I never heard of authors *striking work*. 私は作家がストをやるという話は聞いたことがない.

string[1] /strɪŋ/ 名 ***another*** [***a second***] ***string*** (***to*** *one's* ***bow***) 第二の策, 別の手 ▪ It would be *a* good *second string* in case the Parliament should miscarry. それは議会が失敗した場合には第二の良い策となるだろう.

get [***have, keep***] *a person* ***on a string*** 人を自分の手へ引きつけておく; 人を不安な状態に置く; 人を思いのままにあやつる ▪ What's the point of *having* me *on a string* like that? あんなふうに僕を不安な状態にさせてどういうつもりなのかね ▪ They *had* him *on a string* and he was in serious difficulties. 彼らが彼をあやつっていて彼は困難な状況に陥っていた.

harp on a damp string 効き目がない ▪ Now you are *harping on a damp string*, you can no longer hurt my feelings. もう効き目はないから, これ以上私の感情を傷つけることはできませんよ.

harp on one string →HARP on a string.

have ... in [***on***] ***a*** [***the***] ***string***/ ***lead ... in a string*** …を意のままにあやつる ▪ They believed they *had* the world *in a string*. 彼らは世界を意のままにあやつっていると思いこんでいた. ☞string「人・動物を導いたり引っぱったりするひも」.

have [***there are***] ***no strings*** (***attached***) (資金などが)ひもつきでない ▪ I hope that you'll accept the money—*there are no strings attached*. その金を受け取ってください—ひもつきではありません.

have two [***many***] ***strings to*** *one's* ***bow*** → BOW[1].

in [***on***] ***a string*** 人の意のままになる; ひもつきの ▪ They govern me as a child *in a string*. 彼らは私をまるで意のままにできる子供みたいに牛耳っている ▪ I am not a candidate *on a string*. 私はひもつきの候補ではありません. ☞string「人・動物を引っぱるひも」.

keep *a person* ***on a string*** →get a person on a STRING.

pull every string 全力を尽くす ▪ He *pulled every string* in order to attain the end result. 彼はその目的を達するために余力を尽くした.

pull (***the***) ***strings*** →PULL[2].

sweep the strings (弦)楽器をかなでる ▪ He began to *sweep the strings*. 彼は楽器をかなで始めた.

the first string Aチーム ▪ He is on *the first string*. 彼はAチームに属している.

there are no strings (***attached***) →have no STRINGs (attached).

with a string [***no strings***] ***attached*** 《口》条件つきで[無条件で] ▪ He inherited a large fortune but *with a string attached*. 彼は大きな財産を受けついだがそれには条件がついていた ▪ He was ready to sell the business for five thousand dollars *with no strings attached*. 彼はその店を全く無条件で5千ドルで喜んで売るつもりだった《with no strings = without strings》.

string[2] /strɪŋ/ 動 ***be*** (***highly***) ***strung*** (***out***) (ひどく)興奮[緊張]している; (麻薬などを)常用している (*on*) ▪ But Sylvia *was* too *highly strung* for banter. しかしシルビアはあまり興奮していたのでひやかしなどできなかった ▪ He *was strung out on* alcohol. 彼はアル中だった.

string *oneself* ***up to*** *do* 《口》やっきになって…する ▪ He *strung himself up to* finish the work. 彼はその仕事を終えるためにやっきになった.

strip[1] /strɪp/ 名 ***into strips*** ずたずたに ▪ He tore the cloth *into strips*. 彼はその布をずたずたに裂いた.

tear *a person* ***off a strip***/ ***tear strips*** [***a strip***] ***off*** *a person* 《英口》人をきびしくとがめる, 訓戒する, ガミガミしかる ▪ The boss *tore* her *off a strip*. 社長は彼女をきびしくとがめた. ☞むち打って皮膚を傷つけることから.

strip[2] /strɪp/ 動 ***strip*** *oneself* 裸になる ▪ The nymph *stripped herself* naked to the skin. そのニンフは丸裸になった.

strip a peg 《俗》(服の)つるしを買う ▪ You have *stripped a peg*, though I told you not to. 君は僕が買うなと言ったのに, つるしを買っちゃったね.

strip bare **1** 裸にする ▪ Winter *stripped bare* all the trees save the evergreens. 冬は常緑樹を除くすべての木を裸にした.

2 (持ち物を)全部奪い取る ▪ Moneylenders *stripped* him *bare* of all his property. 金貸しは彼の財産を全部奪い取った.

strip *a person* ***naked*** [***to the skin, to the buff***] 人を丸裸にする ▪ The bandits *stripped* him *to the skin*. 山賊らは彼を丸裸にした.

stripe /straɪp/ 名 ***earn*** *one's* ***stripes*** (人の仕事・地位・階級にふさわしい)業績を上げる ▪ He *earned his stripes* at the former office. 彼は前の会社では業績を上げた.

get [***lose***] *one's* ***stripe*** 昇進する[降級される] ▪ The cadet *got his stripe*, but *lost it* the week after that for being rude. その幹部候補生は昇進したが, その1週間後に無作法であったために降級された.

of every stripe and color あらゆる種類[タイプ]の ▪ People *of every stripe and color* attended the international conference. あらゆるタイプの人々がその国際会議に出席した.

wear the stripes 《米口》刑務所へ行く ▪ Thomas will have to *wear the stripes* for this. トマスはこのために刑務所へ行かねばならないだろう. ☞囚人の着るしま服から.

stroke[1] /stroʊk/ 名 ***a stroke above*** …より一枚うわて (= a CUT above) ▪ It was but natural she should be *a stroke above* the girls of the place. 彼女が土地の娘たちより一枚うわてであるのはごく当然のことだった.

a stroke of bad luck (思いがけない)不運 ▪ It was *a stroke of bad luck* for Bill to get married to a dancer. ビルがダンサーと結婚したのは不運だった.

a stroke of (good) luck (思いがけない)幸運 ▪ He jumped for joy at *this stroke of luck*. 彼はこの思いがけない幸運に欣喜雀躍した.

a stroke of wit [pleasantry, etc.] すばらしい機知[冗談, など](の一つ) ▪ It was one of the best *strokes of wit* I can remember in my time. それはこれまで知っている最もすばらしい機知の一つだった ▪ This *stroke of pleasantry* is aimed at me. このすばらしい冗談は私に向けられたものだ.

at one [a] stroke [blow]/ in one stroke [blow] 一撃で; 一挙に ▪ *At a stroke* he severed the head from the body. 彼は一撃で首をはねてしまった ▪ *At one stroke* he had lost all his old friends. 一挙に彼は旧友を全部失った.

at the stroke =on the STROKE 2.

at the stroke of (時計が)ちょうど…を打とうとして ▪ It is *at the stroke of* six. 時計がちょうど6時を打つところだ.

Different strokes for different folks. 《米・諺》十人十色.

Many [Little] strokes fell great oaks. 《諺》(ささやかでも)何度もおのを入れればカシの大木を切り倒せる,「千里の堤もアリの穴から」,「雨だれも石をうがつ」,「ちりも積もれば山となる」(Erasmus, *Adagiorum Opus*).

not a stroke of work 《口》少しの仕事も…しない ▪ I have *never* done *a stroke of work* since I was born. 生まれてこのかた仕事というものはこれっぽちもしたことがない.

on [upon] the stroke **1** (時計・鐘が)ちょうど鳴りかけて, 今打とうとして ▪ It is *on the stroke* of twelve now. 今12時が打とうとしています.
2 きちんと, 時をたがえずに ▪ I was there *on the stroke*. 私は時をたがえずにそこへ行った.

paint [draw, sketch]... in broad [brush] strokes …を大まかに描く ▪ The documentary *painted* the Maori people *in broad strokes*. その記録番組はマオリの人々のことを大まかに描き出していた.

pull [row] stroke 整調をこぐ ▪ He *pulls stroke* in the race. 彼はそのレースでは整調をこぐ. ☞stroke「他のこぎ手を統制するこぎ手」.

put** a person **off** his **stroke 人のリズム[調子]を狂わせる ▪ My question seemed to *put* the speaker *off his stroke*. 私の質問で演説者は調子が狂ったようだった.

strike a stroke 一撃を加える ▪ You will never *strike a* smart *stroke*. 君はきつい一撃を加えることは決してできない.

stroke and strife 無法な乱暴 ▪ Her husband lived in *stroke and strife*. 彼女の夫は無法で乱暴な生活をしていた.

stroke by stroke 一こぎ一こぎ ▪ The second boat is gaining *stroke by stroke*. 2番目のボートが一こぎ一こぎ追い迫っている.

with a stroke of the pen 一筆で; 一気に《しばしば誇張表現》 ▪ In acting so, he changed the general aspect of affairs *with a stroke of the pen*. その行為によって彼は一気に大勢を変えてしまった.

stroke[2] /stroʊk/ 動 ***stroke** a person **against the hair/ stroke** a person's **hair the wrong way/ stroke** a person **the wrong way (of the hair)*** 人をいら立たせる, 怒らせる ▪ You *stroked* father *the wrong way* by asking for five shillings. お前が5シリングくれと言ったからおとうさんが怒った ▪ Somebody's been *stroking* him *the wrong way of the hair*. 誰かが彼をいら立たせていたのだ. ☞動物の毛を逆なですると怒ることから.

stroll /stroʊl/ 名 ***go for a stroll*** (短い)散歩に出かける ▪ We usually *go for a stroll* in the morning. 我々はたいてい朝散歩に出かける.

have [take] a stroll (短い)散歩をする ▪ We *took a stroll* to the park. 我々は公園まで散歩した.

strong /strɔːŋ|strɒŋ/ 形副 ***(as) strong as a horse [an ox, a bull]*** とても強い, すごく丈夫で ▪ He is grown heavy, and *as strong as a horse*. 彼は体重がつきとても丈夫だ.

be (still) going strong 《口》(いまだに)強健である; 繁盛している ▪ The old man *is still going* very *strong*. あの老人はまだ元気だ ▪ The play *is going* very *strong*. その劇は大いに受けている.

be strong in …が強い, 得意だ ▪ He *is strong in* design. 彼はデザインが得意だ.

be strong on **1** …が得意である, に強い ▪ Security *is strong on* this campus. このキャンパスでの安全は大丈夫だ.
2 …を多量に所有している, がたくさんある ▪ His writings *are strong on* critical observations about terrorism. 彼の書き物にはテロに関する批判的な意見が多く含まれる.

be** one's **strong point [suit] →one's strong POINT; one's strong SUIT.

be strong with 《米》…の気に入っている ▪ She's powerful *strong with* the Judge. 彼女はひどく判事の気に入っている.

come [go] it strong 《口》猛烈にやる, 極端にやる; 誇張する ▪ It was *coming it* too *strong* to allow no tobacco. タバコを許さないなんて少しひどすぎた ▪ They say she can speak several foreign languages, but that is *coming it* a little too *strong*. 彼女は数か国語を話せるということだが, そいつは少し大げさすぎるというものだ.

come on strong 《米》 **1** 奮闘する, 全力を尽くす, 快調にふるまう ▪ In the playoffs she has *come on strong* and become a more forceful leader. 決戦投票で彼女は奮闘し, より強力に首位を走っている.
2 言い寄る, 口説く ▪ Axel Rose reportedly *came on strong* to Kelly Osbourne at a party. アクセル・ローズはパーティーでケリー・オズボーンに言い寄ったと伝えられている.

come on strong (with) 《口》 **1** 《米》(…に)感

情をあらわにする ▪ She has a habit of *coming on* too *strong with* men. 彼女は男性に感情をあらわにしすぎる癖がある.

2 (性的に…に)強引に迫る ▪ He was *coming on strong with* Susie. 彼はスージーに強引に迫っていた.

come out strong 《口》 **1** 大いに気勢をあげる; 思うことをどしどし言う ▪ They've taken a house in Grosvenor Place, and are *coming out strong*. あの連中はグローブナー地区に家を構えて, 大いに気勢をあげている ▪ Farrar *came out* rather *strong* at the meeting. その会合でファーラーはかなりどしどし思うことを言った.

2 《パブリックスクール》 気前よく金を出す ▪ Uncle *came out* fairly *strong*. おじはかなり気前よく金を出してくれた.

go* (*it*) *strong on 《米口》 …を力強く[熱烈に]支持する ▪ We *go strong on* the Church. 我々は教会を力強く支持する ▪ I am disposed to *go it strong on* the theory. その理論を熱烈に支持したい気持ちだ.

have a strong hold upon/ take a strong hold of …をしっかり握る, 把握する ▪ Her unusual finery had *taken a strong hold of* his imagination. 彼女のいつにない美服が彼の想像力をしっかりとつかんでいた.

have a strong stomach →STOMACH.

pitch it strong →PITCH[3].

strong as death 死のように強い (《聖》 *Solom*. 8. 6) ▪ Love, *strong as death*, is dead. 死のように強い愛は死んだ.

strong for 《米》 …を著しくひいきして, 大いに重んじて ▪ I am *strong for* smartphone just now. 目下ひどくスマホびいきなのだ.

strong head 酒に強いこと ▪ He is a man of a *strong head*. 彼は酒に強い人だ.

strong in numbers (政党・宗派などが)大勢で, 頭数の多い ▪ The kennel was pretty *strong in numbers*. 猟犬の群れはかなりたくさんだった.

strong meat →MEAT.

strong of …の味を多分に含んだ ▪ These German sausages are very *strong of* garlic. このドイツのソーセージはひどくニンニクの味がする.

take a strong hold of →have a STRONG hold upon.

think strong beer of *oneself* 我ながら途方もない偉い者だと思う (→think no small BEER of oneself) ▪ I am more inclined to *think strong beer of myself*. 僕はむしろ自分は途方もない偉いやつだと思いたい気持ちだ.

struggle[1] /strʌ́gəl/ 名 ***the struggle for existence*** [***life***] 《生物》 生存競争 《一般的にも用いる》 ▪ *The struggle for existence* is not confined to animals, but appears in the kingdom of thought. 生存競争は動物にのみ限られているのではなくて, 思想の世界にも現れる.

struggle[2] /strʌ́gəl/ 動 ***struggle for breath*** (死に際に)呼吸しようとしてもがく ▪ He was now in pain and *struggling for breath*. 彼は今や苦しみ, 息をしようとしてもがいていた.

struggle for existence 生存競争する ▪ The same types of flowers were *struggling for existence* in the beds. 同様の種類の花が花壇で生存競争していた.

struggle *one's* ***way*** もがきながら進んでいく ▪ I saw him *struggling his way* towards me. 見ると彼は私の方へもがきながら進んで来ていた.

strung /strʌŋ/ 形 ***be strung out*** **1** 《俗》 (麻薬などで)いらいらしている ▪ Judging from his behavior, he must *be strung out*. 彼のふるまいから判断して, どうも薬でいらいらしてるね.

2 (愛する人が)いなくて辛い ▪ As we've just split up, I'*m strung out* for him. 私たちは別れたばかりで, 私は彼がいなくて辛い思いをしている.

strut /strʌt/ 動 ***strut*** *one's* ***stuff*** →STUFF[1].

stub /stʌb/ 動 ***stub*** *one's* ***toe against*** [***on***] つま先を…にぶつける ▪ I *stubbed my toe against* the kerb. 私は縁石につま先をぶつけた.

stubborn /stʌ́bərn|-bən/ 形 (***as***) ***stubborn as a mule*** [***donkey***] 非常に強情で ▪ His uncle is *as stubborn as a mule*. 彼のおじはすごく強情だ.

Facts are stubborn things. 《諺》 事実は理屈通りにいかない.

stuck[1] /stʌk/ 名 ***in*** [***for***] ***stuck*** 《口》 困って (↔out of stuck) ▪ I am *in* terrible [dead] *stuck*. 私は今ひどく困っている. ☞イディッシュ語から.

stuck[2] /stʌk/ 形 ***be stuck up*** 高慢である, うぬぼれている ▪ He has a reputation for *being stuck up* and won't speak to the poor. 彼は高慢だとの評判で貧しい人には話しかけようとしない.

squeal like a stuck pig →PIG[1].

stud[1] /stʌd/ 名 ***take the stud***(***s***) 《米口》 強情を張る ▪ If I was to *take the studs* and lie down in the road, you'd have some trouble. もし私が強情を張って道で横になったなら, ちょっと面倒でしょうよ.

stud[2] /stʌd/ 動 (***be***) ***studded with*** …が点々と散らばっている ▪ The darkness *is studded with* red points. その暗やみには点々と赤い灯が見えている.

studious /stjúːdiəs/ 形 ***be studious of*** …に勤勉である; に注意している ▪ He *is studious of* his business. 彼は仕事に勤勉だ ▪ He *is studious of* outward decorum. 彼は外面的な礼儀作法に気を使っている.

be studious to *do* 努めて…する ▪ I *am studious to* compare the idiom of one language with that of another. 私はある言語のイディオムを他の言語のそれと比較することに努めている.

study[1] /stʌ́di/ 名 ***be in a study*** 深く考えこんでいる ▪ He appeared to *be in a* deep *study*. 彼は深く考えこんでいる様子だった.

be lost in study 考えにふけっている ▪ The long silence meant that he *was lost in study*. その長い沈黙は彼が考えにふけっていることを物語っていた.

have [***be***] ***a quick*** [***slow,*** etc.] ***study*** 暗記が早い[遅い, など] ▪ She *has a* very *quick study*.

S

彼女は暗記がとても早い ▪ Powell *was a* confounded *slow study*. パウエルはべらぼうに暗記が遅かった. ☞study はもと演劇用語でせりふを暗記すること.

in a brown study →BROWN[1].

make a study of …をつぶさに観察する; を研究する ▪ Tom was *making a study of* the girl. トムはその少女をつぶさに観察していた ▪ I am *making a* special *study of* biology. 私は生物学を専攻している.

make it *one's* ***study to*** *do* 努めて…しようとする ▪ He *made it his study to* please me. 彼は努めて私の気に入ろうとした.

under study 検討中で ▪ Further reductions are *under study*. さらなる値引きを検討中だ.

study[2] /stʌ́di/ 動 ***study*** *oneself* ***dumb*** [***to death***] 勉強しすぎて無口になる[死んでしまう] ▪ I know of a man who *studied himself dumb*. 私は勉強しすぎて無口になった男のことを知っている ▪ I don't approve of *studying yourself to death*. 君が死ぬほど勉強するのは感心しない.

study *one's* ***head off*** →do one's HEAD off.

stuff[1] /stʌf/ 名 ***... and stuff***《口》その他そういうくだらぬもの ▪ They are scared of ghosts and spooks *and stuff*. 彼らは幽霊やお化けなんかを怖がっている.

be made of sterner stuff いっそう強い性格をしている (cf. Sh., *Jul. Caes*. 3. 2. 97) ▪ Alfred *was made of sterner stuff* than early British princes. アルフレッドは初期のイギリスの王侯よりも強い性格だった.

do *one's* ***stuff***《口》自分の仕事をさっさとやる; おはこを出す ▪ Come on, *do your stuff*! さあ, 仕事をさっさとやれ.

know *one's* ***stuff***《口》有能である, やり手である ▪ Mr. Roberts *knows his stuff*, all right. ロバーツ氏は確かにやり手だ.

None of your stuff! くだらぬことを言うな!

not give a stuff《英俗》ちっともかまわない, 無関心である ▪ He does*n't give a stuff* what I think! 彼ったら, 私の考えていることには無関心なんだから!

strut *one's* ***stuff***《戯》(特にダンスの)腕前を見せつける[見せびらかす] ▪ He used to show off and *strut his stuff*. 彼はよく自分の腕前を見せびらかしたものだ.

stuff and nonsense《口》〚主に間投詞的に〛たわごと ▪ It's all *stuff and nonsense*. それはまるでたわごとだ ▪ *Stuff and nonsense*! I won't believe a word of it. ばかばかしい. そんなことを一言も信じるものか.

sweat the small stuff《米》些細なことにくよくよする ▪ Here's the best formula for handling stress: Don't *sweat the small stuff*. ストレスに対処する最善の方法は, 些細なことにくよくよするな, ということだ.

That's the stuff (***to give them*** [***the troops***]).《俗》それこそぴったりのものだ《同意・是認を表す》 ▪ I'd like a drop of tea with some rum in it.—*That's the stuff*, mate. ラムを入れたお茶がほしいね—それに限るよ, 君 ▪ You told them they were rogues, did you? Good! *That's the stuff to give'em*. やつらに悪党だと言ってやったのかね. そいつはいい. それこそぴったりだよ.

the stuff that dreams [***heroes,*** etc.] ***are made of*** 夢[英雄, など]の真髄 (cf. Sh., *Temp*. 4. 1. 156) ▪ I'm not *the stuff that dictators are made of*. 私には独裁者になれるような器量はない.

what stuff *one* ***is made of*** …の人物, 人柄 ▪ We must see *what stuff* he *is made of*. 彼の人柄を見なければならない.

stuff[2] /stʌf/ 動 ***a stuffed shirt*** →SHIRT.

Get stuffed!/Stuff it [***you***]***!***《英俗》行っちまえ, うるさい《いらだち・怒り・軽蔑などを表す》.

stuff *oneself* がつがつ腹いっぱい食べる (*with*) ▪ He *stuffed himself* (*with* food). 彼は(食べ物を)腹いっぱい食べた.

stuff *one's* ***ears with wax*** [***wool***] 耳にせんをする ▪ You can *stuff your ears with wax* if you like, but I shall say what I have to say. なんなら耳にせんをしてもいいが, 僕は言いたいことだけは言うよ.

stuff *a person's* ***head with*** 人の頭に(下らぬこと)を詰め込む ▪ Why *stuff the child's head with* such nonsense? なぜその子の頭にそんなたわごとを詰め込むのか.

stuff it《俗》= LUMP it.

stuffing /stʌ́fɪŋ/ 名 ***knock*** [***beat, lick, take***] ***the stuffing out of***《口》…をへたばらせる; のうぬぼれの鼻を折る ▪ Get up, or I'll *beat the stuffing out of* you. 起きるんだ, さもなきゃへたばらせてやるぞ ▪ There is nothing to compare with a mesalliance for *taking the stuffing out of* anyone. 人のうぬぼれの鼻を折るのには身分の卑しい者との結婚に勝るものはない.

stultify /stʌ́ltəfàɪ/ 動 ***stultify*** *oneself* **1**《法》(責任を逃れるために)自分は正気でないと申し立てる ▪ No one shall be allowed to *stultify himself*. 何びとも責任逃れに自分は正気でないと申し立てることを許されるべきではない.

2 ばかをさらす ▪ This witness *stultified himself* by admitting it. この証人はそれを認めてばかをさらした.

stumble /stʌ́mbəl/ 動 ***stumble at*** [***on***] ***the threshold*** (事業の)手始めにつまずく ▪ I lately began to read Seneca's Epistles, and *stumbled at the* very *threshold*. 私は最近セネカの書簡を読み始めたが手始めからつまずいてしまった.

stumble over *one's* ***words*** とちり[つかえ]ながら言う ▪ He *stumbled over his words*. 彼はとちりながら言った.

stumbling /stʌ́mblɪŋ/ 形 ***a stumbling block*** つまずきの石, 障害 (《聖》*Rom*. 14. 13) ▪ He sought employment, but his age turned out to be *a stumbling block*. 彼は仕事を探したが年齢がネックであることが分かった. ☞「人がつまずく木の株」が原義.

stump[1] /stʌmp/ 名 ***at the stump*** →in the STUMP.

buy (***timber***) ***on the stump*** (木)を立ち木のままで買う ▪ He *bought* all that *timber on the*

S

stump for $10,000. 彼はその木を全部立ち木のままで1万ドルで買った.

draw (***the***) ***stumps*** 《クリケット》ウィケットの棒を抜く《試合を終わる印》; (事を)中断する ▪ At half-past six *the stumps were drawn.* 6時半にクリケットの試合が終わった.

fight to the stumps あくまで戦う ▪ I feel sure that the English people would *fight to the stumps* for the honor of England. イングランド人はイングランドの名誉のためにはあくまでも戦うだろうと私は確信する. ☞「足を切られたら残った部分で立って戦う」が原義.

fool around the stump 《米》ぐずぐずする, 遠回しに探る ▪ There's no use *fooling around the stump.* 遠回しに探ったってだめだ.

go on [***take***] ***the stump*** 政談演説をして回る, 遊説して回る ▪ The minister *goes on the stump* in the provinces. 大臣が地方を遊説して回る ▪ He will *take the stump* shortly. 彼はまもなく遊説して回る. ☞もと巨木の切り株を演壇に用いたことから.

in [***at***] ***the stump*** 《米口》(木が)立木のままで ▪ He sold the wood to the man *at the stump.* 彼はその男性に木を立木のままで売った.

on a stump →up a STUMP.

put *a person* ***to his stumps*** 《米口》人に非常な努力を強いる ▪ He could do anything when *put to his stumps.* 彼は非常な努力を強いられるとどんな事でもできた.

run against a stump 《米口》困難にぶつかる ▪ He *ran against a stump* where he was least expecting it. 彼は一番予期していない所で困難にぶつかった.

stir *one's* ***stumps*** 《口・戯》てきぱきと歩く[踊る]; すばやく行動する ▪ Come this way, my hearty, *stir your stumps.* こっちへ来いよ, 君, てきぱき歩くんだ ▪ They'd *stir their stumps* to the sound of a drum. 彼らは太鼓の音に合わせててきぱきと踊ることだろう. ☞stump = leg.

take (***to***) ***the stump*** →go on the STUMP.

up [***on***] ***a stump*** 《米口》 **1** 途方にくれて, 困って ▪ Look here, Uncle Soames, I'm *up a stump.* いいですかソームズおじさん, 私は困っているんですよ.

2 ほろ酔いで ▪ Brooks was considerably *up a stump.* ブルックスはかなり酔っていた.

stump[2] /stʌmp/ 動 ***be stumped*** [***stuck***] ***for words*** [***a reply***] 言葉[返答]につまる ▪ He *was stumped for a reply* to her question. 彼は彼女の質問の答えに窮した.

be stumped up 《俗》無一文になる ▪ He *is stumped up.* 彼は無一文だ.

stump it **1** 《俗》歩いて行く; 逃げだす ▪ To the devil with cabs. I must *stump it.* タクシーなどくそくらえだ. おれは歩いていかなくちゃいけないんだ ▪ *Stump it*, my cove. 逃げだしなよ, 君.

2 《主に米》遊説して回る ▪ *Stumping it* through England for seven years made Cobden a consummate debater. イングランドを7年間遊説して回ったことがコブデンを無比の論客に仕立てた.

style[1] /staɪl/ 名 ***be*** (***not***) *one's* ***style*** 人の流儀に合う[合わない] ▪ His thinking *isn't my style.* 彼の考え方は私の流儀に合わない.

come into style 流行になる ▪ That style of evening dress *came into style* shortly after the war. その型の夜会服は戦後まもなく流行した.

cramp *a person's* ***style*** →CRAMP.

do ... in proper style **1** ...を立派に[きちんと]やってのける ▪ The reception *was done in proper style.* 歓迎会は立派にやってのけられた.

2 《反語》...をまんまとだます ▪ The man *did* her *in proper style* over those antique brasses. その男はその時代ものの真ちゅう製品で彼女をまんまとだました.

in fine style **1** ゆうゆうと ▪ He won *in fine style.* 彼はゆうゆうと優勝した.

2 盛んに ▪ They bantered him *in fine style.* みなが彼を盛んにからかった.

in style **1** 流行にかなって ▪ She dresses *in style.* 彼女の着こなしはいきだ.

2 はでに, 豪奢に ▪ This is what the modern British public considers "living *in style*." これが現代イギリスの一般大衆が「豪奢な暮らし」と考えていることなのだ.

3 立派に ▪ Let's do it *in style* if we do it at all. 仮にやるなら立派にやろう.

like it's going out of style = like it's going out of FASHION.

live in style →in STYLE 2.

out of style 流行にはずれて ▪ His frock is *out of style* now. 彼のフロックコートは今では流行はずれだ.

put on style 《米口》高慢ぶる ▪ Don't be trying to *put on* so much *style.* そんなに高慢ぶろうとするな.

there is a [***no***] ***style about*** ...には上品さがある[ない], 気のきいた風がある[ない] ▪ *There is no style about* him. 彼には気のきいた風がない ▪ *There's a style about* her. 彼女には品位がある.

under the style of ...という名義で ▪ This business was established in 1856 *under the style of* Rich & Sons. この商売は1856年にリッチ親子商会という名義で設立された.

style[2] /staɪl/ 動 ***style*** *oneself* (...と)自称する ▪ He *styled himself* Doctor. 彼は博士と自称した.

stylish /stáɪlɪʃ/ 形 (***as***) ***stylish as a spotted dog under a red wagon*** 《米》きわめてハイカラで ▪ The mother was pretty, and *as stylish as a spotted dog under a red wagon.* その母親は美人ですこぶるハイカラだった.

subject /sʌ́bdʒekt/ 形副名 ***a good*** [***bad***] ***subject*** 本復の見込みのある[ない]患者 ▪ The patient is *a bad subject.* 患者に本復の見込みはない.

be a subject for ...の種になるものだ ▪ I *am* no *subject for* your mirth. 僕は君に笑いものにされるいわれがない ▪ His suggestions at the meeting *are a subject for* laughter. 会合での彼の提案はお笑い草だ.

change the subject 話題を変える ▪ Let's *change the subject*. 話題を変えよう.

not to change the subject, but 話は変わるが ▪ *Not to change the subject, but* have you seen Jim recently? 話は変わるが, 最近ジムに会ったかい.

on** a person's **subject 人のことについて(の) ▪ I have received two letters from him *on your subject*. あの人から君に関する手紙を最近2通受け取りました. ☞F sur son suject のなぞり.

on the subject of …という題目で, について ▪ He spoke *on the subject of* Japanese arts. 彼は日本美術について話をした.

subject to **1** (主権者など)に隷属する ▪ The Empire of India became *subject to* that of Persia. インド帝国はペルシャ帝国に隷属するようになった.
2 (法律・命令など)に従う ▪ The military power ought always to be *subject to* the civil. 武の力は常に文の力に従うべきである.
3 (損失・天候の害・病気など)を受けやすい, 被りやすい ▪ Japan is very *subject to* earthquakes. 日本は非常に地震の害を受けやすい.
4 …を条件とする, ただし…を必要とする ▪ The treaty is *subject to* ratification. 条約は批准を必要とする.
5 〚副詞的に〛…を条件として, と仮定して ▪ *Subject to* your consent, I will try again. 承諾してくださるなら, もう一度やってみます.

the human subject (研究・観察の対象としての)人間 ▪ The phenomena are presented by *the human subject*. この現象は人間が起こしているものだ.

while** one **is on the subject そのことを話して[考えて]いる間に ▪ *While* we *are on the subject* of books, can you tell me the price of Fraser's "Golden Bough"? 本のことを話している間にお聞きするが, フレイザーの「金枝編」の値段はいくらですか.

subjection /səbdʒékʃən/ 名 ***bring*** [***put***]***... in*** [***into***] ***subjection*** …を従属させる ▪ You have *brought* Rhodes *in subjection*. あなたはローズを従属させました.

hold [***keep***]***... in subjection*** …を従属させておく ▪ Imagination should *be kept in subjection* to judgment. 想像力は判断力に従属させておくべきだ.

sublime /səbláɪm/ 名 ***From the sublime to the ridiculous is only a step.*** 《諺》崇高から滑稽へはひとっ跳び.

submerge /səbmə́ːrdʒ/ 動 ***be submerged in*** …に没頭している ▪ He *is submerged in* reading now. 彼は今読書に没頭している.

the submerged tenth どん底階級 ▪ There are always those who seek to ameliorate the conditions of *the submerged tenth*. どん底階級の境遇を改善しようとする人々がいつもいる.

submission /səbmíʃən/ 名 ***crush ... into submission*** …を力で屈服させる ▪ The hostile minority has *been crushed into submission*. 少数の敵対者は力で屈服させられた.

submit /səbmít/ 動 ***submit** oneself **to*** **1** (権力・支配など)に服従[屈服]する ▪ We must *submit ourselves* entirely *to* the Divine Will. 我々は全く神意に従わねばならない.
2 (批判・待遇など)を甘んじて受ける ▪ I *submitted myself to* these conditions. 私はこれらの条件を甘んじて受けた.

subordination /səbɔ̀ːrdənéɪʃən/ 名 ***in subordination to*** …に従属して ▪ The porticos are *in subordination to* the vast fabric which they enclose. その柱廊玄関はそれが取り囲んでいる巨大な建築物に付随している.

under subordination 統御されて ▪ His forces were more *under subordination*. 彼の軍隊のほうがさらに統御されていた.

subscribe /səbskráɪb/ 動 ***subscribe** oneself* …と署名する ▪ He *subscribes himself* L. P. Smith. 彼はL. P. スミスと署名する.

subscription /səbskrípʃən/ 名 ***by subscription*** 予約で《書籍について言う》 ▪ In 1930 he published, *by subscription*, a quarto volume of miscellanies. 1930年に彼は四つ折り版の雑文集を予約出版した.

make [***take up***] ***a subscription*** 《米》寄付を募る ▪ Let's *make a subscription* to relieve the army. 軍隊を救助するために寄付を募ろうじゃないか.

subsistence /səbsístəns/ 名 ***means of subsistence*** 生計の資 ▪ Selling papers is his only *means of subsistence*. 新聞売りが彼のただ一つの生計の資だ.

substance /sʌ́bstəns/ 名 ***in substance*** **1** 実際に(は) ▪ The monarchy did not survive the hierarchy, *in substance*, for a single hour. その君主政治は聖職階級制度よりも実際にはたった1時間も長くは続かなかった.
2 大体において ▪ Her account was *in substance* correct. 彼女の話は大体において正確だった.
3 要するに (= in EFFECT) ▪ My answer will be "no" *in substance*. 私の返事は要するに「ノー」です.

mistake [***take***] ***the shadow for the substance*** にせ物を本物とまちがえる ▪ If you listen to him you will be *taking the shadow for the substance*. 彼の言うことを聞いていたらにせ物を本物とまちがえてしまうよ.

of (***good, great***) ***substance*** 《文》資産のある, 金持ちの, 有力な ▪ He is a man *of substance* and influence. 彼は資産家で有力者だ.

the pith and substance of …の核心 ▪ *The pith and substance of* your idea is the old theory of perpetual motion. 君の考えの核心は古い永久運動の学説だ.

waste** one's **substance 金を浪費する (《聖》*Luke* 15. 13) ▪ French monarchs *wasted their substance* in interminable wars on the Continent. フランス王たちは大陸での果てしのない戦争に金を浪費した.

suburb /sʌ́bəːrb/ 名 ***in the suburbs of*** …の郊外に ▪ He lives *in the suburbs of* London. 彼はロンドンの郊外に住んでいる.

S

succeed /səksíːd/ 動 ***succeed*** *oneself* 《米》再選される，留任する ▪ He was elected to *succeed himself*. 彼は選挙されて留任した.

success /səksés/ 名 ***a howling success*** 《口》大成功 ▪ The general meeting of stockholders was *a howling success*. 株主総会は大成功だった.

make a success of …を成功させる，首尾よくやる ▪ This book teaches you how to *make a success of* your life. この本はどうすれば君の人生を成功させるかを教えてくれる.

meet with [***achieve***] ***success*** 成功する ▪ Whoever is most diligent will *meet with* most *success*. 大勉強家は大成功する.

Nothing succeeds like success. 《諺》一事なれば万事なる.

with [***without***] ***success*** 首尾よく[不首尾で] ▪ He tried several lines of business *with* no great *success*. 彼はいろいろの商売をやったが，あまり成功しなかった ▪ I tried to persuade him, but *without success*. 私は彼を説きつけようとしたがだめだった.

succession /səkséʃən/ 名 ***a succession of*** 一連の，一続きの ▪ He met with *a succession of* disasters. 彼は不幸続きに出あった.

by succession 世襲[継承権]で ▪ I am only a champion *by succession*. 私は世襲でなったチャンピオンにすぎない ▪ Truman became President *by succession*. トルーマンは継承権で大統領になった.

in succession **1** 次々に，相次いで ▪ Many soldiers *in succession* fell in the attempt. その攻略戦で多くの兵士が相次いで倒れた ▪ Misfortunes came *in* rapid *succession*. 不幸が矢つぎ早に来た.

2 世襲して ▪ Such a corporation cannot hold property *in succession*. そのような団体は世襲して財産を持つことはできない.

in succession to …の後任として ▪ He became editor *in succession to* Mr. Smith. スミス氏の後任として彼が主筆となった.

such /sətʃ, sʌtʃ/ 形代 ***all such*** かかる人たち; そういうすべてのもの ▪ Down with anarchists and *all such*! 無政府主義者やそのたぐいの人間をやっつけろ.

and such その他この種のもの ▪ A smaller table held ices, squashes, *and such*. 小さい方のテーブルにはアイスクリーム，スカッシュなどが置いてあった.

another such →SUCH another.

any such 〚否定文・疑問文で〛そのような人 ▪ I haven't heard of *any such*. そのような人のことは聞いたことがない.

as such **1** そのまま，その姿をして ▪ Gelatine does not exist *as such* in the body. ゼラチンはそのままの形で体の中にあるのではない.

2 その名義[資格]で ▪ He was a foreigner and was treated *as such*. 彼は外国人なので外国人として扱われた.

3 それだけ[自体]では ▪ Wealth, *as such*, does not matter much. 富はそれだけではたいしたものではない.

ever such 《口》とてつもなく ▪ It is *ever such* a way off. そこはとてつもなく遠い.

in such a way that …のような具合に ▪ He speaks *in such a way that* I don't understand him. 彼は言うことが私にはわからないような話し方をする.

no such **1** 〚代名詞的に〛そのような人[物]は…ない ▪ It is plain enough he is *no such*. 彼がそのような人でないのは明白至極だ ▪ We know of *no such*. そのような人は知りません.

2 そのような…は…ない ▪ There is *no such* religion. そのような宗教はない.

3 〚形容詞に伴って〛それほど…でない ▪ He is *no such* haughty man. 彼はそれほど高慢な男ではない.

no such thing **1** そんなことは…ない ▪ I shall do *no such thing*. そんなことはしない.

2 〚間投詞的に〛なかなかもって，とんでもない ▪ They thought me rheumatic and feverish, but *no such thing*! みんな私がリューマチで熱があると思いましたが，とんでもありません ▪ We are not here to quarrel.—There's *no such thing*, Bill. 我々は口論するためにここにいるのではない—そうだとも，ビル.

none such そのような人[物]は…ない ▪ *None such* shall inherit the kingdom of God. そのような人は神の国を継ぐことはできない.

not such (***a***) 〚形容詞に伴って〛それほど…でない ▪ He is a very industrious student, and *not such a* bad critic. 彼はとても勉強家であり，またそれほどまずい批評家でもない.

some such 何かそんな ▪ *Some such* plan was in my mind. 何かそんな計画が私の心にはあった.

such a few [***many***] 《口》そんなに少しの[多くの] ▪ He cannot have done *such many* things in that time. 彼はその間にそんなに多くのことをやったはずがない.

such a one そのような人[物]《an は聖書に多い形》▪ *Such a one* is by common consent a blackguard. そのような人は誰しも悪党と認めるところである.

such a second またとそのような ▪ I would not run the risk of *such a second* night. 私はまたとそのような夜の危険を冒したくない.

such and such **1** しかじかの ▪ Every event has a character, is *such and such* an event. すべての出来事には特性があり，しかじかの出来事なのである.

2 しかじかの人[物]《単複どちらの意にも用いる》▪ He said that *such and such* had seen her do it. しかじかの人々が彼女がそうするのを見たと彼は言った ▪ We have done *such and such*. 我々はしかじかのことをやった.

such another/***another such*** そのようなもう一つ[一人](の) ▪ She will not easily get *such another*. 彼女は楽にそんなものをもう一つ手に入れることはできまい ▪ I shall never get *another such* master. もうそんな主人は二度と見つかるまい.

such as **1** …のような人[物] ▪ His conduct is *such as* deserves praise. 彼のふるまいは賞賛に値するていのものだ.

2 たとえば《ある種類の例をあげるときに用いる》▪ Birds of prey, *such as* the eagle and the hawk, don't lay many eggs. 猛禽，たとえばワシとかタカはたくさんの

卵は産まない. ☞この用法は liquors such as beer「ビールのような酒」のような名詞の後に用いられる用法から生じたもの.

3 …する人[物] ▪ *Such as* are rich will not want for friends. 金のある人は友人にこと欠かない.

such … as **1** …のような ▪ I'll give you *such* a thrashing *as* you'll remember. いつまでも忘れないようなむち打ちをお前にくれてやろう.

2〚主文に such＋名詞のみを残して感嘆文的に〛…といったらない ▪ *Such* a dinner *as* we had today! きょう食べた夕食といったらなかった ▪ Oh, dear! *Such* a fuss *as* never was! あらまあ, こんな騒ぎといったらないね!

3…する人[物] ▪ *Such* men *as* heard him praised him. 彼の言葉を聞いた人々は彼をほめた.

such as it [*one*] ***is*** こんなものだが, お粗末ながら《軽蔑, または申し訳の文句》 ▪ *Such as* his mind *was*, it had been assiduously cultivated. 彼の頭はお粗末ながらも一生懸命に修練してあった ▪ You may use my car, *such as it is*. こんなものですが私の車をお使いください. ☞such は is の補語; as は though の意.

such **(…)** ***as to*** *do* …するほど…で ▪ I am not *such* a fool *as to* believe that. 僕はそれを信ずるほど大ばかではない ▪ His eloquence was *such as to* move us to tears. 彼の雄弁はたいしたものなので我々は感動して涙を流した.

such being the case こういうわけだから ▪ *Such being the case*, we were very lucky to have a house of our own. こういうわけだから自分の家ができたのはとても運がよかった.

Such is life [***the world***]. 世の中はそういうものだ《軽いあきらめを表す言葉》 ▪ Here is another creature come to dinner; *such is life!* またみじめな人間が夕食にやってきた. 世の中とはそういうものだ.

such many →SUCH a few.

such much for …のことはこれでおしまい (＝so MUCH for) ▪ *Such much for* him. 彼のことはこれでおしまい.

such others 他のそういう人[物] ▪ He read Dante, Shakespeare, or *such others*. 彼はダンテ, シェイクスピア, または他のその手の人たちの作品を読んだ.

such *A* ***…, such*** *B* このAにしてこの B, AもBも相似ている《次のような諺にだけ用いる》 ▪ *Such* father, *such* son. 《諺》この父にしてこの子あり ▪ *Such* master, *such* servants. 《諺》この主にしてこの使用人.

such **(…)** ***that*** 〚結果用法〛非常な…なので ▪ She had *such* a fright *that* she fainted. 彼女は驚きのあまり卒倒した ▪ His behavior was *such that* [*Such* was his behavior *that*] everyone disliked him. 彼のふるまいがあまりにひどかったので, みんな彼をきらった.

there is such a thing as …なんてこと[もの]があるからね(油断はならない)《口語ではしばしば遠回しのおどしに用いる》 ▪ *There is such a thing as* a letter miscarrying. 手紙が着かないなんてことがあるからね ▪ *There are such things as* horsewhips, and men have backs. 馬のむちなんてものがあるんだし, 人間には背中があるからね《ぶってやるぞ》.

suck[1] /sʌk/ 名 ***at suck*** 乳を飲んでいる ▪ It was but a child *at suck*. それはほんの乳飲み児だった.

give suck (子供に)乳を飲ませる ▪ Mothers ought to *give* their own children *suck*. 母親は当然わが子に乳を飲ませるべきである. ☞nurse, suckle が普通の言い方.

take [***have***] ***a suck at*** …をひと吸いする ▪ The child *took a suck at* a lollipop. その子は棒つきキャンディーをひとしゃぶりした.

What a suck! 《俗》ざま見ろ!

suck[2] /sʌk/ 動 ***suck dry*** 吸い尽くす《比喩的にも》 ▪ Some bees *suck* each blossom *dry*. ミツバチがそれぞれの花の蜜を吸い尽くす ▪ A crew of plunderers would *suck* me *dry* by driblets. 略奪者の一団が少しずつ私の金を吸い尽くしてしまうだろう.

suck *one's* ***fill*** 腹いっぱい乳を飲む ▪ The baby has almost *sucked its fill*. 赤んぼうはほとんど腹いっぱい乳を飲んでいる.

suck it and see 《英口》実際に試してみる ▪ It was very much a case of "*suck it and see*." それこそ「実際に試してみる」べき事例であった.

suck it up 《米口》(痛み・感情を抑えて)続ける, がんばる ▪ He *sucked it up* though he had been ill. 彼はずっと病気だったががんばった.

suck the blood of …の膏血をしぼる ▪ He had acquired the wealth by *sucking the blood of* his miserable victims. 彼は不幸な犠牲者の膏血をしぼってその富を手に入れたのだった.

suck the marrow from …から一番よい所を取る ▪ They'll *suck the marrow from* the idea. 彼らはその考えの一番よい所を取ってしまうよ.

Sucks (***to you***)***!*** 《英俗》いい気味だ, ざまあ見ろ.

sucker /sʌ́kər/ 名 ***a sucker for*** 《口》…に弱い人, 目のない人 ▪ He is *a sucker for* sweet things. 彼は甘い物に目がない.

play *a person* ***for a sucker*** 《米口》人をばかにする ▪ Don't *play* me *for a sucker*. おれをばかにするな.

There's a sucker born every minute. 《諺》だまされやすい人はうんといる《とても保護できない, など》.

sudden /sʌ́dən/ 名 ***all of a sudden***/ ***on*** [***upon***] ***a*** [***the***] ***sudden*** 不意に, 急に《シェイクスピア(1564–1616)の時代は of a sudden がふつう》 ▪ He saw, *all of a sudden*, a man steal forth from the wood. 彼は急に一人の男が森からそっと出て来るのを見た ▪ *On a sudden* a gleam of hope appeared. にわかに一縷(る)の希望が見えてきた.

sudden death 急死; (先に得点した方が勝ちになる)サドンデス ▪ The game went to *sudden death*. その試合はサドンデスになった.

suds /sʌdz/ 名 ***in the suds*** 《俗》困って, 途方にくれて ▪ He was for a time left *in the suds*. 彼はしばらくの間困っていた.

sue /sjuː/ 動 ***sue*** *a person* ***at law*** 人を相手取って訴訟を起こす ▪ A partner cannot *sue* a co-partner *at law* in respect of anything connected with the partnership accounts. 商売仲間は共同会計に関することでは共同経営者を相手取って訴訟を起こすことはできない.

suffer /sʌ́fər/ 動 ***suffer fools gladly*** →FOOL[1].

suffer ... to *do* …が…するのを黙って許す ▪ He did not *suffer* his authority *to* be set at naught. 彼は自分の権威が無視されるのを許さなかった.

suffer *oneself* ***to be*** 黙って…される ▪ His horse never *suffered himself to be* backed but by his master. 彼の馬は主人が下がらせるのでなければ黙って後ろへ下がらなかった.

sufferance /sʌ́fərəns/ 名 ***on*** [***upon***] ***sufferance*** 黙許されて, お情けで ▪ They are employed only *on sufference*. 彼らはただお情けで在職している.

suffice /səfáɪs/ 動 ***suffice it*** (***to say***) (***that***)/***suffice*** (***it***) ***to say*** (***that***) 《文》…と言えば十分だ, と言うにとどめておこう ▪ *Suffice it* (*to say*) *that* he left his family in poverty. 彼が死んで家族が貧乏になったと言えば十分だ.

sufficient /səfíʃənt/ 形 ***sufficient for*** [***to***] …に十分な ▪ The pension is not *sufficient for* living expenses. その年金では生活費に足りない ▪ It was *sufficient to* that purpose. それはその目的に十分だった.

sufficient for [***unto***] *oneself* 人に求めることがない ▪ The English people are *sufficient unto themselves*. イギリス人は人に求めることがない.

Sufficient unto the day is the evil thereof. 一日の苦労は一日だけで十分である (《聖》 *Matt.* 6. 34) ▪ We've met today's difficulties satisfactorily and *sufficient unto the day is the evil thereof.* 我々はきょうの困難には満足に立ち向かった. 一日の苦労は一日だけで十分だ.

suffuse /səfjúːz/ 動 ***be suffused with*** …でいっぱいである ▪ Her eyes *were suffused with* tears. 彼女の目には涙がいっぱいたまっていた.

sugar[1] /ʃʊ́gər/ 名 ***a sugar daddy*** 《口》甘いパパ; 金持ちの年配男, パトロン, 愛人《相手の女性よりもはるかに年上のことが多い》 ▪ She got a Jaguar from her *sugar daddy*. 彼女はパトロンからジャガーを1台もらった ▪ My *sugar daddy* is very responsible, knowledgeable, and very charming. 私のパトロンはとても信頼でき, 物知りで, とても素敵だ.

be all sugar 《口》お世辞たっぷりだ ▪ She *was all sugar*. 彼女はお世辞たっぷりだった.

be neither sugar nor salt/be not made of sugar or salt 張り子ではない, 雨降りぐらいにへこたれない ▪ I *am not made of sugar or salt*. Do you call this rain? 僕は張り子じゃない. これが雨と言えるかい.

sugar[2] /ʃʊ́gər/ 動 ***sugar the pill*** →PILL.

suggest /səgdʒést|sədʒést/ 動 ***I suggest that*** 《法》…だと思うがどうかね ▪ *I suggest that* you were not there at that time. あなたはその時そこにいなかったと思うが, どうかね.

suggest itself (考えなどが)心に浮かぶ (*to*) ▪ The question naturally *suggested itself to* me. その問題が当然私の心に浮かんだ.

suggestion /səgdʒéstʃən|sədʒés-/ 名 ***a suggestion of*** 少しの…; …の気味 ▪ He speaks French with *a suggestion of* an English accent. 彼は少し英語なまりのあるフランス語を話す.

on [***at***] *a person's* ***suggestion*** 人の提言に従い ▪ She wrote a novel *on his suggestion*. 彼女は彼の提言に従って小説を書いた.

suggestive /səgdʒéstɪv|sədʒés-/ 形 ***suggestive of*** …を思わせる, 示唆する ▪ The area was a land *suggestive of* paradise. その地域は楽園を思わせるような所であった.

suicide /súːəsàɪd/ 名 ***commit suicide*** 自殺する ▪ He may *commit suicide*. 彼は自殺するかもしれない.

suit[1] /suːt/ 名 ***a suit at*** [***in***] ***law*** 訴訟 ▪ She had *a suit in law* against the man. 彼女はその男を相手取って訴訟を起こした.

at suit 訴訟して ▪ The parties were *at suit* in the civil court of justice. 当事者たちは民事裁判所で訴訟していた.

be all starched front and dress suit 全くの見かけ倒しである ▪ We know Mr. Banker very well, he's *all starched front and dress suit*. バンカーさんはよく知っている. あの人は全くの見かけ倒しだ.

bring [***institute***] (***a***) ***suit against*** …を相手取って訴訟を起こす ▪ He has *brought suit against* the firm. 彼はその会社を相手取って訴訟を起こした.

follow suit **1** 《トランプ》最初打たれた札と同じ組の札を出す ▪ He put down a spade and I *followed suit* with another. 彼がスペードを出したので私もそれと同じ組の別の札を出した.

2 先例にならう, 人のまね[した通り]をする ▪ Burke resigned from the club, and Jones immediately *followed suit*. バークがクラブをやめたので, ジョーンズもすぐその通りにした.

go to suit 訴訟する ▪ I have a great mind to *go to suit*. 訴訟しようかと大いに考えている.

have a suit to …に請願する ▪ I *have a suit to* the director. 私はその理事に請願している.

in suit with …と一致[調和]して ▪ His manual strength was *in suit with* the ferocity of his manners. 彼の腕力はそのどう猛な態度と調和していた.

make suit 懇願する ▪ She *made suit* to the king. 彼女は王に懇願した.

of a suit with …と同一種類で ▪ The incident is precisely *of a suit with* the previous ones. その事件は以前のと全く同一種類のものだ.

out of suit with …と不調和で ▪ His old books were totally *out of suit with* the furniture. 彼の古い本は家具とは全く不調和であった.

plead *one's* ***suit*** =press one's SUIT 2.

press *one's* ***suit*** **1** しきりに嘆願する ▪ He *pressed his suit* but to no avail. 彼はしきりに嘆願

したがうまくいかなかった.

2《雅》求婚する ▪ He *pressed his suit* with a young woman. 彼は若い女性にしきりに求婚した.

one's ***strong*** [***long***] ***suit*** 得意 ▪ Mathematics is *his strong suit*. 数学は彼の得意とするところだ.

suit² /su:t/ 名 ***an empty suit*** まやかし者, 小もの ▪ He's just *an empty suit*, so you needn't pay any attention to him. 彼はただのまやかし者にすぎないから, 注意を払う必要などないよ.

the men in (***grey***) ***suits*** 《主に英》グレーのスーツの男たち; 黒幕, 政界の大立者《一般人に知られていないが権力のある, 政治・法律関係者》 ▪ Young people are generally detached from *the men in grey suits*. 若者は一般に政治の世界の大物から切り離された存在だ ▪ Everyone has been waiting for *the men in grey suits* to decide Mr. Brown's fate. グレーのスーツの男たちがブラウン氏の運命を決めてくれることを誰もが待ち望んでいた.

suit³ /su:t/ 動 ***be suited to*** [***for***] …に適している ▪ The title of this book *is* well *suited to* its contents. この本の表題はその内容によく適している ▪ The young man *is* quite *suited for* the position. その青年はその地位にうってつけだ.

(***It***) ***suits me fine.*** 《口》それは結構, 好都合だ.

it suits *a person* ***to*** *do* **1** …するのは人にふさわしい ▪ *It* doesn't *suit* you *to* have your hair cut short. 髪を短くするのはあなたに似合いませんよ.

2 …するのは人に都合がよい ▪ When will *it suit* you *to* start? 出発はいつがご都合よろしいですか.

suit *oneself* **1**《口》勝手にする ▪ You can *suit yourself* about going or remaining. 行くなりとどまるなり君の勝手にしたらいい ▪ *Suit yourself*. 勝手にしたら[お好きなように].

2 (望みのものを)手に入れる (*with*) ▪ I can *suit myself with* a cottage. 私は田舎家を手に入れられるんです.

suit *a person* (***down***) ***to the ground*** 《英口》人に全くおあつらえ向きだ ▪ This room *suits* me *down to the ground*. この部屋は僕に全くおあつらえ向きだ.

suitable /sú:təbəl/ 形 ***suitable to*** [***for***] …に適している ▪ This dress is more *suitable to* her age. このドレスのほうが彼女の年にいっそうふさわしい ▪ It is *suitable for* the purpose intended. それはおあつらえ向きだ.

sulk /sʌlk/ 名 ***be in the sulks/have*** (***a fit of***) ***the sulks*** ふくれている, 不きげんである ▪ When you are tired of *being in the sulks*, let me know. ふくれているのにあきたら, そう言っておくれ.

sulky /sʌ́lki/ 形 (***as***) ***sulky as a bear*** 非常に不きげんで ▪ He moved about the room *as sulky as a bear*. 彼はひどく不きげんに部屋の中を歩き回った.

be [***get***] ***sulky with*** …に不きげんである[になる] ▪ He *got sulky with* me about a trifle. 彼はちょっとしたことで私に不きげんになった.

sum¹ /sʌm/ 名 ***a*** (***good***) ***round sum*** 相当よい値 ▪ You can sell it for *a good round sum*. それは相当よい値で売れるよ.

a tidy sum 大金 ▪ His new home cost him *a tidy sum*. 彼の新居には多額の金がかかった.

do a sum/do sums 《口》算数をやる, 計算をする ▪ A calculating machine is one that *does sums* automatically. 計算機は自動的に計算する機械だ.

greater [***better, more***] ***than the sum of its parts*** (全体では)部分[個々]の力以上で ▪ The whole is *greater than the sum of its parts*. 全体は部分の総和以上になる.

in sum 要するに ▪ *In sum*, he is a sacrifice to his own rashness. 要するに, 彼は自身の無鉄砲さのために身を滅ぼしたのだ. ☞ L in summa のなぞり.

the sum and substance 真髄, 要点 (*of*) ▪ The Sermon on the Mount contains *the sum and substance of* Christianity. 山上の垂訓にはキリスト教の真髄が含まれている.

the sum of things 公の福祉; 森羅万象, 宇宙 ▪ Concessions such as these are of little moment to *the sum of things*. このような譲歩は公の福祉にとってあまり重要ではない ▪ The glory of *the sum of things* will flash along the chords. 宇宙の栄光がさっと弦を伝わる. ☞ L summa rerum のなぞり.

the sum total 全体, 総体, 総計 (*of*) ▪ *The sum total of* the damage cannot be calculated. 被害の総額は測り知れない.

work sums 《口》計算をする ▪ Some of you boys are very clever at *working sums*. 君たち少年の中には計算のとてもうまい者がいる.

sum² /sʌm/ 動 ***to sum up*** 約言すれば ▪ *To sum up*, he is true, kind, and honest. 約言すれば彼は誠実で親切で正直なのだ.

summer¹ /sʌ́mər/ 名 ***summer and winter/winter and summer*** 一年中 ▪ *Winter and summer*, steamboats leave Westminster half-hourly. 一年中汽船がウェストミンスターから半時間ごとに出る.

summer² /sʌ́mər/ 動 ***summer and winter*** まる1年を送る; 年がら年中暮らす (*with*) ▪ My cousins have *summered and wintered with* us. いとこたちは私たちの所で年がら年中暮らしてきた.

summit /sʌ́mət/ 名 ***at the summit*** 首脳者の ▪ It was a meeting *at the summit*. それは首脳者会談であった.

sun¹ /sʌn/ 名 ***a place in the sun*** 日の当たる場所, 順境 ▪ He is ambitious of *a place in the sun*. 彼は日の当たる場所を熱望している.

adore [***hail, worship***] ***the rising sun*** 日の出の勢いの人にこびる ▪ The clerks *worship the rising sun*. 事務員らはこの日の出の勢いの人にこびる.

(***as***)***... as the sun shines on*** 確かに《賞賛の文句》 ▪ He is *as* fine a gentleman *as the sun shines on*. 彼は確かに立派な紳士だ.

beneath the sun この世で ▪ Let us enjoy ourselves while we breathe *beneath the sun*. この世に生きているうちは楽しもうではないか.

catch the sun 日のあたる位置にいる; 日焼けする ▪ I've *caught the sun* on the beach. 私は浜で日焼けした.

from sun to sun 日の出から日の入りまで ▪ The man works *from sun to sun*. その男は朝から晩まで働く.

get the sun of 日を背にして(敵)に向かう ▪ In conflict see that you *get the sun of* an enemy. 戦闘のときには日を背にして敵に向かうように気を配ること.

hail the rising sun →adore the rising SUN.

have been in the sun/***have the sun in*** *one's* ***eyes*** 《俗》酔っている ▪ He *has been in the sun*. 彼は酔っている ▪ Last night he *had the sun* very strong *in his eyes*. ゆうべ彼はひどく酔っていた. ☞「日やけしている」が原義.

hold a candle to the sun 余計な[むだな]ことをする ▪ It is like *holding a candle to the sun*. それは全く余計なことだ.

in the sun **1** 日なたで ▪ A cat likes to sit *in the sun*. 猫は日なたぼっこが好きだ ▪ The clothes are drying *in the sun*. 衣類は日なたで乾いている.
2 衆目に見られて (↔in the SHADE) ▪ The effects of physicians' skill lie *in the sun*. 医者の腕前の結果は衆目に見られる.
3 のんきに ▪ He loves to live *in the sun*. 彼はのんきに暮らすのが好きだ.

keep the sun out of …に日が当たらないようにする ▪ *Keep the sun out of* your eyes. 太陽が目に当たらないようにしなさい.

Let not the sun go down upon your wrath [***anger***]. 翌日までも怒るな (《聖》*Ephes.* 4. 26) ▪ It is *not* well to *let the sun go down upon your wrath*. 翌日までも怒るのはよくない.

let the sun shine through *one* 傷を受ける ▪ I will not *let the sun shine through* me. おれは傷を負わされはしないぞ. ☞次の句から.

make the sun shine through …に穴をあける ▪ We *made the sun shine through* some of the walls. 我々は壁のいくつかに穴をあけた.

on which the sun never sets その領地に太陽の没しない《17世紀にはスペイン, 19世紀にはイギリス帝国について言った》 ▪ Snobs are recognized throughout an Empire *on which the sun never sets*. 領地に太陽の没しない国ではいたる所に俗物が見いだされる.

one's ***place in the sun*** 当然受けるべき分け前; はなばなしい地位 ▪ Mendel was an abbot of a monastery, but *his place in the sun* is due to his contributions to genetics. メンデルは修道院長だったが, 彼のはなばなしい地位は発生学への貢献によるものである. ☞Pascal, *Pensées* 73の "ma place au soleil" のなぞり.

rise with the sun 早起きする ▪ The marigold *rises with the sun*. マリーゴールドは朝早く咲く.

see the sun 生きている ▪ I'm now 85. I wonder how much longer I shall *see the sun*. 今85歳だ. あとどれだけ生き長らえられることやら.

One's [***Its***] ***sun is set.*** 全盛は過ぎた ▪ *The sun* of Rome *is set*. ローマの全盛は過ぎた.

take the sun **1** 日なたぼっこをする ▪ He *took the sun* on the grass. 彼は芝生の上で日なたぼっこした.
2《海》(六分儀で)正午に緯度を測定する ▪ They watched the Captain daily *take the sun*. 彼らは船長が毎日正午に緯度を測定するのをながめた.

The sun is over the yardarm. 《口》酒を飲み始めていい頃合いだ. ☞yardarm《海》「ヤーダム, 桁端」.

the Sun of Righteousness 正義の太陽《キリストのこと》(《聖》*Mal.* 4. 2) ▪ Yonder shines *the Sun of Righteousness*. かなたに正義の太陽が輝いている.

There is nothing new under the sun. 《諺》日のもとに全く新しいものは何ひとつない (《聖》*Eccles.* 1. 9).

think the sun rises and sets on *a person* 人をこの世で一番の宝[世界一大切な人物]と考える ▪ I *think the sun rises and sets on* my daughter. 私にとっては娘はこの世で一番の宝だ.

think the sun shines out of *a person's* ***bum*** [***behind, backside, bottom***] 《卑》人のことをこの上ないように思う ▪ Just because her husband is the Mayor, she *thinks the sun shines out of his bum*. 夫が市長だというので彼女は夫のことをこの上ないように思っている.

under the sun **1** この世で ▪ He pretends to know everything *under the sun*. 彼はこの世のありとあらゆることを知っているようなふりをする.
2 [[疑問詞を強調して]] 一体全体 ▪ What *under the sun* were they placed here for? 一体全体何のためにそれらはここに置かれたのだろうか.

worship the rising sun →adore the rising SUN.

sun[2] /sʌn/ 動 ***sun*** *oneself* 日なたぼっこする《比喩的にも》 ▪ They used to *sun themselves* in that place after breakfast. 彼らは朝食後その場所で日なたぼっこをするのが常であった ▪ He *sunned himself* in the smiles of the court. 彼は宮廷中の微笑に包まれて楽しく過ごしていた.

Sunday /sʌ́ndeɪ/ 名 ***a month*** [***week***] ***of Sundays*** 《口》長い間 ▪ I haven't been out of this blessed hole for *a month of Sundays*. もう長いことこのありがたい穴から外へ出たことがないんだ.

have *one's* ***Sunday out*** (暇をとって)日曜日に外出する ▪ He *had his Sunday out* with his sister. 彼は日曜日に妹といっしょに外出した.

last [***next***] ***Sunday***/***on Sunday last*** [***next***] 前[次]の日曜日に ▪ I met him *last Sunday*. 先週の日曜日に彼と会った ▪ The meeting will be held *next Sunday*. 会は来週の日曜日に開かれる.

look nine ways for Sunday, at once/***look two ways for*** [***to find***] ***Sunday*** →WAY.

six ways to [***for***] ***Sunday*** 《米俗》あらゆる点で; 完全に ▪ I was deceived *six ways to Sunday*.

僕はすっかりだまされた.

one's ***Sunday best*** [***clothes***]《口》晴れ着, 一丁羅 ▪ She was in *her Sunday best.* 彼女は晴れ着を着ていた ▪ She was off in *her Sunday clothes.* 彼女は晴れ着で出かけた. ☞古くは Sunday-go-to-meeting CLOTHES. (meeting = church meeting).

(*one's*) ***Sunday out*** 《口》(使用人の)公休日曜日 ▪ You can't stir, because it's not *your Sunday out.* お前は一歩も動けませんよ, お前の公休日曜日ではないのですからね.

when two Sundays meet [***come together, come in one week***]《口》決して…ない,「盆と正月がいっしょに来たら」 ▪ He'll pay his debt *when two Sundays come in one week.* 彼は決して借金を払わないだろう.

sunder /sʌ́ndər/ 名 ***in sunder*** 《詩》 **1** 別々に ▪ The power of parents tore them *in sunder.* 親の力で二人は別々に裂かれた.

2 (一つの物が)ばらばらに ▪ Their bodies were torn *in sunder.* 彼らの体はばらばらに裂かれた.

sundry /sʌ́ndri/ 形 ***all and sundry*** →ALL.

sunny /sʌ́ni/ 形 ***on the sunny side of*** →on the right SIDE of.

sunset /sʌ́nsèt/ 名 *one's* ***sunset years*** 《婉曲》老齢期 ▪ Some people in *their sunset years* are lonely. お年寄りのなかには孤独な人もいる.

sunshine /sʌ́nʃàɪn/ 名 ***have been in the sunshine*** 《俗》酔っている (→have been in the SUN) ▪ His groom said that Master *had been in the sunshine.* 彼の馬丁は主人は酔っておられたと言った.

sup /sʌp/ 動 ***sup sorrow*** 憂き目を見る ▪ I'll make you one day *sup sorrow* for this. いつかこのお返しにお前に憂き目を見させてやるぞ.

superior /səpíəriər|sju-/ 形名 ***be*** *a person's* ***superior in*** …の点で人よりすぐれている ▪ He *is my superior in* every way. 彼はあらゆる点で私よりも一枚上だ.

have no superior 右に出る者がいない (*in, as*) ▪ He *has no superior in* artistic skill [*as* an artist]. 芸術的技能で[芸術家として]彼の右に出る者はいない.

rise superior to (誘惑など)に動かされない ▪ He *rises superior to* temptation. 彼は誘惑に負けない.

superior to **1** …よりも優れて[まさって] ▪ He seems so *superior to* the people round him. 彼は周囲の人々よりずっと優れているように見える.

2 …に屈しない ▪ He is *superior to* temptation. 彼は誘惑に屈しない.

superlative /səpə́ːrlətɪv|sju-/ 名 ***be all superlatives*** (話が)誇張ずくめだ ▪ His talk *is all superlatives.* 彼の話は誇張ずくめだ.

in the superlative/in superlatives この上もなく大げさな言葉で ▪ He spoke *in superlatives* about everything. 彼は何につけてもこの上もなく大げさな言葉うかいをした.

supervision /sjùːpərvíʒən/ 名 ***under the supervision of*** …の監督のもとに ▪ The road was constructed *under his supervision.* その道路は彼の監督のもとに建設された.

supper /sʌ́pər/ 名 ***a covered-dish*** [***pot-luck***] ***supper*** 食べ物を各自持ち寄る食事会 ▪ She made open sandwiches for *the covered-dish supper.* 彼女は食事会用にオープンサンドを作った.

sing for *one's* ***supper*** 口をあずけるお返しに何か仕事をする ▪ He'll have to *sing for his supper* if he comes to stay with us. 彼がうちへ来て同居するのなら口をあずける返しに働かねばならない.

supply /səplái/ 名 ***in short supply*** 乏しい ▪ Goods are *in short supply.* 商品は乏しい状態だ. ☞scarce のほうが普通.

on supply (牧師などが)代理として ▪ Father Hallet was stationed *on supply* at Melior Street. ハレット神父が代理としてメリオール街に配置された.

support[1] /səpɔ́ːrt/ 名 ***give support to*** …をささえる; を支持する ▪ That chair will *give support to* your back. そのいすが君の背をささえてくれるだろう ▪ We *give* our hearty *support to* the plan. 我々はその案を心から支持する.

in support of (陳述など)を確証するために; (意見など)に賛成して ▪ The evidence is to be called *in support of* their statements. 彼らの陳述を確証するために証拠提出が求められることになっている ▪ I am willing to speak *in support of* his opinions. 私は喜んで彼の意見に賛成演説をします.

support[2] /səpɔ́ːrt/ 動 ***support*** *oneself* 自活する ▪ She decided to *support herself* on her musical talents. 彼女は音楽の才で自活しようと決心した.

suppose /səpóuz/ 動 ***be not supposed to*** *do* **1** …する必要はない ▪ She *is not supposed to* do any hard work. 彼女は骨の折れる仕事はしなくてよい.

2 …することを許されていない ▪ Well, he's *not supposed to* go into the kitchen. とにかく, 彼は台所へ入って行くことを許されていない ▪ You *are* not *supposed to* park here. ここに駐車してはいけないことになっています.

be supposed to *do* **1** …することになっている ▪ You *are supposed to* be here at eight every day. 毎日8時にここに来ることになっている.

2 …するものと考えられている ▪ Everyone *is supposed to* know the rules. 誰もがその規則を知っているものと考えられている.

Do you suppose ...? …とでも思っているのかね《ほのめかし・提案を憤慨してしりぞける文句》 ▪ *Do you suppose* that I want you to remain unmarried in order to secure my own position? お前は私が地位の確保のためお前に結婚させたがらないと思っているのか.

I don't suppose 《口》もしかして《丁寧な依頼を導く》 ▪ *I don't suppose* you could lend me your car tomorrow, could you? もしかして明日車を貸してもらえませんか.

I suppose/it is supposed 〚挿入句として〛…だ

ろう，たぶん… ▪ You are Mr. Smith, *I suppose*? あなたはスミスさんでしょうね ▪ He fell and *it is supposed* that he was instantaneously killed. 彼は倒れてたぶん即死したのだろう．

I suppose so. ええ，そうですね；(気のない返事として)はあ，そうですね ▪ Can I invite her to the party?―*I suppose so*. 彼女，パーティーに呼んでもいい?―うん，そうだね．

What's that supposed to mean? 《口》(当惑して[怒って])それはどういう意味だ? ▪ You're a nice guy.―*What's that supposed to mean?* 君って，ナイスガイだね―それって，どういう意味?

you may suppose もちろん ▪ I heard him shouting. But *you may suppose* I paid no heed. 彼が叫んでいるのが聞こえた．だがもちろん僕は耳をかさなかった．

supposition /sʌ̀pəzíʃən/ 名 ***on the supposition that*** …と仮定して ▪ I am preparing *on the supposition that* you will come. 君が来るだろうと仮定して準備しています．

sure /ʃʊər|ʃɔː/ 形副 ***as* [*so*] *sure as*** …すると必ず ▪ *As* [*So*] *sure as* I make arrangements for a picnic, it rains. 私がピクニックの準備をすると必ず雨が降る．

(*as*) *sure as death* [*fate, hell, a gun, sixpence, eggs* (*is* [*are*] *eggs*), *I live,* etc.] 確かに ▪ *As sure as death*, this is one of the rogues. 確かにこいつは例の悪党の一人だ ▪ That's true *as sure as eggs*. それは確かに本当だ．

be sure 〚挿入句〛確かに ▪ The King, *be sure*, would never grant them the privilege. 王は確かに彼らにその特典を許さないだろう．

be* [*feel*] *sure of **1** (主観的に)…を確信している ▪ I *am sure of* living to ninety years of age. 私はきっと90歳まで生きられると思っている ▪ I *feel sure of* his permission. 彼の許可が得られると確信している．

2 (客観的に)…するにきまっている ▪ My daughters *are sure of* getting good husbands. うちの娘たちはいい夫を得るにきまっている．

be* [*feel*] *sure of oneself 自信たっぷりだ ▪ I *felt* quite *sure of myself*. 私は全く自信たっぷりだった．

***be* [*feel*] *sure* (*that*)** (主観的に)…と確信している ▪ I *am sure that* he is innocent. 彼は無実だと確信している．

be sure to do (客観的に)きっと…する ▪ He *is sure to* return. 彼はきっと帰ってくる ▪ If they have any wit or sense, they *are sure to* show it. 彼らに機知か分別があれば，きっと見せるにきまっている．

be sure to* [《口》*and*] *do*/*be sure that きっと…せよ ▪ *Be sure to* come tomorrow. きっとあす来てください ▪ At least *be sure that* you go to the author. 少なくとも必ず著者の所へ行ってくれたまえ ▪ *Be sure and* lock the door. 必ずドアをロックしてくださいよ．

feel sure of →be SURE of.

for sure 《口》確かに ▪ I know *for sure* they want powder. 彼らは確かに弾薬をほしがっているのだ．

I am sure **1** 《口》本当に《強く言明するとき》 ▪ *I'm sure* I don't know. (＝I don't know, *I'm sure*.) 本当に知らないんですよ．

2 〚挿入句〛確かに ▪ His lordship cannot, *I am sure*, object to your presence. 閣下はあなたが出席することに確かにご異存ありますまい．

make sure **1** 確実にする，念を押す (*of*) ▪ To *make sure*, he shot another shot at the tiger. 念のため彼はトラをもう一発ねらい撃った ▪ It is difficult to *make sure of* finding the birds. その鳥を必ず見つけられるようにすることはむずかしい．

2 確保する，手に入れる (*of*) ▪ They *made sure of* the country north of the Ebro. 彼らはエブロ川の北にあるその国を手に入れた．

3 確かめる (*of, that*) ▪ He just waited for a few hours to *make sure of* his position. 彼は自分の立場を確かめるために数時間待っていただけだった ▪ He came back to *make sure* she was away. 彼は彼女が留守であるのを確かめに帰って来た．

4 確信する (*of, that*)《ずさんな使い方》 ▪ He suspected nothing, and *made* quite *sure of* succeeding. 彼は何一つ疑わず，うまくいくものと確信しきっていた ▪ I *made sure* (*that*) it would rain, but it didn't. きっと雨が降ると思っていたが降らなかった．

so sure as →as SURE as.

sure and certain hope (根拠のある)確かな希望 (Prayer Book, "*The Burial of the Dead*") ▪ The children were in the *sure and certain hope* of ices to follow. 子供たちは次にアイスクリームが必ず出るものと期待していた．

Sure do! 《口》うん，もらうよ[ああ，たのむよ]! ▪ Wanna have something to drink?―*Sure do!* なにか飲み物でもどう?―うん，もらうよ．

sure enough 《口》果たせるかな；確かに ▪ I said you'd come, and *sure enough* here you are. 君は来ると僕は言ったが，果たせるかな来たねえ ▪ I saw it, *sure enough*. 確かにそれを見たよ．

sure thing 《口》 **1** 〚a を伴って〛確かなこと ▪ That's *a sure thing*. そりゃ確かなことだ．

2 〚しばしば間投詞〛もちろん，確かに，きっと ▪ Shall you be at Jean's wedding tomorrow? ―*Sure thing*! あすジーンの結婚式へ行くかね―もちろんだ．

3 (お礼の言葉に対して)どういたしまして ▪ Thanks a lot!―*Sure thing*! 本当にありがとう―どういたしまして．

that's for sure →THAT.

to be sure **1** 《文》〚譲歩句〛なるほど，いかにも ▪ The wind is contrary, *to be sure*, but it is far from a storm. 風は確かに逆風だが，あらしほどではない．

2 《口》〚well を伴って〛なるほど，ほんとに《驚きの叫び》 ▪ *Well, to be sure*, this is a large room. いや確かにこれは広い部屋だ．

3 《口》確かに，もちろん ▪ Will you come?―*To be sure*! 来るかい?―もちろんだよ．

Well, I'm sure! 《口》おやまあ!《驚きの叫び》 ▪ "*Well, I'm sure!*" said Becky at this. 「おやまあ!」とベッキーはこれを聞いて言った．

S

you may be sure ⟦挿入句⟧ 確かに ▪ He will, *you may be sure*, accept it. 彼は確かにそれを受け取るだろう.

surely /ʃúərli|ʃɔ́ː-/ 副 ***as surely as*** **1** …と同様確かに ▪ *As surely as* I live, I'll be revenged on him. きっとあの男に仕返ししてやるぞ ▪ *As surely as* the leaf fades, so surely shall we fade. 木の葉が色あせると同じように確かに, 我々も色あせていく.

2 …のたびごとに (as often as) ▪ *As surely as* they stopped, the old man's vigor sank again. 彼らがやめるたびごとに, 老人の元気もまたなくなった.

slowly but surely 徐々に確実に ▪ These things are *slowly but surely* coming about. こんな事柄が徐々に確実に生じかけている.

surety /ʃúərəti|ʃɔ́ːrəti/ 名 ***find surety*** [***sureties***] 保証人を立てる ▪ He was obliged to *find* two *sureties*. 彼はやむなく二人の保証人を立てた.

stand [***go***] ***surety for*** *a person* 人の保証人になる ▪ I will *stand surety for* him. 私が彼の保証人になろう.

surf /səːrf/ 名 ***surf and turf*** (高価な)シーフードつきステーキ ▪ Father ordered the *surf and turf* but the rest of the family ordered humburgers. 父はシーフードつきステーキを注文したが, 家族の残りの者はハンバーガーにした.

surface /sə́ːrfəs/ 名 ***below the surface*** 内面は[に] ▪ He is kind *below the surface*. 彼は内面は親切だ ▪ Try to look *below the surface* of the controversy. その議論の内面を見ようとしたまえ.

come [***rise***] ***to the surface*** 浮かび上がる《比喩的にも》 ▪ Wickedness is sure to *come to the surface* in time. 悪事はいつか必ず浮かび上がってくる.

get below the surface 裏面[心の中]を探る ▪ One never *gets below the surface* with him. 彼の心の中を探ることはできない.

of the surface =on the SURFACE 1.

on the surface **1** 皮相的な, うわべの ▪ His politeness was all *on the surface*. 彼のいんぎんさはうわべだけだった.

2 表面上[うわべ]は ▪ *On the surface* everything was honorable. うわべは何もかも立派だった.

3 明白で ▪ His faults are *on the surface*. 彼の過失は明白だ.

S

raise ... to the surface (沈没船など)を引き揚げる ▪ The divers managed to *raise* the wreck *to the surface*. 潜水夫らは何とかして難破船を引き揚げた.

rise to the surface 水面に出てくる; 見えるようになる ▪ The submarine *rose to the surface*. 潜水艦が水面に出て来た ▪ The fact is now *rising to the surface*. その事実が今や明るみに出つつある.

scratch the surface of →SCRATCH[2].

surmount /sərmáʊnt/ 動 (***be***) ***surmounted by*** [***with***] …を上に置いて(いる) ▪ The spire *was surmounted by* a weathervane. 尖塔のてっぺんには風見がついていた.

surpass /sərpǽs|-pɑ́ːs/ 動 ***surpass*** *oneself* 今までよりよくやる ▪ You have *surpassed yourself* this time. 今度は今までよりよくやったね.

surprise[1] /sərpráɪz/ 名 ***a surprise packet*** 《口》びっくり包み《比喩的にも》 ▪ Here's *a surprise packet* for you. このびっくり箱, 君にあげる.

by surprise 不意打ちして ▪ The truth must be elicited *by surprise*. 真相は不意打ちして聞き出さなければならない.

come as no surprise …が分かっても驚くには当たらない ▪ It *came as no surprise* that he had lost his job. 彼が失業していたのが分かっても驚くには当たらなかった.

have a surprise for *a person* 人をびっくりさせるものがある《知らせ・贈り物など》 ▪ I *have a surprise for* you. 君をびっくりさせること[もの]があるんだよ.

in surprise 驚いて ▪ I watched it *in surprise*. 私は驚いてそれを見つめた.

Surprise, surprise! **1**《口》驚いちゃいけないよ ▪ *Surprise, surprise!* It's a present for you! 驚いちゃいけないよ, 君へのプレゼントだ.

2《皮肉》当然のことながら, 案の定 ▪ We didn't think he'd succeed, and—*surprise, surprise!*—he failed. 彼が成功するとは思っていなかったが, 案の定失敗した.

take ... by surprise **1** (一人で町など)の不意を襲う, (人など)をいきなり襲う ▪ Richard *took* the kingdom *by surprise*. リチャードはその王国の不意を襲った ▪ The rainshower *took* us *by surprise*. にわか雨が私たちをいきなり襲った.

2 (人)に不意打ちをくわせる ▪ This statement, I confess, *took* me *by surprise*. この申し立ては正直私をあっと言わせた.

the surprise of *one's* ***life*** [***time***] この上もない驚き ▪ You will have *the surprise of your life*. 君はこの上もなく驚くことだろうよ.

to *one's* ***surprise*** 驚いたことには ▪ Much *to his surprise* he found his dog dead. ひどく驚いたことに彼の犬は死んでいた ▪ *To the surprise of* everyone, his plan succeeded. みんなが驚いたことに彼の計画は成功した.

with surprise 驚いて, 驚きのあまり ▪ He turned pale *with surprise*. 彼は驚いて青くなった.

surprise[2] /sərpráɪz/ 動 ***be surprised at*** **1** …に驚く, びっくりする ▪ He *was* greatly *surprised at* the news. 彼はその知らせにひどくびっくりした.

2《口》…をけしからんと思う ▪ Fancy your being rude to the vicar. I *am surprised at* you! 君が牧師さんに無礼を働いたなんて. 君にはあきれたよ.

be surprised by **1** …にびっくりする ▪ I *was surprised by* the man's abilities. 私はその男の才能にびっくりした.

2 …に不意打ちをくわされる ▪ The household *was surprised by* a sudden Indian attack. その家は突然先住民の不意打ちを受けた.

be surprised to *do* …してびっくりする ▪ I *was* much *surprised to* hear about it. そのことを聞いてとてもびっくりした.

I shouldn't be surprised if …だとしても別に驚かない ▪ *I shouldn't be surprised if* it rained this afternoon. きょうの午後雨が降っても別に驚かないよ《どうも降りそうだ》.

surprised out of *oneself* びっくり仰天して ▪ Enfield began, *surprised out of himself.* エンフィールドはびっくり仰天して切り出した.

surrender /səréndər/ 動 ***surrender*** *oneself* **1** (特に敵に)身を投じる, 投降する ▪ He *surrendered himself* as a prisoner. 彼は捕虜として投降した.

2 (感動・影響・仕事などに)身を任せる, 専心する (*to*) ▪ He *surrendered himself to* grief. 彼は悲しみの涙に沈んだ ▪ We must *surrender ourselves to* our duties. 我々は仕事に専心しなければならない.

3 (破産者が)破産裁判所に出頭する ▪ The man was required to *surrender himself.* 男は破産裁判所に出頭を求められた.

surrender *oneself* ***to justice*** 自首する ▪ He desired to appease his mind by *surrendering himself to justice.* 彼は自首することによって心の安らぎを得たいと願った.

surround /səráʊnd/ 動 ***be surrounded by*** [***with***] …に取り巻かれている ▪ The castle *is surrounded with* a moat. 城は堀で取り巻かれている.

surround *oneself* ***with*** 自分の周りに…を集める ▪ They *surrounded themselves with* people who shared their beliefs. 彼らは自分たちの周りに信条を同じくする人々を集めた.

survey /sərvéɪ/ 名 ***make a survey of*** **1** …を測量[検分]する ▪ They *made a survey of* the prospective town site. 彼らは将来の都市指定地を検分した.

2 …を概観する ▪ Let us *make a survey of* education in Japan. 日本の教育を概観してみよう.

take a survey of …を概観する ▪ We have already *taken a survey of* the legends. 我々はその伝説をすでに概観した.

survival /sərváɪvəl/ 名 ***the survival of the fittest*** 《生物》適者生存 ▪ This *survival of the fittest* is what Darwin called "natural selection." この適者生存とはダーウィンのいう「自然淘汰」のことだ.

survive /sərváɪv/ 動 ***I'll survive.*** =I'll LIVE.

survive *one's* ***usefulness*** 無用の長物となる ▪ Though old, I shall never *survive my usefulness.* 私は老人だが決して無用の長物にはならないぞ.

susceptible /səséptəbəl/ 形 ***be susceptible of*** **1** (作用など)を受けうる ▪ Coal *is susceptible of* fusion. 石炭は融解する ▪ The word *is* often *susceptible of* both uses. この語はよく二様に用いられる.

2 (感情など)を感じることができる ▪ Her young heart *was susceptible* only *of* pleasure and curiosity. 彼女の若い心はただ喜びと好奇心しか感じられなかった.

be susceptible to **1** (病気)にかかりやすい ▪ Children *are* so *susceptible to* inflammations. 子供はとても炎症にかかりやすい.

2 (外的印象・危害など)に感じ[被り]やすい ▪ He *was susceptible to* the ridiculous. 彼はこっけいなものに感じやすかった.

suspend /səspénd/ 動 ***suspend*** *a person* ***from*** 人に(一時)…を与えないようにする, 人から(一時)…を取り上げる ▪ The boy *is suspended from* school for an indefinite period. その少年は無期停学にされている ▪ The society *suspended* him *from* his vote. 協会は彼から選挙権を一時取り上げた.

suspend payment (破産のため)支払いを停止する ▪ The firm had to *suspend payment.* その会社は支払いを停止しなくてはならなかった.

suspender /səspéndər/ 名 ***hoist*** *oneself* ***by*** *one's* ***own suspenders*** 自力で向上[進歩]する ▪ We have all tried many times to *hoist ourselves by our own suspenders.* 我々はみな何度も自力で向上しようと努めてきた.

suspense /səspéns/ 名 ***hold*** [***keep***] ***… in suspense*** **1** …を未決定のままにしておく ▪ In this case we must *hold* our judgment *in suspense.* この件については判定を保留しなければならない.

2 (知りたいことを知らせないで)…に気をもませておく ▪ This is a story that *keeps* you *in suspense* until the last chapter. これは最後の章まで読者に気をもませておく小説だ.

in suspense **1** 未決定のままで ▪ The matter now hangs *in suspense.* その問題は目下未決定のままになっている.

2 気をもみながら ▪ They were waiting *in* great *suspense* for his arrival. 彼らは彼の到着をひどく気をもみながら待っていた.

suspicion /səspíʃən/ 名 ***a suspicion of*** …の気味 ▪ There was *a suspicion of* sadness in her voice. 彼女の声にはやや悲しそうなところがあった.

above [***beyond***] ***suspicion*** 容疑をかける余地がない ▪ His character is *above suspicion.* 彼は容疑をかける余地のない人柄だ.

have a sneaking suspicion 密かに思う ▪ I *have a sneaking suspicion* that he may be right. 私は彼が正しいかも知れないと密かに思っている.

on suspicion 容疑で (*of*) ▪ He was held *on suspicion of* being a spy. 彼はスパイの容疑で拘留された.

on the suspicion of …の容疑を受けると[受けて] ▪ *On the suspicion of* dishonesty they will be shot offhand. 不正行為の容疑をかけられると彼らは即座に射殺されるだろう.

under suspicion 容疑をかけられて ▪ He is *under suspicion* as one of the murderers. 彼は殺人者の一味との容疑をかけられている ▪ He came *under suspicion* for other crimes. 彼は他の犯罪で容疑をかけられた.

suspicious /səspíʃəs/ 形 ***be*** [***feel***] ***suspicious of*** [***about***] …を疑う ▪ He *is suspicious of* superior people. 彼は目上の者を疑っている.

suspiciously /səspíʃəsli/ 副 ***look*** [***sound***] ***suspiciously like*** …にひどく似ている ▪ This

S

car *looks suspiciously like* my stolen one. この車, 私の盗まれた車とよく似てるんだよね.

swaddling-clothes /swάdəlɪŋklòʊz|swɔ́dəlɪŋ-klòʊðz/ 名 ***still in*** *one's* ***swaddling-clothes*** まだほんの子供で; まだ独り立ちできないで ▪ He is *still in his swaddling-clothes.* 彼はまだ独り立ちできない.

swagger /swǽgər/ 動 ***swagger*** *a person* ***into*** [***out of***] いばりちらして人に…させる[をやめさせる] ▪ He would *swagger* the boldest men *into* a dread of his power. 彼はいばりちらしてどんな大胆な人間でも彼の力を恐れさせるようにするのだった ▪ He *swaggered* them *out of* opposition. 彼はいばりちらして彼らの反抗の手を引かせた.

swallow[1] /swάloʊ|swɔ́l-/ 名 ***One swallow does not make a summer.*** 《諺》ツバメ1羽で夏にはならない《早合点は禁物》.

swallow[2] /swάloʊ|swɔ́l-/ 名 ***at one swallow*** ひと飲みに ▪ He drank it *at one swallow.* 彼はひと飲みにそれを飲んだ.

swallow[3] /swάloʊ|swɔ́l-/ 動 ***be hard*** [***difficult***] ***to swallow*** …は信じがたい ▪ His story *is hard to swallow.* 彼の話は信じがたい.

swallow down *one's* ***spittle*** (怒りを抑えて)つばを飲み下す(《聖》*Job* 7. 19) ▪ If they insult you, sit still and *swallow down your spittle.* 人々が君を侮辱したら, じっと動かず座ってつばを飲み下すがいい.

swallow hook, line, and sinker …を鵜呑みにする ▪ Mother *swallowed hook, line and sinker* her son's excuse. 母親は息子の弁解を鵜呑みにした.

swallow *one's* (***own***) ***words*** **1** 前言を取り消す ▪ I have *swallowed my words* already. 私はもう前言は取り消しました.

2 はっきり言わない ▪ I couldn't understand Tom because he *swallowed his words.* トムははっきり言わなかったので何を言っているのか分からなかった.

swallow *one's* ***pride*** → put one's PRIDE in one's pocket.

swallow the apple [***olive***] 《米俗》(スポーツで)緊張して堅くなる[あがる] ▪ You have to keep your poise, and not *swallow the apple.* 君たちは泰然自若として, あがってはならない.

swallow the bait →BAIT[1].

swallow ... whole …を丸ごと信じる ▪ She always makes a fantastic excuse, expecting me to *swallow* it *whole.* 彼女はいつも途方もない弁解をして, 私がそれをまるごと信じるものと思っている.

swamp /swαmp|swɔmp/ 動 ***be swamped with*** (困難・量など)で圧倒[忙殺]される ▪ The firm *is swamped with* orders. その会社は注文に忙殺されていた.

swan /swαn|swɔn/ 名 ***a black swan*** まれ[珍奇]なもの(Juvenal, *Sat.* 6. 164) ▪ He is *a black swan*, an honest lawyer! 彼はまれな人物だ, 正直な弁護士だなんて!

(***as***) ***graceful as a swan*** 大変優雅な, 実に上品な ▪ Her grandmother is *graceful as a swan.* 彼女のおばあさまは実に上品だ.

one's ***swan song*** 白鳥の歌《最後の作・辞世など》 ▪ His speech to the Reichstag in July was really *Hitler's swan song.* 7月のドイツ議会での彼の演説はなんとヒットラーの辞世であった.

swank[1] /swæŋk/ 名 ***for swank*** 見栄のため ▪ She wears a diamond ring just *for swank.* 彼女はただ見栄のためにダイヤの指輪をはめているのだ.

swank[2] /swæŋk/ 動 ***swank it*** 《俗》もったいぶって歩く ▪ The boy *swanked it* down the road in his new school uniform. 少年は新しい学校の制服を着て見せびらかしながら道を歩いて行った.

swap[1], **swop**[1] /swαp|swɔp/ 名 ***get*** [***have***] ***the swap*** 《俗》首になる ▪ I've *had the swap* several times. 私は数回首になった.

swap[2], **swop**[2] /swαp|swɔp/ 動 ***no time to swap knives*** 《米口》方針を変える余裕がない ▪ There was *no time to swap knives.* 方針を変える余裕はなかった.

swap horses while crossing the stream 中途でくら替えする ▪ It is never wise to *swap horses while crossing the stream.* 中途でくら替えするのは決して賢明ではない.

swap lies 《米口》おしゃべりする ▪ Most men came here to *swap lies.* たいていの人はここへ来ておしゃべりした.

swap stories [***yarns, words***] 《米口》会話をする, 話をする ▪ The older men stayed at home and *swapped stories.* 年寄りは家にいて話をした.

swath /swαθ|swɔθ/, **swathe** /sweɪð/ 名 ***cut a*** (***wide***) ***swath***(***e***) **1** 《米俗》見栄を張る; 人目を引く ▪ Gee! didn't he *cut a swath!* いやはや, 彼が見栄を張ったのなんのって. ☞「かまで大きく一なぎする」が原義.

2 草を刈って道をつける ▪ He *cut a swathe* through the high grass with his scythe. 彼は鎌で丈の長い草を刈って道をつけた.

3 なぎ倒す, ひどく破壊する(*in, through*) ▪ The bulldozer *cut a swathe in* the lines of small old houses. ブルドーザーで小さな古い家並みをなぎ倒した.

swathe /sweɪð/ 動 ***be swathed in*** …にくるまる[包まれる] ▪ He *was swathed in* a towel. 彼はタオルにくるまっていた.

sway[1] /sweɪ/ 名 ***have a great sway*** (***and say***) 大勢力を持つ ▪ He *has a great sway* in the House. 彼は議院で大勢力を有している.

hold [***bear, have***] (***the***) ***sway*** 《文》支配する, 力を握る(*over*) ▪ The two men *held* chief *sway* in the kingdom. その二人が王国で主要な勢力を握っていた ▪ Once the Church *bore sway over* every action of life. 昔は教会が人生の全活動を支配していた.

lose *one's* ***sway over*** …への支配力を失う ▪ The author has *lost his sway over* public opinion. 著者は世論を支配する力を失っている.

under the sway of …の支配を受けて ▪ The

people was *under the sway of* Rome. その民族はローマの支配を受けていた.

sway[2] /sweɪ/ 動 ***sway the scepter*** 統治[支配]する ▪ Charles I continued to *sway the* English *scepter*. チャールズ1世が依然としてイギリスを統治していた. ☞scepter「しゃく」は王位の象徴.

swear /sweər/ 動 ***enough to swear by*** 《俗》ほんの少し ▪ The two ships touched with a shock which was just *enough to swear by*. 2隻の船は触れ合ってほんの少しばかりの衝撃を受けた.

I'll be sworn. きっとだ, 誓ってもよい ▪ *I'll be sworn*, it is true. 太鼓判を押してもいいが, 本当なのだ.

swear black is white →BLACK[1].

swear blind (***that***) 《英口》(嘘だと知っていても本当だと)強調する, 言い立てる ▪ Peter broke the vase, but he *swears blind that* it wasn't him. ピーターは花びんを割ったのに, 自分ではないと言い立てる.

swear by all that is holy [***sacred***]/***swear by all the gods*** 断固として誓う ▪ He *swore by all that is holy* that it was true. 彼はそれは本当だと断固として誓った.

swear home [***through a two-inch board,*** *one's* ***way through a stone wall***] 激しく誓う ▪ He'll *swear his way through a stone wall*. 彼は激しく誓うだろう.

swear like a trooper [***a bargee, a lord, blazes, a tinker***] ひどくののしる, ひどく毒づく ▪ The fellow *swore like a trooper*. その男はひどく毒づいた.

swear the peace against *a person* → PEACE.

swear through a two-inch board → SWEAR home.

swear *a person* ***to secrecy*** [***silence***] 人に秘密を誓わせる ▪ Holmes insisted on *swearing* us *to secrecy* before he gave us the plans. ホームズは我々に計画を授ける前に誓って秘密にするように主張した.

swear up and down 《米》…を[と]断言する, 言い張る ▪ The student *swore up and down* that he hadn't shoplifted. その生徒は万引きしていないと言い張った.

swear *one's* ***way through a stone wall*** → SWEAR home.

sweat[1] /swet/ 名 ***all of a sweat*** 《口》ひどく心配して[おびえて] ▪ She stood *all of a sweat*, looking at the intruder's face. 彼女は乱入者の顔を見つめ, ひどくおびえて立ちすくんでいた.

an old sweat 老兵 ▪ You're *a* level-headed *old sweat*. あなたは沈着な老兵だ.

break (***a***) ***sweat*** 《口》汗をかく, 骨を折る《break a sweat は《米》》 ▪ She *broke sweat* to reach the final. 彼女は決勝進出にむけて汗をかいた[努力した].

by the sweat of *one's* ***brow*** 《文》額に汗して, せっせと働いて ▪ She is growing all kinds of flowers in her garden *by the sweat of her brow*. 彼女は額に汗して庭であらゆる種類の花を育てている.

in a cold sweat (恐怖・不安のために)冷や汗をかいて, ひどくおびえて[不安で] ▪ I woke up *in a cold sweat*, shaking from the nightmare. 私は悪夢を見て震えながら冷や汗をかいて目ざめた.

in a sweat **1** 汗を流して ▪ I was *in a* cold *sweat* from fear. 私は恐怖のために冷汗をかいていた.
2《口》いらだって, あせって (*to do*) ▪ This put our conjurer *in a* deep *sweat*. これでわが手品師はひどくいらだった ▪ He was *in a sweat to* get there right off. 彼はすぐそこへ着こうとあせっていた.

no sweat 《口》楽々と[の]; 〖間接的に〗へっちゃらだよ, わけないよ ▪ Anybody can do that, *no sweat*. 誰にだって楽々とそんなことはできる ▪ Such a job is *no sweat*. そんな仕事, 楽なもんだよ.

stand the sweat 《口》骨折りに耐える ▪ I cannot *stand the sweat* of it. その骨折りには耐えられない.

take the sweat 《口》骨の折れる仕事をやる ▪ He will not *take the sweat*. 彼は骨折り仕事はやるまい.

the sweat of (*one's*) ***brow*** [***face***] 《文》額の汗, 労働 (《聖》*Gen*. 3. 19) (→by the SWEAT of one's brow) ▪ You have earned it with [by, in] *the sweat of your brow*. 君は額に汗してそれを得たのだ.

sweat[2] /swet/ 動 ***Don't sweat it.*** 《米口》心配しなくていい ▪ *Don't sweat it*! We'll provide after-sales service. ご心配には及びません. 私どもがアフターサービスをさせていただきます.

sweat blood →BLOOD.

sweat bullets →BULLET.

sweat for it 後悔する ▪ I will make you *sweat for it*. お前を後悔させてやるぞ.

sweat *one's* ***guts out*** →GUT[1].

sweat it out **1**《口》(不安そうに)待ちわびる ▪ The disbanded soldiers were *sweating it out* for a boat to carry them home. 除隊兵たちは帰国のための輸送船を待ちわびていた.
2《口》＝STICK it out.
3《米俗》きびしく尋問する ▪ The cops *sweated it out* of me for three hours. 警官たちに3時間きびしく尋問された.

sweat like a pig 《口》(仕事・恐怖などで)大汗をかく ▪ He was working hard, *sweating like a pig*. 彼は大汗を流しながら懸命に働いていた.

Sweeney /swíːni/ 名 ***Tell it to Sweeney!*** 《俗》そんなこと誰が信じるものか!, 嘘をつけ!《Sweeney Todd (特別機動隊): イギリス ITV テレビの警察ドラマ (1974–78)から》.

sweep[1] /swiːp/ 名 ***as black*** [***sooty***] ***as a sweep*** 真っ黒な ▪ Our faces soon became *as black as sweeps*. 我々の顔はすぐ真っ黒になった.

at one [***a***] ***sweep*** 一撃に, 一挙に ▪ The mine exploded, killing hundreds of men *at a sweep*. 鉱山が爆発して一挙に何百人という人が亡くなった.

beyond the sweep of →within the SWEEP of.

give a good sweep [***sweep-out, sweep-up***] (部屋)を十分に掃く ▪ The maid *gave* the room *a good sweep-up*. お手伝いが部屋をしっかり掃いてくれた.

make a clean sweep of **1** …を余さず一掃する, 大整理する ▪ The fire *made a clean sweep of* the village. その火事は村中を焼き払った ▪ The new manager is going to *make a clean sweep of* the old staff. 新しい支配人は古い社員を大整理するつもりだ.

2 …に完全な勝利を占める ▪ In the 1948 elections Truman *made a clean sweep of* all the Western states. 1948年の選挙でトルーマンは西部諸州を完全に押さえた.

within [***beyond***] ***the sweep of*** …の及ぶ範囲内[外]の ▪ The knight killed everyone who came *within the sweep of* his sword. 騎士は剣の及ぶ範囲にやって来た者をことごとく倒した.

sweep[2] /swi:p/ 動 ***be swept off*** *one's* ***feet*** →carry a person off his feet (→FOOT[1]).

sweep all before *one* = CARRY all before one.

sweep *a person's* ***decks*** →SWEEP the decks.

sweep everything into *one's* ***net*** 何もかも取り込む ▪ *Everything* he can lay hold of *is swept into his net*. 彼は手当たり次第に自分のものにしてしまう.

sweep into office [***power***] 楽勝して政権をとる ▪ The party hopes to *sweep into office*. その党は楽勝して政権をとりたいと思っている.

sweep the board (***clean***) →BOARD[1].

sweep the city [***country, nation, world***] (町中・国中・世界中で)注目を集める, 人気になる ▪ His wonderful performance *swept the world*. 彼の出来栄えの良さは注目を集めた.

sweep the [*a person's*] ***decks*** [***deck***] (砲・波が)甲板を一掃する ▪ The Commodore's grapeshot *swept their decks* effectively. 艦隊司令官のブドウ弾が敵の甲板を効果的に一掃した.

sweep the seas 海上の敵を一掃する ▪ They *swept the seas* (of their enemies). 彼らは海上の敵を一掃した.

sweep the stakes 賭金全部をさらい込む ▪ I have already *swept the stakes*. 私はもう賭金全部をさらい込んだ.

sweep [***brush, push***]***…under*** [***underneath, beneath***] ***the carpet*** [***mat, rug***] (失敗など)を隠そうとする ▪ They are trying to *sweep* their mistake *under the carpet*. 彼らは失敗を隠そうとしている.

swept and garnished 掃き清め飾り立てて; 面目を一新して (《聖》*Matt*. 12. 44; *Luke* 11. 25) ▪ The room was *swept and garnished* against our coming. その部屋は我々が来るので掃き清め, 飾り立ててあった.

sweet[1] /swi:t/ 名 ***the sweets and bitters of life*** 人生の辛酸 ▪ I know *the sweets and bitters of life*. 人生の酸いも甘いも知っている.

sweet[2] /swi:t/ 形 ***a sweet deal*** 《米口》うまい[おいしい]取引 ▪ It's *a sweet deal* for us. それって, 我々にはおいしい取引だね.

a sweet one 《俗》痛い一撃 ▪ I gave him *a sweet one* on the head. 彼の頭に痛い一撃を食わした.

(***as***) ***sweet as pie*** 《口・しばしば皮肉》とても可愛い, 極めて愛想がいい ▪ He could be *as sweet as pie* if he wanted to get something out of me. 私から何かを聞き出したいと思うようであれば, あいつにも可愛いところがあるんだが.

at *one's* ***own sweet will*** →WILL[1].

be sweet on [***upon***] 《口》…にほれている ▪ I think he *is sweet on* your daughter. あの男はあなたの娘さんにほれているのだと思います ▪ I *am sweet on* the suggestion. 私はその提案にほれこんだ.

cop it sweet **1** 《主に米》厳しい罰を甘んじて受ける ▪ As his plan ended in failure, he *copped it sweet*. 彼は自分の企画が失敗に終ったので罰を甘んじて受けた.

2 《豪口》たなからぼたもちである; 不快なことに耐える ▪ We *copped it sweet* today. The boss went on business. 今日はラッキーだったよ. 部長が出張してね.

have (***got***) ***a sweet tooth*** →TOOTH.

in *one's* ***own sweet time*** [***way***] 《口》都合のよい時に[やり方で] (→in one's own TIME) ▪ I'll do it *in my own sweet time* afterwards. あとで都合のいい時にやるよ.

keep *a person* ***sweet*** 《口》人に取り入る ▪ He tried hard to *keep* the boss *sweet*. 彼は社長に取り入ろうと懸命に努めた.

seem as sweet as sugar [***honey***] この上もなくあいそよい様子をする ▪ When he wants something done for him, Mr. Crake can *seem as sweet as sugar*. クレイク氏は人に何かしてもらいたいときには, この上もなくあいそよい様子ができる.

sweet damn all 《口》全然ないこと ▪ What do you think he gave me as a reward? —*Sweet damn all*! あの男が報酬としていくらくれたと思う—びた一文もくれなかったんだぜ.

sweet nothing 《口》(恋人同士の)甘いささやき ▪ The couple were whispering *sweet nothings* each other. そのカップルは互いに甘い言葉をささやきあっていた.

sweet sixteen うぶな16歳 ▪ She is just *sweet sixteen* and has never been kissed. 彼女はまだうぶな16歳でキスされたこともない.

sweeten /swí:tən/ 動 ***sweeten the kitty*** [***deal***] →sweeten the POT.

sweetly /swí:tli/ 副 ***pay*** [***cost***] ***sweetly*** 《皮肉》高い代価を払う, 高くつく ▪ He has *paid sweetly* for this honor. 彼はこの名誉に高い代価を払った ▪ This high place of his will *cost* him *sweetly*. この高い地位は彼にとって高くつくことだろう.

sweetness /swí:tnəs/ 名 ***all sweetness and light*** 《しばしば戯》(人が)すこぶる快適で[ごきげんで],

S

優しくて礼儀正しい; (状況が)好ましい ▪ The boss was *all sweetness and light* this morning. 社長は今朝はすこぶるごきげんだ. ☞sweetness and light「甘美と光明, 優美と明知」は Swift が *The Battle of Books* において人間の持つべき最も高貴な特質とし, M. Arnold が *Culture and Anarchy* において教養の理想とした言葉.

sweet-talk /swíːttɔ̀ːk/ 動 ***sweet-talk*** *a person* ***into*** 《口》人におべっかを使って…させる ▪ I *sweet-talked* him *into* buying it. 私は彼におべっかを使ってそれを買わせた.

swell[1] /swel/ 名 ***be a swell at*** [***on, in***] …の一流人である, 名人である ▪ He *is a* terrific *swell at* cricket. 彼はクリケットの名手だ ▪ He *is a swell in* politics. 彼は政界で一流の人だ.

come [***do, play***] ***the heavy*** (***swell***) 《俗》いばる, 気取る ▪ He may *do the heavy* while the luck lasts. 幸運の続く間は彼はいばるがいい.

swell[2] /swel/ 動 ***get*** [***have, suffer from***] ***a swelled*** [***swollen***] ***head*** 《口》慢心してくる[している], うぬぼれてくる[ている] ▪ He is *suffering from a swelled head*. 彼はひどくうぬぼれている ▪ Charm is a thing he will lose, if he *gets a swollen head*. 彼が慢心してきたら魅力がなくなってしまう.

swell it いばる, 肩で風を切る ▪ He was *swelling it* in the town among the big bugs. 彼は町の名士連の間でいばっていた.

swell like a turkey-cock 《口》(七面鳥のように)いばりちらす ▪ He's always *swelling like a turkey-cock*. 彼はいつもいばりちらしてばかりいる.

swell the ranks of →RANK.

swelter /swéltər/ 名 ***do a swelter*** 《俗》汗だくになる ▪ So I let them *do a swelter*. そこで彼らを汗だくにさせてやった.

in a swelter **1** うだるような暑さの中で ▪ The officers ate *in a swelter*. 士官たちはうだるような暑さの中で食事した.

2 興奮して ▪ For all the bitter cold, I was all *in a swelter*. 厳しい寒さだったが私はすっかり興奮していた.

swift /swɪft/ 形 ***be swift of foot*** 《雅》足が速い ▪ He *is swift of foot* like a hare. 彼はウサギのように足が速い.

be swift to [***to*** *do*] すぐ…する ▪ He *is swift to* mischief. 彼はいたずらをすぐやる ▪ All *were swift to* follow him. みながすぐ彼に従った.

swig /swɪɡ/ 名 ***take a swig*** 《口》ぐいぐい飲む ▪ He *took a swig* of beer and sighed with relief. 彼はビールをぐいぐい飲んでからふーっとため息をついた.

swill /swɪl/ 名 ***give … a swill*** (***out***) …を水で洗う, すすぐ ▪ *Give* the bucket *a* good *swill out*. バケツを十分すすいでおきなさい.

swim[1] /swɪm/ 名 ***have*** [***take***] ***a swim*** ひと泳ぎする ▪ Let's *have a swim* in the river. 川でひと泳ぎしよう.

in [***out of***] ***the swim*** (***of things***) 《口》好地位に[不利な地位に]; 時勢に明るく[暗く] ▪ He is to all appearance *out of the swim*. 彼はどう見ても実情に暗い様子だ ▪ She is *in the swim* of the world. 彼女は世間の実情に明るい.

in the swim with …と交わって; と相提携して ▪ I saw myself *in the swim with* such good company. 私は自分がとてもよい仲間と交わっているのに気づいた.

swim[2] /swɪm/ 動 ***sink or swim*** →SINK[2].

swim a stroke ひとかき泳ぐ ▪ He can't *swim a stroke*. 彼はまるで泳げない.

swim against the stream [***the current, the tide***] 世の風潮に逆らう ▪ He was endeavoring to *swim against the stream*. 彼は世の風潮に逆らおうと努めていた.

swim before *one's* ***eyes*** [***sight***] 目の前で回る, 回るように見える ▪ His face *swam before her eyes* before she fainted. 失神する前に彼の顔が彼女の目の前でくるくる回るように思えた.

swim for it [*one's* ***life***] 命からがら泳ぐ ▪ He was *swimming for his life*. 彼は必死に泳いでいた.

swim like a stone [***a brick, a millstone, a tailor's goose***]/***swim to the bottom*** 《戯》沈む, 金づちである ▪ I used to *swim to the bottom*. 昔はまるで泳げなかったんだ.

swim with [***down***] ***the stream*** [***current, tide***] 時勢に順応する ▪ A popular man always *swims down the stream*. 人気者はいつも時勢に順応する ▪ There is no help for it, we must *swim with the tide*. 仕方がない, 時勢には順応しなくてはな.

swimming /swímɪŋ/ 名 ***be like swimming through porridge*** 非常に困難である ▪ Trying to understand the complicated theory *was like swimming through porridge* for me. その複雑な理論を理解しようとしても私には全く無理であった.

swimmingly /swímɪŋli/ 副 ***go swimmingly*** (計画が)トントン拍子に進む ▪ Everything has been *going swimmingly*. すべて, トントン拍子に進んでいる.

swing[1] /swɪŋ/ 名 ***a swing around the circle*** 《米》選挙区遊説旅行 ▪ Who had been with Taft on his *swing around the circle*? タフトの選挙区遊説旅行には誰がついて行ったのか.

(***at***) ***full swing*** 全速力で; 全力を奮って ▪ Every hound went, *full swing*, throwing out his tongue. どの猟犬も舌を突き出して全速力で走った.

get into the swing of 《口》…に脂が乗ってくる ▪ He began to *get into the swing of* his class work. 彼は授業に脂が乗ってきだした.

get into the swing of it [***things***] コツを飲みこんでうまくできるようになる ▪ It took me a while to *get into the swing of things*. コツを飲みこんでうまくできるようになるのにしばらくかかった.

give free swing (…を)自由に働かせる[ふるまわせる] ▪ He *gave free swing* to his instincts. 彼は本能を自由に働かせた ▪ Her parents *gave* the girl *free swing*. 少女の両親は彼女を自由にふるまわせた.

go with a swing 《英》 **1** 調子よく[すらすら]運ぶ;

(会などが)盛会である ▪I am sure your party will *go with a swing*. 君のパーティーはきっと盛会だろう.
2 (歌が)調子がよい ▪The song *goes with a swing*. この歌は調子がよい.

have** one's* (full***) ***swing*** →take one's (full) SWING.

in full swing **1** たけなわで, まっ盛りで ▪The fishing was *in full swing*. 漁業はたけなわだった.
2 盛んに働いて ▪He knew a barrister *in full swing* of practice. 彼は盛んに仕事をしている弁護士を知っていた.

in the full swing of …のまっ最中で ▪Athens was *in the full swing of* hope. アテネは希望のまっ最中にあった.

on the swing 左右に揺れて ▪The doors were *on the swing*. ドアは左右に揺れていた.

swings and roundabouts 《英》一方で損をしても他方で儲けて埋め合わせをすること, いいことと悪いことのバランスがとれていること ▪It's just *swings and roundabouts* in politics. 政治の世界は一方で損をしても他方で儲けて埋め合わせができるようになっている.

take a swing at …に殴りかかる ▪He *took a swing at* me, but I was safe. 彼は私に殴りかかったが, 私は無事だった.

take [***have***] *one's* (***full***) ***swing*** したい放題にする ▪He *had his full swing* at this poem. 彼はこの詩で言いたい放題を言った ▪We let things *take their swing*. 我々は事態を成り行きに任せた.

the swing of the pendulum →PENDULUM.

What** one **loses on the swings** one **makes up [***gains***] ***on the roundabouts.*** 一方で損をしても他方で儲けて埋め合わせる (→SWINGs and roundabouts) ▪*What* the government have *lost on the swings* they are *gaining on the roundabouts*. 政府は一方で損をしてもほかで儲けて埋め合わせている. ☞次の諺も参照.

You lose on the swings what you make on the roundabouts. 《諺》儲けたり損したりして元のもくあみになる.

swing[2] /swɪŋ/ 動 ***not room*** (***enough***) ***to swing a cat*** (***in***) 実に狭苦しい ▪There *isn't room to swing a cat* here. ここは実に狭苦しい ▪They had *not room enough to swing a cat in*. 彼らの所は実に狭苦しかった. ☞猫の尾をつかんで振る余地もない, または cat＝a cat of nine tails の意から.

swing a wide loop 輪[射程]を広げる ▪We *swing a wide loop* all over Texas. 我々はテキサス州全体で手広く商売をしている ▪I *swing a wide loop* and have always been an advocate of Gnosticism. 私は知の射程を広げて, いつもグノーシス説を唱道してきた.

swing around the circle 《米》選挙区内を遊説する ▪He was induced to *swing around the circle*. 彼は選挙区内を遊説するように説きつけられた. ☞A. Johnson 大統領が1866年9月シカゴへ旅行したとき使った言葉.

swing both ways →WAY.

swing for it 《口》絞首刑になる ▪If convicted of that murder, he will certainly *swing for it*. もしあの殺人が有罪となれば彼はきっと絞首刑になるだろう.

swing (*oneself*) ***into*** …に飛び込む ▪He *swung* (*himself*) *into* the saddle. 彼はひらりと鞍にまたがった.

swing [***go***] ***into action*** →ACTION.

swing it 《口》(しばしば普通は許されない手段で)うまくやる ▪Work visas were hard to get, but I was able to *swing it*. ワークビザは入手しにくかったが, 私はうまく手に入れられた.

swing open [***wide***] (戸が)くるりと開く ▪The door *swung open*. ドアがくるりと開いた.

swing seconds (振り子が)毎秒1回ずつ振れ動く ▪This little clock has a pendulum *swinging seconds*. この小さい時計には毎秒1回ずつ振れ動く振り子がついている.

swing the lead →LEAD[1].

swing wide →SWING open.

swipe /swaɪp/ 名 ***have*** [***take***] ***a swipe at*** …を強打する ▪He *took a swipe at* the ball. 彼はボールを強打した.

Swiss /swɪs/ 名 ***have more holes than Swiss cheese*** 《主に米》穴だらけで話しにならない ▪The law *had more holes than Swiss cheese*. その法律は穴だらけで話しにならなかった.

switch[1] /swɪtʃ/ 名 ***be*** [***fall***] ***asleep at the switch*** [***wheel***] 《米俗》うっかりしている[する], 油断している[する], さぼっている[さぼる] ▪He *wasn't asleep at the switch*. 彼は油断してはいなかった.

switch[2] /swɪtʃ/ 動 ***I'll be switched.*** 《米口》おったまげてしまう《否定・驚きを表して》 ▪*I'll be switched* if he lives. 彼が生きていたらおったまげてしまわあ ▪Well, *I'll be switched*! いや, おったまげたなあ.

switch** a person **on (内線)電話を人につなぐ ▪Please *switch* Bill *on*. ビルにつないでください.

swoon /swuːn/ 名 ***fall*** (***down***) ***in a swoon***/ ***go off in a swoon*** 気絶する ▪She *fell down in a swoon*. 彼女は気を失った.

lie in a swoon 気絶している ▪They had *lain in a swoon* a good while. 彼らはかなりの間人事不省だった.

swoop /swuːp/ 名 ***at*** [***in***] ***one*** (***fell***) ***swoop***/ ***at a*** (***single***) ***swoop*** さっと舞い降りて; 一挙に ▪The eagle carried away the whole litter of cubs *at one fell swoop*. ワシは一襲のもとに子ギツネたちを全部ひっさらって行った ▪He lost three of his men *at a swoop*. 彼は3人の部下を一挙に失った.

in a swoop 急降下して ▪The airplane descended *in a swoop*. 飛行機は急降下した.

swop /swɑp|swɔp/ 動 ＝SWAP[2].

sword /sɔːrd/ 名 ***a double-edged*** [***two-edged, twin-edged***] ***sword*** 両刃の剣 ▪For me, the proposal was *a double-edged sword*. 私にとってその提案は両刃の剣であった.

at the point of the sword →at the POINT of

S

the bayonet.

be at swords'* [*swords'*] *points*/ *be at swords drawn (…と)ひどく仲が悪い, 不和である (*with*) ▪ They *were at swords' points* at once. 彼らはすぐにひどく仲が悪くなった ▪ The family had *been at swords drawn with* the school. その一家は学校とひどく険悪な関係だった.

***beat* [*turn*] *one's* *swords into plowshares* [*ploughshares*]** 剣を打ってすきの刃に変える, 武器を平和の用具に変える (《聖》*Isa.* 2. 4) ▪ The warlike city could not often afford to *beat her swords into plowshares.* その戦争好きな都市が武器を平和の用具に何度も変えるわけにはいかなかった.

cross swords (…と)剣を交える, 決闘する; (と)討論する (*with*) ▪ He *crossed swords with* the spark. 彼はそのだて男と決闘した ▪ They often *crossed swords* on the matter. 彼らはその件についてよく討論した.

***draw the* [*one's*] *sword against* [*at*]** …を攻撃する ▪ He *drew the sword against* the government. 彼は政府を攻撃した ▪ He *drew his sword at* the king. 彼は王に刃向かった.

Live by the sword, die by the sword.*/*He who lives by the sword dies by the sword. 《諺》暴力に生きる者は暴力で死ぬ.

measure swords →MEASURE[2].

put to* (*the edge of*) *the sword 《文》斬り殺す ▪ The Turks *put to the sword* all that came in their way. トルコ軍はじゃまをする者はすべて斬り殺した.

put up* [*sheathe*] *the sword 剣を納める; 和睦する ▪ The foes *sheathed the sword* and made terms. 敵同士は剣を納めて仲直りした.

They that live by the sword shall perish* [*die*] *by the sword. 《諺》剣をとる者は剣によって滅びる (《聖》*Matt.* 26. 52).

***throw* *one's* *sword into the scale*(*s*)** …の武力で決定を左右する ▪ It was not long before he *threw the American sword into the scales.* まもなく彼はアメリカの武力で決定を左右した.

syllable /síləbəl/ 名 ***to the last syllable*** とことんまで ▪ I am going to say my say *to the last syllable.* 私はとことんまで言いたいことは言うつもりだ.

symbolic /sɪmbάlɪk|-bɔ́l-/ 形 ***be symbolic of*** …を象徴する ▪ The eye *is symbolic of* sight and knowledge. 目は視力と知識を象徴する.

sympathy /símpəθi/ 名 ***extend* *one's* *sympathy to*** …に同情[弔意]を表す ▪ We *extended our sympathy to* him when his wife died of cancer. 彼の妻ががんで死んだ時, 我々は弔意を表した.

have no sympathy with …に賛成[同感]しない ▪ He *had no sympathy with* the Liberal Party. 彼は自由党に賛成しなかった.

have* [*feel*] *sympathy for …に同情を持つ[感じる] ▪ He *had simpathy for* poor people. 彼は貧しい人々に同情を抱いていた.

in sympathy with **1** …に賛成して ▪ I am quite *in sympathy with* your opinions. 君の意見には大賛成だ.

2《商》(物価の上がり下りなど)に伴って ▪ Corn recovered *in sympathy with* wheat. トウモロコシは小麦とともに持ち直した.

3 …に同情して ▪ I lent her some money *in sympathy with* her. 彼女に同情して金を貸してやった.

out of sympathy with …に不賛成で ▪ They were *out of sympathy with* the policy. 彼らはその政策には不賛成であった.

symptomatic /sìmptəmǽtɪk/ 形 ***be symptomatic of*** …の徴候を示す; の印である ▪ Headaches *are symptomatic of* many kinds of trouble. 頭痛はいろんな病気の徴候を示すものだ.

sync /sɪŋk/ 名 ***in sync* (*with*)** 《口》(…に)同期[同調]して (↔out of SYNC) ▪ Who doesn't want to be *in sync with* each other? 互いに同調していたいと願わない者がいるだろうか. ☞sync = synchronization.

out of sync 調子がずれて, 調和せずに (↔in SYNC (with)) ▪ Your step and my step are *out of sync.* 君の歩幅とぼくのは合わないね ▪ The sound on my TV is *out of sync* with the picture. 私のテレビの音は映像と同調していない.

system /sístəm/ 名 ***All systems* (*are*) *go!*/(*It's*) *all systems go.*** 《口・戯》準備万端完了! ▪ *It's all systems go* for launching the rocket. ロケット打ち上げ準備完了. ☞宇宙用語から.

beat the system 体制を打破する ▪ He was able to *beat the system* by getting a loan from the bank. 彼は銀行からの融資で現況を切り抜けられた.

buck the system 体制に逆らう ▪ He secretly admires her obstinacy to *buck the system.* 体制に逆らおうとする彼女の強情さを彼は密かに称賛している.

get … out of* *one's* *system 《口》(心配・悩み・人など)を心から追い払う, 忘れる ▪ I went for a long walk to try to *get* my worry *out of my system.* 悩みを忘れるために遠道の散歩に出かけた ▪ She couldn't *get* him *out of her system.* 彼女は彼のことを忘れることができなかった.

go* [*work*] *on a system 組織的にやる ▪ You will find your work easier if you *go on a system.* 組織的にやれば仕事が楽になるよ.

S

T

T, t /tiː/ 名 ***cross the*** [*one's*] ***t's*** (言行に)細心の注意を払う; 念を入れる ▪ He dotted his i's and *crossed his t's* and polished up his manuscript. 彼は細心の注意を払って草稿を推稿した. ☞横棒を引いて t の字を完成することから.

T.G.I.F./TGIF やれやれやっと金曜日だ ▪ What are you so happy about?—*T.G.I.F.* どうしてそんなにうきうきしているんだ—やっと金曜だからさ. ☞Thank God it's Friday. の略.

to a T [***tee***] 正確に, ぴったりと; 〚done to a Tで〛(肉が)適度な焼き加減の ▪ This suits me *to a T.* これは私にぴったり合う ▪ I understand the practice *to a tee.* そのしきたりは正確に知っている ▪ I like my beefsteak *done to a T.* ステーキは適度な焼き加減がいいねえ. ☞直角を測るT定規から, または横棒を引いて t の字を完成することから, または tittle から.

tab /tæb/ 名 ***keep*** (***a***) ***tab*** [***tabs***] ***on*** 《口》…を勘定する; に注目する, を見張る ▪ She has been *keeping tabs* in her family *on* the baking for a year. 彼女は1年前から一家のパン焼きの量を勘定してきた ▪ You can't get away because he is always *keeping tabs on* you. 彼がいつも君に注目しているのだから逃れることはできないよ. ☞tab＝table「勘定」.

pick up the tab 《米口》勘定を払う ▪ It includes *picking up the tab*, as well as tipping. それにはチップはもちろん勘定の払いも含まれている.

put the tab on 《米》…をほめる ▪ He also *put the tab on* Hungarian dogs. 彼はまたハンガリー犬をほめた.

raise the tab for 《米》…の負担を増大させる ▪ The cost may *raise the tab for* taxpayers. その費用は納税者の負担を増大させるかもしれない.

run up a tab (***of***) (店での勘定を)つけにする ▪ The officials *ran up a* bar *tab of* $3,500—paid for by the office. 役人たちは3,500ドルのバーの勘定を役所払いのつけにした.

throw up a tab 借金を重ねる ▪ He *threw up a tab* until luck should turn. 彼は運が向いてくるまで借金を重ねた.

T

table /téɪbəl/ 名 ***at table***/《米》***at the table*** 食事中 ▪ They were *at* (*the*) *table* when I called. 私が訪問したとき彼らは食事中だった ▪ Don't talk politics *at table.* 食事中に政治を論じてはだめだ.

bring ... to the table …を議事にかける ▪ It's time to *bring* that matter *to the table.* そろそろその問題を議事にかけてもいい頃だ.

bring *a person* ***to the table*** 人を説得して話し合いの席につかせる ▪ We hope to *bring* them *to the* negotiating *table.* 彼らを何とか交渉の席につかせたい.

clear the table 食卓のものをかたうける ▪ Doris always *clears the table.* ドリスがいつも食卓のものをかたうける.

drink *a person* ***under the table*** 《口》(人を)飲みつぶれさす ▪ I could *drink* the devil *under the table.* 僕は悪魔でも飲みつぶれさすことができる.

fix the table ＝lay the TABLE.

for (***the***) ***table*** 食用として ▪ They are a very good dish *for the table.* それはとてもうまい料理だ.

get [***come, go***] ***back to the table*** 再び和解の会談の席につく ▪ We'll have to *get back to the table* and overcome our differences. 我々は再び和解の会談の席について意見の相違を克服すべきだろう.

get round the table (話し合いの)テーブルにつく[つかせる] ▪ They *got round the table* with the employers. 彼らは雇用者と話し合いのテーブルについた ▪ You must *get* the two sides *round the table* and talking. あなたは両者をテーブルにつかせて話し合いをさせるべきだ.

go into tables 九々表などを覚え始める ▪ He had *gone into tables*, and was given new pencils. 彼は九々表を覚え始め, 新しい鉛筆をもらった.

High Table (学長・貴賓用に確保されている)大学内の食卓 ▪ He sat at *High Table* as an honored guest. 彼は来賓として貴賓席の食卓に着いた.

keep a good table いつも上等の食事をする ▪ He always *keeps a good table.* 彼はいつも高級な食事をしている.

keep an open table (食卓を開放して)客を歓迎する (*for*) ▪ He *keeps an open table for* all kinds of dogs. 彼はすべての種類の犬を歓迎する.

keep the table in a roar →set the TABLE in a roar.

keep the table laughing 食事中の客をずっともてなす ▪ At the dinner party we *kept the table laughing.* ディナーパーティーでは我々がずっと客を接待した.

lay ... on [***upon***] ***the table*** 《米》(議案など)を無期延期する; 《英》を上程する ▪ The bill *was laid on the table.* その法案はたな上げ[上程]された.

lay [***set, spread***] ***the table*** 食卓の用意をする ▪ She *set the table* for five men. 彼女は5人分の食卓の用意をした.

lie on the table (議案などが)無期延期[たな上げ]になっている ▪ The petition was ordered to *lie on the table.* その請願書はたな上げするように命じられた.

off the table (議題として)審議されないで (↔on the TABLE) ▪ Pay raises at our university are to be *off the table* for the next two years. 本学での増俸は向こう2年間審議されないことになっている.

on the table はっきり見える所に; (議案が)審議中で (↔ off the TABLE) ▪ Put your cards *on the* *table*. 札をはっきり見える所に置きなさい ▪ The editors put both sides *on the table*. 編集者たちは双方の立場をはっきりさせた ▪ The bill will soon be *on the table*. その議案はまもなく審議されるだろう.

put* [*have*]*... on the table ...を議題にする[審議する] ▪ They *put* the question of a separate Palestinian state *on the table*. パレスチナ国家の分離問題が審議された.

put** a person **under the table 人を酔いつぶす ▪ The drink was enough to *put* him *under the table*. その酒は彼を酔いつぶすほど強かった.

set* [*spread*] *the table →lay the TABLE.

set* [*keep*] *the table in a roar 食卓についた人々を大笑いさせる[させ続ける] ▪ His flashes of wit and humor *kept the table in a roar*. 彼のきらめく機知とユーモアが食卓についた人々を絶えず笑わせた.

sit* (*down*) *at* [*to*] *table 食卓につく ▪ They were just *sitting down to table*. 彼らはちょうど食卓につくところだった.

table manners テーブルマナー ▪ Most parents teach children *table manners* before school age. たいていの親は子供たちが就学年齢に達するまでに食卓での作法を教える. ☞必ず複数形.

table talk (深刻な[悲惨な]話題を避けた)軽い雑談, 食卓での気楽なおしゃべり ▪ We had some *table talk* over dinner. 私たちは夕食をとりながら, たわいもないおしゃべりをした.

***turn the tables on* [*upon*]** ...に対して形勢を逆転させる, さかねじをくわせる ▪ They had won the first match, though I hoped I might *turn the tables on* them in the return. 彼らは第1試合で勝ったが, 私は復しゅう試合では形勢を逆転させたいと思っていた. ☞すごろくの競技者が位置を転換するところから.

under the table [《主に英》***counter***] **1** 酔いつぶれて ▪ He was *under the table* then. 彼はその時酔いつぶれていた.

2 こっそりと, 賄賂として ▪ He gave me some money *under the table*. 彼は袖の下をくれた.

upon the table **1** 審議[検討]されて ▪ The question never came *upon the table*. その問題は1度も審議されなかった.

2 広く知れわたって ▪ The facts are all *upon the table*. それらの事実はどれも広く知れわたっている.

wait* (*at* [《米》*on*]) *table 給仕する ▪ He *waits* well *at table*. 彼は給仕がうまい ▪ He worked his way through college by *waiting table*. 彼は給仕をして働きながら大学を出た.

tablet /tǽblət/ 名 ***Keep taking the tablets!*** 《戯》錠剤を飲み続けるんだよ《正気を失ったような言動をする人に対して》.

tabloid /tǽblɔɪd/ 形 ***in tabloid form*** タブロイド版で; 要約されて ▪ He intends to give *in tabloid form* all the news printed by other papers. 彼は他の新聞に印刷されたすべてのニュースをタブロイド版で出そうと思っている.

taboo /təbúː/ 名 ***put* [*place*] *a taboo on ...*** を禁制にする ▪ The principal *placed a taboo on* smoking in school. 校長は学校での喫煙を禁じた.

put ... under taboo ...を禁制にする ▪ Gambling has *been put under taboo*. とばくは厳禁されてきた.

tack[1] /tæk/ 名 ***change** one's **tack*** 方針を変える ▪ You are wrong to vex him; *change your tack*. 彼をじらすのはまちがっている. 方針を変えなさい.

come* [*get*] *down to* (*brass*) *tacks 要点に触れる ▪ Let's cut out the polite preliminaries and *come down to tacks*. 外交辞令は切り上げて要点に触れようではありませんか.

Go sit on a tack! 《俗》つべこべ言わずに失せろ ▪ *Go sit on a tack*. Don't ever come back again. 文句を言わずに出て行け. 決して二度と戻ってくるな.

on the right* [*wrong*] *tack 方針を誤っていない[いる] ▪ You're quite *on the wrong tack* there. 君はその点ですっかり方針を誤っている ▪ I was *on the right tack*. 私は方針を誤っていなかった. ☞tack「行動の方針」.

on the tack 《俗》酒をやめて ▪ I am *on the tack* now. 今は酒をやめています.

sharp as a tack **1** →(as) SHARP as a needle.

2 非常に頭がよい ▪ He is *sharp as a tack* and doesn't miss a thing. 彼は非常に頭がいいので何も失敗しない.

3 粋でおしゃれな ▪ She always looks *sharp as a tack* at our meeting. 私たちの会に来るときの彼女はいつも粋でおしゃれだ.

***take a different tack* (*to*)** (...を)別な方法で解決する ▪ He *took a different tack to* the mathematical question. 彼は別のやりかたでその数学の問題を解いた.

try another* [*a new*] *tack 別の方針を試みる ▪ You'd better *try a new tack*. 別の方針を試みるほうがいいよ.

tack[2] /tæk/ 名 ***hard* [*soft*] *tack*** 固い[柔かい]パン; 粗[美]食 ▪ He lives on *hard tack*. 彼は粗食している.

tackle /tǽkəl/ 名 ***a flying tackle*** 《アメフト・ラグビー》フライングタックル; 宙に飛んで相手にタックルすること; 飛びかかること ▪ The police officer stopped the burglar with *a flying tackle*. 警察官は飛びかかって強盗を取り押さえた.

tactic /tǽktɪk/ 名 ***bully-boy tactics*** どなったり暴力に訴えたりの策略; ごろつき的な作戦 ▪ The crowd used *bully-boy tactics* to prevent the speaker from being heard. 群衆は大騒ぎの妨害行為をして演説者の声が聞こえないようにした.

tag /tæg/ 名 ***keep a tag on*** = keep (a) TAB on.

tag-rag /tǽgræg/ 名 ***tag-rag and bobtail*** 《軽蔑》有象無象 ▪ We don't take in any *tag-rag and bobtail* at our house. うちには有象無象は入れません.

tail[1] /teɪl/ 名 ***a tail-off*** 減少, 漸減, 下落 ▪ In recent years there has been *a tail-off* in the number of visitors. 近年は訪問客の数が徐々に減ってきている.

T

at the tail end (***of***) (…の)最後の部分に, 最終段階で; (の)最後尾で ▪ I didn't hear most of the speech—I only came in *at the tail end.* 演説の大部分は聞きそびれた. 終わりのところで入っただけなので.

at the tail of …のあとから, について ▪ She had come to Morocco *at the tail of* a Spanish embassy. 彼女はスペイン大使一行随伴でモロッコへ来た.

carry *one's* ***tail between*** *one's* ***legs*** →have one's TAIL between one's legs.

chase *one's* (***own***) ***tail*** 徒労に終わる, むだに行動する ▪ Any exposing of their injustice by yourself means *chasing your own tail.* 君が一人で彼らの不正をあばこうとしても徒労に終わるだけだ.

close on *a person's* ***tail*** 人のすぐ後ろに迫って ▪ There was another car *close on my tail.* 車がもう1台私のすぐ後ろに迫っていた.

fan *one's* ***tail*** 走る ▪ *Fan your tail* for home! 走って家へ帰るんだよ.

freeze *one's* ***tail off*** 凍える, 非常に寒くなる ▪ If you stand out there in the cold wind, you'll *freeze your tail off.* そんな寒風のなかに立っていたら凍えるぞ.

get off *one's* ***tail*** 《米俗》仕事にとりかかる ▪ Now let's *get off our tails.* さあ仕事にとりかかろうぜ. ☞tail「しり」.

get *one's* ***tail up*** [***down***] 元気づく[しょげる] ▪ They will *get their tails down* over this. 彼らはこのことでしょげるだろう.

go into tails (子供が成長して)燕尾服を着始める ▪ I first *went into tails* at sixteen. 私は16歳のときに初めて燕尾服を着た.

have … by the tail 《米俗》…を自分のものにする ▪ All young people can *have* happiness *by the tail.* 若い人たちはみな幸福を完全にわがものにできる.

have [***carry***] *one's* ***tail between*** *one's* ***legs*** しっぽを巻いている, 縮み上がっている (→with the TAIL between the legs) ▪ He slunk away, *carrying his tail between his legs.* 彼はしっぽを巻いてこそこそと逃げ去った.

have *one's* ***tail down*** [***up***] 《口》しょげている[意気盛んである, 自信満々である] ▪ The troops *had their tails up.* その軍勢は意気盛んであった.

in the tail of …の後ろから ▪ *In the tail of* the horses marched the foot regiment. 騎兵隊の後ろから歩兵隊が進軍した.

keep *one's* ***tail up*** 元気でいる ▪ I must try and *keep my tail up.* 元気でいるように努めねばならない.

on *one's* ***tail*** 接近して, 近くまで尾行して ▪ She heard his laugh and knew he must be *on his tail* at last. 彼女は彼の笑い声を聞いたので彼はもうそこまで来ているにちがいないと思った.

out of [***with***] ***the tail of the eye*** 横目で ▪ Miss Lucy noticed this *out of the tail of the eye.* ルーシー嬢はこれを横目で見てとった.

put a tail on …を尾行する[見張る] ▪ The police *put a tail on* some suspicious characters. 警察は何人かの不審人物を尾行した.

roll *one's* ***tail*** 《米俗》急いで行く ▪ They *rolled their tails* for Bavicola. 彼らはバビコラへ急行した.

sit on *a person's* ***tail*** (追い越そうとして)他の車のすぐ後にぴったりつく ▪ That car's been *sitting on my tail* for the past five minutes. あの車は5分前からこの車の後にぴったりついている.

tail(***s***) ***up*** (犬が)尾を立てて; (人が)とても元気で ▪ His *tail* is *up* still. 彼はまだとても元気だ ▪ It's *tails up* with them since then. 彼らはそれ以来至極元気だ.

the tail end (***of***) (…の)最後の部分 ▪ She just caught *the tail end of* the news. 彼女はニュースの最後のところを聞きかじっただけだった.

The tail wags the dog. 下の者が上の者を支配する, 主客が転倒する, 下剋上 ▪ We can't have *the tail wagging the dog.* 下の者に上の者を支配させてはならない.

turn tail **1** (背を向けて)逃げ去る ▪ He *turned tail* and fled. 彼は尻に帆をかけて逃げ去った.
2 (…を)見捨てる (*on, upon*) ▪ You are going to *turn tail on* your former principles. あなたは以前の主義を捨てようとしておられる. ☞タカ狩りでタカが獲物を追うのをあきらめて背を向けることから.

twist the tail of …にいやみなことをする ▪ He *twisted the tail of* a Connecticut insurance company. 彼はコネティカットのある保険会社にいやみなことをした.

with *one's* ***tail***(***s***) ***up*** 胸を張って, 自信満々で ▪ He went to the classroom *with his tail up* as a new teacher. 彼は新任教師として胸を張って教室に出向いた.

with the [*one's*] ***tail between the*** [*one's*] ***legs*** しっぽを巻いて, 縮みあがって (→have one's TAIL between one's legs) ▪ We sent the bully away *with his tail between his legs.* 我々は暴漢をしっぽを巻いて逃げさせた. ☞犬などがしっぽを巻いて逃げることから.

with the tail of the eye →out of the TAIL of the eye.

work *one's* ***tail off*** 猛烈に働く ▪ He *worked his tail off* to get done on time. 彼は時間通りに仕上げようとして必死で働いた.

tail[2] /teɪl/ 名 ***in tail*** 《法》限嗣相続の ▪ He was an heir *in tail.* 彼は限嗣相続人であった.

tailor /téɪlər/ 名 ***be tailor-made*** (…に)ぴったり合っている (*for*) ▪ The role of Eliza *was tailor-made for* her. イライザの役は正に彼女のはまり役だった.

Nine tailors make [***go to***] ***a man.*** 《諺》仕立て屋は9人で男一人前《仕立て屋の柔弱さをあざけって言う》.

The tailor makes the man. 《諺》仕立て屋が立派な男を作る,「馬子にも衣裳」.

tailspin /téɪlspìn/ 名 ***go*** [***send***] ***into a tailspin*** **1** (飛行機が)きりもみを始める[始めさせる] ▪ We *went into a tailspin.* 我々の機はきりもみを始めた.
2 がっかりする[させる] ▪ His wife's death *sent* him

into a tailspin. 妻の死で彼は落ち込んでしまった.

3 不景気になる[する], 混乱に陥る[陥れる] ▪ The oil crisis *sent* Japan's economy *into a tailspin.* 石油危機で日本の経済は混乱に陥った.

take[1] /teɪk/ 名 ***do a double take*** 《口》(ジョークなどが)しばらくしてやっとわかる ▪ People *do a double take* when I tell that joke. 私がそのジョークを言うと, みなしばらく考えてやっとわかってくれる.

do a takeoff of [***on***] …の物まねをする (→TAKE-off 2) ▪ He *did a* wonderful *takeoff on* Hitler. 彼はヒトラーの物まねを見事に演じた.

on the take 機会をねらって; 《口》賄賂がきく ▪ The big fish must be *on the take* in the water. その大きな魚は水の中で機会をねらっているにちがいない ▪ The policeman was *on the take.* その警官には賄賂がきいた.

take-off/ takeoff **1** (航空機などの)離陸 ▪ A drunken pilot was held at Heathrow just before *take-off* to Narita. ヒースロー空港で酒気を帯びたパイロットが成田への離陸直前に押さえられた.

2 物まね, パロディー (→do a TAKEoff of) ▪ It was a *takeoff* of the song "Hey Paula" by Paul & Paula. それはポールとポーラの「ヘイ・ポーラ」という歌のパロディーだった.

3 (跳躍するときの)踏み切り ▪ She seems to have twisted her ankle at *take-off.* 彼女はジャンプで踏み切るときに足首をひねったようだ.

takeout/《英》***takeaway*** 《米》 **1** 持ち帰り用の料理店 ▪ We usually call Samantha's, an Italian *takeout.* うちではふだん持ち帰りイタリア料理店のサマンサに電話する ▪ There's a Chinese *takeaway* on the corner. 街角に持ち帰り用の中華料理店がある.

2 持ち帰り用の料理 ▪ Give authentic Indian *takeout* a try. お持ち帰り用本場インド料理をお試し下さい.

3 ［限定的］ 持ち帰り用の ▪ Let's get a *takeaway* pizza. 持ち帰り用のピザを頼もうよ.

takeover (会社の)乗っ取り ▪ Sometimes a hostile *takeover* isn't as bad as it sounds. ときとして敵対的買収はその名の響きほど悪くないことがある.

take[2] /teɪk/ 動 ***as I take it*** 私の考えるところでは ▪ He is dissatisfied, *as I take it.* 私の見るところでは, 彼は不満足のようだ.

be taken 《戯》すでに結婚している, もういい人がいる ▪ He *is taken* and has three children. 彼はすでに結婚していて3人の子がいる.

be taken aback →ABACK.

be taken ill →ILL.

be taken short →SHORT.

be taken (***up***) ***with*** …に心を惹かれる, が好きになる ▪ He *was* much *taken with* my little child. 彼は私の子供がひどく好きになった.

have what it takes →WHAT it takes.

(***Is***) ***This*** (***seat***) ***taken?*** この席は空いていますか ▪ Excuse me. (*Is*) *This* (*seat*) *taken?*—No. Help yourself. 失礼. この席, どなたか?—いいえ, どうぞ.

It takes a thief to catch a thief. 《諺》泥棒は泥棒に捕まえさせろ, 「蛇(じゃ)の道は蛇(へび)」.

It takes all sorts [***kinds***] (***to make a world***). 《諺》世の中には様々な人がいなければならぬ.

It takes one to know one. 君も同類だよ ▪ Peter is a fool.—*It takes one to know one.* ピーターはばかだ—ばかはばかでなきゃ分からないよね.

it takes (***some***) ***getting used to*** 慣れる必要がある; 慣れたら何とかなる ▪ I never ate fish raw before. *It takes getting used to.* 刺身は食べたことがないんだ. 慣れないとな.

it takes (*A*) *B* (***to*** *do*) (Aが)…するのにBを要する[がかかる] ▪ *It* only *takes* (me) ten minutes *to* walk there. (私が)そこへ歩いて行くのに10分しかかからない.

take *a person* ***a blow*** [***whack***] 人に打撃を加える ▪ I *took* him *a blow* in the pit of his stomach. 私は彼のみぞおちにパンチを見舞った.

Take a hike [***walk***]***!*** 《米口》失せろ, あっちへ行け (→take a WALK 2) ▪ I've had enough of your excuses—just *take a hike.* 弁解はもうたくさんだ. 消えてくれ.

take a lot [***a bit, some***] ***of doing*** なかなか骨だ ▪ The work *takes a lot of doing.* その仕事はなかなか骨だ.

take a lot out of *a person* =TAKE it out of a person.

take adieu [***farewell***] 別れを告げる (*of*) ▪ Thus saying, he *took farewell.* こう言って彼は別れを告げた ▪ We *took* a last *adieu of* him. 我々は彼に最後の別れを告げた.

take and *do* 《米》進んで…する ▪ I'll *take and* bounce a rock off on your head. お前の頭に石をぶっつけるぞ.

take *a person* ***as*** *one* ***find*** *him* [***as*** *he* ***is, as*** *he* ***comes***] 人はこんなものだと受け取る ▪ You must *take* us *as* you *find* us. 私たちはこんな人間だと受け取ってくださらなくてはいけません.

take … as it comes ことをその場その場で処理する ▪ She likes to *take* life *as it comes* without worrying too much. 彼女は人生の苦難をあまり取り越し苦労せず, その都度対処したいと思っている.

take … as read →READ[3].

take … aside →take a person ASIDE.

take farewell →TAKE adieu.

take *one's* ***hat off to*** →HAT.

take home to *oneself* …をすっかり理解する ▪ He *took home to himself* the peculiar meaning of his friend's words. 彼は友人の言葉の特殊な意味がすっかりわかった.

take … in [***on***] *one's* ***way*** (人・場所)を途中訪問する, 寄る ▪ He did not *take* Rome *in his way.* 彼は途中ローマへ寄らなかった ▪ I *took* him *on my way.* 私は途中彼を訪問した.

take it ［can(not) を伴って否定文で］ (困難などに)耐える, 忍ぶ ▪ I *can't take it.* それはがまんできない ▪ That tire *could take it.* そのタイヤはどんな悪い道でも平気だった. ☞ボクシングから.

Take it away! (歌・演奏を)始めなさい ▪ *Take it away*. I wanna hear you play. 始めてくれ. 君の演奏を聞いてみたい.

take it easy →EASY.

take it easy on **1** …に優しくする ▪ *Take it easy on* my brother. He's been ill. 弟には優しくしてあげて. ずっと病気なんだもの.

2 …を使い[食べ, 飲み]過ぎない ▪ *Take it easy on* the coffee. Just one serving for each person. コーヒーは余分に飲まないでよ. ひとり1杯だけなんだから.

take it from here [there] (仕事を)途中で引き継ぐ ▪ I've corrected the errors I can find so you'll have to *take it from here*. 目にとまる誤りは訂正しておいたから, ここからは君が引き継ぎたまえ ▪ I explained how to do it, and let him *take it from there*. やり方を説明してから彼にあとを引き継がせた.

take it from me (that) = you may TAKE it from me that.

take it [things] hard →HARD.

take it ill [well] 悪く[よく]取る ▪ You must not *take it ill* of him. 彼のことを悪く取ってはいけません.

take it in 《米俗》パトロール中にひと休みする ▪ It's great to *take it in*, and smoke. パトロール中にひと休みして一服するのは楽しい.

take it on [upon] *oneself* ***to do*** …することを引き受ける; する責任を負う ▪ He *took it upon himself to* give orders. 彼は命令を下すことを引き受けた ▪ I will *take it upon myself to* solve this problem quickly. 私が責任を持って早急にこの問題を解決しましょう.

take it or leave it **1** (申し出を)そのまま受けるか拒むかのどちらかにする ▪ The price is $30. (You can) *take it or leave it*. 値段は30ドルです. それで諾否を決めてください.

2 どちらでもけっこうだ ▪ Do you like sugar in your coffee?—Well, I can *take it or leave it*. コーヒーに砂糖を入れますか?—いや, どちらでもけっこう.

take it out of *a person* **1** 人に腹いせする ▪ I *took it out of* him on the spot. 彼にその場で腹いせしてやった.

2 人を疲れさせる ▪ It was just the sort of day that *takes it out of* a man. まさに人を疲れさせるといった日だった.

take it out on *a person* 《米口》人に八つ当たりする, 返報する ▪ Look, *take it out on* me. さあ, 当たるなら私に当たってくれ.

take it (that) …と思う, 仮定する ▪ I *take it that* we are to come early. 私たちは早目に来なくてはいけないんですね.

take kindly to →KINDLY.

take … lying down →LIE[4].

take *oneself* ***off*** **1** 立ち去る ▪ He *took himself off* on tiptoe. 彼は抜き足差し足で立ち去った.

2 自殺する ▪ They may *take themselves off*. 彼らは自殺するかもしれない.

take on [upon] *oneself [one]* **1** (役目・責任などを)引き受ける, 負う ▪ Helen *took* the blame *upon herself*. ヘレンはその責めを負った.

2 思いきって…する (*to do*) ▪ I *took upon* me *to* go to Leeds. 私は思いきってリーズへ行った.

take one thing with another →ANOTHER.

take or leave 取るか捨てるかのいずれかに決める (→TAKE it or leave it 1) ▪ They must *take or leave* the proposal. その提案を取るか捨てるかいずれかに決めねばならない.

take *a person* ***out of*** *himself* 人に悩みなどを忘れさせる ▪ A change of air will *take* her *out of herself*. 転地すれば彼女は悩みを忘れるだろう.

take some doing →take a bit of DOING.

take *oneself [one]* ***to*** **1** …に身をゆだねる ▪ At last she *took* her *to* crying. 遂に彼女はひたすら泣いた.

2 …に赴く ▪ He will *take himself to* bed. 彼は床につくだろう.

take *a person* ***to be [for]*** *one's* ***husband [wife]*** 人を夫[妻]として受けいれる ▪ Will you *take* this man *to be [for] your husband*? あなたはこの人を夫として受けいれますか.

take to the air →AIR[1].

take to the boats [water] 船に乗る ▪ We *took to the water* and sailed down the river. 私たちは船に乗って川を下った.

taken altogether →ALTOGETHER.

taking all in all →ALL.

taking one (thing) with another 《英》あれこれ考えると, すべてを考慮すると ▪ *Taking one thing with another*, the design will be outmoded in three years. あれこれ考えると, そのデザインは3年もたてば時代遅れになるだろう ▪ These novelists, *taking one with another*, are masters of prose. これらの小説家は全体としては名文家だ.

We [I] can't take you anywhere! お前はどこへも連れて行けないね《行儀悪くした子供に向かって言う言葉》 ▪ *We can't take you anywhere*. —I didn't do anything. I'm innocent. どこへも連れて行ってやれないな—悪いことなんか何もしてないよ, 僕は無実だ ▪ You've got milk all over your shirt. *I can't take you anywhere*, can I? シャツにミルクをいっぱいこぼして. これじゃ, どこへも連れて行けないでしょ.

What do you take me for? 私をどんな人間だと思っているのか, 私を信用できないのか ▪ Just *what do you take me for*, an idiot? 一体わしをどんな人間と思っているのか, 間抜けだとでも? ▪ Did you have anything to do with this loss?—*What do you take me for?* この損失に君は関わりがあったのか?—この私を信用できないのか, 君は.

what it takes →WHAT.

You can't take it with you. 《諺》あの世まで金を持って行くことはできない.

you may [can] take it from me that …と信じてよい ▪ *You can take it from me that* he has not been idle. 彼は怠けていなかったと信じてよろしい.

taking /téɪkɪŋ/ 名 ***be*** *one's* ***for the taking/be there for the taking*** わけなく[無料で, 自由

に]手に入る ▪The gold medal *was hers for the taking*. 金メダルは楽に彼女の手に届くところにあった ▪If you're interested in the job, it's *there for the taking*. この仕事に関心があるのなら簡単に就職できるよ.

for the taking いつでも[無料で, 自由に]利用できる ▪He seemed to think the world all his *for the taking*. 彼はこの世はすべて自由に利用できる自分のものと思っているみたいだった.

in (a) taking **1**《主にスコ》困った立場で ▪We are *in* sad *taking* with influenza. 我々はみんなインフルエンザでひどく困っている.
2 気をもんで ▪By this time your mother is *in a* fine *taking*. 今頃お母さんはひどく気をもんでいるよ.

like taking candy from a baby →CANDY.

tale /teɪl/ 名 ***A tale never loses [tines] in the telling [carrying].***《諺》話は語ることによって減りはしない,「人の噂は倍になる」.

a tale of a tub [a roasted horse] たわいのないつくり話 ▪He entertained them with *a tale of a tub*. 彼はその連中をたわいのないつくり話で楽しませた. ☞a tale of a tub は Swift の風刺物語からとされるが, 実は16世紀ごろから使われている.

a tale of woe 悲しい身の上話, 泣き言 ▪They all had *tales of woe*. 彼らはみな泣き言をかかえていた.

a tale that is told はかないこと (《聖》*Ps.* 90. 9) ▪My troubles will roll away like *a tale that is told*. 私の悩みは夢のように消え去るだろう.

a tell-tale 人の秘密を言いふらす[告げ口をする]人, 密告者 ▪I don't want to be seen as *a tell-tale*. 人に告げ口屋と見られたくない.

bear [bring, carry] tales →tell TALEs.

by tale (重さ・長さではなく)数で ▪There oysters are sold *by tale*. そこではカキは数で売られている.

Herein [Therein] lies a tale.《戯》これに関連した話がある[これにはいささかわけがある] (→thereby hangs a TALE).

live to tell the tale 九死に一生を得る, 困難な状況にうまく対処する ▪He was attacked by a shark but he *lived to tell the tale*. 彼はサメに襲われたが九死に一生を得た.

old wives' tale →WIFE.

one's ***tale is told*** …は万事休す, の運はすでに尽きた ▪Poor lass, at last *her tale is told*. あの娘もかわいそうに, ついに彼女も万事休すだ.

tell *one's* ***own tale*** 説明をまたずして明らかだ ▪These withered crops *tell their own tale*. この枯れた作物を見れば(日照りのことは)言わずともわかる.

tell *one's* ***tale*** (…と)自分の話をする; 自分の言い分を述べる, 口上を言う ▪Every shepherd *tells his tale* under the hawthorn in the dale. すべての羊飼いは谷間のサンザシのもとで話をする ▪He *told his tale* without comment. 彼は説明抜きで口上を言った.

tell [bear, bring, carry] tales 告げ口をする ▪He *told tales* about me. 彼は僕の告げ口をした ▪Don't *tell tales* to mother. 母さんに告げ口をするなよ ▪She is always *telling tales* about other kids. 彼女は他の子供たちの告げ口ばかりしている.

tell tales out of school →SCHOOL[1].

tell the tale《俗》とほうもない話をする, (特に同情を呼ぶために)哀れっぽく話す ▪The temptation to *tell the tale* to the newcomer was too strong. その新参者にとほうもない話をしたいという誘惑はあまりにも強かった ▪We all *tell the tale* when we want money. 金がいるときには我々はみんな哀れっぽく話す.

thereby hangs a tale それには少しわけ[いわく]がある ▪Yet, though I say it, *thereby hangs a tale*. しかし私が言うのはおかしいが, それには少しわけがあるんだ. ☞Shakespeare の劇によく出る句だが, それ以前から使用されている.

talent /tǽlənt/ 名 ***a man of talent*** 才人 ▪We have *men of talent* here also. ここにだって才人はいる.

a talent scout スカウト《芸能・スポーツ界で才能のある新人を発掘する人》 ▪He currently works as *a talent scout* for the San Diego Padres. 彼は現在サンディエゴ・パドレスのスカウトをしている ▪She introduced herself as *a talent scout* for a television program. 彼女はあるテレビ番組の新人スカウトの仕事をしていると自己紹介した.

a talent show アマチュアの芸能コンテスト ▪She won the *talent show* by her dancing. 彼女はダンスをして芸能コンテストで優勝した.

have a talent for …の才がある ▪He *has a talent for* languages. 彼には語学の才がある.

hide *one's* ***talent in a napkin*** →hide ... in a NAPKIN.

talk[1] /tɔːk/ 名 ***all talk and no cider***《米口》しゃべるばかりでなんにもならないこと ▪The society is *all talk and no cider*. その協会はしゃべるばかりでなんにもならない.

all talk (and no deed [action]) ただ口先ばかり, 口先だけ ▪His politics are *all talk*. あの男の政治はただ口先ばかりだ ▪He is *all talk and no deed*. 彼はただ口先ばかりだ.

back talk →BACK chat.

big [tall] talk《口》大ぼら ▪There's nothing like *big talk* to draw contributions from peasantry. 農民たちから寄付を募るには大ぼらに勝るものはない.

end in talk 何の実も結ばない ▪Whether it will *end in talk* or not I can not say. 何の実も結ばないかどうかは分からない.

give a talk 話[講演]をする ▪He *gave a talk* on modern English literature. 彼は現代英文学について講演をした.

have a talk (…と)話をする (*with*) ▪I *had a* good [heart-to-heart] *talk with* him on the matter. その件について彼とよく[腹を割って]話し合った.

make a talk 人の口の端(は)にのぼる ▪That would *make a talk*. そんなことをしたら人のうわさになるだろう.

more cider and less talk《米口》おしゃべりよりも質 ▪What we want is *more cider and less*

T

talk. 我々がほしいのはおしゃべりよりも実質だ.

scotch talk 噂にふたをする ▪ She was keen to *scotch talk* that she had divorced her husband. 彼女は夫と離婚したという噂にふたをするのに大わらわだった.

small talk 世間話, 雑談 ▪ I engaged in *small talk* with a friend. 友人との雑談に加わった.

straight talk 率直な話 ▪ We will have some *straight talk* with them. 彼らと率直な話し合いをもとう.

sweet talk 《口》おあいそ, おべっか ▪ He tried a bit of *sweet talk*. 彼は少々おべっかを言ってみた.

Talk is cheap. 《諺》口で言うほうがたやすい,「口では何とでも言える」.

talk the talk 《口》人を喜ばせる[人が期待する]ことを言う ▪ You should *talk the talk* and walk the walk. 言うべきことは言い, やるべきことはやればいい.

tall talk →big TALK.

That's the talk! 《米》そうだ, そうだ, その通り ▪ No surrender. *That's the talk!* 降伏はしない. そうだ, そうだ.

the talk of the town 世間の評判[取りざた] ▪ Their divorce was *the talk of the town*. 彼らの離婚は世間の評判になっていた.

walk *one's* [***the***] ***talk*** 《口》言行を一致させる; うまく折り合って暮らす ▪ We should *walk our talk*. 私たちは言行を一致させるべきだ.

talk² /tɔːk/ 動 ***get*** (*oneself*) ***talked about*** 噂の種になる ▪ You'll *get yourself talked about* if you behave badly. 無作法な態度をとれば噂の種になる.

Look [***Hark***] ***who's talking!*** 《口》よく言うよ, 人のことを言えないだろ! ▪ Jimmy's a terrible driver. —*Look who's talking!* ジミーってなんてへたくそな運転なんだ—人のことを言えた義理かい.

Now you're talking! 《口》全くだ; そうこなくちゃ ▪ Jazz has a beauty of its own. —*Now you're talking!* ジャズには独特の美がある—全くだ. ☞目上の者に対しては使えない.

People will talk. 世間は口がうるさいもの ▪ You can't stay here—*people will talk*. ここにいてはだめだ. 人の口に戸は立てられない.

talk a mile a minute 《口》のべつにしゃべりまくる (→a MILE a minute) ▪ When he opens his mouth, he always *talks a mile a minute*. 彼は口を開くといつものべつにしゃべりまくる.

talk above *a person's* ***head*** = TALK over a person's head.

talk against time 時間つぶしにしゃべる;《米口》話を引き延ばして時間切れにする ▪ A minority may determine to *talk against time*. 少数派は討議を引き延ばして時間切れにしようと決心するかもしれない.

talk baby(***-talk***) 《米口》(...に)赤んぼう口調で話す, 赤んぼうに話しかけるような口調で話す (*to*) ▪ She never let him *talk baby-talk*. 彼女は彼が赤んぼうに話しかけるような口調で話しかけるのを許さなかった ▪ Don't *talk baby to* us any longer. もう我々に赤ちゃん言葉で話しかけるのはよしてくれ.

talk big [***large, tall***] 《口》大言をはく, ほらを吹く, 偉そうな口をきく ▪ Take that with a grain of salt; he always *talks big*. それは眉につばをつけて聞くがいい. あの男はいつもほらを吹くから ▪ Al *talks big*, does little. アルは大口をたたくが, ほとんど何もしない.

talk business まじめな話をする ▪ I'm willing to listen if you are going to *talk business*. 君がまじめな話をするのなら喜んで傾聴するよ.

talk cold turkey →TURKEY.

talk daft ばかなことを言う ▪ You're *talking daft*, dad. パパ, ばか言っちゃいけないよ. ☞非標準語法.

talk dirty →DIRTY¹.

talk Greek [***Hebrew, Double-Dutch, gibberish***] ちんぷんかんぷんなことをしゃべる ▪ The poor old woman *talked Greek* in her delirium. かわいそうにそのおばあさんは錯乱状態でわけの分からないことを口走った ▪ Stop *talking Double-Dutch*! 寝言みたいなことを言うのはよせ.

talk *a person's* ***head*** [***arm, ear***(***s***)***, leg, pants***] ***off*** 人がうんざりするほどしゃべる ▪ Once he gets to know you, he'll *talk your head off*. 彼はいったん君を知るようになったら, うんざりするほどしゃべるだろうよ ▪ Whenever I come across her she *talks my arm off*. 彼女とばったり会うといつもべらべらしゃべられる ▪ Grandma *talks my leg off*, but it is nice to just let her talk and listen to her. 祖母はぺちゃくちゃ話すが, 一人でおしゃべりをさせて聞き役に回るのはいいもんだ ▪ I'm afraid I almost *talked her pants off*. 自分ばかりがしゃべって危うく彼女をうんざりさせるところだったと思う.

talk *one's* ***head*** [***arm, ear***] ***off*** 《俗》のべつ幕なしにしゃべる ▪ Dona *talked her ear off*. ドーナはのべつ幕なしにしゃべった.

talk *oneself* ***hoarse*** →shout oneself HOARSE.

talk in *one's* ***sleep*** 寝言を言う ▪ He often *talks in his sleep*. 彼はよく寝言を言う.

talk large →TALK big.

talk nineteen to the dozen →nineteen to the DOZEN.

talk *oneself* ***out of*** ...からうまく言い逃れる ▪ You'll have a job to *talk yourself out of* this. これからうまく言い逃れるのは一仕事だろうよ.

talk out of *one's* ***backside*** 《英卑》くだらないことを言う; ほらを吹く (→talk out of one's ARSE) ▪ Don't *talk out of your backside* at your age. いい歳をしてくだらないことを言うな.

talk out of the top of *one's* ***head*** 全くばかげたことを話す, 愚にもつかぬことを言う ▪ He *talked out of the top of his head* at the conference. 彼はその会議で全くばかげたことをしゃべった.

talk over *a person's* ***head*** 人に理解できないような高尚なことを話す ▪ He may be very clever, but he always *talks over our heads*. 彼はとても賢いのかもしれないが, いつも我々には理解できないような高尚な話をする.

talk posh [***well-off***] 上流階級の言葉を使う

▪ He likes to *talk posh*. 彼は上流の言葉うかいをするのが好きだ.

talk** a person **ragged 人をうんざりさせるほどしゃべりまくる ▪ He *talked* us *ragged* at the meeting. 会議では彼が一人でしゃべりまくった.

talk sailor 船乗り言葉を使う ▪ I could *talk sailor* like an old salt. 私は老水夫のように船乗り言葉が使えた.

talk tall →TALK big.

talk the bark off a tree →BARK[2].

talk the hind leg(s) off a donkey [a dog, a horse] →HIND LEG.

talk through** one's **hat →HAT.

talk through (the back of)** one's **neck [head] → speak through (the back of) one's NECK.

talk till** one **is blue in the face →till one is BLUE in the face.

***talk to** oneself* ひとりごとを言う ▪ He began to examine me carefully, *talking to himself*. 彼はひとりごとを言いながら, 私を綿密に調べ始めた.

talk to a brick wall →WALL.

talk…to death うんざりするほど…に談じこむ ▪ I *talked* them *to death*. 彼らがうんざりするほどしゃべりまくってやった.

talk tough (on) (…について)厳しい口調で意見を言う ▪ She always *talks tough* but she is soft at heart. 彼女はいつもは厳しく言うが本当は優しい人だ.

talk turkey →TURKEY.

talk** one's **way 説きつけて進む ▪ He *talked his way* past a detective. 彼は探偵を説きつけてそばを通り過ぎた.

talk** one's **way out of →WAY.

talk well-off →TALK posh.

talk wise 生意気な口をきく ▪ Don't *talk wise*, now that you've quit. もうお前はやめたのだから偉そうな口をたたくな.

talking of …と言えば ▪ *Talking of* Switzerland—have you ever been there in winter? スイスと言えば, 冬おいでになったことがありますか.

the most talked of man 最も話題となった人 ▪ Oscar Wilde was *the most talked of man* of his day. オスカー・ワイルドは当時最も話題の人だった.

You can talk. 《口》 **1** 結構なご身分だねえ. **2** =You can't TALK.

You can't talk./ Look who's talking!/ You're a (fine) one to talk. 《口》君だってひどいもんだ, 君だって大きなことは言えない ▪ I can't believe he isn't done with his homework yet.—*You can't talk*. When are you going to finish yours? 彼が宿題をまだ終えていないなんて信じられないな—君だって大きなことは言えないよ. 君のはいつ終わらせるつもり?

talker /tɔ́ːkər/ 名 ***a fast talker*** 《米口》口先の巧みな人, 詐欺師 ▪ Don't trust him. He's *a fast talker*. 彼の話を信じてはだめだ. 口先がうまいから.

The greatest talkers are always the least doers. 《諺》一番口数の多い者に限って一番仕事をしない《口先ばかりで実行が伴わない》.

talking /tɔ́ːkɪŋ/ 名 ***do the talking*** スポークスマン[代弁者]をやる ▪ I always have to *do the talking* for my stubborn hubby! いつだって私ががんこな亭主を代弁しなくてはならないのよ.

give** a person **a talking to [talking-to] 《口》人を叱責する, にお目玉をくわす ▪ He is a person capable of *giving* a seaman *a talking to*. 彼は水夫にお目玉をくわすことのできる人だ.

tall /tɔːl/ 形副 ***a tall order*** →a large ORDER.

a tall story [tale] ほら話 ▪ Nobody will believe his *tall tales*. 彼のほら話なんか誰も信じまい.

stand tall 自信たっぷりにことを処理する ▪ My former manager's advice to *stand tall* was what helped me to succeed. 私が成功したのは, 自信を持てという元の監督の助言のお陰だった.

talk tall →TALK big.

walk tall 《米口》いばって歩く, さっそうと歩く ▪ I'm proud of it. I tell you I *walk tall*. 僕はそれが得意なんだ. ほんとに大手を振って歩けるんだ.

tally /tǽli/ 名 ***by the tally*** (野菜など)5ダース束ずつ ▪ I buy turnips *by the tally*. 私はカブを5ダース束ずつ買います.

live (on) tally 《俗》(結婚せずに)同棲(せい)する (*with*) ▪ He had for years been *living (on) tally with* a woman. 彼は何年もある女性と同棲していた.

tan[1] /tæn/ 名 ***get a good tan on*** …をうんと日やけさせる ▪ She *got a good tan on* her skin. 彼女の肌はうんと日やけした.

tan[2] /tæn/ 動 ***tan** a person's **hide*** →dress a person's HIDE.

tandem /tǽndəm/ 副 ***drive [ride] tandem [in tandem]*** (2頭の馬を)縦につないで駆る ▪ The horses, *driven tandem*, were dragging a heavy barge down the canal. 縦につないで駆られている2頭の馬が重い荷船を引っぱって運河を下っていた.

in tandem (with) (…と)協力して ▪ She ran the business *in tandem with* her husband. 彼女は夫と力を合わせて事業を経営した.

tangent /tǽndʒənt/ 名 ***fly [go] off at [in, on, upon] a tangent*** (考えが)突然わき道へそれる ▪ He *flew off at a tangent* from his main subject. 彼は主題から突然わき道へそれた.

tangle[1] /tǽŋgəl/ 名 ***get into a tangle*** もつれる; 混乱する ▪ The traffic *got into a tangle*. 交通は混乱した.

in a tangle もつれて; 混乱して ▪ This string is all *in a tangle*. この糸はすっかりもつれている ▪ The traffic was *in a* frightful *tangle*. 交通はひどく混乱していた.

tangle[2] /tǽŋgəl/ 動 ***a tangled web*** →WEB.

be tangled with (主に悪い仲間)とつき合っている ▪ He has *been tangled with* some bad friends. 彼は悪い仲間とつき合っている.

get tangled up in **1** …に絡む ▪ Nets have *got tangled up in* the fishing boat's propeller. 網が

T

漁船のスクリューに絡んでいる.

2 …に巻き込まれる[関わる] ▪ I wouldn't *get tangled up in* a crime. 犯罪に関わるなんてごめんだ.

tango /tǽŋgoʊ/ 動 ***It takes two to tango.*** →TWO.

tank[1] /tæŋk/ 名 ***be built like a tank*** [***castle***] →BUILT like a tank.

go in the tank 《米俗》試合を投げる ▪ In the third round the fighter *went in the tank*. 第3ラウンドでそのボクサーは試合を投げた.

in the tank 《米口》(株価が)急落して ▪ Auto and metal stocks are doing well, but everything else is *in the tank*. 自動車と金属の株は好調だが, それ以外は株価が急落している.

tank[2] /tæŋk/ 動 ***be tanked up*** 《英口》泥酔している ▪ He *was tanked up* on gin and orange juice. 彼はオレンジジュース割りのジンで泥酔状態だった.

tantamount /tǽntəmàʊnt/ 形 (***be***) ***tantamount to*** ほとんど…に等しい ▪ The Queen's request *was tantamount to* a command. 女王の願いはほとんど命令に等しかった.

tantrum /tǽntrəm/ 名 ***be in*** *one's* ***tantrums/be in a tantrum*** 《口》かんしゃくを起こしている ▪ He *was* always *in a tantrum* if interrupted. 彼はさえぎられるときまってかんしゃくを起こした.

go [***get***] ***into*** *one's* [***a***] ***tantrums*** 《口》かんしゃくを起こす ▪ He told her not to *get into a tantrum*. 彼はかんしゃくを起こすなと彼女に言った.

throw [***have***] ***a tantrum*** 急に怒り出す ▪ Don't *throw a tantrum* if they say no. 彼らが断ってもかっとなったらだめだぞ.

tap[1] /tæp/ 名 ***in tap*** 飲み口がついて; いつでも使えるようにして (=on TAP 1) ▪ There's a pretty brew *in tap* at the bar. あのバーではすてきな酒がいつでも飲める.

on tap **1** 飲み口がついて; いつでも使えるようにして ▪ He has eloquence always *on tap*. 彼は雄弁をいつでもふるえるようにしている.

2 《英・株式》(大蔵省証券などが)いつでも定価で買える ▪ Additional Treasury Bills are *on tap* at a low rate. 追加の大蔵省証券は安い値段でいつでも買える.

turn on the tap 《口》泣きだす ▪ She began to *turn on the tap* at the news. その知らせを聞くと彼女は泣きだした.

tap[2] /tæp/ 名 ***blow*** [***sound***] ***taps*** 《米》消灯らっぱを吹き鳴らす ▪ *Taps* had *been sounded* long since. 消灯らっぱはずっと前に吹き鳴らされていた.

on *one's* ***taps*** 立って, 動き回って ▪ They have to be *on their taps* almost all the time. 彼らはほとんど始終立っていなければならない. ☞tap「靴のかかと」.

tap[3] /tæp/ 動 ***tap the wire*** [***cable***] 通信を傍受する ▪ The telephone presents facilities for the dangerous practice of *tapping the wire*. 電話は通信傍受という危険な作業の便宜を与える.

tape[1] /teɪp/ 名 ***breast the tape*** (競走で)テープを切る, 1着になる ▪ The sprinter *breasted the tape*. そのスプリンターが1着になった.

cut (***through***) (***the***) ***red tape*** お役所風を除く, 形式的な手続きをやめる (→red TAPE) ▪ There is a lot of *red tape* to *be cut*. 除くべきお役所風はたくさんある ▪ How can we *cut red tape*? どうすれば面倒な手続きをやめられるか. ☞昔英国で公文書をとじるのに赤いひもを用いたことから.

masking tape 保護テープ《ペンキを塗る際に周囲が汚れるのを防ぐ粘着テープ》 ▪ Put *masking tape* around windows so you don't get paint on them. ペンキがつかないように窓の周囲に養生テープを張りなさい.

red tape 《軽蔑》 **1** お役所気質, 官僚主義 ▪ I've had enough of *red tape*. 官僚主義はもうこりごりだ.

2 お役所的で面倒な手続き ▪ It took weeks to get a visa owing to *red tape*. 形式的な手続きのせいでビザをとるのに何週間もかかった ▪ I had to go through a lot of *red tape* to get the repair work done. 修理をしてもらうのにいろいろと面倒な役所での手続きをしなければならなかった.

tape[2] /teɪp/ 動 ***have*** [***get***]***…taped*** (***out***) 《主に英》…を見抜く; を理解する ▪ You *had* this world all *taped*. 君はこの世の中をすっかり見抜いていた ▪ You*'ve got* all this *taped out* wrong. 君はこれをすべてまちがって理解している.

taper /téɪpər/ 名 ***hold a taper to the devil*** 悪人のちょうちん持ちをする ▪ He stooped so low as to *hold a taper to the devil*. 彼は悪人のちょうちん持ちをするほど卑劣な行いをした.

tapis /tǽpi/ 名 ***be*** [***come***] ***on*** [***upon***] ***the tapis*** 審議されている[される] ▪ The question has for a long time *been upon the tapis*. この問題はずっと前から審議されてきている. ☞F sur le tapis 'on the tablecloth'.

tar[1] /tɑːr/ 名 ***a touch of tar*** 《侮蔑》黒人の血の混じっていること ▪ There was *a touch of tar* in her. 彼女には黒人の血が混じっていた.

(***as***) ***brisk as bees in a tar bucket*** 《米口》とても活発な ▪ Things are *as brisk as bees in a tar bucket*. 景気はとても活発だ.

(***as***) ***busy as a bee in a tar barrel*** 《米口》とても忙しい ▪ He made himself *as busy as a bee in a tar barrel*. 彼は自分からとても忙しくした.

have *one's* ***head in a tar barrel*** 《米口》困っている ▪ Pete *had his head in a tar barrel* sure enough. ピートは確かに困っていた.

knock [***beat, whale***] ***the tar out of*** *a person* 《米口》人を情け容赦なくなぐる ▪ He *beat the* living *tar out of* me two weeks ago. 彼は2週間前僕をさんざんにぶんなぐった.

lose the ship [***sheep***] ***for a halfpennyworth of tar*** →HALFPENNYWORTH.

tar[2] /tɑːr/ 動 ***be tarred with the same stick*** [***brush***] **1** 同様な欠点を持っている ▪ Now this Jerard *is tarred with the same stick*. ところでこのジェラードも同様な欠点を持っている.

2 他人のせいで不当に非難される ▪ My big brother had been a troublemaker at school, so I *was tarred with the same brush*. 兄が学校で問題児

だったせいで僕まで不当に色眼鏡で見られた. ☞羊の放牧から, 同じ群れの羊の傷は同じ色のタールを塗って治療された.

tar and feather *a person* 人にタールを塗りその上に鳥の羽をなすりつける《特にアメリカで評判のよくない人物に暴徒の加える私刑》 ▪ If I escape from town without *being tarred and feathered*, I shall consider it good luck. タールを塗られその上に鳥の羽をなすりつけられずに町から逃れられれば幸運だと思う.

tar-brush /tά:rbrʌ̀ʃ/ 名 ***a lick*** [***touch***] ***of the tar-brush*** 《侮蔑》黒人の血の混じっていること ▪ There's *a* strong *touch of the tar-brush* in her. 彼女には黒人の血が濃く混じっている.

be touched with the same tar-brush 同様な欠点を持ってる ▪ All alike *were touched with the same tar-brush*. みな残らず同様な欠点があった.

be touched with the tar-brush 《侮蔑》黒人の血が混じっている ▪ The boy *is* very slightly *touched with the tar-brush*. その少年にはごくわずか黒人の血が混じっている.

tardy /tά:rdi/ 形 ***tardy at*** [***for***] 《米》…に遅れる ▪ We were *tardy at* our matins. 私たちは朝の祈りに遅れた.

tare[1] /teər/ 名 ***tare and tret*** 風袋算定法 ▪ We learnt *tare and tret* together, at school. 私たちは学校でいっしょに風袋算定法を学びました.

tare[2] /teər/ 名 ***sow tares among*** *people* [*a person's* ***wheat***] 人をだまして害を加える《《聖》*Matt.* 13. 25》 ▪ They will not suffer a foe to *sow tares among* us. 彼らは敵が我々をだまして害を加えるのを許さない.

target /tά:rgət/ 名 ***an easy target*** =a soft MARK.

on target 正確な, 的を射た ▪ Their criticisms were *on target*. 彼らの批判は的を射ていた.

shoot the same target 意見が一致する, 一致団結する ▪ Let's go ahead for our goal because we're *shooting the same target*. 我々の意見は一致しているのだから目標に向かって進もう.

task /tæsk|tɑ:sk/ 名 ***be at*** *one's* ***task*** 仕事をしている ▪ He *was* busy *at his task*. 彼は忙しく仕事をしていた.

set *a person* ***a task*** 人に仕事[課業]を課する ▪ My master *set* me *a task*. 先生が僕に課題を出した.

take [***call, bring***] *a person* ***to task*** 人をとがめる, 非難する (*for, about*) ▪ My employer *took* me severely *to task for* neglecting my duty. 雇主は務めを怠ったと言って私をきつくとがめた.

tassel /tǽsəl/ 名 ***in tassel*** 《米》(トウモロコシが)房をつけて ▪ Early corn is *in tassel* now. 早生のトウモロコシは今房をつけている.

taste /teɪst/ 名 ***a matter of taste*** 趣味の問題, 人の好き好き ▪ Music is a hard thing to review because it is all *a matter of taste*. 音楽は全く人の好みの問題なので批評しうらい代物だ.

a taste 《口》〚副詞的に〛ちょっぴりと ▪ Nancy will tidy the room *a taste*. ナンシーがちょっぴり部屋の掃除をしてくれるでしょう.

an acquired taste (初めきらいだったが)何度か食べて[飲んで]みて好きになるもの; 次第に好きになった人[物] ▪ Beer is *an acquired taste* with me. ビールは私にとって次第に好きになったものです. ☞acquire a taste for「…を好きになる」から.

big taste 麻薬注射への欲求 ▪ Your *big taste* is going to get worse unless you get treatment. 麻薬注射への欲求は治療をしないとますますひどくなるよ.

get a taste of …の味を知る, をちょっぴり経験する ▪ You will *get a taste of* it one of these days. 近いうちにその味がわかるでしょうよ.

give *a person* ***a taste of*** 人に…の味を知らせる, をちょっぴり経験させる ▪ I *gave* him *a taste of* the whip. 彼にむちの痛さを知らせてやった.

have a taste for …に趣味を持っている, が好きだ ▪ He *has a taste for* true humor. 彼は真のユーモアの趣味がある ▪ He *has a taste for* Manila cigars. 彼はマニラ葉巻きが好きだ.

have a taste of …を味わってみる, ちょっぴり経験してみる ▪ Won't you *have a taste of* this cake [wine]? このケーキ[ワイン]を味わってみませんか.

in bad [***poor***] ***taste*** 下品で ▪ His behavior was *in bad taste*. 彼のふるまいは下品だった.

in good [***excellent***] ***taste*** 上品で ▪ His literary work is *in good taste*. 彼の文芸作品は上品だ.

leave a bad [***nasty, sour***] ***taste in the*** [*one's*] ***mouth*** あと味が悪い, いやな印象を残す ▪ The poems *leave a nasty taste in the mouth*. これらの詩はいやな印象を残す.

out of taste (舌が)味がわからない ▪ After such bitterness, my mouth is *out of taste*. あんなに苦い物を食べたので, 私の口は味がわからない.

There is no accounting for taste(***s***)./ ***Tastes differ.*** 《諺》人の好みは説明できない[それぞれ],「たで食う虫も好き好き」.

to taste 好みに応じて ▪ Please add sugar *to taste*. 好みに応じて砂糖をお入れください.

to *one's* ***taste*** 好みに合って ▪ The other girl is more *to my taste*. もう一人の娘のほうがいっそう僕の好みに合う.

to the [***a***] ***King's*** [***Queen's***] ***taste*** 申し分なく, 完全に ▪ You worked him *to a Queen's taste*. 君はあの男を完全に働かしたね.

tater /téɪtər/ 名 ***nuke a tater*** 《主に米豪》電子レンジでポテトを焼く ▪ I don't have an oven for baked potatoes, so I'll *nuke a tater*. ベイクドポテトを作るのにオーブンがないので電子レンジでポテトを焼くわ.

tatter /tǽtər/ 名 ***in*** (***rags and***) ***tatters*** ぼろを着て; 〚in tatters で〛(希望・夢・計画が)ぼろぼろ[粉々]になって ▪ They go barefoot, and all *in tatters*. 彼らははだしの上すっかりぼろを着て歩き回る ▪ My dream of a world cruise lay *in tatters*. 世界一周の船旅の夢は粉々に砕け散った.

tear ... to tatters …をずたずたに裂く; (議論など)を徹底的に論破する ▪ These philosophers *tear* arguments *to tatters*. こういう哲学者たちは議論を徹底的に論破する.

tattoo /tætúː, tə-/ 名 ***beat a tattoo on*** …をコツコツたたく ▪ He was *beating a tattoo on* the table with his fingers. 彼は指先きでテーブルをコツコツたたいていた.

beat* [*play*] *the devil's tattoo 指で卓上(など)をコツコツたたく《不快・焦燥などの表示》 ▪ She *beat the devil's tattoo* for some moments. 彼女はしばらくの間指で卓上をコツコツたたいた. ☞tattoo「物をどしどし打ち鳴らすこと」.

taw /tɔː/ 名 ***bring*** *a person* ***to taw*** 人を(競技の)出発点に立たせる《比喩的にも》 ▪ If you don't do so, I'll *bring* you *to taw*. 君がそうしなければ私がふんぎりをつけさせるぞ.

come up to taw 出発点につく ▪ The children *came up to taw* to begin their game of marbles. 子供たちはビー玉遊びを始める出発点についた.

tax /tæks/ 名 ***after taxes***《米》税金を差引いて ▪ *After taxes* his take home pay is only $300. 税金を差引いて彼の手取り給料はわずか300ドルである.

crippling taxes 法外に高い税金 ▪ All the populace were suffering from *crippling taxes*. 全民衆は法外な重税に苦しんでいた.

in taxes 税金に ▪ He paid £50 *in taxes*. 彼は税金に50ポンド払った.

tax trap《口》税金の落とし穴 ▪ Be careful not to be caught in a *tax trap*. 税の落とし穴にはまらないように注意しなさい.

taxi /tǽksi/ 名 ***a Tijuana taxi***《俗》ティファナ・タクシー《パトカーを指す隠語》 ▪ I've got *a Tijuana taxi* in sight. パトカーが目に入ったぞ.

tea /tiː/ 名 ***afternoon* [*five-o'clock*] *tea*** 午後のお茶, おやつ ▪ My first introduction to "*afternoon tea*" took place during this visit. 私が初めて「午後のお茶」を知ったのはこの訪問の間のことであった.

another cup of tea →CUP.

at tea ティーを取って ▪ They were *at tea* when I called. 訪問してみると彼らはティーを取っていた.

a person's ***cup of tea***《口》〖主に否定文で〗人の好み ▪ She is not *my cup of tea*. 彼女はぼくのタイプじゃないな.

have* [*take*] *tea ティーを取る ▪ We *take tea* at four. 私たちは4時にティーを取る.

make* (*the*) *tea 茶を入れる ▪ Will you *make* some fresh *tea*, please? 茶を入れ替えてくれませんか.

not for all the tea in China 中国の茶を全部もらっても[絶対に]…しない ▪ I would *not* marry him *for all the tea in China*. 彼とは絶対に結婚しないわ.

read the tea-leaves (カップに残った)茶殻の模様で運勢を占う, 紅茶占いをする ▪ Can anyone *read the tea-leaves* here? ここに誰か紅茶占いのできる者はいないか.

take* [*have*] (*a*) *high tea →HIGH.

tea and sympathy お茶と共感, 悩んでいる人への思いやりと慰め ▪ Could be you need some *tea and sympathy*. 君は思いやりと慰めを必要としているのじゃないかな, 多分《主語 it の省略》 ▪ A woman used *tea and sympathy* to calm down a knife-wielding thief. ある女性がナイフを振りかざした盗賊の気を静めるのにお茶といたわりでもてなした.

teach /tiːtʃ/ 動 ***I'll teach you* (*how*) *to*** *do* …するとひどい目にあわせてやるぞ ▪ *I'll teach you how to* brag another time. 今度ほらを吹いたらひどい目にあわせてやるぞ ▪ *I'll teach you to* meddle in my affairs. 余計な世話をやくとひどい目にあわせてやる.

teach *oneself* 独学する ▪ He *taught himself* English. 彼は英語を独学した.

teach* (*a*) *school →SCHOOL[1].

teach your grandmother to suck eggs →GRANDMOTHER.

team /tiːm/ 名 ***a* [*the*] *whole* [*full*] *team* (*and the yellow dog under the wagon*)**《米口》すぐれた人物 ▪ You'll find him *a full team* at anything. 彼は何をやらしてもすぐれた人物だということがわかりましょう ▪ Mother's *the whole team and the yellow dog under the wagon*! おふくろはすぐれた人物だよ.

drive too much team《米口》手に余ることをやろうとする ▪ But I undertook to *drive too much team*. だが私は手に余ることをやろうと企てたわけだった.

tear[1] /tɪər/ 名 ***bathed* [*drowned, dissolved*] *in tears*** 涙にかきくれて ▪ The unhappy woman, *drowned in tears*, told her story. 不幸な女性は涙にかきくれて身の上話をした.

be bored to tears 非常に退屈している, 全く関心がない (→bore a person to TEARs) ▪ I *am bored to tears* by the latest TV dramas. 最近のテレビドラマにはうんざりしている.

be prone to tears すぐに泣く ▪ My sister *is* very shy and *prone to tears*. 妹はすごくはずかしがりですぐに泣くの.

bore *a person* ***to tears*** 人をあきあきさせる (→be bored to TEARs) ▪ The principal's talk *bored* us *to tears*. 校長の話に僕たちはあきあきした.

bring tears to *a person's* ***eyes*** 人の目に涙を催させる ▪ These words *brought tears to her eyes*. この言葉が彼女の目に涙を催させた.

bring *a person* ***to tears*** 人を泣かせる ▪ The story *brought* them *to tears*. その話で彼らは泣いた.

burst into tears*/*break out in* [*into*] *tears わっと泣きだす ▪ She could not help *bursting into tears*. 彼女はわっと泣きださずにはいられなかった ▪ When I heard this song I *broke out in tears*. この歌を耳にしたとき私は泣き崩れた.

draw* [*wring*] *tears from …の涙を誘う ▪ Her pitiful story *drew tears from* all who heard it. 彼女の哀れな身の上話は聞く者すべての涙を誘った.

end in tears《英》結局まずい結果に終わる ▪ My friendship with him *ended in tears*. 彼と私の友情は結局まずい結果に終わった.

in tears (悲しみ・同情の)涙を流して ▪ The people

T

were all *in tears.* 人々はみんな涙を流していた.

move [***reduce***] *a person* ***to tears*** 人を感動させて泣かせる ▪ The sad story *moved* us *to tears.* その悲しい話に私たちは心打たれて泣いた.

shed tears over 〚主に否定文で〛…のことで悲しむ ▪ I won't *shed tears over* one little failure. 1回のささいな失敗のことで悲しんだりしないぞ.

with tears in *one's* ***eyes*** [***voice***] 涙を浮かべて[にむせんで] ▪ She answered *with tears in her voice.* 彼女は涙にむせんで答えた.

French [etc.] ***without tears*** 楽しいフランス語[など]の学び方 ▪ Please click the links to Latin *without Tears* to find out more. さらに詳細は「楽しく学ぶラテン語」へのリンクをクリックしてください.

tear[2] /teər/ 名 ***full tear*** 〚副詞的に〛まっしぐらに ▪ He galloped away, *full tear*, to the next stage. 彼は次の宿場に向けてまっしぐらに馬を疾駆させて行った.

get [***go***] ***on a tear*** 《米口》浮かれ騒ぐ, あばれ回る ▪ The small river *went on a tear* once in a while. その小川はときどき荒れ狂った.

tear and wear/wear and tear 裂け損じること; (心身の)消耗 ▪ The *tear and wear* of the campaign was telling severely on the yeomanry. その遠征の消耗が郷士階級にひどくこたえていた.

tear[3] /teər/ 動 ***be torn between*** (相反する欲望)のどちらにしようかと迷う, の間で板ばさみになっている ▪ She *was torn between* the two choices. 彼女はその二つの選択肢のどちらにしようかと迷った ▪ He's *torn between* going to the mountains or going to the seashore. 彼は山に行くか海にするかで迷っている.

tear *oneself* ***away*** 身を裂かれる思いで[しぶしぶ]立ち去る[離れる] ▪ She couldn't *tear herself away* from that painting. その絵を前にして彼女はなかなか立ち去りがたかった.

tear … in two [***half***] 二つに引きちぎる ▪ He *tore* her letter *in two.* 彼は彼女の手紙を二つにちぎった.

tear *oneself* ***loose*** (***from***)/***tear loose*** (…から身を)ふりほどく (= break LOOSE) ▪ He caught me by the arm but I *tore myself loose* and ran for help. 彼は私の腕をつかんだが私は身を振りほどき走って助けを求めた.

tear *a person* ***off a strip/tear strips off*** *a person* →STRIP[1].

tear (***out***) *one's* ***hair*** 髪をかきむしる《怒り・悲しみの表示》 ▪ He beat his breast, he *tore his hair.* 彼は胸をたたき, 髪をかきむしった.

tear to pieces [***bits, shreds***] **1** ずたずたに引き裂く ▪ Eight cars *were torn to pieces* by the explosion. 車が8台爆発でバラバラになった.
2 散々にやっつける ▪ His latest novel *was torn to pieces* by a critic. 彼の最近の小説はある批評家によってめちゃめちゃに批評された ▪ It *tore* his reputation *to shreds.* それは彼の評判をめちゃめちゃにしてしまった.

tear *one's* ***way*** しゃにむに進む ▪ He *tore his way* toward his idol. 彼は自分の偶像の方へしゃにむに進んで行った.

That's torn it. →THAT's done it.

tee /tiː/ 名 ***to a tee*** →to a T.

teen /tiːn/ 名 ***in*** *one's* ***first*** [***last***] ***teen*** 13 [19]の年に ▪ I was as inquisitive as a boy *in his first teen.* 私は13歳の少年のように好奇心が強かった.

in [***out of***] *one's* ***teens*** 10代で[を過ぎて] ▪ The chamber-maid was not exactly *in her teens.* 客室係の女性は正確に言えば10代ではなかった.

teenager /tíːnèɪdʒər/ 名 ***status-zero teenagers*** (教育・職・収入がなく犯罪・麻薬に手を出す)社会的地位ゼロの10代の若者 ▪ The youth leader managed to get some *status-zero teenagers* interested in gardening. 青年指導員は悪に染まった10代の若者らに何とか園芸に興味をもたせることができた.

teeter /tíːtər/ 動 ***teeter on the brink*** [***edge***] (***of***) (…という)困難な[危険な]状況が迫っている ▪ Our country is *teetering on the brink of* an economic crisis. わが国に経済危機という苦境が迫っている.

teething /tíːðɪŋ/ 名 ***have*** [***go through***] ***teething problems*** [***troubles, pains***] (仕事などの)初期段階の困難を経験する, 創業の苦労がある, 初めは操作が難しい ▪ We *had teething troubles* with our new television. 新しいテレビの操作が初めの間はやっかいだった ▪ My new car is *having teething troubles*, so I'll take it back to where I bought it. うちの新車は当初の不具合が出ているので, 買った店で見てもらってこよう ▪ We *went through* the usual *teething problems* at the start of the project. プロジェクトの実施当初にはお決まりのちょっとした問題が起きた. ☞「歯生期のむずかり」,「歯の発生に伴う障害」が原義.

teetotum /tìːtóʊtəm/ 名 ***like a teetotum*** (角ごまのように)ぐるぐる回って ▪ She turned round *like a teetotum.* 彼女は角ごまのようにぐるぐる回った.

telegram /téləgræ̀m/ 名 ***by telegram*** 電報で ▪ He was called away *by telegram* to London. 彼は電報でロンドンに呼ばれた.

send a telegram 電報を打つ ▪ Please *send* me *a telegram.* 電報を打ってください.

telegraph /téləgræ̀f|télɪgrɑ̀ːf/ 名 ***by telegraph*** 電信で ▪ The admiral conveyed the orders *by telegraph* to the fleet. 提督はその命令を電信で艦隊に伝えた.

telepathy /təlépəθi/ 名 ***mental telepathy*** 精神感応, テレパシー; 以心伝心; 読心術 ▪ I'll show you how to practice *mental telepathy* with cards. カードを用いたテレパシーの実演をお見せしよう.

telephone /téləfòʊn/ 名 ***by*** [***over the***] ***telephone*** 電話で ▪ I spoke to him *by telephone.* 電話で彼と話した ▪ The matter was arranged *over the telephone.* その件は電話で取り決められた.

on the telephone **1** 電話口に出て ▪ I called him *on the telephone.* 彼を電話に呼び出した ▪ Miss Brown *on the telephone.* ブラウン嬢からお電話です.

2 電話を引いて ▪ Are you *on the telephone*? 君は電話を引いていますか.

talk on the big white telephone 《俗》便器の中に吐く ▪ He was *talking on the big white telephone* because he'd been drinking too much. 彼は飲み過ぎて便器の中に吐いていた.

television /téləvìʒən/ 名 ***on television*** **1** テレビに出て ▪ He will probably be *on television* shortly. 彼はたぶんまもなくテレビに出るだろう.

2 テレビで ▪ Did you see the boat-race *on television*? そのボートレースをテレビで見ましたか.

watch television テレビを見る ▪ The boy *watches television* too much. その少年はテレビを見すぎる.

tell /tel/ 動 ***all told*** **1** 全部で ▪ He owns fifteen horses *all told*. 彼は馬を全部で15頭持っている.

2 《口》結局 ▪ But you are only a boy, *all told*. でも君は結局子供にすぎんじゃないか. ☞「全部数えて」が原義.

Do tell! **1** 《米俗》何とおっしゃる!, まさか! ▪ The man, after hearing the story through, exclaimed, "*Do tell!*" 男はその話を最後まで聞いてから,「まさか」と大声で言った.

2 《英口》(おもしろそうな話だね)ぜひ聞かせてくれ ▪ A rumor about Pauline, you say? *Do tell!* ポーリンの噂話だって? ぜひ聞かせてよ!

Don't tell me! →Never TELL me!

Don't tell me—let me guess. 言わないで—当ててみましょう ▪ *Don't tell me—let me guess*—you've passed the exam. 言わないで—当ててみましょう—試験に合格したでしょ.

hear tell (of, that) →HEAR.

I (can) tell you/let me tell you 実際, 全くのところ ▪ *I tell you*, it got on my nerves. 全く神経にこたえたよ.

I (just) can't tell you 〚疑問詞節を伴って〛十分には言い尽くせない ▪ *I can't tell you* how glad I am. どんなにうれしいかとても言い尽くせません.

I told you so!/Did I not tell you so? 言わないことじゃない; それごらん.

I('ll) tell you what (it is)/I will tell you something 《口》あのねえ; 話があるんだが ▪ *I'll tell you what*, we'll row down. いいかい, こぎ下るぞ.

I'm not telling! 言いたくないね《質問に答えたくない》.

I'm telling you! ほんとに ▪ You ought to get married, Jim, *I'm telling you!* 君はほんとに結婚するべきだよ, ジム.

it tells …と言ってある[書いてある] ▪ *It tells* in the Bible how David slew Goliath. ダビデがゴリアテを殺したと聖書に語られています. ☞how《古》= that.

let me tell you →I (can) TELL you.

Never [Don't] tell me! 《口》 **1** まさか; ばかを言うなよ《不信・じれったさを表す》 ▪ Error of judgment! *Don't tell me.* 判断違いだって! ばかを言うなよ.

2 おやおや, やれやれ ▪ *Don't tell me!* I've forgotten to turn off the water. おや! 水道を止めるのを忘れた.

Nobody can tell./Who can tell? 誰にもわからない ▪ *Nobody can tell* who wrote it. それを誰が書いたか誰にもわからない.

Now it can be told. (極秘事項も)今なら話せる.

tell a different [another, etc.] tale [story] 別の情報を伝えている ▪ She says she feels fine, but her face *tells a different story*. 彼女は口では気分がよいと言っているが, 顔にはそうでないと書いてある.

tell a tale 話をする; 何かを物語る ▪ That *tells a tale*. それは何かを物語っている.

tell all (自分の恥になることまで)洗いざらい話す ▪ Some homosexuals are ready to *tell all*. 同性愛者の中には進んで何もかも洗いざらい話す者がいる.

tell *a person* ***different*** 人に反論する ▪ There's some people who would *tell* you *different*. そうではないと言う人もいるぜ. ☞非標準語法.

tell *a person* ***flat out*** 人に…をきっぱりと断る ▪ I *told* him *flat out* that I wouldn't go out with him. 彼とはつき合いたくないときっぱりと断った.

tell for [in favor of] …に有利である ▪ It is a transaction which *tells in our favor*. これは我々に有利な取引だ.

tell *a person* ***good-by*** 《米》人にさよならを言う ▪ You aren't going without *telling* me *good-by*? さよならも言わずに帰りはしないでしょうね.

tell it like [how] it is 《米俗》ありのままに話す, ありのままに書く ▪ The writer *tells it like it is*. 著者はありのままに書いている.

Tell me. 《口》〚疑問文を伴って〛あの, 聞きたいのだが ▪ *Tell me*, have you finished your homework yet? 教えて, もう宿題終わった?

Tell me about it. 《口》それはこっちのせりふさ, 全くその通りだ ▪ Nasty weather, isn't it?—Yeah, *tell me about it!* いやな天気だな—いや, 全く.

Tell me another. 《口》もっともっともらしいことを言え, 嘘を言うのはよせ.

tell *a person his* ***own*** 《口》人に率直に欠点を言ってきかせる ▪ I shall *tell* him *his own*. 彼に率直に欠点を言ってきかせてやろう.

tell porkies 《英・戯》嘘をつく ▪ Can this be true, or is somebody *telling porkies*, I wonder? 一体これは本当なのか, それとも誰かが嘘をついているのだろうか. ☞lies の押韻俗語 porky-pies の代用に porkies を用いたもの.

tell *one's* ***prayers*** 祈とうする ▪ The woman *told her prayers*. その女は祈とうした.

tell the (whole) world **1** 《俗》強く断言する ▪ I'll *tell the world* that nobody would be able to make him talk. 強く断言するが, あの男は誰が何と言っても口をききはせんだろう.

2 公言する ▪ Reply directly to me if you don't want to *tell the world* about it. それをみなに知られたくなければ私にじかに返事をください.

tell *a person* ***to*** *do* 人に…せよと言う ▪ *Tell* him *to* wait. 彼に待つように言ってください.

tell *a person* ***where to get*** [*he* ***gets***] ***off*** →GET.

tell *a person* ***where to put*/*tell*** *a person* ***what to do with*** 《口》…をきっぱりとはねつける ▪ I *told* him *where to put* his advice. 彼のアドバイスはきっぱりとはねつけた.

What did I tell you? 言った通りでしょう ▪ There, now! *What did I tell you?* そらどうです. 言った通りでしょう.

Who can tell? →Nobody can TELL.

You can't tell him [***her,*** etc.] ***anything.*** 彼[彼女, など]には何も話せないよ《秘密が守れない》.

You never can tell. わからないもんですよ《外見はしばしば人をあざむく》.

You tell 'em! そうだ, そうだ; いいこと言うぞ《弁士を励ます言葉》 ▪ "*You tell 'em,*" he yelled out to the politician making the speech. 「その通りだ」と彼は演説中の代議士に向かって叫んだ.

You tell me. (私には)わからないね ▪ What shall we do next?—*You tell me.* 次はどうしよう—わからんね. ☞you と me に強勢を置く.

You're telling me! 《俗》百も承知だ; 全くその通りだ ▪ I hope he won't come.—*You're telling me.* 彼が来なければいいのに—全くだね. ☞me に強勢を置く.

telling /télɪŋ/ 名 ***give*** *a person* ***a telling-off*** …を叱責する ▪ His mother *gave* him such *a telling off* about the broken doll when he got home. 彼が家に帰ると壊れた人形のことで母親からこっぴどくしかられた.

That's telling(s).*/*That would be telling. 《口》それを言えば秘密がばれる ▪ How do you get your information?—*That's tellings.* どうやって情報を集めているのですか?—それを言えば秘密がばれるよ.

temper[1] /témpər/ 名 ***control*** *one's* ***temper*** →keep one's TEMPER.

fly [***get***] ***into a temper*** かっと怒りだす ▪ At that the woman *flew into a temper.* それを聞くとその女性はかっと怒りだした.

frayed tempers 磨り減った神経, いらだち ▪ Traffic jams inevitably lead to *frayed tempers.* 交通渋滞に引っかかると決まってしまいにはいらいらしてくる.

have a good [***bad***] ***temper*** がまん強い[気が短い] ▪ He *has a bad temper*, and when angry, says things he doesn't mean. 彼は短気で, 怒ると心にもないことを言う.

have (***got***) ***a quick*** [***short***] ***temper*** すぐにかっとなる, 短気である, 怒りっぽい ▪ Our boss *has a quick temper* and doesn't mind letting other people see it. うちのボスはすぐにかっとなるが他人に見られてもお構いなしさ ▪ My mum *has got a* very *quick temper.* おふくろはひどく怒りっぽい.

in a good [***bad***] ***temper*** 上[不]きげんで ▪ He is *in a bad temper.* 彼は不きげんだ.

in a temper かんしゃくを起こして ▪ I cannot tell you what *a temper* I was *in.* 僕がどんなにひどくかんしゃくを起こしたか君には言えない.

keep [***control, hold, restrain***] *one's* ***temper*** 怒りを抑える, じっとがまんする ▪ You will lose your position if you don't *keep your temper.* 怒りを抑えないと君は首になるぞ ▪ She usually managed to *hold her temper.* 彼女はたいてい何とかじっと感情を抑えることができた.

lose *one's* ***temper*** (…に)腹をたてる (*with*) ▪ He entirely *lost his temper with* me. 彼は私にすっかり腹をたててしまった.

out of temper 不きげんで, (…に)腹をたてて (*with*) ▪ It would put me *out of temper.* そんなことになれば私は不きげんになるだろう ▪ The man was *out of temper with* her. その人は彼女に腹をたてていた.

show temper 怒りの色を見せる ▪ He refrained from *showing temper.* 彼は怒りを見せるのを押えた.

one's ***temper rises*** [***frays***] 腹が立ってくる ▪ *My temper rose* at every word he spoke. 彼が一言言うたびに腹が立ってきた.

tempers fray*/*tempers become frayed 神経が磨り減る, いらいらする, 怒る ▪ *Tempers frayed* when we waited three hours, only to be told there was no plane. 3時間も待たされたあげく便はないと言われてみな頭にきた.

temper[2] /témpər/ 動 ***God tempers the wind to the shorn lamb.*** →GOD.

temperature /témpərətʃər/ 名 ***have*** [***run***] ***a temperature*** 《口》(病人が)熱がある ▪ He has *had a temperature* for nearly a week. 彼はほとんど1週間も熱があった.

raise [***lower***] ***the temperature*** 緊張を高める[和らげる] ▪ His flat refusal *raised the temperature* of the meeting. 彼がにべもなく拒絶すると会議に緊張が高まった ▪ The move will help *lower the* political *temperature.* その措置は政治的緊張を緩和するのに役立つだろう.

take *a person's* ***temperature*** 人の体温を計る ▪ I *took their temperatures* this morning. 私はけさ彼らの体温を計ってやった.

tempest /témpəst/ 名 ***a tea-pot tempest*/*a tempest in a tea-pot*** 《米》内輪のごたごた, ささいなことでの大騒ぎ ▪ What *a* ridiculous *tea-pot tempest!* 何とばかげた些細なことでの大騒ぎなんだろう.

tempt /tempt/ 動 ***be tempted to*** *do* …したくなる ▪ I *am tempted to* question that. それを疑いたくなる.

tempt fate*/*tempt the fates →FATE.

tempt (*one's*) ***fortune*** 運を試す ▪ He wisely resolved to *tempt his fortune* no more. 彼は賢明にももう運を試すのはよそうと決心した.

tempt God [***providence***] 神の力を試す; 神意に逆らう ▪ Religion teaches us that *God* ought not to *be tempted.* 神の力を試すべきでないことを宗教は教えてくれる ▪ It is *tempting providence* to go in that old boat. あんなぼろ船で行くことはむちゃだ.

tempt the storm [***flood, sea,*** etc.] 《主に詩》あらし[洪水, 海, など]の危険を冒す ▪ They preferred to *tempt the sea* rather than remain in their own dwellings. 彼らは家にとどまるよりはむしろ

海の危険を冒すことを選んだ.

ten /ten/ 形名 ***eight or ten*** [***ten or twelve***] 8か10の[10か12の] ▪I was talked to by a boy of *eight or ten*. 8歳か10歳の男の子に声をかけられた ▪He is a reader of only *ten or twelve* years of English literature. 彼は英文学の読者としてほんの10年か12年たったばかりだ. ☞英語には数をあげるのにこのようにとばして言う癖がある.

hang ten **1**《俗》(サーフィン・スケートボードで)目立ったパーフォーマンスをする ▪He could *hang ten* on his skateboard. 彼ならスケートボードで目立つパーフォーマンスができるだろう.

2 困難を切り抜ける ▪Don't worry about me. I can *hang ten* overseas. ぼくのことは心配ご無用さ. 海外でもうまくやっていけるから.

ten feet tall 身長10フィートで; 自分を大巨人[偉い]と思って, うぬぼれて得意で ▪I came home feeling *ten feet tall*. 私は得意な気分で帰宅した ▪The outlaw biker bragged to police that he was *10 feet tall* and invincible. アウトローの暴走族は警察に対して, 自分は大物で無敵だとうそぶいた.

ten out of ten 満点, 上出来 ▪He was given *ten out of ten* for his report. 彼のレポートには満点がつけられた.

ten times 10倍も, ずっと《誇張表現》 ▪It was *ten times* worse than a flood. それは洪水よりもずっと悪かった.

ten to one 十中九まで, 九分九厘まで ▪*Ten to one* that happens to be the very thing I want. 十中九までそれはまさに私がたまたま求めているものだ.

tens of thousands 幾万も ▪*Tens of thousands* of books are published every year. 毎年何万という本が出版されている.

tenacious /tənéɪʃəs/ 形 ***be tenacious of*** ... をねばり強く保つ ▪The frog *is* remarkably *tenacious of* life. カエルは著しく生命力がある ▪He *is tenacious of* his opinion. 彼は己の意見に固執する.

tender[1] /téndər/ 名 ***put in*** [***send in, make***] ***a tender for*** ...の入札をする ▪He *put in a tender for* the picture. 彼はその絵の入札をした.

put ... out to tender ...を入札に付す ▪He *put* the building *out to tender*. 彼はその建物を入札に付した.

tender[2] /téndər/ 形 ***a tender spot*** →SPOT[1].

go tender (馬が)足が痛そうに進む ▪The horse *goes tender* while galloping. その馬は疾駆しながら足が痛そうに進む.

tender age [***years***] いとけない年ごろ, 世慣れない年ごろ ▪It is a great evil to imprison boys and girls of *tender age*. 世慣れない少年少女たちを投獄するのは大きな悪だ.

tender loving care 優しい気配り ▪Nurses try to give *tender loving care* to the sick. 看護師は病人に優しい気配りを与えようとする. ☞よく TLC と略される.

tender of [***for, on behalf of***] ...を心にかけて; をいとしがって ▪I am too *tender of* his reputation to publish them. 私は彼の世評を心にかけているので, それらのことを公にできない.

tender of [***in***] *doing* ...しないようにして, を避けたがる ▪He is *tender of giving* offence. 彼は人を怒らせることをきらっている.

the tender passion [***sentiment***] 恋愛, 恋情 ▪I delight in *the tender passion*. 私は恋が大好きだ ▪I am a martyr to this *tender passion*. 私はこの恋情のとりこになっている.

tender[3] /téndər/ 動 ***tender an*** [***the***] ***oath*** 宣誓させる ▪The authorities vainly *tendered* him *the oath*. 当局は彼に宣誓させられなかった.

tenor /ténər/ 名 ***get the tenor of*** ...の主旨[大意]がわかる ▪He *got the tenor of* what was being said. 彼は言われていることの大意がわかった.

the even tenor of *one's* ***way*** 平穏な人生行路 ▪He kept on *the even tenor of his way* for sixty years. 彼は60年間平穏な人生行路をたどり続けた.

tenpins /ténpɪ̀nz/ 名 ***roll tenpins***《米》十柱戯をやる ▪He lost $10 *rolling tenpins*. 彼は十柱戯をやって10ドル失った.

tent /tent/ 名 ***have*** [***pitch, put up***] *one's* ***tent***(***s***) 居を構える (《聖》*Gen*. 12. 8) ▪Roscoe invited him to *pitch his tent* in Liverpool. ロスコーはリバプールに居を構えるように彼に勧めた.

pitch [***strike***] ***a*** [*one's*] ***tent*** テントを張る[たたむ] ▪We *pitched our tent* by the river. 我々は川のそばにテントを張った.

tenterhook /téntərhʊ̀k/ 名 ***on*** (***the***) ***tenterhooks*** ひどく気をもんで ▪I left him *on tenterhooks* of impatient uncertainty. 私は彼を不安でじりじりと気をもませておいた. ☞tenterhook「張りわく(tenter) のくぎ」.

tenth /tenθ/ 名 ***the submerged tenth*** → SUBMERGE.

tenure /ténjər, -njʊər/ 名 ***hold ... on a precarious tenure*** いつ期限が切れるかわからない条件で...を保有している ▪He *holds* his life *on a precarious tenure*. 彼はいつ死ぬかわからない命だ.

one's ***tenure of life*** 寿命 ▪He was warned of *his* slight *tenure of life*. 彼は余命がいくらもないぞと言われた.

term /təːrm/ 名 ***be an elastic term*** 融通がきく, 定まっていない; (職務内容が)広い ▪Being secretary at this office *is a* highly *elastic term*. このオフィスでの秘書の職務内容は非常に広範です.

bring *a person* ***to terms*** 人を降参[承服]させる ▪We finally *brought* the enemy *to terms*. 我々はついに敵を降服させた. ☞terms はここでは「合意条件」の意.

come to terms 折り合う, 相談[協定]がまとまる (*with*) ▪He had no choice but to *come to terms with* the enemy. 彼は敵と折り合うよりほかに道がなかった.

for terms of (*one's*) ***life***《主に法》終身 ▪What people draw from their education generally

T

sticks by them *for terms of life*. 人が教育から得るものは一生涯身から離れないのが通例である.

in glowing terms 肯定的に, 好意的に ▪ Hill talked *in glowing terms* of her former boss. ヒルは元の上司のことを好意的に話した.

in no uncertain terms ＝in so many WORDs.

in terms 商談[談判]中で (*with*) ▪ The booksellers and I are *in terms*. 本屋と私は商談中だ ▪ He was *in terms with* Mr. Vaudal. 彼はボーダル氏と談判中だった.

in terms of **1**《数》(特殊の量を含む)項で表す級数または式にして; (一般に…に特有)の表現[言葉]で ▪ The continuity of motion is really known to us *in terms of* Force. 運動の継続は我々には実は「力」という言葉で知られている.

2 …によって, 換算して, 関して, の点から ▪ It is wrong to try to reckon happiness *in terms of* worldly success. 幸福というものを世俗的な成功という点から考えるのはまちがっている.

in the long [short, medium] term 長[短, 中]期的に(見れば) ▪ *In the short term* we may lose money, but *in the longer term* we will gain. 短期的には損をするかもしれないが, 長期的には儲かるだろう.

keep terms 規定の学期間在学する ▪ He was admitted to the degree of Master of Arts without *keeping terms*. 彼は規定の学期間在学しないで文学修士の称号を与えられた.

keep terms with …と交渉を続ける, 関係がある ▪ The king need *keep terms* no longer *with* the popular assemblies. 王は民衆の集まりともう交渉を続けるには及ばない ▪ Such a profusion of finery *keeps* no *terms with* simplicity. そのようなおびただしい美装は簡素さとは少しも関係がない.

make terms (…と)話[協定]がまとまる (*with*) ▪ We have *made terms with* them, giving them a number of cattle. 我々は彼らと協定がまとまって, 彼らにたくさんの牛を与えることとなった.

not on any terms/on [upon] no terms どうあっても…しない ▪ I would *not* have seen the letter *on any terms*. 私はその手紙をどうあっても見はしなかっただろう.

on [upon] bad [equal, good, friendly, speaking, visiting, etc.***] terms*** 仲の悪い[同等の, 仲のよい, 親しい, 言葉を交わすほどの, 行き来する, など]間柄で (*with*) ▪ I could live *upon good terms* even *with* a deist. 私は理神論信奉者とだって仲よく暮らしていけるさ.

on high [low] terms 高く[安く] ▪ The article was sold *on high terms*. その品は高く売れた.

on** a person's **own terms 人の望み通りの条件で ▪ He allowed me to paint his portrait *on my own terms*. 彼はこちらの望み通りの条件で肖像画を描くことを許してくれた.

on terms **1** 親密な間柄で ▪ The earl and Lord Porlock were not *on terms*. 伯爵とポーロック卿は親密な間柄ではなかった.

2《狩俗》五分五分で (*with*) ▪ The hounds quickly got *on terms with* the fox. 猟犬たちは素早くキツネに追いついた.

3 商議中で, 談判中で (*with*) ▪ He was *on terms with* the publisher for the copyright. 彼は版権のことで出版社と交渉中であった.

on [upon] (...) terms (…の)条件で; 条件つきで ▪ A peace was made with both *upon* better *terms*. もっとよい条件で双方と和睦した ▪ The fortress had surrendered *upon terms*. とりでは条件つきで降伏していた.

termination /tə̀ːrmənéɪʃən/ 名 ***bring ... to a termination/put a termination to*** …を終わらせる ▪ She abruptly *put a termination to* her flirtation. 彼女は突然恋愛遊戯にけりをつけた.

terrify /térəfàɪ/ 動 ***be terrified at [by, with]*** …にたまげる ▪ He *was terrified by* lightning. 彼は稲光にびっくりさせられた.

be terrified of …におびえる ▪ The child *was terrified of* being left alone in the house. その子供は家に一人残されたのにおびえた.

territory /térətɔ̀ːri|-təri/ 名 ***go [come] with the territory*** (ある特定の仕事・状況などには)問題がいくつもある[避けられない] ▪ As she is a celebrity, people are interested in her private life, but that *goes with the territory*. 彼女は有名人なので私生活に関心がもたれているが, それも避けられないことだ.

take in too much territory 極端に走る; 一概に言いすぎる ▪ But I am sure I *took in too much territory* when I said so. しかしそう言ったのは確かに大ざっぱすぎた.

terror /térər/ 名 ***a holy terror*** ひどくおっかない人; 大変な厄介者 ▪ That child is *a holy terror*. あの子は大変な厄介者だ.

be a terror to …を怖がらせる ▪ He *is a terror to* his wife. 彼は細君の恐怖の的である.

flash terror into the heart of →FLASH[2].

have a holy terror of …をひどく恐れる ▪ He *has a holy terror of* fire. 彼は火をひどく恐れている.

have [hold] no terrors for …にとって易しい ▪ English *has no terrors for* me. 英語はちっとも難しくない.

in terror びっくり仰天して ▪ He ran away *in terror*. 彼はびっくり仰天して走り去った.

in terror of …をひどく恐れて ▪ He was *in terror of* his life. 彼は命を落としはしないかとひどく恐れていた.

strike (a) terror into …をふるえ上がらせる ▪ This remark *struck a terror into* them. この言葉は彼らをとほうもなくふるえ上がらせた ▪ A lion's roar will *strike terror into* our hearts. ライオンの咆哮は我々のどぎもを抜く.

the king of terrors 死神 (《聖》*Job* 18. 14) ▪ Job calls it *the king of terrors*. ヨブはそれを死神と呼んでいる.

terrorist /térərɪst/ 名 ***a total terrorist***《俗》(教師・親など)厳格な人物 ▪ My dad is *a total terrorist* and doesn't allow me to go out at night. 父は厳格な人で私の夜間外出は許さないの.

test[1] /test/ 名 ***be a test of*** [***for***] …を試す ▪ The long climb *was a test of* our powers of endurance. その長い登山が我々の忍耐力を試した.

bear [***pass, stand***] ***the test of*** …の試験に耐える, 試験に合格する ▪ These methods have *stood the test of* time. これらの方法は時の試練に耐えたものだ.

bring [***put***]***… to the test*** …を試験する ▪ I will not *put* them *to the test.* 彼らを試験すまい.

give [***have***] ***a test*** 試験をする[受ける] ▪ I will *give* you *a test* in history. 歴史の試験をしてやろう.

take the test 審査条例 (Test Act) によって宣誓する ▪ The man demurred to *take the test* appointed by act of parliament. 男は法令に定められた審査条例によって宣誓するのに異議を唱えた.

test[2] /test/ 動 ***just testing*** 試しに言ってみただけさ《自分の発言の誤りを訂正されたときに言う》 ▪ The Norman Conquest was 1166, wasn't it?—No, 1066.—Oh, yes, *just testing*! ノルマン征服は1166年だったね—いや, 1066年だ—そうそう, 試しに言ってみただけさ.

test the water(***s***) →WATER[1].

testimony /téstəmòʊni|-tɪməni/ 名 ***bear testimony to*** …を証言する ▪ I can *bear testimony to* his good character. 彼が立派な人物であることを私は証明できる.

call *a person* ***in testimony*** 人を証人に立たせる ▪ Several men *were called in testimony*. 数人が証人に立たされた.

tether /téðər/ 名 ***be at*** [***reach***] ***the end of*** *one's* ***tether*** 行きうまって ▪ The speaker *was* soon *at the end of his tether*. 代弁者はすぐ行きうまってしまった.

beyond *one's* ***tether*** 能力[権限]以上で ▪ This is *beyond my tether*. これは私の力に及ばない ▪ He will not be able to go an inch *beyond his tether*. 彼は一歩も権限を越えることはできないだろう.

get [***go***] ***to the end*** [***length***] ***of*** *one's* ***tether*** 方策が尽きる ▪ They had *got to the length of their tether*. 彼らは方策が尽きてしまった.

text /tekst/ 名 ***stick to*** *one's* ***text*** (話などが)脱線しない; 考え[主義]を変えない ▪ Still I *stick to my text* as regards that. そのことについては私はまだ考えを変えていない.

T

Thames /temz/ 名 ***set the Thames on fire***/***burn the Thames*** 〚主に否定文で〛 華々しいことをして名をあげる ▪ I hardly expect him to *set the Thames on fire*. あの男が華々しいことをして名をあげるとはまず思われない ▪ His pictures are going to *burn the Thames*. 彼の絵はすばらしい評判を取ろうとしている.

than /ðən, ðæn/ 接 ***no other than*** …にほかならない ▪ It was *no other than* the king. それは国王にほかならなかった.

nothing else than ただ, 全く ▪ What he told you was *nothing else than* nonsense. 彼があなたに言ったことは全くのたわごとだった ▪ He did *nothing else than* laugh. 彼はただ笑うばかりであった.

other [***another,*** 《米》 ***different***] ***than*** …より以外の ▪ I have a *different* plan *than* yours. 私は君のとは別の案を持っている ▪ I have no *other* friend *than* you. 君のほかに友人はいない.

thank[1] /θæŋk/ 名 ***bow*** *one's* ***thanks*** おじぎをして謝意を表する ▪ The lady *bowed* him *her* most profuse *thanks*. その婦人は彼におじぎをしていかにも丁重に謝意を表した.

express [***offer, extend***] *one's* ***thanks*** 礼を述べる ▪ I don't know how to *express my thanks*. なんとお礼を申しあげてよいかわかりません.

give thanks **1** (特に食卓の祈りで)神に感謝を捧げる (*to*) ▪ He knelt and *gave thanks to* God. 彼はひざまずいて神に感謝を捧げた.

2 感謝する (*for*) ▪ He *gave thanks* to me *for* helping him with French. 彼は私がフランス語を教えたことに対して感謝した.

Many [***Best, A thousand***] ***thanks.***/***I give you my thanks.***/***My thanks to you.*** (どうも)ありがとう ▪ *Many thanks* for your letter. お手紙どうもありがとう. ☞用法については THANK you (very much) を参照.

No, thanks. いやけっこうです ▪ Would you like to read the letter?—*No, thanks.* この手紙を読みたいかね?—いやけっこうです.

no thanks to …のせい[おかげ]ではなく ▪ It is *no thanks to* you that the house wasn't burnt down. 家が全焼しなかったのは君のおかげじゃない.

offer *one's* ***thanks*** →express one's THANKs.

return thanks (恩恵に対して)礼を述べる, 感謝を捧げる《主に儀式ばった場合または食後の祈りにおいて用いる》 ▪ I *returned* her *thanks*, and took my leave. 私は彼女にお礼を述べていとまを告げた ▪ "Let us *return thanks*," said he. 「神に感謝を捧げよう」と彼は言った.

Small [《反語》 ***Much***] ***thanks I got for it!*** お礼なんか言われなかった ▪ I really helped him, but *small thanks I got for it!* 本当に彼を助けたのに, お礼なんか一言もなかった.

small thanks to 《反語》 …のおかげじゃない ▪ We were successful, but *small thanks to* you. 私たちは成功したが君のおかげじゃない.

Thanks a lot [***million***]. 《口》 ほんとにありがとう ▪ I'll bring a bottle of wine.—*Thanks a lot.* ワインを1本持ってこよう—どうもありがとう.

Thanks, but no thanks. 《口》 ありがとう, でも結構よ ▪ How about a beer?—*Thanks, but no thanks.* ビールを1杯どう?—どうも. でもいらない.

Thanks for the buggy ride. 《米》 手伝ってくれてありがとう ▪ *Thanks for the buggy ride*—it was great. 手伝ってくれてありがとう. とても助かった.

thanks to 《しばしば反語》 …のおかげで, のため ▪ *Thanks to* television, boys and girls are neglectful of their studies. テレビのおかげで子供たちは勉強を怠る.

Thanks very much [***awfully***]. 《口》 どうもあり

がとう.

thank[2] /θæŋk/ 動 ***God be thanked!*** →THANK God!

have only** oneself **to thank for/ may thank** oneself **for 《皮肉》…は自分のせいである ▪ You *have only yourself to thank for* it. それは君の自業自得だ.

***have** a person **to thank** (**for**)* (…は)人のおかげ[せい]である ▪ She *has* her parents *to thank for* her success. 彼女が成功したのは両親のおかげだ.

***I thank you to** do* どうか…してください ▪ *I thank you* not *to* walk on the grass. どうか芝生の上を歩かないでください.

(I will) thank you for …を(取って)ください ▪ *I will thank you for* a glass of water. 水を1杯ください ▪ *Thank you for* that ball. そのボールをこちらへ放(ほう)ってください.

***I will thank you to** do* **1** …してください ▪ *I will thank you to* shut the door. ドアを閉めてください.

2《反語》…したってばちは当たるまい ▪ *I will thank you to* be a little more polite. もう少しいんぎんにしてもばちは当たるまい.

No, thank you. いいえけっこうです ▪ Will you have some tea?—*No, thank you.* お茶を召しあがりませんか?—いいえけっこうです.

thank** a person **for nothing 《反語》大きなお世話だ《ろくなことはしてもらっていないと考える場合の文句》 ▪ Part with that horse!—No, I *thank* you *for nothing*. あの馬を手放せって!—いや大きなお世話だよ.

Thank fortune! 《米口》ありがたいことに! ▪ She was in her own coupe, *thank fortune!* 彼女はありがたいことに自分のクーペに乗っていた.

Thank God* [*goodness, Heaven*]*!/God be thanked! ああありがたい (*for, that*) ▪ *Thank goodness* she's alive. 彼女が生きていてありがたい ▪ *Thank heaven for* that. それはありがたい.

thank** one's **(lucky) stars →STAR[1].

Thank you (very much). (どうも)ありがとう ▪ He is much better, *thank you.* 彼はおかげさまでずっとよくなりました. ☞この表現はさらに次のような場合にも用いられる. (1)丁寧な依頼の後で: Would you mind slowing down? *Thank you very much.* スピードを落としていただけませんか. どうかお願いします. (2)丁寧な拒絶の後で: I prefer to stay in London, *thank you.* 私はロンドンにいるほうがいい, 折角だが. (3)皮肉として: I can't lend you money.—*Thank you*, pal. 金は貸せないね—どうもありがと.

***Thanks* [*Thank you*] *for having me* [*us*].** どうもごちそうさまでした《パーティーなどでの別れの挨拶》.

that /ðæt/ 代副接 ***all that*** **1** その種類のすべてのもの ▪ It is past *all that* with me. そういうことはすべて私には手遅れだ.

2《口》〚形容詞・副詞の前で not を伴って〛それほど ▪ He is*n't all that* foolish. 彼はそれほどばかではない.

3《口》魅力いっぱいの, 実にすばらしい ▪ I think Peter is *all that.* ピーターはかっこいいと思う.

and all that **1** …や何やかや ▪ He talks of rights and duties, *and all that.* 彼は権利だの義務だの, なんとかかんとか言っている.

2 全く, どうか《感謝・祝賀などのきまり文句》 ▪ Very many happy returns of the day, *and all that!* どうか幾久しくこの良き日のめぐり来ますように.

and that **1** しかも ▪ He makes mistakes *and that* very often. 彼は間違いをする, しかもしょっちゅうだ.

2 など, その他 ▪ Dob reads Latin and French *and that.* ドブはラテン語やフランス語その他も読みこなす.

(and* [*so*]*) that's that 《口》そのことはそれで済んだ[決まった]《物語・討論を終えるときの文句》 ▪ I won't marry Peter, *and that's that.* ピーターと結婚したくないと言ったらしたくない ▪ But he is dead, *so that's that.* しかし彼は死んだのだから, それはそれでおしまいさ.

and those 〚前の複数名詞を受ける場合〛しかも ▪ I have only three rings, *and those* not of the best. 指輪は三つしかない, しかも上等なものではない.

at that →AT.

be like that 《口》 **1** そんな態度をとる(かたくなにしたり, ふくれたりする) ▪ Don't *be like that*, Mary! そんな態度をとらないでおくれよ, メアリー.

2 こんなに親密である ▪ You're a friend of Martin.—You bet. We*'re like that.* 君はマーティンの友人かい—そうとも. こんな具合さ. ☞通例, 人差し指と中指を交差させて, あるいは両手の人指し指2本を合わせて.

Come* [*Get*] *out of that! 《俗》どけろ!, 行ってしまえ!, やめろ! ▪ Oh, hands off! *Come out of that!* おい, 手を放せよ. やめろったら.

Fool* [*Miserable man,* etc.] *that** one **is! 〚感嘆文の挿入節として〛自分はなんというばか[みじめな人間, など]なんだろう ▪ O *miserable man that* I *am!* ああ私はなんというみじめな人間なんだろう ▪ *Fool that* I *was*, I thought I was loved*!* 私はなんというばかだったのだろう, 私は愛されていると思っていたのだ.

for all that それにもかかわらず ▪ This news is strange, but it is true *for all that.* このニュースは変だが, それでも事実だ.

in that →IN[2].

in those days あの頃は ▪ *In those days* life was easy. あの頃は暮らしが楽であった.

(Is) that so? **1** そうですか ▪ He's an old friend of mine.—*Is that so?* 彼は旧友の一人だ—そうか.

2 まさか ▪ There's life on Mars.—*Is that so?* 火星には生物がいる—まさか. ☞→Is that a FACT?

It* [*A person*] *ain't all that. 《俗》(…が)他の人が思うほどよくない ▪ Next time he tries to cheat money out of you, you just tell him he *ain't all that.* 今度彼があなたからお金をだまし取ろうとしたら, 君は他の人が思うほどよくないねと言ってやりなさい.

it is not that →not THAT.

It is that./That it is. その通りだ ▪ It's cold out, isn't it?—*It is that.* 外は寒いだろう?—その通り.

just like that **1** 手軽に, あっさりと, 無造作に, やすやすと ▪ I became a non-smoker *just like that.*

私はいとも簡単にタバコをやめた.

2 (そのように)突然に ▪ The alarm went off, *just like that.* (そんなに)出し抜けに警報が鳴った.

3 (こんなに)親密に ▪ They are always together, they're *just like that.* 二人は(こんなに)親密にいつもいっしょにいる. ☞通例, 人差し指と中指を交差させて, あるいは両手の人差し指２本を合わせて.

not care* [*give*] *that (パチンと指を鳴らしながら)これっぽちもかまわない[値うちはない] ▪ I would *not give that* for it. そんなものにこれっぽちも出せないね.

not so* [*as*]... *as all that それほどまでは…でない ▪ It is *not as* cold *as all that* in Michigan. ミシガンはそれほどまでは寒くない.

not that/it is not that だからといって…というのではない ▪ Where is he staying now? *Not that* I care. あの男は今どこに滞在しているのだろう. どこにいたってかまうのではないが ▪ *Not that* I am dissatisfied, but (that) I have my own business to attend to. なにも不平があるわけではないが, 私には私の用事があるのだ ▪ If he said so—*not that* he ever did—he lied. もしも彼がそう言ったのなら—そう言ったというのではないが—嘘を言ったのだ.

***not*... *that* one *knows* [*can learn,* etc.]** 自分の知るところでは…ない ▪ He is *not* here, *that* I *can learn.* 僕の知るところでは彼は当地にいない ▪ *No* one knows anything about it *that* I *can find.* 私の気ういたところでは誰もそのことは知らない.

***oh, that*...** **1** …したらよいのになあ ▪ *Oh, that* I could be with you again! あなたとまたいっしょになれたらよいのになあ.

2 ああ…とは ▪ *Oh, that* I should live to see my own son sent to prison! ああ生きていて息子が刑務所へ入れられるのを見ようとは!

(*so, in order*) *that* one *may* [*can, might, should*] 〚目的・願望の従節を導いて〛…するように ▪ We go to school (*so*) *that* we *may* learn. 我々は学ぶために学校へ行く ▪ Christ had prayed *that* Peter's faith *should* not fail. キリストはペテロの信仰が失われぬように祈った.

so* [*such*]... *that →SO, SUCH (…) that.

(*so*) *that* one *may* [《口》 *will*] *not* …しないように ▪ Work hard *so that* you *may not* fail. 落第しないよう懸命に勉強しなさい.

(*so*) *that's that* →(and) THAT's that.

Take that! これでもくらえ!《人を打つときなど》 ▪ I must do my duty, Sir, so *take that*—and *that!* 義務は果たさねばなりませんので, 一発—もう一発!

That does it! 《口》 もうやめた ▪ *That does it!* You can fix this on your own. もうやめた. これ, 自分で直してよ.

that is すなわち, つまり ▪ I often wish I could read—*that is,* read easily. 私は自分が読めれば—つまり, すらすら読めればいいとよく思う.

that is to say →SAY².

That it is. →It is THAT.

that said/ having said that とは言っても ▪ *That said,* there is little to criticize in the performance. とは言っても, その上演には批判すべき点は少なかった.

That takes care of that. これで全部すんだ (= (and) THAT's that) ▪ I've dealt with this matter all morning, and *that takes care of that.* 午前中かかってこの問題を処理した. これで万事解決だ.

***that's a good boy* [*a dear*]** 《口》 いい子だから ▪ Hurry up, *that's a good boy.* 急いでおくれ, いい子だから.

That's about it. 《口》 まあそんなところだ; (仕事は)あらかた済んだ.

that's all それでおしまい; それだけのことだ ▪ I've been a little uneasy, *that's all.* ちょっと心配だっただけのことです ▪ *That's all* for today. きょうはこれでおしまい.

That's done* [*torn*] *it. 《口》 (計画・事業などが)それでだめになった, それでおじゃんだ ▪ I forgot to post it. Good Lord, *that's torn it.* あれを投函するのを忘れた. いやはや, これでおじゃんだ.

***that's for sure* [*certain*]** 〚文尾につけて〛 それは請け合ってもいい ▪ No, he won't come, *that's for sure!* いや, 彼は来ないよ, そりゃもう請け合ってもいい.

That's* a person *for you. 《口》 (特定の人間について)人間なんてそんなもんさ ▪ *That's* teenagers *for you.* 十代の若者ってそんなもんさ.

that's how →THAT's why.

that's how* [*the way*] *it goes. = That's the way the COOKIE crumbles.

That's how it is. そういう次第だ.

that's how* [*the way*] *the cookie crumbles/ that's how* [*the way*] *the ball bounces →That's the way the COOKIE crumbles.

That's it. ああそれだ, そこだ ▪ A hierarchy—*that's it.* That's exactly it. 階級組織—そうだ. まさにそれだ ▪ I'm sure *that's* not *it.* きっとそうじゃない.

***That's my boy* [*girl*].** それでこそいい子だ ▪ I won't do it again. I promise.—*That's my boy.* そんなこと二度としないよ. 約束するから—それでこそいい子だ. ☞主に子供の行儀へのほめ言葉.

That's right. **1** 《英口》 そうです ▪ Are you Mr. Smith?—*That's right.* スミスさんですか?—そうです.

2 《米》 謹聴 ▪ The President's address was frequently interrupted with cries of "*That's right!*" 大統領の演説は「謹聴!」という叫びで何度も中断された.

That's* [*That is*] *so. 《口》 その通り.

That's that. →(and) THAT's that.

That's torn it. →THAT's done it.

That's what I want* [*I'd like*] *to know. そこが知りたいところだ, 気になるところだ ▪ Who broke the vase, I wonder?—*That's what I want to know.* 誰が花瓶を割ったんだろう—こっちもそいつを知りたいんだ.

That's what it is. だからそうなんだ; その通りだ ▪ Hungry like a wolf?—*That's what it is.* 腹ペコなんだろ?—まさにその通り.

***that's why* [*how*]** そういうわけで[そういうふうにして]

▪ *That's why* I dislike him. それだから彼がきらいなんだ ▪ *That's how* a man loves a woman. そのようにして男は女を愛するものなのだ.

There is that. →THERE.

this* [*that*] *and* [*or*] *that →THIS.

Those were the days! あの頃は良かった[楽しかった]なあ ▪ He said he'd give me a job! *Those were the days*. 働かせてやると彼は言ってくれたんだ. よかったなあ, あの頃は.

upon* [*with*] *that そう言って, それから(すぐ) ▪ A proclamation was *upon that* issued out. 布告がそれからすぐ発布された ▪ *With that* he went out of the room. そう言って彼は部屋から出て行った.

Thatcher /θǽtʃər/ 名 ***do a Thatcher*** 首相の座に連続3期留まる ▪ He also *did a Thatcher*. 彼もまた首相を連続3期務めた. ☞英国の女性の政治家 Margaret H. Thatcher (1925–2013) が首相の座に3期(1979–90)留まったことから.

the /ðə, ði, ðiː/ 副 **(*all*) *the better* [*worse*,** etc.] ***for* [*because*]** ...のため[であるから]それだけよい[悪い, など] ▪ You are *all the better for* your failure. 君は失敗してかえってよくなった ▪ I love him *all the more because* he has faults. 彼には欠点があるのでかえって好きだ.

the more, the more ...すればするほどますます ▪ *The more* one has, *the more* one wants. = One wants *the more*, *the more* one has. 持てば持つだけ欲が出る ▪ *The higher* the tree, *the stronger* the wind. 木は高いほど風あたりは強い ▪ *The sooner, the better*. 早ければ早いほどよい.

theater, 《主に英》 **theatre** /θíːətər|θíətə/ 名 ***be good theater*** 上演ばえがする ▪ The play *is* very *good theater*. その芝居はとても上演ばえがする.

do a theater*/*go to the theater 芝居見物に行く ▪ We *went to the theatre* to see "Hamlet." 我々はハムレットの芝居を見に行った.

them /ðəm, ðem/ 代 ***them and us*** 連中と我々[上流階級と庶民, 雇用者と給料生活者, など] ▪ It's not easy to eliminate the old *Them and Us* attitude. 古くからの「連中と我々」といった態度を除去するのは容易ではない.

then /ðen/ 副 ***and then*** **1** それから ▪ We'll have fish first, *and then* roast chicken. まず魚を食べそれからローストチキンにしよう.

2 その上 ▪ I haven't the time, *and then* it isn't my business. その時間がないし, それにこっちの知ったことじゃない.

and* (*then*) *some →AND.

but then しかし同時に, それにしても ▪ *But then* why did you take it? それにしても, なぜそれを取ったのかね.

by then (過去・未来の)その時までに ▪ He had finished the work *by then*. 彼はその時までに仕事を終えていた.

***from then on*(*wards*)** その時以来 ▪ They were friends *from then on*. 彼らはその時以来友人となった.

now then →NOW.

now ... then →NOW ... now.

then again →AGAIN.

then and* [*but*] *not till then その時初めて ▪ *Then, but not till then* should you come. その時初めて君は来るべきです.

then and there*/*there and then その時その場で, たちどころに ▪ It was *then and there* concluded by a general consent. それはその時その場で満場一致で決められた ▪ We insisted on having it *there and then*. 我々はそれをただちにもらうことを主張した.

well then それでは, では ▪ If you want to go, *well then*, go! 行きたいのなら, じゃあ行きなさい.

What then? →WHAT.

theory /θíːəri|θíə-/ 名 ***in theory*** 理論的には ▪ Your plan is excellent *in theory*. 君の案は理論的にはすばらしい.

there /ðeər/ 副間名 ***all there is to do*** → ALL.

(*and* [*but, so*]) *there it is* [*there you go, there we* [*you*] *are*] (それで[でも, だから])それが実情だ; 仕方がない ▪ I don't like my job, but I need the money, *so there it is*. 仕事は気に入らないが金はいる, だから仕方ないんだ.

Are you there? もしもしあなたですか《電話口で》.

away there 向こうに ▪ You can see it *away there* in the park. それが向こうの公園に見えるだろう.

be all there 《口》〖主に否定文で〗(能力・精神が)しっかりしている, 正気である, 抜け目がない ▪ He *is all there* and knows what he is about. 彼はしっかりしていて万事心得ている ▪ Since then he has not been quite *all there*. 彼はその時以来少し頭が変になっている. ☞普通の人間としての「全能力が備わっている」の意から.

be right there 《米俗》とてもうまい ▪ When it comes to telling a joke, he's *right there*. 冗談を言う段になると, 彼はとてもうまい.

be there (現に)いる ▪ But the critic *is there* not to feel but to judge. しかし批評家は感じるためではなく, 目ききをするためにいるのだ.

be there for a person 《口》人が困ったときの助けになる ▪ Jimmy *is* always *there for* me. ジミーはいつも私が困っているときに助けてくれる.

But there! しかしまあ!《がまんしなさい, など》 ▪ *But there*, what's the good of talking about it? しかしまあ, そんなことを言ってもはじまるまい.

get there →GET.

get there with both feet →GET.

have been there 《俗》実地を踏んできた, 知り尽くしている ▪ Her hold on actuality is firm. She *has been there*. 彼女の現実把握はしっかりしている. 彼女は実地を踏んできたのだ.

in there **1** そこの中へ ▪ Put it *in there*. そこの中へ入れなさい ▪ He sat *in there*. 彼はそこに座った.

2 《俗》誠実な, 好ましい ▪ She is really *in there* and everybody likes her. 彼女は実に誠実でみんなに好かれている.

in there *doing* 《米口》全力を尽くして…している ▪ They are *in there fighting* for peace. 彼らは全力を尽くして平和のために戦っている.

I've been there before. (経験してきて)よく知っているよ ▪ There's so much that I could tell 'cause *I've been there before*. 経験を積んできたから色々わかるんだ.

let there be …あれ ▪ *Let there be* light. 光あれ.

neither here nor there →HERE.

out there **1** あそこに[は] ▪ It's warm *out there*. あそこは暖かい.

2 海外[戦地]に ▪ I'm sending you *out there* to break ground. 新天地を開拓させようと君たちを海外へ送り出すのだ.

3 世間(一般)の[で], 世の中の[には] ▪ Please tell all those mothers *out there* to stop being so critical. そういう世間一般の母親たちにあんまりあら探しをするなと言ってください ▪ There are so many lonely people *out there*. 世の中には孤独な人々は大勢いる.

put it there →PUT.

So there! さあどうだ《挑戦的気分を表す》 ▪ I'm sick of you too—*so there!* 君なんかにもうんざりしているんだ—さあどうだ.

That [***This***] ***is all there is to it.*** それ[これ]だけのことだ ▪ Well, *that was all there was to it*. He saved me. まあ, それだけの話だったのさ. 彼が僕を救ってくれたのだ.

there and back 往復 ▪ Can I go *there and back* in one day? 1日でそこへ往復できますか.

there and then →THEN.

There but for the Grace of God go I. →GRACE.

there came …が来た ▪ *There came* to Japan a foreigner. 日本へ一人の外国人がやって来た ▪ At last *there came* a time when his wisdom was needed. ついに彼の知恵が必要とされる時が来た.

there comes ほら[あれ]…が来た《眼前の出来事》 ▪ See, *there comes* the train. ごらん, 列車が来た.

there goes あれ(鐘など)が鳴っている《今聞こえているものについて》 ▪ Hark! *There goes* the bell! お聞き! 鐘が鳴っているよ.

There he [***she***] ***goes.***/***There they go.*** **1** ほら[あれ]あの人(たち)が通る ▪ *There goes* Friday, running to the river! あそこをフライデーが行くぞ, 川の方へ走って.

2 あれあの人(たち)があんなことをする, 言う《通例驚き・非難をこめて》 ▪ *There he goes*, grumbling again! ほら彼がまたぶつくさ言いだしたぞ.

there is [***are***] …がある ▪ *There was* no moon. 月は出ていなかった ▪ *There's* a man at the door wants to see you. 君に会いたいという人が玄関にきているよ.

there is ... *doing* …が…している ▪ *There is* a page *missing*. 1ページ欠けている ▪ *There's* mother *coming*. お母さんがやって来る.

There is ... for you! →FOR.

there is no *doing* …することはできない ▪ *There is no telling* when he will arrive. 彼がいつ来るかわからない.

there is no mistaking →there's no mistaking a thing (→MISTAKE²).

There is that. そりゃその通りだ, それはそうだね《考慮しなければならない, 忘れてはならない》 ▪ Flying is fast, but boring.—Yes, *there is that*. 飛行機は速いけど退屈だ—いや, 全く ▪ Wait for the breeze to change direction? Well, yes, *there is that*. 風向きが変わるのを待てだって? なるほど, そりゃそうだ. ☞is に強勢を置く.

There it goes! あれあれ落ちる[こわれる, 見えなくなる, 行く, など]! ▪ The music is about to begin. —*There it goes!* 音楽がじき始まるぞ—さあ始まった.

There it is. 事実は事実だ; どうしようもない ▪ He wished to forget her. But *there it was*. He loved her desperately. 彼女のことを忘れたいと思った. しかし, どうしようもなかった. 彼は死ぬほど彼女を愛していた.

There now! それどうだ! ▪ *There now*, it's just as I expected. そうらみろ, 私の思っていた通りだ.

there or thereabouts (場所・数量が)その辺のところ ▪ Was it two years ago?—*There or thereabouts*. 2年前のことかね?—その辺のところだ.

there remains to *do* あとは…するだけだ ▪ *There remains* for me *to* apologize. あとは私が謝るだけだ.

There! There! まあまあ!, よしよし!《慰め》 ▪ *There! There!* You'll soon be better. まあまあ, じきよくなりますよ.

There we are. =THERE you are! 2.

There you are! 《口》 **1** あれあんなことをする[言う]! ▪ *There you are* again. そらまた始まった.

2 そらどうだ, それごらん《仕事・議論・予言がうまくいったことに対するコメント》 ▪ That's quite easy; just press that button and *there you are!* そりゃ手もないことさ. ちょっとそのボタンを押せばそれまでだよ ▪ I waited nearly an hour for Tom.—*There you are!* I told you he would be late. 1時間近くもトムを待った—それごらん. 遅れて来るぞと言っただろう.

3 =THERE it is.

there you go (***again***) =THERE you are! 1.

There's a good fellow [***boy, girl,*** etc.]. 〚命令文に後置して〛よい子だからね, お願いだ《相手は子供とはかぎらない》 ▪ Tom, go and fetch the wine for your sister, *there's a dear love*. トム, お姉さんにワインを持ってきておくれ, いい子だから ▪ Don't hurry, *there's a good fellow*. あわてないでくれ, 頼む.

There's *books* ***and*** *books*. 《口》本[など]にもいろいろある, いい本もあれば悪い本もある ▪ *There's* women *and* women. 女性にもいろいろある.

There's for you. さあこれをあなたに差しあげます ▪ *There's for you*, dear Mary. さあこれをあげますよ, メアリー.

(***there's***) ***nothing*** [***little, not much***] ***in it*** →IN².

(***there's***) ***something in it*** 《口》それはある程度本当だ[本当ではない] ▪ Yes, I guess *there's something in it*. うん, ある程度その通りだと思う ▪ I'm

T

afraid *there's nothing in it.* その話は嘘だと思う.

Where is there ...? …はどこにあるか ▪ *Where is there* a hotel?—There is one over there. ホテルはどこにありますか?—向こうに一つあります. ☞非特定な物の存在を聞く言い方; 特定の物なら Where is the hotel? のように there が落ちる.

You've got me there. 《口》何と答えていいのかわからない ▪ No, sorry; *you've got me there.* Don't understand a thing. いや, 申し訳ない. 何と答えればいいか. さっぱり分からない.

therein /ðéərín/ 副 ***therein lies*** 《文》そこに…がある ▪ My uncle works extremely hard and *therein lies* the key to his success. 叔父は実によく働く. 彼の成功はそこにあるのだ.

these /ði:z/ 代 →THIS.

thews /θju:z/ 名 ***have thews of steel*** 非常に頑健だ ▪ He *has thews of steel.* 彼は実に頑健だ.

thick /θɪk/ 形名副 ***a bit [rather, a little too] thick*** 《口》ちとひどすぎる ▪ Tom was *a bit thick.* トムはちょっとひどすぎた ▪ Three weeks of heavy rain is *a little too thick.* 3週間も大雨が降るなんて少々ひどすぎる.

(as) thick as glue [peas in a shell, (two) thieves, three in a bed, inkle-weavers] 《口》きわめて親密な ▪ She and my wife are *as thick as thieves.* 彼女と家内はきわめて親密なのです ▪ We soon grew *as thick as inkle-weavers.* 我々はやがて離れられない仲になった.

(as) thick as hops →HOP[2].

(as) thick as two (short) planks 《英口》非常に頭が悪い ▪ Some of them are *as thick as two short planks.* 彼らの何人かは大ばかだ.

get [give] a thick ear →EAR.

have a thick head 頭が痛い[ぼーっとしている] ▪ I'd love to go, but I*'ve got a* very *thick head* this morning. ぜひ行きたいところだが, けさはひどく頭痛がするので.

have a thick skin →SKIN[1].

in the thick of (行為の)最中[たけなわ]で ▪ We are now *in the thick of* a Cabinet crisis. 今や内閣の危機の最中だ ▪ He was *in the thick of* these splendid projects. 彼はこのすばらしい計画を立てている最中だった.

lay [spread] it on thick 《口》大げさに言う, ほらを吹く ▪ Don't *spread it on thick.* 大げさな言い方はやめろ ▪ Don't you think he is *spreading it on* rather *thick*? 彼は少しほらを吹いていると思わんか.

put it on thick →LAY it on thick.

the thick of …の一番太い[厚い]部分, 最も賑やかな[混み合った]場所 ▪ This is *the thick of* the city. ここが町で一番賑やかなところだ ▪ Late November is *the thick of* fall wine releases. 11月の末といえば秋のワイン発売の真っ盛りだ ▪ It is *the thick of* fall and pumpkins seem to be on everyone's mind. 今は秋たけなわでパンプキンがみなの心を占めているようだ.

thick and fast/fast and thick しきりに, 激しく ▪ It was snowing *thick and fast.* 雪がしきりに降っていた ▪ The events came *thick and fast.* 事件はしきりに起こった.

thick on the ground → be thick on the GROUND.

thick with **1** …が群がっていて[いっぱいで] ▪ The path was *thick with* dangers. その道は危険が多かった ▪ The air was *thick with* dust. 空気はほこりでいっぱいだった.
2 《口》…と親しい ▪ John is very *thick with* Tom now. ジョンは近ごろトムととても親しい.

through thick and thin 万難を排して, 水火をいとわず ▪ There're five hundred men here to back you up *through thick and thin.* ここには水火をいとわずあなたを支持する者が500人います. ☞「茂みや木のまばらな所を通って」が原義.

thief /θi:f/ 名 ***a thieves' kitchen*** 犯罪者の溜り場 ▪ The place turned into *a thieves' kitchen.* その場所は犯罪者の溜り場になった.

like a thief in the night 盗人(ぬすびと)が夜来るように(だしぬけに, こっそりと)(《聖》*1 Thess.* 5. 2) ▪ Old age creeps up *like a thief in the night.* 老年は盗人が夜来るように忍び寄る.

Little thieves are hanged, but great ones escape. 《諺》筋金入りの犯罪人は決して捕まらない.

Set a thief to catch a thief. 《諺》泥棒は泥棒に捕らえさせよ,「蛇(じゃ)の道は蛇(へび)」.

Stop thief! →STOP[2].

thin /θɪn/ 形 ***(as) thin as a lath [rake, stick,*** 《主に米》***rail]*** やせこけて ▪ The child is *as thin as a lath.* その子はやせこけている ▪ She was *thin as a rail* and weighed next to nothing. 彼女はやせこけていて体重も著しく軽かった.

as thin as thin とても薄い ▪ The pancake was *as thin as thin.* そのパンケーキはすこぶる薄かった.

be too thin 見えすいている ▪ His excuse *was* a bit *too thin.* 彼の言い訳は少し見えすいていた.

give *a person* ***a thin time*** 《口》人にさんざんな思いをさせる ▪ If you don't go, she will *give* you such *a thin time.* 行かないと彼女にさんざんな目にあわされるよ.

have a thin skin →have a thick SKIN.

have a thin time (of it) 《英口》さんざんな思いをする ▪ He must have *had a thin time of it.* 彼はさんざんな思いをしたにちがいない.

not grow any thinner 太る ▪ You have*n't grown any thinner.* 君は太ったね.

out of [from] thin air →AIR[1].

thin on the ground → be thin on the GROUND.

thin on top 頭髪が薄くなって ▪ He is getting *thin on top.* 彼は髪の毛が薄くなりかけている.

vanish into thin air →AIR[1].

thing /θɪŋ/ 名 ***a bright young thing*** 快楽を求め流行の先端を行く富める若者 ▪ Our boss is *a bright young thing* who's only half my age. わが社の社長は私の年齢の半分しかない野心的で流行の先端を行く青年である.

T

a close [***close-run***] ***thing*** ＝a NEAR escape.

A thing of beauty is a joy forever. 《諺》美しきものは永遠(とわ)の喜びなり (Keats, *Endymion* (1818)).

a thing of shreds and patches 《雅》布の切れっ端を継ぎはぎしたもの ▪ The bugs have made the program *a thing of shreds and patches*. バグのせいでプログラムがモザイク模様の代物になってしまった ▪ His history was *a thing of shreds and patches*, casually, almost randomly, assembled. 彼の著した歴史書は気の向くままほとんど手当たり次第に集めた雑多な資料を継ぎはぎしたものだった ▪ New York is said to be *a thing of shreds and patches*. ニューヨークは人種[文化]の寄せ集めであると言われている.

a thing of the past 過去の[時代遅れの]人[物] ▪ Hatpins are *things of the past*. ハットピンなんて時代遅れの代物だ.

A thing you don't want is dear at any price. 《諺》安いというだけでものを買ってはいけない,「安物買いの銭失い」.

All good things must (***come to an***) ***end.***/ ***All things*** (***must***) ***come to an end.*** 《諺》楽しくてもあらゆる体験はいつかは終わる,「楽しみ[喜び]は束の間」.

all things considered →CONSIDER.

All things must [***will***] ***pass.*** 何事もついには終わりがくる ▪ Know that nothing lasts forever and *all things will pass*. 永遠に続くものはなく万事はいずれ過ぎ去っていくことを知りなさい.

and things (***like that***) 《口》…など ▪ Grace would mend her father's nets *and things*. グレイスは父親の網などを繕うのだった ▪ Mom's been busy shopping *and things*. ママはお買い物や何かで忙しくしています ▪ My boyfriend likes skateboarding *and things like that*. ボーイフレンドはスケートボードや何かが好きなの.

any fool thing どんなばかばかしい[つまらない]もの(でも) ▪ He would buy his wife *any fool thing* she wanted. 彼は妻が欲しがればどんなくだらないものでも買ってやるのだった.

as things are [***stand***] 現状では ▪ *As things are* I will not invest any money in Indian market. 現状ではインド市場には投資すまい ▪ *As things stand*, we won't finish the job on time. このままだと仕事は時間通りには終わらないだろう ▪ *As things go*, it is very unlikely that she will win the election. 今のところ彼女が当選する可能性は低い.

T

as things go 今の状態では, 世の常として ▪ That's not dear *as things go*. それは今時では高くない.

be (***all, quite***) ***the thing*** 《口》流行しているものである (→the THING) ▪ Her dress *is* not *quite the thing*. 彼女のドレスは流行しているものではない.

be all things to all people [***men***] (人が)すべての人の期待に応えられる (《聖》*1 Cor.* 9. 22); みなに気に入られる, 八方美人になる ▪ The President should *be all things to all men*. 大統領は万人の期待に応えるべきだ.

be no great things 《俗》(…が)たいしたものじゃない ▪ He'*s no great things*, between us, sir. ここだけの話ですが, あの男はたいしたものじゃありません ▪ His scholarship *was no great things*. 彼の学識はたいしたものではなかった.

be [***feel***] ***not quite the thing*** 《主に英》体の具合がよくない ▪ I *am not quite the thing* this morning. けさはどうも調子がよくない.

be not the thing 不適切(なふるまい)である ▪ It'*s not the thing* to wear a white suit at a funeral. 葬式に白いスーツを着るのは場にそぐわない.

be one damn thing after another [***ODTAA***] 次から次へ問題が起きる ▪ In the sumo world these days it'*s one damn thing after another*. Trouble never goes away. 相撲界では近頃次から次に問題が起こり, トラブルがなくならない.

be onto a good thing 《口》うまい儲け口にありついている ▪ Like any successful entrepreneur, he knew when he *was onto a good thing*. 成功した起業家と同様, 彼もいつうまい儲け口にありついているかが分かっていた.

be the done thing →the DONE thing.

be up to** a thing **or two →KNOW a thing or two.

come [***amount***] ***to*** (***much***) ***the same thing*** (***at the end***) →come to the SAME thing.

dear old thing 《口》おじいちゃん; おばあちゃん《親しみをこめて初老の人をさして》 ▪ Give the *dear old thing* a new shawl. おばあちゃんにショールの新しいのをあげなさい.

do** one's* (own***) ***thing*** 最も好きな[得意な, 変わった]ことをする; 気の向くままにやる ▪ Emerson said, "*Do your thing*!" エマソンは「最も好きな仕事をせよ」と言った.

do the other thing 《口》好きなようにする ▪ You won't come? Well, you can *do the other thing*. 君は来ないって? じゃあ勝手にしたらいい. ☞通例「勝手にしろ」の意味に用いる.

do the right [***wrong, sensible***] ***thing*** 正しい[誤った, 分別のある]ことをする ▪ I'm afraid of *doing the wrong thing*. まずいことをしはしないかと心配だ.

do the wild thing 《俗》セックスする ▪ I wanna *do the wild thing*, honey. おい, セックスしたいんだ.

expect great things of …に大いに期待する ▪ We *expect great things of* the new treatment. 我々は今度の治療に大いに期待している.

feel out of things 疎外感を味わう, 疎まれる ▪ I *feel out of things* lately because people are ignoring me. みんなぼくに知らんぷりをしていて近頃疎まれている気がするんだ.

for one [***another***] ***thing*** 一つ[また一つ]には, まず第一[また次]には, 一例をあげると ▪ *For one thing* I'm busy; *for another* I haven't the money. 一つには暇がないし, また一つにはその金もない ▪ *For one thing*, he drinks. 一例をあげると彼は酒を飲む.

have a good thing going 《口》大儲けしている, 優位な立場にいる ▪ Nobody noticed that he *had* *a good thing going.* 誰も彼が大儲けしているなど気うかなかった.

have (***got***) ***a*** [***this***] ***thing about*** 《口》 **1** …を毛嫌いする ▪ My father *has got a thing about* dyed hair. 父は髪の毛を染めるのを毛嫌いしている. **2** …をひどく好む ▪ John *has this thing about* her. ジョンは彼女が大好きだ.

How are [《俗》 ***How's***] ***things?*** →HOW.

If you want a thing done well, do it yourself. 《諺》 物事をきちんと処理するには他人に頼らないことである,「他人を当てにするな」.

imagine things →IMAGINE.

in all things どんな場合でも, いつでも ▪ I believe in tolerance *in all things.* 常に辛抱が肝心だと思っている.

it's a ... thing …だけにわかることだ ▪ You wouldn't understand the thrill of fast cars—*it's a* man *thing.* 君には足の速い車のスリルはわかるまい—男にしかわからないものだから.

It's (***just***) ***one thing after another!*** いやな[思いもかけない]ことが続く, 一難去ってまた一難である ▪ I was late for work. And I had my bike stolen. *It was just one thing after another.* 会社に遅刻するわ自転車を盗まれるわと, 踏んだり蹴ったりだった.

(***just***) ***one of those things*** →ONE.

keep things humming 事を円滑に進める ▪ He's really been *keeping things humming* since he joined us. 彼が私たちに加わってくれて以来, 実に物事が円滑に進んできている.

know [***be up to***] ***a thing or two*** →KNOW[2].

last thing →LAST thing (at night).

learn a thing or two 多少世間を知る ▪ They have *learnt a thing or two* in their lives. 彼らはこれまでに多少世間を知ってきた.

Little [***Small***] ***things please little*** [***small***] ***minds.*** 《諺》 賢くない者は些細なことで気をよくする.

make a (***big***) ***thing of*** [***about***] …を重大視する; で大騒ぎする ▪ He *made a thing of* her abusive language. 彼は彼女の悪態でいきまいた.

make a good thing of …を利用する; で利を占める ▪ I hope my son will *make a better thing of* his life than I have done. 息子が私よりもうまく人生を利用するよう望んでいる ▪ He *makes a good thing of* his spare-time hobbies. 彼は余暇の趣味で利益を得ている.

make things go →GO[2].

not feel quite the thing →be not quite the THING.

not know a thing about …のことは少しも知らない ▪ I do*n't know a thing about* algebra. 私は代数は少しも知らない.

of all things こともあろうに ▪ We're told—*of all things!*—that we shall have to leave the house. 我々は—こともあろうに—家を出なければならないと言い渡されたのだ.

old thing 《口》 君, お前さん 《親しい人へのふざけた, または親しみをこめた呼びかけ; 若い人々がよく用いる》 ▪ So long, *old thing.* じゃあね, 君.

one thing, ... another (***thing***) →ONE.

One thing leads to another. 次から次にいろんなことが起こる; ものごとがお定まりの結果になる, あれこれあって結局…になる ▪ He dropped me home and *one thing led to another* and we ended up in bed. 彼は私を家まで送ってくれたが, 自然の成り行きで, 私たちは結ばれた ▪ We met his father, and *one thing led to another* and we ended up adopting that child. 私たちは彼の父親に会い, とんとん拍子に話が進んで結局その子を養子にすることにした.

other things being equal →EQUAL.

one's (***own***) ***thing*** 自分の一番好きなこと ▪ Bars, clubs aren't really *my thing.* バーやクラブなんかはあまり好きではないんだ.

see [***hear***] ***things*** まぼろしを見る[聞く], 幻覚[幻聴]をおぼえる ▪ When I saw a face at the window, I thought I was *seeing things.* 窓辺に人の顔が見えたとき, まぼろしを見ているのだと思った ▪ At first I thought I was *hearing things*, but then I heard a cop come to the door. 初めは空耳かと思ったが, やがて警察官が戸口に立つのが聞こえた.

show *a person* ***a thing or two/put*** *a person* ***up to a thing or two*** 人を世間知らずでなくする ▪ Jackey *showed* Robinson *a thing or two.* ジャッキーはロビンスンに多少世間のことを教えた.

Stranger things have happened. 《諺》 もっとひどいことはいくらでもある ▪ Like the old saying goes, "*Stranger things have happened.*" 古い諺にあるように「もっとひどいことだってざらにある」のだ.

tell *a person* ***a thing or two*** 人に小言を言う ▪ If he does it again I'll certainly *tell* him *a thing or two.* 彼がもう一度そんなことをしたら必ず小言を言ってやる.

that very thing まさに[ほかならぬ]それ ▪ I was just about to say *that very thing.* まさにそう言おうとしてたんだ.

The best [***Good***] ***things come in small packages.*** 《諺》 貴重なものこそ小さな包みに入ってくる,「胴より胆が張る」.

The best things in life are free. 《諺》 世の中にただよりすてきなものはない.

the done thing/《米》 ***the thing to do*** →DONE.

(***the***) ***first*** [***second, next, last***] ***thing*** まず第一に[第二に, 次に, 最後に] ▪ I must do it *the first thing* in the morning. 朝まず第一にそれをせねばならない ▪ He often goes round *the last thing* to make sure that all is right. 彼はしばしば最後に見回って異常がないことを確かめる.

(***the***) ***first*** [***next***] ***thing*** *one* ***knows*** 《口》 たちまち, やがて ▪ *Next thing* I *knew*, I was deeply in debt. たちまち私は大借金をしていた.

the good things in [***of***] ***life*** 人生のよきもの 《贅沢品や快楽》 ▪ His money brought him *the good things in life* but not happiness. 金は彼に贅沢や快楽をもたらしたが, 幸せをもたらしはしなかった.

the greatest* [*the best*] *thing since sliced bread →BREAD.

the thing/the in thing 最新流行のもの ▪ Vegetarianism is *the thing* in vogue these days. 菜食主義が最近のはやりだ ▪ Blogging has been *the "in thing"* for some time now. しばらく前からブログが流行している.

the thing in itself 物自体, 実在 ▪ He recognizes substance, or, as we might say, *the thing-in-itself*. 彼は実体, あるいは言うなれば物自体を認める. ☞Ⓖ Ding an sich のなぞり《Kant の哲学用語》.

the thing is 問題は…である ▪ *The thing is*, can we get there in time? 問題は, そこへ間に合うように着けるかということだ.

the very thing うってつけの物 ▪ It's *the very thing* for you. それは君にうってつけの物だ.

there's no* (*such thing as a*) *free lunch → LUNCH.

There's only one thing for it. とるべき道はこれだけである ▪ Well, *there's only one thing for it*, I'm afraid ... run! まあ, こうするしかないと思うな…逃げるんだ!

These things* (*will*) *happen. こんなことはよくある(から心配しないでよい) ▪ Sorry. I've spilt some coffee.—Never mind, *these things happen*. ごめん. コーヒーをこぼしちゃった—気にするな, よくあることさ.

Things are seldom* [*not*] *what they seem. 《諺》人は見かけによらぬもの.

things that go bump in the night 《口》夜中にバタンと音を立てるもの《幽霊・おばけ・妖怪・怪奇現象》 ▪ In the castle the children checked out the *things that went bump in the night*. その館の中で子供たちは幽霊を探索した ▪ Cynics say there are no ghosts, but little boys and girls believe in *things that go bump in the night*. 皮肉屋は幽霊なんかいないと言うけれど, 幼い男の子や女の子は夜中にバタンと音を立てるものの存在を信じている.

what with one thing and another → WHAT with A and (what is) B.

think[1] /θɪŋk/ 名形 ***a think piece*** **1** 頭脳, 知性 ▪ She's got *a* powerful *think piece*. 彼女は高い知性を具えている.

2 (問題提起する)新聞記事; (事件の分析・背景・記者の意見が入った)ニュース解説 ▪ That article by Brady Dennis on population explosion in the Washington Post sure was *a* big *think piece*! ワシントン・ポスト紙の人口激増に関するブレイディー・デニス記者の例の記事は確かに大きな問題提起をした ▪ It's *an* interesting *think piece*. それは興味深い解説記事だ.

have a think 《口》考える ▪ I *had a* quiet *think*. 私は静かに考えた.

have* (*got*) *another think coming 《口》(…と思っているなら)大間違いだ[考え直さないといけない] (→if you THINK (that)..., (then) you have got another think coming) ▪ If he thinks he'll be able to graduate, he's *got another think coming*. 彼が卒業できる思っているなら大間違いだ.

think[2] /θɪŋk/ 動 ***and to think* (*that*)** → AND.

come to think of it →COME[2].

dread* [*shudder*] *to think → SHUDDER to think.

give** a person* ***furiously to think →GIVE.

I don't think. 《俗》〚反語表現に伴って〛いやはや全く, とは全く思わないね ▪ You're an amicably-disposed young man, sir, *I don't think*. 君は気立てのいい青年だよ, いやはや全く. ☞don't に強勢を置く.

I should think **1** まあ…だと思います《控え目な言い方》 ▪ *I should think* you'd love it. それがお気に入ると思いますよ.

2 〚think に強勢を置いて〛むろん…だと思う《皮肉・軽蔑などを含めて》 ▪ Would she suffer?—Badly, *I should think*. 彼女は困るだろうか?—むろんひどく困ると思うよ.

I thought as much. そんなことだと思ったよ ▪ Tom and Beth have split up.—*I thought as much*. トムとベスが別れたんだ—そうなるだろうと思っていたよ ▪ He's resigning? *I thought as much*. 彼が辞めるって? そんなことだろうと思っていたよ.

I thought I told* [*asked*] *you to *do* …するように言って[頼んで]おいたはずだが《不履行をなじる言葉》 ▪ *I thought I told you to* come early. 早く来るように言っといたはずだが.

if* [*when*] *you think about it 考えてみれば ▪ It must have been wonderful *if you think about it*. 考えてみれば, それはすばらしいことであったにちがいない.

if you think* (*that*)..., (*then*) *you have got another think coming 《口》…と考えているなら, とんだ了見違いだ (→have (got) another THINK coming) ▪ *If you think* I will help you, *you have got another think coming*. 僕が君を援助するなんて考えているなら, とんだ了見違いだよ.

It makes you think. それは少々異常だ ▪ Children starving in our days? *It makes you think*. 今どき子供が飢え死にする? そりゃちと異常だね.

just think 考えてもみろよ ▪ I'll be on television tomorrow! *Just think*! 私, 明日テレビに出るのよ! 考えてもごらん.

let me think 考えさせてくれ; ええっと ▪ *Let me think* a moment. ちょっと考えさせてくれたまえ ▪ His name was—*let me think*—there, I've forgotten. その人の名は—ええっと—あれ, 忘れちゃった.

make** a person* ***think 人を(真剣に)考え込ませる ▪ When you hear of such accidents, it *makes* you *think*. そういう事故の話を聞くと, 考えさせられる.

Makes you think, doesn't it? よく考え直してみて ▪ About this design. *Makes you think, doesn't it?* このデザインだが, 考え直してみてくれないか.

Only think! 《口》考えてもごらんなさい(驚くでしょう) ▪ *Only think!* I get my new milk again, at eight. 考えてもごらん, 8時にまた新しい牛乳をもらうのよ.

That's what you think. 君がそう考えているにすぎ

ない《嘲笑的に不信を表す》. ☞you に強勢を置く ▪ You are going to lose! —*That's what you think*! 君は負けるぞ―あんたがそう思っているだけさ.

think a lot [***a great deal***] ***of*** …を重んじる, 愛する ▪ His friends *think a lot of* Bob. 友人たちはボブを愛している.

think aloud 考え事を口に出して言う ▪ He has a habit of *thinking aloud*. 彼は考え事を口に出して言う癖がある.

think better of **1** (意向・決心など)を考え直してやめる ▪ I hope you'll *think better of* it. 考え直してほしいんだが.

2 …をもっとよいと思う, 見直す ▪ I *think better of* him than that. 彼はそれよりはましだと思う ▪ I *think better of* him for his present conduct. 私は今度のふるまいで彼を見直した.

think big [***positive, young,*** etc.] 《口》野心的な[積極的な, 若々しい, など]考え方をする, でっかいことをやろうとする ▪ It's true you were fired but *think positive*. 君は確かに首にはなったが, 前向きに考えることだな ▪ He does not try to dress young but he *thinks young*. 彼は若ぶりな身なりこそ試さないが考え方は若々しい ▪ *Think big*, act small. 構想は大きく, 実行は着実に.

think fit [***good, proper***] ***to*** *do* 《しばしば反語》…するのがよいと思う ▪ I *thought good to* go to the philosophers. 私は哲学者のもとへ行くのがよいと思った ▪ He *thought fit to* address me in insulting language. 彼は無礼な言葉で私に話しかけてもよいと思った ▪ He didn't *think fit to* recognize me. 彼は都合が悪いので私にそしらぬ顔をした.

think for *oneself* 自分で考える[決心する] ▪ Many young people can't *think for themselves*. 若い人々の中には自分で考えることのできない者が多い.

think hardly of →speak HARDLY of.

think highly of …を尊重する ▪ The directors *think highly of* Smith. 重役らはスミスを買っている.

think lightly of …を軽蔑する ▪ He *thinks lightly of* wealth. 彼は富を軽蔑している.

think little of …をつまらないと思う ▪ Few women *think little of* fashion. 流行を軽視する女性はまずいない.

think much of …を重んじる ▪ I didn't *think much of* her. 私は彼女を重んじなかった.

think no end of …を非常に高く評価する ▪ We *think no end of* our new chauffeur. 今度の運転手をとても高く評価しています.

think no harm 悪いとは思わない ▪ The child *thought no harm* in doing it. その子は悪いとは思わずにそうしたのだ.

think no more of *A* ***than*** *B* Bと同様Aを何とも思わない ▪ We *think no more of* you *than* you think of us. 君が我々のことを何とも思わないのと同様に我々も君を何とも思っていない.

think nothing of **1** …を何とも思わない ▪ She said she *thought nothing of* the walk. 彼女は歩くことなど何とも思わないと言った.

2 …を無価値だと考える ▪ I *think nothing of* that man. あの男はてんでだめだと思う.

Think nothing of it. (わびに対して)何でもありませんよ ▪ I'm sorry for being late.—*Think nothing of it.* 遅くなってすみません―かまいませんよ.

think out of the box →BOX[1].

think outside the box →BOX[1].

think proper to *do* →THINK fit to do.

think straight →STRAIGHT.

think to *oneself* ひそかに考える ▪ I was *thinking to myself* how pretty she was. 彼女はなんてきれいなんだろうとひそかに考えていた.

think twice →TWICE.

think well [***ill, badly***] ***of*** …をよく[悪く]思う ▪ He *is thought well of*. 彼は人からよく思われている ▪ I hope you won't *think badly of* me because I did so. 私がああしたからと言って悪く思わないでほしい.

A person ***thinks*** *he'****s*** [*she'****s***] ***it.*** 自分を特別だと思っている《実際は違う, というニュアンスで》 ▪ Look at that punk. He really *thinks* he'*s it*. あの不良を見てみろよ. ほんと自分は特別だと思ってやがる.

To think that …! …と思うと; …とは(驚く, 悲しい, など) ▪ *To think that* he is only twenty*!* 彼がほんのはたちだとは(驚く)!

What will they think of next? [***!***] 《口》今度は何を考えつくやら《驚きだ, ばかばかしい》.

Who [***What***] ***do you think?*** 《口》それが誰[どう]だと思う《挿入節として驚くようなことを述べる前に》 ▪ There was an old woman; and *what do you think?* She lived upon nothing but victuals and drink. あるおばあさんがいたんだが, それがどうだと思う? 食物と酒ばかりで暮らしていたんだよ ▪ *Who do you* [*does he*] *think* you are [he is]*?* 君[彼]は自分を何様だと思っているのか.

You can't think! 《口》 **1** あなたには想像もつかないでしょう ▪ *You can't think* how I'm encumbered with these quarrels! 私がこういうけんかでどんなにじゃまされているか, あなたには想像もつかないでしょう.

2 信じられないほど ▪ She is such a saucy girl, *you can't think*. 彼女は途方もなく生意気な女の子ですよ.

thinking /θíŋkɪŋ/ 名形 ***be of*** *a person's* ***way of thinking*** 人と同じ考えである ▪ You *are of my way of thinking*. 君は私と同じ考えだ.

Good thinking! 名案だね.

have *one's* ***thinking-cap on*** 《口》考えこんでいる ▪ I think Mr. Nevills really *has his thinking-cap on* and hit upon a wonderful idea. ネビルズ氏が実際に考え込んでいて, 名案を思いつくと思う.

put on *one's* ***thinking cap*** →CAP[1].

to my (***way of***) ***thinking*** 私の考えでは ▪ The music, *to my thinking*, pleased the King. その音楽は私の考えでは国王の気に入った.

third /θəːrd/ 形名副 ***play third fiddle*** 《米口》非常に下っぱ役をする (*to*) ▪ America does not even *play third fiddle to* this European element. アメリカはこのヨーロッパ的要素に端役的役割すら果たしていない.

put** a person **through the third degree**/ **give** a person **the third degree 《米口》人に(警察の)厳しい尋問をする, 過酷な取調べをする ▪ He *was put through the third degree* at the station. 彼は警察署で厳しい尋問をくわされた ▪ When Jim gets home, I want you to *give* him *the third degree*. ジムが帰宅したら, あなた, 彼を厳しく問いつめてくださいね ▪ Stop *giving* me *the third degree*. 僕に強引に質問するのをやめてくれ. ☞third degree はもと「警察の拷問」.

***Third time does the trick** [**(is) lucky, pays for all, is the charm**].* 《諺》3度目にはめが出る,「3度目の正直」.

***travel third**(**-class**)* 3等で旅行する ▪ They almost invariably *travel third-class*. 彼らはほとんどきまって3等で旅行する.

thirst /θəːrst/ 名 ***get** [**work**] **up a** [one's] **thirst*** のどがかわく ▪ I've *got up* such *a thirst* jogging. ジョギングをしてひどくのどがかわいた ▪ Such work always *gets up a thirst* with me. こういう仕事をするといつものどがかわく.

thirty /θə́ːrti/ 形 ***in** [**out of**] one's **thirties*** 30代で[を出て] ▪ I am just *out of my thirties*. 私は30代をちょうど出たところです.

the Hungry Thirties 恐慌と失業[食糧難]の1930年代 ▪ They were in and out of relief camps in *the Hungry Thirties*. 空腹の30年代に彼らは貧民救済キャンプを出たり入ったりした.

this /ðɪs/ 代形副 ***all this*** **1** すべてのこの種のもの ▪ *All this* is distasteful to me. こういうものはすべて私にはいとわしい.

2 一体この ▪ What's *all this* noise about? 一体この騒ぎはどうしたというのだ.

at this ここにおいて, これを見て ▪ *At this*, he got up and went out. ここで, 彼は立ち上がって出て行った.

before this 今までに ▪ I had heard of it *before this*. そのことは今までに聞いたことがあった.

by this この時までに, 今ごろは ▪ *By this* the sun is setting. 今ごろは日が沈んでいる ▪ They ought to be here *by this*. もう今ごろはここに来ているはずだ.

Get out of this. ここから出て行け ▪ You filthy beast, *get out of this*. この野郎め, ここから出て行け.

like this このように[な] ▪ Do it *like this*. それをこのようにしなさい ▪ Of what could we talk on an evening *like this*! このような晩に何の話ができようか.

put this and that together あれこれ総合して考える ▪ I also could *put this and that together*. 私もあれこれ考え合わせることができた.

these days 近ごろは ▪ Life is easier *these days*. 近ごろの方が暮らしやすい.

this and** [**or**] **that あれやこれや(の) ▪ We sat speaking of *this or that*. 我々は座ってあれやこれやの話をした ▪ Truth must not be measured by the convenience of *this or that* man. 真理は誰彼の便宜によって測られるべきものではない.

*Tom **this and** Tom **that*** 一にも二にもトム ▪ It was Mary *this and* Mary *that*. 一にも二にもメアリーで持ち切りだった.

***this day** [**morning, afternoon, evening**]* きょう[けさ, きょうの午後, 今晩] ▪ Where were you *this day* last year? 去年のきょうどこにいましたか.

This is how it is. (実は)こういう訳なんだ《説明の前置き》.

This is it. そこ(が困った[大事な]ところ)なんだ.

This is where we** [**I**] **came in. これは前見たところ[やったこと]だ. ☞映画が途中から見始めた所に戻ることから.

***this many a day** [**year**]* きょうまでの幾日[幾年]間 ▪ This has made my heart heavy *this many a day*. このことできょうまでの幾日間私の心は重かった.

this much →MUCH.

this ... that/these ... those 《雅》後者は…前者は ▪ Health is above wealth, for *this* cannot give so much happiness as *that*. 健康は富に勝る. 後者は前者ほど多くの幸福を与えることができないからだ.

this, that, and** [**or**] **the other あれやこれや, ありとあらゆる(もの) ▪ She must have *this, that, and the other*. 彼女はあれやこれや手に入れないと承知しない.

with this こう言って[して] ▪ *With this*, he went out. こう言って彼は出て行った.

Thomas /tɑ́məs|tɔ́m-/ 名 ***a doubting Thomas*** →DOUBTING.

thorn /θɔːrn/ 名 ***a bed of thorns*** →BED[1].

***a thorn in the** [one's] **flesh** [**side**]* 苦労, 心配, 悩みの種(《聖》*2 Cor.* 12. 7; *Judges* 2. 3) ▪ The Eastern Church was *a thorn in the side* of the Papacy. ギリシャ教会はローマ教皇にとって悩みの種であった.

be** [**sit, stand, walk**] **on** [**upon**] **thorns 絶えず不安におののく ▪ He was *sitting on thorns*, afraid lest she should refer to the late event. 彼は彼女が今度の事件を言い出しはしないかと心配して絶えずびくびくしていた.

Every rose has its thorn./No rose without a thorn. →ROSE.

***take a thorn out of** a person's **pillow** [**flesh**]* 人の心配の種を一つ除く ▪ You have *taken a thorn out of my pillow* in so doing. 君はそうして私の心配の種を一つ除いてくれたのだ.

thorny /θɔ́ːrni/ 形 ***a thorny question** [**problem, issue**]* やっかいな問題, 難問 ▪ Many scholars have discussed the *thorny question* of abortion. これまで多くの学者が妊娠中絶という難問を論じてきた ▪ The invasion of privacy here is *a thorny problem*. 当地ではプライバシーの侵害がやっかいな問題になっている ▪ Unemployment has long been *a thorny issue*. 失業が頭痛の種になって久しい.

thoroughfare /θə́ːroʊfèər|θʌ́rə-/ 名 ***No thoroughfare.*** 通行止め《掲示》.

those /ðoʊz/ 代 →THAT.

though /ðoʊ/ 接 ***as though*** →AS if.

though you never know だが，どうかわからない ▪ It must be so—*though you never know*. それにちがいあるまいが，さてどうかな.

What though →WHAT though ...?

thought /θɔːt/ 图 ***(a) penny for your thoughts*** →PENNY.

a second thought 再考，再検討，熟慮 ▪ Your *second thoughts* are often wiser than your first ideas. 再考後の考えのほうが最初の着想よりもすぐれていることがよくある.

a thought 〚副詞的に〛少し，心もち ▪ He seems *a thought* rash. 彼はちょっと向こう見ずのようだ.

(as) swift [quick] as thought/ at [like, upon, with] a thought たちまち，ただちに ▪ *Quick as thought* the skipper hurled his weapon. あっと言う間に船長は武器を投げつけた ▪ Come *with a thought*. ただちに来なさい.

at the (very) thought of [that] ...と考えただけで ▪ I shudder *at the thought of* it [*that* I might fail]. そう[失敗するかもしれないと]思っただけでぞっとする.

(be) lost [sunk, wrapt] in thought もの思いに沈んでいる ▪ I found her *lost in thought*. 見ると彼女はもの思いに沈んでいた ▪ He just sat there, *sunk in* deep *thought*. 彼はただそこに座って深くもの思いにふけっていた.

give a thought to/ bestow a thought on ...を一考する ▪ Have you *given any thought to* the question? その問題を一考してみましたか.

give it some thought 成り行きを見る ▪ Will you move house? —Let me *give it some thought*. 引っ越しする?—成り行きを見させてよ.

have second thoughts (about) **1** (...を)考え直す，再考する ▪ I'm *having second thoughts about* buying a new car. 新車の購入を考え直しているところだ ▪ We *had second thoughts* about the problem. 我々はその問題を再考した.

2 決心を変える，気が変わる ▪ I was going to buy the T-shirt, but when I saw another one for only $5, I *had second thoughts*. 私はそのTシャツを買うつもりだったが，たった5ドルの別のを見ると気が変わった.

have thought(s) of **1** ...のことを考えている ▪ I *had* some *thought of* going, but found I could not manage it. 行こうかとも思ったが，そうできないのがわかった ▪ I *had* no *thoughts of* it then. そうする考えはその時少しもなかった.

2 (...すること)を予期している (*doing*) ▪ I *had* no *thought of meeting* him there. あそこで彼に会うことは予期していなかった.

in thought 思案[思索]して ▪ He spent several hours *in thought*. 彼は数時間を思案に費やした.

in** a person's **thoughts 人の念頭にあって ▪ You are much *in our thoughts*. あなたのことは大いに私たちの念頭にあります.

It's the thought that counts. 《諺》(行為よりも)気持ちが肝心.

***keep** one's **thoughts to** oneself* 考えを人に知らせない ▪ He *keeps his thoughts to himself*. 彼は考えを人に明かさない.

like a thought →(as) swift as THOUGHT.

not give it a second thought 考え直さない，自分の考えに自信を持つ ▪ And there's not too many of them, so do*n't give it a second thought*. それにあとわずかしかないので，あとで考え直さないでください.

on second thought →SECOND[2].

Perish the thought! →PERISH.

take no thought for ...のことを思いわずらわない ▪ *Take no thought for* your future needs. 将来の必要品のことは心配するな.

take thought 思いめぐらす ▪ He *took thought* how to escape from it. 彼はそれからどうやって逃れようかと思いめぐらした.

take** one's **thoughts off ...のことを思いわずらうのをやめる ▪ She could never *take her thoughts off* John. 彼女はジョンのことを忘れることができなかった.

Thought is free. 考えることは自由である ▪ I dare say nothing, but *thought is free*. 私は何も言う勇気はありませんが，しかし考えることは自由ですからね.

upon [with] a thought →(as) swift as THOUGHT.

***with the thought of** doing* ...しようと考えて ▪ He went to Paris *with the thought of becoming* an artist. 彼は画家になるつもりでパリへ行った.

thoughtful /θɔ́ːtfəl/ 形 ***be thoughtful of*** ...に思いやりがある ▪ She *is* very *thoughtful of* others. 彼女はとても他人に思いやりがある.

thousand /θáʊzənd/ 形名 ***a thousand and one*** おびただしい ▪ He made *a thousand and one* excuses. 彼はおびただしい言い訳をした.

a thousand thanks [pardons, apologies] ほんとにありがとう[どうもすみません] ▪ I give you *a thousand thanks*. 幾重にもお礼を申しあげます.

a thousand times 千倍も，はるかに ▪ A machine is *a thousand times* more alive than a rock or a tree. 機械は岩や木よりもはるかに活動的だ.

a thousand to one ほとんど絶対的に ▪ *A thousand to one*, they have some care that defeats their comfort. まずまちがいなく，彼らには安楽をぶちこわす心配がある.

be batting a thousand 完全にうまくいっている ▪ We've made every contract, so we*'re batting a thousand* now. すべての契約を結び終えたいまは文句なしにうまくいっています. ☞「(野球で) 10割の打率をあげている」が原義.

by the thousand 千を単位で ▪ Bricks are sold *by the thousand*. れんがは千個いくらで売られる.

by [in] (the) thousands 幾千となく，無数に ▪ And ships, *by thousands*, lay below. そして船が幾千隻となく眼下に浮かんでいた.

hundreds of [and] thousands (of) 何十万(という); 無数(の) ▪ *Hundreds of thousands of* homes were flooded in Mexico. メキシコで何十万もの世帯が洪水の被害に見舞われた ▪ In Ethiopia people died in *hundreds of thousands* due to starvation. エチオピアでは飢餓で無数の人々が命を落とした.

in their thousand →IN their hundreds.

of ten thousand ずば抜けてすぐれた ▪ She herself was a woman *of ten thousand*. 彼女自身がずば抜けてすぐれた女性であった.

one in a thousand →ONE.

thousands of …何千という ▪ *Thousands of* books are published every year. 毎年何千冊という本が出版される.

thrall /θrɔːl/ 名 ***(be) a thrall to [of]*** …のとりこ(になっている) ▪ He *is a thrall to* his passions. 彼は情熱のとりこになっている.

hold ... in thrall …をとりこにする ▪ She *held* him *in* such fascinated *thrall*. 彼女は男をすっかり魅惑してとりこにしてしまった.

thrash /θræʃ/, **thresh** /θreʃ/ 動 ***thrash** a person's **jacket*** →dust a person's JACKET.

thrash (over old) straw 何にもならないことをする ▪ Why plague yourself with *thrashing straw* forever? なぜいつまでもつまらないことをして苦労するのか.

***thrash the life out of** a person* 《口》人を死ぬほどなぐる ▪ I would *thrash the life out of* you. お前を死ぬほどぶちのめしてやるんだが.

thrashing /θræʃɪŋ/ 名 ***give [get] a good thrashing*** したたか打つ[打たれる] ▪ He *gave* me *a good thrashing*. 彼は私をしたたか打った.

thread[1] /θred/ 名 ***bare [worn] to a thread*** よれよれにすり切れて ▪ The coverings were *worn to a thread*. カバーはよれよれにすり切れていた.

break the thread of (話・議論)の筋[続き]を断ち切る ▪ He keeps on *breaking the thread of* his speech by irrelevant remarks. 彼は脱線して絶えず話をとぎらせている.

gather up the threads of **1** (別々に取り扱った問題・部分など)を統一する ▪ Then he began to *gather up the threads of* the story. それから彼はその話をまとめにかかった.

2 =pick up the THREADs of.

hang by [on, upon] a thread きわめて危い状態にある ▪ Life and joy *hang by a* slender *thread*. 生命や喜びはきわめて危い状態にある. ☞頭上に1本の糸で剣をつるされたという Damocles の伝説にかけて用いられることが多い.

***have not a dry thread on** one* ずぶぬれだ ▪ The women *had not a dry thread on* them. 婦人たちはずぶぬれだった.

lose [miss] the thread of (話など)の筋がわからなくなる ▪ He seemed to have *lost the thread of* his argument. 彼は議論の筋が見えなくなったらしかった.

pick up [take up] the threads of 《口》(仕事・生活など)に再び慣れる, を再び始める ▪ I've been away from the job for some time, but I will try to *pick up the threads of* it. 私はしばらくこの仕事から離れていたが, 再び慣れるよう努めます.

take up [resume] the thread of (話)の穂をつぐ ▪ The matron then *resumed the thread of* her discourse again. 夫人はそこでまた話の穂をついだ.

thread and thrum 糸と糸くず; いっさいがっさい; 玉石混交 ▪ A woman is something made of *thread and thrum*. 女性とは美点と欠点を兼備しているものだ.

threads and thrums 種々雑多なはしくれ ▪ By those *threads and thrums*, the reader may judge of the whole. こういう種々雑多な断片から読者は全体を判断できよう.

thread[2] /θred/ 動 ***thread its way*** (道が)縫うように続く ▪ The path *threads its way* between the hedges. 道は生垣の間を縫って続いている.

thread** one's **way [course] (難路・群衆などを)くぐり抜けて行く ▪ He *threaded his way* through the thicket into open spots. 彼は茂みをくぐり抜けて広い場所へ出て行った.

threat /θret/ 名 ***a triple threat*** 3分野にすぐれた人,《サッカー・ラグビー》パス・キック・ランニングの3拍子そろった選手 ▪ He's *a triple threat* on the editorial staff—he can edit, write, and design pages. 彼は編集スタッフの中で3拍子そろった逸材だ. 編集も執筆も割付もこなせる ▪ The *triple threat* halfback is the star of the team. 3拍子そろったハーフバックはチームの花形だ.

be under the threat of …するとおどされている ▪ He *was under the threat of* expulsion. 彼は追放するぞとおどされていた.

Never make a threat you cannot carry out. 《諺》自分にできないことをするぞと言って人をおどすな《さもないと, おどしても本気だと思われなくなるぞ》.

threaten /θrétən/ 動 ***be threatened with*** …の恐れがある ▪ The race *is threatened with* extinction. その種族は絶滅の恐れがある.

three /θriː/ 形名 ***by three(s)/in threes*** 3人ずつ ▪ We entered *by threes*. 我々は3人ずつ入った.

the three R's →R.

the Three in One/One in Three 三位一体 (the Trinity) ▪ There is *One* God *in Three* persons: Father, Son and Holy Spirit. 父, 子, および聖霊という三人の人格を成す, つまり三位一体の神が存在する.

three parts **1** 4分の3 ▪ Conduct is *three parts* of life, they say. 行為が人生の4分の3を成すと言われる.

2 〖副詞的に〗ほとんど ▪ I was *three parts* asleep when he came. 彼が来たとき私はほとんど眠っていた.

three quarters =THREE parts 1.

three sheets in [to] the wind →SHEET[2].

three times three 万歳三唱を3回繰り返すこと ▪ Next followed *three times three*. 次に万歳三唱が3回繰り返された.

three vowels 《俗》借金証文 (an IOU) ▪ He was in the habit of paying his losses with *three vowels*. 彼は借用証で欠損の支払いをする習慣だった.

Three's a crowd. (二人がいっしょにいたいときに)3人目はじゃまだ.

(Yes sir, no sir,) three bags full (sir). 《戯》

ええ，もちろんですとも ▪ What our new manager wants is, "*Yes sir, no sir, three bags full sir.*" 今度の部長が求めているのは「はい，そのとおりでございます」というへりくだった返答だ. ☞Mother Goose: Baa, baa, black sheep から.

threescore /θrì:skɔ́:r/ 名形 ***threescore* (*years*) *and ten*** 70歳《通例人間の寿命とされる》(《聖》*Ps.* 90. 10) ▪ He has long passed the *threescore and ten*. 彼はもうとっくに70歳の坂を越えていた.

three-sixty /θrì:síksti/ 名 ***do a three-sixty/turn three-hundred and sixty degrees*** **1** ぐるりと一回りする ▪ I *did a three-sixty* around the park. 公園の周りをぐるりと一回りした.
2 (決定・意見を)一旦逆転させてからまた元に戻す ▪ He *did a three-sixty* in his words and deeds. 彼の言動は当初とは正反対になってからまた元に戻った.

thresh /θreʃ/ 動 ＝THRASH.

threshold /θréʃhoʊld/ 名 ***at the threshold of*** …の当初に ▪ We were *at the threshold of* a new era. 我々は新時代のかどでに立っていた.
cross the threshold 敷居をまたぐ ▪ A tall figure *crossed the threshold*. 背の高い人が敷居をまたいだ.
on the threshold of **1** 今にも…しようとして ▪ I was *on the threshhold of* solving a tremendous mystery. 私はまさにとてつもない謎を解きかけていた.
2 ＝at the THRESHOLD of.

thrill[1] /θrɪl/ 名 ***Big thrill!*** 《俗》それは大感激だな《相手が言うほど感激的なものではない》.
(***the***) ***thrills and spills*** (スポーツ・余興などの)はらはらするような興奮 ▪ He has learnt a bit about *the thrills and spills* of running smaller businesses. 彼は小会社経営というはらはらする興奮を少し味わった.

thrill[2] /θrɪl/ 動 ***be thrilled to bits*** [***death, pieces***] 《口》ひどく興奮して[喜んで]いる (→to PIECEs 2) ▪ I *was thrilled to bits* when I first saw a platypus. 初めてカモノハシを見たときうれしくてぞくぞくした ▪ We *were thrilled to pieces* with our new granddaughter. 孫娘が生まれてみな大喜びだった.

throat /θroʊt/ 名 ***at the top of one's throat*** 声を限りに ▪ The dogs were barking *at the top of their throats*. 犬たちは声を限りにほえ立てていた.
be at each other's throat*(*s*)*/be at one another's throats 互いにいがみ合ってばかりいる ▪ They've just got married but they *are at each other's throat*. 彼らは新婚早々いがみ合ってばかりいる.
clear one's* [*the*] *throat せき払いをする ▪ He *cleared his throat* before he spoke. 彼は話す前にせき払いをした.
cram ... down a person's throat →thrust ... down a person's THROAT.
cut one another's* [*each other's*] *throats 猛烈に相争う;《口》共倒れになるようなことをする ▪ They are perpetually quarreling among themselves, and *cutting one another's throats*. 彼らはいつもけんかをしては共倒れになるようなことをしている.
***cut* [*slit*] *one's own throat* (*with one's own knife*)** 自滅を招く ▪ They had effectually *cut their own throats with their own knife*. 彼らはまんまと自滅を招いたのだった.
cut the throat of …ののど笛を切って殺す;(計画など)を台なし[おじゃん]にする ▪ That *cuts the throat of* your solution. それで君の解決法は台なしになってしまう.
fly at a person's throat →spring at a person's THROAT.
force ... down a person's throat →thrust ... down a person's THROAT.
give a person the lie in his throat 人の嘘の皮をひんむく ▪ I *gave* him *the lie in his throat*. 彼の嘘の皮をひんむいてやった. ☞「嘘を出場所に戻す」が原義.
have a frog in the throat →FROG.
have a sore throat のどが痛い ▪ I *have a sore throat* and a dry cough. のどが痛くて空せきが出る.
jump down a person's throat →JUMP[2].
lie in one's throat →LIE[3].
pour* [*send*] *... down the throat 飲食に(財産・金)を浪費する ▪ They delight to *send* their estates *down the throat*. 彼らは飲食に財産を浪費するのを快(こころよ)しとしている.
slit one's own throat → cut one's own THROAT (with one's own knife).
spring* [*fly*] *at a person's throat 躍りかかって人ののどをしめようとする ▪ They are ready to *fly at each other's throats*. 彼らは躍りかかってお互いののどをしめようとかまえている.
stick in one's throat →STICK[2].
thrust* [*cram, force, push, ram, shove,* etc.]*... down a person's throat **1** (食べ物)を人ののどに無理に押し込む ▪ They *crammed* food *down the madman's throat*. 彼らは食べ物をその狂人ののどに無理に押し込んだ.
2 人に(意見など)をむりやりに押しつける ▪ They *thrust* the bill *down the throat of* the king. 彼らはその法案を王に押しつけた ▪ I'll *force* the facts *down their throats*. その事実を彼らの鼻先につきつけてやる.
(***up***) ***to the throat*** 満腹するまで《比喩的にも》 ▪ The place was already full *to the throat*. 場所はすでに満員だった.
wet one's throat →WET one's whistle.

throe /θroʊ/ 名 ***in the throes of*** **1** …にひどく苦しんで ▪ He was *in the throes of* seasickness. 彼は船酔いにひどく苦しんでいた.
2 《口》…のまっ最中で ▪ England was *in the throes of* a general election. イギリスは総選挙のまっ最中であった.

throne /θroʊn/ 名 ***mount* [*ascend, come to, take*] *the throne*** 王座に着く《比喩的にも》 ▪ John had a mind to *take the throne*. ジョンは王位につく気持ちがあった ▪ Newton was destined to *ascend the throne*. ニュートンは王座に着くように運命づけられていた.

throttle /θrɑ́tәl|θrɔ́tәl/ 名 **(*at*) *full throttle*** 全速力で ▪ We drove on *full throttle*. 我々は全速力で車を飛ばした.

through /θru:/ 前副 ***all through*** 始終 ▪ I knew that *all through*. 始終そのことは承知していた.

be through to 《英》(電話で)…につながれている ▪ You*'re through to* New York. ニューヨークにおつなぎしました.

be through with **1** …を終わる; を仕上げる ▪ I *am through with* the lessons. 私は課業をすませた. **2** (人)と関係がない ▪ I *am through with* him. あの男とは手を切っている. **3** 《口》…にはうんざりだ ▪ I*'m through with* this job. この仕事にはうんざりだ.

put** a person **through it 《口》人をきびしくしかる[罰する] ▪ The Director sent for him and *put* him *through it*. 重役が彼を呼びつけてひどく叱った.

through and through **1** …をすっかり通って ▪ Your slander has gone *through and through* her heart. あなたの中傷は彼女の心にすっかりこたえた. **2** すっかり, 徹頭徹尾 ▪ I know him *through and through*. 私は彼を知りぬいている.

throw[1] /θroʊ/ 名 ***$50*** [***£20,*** etc.] ***a throw*** (商品の)1個50ドル[20ポンド, など]で ▪ The tickets for the concert are sold for 60 bucks *a throw*. コンサートのチケットは1枚60ドルで発売されている.

free throw 《バスケ》フリースロー ▪ He scored the winning point on a *free throw*. 彼はフリースローを決めて決勝点をあげた.

have a throw at …をやってみる(=have a FLING at) ▪ We will *have a throw at* it. それをやってみよう.

throw[2] /θroʊ/ 動 ***throw a bluff*** 《米口》はったりをかける ▪ I can't *throw a bluff* with those kids I've known always. 昔なじみにははったりをかけられない.

throw a fit →FIT[1].

throw a fly 毛ばり釣りをする ▪ He learnt to *throw a fly*. 彼は毛ばり釣りの仕方を学んだ.

throw a glance [***look***] → THROW one's eye(s).

throw a shadow [***cloud, gloom***] ***over*** …をかげらせる; を陰気にする ▪ Showers of rain *threw a gloom over* the gaieties. にわか雨が浮かれ騒ぎに水をさした.

throw apart [***asunder***] =THROW open 1.

throw** oneself **at **1** 気があるようなそぶりをする; やたらと気を引こうとする ▪ As for the girls, they just *throw themselves at* a man. 娘どもときたら, 男に気があるようなそぶりをしているだけだ. **2** …に飛びかかる ▪ A bear *threw itself at* the fence. 1頭のクマが塀に飛びかかった ▪ He abruptly *threw himself at* the burglar and seized the gun from him. 彼は急に盗賊に飛びかかって銃を奪った. **3** …に従事する[没頭する] ▪ We *threw ourselves at* the job until it was completed. 私たちはその仕事が完結するまで従事した.

throw** oneself **away (つまらない男の)妻になる(*on*) ▪ She had *thrown herself away on* one utterly unworthy of her. 彼女は全く彼女にはふさわしくない男の妻になっていた.

throw doubt [***suspicion***] ***on*** [***upon***] …に疑いを抱かせる ▪ Recent research has *thrown doubt on* this accepted wisdom. 最近の調査研究によってこの確立した学問的知識に疑念が生じた.

throw** oneself **down 身を投げる, 横になる ▪ Tired and worn, he *threw himself down* on his bed. へとへとになって彼はベッドに倒れこんだ.

throw down** one's **arms 武器を投げ捨てる, 降参する ▪ The soldiers immediately *threw down their arms*. 兵士たちは直ちに戦闘をやめた[武器を捨てて投降した].

throw down** one's **brief (弁護士が)弁護を続けることを断る ▪ The defence counsel *threw down his brief* in disgust. 被告側弁護士はうんざりして弁護を続けることを断った.

throw down the gauntlet →cast (out) the GAUNTLET.

throw down** one's **tools →TOOL.

throw dust in** a person's **eyes →DUST[1].

throw** one's **eye(s)/ throw a glance [***a look***] ちょっと目を向ける, ちらと見る ▪ The mother instantly *threw her eyes* to the ground. 母親はすぐ地面にちょっと目を向けた ▪ She *threw* inquiring *glances* across the table. 彼女はテーブル越しにいぶかしげにちらと見た.

throw fetters on →THROW reins on.

throw fire (機関車が)煙突から火を出す ▪ Bad stoking may be the cause of a locomotive *throwing fire*. 火のたき方がまずいと機関車が煙突から火を出す原因になる場合がある.

throw** a person **in at the deep end 人を困難に導く ▪ I had no idea I would *be* literally *thrown in at the deep end*. 文字通り困難な目にあおうとは思ってもいなかった.

throw in** one's **hand [***cards***] →HAND[1].

throw in** one's **lot [***fortune, interest***] ***with*** (しばしば悪い企てに参加するために)…と交際を始める ▪ He would have *thrown in his lot with* the Hyde. 彼はハイド一家と交際を始めたいところだった.

throw in the towel →TOWEL[1].

throw** oneself **into **1** …に身を投げ入れる ▪ He *threw himself into* a chair. 彼はいすに身を投げた. **2** …に身を打ちこむ ▪ He was prepared to *throw himself into* any project. 彼はどんな計画にも身を打ちこもうとしていた. **3** (とりでなど)に乗り込む ▪ He *threw himself into* the fort with his men. 彼は部下を連れてとりでに乗り込んできた.

throw ... into question [***doubt***] …に疑問を投げかける ▪ His behavior *was thrown into question*. 彼の行動には疑問が投げかけられた.

T

throw into shape →put ... into SHAPE.
throw *oneself* ***into the arms of*** ...の妻[めかけ]になる ▪ Those women were *throwing themselves into the arms of* other men. その女性たちは他の男たちのめかけになっていた.
throw it up against [***at, to***] *a person* 《俗》人をしかる, 非難する (*that*) ▪ The children in the street *throw it up against* me (*that*) I ain't got no father. 街の子らは僕には父親がないと言ってなじる.
throw (***a***) (***new***) ***light on*** →LIGHT[1].
throw *a person's* ***mind back*** 思い出させる ▪ The tune *threw my mind back* to my schooldays. その曲で学生時代を思い出した.
throw (*one's*) ***money around*** →throw one's MONEY about.
throw ... off the track [***scent***] →TRACK.
throw *oneself* ***on*** [***upon***] **1** (危急の場合)...に助けを求める; (慈悲など)にすがる ▪ In time of temptation, *throw yourself upon* God. 誘惑のある場合には神の助けを求めるがよい ▪ I must *throw myself upon* your mercy. 君のご慈悲におすがりするほかない.
2 ...を攻撃する ▪ He *threw himself upon* the ragout, and the plate was presently vacant. 彼はすごい勢いでシチューを食べ始め, 皿はすぐ空になってしまった.
3 ...に飛び乗る ▪ He *threw himself upon* his horse. 彼は馬に飛び乗った.
throw open [***apart, asunder***] **1** (戸など)を押し開く ▪ He *threw open* the shutters. 彼は雨戸を押し開いた.
2 公開する ▪ The railway will *be thrown open* in August. 鉄道は8月に公開されるだろう.
throw open *one's* ***doors to*** ...を歓迎する ▪ I will *throw open my doors to* any of your friends. あなたのお友だちなら誰でも歓迎します.
throw open the gates of ...の門戸を開く ▪ They are laboring to *throw open the gates of* commerce. 彼らは通商の門戸を開こうと努力している.
throw out the baby with the bath water →empty the BABY out with the bath(water).
throw overboard →OVERBOARD.
throw reins [***fetters***] ***on*** ...を制御する ▪ *Throw reins on* your passions. 激情を制御せよ ▪ Pride *throws fetters on* love itself. 誇りは愛までも制御する.
throw *one's* ***soul*** [***heart, spirit, energy, efforts***] ***into*** ...に全力を傾ける ▪ She *threw her* whole *soul into* her voice. 彼女は声に全力を注ぎこんだ ▪ He continued to *throw* all *his energy into* the distasteful duty. 彼はそのいやな仕事に相変わらず全力を傾けた.
throw the race [***fight***] 《米》(八百長(やおちょう)で)レース[試合]に負ける ▪ He arranged with Strong that he would *throw the race*. 彼は競走に負けてやるとストロングと取り決めた.
throw *oneself* ***to the floor*** [***ground***] 床[地面]に素早く身を伏せる ▪ I *threw myself to the floor* as the man fired a shot. 男が一発撃ったとき私はがばと身を伏せた.
throw ... to the winds → fling ... to the WIND(s).
throw true (家畜が)親の種に違わぬ子を産む ▪ This variety of the rabbit *throws true*. この種類のウサギは親の種に違わぬ子を産む.
throw up *one's* ***accounts*** 《俗》もどす ▪ My blow made him *throw up his accounts*. 私の一撃は彼にもどさせた.
throw up *one's* ***hands*** [***arms***] 手を上げる《特に降参・絶望の印に》 ▪ *Throw up your hands* now, or I'll shoot every man jack of you. さあ手を上げるんだ, さもなきゃどいつもこいつも撃ち殺すぞ ▪ He *threw up his hands* in despair. 彼は絶望して両手を上げた.
throw up in [***into, on***] ***the wind*** 《海》(船)を風上に向ける; (人が船)を風上に向ける ▪ The ship *was thrown up on the wind*. 船は風上に向けられた ▪ We *threw up in the wind*. 我々は船を風上に向けた.
throw *one's* ***weight about*** [***around***] → WEIGHT.

thrust[1] /θrʌst/ 名 ***make a thrust at*** ...に突きかかる ▪ I *made a thrust at* him. 私は彼に突きかかった.
the cut and thrust (***of***) →CUT and thrust.
thrust and parry 突きと受け《比喩的にも》 ▪ His *thrust and parry* recalls the days of the hustings. 彼の鋭い言葉の応酬は昔の国会議員選挙場のころを思い出させる.

thrust[2] /θrʌst/ 動 ***thrust*** *oneself* ***forward*** [***past***] 強引に前へ出る[通り過ぎる] ▪ They *thrust themselves forward* to see the procession. 彼らは行列を見ようとして強引に前へ出た.
thrust *oneself* ***into*** **1** (危険など)に身をさらす ▪ I will not *thrust myself into* danger. 私は危険に身をさらそうとは思わない.
2 ...に割り込む ▪ They would *thrust themselves into* my company. 彼らは強いて私との交際を求めようとするのだった.
thrust *one's* ***way*** 押し通る ▪ They *thrust their way* through the crowd. 彼らは群衆の間を押し通った.

thud /θʌd/ 名 ***with a thud*** ドシンと ▪ He fell *with a thud* to the carpet. 彼はじゅうたんの上にドサッと倒れた.

thumb[1] /θʌm/ 名 ***be all thumbs*** 無器用だ ▪ Your educated man *is all thumbs*. 君の教養ある人というのは無器用者だ.
bite *one's* ***thumb*** 怒って[いらいらして]親指をかむ ▪ The Spaniards were nettled, and *bit their thumbs* in private. スペイン人たちは怒ってひそかに親指をかんだ.
bite *one's* ***thumb at*** ...をばかにして親指をかんでみせる ▪ I do not *bite my thumb at* you. 私はあなたをばかにして親指をかんでみせているのではない.
get [***receive***] ***the thumbs up*** [***down***] 賛成

[反対]される ▪ His proposal *got the thumbs up* from the party. 彼の提案は党の賛成を得た.

get *one's* ***thumb out of*** *a person's* ***mouth*** 人の爪牙(そうが)を免れる ▪ I have now *got my thumb out of his mouth.* もうあの男の爪牙を免れた.

give the thumbs up [down] 賛成[反対]する ▪ When the play opened, the papers *gave* it *the thumbs down.* その芝居が開演されると新聞はそれに不満の報道をした.

have a green thumb →GREEN.

keep *a person* ***under*** *one's* ***thumb*** 人を厳しく管理する ▪ She *keeps* her children *under her thumb.* 彼女は子供を厳しく管理している.

(*Put your*) *thumbs up!* 《俗》しっかりしろ, 元気を出せ; いいぞ, すてきだ.

stand out like a sore thumb 不適当な[場違いの]ようだ ▪ Dressed like that, you'll *stand out like a sore thumb.* そんな格好では場違いに映るぞ.

stick [stand] out like a sore thumb →STICK[2].

thumbs down 不同意[不満足](の合図) ▪ It will be *thumbs down* to our proposal. 我々の提案には不同意ということになるだろう.

thumbs up 同意[満足](の合図) ▪ It's *thumbs up*, old chap. You've drawn the winner this time. ごきげんだよ, 君. 今度は優勝馬を引き当てたね.

turn up [down] *one's* ***thumb(s)*** 同意[不同意]の意を表す ▪ They unanimously *turned their thumbs up.* 彼らは異口同音に同意の意を表した. ☞古代円形闘技場で親指を起こしまたは伏せて同意・不同意を示したことから.

twiddle *one's* ***thumbs*** →TWIDDLE.

twirl *one's* ***thumbs*** →TWIRL.

under the thumb of (人)にあごで使われて, の言いなりになって ▪ Authors are *under the thumb of* booksellers. 著者は本屋にあごで使われている ▪ She's got him right *under her thumb.* 彼女は彼をすっかり自分の言いなりにしている.

weigh the thumb →WEIGH[2].

thumb[2] /θʌm/ 動 ***thumb a ride*** →hitch a RIDE.

thumb *one's* ***nose at*** 鼻に親指をあて他の指を広げてみせる《反抗・侮辱のしぐさ》 ▪ Underlings in the studio *thumbed their noses at* his back. スタジオの下っぱどもは彼の背中に向かって鼻に親指をあて他の指を広げてみせた.

thumb *one's* ***way*** 《米口》(親指で合図して)通りがかりの車に乗せてもらう, ヒッチハイクする ▪ He *thumbed his way* to New York. 彼はニューヨークまで便乗させてもらった.

thumbnail /θʌ́mnèɪl/ 名 ***a thumbnail sketch*** (親指の爪に描けるほどの)小さなスケッチ, (的確な)寸描, ラフスケッチ ▪ Let me give you *a thumbnail sketch* of what happened. ことの様子をざっと説明しよう ▪ He is good at giving *a thumb-nail sketch* of persons. 彼は人物の寸描にたけている.

thump[1] /θʌmp/ 名 ***with a thump*** ドシンと ▪ He fell down on his face *with a thump.* 彼はドシンとうつ伏せに倒れた.

thump[2] /θʌmp/ 動 ***thump a [the] cushion/ thump the pulpit*** (説教者が)卓をたたいて説教する ▪ He *thumped a cushion* in that congregation. 彼はその集会で卓をたたいて説教した.

thunder /θʌ́ndər/ 名 ***(as) black as thunder*** →BLACK[1].

By thunder! 《米口》全く, まあ, ちくしょう! ▪ Well, you are a big noise now, *by thunder!* いや, 君は今は全く大物だねえ. ☞thunder＝hell.

for thunder's sake 後生だから ▪ Don't go *for thunder's sake.* 後生だから行かないで.

give [catch] particular thunder 《米口》ひどい目にあわせる[あう] ▪ I'll *give* you *particular thunder* someday. いつかお前をひどい目にあわせてやるぞ. ☞thunder＝hell.

Go to thunder! 《米口》くたばってしまえ!

in thunder 《口》[[疑問詞を強調して]] 一体 ▪ Where *in thunder* did he get the money? 彼は一体どこでその金を手に入れたのだろうか.

look like (a) thunder/ have a face like thunder 《口》ひどく怒っている ▪ When I came home late, my father was *looking like a thunder.* 遅く帰宅したら父がひどく怒っていた.

steal [run away with] *a person's* ***thunder*** 人のお株を奪う, 人をだしぬく ▪ I apologize for *stealing your thunder* at the meeting. あの会合であなたのお株を奪って相すみませんでした.

thunder and lightning 弾劾, 非難 ▪ They speak nothing but *thunder and lightning* to us. 彼らは我々にただ非難を浴びせかけるだけだ.

Thunder turns the milk. 雷が鳴ると牛乳が腐る《迷信》.

thunderbolt /θʌ́ndərbòʊlt/ 名 ***be a thunderbolt to*** …にとって青天のへきれきである ▪ The news *was a thunderbolt to* her. このニュースは彼女には青天のへきれきだった.

like a thunderbolt 青天のへきれきのように ▪ The information came upon me *like a thunderbolt.* この知らせは私には青天のへきれきだった.

thunderclap /θʌ́ndərklæ̀p/ 名 ***like a thunderclap*** 青天のへきれきのように ▪ The news came *like a thunderclap.* その知らせは青天のへきれきのように伝わってきた.

thus /ðʌs/ 副 ***as thus*** このように ▪ I kissed her *as thus.* 私は彼女にこのように口づけした.

thus and so 《米口》そういうふうに (＝SO and so 3) ▪ Matters will result *thus and so.* 事態はそういうふうな結果に終わるだろう.

thus and thus このように ▪ He writes *thus and thus.* 彼はこういう手紙をよこしている.

thus far これ[今]まで(は) ▪ *Thus far* it is duty. ここまでは義務である.

Thus far and no further. ここまででそれ以上はだめ《禁止・警告》. ☞Canute王が潮に命じた言葉と

して有名.

thus much →this MUCH.

tick[1] /tɪk/ 名 ***in a tick/ in two ticks/ in half a tick*** 《口》たちまち, すぐに ▪I can explain it *in two ticks*. 今すぐにもそれを説明してみせよう ▪I should have been spotted *in a tick* by a spy. 私はたちまちスパイに見つかっていたことだろう.

on the tick of 《口》きっかり…時に ▪He arrived *on the tick of* six. 彼はきっかり6時にやって来た.

to* [*on*] *the tick 《主に英口》きっかりに ▪At eight o'clock *to the tick*, the day's regular lessons began. 8時きっかりに1日のきまった勉強が始まった.

tick[2] /tɪk/ 名 ***go* (*on*) *tick/ run on* [*upon*] *tick*** 《口》掛けで買う, 借金をこしらえる ▪When he had no funds he *went on tick*. 資金のないときには彼は掛けで買った ▪He *ran on tick* with Piggin for paper. 彼はピギンから紙を掛けで買った.

on* [*upon*] *tick 《口》掛けで ▪He has a bad habit of living *on tick*. 彼は掛けで生活するという悪い癖がある.

tick[3] /tɪk/ 動 ***be ticked off*** 《口》怒っている ▪He *was ticked off* because she didn't turn up. 彼女が姿を現さなかったので彼は怒っていた.

tick ... off on *one's* ***fingers*** 指を1本ずつ押さえながら(声に出して)リストの項目をチェックする ▪She *ticked* their names *off on her fingers*. 彼女は彼らの名前を一人ずつ指を押さえながら確認した.

What makes ... tick? 《口》何が…にそうさせているのか ▪I should like to know *what makes* American society *tick*. 何がアメリカの社会にそうさせているのか知りたいものだ. ☞時計がカチカチ動くことから.

ticket[1] /tíkət/ 名 ***a hot ticket*** 《米》 **1** 引っ張りだこの人[物], 人気者, 売れっ子 ▪He was *a hot ticket* as a rookie last season. 彼は昨シーズン新人選手として人気があった ▪Miniskirts will be the *hot ticket* again next spring. 来春はミニスカートがまた流行するだろう ▪Singers who can dance are *a hot ticket* these days. 昨今はダンスができる歌手がひっぱりだこだ.

2〚限定的〛引っ張りだこの, とても人気のある ▪Skateboards are *a hot ticket* item among young sports enthusiasts. スケートボードはスポーツに熱中する若者の間の人気種目である.

a split ticket 複数政党の候補者に投じられた票, 分割投票 (↔a straight TICKET) ▪She voted *a split ticket*. 彼女は分割投票の1票を投じた.

a straight ticket 全票が同一政党の候補者ばかりに投じられた票 (↔a split TICKET) ▪My uncle tends to vote the *straight ticket*. 叔父はとかく同一党の候補者ばかりに票を入れがちだ.

a ticket tout 買い占めたイベントの券を高値で売りさばく人物, ダフ屋, (競馬の)予想屋 ▪Many *ticket touts* are commonly seen outside big sports events and rock concerts. スポーツ大会やロック・コンサート会場の外には多くのダフ屋の姿がざらにみられる.

Admission by ticket only. 切符のない方はお断り《掲示》.

be the ticket 《俗》 **1**〚主に that's the ticket の形で〛適当な[あつらえ向きの]ものである (→That's the TICKET!) ▪Somehow she's not *the ticket*. どうも彼女はまずい.

2 (行動の)段取りである ▪Well, what's *the ticket*? ところで, これからどうする段取りかね.

carry *one's* ***ticket*** 《米》候補者名簿の候補者を選ぶ《公認選挙》 ▪We *carried our ticket*, but we had a close job of it. 我々は候補者名簿の候補者を選んだが, 接戦だった.

get a ticket 交通違反カードを手渡される ▪If you keep racing along at this speed, you will *get a ticket*! こんなに飛ばしているとスピード違反切符を切られるぞ!

go the clean ticket →CLEAN[1].

run behind* [*ahead of*]** *one's* ***ticket 《米》自党の他候補よりも少なく[多く]得票する ▪He *ran* 35,000 *ahead of his ticket*. 彼は自党の他候補よりも35,000多く得票した.

That's the ticket! 《口》それだ!, それはおあつらえむきだ ▪First, we'll have dinner and then we'll have a game of chess.—Yeah, *that's the ticket!* まず晩飯にして, それからチェスを一勝負やろうか—そうだ, それがいい ▪*That's the ticket!* That's the winning game. そうこなくちゃ嘘だ! それでこそ勝負に勝てる.

vote* [*go*] *a ticket 《米》ある政党の公認候補者に投票する ▪I hope they'll *go* the Webster *ticket*. みんながウェブスターに投票してくれればいい.

work *one's* ***ticket*** **1**《俗》(仮病など使って)除隊する; (一般に)仮病を使う, 口実を設けて(仕事から)逃げ出す ▪He hates the job and is trying to *work his ticket*. 彼はその仕事がいやで口実を設けて逃げ出そうとしている.

2 船賃代わりに船内で働く ▪He got home by *working his ticket*. 彼は船賃代わりに船内で働いて帰国した.

write *one's* ***own ticket*** 自分で将来の方針を立てる ▪I find it hard to *write my own ticket*. 僕は自分で将来の方針を立てるのがむずかしい.

ticket[2] /tíkət/ 動 ***be ticketed through to*** 《米》切符を発行してもらって…へ行く ▪We *were ticketed through to* the other place. 我々は切符を発行してもらって別の場所へ行った.

ticking-off /tìkɪŋɔ́ːf|-ɔ́f/ 名 ***give*** *a person* [***get***] ***a ticking-off*** 人をしかる[しかられる] ▪A police officer *gave* me *a ticking-off* for jaywalking. 信号無視で道路を横切ったことで警察官にしかられた ▪I'm used to *getting a ticking-off* from Mom. ママから小言をくらうのには慣れっこだ.

tickle /tíkəl/ 動 ***be tickled* (*pink*) *to death*** **1** 大いにおもしろがる ▪He will *be tickled to death* to hear that. それを聞けば彼はひどくおもしろがるだろう.

2《口》とてもうれしい ▪I *was tickled to death* at the news. そのニュースを聞いてとてもうれしかった. ☞顔が赤くなるまで笑うことから.

tickle *a person's* ***fancy*** →FANCY[1].

tickle *a person* ***in the palm/ tickle the***

T

***palm of** a person* 人にチップをやる ▪ We *tickled* the men *in the palm.* 男たちにチップをやった.

tidalwave /táɪdəlwèɪv/ 名 ***a tidalwave of*** …の洪水, 大量の… ▪ *A tidalwave of* pornography could sweep the country pretty soon. 今に大量のポルノが国中に氾濫しかねない.

tide[1] /taɪd/ 名 ***a growing tide*** 徐々に増していく風潮, 漸増傾向 ▪ There has been *a growing tide* of interest in this area. このところこの分野への関心が高まってきている.

A rising tide lifts all boats. 《米・諺》上げ潮のときはみな儲かる. ☞John F. Kennedy の言葉とされる.

a tide of joy 幸福の絶頂 ▪ When he proposed to her, *a tide of joy* swept over her. 彼にプロポーズされると歓喜が彼女の全身を駆け巡った.

a turn* [*change*] *of the tide 潮の変わり目; 形勢一変; 危機 ▪ The Socialists hoped for *a turn of the tide.* 社会主義者たちは形勢一変を希望した.

at high* [*low*] *tide 満潮[干潮]時に ▪ The rock is under water *at high tide.* その岩は満潮時には水中に没している.

Every tide has its ebb. 《諺》満ちれば欠ける世の習い.

go* [*swim*] *with* [*against*] *the tide 時勢に従う[逆らう] (→ SWIM with the stream; SWIM against the stream) ▪ It's much easier to *go with the tide* than to try to force one's way against public opinion. 世論に反抗しようとするよりも時勢に従うほうがずっとやさしい.

stem the tide →STEM.

The tide turns. 形勢が一変する ▪ We must wait till *the tide turns.* 形勢が一変するまで待たなくてはならない.

There is a tide in the affairs of men. 《諺》何事にも潮時がある.

Time and tide wait for no man. →TIME[1].

turn the tide 形勢を一変させる ▪ The arrival of fresh reinforcements *turned the tide* in the battle. 新手の援軍がやって来たので戦いの形勢が一変した.

work double tides 大車輪で働く ▪ The artisans *work double tides.* 職人たちは大車輪で働く. ☞「1日2回の潮流を利用するように」という意味から.

tide[2] /taɪd/ 動 ***tide** one's **way*** 潮を利用して進む《比喩的にも》 ▪ We *tided our* slow *way* north. 我々は潮を利用してゆっくりと北に進んだ ▪ Ministers are now endeavoring to *tide their way* through the session. 大臣らは勢いに乗じて会期を切り抜けようとやっきである.

tidy /táɪdi/ 動 ***tidy** oneself* 《口》身づくろいする ▪ She went upstairs to *tidy herself.* 彼女は身づくろいするために2階へ上がった.

tie[1] /taɪ/ 名 ***count* [*hit*] *the ties*** 《米口》(特に切符の買えない浮浪者などが)線路伝いに歩く ▪ I've *counted the ties* and slept in the jungles. 私は線路伝いに歩き, またジャングルの中に寝た. ☞tie《米》「まくら木」.

play* [*shoot*] *off a tie (引き分けの試合の)決勝戦をする ▪ *The tie was played off* last Saturday. 前の土曜日に決勝戦が行われた.

(*the*) *old school tie* 《軽蔑》母校の色柄のネクタイ; パブリックスクールの出身者(であること), 学閥意識 ▪ I just met an *old school tie* in the cloakroom. さっきクロークでパブリックスクールの出身者に会った.

tie[2] /taɪ/ 動 ***be tied to* [*for*] *time*** 期限を切られている ▪ Unfortunately I *am tied to time.* あいにく私は期限を切られているのです.

fit to be tied **1**《俗》ひどく怒って ▪ Dad was *fit to be tied* when my sister came home late that night. 姉がその夜遅く帰ってくるとパパはカンカンだった. **2**《米俗》ひどく, すごく ▪ He laughed *fit to be tied.* 彼はひどく笑った.

get tied up 結婚する ▪ When are the two young people *getting tied up*? いつあの二人の若者はいっしょになるのか.

tie one on 《米俗》酔っ払う ▪ You really *tied one on* the other night. 先夜はほんとに酔っていたね.

tie the hands of …の行動の自由を奪う ▪ It seems very unjust to *tie the hands of* the directors in so important a matter. そんな重要な問題で理事の行動の自由を奪うのはきわめて不当に思われる.

tie the knot 縁結びする; 結婚する ▪ The priest *tied the knot.* その牧師が縁結びした ▪ We *tied the knot* only last month. 私たちはつい先月結婚したばかりです.

tie** a person's **tongue 人にものを言わせない, 口止めする ▪ Very shame *tied her tongue.* 恥ずかしさだけで彼女はものが言えなかった.

tie up the loose ends →LOOSE[1].

tier /táɪər/ 名 ***in tiers*** 段々になって, 列をなして ▪ The casks were arranged *in tiers.* たるは段々に並べられていた.

tiff /tɪf/ 名 ***have a tiff with*** (恋人・友人)と小さいけんかをする ▪ Alice *had a tiff with* her boyfriend. アリスはボーイフレンドとささいなけんかをした.

in a tiff むっとして ▪ At last he went off *in a tiff.* とうとう彼はむっとして去った.

tiger /táɪgər/ 名 ***a paper tiger*** → PAPER tiger.

a tiger in** one's **tank 活力, 精神力 ▪ A bloke like that with *a tiger in his tank* could do it with his eyes closed. 元気のいいあの野郎ならそんなことは朝飯前さ.

buck the tiger 《米俗》(トランプの)銀行[ファロ]をやる ▪ He had the luck that day *bucking the tiger.* 彼はその日は銀行をしていてついていた.

fight* [*whip, hit, hunt, spread*] *the tiger 《米俗》(トランプの)銀行[ファロ]でかける ▪ Simon believes that he can *fight the tiger.* サイモンは銀行でかけることができると信じている.

have a tiger by the tail 手に負えない[予期せぬ]苦境に陥る ▪ As you bit off more than you could chew, you *have a tiger by the tail.* 柄にもないことを始めたから, のっぴきならぬ状況に陥ったのだ.

ride a [***the***] ***tiger*** 危い橋を渡る ▪ If he experiments with drugs, he is *riding a tiger*. もし彼が麻薬をやってみたりしているのなら，危い橋を渡っていることになる ▪ He who *rides a tiger* is afraid to dismount. 《諺》危険なことを続けるより，やめる方が危険.

The tiger cannot change its stripes./The leopard cannot change its spots. 《諺》人の性格は代わらない，「三つ子の魂百まで」.

tight /taɪt/ 形副 ***a tight fit*** 《口》窮屈な衣服《比喩的にも》 ▪ It's rather *a tight fit*. それは少し窮屈だ.

a tight place [***corner, spot***] 《口》難局，窮地 ▪ I felt myself in *a tight spot*. 私は窮地に陥ったのを感じた ▪ They found they were getting into *a tight place*. 彼らは進退きわまってきているのを知った.

a tight squeeze **1** =a TIGHT place.

2 すし詰め状態，押し合い ▪ We managed to get into the bus, but it was *a tight squeeze*. 我々は何とかバスに乗りこんだが，身動きできなかった.

(***as***) ***tight as a brick*** [***a drum, a lord, an owl, a goat, a mink, a ten-day drunk, a tick***] 《俗》ひどく酔って ▪ He's *tight as a drum*. 彼はひどく酔っている ▪ I felt *tight as a tick*. ひどく酔った感じだった.

(***as***) ***tight as a drum*** **1** = (as) TIGHT as a brick.

2 はちきれそうで，パンパンに張って ▪ I've eaten so much that the skin on my belly is *tight as a drum*. 食べすぎて腹の皮が破れそうだ.

3 防水で ▪ Don't worry about leaks. This tent is *tight as a drum*. 水漏れの心配はない. このテントは防水だ.

as tight as wax (ろうのように)ぴったりついて離れない ▪ I pulled and strained, but it was *as tight as wax*. 私は引っぱって力んだが，それはぴったりとくっついて離れなかった.

be tight-lipped **1** 口数が少ない，無口な ▪ She *was* very *tight-lipped* about her future plans. 彼女は将来の計画についてどうしても話したがらなかった.

2 怒った顔をして ▪ Dad *is tight-lipped*. He is going to lose his temper soon. 親父の顔が怒っている. 今にかんしゃく玉を破裂させるぞ.

get tight 《口》酔っぱらう ▪ He *gets tight* every pay-day. 彼は給料日にはいつも酔っ払う.

hold tight **1** しっかりつかまえる ▪ *Hold* it *tight*. それをしっかりつかまえなさい.

2 しっかりつかまる ▪ *Hold tight* to the railings. 手すりにしっかりつかまりなさい.

3 がまんする ▪ You will have to *hold tight* till you find things improving. 事情が好転するまでじっとがまんしなければなりますまい.

4 〚命令文で〛ちょっと待て ▪ Here, *hold tight*, your brother never said such a thing. これ，ちょっとお待ち. 兄さんはそんなことを言ったことは一度もないよ.

keep a tight hand [***hold***] ***on*** …を厳しく取り扱う ▪ He *kept a tight hand on* all his affairs. 彼はすべての事務を厳しく取りしきっていた.

keep a tight rein on/keep…on a tight leash →hold a tight REIN on.

run a tight ship →SHIP[1].

sit tight **1** 《口》じっと座る，腰をすえる; がんばる ▪ "*Sit tight*!" she exclaimed. 「じっと座ってらっしゃい!」と彼女は叫んだ ▪ But she *sat tight* and I couldn't get a word from her. しかし彼女はがんばって私は一言も聞き出せなかった.

2 じっと耐えて時期を待つ ▪ Shareholders are being advised to *sit tight* until the crisis passes. 今はじっとがまんして経済危機が去るのを待つようにと株主は助言を受けている.

tightrope /táɪtròʊp/ 名 ***walk a tightrope/be on a tightrope*** 綱渡りをする，危ない橋を渡る; 慎重に行動する，言動に十分注意する ▪ They are always quarreling, so I need to *walk a tightrope* between them. 彼らはしょっちゅう口げんかばかりしているので，彼らの扱いには慎重を期す必要がある ▪ Young cops *walk a tightrope* in the world of crime. 若い警官たちは犯罪の世界であぶない橋を渡っている.

tile /taɪl/ 名 ***drop a tile*** 《俗》気が変になる ▪ Has he *dropped a tile*? 彼は気が変になったのか.

have a tile loose 《俗》気が変だ ▪ Do you think I *have a tile loose*? 僕が気が変だとでも思っているのかね. ☞「屋根瓦が1枚ゆるんでいる」が原義.

on the tiles 《口》放蕩して ▪ Have you been spending a few nights *on the tiles*? 2, 3夜放蕩して過ごしていたのかい. ☞交尾期の猫が屋根へ上がることから.

till /tɪl/ 名 ***rob the till/have*** *one's* ***hand*** [***fingers***] ***in the till*** 《主に英》店の金に手をつける[着服する] ▪ He found that the treasurer *had his hand in the till*. 彼は経理係がレジの金に手をつけたのを発見した. ☞till「現金箱」.

tiller /tílər/ 名 ***at the tiller*** = (be) at the HELM.

tilt[1] /tɪlt/ 名 (***at***) ***full tilt*** まっしぐらに，全速力で ▪ Every participant was running on *full tilt*. 参加者はみな全速力で走っていた. ☞tilt「剣ややりの突き」.

give a tilt 傾ける ▪ He *gave* the cask *a tilt*. 彼はそのたるを傾けた.

have a tilt at [***against***] (風刺などで人)を攻撃する ▪ She *has a tilt at* him, jeering and mystifying him. 彼女は彼を攻撃し，彼をからかい，けむにまいてしまう. ☞tilt「馬上のやり試合」.

on [***upon***] ***the tilt*** (からになりかけのたるなど)傾いて《比喩的にも》 ▪ Her natural strength was *on the tilt*, as it were. 彼女の生来の体力はいわば傾いていた.

run (***a***) ***tilt*** **1** やり試合をする ▪ The picture exhibits two knights *running a tilt* in the foreground. その絵は前景でやり試合をしている二人の騎士を示している.

2 (人・偽善などを)攻撃する，やり玉にあげる (*against*) ▪ He *runs tilt against* the hypocrisies of life. 彼は人生の偽善をやり玉にあげる.

run at (the) tilt やり試合をする ▪ Henry II was killed *running at tilt*. ヘンリー2世はやり試合をしているときに死んだ.

tilt[2] /tɪlt/ 動 ***tilt at windmills*** →fight (with) WINDMILLs.

timber /tímbər/ 名 ***break [pull, put, strike] for (the) tall timber/ break for high timber*** 《米口》そそくさと立ち去る, あたふたと逃げる ▪ He'll *put for tall timber* one of these days. 彼は近いうちそそくさと立ち去るだろう.

leave for bigger timber 《米口》もっと才能を生かせる大きい場所へ行く ▪ I'd be a fool to stay here any longer; I'll *leave for bigger timber*. こんな所にこれ以上いるのはばかげている. もっと才能を生かせる大きい場所へ行こう.

put ... under timber (土地)に材木用の木を植える ▪ They *put* that land *under timber*. 彼らはその土地に材木用の木を植えた.

Shiver my timbers! →SHIVER[3].

time[1] /taɪm/ 名 ***a dozen times*** 何度も ▪ I've told you *a dozen times*. 何度も君に言ったよ.

a fine time to *do* 《皮肉》...するのに不適当な[遅すぎる]時 ▪ (This is) *a fine time to* ring one up. 人に電話をするには不適当な時刻だ.

a good time →GOOD.

A good time was had by all. 《陳腐》みなが楽しく過ごした ▪ How was the party?—*A good time was had by all*. パーティー, どうだったかい?—みな楽しく過ごしたよ.

a race [fight] against time 時間との競争[闘い] ▪ It became *a race against time*. 今や時間との競争となった ▪ It looked as if his whole life were *a race against time*. 彼の一生は時間との競争のようなものだった.

About time, too. そうしてもいい頃だ(大分遅い) ▪ They got married last week. —*About time, too*. 二人は先週結婚した—そうしてもいい頃だね.

against time [the clock] **1** 時計とにらめっこして; 時限までに仕上げようとして ▪ He was often compelled to write *against time*. 彼はしばしば時と競って筆を駆ることを余儀なくされた.

2 記録を破ろうとして ▪ They raced not against each other, but *against time*. 彼らはお互いに競ったのではなく, 記録を破ろうとしてレースした.

3 時間かせぎに ▪ The thief was talking away *against time* with the policemen. その泥棒は時間かせぎにだらだらと警官と話した.

ahead of time (約束の)時間よりも早く ▪ I always arrive a little *ahead of time*. 私はいつも約束の時間よりも少し早く着く.

ahead of *one's* ***time*** =before one's TIME 2.

all in good time →in good TIME 1.

all the time **1** その間ずっと, 終始 (=all the WHILE) ▪ I was looking at her *all the time*. 私はその間ずっと彼女を見ていた.

2 連続して, 中断なく ▪ Our old refrigerator is running *all the time*. うちの古い冷蔵庫は今でも動いている.

3 《米》常に, いつも ▪ He acts *all the time*. 彼はいつも芝居している.

ancient time(s) →old TIME(s).

Any time! いつでもご遠慮なく《親切のお礼を言われたときの答え》.

as times go 《口》この時勢では, 時節柄 ▪ He is progressive *as times go*. この時勢では彼も進歩的だ.

at a set time 指定時刻に ▪ We had to eat in that hotel *at a set time*. あのホテルでは指定された時間に食事をしなくてはならなかった.

at a time 一度に, 同時に ▪ Do not speak to more than one man *at a time*. 同時に二人以上の人に話しかけるな.

at all times いつでも ▪ Surely man is the same *at all times*. 確かに人間はいつでも変わらないものだ.

at any time いつでも, いつなん時 ▪ He may turn up *at any time*. 彼はいつなん時現れるかもしれない ▪ You will be welcome *at any time*. いつでも大歓迎ですよ.

at no time 決して...ない ▪ He was *at no time* allowed to use the attic. 彼は決して屋根裏部屋を使うことを許されなかった.

at one time 一時は; 同時に, 一斉に ▪ *At one time* I used to go skiing every winter. 一時は毎年の冬スキーへ行ったものだった ▪ Let's start again *at one time*. 再び一斉に始めよう.

at one time or another **1** いつか, かつて ▪ I have read all these books *at one time or another*. これらの本はみな, いつとは言えないが前に読んでいる.

2 さまざまな折に, 幾たびか ▪ *At one time or another* I've considered moving somewhere, but so far I haven't done so. どこかへ引っ越そうかと何度か考えたが, まだしていない.

(at) one time with [and] another いろいろの折に; 前後合わせて ▪ He had seen a good deal of her *one time and another* in his life. 彼はそれまでにいろいろな折に彼女に何度も会っていた ▪ Winthrop was governor, *at one time with another*, eleven years. ウィンスロップは前後合わせて11年間知事をしていた.

at other times **1** ふだんは ▪ If you work hard *at other times*, you won't have to sit up all night before the exam. ふだんよく勉強していれば試験の前に徹夜しなくてもいいだろう.

2 また別の時は ▪ He says sometimes one thing and *at other times* the exact opposite. 彼はある時はあることを言いまた別の時は正反対のことを言う.

at the same time →SAME.

at the time その時は ▪ This trick escaped detection *at the time*. このぺてんはその時は見つけ出されなかった.

at this time of day 《口》今ごろに, 今さら ▪ I will not begin *at this time of day* to distress my tenants. 私は今さら借家人たちを悩ますようなことは始めまい.

T

at time(s)/at times and again 折々, たまに ▪ Away from home for the first time, I'm homesick *at times*. 初めて家を離れて, 時々家が恋しくなる.

at your [his, etc.***] time of life*** 君[彼, など]の年ごろでは ▪ I was a regular dandy *at your time of life*. 私は君の年ごろには全くのだて男でした.

(be) equal to the time of day 《口》万事心得ている ▪ He *is equal to the time of day*. 彼は万事心得ている.

be in with the times 《米口》時世に遅れていない ▪ He knows everything because he *is in with the times*. 彼は時世に沿っているので何でも知っている.

be (stuck) in a time warp 10年1日のごとく変化がない ▪ My whole life seems to *be stuck in a time warp*. どうも私の生活は何もかも以前と全く変わっていないようだ.

before** one's **time **1** 時ならず, 尚早に ▪ He was born *before his time*. 彼は月足らずで生まれた ▪ He died *before his time*. 彼は天寿を全うせずに死んだ.
2 時代に先んじて ▪ Such a man was born *before his time*. このような人は時代に先んじて生まれたのだ.
3 時刻より早く ▪ He came *before his time*. 彼は時刻より早く来た.
4 生まれる[関与する]前のことで ▪ The Watergate scandal was *before my time*. ウォーターゲイト事件は私が生まれる前に起きたことだ.

behind the time 時間が遅れて ▪ Your watch is two minutes *behind the time*. 君の時計は2分遅れている.

behind the times 時代[流行]に遅れて ▪ You are *behind the times* with your information. 君の情報は古い ▪ Her dress was extremely *behind the times*. 彼女のドレスはひどく流行遅れだった.

behind time **1** 遅刻して ▪ I was *behind time* yesterday. きのう遅刻した.
2 (…が)遅れて (*with*) ▪ He is always *behind time with* his payment. 彼は常に支払いが遅れている.

behind** one's **time 遅刻して ▪ He was full eighteen minutes *behind his time*. 彼はまる18分間遅刻した.

between times 合い間合い間に; 折々 ▪ She served me faithfully till the last, packing her belongings in *between times*. 彼女は最後まで私に忠実に仕えてくれ, 合い間に自分の持ち物の荷うくりをした.

bide** one's **time →BIDE.

bring ... to time →call ... to TIME.

buy time 時間をかせぐ ▪ *Buy time* to finish tracing the call. 逆探知が終わるまで時間をかせげ.

by the time …する時までには ▪ It will be nearly two *by the time* you get there. そこに着くころまでには2時近くになっているでしょう.

by this time この時はもう ▪ *By this time* he was undeceived. この時はもう彼は迷いがさめていた.

By time! 《米口》全く, 確かに《穏やかな誓言》 ▪ *By time*, don't that taste good! 全く, そのうまいことと言ったら.

call time (on) (ボクシングなどで…に)試合の開始[終了]を知らせる ▪ George was the first to *call time*. ジョージが最初に試合の終了を知らせた.

call [bring] ... to time 《米口》 **1** …を取り上げる ▪ He was absent when the bill *was called to time*. 彼はその法案が取り上げられたとき欠席していた.
2 …をしかる ▪ She *called* him *to time* sharply. 彼女は彼を激しくしかった.

change [keep up] with the times 時勢とともに変化する[に遅れずについていく] ▪ I don't really like using a mobile phone, but you have to *change with the times*. 本当はケータイを使うのはいやなんだが, 時代とともに変わらないとな.

come to time **1** 義務を果たす.
2 (ボクシングなどで)負ける ▪ It's a finisher. I can't *come to time*. 決勝戦なのだ. 負けるわけにいかない.

come up to time = come ... to TIME 2.

do (**one's**) time 《口》刑期を務める ▪ He *did his time* without protest. 彼は抗議せずに刑期を務めた.

double (quick) time →DOUBLE[1].

draw** one's **time (やむなく)職をやめる ▪ He'll have to *draw his time* and look for a decent job someplace. 彼は職を辞しどこかのまともな勤め口を探さねばなるまい.

each [every] time …のたびごとに ▪ He was out *each time* I called. 訪問のたびごとに彼は留守だった.

empty time むなしい時間, 退屈な時間 ▪ I don't know what to do with all the *empty time* you've left me with. あなたが去ったあとの気の抜けた時間をどう過ごせばよいのかわからない.

every time** one **turns around しょっちゅう, 頻繁に ▪ Something in our house breaks down *every time* I *turn around*. うちでは何かがしょっちゅう故障するな.

fall on hard times 不運[不幸]に陥る ▪ I am sorry to hear that he has *fallen on hard times*. 彼が不幸に陥ったそうで, 気の毒だ.

find time 余暇がある ▪ I can never *find time* to do it. それをする暇がどうしてもない.

first, last, and all the time →FIRST.

for a long time past [to come] これまで[今後]長い間 ▪ I haven't seen him *for a long time past*. 彼とはこれまで長いこと会ってない ▪ We shall not see him *for a long time to come*. 我々は今後長い間彼に会わないだろう.

for a time 一時は, 当分 ▪ He stayed in London *for a time*. 彼は一時はロンドンに滞在していた.

for old times' sake/for old times 昔のよしみで ▪ I called on him *for old times' sake*. 昔のよしみで彼を訪ねた.

for the first [second, last] time 最初[2度目, 最後]に ▪ I met him then *for the first time*. その時初めて彼と会った ▪ I heard from him *for the last time*. 彼からのたよりはそれが最後だった.

for the time being/for the time 当分(の間), 当座 ▪ This will do *for the time being*. 当分これ

で間に合う.

(from [since, for]) time immemorial 大昔から ▪ They have been in the possession of the island *for time immemorial.* 彼らは大昔からその島を所有してきた ▪ It had been the custom, *time immemorial.* それは大昔からの習わしになっていた ▪ These ruins have stood here *since time immemorial.* これらの廃墟は大昔からこの地に建っている.

from time to time 時々 ▪ It was used only *from time to time.* それは時々使用されるだけだった.

gain time **1** (時計が)進む ▪ The clock on my son's PC keeps *gaining time.* 息子のパソコンの時計は進んでばかりいる.

2 (言い訳やぐずぐずしたりして)時をかせぐ (↔lose TIME 2) ▪ Ambiguous answers may serve to *gain time.* あいまいな返答は時をかせぐに役立つこともある. ☞[F] gagner du temps のなぞり.

give** a person **a hard [rough, tough] time 《口》 **1** 人につらい思いをさせる; に不平を言う ▪ The boy *gave* his mother *a hard time* by behaving wildly. 少年は放埒に振る舞って母親につらい思いをさせた.

2 人をからかう, からかってじゃまをする ▪ Don't *give* me *a hard time.* I'm writing my essay. 僕をからかってじゃましないでくれ. エッセイを書いているんだ.

give** a person **a hot time (of it) →give a HOT time (of it).

give** a person **the time of day 《口》 人にあいさつをする ▪ There was not one in the parish who would not *give* him *the time of day.* 教区の中で彼にあいさつをしない者は一人もいなかった.

***give the time to** a person* 《米俗》 人をくどき落とす ▪ He *gave the time to* two girls. 彼は二人の女の子をくどき落とした.

give time 猶予を与える ▪ *Give* me *time* and I will pay. ご猶予くだされば支払います.

go down for the third time 失敗[破産]寸前である ▪ I was *going down for the third time* when I was helped by his offer. まさに破産寸前のとき彼からの申し出によって救われた.

half the time **1** 半分の時間 ▪ I could have done it in *half the time.* 私ならその半分の時間でやってのけただろう.

2 たいてい, しょっちゅう ▪ He is daydreaming *half the time.* 彼はたいてい空想にふけっている.

hard times 不景気, 困難な時代 ▪ The 1930s were *hard times* for many people. 1930年代は多くの人にとって苦難の時代だった.

have a big time →BIG TIME.

have a good [bad, etc.] time (of it) おもしろい思いをする[ひどい目にあう, など] ▪ It seems his servants *had a good time of it.* 彼の使用人たちはおもしろい思いをしたらしい ▪ Those poor people *had a bad time of it.* その貧しい人々はひどい目にあった.

have a hard [rough, bad] time (of it) → HARD, ROUGH[1].

have a high old time 《俗》 大いに楽しむ, 大変楽しく過ごす ▪ We *had a high old time* that night. 私たちはその夜大いに楽しんだ ▪ We're *having a high old time.* 我々はとても楽しくやっている.

have a lively time of it →LIVELY.

have a lot of time for …を称賛する, が好きである ▪ I*'ve got a lot of time for* Betty. She often comes to see me. ベティーって好きよ. よく遊びにきてくれるし.

***have a time** doing* …するのに骨が折れる ▪ I *had* quite *a time locating* your office. あなたの事務所を見つけるのに全く骨が折れました.

have** oneself **a time 愉快に過ごす ▪ You've been *having yourself a time.* 君は愉快にやってきたね.

have a time with 《米口》 …ともめごとを起こす ▪ I've *had a time with* Mr. Bennet. 私はベネット氏ともめごとを起こした.

have all the time in the world たっぷり時間はある ▪ I *have all the time in the world* because of my retirement. 退職したので時間はたっぷりある.

have an easy time of it 安楽に暮らす ▪ He has *had an easy time of it* since his father left him a fortune. 父親が財産を残してくれて以来彼は安楽に暮らしてきた.

have no time for …を軽蔑する; が嫌いである ▪ He's a cheat. I *have no time for* him. 彼はぺてん師だ. あんな男は軽蔑する ▪ I *have no time for* lazy people like you. お前みたいな怠け者はきらいだ.

have no time to lose 一刻も猶予できない ▪ It's urgent. We *have no time to lose.* ことは緊急を要する. ぐずぐずしてはいられない.

have the time of** one's **life 《口》 かつてない愉快な思いをする ▪ He *had the time of his life* when he went to the party. 彼はそのパーティーへ行ったときかつてない愉快な思いをした.

have time on** one's **hands 暇をもてあましている ▪ Old people often *have time on their hands.* 老人はよく暇をもてあましている.

have time on** one's **side →TIME is on the side of.

have time to** do **[for] …する[の]時間がある, に間に合う ▪ He must *have time to* consider it. 彼はそれを考えてみる時間がなくてはいけない ▪ I *have* no *time for* sports. 運動をする時間がない.

have time to kill 暇である ▪ I*'ve got* some *time to kill.* いくらか暇なんだよね.

have time to turn round 〚主に否定文で〛 暇がある ▪ I *have* scarcely *time to turn round* these days. 近ごろはほとんど暇がない.

High time, too! 当然そうしていい頃だ ▪ Two more days to the election, and *high time, too.* 選挙まであと2日. いよいよ機が熟した ▪ Great news, and it's *high time, too.* He is among the inductees into the Hall of Fame. 朗報だ. 当然その時期だが. 彼も野球の殿堂入りする.

How time drags! 何て退屈なんだろう[時が経つのって何て遅いんだろう]! ▪ It's funny *how time drags* when you're waiting. 待っていると不思議になかなか時間が経たない.

How time flies! 時間が経つのは何て早いんだろう ▪ It's nearly midnight! *How time flies!* もうすぐ真夜中だ! あっという間だな, 全く.

in between times =between TIMEs.

in due time →DUE.

in good time **1**〚all を伴って〛そのうちに, そうせくな ▪ I'll tell you *all in good time.* いずれ話すよ.
2 すぐに, 早く ▪ My aunt wants to be well *in good time.* おばは早く元気になりたがっている.
3 時をたがえずに, 時間通りに ▪ He arrived *in good time.* 彼は時間通りにやって来た.

in *one's* ***good time*** =in good TIME 1.

in (next to) no time (at all)/in less than no time すぐに, たちまち ▪ *In less than no time* you shall hear. すぐにおたよりします ▪ He was ready *in no time.* 彼はたちまち用意した.

in *one's* ***own good time*** 気の向くままに, 自分の都合のよいときに ▪ Babies like to do what they want *in their own good time.* 赤んぼうは気の向くままにしたいことを好んでする ▪ Spring arrives *in its own good time.* 春の訪れは年によってまちまちだ.

in [on] *one's* ***own time*** 余暇に, 都合のよい時に ▪ Write it in your own home, *on your own time.* お暇な時にお宅でお書きなさい.

in *one's* ***spare time*** 余暇に ▪ What do you do *in your spare time?* 余暇には何をするのか.

in (the) course [fullness] of time そのうちに, やがては ▪ *In course of time* they married. そのうちに彼らは結婚した.

in the nick of time →NICK[1].

in time **1** やがて, 早晩 ▪ Consolation will come to you *in time.* 慰めはやがて来るだろう.
2 ちょうどよい時に, 間に合って (*to do, for*) ▪ He was just *in time for* the last train. 彼は終電にやっと間に合った.
3 調子が合って[た] (↔out of TIME 3) ▪ He heard a brisk tramp of feet *in time.* 彼は歩調のとれたきびきびした足音を聞いた.
4《口》一体 ▪ Why *in time* don't you come our way? 一体なぜ遊びに来てくれないのかね.

in *one's* ***time*** 自分の時代には ▪ Mr. Arnold was head of the school *in my time.* 私の時代にはアーノルド氏が校長でした.

in time(s) to come 将来, 未来 ▪ It may become necessary to decide this point *in time to come.* 将来この問題を解決する必要が生じるかもしれない.

It happens all the time. いつものことだ(から心配しないでよい) ▪ Oh, that's nothing. In a big city like Paris, *it happens all the time.* ああ, 大したことはない. パリのような大都市では日常茶飯事さ.

it is (high) time もう…の時分だ ▪ *It is time* I was [were] going [for me to go]. もうおいとますべき時分です.

it's about time... もう…してもいいころだ ▪ *It's about time* you knew how to behave yourself. お前ももう行儀作法のわかっていいころだ.

it's only [just] a matter [question] of time (before) …のも時間の問題にすぎない, 遅かれ早かれ…する, そのうち…になる ▪ *It's only a question [matter] of time before* he is caught. 彼が捕まるのもあとは時間の問題だ.

keep good [bad] time (時計が)時間が正確である[ない] ▪ My watch *keeps* very *good time.* 私の時計は時間がとても正確だ.

keep time **1**《音》(手・指揮棒で)拍子を取る; 調子を合わせる (*with*) ▪ They *kept time* to this tune. 彼らはこの曲に合わせて拍子を取った ▪ To dance correctly you must *keep time with* your partner. 正しくダンスするためにはパートナーと調子を合わさねばならない.
2 (時計が)時間が正確だ ▪ The clock has *kept time* for three years. その時計はこの3年間時間が正確に合っている.
3 時間をたがえずに来る ▪ I'll meet you if you'll *keep time.* 時間通りに来るなら出迎えてやろう.

keep time and tune →KEEP[2].

kill time 《口》時間をつぶす ▪ Some read books just to *kill time.* ただ時間つぶしに読書する人もいる.

know the time of day 万事心得ている ▪ He has been here long enough to *know the time of day.* 彼はここに長くいるから万事心得ている.

live [be] on borrowed time **1** (重病人が)医者の診断よりも長生きする, 思ったより長生き[長続き]する ▪ Our fifteen-year-old bike is *living on borrowed time.* 買って15年になるうちの自転車はまだ使われている ▪ The invalid is *living on borrowed time.* 病人は医者の診断よりも長生きしている.
2 風前の灯である ▪ The union's executive *is on borrowed time.* 組合執行部の任期も残りわずかだ.
3 他の人々がやめろと言うことをやっている ▪ The government *is on borrowed time.* 政府は長く政権を握ってはいないだろう.

Long time no see. →LONG.

lose [waste] no time (in) *doing* 機を失せずに…する, 早速…する ▪ He *lost no time in going* there. 彼は機を失せずにそこへ行った ▪ I *lost no time reading* your book. 早速貴著を読みました.

lose time **1** (時計が)遅れる ▪ Our problem is that the clock *loses time.* あの時計が遅れるので困っている.
2 時を失する (*in*) (↔gain TIME 2) ▪ There is no *time to lose* [*to be lost*]. 一刻も猶予できない ▪ Don't *lose time in* useless discussion. むだな議論に時を失うな.

make a time over [about] 《米口》…のことで大騒ぎする ▪ We *made* such *a time about* water. 我々は水のことでとても大騒ぎした.

make good [poor] time (速度・仕事が)速い[遅い] ▪ The subway is supposed to *make better time.* 地下鉄のほうが速いことになっている.

make time (急いで)行く; 都合をつける ▪ I *made*

T

fast *time*. 私は急いで行った ▪I know you are busy, but you must *make time* for me. 忙しいのは分かっているが, 何とかして都合をつけろよ.

***make time to** do* 繰り合わせて…する ▪Could you *make time to* copy it for me? 繰り合わせてそれを写してくださいませんか.

***make time with** a person* 《米俗》人に言い寄る, をくどく ▪He was trying to *make time with* the waitress. 彼はそのウェイトレスをくどこうとしていた.

make up for lost time/make up ground 遅れを取り戻す, 追いつく ▪We'll just have to *make up ground* as best we can. 何とか精一杯がんばって遅れを取り戻さなくてはなるまい.

make up the time (定時にできなかった仕事を)あとで補う ▪I'll *make up the time* by working late tomorrow. 明日残業して埋め合わせます.

many a time/ many a time and oft [often]/many times 幾度も; しばしば ▪Englishmen have done it *many a time*. イギリス人は幾度もそれをしてきた ▪*Many a time and oft* you carried me in your arms. 幾度もあなたは私を抱いてくれました.

many's the time 〚文の書き出しで〛しばしば ▪*Many's the time* I experienced failures when I was a young man. 若い頃はよく失敗した.

mark time →MARK².

move [march] with the times 時勢と共に進む ▪The nation has *moved with the times*. その国民は時勢と共に進んできた.

Moving three times is as bad as a fire. 《諺》3度の引っ越しは火事に1度あうのと同じ,「引越貧乏」.

near** one's **time 臨終[分娩時]が近い ▪The Queen was with child, and *near her time*. お后(きさき)はみごもっておられ, 分娩時が近かった.

nine times out of ten →NINE.

No, no, a thousand times no. 《戯》だめと言ったらだめです[何度言ってもノーです] ▪Here, have some wine.—No, thanks.—Oh, come on!—*No, no, a thousand times no*! さあ, ワインを—いや, 結構—まあ, そう言わずに—いや, ほんとに結構.

not before time 大分遅れて ▪Bill has been promoted, and *not before time*. ビルは昇進したが, 大分遅れてるね. ☞前文へのコメントとして用いる.

not for the first time 前にも時々[しばしば]あった ▪The police are baffled, *not for the first time*. 警察は裏をかかれたが, これが初めてではない.

not give [get]... the time of day …を無視する[される] ▪His posh friends would*n't give* any of you *the time of day*. 彼の上流の友人たちは君たちの誰にも見向きもしないだろう.

not know the time of day 何も知らない ▪Don't ask him the result of the baseball match—he *never knows the time of day*. 彼に野球の試合の結果を聞いてもむだだよ—何も知らないから.

now is the [your] time 今こそ潮時だ ▪*Now's your time* to go in. 今こそ入って行く潮時だ.

of all time 空前絶後の, 古今の ▪He is the greatest genius *of all time*. 彼は古今無双の大天才だ.

of the time(s) 当時の; (特に)当代の ▪The act ran counter to the religious feeling *of the time*. その行為は当時の宗教感情にさからっていた ▪He is one of the greatest men *of the time(s)*. 彼は当代きっての偉人だ.

old before** one's **time 実際よりも年上のようにふるまって[見えて] ▪Hubby is *old before his time*. ハッビーは実際よりも年上に見える.

old [olden, ancient] time(s) 昔, 古代 ▪It was a town of great fame in *ancient time*. そこは古代には非常に有名な町であった.

on a time 《米俗》浮かれ騒いで ▪He was out *on a time*. 彼は外で浮かれ騒いでいた.

on** one's **own time 金をもらわずに; 暇な時に, 勤務時間外に ▪He has done extra work *on his own time*. 彼は金をもらわずに余分の仕事をした ▪Do it *on your own time* if you want to play baseball. 野球がしたいのなら暇な時にやれ.

on time **1** 時間通りに[で] ▪The train arrived *on time*. 列車は定刻に着いた.

2 (一定期間)分割払いで ▪We bought a bed *on time*. ベッドを分割払いで買った.

once upon a time →ONCE.

one at a time (続けて)一度に一つ[一人]ずつ ▪*One at a time* we went into the headmaster's office. 僕たちは一人ずつ校長室に入った.

(Only) time can [will] tell. 時が経ってみなければ分からない[時間が証明してくれる] ▪*Only time will tell* if you are right. 君の言う通りかどうかは時が経たねば分からない.

out of time **1** 遅すぎて ▪The appeal was *out of time*. その訴訟は遅すぎた.

2 時世をまちがえて ▪The novelist seems to have been born *out of time*. その小説家は時世をまちがえて生まれたように思われる.

3 調子がはずれて (↔in TIME 3) ▪The man played *out of time*. 男は調子はずれに演奏した.

out of** one's **time 徒弟奉公を終えて ▪He is not yet *out of his time*. 彼はまだ徒弟奉公を終えてない.

pass (the) time (退屈しのぎに)時間を過ごす ▪I *passed the time* by watching TV. テレビを見て時を過ごした.

pass the time of day with (人)にあいさつする ▪The police will *pass the time of day with* me. 警官たちは私にあいさつをするだろう.

past times →TIME(s) past.

play for time →PLAY².

play out time →PLAY².

prime time テレビの視聴率が最も高い時間帯, ゴールデンタイム ▪It beat every *prime-time* program on Saturday night. その番組の視聴率が土曜夜のゴールデンタイムの他番組を上回った.

quality time 家族[友人]と過ごすくつろぎの時間, 最も楽しくかけがえのない時間 ▪Let's have some *qual-*

T

ity time together. さあ, 家族そろって楽しく過ごそう.

run like time 《米口》速く走る ▪ The current was *running like time*. 流れは速く走っていた.

run out of time 時間切れになる ▪ I *ran out of time* before I could finish the mock exam. 模試を解き終えないうちに時間切れになった.

one's ***second*** [***third***] ***time around*** [***round***] →the second TIME around.

serve the time →SERVE².

serve time =do (one's) TIME.

show *a person* ***a good time*** 人を楽しく過ごさせる, 楽しませる ▪ He knew how to *show* a girl *a good time*. 彼は女の子を楽しく過ごさせる方法を知っていた ▪ She will *show* you *a good time* when you visit Kobe. あなたが神戸を訪れるときには彼女がもてなしてくれるでしょう.

slow time (サマータイムに対して)標準時 ▪ On Sunday we will be on *slow time* again. 日曜日からまた標準時に戻る.

some time **1** いつか ▪ I'll call on you *some time*. いつかお訪ねします.
2 しばらく ▪ It will be *some time* before he gets well. 彼が全快するまでにはしばらくかかるだろう.

take a long time 長くかかる ▪ He *took a long time* over the work. 彼はその仕事にずいぶん手間取った.

take all *one's* (***own***) ***time*** ずいぶん骨を折らせる ▪ It *takes* us *all our time* to make both ends meet. 収支を合わせるのにずいぶん骨が折れる.

take (***the***) ***time*** (***off*** [***out***]) ***to*** *do* 時間をさいて…する ▪ He *took time off to* visit his parents. 彼は時間をさいて両親を訪ねた.

take time **1** 時間がかかる ▪ That will *take time*. それは時間がかかる.
2 ゆっくりする (= take one's TIME) ▪ He *took time* to answer the question. 彼はゆっくりかまえてその質問に答えた.

take *one's* ***time*** **1** ゆっくりする ▪ Pray *take your* own *time*. I am not in any haste. どうかゆっくりしてください. 私は少しも急いでいませんから.
2 ぐずぐずする, あまりにのんびりやる ▪ The shop assistant *took his time* serving us. その店員はのらりくらりと接客した.

take time by the forelock →FORELOCK.

tell the time 時間が分かる, 時計の見方を知っている ▪ The child is only four, but he can already *tell the time*. その子はまだ4歳なのに時計の見方が分かる.

that time of the month 《口》生理の期間 ▪ I'd rather not go out. It's *that time of the month*. 外出したくないの. 生理だから.

the good old times (よき)昔 ▪ Life was easier in *the good old times*. 昔は生活が楽だった.

the next time 今度(…する時は) ▪ *The next time* you come, bring your sister with you. 今度おいでの時は妹さんをお連れください.

the [*one's*] ***second*** [***third***] ***time around*** [***round***] 第2[第3]の機会 ▪ *The second time around* was even better. 第2の機会の方がなおよかった.

The third time is a [***the***] ***charm.*** 《しばしばスポーツ》三度目の正直だ ▪ This year our team is hoping *the third time's a charm*. 今年はわがチームは三度目の正直に期待している.

the time has come (***for*** *a person*) ***to*** *do* (人が)…すべき時が来た ▪ *The time has come for* him *to* take control of the situation. 彼が事態を収拾すべき時が来た.

the time is ripe for *a person* ***to*** *do* 人が…する時機が熟した ▪ *The time is ripe for* us *to* attack. 我々が攻撃すべき時機が熟した.

the time of day **1** 時刻 ▪ How runs *the time of day*?—Past ten. 今何時ですか?—10時過ぎです.
2 《俗》情勢, 事態; 正しいやり方 ▪ No, friend, it is not *that time of day*. いや, 君, そういう事態じゃないんだ ▪ Steady, sir! That's *the time of day*! 落ち着いてください! それでけっこうです.

(***the***) ***time shall be when*** 将来…という時が来るだろう ▪ *Time shall be when* Achilles shall be missed. アキレスがいないのに気づく時も来るだろう.

(***the***) ***time was*** [***hath been***] (***when***) …という時もあった ▪ *Time was when* we had a national style. 我々が国民的風格というものを持っていたころもあった ▪ *Time was*, the city streets were safe at midnight. 町の通りが真夜中でも安全な時代もあった.

(***The***) ***times change.*** 時勢は変わる ▪ *Times change*, but rivalries don't. 時勢は変わっても抗争は変わらない ▪ These give an indication of how *times change*. これらで時勢が変わる様子がわかる.

the times that try men's souls 《米口》危険と苦難の時代《独立戦争のころ》 ▪ He was the only remaining relict of "*the times that tried men's souls*." 彼は「危険と苦難の時代」の唯一の生き残りであった. ☞Thomas Paine (1737–1809)のエッセイの題から.

There is a time for everything. 何事にも潮時というものがある(《聖》*Eccles*. 3. 1) ▪ The Bible tells us that *there is a time for everything*—good and bad. 良きも悪しきも万事に潮時があると聖書にある.

(***There is***) ***no time to lose.*** →LOSE.

there was a time when …以前[昔]は… ▪ *There was a time when* I was unhappy. 以前は不幸だった.

There's a time and a place. 時と場所をわきまえるべきだ ▪ You can't wear a dress like that to a funeral. *There's a time and a place*. 葬儀にそんな格好で行ってはいかん. 時と場所ということがある.

There's always (***a***) ***next time.*** 《諺》(失敗しても)いつだって次があるさ《励ましの言葉》 ▪ Life doesn't end after failure, *there is always a next time*. 人生は失敗のあとで終わりはしない, いつだって次があるさ.

There's (***got to be***) ***a first time for everything.*** 《諺》何事にも初めというものがある《今まで起こらなくても, 今後起こるかもしれない》.

(There's) no time like the present. 《諺》現在くらい絶好の機会はない,「思い立ったが吉日[好機逸すべからず]」.
there's no time to lose = have no TIME to lose.
this is no time for [***to*** *do*] 今は…の場合ではない ▪ *This is no time for* trifling. 今は冗談を言っている場合ではない.
this time last [***next***] ***year*** 去年[来年]の今ごろ ▪ I was in America *this time last year*. 去年の今ごろはアメリカにいた.
through good times and bad (***times***) 良いときも悪いときも変わらず ▪ We have supported each other *through good times and bad*. 順風のときも逆風のときも変わらずお互いに支えあってきた.
time and a half 《米》1倍半 ▪ I got *time and a half* last month. 先月は1倍半の給料があった.
Time and tide wait [***stay***] ***for no man.*** 《諺》歳月人を待たず.
time and (***time***) ***again/time after time*** 何度も, 繰り返し ▪ *Time after time* we have warned you. 何度も我々はあなたに警告してきた ▪ *Time and again* he eluded the enemy. 何度も彼は敵から逃れた.
time enough すぐ間に合って, 十分早い (*for, to do*) ▪ You shall see him *time enough*. 彼にすぐ会わせてあげよう ▪ Tomorrow will be *time enough to* hear such stuff. そんなことを聞くのはあすで十分だ.
Time flies. 《諺》光陰矢のごとし.
time hangs heavy on *a person's* ***hands*** → HANG heavy on a person.
time immemorial →(from) TIME immemorial.
Time is a great healer. 《諺》時は偉大ないやし手《時がたてば悲しみ・憎しみなどが薄らぐ》.
time is getting on 時がどんどん経っている; 時刻が遅くなっている; 残り時間が少なくなっている ▪ Let's hurry up and finish; *time's getting on*. 急いで済まそう. 残り時間はあとわずかだ.
Time is money. 《諺》時は金なり. ☞Franklin, *Advice to Young Tradesman* から.
time is on the side of/have time on *one's* ***side*** 時は…の味方である; 時間的な余裕がある ▪ If you wait, *time is on your side*. 待っていれば時が味方をしてくれる ▪ Don't worry. You still *have* plenty of *time on your side*. 心配するな. まだ時間の余裕はたっぷりある ▪ She failed the exam, but *time is on her side*; she can take it again next year. 彼女は試験に落ちたがあせることはない. 来年また受ければよいのだから.
Time is up. 時間が切れた ▪ *Time is up*! Put down your pencils. はい, 時間です. 鉛筆を置いて.
time off 休み, 休憩 ▪ She took *time off* to make some phone calls. 彼女は休憩を取ってあちこちへ電話した.
time out of mind **1** 大昔から ▪ The goblet has belonged to the Musgraves *time out of mind*. そのゴブレットは大昔からマスグレーブ家のものであった. **2** 非常に長い間 ▪ This will last *time out of mind*. これは非常に長い間もつでしょう.
time will tell 時が経てばわかる ▪ It is hard to tell now, but *time will tell*. 今それは判断しうらいが, そのうち明らかになるだろう ▪ Only *time will tell* if the plan will be successful. その計画がうまくいくかどうかは時が経たねばわからない.
Time works wonders. 《諺》時は奇跡を生む.
Times change and we with time. 《諺》時勢は変わり我々もそれとともに変わる,「時移り俗変わる」.
times out of [***without***] ***number/times and often*** 幾度となく ▪ *Times without number* they have been called upon to decide the question. 幾度となく彼らはその問題を解決することを要求されてきた ▪ He has been here *times and often*. 彼はしばしばここへやって来た.
time(***s***) ***past/past times*** 過去の時代 ▪ It was fortified in *times past* with a castle. そこは昔は城で固めてあった.
to time **1** 期限までに(終わるように) ▪ He disliked writing *to time*. 彼は期限までに書きあげるのを嫌った. **2** =up to TIME.
up to time 《英口》時間通りに[で] ▪ See that you are *up to time*. 時間通りにするよう心がけなさい.
waste no time (***in***) *doing* →lose no TIME (in) doing.
What a time you have been! ずいぶん手間どったね ▪ *What a time you have been* at it!—Nearly three months. それにずいぶん手間どったな—3ヶ月近くかかったよ.
what time 何時に ▪ Find out *what time* he intends to breakfast. 彼が何時に朝食を取るつもりでいるか調べろ.
What time is it?/What is the time? 今何時ですか.
with time 時が経つにつれて; やがて ▪ Ambition increases *with time*. 野心は時が経つにつれて増していく ▪ *With time* it will come all right. やがてそれは元通りになるだろう.
You're a long time dead. →DEAD.

time[2] /taɪm/ 動 ***be well*** [***ill***] ***timed*** 時機を得ている[得ていない] ▪ His remark *was ill timed*. 彼の言葉は時機を逸していた.

time out, timeout /tàɪmáʊt/ 名 ***take time out*** 一時休憩する ▪ He *took time out* from directing the movie. 彼は映画の監督を一時休んだ.
take time out for …で時を過ごす ▪ He has *taken time out for* reflection. 彼は反省して過ごした.

Times /taɪmz/ 名 ***write to the Times*** タイムズ紙に投稿する; 苦情などを世に訴える ▪ "I shall *write to the Times*" is a favorite threat of Britons. 「タイムズ紙に投書するぞ」というのがイギリス人のおきまりのおどし文句である.

timid /tímɪd/ 形 (***as***) ***timid as a rabbit*** [***hare***] 非常に内気で ▪ That fellow is *as timid as a rabbit*. あの男はすごく内気だ.

T

tin /tɪn/ [名] ***a little tin god*** 《文》→GOD.

a tin ear 騒音に敏感でない[音感がない]こと ▪ I've got *a tin ear* and make a poor choir member. 音痴なので私は合唱メンバーには不向きなの.

have a tin ear for …の才能がない, 理解力に欠ける; に音痴である ▪ He *has a tin ear for* languages. 彼には語学の才能がない ▪ Congress *has a tin ear for* the plight of the working class. 議会は労働階級の窮状を聞こうとしない ▪ Unfortunately, Mr James *has a tin ear for* history. 不幸にして, ジェイムズ氏は歴史音痴である《歴史がわかっていない》 ▪ She is a marvelous musician; I *have a tin ear*. 彼女はすばらしい音楽家だが, 私は音痴だ.

make a (***little***) ***tin god*** (***out***) ***of*** (誤って)…を神聖視する ▪ We shouldn't *make a little tin god out of* Calvin. 我々はカルバンを神格化すべきでない.

put the tin hat on =put the LID on (it) 1.

put the tin lid on =put the LID on (it) 1.

straight from the tin 源からすぐに, ま新しい ▪ What they want here is Yankee twang *straight from the tin*. 彼らがこの場合に求めているのは本場のヤンキーなまりである.

tinker /tíŋkər/ [名] ***as drunk*** [***quarrelsome***] ***as a tinker*** ひどく酔っ払って[けんか好きで] ▪ The man was *as drunk as a tinker*. その男はひどく酔っ払っていた. ☞回り歩く tinker (鋳掛け屋)が酒やけんかが好きで不評判であったことから.

have a tinker at …をへたにいじくる ▪ They spent their time and money in *having a tinker at* it. 彼らはそれをへたにいじくるのに時間と金をかけた.

not care a tinker's curse [***damn***]/《口》***not give a tinker's damn*** [***cuss***] ちっともかまわない ▪ I do*n't care a tinker's curse* if you do. 君がそうしたところでちっともかまわない.

not worth a tinker's curse [***damn***] ちっとも値うちがない ▪ This urn is*n't worth a tinker's curse*. この壺はちっとも値うちがない ▪ I'll *not* be *worth a tinker's damn* tomorrow if I don't get some more sleep tonight. 今夜もっと眠っておかないと, 明日は全く役に立てないだろう. ☞tinker (鋳掛け屋)が盛んにののしる (curse) とされているが,「そのののしり文句ほどの価値もない」の意から.

swear like a tinker →SWEAR like a trooper.

tinkle /tíŋkəl/ [名] ***give*** *a person* ***a tinkle*** 人に電話をかける ▪ I'll *give* you *a tinkle* when I get home. 家に帰ってから電話するよ.

tin-tack /tíntæk/ [名] ***come down to tin-tacks*** 実際問題[要点]に触れる ▪ He avoided *coming down to tin-tacks*. 彼は実際問題[要点]に触れるのを避けた.

tintype /tíntàɪp/ [名] ***Not on your tintype.*** 《米俗》確かにそうじゃない ▪ Is modern art revolutionary? *Not on your tintype*. 現代の芸術は革命的であるか. 断じてそうではない.

tiny /táɪni/ [形] ***little tiny/tiny little*** ちっちゃな, とても小さい ▪ This Cupid was a *little tiny*, peevish fellow. このキューピッドはちっちゃな気むずかしいやつだった.

tip[1] /tɪp/ [名] ***at the tips of*** *one's* ***fingers/at*** *one's* ***finger tips*** お手のもので, 精通して ▪ All the modern accomplishments are *at the tips of her* delicate *fingers*. 近代的な才芸はすべて繊細な彼女のお手のものだ.

from tip to tip 翼の端から端まで ▪ The bird measures 15 inches *from tip to tip*. その鳥は翼の端から端まで15インチある.

from tip to toe 頭のてっぺんからつま先まで, すっかり ▪ She is fashionably dressed *from tip to toe*. 彼女は頭のてっぺんからつま先まで流行の身なりをしている. ☞from TOP to toe のほうが普通.

have ... on [***at***] ***the tip of*** *one's* [***the***] ***tongue/... be on the tip of*** *one's* ***tongue*** …が口から出かかっている ▪ She *had* arguments *at the tip of her tongue*. 彼女は危うく論拠が口をついて出るところだった ▪ I *have* it *on the tip of my tongue*, but can't exactly recall it. それが口から出かかっているのだが, はっきりと思い出せない ▪ His name *was on the tip of my tongue* but I couldn't quite get it. 彼の名前が出かかっていたんだが, どうも思い出せなかった.

on the tips of *one's* ***toes*** =on (the) TIPTOE.

the tip of the iceberg →ICEBERG.

to the tips of *one's* ***fingers/to*** *one's* ***finger tips*** すっかり ▪ He is an artist *to his finger tips*. 彼は徹頭徹尾芸術家だ.

tip[2] /tɪp/ [名] ***give*** *a person* ***the tip*** 《口》人に情報を流す ▪ He *gave* us *the tip* beforehand. 彼が我々に前もって情報を流してくれた.

miss *one's* ***tip*** へまをやる; 失敗する ▪ The clown has *missed his tip* very often, lately. その道化は最近しょっちゅうへまをやっている. ☞もとサーカスの俗語から;「演技せよという暗示 (tip) が通じない」が原義.

put *a person* ***up to all the tips*** 人に情報を知らせる ▪ He will *put* me *up to all the tips*. 彼が私に情報を知らせてくれるだろう.

Take my tip./Take a tip from me. 私の言う通りにしなさい ▪ *Take my tip* and leave this gal alone. 私の言う通りにしてこの女の子をそっとしておきなさい ▪ *Take a tip from me*. Try to stop smoking. 言う通りにしろよ. タバコはやめなさい.

the straight tip 確かな内報 ▪ We've got *the straight tip*. 我々は確かな内報を得ている.

tip[3] /tɪp/ [動] ***tip*** *one's* ***hat*** 帽子をちょっと上げてあいさつする (*to*) ▪ He solemnly *tipped his hat to* her. 彼は帽子をちょっと上げて彼女に厳かに会釈をした.

tip (***over***) ***the perch*** →PERCH[1].

tip the balance =TIP the scales 1.

tip the scales [***beam***] **1** 天びんの一方を重くする, 一方を優勢にする, (力の)釣合いを破る ▪ His view will *tip the beam*. 彼の見解が一方を優勢にするだろう ▪ Americans *tipped the scales* decisively in two world wars. アメリカ人は2回の世界戦争において決定的に釣り合いを破った.

2 (…の)重さがある (*at*) ▪ She *tips the scales at*

150 pounds. 彼女は150ポンドの体重がある.

tip[4] /tɪp/ 動 ***tip a nod*** (人に)うなずいてみせる ▪I *tipped* him *a nod*, and he was in great spirits. 彼にうなずいてみせると, 彼は大はりきりだった.

tip** a person one's **fin →give a person one's FIN.

tip the** [**a**] **wink (人に)目くばせする, そっと知らせる ▪I came as soon as you *tipped* me *the wink*. あなたの目くばせにすぐとんでまいりました.

tiptoe /típtòʊ/ 名 ***on*** [***upon***] (***the***) ***tiptoe/on*** [***upon***] (*one's*) ***tiptoes*** **1** つま先で ▪He followed his cousin *on tiptoe*. 彼はぬき足さし足でいとこの後をつけた ▪Standing *on tiptoes*, he looked into the window. 彼はつま先立ちで窓の中をのぞいた.
2 熱心に待望して ▪All stood *on the tiptoes* of expectation [expectancy]. みなが今か今かと待っていた.

tire[1], 《英》**tyre** /taɪər/ 名 ***a spare tire*** **1** スペアタイヤ ▪You should put *a spare tire* on your truck. トラックにはスペアタイヤをのせておくのがいい.
2 《口》腰の周りのぜい肉, おなかが出ること, 太鼓腹, 中年太り ▪I've got to get rid of this *spare tire*. このおなか周りのぜい肉を落とさなくっちゃ ▪He went on a diet to lose his *spare tire*. 太鼓腹をなくすため彼はダイエットを続けた.
3 《米俗》無用の輩(やから), 怠け者, 役立たず, 余計なやつ ▪You *spare tires* over there! Get to work. そこの怠け者! 仕事にかかれ ▪He's really *a spare tire*. 彼って, ほんと, 余計だよ.

tire[2] /taɪər/ 動 ***never tire of*** (*doing*) (いくら…しても)…に飽きない ▪We could *never tire of* Disneyland attractions. ディズニーランドのアトラクションには全然飽きなかった ▪My colleagues and I *never tire of talking* about children and books. 同僚たちとは全く飽きずに子供たちや本の話をする.

tire to death …をへとへとに疲れ果てさせる ▪He *was tired to death*. 彼はへとへとに疲れ果てていた.

tired /taɪərd/ 形 ***be tired and emotional*** 酔っ払っている ▪He must have *been tired and emotional* when he wrote this. 彼がこれを書いたときは酔っ払っていたにちがいない.

(***be***) [***get***] ***tired of*** …に飽きている[飽きる] ▪I *am tired of* boiled eggs. ゆで卵にあきあきしている ▪I'*m tired of* listening to her complaints. 彼女の愚痴はほとほと聞き飽きた.

(***be***) ***tired with*** **1** …で疲れて(いる) ▪I *am tired with* standing. 立っていたので疲れた.
2 …がじれったくなって(いる) ▪I got *tired* out *with* him at last. とうとう彼がじれったくなってきた.

make** a person **tired 《口》人をうんざりさせる ▪Stop complaining; you *make* me *tired*. ぶつくさ言うのはよせ. 君にはうんざりさせられるよ.

tissue /tíʃuː/ 名 ***a tissue of lies*** でたらめだらけ, 嘘八百 ▪All of the explanations about his death proved to be *a tissue of lies*. 彼の死についての説明はすべて嘘八百だったとわかった.

tit[1] /tɪt/ 名 ***tit for tat*** しっぺ返し; 〚副詞的に〛しっぺ返しとして ▪I gave her a *tit for tat*. 彼女にしっぺ返しをしてやった ▪Mary tore her brother's book and *tit for tat* he hid her doll. メアリーは兄の本をやぶった. そこでしっぺ返しに兄はメアリーの人形を隠した.

tit[2] /tɪt/ 名 ***get on** a person's **tit*(*s*)** 《英口》人の神経にさわる, いらいらさせる (=get on a person's NERVEs) ▪This guy has been *getting on my tits* recently. こいつには近頃いらいらさせられる.

tithe[1] /taɪð/ 名 ***not ... a tithe of*** …を少しも…しない ▪I do*n't* believe *a tithe of* what he says. 彼の言うことなんか少しも信用しない.

tithe[2] /taɪð/ 動 ***tithe mint and cummin*** 末節に拘泥(こうでい)して大綱をなおざりにする (《聖》*Matt*. 23. 23) ▪It is natural for some to *tithe mint and cummin* in religion. 宗教の枝葉末節にこだわって大綱をなおざりにする者も当然いる.

tittle /títəl/ 名 ***not one jot or tittle*** →not a JOT.

to a tittle 正確に, きちんと (=to a T) ▪He's Judas *to a tittle*. あいつはまさしくユダ[裏切り者]だ ▪I'll quote him *to a tittle*. 彼の言ったことを正確に引用しよう.

tizzy /tízi/, **tizz** /tɪz/ 名 ***be*** [***get***] ***in*** [***into***] ***a tizzy*** [***tizz***] (***about***) 些細なことでうろたえている[うろたえる] ▪He *is in* such *a tizz about* his homework. 彼は宿題のことでおろおろしている ▪The local press *was in a* complete *tizzy about* the murders. 地方紙はその殺人事件で全くおたおたしていた.

***send** [**throw**] a person **into a tizzy** [**tizz**]* 人をうろたえさせる ▪A recent news item *threw* me *into a tizzy*. 最近ある新聞記事を見て狼狽した ▪His sudden appearance literally *sent* me *into a tizz*. 急に彼が現れたので本当にどぎまぎしてしまった.

to /tə, tu, tuː/ 副 ***to and fro*** /túːənfróʊ/ あちらこちらへ ▪His eyes went *to and fro*. 彼の目はあちらこちらへ動いた ▪The pendulum has been swinging *to and fro*. 振り子はあちこちと揺れていた.

toad /toʊd/ 名 ***a toad under a harrow*** 常に苦しめられている人 ▪They were kept like *toads under a harrow*. 彼らは常に苦しめられていた.

eat** a person's **toads 人にへつらう ▪They were forced to *eat his toads* through life. 彼らは一生涯彼にへつらわねばならなかった. ☞香具師(やし)の助手が解毒の力があることを示すためにヒキガエルを食うまねをしたことから.

the biggest toad in the puddle 《米口》一番偉い人 ▪He thought he was *the biggest toad in the puddle*, but he wasn't. 彼は自分が一番の大物だと思っていたが実際はそうではなかった.

toast /toʊst/ 名 (***as***) ***warm*** [***hot, dry***] ***as a toast*** (トーストのように)温かい[熱い, 乾いた] ▪Keep yourselves *as hot as toast*, d'ye hear? 体をぽかぽかにさせておくんだぞ, いいかい.

be the toast of …の賞賛の的である, に喝采を浴びる ▪Her charm and wit made her *the toast of* Paris. その魅力と機知で彼女はパリに賞賛された.

be toast **1**《俗》非常に困ったことになる ▪ If the boss finds out about this, we*'re toast*! ボスにばれたら俺たちヤバイぞ.
2 もはや重要でなくなる, お役ごめんになる, だめになる ▪ His reputation will soon *be toast*. 彼の名声も今に地に落ちるだろう.
3《主に米口》死んで[死にかけて]いる, だめになっている ▪ My brain *is* almost *toast* due to lack of sleep. 睡眠不足で頭がほとんど働かない ▪ I don't want to be a complainer—but my computer *is toast* right now. 愚痴は言いたくないけど今コンピューターが故障しているんだ.

drink a toast 乾杯する ▪ To his memory let us *drink a toast* of honor. 彼の霊につつしんで乾杯いたしましょう.

give a toast 乾杯する (*to*) ▪ He then *gave* us *a toast*, "Success to England!" 彼はそれから「イギリスの成功を祈念して!」と言って, 私たちに乾杯した.

have [***get***] *a person* ***on toast***《俗》**1** 人をやっつける, だます ▪ We*'ve got* him *on toast* now. 今度はあいつをやっつけてやったぞ.
2 人の弱味を握る ▪ I saw him steal something. Now I *have* him *on toast*. 彼が何かを盗むのを見た. もう弱味を握ったぞ.

on toast (調理品を)トーストにのせて ▪ Delicate woodcocks were served up *on toast*. おいしそうなヤマシギの肉がトーストにのせて出された.

toboggan /təbɑ́gən|-bɔ́g-/ 名 ***on the toboggan***《米俗》急落して; 下り坂で ▪ Wheat is *on the toboggan*. 小麦は急落している. ☞toboggan「滑降用平底そり」.

toco, toko /tóʊkoʊ/ 名《英俗》***catch*** [***give***] ***toco*** 体罰をくらう[くわす] ▪ They both *caught toco* when they went back. 彼らは二人とも帰ったときに体罰をくらった.

tod /tɑd|tɔd/ 名 ***on*** *one's* ***tod***《英口》一人で, 独力で ▪ He was eating supper *on his tod*. 彼は一人で夕食を食べていた. ☞tod<Tod Sloan: own の押韻俗語.

today /tədéɪ/ 副 ***here today*** (***and***) ***gone*** [***away***] ***tomorrow*** 今日来たかと思うと明日は帰ってしまう;《諺》今日ありて明日なき身 ▪ Our son seems very busy and always *here today and gone tomorrow*. 息子はとても忙しいらしくて, 今日来たかと思うと明日は帰ってしまう.

Today here, tomorrow the world.《諺》今この地での成功はやがて他所へ広まりゆく.

to-do /tədúː/ 名 ***make a to-do***《口》大騒ぎする (*about*) ▪ The papers *made a* great *to-do about* it. 新聞はそのことで大騒ぎした.

toe[1] /toʊ/ 名 ***a toe-rag*** ならず者, ろくでなし, 人間のくず ▪ Have nothing to do with those *toe-rags*. あのろくでなし連中と関わりをもつな.

cock *one's* ***toes*** (***up***) →turn one's TOEs up.

go [***stand***] ***toe-to-toe*** (***with***) つま先を合わせて立つ《試合などで威嚇する態度》, (…と)真っ向勝負をする ▪ Are you sure you can *go toe-to-toe with* him and win? 彼に真っ向勝負を挑んで勝てる自信はあるか.

keep *a person* ***on*** *his* ***toes*** 人に油断させないでおく, 慎重に構えさせる ▪ Such freedom *kept* the government *on its toes*. このような自由が与えられたので政府はいつも慎重に構えた.

keep on *one's* ***toes*** 油断しない ▪ The principal is coming. *Keep on your toes*. 校長がこっちへ来る. 油断するな.

kiss the pope's toe 教皇の右足のサンダルの黄金の十字架にキスする《謁見に普通のあいさつ》 ▪ I *kissed the pope's toe* yesterday morning. 私は昨朝教皇に謁見した.

light fantastic toe《戯》踊り (Milton, *L'Allegro* 35) ▪ He prided himself on his *light fantastic toe*. 彼は自分の踊りを自慢していた.

make *a person's* ***toes curl*** 人をのけぞらせる, 楽しい[嫌な]気分にさせる ▪ In the drama there were some scenes that *made my toes curl*. そのドラマには私をのけぞらせるような場面がいくつかあった.

on *one's* ***toes*** 元気で; 抜け目のない ▪ The nip in the air puts a fellow *on his toes*. 風の身を切るような冷たさが人を元気にしてくれる ▪ The salesman is *on his toes*. そのセールスマンは抜け目がない.

put [***dip, stick***] ***a toe in the water***(***s***) おそるおそる[試しに]ちょっとやってみる ▪ He finally *put a toe in the* commercial *waters* last year. 彼はとうとう昨年広告(放送)業界におそるおそる足を踏み入れた.

toe's length ごく短い距離 ▪ He was not fit to walk his *toe's length*. 彼はまだほんの 1 歩も歩けないくらいだった.

toes up《俗》死んで (→turn one's TOEs up) ▪ I thought I'd be by this time *toes up* in Stepney churchyard. 自分は今ごろは死んでステップニー墓地に入っていることだろうと思っていた.

tramp on the toes of …の権利を侵害する ▪ I do not *tramp on my neighbor's toes*. 私は隣人の権利を侵害しない.

tread [***step***] ***on the toes of*** …のつま先を踏む; の感情を害する, を怒らせる ▪ The cocky young fellow *treads on the toes of* his elders. その生意気な若者は目上の者を怒らせる.

turn *one's* ***toes out*** [***in***] 外わ[内わ]にする ▪ Don't try to *turn your toes in*. Try to turn your entire leg in. つま先だけを内わにしようとせず, 脚全体を内股にしてみなさい.

turn *one's* ***toes up***/***turn up*** *one's* ***toes***《俗》死ぬ ▪ Some of them *turned their toes up*. 彼らの何人かは死んでしまった.

turn (***up***) *one's* ***toes to the daisies*** →DAISY.

toe[2] /toʊ/ 動 ***toe and heel*** (***it***) 踊る ▪ Fiddler, tune up merrily! *Toe and heel it* happily. バイオリン弾き, 陽気に歌を始めてくれ! 楽しく踊るんだ.

toe the [***a***] ***line*** [***mark, scratch, crack, trig***]/《米・まれ》***toe the chalk*** **1** (競技で)スタートラインにつく, スタートラインにつま先を触れて立つ; 一列に並ぶ ▪ He marked a line on the deck, and made them *toe the mark*. 彼は甲板に線を引いて彼らを一列に並ばせた ▪ The boys were ordered to *toe the line*. 少年らはスタートラインに並べと命ぜられた.

2 (党・集団の)規律[方針, 命令, 統制, 政綱]にきちんと従う ▪ They *toe a* party *line* without protest. 彼らは党の政綱に文句を言わずに従う ▪ As he is in authority we shall have to *toe the line*. 彼が権力者だから, 彼の命令にきちんと従わなければならないだろう ▪ Ministers who refused to *toe the* Party *line* were instantly got rid of. 党の方針に従わない大臣はただちに除籍された.

toffee /tάfi|tɔ́fi/ 名 ***cannot** do **for toffee*** 《英口》からきし[さっぱり]...できない ▪ He *can't* shoot *for toffee*. 彼はからきし銃が撃てない.

toffee-nosed 俗物の, 上流気取りの ▪ He didn't like that *toffee-nosed* sister of hers. 彼はあの気取り屋の彼女の姉が気に入らなかった ▪ He's very nice, but his brother is very *toffee-nosed*. 彼はとてもすてきだが, 彼の兄はひどく俗物だ.

together /təgéðər/ 副 ***all together*** みないっしょに ▪ They sang *all together*. 彼らはみないっしょに歌った.

get it together 《口》 **1** 何とかうまくやりとげる ▪ We talked about doing this last summer but we never *got it together*. 去年の夏これをやろうと話し合ったが, まだ実行していない.

2 性的関係を持つ ▪ Not until Jim's party did we really *get it together*. ジムのパーティーのときに初めてぼくたちは結ばれた.

together with ...と共に; とあわせて; と同時に ▪ He is selling the house, *together with* the furniture. 彼は家を家具と共に売るつもりだ.

toil[1] /tɔɪl/ 名 ***in the toils*** わなにかかって; 魅惑されて ▪ They may catch me like a fox *in the toils*. 彼らは私をわなにかかったキツネのように捕えるかもしれない.

toil[2] /tɔɪl/ 動 ***toil and moil*** あくせくと働く ▪ For worldly wealth, men can *toil and moil* all the week long. 現世の富を得るために人々は1週間じゅう働くこともできる.

toilet /tɔ́ɪlət/ 名 ***go to the toilet*** 《婉曲》用便する, トイレに行く ▪ My daughter is three years old and washes her hands after she *goes to the toilet*. 娘は3歳で, 用を済ますと手を洗うんだ.

make** one's **toilet 化粧する, 身ごしらえする ▪ He was *making his toilet* before dinner. 彼は晩餐(さん)の前に身ごしらえをしていた.

pray to the toilet 酒に酔って嘔吐する ▪ He was *praying to the toilet*, as usual. 彼はいつものように吐いていた.

toing /túːɪŋ/ 名 ***toing and froing*** **1** 繰り返し, 行ったり来たりすること ▪ The job involved a lot of *toing and froing* between London and Paris. その仕事ではロンドン・パリ間を何度も往復せねばならなかった.

2 無益な活動, むだな論争 ▪ After a great deal of *toing and froing*, we decided not to change our plan after all. さんざん話し合ったあげく, 結局は計画を変えないことに落ち着いた.

token /tóʊkən/ 名 ***as a token of*** ...の印に ▪ A white flag is used *as a token of* surrender. 白旗は降服の印に使用される.

by the same* [*this, that*] *token **1** その証拠には; それで思い出すが; その上 ▪ Max was a staunch Roman Catholic. *By this token*, many an argument have I had with him on religion. マックスは忠実なローマカトリック教徒であった. その証拠に, 私は何度も彼と宗教論を戦わせたのであった ▪ The thieves were caught, and *by the same token* sent to prison. 泥棒らはつかまり, しかも刑務所へ送られた.

2 同様に ▪ This rule applies to all the students, and, *by the same token*, it should apply to you. 本規則は全学生に適用される. 同様に, 君にも当然当てはまる.

in token of ...の印に, 証拠に ▪ They were bearing a satchel full of hay *in token of* their bondage and service. 彼らは奴隷の身分と奉仕との印に干し草をいっぱい入れたかばんをかついでいた.

tolerance /tάlərəns|tɔ́l-/ 名 ***have* [*show*] *zero tolerance* (*towards*)** ...に一切情け容赦しない ▪ The police *showed zero tolerance towards* the thieves. 警察は窃盗犯に一切情け容赦しなかった.

tolerant /tάlərənt|tɔ́l-/ 形 ***tolerant of*** **1** ...をがまんして ▪ You are not *tolerant of* little mannerisms. あなたはちょっとしたマンネリズムをがまんしない.

2 《医》(薬剤など)に抵抗力のある ▪ The skin in two or three weeks became *tolerant of* the drug. 皮膚は2, 3週間もするとその薬に抵抗力ができてきた.

tolerant to ...に寛容で ▪ His own early errors made him *tolerant to* the faults of others. 彼自身が以前にまちがいをしたために, 他人の欠点を大目に見るようになった.

toll /toʊl/ 名 ***a toll call*** 長距離通話 ▪ We had several *toll calls* on last month's telephone bill. 先月の電話料金請求書に長距離電話が数本あった.

***take its toll on/take a* (*heavy*) *toll* (*of*)** ...に大きな損失[被害]をもたらす, (人命など)を大量に失わせる (*of*) ▪ The epidemic *took a heavy toll of* the lives of people. その疫病で多くの人命が奪われた.

toll free (電話が)無料で; 無料電話の ▪ You can call us day and night, seven days a week, *toll free*. 当社へは年中昼夜無料でおかけいただけます ▪ Would it be all right to use your phone to make a *toll-free* call? 無料電話をかけたいんだけど君の電話を使っていいかい.

Tom /tɑm|tɔm/ 名 ***a Tom o' Bedlam*** 狂人; 精神病院を出て物乞いをすることを許された狂人 ▪ I won't answer such *a Tom o' Bedlam*. 私はそんな狂人には返事をしない.

every Tom, Dick and Harry 《口》誰(に)でも, 猫もしゃくしも ▪ They invited *every Tom, Dick and Harry*. 彼らは猫もしゃくしも残らず招いた.

T

make** oneself **a Tom-noddy ばかなまねをする ▪ What *a Tom-noddy* you have *made yourself*! なんというばかなまねをしたんだね.

More folk know Tom Fool than Tom Fool knows. 《諺》ばか者が知っているよりも多くの人たちがばか者を知っている《ばかなことで名が売れているのは名誉ではない》.

Tom Tiddler's ground **1** 陣取り《子供の遊び》 ▪ Squalid children made *Tom Tiddler's ground* of the steps and street. きたない子供たちが階段や通りで陣取りをした.

2 宝の山 ▪ He had come on to *Tom Tiddler's ground*. 彼は宝の山へ踏み込んだのだった.

tomahawk /tάməhɔ̀:k|tɔ́m-/ 名 ***blow tomahawks*** 風が身を切るように吹く ▪ The weather is boisterous; it's *blowing tomahawks* and tornadoes. 天気は荒れ狂っている. 風が身を切るように渦巻いて吹いている.

bury [***lay aside***] ***the tomahawk*** ほこを収める, 和睦する ▪ I was grateful that the two nations had *laid aside the tomahawk* at my request. 両国民が私の願いを入れて和睦してくれてありがたかった. ☞次項も参照.

dig up [***raise, take up***] ***the tomahawk*** 戦端を開く ▪ I persuaded them to *take up the* bloody *tomahawk* against those perfidious French. 私はこれらの裏切り者のフランス人たちに対して血に飢えたほこを取るように彼らを説きつけた. ☞tomahawk は北米先住民の戦(いくさ)おので, 彼らは和睦するときにはおのを埋め, 戦うときにはまた掘り出す習わしであった.

tomb /tu:m/ 名 ***(as) quiet*** [***silent***] ***as the tomb*** ひどく静かで, (人が)少しも口をきかないで ▪ All [He] was *quiet as the tomb*. どこも静まり返って[彼は黙りこくって]いた.

give** a person **hark from the tomb 《米口》人にさんざん小言を言う ▪ If you'll believe me, she did *give* him *hark from the tomb*. 実の話彼女は彼に大目玉をくわせたんだ. ☞Isaac Watts の賛美歌の 1 行 "Hark! from the tombs a doleful sound" から.

tommy-rot /tάmirὰt|tɔ́mirɔ̀t/ 名 ***talk tommy-rot*** 《俗》全くのナンセンス[たわごと]を言う ▪ He's *talking tommy-rot* as usual. 彼は例によってたわごとを並べている.

tomorrow /təmάroʊ|-mɔ́r-/ 名 ***as if*** [***like***] ***there was*** [***were***] ***no tomorrow***/ ***like there's no tomorrow*** 《口》がむしゃらに, どんどん ▪ It is not advisable to spend all your money *like there was no tomorrow*. どんどん金を使い果たすのは賢明ではない.

Never leave [***put off***] ***till tomorrow what you can do today.*** 《諺》きょうできることをあすに延ばすな.

tomorrow comes never (いつになっても)決して…ない ▪ He may come tomorrow. —*Tomorrow comes never*, I believe. 彼はあす来るかもしれない—きっと金輪際来やしないでしょうよ.

Tomorrow is another [***a new***] ***day.*** 《諺》あすという日もある.

tomorrow morning [***afternoon, evening,*** etc.] あすの朝[午後, 晩, など] ▪ I will come to you *tomorrow morning*. あすの朝お伺いします ▪ Can you spend *tomorrow evening* with us? あすの晩遊びにおいでになりませんか.

Tomorrow never comes. 《諺》あすは決して来ない《きょうすべきことをあすに延ばすな》.

Tomorrow will [***can***] ***take care of*** [***look after***] ***itself.*** 《諺》あすのことはあす自身が面倒を見る(《聖》*Matt.* 6. 3 4).

ton[1] /tʌn/ 名 ***have** a person **down on** one **like a ton of bricks*** 人にひどく非難される ▪ If I start gambling again I'll *have* all the family *down on* me *like a ton of bricks*. またギャンブルを始めたら家族みんなから総すかんを食うだろう.

hit** a person **like a ton of bricks **1** = come down on a person like a thousand of BRICKs.

2 《米口》人をひどく驚かす ▪ Suddenly, the truth *hit* me *like a ton of bricks*. 突然本当のことがわかって愕然とした.

like a ton of bricks →like a BRICK.

tons of 《口》多量の ▪ Is there any culture at Chicago?—*Tons of* it. シカゴに文化がありますか—ごまんとありますよ ▪ I have seen it *tons of* times. それは何度も見たことがある.

weigh a ton ひどく重い ▪ This suitcase *weighs a ton*! このスーツケースはやけに重いな.

ton[2] /tɔ:n/ 名 ***be all the ton*** 流行して ▪ A mantle, too, *is all the ton*. マントも流行している. ☞F ton 'manner in general'.

tone /toʊn/ 名 ***give tone to*** …を高める[強める] ▪ The presence of his name *gives tone to* the whole society. 彼の名前があれば社会全体が高まる.

raise [***lower***] ***the tone*** 気風・風潮を高める[下げる] ▪ A preface from the president has *raised the tone* of his book. 学長の序文のおかげで彼の著書の風格が上がった ▪ That horrible building *lowers the* whole *tone* of the neighborhood. あのひどいビルのせいで辺りの景観がすっかり損なわれてしまった.

set the tone (…の)傾向[気分, 調子]を決める(*of, for*) ▪ His enthusiasm *set the tone of* the meeting. 彼の熱情が会の気分を決定した.

take a high tone 高言を吐く ▪ He suddenly *took a high tone*. 彼は突然横柄な言い方をした.

tongs /tɑŋz|tɔŋz/ 名 ***hammer and tongs*** → HAMMER.

not touch with a pair of tongs 触れることさえいやだ ▪ I would*n't touch* the affair even *with a pair of tongs*. その事件には触れることさえいやだ.

tongue /tʌŋ/ 名 ***a sharp tongue*** 辛辣(らつ)な言葉 ▪ He has *a sharp tongue* and is very strict with everyone. 彼は毒舌家で誰にも実に厳しい.

a silver [***smooth***] ***tongue*** 雄弁さ, 説得力 ▪ His *silver tongue* got him the job. さわやかな弁舌のおかげで彼はその職に就けた.

A still tongue makes a wise head. 《諺》賢

T

者は寡黙.

a tongue twister 早口言葉 ▪ This one is said to be the toughest *tongue twister* in English. これが英語で一番難しい早口言葉だと言われている.

all tongues 《聖》自国語を持つすべての国民 (*Isa*. 66. 18, etc.) ▪ I will gather *all* nations and *tongues*. 私はすべての国とすべての民族とを集める.

bite** one's **tongue off 《口》舌をかみ切る《言ったことを後悔する》 ▪ When I realized that he was listening, I could have *bitten my tongue off*. 彼が聞いていたと知ったとき, 私は舌をかみ切りたいほどだった.

***bridle* [*watch*] *one's* tongue** 言葉を慎む ▪ It would pay you to *bridle your tongue*. 言葉を慎んだ方が身のためだぞ.

cause* (*some*) *tongues to wag = set (the) TONGUEs wagging.

click** one's **tongue 舌をチッチッと鳴らす《非難・いらだちの表現》 ▪ He *clicked his tongue* in disapproval. 彼は舌をチッチッと鳴らして非難を表した.

find** one's **tongue (びっくりしたり, 恥ずかしかったりした後で)やっと口がきけるようになる ▪ He was *finding his tongue*. 彼はやっと口がきけるようになりかけていた.

get** one's **tongue** (**a**)**round 〚主に否定文で〛(名前など)を正しく発音する ▪ I can't *get my tongue around* Welsh place names. 私はウェールズ語の地名がうまく発音できない.

give** a person **the** (**rough**) **edge of** one's **tongue →EDGE[1].

give tongue/throw** (one's) **tongue (猟犬が, 特に臭跡・獲物を発見して)ほえる; (転じて人が)わめく; はっきり言う ▪ Ringwood never *threw his tongue* but where the scent was undoubtedly true. リングウッドは臭跡がまぎれもなく本当である場合のほかはほえなかった ▪ To speak in the sportsman's style, he has not *given tongue* often. 猟人用語で言えば, 彼はあまりわめいたことはなかった.

give tongue to ...を口に出して言う ▪ He decided to *give tongue to* his suspicions. 彼は自分の疑惑を口に出して言おうと決心した.

guard** one's **tongue 発言に気をつける ▪ I think I must *guard my tongue* about everything. 全てのことについて発言には気をつけなければと思う.

have a loose tongue 口が軽い ▪ She *has a* very *loose tongue* and wags it all the time. 彼女は非常に口が軽く, しょっちゅう言いふらしている.

have a silver tongue 雄弁である, 弁舌がさわやかである, 説得力がある ▪ He is a famous professor at this university and *has a silver tongue*. 彼はこの大学の有名教授で弁舌さわやかだ.

have a tongue like a whip 毒舌を吐く, 口が悪い ▪ My mother-in-law *has got a tongue like a whip*, and no common sense. うちの姑ときたら口は悪いし, 常識はないし.

have a wicked* [*malicious, spiteful*] *tongue 口が悪い ▪ We all know she *has a wicked tongue*. 彼女が口が悪いのはみんな知っている.

have** one's **tongue in** one's **cheek →speak with one's TONGUE in one's cheek.

***hold* [*bite*] *one's* tongue** 口をつぐんでいる ▪ *Hold your* impertinent *tongue*, sir. 生意気な口を慎みたまえ ▪ He thinks it best to *hold his tongue*. 彼は黙っているにかぎると考えている.

keep a civil tongue in** one's **head 丁寧な口をきく ▪ You may as well *keep a civil tongue in your head*. 丁寧な口をきいたほうがいいだろう.

***keep a quiet* [*still*] *tongue* (*in* one's *head*)** 黙っている ▪ You'll *keep a quiet tongue in your head*, will you? 黙っているんだぞ ▪ I believe you can *keep a still tongue in your head*. 君はきっと口数を多くきかないと思うね.

lash** a person **with** one's **tongue/give** a person **a tongue-lashing 人をこっぴどくしかる, ののしる, 非難する ▪ The manager will *give* us *a tongue-lashing* if we lose this game. この試合を落とすと監督にこっぴどくしかられるぞ ▪ The orator *lashed* us *with his tongue*. 演説者は我々を激しくののしった.

lay tongue to ...を表現する, 口に出す ▪ He used the strongest words he could *lay tongue to*. 彼は口に出せるかぎりの激烈な言葉を使った.

loosen** a person's **tongue →LOOSEN.

lose** one's **tongue (恥ずかしさなどで)口がきけなくなる ▪ Have you *lost your tongue* all at once, Jack? 急に口がきけなくなったのかい, ジャック?

mind** one's **tongue =bridle one's TONGUE.

on* [*at*] *the tip of* one's [*the*] *tongue →have ... on the TIP of one's tongue.

on the tongues of men/on everyone's tongue 人の噂にのぼって ▪ It's a new phrase now *on the tongues of men*. それは今みなが口にしている新しい成句だ.

put out** one's **tongue/put** one's **tongue out 舌を突き出す ▪ Don't *put your tongue out* at me, you saucy child! 私に向かって舌を突き出すんじゃない, 生意気な子供だ.

roll* [*slip, trip*] *off the tongue (名前・語句が)言いやすい, 語呂がよい ▪ His name doesn't exactly *roll off the tongue*. 彼の名前はどうも発音しにくい.

set* [*start*] (*the*) *tongues wagging 噂話の種になる ▪ His scandal *set the tongues wagging*. 彼のスキャンダルは噂話の種になった ▪ The affair between the boss and his secretary *started tongues wagging*. 社長と秘書の情事の噂が立った.

speak in tongues 意味不明のことを言う ▪ He often *speaks in tongues* while working. 彼は仕事中にしばしば意味不明の言葉を発する.

speak* [*talk*] *with* (*a*) *forked tongue 二枚舌を使う, 嘘をつく ▪ I don't trust his promises because he *speaks with a forked tongue*. 彼は二枚舌を使うので彼との約束のことは信じていない.

speak* [*talk*] *with* one's *tongue in* one's *cheek/put* one's *tongue in* one's *cheek (本心と)裏腹のことを言う; 皮肉に言う ▪ Shaw often

T

talked with his tongue in his cheek. ショーはよく本心とは裏腹のことを言った ▪ That man, so to speak, *puts his tongue in his cheek.* あの男はいわば本心と裏腹のことを言う.

stick [***thrust***] *one's* ***tongue in*** *one's* ***cheek*** 舌先でほおをふくらませる《軽蔑・ひょうきんのしぐさ》 ▪ I signified my contempt of him by *thrusting my tongue in my cheek.* 私は舌先でほおをふくらませて, 彼を軽蔑している気持ちを見せつけてやった.

the gift of tongues 未知の外国語を話す能力《特に初期キリスト教徒に奇跡的に与えられたもの》(《聖》*Acts* 2. 1-13); 語学の才 ▪ He possessed *the gift of tongues.* 彼には語学の才があった.

throw (*one's*) ***tongue*** →give TONGUE.

A person's ***tongue is hanging out.*** とても喉が渇いて[酒を飲みたがって]いる ▪ *That poor fellow's tongue* looked to *be hanging out.* そのかわいそうなやつは喉が渇いているようだった.

tongue-tied (羞恥・恐怖で)口が利けないで, ものが言えずに ▪ I just stood *tongue-tied* in front of the examiners. 試験官たちを前にして口も利けずにただ突っ立っていた.

wag *one's* ***tongue*** →WAG one's chin.

watch *one's* ***tongue*** =bridle one's TONGUE.

(***with*** *one's*) ***tongue in*** (*one's*) ***cheek*** 皮肉たっぷりに ▪ He seems to have painted his flippant picture *with his tongue in his cheek.* 彼はその軽薄な絵を皮肉たっぷりに描いたもののようだ.

tonic /tánɪk|tɔ́n-/ 名 ***act as a tonic on*** *a person* 人を元気づける ▪ The good news *acted as a tonic on* us all. その吉報は我々みなを元気づけた.

too /tuː/ 副 ***all too*** あまりにも ▪ The holidays ended *all too* soon. 休みはあまりにも早く終わった.

be too bad →(It's) too BAD.

but too 遺憾ながら (= ONLY too 2) ▪ It is indeed *but too* true. それはまことに遺憾ながら本当です.

none too →NONE.

only too →ONLY.

quite too →QUITE.

too much (***of a good thing***)《口》とてもたまらない, あんまりで ▪ Oh *too much*! I can't stand it! ああ, あんまりだ, とてもがまんができない ▪ This is surely *too much of a good thing.* これは確かにあんまりというものだ.

too ... to *do* [***for***] あまり…で…できない ▪ The news is *too* good *to* be true. その知らせはあまりよすぎて本当とは思われない ▪ It's *too* hot *for* work [*to* work]. あまり暑くて仕事ができない.

too too **1**〚副詞的に〛あまりにも甚だしく ▪ It is *too too* apparent. あまりにも見えすいていた ▪ It was *too too* bad. それはあまりにもひどかった.

2〚形容詞的に〛甚だしい; とてもすばらしい ▪ My frocks are *too too*! 私のフロックはとてもすばらしい.

tool /tuːl/ 名 ***be not the sharpest*** [***smartest***] ***tool in the box*** [***drawer, shed***] (他の人と比べて)あまり賢くない ▪ She's *not the sharpest tool in the box,* but she is vey cute. 彼女はあまり賢くはないがとてもかわいい.

down tools/throw [***chuck, lay, put***] ***down*** *one's* ***tools***《英》**1**(1日の)仕事を終える ▪ We aim to *down tools* at about 5 p.m. each day. 毎日ほぼ午後5時終業を目安にしている.

2 ストライキを行う ▪ Thousands of workers *downed tools* to demand more pay. 賃上げを要求して何千という労働者がストを打った ▪ The union will certainly *down tools* if no settlement is reached. 示談にならないと組合はきっとストをやるだろう.

play with edge(***d***) ***tools*** →EDGE(D) TOOL.

the tools of the [*one's*] ***trade*** 商売道具 ▪ He is a scholar and *the tools of his trade* are books. 彼は学者だから商売道具は本だ.

toot[1] /tuːt/ 名 ***on a toot***《米俗》飲み騒いで ▪ He went off *on a* four-day *toot.* 彼は4日間飲み騒いだ.

toot[2] /tuːt/ 動 ***toot*** (***it***) ***on*** [***upon***] (らっぱなど)を吹き鳴らす ▪ A great many of them can *toot it upon* a pipe. 彼らの中には笛を吹き鳴らすことができる者が非常に多い.

toot on *one's* ***own trumpet*** 手前みそを並べる ▪ We can all *toot* a little *on our own trumpet.* 誰でも少しは手前みそが言える.

toot *one's* (***own***) ***horn*** → blow one's own HORN.

tooth /tuːθ/ 名 ***a tooth for a tooth*** 歯には歯(でする仕返し)(《聖》*Exod.* 21. 24) ▪ An eye for an eye, *a tooth for a tooth*—that is what we expect. 目には目を, 歯には歯を—それこそ我々が期待しているものだ.

(***as***) ***scarce as hen's teeth/scarcer than hen's teeth*** →HEN.

bare *one's* ***teeth*** = show one's teeth (→TOOTH).

(***be***) ***armed to the teeth*** →ARM[2].

be born with a dainty tooth →DAINTY.

be like pulling teeth 至難の業である ▪ In this country, keeping radicals under strict control *is like pulling teeth.* この国では過激派を厳重に取り締まるのは至難の業である.

between *one's* ***teeth*** (怒り・苦痛などで)歯をかみしめて ▪ "Get lost!" he spat out *between his teeth.* 「失せろ」と彼は歯をかみしめたまま吐き出すように言った.

by [***with***] ***the skin of*** *one's* ***teeth*** →SKIN[1].

carry a bone in the teeth →carry a BONE in the mouth.

cast [***throw***]***... in*** *a person's* ***teeth*** (過失など)で人を非難する, とがめる(《聖》*Matt.* 27. 44) ▪ This neglect of family devotions *is* often *thrown in our teeth.* このように家庭のお祈りを怠ることでしばしば私たちは非難される ▪ He was perpetually *throwing in the teeth of* his second wife the unrivaled virtues of his first. 彼は始終最初の妻の無類の美徳をあげて二度目の妻を責めていた.

clench *one's* ***teeth*** →set one's TEETH.

cut teeth (乳)歯が生える ▪ My baby has already *cut teeth.* うちの子, もう歯が生えてるの.

cut** one's **teeth on**/《米》**cut** one's **eyeteeth on 《口》…で最初の経験をする, から始める ▪ Let him *cut his teeth on* a smaller car. 彼には小さい車から始めさせるがいい ▪ His grandfather taught him how to fish, so he *cut his eyeteeth on* fishing. 祖父に釣り方を教わって, 彼は魚釣りを始めた.

draw* [*pull*] *a person's teeth 人の不平[悩み]の原因を除く; 人を無力[無害]にする, 危険な[手ごわい]人物を骨抜きにする, 手なずける ▪ These new regulations will effectually *draw his teeth.* これらの新規則がてきめんに彼を無害にするだろう ▪ The boss *pulled the teeth of* the workers by offering them a new kind of benefit. 社長は新しい特典を出すと持ちかけて労働者をなだめた.

drop** one's **teeth ひどく驚く[たまげる] ▪ I almost *dropped my teeth* when I heard the news. その知らせを聞いてたまげそうになった.

fasten** one's **teeth on …にかみつく, 食いつく ▪ She *fastened her teeth on* her attacker's hand. 彼女は暴漢の手にかみついた.

get* [*sink*] one's *teeth into **1** …にかぶりつく ▪ The hungry boy *sank his teeth* deep *into* a sandwich. 腹をすかせた少年はサンドイッチにかぶりついた.

2 (仕事など)にかなり乗り出す; (仕事)を夢中で始める; と真剣に取っ組む ▪ Wait till you *get your teeth into* the work. その仕事にかなり乗り出すまで待っていたまえ ▪ I just can't wait to *sink my teeth into* this job. この仕事を始めるのが待ち遠しくてたまらない.

give teeth/give teeth to 《口》(法律など)を強化する ▪ It is desirable to *give teeth to* the law. その法律にてこ入れすることが望ましい.

gnash the* [one's] *teeth →GNASH.

grind** one's **teeth →GRIND[2].

grit** one's **teeth →GRIT[2].

***have a tooth out* [《米》*pulled*]** 歯を1本抜いてもらう ▪ I want to *have a tooth out.* 歯を1本抜いてほしいのです.

have* (*got*) *a sweet tooth 甘党である ▪ Tom *has a sweet tooth* and prefers fruity, sweet tasting tomatoes. トムは甘党で, フルーティな甘い味のトマトが好きだ.

have teeth (法律・規則などが)効力をもつ; (組織が)力をもつ ▪ Our union *has teeth* and isn't under the management's thumb. わが組合は強力で経営者の言いなりにはならない.

in the* [one's] *teeth まともに, 真正面から ▪ Others met the enemy *in the teeth.* 他の者は真正面から敵に立ち向かった ▪ The wind is right *in our teeth.* 風は我々の真正面から吹いてくる.

in the teeth of **1** …にまともに向かって ▪ He had run across *in the teeth of* the rising gale. 彼は吹き始めた強風にまともに向かって駆け抜けたのだった.

2 …に歯向かって, をものともせず, にもかかわらず ▪ A judge has no right to enter judgment *in the teeth of* the finding of a jury. 裁判官は陪審員の調査結果に反対して判決を下す権限はない ▪ Why do you continue to live here, *in the teeth of* these repeated warnings? このように繰り返して警告したのに, どうしていつまでもここに住んでいるのですか.

3 (危険など)に直面して ▪ They were in fact *in the* very *teeth of* starvation. 彼らは事実まさに餓死に直面していた.

kick ... in the teeth 《口》(人)をひどくがっかりさせる ▪ He *kicked* me *in the teeth* by refusing it. 彼は私にそれをにべもなく拒絶した.

lie in** one's **teeth →LIE[3].

lie through** one's **teeth →LIE in one's teeth.

long in the tooth (馬が)歯が浮いた; 年老いた ▪ He is a bit *long in the tooth* for the army. 彼は軍隊へ入るには少し年を食っている.

make** a person's **teeth chatter (寒さ・恐怖などで)人の歯をガチガチいわせる ▪ This cold weather *makes my teeth chatter.* この寒さで歯がガチガチ鳴る.

milk teeth 生え替わる前の歯, 乳歯 ▪ Most pupils had dental decay in their *milk teeth.* 学童の大半は乳歯が虫歯になっていた.

pick** one's **teeth 爪楊枝(ﾂﾏﾖｳｼﾞ)で歯をつつく[きれいにする] ▪ It's bad manners to *pick your teeth* in public. 人前で爪楊枝で歯をつつくのは行儀が悪い.

put teeth in (法律など)を強化する, 施行(しやすいように)する ▪ The legislature *put teeth in* the traffic law by increasing the penalties. 州議会は科料を上げて交通法を強化した.

set* [*clench*] one's *teeth (怒り・決心で)歯をくいしばる ▪ She *set her teeth* when she thought of Arthur. 彼女はアーサーのことを考えて歯をくいしばった.

set** one's **teeth against …に断固反対する ▪ They will surely *set their teeth against* the project. 彼らはきっとその計画に断固反対するだろう.

set* [*put*] a person's *teeth on edge →set the teeth on EDGE.

show** one's **teeth 歯をむき出す; 威嚇する ▪ It would be to no purpose to *show our teeth* unless we could bite. かみつくことができないかぎり歯をむき出しても何にもなるまい ▪ The law *shows her teeth*, but dare not bite. その法律は歯をむき出すが, あえてかみつかない. ☞ 犬が歯をむき出してうなることから.

sink** one's **teeth into = get one's teeth into (→TOOTH).

sink tooth into 《米口》…を食べる ▪ They will *sink tooth into* genuine turkey meat on Thanksgiving Day. 彼らは感謝祭の日に本物の七面鳥の肉を食べる.

something to get* [*sink*] one's *teeth into 真剣に取り組めるもの ▪ This work gave me *something to get my teeth into.* この仕事で真剣に取り組むものができた.

take the bit between** one's **teeth →get the BIT between one's teeth.

One's ***teeth water.*** →The TEETH water.

The [*One's*] ***teeth water.*** よだれが出る(ほしくてたまらない) (→one's MOUTH waters) ▪ *My teeth water* at the gooseberries. そのグズベリーを見るとよだれが出る.

throw ... in *a person's* ***teeth*** →cast ... in a person's TEETH.

to the [*one's*] ***teeth*** 十分に, 寸分のすきなく ▪ The robbers were armed *to the teeth* when they robbed the bank. 強盗たちは銀行を襲ったとき完全武装していた.

tooth and nail [***claw***] (食いついたり, 引っかいたりして)必死に, 死力を尽くして, 猛烈に ▪ I am ready to oppose any such project *tooth and nail.* 私はいつだってそのような計画には死力を尽くして反対してやる ▪ Tomorrow I resume the novel, *tooth and nail.* あすから私は必死になってあの小説をまた書き始める ▪ The two boys were going for each other *tooth and nail.* 二人の少年は必死になって互いにつかみかかっていった ▪ We fought *tooth and claw* to get our plan accepted. 我々の計画を通そうと必死にがんばった. ☞[L] unguibus et rostro のなぞり; もと with tooth and nail で「歯でかみついたりつめで引っかいたりして」が原義.

toothbrush /túːθbrʌ̀ʃ/ [名] ***a toothbrush moustache*** 短く刈り込んだ口ひげ, ちょびひげ ▪ Hitler has made the *toothbrush moustache* infamous. ヒトラーのせいでちょびひげは悪名高くなってしまった.

toothcomb /túːθkòʊm/ [名] ***go over*** [***through***]***... with a toothcomb*** → go through ... with a fine (tooth) COMB.

top[1] /tɑp|tɔp/ [名] ***a top-up*** (グラスへの飲み物の)注ぎ足し ▪ Would you like *a top-up*? お飲み物を注ぎ足しましょうか.

at the top of …のてっぺん[上部]に ▪ Our host placed us *at the top of* the table. 主人は私たちをテーブルの上席に着けてくれた ▪ Jim is *at the top of* his class. ジムはクラスの主席だ.

at the top of *one's* ***game*** 《スポーツ》絶好調で ▪ I'm *at the top of my game* this year. 今年は絶好調です.

at the top of *one's* ***speed*** [***voice, lungs***] 全速力で[声を限りに] ▪ They were swearing at each other *at the top of their voices.* 彼らは声を限りにののしり合っていた.

at the top of the agenda →AGENDA.

at the top of the hour (毎)正時に ▪ Every class in this school starts *at the top of the hour.* この学校での授業は毎正時に始まります.

at top 上に, てっぺんに ▪ It had this inscription, *at top.* それには上に次の碑文がついていた.

be on top of =get on TOP of.

be (***the***) ***tops*** 《口》最高のものである, ずばぬけてうまい ▪ He *is tops* at tennis. 彼はテニスがずばぬけてうまい.

be tipped for the top トップの地位に推挙される ▪ As he's *been tipped for the top*, he won't be a vice-president soon. 彼はトップの座に推挙されたのでまもなく副社長はやめるだろう.

blow *one's* ***top*** 《口》かんかんにしかる, 気が狂う; ピストル自殺する (→BLOW[2]) ▪ He got so upset that I thought he was going to *blow his top.* 彼はひどく取り乱していたので気が狂うのじゃないかと思った. ☞top =head.

bottom to top =TOP to bottom.

climb [***get***] ***to the top of the*** (***career***) ***ladder*** トップの座に登りつめる ▪ You must work like a demon if you want to *get to the top of the ladder.* トップの座に登りつめたければ, 必死に働くのみだ.

come on top of (よくないこと)の上に重なる (→on TOP of 2) ▪ Then poverty *came on top of* his illness. 彼が病気のところへさらに貧乏が重なった.

come out (***at the***) ***top*** 首位を占める, 一番になる ▪ He *come out* (*at the*) *top* of the school. 彼はその学校の一番になった.

come out on top (競技・訴訟に)勝つ; 優勢になる ▪ I see you *came out on top* in the law suit. 訴訟の結果勝ったと見えますね.

come to the top **1** 上に上がって来る ▪ In jam making the scum always *comes to the top.* ジャム作りではかすはいつも上に上がって来る.
2 他にぬきんでる ▪ They had *come to the top* by virtue. 彼らは美徳によって他にぬきんでていた.

from the top (歌・演奏・台本などの)はじめ[最初]から ▪ Let's try it again *from the top.* もう一度最初からやってみよう.

from top to bottom [***toe, tail***] 頭のてっぺんから足のつま先まで; すっかり, 全部 ▪ The camels were covered *from top to toe* with silk. ラクダは頭のてっぺんから足のつま先まで絹布でおおわれていた ▪ Tell him *from top to tail.* 彼に全部話してやれ ▪ They are English *from top to toe.* 彼らは徹頭徹尾イギリス人だ.

get on top of **1** (仕事)をうまく処理する, 掌握[支配]する ▪ The police are trying to *get on top of* the terrorists. 警察はテロリストの掌握に努力している.
2 (仕事などが人)を悩ませる ▪ His work is *getting* badly *on top of* him. 仕事で彼は大分悩んでいる.

get to the top of the ladder [***tree***] →reach the TOP (of the ladder).

go on top 先頭を切る ▪ The horse *went on top* in the backstretch. その馬はバックストレッチで先頭を切った.

go over the top **1** ざんごうの胸壁を越えて攻撃する; (愚かなほど)大胆なことをする ▪ Tomorrow she was *going over the top.* あす彼女は大胆なことをするはずだった.
2 目標を上回る ▪ The drive had *gone over the top* and 100 dollars were collected. (募金)運動は目標を上回り, 100ドル集まった.
3 はめをはずす ▪ The children *went over the top* when they knew there was no school in the afternoon. 午後からは授業がないということを知ると, 子供たちははめをはずして騒いだ.

T

neither top nor tail/neither top, tail, nor mane [***root***] 少しも…ない ▪ His sermon had *neither top, tail, nor mane.* 彼の説教はさっぱりわからなかった ▪ They will make *neither top, tail, nor root* out of it. 彼らにはそれがさっぱりわかるまい.

not have much up top あまり頭がよくない ▪ He does*n't have much up top*, I'm afraid. 彼は大して賢くないようだ.

off the top of *one's* ***head*** 《口》思いつきで, 準備なしで; 何も見ないで ▪ I made a speech *off the top of my head.* 私は即席でスピーチをした.

on (***the***) ***top*** 《英俗》高速ギアにして ▪ Most of the run was done *on the top.* 運転の大半は高速ギアにして行われた.

on [***upon***] (***the***) ***top of*** **1** …の上に ▪ One thing was heaped *on top of* the other. 一つのものが他の上に積み上げられていた.

2 …に加えて ▪ He had two heavy falls in a week, and a bad cold *on the top of* them. 彼は1週間に2度ひどくころび, その上に大風邪をひいてしまった.

3 …に近い ▪ He was *upon the top of* his marriage. 彼はもうすぐ結婚するところだった.

4 …を管理して ▪ He acted like a man *on top of* his job. 彼は自分の職場の管理者のようにふるまった.

5 …に通じて ▪ He's right *on top of* all the news. 彼はすべてのニュースにすっかり通じている.

on top **1** 上に; (バスなどの)2階の席に ▪ The green book is *on top.* 緑の本は上にある.

2 優位に立って, 優勝して ▪ The boy finished *on top.* その少年が優勝した.

3 雲の上を ▪ When flying *on top*, the plane is in brilliant sunshine. 雲の上を飛ぶときには, 飛行機は輝かしい日ざしを浴びている.

on top of the heap とてもうまい具合に ▪ He came out *on top of the heap.* 彼はまんまと抜け出した.

on top of the world 成功[幸福, 有名]の絶頂に ▪ She was prettier than the sea, and I was *on top of the world.* 彼女はすごく美人だったので私は幸福の絶頂にあった ▪ This stool makes you feel like you're sitting *on top of the world.* このスツールは最高の座り心地が得られます.

over the top 度が過ぎた ▪ Her reaction to my saying was *over the top.* 私の言ったことに対する彼女の反応はオーバーだった. ☞《英口》では OTT と略すことがある.

T

pay [***earn, charge***] ***top dollar*** 最高額を支払う[かせぐ, 請求する] ▪ If you want the best of anything, you have to *pay top dollar.* 何でも最良のものを望むなら最高額を出す必要がある.

push [***put***] *a person* ***over the top*** (試合・競技などで)人を有利にする[勝利に導く] ▪ The manager made one last attempt to *put* the team *over the top.* 監督はチームを勝利に導こうと最後の試みを行った ▪ It was the "Thriller" video that *pushed* Jackson *over the top.* ジャクスンが頂点を極められたのはビデオ「スリラー」の成果だった.

reach [***get to***] ***the top*** (***of the ladder*** [***tree***]) (ある職業分野の)トップにのし上がる, 第一人者となる ▪ He has every chance to *reach the top.* 彼は第一人者になる見込みが十分ある.

rise to the top 表面に浮かび上がる ▪ Cream, being lighter than milk, will *rise to the top.* クリームはミルクよりも比重が軽いので表面に浮いてくるだろう.

Take it from the top. 《口》(せりふ・演技・演奏などを)初めからやってみてくれ ▪ We must try it once again. *Take it from the top* and watch my baton. もう一度やり直しだ. 初めからやってくれ. 私の指揮棒をよく見て.

talk out of the top of *one's* ***head*** →TALK[2].

the big top **1** サーカスの大テント ▪ The high-wire act is almost always in *the big top.* 綱渡りや空中ブランコはたいてい大テントの中で行われる.

2 《俗》最も警戒が厳しい刑務所 ▪ He was sentenced to ten years in *the big top.* 彼は10年の厳重な禁固刑を宣告された.

the top and bottom 結局のところ ▪ That's *the top and bottom* of it. かいつまんだところはそうだ.

be top dog →DOG[1].

the top of *one's* ***mind*** [***head***] 半ばうわの空 ▪ With *the top of his mind* he listened to them. 半ばうわの空で彼は彼らの話を聞いた.

the top of the heap [***pile***] 《米口》最も有利な位置; (社会・組織の)頂点, 最上位 ▪ At *the top of the heap* is the person who owns the theater. 最も有利な位置には劇場の持ち主がいる ▪ She fought her way to *the top of the pile.* 彼女は苦闘の末に組織の長に上りつめた.

the top of the hour (テレビ・ラジオ番組で時計の)1時間の初め ▪ We have more news coming up at *the top of the hour.* 次のニュースは時報に続いてお伝えします.

the top of the market 最高値 ▪ They'll insure me *the top of the market.* 彼らは私に最高値を保証してくれるだろう.

the top of the tide [***high water***] 満潮; 一番調子のよい時 ▪ It was just at *the top of high water* when these people came on shore. これらの人々が浜辺へ来たときちょうど満潮だった ▪ At *the top of the tide* she turned off the stocks. 彼女は一番調子のいい時に株を売った.

the top of the tree [***ladder***] 最高の地位 ▪ Brilliancy and determination brought them to *the top of the tree.* 才気と決断力が彼らを最高の地位につかせた ▪ In surgery, he's quite at *the top of the tree.* 外科では彼が第一人者だ.

the top ten [***twenty,*** etc.] トップ10[20, など]《楽曲などの売れ行きランキング》 ▪ The song didn't even make [get into] *the top twenty.* その歌はトップ20位までにすら入らなかった.

to the top of *one's* ***bent*** →BENT[2].

top and tail **1** 全体, 全部 ▪ It is the *top and tail*, length and breadth. それが一切がっさいだ.

2 結局のところ ▪ The *top and tail* of it is this. それは結局のところこうなのだ.

3 すっかり, 全く ▪ Go to hell, both *top and tail*. すっかりくたばってしまうがいい.

top drawer →the top DRAWER.

top flight **1** (職・スポーツでの) 最高位, 一流 ▪ What soccer team has been in the *top flight* the longest in England? イングランドではどのサッカーチームが一番長くトップにいるか.

2 最高位の, 一流の ▪ He was a *topflight* shortstop who took part in three triple plays. 彼は3度の三重殺に関わった超一流の遊撃手だった.

top-notch 最高の, 一流の ▪ People will pay a fortune for really *top-notch* wines. 客は本当に最高級のワインには大金をはたく.

top-of-the-line 最上級の, 一流の ▪ The Cadillac is a *top-of-the-line* American automobile. キャデラックは米国産の最高級車である.

top of the pops 《口》ポップスのベストセラー; 最も人気のある人[物] ▪ What's *top of the pops* this week? 今週のポップス・ベストセラーは何か? ▪ She's always *top of the pops* among the boys at school. 彼女はいつだって男子生徒に校内で一番の人気がある.

top to bottom さかさまに, 逆に ▪ The barrel was turned *top to bottom*. たるはひっくり返された.

top[2] /tɑp|tɔp/ 名 ***(as) sound [fast] as a top*** ぐっすり眠って ▪ I took a nap *as sound as a top*. 私はぐっすり眠った ▪ In two minutes I was *as fast as a top*. しばらくすると私はぐっすり眠った.

old top 《俗》君, お前(親しい間柄の呼びかけ).

sleep like a top ぐっすり眠る ▪ For the first time in ages I *slept like a top* last night. 昨夜は久しぶりにぐっすり眠った. ☞こまが回っているときじっとしているように見えることから.

top[3] /tɑp|tɔp/ 動 ***be topped with*** 頂上を…で覆われている; でトッピングされている ▪ The hills *were topped with* clumps of trees. その丘のてっぺんにはこんもりとした森があった ▪ I'd like my pizza *topped with* pepperoni. ピザはペパローニのトッピングがいい.

to top [cap, crown] it all (off) あげくの果てに, なおその上に (→to CAP it all; to CROWN (it) all) ▪ *To top it all*, he fell ill and died. あげくの果てに, 彼は病気になって死んだ ▪ *To top it all off*, he won the Rookie of the Year award. その上彼はその年の新人王を勝ちとった.

top a ball/top** one's **drive 《ゴルフ》球の中心より上を打つ ▪ My cleek seems to have *topped a ball*. 私の1番アイアンは球の中心より上を打ったらしい.

top and tail 《英》(野菜・果物の)両端[上下]を切り取る; (赤んぼう・幼児の)顔と尻を洗う ▪ Peel a carrot and, after *topping and tailing* it, put it in boiling water. ニンジンの皮をむいて, 両端を切ったら, 沸騰したお湯に入れてください ▪ *Top and tail* the baby before the bath. 赤ちゃんに湯を使う前に顔とお尻を洗いなさい.

top** one's **part 《劇》役を最上に演じる; 演じすぎる; 首尾よくやってのける ▪ Ay, and *top my part* too. ええ, しかも最高に演じてみせますよ ▪ The Opposition are acting up to their character—nay, *topping their parts*. 野党は立派に役を演じている—いや演じすぎている ▪ England was once more *topping her part* on the Continent. イギリスはまたもや大陸で首尾よくやってのけていた.

top (up)** one's **fruit [punnet] 《市場俗》一番上等の果物をかごの上部に置く ▪ You've been *topping your punnets*. あんたは一番上等の果物をかごの上部に置いていたんだね.

topple /tɑ́pəl|tɔ́p-/ 動 ***topple up** one's **heels*** →kick up one's HEELs.

topsy-turv(e)y /tɑ̀psitə́ːrvi|tɔ̀p-/ 副形 ***turn topsy-turvy*** 逆さまにする[なる], めちゃめちゃにする[なる] ▪ The whole world has *turned topsy-turvy*. 世界中がめちゃめちゃになった.

torch /tɔːrtʃ/ 名 ***carry the [a] torch*** **1** 指導者となる ▪ They called in Mr. Smith to *carry the torch*. 彼らは指導者としてスミス氏を招いた.

2 支持する, 提灯を持つ (*for*) ▪ The paper *carried the torch* monthly *for* his progressive movement. その新聞は毎月彼の進歩的運動を支持した.

3 (片思いの)恋をする ▪ Ray *carried the torch* till she returned his love. レイは彼女が愛に応えるまで片思いをしていた. ☞たいまつは昔愛の象徴と考えられていた.

hand on the torch **1** たいまつを渡す ▪ The runners *handed on the torch* in turn. 走者は順番にトーチを渡した.

2 知識[伝統]の灯火を後世に伝える ▪ They were all engaged in *handing on the torch* of literary tradition. 彼らはすべて文学上の伝統の灯火を後世に伝えることに従事していた. ☞古代ギリシャのたいまつ競走から.

put ... to the torch/put a torch to ... …を火にくべ(て破棄す)る; に放火する ▪ A man *put a torch to* the house before he ran away. 一人の男が走って逃げ去る前にその家に放火した.

torment /tɔ́ːrment/ 名 ***in torment*** (精神的・肉体的に)苦しんで ▪ He lay *in* great *torment*. 彼は非常に苦しみつつ横たわっていた.

torrent /tɔ́ːrənt|tɔ́r-/ 名 ***in torrents*** (雨が)滝のように ▪ The rain came down *in torrents*. 雨が滝のように降ってきた.

torture /tɔ́ːrtʃər/ 名 ***in torture*** 責めさいなまれて ▪ They were *in* such great *torture*, wishing they had never come to sea. 彼らは大いに責めさいなまれて, 水夫にならなかったらよかったと思った.

put ... to (the) torture …をごう問にかける ▪ He moved that the persons should *be put to the torture*. その連中をごう問にかけることを彼は提議した.

toss[1] /tɔːs|tɔs/ 名 ***argue the toss*** 決定済みのことをくどくど言う ▪ It's no use your *arguing the toss*. You're not going this time. 決定済みのことをくどくど言っても仕方がない. 今回は君は行かないんだ. ☞コインを投げて順番などを決定することから.

T

not give [***care***] ***a toss*** 《英口》〚否定文で〛全く気にしない ▪ He is a person who doesn't *give a toss* about society. 彼は世間を全く気にしない人です.

take a toss ころぶ,(特に)落馬する ▪ He *took a toss* in the second race. 彼は第2レースで落馬した.

toss and catch 《米》コイン投げ遊び ▪ They were playing *toss and catch*. 彼らはコイン投げ遊びを楽しんでいた.

win [***lose***] ***the toss*** コイン投げ[トス]で勝つ[負ける]; うまくいく[いかない] ▪ The captain has *won the toss* for Australia and they'll be batting first against Sri Lanka. 主将がトスで勝ってオーストラリアチームは対スリランカ戦の打撃番を取った.

toss[2] /tɔːs|tɔs/ 動 ***toss*** *oneself* 寝返りを打つ ▪ He *tossed himself* about in bed. 彼はベッドであちこち寝返りを打った.

toss a coin →COIN[1].

toss a pancake パンケーキを(なべの上で)ぽんと投げて裏返す ▪ *Toss a pancake* if you can. パンケーキをできればぽんと投げて裏返してごらんなさい.

toss and turn (ベッドで)輾転(てん)反側する ▪ He *tossed and turned* feverishly. 彼は熱に浮かされて輾転反側した.

toss *one's* ***head back*** [***up***] 頭を後ろへ[上へ]つんとそらす《軽蔑・無関心のしぐさ》 ▪ He *tossed his head back*. 彼は頭をつんと後ろへそらした.

tote /toʊt/ 動 ***tote fair*** 《米口》自分の運ぶべき分を運ぶ; 公明正大にふるまう ▪ Inspectors kept them *toting fair*. 検閲官が彼らを公明正大にふるまわせた.

tote tales 《米口》告げ口をする ▪ I never *toted tales*. 私は告げ口をしたことはない.

tother /tʌ́ðər/ 代 《戯》 ***tell tother from which*** どれがどれかを区別する ▪ I can't *tell tother from which*. どれがどれだか区別できない. ☞tother = the other.

touch[1] /tʌtʃ/ 名 ***a magic touch*** 特殊な才能, 巧みさ (*with*) ▪ Some people have *a "magic" touch with* their dogs. 犬を訓練するすばらしい技量を具えた人もいる ▪ Tiger Woods appeared to have lost his *magic touch*. タイガー・ウッズは持ち前の神通力を失ったかのようだった.

a soft [***easy***] ***touch*** 《口》甘い相手, カモ ▪ We all regard him as *a soft touch*. みんな彼のことをいいカモだと思っている.

T

a touch 〚副詞的に〛少し (→ a THOUGHT) ▪ They are *a touch* more sensible. 彼らはもう少し話がわかる.

a touch of 少しの..., の気味 ▪ I have *a touch of* fever. 私は少し熱がある.

a touch of class センスのよさ, 上品さ, 気品 ▪ Her behavior really has *a touch of class*. 彼女のふるまいは実に上品だ.

at a touch ちょっと触れただけで ▪ *At a touch* he yielded. 一押しで彼は折れた ▪ The sharp knife cut it *at a touch*. その鋭いナイフがちょっと触れるとそれは切れた.

come to the touch 試される ▪ Verity is not afraid to *come to the touch*. 真実は試されるのを怖がりはしない.

get in touch with ...と連絡を取る ▪ I can not *get in touch with* the police. 警察と連絡がつかぬ.

have a touch of class 気品がある ▪ The old house *had a touch of class*. その古い建物には気品があった.

have a touch of the sun 軽い日射病にかかる ▪ He *had a touch of the sun*, playing tennis. 彼はテニスをしていて軽い日射病にかかった.

have the [***a***] ***magic touch*** 不思議な才能がある (*with*) (→ a magic TOUCH) ▪ Kindergarten teachers *have a magic touch with* young children. 幼稚園の先生は幼児の扱いがうまい ▪ He *has the magic touch*: he can compose, paint, and write novels. 彼には不思議な才能があって, 作曲もできるし絵も小説もかける.

in touch **1** 手を触れうるほど近い所に, 手の届く所に (*of*) ▪ He was tottering *in touch of* the inestimable prize. 彼は測り知れないほど高価な賞に手の届く所でまごまごしていた.

2 《スポーツ》側線外に ▪ The ball is *in touch*. ボールは側線外にある.

in touch with ...に接触[同情, 一致]して ▪ The Kingship of the Tudors always sought to be *in touch with* popular feeling. テューダー王家はいつも民衆の感情と接触を保とうと努めた.

Keep in touch. さよなら[じゃ, またね] ▪ Nice talking to you. *Keep in touch*. お話できて楽しかったよ. では, また.

keep [***be, stay***] ***in touch with*** ...と接触を保つ[保たせる]; の事情に通じている ▪ Sir Henry has always *kept* himself *in touch with* English public opinion. サー・ヘンリーは常に英国の世論と接触を保ってきた.

kick ... into touch 《主に英》...を拒絶する; を延期する ▪ He *kicked* the booze *into touch* and came back from the brink. 彼は酒を断ち, 絶望の淵から生還した.

light the (***blue***) ***touch paper with*** 《英》...の怒りをかう ▪ His speech *lighted the blue touch paper with* people. 彼の演説は人々の怒りをかった.

lose *one's* ***touch*** 技量が落ちる, 上手でなくなる ▪ The tennis player seems to have *lost his touch*. あのテニスの選手は技量が落ちたようだ.

lose touch with ...と接触を失う ▪ He had never *lost touch with* his friends. 彼は友人との接触を失ったことは一度もなかった.

make a touch 金を借りようとする ▪ Jones tried to *make another touch* yesterday. ジョーンズはきのうまた金を借りようとした.

no [***not a***] ***touch to*** 《米口》...と比べものにならない ▪ This version is *not a touch to* the original. この翻訳本は原作とは比べものにならない.

out of touch with **1** ...と接触[同情, 一致]しないで ▪ But they are *out of touch with* all the information. しかし, 彼らはすべての情報に通じていない.

2 …の認識が欠けて ▪ He is *out of touch with* what's going on in the arts world. 彼は芸術界の現状認識に欠けている.

***put** A **in touch with** B* AをBと接触させる ▪ It *put* him *in touch with* the writer. それで彼はその作家と接触するようになった.

put the finishing* [*final*] *touches to (事)を仕上げる ▪ We will soon *put the final touches to* the contract. じきにその契約を完全に結べるだろう.

put the touch on 《touch は theft を表す俗語》=put the ARM on 1.

put…to the touch …を試してみる ▪ I had *put* the matter *to the touch* of proof. その問題を試してみました.

the common touch →COMMON.

the* [*a*] *personal* [*human*] *touch (機械ではなく)人間らしい感触 ▪ The paintings added *a personal touch* to the waiting room. その絵が待合室に人間らしさを付け加えていた.

touch and go/touch-and-go **1**〚名詞的に〛一触即発の[不安定な]状況 ▪ It's *touch and go* as to whether he will live. 彼が生きるかどうか不安定だ.

2〚形容詞的に〛一触即発の, きわどい; はっきりわからない, 見当がつかない ▪ The city was in a *touch-and-go* situation. 町は一触即発の情勢だった ▪ It was a *touch and go* kind of day weather-wise. その日は天候が不順気味ではっきりしない1日だった.

within touch 手の届く所に (*of*) ▪ The roof was *within touch*. 屋根は手の届く所にあった ▪ He is not yet *within touch of* the telegraph. 彼はまだその電信を受け取っていない.

touch[2] /tʌtʃ/ 動 ***be touched with* [*by*]** **1** (ある感情)を催す ▪ He *was touched with* remorse. 彼は悔悟の念にかられた.

2 …に感動する ▪ I *was touched with* this story [*by* his kindness]. 私はこの話[彼の親切]に感動した.

not touch…with a ten-foot pole/《英》***not touch…with a barge pole*** →POLE[1].

touch and go **1** ちょっと触れてすぐ立ち去る; ちょっと扱う ▪ It is enough for me now to *touch and go*. 今はちょっと触れるだけで十分だ.

2 かろうじて成功する ▪ He did his best to *touch and go*. 彼はベストを尽くしてかろうじて成功した.

touch base with →BASE[1].

touch bottom →BOTTOM[1].

***touch** one's **hat* [*cap*]** 帽子に手をかけて会釈する (*to*) ▪ We *touch our hats* with much formality. 我々はひどく形式ばって帽子に手をかけて会釈する ▪ So Mr. Grimes *touched his hat to* him. そこでグライムズ氏は帽子に手をかけてその男に会釈した.

touch it off to the nines 《俗》申し分なくやってのける ▪ If I didn't *touch it off to the nines*, it's a pity. 申し分なくやってのけなかったなら, それは残念だ.

touch lucky 好運をつかむ ▪ He *touched lucky* over those shares. 彼はその株で好運をつかんだ.

***touch…on a raw* [*sore, tender*] *place* [*spot*]** →TOUCH…to the quick.

touch** a person **on the raw →RAW.

touch the spot →SPOT[1].

***touch…to the quick* [*on the raw*]*/touch…on a raw* [*sore, tender*] *place* [*spot*]** …の痛い所に触れる; を怒らせる, いらいらさせる ▪ It *touched* them *on the raw*. それは彼らの痛い所に触れた ▪ The last remark *touched* him *on a sore spot*. 最後の言葉が彼の痛い所をついた.

touch wood →WOOD.

touched in** one's **mind* [*brain, wits*]*/touched in the head 少し気がふれて ▪ He seems to be a bit *touched in his mind*. 彼は少し気がふれているようだ ▪ The war left him a little *touched in the head*. 戦争のせいで彼は少し頭がおかしくなった.

touched in the wind →WIND[1].

toucher /tʌ́tʃər/ 名 ***a near toucher*** 《俗》危機一髪 ▪ It was *a near toucher*, though! それにしても, それは危機一髪だった!

(as) near as a toucher 《俗》すんでのことで, 危うく ▪ He was *as near as a toucher* falling into the stream. 彼は危うく川の中に落ちるところだった.

touching /tʌ́tʃɪŋ/ 前 ***as touching*** 《古》…に関して ▪ *As touching* the gulls, they build in rocks. カモメについて言えば, 彼らは岩の間に巣を作る.

tough[1] /tʌf/ 形 ***a tough break/tough luck*** 《口》ちょっとした不運, つきのなさ ▪ Sorry to hear about your accident. *Tough break*. 事故のこと, 聞いたよ. 運が悪かったね ▪ The loss was *tough luck* for your team last night. ゆうべ君のチームが負けたのはついてなかったせいだ ▪ He got *a tough break* when he was denied a raise. 昇給を拒否されたのは彼は運が悪かった.

***a tough customer* [*cookie*]** →an ugly CUSTOMER.

(as) tough as leather 非常に強じんな ▪ This beefsteak is *as tough as leather*. このステーキはとても固い.

(as) tough as nails =(as) hard as NAILs.

(as) tough as old boots **1** (食物が)固くて噛み切れない ▪ That steak I had was *as tough as old boots*. 僕が食べたあのステーキはひどく固かった.

2 (苦痛・非難に)耐えられる, 粘り強い ▪ Don't worry, he'll soon recover. He's *tough as old boots*. 心配いらない. 彼はそのうち立ち直るさ. タフなやつだから.

get tough with …に強硬な態度をとる ▪ They *got tough with* their workers. 彼らは労働者たちに強硬な態度をとった.

That's tough. それは気の毒だ ▪ I lost ten bucks. —*That's tough.* 10ドルなくしちゃった—お気の毒に.

tough love (故意にとる)厳しい態度, 愛の鞭 ▪ I believe in *tough love* for dealing with problem children. 問題児の扱いには「愛の鞭」が一番と思う.

tough titty/tough titties 《口》そいつは気の毒だ ▪ I'm turning the television off, so *tough titty*. テレビは切るよ. 悪いけど ▪ You may be hurt by this but *tough titties*. 君はこれで傷つくかもしれないが, おあ

いにくさま.

When the going gets tough(, the tough get going). 《諺》状況が厳しくなると強者はいっそう活動する.

tough[2] /tʌf/ 動 ***tough it out*** 《米口》困難を忍ぶ ▪ He has *toughed it out* three years with Judy. 彼は3年間ジュディーと困難を忍んできた.

tour[1] /tʊər/ 名 ***go on a tour*** 周遊に出かける ▪ He *went on a tour* abroad. 彼は外国へ周遊に出かけた.

go on tour (演芸などで)周遊する ▪ The theatrical company *goes on tour* every year. その劇団は毎年巡業する.

make the tour of …を一巡[周遊]する ▪ We set out together to *make the tour of* Europe. 我々はヨーロッパを周遊するためにいっしょに出かけた.

on tour 周遊中で[の] ▪ He was *on tour* in France. 彼はフランスを周遊中だった ▪ He was an actor *on tour* in the company. 彼はその一座に加わって巡業中の役者であった.

take ... on tour …を巡業に連れて行く ▪ We *took* the company *on tour* on the Continent. 我々はその一座を大陸巡業の旅に連れて行った.

tour[2] /tʊ́ər/ 名 ***a tour de force*** (芸術的)力作, 見事な手腕 ▪ His performance as Hamlet was *a* brilliant *tour de force*. 彼のハムレット役は実に名演だった. ☞F 'an act of strength'.

tout /taʊt/ 名 ***keep (the) tout (on)*** 《俗》(…を)見張りする ▪ They *kept the tout on* each other. 彼らはお互いを見張りあった.

on the tout for …を見張って ▪ The pickpocket was *on the tout for* a careless stroller. すりはぶらぶら歩くうかつ者を物色していた.

tow /toʊ/ 名 ***in tow*** **1** (引き船に)引かれて (*of, by*) ▪ Our ship was *in tow by* the towing vessel. 我々の船は引き船に引かれていた.
2 …を従えて[連れて] ▪ She arrived with her five children *in tow*. 彼女は5人の子供を引き連れてやってきた.

take [have] ... in tow (船などが)…を引いて行く; を導く; を支配する ▪ We *took* the hippopotamus *in tow*. 我々はカバを引いて行った ▪ Providence *takes* us *in tow*. 神は我々を導きたもう ▪ Already she has *taken* him *in tow*. 彼女はもう夫をしりにしいている.

T

towel[1] /táʊəl|táʊəl/ 名 ***throw [toss, fling,*** 《口》 ***chuck] in the towel*** (ボクシングで敗北の承認として)タオルを投げ入れる; 降参する (→throw in the SPONGE) ▪ I've done my limit, and *tossed in the towel*. 私は根かぎりのことをやった. そして降参した.

towel[2] /táʊəl/ 動 ***towel*** *oneself* タオルで体をふく ▪ He was *toweling himself* before the mirror. 彼は鏡の前でタオルで体をふいていた.

tower /táʊər/ 名 ***a tower of strength*** →a pillar of STRENGTH.

tower and town/town and tower 《詩》人家のある所, 町 ▪ Ring out the bells from every *town and tower*! あらゆる町から鐘を鳴らせ.

towering /táʊərɪŋ/ 形 ***in a towering passion [rage]*** 激怒して (cf. Sh., *Haml.* 5. 2. 80) ▪ He came down *in a towering rage*. 彼は激怒して降りてきた.

town /taʊn/ 名 ***a man about town*** (ロンドンの)高等遊民, 通人; (クラブ・劇場などに絶えず出入りする)社交家, 遊び人 ▪ I was *a man about town* when he undertook that expedition. 彼がその遠征をしたころ私は高等遊民だった ▪ He's just *a man about town*—nothing to do except dress and amuse himself. 彼はまさに遊び人だ—着ることと遊ぶこと以外何もすることがない.

a man [woman, girl] of the town 町の男[女] 《放蕩者や夜の女など》 ▪ He has been *a man of the town*. 彼は放蕩者であった ▪ You'll never see *a girl of the town* in those streets. その町では町の女は決して見られない.

a night (out) on the town [tiles] 夜の町で遊ぶこと, 夜遊び ▪ I take my wife out for *a night on the town* from time to time. 私はときどき妻を夜の町へ遊びに連れて行く ▪ We went for *a night on the tiles*. 我々は夜の町へ繰り出した.

a one-horse town →ONE-HORSE.

come to town 現れる, 登場する ▪ Londoners were delighted that J. M. Barrie had *come to town*. ロンドンっ子たちは J. M. バリーが登場したことを大喜びした.

down town →DOWN[1].

go down town →DOWN[1].

go out on the town 夜の町へ遊びに出かける ▪ They *went out on the town* and didn't get home till the morning. 彼らは夜の町へ遊びに行き, 朝まで帰らなかった.

go to town **1** 町へ行く ▪ I *went to town* to do some shopping. 買い物をしに町へ行った.
2 《口》浮かれ騒ぐ ▪ He never *goes to town* out of sentiment. 彼は感傷的に浮かれ騒ぎはしない.
3 《米口》てきぱき能率的に[さっさと, 意気込んで, 思いっきり]やる ▪ Your friends were *going to town* on it. 君の友人たちはそれをてきぱき能率的にやっていた.
4 《米口》大成功する ▪ That boy is really *going to town* some day. あの少年はほんとにいつか大成功するぞ.
5 《口》(…に)大金を使う (*on*) ▪ He has been *going to town on* cars. 彼は車に大金を使っている.

go up to town 上京する ▪ He *went up to town* from Leeds. 彼はリーズから上京した.

hit town →HIT[2].

in [out of] town 〚無冠詞で〛在京して[退京して] 《今考えている, または話者が今いる町; 特に地方の主要な町や首都をさす》 ▪ A friend of mine was lately *in town*. 私の一友人が最近在京していました ▪ He went *out of town* on purpose. 彼はわざと退京した.

on the town **1** 町へ遊びに出かけて《レストラン・クラブなどへ行く》 ▪ They were out *on the town*. 彼らは町へ出て遊び回った.

2 売春[悪事]をして日を送って ▪ Those prostitutes had been a long time *on the town.* その売春婦たちは長いこと売春していた ▪ Jack was *on the town* again. ジャックはまた悪事をして日を送っていた.
3《米》町の厄介になって ▪ The family is *on the town.* その一家は町の厄介になっている.
paint the town (red) →PAINT².
run** a person **out of town 《主に米》人を追い出す[立ち退かす] ▪ If he causes trouble, you'd better *run* him *out of town.* もし彼が面倒なことを起こせば, 追い出したほうがいい.
strike town →STRIKE².
town and gown 市民と大学側の人 ▪ I wish to disclaim all sympathy with *town and gown* rows. 市民と大学側の人とのけんかに同情することはいっさい拒否したいと思う. ☞Oxford と Cambridge で.

toy /tɔɪ/ 名 ***a toy boy*** (年長の女性に愛される)若い男性 ▪ She seems to have *a* new *toy boy* every week. 彼女は毎週別の若いツバメと取り替えているらしい.
make a toy of …をもてあそぶ, おもちゃにする ▪ He *makes a toy of* his car. 彼は自分の車を乗りまわす.

trace¹ /treɪs/ 名 ***keep trace of*** …の跡をつける ▪ His object is to *keep trace of* a national legend. 彼の目的は国民的伝説の跡をつけることである.
lose trace of =keep TRACK (of).
on** a person's **trace(s) 人を追跡して ▪ Two dogs came *on the stag's traces.* 2匹の犬が雄ジカを追跡してやってきた.
sink [vanish] without (a) trace 跡形もなく消え去る ▪ The huge tanker *sank without trace* within minutes. その巨大なタンカーは数分のうちに完全に水没した ▪ The young singer enjoyed brief success and then *sank without trace.* その若手歌手の人気はしばらく続いたあと完全に衰えた.

trace² /treɪs/ 名 ***break [burst] a trace*** 根かぎり精を出す ▪ I'd *burst a trace* trying to go. 私は根かぎり精を出して行こうとします.
force ... into the traces …をむりやりに常の仕事につかせる ▪ He was too fond of my genius to *force* it *into the traces.* 彼は私の才能を大いに買っていたのでそれを強いて常の仕事につかせはしなかった.
get one leg over the traces 道を誤る ▪ I may have *got one leg over the traces.* 私は道を誤ったのかもしれない.
jump the traces →JUMP².
kick over the traces →KICK².

track /træk/ 名 ***a track record*** 《米》陸上競技の成績; (過去の)業績, 実績 ▪ Your *track record* is more important than your qualifications. 実績が資格よりもものをいう ▪ This applicant has *an* excellent *track record* as a manager. この応募者はマネージャーとして優れた実績を有している.
across the tracks = on the right side of the TRACKs.
back on track 再び軌道に乗って ▪ They had the project *back on the track* by the end of the month. 彼らは月末までにそのプロジェクトを元の軌道に戻した ▪ At last the peace process was *back on track* after many weeks of rows. 何週間も決裂が続いたのち, ようやく紛争処理交渉が再開された.
be on a fast track to →(be on) a FAST track.
be on the fast track (to [for]) →FAST.
be on the inside track → have the inside TRACK.
be on track (for) 軌道に乗っている; (…に向かって)順調に進んでいる ▪ This project *is on track for* its goal. この企画は目標に向かって順調に進んでいます.
clear track 道をあける; 〚命令文で〛そこのけ! ▪ *Clear track!* We're coming through! 道をあけろ! 俺様たちのお通りだ!
cover (up) one's tracks 1 足跡をくらます ▪ The thief who broke into my house *covered his tracks.* うちに押し入った泥棒は足跡をくらました.
2 行動[意図]をくらます ▪ Whatever else he lacks, he has the art of *covering up his tracks.* 他に何がないにせよ, 彼は自分の行動をくらます術を心得ている.
flirt with a muddy track on Black Friday 魔の金曜日に火遊びをする ▪ If he has fallen in love with a woman who has three children, then he is *flirting with a muddy track on Black Friday.* 彼が子供の3人いる女と恋をしたのなら, 魔の金曜日に火遊びをしていることになる.
fly the track 《米》常軌を逸する ▪ The oldest man will sometimes *fly the track.* いくら年をとっても常軌を逸することはあるものだ.
freeze in one's tracks 驚いて[おびえて]立ちすくむ (→ stop one (dead) in their TRACKs) ▪ My horse *froze in its tracks* and refused to move. 馬がおびえてその場に立ちすくみ, 動こうとしなかった.
get on the track of …を開始する ▪ He *got on the track of* these findings. 彼はこの調査を始めた.
have [be on] the inside track 走路の内側を走る; 有利な立ち場にある (*with*) ▪ He *has the inside track* to getting that contract. 彼はその契約を取るのに有利な立ち場にある ▪ She *has the inside track with* the Obama administration. 彼女はオバマ政権に重んじられている.
in the track of …を追って ▪ My pen goes *in the track of* my thoughts. 私のペンは思想を追って動く.
in one's tracks 《口》その場で; たちどころに ▪ He fell dead *in his tracks.* 彼はその場で死んで倒れた ▪ He stopped dead *in his tracks.* 彼はその場にぴたりと立ち止まった.
jump [leave] the track 1 脱線する ▪ The train *left the track.* 列車は脱線した.
2 本題・本筋からはずれる ▪ The speaker *jumped the track* to talk about women's lib. 講演者は本題をはずれてウーマンリブのことを話しだした.
keep [lose] track (of) (…の)跡をつける[見失う]; (を)覚えている[忘れる]; (との)接触を保つ[失う] ▪ The noise made it difficult to *keep track of* what

was going on. その騒音で起こっていることの見当がつきにくくなった ▪ Day after day passed in precisely the same manner, until one *lost* all *track of* the days of the week. 毎日毎日が全く同じように過ぎていくので, しまいには何曜日かわからなくなってしまった ▪ He tried to *keep track of* all his old school friends. 彼は昔の学友全員の消息を失わないように努めていた.

make [***take***] ***tracks*** (***for***) 《口》(...へ)去る, 進んで行く; (へ)急いで行く ▪ I'm going to *make tracks for* the post office at once. すぐ郵便局へ急ごうと思っている.

make tracks (***for home***) 《口》おいとまする ▪ It's time we were *making tracks for home*. もうおいとまするときです.

off the beaten track →BEATEN.

off the track **1** (猟犬が)臭跡を失って; 犯人の手がかりを失って ▪ The police seem to have gone *off the track* in this case. この事件では警察は犯人の手がかりを失ってしまったようだ.

2 本題をはずれて; 誤って ▪ Guess again. At present you are very much *off the track*. もう一度当ててみなさい. 目下君はひどく見当ちがいしているよ.

on the right [***wrong***] ***side of the tracks*** 金持ち[貧乏人]の住んでいる区域に ▪ He was born *on the wrong side of the tracks*. 彼は貧乏人の住んでいる区域に生まれた. ☞アメリカのたいていの町は鉄道線路を境に階級が分かれていたところから.

on the right [***wrong***] ***track*** 正しい[誤った]臭跡をたどって; 正しく[まちがって] ▪ It is a consolation to find that one is *on the right track*. 自分がまちがっていないということがわかると気が休まる.

on the track **1** 追跡して; 手がかりを得て (*of*) ▪ The men are *on the track of* the thief. その男たちは泥棒を追跡している.

2 本題をはずれずに, 正しく ▪ I think we are *on the track* now. 今度は正しいと思います.

on *a person's* ***track*** 人を追跡して ▪ He's always *on my track*. 彼はいつも私を追い回している.

put *a person* ***on the inside track*** (人を)有利な地位[立場]におく ▪ This book aims to *put* you *on the inside track*, with tips for traveling safely. 本書の目的は安全旅行の秘訣を提供して読者が難にあわないようにすることである.

stop (***dead***) ***in*** *one's* ***tracks/be stopped in*** *one's* ***tracks*** 活動を突然やめる; 驚いて立ちすくむ ▪ He *stopped in his tracks* with a look of amazement on his face. 彼は驚いた様子で突然手をとめた ▪ When I saw her coming my way I *stopped dead in my tracks*. 彼女がこっちへ来るのを見て足がすくんだ.

stop *one* (***dead***) ***in*** *their* ***tracks*** 活動を突然やめさせる ▪ This is how to *stop* terrorists *dead in their tracks*. こうすればテロリストどもの活動を抑えられる ▪ She felt she would like to *stop* his talk *in its tracks*. 彼女は彼の話をすぐに終わらせたいと思った.

take tracks (***for***) →make TRACKs (for).

throw [***put***] ***... off the track*** (追手)をまく, ごまかす ▪ The police *were thrown off the track* by the man's false alibi. 警察はその男の偽のアリバイにごまかされてしまった.

tract /trækt/ 名 ***a tract for the*** [***our***] ***times*** 現代のための小冊子 ▪ This book is truly *a tract for our times*. 本書はまさに現代のための小冊子だ.

trade /treɪd/ 名 ***a trade secret*** **1** 企業秘密 ▪ The ingredients of this sauce are *a trade secret*. このソースの原料は企業秘密です.

2 《戯》(一般に)秘密 ▪ Can I have a recipe for this pumpkin pie?—Sorry, it's *a trade secret*. このパンプキン・パイのレシピ, 教えてくれない?—ごめん. 内緒なの.

be good [***bad***] ***for trade*** 買い気を起こさせる[起こさせない] ▪ Good domestic policy *is good for trade*. 優れた国内政策は国民の買い気を起こさせる.

by trade 商売は ▪ He was a butcher *by trade*. 彼は商売は肉屋であった.

drive [***make, do***] ***a roaring trade*** →ROARING.

Every man for his own trade./Every one to his trade. 《諺》もちはもち屋.

in the ... trade ...商を営んでいる ▪ He is *in the* book [furniture] *trade*. 彼は書店[家具商]を営んでいる.

in trade **1** 商売を営んで ▪ Mr. Smith is *in trade*. スミス氏は商売を営んでいる.

2 《米》物々交換用の ▪ These things are *in trade*. これらの物は物々交換用だ.

make a trade of *A* ***for*** *B* AをBと交換する ▪ I *made a trade of* my camera *for* his antique typewriter. 僕は自分のカメラを彼の年代物のタイプライターと交換した.

of a trade 同業の ▪ We are three *of a trade*. 我々は3人とも同業だ.

ply *one's* ***trade*** 《文》商売を営む, 商売に励む ▪ Pickpockets *ply their trade* in Milan's main shopping areas and train stations. すりたちはミラノの目抜き商店街と駅を根城にしている ▪ The old baker has been *plying his trade* for close to sixty years. パン屋のじいさんはかれこれ60年近く商売をしている ▪ He *plied his trade* at the smithy. 彼は鍛冶屋の仕事に励んだ.

put *a person* ***to a trade*** 人に仕事を学ばせる ▪ I must *put* my son *to a* useful *trade*. 息子に役に立つ仕事を覚えさせなければならない.

Two of a trade never [***seldom***] ***agree.*** 《諺》商売敵は決して[めったに]合わない.

tradition /trədíʃən/ 名 ***by tradition*** 言い伝えで; しきたりで ▪ The old songs had been delivered to them, *by tradition*, from their fathers. その古い歌は祖先から言い伝えで彼らに伝えられてきていた.

traffic /trǽfɪk/ 名 ***as much as the traffic will bear*** 現状が許す限り; 市場がもつ限り ▪ *As much as the traffic will bear*, you can charge them to your credit card. 現状が許す限り, 代金はカード払いでいいです.

T

be open to traffic 開通する ＊The railway *is open to traffic*. その鉄道は開通した.

trail[1] /treɪl/ 名 ***be hot on the trail of*** →HOT.

blaze a [the] trail →BLAZE a way.

camp on the trail of 《米》 …をしつこく追跡する ＊He *camped on the trails of* all sorts of beasts. 彼はあらゆる種類の動物をしつこく追跡した.

get on the trail of …の手がかりを得る ＊The detective very soon *got on the trail of* the burglars. 探偵はじきに強盗一味の足どりをとらえた.

(hard) on the trail of …を(ぴったりと)追跡して ＊They were coming full speed *on our trail*. 彼らは全速力で我々を追跡して来ていた.

hit the trail →HIT[2].

in trail 1列になって ＊The party marched *in trail*. 一行は1列になって前進した.

off the trail 臭跡を失って; 迷って ＊The dogs seem to be *off the trail* of the deer. 犬どもはシカの臭跡を失ったらしい ＊We've got *off the trail* somehow. どうやら道に迷ってしまったぞ.

put** a person **off the trail =put a person off the SCENT.

trail[2] /treɪl/ 動 ***trail** one's **coat*** →COAT.

train[1] /treɪn/ 名 ***a through train*** (乗り換え不要の)直通列車 ＊I took the *through train* from Chicago to Boston. シカゴからボストンまでの直通列車に乗った.

board [ride] the gravy train →GRAVY.

by train 列車で ＊I went to Rome *by train*. 列車でローマへ行った.

catch [make]** one's **[a] train 列車に間に合う ＊He has just *made the train*. 彼はやっとその列車に間に合った.

in its train …を伴って ＊War brings famine *in its train*. 戦争はききんを伴ってくる.

in the train of …に続いて ＊Education came *in the train of* other good things. 教育は他のよいものに続いて行われた.

in train (手順が)整って ＊We have put matters *in train* for the election. すっかり選挙の手順を整えた.

join [get] on the gravy train 甘い汁の分け前を受け取る ＊There was a scramble to *join on the gravy train*. 甘い汁が吸える役職の奪い合いが起きた ＊There was an influx of migration to *get on the gravy train* in California. 一攫千金の分け前にあずかろうと大勢がカリフォルニアに殺到した.

miss [lose]** one's **train 列車に乗り遅れる ＊I *missed my train* by two minutes. 私は2分違いで列車に乗り遅れた.

ride the gravy train → board the GRAVY train.

take (a) train to …に列車で行く ＊I *took* the 12:30 *train to* town. 12時半の列車で町へ行った.

the gravy train →GRAVY.

one's [a] train of thought 思考の流れ ＊A knock on the door checked *my train of thought*. ドアのノックの音で思考の流れが中断された.

train[2] /treɪn/ 動 ***train fine*** 厳密に訓練する.

train it 《口》 列車で行く ＊We *trained it* from Aberdeen to Edinburgh. 我々はアバディーンからエディンバラまで列車で行った.

training /tréɪnɪŋ/ 名 ***be in [out of] training*** 練習中である[でない]; コンディションが良い[悪い] ＊The boxer *is* always *in training*. そのボクサーはいつも練習している ＊I *was in* good *training*. 私は絶好調だった.

go into training (競走などのために)練習する ＊He was determined to win and *went into training* for 6 days. 彼は勝とうと心に決め6日間練習をした.

tram[1] /træm/ 名 ***by tram*** 電車で ＊I go to school *by tram*. 私は電車で通学します.

tram[2] /træm/ 動 ***tram it*** 電車で行く ＊On Sundays we *tram it* to Kew. 日曜日には私たちは電車でキューへ行く.

tramp[1] /træmp/ 名 ***go for a tramp*** 徒歩旅行に行く ＊Let's *go for a tramp* in the country. 田舎へ徒歩旅行に行きましょう.

on (the) tramp (職を求めたり, 浮浪者として)放浪して, 渡り歩いて ＊She seems to have been just *on tramp*. 彼女はただ渡り歩いていたらしい.

tramp[2] /træmp/ 動 ***tramp it*** 《口》 歩く, 徒歩で行く ＊I missed the train and had to *tramp it*. 列車に乗り遅れたので歩かねばならなかった.

trample /trǽmpəl/ 動 ***trample ... to death*** …を踏みつけて殺す ＊The elephant *trampled* the jackal *to death*. ゾウはジャッカルを踏みつけて殺した.

trample ... under foot [one's feet] …を踏みにじる《比喩的にも》 ＊He would *trample* us *under foot* if he could. 彼はできるものなら我々を踏みにじるだろう ＊They *trample* all learning *under foot*. 彼らはすべての学問を踏みにじる.

trance /træns|trɑːns/ 名 ***go (off) into a trance*** 忘我の境に入る, 失神する ＊The woman seemed to *go off into a trance*. その女性は忘我の境に入るように見えた.

transit /trǽnsət/ 名 ***in (one's) transit*** 通過[輸送]中に ＊I lay at Gloucester *in my transit*. 私は通過中にグロスターに泊まった ＊Agricultural products lose their quality *in transit*. 農産物は輸送中に品質が悪くなる.

transom /trǽnsəm/ 名 ***over the transom*** 《米口》 依頼[取り決め]なしに, 勝手に ＊He sent his manuscript to a publisher *over the transom*. 彼はある出版社に自分の原稿を勝手に送りつけた.

transport[1] /trǽnspɔːrt/ 名 ***in transport*** 輸送中に ＊The article was lost *in transport*. その品物は輸送中に紛失した.

in transports/in a transport 有頂天になって ＊He was *in a transport* at possessing a fortune. 彼は大財産を手に入れて有頂天になっていた.

in transports of …で狂って ＊She was *in*

transports of joy [rage]. 彼女は狂喜して[怒り狂って]いた.

with transport 狂喜して ▪ He was hailed *with transport* wherever he appeared. 彼はどこへ姿を見せても狂喜して迎えられた.

transport[2] /trænspɔ́ːrt/ 動 ***(be) transported with*** …のために夢中になって(いる) ▪ I *was transported with* joy [anger]. うれしくて夢中になった[怒りで逆上した].

trap /træp/ 名 ***(be) up to trap*** 《口》心得て(いる), こすい ▪ He *was* too much *up to trap* to be cheated. 彼はとても抜け目がないのでだまされなかった.

fall [walk] into a trap/ be caught in a trap わなにかかる, わなに陥る ▪ He *walked* straight *into the trap*. 彼はまっしぐらにそのわなに陥った ▪ He *was caught in his* own *trap*. 彼は自分でしかけたわなにかかった.

Keep your trap shut! 《俗》黙っていろ.

lay [set] a trap for …をわなにかける ▪ The employer *set a trap for* the man. 主人はその男をわなにかけた.

open** one's **trap 《俗》 =open one's MOUTH.

shut** one's **trap 《俗》 =close one's MOUTH.

understand trap 《口》抜け目がない ▪ Well, brother, I *understand trap*. そりゃ, 君, 私も抜け目はないよ.

trash /træʃ/ 名 ***steal trash*** 金を盗む (cf. Sh., *Oth*. 3. 3. 157) ▪ He was sent to jail for *stealing trash*. 彼は金を盗んで刑務所へ送られた.

talk trash 《俗》むだ話をする, 人のことをあれこれ言う ▪ Some women like *talking trash* on the roadside. 道端でむだ話をするのが好きな女性もいる.

travail /trəvéɪl/ 名 ***in travail*** 産みの苦しみをして ▪ The nation had been long *in travail*. 国民は長く産みの苦しみをしていたのだった.

travel[1] /trǽvəl/ 名 ***get the travel bug*** 旅行がしたくてたまらない (→be bitten by the BUG) ▪ I like traveling and always *get* [am bitten by] *the travel bug*. 旅行好きでいつも旅行がしたくてたまらない.

on** one's **travels 旅行中で ▪ Is he still *on his travels*? 彼はまだ旅行中ですか.

Travel broadens the mind. 《諺》旅は訪れる地と人のことがわかる.

travel[2] /trǽvəl/ 動 ***Have ..., will travel.*** 《戯》…を所持しており, いつどこへでも出向きます ▪ *Have* teaching qualification, *will travel*! 当方, 教員資格あり, いついずこへも参上. ☞タイムズ紙の個人広告から.

He travels fastest who travels alone. 《諺》身内がいない方がことを成し易い《独り身が一番腰が軽い》.

It is better to travel hopefully than to arrive. 《諺》到着するよりも希望を抱いて旅をするほうが楽しい.

travel it 旅行する; (特に)徒歩で行く ▪ He *traveled it* through the district. 彼はその地方を旅行した ▪ I wanted to hear from anyone who's *traveled it* without a car. 誰でも車に乗らず徒歩で行った人からの話を聞きたかった.

travel light 軽装で旅行する《比喩的にも》 ▪ I prefer *traveling light*. 軽装で旅をするほうが好きだ.

travel out of the record →RECORD.

traveler, 《英》**traveller** /trǽvələr/ 名 ***a traveler's tale*** (旅行者の)ほら話 ▪ The sailor delights in *travelor's tales*. その水夫はほら話をするのが大好きだ.

play the traveler upon** a person*/《俗》tip** a person **the traveler*** 人にほらを吹く; 人をだます ▪ Do you *tip* me *the traveler*, my boy? 私にほらを吹こうというのかね, 君 ▪ I am not *playing the traveler upon* you. あなたをだましているのではない. ☞旅行者がほら話をすることから.

traverse /trəvə́ːrs/ 動 ***traverse** one's **ground*** (フェンシング・けんかなどで)右に左に動き回る ▪ He *traversed his ground*, tiring his enemy with change of play. 彼は右に左に動き回り, 攻め方を変えて敵を疲れさせた.

travesty /trǽvəsti/ 名 ***make a travesty of*** =make a MOCKERY of.

treacle /tríːkəl/ 名 ***like thinking through treacle*** はっきり頭が働かずに, はっきり考えられずに ▪ I drank too much and I had trouble with my job. It was *like thinking through treacle*. 飲み過ぎで仕事が思うようにいかなかった. はっきり頭が働いていなかったんだ.

tread /tred/ 動 ***tread a path to*** …への道を踏み作る ▪ He *trod a path to* psychology. 彼は心理学への道を切り開いた.

tread carefully [warily] 慎重に扱う, 用心して行動する ▪ You will have to *tread* very *carefully* in handling this issue. この問題は慎重に扱う必要があるだろう.

tread on air →walk on AIR.

tread on** a person's **heels = tread on the HEELs of.

tread on** one's **own tail 人を打とうとしてかえって自ら傷つく ▪ His criticism was in the nature of *treading on your own tail*. 彼の批判は天に向かってつばするといった感があった.

tread on sure ground 確信を持って話す ▪ Now I am *treading on sure ground*. 私の今言っていることは確かです.

tread on the toes of →TOE[1].

tread on** a person's **toes = tread on the TOEs of.

tread the boards →walk the BOARDs.

tread the deck 船に乗っている, 船乗りをする ▪ They were as skillful seamen as ever *trod the deck*. 彼らはかつてないほど腕ききの水夫たちだった.

tread the ground 歩く ▪ I thought she *trod the ground* with greater grace. 彼女はいっそう優美に歩いているように私には思えた.

tread the path of …の道をたどる ▪ I will not cease *treading the path of* labor. 私は労働の道を

たどるのをやめはしない ▪ They have *trod the paths of* the world before him. 彼らは彼より以前に浮世の道をたどってきた.

***tread the stage* [*boards*]** 舞台に立つ, 俳優である; 脚本を書く (= walk the BOARDs) ▪ He now *treads the stage*. 彼は今舞台に立っている.

tread this earth/tread shoe-leather 生きている ▪ A better man never *trod shoe-leather*. これ以上立派な人はこれまでになかった.

tread ... to the ground …を踏みにじる《比喩的にも》(→trample ... under FOOT) ▪ The horse *trod* him *to the ground*. 馬は彼を踏みにじった.

tread water **1** 立ち泳ぎする ▪ I always raised myself by *treading water*. 私は立ち泳ぎをしていつも体を持ち上げた.

2 進歩がない, むなしく時間をつぶす, ぼんやりと過ごす ▪ I've been *treading water* for the past two years. 過去2年間むだに日々を送ってきた ▪ He's done nothing but *tread water* these days. 彼はこのところむなしく時間をつぶしてばかりいる.

treadmill /trédmìl/ 名 ***be on a treadmill*** 働きうめである ▪ She *was on a treadmill* and worn out. 彼女は働きうめでくたくただった.

treat[1] /triːt/ 名 ***a treat*** 〚副詞的に〛《俗》非常によく; 非常に ▪ This air makes your liver work *a* fair *treat*. ここの空気は肝臓の働きをとてもよくしてくれる.

be a treat 《口》非常にけっこうなものである (*to*) ▪ His speeches *were an* intellectual *treat to* them. 彼の演説は彼らには知的な喜びであった.

get on a fair treat 《俗》とても進歩が速い, うまい具合にいく ▪ He's *getting on a fair treat* in German. 彼はドイツ語がめきめき上達している.

go down a treat (物が人々に)大いに受ける ▪ The lucky dip stall *went down a treat* with the children. つかみ取りの露天は子供たちに大人気だった ▪ A cup of coffee would *go down a treat*. コーヒーを1杯いただけると実にありがたい.

stand treat 《口》おごる ▪ Who is going to *stand treat*? 誰がおごるのか.

work a treat うまくいく, よく効く ▪ If you put some salt on wine stains, it *works a treat*. ワインのしみに塩を使うと, きれいに落ちる.

treat[2] /triːt/ 動 ***treat** a person **like** (**a piece of**) **dirt*** →DIRT.

treat** oneself **to …を楽しむ, (飲食物・衣服など)を奮発する ▪ I shall *treat myself to* a good holiday. 私はすてきな休みを楽しむことにしよう.

treatment /tríːtmənt/ 名 ***give** a person **the silent treatment*** 人に全く口をきかない, 人を冷たく無視する ▪ My wife *gave* me *the silent treatment* during the ride home. 妻は家への車の中では私に一言も口をきかなかった.

under treatment 治療を受けて ▪ She is still *under treatment* in hospital. 彼女はまだ病院で治療を受けている.

treaty /tríːti/ 名 ***in treaty*** 談判[交渉]中で (*with a person, for*) ▪ It appears he is *in treaty for* a place in the North. 彼は北部の土地を交渉中らしい ▪ I was *in treaty with* the firm. 私はその会社と交渉中だった.

tree /triː/ 名 ***a man up a tree*** 《米口》公平な第三者 ▪ It seems mighty funny to *a man up a tree*. 公平な第三者にはすこぶるこっけいに見える.

at the top of the tree →the TOP of the tree.

bark up the wrong tree →BARK[3].

grow on trees (… は)容易に多く得られる ▪ Money doesn't *grow on trees*. 金のなる木はない.

***in the green* [*dry*] *tree* [*wood*]** 順[逆]境で; 青年[老年]時代に (《聖》*Luke* 23. 31) ▪ If this was done *in the green tree*, what would be done *in the dry*? もしこれが順境でなされるのであれば, 逆境ではどうされるであろうか ▪ If he is like that *in the green tree*, what will he be like *in the dry tree*? 若い時にそのようでは, 彼は年老いたらどんなになるだろうか.

not see the wood for the trees → cannot see the WOOD for the trees.

out of** one's **tree 《俗》気が狂って, 大ばかで ▪ That man must be *out of his tree* behaving like that. あんなふるまいをするなんてあの男は狂っているに違いない. ☞tree = head.

take a tree 《米口》木の上[後ろ]に逃れる ▪ The bear *took a tree*. クマは木の上に逃れた.

***the tree of knowledge* (*of good and evil*)** 知恵の木 (《聖》*Gen*. 31. 19) ▪ Man has eaten of *the Tree of Knowledge*. 人間は知恵の木(の実)を食べてしまった.

the tree of life 生命の木 (《聖》*Gen*. 2. 9, etc.) ▪ But *the tree of life* will not let her die. しかし生命の木は彼女を死なせはしまい.

up a* (*gum*) *tree 《口》追いつめられて, 進退きわまって ▪ I'm *up a tree* with the algebra homework. 代数の宿題で困り果てているんだ ▪ I have her *up a tree*, as the Americans say. アメリカ人の言い方で言えば, 私は彼女を進退きわまらせているのだ. ☞獣が木に逃れて逃げ場を失うことから.

tremble[1] /trémbəl/ 名 ***all of a tremble/* (*all*) *in a tremble/on* [*upon*] *the tremble*** 《口》(心配・興奮で)ぶるぶる震えて ▪ I am already *all of a tremble*. 私はもうぶるぶる震えています ▪ Why should I be *in* such *a tremble* all the while he talked? 彼がしゃべっている間じゅう, なんだってこうぶるぶる震えていなければならないのか.

tremble[2] /trémbəl/ 動 ***Hear and tremble!*** 聞いて驚くな.

tremble in the balance → be in the BALANCE.

tremble to think 考えると身ぶるいする ▪ I *tremble to think* what has become of him. 彼がどうなったかと思うと身震いする.

trembling /trémblɪŋ/ 名 ***with* [*in*] *fear and trembling*** →FEAR[1].

trench[1] /trentʃ/ 名 ***mount the trenches*** ざんごう内の任務につく ▪ At ten we *mounted the*

T

trenches. 10時にざんごう内の任務についた.

relieve the trenches ざんごう内の兵と交替する ▪ Send them to *relieve the trenches.* 彼らをやってざんごう内の兵と交替させよ.

trench[2] /trentʃ/ 動 ***trench*** *one's* ***way*** 切り開いて進む ▪ They were *trenching their way* through the place. 彼らはそこを切り開いて進んでいた.

trencher /tréntʃər/ 名 ***lick*** *a person's* ***trencher(s)*** 人にへつらう; 人の食客になる ▪ You began to *lick a Cardinal's trencher.* あなたはある枢機卿にへつらい始めた ▪ He will *lick my master's trenchers* at supper. 彼は夕食時に私の主人の食客になるだろう. ☞trencher「食事をのせる木皿」.

trespass /tréspəs/ 動 ***No trespassing.*** 立ち入るべからず《掲示》.

trial /tráɪəl/ 名 ***a sore trial*** 困った[苦しい]こと, うるさい[やっかいな]もの ▪ The long waiting was *a sore trial.* 長いこと待たされるのはつらかった ▪ The naughty boy is *a sore trial* to his parents. そのいたずらっ子に両親は手を焼いている ▪ You've had *a sore trial,* but some day you will see how necessary it was. 君はこれまで厄介な目にあってきたが, それがいかに必要だったかがわかる日がいつか来るさ.

a trial balloon →BALLOON.

a trial by fire 試練 ▪ Finishing such a huge amount of work in time is really *a trial by fire.* これだけの分量の仕事を期限内に済ませるのは実に至難の業であった.

a trial of strength 力の強さを競うコンテスト, 力比べ ▪ The rivalry of the males is always decided by *a trial of strength.* オスの抗争の決着は常に力比べでつけられる.

be on (*one's*) ***trial*** 試されて[審理されて]いる ▪ He declared that constitutional government *was on its trial.* 彼は立憲政治は試されていると断言した.

bring ... to trial/bring ... up for trial (人・訴訟)を審理[裁判]する ▪ He *was brought to trial.* 彼は裁判にかけられた.

call the trial 裁判[審理]にかける ▪ *The trial* must *be called* over again. もう一度審理にかけなければならない.

give ... a trial ...を試してみる ▪ He *gave* the new typist *a trial.* 彼は新しい入力担当者を試しに雇ってみた.

give ... a trial run →RUN[1].

make (***a***) ***trial of*** (物)を試す, 試験する ▪ He *made trial of* his strength against the man. 彼はその男と力を試してみた.

on trial **1** 試しに ▪ I will take the maid for a month *on trial.* そのお手伝いを試しにひと月置いてみよう.

2 試してみると ▪ The new clerk was found *on trial* to be incompetent. 新しい事務員は試してみると無能であることがわかった.

3 裁判中で ▪ The murderer is now *on trial.* その殺人者は今公判中だ.

put *a person* ***on*** *his* ***trial*** 人を審理[裁判]する ▪ In this case the parties *were* first *put on their trial.* この訴訟では当事者たちがまず審理された.

put ... to trial ...を試してみる ▪ I shall *put* the machine *to* further *trial.* その機械をさらに試してみましょう.

stand [***undergo***] (*one's*) ***trial*** 審理・裁判・試験を受ける (*for*) ▪ He went to *stand trial for* his licence as a preacher. 彼は説教師の免許試験を受けに行った ▪ He *underwent trial for* murder. 彼は殺人の裁判を受けた.

stand upon *one's* ***trial*** 裁判を受ける ▪ The prisoner *stands upon his trial.* 被告は裁判を受けている.

trial and error 試行錯誤, 手探り ▪ I'm learning to use my computer by *trial and error.* 私は手探りでコンピューターの使い方を覚えている.

trials and tribulations 辛苦 ▪ This book is about the *trials and tribulations* of the Jewish people. この本はユダヤ民族の辛苦を扱ったものである.

under trial 公判中で ▪ The case is now *under trial.* その訴訟は今公判中である.

triangle /tráɪæŋgəl/ 名 ***the eternal triangle*** 男女の三角関係 ▪ I'm tired of *the eternal triangle,* but she doesn't care about it. 私は三角関係にはうんざりだが, 彼女は平気なんだ.

tribute /tríbju:t/ 名 ***floral tributes*** 葬儀用に届けられた献花 ▪ The church was filled with *floral tributes.* 教会一杯に葬儀の献花が供えてあった.

lay a tribute on ...に貢を納める義務を負わせる《比喩的にも》 ▪ A fast only *laid a tribute on* our eyes. 断食は我々の目に負担をかけたにすぎなかった.

lay [***bring***] ***... under tribute*** ...に貢物を納めさせる ▪ The king *brought* British tribes *under tribute.* 王はイギリスの各種族に貢物を納めさせた.

pay a (***high***) ***tribute to*** ...を(大いに)賞賛する (= pay (a) TRIBUTE to 2) ▪ They *paid a high tribute to* his merits. 人々は彼の功績を大いに賞賛した.

pay (***a***) ***tribute to*** **1** ...に進貢する ▪ The conquered nation had to *pay tribute to* Rome. その征服された国はローマに進貢せねばならなかった.

2 ...に賛辞を呈する ▪ I *pay tribute to* what Mrs. Smith has done for the parish. スミス夫人が教区のためにしてくださったことに賛辞を呈します.

under tribute 貢を納める義務を負って《比喩的にも》 ▪ The idle shall be *under tribute.* 怠け者には貢を納める義務を負わせよう.

trick /trɪk/ 名 ***a bag*** [***box***] ***of tricks*** 《口》精巧な仕掛け[装置], 七つ道具; (目的達成に必要な)あの手この手 ▪ Every good magician has *a bag of tricks.* すぐれたマジシャンはみな七つ道具を具えている.

a con [***confidence***] ***trick*** 信用詐欺 ▪ This sort of offer is little better than *a con trick.* この種の申し込みはほとんど信用詐欺と言ってよい.

a dirty trick 卑劣な策略[まね], 不正行為; 〚複数形で〛(政治上の)不正工作 ▪ They played *a dirty trick* to get rid of us. やつらは僕たちを追い払おうと

汚い手を使った ▪ That was *a dirty trick* he played on her when he ran away with her younger sister. 彼はその妹と駆け落ちして彼女に卑劣な行為をとった ▪ Both sides used *dirty tricks* on each other. 両陣営は互いに不正工作をし合った.

a hat trick **1**《サッカー》ハットトリック《1試合に1人が3点(以上)得点すること》 ▪ He scored three goals for *a hat-trick* on his international debut. 彼は国際試合の初戦で3ゴールをあげてハットトリックを達成した. ☞クリケットで三者連続アウトにした投手に帽子が贈られたことから.

2《野球》サイクルヒット《1試合に単打, 二塁打, 三塁打, 本塁打を打つこと》; 1試合に3本塁打を打つこと ▪ He belted *a hat trick* Monday against the Giants. 彼は月曜日のジャイアンツ戦でサイクルヒットを打った ▪ We watched him hit *a hat trick*—three home runs in a ballgame. 我々は彼がハットトリック, つまり野球の1試合に3ホーマーを打つのを見た.

3 きわめて巧妙な手[術策] ▪ At the last minute of the elections the liberals will try *a hat trick*. 選挙のまさに終盤に自由党はきわめて巧妙な策を試行するだろう.

a trick worth two of that 《口》それよりはるかにまさった方策[方法] (cf. Sh., *1 Hen. IV* 2. 1. 41) ▪ No, no. We know *a trick worth two of that*. いやいや, それよりずっといい方策を知っている.

be up to every trick =KNOW a thing or two.

be up to *one's* **(*old*) *tricks* (*again*) (*of*)** (...の)また悪い癖を出す[昔の手を使う] ▪ He's *up to his old tricks of* having lunch during class. 彼は授業中に弁当を食べるという悪い癖がまた出ている.

do a vanishing trick 突然姿をくらます[ドロンを決める] ▪ He *did* one of his *vanishing tricks* before the deadline for the payment. 彼は支払の締め切り前にお得意のドロンを決めた.

do **[*turn*]** ***the trick*** 《口》目的を達する, うまくいく ▪ A pail of whitewash and a can of paint will *do the trick*. 石灰塗料の手おけとペンキが一缶あればうまくいく.

get **[*learn*]** ***the trick of it*** そのこつを知る ▪ I shall soon *get the trick of it*. やがてそのこつがわかるだろう.

have a trick of *doing* ...する癖がある ▪ He *has a trick of repeating* himself. 彼は同じことを繰り返して言う癖がある.

How's tricks? 《口》元気?《友人同士のあいさつ》 ▪ *How's tricks?*—Can't complain. どう, 元気かい—まあまあってとこさ.

in trick 《紋章》ペンで描かれた ▪ The flags are shown *in trick*. 旗はペン画で示されている.

know a trick or two/be up to every trick =KNOW a thing or two.

know the trick of the trade 商売のかけひき[こつ]を心得ている ▪ The novelist *knows* all *the tricks of the trade*. その小説家は自分の商売のこつをすべて心得ている ▪ The champion *knows* all *the tricks of the* boxing *trade*. チャンピオンはボクシングのあらゆる巧みな技を心得ていた.

not **[*never*]** ***miss a trick*** **[*move*]** →MISS[2].

play **[*serve*]** *a person* ***a trick/play a trick on*** *a person* **1** 人をたぶらかす, ぺてんにかける ▪ He shall not *serve* me *that trick* twice. やつのあんなぺてんには二度とかからないぞ ▪ *Play* me no *tricks*. 私をたぶらかさないでください.

2 人にいたずら[悪ふざけ]をする ▪ He *played a* nasty *trick on* me. 彼は僕にひどいいたずらをした ▪ His classmates *played tricks on* him by hiding his clothes while he was swimming. 彼の級友たちはふざけて彼が泳いでいるときに服を隠した.

play tricks 手品をする ▪ Black shadows of the trees *play tricks* with the familiar scenes. 木々の黒い影は見慣れた景色を一変させる.

put a trick **[*tricks*]** ***upon*** ...をたぶらかす, ぺてんにかける ▪ They watched their opportunity to *put a trick upon* us. 彼らは我々をぺてんにかける機会をうかがっていた.

take **[*win*]** ***a*** **[*the*]** ***trick*** 《トランプ》ひと回り分の札を手に入れる《通例4枚》 ▪ I hardly *took a trick* all evening. ひと晩中ひと回り分の札が手に入らなかった.

the oldest trick in **[*on*]** ***the book*** 人を欺くための常套手段 ▪ It's *the oldest trick on the book* to blame someone else for your problems. 君の問題を他人のせいにするなんて古い手だ ▪ Even though this is *the oldest trick in the book*, it still works like a charm. こいつは使い古された汚い手だが, それでもみなみごとに引っかかる.

the whole bag of tricks **1** あらゆる手段[術策] ▪ Well, you've tried *the whole bag of tricks*. とにかく, 君はあらゆる手段を試みたわけだ ▪ Hotel managers are using *a whole* new *bag of tricks* to attract their guests. ホテルの経営者たちは客引きのためにあらゆる新しい手を使っている ▪ He's brought the man to his knees by using his *whole bag of tricks*. 彼は術策を用いて男を屈服させた.

2 猫もしゃくしも, 一切がっさい ▪ How many people has he invited?—*The whole bag of tricks*, I believe. 彼は何人招待したのかね?—猫もしゃくしもだと思うよ, きっと.

There are tricks in every trade. 《諺》どんな商売にもコツがある.

trick or treat **1** お菓子をくれないといたずらするぞ ▪ The children went from house to house, shouting "*Trick or treat*!" 子供たちは「お菓子をくれないといたずらするよ」と言いながら家々を回った.

2 〚動詞的に〛(ハロウィーンに子供が)菓子をねだりながら1軒ずつ回る ▪ When was the last time you went *trick-or-treating* and what was your costume? この前に君がお菓子ちょうだいと言って回ったのはいつで, どんな扮装をしていたかい?

turn a trick **[*tricks*]** 売春する ▪ She even considered *turning tricks* to pay the rent. 家賃を払うために彼女は売春することまで考えた. ☞trick「性行為」.

turn the trick →do the TRICK.

use [***try***] ***every trick in the book*** 《口》あらゆる手を尽くす ▪ We are *using every trick in the book* to stay one step in front of our competitors. 我々は競争相手より1歩リードするためにあらゆる手を尽くしているところだ.

win a [***the***] ***trick*** →take a TRICK.

tried /traɪd/ 形 ***tried and true***/《英》***tried and tested*** [***trusted***] 立証済みの, 当てになる ▪ I have *tried and true* friends. 私には当てになる友人たちがいる ▪ I'll teach you a *tried and tested* method of ensuring your data protection. データ保護を確実に行う立証された方法をお教えしましょう.

trifle /tráɪfəl/ 名 ***a trifle*** 〚副詞的に〛少しばかり, やや ▪ He seems *a trifle* angry. 彼はいささか怒っているらしい.

trig /trɪg/ 名 ***toe the trig*** →TOE the line.

trigger /trígər/ 名 ***easy on the trigger*** 《米口》すぐ引き金を引く, すぐ行動に出る ▪ I'm mighty *easy on the trigger*. 僕はすぐ行動に出るたちだ.

in the drawing of a trigger たちまち ▪ This is the cap of honor; it dubs a man a gentleman *in the drawing of a trigger*. これは名誉の帽子だ. これはたちまち人を紳士に仕立てあげる.

pull (***the***) ***trigger*** (***at, on***) (…をねらって)引き金を引く ▪ Not once or twice you've *pulled trigger on* me. 君が私をねらって引き金を引いたのは1度や2度ではない.

quick on the trigger すばしこい, 抜け目のない; 《米口》早撃ちの, すぐ発砲する (trigger-happy) ▪ The man is a born musical leader, *quick on the trigger*. その男は抜け目のない, 天才的な音楽指揮者だ ▪ Wyatt Earp was known to be *quick on the trigger*. ワイアット・アープは早撃ちの名手として知られていた. ☞引き金を引くのが早いことから.

trigger happy =quick on the TRIGGER.

trim[1] /trɪm/ 名 ***be in no trim for*** …に適当な状態でない ▪ I *am in no trim for* rough work. 私は荒仕事をやれる状態ではない《服装・健康などが》.

get into trim 調子がよくなる ▪ I will give him a dose of that remedy when once I *get into trim*. 私が調子よくさえなったら, 彼にもその薬を一服飲ませてやろう.

give *a person* ***a trim*** 《口》人の髪を刈る ▪ The barber will *give* you *a trim*. 理髪師が髪を刈ってくれましょう.

in fighting trim 《主に米》絶好調で, 意欲十分で, 極めて良い状態で ▪ The player was *in fighting trim* despite his long spell away from the game. 選手は長い間, 試合から遠ざかっていたにもかかわらず極めて調子が良かった ▪ The Harvard football players are *in fighting trim*. ハーバード大のフットボール選手たちは絶好調だ ▪ It was a challenging performance, but the dancers were *in fighting trim*. むずかしい公演だったが, ダンサーたちはやる気満々だった.

in (…) ***trim*** **1** 《海》(船が)…の状態で ▪ They must always be *in* sailing *trim*. それらの船はいつも出帆準備を整えていなければならない.

2 適当な状態で, 調子がよい, 整って ▪ My eyes, head, feet, all fairly *in trim*. 私の目も頭も足もいずれもかなり調子がいい ▪ The whaling gear was *in trim*. 捕鯨道具は整っていた.

trim[2] /trɪm/ 動 ***trim*** *one's* ***course*** 帆を整えて進む《比喩的にも》 ▪ The Mars Polar Lander successfully *trimmed its course*. 火星極着陸船は順調に飛行を続けた.

trim *a person's* ***jacket*** →dust a person's JACKET.

trim the [*one's*] ***sails*** (***to the wind***) →SAIL[1].

trim *oneself* (***up***) 身なりをきれいにする, めかす ▪ She hastened to *trim herself*. 彼女は急いで身じまいをした.

trine /tráɪn/ 名 ***in trine with*** (二つの天体が)…と三分一対座をなして ▪ The moon was *in trine with* the sun. 月は太陽と三分の一対座をなしていた. ☞占星術から.

trip[1] /trɪp/ 名 ***a bad trip*** 《俗》不快な旅《麻薬を飲んで気分が悪くなること》; いやな経験 ▪ He had *a bad* LSD *trip*. 彼は LSD を飲んで気分が悪くなった.

a round trip 往復(旅行); 往復旅行券 ▪ The fare for *a round trip* is generally lower than for two one-way journeys. 往復旅費1枚分は片道旅費2枚分よりもふつう安い ▪ Two *round trips* to Denver, please. デンバーまで往復2枚ください.

(***a trip***) ***down memory lane*** →LANE.

do the trip (…へ)船旅をする (*to*) ▪ I have never *done the trip to* Venice. ベニスへ船旅をしたことがない.

go for a trip 旅行に行く ▪ We *went for a trip* round the lake. 我々は湖水一周旅行に行った.

go on a trip (短い)旅行をする ▪ We *went on a trip* round the lake. 我々は湖水一周旅行をした.

in a trip of a minute 1分のうちに ▪ They finished it *in a trip of a minute*. 彼らはそれを1分のうちに仕上げた.

take [***make***] ***a trip to*** …に旅行する ▪ I am thinking of *making a trip to* the seaside. 海へ遊びに行こうかと思っている.

trip[2] /trɪp/ 動 ***catch*** *a person* ***tripping*** 人のあげ足を取る ▪ I *caught* him *tripping* in his story. 私は彼の話であげ足を取ってやった.

trip it **1** 踊る ▪ The young folks *tripped it* away on the grass. 若者達は芝生の上で踊り続けた.

2 軽快に歩く ▪ I *tripped it* down to my office. 私は軽快に歩いて事務所まで行った.

3 小旅行をする ▪ I *tripped it* to Brighton for the good of my health. 私は保養のためにブライトンへ小旅行をした.

trip the light fantastic 《戯》ダンスをする (Milton, *L'Allegro* 35) (→light fantastic TOE).

trip up *a person's* ***heels*** →HEEL.

tripe /traɪp/ 名 ***a bag of tripe*** 《軽蔑》人間, やつ ▪ He was *a* squeaking *bag of tripe*. 彼はキー

キー声をした男だった.

talk tripe 全くのたわごとを言う ▪ He was *talking tripe* in front of the audience. 彼は聴衆を前にしてたわごとばかり並べていた.

triplicate /tríplɪkət/ 名 ***in triplicate*** 同文が3通作成された ▪ The constitution was written *in triplicate*. その憲法は3通から成っていた.

tripod /tráɪpɑd|-pɔd/ 名 ***the tripod of life***/***the vital tripod*** 生命のかなえ《心臓・肺・脳》 ▪ The heart, lungs, and brain constitute "*the tripod of life*." 心臓と肺と脳が「生命のかなえ」を構成する.

Triton /tráɪtən/ 名 ***a Triton of*** [***among***] ***the minnows*** ざこの中のエビ, 鶏群の一鶴(かく) ▪ On his own side he is *a Triton among the minnows*. 彼自身の側では彼も鶏群の一鶴だ.

triumph /tráɪəmf/ 名 ***in triumph*** 勝ち誇って, 意気揚々として ▪ Hail to the chief who advances *in triumph*. 勝ち誇って進み出てくるかしらに万歳.

trivet /trívət/ 名 (***as***) ***right as a trivet*** → (as) RIGHT as my glove.

Trojan /tróʊdʒən/ 名 ***a Trojan horse*** トロイの木馬《内部から崩壊を促すもの》 ▪ The Japanese company in England seemed *a Trojan horse* to the EC. イングランドにあるその日本の会社は EC にとってはトロイの木馬と思われた.

a true [***trusty***] ***Trojan*** 《口》本当の[頼みがいある]好漢 ▪ He was a kind good fellow, *a true Trojan*. 彼は親切ないい男で, 本当の好漢だった.

like a Trojan 《口》(トロイ人のように)元気よく, せっせと ▪ He was working *like a Trojan*. 彼は元気よく働いていた.

trolley /tráli|tróli/ 名 ***be off*** [***slip***] *one's* ***trolley*** 《米俗》気が狂っている[狂う] ▪ Square watermelons? You must *be off your trolley*. 四角いスイカだと? 気は確かか. ☞trolley「頭」.

trooper /trú:pər/ 名 ***like a trooper*** 《口》甚だしく ▪ The fellow swore [ate] *like a trooper*. 男は盛んにののしった[食べた].

trophy /tróʊfi/ 名 ***a trophy wife*** (夫の高い地位にふさわしい)若くて美しい妻, 箔つけワイフ ▪ Do you really want to become *a trophy wife* and live a life of luxury? 年配の富豪の若妻になって贅沢三昧の生活をしたいと本気で考えているのかね.

trot[1] /trɑt|trɔt/ 名 ***at a trot*** 速足で ▪ The cavalry advanced *at a trot*. 騎兵隊は速足で進んだ.

go for a trot 速足散歩に行く ▪ It is pleasant to *go for a trot* in the morning. 朝速足散歩に行くのは楽しい.

on the trot **1** 絶えず動き回って, いつも忙しくして (= on the GO) ▪ He is one of those who keep the waiter *on the trot*. 彼は給仕人を絶えず動き回らせる手合いの一人だ.

2 たてつづけに ▪ He had three wins *on the trot*. 彼はたてつづけに3回勝った.

trot[2] /trɑt|trɔt/ 動 ***hot to trot*** →HOT.

trot *oneself* ***off*** 《口》ちょっと出かける ▪ I will *trot myself off* for the moment. ちょっと出かけます.

trot *a person* ***off*** *his* ***legs*** (見物などに)人を歩かせてへとへとに疲れさせる ▪ He *trotted* me *off my legs*. 彼は私を歩いてくたびれ果てさせた ▪ Toby *was trotted* nearly *off his legs* in the chase. トビーは追跡でさんざん歩かされてへばった.

trot ... on *one's* ***knee*** (幼児)をひざにのせてゆすぶる ▪ He *trotted* the baby *on his knee*. 彼は赤ちゃんをひざにのせてゆすぶった.

troth /trɔ:θ|trəʊθ/ 名 ***plight*** *one's* ***troth*** 誓約する; 夫婦の約束をする ▪ They *plighted their troths* together. 彼らは共に誓いを交わした ▪ Betrothal rings are worn by maidens who have *plighted their troth*. 婚約指輪は夫婦の約束をした娘たちがはめる.

trouble[1] /trʌ́bəl/ 名 ***A trouble shared is a trouble halved.*** 《諺》悩みは話せば軽くなる.

a trouble-shooter 紛争の調停人 ▪ He has acted as *a trouble shooter* and successfully settled many disputes. 彼はこれまで調停者をつとめ, みごとに多くの争議に決着をつけた.

ask [***look***] ***for trouble***/***seek trouble*** 《口》求めて災難を招く ▪ It's *asking for trouble* to associate with criminals. 犯罪者とつき合うのは求めて災難を招くことになる.

be at the trouble to *do* [***of*** *doing*] 面倒ながら…する ▪ Would you *be at the trouble to* write that to him? ご面倒でもそう彼に書いてやってくださいませんか.

be in trouble **1** 困っている ▪ He *is in* great *trouble* about it. 彼はそのことでひどく困っている.

2 (…と)もめている, ごたごたを起こしている (*with*) ▪ The establishment *is in trouble with* the police. その店は警察とごたごたを起こしている.

3 かかり合いになっている;《俗》入牢している ▪ This gentleman has lately *been in trouble* in the Tower of London. この方は最近までロンドン塔に入牢しておられました.

4 (未婚女性が)妊娠している ▪ She consented to be married to the prisoner as she believed she *was in trouble*. 彼女は妊娠していると信じていたので, その囚人との結婚に同意した.

borrow trouble/***meet trouble halfway*** 取り越し苦労をする ▪ You're just *meeting trouble halfway*. 君は取り越し苦労をしているにすぎない ▪ Being a coward, he is apt to *borrow trouble*. 憶病者だから彼は取り越し苦労をしがちだ.

cause trouble =make TROUBLE(s).

get into trouble/***bring*** *oneself* ***into trouble*** もんちゃくを起こす《特に警察に呼ばれたり, 検挙されたり, 刑務所に入れられたりするようなことを言う》 ▪ Take care what you say, or you'll *get into trouble*. めったなことを言うと, ごたごたを起こすことになるぞ ▪ He offended the Mayor, and *brought himself into trouble*. 彼は市長を怒らせて刑務所に入れられた.

get *a person* ***into trouble*** 人にもんちゃくを起こさ

せる; (女性)を妊娠させる ▪ This will *get* you *into trouble*. これで面倒なことになるぞ ▪ He had *got* girls *into trouble* more than once. 彼は何度も女の子を妊娠させていた.

get out of trouble ごたごたを免れる[免れさせる] ▪ How can you *get out of trouble* if you get in trouble? 面倒に巻き込まれたら, どうやればそれから抜け出せるんだ.

give** a person **trouble 人に面倒をかける ▪ We hope your vehicle will never *give* you *trouble*. お求めの車でご面倒をおかけすることはなかろうと思います ▪ I beg you will not *give* yourself any *trouble*. どうかご心配なさらないように願います.

***go to the trouble of** doing* わざわざ...する ▪ Some people *go to the trouble* and expense *of traveling* out of snobbery. 人によっては俗物根性から金を出してわざわざ旅行する者もいる.

***go to trouble to** do* 骨折って...する ▪ He *went to trouble to* complete the work. 彼は骨折ってその作品を完成した.

have teething trouble(s) →have TEETHING problems.

***have trouble to** do* ...するのに骨が折れる ▪ I *have* much *trouble to* keep out of debt. 借金をしないようにするのにずいぶん骨が折れます.

have trouble with **1** (病気)で困っている ▪ I am *having trouble with* my teeth. 歯痛で参っている. **2** ...ともめる ▪ You will *have trouble with* him. 彼ともめることだろう.

keep out of trouble ごたごたに巻き込まれないようにする ▪ We must *keep out of trouble* somehow. どうにかしていざこざに巻き込まれないようにせねばならない.

look for trouble →ask for TROUBLE.

***make trouble for** a person* 人に迷惑をかける, をかかり合いにする ▪ He's always *making trouble for* his friends. 彼はいつも友人に迷惑をかけている.

make trouble(s) 騒ぎを起こす; ごねる ▪ She is always *making troubles*. 彼女は騒ぎを起こしてばかりいる.

meet trouble halfway →borrow TROUBLE.

more trouble than a cartload of monkeys 《口・戯》大変な面倒 ▪ The five children were *more trouble* to their mother *than a cartload of monkeys*. その5人の子供たちは母親には大変な面倒だった.

more trouble than** one [it] **is worth 役に立つよりも面倒になって ▪ Some servants are *more trouble than* they *are worth*. 使用人の中には役に立つよりも面倒になるものもいる.

No trouble (at all). お安いご用です ▪ Sorry to inconvenience you.—*No trouble at all*. 不便をかけて申し訳ない—お安いご用さ.

put** a person **to trouble 人に骨を折らせる ▪ I'm sorry I've *put* you *to* so much *trouble*. 大変ご迷惑をおかけしてすみません.

save [spare]** a person **trouble 人の労を省く ▪ That will *spare* me much *trouble*. これで私はだいぶ助かる.

seek trouble →ask for TROUBLE.

spell (big) trouble 面倒[厄介]なことになりそうである ▪ His remark *spells trouble*. 彼の発言は面倒なことになりそうだ.

***take the trouble to** do* 労を惜しまず...する ▪ Don't *take the trouble to* come and meet me. わざわざ迎えに来ないでください.

take trouble 労を取る, 骨を折る (*over, about*) ▪ You need not *take* any *trouble about* it. そのことは少しもご心配くださるに及びません.

the trouble (with** one**) is (that) (...の)困ったことは...である ▪ *The trouble with* us *is that* we have no funds. 我々の困ったことは資金がないことだ.

there's trouble brewing 《口》厄介なことが生じている, ごたごた[面倒なこと]が起こりそうだ ▪ *There's trouble brewing* in the car industry. 自動車産業界でもめごとが起きている ▪ *There's trouble brewing* in the toy factory. 玩具工場で面倒が起きそうだ.

Troubles [Misfortunes] never come singly. 《諺》不幸は重なるものだ.

What is the trouble with ...? ...はどうしたのだ, どこが悪いのか ▪ Well, *what's the trouble with* you today, Mary? さて, 今日はどこが悪いの, メアリー.

trouble[2] /trʌ́bəl/ 動 ***be troubled about [over]*** ...のことで困っている ▪ I *am* much *troubled about* the affair. その件では大いに困っている.

be troubled with (病気など)で困っている ▪ He *was troubled with* a severe headache. 彼はひどい頭痛で困っている.

trouble** oneself **about ...を心配する ▪ Don't *trouble yourself about* the future. 将来のことを心配なさるな.

***trouble** oneself **to** do* 労を惜しまずに[わざわざ]...する ▪ He had never *troubled himself to* understand the question. 彼はその問題を理解しようと骨折ったことはなかった.

troubled /trʌ́bəld/ 形 ***fish in troubled waters*** →FISH[2].

troubled waters 混乱状態 ▪ The inadvertent inquiry brought us into *troubled waters*. その不注意な詮索のために我々は混乱に陥った.

trough /trɔːf|trɔf/ 名 ***dance in the hot trough*** →DANCE[2].

trough of the sea 波くぼ《二つの波の間の谷》 ▪ The ship lay rolling in the *trough of the sea*. 船は波くぼで横揺れに揺れていた.

walk [bring] up to the trough, fodder or no fodder 《米口》運命・責任を(不平を言わずに)受けいれる[受けいれさせる] ▪ That will surely *bring* him *up to the trough, fodder or no fodder*. それできっと彼も文句を言わずに責任を受けいれるだろうよ.

trouser /tráuzər/ 名 ***get too big for** one's **trousers*** →be too BIG for one's boots.

wear the trousers [《米》pants] 《英》夫を尻に敷いている (→wear the PANTS) ▪ There is no doubt that Mrs. Smith *wears the trousers*. スミス夫人が夫を尻に敷いているのはまちがいない.

with** one's **trousers down = with one's PANTS down.

trout /traʊt/ 名 ***an old trout*** 《口》不きげんな老女, 気むずかしい婆さん ▪ If ever there was *an old trout* surely Queen Vickster was it. この世にガミガミばばあがいるとすればビックスター女王こそその人だった.

trove /troʊv/ 名 ***a treasure trove*** (多く所有者不明の)貴重な埋蔵物 ▪ I found *a treasure trove* of antique furniture in an old farmhouse. ある古い農家で骨董家具の掘り出し物を見つけた.

trowel /tráʊəl/ 名 ***lay it on with a trowel*** →LAY it on thick.

truant /trú:ənt/ 名 ***play truant*** 《英》(学校などから)ふける, (を)サボる (*from, to*)(=《米》play HOOK(E)Y) ▪ He used to *play truant from* school. 彼はよく学校からふけていた ▪ Let wearied eyes *play truant to* toil. 疲れた目には仕事をサボらせるがいい.

truce /tru:s/ 名 ***(a) truce to [with]*** 〚間投詞的に〛…はもうたくさんだ, をやめろ ▪ A *truce to* this light conversation. こんな軽い話はもうたくさんだ ▪ *Truce with* toying for this once! 今度だけは戯れるのはやめてくれ!

truck /trʌk/ 名 ***by truck*** 物々交換によって ▪ Their trade is managed *by truck*. 彼らの取引は物々交換によって行われている.

have no truck with 《古風》…と取引[交際]しない ▪ I will *have no truck with* him. あの男とは交際すまい.

in truck (for) (…と)交換に ▪ They sold weapons *in truck for* diamonds. 彼らはダイヤと交換に武器を売った.

stand no truck 《口》ばかなまねをがまんしない ▪ I shall *stand no truck*. 私はばかなまねはがまんしないぞ.

trudge /trʌdʒ/ 動 ***trudge it*** てくてく歩く ▪ Give me your arm, we'll *trudge it*. 腕を貸してくれ, てくてく歩こうじゃないか.

true /tru:/ 形名副 ***a true bill*** →BILL[1].

(all) good men and true 《主に戯》立派な人たち(みんな); 正義の士; 陪審員 (cf. Sh., *Much Ado* 3. 3. 1) ▪ Trial by twelve *good men and true* is a sound system. 12人の陪審員による裁判は健全な制度である ▪ An English jury is traditionally composed of *all good men and true*. 英国の陪審は伝統的にすべて立派な人々で構成されている.

(as) true as steel [flint, touch] 非常に忠実な, あくまで誠実[真実]で ▪ His wife was *as true as steel*. 彼の妻は非常に操の堅い女であった ▪ He is *as true as steel* to his word. 彼は約束はあくまで守る.

breed true 《生物》正しく祖先の型を伝える ▪ The Spanish breed has long been known to *breed true*. スペイン種はだいぶ前から正しく祖先の型を伝えるものと知られてきた.

come true **1** (予言などが)適中する, 当たる ▪ His prediction has *come true*. 彼の予言は適中した.
2 =breed TRUE.

hold true **1** 有効である, 当てはまる ▪ The logic will *hold true* of him. この理屈は彼にも当てはまる.
2 真である, 本当で通る ▪ It does not always *hold true*. それは必ずしも真ではない.

in [out of] (the) true 正確[不正確]で; きちんとして[しないで] ▪ The door is *out of true*. ドアは少し狂っている.

it is true/true (it is) いかにも, 確かに《後に but を伴って; 譲歩を表して》 ▪ *It is true*, he is young, but he is wise. なるほど彼は若いが賢明だ.

it just isn't true 《口》〚前文を強調して〛本当だ ▪ I'm so happy, *it just isn't true*! とてもうれしい, 本当だぜ.

keep true 忠節を守る ▪ The Forty-seven *kept true*. 四十七士は忠節を守った.

prove true 本当だと判明する, 当たる ▪ The report *proved true*. 報告は本当だった.

ring true →RING[3].

run true to form →FORM[1].

show** one's **(true) colors →COLOR.

tell [speak, say] true 正直に言う, 本当のことを言う ▪ *Tell* me *true*. 正直に言ってごらん ▪ He knows that she *says true*. 彼は彼女が本当のことを言っていると分かっている.

There's many a true word spoken in jest. 《諺》冗談で言ったことが本当になることが多い,「嘘から出たまこと」.

Too true! 《口》その通り ▪ Elvis is great.—*Too true*. エルビスは最高だ—その通りだ.

true enough 《口》確かに ▪ She is a nice girl, *true enough*. 彼女は確かにいい娘だ.

true it is →it is TRUE.

true of …について本当で[当てはまって] ▪ And what is *true of* individuals is equally *true of* nations. そして個人に当てはまることは国家についても当てはまる.

true to **1** …に一致して, 違わず, 忠実で ▪ His representation of the bird is *true to* nature. 彼によるその鳥の描写は真に迫っている ▪ The translation was nicely *true to* the original. その翻訳は厳格に原文に忠実であった.
2 (友・主義・約束など)に誠実な, そむかない ▪ He was *true to* his word. 彼は自分の約束にそむかなかった ▪ I will be *true to* you. あなたに誠意を尽くします.

true to form →FORM[1].

true to life (話・劇が)真に迫った, (絵が)本物にそっくりの ▪ This portrait of him is very *true to life*. 彼のこの肖像画は本人に生き写しだ ▪ This story is *true to life* because these things actually can happen. この物語はまるで実話だ. こういったことは現実に起こることがあるから.

true to type **1** 〚副詞的に〛例のごとく, 予想通り (= true to FORM) ▪ *True to type*, he died while working at his desk. 案の定彼は執務中に死亡した ▪ The team's winning *was true to type*. そのチームの勝利は予想通りだった.
2 〚形容詞的に〛型通りの, 典型的な; 純(血)種の

T

▪ We are striving to breed *true to type* Siberians. 純種のシベリアン・ハスキーのブリーディングに励んでいる.

truly /trúːli/ 副 ***yours truly*** 敬具《手紙の結句》;《戯言》小生 (myself) ▪ *Yours truly*, A. De Morgan. 敬具, A. ドモーガン ▪ Give the young one a glass, and score it up to *yours truly*. あの若い衆に1杯飲ませて, 勘定は私につけておいてくれ.

trump /trʌmp/ 名 ***come up trumps*** **1** 気前のいいところを見せて人を驚かす ▪ He *came up trumps* and paid for our drinks. 彼は気前のいいところを見せて我々の酒代を払ってくれた.

2 =turn up TRUMPs 1.

go trumps (on) (…よりも)強い切り札を出す; (…を)しのぐ ▪ *Go trumps on* others by this method. この方法で他をしのぎなさい.

hold (all the) trumps まだ切り札を持っている; 奥の手がある ▪ You never *hold trumps*, you know. 君は切り札なんてないんだよ ▪ He *holds all the trumps* in the race. そのレースでは彼が断然有利だ.

play *one's* ***trump card/ play*** *one's* ***last trump*** 切り札[奥の手]を出す ▪ He had still *his trump card* to *play*. 彼にはまだ切り札があった.

put *a person* ***to*** *his* ***trump(s)*** 人を最後の切り札を出す立場に追い込む; 人を策に窮させる ▪ We *are* now *put to our* last *trump*. 我々はもう最後の手段を取るはめになった ▪ The strangeness of her dress *put* me *to my trumps*. 彼女の服があまり奇妙なのでほとほと困ってしまった.

turn up [out] trumps 《口》 **1** 上首尾にいく ▪ There are instances of speedy marriages which have *turned up trumps* after all. 早まった結婚で結局上首尾にいった例もいくつかある.

2 非常に役に立つ ▪ We couldn't have got married if John's uncle hadn't *turned up trumps*. ジョンのおじさんが奔走してくれなかったら私たちは結婚できなかっただろう. ☞早めに勝ち札を拾うことから.

trumpet /trʌ́mpət/ 名 ***blow*** *one's* ***own trumpet*** 自画自賛する ▪ He is not liked by anyone as he *blows his own trumpet*. 彼は手前みそを並べるので誰にも好かれない.

trumpeter /trʌ́mpətər/ 名 ***be*** *one's* ***own trumpeter*** =blow one's own TRUMPET.

Your trumpeter's dead! 《俗》怪しいもんだぞ《人がほらを吹くときに言い返す》 ▪ I shouldn't like to call you a liar, but certainly *your trumpeter's dead!* 君を嘘つきとは言いたくないが, 確かに怪しいもんだ.

trunk /trʌŋk/ 名 ***live in*** *one's* ***trunks*** 旅装を解けずにいる ▪ I have been *living in my trunks* for the past six days of the voyage. 私はここ6日間の航海の間旅装を解けずにいる.

trust[1] /trʌst/ 名 ***have trust in*** …を信用している ▪ He *has* perfect *trust in* me. 彼は私をすっかり信用している.

hold ... in trust …を保管している ▪ I am *holding* the property *in trust* for my niece. 私はその財産をめいのため保管しています.

in trust 委託して[されて] ▪ Put your money *in trust*. 金を預けなさい.

in *a person's* ***trust/in the trust of*** …に預けられて ▪ Our dog is left *in the trust of* a neighbour. うちの犬は近所の人に預かってもらっている.

on trust 信用で, 掛けで ▪ He lived *on trust* at an ale-house. 彼はある酒屋で掛けで暮らしていた.

put [place, repose] (*one's* ***) trust in*** …を信用する ▪ Don't *put trust in* money. 金を信用するな.

take ... on [upon] trust …を人の言うがままに信じる ▪ He *takes* things *on trust*. 彼は物事を人の言うがままに信じる.

to *a person's* ***trust*** 人に託して ▪ I should never have committed such letters *to his trust*. そんな手紙を彼に託すべきではなかった.

trust[2] /trʌst/ 動 ***not trust*** *a person* ***an inch [as far as*** *one* ***could throw*** *him***]** 《口》人を少しも信用しない ▪ I would*n't trust* him *as far as* I *could throw* him. 彼を少しも信用しないね.

trust *a person* ***to*** *do* 安心して人に…させられる ▪ *Trust* him *to* do the work well. 大丈夫, 彼ならその仕事を立派にやってのけるさ.

truth /truːθ/ 名 ***a home truth*** 胸にこたえる事実, 知られたくない(不快な)事実; 相手を傷つける申し立て ▪ You need to be told a few *home truths*, whether you like it or not. 君が何と言おうと, いやなことだが少々耳に入れておかなくてはならないんだ ▪ The problem of youth unemployment has become *a home truth*. 若者が職に就けないという問題は確たる事実となっている.

be economical with the truth →ECONOMICAL.

bend the truth (都合のよいように)事実[真実]を曲げる ▪ Is it acceptable to "*bend the truth*" about yourself in order to secure a job? 職に就くために自分に関する「事実を曲げて」も許されるのだろうか.

Half the truth is often a whole [great] lie. 《諺》真実の半分だけを語るのはしばしば大嘘をつくのに等しい.

if (the) truth be known [told] 本当のことを言うと ▪ Nobody likes him. In fact, *if the truth be told*, everyone is rather afraid of him. みな彼がきらいだ. つまり, 実を言うとみな彼を怖がっているんだ.

in truth 実は; 本当に, 実際に《通例陳述を強める》 ▪ But *in truth* they ought only to blame themselves. しかし実は彼らは自分たちだけを責めるべきなのだ.

Isn't it the truth! 《米》全くね ▪ It seems to rain every Sunday.—*Isn't it the truth!* 日曜にはいつも雨が降るようだね—全くね.

out of truth 調子が狂って ▪ The door is *out of truth*. ドアは調子が狂っている.

tell [say, speak] the truth 本当のことを言う ▪ It pays to *tell the truth*. 真実を語って損はない.

tell the truth and shame the devil →

SHAME².

the bald truth 偽らざる真相，ありのままの状態 ▪It is *the bald truth* that he cheated on his taxes. 彼が脱税したというのは偽らざる真相である.

The greater the truth, the greater the libel. 《諺》誹毀したことが事実であればあるほどその誹毀は大きくなる.

the truth is (***that***) 実は…である ▪*The truth is*, I forgot it. 実は忘れたのです.

the truth, the whole truth, and nothing but the truth 全く嘘偽りのない真実 ▪Do you promise to tell *the truth, the whole truth, and nothing but the truth*? 全く嘘偽りのない真実だけを述べると約束するかね? ☞法廷で宣誓するときの決まり文句から.

the unvarnished truth ありのままの真実 ▪We must have *the unvarnished truth* about our sales. わが社の販売取引の実態をつかまねばならない.

there is (***some***) ***truth in*** …には(いくぶんか)道理がある ▪*There is some truth in* what you say. 君の言うことにもいくぶん道理がある.

to tell (***you***) ***the truth/truth to tell*** 実を言えば ▪*To tell the truth*, I forgot all about your request. 実を言えば君の頼みはすっかり忘れていた.

Truth is stranger than fiction. →Fact is stranger than FICTION.

Truth will out. 《諺》真実はいつかあらわれる.

try¹ /traɪ/ 名 ***a try-out*** [***tryout***] (選手・俳優などの)適性検査，トライアウト，オーディション ▪I went to the *try-outs* for the basketball team yesterday. きのうバスケチームの新人テストを受けに行った.

give *a person* ***a try*** 《口》人を試しに使ってみる ▪I'll *give* him *a try*. 彼を試みに使ってみよう.

give it a try 試してみる; 使ってみる ▪Let me *give it a try*. ひとつ僕がやってみよう ▪How about this drink? *Give it a try*. この酒はどうだ. 試しに飲んでみろ.

have a try at [***for***] 《口》…をやってみる ▪Let's *have a try at* it. それをひとつやってみようじゃないか.

worth a try 試してみる価値がある ▪This plan seems *worth a try*. この計画は試してみる値打ちがありそうだ.

try² /traɪ/ 動 ***be tried and found wanting*** →be weighed and found WANTING.

Do try more. さあもっといかが《物を勧めて》.

not for lack [***want***] ***of trying*** →not for WANT of trying.

try a door [***window***] ドア[窓]の締まりを調べてみる ▪He *tried* all the *doors and windows* before going to bed. 彼は寝る前にすべてのドアと窓の締まりを調べてみた.

try and *do* 《口》…するように努める ▪I'll *try and* come tomorrow. あす来るようにしましょう.

try anything once 何でも一度はやってみる ▪I will *try anything once* except murder. 僕は人殺しのほかは何でも一度はやってみたい.

try as *one* ***may*** どんなに努力しても ▪He could not pass the examination, *try as* he *might*. 彼はどんなに努力してもその試験に通らなかった.

try *one's* ***best*** [***hardest***] 全力を尽くす ▪I *tried my hardest* to save him. 彼を救うために全力を尽くした ▪I will *try my best*. 全力を尽くしてやってみましょう.

try *one's* ***hand*** (***at***) →HAND¹.

try it on 《俗》 **1** (…を)ぺてんにかける，かつごうとする (*with*) ▪No use to *try it on with* me. 僕をかつごうたってむだだよ.

2 (わざと)ずうずうしく[反抗的に]ふるまう ▪A teacher should punish his pupils as soon as they start *trying it on*. 教師は生徒が反抗的なふるまいをしたらすぐ罰しなければならない.

try it on the dog 食物を犬に食べさせてみる《毒味させる》; 《劇》新しい劇を地方[マチネ]で打って様子を見る ▪Arrangements have been made to *try it on the dog*. 新しい劇を地方で打って様子を見る手筈が整った.

tryst /trɪst/ 名 ***break*** [***keep, make***] ***tryst*** 《雅》(特に恋人同士が)会合の約束を破る[守る，する] ▪He *made tryst* with her. 彼は彼女と逢い引きの約束をした.

tub /tʌb/ 名 ***a tale of a tub*** →TALE.

a tub of lard [***guts***] 《口・軽蔑》でぶ，太っちょ ▪I don't like *that tub of lard*. あんな太っちょ，きらい《しばしば子供が使う》.

Every tub must [***Let every tub***] ***stand on its own bottom.*** 《諺》何びとも自己を頼まねばならない.

throw out a tub to the whale (差し迫った危険を逃れるため)相手の気をそらせようとする ▪He *throws out a tub to the* High Church *whale*. 彼は高教会派の気をそらせようとする. ☞クジラに出会ったとき，船を転覆させられないように水夫がおけを投げてクジラの気をそらせたことから.

thump the tub 《英》強烈に支持する ▪The advocates of nuclear nonproliferation are *thumping the tub* for the Prime Minister. 核兵器拡散防止の主導者たちは首相を強力に支持している.

tube /tjuːb/ 名 ***go down the tube***(***s***) 《口》(会社・計画・制度などが)だめになる，成り立たない ▪Our company *went down the tube*. わが社は倒産した.

tuck¹ /tʌk/ 名 ***a tuck shop*** (校内・学校近くの)学童相手の小さな売店[菓子屋] ▪There used to be *a tuck shop* around here. 昔このあたりにお菓子屋さんがあったんだよ.

make [***put, take up***] ***a tuck in*** (服)に縫い上げをする ▪She *made a tuck in* the sleeves. 彼女はそでに縫い上げをした.

tuck² /tʌk/ 動 ***be tucked away*** (建物などが)人里離れたところに静かに建っている ▪The cabin *was tucked away* in the woods. その小屋は森の中にひっそりと立っていた.

tuck *one's* ***tail*** 恥をかく ▪He hated to *tuck his tail* now. 彼はもう恥をかくのはいやだった.

tuck *oneself* ***up*** (居心地よく)くるまる ▪He

tucked himself up in bed. 彼はベッドで毛布にくるまった.

tucker[1] /tʌ́kər/ 名 (***as***) ***mad as tucker***《米口》非常に怒って ▪ Bill got *mad as tucker* when he heard it. ビルはそれを聞くとかんかんに怒った.

one's ***best bib and tucker*** →BIB.

tucker[2] /tʌ́kər/ 動 ***be tuckered out***《米口》へとへとに疲れる ▪ I can't go any further. I'*m tuckered out*. これ以上歩けない. へとへとだ.

tug[1] /tʌg/ 名 ***a tug of love***《英口》親権争い ▪ There was *a tug of love* about a girl between the warring couple. そのいがみ合っている夫婦間には一人の女の子をめぐる親権争いがあった.

be [***feel***] ***a tug at*** *one's* ***heartstrings*** 後ろ髪を引かれる思いである ▪ Parting from his family *was a tug at his heartstrings*. 彼には家族の者と別れるのは後ろ髪を引かれる思いであった.

feel a great tug 非常につらい ▪ We *felt a great tug* at parting. 別れがひどくつらかった.

give a tug at ...をぐいと引く ▪ He *gave a tug at* the cord. 彼は綱をぐいと引っぱった.

have a great tug 大骨を折る ▪ I *had a great tug* to persuade him. 彼を説得するのに大骨を折った.

the tug of war **1** 決戦 ▪ When Greeks joined Greeks, then was *the tug of war*. 両雄相会すと決戦が起こった.

2 綱引き ▪ *The tug of war* was the most popular item in Saturday's entertainment. 綱引きが土曜日の娯楽の一番人気のある種目だった.

tug[2] /tʌg/ 動 ***tug at*** *a person's* ***heartstrings*** →HEARTSTRINGS.

tug at the [***an***] ***oar*** ガリー船の奴隷としてこぐ; 絶え間なく働く, あくせく働く ▪ It kept him *tugging* away *at the oar*. そのため彼は絶え間なく働き続けねばならなかった.

tumble[1] /tʌ́mbəl/ 名 (***all***) ***in a tumble*** ごちゃごちゃになって ▪ Things are *all in a tumble*. 何もかもごっちゃになっている.

have a tumble ころぶ ▪ He *had a* slight [nasty] *tumble*. 彼はちょっと[ひどく]ころんだ.

take a tumble **1** =have a TUMBLE.

2 (価値・影響力などが)急に下落[低下]する ▪ Dividends *took a* bad *tumble*. 配当が急下落した.

3《米俗》賢くなる, 行いを改める (*to*) ▪ Why don't you *take a tumble to* yourself? 君はなぜ賢くなれないのかね ▪ We had to *take a tumble*. 僕たちは行いを改めねばならなかった.

tumble[2] /tʌ́mbəl/ 動 ***toss and tumble*** のたうち回る ▪ The sick child *tossed and tumbled* in his bed. 病気の子供はベッドの中をのたうち回った.

tumble home (舷側が)内側に傾斜する《比喩的にも》 ▪ The old man's mouth *is tumbled home*. 老人の口は内側へ曲がっている.

tumble to pieces 倒れてばらばらになる ▪ The building is *tumbling to pieces*. その建物は倒れてばらばらになりかけている.

tune[1] /tjuːn, tʃuːn/ 名 ***call the*** [*one's* ***own***] ***tune*** 自分の思う通りの指図をする (→pay the PIPER) ▪ He insists on *calling the tune*. 彼は自分の思う通りの指図をすると言い張っている.

can't carry a tune (***in a bushel basket*** [***in a bucket, in a paper sack***]) 音楽の才能がまるでない ▪ He *can't carry a tune* and his singing is a pain to listen to. 彼は音痴なので歌うのを聞くのは苦痛だ.

change *one's* ***tune/sing another*** [***a different***] ***tune/sing a new tune/whistle a different tune*** (特に, いばった態度から謙遜に)調子を変える, 話しぶりを変える ▪ When he hears that his partner has been arrested, he'll *sing a different tune*. 相棒が捕まったと聞けば, 彼は態度を変えるだろう.

dance to a different tune →DANCE[2].

dance to *a person's* ***tune*** 人のいいなりになる ▪ He made the villagers *dance to his tune* without their knowledge. 彼は村人たちをこっそり自分のいいなりになるように仕向けた.

in [***out of***] ***tune*** 調子が合って[はずれて]; 調子よく[悪く]; 和合して[せずに] (*with*) ▪ My voice is harsh here, not *in tune*. 私の声はここで耳ざわりになって, 調子が合っていない ▪ This piano is *out of tune*. このピアノは調子が狂っている ▪ Her mind was not quite *in tune with* the profundities of that journal. 彼女の頭はどうもその雑誌の深遠な記事と噛み合わなかった.

sing another [***a different***] ***tune*** → change one's TUNE.

the tune the (***old***) ***cow died of***《戯》不快音の連続, 恐ろしく退屈な音楽 ▪ It was just *the tune the old cow died of* throughout. それは終始恐ろしく退屈な音楽だった.

to some [***every***] ***tune*** 相当に[ひどく] ▪ The news surprised him *to some tune*. その知らせは彼を相当びっくりさせた ▪ They have been whipped *to every tune*. 彼らはひどくむち打たれた.

to the tune of《口》大枚...も ▪ I had demands on me yesterday *to the tune of* £300. きのう大枚300ポンドも請求された.

tune[2] /tjuːn, tʃuːn/ 動 ***be tuned into*** ...に理解を示す, がわかっている ▪ I felt stiff and lethargic, and my mind *was*n't *tuned into* the job. 体はこわばり, けだるかったし, 頭は仕事のことがわかっていなかった.

tunnel /tʌ́nəl/ 動 ***tunnel*** *one's* ***way*** トンネルを掘って進む ▪ The stream *tunnels its way* out near there. その小川はその近くから湧き出ている.

tuppence /tʌ́pəns/ 名 ***not care*** [***give***] ***tuppence*** (***for, about***)《英口》(...のことを)少しもかまわない, 気にしない (→care TWOPENCE) ▪ Do whatever you like. I do*n't care tuppence*. 何でも好きなことをしていいよ. こっちは一向にかまわないから ▪ He did*n't give tuppence for* my feelings or what I wanted. 彼は私の感情も要望もおかまいなしだっ

た.

turf[1] /tə:rf/ 名 ***on the turf*** **1** 競馬が商売で ▪ We are all of us *on the turf.* 我々はみな競馬が商売だ.
2《米俗》売春をして ▪ During her early years *on the turf,* Kate was thrifty. 売春をしていた若いころはケイトはつましかった.

turf[2] /tə:rf/ 動 ***turf it*** 死んで埋葬される ▪ He has *turfed it* at last. 彼はついに死んで埋葬された.

Turk /tə:rk/ 名 ***a young [little] Turk*** 手に負えない腕白小僧 ▪ You are indeed *a young Turk.* お前はほんとに手に負えない小僧だ.

like a Turk =like a TROJAN.

turn [become] Turk (トルコ皇帝支配下で)イスラム教徒になる ▪ He offered to *turn Turk* if they would spare him. 彼は命を助けてくれるならムスリムになろうと言った.

turkey /tə́:rki/ 名 ***a turkey shoot*** たやすいこと, 楽勝《実力の差が歴然で一方には楽勝, 他方には勝ち目のない状態》 ▪ That's not difficult, but not *a turkey shoot* either. それは難しくはないけれど, 簡単なことでもない.

(as) proud as a lame turkey《米口》大変謙遜で ▪ The creature got *as proud as a lame turkey.* そいつはひどく謙遜になった.

(as) red as a turkey-cock (怒り・恥ずかしさで)顔が火のように赤くなって ▪ He turned *as red as a turkey-cock* with rage. 彼は怒りで顔が火のように赤くなった.

be like turkeys voting for Christmas 自滅するようなものである, 明らかに不利である ▪ If you go on doing nothing, it'll *be like turkeys voting for Christmas.* 手をこまねいていては自滅するようなものだ.

cold turkey《俗》突然に, いきなり ▪ He gave up his drinking habit *cold turkey.* 彼は飲酒癖をスパッとやめた.

go cold turkey/do a cold turkey《口》麻薬[酒, タバコ]をきっぱりと[ひと思いに]断つ ▪ I had to stop smoking, so I *went cold turkey.* 禁煙しなくてはならなかったので, ひと思いにやめた.

not say (pea-)turkey《米口》一言も言わない (*about*) ▪ She *never said pea-turkey about* it. 彼女はそのことについては一言も言わなかった.

say turkey《米口》あいそのいいことを言う (*to*) ▪ You never once *said turkey to* me. あなたは一度も私にあいそのいいことを言ったことはない.

say turkey to *A* ***and buzzard to*** *B*《米口》BよりもAに利点を与える ▪ Why do they insist on *saying turkey to* the Canadians *and buzzard to* the Americans? なぜ彼らはアメリカ人よりもカナダ人に利点を与えることを主張するのか.

talk cold turkey《米俗》(いやなことなどを)率直に[ずけずけ]話す ▪ She *talked cold turkey* about sex. 彼女は性についてずけずけ話した.

talk turkey《米口》 **1** あいそのいいことを言う ▪ I was very apt to *talk turkey.* 私はあいそのいいことを非常に言いがちだった.
2 =talk cold TURKEY.

turkey's nests [dust bunnies, dust kittens] 綿ぼこり, 綿ごみの塊り, 綿毛の玉 ▪ He hasn't cleaned in weeks. There are *turkey's nests* in every corner. 彼は何週間も掃除をしていない. 部屋の四隅に綿ごみがたまっている.

walk turkey《米口》(船が)縦横に揺れる ▪ The north wind commenced to make the ship *walk turkey.* 北風で船は縦横に揺れ始めた.

turmoil /tə́:rmɔɪl/ 名 ***be in turmoil*** (心配で)動揺[おろおろ]している ▪ Her only son has met with a car accident and her mind *is in turmoil.* 一人息子が交通事故にあって, 彼女はおろおろしている.

turn[1] /tə:rn/ 名 ***a bad [evil, ill] turn*** 不親切, 非道な仕うち ▪ I did the lass *a bad turn* when I took her away. あの娘を連れ去ったのはひどい仕うちをしたわけだった.

a good turn 親切 (→One good TURN deserves another.) ▪ He did me *a good turn.* 彼は私に親切にしてくれた.

a turn of events (意外な)事件の成り行き ▪ He thought it *a* strange *turn of events.* 彼はそれを不思議な事の成り行きだと思った.

a turn of phrase 言い回し ▪ It was *a* very expressive *turn of phrase.* それはとても表現力のある言い回しだった.

a turn of speed 急に速度を上げること; スピードを出す力 ▪ I put on *a turn of speed* and grabbed him. 私は急に速度を上げて彼をつかまえた ▪ The car showed *a* remarkable *turn of speed.* 車はすばらしいスピード力を発揮した.

a turn of the screw →SCREW[1].

at every turn 絶えず; どこでも ▪ He says such uncouth things *at every turn.* 彼は絶えずそんな野暮なことを口にする ▪ Such a castle meets us *at every turn.* そんな城にはどこでもお目にかかる.

by the [a] turn of a hair 危機一髪のところで ▪ He missed the approaching car *by a turn of a hair.* 彼は近づいて来る車を危機一髪のところで逃れた.

by turns 代わり番に, かわるがわる ▪ They slept only *by turns* in order to guard against wild beasts. 彼らは野獣を警戒するため代わり番にしか眠らなかった ▪ He became pale and red *by turns.* 彼は青くなったり赤くなったりした.

call the turn →CALL[2].

do a good turn to/do *a person* ***a good turn*** 人に親切にする, 人を助ける ▪ The new doctor *does* the poor people *a good turn* by treating them free. 今度来た医師は貧しい人たちを無料で診察して彼らを援助する.

full of turns and twists ひどく曲がりくねって; 曲折が多く ▪ His life was *full of turns and twists.* 彼の人生は曲折が多かった.

get a turn《口》ぎょっとする ▪ I *got* quite *a turn* when I saw her standing there so quiet. 彼女がそこにじっと立っているのを見たとき全くぎょっとした.

give a turn **1**《口》(人を)ぎょっとさせる ▪ It was

only a dream; but it *gave* me *a* terrible *turn*. 夢にすぎなかったが, 私はひどくぎょっとした.
2 (猟犬が野ウサギを)急に曲がって反対の方へ逃げさせる ▪ At last the greyhound *gave* her *a turn*. とうとう猟犬はそのウサギに急に曲がって反対の方へ逃げられた.
3 ひねった解釈をする ▪ Do not *give* so cruel *a turn* to my silence. 私が黙っているのをそんなに残酷にひねって取らないでください.
4 (ねじを)回す ▪ *Give another turn* to the screw. ねじをもう一度回せ.

have a turn 《口》 **1** (急に)気分が悪くなる ▪ I've just *had a* nasty *turn*. さっきからひどく気分が悪い.
2 ＝get a TURN.

in turn **1** かわるがわる, 順番に (＝by TURNs) ▪ The daughters *in turn* rode on pillionseat. 娘たちはかわるがわるバイクの後部座席に乗った.
2 たち代わって, 今度は自分が, 次には ▪ He that shuts love out, *in turn* shall be shut out from love. 愛情を締め出す者は次は愛情から締め出される.

in* one's *turn **1** 番[順番]に当たって ▪ They all spoke, each *in his turn*. 彼らはそれぞれ順に当たって話した.
2 たち代わって, 今度は自分が ▪ Germany became *in its turn* the instructress of the neighboring tribes. 今度はドイツが近隣の諸族の指導者となった.

in turns かわるがわる ▪ The students would do it *in turns*. 生徒たちはかわるがわるそれをやるのだった.

on the turn **1** 変わり目で, (特に)好転して ▪ Our fortune is *on the turn*. 私たちの運命が変わろうとしている.
2 (食物が)酸敗しかけて; (天候・季節が)変わりかけて ▪ The milk is *on the turn*. この牛乳は腐りかけている ▪ The weather was *on the turn*. 天候が変わりかけていた.

One good turn deserves another. 《諺》 善行を施せば他人からも善行を施される, 「情けは他人(ひと)のためならず」.

out of* (one's) *turn **1** 順番をちがえて ▪ You must not play *out of turn*. 演技の順番をちがえてはいけない.
2 場所柄をわきまえずに, 軽率に ▪ I thought she was laughing *out of turn*. 彼女は場所柄をわきまえず笑っていると私は思った.

serve* one's (*own*) *turn*/*serve a turn (人が)自己の役に立てようとする, 自己のためを図る ▪ He caught hold of it to *serve his own turn*. 彼は自分の用に立てようとしてそれをつかんだ ▪ He is affecting zeal for religious liberty merely to *serve a turn*. 彼はただ自己のためを図って信教の自由への情熱があるように装っているのだ.

serve* a person's [*the*] *turn 人の役に立つ, 十分間に合う ▪ Nothing would *serve his turn* but tea. お茶でなければ彼には間に合わなかった ▪ A little yeast may *serve the turn*. イースト菌が少しあれば役に立つかもしれない.

serve* one's [*its*] *turn それなりに役に立つ ▪ This stove has *served its turn* well. このストーブはそれなりに役に立った.

speak out of* (one's) *turn → talk out of (one's) TURN.

take a favorable turn 好転する ▪ Foreign trade *took a favorable turn*. 外国貿易は好転した.

take a new turn 新たな転機を迎える ▪ Our company *took a new turn* under the new president. わが社は新社長のもと新たな転機を迎えた.

take a short turn 飛行機が急旋回する ▪ The plane *took a short turn* left to avoid some turbulence. 機は乱気流を避けるために左へ急旋回した.

take a turn **1** ちょっと散歩する ▪ He *took a turn* in the garden. 彼は庭をちょっと散歩した.
2 (…を)ひとしきりやる ▪ I'll *take a turn* at the oars now. 今度は僕がひとしきりこいであげよう.

***take a turn for the better* [*worse*]** (患者が)良い[悪い]方へ向かう ▪ The patient suddenly *took a turn for the worse*. 病人は急に容態が悪くなった.

take it in turn*(*s*) *to do 交替で…する ▪ They *took it in turns to* watch. 彼らは交替で見張った.

take* one's *turn 自分の番を勤める ▪ We *took our turn* at sitting up. 我々は番を決めて起きていた.

***take turns about* [*with*]** (物事)を輪番にする ▪ They *took turns about* cooking. 彼らは輪番で煮炊きした.

***take turns at* [*in, to* do]** …を交替でする ▪ We *took turns at* sleeping and watching. 我々は交替で眠ったり見張ったりした.

talk* [*speak*] *out of* (one's) *turn 軽率なことを言う ▪ You *spoke out of turn* in criticizing her modern furniture. 君が彼女のモダンな家具を批評したのは軽率なことを言ったことになる.

the turn of a hair 危機一髪 ▪ It was *the turn of a hair* that they didn't bury him alive. 彼らは危機一髪のところで彼を生き埋めにしないですんだ.

the turn of events →a TURN of events.

the turn of life (女性の)更年期 ▪ When menstruation is about to cease, the period is called "*the turn of life*." 月経が閉止しかける時期は「更年期」と呼ばれる.

to a turn ほどよく, 申し分なく(焼けて, できて) ▪ The beef was roasted *to a turn*. 牛肉はほどよく焼けていた ▪ The pie is done *to a turn*. パイは申し分なくできている. ☞焼きぐしを回すことから.

turn* (*and turn*) *about かわるがわる ▪ We took it *turn and turn about* to sit up and rock the baby. 我々はかわるがわる起き上がって赤んぼうをゆすってやった.

wait* one's *turn 自分の番を待つ ▪ I'm *waiting my turn* to speak. 私は自分が話す番を待っている.

with a round turn 急に, ぐっと ▪ It brought him up *with a round turn*. それは急に彼を止めた.

turn[2] /təːrn/ 動 ***as it turned out*** 結局のところ ▪ But *as it turned out* he was more prosperous than before. しかし結局のところ彼は以前よりも羽振りがよかった.

(be) turned of (何歳)の坂を越えて(いる) ▪ He *was turned of* seventy years. 彼は70歳の坂を越えていた.

not know which way [where] to turn どうしたらよいかわからない ▪ She did *not know which way to turn* to find means. 彼女は金を工面するためにどうしたらよいかわからなかった.

not turn a hair →HAIR.

Right [Left, Right about] turn! 《号令》右向け右[左向け左, 回れ右]!

turn about in *one's* ***mind*** 思いめぐらす ▪ *Turn* these ideas *about in your mind*. これらのことを心の中で思いめぐらすがいい.

turn and rend (友人を)さんざん罵倒する ▪ His adulators of yesterday are prepared to *turn and rend* him. きのう彼にお追従を言った人たちが今は彼をさんざんにこきおろそうとしている.

turn in on [upon] *oneself* 内向的になる, (国が)孤立主義的になる ▪ Are Americans *turning in upon themselves*? アメリカ人は孤立主義的になっているのだろうか.

turn inside out **1** 裏返しにする[なる] ▪ The wind *turned* my umbrella *inside out*. 風で傘がおちょこになった.

2 (場所)をひっかき回して捜す ▪ I *turned* my desk *inside out* looking for a paper. 机をひっかき回してある書類を捜した.

3 大きな変化をもたらす, 混乱させる ▪ The earthquake *turned* my viewpoint *inside out*. 地震で私のものの見方は大きく変わった.

turn *oneself* ***inside out*** 精いっぱい努力する ▪ I've *turned myself inside out* to do them favors. 私は彼らに便宜を与えるために精いっぱい努力した.

turn it in 《口》(おしゃべりなどうるさいことを)やめる ▪ *Turn it in*, John. ジョン, そんなことおよしよ.

turn it up **1** 《口》仕事をやめる ▪ I'll *turn it* all *up*. 僕は仕事をすっかりやめてしまおう.

2 =TURN it in.

turn left 左に曲がる, 左折する ▪ *Turn left* at the next corner. 次の角で左折しなさい.

turn loose →LOOSE[1].

turn on the waterworks →WATERWORKS.

turn out well 出世する ▪ He's a diligent boy, and ought to *turn out well*. 彼は勤勉な少年だから出世するはずだ.

turn right 右に曲がる, 右折する ▪ *Turn right* at the next crossing. 次の十字路で右折しなさい.

turn round and *do* 《口》驚いた[あきれた]ことに…する ▪ The owner *turned round and* said, "I won't sell you the house." 驚いたことに所有者は「あなたにその家は売らない」と言った.

turn the balance [beam, scale] **1** (…の)重さがある (*at*) ▪ He *turns the scale at* 16 stone. 彼は体重が16ストーン[約102キロ]ある.

2 天びんの一方を下がらせる; 事を決定する ▪ A straw will often suffice to *turn the balance*. わら1本でも天びんの一方を下がらせるのに十分の場合がよくある ▪ His casting vote would *turn the scale*. 彼の決定投票で事が決まるだろう.

turn the edge of …の刃がまくれる, の刃をなまくらにする《比喩的にも》 ▪ It *turns the edge of* their knives. そのため彼らのナイフの刃がなまくらになる ▪ It was a difficulty sufficient to *turn the edge of* the finest wit. それは最もすぐれた才知の刃をもなまくらにするほどの難問であった.

turn the milk (sour) (雷・あらしで)牛乳が酸敗する《迷信》 ▪ The storm *turned the milk (sour)*. あらしで牛乳が腐った.

turn up like a bad penny →PENNY.

turn (up) *one's* ***toes to the daisies*** →DAISY.

turn ... upside(-)down →UPSIDE(-)DOWN.

Whatever turns you on! 《俗》てんで興味ないね え, 何がおもしろいのかねえ ▪ Some people truly enjoy gambling. Great! *Whatever turns you on*. ギャンブルが楽しくて仕方ないやつもいるが, 結構なことだ. 好きにすれば.

turning /tə́ːrnɪŋ/ 名 ***It's a long lane [road] that has [knows] no turning.*** 《諺》曲がり角のない道はない, 「待てば海路(かいろ)の日よりあり」《不幸・災いはいつまでも続かない》.

turn-out /tə́ːrnàʊt/ 名 ***tea and turn-out*** 茶とそれに添えた食物 ▪ They only gave *tea and turn-out*. 彼らは茶と茶請けしか出さなかった.

turn-up /tə́ːrnʌ̀p/ 名 ***a turn-up for the book(s)*** 《英》全く予期せぬこと, 突然のびっくりする出来事 ▪ What *a turn-up for the book*! I won in the lottery. なんとびっくり! 宝くじに当ったんだ ▪ An alcoholic coming home sober would be *a turn up for the books*. アルコール中毒者がしらふで帰宅したりすれば驚きだ. ☞競馬において, 思いがけない馬が優勝するとか, 本命馬がふるわなかったりするような場合に使われた.

turpentine /tə́ːrpəntàɪn/ 名 ***talk turpentine*** 《口》絵画を論じる ▪ Everybody here *talked turpentine*. 当地の人が残らず絵画を論じた. ☞turpentine「油絵に使うテレビン油」.

turtle /tə́ːrtəl/ 名 ***turn turtle*** **1** ウミガメをひっくり返して捕える ▪ *Turtle were turned* in considerable numbers. ウミガメがかなりたくさんひっくり返して捕えられた.

2 (ボート・自動車などが)転覆[逆転]する ▪ Two trucks had *turned turtle* on the embankment. トラックが2台堤防の上でひっくり返っていた ▪ The airplane *turned turtle*. その飛行機は逆さまになった.

tutor /tjúːtər/ 動 ***tutor*** *oneself* 自己を鍛える ▪ You must *tutor yourself* to be patient. 辛抱強くなるように自己を鍛えなくてはだめだ.

twain /tweɪn/ 名 ***in twain*** =in TWO.

never the twain shall meet 両者はあまりに違っていて共存できない, 水と油だ ▪ East is East, and West is West, and *never the twain shall meet*. 東は東, 西は西で, 両者は決して共存できるものではない.

tweedledum /twìːdəldʌ́m/ 名 ***tweedledum***

and tweedledee 似たり寄ったりの二つのもの ▪ By no effort of the mind can we separate *tweedledum and tweedledee.* どんなに頭を働かしてもうり二つのものを区別することはできない. ☞「互いに競う二人の楽人」の意から.

twelve /twelv/ 名 ***in twelves*** 12折りの[に] ▪ The second edition of The "Vicar of Wakefield" was published in two volumes *in twelves.* 「ウェイクフィールドの副牧師」の再版は12折りの2冊本の形で出版された.

strike twelve the first time [***all at once***] 最初から[たちまち]ありったけの才能をさらけ出してしまう ▪ They did not *strike twelve the first time.* 彼らは最初からありったけの芸をさらけ出しはしなかった ▪ There are some writers who *strike twelve all at once.* たちまちありったけの才能をさらけ出してしまう作家もある.

twenty /twénti/ 形名 ***a 21st-birthday party*** 21歳の誕生日の祝い《伝統的な成人祝賀パーティー》 ▪ Her parents and her brother celebrated *a 21st-birthday party.* 彼女の21歳の誕生日を両親と弟が祝った. ☞現在では法規上は18歳で成人となるが依然としてしきたりとして行われている.

a twenty-four seven/a 24-7 週7日24時間営業[無休]の店[レストラン] ▪ Why can't there be more *24-7s*? They're such a good idea. 年中無休24時間営業の店がもっとあったらいいのだが. 実に素敵な思いつきなのに ▪ We are *a twenty-four seven* store. うちの店は24時間営業です.

in *one's* ***twenties*** 20代に[で] ▪ He is *in his* late [early] *twenties.* 彼は20代の末[初め]だ.

like twenty 《米口》ひどく, 甚だしく ▪ She kicked *like twenty.* 彼女はひどく足をばたつかせた.

the Roaring Twenties 狂騒の1920年代《第一次世界大戦直後の若者と女性が自由を謳歌した時代》 ▪ In *the Roaring Twenties,* women bared their knees for joy. 狂騒の20年代に女性は戯れにひざ小僧を露わにした.

twenty and twenty 多数の ▪ I talked of *twenty and twenty* fond things. 私はかずかずのむだ話をした.

twice /twaɪs/ 副名 ***a twice-told tale*** 二度繰り返された[陳腐]な話 (cf. Sh., *John* 3. 4. 108) ▪ It was *a twice-told tale,* but he embarked upon it without hesitation. それは陳腐な話だったが, 彼はちゅうちょなくそれを始めた.

at twice **1** 二度に ▪ Did Mr. Tulliver let you have the money all at once?—No, *at twice.* タリバー氏は一度に金をくれたか?—いや, 二度に分けたよ.
2 二度目に ▪ He succeeded *at twice.* 彼は二度目に成功した.

be twice the man [***woman***] (***that*** *a person* ***is***) 以前[他の人]より2倍も[ずっと]立派に[たくましく, 健康に]なっている ▪ He feels that he *is twice the man* he *used to be.* 彼は以前よりもずっと元気になったと感じている ▪ For your information, she's *twice the woman that* you *are*! 言っておくが, 彼女はお前よりもはるかに優れた女性なんだぞ ▪ My cousin *is twice the man* he *used to be.* 従弟は昔より倍も大人になっている.

in twice 《口》2回にわたって ▪ I did it *in twice.* それを2回にわたってした.

once or twice [***twice or thrice***] 1, 2回[2, 3回]《漠然と用いる》 ▪ He has caught me *twice or thrice.* 彼は2, 3度私をつかまえた ▪ He made me angry *once or twice.* 彼は1, 2回私を怒らせた.

think twice 再考する, 熟慮する (*about*) ▪ Do not *think twice about* it, but say "No." そのことを再考しないで,「ノー」と言いなさい.

twice as ... as ...の2倍も ▪ He is about *twice as* old *as* I am. 彼は私の倍も年をとっている.

twice over (1回でなく)2回 ▪ He said the word *twice over.* 彼はその言葉を2回言った.

twiddle /twídəl/ 動 ***twiddle*** *one's* ***thumbs*** [***fingers***] (手持ちぶさたに)指をひねり回す; ぶらぶらしている ▪ He *twiddled his thumbs* and looked down on the deck. 彼は指をひねり回し甲板に目を伏せた ▪ We didn't *twiddle our fingers* much that week. その週はあまりぶらぶらしなかった.

twig /twɪɡ/ 名 ***As the twig is bent, so is the tree inclined.*** 《諺》小枝が曲がると木も傾く.

hop the twig →HOP³.

work the twig 占い棒を使う ▪ The man sought for water *working the twig.* 男は占い棒を使って水を探した.

twilight /twáɪlàɪt/ 名 ***the twilight zone*** (境界がはっきりしない)中間的な領域 ▪ She's been unconscious, trapped in *the twilight zone* between life and death. 彼女はずっと意識が戻らず生死の間をさまよっている.

twinkle /twíŋkəl/ 名 ***a twinkle in*** *one's* ***eye*** →a gleam in one's EYE.

in a twinkle/in the twinkle of an eye 瞬く間に, たちまち ▪ I'll be with you *in a twinkle.* すぐごいっしょします ▪ *In the twinkle of an eye* we were rolling to Willis's. 瞬く間に我々はウィリスの家へ馬車で急いでいた.

when you were just [***no more than***] ***a twinkle in your father's eye*** 《口・戯》君が生まれる以前から ▪ I was a writer *when you were just a twinkle in your father's eye.* 私は君が生まれる以前から作家だった.

twinkling /twíŋklɪŋ/ 名 ***in a twinkling/in the twinkling of an eye*** [***a bedpost, a bedstaff***] 瞬く間に, たちまち (《聖》*1 Cor.* 15. 52) ▪ The liquor was out of sight *in a twinkling.* 酒は瞬く間に見えなくなった.

twirl /twəːrl/ 動 ***twirl ... round*** *one's* ***finger*** →twist ... round one's (little) FINGER.

twirl *one's* ***thumbs*** (手持ちぶさたに)指をひねり回す (→TWIDDLE one's thumbs) ▪ Anything is better than sitting *twirling your thumbs* like a fool. ぼんやり座って指をひねり回しているよりはどんなことだってましだよ.

twist[1] /twɪst/ 名 ***a twist in one's tongue*** 舌もつれ ▪I have *a* small *twist in my tongue.* 私は少し舌もつれがする.

drive [***send***] *a person* ***round the twist*** 人を逆上させる ▪His lack of consideration is *driving* me *round the twist.* 彼の思いやりのなさには全く頭にくる ▪No wonder it nearly *sent* him *round the twist.* そのため彼がカッとなる寸前だったのも無理はない.

out of twist ねじれていない ▪The ladder is *out of twist.* このはしごはねじれていない.

round the twist 《英》狂った, 怒った ▪It's common talk that he is *round the twist* and that he's got worse recently, since his mother died. 母親が亡くなって以来, 彼はおかしくなって, 最近はさらにひどくなっているというのはよく知られた話さ.

the twist of the wrist 手練, こつ ▪It takes months to learn *the twist of the wrist.* こつを知るには何か月もかかる.

the whole twist and tucking 《米口》全部, 全員 ▪*The whole twist and tucking* of them went away. 彼らの全員が立ち去った.

twists and turns 曲がりくねり; 紆余(うよ)曲折 ▪After various *twists and turns*, I found myself by the side of a pond. いろいろと曲がりくねったあげく池のそばに来ていた.

twist[2] /twɪst/ 動 ***twist and turn*** 曲がりくねる ▪The road *twists and turns* up the side of the mountain. 道は山腹を曲がりくねって上っている.

twist *a person's* ***arm*** 人に強いる ▪He *twisted my arm* till I consented to drink. 彼は私に強いて1杯やることに同意させた.

twist in the wind (屈辱・汚名に)長く苦しむ, 大いにもだえ苦しむ ▪The company has left him to *twist in the wind.* 会社は彼に汚名を着せて苦しむままに放置した. ☞絞首刑から.

twist *a person* ***round*** [***around***] *one's* (***little***) ***finger*/*turn, twist, and wind*** *a person* →twist ... round one's (little) FINGER.

twist the tail of →TAIL[1].

twist *one's* ***way*** 縫うように歩く ▪We *twisted our way* through the crowd. 我々は人ごみの間を縫うように歩いて行った.

twit /twɪt/ 名 ***in a twit*** 動転して, 狂わんばかりになって ▪She lost her handbag and she was all *in a twit.* ハンドバッグをなくして彼女はすっかり気が動転していた.

twitch /twɪtʃ/ 名 ***all of a twitch*** =all of a TREMBLE.

at a twitch たちまち ▪He is afraid that his fame will break *at a twitch.* 彼は自分の名声がたちまち地に落ちはせぬかと心配している.

twitter /twítər/ 名 (***all***) ***in*** [***of***] ***a twitter*** 《口》そわそわして ▪The news set me *all in a twitter.* その知らせで私はそわそわした.

two /tu:/ 形名 ***a*** [***one***]***... or two*** 一つか二つの; いくらかの ▪*A* year *or two* are needed for research. 研究に1, 2年要する. ☞複数動詞で呼応する.

a two-by-four (厚さ2インチ幅4インチの)ツーバイフォー材木 ▪He hit the burglar on the head with *a two-by-four.* 彼は賊の頭をツーバイフォーの角材で一撃した.

a two-up, two-down 上下それぞれ2室から成る家屋 ▪There are three families living in *a* small *two-up, two-down.* 上下それぞれ2室の狭い家に3世帯が住んでいる.

a two-way street →STREET.

be in two minds →MIND[1].

be two-faced 表裏[二心]がある, 二枚舌を使う ▪That guy has the reputation of *being two-faced.* あいつは言動に表裏があるととかくの噂がある.

be two of a kind (二人が)似た性格をしている; 似たもの同士, うりふたつで ▪He and I *are two of a kind*, so we've stayed friends for so long. 彼とは似たもの同士だからずっと仲良しでいる ▪Beth and Tom *are two of a kind*; they both love traveling. ベスとトムは似合いのカップルで二人とも旅行好きだ ▪My father and my uncle *are two of a kind.* 父とおじはとても似ている.

by [***in***] ***twos and threes*** 三々五々, ちらほら ▪They would lodge *by* [*in*] *twos and threes* in the lonely farmhouse. 彼らはあの寂しい農家に三々五々泊まるだろう.

fall between two stools →STOOL.

for two pins 《英》→PIN[1].

have two left feet 《口》→ have two LEFT hands.

in two (まっ)二つに ▪He cut the apple *in two* and ate half of it. 彼はリンゴを二つに切って半分食べた ▪The toy broke *in two* when I trod on it. 私が踏んだら玩具は二つに割れてしまった ▪The timber shivered *in two.* 材木はまっ二つに裂けた.

in two twos [***ticks***] 《口》たちまち ▪The business was over *in two twos.* 仕事はすぐに終わった.

It takes two to make a bargain. →BARGAIN[1].

It takes two to tango./It takes two to make a quarrel. 《諺》タンゴを踊る[けんかをする]には二人必要; 当事者二人が関与する[必要である]; 「けんか両成敗」 ▪*It* will *take two to tango*, if we try to settle this problem. この問題を解決しようとするなら, どうしても二人必要だろう.

one ... or two →a ... or TWO.

(***put*** [***stick***] ***in***) *one's* ***two pennyworth***/《米》*one's* ***two cents' worth*** =get in one's twopence WORTH.

put [***lay***] ***two and two together*** あれこれ考え合わす ▪*Putting two and two together*, he realised what was going to happen. あれこれ考え合わせてみて, 彼は何が起きようとしているかをはっきり理解した.

put [***stick***] ***two fingers up at*** 《英》(人差し指と中指を立て手の甲を相手に向けて)人に怒り[軽蔑]を表す ▪He *stuck two fingers up at* me and walked out in anger. 彼は私に向かって2本指を立て,

プリプリして出て行った.

That makes two of us. 《口》私の場合もそうなんですよ ▪ I like skiing very much.—*That makes two of us.* 私はスキーが大好きです—私もそうですよ.

There are no two ways about it 《口》→WAY.

two and [by] two 二つずつ, 二人ずつ ▪ We started on foot, *two and two.* 我々は二人ずつ歩いて出発した.

Two and two make(s) four. 2足す2は4《自明の理》 ▪ The notion is as clear as that *two and two make four.* この考えは2足す2は4と同じくらい自明だ.

Two can live as cheaply as one. 《諺》二人なら一人と同様安く暮らせる.

two can play at that game →GAME.

Two heads are better than one. →HEAD[1].

two or three 2, 3の, いくらかの (a few) ▪ The walls were covered with books except in *two or three* places. 周囲の壁は2, 3か所を除いてはどこも本におおわれていた.

two sides of the same coin →(the) two SIDEs of the same coin.

***two-time** a person* 不倫をして配偶者を裏切る, 同時に二人のボーイ[ガール]フレンドとデートする ▪ She refused to believe he was *two-timing* her. 彼女は彼が浮気をしているとは信じなかった ▪ If I ever found out he was *two-timing* me with that girl, I'd kill him. 彼が私とあの娘と二股かけて付き合っているとわかったら, ただではおかないから.

two times 2度 ▪ The other *two times* he was away. 彼は他の2回は留守だった. ☞常に修飾語とともに用いられ, その他の場合は twice を用いる.

Two's company, three's none [a crowd]. →COMPANY.

twopence /tʌ́pəns/ 名 ***care twopence*** 〚否定文・疑問文で〛かまう, 気にする ▪ He asked me if you really *cared twopence* for Kate. 彼はあなたがケイトのことを本当に少しでもかまっているのかと私に聞いた.

twopence colored 安くてはでな ▪ She has been all her life very *twopence colored.* 彼女はこれまでずっととても安くてはでにしてきた.

twopenny /tʌ́pəni/ 名 ***not care a twopenny damn*** 《口》少しも気にしない ▪ I *don't care a twopenny damn* if he did so. 彼がそうしたところで少しも気にしない.

tuck in** one's **twopenny (かえる跳びで)頭を下げる ▪ *Tuck in your twopenny,* Tom. 頭を下げなよ, トム. ☞twopenny = head.

twopenny halfpenny 安っぽい, つまらない ▪ What she lost was a *twopenny halfpenny* pendant. 彼女がなくしたのは安っぽいペンダントだった.

type /taɪp/ 名 ***be true to type*** →TRUE to type.

in (the) type (of) (…を)象徴して ▪ He offered wine *in the type of* his blood. 彼は彼の血を象徴しているようなワインをさし出した.

in type(s) 活字に組まれて ▪ The work had been kept *in type* for nearly a year. その作品は1年近くも活字に組まれたままだった.

(not) be** a person's **type 好みのタイプである[ない] ▪ Mark *isn't* really *my type,* but I like him as well. マークは本当はタイプじゃないけど, 彼も好きよ ▪ The one on the right *is* more *my type.* 右側の子のほうが僕の好みのタイプだ.

revert to type **1** 元の木阿弥(もくあみ)になる, 元[本来]の(悪い)姿に戻る ▪ Just a few weeks later, he seemed to have *reverted to type.* ほんの数週間も経つと彼は化けの皮がはがれたようだ ▪ They *reverted to type* and started their dirty tricks. 彼らはもとのやり方に戻って, 汚い手を使い始めた.

2《生物》先祖返りする; もとに戻る ▪ Garden plants sometimes *revert to type.* 園芸植物はときに先祖返りすることがある.

the strong silent type 感情を表に出さないが行動的な人[男性] ▪ She finds herself attracted to *the strong, silent type.* 控え目だが行動力のある男性に彼女は惹かれていた.

typhoid /táɪfɔɪd/ 名 ***a typhoid Mary*** 不運を運ぶ[広める]人 ▪ He's such *a typhoid Mary.* Everything has gone wrong since he has been here. 彼はひどい疫病神だ. 彼がここに来てから何もかもうまくいかない. ☞「腸チフス菌保有者」から.

typical /típɪkəl/ 形 ***(be) typical of*** **1** …を代表[象徴]する ▪ These students *are typical of* their class. この学生たちはクラスを代表する ▪ He *was* most *typical of* the times in which he lived. 彼はその生きていた時代を最もよく象徴する人であった.

2 …を予表する ▪ It *was typical of* Christ's second coming. それはキリストの再来を予表していた.

T

U

U /juː/ 名 ***U and Non-U*** 上流階級的と非上流階級的 ▪ She coined the terms *U and non-U*—to speak of spectacles is U, of glasses non-U. 彼女はUおよび non-U という造語を考案した. 眼鏡を spectacles と言えばU(上流階級), glasses と言えば non-U (非上流階級)というわけだ. ☞Nancy Mitford が考案した言葉づかいによって上流階級 (upper class) か非上流階級 (non upper class) かを判別する体系.

ugly /ʌ́gli/ 形 ***an ugly customer*** → CUSTOMER.

an ugly duckling 醜いアヒルの子《家中からばかにされるが後にえらくなる子供》 ▪ We'll hope you'll turn out more in the *ugly duckling* line. あなたがむしろ醜いアヒルの子といったふうにおなりになることを望んでいます. ☞Andersen の童話から.

(as) ugly as sin 《口》(…が)ひどく不器量[不格好]で ▪ That new building is *as ugly as sin*! あの新しい建物はすごく不格好だ.

cut up ugly 《口》怒る ▪ He *cut up* uncommonly *ugly*. 彼はひどく怒った.

feel ugly 《米口》腹だたしく思う ▪ Don't say that; it makes me *feel ugly*. それを言うな, 腹がたってくるから.

turn ugly 気が荒くなる ▪ The dog *turned ugly*. その犬は気が荒くなった.

ullage /ʌ́lɪdʒ/ 名 ***on ullage*** (ワインをたるに)いっぱい詰めないで ▪ The wines should not remain long *on ullage*. ワインはいっぱい詰めずに長くおいてはいけない.

um /ʌm/ 動 ***um and aah*** =HUM and haw.

umbrage /ʌ́mbrɪdʒ/ 名 ***give umbrage to** a person* 人を立腹させる ▪ The sermon *gave* great *umbrage to* the Duke. その説教は公爵を大いに立腹させた.

***take umbrage at* [*about*]** 《文・戯》…に立腹する ▪ He *took umbrage at* the tone of this letter. 彼はこの手紙の調子に腹を立てた.

umbrella /ʌmbrélə/ 名 ***under the umbrella of*** …の傘下に ▪ They were combined *under the umbrella of* Fascism. 彼らはファシズムの傘下に連合した.

umpteenth /ʌ̀mptíːnθ/ 形 ***for the umpteenth time*** 《口》十何度目かに ▪ I'm telling you so *for the umpteenth time*. こんなことを言うのはこれで十何度目かじゃないか.

un, 'un /ən/ 代 ***That's a good 'un.*** 《口》そいつはうまいもんだな《しゃれ・嘘などが》 ▪ Well, *that was a good 'un*. いや, そいつはうまく言ったもんだな.

unable /ʌnéɪbəl/ 形 ***(be) unable to** do* …することができない ▪ He *was unable to* move. 彼は動くことができなかった.

unaccounted /ʌ̀nəkáʊntəd/ 形 ***unaccounted for*** 説明されていない, 原因不明で ▪ His disappearance remains *unaccounted for*. 彼の失踪は依然として原因不明である.

unaccustomed /ʌ̀nəkʌ́stəmd/ 形 ***be unaccustomed to*** (*doing*) (…すること)に慣れていない ▪ He *was unaccustomed to* fear. 彼は怖がることに慣れていなかった ▪ I *am* quite *unaccustomed to speaking* in public. 人前で話すのは全く慣れていない.

unacquainted /ʌ̀nəkwéɪntəd/ 形 ***unaquainted with*** (人)を見知らぬ, (物)に不案内な ▪ I am *unacquainted with* him. 彼とは面識がない ▪ I am quite *unacquainted with* English. 英語は全くわからない.

unaided /ʌnéɪdəd/ 形 ***the unaided eye*** 肉眼 ▪ The defect can be detected by *the unaided eye*. そのきずは肉眼でも見つけられる.

unanimity /jùːnənímәti/ 名 ***with unanimity*** 満場一致で ▪ Parliament spoke *with unanimity* on that question. その問題については議会の意見は満場一致であった.

unanswerable /ʌnǽnsərəbəl|-ɑ́ːn-/ 形 ***unanswerable for*** …の責任がない ▪ He was *unanswerable for* his acts. 彼にはその行為の責任がなかった.

unapt /ʌnǽpt/ 形 ***(be) unapt at*** …がへたで(ある) ▪ I *am unapt at* games. 私はゲームはへたです.

(be) unapt for (用途・目的)に不向きで(ある) ▪ The old man *was unapt for* active exercise. 老人は活発な運動には向いていなかった.

***(be) unapt to** do* **1** (物が)容易に…しそうもない ▪ His mind *was unapt to* apprehend danger. 彼の心はなかなか危険を感じそうもなかった.

2 (人が)…する気がない ▪ I *am unapt to* take up ideas suggested to me. 私は人が示唆してくれる考えを受けいれる気がない.

unasked /ʌnǽskt|-ɑ́ːskt/ 形 ***unasked for*** 求められない ▪ The contributions were *unasked for*. その寄付金は求められないで出されたものである.

unattached /ʌ̀nətǽtʃt/ 形 ***an unattached young lady*** 婚約者のいない自由な若い女性 ▪ They invited some charming *unattached young ladies*. 彼らは何人かの婚約者のいない自由な身の若くて美しい女性たちを招いた.

unavailable /ʌ̀nəvéɪləbəl/ 形 ***unavailable for*** **1** …に利用[適用]できない ▪ Your ticket is *unavailable for* express trains. あなたの切符では急行列車は利用できません.

2 《米》(選挙)に出馬しない ▪ He declared himself *unavailable for* the Senate contest. 彼は上院議員選挙戦に出馬しないと表明した.

unaware /ʌ̀nəwéər/ 形 ***(be) unaware of*** … を知らない ▪ He seemed *unaware of* the mistake. 彼はその誤りに気づいていないらしかった.

unawares /ʌ̀nəwéərz/ 副 ***all unawares*** 全くうっかりと ▪ *All unawares*, I had played into his hand. 全くそれと知らずに彼の思うつぼにはまってしまっていた.

at unawares **1** 知らずに; 知られずに ▪ He feared lest some word should escape him *at unawares*. 彼は知らず知らずにある言葉が口から漏れはしないかと心配していた ▪ It stole into the world *at unawares*. それは人知れずこの世に現れた.
2 不意に ▪ He had come to the edge of a precipice *at unawares*. 彼は不意にがけの端に来ていた.

take [***catch***] *a person* ***unawares*** 人に不意打ちをくわせる ▪ No man ever *took* him *unawares*. 彼に不意打ちをくわせた者は誰もいなかった.

unawares to …に気づかずに; に知られずに ▪ *Unawares to* myself, I had moved forward. 私は自分でも気づかずに前へ出ていた ▪ I kissed his hand *unawares to* him. 彼に気づかれずに彼の手にキスした.

unbeaten /ʌ̀nbíːtən/ 形 ***the unbeaten track*** [***path, way***] 前人未踏の道; 未開発の領域 ▪ *The unbeaten ways* make distance seem longer. 前人未踏の道は距離が遠く思われる ▪ I like exploring *the unbeaten path* of life. 人生の未知の領域を探索するのが好みだ.

unbecoming /ʌ̀nbɪkʌ́mɪŋ/ 形 ***(be) unbecoming to*** [***for, of***] …に不適当で(ある) ▪ The behavior *was* utterly *unbecoming to* a woman of her birth. そのふるまいは彼女のような高貴な女性には全く似つかわしくなかった ▪ You must not do what *is unbecoming for* [*of*] your situation. 君の立場にふさわしくないことをしてはいけない.

unbeknown /ʌ̀nbɪnóʊn/ 形 ***unbeknown to*** …に知られない(で) ▪ I was there *unbeknown to* her. 彼女に知られずに私はそこへ行っていました.

unbeknownst /ʌ̀nbɪnóʊnst/ 形副 ***unbeknownst to*** 《口》…に知られない(で) ▪ He did it *unbeknownst to* me. 彼は私に知られずにそうした.

unbend /ʌ̀nbénd/ 動 ***unbend*** *one's* ***brow*** ほっとする, 陽気になる ▪ A smile *unbent his brow*. 彼は微笑してほっとした顔をした.

unbosom /ʌ̀nbʊ́zəm/ 動 ***unbosom*** *oneself* 胸のうちを漏らす (*of a thing to a person*) ▪ He was led to *unbosom himself of* the secret *to* several friends. 彼はその秘密を数人の友人に漏らすように仕向けられた.

unbowed /ʌ̀nbáʊd/ 形 ***bloody*** [***battered, bloodied***] ***but unbowed*** 《雅》(不愉快な状況・競争で痛めつけられたが)へこたれない, 負けないで ▪ He was *bloody but unbowed* and would fight to the last. 彼はへこたれずに最後までやり抜く覚悟だった ▪ *Bloodied but unbowed*, the Western novel is not entirely dead. 痛めつけられたが負けず, 西洋の小説はすっかり滅びたわけではない. ☞英国の詩人 William Ernest Henley (1849?–1903)の詩 *Invictus* の1行 My head is bloody but unbowed から.

unburden /ʌ̀nbə́ːrdən/ 動 ***unburden*** *oneself* 心の中を打ち明ける (*of a thing to a person*) ▪ At last he *unburdened himself to* a confidant. ついに彼は腹心の友に意中を打ち明けた ▪ She *unburdened herself of* the whole story. 彼女は一部始終を打ち明けた.

uncalled /ʌ̀nkɔ́ːld/ 形 ***uncalled for*** 不用で, 余計で ▪ Such comments are *uncalled for*. そのような批評は余計なものだ ▪ The thought comes *uncalled for* into my mind. その思いが用もないのに心の中に浮かんでくる.

uncertain /ʌ̀nsə́ːrtən/ 形 ***in no uncertain terms*** →in so many WORDs.

uncertain of [***about, as to***] …についてはっきり知らない, 確信がない ▪ I am *uncertain of* the outcome. 結果についてははっきりしたことはわからない ▪ He was *uncertain about* his plans for future. 彼は将来の計画については確信がなかった.

unchallenged /ʌ̀ntʃǽləndʒd/ 形 ***go unchallenged*** (人・陳述などが)問題にならずに通る ▪ He *went unchallenged* and was not brought into question. 彼のことは問題にならずに通り, 審議されなかった.

uncle /ʌ́ŋkəl/ 名 ***a funny uncle*** 《口》変なおじさん《親類の子供に性的ないたずらをする男》 ▪ I have read about child molesting, "*funny uncles*," etc. 私は児童への性的いたずらや「変なおじさん」などのことを読んだことがある.

be at my uncle's 《俗》質入れしてある ▪ My watch *is* at present *at my uncle's*. 私の時計は今質入れしてある.

come the uncle over *a person* (しかるときなどに)人に対しておじさん風を吹かせる (→talk to a person like a DUTCH uncle) ▪ My tutor has the cheek to try and *come the uncle over* me. 僕の家庭教師は厚かましくも僕におじさん風を吹かせようとするんだ.

cry [***say***] ***uncle*** 《米口》参ったと言う, 降参する (→cry CRAVEN) ▪ I will make him *say* "*Uncle*." 彼に「参った」と言わせてやるんだ.

go [***take***] ***to*** (***my***) ***uncle's*** 《俗》質入れする ▪ What's happened to your watch? *Gone* [*Taken*] *to uncle's*? 時計はどうしたんだ. 質に入れたのか?

I'll be a monkey's uncle! →MONKEY.

old Uncle Tom Cobbleigh and all すべての人, みんな ▪ I am ready to co-operate with *old Uncle Tom Cobbleigh and all*. 私は進んであらゆる人と協力する. ☞ballad から.

Uncle Sam 《口》アンクル・サム《米国(政府)を擬人化した呼称, 典型的アメリカ人のニックネーム》 ▪ The Kremlin changed her policy and started to get close to *Uncle Sam*. ロシア政府は政策を変更し米国に歩み寄り始めた.

Uncle Tom 権威のある白人に協力する黒人 ▪ He refused to be an *Uncle Tom* and fought against racial discrimination. 彼は白人に従順な黒人となるこ

とを拒み人種差別と闘った. ☞H. B. Stowe, *Uncle Tom's Cabin* (1852).

unclean /ʌ̀nklíːn/ 形 ***the unclean spirit*** (特に人の心に宿る)悪霊, 悪魔 ▪ *The unclean spirit* is gone out of the man. その男の中から悪魔が出ていった.

uncommitted /ʌ̀nkəmítəd/ 形 ***uncommitted to*** (ある方針)に踏み切っていない ▪ I am *uncommitted to* any course of action. 私はどんな行動方針にも踏み切っていない.

uncommonly /ʌnkámənli|-kɔ́m-/ 副 ***not uncommonly*** まれではなく, かなりしばしば ▪ It is *not uncommonly* said so. かなりよくそう言われている.

unconcerned /ʌ̀nkənsə́ːrnd/ 形 ***(be) unconcerned about [at]*** …に冷淡で(ある) ▪ He *is unconcerned about* personal appearance. 彼は身なりにはむとんちゃくだ ▪ He *was unconcerned at* her loss. 彼は彼女を失ったことにも平気だった.

(be) unconcerned in …にかかり合っていない ▪ He *was unconcerned in* the conspiracy. 彼はその陰謀にはかかり合っていなかった.

(be) unconcerned with …に無関心で(ある) ▪ They were indolent gods, *unconcerned with* human affairs. 怠惰な神々で, 人事には無関心であった.

unconnected /ʌ̀nkənéktəd/ 形 ***unconnected with*** …と関係[関連]のない ▪ He was entirely *unconnected with* the neighborhood. 彼はその界わいとは全く近所うき合いがなかった.

unconscious /ʌ̀nkánʃəs|-kɔ́n-/ 形 ***(be) unconscious of*** …を意識していない ▪ I *am unconscious of* having said so. そんなことを言った覚えはない.

uncover /ʌ̀nkʌ́vər/ 動 ***uncover*** *oneself* 身につけた物を脱ぐ ▪ The patient *uncovered himself* in bed. 病人はベッドで身につけた物を脱いだ.

uncrowned /ʌ̀nkráʊnd/ 形 ***(be) the uncrowned king [queen] (of)*** (特定の分野での)最高の男性[女性](である) ▪ He *is the uncrowned king of* light music. 彼は軽音楽界の無冠の帝王だ ▪ She is regarded as *the uncrowned queen of* women's tennis. 彼女は女子テニス界の女王とみなされている.

unction /ʌ́ŋkʃən/ 名 ***extreme unction*** 終油の秘跡 ▪ The priest administered *extreme unction* to the dying woman. 牧師は死にかけている女性に終油の秘跡を施した.

lay a flattering unction to *one's* ***soul*** うれしがらせの甘言[気休め]でいい気になる (cf. Sh., *Haml.* 3. 4. 145) ▪ We could not *lay* some *flattering unction to our souls.* 我々はうれしがらせの甘言でいい気になることができなかった ▪ I *lay* that *flattering unction to my soul.* そう思って気休めにしています.

with unction 感激した語調で ▪ He delivered the speech *with unction.* 彼は感激した語調でその演説をぶった.

undeceive /ʌ̀ndɪsíːv/ 動 ***be undeceived of*** …の目[迷い]がさめる ▪ He *was undeceived of* his error. 彼は自分のまちがいに気がついた.

under /ʌ́ndər/ 前副 ***and [or] under*** またはそれ以下の(大きさ・価格など) ▪ He left property worth only £500 *or under.* 彼は500ポンドまたはそれ以下の財産を残しただけだった.

from under (…の)下から ▪ The waters came down *from under.* 水の流れはその下から落ちてきた ▪ Her curls came out *from under* her hat. 帽子の下から彼女の巻き毛が出ていた.

half under 多少[半ば]意識のある ▪ He was *half under* and could understand what we were saying. 彼は半ば意識があり我々の言っていることがわかった.

one degree under 《口》体調がすぐれない ▪ I am feeling *one degree under* this morning. けさは体調がすぐれない.

underground /名 ʌ́ndərgràʊnd; 副 ʌ̀ndərgráʊnd/ 名副 ***by underground*** 地下鉄で ▪ We went to Baker Street *by underground.* 我々は地下鉄でベイカー街まで行った.

go underground (禁止された政党などが)地下へもぐる ▪ It is said that the banned political party has *gone underground.* 例の禁止された政党は地下にもぐったそうだ.

underplay /ʌ̀ndərpléɪ/ 動 ***underplay*** *oneself* 力量以下の勝負する ▪ No person is ever known to flatter at chess, by *underplaying himself.* チェスで力量以下の勝負をして, いい気になる人はいたためしがない.

understand /ʌ̀ndərstǽnd/ 動 ***a tongue not understanded of the people*** 外国語 (Prayer-book, "*Articles of Religion*" 24) ▪ The practice began of having divine service in *a tongue not understanded of the people.* 礼拝を外国語で行う習慣が始まった. ☞of＝by.

as I understand 私の聞き及んでいるところでは ▪ He is coming from Ceylon *as I understand.* あの方は確かセイロンからおいでになるのだと聞いています.

Do I [Am I to] understand that ...? …と言われるのですか ▪ *Do I [Am I to] understand that* you refuse? いやだと言われるのですか.

give *a person* ***to understand*** →GIVE.

make *oneself* ***understood*** 自分の考え[言葉]を人にわからせる ▪ Can you *make yourself understood* in English? あなたは英語で意思を伝えることができますか.

(now,) understand me (さて)よく聞くんだぞ《警告・おどしの前置き》 ▪ *Now, understand me,* I am resolved to give you a very bad report. さあ, よく聞きなさい, 君にひどく悪い通知表をあげることにしたのだ.

pass all understanding 人智を越える; 到底理解できない (《聖》 *Philip.* 4. 7) ▪ Why he should have done it *passes all understanding.* 彼がなぜそんなことをしたのかどうしても分からない.

To understand all is to forgive all. 《諺》一切を理解すれば一切を許せる.

understand each other [one another] (二

人が)心を合わせている; ぐるになっている ▪ It's so apparent that they *understand each other*. 彼らが心を合わせていることはとても明らかである.

understanding /ʌ̀ndərstǽndɪŋ/ 名 ***a good understanding*** (二者間の)和親 ▪ He strove to bring about *a good understanding* between the two countries. 彼は両国間に和親をもたらそうと努力した.

come to* [*arrive at, reach*] *an understanding 話し合いがつく(*with*) ▪ I *came to an understanding with* him before parting. 別れる前に彼と話し合いがついた.

have an understanding with …と話し合いをつける ▪ I should like to *have an understanding with* you about this matter. この件についてあなたと話し合いをつけたい.

of understanding 理解力ある, もののわかった ▪ They went astray as children *of* no *understanding*. 彼らは少しも理解力のない子供たちのように話が脱線した.

on the understanding that 《文》…という条件で ▪ You may go to the dance, *on the understanding that* you are back before midnight. 真夜中以前に帰るという条件でならダンスへ行ってもよい.

on* [*with*] *this* [*that*] *understanding こう[そう]いう話し合いで ▪ *With* [*On*] *this understanding*, we parted for the night. 我々はこういう話し合いでその晩は別れた.

reach an understanding →come to an UNDERSTANDING.

undertake /ʌ̀ndərtéɪk/ 動 ***I* (*dare*) *undertake*** 確かに《陳述に添えて》 ▪ You have gallants among you, *I dare undertake*. あなたがたの中には確かに勇者がおられる.

undertone /ʌ́ndərtòʊn/ 名 ***in undertones*** 小声で ▪ They talked *in undertones*. 彼らは小声で話していた.

underway /ʌ̀ndərwéɪ/ 形 ***get underway*** 始まる; 旅に出る ▪ Our new project finally *got underway*. 我々の新しいプロジェクトがついに始まった.

undeserving /ʌ̀ndɪzə́ːrvɪŋ/ 形 ***undeserving of*** …に値しない ▪ Such influences certainly were *undeserving of* our attention. そのような影響は確かに注目に値しなかった.

undivided /ʌ̀ndɪváɪdəd/ 形 ***get* [*have*] *a person's undivided attention*** 《主に戯》人の注意のすべてを受ける[受けている] ▪ When I'm gone you can *have his undivided attention*. 私がいなくなっても彼がしっかり君の面倒をみてくれるよ.

undo /ʌ̀ndúː/ 動 ***What is done cannot be undone.*** 《諺》一度したことは元に返らない,「覆水盆に返らず」.

undoing /ʌ̀ndúːɪŋ/ 名 ***be a person's undoing*** 人の身の破滅になる ▪ Drink *was his undoing*. 酒が彼の破滅の元となった.

to one's undoing 零落してしまうように; その結果零落して ▪ He went to the moneylenders, *to his utter undoing*. 彼は金貸しから金を借りた末すっかり零落してしまった.

undone /ʌ̀ndʌ́n/ 形 ***come undone*** ほどける ▪ The bandage on my left hand had *come undone*. 私の左手の包帯がほどけていた.

I am undone. 私はもうだめだ, おしまいだ ▪ Whichever way I turn, *I am undone*. どちらへ行っても私はもうおしまいだ.

leave ... undone →LEAVE[2].

remain undone なされないままである ▪ Nothing *remained undone*. なされないままになっているものは何ひとつなかった.

undreamed /ʌ̀ndríːmd/, **undreamt** /ʌ̀ndrémt/ 形 **(*be*) *undreamed of*** 想像だにしない, 夢にも思わない ▪ The printing press *was undreamt of* at that time. その時分には印刷機などは思いもよらなかった.

undress /ʌ̀ndrés/ 動 ***undress oneself*** 衣服を脱ぐ ▪ She then *undressed herself* and went to bed. 彼女はそれから服を脱いで床についた.

undue /ʌ̀ndjúː/ 形 ***an undue influence*** 《法》不当圧迫 ▪ They are exercising *an undue influence* upon you. 彼らは君に不当圧迫を加えている.

undulation /ʌ̀ndʒəléɪʃən/ 名 ***by undulation*** 体をくねらせて ▪ Worms move *by undulation*. イモムシは体をくねらせて動く.

in undulations (丘が)うねうねと ▪ The hills are raised *in undulations*. 丘陵がうねうねと起伏している.

uneasiness /ʌ̀níːzinəs/ 名 ***be under some uneasiness at*** …に少々不快[不安]を感じている ▪ I have lately *been under some uneasiness at* your silence. このところあなたから便りがないのでちょっと心配していました.

cause* [*give*] *a person uneasiness 人を不快にする, 不安にする ▪ My visit did not *cause* him the least *uneasiness*. 私の訪問は彼を少しも不快にさせはしなかった.

uneasy /ʌníːzi/ 形 ***uneasy about*** …のことが心配[不安]で ▪ I feel *uneasy about* my health. 私は健康について不安を感じている.

uneasy at …が不安で ▪ We grew *uneasy at* his long absence. 彼が長く家をあけているのが不安になってきた.

unemployment /ʌ̀nɪmplɔ́ɪmənt/ 名 ***go on unemployment*** 《米口》=go on WELFARE.

unencumbered /ʌ̀nɪnkʌ́mbərd/ 形 ***unencumbered by* [*with*]** …に妨げられない ▪ Such people were *unencumbered with* [*by*] trades and business. そのような人々は商売や業務にじゃまされることはなかった.

unequal /ʌníːkwəl/ 形 ***unequal to* [*to doing*]** …に[するに]耐えない ▪ I feel *unequal to* the task. 私にはその仕事はできないような気がする ▪ I was *unequal to* personally *opposing* that dear friend. あの親友にじきじき反対することはできなかった.

unfamiliar /ʌ̀nfəmíljər|-iə/ 形 ***unfamiliar***

U

to (物が人)によく知られていない ▪ His face did not seem *unfamiliar to* me. 彼の顔は私には初めてとは思われなかった.

unfamiliar with (人が物)をよく知らない; と親しくない ▪ He is totally *unfamiliar with* this neighborhood. 彼はこの土地のことは全く知らない ▪ I am *unfamiliar with* Latin. ラテン語はよくわからない.

unfavorable, 《英》 **unfavourable** /ʌ̀nféɪvərəbəl/ 形 ***unfavorable to*** [***for***] …に都合の悪い, 不利な ▪ These situations were *unfavorable to* their growth. こういう状況はそれらの発育に不利であった ▪ The weather was *unfavorable for* shooting. 天気は猟に不向きであった.

unfit /ʌ̀nfít/ 形 ***unfit for*** [***to*** *do*] …に[するには]不適当な, 不似合いな ▪ He is a man *unfit for* such a trust. 彼はそのように信頼されるにはふさわしくない人物だ ▪ The flame is *unfit to* read by. その炎は本を読むのには向いていない.

unfitted /ʌ̀nfítəd/ 形 ***unfitted to*** *do* [***for***] …するに[…に]不適任の ▪ He felt himself *unfitted for* the ministry. 自分は大臣職に不適任と彼は思った.

unfitted with …の設備がない, を取りつけていない ▪ My house is *unfitted with* a bath. 私の家では風呂を取りつけていない.

unfitting /ʌ̀nfítɪŋ/ 形 ***unfitting for*** …に不適当な ▪ They were *unfitting for* naval warfare. それらは海戦に向いていなかった.

unfix /ʌ̀nfíks/ 動 ***Unfix bayonets*** [***swords***]***!*** 《号令》取れ剣!

unfold /ʌ̀nfóʊld/ 動 ***unfold itself*** 展開する ▪ Slowly the scene *unfolded itself*. 徐々に風景が繰り広げられた.

unfortunate /ʌ̀nfɔ́:rtʃənət/ 形 ***unfortunate in*** …の点で不しあわせな ▪ He is *unfortunate in* his children. 彼は子供運に恵まれていない.

unglued /ʌ̀nglú:d/ 形 ***come unglued*** 《米》 **1** 慌てふためく ▪ He *came unglued* over his wife who was pregnant. 彼は妊娠した妻に慌てふためいた.
2 失敗する, うまくいかない ▪ I knew that everything was *coming unglued* [《英》 unstuck]. すべてがうまくいっていないことは私にはわかっていた.

ungrateful /ʌ̀ngréɪtfəl/ 形 ***ungrateful to*** …をありがたく思わない ▪ She is *ungrateful to* her brother in spite of all that he has done for her. これまでいろいろとしてもらったのに, 彼女は兄をありがたいと思っていない.

unhappy /ʌ̀nhǽpi/ 形 ***unhappy in*** **1** …に恵まれていない ▪ She is *unhappy in* her servants. 彼女は使用人に恵まれていない.
2 …が不手ぎわな[まずい] ▪ He was *unhappy in* his choice of words. 彼は言葉の選択がまずかった.

unheard /ʌ̀nhə́:rd/ 形 ***be unheard of*** **1** 前代未聞である ▪ Such a scandal *is* quite *unheard of*. そんなスキャンダルは前代未聞だ.
2 無名である ▪ Then the author *was unheard of* here. その頃当地ではその著者は名が知られていなかった.

go unheard →GO².

uniform /jú:nəfɔ̀:rm/ 名形 ***in*** [***out of***] ***uniform*** 制服[私服]で ▪ He looks handsome *in uniform*. 彼は制服を着ると立派に見える.

uniform with …と同じ形[様子]をした, そろいの ▪ They are *uniform* in size *with* each other. それらは大きさが同じだ.

union /jú:njən|-niən/ 名 ***in union*** 共同で; 和合して ▪ They have been living together *in union*. 彼らは和合して暮らしてきた.

unison /jú:nəsən/ 名 ***in unison*** **1** 一斉に, 一致して ▪ The show girls were hopping *in unison*. 踊り子たちはそろってはね回っていた ▪ Set the class to repeat them *in unison*. クラスの者にそれを一斉に繰り返して言わせよ.
2 (…と)一致[調和]して (*with*) ▪ His opinions were not *in unison with* those of the majority of men. 彼の意見は大多数の人々の意見と一致していなかった ▪ Their voices were *in unison with* the music. 彼らの歌声はその音楽と調和していた.

unit /jú:nət/ 名 ***be a unit*** 《米》一致する ▪ We *were a unit* on the question. その問題では我々は一致していた.

united /junáɪtəd/ 形 ***talk United States*** 《米口》激しい言葉うかいをする ▪ I'd *talk United States* to him if I lost my job by his disparaging comments. 彼の誹謗で失業でもしたら, 彼に激しい言葉うかいで食ってかかってやろう.

United we stand, divided we fall. 《諺》団結すれば栄え, 分裂すれば倒れる.

unity /jú:nəti/ 名 ***at unity*** 一致して, 和合して (*with*) ▪ The bad are never *at unity with* one another. 悪人はお互いに和合していることは決してない.

in unity (…と)一致[調和]して (*with*) ▪ He can work *in unity with* others. 彼は他人と協力して働ける ▪ The Smiths are living *in unity*. スミス夫妻は仲よく暮らしている.

university /jù:nəvə́:rsəti/ 名 ***the university of life*** 人生という大学, (教訓を学ぶ手段としての)人生体験 ▪ Time flew and he continued to learn through *the university of life*. 時は瞬く間に流れ, 彼は人生体験を通して学び続けた.

unkind /ʌ̀nkáɪnd/ 形 ***it's*** [***that's***] ***unkind of*** *one* (***to*** *do*) (…するとは)…も不親切だ ▪ *It was* very *unkind of* you *to* tell her that. 彼女にそれを言うなんて君もあまり思いやりがなかったね.

the (***most***) ***unkindest cut of all*** この上ない無情な仕打ち (cf. Sh., *Jul. Caes.* 3. 2. 187) ▪ This was *the most unkindest cut of all*, coming on the top of failure. これは失敗した上に加えられたのでこの上もない無情な仕打ちであった.

unkindly /ʌ̀nkáɪndli/ 副 ***look unkindly at*** [***on***] …に不親切な顔つきをする ▪ She has *looked unkindly on* you. 彼女は君にきつい顔つきをしてきた.

take … unkindly …を悪く取る ▪ I hope you will not *take* it *unkindly*. それを悪くお取りになりませんように.

unknit /ʌnnít/ 動 ***unknit*** *one's* ***brow*** 寄せた眉を開く ▪ *Unknit* that threatening unkind *brow.* そんなにおっかない顔をして額にしわを寄せるのはおよしなさい.

unknowing /ʌnnóʊɪŋ/ 形 ***unknowing of*** ... を知らない ▪ He was simple, and *unknowing of* matters of State. 彼は単純な人間で政治問題には無知であった.

unknown /ʌnnóʊn/ 形 ***an unknown quantity*** →QUANTITY.

unknown of (人)に知られずに ▪ They met *unknown of* any. 彼らは誰にも知られずに会った.

unknown to **1** ...に知られないで, 不案内で ▪ These things are often *unknown to* the world. こういうことは世間に知られていないことがよくある ▪ They didn't kiss, because kissing was *unknown to* them. 彼らにはその習慣がなかったのでキスはしなかった.

2 ...に知られないで ▪ He stole, *unknown to* anybody, on board a ship. 彼は誰にも知られずにこっそり船に乗った.

unless /ənlés/ 接 ***unless and until*** →UNTIL.

unless it be for ...のほかには ▪ *Unless it be for* Henry nobody saw it. ヘンリーのほかには誰もそれを見た者はいなかった.

unless when [***where***] ...の時[ところ]を除いては ▪ He passed the day by himself, *unless when* relieved by the company of Partridge. 彼はパートリッジと同座して慰められた時を除けば, ひとりぼっちでその日を過ごした ▪ The horse was jet black, *unless where* he was flecked by spots of foam. 馬は点々とあわ汗が出ているところを除けば真っ黒だった.

unlicked /ʌnlíkt/ 形 ***an unlicked cub*** [***whelp***] 無作法な若者[少女] ▪ You know, Polly, what *an unlicked cub* I was when I married you. ポリー, 君と結婚したころの私がどんなに無作法な若者だったか君も知っているだろう.

unlikely /ʌnláɪkli/ 形 ***be unlikely to*** *do* ...しそうもない ▪ He *is unlikely to* come. 彼は来そうもない.

unlooked /ʌnlʊ́kt/ 形 ***unlooked for*** 予期されていない, 思いがけない ▪ The chance was quite *unlooked for.* そのチャンスは全く思いがけないものだった.

unmindful /ʌnmáɪndfəl/ 形 ***unmindful of*** ...を念頭におかない, にむとんちゃくな ▪ He is *unmindful of* his health. 彼は健康にむとんちゃくだ ▪ Every person was willing to save himself, *unmindful of* others. 誰もが他人のことは念頭におかずに自分が助かろうとしていた.

unnamed /ʌnnéɪmd/ 形 ***go unnamed*** 名前をふせる ▪ A man who shall *go unnamed* is willing to help you. 名前はふせるが, ある人が君を進んで援助してくださるのだ.

unnaturally /ʌnnǽtʃərəli/ 副 ***not unnaturally*** 無理もないことで ▪ He expected, *not unnaturally*, that his father would help him. 無理もないことだが, 彼は父親が助けてくれるものと思っていた.

unnoticed /ʌnnóʊtəst/ 形 ***leave ... unnoticed*** ...を無視する ▪ The masses of cloud sailed stately by all day, and *left* me *unnoticed.* 雲のかたまりは終日悠然と流れていき, 私などには目もくれなかった.

pass unnoticed 見落とされる, 見のがされる ▪ His mistake *passed unnoticed.* 彼の過失は見落とされた.

unobservant /ʌnəbzə́:rvənt/ 形 ***unobservant of*** ...に注目していない; (規則など)を守らない ▪ Some of us are *unobservant of* lawful authority. 私たちの中には法を守らない者もいる ▪ She seemed *unobservant of* his presence. 彼女は彼がいることに気づいていない様子だった.

unpleasantness /ʌnplézəntnəs/ 名 ***have an unpleasantness with*** *a person* 人との仲がおもしろくない ▪ I *had a* slight *unpleasantness with* him. 彼との仲が少しおもしろくなかった.

the late [***recent***] ***unpleasantness*** 《米戯》最近のいやな出来事; 南北戦争 ▪ During our "*late unpleasantness*" a convalescent hospital was established here. 「最近のいやな出来事」の間に病後保養所が当地に建てられた.

unprepared /ʌnprɪpéərd/ 形 ***unprepared for*** [***to*** *do*] ...の[する]用意ができていない ▪ We were all *unprepared for* the news. 我々はみなその知らせを予期していなかった ▪ I am rather *unprepared to* see you. あなたにお目にかかろうとはちょっと意外でした.

unprovided /ʌnprəváɪdəd/ 形 ***unprovided for*** 不自由で ▪ The widow was *unprovided for* after her husband's death. その未亡人は夫の死後不自由した.

unprovided with ...を供給されない, 備えつけない ▪ The drone is *unprovided* by nature *with* a sting. ミツバチの雄は生まれつき針を持っていない ▪ He was found *unprovided with* a ticket. 見ると彼はチケットを持っていなかった.

unput /ʌnpʊ́t/ 形 ***come unput*** はずれる, くずれる, 崩壊する; 失敗する, 災難にあう ▪ The last remaining bomb *came unput* and fell into the water. 最後に残った爆弾が(機体から)離れて海中に落ちた.

unqualified /ʌnkwɑ́ləfàɪd|-kwɔ́l-/ 形 ***unqualified for*** [***to*** *do*] ...に[するのに]不適任で ▪ He is *unqualified for* his situation. 彼はその地位に不適任だ ▪ The King was *unqualified to* rule. 王は統治するにふさわしくなかった.

unruly /ʌnrú:li/ 形 ***the*** [***an***] ***unruly member*** →MEMBER.

unsaid /ʌnséd/ 形 ***consider ... unsaid*** ...を言わなかったと考える ▪ I think we'll *consider* that *unsaid.* それは言わなかったことにしようと思う.

leave ... unsaid →LEAVE ... undone.

unsatisfied /ʌnsǽtəsfàɪd/ 形 ***be unsatisfied with*** ...に満足していない ▪ He *was unsatis-*

U

fied with the result. 彼はその結果に不満だった.

unskilled /ʌ̀nskíld/ 形 ***unskilled in*** …に未熟な ▪ He was yet *unskilled in* debate. 彼はまだ討論が未熟であった.

unskilled of …を知らない ▪ Thus he spoke, *unskilled of* what the Fates provide! 運命が何を用意しているかも知らず, 彼はこう話した.

***unskilled to** do* …しえない ▪ Down he goes at once, *unskilled to* swim. 彼は泳げないので, すぐ沈んでしまう.

unsparing /ʌ̀nspéərɪŋ/ 形 ***unsparing in*** [***of***] …を惜しまない ▪ He was *unsparing of* praise. 彼は賞賛を惜しまなかった.

with unsparing hand 惜しげもなく (Milton, *Paradise Lost* 5. 344) ▪ She heaped fruit on the board *with unsparing hand*. 彼女は果物を惜しげもなく食卓の上に積み上げた.

unspoken /ʌ̀nspóʊkən/ 形 ***unspoken to*** (人から)話しかけられない ▪ She sat there not speaking, and *unspoken to*. 彼女は口もきかず, 話しかけられもせずにそこに座っていた.

unspotted /ʌ̀nspɑ́təd|-spɔ́t-/ 形 ***remain*** [***keep** oneself*] ***unspotted from the world*** 世の汚れに染まらない (《聖》 *Jas*. 1. 28) ▪ It's next to impossible to *keep oneself unspotted from the world*. 世の汚れに染まらずにいるなんてまず不可能だ.

unstable /ʌ̀nstéɪbəl/ 形 ***(as) unstable as water*** 非常に頼りない (《聖》 *Gen*. 49. 4) ▪ These women were all the same, *unstable as water*. この女性はみな同じで, 水のように頼りなかった.

unstuck /ʌ̀nstʌ́k/ 形 ***come unstuck*** **1** (くっついていたものが)取れる ▪ Over time, my wallpaper has *come unstuck*. 時が経ち壁紙がはがれてしまった.
2 《俗》(計画などが)くずれる, 失敗する ▪ I thought my theory had *come unstuck*. 私の理論はくずれたと思った ▪ I *came unstuck* over a horse. 私は馬のことで災難にあった ▪ She is proud of her cooking, but she will *come unstuck* someday. 彼女は料理を自慢しているがいつか失敗するだろう.

unsuitable /ʌ̀nsúːtəbəl/ 形 ***unsuitable to*** [***for***] …に不適当な, 不似合な ▪ The means was quite *unsuitable to* his end. その手段は彼の目的には全くふさわしくなかった ▪ It is *unsuitable for* practice. それは実行には向いていない.

unsuited /ʌ̀nsúːtəd/ 形 ***unsuited to*** [***for***] …に不適当な ▪ His garment is *unsuited to* the climate here. 彼の着衣は当地の気候に向いていない ▪ He is clearly *unsuited for* historical research. 彼は明らかに歴史調査には向いていない.

unsure /ʌ̀nʃʊ́ər|ʃɔ́ː/ 形 ***unsure of*** [***about***] …が確かでない ▪ I am *unsure of* the date. その日付は確かではない.

unthinkable /ʌ̀nθíŋkəbəl/ 形 ***think the unthinkable*** 思い切った行動を考える[措置を講じる] ▪ The government *thought the unthinkable* on welfare. 政府は福祉関係の思い切った措置を講じた.

until /əntíl/ 前 接 ***it is not until** A **that** B* Aして初めてBする ▪ *It was not until* last night *that* I got the news. 昨夜になってやっとその知らせを聞いた ▪ *It was not until* it had grown dark *that* he made preparations to start. 暗くなって初めて彼は出発の用意をした.

not until …して初めて ▪ Votes for women came in recent times, *not until* after World War I. 女性の選挙権は最近, つまり第一次大戦後に初めて与えられた.

unless and until …するまで《until のもったいぶった言い方で unless and は冗語》 ▪ *Unless and until* I receive a full apology, I shall not forgive him. 正式なわびを入れるまでは彼を許さない.

untimely /ʌ̀ntáɪmli/ 形 ***come*** [***bring***] ***to an untimely end*** 若死にする[させる] ▪ Heaven *brought* them all *to an untimely end*. 天は彼らすべてを若死にさせた.

untouched /ʌ̀ntʌ́tʃt/ 形 ***remain untouched upon*** 言及[論及]されないままである ▪ The question *remains untouched upon*. その問題は相変わらず論及されていない.

untried /ʌ̀ntráɪd/ 形 ***leave nothing*** [***no means, no remedy***] ***untried*** あらゆることをやってみる, 手段を尽くす ▪ We have *left nothing untried*. 我々はあらゆる手段を尽くした ▪ We *left no means untried* to find it. 我々はそれを見つけるためにあらゆる手段を尽くした.

unused /ʌ̀njúːst/ 形 ***unused to*** [***to** doing*] …に慣れていない ▪ I am *unused to* written examinations. 私はペーパーテストに慣れていない.

unwashed /ʌ̀nwɑ́ʃt|-wɔ́ʃt/ 形 ***the great unwashed*** 下層民 ▪ Their ancestors were *the great unwashed*. 彼らの祖先は下層民であった.

unwept /ʌ̀nwépt/ 形 ***unwept, unhonored and unsung*** 泣く人も, 敬う人も, 歌う人もなく (Scott, *The Lay of the Last Minstrel*) ▪ The man died *unwept, unhonored and unsung*. その男は泣く人も, 敬う人も, 歌う人もなく死んでいった.

unwilling /ʌ̀nwílɪŋ/ 形 ***unwilling to** do* …したくない ▪ We should be very *unwilling to* offend him. 我々はあの人の感情を傷つけることなどとてもしたくありません.

unworthy /ʌ̀nwə́ːrði/ 形 副 ***unworthy of***
1 …に値しない ▪ I felt myself *unworthy of* her love. 私は彼女の愛に値しないと感じた.
2 (人)として恥ずべき, にあるまじき ▪ Such unfair practices are *unworthy of* reputable business men. そんな不正なことをするとは立派な実業家として恥ずべきことだ.
3 〚副詞的に〛 …にふさわしくなく ▪ Let us not act *unworthy of* our good education. 立派な教育にふさわしくないふるまいはしないようにしよう.

up[1] /ʌp/ 副 前 名 ***be all up*** / ***be all UP*** /juːpíː/ 万事終わって[休して] (*with*) ▪ It *is all up with* him by this time. 今ごろはもう彼は万事休すだ ▪ It's *all UP*! I haven't got a chance! 万事休すだ.

U

もうチャンスはない.

be hard up (***for, to***) →HARD.

be on an up 《口》上り調子である; きげんがいい ▪ He's *on a* definite *up* now. 彼はいま確かに上り調子だ.

be (***right***) ***up there with*** …に負けない, 匹敵する ▪ He *is right up there with* the very best cricketers of our age. 彼は現代最高のクリケット選手にだって負けはしない ▪ Aluminium *is up there with* the foremost conductors of heat. アルミは熱の伝導体として何物にも引けを取らない.

be up *oneself* 《英口》非常にうぬぼれている ▪ She *is* so *up herself*, it's unbearable. 彼女はすっかり天狗になってどうにも鼻持ちならない.

be up and about [《米》***around***] 《英》(病人が)床を離れている; ぶらぶら歩き回っている ▪ The patient *is* now *up and about* again. 病人はもう元のように起きて動き回っている ▪ There *were* a good many *up and around*. かなり多くの人たちがぶらぶら歩き回っていた.

be up and at them [***'em***] 積極的[精力的]である[に取り組んでいる] ▪ He *is up and at them* like no one else. 彼は他の誰にも負けないほど積極的だ.

be up and doing **1** 大いに活動している, 立ち働いている ▪ We must *be up and doing* if we are to catch the train. その列車に乗るつもりならてきぱきしなくちゃだめだ.

2 =be UP and about.

be up and running →RUNNING[2].

be up for **1**《米口》(選挙など)に出馬している, (試験など)を受けている ▪ He *is up for* reelection. 彼は再選挙に出馬中だ ▪ Those problems *are up for* discussion. それらの問題は討議に付されている.

2 (活動など)に参加したい; …ができる ▪ We're going on a hike next Sunday. *Are* you *up for* it? 僕たち今度の日曜にハイキングに行くんだ. 君も来るかい? ▪ After a long day of hard work, he *was*n't really *up for* a party. 長い一日の激務のあと彼はどうもパーティーに行く気はしなかった ▪ The question is: *are* you *up for* it? 問題は君にそれができるかということだ.

be [***come***] ***up for auction*** [***sale***] 競売[売り]に出されている ▪ A gorgeous 3-story house *is up for sale*. 3階建ての豪邸が売りに出されている ▪ The furniture will *be up for auction* today. 家具は本日競売にかけられる.

be up in [《米》***on***] 《口》…に精通している, をよく知っている ▪ He *was* most *up in* those subjects. 彼はそれらの学科に一番精通していた ▪ My brother-in-law *is* really *up on* computers. 義理の兄は実にコンピューターにくわしい.

be up to **1** …ができる ▪ He *was up to* any villainy. 彼はどんな悪事でもやれた.

2 …に対処することができる ▪ We *were up to* their tricks. 我々は彼らのぺてんなどに乗りはしなかった.

3 …に精通している ▪ Sam *was* not *up to* many things about horses. サムは馬のことは多くは知っていなかった.

4 …に達して[伍して]いる ▪ The harvest of this year *was up to* a full average. 今年の収獲は十分平年作に達していた.

5 (悪事など)をしきりにしようとしている; …に従事している ▪ He*'s up to* no good. 彼はよからぬことをやっている ▪ What's the old 'un *up to*, now? おやじは一体今何をやらかしているのだろう ▪ What have you *been up to* lately? 近頃はどうしているかい.

6《英・方》(人)に仕返しする ▪ I'll *be up to* you. おまえに仕返ししてやるからな.

7《口》…の義[責]務となっている, 次第である ▪ It *was up to* him to do this thing. それをやるのが彼の義務だった ▪ The success of this project *is* entirely *up to* you. この計画の成功はすべて君にかかっている.

8《パブリックスクール》…のクラスにいる ▪ He *is up to* Mr. Star. 彼はスター先生のクラスにいる. ☞Eton 校の用語.

be up (***with***) 《口》(…に)面倒が起きて, 故障して ▪ I can tell something *is up* from the look on her face. 彼女の表情からしてきっとどこか調子が悪いのだろう ▪ What*'s up with* my laptop? Please help! 私のラップトップ, どうなったのかしら. お願い, 助けて.

be up with the lark →up with the LARK.

from … up (ある時)から ▪ He has been her assistant *from* his youth *up*. 彼は青年時代からずっと彼女の助手を務めてきた ▪ *From* my childhood *up* I had known him. 子供のころから彼を知っていた.

Is anything up with …? 《口》…はどうかしたのか ▪ *Is anything up with* John? ジョンはどうかしたのか. ☞up=the matter.

not up to much 《英》たいしたものでない ▪ I do*n't* think his work is *up to much*. 彼の作品はたいしたものじゃないと思う.

on the up and up →UP AND UP.

show *a person* ***up*** 人を2階に案内する ▪ *Show* them *up*. あの人たちを2階へ案内しておくれ

something [***nothing***] ***is up with*** 《口》…はどうかしている[どうもしていない] ▪ *Something is up with* him today. 彼は今日はどうかしている.

there is something up with …はどうかしている[どこかおかしい] ▪ *There's something up with* that girl. あの娘はどうかしている.

up against 《口》(困難など)にぶつかって, 直面して ▪ All he's *up against* is a case of grand larceny. 彼が壁にぶつかっているのは重窃盗罪事件だけだ.

up against it 《口》(経済的に)苦境に陥って, 困って ▪ We're *up against it* with a vengeance! 我々は実に困っている.

up and *do* **1** 立って…する ▪ Refreshed, I *up and* plod on again. 元気を回復すると, 私はまた立ってこつこつ歩き続けるのだ.

2 突然に[公然と]言い放つ ▪ Whereupon she *up and* told him all that had passed between them. そこで彼女は彼らの間に起こったことをきっぱり彼に言った.

up and coming 《米口》 **1** (人が)元気いっぱいで;

(町などが)活気づいて, 進取的で ▪ The town is pretty *up and coming* for a place of its size. 町はその大きさにしては活気づいている.
2 成功の見込みがある, うまくいきそうな; やり手の ▪ She is one of the *up-and-coming* young actresses. 彼女は前途有望な若手女優の一人である ▪ He was one of the *up and coming* young architects. 彼は活動的な若手建築家の一人に数えられた.

up and down **1** 上がったり下がったり, 上下に ▪ He paused, and took a survey *up and down*. 彼は足を止めて上下をながめた ▪ The action is *up and down*, without vibration. その運動は振動のない上下の運動である.
2 行きつ戻りつ; あちこちと ▪ He was pacing moodily *up and down*. 彼はむっつりして行きつ戻りつしていた ▪ We looked for it *up and down*. それをあちこち捜し回った.
3 ここかしこに ▪ They gathered *up and down* into little sets. 彼らはここかしこに集まって小さな群れをなした.
4 《米口》あからさまに[の], 無愛想に[な] ▪ He's pretty *up and down* with us. 彼は私たちにかなりあからさまにものを言う ▪ I told her so, *up and down*. 私は彼女にあからさまにそう言ってやった.
5 (健康・仕事が)よかったり悪かったりで ▪ Things are *up and down*. 景気はよかったり悪かったりだ.

up and down the country [***land***] 国のあちこちで ▪ The product is prepared in plants *up and down the land*. この製品は国のあちこちにある工場で作られている.

up before (裁判所に)出廷して ▪ His son came *up before* the magistrate for speeding. 彼の息子はスピード違反のとがで治安判事の面前で聴聞を受けた.

up south [***north, east***] 《米口》南部[北部, 東部]に ▪ I've been away *up south*. 南部へ行っていた ▪ Money is tight *up East*. 東部では金づまりだ.

up there **1** あそこで ▪ Is that you *up there*? 君かい, そこにいるのは.
2 天国で ▪ Somebody likes me *up there*. 誰かが天国では私を愛してくれるさ.

up till =UP to.

up to **1** (…の高さ)まで ▪ I found an ascent *up to* the market-place. 私は市場までの上り道を見つけた.
2 高く…の方へ ▪ *Up to* the hills I lift my eyes. 山の高みに私は目をあげるのだ.
3 …の所[時]まで ▪ When he came *up to* me, he took me by the hand. 私の所まで来ると彼は私の手を取った ▪ This has been kept *up to* the present day. これは今日まで保存されている.
4 《口》(顔)の前で ▪ She told me so, *up to* my face. 彼女は私に面と向かってそう言った.
5 (ある程度)に達するまで; (ある数量)までも ▪ He had lived *up to* his income. 彼は収入ぎりぎりの生活をしていた ▪ The canoes carried *up to* thirty-six men. それらのカヌーは36人もの人を乗せていた.

up to much たいしたもの ▪ The shoes were not *up to much*. 靴はたいしたものではなかった.

up to something 何かたくらんで ▪ When she is quiet—watch out—she is *up to something*. 彼女がおとなしくしていたら気をつけろ. 何かたくらんでいるから.

up to the [*one's*] ***ears*** [***eyes, eyeballs, neck,*** 《米》***chin***] (***in***) → EAR; EYE; NECK; CHIN[1].

up to the minute →MINUTE.

up with **1** (人・場所など)…と相並んで ▪ She made for the vestry, but we were *up with* her. 彼女は礼拝堂の方へ向かったが, 我々も彼女について行った ▪ When the day appeared, we were *up with* the cape. 朝になったとき我々はみさきの所まで来ていた.
2 (功績・成功などが)…に匹敵して, 近似して ▪ He is not *up with* his father as a scholar. 彼は学者としては父親にかなわない.
3 〚主に命令文で〛…を立てる, 引き上げる ▪ *Up with* the helm! うわ手かじ! ▪ *Up with* you! 起きろ!
4 《米》…がはかどって ▪ He is well *up with* his program. 彼の計画はかなり進捗している.

up with the times =up to the MINUTE.

ups and downs **1** (道などの)上り下り, 起伏 ▪ The street was full of *ups and downs*. 通りにはいたるところ上り下りがあった.
2 栄枯盛衰, 浮き沈み (*of*) ▪ They had their *ups and downs of* fortune. 彼らにも運の浮き沈みがあった.

What's up? 《口》何事が起こったのか, (近頃)どうしているのか ▪ *What's up* with you? 君, どうかしたの? ▪ Hi, *what's up?* やあ, 元気かい?

up[2] /ʌp/ 動 ***up and leave*** [***go,*** etc.] 《口》急に去る[行く, など] ▪ He just *upped and left* without a word. 彼は一言も言わずにぷいと立ち去った ▪ The actress *up and married* her director. その女優は監督と電撃結婚した. ☞このように up が無変化で単に次の動詞を強める場合もある.

up stakes [***sticks***] (ある場所を)立ち去る, 移転する ▪ They *upped stakes* and moved again. 彼らはまた移転して立ち去った ▪ I can *up stakes*, and go home in the old boat. 私は立ち去り古い船で国に帰れるのだ.

up and up /ʌ̀pənʌ́p/ 名 ***on the up*** (***and up***) **1** 《米口》公正に[な] ▪ The show is run *on the up and up*. そのショーは公正に行われている.
2 《英》次第に上向いて, 好調で, 上り調子で ▪ Things are *on the up* again now. 事態は再び持ち直している ▪ From now on everything is *on the up and up*. 今後万事上向いてくる.
3 《米口》正直な ▪ We can trust John—he's *on the up and up*. ジョンは信頼していい. 正直だから.

upbringing /ʌ́pbrìŋɪŋ/ 名 ***have a… upbringing*** …なしつけを受ける ▪ I *had a* strict Catholic *upbringing*. 私は厳格なカトリックのしつけを受けて育った. ☞upbringing「子供のしつけ(方)」.

upgrade /ʌ́pgrèɪd/ 名 ***on the upgrade*** 《米口》上昇[向上]して ▪ In the iron trade demand

U

seems to be *on the upgrade*. 鉄器業界では需要が上昇しているらしい.

uphill /ʌ̀phíl/ 形 ***an uphill battle*** [***fight, struggle, job, task***] 苦闘, 厄介な仕事; 労多くして功少なきこと ▪ It is *an uphill battle* trying to start a business in Africa. アフリカで事業を興そうとするのは至難の業だ ▪ It's *an uphill struggle* teaching him Latin; he has no aptitude for languages. 彼にラテン語を教えるのは全くの骨折り損だ. 彼には語学の才能がないのだから.

uplift /ʌ́plìft/ 名 ***on the uplift*** 《米口》向上して, 上向いて ▪ The summer season is *on the uplift*. 夏のシーズンは景気が上向いている.

upon /əpɑ́n|əpɔ́n/ 前 ***be*** (***almost***) ***upon one*** (***for***) 《文》(...にとって時が)近づいている ▪ Ramadan *was almost upon* us again. ラマダーンがまた近づいていた.

A ***upon*** *A* Aの累積, AまたA ▪ For mile *upon* mile the desert plain stretches out. 砂漠の平原が何マイルも何マイルも広がっている ▪ His novels have captivated millions *upon* millions of readers. 彼の小説は何百万もの読者の心をとりこにした.

upper /ʌ́pər/ 形名 ***be*** (***down***) ***on*** *one's* ***uppers*** 《英口》ひどく貧乏して[困って]いる ▪ *I'm down on my uppers*. I want money. 私はひどく困っている. 金がほしい ▪ Greener *is on his uppers*. グリーナーはひどく貧乏している. ☞「靴底をすりへらしてしまって」が原義.

get [***gain***] ***the upper hand*** (***of, over***) →HAND[1].

upper crust **1**(パンなどの)上皮 ▪ The *upper crust* of a fine loaf of bread was served to the most important guest. 主賓にはみごとなパンの上皮が供された.

2《俗》頭; 帽子 ▪ Tom completely tinkered his antagonist's *upper crust*. トムは相手の頭をすっかりおもちゃにした.

3《口》上流階級 ▪ Those families are our *upper crust*. これらの家柄の者がわが国の上流階級なのだ.

upper works **1**《海》乾舷(かんげん) ▪ The ship was set on fire to burn her *upper works*. 船は乾舷を焼くために火をつけられた.

2《俗》頭 ▪ They were not strong in their *upper works*. 彼らはおつむが強くなかった.

walk on *one's* ***uppers*** 《米口》**1** 底に穴のあいた靴をはく ▪ He was by this time *walking on his uppers*. 彼はこのときには底に穴のあいた靴をはいていた.

2 ひどく金が足りない[貧乏する] (= be (down) on one's UPPERs) ▪ This month he is *walking on his uppers* and next month he is driving a brand new car. 彼は今月ひどく貧乏しているかと思うと翌月はピカピカの新車を乗り回している.

uppermost /ʌ́pərmòʊst/ 副 ***come uppermost*** 最初に心に浮かんでくる ▪ It is not always wise to say whatever *comes uppermost*. 何でも最初に心に浮かぶことを言うのは必ずしも賢明ではない.

uppish /ʌ́pɪʃ/ 形 ***get uppish*** 《口》高ぶる, 偉そうにする ▪ Don't *get uppish*! 偉そうにするなよ.

upright /ʌ́pràɪt/ 名 ***out of*** (***an***) ***upright*** 傾いて ▪ The wall is a little bit *out of an upright*. 塀は少々傾いている ▪ The mullion was much *out of upright* and had an iron stay. 縦仕切りはひどく傾いていたので, 鉄の支えがしてあった.

uproar /ʌ́prɔ̀ːr/ 名 ***in*** (***an***) ***uproar*** 大騒ぎで ▪ The street was *in* such *an uproar*. 通りはひどい大騒ぎだった.

upset[1] /ʌ̀psét/ 形 ***an upset price*** 売り唱え値《競売開始のときにつける最低値段》 ▪ *The upset price* was one pound an acre. 売り唱え値は1エーカーにつき1ポンドだった.

upset[2] /ʌ̀psét/ 動 ***upset the apple-cart*** → APPLE-CART.

upshot /ʌ́pʃɑ̀t|-ʃɔ̀t/ 名 ***bring*** [***come***] ***to the*** [***an***] ***upshot*** 終結させる[する] ▪ We *brought* the matter *to a* speedy *upshot*. 我々は事件をすみやかに終結させた ▪ When it *came to the upshot* he had all burnt. 事が終わったとき彼は一切を焼かれていた.

in [《まれ》***at***] ***the upshot*** 終わりに, とどのつまり ▪ We may be sure that all come to this *in the upshot*. きっと誰も終わりにはこういうふうになるのだろう ▪ They shall pay dear for it *at the* last *upshot*. とどのつまりは彼らをひどい目にあわせてやるんだ.

upshots /ʌ́pʃɑ̀ts|-ʃɔ̀ts/ 副 ***be upshots with*** ...に仕返しする ▪ He resolved to *be upshots with* Jim Laceby. 彼はジム・レイスビーに仕返ししてやろうと決心した.

upside /ʌ́psàɪd/ 名 ***upside of*** ...を越えた ▪ Their ages are *upside of* forty. 彼らは40歳を越えている.

upside(-)down /ʌ̀psaɪddáʊn/ 副 ***hold ... upside(-)down*** ...をさかさまに持つ ▪ He was *holding* the barometer *upside down*. 彼は晴雨計をさかさまに持っていた.

turn ... upside(-)down ...をひっくり返す《比喩的にも》 ▪ All our things *were turned upside down*. 我々の道具はすべてひっくり返されてしまった ▪ It *turned* her poor little brains *upside down* forever. それでかわいそうに彼女の頭は永久に狂ってしまった.

upsides /ʌ́psàɪdz/ 副 ***get upsides of*** 《口》...に追いつく ▪ He never let any horse *get upsides of* him if he could help it. 彼はできればどの馬にも自分に追いつかせたくなかった.

upsides with **1**《英口》(復しゅうなどして)五分五分になって, 恨みを晴らして ▪ He considered it his duty to be *upsides with* him. 彼はその男に恨みを晴らすのを自分の義務と考えた ▪ I'll be [get] *upsides with* him some day. いつか彼にお礼をしてやる.

2《口》...と互角[同格]で ▪ Baron Farney must finish at least *upsides with* his then conqueror. ファーニー男爵はその時彼に勝っている相手とは少なくとも互角で終わらねばならない.

3 …をよく知って ▪ You must be *upsides with* all these new regulations. 君はこういう新規則をすべて知っているにちがいない.

upstairs /ʌ̀pstéərz/ 副 ***go upstairs*** **1** 2階へ上がる ▪ I'm about to *go upstairs*. これから2階へ上がるところです.

2《口》空中へ上がる ▪ The plane *went upstairs* at speed. 飛行機はぐんぐん上空へ上がった.

kick ... upstairs《戯》(うるさい人)を空名的な高位に祭りあげる, 昇進の名目で追い出す ▪ He is about to *be kicked upstairs* to be Secretary of State. 彼は国務長官という空名的な高位に祭りあげられようとしている.

not have much* [*a lot*] *upstairs《口》あまり利口ではない ▪ He does*n't have a lot* going on *upstairs*. 彼はあまりおつむがよくない.

show** a person **upstairs 人を2階に案内する ▪ I *was shown upstairs* into his den. 私は2階の彼の部屋へ案内された.

step upstairs = go UPSTAIRS 1.

uptake /ʌ́ptèɪk/ 名 ***be quick* [*slow*] *on* [*at, in*] *the uptake***《口》理解が早い[のろい] ▪ Children *are* very *quick in the uptake*. 子供は理解が非常に早い ▪ I *am slow at the uptake* for learning new things. 新しいことを憶えるのに理解に手間取るんだ ▪ She's hardworking, but a bit *slow on the uptake*. 彼女は熱心だが, 少々飲み込みが遅い.

uptight /ʌ̀ptáɪt/ 形 ***get* [*be*] *uptight about***《口》…のことで神経をピリピリさせる[ている] ▪ He *gets uptight about* noise. 彼は騒音については神経をピリピリさせる ▪ Why *are* you so *uptight about* what people say about you? どうして君についての人の噂にそんなに神経をとがらせているの?

uptrend /ʌ́ptrènd/ 名 ***on the uptrend***《米》(景気が)上り坂で ▪ Business would soon be *on the uptrend*. 間もなく景気は上向くだろう.

upward /ʌ́pwərd/ 副 ***and* [*or*] *upward*** またはそれ以上 ▪ Some of them are worth as much as £30 *and upward*. それらの幾つかは30ポンドまたはそれ以上の価値がある.

from ... upward **1** (ある部分)から上 ▪ These men go naked *from* the girdle *upward*. これらの人は帯から上は裸でいる.

2 (ある時)からこれまで ▪ He had nursed the great idea *from* his youth *upward*. 彼は青年時代からこの方, その大きな理想をいだいてきたのだった.

upward of **1** …の上で ▪ *Upward of* this, the hill is covered with heather. ここから上はこの山はヒースにおおわれている.

2 …より以上 ▪ He is *upward of* seventy. 彼は70の坂を越えている.

urge /əːrdʒ/ 動 ***urge** a person **to** do* 人を駆り立てて…させる ▪ His patriotism *urged* him *to* serve his country. 彼は愛国心に駆られて祖国に尽くした.

urgent /ə́ːrdʒənt/ 形 ***urgent of*** (感情などが)…をせきたてて ▪ The miseries of Ireland are *urgent of* redress. アイルランドの不幸な事態が救済をせきたてている.

***urgent* (*with** a person*) *for* [*to** do*]** (人に)…を[することを]切望する ▪ He is very *urgent to* see her. 彼はしきりに彼女に会いたがっている ▪ He was *urgent with* me *for* [*to* disclose] further particulars. 彼はさらに詳細を教えろと私にせがんだ.

usage /júːsɪdʒ/ 名 ***come into* [*go out of*] *usage*** 使用される[されない]ようになる ▪ Those expressions have *gone out of usage*. そういう言い回しは使用されなくなっている.

under rough usage 手荒く使われて ▪ This machine has broken *under rough usage*. この機械は手荒く使われてこわれた.

usance /júːzəns/ 名 ***at usance*** 慣例日付け払いで ▪ No bills are now drawn in London *at usance*. 現在ロンドンでは手形は慣例日付け払いで振り出されることはない.

use[1] /juːs/ 名 ***as was** one's **use*** 例によって ▪ He called on us that Sunday *as was his use*. 彼は例によってその日曜日に訪問してきた.

bring* [*come*] *into use 使用し始める[されるようになる] ▪ The machine *was brought into* common *use*. その機械は一般に使用されるようになった ▪ This word has lately *come into use*. この語は最近使用されるようになった.

find a use for …の利用法を見つける ▪ I have *found a use for* banana-skins. 私はバナナの皮の利用法を見つけた.

for the use of …が使うために, …用として ▪ This is a room *for the use of* ladies only. これは女性専用の部屋です ▪ His is an English grammar *for the use of* students. 彼のは学生用の英文法書だ.

for use 使うために ▪ Books are *for use* not for ornament. 書物は使うもので飾りではない.

go* [*fall*] *out of use 使用されなくなる, すたれる ▪ The custom has *gone out of use*. その習慣はすたれた.

have no use for **1** …を要しない, の用はない ▪ We *have no use for* his services. 彼に助けてもらう要はない ▪ He doesn't smoke, so he *has no use for* a lighter. 彼はタバコを吸わないからライターはいらない.

2《俗》…はごめんだ, きらいだ ▪ I *have no use for* him—don't like him. あの男はごめんだ—虫が好かん ▪ He *had no use for* French. 彼はフランス語はきらいだった.

have the use of …を用いる習慣がある ▪ They *had the use* and knowledge *of* iron. 彼らは鉄を用いる習慣も知識もあった.

have use for …を必要とする ▪ The world will still *have use for* you and me. この世の中はまだ君や私を必要とするだろう.

have** one's **uses《口・主に戯》役に立つことがある ▪ We didn't like him, but he *had his uses*—he was a great cook! 彼のことは気に入らなかったが役立つ面もあった. 何しろ料理がとびきりうまかった.

in use 用いられて, 行われて (↔out of USE) ▪ This is a low word not *in use* now. これは現在用いられていない卑語である.

it is (of) no use *doing* [***to*** *do*] …してもむだだ, 役に立たない ▪ *It* would *be of no use* for you *to* try. 君がやってみてもむだだろう ▪ Ah, well, *it is no use going* back now. 仕方がない, もう後戻りしてもむだだ.

lose the use of …が使えなくなる ▪ He has *lost the use of* his left arm. 彼は左腕が使えなくなった.

make use of …を使用する, 利用する ▪ We *made use of* all our strength. 我々はありったけの力を使った.

of great [***some, little***] ***use*** 大いに役に立つ[少し役に立つ, ほとんど役に立たない] ▪ Snow is *of great use* in winter. 雪は冬には大いに役に立つ ▪ It will be *of some use* in the future. それは将来何かの役に立つだろう.

(of) no use 役に立たない, 無益で ▪ Talking is *no use*. 話してもむだだ ▪ I feel *of no use* to anybody. 私は誰の役にも立たないような気がする.

(of) no use [***good***] ***to man or beast*** 何の役にも立たない ▪ The goods are *of no use to man or beast* practically. その品は実用面では何の役にも立ちません ▪ This machine is so old it's *no use to man or beast*. この機械は古くて使い物にならない.

of... use …に用いられる ▪ The words are *of* very frequent *use* in the New Testament. これらの語は新約聖書では頻繁に用いられている.

Once a use, forever a custom. 《諺》習い性となる.

out of use 用いられなくなって, すたれて (↔in USE) ▪ The word is now wholly *out of use*. その語は今では完全にすたれている.

put... to (a) good [***bad***] ***use*** …を善用[悪用]する ▪ I love to fix up old computers and *put* them *to good use*. 古いコンピューターを修理してそれをうまく利用するのが大好きだ.

put... to use …を用いる, 利用する ▪ Every moment may *be put to* some *use*. 一瞬一瞬を何かに利用することもできる.

there is no use in …はむだである ▪ *There is no use in* crying. 泣いても始まらない.

use and wont 慣習, 慣例 ▪ Privileges belonging to the said lands conform to *use and wont*. 前記の土地に付随する特典は慣習と一致するものである ▪ Bosnian *use and wont* were taken into full consideration. ボスニアの慣習が十分に考慮された.

Use makes perfect. 《諺》習うよりは慣れよ.

What is the use of [***in***] *doing...?* …したって何になるものか ▪ *What is the use of being* so proud? そんなに自慢して何になるんだ.

with use 絶えず使用して ▪ The table was worn and polished *with use*. そのテーブルは絶えず使用されたためすり減ってつやが出ていた ▪ The machine will soon be easier *with use*. この機械は使用していればじきにもっと使いやすくなる.

use[2] /juːz/ 動 ***could*** [***can***] ***use*** 《口》…がほしい, あるといい; 必要である ▪ I *could use* a drink. 1杯ほしいな ▪ I *could use* a worker like him. 彼のような働き者がほしい.

use *oneself* ふるまう, 身を処する ▪ Do you know how he has been *using himself* in the last half-year? 彼がこの半年ほどどのようなふるまいをしてきたか知っていますか.

use *one's* ***bean/use*** *one's* ***noodle*** [***noddle***]/***use*** *one's* ***noggin*** 《俗》頭を使う (= use the (old) NOGGIN) ▪ I just *used my bean*, that's all. ちょっと頭を使っただけだ. それだけさ ▪ Go to many sources and *use your noodle* to decide what's true. 多くの情報源に当たり何が正しいかを決めるのに頭を使え ▪ You can do better in math if you just *use your noddle*. 頭を使いさえすれば数学の成績がずっとよくなる.

use the bathroom [***toilet***] 《婉曲》トイレを使う, 用便する ▪ May I be excused to *use the bathroom*? お手洗いを使わせていただいてもよろしいですか?

use the sea 水夫をする ▪ John continued for some time to *use the sea*. ジョンはしばらく引き続いて水夫をやった.

Use your pleasure. ご随意に, ご自由に.

used /juːst/ 形 ***be*** [***get***] ***used to*** [***to*** *doing*] …に[…することに]慣れている[慣れる] ▪ I'*m* quite *used to* hard work [*to working* hard]. 激しい仕事にはじゅうぶん慣れています ▪ You will soon *get used to* it. じきそれに慣れますよ. ☞to の後には名詞・動名詞が来るが, まれにI have been used to watch them.「それは見慣れてきました」のように不定詞が来る場合もある.

used to /juːstə, juːstu/ 助 …するのが常であった; 以前は…した ▪ I *used to* go to school with him. 私は彼と学校へ行くのが常でした ▪ What did he *use to* say? 彼はいつも何と言っていましたか ▪ I like him now, but I *used* not *to* [《口》didn't *use to*]. 《文》今は彼が好きだが以前はそうではなかった. ☞usen't to, usedn't は《古風》.

as *one* ***used to was*** 《俗》以前のように ▪ I'm not so young *as* I *used to was*. 私は昔のように若くない.

did use to 〚否定文・疑問文で〛以前は…した ▪ I *did*n't *use to* like her, but now I have fallen madly in love with her. 以前は彼女が好きではなかったが, 今は首ったけだ ▪ *Did* you *use to* work here? 以前はここで働いていましたか. ☞did used to を使う人もあるが, 多くの人は誤りと考えている.

did use to be 〚疑問文で〛以前は…であった ▪ *Did* he *use to be* a musician or something? 彼, 以前はミュージシャンか何かだったのか? ▪ *Did* this building *use to be* a hotel? この建物は以前はホテルでしたか?

there used to be 以前…があった ▪ *There used to be* some trees in this field. この畑には以前は木が何本かあった.

useful /júːsfəl/ 形 ***come in useful*** →COME

U

in handy.

make** oneself **useful 手伝う ▪I was careful to *make myself* generally *useful*. 私は何かと手伝うように気を配った.

useless /júːsləs/ 形 ***feel useless*** 《俗》調子が悪い, 元気がない ▪I am *feeling useless* today. きょうは調子がよくない.

usher /ʌ́ʃər/ 動 ***usher … into the world*** …を世の中へ出す ▪He *ushered* the theory *into the world* in 1913. 彼はその説を1913年に世に問うた.

usual /júːʒuəl/ 形 ***as is usual with*** …にはよくあることだが ▪*As is usual with* picnickers, they left a lot of litter behind them. ピクニックをする人たちの常として, 彼らは後にごみをたくさん残していった.

(as) per usual →PER.

as usual いつものように[で] ▪He was late *as usual*. 彼は例によって遅刻した ▪The business is *as usual*. 商売は相も変わらずです.

do the** [one's] **usual 《口》いつもの通りにする ▪He *did his usual* and spoke too long. 彼は例によって例のごとくひどく長話をした.

***it is usual with** one **to** do* …は…するのが普通である ▪*It is usual with* him *to* be late. 彼の場合遅れるのが普通だ.

out of the usual 異常な ▪It's nothing *out of the usual* for Jim to be late. ジムが遅刻するのはちっとも異常ではない.

than usual いつもよりも ▪He got up later *than usual*. 彼はいつもよりも遅く起きた.

usurp /jusə́ːrp|-zə́ːp/ 動 ***usurp the place of*** …に取って代わる ▪Copper began to *usurp the place of* other metals. 銅が他の金属に取って代わり始めた.

usury /júːʒəri/ 名 ***at** [**on, upon**] **usury*** 高利で ▪He lent his capital *upon usury*. 彼は高利で資金を貸しつけた ▪I borrowed money *at usury*. 高利で金を借りた.

with usury 利子[おまけ]をつけて ▪The service was repaid *with usury*. その奉仕はおまけつきで返ってきた.

utility /jutíləti/ 名 ***a utility room*** ユーティリティールーム《洗濯機などの家電機器を設置した小部屋》 ▪Mother is doing the laundry in *the utility room* upstairs. 母は2階の小部屋で洗濯をしている.

of great utility 非常に役に立つ ▪It will be found *of great utility* by its users. それは非常に役に立つことが使用者にわかるだろう.

of little** [**no**] **utility ほとんど[少しも]役に立たない ▪It is *of little utility*. それはほとんど役に立たない.

utmost /ʌ́tmòust/ 名 ***at the utmost*** いくら多くても, たかだか (→at (the) MOST) ▪This watch is worth a thousand yen *at the utmost*. この時計はたかだか1,000円の価値しかない.

do** one's **utmost 全力を尽くす ▪Will you *do your utmost* to obtain justice? 正義を得るために全力を尽くしてくれますか?

get the utmost of =get the BEST of.

to the utmost 極度に, 極力 (*of*) ▪The stepmother tormented her *to the utmost*. 継母は彼女をとことんまでいじめぬいた ▪He would keep his pledge *to the utmost of* his power. 彼は極力約束を守るだろう.

utterance[1] /ʌ́tərəns/ 名 ***find utterance*** (話・感情などが)出る, 表現される (*in*) ▪Some unwise suggestions *found utterance*. ばかげた話が持ち出された ▪The souls of mighty poets *found utterance in* the music of English words. 大詩人の魂が英語の美しい調べとなって表現された.

give utterance to (怒りなど)を表現する, もらす ▪He has recently *given utterance to* his views as follows. 彼は先ごろ次のように自分の見解を述べた.

utterance[2] /ʌ́tərəns/ 名 ***to the utterance*** 《雅》いまわのきわまで, 死ぬまで ▪I will fight him *to the utterance* upon this quarrel. このけんかに関しては彼と死ぬまで戦ってやる.

uttermost /ʌ́tərmòust/ 形 ***to the uttermost farthing*** 最後の一文まで ▪The debt shall be paid *to the uttermost farthing*. 借金は最後の一文まで払わせてやるぞ.

U-turn /júːtə̀ːrn/ 名 ***make** [**do**] **a U-turn***
1 (車両が)Uターンする ▪Officer, may I *make a U-turn* here?—No. おまわりさん, ここでUターンできますか?—だめだ.
2 《報道》考え[計画]を完全に変える ▪Britain has *made a U-turn* in its policy on satellite TV. 英国は衛星テレビに関する政策をがらっと変えた.

U

V

vacant /véɪkənt/ 形 ***fall vacant*** あく ▪ Three places had *fallen vacant*. 3箇所があきになっていた.

vacant of 全然…のない ▪ The hour being *vacant of* business, he got upon his legs. その時は仕事もなく, 彼はけんか腰になった.

vacation[1] /veɪkéɪʃən, və-/ 名 ***on*** (***a*** [*one's*]) ***vacation*** 《主に米》休暇で ▪ Those students were hired to fill in for workers *on vacation*. その学生たちが休暇中の作業員の補充として雇われた ▪ He was away *on a vacation*. 彼は休暇で旅へ出ていた ▪ I was then *on my vacation*. 私は当時休暇をとっていた.

take [***get***] ***a vacation*** 《主に米》休暇をとる ▪ I never *get a vacation* nowadays. 私はこのごろは決して休暇をとらない.

vacation[2] /veɪkéɪʃən, və-/ 動 ***go vacationing*** 《米》休暇で遊びに行く ▪ Despite hard times, people will *go vacationing*. 不景気にもかかわらず, 人々は休暇には遊びに行く.

vacuum /vǽkjuəm/ 名 ***in a vacuum*** 〚しばしば否定文で〛周囲から孤立して, 絶縁して ▪ No poem is written *in a vacuum*. There are always influences from past poets. どんな詩も他の詩と無関係に書かれはしない. 過去の詩人からの影響が常にあるものだ ▪ We will not make a decision about when to start *in a vacuum*. いつ出発するかを唐突に決めるつもりはありません.

Nature abhors a vacuum. 自然は真空を嫌う (Spinoza, *Ethica*).

vague /veɪg/ 名 ***in the vague*** 漠然として ▪ My plans are still *in the vague*. 私の計画はまだ漠然としている.

vain /veɪn/ 形名 (***as***) ***vain as a peacock*** すごくうぬぼれが強い ▪ She's been *vain as a peacock* since she won that award. 彼女はその賞を取ってからというもの, すっかりうぬぼれてしまっている.

be vain of …を自慢する ▪ Between you and me, he *was* not a little *vain of* his legs. ここだけの話だが, 彼は少なからず脚がご自慢だったんだよね ▪ She *is vain of* her face. 彼女は自分の顔が自慢である.

in vain むだに[で], むなしく ▪ All our efforts were *in vain*. 我々の努力はすべてむだだった ▪ He tried *in vain* to please her. 彼は彼女を喜ばそうとしたがだめだった.

take (*a person's* ***name***) ***in vain*** 《戯》(神の名を)軽々しく[みだりに]口にする; 何気なく口にする (《聖》*Exod*. 20. 7) ▪ I always call Chancery "it." I wouldn't *take its name in vain* for worlds. 私は大法官庁のことをいつも「あそこ」と呼んでいる. どうあってもその名を軽々しく口にするなんてことはしないのだ ▪ Who's that *takes my name in vain*? 何気なく私の名を口にしているのは誰かね? (人が自分の名をあげて噂しているとき部屋へ入ってきた場合など).

vale /veɪl/ 名 ***the vale of years*** 老年 (cf. Sh., *Oth*. 3. 3. 266) ▪ He is sunk deep into *the vale of years*. 彼はすっかり老いこんでしまっている.

this vale of tears [***misery, sorrow, woe***] この涙[不幸, 悲しみ, 悩み]の谷間, 浮き世 ▪ I long to leave *this vale of tears* and enter heaven. 私は浮き世におさらばして極楽入りを待ちこがれている.

valet /vǽlət, vælé ɪ/ 名 ***No man is a hero to his valet.*** →HERO.

valley /vǽli/ 名 ***the*** [***this***] ***valley of tears*** 涙の谷, 浮き世 (=this VALE of tears) ▪ In *this valley of tears* there come many evil things. この涙の谷ではかずかずの悪がやって来る.

the valley of the shadow of death → SHADOW.

valor, 《英》**valour** /vǽlər/ 名 ***the better part of valor*** 慎重, 用心 ▪ The general decided on *the better part of the valor*, and surrendered. 将軍は慎重にやるにこしたことはないと決めて降伏した. ☞《諺》DISCRETION is the better part of valor から.

valuable /vǽljəbəl|-jʊb-/ 形 ***valuable for*** (目的)にとって貴重[大切]な ▪ Water is *valuable for* putting out fires. 水は火事を消すのになくてはならない.

valuation /vӕljuéɪʃən/ 名 ***make a valuation of*** …を値踏みする ▪ They *made a* new *valuation of* all private property. すべての個人財産が新たに値踏みされた.

set too high [***low***] ***a valuation on*** …に高[安]すぎる評価をつける ▪ I think you *set too high a valuation on* the building. あなたはあの建物に高すぎる評価をつけておられると思います.

take [***accept***] *a person* ***at*** *his* ***own valuation*** 人をその人自身の評価通りに取る ▪ They appear disposed to *take* him *at his own valuation*. 彼らは彼を彼自身の評価通りに買うつもりらしい.

value[1] /vǽlju:/ 名 ***a value judgment*** [《英》***judgement***] (事実ではなく個人的な意見に基づく)価値判断《非難して》 ▪ All human suffering is an experience based on *value judgements* of what is good and bad. 人間が苦しむのはすべて主観的に善悪の価値判断をするからである ▪ You are always making *value judgements*. 君はいつも主観的な価値判断をしている.

give [***get***] ***good value for*** …に対して十分値うちのある物を与える[受け取る] ▪ He *got good value for* his money. 彼は払った金に十分値するものを得た.

V

give value for value 値うちだけのものを支払う ▪ It is a good piece of furniture and I want to *give value for value*. 立派な家具だから，値うちに合うだけのものを支払いたい.

market value 市場価値 ▪ *Market value*s rose sharply last week. 市場価値が先週急に上がった.

of great* [*some, little, no*] *value 価値が大いにある[少しある，少ない，ない] ▪ This book is *of great value*. この本は非常に価値がある ▪ Gold is *of no value* to them. 金は彼らにとって価値はない ▪ This research is *of some value* to me. この調査は私には少々価値のあるものです.

of value 貴重な; 有用な ▪ They removed everything *of value* from the vessel. 彼らはその船から貴重品はいっさい他へ移した ▪ It is reputed *of value* in kidney diseases. それは腎臓病にきくという評判だ.

***set* [*put*] *a high* [*much, little*] *value on* [*upon*]** …を高く買う[大いに買う，あまり買わない] ▪ He *set* too *great a value on* the services that he had rendered us. 彼は我々のために尽くしたことを恩にきせすぎた ▪ He *set much value upon* the study of Greek. 彼はギリシャ語研究を高く買っていた.

set* [*put*] *a value on …を値踏みする ▪ I asked him to *set a value on* the pictures. 私は彼にその絵を値踏みしてくれるように頼んだ.

to the value of 価格が…の ▪ He has gained a prize *to the value of* £10,000. 彼は価格で1万ポンドの賞を得た.

under value 価格[額面]以下で ▪ Foreign money is changed *under value*. 外貨は額面以下に両替えされる.

value for money 払った金に見合う価値，金相応のもの ▪ This book will give *value for money*. この本は払った金に見合う値打ちがあるよ.

value[2] /vǽlju:/ 動 ***value** oneself **for*** (自分のしたことなど)を相当のものだろうとうぬぼれる ▪ Everyone is in danger of *valuing himself for* what he does. 人はみなおのれの所業を相当なものだとうぬぼれる危険がある.

value** oneself **on [***upon***] …を誇る ▪ He *values himself on* his birth. 彼は門地を自慢している.

vamoose /vəmú:s/ 動 ***vamoose the ranch* [*camp, kitchen*]** 《米口》立ち去る ▪ I proposed to quietly *vamoose the ranch*. 私はそっと立ち去ることを提案した.

van /væn/ 名 ***in the van* (*of*)** 《英・文》(…の)先頭に立って ▪ Our firm is always *in the van* with improvements. わが社は改善にかけては常に先頭を切っている ▪ France is *in the van of* the movement. フランスがその運動の先頭に立っている.

***lead the van* (*of*)** (…の)先駆を務める ▪ He *leads the van of* this great movement. 彼がこの大運動の先駆を務めている.

vanguard /vǽngà:rd/ 名 ***in the vanguard* (*of*)** (運動の)先頭に立って ▪ At length Germany was *in the vanguard of* civilization. ついにドイツが文明の先頭に立った.

vanish /vǽnɪʃ/ 動 ***vanish from* [*out of*] *sight*** 見えなくなる ▪ He ran into the wood and *vanished from sight*. 彼は森の中へ駆け込んで見えなくなった.

***vanish into air* [*smoke, wind*]** 空[煙，風]の中に消散する ▪ Wreaths of smoke *vanished into air*. うずを巻いた煙が空中に消えうせた ▪ All his frauds will *vanish into wind*. 彼のいかさまはことごとく風の中に消散するだろう.

vanish into the blue → disappear into the BLUE.

vanishing point /vǽnɪʃɪŋpɔ̀ɪnt/ 名 ***to a* [*the*] *vanishing point*** 《口》(物が尽きて)消滅点に達するまで ▪ The danger of operation is retreating *to a vanishing point*. 手術の危険は少なくなりゼロに近づいている ▪ Profits have dwindled *to the vanishing point*. 利益はだんだん減ってゼロになってしまった.

vanity /vǽnəti/ 名 ***All is vanity.*** いっさいは空(くう)である (《聖》*Eccles*. 1. 2).

out of vanity 虚栄心から ▪ He did it *out of vanity*. 彼は虚栄心からそうした.

the pomps and vanities 虚栄 ▪ He renounced *the pomps and vanities* of this wicked world. 彼は浮世の虚栄を捨てた.

Vanity Fair 虚栄の市; 虚栄の世の中 (Bunyan, *Pilgrim's Progress* 1) ▪ But how preach at all in such a *vanity fair* as this? だが，このような虚栄の市でそもそもどのようにして説教したらいいのか.

vanity of vanities 空(くう)の空(くう)(《聖》*Eccles*. 1. 2) ▪ The book is a varied study of the *vanity of vanities* of all the societies. その本は全社交界の空の空に関する多彩な研究書である.

vantage /vǽntɪdʒ|vá:n-/ 名 ***catch* [*have, hold, take*] *a person* at vantage** 人よりも有利な地位に立つ，人の不意を打つ ▪ At last she *had* him *at vantage* again, and was before him. とうとう彼女はまた彼よりも有利な地位に立ち，彼を抜いてしまった ▪ You have *taken* me *at vantage*. あなたには不意をつかれました.

***place* [*point, coign*] *of vantage*/*vantage ground* [*point*]** 有利な地位，地の利 ▪ From the *vantage point* of a window seat, one surveys the slums. 窓側席の地の利を利用してスラム街がながめられる.

variance /véəriəns/ 名 ***at variance*** **1** (人が)相争って，不和で (*with, among, between, from*) ▪ He was *at variance with* his father. 彼は父親と不和だった ▪ They were *at variance among* themselves. 彼らは互いに争っていた ▪ He is totally *at variance from* the Government. 彼は政府と全くもって不和である.

2 (物が)相違して，一致しないで，矛盾して (*with*) ▪ The brow and the mouth are *at variance*. 額と口がちぐはぐである ▪ His conduct was not a little *at variance with* his professions. 彼のふるまいは口で言っているところとは少なからず矛盾していた.

set** a person **at variance 人を不和にする[離間する] ▪ I am come to *set* a man *at variance* against his father. 私はある人をその父親と仲たがいさせるために来ているのだ.

variant /véəriənt/ 形 ***variant from*** …と相違した ▪ The publication in the papers was *variant from* that which he sent home. 新聞に発表された文章は彼が故国に送ったものとは相違していた.

variation /vèəriéɪʃən, vǽr-/ 名 ***variations on the theme of*** …のいろいろな変種 ▪ He thought out new *variations on the theme of* blackmailing. 彼はゆすりにおけるいろいろな新手の変種を考え出した. ☞「主題をめぐる変奏曲」が原義.

variety /vəráɪəti/ 名 ***a variety of*** さまざまの ▪ We discussed *a variety of* topics. 我々はさまざまな話題について話し合った ▪ A school teacher has *a* wide *variety of* duties. 学校教師には実にさまざまの仕事がある.

give variety to …に変化をつける ▪ Those hillocks *give variety to* the landscape. あれらの小山が風景に変化をつけている.

of the ... variety 《戯》…のタイプの[で] ▪ He is a man *of the* confident *variety*. 彼は自信たっぷりのタイプの男性だ.

Variety is the spice of life. 《諺》変化は人生の薬味, いろいろあってこそ人生は楽しい.

variety show バラエティー番組 ▪ The Jackson 5 got its own *variety show*. ジャクスンファイブは自身のバラエティー番組を持っていた.

various /véəriəs, vǽr-/ 形 ***various and sundry*** 種々雑多な ▪ There are a tiny handful of naysayers on *various and sundry* points. 少数ながらさまざまな点に関していつも反対する人たちがいる.

varnish /vɑ́ːrnɪʃ/ 名 ***put a varnish on/give a varnish to*** …を紛飾する, 巧みに繕う ▪ He *put a varnish* of legality *on* his actions. 彼は自分の行為を合法であるとして紛飾した ▪ Women will always *give a varnish* of duty *to* their inclinations. 女性はいつも自分のやりたいことを義務でするのだと言い繕う.

vault /vɔːlt/ 動 ***vaulting ambition*** はやりたつ野心 (cf. Sh., *Macb*. 1. 7. 27) ▪ Sometimes his *vaulting ambition* overleaps itself. ときどき彼のはやり立つ野心はやり過ぎてしくじることもある.

veer /vɪər/ 動 ***veer and haul*** 《海》 **1** 綱をゆるめたり張ったりする《比喩的にも》 ▪ Here is a sum on which the Government may fairly *veer and haul*. これは政府が使用をゆるめたり締めたりしてもさしつかえない金額である.

2 (風向きが)交互に変わる ▪ The wind *veers* aft *and hauls* forward. この風は船尾へ次に船首へと交互に変わっている.

vegetable /védʒətəbəl/ 形名 ***be a vegetable*** 生きてはいるが機能をまともに使っていない, 植物人間状態である ▪ She had *been a vegetable* for the past 10 years. 彼女は過去10年間植物人間であった.

become a mere vegetable じっと座ったきりの生活をする ▪ I am *becoming a mere vegetable*. 私はじっと座ったきりの生活をしています.

vegetable life **1** 〚総称的〛植物 ▪ The island had almost no animal or *vegetable life*. その島には動植物はほとんど見られなかった.

2 草木のような生活 ▪ The patient was weary of a merely *vegetable life*. その病人は単に草木のような生活をすることにうんざりしていた.

veil /veɪl/ 名 ***beyond [behind, within] the veil*** あの世に (《聖》*Heb*. 6. 19) ▪ He is past *behind the veil*. 彼はあの世へ行っている ▪ He passed on *within the veil*. 彼はあの世へ去って行った.

draw [throw, cast] a veil over 《文》…をおおい隠す, 隠ぺいする ▪ It *throws a veil over* the grossness of its error. それでその誤りのひどさがおおい隠されている.

raise [drop, lower]** one's **veil ベールを上げる[下げる] ▪ She *lowered her veil* to escape detection. 彼女は人に見つからないようにベールを下ろした.

renounce the veil 修道女の生活をやめる ▪ By twenty she had quite *renounced the veil*. 20歳になるころまでには彼女は修道女の生活をすっかり絶っていた. ☞修道女のかぶるベールから.

take the veil 修道女になる, 修道院に入る ▪ My father intended I should *take the veil*. 父は私を修道院に入れるつもりでした.

under the veil of …の名に隠れて, にかこつけて ▪ They are committing murder *under the veil of* patriotism. 彼らは愛国心にかこつけて人殺しをしているのだ.

within the veil →beyond the VEIL.

vein /veɪn/ 名 ***in the (right) vein*** 気が向いて (*for*) (↔ out of the VEIN) ▪ Nobody can be more amusing when she is *in the vein*. 気が向いたときの彼女ほどおもしろい人はまたとない ▪ I am not *in the vein for* work. 私は働く気がしない.

in the same vein 同じ調子の[で] ▪ He made other remarks *in the same vein*. 彼は他のことも同じ調子で言った.

of a ... vein …の気質の ▪ He is *of an* imaginative *vein*. 彼は空想にふけるたちの人だ.

out of the vein 気が向いていない (↔in the (right) VEIN) ▪ He makes it a rule to study whether in the vein or *out of the vein*. 彼は気が向いても向かなくても勉強することにしている.

velvet /vélvət/ 名形 ***be [stand] on velvet*** (一般的に)楽な地位にある, 有利な地位にある; 《主にとばく俗》必ず儲かる地位にある ▪ We *stand on velvet* as to finance. 財政面では我々は楽な地位にある ▪ Success is placed. Now we *stand on velvet*. サクセス号は入賞した. さあ儲けにありつけるぞ.

the [an] iron hand [fist] in the velvet glove/the iron beneath** one's **velvet glove 表面だけ優しいこと, 外柔内剛 ▪ He's one of those men who have *an iron hand in the velvet glove*. 彼は外柔内剛型の一人だ ▪ The people did not have a chance to feel *the iron beneath their velvet glove.* 人民は彼らの外柔内剛ぶりを感じる機会がなかった. ☞元プロイセンの首相 Bismarck について言ったもの.

to the velvet 純益として, 儲けて ▪ I was several hundred pounds *to the velvet.* 数百ポンド儲けた.

veneration /vènəréɪʃən/ 名 ***have* [*hold*]... *in veneration*** ...を尊敬する, 崇拝する ▪ He *held* my judgment *in* high *veneration.* 彼は私の判断を大いに尊重していた.

vengeance /véndʒəns/ 名 ***feel*** *a person's* ***vengeance*** 人の恨みを思い知る ▪ He shall *feel my vengeance.* 彼に私の恨みを思い知らせてやる.

Heaven's vengeance is slow but sure. 《諺》天罰は遅いが必ず来る,「天網恢々(かいかい)疎(そ)にして漏らさず」.

***seek vengeance on* [*upon*]** ...に復しゅうしようとする (*for*) ▪ He *sought vengeance upon* us *for* the injury. 彼は我々に危害の復しゅうをしようとした.

take a bloody vengeance on ...を殺して復しゅうする ▪ He *took a bloody vengeance on* the murderer. 彼はその殺人者に血の復しゅうをした.

***take* [*inflict*] *vengeance on* [*upon*]** ...に復しゅうする ▪ A venger is one who *takes vengeance on* an offender. 復しゅう者とは加害者に復しゅうする人のことである.

with a vengeance 《口》[[強意的に]] ひどく, やけに, いやと言うほど; まさしく ▪ When it does rain here, it rains *with a vengeance.* ここでは雨が降るとなるととてもひどい ▪ He is a genius, *with a vengeance.* 彼はまさしく天才だ.

wreak *one's* ***vengeance*** 恨みを晴らす ▪ She at last determined to *wreak her vengeance* by setting fire to his house. 彼女はついに彼の家に火をつけて恨みを晴らそうと決心した.

***wreak vengeance on* [*upon*]** = take VENGEANCE on.

Venice /vénəs/ 名 ***the Venice of the North*** 北のベネチア《アムステルダムの異名》 ▪ I paid a one-day visit to Amsterdam, *the "Venice of the North."* 別名北のベネチアのアムステルダムを1日訪れた.

vent[1] /vent/ 名 ***find* [*get, have, make, want*] (*a*) *vent*** 出口[はけ口]を見いだす[得る, もつ, つくる, 求める] ▪ Their admiration *found vent* in deep-chested cheers. 彼らの賞賛の念は満腔の歓呼となって現れた ▪ New wine, *wanting vent,* blows up the bung. 新しいワインは出口を求めてたるを破裂させるのだ ▪ He *found a vent* for his anger in smashing it. 彼はそれを砕いて怒りのはけ口を見つけた.

give vent to 《口》...に出口[はけ口]を与える; (感情など)をぶちまける, もらす ▪ He is apt to *give vent to* his feelings. 彼はとかく感情を表しがちだ ▪ This enraged me and I *gave* full *vent to* my anger. このことで私は激怒し, かんしゃくを爆発させた ▪ He *gave vent to* the following reflections. 彼は次のような感想をもらした.

take vent **1** (火薬が)爆発力を失う ▪ Gunpowder, having *taken vent,* cannot take fire. 火薬は爆発力を失うと火がつかない.

2 もれる ▪ Stop it well so that nothing may *take vent.* 何ひとつもれないようにそれを十分に止めておけ.

vent[2] /vent/ 動 ***vent itself*** もれ出る; 現れる ▪ The lake *vents itself* into the sea at Galway. その湖はゴールウェイで海に注いでいる ▪ This cheerfulness has *vented itself* in his playful poetry. この陽気さが彼のおどけた詩に現れている.

venture[1] /véntʃər/ 名 ***at a venture*** でたらめに, 偶然に ▪ A certain man drew a bow *at a venture.* 一人の男が何心なく弓を引いた ▪ He chose the book *at a venture* from the shelves. 彼は棚からでたらめにその本を選んだ.

venture[2] /véntʃər/ 動 ***Nothing* [*Nought, Naught*] *venture, nothing* [*nought, naught*] *have* [*win*]./ *Nothing ventured, nothing gained.*** 《諺》虎穴に入らずんば虎児を得ず.

venture *oneself* 危険を冒す, 思いきって進む ▪ Dare you *venture yourself* alone with me? 思いきって私と二人だけで出かける勇気がありますか.

venue /vénjuː/ 名 ***change the venue*** 《法》裁判地を移転する ▪ Here they *changed the venue* to ensure justice. ここで彼らは公正を期すために裁判地を変えた.

lay* [*fix, place*] *the venue 《法》裁判地を指定する ▪ The plaintiff *laid the venue* in Warwickshire. 被告は裁判地をウォリック州に指定した.

verbal /vɔ́ːrbəl/ 形 ***have a good verbal memory*** 言葉に対する記憶がよい ▪ Dr. Johnson *had a good verbal memory.* ジョンスン博士は言葉に対する記憶がよかった.

verbal diarrh*(*o*)*ea 《戯》病的なおしゃべり, 言葉下痢 (→have verbal DIARRHEA) ▪ Are you saying I've got *verbal diarrhoea?* 私が饒舌病にかかっているというのですか?

verdict /vɔ́ːrdɪkt/ 名 ***bring in* [*deliver, give, render, return*] *a verdict of*** 陪審員が...の答申をする[評決を下す] ▪ The coronor *brought in a verdict of* death by suicide. 検死官はその死が自殺によるものと答申した ▪ The jury *returned a verdict of* guilty. 陪審員は有罪の評決を下した.

pass a* [*one's*] *verdict 判決を下す (*upon*) ▪ The jury were about to *pass their verdict upon* it. 陪審員はその判決を下そうとしていた.

the popular verdict 一般大衆の意見 ▪ *The popular verdict* was that it served him right. 彼はいい気味だというのが一般大衆の意見だった.

verge /vəːrdʒ/ 名 ***on the verge of*** **1** ...の間ぎわに ▪ He is now tottering *on the verge of* the grave. 彼は今にも死にかけている ▪ The nation seemed *on the verge of* a civil war. その国家は内乱の瀬戸ぎわにあるように思われた.

2 今にも...せんとして (*doing*) ▪ Twice she was *on the verge of telling* all. 二度も彼女はまさに一切を

話すところだった.

to the verge of …の間ぎわまで《比喩的にも》 ▪ He has been driven *to the* very *verge of* despair. 彼は絶望の間ぎわまで追いつめられた ▪ He was jealous *to the verge of* insanity. 彼は狂気と言ってよいほどに嫉妬深かった.

versatile /vəːrsətəl|-tàɪl/ 形 ***versatile in*** …が多才の, 多方面の ▪ He is *versatile in* his genius. 彼の才は多方面にわたっている.

verse /vəːrs/ 名 ***chapter and verse*** →CHAPTER.

in verse 韻文で ▪ The play is written partly *in verse* and partly in prose. その劇は一部は韻文で一部は散文で書かれている.

put* [*turn*]*… into verse …を韻文にする ▪ In ancient time, the laws *were* many times *put into verse*. 古代には法律はたびたび韻文にされた.

versed /vəːrst/ 形 ***be versed in*** …に精通している ▪ He *is* deeply *versed in* Japanese literature. 彼は日本文学に深く通じている.

vertical /vəːrtɪkəl/ 名 ***out of the vertical*** 垂直でない, 傾斜して ▪ The wall is *out of the vertical*. 壁は傾斜している.

vessel /vésəl/ 名 ***Empty vessels make the most* [*great*] *sound* [*noise*].** 《諺》空の容器は一番音を立てる,「空だるは音が高い」,「浅瀬に仇波(あだなみ)」《頭の空っぽの者が一番多弁である》.

vest[1] /vest/ 名 ***play it close to the vest*** 手の内を見せない (→play one's CARDs close to one's chest) ▪ The boss is *playing it close to the vest* that nobody knows who will be the next head. 上司は次の主任が誰になるか分からないと言って手の内を見せないでいる.

vest[2] /vest/ 動 ***vest** oneself* 祭服を着る ▪ The Bishop *vested himself* to say Mass. 司教はミサを読むために祭服を着た.

vested /véstəd/ 形 ***have a vested interest*** (***in***) 既得権がある; 持続的興味を持つ ▪ America *has a vested interest in* India's success. アメリカはインドの成功に強い関心がある.

vestige /véstɪdʒ/ 名 ***not a vestige of*** みじんの…もない ▪ There is *not a vestige of* truth in the report. その報告書にはみじんの真実もない.

vestured /véstʃərd/ 形 ***vestured with* [*in*]** (衣服)をまとった《比喩的にも》 ▪ We were *vestured with* poor clothes. 我々は見すぼらしい服をまとっていた ▪ They will be *vestured with* life. 彼らは生命の衣をまとうだろう.

veto /víːtoʊ/ 名 ***pocket veto*** (合衆国大統領・州知事などが持つ)議案拒否権, 議案の握りつぶし ▪ President Reagan issued a *pocket veto* late in 1981 and 1983. レーガン大統領は1981年, 1983年の後半に拒否権を発動した.

***put* [*place, set*] *a* [*one's*] *veto on* [*upon*]** …を拒否する ▪ He *put a veto on* the proposal at once. 彼はすぐその提案を拒否した.

vex /veks/ 動 ***a vexed question*** 盛んに論じられた問題, やかましい問題 ▪ I do not mean to meddle in so *vexed a question*. そのようにやかましい問題に口ばしを入れるつもりはありません.

be* [*feel*] *vexed 腹がたつ, じれったがる (*by, at, with a person for, that*) ▪ I *am vexed at* his idleness. 彼の不勉強にはごうを煮やしている ▪ I *am* always *vexed with* people who don't care what they eat. 私は何を食べようとかまわないという連中にはいつも腹がたつ ▪ He *was vexed with* his son *for* his laziness. 彼は息子が怠けるのでじりじりしていた ▪ She *was vexed that* I did not help her. 彼女は私が助けてやらないのでじれったがっていた.

***vex** oneself* 悩む, じれる ▪ Why will you *vex yourself* about your father? どうしておとうさんのことで悩んでおられるのですか.

vex a saint 聖人[君子]をも怒らせる ▪ This would *vex a saint* all right. これではまず君子でも怒るだろう.

vial /váɪəl/ 名 ***pour out the vials of** one's **wrath on* [*upon*]** …に復しゅうする;《口》怒りをぶちまける (《聖》*Rev.* 16. 1) ▪ The almighty Creator *pours out the* utmost *vials of his wrath upon* them. 全能の神は彼らに根かぎり復しゅうする ▪ She *poured out the vials of her* mental *wrath on* the head of Mrs. West for the insult. 彼女は侮辱に対してウェスト夫人に心の怒りをぶちまけた.

vice[1] /váɪs/ 名 (***as***) ***firm as a vice*** 万力でつかんだようにしっかりと ▪ His grasp was *as firm as a vice*. 彼がつかんだ手はぴくりとも動かなかった.

grip like a vice 万力のように[むんずと]つかむ ▪ He *gripped* my hand *like a vice*. 彼は私の手を万力のように握りしめた.

vice[2] /váɪs/ 名 ***have the vices of** one's **virtues*** =have the DEFECTs of one's qualities.

vice versa /vàɪsivəːrsə/ 副 逆に;〚省略文で〛逆もまた同じ ▪ The man blames his wife and *vice versa*. 夫は妻をとがめ, 妻は夫をとがめる ▪ He calls black white and *vice versa*. 彼は黒を白と言い, 白を黒と言う. ☞L 'position turned'.

vicinage /vísənɪdʒ/ 名 ***in the vicinage of*** 《文》…の付近の[に] ▪ The Canadians *in the vicinage of* Quebec lived comfortably. ケベック付近のカナダ人たちは安楽に暮らしていた.

vicinity /vəsínəti/ 名 ***in close vicinity to*** 《文》…のすぐ近くに ▪ He lives *in close vicinity to* the church. 彼は教会のすぐ近くに住んでいる.

in the vicinity of …の付近に[の] ▪ He has his snug retreat *in the vicinity of* the metropolis. 彼は首都の付近に住み心地のよい隠退所を持っている.

vicious /víʃəs/ 形 ***a vicious circle*** 《論》循環論法;《経》悪循環 ▪ This is arguing in *a vicious circle*. これでは循環論法で論じていることになる ▪ Rising costs and rising wages—*a vicious circle*. 物価があがって給料があがる—悪循環というものだ.

victim /víktəm/ 名 ***be a victim of** one's **own success*** 成功はしたが, かえって皮肉[最悪]な結果となる ▪ His shop *is* kind of *a victim of its*

V

own success as a discount shop. 彼の店は, 安売り店としてはいわば成功したが, かえって皮肉な結果になっている.

be made a victim of …の犠牲にされる ▪ We *were made victims of* economic depression. 我々は不景気の犠牲にされた.

fall a victim to/become a victim of 《文》…の犠牲になる ▪ He *fell a victim to* an assassin. 彼は暗殺者の犠牲になった ▪ He *became a victim of* his own ambition. 彼は自らの野心の犠牲になった.

victor /víktər/ 名 ***To the victors belong the spoils.*** 《諺》勝者は人と財産の支配権を得る, 勝者がすべてを手にする ☞ 選挙で勝った政党が支持者を公職に望むように任命するアメリカの政治制度から.

victorious /vɪktɔ́:riəs/ 形 ***be victorious over*** …に勝利を得る, 勝つ ▪ He *was victorious over* the Turks in war, and *over* himself in peace. 彼は戦時にはトルコ人に勝ち, 平時には自己に勝った.

victory /víktəri/ 名 ***be a victory for common sense*** (争いの解決策が)えこひいきのない立派なものである ▪ We welcomed the decision as *being a victory for common sense*. 我々はその決定がどちらにもくみしない立派なものであると歓迎した.

cruise to victory 悠々と勝つ ▪ Once again Usain Bolt *cruised to victory* in the 100 meters. またしてもウサイン・ボルト選手は100メートル走で楽勝した.

have* [*get, win*] *the victory 勝利を得る (*over*) ▪ The Greeks fought strenuously, and *got the victory over* the Persians. ギリシャ人は奮闘し, ペルシャ人に対して勝利を得た.

Vietnam /vi:ètnɑ́:m, -nǽm/ 名 ***Vietnam syndrome*** 《口》ベトナム・シンドローム[症候群]《ベトナム戦争に起因する, 国際紛争への軍事介入などの政策に対する不信》 ▪ American foreign policy still suffers from what some have called the "*Vietnam Syndrome*." アメリカの外交政策はいまだにいわゆる「ベトナム・シンドローム」に悩まされている.

view[1] /vju:/ 名 ***a view halloa* [*halloo*]** (キツネ狩りで)キツネが隠れ場所から飛び出すのを見つけて叫ぶ声 ▪ He gave *a view halloa*, and the hounds immediately ran to him. 彼が見つけたぞと叫ぶと犬どもが駆け寄った.

a worm's-eye view →WORM[1].

air one's view →AIR one's opinion.

at first view →at FIRST sight.

bring ... into view …を見えるようにする ▪ The telescope can *bring into view* objects a mile distant. 望遠鏡で1マイル先の物が見える.

come into view 見えてくる ▪ At last a hotel *came into view*. とうとうホテルが見えてきた.

come within view of =within SIGHT of.

do* [*take*] *some views of …の風景を描く[写す] ▪ I *did some views of* the lake. その湖水の風景を描いた.

exposed to view 現れて, 見えるようになって ▪ A clear green lake was *exposed to view*. 澄んだ青い湖が見えてきた.

get* [*have*] *a grandstand view of …の全貌が見渡せる ▪ From here you can *get a grandstand view of* the city. ここから町がすっかり見える.

go out of view =go out of SIGHT.

have ... in view 《文》 **1** …を心に留めている, に注目している ▪ I *have* a quantity of work *in view*. たくさんの仕事に気を配っています.

2 …をもくろんでいる ▪ They *had* a deep political object *in view*. 彼らは深い政治目的を抱いていた.

have* one's *views colored by 見解[意見]が…の影響を受ける ▪ He *had his views colored by* his own background and upbringing. 彼の見方には彼自身の出自と生い立ちの影響が色濃く及んでいた.

***have views on* [*upon*]** …に目をつける, をねらう ▪ The cat *has views upon* the larder. その猫は食料品室をねらっている ▪ I *have views on* a meal at the next town. 次の町で食事をするつもりでいる.

in my view 私の意見では ▪ *In my view*, war is a game in which both sides lose. 私に言わせれば, 戦争とは双方が負けるゲームである.

in the long* [*short*] *view 長い[短い]目で見ると ▪ *In the long view* the victory means even more to the country. 長い目で見ると, 勝利はその国にとっていっそう重要な意味を持っている.

in the view of …の[から]見える所に ▪ He was smiling *in the view of* all persons. 彼はすべての人から見える所でにこにこしていた.

in* [*within*] *view **1** 見えて, 見える所に ▪ There was nothing *in view* except a tall tree. 高い木のほかには何ひとつ見えていなかった ▪ If Bill ventured outside, his mother expected him to stay *within view*. もしビルが危険を冒して外に出ても, 母親は自分から見えるところにいて欲しかった.

2 期待して, 希望して ▪ Lady Goblins still have playoffs *in view*. レディーゴブリンズには引き分け再試合の望みがまだある ▪ With the coming election *in view*, the party leader explained the party policies. 来る選挙を目当てにして党首は政策を説明した.

3 もくろんで, 考慮に入れて ▪ And with this *in view*, the saddles are very generally left on. そしてこのことを見込んで馬の鞍(くら)は通例つけたままにしておく.

in view of **1** …の[から]見える所に ▪ We came *in view of* a church spire. 我々は教会の尖塔の見える所にやって来た ▪ He stood *in* full *view of* the crowd. 彼は群衆からすっかり見える所に立っていた.

2 《卑》…を予想[期待]して (=with a VIEW to 1) ▪ Let us cheerfully loose the reins, *in view of* attaining the end. その目的を成就するために快活に手綱をゆるめようではないか ▪ He did so *in view of* marrying Ethelinda. 彼はエセリンダと結婚しようと思ってそうしたのだ.

3 …を考慮して, にかんがみて ▪ *In view of* the readiness she showed, all appeared to be forgiven. 彼女がいそいそした様子を示したことを考えると何もかも赦してくれたらしかった.

4 …のために ▪ *In view of* the excellencies of the works embodied in it, the language continued to be occasionally used. それで表現されている作品がすばらしいところから, その言語は依然として時おり使用された.

keep … in view =have … in VIEW 1.

lost to view 見えなくなって ▪ Tom was already *lost to view* among the trees. トムの姿はもう木立の間に見えなくなっていた.

meet** a person's **view(s) 人の意向に添う ▪ I will try to *meet your views* in every way. 全面的にご意向に添うようにしましょう.

on the view 見ただけで ▪ That may be accomplished first *on the view*. それはまず見ただけでできる.

on [upon] (the) view of …を観察して, 検視して ▪ An inquest was held *on view of* the body. その死体を見て検視が行われた.

on view 展示して, 公開して ▪ The exhibition will be *on view* until September 30. その展覧会は9月30日まで公開されます ▪ It shall be *on view* in the drawing-room. それは応接室でお目にかけよう.

take a dim view of →DIM.

take a favorable [dark, just,** etc.**] view of …を好意的に[悲観的に, 公正に, など]見る ▪ He *took a favorable view of* her conduct. 彼は彼女のふるまいを好意的に見た.

take a general view of …を概観する ▪ Let us *take a general view of* the subject. その問題を概観してみよう.

take a poor view of …に感心しない, 不賛成である; を悲観する ▪ I *take a poor view of* his action at that time. あの時の彼のとった行動には感心しない ▪ He *took a poor view of* the plan. 彼はその計画に不賛成だった.

take a view of …を見る; を視察[検分]する ▪ He had *taken a view of* the monuments. 彼はもうそれらの記念碑を見ていた ▪ The next day he *took a view of* all Darius's money. その翌日彼はダリウスの財産すべてを検分した.

take long views/take the long view 遠い将来のことを考える ▪ Those who *took the long view* are now reaping the benefit of such a policy. 遠い将来のことを考えた人々はそのような政策の利益を今得ている.

take short views/take the short view 近い将来だけのことを考える ▪ We must not *take short views*, we must take long views. 近い将来だけのことを考えてはいけない, 遠い将来のことを考えなくてはだめだ.

take some views of =do some VIEWs of.

take the view that …という見解を取る ▪ I *take the view that* current and future harmful animal testing should be eliminated. 現在および将来の有害な動物実験は廃止されるべきであるとの見解である.

to the view 視界に, 見える所に ▪ It seemed as if heaven was opening *to the view*. まるで天が開いて見えているかのようだった ▪ It is half invisible *to the view*. それは半ば隠れて見えなかった.

with a view to 1《文》〚名詞・代名詞・動名詞を伴って〛…の目的で, を目当てにして ▪ Providence has constituted us *with a view to* activity. 神は活動させようとして人間を作りたもうた ▪ She was educated *with a view to* becoming a governess. 彼女は家庭教師になる目的で教育された.

2 …に関して ▪ War may be considered *with a view to* its causes and its conduct. 戦争はその原因と行動について考察の対象とすることができる.

3《俗》…を考えて (= in VIEW of 3) ▪ *With a view to* his approaching nuptials, she presented him with a handsome service of plates. 彼の結婚式が近づいてきたのにかんがみて, 彼女は立派な食器をひとそろい彼に贈った.

***with a view to** do* 《俗》…する目的で ▪ The troops had been embarked *with a view to* retake the island of Grenada. 軍隊はグレナダ島を再び占領する目的で船出していた.

***with the [《俗》a] view of** doing* …するつもりで, する目的で ▪ Religion must be formed *with the view of securing* a future happiness. 宗教は未来の幸福をしっかりとつかむ目的で作らなければならない.

with this [that] view この[その]目的で, この[その]ために ▪ *With this view* he dispatched a courier to Bourbon. この目的で彼はブルボンに急使を派遣した ▪ He went to London *with that view*. 彼はそのためにロンドンへ出向いた.

view[2] /vju:/ 動 ***an order to view*** → ORDER[1].

vigil /vídʒəl/ 名 ***keep (a, one's) vigil/keep (one's) vigils*** 寝ずの番をする, (看病などで)徹夜する ▪ Her angels *kept their vigils* round her bed. 彼女の守護天使たちが彼女の床の回りで寝ずの番をしていた ▪ She *kept vigil* over a sick child. 彼女は病児の看病で徹夜した.

vigor, 《英》**vigour** /vígər/ 名 ***in vigor*** (法律が)実施されて ▪ The act was *in* full *vigor*. その法律は完全に実施されていた.

with vigor 勢いよく, 元気よく ▪ The war continues *with* increasing *vigor*. 戦争はいよいよ勢いよく続いている.

village /vílɪdʒ/ 名 ***a global village*** 地球村《IT 技術の発達により情報の共有とコミュニケーションが容易になり一つの村のようになった地球》 ▪ Marshall McLuhan was the first person to popularize the concept of *a global village*. マーシャル・マクルーハンは地球村の概念を一般化した最初の人だった.

a Potemkin** /poʊtémkɪn/ **village 見せかけ, 虚飾 ▪ This country's borrowed prosperity is nothing less than *a Potemkin village*. この国の借り物の繁栄は, 見せかけにほかならない. ☞ロシアの Catherine 2世の寵臣 Potemkin が女帝のクリミア地方の視察の折りに急造したといわれる見せかけだけの村.

a village idiot まぬけ, 田吾作 ▪ He is playing *the village idiot*. 彼はまぬけのまねをしているんだ.

villain /vílən/ 名 ***the villain of the piece***

劇の悪役;(問題を起こした)張本人, 元凶 ▪ *The villain of the piece* was suspected to be the manager. 張本人は支配人ではないかと疑われていた.

vim /vɪm/ 名 ***vim and vigor*** 《陳腐》活気, 元気 ▪ My gandfather's got a lot of *vim and vigor*. うちのおじいちゃんは元気いっぱいだ.

vindicate /víndəkèɪt/ 動 ***vindicate*** *oneself* 弁明する, 申し開きする ▪ He could have *vindicated himself*, if his enemies had chosen to be his listeners. 彼の敵が耳を借す気になっていたら, 彼は申し開きをすることができるところだった.

vindication /vìndəkéɪʃən/ 名 ***in vindication of*** …を擁護して ▪ Then Lord Sandwich spoke *in vindication of* the measure. それからサンドウィッチ卿がその法案の擁護演説をした.

vine /vaɪn/ 名 ***a clinging vine*** 男性に頼りっきりの女性 ▪ I don't like Mary. She's such *a clinging vine*. メアリーはきらいだ. 男に頼りっきりなんだもの.

under *one's* ***(own) vine and fig-tree*** わが家で安らかに (《聖》*1 Kings* 4. 25) ▪ He sits secure *under his own vine and fig-tree*. 彼は何の心配もなくわが家で安らかに暮らしている.

wither [die] on the vine 《文》実を結ばずに終わる ▪ The book he was writing *withered on the vine*. 彼が書いていた本は未完で終わってしまった. ☞「摘まれないブドウがつるについたまま枯れる」が原義.

violation /vàɪəlèɪʃən/ 名 ***in violation of*** …に違反して ▪ Some act *in violation of* laws and regulations. 法令違反の行動をする者もいる.

violative /váɪəlèɪtɪv/ 形 ***(be) violative of*** …に違反する ▪ The act *is violative of* the amendments and therefore invalid. その行為は憲法補則に違反するものであるから無効である.

violence /váɪələns/ 名 ***do violence to*** **1** …に暴行を加える, をしいたげる ▪ They have *done violence to* her tomb. 彼らは彼女の墓を暴いた.

2 …を犯す, に違反する; を冒とくする ▪ They *did violence to* the majesty of the law. 彼らは法の尊厳を犯した ▪ By so doing he *did* great *violence to* his conscience. そうすることによって彼ははなはだしく自己の良心にそむいた.

offer violence to …に暴力を加える ▪ They intend to *offer violence to* the Lombards. 彼らはランバード一家に暴力を加えるつもりだ.

use [resort to] violence 暴力を用いる[に訴える] ▪ He could not bring himself to *use violence* toward his best friend. 彼は一番の親友に暴力を用いる気にはなれなかった.

with violence 乱暴に ▪ He knocked a fourth time, and *with violence*. 彼は4度目にしかも力まかせに戸をたたいた.

violent /váɪələnt/ 形 ***lay violent hands on*** …に暴力をふるう, を殺す ▪ He *laid violent hands on* the collar of poor Partridge. かわいそうに彼はパートリッジのえり首を荒々しくつかんだ ▪ He has *laid violent hands on* himself. 彼は自害した.

violet /váɪələt/ 名 ***a shrinking [blushing] violet*** 《戯》内気な人, はにかみや ▪ We all saw him as *a shrinking violet*. 我々はみな彼のことをはにかみやだと見ていた.

violin /vàɪəlín/ 名 ***play first violin*** 牛耳る ▪ He chose to *play first violin* without further ceremony. 彼はそれ以上遠慮せずに牛耳ろうとした.

viper /váɪpər/ 名 ***a generation of vipers*** マムシの子ら《邪悪な人々》(《聖》*Matt.* 3. 7) ▪ It is not for you, *a generation of vipers*, to lay hands on this girl. この娘を捕えるのはマムシの子らである君たちの役目ではない.

cherish [nourish, warm] a viper in *one's* ***bosom*** = warm a SNAKE in one's bosom.

virgin /vɔ́ːrdʒən/ 名 ***a virgin page*** 空白のページ ▪ There is *a virgin page* in the middle of the book. その本のまん中には空白の1ページがあります.

like a virgin comes to a child 何も知らずに ▪ My uncle came to his wealth *like a virgin comes to a child*. おじは自分では何もわからぬままに莫大な財産を手に入れた.

virgin earth [soil] 処女地《比喩的にも》 ▪ Hence the astonishing fertility of all *virgin earth*. それゆえすべての処女地は驚くほど肥よくなのである ▪ Comic opera may be called *virgin soil*. コミックオペラは未開拓地と言ってもよい.

Virginia /vərdʒínjə|-niə/ 名 ***make a Virginia fence*** 《米》酔っ払ってジグザグに歩く, 千鳥足で歩く ▪ He was *making a Virginia fence* along the street. 彼は通りを千鳥足で歩いていた. ☞Virginia fence がジグザグ模様になっていることから.

virtue /vɔ́ːrtʃuː/ 名 ***by [in] virtue of*** …の力で; によって, のおかげで ▪ They won the day, but only *by virtue of* hard fighting. 彼らは勝ちはしたが, それは全く悪戦苦闘によってであった ▪ He remained a senator *in virtue of* his birth. 彼は生まれがよかったおかげでずっと元老院議員でいられた.

extoll the virtues of 《文》…の美点を褒めたたえる ▪ The Republican Party have *extolled the virtues of* capitalism as the door to a prosperous future. 共和党は資本主義を繁栄する未来へのとびらを開くものとして褒めたたえた.

make a virtue of (行為などで)手柄顔をする, 面目を施す ▪ Mat thought he might *make a virtue of* telling Tom. マットはトムに教えてやって手柄顔をしようかと思った.

make a virtue of necessity やむをえずすることを進んでするかのように装う; 当然しなければならないことをして手柄顔をする ▪ *Making a virtue of necessity*, Peter invited his mother-in-law to stay for dinner. やむをえずすることを進んでするかのように装って, ピーターは義母に夕食にとどまってくれませんかと言った.

of easy virtue (女性が)節操のない ▪ She was a woman *of easy virtue*. 彼女は尻の軽い女だった.

of virtue 徳の高い, 節操のある ▪ He is a man *of virtue*. 彼は徳の高い人だ.

Virtue is its own reward. 《諺》善行の報いはその中にあり. ☞Ⓛ Ipsa sui pretium virtus sibi のなぞ

り.

vision /víʒən/ 名 ***come within*** [***go out of***] *one's* ***vision*** 見えてくる[見えなくなる] ▪ Soon the star *went out of our vision.* やがてその星は見えなくなった.

have tunnel vision 偏狭である; 視野が狭い ▪ We don't want to be accused of *having tunnel vision.* 周りが見えていないといって非難されたくない ▪ Those people *have* absolute *tunnel-vision* about each other. あの人たちは互いに関して極端に視野が狭い.

have visions of (*doing*) …する夢を描く ▪ Audi *has visions of becoming* the world's leading luxury car producer. アウディは世界第1位の高級車の生産者になる夢を描いている.

visit[1] /vízət/ 名 ***a flying*** [***lightning***] ***visit*** 大急ぎの旅行 ▪ He paid *a flying visit* to London. 彼はロンドンまであわただしい旅をした.

a visit from the stork 赤んぼう[子供]の誕生 ▪ My wife is expecting *a visit from the stork.* 妻が出産予定なんだ. ☞stork「コウノトリ」.

go on a visit to …へ旅行する, 出かける ▪ He *went on a visit to* the seaside. 彼は海岸へ出かけて行った.

on a visit to …を訪問するため; の家に滞在中で ▪ He left here *on a visit to* London. 彼はロンドンへ向け当地を出発した ▪ George was *on a visit to* a friend. ジョージは友人の家に滞在中だった.

pay [***make***] ***a visit*** 訪問する, 訪れる (*to*) ▪ You have not *made* us *a visit* for a long time. 長いことおいでになりませんでしたね ▪ Yesterday I *paid a visit to* the shrine. きのうその神社へ参拝した.

receive [***have***] ***a visit from*** (人)の訪問を受ける ▪ He *received* frequent *visits from* the ghost. 彼はしばしばその亡霊に襲われた.

return *one's* [*a person's*] ***visit*** 答礼の訪問をする ▪ I *returned my visit* at three weeks' end. 3週間後に私は答礼の訪問をした ▪ I was out the other day when he came to see me, and I am going to *return his visit.* この間彼が訪ねて来てくれたときに留守だったので, 彼に答礼の訪問をするつもりだ.

the right of visit = the right of VISITATION (and search).

visit[2] /vízət/ 動 ***be visited with*** [***by***] (病気・災害など)に襲われる ▪ Cornwall *was visited with* the plague. コーンウォル地方はペストに襲われた ▪ To make matters worse, he *was visited by* a severe illness. 更に悪いことに彼は重い病気に見舞われた.

go visiting 訪問に行く ▪ All ages and sexes *went visiting.* 老若男女ことごとく訪問に行った.

V

visitation /vìzətéɪʃən/ 名 ***a visitation of God*** [***Providence***] 神罰, 天の怒り ▪ The famine was *a visitation of God* for their sins. その飢饉は彼らの罪に対する神罰であった.

the right of visitation (***and search***) (船舶の)臨検(捜索)権 ▪ The law of nations gives to every belligerent cruiser *the right of visitation and search* of all merchant ships. 国際法はすべての交戦国の巡洋艦にあらゆる商船の臨検捜索権を与えている.

visiting /vízətɪŋ/ 形 ***have a visiting acquaintance*** (***with***)/ ***be on visiting terms*** (***with***) (…と)往来する間柄である ▪ I *have a visiting acquaintance with* them. 私は彼らと往来する間柄だ ▪ We *are* not *on visiting terms.* 我々は往来し合う間柄ではない.

vista /vístə/ 名 ***in vista*** 見通しになって ▪ The rooms lie *in vista* as a great gallery. それらの部屋は大きな画廊のように見通しになって連なっている.

vital /váɪtəl/ 形 ***a vital part*** (体の)急所 ▪ He was wounded in *a vital part.* 彼は急所を負傷した.

vital statistics **1** (生死・婚姻などの)人口統計 ▪ *Vital statistics* is data relating to births, deaths, health, diseases and marriages. 人口統計とは出生, 死亡, 健康, 疾病, 結婚等に関するデータだ.

2 〚one's を伴って〛《口》女性のバスト・ウェスト・ヒップの寸法 ▪ *Her vital statistics* are as follows. 彼女のスリーサイズは次の通り.

vital to …に絶対必要で ▪ Secrecy is *vital to* the success of the scheme. その企てが成功するためには秘密厳守が絶対必要だ.

vitamin /váɪtəmən|vít-/ 名 ***a vitamin bomb*** →BOMB.

vocal /vóʊkəl/ 形 ***become vocal about*** …についてやかましくなる ▪ Public opinion has *become vocal about* the question. その問題について世論がやかましくなった.

make *a person* ***vocal*** 人に口をきかせる ▪ Anger *made* the shy girl *vocal.* 怒りのため内気な少女も口をきいた.

vocal by [***with***] …の声で満ちわたって ▪ All the air is *vocal with* whispering trees, and singing birds. あたり一帯の大気は木の葉のさわさわいう音と小鳥のさえずりに満ちわたっている.

vocation /voʊkéɪʃən/ 名 ***by vocation*** 職業は ▪ He is a physician *by vocation.* 彼の職業は医師だ.

feel no vocation for (仕事)をしたい気が強くしない ▪ I *feel no vocation for* the task. その仕事をする気が少しもしない ▪ She *felt no vocation for* the cloister. 彼女は修道院へ入りたい気は少しもしなかった.

find *one's* ***vocation*** (色々の仕事の後で)天職を見つける ▪ He *found his vocation* late in life. 彼は晩年に天職を見いだした.

have no vocation for [***to***] …の適性がない ▪ He *has* little or *no vocation for* teaching. 彼に教師の適性はまずない.

miss *one's* ***vocation*** 天職を誤る ▪ I may have *missed my vocation.* I should have been a teacher. 私は天職を誤ったのかもしれない. 私は教師になるべきだった.

vogue /voʊg/ 名 ***be*** (***all, quite***) ***the vogue*** 最新の流行である ▪ Small hats *were quite the vogue*. 小さい帽子が最新の流行だった.

bring [***put***]***... into vogue*** ...を流行させる, はやらせる ▪ It *was brought into vogue* by Mr. Tudor. それはチューダー氏がはやらせた.

come [***start***] ***into vogue*** はやりだす ▪ When did plus fours *come into vogue*? ゴルフ用の半ズボンはいつはやりだしたのか.

give vogue ...を流行させる, もてはやさせる (*to*) ▪ Her wealth *gave* her *vogue*. 富が彼女を人気者にした ▪ Those letters *gave vogue to* the book. それらの手紙がその本をはやらせた.

go out of vogue はやらなくなる ▪ The phrase *went out of vogue* a short time ago. その言い方は少し前にはやらなくなった.

have a great vogue 大流行[大人気, 大好評]である ▪ The novel *had a great vogue* in its day. その小説は当時大好評を博していた.

have a short vogue 一時はやる ▪ Long skirts *had a short vogue*. ロングスカートは一時はやった.

in vogue 流行して, 人気があって ▪ Cycling is much *in vogue*. サイクリングは大いにはやっている ▪ Those novelists are *in vogue*. こういう作家たちが人気がある.

out of vogue はやらないで, 人気がなくなって ▪ My book would be *out of vogue* with the first change of fashion. 私の本は流行が変わり次第はやらなくなるかもしれない.

put ... into vogue →bring ... into VOGUE.

start into vogue →come into VOGUE.

there is a vogue for ...がはやっている, 流行している ▪ *There is a vogue for* very high heels on women's shoes. 非常に高いかかとの婦人靴が流行している.

voice /vɔɪs/ 名 ***a voice crying in the wilderness*** 荒野に呼ばわる者の声; 世にいれられない改革家などの叫び (《聖》 *Matt.* 3. 3) ▪ All my life I have been *a voice crying in the wilderness*. 私はこれまでずっと荒野に呼ばわる者の声となってきました.

at the top of *one's* ***voice*** →at the TOP of one's speed.

be in good [***poor,*** etc.] ***voice*** 上手に[下手に, など]歌っている ▪ The baritone *was in excellent voice*. バリトン歌手はとても上手に歌っていた.

count on *a person's* ***voice*** 人の声援を当てにする ▪ You know I *count on your voice*. ご存じのように僕は君の声援を当てにしています.

find *one's* ***voice*** 口に出して言う; 声が出る ▪ At last I *found my voice*. ようやく声が出るようになった ▪ The patriotic muse *finds her voice* in times of war. 愛国詩人は戦時に歌いだす.

find voice in (感情などが)...となって現れる ▪ Hero-worship *found voice in* song. 英雄崇拝が歌となって現れた.

general [***popular, public***] ***voice*** 世論 ▪ The *popular voice* encouraged them to persist. 世論に励まされて彼らはがんばった.

give voice (感情などを)口に出す, 漏らす (*to*) ▪ Finally he *gave voice to* his thoughts. ついに彼は自分の考えを漏らした.

have (***a***) ***voice in*** (決定)に発言[投票]権がある ▪ We should *have a voice in* the thing that is to be decided. 我々は決定される事柄に発言権がなくてはならない.

in (***a***)***... voice*** ...な声で ▪ She replied *in* faint *voice*. 彼女はかすかな声で答えた ▪ He added *in a* lower *voice*. 彼は声を落としてつけ加えた.

in [***out of***] ***voice*** (話す・歌うのに)声がよく出て[出なくて] ▪ I was *in* wonderful *voice* last night. 私はゆうべはすばらしく声がよく出た ▪ The speaker was *out of voice*. 弁士は声がよく出なかった.

keep *one's* ***voice down*** もっと静かに話す ▪ *Keep your voice down* and stop yelling! もっと静かに話し, 怒鳴るのをやめてくれ!

lift (***up***) ***a*** [*one's*] ***voice*** (賛成・抗議などの)声をあげる (*in favor of, against*) (《聖》 *Num.* 14. 1, *Ruth* 1. 9) ▪ They *lifted up their voice* in prayer. 彼らは声をあげて祈った ▪ The people *lifted up their voice against* his tyranny. 人民は声を大にして彼の暴政に抗議した.

lose the [*one's*] ***voice*** (話す・歌うための)声が出なくなる ▪ In one case *the voice is lost* completely. ある場合には声が全然出なくなってしまう.

make *one's* ***voice heard*** → make oneself heard (→HEAR).

out of voice →in VOICE.

popular [***public***] ***voice*** →general VOICE.

raise *one's* ***voice*** →RAISE[2].

recover *one's* ***voice*** 口がきけるようになる ▪ At length he *recovered his voice*. やっと彼は口がきけるようになった.

speak with [***in***] ***one voice*** (特に政治で)全員一致した意見を言う ▪ Parliament *spoke in one voice* in support of the proposed constitution. 議会は提案された法令を全員一致で支持した.

talk to hear *one's* ***own voice*** 自分本位[必要以上]にしゃべる ▪ He's just *talking to hear his own voice*, so let him have his own way. 彼は自分勝手にべらべらしゃべっているだけだから, ほっておけ.

the still small voice →STILL.

the voice of conscience 良心の声 ▪ Politicians should be made to listen to *the voice of conscience* from time to time. 政治家にはときどき良心の声に耳を傾けさせるべきだ.

The voice of the people is the voice of God. 《諺》民の声は神の声, 天声人語. ☞Ⓛ Vox populi, vox Dei のなぞり.

throw *one's* ***voice*** 腹話術を使って話す[言う] ▪ As a ventriloquist, he is good at *throwing his voice*. 腹話術師としての彼の腹話術での語りはうまい.

under *one's* ***voice*** 小声で ▪ He spoke *under his voice*. 彼は小声で話した.

one's ***voice breaks*** **1** 声変わりする ▪ *The boy's*

voice has *broken*. その少年は声変わりした.

2 涙声になる ▪ I can't read this poem without *my voice breaking*. この詩を読むときまって涙声になってしまう.

One's ***voice is as smooth as syrup.*** 話しぶり[あたり]がソフトである ▪ He is tall and handsome; besides, *his voice is as smooth as syrup*. 彼は背が高くてハンサムだし, その上あたりもやわらかだ.

with (a)... voice …な声で ▪ The old man was muttering *with* hoarse, harsh *voice*. 老人はしゃがれたとげとげしい声でぶつぶつ言っていた.

with one voice 異口同音に, 満場一致で ▪ *With one voice* they all condemn you. 異口同音に彼らはみなあなたを非難している ▪ He was chosen *with one voice*. 彼は満場一致で選ばれた.

void /vɔɪd/ 形名 ***an aching void*** 痛切な寂しさ (Cowper, *Olney Hymns* 1. 11) ▪ There was *an aching void* in his heart. 彼の胸の中には痛切な寂しさがあった《愛する者が死んで》.

fall void 空席になる ▪ A bishopric *fell void*. 司教の職が一つ空席になった.

fill the void 空虚を満たす ▪ Nothing can *fill the void* made by his death. 彼の死によって生じた空虚を満たすことはできない.

null and void →NULL.

void of (欠点・徳など)のない ▪ It is by no means *void of* imperfections. それは決して不備な点がないわけではない ▪ He was totally *void of* discretion. 彼は全然分別がなかった.

volcano /vɑlkéɪnoʊ|vɔl-/ 名 ***sit on a volcano*** 一触即発の場にいる ▪ People living by a nuclear base know they are *sitting on a volcano*. 核基地の近くに住む人々は一触即発の場にいることを知っている.

vole /voʊl/ 名 ***go the vole*** 一か八かやってみる; あれもこれもみんなやってみる ▪ He *went the vole*, he would be colossal, or a blank failure. 彼は一か八かやってみた, どえらい人物になるか, すっかり失敗するかのどっちかだった ▪ He has *gone the vole*—has been soldier, singer, tinker, and is now a beggar. 彼はあれもこれもみんなやってみた—兵士にも歌手にもいかけ屋にもなり, そして今では物乞いなのだ. ☞vole「トランプで一勝負中の出札をみな取ること」.

volition /voʊlíʃən/ 名 ***of*** *one's* ***own volition*** 自ら進んで ▪ He went *of his own volition*. 彼は自ら進んで出かけた.

volley /váli|vɔ́li/ 動 ***volley forth [off, out]*** (言葉などを)急に発する ▪ She *volleyed forth* a horrid cry. 彼女は急に恐ろしい叫びをあげた ▪ Sir Julius *volleyed out* silver laughter. サー・ジュリアスは急に銀をころがすような笑い声を立てた.

volume /váljəm|vɔ́lju:m/ 名 ***gather volume*** (程度が)増す, 増大する ▪ His anger was *gathering volume*. 彼の怒りは次第に募ってきた.

pump up the volume 《俗》大音量で演奏する, ばか騒ぎをする ▪ The fans *pumped up the volume* before the kick-off. ファンたちはキックオフの前に大騒ぎした.

speak [express, tell] volumes 大いに意味深い, 意味深長である ▪ Her look *spoke volumes*. 彼女の目つきは意味深長だった.

speak volumes for …を証して余りがある ▪ His donations to charity *speak volumes for* his generosity. 彼が慈善に寄付したことは彼の気前のよさを証して余りがある.

volunteer /vὰləntíər|vɔ̀l-/ 動 ***volunteer to serve*** 兵役に志願する ▪ He *volunteered to serve* at sea against the Dutch. 彼はオランダ軍と戦うため海軍に志願した.

vomit /vámət|vɔ́mɪt/ 名 ***return (back) to*** *one's* ***vomit*** 元の悪習に戻る (《聖》*Prov*. 26. 11; *2 Pet*. 2. 22) ▪ They likewise *returned to the vomit* of their abominable idolatory. 彼らもまた忌まわしい偶像崇拝という元の悪習に戻っていった.

vote[1] /voʊt/ 名 ***a vote of confidence [censure]*** 信任[不信任]投票 ▪ The Government received *a vote of confidence*. 政府は信任投票を得た ▪ *The vote of censure* was defeated. その不信任決議は通らなかった.

a vote of thanks 感謝の決議 ▪ I'd like to propose *a vote of thanks* to Dr. Brown for his interesting and instructive talk. ブラウン博士の興味深く, 有益なお話に対して感謝の決議を提案したいと存じます.

by a voice vote =in a voice VOTE.

cast a vote 一票を投じる (*for*) ▪ I shall *cast a vote for* the Labor candidate. 私は労働党候補に1票を投じよう.

come [go, proceed] to the vote (議案などが)採決に付される ▪ The question *came to the vote*. その問題は採決に付された ▪ He implored the House to let the question *go to the vote*. 彼はその議題が採決に付されるように議会に懇願した.

dodge a vote 《米》(故意に)投票を避ける ▪ It has been suggested I *dodged the vote*. 私がその投票を避けたとほのめかす者がいた.

get out the vote 《米》(特定の件について)有権者が全部投票するようにする ▪ No one knows what it costs Smith to *get out the vote*. 有権者が全部投票するようにするためにスミスにどれだけの金がかかるか誰も知らない.

give a [*one's* ***] vote*** 投票する (*to, for*) ▪ Every man should *give his vote* freely and without influences. 誰もが自由に他から左右されずに投票すべきである ▪ I'm resolved to *give a vote for* the Labor Party. 私は労働党に投票しようと決心している.

have votes [the vote] 選挙権を持つ ▪ Today women *have the vote*. 今日では女性は選挙権を持っている ▪ They ceased to *have votes*. 彼らは選挙権を持たなくなった.

in a voice vote 《米》満場一致の投票で ▪ The delegates roared approval *in a voice vote*. 代議員らは満場一致で, 賛成だという声をどっとあげた.

proceed to the vote →come to the VOTE.

V

put ... to the vote ...を票決に付する ▪ We *put* the matter *to the vote*. その問題を票決に付した.

record a [*one's*] ***vote*** 投票する (*to, for*) ▪ He *recorded his vote for* the party. 彼はその党に投票した.

take a vote 採決を行う (*on*) ▪ The judges *took a vote on* the question. 審査員はその問題について採決を行った.

vote[2] /voʊt/ 動 ***vote with*** *one's* ***feet*** 政治体制の気に入らない土地を去る ▪ Many people are leaving the place, *voting with their feet*. 多くの人々がその土地を去るのは, 政治体制が気に入らないことを示している.

vote with *one's* ***pocketbook*** [《英》 ***wallet***] 一番儲けさせてくれそうな人に投票する ▪ The spirit of capitalism is to *vote with one's pocketbook*. 資本主義の精神は一番儲けさせてくれそうな人に投票することだ.

voter /vóʊtər/ 名 ***a floating voter*** 浮動票投票者 ▪ *Floating voters* are apt to play a decisive role in an election. 浮動票投票者は選挙において決定的な役割を演じることが多い.

vow[1] /vaʊ/ 名 ***be under a vow*** 誓いを立てている (*to do, of*) ▪ I *am under a vow to* drink no wine. 私は禁酒の誓いを立てている.

break a [*one's*] ***vow*** 誓いを破る ▪ I would not *break my vow*. 私は誓いを破りません.

keep [***hold***] ***a*** [*one's*] ***vow*** 誓いを守る ▪ He did not mean to *keep his vow*. 彼は誓いを守るつもりはなかった.

make a vow 誓いを立てる ▪ I *made a vow* to kill the man. 私はその男を殺す誓いを立てた.

pay *a person* ***a vow*** 人に誓いを立てる ▪ How should she *pay* you *a* grateful *vow*? どうして彼女がありがたがってあなたに誓いを立てるだろうか.

take the vows 修道者となる ▪ He *took the vows* of the Augustinian order. 彼はアウグスティノ会修道士となった.

vow[2] /vaʊ/ 動 ***I vow*** 《口》 誓って言うが, 確かに ▪ You'd break a man's sides with laughing, *I vow*. 君の話はおかしくて腹の皮がよじれそうだよ, 全く ▪ *I vow* and declare I am ashamed for it. 誓って断言するが, そのことは恥じている.

voyage[1] /vɔ́ɪɪdʒ/ 名 ***go on*** [***make, take***] ***a voyage*** 航海する ▪ We *made a voyage* to Denmark. 我々はデンマークに航海に出た.

on a voyage 航海中で[に] ▪ He is away *on a voyage*. 彼は航海中で不在だ.

wish *a person* ***bon*** [***a pleasant, a happy***] ***voyage*** 人に航海中ごきげんようと言う ▪ I *wished* him *bon voyage* /bɔvwɑjɑ́ːʒ/. 彼に航海中ごきげんようと言った ▪ I *wish* you *a pleasant* [*happy*] *voyage*. 航海中ごきげんよう.

voyage[2] /vɔ́ɪɪdʒ/ 動 ***voyage out*** [***forth***] 航海に出て行く ▪ They *voyaged out* to see the world. 彼は世界を見るために航海に出て行った.

vulgar /vʌ́lgər/ 形 ***the vulgar herd*** 《軽蔑》 大衆 (→ the common HERD) ▪ *The vulgar herd* cannot be expected to appreciate my poems. 大衆には私の詩を鑑賞することはできまい ▪ He rose above *the vulgar herd*. 彼は俗衆を超越した.

vulnerable /vʌ́lnərəbəl/ 形 ***a vulnerable part*** [***point, portion, spot***] **1** 弱味, 弱点 ▪ Calumny attacks the most *vulnerable part*. 中傷は一番の弱点を見いだして攻撃するものだ.

2 =a VULNERABLE side.

a vulnerable side (場所などが)攻撃されやすい部分 ▪ Every *vulnerable side* was guarded. 攻撃されやすい部分はどこも防備された.

vulnerable to **1** (批判・攻撃)を受けやすく ▪ His mind is *vulnerable to* temptation. 彼の心は誘惑に惑わされやすい.

2 ...に傷つきやすく ▪ Are you *vulnerable to* ridicule? あなたはひやかされるとすぐ怒りますか?

W

W /dʌ́blju:/ 名 ***the three W's*** 3つのW《子供が外出するとき親に伝えるべきWで始まる3つのことがら,「誰と(Who with?)」「どこへ(Where?)」「いつ帰るか(When?)」》 ▪ The section tells children that before they go out they should remember *the three W's.* その欄には子供らは出かける前には「誰とどこへ行きいつ帰るか」をちゃんとわきまえるようにと記してある.

wad[1] /wɑd|wɔd/ 名 ***blow*** [***shoot***] *one's* ***wad*** **1**《米口》あり金を全部はたく ▪ He's going to *shoot his wad* on his night out. 彼は一晩の夜遊びであり金を全部はたくつもりだ ▪ We'd rather not *blow* the whole *wad* on one fancy meal. 豪華な一回の食事にありったけの金をはたくようなことはしたくない.
2《米口》言いたいことを全部言う ▪ He *shot his wad* at the meeting. 彼は会で思いのたけをぶちまけた.

wad[2] /wɑd|wɔd/ 動 ***be wadded with conceit*** 慢心している ▪ He *is* well *wadded with conceit.* 彼はすっかり慢心している.

wade /weɪd/ 動 ***wade through slaughter*** [***blood***] 血潮を踏み渡る ▪ The baron has *waded through slaughter* to a throne. 男爵は戦場の血潮を渡って王位を得た ▪ France *waded through* seas of *blood* to destroy the monarchy. フランスは血潮の海を踏み渡って専制政治を破壊した.

wafer /wéɪfər/ 名 (***as***) ***thin as a wafer*** ひどく薄い ▪ His lips are *as thin as a wafer* with age. 彼のくちびるは年のためにひどく薄くなっている.

wag[1] /wæg/ 名 ***hop the wag*** =play the WAG 2.

play the wag **1** おどける ▪ We were *playing the wag* daily. 我々は毎日のようにおどけていた.
2《俗》ずる休みする, サボる ▪ They often persuaded me to *play the wag* from school. 彼らはよく学校をサボるように私を説きつけた.

play wag =play the WAG 2.

wag[2] /wæg/ 動 ***How wags the world?*** 景気はどうですか ▪ *How wags the world* with you? 君, 景気はどう ▪ But you shall hear *how the world* has *wagged* with me. しかし私の景気具合がどんなかお知らせしましょう. ☞How does the world wag? よりも普通.

let the world wag (***as it will*** [***may***]) 成り行きに任せる ▪ *Let the world wag* on *as it may.* 成り行きに任せておけ ▪ I *let the world wag* for that night. その晩は成り行きに任せておいた.

not wag a finger《口》指1本動かさない, 横のものを縦にもしない ▪ I'll wager, now, that she has*n't wagged a finger.* きっと彼女は横のものを縦にしたためしもないんだろうよ.

The tail wags the dog. →TAIL[1].

one's ***tongue wags*** 舌がよく回る, べらべらしゃべる ▪ *His tongue* was beginning to *wag.* 彼の舌はべらべら回り始めていた.

wag *one's* ***chin*** [***tongue, jaws***] (軽率に・意地悪く)ペラペラしゃべる ▪ Everyone eagerly began to *wag his tongue.* みんな熱心にペラペラしゃべり始めた.

wag *one's* ***finger at*** *a person* 人に向かってゆっくり指を振る《軽い非難のしぐさ》 ▪ Don't *wag your finger at* me. 指を振って私を非難しないでください.

wag *one's* ***head*** 頭を振り動かす《あざけり・おもしろがりのしぐさ》 ▪ Tidd *wagged his head* at the captain knowingly. ティッドはわけ知り顔をして船長に向かって頭を振り動かした.

wag it 《俗》(学校などを)サボる(→play the WAG 2) ▪ They had *wagged it* from school. 彼らは学校をサボっていた.

wage[1] /weɪdʒ/ 名 ***freeze*** *a person's* ***wages*** 賃金[給料]を凍結する《現状のまま留め置く》 ▪ The firm *froze everyone's wages* when the economy went sour. 景気が悪化すると会社は全員の賃金を凍結した.

the wages of sin 罪の報い ▪ He ate all the strawberries and ended up with a stomachache—*the wages of sin,* no doubt. 彼はイチゴを全部食べたあげく腹痛を起こした—まさに天罰だった.

The wages of sin is death. 罪の報いは死である(《聖》*Roms.* 6. 23) ▪ He wanted to bring home to the reader that *the wages of sin is death.* 彼は罪の報いは死であるということを読者にしみじみと悟らせたいと思ったのだ.

wage[2] /weɪdʒ/ 動 ***wage war on*** [***with, against***] →make WAR on.

wager /wéɪdʒər/ 名 ***have a wager on*** ...に賭ける ▪ Will you *have a wager on* it? それに賭けますか.

lay [***make***] ***a wager*** 賭けをする ▪ I *laid a wager,* and Mr. Poole held the stakes. 私が賭けをして, プール氏が賭け金を持っていた.

win [***lose***] ***a*** [*one's*] ***wager*** 賭けに勝つ[負ける] ▪ I've *lost the wager.* その賭けに負けた ▪ By this performance, she *won her wager.* このようにやって彼女は賭けに勝った.

wagon /wǽgən/ 名 ***be*** [***go***] ***on the wagon*** 《口》禁酒している[する] ▪ He *is* lean and *on the wagon.* 彼はやせていて禁酒中だ ▪ He *went on the wagon* once and for all. 彼はきっぱりと禁酒した. ☞(water) wagon (水を運ぶ荷馬車)の「水を飲んで」が原義.

circle the wagons/draw [***pull***] *one's* ***wagons into*** [***in***] ***a circle*** 《米口》(集団が) 互いに共通する利益を守って一致団結する, 防御[対抗] するため

に円陣を組む ▪ We *drew our wagons in a circle* and tided over the crisis. 我々は一致団結してその難局を切り抜けた. ☞西部開拓時代, 幌(ほろ)馬車隊が円陣を組んで先住民の襲撃を防御したことから.

fall off the wagon 《口》(禁酒していて)また酒を飲み始める (→off the WAGON) ▪ Like the bartenders, they *fall off the wagon*. そのバーテンダーたちのように, 彼らはまた酒を飲み始める.

fix** a person's **little red wagon = fix a person's WAGON 1.

fix** a person's **wagon 《口》 **1** しりをぴしゃりとぶつ 《子供へのおどしに使う》 ▪ Stop that right away or I'll *fix your wagon*. そんなことはすぐやめなさい. でないとおしりをぴしゃりとぶちますよ.

2 相手の裏をかく ▪ This counterplan will *fix his wagon*. この対策で彼も裏をかかれるだろう.

hitch** one's **wagon to** a person* [a star***] コネを利用して成功しようとする, お裾分けしてもらう (→HITCH[2]) ▪ He *hitched his wagon to* a rising young star. 彼は新進の若手スターにコネをつけた ▪ There's no reason why you shouldn't *hitch your wagon to* your elders. 先輩のおこぼれを頂戴したっていいじゃないか. ☞Emerson の随筆 *Civilization* (1870)から.

jump on the wagon = climb on the BANDWAGON.

off the wagon 《口》禁酒を破って (→fall off the WAGON) ▪ A glass of whiskey is enough to drive him *off the wagon*. ウィスキーを1杯飲んだだけで彼はまた飲み始めるだろう.

wait for the wagon もっとよい折を待つ ▪ You'll have to *wait for the wagon*. 君はもっとよい折を待たねばなるまい.

waif /weɪf/ 名 ***waifs and strays*** **1** (がらくたの)寄せ集め ▪ All I have are *waifs and strays*. 私が持っているのはがらくたの寄せ集めだけだ.

2 ホームレス, (特に)都市の浮浪児たち ▪ They are the *waifs and strays*, and cast-aways of society. 彼らは浮浪児や社会から捨てられた人たちである.

3 《戯》どこにも行き場のない寂しい人たち ▪ My wife always invites some *waifs and strays* from work to our house. 家内は会社の孤独な同僚を家にしょっちゅう招く.

wail /weɪl/ 動 ***wail like a banshee*** 泣き叫ぶ ▪ Terrified, the girl *wailed like a banshee*. 少女はおびえて泣き叫んだ. ☞アイルランド民話に出てくる泣き叫ぶ女の姿をした妖精から. 家族の一人が死ぬ前兆とされた.

waist /weɪst/ 名 ***have no waist*** 《口》(胴も腰も同じくらいに)太っている ▪ That man *has no waist* at all. あの男はよく太っている.

wait[1] /weɪt/ 名 ***have a wait for*** ...を待つ ▪ I *had a* long *wait for* the bus. 私はバスを長いこと待った.

lie in [***lay***] ***wait for*** **1** (敵)を待ち伏せする ▪ The detective was *lying in wait for* the suspected man. 探偵は犯人と思われる人物を待ち伏せていた.

2 (困難などが)待ちかまえている ▪ He needed determination to meet all the challenges *lying in wait for* him. 彼は前途に控える難題に対処する決意を固めなければならなかった.

wait[2] /weɪt/ 動 ***can't wait to** do* 《口》...したくてたまらない, (うれしくて)待ちきれない ▪ She *can't wait to* enter high school. 彼女は早く高等学校へ入りたくてたまらない.

Everything comes to those who wait. 《諺》待つ人にはすべての物が手に入る, 「待てば海路[甘露]の日よりあり」, 「果報は寝て待て」.

have always to be waited for いつも人を待たせる, 時間を守らない ▪ He almost *always has to be waited for*. 彼は大抵いつも人を待たせる.

I can hardly wait/I can't wait 《皮肉》待ち遠しいね ▪ *I can hardly wait* for the spring. 春が待ち遠しい ▪ *I* just *can't wait* for Christmas! クリスマスが待ち遠しくてたまらない.

(***Just***) ***you wait.*** 今に見ていろ《おどし文句》 ▪ *Just you wait*! You'll be broke and I'll have money. 今に見ていろ! あんたは文なし, 私は金持ちになるから.

keep** a person **waiting 人を待たせる ▪ I am sorry to have *kept* you *waiting*. お待たせしてすみません.

Wait a moment [***a minute,*** 《口》 ***a bit, a second***]. **1** ちょっとお待ちください ▪ Please *wait a moment* or two. しばらくお待ちください ▪ *Wait a minute*, what did you say her name was? ちょっと待って, 彼女の名前はなんですって?

2 (何かに気づいたり思い出して)ちょっと待てよ ▪ *Wait a minute*—this isn't the right key. 待てよ—こいつは違う鍵だぞ.

wait and see 成り行きを待つ, 静観する ▪ The minister says *wait and see* on the new transport plan. 大臣は新交通計画に関しては成り行きを待てと言う. ☞英国首相 Asquith が1910年の国会の答弁で何度もこの文句を使ったことにかけてよく使われる; ただし, 初例は1719年ごろからある.

wait (***at*** [***on***]) ***table*** →TABLE.

wait** a person's **convenience 人の都合を待つ ▪ He always expects me to *wait his convenience*. 彼は常に私が彼の都合を待つものと当てこんでいる.

wait dinner [***supper***] ***for** a person* 人のために正餐(さん)[夕食]を遅らせる ▪ Don't *wait dinner for* me. 私のために正餐を遅らせないでくれ.

Wait for it! **1** 《英口》(時機が来る[命令・指示がある]まで)待て ▪ How have I escaped this? *Wait for it ... wait for it!* 僕がどうやってこれを逃れたかって? まあまあ, 待ちたまえ ▪ Are you ready? *Wait for it!* Now! みんな用意はいいか. まだまだ! 今だ!

2 聞いてびっくりするな ▪ We had roast duck and—*wait for it*—caviar! 僕らが食べたのはローストダックと—それに, 聞いて驚くなよ—キャビアだ!

wait for the other shoe to drop 避けられそうにない出来事を待ちかまえる, 続いて起こることを覚悟する

▪ She has decided to leave her husband, so we're just *waiting for the other shoe to drop.* 彼女が夫のもとを去ろうと決意したからには，覚悟して成り行きを待つのみだ.

wait on [***serve***] *a person* ***hand and foot*** (人の)手足となって[まめまめしく]万事の世話をする (→HAND and foot 2) ▪ He loves her, and *waits on* her *hand and foot.* 彼は彼女を愛していて，かいがいしく何から何まで身の回りの世話を焼く.

wait supper for *a person* →WAIT dinner for a person.

wait (***the***) ***table*** 《米》食事の給仕をする ▪ She *waited the table* with nonchalance. 彼女は無関心に食事の給仕をした ▪ I earned a few dollars *waiting table.* 食事の給仕をして数ドルかせいだ.

wait till [***until***] *one* ***sees*** 《口》成り行きを待つ; 今に見ろ…だからな ▪ You boys, just *wait till* you *see.* 君たち，まあ成り行きを待ちたまえ ▪ *Wait until* you *see* what I've found! いいか，僕が見つけたものを今見せてやるからな.

wait *one's* [***a, the***] ***time*** [***hour, opportunity, season***] 機会の来るまで控えている ▪ Cassius was obliged to *wait his opportunity.* カッシウスは機会の来るまで控えているより仕方がなくなった ▪ Well, I'll *wait a* better *season.* まあもっとよい機会が来るまで控えていましょう.

What are we waiting for? 《口》何を待ってるんだ; さっさとやろうじゃないか，何をぐずぐずしているのだ ▪ *What are we waiting for?* Let's get started! 何を待ってるんだ? さっさとやろうよ ▪ If your car needs cleaning, *what are you waiting for?* 自分の車を洗わねばならないのなら，さっさとやれよ.

waiting /wéɪtɪŋ/ 名形 ***an accident*** [***a disaster***] ***waiting to happen*** →ACCIDENT, be a DISASTER waiting to happen.

in waiting **1** (王・女王などに)侍して，仕えて ▪ He was officially one of Her Majesty's Lords *in Waiting.* 彼は正式な皇后陛下の侍従の一人であった ▪ Lady Penbroke is *in waiting* at Windsor. ペンブローク夫人はウィンザー宮殿で女官をしている.

2 待って (*for*) ▪ A closed carriage was at the door *in waiting for* her. 屋根つきの馬車が玄関で彼女を待っていた.

on the waiting list 補欠になって，番の来るのを待って ▪ There were others *on the waiting list* who wanted the Senatorship. 他にも上院議員の職を望んでいる人々が番の来るのを待っていた.

wake[1] /weɪk/ 名 ***in the wake of***/***in*** *a person's* [*thing's*] ***wake*** **1** 《海》(船)の通った跡について ▪ We were *in the wake of* a frigate. 我々はフリゲート艦の通った跡について進んだ.

2 《しばしば戯》…のすぐ後について ▪ She was following *in the wake of* her stately parents. 彼女は恰幅のよい両親に従っていた.

3 …にならって ▪ Orphans cried, and women followed *in their wake.* 孤児たちはおんおん泣き，女性たちもそれにならった.

4 …の後に，の直後に ▪ Miseries follow *in the wake of* a war. 戦争の後には不幸が続く ▪ The other diseases that followed *in smallpox's wake* wiped out the inhabitants. 天然痘に続く他の疾病で住民は絶滅した.

leave [***bring***] ***… in its wake*** あとに…の痕跡を残す[もたらす] ▪ The tornado *left* $20 million worth of destruction *in its wake.* 竜巻は2,000万ドル相当の被害の爪あとを残した.

wake[2] /weɪk/ 名 ***sleep and*** [***or***] ***wake*** 目ざめと眠り ▪ I was in that half-conscious state between *sleep and wake.* 私は目ざめと眠りの中間のあのぼうっとした状態にあった ▪ The thought never left her in *sleep or wake.* その考えは寝てもさめても彼女の念頭から去らなかった.

wake and dream 夢とうつつ ▪ Their beauty is such as haunts the borders between *wake and dream.* その美しさは夢とうつつの境によく現れるものだ.

wake[3] /weɪk/ 動 ***enough to wake the dead*** 死人の目をさますほど(やかましい音を立てる) ▪ They were making *enough* noise *to wake the dead.* 彼らは死人の目をさますほど騒ぎ立てていた ▪ The doorbell was loud *enough to wake the dead.* 呼び鈴がけたたましい音で鳴った.

wake it 起きている ▪ He has nothing to do but to *wake it.* 彼は起きているよりほかすることがない.

wake snakes, (***and walk your chalks***) →SNAKE.

wake the [***a***] ***night*** 《詩》夜寝ずにいる ▪ I could *wake a* winter *night* for the sake of somebody. 私は人のために冬の夜を寝ずにいることもできる.

wake up and smell the coffee 《主に米口》(迷いから)目をさまして正気に返る[行動を起こす] ▪ You've already had enough bad luck. *Wake up and smell the coffee.* あなたはとうに十分ひどい目にあった. 目をさまして正気に返りなさい ▪ Anybody who hasn't started saving by their mid-40s should *wake up and smell the coffee.* 40代半ばまでに貯金を始めていない人は，目を覚まして行動を起こすべきだ.

waking or [***and***] ***sleeping*** 寝てもさめても ▪ *Waking and sleeping* she had pictured his arrest. 寝てもさめても彼女は彼の逮捕される有様を心に描いていた.

walk[1] /wɔːk/ 名 ***a walk in the park*** 《主に米》極めて簡単なこと，わけなくできること，朝飯前 ▪ This job is *a walk in the park* compared to the old one. この仕事は骨が折れるが，前のに比べればなんてことはない ▪ I succeeded, but it was not *a walk in the park* for me. 成功するにはしたが，私には並大抵のことではなかった ▪ Is it difficult to surf the net?—No, not at all, it's *a walk in the park.* ネットサーフィンって難しいの?—いいや，全然，朝飯前さ.

at a walk (馬が)並み足で ▪ The horse proceeded *at a walk.* 馬は並み足で進んだ.

be … minutes' walk (…から)歩いて…分のところである (*from*) ▪ The school *is* 15 *minutes' walk*

from my house. 学校は家から歩いて15分のところだ.
by *a person's* ***walk*** 人の歩きぶりで ▪ I know him a mile off *by his walk*. 1マイル先からでも歩きぶりで彼とわかる.
drop into a walk (走っていたものが)歩きだす ▪ After running for a mile he *dropped into a walk*. 1マイル走ってから彼は歩きだした.
fall into a walk (駆けていた馬が)並み足になる ▪ He let his horse *fall into a walk* as he approached the house. 彼はその家に近づくと馬を並み足にした.
from all walks of life/in every walk of life さまざまなタイプの職業[階級]の ▪ The association has over 2,000 members *from all walks of life*. その協会にはあらゆる職業の二千人以上の会員がいる.
go [***go out***] ***for a walk*** 散歩に行く[出かける] ▪ I *went for a walk* in the park. 公園に散歩に出かけた ▪ He *went for a walk* across the park to the wood. 彼は公園を横切って森まで散歩に行った.
have a walk 散歩する, 歩く ▪ All of us *had a walk* in the garden. 我々はみんな庭を散歩した.
in a walk 楽々と, 易々と ▪ The top players got through the first rounds *in a walk*. トップ選手たちは最初のラウンドを軽々とクリアした. ☞野球で, 安打でなく四球でも一塁に出られることから.
take a walk **1** 散歩する, 歩く ▪ I *took a walk* in the park. 公園を散歩した ▪ Let's *take a walk* to the station. 駅まで歩きましょう.
2《米口》去る ▪ His breath *took a walk*. 彼は息が切れてしまった ▪ They had to *take a walk*. 彼らは去らねばならなかった.
take a walk on *a person* 《米》人をきらう ▪ Senator Byrd *took a walk on* Stevenson. バード上院議員はスティーブンスンをきらった.
take ... for a walk ...を散歩に連れて行く ▪ I *took* my brother *for a walk* in the park. 弟を公園へ散歩に連れて行った.
walk of [***in***] ***life*** **1** 社会的身分, 社会的地位 ▪ Grief is something that people in every *walk of life* experience. 嘆きはあらゆる階級の人が体験するものである ▪ It is not easy to tell from what *walk in life* women may come. 女性がどの社会的身分の出であるかはわかりにくい.
2 職業, 定職 ▪ There are men of genius in very objectionable *walks of life*. きわめて忌まわしい職業においても天才はいる.
walk of society =WALK of life 1.
walk the walk 約束を実行する, 実際に経験する ▪ If you're going to talk the talk, you've got to *walk the walk*. 言うべきことを言うつもりなら, なすべきことをなさねばならない.
win in a walk (競走などで)楽勝する ▪ I can *win* the case *in a walk*. この裁判には楽に勝てる.

walk[2] /wɔːk/ 動 ***run before*** *one* ***can walk*** 歩ける前に走る《比喩的にも》(→WALK before one can run) ▪ You are trying to *run before* you *can walk*. 君は歩ける前に走ろうとしているんだね.
walk a chalk line →WALK (the) chalk.
walk a hospital →WALK the hospitals.
walk a tightrope →TIGHTROPE.
walk a turn 1回行き戻りする ▪ They *walked a turn* through the hall. 彼らは会場を1回行き戻りした.
walk abroad 《文》広がる ▪ The pestilence is *walking abroad*. その疫病は広がりつつある.
walk all over *a person* **1**《口》人をいじめる; 人をこき使う ▪ His wife *walks all over* him. 奥さんは彼をこき使う.
2 人に楽勝する, を簡単にうち負かす ▪ I played chess with my wife, and she *walked all over* me. 家内とチェスをしたら苦もなくひねられた ▪ I *walked all over* him, making him run for his life. 僕が苦もなくやっつけると, 彼は命からがら逃げ去った.
walk before *one* ***can run*** 走れるようになる前にまず歩く《比喩的にも》(→run before one can WALK) ▪ Don't hurry. You must learn to *walk before* you *can run*. 急いではいけない. 走れるようになる前にまず歩けるようにならなくちゃ.
walk free 晴れて[無罪で]退廷を許される ▪ The man who they believed was guilty *walked free*. 有罪間違いなしと見られた男が無罪で退廷した.
walk in darkness 暗い[罪の]生活を送る (《聖》*John* 12. 35) (↔WALK in the light) ▪ Till then I had *walked in darkness*, yet knew it not. それまで私は罪の生活を送っていたのだが, それがわからなかった.
walk in *a person's* ***footsteps*** →follow in a person's FOOTSTEPs.
walk in *one's* ***sleep*** 夢遊病である ▪ He has a history of having *walked in his sleep* as a child. 彼には子供のとき夢遊病であった経歴がある.
walk in the light 正しい生活をする (《聖》*1 John* 1. 7) (↔WALK in darkness) ▪ We should *walk in the light* as Christ did. キリストがなさったように私たちも正しい生活をするべきだ.
walk it **1**《口》歩いていく ▪ I resolved to *walk it* out of Cheapness. 私は歩いてチープネスから出て行く決心をした.
2《英俗》(馬などが)楽勝する ▪ They appeared to *walk it* in vain. 彼らは楽勝しそうに見えたがダメだった.
walk off *one's* ***legs*** →LEG[1].
walk *a person* ***off*** *his* ***legs*** [***feet***] 《口》人を歩き疲れさせる ▪ You have *walked* me *off my legs*. 君は僕を歩かせてくたくたにさせたね ▪ She's over seventy, but she could *walk* you younger ones *off your feet*. 彼女は70過ぎだが, いっしょに歩いたら年下の君たちがへとへとにされるだろう.
walk off the job 《米》ストをする ▪ They turned down his request and *walked off the job*. 彼らは彼の要求を拒絶してストを起こした.
walk off with the show →steal the SHOW.
walk on eggs →tread on EGGs.
walk on foot 歩く ▪ The King *walked on foot*

among the infantry. 王は歩兵といっしょに歩いた.

walk soft 優しく[つつましく]ふるまう ▪ Try to *walk soft* and not to rock the boat. 控え目にふるまい, 波風を立てないようにしなさい.

walk Spanish 《米口》 **1** 首筋としりを押さえられて歩く[押さえて歩かせる]; しぶしぶ歩く[歩かせる] ▪ He moved, *walking Spanish* like the boy in the school-yard. 彼は校庭を首筋を押さえて歩かされる男の子みたいにしぶしぶ歩いた.

2 逃亡する ▪ They were made to *walk Spanish*. 彼らは逃亡させられた.

walk tall →TALL.

walk the boards →BOARD[1].

walk* (*the*) *chalk*/*walk the chalk mark*/*walk the* [*a*] *chalk line **1** 《俗》 (酔っていないことを証明するために)床に引いた白線の上をまっすぐに歩く ▪ He swore he was not drunk and offered to *walk the chalk* to prove it. 彼は自分は酔っていないと誓い, その証拠に床に引いた白線の上をまっすぐに歩いてもいいと言った.

2 《米口》 指令通りに行動する; いつもきちんと行動する ▪ All of them *walk the* Communist *chalk line*. 彼らはみな共産党の指令通りに行動する.

walk the floor 床の上を歩き回る ▪ He *walked the floor*, trying to solve the question. その問題を解こうとして床の上を歩き回った.

***walk the hospitals* [*a hospital, the wards*]** インターンをやる ▪ He became a medical student, came up to London to *walk the hospitals*. 彼は医学生になり, インターンをやるためにロンドンへ上京してきた.

walk the plank →PLANK[1].

***walk the street*(*s*)** →STREET.

walk with God 神とともに歩む (《聖》 *Gen*. 5. 22) ▪ It was the desire and delight of his soul to *walk with God*. 神とともに歩むことは彼の願いであり喜びであった.

walkabout /wɔ́ːkəbàʊt/ 名 ***go walkabout*** ふらふらうろつき回る ▪ Our cat *went walkabout* for two long weeks once. うちの猫は2週間もの間うろつき回ったことがあった.

walking /wɔ́ːkɪŋ/ 名 ***a walking dictionary* [*encyclopedia*]** 生き字引, 大変な物知り ▪ He is *a walking dictionary* of video game terms. 彼はビデオゲーム用語にとてもくわしい ▪ He is *a* veritable *walking encyclopedia* when it comes to the local history. 彼は郷土史にかけては実に物知りである.

***get* *one's* *walking papers* [*orders, ticket*]** 《米口》 首になる, 振られる ▪ Two baseball veterans *got their walking papers* today. きょう野球のベテラン選手が二人首になった.

give* *a person his* *walking papers 《米》 人を首にする, 振る ▪ She *gave* Jim *his walking papers*. 彼女はジムを振った. ☞walking papers [orders, ticket]「解雇通知」.

go walking 《米》 散歩に行く ▪ Let's *go walking* in the park. 公園へ散歩に行こうよ.

take* *a person* *walking 《米》 人を散歩に連れて行く ▪ He *took* Bonnie *walking*. 彼はボニーを散歩に連れて行った.

within walking distance of ...から歩いて行ける所に ▪ My house is *within walking distance of* the school. 僕の家は学校から歩いて行ける所にある.

walk-over /wɔ́ːkòʊvər/ 名 ***have a walk over*** 《口》 楽勝する ▪ I'll *have a walk-over* in the next round. 次のラウンドでは楽勝してみせる.

wall /wɔːl/ 名 ***a wall of silence*** 沈黙の壁, 反応が全くない状態 ▪ When I made a new proposal, I was met with *a wall of silence*. 私が新しい提案をしても, 聴衆からは何の反応もなかった.

beat* [*bang, run*] *one's* *head against a* (*stone,* 《主に英》 *brick*) *wall →HEAD[1].

bounce off the walls 《米口》 ひどく興奮[動揺]する, そわそわする ▪ He was nervous enough to *bounce off the walls* just before his final exams. 最終試験の直前で, 彼は気もそぞろだった.

climb* (*up*) *the wall **1** =go up the WALL.

2 逃げ出したくなるほど退屈になる ▪ If she doesn't stop talking, I'll *climb the wall*. 彼女が口を閉じなければ, 私は退屈で逃げ出したくなるだろう.

come* [*run, go*] *up against a brick wall*/*hit a* [*the*] *stone* [*brick*] *wall じゃまや妨害にあう, 障害に出くわす, ことが進展しない ▪ I tried everything but each time I *came up against a brick wall*. 万策を講じてみたが, その都度壁に突き当たった.

drive* [*push, send*] *a person* *to the wall 《口》 人を窮地に陥れる, 進退きわまらせる ▪ I see what you are *driving* me *to the wall* about. 君が何で私を窮地に陥れようとしてるのかわかったよ ▪ This bank smash has *driven* him *to the wall*. この銀行破産のため彼はすっかり困窮した.

drive* *a person* *up the wall →send a person up the WALL.

give* *a person* *the wall 人に道を譲る, 有利な立場を譲る ▪ The Persians *gave* an elder *the wall* when they met him in the streets. ペルシャ人たちは通りで年長者に会うと道を譲った. ☞昔道路の悪かったころは, 壁ぎわの歩道がきれいであったところから.

go over the wall 《口》 監禁生活から脱出する, 脱獄する ▪ The nun has *gone over the wall*. その修道女は修道院を脱出した.

go to the wall 《英口》 **1** (闘争などで)負ける; 席を譲る; (事業などに)失敗する, 行き詰まる, 破産する ▪ The weakest always *go to the wall*. 《諺》 一番弱い者がいつも負ける ▪ His honor *went to the wall*. 彼の面目が丸つぶれになった ▪ Since the war, several magazines have *gone to the wall*. 戦後いくつかの雑誌がつぶれた ▪ After ten months of massive losses, the firm finally *went to the wall*. 10か月も大損失が続いた後, 社は遂に破産した.

2 何があっても支持する, 身を削っても助ける ▪ I was ready to *go to the wall* for Bob, but he didn't want anyone's help. 喜んでボブを全面的に支持しよう

としたが，彼は誰の援助も望まなかった．☞「壁に追い詰められた人」が原義．

go up the wall 《口》(挫(ざ)折などで)狂気のようになる ▪ I found my wife *going up the wall.* 私は妻が狂気のようになっているのを知った．

have [***take***] ***the wall*** (***of*** *a person*) (人に)道を譲らせる，(人よりも)有利な立場を取る ▪ He *took the wall of* me in the streets. 彼は通りで私に道を譲らせた ▪ They *had the wall* there. 彼らはそこで有利な立場に立った．

jump [***leap***] ***over the wall*** 教会[宗旨]を離脱する ▪ A lot of young people are *jumping over the wall.* 多くの青年が教会を離脱しつつある．

nail *a person* ***to the wall*** 怒って苦しめる，(報復として)懲らしめる，痛い思いをさせる ▪ Stop teasing her, or her brother will *nail* you *to the wall.* 彼女をいじめるのをやめないと，彼女の兄に仕返しをされるぞ．

off the wall 《米口》 **1** 風変わりな，伝統にとらわれない，突飛な ▪ All her designs are completely *off the wall.* 彼女のデザインはことごとく常軌を逸している ▪ He has been making *off-the-wall* remarks all day. 彼は朝からずっと突飛な発言ばかりしている．
2 狂気の，怒った ▪ He was *off the wall* at first, but calmed down pretty soon. 彼は最初かっかしていたが，やがて落ち着いた．
3 (非難が) 根拠のない ▪ This sexual harassment accusation is totally *off the wall.* このセクハラの告訴は全く事実無根である．☞スカッシュなどで「壁に当たったボールが予期せぬ方向に弾む」が原義．

push *a person* ***to the wall*** →drive a person to the WALL.

run into a stone [***a brick***] ***wall*** 大きな障害につき当たる，克服しがたい障壁にぶつかる ▪ I *ran into a brick wall* when it came to publishing the book. いざその本を出版する段になって，大きな障害につき当たった．

see through a brick wall →SEE.

send *a person* ***to the wall*** 人を押しのけて無視する ▪ During the later fifties he *was sent to the wall* by her superior talents. 50年代の終わり頃は彼は彼女のすぐれた才能によって窓際に追いやられていた．

send [***drive***] *a person* ***up the wall*** 人を逆上させる ▪ The noise is enough to *send* anyone *up the wall.* その騒音は誰でも逆上させるほどひどいものだ．

take the wall (***of*** *a person*) → have the WALL (of a person).

talk to a brick wall 壁に向かって話す(ようなものだ); 聞く耳を持たぬ人を相手にする，骨折り損の説得をする ▪ You might as well *talk to a brick wall.* (そんなことをするくらいなら)壁に向かって話すほうがましだよ ▪ It's like *talking to a brick wall* arguing with him. 議論をしようとしても，彼は全く耳を貸そうとしない．

the handwriting [《英》 ***the writing***] ***is on the wall*** (***for*** *a person*) 《米》(人が)失敗する[続けられない] 不吉な前兆がはっきりある ▪ *Is the handwriting on the wall for* America? アメリカの前途に凶相が現れているか ▪ The team has lost its final game and *the writing is on the wall for* the manager. チームが最終戦に敗れ，監督の更迭は明白だ．

the handwriting [《英》 ***the writing***] ***on the wall*** 《米》 壁に書かれた文字; 災いの前兆 (《聖》 *Dan.* 5. 5) ▪ Before the stock-market crash he saw *the handwriting on the wall* and sold all his securities. 株式市場の総崩れの前に彼はその前兆を見て，自分の証券を全部売ってしまった ▪ He saw *the writing on the wall* and decided to behave better. 不吉な兆しがみられたので彼は品行を正すことにした．

these four walls 《口》(自分がいる)この部屋，(自分だけの)この空間 ▪ I'm gonna die in *these four walls.* 私は今いるこの部屋で死ぬつもりだ．

turn *one's* ***face to the wall*** 顔を壁の方に向ける 《死期の迫ったことを意識する人に使う》(《聖》 *2 Kings* 20. 2; *Isa.* 38. 2) ▪ He would *turn his face to the wall*, and die with that word unsaid. 彼は顔を壁の方に向け，その言葉は言わずに死んでいくだろう．

up against the wall 窮地に追い込まれて，非常に困って，八方ふさがりで ▪ Before I knew it, I was *up against the wall* in cuffs. 知らぬ間に私は手錠をはめられて，打つ手がなかった．

up the wall かんかんに怒って，いらいらして; 気が動転して，気が狂いそうになって ▪ He'll go *up the wall* if he finds out. 彼に知れたらかんかんになるぞ ▪ She's really *up the wall* about her son's illness. 彼女は息子が病気になって全く動転している．

wall to wall (敷物が)床の全面をおおう; どこにでもいる ▪ I'm not interested in *wall to wall* men. どこにでもいるような男に私は興味はない．

Walls have ears. 《諺》 壁に耳あり．

with *one's* ***back to the wall*** →BACK[1].

within four walls 室内で; ひそかに ▪ This information must be kept *within four walls.* この情報は秘密にしておかねばならない．

wallaby /wάləbi|wɔ́l-/ 名 ***on the wallaby*** (***track***) 《口》(求職・放浪のため)歩き回って，失職して ▪ I have heard it sung when I was *on the wallaby.* 私が歩き回っていたころにその歌が歌われるのを聞いたことがある ▪ He wanted a summer *on the wallaby track* to open his mind. 彼は放浪のひと夏が心を広げてくれることを願った．☞wallaby「ワラビー(小型カンガルー)」.

wallet /wάlət|wɔ́l-/ 名 ***be hit hard in the wallet*** 多額の金を支払わされる ▪ I stopped for fuel and *was hit hard in the wallet!* 給油のために停車したが，べらぼうな値段だった．

vote with *one's* ***wallet*** (法外な価格にうんざりして)他の場所で買い物をする ▪ We *voted with our wallets* because petrol prices were too expensive there. そこではガソリンの値段がべらぼうに高かったので，他の場所で買った．

wallop /wάləp|wɔ́l-/ 名 ***fall with a wallop***/ ***go*** (***down with a***) ***wallop*** ドサッと倒れる ▪ Murray followed, but he *went down with a* *wallop*. マリーはついて行ったが, ばったり倒れてしまった.

wallow /wɑ́loʊ|wɔ́l-/ 動 ***wallow in money*** [***wealth***]《口》金がうなるほどある ▪ They literally *wallow in money* when business is good. 彼らは景気がよいときには金が文字通りうなるほどある ▪ The current government *wallows in wealth* while the citizens wallow in misery. 現政府にはうなるほど金があるが, 一方, 国民は悲惨な生活にあえいでいる.

walnut /wɔ́ːlnʌ̀t/ 名 ***as crinkled*** [***wrinkled***] ***as a walnut*** 皺だらけで, 皺くちゃの ▪ The old farmer's face was *as crinkled as a walnut*. 老農夫の顔には深い皺が刻まれていた.

over the walnuts and wine デザートで, 食後の談話で ▪ *Over the walnuts and wine*, the old professor became chatty. 食後の談話で老教授は多弁になった.

waltz /wɔːlts|wɔːls/ 動 ***waltz home*** 楽勝する ▪ With two of the other team off the field with injuries, we should have *waltzed home*. 相手チームの選手が二人けがで退場したので, 我々は楽勝するはずだったのだが.

wand /wɑnd|wɔnd/ 名 ***wave a*** [*one's*] (***magic***) ***wand*** 魔法の杖を振る ▪ If only I could *wave a wand* and make you better again! 魔法の杖を振ってお前をまともな人間に戻せたらいいのだがなあ!

with a wave of *one's* (***magic***) ***wand*** 魔法の杖をひと振りして ▪ He wished he could put everything right *with a wave of his wand*. 彼は魔法の杖をひと振りすれば万事がうまくいけばいいのにと思った.

wander /wɑ́ndər|wɔ́n-/ 動 ***wander back to the past*** (考えが)ぼんやりと過去のことに及ぶ ▪ His thoughts *wandered back to the past*. 彼の思いはぼんやりと過去のことに及んでいった.

wander in to see *a person* 人をぶらっと訪ねる ▪ He *wandered in to see* me this afternoon. きょうの午後彼がぶらっと訪ねてきた.

wander in *one's* ***wits*** 頭が少しおかしい ▪ The old man was inclined to *wander in his wits*. その老人はともすれば頭が少しおかしくなった.

wander the world (***through***) 世界中をさまよい歩く ▪ You may *wander the world* and not find such another. 君が世界中をさまよい歩いてもそのような人間はまたと見つかるまい.

wandering /wɑ́ndərɪŋ|wɔ́n-/ 形 ***a wandering fire*** [***light***] キツネ火 (will-o'-the-wisp) ▪ The little boy was lost in the fen, led by the *wandering light*. 男の子はそのキツネ火にだまされて沼地で道に迷った.

have wandering hands 《英戯》(通例男性が)女性の体に触れる, セクハラをする ▪ Bob is notorious for *having wandering hands*. ボブはすぐ女性に触ると悪名が高い.

wane /weɪn/ 名 ***in*** [***at***] ***the wane of the moon*** 月の欠けるころに《農業などで縁起のよい, または不吉な時期とされる》 ▪ In Suffolk it is considered unlucky to kill a pig *in the wane of the moon*. サフォーク州では月の欠けるころにブタを殺すのは不吉と考えられている.

on [***upon***] ***the wane/ in*** (***the, her, its***) ***wane*** (月が)欠けかかって; 衰えかけて, 落ち目になって ▪ The moon is *on the wane* [*in her wane*]. 月は欠けかかっている ▪ His prosperity is *on* [*in*] *the wane*. 彼の繁栄は落ち目になっている.

on the wane and on the wax (月が)満ち欠けして (→WAX and wane 1) ▪ The moon is regularly *on the wane and on the wax* at regular intervals. 月は一定の間隔で規則的に満ち欠けする.

wangle /wǽŋgəl/ 動 ***wangle*** *one's* ***way out of*** →WAY.

want[1] /wɑnt|wɔnt/ 名 ***above want*** 生活に困らないで ▪ He found himself barely *above want*. 彼はやっと生活に困らない程度であった.

be reduced to want 困窮する ▪ He *was reduced to* great *want*. 彼は大いに困窮した.

come to want/fall into want 貧困になる ▪ Who could have thought of his *coming to want*! 彼が貧困になるなんて誰に考えられただろうか.

feel the want of ...がなくて寂しい ▪ I *feel the want of* friends. 私は友人がいなくて寂しい.

for want of ...の不足のため, がないので ▪ This plant is dying *for want of* water. この植物は水がないので枯れかかっている.

for want of a better word 他によい言葉が見つからないで ▪ The autopilot kept hiccupping, *for want of a better word*, causing a number of jolts. 自動操縦装置がしゃっくりを—どうもうまく言えないのだが—続けて, 機体ががたがた揺れた.

For want of a nail the shoe was [***is***] ***lost; for want of a shoe the horse was*** [***is***] ***lost;*** (***and***) ***for want of a horse the man*** [***rider***] ***was*** [***is***] ***lost.*** 《諺》釘1本がないために蹄鉄がなくなり, 蹄鉄が一つないために馬が使えなくなり, 馬がだめになったため御者がいなくなった[なる],「千丈の堤も蟻の穴より崩れる」. ☞細かいことを見過ごすと, ひどい結果を招くことがある, の意. この諺は3文から成っているが, そのいずれもが単独でも引用される.

in no want of ...が十分あって ▪ She is *in no want of* words to shower upon Rosa. 彼女がローザに浴びせる言葉はどっさりある.

in want 窮乏して ▪ They are living *in want*. 彼らは貧乏暮らしをしている ▪ He was *in* great *want*. 彼はひどく困っていた.

in want of **1** ...を必要として ▪ He is *in want of* good assistants. 彼はよい助手を必要としている ▪ Our house is *in want of* repair. うちの家は修繕の必要がある.

2 ...に窮して ▪ He is always *in want of* money. 彼はいつも金に窮している.

meet a long-felt want 長い間の欠乏を満たす ▪ The book *meets a long-felt want*. 本書は長い間の切実な欲求を満たすものである.

no want of たくさんの ▪ There is *no want of* anything [money]. 何もかも[金は]たくさんある.

not for want of trying 努力が足りなかったからではない ▪ He has failed, but it is*n't for want of trying*. 彼は失敗したが, それは努力不足のためではない.

Then want must be your master. まっぴらごめんだ《I want で始まる命令を断る文句》 ▪ Come upstairs: I want you. ―*Then want must be your master.* I'm busy. 2階へ来ておくれ. 用事があるんだ―まっぴらごめんですよ. こっちは忙しいんだから.

Want is the mother of industry. 《諺》貧困は勤勉の母.

Wilful waste makes woeful want. → WASTE[1].

want[2] /wɑnt|wɔnt/ 動 ***be wanted by the police*** お尋ね者だ ▪ He *is wanted by the police* on two charges. 彼は二つの罪で指名手配中だ.

do not want to *do* …すべきではない ▪ You *don't want to* scribble on the wall. 壁に落書きをすべきではない.

(***How much***) ***do you want to bet?*** 《口》賭けるか; それは確かか ▪ I'm sure he'll win. ―*How much do you want to bet?* 彼がきっと勝つと思う―嘘だろう.

if you want ..., *a person* ***is your*** [***the***] ***man*** [***woman***] 《口》…したいなら(ある人)が最適任者[もってこいの人]だ ▪ *If you want* the job done fast, then Jones *is your man.* 仕事を早く片うけたいなら, ジョーンズがぴったりの人物である.

it wants ... minutes to …にはあと何分である ▪ *It* only *wants* five *minutes to* dinner. 夕食にはあと5分しかない. ☞ 今は通例 It is five minutes to ten. のような言い方をする.

it wants *A* ***of*** *B* BにAだけ足りない ▪ *It wants* one inch *of* the regulation length. それは規定の長さに1インチ足りない.

not want to know 《口》少しも興味を示さない, 知らん顔をしている ▪ I talked about philosophy, but she did*n't want to know*. 私は哲学の話をしたが, 彼女は知らん顔をしていた.

want for nothing 何も不自由しない ▪ You shall *want for nothing* as long as I live. 私の生きている間はお前に何も不自由はさせない.

want nothing to do with →NOTHING.

want rid of 《英口》…を免れたいと思う; (人から)自由になりたい ▪ Does she really *want rid of* him? 彼女は本当に彼から逃れたがっているのか.

want some doing 《口》(むずかしくて)少し手がかかる ▪ That sort of thing *wants some doing*. そういうことは少し手がかかる.

What does *one* ***want with ...?*** …は…をどうしようと言うのか ▪ *What does* he *want with* the money? 彼はその金をどうしようと言うのか ▪ *What do* you *want with* me? 私をどうしようと言うんです.

wanting /wɑ́ntɪŋ|wɔ́nt-/ 形 ***be a little wanting*** (頭が)少し足りない ▪ That man *is a little wanting*. あの男は少し足りない.

be wanting to …の期待に添わない ▪ The Earl was not a man to *be wanting to* his country at such a moment. 伯爵はそのような時に祖国の期待にそむくような人ではなかった.

be weighed [***tried***] ***and found wanting*** 試されて不合格とされる, まさかの時の試練に耐えない(《聖》*Dan.* 5. 27) (→weighed in the BALANCE and found wanting) ▪ When serious trouble came, he *was tried and found wanting*. 大きな面倒が持ち上がったとき, 彼はその試練に耐えなかった.

find ... wanting (…が)基準に達しないと判断する ▪ I *found* him *wanting* as a poet. 彼は詩人としては力量不足だと思う.

wanting in …に欠けて, 不十分で ▪ He is not *wanting in* the knowledge of his profession. 彼は自分の職業の知識に欠けてはいない.

wanton /wɑ́ntən|wɔ́ntən/ 名 ***play the wanton/play the wanton's part*** ふざける ▪ I am *playing the wanton* in these sketches. 私はこの小品の中でふざけているのだ.

wantonness /wɑ́ntənnəs|wɔ́ntən-/ 名 ***in wantonness*** 気ままに, いたずらで ▪ You have torn up that book *in wantonness*. お前はいたずらでその本をやぶいてしまった.

war /wɔːr/ 名 ***a shooting war*** (冷戦と対比して) 撃ち合いの戦争, 実戦 ▪ The two countries are on the verge of *a shooting war*. 両国は今にも砲火を交える寸前にいる.

a turf war 《口》縄張り争い ▪ *A turf war* between rival hedgehogs was caught on film. 勢力を張り合うハリネズミ同士の縄張り争いの様子が映像に記録された ▪ *Turf wars* are inevitable when two departments are merged. 二つの部署が統合されると勢力争いが避けられない.

a war baby 《口》戦時中に生まれた子《とくに私生児》 ▪ Many of the *war babies* were adopted by families in Canada. 戦争の落とし子の多くはカナダの家庭に養子縁組された.

a war chest (戦争・選挙戦に当てられる) 活動資金, 軍資金, 運動資金 ▪ The Minister took £10 billion from his *war chest* to fight the next election. 大臣は次の選挙戦のために自らの運動資金から100億ポンドを当てた.

a war [***battle***] ***of nerves/a nerve war*** (暴力ではなく, 脅しなどによる) 神経戦, 心理的手段を使って競争相手の神経を摩耗させあう抗争 ▪ He and his neighbor have been fighting *a war of nerves* against each other. 彼とその隣人はこのところ互いに神経戦の応酬を続けている.

a war of words (***between, over***) 《報道》言葉による戦い, (特に新聞で) 舌戦, 論争 ▪ The *war of words between* the two countries over acid rain heated up. 酸性雨に関する両国の論争が激しくなった ▪ Their amicable discussion soon degenerated into *a war of words*. 彼らの親しい話し合いがやがてとげとげしい口論になった.

a war to end war 戦争を終わらせるための戦争 ▪ The Great War was supposed to be *a war to end war*. 世界大戦は戦争を終わらせるための戦争だと

考えられていた.

(a) war to the death [knife] → DEATH; KNIFE.

an all-out war (市民をも巻き込む)全面戦争, 総力戦 ▪ He waged *an all-out war* when he invaded Poland. 彼はポーランドに侵入して全面戦争を遂行した.

an old war horse (過去の戦歴を好んで回顧する)歴戦の強者(つわもの), 退役軍人, 老兵 ▪ My great grandfather was *an old war horse* for the Union. うちの曽祖父は北軍の退役軍人だった.

at war (with) (ある国と)戦って, 戦争中 (↔at PEACE 1); (人と)争って; (思想などが…と)相いれない ▪ The two nations were *at war with* each other. その両国は交戦中であった ▪ Sentiments of liberty were not *at war with* order, virtue, and religion. 自由の感情は秩序や美徳や宗教と相いれないものではなかった.

be at war with weight やせようと奮闘している ▪ Constantly *at war with weight*, I have gone on and off diets. 私はこれまでずっとやせようとして, ダイエットを繰り返している.

carry the war into Africa 《米口》 = carry the WAR into the enemy's camp.

carry the war into the enemy's camp [country] 防衛から攻勢に転じる; 同じ苦情などで相手に逆襲する ▪ Her smile annoyed John. He *carried the war into the enemy's country.* "Are you aware that Bill takes morphine?" 彼女がにやりとしたのでジョンは腹を立てた. 彼は逆ねじを食わせた. 「あなたはビルがモルヒネを飲むのを知っていますか」.

declare war against [on, upon] **1** (他国)に宣戦を布告する ▪ The Reds *declare war on* organized society. 共産主義者は効率化された社会に宣戦する.

2 (犯罪など)の一掃を宣言する ▪ The police have *declared war against* violent crime. 警察は凶悪犯罪を一掃すると宣言した.

go on the war trail 《米》 戦いに行く ▪ He doesn't *go on the war trail.* 彼は戦いに行かない.

go to the wars (外地に)出征する ▪ The minstrel boy *is gone to the wars.* あの歌手は出征している.

go to war **1** 戦争を始める (*with, against*) ▪ She has too much common sense to *go to war with* Russia. その国は常識があるからロシアと戦争を始めるようなことはしない.

2 戦争に行く ▪ How can we let you *go to war*? どうしてお前を戦争へなどやれましょう.

3 =go to the WARs.

have been in the wars **1** 《英口》 (主に子供がけんか・事故などで)けがをしている, ひどい目にあっている ▪ Little Johnny *has been in the wars.* He broke his arm yesterday. ジョニー坊やはけがをしている. きのう腕を折ったのだ ▪ We *have been in the wars* with three guys. 3人のやつらとやり合ってけがをした.

2 《口・戯》 虐待された跡がある ▪ Sundry other marks upon his body showed him to *have been in the wars.* 彼の体には他にもいろんな傷があって, 虐待されたことを物語っていた.

make war medicine 《米》 (北米先住民が)必勝のまじないをする; 好戦的になる ▪ Senator Dolliver was outside, *making war medicine.* ドリバー上院議員は外に出て好戦的になっていた.

make [《雅》 wage, 《文》 levy] war on [upon, with, against] …と戦争する, 戦う ▪ The colonists were accustomed to *making war on* the creatures of the forest. 植民地の人々は森の生き物と戦うのに慣れていた.

open war 公然たる敵意 ▪ It is *open war* between them. 彼らは公然たる敵意をいだいている.

strike the war pole 《米》 戦いに行く ▪ 250 warriors *struck the war pole.* 250人の戦士が戦いに行った. ☞war pole 「北米先住民が戦いに関係した公の儀式に建てる柱」.

the tug of war →TUG[1].

This means war! 《口・戯》 これでは戦争をやるしかない, よし戦ってやる ▪ They are going to sell us out. *This means war!* 彼らは我々を裏切ろうとしている. こうなったら戦うまでだ.

ward /wɔːrd/ 名 ***be in ward to*** …に後見されている ▪ The child *is in ward to* my uncle. その子供は私のおじに後見されている.

place [put] (a child) in ward (子供を)後見する ▪ The aged grandparents *placed* the child *in ward.* 年をとった祖父母がその子を後見した.

watch and ward →WATCH[1].

wardrobe /wɔ́ːrdròʊb/ 名 ***have a large [small, limited, slender] wardrobe*** 衣装持ちである[でない] ▪ She *has a large wardrobe* of fine clothes. 彼女にはりっぱな衣装がどっさりある.

wardship /wɔ́ːrdʃìp/ 名 ***be under** a person's **wardship*** 人に後見されている ▪ The child *is under her uncle's wardship.* その子はおじに後見されている.

have the wardship of …を後見している ▪ I *have the wardship of* a minor. 私は未成年者を一人後見している.

ware /weər/ 名 ***cry [shout]** one's **wares*** 商品を呼び売りする ▪ Peddlers *cry their wares* aloud. 行商人は大声で商品を呼び売りする.

puff** one's **wares 自画自賛する ▪ Beware of people who *puff their wares.* 自画自賛する人には用心せよ.

warm[1] /wɔːrm/ 形名 ***a warm corner*** **1** 激戦地 ▪ It was *the warmest corner* of the battle. そこが最大の激戦地であった.

2 不愉快な立ち場 ▪ We found ourselves in *a* very *warm corner.* ひどく不愉快な立場に陥った.

a warm reception **1** 心からの歓迎 ▪ He gave me such *a warm reception.* 彼は心から歓迎してくれた.

2 《皮肉》 (敵に対する)猛烈な抵抗 ▪ We must give the rival *a warm reception.* 競争相手には猛烈に

抵抗してやらねばならない.

(as) warm as a toast →TOAST.

be getting warm(er) 《口》(かくれんぼなどで)見つけそうになっている ▪ You*'re getting warm.* 見つけそうになっているよ ▪ Indicative words show the searcher that he *is getting warm.* 指示語は捜す人に今にも捜し当てそうだと教える機能がある.

get a warm →have a WARM.

get warm **1** 暖かくなる, 暖まる ▪ It is *getting warmer* day by day. 日ましに暖かくなってきた ▪ Come and *get warm* by the fire. こっちへ来て火のそばで暖まりなさい.

2 暑くなる, ほてる ▪ I *got warm* playing in the sun. 日なたで遊んで暑くなった.

3 熱中する, 興奮する ▪ The argument is *getting warm.* 議論は白熱してきている.

give... a warm 《口》...を温める ▪ *Give* this milk *a warm.* この牛乳を温めてくれ.

give** a person **a warm time (議論などで)人を激しくつるし上げる ▪ The heckler *gave* the speaker *a warm time.* そのやじ馬は弁士を激しくつるし上げた.

grow warm 熱中[興奮]する ▪ They *grew warm* over the debate. 彼らは議論に熱中した ▪ The debate *grew warm.* 議論が白熱した.

have [get, take] a warm 《口》暖まる ▪ I *had a* good *warm* by the fire. 火のそばで十分暖をとった.

in warm blood →in hot BLOOD.

keep** a person's **[the] seat [place] warm (for him [her]) 《口》ある人が資格を得るまで代わってその地位についている ▪ The Cranworths determined who should *keep the seat warm* till the eldest son came of age. クランワス夫妻は長男が成年に達するまで誰が代わってその地位につくかを決定した.

***make it [things,** etc.**] warm for** a person* 人を攻撃する, いたたまれなくする(→make a place too HOT for a person) ▪ He became aggressive and *made things warm for* me. 彼は僕にけんかをふっかけてかかってきた ▪ I will *make* the country too *warm for* him to stay in. 彼がこの国にいたたまれなくしてやるぞ.

take a warm →have a WARM.

warm with →hot WITH.

warm work **1** 激戦 ▪ Nelson said, "This is too *warm work*, Hardy, to last long." 「これはあまりの激戦だからいつまでも続きはすまいよ, ハーディー君」とネルスンは言った.

2 骨の折れる仕事 ▪ I had *warm work* in doing it. それをするのには骨が折れた.

warm[2] /wɔːrm/ 動 ***get warmed up*** **1** 暖まる ▪ We built a fire to *get warmed up.* 暖まるために炉の火を燃した.

2 体調を整える, (運動選手が)ウォーミングアップをする ▪ A pitcher must always throw several practice balls to *get warmed up.* ピッチャーは肩ならしのためにいつも数回練習のボールを投げねばならない.

3 怒る ▪ He *got warmed up* in his dispute. 彼は論争をしていて腹をたてた.

***warm** oneself* 体を暖める ▪ *Warm yourself* by the fire. 炉のそばで体を暖めなさい.

warm** a person's **blood 人を暖める; 人を興奮させる ▪ A glass of brandy *warmed my blood.* ブランデーを1杯飲んだので体が暖まった.

warm** a person's **jacket → dust a person's JACKET.

warm [ride] the bench 《俗》(野球・フットボールの選手が)ベンチを暖めている; 2番手として待つ ▪ Jim patiently *warmed the bench* while his teammates played. ジムはチームの仲間が試合をしている間辛抱強くベンチを暖めていた ▪ I can't wait till he retires; I've been *warming the bench* for years. 彼の退職が待ち遠しい. 後釜に座るのを何年も待ってきたから.

warm the cockles of** a person's **heart 《英》→COCKLE.

warm wise to 《米俗》...を知る[感うく]ようになる ▪ We young fellows begin to *warm wise to* ourselves. おれら若い者は自分というものを知り始めている.

warming /wɔ́ːrmɪŋ/ 名 ***get [give] a warming*** ぶんなぐられる[なぐる] ▪ I'll *give* your hide *a warming.* お前をぶんなぐってやるぞ.

warning /wɔ́ːrnɪŋ/ 形名 ***a warning shot across the bows*** (計画を中止・変更させる)警告, 威嚇射撃 ▪ They fired *a warning shot across the bows* of the intruder. 彼らは不法侵入船に威嚇射撃を行った. ☞停船させるか進路を変えさせる目的で, 当たらないように船首の前方を狙った威嚇射撃から.

at a moment's warning ただちに ▪ All the troops were ready to march *at a moment's warning.* 全軍はただちに進軍の用意が整っていた.

give** a person **fair warning 人にあらかじめ断る《あとで苦情のないように》 ▪ I *give* you *fair warning.* 君にあらかじめ断っておく.

give warning **1** 警告する(to) ▪ He *gave* his master *warning* of the danger. 彼は主人に危険の迫っていることを知らせた.

2 訓戒する ▪ The president *gave warning* to them for behaving beyond the limit. その逸脱した行為に対して社長が彼らを訓告した.

3 (解雇・辞任の)予告をする ▪ I have *given* the cook a month's *warning.* 料理人に1か月後の解雇の予告をした ▪ The gardener has *given* me *warning.* 庭師は暇をくれと申し込んできた.

sound a note of warning/sound a warning note 《口》危険の恐れを警告する(*to*) ▪ The speaker *sounded a note of warning to* those who would go too fast. 講演者は速度を出しすぎる人々に危険の恐れを警告した.

take warning (by) (他人の不運などを)戒めとする ▪ He *took* no *warning by* my coming. 彼は私が来たことをもって戒めとしなかった.

without warning 前ぶれ[前兆]なしに ▪ The enemy attacked *without warning.* 敵は前ぶれなしに攻撃してきた ▪ The tree fell *without warn-*

ing. その木は突然倒れた.

warp /wɔːrp/ 名 ***the warp and woof of*** …の縦糸と横糸; 基礎 ▪ Meaning and sound are *the warp and woof of* speech. 意味と音声が言葉の基本的な要素だ.

war-paint /wɔ́ːrpèɪnt/ 名 ***in full war-paint*** 《口》盛装して ▪ Do you mean the man *in full war-paint*? 君が言ってるのは盛装しているあの男のことかい. ☞war-paint「北米先住民の出陣化粧」.

warpath /wɔ́ːrpæ̀θ|-pɑ̀ːθ/ 名 ***be*** [***go***] ***on the warpath*** **1** 戦いに行く ▪ He has never *been on the warpath*. 彼は一度も戦いに行ったことがない ▪ He *went out on the warpath*, and added scalp to scalp. 彼は戦いに行き, (戦利品の) 頭皮を何枚もふやした.

2《口・戯》気負いたっている, けんか腰になっている; 怒っている ▪ Bobby *was* again *on the warpath*. ボビーはまたけんか腰になっていた ▪ Look out—the boss *is on the warpath* again! 気をつけろ! ボスがまた頭にきている. ☞warpath「北米先住民の出征路」.

warrant[1] /wɔ́ːrənt|wɔ́r-/ 名 ***be a warrant for*** …の保証となる ▪ Diligence *is a* sure *warrant for* success. 勤勉は成功を確実に保証してくれる.

be** a person's **warrant 人の保証になる[立つ] ▪ His promise *is our warrant*. 彼の約束が私たちの保証だ ▪ I will *be your warrant*. 私が君の保証に立とう.

have warrant for …の正当な理由[権能]を持つ ▪ What *warrant* do you *have for* saying so? 君にはそう言う正当な理由があるのか ▪ You *have* no *warrant for* what you do. 君にはそんなことをする権能はない.

without warrant いわれもなく ▪ People spoke slightingly of his ability *without warrant*. 人々は彼の才をいわれもなくけなした.

warrant[2] /wɔ́ːrənt|wɔ́r-/ 動 ***I('ll) warrant*** (***you***)《主に口》請け合って, 確かに ▪ *I warrant* she kissed him. 確かに彼女は彼にキスしたのだ ▪ He is a true-blue Scot, *I'll warrant you*. 彼は生粋のスコットランド人だ, 請け合ってもいい.

not warranted in** doing* [to** do*] …するのは正当ではなく ▪ We are *not warranted in referring* our sensations to a cause. 感覚を一つの原因に帰するのは正当ではない.

wart /wɔːrt/ 名 ***paint** a person **with his warts*** 《口》人の欠点も隠さずありのままに描く ▪ Cromwell wished to *be painted with* all *his warts*. クロムウェルはすべての欠点も隠さずありのままに描いてもらうことを望んだ.

warts and all 《口》(美点ばかりでなく)欠点も隠さずに ▪ The writer's subject is the British party system, *warts and all*. その作家の主題はイギリスの政党組織を欠点も隠さずに論じることである ▪ The girl still loves him, *warts and all*. 少女は彼を欠点も含めてまだ愛している.

war whoop /wɔ́ːrhùːp|-wùːp/ 名 ***give*** [***raise, set up***] ***the*** [***a***] ***war whoop*** 《米》ときの声をあげる, 戦いに行く ▪ In marching they *set up the war whoop*. 進軍の際彼らはときの声をあげた.

wary /wéəri/ 形 ***be wary of*** (*doing*) (…するの)に用心深い ▪ *Be wary of* strangers. 見知らぬ人には用心しなさい ▪ He *is wary of telling* secrets. 彼は秘密を話すのに用心深い.

wash[1] /wɑʃ|wɔʃ/ 名 (***be***) ***at the wash*** 洗濯に出して(ある) ▪ She knew how much linen *was at the wash*. 彼女はどれだけのシャツ・シーツ類が洗濯に出ているか知っていた.

come out in the wash 《口》 **1** 明るみに出る, ばれる ▪ The mistakes will all *come out in the wash*. そのまちがいはすべてばれるだろう.

2 (結局)うまく収まる ▪ Things will *come out in the wash*. 事態は結局うまく収まるだろう.

get a wash =have a WASH 1.

give ... a wash …を洗濯する ▪ *Give* it *a* good *wash*. それをよく洗いなさい.

have a wash **1** (手・顔を)洗う ▪ We must *have a wash* and eat some breakfast. 手を洗って何か朝食を食べなければならない.

2 洗濯物がある ▪ She *has a* large *wash* today. 彼女は今日は洗濯物がたくさんある.

in the wash 洗濯中に ▪ Our shirts were damaged *in the wash*. 私たちのシャツは洗濯中に痛んだ.

send ... to the wash …を洗濯に出す ▪ I *sent* my shirts *to the wash*. シャツを洗濯に出した.

wash and wear 洗ってすぐ着られる, アイロンがけの必要がない ▪ Helen's dress was made of a *wash and wear* fabric. ヘレンのドレスはノーアイロンの生地でできていた.

wash[2] /wɑʃ|wɔʃ/ 動 ***be*** (***a-***)***washing*** 洗濯されている ▪ Their shirts *were washing* below. 彼らのワイシャツは下で洗濯されていた.

be [***feel***] ***washed out*** [***up***] **1**《口》疲れて青ざめている, 元気がない ▪ I *feel* completely *washed out*. すっかりくたびれてしまった ▪ I returned home, *washed-out* and depressed. 疲れ果てて落ち込んで故郷へ戻った.

2《口》完全に失敗した, もう人気が出ない ▪ He'll never go on stage again. He's all *washed-up* as an actor. 彼が舞台に立つことはもう二度とあるまい. 役者としてすっかり用済みだ.

***wash** oneself* 体を洗う; (しばしば単に)手や顔を洗う ▪ We *wash ourselves* every day. 我々は毎日体を洗います ▪ *Wash yourself* speedily and follow me. 素早く手や顔を洗ってついて来なさい.

wash an [***the***] ***Ethiop*** [***a blackamoor***] (***white***)/***wash an ass's head*** [***ears***] むだ骨を折る ▪ She labors to *wash the Ethiop white*. 彼女はむだ骨を折ろうとしている ▪ It is loss of time and soap to *wash an ass's head*. むだ骨を折るのは時間と金の浪費だ.

wash ... clean …をきれいに洗う ▪ *Wash* your hands *clean*. 手をきれいに洗いなさい.

wash** one's **dirty linen at home [***in pub-***

W

lic] →LINEN.

wash** one's **hands of →HAND[1].

wash** one's **spears 戦いに行く ▪ The young men, like Zulu warriors, wished to *wash their spears.* 若者たちはズールー人の戦士のように戦いに行くことを望んだ. ☞南ア先住民は戦いに行くとき槍(やり)を血で洗うとされていたところから.

Where can I wash up?/Is there some place I can wash up? 《婉曲》お手洗いはどこですか ▪ Welcome. Do come in.—Oh, *where can I wash up?* よくきたな. さあ, 入ってくれ—ええと, お手洗いはどこ?

will not wash 《口》(調査・実験などに)耐えない, 当てにならない, (人には)信じられない (*with*) ▪ His patriotism [story] *won't wash.* 彼の愛国心[話]は当てにならない ▪ Your story about sighting a UFO just *won't wash with* me. 君は UFO を見たというけど, どうも私には眉つばものに思える.

washing /wɑ́ʃɪŋ|wɔ́ʃɪŋ/ 名 ***do the washing-up*** 《英》(食後の)食器洗いをする ▪ She doesn't mind doing the cooking, but she hates *doing the washing-up.* 彼女は料理をするのはいとわないが食後の皿洗いは大嫌いだ.

washing-up 食後の汚れた食器類 ▪ Where did all this *washing-up* come from? よくこれだけの汚れた食器が出たものだ.

wasp /wɑsp|wɔsp/ 名 ***a waist like a wasp's*** 細い[くびれた]腰 ▪ Jane has *a waist like a wasp's.* ジェインはくびれた腰をしている.

a wasp's nest 敵の多い所 ▪ Louise thrust herself into *a wasp's nest.* ルイーズは敵の多い所へ頭を突っ込んでしまった.

sting like a wasp (舌に)毒がある ▪ Mrs. Brown's tongue *stings like a wasp.* ブラウン夫人の舌には毒がある.

waste[1] /weɪst/ 名形 ***a waste of space*** 《英口》全く役に立たない人, 能なし, 粗大ゴミ ▪ The new clerk is *an* absolute *waste of space.* 新入りの事務員は全くの役立たずだ ▪ My husband's *a* complete *waste of space.* うちの主人ときたらまるきり粗大ゴミよ.

a waste of waters/a watery waste 大海原 ▪ A raft is floating upon *a waste of waters.* いかだが大海原に浮かんでいる.

cut to waste (布を)むだな断ち方をする; (時間を)むだに割り当てる ▪ An hour and a half had *been cut to waste.* 1時間半がむだに割り当てられていた.

go to waste むだになる, 浪費される ▪ There is not a particle of vapor in the universe that *goes to waste.* 宇宙にはむだになる水蒸気は一滴もない.

lay waste 《文》(土地・国を)荒らす, 荒廃させる ▪ Villages *were* burnt and *laid waste.* 村々は焼かれて荒らされた.

lie waste (土地が)荒れている, 耕されずにいる ▪ The village has been *lying waste* for more than ten years. その村は10年以上も前から荒れている.

make waste むだになる ▪ Haste *makes waste.* 《諺》急がば回れ.

run to waste (酒が)流れてむだになる; (富・権力などが)浪費される ▪ The sewage *ran to waste* on the seashore. 下水は海岸に流れてむだになった ▪ The faculties of the mind *run to waste* if neglected. 精神の機能は顧みずにおくと浪費されてしまう.

Wilful waste makes woeful want. 《諺》気ままに使って泣く貧乏. ☞意図的な頭韻.

waste[2] /weɪst/ 動 ***be wasted on*** …にはむだである ▪ Experience *is wasted on* a fool. 経験も愚か者にはむだだ ▪ All my advice *was wasted on* him. 私の忠告も彼にはすべてむだだった.

***waste** (one's) **breath** [**words**]* むだなことを言う ▪ Why do you *waste your breath* arguing with such a stubborn fellow? どうしてあんながんこ者とむだな議論をするのか ▪ We need not *waste words* in coming to our point. 我々は要点に触れるのにむだなことを言う必要はない.

Waste not, want not. 《諺》むだをしなければ不自由はしない.

waste one 《野球》わざとボール(球)を投げる ▪ He *wasted one* in the hope of getting the hitter to swing. 彼はバッターにバットを振らせてやろうと思ってわざとボールを投げた.

waste** one's **substance →SUBSTANCE.

watch[1] /wɑtʃ|wɔtʃ/ 名 ***in the night watches/in the watches of night*** 夜眠らずにいるときに (《聖》*Ps.* 63. 6) ▪ I have read him *in the night watches.* 私は夜眠らずにいるときに彼の本を読んだ.

***keep** (**a**) (**close, sharp**) **watch on** [**of, over**]* …を(油断なく)張り番する ▪ I *kept a sharp watch on* him all the time. 私は始終彼を油断なく張り番していた ▪ He *kept watch of* you even after the money was stolen. その金が盗まれた後でさえ彼は君を張り番していた ▪ They *kept a close watch on* the harbor. 彼らは港を厳重に見張った.

keep** (**a**) **watch for …を待ちかまえる, 警戒する ▪ We *kept watch for* a thief. 泥棒を警戒した.

***on** [**upon**] **the watch for** [**to** do]* …を[しようと]見張って, 警戒して ▪ He was *on the watch for* indications of a coming reaction. 彼は反動のくる徴候を見張っていた.

on** a person's **watch 《米》(権力者・責任者)の管理下で ▪ He as a leader should be judged for what happens *on his watch.* 彼はリーダーとして, 自らの管理下で起きる出来事によって評価されるべきだ. ☞「夜間の見張り役」から.

pass as a watch in the night つかの間に過ぎ去ってしまう (《聖》*Ps.* 90. 4) ▪ Ten years have *passed as a watch in the night.* 10年間がつかの間に過ぎ去ってしまった.

set a watch 見張りを立てる ▪ If we *set a watch,* we shall probably catch the thief. 見張りを立てれば, たぶん泥棒はつかまるだろう.

stand** (**a,** one's) **watch 見張りに立つ; 《主に海》当直する ▪ I *stood my watch* upon the hill. 私は

W

山の上で見張りをしていた ▪ He *stands watch* as second officer. 彼は2等航海士として当直する.

stand upon** one's **watch 見張りに立つ (《聖》 *Habak*. 2. 1) ▪ I will *stand upon my watch*, and set me upon the tower. 私は見張りに立ち, 物見やぐらに身を置こう. ☞聖書語法.

watch and ward きびしい警戒; 不断の監視 《今は watch の修辞的かつ強意的な同意語としてのみ用いる》 ▪ We must keep some *watch and ward* over his tongue. 我々は彼の口を厳しく警戒する必要がある.

watch[2] /wɑtʃ|wɔtʃ/ 動 ***A watched pot never boils.*** →POT.

be like [as interesting as] watching grass grow/ be like [as interesting as] watching paint dry 《戯》ひどく退屈である, あくびが出るほどおもしろくない ▪ To watch somebody fly-fishing *is* about *as interesting as watching grass grow*. 人の毛ばり釣りを見ているとあくびが出る ▪ Watching golf on television *is like watching paint dry* to me. テレビでゴルフを見るのは退屈で仕方がない.

bear watching →BEAR[2].

***watch** oneself* =WATCH it.

watch and pray (誘惑に陥らぬように)目を覚まして祈る (《聖》 *Matt*. 26. 41; *Mark* 14. 38) ▪ *Watch and pray* that you enter not into temptation. 誘惑に陥らぬように目を覚まして祈りなさい.

watch it 《口》用心する, 注意する ▪ You'll be cheated if you don't *watch it*. 用心しないとだまされるぞ. ☞常に命令文か不定詞形で用いる.

watch** one's **language [mouth, tongue] 《口》言葉を慎む ▪ It would pay you to *watch your tongue*. 言葉を慎むほうが身のためだぞ ▪ *Watch your mouth* before I knock you out. なぐり倒されないうちに口を慎め.

watch** a person **like a hawk 《口》ウの目タカの目で人を監視する ▪ He was *watching* his daughter all the time *like a hawk*. 彼は始終自分の娘をウの目タカの目で監視していた.

watch** one's **opportunity [time] 機会を待つ ▪ You had better *watch your time* and then act. 君は機会を待ってから行動するほうがいい.

watch** one's **step →STEP[1].

Watch this space. 《口》(新聞[雑誌]記事で)明日[次号]のこの欄にご注目を; 乞うご期待 ▪ We can't tell you any more right now, but *watch this space*. ここまでは以上ですが, 続報にご期待ください.

watch what** one **says [does] 注意深く話す[振舞う] ▪ That cheap daughter of yours ruined my son.—*Watch what* you *say* about my daughter. お前のはすっぱ娘がうちの息子をだめにしやがった—うちの娘のことを言うときは言葉を慎め ▪ He got himself into trouble at work because he didn't *watch what* he *did*. 注意深く行動しなかったので, 彼は仕事で面倒に巻きこまれた.

watchful /wɑ́tʃfəl|wɔ́tʃ-/ 形 ***be watchful against [for]*** …に用心する ▪ You must *be watchful for* mistakes. 誤りに用心しなくてはいけない.

be watchful of …に注意する ▪ You must *be watchful of* your behavior. 行動に注意しろよ.

water[1] /wɔ́:tər/ 名 ***A lot of water has run under the bridge.*** →Much WATER has run under the bridge.

above water **1** 水面上に出て ▪ The log kept him *above water*. その丸太によって彼は水面に顔を出していられた.

2 (経済上などの)困難を免れて ▪ It is all I can do to hold my head *above water*. 借金をしないでやっていくのが精一杯のところだ.

back water →BACK[2].

be (all) water under the bridge 《口》(とうに)すんだことだ ▪ We had a quarrel three months ago but that's *all water under the bridge*. 3か月前に口論したが, もうすっかり昔の話だ.

be in [get into] murky [uncharted] waters 未知の困難に遭遇している[する] ▪ I *got into* completely *uncharted waters* and decided to leave it to the experts. 全く分からなくなり, 専門家にまかすことにした.

believe that water can [will] flow uphill 《反語》水が丘に流れ上がると信じる ▪ I could no more believe his word than I could *believe that water would flow uphill*. 水が流れて丘に上がることを信じられないように, 彼の約束も信じられなかった.

blow ... out of the water (組織)をぶち壊す, (人)を完全に打ち負かす, 全く信用を失わせる ▪ The government's main economic policies have *been blown out of the water*. 政府の主要な経済政策は壊滅的な破綻をきたしている ▪ This evidence will *blow* the prosecution's case completely *out of the water*. この新しい証拠でその告訴を完全に退けられるだろう. ☞「ミサイル・魚雷によって粉々に破壊された船」から.

bread and water →BREAD.

bring the water to** a person's **eyes [mouth] 目に涙[口によだれ]を催させる ▪ The blow *brought the water to his eyes*. その打撃で彼は目から涙が出た.

by water 船で, 水路で (→by LAND, by AIR) ▪ Conveyance is cheaper *by water* than by rail. 輸送は鉄道よりも船のほうが安上がりだ ▪ They prepared for an assault *by water*. 彼らは水路からの攻撃の準備をした.

chart unknown waters 人跡未踏の地を探検する; 未知の分野を探索する ▪ She spends hours *charting unknown waters* on the Internet. 彼女は何時間もかけてインターネットで未知の領域を調べる.

Come on in, the water's fine. →COME[2].

cross the water 海を渡る ▪ He *crossed the water* to see his son in Ireland. 彼はアイルランドにいる息子に会うために海を渡った.

cut off the water 断水させる ▪ At last the

company's man came to *cut off the water.* とうとう会社の人が断水させにやって来た.

dash cold water on →throw cold WATER on.

dead in the water 座礁して, 立ち往生して, 全く動かない[機能しない]で, 成功の見込みなく ▪ The talks are now *dead in the water.* その会談は現在行きうまっている ▪ If we don't work with big names, we're *dead in the water.* わが社は大手企業と提携しないと成り立っていかない. ☞「風が吹かずに動けない帆船」が原義.

disappear like water on sand 跡形もなく消える ▪ Those bank robbers *disappeared like water on sand.* あの銀行強盗たちは煙のように姿を消してしまった.

draw water to *one's* **(*own*)** ***mill*** →MILL[1].

drink the waters 鉱泉水を服用する, 湯治する ▪ He went to Bath, intending to *drink the waters.* 彼は湯治するつもりでバースへ行った.

fish in troubled waters →FISH[2].

get into deep water 深みにはまる《自分で処理できないことに手を出す》 ▪ Don't dabble in stocks, or you will *get into deep water.* 株に手を出したら, 深みにはまってしまうぞ.

get into hot water 困る, 苦境に陥る ▪ You'll *get into hot water* at school tomorrow. あす学校でしかられるぞ.

get into smooth water 軌道に乗る ▪ The scheme now seemed to have *got into smooth water.* その計画は今や軌道に乗ったように思われた.

get out of hot water 苦境から脱する ▪ She's finally paid her tuition and is *out of hot water* with the school. 彼女はやっと授業料を納めて学校の心配事を切り抜けた.

go in the water 《米口》改宗して洗礼を受ける ▪ Katrine is "*going in the water.*" カトリンは「改宗して洗礼を受け」ます.

go on the water ボートで水上に出る; 島流しになる ▪ Let's *go on the water* this warm afternoon. こんな暑い午後だからボートに乗って水上に出ようよ.

go over the water 渡航する ▪ He *went over the water* in his youth. 彼は若いときに渡航した.

have **[*have got*]** ***water on the brain*** **[*in the head*]** 脳水腫(しゅ)にかかっている;《皮肉》少々頭が悪い ▪ Tommy's *got water on the brain.* トミーは少し頭がいかれている.

hold water **1**(容器が)水を漏らさない ▪ Sponges *hold water.* 海綿は水を漏らさない.

2《口》〚主に否定文で〛(計画・陳述・理論などが)つじつまが合う, すきがない (《聖》*Jer.* 2. 13) ▪ His arguments do not *hold water.* 彼の議論はつじつまが合わない ▪ The plan does not *hold water.* その計画にはすきがある.

3(ボートを止めるとき)オールの水かきを垂直にして水に逆らう ▪ The men in the boat *held water* instantly. ボートの人々はすぐオールの水かきを垂直にして水に逆らった.

hold (*one's*) ***water*** 小便をこらえる ▪ He can never *hold his water.* 彼はどうしても小便をこらえることができない.

in deep water(s) 非常に困って, 苦しんで (《聖》*Ps.* 69. 2) ▪ The firm is *in deep water.* あの会社は非常に困っている.

in hot water 困って ▪ He seems to be usually *in hot water* about something or other. 彼はたいてい何かしら心配事があるようだ.

in low water 《俗》金に困って ▪ At the end of each month he is *in* dead *low water.* 毎月末には彼はひどく金づまりになる.

in smooth water(s) 順調に, すらすらと ▪ This year we are *in smooth water.* 今年は順調にいっている.

in water 《口》水彩(画)の ▪ The portraits are done *in water.* それらの肖像画は水彩で描かれている.

keep (*oneself*) ***above water*** 借金せずにいる ▪ He managed to *keep above water* during the bad seasons. 彼は不景気時代に何とか借金せずにいた.

keep *one's* ***head above water*** →HEAD[1].

let **[*take*]** ***in water*** 水が染み込む ▪ My broken shoes *let in water.* 私のやぶれぐつには水が染み込む.

lift *a person* ***onto the water wagon*** **[*cart*]** 人に酒を断たせる ▪ His experience *lifted* him *onto the water wagon.* 自分の体験から彼は酒を断った.

like water 《口》湯水のように, どんどん ▪ He spends his money *like water.* 彼は湯水のように金を使う ▪ The sweat poured off my face *like water.* 汗が顔からどんどん吹き出してきた.

(*like* **[*just*])** ***water off a duck's back*** 《口》カエルの面(つら)に水で, 何の反応もなく ▪ I felt my arguments were *like water off a duck's back.* 私の議論は何の反応もないのを感じた ▪ His book got bad reviews, but it was all *water off a duck's back.* 著書は酷評されたが, 彼は全く気にもとめなかった.

make water **1**(船が)水漏れする ▪ The ship was *making water* fast. 船はどんどん水漏れしていた. ☞[F] faire eau, [It] far acqua, [G] Wasser machen のなぞり.

2 小便する ▪ No prisoner shall *make water* against any part of the building. いかなる囚人も建物のどの部分にも小便をかけてはならない. ☞[F] faire de l'eau のなぞり.

Much **[*A lot of*]** ***water has run*** **[*passed, flowed*]** ***under the bridge.*** 多くのことが起こった ▪ What *a lot of water has run under the bridge* since the death of Aunt Ann! アンおばさんの死後何と多くのことが起こったことか.

muddy the waters 混乱を起こす ▪ I hope you don't *muddy the waters* by your own decisions. 自分一人で決定して混乱を起こしたりしないでほしい.

of the first water **1**(宝石が)最上級の ▪ He wore a brilliant *of the first water* on the fourth finger of his left hand. 彼は左手の薬指に最上級のブリリアント型のダイヤをはめていた.

2 徹底した, 全くの ▪ He assumed the air of a

lady-killer *of the first water*. 彼は全くのプレイボーイのふりをしていた. ☞water「(宝石の)品質」.

on the water **1** 水上に; 船に乗って ▪ The country had another enemy *on the water*. その国は水上にもう一つの敵がいた ▪ Great numbers of men are *on the water*. たくさんの人々が船に乗っている.
2 海路を輸送中で ▪ There is a large quantity of tea *on the water* on its way from the East. たくさんの茶が東洋から海路を輸送中である.

on the water wagon [***cart***] 酒を断って (→be on the WAGON) ▪ I'm [I've got] *on the water cart*. 私は酒を断っている[断った].

pass water 排尿する《通例障害を伴うような場合に使う》 ▪ He has had much difficulty in *passing water*. 彼は排尿するのにひどく骨が折れるのだった.

pour cold water on →throw cold WATER on.

retain (*one's*) ***water*** =hold (one's) WATER.

(***so much***) ***water over the dam*** →WATER under the bridge.

Still waters run deep. →STILL.

stir the waters =muddy the WATERs.

take (***the***) ***water*** **1** (動物・水鳥・人が)水に入って泳ぐ ▪ I saw a deer *take the water* 300 yards or so above me. 1匹のシカが300ヤードかそこら上流を水に入って泳ぐのが見えた.
2 (船が)進水する; (飛行機が)着水する ▪ The vessel *took the water* without a hitch. 船は首尾よく進水した.
3 乗船する ▪ They *took water*, but were seized on the way to Brighton. 彼らは乗船したが, ブライトンへ行く途中でつかまった.

take the waters 湯治する ▪ He is *taking the waters* at Bath. 彼はバースで湯治している.

take to the water →TAKE to the boats.

take water 《米口》 逃げる ▪ The fellow *took water* at once. その男はすぐ逃げてしまった.

talk under water 《主に米》 とめどなくしゃべる, しゃべりまくる ▪ He tells me that she *talks under water*. 彼が言うには, 彼女はしゃべりだしたら止まらないそうだ.

test the water(***s***) 成り行きを見る, 様子[反応]をうかがう, さぐりを入れる ▪ I decided to *test the waters* first before opening a new restaurant here. ここでレストランを開業する前にまず人々の反応を当たることにした ▪ I mentioned my idea to some friends as a way of *testing the water*. 反応を調べようと自分の考えを数人の友人に話した ▪ Be sure to *test the waters* before you decide on anything. 何事も決める前に必ず周囲の状況を見ること.

The waters are out. 大水が出ている ▪ *The waters are out* in Lincolnshire. リンカンシャー州では洪水が起きている. ☞waters=floods.

throw [***dash, pour***] ***cold water on*** [***upon***] (企てなど)をじゃまする, に水を差す ▪ He *threw cold water upon* the scheme. 彼はその計画をじゃました ▪ He *poured cold water upon* the zeal of his friends. 彼は友人たちの熱意に水を差した ▪ You shouldn't *dash cold water on* their enthusiasm. 彼らの情熱に水を差すようなことをしてはいかん.

tread water →TREAD.

turn on the water せんをひねって水を出す ▪ The turncock *turned on the water*. 水道給水栓係がせんをひねって水を出した.

under water 水面下に没して; 生活に失敗して ▪ A large part of the suburbs was *under water*. 郊外は大部分水びたしになっていた ▪ Lord Evandale's head was *under water*. エバンデイル卿は失脚した.

water bewitched 《口》 ひどく薄めた酒; (今は主に)薄い茶 ▪ She is very sparing of tea. The last I took was no more than *water bewitched*. 彼女はひどくお茶をけちけちする. この前飲んだのなんかひどく薄い茶にすぎなかった.

water of life 生命の水 (《聖》 *Rev.* 22. 1); 不老不死の水 ▪ The East is haunted by dreams of a *water of life*. 東洋には生命の水の夢がつきまとっている.

water off a duck's back →(like) WATER off a duck's back.

water under the bridge/(***so much***) ***water over the dam*** 過ぎ去ったこと ▪ Oh well, that's all *water under the bridge* now. なにいいさ, もうみんな過ぎ去ったことだから.

writ(***ten***) ***on*** [***in***] ***water*** (名声・業績などが)はかない, すぐ消えてしまう ▪ Here lies one whose name was *writ in water*. 水にその名を書きし者ここに眠る《Keats 自作の墓碑銘》 ▪ Her fame is *written on water*—no one will remember her in ten years' time. 彼女の名声はすぐに消えてしまう. 10年もすれば誰も憶えている者などいないだろう. ☞[L] in acqua scribere のなぞり.

You may [***can***] ***take*** [***lead***] ***a horse to*** (***the***) ***water*** (***, but you can't make him*** [***it***] ***drink***). →HORSE[1].

You never miss the water till the well runs dry. 《諺》 井戸が涸(か)れてはじめて水のありがたさを知る《ものを失うまでその価値に気づかないものだ》.

water[2] /wɔ́:tər/ [動] ***a watering hole*** [***place***] 居酒屋, バー, パブ ▪ This is my favorite *watering hole* in this town. ここがこの町で私のなじみのバーだ.

make** a person's **mouth water →MOUTH[1].

water** one's **clay →wet one's CLAY.

waterfront /wɔ́:tərfrʌ̀nt/ [名] ***cover the waterfront*** (問題を)論じ尽くす ▪ The speaker *covered the waterfront* on recent politics. 講演者は最近の政治について論じ尽くした.

water's edge /wɔ́:tərzèdʒ/ [名] ***beyond the water's edge*** 《米》 限度以上に ▪ How far *beyond the water's edge* will the Republicans carry opposition? 共和党はどの程度まで限度以上に不同意を唱えるだろうか.

stop at the water's edge 《米》 止まる時を知る ▪ Partisan politics should *stop at the water's edge*. 利党的政治は止まる時を知らなければならない.

waterworks /wɔ́ːtərwə̀ːrks/ 名 ***turn on the waterworks*** 《俗》わっと泣く ▪ She hurt her knee and *turned on the waterworks.* 彼女はひざにけがをしてわっと泣き出した.

wave[1] /weɪv/ 名 ***a heat wave*** 猛暑の時期 ▪ This district is experiencing *an* unusually severe *heat wave.* 当地は異常な猛暑に見舞われている.

a Mexican wave ウェーブ《スタジアムで観客が縦列毎に一斉に手を挙げながら立って座る動作でできる波のような動きの応援パフォーマンス》 ▪ When the captain scored another goal, *a Mexican wave* went across half the stadium. 主将がまた1ゴールを決めると, ウェーブがスタジアムを半周した. ☞1986年のサッカー・ワールドカップの際にメキシコで行われたのがはじまり.

a wave of controversy 論争の高まり ▪ The expensive new art gallery opened this spring on *a wave of controversy.* 巨額を投じた新しい画廊が賛否両論のうねりの中を今春開館した.

a wave of crime 犯罪が増加する傾向 ▪ There has been *a wave of crime* in urban areas lately. 最近都市圏で犯罪が増えてきている.

catch the wave 《米》好機をとらえる, (新しいことを行う)機会を活かす ▪ Politicians are planning to *catch the wave* of raising income taxes. 政治家は所得税を上げる絶好のチャンスを活かそうともくろんでいる. ☞サーフィンで「よい波に乗る」が原義.

in waves 波状に[の] ▪ The water moved *in waves.* 水は波をなして動いた ▪ The enemy attacked *in waves.* 敵は波状攻撃をしてきた.

make waves **1**《俗》〚主に否定命令文で〛波風を立てる ▪ We must remain friends, so don't *make waves.* 私たちは友人同士でいなければならないのだから, 波風を立てないでくれ.

2 (不平を訴えて) 騒動を起こす ▪ Those employees who *made waves* were not appreciated. 争議を起こした従業員たちは不評だった.

ride **(*on*)** ***a*** **[*the*]** ***wave*** **(*of*)** (…の)人気の波に乗る ▪ He came to power *riding on a wave of* personal popularity. 彼は個人的な人気を利用して権力の座についた.

ride **(*the crest of*)** ***the waves*** = RIDE the waves 2.

the wave of the future (未来に向けた)時代の波[趨勢(すうせい)], 将来支配的地位を占めそうなもの ▪ Hybrid cars seem to be *the wave of the future.* ハイブリッド車が今後の主流になりそうだ.

wave[2] /weɪv/ 動 ***wave good-by to*** …に手を振ってさよならを告げる ▪ We *waved good-by to* our friends. 我々は手を振って友人たちに別れを告げた.

wave *one's* ***hand to*** …に向かって手を振る ▪ They *waved their hands to* us as the car went by. 彼らは車が通り過ぎるとき私たちに手を振った.

wavelength /wéɪvlèŋkθ/ 名 ***on different wavelengths*** 《口》波長[意見, 感情など]が異なって ▪ They're *on* completely *different wavelengths.* 彼らは意見が全く異なっている.

on the same wavelength 《口》波長[意見, 感情など]が同じで (*as*) ▪ He's *on the same wavelength as* the board. 彼は委員会と同じ意見だ ▪ I feel awkward with Jim because we are not *on the same wavelength.* 僕とジムとは波長が違うので彼といると気まずい思いをする ▪ She and I are *on the same wavelength* on the subject of marriage. 結婚ということについては彼女と同じ考えだ.

waver /wéɪvər/ 名 ***be on*** **[*upon*]** ***waver*** ためらっている ▪ Does she mean to accept him? —Well, she's *on* the *waver.* 彼女は彼の申し込みを承諾するつもりかね—いや, ためらっているんだ.

wax[1] /wæks/ 名 ***a nose of wax*** →NOSE[1].

(*as*) ***close*** **[*neat, tight*]** ***as wax*** 非常に無口で[きれいで, きっちりしていて] ▪ I tell you everything, and yet you are *as close as wax* with me. 僕は君に何でも話すのに, 君は僕に何も言ってくれないな ▪ The furniture was common, but *neat as wax.* 家具はありふれたものだったが, 非常にきれいだった ▪ I pulled and strained, but it was *as tight as wax.* 私は引っ張ったり力んでみたが, それはすごく窮屈だった.

be like wax 思いのままになる ▪ He *was like wax* in their hands. 彼は彼らの手にかかり意のままにされた.

be wax in *a person's* ***hands*** 人に屈従的である, の言いなりになる ▪ He *is wax in his wife's hands.* 彼は妻にへいこらしている.

fit like wax ぴったりと合う ▪ His coat *fits* him *like wax.* 上着がぴったりと彼に合っている.

mold *a person* ***like wax*** 《口》人の性格を思いのままに形作る ▪ You can *mold* him *like wax.* 君なら彼の性格を意のままに形成することができる.

put ... on wax 《米俗》(レコードに)…を録音する ▪ The recording companies *put* it *on wax.* レコード会社がそれを録音した.

stick to *a person* ***like wax*** 人の腰ぎんちゃくである ▪ They *stuck to* him *like wax.* 彼らは彼の腰ぎんちゃくだった.

wax[2] /wæks/ 名 ***be in a wax*** 《俗》かっとなっている ▪ Don't *be in a wax* with me. 私に腹をたてないでください.

get into a wax 《俗》かっとなる ▪ Can't you *get into a wax*, old girl? かっとなれないのかい, おばさん.

put *a person* ***in a wax*** 《俗》人をかっとさせる ▪ Her retort *put* him *in a wax.* 彼女の口答えで彼はかっとなった.

wax[3] /wæks/ 動 ***wax and wane*** **1** (月が)満ちたり欠けたりする (→on the WANE and on the wax) ▪ As the moon *waxes and wanes*, so does the height of the tide change. 月が満ち欠けするにつれて潮位も上下する.

2《雅》盛んになったり衰えたりする ▪ All life's glamors *wax and wane.* 人生のすべての魅惑には栄枯盛衰がある ▪ The government's popularity has *waxed and waned* over the past year. この1年間で政府の人気は上がったり下がったりした.

wax fat and kick 増長して手に負えなくなる (《聖》*Deut.* 32. 15) ▪ The spoiled child has *waxed* *fat and kicked.* 甘やかされた子は手に負えなくなった.

wax lyrical about [***over***] →LYRICAL.

way /weɪ/ 名 ***a long*** [***good, great, little***] ***way*** (***off***) 〚しばしば副詞句として〛遠い[かなりの, 非常な, わずかの]距離 ▪ A mile is *a long way.* 1マイルというと遠道だ ▪ The sandbanks reach out *a good way* into the sea. 砂州はかなり遠くまで海へ延びている ▪ That day may be *a good way off.* その日はかなり先のことかもしれない ▪ It's only *a little way* to the station. 駅はほんのすぐそこだ.

a parting of the ways **1** →the PARTING of the ways.

2 人生[行動]の分かれ目 ▪ The comedy duo finally came to *a parting of the ways.* お笑いコンビの二人はいよいよ今後は別々の道を進むことにした.

a way around **1** 回り道 ▪ We found there was no easy *way around.* 我々には楽な回り道はないのがわかった.

2 …を回避する方法 ▪ Is there any *way around* the dilemma? このジレンマを回避する方法がありますか.

a [*one's*] ***way of life*** 生き方, 暮らし方 ▪ I am not familiar with *their way of life.* 彼らの暮らし方についてはよくは知らない.

a way out of (困難)から脱する道 ▪ We have discovered *a way out of* the difficulty. 我々は困難から脱する手段を見いだした.

a way through 通り抜ける道 ▪ There is no *way through.* 通り抜け出る道はない.

across the way →over the WAY.

all the way **1** 途中ずっと; はるばる; わざわざ ▪ He ran *all the way* to the station. 彼は駅までずっと走った ▪ He has come *all the way* from York. 彼ははるばるヨークからやって来た ▪ You need not have come *all the way* in the rain. 雨の中をわざわざ来てくださらなくてもよかったのに.

2 全部 ▪ If it is right this far, it is probably right *all the way.* ここまで正しいのなら, たぶん全部正しいのだろう.

all the way from *A* ***to*** *B* 《米口》AからBまでさまざまに ▪ The population is estimated *all the way from* fifteen *to* forty thousand. 人口は1万5千から4万までさまざまに概算されている.

all the way through 初めから終わりまで; 全行程を ▪ I have read the article *all the way through.* その論文は通読した ▪ Students go *all the way through* college without learning what their aptitudes are. 学生たちは自分の適性が何であるかを学ばずに大学の全課程を終える.

along [***on***] ***the way*** **1** (行く)途中で ▪ Buy a burger and eat it *on the way.* ハンバーガーを買って途中で食べなさい.

2 (あることを)しながら; その間に ▪ I've been in this job for forty years and picked up a lot of expertise *along the way.* 40年この仕事をして, その間に多くの専門的技術を身につけた.

any old way **1** 《口》乱雑に, 無造作に ▪ Don't do your homework *any old way.* 宿題をいい加減にやってはいけない.

2 〚接続詞的に〛どんな方法で…しても ▪ I love you *any old way* you do. 君がどんなやり方をしようとも君が好きだ.

any way you can fix it ＝NOHOW you can fix it.

any way [***no matter how***] ***you slice it***/***whichever way you slice it*** 《米口》どのように考えても ▪ You can't stay innocent forever *any way you slice it.* どう考えても, ずっとしらを切りとおすことはできまい.

be a long way from [***off***] …どころではない, 決して…ではない ▪ He *is a long way from* being rich. 彼は金持ちどころではない ▪ Your English *is a long way off* perfection. 君の英語は完全には程遠い.

be behind [***with***] *a person* ***all the way*** …を全面的に支持している ▪ He's doing well here, and we*'re behind* him *all the way.* 彼はここでよくやっており, 我々は彼を全面的に支持している.

be born [***made***] ***that way*** 生まれつきそうする ▪ It's not his fault he's so shy—he *was born that way.* 彼の人見知りは生来のものであって, 彼のせいではない.

be fond of *one's* ***own way*** →love one's own WAY.

be in a fair way to [***to*** *do*] →FAIR.

(***be***) ***in the family way*** →in a FAMILY way 2.

be in the way with →walk in the WAY with.

(***be***) ***on your way*** あっちへ行け ▪ Take what you need and *be on your way.* 要るものを持ってとっとと失せろ.

be that way →GET that way.

both ways 往復とも; 両方に ▪ The argument cuts *both ways.* その議論は両方に通じる.

(***by***) ***a long way*** 〚主に否定文で〛はるかに ▪ He is not clever *by a long way.* 彼は断然利口ではない ▪ I was his junior *by a long way.* 私は彼よりもはるかに年下だった.

by the way **1** 途中で ▪ We met several officers *by the way.* 我々は途中で数人の士官に会った.

2 道ばたで ▪ The man begged *by the way.* 男は道ばたで物乞いをしていた.

3 ついでながら ▪ I can tell you that *by the way.* ついでながらそのことを話しておくよ ▪ But this is *by the way.* しかし, これはついでの話だよ.

4 ところで, ときに《話題を変えるときなどの断り文句》 ▪ Johnson, *by the way*, was dead at that time. ところで, ジョンスンは当時は亡くなっていた ▪ *By the way*, have you seen him lately? ときに最近あの男に会いましたか.

5 片手間に ▪ It is not to be done *by the way*, but with all our might. それは片手間にすべきものではなく, 全力を尽くしてすべきものだ.

by way of **1** …を通って, 経由して (via) ▪ He went to Europe *by way of* Siberia. 彼はシベリア経由でヨーロッパへ行った.

2 …のために, として, のつもりで ▪ I employed him

W

by way of experiment. 試みに彼を使ってみた ▪ I said so *by way of* a joke. 冗談にそう言ったのだ.

by way of *doing* 《口》 **1** いつも…して ▪ The Gibsons were *by way of spoiling* me. ギブスン家の人たちはいつも私をちやほやしすぎた.

2 …のように見せかけて; で売り出そうとして ▪ He is *by way of knowing* everybody. 彼はみんなを知っていると公言している ▪ She is *by way of becoming* a fine pianist. 彼女は立派なピアニストになって売り出そうとしている.

3 …といったようなもので ▪ She's *by way of being* a beauty. 彼女はまあ美人と言ったところだ ▪ I am *by way of being* Lord Emsworth's son. 私はエムスワス卿の息子といったところです.

4 …するようになって ▪ He is *by way of doing* better work than formerly. 彼は前よりもいい仕事をするようになっている.

can't blow [***fight***] *one's* ***way out of a*** (***wet***) ***paper bag*** 《戯》けんかがすこぶる弱い, 全く無力である ▪ Those weaklings *couldn't fight their way out of a paper bag* if they tried. あの弱虫たちが頑張っても歯がたたないだろう ▪ We *couldn't fight our way out of a paper bag* with just a map and a flashlight. 我々は地図と懐中電灯だけではどうすることもできなかった.

change *one's* ***ways*** 生き方を変える ▪ She's too old to *change her ways*. 彼女は生き方を変えるには年をとりすぎている.

claw *one's* ***way back from*** 大いに努力して苦難を超える ▪ We *clawed our way back from* almost certain defeat and won by a single point. 私たちはほとんど負けていたところを奮起して切り抜け, わずか1点差で勝った.

come a long way 著しく進歩する ▪ She has really *come a long way* since she started learning French. 彼女はフランス語を習い始めてから実にめざましい進歩を遂げた.

come out of *one's* ***way*** (***to*** *do*) わざわざ(…する) ▪ He *came out of his way to* pay you a visit. 彼はわざわざあなたを訪問したのです.

come *a person's* ***way*** **1** (事が)人に起こる ▪ All this *came his way*. こうしたことがすべて彼に起こった. **2** 《俗》(事が)うまく運ぶ, 思うつぼにはまる ▪ Things started *coming my way* again. 事情がまた思うつぼにはまり始めた.

cry all the way to the bank 《口》(金持ちのおばが死ぬとか, 恥ずべきことをするとかで)泣きながら大金を儲ける ▪ When his rich aunt died, he was *crying all the way to the bank*. 金持ちのおばが死んだとき, 彼は泣きながら大金を手にした. ☞米国のピアニスト, リベラーチェ (Liberace) が自分のショーの酷評を読んだときに出た言葉とされる.

cut both ways →CUT².

discover the hard way → learn the hard WAY.

down **...** ***way*** 《口》…あたりに ▪ He lives *down* Essex *way*. 彼はエセックスあたりに住んでいる.

each way 《英》(競馬が)優勝しても入賞してもいいように ▪ Put £5 *each way* for me on Fol-de-rol please. フォルデロルに優勝しても入賞してもいいように5ポンド賭けておいてください.

either way どっちみち ▪ There is but a few years' difference between them, *either way*. 彼らの間にはどのみち2, 3年の差があるだけだ.

every which way 《口》 **1** 四方八方に ▪ I heard a crash and saw pieces of glass flying *every which way*. ガチャンと音がして, 見るとガラスの破片が四方八方に飛び散っていた.

2 あらゆる可能な方法で ▪ The statue of the former dictator has been vandalized *every which way*. 前の独裁者の銅像はあらゆる手を使ってめちゃめちゃに破壊された.

face both ways 競技者の両方を同時に支持する ▪ It is rather awkward you having to *face both ways*. 試合の両チームを同時に応援しなければならないのは, 相当ばつが悪い.

fall into the way of *doing* …する癖がつく ▪ I have *fallen into the way of smoking*. 私はタバコを吸う癖がついた.

feel *one's* ***way*** →FEEL².

find out the hard way → learn the hard WAY.

find [***make***] *one's* ***way about*** [***around***] あたりの方角がわかる; 事情がわかってくる ▪ If we study the literature of the past, we shall *find our way about* better in the present. 過去の文学を研究すれば, 現在の事情がさらによくわかってくるだろう.

find [***make***] *one's* ***way along*** →ALONG.

for once in a way たまには ▪ Now I like this kind of thing *for once in a way*. 私はたまにはこういうことが好きなのです.

from way back 《米口》ずっと昔から ▪ I've known him *from way back*. 彼とはずいぶん前からの知り合いだ.

gather way **1** (船などが)動き始める, 速度を増す (↔ lose WAY) ▪ A light breeze was blowing and the schooner soon *gathered way*. そよ風が吹いていて帆船はやがて動き出した.

2 (動く物が)勢いを増す ▪ The train rapidly *gathered way*. 列車は急速にスピードを増した.

get [***be***] ***in the*** [*a person's*] ***way*** 人のじゃまをする[になる], 妨害する[になる], (道などを)ふさぐ[いでいる] ▪ Oh, I'm terribly sorry, *am I in your way*? あら, ほんとにごめんなさい. おじゃまでしょうか ▪ He is always *getting in my way*. 彼はいつも私のじゃまばかりしている ▪ The old man is always *getting in the way* of busy people. その老人は忙しい人々のじゃまばかりしている.

get into *one's* ***own way*** うろたえて自分のじゃまをする ▪ I was always *getting into my own way*. 私はいつもうろたえて自分のじゃまをしていた.

get into the way of *doing* **1** …する癖がつく ▪ You'll soon *get into the way of walking* barefoot. やがてはだしで歩く癖がついてしまうよ.

2 …できるようになる ▪ He *got into the way of getting* his own living. 彼は自活できるようになった.

get into** a person's **ways 人のやり方に慣れる ▪ I soon *got into his ways.* じき彼のやり方に慣れた.

get it all** one's **own way =have it (all) one's WAY.

get (...) out of the way **1** (じゃまにならないように)…をよける; を除く, 処分する ▪ *Get* it *out of the way.* それをどけてくれ ▪ I've *got* the chore *out of the way.* その仕事を片うけた.

2 じゃまにならないようによける ▪ *Get out of the way* of the car. 車のじゃまにならないようにどいてくれ.

***get out of the way of** doing* …の仕方を忘れる ▪ I *got out of the way of keeping* books. 帳簿のつけ方を忘れてしまった.

get out of** a person's **way 人のじゃまにならぬようにどく ▪ Please *get out of my way.* どうか僕が通れるようにどいてくれ.

get** one's **(own) way →have one's (own) WAY.

get that way →GET.

get under way →under WAY.

give way →GIVE.

go a long [good, great] way →GO^2.

go a long way round →ROUND.

go a short [little] way (to, towards) →GO^2.

go all the way **1** 《俗》最後まで[徹底的に]やる ▪ We finally decided to *go all the way* and remodel the entire house. とことんやって家全体をリフォームしようとやっと決めた.

2 《スポーツ・口》トーナメントで全勝する ▪ She *went all the way* at Wimbledon last year. 彼女は去年ウィンブルドンですべての試合に勝った.

***go all the way with** a person* **1** 人に全面的に同意する ▪ I cannot *go all the way with* him in this matter. この件で彼に全面的には同意しかねる.

2 人と深い仲になる ▪ She *went all the way with* him. 彼女は彼と行くところまで行った.

go back a long way **1** (人・集団が相互に)長い間知っている ▪ We were at college together so we *go back a long way.* 僕たちは大学がいっしょだったからもう長いつき合いだ.

2 (活動・考え方などが)かなりの歴史がある, …まで遡る ▪ Nagasaki's ties with Vietnam *go back a long way* as far as the 16th century. 長崎とベトナムの絆ははるか16世紀にまで遡る.

go on** one's **way (一時立ち止まって)また進んで行く, 道を進む ▪ I *went on my way* to the village. 私はさらに歩いてその村まで行った.

go out of** one's **way **1** 回り道をする ▪ We *went out of our way* as far as Venice. 回り道をしてベネチアまで行った.

2 取り乱す ▪ He answered without *going out of his way.* 彼は取り乱さずに返事をした.

***go out of** one's **way to** do* わざわざ[故意に]…する ▪ He *went out of his way to* assist me. 彼はわざわざ私の手伝いをしてくれた ▪ He *went out of his way to* be rude. 彼は故意に無作法にした.

go [take]** one's **(own) way わが道を行く, 自分の思う通りにふるまう ▪ Let him *go his own way.* 彼に思う通りにさせてやれ ▪ He always *takes his own way.* 彼はいつも思う通りにふるまう.

go** one's **separate ways **1** 仲間と違った方向へ向かう, 別々の道を行く ▪ Nancy and I *went our separate ways* to college. ナンシーと僕はそれぞれ別の大学へ進んだ.

2 愛情関係[企業提携]をご破算にする ▪ We broke up and *went our separate ways* last month. 私たちは先月これまでの関係をご破算にして別れた ▪ The two companies *went their separate ways* owing to financial difficulties. 両社は財政困難のため提携を解消した.

go the right way about it 正しいやり方をする ▪ It's easy to persuade him, if you *go the right way about it.* 正しくやれば彼を説得するのは易しい.

go the right way to work 正しいやり方をする ▪ You are *going the right way to work* to make him angry. 彼を怒らせるのはそのやり方にかぎるよ.

go the way of …と同じ道をたどる, 同じ結果になる ▪ The United Nations would have *gone the way of* the League of Nations. 国連は国際連盟と同じ運命をたどっていたことだろう.

go the way of all flesh [nature, all the earth, all living] 世の人のみな行く道を行く, 死ぬ (《聖》*Josh.* 23. 14; *1 Kings* 2. 2) ▪ I heard that Don Rodrigo had *gone the way of all flesh.* ドン・ロドリゴは死んだとのことだった ▪ He had long *gone the way of nature.* 彼はとうの昔に死んでいた.

go the way of the dodo [the horse and buggy] すたれる, 古くさくなる, 絶滅する ▪ The floppy disk has already *gone the way of the dodo.* フロッピーディスクはもう時代遅れになった.

go the wrong way **1** (食物が)気管に入る ▪ He was killed by a piece of chestnut, which *went the wrong way.* 彼はクリの小片が気管に入って死んだ.

2 まちがったやり方をする ▪ I *went the wrong way* to work. 私は仕事のやり方をまちがえた.

go** a person's **way **1** 人といっしょに行く ▪ He asked if I were *going his way.* 彼は私が彼といっしょに行くのかと尋ねた.

2 (人と)同じ方向に行く, 同じ道を進む ▪ I'm *going your way.* Do you want a lift? 君と同じ方向だから車に乗せてやろうか.

3 人の思い通りになる ▪ Things are *going his way.* 事態は彼の思い通りになっている.

go** one's **way **1** 行く, 出て行く ▪ Now *go your way.* さあ行きなさい ▪ Muttering to himself, he *went his way.* 一人でつぶやきながら彼は出て行った.

2 =have one's (own) WAY.

go way back/《主に英》***go back a long way*** 《主に米》お互い昔から知っている, 旧知の ▪ Henry and I *go back* quite *a long way* and we're very

W

good friends. ヘンリーとはかなり長いつき合いであり，とても仲良しである.

go *one's* ***way(s)*** 〚命令文で〛立ち去れ ▪ *Go thy ways* with him, sir. 彼といっしょにお行きなさい.

happen *a person's* ***way*** = come a person's WAY.

have a long way to go まだ長い道のりがある ▪ We still *have a long way to go* before we can claim to have AIDS under control. エイズを撲滅したと主張できるまでにはまだ相当かかる.

have a short way with …をぞんざいに扱う ▪ The mystics have often *had a* very *short way with* dogmas. 神秘家たちは教義をしばしばぞんざいに扱ってきた.

have a way of *doing* …する癖がある ▪ He *has a* little *way of leaving* his bills unpaid. 彼は勘定を払わないでおくちょっとした癖がある.

have a way with …を扱うのがうまい ▪ He *has a way with* animals. 彼は動物の扱いがうまい ▪ Ask Betty to explain it. She *has a way with* words. 説明はベティーに頼みなさい. 言葉の選び方がうまいから.

have a way with *one* 口がうまい，魅力がある ▪ Say what you like, he *has a way with* him. 君が何と言おうと彼には魅力がある.

have come a long way (since) →LONG.

have everything *one's* ***own way/have it (all)*** *one's* ***way*** 思うままを押し通す; 思う通りにやってのける ▪ He loves to *have everything his own way*. 彼は思うままを押し通すのが好きだ ▪ You can't *have it all your* own *way*. 思う通りにやってのけられるものではない.

have it both ways 両天びんにかける，両方よいことをする ▪ Either there is a valid contract or there is not; you can't *have it both ways*. 有効な契約をするかしないかだ. 両天びんにかけることはできないよ.

Have it your own way! 《口》勝手にするがいい ▪ *Have it your own way*. I'm tired of arguing. お前の好きなようにしろ. 言い合いはもううんざりだ.

have [get] *one's* ***(own) way*** 思い通りにする ▪ You cannot *have your way* in everything. 何でも思い通りにするわけにはいかない.

have way (感情が)外に現れる ▪ His apprehensions would *have way*. 彼の心配は顔色に現れるのだった ▪ A scalding tear or two *had way* in spite of him. 彼は熱い涙が我知らずこぼれた.

have *one's* ***(wicked) way with*** *a woman* 《戯》(処女)とセックスをする ▪ He invited her there so that he could *have his wicked way with* her. 彼は邪(よこしま)な目的で彼女をそこへ誘った.

hold [keep] *one's* ***(own) way*** 続けて進む; 続行する，維持する ▪ A shark was *holding its way* near the surface of the ocean. フカが海面の近くをどんどん進んでいた ▪ They have much to do to *hold their own way*. 彼らは現状を維持するのが大変だ.

if I had my way もし思い通りになるなら ▪ *If I had my way*, I would change a few things. もしできることなら，いくらか現状を変えたいものだ.

in a bad way (健康・財政・事業などが)危い状態で ▪ He is *in a bad way*. He's not expected to live through the night. 彼は命が危い. 今晩中もつ見込みはない ▪ Here you are *in a bad way*. この点で君はおもしろからぬ状態に陥っているわけだ.

in a big way **1**《米俗》大張り切りで ▪ They went for pin-ups *in a big way*. 彼らは大張り切りでピンナップ写真を買いに行った.
2 大々的に ▪ I can fruit *in a big way*. 私は大々的に果物のかん詰めを行っている.

in a good [poor, forlorn, rising] way よい[情ない，寂しい，日の出の]状態で ▪ I am *in a good way* for salvation. 私は救済されるにうってつけの状態にある ▪ All the families were *in a poor way*. 全世帯が悲惨な状態にあった ▪ The writer is *in a rising way*. その作家は新進だ.

in a great [good, large] way 大規模に; 派手に ▪ His business is *in a* very *large way*. 彼は商売を手広くやっている ▪ We lived *in a good way*. 私たちは派手に暮らしていた.

in a small way 小規模に; つましく ▪ He started the business *in a small way*. 彼は小規模に商売を始めた ▪ His aunt lived *in a* very *small way*. 彼の伯母はきわめてつましく暮らしていた.

in a sort [kind] of way 《口》いくぶん，ある意味では ▪ Yet, *in a kind of way*, it was the grandest. しかし，ある意味ではそれは最も壮大なものであった.

in a way **1** いくぶん，ある意味では ▪ He is handsome *in a way*. 彼はまずまずの好男子だ.
2《英口》悩んで，心配して ▪ She was *in a* dreadful *way* about it. 彼女はそのことでひどく心配していた.

(in) all ways/(in) any way どの面でも ▪ He is better *in all ways* than I. 彼はどの面でも私よりすぐれている.

in every way あらゆる点で ▪ He is a gentleman *in every way*. 彼はどの点から見ても紳士だ.

in more ways than one いろいろな点[意味]で ▪ The twins are different *in more ways than one*. その双子はいろんな点で違っている ▪ Wearing black leather is hot *in more ways than one*. 黒革の服を着るといろんな意味ですばらしい.

in no way どの点においても[決して]…ない ▪ He is *in no way* to blame. 彼は少しも悪くない.

(in) one way ある点から見て ▪ The work is well done *in one way*. その仕事はある程度よくできている.

in one way or another どうにかして ▪ The work must be finished *in one way or another*. その仕事はどうにかして終えねばならない.

in other ways 他の点では ▪ He is a remarkable man *in other ways*. 彼は他の点では非凡な人だ.

in *one's* ***own way*** **1** 独自のやり方で ▪ She allowed her son to act *in his own way*. 彼女は息子を勝手気ままにさせておいた.
2 自分なりに ▪ He is happy *in his own way*. 彼は彼なりに幸福なのだ.

in some way 何とか(して) ▪ I must try to help him, *in some way.* 何とか彼を助けてやりたいものだ.
in some ways いろんな点で ▪ He is, *in some ways*, a better businessman than you are. 彼はいろんな点で君よりもすぐれた実務家だ.
in the usual* [*general, ordinary*] *way たいてい, 通例 ▪ *In the usual way*, I am home by five o'clock. たいてい5時には帰宅しています.
in the way **1** 行く道に, 途中に ▪ He died, and was buried *in the way* to Bethlehem. 彼は死亡し, ベツレヘムへの途中で埋葬された.
2 じゃま[妨害]になって ▪ Is this the only difficulty *in the way*? じゃまになっている困難はこれだけですか ▪ He would have been *in the way*. 彼はじゃまになったことだろう.
3 …しそうで, 手に入れそうで (*of, to, to do*) ▪ Now I am *in the way of* getting well again. 今私はまたよくなりそうです ▪ He is *in the way to* earn a little money. 彼は多少の金を儲けられそうだ ▪ He is now *in the way to* recovery. 彼はもう回復しそうだ.
4 《英》 手近に ▪ I was not *in the way* at first. 私は初めは手近にいなかった.
in the ... way **1** …商を営んで ▪ He is *in the* grocery *way*. 彼は食料品商を営んでいる.
2 …の種類[型]の ▪ From a child he was fond of everything *in the* military *way*. 彼は子供のころから武張ったことを何でも好んだ.
in the way of **1** …のじゃまになって ▪ Great difficulties stand *in the way of* its achievement. その完成には大きな困難が立ちふさがっている ▪ His pride stood *in the way of* success. 彼の高慢が成功のじゃまをした.
2 …の間に ▪ He remembered that he had come *in the way of* business. 自分は仕事の間にやって来たのだということを彼は思い出した.
3 …の点で, としては ▪ There is nothing remarkable *in the way of* scenery. 景色の点ではたいしたことはない ▪ He is something special *in the way of* a teacher. 彼は教師としては少し変わった方だ.
4 …の種類[型]の ▪ He did a good deal *in the way of* ravaging. 彼はおびただしく掠奪的なことをやった ▪ Do you want anything *in the way of* ties? ネクタイのようなものがいりますか.
5 …の癖があって ▪ I am *in the way of* reading in bed. 私は寝ころんで読書する癖がある.
in the way one should go 適切に (《聖》 *Prov.* 22. 6) ▪ A child should be brought up *in the way* he *should go*. 子供は適切に育て上げねばならぬ.
(***in***) ***the worst way*** ひどく, とても, 特に ▪ I want a new computer *in the worst way*. 新しいコンピューターが欲しくてたまらない.
in this* [*that*] *way 《口》 この[あの]ように ▪ I can't let you cut an old friend *in this way*. 君にこんなふうに昔なじみと絶交させるわけにいかない.
in a person's way **1** 人が…できるように, を得られるように ▪ He has a cousin who puts a good many little things *in his way*. 彼にはちょっとしたものをたくさん得られるようにしてくれるいとこがいる ▪ I write to none but those who lay it *in my way* to do so. 私は手紙を書けるようにしてくれる人以外には書かない ▪ We have now nothing to live on but what Providence throws *in our way*. 我々は今や神様が与えてくださるもの以外には生活の資とするものがない.
2 人のじゃまになって ▪ The smaller girls managed to be *in everybody's way*. 小さい女の子たちは何とかしてみんなのじゃまをした ▪ She considers that I stand *in her way*. 彼女は私が彼女のじゃまになっていると考えている.
3 人の前途に ▪ A good opportunity lies *in my way*. 好機が私の前に控えている.
4 (品物が)人に取り扱われて ▪ Such goods do not lie *in our way*. そのような品は私どもは扱っていません.
in one's way **1** 〚主に否定文で〛 お手のもので, 専門で ▪ Research was not *in his way*. 研究は彼のお手のものではなかった.
2 それなりに, それはそれとして ▪ He is a poet *in his way*. 彼は彼なりに詩人だ ▪ The picture is beautiful *in its way*. その絵はそれなりに美しい.
3 途中で ▪ He met them *in his way*. 彼は途中で彼らと会った.
4 見られる[利用できる, 得られる]ようになって ▪ It had fallen *in my way* to know every one of them. 私は彼らの一人一人を知ることができるようになった ▪ They did not come *in his way*. それらは彼に見られるようにならなかった.
it is* (*only*) *one's way …の癖だ(から仕方がない) ▪ But *it's my way* to make short cuts at things. だが何でも手っ取り早くやるのが私の癖なんです.
(***it's* [*that's*]**) ***always the way* (*with*)** 《口》 …はいつでもそうする ▪ But then *it is always the way with* those well-off people. それにしても, そういう裕福な人々はいつもそうするのだ ▪ I was late, and I got stuck in a traffic jam.—Yes, *that's always the way*. 遅れた上に交通渋滞に引っかかった—そう, いつもそんな風なのさ.
keep out of the way →out of the WAY.
keep out of a person's way →out of a person's WAY.
keep one's way →hold one's (own) WAY.
know* [*see, find* (*out*)] *how* [*which way*] *the wind blows →WIND[1].
***know* [*learn*] *one's way about* [*around*]** 《口》 (ある場所の)地理に明るい; (危急の場合に)どうふるまうべきかを知っている ▪ He has lived there for many years and really *knows his way around*. 彼は長年そこに住んでいるのでほんとに地理に明るい ▪ I hadn't really had time to *know my way about*. どうふるまうべきかを考える余裕はほんとになかった.
laugh all the way to the bank 《口》 楽々と大儲けする, 大儲けで笑いが止まらない ▪ Drug makers must be *laughing all the way to the bank* with flu raging nationwide. インフルエンザの全国的大流行で製薬会社は濡れ手に粟にちがいない ▪ After we sold the house, my wife cried and I *laughed*

all the way to the bank. 家を売ったあと，妻は泣き，私は大金を手にして笑った.

lead the way →LEAD[3].

learn [***discover, find out***] ***the hard way*** 《口》(特に不愉快なことを)苦労して学ぶ[発見する] ▪ I've *learned* it all *the hard way.* 私は何もかも苦労して覚えた ▪ He has *found out the hard way* who his real friends are. 彼は真の友人が誰かが苦労の末わかった.

lie *one's* ***way into*** [***out of***] 嘘をついて…する[から逃れる] ▪ He *lied his way into* the concert by claiming to be a pressman. 彼は報道記者と偽ってコンサート会場に入った ▪ You can't *lie your way out of* the trouble. 嘘をついて難を逃れられない.

light *a person* ***the way*** 明かりを持って人の道案内をする ▪ He hastened to *light* her *the way.* 彼は急いで明かりを持って彼女の道案内をした.

look nine [***seven***] ***ways*** (***for Sunday, at once***)/ ***look two ways for*** [***to find***] ***Sunday*** ひどい斜視である ▪ He seemed to be *looking two ways for Sunday.* 彼はひどい斜視のようだった.

look the other way そっぽを向く，見て見ぬふりをする ▪ The mother *looked the other way* when the boy was naughty. 母親は息子がいたずらをしているとき見て見ぬふりをした.

lose way 《海》(船が)速力を失う (↔gather WAY 1) ▪ The boat slowly *lost way.* 船は徐々に速力を失った.

lose *one's* [***the***] ***way*** 道に迷う ▪ They *lost their way* in the dark. 彼らは暗やみで道に迷った.

love [***be fond of***] *one's* ***own way*** 思い通りにするのを好む ▪ He *is* more *fond of his own way* than of anything else in the world. 彼は何にもまして思い通りにするのが好きだ.

make *one's* ***own way*** (自分で努力して)出世する，(…でとくに)仕事に成功する (*in*) ▪ They *make their own way in* every quarter of the globe. 彼らは地球上のいたる所で成功する ▪ He's trying to *make his own way in* the IT business. 彼は IT 事業で名を成そうとがんばっている.

make the best of *one's* ***way*** 《英》できるだけ速く行く，道を急ぐ ▪ Then we'll *make the best of our way* home, and have a glass of wine there. それからできるだけ早く家へ帰って，そこで1杯やりましょう.

make way **1** 道をあける[譲る] (*for*) ▪ Everybody *made way for* him. みんなが彼に道をあけてくれた.
2 (後継者･代用物などのために)席をあける[譲る] (*for*) ▪ I shall *make way for* a younger man. 後進のために席を譲ろう ▪ The old house has been destroyed to *make way for* a modern building. その古い家は取りこわされて現代建築に取って代わられた.
3 (船･計画などが)進む，はかどる ▪ The plan has *made* no *way.* 計画は少しもはかどらない ▪ Our vessels *made* better *way* in a rough sea. 我々の船は荒海のほうがよく進んだ.

make *one's* ***way*** **1** (…が)進む，行く ▪ He *made his way* to Oxford. 彼はオックスフォードへ進んで行った ▪ It rapidly *made its way* into universal favor. それは急速に世間一般の人気を博するにいたった.
2 ＝make one's own WAY.

make *one's* ***way about*** [***around***] → find one's WAY about.

make *one's* ***way in life*** [***the world***] ＝make one's own WAY.

make *one's* ***way through*** …を通り抜ける ▪ He *made his way through* the forest. 彼はその森を通り抜けた.

mend *one's* ***ways*** →MEND one's manners.

my way or the highway 《米口》何があろうとこっちの思い通りにする[せよ]，議論の余地はない ▪ There is only one rule here. It's *my way or the highway.* ここではルールは一つだけ. つまり，当方に同意してもらうしかない ▪ It's *my way or the highway*—what I say goes, period! 議論の余地なし. 僕の言うことが通る，以上終わり!

no two ways about it [***that***] それは疑いの余地がない ▪ That's a fact, and *no two ways about it.* それは事実で，疑いの余地はない.

no way **1** 少しも…でない ▪ He is *no way* inferior to me. 彼は少しも私より劣っていない.
2 《米口》まっぴらだ ▪ Won't you come with me?—*No way!* ごいっしょしませんか—いやだよ.

no way of *doing* …する方法[すべ]はない ▪ Is there *no way of stopping* war? 戦争をやめさせるすべはないのか.

not … in any way(***, shape, or form***) どの点からも…ない; 少しも[全然]…ない ▪ X-rays do *not in any way* harm the article. エックス線は少しもその品を害さない ▪ He's *not* involved *in any way,* shape, or form in the scandal. その疑獄に彼は全く関わり合いはない.

not know which way to look 《口》途方にくれる ▪ I was so surprised that I did *not know which way to look.* とてもびっくりして途方にくれた.

not know which way to turn [***jump***] → TURN[2].

on the way down 降りる途中で; 落ち目で ▪ The fighter is over the hill and *on the way down.* そのボクサーは人気の絶頂を過ぎて落ち目になっている.

on the [*one's*] ***way out*** **1** 《口》出る途中で，去りかかって; 《口》すたれかかって，消えかかって ▪ She kissed me *on the way out.* 彼女は帰りがけに私にキスした ▪ Big scale "giveaways" are *on the way out.* 大規模な援助費は与えられなくなりつつある ▪ The local industry was *on the way out* anyway. どっちみち地場産業は先が見えていた.
2 死にかかって ▪ The patient was *on the way out* when I arrived. 私が着いたときには患者は息を引き取ろうとしていた.

on the [*one's*] ***way up*** 上昇中で; 進行中で; 成功の途上にある ▪ Metal prices are *on the way up.* 金属の相場が上がっている ▪ We're *on our way up!* 私たちに目が出てきたぞ.

on** one's **way 立ち去ろうとして ▪ I should be *on my way* now. もう帰らねばなりません ▪ *On your way*! あっちへ行け ▪ If he phones again, tell him I'm *on my way*. 彼からまた電話があったら僕は今そっちへ向かうと伝えてくれ.

on** one's* [the***] ***way*** **1** 途中で ▪ I saw it *on my* [*the*] *way* to school. 学校へ行く途中それを見た ▪ Buy some bread *on the way* home. 家に帰る途中でパンを買ってきて.
2 進行中で, …しそうになって (*to*) ▪ He is well advanced *on the way to* recovery. 彼はどんどん回復中だ ▪ Prices are *on the way to* becoming still higher. 物価はさらに上昇しつつある.
3 やって[送られて]来て, 起ころうとして; 赤んぼうができて[まだ生まれないで] ▪ The books you ordered are *on their way*. ご注文の本はお送りしてあります ▪ She has a child and another one *on the way*. 彼女には子供が一人いて, もう一人がお腹にいる.

once in a way たまには ▪ *Once in a way* I don't mind it. たまにはそれもかまわない.

one way and another ＝one WAY or another 2.

one way or another **1** どうにかして ▪ I will do it *one way or another*. どうにかしてやってみましょう.
2 あれやこれやで ▪ He makes much money *one way or another*. 彼はあれやこれやで金をうんと儲ける.

one way or (***the***) ***other*** どのみち, いずれにしても ▪ They seemed to have no opinion about it, *one way or other*. 彼らはどっちみちそれについては意見がない様子だった.

open the way for [***to***] …に進路を開く, 道をあける, を引き起こす ▪ That would *open the way to* an increase in drug smuggling. そんなことをしたら麻薬密輸の増加に道を開くことになろう ▪ New regulations *opened the way for* more people to live and work here. 新しい法規によってより多くの人が当地に住み着いて働くようになった.

out of harm's way →HARM.

out of the way **1** 道を離れて[はずれて] ▪ He stepped *out of the way* and she hurried on. 彼は回り道をし, 彼女はどんどん先へ行った.
2 世を離れて; 人里離れて, 辺ぴな ▪ He had speculated too much and was keeping *out of the way*. 彼はあまりにも思索にふけりすぎ, ずっと世離れしていた ▪ The place was so much *out of the way*. そこはあまりにも辺ぴだった.
3 じゃまにならない所に; 片づいて, 終了して ▪ Get *out of the way*! どけ ▪ Keep *out of the way*. 近寄るな ▪ Move your legs *out of the way* so she can get past. 彼女が通れるように君の足をどけなさい ▪ Now the question is *out of the way*. 今やその問題はけりがついた ▪ The election is *out of the way* at last. やっと選挙が終わった.
4 死んで ▪ The man is *out of the way* now. その人はもう死んでいる.
5 〚否定文で〛 常軌を逸した, 異常な ▪ I have noticed nothing *out of the way*. これまで何も異状な気づきはない ▪ There is nothing *out of the way* about him. 彼には何も異常な点はない.

out of** a person's **way 人を避けて ▪ The fellow kept *out of my way*, and I could not see him. その男は私を避け続けたので, 会えなかった.

out of** one's **way 道を離れて, 道をはずれて ▪ It was a good mile *out of his way*. それは彼の行く道筋から1マイルはじゅうぶん離れていた ▪ Let us step a little *out of our way*. 少し回り道をして行きましょう.

over [***across***] ***the way*** 道の向こう側に ▪ His house stands *over the way*. 彼の家は道の向こう側に建っている ▪ He lives just *across the way* from our house. 彼はうちの真向いに住んでいる.

*one's **own way*** 自分独自のやり方で ▪ Do it *your own way*. それを君の勝手にやってみたまえ.

pave the way for [***to***] →PAVE.

pay** one's* (own***) ***way*** →PAY².

pick** one's **way →PICK².

point the way (***to***) (…へ)将来なすべき[できる]ことを示す ▪ His speeches *pointed the way to* an important social reform. 彼の演説は重要な社会改革へのなすべき道を示した.

put another way 〚put は過去分詞〛 言い換えれば ▪ Go back to your own room. *Put another way*, get out of here! 自分の部屋へ戻れよ. 早い話が, ここから出て行ってくれということだ.

put** a person **in the way of**/**put**…*(in***) *a person's **way*** 人に…ができる[得られる]ようにしてやる ▪ I soon *was put in the way of* earning a living. 私はやがて生計を立てるようにしてもらった.

put** a person **out of the way (じゃまな)人を片づける, 殺す ▪ Richard determined to *put* her *out of the way*. リチャードは彼女を亡き者にしようと決めた.

put** oneself **out of the way 骨を折る (*for, to do*) ▪ He *put himself out of the way for* my sake. 彼は私のために骨を折ってくれた ▪ Why should she *put herself out of the way to* welcome such a youth? なぜ彼女がそんな若者を歓迎するために骨を折らねばならないのか.

right of way **1** (他人の土地の)通行権 ▪ Hikers have had the *right of way* through these woods for decades. ハイカーたちは何十年も前からこの森を自由に通ってきた.
2 (人・乗物の)通行優先権 ▪ Pedestrians always have the *right of way* over any kind of vehicle. 歩行者の方が常にどんな車両よりも優先される.

rub** a person* (up***) ***the wrong way*** →RUB².

see** one's **way (***clear***) (行動・結果の)見通しがつく (*to*); 〚主に否定文・疑問文で〛 できるように思う (*to do*) ▪ I feel that I begin to *see my way* (*clear*). 私は見通しもつきかけてきたような気がする ▪ They do not *see their way to* altering it. 彼らはそれを変更する見通しがつかない ▪ I do not *see my way to* get you an invitation. どうもあなたを招待できないようです.

set in** one's **ways (年とって)自分の流儀に凝り固まって ▪ You can't change his mind—he's too *set in his ways*. 彼に考えを変えさせることはできないよ, あ

まりにも自分の流儀に凝り固まってるからね.

set** a person **on his** [**in the**] **way 人に道をたどれるようにしてやる ▪ The man took the boy to the signpost and *set* him *on his way*. その人はその少年を道標の所へ連れて行って, 先へ行けるようにしてやった.

smooth** one's* [the***] ***way*** →SMOOTH a person's path.

some way しばらくの間 ▪ The tradition was preserved *some way* into the sixteenth century. そのしきたりは16世紀までしばらく維持されていた.

stand in the way of →in the WAY of 1.

stroke** a person's **hair the wrong way →STROKE[2].

swing both ways 《口》両刀を使う, 男にも女にも関心がある, 男女両方とセックスをする ▪ Is he gay?—Well, I guess he *swings both ways*. 彼はゲイなのか?—うーん, 両刀使いだろう ▪ She *swings both ways*. 彼女って, 両刀使いなんだよ.

take** (a place) **in** one's **way 道すがら(ある場所へ)立ち寄る ▪ We may *take* Chatsworth *in our way*. 道すがらチャッツワスへ立ち寄るかもしれない.

take** one's* (own***) ***way*** →go one's (own) WAY.

take the easy way out 自殺する ▪ It's against nature to *take the easy way out*. 自殺するのは大自然の掟に反する.

take the easy [***quick,*** etc.] ***way out*** (***of***) (…から)楽に[さっさと, など]逃れる ▪ You *took the quick way out of* the difficulty. 君はその苦境からさっさと逃れた.

take the way (ある場所への)道につく (*to, towards*) ▪ They departed and *took the way towards* Rome. 彼らは出発してローマへの道についた ▪ He *took the way to* his hut. 彼は自分の小屋への道についた.

take ... the wrong way 誤解して腹を立てる (= take ... AMISS) ▪ I don't want you to *take* this *the wrong way*, but you have to quit talking. こう言っても怒らないでほしいが, おしゃべりをやめてくれないか.

take** one's **way (…の方へ)行く; 旅する ▪ He *took his way* towards the city. 彼はその町へ出かけた ▪ Still he *took his way* onward. なおも彼はどんどん旅をし続けた.

talk** one's **way out of うまく話をして(困難・苦境)から逃れる ▪ I *talked my way out of* having to give a speech. うまく言い逃れてスピーチをしなくてすんだ ▪ She *talked her way out of* the trouble. 彼女はうまく話をしてそのいざこざを切り抜けた.

that is the way **1** 道はあちらです ▪ *That is the way*; along that path to the left. 道はあちらです. あの左の道です.

2 そう, そう《相手のしていることをほめて》 ▪ *That is the way*; you are doing it well. そう, そう. うまくやっているぞ.

that way **1** あちらへ ▪ Are you going *that way*? あちらへお行きですか.

2 そんなふうに[で] ▪ I ain't given *that way*. 私はそういうふうにはできていない.

3《俗》ほれて ▪ Those two are *that way* about each other. この二人はお互いにほれあっている.

That's [***It's***] ***always the way.*** 《口》(悪い事が)いつもこうなる, (よくない事が)きまったように起きる ▪ *That's always the way*. When you forget your umbrella, it rains. いつもきまってこうだ. 傘を忘れたときに限って雨が降るんだから ▪ *It's always that way* in damaged relationships—love and hate forever intertwine. 関係が破綻を来たすときまって愛憎が果てしなく絡み合う.

That's (***just***) ***the way it goes.*** 《口》そんなことはよくあるものだ; それが運命だからあきらめなさい ▪ It sure isn't fair, but *that's just the way it goes*. 確かに公平ではないが, それって, よくあることさ.

That's no way to behave. それは無作法だ ▪ Fancy answering back! *That's no way to behave*. まあ口答えするなんて! それは無作法ですよ.

That's the way the cookie crumbles [《口》***the mop flops, the ball bounces***]. 《米口》(人を慰めて)そんなことはよくあることだ, 世の中はそんなものさ (→COOKIE) ▪ Too bad you failed again, but *that's the way the ball bounces*. 君がまた失敗したのは残念だが, なあに, よくあることさ.

(***That's the***) ***way to go!*** 《米口》 **1** よしその調子だ, いいぞよくやった, でかした ▪ Are you through? *That's the way to go*. It looks great! 終わったか. いいぞ, よくやった. みごとだ ▪ That was a great lecture. *Way to go!* でかした, みごとな演説だったよ ▪ "*That's the way to go!*" said Jim when I finally got the car started. やっとのことで車のエンジンがかかると「おみごと, よくやった」とジムが言った.

2《戯》ばかねえ ▪ *Way to go*. Now there are papers all over the floor. ひどいわねえ. 床中に書類が散らかっているじゃないの.

the easy way out ずる(をすること) ▪ It is *the easy way out* to blame others for our failure. 自分の失敗を他人のせいにするのはずるいことだ.

The farthest way about is the nearest way home. / ***The longest way round is the shortest way.*** 《諺》急がば回れ.

the hard way →HARD.

the other way 〚all, quite, very much などを伴って〛正反対で ▪ They are patterns of excellence. I am *all the other way*. 彼らは典型的にすぐれた人たちです. 私は全く正反対です.

the other [***wrong***] ***way about*** [***round, around***] 逆に, 反対に ▪ Sometimes a verb is derived from a noun and sometimes it is *the other way about*. 動詞が名詞から派生していることもあるし, その反対のこともある ▪ I thought he had hit her, but it was *the other way around*. 彼が彼女をたたいたとばかり思っていたら, その逆だった.

the parting of the ways →PARTING.

the right [***wrong***] ***way up*** 上下正しく[転倒して] ▪ He stood *the wrong way up*. 彼はさかさまになった.

the way 〚連結詞なしに節を導いて〛 **1** …のやり方

▪ *The way* she spoke hurt me. 彼女の話し方がしゃくにさわった.

2 …のように (*as*) ▪ He doesn't do it *the way* I do. 彼は私がやるようにはやらない.

3 …によれば ▪ *The way* I look at [see] it there's still room for that. 私の見るところまだその余地はある.

4 …であるから ▪ No wonder that girl despises me, *the way* you encourage her. あの子が私を軽蔑するのも当たり前です, あなたがけしかけるんですから.

5 …で判断すると ▪ It might be a novel *the way* it's selling. 売れ方から見るとそれは小説といったところだ.

the way *one's* ***mind works*** 心の働き方 ▪ This letter shows *the way his mind worked.* この手紙は彼の心の働き方をよく示している.

the way of the world 世の習わし ▪ I was ignored when I was poor, as is *the way of the world.* 私は貧乏なとき人から無視されたが, それが世の習わしというものだ.

the way to *a person's* ***heart*** 人を喜ばす方法 ▪ *The way to a man's heart* is through his stomach. 《諺》人を喜ばす方法はごちそうを食べさせることにある.

the way(s) of God [the Lord] 神[主]の道, 天道 (《聖》*2 Sam.* 22. 22) ▪ A day will come when *the ways of God* will be cleared up. 天道を妨げるものがなくなる日がくるだろう. ☞聖書語法.

the whole way ずっと, 初めから終わりまで (→all the WAY) ▪ I can't go *the whole way* with the book. この本には全面的に賛成することはできない.

the wrong way about [round, around] → the other WAY about.

the wrong way up →the right WAY up.

There are [There's] no two ways about it [that]. 少しの疑いもない ▪ That's a fact, and *there are no two ways about it.* それは事実で, 疑いは全然ない.

There is more than one way to skin a cat [get a pig to market, flay a fox]./There's more ways than one to kill [skin] a cat. 《諺》やり方[手段]はいろいろある; 猫の皮をはぐ[ブタを市場へ出す, キツネの皮をはぐ]方法は一通りだけではない《事をするにはいろいろなやり方がある》. ☞異常・非合法なやり方をするときの弁解.

this way **1** こちらへ ▪ Please step *this way.* どうぞこちらへ.

2 こんなふうに ▪ I did it *this way.* こんなふうにそれをやりました.

this way and that あちこち; あれこれと ▪ He turned his head *this way and that.* 彼はあちこち頭を向けた ▪ I've tried *this way and that* to please him. 彼の気に入るようにあれこれと努めた.

to *one's* ***way of thinking*** …の考えでは ▪ *To his way of thinking,* mobile phones should be banned on the street. 彼に言わせると, 通りでは携帯電話を禁止すべきとのこと.

under way (船が)航行中で; (一般に)始めて, 進行中で ▪ He went on board, and got the brig *under way.* 彼は乗り込んで帆船を航行させた ▪ He is getting *under way* for Necker. 彼はネッカーへ出発しようとしている ▪ We have several plans *under way.* 我々はいくつかの計画を始めている.

walk [be] in the way with …とともに旅をする; とつき合う (《聖》*Prov.* 1. 15) ▪ My son, *walk* not thou *in the way with* them. わが子よ, 彼らの仲間になってはならない. ☞聖書語法.

wangle *one's* ***way out of*** まんまと[うまく]…から抜け出す ▪ I managed to *wangle my way out of* poverty. なんとか首尾よく貧困から抜け出せた ▪ He *wangled his way out of* doing the job. 彼はうまくその仕事をせずに逃れられた.

want *one's* ***own way*** 思い通りにしたがる ▪ He *wants his own way* in everything. 彼は何かにつけて自分の思い通りにしたがる.

a person's ***way*** 人の方へ; 人の家の近所へ ▪ The cry drew all eyes *her way.* その叫び声ですべての人の視線が彼女の方へ向けられた ▪ I seldom come *your way* now. 今頃はめったにお宅の近くへ行かない.

way back 《米口》ずっと離れて, ずっと昔に ▪ This occurred *way back,* when the Native Americans had no horses. これはずっと昔の, 北米先住民が馬を持っていなかった時代に起こった.

way down 《米口》ずっと下って ▪ He is bound for a city *way down* south. 彼ははるか南部の町へ向かっている.

Way enough! 《海・号令》こぎ方やめ! ▪ *Way enough* in three. Three…two…one, *way enough!* 3つ数えたらこぎ方やめだ. 3, 2, 1, やめ!

way of business 仕事, 職業 ▪ He was in the same *way of business* before the war. 彼は戦前同じ仕事をしていた ▪ He is in a small *way of business.* 彼の商売は小さい.

one's ***way of life*** →a WAY of life.

way of living [life] 暮らし方 ▪ Their *way of life* gives them leisure to pursue those arts. 彼らの暮らし方があの芸術を追求する余暇を彼らに与える.

way off 《米口》ずっと遠くに; 大違いで ▪ I found him *way off* in that wood. 彼をずっと遠くのあの森で見つけた ▪ The papers are generally *way off* in some things. 新聞は事により大違いしているのが通例だ.

way out **1** 《米口》(中心から)ずっと離れた ▪ Catalina is an island out at sea—*way out.* カタリナは洋上の島で—ずっと離れたところにある.

2 《俗》急進的な, とっぴな ▪ This picture is too *way out* for me. この絵はとっぴすぎて僕には分からん.

way over 《米口》ずっと向こうの (far over); …まで (*to*) ▪ *Way over* yonder! ずっと向こうの方です ▪ It caused a stench *way over to* Broadway. それはブロードウェイの方まで悪臭をただよわせた.

way up 《米口》 **1** 〚副詞的に〛ずっと高く ▪ Do you live *way up* there? 君はそんな高い所に住んでいるのか.

2 〚限定的〛すぐれた ▪ I think of her as one of

those *way up* girls. 彼女は例のすぐれた女の子の一人だと思う.

way up north 《米》ずっと北では ▪It snows much *way up north.* ずっと北では大雪が降る.

ways and means **1** 方法, 手段 ▪I hope we can find *ways and means* of getting to the seaside. 海岸へ行く手段が見つかればいいと思う.

2 財源, 歳入の道 ▪The next thing to consider is the *ways and means.* 次に考えねばならぬのは財源だ.

well on *one's* ***way*** だいぶ進んで ▪He is *well on his way* to becoming an officer of the company. 彼はその会社の役員になる道をだいぶ進んでいる.

wend *one's* ***way*** →go one's WAY.

What a way to *do!* 《口》…とは何というすばらしい[ひどい]ことか ▪Hawaii. *What a way to* spend a week or two! ハワイ. 1, 2週間過ごすのは何とすばらしいことか ▪No money? *What a way to* spend a weekend! 金がないって? 週末を過ごすのに何たることだ.

win *one's* ***way*** →WIN.

wise in the ways of …についてよく知って, に精通して ▪My uncle is not too *wise in the ways of* the world. 叔父は世間のことはあまりよく知らない.

with ... out of the way …が除去されたので ▪*With* the party *out of the way*, aren't you happy? パーティーがすんでうれしいだろう.

work *one's* ***way*** →WORK[2].

work *one's* ***way through college***(, etc.) →WORK[2].

work *one's* ***way up*** →WORK[2].

wayback /wéɪbæk/ 名 ***a wayback from wayback*** 《米口》田舎者 ▪We were, in Western terms, "*waybacks from wayback.*" 我々は西部の言葉で言えば「田舎者」であった.

from wayback 《米口》辺境の森林地からの ▪I tell you, he's an artist *from wayback*! 確かに, 彼は辺境の森林地出身の画家だよ.

wayside /wéɪsàɪd/ 名 ***fall*** [***drop***] ***by the wayside*** 中途で没落する, 負ける (→FALL[2]) ▪They won't *drop by the wayside* so easily. 彼らが中途でそうやすやすと脱落することはあるまい.

wazoo /wəzúː/ 名 ***up*** [***out***] ***the wazoo*** 《米俗》非常に数多く, 多量に ▪We have had snow *up the wazoo* this winter. この冬には雪がどっさり降った ▪My computer has unwanted software *out the wazoo.* 僕のコンピューターには, いりもしないソフトが山ほど入っている.

weak /wiːk/ 形 ***a weak sister*** 《米口》(困ったときに)当てにならない人 ▪There is always *a weak sister* who turns yellow. 臆病風を吹かす当てにならないやつがいつもいるものだ.

(***as***) ***weak as a cat*** [***kitten***] 《口》(体が)非常に弱い ▪We must get food somewhere. I feel *as weak as a cat.* どこかで食べものにありつかなくちゃ. へたばりそうだ.

(***as***) ***weak as dishwater*** 《口》(紅茶が)とても薄い ▪The tea she made was *as weak as dishwater.* 彼女が入れた紅茶はとても薄かった.

(***as***) ***weak as water*** (体・精神が)非常に弱い ▪I am only just getting well of a fever, and I am *as weak as water.* 私は熱病がやっと治りかけたところで, とても衰弱している ▪Away from you I am *as weak as water.* 君から離れると, 私は実に弱い存在だ.

go weak at the knees **1** (恐怖・病気で)ひざがガクガクする ▪I *went weak at the knees* and I was on my knees within seconds. ひざがガクガクして, あっという間にひざをついた.

2 恋に落ちる, 好きになる ▪He smiled at her again and she has *gone weak at the knees.* 彼がまた微笑みかけると, 彼女はころりと参ってしまった.

in a weak moment/in a moment of weakness 弱腰になっているときに ▪*In a moment of weakness* I agreed to let him stay at our house. 弱腰になって彼にうちへ泊まってもいいと言った ▪I was on a diet but *in a weak moment* I ate a cream cake. ダイエット中なのについ気がゆるんでクリームケーキを食べてしまった.

the weak(***er***) ***sex*** →the fair(er) SEX.

The weakest goes to the wall. →go to the WALL.

weak in …が弱い ▪I am *weak in* algebra. 僕は代数が弱い.

weak in the head →soft in the HEAD.

weak in the upper story →STOR(E)Y.

one's ***weak side*** (とりでなどの)防備の弱い側; 弱み, 弱点 ▪Satan soon after got in upon *my weak side.* 悪魔はまもなく私の弱味につけ込んできた. ☞F côté faible のなぞり.

weakness /wíːknəs/ 名 ***have a weakness for*** …に目がない ▪I *have a weakness for* coffee. 私はコーヒーには目がない.

weal /wiːl/ 名 ***come weal or woe*** どんなことがあっても ▪*Come weal or woe*, I will never desert my friend. 何があっても友を見捨てはしない.

in weal and woe 幸不幸いずれのときも ▪*In weal and woe* I have ever had the true sympathy of all my people. 幸不幸いずれのときにも私はいつも人民全体の真の共感を得てきた.

whether for weal or woe よかれあしかれ ▪She had always taken her own course, *whether for weal or woe.* 彼女はよかれあしかれ我が道を歩んできた.

wealth /welθ/ 名 ***a wealth of*** 豊富な ▪She has *a wealth of* curly black hair. 彼女は豊かな黒い巻き毛をしている ▪*A wealth of* words is not eloquence. 言葉が多いのは雄弁ではない.

come to wealth 金持ちになる ▪He suddenly *came to wealth* by his aunt's death. 彼は伯母が死んだため急に金持ちになった.

liquid wealth 流動資本, (株・土地など)容易に換金できる資産 ▪The shrewd businessman's *liquid wealth* increased every year. 抜け目のないビジネスマンの流動資本は年々増えていった.

wean /wiːn/ 動 ***wean** oneself **from*** …から遠ざかる; を捨てる ▪ He tried to *wean himself from* Mary by degrees. 彼は徐々にメアリーから遠ざかろうとした.

weapon /wépən/ 名 ***a double-edged weapon*** 使い手に役立つが傷も負わせる武器, 二様に解釈できる状態, 諸刃(もろは)の刃(やいば) ▪ Love is *a double-edged weapon*; it can heal and it can hurt. 愛は諸刃の刃である. 癒すこともあれば傷つけることもある.

at all* [*any*] *weapons どんな種類の武器でも ▪ He was expert *at all weapons*. 彼はどんな武器でもお手のものであった.

at** a person's **own weapon(s) 人に得意の武器を取らせて; 得意の手を使って ▪ This was truly foiling the Devil, *at his own weapons*. これはまさに悪魔に得意の武器を取らせてその裏をかくというやつだった.

wear[1] /weər/ 名 ***be in wear*** (衣類・飾りが)着用されている, はやっている ▪ Serges *were in* general *wear*. みんなサージを着ていた ▪ *Are* trimmings much *in wear* this year? ことしはふち飾りがかなりはやっていますか?

come into wear (服飾などが)流行してくる ▪ Do you know patches are *coming into wear* again? つけぼくろがまた流行しかけているのを知っていますか.

have ... in wear (人が)…を着用している ▪ She *had* a silk dress *in wear*. 彼女は絹のドレスを着ていた.

show wear 使い[着]古されている; くたびれている ▪ The carpets are *showing wear*. そのじゅうたんはいたみが見える.

stand wear (布などが)長持ちする, 強い ▪ This cloth will *stand* much *wear*. この布は非常に長持ちする.

the worse for wear **1** 着て[使って]いたんで ▪ The hat is *the worse for wear*. この帽子はくたびれている ▪ The statuette never seemed *the worse for wear*. その小像は使い古されていたんでいるようには少しも見えなかった.

2 《口》ひどく酔って ▪ She seemed very much *the worse for wear* after the party. 彼女はパーティーの後すっかり酔っ払っているようだった.

wear and tear →TEAR².

wear[2] /weər/ 動 ***wear a crown* [*a diadem, the purple*]** 王位についている ▪ Uneasy lies the head that *wears a crown*. 王位についている身ほど安からぬ者はない ▪ The King has the misfortune to *wear the purple*. その王は不幸にして王位についているのだ.

wear** one's **age* [*years*] *well (年の割りに)若々しく見える ▪ My aunt *wears her age well*. 私の叔母はなかなかふけない.

***wear** one's **arm in a scarf* [*sling*]** (けがをした)腕を包帯でつるす ▪ He *wore his arm in a scarf* for two months. 彼は2か月間腕を包帯でつるしていた.

***wear blinders* [*blinkers*]** 視野が狭い, 偏狭な考えを持つ ▪ Anyone who thinks otherwise is surely *wearing blinders*. これと違った考え方をするやつは視野が狭いといわざるを得ない.

wear** one's **heart on** one's **sleeve →HEART.

wear in** one's **heart (主義などに)打ち込んでいる; (人を)熱愛している ▪ He *wears* his work *in his heart*. 彼は仕事に打ち込んでいる.

wear it 《英俗》がまんする ▪ I won't *wear it*! そんなことはがまんしないぞ. ☞「安っぽい服を着る」が原義.

wear late (時が)遅くなる ▪ It was now *wearing late* in the day. もう日も遅くなりかけていた ▪ As the evening *wore late*, the uproar grew louder. 夜がふけるにつれて, 大騒ぎはいよいよやかましくなった.

wear** one's **learning* [*culture, brightness*] *lightly 学識[教養, 頭の良さ]を誇ろうとしない ▪ He is never one to *wear his learning lightly*. 彼は学識を誇ろうとしないというたぐいの人間ではない.

***wear on** a person's **nerves* [*patience*]** 人の神経にさわる, 人をいらいらさせる ▪ Her incessant nagging was *wearing on his nerves*. 彼女の絶え間のない小言が彼の神経にさわっていた.

***wear the trousers* [《米》 *pants*]** → TROUSER; PANTS.

wear thin **1** すり減って薄くなる ▪ The coin has *worn thin*. 硬貨がすり減って薄くなっている ▪ My patience is *wearing thin*. だんだんがまんができなくなってきた.

2 (話などが)新味を失う, 飽きられる ▪ Pacifism is *wearing* a little *thin*. 平和主義は少し新味を失いかけている.

wear ... to death …を死ぬほど疲れさせる ▪ She has been *wearing* herself *to death*! 彼女は死ぬほどわれとわが身を疲れさせていた.

wear to** a person's **shape (衣服が)着ていると体によく合ってくる ▪ Clothes *wear to one's shape*. 衣服は着ていると体によく合ってくる.

wear well **1** もちがよい ▪ This coat has *worn well*. この上着はもちがよかった.

2 (人が)年をとらない, ふけない, 若く見える ▪ Old Tomkins *wears well*. トムキンズ老人はふけない.

win and wear (女性を妻として)得てわがものとする ▪ As for his daughter, you have yet to *win* her *and wear* her, as the saying is. 彼の娘については, 君がいわゆる「得てわがものとする」のはまだ先のことだ.

weary[1] /wíəri/ 形名 ***get the wearies*** 《米俗》気うつになる ▪ I'm *getting the* evening *wearies*. 夕方には気うつが出てくる.

weary for …に(待ち)こがれて疲れて ▪ He sighed, so *weary for* one so young. そんなに若い人にひどくこがれ疲れて, 彼は吐息をついた.

weary of …に飽きはてて ▪ I grew *weary of* the sea. 海にはもううんざりしてしまった ▪ Plato is never *weary of* speaking the honor of the soul. プラトンは魂の誉れについて語るのに決して飽きない.

weary Willie 《俗》いつも疲れている人; 浮浪者 ▪ *Weary Willie* may say that he hates work. いつも疲れている人は仕事はきらいだと言うかもしれない.

W

weary with …で疲れて ▪ My hand is *weary with* writing. 書き物で手がくたびれた.

weary[2] /wíəri/ 動 ***weary ... to death*** …を死ぬほどうんざりさせる ▪ He *wearies* us *to death* with his stories. 彼はいろんな話をして我々を死ぬほどうんざりさせる.

weasel /wíːzəl/ 名 ***(as) cunning as a weasel*** 非常にずるい ▪ I'm as sharp as a ferret, and *as cunning as a weasel*. 私はとても厳しくとても狡猾なんだ.

catch a weasel asleep 抜け目のない人を欺く, 生き馬の目を抜く ▪ Catch me? *Catch a weasel asleep*! おれをつかまえるって? そいつは生き馬の目を抜くようなものだ!

weasel words 《主に米》あいまいな逃げ口上, すっとぼけ ▪ She is easily taken in by the *weasel words* of crafty merchants. 彼女は巧妙な商人の逃げ口上に手もなくひねられる.

weather[1] /wéðər/ 名形 ***a fair weather friend*** 《口》幸運の時だけの友人 ▪ How many *fair weather friends* I had made in my life! それまでに何と多くの幸運の時だけの友人を作ったことか ▪ Don't rely on him—he's *a fair-weather friend*. 彼に頼ってはだめだ. まさかのときには当てにならないから.

above the weather 《航空》雲より上を[に] ▪ The plane flew *above the weather*. 飛行機は雲より上を飛んだ.

all kinds of weather →(in) all WEATHER(s).

dance and sing all weathers 日よりを見る, 時勢に順応する ▪ He is not a person to *dance and sing all weathers*. 彼は日より見主義者ではない.

drive with the weather 風波のままに漂う ▪ We let her go and *drive with the weather*. 我々は船を放し, 風波のままに漂わせた.

freak weather conditions 例年と異なる気象状況, 異常気象 ▪ Are *freak weather conditions* in recent years the work of global warming? 近年の異常気象は地球温暖化のせいなのか.

go into the weather 風雨の中へ出て行く ▪ The captain *goes into the weather* as merrily as to a birthday. 船長は誕生日の集まりへでも行くように陽気に風雨の中へ出て行く.

have the weather gage of →GA(U)GE.

(in) all weather(s)/all kinds of weather 《英》雨が降ろうが風が吹こうが; どんな天気でも ▪ He goes out *in all weathers* to work. 彼はどんな天気でも仕事に出かけていく ▪ Fred keeps the house *all kinds of weather*. フレッドは雨が降ろうが風が吹こうが, 家に閉じこもっている. ☞weather の複数は (in) all WEATHERs 以外はまれ.

in fair weather or foul 晴雨にかかわらず ▪ We will set off tomorrow, *in fair weather or foul*. 晴雨にかかわらず我々はあす出発する.

in the weather 風雨にさらされて; 戸外で ▪ The outside of the building lies *in the weather*. その建物の外部は風雨にさらされている ▪ She longed to be *in the weather* after an illness. 彼女は病後戸外へ出たがった.

keep a [one's] weather(-)eye open [awake, lifted] 《口》絶えず注意している, 抜け目がない ▪ You look out. *Keep your weather-eye awake*. 君は警戒しろ. 絶えず注意しているんだぞ. ☞海語から.

keep the weather gage of → have the weather GA(U)GE of.

keep the weather of **1**《海》…の風上にいる ▪ The vessel *kept the weather of* us. その船はずっと我々の風上にいた.
2 …を牛耳る, 司る ▪ My honor *keeps the weather of* my fate. 私の名誉が私の運命を司る.

King's [Queen's, royal] weather (晴れの儀式の日の)快晴 ▪ It was altogether *royal weather* for the fete. 全くその祝典には申し分のない快晴だった.

Lovely [Nice] weather for ducks! 《戯》ひどい雨だねえ ▪ Nasty weather.—Yes. *Nice weather for ducks!* いやな天気だね—本当に. ひどい雨だこと.

make heavy weather of 《口》(小事)を大げさに考えすぎる ▪ Those muddle-headed persons *make heavy weather of* the simplest tasks. そういう頭の混乱した連中はとても簡単な事でも大げさに考える.

make heavy weather with …で四苦八苦する ▪ He is *making heavy weather with* his algebra. 彼は代数で四苦八苦している.

Nice weather for ducks! →Lovely WEATHER for ducks!

Nice weather we're having. **1**《初対面の人との話の口切りに》よいお天気ですね ▪ *Nice weather we're having.*—Yeah. It's great. いい天気ですな—さよう. よい日よりで.
2《皮肉》悪い天候ですね ▪ *Nice weather we're having*!—Sure. Lovely weather for ducks. ひどい天気だこと—本当に. よく降るわね.

Queen's [royal] weather →King's WEATHER.

seasonable weather 季節に合った天候 ▪ We are having *seasonable weather* this spring here. 当地では今年は春らしいうららかな天気だ.

stress of weather →STRESS.

stretch wing to weather 飛ぶ (fly) ▪ A falcon was *stretching wing to weather* high in the sky. ハヤブサが空高く飛んでいた.

the weather breaks [holds] 天気がくずれる[続く] ▪ Next day *the weather broke*. 翌日天気がくずれた ▪ I hope *the weather holds*. いい天気が続くといいが.

through the weather 風雨をついて ▪ They started *through the weather* for his house. 彼らは風雨をついて彼の家へと出発した.

under the weather **1**《口》時候あたりがして, 不快で ▪ What, mother, are you *under the weather*? おや, おかあさん, 具合が悪いのですか ▪ How have you been? —I've been *under the* *weather*, but I'm better. 近頃, どうだい?―このところ調子が悪くてね, でもだいぶよくなったよ.

2《俗》酔っぱらって ▪ I'm a little *under the weather*. 少し酔っているんだ.

weather eye **1** 天候が読める目, 訓練された人の天候観測眼 ▪ Grandfather's *weather eye* always tells him whether it will be wet or dry. 祖父は降るか晴れるかをいつも当てることができる.

2 注意, 警戒 (→keep a WEATHER(-)eye open) ▪ We kept a *weather eye* on the man to make sure he didn't escape. 逃亡しないように彼をずっと監視し続けた.

weather permitting 〚文尾につけて〛天気さえよければ ▪ The ship will be ready to sail, *weather permitting*. 船は天気さえよければいつでも出帆します.

What do you think about [of] this weather? (会話の切り出しに) 何という天気でしょうね ▪ Nice to see you again.―*What do you think about [of] this weather?*―Lovely weather for ducks. また会えてうれしいよ―この天気, どう思う?―アヒルにとっては上天気だね《よく降るね》.

weather[2] /wéðər/ 動 ***weather a point*** 《海》みさきの風上を通る; 難局を乗り切る ▪ But, through mercy, he *weathered this point* also. しかし神の助けで彼はこの難局をもまた乗り切った.

weather a storm **1**《海》(船が)暴風雨を乗り切る ▪ The ship has *weathered* so many *storms* without loss. その船は損失もなく何回もしけを乗り切ってきた.

2 難局を乗り切る ▪ The enterprise has successfully *weathered the storm*. その企業は首尾よく難局を切り抜けた.

weather the storm →STORM.

weather-cock /wéðərkɑ̀k|-kɔ̀k/ 名 ***change [spin] like a weather-cock*** (風見のように) しょっちゅう気が変わる, 感化されやすい ▪ His mind has *changed like a weather-cock* in the shifting winds of public opinion. 世論の風向きの変化につれて彼の決心はぐらぐらと揺らいだ.

weave /wiːv/ 動 ***get weaving*** 《英俗》〚主に命令文で〛急ぐ, てきぱきやる ▪ *Get weaving*, boys! 急ぐんだ, みんな.

weave a [one's] spell 《主に英》→SPELL[1].

weave in and out of (障害物)の中を縫うように進む ▪ He walked on, *weaving in and out of* the crowd. 彼は人込みの中を縫うように前進した.

weave one's way 縫うように進む ▪ We two *weaved our way* through the forest. 我々二人は森の中を縫うように進んだ.

web /web/ 名 ***a spider's web*** クモの巣; わな ▪ The youth was caught in *a spider's web* when he joined that club. その青年はそのクラブの一員になったときわなに陥ってしまった.

a tangled web 非常に込み入った状況, 複雑で困惑させる状態 ▪ His life was *a tangled web* of intrigues and reversals. 彼の人生は陰謀とどんでん返しのもつれた糸であった ▪ Our inquiry revealed *a tangled web* of corruption and greed. 我々の調査の結果, 汚職と貪欲の絡み合った状況が明るみに出た.

a web of lies 嘘で固めた話 ▪ What he told me was *a web of lies*. 彼が私に言ったことは嘘で固めた話だった.

surf the Web 《電算》サイトをあちこち見て回る, ネットサーフィンする ▪ My son can *surf the Web* like a professional. 息子のネットサーフィンの腕前はプロ級だ.

wed /wed/ 動 ***be wedded to*** …と結婚する ▪ Cecily *was wedded to* Thomas Brown. セシリーはトマス・ブラウンと結婚した.

wedding /wédɪŋ/ 名 ***a white wedding*** 教会で挙げる結婚式 ▪ They spent just £1,000 on their *white wedding* to avoid getting into debt. 二人は借金を避けて教会で式を挙げ, 経費わずか1,000ポンドだった. ☞花嫁が着る貞節のシンボルである真っ白いウェディングドレスの色から.

hear wedding bells for …が結婚する(のを知る) ▪ You will *hear wedding bells* soon *for* Kate and Fred. ケイトとフレッドはもうじき結婚すると思う.

like a spare prick [wick] at a wedding 《英卑》(パーティーなどで)全く余分で, お呼びでない ▪ Nobody spoke to me at the party. I felt *like a spare prick at a wedding*. そのパーティーでは誰も話しかけてくれなかった. 私なんぞお呼びでないといった感じだった. ☞prick, wick＝penis.

one's ***wedding tackle*** 《英戯》男性の性器 ▪ He then took hold of *my wedding tackle*. 彼はそれから僕の一物を握った.

wedge[1] /wedʒ/ 名 ***drive a wedge into [between]*** …を分裂させる; の間の仲を割く ▪ Maurice *drove a wedge into* the company by selling his block of shares to the enemy. モーリスは大量の持ち株を敵に売って会社を分裂させてしまった ▪ The differences of personalities *drove a wedge between* them. 性格の違いで二人の間にひびが入った.

in a wedge/in wedges くさび[V字]形に ▪ He drew up his men *in a wedge*. 彼は部下をV字形に集合させた ▪ The seats are disposed *in wedges*. 座席はくさび形に配置されている.

knock out the wedges 《米口》人を苦境に陥れて見捨てる ▪ You ought not to go *knocking out the wedges*. 人を苦境に陥れて見捨ててはいけない.

the thin [little, small] end of the wedge/the thin edge of the wedge 大事に至る小さな発端《よい場合にも悪い場合にも使う》 ▪ The rule was but *the small end of the wedge*. その統治は大事に至る小さな発端にすぎなかった ▪ He only takes one glass every evening but it is *the thin edge of the wedge*. 彼は毎晩1杯やるだけだが, それが大事に至る小さなきっかけになる.

wedge[2] /wedʒ/ 動 ***wedge*** *oneself* 割り込む ▪ He *wedged himself* into the crowd. 彼は群衆の中へ割り込んだ.

wedge apart [asunder] (くさびを打ち込んで)…を押し分ける ▪ Little things *wedge* pastor and people *apart*. 小さな事柄が牧師と衆人とを押し分ける.

wedlock /wédlɑ̀k|-lɔ̀k/ 名 ***(be) born in [out of] wedlock*** 嫡出の[庶出の] ▪ Little Bessy *was born in wedlock*. 小さいベシーは嫡出の子だった ▪ One would suspect him *born out of* lawful *wedlock*. 人は彼を私生児ではないかと思うだろう.

wee /wiː/ 形 ***a wee bit*** 《主にスコ》ほんの少し, ちょっぴり ▪ The champagne has given me just *a wee bit* of a migraine. あのシャンパンでほんのちょっぴり頭が痛い ▪ She is *a wee bit* jealous. 彼女はちょっぴり嫉妬深い.

the wee folk 妖精たち ▪ He saw some hundreds of *the wee folk* dancing round these trees. 彼は数百人の妖精たちがその木の回りで踊っているのを見た.

the (wee) small hours →HOUR.

weed /wiːd/ 名 ***grow like weeds*** むやみに生長する ▪ These plants *grow like weeds*. この植物はむやみに生長する.

Ill weeds grow apace. 《諺》悪草は生長が早い,「憎まれっ子世にはばかる」.

One year's seed makes seven years weeds. 《諺》雑草に1年種を落とさせると7年間雑草が絶えない.

run to weeds (...に)雑草がはびこる ▪ The garden is *running to weeds*. 庭には雑草がはびこっている.

week /wiːk/ 名 ***a week of days*** まる1週間 (《聖》*Dan.* 10. 2) ▪ They dared not keep me *a week of days*. 彼らは私をまる1週間引き留めておく勇気はなかった.

a week of Sundays [weeks] 《口》7週間(もの間); 非常に長い間 ▪ Why, I haven't seen you for *a week of Sundays*! まあ, ほんとに久しぶりですね.

a week today/a week from now 来週のきょう ▪ School begins *a week today*. 学校は来週のきょうから始まる.

a week tomorrow [on Tuesday, etc.***]/***《主に英》***a week from tomorrow [Tuesday,*** etc.***]*** 来週のあす[火曜日などに] ▪ It's my birthday *a week on Friday*. 来週の金曜日は僕の誕生日だ.

a week yesterday [last Sunday, etc.***]*** 《主に英》先週のきのう[日曜日などに] ▪ It was *a week yesterday* that I heard the news. その知らせを聞いたのは先週のきのうだった.

by the week 週いくらで ▪ I used to get paid *by the week*. 以前は週給払いだった ▪ We rented a cottage *by the week*. 山荘を週いくらで借りた.

for weeks 何週間も ▪ I haven't seen you *for weeks*. しばらくぶりですね.

into next week ひどく, 致命的に ▪ I knocked him down *into next week*. 彼をひどく打ちのめした.

knock [send] *a person* ***into the middle of next week*** 《俗》**1** 人をひどく打ちすえる, やっつける ▪ Had I done it, he probably would've *knocked* me *into the middle of next week*. そうしていたら彼にひどくどやされていただろう.
2 人を仰天させる, 困惑させる ▪ When he found we knew all about it, he *was knocked into the middle of next week*. 我々がそのことを全部知っていることがわかると, 彼は閉口してしまった.

Sunday [Monday, etc.***] week*** 《主に英》先週または来週の日曜[月曜, など] ▪ I came back last *Saturday week*. 先週の土曜日に帰って来ました ▪ Let us say *Monday week*, dear. 来週の月曜にしようよ.

this day [today, yesterday, tomorrow, etc.***] week*** 《主に英》先週または来週のきょう[きのう, あす, など] ▪ I saw her *this day week*. 彼女と先週のきょう会った ▪ Can you make it convenient to be there *this day week*? 来週のきょうそこへ来る都合がつけられますか ▪ Send Charley to me *this night week*. 来週の今晩チャーリーをよこしてくれ.

too late a week 遅すぎて, 後の祭りで (cf. Sh., *A. Y. L.* 2. 3. 74) ▪ But I fear it is *too late a week*. しかしもう後の祭りではないかしら.

week after week 《口》何週間もずっと ▪ The drought continued *week after week*. 日照りが何週間も続いた.

week and week about 隔週に ▪ The girls were supposed to market *week and week about*. 少女たちは隔週に買い物をすることになっていた.

week by week 一週一週と経つうちに, 週を重ねるごとに ▪ She got a little better *week by week*. 何週も経つうちに彼女は少しずつ回復した.

week in(,) week out いつも, 絶えず (→DAY in, day out; YEAR in, (and) year out) ▪ *Week in, week out*, the old bus lumbered through the village at 8 a.m. いつもその古バスは午前8時に村をガタガタ通った.

weekend /wíːkènd/ 名 ***a wet weekend*** みじめなもの ▪ He's going about with a face like *a wet weekend*. 彼はみじめな顔をして歩き回っている. ☞「雨降りの週末」が原義.

look like a wet weekend 《口》ひどく浮かない顔をしている ▪ What's up? You *look like a wet weekend*. どうかしたの. ひどく浮かない顔をしてるけど.

make a weekend of it 《口》(パーティー・外出・娯楽で)週末を楽しく過ごす ▪ Let's *make a weekend of it*, shall we? 週末をいっしょに楽しく過ごそうよ.

on [《英》at] the weekend 週末に ▪ I never work *on the weekend*. 週末には仕事をしない.

weep /wiːp/ 動 ***could have wept*** 《口》(失望して)泣きたいほどだった, とてもがっかりした ▪ I *could have wept* thinking what I'd missed. 取り逃がしたものを考えると泣きたい気がした ▪ She *could have wept* when she found out it was canceled. それが取りやめになったと知って彼女はひどくがっかりした.

weep a little weep 《米口》ちょっと泣く ▪ I sat down by my desk and *wept a little weep*. 私はデスクのわきに座って, ちょっと泣いた. ☞ Alcott, *Little Women* の Jo の言葉から.

weep blood →WEEP (tears of) blood.

weep *one's* ***fill [bellyfull]*** 思う存分泣く ▪ She had gone to the grave, and there *wept her fill*. 彼女は墓の所へ行って, そこで思う存分泣いた.

weep *one's* ***heart out*** → WEEP out one's

W

heart.

weep** oneself **out 心ゆくまで泣く ▪ It is better for you to *weep yourself out.* 心ゆくまで泣くといい.

weep out** one's **eyes 目を泣きはらす ▪ I have *wept out my eyes* for grief. I cannot read. 私は悲しみのために目を泣きはらしてしまった. 字が読めない.

weep out** one's **heart**/ **weep** one's **heart out 胸もつぶれんばかりに泣く ▪ It seemed unspeakably pathetic to hear her *weeping her heart out.* 彼女が胸もつぶれんばかりに泣いているのを聞くのは言いようもなく哀れだった.

weep (tears of) blood (心・傷が)血の涙を流す ▪ My heart *weeps blood* to see your glory lost! 君の光栄が失われたのを見て私の心は血の涙を流すのだ.

weep** oneself **to sleep →SLEEP[1].

weep with [over] an onion 空涙を流す ▪ He was *weeping* ruefully *with an onion.* 彼は悲しげに空涙を流していた.

weeping cross /wíːpɪŋkrɔ́ːs|-krɔ́s/ 名 ***come home [return] by weeping cross*** ひどく後悔する, 失敗する ▪ Making an irruption into Provence, he *came home by weeping cross.* プロバンスに侵入して彼はひどく後悔した. ☞weeping cross「ざんげの涙を捧げる路傍の十字架」.

weigh[1] /weɪ/ 名 ***under weigh*** (船が)航行中で; 進行中で ▪ The packet got *under weigh.* 郵便船は出帆した ▪ We were soon *under weigh* again. 我々はすぐまた動きだした. ☞under WAY の誤用.

weigh[2] /weɪ/ 動 ***be weighed (in the balance(s)) and found wanting*** →weighed in the BALANCE and found wanting; be weighed and found WANTING.

weigh anchor →ANCHOR[1].

weigh (half) a ton 《口》(持ち運ぶのに)ひどく重い ▪ My suitcase *weighed a ton.* 私のスーツケースはひどく重かった ▪ This suitcase *weighs half a ton!* What have you got in it? このスーツケースはずいぶん重いけど中に何が入っているの.

weigh in** a person's **favor 人にとって有利に働く ▪ His shyness *weighed in his favor.* 彼の内気さが彼にとって有利に働いた.

weigh on** a person's **mind = prey on a person's MIND.

weigh the thumb 《俗》(親指ではかりを押さえて)重量をごまかす ▪ The store clerk tried to *weigh the thumb* when selling sugar. 店員は砂糖を売っているとき親指ではかりを押さえて重量をごまかそうとした.

weigh** one's **words よく考えてものを言う, 一言一句をおろそかにしない ▪ *Weigh your words* when you speak. 話すときにはよく考えてものを言いなさい.

W

weight /weɪt/ 名 ***a dead weight*** 非常な重荷になる人[物], 足かせ ▪ You can't join the rescue party. You would just be *a dead weight.* お前が救助隊に加わるのは無理だ. 足手まといになるだけだろう.

a weight off** one's **mind →MIND[1].

be a weight off** one's **shoulders もう心配しなくてよい, 肩の荷が下りる ▪ That *was a* great *weight off my shoulders.* それですっかり肩の荷が下りた ▪ If you could take it over, that would *be a* tremendous *weight off my shoulders.* もし君がそれを引き継いでくれたら, 私はもう心配せずにすむのだが.

by weight 重さで[が] ▪ Bread is sold *by weight* rather than by the loaf in Europe. ヨーロッパではパンは1斤単位ではなく重さで売られる ▪ The proportions of acid and water were equal *by weight.* 酸と水の割合は重量が同じであった.

carry [have] (the weight of) the world on** one's **shoulders [back] 重い責任を負わされている ▪ He is so egocentric that he acts as if he is *carrying the world on his shoulders.* 彼はすごく自己中心的で, まるで地球の重みを一人で背負っているようにふるまっている.

carry weight 影響力がある, 重要である (*with*) ▪ Her opinion *carries* great [no] *weight with* him. 彼女の意見は彼には非常に力がある[全く無力だ].

feel the weight of (打撃・圧迫など)に苦しむ ▪ He had *felt the weight of* her Majesty's power. 彼は女王の権力に苦しんできた.

fling** one's **weight about [around] →throw one's WEIGHT about.

gain [lose] weight 体重がふえる[減る] ▪ He has *lost* much *weight.* 彼はだいぶ体重が減った.

get [take] the weight off** one's **feet [legs] 《口》(疲れた人などが)座って足の疲れをとる ▪ She sat down and *got the weight off her feet.* 彼女は座って足の疲れをとった.

give weight to (意見・事情など)に重きを置く, を重要視する ▪ We have *given* due *weight to* the statement. 我々はその声明には十分重きをおいた.

have (the weight of) the world on** one's **shoulders [backs] →carry (the WEIGHT of) the world on one's shoulders.

have weight 重要である, 重きをなす (*with*) ▪ It *has* no *weight with* me. それは私には何でもないことだ.

in weight 重量が… ▪ It is heavy [light] *in weight.* それは目方が重い[軽い].

keep** one's **weight down 太るのを防ぐ ▪ The athlete *kept his weight down* by constant exercise. そのアスリートは絶えず運動して太るのを防いだ.

lay weight on [upon] …に重きを置く, を重要視する ▪ Perhaps we *lay* too much *weight on* dress and outward things. たぶん我々は衣服や外見上の事柄を重要視しすぎるのだろう.

lose weight →gain WEIGHT.

of weight 重要な ▪ He is a man *of weight.* 彼は有力者だ ▪ This argument is *of* great *weight.* この議論は非常に重要だ.

pull (**one's**) weight →PULL[2].

punch above** one's **weight 《英・報道》自分の能力を超える活動をする, 思った以上に影響力がある ▪ The small city has always *punched above its* *weight* when it comes to sport. その小さな市は，スポーツとなると常に実力以上に他を圧倒してきた ▪ He *punched above his weight* by finishing in third place. 彼は3位入賞と健闘した.

punch** one's **weight 《英・報道》能力通りの仕事をする，期待通りの影響力がある ▪ It's high time you *punched your weight*. そろそろ君の力に見合った成果を挙げてほしい.

put on weight 体重が増す ▪ He has *put on weight*. 彼は体重がふえた.

put** one's **weight behind → throw one's WEIGHT behind.

put weight on …を強調する ▪ The director *put weight on* the urgency of the work. 所長はその仕事が緊急を要するものであることを力説した.

short weight 重量の不足; 不正なはかり ▪ They give *short weight* and short measure in that store. あの店でははかりとます目が足りない.

swing** one's **weight 権力を行使する，顔をきかす ▪ Mr. Martin *swung his weight* to get his son a job with the firm. マーティン氏は息子をその会社に入れるために顔をきかせた.

***take the weight off** one's **feet** [**legs**]* →get the WEIGHT off one's feet.

throw in** one's **weight 支持[援助]する ▪ I shall *throw in my weight* wherever I can. 私はできる場合はいつでも援助します.

***throw** [**toss, fling**] one's **weight about** [**around**]* 《口》いばりちらす; 職権を乱用する ▪ He enjoys *throwing his weight about* and getting his way. 彼はいばって思い通りにするのを楽しんでいる.

throw** [**put**] one's **weight behind …を支持して力こぶを入れる ▪ They will *throw their weight behind* the new drive. 彼らはこの新運動を力こぶを入れて支持するだろう.

under the weight of …の重みを受けて ▪ The table groans *under the weight of* delicacies. 食卓は山海の珍味の重みに耐えかねている《ごちそうがどっさり並べてある》 ▪ The whole edifice broke down *under its own weight*, so to speak. その大建築はいわば自らの重みで崩壊したのだ.

*one's **weight in** [**of**] **gold** [**silver**]* それと同じ目方の金[銀]《価値などを大げさにほめるときに用いる》 ▪ He is worth to her *his weight in gold*. 彼は彼女にとっては同じ重さの金ほどの価値がある ▪ He would have paid the nurse with *her weight in gold* for taking care of his daughter. 彼は娘の面倒を見てくれたことに対して乳母(ぅ)に彼女と同じ目方の金を支払いたいくらいだった.

weight of numbers 数の多さ，集団の力 ▪ They would get what they wanted by sheer *weight of numbers*. 彼らは多勢を頼んで望みのものを手に入れたものだった.

worth** one's **weight in gold →one's WEIGHT in gold.

weird /wɪərd/ 形動 ***the weird Sisters*** 魔女 ▪ He had rather see one of *the weird Sisters* flourish through his keyhole on a broom-stick. 彼はむしろ魔女の一人がほうきの柄に乗って鍵穴からはでに入ってくるのを見たかった.

weird and wonderful 《口》巧妙新奇な ▪ I am allergic to those *weird and wonderful* machines. 僕はこういう巧妙新奇な機械は苦手だ.

welcome[1] /wélkəm/ 形名間 ***a royal welcome*** 王さまにふさわしいほどの大歓迎 ▪ I was surprised at the *royal welcome* the villagers gave me. 村人の盛大な歓迎を受けて私は驚いた.

a warm welcome 温かい歓迎 ▪ They got *a* very *warm welcome* when they arrived. 彼らが着くと心から温かく迎えられた.

a welcome mat **1** Welcome の文字が入ったドアマット ▪ Father bought *a welcome mat* for our new house. 父は新しい家の(歓迎の文字入りの)ドアマットを買った.

2《口》⟦the welcome mat is out, put out the welcome mat の句で⟧ 心からの歓迎 ▪ Our *welcome mat is* always *out* to our friends. 我が家ではいつでも友人の来訪は大歓迎である.

and welcome ⟦文尾につけて⟧ それでけっこう; どうぞ ▪ Here are some cakes; take them *and welcome*. お菓子があります. どうぞお取りください ▪ He may go bankrupt *and welcome*. 彼が破産しようとこっちの知ったことじゃない.

(as) welcome as flowers in May 大歓迎で ▪ Why, we haven't seen you for months, you're *as welcome as flowers in May*. まあ，何か月ぶりかですね，大歓迎ですよ.

***(as) welcome as snow in harvest** [**water into** one's **shoes**]* 《反語》一向にありがたくない ▪ His lecture was *as welcome as snow in harvest*. 彼の講演は一向に魅力がなかった.

bid** [**wish**] a person **welcome 人にようこそと言う ▪ I'd like to *bid* you *welcome* to my humble abode. むさくるしい我が家へようこそ ▪ I sent Ned to Wooton to *wish* my sister *welcome* home. 私はネッドをウートンへやって妹にようこそお帰りと言わせた.

give (a) warm welcome (…を)大歓迎する (*to*); 《反語》(…に)激しく抵抗する (*to*) ▪ They *gave a warm welcome to* the general. 彼らは将軍を大歓迎した ▪ We *gave a warm welcome to* the enemy. 我々は激しく敵に抵抗した.

make** a person **welcome 人を歓迎[歓待]する ▪ He will not *make* me *welcome*. 彼は私を歓迎してくれないだろう.

more than welcome (人・助言・改革など)大歓迎で，大いに求められて ▪ Any comments would be *more than welcome*. どんなコメントでも大歓迎です.

outstay** [**overstay, wear out**] one's **welcome 長居をしてきらわれる[あきられる] ▪ He has *overstayed his welcome*. 彼は長居をしてきらわれた ▪ He has no fear of *overstaying his welcome*. あの男は長居してあきられはしないかという心配などしない.

***say welcome to** a person* = bid a person WELCOME.

welcome home 帰宅, 帰国; 〚間投詞的に〛お帰りなさい ▪ She invited me to a supper for my *welcome home*. 彼女は私の帰還を祝って夕食に招待してくれた ▪ *Welcome home*, gentlemen! お帰りなさい, みなさん.

welcome to [***to*** *do*] ...を自由に使ってよい; 《皮肉》勝手に...するがよい ▪ You are *welcome to* any book in my library. 私の書斎の本はどれでも自由に使ってよろしい ▪ You are *welcome to* take what steps you please. 勝手に好きなようにするがよい.

wish** a person **welcome →bid a person WELCOME.

(***You are***) ***welcome.*** **1** よくおいでなさいました; さあどうぞご自由に(お取りください) ▪ (*You are*) *welcome*, Moses! よく帰って来たな, モーゼズ! ▪ *You are welcome* to it. それをご自由にお取りください.
2 《米》どういたしまして《謝礼に対して》 ▪ Much obliged.—*You're welcome*. お世話になりました—どういたしまして.

welcome[2] /wélkəm/ 動 ***welcome** a person **back*** [***home***] 人の帰宅[帰国]を喜んで迎える ▪ No one *welcomed* him *back*. 誰も彼の帰宅を喜んで迎える者はいなかった ▪ He *was welcomed home* to Japan by his friends. 彼は友人たちから帰朝の歓迎を受けた.

welcome ... with open arms → with open ARMs.

welfare /wélfèər/ 名 ***go on welfare*** 《米口》失業手当を受けている ▪ Lots of people *go on welfare*. 多くの人が失業手当を受けている.

well[1] /wel/ 名 ***The well's run dry.*** 材料[資源]が枯渇してしまった ▪ There's not another novel in him, *the well's run dry*. 彼には小説の構想はもう一つもない. 種は尽きた.

Truth lies at the bottom of a well. 《諺》真相は探りにくい.

well[2] /wel/ 副形 ***all being well*** 万事うまくいけば, 思い通りになれば ▪ I'll see you again in June then, *all being well*. では万事順調に運べば6月にまたお会いしましょう.

all well and good 《口》いかにもけっこうだ(が不満足だ) ▪ Cars are *all well and good*, but I prefer bikes. 車も大いにけっこうだが, 僕はバイクの方がいい.

All's well. 異常なし《歩哨(ほしょう)が誰何(すいか)して合言葉を聞いてから言う文句》.

All's well that ends well. →ALL.

as well **1** ...もまた ▪ I can do it *as well*. 私もそれができます ▪ He has knowledge, and experience *as well*. 彼には知識もまた経験もある.
2 ...のほうがよい (*that, if*) ▪ It was just *as well* he did so. 彼はそうしたほうがよかったのだ ▪ I think it would be *as well if* John was to go off this afternoon. ジョンはきょうの午後出かけるほうがいいと思う.

as well as **1** ...と同じようによく ▪ He knows English *as well as* I. 彼は私と同じように英語をよく知っている.
2 ...と同様に, だけでなく ▪ He has experience *as well as* knowledge. 彼は知識だけでなく経験もある ▪ You *as well as* I are wrong. 私と同様に君もまちがっている.
3 ...に加えて, その上に ▪ The editors *as well as* the proofreaders were working overtime. 校正係に加えて編集者たちも残業していた.

be in well (***with***)/《英口》***be well in*** (***with***) 《米》要人[有力者]に信頼されている, に受けがよい, と親しい ▪ He's *in well with* the manager of his company. 彼は社長の覚えがめでたい ▪ She seems to *be well in with* all the important people here. 彼女は当地のお偉方と親しいようだ.

(***be***) ***well away*** **1** 出発して(いる), かなり進んでいる ▪ Andrew got *well away* but Henry pulled him up. アンドリューはかなり進んだが, ヘンリーがそれを引き留めた ▪ He again seemed *well away* for the home side. 彼はまた決勝点の側へかなり進んでいるように見えた.
2 良い出発をする ▪ The runner *was well away* at the start. その走者はスタートをうまく切った.
3 《口》酒が回りかけて, 酔って ▪ When we arrived at the party, he *was well away*. 我々がパーティーに行った時は, 彼はもうでき上がっていた.
4 《英口》...に夢中になって, のめりこんで ▪ He started talking about taxes and *was soon well away*. 彼は税金の話を始めると, やがて熱中した.
5 《英口》眠って ▪ Grandma's head started to nod and soon she *was well away*. おばあちゃんはうとうとし始め, やがて寝入ってしまった.

be well left →LEAVE[2].

be well off →OFF[1].

be well on (夜・時が)ふけて; 年をとって ▪ It *was well on* in the evening. 夜もだいぶふけていた ▪ He *is well on* into his eighties. 彼は年をとり80歳代だ.

be well on in years [***life***] よほど年をとっている ▪ He *is well on in years*. 彼はかなり年をとっている.

be well out of 《英口》(仕事など)を損をせずに免れる ▪ I wish I *was well out of* this business. この仕事から損をせずに免れられたらいいのだが.

be well up in 《口》...に通じている ▪ He *is well up in* the law. 彼は法律に通じている.

be well up on ...を熟知している; に通じている ▪ I'm not very *well up on* Ancient Roman history. 私は古代ローマ史にはあまり詳しくない ▪ She's very *well up on* modern American literature. 彼女は現代米文学に造詣が深い.

can [***could***] (***very***) ***well** do* 《口》→may (very) WELL do.

deserve well of →DESERVE.

do well →DO[2].

do** oneself **well →DO[2].

***do well by** a person* 人に寛大に接する, 優遇する (→DO ... by a person) ▪ He *did well by* me when I needed money. 私が金に窮していたとき彼は優しく応じてくれた.

***do well for** oneself* →DO[2].

foot well (馬が跳ぶ前に)良い足場を得る ▪ He allowed the horse to *foot well* before he sprang. 彼は馬に跳ぶ前に良い足場を得させた.

get well (病気が)治る, 全快する ▪ He *got well* soon. 彼はまもなく全快した.

***go well* 1** うまくいく, 無事である (*with, on*) ▪ Everything *goes well with* me. 私は万事うまくいっている ▪ The boat *went well on* her trial. そのボートは試運転でうまくいった.

2 よく似合う, うまくつり合う (*with, on*) ▪ The furniture *goes* very *well with* the room. その家具は部屋と非常にうまく調和している.

3 (品物が)よく売れる ▪ These goods are *going well*. この品はよく売れている.

4 人気を得る, 評判になる ▪ The records *went well*. そのレコードは評判になった.

it [etc.] ***is all very well, but/it*** [etc.] ***is well*** (***enough***)***, but*** それ[など]はいかにもけっこうだが《不満の反語的表現, または相手の議論をはねつける言い方》 ▪ *It is all very well*, Amelia. それはいかにもけっこうだけどね, アミーリア ▪ He's *all very well* in his way. *But* we're not fools. 彼は彼なりにいかにもけっこうだ. だが我々はばかじゃないんだ ▪ *This is well enough, but* nevertheless I cannot accept it. それはいかにもけっこうなんだが, 私はやはり受けいれることはできない ▪ Get a new hoover.—*It's all very well* to say so, *but* how can I possibly afford it? 新しい掃除機を買ったら?—そう言ってくれるのはうれしいけど, そんな余裕はないよ.

it is well with …は元気である ▪ *It is well with* my father. 父は元気です.

it's (***just***) ***as well*** (***that…***) …は幸運[好都合]である ▪ *It's as well that* I brought an umbrella. 傘をもってきてよかった ▪ He was wearing a crash helmet, *which was just as well*. 彼はそのときヘルメットをかぶっていた, 運がよかったことに.

jolly well 《英口》 **1** とても上手に ▪ You did the work *jolly well*. その仕事をとてもうまくやってのけたね.

2 〚動詞の前で〛 確かに, 絶対に ▪ You can *jolly well* succeed. 君はきっと成功するさ.

just as well →as WELL 2.

keep well with *a person* →stand WELL with a person.

let [***leave***] ***well*** (《米》 ***enough***) ***alone*** 良いことはそのままにしておく, いらぬおせっかいをしない ▪ Why can't you *leave well alone*? どうして良いことはそのままにしておけないのか ▪ Tom was very near yielding, but she could not *let well alone*. トムはもうすぐ折れるところだったのに, 彼女がいらぬおせっかいをした.

***live well* 1** 裕福に暮らす ▪ I shall *live well* without you. 私はあなたがいなくても裕福に暮らせるでしょう.

2 飲食物が豊富である, 美食する ▪ If you would *live well* for a week, kill a hog. 1週間美食したければ, ブタを1頭ほふりなさい.

3 道徳的な生活をする ▪ If you would *live well* all your life, turn priest. 一生道徳的な生活がしたければ, 牧師になりなさい.

***look well* 1** 健康に見える ▪ He *looks well*, but he is really very sick. 彼は見かけは元気そうだが, 実はひどく病んでいる.

2 魅力的に見える ▪ Blue *looks well* on you. 青色はあなたによく似合う.

may as well A as B Bと同様Aしてもよい, BよりAのほうがよい ▪ You *may as well* call a cat a little tiger *as* call a tiger a big cat. トラを大きな猫と言うなら, 同様に猫を小さいトラと言ってもいい ▪ One *may as well* not know a thing at all *as* know it imperfectly. なま半可に知るくらいなら, 全く知らないほうがましだ.

may [***might***] ***as well*** *do* (***as not***) …したほうがよい (had better) ▪ We *may as well* begin at once. すぐに始めるほうがよい ▪ You *may* just *as well* go (*as not*). 君は行ったほうがいい ▪ Since nobody else wants her souvenir, I *might as well* accept it. 彼女の土産を他の誰もほしがらないので, 僕がもらったほうがいいだろう.

may [***might, could***] (***very***) ***well*** *do* たぶん…だろう ▪ It *may well* rain in the afternoon. 午後からはたぶん雨だろう ▪ The team *may well* have won yesterday. 昨日はたぶんそのチームが勝ったのだろう ▪ If he were alive, he *might very well* have become a good teacher. 彼が生きていればたぶん良い教師になっていただろうが. ☞might, could は仮定法.

may well *do* …するのはもっともだ ▪ She *may well* be proud of her son. 彼女が息子を自慢するのも無理はない ▪ The people were afraid, and *well* they *might* be. 人々は怖がっていたが, 無理もなかった.

might as well *do* **1** (…するくらいなら)…したほうがましだ, (…するのは)…するようなものだ ▪ You *might as well* go up a tree for fish. (そんなことをするのは)木によって魚を求めるようなものだ ▪ If a man sinks discouraged upon the threshold of a life of fierce competition he *might as well* be a dead man. もし人が競争の激しい人生への門出に意気阻喪(ｿｿｳ)してしまうようなら, 死んだほうがいいくらいだ. ☞下の項目 might as WELL A as Bの as B以下が略された形; might は仮定法.

2 …してください ▪ You *might as well* put out an extra cup. カップを余分に一つ出しておいてちょうだい.

might as well A as B BするくらいならAするほうがましだ, BするのはAするようなものだ《不可能だ, ばかげている; 論外のことを否定するために, 明らかに否定できる事柄を引き合いに出した言い方》 ▪ You *might as well* advise me to give up my fortune *as* my argument. 私に議論をやめようと勧めるくらいなら, 財産を捨てろと勧めたほうがましだ ▪ You *might as well* reason with the wolf *as* try to persuade that man. あの男を説き伏せようとするのは, オオカミに道理を説いてきかせるようなものだ.

Oh well. まあいいさ《あきらめの言葉》 ▪ *Oh well*, it can't be helped. まあいいさ, 仕方がない.

only too well (好ましくないものを)すでによく知って ▪ Do you know that bully named Nick?—*Only too well*. ニックという名のいじめっ子を知ってるかい—

知ってるとも.

pretty well ほとんど ▪ You're *pretty well* the only person who's willing to help. 喜んで援助してくれるのはまず君一人だ.

shape well 《口》うまく発達する ▪ He's certainly *shaping well* at present. 確かに今のところ彼の発達状態は良好だ ▪ Our plans are *shaping well*. 我々の計画はうまくいっている.

speak well of ...をほめる (↔SPEAK ill of) ▪ The boys *spoke well of* the master. 少年たちはその先生をほめた ▪ He *is well spoken of* [*spoken well of*]. 彼は評判がよい.

stand [***keep***] ***well with*** *a person* 人の気に入る, 受けがよい ▪ He *stood well with* his neighbors. 彼は隣人に受けがよかった ▪ He desired to *keep well with* Stella's father. 彼はステラの父親に気に入られたいと思った.

take well 写真写りがよい ▪ He does not *take well*. 彼は写真写りがよくない.

think well [***ill, badly***] ***of*** →THINK[2].

very well **1** すこぶる健康で ▪ How are you?—*Very well*, thank you. ごきげんいかがですか—すこぶる快調です.

2 とても上手に ▪ He manages that skateboard *very well*. 彼はスケートボードの扱いがとてもうまい.

Very well. 《英・文》よろしい《同意・承諾の意に》 ▪ *Very well*, then, I will say no more. よろしい, それならもう何も言いますまい ▪ *Very well*, if you really must. どうしてもというなら仕方がないな.

Well and good. よろしい, 仕方がない《皮肉な同意》 ▪ If you bow and scrape to rich people, *well and good*. 金持ち連中にぺこぺこ頭を下げるなら, 仕方ないな.

well and truly 《口》完全に, 全く ▪ He was *well and truly* drunk. 彼は全く酔っ払っていた ▪ We were *well and truly* lost in the middle of the forest. 我々は森の中ですっかり迷っていた.

Well begun is half done. →BEGIN.

well day 病気の出ない日 ▪ As it was one of his *well days*, he walked in without help. その日は病気の出ない日だったので, 一人で歩いて部屋に入った.

Well done! うまいぞ!, でかした! ▪ *Well done*, Jim. Excellent speech. よくやった, ジム. 見事なスピーチだったよ.

well enough **1** 十分よく, 十分に ▪ I deserved his kicks *well enough*. 私は彼にけられるだけのことは十分あった ▪ It is known *well enough*. それは十分よく知られている.

2 かなり元気で ▪ She is *well enough*. 彼女はかなり元気だ.

3 かなりよく ▪ She sings *well enough*. 彼女は歌がかなりうまい.

W

Well, I don't know. 〚間投詞的に〛さあ, どうだかね《疑いを表す》 ▪ *Well, I don't know*, nothing seems to me as it was twenty years ago. さあ, どうだかね, 私には何ひとつ20年前のようには見えないよ.

Well, I never (***did***)***!*** 《口》これは驚いた, まさか (→I NEVER did!) ▪ *Well, I never!* Fancy meeting you here! これはこれは. こんな所で君に会おうとは.

Well may you ask! 《反語》よくもそんなことが聞けたものだね, こちらが聞きたいくらいだ ▪ What happened to the money you gave him?—*Well may you ask!* He says he lost it. 君が彼にやった金はどうなった?—こっちが聞きたいよ. 彼はなくしたと言ってるけど.

Well met! →(be) well met (→MEET).

well out of it [***that***] 《口》関係がなくて幸運で ▪ Some of my friends got involved in the scandal. I was *well out of it*. そのスキャンダルに巻き込まれた友人もいた. 私は関わりがなくてよかった.

Well said! 《口》まさにその通り, 大賛成, ご名答 ▪ We must stand up for ourselves.—*Well said*. 我々は自立しなくてはいかん—その通りだ.

well taken 《米》適切な ▪ One of his points seems to us *well taken*. 彼の示唆の一つは私たちには適切なもののように思われる.

well then →THEN.

Well, well. まあ, やれやれ, よしよし《驚き・あきらめ・同意など》 ▪ *Well, well*, you may banter as long as you like. やれやれ, 好きなだけひやかしていらっしゃい ▪ Father, you mustn't talk like that. —*Well, well*, my dear. パパ, そんなふうに言うものじゃないわ—うん, よしよし.

well-off /wèlɔ́ːf|-ɔ́f/ 形 ***well-off for*** ...の豊富な ▪ We are *well-off for* wild-flowers here. 当地は野花が豊富です.

welly /wéli/ 名 ***Give it some welly.*** 《口》もっとがんばれ[努力せよ] ▪ It's up to you! *Give it some welly*! 君次第だ, もっとがんばれ. ☞welly「加速」.

wen /wen/ 名 ***the great Wen*** ロンドン市 ▪ But what is to be the fate of *the great Wen* of all? しかしロンドン市の運命はどうなるのであろうか. ☞wen「大都市」; Cobbett が *Rural Rides* (1821)でこう呼んだことから.

west /west/ 副名 ***due west*** 真西に ▪ We sailed *due west*. 我々は真西に航行した.

go west **1** (太陽が)西に傾く ▪ The sun had *gone west*. 太陽は西に傾いていた.

2 《英》死ぬ; (物が)だめになる, (金などが)なくなる ▪ She *went west* in a plane crash. 彼女は墜落事故で死んだ ▪ My old raincoat has *gone west*. 古いレインコートがだめになった ▪ My watch *went west* when I dropped it on the floor. 床に落として時計が壊れた ▪ There's valuable evidence *gone west*. 貴重な証拠がなくなってしまった. ☞太陽が西に沈むことから, 第1次世界大戦中にできた句.

3 《米》金儲けに西部へ行く ▪ *Go West*, young men! 西部に行きたまえ, 若い衆(しゅう)!

in the west **1** 西方[西部]に ▪ The sun is *in the* low *west*. 太陽は西に傾いている ▪ Spain is *in the west* of Europe. スペインはヨーロッパの西部にある.

2 (風が)西から吹いて ▪ The wind was *in the west*. 風は西から吹いていた.

lie east and west →EAST.

on the west of ...の西に接して, の西端に ▪ Germany is *on the west of* Poland. ドイツはポーランドの西に接している ▪ England is *on the west of* Europe. イギリスはヨーロッパの西端にある.

out West 《米》(東部から見て)西部(地方)で[へ] ▪ They'd lived *out West* for nearly twenty years. 彼らは西部で20年近く暮らしたのだった ▪ We're moving *out West* pretty soon. 我々はもうじき西部へ移住するんだ.

(*to the*) *west of* ...の西方に ▪ China lies *to the west of* Japan. 中国は日本の西方にある ▪ The town is *west of* Lexington. その町はレキシントンの西方にある.

wet[1] /wet/ 形名 ***a wet dream*** **1** 夢精, 性夢 ▪ Most boys start getting *wet dreams* in their early teens. たいていの男の子は十代前半で夢精が始まる.

2 《口》興奮させる[すばらしい]もの ▪ This new machine is *a* car maniac's *wet dream*. この新車種はカーマニアの垂涎(すいぜん)の的だ.

a wet smack 《米俗》座興をそぐ人, 興ざまし ▪ The other girl said he was *a wet smack*. もう一人の少女が彼は興ざましだと言った.

act wet 《口》ばかなまねをする ▪ He *acts* so *wet* when he is a little drunk. 彼は少し酔うと, とてもばかなまねをする.

all wet 《米俗》大いに誤って, まちがって ▪ You're *all wet* about that. それについては君はまちがっているよ ▪ The new administration's environmental policy is *all wet*. 新政権の環境政策は見当はずれだ.

(*be*) *wet through*/(*be*) *wet to the skin* ずぶぬれになる ▪ In half an hour I *was wet to the skin*. 30分もたつと私はずぶぬれになっていた ▪ I reached Hartford *wet through*. 私はずぶぬれになってハートフォードへ着いた.

come with a wet sail 急いで勝利を得ようとする ▪ Rick, *coming with a wet sail*, rushed by and was ultimately killed. リックは急いで勝利を得ようとして突進し, ついに殺されてしまった. ☞帆に十分風をはらませるために帆をぬらして走ることから.

dripping* [*wringing, soaking*] *wet ずぶぬれになって ▪ I was *dripping wet* having fallen into the river. 私は川へ落ちたので, ずぶぬれになっていた.

get wet ぬれる ▪ We *got wet* to the skin. 我々はずぶぬれになった.

go wet 《米口》酒類の販売を許すようになる; 非禁酒主義になる ▪ The county has *gone wet*. その郡では酒類の販売を許可するようになった.

have a wet night (***of it***) 《口》一晩中飲む ▪ Come, boys, let's *have a wet night*. さあみんな, 一晩飲みあかそうぜ.

out of the wet 雨の降る戸外から ▪ We came in *out of the wet*. 我々は雨の降る戸外から中へ入った.

wet behind the ears →EAR.

wet from the press 刷りたてで ▪ The sheets arrived *wet from the press*. 印刷物は刷りたてで届いた.

wet goods 《米口》酒類 ▪ We sampled our stock of *wet goods*. 店にある酒類の見本を作った.

wet or fine 降っても照っても ▪ I take my umbrella, *wet or fine*. 降っても照っても傘を持って行く.

Wet Paint. 「ペンキ塗り立て」《掲示》 ▪ Caution: *Wet Paint*. ペンキ塗り立てにつきご注意ください.

wringing wet →dripping WET.

wet[2] /wet/ 動 ***be wetted through*** = be WETted to the skin.

be wetted to the skin ずぶぬれになる ▪ I had *been wetted to the skin* in the afternoon. 私はその日の午後ずぶぬれになっていた.

wet** oneself/ **wet** one's **pants [***knickers***] 《口》失禁する, お漏らしをする ▪ I laughed so much I almost *wet myself*! 大笑いして漏らしそうになった.

wet** one's **line 釣糸をたれる, 釣りをする ▪ I have not yet *wet my line* since then. その時以来まだ釣りをやっていない.

wet the baby's head →HEAD[1].

wet the [*one's*] ***bed*** 寝小便する ▪ The boy has *wetted his bed* again. 坊やがまた寝小便をしている.

wet the colors 《米口》乗組員に酒をふるまう ▪ The bridegroom is generally supposed to "*wet the colors*." 花婿は乗組員に酒をふるまうものと一般に考えられている.

wet the other [***t'other***] ***eye*** 何杯も立て続けに飲む ▪ Moisten your clay, *wet the other eye*. 1杯やりたまえ, 何杯だっていいよ.

wet** a person **through =WET a person to the skin.

wet** a person **to the skin 人をずぶぬれにさせる ▪ The rain *wetted* us *to the skin*. その雨で我々はずぶぬれになった.

wet** one's **whistle [***mouth, throat, weasand***] 《口》(酒で)のどをしめらせる ▪ The wine shall be kept to *wet your whistle*. その酒はあなたに1杯やっていただくために取っておきましょう.

whack[1] /*h*wæk/ 名 ***a fair whack*** 《俗》平等な分け前, 公平な取り分 ▪ I've finally had *a fair whack* of money transferred to my bank account. やっと平等な取り分が銀行口座に振り込まれた.

at [***in***] ***one whack*** 《米口》一度に, 一気に ▪ Dan lost $500 *in one whack*. ダンは一度に500ドル失った ▪ They built 25 houses *at one whack*. 彼らは25軒の家屋を一斉に建てた.

get [***have, take***] *one's* ***whack*** 《口》 **1** 分け前にあずかる ▪ I have *had my whack* of pleasure. 私も人並みの楽しみは味わいました ▪ I'll *take my whack* today. きょうは分け前にあずからせてもらおう.

2 1杯やる ▪ You might give me a chance to *take my whack*! 僕に1杯やらせてくれてもいいじゃないか.

go whacks 《口》山分けする ▪ I *went whacks* with him. 私は彼と山分けした.

have [***take***] ***a whack at*** 《口》...をやってみる ▪ I *had a whack at* skating. スケートをやってみた ▪ He even *took a whack at* the dish. 彼はその料理を口にさえした. ☞whack「強打」; たぶん木を倒すことから.

in whack 《米口》調子がよい ▪ I am *in* fine *whack*. 僕はぴんぴんしている.

out of whack **1**《米口》調子が悪い ▪ My stomach seems to be *out of whack*. どうも胃の調子が悪い ▪ Our wireless is *out of whack*. うちのラジオは調子が悪い.

2 一致しない (*with*) ▪ The weather forecast was *out of whack with* the today's weather. 天気予報は今日の天候と一致しなかった.

That's* [*It's*] *a whack. 《米口》承知した, 約束した ▪ When I asked her to marry me, she said *it was a whack*. 彼女に結婚してくれと言ったら, いいわと言われた.

the full whack 《英口》全額, 全部, めいっぱい ▪ We had to pay *the full whack* the next day. 翌日に全額を支払わねばならなかった.

top* [*full*] *whack 最高値, 最高率 ▪ I'm not going to offer *top whack* for anything at a classic car auction. クラシックカーの競売では, どの物件にも最高額をつけるつもりはない.

whack[2] /*h*wæk/ 動 ***be whacked to the wide*** →WIDE.

whale[1] /*h*weɪl/ 名 ***a whale of*** 《口》際限ないほどの, たくさんの ▪ It had taken him *a whale of* time to arrive. 彼が来るのにひどく時間がかかった. ☞クジラが巨大なことから.

***a whale of a* [*an*]** 《米》 **1** 非常に大きな ▪ There's *a whale of a* difference between the two. 両者の間にはたいした相違がある.

2 非常にすばらしい ▪ We had *a whale of a* good time at the party. パーティーではすごく楽しく過ごした ▪ You've done *a whale of a* job as the managing editor. 君は編集長として実に立派にやったね.

be a whale on …に非常に巧みである, 非常に熱心である ▪ He *was* not *a whale on* geography. 彼は地理はたいして得意ではなかった.

have a whale of a* (*good*) *time 《口》非常に楽しむ (→a WHALE of a 2) ▪ We took our holidays in Cornwall and *had a whale of a time*. 我々はコーンウォルで休みを過ごしてとても楽しかった.

throw out a tub to the whale →TUB.

very like a whale いかにも仰せの通り《不合理な話に対する反語》(cf. Sh., *Haml.* 3. 2. 398) ▪ Methinks it is *very like a whale*. いかにも仰せの通りと存じます.

whale[2] /*h*weɪl/ 動 ***whale it at*** 《米口》…に激しく食ってかかる ▪ In tones of wrath he *whaled it at* his opponent. 怒った調子で彼は激しく相手に食ってかかった.

wham /*h*wæm/ 名 ***wham, bam*(*, thank you ma'am*)** **1**《口》(愛情もなく二度と会わない相手と)さっさとすませるセックス ▪ It was just *wham, bam, thank you ma'am* all the way through. 終始さっさとねんごろに及んだ.

2 急速に事が進むこと, 急展開 ▪ Heat a chocolate pudding with some custard in the microwave and *wham, bam*! You've got a good dessert. チョコレートプリンにカスタードソースをかけて電子レンジでチン! をしたら, さっとおいしいデザートのできあがり.

whammy /*h*wǽmi/ 名 ***a double whammy*** 《報道》(しばしば新聞・テレビニュースで)二重の打撃 ▪ The city was hit with the *double whammy* of scandal and economic crisis. その都市は醜聞と経済危機のダブルパンチを受けていた.

what /*h*wɑt|wɔt/ 代形副 ***and* [*or*] *what not*/ *and what have you*/ *and I don't know what all*** 《口》その他何やかや[それに類するもの], …など《列挙したあとに》 ▪ There were many pots, pans, dishes, *and what not* in the kitchen. 台所には深なべ, 平なべ, 皿などがたくさんあった ▪ The store sells nails, screws, hammers, *and what have you*. その店では釘, ねじ釘, 金うちなんかを売っている ▪ I value the grandeur, neatness, *and I don't know what all*, of an author's expression. 私はある作家の表現の華麗さ, 巧妙さなどを重んじる.

be ... what it may …は何であれ ▪ *Be* the matter *what it may*, always speak the truth. 事は何であれ, 常に真実を話すがいい.

but what 〚否定文で〛…でない(ところの) ▪ There is no man *but what* is liable to some fault. とかく過失を犯しがちでない者などはいない.

***come what will* [*may*]** 何事があろうと ▪ *Come what will* I am prepared for it. 何事があろうと覚悟はできている.

Do you see what I see? まさか ▪ "*Do you see what I see?*" she yelled in amazement, seeing a UFO hovering overhead. 「これって, まさか」と UFO が頭上で空中静止しているのを見て, 彼女は驚いて叫んだ.

Do what? 何とおっしゃいましたか (What did you say?) ▪ Let's perambulate. —*Do what*? —Let's take a walk. パランビュレイトしようよ—何をしようだって?—散歩しようってことさ.

do what comes naturally 《口》もって生まれた能力でことをする, 本能のままにやすやすと…をする ▪ Animals will *do what comes naturally*. 動物は本能の命ずるままに行動するものだ.

Eh, what? そう思わないか ▪ She's a nice girl, *eh, what?* 彼女はいい子だと思わないかい.

***for what I know* [*care, can tell*]** (…しようと)かまわない; ことによると (perhaps) ▪ She may die *for what I care*. 彼女が死のうとこっちの知ったことか ▪ He may have been murdered, *for what I can tell*. 彼はことによると殺されたのかもしれない.

for what it* [*he*, etc] *is ありのままに, 実質通りに ▪ Sometimes you have to accept the situation *for what it is*. ときには状況をありのままに受け入れなければならないことがある ▪ We thought we saw the man *for what he was*. 彼の正体が知れたと思った.

get what for 《英口》(自分のしたことで)しかられる, 懲らしめられる ▪ You'll *get what for* when your father comes back. 父さんが帰って来たらしかられるよ.

***get* [*take*] *what's coming to* one** 《口》(非行・愚行などの)まいた種を刈る ▪ You *get what's coming to* you, whatever you do. 君は何をしようと, 自

分でまいた種は自分で刈ることになる.

give *a person* ***what for*** 《英口》人をひどく痛い目にあわせる, 懲らしめる ▪ I'll *give* you *what for* if you do that again. 二度とそれをしたらひどい目にあわせるぞ. ☞痛い目にあわせると, 相手が What for? と聞き返すことから.

Guess what! (会話の切り出しに) あのね, いいかい ▪ *Guess what!*—What?—Kate is going to have a baby.—Oh, that's great! あのね—なあに—ケイトに赤ちゃんができたんだって—まあ, 素敵!

I don't know what/ Lord [***God***] ***knows what/Who knows what?*** 何だかわからないもの ▪ He called me many *God-knows-whats*. 彼は何とかかんとか私をあしざまに言った.

I know what よい考えがある ▪ *I know what*—let's go to London. いい考えがある—ロンドンへ行こうじゃないか.

I('ll) tell you what (***it is***) →TELL.

A ***is to*** *B* ***what*** *C* ***is to*** *D.*/***What*** *C* ***is to*** *D A* ***is to*** *B.* AのBに対する関係はCのDに対する関係に等しい ▪ Leaves *are to* the plant, *what* lungs *are to* the animal. 葉の植物におけるは肺の動物におけるがごとし ▪ *What* beauty *is to* a woman, civility *is to* a man. 男子の礼儀は, 女子の美しさに相当する.

know what's what 《口》ものの道理をわきまえている, 事理に明るい ▪ When it comes to wines, he *knows what's what*. ワインのことになると彼は何でも知っている.

Let others say what they will. 他人は何と言おうと ▪ *Let others say what they will*, I always speak the truth. 他人は何とでも言え, 私はいつも真実を言うのだ.

Like what? たとえば(どんなの)? ▪ You should pick another song.—*Like what?*—Anything that fits your deep voice. 別の歌を選んだら?—たとえば?—君の低い声に合う歌ならなんでも.

(***now***) ***that's what I*** (***would***) ***call ...*** 《口》これこそ本物の…だ, これぞまさしく…だ ▪ Mmm, that smells delicious. *That's what I call* home cooking. うーん, うまそうなにおいがする. これぞまさしく家庭料理だ.

Now what? ＝WHAT now?

or what(***?***) 《口》 **1** …か何か ▪ I don't know whether he wants to come, *or what*. 彼が来たいのかどうか分からない.
2 (相手に尋ねて)…か何か ▪ Is this book an autobiography *or what?* この本は自叙伝か何かなのか.
3 (確認して)…だよな ▪ Is this a good movie *or what?* これはいい映画だよな.

or what not →and WHAT not.

Say what?/What say? 《口》 何と言いましたか (＝What did you say?) ▪ Take this downstairs.—*Say what?*—Never mind, I'll do it myself. これを下へ持って降りてくれないか—えっ, 何だって?—いいよ, 自分でするから.

So what? →SO.

take what's coming to *one* →get WHAT's coming to one.

That's what it's all about. それがすべて[重要]である, 結局そういうことなのだ ▪ Speak your mind. *That's what it's all about.* 率直に意見を述べること, それが大切なのです.

That's what you think. 《口》(相手の考えが間違っていることを指摘して)それは君が考えているだけのことだ ▪ Jack is in bed with the flu.—*That's what you think.* I saw him walking in the park just now. ジャックはインフルエンザで床に就いている—君がそう考えているだけで, 彼が公園を歩いているのをさっき見たぜ. ☞you に強勢が置かれる.

(***Well,***) ***what do you know about that!*** 《口・戯》(いや)驚いたね!, どうだい《驚きの表現》 ▪ Well, *what do you know about that!* I found it in my pocket. いや驚いたね. それがポケットの中にあったんだよ ▪ And they're getting married? Well, *what do you know!* それで二人は結婚するんだって? いや, こいつはたまげたな ▪ *Well, what do you know*, the Iranians don't really want a stable Iraq after all. いや驚いたね, イラン人は結局安定したイラクなんて実は欲していないんだって.

What about ...? **1** …はどうだね ▪ *What about* a game of bridge? ブリッジの一勝負はどうかね ▪ *What about* inviting him here? 彼をうちに招待してはどうだろう.
2 …はどうしたのか ▪ *What about* the ten shillings I lent you? 君に貸した10シリングはどうしたのかね.

What about it? どうかね?《相手の意見を求めて》 ▪ Well, here's an inn. *What about it?* Shall we have something to eat and drink here? おや, ここに宿屋がある. どうだい. ここで何か飲み食いしようか.

what beats *one* 理解できないこと, 分からないこと ▪ *What beats* me is how you two ever got in touch. どうにも分からないのは, 君たち二人がどうやって連絡を取り合ったかだ.

what between [***by***] *A* ***and*** (***what between*** [***by***]) *B* →WHAT with A and (what with) B.

what *one* ***can*** 《口》できるだけ ▪ He helps me *what* he *can*. 彼は極力私を援助してくれる.

What do you know? **1** 《米俗》どうだい, やあ《あいさつ》 ▪ Hi, *what d'you know?*—Oh, nothing much. やあ, どう?—まあまあだよ.
2 ＝(Well,) WHAT do you know about that!

What do you say to [(***that***)]***...?*** …(して)はどうでしょうか《相手の意向を尋ねる》 ▪ *What do you say to* a trip to Hakone? 箱根行きはどうだい? ▪ *What do you say to* going fishing with me Sunday? 日曜日にいっしょにつりに行くのはどうだい? ▪ *What do you say* we go swimming? 泳ぎに行かないかい?

What do you think of ...? …はいかがですか ▪ *What do you think of* some eggs and bacon? ベーコンエッグはいかがですか.

What do you think you're doing? 《口》何をやっているつもりなのかね, どうしてそんなまねをするのか《非難の言葉》 ▪ Just *what do you think you're* *doing?* You're supposed to be fixing the trucks. 一体何をやっているのだ. トラックの修理をしているはずだろ.

What do you want me for? 何のご用ですか ▪ *What do you want me for* anyway, Harry? とにかく僕に何の用だい, ハリー.

what does** one* (go and*** [***have to***]) ***do but** do* いまいましくも人が…する ▪ I was going to dance with Mary when *what do* I *have to do but* fall on my face. メアリーとダンスしようとしていて, 僕はいまいましくもばったり前にこけてしまった.

what-d'ye-call-'em [***-him, -her, -it***] 《口》あの何とかといった人たち[人, 女の人, もの]《名前を忘れたときに用いる》 ▪ It was a great blow to break up old associations and *what-d'ye-call-'ems* of that kind. 古くからの交際やそのたぐいの何やかやを捨てるのは大きな衝撃であった.

What (***...***) ***for?*** 《口》何のために, なぜに ▪ *What* are you staring at a fellow like that *for*? なぜあんな男をじろじろ見ているのかね.

What gives? 《米俗》 **1** どうかね《普通のあいさつ》 ▪ Hi. *What gives?*—Oh, hi. やあ, どうだい—ああ, どうも.

2 どうしたのか ▪ *What gives?*—Nothing, just a little misunderstanding. どうしたの?—いや, なに, ちょっとした行き違いがあってさ.

What goes around comes around. 《諺》起こることはどうしたって起こるものだ《なるようにしかならない》,「因果応報」.

What has he got that I haven't (***got***)***?*** (あんなに成功し人気があるのは)彼には私にないどんなものがあるのか ▪ Why do all you women love him? Jeez, *what has he got that I haven't got?* 君たち女性はなぜみんな彼が好きなのか. くそっ, 僕にない何がやつにあるというのだ.

what have you 《口》他のそのようなもの ▪ He sells books, toys or *what have you*. 彼は本や玩具その他そのようなものを売っている.

What if...? **1** …としたらどうなるだろうか ▪ *What if* we were to try? やってみるとしたらどうなるだろうか.

2 …したってかまうものか ▪ *What if* we are poor? 貧乏が何だって言うんだ.

What in the world...?/What on earth...?/What the deuce [***devil, dickens***]***...?*** 一体全体 ▪ *What on earth* does he mean by that? 彼はあんなことを言って一体どういうつもりなのか ▪ I wonder *what in the world* you mean. 一体君はどういうつもりなのかね.

what... is [***was, used to be***] …の現在[過去]の姿 ▪ He has made me *what* I *am*. 私がこうなったのも彼のおかげだ ▪ Today's China is not *what* she *was* ten years ago. 今日の中国は10年前の中国とはちがう.

what is called/what we [***you, men***] ***call*** いわゆる ▪ I am still *what men call* young. 私はまだいわゆる若いのだ ▪ He is *what we call* a walking dictionary. 彼はいわゆる生き字引だ.

***What is** he **for** a man?* →FOR.

What is it to...? 《口》(人)にとって何だと言うのか(関係ない) ▪ *What is it to* you if thousands starve elsewhere? 何千人の人がよそで餓死したって君にとってどうだって言うのか ▪ *What's it to* you how I spend my money? 私が自分の金をどう使おうとお前には何の関わりもないことだ.

What is... like? …はどんなふうですか ▪ *What's* the weather *like* this morning? 今朝の天気はどんなふうですか ▪ *What's* the new teacher *like?* 新任の先生はどんな人ですか.

what is more [***better,*** etc.] その上[さらによいことには, など] ▪ He is hard-working, and, *what is more*, honest and punctual. 彼はよく働く, おまけに正直でよく時間を守る ▪ He is a good scholar, and, *what is better*, a good teacher. 彼は学問ができて, さらによいことには授業がうまい.

***What** C **is to** D A **is to** B.* →A is to B WHAT C is to D.

***what it is like to** do* 《米》…するとどんな気味[味]がするか ▪ *What is it like to* take that medicine? その薬を飲むと, どんな味がするかね.

what it is (***to** do*) それがどんなものであるか, その味を ▪ I do not know *what it is to* be melancholy. 憂鬱がどんなものであるか知らない ▪ Many a father has learnt to his sorrow *what it is to* have his boy idle. 父親の中には息子を怠けさせることの味を知って悲しんだ者が多い.

what it takes 《米口》成功する[人気を集める]のに必要なもの《金・知恵・性的魅力など》 ▪ He certainly has more of *what it takes* than anybody else. 彼は必要なものを確かに誰よりも多く持っている ▪ She has *what it takes*. 彼女には必要なものがある. ☞1940年ごろから「性的魅力」の意味が最も普通;「状況が必要としているもの」が原義.

what little わずかだが全部(の) ▪ I gave *what little* money I had. 持っていたなけなしの金を全部出した ▪ *What little* he said on the subject was full of wisdom. 彼がその題目について言ったことは, わずかだが英知にあふれていた.

What more can one ask [***want***]***?*** これ以上望むことがあろうか ▪ It's low-fat, nutritious and delicious! *What more can one want*? それは低脂肪で栄養価があり美味である. これ以上のものは望めない.

What next? →NEXT.

What now? 今度は何か ▪ I've given you the money already. *What now?* 君にもう金はあげた. 今度は何かね.

What of...? 《口》 **1** …はどうしたのか ▪ And this fellow, *what of* him? それにこの男, 彼がどうしたんだ ▪ *What of* your cat? お宅の猫はどうなったのか.

2 …がどうしたと言うのだ ▪ The VOA? Well, *what of* it? VOAだって? で, それがどうしたと言うのだ ▪ Yes, I wrote the article. *What of* it? 確かにあの記事を書いたのは私だが, それがどうかしたか.

What on earth...? →WHAT in the world...?

what one is [***has***] (現在の)人となり[人の財産] ▪ A man's worth lies not so much in *what one* *has* as in *what one is*. 人の価値はその財産よりも人となりにある.

What say? 《米》何ですって《わからない部分を聞き返す言葉》 ▪ Was he hurt, uncle?—*What say?* 彼はけがをしたのですか, おじさん—何だって.

***What say we** do...?* = WHAT do you say to ...?

What the deuce [***devil, dickens***]***...?*** → WHAT in the world ...?

What then? ではどうなるのだ; それでどうだと言うのか (What of that?) ▪ But if they left me one by one, *what then?* しかし彼らが一人ずつ私から離れたとしても, それがどうしたと言うのだ.

what there is of it そのありったけのもの ▪ All the evidence, or *what there is of it*, seems to suggest otherwise. 証拠のすべて, そのありったけのものが, そうではないと示唆しているようだ.

What though...? ...としても何だ (= WHAT if...? 2) ▪ *What though* the task is difficult? 仕事がむずかしいとしても何だって言うんだ.

what we [***you***] ***call*** →WHAT is called.

what with [***between, by***] *A* ***and*** (***what with*** [***between, by***]) *B* AやらBやら(の理由)で ▪ *What with* hunting *and* bad weather, the progress of the travelers was so slow. 狩りやら悪天候やらで, 旅人たちの前進はきわめて遅々たるものだった ▪ *What by* good fortune *and what by* exertions, he made a large sum of money. 幸運や努力やらで, 彼は大金をこしらえた. ☞what with [between, by] は省くほうが普通.

what with one thing and another 《口》(できなかったことを言い訳して) あれやこれやで, なんやかやで ▪ I was a little tired *what with one thing and another*. あれやこれやで私は少々疲れていた ▪ *What with one thing and another*, he couldn't get home until after midnight. あれやこれやの理由で, 彼は真夜中過ぎまで帰宅できなかった.

***What would I not give to** do!* ...できるなら何だって惜しくない ▪ *What would I not give to* see her! 彼女に会えるなら何だってくれてやるのに.

What you don't know won't [***can't***] ***hurt you.*** 《諺》いやなことを知らなくても, それで損することはない《いやなことを知らせなかったときの言い訳》.

What's all this? 《口》どうしたのか ▪ *What's all this?* Not convinced? どうしたの. 納得がいかないの?

What's bugging [***eating***] ***you?*** 何を悩んでいるのか ▪ Aw, come on, cheer up. *What's eating you*, anyway? さあさあ, 元気を出せ. 一体何をくよくよしているんだ ▪ You look unhappy. *What's bugging you?* 悲しそうな顔をしてるが, 何を悩んでいるのか.

What's by...? 《俗》...はどうなのか ▪ I'm through. *What's by* you? 僕は終わった. 君はどうだい.

What's cooking?/What's new (***with you***)***?*** どうしてるか, 変わったことないか ▪ Hey, you guys. *What's cooking?* やあ, 君たち. どうしてる? ▪ Hi, Jack. *What's new*?—Nothing much. やあ, ジャック. 変わったことない?—まあまあさ ▪ *What's new with you*, Eric? —Same as always. Anything happening with you? 元気か, エリック—相変わらずさ. そっちはどうだ.

What's doing? →DO[2].

What's done is done. すんだことはすんだことさ; もう取り消しできない ▪ I forgot to include it, but *what's done is done*—I've already mailed the letter. それを同封し忘れたけど, どうしようもない. もう投函しちゃったから.

***What's got into** a person?* 《口》(以前と態度が変わったときに)...は一体どうしてしまったのか ▪ *What's got into* you all of a sudden? 君, 急に一体どうなったのだ.

what's his name [***face***] 《口》(名前が思い浮かばないで)あの何とかいう人, 例の何とかさん ▪ This morning I met that tall man with red hair—old *what's-his-name*. けさ, あの赤毛の背の高い人—何とかという老人と会ったよ ▪ Was *what's his name* [*face*] there at the party? 例の何とかさんはパーティーに来ていたかい.

What's it to you? 《口》それが何だと言うんだ, 君には関係ないことだ ▪ Where are you going?—*What's it to you?* どこへ行くの?—大きなお世話だ.

What's on? (テレビ[映画館]では)今何を放映[上映]しているのか ▪ *What's on* at Nottingham Playhouse? ノッティンガム劇場では今何をやっているのかい?

What's the (***big*** [***great***]) ***idea?*** →IDEA.

What's up? 《口》 **1** (...は)どうしたのか (*with*) (→UP[1]) ▪ You're very quiet. *What's up?* えらくおとなしいが, どうしたのだ ▪ *What's up with* her? She looks furious. 彼女はどうしたんだ. 頭にきているようだが.

2 《主に米》どうしてるか, 変わりないか ▪ Hey, Hal, *what's up?*—Not a whole lot. How's it going? やあ, ハル, どうだい—まあまあさ. そっちは.

what's what 《口》ものの道理, 事の真相 ▪ My friend told me *what was what*. 友人が事の真相を教えてくれた.

What's with...? 《米俗》...はどうしたのか, どういうことなのか ▪ Nick, *what's with* the free food? ニック, 無料食品とはどういうことなのかね.

What's yours? →YOURS.

Who knows what? →I don't know WHAT.

You got to do what you got to do./A man's gotta do what a man gotta do. いやでもしなければならない ▪ I know it's disgusting, but *you gotta do what you gotta do*. いやなのは分かるが, しなければならないことはしなければならない.

you know what →KNOW[2].

You know what? (会話の切り出しに)あのね ▪ *You know what?* —No, what? —I think this rice is half-cooked. あのな—なあに?—このご飯, 生煮えみたいだけど.

You what! 《口》君がどうだって《不信・ショック・怒りなどの表現》 ▪ I love John.—*You what!* ジョンを愛しているわ—君がどうだって!

whatever /*h*wɑtévər|wɔt-/ 関代 ***or whatever***

W

《口》何かそのようなもの ▪ Bring me a cup, a glass, *or whatever.* カップかグラスか何かを持ってきてくれ.

Whatever is, is right. 《諺》存在するものはすべて正しい. ☞Pope, *An Essay on Man* (1732–34).

Whatever turns you on. 《戯》君が好きならいいじゃないか《それって何がおもしろいのかね》 ▪ So you polish old coins in your spare time? Oh well, *whatever turns you on.* それで暇なときに古銭を磨くんだって? いや, なに, 好きにするがいいさ.

whatever you do どんなことがあっても(...するな) ▪ *Whatever you do,* don't tell Mary. どんなことがあっても, メアリーには言うなよ.

whatever you say [***think***] (相手の言うことをしぶしぶ受け入れて)わかったよ, 言う通りにするよ ▪ We'd better stop the game here.—Ummm. O.K. *Whatever you say.* このあたりでゲームをやめようか—うーん, わかった. そうしよう.

wheat /*h*wiːt/ 名 ***good as wheat*** 《米口》けっこうだ, よろしい ▪ Suppose we make it up!—*Good as wheat.* 仲直りしてはどうだろう—よかろう.

it is (***all***) ***wheat*** 《米口》大丈夫だ ▪ *It is wheat* with him. 彼は大丈夫だ.

separate [***sift***] ***the wheat from the chaff*** =separate the GRAIN from the chaff.

wheedle /*h*wíːdəl/ 動 ***wheedle*** *oneself* ***into*** ...に甘言で取り入る ▪ He *wheedled himself into* the good graces of his boss. 彼は甘言で社長のきげんを取り結んだ.

wheedle *one's* ***way*** 甘言で進んで行く ▪ He *wheedled his way* onto the stage. 彼は甘言を弄して舞台に立った.

wheel[1] /*h*wiːl/ 名 ***a big wheel*** 大立物 ▪ He is *a big wheel* in the party. 彼は党内の大立物だ.

a fifth [***third***] ***wheel*** 《米》歓迎されない[余計な]人[物], 無用の長物, 足手まといの人 ▪ I hate living with my son and his wife. I feel like *a fifth wheel.* 息子夫婦との同居はいやだ. 厄介者扱いされるようで.

a wheelhorse まじめに働いて頼りになる人, 忠勤者 ▪ Mr. Harris is the *wheelhorse* of our firm. ハリス氏はわが社の勤勉で信頼のおける人物だ.

asleep at the wheel 《口》不注意で, 油断して, 不活発な ▪ I was *asleep at the wheel* then. I'll try to do better next time. あの時は油断していた. 次はもっとうまくやってみせる. ☞「居眠り運転をして」が原義.

at the next turn of the wheel 今度運が向けば ▪ We may be rich *at the next turn of the wheel.* 今度運が向けば金持ちになれるかもしれない. ☞wheel「運命の車」.

at the wheel **1** 舵輪[ハンドル]を取って; 支配[管理]権を握って ▪ Do not speak to the man *at the wheel.* 運転士に話しかけないでください.

2 (馬が)あと馬になって ▪ I took my carriage with five horses attached, three *at the wheel* and two leaders. 私は5頭立ての馬車に乗った, 3頭はあと馬にして2頭が先頭馬だった.

behind the wheel =at the WHEEL 1.

break a butterfly on the wheel/ break [***crush***] ***a fly on the wheel*** つまらぬことに大骨を折る, 鶏を裂くに牛刀をもってする (Pope, *Prologue to the Satires* 308) ▪ To apply any more elaborate criticism to it would be to "*break a fly on the wheel.*" それをこれ以上念入りに批評するのは「鶏を裂くに牛刀をもってする」ことになる. ☞次の句から.

break *a person* ***on the wheel*** 人を車裂きの刑に処する ▪ Rack him first, and after *break* him *on the wheel.* やつをまず拷(ごう)問にかけ, 次いで車裂きの刑に処すがいい.

fortune's wheel 運命, 栄枯盛衰 ▪ The turn of *fortune's wheel* was distinctly favorable. 運命の動きははっきりと有利であった. ☞wheel「運命の女神が回すと言われている輪」.

grease [《英》***oil***] ***the wheels*** 《米》 **1** (賄賂を使ったりして)事を円滑に運ばせる ▪ A hundred pounds would *grease the wheels.* 100ポンド出せば事が円滑に運ぶだろう.

2 もてなしをする; 経費をまかなう ▪ Today *the wheels are greased* by me. きょうは私が経費をまかないます. ☞「車に油をやる」が原義.

in the wheel =at the WHEEL 2.

keep the cart on the wheels →CART.

oil the wheels →grease the WHEELs.

on the wheel **1** =on WHEELs.

2 製造[形成]中で ▪ Our Reformation was *on the wheel.* 我々の改革は進行中であった. ☞wheel「陶工のろくろ」.

on wheels **1** 車で, 車に乗って ▪ They have moving houses built *on wheels.* 彼らは車で動くように作った家を持っている ▪ They followed the chase *on wheels.* 彼らは車で狩猟をした.

2 〚主に go, run を伴って〛すらすらと, 順調に ▪ Thus his tongue *ran on wheels.* このように彼の舌はぺらぺらと動いた.

3 (時計が)進みすぎて ▪ I think my watch runs *on wheels.* 私の時計は進みすぎているのだと思う.

4 《米俗》大はりきりで ▪ I'll come to the party *on wheels.* 大はりきりでパーティーへ行くよ.

put [***throw***] ***sand in the wheels*** →SAND.

reinvent the wheel (誰かがしたことの)焼き直し[二番煎じ]をする ▪ Try this if you don't want to *reinvent the wheel.* もし人の二番煎じがいやなら, これをやってごらん.

see the [*a person's*] ***wheels go round*** 事の運び具合いを見る ▪ I want to watch a supercargo and *see his wheels go round.* 私は船荷監督を見ていて彼の事の運び具合いを見たいのです.

set [***put***] (***the***) ***wheels in motion/start the wheels turning*** 事を実行に移す, 行動にかかる ▪ We need more money to *set the wheels in motion.* 事を実行に移すためにはもっと資金が必要だ.

spin like a Catherine wheel 速く回る ▪ The boy's top *spun like a Catherine wheel* on the hard stone. 男の子のこまは堅い石の上で速く回った.

☞St. Catherine of Alexandria が殉教した際の刑具スパイクつき車輪の形から.

spin** one's **wheels 《主に米口》 **1** (雪・ぬかるみにはまって)車輪が空回りする ▪ My car's *wheels* were *spinning* in the deep snow. 車輪が深い雪にはまって空回りしていた.

2 (ほとんど進展がない状況で)行動が空回りする, むだ骨を折る, 時間[努力]を浪費する ▪ I feel I am merely *spinning my wheels*. 私はただむだ骨を折っているだけのような気がする ▪ He is not getting anywhere. He's just *spinning his wheels*. 彼は何の成果も得られていない. ただ空回りしているだけだ.

take the wheel 支配[管理]権を握る ▪ A general *took the wheel* and governed the state. 一人の将軍が支配権を握り, 国を治めた.

***the fifth wheel of a coach* [*wagon*]** →FIFTH.

the full whack 《英口》 全額, 全部, めいっぱい ▪ We had to pay *the full whack* the next day. 翌日に全額を支払わねばならなかった.

The squeaking* [*squeaky*] *wheel gets the oil. 《諺》きしむ車輪は油を差してもらえる《大声で不満を言わないと誰の注意も引かず, 何も手に入らない》.

The wheel has come full circle. 車(運命)の車輪はすっかり1回転した; 事態は1回転して振り出しに戻った (cf. Sh., *Lear* 5. 3. 174) ▪ *The wheel had come full circle*. The English Drama had returned to its place of origin, the Christian Church. 事態はまた振り出しに戻った. イギリスの演劇はその発生地, キリスト教の教会に立ち戻ったのだ.

The wheels are turning. 《口》事が進行中である, 難問を考えている最中である ▪ *The wheels are turning* on plans to convert the hospital into a shopping mall. その病院をショッピングセンターに改築するという計画を構想中である.

turn* (*Catherine*) *wheels とんぼ返りを打つ (→spin like a Catherine WHEEL) ▪ The boy was *turning wheels* upon the pavement for a penny. 少年は小銭をもらおうと舗道でとんぼ返りをしていた.

wheel of fortune **1** 回転式抽せん器 (lottery wheel) ▪ My mom once hit a jackpot on a *wheel of fortune* machine. 以前ママは回転抽せん器で大当たりを取ったことがある.

2 運命, 栄枯盛衰 (= fortune's WHEEL) ▪ The *wheel of fortune* turns incessantly round. 運命の輪は絶えまなく回る ▪ India is now riding high on the *wheel of fortune*. インドは今幸運の絶頂にある.

wheels within wheels こみいったからくり[事情], 底に底のある魂胆 (《聖》*Ezek*. 1. 16) ▪ There are *wheels within wheels* in the social world of Paris. パリの社交界にはこみいったからくりがある.

wheel[2] /hwiːl/ 動 ***Right* [*Left*] *wheel!*** 《号令》右[左]に向きを変え進め! ▪ *Left wheel* into line. 左に向きを変え整列せよ ▪ The Captain called out, "*Right wheel*." 隊長は「右に向きを変え進め」と呼ばわった.

wheel and deal 敏腕をふるう ▪ It showed the town how an absolute dictator *wheels and deals*. それはその町で絶対独裁者がいかに敏腕をふるうかを示した.

wheeling and dealing (政治・取引での)複雑で巧妙な策略 ▪ This is an article about all the *wheeling and dealing* in financial markets. これは金融市場でのいろんな手の込んだ策略についての記事だ.

wheelbarrow /hwíːlbæroʊ/ 名 ***(as) drunk as a wheelbarrow*** ぐでんぐでんに酔って ▪ He came to us *as drunk as a wheelbarrow*. 彼はぐでんぐでんに酔って我々の所へやって来た. ☞手押し車が揺れることから.

when /hwen|wen/ 副接 ***as and when*** /《米》 ***if and when*** (通常ではなく)もし…するときは ▪ We can just pick up some food *as and when* we need it. 必要なときにはちょっと買って食べればよい.

***if* [*when*] *it comes* (*right*) *down to it* [*that*]** そういうことになると, そういう事情なら ▪ *If it comes right down to it*, you can visit us any time you like. そういうことになれば, いつでもお好きなときにおいでください ▪ *When it comes down to that*, we can lend you the fare. そういう事情になれば, 金を用立てしましょう.

say when 《口》いいときに言いたまえ《酒をついでやるときの文句》 ▪ "*Say when*," said Bonko, commencing to pour out the spirit into my glass. 「いいときに言ってくれ」とバンコーは私のグラスにウィスキーを注ぎながら言った ▪ "*Say when*, Aaron." — "When," said Aaron. 「いいときに言えよ, アーロン」—「いいよ」とアーロンが言った.

since* [*till*] *when いつから[まで] ▪ *Since when* has he been missing? いつから彼は行方不明なの? ▪ *Till when* can you stay? いつまでいられますか.

when it comes to →COME[2].

when least expected 全く予期していないときに ▪ He always calls *when least expected*. 彼はいつも思わぬときに電話してくる.

when pigs fly →PIG[1].

when the chips are down →The CHIPs are down.

whence /hwens/ 副 ***Whence comes it that …?*** 《詩・雅》どうして…なのか ▪ *Whence comes it that* you are late? どうして遅刻したのだ? ☞do を用いない疑問文.

where[1] /hweər|weə/ 副 ***get** a person **where he lives*** 人の痛いところを突く ▪ This really *gets* Smith *where he lives*. これはきっとスミスの痛いところを突くぞ.

get** a person **where** one **wants him 《口》人を好きなように操る ▪ I've *got* that fellow *where* I *want him*. おれはあいつを好きなように操れる.

***that's where … come in* [*into it*]** 《口》これが(人の)言わんとする[(物の)意味する]ところだ ▪ See, *that's where* I *come in*. I'm creating this site for people to use. いいか, これが僕の真意だ. みんなが使えるようにこのサイトを開設しようとしているのだ.

That's where it is. 《口》それが本当のところだ ▪ She's frightened of him, *that's where it is.* あの子は彼を怖がっています, それが本当のところです.

this is* [*that's*] *where we came in*/ *... which is where we came in 《口》ここが出発したところだ, これでまた話の出発点に戻った ▪ And *that's where we came in.* It's a cycle that can't be broken. これでまた話が振り出しに戻った. いつまでも堂々巡りだ.

Where am I? ここはどこですか ▪ We stood in front of a large building. "*Where am I?*" I asked. 大きなビルの前に立った.「ここはどこですか」と私は尋ねた.

Where are we? **1** ここはどこですか ▪ *Where are we*, I wonder? ここはどこかしら.
2 どこまで話をしていたのかな, (授業で)どこまで進んだのでしたか; さっき[この前は]何の話をしていたっけ ▪ Let's see, *where are we?* えーっと, どこまで話したのかな[どこまで進んだんだっけ] ▪ *Where were we* last time? Oh yes, we talked about the yellow sand. この前は何の話しをしていたっけ? ああ, そうだ. 黄砂の話だったな.

Where do we go from here? 次はどうするのか; 次の段取りは ▪ Now tell me, *where do we go from here?* さあ, 教えてくれ, 次はどうするのか.

***Where does** a person **get off** (doing ...)?* 《口》(不当な発言・行為に怒って)...するなんてどういうことか ▪ *Where does* he *get off* calling me lazy? I've been working hard all week. 彼が私を怠け者と言うなんてひどいや. こっちは1週間働き通しなのに.

***Where ... from* [*to*]?** 《口》どこから[どこへ] ▪ *Where* does he come *from?* 彼はどこの出身か ▪ *Where* are you going *to?* どこへお出かけですか ▪ "*Where to?*" asked the cab driver.「どちらまで?」とタクシーの運転手が尋ねた.

where** one [a person] **is coming from 《口》自分[人]が言わんとすること, 自分[人]の気持ち[意図] ▪ He understands *where* I'*m coming from* if I scold him. 彼は私がしかっても真意は分かってくれる.

Where is ... going to stop? ...は止めようがなくなる ▪ If we let this petty theft pass, *where is* it *going to stop?* このささいな盗みを見逃したら, とどまるところがなくなるではないか.

where it's* (*all*) *at 《米俗》最もおもしろい[重要な]場所, 本場 ▪ If you're interested in pop art, New York is *where it's all at.* 君がポップアートに関心があるなら, ニューヨークが本場だよ.

where the action is 活動の中心, 核心 (= WHERE it's (all) at) ▪ The brokerage business is *where the action is* these days. 仲介業が最近は脚光を浴びている.

Where's the other* (*ninety-*)*nine? = YOU and the other (ninety-)nine?

where[2] /*h*weər|weə/ 名 ***the where and when* [*how*]** 場所と時[方法] ▪ The invitation announced *the where and when* of the wedding. 招待状で結婚式の場所と日時が公表された.

whether /*h*wéðər/ 接 ***I don't know whether to eat it or rub it on.*** (初めての食物を) どうやって食べるのか ▪ What kind of dessert is this? *I don't know whether to eat it or rub it on.* これは何のデザートだろう. 食べ方がわからないや.

whether or no **1** ...かどうか, のどちらにしても ▪ *Whether or no* it is true I cannot tell. それが本当かどうか私にはわからない.
2 《口》どっちみち ▪ We must stick to it *whether or no.* どっちみちそれを固守しなければならない.

whether or not ...のどちらにしても ▪ *Whether or not* the picture is a genuine one, it makes me happy to look at it. その絵が本物であろうとなかろうと, それを見ると楽しくなる.

whether ... or not ...かどうか; であろうとなかろうと ▪ I don't know *whether* it is raining *or not.* 雨が降っているかどうかわからない ▪ You must do it, *whether* you like it *or not.* いやでも応でも君はそれをしなければならない.

whew /fjuː, *h*wjuː/ 名 ***all of a whew*** 急いで; あわてて ▪ He wants me to go *all of a whew.* 彼は私に大急ぎで行かせたがっている.

which /*h*wɪtʃ|wɪtʃ/ 代 ***which is which*** どれがどれか ▪ I can hardly remember *which was which.* どれがどれだったかとても思い出せない.

whiff /*h*wɪf/ 名 ***catch* [*get*] *a whiff of*** ...のプンとくるにおいをかぐ; の気配を感じ取る ▪ I *caught a whiff of* hostility in his attitude. 彼の態度にどことなく敵意を感じた.

take* [*have*] *a whiff (タバコを)1服やる ▪ He *took a whiff* or two. タバコを1, 2服すぱすぱ吸った ▪ He stopped work to *have* a few *whiffs.* タバコを1服するために仕事の手を休めた.

the whiff of grapeshot ブドウ弾の2, 3発《民衆運動抑圧に銃を用いること》 ▪ The cold war between himself and Bertrand was over at last. This was *the whiff of grapeshot.* 彼とバートランドとの間の冷戦はついに終わった. これはブドウ弾の2, 3発といったものだった. ☞1795年の Napoleon の行動から.

while /*h*waɪl|waɪl/ 名接 ***a little* [*short*] *while*** ちょっとの間 ▪ The rain lasted only *a little while.* 雨はほんのちょっとの間続いただけだった.

a long* [*good*] *while →(for) a long WHILE.

a while しばらくの間 ▪ Pleasantly they passed *a while* together. 楽しく彼らはひと時を共に過ごした ▪ I will sit down *a while.* しばらくの間座っていよう.

***a while ago* [《米》 *back*]** ちょっと前に ▪ He wrote me *a while ago* about his new job. 彼は今度の仕事のことをついこの前に手紙で知らせてきた ▪ She was in the hospital *a while back.* 彼女は少し前に入院していた.

after a while しばらく[少し]して ▪ They began to walk again *after a while.* 彼らはしばらくしてまた歩き始めた.

all the while その間ずっと, 始終 ▪ The weather was fine *all the while.* 天気はその間ずっとよかった ▪ She was shut up *all the while* we were there. 我々がそこにいる間ずっと彼女は閉じ込められていた.

all this* [*that*] *while この[その]間ずっと ▪ I have

been waiting *all this while.* 今までずっと待っていました ▪ He had been mistaken *all that while.* 彼はその間ずっとまちがえられていた.

at whiles 折々, 時々 ▪ Gloom hung *at whiles* upon his brow. 憂鬱の影がときどき彼の額にさした.

between whiles 合い間に, 折々 ▪ There was, *between whiles*, a noise like that of thunder. 折々雷のような音が聞こえた.

(for) a long [good] while 長いこと ▪ I have not seen him *(for) a long while.* 長いこと彼に会っていない.

for a [one] while しばらくの間 ▪ That's enough *for one while.* しばらくはそれで十分だ ▪ I forget it *for a while.* いっときそれを忘れた.

in a (little) while 間もなく ▪ I'll phone you *in a little while.* 間もなくお電話します.

it is worth while *doing* →WORTH.

make it worth *a person's* ***while*** 人の労に十分に報いる ▪ Keep dark upon it. I will *make it worth your while.* そのことは秘密にしておいてくれ. 君の労に十分に報いてやるから.

once in a [every] while →(for) ONCE in a way.

quite a while 《口》かなり長い間 ▪ It was *quite a while* before he elicited the facts from me. 彼が私からその事実を聞き知ったのはかなり経ってからのことだった.

the while その間 ▪ We rowed the boat and sang *the while.* 我々はボートをこぎながら歌を歌った.

while I think of it 思いだしたついでに ▪ I want to ask you something *while I think of it.* ついでにあなたに尋ねたいことがある.

while you are about it 君が今しているついでに ▪ Get me one more *while you are about it.* ついでにもう一つ頼む.

worth *(one's)* ***while*** *(**to** do, doing)* → WORTH.

whim /*h*wɪm/ 名 ***follow*** *one's* ***whims*** 気の向くままにする ▪ I permitted them to *follow their whims.* 彼らに気の向くままにさせておいた.

full of whim (and fancies) 気まぐれな, 酔狂な ▪ He is *full of whims* at such times. そんなとき彼は気まぐれだ ▪ You are *full of whims and fancies*, but you can also be a great support to me. 君は気まぐれだが大いに僕の支えになってくれることもある.

on a whim よく考えずに, 衝動的に, 思いつきで ▪ Don't buy things *on a whim.* 衝動買いをしてはいけない.

take [have] a whim for [to** do**] ふと…してみる気になる ▪ He *took a whim to* read his old diary. 彼はふと古い日記を読んでみる気になった.

the whim strikes *a person* ***to*** *do* ふと気まぐれから…する ▪ *The whim struck* him *to* become an army flier. 彼は気まぐれから陸軍航空兵になった.

whimper /*h*wímpər/ 名 ***not with a bang but (with) a whimper*** 期待はずれで, 予想したほどわくわくしない ▪ *Not with a bang but a whimper.* They may have excited us as kids. 期待はずれだった. 子供の頃だったらわくわくしたかも知れないが.

whip[1] /*h*wɪp/ 名 ***as thin as a whip*** やせているが強靱な, しなやかにやせた ▪ The new PE teacher is *as thin as a whip* and looks very strict. 新しい体育の先生は鞭のようにやせていてとても厳しそうだ.

crack the whip 《口》采配を振るう; いばり散らす, 高圧的にふるまう ▪ The boss wants me to *crack the whip* while he is away. 社長は自分の留守中は私が采配を振るうことを望んでいる.

have [hold] the whip(-)hand of …を支配する, 左右する ▪ A silent woman *has* always *the whip-hand of* a talker. 無口な女性はいつもおしゃべりな人を支配する ▪ In the art of conversation I *have the whip-hand of* him. 話術では彼よりも私のほうがうわ手だ.

have [hold] the whip over …を操る, 支配する ▪ He has always *held the whip over* his younger colleagues. 彼はずっと年下の同僚を牛耳ってきた.

(ride) whip and spur 大急ぎで(馬を飛ばす) ▪ I *rode whip and spur* to fetch them. 私は彼らを連れてくるために大急ぎで馬を飛ばした.

Whip behind! 後ろに誰か乗っているよ《馬車の後ろにだれかが乗っているのを御者に知らせる言葉》 ▪ Someone cried, "*Whip behind!*" 「後ろに誰か乗っているよ!」と誰かが叫んだ.

whips and jingles 《米俗》二日酔い ▪ I woke up with a case of the *whips and jingles.* 目がさめてみると二日酔いというやつだった.

whip[2] /*h*wɪp/ 動 ***like a whipped dog*** (罰され[敗れ]て)恥じ入った様子で, 悲しそうに ▪ He came in looking *like a whipped dog.* 彼はうなだれた様子で入ってきた.

whip all creation 《米口》どんなものにも勝る, 比類がない ▪ We can *whip all creation* so easily. 我々はまさに天下無敵だ.

whip an acre of wild cats → WHIP one's weight in wild cats.

whip ... into a frenzy [fervor, fury] …をあおって熱狂[興奮, 激怒]させる ▪ He *whipped* the crowd *into a frenzy* of excitement. 彼は群集をあおって, 興奮の渦に巻き込んだ ▪ The players *whipped* each other *into a frenzy* of enthusiasm. 選手たちは互いに鼓舞し合って奮い立った.

whip ... into line 人を強硬に自分の思うままにさせる ▪ The government tried to *whip* teachers *into line.* 政府は教員団を強引に操ろうとした.

whip ... into shape …をたたき上げる, 向上させるために鍛える (= KNOCK ... into shape) ▪ The new coach *whipped* the team *into shape.* 新コーチはチームを鍛えて立て直した.

whip round for a subscription 寄付を集めに回る ▪ We'll *whip round for a subscription* for the injured workman. けがをした作業員のために寄付を集めに回ろう.

whip *one's* ***weight in wild cats [in wild cat skins]/whip an acre of wild cats*** 《米

口》すごくどう猛にうまく戦う ▪ I can usually *whip my weight in wild cats.* 私はいつもすごくどう猛にうまく戦える ▪ He had courage enough to *whip an acre of wild cats.* 彼はすごくどう猛にうまく戦うだけの勇気があった.

whirl /*h*wəːrl/ 名 ***give ... a whirl*** 《口》...を試してみる ▪ Bill wanted to *give* my suggestion *a whirl.* ビルは私の提案を試してみたがった.

in a whirl **1** ぐるぐる回って, 旋回して ▪ The snow fell *in a whirl.* 雪は卍巴(まんじともえ)と降った.

2 (思想などが)千々(ちぢ)に乱れて ▪ My thoughts are *in a whirl.* 私の心は千々に乱れている ▪ His head was *in a* complete *whirl.* 彼の頭は全く混乱していた.

whirligig /*h*wə́ːrligìg/ 名 ***the whirligig of time*** 時運の変転 (cf. Sh., *Twel. N.* 5. 1. 385) ▪ Our feelings of happiness and sorrow are soon lost in *the whirligig of time.* 我々の幸福とか悲しみとかの感情は, 時運の変転の中にすぐ紛れてしまう.

whirlwind /*h*wə́ːrlwìnd/ 名 ***ride the whirlwind*** (天使が)旋風を御する; 動乱を乗り切る ▪ Today the human race is trying to *ride the whirlwind.* 今日人類は動乱を乗り切ろうとしている.

(*sow the wind and* [*to*]) *reap the whirlwind* 《米・雅》(悪事をして)幾倍もひどい罰を受ける (《聖》*Hos.* 8. 7) ▪ Having fired his best salesperson, he's *reaping the whirlwind* with declining sales. 一番優秀な販売員を解雇したので売り上げが減り, 彼はその報いを受けている.

whisk /*h*wɪsk/ 名 ***with*** [***in***] ***a whisk*** すぐに, 即座に ▪ You see it all *in a whisk.* それは全部すぐにわかりますよ.

whisker /*h*wískər/ 名 ***all my whiskers*** 《俗》たわごと ▪ All that stuff about his being so upset was *all my whiskers.* 彼がびっくり仰天したなどというのはすべて私のたわごとだった.

be [***come***] ***within a whisker of*** (*doing*) 《英口》(...する)ほんの一歩手前である[までくる] ▪ He *was within a whisker of* flooring the world champ. 彼は世界チャンピオンをノックアウト寸前まで追い込んでいた ▪ The flying plate *came within a whisker of* his head. 皿が飛んできて危うく彼の頭に命中するところだった.

by a whisker 《口》かろうじて, 僅少差で ▪ Our team lost *by a whisker.* わがチームは僅かの差で敗れた.

have [***have grown***] ***whiskers*** 《口》(話が)時代遅れになる, 古くさくなる ▪ Most of his gags *have grown whiskers.* 彼がとばすギャグの大半はもう受けなくなってしまった.

whisper[1] /*h*wíspər/ 名 ***a stage whisper*** 聞こえるように, 聞こえよがしのひそひそ話 ▪ Some jokes shouldn't be told in *a stage whisper.* 冗談のなかには人前で言わないほうがいいものもある ▪ Our three-year-old son asked in *a stage whisper,* "Why is that lady so short?" 3歳の息子が「あのおばちゃん, どうしてあんなにちっちゃいの?」とみんなに聞こえる小声で言った. ☞「(観客に聞こえるように言う)わきぜりふ」が原義.

give the whisper 《口》そっと耳打ちする ▪ Just *give* him *the whisper* to that effect. 彼にその旨をそっと耳打ちしてやりなさい.

in a whisper/in whispers 声をひそめて, ひそひそと ▪ He always talks *in a whisper.* 彼はいつもひそひそ声で話す.

whisper[2] /*h*wíspər/ 動 ***whisper in*** *a person's* ***ear*** 人にこっそり教える ▪ He *whispered in my ear* that it would be wise to hold the shares for a rise. 株が上がるから持っているのがいいと彼がこっそり教えてくれた.

whistle[1] /*h*wísəl/ 名 ***a whistle-stop tour*** (小駅ごとの)地方遊説 ▪ He left on *a whistle-stop tour* of the Lake District. 彼は湖水地方の選挙遊説に出発した. ☞「(信号がある時だけ列車が停止する)小さな町をめぐる旅」が原義.

(*as*) *clean* [***clear, dry***] ***as a whistle*** すばらしくきれいで[明白で, 乾いて]《しばしば形容詞の他の意味にかけて使用される》 ▪ There is no drugs or gambling. My private life is *as clean as a whistle.* 麻薬もやらず賭けごともしない. 私の私生活は清廉潔白だ ▪ My throat is *as clear as a whistle.* 私ののどはすばらしく澄んでいます ▪ By the time we reach the manse we are *as dry as a whistle.* 牧師館に着くころには我々の体はすっかり乾いている.

blow the whistle on **1** (賛成できないもの)に待ったをかける, やめさせる ▪ If my father finds out that I smoke, he'll *blow the whistle on* it. 僕がタバコを吸うことを父が見つけたら, やめさせるだろう.

2 《口》...の犯罪を暴露する, を密告する ▪ She *blew the whistle on* him for installing illegal wiretaps. 彼女は不法に電話盗聴器を設置したとして彼をたれこんだ. ☞「笛を吹いて工場の作業をやめさせる」が原義.

not worth a whistle 全くつまらないこと ▪ His latest story is *not worth a whistle.* 彼の最近の小説は全くつまらない.

pay (***too dear***) ***for*** *one's* ***whistle*** 《米口》つまらぬものに高い代価を払う; (くだらぬことをして)ひどい目にあう ▪ I should not like to *pay too dear for my whistle.* 私はつまらぬものに高い代価を払いたくない ▪ If a man likes to do it he must *pay for his whistle.* そんなことをしたがる人はひどい目にあわねばならない. ☞Franklin のおいがつまらない笛をほしがって4倍もの代金を出した話から.

wet [***whet***] *one's* ***whistle*** 《口》のどを潤す, 1杯やる ▪ Let's drink the other cup to *wet our whistles.* のどを潤すためにもう1杯やろうじゃないか ▪ Would you care to *wet your whistle,* Jim? 1杯やらないか, ジム. ☞whistle 《戯》「のど」; whet は《誤用》.

whistle[2] /*h*wísəl/ 動 ***bid*** [***let***] ***... go whistle*** ...に勝手にさせる ▪ Your fame is secure—*bid* the critics *go whistle.* 君の名声は確固たるものだ—批評家たちにはおとといい来いと言ってやるがいい ▪ This being done, *let* the law *go whistle*. これがすんだのだから，法律なんかもうどうでもいい．

can whistle for it 《英口》それを望んでもむだである，与えるつもりはない ▪ If he wants money, he *can whistle for it*. 彼が金をほしがっても，やるものか．

go whistle 勝手にする，ぶらぶらする ▪ When danger's past, the saint may *go whistle*. 《諺》危険が過ぎれば聖徒は勝手にするがいい，「のど元過ぎれば熱さ忘れる」．

whistle ... down the wind …を放す，放棄する ▪ You cannot *whistle* me *down the wind* as though I were of no account. 私を能なしみたいに捨てることはできませんよ． ☞タカは普通獲物を追わせるときには風上へ飛ばせるが，自由にしてやるときは風下へ放つことから．

whistle in the dark **1** (暗やみで)口笛を吹いて元気を出す ▪ He says he's not afraid of being fired, but I think he's just *whistling in the dark*. 彼は首にされたって平気だと言っているが，から元気を出しているだけだと思う．

2 当て推量をする，憶測で結果を推測する ▪ Is he close, or is he just *whistling in the dark*? 彼の推測は当たりに近いか，それともただの当てずっぽうか．

whistle *one's* ***way*** 笛を鳴らし[口笛を吹き]ながら進む ▪ The steamer *whistled its way*. 蒸気船は汽笛を鳴らしながら進んだ ▪ He *whistled his way* to the front-door. 彼は口笛を吹きながら玄関に向かった．

whit /hwɪt/ 名 ***any*** [***one***] ***whit*** いささかでも ▪ Every child that can *any whit* speak knows it. 少しでもものを言える子供はすべてそのことを知っている．

white /hwaɪt/ 形名 ***a white ball*** すべての婦人が白衣を着た舞踏会 ▪ Lidian gave *a white ball* in her honor. リディアンは彼女のためにすべての婦人が白衣を着た舞踏会を催した．

a White Christmas 雪の降ったクリスマス ▪ We celebrated *a White Christmas* in New England. ニューイングランドで雪のクリスマスを祝った．

a white knight (会社が乗っ取られないよう出資する)救済会社，白馬の騎士 ▪ Hope has faded that *a white knight* will appear to stop the takeover bid. 株式の公開買いつけを防ぐのに白馬の騎士が現れる望みが薄れた．

a white man **1** 白人 ▪ We *white men* have been spoiled by education. 我々白人は教育によって損われている．

2 《米口》(白人のように)立派な人 ▪ You've behaved to me like *a white man* from the start. あなたは初めから立派な人のように私に対してふるまってくださいました． ☞今は差別的．

a white man's chance 《米口》(白人にふさわしい)ちゃんとした機会 ▪ To give him *a white man's chance*, I proposed alternatives to him. 彼にちゃんとした機会を与えるために，彼に二者択一を提案した． ☞今は差別的．

a white night 白夜; 眠れぬ夜 ▪ The almost entirely *white night* she had just passed. そのほとんど全く眠れぬ夜を彼女はやっと明かしたところだった． ☞F nuit blanche のなぞり．

a white van man 《英口》(乱暴な運転をする)白いバンの運転者 ▪ I hate driving to work with the impatient hooting of *white-van men*. 白バンの無謀運転手どもにいらいらと警笛を鳴らされて車で通勤するのはいやだ．

a whiter shade of pale 《戯》真っ青 ▪ He turned *a whiter shade of pale* when he saw a bear. クマを見たとき彼は真っ青になった．

act white by *a person* 《口》人に公明正大[公平]にふるまう ▪ I meant to *act white by* you. 君には公平にふるまうつもりだった．

(*as*) *white as a sheet* [***cloth, ghost***] 《口》(病気・恐怖・衝撃で)真っ青で，すっかり青ざめて ▪ She looked *as white as a cloth*. 彼女は真っ青な顔をしていた ▪ He went *as white as a sheet* when he heard the news. 彼はその知らせを聞くと顔色を失った．

(*as*) *white as* (*driven*) *snow* [***milk, lily flower, glass, a swan, whale's bone, flour, a neap, wool, curds***] 真っ白で; 潔白で ▪ The king had a daughter *as white as a swan*. その王にはハクチョウのように色の白い娘がいた ▪ I am *as white as snow* compared to some blackguards. 私は一部の悪党と比べると雪のように潔白だ．

be in white terror [***a white rage***] 恐怖[怒り]で真っ青になっている ▪ He *was in a white rage* at me. 彼は私への怒りで真っ青になっていた ▪ The man *was in white terror* of a similar destiny. 男は同様の運命への恐怖で真っ青になっていた．

bleed white →BLEED.

call white black/turn white into black/prove that white is black, and black is white/talk black into white 白を黒と言いくるめる，サギをカラスと言いくるめる ▪ He tries to *prove that white is black, and black is white*. 彼は白を黒，黒を白と言いくるめようとする．

go white 真っ青になる ▪ She *went white* to her lips. 彼女は唇まで真っ青になった．

in the white (布が)白生地のままで; (製品が)未完成の状態で ▪ The articles are sent *in the white* to London, where they are dyed. 品物は白生地のままでロンドンへ送られ，そこで染められる ▪ The furniture was made in London, but *in the white*. その家具はロンドンで作られたが，まだ未完成だ．

in white 白衣を着て[た] ▪ She was (dressed) *in white*. 彼女は白衣を着ていた．

make *one's* ***name white again*** 汚名をそそぐ ▪ Your *name* must *be made white again*. あなたは汚名をそそがれねばならない．

mark ... with a white stone …を特筆大書する ▪ I have *marked* that day *with a white stone* as being the one on which I ate my first caviar. 私は初めてキャビアを食べたとあってその日を特筆大書した． ☞古代ローマ人が白チョークで暦の幸福な日に印をつけた故事から．

pearly whites 《英口》真っ白な歯 ▪ Smile, and show off those *pearly whites*. 笑って，そしてその真っ白い歯をみせなさい．

say black is the white of *a person's* ***eye*** →BLACK¹.

talk black into white →call WHITE black.

treat *a person* ***white*** 《米口》人を公平に扱う ▪ You *treated* me *white* all the same. あなたは私をやはり公平に扱ってくれた．

turn up [***show, throw up***] ***the whites of*** *one's* ***eyes*** (偽りの信心，死んだとき，驚き・恐怖などで)白目を見せる ▪ The Professor *showed the whites of his eyes* devoutly. 教授は信心深そうに白い目を見せた ▪ She *turned up the whites of her eyes*, as if about to scream. 彼女はまるで絶叫する寸前のように白目をむいた．

turn white ＝go WHITE.

turn white into black →call WHITE black.

white-bread 《米》〘限定的〙平凡な，ありきたりの．育ちはよいがおもしろみに欠ける ▪ It's a movie about *white-bread* characters living *white-bread* lives. 退屈な生活をしている退屈な主人公の映画だ．

white heat 白熱《1500〜1600℃》; かんしゃく，激情 ▪ It is heated at a red heat, and then to an incipient *white heat*. それは赤熱，次いでもうすぐ白熱になる温度まで熱せられる ▪ There are politicians always at a *white heat*. いつも激情をたぎらせている政治家がいる ▪ At that he got into a *white heat*. それを聞くと，彼はかっとなった．

white hot 《米俗》大罪を犯してお尋ね者になって ▪ Floyd became *white hot*. フロイドは大罪を犯してお尋ね者となった．

White or black? (コーヒーに)ミルクを入れますか，入れませんか ▪ How would you like your coffee, *white or black?*—Black, please, and no sugar, thanks. コーヒーはミルク入り? それともブラック?—ブラック，そして砂糖なしにして．

white trash 《米卑》無学で貧しい白人たち ▪ I wish to know more about the poor *white trash*. 無学で貧乏な白人のことをもっと知りたいものだ．

whiter than white **1** 限りなく真っ白に ▪ The hero is depicted, morally, *whiter than white*. 主人公は道徳的に限りなく真っ白に描かれている. ☞石けんなどの広告から．

2 あまりに純粋すぎてうさんくさい，偽善的な ▪ He looks *whiter than white*. I can't trust him. 彼は誠実すぎて，かえってうさんくさく信用しかねる．

whited /*h*wáɪtəd/ 形 ***a whited sepulcher*** → SEPULCHER.

whizz /*h*wɪz/ 名 ***a whizz-kid/a whiz-kid*** 《口》神童，若い切れ者 ▪ The new manager is *a* financial *whizz-kid* from Harvard Business School. 新支配人はハーバード経営学大学院出の若手エリート実業家だ．

who /huː/ 代 ***and I don't know who all*** 《口》その他誰やかれや ▪ There was Mason, Burns, *and I don't know who all*. メイスン，バーンズ，その他誰やかれやがいた．

as who should say →SAY².

I don't know [***I know not, Lord knows***] ***who*** 誰やら知らぬ人; 身分のわからぬ人 ▪ Mamma's father was a lord, and her mother *I don't know who*. 母の父親は貴族でしたが，母親は身分のわからぬ人でした．

Look who's here! (今来た人に注意を促して)ご覧なさい，誰だと思うかい ▪ *Look who's here!*—Yeah. Isn't that Bill Jones? 見ろよ．誰かと思ったら—本当に．ビル・ジョーンズじゃないか．

Look who's talking. 《口》文句を言った誰かさんが同じ事をしている，君も同罪だ，大きな事は言えないよ ▪ You criticized me for being late. *Look who's talking.* You just missed your flight! 僕が遅刻したと小言を言われたことがある．ところがどうだ．その君が飛行機に乗り遅れたじゃないか．

Says [***Sez***] ***who?—Says*** [***Sez***] ***me.*** 《口》まさか，そんなことが—そのまさかなんだ ▪ *Says* [*Sez*] *who?*—*Says* [*Sez*] *me*, that's who! まさか—その，まさかさ．☞Says who? は不信を表す決まり文句．Says me. はそれに応答する決まり文句．

Those who can, do; those who can't, teach. 《諺》上手に事をなす者はそれを生業(なりわい)にできるが，なせない者は教師になる (G. B. Shaw, *Man and Superman*). ☞教師をけなすのに用いられる．

who all 《米口》…のすべての人々 (all who) ▪ I forget *who all* were there. そこにいた人をみな忘れた．

Who are you to *do* ***…?*** …するなんて君は何さまなのか ▪ *Who is he to* decide what's best? どうすれば一番よいかを決定するなんて彼は何さまなのか．

who is who/who's who 《口》誰かれの見分け，各人の性格[地位] ▪ She could not distinguish *who was who*. 彼女は誰かれの見分けはつかなかった ▪ I knew nothing of *who was who* in London. 私はロンドンの各人の性格・地位などは全く知らなかった．

whole /hoʊl/ 形名 ***a whole lot of*** 《口》たくさんの (lots of) ▪ He talks *a whole lot of* nonsense. 彼は愚(ぐ)にもつかぬことばかり言う．

as a whole 総括して，全体として ▪ The climate of Asia can hardly be spoken of *as a whole*. アジアの気候を総括的に語ることはまずできない．

(***as***) ***whole as a fish*** [***a trout***] 非常に元気で ▪ They are both *as whole as fishes*. 彼らは二人ともとても元気です．

go (***for***) ***the whole*** 《米口》全く受けいれる ▪ Don't meet him half-way but *go the whole* for him. 彼に歩み寄るのではなくて，全面的に受けいれなさい．☞<go the whole HOG.

go the whole animal [***creature***] 《米口》(事を)徹底的にやる ▪ Then of course you mean to *go the whole creature*. では，もちろん君は徹底的にやるつもりなんだね．☞<go the whole HOG.

in [***with***] ***a whole skin*** →with a whole SKIN.

in (***the***) ***whole*** **1** 〘the なしで〙全部，まるごと (↔in PART) ▪ This work ought to be printed *in* *whole*. この作品は全部印刷すべきものである ▪ He has rejected their claim *in whole* or in part. 彼は彼らの要求をまるごと，もしくは部分的に拒絶した.

2〚the をつけて〛全部で ▪ The poem contains 500 lines *in the whole*. この詩は全部で500行ある.

make up out of whole cloth《米》全く事実無根である ▪ His story *is made up out of whole cloth*. 彼の話は全くでたらめだ ▪ The explanation was too strange for him to have *made up out of whole cloth*. その説明は彼がでっち上げたとは思えないくらい不可思議な内容だった.

on [***upon***] ***the whole*** **1** 概して ▪ He is, *on the whole*, a satisfactory student. 彼はまずまず申し分のない学生だ.

2 大体 (= (for) the most PART) ▪ *Upon the whole* he was sentenced to die. ほぼ満場一致で彼は死刑を宣告された.

the whole enchilada/ the whole ball of wax 全体, 全部, すべて ▪ She was responsible for *the whole ball of wax*. 彼女は全体責任を負っていた ▪ We've got pots, pans and *the whole ball of wax*. 鍋釜など炊事道具が一切そろっている ▪ Tell me about your family, friends and *the whole enchilada*. あなたの家族, 友人その他もろもろについて話してください.

the whole lot (***of***) (…の)何もかも ▪ He has sold *the whole lot* at a garage sale. 彼はガレージセールで一切合財(がっさい)を売り払った ▪ I sold *the whole lot of* my collection for just $50. 僕のコレクション全部をたった50ドルで売った.

the whole megillah/《米俗》***the whole schmeer*** [***schmere, scheemer***] 全体, 全部, すべて ▪ The accountant went through *the whole megillah* all over again. 会計士はすべてを初めからすっかりやり直した ▪ The divorce lawyer took me for the house, the yacht and *the whole schmeer*. 離婚訴訟弁護士は私から家もヨットも何もかも取り上げた.

the whole shooting match →MATCH[1].

with a whole skin →SKIN[1].

wholesale /hóʊlsèɪl/ 名副 ***by*** [《米》***at***] ***wholesale*** **1** 卸し売りで (↔by RETAIL) ▪ Great merchants sell *by wholesale*. 大商人は卸し売りで売ってくれる ▪ They are worth ten dollars *at wholesale*. それは卸し売りで10ドルする.

2 大量に, 十把一からげに ▪ The Bashkirs slaughtered them *by wholesale*. バシキール人はそこの人たちを大量に殺戮(さつりく)した.

sell [***buy***] ***wholesale*** 卸し売りで売る[買う] ▪ These shoes *are sold wholesale* in boxes. この靴は箱に入れて卸し売りで売られる.

whoop[1] /huːp|wuːp/ 名 ***a whoop and a holler***《米》かなり短い距離 ▪ He lives *a whoop and a holler* down the road. 彼はこの道のちょっと向こうに住んでいる.

not care [***worth***] ***a whoop***《米》ちっともかまわない[価値がない] ▪ They *don't care a whoop* about the question. 彼らはその問題にはちっともかまわない ▪ So far they have *not* had an item *worth a whoop*. 今までのところ彼らには少しでも価値のある品目は一つもなかった.

whoop[2] /huːp|wuːp/ 動 ***whoop it*** [***'em,*** etc.] ***up***《口》**1** 大声をあげて騒ぎ立てる, 大いにはしゃぐ ▪ He *whoops it up* with the plain people. 彼は教養のない人たちと大声をあげて騒ぎ立てる.

2 むやみにほめ立てる ▪ These Californians are eternally *whooping up* the glorious climate. これらのカリフォルニア人ときたら, 始終すばらしい気候をむやみにほめ立てている.

whoopee /*h*wʊ́piː|wʊpíː/ 名 ***make whoopee*** **1**《米俗》〚主に進行形で〛(飲めや歌えの)大騒ぎをする ▪ English newspapers *are making whoopee* about it. イギリスの新聞はそのことで大騒ぎしている ▪ Here's a photo of us *making whoopee* at Ted's party. ここにテッドのパーティーで僕たちが大騒ぎをしている写真がある.

2《米口》セックスをする ▪ The most unusual place they *made whoopee* was in the ICU. 彼らがやったもっとも珍しい場所は集中治療室の中だった.

whore[1] /hɔːr/ 名 ***play the whore*** (女性が)私通する ▪ She was asked why she *played the whore*. 彼女はなぜ私通したのかと聞かれた.

whore[2] /hɔːr/ 動 ***go a-whoring after*** …への邪欲に迷う(《聖》*Exod*. 34. 15; *Deut*. 31. 16) ▪ So must you ever *go a-whoring after* my own sons! では, お前はいつも私の息子への邪欲に迷わずにはいられないのだね.

why /*h*waɪ/ 名副 ***the why***(***s***) ***and*** (***the***) ***wherefore***(***s***) 理由, いわく因縁 ▪ I never understood *the why and wherefore* of their marriage. 私は彼らの結婚のいわく因縁がどうしてもわからなかった ▪ I don't know much about *the whys and the wherefores* of his objection. 彼が反対する理由があまりよく分からない.

Why don't I…? (私が)…しましょうか, してあげようか《提案》 ▪ *Why don't I* give you a lift home? 家まで車で送ってあげようか.

Why don't we…? (いっしょに)…しましょうか, しようか, しませんか《勧誘》 ▪ *Why don't we* take a five minute break? 5分だけ休憩しようか.

Why don't you…? …してはどうですか, したら, しなさいよ《提案》 ▪ *Why don't you* ask her yourself? 君が自分で彼女に聞けよ.

Why ever…? 一体なぜ ▪ *Why ever* didn't you tell me? 一体どうして私に話してくれなかったのか.

Why not (***do***)***?***《口》**1** なぜいけないのだ; いいじゃないか ▪ We've got to do it eventually, so *why not* now? 結局それをしなくちゃならない, だったらなぜ今しないのか ▪ "*Why not?*" he said when the idea was presented. 彼はその案が提出されたとき,「いいじゃないか」と言った.

2 (提案して)…しようよ; (提案を承諾して)うん, そうしよう ▪ *Why not* go and see Tom?—OK. トムのところへ遊びに行こうよ—うん, 行こう ▪ Let's go jogging in the park.—OK, *why not?* 公園へジョギングに行こうよ—いいとも, そうしよう.

wick /wɪk/ 名 ***dip** one's **wick*** 《卑》(男性が)性交する ▪ He's incredibly promiscuous—he'll *dip his wick* anywhere. 彼は全く相手かまわずで, 場所も選ばない. ☞wick = penis.

get on** a person's **wick 《俗》人のしゃく[神経]にさわる ▪ The boss *gets on my wick.* 社長はおれのしゃくにさわる.

wicked /wíkəd/ 形 ***go where the wicked cease from troubling*** →GO².

have** one's **wicked way with 《戯》…と性交する ▪ Jack had *had his wicked way with* Jill. ジャックはジルとやっていたのだ.

(There's) no peace [rest] for the wicked. 《主に戯》悪人に平穏[安らぎ]はない《多くの仕事に不平を言うときに用い, 忙しくて目が回りそうだ, の意》(《聖》*Isa.* 48. 22).

wicket /wíkət/ 名 ***be [bat] on a sticky wicket*** 《英口》苦しい立場に置かれる ▪ If we're late again, we'*re* (*batting*) *on a sticky wicket.* また遅刻したら, おれたち苦しい立場に置かれるぞ. ☞sticky wicket「雨上がりの, ボールのはずまないフィールド」. 打者に不利なことから.

keep** one's **wicket up 《クリケット》(打者が)アウトにならずにいる; くじけない ▪ You'll meet with all kinds of difficulties, but *keep your wicket up.* いろいろな困難に出くわすだろうが, くじけちゃだめだ.

on a good [bad] wicket 有利[不利]な立場で ▪ They are *on a* fairly *good wicket* as regards their share in the national income. 彼らは国民総所得の分け前という点ではかなり有利な立場にある ▪ He was forced to fight a by-election *on a bad wicket.* 彼は不利な立場で補欠選挙を戦わざるをえなかった.

wide /waɪd/ 形副名 ***a wide boy*** 《英口》不正に金儲けする男, 抜け目のないやつ ▪ Say no. He's a bit of *a wide boy.* いやだと言え. あいつはどうも油断ならんやつだから.

be whacked [broke, done] to the wide すっかり疲れる[一文なしになる, へたばる] ▪ I'*m* just *whacked to the wide.* 僕は全くくたくたになってしまった ▪ I *was* about *broke to the wide* when they took me on. 私は保護されたときには, ほとんど一文なしになっていた ▪ He *was done to the wide* by the end of the fifth round. 彼は第5ラウンドの終わりまでにすっかりへたばっていた. ☞to the wide は to the wide world の略; →to the WORLD.

(be) wide awake →AWAKE¹.

blow wide open →BLOW (wide) open.

far and wide →FAR.

wide of …から遠く離れた[て] ▪ His remark is *wide of* the truth. 彼の言ったことは真相に遠い ▪ He is speaking *wide of* the mark. 彼は要領を得ないことを言っている ▪ The arrow fell *wide of* the target. 矢は的をはずれて落ちた.

wide open **1** 《米俗》公然と ▪ Gambling houses were run *wide open.* 賭博宿が公然と経営されていた.
2 未解決で ▪ The bank robbery is still *wide open.* その銀行強盗事件はまだ解決していない.
3 できるだけ速く, 全速力で ▪ I was driving along *wide open* when a tire burst. エンジン全開で飛ばしていたら, タイヤがパンクした.
4 (場所に)犯罪[堕落]があふれて, 罪悪がのさばって ▪ The prison was *wide open* because it was understaffed. 看守の人員不足のため, その刑務所は無法状態だった.

widow /wídoʊ/ 名 ***a golf [tennis, computer, etc.] widow*** ゴルフ[テニス, コンピューター]未亡人《夫がスポーツなどに熱中して顧みられない妻》 ▪ I'm *a football widow*, and you a couch potato. フットボールのせいで私はそっちのけ, あなたはテレビに夢中というわけね.

the widow's cruse →CRUSE.

widow's mite 貧者の一灯, 微力 (《聖》*Mark* 12. 42) ▪ He gave his *widow's mite* to the cause. 彼はその運動に貧者の一灯を献じた.

widow's weeds 未亡人が葬儀で着る喪服 ▪ Her *widow's weeds* really became her. 未亡人の喪服が彼女にじつに似合った.

wife /waɪf/ 名 ***a wife of the left hand*** → LEFT.

all the world and his wife → (all) the WORLD and his wife.

have a woman to wife = take a woman to WIFE.

make a good wife (将来)良妻になる ▪ She will *make* him *a good wife.* 彼女は彼のよき妻となるだろう.

old wife 《主に軽蔑》老婆, ばあさん ▪ *Old wives* lighten their spinning by songs. ばあさん連中は歌で糸紡ぎの仕事を軽くする.

old wives' tale [fable, story] (おしゃべりばあさんのするような)たわいのない話; 迷信 ▪ These are the sort of *old wives' tales* which he recites to us. 彼が私たちに聞かせてくれる話はたわいのない話だ ▪ Don't worry. It's medically proven that's an *old wives' tale.* ご心配なく. それが迷信だということは医学的にも証明されているんだから.

take** a woman **to wife …をめとる, 妻として迎える ▪ She was very young when *taken to wife.* 彼女はめとられたときには非常に若かった.

wig /wɪg/ 名 ***a big wig*** 《口》高官, おえら方 ▪ One of the *big wigs* will take it up. 早晩おえら方が誰かその問題を取り上げるだろう.

Dash my wig(s)! 《口》いまいましい!, くそ!《軽いののしり言葉》 ▪ *Dash my wig* if I am mistaken! いまいましい, まちがってなんかいるものか. ☞怒ってかつらをつぶすことから.

flip** one's **wig 《米口》かんしゃくを起こす ▪ Stop whistling. You make me *flip my wig.* 口笛を吹くのをやめろ. いらいらしてくる.

have** one's **wig sorted 《俗》しかられる ▪ I'll

W

have my wig sorted by the captain. おれは船長にしかられるだろう.

in wig and gown かつらとガウンを着けて, 法官服を着て ▪ There is the register below the Judge *in wig and gown*. 法官服を着た裁判官の下に登録簿がある.

keep *one's* ***wig on*** = keep one's HAIR on (one's head).

My wig(s)! 《口》いやはや《無意味な驚きなどの表現》 ▪ *My wig!* but she is garrulous. いやはや, おしゃべりな女だな.

wigs on the green 《口》つかみ合い, 激論 ▪ They felt there would be *wigs on the green*. 彼らはつかみ合いが始まるだろうと感じた. ☞つかみ合いをすればかつらが草の上に落ちることから.

wigging /wíɡɪŋ/ 名 ***get a wigging*** 《俗》ひどくしかられる ▪ You'll *get a wigging* for leaving the door open. ドアをあけっぱなしにしておくと, ひどくしかられるぞ.

wiggle /wíɡəl/ 名 ***get a wiggle on*** 《米俗》急ぐ(= get a MOVE on) ▪ Tell him to damn well *get a wiggle on*. 彼に根かぎり急げと言ってくれ.

wild /waɪld/ 形名副 ***be wild about*** 《米口》…に夢中になっている ▪ He *is wild about* fishing. 彼は釣りに夢中になっている ▪ He *is wild about* Mary. 彼はメアリーに夢中になっている.

be wild to *do* [***for***] ひどく…したがっている ▪ He *was wild to* see her. 彼は彼女にひどく会いたがっていた ▪ I *was wild for* revenge. 私は復しゅうの鬼になっていた.

beyond *one's* ***wildest dreams*** 予想をはるかに超えて ▪ The success of her first album was *beyond her wildest dreams*. 最初のアルバムの成功は彼女の予想以上のものだった.

blow wild (油井(ゆせい)が)もて余すほど盛んに噴出する ▪ When the wells *blow wild* the city is enveloped in a dark spray of oil. 油井がもて余すほど盛んに噴出するときには, その町は黒い石油のしぶきに包まれる.

drive *a person* ***wild*** 人を夢中にさせる, 発狂させる ▪ Her misery had actually *driven* her *wild*. 不幸が本当に彼女を乱心させた.

go (hog) wild 狂乱する, ひどく怒る, 夢中になる ▪ He *went wild* with joy. 彼は狂喜した ▪ The audience *went hog wild* as soon as the pop star began to sing. ポップスターが歌いだした途端に聴衆は熱狂した. ☞hog「ブタ」がときに抑制がきかず攻撃的になることから.

go wild over **1** …で大騒ぎする ▪ The children *went wild over* the rabbit. 子供たちはそのウサギで大騒ぎした.

2 …が大変気に入る ▪ They *went wild over* her cake. 彼らは彼女のケーキが大変気に入った.

grow wild 野生している ▪ Trees of this kind *grow wild* in his woods. この種の木は彼の森の中に自生している.

in the wilds 未開地に ▪ He spent seven years *in the wilds* of N. Africa. 彼は北アフリカの未開地で7年間を過ごした.

not in *one's* ***wildest dreams*** 夢にも…ない ▪ *Never in my wildest dreams* did I imagine Canada winning. カナダが優勝するとは全く予想していなかった.

play the wild 《米口》勝手気ままに[乱暴に]ふるまう (*with*) ▪ I have been *playing the wild* in St. Louis. 僕はセントルイスで勝手気ままにふるまってきた ▪ Love can *play the wild with* any young man. 恋はどんな若者をもむちゃにもてあそぶことができる.

run wild **1** (動植物が)野育ちである, やたらにはびこる ▪ The horse *runs wild* in Arabia. アラビアには野育ちの馬がいる ▪ The weeds are *running wild* over the garden. 雑草が庭にはびこっている.

2 放らつにする, したい放題にする ▪ He *ran* a little *wild*, and went for a soldier. 彼は少し放らつにやり, 兵士になった.

wild and woolly **1** 《米口》(無法の辺境開拓者のように)粗野で, 野育ちで ▪ Clarke is a *wild and woolly* county. クラークは粗野な郡だ.

2 手に汗を握らせる, スリリングな ▪ I found the martial arts world really *wild and woolly*. 武道の世界は実にわくわくさせてくれるとわかった.

wild and woolly [***lawless***] ***West*** 《米口》未開で無法の西部 ▪ I wish I had lived in the *wild and woolly West*. 未開で無法の西部に生きていたらなあ.

wild card **1** 予想がつかないこと[人] ▪ The real *wild card* is the undecided vote. 全く予想がつかないのは浮動票の行方だ.

2 《スポーツ》(予選免除の)特別枠 ▪ He was selected as a *wild card* via fan vote. 彼はファン投票で特別枠として選出された.

3 〚限定的〛特別枠の ▪ The ex-champion is among eight *wild-card* entries to the US open. 前チャンピオンは全米オープンの8人の特別枠参加者の一人だ.

wild horses would [***could***] ***not make*** (etc.) *one*… 《口・戯》何ものにも…するよう説得されない, どんなことがあっても…したくない ▪ *Wild horses wouldn't keep* me at home on a Friday night. 金曜の夜は何としても家にじっとしていられない ▪ *Wild horses couldn't drag* me to church this morning. 誰が何と言ってもけさは教会へは行かない.

wildcat /wáɪldkæt/ 名 ***a wildcat strike*** 《口》(本部の指令によらない)組合員の自発的なストライキ ▪ Some 200 workers have gone on *a wildcat strike* and occupied the factory. 200人ばかりの労働者が山猫ストを打って工場を占拠した.

wilderness /wíldərnəs/ 名 ***a voice crying in the wilderness*** →VOICE.

a wilderness of **1** (荒野のように)だだっ広い ▪ He looked out over *a wilderness of* roofs. 彼はごたごたと続く屋根を見はらした.

2 おびただしい数[量]の ▪ They have committed *a wilderness of* faults and follies. 彼らは無数の過失や愚行を犯した.

in the wilderness (政治家が要職を離れて)権力[人望]を失って ▪ He spent several years *in the* political *wilderness*. 彼は数年間政界での影響力を失っていた.

wander in a wilderness 荒野をさまよう; (政党が)在野である (《聖》*Num*. 14. 33) ▪ The party had been *wandering in the wilderness* since 1990. その党は1990年以来在野であった.

wildfire /wáɪldfàɪər/ 名 ***like wildfire*** 野火のような[すさまじい]勢いで ▪ The report spread *like wildfire* through the town. その噂は野火のような勢いで町じゅうに広まった ▪ Such thoughts were running *like wildfire* through her mind. そのような考えがすさまじい勢いで彼女の頭の中を駆けめぐっていた.

wild-goose /wàɪldgúːs/ 名 ***a wild-goose chase*** (雲をつかむような)当てのない追求, むなしい探索 ▪ His journey to London on such slender encouragement is *a wild-goose chase*! そんなわずかの励ましで彼がロンドンへ旅立つと思うのはむなしい骨折りというものだ. ☞ガンはめったに撃ち落とせないことから.

wild horse /wáɪldhɔ́ːrs/ 名 ***draw with wild horses*** 野生の馬を使って八つ裂きにする《中世の刑罰》 ▪ Or else they would *draw* him forth *with wild horses*. さもなければ彼は野生の馬を使って八つ裂きにされるだろう.

Wild horses would not drag it out of me. (秘密などを)どんなことがあってもしゃべらないぞ ▪ I do know where he has gone, but *wild horses would not drag it out of me*. 彼がどこへ行ったかちゃんと知っている. だが, どんなことがあってもしゃべるもんか. ☞上の処刑から.

wildly /wáɪldli/ 副 ***talk wildly*** **1** 無責任なことを言う ▪ Except on his own subject, he's inclined to *talk wildly*. 自分の専門以外のことでは彼は無責任なことを言いがちだ.

2 むなしいおどし文句を並べる ▪ He *talked wildly* of refusing to pay his taxes. 彼は税金を払わないなどとむなしいおどし文句を並べた.

will[1] /wɪl/ 名 ***a living will*** 生前遺言書, (尊厳死を希望する[人工的延命措置を望まない])末期患者の遺言書 ▪ I'll state in my *living will* that I don't want a feeding tube if unable to swallow food. 私は食物が嚥下(えんげ)できなくなっても摂食用チューブを望まない旨を遺言状に記すつもりだ.

a will o' the wisp **1** 鬼火, キツネ火 ▪ I have never seen *a will o' the wisp* in my life. 生まれてこのかた鬼火を見たためしがない.

2 とらえどころのない[人を惑わす]人物[考え] ▪ He is *a will-o'-the-wisp* who does the unexpected thing at the unexpected time. 彼はふいに思いがけないことをするとらえどころのない男だ.

a will of iron 鉄の意志 ▪ He has got *a will of iron*. 彼は鉄の意志を持っている.

a will of *one's* ***own*** 頑固な意志; 《婉曲》我意 ▪ I am not allowed any *will of my own*. 私は自分の意志というものを許されていない ▪ She has *a will of her own*. 彼女は我が強い.

against *a person's* ***will*** 人の意志に反して ▪ He married her *against the will of* her parents. 彼は彼女の両親の意志に反して彼女と結婚した.

against *one's* ***will*** 心ならずも ▪ He forced us to come *against our will*. 彼は私たちがいやがるのを無理に来させた.

an estate [***a tenant***] ***at will*** 地主の随意でいつでも立ちのかせる借地[借地人] ▪ Under *an estate at will*, the landlord may evict the tenant at any time. 随意借地では地主は随意に借地人を立ちのかせることができる.

at *one's* (***own sweet*** [***free***]) ***will*** 意のままに, 随意に; 《皮肉》勝手気ままに ▪ He revised it *at his own sweet will*. 彼はそれを意のままに改訂した ▪ The river glides *at his own sweet will*. 川は勝手気ままに流れていく.

at will 意のままに, 随意に ▪ You may go or stay *at will*. 行くもとどまるも自由にしなさい ▪ The vocal cords can be opened or shut *at will*. 声帯は意のままに開閉できる.

at *a person's* ***will*** 人の意のままに ▪ My life is yours. I set it *at your will*. 私の命はあなたのものです. あなたの意のままに委ねます.

cut *a person* ***out of*** *one's* ***will*** (遺言を変更して)人を遺産相続から外す ▪ He *cut* Jimmy *out of his will*. 彼はジミーを遺産相続から外した.

do the will of *a person* (人)の望み[命令]に従う, 言う通りにする ▪ We strive to know and *do the will of* God. 神の御心を体しそれを行うよう努めます.

good [***ill***] ***will*** 好意[悪意] ▪ Japan's course is being regarded with ever increasing *good will*. 日本の針路は日ましに好意をもって見られるようになっている ▪ He has never manifested the slightest *ill will* toward it. 彼はそれに少しもいやな様子は見せたことはない.

have *one's* ***will*** 意地を通す, 思う通りにする ▪ He must always *have his will*. 彼はいつも我を通さないではおかない.

if it be [***is***] ***your*** [***his,*** etc.] ***will*** そういうおぼしめしなら ▪ *If it is your will*, I'll have my starship prepared immediately. そういうおぼしめしなら, わが恒星間宇宙船を直ちに準備させましょう.

one's (***last***) ***will and testament*** 遺言 ▪ The old man dictated *his last will and testament* on his deathbed. 老人は今わのきわに遺言を口述筆記させた.

of *one's* ***own free will*** 自ら進んで ▪ He did it *of his own free will*. 彼はそれを自ら進んでやった.

remember *a person* ***in*** *one's* ***will*** 遺言状に書いて人に遺産を分ける ▪ He *remembered* each of the servants *in his will*. 彼は遺言状に書いて使用人の一人一人に遺産を分けた.

take the will for the deed 志を行いと同じようにありがたく思う ▪ We will *take the will for the deed*. そうしようとする志はありがたく思う ▪ You must *take the will for the deed*. こんなにする志は多としていただきたい.

The will is as good as the deed. 《諺》何事にも志が大切.

Where there's a will, there's a way. 《諺》決意があれば道は開ける,「精神一到何事か成らざらん」.

will to power 権力への意志 ▪ Life itself is *will to power.* 人生そのものが権力への意志なのだ. ☞ Nietzsche, *Der Wille zur Macht* (1888–94)のなぞり.

with a will 《文》身を入れて, 本気で ▪ He set to work *with a will.* 彼は真剣に仕事に取りかかった ▪ I threw the stone *with a will.* 私は本気で石を投げた.

with the best will (in the world) いくら本気になっても, いくら身を入れても ▪ *With the best will* we found it impossible to eat any of her cooking. 我々はがんばってみたが彼女が作った料理は何も食べられなかった.

work** one's **will 自分の欲するところを行う, 目的を遂げる ▪ He left misrule and violence to *work their will* among men. 彼は悪政と暴力が人民の間でほしいままにふるまうのに任せた ▪ He *worked his* wicked *will* upon them. 彼は彼らに対してよこしまな目的を達した.

will[2] /wəl, wɪl/ 助動 *do* ***as ... as you will*** どれほど...しようとも ▪ No one will hear you, shout *as* loud *as you will.* どんなに大声でどなっても, 誰にも聞こえないでしょう.

as ... will →AS.

be that as it will それがどうあろうとも (however that may be) ▪ *Be that as it will*, he never returned to recover his wealth. それがどうあろうとも, 彼はついに富を取り戻しに帰って来なかった.

come what will →WHAT.

if you will **1** あるいは, つまり, 言うなれば ▪ He is my senior advisor—my deputy, *if you will.* 彼は私の首席顧問つまり代理人である.
2 よろしければ ▪ Tell us about yourself a bit *if you will.* よろしければご自身のことを少しお話しください.

***whether** one **will or no/will** one **or not/will** one **nil** one* いやでも応でも ▪ They will fetch her away, *whether* she *will or no*, out of my tent. 彼らは彼女をいやでも応でも私のテントから連れ去るだろう ▪ The consequences have to be borne, *will* he, *nil* he. この結果は彼がいやでも応でも忍ばねばならない.

***will** oneself* 固く決意する, 自分に言い聞かせる, 意志の力で...する ▪ I looked straight ahead and *willed myself* to stay awake. まっすぐ前方を見つめて眠り込まないよう気力でがんばった.

willies /wíliz/ 名 ***get [have] the willies*** 《口》いらいらする, おどおどする ▪ I *got the willies* the first time I rode on a roller coaster. 私は初めてジェットコースターに乗ったときはらはらした.

give** a person **the willies 《口》人をいらいらさせる ▪ This damned country *gives* me *the willies.* このけしからん国にはいらいらさせられる.

willing /wílɪŋ/ 形 ***a willing horse*** 心から進んでやる人 ▪ All lay their load on *a willing horse.* 心から進んでやる人にはすべての人が重荷を背負わせる.

***be willing to** do* 喜んで[進んで]...する ▪ He *was willing to* comply with that. 彼は喜んでそれに応じた ▪ I *am* quite *willing to* do anything for you. 君のためなら喜んで何でもします.

show willing 協力的であることを示す ▪ I wanted to *show willing* to Jim. 自分が協力を惜しまないことをジムに示したかった.

spur a willing horse いそいそと進む馬に拍車をかける, 余計な世話をやく ▪ Do not *spur a willing horse.* 《諺》いそいそと進む馬に拍車をかけるな《余計な世話はやくな》.

willow /wíloʊ/ 名 ***wear (the) willow [the willow garland, the green willow]*** **1** 恋人の死を悲しむ ▪ She had *worn the willow* long enough. 彼女は心ゆくまで長く恋人の死を嘆き悲しんだ.
2 恋人に捨てられる ▪ The young man is unhappy—in fact, he is *wearing the willow.* その青年は悲しんでいる. 実は失恋しているのだ. ☞ 柳は失恋・配偶者の死に対する悲しみの象徴.

win /wɪn/ 動 ***win** one's **bread [livelihood, living]*** パンをかせぐ, 糊口の資をかせぐ ▪ I have for many years *won my living* by fishery. 私は多年漁業で生計を立ててきた.

win free [clear] 自由になる (*of*) ▪ At last the prisoner *won free.* やっと囚人は自由の身となった.

win hands down 楽勝する (→HANDs down) ▪ Jones *won* the election *hands down.* ジョーンズは選挙で楽勝した.

win in walk →win in a WALK.

win or lose 勝っても負けても, 成功してもしなくても ▪ *Win or lose*, we must fight. 勝とうと負けようと戦わねばならない.

win** one's **spurs →SPUR[1].

win the day/win the [a] field 戦いに勝つ; 成功する ▪ His courage *won the day.* 彼の勇気のおかげで戦いに勝った ▪ He *won* two *fields* of the sultan. 彼はイスラム国の君主と戦って2回勝った ▪ The girl always *won the day.* その女の子は常に成功した.

***win** a person **to** do* 人を説きふせて...させる ▪ I have *won* him *to* consent. 彼を説得して同意させた.

win** one's **way うまく進んで行く; うまくたどり着く《比喩的にも》 ▪ He *won his way* through the storm. 彼はあらしの中をうまく進んで行った.

You (just) can't win. 全くうまくいかない, もうお手上げだ ▪ Every time I block a rabbit's holes, I find another. *You just can't win.* ウサギの穴を一つふさぐと, きまって別のが見つかる. もうお手上げだ.

You (just) can't win them ['em] all. 《口・戯》いつも勝つことはできない; 万人の気に入るわけにはいかない ▪ No matter how good you are, *you can't win 'em all.* いくらうまくても, いつも勝つわけにはいかないさ. ☞ 落胆・失敗した人が言ったり言われたりする言葉.

You win. 《口》君の勝ちだ, 君の言う通りにする ▪ OK, *you win.* We'll stay home tonight. わかった, 君の言う通りにするよ. 今夜は家で過ごそう.

(You) win some [a few], (you) lose some [a few]. 勝つこともあれば負けることもある; いつもうまくいくとは限らない ▪ *You win some, you lose some,* that's how it goes. いつもうまくはいかないよ. 物事ってそんなものさ ▪ *You win a few, you lose a few,* and sometimes you lose badly. 勝ったり負けたり, ときには大負けだってあるさ. ☞自らの失敗の弁解や失敗した人への慰めに用いられる陳腐な表現.

wince /wɪns/ 動 ***Let [Make] the galled jade wince.*** 侮辱されたと思う人は怒ってみろ (cf. Sh., *Haml.* 3. 2. 253) ▪ The words had been written with no suspicion that they could *make the galled jade wince.* その言葉は侮辱されたと思う人を怒らせるとは夢にも考えないで書かれていた.

wind[1] /wɪnd/ 名 ***a fair wind*** 順風, 追い風 ▪ He set sail with *a fair wind* behind him. 彼は順風を背に受けて出航した.

against the wind **1**《海》風に逆らって ▪ Our boat sailed *against the wind.* 我々の船は風に逆らって帆走した.
2 時流に逆らって, 時の世論に抗して ▪ He never minds what others say; he likes sailing *against the wind.* 彼は他人が何と言おうと全く気にせず, 好んで大勢に逆らう.

as swift as the wind/swifter than the wind (風のように)非常に早く ▪ He went away *swifter than the wind.* 彼は風より早く立ち去った.

beat the wind →BEAT the air.

before the wind 《海》(船が)追い風を受けて; 順調に ▪ We got *before the wind* to the Cape of Good Hope. 我々は追い風を受けて希望峰へ着いた ▪ The ship drove [ran] *before the wind.* 船は順風を受けて快走した.

between [betwixt] wind and water **1**《海》(船の)喫水線を; 急所を ▪ They had received a shot *between wind and water* and the ship leaked dangerously. 彼らは喫水線に弾丸を受け船は水漏れして危険な状態にあった ▪ The Congress was hit seven times *between wind and water.* 議会は7回急所をたたかれた.
2 湿地で, 水に触れる所で ▪ An oaken gate-post always decays *between wind and water.* カシの木の門柱は水に触れる所ではいつも腐る.

blow in the wind 議論の最中である, 未決定である ▪ The answer to the housing problem is still *blowing in the wind.* 住宅問題の解決策は依然として出ていない.

blow with the wind 風まかせに[気の向くままに]行動する ▪ He's a man of conviction, and he does not *blow with the wind.* 彼は信念のある人で, 一貫性のない行動はとらない.

break wind おならをする ▪ He belches or *breaks wind.* 彼はげっぷをしたりおならをしたりする.

cast ... to the winds →fling ... to the WIND(s).

catch** a person **in the wind →hit a person in the WIND.

catch** one's **wind →get one's WIND.

catch wind of 《口》…に感づく ▪ They *caught wind of* our secret plan and left the town. 彼らは我々の密かな計画を嗅ぎつけて町を立ち去った. ☞猟師や天敵の存在を風を頼りに匂いで察知する野生動物から.

close to [by, on, upon] a [the] wind **1**《海》ほとんど風上に向かって ▪ They lay *close by a wind.* 彼らはほとんど風上に向かって航行した.
2 きわどい所を ▪ He has sailed too *close to the wind* at home. 彼は故国であまりにもきわどいことをやってきた.

down (the) wind 風下に (↔ up (the) WIND) ▪ The hare will run *down the wind.* その野ウサギは風下へ逃げるだろう.

feel the wind →feel a DRAUGHT.

find how [which way] the wind blows [lies, sits] →know how the WIND blows.

fling [cast, give, scatter, throw] ... to the wind(s) …を捨て去る, 全く捨ててしまう (《聖》*Ezek.* 17. 21) ▪ You must *throw* your fears *to the winds.* 心配なんか捨てておしまいなさい ▪ She *cast* prudence *to the winds.* 彼女は慎重さを捨ててしまった ▪ I *threw* caution *to the wind* and ordered two desserts. 思い切ってデザートを二つ注文した.

gain [get, take] the wind of **1**《海》(他船)の風上に出る; …よりも有利な地位を占める ▪ We made all haste to *gain the wind of* the ship. 我々はその船の風上に出るため大いに急いだ ▪ They did all they could to *take the wind of* us. 彼らは我々よりも有利な地位を占めるためにできるかぎりのことをした.
2 …をかぎつける ▪ The two rhinoceroses thus *gained our wind.* その2匹のサイはこうして我々をかぎつけた.

get** one's **second wind 調子を取り戻す, 立ち直る ▪ The lecture was dull in the middle, but the speaker *got his second wind* toward the end. 講演は中ほどはおもしろくなかったが, 講演者は終わりごろまた調子を取り戻した. ☞wind「呼吸」.

get the wind up 《英口》どきっとする ▪ I *get the wind up* every time I walk along that road in the park. 公園のあの道を歩くたびに僕はどきっとする. ☞昔, 風が強すぎると飛行を妨げたことから.

get wind →take WIND.

get [catch, recover]** one's **wind 息をつく ▪ You had better *get your wind* now, and change your clothes. もう息をついて着替えをしたほうがいいでしょう.

get [have] wind of …をかぎつける, 知るようになる ▪ The mayor *got wind of* our correspondence. 市長は我々の文通をかぎつけた ▪ The government *had* some *wind of* this. 政府はこれを多少知っていた.

give ... to the winds →fling ... to the WIND(s).

W

give ... one's wind (動物)にかぎつけられる ▪ I *gave* the large herd *my wind.* 私はその動物の大群にかぎつけられてしまった.

go to the winds すっかりなくなる ▪ At this all his self-restraint *went to the winds.* これを聞くと, 彼の自制心はすっかりなくなってしまった.

gone with the wind 跡かたもなく消え去る(E. Dowson, *Non Sum Qualis Eram* 3) ▪ Saying goodby, he was *gone with the wind.* さよならを言うと, 彼は風とともに消えてしまった.

hang in the wind 腰が決まらないままでいる ▪ They *hang in the wind*, as neuters. 彼らは中立者として腰が決まらないままでいる. ☞風次第でどう進むかわからないことから.

have a bad [good, long] wind 息が続かない[続く] ▪ Revolutions *have a long wind*, like marathon runners. マラソン選手のように改革も息が長く続く.

have in the wind =gain the WIND of 2.

have the wind of **1**《海》(他船)の風上にある; ...よりも有利な地位を占めている ▪ We *had the wind of* the Spanish ships. 我々はスペインの船の風上にあった.

2 =gain the WIND of 2.

have the wind up《俗》=get the WIND up.

hit [catch] a person in the wind《ボクシング》人のみぞおちを打つ ▪ He *hit* the opponent *in the wind.* 彼は相手のみぞおちを打った.

hurl ... to the wind(s) → fling ... to the WIND(s).

in the wind **1** 風上に ▪ Oh! How he holds his nose up, like a stallion *in the wind* of a mare! ああ, 彼はまるで雌馬の風上にいる雄馬みたいに鼻を上へ向けているではないか.

2 かぎつけ(られ)るように, 見つけ(られ)るように ▪ They scent danger *in the wind.* 彼らは危険をかぎつけることができる ▪ A bailiff was *in the wind.* 執行官補佐人が見つけられた.

3〚述語的に〛(事が)起ころうとして ▪ There must be something *in the wind*, perhaps a war. 何か起こりかけているにちがいない, おそらく戦争だろう.

4 (起こっている事件の)張本人になって ▪ There's a woman *in the wind.* I'll lay my life on it. 女が張本人になっているんだ. 首をかけてもいいよ.

5《海俗》〚述語的に〛酔っ払って ▪ He was a little *in the wind.* 彼は少し酔っ払っていた.

into the wind 風上に向かって; 風に面して ▪ The pilot turned *into the wind* to land. パイロットは着陸するため風上に向かって方向を変えた.

It is an ill wind that blows nobody good [no one any good].《諺》誰の得にもならぬような風は吹かない; 泣く者があれば笑う者がある, 「甲の損は乙の得」.

knock the wind out of a person 人の息の根を止める ▪ The bitter cold had nearly *knocked the wind out of* me. 私は極寒で息の根が止まりそうだった.

know [see, find (out)] how [which way] the wind blows [lies, sits] 風向きを知る, 形勢を知る ▪ Miss Sprong, *seeing how the wind lay*, tried to praise him. スプロング嬢は風向きを見てとって彼をほめようとした ▪ Caleb now *found how the wind sat.* ケイレブは今や形勢がわかってきた ▪ Who *knows which way the wind blows?* 今後の成り行きは誰にも読めない ▪ I'm going to *find out how the wind blows* concerning a promotion. 昇給がどうなるか状況をさぐってみよう.

leave a person twisting [swinging, turning] in the wind/ let a person twist [swing, turn] in the wind《主に米》(苦しい状況にある人)を助けずに放置する, いつまでも思い悩ませておく ▪ The music industry has abandoned him and *left* him *twisting in the wind.* 音楽業界は彼を見離したあげく見殺しにしてしまった ▪ They *left* him *swinging in the wind* to cover up their mistakes. 彼らは自らの過失を隠蔽するために彼を苦しい状況に放置した.

like the wind (風のように)速く ▪ The boy flew *like the wind* to buy the toy. 男の子はおもちゃを買いに速く走って行った ▪ She's slight in build and she can run *like the wind.* 彼女はほっそりした体格で走るのがとても速い.

limb and wind →LIMB.

lose one's wind 息が切れる ▪ A man without spirit is like a horse who has *lost his wind.* 気迫のない者は息切れした馬のようなものだ.

near the wind **1** ほとんど風上に向かって ▪ The ship can lie *near the wind.* 船はほとんど風上に向かって進むことができる.

2 きわどい所を ▪ He may sail very *near the wind* indeed, and be pardoned. 彼は全くきわどいことをやっても許されるかもしれない.

on the wind 風に乗って ▪ Scent is carried *on the wind.* においは風に乗って運ばれる.

piss against [into] the wind →PISS².

put the wind up《主に英》**1** = get the WIND up.

2 人をぎょっとさせる, おびえさせる ▪ I tell you you've absolutely *put the wind up* Peter! いいかい, 君はほんとにピーターをぎょっとさせたんだよ ▪ I tried to *put the wind up* them by threatening to call the police. 警察を呼ぶぞと脅して彼らを怯(ひる)ませようとした.

raise the wind《俗》金を工面(くめん)する ▪ I can't *raise the wind* for a holiday this year. ことしは休暇の金を工面することができない. ☞風が出ないと船が走らないことから.

recover one's wind →get one's WIND.

sail before the wind →SAIL².

sail near [close to] the wind →SAIL².

sail with every (shift of) wind どんな境遇をも自己に有利に導く ▪ The Dissenters can *sail with every wind.* 非国教徒たちはどんな境遇をも自己に有利に導くことができる.

save one's wind 黙っている ▪ You'd better be

saving your wind. 君は黙ってるほうがいいだろう.

scatter ... to the winds → fling ... to the WIND(s).

second wind 息つぎ, 元気の回復 ▪ A bull if allowed to get its *second wind* will go on almost forever. 雄牛は息つぎをするのを許されればほとんどいつまでもやり続ける.

see how* [*which way*] *the wind blows → know how the WIND blows.

sink the wind 風に逆らって行く ▪ *Sinking the wind* all the way, the hare ran to Silverspring. ずっと風に逆らいながら, 野ウサギはシルバースプリングへ走って逃げた.

Sits the wind there* [*in that quarter*]*? 風向きはそちらからか; 形勢はそうなのか ▪ *Sits the wind there?* Pray you tell me. 形勢はそうなのか. どうか教えていただきたい.

something in the wind ひそかに準備されたこと, 秘密の計画 ▪ I'm sure there's *something in the wind* for Mom and Dad's anniversary. ママとパパの結婚記念日の行事がこっそり計画されているはずだ. ☞香りが風に運ばれることから.

sound in wind and limb →SOUND².

sow the wind and* [*to*] *reap the whirlwind →WHIRLWIND.

speak* [*talk*] *to the wind 言ってもむだである ▪ Speak to her? You might *talk to the wind.* 彼女に話すって? 風に話しかけたほうがまだましだよ.

spit against* [*in, into*] *the wind = PISS against the wind.

split the wind 《米口》全速力で行く[走る] (→ BURN the earth) ▪ He *split the wind*, showing the crowd that age had not crept into his heels. 彼は猛スピードで走って, 年はとっても足は遅くなっていないことを群衆に示した.

swifter than the wind → as swift as the WIND.

take the wind of →gain the WIND of.

take the wind out of the sails of 《口》 **1** (人)を面くらわせる ▪ He suddenly *took the wind out of Tom's sails* by asking when he was getting married. 彼はトムにいつ結婚するのかと尋ねていきなりトムを面くらわせた.

2 ...の鼻をあかす, だしぬく ▪ He *took the wind out of Jim's sails* by becoming mayor. 彼は市長になってジムの鼻をあかした. ☞他船の風上へ回ってその風を奪うことから.

take* [*get*] *wind 世間の噂になる, 知れ渡る ▪ Do you know the Review begins to *get wind* here? 「評論」が当地で噂になりかけているのを知っていますか ▪ Long before that time, the project had *taken wind.* その時よりずっと前にその計画は知れ渡っていた.

talk to the wind →speak to the WIND.

***the four winds* (*of heaven*)** 四方八方 (《聖》 *Ezek.* 37. 9) ▪ The remains had been scattered to *the four winds.* その遺物は四散されてしまった ▪ The infantry headed off for *the four winds* in the city. 歩兵隊はその都市の八方へ進攻した.

The wind has changed. 風向きが変わった ▪ Since then *the wind has* gradually *changed.* それ以来風向きが徐々に変わってきている.

the wind of change (政治・社会情勢の)変革への動き ▪ The party requires a waft of *the wind of change.* その党は少々変革への動きを必要としている. ☞1960年に Macmillan イギリス首相が使った言葉.

***the wind rises* [*falls*]** 風が立つ[やむ] ▪ *The wind* has *risen* tonight. 今夜は風が立ってきた ▪ *The wind fell*, and there was a great calm. 風がやみ, すっかり凪(なぎ)になった.

throw ... to the winds → fling ... to the WIND(s).

throw ... up in* [*into*] *the wind **1** = THROW up in the wind.

2 《米口》 ...を未解決にする ▪ He *threw* the whole business *up into the wind.* 彼はその業務を全部未解決の状態にしてしまった.

throw ... up on the wind →THROW up in the wind.

touched in the wind (馬などが)息切れがして ▪ His face was red and he was *touched in the wind.* 彼は真っ赤な顔をし息切れがしていた.

up* (*the*) *wind 風の中へ, 風に逆らって (↔ down (the) WIND) ▪ The airplane landed *up the wind.* 飛行機は風に逆らって着陸した.

What wind blows you here? どういう風の吹き回しでここへ来たのか ▪ Ask him *what wind blew* him *here.* 彼がどういう風の吹き回しでここへ来たのか聞いてみなさい.

whistle ... down the wind →WHISTLE².

whistle in the wind むだな努力をする, ちゃんとした答えが返ってこない ▪ You might just as well *whistle in the wind* as talk to Frank. フランクに話しかけてもまともな返事は返ってこない.

wind and weather 風雨 ▪ It is a great house still, proof against *wind and weather.* それはまだ風雨に耐えうる大きな屋敷だ.

wind in the head うぬぼれ ▪ He has probably got *wind in the head* through living in that gorgeous Gothic pagoda. 彼はたぶんあの立派なゴシック風の塔に住んでいるのでうぬぼれているのだろう.

with the wind **1** 風とともに, 風のまにまに ▪ A stag came running *with the wind.* 雄ジカが1頭, 風とともに走って来た ▪ The boat shifted *with the wind.* ボートは風のまにまに漂った.

2 = before the WIND.

within wind of ...に見つけられるほど近くに ▪ Here are the Prussians *within wind of* us! ここには我々に見つかるほど近くにプロイセン軍がいる.

wind² /waɪnd/ 名 ***out of wind*** (板などが)曲がっていない ▪ Make sure the piece of wood is *out of wind.* その木切れが曲がっていないことを確かめなさい.

wind³ /waɪnd/ 動 ***be wound up in*** ...に夢中になっている ▪ My husband *is* all *wound up in* his research project. 主人は研究計画にすっかり熱

中しておりますの.

wind** oneself **into …に巧みに取り入る ▪ He has *wound himself* almost *into* my brother's confidence. 彼は私の兄に巧みに取り入ってその信頼をほとんど得ている.

wind … round** one's **(little) fingers → twist … round one's (little) FINGER.

wind up nowhere 成功しない ▪ If you are so lazy, you'll *wind up nowhere.* そんなに怠けていたら成功しないよ.

wind** one's **way うねって進む《比喩的にも》 ▪ We *wound our way* through the colony. 我々は植民地をうねって進んだ ▪ He *wound his way* into my affections. 彼はうまく取り入って私の愛情を得た.

winding /wáɪndɪŋ/ 名 ***in* [*out of*] *winding*** (板などが)曲がっていて[いない] ▪ The tiles themselves must be *out of winding.* タイル自体が曲がっていてはいけない.

windmill /wíndmìl/ 名 ***fight* (*with*) [*tilt at*] *windmills* [*a windmill*]** 《雅》仮想の敵と戦う ▪ Dr. Burney is again *fighting a windmill.* バーニー博士はまたぞろ仮想の敵と戦っている ▪ The Quixotes of this age *fight with windmills* of their own heads. 当代のドンキホーテたちは自分の頭で考え出した仮想の敵と戦っている ▪ One should never *tilt at windmills.* 決して独り相撲をとってはならない. ☞Don Quixote が風車を巨人と思ってこれと戦った話から.

fling* [*throw*]** *one's* ***cap* [*bonnet*] *over the windmill 無鉄砲な行動をする, 因襲に逆らう; (特に女性が)習俗を無視して恋愛に身を投じる ▪ He has enjoyed his youth too freely and *flung his cap* too far *over the windmill.* 彼はあまりにも自由に青春を楽しみ, あまりにも無鉄砲な行動をしてきた ▪ You're going to make a bolt with Godfrey and *throw your bonnet over the windmill.* あなたはゴッドフリーと駆け落ちして恋愛に身を投じようとしているのです. ☞F jeter son bonnet par-dessus les moulins のなぞり.

window /wíndoʊ/ 名 ***a window of opportunity*** (特にビジネスで) またとない瞬時の好機, (逃してはならない)この一瞬の好機 ▪ This is *a window of opportunity* to invest in real estate. 今が不動産に投機する絶好のチャンスだ.

a window on the world 世界の窓, 他国(民)を知る手段 ▪ The English language has been *a window on the world.* 英語はこれまでずっと世界の窓であった.

come in by the window こっそり入る ▪ We knew that you *came in by the window.* 君がこっそり入って来たのは知っていた. ☞F entrer par la fenêtre のなぞり.

go* [*fly*] *out* (*of*《英》) *the window 《口》完全になくなる, 捨て去られる, すたれる ▪ Cursive writing has *gone out the window* as more and more kids use computers. コンピューターを使う子供の数が増えるにつれて, 筆記体が使われなくなってきた ▪ Kids become addicted to TV and all good intentions to study *fly out of the window.* 子供たちはテレビ漬けになって, せっかくの勉強のやる気がすっかり失せてしまう.

have* [*put*] *all *one's* ***goods in the* (*front-, shop-*)*window*** 《口》見かけ倒しだ ▪ He isn't really reliable; he only *puts all his goods in the window.* 彼は本当は当てにならず, 見かけ倒しに過ぎない.

in the window (掲示・広告などを)窓に出して, (商品を)ショーウインドーに陳列して ▪ A sign *in the window* said: Sale of Men's Shirts. ウインドーに「男物シャツ特売」と出ていた ▪ The articles in stock are displayed *in the window.* 在庫品がウインドーに陳列されている.

***open a window to* [*into*]** …に[を知る]機会を与える ▪ His letters *open a window into* the very emotions of his heart. 彼の手紙は彼の心の内までも知る機会を与えてくれる.

out of the window 《口》もう考慮に入れられないで ▪ The plan to launch another satellite is *out of the window.* 別の衛星を打ち上げる計画はもう考慮に入れられていません.

the window of the soul 《雅》心の窓, 目 ▪ A smile is a light in *the window of the soul.* 微笑みは心の窓に点(と)る明かりである.

the window of vulnerability 攻撃されるともろい箇所, 弱点[泣きどころ](を見せてしまうこと) ▪ Our attack on *the* enemy's *window of vulnerability* was very successful. 敵の手薄な布陣へのわが軍の攻撃は大成功であった.

the windows of heaven 天の戸《ここから雨が降ると考えられた》 ▪ The wind was not cold, but *the windows of heaven* were opened. 風は冷たくなかったが, 天の戸は開けられていた. ☞ヘブライ語法.

throw the house out at* (*the*) *window 大混乱に陥れる, 上を下への大騒ぎを起こさせる ▪ The enraged marquis *threw her* whole *house out at window.* 激怒した侯爵は彼女の家を大混乱に陥れた ▪ Sometimes she *throws the house out at the window* with banquettings. ときどき彼女は宴会でどんちゃん騒ぎをする. ☞F jeter la maison par la fenêtre のなぞり.

window dressing 見せかけ ▪ All those invitations were just so much *window dressing.* そういう招待はすべて見せかけだけだった.

windward /wíndwərd/ 名 ***cast* [*keep, lay*] *an anchor to the windward*** 安全を図る ▪ This policy is based on a desire to *keep an anchor to the windward*, to secure the United States for a friend. この政策は安全を図りたい, つまりアメリカ合衆国をしっかり味方につけておきたいという望みに基づいている. ☞「風上に投錨する」が原義.

get to windward of …をだしぬく, より優勢の地歩を占める ▪ We managed to *get to windward of* the situation. 我々はなんとか優勢に立った. ☞「他船の風上に出る」が原義.

keep to windward of …を避けている ▪ With great difficulty he has *kept to windward of* the English fleet. やっとのことで彼は英国艦隊を避けた.

on the windward side of …の風上側に ▪ There was a hut *on the windward side of* the trees. 森の風上側に小屋があった.

to* (*the*) *windward 風上の方に ▪ The ship beat *to the windward.* 船は風上に間切った ▪ The heavens were gray, and there was a very dark line *to windward.* 空は曇っていて, 風上の方にひどく暗い筋が見えた.

windy /wíndi/ 形 ***on the windy side of*** (法律など)の手の及ばぬように (cf. Sh., *Twel. N.* 3. 4. 181) ▪ No, they are not honest, but they manage to keep *on the windy side of* the law. いや, 彼らは正直ではないが, なんとかして法の手の及ばぬようにしているのだ.

wine[1] /waɪn/ 名 ***Good wine needs no* (*ivy*) *bush.*** 《諺》良酒に看板はいらない. ☞bush (ツタの枝)は昔の酒屋の看板.

in wine 酒に酔って ▪ He was brought home *in wine.* 彼は酒に酔って家に連れて来られた.

look on the wine when it is red 酒を飲みすぎる (《聖》 *Prov.* 23. 31) ▪ We knew he had *looked on the wine when it was red.* 我々は彼が酒を飲みすぎたのがわかった.

new wine in old bottles 古い皮袋に盛った新酒 《旧来の形式では律しえない新原理; 著しく場違いなもの》 (《聖》 *Matt.* 9. 17) ▪ It is no use for a family like that to live in that big house. It's an instance of *new wine in old bottles.* あんな一家があの大きな家に住んで何になるというのか. 著しく場違いなものの見本だ.

over the walnuts and wine →WALNUT.

put new wine into old bottles 古い皮袋に新酒を盛る《旧来の形式に新原理を当てはめる; 矛盾したことをする》 (《聖》 *Matt.* 9. 17) ▪ He has to work in an alien tradition—to *put new wine into old bottles.* 彼はなじみのない伝統に従って働く—つまり旧来の形式に新しい考えを盛る必要があるのだ.

take wine with (友情などの印に)…と乾杯する ▪ The stranger *took wine with* the whole party together. その見知らぬ人は一座の全員と乾杯した.

When wine is in, wit* [*truth*] *is out. 《諺》酒が入れば知恵はお留守になる.

wine and dine =DINE and wine a person.

wine, woman and song 酒と女と歌 ▪ Who loves not *wine, woman and song*, he is a fool his whole life long. 酒と女と歌とを愛さない者は一生涯愚か者だ. ☞Luther の言葉 (G Wein, Weib und Gesang) とされるもののなぞり.

wine[2] /waɪn/ 動 ***dine and wine*** 《口》酒食を供する ▪ He has *dined and wined* everybody who has had anything to do with his success. 彼は己の成功に少しでも関係のある人全員に酒食を供した.

wing[1] /wɪŋ/ 名 ***add wings*** →lend WINGs.

clip the wings of …の活躍の力を奪う, を無力にする ▪ I'll halve his allowance; that will *clip his wings* effectually. 彼の手当を半分にしてやろう. そうすればきっと活躍できなくなるだろう ▪ Is it possible to *clip the wings of* his conceit? 彼のうぬぼれをくじくなんてできるだろうか. ☞鳥の羽を切って飛べなくすることから.

hit under the wing 《俗》酔って ▪ It was easy to tell when he was *hit under the wing.* 彼が酔っていたらすぐ分かる. ☞「翼の下を撃たれた鳥のように動けなくなって」が原義.

in the wings 近くに待機して, 今にも起こりそうで ▪ More bad news could be *in the wings.* さらに悪いニュースが入ってくるかもしれない. ☞wings「舞台のそで」で出番をまつ役者から.

lend* [*add*] *wings 促進する (*to*) ▪ This sound of danger *lent* me *wings.* この危険を告げる音を聞いて私は一目散に走った.

on a wing and a prayer 成功の望み薄で, うまくいきそうもなく ▪ Tonight's show is *on a wing and a prayer.* 今夜のショーは大して入りがよくあるまい ▪ We could see a plane coming in *on a wing and a prayer.* 今にも墜落しそうになって接近してくる機影が見えた. ☞1943年作の H. Adamson の歌のタイトルから. 飛行機の緊急不時着を指す.

on* [*upon*] *the wing **1** 飛んで, 飛翔中で ▪ I have been as happy as a bird *on the wing.* 私は飛んでいる鳥のようにしあわせでした ▪ The trees are in bloom, the grass is green, and the lark is *on the wing.* 木には花が咲き, 芝生は青く, ヒバリが飛んでいる. **2** 動き回って; 旅をして ▪ His thoughts were always *on the wing.* 彼の考えはいつも動き回っている ▪ Nobody was *on the wing*; hardly a single traveler. 誰も旅をしていなかった. まず一人の旅人もいなかった.

3 立ち去ろうとして, 出発しようとして ▪ Look you, they are already *on the wing.* 気をつけてください, 彼らはもう立ち去ろうとしています ▪ The squad was *on the wing* for Namibia last Saturday. チームは先週の土曜にナミビアへ出発しようとしていた.

on the wings of the wind 風の翼に乗って, 迅速に (《聖》 *Ps.* 18. 10) ▪ The foe seems to come and go *on the wings of the wind.* 敵は風の翼に乗って行き来するように思われる ▪ You travel *on the wings of the wind.* 君は迅速に旅をするのだね.

on wings (心も浮々と)足も軽やかに ▪ Gerard went home *on wings.* ジェラードは足どりも軽く家に帰った.

show the wings (平時の訪問旅行によって)空軍力を誇示する ▪ The U.S. Air Force *showed the wings* in Seoul. 米空軍はソウルで空軍力を誇示した.

singe one's wings →SINGE one's feathers.

spread* [*stretch*] *one's wings **1** 活動[関心]を広げる; 能力を伸ばす ▪ You must *spread your wings* a bit. 少し関心を広げなければだめだ.

2 (生まれて初めて)わくわくする生活を始める, 羽を伸ばす ▪ The kids had all left home and I thought it was time to *spread my wings.* 子供たちも家を出

W

たことだし，少し人生を楽しんでもよい頃かなと思った．

sprout wings **1** 羽化する ▪ One butterfly after another *sprouted wings* and fluttered away. チョウが次々に羽化して，飛んでいった．
2 天使のような性格になる ▪ He seems almost to have *sprouted wings* lately. 彼は最近天使のような性格になったと言えるくらいだ．

take to itself wings (金などが)羽がはえたように飛び去る ▪ My cigarette case must have *taken to itself wings*. 私のシガレットケースは羽がはえて消えたんだ，きっと．

take ... under *one's* ***wing*** →under the WING of.

take wing 飛び去る，立ち[逃げ]去る ▪ Success, like Fame, has *taken wing*. 成功は名声と同様に飛び去った ▪ Fame is a vapor and money *takes wing*. 名声は蒸気のように消えていき，金銭は羽がはえて逃げていく．

take wings 急速に進捗する ▪ From that day on the excavation *took wings*. その日から発掘は大いに進捗した．

try *one's* ***wing(s)*** 腕を試してみる ▪ He began to *try his wings* as a musician. 彼は音楽家として腕を試してみ始めた．

under the wing of …にかばわれて; をかばって ▪ I have been brought up *under my mother's wing*. 私は母にかばわれて育ってきた ▪ I took him *under my wing*. 私は彼を保護してやった．☞鳥がひなを羽の下にかばうことから．

wait [stand] in the wings (後継者として)控えている ▪ The president is getting old, but fortunately there are several younger men *waiting in the wings*. 社長は年をとってきたが，幸い年下の後継者が何人か控えている ▪ Many younger tennis players were *standing in the wings* behind him. 多くの若いテニス選手が彼のあとに控えていた．☞wings「(観客からは見えない)舞台の袖」で俳優が出番を待つことから．

wing[2] /wɪŋ/ 動 ***wing it*** 《口》即興でする ▪ Do you have a plan or are you going to *wing it*? 何か用意してあるのか，それとも即興でやるつもりか．

wing *one's* ***way [flight]*** 飛んで行く ▪ The parting year prepares to *wing its way*. 去りゆく年は飛んで行く準備をする ▪ The week had nearly *winged its flight* away. その週はほとんど飛ぶように過ぎて行った．

wink[1] /wɪŋk/ 名 ***A nod is as good as a wink (to a blind horse).*** →NOD[1].

(as) quick as a wink →as QUICK as lightning.

forty winks 《口》(特に食後の)うたた寝 (nap) ▪ He took [had] *forty winks* after dinner. 彼は夕食後うたた寝をした．

get the wink 目くばせを受ける ▪ She's *got the wink*, the smile, and the thumbs up. 彼女は目配せと微笑みと親指を立てた承諾のジェスチャーを受けた．

in a wink 瞬く間に，たちまち ▪ He was gone *in a wink*. 彼は瞬く間に行ってしまった．

not a [one] wink 一睡もしない ▪ She did *not* sleep *a wink* last night. 彼女はゆうべ一晩中まんじりともしなかった ▪ I did *not* get *a wink* of sleep. 私は一睡もしなかった．

tip [give] *a person* ***the wink*** 《英》 **1** 人に目くばせする ▪ I only *tip* him *the wink*, and he understands. 彼に目くばせさえすればわかってくれる ▪ He *gave* me *the wink* that the lady was a friend of his. 彼は私に目くばせしてその女性が彼の友人であることを教えた．
2 人にひそかに知らせる ▪ If you hear of anything about him, just *tip* me *the wink*. もし彼のことを耳にしたら，こっそり教えてくれ．

wink[2] /wɪŋk/ 動 ***wink the other eye*** 《俗》鼻であしらう ▪ Policemen and other matter-of-fact persons *winked the other eye* when the UFO was mentioned. 警察官と他の事務的な連中は未確認飛行物体の話が出たとき鼻であしらった．

winking /wíŋkɪŋ/ 名 ***as easy as winking*** (まばたきすることぐらいに)実に容易に ▪ She'll make a hundred and fifty pounds a week *as easy as winking*. 彼女は週150ポンド儲けるなど朝飯前だ．

in the winking of an eye = in the TWINKLING of an eye.

like winking 瞬く間に; ひどく ▪ He can sum up *like winking*. 彼は瞬く間に合計することができる ▪ Both my legs began to bend *like winking*. 私の両足はひどく曲がり始めた．

winner /wínər/ 名 ***on to [onto] a winner*** 《口》金のなる木を見つけて ▪ I realized I was *on to a winner* when I first saw him box. 彼がボクシングをするのを初めて見たとき，金のなる木を見つけたことが分かった ▪ He is the sole importer of the product, and he thinks he's *onto a winner*. その製品の輸入は自分だけなので，彼は金の卵をつかんだと思っている．

pick a [the] winner 《口》えりすぐりのものを当てる[選ぶ] ▪ Since all three are similarly pricey, it's difficult to *pick a winner*. 3機種とも同じように価格が高いので，どれを選べばいいのか難しい．

wipe[1] /waɪp/ 名 ***fetch*** *a person* ***a wipe/ fetch [take] a wipe at*** *a person* 《俗》人にぴしゃりと一つくらわす ▪ He used to *fetch* me *a wipe* with his stick. あいつはいつもステッキでおれをぴしゃりとなぐったものだ．

give ... a wipe …をぬぐう ▪ *Give* this plate *a wipe* with cloth. この皿を布巾でぬぐいなさい．

wipe[2] /waɪp/ 動 ***wipe*** *one's* ***boots on*** …にこの上ない侮辱を加える ▪ He has often *wiped his boots on* a man. 彼は人にこの上ない侮辱を加えたことが何度もあった．

wipe *one's* ***eyes*** 涙をぬぐう ▪ She *wiped her eyes* with her hand. 彼女は手で涙をぬぐった．

wipe *one's* ***hands [lips] of*** …と手を切る ▪ I was determined to *wipe my hands of* it. 私はそれと手を切る決心をしていた．

wipe off (old) scores →clear a SCORE.

wipe ... off the face of the earth →FACE[1].

wipe the eye of *a person* →wipe a person's EYE.

wipe the [***that***] ***smile*** [***grin***] ***off*** *a person's* ***face*** →FACE[1].

wiped out 酔っ払って ▪ Last night I was *wiped out*. ゆうべ僕は酔っ払っていた.

wire /waɪər/ 名 ***a live wire*** **1** 電流の通じている電線 ▪ He was severely burned by the *live wire*. 彼は裸電線に触れて大やけどをしてしまった.

2 《口》活発な人, 活動家 ▪ We need several salespeople who are *live wires*. わが社には元気のよい販売係が数人必要だ.

be (***all***) ***on wires*** 興奮して, いらいらして ▪ I *was all on wires* that time. 私はそのとき興奮していた.

by wire 電報で ▪ Let me know *by wire*. 電報で知らせてください.

cross the wire 競争を終える[やめる], ゴールインする ▪ We couldn't tell who the winner was until they *crossed the wire*. 勝負がつくまでどちらが勝つかわからなかった.

down to the wire 《米俗》 **1** 締め切りに近づいて ▪ He is *down to the wire* on his term paper. 彼は期末レポートの締め切りが近づいている.

2 金が底をついて ▪ He hasn't eaten anything since morning. He's *down to the wire*. 彼はけさから何も食べていない. 財布がからっぽなのだ.

get under the wire of 《米口》(部類)に入れられるに値する ▪ They may just *get under the wire of* the above definitions. 彼らはやっと上記の定義に入れられるに値する.

get [***have***] *one's* ***wires crossed*** 《口》 = get the LINEs crossed.

lay wires for 《米口》...の準備をする ▪ Woodruff began to *lay wires for* the coming senatorial vacancy. ウッドラフは次の上院議員の空席への準備をし始めた.

on another wire 他の電話で話し中 ▪ He is busy *on another wire*. 彼は他の電話に出ている.

pull [***move***] (***the***) ***wires*** 《口》(特に政治的に)糸を引く, 陰であやつる ▪ He was perfectly aware who *moved the wires*. 彼は誰が糸を引いているかよく知っていた ▪ He may practically *pull the wires* of a President. 彼は事実上会長を陰であやつるかもしれない. ☞あやつり人形から.

under the wire 《米》 **1** 決勝線の所で ▪ The third horse *under the wire* was placed second after they disqualified the winner. 優勝馬が失格となって3着の馬が2着に繰り上がった.

2 締め切り間ぎわに; いよいよという時になって ▪ He paid his taxes just *under the wire*. 彼はいよいよという時になって税金を払った.

under wire 《米》鉄条網をめぐらして[た] ▪ The house is all *under wire*. その家はぐるりと鉄条網をめぐらしている.

wireless /wáɪərləs/ 名 ***by wireless*** 無電で ▪ A message was sent *by wireless*. 無電でメッセージが送られた.

listen to the wireless 《英》ラジオを聞く ▪ I was up *listening to the wireless*. 私は起きてラジオを聞いていた. ☞今ではイギリスでも radio の方が普通.

on [***over***] ***the wireless*** 《英》ラジオで(聞く, 話す, 歌うなど) ▪ I listened to baseball *on the wireless*. ラジオで野球の試合を聞いた ▪ He speaks occasionally in lecture halls or *over the wireless*. 彼はときどき講堂やラジオで講演する.

wisdom /wízdəm/ 名 ***conventional*** [***received***] ***wisdom*** 一般に正しいとされている通念 ▪ *Conventional wisdom* has it that riots only happen in big cities. 一般には暴動は大都会にしか起きないと考えられている ▪ The *conventional wisdom* is that marriage makes a relationship more secure. 昔からの通念では結婚によって絆はいっそう固まるとされている.

cut *one's* ***wisdom teeth*** (通例20歳以上になって)知恵歯がはえる; 分別のつく年齢になる ▪ He has not *cut his wisdom teeth* yet. 彼はまだ分別のつく年齢になっていない.

in *one's* (***infinite***) ***wisdom*** 《戯》自分だけの判断で, よく考えもせずに ▪ He tends to act *in his wisdom*. 彼はあまり考えずに行動しがちだ ▪ The council, *in their wisdom*, have decided to close the public library. 委員会が勝手に公共図書館を閉鎖すると決めた.

wise[1] /waɪz/ 形 ***a wise***(-)***guy***/ 《米卑》 ***a wise***(-)***ass*** 《米口》知ったかぶりの男, 思い上がった[生意気な]やつ ▪ He's just some *wise-ass* who thinks he knows everything. やつは何でも知っていると思い上がったどこかの馬の骨だ ▪ Okay, *wise guy*, what do you think we should do then? わかったよ, うぬぼれ屋さん, だったら僕たちはどうしたらいいと思う?

A wise man changes his mind sometimes, a fool never. 《諺》賢者はときとして考えを変えるが, 愚者は決して変えない,「君子は豹(ひょう)変す」.

a word to the wise (***is sufficient***) → WORD.

(***as***) ***wise as an owl*** 非常に賢い, とても賢明な ▪ Grandad knows many things. He is *as wise as an owl*. うちのじいちゃんはいろんなことを知っている. すごく賢い. ☞フクロウはギリシャ神話の女神アテナおよびローマ神話のミネルバの象徴(emblem).

as wise as before 以前と同じく何も知らずに ▪ They came again *as wise as before*. 彼らは相変わらずわからずに戻ってきた.

(***as***) ***wise as Solomon*** →SOLOMON.

(***be***) ***none the wiser*** [***no wiser***]/ ***not*** (***be***) ***any the wiser*** **1** 相変わらずわからない ▪ I've read the instructions, but I'm still *none the wiser*. 説明書を読んだがやっぱりわからない ▪ I was *none the wiser* for his explanation. 彼の説明を聞いても少しもわからなかった ▪ He came away *none the wiser*. 彼はやはりわからずに帰ってきた.

2 (悪事に)気づかない ▪ If only you put the money back, *nobody* will *be any the wiser*. 金をそっと返

しておきさえすれば誰にも気うかれまい.

be wise after the event (人が)事のあとで気うく, 下司(げす)のあと知恵で ▪ It's no good *being wise after the event.* あと知恵は何の役にも立たない.

be [***get***] ***wise to*** [***on***] 《口》 …を知っている[知る] ▪ I *am wise to* your game. その手は食わない ▪ Dealers *got wise to* the trend and increased their prices accordingly. 販売業者はその流行を察知し, それに応じて売値を上げた.

get wise with 《米俗》 …となれなれしくなる ▪ Has he ever tried to *get wise with* you? 彼はあなたとねんごろになろうとしたことがありますか.

put *a person* ***wise*** 《米俗》 …を人に知らせてやる (*to, on*) ▪ Didn't he *put* you *wise to* me? 彼が僕のことを君に知らせなかったかい.

Where ignorance is bliss, 'tis folly to be wise. →IGNORANCE.

wise after the event (下司(げす)の)あと知恵 ▪ It's easy to be *wise after the event.* あと知恵はわけなくつく.

worldly wise 世故にたけて ▪ He appears *worldly wise.* 彼は世故にたけているようだ.

wise[2] /waɪz/ 名 ***in any wise*** どうしても ▪ This road is *in any wise* necessary. この道路はどうしても必要である.

in like wise 同じように ▪ I shall pray for you *in like wise.* 私も同じようにあなたのために祈りましょう.

(***in***) ***no wise*** 決して…ない ▪ He is *in no wise* a gentleman. 彼はどう見ても紳士ではない ▪ To tell lies will *in no wise* help you. 嘘を言うのは決してためにならないよ.

in some wise どうにか; どこか ▪ The father's love was changed *in some wise.* 父親の愛情がどこか変わった.

(***in***) ***this wise*** このように ▪ The birth of Jesus was *in this wise.* イエスはこのようにして誕生した ▪ He soon arranged it *this wise.* 彼はやがてそれを次のように手配した.

wish[1] /wɪʃ/ 名 ***a wish list*** 願い事のリスト[一覧] ▪ Families with kids have a larger house on their *wish list.* 子供のいる家庭が望むものの中にはもっと広い家が挙げられる.

at *one's* ***own wish*** 自分の希望で ▪ He went there *at his own wish.* 彼は自分の希望でそこへ行った.

one's ***best wishes*** 祝福のあいさつ ▪ Please accept *my best wishes* for your happiness. ご幸福をお祈りいたします ▪ Please send her *my best wishes.* 彼女によろしくお伝えください.

carry out [***attend to, further***] *a person's* ***wishes*** 人の希望に添う ▪ I am sorry I cannot *further your wishes.* お気の毒ですが, ご希望に添いかねます.

get *one's* ***wish*** 望むものを得る ▪ He *got his wish* at long last. 彼はとうとう望むものを得た.

good wishes 好意 ▪ You have our *good wishes.* ご幸福[ご成功]を祈っています.

If wishes were horses, beggars would ride. 《諺》 願望が馬なら物乞いも乗ろう,「とかく浮き世はままならぬ」.

The wish is father to the thought. 《諺》 望みは考えの父である《そうあれかしと願っているとやがて願い通りになると思うようになる》.

to *one's* ***wish***(***es***) 望み通りに ▪ The people were rewarded *to their wish.* 人々は望み通りに報いられた.

Your wish is my command! 《口・戯》 なんなりとご希望通りにいたします ▪ What would you like me to do for you next? *Your wish is my command.* 次に何をしてさしあげましょうか. お望み通りにいたします ▪ Put the kettle on.—*Your wish is my command.* やかんを火にかけて—かしこまりました.

wish[2] /wɪʃ/ 動 ***couldn't wish for a more*** [***better,*** etc.] ***…*** これ以上の[これほどすぐれた]…は望めないだろう, (望める限りで)最高の…である ▪ You *couldn't wish for a better* friend. 彼[女]に勝る親友は得られまい ▪ We *could not have wished for a more pleasant* holiday. あれ以上楽しい休暇は望めなかっただろう.

I [***You***] ***wish!*** 《口》 そうなればいいと思っているが, だったらいいのに ▪ You seem to have lost considerable weight.—*I wish!* ずいぶん体重が減ったようね—そうならいいけど ▪ Do you think I'll make it?—*You wish!* 私, うまくいくかしら—そうだったらいいね.

I wish I had a pound [***shilling, dollar***] ***for every*** …はなんてたくさんだろう ▪ *I wish I had a shilling for every* book on these shelves. このたなにはなんてたくさんの本があるのだろう ▪ *I wish I had a pound for every* time I've heard him say that. 何回彼がそう言うのを聞いたことだろう.

it is to be wished (***that***) …は望ましい[願わしい]ことだ ▪ *It is to be wished that* the war would soon be over. 戦争が早く終わることが望ましい.

(***just***) ***as you wish*** 《主に英・文》 あなたの望み通りに ▪ We can meet at my place or yours, *as you wish.* 私の家とお宅とどちらでお会いしてもよろしい, あなたの望み次第で.

wish … at the bottom of the sea …が海底のもくずになればいいと思う; どこへでも行ってしまえと願う ▪ I *wished* both magazine and review *at the bottom of the sea.* 雑誌も批評も消えてしまえと願った.

wish *oneself* ***dead*** [***home, at home***] 死んでいたら[帰宅していたら, 家にいたら]と思う ▪ He *wished himself dead.* 彼は自分が死んでいたらと思った ▪ I *wished myself home* again. また家に帰れたらと思った.

wish evil →WISH well.

wish *a person* ***further*** [***farther, at the devil***] 《口》 人が早く行ってしまえばいいのにと思う ▪ Whenever I see him, I could *wish* him *at the devil!* 彼に会うといつでも, 早く行っちまえばいいと思う.

wish *a person* ***happy*** 人が幸福であることを望む ▪ We all *wish* her very *happy.* 私たちはみな彼女が

W

とても幸福であることを望んでいる.

wish ill →WISH well.

wish *a person* ***to*** *do* 人に…してもらいたいと望む ▪ Do you really *wish* me *to* go? ほんとに私に行ってほしいのですか.

wish to God [***goodness, heaven***] …ということを心から願う ▪ I *wish to heaven* I did. ほんとにそうすればよかったのになあ ▪ I *wish to God* I were now in London. 今ロンドンにいたら実によいのだが.

wish well [***ill, evil***] 《文》幸福を祈る[不幸であれとのろう] (*to*) ▪ He *wished well to* all men. 彼はあらゆる人の幸福を祈っていた ▪ I *wish* you *well* in your new job. あなたが新しい仕事でうまくいくように祈っている ▪ She said she *wished* nobody *ill*. 彼女は誰の不幸も願っていないと言った.

Wish you were here. あなたもこちらへ来ていたらいいのに《旅先からのあいさつ》 ▪ Enjoying our holidays. *Wish you were here* with us. Love from Vicky. 私たち休暇を満喫しています. あなたもいっしょならいいのに. ヴィッキーより.

wouldn't wish … on *one's* ***worst enemy*** 《口》…を誰にも体験させたくない, どんな憎いやつにも押しつけたくない ▪ I *wouldn't wish* a terrible job like that *on my worst enemy*. あんなひどい仕事は誰にもさせたくない.

wishful /wíʃfəl/ 形 (***be***) ***wishful to*** *do* [***for***] …したいと[…を]望んでいる ▪ I *was wishful to* say a word to you, sir. あなたに一言お話ししたいと思っていました ▪ I dwell here alone *wishful for* happy days. 私はしあわせな日を望んでここに一人で住んでいる.

wishful thinking 希望的観測 ▪ That line of thought is *wishful thinking*. そのような考え方は希望的観測だ. ☞Freud の心理学から.

wishing /wíʃɪŋ/ 名 ***can*** [***may***] ***be got*** [***had***] ***for the wishing*** 望むままに得られる ▪ Nothing valuable *may be had for the wishing*. 望みさえすれば得られるものにろくなものはない.

wit[1] /wɪt/ 名 ***at*** *one's* ***wits' end*** 途方にくれて (《聖》*Ps.* 107. 27) ▪ The two ladies are quite *at their wits' end*. 二人の女性は全く途方にくれている.

bring [***drive, put***] *a person* ***to*** *his* ***wits' end*** **1** 人を途方にくれさせる ▪ The task *drove* me *to my wits' end*. その仕事には途方にくれた ▪ You've *brought* him *to his wits' end*. あなたは彼を途方にくれさせてしまった.

2 人を憤激させる ▪ The child *drives* me *to my wits' end*. その子供には全く腹が立つ.

collect [***gather***] *one's* ***wits*** (驚き・ショックの後で)気持ちを落ち着ける ▪ I must *gather my wits* a bit before I act. 行動する前に少し気持ちを落ち着けなければならない.

frighten [***scare***] *a person* ***out of*** *his* ***wits*** 人を気も狂うほどびっくり仰天させる, 人の正気を失わせる ▪ Don't shout so suddenly—you *scared* me *out of my wits*! そんなにだしぬけに大声を出すな. たまげるではないか ▪ The governor *was frightened out of his wits*. 知事はびっくり仰天した.

have quick [***slow***] ***wits*** 機転がきく[きかない] ▪ I'm looking for a kind person who *has quick wits*. 機転のきく優しい人物を探している ▪ A good softball fielder *has quick wits*. ソフトボールのうまい野手はとっさの判断ができる ▪ They are first-rate people even if they *have slow wits*. 機転はきかなくても彼らは飛び切りの人物だ.

have the wit to *do* …するだけの分別がある ▪ But they *had the wit to* recall him. しかし彼らは彼を呼び戻すだけの分別があった.

have [***keep, need***] *one's* ***wits about*** *one* 抜け目がない; (まさかの場合などに)度を失わない ▪ One needs to *have one's wits about* one in crossing a street in London. ロンドンの通りを横切るときには抜け目なくしなくてはならない ▪ You *need your* sharpest *wits about* you driving in New York. ニューヨークで運転するときは細心の注意が必要だ.

in *one's* (***right***) ***wits*** 正気で ▪ It is impossible for a person *in his wits* to do such a thing. 正気な人にはそんなことはとてもできない.

live by [***on***] *one's* ***wits*** (一定の生業(なりわい)がなく)小才を働かせて[やりくりで]どうにか暮らす; 巧みに一時しのぎする ▪ He is *living by his wits* as the saying goes. 彼はいわゆる小才を働かして暮らしている ▪ He had no job and was *living by his wits*. 彼は仕事がなく, やりくりでどうにかしのいでいた.

match wits with …と張り合う, 知恵くらべする ▪ I managed to *match wits with* the chess player. 私はチェスの相手とどうにか張り合えた.

measure *one's* ***wits*** (***against …***) (…と)知恵比べをする ▪ I have *measured my wits against* theirs. 私は彼らと知恵比べをした.

pit *one's* ***wits against*** 《英》(頭を使って)…と競う[戦う], …を打ち負かそうと知恵を絞る ▪ You *pit your wits against* the computer in a computer chess game. コンピューター・チェスのゲームではコンピューターを相手に知恵を絞る ▪ That's the pleasure of fishing—*pitting your wits against* these clever fish. それが—賢い魚たちと知恵比べをする—釣りの醍醐味(だいごみ)だ.

put *a person* ***to his wits' end*** →bring a person to his WITs' end.

set *one's* ***wits to work*** 注意深く考え始める ▪ You'd better *set your wits to work* at once. 君はすぐ注意深く考え始めたほうがいい.

the wit of man 人知 ▪ It is past *the wit of man* to know the beginning of the universe. 宇宙の始まりを知ることは人知の及ばぬことだ.

wit[2] /wɪt/ 動 ***to wit*** 《主に法》すなわち ▪ In certain degrees of heat, *to wit*, at thirty-three degrees of Fahrenheit's, water is always fluid. ある一定の温度, すなわち華氏33度では, 水は常に液状である.

witch /wɪtʃ/ 名 ***a white witch*** (人の幸福のためにのみ力を行使する)善魔女 ▪ When he had warts or burns, he went to the *white witch* at Northam to charm them away. 彼はいぼややけど跡ができ

ると, ノーサムの善魔女の所へ行ってまじないで取ってもらった.

a witch-hunt 反体制の人への迫害 ▪ He was engaged in *a witch-hunt* against communists after the war. 戦後彼は赤狩りに携わっていた. ☞中世の魔女狩りから.

an old witch 《軽蔑》意地悪[くそ]ばばあ ▪ The owner of the shop is *an old witch.* あそこの店主は意地悪ばばあだ.

(as) cold as [colder than] a witch's tit 《口》とても寒い[冷たい] ▪ It's *as cold as a witch's tit* here in February. 当地では2月は非常に寒い ▪ She gave me a look *colder than a witch's tit.* 彼女はとても冷ややかな眼差しを私に向けた.

(as) nervous as a witch ひどくそわそわして ▪ He's *nervous as a witch.* He can't keep still a minute. 彼はひどくそわそわしている. 1分もじっとしていられない.

The witch is in it. それは妖術にかけられているのだ ▪ She said aloud to herself, "Well, *the witch is in it.*" 彼女は「やれやれ, これは妖術にかけられているのだ」と独り言を言った.

witching /wítʃɪŋ/ 形 ***the witching time of night/the witching hour*** (魔物の横行する)丑(うし)三つどき, 真夜中 (cf. Sh., *Haml.* 3. 2. 406) ▪ It draws near to *the witching time of night.* もう丑三つどきに近い ▪ It's already past *the witching hour.* もう真夜中過ぎだ.

with /wɪθ/ 前 ***get with it*** 〚命令文で〛てきぱきやる ▪ Wake up and *get with it.* 目をさましててきぱきやれ.

hot [warm, cold] with 《俗》砂糖を入れた熱い[温かい, 冷たい]酒 (→cold WITHOUT) ▪ Take a glass of brandy.—*Hot with*? ブランデーを1杯やれ—砂糖を入れた熱いやつかい.

I'm with you on that./I'm with you, pal. (それについては)その通りだ ▪ It seems like a waste of time.—*I'm with you on that.* 時間のむだのようだな—僕もそう思う.

not with it **1** モダンでない; 頭が古い ▪ Trouble with my father is, he is *not with it.* 父のまずいところは頭が古い点だ.

2 ものわかりがよくない, てきぱきやって[集中して]いない ▪ Jack's *not with it* yet. He's only just recovered from the anesthetic. ジャックはまださっさとできない. 麻酔から覚めたばかりだから ▪ What's the matter? You're *not with it* today. どうしたんだ. 今日は注意散漫だが.

with all →ALL.

with it 《口》 **1** ものわかりがよい; てきぱきやって, 集中して ▪ You are really *with it* today, girls. みなさん, 今日はてきぱきやっていますね.

2 (服装・考え方などが)現代的で. 進んでいる ▪ My uncle is middle-aged, but quite *with it.* おじは中年だがなかなかモダンだ.

3 その上 ▪ This book is very interesting—instructive *with it.* この本はとてもおもしろい—その上ためにもなる.

With or without? (コーヒー・紅茶に)砂糖やミルクを入れますか, 入れませんか ▪ How do you like your coffee? *With or without?* コーヒーのお好みは? 何か入れましょうか, それともブラック?

with that そう言って ▪ *With that* he went away. そう言って彼は立ち去った.

with this こう言って, ここにおいて ▪ And *with this* I bid you farewell. ではこれでお別れします.

withdraw /wɪðdrɔ́ː/ 動 ***withdraw into*** *oneself* 自分の中に閉じこもる ▪ Mary hates parties and is apt to *withdraw into herself.* メアリーはパーティーが大嫌いで, 自分の殻に閉じこもりがちだ.

within /wɪðín/ 前副名 ***from within*** 内部から (↔ from WITHOUT) ▪ The door opens *from within.* そのドアは内側から開く ▪ Seen *from within,* the cave looks larger. 内部から見ると, そのほら穴は大きく見える.

within *oneself* **1** 全力を傾けずに, 力を出し切らないで ▪ They are rowing quite *within themselves.* 彼らは全く余裕しゃくしゃくとボートをこいでいる.

2 〚say, think などを伴って〛心の中で ▪ He laughed *within himself.* 彼は心の中で笑った ▪ I prayed *within myself* for her. 私はひそかに彼女のために祈った.

within and without 内外ともに ▪ His house is clean *within and without.* 彼の家は内外ともにきれいだ.

without /wɪðáʊt/ 前副名 ***cannot*** *do A* ***without*** *doing B* →CAN³.

cold without 《俗》砂糖を入れない冷たい酒 (→hot WITH) ▪ There was punch, *cold without,* etc. ポンチや砂糖を入れない冷たい酒などがあった.

from without 外部から (↔ from WITHIN) ▪ Help came *from without.* 助けは外部から来た ▪ The door opened *from without.* ドアは外から開いた.

not without 多少...ないでもなく ▪ *Nor* were we *without* guests. またお客もなきにしもあらずだった ▪ She remembered it *not without* a pang. 彼女はそれを思い出して苦痛をおぼえないわけではなかった.

not [never] *do A* ***without*** *doing B* Aすれば必ずBする ▪ I *never* see you *without thinking* of my brother. 私はあなたを見ると必ず弟を思い出します.

those (that [who] are) without 局外者, 他の社会などの人 (《聖》*1 Cor.* 5. 12) ▪ The secrets of my trade are not to be communicated to *those who are without.* 私の商売の秘訣は局外者に伝えることはできない.

without wanting [wishing] to *do* (批判めいた話題を切り出す前に, 発言を弱めて)...しないといいのだが, したくないのだが ▪ *Without wanting to* sound dismissive, you seem to be in the wrong. 生意気に聞こえなければいいのだが, どうも君は間違っているようだ ▪ *Without wishing to* offend you, you have no idea what you are talking about. 君の感情を害したくはないんだが, 君は自分が言っていることが分かっていない.

witless /wítləs/ 形 ***be scared* [*bored*] *witless*** 《口》 怖くて肝がつぶれ[退屈で気が狂い]そうになる ▪I *was scared witless* when I first arrived in New York. はじめてニューヨークに着いたとき, 恐ろしくて度肝を抜かれた.

witness[1] /wítnəs/ 名 ***be a witness to*** …の証拠である ▪My clothes *are a witness to* my poverty. 私の衣服を見れば貧しさがおわかりでしょう.

be witness to …を目撃する ▪I have *been* twenty times *witness to* that. 私はそれを20回も目のあたりに見た.

bear* [*take*] *false witness 虚偽の証言をする ▪She came to *bear false witness* in her sister's cause. 彼女は妹のために虚偽の証言をしにやって来た.

bear** a person **witness 人の証人となる, 人の言ったことを証明する ▪He *bears* me *witness* that I never said that. 私がそんなことを言わなかったことは彼が証人になってくれている.

bear* [*give*] *witness to …の証言をする, 証拠となる ▪I can *bear witness to* his innocence. 彼の無実を証言することができる ▪Your compassion *bears witness to* your noble spirit. あなたのご同情はあなたが高潔な精神の持ち主である証拠です ▪They all *gave witness to* the popularity of this man. 彼らはこぞってこの人物の人望を証言した.

call* [*take*]*… to witness …に証人に立ってもらう ▪He *took* his neighbors *to witness* that he was weaving. 彼は近所の人たちを証人に立てて, 自分は織工であると言った.

give witness on behalf of …のために証言する ▪He *gave witness on behalf of* the accused person at his trial. 彼は裁判で被告のために証言した.

God is my witness 神も照覧あれ ▪*God is my witness*, there's no spite in me. 神も照覧あれ, 私には悪意はありません.

***in witness of* [*hereof, whereof*]** …の[その]あかしとして ▪*In witness whereof* I have hereunto set my seal. そのあかしとして私はここに署名押印する.

take false witness →bear false WITNESS.

take … to witness →call … to WITNESS.

with a witness 明白に, 確かに ▪At night, it blew great guns, *with a witness*. 夜確かに大風が吹いた.

witness[2] /wítnəs/ 動 ***(as) witness*** その証拠としては, たとえば ▪I am innocent, *(as) witness* my poverty. 私は潔白だ, 貧乏しているのがその証拠だ ▪Novels offer nothing new; *(as) witness* every month's review. 小説にはなんら新味がない. たとえば毎月の批評を見よ.

wobbler /wábələr|wɔ́b-/ 名 ***throw a wobbler*** →throw a WOBBLY.

wobbly /wábli|wɔ́b-/ 名 ***throw a wobbly* [*wobbler*]** 《英口》 突然興奮する, 急に怒りで逆上する ▪She *threw a wobbly* when she found him reading her diary. 彼が自分の日記を読んでいるところを見つけて彼女はカッとなった.

woe /wou/ 間副名 ***in weal and woe*** →WEAL.

woe be to 《主に詩・戯》 …に災いあれ, は災いなるかな ▪*Woe be to* him that reads but one book. 《諺》 一冊の書物しか読まない者に災いあれ.

woe betide you* [etc.] *if 《口》 …なら困ったことになるだろう ▪*Woe betide you if* you do it without my permission. 私の許可なしにそんなことをしたら, 困ったことになるぞ.

***Woe is him* [*the day*].** 《主に詩・戯》 彼[この日]はのろわれてあれ ▪*Woe is him* whose bed is made in hell. 地獄に床を持つ人はのろわれてあれ ▪Thou art welcome—yet *woe is the day*! よくおいでくださいました—しかし, この日はのろわしいかな.

Woe is me. 《口》 ああ悲しいかな ▪*Woe is me* if I preach not the gospel. 福音を説かないとすれば, ああ悲しいかな ▪Now *woe worth me* but I feared it! ああ悲しいことだ. でもこうなるのを恐れていた.

wolf[1] /wulf/ 名 ***a wolf in sheep's clothing* [*in a lamb's skin*]** ヒツジの皮をかぶったオオカミ; 温順を装った危険な人物 (《聖》 *Matt.* 7. 15) ▪What have we here then? *A wolf in a lamb's skin*? ではここにいるのは誰だろう. 温順を装った危険な人物なのか. ☞イソップ寓話から.

(a) wolf-whistle **1** 〚名詞的に〛 (通りを行く)魅力的な女性の注意を惹くために男性が吹く口笛 ▪They both gave *a wolf-whistle* at the pretty young girl in hot pants. 二人ともホットパンツのかわいい女の子に向かって口笛をヒュッと鳴らした ▪You'll get a few *wolf-whistles* if you walk through town in such a miniskirt. そんなミニスカ姿で通りを歩いたら何度か口笛を吹かれるぞ.

2 《英》 〚動詞的に〛 (魅力的な女性に対して)口笛を吹く ▪I *was wolf-whistled* by a group of youngsters as I crossed the street. 通りを歩いていると若者の一団に口笛を吹かれた.

(as) greedy* [*hungry*] *as a wolf (オオカミのように)あくまで貪欲で[空腹で] ▪I'm *as hungry as a wolf*; run, or I shall eat thee! 私はひどく空腹だ. 逃げないと, 食べてしまうぞ.

cry wolf オオカミが出たと叫ぶ; 虚報を伝える ▪Politicians often *cry wolf* in order to obscure the real dangers that exist. 政治家は現にある本当の危険をぼかすためによく虚報を伝える. ☞イソップ寓話から.

have* [*hold, take*] *a wolf by the ears 危険な立場に立つ, 進退きわまる ▪I *have a wolf by the ears*; what shall I do? 私は危険な立場に立っている. どうしたらいいだろう.

have a wolf in the** [one's] **stomach ひどくひもじい; 猛烈に食欲がある ▪A growing youth *has a wolf in his stomach*. 《諺》 育ち盛りの若者の胃袋の中にはオオカミがいる《育ち盛りの少年は食欲旺盛である》.

howl with the wolves 有力者に賛同する ▪The Church never *howled with the wolves*. 教会は権力者に決して迎合しなかった.

keep the wolf from the door 《口》 飢えをしのぐ ▪Our wages are just enough to *keep the* *wolf from the door.* 我々の賃金では飢えをしのぐのが精いっぱいだ.

see* [*have seen*] *a wolf 口がきけなくなる ▪ Why is she mute?—Perhaps she *has seen a wolf.* なぜ彼女は黙っているんだ?—たぶん口がきけなくなったのだろうよ. ☞オオカミを見ると, 口がきけなくなるという古い言い伝えから.

take a wolf by the ears →have a WOLF by the ears.

the big bad wolf 性悪のオオカミ《脅威となる人・物》 ▪ A rumor of war was *the big bad wolf* at that time. 戦争になる噂が当時人々をおびえさせていた.

the wolf is at the door 飢餓に瀕する ▪ At last *the wolf was at the door* and he was still unable to work. ついに飢餓に瀕するようになったが, 彼はまだ働くことができなかった.

throw to the wolves =throw ... to the LIONs.

To mention the wolf's name is to see the same. 《諺》 噂をすれば影(がさす).

ugly enough to tree a* (*barking, gray, white, she-, an early*) *wolf 《米口》 (オオカミも恐れて木に登ってしまうほど)恐ろしく不器量な ▪ She was small and *ugly enough to tree a wolf.* 彼女は小柄で恐ろしく不細工だった.

wake a sleeping wolf やぶをつついてヘビを出す ▪ Keep it so: *wake* not *a sleeping wolf.* そっとしておきなさい. やぶをつついてヘビを出さんことだ.

Ware wolves! オオカミ[危険]に気をつけろ ▪ The children cried out "*Ware wolves!*" as soon as the nurse came in sight. 子供たちは乳母(うば)の姿が見えるとすぐ, 「オオカミに気をつけろ」 とどなった.

wolf[2] /wʊlf/ 動 ***wolf it*** オオカミのようにふるまう ▪ He was *wolfing it* in Kaseem. 彼はカシームでオオカミのようにふるまっていた.

wolfy /wʊ́lfi/ 形 ***wolfy about the head and shoulders*** 《米口》 (西部の辺境開拓者のように)大ぼらを吹く ▪ Side to side, I'm ten feet wide. A bit *wolfy about the head and shoulders.* 僕の横幅は10フィートある. ちょっぴりほらが混じっているが.

woman /wʊ́mən/ 名 ***a loose woman*** ふしだらな女性, 身持ちの悪い女性 ▪ Keep away from that girl. She's *a loose woman.* あの娘に近寄るなよ. あれは身持ちが悪いからな.

a woman of pleasure →a man of PLEASURE.

a woman of the town →a man of the TOWN.

a woman of the world →a man of the WORLD.

A woman's place is in the home. 《諺》 女性は家にいて家事と子育てをすべきだ. ☞現代では古い概念とされる.

a woman's wit 女性の知恵《本能的な洞察力》 ▪ Make the door upon *a woman's wit,* and it will out at the casement. 女性の知恵を閉じこめれば窓から出てしまう.

***A woman's* [*Women's*] *work is never done* [*at an end*].** 《諺》 女性の仕事は決して終わりにならない《家事と子育てはいくらやってもきりがない》.

born of woman およそ人間に生まれた (cf. Sh., *Macb.* 4. 1. 80) ▪ No man *born of woman* is so strong. およそ人間に生まれた者でそんなに強い者はいない.

hide behind a woman's skirts 自分の責任を女性になすりつけ(て避け)ようとする ▪ I can't respect a man who tries to *hide behind a woman's skirts.* 女性に責任をなすりつけようとするような男を尊敬などできない.

little woman 少女; お嬢さん《呼びかけ》 ▪ Come in, *little woman,* and have some tea! お嬢さん, お入りになってお茶を召し上がれ!

make a woman of 《米》 (人)に女性の仕事をさせる ▪ We conquered you; we *made women of* you. 我々はお前たちを征服した. お前たちに女性の仕事をさせた. ☞女性の仕事に対する北米先住民の考えから.

make an honest woman of 《戯》 (関係した女性)を正式の妻とする, 相手が妊娠したため結婚する ▪ Hitler decided to *make an honest woman of* Eva just before both committed suicide. ヒトラーはエバと二人で自殺する直前に彼女を正妻に直す決心をした ▪ He has recently *made an honest woman of* his sweetheart. 彼は最近恋人とできちゃった婚をした.

one's ***old woman*** 妻, 細君 ▪ *His old woman* is in hospital. 彼の細君は入院している.

one's ***own woman*** 独立した判断と人格を持った女性 ▪ I'm *my own woman* and I choose my own friends. 私は自立した女性だから自分の友だちは自分で選びます.

play the woman (泣いたり怖がったりして)めめしいふるまいをする ▪ It's no use *playing the woman.* めめしいふるまいをしてもだめだ.

the new woman 新しい女性《男女同権などを唱道する》 ▪ *The new woman* is a little above him. 新しい女性は少々彼には理解できない.

the old woman **1** =one's old WOMAN.
2 女性の雇い主 ▪ My *old woman* is strict but nice to all her workers. 私の雇い主の女性は従業員全員に厳しいがよくもしてくれる.

the old women in the Cabinet 優柔不断な大臣連中 ▪ *The old women in the Cabinet* should resign. 優柔不断な大臣どもは辞職せよ.

the other woman →the OTHER man.

There's a woman in it. 《口》 この裏面には女がいる, 女を捜せ ▪ He realizes that *there's a woman in it* somewhere. 事件の陰のどこかに女がいると彼は気づいている.

womb /wu:m/ 名 ***from the womb to the tomb*** =from the CRADLE to the grave.

in the womb of time 未来に, 将来起こるべき ▪ The fulfilment of her destiny is *in the womb of time.* 彼女の運命の達成は将来起こるべきことだ ▪ It still lies *in the womb of time.* それはまだ後になってみなければわからない.

the fruit of the womb →the FRUIT of the

body.

wonder[1] /wʌ́ndər/ 名 ***a chinless wonder*** 《英口》上流階級のばか息子 ▪I am sick of the sight of *a chinless wonder* type. 上流階級のばか息子タイプときたら見るのもうんざりだ.

a nine* [*seven*] *days'* [*day*] *wonder →NINE.

a one-hit wonder ヒット曲1曲限りで消えてしまう流行歌手, 一発屋 ▪She proved to be a major star, not *a one-hit wonder*. 彼女は1曲のヒットだけで消える歌手ではなく, 花形スターとなった.

(*and*) *no* [*small*] *wonder* それも不思議ではない ▪He has got the prize, *and no wonder*. 彼がその賞を得たが, それもそのはずだ ▪He is ill, *and small wonder*. 彼は病気だが, それも当然だ.

and what wonder 不思議ではない ▪I was alarmed, *and what wonder*! 私は胆をつぶしたが, 無理もなかった.

do wonders →work WONDERs.

for a wonder 不思議にも ▪*For a wonder* he was not seasick. 不思議にも彼は船酔いしなかった.

hear* [*read, speak, talk*] *wonders 驚くべきことを聞く[読む, 語る, 話す] ▪They *talk wonders* of her beauty. 人は彼女の驚くべき美しさを噂している ▪I have *read wonders* of it. そのことについて驚くべきことを読みました.

in the name of wonder 〚疑問文を強調して〛一体全体 ▪What *in the name of wonder* do you mean? 一体全体それはどういう意味なのか ▪*In the name of wonder*, what's Caesar's purpose? 一体全体カエサルの目的は何なのか.

in wonder 驚いて, 驚嘆して ▪All looked on *in wonder*. みんなは驚きあきれて眺めていた.

it is a wonder*/*wonder it is 不思議なことだ (*that*) ▪*It is a wonder* there is no notice taken of it. それに全然注意が払われないとは不思議なことだ.

(*it is*) *no wonder* 少しも不思議ではない (*that, if*) ▪(*It is*) *no wonder* (*that*) he did not come. 彼が来なかったのは少しも不思議ではない ▪*It is* therefore *no wonder*, *if* he attempted many things. そこで彼がいろんなことを試みたとしても不思議ではない.

(*it is*) *small* [*little*] *wonder* (*that*) …はたいして不思議ではない ▪*Small wonder* (*that*) disease is domesticated there. そこに病気が巣くっているのはさしても不思議ではない.

perform wonders →work WONDERs.

read* [*speak, talk*] *wonders →hear WONDERs.

***the wonder is,* (*that*)** 不思議なことは…だ ▪*The wonder is, that* he did not come. 不思議なのは彼が来なかったことだ.

What wonder if…? …としても何の不思議があろうか ▪*What wonder if* he failed? 彼が失敗したとしても何の不思議があろうか.

what wonder, that …は不思議ではない ▪*What wonder, that* the scheme failed. その計画が失敗したのは不思議ではない.

wonder it is →it is a WONDER.

Wonders will never cease. 《皮肉》これは本当に驚いた ▪He's a general! Well, *wonders will never cease*. 彼が将軍だって! いやあ, これは実に驚いた.

work* [*do, perform*] *wonders 驚くべきことをする; 驚くほどうまくいく ▪My steward has really *done wonders*. うちの執事はほんとに驚くべきことをやってのけた ▪A change of medicine sometimes *works wonders*. 薬を変えると, ときどき驚くほどよくきくことがある.

wonder[2] /wʌ́ndər/ 動 ***be wondered at*** 不思議に思われる ▪It cannot *be wondered at* if he took such opportunities as offered. 彼が出てきた機会を利用したとしても不思議ではない.

***I shouldn't wonder* (*if*)** 《口》(…としても)驚きはしない ▪*I shouldn't wonder if* he did not understand what he was saying. 彼が自分の言っていることをわかっていないとしても驚きはしない.

I wonder **1**〚疑問文を伴って〛…かしら ▪*I wonder* who invented gas-lamps. 誰がガス灯を発明したのかしら ▪How can that be, *I wonder*? どうしてそんなことがありうるのかしら.
2《口》どうだか(怪しいものだ) ▪Oh, it was entirely his own idea.—*I wonder*! いや, それは全く彼自身の考えだったのだ—どうだかね.

I wonder if …でしょうか《丁寧な依頼》 ▪*I wonder if* I could see you this afternoon. きょうの午後会っていただけるでしょうか. ☞I was wondering if …とすればなお丁寧.

wonder if …かしら(と思う) ▪I *wonder if* it will rain tomorrow. あす雨が降るかしら ▪He *wondered if* it would rain the next day. 彼は翌日雨が降るかしらと思った.

wont /wɑːnt|wəʊnt/ 名形 ***be wont to*** *do* …するのを常としている ▪We two *were wont to* meet at that pleasant spot. 我々二人はその楽しい場所で会うのを常としていた.

it is *one's* ***wont to*** *do* …する習わしである ▪*It was my wont to* ride there. そこへ馬で行くのが私の習わしであった.

of wont 普通の ▪His commemoration was *of* daily *wont* in this neighborhood. 彼を称賛するのはこの界わいでは毎日普通に見られることであった.

use and wont →USE[1].

wood /wʊd/ 名 ***a dead wood*** 無用の人, 役立たず ▪Get rid of all the *dead wood* and recruit able young people. 役に立たない連中をすべてお払い箱にして, 有能な若者を入れよ.

a man of the woods オランウータン ▪You are shown in this yard *a man of the woods*. この囲いにはオランウータンが見られます. ☞orangutanはマレー語orang utan (man＋forest)の意.

be* [*get*] *out of the wood [《米》***woods***]《口》危機を免れる, 困難を切り抜ける ▪They are shouting before they *are out of the wood*. 彼らは危機を免れないうちから喜んでいる ▪When a patient reaches this stage, he *is out of the woods.* 患者がこの段階に達すると危機を脱したのだ. ☞森は道に迷いやすいところから.

beat the woods 森の獲物を追い出す ▪ They were told to *beat the woods.* 彼らは森の獲物を追い出せと言われた.

cannot see the wood [《米口》 ***forest***] ***for the trees*** 《英口》木を見て森を見ない《一部に気を取られて大局が見えない》 ▪ I see you *cannot see the wood for the trees.* 君は木を見て森を見ないね.

crow before *one* ***is out of the woods*** 危険から脱する[決着がつく] 前に喜ぶ ▪ I think our team will win, but I don't want to *crow before* we *are out of the woods.* わがチームが勝つと思うが, 勝負がつくまでは糠(ぬか)喜びはすまい.

Don't halloo [***whistle***] ***till you are out of the wood.*** 《諺》早まって喜ぶな.

go to the woods 社会的地位を失う, 社会から追放される ▪ Two other gamblers have *gone to the woods.* 他の二人のばくち打ちも社会から追放された.

knock (***on***) ***wood*** →touch WOOD.

out of the wood 危険[苦境]を脱して ▪ The doctor says that she is not yet *out of the wood.* 医師の意見では彼女はまだ危険を脱してはいない.

saw wood →SAW^2.

take in wood **1** 《米口》(蒸気船に)たきぎを積む ▪ We stopped three miles below, to *take in wood.* たきぎを積むために3マイル川下に止まった.
2 1杯やる ▪ Stranger, will you *take in wood*? 見知らぬ方, 1杯やりませんか.

take *a person* ***to the wood shed*** 《米口》慎重に咎(とが)める, よく考えて罰する ▪ We'll have to *take* him *to the wood shed.* 彼を慎重に処罰せねばなるまい.

take to the woods 《米口》 **1** 森に逃げ込む; 野に下る ▪ Farmers' wives *took to the woods* when the buggy came upon them. 農夫の妻たちは自動車が突然近づいて来たとき森に逃げ込んだ ▪ William C. Morland, Idaho Republican, *took to the woods* in 1932. アイダホの共和党員のウィリアム C. モーランドは1932年に野に下った.
2 逃げ隠れる ▪ When he saw the girls coming, he *took to the woods.* 女の子たちが来るのを見ると, 彼はこそこそと逃げた.

to the woods for it 《米口》それを追い出せ ▪ We'll give rag-time a few months more, then *to the woods for it.* ジャズ音楽をもう2, 3か月はやらせて, その後はそれを追い出そう.

touch wood/《米》***knock*** (***on***) ***wood*** 木にさわれ; たたりがありませんように, うまくいきますように ▪ I have never been in danger of drowning.—Better *knock on wood.* 僕は水におぼれかけたためしがない—大きな口はたたかないほうがいいよ ▪ This is the safest ship in the world, I hear.—*Touch wood.* これは世界一安全な船—たたりがありませんように—だそうだ ▪ It's been fine so far and, *touch wood*, it'll stay fine for the weekend. これまで好天だったので, どうか週末も続きますように. ☞自慢などしたあとに復しゅうの女神 Nemesis の怒りを和らげるために木にさわる迷信から.

woodbine /wʊ́dbàɪn/ 名 ***go where the woodbine twineth*** 《米口》だめになる ▪ The bill *goes where the woodbine twineth.* その法案はだめになる.

woodchuck /wʊ́dtʃʌ̀k/ 名 (***as***) ***sound as a woodchuck*** 《米》非常に健康で ▪ He will come all right by and by—*as sound as a woodchuck.* 彼はやがて元通りに—すっかり元気になりましょう.

the land of woodchucks 《米》田舎 ▪ But what could a greenhorn, right from *the land of woodchucks* do? しかし, 田舎から出たての青二才に何ができるだろうか.

wood sawyer /wʊ́dsɔ̀ːjər/ 名 (***as***) ***independent as a wood sawyer*** [《戯》 ***a wood sawyer's clerk***] 《米》全く独立して ▪ If you live in the forecastle, you are *as independent as a wood sawyer.* 水夫部屋に住んでいれば全く気ままにしていられるよ.

woodwork /wʊ́dwə̀ːrk/ 名 ***blend*** [***fade, vanish***] ***into the woodwork*** 《口》どこへともなく姿を消す, 目立たないように行動する ▪ He had to *vanish into the woodwork* for his own safety. 彼は身の安全のため行方をくらます必要があった ▪ The best thing to do is to try and *fade into the woodwork.* 目立たないように行動するに限る.

come [***crawl***] ***out of the woodwork*** 《口》 **1** どこからともなく姿を現す ▪ The terrorist leader *crawled out of the woodwork* again. テロリストの首領が再びどこからともなく姿を見せた.
2 《軽蔑》突然何かを始める, 急に言い始める ▪ Then people *came out of the woodwork* and started being friendly to us. するとみなは手のひらを返したように我々になれなれしくし始めた. ☞「木製品から白アリがわいて出る」が原義.

wool /wʊl/ 名 ***against the wool*** 逆毛に; 性に合わないで ▪ Working goes *against the wool.* 働くことは性に合わない.

all wool and a yard wide/ all wool, a yard long and a yard wide 《米口》全く大丈夫で, 本物で ▪ Now you're a live one, *all wool, a yard long and a yard wide.* さて, 君は威勢のいい人だ, 正真正銘にだ.

(***as***) ***soft*** [***white***] ***as wool*** 羊毛のように柔かい[白い] ▪ The waves looked *soft as wool.* 波は羊毛のように柔かく見えた ▪ His hair is *as white as wool.* 彼の髪の毛は羊毛のように白い.

be wool-gathering →go WOOL-gathering.

draw [***pull***] ***the wool over*** *a person's* ***eyes*** 《口》人の目をくらます, 人をだます ▪ He ain't so big a fool as to have *the wool drawn over his eyes* in that way. 彼はそんなふうに目をくらまされるほど大ばかじゃない.

dye in (***the***) ***wool*** →DYE^2.

go for wool and come home shorn ミイラ取

W

りがミイラになる ▪ Sancho Panza says, many *go for wool and come home shorn.* サンチョ・パンサいわく, ミイラ取りがミイラになることは多い.

go* [*run, be*] *wool-gathering とりとめもない空想にふける, うわの空になる ▪ His wits *went wool-gathering* at that instant. 彼の頭はその瞬間うわの空になった ▪ You *are wool-gathering* a little, eh? 君は少しうわの空になっているようだね. ☞「垣根などについた羊の毛のような価値のないものを集めに行く」が原義.

keep *one's* ***wool on*** 《俗》怒らない ▪ *Keep your wool on*! There's no need to get so excited! 怒りたもうな. そんなに興奮しなくてもいいさ. ☞< keep one's HAIR on.

lose *one's* ***wool*** 怒る ▪ Last night he *lost his wool* and made an awful fool of himself. ゆうべ彼は怒ってひどくばかなまねをした.

***Much cry and little wool* (*as when pigs are shorn*).** →CRY[1].

out of the wool (羊が)毛を刈り取られて ▪ He left town to see the sheep just *out of the wool* after shearing. 彼は刈り込みのあと裸になったばかりの羊を見に町を去った.

pull the woof over *a person's* ***eyes*** →draw the WOOL over a person's eyes.

run wool-gathering →go WOOL-gathering.

send* [*set*]*...* (*a*) *wool-gathering ...をうわの空にさせる ▪ He *sends* his father-in-law almost *a wool-gathering.* 彼は奥方の父親をほとんどうわの空にさせている.

wool on the back 金, 財産 ▪ He has a sufficiency of *wool on the back.* 彼は金がたんまりある.

wrap* (*up*) *in cotton wool 《口》(人を)大事にしすぎる, 過保護にする ▪ She keeps her son *wrapped up in cotton wool.* 彼女は息子を過保護にしている.

woolly /wóli/ 形 ***the woolly West*** 《米口》粗野な西部 (→WILD and woolly West) ▪ This was roughing it, was it? Life in *the woolly West*! これは困難に耐えるというやつだったな, 粗野な西部の生活は.

word /wəːrd/ 名 ***a dirty word*** **1** 下品な[野卑な] 言葉 ▪ You shouldn't use such *dirty words.* そんな下品な言葉を使ってはいけません.

2 好まれない考え[言葉], 不愉快な言葉 ▪ Marriage seems to be *a dirty word* to young men these days. 近頃では結婚は若い男性には禁句のようだ.

a good word **1** 好意[称賛]の言葉 ▪ He has *a good word* for every one. 彼は誰でもほめる ▪ I know I shall always have your *good word.* あなたからはいつも好意ある言葉がいただけるものと存じています.

2 とりなしの言葉 ▪ He spoke *a good word* for me to the Mayor. 彼は市長に私のためにとりなしてくれた.

3 吉報 ▪ Hello, there; what's the *good word*? —Why, much as usual. やあ, 君. 何かいいことないかい—なに, 相変わらずさ.

a household word →HOUSEHOLD.

a man* [*woman*] *of few words 口数の少ない人, 無口な人 ▪ Like most heroes, he was *a man of few words.* たいていの英雄がそうであるように, 彼も口数が少なかった.

a man of his word/a woman of her word 約束を守る人 ▪ As for himself, he is *a man of his word.* 彼はと言えば, 約束の堅い人だ.

a word and a blow 言うが早いかなぐりつけること; (一般に)あっと言う間にしてしまうこと ▪ With them it is "*a word and a blow.*" 彼らにあっては「言うが早いかなぐりつける」というやつだ ▪ They did not expect that I would be *a word and a blow.* 彼らは私があっと言う間にしてしまうとは予期しなかったのだ.

a word in* [*out of*] *season 時宜(じぎ)を得た[得ない]助言 (《聖》*Isa.* 50. 4) ▪ It is wonderful what *a word in season* from a man of genius may do. 天才からの時宜を得た助言がどれだけ役に立つかは驚くばかりだ.

A word in your ear. ちょっと一言 ▪ *A word in your ear.* Do not forget how to cook. ちょっと一言. 料理法を忘れちゃいけないよ.

A word* (*once*) *spoken is past recalling. 《諺》口から出た言葉は呼び戻すことはできない《一旦言ってしまったらもう取り返しがきかない》.

a word or two 一言二言 ▪ I entreated them to let me say *a word or two.* 私は一言二言言わせてほしいと彼らに頼んだ.

***a word to the wise* (*is sufficient*)** 賢人には一言(言えば足る) ▪ "*A word to the wise,*" said our host. "Don't go into the haunted room at midnight."「賢人には一言」と我々の主人役の人が言った.「真夜中に幽霊の出没する部屋に入ってはなりません」 ▪ I assumed that *a word to the wise was sufficient.* 私は賢人には一言で足りるものと思っていた. ☞ L verbum sapienti のなぞり.

an operative word 重要な言葉 ▪ You can go wherever you like but drive carefully. The *operative word* is carefully. どこでも好きなところへ行って構わないが, 慎重に運転しろよ. 大切なのは「慎重に」だ ▪ I want more time for my private life, private being the *operative word.* 私生活にもっと時間がほしい.「私(生活に)」が肝心なところだ.

at a* [*one*] *word **1** 言下に, ただちに ▪ *At a word* I would have flung it away. ただちに私はそれを投げ捨てたことだろう.

2 かいつまんで, 一言で ▪ Tell me *at one word* what you wish with me. 私に何をしてもらいたいのか一言で言ってみなさい.

bandy words with →BANDY.

be as good as *one's* ***word*** 約束を果たす, 言ったことを実行する ▪ Scrooge *was as good as his word.* スクルージは約束を果たした.

be better* [*worse*] *than *one's* ***word*** 約束以上のことをする[約束を破る] ▪ Scrooge *was better than his word.* スクルージは約束以上のことをした ▪ Will you *be worse than your word*? あなたは約束を破るのですか.

be lost* [*stuck, at a loss*] *for words (驚き[混乱, 動転]のあまり)言葉も出ない, 言葉に詰まる

W

▪ They asked me to make a speech, but I *was* completely *lost for words*. スピーチを求められたが，全く言葉が出なかった ▪ She was so shocked by his behavior that she *was at a loss for words*. 彼女は彼の行動があまりにショックで，何と言っていいか分からなかった ▪ For the first time in my life I *was stuck for words*. 生まれてはじめて私は言葉に詰まった．

be not the word for it [***him,*** etc.] 〚主語は形容詞など〛ぴったりした言葉とは言えない，…どころではない ▪ Cold *isn't the word for it* today. It's freezing. 今日は寒いなんてものではない．凍えそうだ ▪ Talented *is not the word for him*. 才能があるという言葉では彼には足りない[天才といってよい]．

be the word for 《口》…に当てはまる言葉[適評]だ ▪ Ladylike *was the word for* her. しとやかというのがまさに彼女に当てはまる言葉だった ▪ Warm's not *the word for* it. これは暖かいといったものじゃないよ《暑いと言ったほうがいい》 ▪ Our victory was pure luck. Well, luck *isn't the word for* it. 我々が勝ったのはまさについていたから，いや，つき以上の何かのお陰だった．

beyond words なんとも言えないほど ▪ Her tact is *beyond words*. 彼女の如才なさは筆舌に尽くし難い．

break *one's* ***word*** 約束を破る ▪ A gentleman never *breaks his word*. 紳士に二言(ごん)はない．

break words with →BREAK[2].

bring word 知らせをもたらす ▪ A servant *brought word* that his master had returned. 主人が帰ったと使用人が知らせてきた．

by word of mouth →MOUTH[1].

come to high words 言葉が荒くなる，口論になる ▪ They soon *came to high words*. 彼らはすぐに言葉が荒くなった．

eat *one's* ***words*** →EAT[2].

empty words 無味乾燥な言葉 ▪ The lawmaker gave us nothing more than handshakes and *empty words*. 政治家は我々と握手をし空々しい言葉をかけてくれただけだった．

fair words 甘言 ▪ He gave his men *fair words*. 彼は兵たちに甘言を弄した．

Fair [***Fine***] ***words butter no cabbage*** [***parsnips***]. 《諺》美辞巧言はキャベツにバターをつけない《口先だけのお世辞は何の役にも立たない》．

Famous last words! おっしゃいましたね; とか何とか言っちゃって(そんなことを信じるものか) ▪ This is the war to end all wars.—*Famous last words!* この戦争ですべての戦争が終わる—とか何とか言っちゃって．☞「臨終名言集」が原義．

four-letter words 四文字語，(性・排泄に関する4文字から成る)下品なタブー語 ▪ It is bad manners to use *four-letter words* in front of ladies. 女性の前で四文字語を使うのは不作法である．

from the word "go" →GO[1].

get in a word →put in a WORD.

get [***slide, push***] ***in a word*** 《英口》***edgeways*** [《米口》***-wise, -way***] →EDGEWAY(S).

get into words 口論する ▪ We had *got into words* about the invitations. 我々は招待のことで口論していた．

get the word ＝get the MESSAGE.

get word ＝have WORD.

give *a person* ***a good word*** 人をほめる ▪ He *gave* you *a good word*. 彼は君のことをほめていたよ．

give the word 合言葉を言う ▪ He *gave the word*, and the gate was opened. 彼が合言葉を言うと，門が開かれた．

give the word for [***to*** *do*] …の[する]命令を下す ▪ I *gave* him *the word to* lower the long-boat. 大ボートを降ろせと彼に命じた．

give [***pledge, pass***] *one's* ***word*** 約束する ▪ You *gave* us *your word*! 約束をしてくれたじゃありませんか ▪ He *pledged his word* not to attempt it. 彼はそれを試みないと約束した．

give *a person one's* ***word for*** [***that***] …を[…と]人に保証する ▪ I *give* you *my word for* it. それは私が保証します ▪ I *give* you *my word that* my brother did not leave a shilling to his son. 嘘偽りのないところだが，兄は息子に1シリングも残さなかった．

give words to …を言い表す ▪ He was at a loss to *give words to* his indignation. 彼は憤りをどう言い表してよいか途方にくれた．

God's word/the word of God [***the Lord***]
1 神のみ告げ，福音 ▪ They spoke *the word of God* boldly. 彼らは大胆に神のみ告げを語った．
2 聖書 ▪ I like to hear *God's word*. 聖書を読んで聞かせてもらいたい．

half a word ほんの一言 ▪ Might I have *half a word* with you? ほんの一言お話ししたいのですが．

hang on *a person's* ***word*** →HANG on a person's lips.

hard [***high, sharp***] ***words*** 激語，口論 ▪ They had *hard words* with each other. 彼らは口論しあった．

have a quiet word (人と)内密の話をする ▪ Could I *have a quiet word* with you about it? それについて君と内密の話をしたいのですが．

have a way with words しゃべりがうまい，雄弁な (→have a WAY with) ▪ He is young, but really *has a way with words*. 彼は若いが実に弁が立つ．

have a word **1** 一言話をする (*with*) ▪ I wanted to *have a word with* him. 私は彼と一言話したいと思った．
2 口論する ▪ You and I never *had a word*. 君とは一度もけんかをしたことがなかったね．

have a word in *a person's* ***ear*** 《英》内々で話をする，内密に耳に入れる ▪ Can I *have a word in your ear*, Jim? ジム，ちょっと話があるのだが．

have no words for [***to*** *do*] …の表現のしようがない ▪ I *have no words to* express my gratitude. お礼の言葉もありません．

have not a word to throw to [***at***] ***a dog*** 一言も口をきかない (cf. Sh., *A. Y. L.* 1. 3. 3) ▪ Why, on that ship you *hadn't a word to* *throw to a dog.* だって，あの船では君は一言も口をきかなかったじゃないか．

have the final [***last***] ***word*** **1** (議論で)どこまでも譲らない，人をやりこめる; へらず口をたたく ▪ I am determined to *have the last word.* 僕はどこまでも譲らない決心だ ▪ She manages to *have the last word.* 彼女はどうにかうまく相手をやりこめる ▪ That woman always *has the last word.* あの女性はいつもへらず口をたたく．

2 (…についての)最終決定をくだす，決定権がある ▪ The head chef *has the final word* on what is served each week. 料理長に毎週の提供料理を決定する権限がある．

have word 知らせを受ける ▪ We *had word* that Mr. Dombey was doing well. ドンビー氏は元気だという知らせを受けた．

have [***exchange***] ***words*** (***with***) 《主に英》(…と)口論する ▪ I *had words with* my wife. 妻と口論した ▪ They *had words* together. 彼らは言い争った ▪ They both got angry and *exchanged words.* 二人とも腹を立てて口論した．

high words →hard WORDs.

I give you my word 請け合ってもよい ▪ I'll pay you back next week, *I give you my word.* 来週支払うよ，請け合ってもいい．

in a word 《口》一口に言えば，要するに (= in SHORT) ▪ *In a word,* he tires of everything. 要するに彼は何にでも飽きるのだ．

in other words 言い換えれば ▪ He became, *in other words,* a great hero. 言い換えれば，彼は大英雄になったわけだ．

in so many words それだけの言葉で; はっきりと，あからさまに ▪ William told us *in so many words* that it was impossible. ウィリアムはそんなことは不可能だとはっきりと言った ▪ She said yes, but not *in so many words.* 彼女は承知したよ．はっきりとではないけどね．

in word 口では，口先では (↔in (very) DEED 2) ▪ He is bold *in word* only. 彼は口先だけ威勢がよい ▪ He is honest *in word* and deed. 彼は言行ともに正直だ．

in words of one syllable 簡単な言葉で; 一口に言えば ▪ He explained it to her *in words of one syllable.* 彼はそれを簡単な言葉で彼女に説明した ▪ *In words of one syllable,* he's a cheat. 一口で言えば，彼はぺてん師だ．

It's my word against his. 彼にも私にも証人がいない ▪ How can you know for certain? *It's my word against his.* 君にどうして確かにわかりましょう．彼にも私にも証人がいないのですから．

(***just***) ***say the word*** そう命じる[言う] ▪ If you *say the word,* we go. 行けとおっしゃれば，参ります．☞"Go!" という命令で競走を始めることから．

keep *one's* ***word*** 約束を守る ▪ I will *keep my word* with you. あなたとの約束は守ります．

one's [***the***] ***last*** [***final***] ***word*** (***on, about***) (…についての)決定的な発言，最終決定 ▪ Is that *your final word on* the matter? それがその問題についての君の結論なのか．

leave word with →LEAVE[2].

let the words stand 表現を変えない，元のままにしておく ▪ I'm satisfied with the wording of your article. *Let the words stand.* 君の記事の言葉うかいが気に入った．変更しないでおこう．

make words 〚否定文で〛言う ▪ Let's *make* no more *words* about it. もうそのことは言いますまい．

My word! 《口》〚間投詞的に〛全く!，これはこれは!《驚きを表す》 ▪ *My word!* that's something like a mob! 全く，それは大したやじ馬だ．

never said [***spoke***] ***a truer word*** …のおっしゃる通りだ ▪ Yes, you *never said a truer word.* さよう，あなたのおっしゃる通りです．

not a word of truth in …は全くの偽りで ▪ There is*n't a word of truth in* this rumor. この噂は全くの偽りです．

not a word (***to***) (…に)一言も言うな ▪ Above all, *not a word to* Bessie about it. わけてもベッシーにはそのことを一言も言っちゃだめだ．

Not another word! もう言うな! ▪ *Not another word!* It's a pleasure. もうおっしゃいますな．何でもないことです．

not believe a word of it そんなことは全く信じない ▪ I've heard a lot about him but I do*n't believe a word of it.* 彼の噂はいろいろ聞いているが，私は全然信じないね．

not breathe a word →BREATHE.

not [***never***] ***have a good word to say for*** [***about***] 《口》…を(全く)ほめない ▪ He *rarely has a good word to say about* his colleagues. 彼は滅多に同僚をほめない ▪ *Nobody has a good word to say for* either of them. 二人ともみなに受けが悪い．

not (…) ***in so many words*** 《口》はっきりと(…)ではない ▪ The talk was*n't* a success *in so many words,* but it was useful. 話し合いははっきりと成功したとは言えないが，有益だった．

not mince *one's* ***words*** → not MINCE matters.

not waste words 言葉をむだにしない，簡潔に話す ▪ He did*n't waste words* telling them what to do. 彼は言葉少なに彼らに仕事を言いつけた．

of few [***many***] ***words*** 口数の少ない[多い] ▪ He had always been a man *of few words.* 彼はかねてから口数の少ない人であった ▪ She was not a woman *of many words.* 彼女は口数の多い女ではなかった．

on [***upon***] ***my word*** 確かに，誓って ▪ He is a very good boy, *upon my word.* 彼は確かによい少年だ．

on [***with***] ***the word*** 言下に，そう言ってすぐ ▪ *With the word,* he dismissed me. そう言ってすぐ，彼は私を解雇した．

on the word of (王など)としての約束にかけて ▪ *On the word of* a king he promised to do the same. 王としての約束にかけて彼は同様のことをすることを約した．

on [***upon***] *one's* ***word*** 誓って ▪ You promised me *on your word*. 君は誓って私に約束したんだぞ.
on *one's* ***word of honor*** →HONOR[1].
one more word out of you, and... 《口》もう一言でもしゃべったら; 黙らないと... ▪ *One more word out of you, and* I'll spank you. 黙らないと, ひっぱたくぞ.
or words to that effect (つまり)その趣旨の発言を, ざっと言い換えるとそういう内容を ▪ He said he was very worried, *or words to that effect*. 彼はとても心配している, というようなことを言っていた.
play on words しゃれを言う ▪ Don't *play on words* or use humor to cover up the issue. 問題をもみ消そうとしゃれを飛ばしたりユーモアを用いたりするな.
pledge [***pass***] *one's* ***word*** → give one's WORD.
put in a good word for ...をほめる ▪ If only someone would *put in a good word for* John, I am sure he would get that promotion. 誰かがジョンを称賛しさえすれば, きっとその昇進にありつけるのだが.
put [***get***] ***in a word*** 口を出す ▪ I tried to *put in a word* but to no avail. 私は口を出そうとしたが果たせなかった.
put ... into words ...を(言葉に)言い表す ▪ She could not *put* her fear *into words*. 彼女は自分の恐怖を言い表すことができなかった.
put the word out ニュース[噂]を広める ▪ They *put out the word* that she was fired. 彼女は首になっているという噂が広がった.
put the words into *a person's* ***mouth*** → MOUTH[1].
put *one's* ***word in*** 差し出口をきく ▪ He's always *putting his word in*. 彼はいつも差し出口をきいてばかりいる.
put words into *a person's* ***mouth*** 人が言いもしないのに言ったことにする ▪ I didn't say so. Don't *put words into my mouth*. 僕はそんなことは言っていない. 言いもしないことを言ったことにしないでくれ.
say a few words →SAY[2].
say [***speak***] ***a good word for*** ...をよく言う, ほめる ▪ It is customary to *say a good word for* the departed. 故人のことはよく言うのが慣例だ.
say *one's* ***last word*** 最終的な意見[決定, 命令]を言う ▪ I've *said my last word* on the subject. その件については結論を出しておいた.
say the last word →LAST[2].
say the word 開始の指示を出す; 遠慮なくはっきり言う ▪ We'll all shout "Happy Birthday!" when I *say the word*. 僕が合図したらみなで「お誕生日おめでとう!」と大声で言うことにしよう ▪ Just *say the word* and I'll be there right by your side. 一言言ってくれたら, 早速飛んで行ってやる.
send word 伝言する, 申し送る ▪ *Send* me *word* whether he has so great an estate. 彼がそんな大きな地所を持っているのかどうかことづけしてくれ ▪ He has *sent word* to excuse himself. 彼は(招待などを)失礼すると断りの伝言をした.
Sharp is the word! →SHARP.
sharp words →hard WORDs.
speak a good word for →say a good WORD for.
spread [***preach***] ***the word*** みなに伝える, 周知徹底させる ▪ Our boss will be speaking at the hall at 1.30. *Spread the word*. 1時半から講堂で社長からの話がある予定だ. みなにそう伝えてくれ.
stand by *one's* ***word*** 自分の約束を守る ▪ I'll *stand by my word* and do anything for you. 約束通り何だってしてあげるよ.
suit the action to the word(s) →ACTION.
take *a person* ***at*** *his* ***word*** 人の言う通りを信じる ▪ Old as I am I *take* you *at your word*. 私は年をとってはいるが, 君の言う通りを信じよう.
Take my word for it. 私の言うことを本当だと思ってよい ▪ *Take my word for it*, there is nothing in it. 本当なんですよ, それは何でもないんです.
take the words (***right***) ***out of*** *a person's* ***mouth*** 人の言おうとしていることを先に言う ▪ You have *taken the* very *words out of my mouth*. 君は私がちょうど言おうとしていることを先に言ってしまった ▪ I agree completely! You've *taken the words right out of my mouth*! 全くその通り. 今そう言おうとしていたんだ.
take (***up***) ***the word*** 話し始める《誰か他の人の直後または代わりに》 ▪ The Colonel, left alone with his wife, made haste to *take the word*. 大佐は妻と二人きりになると急いで話し始めた.
take *a person's* ***word*** 人の言葉を信じる (*for*) ▪ You can *take Harris's word for* that. そのことではハリスの言葉を信じてよい ▪ When he said he was all right, I *took his word for* it. 彼が大丈夫と言うものだから, 真に受けてしまった.
the F-word [***the B-word,*** etc.] (その文字で始まる) 口に出して言えない無作法な言葉[話題]《例えば fuck = F-word, bitch = B-word など》 ▪ He doesn't use *the F-word* in his house. 彼は家では(Fではじまる)例の下品な言葉を使わない.
the last word **1** (談話, 特に論争における)最後の言葉 ▪ It was plain she would have one *last word* more. 彼女がもう一言最後の言葉を言いたがっているのは明らかだった.
2 〚複数形で〛 臨終の言葉 ▪ "More light!" were *the last words* of Goethe. 「もっと光を!」がゲーテの臨終の言葉だった.
3 決定的な言葉; 最高権威 ▪ He is *the last word* in architecture. 彼は建築学の最高権威だ.
4 最新流行のもの ▪ The long mantles are *the last word* of Paris fashions. 長いマントがパリで最新流行のものだ.
the latest word = the last WORD 4.
the word came that ...との知らせがあった ▪ *The word came that* he could not come. 彼から来られないとの知らせがあった.
(***the***) ***word is that*** ...と言われている ▪ *The word is that* the house will be sold. その家は売ら

れるそうだ.

the word of God →God's WORD.

the word on the street 《口》噂, 情報 ▪ *The word on the street* is that the leading construction firm is going bankrupt. その一流建設会社が倒産するという噂でもちきりだ.

the word spreads あっという間に噂[情報]が広まる ▪ *The word* quickly *spread* and soon everyone knew. 噂が瞬く間に広がってみなに知れ渡った.

Them's fighting words. そいつは(けんかをふっかける)売り言葉だ ▪ Your father's smarter than mine? *Them's fighting words.* お前のおやじの方がおれのより賢いだと? やる気か? ☞those are を表す非文法表現の them's は意図的.

too ...for words …すぎて言葉で言い尽くせない ▪ The scenery was *too* beautiful *for words.* その景色はあまりにも美しくて言葉で言い表せなかった.

upon my word =on my WORD.

weasel words 《口》曖昧な逃げ口上(こうじょう), とぼけること, 知らんぷり ▪ The criminal tried to fool the police with *weasel words.* 容疑者はのらりくらりととぼけて警察をだまそうとした. ☞イタチが鳥の卵の中身を吸って殻だけを残すことから.

weigh *one's* ***words*** →WEIGH[2].

What's the (good) word? 《俗》お元気ですか ▪ Hi, Jack! *What's the (good) word?* あら, ジャックじゃないの. 元気?

winged words 《雅》翼ある言葉, きわめて重要な[適切な]言葉 ▪ He addressed the crowd with *winged words.* 彼は群集に向かって実に適切な言葉を駆使して演説した. ☞Homer の叙事詩, 特に *Odyssey* に頻出する épea pteróenta のなぞり.

with the word →on the WORD.

without a word 一言も言わずに ▪ She held out her hands, *without a word.* 彼女は一言も言わずに両手を差し伸べた.

without a word of a lie 《口》嘘偽りなく ▪ *Without a word of a lie,* I saw it with my own eyes. 嘘偽りなく, この目で見たのです.

won't hear a word (said) against …の悪評を信じない ▪ He's madly in love with her and *won't hear a word said against* her. 彼は彼女にぞっこんで, 彼女への悪口は聞こうともしない.

word for [by] word 一語一語, 逐語的に ▪ I will repeat it to you *word for word.* それを一語一語繰り返して話してあげます ▪ He declared *word by word* what she had said. 彼は彼女の言ったことを言葉通りにきっぱりと言った.

One's ***word is (as good as)*** *his* ***bond.*** …の約束は契約書[証文]と同じくらい確実だ, は約束を違えない《絶対に守る》 ▪ So, *is your word your bond?* ということは, 武士に二言はないな? ▪ Don't worry, Bob. *Your father's word is as good as his bond.* 心配するな, ボブ. 父さんは必ず約束を守るぞ.

One's ***word is law.*** 人が絶対的な権力を持っている ▪ In private schools *the parents' word is law.* 私立学校では親が絶対的な権力を持っている ▪ *His word was law* inside the firm. 彼の言葉はその会社内では鶴の一声であった.

word of honor 名誉をかけての誓い ▪ I give you my *word of honor.* 私の名誉にかけて誓う ▪ *Word of honor,* I never saw such a beauty in my life. 全くのところ, こんな美人は今までに見たことがない.

word or [nor] sign 〚主に否定文で〛言葉か身ぶりで ▪ He gave neither *word nor sign* that he was not alone. 彼は自分が一人ではないということを言葉でも身ぶりでも示さなかった.

word splitting 《軽蔑》細かすぎるほどの言葉の区別 ▪ I'm tired of her *word-splitting.* 彼女の言葉うかいのやかましさにはうんざりする.

words fail *a person* (感動・怒りなどで)言葉に詰まる, 絶句する ▪ Here *words failed* him. ここで彼は言葉に詰まってしまった.

words go through *one* ***like a knife*** 言葉が耳に痛い[心を傷つける] ▪ His *words went through* me *like a knife,* and I cried all day. 彼の言葉が私の胸を切り裂き, 終日泣き暮らした.

words of wisdom 《しばしば皮肉》賢明な言葉[助言] ▪ These *words of wisdom* were lost on the young man. この賢明な助言もその若者に通じなかった.

write word 手紙で知らせてやる ▪ She *writes word* that the lad will come today. その若者がきょう来ると彼女が手紙で知らせてきている.

You have my word. 《口》(約束して)信じてください, 大丈夫です ▪ It's true. *You have my word.* それは本当だ. 私が保証する.

(You) mark my words. →MARK[2].

work[1] /wəːrk/ 名 ***a good work*** 善行; 功徳 ▪ He has done but two *good works* in all his life. 彼は生まれてこのかた善行を二つしかしたことがない.

A little (hard) work never hurt [killed] anyone. 《諺》ささやかな(辛い)仕事は決して人を傷つけない《辛い仕事も進んで行え》.

a work-in (労働者の)職場占拠 ▪ The workers staged *a work-in* that lasted for 2 weeks. 労働者たちは職場占拠を決行し, それが2週間続いた.

a work of time 時間のかかる仕事 ▪ This is apt to be *a work of time.* これは時間のかかる仕事になりがちだ.

(all) in the [a] day's work 当たり前のこと, 少しも厄介でない ▪ Heroic conduct of this type is regarded by British officers as "*all in the day's work.*" この種の英雄的行為をイギリスの士官は「当たり前のこと」とみなしている. ☞day's work《海》「正午から翌日の正午にわたる24時間の船位の算出」.

All work and no play makes Jack a dull boy. 《諺》勉強ばかりして遊ばないと子供はばかになる,「よく学びよく遊べ」.

at work **1** 仕事をして; 活動中で ▪ He is *at work* on a novel. 彼は小説を書いている ▪ The engines are *at work.* エンジンは作動している ▪ The same influence was already *at work.* 同じ影響がすでに働いていた.

2 職場[会社]にいる, 仕事中で ▪ Is it all right if I call you *at work*? 仕事中に電話してもかまわないか?

be too much like hard work 《口》(仕事・スポーツなどが)ちょっときつすぎる ▪ A dance marathon would *be too much like hard work*. ダンスの長時間競技なんて, ちときつすぎるね.

bung* [*gum*] *up the works →GUM up the works.

busy work 時間つぶしの仕事, 忙しく見せているだけの仕事 ▪ Still 15 minutes left before class was over. So she gave them a test for *busy work*. 授業終了までまだ15分あったので, 時間つぶしに試験をした.

By their works you shall know them. 行為によって人柄がわかる ▪ The statement, "*By their works you shall know them*," is true! 行為によって人柄がわかるというのは本当だ.

dirty work at the crossroads →DIRTY[1].

do *a person's* ***dirty work for him*** →DIRTY[1].

do *its* ***work*** きく, 作用を及ぼす ▪ The brandy-and-water had *done its work*. 水割りのブランデーがきいてきていた ▪ Famine and heat had *done their work* on them by turns. 飢きんと暑さが彼らにかわるがわる作用を及ぼしていた.

fall* [*get, go*] *to work 仕事にとりかかる (*on*) ▪ His wits *went* instantly *to work*. 彼の才知はすぐ働き始めた ▪ The four *fell to work on* the breakfast. 4人は朝食にとりかかった.

get the works 《口》ひどい目にあう, 殺される ▪ He'll *get the works* if he goes near them. 彼らに近づいたら彼はひどい目にあうだろう.

give ... the full works (…に)できるだけのことをする, 十分にもてなす ▪ The restaurant will *give* you *the full works*. そのレストランは十分にもてなしてくれるよ.

give ... the works **1**《口》…をひどい目にあわせる, (特に銃で)殺す ▪ They may *give* you *the works*. 彼らは君をひどい目にあわせるかもしれない.

2 =give ... the full WORKs.

go* [*set*] *about *one's* ***work*** 仕事を始める ▪ I *went* cheerfully *about my work*. 楽しく仕事を始めた.

go to work →fall to WORK.

good works 慈善行為 (《聖》*Acts* 9. 36) ▪ She had no shyness in the cause of *good works*. 彼女は慈善行為のためには内気など投げ捨てていた.

gum up the works →GUM[2].

have *one's* ***work cut out*** (***for*** *one*) 《口》→CUT[2].

in good* [*full*] *work 収益のある[忙しい]仕事をして ▪ When *in good work* he earned about 300 pounds weekly. 収益のある仕事をしているときには, 彼は1週300ポンドほど儲けた ▪ The mine is now *in full work*. 鉱山は今盛んに活動している.

in the works 《米口》完成の途上にある, 進行中で ▪ The prints are *in the works*. 印刷は進行中だ ▪ Final decisions on these problems are still *in the works*. この問題の最終的決定はまだ審議中だ.

in work 就業して, 仕事を持って (↔out of WORK) ▪ He has been *in work* only two weeks. 彼が仕事についてから2週間にしかならない.

It is not work that kills, but worry. 《諺》命取りになるのは労役ではなくて気苦労である《せっせと働くのは害にならないが取り越し苦労は健康によくない》, 「心配は身の毒」.

make* (*a*) *work 混乱させる, 大騒ぎする ▪ They are *making* no end of (*a*) *work*. 彼らは途方もなく大騒ぎしている.

make hard work of …を難しく[する]見せる, に骨を折る ▪ They *made hard work of* what should have been an easy game. 彼らは楽勝のはずの試合で手こずった ▪ My son's *making* such *hard work of* his maths homework. 息子は数学の宿題に四苦八苦している.

make light work of …を手軽にする, 楽にする ▪ He *made light work of* it. 彼はそれを軽くやってのけた.

make sad work of it へまなやり方をする, みそをつける ▪ If he writes a book, he will *make sad work of it*. 彼が著述したらみそをつけるだろう.

make short work of …を手早く片うける, さっさと始末する ▪ He *made short work of* the task to leave the office earlier. 彼はもっと早く職場を出るため, その仕事をさっさと終わらせた.

make sure work with …を確保する ▪ The spider *made sure work with* her prey. クモはそのえじきを確保した.

make* (...) *work **1** (人などに)仕事を当てがう (*for*) ▪ By so doing I might have *made work for* the hangman. そんなことをすれば絞首刑執行人に仕事を当てがうことになったかもしれない.

2〚形容詞を伴って〛(…の)仕事をする ▪ Come with me, and we will *make* short *work*. いっしょに来なさい, さっさと片うけましょう ▪ He was *making* good *work* of it across the plains on his mare. 彼は雌馬に乗って平原をどんどん突っ走っていた.

of all work (使用人など)雑役の《比喩的にも》▪ We must get a stout maid *of all work*. 丈夫な雑役係を雇わねばならない ▪ Mine is a pen *of all work*. 私のは何にでも使うペンです.

off work 仕事を休んで, 休暇を取って ▪ British workers were reported to be *off work* in droves that day. 英国の労働者が当日大挙して休暇を取っていると報じれられた.

oil the works =grease the WHEELs.

out of work 失業して (↔in WORK) ▪ About 300 men have been thrown [put] *out of work*. 約300人が首になった.

put to work (人に)…を始めさせる (=set to WORK 2) ▪ They *put* me *to work* on some typing on my first day in the office. 入社の初日にタイピングを始めさせられた.

set to work **1** 仕事[作業]を始める ▪ I *set to work* at another novel. 私はもう一つの小説にとりか

かった ▪ Charles *set* seriously *to work* to govern alone. チャールズは真剣に一人で治めにかかった.
2 …を始めさせる ▪ They *set* their wits *to work*. 彼らは頭を働かせ始めた ▪ I *set* him *to work* on the proof. 私は彼に校正の仕事にとりかからせた.
set** oneself **to work (ある仕事を)やり始める ▪ I *set myself to work* to learn Latin. 私はラテン語の勉強にとりかかった.
shoot the works **1** あり金を全部賭ける ▪ What do you want to bet?—*Shoot the works*. 何を賭けたいのかね—あり金全部だ.
2 全力を尽くす, 危険を冒す (*on*) ▪ He cheerfully *shot the works on* it. 彼は割り切ってそのことに全力を尽くした.
3 《俗》 嘔吐する, へどを吐く ▪ I knew she was going to *shoot the works*. 彼女は吐きそうなのだと分かった.
the donkey [《米》 ***grunt***] ***work*** 《口》 退屈で骨の折れる仕事 ▪ Why do I have to do all *the donkey work*? なぜこんな退屈な仕事をせねばならないのか.
the (***whole***) ***works*** 《口》 ありったけ全部, 一つも残さず ▪ They had guns, grenades, rockets, *the whole works*. 銃も手榴弾もロケット弾も何もかもそろっていた ▪ One pizza with *the whole works*, please. トッピングを全部のせたピザを1枚ください.
work of mercy [***charity***] 慈悲の行為 ▪ It is *work of mercy* to bury dead men. 死者を葬ることは慈悲の行為である.

work[2] /wəːrk/ 動 ***get to work on*** **1** (仕事など)にとりかかる ▪ Children *got to work on* food. 子供たちは食べ物を食べにかかった.
2 (人)に働きかける ▪ I'll *get to work on* my chief. 上司に働きかけてみよう.
make … work 有効に動かす[作用させる] ▪ Can you *make* this machine *work*? この機械をうまく動かせますか ▪ We must *make* the scheme *work*. この企てをうまく成功させなければならない.
Things work themselves out. 《口》 物事は自然に解決する《困っている人への慰め》 ▪ Do you believe that all *things work themselves out* in the end? 物事はすべて最後には自然に解決すると信じますか?
***work** oneself* 進んで行く ▪ He *worked himself* into the center of the crowd. 彼は群衆のまん中へ進んで行った ▪ Tom *worked himself* into his great coat. トムはコートを着こんだ ▪ He made the boat *work itself*. 彼はボートを進ませた.
work a miracle 奇跡を行う ▪ Spanish saints *worked the miracles*. スペインの聖徒がその奇跡を行ったのだ.
work** one's **ass [***butt***] ***off***/《英卑》 ***work** one's **arse*** [***backside***] ***off*** 《米卑》 一生懸命に働く ▪ Her father *worked his backside off* to pay for her education. 彼女の父は彼女の教育費を支払うため懸命に働いた.
work at [***on***] ***it*** 努力を続ける ▪ You can solve this problem if you *work at it*. ねばっていればこの問題が解けるよ.
work both sides of the street 詐欺を働く, 二枚舌を使う ▪ That real estate agent always *works both sides of the street*. あの不動産業者はきまって二枚舌を使い分ける.
work double tides →TIDE[1].
work** one's **fingers to the bone →FINGER[1].
work** one's **hands off 《米俗》 一生懸命に働く ▪ Give any person this kind of break in the South, and he'll *work his hands off*. 南部では誰にでもこのような機会を与えれば一生懸命に働くだろう.
work** one's **head off 《米俗》 猛烈に勉強する ▪ You *worked your head off* for it. 君はそれを得ようとして猛烈に勉強したね.
work** oneself **ill [***to death***] 働きすぎて病気になる[死ぬ] ▪ She *worked herself to death*. 彼女は働きすぎて死んでしまった.
work** oneself **in 仕事に慣れる ▪ It takes some time to *work yourself in*. 仕事に慣れるには少し時間がかかる.
work it [***things***] **1** 《口》 うまくやる[算段する] ▪ I'll *work it* if I can. できればうまく算段してみよう ▪ I'll *work it* (so) that I can take a holiday. 休暇が取れるようにうまく算段してみよう.
2 《俗》 (性的魅力を振りまいて) 自信たっぷりにふるまう ▪ She was up on the platform dancing, and she was *working it*. 彼女はステージで踊っており, 自信たっぷりだった.
work itself clear [***right***] 徐々に澄んでくる[元通りになる] ▪ The turbid stream *works itself clear*. 濁流も徐々に澄んでくる ▪ It would take some time for the trade to *work itself right*. 商売が徐々に元通りになるには少し時間がかかるだろう.
work itself out (事が)自然にうまくおさまる, おのずと成就する ▪ Don't worry. This will *work itself out*. 心配するな. こいつはおのずとうまくいくさ.
work like a beaver [《口》 ***a dog, a Trojan***] せっせと働く ▪ I've been *working like a beaver* weeding the garden. 庭の草取りをしてせっせと働いた ▪ She *worked like a dog* to pass her exams. 彼女は合格しようと必死に勉強した ▪ I'll *work like a Trojan* to win. 勝つために身を粉にして働くつもりだ.
work like a charm (薬が)効き目がすばらしい; (計画などが)実にうまく行く ▪ This medicine *works like a charm*. この薬は効き目がすばらしい ▪ The scheme *worked like a charm*. その計画は実にうまく行った. ☞charm「呪文」.
work like a dog ＝WORK like a beaver.
work loose ゆるむ ▪ The hinges *worked loose* in a very short time. 蝶番(ちょうつがい)はすぐにゆるんだ.
work** oneself **off as 《米口》 (ぎまんの目的で)…のふりをする ▪ He was *working himself off as* a Methodist parson. 彼はメソジストの牧師を装っていた.
work on it ＝WORK at it.
work or want 働かなければ貧乏する ▪ It was *work or want* in those days. 当時は働かなければ貧乏するという有様だった.

W

***work** one's **passage** [**way**] (**out**)* 船賃の代わりに乗船中働く ▪ He *worked his passage* as a coal-passer. 彼は船賃の代わりに乗船中に石炭繰りとして働いた ▪ He has *worked his way out* before the mast from Calcutta. 彼は船賃の代わりにカルカッタから平(ひら)水夫として乗船中働いてきた.

work some fat** [**weight**] **off 努力して体脂肪を燃焼させる ▪ You need to *work off some fat*. がんばって体脂肪を落とさなくっちゃだめよ.

work the oracle →ORACLE.

work the ropes 事をあやつる ▪ How our mutual friend *worked the ropes* is unknown. 我々の共通の友人がどのように事をあやつったかはわからない.

work things →WORK it.

work things out 《口》 個人的な問題を解決する ▪ A married couple should *work things out* for themselves. 夫婦は個人的な問題は自分たちで解決すべきだ.

work** one's **ticket →TICKET[1].

work up a head of steam 活発になり始める, うまくいきだす ▪ It will take this project a while to *work up a head of steam*. この計画が軌道に乗り始めるにはしばらくかかるだろう.

work up an appetite 食欲を増進させる ▪ Why don't you clean up the shed and *work up an appetite*? 物置きでも掃除して, おなかをすかせたら?

work** oneself (**up**) **into だんだん興奮して(ある状態)になる ▪ He *worked himself into* a temper. 彼はだんだん興奮して怒りだした.

work** one's **way (骨折って)進んで行く ▪ I *worked my way* through the crowd. 人ごみの中を押し分けて行った.

work** one's **way round 苦労して回り道をして行く ▪ He *worked his way round* to face his attacker. 彼は苦労して回り道をし, 自分を襲った者に面と向き合った.

***work** one's **way through college**(, etc.)* 働きながら大学(など)を卒業する, 苦学する ▪ He had to *work his way through* law school. 彼は働きながら法科大学院を出た.

work** one's **way up 徐々に出世する ▪ He's *worked his way up* from an office junior. 彼は走り使いから身を起こして少しずつ昇進していった.

work** one's **will →WILL[1].

workaday /wə́ːrkədèɪ/ 形 ***this** [**a**] **workaday world*** このあくせくした世の中 ▪ We've got to live in *a workaday world*. 我々はこせこせした世の中で暮らさねばならないのだ.

worker /wə́ːrkər/ 名 ***a fast worker*** 《口》(色事で)すご腕の人 ▪ Norton was known among them as *a fast worker*. ノートンは彼らの間では色事師として知られていた.

working /wə́ːrkɪŋ/ 名 ***have a working knowledge of*** …を使えるだけの知識がある ▪ She speaks good French and she *has a working knowledge of* Italian and Spanish. 彼女はフランス語をうまく話せるしイタリア語とスペイン語も使える.

in** (**full, good**) **working** [**running**] **order (実に)円滑にいって, (機械が全く)正常に動いて ▪ Everything is *in working order*. 万事円滑にいっている ▪ Put the machine *in working order*. 機械をうまく動くようにしなさい ▪ For Sale: Fridge *in good working order*, £600. 売り物: 状態のよい冷蔵庫を600ポンドでお譲りします《掲示》 ▪ The machine is certainly old but it is still *in full working order*. その機械は確かに古いがまだ調子よく作動している.

workman /wə́ːrkmən/ 名 ***Bad workmen blame their tools.*** →BLAME[2].

workout /wə́ːrkàʊt/ 名 ***have a workout*** 《米口》(運動などを)一生懸命にやること ▪ Well, we sure *had a workout*. そうだな, 僕らは確かに精一杯やった.

world /wəːrld/ 名 ***a better world*** あの世, 来世 ▪ A Christian's chief care is to pass quietly to *a better world*. キリスト教徒の主な関心はあの世へ静かに移ることである.

a brave new world 《皮肉》すばらしい新世界; (大変革を伴う)希望に満ちた歴史上の一時期 (cf. Sh., *Temp*. 5. 1.183) ▪ We are approaching *a brave new world* of nanomedicine. 我々は電顕医学というすばらしい新世界に足を踏み入れようとしている. ☞ Aldous Huxley, *Brave New World* (1932)の題名となった. 皮肉な意味で多く用いられる.

a man** [**woman**] **of the world 世故にたけた人[婦人], 世慣れた人[婦人] ▪ He has always shown himself *a man of the world*. 彼はいつも自分が世故にたけた人であることを示してきた ▪ With all the skill of *a woman of the world*, she shuffled away the subject. 世故にたけた女の腕を見せて, 彼女はその題目を言い紛らした.

a phony world まがいものの世界, 偽りに満ちた世の中 ▪ I've had enough of this *phony world* of the upper classes. 上流社会というこのまやかしの世界にはもううんざりだ.

a** [**the**] **twilight world 薄明かりの世界; はっきりしない状況; 法を避ける生き方 ▪ They live in *a twilight world* where drugs and sleeping rough are usual. 彼らは麻薬と野宿が日常の, 法を避ける生活をしている.

a whole world of 無数[量]の《a WORLD of の強意形》 ▪ I have *a whole world of* business to do today. 今日はする仕事が山ほどある.

a world away from …とはるかに異なって[隔たって] ▪ Her interests are *a world away from* his. 彼女の興味は彼のとはまるで異なっている.

a world of 無数[量]の ▪ This air is doing you *a world of* good. この空気は大変あなたのためになっています ▪ I had *a world of* things to say to you. あなたに言うことがどっさりあった.

***a world of difference** (**between** A **and** B)* 《口》 **1** (AとBとの)大きな違い, 天と地の開き, 雲泥の差 ▪ There's *a world of difference between* seeing a film on video *and* seeing it in the theater. 映画をビデオで見るのと劇場で見るのとは大違いだ.

W

2 大いなる前進，大きな影響，顕著な感化 ▪ A little sympathy makes *a world of difference* to someone badly treated. 虐待を受けた者にはちょっとした思いやりでも大きな救いだ.

above the world 俗世間を超越して ▪ He is *above the world* and, so to speak, extramundane. 彼は俗世間を超越し，いわば浮世離れしている.

against the world 全世界を敵に回して ▪ I will hold thee with my life *against the world*. 私は全世界を敵に回しても命がけでそなたを防ぎ守ろう.

all ... in the world (特に時間が)たっぷりの ▪ Come any time tomorrow. I'll have *all* the time *in the world*. 明日いつでも来いよ．時間はたっぷりある.

all the world **1** 全世界 ▪ London is the fairest capital of *all the world*. ロンドンは全世界で一番美しい首都である.

2 生存しているすべての人々；(狭義では)世間(のすべての人々) ▪ *All the world* loves him. すべての人々が彼を愛している ▪ I will faithfully serve her against *all the world*. 私は世間すべての人を向こうに回して彼女に忠実に仕えよう.

3 上流社会のすべての人々 ▪ Oh, *all the world*'s here. ああ，上流社会のすべての人々がここにいます.

4 ありとあらゆるもの；(しばしば感情的に)すべての[かけがえのない]もの (*to*) ▪ I may forsake mankind, and *all the world*. 私は人間もありとあらゆるものも捨ててよい ▪ She is *all the world to* me. 彼女は私にとってかけがえのないものだ.

(all) the world and his wife 《英戯》(男も女も)誰もかれもみな，猫もしゃくしも，非常に多くの人 (Swift, *Polite Conversation*, Dialogue 3) ▪ *All the world and his wife* were trying to trample upon me. 誰もかもが私を踏みつけにしようとしていた ▪ *The world and his wife* will be at the huge outdoor concert. その野外大コンサートには大勢が押しかけるだろう.

all the world over/all over the world 世界中で ▪ A girl who is both pretty and charming is popular *all the world over*. きれいで魅力のある少女はいたる所で人気がある.

All's right with the world. →RIGHT[1].

another world あの世；別世界 ▪ She preferred death in *another world* to life in this. 彼女はこの世で生きているよりもいっそ死んであの世へ行くほうがいいと思った ▪ It is like entering *another world*. それは別世界に入るような思いだ.

as long as the [this] world lasts この世の続くかぎり ▪ There will be war *as long as the world lasts*. この世の続くかぎり戦争は絶えないだろう.

as the [this] world goes 世間並みに言えば ▪ *As the world goes*, this is no small assurance I repose in you. 世間並みに言えば，私が君に寄せているこの信頼はたいしたものですよ.

be born into the [this] world 生まれる ▪ He *was* then not yet *born into this world*. 彼は当時まだ生まれていなかった.

be sent into the world →SEND.

be worlds apart →APART.

begin [go out into] the world 世の中へ出る ▪ You are *beginning the world* as you call it. 君はいわゆる世の中へ出始めているわけだ.

bring ... into the world **1** →BRING.

2 (助産師などが)子供を取り上げる ▪ The doctor who *brought* me *into the world* died yesterday. 僕が生まれた時に取り上げてくれた医師が昨日亡くなった.

broke to the (wide, wide) world →BROKE.

carry the world before one →CARRY all before one.

come down in the world = go down in the WORLD.

come into [to] the world 《雅》生まれる；出版される ▪ Our lives changed completely when little Jimmy *came into the world*. ジミー坊やが生まれて，私たちの生活はすっかり変わった ▪ All of us *came to the world* with nothing. 我々はみな何も持たずにこの世に生まれた ▪ A little treatise has lately *come into the world*. ある小論文が最近出版された.

come [go, move] up in the world = get up in the WORLD.

dead to the world →DEAD.

depart out of this world → go out of this WORLD.

do ... the world of good (人を)ずっと気分よく[元気に]させる ▪ We had a week off at the beach and it's *done* us both *the world of good*. 海辺で1週間休暇を過ごしたら二人ともすっかり元気になった.

enter the world **1** 世に出る，生まれる ▪ God *entered the world* through the womb of the Blessed Virgin Mary. 神は聖母マリアの胎内から生まれた.

2 世の中へ出る ▪ You must *enter the world* soon. 君はやがて世の中へ出なければならない.

for (all) the world 〚否定文で〛どうあっても ▪ I would not do such a thing *for all the world*. そんなことは絶対にするもんか. ☞「全世界をくれても」が原義.

for all the world like [as if] 《文》どう見ても…のようで，まるで…のようで ▪ He is, *for all the world*, *like* a monkey. 彼はどう見てもサルにそっくりだ ▪ She looked *for all the world as if* she were a boy. 彼女はまるで男の子のようだった ▪ Love can look *for all the world like* mental illness. 恋をすると，ちょうど心の病にかかったのとそっくりの様相を呈する. ☞「世界中のあらゆるものを考慮しても」が原義.

for the world/for anything in the world どうあっても ▪ I would not do it *for the world*. どうあってもそんなことをするもんか.

get on in the world 出世する ▪ He is *getting on* a little *in the world*. 彼は少し出世しかけている.

get the best of both worlds →BEST.

get the worst of both worlds = make the worst of both WORLDs.

get [come, go, move] up in the world 社会

的位置が向上する ▪ His family is now *getting up in the world.* 彼の家族は目下，社会的地位が向上している ▪ He must be *moving up in the world* to live in Beverly Hills. ビバリーヒルズに住んでいるところを見ると，彼は出世しているにちがいない.

give the world .../give ... to the world (物)を作って[発明して]世に送り出す，出版[公表]する ▪ England *gave* soccer *to the world* in the 19th century. イングランドは19世紀にサッカーを考案して世に広めた.

give worlds [the world] (...のためなら)どんなことでもする，いとわない (*for, to do*) ▪ The man would *give worlds for* a glass of beer. あの男は1杯のビールにありつけるなら何ものもいとわない ▪ I'd *give the world to* be there but alas, I can not be. 何としてもそこへ行きたいのだが，残念ながら行けない.

go down in the world 社会的位置が下がる，落ちぶれる ▪ He has *gone down in the world* of late. 彼は最近落ちぶれてきた.

go out into the world →begin the WORLD.

go [depart] out of this world 世を去る，死ぬ ▪ She *went out of this world* last week at age 46. 彼女は先週46歳でこの世を去った.

go to the better world あの世へ行く，死ぬ ▪ The novelist has *gone to the better world.* その小説家はあの世へ行った.

Half [One half of] the world knows [kens] not how the other (half) live [lies]. 《諺》世人の半分は他の半分の人々の生活を知らない《安逸贅沢な生活をしている者には貧しい人々の生活は分からない》.

have the best of both worlds = get the BEST of both worlds.

have the cares [weight] of the world on one's shoulders 大きな心配をかかえている ▪ She looks as if she's *got the cares of the world on her shoulders.* 彼女は大きな悩みをかかえているみたいな様子だ.

have the world at one's feet [before one] **1** 洋々たる前途がある ▪ He will *have the world at his feet* in another five years. 彼はもう5年もすれば洋々たる前途が開けるだろう ▪ He *has the world before* him. 彼は前途洋々だ.
2 大成功をおさめている，きわめて人気がある ▪ The young film star already *has the world at her feet* only a year after her debut. その若手映画スターはデビュー後わずか1年でもう絶大な人気を博している.

How goes the world with ...?/How is the world using [treating] ...? ...の景気はどうか，どう暮らしているか ▪ *How goes the world with* him? 彼はどうしていますか ▪ *How is the world using* you? いかがお暮らしですか.

how the world goes 事情がどうなっているか ▪ Let us go and see *how the world goes* with him. 彼がどうしているか見に行ってみよう.

(I don't know) what's the world [what the world's] coming to. (人のしたことを非難して)一体どうなっているのやら; 一体この世の中どうなって行くのだろう《世も末だ》 ▪ Instant stew? *What is the world coming to?* インスタント・シチューだって? 世も末だな ▪ When I read the news these days I wonder *what the world's coming to.* 最近ニュースを読むと世の中は一体どうなるのだろうかと思う ▪ Video games in the library? *What is the world coming to?* 図書室にビデオゲームを設置してあるとは，一体何を考えているのだろう.

I would give worlds [the world] to do どんなにしても...したい ▪ *I would give the world to* know what they are talking about. どんなにしても彼らが話していることが知りたいものだ.

in a (little) world of one's own/in one's own (little) world/in a (little) world by oneself **1** 自分一人の世界に閉じこもって ▪ Since her husband died, she has been living *in a world of her own.* 夫が死んで以来，彼女は自分一人の世界に閉じこもって生活している ▪ He is *in a little world of his own* in a cabin in the mountains. 彼は山奥の小屋でひっそりと暮らしている ▪ She was really *in her own world* at the meeting. 彼女は会合で全くぽつんとしていた.
2 非常に集中して，深い瞑想に入って ▪ She is *in a world of her own* when she is reading. 彼女は読書中にはそれに没頭する.
3《俗》独りよがりで ▪ He is *in a world* all *by himself* and doesn't care what people think of him. 彼は全く独りよがりで，人が何と言おうと気にしない.

in an ideal [a perfect] world 理想的な世界では ▪ *In an ideal world* we would be recycling everything. 理想を言えばあらゆる物をリサイクルできるようになればと思う.

in another world 他のことを考えて，茫然(ぼうぜん)自失して ▪ She just sat there—she seemed to be *in another world.* 彼女はただじっと座っていてぼんやりとした様子だった.

in the world **1** 世界中で ▪ He is the greatest man *in the world.* 彼は世界中で一番偉い人だ.
2〚疑問文・否定文を強調して〛一体全体，いやしくも ▪ What *in the world* does he mean? 一体彼はどういうつもりなのか ▪ He had not a debt *in the world.* 彼は借金は全然なかった.

in the world but not of it 世俗的でない，浮世離れした ▪ He is a strange visionary, *in the world but not of it.* 彼は一風変わった空想家で浮世離れしている.

It's a funny old world. 偶然の一致[不思議な出来事]がいろいろと起きる ▪ Fancy meeting you here of all places! *Isn't it a funny old world?* よりによってこんな所であなたにばったり会うなんて! まさに奇遇ね.

It's a small world. 世の中は狭いね ▪ Well, well, well, *it's a small world*, isn't it? 全く世の中って狭いね.

know the world 世間を知る ▪ Old folks have discretion, and *know the world.* 老人は分別があ

り，世間を知っている.

lead the world 世界をリードする，世界一である ▪ America undoubtedly *leads the world* in motion pictures. 米国は映画にかけては確かに世界一だ.

let the world wag (***as it will***) →WAG[2].

live out of the world 世間を避ける ▪ Since he retired from business he has *lived out of the world*. 彼は仕事をやめてからは隠とんしている.

make a noise in the world →NOISE.

make the best of both worlds **1** 世俗的利害と精神的利害の一致を図る; 二つの相反する要求を満たす ▪ He loves his family, but he also likes golf, and tries to *make the best of both worlds*. 彼は家庭を愛しているが，同時にゴルフも好きなので，できる限り両者を生かそうと努力している.
2 異なる両陣営からよいことをせしめる ▪ There have been statesmen seeking to *make the best of both worlds*. 双方からうまい汁を吸おうとする政治家たちがこれまでにいた.

make the world go round 世の中をうまく動かす ▪ It's love that *makes the world go round*. 世の中をうまく動かすのは愛だ.

make the worst of both worlds 二つの考え方[やり方，暮らし方]の一番悪いところをあわせ持つ ▪ Smoking as well as drinking much is *making the worst of both worlds*. 大酒を飲んでタバコを吸っていれば，両方の一番悪いところをつかむことになる.

mean [***be***] (***all***) ***the world to*** ...にとってかけがえのないものである (→all the WORLD 4) ▪ This job *means the world to* me, and I love it very much. この仕事は私にとってかけがえのないもので，強く愛着を感じています ▪ We've only got one child and he'*s all the world to* us. 私たちにはたった一人しか子供がいないので目に入れても痛くない.

Never in the world! 絶対に(...)しない ▪ Will he succeed?—*Never in the world!* 彼は成功するだろうか—絶対だめだね.

not ... for worlds どうあっても...しない ▪ I would*n't* stand in his way *for worlds*. 私はどうあっても彼のじゃまはしない.

not set the world on fire あまりわくわくさせない，大してうまくいっていない ▪ The restaurant offers a decent menu, but it does*n't set the world on fire*. そのレストランはそこそこのメニューを提供するが，あまりぱっとはしない.

of the world 世俗の，俗な (secular) ▪ Be not *of the world*. 俗界を脱せよ.

on top of the world →TOP[1].

one of the world's worst 《口》この上もなくいやなやつ ▪ He's quite *one of the world's worst*. 彼は全くこの上もなくいやなやつだ.

out of this [***the***] ***world*** **1**《米俗》特別上等の，とびきりの，すてきな ▪ It's a simple recipe but tastes *out of the world*. それは簡単なレシピだがとびきりおいしい ▪ Patsy's cooking is really *out of this world*. パッツィの料理はほんとにすてきだ.
2《俗》(麻薬[酒]に) 酔って ▪ Is she ever *out of this world*! What did she drink? 彼女，酔ってふらふらじゃないか. 何を飲んだんだ?

put ... into the world ...を世の中へ出す ▪ They are old enough to *be put into the world*. 彼らは世の中へ出してよい年ごろだ.

rock the world of ... 内で強烈な印象を与える ▪ The DVD recorder had *rocked the world of* TV. DVDレコーダーはテレビ業界で異彩を放った.

see the world 世界[世間]を知る ▪ He has traveled, and *seen the world*. 彼は旅行をして，世間を見てきた.

set the world on fire →set the THAMES on fire.

set the world to rights 《口》天下国家を論じる ▪ They sat by the fire, *setting the world to rights*. 彼らは炉端に座って天下国家を論じた.

take the world as it is [***as** one **finds it***] 世の中をありのままに受けいれる ▪ I think we ought to *take the world as it is*. 世の中はこうしたものだとそのまま受けいれるべきだと思う.

the best of all possible worlds →BEST.

the end(***s***) ***of the world*** →END[1].

the fourth world 《口》第四世界，資源[工業技術]がなく貧しい発展途上の国々 ▪ Their collective standard of living is reduced to a *Fourth World* nation. 彼らの総体的生活水準は第四世界の国のレベルまで落ちている.

the lower [***nether***] ***world*** 黄泉，冥府，地獄 ▪ Dante visited *the nether world* of woe. ダンテは苦しみの地獄を訪れた.

the New World 新世界《特に南北アメリカ》 ▪ *The New World* poured in many objects hitherto unknown to Europe. 新世界は今までヨーロッパに知られていなかった多くのものを続々と取り入れた.

the next world →the other WORLD.

the Old World 旧世界《特にヨーロッパ・アジア》 ▪ American freedom exerts great influence upon *the Old World*. アメリカの自由は旧世界に大きな影響を及ぼす.

the other [***next***] ***world***/***the world to come*** [***to be***] あの世，来世 ▪ Will there be no jealousies in *the other world*? あの世には嫉妬などないのだろうか.

the outside world (自分の住んでいる)外の世界 ▪ The snow cut them off from *the outside world*. その雪で彼らは外の世界から孤立してしまった.

the** Smith**s of this world 《口》〖...s は複数形の人名〗一般に(スミス)という名前の人 ▪ What makes many of *the* Johnson*s of this world* so successful, I wonder? ジョンスンという名の人が多く出世するのはなぜだろう.

the third world **1** (旧米ソ[資本主義諸国と共産圏]に対して) 中立国 ▪ The two superpowers feared *the third world* nations might fall into alignment with the enemy. 両超大国は非同盟諸国が相手国に加担しはすまいかと恐れていた.
2 (アジア・アフリカなどの)発展途上国 ▪ *The third*

world must be freed from starvation and illiteracy. 発展途上国から飢餓と非識字をなくさねばならない.

the way of the world →WAY.

the whole world 1 全世界 ▪ Once beyond Whitford, *the whole world* was new to her. ひとたびウィットフォードの外へ出ると, 全世界が彼女にとっては新しかった.

2 (世間の)すべての人々 ▪ *The whole world* is beggaring itself by war. 万人が戦争で貧乏になっている.

The world is *one's* ***oyster.*** 世の中は我が意のままだ (cf. Sh., *Merry W.* 2. 2. 2) ▪ If you've got a good education, *the world is your oyster.* しっかりとした教養があれば世の中は思いのままになる.

the world over =all the WORLD over.

the world, the flesh, and the devil 名利と肉欲と邪心《もろもろの誘惑》(Prayer Book, "the Litany") ▪ He renounces *the world, the flesh, and the devil*, preaching and praying every day. 彼は名利と肉欲と邪心を捨てて, 毎日説教したり祈ったりしている.

the world to come [***to be***] → the other WORLD.

the world will [***would***] ***be the poorer*** [***a poorer place***] ***for*** 世界は...の分だけ貧しくなるだろう ▪ *The world will be a poorer place for* his death. 彼の死によって世界はその分だけ貧しくなろう.

the world's end 世の果て (→to the WORLD's end) ▪ He lives at *the world's end.* 彼は世の果てに住んでいる.

think the world of ...を非常に重んじる, とても愛している ▪ She *thinks the world of* Beth. 彼女はベスをかけがえのないものに思っている ▪ My son *thinks the world of* you. 息子はあなたをとても愛していますよ.

(***think*** [***consider***]) ***the world owes*** *one* ***a living*** (自分はすぐれた人間だから, あるいは生きているのだから)世間から食べさせてもらう権利がある(と考える) ▪ Many people *think the world owes* them *a living.* 自分は世間から食べさせてもらう権利があると考えている人が多い.

(***think***) ***the world revolves around*** *one* 《口》世界が自分を中心に回っている(と考えている) ▪ I hate working with George. He thinks *the world revolves around* him. ジョージと仕事を組むのはごめんだな. あいつは自分を何さまだと思っているんだ.

to the world 《俗》全く, すっかり (→be whacked to the WIDE) ▪ I am tired [drunk] *to the world.* すっかり疲れて[酔って]しまった.

to the world's end 世の終わり[果て]まで ▪ Human nature will never change *to the world's end.* 人情は世の終わりまで変わるまい ▪ I resolved to follow her *to the world's end.* 私は世の果てまで彼女を追って行こうと決心した.

watch the world go by 世の中の動きを傍観する ▪ He was content to just sit back and *watch the world go by.* 彼はいすにゆったりと腰かけて世の中の動きを傍観することに満足していた.

What is the world coming to? →(I don't know) what's the WORLD coming to.

while the world goes round この世のあらんかぎり ▪ Their fame shall last *while the world goes round.* 彼らの名声はこの世のあらんかぎり続くことになろう.

one's ***whole world comes crashing down around*** *one*/*one's* ***whole world turns upside down*** 自分の全世界が音を立てて崩れ落ちる[ひっくり返る]; (不快な出来事で)うろたえる ▪ She said she didn't love me anymore, and *my whole world came crashing down around* me. もう愛していないと彼女に言われて私はおろおろした ▪ When she found out he'd had an affair, *her whole world turned upside down.* 彼の浮気を知ったとき彼女はすっかり取り乱した.

world without end 永久(に[の])《誇張表現》(《聖》*Isa.* 45. 17; Prayer Book, "*Morning Prayer*") ▪ He talks *world without end.* 彼はいつまでもしゃべる ▪ He has a *world-without-end* of things to do. 彼にはしなければならないことが無限にある.

worlds away from =a WORLD away from.

worlds too あまりにも ▪ I was *worlds too* shy. 私はあまりにも内気だった.

would give the world for →GIVE.

worm[1] /wəːrm/ 名 ***a can*** [***bag***] ***of worms*** 見かけよりも複雑[困難]な状況, 触らない方が無難なもの ▪ This problem may look simple, but in fact it's *a can of worms.* この問題は一見単純そうだが, 実は非常に厄介なものだ.

a worm's-eye view 《英》虫瞰図; 近視眼的[現実的]印象[見解]; 下から見上げた部分的な眺め, 低い地位からの限られた見方 (→a BIRD'S-EYE view) ▪ Let me offer you *a worm's-eye view* based on my own experience. 私自身の経験に基づく卑見を述べさせていただきます ▪ The novel provides us with *a worm's eye view* of society. その小説には下位層から見上げた社会の一部が描かれている ▪ They gave *a worm's eye view* of the situation as they saw it. 彼らはその状況について見た通りの現実的な印象を述べた.

be a worm 憂鬱である, 元気がない (《聖》*Ps.* 22. 6) ▪ I *am a worm* today. きょうは元気がない.

(***Even***) ***a worm will turn.***/ ***Tread on a worm and it will turn.*** 《諺》一寸の虫にも五分の魂.

idle worms 怠け者の指にできると思われている虫 ▪ Warm the *idle worms* in your fingers' ends. あなたの指先にできた怠けの虫を暖めなさい《怠けるな》.

meat [***food***] ***for worm***/ ***worm's*** [***worms'***] ***meat*** (人間の)死体; 死すべき人間 ▪ By Heaven, he shall be *worms' meat* within these two hours. 誓って, あの男をこの2時間内に殺してやろう.

(***must have***) ***had worms for breakfast*** 《口》じっとして[座って]いられない ▪ What's the matter? Did you *have worms for breakfast*? 一体ど

うしたの. 何をそんなにそわそわしているのよ.

the son of a worm みじめな人間 (《聖》*Job* 15. 14) ▪ He that affronts me is *the son of a worm.* 私を侮辱する人はみじめな人間だ.

the worm of conscience 良心のとがめ ▪ *The worm of conscience* still gnaws thy soul. 良心のとがめがいつもお前の心を刺している.

***the worm turns* [*may turn*]** 《口》(従順な人が)急に強気に出る, (辛抱強い人が)突然がまんできなくなる ▪ She has dominated her husband, but some day *the worm may turn.* 彼女は夫をずっとしりに敷いてきたが, いまに噛みつかれるぞ.

worm[2] /wəːrm/ 動 ***worm** oneself **into*** **1** くねくねと入って行く ▪ Gale *wormed himself into* the little passage. ゲイルはくねくねとその小さな通路へ入って行った.

2 巧妙に取り入って(信用・地位など)を得る ▪ He *wormed himself into* cabin boy. 彼は巧妙に取り入ってキャビンボーイになった.

worm** one's **way into **1** くねくねと入って行く (= WORM oneself into) ▪ Her pet chihuahua *wormed his way into* my yard. 彼女のペットのチワワが身を捩じらせてうちの裏庭に入ってきた.

2 巧妙に取り入って(信用・地位など)を得る ▪ She *wormed her way into* favor with Lord North. 彼女は巧妙に取り入ってノース卿の寵愛を得た.

wormwood /wə́ːrmwʊ̀d/ 名 ***be* (*gall and*) *wormwood to*** …にとってきわめて不快である, 非常にくやしい (《聖》*Lam.* 3. 19) ▪ The accounts *were wormwood to* the Duke. その話は公爵にはひどくいやだった ▪ The sight of other people's good fortune *is gall and wormwood to* a vast number of people. 他人の幸運を見るのは, 非常に多くの人々にとってくやしさの種となる.

worn /wɔːrn/ 形 ***worn threadbare/worn to a shred* [*shreds*]** (服・考えなどが)使い古しの, くたびれた ▪ He loves his old jeans *worn to shreds.* 彼ははき古したジーンズが大のお気に入りである.

worry[1] /wə́ːri|wʌ́ri/ 名 ***No worries!*** 《口》(依頼に対して)承知した ▪ Will you help me with my homework?—Sure, *no worries.* 僕の宿題を手伝ってもらえないか—いいとも, お安い御用だ.

worry[2] /wə́ːri|wʌ́ri/ 動 ***be worried sick about* [*over*]** = WORRY oneself sick about.

be worried to death **1** = WORRY ... to death 1.

2 …のことでひどく心配している ▪ We *are worried to death* about the sudden drop in the stock market. 株価の急落が心配でたまらない.

I should worry. 《反語》ちっともかまわないよ, それはいいね ▪ Now I can say *I should worry.* 言っとくけど, こっちはちっともかまわないよ.

not to worry 《口》心配ご無用 ▪ *Not to worry,* Ed. We are in the same boat. 心配するなよ, エド. 僕たち二人とも立場は同じさ.

***worry** oneself* くよくよする, 気をもむ ▪ Don't *worry yourself* about it. そのことでくよくよするな.

***worry** oneself **sick* [*silly*] *about* [*over*]** …のことでひどく心配する ▪ She *worried herself silly over* her profligate son. 彼女はどら息子のことをひどく心配した.

worry the sword 《フェンシング》しきりに剣を動かして相手を悩ます ▪ While the beast is *worrying the sword* he slips into the church. 人でなしが剣を振り回している間に彼は教会にすべり込んだ.

worry ... to death **1** …を死ぬまで苦しめる ▪ He *was worried to death* by those ungrateful nations. 彼はその恩知らずな諸国民に死ぬまで苦しめられた.

2 死ぬほど悩ます ▪ You *worry* me *to death* with your chattering. 君のおしゃべりにはほとほと閉口する.

worry** one's **way 苦心して進む ▪ Scott *worried his way* into some understanding of the language. スコットは苦心してその言語を多少理解するにいたった.

You had me worried. 《口》君の話を取り違えて心配したよ ▪ *You had me worried*—I thought you were going to resign! 心配するではないか. 君が辞めるとでもいうのかと思ったよ.

You should worry! 《口・戯》あなたには心配なんかないはずだ, 心配しなくてもよい ▪ Even if you're not in the USA, *you should worry.* たとえ米国にいなくても君には心配などないはずだ ▪ *You should worry!* You're the best in the class and you won't fail the exam. 心配ご無用. 君はクラスでトップだから試験に落ちはしないさ.

worse /wəːrs/ 形副名 (***and***) ***what is worse*** →to make matters WORSE.

and worse →or WORSE.

be in a worse way than …よりも病気が重い ▪ He *is in a worse way than* you. 彼は君よりも病気が重い.

be taken worse 病気が悪くなる ▪ He has *been taken worse.* 彼は病気が悪くなった.

be worse off 暮らし向きが悪い ▪ He *is* far *worse off* than his brother. 彼は兄よりもずっと暮らし向きが悪い.

be worse than uselss 有害無益である ▪ Your remedy *is worse than useless.* 君の救済策は有害無益だ.

be worse than** one's **word →be better than one's WORD.

can* [*could*] *do worse than *do* 《口》…するのも悪くない ▪ You *could do worse than* go into teaching as a profession. 教師を職業とするのも悪くない. ☞この句は understatement だから「…するのはすばらしい」の意を含む.

come off worse (けんか・競争に)負ける ▪ The police *came off worse* in that chase. その追跡劇では警察の方が振り切られた.

do worse いっそうひどいことをする (*to*) ▪ To *do worse to* you would be fell cruelty. あなたにいっそうひどいことをするのは, 恐るべき残忍というものでしょう.

for better or for worse/for better, for

worse →BETTER[1].

for the worse (変化などが)悪い方へ，いっそう悪く ▪ We swapped *for the worse*. 我々は交換して悪いものを取ってしまった ▪ The patient took a turn *for the worse*. 病人は悪化した.

go from bad to worse →BAD.

have the worse (試合などで)負ける; (一般に)不利な立場にある ▪ In that battle the heathen people *had* greatly *the worse*. その戦闘で異教徒が大敗した ▪ He divined that he should *have the worse* of this. 彼はこれで自分が不利な立場に立つだろうと推測した.

if worse comes to worst →if the WORST comes to the worst.

(it) could be worse まずまずというところだ，上を見ればきりがない ▪ I know things *could be worse* with me, but it is still very bad. 私の現状はまあまあだとは分かっているが，それにしても実にひどい.

(it) could have been worse まずまずというところだった，不幸中の幸いだった ▪ The damage was pretty bad, but *it could have been worse*. 損害はかなりひどかったが，でもあれだけで済んでよかった.

it might have been worse あれくらいで済んでよかった ▪ All one can say is that *it might have been worse*. あれくらいで済んでよかったとしか言えない.

make matters [things] worse 事態を悪くする ▪ The fact that he spent the money *made things worse*. 彼がその金を使ったため事態が悪化した.

no worse than …と変わらない[同じ]くらい良い ▪ If need be, I shall do it *no worse than* others. 必要とあれば他の者に負けないくらいにやってやる.

none the worse for **1** …にもかかわらず同じ状態で ▪ He was *none the worse for* his accident. 彼は事故にあってもどうもなかった.

2 《口》…でよくなって ▪ His coat would be *none the worse for* a good brushing. 彼の上着は十分ブラシをかけたらよくなるだろう.

3 …にもかかわらずやはり，同じように ▪ I like him *none the worse for* being outspoken. 彼は思うことをずばりと言うが，それでもやはり私は彼が好きだ.

or [and] worse さらに悪いもの ▪ It is a disgrace *or worse*—perhaps a crime. それは不面目よりもさらに悪いもの—おそらく犯罪である ▪ He slandered them for drunkards *and worse*. 彼は彼らのことを酔いどれとか，さらにひどいことを言って中傷した.

put ... to better and to worse …をあらゆる運命にさらす ▪ I will *put* my body *to better and to worse*, to fight for the queen. 私はわが身をあらゆる運命にさらして，女王のために戦おう.

so much the worse for …によっていっそう悪くなって，…した分だけかえってひどくなって ▪ I got *so much the worse for* the change of air. 転地したらかえって病状が悪化した ▪ The show is *so much the worse for* the change. ショーは手を加えたためにかえって悪くなっている.

the worse for drink [liquor] 酒に酔って ▪ He was run over because the driver was *the worse for drink*. 彼がはねられたのは，運転者が酒気帯びだったからだ.

the worse for wear →WEAR[1].

(Things [It]) could be worse. まあまあだよ ▪ How are things with you these days? Well, *could be worse*, I guess. 調子はどうだい—まあまあってとこさ. ☞How are you? などの応答.

think none the worse of …をやはり重んじる[尊敬する] ▪ I *think none the worse of* him because he is ill-dressed. 私は彼が身なりが悪くてもやはり尊敬する.

to make matters [things] worse/(and) what is worse その上悪いことには ▪ *To make matters worse*, her husband became ill. その上彼女が困ったことには，夫が病気になった ▪ *What is worse*, he did not leave his address. さらに悪いことには，彼は宛名書きを残さなかった.

worse and worse いっそう[いよいよ]悪く ▪ The patient is getting *worse and worse*. 病人はいよいよ悪くなっている.

one's ***worse half*** →HALF.

worse kind 《米口》ひどく (=(the) WORST kind) ▪ Then he begged *worse kind* just to let him go out. それから，彼はちょっと外へ出させてくれと懇願した.

worse luck →LUCK[1].

worse than all 何よりも困ったことには ▪ *Worse than all*, his father has gone bankrupt. 何よりも困ったことに，彼の父親が破産した.

worse than ever ますます悪く[ひどく] ▪ He behaves *worse than ever*. 彼のふるまいはますます悪くなってきた ▪ It is raining *worse than ever*. 雨がますますひどく降っている.

worse than useless 有害無益で，全然役に立たない ▪ Those movies are *worse than useless*. そういう映画は有害無益だ.

Worse things happen at sea. →SEA.

worship[1] /wə́ːrʃəp/ 名 ***a place [house] of worship*** 礼拝所 ▪ They went to their different *places of worship*. 彼らはそれぞれ異なった礼拝所へ出かけた.

the worship of Mammon 金銭崇拝，過度の金銭欲 ▪ He has confused the worship of God with *the worship of Mammon*. 彼は神の崇拝を金銭欲の礼賛と混同していた. ☞Mammon は貪欲と金銭崇拝の象徴(《聖》*Luke* 16. 13).

your [his] worship 《英》閣下《特に市長について》 ▪ *His Worship* the Mayor of Wells today made a visit to the hospital. ウェルズ市長閣下が本日病院を訪問された ▪ I have got a letter for *your worship*. 閣下宛ての手紙を持っています.

worship[2] /wə́ːrʃəp/ 動 ***worship at the alter [shrine] of*** …を支持する，信奉する ▪ We tend to *worship at the altar of* technology. 我々はとかく科学技術を信奉しがちである.

worship the ground *a person* ***walks [treads] on*** 人をこの上もなく愛する[賛美する]

▪ She *worships the ground* her son *walks on.* 彼女は息子をこの上もなく愛している.

worship the rising sun →adore the rising SUN.

worshipful /wə́ːrʃəpfəl/ 形 ***the Most*** [***Right***] ***Worshipful*** 閣下《市長・州長官などについて》 ▪ The letter was addressed to *the Right Worshipful* the mayor. 手紙は市長閣下宛てになっていた ▪ "Thanks, *Most Worshipful*," returned Miss Vernon.「ありがとうございます, 閣下」とバーノン嬢は答えた.

worst /wəːrst/ 形副名 ***at*** (***the***) ***worst*** **1** 最悪の状態で ▪ You are *at the worst* now, and things will begin turning up. 君は今が最悪の状態で, これから好転しだすだろう ▪ When the world is *at worst* it will mend. 世界は最悪の状態になると好転していく. **2** 最悪の場合でも, いくら悪くても ▪ *At the worst*, he will not come off a loser. いくら悪くても彼は負けはしないだろう.

at *one's* ***worst*** 最悪の状態で, 最も不できの場合で ▪ The storms are *at their worst* in February. あらしは二月が一番ひどい ▪ Even *at his worst*, he was better than any of them. 彼は最悪のできの場合でも彼らの誰よりもじょうずだった.

be prepared for the worst 最悪を覚悟している ▪ I *am prepared for the worst*, even recall. 私は最悪を覚悟しています, 取り消しさえも.

bring out the worst in →BRING out the best in a person.

come off worst (競争・けんかで)負ける, 大敗する, 最下位になる ▪ He *came off worst* in the TV debate. テレビ討論会で彼がビリになった.

come to the worst 最悪の事態になる ▪ Things never *come to the worst* but they mend. 物事は最悪の事態になれば必ず改まる.

do *one's* [***the***] ***worst*** 最もひどいことをする ▪ Now you may go away and *do your worst.* さあ行って最もひどいことをするがいい ▪ Let the wind *do its worst.* 風にどれほどでもひどく吹かせてみるがいい.

fear the worst →FEAR².

get the worst of both worlds →make the worst of both WORLDs.

get the worst of it (けんかなどで)負ける, やっつけられる ▪ This is the first time I ever *got the worst of it.* これまでに負けたのは今回が初めてだ.

give *a person* ***the worst kind of*** 《米口》人にこっぴどく…を与える ▪ I *gave* him *the worst kind of* a licking. 彼をこっぴどくなぐってやった.

have the worst (***of it***) 負ける ▪ George decidedly *had the worst* in the fight. ジョージはそのけんかでこっぴどく負けた ▪ The Auckland players *had the worst of it* in that game. オークランドの選手たちがその試合で負けた ▪ We *had the worst of it* at first, for the game was a new one to us. そのゲームに慣れていなかったので我々は初めのうちは負けていた.

if the worst comes to the worst 最悪[万一]の場合には ▪ *If the worst comes to the worst,* you can declare bankruptcy. 最悪の場合は破産宣告をすればいい ▪ *If worse comes to worst,* we will send you home. いざとなったらお宅までお送りします.

if worst [***worse***] ***comes to worst*** 《主に米》 =if the WORST comes to the worst.

(***in***) ***the worst way*** 《米口》大いに, ひどく ▪ It was wanted *in the worst way.* それが大いに求められていた.

make the worst of …を悲観する, の最悪の面だけを考える ▪ But it's over, you know; so what's the point of *making the worst of* it? しかし, それはすんだことだよ. だから, それを悲観してどうなるというんだ.

make the worst of both worlds →WORLD.

speak [***talk***] ***the worst of*** …をこきおろす ▪ Let princes *speak the worst of* me. 諸公に私をこきおろさせるがよい.

(***the***) ***worst kind*** 《米口》非常に, ひどく, とても ▪ He loves Sally *the worst kind.* 彼はサリーをこよなく愛している ▪ I licked him *the worst kind.* 彼をこっぴどくなぐってやった.

the worst of **1** …の一番よくない性格 ▪ Do you know *the worst of* your father? 君はお父さんの一番よくない性格を知っているかね. **2** …の一番困ったこと ▪ But that was not *the worst of* it. しかし, それがそのことの一番困ったことではなかった.

the worst (***of it***) ***is*** (***that***) 一番悪い[困った]ことには ▪ *The worst was,* all the ladies cried in concert. 一番困ったことには, すべての女性たちが一斉に泣きだした.

think the worst of …を最も悪く考える ▪ She will not *think the worst of* me. 彼女は私のことをこの上もなく悪く考えはしないだろう.

worst of all 何よりも悪いことには, 一番困るのは ▪ The story is predictable, cliched, and *worst of all*, boring. その物語は話の筋が見え見えで, 陳腐な表現だらけで, それに最悪なことに退屈だ.

wouldn't wish ... on *one's* ***worst enemy*** いやなやつにも押しつける気になれない, きわめて不快である ▪ The aftereffects of the medicine are horrible. You *wouldn't wish* them *on your worst enemy.* その薬の後作用はひどく, 不快きわまりない.

worth /wəːrθ/ 形名 ***as much as ... is worth*** …の価値に匹敵する ▪ It is *as much as* his life *is worth.* それは彼としては命がけのことだ ▪ It is *as much as* my place *is worth* to let you see it. 君にそれを見せると私の地位が危うい.

for all *one* ***is worth*** **1** 全力を尽くして ▪ He ran *for all* he *was worth.* 彼は一生懸命に逃げた ▪ The steamer is driving, *for all* she *is worth*, down the waters. 汽船は全速力で川を下っている. **2** それだけのこととして (=for what it is WORTH) ▪ Yet you love me *for all* I *am worth.* なのにあなたはこんな私を愛してくれるのね.

for what it is worth 《口》 **1** (真偽はわからないが)それだけのこととして ▪ I took the story *for what it was worth.* 私はその話をそのままに受け取った.

2 価値があるか[役に立つか]どうかはわからないが ▪ *For what it's worth*, I'll always be here for you. お役に立てますかどうか, でも, ずっとここで待機しております ▪ That's my opinion *for what it's worth*. 大したものではないが以上が私の意見だ.

get in [***weigh in, have***] *one's* ***twopence*** [***fourpence***] ***worth*** 《口》(討論・会議などで)自分の意見を述べる ▪ You should have *got in your twopence worth* earlier. 君はもっと早く自分の意見を述べるべきだった.

get *one's* ***money's worth*** 金だけの値うちのものを得る ▪ The tour wasn't a great bargain, but I feel that we *got our money's worth*. 旅行はたいして安くはなかったが, 使った金だけの値うちはあったと思う.

it is worth *doing* …する価値がある ▪ *It is worth reading* this book. この本は読む値うちがある. ☞破格構文だが, 一流の文筆家が使用している.

it is worth while *doing*/***it is worth*** (*a person's*) ***while to*** *do* (人が)…する(ことに時間をかける)だけの価値がある ▪ When in Liverpool, *it is worth while visiting* the Anglican Cathedral. リバプールへ行ったら聖公会大聖堂は訪ねるだけの価値がある ▪ *It is worth your while to* read that book. あの本は読む価値があるよ.

make ... worth *a person's* ***while*** 《口》時間[労力]をかける価値を保障する, 時間[労力]に見合う金を支払う ▪ If you can work on Saturdays, we'll *make* it *worth your while*. 土曜日に勤務してもらえればそれ相当の賃金を支払います.

not worth a dime 全く価値[値うち]がない, 取るに足りない ▪ This swampy land is *not worth a dime*. このじめじめした土地は三文の値うちもない. ☞dime「米国の10セント硬貨」.

not worth a (***red***) ***cent*** →CENT.

not worth the paper it's [***they're***] ***printed*** [***written***] ***on*** (書類・契約書が)全く法的価値がない ▪ The promises in this letter are*n't worth the paper they're written on*. この書簡に書かれている約束に法的価値は全然ない.

of great [***little, no***] ***worth*** 価値の大きい[少ない, ない] ▪ He is a man *of great worth*. 彼はとても立派な人物だ ▪ It was a jewel *of little worth*. それはあまり価値のない宝石だった.

of worth すぐれた, 立派な ▪ Her thin white hand wore a ring *of worth*. 彼女の細い白い手には立派な指輪がはめてあった ▪ Women *of worth* and sense are to be found everywhere. 立派な分別のある女はいたる所にいる.

The worth of *a thing* ***is what it will bring.*** 《諺》物の価値はその物によって得られる金額の多寡で決まる.

weigh in *one's* ***twopence*** [***fourpence***] ***worth*** →get in one's twopence WORTH.

What is worth doing at all is worth doing well. 《諺》いやしくもする価値のあることなら立派にやるだけの価値がある.

What's it worth (***to*** *a person*)***?*** (それは)どれだけの価値があるか, (そうしてやったら)いくらくれるのか ▪ Can you help me?—I might. *What's it worth to you?* 手を貸してくれるかい?—やってもいいが, いくら寄こすか.

worth it 《口》骨折りがいのある ▪ Will the effort be *worth it*? その努力は骨折りがいがあるのか.

worth *doing* …するだけの価値がある, するに足る ▪ Is life *worth living*? 人生は生きていく価値があるのか ▪ The book is well *worth reading*. その本は十分読む価値がある ▪ It's hardly *worth troubling* about. それはほとんど気を使うだけの値うちがない.

worth the name 《文》…の名にふさわしい (=WORTHY of 1) ▪ Any artist *worth the name* could draw better than that. 画家の名にふさわしい者ならもっとましに描けるだろう.

worth *one's* ***weight in gold*** →one's WEIGHT in gold.

worth (*one's*) ***while*** (***to*** *do, doing*) (…するだけの)価値がある, 骨折りがいのある(「時間をかけるだけの」という意味はほとんど含まれない) ▪ I must do something *worth while*. 私は何か価値のあることをしなければならない ▪ It is *worth while reading* [*to* read] this book. この本は読むだけの価値がある ▪ The work is *worth our while*. その仕事は骨折りがいがある. ☞This book is worth while reading. は破格構文.

worthy /wə́ːrði/ 形副 ***worthy of*** **1** …にふさわしい, に足る ▪ He is a poet *worthy of* the name. 彼は詩人の名にふさわしい詩人だ ▪ The place is quite *worthy of* a visit. そこは一度行ってみるだけの価値が十分ある.

2《詩》…にふさわしく ▪ He acts *worthy of* himself. 彼は身にふさわしくふるまう.

worthy (***the***) *doing* …する値うちがある ▪ Nothing *worthy noticing* occurred. 何も注目するに足ることは起こらなかった ▪ His words are *worthy the inserting*. 彼の言葉は挿入する値うちがある.

worthy to *do* …するに足る ▪ This is surely a matter *worthy to* be considered. これは確かに考慮するに足る問題だ.

would /wəd, wʊd/ 助 ***I would*** 《口》君は…するがいい ▪ If possible, *I would* take an Herodotus with me. できればヘロドトスを1巻持って行くがいい ▪ *I would*n't go skating today; the ice isn't safe. きょうはスケートに行かないほうがいい. 氷が危険だから. ☞「私なら…する」という意味から発展したもの.

I would fain [***gladly, willingly***] *do* 喜んで…したい ▪ *I would gladly* be acquainted with her. 喜んで彼女と知り合いになりたい ▪ *I would fain* die a dry death. 溺れたり血を流したりする死に方はしたくない.

(***I***) ***would to God*** [***to Heaven***] (***that***) 〚仮定法の文を伴って〛どうか…であってほしい(I wish) ▪ *Would to God* it were true. それが本当であればよいがなあ ▪ *I would to God* I had more. もっとたくさんあればよいのだが.

one would think [***suppose***] …と思われる

W

▪ *One would think* she was keeping company with him. 彼女は彼とつき合っていたように思われる.

would have *a person do* 人に…させたいと思う ▪ What *would* you *have* me do? 私に何をさせたいのですか.

would not *do* どうしても…しなかった《過去の固執》 ▪ The door *would not* open. ドアはどうしても開かなかった ▪ He *would not* go any further. 彼はそれより先へは行こうとしなかった.

would rather [***sooner***] *do* →had RATHER; would SOONer do ... than do.

would that... 《雅》〚仮定法の文を伴って〛…であったらよいのに ▪ *Would that* I had seen the temple before it was burnt down. 焼失する前にその寺院を見ることができていたらなあ.

wouldn't be seen dead (***in a ditch***) ***with*** [***in***] 《口》…は死ぬほどいやだ ▪ I *wouldn't be seen dead with* him [*in* such clothes]. あんな男[あんな服]は死んだってごめんだ.

wouldn't know [***recognize***]***... if*** *he* ***saw one*** 《口》…のことなどまるで知らない ▪ I *wouldn't know* a musk duck *if* I *saw one*. 僕はニオイガモなんてまるで知らないね.

wound /waʊnd/ 名 ***By Christ's*** [***His***] ***wounds!/ His arms and wounds!/ Wounds of God!/ God's wounds!/ Blood and wounds!*** 誓って!, なむさん!, これはしたり!《誓言・呪詛》 ▪ *By His wounds*, false traitor, thou shall die. 裏切者め, 誓って殺してくれる ▪ *Blood and wounds!* do you question the honor of my wife! 驚いた, あなたは私の家内の名誉を疑われるのですか.

heal *one's* ***wounds*** 傷ついた感情が癒える ▪ It took a long time to *heal her wounds* after her husband passed away. 夫が亡くなってから彼女の心の傷が癒えるのに長いことかかった.

lick *one's* ***wounds*** →LICK².

like a wound/ like an open [***internal***] ***wound*** (悲しみ[苦悩]に)傷ついて ▪ This memory festered *like an open wound*. これを思い出しては悲しみで心がうずいた.

open [***reopen***] ***old wounds*** 心の古傷に触る, 昔の苦痛[悲しみ]を新たにする ▪ The news of the suspect's arrest *reopened old wounds* for the victim's family. 容疑者逮捕の知らせに, 犠牲者の遺族の心にあのときの悲しみが再び蘇ってきた.

wrack /ræk/ 名 ***bring*** [***put***]***... to wrack*** (***and ruin***) …を破滅させる ▪ The greater part of his army *were* all *put to wrack*. 彼の軍隊の大部分は残らず破滅させられた.

go [***run***] ***to wrack*** (***and ruin***) 破滅する ▪ All things were *going to wrack*. すべてのものが破滅に向かっていた ▪ This Ark by divine Providence was held from *running to wrack*. この箱船は神意によって破滅するのを免れた.

wrap¹ /ræp/ 名 ***be*** [***lie***] ***under wraps*** 秘密になっている ▪ The design for the new museum *is* still *under wraps*. 新美術館の建築設計はまだ内緒にされている ▪ These letters have *lain under wraps* since then. これらの書簡はそれ以来非公開になっている.

keep ... under wraps 《口》(計画を)秘密にしておく, (人を)隠しておく ▪ Their plans *are kept under wraps*. 彼らの計画は秘密にされている.

take [***remove***] ***the wraps off*** [***from***] …を公開する ▪ *The wraps* will soon *be taken off* our new machine. わが社の新しい機械はじきに公開される.

the wraps come off …が公開される ▪ *The wraps came off* BMW's latest model today. BMW の最新モデルが今日お披露目された.

wrap² /ræp/ 動 ***be wrapped*** (***up***) ***in*** **1** …に夢中になる, にすっかり心を奪われる ▪ He *was wrapped up in* thought. 彼は夢中で考えこんでいた ▪ He *is wrapped up in* himself. 《米俗》彼はうぬぼれている ▪ He *is* completely *wrapped up in* his work. 彼は仕事に没頭しきっている.
2 深く関係[関連]している ▪ We learned our neighbors *were wrapped up in* criminal activities. 近くの住人たちが犯行に深く関わっていることが分かった.

wrap *one's* ***brain*** [***mind***] ***around*** 《俗》理解する ▪ I just can't *wrap my brain around* what you say. おっしゃることが分かりかねますが.

Wrap (***it***) ***up!*** だまれ ▪ *Wrap it up*, you boys! しゃべるな, おまえたち.

wrap (***up***) ***in cotton wool*** →WOOL.

wrath /ræθ|rɔθ/ 名 ***A soft answer turneth away wrath.*** 《諺》穏やかな答えは怒りをそらす(《聖》*Prov*. 15. 1).

children [***vessels***] ***of wrath*** 《雅》神罰を受くべき人々 ▪ Are all of Adam's descendants *vessels of wrath*? アダムの子孫はすべて神罰を蒙るべきなのか.

in wrath 激怒して ▪ Do not come near me, while I'm *in wrath*. 私が激怒しているうちは近寄るな.

slow to wrath なかなか怒らない ▪ He is *slow to wrath*. 彼はなかなか怒らない.

the day of wrath 天罰の下る日 ▪ *The day of wrath* is so near. 天罰の下る日はとても近い.

the grapes of wrath 怒りのブドウ《神の怒りの象徴》(《聖》*Isa*. 63. 2–3; *Rev*. 14. 19–20) ▪ Will *the grapes of wrath* come to another harvest? また次の収穫に怒りのブドウが取れるだろうか.

the wrath to come 《文》迫り来る怒り(《聖》*Matt*. 3. 7.) ▪ Nuclear weapons seem to me *the wrath to come*. 核兵器は私には迫り来る怒りのように思われる.

wreak /riːk/ 動 ***wreak itself*** (感情などが)漏れ出る, 注ぐ(*on, upon*) ▪ The indignation of mankind *wrecked itself upon* them. 人類の憤りが彼らに注がれた.

wreathe /riːð/ 動 ***be wreathed in*** 満面に(微笑など)を浮かべている ▪ Her face *was wreathed in* smiles as she ran to meet me. 私を迎えに走り出て来たとき彼女は満面に笑みを浮かべていた.

wreathe (*oneself*) ***around*** [***round***] …に巻きつく ▪The snake *wreathed itself around* the trunk of a tree. ヘビは木の幹に巻きついた.

wreck /rek/ 名 ***be a*** [***the***] (***mere***) ***wreck of*** *one's* ***former self*** 昔のおもかげもない哀れな姿になる ▪It *was*, indeed, *the wreck of his former self*. それは確かに昔のおもかげもない哀れな彼の姿であった.

go to wreck (***and ruin***) 破滅する ▪His whole business is *going to wreck and ruin*. 彼の仕事は全部がめちゃめちゃになりつつある.

make a wreck of …を台なしにする ▪This beautiful fiend had *made a wreck of* her life. この美しい魔性の人物は彼女の一生を台なしにしてしまった.

wrench[1] /rentʃ/ 名 ***throw a*** (***monkey***) ***wrench into*** …をぶちこわす ▪Hard luck *threw a wrench into* his plans. 不運が彼の計画をぶちこわした.

wrench[2] /rentʃ/ 動 ***wrench open*** ねじってあける ▪*Wrench* the lid *open* straight. ふたをすぐねじって開けろ.

wrestle /résəl/ 動 ***wrestle with God*** (***in prayer***) 一心不乱に神に祈る (《聖》*Gen.* 32. 24) ▪The mother *wrestled with God* in earnest prayer. 母親は一心不乱に神に祈った.

wretch /retʃ/ 名 (***a***) ***wretch of a*** かわいそうな, 哀れな ▪It was her *wretch of a* husband. それは彼女の哀れな夫であった.

the little wretch ちび助《小鳥・動物などについて》 ▪Fanny was wonderfully pleased with *the little wretch*. ファニーはそのちび助がひどく気に入っていた.

wriggle /rígəl/ 動 ***wriggle*** *oneself* のたくる ▪I *wriggled myself* out at a small hole. 私は小さな穴から身をよじって出た.

wriggle (*oneself*) ***into*** 巧みに…に取り入る ▪He *wriggled himself into* my father's favor. 彼は巧みに私の父に取り入った ▪He *wriggled himself into* a peerage. 彼は巧みに貴族になりおおせた.

wriggle off the hook (責任・仕事を)うまいこと逃れる ▪I *wriggled off the hook* when they wanted to make me do the work. 彼らは私にその仕事を押しつけようとしたが, 何とかうまく逃れられた.

wriggle *one's* ***way*** くねくねして進む ▪The eel *wriggled its way* into the water. ウナギはくねくね這って水にとび込んだ.

wring /rɪŋ/ 動 ***know*** [***see***] ***where the*** [*one's*] ***shoe wrings*** (*one*) 痛いところを知っている ▪Every man *knows* best *where his shoe wrings*. わが身の痛さは自分が一番よく知っている ▪They *see where the shoe wrings* him. 彼らは彼の痛いところを知っている.

wring *a person's* ***hand*** 感激して人の手を握る ▪The President *wrung the astronaut's hand*. 大統領は宇宙飛行士と感激の握手をした.

wring *one's* [***the***] ***hands*** [***fingers***] 手をもみ絞る《苦痛・悲しみ・絶望などのしぐさ》 ▪Persons in violent grief *wring their hands*. 激しい悲しみに沈んだ人々は手をもみ絞る.

wring *a person's* ***heart*** 人の心を苦しめ悩ます ▪It *wrings my heart* to hear your story. 君の身の上話を聞くと胸が痛む.

wring *a person's* ***neck*** 《口》人を絞め殺す ▪If he ever makes a pass at you, I'll *wring his neck*. もしあいつが君をくどこうとしたら, 絞め殺してやる. ☞ニワトリの首をひねって殺すことから.

wringing wet →dripping WET.

wringer /ríŋər/ 名 ***go*** [***be put***] ***through the wringer*** 苦い試練を経る, ひどい目にあう ▪I *went through the wringer* trying to find out the truth. 真相を究明しようとしてひどい目にあった.

wrinkle /ríŋkəl/ 名 ***a new wrinkle*** 新案, 妙案 ▪The military junta has hit upon *a new wrinkle* to keep the news from its people. 軍事政権は情報を人民に流さない新しい手を思いついた.

give *a person* [***put*** *a person* ***up to***] ***a wrinkle*** (***or two***)/***give*** *a person* [***put*** *a person* ***up to***] ***a wrinkle on*** *one's* ***horn*** 《口》人に(少々)よい知恵をつける ▪He could *put* her *up to a wrinkle or two*. 彼は彼女に少々よい知恵をつけることができた ▪I'll *give* you *a* new *wrinkle on your horn*. 君にひとつ新しくてよい知恵をつけてやろう.

iron out the wrinkles 些細な問題をすべて解決する, あらゆる困難をすっかり処理する ▪She is willing to *iron out the wrinkles* of our daily life. 彼女は私たちの日常生活の諸問題を喜んで解決してくれる.

know a wrinkle of 《口》…のこつを知っている ▪He *knows a wrinkle of* everything. 彼はあらゆるもののこつを知っている.

writ /rɪt/ 名 *one's* ***writ runs*** 自分に権限がある ▪*My writ runs* no more. もう自分には何の権限もない. ☞writ「令状」.

write /raɪt/ 動 ***be written all over*** *a person's* ***face*** (人の感情が)はっきり顔に表れている ▪Disappointment *was written all over her face*. 彼女の顔に失望の色がありありと見えた ▪I see you're not happy; it *is written all over your face*. うれしくないようだね. 顔にちゃんと描いてある.

A ***is written on*** [***in, over***] *B* BにはAと書いてある, BにはAの印がある ▪Cook *is written on* her round face. 彼女の丸い顔には料理人と書いてある ▪Duty *is written* all *over* him. 彼はどこから見ても義理がたい人のようだ.

it's written in the stars (***that***) …する運命である ▪*It was written in the stars that* they should meet and fall in love. 二人は出会って恋をする運勢の下にあった.

not much to write home about/***not much to shout about*** 《口》あまり大したものではない (→nothing to WRITE home about) ▪The food was *not much to write home about*. 料理はあまり大したものではなかった ▪The film was OK, but it was*n't much to shout about*. その映画はまあよかったが, 取り立てて佳作というほどではなかった.

nothing [***not anything***] ***to write home about*** 《口》たいしたことではない ▪My book is *nothing to write home about.* 私の本はたいしたものではない ▪ They were*n't anything to write home about.* 彼らはたいした連中ではなかった.

something to write home about 《口》たいしたもの ▪ The party was *something to write home about.* パーティーはたいしたものだった.

that's all she wrote 《米口》以上で終わりだ, それだけである ▪ And *that's all she wrote* for today, folks. それで, 諸君, 今日は以上でおしまいだ ▪ All you have to do is press the button and *that's all she wrote.* ボタンを押すだけでよい. たったそれだけだ.

writ [***written***] ***large*** 《文・雅》 **1** 特筆大書して ▪ Let us see it *writ large* upon the history of nations. それが諸国民の歴史に特筆大書してあるのを見ようではないか ▪ New Presbyter is but Old Priest *writ large.* 新しい長老は古い司祭を大きく書いたにすぎない ▪ The man was no more than the boy *writ large.* その男は大きくなった少年にすぎなかった.

2 明白で, はっきりして ▪ Anger is *writ large* in his face. 彼の顔にはありありと怒りの色が見える ▪ Genomics is genetics *writ large.* ゲノム[染色体遺伝子]学は遺伝学を明解にしたものである.

writ small 小規模の ▪ Personality is culture *writ small.* 個性は小規模の文化だ.

write *oneself*... **1** (文書・手紙で)...と称する ▪ He took his degree, and *wrote himself* B.A. 彼は学位を取って文学士と称した ▪ He *wrote himself* consul. 彼は自らを領事と称した.

2 ...と署名する ▪ James Hook *wrote himself* Jas. Hook. James Hook は Jas. Hook と署名した.

3 書いて...の状態になる ▪ He *wrote himself* into contempt. 彼はものを書いて軽蔑された.

write *oneself* ***down*** **1** ...であると書く[名乗る] (*as*) ▪ He *writes* himself *down as* M.P. 彼は国会議員と名乗っている ▪ By saying so you *write* yourself *down as* an ass. そんなことを言うと君は自分を愚か者だと言いふらすことになる.

2 (駄作を書いて)文名を落とす ▪ He has *written himself down* at a terrible rate by his last novel. 彼はこの前の小説で著しく文名を落とした.

write fine (ペンが)きれいに書ける ▪ This pen *writes fine.* このペンはきれいに書ける.

write home 家に手紙を書く ▪ My son *writes home* once a week. 息子は週1回家に手紙をよこす.

write in pen and ink →WRITE with pen and ink.

write in pencil →WRITE with a pencil.

write in the dust/write in [***on***] ***sand*** [***air, water, the wind***] 跡形も残らない, はかない (→writ(ten) on WATER) ▪ Oh! let not your vow have *been written in sand!* ああ, あなたの誓いが跡形も残らないものになりませんように ▪ Her virtues *are written on air.* 彼女の美徳ははかないものだ.

write *oneself* ***man*** [***woman***] 成年に達する ▪ You will be mad with vanity before you *write yourself man.* お前は成年に達しないうちに虚栄心でのぼせあがるだろうよ.

write on and on だらだらと書き続ける, とめどなく書く ▪ Never *write on and on* just to fill up space. ただ埋め草にだらだらとは決して書かないように.

write on sand [***air, water, the wind***] →WRITE in the dust.

write *oneself* ***out*** (作家などが)書き尽くして種切れになる ▪ The writer has *written himself out.* その作家は書き尽くして種切れになってしまった.

write out fair 清書する ▪ I offered to *write* his memorials *out fair.* 私は彼の記録を清書してあげようと申し出た.

write (***to***) *a person* ***that*** [***how***] 人に...と言ってやる ▪ She *writes* me *that* she is much better. 彼女はずっとよくなったと言ってきている ▪ I have *written to* Rose *how* we had best start. 私は我々は出発するのが一番よいとローズに手紙で知らせた.

write with a pencil/write in pencil 鉛筆で書く ▪ Don't *write* a letter *with a pencil.* 手紙を鉛筆で書くな ▪ I am *writing in pencil*, as I have no ink at hand. インクが手もとにないので, 鉛筆で書いています. ☞with は鉛筆を道具と見, in はその素材に重点をおく. そのため write with [in] ink の場合, in ink の頻度が高い.

write with [***in***] ***pen and ink*** ペンで書く ▪ He *wrote* the letter *with pen and ink.* 彼はその手紙をペンで書いた.

writer /ráɪtər/ 名 ***a writer to the signet*** 《スコ》高等弁護士 《略は W.S.》 ▪ *A writer to the signet* is the highest grade of the profession of solicitor, as practised in Scotland. 高等弁護士はスコットランドで開業している弁護士の最上位である.

writer's block (作家などが)ものが書けなくなるスランプ ▪ He often suffered from *writer's block.* 彼はよく(心理的要因で)筆が進まなくなった.

writer's cramp [***palsy, paralysis***] (作家などの)指けいれん, 書痙(けい) ▪ This is known under the name of *writer's cramp.* これは書痙という名で知られている.

writing /ráɪtɪŋ/ 名 ***at*** [***up to***] ***this*** (***present***) ***writing*** 今これを書いているとき[まで] ▪ I am, *at this present writing*, not very much for it. 私はこれを書いている現在, それにあまり賛成ではない.

by writing 文書によって (↔by word of MOUTH) ▪ He made proclamation *by writing.* 彼は文書によって布告した.

in writing 書面で ▪ The contract should be *in writing.* 契約は書面によらねばならない ▪ The author's agreement is *in writing.* その著者の同意は書面によるものだ.

the writing [《米》 ***handwriting***] ***on the wall*** →the handwriting is on the WALL (for a person).

wrong /rɔːŋ|rɒŋ/ 形 副 名 ***a wrong'un*** [***wrong 'un***] 悪党; (競馬で)負けそうな馬; 《クリケット》曲球の一種 (googly) ▪ Why, anyone could have seen he was *a wrong'un*, by his face. 彼の顔を見れば, 誰だって彼が悪党だということがわかっただろう

W

よ ▪ They had often blown a dollar on *a wrong'un*. 彼らは負けそうな馬によく1ドル賭けた ▪ It is very difficult to detect his *wrong'un*. 彼の曲球を見つけるのはとてもむずかしい.

be in the wrong place at the wrong time 思いがけず災難にあう ▪ It wasn't his fault. He *was* just *in the wrong place at the wrong time*. 彼の落ち度ではなく, ただ思いがけず面倒に巻き込まれただけだ.

by wrong 不正にも, まちがって ▪ Woe unto him that buildeth his chambers *by wrong*. 不義をもってその家を建てる者は災いなるかな.

can* [*could*] *do no wrong (とても偉いので)することは何でも正しい ▪ He *can do no wrong* in his wife's eyes. 彼の妻の目から見れば彼は絶対にへまはしない人に見える.

can't* [*couldn't*] *go wrong **1**《口》きっとうまくやる, きっと成功する ▪ With your talent, you *can't go wrong*. 君の才能をもってすればきっとうまく行く.
2 (…が)必ず気に入られる, 喜ばれる (*with*) ▪ For a quick meal you *can't go wrong with* pizza. さっと食事するならピザに限る.

catch *a person* ***on the wrong foot*** →FOOT[1].

come to the wrong shop →come to the right SHOP.

distinguish between right and wrong/know right from wrong 正邪をわきまえる ▪ He was without the means of *knowing right from wrong*. 彼は正邪をわきまえる手段がなかった.

do* (*a, the*) *wrong (…に)不当なふるまいをする, 不法な行為をする (*to*) ▪ She has *done* me great *wrong*. 彼女は私に大いに不当なふるまいをした ▪ She was the person who *did the wrong to* him. 彼女が彼にその不法な行為をした人であった ▪ To say too much might *do* my honor *wrong*. あまり言いすぎると, 私の名誉をそこないかねない.

get* (*hold of*) *the wrong end of the stick →STICK[1].

get* [*put*]** *a person* ***in wrong 《米俗》人をきらわれ者にする (*with*) ▪ He's *got* you *in wrong with* the Governor while you were away. 君の留守の間に彼が君を所長のきらわれ者にしてしまったのだ.

get in wrong with *a person* 《米俗》人にきらわれる, 人を怒らせる ▪ He is always *getting in wrong with* someone or other. 彼はいつも誰かにきらわれている.

get *a person* ***wrong*** **1**《口》人を誤解する ▪ Don't *get* me *wrong*. I'm still thinking of you. 誤解しないでくれ. まだ君のことを思っているのだから.
2《俗》(少女)を妊娠させる ▪ Don't do that, or you'll *get* me *wrong*. そんなことをしたら, 赤ちゃんができるじゃないの.

get *a thing* ***wrong*** **1** (計算などを)誤る ▪ You *got* the calculation *wrong*. 君は計算をまちがえている.
2 (歌・物語などを)誤解する, 誤って覚える ▪ You've *got* the story *wrong*. 君はその話を誤解している.

go the wrong way →WAY.

go wrong **1** 道を誤る; しくじる (*with*) ▪ It is easy to *go wrong* where nobody has beaten the way. 誰も道を踏みならしていない所では道に迷いやすい ▪ You can't *go wrong with* it. それをしくじるはずがない.
2 正道を踏みはずす; (女性が)身を誤る ▪ But I *went wrong* again. しかし私はまたぐれてしまった ▪ She had a vague idea about girls *going wrong*. 彼女は女の子が身を誤るということについてははっきりと知らなかった.
3 (事が)まずくいく, 失敗する (*with*) ▪ Everything seemed to *go wrong with* me. 何もかも私にはうまくいかないように思われた.
4 (人が事業などで)失敗する ▪ I'm really sorry he's *gone wrong*. 失敗したとはほんとに彼は気の毒だ.
5 (機械・時計などの)調子が狂う (*with*) ▪ The water supply has *gone wrong*. 水道の調子が狂った ▪ Something *went wrong with* my watch. 私の時計がどこか故障した.
6 (肉・果物などが)腐る ▪ These apples have *gone wrong*. これらのリンゴは腐っている.

in the wrong (態度・行動などを)誤って (↔be in the RIGHT) ▪ I quarreled with her last night; I was quite *in the wrong*. ゆうべ彼女といさかいをしたが, 全く私の誤りだった.

in wrong 不正にも ▪ Then we met *in wrong*. それから私たちは会ったが, それはまちがいだった.

it is* [*would be*] *wrong to *do* …するのはまちがっている[いるだろう] ▪ *It was* very *wrong* of him *to* make such a request. 彼がそんなことを頼むのは大まちがいだった ▪ *It would be* indeed *wrong to* say so. そう言うのは本当にまちがっているだろう.

know right from wrong →distinguish between right and WRONG.

laugh on the wrong side of *one's* ***mouth* [*face*]** →LAUGH[2].

lead *a person* ***wrong*** 人の方向を誤らせる[迷わせる]; 人にまちがったことを教える ▪ You *led* me *wrong*. 君は僕にまちがったことを教えてくれたね.

on the right* [*wrong*] *side of the tracks 《口》→TRACK.

on the wrong side of →SIDE.

put *a person* [*oneself*] ***in the wrong*** 人の[自分の]誤りを示す, 失態だとする ▪ It *puts* Lord Tennyson so brutally *in the wrong*. それは著しくテニスン卿の誤りを示すものだ ▪ He had now *put* himself *in the wrong*. 彼は今や自分の失態だとしてしまっていた.

put *a person* ***in wrong*** →get a person in WRONG.

right and wrong →RIGHT[1].

something* [*nothing*] *is wrong with …はどこか故障がある[どこにも故障がない] ▪ *Something is wrong with* this machine. この機械はどこか故障している ▪ *Nothing is wrong with* her, I hope? 彼女はどこもいけないところはないのでしょうね.

suffer wrong (他から)害を被る, 不法の処置を受ける ▪ Each had *suffered* some *wrong*. 各人とも不法な処置を多少受けていた.

***take the* [*a*] *wrong turning* [*path, way*]** 道を誤る; 身を誤る ▪ He *took the wrong way* to right himself. 彼は弁明する道を誤った ▪ Here you *take a wrong way*. ここでやり方を誤っていますよ.

take ... the wrong way …を悪く取る, 誤解する ▪ She always *takes* my suggestion *the wrong way* and we end up arguing. 私が提案すると彼女は必ず悪く取って結局は口論になる ▪ Don't *take* this *the wrong way*, but don't you think you're a bit too strict? 悪く取らないでほしいが, 君は少し厳しすぎるとは思わないか.

That's where you are wrong. そこが君の間違っている点だ.

the wrong end あべこべの端《比喩的にも》 ▪ This is beginning at *the wrong end*. これはあべこべに始めるというものだ.

the wrong side **1** (織物などの)裏面; 反対側 ▪ He jumped on to his pony from *the wrong side*. 彼は反対側から小馬に飛び乗った.

2 自分の賛成しない側[党, 主義] ▪ He could argue on *the wrong side* of any question. 彼はどんな問題でも自分の賛成しない面について論じることができた.

3 不利な[望ましくない, 危険な]側 ▪ We were on *the wrong side* of the fence. 我々は防壁の不利な側にいた ▪ The poor house was on *the wrong side* of Oxford Street. その貧乏な家はオックスフォード街の柄の悪い側にあった.

the wrong side of the tracks →on the right side of the TRACKs.

(*the*) *wrong side out* [*before*] 〚副詞的に〛 裏返しに[後ろ前に] ▪ He got his coat *wrong side out*. 彼は上着を裏返しに着た ▪ His hat was on *wrong side before*. 彼の帽子は後ろ前になっていた. ☞ the をつけないほうが多い.

(*the*) *wrong way* 〚副詞的に〛 あべこべの方向[位置]に ▪ The S stands *the wrong way*. そのSはあべこべになっている.

the wrong way round 逆に, 反対に ▪ They teach English *the wrong way round*. 彼らは英語の教え方があべこべだ ▪ You placed it *the wrong way round*. 君はそれをあべこべに置いている.

to* one's *own wrong 自分が害を被って ▪ Be cautious lest you pay it *to your own wrong*. それを自腹を切って払うことのないように注意しなさい.

Two wrongs don't make a right. 《諺》 悪と悪では善にはならない《他人もしているからといって自分のした非行が正当化されるわけではない》.

What's wrong with ...? 《口》 …のどこが悪いのか, どこが気に入らないのか ▪ *What's wrong with* playing here? ここで遊んでいてどうして悪い ▪ I want to know *what's wrong with* a game of bridge? ブリッジの勝負をしたっていいじゃないか.

***wrong in* one's *senses*/*wrong in the head* [*the mind*]** 頭が変で, 正気でなく ▪ This maid was *wrong in the mind*. このお手伝いの娘は頭が変だった ▪ He was *wrong in his senses*. 彼は正気でなかった.

wrought /rɔːt/ 形 **(*be*) *wrought in*** (芸術品などが)…で作られて(いる) ▪ Some columns *are wrought in* marble. 大理石で作られている柱もある.

(*be*) *wrought of* (材料)で作られて(いる) ▪ Good mill stones *are wrought of* the rock. 上等の石うすはその岩で作られている.

(*be*) *wrought up* 緊張して(いる), 神経が高ぶって(いる) ▪ He *is* terribly *wrought up* over it. 彼はそのことで神経がひどく高ぶっている.

(*be*) *wrought with* …の刺しゅうがして(ある) ▪ The napkin *is wrought with* horse and hound. ナプキンには馬と猟犬の刺しゅうがしてある.

wry /raɪ/ 形 ***a wry look* [*twist*]** しかめつら《不興・嫌悪を表す》 ▪ He cast many *wry looks* at the thick logs. 彼はその太い丸太の方を何度もしかめつらをして見た ▪ His features gave *a wry twist*. 彼の顔はしかめつらになった.

a wry smile にが笑い《嫌悪を表す》 ▪ He turned to me with *a wry smile*. 彼はにが笑いしてこっちを向いた ▪ He gave *a wry smile*. 彼はにが笑いした.

***make* [*draw, pull*] *a wry face* [*mouth*]** 顔[口]をしかめる, ゆがめる《まずさ・嫌悪などのため》 ▪ Each guest drank and *made a wry face*. どの客も1杯飲んで, 顔をしかめた ▪ He *made a wry mouth*, and returned it. 彼は口元をゆがめて, それを返した.

X

x /eks/ 名 ***X marks the spot*** Xをつけた所がその場所だ ▪ The treasure hunter said, "Here it is; *X marks the spot.*" 宝探しをする人が言った,「ここだ, Xをつけた所がその場所だ」.

x number [***amount***] ***of...*** 《口》なにがしかの数[量]の… ▪ I want to make *x amount of* dollars. 何ドルか稼ぎたい ▪ You have only *x number of* hours left in your life. あなたの寿命にはなにがしかの時間しか残されていない.

x.y., X.Y. /ékswáɪ/ 名 匿名の人物 ▪ I received a letter from an unknown person, who signed the letter as "*X.Y.*" 無名の人物から手紙を受け取った, その手紙には「X.Y.」の署名があった.

Y

yacht /jɑt|jɔt/ 動 ***go yachting*** ヨット乗りに行く ▪ We *went yachting* in the afternoon. 午後ヨット乗りに行った.

yadda /jǽdə/ 名 ***yadda yadda*** (***yadda***)/ ***yada yada*** (***yada***) 《口》だらだら続くつまらない話 ▪ I got so many phone calls from Mom, all *yadda yadda yadda.* 母から何度も電話をもらった, いずれもうるさいお説教だった.

yank /jæŋk/ 動 ***yank*** *a person's* ***chain*** 《米口》人に嘘を冗談として言う ▪ Are you just *yanking my chain*? 私をからかっているのか. ☞yank「強く, 早く, 急に引っ張る」.

yank on the brake 《米》急ブレーキをかける ▪ He *yanked on the brake* when he saw a stone ahead. 彼は前方に石のあるのを見て急ブレーキをかけた.

Yankee /jǽŋki/ 名 ***as Yankee Doodle as apple pie and baseball*** 《米》全くアメリカ的で ▪ They are *as Yankee Doodle as apple pie and baseball.* 彼らは全くアメリカ的である.

yard /jɑːrd/ 名 ***by the yard*** 長々と ▪ He could talk *by the yard* of what little he did know. 彼は自分の知っているわずかなことを長々と話せた.

in *one's* (***own***) ***back yard*** →BACKYARD.

mind *one's* ***own yard*** 《米》自分の仕事を心がける, 他人のことに口出しをしない ▪ *Mind your own yard.* 他人のことに口出しするな.

Not in My Back Yard! →BACKYARD.

the whole nine yards →NINE.

yard-stick /jɑ́ːrdstìk/ 名 ***measure*** *a person* ***by*** *one's* ***own yard-stick*** 自分の尺度で人を測る ▪ Don't *measure* others *by your own yard-stick.* 自分の尺度で他人を測ってはいけない.

measure ... with a yard-stick 長さで…の価値を判定する ▪ You must not *measure* a man *with a yard-stick.* 体の大小で人の価値を判断してはならない.

yarn /jɑːrn/ 名 ***big yarn*** とても退屈な人[話, 催し] ▪ I love my grandpa very much, but the stories he tells are a *big yarn.* じいちゃんは大好きだが, 彼の話は退屈この上ない.

breast the yarn 《米俗》(競走で)テープを切る, 1着になる ▪ Smith was the seventh but finally *breasted the yarn.* スミスは7番目だったが, ついに1着になった.

spin a yarn 《口》長物語をする; 作り話をする ▪ Come, *spin* us *a* good *yarn.* さあ, 私たちにおもしろい話をしてください ▪ Tell lies! That is, *spin a yarn*; well, I can do that. 嘘をつくって! 作り話をすることだな. それなら僕にもできる. ☞海語から.

yawn[1] /jɔːn/ 名 ***give a yawn*** あくびをする ▪ *Giving a* heavy *yawn*, he looked sleepily about him. 大あくびをして彼は眠そうにあたりを見回した.

make *a person* ***a yawn*** 人にあくびを催させる ▪ His long story *made* me *a yawn.* 彼の長話は私にあくびを催させた.

with a yawn あくびをしながら ▪ He stretched himself *with a yawn.* 彼はあくびをして伸びをした.

yawn[2] /jɔːn/ 動 ***yawn*** *a person* ***good night*** あくびをしながら人におやすみと言う ▪ He *yawned* me *good night.* 彼はあくびをしながら私におやすみと言った.

yawn *one's* ***head off*** 大きなあくびをする; ひどく退屈である ▪ It is a small town where you *yawn your head off.* そこはひどく退屈な小さな町です.

yeah /jeə/ 副 ***Oh yeah?*** 《口・皮肉》(相手が言ったことに対して答えて)さーてどうだか, ふーんそうかい《無礼な不信の表現》 ▪ I'm going to be a millionaire one day.—*Oh yeah?* いつかは百万長者になるぞ—さーてどうだか.

year /jɪər/ 名 ***a year and a day*** 《法》満1年《正味1年と1日の猶予期間》 ▪ Claim copyhold within *a year and a day* after the death of the inheritee. 不動産権は被相続人の死後満1年以内に要求しなさい.

***all* (*the*) *year round* [*around*]** 一年中 ▪ The top of the mountain is covered with snow *all the year around.* その山の頂は一年中雪におおわれている ▪ Thanks to the indoor courts we can play tennis *all year round.* 室内コートのおかげで我々は一年中テニスができる.

be beneath *one's* ***years*** 年甲斐もない ▪ It would *be beneath your years* to do such a thing. そんなことをしては年甲斐もない.

beyond *one's* ***years*** 年齢以上に, 年の割に ▪ He is wise *beyond his years.* 彼は年の割に賢い.

by the year 1年いくらで ▪ He is paid *by the year.* 彼は1年いくらで支払いを受けている《年俸をもらっている》.

die full of years 天寿を全うして死ぬ ▪ My mother *died full of years.* 母は天寿を全うした.

for years 幾年もの間 ▪ I have been in this business *for years.* 私は何年もの間この商売をしている.

for *one's* ***years*** 年[年齢]の割りに ▪ He is young *for his years.* 彼は年の割りに若い.

from year to year 毎年毎年; 年々歳々 ▪ He receives payment *from year to year.* 彼は年々支払いを受けている ▪ He is a tenant *from year to year.* 彼は年々歳々店子(たなこ)だ.

from year's end to year's end 年がら年中 ▪ He is complaining *from year's end to year's end.* 彼は年がら年中不平ばかり言っている.

get along in years 〚主に進行形で〛年をとる, 年老いる ▪ The trouble with *getting along in years* is that you have to take medications. 年をとって困ることは薬の世話にならねばならぬことだ.

in a year's time 一年たてば ▪ He will be back *in a year's time.* 彼は一年たてば帰って来るだろう.

in recent years →of late YEARs.

in* [*from, since*] *the year dot [《米》***one***] 《英口》ずっと昔[太古, 大昔, 西暦1年]に[から, より], ずっと前; 遠い将来に ▪ It seemed that his car was made *in the year one.* 彼の車は大昔に造られたように思えた ▪ People have fallen in love with one another *since the year dot.* 古より男と女は恋をしてきた ▪ I reckon he was born *in the year dot.* 彼はずっと前に生まれたのだと思う ▪ This isn't going to happen *in the year dot.* これは遠い将来に起こることじゃない. ☞the year dot = the year 0; A.D. 1 (西暦1年)より前, すなわち数字1の前の A.D. のDの直後の dot に言及する表現.

***in the year of grace* [*Christ, our Lord*]** キリスト紀元の, 西暦の ▪ It happened *in the year of grace* 55. それは西暦55年に起こった.

(*in*) *the year one* →in the YEAR dot.

in *a person's* ***year*** 人と同学年で ▪ He is *in my year* at college. 彼は大学で私と同学年です.

in *one's fifth* [etc.] ***year*** 満4[など]歳の[で] ▪ He was graduated *in his* 20th *year.* 彼は満19歳で卒業した ▪ I caught a buck *in its* 2nd *year.* 私は満1歳の雄ジカを捕えた.

in years **1**《米》幾年もの間 ▪ I haven't seen him *in years.* もう何年も彼と会わない.
2 年齢が[は] ▪ He is a boy *in years,* but a man in intelligence. 彼は年はまだ子供だが, 知恵は大人だ.

it's years since 《俗》…してからずいぶん長いことだ ▪ *It's years since* I saw him. とんと彼に会わない.

Keep a thing seven years and you'll* (*always*) *find a use for it. 《諺》物も7年とっておけば使い道が出てくる, 「ほうろくの割れも3年おけば役に立つ」.

leap year 閏年(うるうどし) ▪ There are 365 days in a year, and 366 in a *leap year.* 1年は365日だが, 閏年には366日ある ▪ My son is a *Leap Year* baby, born Feb. 29, 2000. 息子は2000年の2月29日生まれの閏年ベビーだ.

next year 来年 (→the next YEAR) ▪ I shall be graduated *next year.* 来年卒業する.

not* [*never*] *in a hundred* [*thousand, million,* etc.] *years 《口》100年[1000年, 百万年, など]経っても…しない; 絶対に…ない ▪ You would never learn to drive, *not in a hundred years.* 君は100年経っても車の運転はできないだろうよ ▪ *Never in a million years* did I think I'd be married a month after meeting somebody. 会ってから1か月で結婚することになるなんて金輪際思わなかった.

of late years/in recent years 近年(に); この数年に ▪ Such a spectacle has never been seen *of late years.* そのような光景は近年見たことがない ▪ Industry in this country has made remarkable progress *of late years.* この国の産業は近年著しい進歩を遂げた.

of mature years 《婉曲》円熟した年齢の, 熟年の, 老齢の ▪ A man *of mature years* stepped from the car. 一人の熟年の男性が車から降りた.

of the year (人・車などが)今年最優秀[最高]の ▪ Renault Clio wins Car *of the Year.* ルノーのクリオ, 今年最優秀の車に選ばれる《新聞の見出し》.

old beyond *one's* ***years*** 実際よりも大人びて[老けて] ▪ Stacy looks *old beyond her years,* yet she's young enough to be considered foolish. ステイシーは実際よりも老けて見えるが, 愚か者と考えられるくらい若い.

on* [*along*] *in years 年老いて ▪ Dad is getting a bit *on in years.* おやじは少し老いぼれてきた ▪ We do not become interested in family history until we are *along in years.* 年が寄るまで家族歴[家系]には関心を持たないものだ.

put years on *a person* 人を老けさせる ▪ Those troubles *put years on* him. それらの苦労のため彼は老けた.

ring in the New Year **1** 鐘を鳴らして新年を迎える ▪ The bell-ringers assembled to *ring in the New Year.* (教会の)鳴鐘者たちが集まって新年を迎える鐘を打ち鳴らした.
2 シャンパングラスで乾杯して新年を迎える ▪ We *rang in the New Year.* シャンパングラスをカチンと鳴らして新年を迎えた.

take years off *a person* 《口》人を若く見せる[若

Y

返らせる］ ▪ An outdoor life has *taken* five *years off* him. 戸外生活で彼は5年は若返った.

The first hundred years are the hardest. 《諺》生涯の最初の100年が最も辛くそれ以後は楽になる《100歳を越えるのはまれだから, 一生を通して苦しいものだ》.

the lost years 失われた年月, むだに過ごして取り戻せない時間 ▪ Somewhere in *the lost years* he failed at his second marriage. 失われた年月のどこかで彼は2度目の結婚にも失敗した.

the next year その翌年(に) ▪ *The next year* he died. その翌年彼は死んだ.

the year before last →LAST[2].

the year dot →in the YEAR dot.

the year of grace [***Christ, our Lord***] 《文》西暦 (→in the YEAR of grace) ▪ Some medieval documents treat 1 January as the first day of *the year of grace*. 一部の中世期の文書は, 1月1日を西暦の元日とみなしている.

twilight years 人生のたそがれ時, 晩年, 死の直前の数年間 ▪ She had a modest home in which to spend her *twilight years*. 彼女には晩年を過ごすささやかな住まいがあった.

with years 年を経て ▪ The stone lamp is green *with years*. 石灯ろうは年を経て青ごけがついている.

year after [***by***] ***year*** 年々歳々, 毎年毎年 ▪ He receives payment *year by year*. 彼は毎年支払いを受ける ▪ Let us look at it *year by year*. それを年ごとに調査することにしよう.

year-around [***round***] 一年中の, 年間通じての ▪ Colorado is a *year-round* resort; there is fishing in the summer and skiing in the winter. コロラド州は一年中楽しめるリゾート地で, 夏は釣り, 冬はスキーができます.

year in, (***and***) ***year out*** 年がら年中(続けて) (→DAY in, day out; WEEK in(,) week out) ▪ You go on working *year in, year out*. 君は年がら年中働き続ける ▪ We live with the tangerine *year in, year out*. 我々は年がら年中ミカンとともに暮らす.

year on year/year-on-year 《商》(主に物価・数値等について)前の年と比べて(の), 対前年比で(の); 毎年(の) ▪ The birthrate has increased *year on year*. 出生率が前年に比べて増加した ▪ For most of the cities, mortality *year on year* is decreasing. ほとんどの都市では死亡率は年毎に減少している ▪ The study showed a *year-on-year* increase in unemployment. その調査で失業率が前年より上昇していることが分かった.

Years bring wisdom. 《諺》歳月は知恵をもたらす, 「カメの甲より年の功」.

yell[1] /jel/ 名 ***raise the yell*** 《米俗》抗議する, 苦情を言う ▪ Hey, man, it's your own fault, so don't *raise the yell*. これこれ, お前の方が悪いのだから, 苦情を言ってはいかん.

yell[2] /jel/ 動 ***yell*** *one's* ***head off*** 大声でどなる ▪ The boys were *yelling their heads off* in the playground. 男の子たちは運動場で大声でどなっていた.

yellow /jéloʊ/ 形 ***a yellow dog*** 《米》つまらない［低級な］人［物］ ▪ Two of the magazines are good. The rest are *yellow dogs*. それらの雑誌の2冊はよい. あとはつまらないしろものだ ▪ I won't allow no *yellow dog* of a Smith to step over me. つまらないスミスのごとき人物に飛び越えて昇進されてたまるものか.

a yellow dog under the wagon ＝a whole TEAM (and the yellow dog under the wagon).

a yellow streak →STREAK[1].

be yellow about the gills →be white about the GILLs.

yen /jen/ 名 ***have a yen for*** [***to*** *do*] 《米》…を［することを］熱望する ▪ I *have a yen for* spicy food. 香辛料のきいた物が食べたい ▪ He *has a yen to* see the world. 彼はしきりに世間を見たがっている. ☞中国語の yen (煙 (opium)) から.

yeoman /jóʊmən/ 名 ***do yeoman***('***s***) ***service*** (まさかの時に)お役に立つ, 忠勤を励む (cf. Sh., *Haml.* 5. 2. 36) ▪ The law has *done* me *yeoman service* in the hour of necessity. その法律は困ったときに私に役立った.

yes /jes/ 副名 ***say yes*** →SAY[2].

yes and no **1** イエスともノーとも言える; さあどうかな ▪ Is John a good teacher?—*Yes and no.* ジョンは良い教師ですか—イエスともノーとも言えるね.

2 もの当て遊び ▪ It was a game called *Yes and No.* It was formerly called Animal, Vegetable, and Mineral. それは「イエスとノー」という遊戯であった. それは以前は「動物・植物・鉱物」と呼ばれた. ☞当てる人の質問に対しては Yes または No としか答えないことから.

3 イエスとノー ▪ Confine yourself to *yes and no*. イエスとノーの一点ばりで通せ.

yesterday /jéstərdèɪ/ 名副 ***need … yesterday*** …を(早く早くと)せきたてる, せっかちに要求する ▪ I need something new and I *need* it *yesterday*! 新しいのがいるのよ, それも今すぐに!

not born yesterday 《口》おぼっちゃんじゃない, 簡単には騙されないぞ; 世故にたけて ▪ "I was*n't born yesterday*," he returned. 「僕はおぼっちゃんじゃないぞ」と彼はやり返した ▪ Father was*n't born yesterday*. 父は世故にたけている.

of yesterday つい昨今の ▪ It was a thing *of yesterday*. それはつい昨今のことだった.

the day before yesterday 一昨日, おととい ▪ I returned home *the day before yesterday*. 私はおととい帰宅した.

yesterday week 先週のきのう ▪ I met him for the first time *yesterday week*. 私は先週のきのう初めて彼に会った.

yesterday's man 全盛期を過ぎた人, 後進に道を譲るべきベテラン［(特に)政治家］ ▪ Mr. Jones is *yesterday's man* and will be retiring soon anyway. ジョーンズ氏はもう落ち目で, どっちみちまもなく退職だろう.

yesterday's news もはや関心を集めなくなった出来事 ▪ That's *yesterday's news*. それは古い情報だ.

yet /jet/ 副 ***and yet*** →AND.

as yet →AS.

be yet to *do* まだ…していない ▪ The time *is yet to* come. まだその時ではない.

(*be*) *yet to be* *done* まだ…してない; まだ…せねばならない ▪ The painting and papering *were yet to be* done. ペンキ塗りや紙張りはまだできていなかった ▪ Much *yet* remains *to be* endured. まだまだ耐えなければならないことがたくさんある.

have yet to *do* まだ…しない; これから…することになっている ▪ But the two *had yet to* become intimate. しかしその二人はまだ親しくなっていなかった.

nor yet また…ない ▪ I don't like the red one, *nor yet* the brown one. 赤いのはきらいだが, 茶色のもきらいだ.

not yet まだ…ない ▪ They have *not yet* heard it. 彼らはまだその事を聞いていない ▪ It is *not* time *yet*. まだ時刻ではない.

yet again/yet once more またもう一度 ▪ He refused me yesterday and now he's refused me *yet again*! 彼は昨日私を拒み, 今また断った ▪ *Yet once more*, my son came asking me for money. 更にもう一度, 息子は金の無心にやってきた.

yield /jiːld/ 動 ***yield*** *oneself* ***prisoner*** 降参して捕虜になる ▪ He gave his sword to the Commanding officer, and *yielded himself prisoner*. 彼は剣を指揮官に渡して降参し捕虜になった.

yield the palm to →PALM[2].

yield the point 論点を譲る ▪ He *yielded the point* in argument. 彼は議論で論点を譲った.

yield to none 誰にも負けない, 最上である ▪ Our watches *yield to none* in the world. わが社の時計は世界最高です ▪ I *yield to none* in appreciation of his merit. 私は彼の長所を認める点において人後に落ちない.

yield *oneself* (***up***) ***to*** …に身を任せる, ふける ▪ They *yield themselves* (*up*) *to* all sorts of extravagances. 彼らはあらゆる種類の贅沢にふける ▪ She *yielded herself up to* the rhythm of a waltz. 彼女はワルツのリズムに身を任せた.

yoke /joʊk/ 名 ***pass*** [***come, fall***] ***under the yoke*** 屈服する ▪ His army was routed and *passed under the yoke*. 彼の軍隊は敗走させられ屈服した ▪ They *came under the yoke* of the English. 彼らはイギリス人の支配を受けた. ☞古代ローマで被征服者に屈服の印としてくびきまたは剣のアーチの下をくぐらせたことから.

send ... under the yoke …を屈服させる ▪ Necessity *sent* them *under the yoke* of tradition. 必要上彼らは慣習に屈した.

shake [***cast, fling, throw***] ***off the yoke*** くびきを振り落とす; 束縛[抑圧]を脱する ▪ In 1783 the American Colonies *threw off the yoke* of England. 1783年にアメリカの植民地はイギリスの支配を脱した ▪ The people *cast off the* tyrant's *yoke*. 国民は暴君の圧制を脱した.

submit to *a person's* ***yoke*** 人の支配に屈する ▪ Spain *submitted to Napoleon's yoke*. スペインはナポレオンの支配に屈した.

yokel /jóʊkəl/ 名 ***local yokel*** 《俗》市警察官《州警察官・ハイウェイパトロール警官に対して》 ▪ There's a *local yokel* eastbound on the move. 市警官が東に向けてパトカーで移動中だ.

yolk /joʊk/ 名 ***in the yolk*** (羊毛が)生(き)のままの[で] ▪ Wool *in the yolk* is fetching about 4d. a lb. 生羊毛が1ポンドにつきおよそ4ペンスで売れている.

yonder /jάndər|jɔ́n-/ 副名 ***here and yonder*** あちらこちらに ▪ Gangs of streetpaviors were seen *here and yonder*. 街路舗装工の群れがあちらこちらに見えた.

into the wide [***wild***] ***blue yonder*** →BLUE.

yore /jɔːr/ 名 ***of yore*** (ずっと)昔, 以前 ▪ They have become wiser than *of yore*. 彼らは以前より賢くなった ▪ Here haunted *of yore* the fabulous Dragon of Wantley. ここは, その昔伝説上のウォントリーの竜が出没した所だ.

Yorkshire /jɔ́ːrkʃər/ 名 ***a Yorkshire bite*** ひどい詐欺行為[詐欺師] ▪ This will turn out to be *a Yorkshire bite*. これはひどい詐欺行為ということになるだろう.

come [***put***] ***Yorkshire on*** [***over***] 《口》…をだます, だしぬく ▪ He has *come Yorkshire over* me. あいつは僕をだましやがった.

you /ju, juː/ 代 ***Are you there?*** →THERE.

There is ... for you! →FOR.

to you **1** あなたに呼んでもらいたい名で ▪ I say, Mr. Jones!—Please, not Mr. Jones, but John *to you*, as we are now friends. あの, ジョーンズさん!—どうかジョーンズさんはよしてくれ. ジョンと呼んでほしいね. 僕たち, もう友だちなのだから.

2 俗にわかりやすく言えば ▪ That's a Primula vulgaris, or a primrose *to you*. あれはプリームラ・ウルガーリス, つまりわかりやすく言うとプリムローズ(サクラソウ)だ.

You and the other (***ninety-***)***nine?/ You and who else*** [***whose army***]***?*** そんなことができるかね《高言・おどしに対する嘲笑的な返事》 ▪ I'm going to thump you.—Oh yes, *you and who else?* ぶっとばすぞ—ほう, そんなことができるのかね.

you and your 《口》またいつもの[例の]…だ《うんざりする》 ▪ *You and your* sob stories! また例のお涙ちょうだい話か!

you and yours あなたとあなたの家族や友人たち ▪ We have a gift for *you and yours*. あなたとあなたの家族, 友人たちへの贈り物があります.

You never can tell. →TELL.

You said it. →SAY[2].

You're another. →ANOTHER.

young /jʌŋ/ 形名 ***a young family*** 小さい子供たち; 小さい子供だけの家族 ▪ How is it living in Bulgaria for *a young family*? 小さい子供たちにとってブルガリアで生活するのはどういうものか.

a young man in a hurry (特に)熱烈な改革者 ▪ Obama is *a young man in a hurry*. オバマ氏は熱烈な改革者である.

a young person →PERSON.

be caught young (野生の動物が)子供のときに捕えられる, 子飼いにされる ▪ A tiger must *be caught young.* トラは子飼いにせねばならない ▪ A sailor must *be caught young.* 水夫は子供のときから鍛え上げねばならない.

be getting younger 《口》(往時に比べて)若年化している ▪ In the NBA, the players *are getting younger.* NBA では選手層は若年化している.

be* [*stay*, etc.] *young at heart (年配の人が)いまだに若者と同じように感じたり行動したりする, 気が若い ▪ I know a lot of people who are older, who *are* very *young at heart.* 年はとっても気が若い人を私はたくさん知っている ▪ My grandfather is over 70 but he still *feels young at heart.* 祖父は70歳の峠を越えているが気分はまだ若い.

not as* [*so*] *young as* one *used to be [(*once*) *was*] 昔のように若くはない ▪ I think you forget I'm *not so young as* I *once was.* 私が昔のように若くはないことを君は忘れてるらしいね.

not be getting any younger*/ *not grow any younger 《口》年をとる, 年がいく ▪ "You*'re not getting any younger*, Daddy," growled Laura.「お父さん, 若くはないのよ」とローラは怒鳴って言った ▪ He forgets he's *not growing any younger.* 彼は自分が年をとっていることを忘れている.

the young idea →IDEA.

the young person (わいせつな話・文学にふれないよう保護を要する)純真な若者; 《法》幼児以外の18歳以下の者 ▪ "*The Young Person*'s Guide to the Opera" is an easy-to-read, entertaining book.「純粋な若者のためのオペラの手引き」は, 読みやすくおもしろい本である.

with* [*in*] *young (動物が)子をはらんで ▪ The cat goes *with young* fifty-six days. 猫は妊娠期間が56日である ▪ The sow, when *in young*, should be kept in good condition. 雌ブタは妊娠中は体の調子をよくしておかねばならない.

young and old 老いも若きも; 老若(を問わず) ▪ Death comes to *young and old.* 死は老若を問わずやって来る.

young blood (ある組織に新しい考え・活力を与えてくれる)若い血 ▪ The board needs some fresh, *young blood.* 委員会は何人かの新鮮で若い人材を必要としている.

***young man* [*gentleman, woman, lady*]** 《口》おい, いいかね《年齢にかかわりなく, 叱責・警告するときの呼びかけ》 ▪ You had better provide yourself with another situation, *young man.* いいかね, 君は他の職についたほうがいいよ ▪ Let me tell you, *young woman*, it is hard on a man. ねえ, 言っておくがね, それは男にもつらいことだよ.

one's ***young ones*** 子供たち; 子孫 ▪ The poor wren will fight, *her young ones* in the nest, against the owl. かわいそうなミソサザイはひなたちを巣に置いて, フクロウと戦うだろう.

young 'un 《口》若者, 子供 ▪ She told all marauding *young 'uns* to keep out of the kitchen. 彼女は食べものを狙う子供ら全員に台所に入るなと言った.

You're only young once. 《諺》若い時は二度とない《楽しみたまえ》.

yours /jʊərz|jɔːz/ 代 ***I am yours to command.*** 《口》何なりとお命じください.

What's yours? 《俗》君は何(の酒)を飲みますか ▪ I'll have another beer. *What's yours?* 僕はビールをもう1杯もらおうか. 君は何にする?

What's yours is mine, and what's mine is mine. 《諺》お前のものはおれのもの, おれのものもおれのもの. みんな自分のもの,「どっちに転んでもこっちのもの」. ☞What's yours is mine, and what's mine is yours. (君のものは僕のもの, 僕のものは君のもの)をもじったもの (cf. Sh., *Meas. for M.* 5. 1.).

you and yours →YOU.

***Yours faithfully* [*sincerely*]** 敬具, かしこ《手紙の結句》. ☞《米》では yours を略すことがある.

yours truly →TRULY.

yourself /jʊərsélf|jɔː-/ 代 ***be yourself*** **1** 常態[健康, 正常]である ▪ You *are* not *yourself* tonight. 君は今夜はどうかしている.

2〚命令文で〛《口》元気を出せ, しっかりしろ ▪ *Be yourself*, John! ジョン君, 元気を出せ.

Go and chase yourself! →Go CHASE yourself!

How's yourself? 《俗》ごきげんいかがですか《特に相手の同様な問いに答えて》 ▪ How are you?—I'm all right. *How's yourself?* ごきげんいかがですか—とても元気です. あなたはいかがですか.

youth /juːθ/ 名 ***from youth upwards*** 若い時分から ▪ *From youth upwards* he showed talent. 彼は若い時分から才能を示した.

in *one's* ***youth*** 若い時分に ▪ He traveled *in his youth.* 彼は若い時分に旅行した.

past *one's* ***first youth*** (女性が)年増(としま)で ▪ She is *past her first youth.* 彼女は年増だ.

the gilded* [*golden*] *youth 金持ちの若紳士(たち) ▪ He was invited to dine with some of *the gilded youth* of the city. 彼は町の富裕な貴公子の幾人かと食事するよう招かれた. ☞F la jeunesse dorée のなぞり.

Youth must be served. 《諺》若い者には楽しい思いをさせてやるべきだ,「若い時はもてるもの」. ☞若い者は若いうちに楽しんでおけ, の意.

Youth's a stuff will not endure. 《諺》青春は長く続かない,「少年老いやすし」. ☞will の前に that を補って考える.

yo-yo /jóʊjoʊ/ 名 ***go* [*pop*] *in and out like yo-yos* [*a yo-yo*]/ *bounce up and down like a yo-yo*** (おもちゃのヨーヨーのように)出たり入ったりする, 跳ね上がったり下がったりする ▪ My mischievous cousin Peter *popped in and out* of my childhood *like a yo-yo.* いたずら好きないとこのピーターは私の子供時代にちょいちょい登場した.

yo-yo dieting 減食と大食[体重の増減]を繰り返すダイエット ▪ None of my *yo-yo dieting* has ever

Y

worked. 体重の増減を繰り返すダイエットはどれもうまく行かなかった.

yo-yo wrist ヨーヨーが原因で起きる手首と腕の筋違い ▪ My *yo-yo wrist* was so bad I went to the hospital. ヨーヨーで手首の筋をひどく痛めて病院へ行った.

Z

Z /zi:|zed/ 名 ***catch*** [***cop, cut, get***] ***some Z's*** [***Zs***]《米口》ひと眠りする ▪ Why don't you try to *cop some Zs*? ちょっと仮眠をとってはどうだい? ☞ /zi:z/ (《英》/zedz/) と読む. z 音がいびきの音に似ていることから; 漫画で, 寝ている人の口からの吹き出しに zzzz と書かれる.

zeal /zi:l/ 名 ***with zeal*** 熱心に, 熱誠をもって ▪ He works *with zeal*. 彼は熱心に働く.

zealous /zéləs/ 形 ***be zealous for*** ...のために熱心である; を熱心に支持する ▪ None *is* more *zealous for* your welfare than I. 私ほどあなたの幸福を熱望する者はありません ▪ The House of Commons *is* more *zealous for* royalty than the king. 下院の方が国王よりも熱心に王権を支持する.

zed /zed/ 名 (***as***) ***crooked as the letter zed*** すごく曲がって, ゆがんで ▪ The way is *crooked as the letter zed*. 道はひどく曲がっている.

zenith /zí:nəθ|zénɪθ/ 名 ***be at the zenith of*** (勢力・幸福・繁栄)の絶頂にある ▪ He *is at the zenith of* his fortune [prosperity]. 彼は幸運[繁栄]の絶頂にある.

be at** one's* [the***] ***zenith*** 絶頂にある ▪ His fame *was* then *at its zenith*. 彼の名声はそのとき絶頂にあった.

zero /zíəroʊ/ 名 ***below zero*** 氷点下 ▪ The mercury stood at 10° *below zero*. 寒暖計は氷点下10度であった.

ground zero **1** (核爆発の)爆心地 ▪ Hiroshima and Nagasaki were *ground zero* after the atomic bombs were dropped on them in August 1945. 広島と長崎は1945年8月に原子爆弾が投下されたあと爆心地となった.

2 (2001年9月11日同時多発テロ以降の) グラウンドゼロ, ニューヨーク市のワールドトレードセンタービル跡地 ▪ Volunteers performed heroic service at *Ground Zero* after the World Trade Center bombings. 世界貿易センタービル爆破のあとグラウンドゼロでボランティアが勇ましい働きをした.

3 ごちゃごちゃと散らかった場所 ▪ Why must you turn your room into a total *ground zero*? どうして部屋をめちゃくちゃに散らかさなきゃならないんだ.

in zero time flat わずかな時間で, たちまち《誇張表現》 ▪ I'll do it *in zero time flat* just for you. あなたのためにそれをすぐにやってあげます.

put in zeros 《米》数字のけたを大きくする; 過大に評価する ▪ People are apt to *put in* too many *zeros*. 人々は過大に評価しがちだ.

the zero hour 《軍》行動開始時間; 《口》予定時刻 ▪ Well, *the zero hour* has come. So long, Japan. さていよいよ出発の時が来た. さらば, 日本.

zest /zest/ 名 ***add*** [***give***] (***a***) ***zest to*** ...の興を増す, に妙味を添える ▪ A little danger *adds zest to* sport. スポーツは少し危険なほうがおもしろい ▪ Spices *give zest to* a dish. 香辛料は料理に風味を添える.

with zest 興味をもって ▪ He ate it *with zest*. 彼はそれをうまそうに食べた.

zigzag[1] /zígzæg/ 名 ***in zigzags*** ジグザグに, 稲妻形に ▪ The party moved *in zigzags*. 一行はジグザグに進んだ.

zigzag[2] /zígzæg/ 動 ***zigzag** one's **way*** ジグザグに進む ▪ He *zigzagged his way* back to the ship. 彼は千鳥足で船へ帰った.

zone /zoʊn/ 名 ***a ...-free zone*** 《口・戯》...がない区域 ▪ Mayor Gordon made the area *an* automobile-*free zone*. ゴードン市長はその地区を自動車乗り入れ禁止区域にした.

in a zone 《俗》ぼんやりして, 空想にふけって ▪ I want to stay *in a zone*. ぼけっとしていたい.

loose the maiden zone of ...の処女を奪う ▪ He *loosed the maiden zone of* the maid. 彼はメイドの処女を奪った.

no-go zone 立ち入りを避けるべき危険地域, 立ち入り禁止区域 ▪ Until as recently as two years ago, the downtown area of the city was a *no-go zone*. ほんの2年前まではその都市の中心部は無法地帯だった.

zone defense ゾーンディフェンス(コート内の各場所を守る) ▪ If teams go into a *zone defense*, it makes it easier for us to shoot threes. ゾーンディフェンスで戦えばこちらは3点シュートが打ちやすくなる.

zoo /zu:/ 名 ***It's a zoo.***/***What a zoo.*** 《俗》(場所が)ごった返している ▪ Honey, *it's a zoo* here at five. ここは, あなた, 5時は押し合いへし合いよ ▪ We're in the midst of moving our office and useless documents are all over the place—*what a zoo*! 今事務所の引越しの最中で不要な書類がいたるところに散らばっている—足の踏み場もない.

2014 年 6 月 10 日　初版発行

クラウン英語イディオム辞典

2014 年 6 月 10 日　第 1 刷発行

編　者　安 藤 貞 雄（あんどう・さだお）

発行者　株式会社 三省堂　代表者 北口克彦

印刷者　三省堂印刷株式会社

発行所　株式会社 三省堂
〒101-8371
東京都千代田区三崎町二丁目 22 番 14 号
電話　（編集）03-3230-9411
（営業）03-3230-9412
振替口座　00160-5-54300
http://www.sanseido.co.jp/

〈クラウンイディオム・1,488pp.〉

落丁本・乱丁本はお取替えいたします

ISBN 978-4-385-10428-7